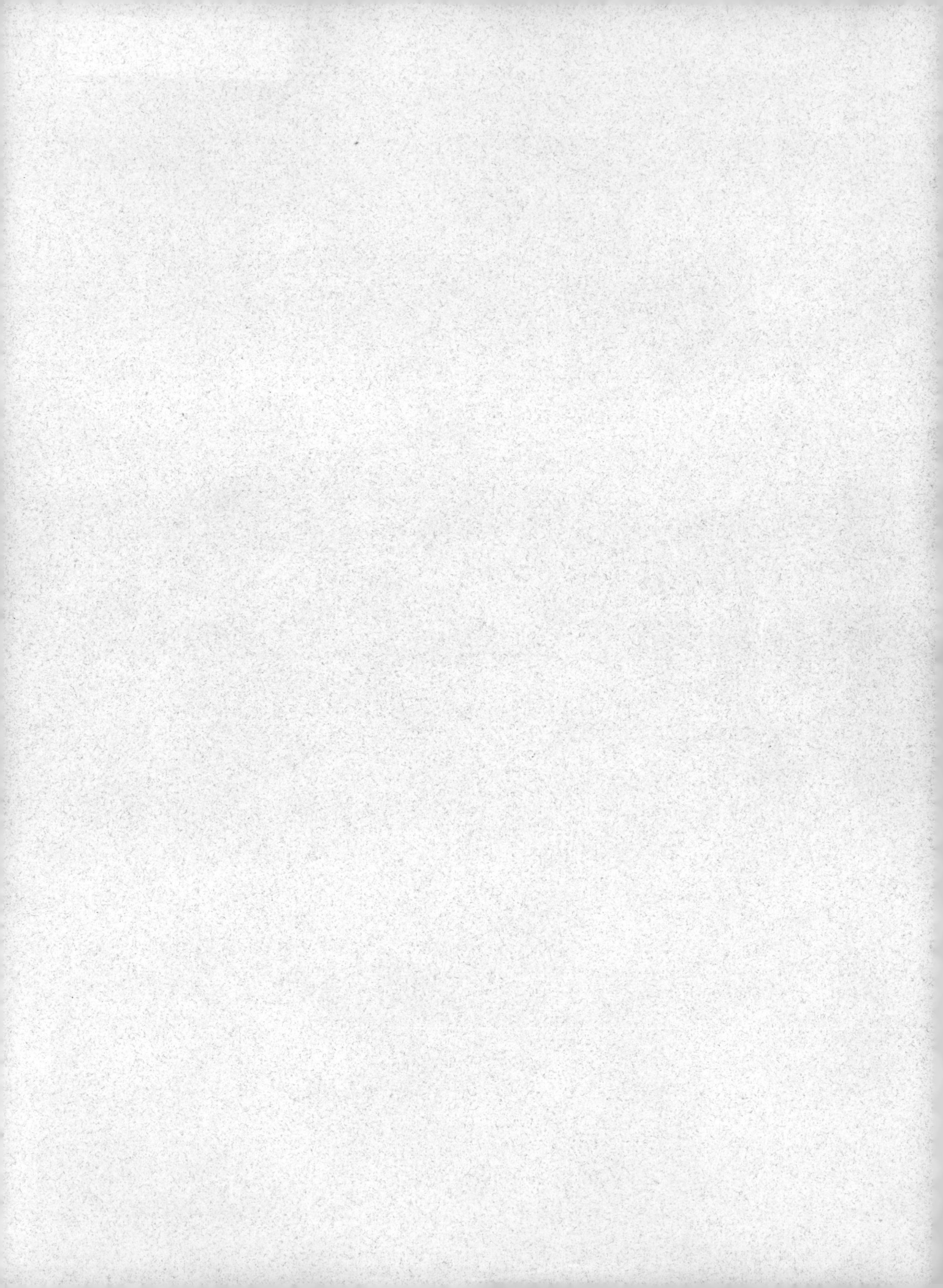

Congress and the Nation

Volume VIII
1989-1992

A Review of Government and Politics

Congressional Quarterly
Washington, D.C.

Congressional Quarterly

Congressional Quarterly Inc., an editorial research service and publishing company, serves clients in the fields of news, education, business and government. It combines the specific coverage of Congress, government and politics contained in the *Congressional Quarterly Weekly Report* with the more general subject range of an affiliated service, the *CQ Researcher.*

Congressional Quarterly also publishes a variety of books, including college political science textbooks under the CQ Press imprint and public affairs paperbacks on developing issues and events. CQ Books researches, writes and publishes information directories and reference books on the federal government, national elections and politics, including the *Guide to the Presidency,* the *Guide to Congress,* the *Guide to the U.S. Supreme Court,* the *Guide to U.S. Elections* and *Politics in America. CQ's Encyclopedia of American Government* is a three-volume reference work providing essential information about the U.S. government. The *CQ Almanac,* a compendium of legislation for one session of Congress, is published each year. *Congress and the Nation,* a record of government for a presidential term, is published every four years.

CQ publishes the *Congressional Monitor,* a daily report on current and future activities of congressional committees, and several newsletters including *Congressional Insight,* a weekly analysis of congressional action. The CQ FaxReport is a daily update available every afternoon when Congress is in session. An electronic online information system, Washington Alert, provides immediate access to CQ's databases of legislative action, votes, schedules, profiles and analyses.

Library of Congress Catalog Number: 65-22351

ISBN: 0-87187-789-9
ISSN: 1047-1324

1414 22nd Street N.W., Washington, D.C. 20037

Editor: Colleen McGuiness
Associate Editor: Kerry V. Kern
Major Contributors: Nadine Cohodas, John R. Cranford, Prudence Crewdson, Daniel C. Diller, Harrison Donnelly, Martha V. Gottron, Kenneth Jost, John L. Moore, Patricia Ann O'Connor
Contributors: Joseph A. Davis, Carroll J. Doherty, Julie Rovner, Pat Towell, Jill Zuckman
Editorial Assistants: Christopher M. Karlsten, Owen Pinkerton, Michelle E. Sobel
Typesetter: Jessica Forman
Index: Jan Danis
Graphics: Hordur Karlsson, Dan Royer

Congressional Quarterly Inc.

Andrew Barnes *Chairman*
Andrew P. Corty *Vice Chairman*
Neil Skene *Editor and Publisher*
Robert W. Merry *Executive Editor*
John J. Coyle *Associate Publisher*
Michael L. Koempel *Director of Information Services*
Robert E. Cuthriell *Director of Development*

Book Division

Patrick Bernuth *General Manager*

Editorial Department
David R. Tarr *Editor-in-Chief*
Brenda W. Carter *Acquisitions Editor*
Jeanne Ferris *Acquisitions Editor*
Shana Wagger *Acquisitions Editor*
Martha Hawley-Bertsch *Assistant Editor*
Charlene Gargasz *Administrative Assistant*

Editorial Design and Production Department
Nancy A. Lammers *Director*
Ann Davies *Senior Editor*
Carolyn Goldinger *Senior Editor*
Jerry A. Orvedahl *Project Editor*
Jon Preimesberger *Project Editor*
Ann F. O'Malley *Senior Production Editor*
Laura Carter *Production Editor*
Christopher M. Karlsten *Production Editor*
Michelle E. Sobel *Editorial Assistant*

Book Marketing and Customer Service Department
Kathryn C. Suárez *Director*
Jacqueline A. Davey *Manager, Library and Professional Marketing*
Kate Quinlin *College Marketing Manager*
Joni Berkley *Marketing Coordinator*
Heather Wilkinson *Marketing Administrator*
Dianne Clack *Administrative Assistant*

Production

Ron Knott *Computers/Production Director*
I.D. Fuller *Production Manager*
Michael Emanuel *Assistant Production Manager*
Jhonnie G. Bailey *Assistant to the Production Manager*

Editor's Note

Congress and the Nation Vol. VIII continues a series launched by Congressional Quarterly in 1965 with the publication of *Congress and the Nation Vol. I*, a 2,000-page reference book covering national government and politics from 1945 through 1964. Each of the succeeding volumes has covered governmental action during a four-year presidential term: *Congress and the Nation Vol. II*, 1965-68; *Congress and the Nation Vol. III*, 1969-72; *Congress and the Nation Vol. IV*, 1973-76; *Congress and the Nation Vol. V*, 1977-80; *Congress and the Nation Vol. VI*, 1981-84; and *Congress and the Nation Vol. VII*, 1985-88.

With the publication of this volume, librarians, historians, political scientists, journalists and students have eight volumes spanning nearly 50 years of Congressional Quarterly's reporting on public policy.

In compiling *Congress and the Nation Vol. VIII*, Congressional Quarterly has condensed its legislative, presidential and political coverage during the 1989-92 period into a 1,200-page volume. Readers are given both an overview of the four-year period and detailed chronologies of governmental action in every major subject area.

This volume chronicles the presidential term of George Bush, which witnessed the end of the U.S.-Soviet Union superpower rivalry and the beginning of the post-Cold War era. Dramatic world events brought the fall of Soviet communist domination of Eastern Europe, the reunification of the two Germanys and the breakup of the Soviet Union. New ways of thinking about the world and about U.S. defense policy were required.

When Iraq invaded oil-rich Kuwait in August 1990, Bush fashioned a multinational coalition, authorized by the United Nations, to respond to the crisis. The U.S.-led forces quickly achieved the goal of ousting Iraq and restoring Kuwait's legitimate government. In the aftermath of the 1991 Persian Gulf War, Bush's approval ratings reached record levels.

When Bush was elected in 1988, he became the first sitting vice president since Martin Van Buren in 1836 to win the presidency. Also like Van Buren, however, he was not returned to office after one term. His dramatic drop in support was attributed to Americans' belief that Bush lacked a domestic policy agenda as well as an understanding of the difficulties many were enduring because of the sluggish economy.

Relations between the Republican White House and the Democratic Congress often were contentious. Few administration initiatives were enacted, and Bush wielded his veto, real or threatened, to block dozens of bills. Meanwhile, Congress' legislative achievements — such as bailout of the thrift industry, overhaul of the Clean Air Act, extension of civil rights for the disabled, revision of legal immigration laws and enactment of a jobs-creating highway funding bill — were overshadowed by scandal and perceived ineptitude.

Two members of the House leadership, including the Speaker, resigned in the face of ethical violations. The public learned that many members routinely overdrew their House bank accounts and that some had converted public funds to cash at the House Post Office. In the Senate, the Keating Five were suspected of doing favors for a wealthy campaign contributor, and the Judiciary Committee's handling of sexual harassment allegations against Supreme Court justice nominee Clarence Thomas caused an uproar.

Congress and the Nation Vol. VIII is a record of these and other congressional activities — from momentous events to routine extensions of programs. Researchers can find the pertinent facts on issues and legislation; descriptions of proposals and bills; succinct accounts of legislative, executive and lobbying action; key votes; and provisions of legislation.

How to Use This Book

The **Summary Table of Contents** following this editor's note shows the overall organization of the volume. The detailed **Table of Contents** *(p. ix)* provides an outline of each chapter, as well as a listing of all the stories contained in a particular chapter. For a specific topic within a story, the reader should consult the **Index** *(p. 1261)*. For example, a reader who is interested in congressional action on foreign aid would find in the Table of Contents that stories on this issue are in the Foreign Policy chapter. A reader who needs more specific information, such as details of executive and legislative action on aid to a particular country or region, could consult the Index and find specific page references under each separate listing of a geographic area.

The first chapter, Politics and National Issues, gives a legislative summary of each session of the 101st and 102nd Congresses and a discussion of the 1990 and 1992 elections. The chapter forms a framework for the legislative chapters that follow.

Note the organization of the legislative chapters — Economic Policy, Foreign Policy, Defense Policy, and so on. Each opens with an introduction providing the reader with an overview. That is followed by a chronology of legislative action, divided by Congress, from 1989 through 1992.

The final chapter assesses the Bush presidency.

The **Appendix** *(p. 999)* contains a variety of supplementary material, including Senate and House key votes (identified in boldface in the legislative chapters) during the four-year period, with charts showing how each member voted; a glossary of congressional terms and an explanation of how a bill becomes law; lists of committee and subcommittee chairmen; biographical data on members of Congress in 1989-92; profiles of Cabinet members and other senior officials; controversial nominations; presidential vetoes; major presidential speeches and messages to Congress; and political charts, including presidential election returns for 1988 and 1992 and House, Senate and gubernatorial returns for 1990 and 1992.

Colleen McGuiness
November 1993

Editor's Note

Summary Table of Contents

Chapter 1	Politics and National Issues	1
Chapter 2	Economic Policy	29
Chapter 3	Trade Policy	163
Chapter 4	Foreign Policy	201
Chapter 5	Defense Policy	333
Chapter 6	Transportation and Commerce	413
Chapter 7	Energy and Environment	465
Chapter 8	Agricultural Policy	533
Chapter 9	Health and Human Services	559
Chapter 10	Education Policy	639
Chapter 11	Housing and Urban Aid	661
Chapter 12	Labor and Pension Policy	701
Chapter 13	Law and Justice	739
Chapter 14	General Government	853
Chapter 15	Inside Congress	911
Chapter 16	The Bush Presidency	989
Appendix		999
Index		1261

Table of Contents

Chapter 1 — Politics and National Issues

Introduction 3
1989 Chronology 5
The Legislative Year 5
The Political Year 6
1990 Chronology 8
The Legislative Year 8
The Political Year 9
1991 Chronology 12
The Legislative Year 12
The Political Year 14
1992 Chronology 14
The Legislative Year 14
The Political Year 17

Chapter 2 — Economic Policy

Introduction 31
The Federal Budget
Introduction 37
1989-90 Chronology 41
Fiscal 1990 Budget 41
Reconciliation, Fiscal 1990 43
Appropriations, Fiscal 1990 52
Fiscal 1991 Budget 53
Reconciliation, Fiscal 1991 55
Appropriations, Fiscal 1991 73
Balanced Budget Amendment 75
1991-92 Chronology 75
Fiscal 1992 Budget 75
Appropriations, Fiscal 1992 77
Fiscal 1993 Budget 79
Appropriations, Fiscal 1993 81
Budget 'Walls' 82
Budget-Control Efforts 84
Tax Policy
Introduction 87
1989-90 Chronology 91
1989 Deficit-Reduction Bill 91
1990 Deficit-Reduction Bill 92
Capital Gains Cut 96
1991-92 Chronology 99
Middle-Class Tax Cut Veto 100
Urban Aid Tax Bill Veto 103
Energy Taxes 108
Other Tax Action 109
Financial Regulation
Introduction 113
1989-90 Chronology 117
Savings and Loan Bailout 117
Securities Market Reforms 130
Bank Fraud Penalties 133
Money Laundering 134
Coin Redesign 135
1991-92 Chronology 136
Banking Overhaul 136
Thrift Bailout Refinancing 148
Government-Sponsored Enterprises 153
Money Laundering 156
Credit Reporting Safeguards 157
Government Securities Dealers 158
Partnership Roll-Ups 158
Investment Advisers Regulation 159
Corporate Auditor Requirements 160
Bank Red Tape Relief 160
Bank Disaster Assistance 161
Coin Redesign, Commemoratives 161

Chapter 3 — Trade Policy

Introduction 165
1989-90 Chronology 169
Soviet, East Bloc Trade 169
China Trade 173
Textile Import Quotas 174
Export Controls 175
Foreign Investment Data 177

Enterprise for the Americas 179
Caribbean Basin Initiative 180
Ex-Im, IDB, IMF Authorizations 184
Multilateral Lending 185
Steel VRAs Extension 186
Fair Trade in Financial Services 187
1991-92 Chronology 187
North American Free Trade Agreement ... 187
China Trade 190
Soviet, East Bloc Trade 192
Enterprise for the Americas 194
Export Controls 195
Trade Expansion Act 196
Minivan Tariffs 197
Fair Trade in Financial Services 198
Customs Law Revisions 198
Ex-Im Bank Authorization 199
OPIC Authorization 199

Chapter 4 — Foreign Policy

Introduction 203
1989-90 Chronology 205
U.S.-Soviet Relations 205
Poland, Hungary Aid 210
German Unification Treaty 214
El Salvador Aid 214
Nicaragua Policy 219
Panama Invasion, Aid 223
1990-91 Aid Authorization 227
1990 Aid Appropriations 228
1991 Aid Appropriations 233
Iran-Contra Legacy 238
1990 Intelligence Authorization 239
1991 Intelligence Authorization 242
State Department Authorization 247
China Policy 250
South Africa Policy 253
Chemical Weapons Sanctions 254
Andean Drug War 255
Food for Peace 256
United Nations Funding 258
Palau Autonomy 258
Torture Treaty 259
Armenian Genocide Resolution 259
1991-92 Chronology 260
Aid to Former USSR 260
1992-93 Aid Authorization 267
1992 Aid Appropriations 269
1993 Aid Appropriations 271
Middle East Peace Talks 277
Aid to Yugoslavian Republics 278
Somalia Relief Effort 278
Revised 1991 Intelligence Bill 280
1992 Intelligence Authorization 281
1993 Intelligence Authorization 283
Iran-Contra Pardons 284
'October Surprise' Probe 287
POW/MIA Investigation 288
State Department Authorization 290
Chemical Weapons Sanctions 292
Nuclear Arms Proliferation 293
Controversial Arms Sales 293
South Africa Policy 294
Cuba Embargo 295
Haitian Refugee Policy 296
Andean Drug War 296
Kurdish Refugee Aid 297
Global Warming Treaty 297
Special Report:
Persian Gulf War 299
Special Report:
End of the Cold War 319

Chapter 5 — Defense Policy

Introduction 335
1989-90 Chronology 339
Tower Nomination 339
1990 Defense Authorization 340
1990 Defense Appropriations 350
1990 Military Construction 352
Military Base Closings 353
U.S.-Japan Plane Deal 354
1991 Defense Authorization 355
1991 Defense Appropriations 363
1991 Military Construction 365
Nuclear Testing Treaties 366
Defense Production Act 368
1991-92 Chronology 369
1992 Defense Authorization 369
1992 Defense Appropriations 380
1992 Military Construction 382
Arms Control Agreements 383
Nuclear Test Ban 392
Military Base Closings 393
1993 Defense Authorization 395
1993 Defense Appropriations 407
1993 Military Construction 409
Philippine Base Closings 411
Defense Production Act 412

Chapter 6 — Transportation and Commerce

Introduction ... 415

1989-90 Chronology ... 417
Aviation Package ... 417
Airport Noise Abatement ... 419
Smoking on Airplanes Ban ... 419
Aviation Security ... 420
Airline Buyouts ... 421
Blind Airline Passengers ... 422
Aircraft Liability Insurance ... 422
FAA Authorization ... 422
Hazardous Materials ... 422
'Backhauling' Regulation ... 423
Amtrak Authorization ... 424
Amtrak Waste Disposal ... 424
Local Rail Assistance ... 424
Drug Testing Transport Workers ... 425
Truck Stop Drugs ... 425
Boat Fees ... 425
Coast Guard Authorization ... 425
NOAA Authorization ... 425
Maritime Authorization ... 426
Marine Fisheries Bills ... 426
Cable Regulation ... 427
Television Violence ... 428
Closed-Captioning ... 428
Children's Television ... 429
Children's TV Grants ... 429
FCC Reauthorization ... 429
Fairness Doctrine ... 430
Radio Spectrum Allocation ... 430
'Dial-A-Porn' Restrictions ... 431
Phone Rates ... 431
Telemarketing Controls ... 432
Telephone Monopolies ... 432
Consumer Product Safety ... 432
'Dolphin-Safe' Tuna ... 433
Fish Inspection ... 434
Product Liability ... 435
Insurance Antitrust Exemption ... 435
SBA Authorization ... 435
Hotel Fire Safety ... 436
'Fire-Safe' Cigarettes ... 436
Fastener Standards ... 436

1991-92 Chronology ... 436
Highway Authorization ... 437
Air Bags ... 444
Transportation Corrections ... 445
Trucking Bankruptcies ... 445
Airline Reservations ... 445
Aviation Worker Fines ... 445
Flight Attendants' Workday ... 446
Aircraft Inspection ... 446
FAA Authorization ... 446
FAA Maps ... 447
Amtrak Authorization ... 447
Railroad Safety ... 447
Rail Strikes ... 447
Drug Testing Transport Workers ... 448
Boat Fees ... 448
Coast Guard Authorization ... 448
Foreign Ship Subsidies ... 449
Ship Inspection ... 449
Cruise Ship Ownership ... 450
Crew Documents ... 450
NOAA Authorization ... 450
Maritime Authorization ... 450
Cable Regulation ... 451
Public Broadcasting ... 457
FCC Reauthorization ... 458
Radio Spectrum Allocation ... 459
Home Digital Recording ... 459
Telemarketing Controls ... 459
900-Number Regulation ... 460
Rural Communications ... 460
Telephone Monopolies ... 461
Caller Identification ... 462
Tourism Promotion ... 462
Consumer Product Safety ... 462
Product Liability ... 462
Insurance Antitrust Exemption ... 463
Small Business Loans and Capital ... 463
High-Tech Small Business ... 464
Women in Business ... 464

Chapter 7 — Energy and Environment

Introduction ... 467

1989-90 Chronology ... 473
Clean Air ... 473
Fuel Efficiency ... 484
Energy Tax Breaks ... 484
Natural Gas Decontrol ... 484
Alternative Power ... 486
Energy Conservation ... 486
Hydrogen Fuel Research ... 486
Octane Labeling ... 487
Pipeline Inspections ... 488
Strategic Oil Reserves ... 488
Antarctica Mining Ban ... 489
Uranium Enrichment ... 489
NRC Fees ... 489
Oil-Spill Liability ... 490
Offshore Drilling Bans ... 491
Coastal Zone Management ... 491
Great Lakes Cleanup ... 491
Tongass National Forest ... 492
Water Projects ... 493
Wetlands Bill ... 494

Northern Spotted Owl ... 494
Global Warming ... 495
Environmental Education ... 495
Irrigation Subsidies ... 495
Grand Canyon Erosion ... 496
Nevada Wilderness ... 496
Arizona Wilderness ... 496
Zebra Mussels Control ... 496
Barrier Islands ... 497
Florida Keys ... 497
Federal Facilities Cleanup ... 497
Pesticide Residues ... 498
EPA Cabinet Status ... 498
National Park Service Autonomy ... 499
Arctic Wildlife Refuge ... 499
Oil Shale Claims ... 499
BLM Reauthorization ... 499

1991-92 Chronology ... 500
Energy Bill ... 500
Arctic Wildlife Refuge ... 512
Yucca Mountain Nuclear Dump ... 512
Irrigation Subsidies ... 513
Oil and Gas Royalties ... 518
Grazing Fees ... 518
Mining Law Overhaul ... 519
BLM Reauthorization ... 520
Northern Spotted Owl ... 520
Endangered Species ... 521
California Desert Protection ... 522
Pesticide Reauthorization ... 522
Solid Waste ... 523
Nuclear Test Ban ... 523
Nuclear Waste Dump ... 524
Federal Facilities Cleanup ... 525
National Park System ... 525
Udall Foundation ... 527
Rocky Mountain Arsenal ... 527
Pacific Yew ... 527
Drift Net Fishing ... 528
Water Projects ... 528
Environment Summit ... 528
Clean Water Revision ... 529
EPA Cabinet Status ... 529
Antarctica ... 529
Indian Electric Project ... 530
Lead Use Restrictions ... 530
Service Station Competition ... 530
Colorado Oil Shale Reserves ... 530
Radon Abatement ... 530
New England Ground Fish ... 530
Mining Restrictions ... 531
Marine Die-Off ... 531
Undersea Research ... 531
Ocean Dumping ... 531
Beach Pollution ... 531
Indoor Air Pollution ... 531
Pipeline Safety ... 531
Energy Labs ... 532
National Map Project ... 532

Chapter 8 — Agricultural Policy

Introduction ... 535

1989-90 Chronology ... 537
Omnibus Farm Bill ... 537
Rural Development ... 547
Farm Program Cuts ... 548
Dairy Price Supports ... 548
Disaster Relief ... 548
Earthquake Aid ... 549
Commodity Futures ... 550
Screwworm Eradication ... 550
Crop Yields ... 550
Farmland Acquisition ... 551

1991-92 Chronology ... 551
Commodity Futures ... 551
New Farmer Loans ... 553
Dairy Production ... 553
Farm Credit ... 554
Export Enhancement Program ... 554
Soviet Credit Guarantees ... 555
Market Promotion Program ... 555
Farm Bill Changes ... 555
Streamlining Agriculture ... 556
Wetlands Funding ... 556
Disaster Relief ... 557
Sugar Allotment ... 557
Tobacco Quota ... 557

Chapter 9 — Health and Human Services

Introduction ... 561

Health

1989-90 Chronology ... 565
Catastrophic Coverage Repeal ... 565
Physician Payments, Referrals ... 567
1989 Medicare Reconciliation ... 571
1990 Medicare Reconciliation ... 573
Medicaid ... 578
Medigap Regulation ... 582
Food Labeling ... 585
'Orphan' Drug Veto ... 585
Medical Device Regulation ... 586
Radiation Victims Compensation ... 586
FDA Consolidation ... 586
Nursing Home Regulation ... 586
Childhood Vaccines ... 587

TB Prevention 587
Health Service Corps 587
Minority Health Programs 588
AIDS 588
Organ and Bone Marrow Programs 590
Emergency Services 590
NIH Reauthorization 590
Anti-Smoking Bills 591
Injury Research 591
Elderly Health, Alzheimer's 592
Mental Health Projects 592
Family Planning 592
Cancer Screening 593
Health Planning Grants 593
Developmental Disabilities 593
Nutrition Monitoring 593
Abortion 594
Disabilities Prevention 595
Research Laboratory 595
Mandated Benefits 595
Adolescent Family Life 595

1991-92 Chronology 595
Health Reform 596
Abortion 597
Medicaid 600
NIH Reauthorization 602
Prescription Drug User Fees 603
'Orphan' Drugs 603
Drug, Mental Health Programs 604
Medicaid Drug Discounts 605
Generic Drug Regulation 606
Infertility Clinics 606
Lead Poisoning 606
Medical Device Regulation 607
Rehabilitation Act 607
DES Research 607
Breast Cancer Screening 608
Disease Prevention 608
Alzheimer's Disease 608
Cancer Registries 608
Drug Licensing 608
Health Policy Agency 608
Medical Training 609
Malpractice Suits 609
Health Care Fraud 609
Medicare Payment Rules 609
Long-Term Care 609
FDA Enforcement 610
Disabilities Prevention 610

Human Services

1989-90 Chronology 611
Child Care 611
Head Start 613
Human Services Reconciliation 614
Community Service 616
WIC Reauthorization 617
Food Stamps 618
Child Abuse 619
Volunteer Programs 619

1991-92 Chronology 620
Older Americans Act 620
Child Welfare Veto 621
Head Start 621
Children with Disabilities 622
Abandoned Children 622
Child Abuse 622
Protections for Mentally Ill 622
Farmers' Markets 622
Infant Formula Price Fixing 523
Meals for Homeless Children 623
Welfare Reform 623
Welfare Tracking 623
Temporary Care 623
Women with AIDS 623

Veterans' Affairs

1989-90 Chronology 625
Omnibus Veterans' Measure 625
Veterans Reconciliation 625
Nurses' Pay 627
Agent Orange 628
Veterans Housing 628
Personnel Retention 629
Medical Research Grants 629
Recruitment and Hiring 629
Employment and Training 629
Educational Services 629
Disability Pay 629
Veterans' Rehabilitation 629

1991-92 Chronology 629
Gulf War Benefits 629
COLA Increases 631
Agent Orange 632
Job, Education Aid 633
VA Doctor, Dentist Pay Raise 633
Veterans Services 634
Reservist Protections 634
Aid for Homeless Veterans 634
Veterans Health 635
Loan Guarantees for Reservists 635
Radiation Compensation 636
Post-Traumatic Stress 636
Minority Veterans Affairs 636
Job Discrimination 636
Hospice Care Pilot Program 637

Chapter 10 — Education Policy

Introduction 641
1989-90 Chronology 643
Bush Education Initiative 643
Vocational Education 644

Education for the Disabled 647
Student 'Right-to-Know' 648
Student Loan Defaults 649
Math, Science Education 650
Taft Institute 651
Chapter 1 Assessment 652
Library Aid 652
Dropout Program 652
Pepper Program 652

1991-92 Chronology 653
Higher Education Aid 653
School Reform 657
Adult Literacy 658
Longer School Year 659
Dropout Prevention 659
Video Programs 659
Education of the Deaf 660
Education Research 660

Chapter 11 — Housing and Urban Aid

Introduction 663
1989-90 Chronology 665
Housing Reauthorization 665
HUD Scandal 676
HUD Reform 685
FHA Mortgage Loans 689
FHA Insurance Fund 690
Mortgage 'Prepayments' 692
Homeless Aid 693
Flood, Crime Insurance 694

1991-92 Chronology 694
Housing Reauthorization 694
Flood Insurance 698
Urban Aid 699

Chapter 12 — Labor and Pension Policy

Introduction 703
1989-90 Chronology 705
Minimum Wage 705
'Section 89' 708
Parental Leave 710
Eastern Strike Veto 712
Job Training 713
Displaced Workers 714
Age-Based Discrimination 714
Age-Discrimination Lawsuit Waivers 716
Housing Benefit Plans 717
Unemployment Benefits 717
Social Security 717
Pension Reversions 719

1991-92 Chronology 720
1991 Unemployment Benefits 721
1992 Unemployment Benefits 725
Job Training 728
Parental Leave 730
Davis-Bacon Revision 732
Women's Employment 732
Child Labor 733
Striker Replacement 733
Black Lung Trust Fund 734
Occupational Safety 734
Construction Safety 736
Social Security 736
ERISA Reforms 737

Chapter 13 — Law and Justice

Law and Law Enforcement
Introduction 741
1989-90 Chronology 743
Americans with Disabilities 743
Immigration Reform 752
Chinese Student Visas 755
Refugee Asylum 756
Nurse Immigration 757
Civil Rights 757
Flag Desecration 760
Civil Rights Commission 762
Lucas Nomination 763
Crime Bill 764
Gun Control 765
Drug Legislation 768
Vertical Price Fixing 770
RICO Limitations 771
Antitrust Measures 772
Artists' Rights 772
Computer Software 773
State, University Copyright Coverage 773
Copyright Fees 773
Copyright Tribunal 773
Legal Services Corporation 773
Judgeships Bill 774
Administrative Law Judges 775
Judicial Impeachments 775
Thomas Nomination 777

Starr Nomination 778
Hate Crime Statistics 778
Violence Against Women 778
Law Agents' Liability 778
Consolidation of Lawsuits 779
Whistleblower Rewards 779
Debt Collection 779
Naturalization Process 779
Philippine War Veterans 779
Military Malpractice 780
Biological Weapons Ban 780

1991-92 Chronology 780
Civil Rights 780
Civil Rights Commission 785
Crime Bill 786
Drug Legislation 789
Carjacking Penalties 790
Child Support 790
Sports Lottery Ban 790
Vertical Price Fixing 791
RICO Limitations 791
'Fair Use' 791
Patent and Trademark Infringement 792
Patent Maintenance Fees 792
Patent Office Reauthorization 792
Semiconductor Chips 792
Patent Extensions 793
Copyright Renewal 793
Aid for Bilingual Voters 793
Aliens in the Armed Forces 793
Naturalization Process 794
Chinese Nationals 794
Soviet Scientists 794
Japanese-American Internees 794
Visa Exemptions 794
Legal Services Corporation 795
Independent Counsel 795
Judicial Nominating Process 795
Ryskamp Nomination 796
Carnes Nomination 796
'Hate Crimes' 797
Battered Women 797
Torture Victims 797
Juvenile Violence 797
Child Abuse 798
DNA Testing 798
Customs' Damages 798
Consolidation of Lawsuits 798
Judicial Administration 798
Military Malpractice 798
Bankruptcy Judges 798
Tobacco Sales Ban 799

The Supreme Court
Introduction 801
Supreme Court Decisions, 1988-92 807
Business Law 807
Courts and Procedure 813
Criminal Law 817
Election Law 829
Environmental Law 830
Family Law 831
Federal Government 832
First Amendment 834
Immigration Law 838
Individual and Civil Rights 838
International Law 844
Labor Law 845
Property Law 848
States 849
Torts 851

Chapter 14 — General Government

Introduction 855

1989-90 Chronology 857
Federal Pay Overhaul 857
Federal Workers 858
Federal Honoraria Ban 858
Lump-Sum Pension Payments 858
Hatch Act Veto 859
'Revolving Door' 861
Lobbying Curbs 862
Financial Centralization 862
Whistleblowers Protection 862
Regulatory Negotiation 864
Fund Transfers 865
NEA Funding 865
Paperwork Reduction 867
Acid-Free Paper 869
Post Office 'Off Budget' 869
Curbs on Deceptive Mail 870
Child-Proof Packaging 870
Anti-Porn Mail 870
'Motor Voter' 871
Uniform Poll-Closing Time 872
D.C. Political Issues 872
D.C. Police Officers 873
D.C. Metro Assistance 873
Puerto Rico Plebiscite 873
Fiscal 1990 NASA Authorization 874
Fiscal 1991 NASA Authorization 876
Space Station 877
Superconducting Supercollider 878
Space Inventions Patent 879
Technology Programs 879
Mining Research 880
Earthquake Hazards 880
Earthquake Research 881
Animal Research Labs 881

Indian Programs Investigation 881
Indian Health and Human Services 883
Indian Education 883
Indian Law Enforcement 883
Indian Environmental Quality 884
Indian Forest Management 884
'Indian Preference' 884
Tribal Remains 884
Indian Museum 885
Seminole Indians 885
Puyallup Settlement 885
Micmac Settlement 885

1991-92 Chronology 886
Federal Honoraria Ban 886
Hatch Act Revisions 886
'Revolving Door' 887
Lobbying Rules 887
Performance Standards 887
Waste-Buster Awards 888
Ethics Office Funds 888
EEOC Revisions 888
White House Spending 888
Defense Workers Relief 888
Gulf War Compensation 889
Supercomputers 889
Fire Administration 889
GSA Overhaul 889
Procurement Rules 890
Paperwork Reduction 890
Energy Efficiency 890
State Aid Disbursement 890
Joint Ventures 890
Competitiveness Council 891
Competitiveness Bills 891
High-Tech Training 892
Kennedy Documents 892
'Motor Voter' 893
Decennial Census Study 895
Election Day Holiday 895
D.C. Legislation 895
Puerto Rico Plebiscite 897
Fiscal 1992-94 NASA Authorization 897
Fiscal 1993 NASA Authorization 898
Space Station 899
Landsat 900
Superconducting Supercollider 901
Commercial Space 902
Technology Programs 902
Fiscal 1992-93 NSF Funding 902
Water Desalination 903
Metric Packaging 903
Debt-for-Science Swaps 903
High-Speed Computer Network 903
Fire Safety 904
Electric Vehicles 904
High-Speed Rail 904
Animal Research Labs 904
Indian Health Services 905
Hawaiian Health Care 906
Indian Self-Governance 906
Indian Criminal Jurisdiction 906
Tribal Courts 906
Indian Lands Management 907
Indian Job Training 907
'Indian Preference' 907
Indian Languages 907
Alaska Native Languages 907
Indian Right-to-Sue 908
Unacknowledged Tribes 908
Indian Research 908
Indian Veterans Memorial 908
Navajo-Hopi Relocation 908
Micmac Indians 908
Lumbee Tribe 909
Mimbres Tribe 909

Chapter 15 — Inside Congress

Introduction 913

Members and Procedures

1989-90 Chronology 915
Organization 915
Wright Resignation 917
Coelho Resignation 918
Ethics Code Rewrite 920
Ethics Probes 921
Pocket-Veto Power 927

1991-92 Chronology 927
Organization 928
House Bank 929
House Post Office 939
Restaurant Bills 942
Traffic Tickets 942
Ethics Probes 942
News Leaks Investigation 946
Ethics Committee Reorganization 947
Professional Administrator 947
Congressional Reform Study 948
House Voting Privileges 948
Closed-Captioned TV 949

Election Issues

1989-90 Chronology 951
Campaign Finance 951
'Grandfather Clause' 952
Political Ads 957
Term Limitations 958

1991-92 Chronology 959
Campaign Finance 959
Term Limitations 963

Pay and Benefits
1989-90 Chronology 965
Congressional Pay 965
Franking Privilege 968

1991-92 Chronology 970
Congressional Pay 970
Madison Amendment 972
Franking Privilege 973
Nuclear Bunker 973

Special Report:
The Keating Five 975

Chapter 16 — The Bush Presidency

Introduction 991
The Bush Persona 991
Bush Appointments 993
The Economy 995
Foreign Policy 995
Domestic Policy 997
Bush and Congress 997
Electoral Defeat 998

Appendix

Glossary of Congressional Terms 1001
The Legislative Process in Brief 1013

Key Votes
1989 Key Votes 1021
1990 Key Votes 1039
1991 Key Votes 1061
1992 Key Votes 1083

Congress and Its Members
Membership Lists 1107
Members of Congress, 1989-92 1115
Congressional Committees 1125
Post-Election Sessions 1137
Senate Cloture Votes, 1917-92 1139

Congressional Reapportionment
Redistricting for the 1990s 1145
Reapportionment History 1151

The Presidency
Bush Appointments to Major Posts 1169
Presidential Vetoes, 1989-92 1181
Selected Presidential Texts 1183

Political Charts
Winning Party in Presidential Races 1225
Presidential Elections, 1860-1992 1226
1988 Presidential Election 1228
1992 Presidential Election 1229
1992 Electoral Votes 1230
Republican Convention Balloting 1231
Democratic Convention Balloting 1232
House Seats and Electoral Votes 1233
Political Parties in Congress, Presidency . 1234
House Election Results, 1948-92 1236
101st Congress Special Elections 1238
1990 Election Returns 1240
102nd Congress Special Elections 1248
1992 Election Returns 1250
Governors, 1989-92 1259

Index 1261

Congress and the Nation

Volume VIII
1989-1992

Politics and National Issues

Introduction 3
1989 Chronology 5
1990 Chronology 8
1991 Chronology 12
1992 Chronology 14

Politics and National Issues

When the history of 1989-92 is written, the signal event will surely be the collapse of Soviet communism and the dissolution of the Union of Soviet Socialist Republics. The world watched as, one by one, the countries of the Warsaw Pact broke away from the Soviet Union to turn toward democracy and market economies and then as the Soviet Union itself broke apart. Seemingly overnight, the superpower rivalry that had dominated U.S. defense and foreign policy for nearly half a century was over.

For many Americans, however, these astounding events were overshadowed by economic recession. Faced with slow economic growth and high levels of unemployment, more and more people began to fear that they and their children would never be able to realize the American dream of a continually improving standard of living.

Those fears were to make Republican George Bush a one-term president. Bush had entered the White House on the popularity of his predecessor, Ronald Reagan, and saw his own public approval ratings soar to record heights after the successful U.S.-led military action against Iraq in 1991. But Bush was never able to convince voters that he had a credible plan for rejuvenating the economy or addressing other domestic problems, including a failing health insurance system and the huge budget deficits caused in part by the Reagan-Bush economic policies.

The Democratic-controlled Congress gave the president little quarter, although the two did cooperate to enact a far-reaching rewrite of the Clean Air Act. Other major achievements of the 101st and 102nd Congresses included measures making public and work places accessible to Americans with disabilities and a restructuring of the thrift industry. But severe image problems overshadowed these achievements. More often than not, the Democratic Congress clashed with the Republican White House, with legislative gridlock the result. This perceived ineptitude combined with numerous scandals to drive congressional approval ratings to record lows.

The Post-Cold War Era

The change in the political order in Eastern Europe occurred with breathtaking speed. By the end of 1989, every state in the Warsaw Pact had begun the difficult transformation from authoritarian rule and a command economy to a market-based democracy. Nowhere was the sense of new freedom more keenly demonstrated than in Berlin, where East and West Germans together tore down the wall that had divided the city since the end of World War II.

Two years later, the Soviet Union reverted to independent republics after Russian President Boris N. Yeltsin defied hard-line communists who had arrested Soviet President Mikhail S. Gorbachev and tried to seize control of the central government. Gorbachev was restored to power but was unable to hold the Soviet Union together. By the end of 1991, the Soviet Union was officially dissolved, Gorbachev had resigned and Yeltsin was the key leader trying to liberalize Russia's economic and political structures.

The turn to democracy was not confined to the former Soviet empire. In Nicaragua and El Salvador, Bush agreed to temper Reagan's hard-line policies, which moved both countries toward a peace they had not experienced in at least a decade. In Panama, Bush mounted a military operation that resulted in the capture of Panamanian dictator Manuel Antonio Noriega, who was brought to the United States and convicted on charges of drug-trafficking. The operation also restored to power the elected leaders of the Panamanian government, who had been ousted by Noriega.

Nelson Mandela, leader of the African National Congress, in 1990 was freed from his prison cell on Robbins Island after 26 years and began to negotiate the end to apartheid in South Africa.

Not all attempts to throw off authoritarian rule were successful; for example, the Chinese government brutally suppressed pro-democracy demonstrators in 1989. And the world in the post-Cold War era seemed as vulnerable to instability and violence as in the past. Civil war erupted in many of the former Soviet republics and in the former Yugoslavia, where ethnic and religious differences resulted in the worst atrocities in Europe since World War II.

Iraq's invasion of oil-rich Kuwait in August 1990 led to the largest U.S. military engagement since the Vietnam War. In a riveting display of modern weaponry, a U.S.-led multinational force quickly pushed Saddam Hussein's forces out of Kuwait. The victory, which entailed far fewer American casualties than had been expected, was a rejuvenating moment for Americans whose faith in the nation's military powers had been shaken by the loss of the Vietnam War.

The military victory in Iraq also was the crowning moment of George Bush's presidency. But the euphoria was fleeting. Almost as soon as the war had ended, Democrats succeeded in turning the nation's attention to the economy's miserable performance. And although Iraq was routed from Kuwait, the action failed to unseat Saddam. The Iraqi dictator's hold on power, together with Democratic questions about the Reagan and Bush administration support for Iraq before the invasion, continued to dog Bush for the rest of his term.

The Economy

When Bush assumed office, the economy was still in what would become the longest peacetime expansion. Unemployment stood at 5.3 percent, and the inflation rate was 4.2 percent. But the expansion slowed during the first quarter of 1989, and the economy slid into recession. Although the 1990-91 recession was neither as long nor as deep as other postwar downturns, the recovery seemed prolonged. Unemployment, which began to go up in mid-1990, stayed high throughout Bush's term. Personal income stopped growing and was at the same level at the end of 1992 as it was when Bush was inaugurated president.

Constrained by the federal budget deficit, Bush could do little about the economy, and indeed, many economists said there was little the president or Congress should do — that the economy should be left alone to correct itself. But the voters were not so patient, and they tended to blame Bush for not leading the country back onto a path of growth and competitiveness. Bush's own actions also may have given his opponents political fodder. His plan for reinvigorating the economy seemed too little and too scattershot. And his opposition to an extension of jobless benefits allowed his detractors to portray him as insensitive to the needs of workers and their families.

Bush also sustained serious political damage on tax matters. Twice he asked Congress for a cut in the tax rate on capital gains and twice he was denied. Democratic opponents argued that the cut would add significantly to the deficit, but the argument that was most damaging to the Bush administration was that a capital gains cut would favor the rich at the expense of the poor and the middle class.

The single action that may have dealt the biggest blow to Bush's political fortunes occurred in 1990 when Bush broke his 1988 campaign promise not to raise taxes. Concerned that a hemorrhaging deficit could severely damage the economy and his own re-election chances in 1992, Bush sought the help of Democrats to work out a bipartisan deficit-reduction deal. Democrats were reluctant to bargain until Bush in late June declared that tax increases would be a necessary component of any meaningful deficit-reduction package. Although conservative Republicans viewed the president's action as treachery and many taxpayers saw it as the ultimate broken campaign pledge, Bush's willingness to accept a tax increase made possible enactment of the first meaningful constraints on the growth of the federal budget since 1985, when Congress enacted what became known as Gramm-Rudman. The 1990 package of tax increases and spending cuts was expected to reduce the deficit by $500 million over the next five years.

Overshadowed by Scandal

The deeply partisan debate that stymied passage of the deficit-reduction package for weeks characterized relations between Capitol Hill and the White House throughout Bush's presidency. Bush offered few of his own initiatives — contributing to the public perception that he had only an incomplete vision for America. Instead, he used his veto power to block dozens of bills, including one extension of unemployment benefits, "motor voter" registration, and family and medical leave. Of all the bills Bush vetoed, Congress was able to override only one — to reregulate the cable industry. Bush successfully used the threat of a veto either to block some bills altogether or to reshape them in a manner more acceptable to him.

The perception of a divided Congress unable to handle public business efficiently because of its own partisan bickering was just one factor in the erosion of public support for the nation's top legislative body. The second, and perhaps more damaging, was a series of scandals that plagued both chambers throughout the four-year period.

In the House, ethics questions and violations even touched the leadership, where, within days of each other in 1989, Speaker Jim Wright, D-Texas, and Majority Whip Tony Coelho, D-Calif., resigned their leadership posts and their congressional seats. Later, twin scandals became symbols of congressional excess and corruption. The first was the disclosure that hundreds of members had routinely overdrawn their House bank accounts; the second, the allegation that some members had converted public funds to cash at the House Post Office and that patronage employees had sold drugs at the federal facility.

In the Senate, an investigation concluded on the Keating Five — four Democratic senators and one Republican suspected of receiving campaign contributions in return for favors they did for Charles H. Keating Jr., who was under indictment for fraud in connection with the failed savings and loan that he owned.

Congress drew public ire in 1989 when it attempted to give itself a big pay raise without taking a recorded vote. Two years later, the Senate Judiciary Committee left women throughout the country outraged with its handling of allegations by law professor Anita F. Hill that she had been sexually harassed by Clarence Thomas, whom Bush had nominated to fill the vacancy created by Justice Thurgood Marshall's retirement from the Supreme Court.

Thomas was one of two justices Bush named to the high court. The other was David H. Souter, who succeeded William J. Brennan Jr. Together with the three appointments made by Ronald Reagan, the Court had a decidedly conservative cast. But it was no more predictable than ever. In a ruling that surprised all sides, the Court in 1992 upheld a woman's fundamental right to abortion.

Politics

Change was the operative word in politics, where a majority of American voters heeded Democrat Bill Clinton's call for change and turned George Bush out of office. The governor of Arkansas took 43 percent of the vote to Bush's 38 percent. The other 19 percent went to Ross Perot, the Texas billionaire who ran a quirky independent campaign in which he talked bluntly to the American people about the need to reduce the federal budget deficit.

Change also reached Congress. A record numbers of women, blacks and Hispanics were elected in 1992. In the Senate, four women, including the first black woman, were elected. At the beginning of the 103rd Congress, a fourth of the House members were beginning their first term in office, a result of retirements and redistricting more than voter rejection of incumbents. Instead of ousting sitting incumbents, voters seemed more comfortable setting limits on how long their legislators in Washington could serve. After the 1992 elections, 15 states had terms limits.

Despite all the new faces, the partisan line-up in Congress remained virtually unchanged, with Democrats still in control — at least nominally — of both the House and Senate. It remained to be seen if the Democratic Congress could work with a new Democratic president to resolve the stubborn economic and social problems facing the country as well as define the American role in the post-Cold War era.

1989

The Legislative Year

Despite momentous events that rocked the world and the nation in 1989, Congress' focus was on internal politics. Abroad, communist power over Eastern Europe collapsed, a pro-democracy movement flowered and was crushed in China, nationalist yearnings threatened to break up the Soviet Union and civil war continued in El Salvador. At home, natural disasters devastated areas of California and South Carolina, narcotics ravaged neighborhoods despite federal anti-drug initiatives and a Supreme Court ruling intensified the debate on what appeared to be the most emotional issue in American politics — abortion.

In all of these events, Congress was consigned to a role that was, if not peripheral, at most reactive. Moreover, the 1988 elections had not given either the new Republican president, George Bush, or the Democratic-controlled Congress any clear mandate, and neither party had a compelling agenda of its own.

For much of the year, congressional attention was focused inward, on events surrounding the resignations of House Speaker Jim Wright, D-Texas — the first time in history a Speaker had quit midterm — and House Majority Whip Tony Coelho, D-Calif. Questions about their personal ethics forced both men out of office.

Even with the turbulence, Congress completed its work in a relatively timely fashion, adjourning in the early morning hours of Nov. 22. For only the second time in two decades, the first session of a Congress adjourned before the end of November.

For the second year in a row, Congress enacted all 13 appropriations bills individually, avoiding an omnibus "continuing resolution," which rolled all government spending into one package and had become increasingly criticized.

But congressional leaders agreed that the session was not especially productive. Measures to raise the minimum wage, to revise Medicare payments to physicians, to achieve modest deficit reduction and to bail out failed savings and loan institutions were the major bills cleared during the year. Most significant measures were put over into the second session.

Leadership Turmoil

Speaker Wright had been under investigation by the House Committee on Standards of Official Conduct (ethics committee) for 10 months for a number of alleged financial improprieties. Six wrenching weeks after the committee announced its conclusion that he might have broken House rules in as many as 69 instances, Wright announced on May 31 that he would resign as Speaker and leave the House. Coelho had announced his intended resignation only days before in the face of allegations of irregularities in his purchase of a $100,000 "junk bond."

On June 6, the day Wright stepped down as Speaker, the House elected the Democratic majority leader, Thomas S. Foley of Washington, the new Speaker. Better known for bringing together warring factions than for drawing up battle plans, Foley seemed a good choice to put the Wright episode to rest.

But Foley could do little to stem the ethics infection that Wright came to symbolize. Wright's principal accuser, Republican Newt Gingrich of Georgia, a strident partisan activist, himself came under scrutiny by the ethics committee for a book promotion deal, and several other House members were accused of sexual misconduct. Ethics problems also surfaced for five senators who had intervened with federal regulators in behalf of an ailing savings and loan institution. The senators became known late in the year as the Keating Five, after the thrift's owner, Charles H. Keating Jr.

The resignations of Wright and Coelho and the election of Foley to the Speakership precipitated several other changes in the House Democratic leadership. Richard A. Gephardt of Missouri was elected majority leader and William H. Gray III of Pennsylvania was named majority whip.

Gephardt's election put on hold, at least temporarily, his national political ambitions. Gephardt, who had run unsuccessfully for president in 1988, promised his colleagues that he would not enter the race in 1992.

Gray's election to the No. 3 leadership job made him the highest-ranking black leader in the history of the House. To win the position, Gray had to overcome concerns that he might be the focus of an ethics investigation. According to reports leaked from the Justice Department, the FBI was looking into possible "no-show" employees on Gray's payroll. Gray put most concerns to rest when he secured a formal statement from Attorney General Dick Thornburgh stating that Gray was not the target of an investigation. Steny H. Hoyer of Maryland was elected to replace Gray as chairman of the Democratic Caucus.

On the other side of the aisle, Republicans in March chose Gingrich to replace Dick Cheney of Wyoming as their party's whip. Cheney had been named secretary of defense.

Gingrich won the election by a bare 87-85 majority over Edward R. Madigan of Illinois. The vote was heavily affected by regional politics — Madigan represented the same state as GOP leader Robert H. Michel. The vote also was seen as a political wake-up call to incumbent GOP leaders from younger members who wanted a more aggressive, activist party.

In the Senate, Democrat George J. Mitchell of Maine was serving his first year as majority leader, where he cautiously proceeded to impose order on the legislative schedule and to find consensus among Democrats. Most senators said Mitchell lived up to his promise to have an open, consultative leadership style. Relations with Republicans were easier than they had been under his predecessor, Robert C. Byrd, D-W.Va. — so much so that the GOP let Mitchell adjourn the Senate by himself for the August recess, a sign that members were not worried that he would pull any legislative shenanigans.

Mitchell also improved senators' working conditions with a more regular and predictable schedule. Few late-night sessions were held. Mitchell continued Byrd's popular practice of conducting three-week legislative sessions and then giving senators a week to take care of business in their states.

Pay Raises and Capital Gains

Congress began and ended the year with legislative wrangles over its own pay. Congressional pay raises are never popular with voters, and this one, which would have raised pay by 51 percent for members of Congress

Congress in 1989

The first session of the 101st Congress ended Nov. 22, 1989, when the House adjourned *sine die* at 4:31 a.m. EST. The Senate had adjourned at 4:06 a.m.

Convened on Jan. 3, the session lasted 324 days — 52 days longer than the last session of the 100th Congress. The Senate met for 136 days in 1989, the House for 150 days. The session was the 29th-longest in history. The longest session was the third session of the 76th Congress, which lasted an entire year, from Jan. 3, 1940, to Jan. 3, 1941.

There were 7,390 bills and resolutions introduced during the 1989 session, compared with 3,740 in 1988 and 7,532 in 1987. A total of 240 bills cleared by Congress in 1989 became public law. President Bush vetoed nine bills; none was overridden. A dispute arose over the status of a 10th bill Bush claimed to have pocket-vetoed while Congress was adjourned for its August recess. *(Public laws, box, p. 14; presidential vetoes, p. 1181)*

During 1989, the House took 368 recorded votes, 83 fewer than in 1988. The Senate took 312 recorded votes, 67 fewer than in 1988. *(Recorded votes, box, p. 16)*

and other top federal officials, was especially controversial given the economic slowdown the nation was experiencing.

A plan to let the raise take effect without a vote on either the House or Senate floor added to the public outcry. As a result, Congress blocked the raise in early February, one day before it was to take effect.

Late in the year, Foley endeared himself to the House rank and file when he helped to engineer adoption of a bipartisan plan that would raise congressional pay by a third over two years and at the same time overhaul ethics rules and ban honoraria payments. The Senate refused to go along with that plan, instead giving itself a 10 percent pay increase.

Foley's success on the pay raise helped him recover from his losing fight with the White House over capital gains taxes. Despite strong opposition by party leaders, a fourth of the House Democrats joined Republicans to pass a Bush-backed proposal to cut capital gains taxes.

In the Senate, however, Mitchell displayed an impressive ability to impose party discipline when he almost single-handedly stopped the capital gains proposal. The Senate also gave the new president two other embarrassing defeats. Early in the year, it refused to confirm Bush's choice of former Republican senator John Tower to be secretary of defense. In September, the Senate rejected a constitutional amendment to ban flag burning. Bush had sought the amendment after the Supreme Court ruled flag desecration laws unconstitutional.

A Few Accomplishments

The first year of the 101st Congress was not without some accomplishments. Most were not new directions in policy, but damage-control moves to correct past mistakes and excesses. Having virtually ignored a mushrooming financial crisis among the nation's savings and loan institutions in 1988, for example, Congress moved swiftly in 1989 to clear a sweeping measure to restructure and refinance the thrift industry and its deposit insurance system.

Congress also bowed to outraged lobbying by the elderly and repealed a catastrophic health insurance law it had enacted only the year before. In other action, Congress took a small step toward reducing the budget deficit, passed legislation to clean up housing programs in the wake of Reagan-era scandals, sought to curb runaway medical costs by changing the way Medicare pays doctors and raised the minimum wage.

Congress did not complete action on a number of other significant measures, including those dealing with clean air, child care and parental leave. Those were put over into the second session. "No football game's ever been decided at halftime, no baseball game after four and a half innings," Mitchell said.

The Political Year

Having won their third straight presidential election in 1988, Republicans looked to the elections of 1989 as a prelude to their battle to wrest control of the 1990 redistricting process from the hands of the Democrats and to propel themselves into a majority in the House.

Early in 1989, their prospects appeared to be rising. New Republican National Committee Chairman Lee Atwater, fresh from his successful stewardship of George Bush's presidential campaign, had persuaded a House member, Bill Grant of Florida, and several state and local officials to switch from the Democratic to Republican Party. Tommy F. Robinson, Ark., also switched from the Democratic to the Republican Party in July 1989. But Republicans were unable to convert this momentum into success at the polls.

Out of 10 high-profile elections in 1989 — two gubernatorial races and eight House special elections — Republicans won two. Democrats not only repelled GOP assaults in the Deep South but also gained ground in areas that had previously been the Republicans' domain.

Gubernatorial Races

In Virginia, the state that billed itself as the "cradle of the Confederacy," Democrat Lt. Gov. L. Douglas Wilder became the nation's first elected black governor. In New Jersey, Democratic Rep. James J. Florio won the right to succeed the state's popular Republican governor, Thomas H. Kean.

Wilder squeezed by former state attorney general J. Marshall Coleman by the slimmest of margins — 6,741 votes out of nearly 1.8 million cast. The Virginia contest was remarkable for its historical significance as well as the relative absence of racial animosity in the campaign.

To Wilder's advantage, Virginia did not have a history of racially polarized voting. The state's black population of nearly 20 percent was a significant voting bloc in

Congressional Leadership 1989-92

101st Congress

Senate

President Pro Tempore — Robert C. Byrd, D-W.Va.
Majority Leader — George J. Mitchell, D-Maine
Majority Whip — Alan Cranston, D-Calif.
Democratic Conference Secretary — David Pryor, D-Ark.

Minority Leader — Bob Dole, R-Kan.
Assistant Minority Leader — Alan K. Simpson, R-Wyo.
Republican Conference Chairman — John H. Chafee, R-R.I.
Republican Conference Secretary — Thad Cochran, R-Miss.

House

Speaker — Thomas S. Foley, D-Wash.[a]
Majority Leader — Richard A. Gephardt, D-Mo.
Majority Whip — William H. Gray III, D-Pa.
Chairman of the Caucus — Steny H. Hoyer, D-Md.

Minority Leader — Robert H. Michel, R-Ill.
Minority Whip — Newt Gingrich, R-Ga.[b]
Chairman of the Conference — Jerry Lewis, R-Calif.
Republican Policy Committee Chairman — Mickey Edwards, R-Okla.

102nd Congress

Senate

President Pro Tempore — Robert C. Byrd, D-W.Va.
Majority Leader — George J. Mitchell, D-Maine
Majority Whip — Wendell H. Ford, D-Ky.
Democratic Conference Secretary — David Pryor, D-Ark.

Minority Leader — Bob Dole, R-Kan.
Assistant Minority Leader — Alan K. Simpson, R-Wyo.
Republican Conference Chairman — Thad Cochran, R-Miss.
Republican Conference Secretary — Bob Kasten, R-Wis.

House

Speaker — Thomas S. Foley, D-Wash.
Majority Leader — Richard A. Gephardt, D-Mo.
Majority Whip — David E. Bonior, D-Mich.[c]
Chairman of the Caucus — Steny H. Hoyer, D-Md.

Minority Leader — Robert H. Michel, R-Ill.
Minority Whip — Newt Gingrich, R-Ga.
Chairman of the Conference — Jerry Lewis, R-Calif.
Republican Policy Committee Chairman — Mickey Edwards, R-Okla.

[a] When the 101st Congress convened, Jim Wright, D-Texas, was Speaker and Tony Coelho, D-Calif., was House majority whip. Both subsequently resigned their posts; Wright on June 6, 1989, and Coelho on June 15, 1989. Before the resignations, Foley served as majority leader and Gray was chairman of the Democratic Caucus.

[b] Gingrich was elected minority whip March 23, 1989, replacing Dick Cheney, R-Wyo.

[c] Bonior succeeded Gray, who resigned Sept. 11, 1991.

1989, but not large enough to be particularly threatening to the white majority. Wilder won roughly 40 percent of the white vote to go along with an estimated 95 percent of the black vote.

Still, Wilder ran well behind his two white Democratic ticket mates. And the actual vote in the governor's race — a virtual dead heat — had not been predicted either by election-eve surveys or election day exit polls, which had indicated that Wilder would win by about 5 to 10 percentage points. Analysts later speculated that a number of white Virginia voters told pollsters they intended to vote for Wilder and then did not.

The same day that Wilder won election in Virginia, Manhattan Borough President David N. Dinkins became the first black ever elected mayor of New York City. Dinkins had defeated incumbent Edward I. Koch in the Democratic primary. Both Wilder and Dinkins had earned their political prominence by projecting mainstream images and speaking in measured tones.

For Wilder, the gubernatorial victory marked the third history-making event of his career. In 1969, he was the first black elected to the Virginia Senate since Reconstruction. His election as lieutenant governor in 1985 made him the first black since Reconstruction to capture a major statewide office in the South. (Wilder was the first black to be elected governor of a state, but he was not the first black governor. That honor went to Pinckney B. S. Pinchback, who served as acting governor of Louisiana for slightly more than a month during the Christmas holiday season of 1872.) In the New Jersey race, Florio scored a crushing victory over GOP Rep. Jim Courter, winning 61.2 percent of the vote in a remarkable turnabout of partisan voting patterns. Just four years earlier, Republican Kean won a second term as governor with 70 percent of the vote, a state record. Kean's coattails in 1985 helped the GOP sweep to a state Assembly majority.

In 1989, Florio's strength — his was the third-best New Jersey gubernatorial showing ever — spurred a five-seat Assembly gain for the Democrats, giving them control of both houses of the legislature in time for the congressional redistricting scheduled to begin in 1991.

Florio entered the race the favorite but was not considered a shoo-in. The issue that turned the election definitively in his favor was abortion. Outspoken in his support of giving women a choice, Florio won strong backing from abortion rights activists enraged by the Supreme Court's July ruling in *Webster v. Reproductive Health Services*. In that decision, the Court upheld a state law sharply restricting abortion rights, giving states new authority to determine abortion policy.

Courter, who in the House had voted consistently in opposition to abortion, wavered on the issue during the campaign, pleasing no one. With state polls showing widespread opposition to restrictive laws on abortion, Courter stated that abortion was not a priority issue for him, a statement that infuriated anti-abortion activists. Later he said he opposed abortion but would not seek to overturn state provisions permitting the procedure.

Special Elections

An unusually high number of House special elections were held in 1989. Four vacancies were caused by deaths. Two seats opened up when Speaker Jim Wright, D-Texas, and Majority Whip Tony Coelho, D-Calif., left Congress amid accusations of ethical wrongdoing. Another two seats were left empty when their occupants accepted other positions.

The seats vacated by Wright and Coelho both remained in Democratic hands. In Wright's Texas district, Pete Geren barely defeated Republican Bob Lanier, winning just 51 percent of the vote. In contrast with the close race in Fort Worth, California Democrat Gary Condit's election to succeed Coelho was a breeze. He took 57 percent of the vote against Republican Clare Berryhill and six other contestants.

In a major embarrassment for the Bush administration, Democrats also took over an Indiana seat formerly held by Vice President Dan Quayle. The seat was vacated in 1989 when its holder, Republican Daniel R. Coats, was appointed to fill Quayle's remaining term in the Senate. Jill L. Long, a Democrat who had lost a 1986 Senate challenge to Quayle and run unsuccessfully in 1988 against Coats, defeated Republican Dan Heath by the narrowest of margins, 50.7 percent to 49.3 percent.

Republicans did hold on to the seat vacated when Rep. Dick Cheney of Wyoming resigned to become secretary of defense. GOP state Rep. Craig Thomas won comfortably. And a Republican, Ileana Ros-Lehtinen, won the Florida district that New Deal Democrat Claude Pepper, who died in May, had represented since 1963. Although taking the seat of a New Deal liberal was clearly a partisan victory for the national GOP, many of those who voted for Ros-Lehtinen were motivated much more by ethnic pride than by party label. She became the first Cuban-American House member.

In another race that Republicans expected to win, Mississippi's 5th District, Democratic state Sen. Gene Taylor decisively defeated Republican Tom Anderson Jr., a longtime aide to popular Sen. Trent Lott, who had left the seat only a year earlier. The vacancy occurred when Republican Rep. Larkin Smith died in a plane crash.

Finally, Democrats retained two seats vacated by the deaths of Democratic incumbents. State Sen. Craig Washington handily won election to replace Texas Rep. Mickey Leland, who had been killed in a plane crash in Ethiopia. In Alabama, Democrat Glen Browder easily won a special election to succeed Democrat Bill Nichols, who had held the seat for 22 years.

1990

The Legislative Year

Exhausted from a year of partisan battles, public recriminations and a final month of marathon floor sessions, the 101st Congress adjourned at 1:17 a.m. EST on Oct. 28, 1990, giving lawmakers just nine days to campaign in a mid-term election widely seen as a test of voters' anti-incumbent sentiment. Not since 1942, when it did not take an official recess, had Congress been in session as close to an election as in 1990.

Congress managed to grind out an impressive stack of laws in its final month, including a plan to reduce the deficit by $495 billion, a massive overhaul of the Clean Air Act, a child care assistance bill and broad revisions of federal housing and farm programs.

These achievements were overshadowed in the minds of many people, however, by Congress' unfinished agenda — notably, its inability to pass campaign finance legislation — and by the yearlong drone of ethics inquiries, partisan caviling and congressional irresolution.

Public opinion polls in late October registered Congress' approval rating at 23 percent — the lowest figure since 1979. "We are the laughingstock of the nation," said Rep. Silvio O. Conte, R-Mass., as Congress was struggling to adjourn.

New Dynamics

The year began with President Bush riding high in public approval after commanding a quick military victory in Panama and overthrowing dictator Manuel Antonio Noriega. Noriega, who had been indicted in 1988 by federal grand juries in Florida on multiple drug charges, surrendered to American troops on Jan. 3, 1990, and was brought to the United States to await trial.

But for much of the year, U.S. policy — and Congress — hardly seemed to keep up with kaleidoscopic world affairs: the two Germanys were reunified; Nelson Mandela, leader of the African National Congress, was released from prison in South Africa; the Sandinistas were voted out of office in Nicaragua; and Soviet President Mikhail S. Gorbachev won the Nobel Peace Prize.

Iraq's invasion of Kuwait on Aug. 2 provoked a huge deployment of U.S. troops to the Persian Gulf region, threatened the economy with higher energy prices and sharpened debate over defense policy in the post-Cold War era. Immediately after Iraq's invasion of Kuwait, the House and Senate passed resolutions supporting Bush's decision to send troops to the Gulf. Congress also approved a $1.9 billion supplemental appropriation to pay for the deployment in fiscal 1990.

Backing for Operation Desert Shield remained strong throughout the fall, but lawmakers aimed increasingly sharp and skeptical questions at the administration concerning its ultimate goals in the Gulf. The White House and many Democrats also were at odds over whether the administration was required to seek advance congressional approval for a military strike against Iraq.

However, the 101st Congress never formally debated U.S. policies in the Gulf and refused to hold a special session after the November elections. Members instead opted to take up the issue when the 102nd Congress convened in 1991.

Budget Fiasco

Congress simply may not have had the stamina for an extended debate on Gulf policy after its ugly and public battle over the budget. Prospects for timely action to address the budget deficit appeared favorable in May, when congressional leaders and Bush agreed to conduct high-level negotiations to develop a deficit-reduction package. They continued to be favorable in June, when Bush abandoned his 1988 campaign pledge of "no new taxes."

But as the budget summit continued, first with 21 members of Congress and eventually only eight, many members left out of the negotiations began to object. "Eight men met in secret for several weeks to prepare this budget. That is not the democratic way to do business," complained Rep. Dan Glickman, D-Kan.

The congressional leadership suffered a humiliating defeat in early October when the House rejected the budget package. Opposition was led by GOP Whip Newt Gingrich of Georgia, who was a party to the budget summit but who, by many accounts, did not actively participate in shaping the final product.

The budget impasse sent the government lurching from one crisis to the next. At one point, the government shut down for three days when Bush vetoed a stopgap spending bill. Another budget agreement was finally hammered out, this time with input from a much larger group of members, and passed. The year ended with the economy in acknowledged recession, the budget deficit at record-high levels, and the standing of Congress and its leaders at a low ebb.

Achievements Overshadowed

The budget fiasco all but overshadowed some major legislative accomplishments. Congress ratified the first rewrite of clean air legislation in 13 years. The bill set up an ambitious program to reduce smog and toxic industrial emissions, to clean up motor vehicle fuels and emissions, and to phase out chemicals that harmed the Earth's protective ozone layer.

Five-year renewals of the nation's farm and housing programs were cleared, as was a bill to help low- and moderate-income families cope with the costs of child care. Congress also enacted the Americans with Disabilities Act, which prohibited job discrimination on the basis of disability and required that all public services and public accommodations be made accessible to the disabled. Congress cleared the most sweeping revision of legal immigration laws in a quarter of a century.

Congress in 1990

The second session of the 101st Congress ended Oct. 28, 1990, when the Senate adjourned *sine die* at 1:17 a.m. EST. The House had adjourned at 1:02 a.m.

Convened on Jan. 23, the session lasted 279 days — 45 days less than the first session. Each chamber met for 138 days in 1990. The second session was the 34th-longest in history, the 11th-longest for an election year.

There were 4,434 bills and resolutions introduced during the 1990 session, compared with 7,390 in 1989 and 3,740 in 1988. A total of 410 bills cleared by Congress in 1990 became public law. President Bush vetoed 10 public bills and one private bill during the year. Congress did not override any of the vetoes. *(Public laws, box, p. 14; presidential vetoes, p. 1181)*

During 1990, the House took 510 recorded votes, 142 more than in 1989. The Senate took 326 recorded votes, 14 more than in 1989. *(Recorded votes, box, p. 16)*

Congressional efforts to reform the campaign finance system failed, however. Both chambers passed measures, but they died in a conference committee that never met. Both bills would have introduced public financing and spending limits, and Bush had threatened to veto any bill that contained such provisions.

Congress also was unable to override the president's veto of a bill to reverse or modify several recent Supreme Court decisions that made filing and winning job-discrimination suits harder for workers. It was the first defeat civil rights activists had sustained in more than 25 years. Bush argued that the legislation would lead employers to adopt hiring and promotion quotas to avoid litigation.

The Political Year

War and recession hovered ominously over the 1990 campaign, but neither figured prominently in its outcome. Instead, the election campaigns looked more like a series of hard-fought city council contests, shaped largely by personalities, local issues and a pronounced absence of clear-cut national themes.

While frustrated voters talked about "throwing the bums out," on Nov. 6 they returned incumbents to Washington en masse. Only one of the 32 Senate incumbents seeking re-election lost, while only 15 of the 406 House members who ran in the general election were defeated.

The election results reinforced two of the traits that had made Congress so hard to lead — the lack of party discipline and the erosion of confidence in government. Incumbents prospered most by blaming the mess on some-

Term Limits

About the only people who fared better than Bill Clinton on election night in 1992 were supporters of term limits. They prevailed in all 14 states that had ballot initiatives to limit the number of years that House and Senate members could serve. In most cases, the support was overwhelming.

Nearly 21 million Americans supported term limits, a 200-year-old concept revitalized by voters disgusted by congressional scandal and discontented with career politicians. *(Details, pp. 958, 963)*

Counting Colorado, which approved an initiative in 1990, 181 members of the 103rd Congress would serve under the specter of term limits. In some states, House members were required to step aside after only three two-year terms in office, while all the states with term limits held senators to two six-year terms.

The following table lists the states that adopted term limits in 1992 and the limitations imposed.

State	Term Limit (In Years) Senate	House	Vote Tally (In Percentages)
Arizona	12	6	74-26
Arkansas	12	6	60-40
California	12	6	63-37
Florida	12	8	77-23
Michigan	12	6	59-41
Missouri	12	8	74-26
Montana	12	6	67-33
Nebraska	12	8	68-32
North Dakota	12	12	55-45
Ohio	12	8	66-34
Oregon	12	6	69-31
South Dakota	12	12	63-37
Washington	12	6	52-48
Wyoming	12	6	77-23

Note: Colorado voters adopted an initiative in 1990 that limited the state's U.S. House and Senate members to 12 years each.

Source: Associated Press.

body else — in effect, running against Washington. And neither party emerged with a mandate.

In reaching a compromise on the federal budget just weeks before the election, President Bush and Congress' Democratic leadership prevented the election from becoming a referendum on economic policy. Divisive issues such as taxes and abortion played out inconsistently across party and state lines. Even the growing prospects for war with Iraq failed to stir a wide-ranging debate over U.S. policy in the Persian Gulf.

Warning shots fired at two high-profile incumbents illustrated the mixed signals voters were sending. New Jersey voters, riled at tax hikes pushed by their Democratic governor, James J. Florio, vented their spleen on Democratic Sen. Bill Bradley, widely regarded as a potential future presidential candidate. They sent Bradley back for a third term, but by only a 3 percentage point margin.

House GOP Whip Newt Gingrich of Georgia led the charge against taxes in Washington, but he escaped defeat in the Atlanta suburbs by fewer than 1,000 votes. His inattentiveness to striking Eastern Airlines workers almost cost him re-election.

Altogether, the Republicans lost one Senate seat and eight House seats, weakening the administration's hand. Bush faced the possibility of tougher fights in the House over vetoes. He had come to depend upon a strategy of governing by veto in dealing with the heavily Democratic Congress. (As it turned out, a Bush veto was not overridden until the final days of the 102nd Congress.) The GOP's greatest damage, however, sprang from failure to meet its own expectations, announced before Bush moved away from his "no new taxes" pledge and when his soaring popularity held out the hope that the Republicans would defy history and gain seats in Congress or at least break even.

Conversely, the Democratic leadership may have emerged slightly stronger, although it still lacked the troops to override vetoes easily. Furthermore, House Democratic incumbents, a significant number re-elected by their thinnest margins in years, were unlikely to act with abandon; many did not know who their constituents would be after redistricting was completed.

The statehouses proved to be the real workshop of democracy in 1990. Anti-incumbent sentiment overtook sitting Republican governors in four states and Democratic governors in two. Seven other statehouse also changed hands, with four going to Republicans and three to Democrats.

Anti-Incumbent Sentiment

Colorado in 1990 became the first state to impose term limits on federal officeholders. (California, Colorado and Oklahoma voters also adopted ballot initiatives capping the service of state legislators.) But the broad anti-incumbent sentiment expressed toward Congress in pre-election polls did not materialize at the ballot box. *(Term limits, box, this page)*

Only one Senate incumbent, Republican Rudy Boschwitz of Minnesota, was defeated. In the House, 96 percent of the incumbents seeking re-election were returned. Total turnover, including retirements, amounted to just 10 percent.

Still, the voters did send incumbents a pointed message. About 85 House incumbents won with less than 60 percent of the vote, roughly double the number in 1988. Fifty-three House members were re-elected with their lowest winning percentage ever; of these, 35 drew less than 60 percent of the vote.

The depressed margins of victory also accounted for an anomaly: Despite winning more House seats (267) in 1990 than in any other election since the recession-year contest of 1982, the Democrats' share of the total, nationwide congressional vote was their lowest for any midterm election since 1966. In 1990, Democratic candidates drew just 52.9 percent of all House votes. By comparison, when Democrats captured 269 seats in 1982, their share of the nationwide congressional vote was 55.2 percent, more than 2 percentage points higher than in 1990.

Senate Races

In real numbers, the Republican Party held its Senate losses to a minimum. The GOP suffered a net drop of one Senate seat — well below the average for the party in the White House in recent off-year elections.

In terms of expectations, however, the 1990 Senate campaign was a major Republican setback. National GOP strategists had initially billed the election as one in which they would cut into the 55-45 Democratic majority, in preparation for a big push in 1992 when Democrats would have to defend 20 seats to the Republicans' 15. Instead, Republicans slipped further into the minority, holding 44 seats to the Democrats' 56.

The Democratic gain came despite a national party strategy aimed at protecting the existing majority by defending incumbents. Only a token effort was made to find challengers to GOP incumbents. Democrats were pleasantly surprised when some of their self-starters did well, especially Paul Wellstone, a college professor with a colorful personality who upset the seemingly invulnerable Boschwitz, a two-term Republican from Minnesota.

The Republican Party invested its hopes — and millions of dollars — in the campaigns of five House members and one former member running against Democratic incumbents in Hawaii, Illinois, Iowa, Michigan, Nebraska and Rhode Island. All lost, some by landslides. The only real GOP threat came in a New Jersey race that Republican officials had written off. Sen. Bill Bradley, heavily favored, was caught in a voter reaction to a Democratic-backed state tax hike and held to under 51 percent by Christine Todd Whitman, a former public utilities commissioner.

The Republicans managed to stave off a deeper net loss only because they played better defense than offense. In North Carolina, conservative Republican Jesse Helms used negative TV ads to overcome a strong challenge from Harvey B. Gantt, a former mayor of Charlotte who was seeking to become the first black sent to the Senate from the South since Reconstruction. Mark O. Hatfield of Oregon and Mitch McConnell of Kentucky also turned back challenges that had put them at unexpected risk in the final weeks of the campaign.

House Races

The 1990 elections reaffirmed the aphorism that a House seat is a very difficult thing for an incumbent to lose. Nonetheless, 15 incumbents — six Democrats and nine Republicans — lost their jobs, and the Democrats won six open seats that had been held by the GOP.

That represented a net gain of nine for the Democrats and a net loss of eight for the Republicans (counting a GOP win of a vacant Ohio seat) over the party lineup at the end of the 101st Congress. In addition, Vermont's Bernard Sanders, a self-described socialist who ran as an independent, defeated freshman GOP Rep. Peter Smith.

Among the 44-member freshman class of the 102nd Congress were:

- The first black Republican House member since 1935 — Gary Franks of Connecticut.
- The first black member of Congress from Louisiana since Reconstruction — Democrat William J. Jefferson.
- The first socialist House member since 1929 — Sanders.
- Two former members of the House — Democrats Ray Thornton of Arkansas (1973-79) and Neil Abercrombie of Hawaii (1986-87).
- Four women (all Democrats) — Maxine Waters of California, Rosa DeLauro of Connecticut, Barbara-Rose Collins of Michigan and Joan Kelly Horn of Missouri.
- Four blacks (three Democrats, one Republican) — Waters, Jefferson, Collins and Franks.

Seven of the 15 losers in the general election, plus one incumbent who lost his primary election, were dogged by some charge of unethical conduct. Public outrage over the increasingly expensive bailout of failed savings and loan institutions helped unseat five incumbents: Republicans John Hiler of Indiana, Denny Smith of Oregon, Charles "Chip" Pashayan Jr. of California and Stan Parris of Virginia, and Democrat Douglas H. Bosco of California.

Personal scandals helped halt the House careers of Democrats Jim Bates of California and Roy Dyson of Maryland and Republicans Arlan Stangeland of Minnesota and Donald E. "Buz" Lukens of Ohio. Lukens lost his primary and resigned from the House before the election.

Other incumbents were hurt by their own abrasive or blustery personalities. Only one incumbent, North Carolina Democrat James McClure Clarke, lost largely because of the extremely competitive nature of his congressional district. Every race in the district since 1980 had been decided by fewer than 5,000 votes. Although in 1988 McClure was the first incumbent since 1978 to win re-election, voters turned him out in 1990 in favor of his Republican challenger.

Statehouses

The real electoral turbulence in 1990 occurred in state races, where 14 governorships switched from one party to another and more incumbent governors were toppled than in any other year since 1970.

Neither party emerged as an overall winner. Democrats dropped from 29 governorships to 28, Republicans from 21 to 19. Two new governors were elected under the banners of independent parties. Arizona's governorship was left temporarily undecided when neither candidate won the majority required by state law.

The GOP picked up that governorship in February 1991, when the Republican candidate Fife Symington won a runoff election. And it gained another statehouse in March 1991 when Louisiana Gov. Buddy Roemer, elected as a Democrat in 1987, switched parties. That left the lineup at 27 Democrats, 21 Republicans and two independents.

Six of 23 gubernatorial incumbents who sought reelection lost their jobs. Two of the losses — Democrats James J. Blanchard of Michigan and Rudy Perpich of Minnesota — came as surprises. On the Republican side, four incumbents widely regarded as vulnerable — Bob Martinez of Florida, Mike Hayden of Kansas, Kay A. Orr of Nebraska and Edward D. DiPrete of Rhode Island — were defeated.

In Connecticut, former GOP senator Lowell P. Weicker Jr. won the seat vacated by Democrat William A. O'Neill. Weicker, a maverick liberal Republican who lost a 1988 Senate re-election bid, chose to run on his own ticket instead of competing for the GOP nomination. He became the immediate favorite against the regular party nominees, Republican Rep. John G. Rowland and Democratic Rep. Bruce A. Morrison.

Alaska voters were similarly unfettered by convention, electing former Republican governor Walter J. Hickel. Hickel had thrown the race into disarray by jumping in on the Alaska Independence Party ticket only six weeks before the election. Republicans had nominated State Sen. Arliss Sturgulewski, but some were uncomfortable with her abortion rights stance, and even her running mate abandoned the ticket to run with Hickel.

Gubernatorial races drew particular attention in 1990 because governors and legislatures were poised to redraw districts for state and federal legislators. Governors typically had veto power over new district maps and could influence the process to aid their party.

No race was more important in this regard than California, which was expected to add seven congressional seats for a total of 52. Republicans won this seat, electing Sen. Pete Wilson. They also won governorships in several states expected to lose House seats in the reapportionment, including Michigan, Ohio and Illinois. But Democrats were able to take back governorships in Texas and Florida, which between them were expected to pick up seven House seats.

Democrats also won control of five new state legislative chambers — the state senates in Arizona, Montana and Nevada and the state houses in Indiana and Kansas. Overall, Democrats controlled 72 chambers, and the GOP controlled 23. Three chambers were tied, and one — Nebraska — was unicameral and non-partisan.

Special Elections

Continuity was the rule in the four special House elections in 1990. None of the seats changed partisan hands.

Two special elections were held in New York City. In the 14th District, voters elected Republican City Council member Susan Molinari to replace her father, Guy V. Molinari, who had resigned his House seat after being elected Staten Island borough president. In the 18th District, Democratic state Rep. Jose E. Serrano swamped his Republican opponent in the race to succeed Robert Garcia, who had resigned after being convicted of influence peddling.

In Hawaii, former representative Patsy T. Mink (1965-77), a Democrat, was returned to Congress to fill the seat vacated when Rep. Daniel K. Akaka was appointed to succeed Sen. Spark M. Matsunaga, D, who died. Akaka subsequently won a special election to fill Matsunaga's remaining term. And in New Jersey's 1st District, Democrat Robert E. Andrews succeeded James J. Florio, who resigned in January to become governor.

1991

The Legislative Year

The year had hardly begun when its signal event arrived on Capitol Hill. After three days of somber but passionate debate, Congress on Jan. 12 gave President Bush authorization to go to war against Iraq. The vote represented the first time since Dec. 8, 1941, that Congress had exercised its constitutional authority to declare war. The debate also demonstrated that Congress retained the capacity to consider issues thoughtfully and expeditiously.

Less than two months later, a triumphant Bush ascended the dais in the House of Representatives to tell the assembled Congress — and the nation — "Aggression is defeated; the war is over."

The end of the shooting war abroad, however, marked the beginning of a shouting war at home, as lawmakers turned their attention from the victory overseas to the sagging economy and other domestic concerns. But the budget deal that the White House and Congress wrote in 1990, combined with partisan politics in 1991, made significant progress on domestic issues nearly impossible. The Republican president used his veto, real and threatened, to stall Democratic measures he did not like, such as civil rights and extended unemployment benefits. Compromises were forged only after Bush's standing in the public opinion polls began to fall.

By Thanksgiving, Congress had sent the president only one major bill to create jobs, a six-year, $151 billion transportation measure. Help for the jobless — $5.8 billion worth of new unemployment benefits — came only after months of partisan bickering.

The session ended after one last quarrel on taxes. Bush Nov. 26 called on the House to pass tax cuts, and Speaker Thomas S. Foley, D-Wash., agreed to bring Congress back in December to do just that. Bush declined, preferring that Congress go home. To cover themselves in case Bush started bashing Democrats in their absence, congressional leaders did not formally adjourn the first session when Congress completed its legislative business on Nov. 27. Instead, they left open the possibility of a quick return by setting formal adjournment for Jan. 3, immediately before the next session started. But Congress did not return in the interim.

The partisanship that had marked Congress for the last several sessions intensified in 1991. "I've been here for 17 years, and I've never seen so much posturing so early" in the election cycle, said Rep. William J. Hughes, D-N.J. House Republican leader Robert H. Michel of Illinois agreed. "The whole session seemed to be steeped pretty bad in politics," he said.

Partisanship was not the only roadblock to accomplishment, however. Although Congress reluctantly agreed to more money to continue the bailout of failing thrift institutions, fear of missteps and competing pressure from the banking, insurance and securities industries scuttled attempts to restructure the ailing banking industry. Congress did the minimum — authorizing $30 billion in new credit to cover losses of failed banks — but refused to increase banks' powers to expand.

War Declared and Eclipsed

The Jan. 12 vote authorizing war with Iraq, which had invaded Kuwait in August 1990, was the first time since World War II that Congress had directly confronted the issue of sending troops into combat before the fact. The debate and vote did not resolve the question whether the president had the authority to wage war without legislative action, a controversial issue since Vietnam. But the president's decision to seek the war resolution and its subsequent passage reclaimed a lost partnership.

Speaker Foley called the 102nd Congress "the most constitutionally important Congress since World War II . . . because of the action on the gulf resolution. This is the first time since World War II that Congress and the president have carried out their constitutional responsibilities on the war-making powers, to the great credit of both. Now it's sort of ho-hum that it happened. But it didn't happen in Vietnam. It didn't happen in Korea. And it didn't happen in any of the other military engagements that have taken place since the end of World War II. It restored Congress to its constitutional primacy and responsibility in the war-making powers."

Once the war was successfully concluded, Operation Desert Storm receded from pre-eminence on the national agenda with startling speed. By late August, in what was likely to be a far more momentous development, the Soviet Union was falling apart.

Many saw the collapse of the Soviet Union as an invitation to shift Pentagon funds to domestic programs. But such a move would have required junking the 1990 budget agreement, and members had little taste for doing that so late in the fiscal 1992 appropriations process. Congress made no significant reduction in the $291 billion for defense spending that Bush had requested in February. But the pressure was clearly building for a major spending realignment in 1992.

Image Problems

While the war debate was Congress' finest hour in 1991, considerable competition existed for its low point. Two leading contenders were the confirmation hearings of Clarence Thomas to be an associate justice of the Supreme Court and the revelation that House members routinely wrote checks on the House bank without having the funds to cover them.

Thomas, a federal court of appeals judge, had been named to succeed Justice Thurgood Marshall, who was retiring. Thomas' conservative credentials had already made his confirmation as the second black to sit on the Court a subject of great controversy, but the hearings turned into a national soap opera in October after law school professor Anita F. Hill alleged that Thomas had sexually harassed her, and lurid details poured out of the hearing room. Thomas was confirmed, but the Senate's handling of the situation left women outraged and led many senators to call the confirmation process flawed.

The check-writing imbroglio stemmed from the House bank's practice of covering members' checks whether or not the writer had sufficient funds in his or her account. The disclosure played into the hands of those who were already criticizing Congress for members-only special privileges. The House Standards of Official Conduct Committee (ethics committee) began an inquiry late in the year, which virtually ensured the issue would remain fresh enough to figure into some 1992 elections.

The two-year Keating Five investigation also came to a conclusion in 1991. The Senate Ethics Committee reprimanded Alan Cranston, D-Calif., a week before the session ended. Nine months earlier, the committee criticized in writing the four other senators — Democrats Dennis DeConcini of Arizona, John Glenn of Ohio, and Donald W. Riegle Jr. of Michigan, and Republican John McCain of Arizona — for their poor judgment in acting in behalf of Charles H. Keating Jr. Keating owned a savings and loan that went bankrupt at a $2 billion cost to federal taxpayers.

Congress in 1991

Although both chambers completed their legislative business Nov. 27, 1991 — the House at 7:03 p.m. EST and the Senate at 7:05 p.m. — the first session of the 102nd Congress did not formally end until 11:55 a.m. Jan. 3, 1992, when Congress reconvened to officially adjourn the first session. It opened the second session five minutes later.

The November adjournment resolution had left open the possibility that the majority and minority leadership could reconvene Congress if necessary.

Convened on Jan. 3, the session lasted 365 days. Two other sessions — the first of the 77th Congress and the second of the 81st Congress — also lasted 365 days. Only the third session of the 76th Congress was longer. It ran from Jan. 3, 1940, to Jan. 3, 1941 — 366 days because of a leap year.

There were 7,758 bills and resolutions introduced during the 1991 session, compared with 4,434 in 1990 and 7,390 in 1989. A total of 243 bills cleared by Congress in 1991 became law. President Bush vetoed three bills; none was overridden. A dispute arose over the status of a fourth bill Bush claimed to have pocket-vetoed between the time Congress completed its legislative business in November and the second session convened in January. *(Public laws, box, p. 14; presidential vetoes, p. 1181)*

During 1991, the House took 428 recorded votes, 82 fewer than in 1990. The Senate took 280 recorded votes, 46 fewer than in 1990. *(Recorded votes, box, p. 16)*

Leadership Changes

Cranston had given up his position as majority whip at the end of 1990. Senate Democrats replaced him with Wendell H. Ford of Kentucky at the beginning of the 1991 session. Democrats on the House side also installed a new majority whip in 1991, when they elected David E. Bonior of Michigan to succeed William H. Gray III of Pennsylvania. Gray had left the House in September to become president of the United Negro College Fund.

Before the 102nd Congress convened, House Democrats ousted two aging committee chairmen whose leadership had been deemed ineffective. At Democratic Caucus meetings in December 1990, Charlie Rose, N.C., toppled Frank Annunzio, Ill., for the chairmanship of the House Administration Committee. Robert A. Roe, N.J., was elected to replace Glenn M. Anderson, Calif., as chairman of the Public Works Committee.

The Senate Republican Conference took the unusual step of ousting an incumbent leader, voting to replace its politically moderate chairman, John H. Chafee of Rhode Island, with the more conservative Thad Cochran of Mis-

Public Laws

Following is a list of the number of public laws enacted since 1975:

Year	Public Laws	Year	Public Laws
1975	205	1984	408
1976	383	1985	240
1977	223	1986	424
1978	410	1987	242
1979	187	1988	471
1980	426	1989	240
1981	145	1990	410
1982	328	1991	243
1983	215	1992	347

sissippi. The 22-21 vote came in November 1990. The last time Republican senators had bounced a leader was in 1982, when they voted in favor of Richard G. Lugar of Indiana over Bob Packwood of Oregon for chairman of the National Republican Senatorial Committee.

The Political Year

Concern about the economy and health care, as well as growing anti-incumbent sentiment, produced a pair of major election upsets in 1991 and had a significant impact on the campaign agenda for 1992.

The upsets came in Mississippi, where voters lashed out at Democratic Gov. Ray Mabus and easily elected conservative Republican Kirk Fordice, and in Pennsylvania, where voters picked Harris L. Wofford Jr., a liberal Democrat, over former U.S. attorney general and governor Dick Thornburgh. Economic issues were a major concern in both states.

Thornburgh started out as the heavy favorite to retake the seat that had been held by popular Republican Sen. John Heinz. After Heinz was killed in an airplane crash in April, Pennsylvania's Democratic governor had appointed Wofford to the Senate seat until a special election could be held in November.

Republicans who campaigned for Thornburgh, including President Bush, initially underestimated the low-key and little-known Wofford, who managed to turn the election into a referendum on Bush's economic record. Wofford also scored major gains by tapping into widespread public concerns over the cost and availability of health care. When the final ballots were tallied, Wofford had won the election with 55 percent of the vote.

In Mississippi, a stagnant economy and a high unemployment rate combined to make Fordice the first Republican elected governor of the state since Reconstruction. Mabus' ouster capped a broader incumbent purge that had begun in the September primary. The three-term lieutenant governor also lost his re-election bid, and 29 state legislators were turned out, either in the primary or the general election.

Anti-incumbent fervor of a different kind became obvious in Kentucky when Democratic Lt. Gov. Brereton Jones scored a crushing victory over GOP Rep. Larry J. Hopkins. Hopkins was hurt badly by revelations that he had floated checks at the House bank. Jones, whose own personal finances also were an issue in the race, won with nearly 65 percent of the vote.

The six special elections for House seats in 1991 produced one turnover: Democrat John Olver picked up the Massachusetts seat of Republican Silvio O. Conte, who had died in February.

Texas state Rep. Sam Johnson, a Republican, beat Tom Pauken to take the 3rd District seat of Republican Steve Bartlett, who had resigned to run for mayor of Dallas.

In Illinois' safely Republican 15th District, GOP state Rep. Thomas W. Ewing breezed to victory to succeed Republican Edward R. Madigan, who had resigned in March to become secretary of agriculture.

Democrat Ed Pastor became Arizona's first Hispanic member of Congress with a comfortable victory over his Republican opponent in the state's 2nd District. Pastor succeeded Democratic Rep. Morris K. Udall, who had represented the district for 30 years before resigning in May because of failing health.

In Pennsylvania's 2nd District, Democrat Lucien E. Blackwell, a former city councilman, beat out a crowd of Democratic challengers to take the seat previously held by William H. Gray III.

And in Virginia, state delegate George F. Allen kept the 7th District in Republican hands. Allen replaced Rep. D. French Slaughter Jr., who resigned because of ill health.

1992

The Legislative Year

Hobbled by partisanship and purse strings, the 102nd Congress produced one of the shortest lists of legislative accomplishments in recent memory. Congress and the president enacted some notable measures, including the first overhaul of energy regulations in a decade, new regulation of the cable television industry and aid to the former Soviet republics. But the number of achievements paled in comparison with the number of bills that were considered but never enacted, among them urban aid, education reform, campaign finance, crime control, family leave and reauthorizations of several environmental protection measures.

Congress did little more than talk about some of the biggest issues facing the country. Health care was severely pinching the budgets of voters and the federal government, but neither party could line up behind any one of the various reform proposals that had been offered. House Appropriations Committee Chairman Jamie L. Whitten, D-Miss., drafted a jobs bill to stimulate the recessionary economy, but the price tag was so high, he never even took it to the committee. And the White House and Congress struggled all year without agreeing on an anti-recession package.

Partisan posturing in a presidential election year accounted for much of the gridlock in Congress and between the Democratic-led Congress and the Republican White House. But the bigger factor may have been the 1990 budget agreement that hung over nearly every decision Congress made. That agreement prohibited Congress from shifting funds between defense and domestic programs and required that new spending be financed with new revenue or spending cuts in other programs. Those restrictions did not prevent the deficit from soaring to record levels, but it did tie Congress' hands.

"The budget is what's grinding the government to a halt," said James A. Thurber, a political scientist at American University. "The 1990 budget deal created a zero-sum game — revenue neutrality — that in itself creates deadlock."

Legislative deadlock, continuing scandal (particularly in the House) and redistricting combined to make members of Congress feel as if they were in a state of siege. Congressional approval ratings fell to new lows. Another record was broken when 53 House members and eight senators decided to retire instead of stand for re-election. And voters rejected 19 representatives and one senator in the primaries. Comparatively few incumbents were turned out in the general election — only 24 in the House and one in the Senate.

Congress in 1992

If the second session of the 102nd Congress was not marked by legislative achievement, it was notable for its brevity. The 102nd Congress officially ended at 10:04 a.m. EST on Oct. 9, 1992, when the House adjourned *sine die*. That was the earliest adjournment in 16 years. The Senate had adjourned *sine die* the night before at 9:46 p.m.

Convened on Jan. 3, 1992, the second session lasted 281 days — two days more than the second session of the 101st Congress but 84 days less than the first session of the 102nd. The Senate was in session for only 129 days, the lowest total since 1956, when senators were in session for 119 days. The House was in session for 126 days, the lowest since 1984. The relatively early adjournment gave members nearly four full weeks to campaign for re-election compared with nine days that separated adjournment and the election in 1990.

There were 4,258 bills and resolutions introduced during the 1992 session, compared with 7,758 in 1991 and 4,434 in 1990. A total of 347 bills cleared by Congress in 1992 became public law. President Bush vetoed 21 bills in 1992 for a total of 44 during his four years in office. Congress overrode only one veto during Bush's entire presidency, the 1992 cable regulation bill (S 12). Bush said he pocket-vetoed two additional bills (one in 1989, one in 1991), but Congress disputed the claim. *(Public laws, box, p. 14; presidential vetoes, p. 1181)*

During 1992, the House took 473 recorded votes, 45 more than in 1991. The Senate took 270 recorded votes, 10 fewer than in 1991 and the least since 1969. *(Recorded votes, box, p. 16)*

From the Heights ...

When the first session ended, Democratic leaders defended their modest accomplishments and said that 1992 would be more productive. But in retrospect, the 102nd Congress reached its zenith with its opening debate on the Persian Gulf War in January 1991. Its two biggest legislative accomplishments, a massive highway bill and a civil rights bill protecting workers from job discrimination, also came in the first session.

Early in 1992, Democratic leaders hoped to bring down the budget "walls" that prevented defense funds from being shifted to popular domestic programs. But the effort faltered in both chambers, when Democrats who represented districts that stood to lose jobs if defense spending was cut joined conservatives in both parties who thought savings in defense should be used to reduce the deficit.

Spurred by that success, Republicans and their conservative Democratic allies tried to move the long-stalled constitutional amendment that would require a balanced budget. But the Democratic leadership dug in its heels. Senate Appropriations Committee Chairman Robert C. Byrd, D-W.Va., threatened a filibuster, which gave House leaders a psychological lift in their efforts to muster the votes to kill the amendment. It died in mid-June.

Perhaps nothing symbolized the gridlock in Washington so much as the debate over urban aid in the wake of the Los Angeles riots in April — the worst incident of domestic violence in 20 years. Congress and President Bush could not agree either on the amount and kind of aid or on how that aid should be funded.

Immediately after the riots, Congress approved a quick boost to help small business and other victims of the riots. Even though the bill's emergency status exempted it from the budget caps, Democrats had to settle for $500 million in aid, a third of what they had proposed.

Congress promised to work out a long-term, far-reaching initiative to help all cities combat crime, poverty and unemployment. That never happened. Instead, near the end of the session, Congress attached a measure creating a limited number of enterprise zones to a tax measure, which Bush pocket-vetoed after Congress adjourned, saying it increased taxes.

Congress also left one big debit item unpaid. The Resolution Trust Corporation, the agency charged with salvaging failed savings and loans, had been out of funds since April. Efforts to provide $43 billion to continue its operations failed, largely because, after approving approximately $80 billion for the bailout in earlier years, members were skittish about the political consequences of appropriating even more money to finish the job. "They've left a terrible booby trap for [President-elect Bill] Clinton," said former representative Bill Frenzel, R-Minn.

... to the Depths

Congress' internal strife complicated matters. Throughout 1992, the House leadership was fending off allegations of institutional malfeasance at the House bank and Post Office, which were likely to leave a lasting impres-

Recorded Vote Totals

Following are the recorded congressional vote totals between 1950 and 1992. The figures do not include quorum calls. The 95th Congress (1977-79) took 2,691 recorded votes, the highest number for an entire Congress. The high for a single year was in 1978, when 1,350 recorded votes were taken. That year also was the high mark for recorded votes in the House — 834. The high for the Senate was 688 recorded votes in 1976.

Year	House	Senate	Total
1950	154	229	383
1951	109	202	311
1952	72	129	201
1953	71	89	160
1954	76	171	247
1955	76	87	163
1956	73	130	203
1957	100	107	207
1958	93	200	293
1959	87	215	302
1960	93	207	300
1961	116	204	320
1962	124	224	348
1963	119	229	348
1964	113	305	418
1965	201	258	459
1966	193	235	428
1967	245	315	560
1968	233	281	514
1969	177	245	422
1970	266	422	688
1971	320	423	743
1972	329	532	861
1973	541	594	1,135
1974	537	544	1,081
1975	612	602	1,214
1976	661	688	1,349
1977	706	635	1,341
1978	834	516	1,350
1979	672	497	1,169
1980	604	531	1,135
1981	353	483	836
1982	459	465	924
1983	498	371	869
1984	408	275	683
1985	439	381	820
1986	451	354	805
1987	488	420	908
1988	451	379	830
1989	368	312	680
1990	510	326	836
1991	428	280	708
1992	473	270	743

sion of congressional excess and corruption in the public's mind.

Revelations that more than 60 percent of House members had routinely overdrawn their House bank accounts without penalty shook the House for months. Although no taxpayer money was involved, the free overdraft protection was a perquisite unavailable to the folks back home. Fallout from the scandal helped persuade several members to retire and played a role in some primary and general election defeats.

House leaders also had to deal with a scandal at the House Post Office involving allegations that legislators had converted public funds into cash and that patronage employees sold drugs at the federal facility. Before the year was out, four clerks, a supervisor and the post office's chief of staff pleaded guilty to various charges. A federal grand jury had subpoenaed expense account records of three House members, including Ways and Means Chairman Dan Rostenkowski of Illinois. The three members denied any wrongdoing. At year's end, the House Committee on Standards of Official Conduct (ethics committee) was reviewing the situation to determine whether the incident merited a full-blown ethics inquiry.

Minority Rule

The shortage of federal funds and the absence of a legislative agenda left Congress and the White House to battle over social policy — issues on which ideology takes precedence and compromises are hard to reach. President Bush continued his successful strategy of vetoing or threatening a veto to stop legislation that he did not want. Vetoes killed the Democrats' family leave bill, which would have let workers take unpaid leave to care for a new child or an ill relative; the "motor voter" bill, which would have allowed people to register to vote when they renewed their driver's licenses; and campaign finance legislation, which would have capped spending and provided public funding of congressional elections.

A veto threat derailed a school reform bill that did not include the president's school choice initiative to allow parents to use federal vouchers at public and private schools. In the Senate, the Democrats could not stop Republican filibusters during consideration of legislation to regulate handgun sales and to limit the ability of employers to replace striking workers.

In the waning days of the session, however, Democrats finally won their first veto fight in the entire four years of Bush's presidency when they mustered enough Republican support to override a veto of the cable television regulation bill. The legislation, which required caps on basic cable service, was popular with cable users. Many members apparently calculated that they risked more by angering their constituents if they let the veto stand than by angering a president who was trailing badly in the election polls.

In many instances, Congress dealt with possible voter retaliation by postponing decisions on controversial measures. Bills to increase federal gas mileage standards, permit oil and gas drilling in Alaska's Arctic National Wildlife Refuge, reauthorize the Endangered Species Act, rewrite the federal law regulating pesticide use and extend a program that provided legal aid to the poor all died when Congress adjourned without completing action on them.

The Political Year

A majority of American voters listened to Democratic presidential candidate Bill Clinton's call for change in 1992 and turned President George Bush out of office after only one term. Clinton, the governor of Arkansas, carried 32 states and the District of Colombia, won 370 of 538 electoral votes and outscored Bush by 5 percentage points — 43 percent to 38 percent.

Clinton's was the most sweeping triumph for any Democrat since President Lyndon B. Johnson in 1964 and the best showing for any Democratic challenger since Franklin D. Roosevelt ousted Republican Herbert Hoover from the White House in 1932. In placing Clinton, 46, and Tennessee Senator Al Gore, 44, at the head of the government, Americans for the first time elected a president and vice president both born after World War II.

The widespread desire for a change in government also benefited independent candidate Ross Perot, the Texas billionaire who spoke bluntly of the need to reduce the federal budget deficit. Perot won 19 percent of the popular vote, the largest vote total for an independent candidate in presidential election history and the biggest vote share since 1912, when Theodore Roosevelt ran under the Progressive Party banner. *(Details, box, p. 21)*

Change also reached Congress, where voters added record numbers of women, blacks and Hispanics. The new Senate would be the most diverse in history, with the addition of four women, including the first black woman ever elected to the body. A fourth of the House members in 1993 would be freshmen, a result of retirements and redistricting as well as voter rejection of incumbents.

Overall, however, the partisan lineup in Congress was virtually the same, with the Democrats firmly in control of both chambers. The lineup in the Senate remained at 57 Democrats and 43 Republicans. At the beginning of the 103rd Congress, the House had 258 Democrats, 176 Republicans and one independent. The Republicans had gained 10 seats.

Presidential Election

A year before the 1992 presidential campaign began, President Bush seemed poised for one of the smoothest reelections in White House history. After leading the nation to victory in the brief Persian Gulf War, the president's popularity soared. Yet when he formally launched his candidacy in Washington on Feb. 12, 1992, Bush faced the prospect of spirited competition not only in the fall from the Democrats but also in the Republican primaries.

In the intervening 11 months, the economy had gone into what even the president called a "free fall." So, too, had Bush's popularity. The president had dropped from a peak of 89 percent approval in the Gallup Poll in March 1991 to 44 in February 1992. Not much that the White House did before or during the campaign helped revitalize either the economy or the president's political standing.

On the Democratic side, Clinton's nomination seemed the most likely outcome as the campaign got under way. His campaign was well-positioned on all major fronts — organization, message development, fund raising and endorsements. Clinton's early primary wins put him far ahead of the other Democratic contenders, but continuing doubts about Clinton's character raised questions about the governor's electability.

Voter dissatisfaction with both the likely Republican and Democratic nominees, coupled with a growing distrust and dislike of Washington politicians, paved the way for Perot's independent and on-again, off-again candidacy. Perot's popularity with the voters peaked in June, reaching the mid-30s in a three-way race, but he remained a factor even during his temporary withdrawal from the campaign. *(Perot, box, p. 25)*

Democratic Primaries

Bush's apparent invincibility in the aftermath of the Persian Gulf War gave many of the more widely known potential Democratic contenders pause. Congressional heavyweights decided to sit out the 1992 elections; so, too, did Jesse Jackson, the leading black spokesman who had sought the presidency in 1984 and 1988, and New York Gov. Mario M. Cuomo. Clinton's prime competition for black votes, Virginia Gov. L. Douglas Wilder, quit the race before the first primary was held.

In addition to Clinton, just four other Democrats actively sought the nomination as the primary season began. Former Massachusetts senator Paul E. Tsongas, former California governor Edmund G. "Jerry" Brown, and Sens. Tom Harkin of Iowa and Bob Kerrey of Nebraska. None of the four had much following beyond their own region, and all of them were long shots for the nomination. Brown, however, ran an innovative campaign, placing a $100 limit on contributions, which could be pledged by dialing a toll-free 800 number.

On the eve of the New Hampshire primary in February, renewed controversies surfaced about Clinton's draft status during the Vietnam War and allegations of marital infidelity. Calls went out for new candidates to enter the race. Some prominent Democrats considered but then dropped the idea because the nominating system seriously handicapped any late entry into the race.

As a result, voters in most states did not have a wide choice. In only five primaries could Democrats choose from a full field of active candidates. Clinton, Brown and Tsongas were the active candidates in just 10 other primaries. As Harkin, Kerrey and then Tsongas dropped out, Clinton's main competition in the last two dozen primaries came from Brown.

Clinton entered the race in the fall of 1991 no better known nationally than the other four candidates. His skills as a candidate and coalition builder enabled him to survive, even thrive, in the primaries. He built a fund-raising operation that quickly outdid his rivals, collected a large array of endorsements from fellow state officeholders across the country and showed a formidable vote-getting ability in spite of his scars.

Clinton finished the primaries with some impressive totals. He drew a higher percentage of the nationwide primary vote (52 percent) than any Democrat since primaries began to dominate the nomination process in the 1970s. Although he lost in New Hampshire, Clinton became the first Democrat to win primary victories in each of the 10 largest states.

He scored more primary victories (32) than any other Democratic candidate ever did. And his nearly 10.5 million primary votes were more than any previous candidate, Democrat or Republican, had ever won in the history of the presidential primaries. In the process, Clinton, who posi-

Number of Black Members In Congress, 1947-93

Listed below by Congress is the number of black members of the Senate and House of Representatives from the 80th Congress through the opening of the 103rd Congress. The figures do not include the non-voting delegate from the District of Columbia.

Congress	Senate	House
80th (1947-49)	0	2
81st (1949-51)	0	2
82nd (1951-53)	0	2
83rd (1953-55)	0	2
84th (1955-57)	0	3
85th (1957-59)	0	4
86th (1959-61)	0	4
87th (1961-63)	0	4
88th (1963-65)	0	5
89th (1965-67)	0	6
90th (1967-69)	1	5
91st (1969-71)	1	9
92nd (1971-73)	1	12
93rd (1973-75)	1	15
94th (1975-77)	1	16
95th (1977-79)	1	16
96th (1979-81)	0	16
97th (1981-83)	0	17
98th (1983-85)	0	20
99th (1985-87)	0	20
100th (1987-89)	0	22
101st (1989-91)	0	24
102nd (1991-93)	0	26
103rd (1993-95)	1	38

Number of Women Members In Congress, 1947-93

Listed below by Congress is the number of women members of the Senate and House of Representatives from the 80th Congress through the opening of the 103rd Congress. The figures include women appointed to office as well as those chosen by voters in general elections and special elections.

Congress	Senate	House
80th (1947-49)	1	7
81st (1949-51)	1	9
82nd (1951-53)	1	10
83rd (1953-55)	3	12
84th (1955-57)	1	16
85th (1957-59)	1	15
86th (1959-61)	1	16
87th (1961-63)	2	17
88th (1963-65)	2	11
89th (1965-67)	2	10
90th (1967-69)	1	11
91st (1969-71)	1	10
92nd (1971-73)	2	13
93rd (1973-75)	0	16
94th (1975-77)	0	19
95th (1977-79)	2	18
96th (1979-81)	1	16
97th (1981-83)	2	21
98th (1983-85)	2	22
99th (1985-87)	2	23
100th (1987-89)	2	24
101st (1989-91)	2	29
102nd (1991-93)	3	29
103rd (1993-95)	6	48

tioned himself as a centrist on policy issues, demonstrated broad acceptability to the array of constituency groups within the Democratic Party without being co-opted by any particular one.

Nonetheless, Clinton's primary victories were regularly overshadowed by exit polls showing that even many Democrats had doubts about his character and preferred Perot. What Clinton lost with the scrutiny of his character was the aura of electability that he possessed at the beginning of the primary season. Perot's remarkably strong charge also reflected Clinton's failure to convince voters of his credentials as the candidate of change.

With his selection of Sen. Al Gore of Tennessee as his running mate and his performance at the Democratic National Convention in New York City in July, Clinton began to alleviate both those concerns.

In choosing Gore, Clinton did not seek regional, ideological or demographic balance. Both men were members of the "baby boom" generation, both were from the South and both were political moderates. But Gore complemented Clinton in some of the ways a vice presidential candidate usually does. While Clinton's political career was based in Arkansas, Gore's was based on Capitol Hill. Gore's knowledge of foreign affairs and arms control lent balance to Clinton's expertise on domestic issues. And while Clinton was the subject of damaging stories about his draft status and alleged womanizing, Gore was a Vietnam veteran whose wife had waged a "family values" campaign against rock music lyrics considered obscene.

Democratic Convention

Clinton arrived in New York July 12 for the start of the Democratic Convention buoyed by a boost in the polls suggesting many Americans were pleased with his choice of a running mate. Later the same day, Jesse Jackson concluded his national television show by endorsing Clinton. Jackson was less than enthusiastic, but, more important, the endorsement came without Clinton having to negotiate with Jackson the way his predecessors had.

Brown remained the lone holdout, but Clinton's people never seemed overly upset about that, and it did not prevent the Democrats from presenting an image of unity and harmony. Brown's delegates, angry that he was not given a prime-time speaking slot, caused some disruptions on the convention floor, and the news-starved media gave them plenty of attention. But the incidents did not detract from the impression that Clinton was firmly in charge.

With the nomination a foregone conclusion, much of the convention formalities were given over to speeches. On opening day, July 13, a large section of the program was designed to give exposure to six female Democrats running for Senate seats. Throughout the week, women played a major role at the convention, and issues important to women — abortion rights, women's health care, sexual harassment — were discussed from the podium, always to loud cheers from the floor.

The Democrats chose three keynote speakers to end Monday's program — Sen. Bill Bradley of New Jersey, Gov. Zell Miller of Georgia and former representative Barbara C. Jordan of Texas. Tuesday night, delegates were moved to tears as two activists with the AIDS (acquired immune deficiency syndrome) virus asked for greater federal commitment to helping people with AIDS and finding a cure for the disease. Former president Jimmy Carter endorsed Clinton, and then Jackson addressed the convention, giving a fiery speech that held delegates in thrall.

Adoption of the Platform. Earlier in the evening of the 14th, the Democrats adopted their platform, but the debate was brief and uninspired. Clinton's overwhelming delegate strength and Democrats' frustration with three straight presidential losses helped mute any complaints over the centrist platform that clearly reflected the Clinton view of how the Democratic Party should present itself to the voters.

The platform emphasized the need for economic growth, pledged to uphold law and order and to use military force overseas where necessary, called for a cutoff in welfare benefits after two years and supported the right of states to enact death penalty statutes. It also included more traditional Democratic viewpoints, such as protecting abortion rights, providing civil rights for homosexuals and taxing wealthy people at higher rates.

By prior agreement, delegates pledged to Tsongas were allowed to offer and debate four minority planks. But it was a debate only in the loosest sense of the word. The speeches on both sides were brief. Three of the planks ultimately were rejected by voice vote. One called for investment-related tax breaks. Another called for limits on government spending, including Medicare and other politically sensitive entitlements. The third proposed increasing the gasoline tax by 5 cents a gallon to raise revenue to rebuild the nation's infrastructure.

The fourth plank, which said that a middle-class tax cut and a tax credit for families with children ought to be delayed until the deficit was under control, was defeated, 953 to 2,287. The platform was then adopted on a voice vote.

Nomination. Wednesday night, July 15, began with a tribute to the late Robert F. Kennedy and speeches by three Democratic also-rans: Kerrey, Tsongas and Brown. Although Brown continued to refuse to endorse Clinton, his speech followed the party's game plan, with most of it directed squarely at the Bush administration.

Then Cuomo came to the podium to nominate Clinton. Considered the party's premier orator, Cuomo did not disappoint his listeners. Cuomo said that Clinton was "someone smart enough to know, strong enough to do, sure enough to lead. The Comeback Kid. A new voice for America."

The official roll call of states began with Alabama passing to give Arkansas the opportunity to cast the first vote. Clinton's mother, delegate Virginia Kelly, told the convention that the state cast all 48 votes for its favorite son. Ohio got the honor of putting Clinton over the top. At the end of the roll call, the tally was Clinton, 3,372; Brown, 596; and Tsongas, 209. Subsequently, the nomination was approved by acclamation.

The evening came to a dramatic and surprising end when the nominee answered chants of "We want Bill" by visiting the convention hall. Clinton had been watching the roll call from a party at Macy's department store two blocks away and walked most of the way to Madison Square Garden after he saw the pandemonium that broke out when he was formally nominated. His appearance on the floor a day early was unusual but not unprecedented and was wildly welcomed by the delegates, who cheered, chanted and stomped in appreciation.

A New Covenant. On the fourth and final day of the convention — six months after the first Democratic primary and more than four months before the election — Bill Clinton addressed the most pressing concern of his candidacy: How to define himself.

In his 54-minute speech, Clinton zeroed in on the themes reflected in the party platform. He described himself as "a product of the American middle class" who would accept the nomination "in the name of all the people who do the work, pay the taxes, raise the kids and play by the rules — the hard-working Americans who make up our forgotten middle class."

To those familiar with Clinton only through the harsh glare of media coverage, the Arkansas governor offered a very different image. He spoke of growing up fatherless and of the small-town values his mother and grandparents instilled in him. The references to his background were aimed at dispelling notions that Clinton had grown up in a privileged environment, to show that he was more in touch with most Americans than Bush was and to address questions about his character.

That point was underscored in a 14-minute biographical portrait that preceded his entrance. Produced by family friend Linda Bloodworth-Thomason, the creator of several successful television programs, the film presented an intimate look at Clinton's life, starting with black and white photos of Hope, Ark., his hometown.

The delegates cheered as Clinton's mother told how Clinton confronted his inebriated and abusive stepfather, and they hushed when Clinton described the ordeal of watching with his young daughter, Chelsea, the "60 Minutes" interview about allegations that he had had extramarital affairs. Through one-on-one interviews with his mother, half brother, Roger, and wife, Hillary, Clinton was portrayed as a devoted husband and caring father.

In his acceptance speech, Clinton distanced himself from the traditional liberal, activist government policies that many Americans associated with the Democratic Party. "My fellow Democrats," he said, "it's time for us to realize that we've got some changing to do too. There is not a program in government for every problem. And if we really want government to help people, we've got to make it work again."

He termed his proposal a "New Covenant, a solemn agreement between the people and their government, based not simply on what each of us can take, but on what all of us must give to our nation." Clinton said he and Gore offered "a new choice based on old values. We offer opportunity. We demand responsibility.... The choice we offer is not conservative or liberal; in many ways it's not even Republican or Democratic. It is different. It is new. And it will work."

Preceding Clinton's address, vice presidential nominee Gore's acceptance speech was shorter but no less energizing than Clinton's. Taking a series of swipes at Bush and Vice President Dan Quayle, Gore accused them of advocating tax policies that favored the rich, ignoring AIDS, embarrassing the country with weak environmental policies and allowing the nation's budget deficit to mushroom out of control. "It is time for them to go," he repeated, leading the crowd in the main refrain of his speech.

For the well-choreographed finale, American flags were passed out by the hundreds. The convention closed with Democratic dignitaries joining the nominees and their families on stage, swaying and singing the refrain of the Clinton campaign song, "Don't Stop Thinking About Tomorrow," by the rock group Fleetwood Mac. The song seemed chosen to emphasize the generational gap between Clinton and Bush.

Republican Nomination

Bush's nomination for a second term was never in jeopardy, despite his sagging popularity. But his campaign never found a theme that resonated with voters, and the president and his staff were slow to show much focus or fire.

Two of the three thematic pillars of the Republican presidential coalition — opposition to communism and resistance to higher taxes — had been negated by the end of the Cold War and Bush's reneging on his 1988 "no new taxes" pledge. The third pillar, support of a conservative social agenda, threatened to alienate the more moderate wing of the GOP. In addition, Bush was hurt by the widespread perception that he had no coherent plan for economic recovery.

The only real challenge to Bush came from the party's conservative wing, which had been suspicious of Bush since at least 1980 when he ran for the nomination against Ronald Reagan, the conservatives' hero. Eight years as Reagan's vice president, coupled with Reagan's explicit blessing, brought conservatives in line behind Bush in 1988. But much of that good will evaporated when Bush broke his 1988 campaign promise and accepted a tax increase in 1990 as part of a budget agreement. Conservative Republicans cried heresy. Seizing what he saw as an opportunity, conservative commentator Patrick J. Buchanan, a former speechwriter for President Richard Nixon and one-time communications director for the Reagan White House, entered the race.

Although he collected fewer than 100 delegates, Buchanan got in his licks. Bush won every primary, but he wound up with fewer than three-fourths of the Republican primary ballots, a far lower share than the last three elected Republican presidents (Reagan, Nixon and Dwight D. Eisenhower) received on their road to re-election.

Former Louisiana state representative David Duke also ran a limited campaign for the presidency. But the former Ku Klux Klan member won little support among Republicans and ended his campaign on April 22.

Republican Convention

Bush came to the Republican National Convention at the Houston Astrodome in need of a good bounce in the polls, which generally showed him trailing Clinton by close to 20 percentage points. On his arrival in Houston, Bush told supporters to prepare "for the most stirring political comeback since Harry Truman gave 'em hell in 1948."

Throughout the four-day convention Aug. 17-20, speaker after speaker exhorted the delegates and the national television audience to remember the past and trust in experience. Bush was hailed for presiding over the fall of communism and winning the Persian Gulf War. The president was portrayed as a level-headed manager and warm family man, while Clinton was described as a classic tax-and-spend liberal, a draft dodger, a neophyte on foreign affairs — in short, the "failed governor of a small state." Voters were asked to ignore the Democrats' attempt to remake themselves in a more moderate image and to recall instead what life was like under Jimmy Carter, the last Democratic president.

The formal opening of the convention came Monday morning, when Republican National Committee Chairman Rich Bond called the first session to order. The main business that day was adoption of the platform, but efforts to force a debate on abortion fell short. A majority in six delegations was required to challenge the platform's call for a constitutional ban on all abortions, but abortion rights supporters said they could muster majorities in only four delegations. Delegates, they said, felt it was more important to avoid embarrassing the president than to force an open debate on the controversial issue.

In the end, the platform was approved by voice vote. Cries of "no!" were heard when the document was put to delegates for a vote, but no public challenge was made.

Speakers. Dozens of speakers addressed the Republican delegates throughout the first three days of the convention. Perhaps the most stirring were former president Reagan, who described his speech as the "last chapter" in his political career, and Mary Fisher, the daughter of a Detroit multimillionaire and longtime GOP fundraiser, who spoke about the AIDS virus, which she had contracted from her former husband. "I ask you . . . to recognize that the AIDS virus is not a political creature," Fisher said, as she implored the delegates to show people with AIDS the same sort of compassion that she said the president and Mrs. Bush had shown to her.

Patrick Buchanan was enthusiastically received during a speech in which he paid tribute to Reagan and called on Republicans to unite behind Bush. He also whipped the crowd into a frenzy with a bitter, scathing attack on Clinton. Buchanan sharply questioned Clinton's patriotism and charged that the Democrat's view of change for America would mean abortion on demand, a litmus test for nominees to the Supreme Court, homosexual rights, women in combat and discrimination against religious schools. "That's change, all right," Buchanan said, but "it's not the kind of change we can abide in a nation that we still call God's country."

Vice President Quayle's wife, Marilyn, called on delegates to abide by traditional values. She said that she and her husband, like the Democratic standard-bearers, were members of the baby boom generation, "but not everyone demonstrated, dropped out, took drugs, joined in the sexual revolution or dodged the draft."

Independent, Third-Party Candidates

Independent Ross Perot failed to carry a state Nov. 3, 1992, but his 18.9 percent share of the popular vote was the highest that any independent or third-party candidate had won since former president Theodore Roosevelt ran as the candidate of the Progressive Party in 1912. Following is a list of third-party and independent candidates who received more than 10 percent of the popular vote. The name of the third party is indicated in parentheses, where applicable.

Candidate	Year	Percentage of Vote
Theodore Roosevelt (Progressive)	1912	27.4
Millard Fillmore (Whig-American)	1856	21.5
Ross Perot	1992	18.9
John C. Breckinridge (Southern Democrat)	1860	18.1
Robert M. La Follette (Progressive)	1924	16.6
George C. Wallace (American Independent)	1968	13.5
John Bell (Constitutional Union)	1860	12.6
Martin Van Buren (Free Soil)	1848	10.1

First Lady Barbara Bush adopted a gentler theme, praising her husband and saying how pleased she was that he believed his greatest accomplishment was "that his children still come home."

The keynote address was delivered by Texas Sen. Phil Gramm, who used the opportunity to bash both Congress and Clinton. He was preceded by Housing and Urban Development Secretary Jack F. Kemp, who, like Gramm, was considered a potential contender for the Republican nomination in 1996. Kemp received a warm reception for his efforts, but the response to Gramm was tepid.

Nomination and Acceptance. The nomination speeches began Wednesday night, Aug. 19, when Labor Secretary Lynn Martin officially nominated Bush. After a series of seconding speeches, balloting was delayed until William J. Bennett, the former drug czar and secretary of education, nominated Quayle for the vice presidency.

The roll call itself was arranged so that Texas, the convention's host state and technically the president's home, put Bush over the top. The final tally was 2,166 votes for Bush, 18 for Buchanan and three for others, before the nomination was approved by acclamation. New Hampshire never cast its 23 votes.

The buildup for both acceptance speeches, delivered on the final night of the convention, had been intense. Quayle, who had survived attempts to dump him from the ticket during the weeks leading up to the convention, was widely perceived as being bumbling, gaffe-prone and ineffective. His acceptance speech was an opportunity to recast himself as a thoughtful, middle-class American fighting for family values. Bush had an even greater task — to give "the speech of his life."

Neither nominee quite lived up to the advance billing, but both delivered speeches that lifted the voices and spirits of the delegates and raised the ticket's standing in the public opinion polls.

Speaking first, Quayle launched an all-out assault on his detractors. "I know my critics wish I were not standing here tonight. They don't like our values. They look down on our beliefs. They're afraid of our ideas.... I say to them: You have failed. I stand — I stand before you, and before the American people — unbowed, unbroken and ready to keep fighting for our beliefs."

After a stirring introduction by Senate Minority Leader Bob Dole of Kansas, Bush came out fighting against Clinton and the Democratic-controlled Congress. The president offered no detailed vision for a second term but said he would propose an unspecified across-the-board tax reduction, provided Congress would cut spending in a manner he found acceptable. He also proposed allowing taxpayers to set aside 10 percent of their taxes to reduce the deficit but did not specify the spending cuts he would call for to make up the revenue.

Responding to delegates who were still angry about his broken pledge on taxes, Bush admitted that he had made a mistake and then posed a question to the electorate. "Who do you trust in this election — the candidate who has raised taxes one time, or the other candidate who raised taxes and fees 128 times and enjoyed it every time?"

Trust also was the issue as Bush highlighted his role as commander in chief in what was widely considered to be his strength — foreign policy. Noting that the "Soviet bear" might be gone but that there were "still wolves in the woods," Bush touted his stewardship of the Persian Gulf War and raised questions about what Clinton would have done. "What about the leader of the Arkansas National Guard," Bush mocked, "the man who hopes to be commander in chief? Well, while I bit the bullet ... he bit his nails."

The Fall Campaign

Bush continued to try to focus voter attention on Clinton's character throughout the fall. But Clinton began the final phase of the campaign as the front runner, and nothing Bush did ever dislodged the Democrat from that position. By the time of the presidential debates in mid-October, the political community had reached virtually unanimous agreement that without a major news development or a Clinton misstep Bush was likely to lose his bid for a second term.

The three presidential debates, all of which included Perot, who had re-entered the race on Oct. 1, were a box office smash. An estimated 81 million viewers watched the first debate, 90 million the second and 99 million the third.

Each debate was conducted under different rules, and the differences mattered. On Oct. 11, the three candidates stood behind lecterns at Washington University in St. Louis and fielded questions from a panel of journalists. The format was perfect for Perot to use his well-practiced one-liners and homilies to advantage. On the subject of experience, for example, he said: "They've got a point. I don't have experience running up a $4-trillion debt."

On Oct. 15, the candidates appeared on a stage at the University of Richmond with stools and a single moderator, who directed the debate but let the audience of 209 undecided voters ask most of the questions. This setting — suggestive of an afternoon TV talk show — put Clinton at ease. The Democrat ambled to the edge of the stage to speak directly to nearby members of the audience. In contrast, the president had some difficulty connecting with the questioners and seemed anxious for the debate to be over.

The third debate on Oct. 19 in East Lansing, Mich., was in two parts. In the first half, the candidates answered questions posed by a single moderator; in the second half, a panel of journalists asked the questions. Bush was widely acknowledged to have had the best 90 minutes of his campaign to date in that debate, but it was not enough to change voters' perceptions. Several post-debate polls found Bush in last place.

In the final weeks before election day, the Bush campaign seemed to spring to life. The president campaigned with nearly manic determination from network chat shows at dawn until rallies well past dark. A Gallup Poll conducted for *USA Today* and CNN found the gap between Clinton and Bush as small as 1 percentage point in the popular vote. That buoyed the president, even though most other national polls showed Clinton leading by 6 points or more.

The late stages of the campaign also were rife with personal attacks and negative advertising. Clinton referred to Bush's campaign tactics as "incredibly dishonest," while Bush on the stump said that "my dog Millie knows more about foreign affairs than those two bozos" — referring to Clinton and Gore. Bush also took to calling Gore "Mr. Ozone," "Ozone Man" or just "Ozone." He said Gore was an environmental extremist: "crazy, way out, far out, man."

Despite Bush's rise in the polls and the uncertainty raised by Perot's presence in the race, the outcome of the election was in little doubt. Clinton still appeared to be firmly in the lead as the fall campaign came to an end.

Changing the Electoral Equation

Clinton won on Nov. 3 in large part because he held the edge in swing groups that were key to victory. He won a plurality among independents — the first time they had broken for a Democrat since 1964 — according to Voter Research and Surveys (VRS), which did exit polling on election day for the television networks.

Clinton ran virtually even with Bush among white voters (again the best showing by a Democrat since 1964), while building large advantages among blacks and Hispanics. He also enjoyed a huge edge among those who viewed their family financial situation as getting worse, one-third of the electorate, according to the survey. That outweighed the hefty pro-Bush edge among those who felt their family's financial situation was improving, a group that made up one-fourth of the voters.

The gender gap appeared in the exit polling, although both sexes backed Clinton, women by 9 percentage points, men by 3 points. Clinton also ran better among the youngest and oldest of voters than he did among fellow baby boomers. He had a 10-point advantage among voters under 30, many in the "MTV generation" that Clinton and Gore had courted. The ticket had an even healthier lead (12 percentage points) among voters aged 60 and over, many of whom had begun voting for the Democrats during the New Deal years and had remained loyal to the Democrats ever since. Clinton carried voters between 30 and 59, but his edge among them was in the low single digits.

Feelings of economic anxiety helped Clinton reclaim nine states that voted Democratic for president for the first time since 1964. The prize among these was California, with 54 electoral votes, the most of any in the country. The economy there was at a half-century low, and the Bush forces conceded the state to the Democrats early in the campaign. The other states were New Hampshire and Vermont in upper New England; New Jersey and Illinois in the industrial Frost Belt; and Colorado, Montana, Nevada and New Mexico in the Rockies.

Clinton swept the East and carried the Midwest, except for Quayle's home state of Indiana and the traditional Republican Plains states of Kansas, Nebraska, and North and South Dakota. Even more surprising, Clinton won the West, except for Alaska and the Republican states of Arizona, Idaho, Utah and Wyoming.

That reduced Bush's base essentially to the South, where he won more than two-thirds of his electoral votes. Even there Clinton was able to pick off five states — Arkansas, Georgia, Kentucky, Louisiana and Tennessee. And he seriously reduced Bush's margins in Florida, North Carolina and Texas. *(Vote by region, box, p. 23)*

Republicans had succeeded in winning five of the previous six presidential elections by conceding the cities to the Democrats but winning the suburbs and rural areas. In 1992, however, the Democrats made deep inroads into the suburban vote. Altogether there are 28 predominantly suburban counties across the country, each with a population of at least 500,000. In 1988, Democratic contender Michael Dukakis carried only six of them; in 1992, Clinton carried at least three times that many.

Turnout and Perot

Conventional wisdom had held that higher turnout would benefit the Democrats, because the additional voters likely would be change-oriented and therefore more supportive of Clinton or Perot than of Bush. That seemed to have happened. Turnout was up to 104.4 million, the first time an American election had exceeded 100 million votes. The bump up from the 1988 figure of 91.6 million voters was the largest increase in turnout in 40 years. First-time voters, according to the VRS, cast 11 percent of the ballots and went heavily Democratic, with 48 percent backing Clinton, 30 percent Bush and 22 percent Perot. But the big turnout probably benefited Perot more than Clinton. The VRS found that about 15 percent of Perot's

Presidential Vote by Region

Bill Clinton swept all of the states in the East (plus the District of Columbia), most of those in the Midwest and West, and enough of those in the South to keep President Bush from being competitive in the electoral vote. The popular vote percentages for 1992 were based on nearly complete but unofficial returns. Candidate percentages for the West do not total 100 because of rounding.

	1992					1988			
	Popular Vote			Electoral Vote		Popular Vote		Electoral Vote	
Region	*Clinton*	*Bush*	*Perot*	*Clinton*	*Bush*	*Bush*	*Dukakis*	*Bush*	*Dukakis*
East	47%	35%	18%	127	0	50%	49%	73	61
Midwest	42	37	21	100	29	52	47	108	29
South	41	43	16	47	116	58	41	155	0
West	43	34	22	96	23	52	46	90	21
National	43	38	19	370	168	54	46	426	111

Note: Total electoral votes do not add to 538 because one West Virginia elector voted for Bentsen for president and Dukakis for vice president.

voters would have stayed home if Perot had not been on the ballot.

With 19.7 million votes, Perot showed impressive strength across the nation. He fell below 10 percent of the vote only in Mississippi and the District of Colombia, and he won at least 20 percent of the vote in 30 states. Perot even finished second ahead of Clinton in Utah and second ahead of Bush in Maine. Perot's weakest region was the South, in part because he won only 7 percent of the black vote — compared with 11 percent for Bush and 82 percent for Clinton, according to the VRS — and only 15 percent of the white fundamentalist Christian vote, both major constituencies in the South. Perot ran best among self-described independents, men under 30 and voters who viewed their family's financial situation as getting worse. But he still was unable to carry a single state and thus was shut out in the electoral vote.

In the three-way race for the presidency, Clinton failed to win a majority of the popular vote, which some Republicans said meant that he did not get a mandate for governing. Clinton's vote percentage was the fourth-lowest of anyone elected president. Yet two of those who won with a lower percentage than Clinton were Abraham Lincoln and Woodrow Wilson, regarded as among the strongest chief executives in the nation's history.

In the end, the most remarkable fact of the election may have been that Bush, whose approval ratings set records in 1991, plummeted to the second-worst finish of any incumbent president who sought re-election. Only William Howard Taft, in 1912, did worse, with 23 percent of the vote. Like Taft, Bush was beset by a reinvigorated Democratic Party on one hand and by a tenacious, charismatic third candidate on the other.

The key question, and one that was impossible to answer, was whether the 1992 election was the start of a new Democratic era in presidential politics as 1968 was for the Republicans, or an aberration, much as Jimmy Carter's victory in 1976 proved to be. With the leadership of both the White House and Congress in their hands, Democrats controlled their destiny.

Senate Elections

The 1992 elections ushered in the most diverse freshman class in Senate history, including record numbers of women and minorities. An institution viewed as an exclusive enclave of white males was made more representative of the country. When the new Senate convened in January 1993, the six women among its 100 members included the first black woman senator, Carol Mosely-Braun of Illinois, and the first pair of women to represent a state, Dianne Feinstein and Barbara Boxer of California. It also included the first American Indian to sit in the Senate in more than 60 years, Ben Nighthorse Campbell of Colorado.

But for all the drama of the historic elections, the Senate as a whole barely shifted in terms of partisanship or ideology. And for all the talk of a seething, anti-incumbent electorate, voters ousted only four of the 26 incumbents on the ballot. Republicans Bob Kasten of Wisconsin and John Seymour of California and Democrat Terry Sanford of North Carolina lost on Nov. 3. A fourth incumbent, Democrat Wyche Fowler Jr. of Georgia, lost a Nov. 24 runoff to Republican challenger Paul Coverdell. A victory by Democrat Kent Conrad in the Dec. 4 special election in North Dakota gave Democrats a 57-43 edge in the 103rd Congress — the same as in the 102nd.

Democrats had hoped to capture a 60-seat majority that could thwart GOP-led filibusters. They fell short of that goal, despite capturing the White House. But with 21 seats to defend against 15 for the Republicans, the Democrats faced longer odds than the GOP going into the campaign season. The Democrats' cause was helped when some of the party's most vulnerable incumbents either retired or lost in primary elections. Others heeded the warning signs and ran aggressive campaigns.

The Republicans also had their share of tenacious, well-funded incumbents who went on the offensive early and never let up. Most notable were four who were initially considered ripe for defeat — Arlen Specter of Pennsylvania, Bob Packwood of Oregon, Frank H. Murkowski of Alaska and Alfonse M. D'Amato of New York.

Clinton's victory appeared to have had a minimal effect on Senate races. His commanding lead in California contributed to Boxer's win in that state. But Clinton's stunning vote tally in rock-ribbed Republican New Hampshire did not pull along Democrats vying for the Senate and governor's seats.

Women's Surge

In an election season dubbed the "Year of the Woman," five of the 11 women nominated (included one incumbent, Democrat Barbara A. Mikulski of Maryland) won Senate races. The October 1991 confirmation hearings of Clarence Thomas to be an associate justice of the Supreme Court provided the initial impetus for the unprecedented gains by women Senate candidates. For many women and some male viewers, the televised image of an all-white, all-male Senate Judiciary panel grilling Professor Anita F. Hill about her harassment charges against Thomas was "the picture worth a thousand words," said Ruth Mandel, director of the Center for the American Woman and Politics at Rutgers University.

Many of the female candidates argued that they would be more sensitive than their male opponents to women's issues. Many of them also had the appeal of being candidates who were outside the normal scope of power in Washington. But like their male counterparts, female challengers learned that the experience, money and name recognition associated with incumbency remain enormous hurdles. The six women who ran against incumbents all lost.

Three of the four women challengers who won were veteran politicians. Feinstein had been the mayor of San Francisco; Boxer was a sitting member of the House; and Mosely-Braun was the Cook County recorder of deeds and had been a state legislator. Only Washington Democrat Patty Murray had not held public office, but she had been active in a score of Democratic causes.

Throughout 1992, much talk was heard about the presumed appeal of "outsider" credentials. The notion generally had less currency in Senate races than in House contests, perhaps in part because House members were tainted by scandals at the House bank and Post Office.

The more successful outsider candidates were those who had considerable political experience. Russell D. Feingold, a Democrat who spent 10 years in the Wisconsin Senate, projected an outsider image in his successful bid to unseat Kasten. And despite Campbell's years as a member of Colorado's House delegation, voters had a hard time seeing the pony-tailed member of the Northern Cheyenne Council of 44 Chiefs as a Washington insider.

The Southern Flank

Much of the Democrat's Southern flank in the Senate seemed exposed and potentially vulnerable going into 1992. Democrats defended seats in eight Southern and border states. Five of these incumbents were freshmen seeking their first re-election, and several had barely won in 1986.

Voter disenchantment with the national Democratic Party and with votes against the Persian Gulf War seemed especially problematic for the Southern Democrats. But both issues were mitigated as the Democrats nominated a moderate Southerner for president and as concern over the wobbly economy eclipsed concern over the war vote.

In the end, five of the Southern Democrats were never seriously threatened. Bob Graham of Florida, Richard C. Shelby of Alabama, Wendell H. Ford of Kentucky and Dale Bumpers of Arkansas each won with at least 60 percent of the vote. John B. Breaux of Louisiana was re-elected with 73 percent of the votes in that state's all-party primary on Oct. 3.

Sen. Ernest F. Hollings of South Carolina won only 56 percent of the vote, his smallest percentage since first being elected to the Senate in 1966. His North Carolina colleague Terry Sanford was not so lucky. He lost to businessman Lauch Fairchild, a Democrat turned Republican and a former close friend. Democrat Fowler of Georgia also was seen as vulnerable because of his slim margin of victory in 1986 and a voting record that was more liberal than that of a typical Southern senator. Fowler ran a percentage point ahead of challenger Coverdell on Nov. 3 but did not win a majority of the vote, which forced a runoff election on Nov. 24. Coverdell edged Fowler with 51 percent in light turnout to win the seat.

Unsinkable Incumbents

Some incumbents won re-election despite earlier indications that their political futures were in doubt. Several of them had to overcome charges of unethical behavior. Two senators won re-election despite their involvement in the Keating Five savings and loan scandal. Republican John McCain of Arizona was never seriously pressed by his opponents. Democrat John Glenn of Ohio encountered more trouble. The Senate Ethics Committee in 1991 found that Glenn, like McCain, had done nothing improper or illegal. But the investigation took some of the luster off Glenn's heroic image as a former astronaut. Glenn managed to maintain a slim lead, however, winning with 55 percent of the vote.

Clinton Firsts

- Bill Clinton was the first Democrat to be elected president without carrying Texas since Texas joined the Union in 1845.
- Clinton was the first candidate of either party since 1952 to be elected without having won the New Hampshire primary.
- Clinton was the first president from the "baby boom" generation, born after World War II.
- Clinton was the first president since Franklin D. Roosevelt who had not served in military uniform.
- Clinton/Gore was the first successful all-Southern ticket since 1828.

The Perot Factor

The wild card of the 1992 presidential election campaign was Texas billionaire Ross Perot, whose on-again, off-again independent candidacy often overshadowed the campaigns of President Bush and Arkansas Gov. Bill Clinton. Perot campaigned on the premise that politicians in the major parties lacked the will to address the pressing issues facing the nation, particularly the budget deficit. If the voters wanted to get down to business, then they should vote for Perot, he often said. But if all they wanted was talk and slow dancing, then they should vote for Bush or Clinton.

Perot's plain talk and call for change struck a chord among many of the nation's voters. For example, more than one-fourth of the Democratic primary voters in New Jersey, nearly one-third in California and nearly one-half in Ohio told exit pollsters June 2 that they preferred Perot to Clinton. And one-third of the Republican primary voters in New Jersey and Ohio and close to half in California indicated a preference for Perot over Bush.

Many of these voters joined Perot's volunteer effort to gather enough signatures to put the Texas businessman on the ballot in all 50 states and the District of Columbia. That drive gained momentum early in June when Perot signed on Democrat Hamilton Jordan and Republican Edward J. Rollins as strategists for his undeclared presidential campaign. Jordan managed Jimmy Carter's presidential runs in 1976 and 1980. Rollins directed President Ronald Reagan's 1984 re-election campaign.

Polls were showing Perot's percentage in the mid-30s in a three-way vote, and pundits began to speculate that none of the three candidates would win a clear majority and that the election would be thrown into the House of Representatives for the first time since 1825, when John Quincy Adams was elected.

Out, Then In Again

By early July, Perot's position had eroded as scrutiny of his career and personality intensified. By mid-July, he was running third, with less than 20 percent in a three-way race. On July 16, just hours before Bill Clinton delivered his acceptance speech to the Democratic convention, Perot announced that he was withdrawing from the race.

Although many of those who had worked to put Perot's name on the ballot in their particular state felt betrayed by his abrupt withdrawal, many others continued the effort. And although he did not actively campaign, Perot continued to bankroll the operation. The volunteer organization, known as United We Stand, America, had more than 60 offices around the country, and each received $7,500 a month from Perot. By Sept 18, when the final petition was filed in Arizona, Perot had spent an estimated $18 million getting his name on state ballots.

Two months after Perot withdrew from the race, national polls continued to show a substantial number of voters still supporting a Perot candidacy. Finally, on Oct. 1, Perot announced that he would indeed run for president. That qualified him to participate in the three presidential debates. Polls taken after each of the debates were mixed, but many showed significant gains for Perot. At a minimum, the debates restored the legitimacy he had lost after dropping out in July.

Perot's Campaign

Other than the debates and some talk-show programs, Perot made no campaign appearances. Instead, he aired a series of slightly quirky, remarkably simple "infomercials," which aired for 30 minutes each in network prime time and were watched by millions.

In these programs, Perot analyzed the federal budget deficit and national debt, and he proposed spending cuts and tax increases to address them. Visually, the programs consisted of Perot sitting at a table, holding up a succession of pie charts and other graphics and stabbing at them with a lecturer's pointer. The script was vintage Perot: "If you don't like [the 50-cents-a-gallon gas tax increase] then come up with something else, but it's got to raise $150 billion," he would say.

A week before the election, Perot's ability to withstand the pressures of a presidential campaign again came into question when he said on a nationally televised news program that he had suspended his presidential efforts in July to keep Republican operatives from disrupting the August wedding of his youngest daughter. Perot admitted from the outset that he had no hard evidence of such a plot. And the following day he said he would honor the denials from Bush's camp.

At the same time, he reacted angrily to suggestions that his charges had been ill-founded or disingenuous. In behavior reminiscent of that which preceded his withdrawal from the race in July, Perot told reporters at his Dallas headquarters that "I am sick and tired of you all questioning my integrity without any basis for it. I don't have to prove anything to you people."

In the wake of the incident, most polls showed that Perot's momentum had stalled or that he had fallen in the polls. Still, on election day, he won 19 percent of the popular vote, the most for any independent candidate since 1912. And by most accounts, his presence in the race forced the two major political party candidates to address issues they would just have soon ignored. *(Independent, third-party candidates, box, p. 21)*

Three Republican incumbents thought to be vulnerable also managed to hold on to their seats. D'Amato of New York, Packwood of Oregon and Murkowski of Alaska turned back challenges from Democrats who had trouble overcoming brutal primary fights. Specter of Pennsylvania had initially been considered vulnerable because of his role as Hill's chief interrogator during the Thomas hearings. But his opponent, Lynn Yeakel, who had staged a stunning win in the Democratic primary, proved to be no match in the fall campaign.

Party Prevails

Although Democrats mounted credible challenges to three open seats in Utah, New Hampshire and Idaho, the GOP relied on a rich tradition of party domination in those states to win all of them. In the remaining races, the incumbents faced little threat and handily won re-election. These included Republicans Don Nickles of Oklahoma, Daniel R. Coats of Indiana, Charles E. Grassley of Iowa and Bob Dole of Kansas. The Democrats included Christopher J. Dodd of Connecticut, Harry Reid of Nevada, Patrick J. Leahy of Vermont, Tom Daschle of South Dakota and Daniel K. Inouye of Hawaii.

In North Dakota, politicians played a game of musical chairs. Democratic Rep. Byron L. Dorgan was elected to the seat left vacant by Democrat Conrad, who had announced his retirement from the Senate after a single term. After Sen. Quentin N. Burdick, D, died, however, Conrad decided to run for election to fill the remaining two years of Burdick's term. Conrad won that special election Dec. 4, succeeding Burdick's widow, who had been appointed to the Senate seat in the interim.

House Elections

A weak economy, overdrafted checks, "outsider" candidates and twisted new district lines were the factors setting the tone for the 1992 House election campaigns. Voter discontent and redistricting did take a toll on members who sought re-election, but the much-discussed possibility of an election day cyclone of anti-incumbent sentiment failed to materialize. Only 24 incumbents were defeated. Several dozen other incumbents had either retired or been defeated in primary elections, so 110 newcomers — a fourth of the House membership — would sit in the 103rd Congress.

Republicans, who began the campaign cycle with high hopes for substantially eroding the Democratic majority in the House, had to settle for a very modest 10-seat gain. The partisan lineup for the 103rd Congress was 258 Democrats, 176 Republicans and one independent.

If the partisan makeup of the House changed only slightly, the demography of the chamber changed dramatically. A record number of women, African-Americans and Hispanics were elected, making the House more representative of the ethnic diversity of the country itself.

Drag at the Top

Only once before, in 1892, had one party gained House seats while the other party captured the White House. That year President Benjamin Harrison lost to Democrat Grover Cleveland, while Harrison's GOP registered big gains in the House.

The GOP gains in 1992 were small comfort to a party that a year earlier had expected a solid presidential victory and a significant number of House pickups. With post-census reapportionment moving House seats from Democratic regions to the more Republican Sun Belt, and with a ticket topped by President Bush, buoyed in public opinion polls by the Persian Gulf War, the GOP seemed poised to challenge the Democrats' 38-year control of the House.

Instead, a sour economy and Bush's evaporated popularity turned into minuses for GOP candidates at lower levels of the ticket. According to one GOP analyst, Republican House candidates outpolled Bush by more than 3 million votes. That was the first time since 1964 that Republicans lower down on the ticket fared better than their party's presidential candidate. Nonetheless, many Republican House candidates, especially those competing for the 91 seats for which no incumbent was running, were unable to overcome the drag at the top of the ticket.

Scandals, Maps and Upsets

By far the most common symptom afflicting the 24 incumbents who lost Nov. 3 was unfavorable publicity over ethically questionable behavior. Eight members with sizable numbers of overdrawn checks at the House bank lost. Two of those eight — Democrats Joseph D. Early of Massachusetts and Mary Rose Oakar of Ohio — were cited by the House Committee on Standards of Official Conduct (ethics committee) for having abused their privileges at the bank. Overdrafts also contributed to the downfall of Democrats Jerry Huckaby of Louisiana, Gerry Sikorski of Minnesota, Thomas J. Downey of New York, Peter H. Kostmayer of Pennsylvania and Albert G. Bustamante of Texas, as well as Ohio Republican Bob McEwen.

After scandal, redistricting was the leading cause of incumbent defeat. Democrats Dave Nagle of Iowa and Tom McMillen of Maryland and Republicans Clyde C. Holloway of Louisiana and Ron Marlenee of Montana lost after redistricting matched them against another incumbent. Huckaby also was pitted against a sitting member.

In addition, Alabama Democrat Ben Erdreich and Georgia Democrat Richard Ray lost in districts that were redrawn to be considerably more Republican. Missouri Democrat Joan Kelly Horn, a winner by 54 votes in 1990, was given a less Democratic district in which to run; she lost to a well-organized GOP opponent.

The most surprising Democratic defeats were those of third-term Reps. Jim Jontz of Indiana and Liz J. Patterson of South Carolina. Although both occupied GOP-dominated districts, they had won re-election in 1988 despite a big Bush presidential vote. This time, with Bush losing the White House, they were ousted by underdog Republican challengers.

A weak primary performance foreshadowed a loss in the general election by Rep. John J. Rhodes III, R-Ariz.

A Boost from Clinton

For the first time since 1976, Democratic House candidates — challengers and incumbents alike — enjoyed a luxury long afforded to GOP candidates in presidential election years: The top of the ticket helped boost their vote. That was particularly noticeable in open-seat contests. But Clinton coattails also helped Democratic challengers oust four of the eight Republican incumbents who lost: Frank Riggs of California, Tom Coleman of Missouri, Bill Green of New York and Don Ritter of Pennsylvania.

Clinton's candidacy was a special blessing for many Southern Democratic incumbents who in recent presidential-election years saw hordes of voters shun their party's White House nominees. In North Carolina, for instance, Clinton helped Democrats re-elect their four most vulnerable incumbents — Stephen L. Neal, H. Martin Lancaster, Tim Valentine and W. G. "Bill" Hefner. All four of those white incumbents had been weakened by redistricting, which transferred loyally Democratic black voters from their districts into one of the two new majority-black districts.

Anti-Incumbency Sentiment

Although the much heralded anti-incumbent sentiment failed to translate into massive losses at the polls, several congressional leaders were singed. The Democratic House leadership was especially chastened. Speaker Thomas S. Foley of Washington, Democratic Congressional Campaign Committee Chairman Vic Fazio of California, Majority Whip David E. Bonior of Michigan and House Democratic Caucus Chairman Steny H. Hoyer of Maryland all were held to 55 percent or less. Ways and Means Committee Chairman Dan Rostenkowski, D-Ill., Minority Leader Robert H. Michel, R-Ill., and Minority Whip Newt Gingrich, R-Ga., won less than 60 percent of the vote in their races.

Other incumbents won largely because anti-incumbent sentiment split among contenders. In Connecticut's 3rd District, the third-party candidacy of Democratic primary loser Lynn Taborsak boosted the re-election bid of freshman Gary Franks, the House's only black Republican. Besieged by personal financial difficulties and staff turnover, Franks survived as Taborsak, running on Gov. Lowell P. Weicker Jr.'s A Connecticut Party line, split the anti-Franks vote with Democratic nominee James Lawlor.

Despite all the hoopla that 1992 would be the year of the outsider, only 31 of the 110 new House members had never held elective office, and several of those had worked in government or party politics.

A More Representative House

Record numbers of women, blacks, Hispanics and other ethnic groups were elected to the House. The new House would include 48 women — 24 of the 27 women who sought re-election and 24 newcomers.

Altogether, women would represent 27 states and the District of Columbia in the 103rd Congress, up from 19 plus the District in the 102nd. The largest contingent came from California, with seven female House members; Florida and New York each elected five women. Despite their record gains, women still made up only about 10 percent of Congress, even though they accounted for more than half the U.S. population.

Sixteen African-Americans were elected to the House for the first time, bringing the total number of blacks in the House to 38. Most of the districts represented by the freshmen were as new as their representatives. Thirteen of the 16 new black members were from predominantly black districts created in 1992 through reapportionment. (The other three replaced retiring or defeated black incumbents from urban districts.)

Age Structure of Congress

(Average ages at start of first session)

Year	House	Senate	Congress
1949	51.0	58.5	53.8
1951	52.0	56.6	53.0
1953	52.0	56.6	53.0
1955	51.4	57.2	52.2
1957	52.9	57.9	53.8
1959	51.7	57.1	52.7
1961	52.2	57.0	53.2
1963	51.7	56.8	52.7
1965	50.5	57.7	51.9
1967	50.8	57.7	52.1
1969	52.2	56.6	53.0
1971	51.9	56.4	52.7
1973	51.1	55.3	52.0
1975	49.8	55.5	50.9
1977	49.3	54.7	50.3
1979	49.8	55.5	50.9
1981	48.4	52.5	49.2
1983	45.5	53.4	47.0
1985	49.7	54.2	50.5
1987	50.7	54.4	52.5
1989	52.1	55.6	52.8
1991	52.8	57.2	53.6
1993	51.7	58.0	52.9

All of the 13 seats created through reapportionment were in a triangle stretching from the Washington, D.C., suburbs to Miami and Dallas. For the first time since the Reconstruction era, a black was among the House delegations from Alabama, Florida, North Carolina, South Carolina and Virginia.

The term "freshman" belied the political experience of the newcomers. All but one of the 16 had previously held public office. About two-thirds of the 25 sitting black members had entered Congress with comparable experience.

Nine new faces boosted Hispanic representation to 19 (including delegates from the U.S. Virgin Islands and Puerto Rico whose voting privileges were limited), the largest Hispanic delegation ever.

Most of the Hispanic freshmen came with strong credentials. Democrat Robert Menendez was a former mayor of Union City, N.J., and a former state senator. Two Los Angeles-area Democrats, Xavier Becerra and Lucille Roybal-Allard, served in the California State Assembly. GOP freshman Lincoln Diaz-Balart was a Florida state senator from Miami.

Previously, most of the Hispanics in Congress were Mexican-American Democrats from the urban areas of the Southwest and Southern California. Although the urban emphasis remained, the Class of 1992 included Cubans, Puerto Ricans and Hispanic Republicans. Several, including Democrats Menendez and Luis V. Gutierrez of Illinois, were the first Hispanics to represent their states.

State Elections

Anti-incumbency and "Year of the Woman" themes may have worked well in some Senate and House elections, but they had little effect in the 12 gubernatorial races in 1992. Voters seemed more concerned about economics and ethics issues. The four incumbent governors running for re-election — all Democrats — were returned to office. And a former Democratic governor won back his job after an eight-year absence. The three women running for governor in Montana, New Hampshire and Rhode Island all lost. Women held the governorships in Kansas, Oregon and Texas.

Altogether, Democrats won three seats formerly held by Republicans, while the GOP picked up one seat held by a Democrat, for a net gain of two seats for the Democrats. That gave the Democrats a total of 30 governorships; the Republicans held 18. Two governors were independents.

Republicans made some inroads in the nation's statehouses on Nov. 3, but the Democrats still held a sizable majority. Before the election, Democrats controlled 70 legislative chambers, Republicans 25. Three chambers were tied, and Nebraska's legislature was unicameral and nominally non-partisan. Republican gains put the GOP in control of 30 of the nation's 99 legislative chambers in January 1993, a net gain of five. Democrats controlled both houses in 25 states, and Republicans controlled both in eight. In 16 states, the chambers were split between the two parties, and three chambers remained tied.

Voters in 14 states in 1992 also approved limits on the number of terms their representatives and senators in Congress could serve. *(Term limits, box, p. 10)*

2

Economic Policy

Introduction	*31*
The Federal Budget	*37*
Tax Policy	*87*
Financial Regulation	*113*

Economic Policy

When President Ronald Reagan turned over the White House keys to George Bush in January 1989, neither likely was aware that Reagan also had handed off a most shaky economy to the man who had been his vice president.

President Bush assumed his predecessor's economic mantle of low taxes, limited government and reduced regulation. And though Bush's role in setting economic policy during the Reagan administration's eight years was not always central, the claim to Reagan's formula for success was undoubtedly of benefit to Bush's successful 1988 presidential campaign. But that inheritance also became a political liability when the economy faltered two years later and slipped into a modest, nine-month recession.

The downturn in economic activity — and the weak recovery that followed — led to an effort by Bush and some members of Congress to find a legislative means to spark sustained growth. What they found, however, was little consensus that government fiscal policy could be changed to provide needed stimulus without exacerbating other problems that had plagued the economy in the recent past — chiefly the budget deficit. Ultimately, Congress and the president failed to agree on any course of action.

That may have been unintentional, but it was a result advocated by most economists, who argued for allowing the economy to right itself. The difficulty for the politicians was the risk that they would suffer at the polls for the economy's having continued to move in a cycle of business expansion and contraction. And to the extent that there were political consequences for the recession, they devolved onto the president.

Bush succumbed in his re-election bid — as did others before him — when voters blamed him for economic problems that were largely beyond his control. Other factors certainly contributed to his defeat, not least among them that Bush had alienated conservatives when he broke his "no new taxes" pledge in 1990 in an effort to strike a deficit-reduction deal with congressional Democrats. But no political party had retained control of the White House since World War II when the unemployment rate rose significantly during an election year.

Incumbent Republican Vice President Richard Nixon lost his presidential bid to Democrat John F. Kennedy in 1960 under those circumstances; likewise did Democratic President Jimmy Carter lose to challenger Reagan in 1980. The unemployment rate climbed steadily for the first six months of 1992 — though it declined somewhat as the election drew nigh — and Bush lost to Democrat Bill Clinton.

Reagan had left an impressive legacy: an unprecedented 74 months of peacetime economic expansion. The period of growth had not yet stalled when Reagan left the White House and would eventually hit 91 months, a record for the United States surpassed only by 106 months of expansion during 1961-69, a time that included the height of the Vietnam War. During the Reagan expansion, the gross domestic product grew an average of 3.9 percent a year — after the effects of inflation were factored out. That level of growth was far from exceptional for the post-World War II era, but it did lead to a strong sense of public optimism. (In 1991, gross domestic product, or GDP, replaced gross national product, or GNP, as the government's basic measure of economic activity. The Commerce Department retroactively recomputed GDP figures to enable historical comparisons.) *(GDP vs. GNP, box, p. 36)*

The 5.3 percent unemployment rate and 4.2 percent inflation rate recorded at the end of Reagan's second term were, he and his advisers said, the direct, positive results of the administration's fiscal policies. The deep 1981-82 recession that also occurred on his watch was forgotten.

Moreover, the days of $200 billion budget deficits appeared to be in the past, even though the federal debt had almost tripled while Reagan was in office and short-term interest rates were higher when Reagan sent his last budget proposal to Congress than at any time since 1984.

In his last budget, issued in January 1989, Reagan projected that the deficit for fiscal 1990 would fall below 2 percent of the gross national product for the first time since 1979. And under the last Reagan administration forecast, the economy was expected to continue to grow, unemployment and inflation rates to fall, and interest rates to drop substantially. The federal budget was expected to be balanced by 1993.

No forecast could have been more wrong.

References

Discussion of economic policy for the years 1945-64 may be found in *Congress and the Nation Vol. I*, pp. 337-458; for the years 1965-68, *Congress and the Nation Vol. II*, pp. 119-182, 253-305; for the years 1969-72, *Congress and the Nation Vol. III*, pp. 53-145; for the years 1973-76, *Congress and the Nation Vol. IV*, pp. 49-149; for the years 1977-80, *Congress and the Nation Vol. V*, pp. 205-287; for the years 1981-84, *Congress and the Nation Vol. VI*, pp. 27-120; for the years 1985-88, *Congress and the Nation Vol. VII*, pp. 27-136.

Economic Team Served Four Years ...

President Bush enjoyed a luxury granted few presidents: The four-person economic team that he assembled at the start of his administration stayed intact through the four years he occupied the White House.

Despite evident disagreements from time to time over what was the proper policy choice, the president's four key economic policymakers presented a united public front and their longevity permitted a rare degree of policy continuity.

Also, when given the opportunity to blame Federal Reserve Board Chairman Alan Greenspan for a recession that hit the United States in mid-1990, Bush chose instead to give Greenspan a strong endorsement and an early reappointment for a second four-year term in charge of the nation's monetary policy.

Three of Bush's four top economic officials — Treasury Secretary Nicholas F. Brady, Office of Management and Budget (OMB) Director Richard G. Darman and U.S. Trade Representative Carla A. Hills — had previously served Republican presidents.

Brady, a longtime Bush friend, was a holdover as the last Treasury secretary of the Reagan administration. He had been tapped by President Ronald Reagan when James A. Baker III resigned the Treasury post to run Bush's election campaign. Brady had been was confirmed 92-2 on Sept. 14, 1988; he did not need to be reconfirmed after Bush assumed office. Brady had spent eight months in 1982 as an appointed Republican senator from New Jersey.

Darman had held a variety of government positions, including that of deputy Treasury secretary under Baker in 1985-87. Hills, an attorney in Washington, D.C., was secretary of housing and urban development in the Ford administration. Only Stanford economics professor Michael J. Boskin, who became chairman of the president's Council of Economic Advisers, held no prior positions in government.

Darman first won unanimous support from the Senate Governmental Affairs Committee. Appearing before the committee on Jan. 19, 1989, he stuck firmly to Bush's campaign pledge of "Read my lips; no new taxes." Darman essentially ruled out any administration effort to reduce the deficit by increasing revenues. In what would become a familiar adage on Capitol Hill, he told the committee that he would apply the "duck test" to proposed revenue-raisers that might be deemed to be tax increases: "If it looks like a duck, walks like a duck and quacks like a duck, then it's a duck."

The Senate confirmed Darman on Jan. 25 by a vote of 99-0.

After a swift confirmation hearing on Jan. 27, the Senate Finance Committee voted 19-0 to approve Hills' nomination as the chief U.S. negotiator on trade and lead guardian against unfair and disruptive foreign trade practices. The hearing focused almost exclusively on trade matters. Hills pledged routine consultations with Congress and tough negotiations with trade partners. She vowed to open foreign markets "with a crowbar or a handshake."

The Senate voted 100-0 on Jan. 31 to confirm her nomination.

On Feb. 2, the Senate voted 100-0 to confirm Boskin to head the Council of Economic Advisers.

Greenspan Wins Second Term

Upon becoming chairman of the Fed in August 1987, Greenspan began immediately to make a name for himself as a staunch inflation-fighter, protesting Reagan administration pleas to cut interest rates and

End of the Reagan Expansion

By many measures, January 1989 was the turning point for an economy that was destined for a correction that became the 1990-91 recession.

Economic growth began to slide in the first quarter of 1989 and, though it recovered slightly in early 1990, the economy was plainly headed for a contraction. At the outset of the Bush administration, unemployment reached its low point following the 1981-82 recession, before starting a significant upturn in mid-1990 that continued through the end of Bush's term. Inflation jumped in 1990, though it subsided during the recession. And interest rates — instead of falling — stayed relatively flat until pressure from the economic slowdown forced them onto a steep downward path at the end of 1990. *(Charts, p. 35)*

Most telling for the voters who would judge the overall economic performance of the Bush presidency, personal income essentially stopped growing and at the end of 1992 was at the same level as the day Bush took office.

Other clouds darkened the economic sky.

Reagan's projection of declining deficits turned out to be wrong for three fundamental reasons. The deficit forecast failed to anticipate the effects of a recession that was less than 18 months out on the horizon. It failed to anticipate the cost of cleaning up the detritus left by a thousand failed savings and loan associations and hundreds of failed banks. And it suffered from a general case of over-optimistic expectations. Instead of declining, the deficit attained its four highest levels in history in fiscal 1990-93.

The savings and loan debacle, and an attendant emergency in the banking industry, amounted to a financial crisis that threatened to rival that of the Great Depression. The Bush administration was left to manage the crisis and mitigate its damage, but its magnitude had been exacerbated by the Reagan administration's inattention.

... With Inflation-Fighter Greenspan

leading the charge to tighten the money supply when it appeared to him that inflation might be resurgent.

Throughout his tenure, Greenspan signaled no shift in his basic view that the Fed must work to keep inflation in check and that long-term economic growth was at least as dependent on prices remaining stable as it was on easy credit. Maintaining a balance between the two had been Greenspan's stated concern from the moment the economy started slowing in 1989, and it caused Brady and other critics within the Bush administration to complain that Greenspan's Fed was too reluctant to cut interest rates to stimulate growth.

The Fed under Greenspan seemed more likely to adjust interest rates downward in response to market pressure than to try to lead the market. So, as Greenspan's term as chairman was coming to an end in August 1991, speculation abounded that he would be sacrificed to divert blame for the continuing recession away from Bush administration policies.

On July 10, days before Bush was to leave for an annual economic summit with the leaders of the six other major industrialized nations, he announced that he would reappoint Greenspan for another four-year term as chairman and for a full, 14-year term on the Fed board, beginning Jan. 31, 1992. Bush said that Greenspan's future had never been in doubt, and the reappointment was viewed as a public show of confidence in the Fed's anti-inflationary stance. "The respect that Alan Greenspan has around the world and in this country, particularly in the financial marketplaces is unparalleled," Bush said.

The Senate Banking Committee was preoccupied at the end of 1991 with a major overhaul of banking laws, and neither the committee nor the full Senate acted on Greenspan's renomination before the end of the year. Having previously been confirmed, he continued to serve.

On Feb. 20, 1992, the committee approved Greenspan's renomination on a 20-1 vote, with Alfonse M. D'Amato, R-N.Y., a vigorous critic of the Fed's tight money policies, casting the lone dissent. The Senate confirmed Greenspan on a voice vote Feb. 27.

In the course of his presidency, Bush was able to name five of the seven members of the Fed board, counting reappointments of both Greenspan and board member Edward W. Kelley Jr., who was confirmed for a full 14-year term in April 1990. Reagan had managed to appoint all seven board members, but it was rare for a president to have that opportunity.

Bush appointments to the Fed included:

- David W. Mullins Jr., confirmed in May 1990 for an unexpired term through Jan. 31, 1996. He was then confirmed in July 1991 for a four-year term as vice chairman. Mullins had been a Harvard finance professor before helping shepherd the savings and loan bailout bill through Congress in 1989 as assistant Treasury secretary for domestic finance.
- Lawrence B. Lindsey, confirmed in November 1991 for an unexpired term through Jan. 31, 2000. A Harvard economics professor before coming to work in the Bush White House, Lindsey was an ardent advocate of supply-side theory, which stressed tax cuts to stimulate economic growth and tended to disregard the effects of budget deficits.
- Susan Meredith Phillips, confirmed in November 1991 for an unexpired term through Jan. 31, 1998. Vice president for finance at the University of Iowa at the time of her appointment, Phillips previously served as chairman of the Commodity Futures Trading Commission.

About the only bright spot on the economic front was a substantial improvement in the nation's trade deficit. Thanks to the dollar's steadily declining value when measured against other currencies, exports surged as foreign buyers were enticed by their ability to buy more goods with the same number of yen or deutsche marks. The same phenomenon put the brakes on the growth of imports, as for a time did declining oil prices and the contracting economy.

The merchandise trade deficit fell in 1991 to its lowest level since 1983. And the current account deficit — the broadest measure of U.S. economic relations abroad — nearly disappeared that same year, aided in no small part by foreign payments to cover the cost of the Persian Gulf War.

Long Slide In, Slow Climb Out

Most economic analysts concluded that the 1990-91 recession was neither as long nor as deep as the average post-war downturn. The National Bureau of Economic Research in Cambridge, Mass., official arbiter of the dates of recessions, decided that, by July 1990, the long Reagan expansion had peaked and that the recession lasted until March 1991.

At nine months, the recession was shorter than the 11-month post-war average, and far shorter than the most recent preceding downturn — the 16-month recession that plagued the country in Reagan's first term. Not only was it shorter, but the 1990-91 recession also had a lesser impact on employment. Unemployment crested above 10 percent for 12 months in 1982-83. But unemployment peaked at 7.6 percent in July-August 1992, suggesting a significantly less onerous impact.

The Congressional Budget Office offered a representative view in January 1992: "This recession, as difficult as it may have been for many individuals and certain regions, has been much less severe for the nation as a whole than the downturns of 1973-75 and 1981-82."

It was a different sort of recession, however, and one whose effects were felt long after the raw numbers suggested that the business cycle had turned up. Several striking contrasts were apparent between the 1990-91 recession and the one nearly a decade earlier. Foremost were the conditions at the onset and the conclusion of both periods of economic contraction.

The 1981-82 recession was immediately preceded by a six-month recession in 1980 and 12 months of feeble growth in the interim. Prior to that, the economy was churning along at a rapid pace, but inflation was hitting double-digit levels. Interest rates jumped to double digits, too, spurred by actions of the Federal Reserve Board to tighten credit and cool the overheated economy. Nothing like that preceded the 1990 recession. In four of the six quarters prior to its start, the economy grew by less than 2 percent, computed on an annual basis after allowing for inflation — hardly a sizzling pace. Inflation had been averaging less than 4.5 percent for three years.

At the conclusion of the 1981-82 recession (and in other post-war recoveries), the economy boomed and unemployment fell sharply. In 1983, for example, the GDP grew an inflation-adjusted 3.9 percent; in 1984, growth was 6.2 percent. As the 1990-91 recession bottomed out, there was no noticeable rebound. It was not until the first quarter of 1992 that growth surpassed 1.5 percent on an annual, inflation-adjusted basis; the growth rate for all of 1992, well after the recession ended, was only 2.6 percent.

One measurable effect of the stagnant economy was the undercurrent of long-term unemployed workers. Although the unemployment rate was not especially high at the most severe point of the 1990-91 recession, the fraction of jobless workers whose period of unemployment exceeded 26 weeks rose from about 10 percent in 1989 to about 18 percent for the entirety of 1992. In contrast, the fraction who were out of work for five weeks or less fell from about 50 percent in 1989 to less than 35 percent at the end of 1992. More than a year and a half after the recession technically ended, jobless workers were still awaiting some sign that a recovery was in process.

The Fed's Role

Not surprisingly, when politicians went looking for someone to blame for recessions, they set the Federal Reserve Board in their sights.

Fed Chairman Paul A. Volcker was made a pariah for having driven up interest rates in the late 1970s and early 1980s in a successful effort to wring double-digit inflation out of the economy — and in so doing contributing to the double recessions of 1980 and 1981-82.

Under Chairman Alan Greenspan, who took control of the Fed in August 1987, inflation-fighting had remained a central — if not the central — objective of the people who managed the nation's monetary policy. Greenspan deviated not a bit from Volcker's tight-money philosophy, arguing repeatedly in his regular trips to Capitol Hill that long-term economic growth and prosperity would flow naturally from stable prices.

Indeed, as the economy began to slow in 1989, Greenspan announced to Congress his concern that the Fed had to balance its role as a brake on inflation — by keeping credit in fairly close check — and a lubricant for continued economic growth — by not allowing the reins to bind.

Greenspan's Fed had actually tightened credit slightly in late 1988 and early 1989, pushing to 7 percent the discount rate charged by the Fed on loans to banks — one of two Fed benchmarks watched closely by financial markets. Greenspan believed that interest rate movements should be market driven, and the Fed did not start ratcheting down the discount rate until almost two years later, in December 1990, when the economy had already stalled.

That step came immediately after the Congress and the president completed work on a huge deficit-reduction package that Greenspan had conceded earlier in the year would have a depressing effect on the economy and require some accommodation in the form of easier credit. But in mid-1990, when Treasury Secretary Nicholas F. Brady and other administration officials were publicly urging Greenspan to ease up on interest rates, Greenspan was plainly reluctant.

"What adjustment might be necessary and how it might be timed cannot be spelled out before the fact," Greenspan told the Senate Banking Committee in July. "I can only offer the assurance that the Federal Reserve will act, as it has in the past, to endeavor to keep the economic expansion on track."

By then, the economy was already contracting — though no official forecasts said so.

The Bush administration complained in its January 1991 budget submission to Congress that the Fed had been slow to react to the recession and to relax credit sufficiently. And Democrats and Republicans on the Joint Economic Committee agreed on but one thing in March 1991 — the Fed should cut interest rates further. But those criticisms did not deter Bush from appointing Greenspan to a second four-year term as chairman later in the year. *(Economic appointments, box, p. 32)*

As the recession deepened, the Fed did react, pushing down both the discount rate and the more finely tuned federal funds rate, which is charged on overnight interbank loans used to meet Fed reserve requirements. Both rates fell throughout 1991. The discount rate stood at 4.5 percent at year's end — and the economy continued to falter.

In mid-December 1991, the Fed sent its strongest psychological signal to the markets — a move in sharp contravention of Greenspan's typical views. It slashed the discount rate a full point — to 3.5 percent. The rate had not been so low since November 1964. "There is a deep-seated concern out there, which I must say to you I have not seen in my lifetime," Greenspan told the House Ways and Means Committee Dec. 18, two days before the Fed chopped the discount rate. It was the clearest sign that policy makers were truly flummoxed by the failure of the economy to rebound strongly from the recession. In mid-1992, as the economy continued to struggle, the Fed cut the discount rate further, to 3 percent.

A Muted Response

Politicians abhor inaction in the face of a crisis, but in the case of the 1990-91 recession, little agreement existed about what the government could, or should, do. In part, the lack of consensus stemmed from a real fear of adverse consequences from a policy misstep. In part, it resulted as lawmakers engaged in high-stakes political poker with the White House up for grabs in 1992.

A failure to agree, however, did not deter Bush or members of Congress from proposing a host of fiscal policy solutions to spark the economy back to life, most of them involving tax cuts.

Comparing Recessions, 1980-92

Economic Growth . . .

Quarterly Percentage Change (Annual Rate)

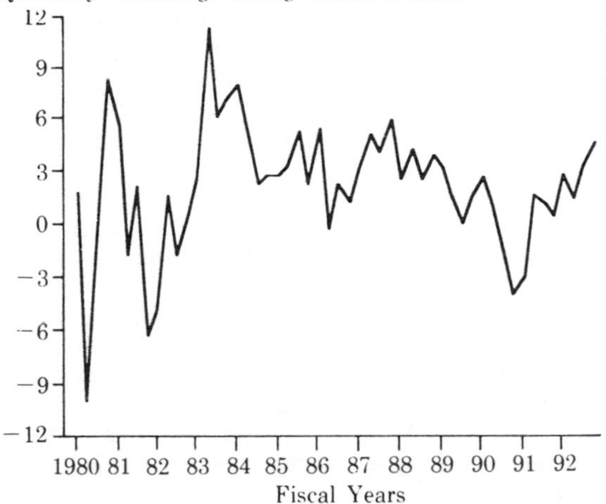

. . . showed a bigger decline during the 1980 and 1981-82 recessions than it did in the 1990-91 recession. Recovery in 1991-92 was weak.

Growth: Quarterly changes in gross domestic product, assessed as a seasonally adjusted annual rate based on constant 1987 dollars.

Source: Commerce Department, Bureau of Economic Analysis.

Inflation . . .

Quarterly Percentage Change (Annual Rate)

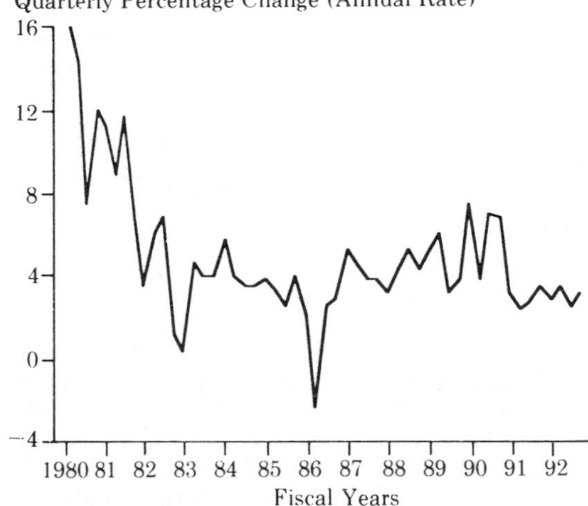

. . . reached historically high levels before the 1980 and 1981-82 recessions began. The Consumer Price Index did not hit similar peaks before the 1990 recession.

Inflation: Quarterly change in the Consumer Price Index for all urban consumers, expressed as a seasonally adjusted compound annual rate.

Source: Labor Department, Bureau of Labor Statistics.

Unemployment . . .

Quarterly Percentage Average

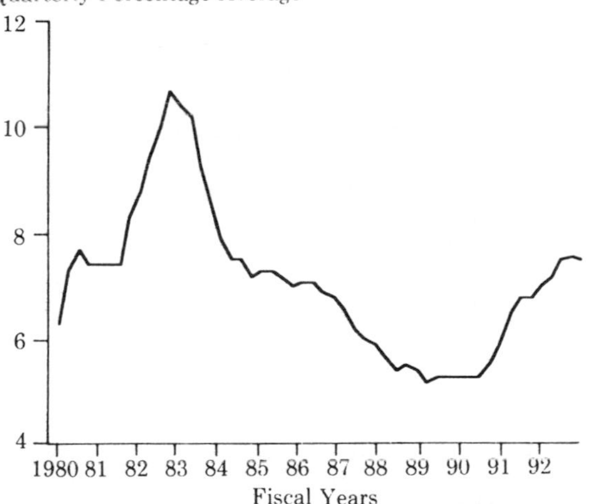

. . . surged in the 1980 and 1981-82 recessions and after a brief, steep drop stabilized at a high level before climbing in 1990.

Unemployment: Quarterly rate of unemployment for all civilian workers (does not include the military).

Source: Labor Department, Bureau of Labor Statistics.

Interest Rates . . .

Quarterly Percentage Average

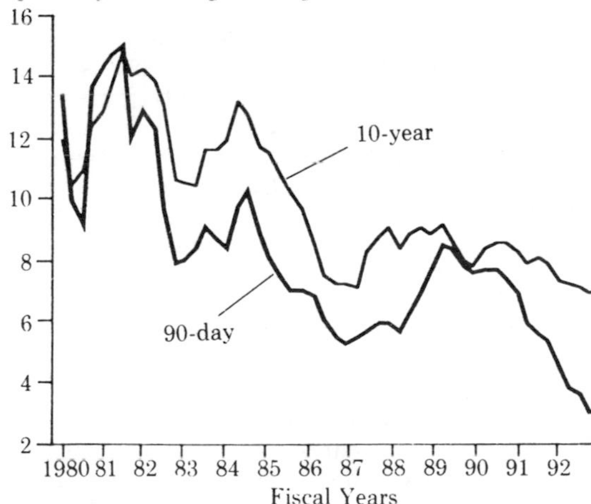

. . . on long- and short-term Treasury securities fell in 1992 to their lowest points in a decade. The slow recovery kept rates down.

Interest Rates: Quarterly average for new issues of 90-day Treasury bills and for 10-year Treasury bonds adjusted to constant maturities.

Source: Treasury Department.

GDP vs. GNP

Beginning in the fall of 1991, the Commerce Department — followed by the government agencies and private businesses that use its data — stopped emphasizing gross national product (GNP) and began using gross domestic product (GDP) as the most common yardstick for measuring performance of the U.S. economy. (Statistics appearing in this edition of *Congress and the Nation* use GDP where a gauge of the broad economy is required.)

The concepts used to calculate GDP and GNP are largely equivalent. And the resulting numbers are similar in composition, size and patterns of change — but important differences do exist between the two.

As taught to generations of schoolchildren and in college economics classes, GNP is the sum of all goods and services produced in the United States. In fact, that definition is best applied to GDP. As a technical matter, GNP measures output produced by labor, capital and property supplied by U.S. residents, regardless of where that labor and capital are located. GDP is the sum of goods and services produced within the borders of the United States, regardless of where the supplier of the means of production resides.

Two principal reasons were cited for the switch. First, data about economic activity within the United States are easier to collect than are data abroad. Therefore, GDP — which involves no foreign data — provides a more timely and accurate measure of economic activity. Second, most other countries measure their economic performance by GDP, not GNP (in part because their residents own much less productive property abroad). Using GDP thus makes comparisons between the United States and other countries simpler and more precise.

Because GNP includes calculations of U.S. earnings overseas — and because U.S.-owned assets abroad produce greater earnings than foreign-owned assets produce in the United States — GNP is typically a slightly larger number than GDP. At the end of 1992, the gross domestic product was calculated to be $6.0385 trillion; the gross national product was $6.0458 trillion, a largely insignificant difference of about 0.1 percent. Also, according to the Commerce Department, GDP grew slightly faster during the 1980s than did GNP.

Because the numbers are different, precise comparisons of new GDP-based statistics with old GNP-based statistics are not possible. To assist such comparisons, the Commerce Department's Bureau of Economic Analysis recomputed most calculations of U.S. economic activity back to before the World War II era.

The Commerce Department continues to calculate and publish GNP, in part because GNP provides a better measure of income to U.S. residents.

Conservatives issued random calls for a cut in the tax on capital gains from the sale of stock and other assets that appreciated in value. The charge for a capital gains cut was lead by Secretary of Housing and Urban Development Jack F. Kemp, an original adherent of the supply-side economic theory that dominated the early Reagan years. Some congressional liberals called for a big increase in spending on road construction and other infrastructure, the sort of classic public works jobs program popular for decades with Democrats. Others sought a tax cut for the middle class that in theory would have boosted consumption and aided the recovery.

Most economists advised Congress and the president to go slow — or do nothing — on the ground that any stimulus provided by a tax cut or a boost in spending would have offsetting negative effects, as interest rates rose in reaction to increased government borrowing. "A tax cut now could hardly be viewed as an anti-recession measure," said Alice M. Rivlin in October 1991. Rivlin was a Brookings Institution economist who had previously been director of the Congressional Budget Office; her view was one widely held at the time by economists.

In early 1992, as the election approached and politicians became more itchy about the stubborn economy, louder calls for middle-class tax cuts came from both ends of the political spectrum. But economists poured more cold water on the idea, and opinion polls showed that even the public seemed uneasy with it.

Some noted economists backed a modest increase in the deficit as a fiscal stimulus, arguing that interest rates would remain low, particularly if the Fed cooperated.

Paul A. Samuelson of the Massachusetts Institute of Technology was among those who urged some legislative response in congressional testimony in January 1992. He favored not only accelerated infrastructure spending, but also enactment of a temporary investment tax credit, which he said would encourage businesses to expand productive capacity — and create jobs. But even Samuelson was cautious: "As yet there is no warrant for election-year crash programs to open the floodgates of fiscal stimulus."

Despite opposition from most Republicans, congressional Democrats exercised their majority will to send two tax bills to the White House in 1992 — one a middle-class tax cut, the other a package of tax cuts to aid businesses in urban areas, with a little middle-class relief on the side.

Early in the year, some perceived that Bush might be receptive to a middle-class tax cut, but that hope waned. Later, some thought that he would support a bill creating urban enterprise zones, an idea long advanced by Kemp and that Bush also had embraced. But Bush was unalterably opposed to Democratic initiatives that had been incorporated into both bills. Both died under his veto.

The Federal Budget

The federal deficit dominated all budget talk in the late 1980s and early 1990s, just as it had during the second presidential term of Ronald Reagan.

Congress created a commission to study the deficit, but the commission was largely ignored and it came to no consensus. Summit meetings were held among congressional leaders of both parties and White House officials. Twice such summits resulted in enactment of deficit-reduction bills that included politically painful spending cuts and tax increases. But the deficit grew ever larger.

Congress also again changed its internal budget procedures (embodied in the Gramm-Rudman-Hollings anti-deficit law), following the Gramm-Rudman canon that lawmakers could not control themselves — or spending — unless their options were severely limited.

The changes, which came in late 1990, were an attempt by Congress to put itself in a different sort of straitjacket than the one imposed by the original Gramm-Rudman law, enacted in 1985, or by its first revision in 1987. The brainchild of Sens. Phil Gramm, R-Texas, Warren B. Rudman, R-N.H., and Ernest F. Hollings, D-S.C., the law had long since failed its purpose in the minds of most observers. Hollings had even disavowed it.

For three straight years under Gramm-Rudman (fiscal 1987-89), the deficit hovered around $150 billion, an amount less than that recorded in fiscal 1985 or 1986. But the deficit blossomed anew during the Bush administration, hitting the four highest totals in history in fiscal 1990-93 and twice threatening to breach the $300 billion mark.

The 1990 rules changes preserved only the vague idea that the deficit should be placed on a declining path. The latest enforcement mechanism was directed not at the overall deficit, but at some of its component parts — in particular those actions that Congress took on a year-to-year basis. The new rules ignored other items that contributed significantly to the red ink but happened more or less on their own.

It was plain to nearly anyone connected to the budget process that most increases in the deficit were "uncontrollable." They came from higher spending on "entitlements" and other "mandatory" spending programs, which typically paid cash assistance to qualified recipients. The only control Congress exercised over mandatory programs was to eliminate them or change the eligibility criteria for beneficiaries. Either option was politically quite difficult; since efforts to reduce the deficit began in the mid-1980s, Congress had recorded only modest successes at best in reducing entitlement spending.

The 1990 budget rules set overall deficit targets that were much higher than those under previous versions of Gramm-Rudman. And instead of requiring changes in mandatory programs to counteract essentially automatic increases in the deficit, the 1990 rules put strict limits on the ability of Congress to spend money on "discretionary" programs — everything from crime control to space exploration. The new rules also made it nearly impossible for Congress to create new entitlements or to make old entitlements more generous, unless lawmakers found a way to pay for the added benefits up front.

The new rules produced several effects that were generally viewed as positive.

First, although the deficit continued to exceed $200 billion a year, the targets allowed for that. The resulting benefit was that congressional budget resolutions were less prone to use phony accounting gimmicks to bring the projected deficit down to a level acceptable on theory — but unattainable in practice.

Second, Congress did not engage in its typical budget fighting in 1991 or 1992. It would be wrong to say there was budget peace, but lawmakers were able to concentrate on priorities within a narrow range of options and did not have to engage in the sort of political posturing that characterized budget fights in the recent past.

Third, the reduced tendency to employ gimmickry required those members who wanted to breach the deficit rules to justify their actions. For instance, some congressional Democrats — particularly members of the Appropriations committees, who chafed most under the discretionary spending caps — tried to change the rules in 1992. Their effort to shift some discretionary defense spending to domestic programs failed, however, when they could not persuade their colleagues that the change was warranted.

References

Discussion of federal budget policy for the years 1945-64 may be found in *Congress and the Nation Vol. I*, pp. 387-395; for the years 1965-68, *Congress and the Nation Vol. II*, pp. 127-140; for the years 1969-72, *Congress and the Nation Vol. III*, pp. 63-75; for the years 1973-76, *Congress and the Nation Vol. IV*, pp. 57-81; for the years 1977-80, *Congress and the Nation Vol. V*, pp. 211-230; for the years 1981-84, *Congress and the Nation Vol. VI*, pp. 33-61; for the years 1985-88, *Congress and the Nation Vol. VII*, pp. 33-74.

Despite these apparent successes in constraining the deficit, as Bush was leaving office in January 1993, the Congressional Budget Office (CBO) estimated that the deficit would show no shrinkage and remain at about $300 billion a year through the mid-1990s. That news was unsettling enough. It was amplified, however, when lawmakers remembered that the discretionary spending caps were to expire in fiscal 1995 — and that it was those caps that had yielded whatever deficit reduction occurred in the years since 1990.

The 103rd and 104th Congresses and the new president, Bill Clinton, would plainly have their work cut out for them, if they were to accomplish on the budget front what Bush and the 101st and 102nd Congresses could not.

National Economic Commission Ignored

The National Economic Commission, a blue-ribbon panel created by Congress in 1988, provided the first failed opportunity in the Bush administration to help solve the deficit crisis. The commission filed its final report March 1, 1989, a little over a month after Bush took office. It then went out of business.

Given one year and $1 million in taxpayer money to come up with a bipartisan fix for the government's chronic deficit-spending habit, the commission was expected to pay for itself many times over. But its deliberations devolved into the same kind of partisan bickering over spending cuts and tax hikes that had long divided Congress and the White House. In the end, the panel's 14 members — seven Democrats and seven Republicans — could not agree on a single solution.

The commission's final report — actually two separate reports, reflecting majority and minority views — offered few specific recommendations for cutting the deficit. The majority — all the Republicans joined by one Democrat — issued a short, 10-page statement endorsing Bush's pledge to avoid raising taxes. They urged more "restraints" on spending but otherwise declined to offer any recommendations. The minority — all Democrats — said Bush's approach to budgeting "leads nowhere" because it "rules out any discussion of additional revenues," but they also offered no specific alternatives.

Created in late 1987 by a minor provision in a massive deficit-reduction bill, the commission was promoted as a means to bridge a longstanding partisan divide. The elite group of government, business and labor leaders who made up the commission were thought to have the clout to force their consensus opinions on Congress and the White House. Its cochairmen were Robert S. Strauss, a former chairman of the Democratic National Committee and former U.S. trade representative, and former transportation secretary Drew Lewis, a Republican.

Their political and business expertise notwithstanding, commission members quickly learned that deep-seated fiscal values were not conducive to neat win-win solutions. The commission ultimately fell victim to Bush's "no new taxes" campaign battle cry. Bush had made no secret of his hostility toward the panel, blasting it during the campaign as little more than a stalking horse for tax increases.

With a White House-congressional budget summit called at the outset of Bush's first term, Office of Management and Budget (OMB) Director Richard G. Darman and Treasury Secretary Nicholas F. Brady insisted the commission be terminated. The president had the authority to extend its mandate until September 1989, but Bush chose not to do so, to avoid sending wrong signals to congressional negotiators.

1989 Summit: A Precursor

The budget summit in 1989 was nothing like the one that was to take place a year later — neither as complex and politically difficult nor as productive. In nine weeks of negotiations, congressional leaders and White House officials settled on a package of budget savings that were projected to yield a deficit of $99.4 billion in fiscal 1990, slightly less than the $100 billion Gramm-Rudman ceiling.

Bush had started the process on Feb. 9, just three weeks into his administration, by proposing the broad outlines of a budget and a series of summit talks to hash out the details. The Democrats who controlled Congress chose to talk, knowing that if they drafted their own budget they would take the blame for any adverse results.

The summit agreement was announced April 14, but the deal was quickly seen as full of one-time windfalls and accounting gimmicks with little bearing on long-range fiscal policy. Moreover, it was based on an extremely optimistic economic forecast that gave no thought to the possibility that within 15 months — before fiscal 1990 was concluded — the economy would be in recession.

The pivotal feature of the agreement — $5.3 billion in "new revenues" — had yet to be negotiated. Indeed, two key figures in the negotiations, Senate Finance Committee Chairman Lloyd Bentsen, D-Texas, and Ways and Means Chairman Dan Rostenkowski, D-Ill., refused to attend the Rose Garden ceremony. Bentsen reportedly told the president he thought the budget deal was "marginal" and that there remained a "great gulf of disagreement" over how to raise the additional revenues called for in the package.

Efforts to put the budget deal into law supplied proof that it was less than a substantive agreement. Working out a deficit-reducing reconciliation bill took from April until Thanksgiving. In the interim, Congress failed to meet the $100 billion Gramm-Rudman target, and $16.2 billion in automatic spending cuts were triggered in mid-October. The reconciliation bill eventually rolled back a portion of those automatic cuts — but its sponsors retained about a third of the cuts so they could claim "real" budget savings of just under $15 billion.

1990 Summit: Both Success and Failure

After limited success at bipartisan deficit negotiations the year before, lawmakers were in no hurry in 1990 to try again. But Gramm-Rudman intervened. As the year began, it was forecast that the fiscal 1991 deficit would exceed $130 billion. But that was before there was a hint of the recession that would begin in July.

As the economy slowed, however, forecasters changed their estimates and said the 1991 deficit would probably be well in excess of $200 billion. Gramm-Rudman would require automatic spending cuts in October to bring the deficit down to the year's target of $64 billion, unless Congress and the president could agree on alternative measures.

Bush broke the ice by inviting congressional leaders to the White House for preliminary talks on May 6. Out of that session came agreement to hold a full-scale summit. The early phase of the negotiations, which lasted from May 15 until Congress left town for its annual August recess, at times resembled a seminar. OMB and CBO officials, and subcommittee and committee chairmen with jurisdiction

Growth of Deficit and Debt

Deficit Fluctuated . . .

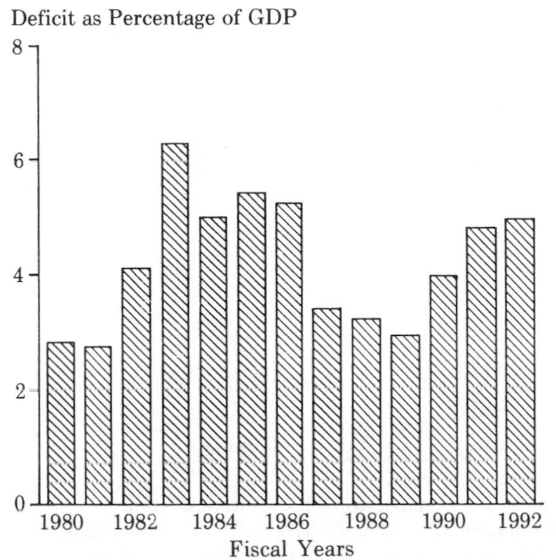

. . . As Debt Rose Steadily

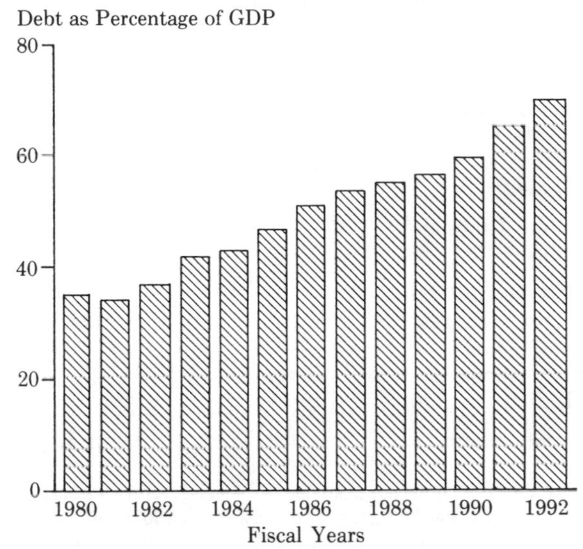

The federal deficit responded fitfully throughout the 1980s and into the 1990s to efforts to control it. Measured against the performance of the economy as a whole, the deficit fell in the late 1980s to just under 3 percent of gross domestic product (GDP). Some economists believed that a deficit of about 2 percent of GDP could be sustained indefinitely and might be beneficial. In 1990 and after, the deficit bounced back, exceeding 5 percent of GDP.

Meanwhile, the total federal debt climbed as a share of GDP, from about 34 percent in 1980-81 to just under 70 percent in 1992.

Source: Office of Management and Budget, *Budget Baselines, Historical Data and Alternatives for the Future* (Washington, D.C.: U.S. Government Printing Office, January 1993).

over specific spending areas, gave detailed briefings to the 17 congressional leaders and three White House negotiators. But after initiating the summit, Bush himself played little direct role in shaping its work.

It was a time marked as well by periodic skirmishing, during which episodes of bipartisan good will were interrupted by nasty bouts of name-calling, reflecting deep disagreement over fundamentals.

The talks began with no clear agenda or direction. Virtually no decisions were made until members returned in September from the summer recess. But early on, negotiators agreed to a deficit-reduction target of $50 billion for fiscal 1991 and $500 billion over five years. The expected jump in the 1991 deficit — and the decision to try to cut it by only $50 billion — assured that any deal also would include a further revision of Gramm-Rudman and its deficit targets. Making the cuts necessary to meet the existing targets would have been politically impossible and, many argued, damaging to the economy.

Democrats were initially fearful that a summit would be a political trap in which they would be forced to take the blame for tax increases. They accepted Bush's invitation to talk on the basis that "no preconditions" be set — a term interpreted to mean that taxes would be on the table.

Conservative Republicans immediately sounded the alarm. And, in late June, Bush proved them accurate in their fears of a tax increase. Taking a step he deemed essential to keep the talks alive, he issued a statement effectively endorsing higher taxes. Bush tried to limit the political damage, holding a news conference to explain his decision. He argued that "getting this deficit down, continuing economic expansion and employment in this country" were more important than his earlier campaign pledges not to raise taxes. "I knew I'd catch some flak on this decision," he said, "but I've got to do what I think is right."

The sense of forward motion generated by Bush's move was quickly interrupted by the July Fourth recess, however. When lawmakers returned, partisan tensions began to mount. Hoping that the threat of Gramm-Rudman cuts in October would force both sides to reach an agreement in September, negotiators recessed for August, after setting an ambitious schedule that would culminate in enactment of a deficit-reducing reconciliation bill by Oct. 2.

When the talks resumed on Sept. 7, a major new factor had entered the equation: the Aug. 2 Iraqi invasion of Kuwait. Now the talk was of higher oil prices, escalating defense needs, war and possible recession.

Negotiators were optimistic, but they made little progress. As the Oct. 1 deadline for compliance with Gramm-Rudman neared, OMB projected that Gramm-Rudman cuts in excess of $100 billion were probable. That would have meant slashing in excess of 40 percent from discretionary spending on both defense and domestic programs. Those amounts were far larger than the biggest Gramm-Rudman cuts ever allowed to stay in effect, which trimmed outlays by less than 5 percent in 1986.

Just hours from the triggering of automatic cuts on Oct. 1 — and a government shutdown that would result

Budget Resolution Totals, 1990-93

(Fiscal years, in billions of dollars)

	1990	1991	1992	1993
Budget Authority	$1,329.4	$1,485.6	$1,590.1	$1,515.9
Outlays	1,165.2	1,236.9	1,448.0	1,500.0
Revenues	1,065.5	1,172.9	1,169.2	1,173.4
Deficit	−99.7	−64.0	−278.8	−326.6
Gramm-Rudman Deficit Targets	−36.0	0.0	—	—
1st Revision Gramm-Rudman Deficit Targets	−100.0	−64.0	−28.0	0.0
2nd Revision Gramm-Rudman Deficit Targets	—	−327.0	−317.0	−236.0
Actual Deficit	−221.4	−269.5	−290.3	−254.9

Note: The 1990 budget-reconciliation bill (HR 5835 — PL 101-508) significantly revised upward the Gramm-Rudman deficit targets (they had previously been revised upward in 1987). But as a practical matter, after 1990, Congress did not intend that the overall targets be used to enforce budget cuts. Instead, the 1990 measure created new methods of budgetary discipline by imposing special targets for discretionary spending and requirements that bills to increase mandatory spending or reduce taxes be offset by spending cuts or other tax increases.

Sources: Congressional budget resolutions; Gramm-Rudman law, as amended; Office of Management and Budget.

because Congress also had failed to clear needed appropriations bills during the summit impasse — budget negotiators began to deal seriously. Finally, on the afternoon of Sept. 30, Bush announce that agreement had been reached. The deal met two of the three requirements established by its authors early on: It claimed to reduce expected government spending by $500 billion over five years, and it contained numerous changes to the congressional budget process designed to prevent the agreement's key provisions from being breached in later years. Negotiators had failed to reach their third goal: cutting $50 billion from the fiscal 1991 deficit. In the end, they settled for savings of $40 billion.

But when the deal was presented for approval by Congress in the form of a budget resolution, it met with resounding, bipartisan defeat in the House. The deep partisan differences that had made it so difficult to reach a summit agreement resurfaced as soon as the rank and file were asked to endorse the effort. Ultimately, a second budget resolution was adopted, for the most part unchanged from the first, and a reconciliation bill incorporating the details was enacted. But the summit left a sour taste in the mouths of many lawmakers and became the grist for political charges and counter-charges throughout the balance of Bush's term.

The Aftermath

Following the 1990 summit, and the enactment of new budget rules, little action was seen on the budget front. Yearly battles over tax cuts and tax increases, or proposals to spend more money on favored domestic programs, were almost non-existent.

Both political parties spent time policing each other for strict adherence to the budget rules, but neither paid much attention to the overall size of the deficit. Nothing drove that point home more starkly than Bush's announcement in his 1992 State of the Union address that he immediately was reducing the amount of income tax withheld from employee paychecks in an attempt to give consumers more spending money. The move was political — in a political year. It amounted to a small increase in workers' take home pay (and a guarantee that tax refunds would be smaller in 1993). But more importantly, it was expected to reduce tax receipts by $15 billion in fiscal 1992 — and increase the deficit by a like amount.

A boost to the deficit of that size would have been unthinkable under the old Gramm-Rudman rules, but the new rules imposed no penalty on a deficit increase that did not result from legislation, and this plan did not require congressional approval.

Some in Congress chafed at the limits that were imposed by the new budget rules. In 1992, Democrats launched an abortive attempt to remove the "walls" that barred using extra large cuts in defense spending to finance domestic initiatives. But that plan failed, in no small part because many lawmakers believed that junking the budget rules would remove the insulation that protected them from charges that they were ignoring the deficit. And the alternative would have been to make another real stab at deficit reduction, something few wanted to try in a presidential election year.

Chronology Of Action On the Budget

1989-90

President Bush took office in 1989 and inherited a budgetary nightmare. Congress and President Ronald Reagan had serious disagreements over budget policy, especially after the Democrats regained control of the Senate in the 1986 elections. And the federal budget deficit, once considered a problem when it was less than $100 billion annually, had swollen to twice or three times that amount. Efforts to control the deficit seemed to have little effect.

But a new spirit of comity prevailed at the outset of work between the new administration and Congress, despite fundamental differences that remained between the Democratic and Republican Parties — proposals to reduce the tax on capital gains, for instance, continued to erect stumbling blocks to budget agreements. Congressional budget leaders and White House officials quickly put together a budget agreement for fiscal 1990, and lawmakers gave strong bipartisan support to the resulting budget resolution.

That mood soon evaporated, however, and strife enveloped a reconciliation bill needed to enact the broad budget outlines into law. Delay and dismay killed expectations for an easy budget year that might have paved the way for a more ambitious year-end deal between Bush and Congress for fiscal 1991.

Instead, 1990 became a budget battleground that required a seemingly endless budget summit to arrive at an agreement. The economy had soured midyear; the savings and loan bailout of 1989 was proving more costly than anticipated; and war was looming in the Persian Gulf. Those factors threw hopeful forecasts into the trash and drove the deficit higher.

Pushed by Sens. Phil Gramm, R-Texas, Warren B. Rudman, R-N.H., and Ernest F. Hollings, D-S.C., Congress had acted five years earlier to impose some additional discipline on the budget process by requiring automatic spending cuts to reduce the deficit if it exceeded a statutory target. The circumstances of 1990 threatened monumental automatic cuts under the 1985 Gramm-Rudman-Hollings anti-deficit law (PL 99-177), revised in 1987 (PL 100-119) and usually referred to as Gramm-Rudman. *(Gramm-Rudman, Congress and the Nation Vol. VII, pp. 44, 67)*

The only alternatives to the pain and disruption of Gramm-Rudman cuts were for Congress and the president to find a way to reduce the deficit substantially or to rewrite the Gramm-Rudman rules. Ultimately, they did both.

The 1990 summit negotiations produced a five-year agreement that promised almost $500 billion in "real" deficit reduction and a chance for budget peace in later years.

Fiscal 1990 Budget

With a new occupant in the White House and a desire by Democrats in Congress not to do battle with George Bush in the first months of his presidency, crafting a federal budget in 1989 took on an accommodationist air.

Bush began the process in early February by offering only the general outlines of a budget proposal and inviting Congress to join him in negotiating the details. Democrats had little choice; if they refused to negotiate a joint plan, they would have been left to draw up their own budget and take the blame for the spending cuts and possibly the tax increases required to pay for new programs.

After nine weeks of informal summit talks, administration and congressional budget negotiators reached agreement on a package of reductions that eventually were incorporated into a budget resolution for fiscal 1990. Later, a deficit-reducing reconciliation bill put most presumed spending cuts from that deal into law.

The agreement produced by the budget summit and announced April 14 in the White House Rose Garden was about equally divided between broad spending cuts and yet-to-be determined revenue increases. A large share of the agreement's proposed spending cuts involved one-time windfalls or other accounting gimmicks that would not carry over into future years. Nearly half of the $2 billion in cuts called for in farm price supports, for example, were to be achieved by speeding up payments to farmers so they would occur early, in fiscal 1989. Another $2 billion would be "saved" by taking the U.S. Postal Service off-budget.

Moreover, the deal was based largely on the administration's premise that the nation's economy would continue to grow — and at a healthier clip than most economists believed possible.

President's Budget Request

Two presidents were in office in January 1989, so two budget requests were presented to Congress. Outgoing President Ronald Reagan on Jan. 9 submitted his eighth formal budget request to Congress — his ninth counting the historic tax and spending cuts he sought and won immediately after taking office in 1981. Reagan called for spending $1.15 trillion in fiscal 1990, raising $1.06 trillion in revenues and leaving a deficit of $92.5 billion, well under the $100 billion target set by the 1985 Gramm-Rudman anti-deficit law, as amended in 1987 (PL 99-177, PL 100-119). It was a budget that Reagan could say upheld his original mandate — and that Bush, who took office 11 days later, could work from, yet amend at will. *(Gramm-Rudman, Congress and the Nation Vol. VII, pp. 44, 67)*

In his first prime-time appearance before Congress and the nation, Bush spoke to a joint session of Congress Feb. 9 and laid out a fiscal agenda that largely had not been discussed during the 1988 campaign. The president's close advisers, led by budget director Richard G. Darman, structured a broad but thinly detailed set of budget proposals for fiscal 1990 to appeal to nearly every Democratic and Republican interest. Darman crafted for Bush a proposal that called for $1.16 trillion in outlays, $1.07 trillion in revenues and a $91.1 billion deficit — slightly smaller than in Reagan's budget.

The plan was not presented as a full-fledged, function-by-function budget, but as an adjustment to Reagan's budget request. As a consequence, the proposal was difficult to evaluate, and members of Congress had to rely heavily on White House interpretations of its details.

The plan included increases in key education, anti-poverty and environmental protection programs; constant (if constrained) spending for defense; and beefed-up efforts to fight illegal drugs. And it projected a deficit that met the Gramm-Rudman target while avoiding the need for new taxes, a central Bush campaign pledge.

Bush's budget also was drafted in comparison with actual fiscal 1989 spending levels, not an inflation-adjusted fiscal 1990 "current services baseline" that was the traditional starting point for federal budgets. That allowed Bush to say that he proposed to "increase" Medicaid (a federal-state health care entitlement program for the poor) by $3.3 billion, an amount that merely reflected what the program would cost anyway if Congress ignored Reagan's earlier proposal to cut back existing benefits.

Bush identified nearly $30 billion in outlays to be spent on "priorities" — defense, drug enforcement, education and environmental initiatives, among others. Although he described all of these programs as increases over fiscal 1989 spending, most turned out to be only nominal changes (or even cuts) from what were later calculated to be current services projections.

And the budget lumped remaining discretionary spending programs into a single category and asked Congress to negotiate over the individual outlay levels. The catch: Programs in this category, which totaled $136 billion in fiscal 1989 outlays, were to be allowed no additional money in 1990. That meant some programs could receive increases to current services levels only if offsetting cuts were made in other programs. Bush refused to say which programs he would cut, offering only casual "illustrations," showing how the Women, Infants and Children (WIC) food program could receive inflation increases if subsidies for mass transit and Amtrak were cut below 1989 levels.

This, it turned out, was the "flexible freeze" that Bush had mentioned often, without defining it, during his election campaign.

Budget Resolution

After just a month of work, the House and Senate easily gave final approval to a fiscal 1990 budget resolution the week of May 15.

The measure (H Con Res 106) conformed to the April 14 budget summit agreement between Congress and the White House. But it gave few specific instructions to Senate and House committees on how to achieve the savings called for in that deal.

H Con Res 106 projected spending of $1.17 trillion, revenues of $1.07 trillion and a deficit just millions of dollars under the $100 billion Gramm-Rudman target for the year.

Final adoption of the budget was made even easier because House and Senate conferees had declined to resolve differences on reconciliation instructions to House and Senate committees, directing them to achieve spending cuts or revenue increases. Instead, the conference report included separate sets of reconciliation instructions for each chamber. The differences were to be worked out later, when House and Senate conferees met on the reconciliation bill. *(Reconciliation, p. 43)*

These and other issues were left unresolved, mainly because the White House agreement itself had been silent on how to raise some $5.3 billion in new revenues needed to keep the deficit from exceeding $100 billion.

House Action. The House Budget Committee April 27 ratified the broad outlines of the budget summit deal — but not without some loud complaints from the rank and file that kept the committee working behind closed doors through much of the week.

By an 18-6 show of hands, a majority of Democratic and Republican committee members approved H Con Res 106. Like the budget agreement, the House measure was designed to restrain growth in defense spending and allow for nearly $4 billion in new spending for domestic programs, most of it earmarked for education initiatives and science and space projects.

When the committee finally opened its doors April 27 for a vote to report the budget resolution to the floor, committee leaders from both sides of the aisle clearly had accommodated enough members to assure approval. All the high-priority, low-income programs long protected by House Democrats — child nutrition, vocational rehabilitation, older Americans' employment, programs for the homeless, among others — were shielded from cuts, with funding provided at least to cover the costs of inflation. H Con Res 106 was formally reported (H Rept 101-42) on May 2.

The House bowed to leadership pleas for fiscal peace and order, giving overwhelming, if grudging, approval on May 4 to the budget resolution. H Con Res 106 was adopted on a **key vote of 263-157 (R 106-61; D 157-96)**. But the large vote margin masked wide dissatisfaction among Democrats and Republicans with the limited terms of the deal. *(1989 key votes, p. 1021)*

House leaders rebuffed a number of guerrilla attacks designed to alter substantially the basic outlines of the April 14 White House agreement.

The Congressional Black Caucus offered an alternative budget that would have cut defense spending by a total of $39.1 billion and raised taxes by $25.3 billion. It was rejected 81-343. Another liberal alternative, offered by Richard A. Gephardt, D-Mo., called for raising $9 billion in revenue through an oil-import fee, most of it to be channeled into domestic programs. The amendment was rejected, 49-373.

Fiscal conservatives fared even worse. John R. Kasich, R-Ohio, offered a spending freeze proposal and was defeated 30-393.

Liberal Democrats were not permitted by the rule governing floor debate to offer amendments that would shift spending from defense to domestic priorities. Unable to get past the Rules Committee, Democratic budget critics took their complaints to a heated May 4 meeting of the Democratic whips' organization. There some members complained that Democratic leaders were making a mistake by cooperating with Republicans and not drawing partisan distinctions more sharply.

Senate Action. While the summit agreement eased the way for adoption of a budget resolution, it also left the Budget panels with little to do. When the Senate Budget Committee met April 18-19, members were presented with the outlines of the deal between administration officials and congressional leaders setting overall ceilings for defense, foreign aid and domestic programs. Chairman Jim Sasser, D-Tenn., announced early on that he and ranking Republican Pete V. Domenici of New Mexico would oppose any effort to change those parameters.

Thus committee members had to either accept their leaders' basic recommendations or scrap the entire deal and send negotiators back to the bargaining table. Indeed, short of rewriting the entire agreement, the only task before the committee was to determine how to divide up discretionary domestic spending totals among the various functions of government — an action that the Appropriations Committee was not bound to follow.

Some committee members nevertheless tried to change the level of the debate. J. Bennett Johnston, D-La., began by offering what he called a "truth amendment," which would require the use of the less rosy economic forecast of the Congressional Budget Office, yielding a bigger projected fiscal 1990 deficit and thus requiring cuts of $47 billion to reach the Gramm-Rudman target. It was defeated, 4-19.

Kent Conrad, D-N.D., tried with an amendment to send negotiators back to the table, but he was defeated, 8-15.

Ernest F. Hollings, D-S.C., who had called the White House agreement "pure sham," came closer to replacing it with an amendment to freeze all spending at fiscal 1989 levels, except for Social Security, Medicare and other entitlement payments that had cost-of-living increases built into their benefits. He was defeated, 10-13, though he vowed to try again when the resolution came to the Senate floor.

In the end, Sasser and Domenici's original proposal was accepted without change on a 16-7 vote, with a majority of Democrats and Republicans voting for it. The Senate Budget Committee formally reported its version of the budget resolution (S Con Res 30 — S Rept 101-20) on April 27.

The Senate gave overwhelming support to H Con Res 106 on May 4, voting 68-31 after substituting the text of S Con Res 30. As in the House, the leadership fought off efforts to alter the basic compromise reached in the budget summit and embodied in the resolution.

Paul Simon, D-Ill., found little favor for a plan to rechannel $3 billion in defense spending to education programs. His amendment was tabled (and thus killed), 64-31.

Hollings repackaged his spending freeze proposal from committee but won only eight additional votes on the floor; it was rejected 18-82.

Final Action. In a victory of style over substance, House and Senate conferees gave quick bipartisan approval to H Con Res 106 on May 11. They haggled only two days before agreeing to disagree on key deficit-reducing reconciliation guidelines for 10 House and eight Senate committees. They instructed the House Ways and Means and Senate Finance committees to come up with $5.3 billion in new revenues — the amount required in the summit agreement. But because the summit had not specified how the money was to be raised, lengthy negotiations were expected.

In all, Senate instructions totaled $13.8 billion in additional revenues and outlay savings through reconciliation; the House total was $13.5 billion.

The House adopted the conference report (H Rept 101-50) May 17 by a 241-185 margin; the Senate adopted it the next day, 63-37. The budget resolution does not require the president's signature.

Reconciliation, Fiscal 1990

Congress ended its 1989 session by clearing a $14.7 billion deficit-reducing reconciliation bill (HR 3299 — PL 101-239) by easy votes that belied the months of contention before agreement was reached. The bill was required under the bipartisan budget deal between Congress and the White House reached in April and the subsequent congressional budget resolution (H Con Res 106) adopted in May. *(Budget, p. 41)*

Congress' tentative schedule had at first called for passage of a reconciliation measure by mid-June, later by mid-July. But final action was delayed until just before Thanksgiving largely because of a serious conflict over Bush's call for a cut in the tax rate on capital gains (profits from the sale of stocks and other assets). *(Capital gains, p. 96)*

The House passed HR 3299 on Oct. 5; the Senate passed a significantly different version on Oct. 13. By then, with difficult negotiations ahead, it was too late to meet the deficit target set in the Gramm-Rudman anti-deficit law (PL 99-177, PL 100-119). Gramm-Rudman required that the projected fiscal 1990 deficit be reduced to $110 billion or less by Oct. 15 (that amounted to a target level of $100 billion plus a $10 billion margin of error). *(Gramm-Rudman, Congress and the Nation Vol. VII, pp. 44, 67)*

Based on legislative action as of Oct. 1, the Office of Management and Budget forecast a fiscal 1990 deficit of $116.2 billion. As a result, on Oct. 16, Bush signed a mandatory order for $16.2 billion in across-the-board cuts, half in defense and half in domestic programs. When HR 3299 was finally enacted, it rolled back some of those cuts but retained a portion to achieve nearly a third of its deficit-reduction goal.

Resolving Disputes

The delay in passing the reconciliation bill was more the result of disputes over unrelated issues than quarrels about how to meet the mandated deficit-reduction goal. Chief among the extraneous items that hitched a ride temporarily or permanently on the 1990 reconciliation bill were:

Capital Gains. The House gave strong approval to a cut in the tax on capital gains, but the Senate balked. Bush's November decision to stop seeking the tax cut lifted the last roadblock to enactment.

Catastrophic Health Costs. The House bill included a full repeal of the 1988 Medicare Catastrophic Coverage Act (PL 100-360), which had sparked a backlash among elderly beneficiaries opposed to a new surtax to pay for the coverage. The Senate had no comparable provision, and conferees ultimately agreed to strip the repeal from the bill. Virtually the entire catastrophic-costs insurance program was repealed in a separate measure (HR 3607 — PL 101-234) at the end of the session. *(Catastrophic coverage, Congress and the Nation Vol. VII, p. 561; repeal, p. 565)*

Medicare. The reconciliation bill served as a vehicle for what may have been the most important health policy accomplishment of the year: overhauling the system for reimbursing doctors under Medicare. Under the new plan, physicians' payments were to be set by a national fee schedule based on the time, training and skill needed to perform a given service. The plan also sought, for the first time, to control the volume of services as well as their price by setting an overall annual target for Medicare spending on doctors' bills. *(Medicare, p. 571)*

Medicaid. Although most of an ambitious expansion of the joint federal-state Medicare program that had been passed by the House as part of the reconciliation bill was

Debt Limit Hit $3.12 Trillion in 1989 ...

Congress' annual exercise in brinkmanship — increasing the limit on total borrowing by the federal government — was routine in 1989 and carried to extremes in 1990.

Bills increasing the so-called debt ceiling were the ultimate in must-pass legislation: Failure to raise the limit would prevent the federal government from selling new bonds to finance its operations and to redeem those bonds that periodically came due. Most of the time, relatively little debate was devoted to increasing the debt limit itself, which more than quadrupled during the 1980s, as the accumulated effects of huge budget deficits increased the total federal debt above $4 trillion in fiscal 1992.

As a consequence of their mandatory nature, debt limit bills often became hostages to other measures with significant political, and usually fiscal, import.

For instance, the 1985 Gramm-Rudman anti-deficit law (PL 99-177) and a major 1987 amendment to that law (PL 100-119) were highly controversial measures. Both were attached to bills increasing the debt limit. *(Debt limit, Congress and the Nation Vol. VII, p. 42; Gramm-Rudman, Congress and the Nation Vol. VII, pp. 44, 67)*

As was typical, passage of a needed debt limit increase in 1989 was held up for a time by efforts to use the bill as an engine to enact unrelated measures into law. And in 1990, a yearlong budget impasse required an unprecedented six temporary increases — some effective for only a few days — until a sweeping budget deal was made. That agreement, in turn, permitted passage of a permanent increase in the debt ceiling to $4.145 trillion, an amount sufficient to carry the government into early 1993 and prevent the need for a debt limit debate in 1991 and 1992. That became the first two-year period not to require a debt limit increase since the years 1946-54.

1989 Action

Congress passed one temporary and one permanent increase in the debt limit in 1989, a largely typical year as debt limit fights went. Borrowing by the Treasury was expected by mid-August to reach the previous $2.8 trillion debt limit, enacted in September 1987.

On May 17, the House had passed a resolution (H J Res 280) permanently increasing the debt ceiling at the same time it adopted the conference report on the fiscal 1990 budget resolution (H Con Res 106). Under a 1979 rule devised by Richard A. Gephardt, D-Mo., House passage of legislation to increase the debt limit was automatic when that chamber adopted the final version of the year's budget resolution.

Senate leaders, however, wanted to defer action on the permanent increase until most of the year's business was complete, to prevent the bill from becoming, in the words of Finance Chairman Lloyd Bentsen, D-Texas, "a lightning rod, a magnet, for every amendment [senators] could think of."

So, on Aug. 1, the House passed 231-185 a short-term extension (HR 3024 — H Rept 101-188) temporarily raising the debt ceiling to $2.87 trillion to permit continued borrowing through Oct. 31, when the limit was to revert to $2.8 trillion. The Senate passed the bill by voice vote on Aug. 4 and President Bush signed it (PL 101-72) Aug. 7. A provision of the short-term bill changed accounting rules for certain bonds sold at a discount. Instead of counting "zero-coupon" bonds at face value (their full worth upon maturity), the Treasury was to count only the purchase value plus any accrued interest when calculating the national debt. The effect was to slow slightly the growth in the debt.

As the Oct. 31 expiration of the temporary increase approached, Treasury Secretary Nicholas F. Brady bought some time with an unscheduled Oct. 30 auction of government securities that raised enough cash to cover government obligations through Nov. 8.

The move was controversial, and critics said it was done to give the administration a few more days to try to enact a cut in the tax on capital gains — income from the sale of stocks and other assets that increase in value. Republicans had hoped to attach a capital gains tax cut to either the permanent debt limit bill or the fiscal 1990 budget-reconciliation bill (HR 3299). Action on both was stymied until Bush and congressional Republicans abandoned the capital gains fight fearing that they would be blamed for inviting governmentwide default. *(1989 reconciliation bill, p. 43)*

Democrats and Republicans dickered for several days more over other amendments, agreeing at the 11th hour to add just one provision — to repeal "Section 89" rules aimed at preventing discrimination in employee benefit plans. The popular provision had just been stripped as extraneous matter from the reconciliation bill. *(Section 89 repeal, p. 708)*

dropped in conference, a few provisions remained. In particular, the bill required states to extend Medicaid eligibility for certain pregnant women and poor, young children. *(Medicaid, p. 578)*

Child Care. The House bill contained competing plans from two different committees to help working parents find and pay for child care. Unable to forge a compromise, the Democratic leadership left the problem of reconciling the two approaches to conferees. The Senate passed a separate child care bill (S 5), but the Senate Finance Committee refused to negotiate on the issue during consideration of the reconciliation bill. In the end,

... And Surpassed $4.14 Trillion in 1990

With federal cash reserves exhausted and the government's credit due to be cut off by Nov. 9, the Senate amended H J Res 280 on Nov. 7 to extend the government's borrowing authority to $3.1227 trillion, good through 1990. The House accepted the Senate amendment later that night on a 269-99 vote, and Bush signed the bill (PL 101-140) the following day. The Treasury Department quickly rescheduled a number of securities auctions to raise money, with the first sale that afternoon.

1990 Action

As Congress prepared for its August recess in 1990, it appeared that the existing debt ceiling might be breached while members were out of town. Because members were unwilling to approve a long-term debt limit extension in the absence of a budget deal, Congress enacted a succession of temporary measures to keep pressure on the budget negotiators.

The House, 247-172, passed the first of those short-term debt extensions (HR 5350 — PL 101-350) on Aug. 3. The Senate acted by voice vote in the early morning hours of Aug. 4, in the session that began Aug. 3. Bush signed the bill into law Aug. 9. The new temporary ceiling was good through Oct. 2.

The House and Senate then both passed by voice vote a second short-term extension (HR 5755 — PL 101-405) on Sept. 30; it was signed Oct. 2 and enabled the government to borrow through Oct. 6.

Four further temporary extensions were included in short-term continuing appropriations resolutions for fiscal 1991 that were needed because the budget impasse blocked enactment of regular appropriations bills. *(Fiscal 1991 appropriations, p. 73)*

The final four short-term increases were:

- H J Res 666 (PL 101-412). The House passed the joint resolution, 305-105, Oct. 8 (in the session that began Oct. 7) and the Senate followed suit by voice vote the same day, after amending it. The House cleared the measure early Oct. 9, and Bush signed it that day. The legislation was good through Oct. 19.
- H J Res 677 (PL 101-444). The House passed the legislation, 379-37, on Oct. 18 to keep the government functioning through Oct. 24. The Senate by voice vote passed, and thus cleared, the resolution Oct. 19. Bush signed the measure the same day.
- H J Res 681 (PL 101-461). The measure passed the House, 380-45, and Senate, by voice vote, on Oct. 24 to keep the government operating through Oct. 27. Bush signed it Oct. 25.
- H J Res 687 (PL 101-467). The House, 283-49, and Senate, by voice vote, passed the resolution on Oct. 27. It was good through Nov. 5, giving Bush time to consider and sign the reconciliation bill and the 13 regular appropriations bills. Bush signed it Oct. 28.

Eventually, a budget deal was brokered that included a five-year plan to reduce the deficit. As part of the budget-reconciliation bill (HR 5835 — PL 101-508) that enacted the terms of the agreement into law, Congress voted to increase the permanent debt ceiling to $4.145 trillion. The House adopted the conference report on the reconciliation bill (H Rept 101-964) early Oct. 27 and the Senate followed suit later that day, clearing the bill for the president. He signed it into law on Nov. 5. *(1990 reconciliation bill, p. 55)*

Budget negotiators at first proposed increasing the debt limit by almost $2 trillion over the previous permanent debt ceiling. That was projected to cover all government borrowing needs for the full term of the five-year deal — through fiscal 1995. The increase was scaled back, however, to about $1 trillion, which congressional staff estimated could last until spring 1993. That forecast held true, requiring no debt limit votes in 1991 or 1992. Another debt limit showdown was expected early in the first year of Bill Clinton's presidency.

Debt Limit Extensions, 1989-90

Date Enacted	Public Law	Amount (In Trillions)
Aug. 7, 1989*	PL 101-72	$2.870
Nov. 8, 1989	PL 101-140	3.123
Aug. 9, 1990*	PL 101-350	3.195
Oct. 2, 1990*	PL 101-405	3.195
Oct. 9, 1990*	PL 101-412	3.195
Oct. 19, 1990*	PL 101-444	3.195
Oct. 25, 1990*	PL 101-461	3.195
Oct. 28, 1990*	PL 101-467	3.230
Nov. 5, 1990	PL 101-508	4.145

* Temporary increases that on specified dates were to revert to lower ceilings.

Source: Office of Management and Budget.

Democrats agreed to drop the child care provisions from reconciliation. *(Child care, p. 611)*

'Section 89.' The House jettisoned provisions included in HR 3299 by the Ways and Means Committee that would have revised "Section 89" rules requiring employers to prove they were providing roughly equal health and other benefits to all employees. The House voted instead to repeal the rules, which had become the focus of intense pressure from business groups. The Senate Finance Committee followed suit, approving full repeal. However, the provision was dropped when extraneous matter was stripped from the Senate bill. It then passed as an amendment to a bill extending the debt limit (H J Res 280 — PL 101-140). *(Section 89, p. 708; debt limit, box, p. 44)*

Fairness Doctrine. An attempt to enact into law the so-called fairness doctrine, which for years required broadcasters to air all sides of important public issues, faltered. The measure was included in the House bill but was later stripped from the bill as extraneous. *(Fairness doctrine, p. 430)*

Legislative Action

House Action. The 10 House committees charged with contributing to the reconciliation measure completed most of their work during the weeks of July 10 and July 17. Delays in Ways and Means held the bill off the floor. Ways and Means on July 13 approved a core package of $5.5 billion in new revenue, but the panel quickly became bogged down in debates over cutting capital gains taxes, paying for costly extensions of expiring tax breaks and modifying or repealing catastrophic costs health insurance.

Before the August recess, the panel voted to modify the catastrophic costs program, but a failed effort by committee Chairman Dan Rostenkowski, D-Ill., to block a capital gains tax cut prevented members from finishing work on revenues until early September.

The Budget Committee on Sept. 19 took the committees' recommendations, wrapped them into one bill (HR 3299) and sent it on to the floor without recommendation, reflecting dissatisfaction with the gimmick-laden measure among members from both parties. Budget Chairman Leon E. Panetta, D-Calif., conceded that without date shifts and other accounting gimmicks, the savings claimed in the bill would have been "several billion dollars" less. HR 3299 (H Rept 101-247) was formally reported Sept. 20.

The House on Oct. 5 passed HR 3299 by a 333-91 vote. The measure had shrunk during floor action from a $16.6 billion deficit-reduction package to one worth just under $11 billion in 1990 savings, even counting its many bookkeeping changes.

The losses primarily stemmed from a vote to repeal the catastrophic costs law, an action that was projected to cost about $4 billion in premiums that had been expected from would-be beneficiaries in 1990. The repeal amendment was adopted easily on Oct. 4, by a **key vote of 360-66 (R 164-10; D 196-56)**. A substitute amendment intended to salvage some of the program's benefits for the elderly then was rejected 156-269. *(1989 key votes, p. 1021)*

In a victory for small businesses Sept. 27, the House by a **key vote of 390-36 (R 172-2; D 218-34)** decided to repeal the Section 89 rules.

The capital gains fight was resolved in the president's favor when Republicans and 64 Democrats joined to defeat a Democratic leadership alternative that combined an expansion of individual retirement accounts (IRAs) with an increase in the top individual income tax rate. The defeat of the alternative retained a capital gains tax cut provision that had been included in the bill by a divided Ways and Means Committee. The leadership amendment was rejected Sept. 28 on a **key vote of 190-239 (R 1-175; D 189-64)**.

Before final passage, the House on Oct. 5 rejected two attempts to trim child care provisions included in the bill by the Ways and Means Committee and the Education and Labor Committee. The House easily rejected 140-285 a GOP child care proposal that relied solely on expansion of the earned-income tax credit for poor families with children. A second amendment, sponsored by Charles W. Stenholm, D-Texas, was similar to provisions in the bill but would not have set standards for child care providers. Stenholm's amendment failed on a **key vote of 195-230 (R 159-16; D 36-214)**.

Senate Action. Most of the eight Senate committees charged with contributing to the reconciliation bill finished their components of the measure by the August recess. But with tough decisions still pending before House Ways and Means, Senate Finance put off its business until after members returned in September.

Committee Chairman Lloyd Bentsen, D-Texas, gave up efforts to modify the catastrophic coverage law Sept. 26, after his committee was unable to draft a bipartisan overhaul that could save the program from repeal. But the committee waited to markup its revenue measures until the House had completed its consideration of capital gains.

In a marathon session that lasted into the early hours of Oct. 4, Bentsen defeated a Republican effort to add a capital gains cut to the bill on a 10-10 tie vote. The committee instead approved a package offered by Bentsen, which included a 50 percent deductibility for IRAs. It also called for a wide array of tax benefits sought by various committee members, along with offsetting tax increases to pay for them. The result was a bill so loaded down that it attracted national media attention and embarrassed some committee members.

The Senate Budget Committee met Oct. 12 and voted 9-7 to send its bill (S 1750), assembled from the committee recommendations, to the floor. Members from both parties took turns bashing the product, complaining about its savings gimmicks and the hundreds of extraneous, non-budgetary items. The dissatisfaction of rank-and-file members helped pave the way to a compromise.

A furious round of maneuvering began even before the Budget Committee reported the bill. Late on Oct. 5, Majority Leader George J. Mitchell, D-Maine, unexpectedly proposed that the massive deficit-reduction measure be stripped of hundreds of extraneous items, including the capital gains cut as well as Democratic initiatives such as child care.

His stated purpose was to rescue a legislative situation gone awry and to pass a scaled-down bill soon enough to avert the looming Gramm-Rudman spending cuts. He also erected a major obstacle to adding the capital gains cut to the Senate bill on the floor: Republicans would have to muster 60 votes to overcome a budgetary point of order to a capital gains amendment.

In a further move to force quick action, Mitchell canceled a long-planned, 10-day recess, and he scheduled a rare weekend session.

House Speaker Thomas S. Foley, D-Wash., had made a similar offer of a stripped-down bill more than a week before to House Minority Leader Robert H. Michel, R-Ill. — with one major difference. Foley's proposal had been conveyed privately and was quietly shot down by the White House. Mitchell boldly posed his offer on the Senate floor, a public challenge that was harder for the administration to refuse without appearing to sacrifice real deficit reduction for a favorite tax cut.

The breakthrough came on Oct. 13, when Republican leaders essentially accepted Mitchell's offer. In working out the deal, they gave up their insistence both on the promise of a simple majority vote on a capital gains tax cut and on assurances that the House likewise would accept a stripped-down package. Late that evening, the Senate passed HR 3299 by a **key vote of 87-7 (R 40-2; D 47-**

5), after first substituting a stripped version of S 1750 for the text of the House-passed bill.

Final Action. The deficit-reduction bill was sent to a mammoth 232-member conference committee, but the final compromise was reached only after days of marathon deliberations involving a small leadership group, with White House officials as participant-observers.

Senate Democrats who had initiated the move for a "clean" bill to help block the capital gains amendment found themselves faced with objections in conference. House Democrats balked at stripping their own extraneous provisions. And Senate Republicans held out, hoping to win agreement for a separate vote on capital gains.

Finally, on Nov. 2, Bush retreated from his demand for a capital gains tax cut, calling in return for a "truly clean" bill with hard savings of at least $14 billion. With pressure growing for adjournment by Thanksgiving, conferees complied with Bush's demands, stripping the bill of the House's many extraneous provisions and ending up with more than $14 billion in savings.

The savings relied heavily on retaining the equivalent of about a third of the $16.2 billion in automatic Gramm-Rudman spending cuts triggered with Bush's Oct. 16 order. The savings preserved from the automatic cuts amounted to $4.55 billion for 1990.

The conference finished its work on Nov. 21, and the House adopted the conference report (H Rept 101-386) late the same day on a vote of 272-128. In the early hours of Nov. 22, the Senate adopted the conference report by a voice vote, clearing HR 3299 for the president. Bush signed the measure on Dec. 19, calling it "Congress' response to my challenge."

Major Provisions

The final version of the Omnibus Budget Reconciliation Act of 1989 (HR 3299 — PL 101-239) was intended to provide one-year savings in fiscal 1990 of $14.7 billion, almost a third of which ($4.55 billion) was achieved by preserving a portion of the Gramm-Rudman across-the-board spending cuts ordered prior to enactment. Another $2.9 billion came from net tax increases, most of which were slight modifications in existing law. The balance came from a host of savings mostly in entitlement or other mandatory spending programs, although some entitlements also were granted narrow spending increases.

Not all of the tax changes generated revenue; the bill renewed 10 popular expiring tax provisions and created some new tax breaks, whose fiscal 1990 cost totaled almost $1.9 billion. *(Taxes, pp. 91, 96)*

HR 3299 provided changes in farm policy *(p. 548)*; Medicare, Medicaid and other health programs *(pp. 567, 571, 578)*; welfare programs *(p. 614)*; veterans programs *(p. 625)*; student loans *(p. 649)*; and the U.S. Postal Service *(p. 869)*. In addition, the final bill included provisions that:

Pension Law Penalties

- Required the labor secretary to assess a civil penalty for certain violations of the Employee Retirement Income Security Act (ERISA). The bill set the penalty at 20 percent of the amount recovered as a result of a settlement or a judicial proceeding involving a breach of fiduciary duty or other responsibility under Part 4 of ERISA, which spelled out the duties of trustees and fiduciaries in managing private pension plans.
- Authorized the secretary to waive the penalty if he determined in writing that the fiduciary acted reasonably and in good faith, or if it seemed likely the fiduciary would not be able to restore all losses to the plan without "severe financial hardship" unless a waiver or reduction of penalty were granted. The bill also reduced the 20 percent penalty by the amount of any tax or other penalty imposed on the fiduciary under other provisions of ERISA.

Regulatory Agency Fees

- Increased charges at the Federal Communications Commission for regulated private radio services, common carriers and broadcast outlets, and for radio operator examinations and ship inspections. Fines for violations, not raised since 1934, also were increased.
- Kept fees in fiscal 1990 for industries the Nuclear Regulatory Commission oversaw to an amount equivalent to cover 45 percent of the commission's operating costs for the year. Set initially in 1985 to recover 33 percent of costs, the target had been raised to 45 percent for fiscal 1988 and 1989.

Revenues

- **Education-Assistance Exclusion.** Restored and extended through Sept. 30, 1990, the exclusion for employer-provided education assistance, which expired Dec. 31, 1988. The limit remained $5,250 a year, and graduate courses remained ineligible.
- **Legal Services Exclusion.** Restored and extended through Sept. 30, 1990, the exclusion for employer-provided group legal services. The exclusion was available for services provided or for taxable years ending after Dec. 31, 1988, when the credit had expired.
- **Targeted-Jobs Credit.** Extended through Sept. 30, 1990, the targeted-jobs tax credit by which employers could deduct 40 percent of the first $6,000 in first-year wages for economically disadvantaged or disabled hires.
- **Mortgage Revenue Bonds, Credit Certificates.** Extended through Sept. 30, 1990, authority for mortgage revenue bonds and mortgage credit certificates issued at state and local levels to assist in financing for middle-income families.
- **Small-Issue Bonds.** Extended through Sept. 30, 1990, tax-exempt status of certain small issues of private activity bonds if at least 95 percent of the proceeds assisted small manufacturing firms or first-time farmers in obtaining start-up financing.
- **Business Energy Credit.** Extended through Sept. 30, 1990, energy-investment tax credits for businesses (solar, geothermal and ocean thermal) equal to 10 percent of the investment in solar or geothermal energy systems and 15 percent of the investment in an ocean thermal system.
- **Self-Employed Health Insurance.** Extended 25 percent deduction for health insurance expenses of self-employed individuals through Sept. 30, 1990. Only expenses for coverage during nine months were eligible for the deduction, and the earned income for an individual for those same nine months was to be determined on a pro-rata basis.
- **Low-Income Housing.** Extended the credit to investors in low-income housing through Sept. 30, 1990, with a three-fourths limit on the value of the credit in calendar year 1990 to reflect a pro-rata application of the nine-month term of the extension.

• **Research and Experimentation (R&E).** Extended the 20 percent tax credit allowed for qualified research expenditures incurred in a trade or business. The credit, which would have expired Dec. 31, 1989, applied to 1990 expenditures but with a three-fourths limit reflecting the nine-month term of the extension.

• **R&E Allocation Rules.** Revised R&E cost allocation rules for corporations paying taxes in more than one country. If expenses were incurred solely for research to satisfy a legal requirement imposed by a government, those expenses were allocated solely to income from within that jurisdiction. Remaining research expenses incurred in the United States were allocated 64 percent to U.S.-source income; expenses incurred outside the United States were allocated 64 percent to foreign-source income.

• **Dividends-Received Deduction.** Modified treatment of dividends on Section 1504(a)(4) stock by certain corporations (parents and subsidiaries) filing consolidated returns so the group of corporations was required to compute its tax on income from such subsidiaries' distributions without offsets for losses or credits of other corporations within the group.

• **'Junk Bonds.'** Modified treatment of certain high-yield original-issue discount obligations, sometimes called "junk bonds," to divide the proceeds into separate categories for interest and return on equity. The interest element was deductible for issuers of the obligations when paid (at the bond's date of maturity), while the return-on-equity element was not deductible except that the dividends-received deduction was allowed.

• **Non-Recognition of Income.** Limited the non-recognition of income for securities received in payment for certain transactions under Section 351. Under that section, no taxable gain or tax loss had been recognized if property were transferred to a corporation solely in exchange for stock or securities that conveyed immediate control of that corporation. But if the transaction involved a debt obligation other than a security, that part of the transaction had been taxable. As amended, the law also treated securities in Section 351 transactions as property, the gain on which was taxable.

• **Mutual Funds.** Altered regulations governing mutual funds — regulated investment companies (RICs) — to require an RIC to distribute 98 percent of its ordinary income, instead of 97 percent, to avoid a penalty excise tax.

• **Load Charges.** Altered regulations governing RICs to exclude load charges (advance charges for sales fees) in determining a shareholder's basis in mutual-fund shares sold or exchanged within 90 days if the shareholder subsequently acquired shares pursuant to a reinvestment right.

• **Dividend Income.** Required RICs to include dividend income received on the date the stock became ex-dividend (the date the value of the dividend leaves the dividend-issuing entity's books), not on the date the RIC received that value as under existing law.

• **Built-In Gain and Loss Thresholds.** Reduced built-in gain and loss thresholds for Sections 382 and 384, tightening restrictions on the use of losses and gains when certain changes took place within the control of the corporation. Instead of a threshold of 25 percent of the fair market value of the corporation's assets, the threshold would be either 15 percent of that value or $10 million, whichever was less.

• **'Wasting' Stock.** Required issuers of self-liquidating stock to reduce the original price for the non-taxed part of dividends and treat dividends from certain preferred stock as extraordinary dividends. The provision would apply when an issue's price exceeded its liquidation rights and shares had a dividend rate at the time of issue that declined in the future. It also would apply when such stock was otherwise structured to reduce shareholder taxes through dividend-received deductions and capital losses on sale of the stock.

• **Excess-Loss Account Rules.** Modified excess-loss account recapture rules to prevent parent corporations from achieving a tax advantage by shifting their excess-loss account in a subsidiary's stock from basis to debt. Under existing law, a parent corporation could dispose of some of a subsidiary's stock and apply the excess loss to reduce the basis of debt the parent held in the subsidiary.

• **Debt/Equity.** Allowed the Treasury to characterize an investment instrument with both debt and equity qualities as being part debt and part equity — with the appropriate tax consequences for each — instead of as entirely debt or entirely equity.

• **Reporting Acquisition, Recapitalization.** Required reporting to the Internal Revenue Service (IRS) of certain acquisition and recapitalization transactions after March 31, 1990. These transactions included acquiring controlling interest in a corporation. The information required included the identities of the parties, the fees involved and any changes in the corporation's capital structure.

• **'S' Corporations.** Required "S" corporations, small corporations taxed like partnerships, to make estimated tax payments for their liabilities on certain forms of income on which such payments had not been required.

• **Interest Deductions.** Limited the deduction for interest a corporation paid to related parties that were not subject to U.S. tax on the interest received — but only to the extent that the interest exceeded certain thresholds relating to the company's taxable income. Disallowed amounts also could be carried over to later tax years.

• **Net Operating Losses.** Limited carrybacks of certain corporate net operating losses when the losses stemmed from interest deductions attributable to certain corporate equity-reducing transactions, such as major stock acquisitions or excess distributions. The carryback that was limited was either the interest expense allocable to the transaction or the excess of the corporation's interest expense in the loss-limitation year over the average of such expenses in three previous tax years, whichever was less.

• **ESOP Interest Exclusion.** Repealed the partial exclusion for interest paid on employee stock ownership plans (ESOPs) when the ESOP did not own more than half of each class of stock or more than half the total value of all the employer's outstanding stock. Options held by the ESOP were not counted toward the 50 percent.

• **ESOP Dividend Deduction.** Limited the deduction an employer could take for dividends paid on securities held by an ESOP to a deduction for those dividends paid on employer securities acquired with a loan to which the partial interest exclusion applied. Dividends could be used to repay an acquisition loan only if those dividends were paid on employer securities acquired with that loan.

• **ESOP 'Rollover' Rules.** Allowed the recognition of gain to be deferred (a tax-free "rollover") on the sale of qualified securities to an ESOP only if the holder owned the securities at least three years before the sale of stock to an ESOP (effective for sales after July 10, 1989).

• **ESOP Additions.** Repealed the special dollars-per-year limit on additions to an ESOP for years beginning after Dec. 31, 1989.

• **ESOP Assumption of Tax Liability.** Repealed the provision by which ESOPs had been allowed to assume the tax liability of an estate, effective for estates of people who died after July 12, 1989.

• **ESOP Estate Tax Deduction.** Repealed the estate tax deduction for certain sales of employer securities to an ESOP, effective for estates of people who died after July 12, 1989.

• **Pension Funds.** Allowed employers to pay their current costs of health coverage for retirees with "excess" pension fund money not needed to cover pension liabilities, but limited employer contributions to pension plans that also pay incidental or subordinate medical benefits for retirees. Treasury regulations had defined this to mean that total employer contributions to provide such medical benefits and life insurance could not exceed 25 percent of the aggregate pension contributions during the same period. The bill codified the 25 percent rule and required that this determination be made on the basis of actual contributions to the plan instead of on costs.

• **Foreign Corporations.** Required the tax year of a controlled foreign corporation or foreign personal holding company to be the taxable year of its U.S. shareholders who owned a majority of the value of the U.S. shareholder-owned stock and who had identical taxable years.

• **'Resourcing' Income.** Authorized the Treasury to recharacterize the source of income of any member of an affiliated group of corporations or to modify consolidated return regulations as necessary to prevent avoidance of the limits on foreign tax credits.

• **Information Reporting.** Improved information reporting by U.S. subsidiaries and branches of foreign corporations, widening existing requirements, adding a requirement to maintain U.S. records, enhancing the enforceability of IRS summonses and increasing penalties for non-compliance.

• **Third World Debt.** Repealed preferential tax treatment for bank loans to Third World countries that had been designated for more U.S. lending under former Treasury secretary James A. Baker III's plan to alleviate developing countries' debts.

• **Aviation Excise Tax.** Suspended for one year the reduction trigger in taxes supporting the Airport and Airway Trust Fund. The trigger otherwise would have reduced affected excise taxes (including the airline ticket tax) from 8 percent to 4 percent on Jan. 1, 1990, because appropriations for airport improvements and other purposes in fiscal 1988 and 1989 were less than 85 percent of authorized amounts.

• **Airline Ticket Tax.** Accelerated collection of the airline ticket tax by modifying the collection period from the second semimonthly period (following the semimonthly period in which the tax was billed) to the first week of same.

• **Oil-Spill Liability Trust Fund.** Imposed a 5-cents-per-barrel tax on each barrel of domestic crude oil and each barrel of foreign crude or petroleum products to finance the Oil-Spill Liability Trust Fund. The tax would be suspended whenever the fund's interest-bearing balance exceeded $1 billion. The new trust fund would eventually subsume the Trans Alaska Pipeline Liability Fund.

• **Departure Taxes.** Increased the international air departure tax from $3 to $6 per departing air passenger as of Jan. 1, 1990, and imposed a new $3 fee on each departing international passenger on commercial ships as of Jan. 1, 1990.

• **CFCs.** Imposed taxes on ozone-depleting chemicals subject to the Montreal Protocol, including chlorofluorocarbons (CFCs) used in producing rigid foam insulation and all halons. The tax per pound of ozone-depleting chemical was set at $1.37 for 1990 and 1991, $1.67 for 1992 and $2.65 for 1993 and 1994. For each year thereafter, the rate would increase by 45 cents per pound.

• **Gasoline Excise Tax.** Accelerated the deposit requirement for collection of the gasoline excise tax, requiring taxpayers with more than $100 per month in gasoline excise tax liability to deposit taxes four times monthly.

• **Cigar Tax.** Modified taxation of bulk cigar imports to impose the tax after repackaging appropriate for consumer sales, allowing transfer of bulk cigars under bond from a foreign trade zone to an importer's business site where repackaging took place.

This corrected an inadvertent deletion of the "transfer in bond" provision from the Internal Revenue Code pursuant to the Reconciliation Act of 1986.

• **'Like-Kind' Exchanges.** Denied tax-free treatment to related parties in a direct or indirect exchange who then hold the property for less than two years.

The provision also barred like-kind treatment under Section 1031 for exchanges of foreign and domestic real property.

• **Completed Contract Accounting.** Repealed the remaining part of the completed contract method of accounting, which allowed long-term contractors to defer taxes on part of their earnings until the entire contract was completed.

Existing rules for certain construction contracts, qualified ship contracts and residential construction contracts were retained.

• **Trademark Purchases.** Changed the treatment of the costs of acquiring franchises, trademarks and trade names, repealing the special treatment accorded payments in discharge of a fixed-sum amount exceeding $100,000. The bill also changed rules that allowed a deduction for contingent amounts paid or incurred on account of the transfer of a franchise, trademark or trade name.

• **Employment Tax.** Imposed income-tax withholding on the wages of agricultural workers whose cash wages had already been subject to withholding for Social Security taxes after Dec. 31, 1989.

• **Deposit of Withholding.** Shortened the time an employer might hold income and Social Security taxes withheld from employees' paychecks and lowered to $100,000 the threshold figure at which this acceleration of deposits took effect.

• **Personal Injury Damages.** Ended the tax exclusion for damages received for personal injury with respect to punitive damages awarded in cases that did not involve physical injury or sickness.

• **In-Kind Partnerships.** Taxed pre-contribution gain on certain in-kind partnership distributions. The contributing partner was treated as recognizing gain or loss on the contributed property. The provision applied only to property distributions within five years after the property was contributed.

• **Cellular Phones.** Treated cellular telephones and other telecommunications equipment as "listed property," granting them the tax consideration given costs incurred to own or rent such property in business or a trade.

• **WIN.** Denied retroactive certification of the work incentive (WIN) credit, which had to be certified on or before the day the person began work.

• **Related Holding of Remainder Interest.** Denied any depreciation of amortization deduction for a term interest in property for any period during which the remainder interest in the property was held directly or indirectly by a related person.

• **Reporting of Loan Origination Fees.** Required lenders to report the percentage points charged on a mortgage and to report whether they were paid directly by the borrower or withheld from the loan disbursement.

• **Life Insurance.** Changed treatment of investment-oriented life insurance contracts known as "modified endowment contracts," which are bought as a tax-sheltered investment. The targeted contracts were those in which the cumulative amount paid under the contract at any time in the first seven years exceeded the sum of the net level premiums that would have been paid had the contract provided for paid-up benefits after the payment of seven level annual premiums.

• **Social Security Wage Base.** Increased the wage base on which Social Security taxes were calculated by including in the base all payments to a tax-deferred savings plan, with the effect of raising the ceiling on wages subject to Social Security taxes in 1990 by about 2 percent.

• **Hedge Bonds.** Limited the tax-exempt status of bonds issued by state and local governments in advance of need (to safeguard against future increases in interest rates). Interest on such bonds would be taxable except when the issuer expected to spend at least 15 percent of the net proceeds for the issue's purposes within 12 months, another 15 percent within 24 months, another 20 percent within 36 months and another 35 percent within 60 months.

• **Arbitrage Rebate Rules.** Lengthened the six-month exception to two years for bonds from which at least 75 percent of the net proceeds were to be used for construction. To qualify, bonds could not be private activity bonds; at least 10 percent of the proceeds of the issue had to be spent within six months of issue, at least 45 percent within 12 months, at least 75 percent within 18 months and 100 percent within 36 months.

• **Corporate Alternative Minimum Tax.** Repealed provisions by which depreciation, intangible drilling costs, depletion and mining expenses could not be written off under adjusted current earnings faster than under the taxpayer's book method (determined by comparing current value of deductions under the prescribed tax method and the book method).

The bill also expanded the use of the dividends-received deduction for adjusted current earnings to cover any dividend for which the deduction was 100 percent to the extent that the earnings were subject to tax, and to dividends from a 20 percent-owned corporation, to the extent that the earnings were subject to tax.

• **Foreign Sales Corporations.** Allowed the dividends-received deduction for dividends received from a foreign sales corporation only if received by a qualified cooperative engaged in marketing agricultural or horticultural products.

• **Discharge of Debt.** Excluded from tax any income from the discharge of indebtedness from adjusted current earnings.

• **Home Construction Contracts.** Excepted all home construction contracts from the alternative minimum tax rule, effective for contracts entered into after Sept. 30, 1990.

• **Individual Research Credits.** Repealed a requirement that individuals' research expenses be amortized over 10 years for purposes of the alternative minimum tax. The repeal applied to individuals who materially participated in the activity in which the expense was incurred.

• **Foreign Tax Credit Offsets.** Allowed certain corporations with 100 percent foreign income to use their foreign tax credits to offset 100 percent of their alternative minimum tax, instead of 90 percent as before.

• **'Orphan' Drug Credit.** Increased the minimum tax credit by the amount of the "orphan" drug credit that was not allowed solely by reason of the alternative minimum tax limitation. Under existing law, the tax credit for orphan drugs (drugs needed by relatively few people) could not reduce a taxpayer's tax to less than the alternative minimum tax.

• **Minimum Tax Credit.** Allowed the minimum tax credit to corporations for the entire minimum tax liability applying to tax credits arising in taxable years after Dec. 31, 1989.

• **IRS Information Reporting Penalties.** Established a three-tier penalty structure for failure to file an information return on time in which the penalty varied depending on when, if at all, the taxpayer corrected the failure. Previously, the penalty was a $50 fine for each failure, with a maximum penalty of $100,000 per year. The bill set fines of $15 per return for those filed within 30 days after a deadline, with a maximum of $75,000; $30 per return for those filed after 30 days but before Aug. 1 of any year, with a $150,000 maximum; and $50 per return, with a maximum of $250,000, for those filed after Aug. 1.

The bill set lower maximum penalties for small businesses (with gross receipts of less than $5 million): $25,000 for returns filed within 30 days, $50,000 for returns filed before Aug. 1 and $100,000 for those filed after Aug. 1.

Any person who failed to furnish a correct payee statement to a taxpayer by the due date was subject to a penalty of $50 per statement, up to $100,000 per year. If the failure was caused by intentional disregard of the requirement, the penalty was $100 per statement or, if greater, 10 percent of the amount required to be shown on the statement.

People filing more than 250 returns per year were required to transmit the returns by magnetic media instead of on paper forms.

• **IRS Accuracy Penalties.** Consolidated accuracy-related penalties, establishing a general 20 percent penalty for negligence or disregard of rules and regulations, for substantial understatement of income tax, for overstatements of the value of property or of pension liabilities and for understatements of the value of estates or gifts.

Existing law authorized a 5 percent negligence penalty, a 25 percent understatement penalty and 10 percent to 30 percent penalties for overstatements and understatements.

In general, the penalty applied only to the part of an underpayment related to the inaccuracy, not to the entire underpayment as under current law.

The bill extended the valuation penalty to all taxpayers and raised the threshold so it applied only if the relevant part of the taxpayer's underpayment exceeded $5,000 (or $10,000 for most corporations). The penalty would double if the face value of the property were overstated by 400 percent or more.

The 75 percent penalty for fraud was retained.

• **IRS Preparer, Promoter, Protester Penalties.** Increased penalties for professionals who prepare tax returns and revised standards that would trigger penalties. A $250 penalty applied if any part of a return or claim for refund were based on a position that the preparer knew, or should have known, to be unreasonable. A $1,000 fine applied to willful understatement or disregard of tax law by a preparer. Existing fines were $100 and $500, respectively.

The bill made each sale of an interest in an abusive tax shelter subject to penalty; existing law was unclear on whether the penalty applied to individual or multiple sales. The penalty was $1,000 per sale but no more than 100 percent of a taxpayer's gross receipts from such sales.

The bill increased from $5,000 to $25,000 the penalty for a taxpayer holding a frivolous or delaying position in Tax Court.

- **IRS Delinquency Penalties.** Increased the penalty for negligent or fraudulent failure to file a return to 15 percent of the net amount of tax due per month, up to a maximum of five months or 75 percent. The existing monthly fine was 5 percent, with a maximum of 25 percent.

The bill set penalties for late deposits of payroll and other taxes at 2 percent if the deposit was made between five and 15 days after it was due, 10 percent after day 15 and 15 percent if the taxpayer failed to correct the problem after day 15 and after receiving some preliminary notice from the IRS. The existing penalty was 10 percent of the underpayment, unless the taxpayer could show reasonable cause.

- **Repeal of Financial Institution Benefits.** Counted as part of the savings under reconciliation the accelerated repeal of tax benefits available to firms that bought failing financial institutions under federal supervision. The repeal was enacted in the savings and loan bailout bill (HR 1278 — PL 101-73). Effective May 10, 1989, that bill repealed special tax breaks that allowed the purchasing firms to exclude from taxable income federal financial assistance received as part of the purchase contract, to engage in tax-free reorganizations that otherwise would not be permitted and to use the net operating losses and built-in losses of a failed bank or thrift. *(Thrift bailout, p. 117)*
- **Marital Deduction.** Allowed the marital deduction for property passing to non-citizen spouses if they became U.S. citizens before the estate tax return of the decedent spouse was filed, so long as the surviving spouse was a U.S. resident at the date of the decedent's death and at all times before becoming a U.S. citizen.
- **Foreign Tax Credit and Lump-Sum Distributions.** Provided that the foreign tax credit was applied separately with respect to any lump-sum distribution (including from a foreign source) on which a separate tax was imposed and for which the amount of the distribution was treated as taxable for purposes of calculating the limitation.

Social Security

- **Elimination of Dependency Test for Adopted Children.** Provided that adopted children were eligible for children's insurance benefits regardless of whether the child was living with a covered worker when the worker became eligible for retirement or disability benefits.
- **Coverage Exemption, Religious Faith.** Extended the exemptions from Social Security coverage for members and employees of certain religious sects.
- **Coverage, U.S. Citizens Abroad.** Eliminated the option of U.S. employers to end Social Security coverage of U.S. citizens who worked abroad for foreign affiliates of a U.S. employer.
- **Continuation of Disability Benefits During Appeal.** Extended for one year, through June 30, 1991, the option of Social Security disability beneficiaries found to be no longer disabled to continue receiving benefit checks (and Medicare coverage) through the hearing stage of their appeal.
- **Social Security Wage Base.** Required that tax-deferred compensation reported to the federal government, including funds deposited into tax-deferred savings plans, be included in the annual calculation of the Social Security earnings base (the earnings taxed for Social Security).
- **Refunds, Medicare Catastrophic Coverage Act.** Provided that refunds for health insurance premiums or for duplicate coverage made to people by employers or former employers as a result of the 1988 Medicare Catastrophic Coverage Act (PL 100-360) not be subject to the Social Security payroll tax or to the federal unemployment tax, nor be included in the annual calculation of the Social Security earnings base. Authorized the Treasury secretary to prescribe how the refunds should be reported.
- **Demonstration Programs, Disability Insurance.** Extended for three years, through June 10, 1993, authority for work-incentive demonstration programs to encourage beneficiaries of the Social Security Disability Insurance program to return to work.
- **Earnings and Benefit Statements.** Required the health and human services (HHS) secretary, beginning no later than Oct. 1, 1990, to provide people aged 25 and older with a statement of their Social Security accounts upon request. The statement would include the amount of earnings, an estimate of Social Security taxes withheld and an estimate of future benefits at retirement. Beginning in 1995, the bill required such statements to be provided automatically at age 60 to all potential Social Security recipients for whom a current address could be determined. Beginning in 1999, the statements had to be provided biennially to people under age 60.
- **Beneficiary Protections.** Provided for a series of alterations in the operations of the Social Security Administration (SSA), including requiring that SSA take into account physical, mental, educational or linguistic limitations of beneficiaries in its interactions with them; that notices of benefit denials include information on options to get legal representation before SSA; and that people going to an SSA field office concerning time-sensitive matters receive a same-day interview with an SSA employee.

Railroad Retirement

- Extended for one more year, to Oct. 1, 1990, the transfer of proceeds from the income taxation of railroad retirement Tier II benefits from the general fund of the Treasury to the railroad retirement trust fund.
- Made employer-paid premiums for group-term life insurance coverage of more than $50,000 subject to the railroad retirement payroll tax, conforming the treatment of such premiums with their treatment under the Social Security payroll tax.
- Made contributions to 401(k) deferred compensation plans subject to the railroad retirement payroll tax, conforming the treatment of such contributions with their treatment under the Social Security payroll tax.
- Codified a 1981 Supreme Court ruling in *Rowan Companies v. United States*, bringing the railroad retirement payroll tax in line with the Social Security payroll tax, thus allowing an exception to the IRS definition of taxable wages for meals and lodging provided for the convenience of the employer, but stipulating that nothing in IRS regulations

for taxable income that provides an exclusion from wages should be construed to require a similar exclusion from compensation in railroad retirement regulations.

Offshore Oil Pollution

• Reimposed the 3-cent-a-barrel fee on oil produced offshore until the Offshore Oil Pollution Compensation Fund reached $200 million, not $100 million as in existing law, thus increasing 1990 receipts by an estimated $9 million.

Miscellaneous

• **Flood and Crime Insurance.** Counted as part of the bill's total savings the $190 million in premiums to be gained in 1990 because of a separate law (HR 3281 — PL 101-137) renewing both the federal flood and crime insurance programs. *(Details, p. 694)*

• **Sequester.** Saved $4.55 billion in 1990 by partly keeping in effect an across-the-board cut in spending triggered in October when the deficit was projected to exceed the Gramm-Rudman target for the year.

Appropriations, Fiscal 1990

Set back by anti-abortion vetoes and a variety of internal disputes, Congress in 1989 completed action on most of the 13 regular appropriations bills for fiscal 1990 nearly two months after the Oct. 1 start of the fiscal year. Only one bill, that for energy and water projects, was enacted on time. So in the meantime, Congress passed three stopgap continuing resolutions that kept the government running until Nov. 20.

Lawmakers struggling to adjourn finished the last of the regular bills just as the third temporary measure was about to expire. Bush approved eight pending measures in a flurry of bill signing the next day.

Among the final eight were new versions of three bills that Bush had previously vetoed — those for foreign aid; the District of Columbia; and labor, health, human services and education. Bush had objected to prior versions of all three because they contained provisions at odds with his anti-abortion stance.

Abortion had become one of the dominant political issues of the year following the Supreme Court's July 3 decision in *Webster v. Reproductive Health Services* that states could impose restrictions on abortions. In what was seen as a seminal event, on Oct. 11, the House reversed course after nearly a decade of opposing the use of taxpayer money to finance abortions, except those necessary to save the life of a woman. In a **key vote of 216-206 (R 41-134; D 175-72)**, the House signaled its desire to accept Senate language in the labor, health and human services bill that also would permit federally financed abortions in "promptly reported" cases of rape and incest. *(Abortion, p. 594; 1989 key votes, p. 1021)*

Following Bush's veto of that bill, the House on Oct. 25 fell 51 votes short of the two-thirds majority needed to override. Intent on quitting before Thanksgiving, lawmakers chose to concede the fight, and new versions of all three vetoed bills were sent to the White House with the restrictive abortion language that Bush preferred.

During House-Senate negotiations on the fiscal 1990 interior appropriations bill (HR 2788 — PL 101-121), another matter of social and political concern arose — the question of federal financing by the National Endowment for the Arts (NEA) of projects that some considered to be obscene or blasphemous. Sen. Jesse Helms, R-N.C., offered a floor amendment to an unrelated measure expressing the Senate's intent that its conferees on the interior bill insist on Senate language barring NEA grants for obscene works. The conference committee was poised to accept vastly watered down language that Helms considered totally unacceptable. The Senate, however, surprised observers by voting to table (thus kill) Helm's amendment on a **key vote of 62-35 (R 19-25; D 43-10)**. *(NEA funding, p. 865)*

The House had an opportunity to weigh in on a fundamental dispute between calls for fiscal austerity and support for big science projects — in this case the superconducting supercollider, the world's biggest atom smasher with a price tag approaching $10 billion. An amendment to the energy and water bill (HR 2696 — PL 101-101) to cut back the first allocation of construction money on the project was rejected on a **key vote of 93-330 (R 28-144; D 65-186)**. It was the first of many floor tests to come on the supercollider. *(Supercollider, pp. 878, 901)*

Supplemental Appropriations

Congressional leaders began 1989 aiming to finish all 13 appropriations bills by the start of the new fiscal year on Oct. 1, as it had in 1988 for the first time in 12 years. But appropriators got a late start when the House, Senate and administration spent three months during the spring battling to pass a supplemental appropriations bill for fiscal 1989.

The $3.3 billion supplemental (HR 2402 — PL 101-45) followed Bush's April request for a "dire emergency" spending increase, most of which was for veterans' benefits and guaranteed student loans. At first the House Appropriations Committee agreed to more than double Bush's $2.2 billion request, adding $822 million for anti-drug activities, among other items. *(Anti-drug bill, p. 768)*

The committee sent its bill (HR 2072 — H Rept 101-30) to the House floor in April, where it drew heavy fire from Republicans and the administration. HR 2072 was pulled from floor consideration, then returned with a leadership plan to pay for the extra spending. Majority Leader Thomas S. Foley, D-Wash., offered an amendment to slice roughly one-half of 1 percent from every appropriations account. Foley's proposal was roundly rejected on a **key vote of 172-252 (R 9-160; D 163-92)**. The bill was pulled from the floor again and later passed 227-197 on May 24 after the House adopted a series of amendments scaling back spending but retaining the anti-drug money. Meanwhile, the House on May 18 by voice vote passed a separate supplemental spending bill (HR 2402), which contained only the veterans' benefits. The Senate passed HR 2402 by voice vote the same day.

In the Senate, Appropriations Chairman Robert C. Byrd, D-W.Va., produced a version of HR 2072 (S Rept 101-41) with no new money for anti-drug efforts. On the Senate floor in June, he had to fend off several drug-related amendments. With a successful motion to table (thus kill) one such amendment on a June 1 **key vote of 77-18 (R 30-11; D 47-7)**, Byrd held the line and was able to resist the House in conference. The full Senate passed HR 2072 by voice vote June 7.

Conferees on HR 2072 quickly agreed upon all issues, except the anti-drug money, which was to go back to the floor as a separate item to face a showdown in both chambers. The House June 21 unexpectedly rejected 201-218 the broader conference agreement (H Rept 101-89), however, forcing yet another round of high-level negotiations. Ultimately, all sides, including the White House, agreed to include $75 million in additional money for anti-drug efforts, which along with the other elements of the conference agreement on HR 2072 were added by the Senate as an amendment to the pending veterans' supplemental (HR 2402), which had been sidetracked. The House then accepted the Senate's amendment, clearing HR 2402. The president signed the measure June 30.

Continuing Resolutions

The drug issue later forced a standoff on the transportation appropriations bill, and other spending measures had their own peculiar but less momentous problems. As a result of the delays, lawmakers resorted to three stopgap continuing appropriations resolutions.

The first (H J Res 407 — PL 101-100), which passed the House (H Rept 101-249) 274-152 on Sept. 26 and the Senate 100-0 on Sept. 28, provided continuing appropriations from Oct. 1 through Oct. 25. The Senate added an amendment providing $1.1 billion in disaster aid to the Carolinas, Puerto Rico and the Virgin Islands for damage from Hurricane Hugo. The House accepted the Senate amendment Sept. 28, and Bush signed the measure the following day.

The second continuing resolution (H J Res 423 — PL 101-130) passed the House (H Rept 101-301) 321-99 Oct. 24, and the Senate amended the measure and passed it 97-1 the following day. The House accepted the Senate amendments late Oct. 25, clearing the bill for the president just hours before the first stopgap bill was due to expire. The new short-term measure, which was signed Oct. 26, kept appropriations flowing through Nov. 15 to programs for which regular bills had not been enacted.

Coincidentally, like H J Res 407, the bill was a vehicle for major disaster aid: $2.85 billion, mostly for damage from an earthquake that hit Northern California on Oct. 17.

On Nov. 15, as the second temporary measure was about to lapse, the House, 296-123, and Senate, by voice vote, passed a third continuing resolution (H J Res 435 — PL 101-154), providing appropriations through Nov. 20. Bush signed the measure that night.

Fiscal 1991 Budget

The battle over the fiscal 1991 budget — which pitted Democrats against Republicans and sometimes the Republicans against themselves — took the entire 1990 session, locked the leadership into seemingly endless meetings, periodically exploded into nasty partisan name-calling and delayed work on other pressing legislation.

A deteriorating economy and its consequence — a fast-rising deficit — led to an increasingly partisan approach to the budget that eventually blocked the normal legislative process and forced the White House and congressional leaders to hold an unprecedented series of budget negotiations.

Work was concentrated in a four-and-a-half-month budget summit that extracted a heavy toll from both sides: President Bush retreated from his 1988 campaign pledge that he would not raise taxes, angering rank-and-file Republicans. House Democratic leaders were spurned by their members, who overwhelmingly rejected the product of the budget summit on the House floor.

In the end, frustrated and angry lawmakers were forced to stay in session closer to the fall elections than at any time since World War II before putting the finishing touches on a budget reconciliation bill, the centerpiece of the year's fiscal work.

The result of their efforts was a budget package that promised to cut $42.5 billion from the deficit in fiscal 1991 and $496.2 billion over five years. The biggest cuts over five years came from discretionary spending, especially defense. The next largest portion was from tax increases totaling $146.3 billion. Entitlement cuts and user fee increases yielded $99 billion over five years. And net interest on the federal debt was expected to drop $68.4 billion because of the other budget savings.

In a bid to establish peace for the next several years, members completely overhauled the fiscal process and scrapped any hope of balancing the budget in the meantime.

President's Budget Request

Bush submitted a fiscal 1991 budget request on Jan. 29, 1990. He proposed spending $1.23 trillion, offset by revenues of $1.17 trillion, yielding a deficit of $63.1 billion. When recalculated to account for specific requirements of the 1985 Gramm-Rudman anti-deficit law (PL 99-177), as amended in 1987 (PL 100-119), the deficit was projected to be $64.7 billion, close enough to the law's $64 billion target to avoid automatic spending cuts. *(Gramm-Rudman, Congress and the Nation Vol. VII, pp. 44, 67)*

In the budget, White House budget director Richard G. Darman predicted that, without any further action by Congress, the fiscal 1991 deficit would be $100.5 billion. That was an estimate of the "baseline" deficit, which assumed no changes in law but did allow for inflation and for demographic changes, such as the number of people eligible for mandatory programs such as Medicare.

To bring the deficit in line with Gramm-Rudman, Bush essentially called for about $36 billion in deficit reduction. More than half, or $19.5 billion, was slated to come from new revenue sources, though Bush denied that any were tax increases by traditional definition.

The top money-raiser was a plan to reduce the tax rate on capital gains income (the sale of stocks or other assets that appreciate in value). The administration projected that a capital gains cut would cause taxpayers to sell assets, which would mean an increase in revenue of $4.9 billion in fiscal 1991. *(Capital gains, p. 96)*

Other projected revenues included $5.6 billion from user fees that were routinely proposed but mostly went unrealized; $3.8 billion from mandating that all state and local government employees pay Medicare payroll taxes, a proposal that Congress repeatedly had rejected; $2.5 billion from unspecified Internal Revenue Service management reforms; and $1 billion from expedited collections of existing telephone and payroll taxes.

About a third of Bush's proposed deficit reduction, or $12 billion, came from cuts in entitlement programs, notably Medicare, farm price supports and federal employees' health and retirement benefits. Medicare took the brunt, $5.5 billion, though Bush stressed that the cuts would affect payments to doctors and hospitals, not patients' benefits.

Bush also proposed killing a number of domestic programs, including several that had been targeted unsuccessfully throughout the Reagan years. Among them were Amtrak, the Economic Development Administration, Small Business Administration disaster loans and mass transit operating subsidies.

Less than 10 percent of Bush's proposed cut in the deficit came from defense programs. The administration sought $303.3 billion in fiscal 1991 spending for defense, a cut of 2.1 percent after inflation was taken into account.

Budget Resolution

Normally, the next step would have been the development and adoption of a congressional budget resolution. But two problems existed. First, Democrats were divided over how much money to shift from defense to domestic programs in the wake of the end of the Cold War and were leery of calling for tax increases while Bush maintained his pledge of "no new taxes." Second, and more importantly, Bush's budget numbers did not hold up under close scrutiny — and with a declining economy.

The administration's budget was hitched to highly optimistic economic assumptions; White House economists projected much stronger growth and far lower interest rates in both 1990 and 1991 than did the Congressional Budget Office (CBO) or many private economists.

When CBO released its annual re-estimate of the president's budget March 5, it projected a $161 billion baseline deficit and a $131 billion deficit. The difference was largely attributable to different economic assumptions and to costs of the savings and loan bailout that were not included in Bush's budget.

Early in 1990, Bush ruled out convening a budget summit — the experience with trying to work a budget deal the year before had left both sides soured. The House went on to adopt a budget resolution, but the Senate managed to produce only a skeletal plan, which the House was unwilling to consider in conference. The two chambers subsequently cleared stopgap measures that allowed appropriations bills to move forward while congressional leaders and administration officials worked to reach a deficit-reduction deal.

That agreement was incorporated into a final budget resolution (H Con Res 310 — H Rept 101-820) that called for $1.24 trillion in outlays, $1.17 trillion in revenues and a $64 billion deficit. The deficit was contrived to meet the then-existing Gramm-Rudman target (which members knew would be scrapped). The budget resolution required a five-year budget-reconciliation bill to reduce the deficit by nearly $500 billion. *(Reconciliation, p. 55)*

The budget was adopted after the House first rejected the conference report and it was resubmitted to conference to remove most of its specific instructions to committees for how to reduce the deficit.

House Action. House Budget Committee Democrats set out gamely in February 1990 to draft a budget that would match Bush's bottom line of $36.5 billion in deficit reduction but reflect party priorities. Generally, that goal was thought to mean cutting more from defense and making room for several billion dollars extra for favored domestic initiatives, including programs for low-income children, housing and transportation. But negotiations broke down as liberals looked for larger defense cuts and heftier domestic hikes than conservatives could stomach.

Weeks went by with Budget Committee Democrats meeting informally but failing to reach agreement. When Congress returned from its spring break on April 18, the committee still had not produced a resolution. By then, however, projections of the deficit were rising fast and the exercise was beginning to seem somewhat academic. And a budget summit appeared ever more likely.

On April 19, the committee finally approved a $1.24 trillion budget resolution (H Con Res 310). The 21-14 vote was strictly on party lines, with all Republicans opposed. The resolution was formally reported (H Rept 101-455) on April 23.

H Con Res 310 provided less for defense and more for domestic programs than did Bush's budget and the same amount in revenues. Like the Bush plan, it claimed to cut about $36 billion from the deficit. It also included about $6.4 billion in new spending initiatives.

The House adopted H Con Res 310 on May 1 by a vote of 218-208. No Republican supported the plan; 34 Democrats voted against it — including both conservatives dissatisfied with the defense spending figure and liberals opposed to the domestic spending cuts. Democratic leaders sold the package primarily as a negotiating position in any future talks with the Senate and the administration.

Republicans had initially planned to offer the president's budget as a substitute but decided at the last minute not to do so, much to the glee of the Democrats. But the House rejected three substitutes for the committee version of H Con Res 310.

Two Republican proposals were defeated. The first, offered by Budget Committee member John R. Kasich of Ohio, called for a freeze of both defense and domestic discretionary budget authority at existing levels. The result would have been higher defense and lower domestic spending than called for in the committee resolution. The plan was defeated 106-305 on April 26. The House the same day also rejected, 48-354, a substitute offered by William E. Dannemeyer, R-Calif., that called for the issuance of gold-backed bonds to refinance the federal debt.

A proposal by the Congressional Black Caucus would have reduced the deficit to $63.8 billion in fiscal 1991 through greater defense cuts and larger revenue increases than called for in the committee plan. It was rejected May 1 by a vote of 90-334.

Senate Action. Democrats on the Senate Budget Committee began meeting privately in March, but they were even more sharply divided than their House counterparts. Unable to count on Republican votes, Chairman Jim Sasser, D-Tenn., had no choice but to try to bridge Democratic differences over defense spending and the size of overall budget cuts.

In late April, still short of the votes needed to approve a budget, Sasser decided to go ahead with formal committee meetings. In an unusual procedure, he tried to forge agreement on an overall budget framework before working out details. In three days of open sessions — which Sasser described as "a way of letting members express their views" — members considered and rejected a series of plans.

On May 2, the committee finally agreed to a $1.23 trillion budget plan (S Con Res 129) that promised to bring the deficit to $58.6 billion, but only after Sasser had made a number of concessions that threatened to prove troublesome on the floor. The resolution was approved 14-9, with the panel's 13 Democrats and one Republican, Charles E. Grassley of Iowa, voting for it. S Con Res 129 was reported (S Rept 101-283) on May 10.

To win approval, Sasser assembled a plan that incorporated the diverse demands of committee Democrats. He scaled back previously proposed defense cuts, shielded farm programs from large reductions and substantially increased the amount of unspecified domestic spending cuts needed to meet his deficit-reduction target.

The package also instructed authorizing committees to raise $25.5 billion in fiscal 1991 through revenues, user fees and entitlement cuts and set an overall domestic discretionary spending ceiling for appropriators that was $3.6 billion below the existing inflation-adjusted level. The plan did not specify how those domestic cuts would be made or how an additional $5 billion increase assumed for a variety of science, space, environmental, transportation, housing, education, health and anti-drug programs would be paid for. While the committee distributed spending increases throughout the budget's functional categories, it lumped most of the required domestic spending cuts under the vague category of "offsetting receipts."

S Con Res 129 appeared in serious trouble on the Senate floor. Republicans argued that it should be dumped in favor of a budget summit. And Democrats remained sharply divided over the level of defense spending. Prospects for bringing the measure to the floor were weakened further when Bush and congressional leaders agreed May 9 to begin top-level budget talks.

Pressure, however, was felt from another corner to move ahead. House and Senate Appropriations committees were eager to get to work on annual spending bills and were urging Budget leaders to finish the budget resolution, which would set overall totals for appropriations. Concern was particularly great in the Senate; unlike the House, Senate appropriations measures were subject to a point of order if brought to the floor before both chambers agreed on a congressional budget plan. *(Appropriations, p. 73)*

With S Con Res 129 effectively dead, the Senate on June 14 attempted a compromise. It adopted H Con Res 310 by voice vote after substituting the text of S Con Res 110, a pared down "policy-neutral" budget resolution, whose sole purpose was to allow the appropriations process to go forward. Senate leaders hoped to have a quick conference with the House that would focus on the overall discretionary spending figure, but House leaders balked.

In the absence of a conference agreement on the budget, each chamber voted to let appropriators go to work. The House adopted H Res 413 on June 19 on a near party-line vote of 276-136. Ostensibly a rule to allow consideration of the energy and water appropriations bill, H Res 413 also deemed H Con Res 310 to be final for all appropriations bills. On July 12, the Senate approved by voice vote its own deeming resolution (S Res 308), enabling appropriations bills to progress.

Final Action. The summit, involving at times as many as 20 people, convened May 15 but at first much of its time was spent in what amounted to seminars on the budget, not serious negotiations. Two events then gave impetus to the talks: On June 26, Bush released a surprise statement that "tax revenue increases" would be needed in any deficit-reduction package, and on July 16, Darman released a forecast that the 1991 deficit could hit $231.4 billion.

Nevertheless, the talks sputtered along, recessing in August, reconvening in early September in seclusion to little avail. Finally, on Sept. 17, the talks were confined to five congressional and three White House negotiators — and they made progress.

On Sept. 30, with automatic spending cuts in the magnitude of $85 billion about to be triggered by Gramm-Rudman the following day, the negotiators announced they had an agreement. The deal met two of the three requirements established by negotiators early on: It claimed to reduce expected government borrowing by about $500 billion over five years, and it contained numerous changes to the congressional budget process designed to prevent the agreement's key provisions from being breached in later years. Negotiators had failed to reach their third goal — cutting $50 billion from the fiscal 1991 deficit. In the end, they settled for savings of $40 billion. The pain of the savings was spread broadly among the parts of the budget:

- Defense and domestic discretionary spending, an ever-shrinking slice of the budget pie, were to be cut $182 billion.
- Entitlements such as Medicare and farm subsidies were to be cut $106 billion.
- New taxes and user fees for government services were to add $148 billion to the government's coffers.
- Interest payments on the federal debt, which was expected to top $4 trillion during the life of the agreement, were reduced by $65 billion.

Bush and congressional leaders from both parties defended the deal against rising opposition when it was brought to the House floor as a conference agreement on H Con Res 310 (H Rept 101-802).

In the early hours of Oct. 5 (in the session that began Oct. 4), the House rejected the conference report on a **key vote of 179-254 (R 71-105; D 108-149).** House Republicans were especially torn, and many blamed Minority Leader Robert H. Michel, R-Ill., for supporting a plan to increase taxes. *(1990 key votes, p. 1039)*

Congress Oct. 5 quickly cleared and sent to Bush a continuing appropriations resolution (H J Res 660) to keep the government in business and block Gramm-Rudman cuts, while the negotiations resumed. But an angry Bush vetoed the bill Oct. 6, forcing a shutdown of non-essential government activities over the three-day Columbus Day holiday — most visibly, museums and other tourist attractions in Washington.

Congress then remained in session, trying to find a way out of the impasse — with many of the disappointed tourists in the House and Senate visitors' galleries. On Saturday afternoon, Oct. 6, the House tried but failed to override the veto of H J Res 660. Meanwhile, House and Senate Budget leaders — minus the deeply divided House Republicans — began trying to patch together a new budget resolution that could win approval.

Their solution was to bring back H Con Res 310, after removing most of the specific requirements for a reconciliation bill to accomplish the needed budget savings. With the government shut down, and more members satisfied that they would have some latitude in committee to refine the reconciliation bill, the revised conference agreement on H Con Res 310 (H Rept 101-820) was reached.

The House adopted the conference report by a vote of 250-164 in the early hours of Oct. 8 (in the session that began Oct. 7); the Senate did likewise by a vote of 66-33 early Oct. 9 (in the session that began Oct. 8), clearing the measure and starting a rush to enact a reconciliation bill to put the budget in force.

Reconciliation, Fiscal 1991

Congress in 1990 took just three weeks to write and clear a budget reconciliation bill (HR 5835), a task that in the past had required months of work.

New Budget Process Provided . . .

One of the biggest selling points of the 1990 budget deal — for Congress and the Bush administration — was a package of procedural changes designed to make the deficit-reducing savings stick.

Included within the budget-reconciliation bill (HR 5835 — PL 101-508) were changes that drastically altered the budget process that Congress had followed since the Gramm-Rudman anti-deficit law was enacted in 1985 (PL 99-177) and modified in 1987 (PL 100-119). Gramm-Rudman had been a major revision of the 1974 Congressional Budget and Impoundment Control Act (PL 93-344), which had set in motion the basic budget process used since by Congress. *(1990 reconciliation bill, p. 55; Gramm-Rudman, Congress and the Nation Vol. VII, pp. 44, 67; 1974 budget act, Congress and the Nation Vol. IV, p. 71)*

Gramm-Rudman had set a goal of a balanced budget by 1991; the 1987 changes pushed the goal to 1993. The law mandated specific deficit targets each year and established a procedure for automatic spending cuts — called sequesters — if Congress and the president could not meet the targets through the ordinary budget process.

By 1990, however, the idea of balancing the budget in short order was dismissed as impossible, and the law was being criticized by budget experts and many lawmakers as leading to accounting gimmickry instead of true deficit reduction.

President Bush supported Gramm-Rudman but pressed for other ways of revising the budget process: a constitutional amendment requiring a balanced budget and a line-item veto of appropriations. However, he could not win enactment of either of them.

The Democratic chairmen of the House and Senate Budget committees decided that 1990 would be an appropriate time to overhaul Gramm-Rudman, focusing on longer-range budgeting and greater flexibility on spending. Many features of their plans, including a "pay-as-you-go" provision for bills that increased entitlement spending or reduced revenues, were eventually adopted.

To some, the final product seemed to signal an end to Gramm-Rudman as it had been known. Though the process changes were cast as amendments to the 1985 law, a key element of that law — the goal of a balanced budget — was abandoned. But in hailing the changes as he signed them into law Nov. 5, Bush said they "extended" and "strengthened" Gramm-Rudman and its enforcement mechanisms.

Legislative History

The Gramm-Rudman sequester procedure had been viewed as such a draconian threat that Congress and the administration were expected to settle any differences to avert it. But in 1989, the across-the-board cuts were triggered when Bush and the Democratic-controlled Congress failed to reach agreement by Oct. 1 of that year on a budget to stay within the law's deficit target of $110 billion.

Bush signed a sequester order on Oct. 16, 1989, which remained in effect until a $14.7 billion deficit-reducing reconciliation bill (HR 3299 — PL 101-239) that relied on some of the automatic cuts to achieve its goal was signed into law on Dec. 19. *(1989 reconciliation bill, p. 43)*

Because of that experience and general frustration with the process, Democrats in Congress stepped up their criticism of the law and drafted plans to overhaul or scrap it. Two principal proposals came early in 1990 from the House and Senate Budget chairmen — Rep. Leon E. Panetta, D-Calif., and Sen. Jim Sasser, D-Tenn. Both wanted to replace the Gramm-Rudman deficit targets and the enforcement procedure of automatic cuts with procedures requiring about $30 billion in annual deficit reduction, enforced with new parliamentary rules and — in Sasser's case — with the reward of payroll tax cuts for compliance.

Office of Management and Budget Director Richard G. Darman responded by issuing a veto threat against repeal of Gramm-Rudman and charging that Democrats wanted to escape the law's discipline.

Lawmakers in both chambers talked about budget process changes through much of the year and held some formal legislative proceedings toward that goal. But once the White House-congressional budget summit got under way in May, it became the real forum for making any decisions about procedural changes. *(1990 budget summit, p. 37)*

While summit negotiators met and made little progress, Democratic leaders decided to keep the regular congressional budget process going while the talks proceeded. Procedural changes were a secondary issue in the talks, but during much of June and July the summit seemed as likely as not to end in an impasse. In that atmosphere, the House took up — and rejected on July 17 — the most prominent of budget process changes: the balanced budget constitutional amendment. *(Balanced budget amendment, p. 75)*

And on July 26, the Senate Budget Committee reported out nine measures to revise the budget process. But aides acknowledged that the markup was held largely because of pressure from members who wanted some action on budget process plans they had authored even if none reached the floor. None did.

The summit recessed for August with no resolution in sight, and when negotiators resumed meeting in September, Republican negotiators kept up pressure to include process changes to tighten the fiscal reins on Congress. The agreement reached Sept. 30 included proposals that did not go quite so far as Republicans wanted in giving the president more

... In 1990 Reconciliation Bill

authority to limit federal spending — such as the line-item veto. But the changes agreed to were generally viewed as likely to impose at least some additional fiscal restraint on Capitol Hill.

The House on Oct. 5 (in the session that began Oct. 4) rejected the conference report on the budget resolution (H Con Res 310 — H Rept 101-802) incorporating the original summit agreement on a **key vote of 179-254 (R 71-105; D 108-149)**. But when negotiators brought back a revised version, the process changes were essentially untouched. They were then incorporated into HR 5835, which cleared Oct. 27. *(1990 key votes, p. 1033)*

Lawmakers and administration officials stressed the new spending controls in the bill. But the final plan also included features that would allow the deficit to grow as long as Congress did nothing overt to cause it to grow. Specifically:

- Discretionary spending would be allowed to increase at the rate of inflation.
- Entitlement spending programs such as Medicare could grow without penalty as more people became eligible for benefits.
- No penalties would be imposed for increases in spending or reductions in revenues that resulted from a deterioration in the economy or a mistake in technical forecasts, such as the estimated rate of revenue growth.

Spending for some special benefits — debt forgiveness for foreign countries, additional IRS agents and the military operations in the Persian Gulf crisis — were exempted from the spending caps.

Lawmakers got several things from the new procedures. The Appropriations committees gained not only the inflation-based increases in domestic spending, but they also snared an additional $20 billion in spending authority spread over fiscal years 1991-93.

Key Changes

Following were the key changes in the congressional budget process provided in the reconciliation bill:

Calendar Changes. The president's budget request to Congress, though rarely delivered on time, was now due the first Monday in February, not the first Monday after Jan. 3. If a budget resolution was not adopted by April 15, the Budget committees would have to report spending limits for the Appropriations committees based on discretionary spending in the president's budget. And while the fiscal year still began Oct. 1, automatic spending cuts would not be triggered until 15 days after Congress adjourned.

Five-Year Budgeting. Budget resolutions and necessary reconciliation bills had to project spending, revenues and deficits for five years.

Automatic Spending Cuts. The Gramm-Rudman procedure — an initial automatic spending cut or sequester that was calculated in mid-August and took effect Oct. 1, followed by a final sequester Oct. 15 — was dropped.

Instead, the bill created a set of three sequesters, each of which would kick in 15 days after Congress adjourned: The first would offset discretionary appropriations for the coming fiscal year that exceeded statutory limits; it only affected discretionary spending. The second would be triggered if Congress enacted entitlement spending increases or revenue decreases during the year and would only affect "non-exempt" entitlements. The third would offset an increase in the deficit above the limit set in the law, if the first two sequesters had not eliminated the excess deficit; it would cover all non-exempt spending. The discretionary and entitlement sequesters also would "look back" to offset spending increases or revenue cuts that affected the prior fiscal year.

Discretionary Spending Caps. Appropriations bills had to stay within specific caps for defense, foreign aid and domestic discretionary spending for fiscal years 1991-93; for fiscal years 1994-95, the law set overall discretionary spending caps, but spending could be shifted among the three broad categories. Bills exceeding the caps would be out of order for floor consideration. Each year these caps were to be adjusted upward to account for inflation.

Deficit Targets. The law set new, higher deficit targets for fiscal years 1991-95. These targets were to be automatically adjusted in fiscal 1992-93 to account for changes in the economy and technical estimates of the cost of entitlements. The president had the option of adjusting the deficit caps for economic or technical changes in fiscal years 1994-95.

Pay-As-You-Go Entitlements and Revenues. Bills containing increases in entitlement or other mandatory spending or reducing revenues had to be deficit-neutral. They would be out of order for floor consideration unless accompanied by offsetting entitlement cuts or revenue increases.

Supplemental Appropriations and Emergencies. Supplemental appropriations enacted before July 1 that exceeded spending caps would trigger sequesters 15 days after their enactment; the automatic cuts would offset the excess within the spending category in which the excess occurred. If requested to do so by the president, Congress could enact emergency appropriations, entitlement increases or revenue cuts without triggering sequesters.

War and Recession. A declaration of war would still cancel the sequester process. Congress also could vote to cancel the sequester process in the event of a projected recession or measured economic growth below 1 percent for two consecutive quarters.

The groundwork for the measure was laid in long budget summit talks that had kept most members far from the action all year. The House voted 228-200 to adopt the conference report on the bill (H Rept 101-964) in the early morning of Oct. 27, in the session that began Oct. 26. The Senate adopted the conference report hours later, by a vote of 54-45, clearing HR 5835 for the president. Despite White House support for the bill, a majority of Republicans in both chambers voted against final passage. President Bush signed the legislation into law (PL 101-508) on Nov. 5, ending a yearlong dance over how to stem the tide of federal red ink.

The measure was intended to cut the deficit by $28 billion in fiscal 1991 and $236 billion over five years. More than half of the deficit reduction — $137 billion over five years — came from revenue increases, the remainder from savings in entitlements and other mandatory spending. An additional $184 billion was to be achieved through cuts in appropriations that were enforced by strict spending caps. Further cuts to bring total savings almost to $500 billion would be realized from lower than anticipated interest payments on the federal debt as the deficit was reduced.

Legislative History

The die was cast for the bill in mid-summer as budget summit negotiators agreed to try to reach agreement on a plan to cut the deficit by $500 billion over five years. The real work did not get under way in crafting the fine points of a reconciliation bill to enact those savings until after a final budget resolution (H Con Res 310) was adopted Oct. 9. *(Budget, p. 53)*

House Action. On Oct. 15, the House Budget Committee assembled the recommendations of 12 different House committees into HR 5835. The bill was formally reported (H Rept 101-881) the next day.

In many ways, the committee version resembled the budget summit package. But on the floor, Democrats abandoned any attempt to compromise with Republicans. On Oct. 16, a substitute amendment drawn up by Democrats on the Ways and Means Committee was pushed through. It was designed to emphasize charges that Republicans were the party of the wealthy, while Democrats were looking out for low- and middle-income taxpayers.

The Democrats' substitute targeted wealthy taxpayers with a 10 percent surcharge on individuals with taxable incomes above $1 million, a boost in the top marginal income tax rate to 33 percent from 28 percent and a jump in the alternative minimum tax rate paid by wealthy taxpayers who took advantage of a large number of deductions from 21 percent to 25 percent. It increased the wage cap for Medicare payroll taxes to $100,000 from $51,300. And it increased premiums and deductibles for Medicare Part B, but at a lower rate than in the summit agreement.

The Democratic alternative included a capital gains tax cut specifically targeted at the middle class, allowing individuals $1,000 in capital gains tax-free each year and a lifetime exclusion of $100,000.

In a bid to ease the burden on low- and middle-income taxpayers, the package did away with the budget summit's proposal to increase the gasoline tax and add a 2-cents-a-gallon tax on refined petroleum products, including heating oil. It made up for the resulting revenue shortfall — nearly $57 billion over five years — by forgoing for one year the indexing of tax brackets and personal exemptions to account for inflation, a change that was expected to yield $36 billion over five years. That opened the way for Republicans to charge the Democrats with aiming at the rich but hitting the middle class.

Bush warned before the measure passed that it would be dead on arrival if it ever got to the White House.

House Republicans came up with an alternative budget package that promised $400 billion to $410 billion in savings over five years, mostly by freezing spending. But the Democratic-controlled Rules Committee refused to let them offer the plan on the floor.

The House Oct. 16 passed the Democratic alternative on a **key vote of 238-192 (R 10-164; D 228-28)**. The House then passed HR 5835 on a closer 227-203 vote. *(1990 key votes, p. 1039)*

Senate Action. The Senate Budget Committee, moving on a parallel fast-track with the House, assembled its reconciliation bill from the recommendations of 10 Senate committees and sent its measure (S 3209) to the floor on Oct. 16.

The Senate bill, unlike its House counterpart, was kept intact by a united bipartisan leadership front. Majority Leader George J. Mitchell, D-Maine, and Minority Leader Bob Dole, R-Kan., were able to keep reluctant troops in line long enough to block all substantive amendments. They argued repeatedly, and sometimes emotionally, that the fragile deficit reduction plan could easily unravel.

The leadership had little choice but to stick together, in large part because of the Democrats' narrow majority. Mitchell and other Democratic leaders had promised to protect the package against potentially fatal amendments to help win passage of a major component of the plan in the Finance Committee, where Democrats held only a two-member majority. Still, Mitchell and others said it pained them to have to oppose a number of amendments they found attractive, especially proposals to shift more of the tax burden onto wealthy taxpayers.

The Senate passed HR 5835 on Oct. 19, in the session that began Oct. 18, by a **key vote of 54-46 (R 23-22; D 31-24)**, after substituting the text of S 3209 for that of the House-passed bill.

Final Action. Buoyed by quick House and Senate passage of HR 5835, conferees met during the Oct. 20-21 weekend with high hopes of cutting a deal that would at last send everyone home. But they quickly fell into partisan wrangling over how to tax the super-rich.

The administration and Senate Republicans rejected the House Democrats' plan to slap a highly visible surtax on millionaires. House Democrats were unhappy about a 5-cents-a-gallon gas tax increase, Medicare cuts that they still considered too high and a host of other problems.

With the fall elections less than two weeks away, prospects for a deal seemed bleak. Then Dole and fellow Senate Finance Committee member Bob Packwood, R-Ore., produced a compromise that resuscitated the agreement. Packwood suggested substituting for the surtax a provision phasing out the personal exemption for wealthy taxpayers above certain income levels. The effect would be to raise the top marginal tax rate on the richest taxpayers, but the mechanism was not nearly so explicit as a surtax on millionaires.

Conferees also agreed to impose a new top marginal tax rate of 31 percent, with a 28 percent top rate on capital gains. They agreed to limit a taxpayer's itemized deductions by 3 percent of the amount his or her income exceeded $100,000.

Whatever reluctance remained among Democrats, it was overcome by their desire to leave town. The conference report subsequently was adopted, and the bill cleared.

Major Provisions

The final version of the Omnibus Budget Reconciliation Act of 1990 (HR 5835 — PL 101-508) was intended to increase revenue collections by about $137 billion over five years and reduce spending by about $99 billion over five years, particularly on entitlements and other mandatory spending programs. Some policy changes resulted in spending increases.

HR 5835 provided changes in transportation policy *(p. 418)*; farm policy *(p. 537)*; health care, including Medicare and Medicaid *(pp. 573, 578, 582, 586)*; child care *(p. 611)*; human services *(p. 614)*; veterans programs *(p. 625)*; student loans *(p. 649)*; and pension payments *(p. 719)*. The bill also included provisions that:

Banking

• **Deposit Insurance Premiums.** Authorized the Federal Deposit Insurance Corporation (FDIC) to set deposit insurance premiums for banks (covered by the Bank Insurance Fund) and savings and loan institutions (covered by the Savings Association Insurance Fund) at whatever level was necessary to maintain a minimum reserve in each of the insurance funds to cover potential losses.

In addition, the FDIC was authorized to adjust insurance premiums twice a year, instead of annually, as under current law. And the law repealed a provision enacted in 1989 as part of the thrift industry salvage bill (HR 1278 — PL 101-73) that required the FDIC to rebate excess bank or thrift premiums once the insurance funds achieved a ratio of 1.25 percent of total liabilities (or 1.5 percent if the FDIC board chose to seek a higher ratio).

• **FDIC Borrowing.** Authorized the FDIC to borrow working capital from the Federal Financing Bank, a Treasury Department entity, instead of from more expensive private sources. Existing law limits on FDIC borrowing from private sources would apply to Federal Financing Bank borrowing.

Housing

• **Increase in Mortgage Limit.** Removed the termination date of fiscal 1990 from the $124,875 Federal Housing Authority (FHA) mortgage limit.

• **Mortgagor Equity.** Prevented homeowners from borrowing more than the value of their home when other fees were financed into the mortgage. Limited the insured principal to 98.75 percent of the appraised value of the property, plus the amount of the mortgage insurance premium paid at the time the mortgage was insured. For properties with an appraised value of more than $50,000, the insured principal obligation was limited to 97.75 percent.

• **Mortgage Insurance Premiums.** Required the secretary of housing and urban development (HUD) to institute a new premium structure to shore up the financially shaky FHA insurance fund for single-family homes. The plan, which used a risk-based premium based on how much money a buyer put into the down payment, was designed to prevent people who were likely to default on loans from receiving them.

For mortgages on single- to four-family homes executed on or after Oct. 1, 1994, required the secretary, at the time of insurance, to collect a single payment equal to 2.25 percent of the amount of the original insured principal of the mortgage.

Required the secretary to refund a portion of the initial premium charge paid upon payment in full of the principal obligation before the maturity date of the mortgage. Allowed HUD to devise a refund schedule laying out how long HUD had to handle the insurance on a loan before the homeowner no longer qualified for the return on the initial premium. The purpose of this was to allow homeowners to recoup some of their initial costs when HUD did not insure the loan for a long period.

Authorized the secretary to collect annual premium payments equal to 0.5 percent of the remaining insured principal balance. For any mortgage involving an original principal obligation that was less than 90 percent of the appraised value of the property, the premium had to be paid for the first 11 years of the 30-year loan. For mortgages greater than or equal to 90 percent of the value, premiums had to be paid for the entire 30-year life of the loan.

For mortgages involving an original principal obligation that was greater than 95 percent of the appraised value of the property, the secretary was authorized to collect an annual premium of 0.55 percent of the remaining insured principal balance during the 30-year loan.

• **Transition Premiums.** Until Oct. 1, 1994, when the new risk-based insurance program was to be instituted, the act provided for a transition period to change the premium structure. For mortgages executed during fiscal 1991 and 1992, the secretary was authorized to collect at the time of insurance a single premium payment equal to 3.8 percent, which was the current upfront premium.

In addition, the secretary was authorized to collect annual premium payments equal to 0.5 percent of the remaining insured principal balance. For any mortgage involving an original principal obligation of less than 90 percent of the appraised value of the property, the annual premium had to be paid for the first five years of the loan. For any mortgage that was originally from 90 percent to 95 percent of the value of the property, the annual premium had to be paid for the first eight years of the loan. And for mortgages greater than 95 percent of the value, annual premiums had to be paid for 10 years.

For mortgages executed during fiscal 1993 and 1994, the secretary was authorized to collect at the time of insurance a single premium payment equal to 3 percent of the amount of the original insured principal obligation.

In addition, the secretary was authorized to collect annual premium payments equal to 0.5 percent of the remaining insured principal balance. For mortgages involving an original principal obligation of less than 90 percent of the appraised value of the property, the premium had to be paid for the first seven years of the loan. For mortgages from 90 percent to 95 percent of the value, premiums had to be paid for the first 12 years. And for mortgages in which the principal obligation was more than 95 percent of the value, premiums had to be paid for the full 30 years of the loan.

Required the secretary to refund all of the unearned premium charges paid during fiscal 1991-94 upon payment in full of the principal obligation of the mortgage before maturity.

Required the secretary to issue regulations to carry out this section no later than 90 days after enactment.

1990 Credit Reforms

In a victory for White House budget director Richard G. Darman, reforms aimed at disclosing and controlling the cost of government loans, loan guarantees and insurance were included in the 1990 budget-reconciliation bill (HR 5835 — PL 101-508). *(1990 reconciliation bill, p. 55)*

The credit reform provisions required that, beginning in fiscal 1992, the net long-term costs of loan and loan guarantee programs be included in the current fiscal year's budget. Also beginning in fiscal 1992, specific congressional appropriations were required for new direct loans or loan guarantees and specific budget authority was required for modifications to loan or loan guarantee programs.

Entitlement loan programs, such as the guaranteed student loan and veterans' home loan guarantee programs, were exempted from the requirements, as were the farm credit activities of the Commodity Credit Corporation. Federal government insurance activities also were exempted, including those in agencies created to protect depositors in the nation's financial institutions: the Federal Deposit Insurance Corporation, the Resolution Trust Corporation and the National Credit Union Administration.

As required by the bill, the Office of Management and Budget and the Congressional Budget Office (CBO) reported in mid-1991 on ways to account for deposit insurance under the credit reform program. And in his fiscal 1993 budget request submitted to Congress in early 1992, President Bush proposed legislative changes to account for the very large liabilities of the deposit insurance system (which had accrued from banks, thrift institutions and credit unions that were expected to fail but had not done so) in the budget process. Those proposals were not acted upon.

Darman had raised the credit reform issue with a provocative warning in sending Bush's fiscal 1991 budget to Congress on Jan. 29, 1990. With the savings and loan bailout fresh in the minds of the public and government officials, Darman said the government faced $5.7 trillion in contingent liabilities under various loan, loan guarantee and insurance programs. *(Savings and loan bailout, p. 117)*

Darman called these future liabilities "hidden Pacmen," a reference to the devouring computerized creature in a popular video arcade game. He said that even though the liabilities would not all fall due at the same time, likely losses on loans and loan guarantees alone were "virtually certain" to total tens of billions of dollars.

Comptroller General Charles A. Bowsher, head of the General Accounting Office, and CBO Director Robert D. Reischauer seconded Darman's warnings in an April 1990 hearing before the House Budget Committee Task Force on Urgent Fiscal Issues. All three officials criticized the growth in loan guarantees, which were not included in calculating the deficit and which had spiraled upward while direct loans were decreasing.

The credit reform provisions were rolled into the reconciliation bill cleared by Congress on Oct. 27 with little public discussion. However, Bush noted them in signing the bill Nov. 5, saying they would "expose and limit previously hidden (and rapidly growing) liabilities."

- **Mutual Mortgage Insurance Fund Distributions.** Required the secretary to consider the actuarial status of the fund in determining whether a surplus of funds existed to distribute to mortgagors.
- **Actuarial Soundness of Mutual Mortgage Insurance Fund.** Required the secretary to ensure that the fund attained a capital ratio of no less than 1.25 percent within 24 months after enactment. The capital ratio was the percentage of the amount of cash on hand out of the total amount of outstanding mortgages. (During a 10-year period, the capital ratio had steadily declined, with cash on hand dropping from $3.4 billion in 1979 to $2.6 billion in 1989. Had it been sound, the fund would have grown to $8 billion during that decade, according to the accounting firm Price Waterhouse.) Required the secretary to ensure that the fund attained a capital ratio of no less than 2 percent within 10 years of the date of enactment and to ensure that the fund maintained that ratio at all times thereafter.

Required the secretary to submit a report to Congress 24 months after enactment describing the actions that would be taken to ensure that the fund attained the required capital ratio.

Required the secretary to conduct an annual independent actuarial study of the fund and to report annually to Congress on its financial status.

Prohibited the secretary from sending mortgagors distributive shares, or excess premiums, if the insurance fund was not meeting operational goals. For example, during the 1970s, FHA-insured loans had a low default rate and HUD returned some premiums when owners paid off their loans. Operational goals included:

- Maintaining the required capital ratio.
- Meeting the needs of home buyers with low down payments and first-time home buyers by providing access to mortgage credit.
- Minimizing the risk to the fund and to homeowners from defaults.
- Avoiding policies that caused low-risk borrowers to go instead to commercial lenders, a phenomenon called "adverse selection."

Also authorized the secretary to adjust the insurance premiums if the fund was not meeting its operational goals. Required the secretary to notify Congress of the proposed change and the reasons for the change. Changes in premiums would take effect no earlier than 90 days after Congress was notified unless Congress acted during that time to increase, prevent or modify the change.

• **Home Equity Conversion Mortgage Insurance Demonstration.** Extended the termination date to Sept. 30, 1995, from Sept. 30, 1991. Limited the total number of mortgages insured under the program to no more than 25,000.

• **Auction of Federally Insured Mortgages.** Required HUD to arrange for the sale of interests in mortgage loans through an auction instead of accepting the multifamily mortgages from the original holders and giving a 10-year market-rate bond. To entice people to invest in multifamily housing during the late 1960s and early 1970s, HUD offered to take over mortgages after 20 years in exchange for an interest-bearing bond. HUD now wanted to buy out these mortgage agreements to save money.

Required HUD to arrange the auction at a price, to be paid to the mortgagee, of the base amount plus accrued interest to the date of sale. Provided that the sale price also include the right to a subsidy payment to the mortgagee that would make up for any improvements on the property.

Required HUD to conduct a public auction to determine the lowest interest rate necessary to accomplish a sale of the mortgage and any benefits accrued to it on the property and insurance.

Required a mortgagee, who decided to assign a mortgage to HUD, to provide the department and bidders at auction a description of the property and mortgage, including the principal mortgage balance, original stated interest rate, service fees, real estate and tenant characteristics, level and duration of federal subsidies and any other information HUD said was appropriate.

Required HUD to provide information regarding the status of the property relating to the Emergency Low-Income Housing Preservation Act of 1989 that had to do with prepayment provisions. (This was to ensure that affordable housing for low-income people was not lost to the market as owners paid off their federally subsidized mortgages.) Required HUD, after receiving the description of the property, to advertise for auction and publish mortgage descriptions in advance of the auction. Authorized HUD to wait up to six months to conduct the auction but prohibited HUD from holding the auction sooner than two months after receiving the mortgagee's written notice of intent to assign its mortgage to HUD.

Required HUD to accept the interest rate bid for purchase that HUD determined to be acceptable and required HUD to publish the accepted bid in the *Federal Register*.

Required settlement to occur no later than 30 business days after the winning bidders were selected in the auction, unless HUD determined that extraordinary circumstances required an extension.

Authorized mortgagees to retain all rights to assign the mortgage loan to HUD if no acceptable bids were received or settlement did not take place within the required time period.

Required HUD, as part of the auction, to agree to provide a monthly interest subsidy payment from the General Insurance Fund to the purchaser of the original property and mortgage securing that property. This was part of the buyout of the mortgagee's right to an interest-bearing bond.

Required HUD to encourage state housing finance agencies, non-profit organizations, tenant organizations and mortgagees participating under an Emergency Low-Income Housing Preservation plan of action to participate in the auction.

Required HUD to put the requirements under this section into effect within 30 days from enactment and not subject them to the requirement of prior issuance of regulations in the *Federal Register*. Required HUD to issue implementing regulations within six months of enactment.

Prohibited any of these provisions from diminishing or impairing the low-income use restrictions applicable to the project under the original regulatory agreement or the revised agreement entered into under the Emergency Low-Income Housing Preservation Act or other agreements to provide federal assistance to the housing or its tenants.

Specified that these provisions would not apply after Sept. 30, 1995, and required HUD to report to Congress on these provisions no later than Jan. 31 of each year beginning in 1992.

Crime, Flood Insurance

• **Crime Insurance.** Reauthorized the federal crime insurance program for four years through Sept. 30, 1995. The law also allowed policyholders to keep their coverage through Sept. 30, 1996, should the program be terminated, and it continued an existing 15 percent limit on premium increases through Sept. 30, 1995.

• **Flood Insurance.** Reauthorized the federal flood insurance program for four years through Sept. 30, 1995. The law also continued an existing 10 percent limit on premium increases through Sept. 30, 1995. But beginning in fiscal 1991, insurance premiums would be increased to include administrative and flood-plain mapping costs. The limit on increases would not apply to fiscal 1991 administrative costs.

Labor

• **Occupational Safety and Health Act Penalties.** Increased maximum civil penalties sevenfold, bringing fines for each willful or repeated violation to $70,000. The bill also imposed a new minimum mandatory penalty of $5,000 for willful violations of Occupational Safety and Health Administration (OSHA) laws. The new fines were expected to produce nearly $900 million in new revenue over five years.

• **Mine Safety and Health Act Penalties.** Increased maximum civil penalties fivefold to $50,000 for violations of mine safety and health laws. The new fines were expected to produce $247 million over five years.

• **Fair Labor Standards Act Penalties.** Imposed a maximum civil penalty of $10,000 for violations of child labor laws. The increase would produce $15 million over five years.

Social Security

• **Continuation of Disability Benefits During Appeal.** Made permanent the option of recipients of Disability Insurance benefits who were found to be no longer disabled to continue to receive benefits during the appeals process. In certain cases in which the appeal failed, the money might have to be returned.

• **Definition of Disability for Disabled Widows or Widowers.** Made the definition of disability the same for widows or widowers of workers covered by Social Security as for workers and applicants for benefits under the Supplemental Security Income program (SSI). Previously, widows or widowers of a worker covered by Social Security were subject to a definition of disability stricter than that for covered workers or SSI applicants.

• **Survivors' Benefits for Adopted Children.** Beginning with applications filed on or after Jan. 1, 1991, made eligible for Social Security survivors' benefits a child adopted by the surviving spouse of a deceased worker so long as the child had either lived with the worker or received one-half support from the worker in the year preceding the worker's death.

• **Representative Payee Reforms.** Made several alterations in the program under which Social Security or SSI checks were paid to a relative or other person, known as a "representative payee," in cases in which the beneficiary was unable to handle his or her finances. The new provisions:

• Required a more extensive investigation of representative payee applicants, including requiring applicants to submit documented proof of identity.

• Required the compilation of a list of payees found to have misused benefit payments.

• Restricted categories of persons who could serve as representative payees.

• Provided for appeals processes for persons for whom the Department of Health and Human Services (HHS) determined a representative payee was needed.

• Permitted, for three years only, certain community-based social service agencies that served as representative payees for five or more beneficiaries to collect monthly fees for such services. The fee, deducted from the beneficiary's Social Security or SSI check, could not exceed 10 percent of the check or $25.

• **Attorneys' Fees.** Streamlined the system under which attorneys representing Social Security beneficiaries in Social Security Administration (SSA) proceedings were paid. For cases in which an application for past-due benefits was approved, the agency would generally approve any petition, signed by both the attorney and client, for an agreed-upon fee not to exceed the lower of 25 percent of the back payments or $4,000. The HHS secretary would be permitted to adjust the maximum figure periodically for inflation. The administrative law judge who decided the case could protest the agreed-upon fee if he or she determined that it was excessive in light of the services rendered.

• **Beneficiary Protections Based on Faulty Information Provided by the SSA.** Provided that, if a person who was denied benefits reapplied instead of appealing the denial based on incorrect, incomplete or misleading information provided by the SSA, the failure to appeal would not constitute a basis for denial of the second application. (Information provided by SSA prior to May 1989 neglected to inform those whose applications for benefits were denied that reapplying instead of appealing the adverse ruling could result in the denial of the claim without further review of the evidence.)

• **SSA Telephone Service.** Required the secretary to re-establish as soon as possible but at the latest within 180 days telephone service to local SSA offices, which was cut off in October 1989, when all calls made to the agency's 800 number began to be routed to one of 37 SSA teleservice centers around the country. The General Accounting Office would have to report within 120 days on the level of telephone access to local offices. Also required the secretary to carry out demonstration projects to test the accountability procedures in three of the teleservice centers. Under the projects, certain callers would have to be provided with written documentation of their phone call, including the name of the SSA employee, a description of any action that the employee said would be taken and of any advice that was given.

• **Earnings and Benefit Statements.** Required, beginning Oct. 1, 1999, that all workers covered by Social Security be sent an annual statement of earnings credited to their account as well as potential benefits payable upon retirement. The fiscal 1990 reconciliation bill required such statements to be sent only once every two years.

• **Trial Work Period for Disabled Beneficiaries.** Made it easier for disabled beneficiaries to test their ability to return to work without threat of losing their disability benefits. Previously, beneficiaries were permitted only a single nine-month trial work period in which earnings were not counted toward elimination or reduction of benefits. The bill required that beneficiaries be allowed to work on a trial basis until a total of nine months had been worked over any five-year period.

• **Elimination of Advance Tax Transfer.** Repealed a provision of the 1983 Social Security overhaul bill (PL 98-21) requiring that estimated Social Security payroll tax receipts be credited to the Social Security trust fund in advance each month based on the estimated amount of taxes due that month. The provision returned to the method under which tax funds were credited to the trust fund only as they were received, although it retained authority for the secretary of the Treasury to use the advance tax transfer mechanism if he determined it was needed for Social Security to meet its payment obligations to beneficiaries. *(1983 act, Congress and the Nation Vol. VI, p. 659)*

• **Repeal of Retroactive Benefits for Certain Beneficiaries.** Eliminated eligibility for six months of retroactive benefits for certain categories of beneficiaries under age 65. (The provision, which would save an estimated $700 million over five years, also would relieve significant administrative burdens on the SSA.)

• **Dependent Benefits for Disabled Workers.** Codified the SSA practice of suspending payment of benefits to dependents of disabled workers in months when the worker was still eligible but did not receive benefits because earnings were too high.

• **Payment of Benefits to 'Deemed' Spouses.** Beginning Jan. 1, 1991, permitted benefits to be paid to both a legal spouse and a "deemed" spouse. Deemed partners were those later found not to have been legally married because of some defect in the marriage ceremony or because the spouse was not legally divorced from a previous spouse.

Previously, deemed spouses could not receive benefits at the same time benefits were paid to a legal spouse.

• **Vocational Rehabilitation Demonstrations.** Required the HHS secretary to establish demonstration programs permitting disabled beneficiaries to select their own vocational rehabilitation programs. Previously, disabled beneficiaries were automatically referred to state-run rehabilitation agencies.

• **Use of Social Security Number by Illegal Aliens Granted Amnesty.** Exempted from prosecution for fraudulent use of Social Security numbers or cards illegal aliens granted amnesty under the 1986 Immigration Reform and Control Act (PL 99-603). The exemption did not apply to individuals who sold Social Security cards, possessed cards with intent to sell them, or counterfeited or possessed counterfeit cards with intent to sell. *(1986 law, Congress and the Nation Vol. VII, p. 717)*

• **Special Minimum Benefit.** Reduced the amount of wages needed to earn a year of coverage toward Social Security's special minimum benefit paid to those who worked many years at low wages.

Instead of having earnings equal to 25 percent of the "old law" contribution and benefit base ($9,900 in 1991), workers would have to earn 15 percent of that amount ($5,940 in 1991).

• **Collection of Employee Social Security Tax on Group Life Insurance.** Beginning Jan. 1, 1991, required former employees who continued to receive taxable group-life insurance benefits from their former employers to pay with their personal taxes the amount of Social Security tax due on the life insurance benefits they received.

• **Waiver of Waiting Period for Certain Divorced Spouses.** Beginning Jan. 1, 1991, waived the two-year waiting period during which a divorced spouse was ineligible for spousal benefits if the worker in question was already receiving benefits before the divorce. (The purpose of the two-year waiting period was to prevent couples from divorcing to allow the worker's spouse to obtain benefits even though the worker would not be eligible because he or she was still working.)

• **Social Security Administration Review of Favorable Disability Determinations.** Lowered from 65 to 50 the percentage of cases that SSA had to review after a state agency judged a person to be disabled and thus eligible for disability benefits. SSA also would have to review as many cases in which a state agency certified that a beneficiary was still disabled as were necessary to maintain a high level of accuracy in such decisions. Formerly the agency was required to review 65 percent of those cases, as well.

• **Recovery of Overpayments from Former Social Security Beneficiaries.** Beginning Jan. 1, 1991, permitted SSA to recover overpayments of benefits from former beneficiaries by arranging with the Internal Revenue Service to deduct the amount owed from a federal tax refund due.

• **Railroad Retirement Tier II Fund.** Required that proceeds from income taxes on railroad retiree Tier II benefits continue to go into the Railroad Retirement Account for two more years, instead of the general fund as previously scheduled for Oct. 1, 1990. The extension was estimated to give an additional $385 million to the railroad account.

Abandoned-Mine Reclamation Fund

• **Reauthorization.** Extended the collection of fees from the coal industry through fiscal 1995. First imposed under a 1977 law (PL 95-87) to finance the restoration and cleanup — or "reclamation" — of abandoned coal mining lands, the fees had been scheduled to expire in August 1992. Extending them would raise an additional $832 million, bringing the total collected under the 1977 law to more than $4 billion. *(1977 act, Congress and the Nation Vol. V, p. 544)*

• **Abandoned Mines — Grant Formula.** Revamped the grant formula under which money from the fund was allocated to coal-producing states to run cleanup programs. The new formula would continue sending states with federally approved reclamation programs 50 percent of the funds collected within their borders (not counting some Indian lands, which were dealt with separately).

The distribution of the remaining money, however, was no longer left completely up to the interior secretary. Twenty percent had to go to the Agriculture Department to fund an existing rural abandoned-mine program. Forty percent had to be set aside for supplemental grants for high-priority health and safety projects in a way that assured that much of that money go to heavily damaged areas in Appalachian and Midwestern states.

The rest of the money would continue to be used by the secretary for emergencies, for cleanup activities in states that did not have approved programs and for administrative costs.

• **High-Priority Mines.** Allowed money from the fund to be used to clean up high-priority mines that were active after 1977 if enough reclamation funds were not available from other sources. The 1977 law prohibited the use of funds to clean up mines abandoned after enactment, but some mining operations and their bonding companies had gone bankrupt, creating a new generation of abandoned mines.

• **Acidic Water Seepage.** Authorized states to set up programs, financed by money from the fund, to halt and mitigate damage caused by acidic water seeping from abandoned mines. Such deposits harmed water quality and other biological resources.

• **Water Treatment Facilities.** Allowed states to use money to protect, repair, replace, construct or enhance water supply and treatment facilities to replace water supplies adversely affected by past coal mining.

• **Other Cleanup Projects.** Continued to allow states that had completed all priority coal mine reclamation projects to use money from the fund to clean up after other mineral mining operations and to protect, repair, replace, construct or improve water-supply utilities, roads and other facilities adversely affected by mining operations.

• **Reclamation Fund Surpluses.** Required the Treasury to invest surplus money from the fund in public-debt securities and credit the earned interest back to the fund.

• **Coal Producer Audits.** Gave the interior secretary expanded authority to audit coal producers to ensure full payment of fees.

Coastal Zone Management Act (CZMA)

• **General.** Expanded, revamped and reauthorized for five years the 1972 law (PL 92-583) providing federal grants to states to encourage them to draft plans for protecting their shore areas from the adverse impacts of development. *(1972 law, Congress and the Nation Vol. III, p. 799)*

• **CZMA Program Authorization.** Authorized appropriations for five years at continually increased levels, totaling $58.75 million in fiscal 1991 and $119.24 million in fiscal 1995.

• **Consistency Provision.** Bolstered the so-called consistency provision by overturning a 1984 Supreme Court decision in *Secretary of the Interior v. California.* The original provision was meant to assure states that federal coastline activities would be consistent with federally approved plans. But the Court ruled that federal outer continental shelf oil and gas-drilling lease sales were not covered by the provision because they had no "direct" affect on state-controlled coastal zones, which did not extend into shelf areas. *(Case summary, Congress and the Nation Vol. VI, p. 754)*

The new provision declared that all federal agency activities, whether in or outside of the coastal zone, were subject to the consistency requirement. The president could grant a waiver if he found that a specific activity was "in the paramount interest of the United States."

• **Coastal Cleanup Loans.** Repealed the Coastal Energy Impact Program, which until 1983 gave states loans to help them mitigate the impact of offshore oil and gas drilling and other energy-related activities. Loan repayments (averaging more than $6 million a year) would now go to a new, more limited Coastal Zone Management Fund, from which the commerce secretary would fund the program's administrative costs, special projects, emergency assistance, grants to help states develop plans and other discretionary activities.

• **Coastal Enhancement Grants.** Enticed states with new Coastal Zone Enhancement Grants to improve their plans in one or more of eight areas: coastal wetlands protection; natural hazards management (including potential sea and Great Lakes level rise); public access improvements; reduction of marine debris; coastal growth and development impact assessments; special area management planning for important coastal areas; ocean resource planning; and siting of coastal energy and government facilities.

• **Achievement Awards.** Authorized the commerce secretary to make annual "Walter B. Jones" achievement awards of up to $5,000 each to recognize individuals and local governments for outstanding accomplishments in the field of coastal zone management. Walter B. Jones, D-N.C., was the chairman of the House Merchant Marine and Fisheries Committee.

• **Coastal Pollution Control.** Established a Coastal Non-Point Pollution Control program, requiring shoreline states to develop plans for protecting their waters from non-point-source pollution from nearby land uses. States would get new grants to help them develop their programs, but the government would withhold parts of their CZMA and Water Pollution Control Act grants starting in 1996 if they failed to submit "approvable" non-point-pollution plans.

• **Coastal Non-Point-Pollution Guidelines.** Required the Environmental Protection Agency (EPA) to establish uniform national guidelines for controlling non-point-source pollution to coastal waters. States were required to follow these guidelines in developing their plans.

Environmental Protection Agency

• **Agency Fees.** Imposed additional fees totaling $28 million in fiscal 1991 and $38 million a year in fiscal 1992-95 on entities regulated or serviced by EPA.

The provision left most of the specifics to the EPA, but it limited new fees charged under the Water Pollution Control Act to $10 million a year.

It also prohibited the EPA from increasing fees for programs under the jurisdiction of the House Energy and Commerce Committee with two exceptions — fees specifically authorized by the 1990 Clean Air Act amendments and fees collected under the Toxic Substances Control Act that were in effect on the date of enactment of the reconciliation bill.

Revenues from the new fees had to be deposited in a special account in the Treasury and, subject to appropriations bills, used for the services for which they were charged.

• **Pollution Prevention.** Created a new $16 million-a-year EPA program aimed at preventing pollution "at the source" by changing production methods in ways that reduced waste.

Called the Pollution Prevention Act of 1990 and authorized in fiscal 1991-93, the provisions were similar to those in three other bills (S 585 — S Rept 101-526; HR 5931; HR 1457 — H Rept 101-555) that were considered by the 101st Congress but did not clear.

The law required the EPA to develop and implement a strategy to promote pollution source reduction, set up a new office to carry out the program, and make matching grants to states to encourage them to create their own source-reduction programs.

The EPA also was required to offer technical assistance to businesses on the subject, including funding for experts; improve public access to source-reduction data collected by the federal government and open a computerized Source Reduction Clearinghouse for that purpose; establish a technical advisory panel on pollution source reduction; create a training program and publish guidance documents on the subject; and give annual awards to companies with outstanding pollution source-reduction programs.

In addition, certain businesses that used toxic chemicals were required to file reports with the government disclosing the level of chemicals they released into the environment; the level recycled; the type of source-reduction techniques they used; and where they learned of such practices.

The EPA was required to issue reports on the new program and detailed analyses of the newly collected data every two years, including an assessment of whether the program was effective and whether the data were useful and valid.

Other Energy, Environment

• **'Superfund' Extension.** Extended the "superfund" hazardous waste cleanup program authorization for three years, from Sept. 30, 1991, when it was set to expire, to Sept. 30, 1994.

• **Nuclear Regulatory Commission (NRC).** Increased NRC user fees to raise an extra $287 million in fiscal 1991 and $1.554 billion through fiscal 1995. The bill accomplished this by requiring the agency to impose fees on its licensees to recover 100 percent of its budget, up from 45 percent in fiscal 1988-90. Without congressional action, the percentage requirement would have reverted to 33 percent, the floor established by the 1985 reconciliation bill (PL 99-272). The same held true for fiscal 1996: Without further action, the 100 percent figure would have reverted to 33 percent. *(1985 reconciliation, Congress and the Nation Vol. VII, p. 40)*

Miscellaneous User Fees

• **Customs Fee.** Extended merchandise processing fees and other user fees through Sept. 30, 1995.

• **Customs Adjustment Authority.** Authorized the secretary of the Treasury to adjust the merchandise processing fee on formal entries to take into account changes in economic conditions or trade flows, to avoid unintended under- or over-collections, and to help ensure that the user fee would continue to conform to the requirements of the General Agreement on Tariffs and Trade (GATT). The provision established a formula for adjusting the fee and set out requirements for the secretary to provide notification, allow for public comment and consult with Congress before adjusting the fee.

• **Small User-Fee Airports.** Provided that user-fee airports that processed fewer than 25,000 informal entries (generally, those valued at less than $1,250) a year would be required to collect an entry-by-entry fee and make a specified reimbursement to the Customs Service but would not have to reimburse Customs in an amount double their current assessment for Customs processing services, as was the existing case. User-fee airports processing 25,000 or more informal entries a year would continue to be exempt from the entry-by-entry fees but would be subject to the double reimbursement requirement. Conferees added a technical amendment that reflected that the double reimbursement requirement worked an unintended hardship on user-fee airports that processed a low volume of informal entries.

• **Technical Corrections.** Corrected technical and drafting errors in the Customs and Trade Act of 1990 (HR 1594 — PL 101-382) and reinstated two statutory provisions of the Customs Forfeiture Fund that were inadvertently deleted from existing law.

• **Patent and Trademark Office.** Placed all receipts raised by the surcharge on patent user fees in fiscal 1991 in a special fund in the Treasury and credited them as offsetting receipts. The special fund was solely for the use of the Patent and Trademark Office. Of this money, $91 million would be available to the Patent and Trademark Office to the extent provided in appropriations acts, and $18.8 million would be available directly to the patent office. In fiscal 1992-95, all receipts would be placed in this fund in the Treasury and credited as offsetting receipts, to be available to the patent office only to the extent provided in appropriations acts. The conferees agreed to raise user fees 13 percent above the House and Senate reconciliation bills and expected to generate $109.8 million in surcharges.

• **National Oceanic and Atmospheric Administration (NOAA).** Increased fees for services provided by NOAA, a division of the Commerce Department that included the National Weather Service. The increases totaled $2 million a year in fiscal 1991-93 and $3 million a year in fiscal 1994-95. The commerce secretary was required to waive the fees if necessary to continue providing emergency weather services, such as warnings and watches.

• **Radon Proficiency Program.** Required EPA to research radon measurement methods. Required that EPA charge a fee sufficient to cover the costs of an existing radon proficiency program, plus an additional $1.5 million a year for the new research. The EPA was required to conduct a study on the feasibility of establishing a mandatory proficiency program, which could require that any measuring device meet minimum performance criteria and any person conducting such measurements meet minimum proficiency criteria. The EPA had to report to Congress by March 1, 1991.

• **Department of Energy Study.** Directed the secretary of energy to study the department's user-fee assessment and collection practices and make recommendations on ways to improve those practices.

• **Department of Transportation.** Required the Transportation Department to report on the assessment and collection of licensing fees under the Commercial Space Launch Act.

• **Travel and Tourism Fee.** Required the commerce secretary to collect a fee from each commercial airline and passenger cruise ship line bringing passengers to the United States. The fee was to be $1 for each alien arriving at any U.S. port via that airline or cruise line during calendar 1991, with fees for later years calculated by the number of alien passengers during the previous year.

• **Coast Guard Fees.** Directed the Coast Guard to set up a system for the collection of $200 million from payments by users of direct and indirect services provided by the Coast Guard. The fee system went into effect immediately and continued through fiscal 1995.

The Coast Guard's authority to collect fees was extended to include direct user fees for inspection and examination of certain vessels and licensing, certification and documentation of personnel.

Indirect fees also were to be collected annually from owners or operators of recreational boats over 16 feet in length. Boats longer than 16 feet but less than 20 feet could be assessed a fee of not more than $25. Fees for boats longer than 20 feet but less than 27 feet could be no more than $50. For vessels 40 feet in length and more, the fee could not exceed $100.

The assessment was limited to vessels operating in navigable waters of the United States where the Coast Guard had a presence. Failure to pay the fees could result in a fine of up to $5,000.

• **Tonnage Duties.** Imposed increased tonnage duty for all vessels entering a port of the United States from any foreign port or place in the Western Hemisphere to 9 cents per ton, not to exceed 45 cents per ton per year, up from 2 cents per ton, not to exceed 10 cents per ton per year.

Duties on vessels entering U.S. ports from other foreign ports were to increase to 27 cents per ton, not to exceed $1.35 per ton per year. The current rate for these vessels was 6 cents, not to exceed $1.35 per ton per year.

After fiscal 1995, the tonnage fees would return to the amount imposed under existing law.

Vessels departing a U.S. port and returning to the same port, without going to another port or place, excepting vessels of the United States, recreational vessels or some barges, would pay 9 cents per ton, not to exceed 45 cents per ton per year for the next five fiscal years. In 1996, the rate for these vessels would be lowered to 2 cents per ton, not to exceed 10 cents per ton per year.

Vessels in distress and fishing boats or vessels not engaged in trade were not required to pay the duties.

• **Railroad User Fees.** Required the transportation secretary to establish a schedule of fees to be assessed to railroads. Fees could be collected by any federal, state or local agency chosen by the secretary and would be used to offset administrative costs incurred to carry out provisions of the Federal Railroad Safety Act of 1970 (PL 91-458). At no time could the aggregate of fees received for any fiscal year exceed 105 percent of the amount appropriated for activities to be funded by the fees. *(1970 act, Congress and the Nation Vol. III, p. 166)*

The secretary was required to report to Congress within 90 days after the end of each fiscal year the impact of the fees on the financial health of the railroad industry and its competitive position relative to each competing mode of transportation — including the total cost of federal safety activities for each such other mode of transportation, and the portion of that total cost, if any, defrayed by federal user fees. If any significant difference in costs and fees existed, the secretary, within 90 days of submitting the report, had to submit recommendations for legislation to correct any such difference.

Individual Income Taxes

• **Tax Rates.** Replaced the previous rate structure with three rates: 15 percent, 28 percent and 31 percent. The new 31 percent rate affected single individuals with taxable incomes of $49,200 or more; joint filers with taxable incomes of $82,050 or more; single heads of households with incomes of $70,350 or more; and married individuals filing separately with incomes of $41,025 or more.

The 31 percent marginal rate replaced the 33 percent paid by those in the "bubble," an anomaly created by the 1986 Tax Reform Act (PL 99-514) as the benefits of the lower 15 percent rate and the personal exemption for upper-income taxpayers were phased out. Those in the bubble — couples with taxable incomes of between roughly $80,000 and $200,000 and single filers with incomes of between $50,000 and $110,000 — paid a 33 percent marginal rate while those with higher incomes paid a flat 28 percent rate. The new 31 percent rate applied to those in and above the bubble range. The 15 percent and 28 percent marginal rates remained in effect for those with lower incomes. *(1986 law, Congress and the Nation Vol. VII, p. 79)*

• **Capital Gains.** Set a maximum tax rate of 28 percent on profits from the sale of appreciated assets, such as real estate, stocks or timber.

• **Alternative Minimum Tax.** Increased from 21 percent to 24 percent the alternative minimum tax rate paid by high-income taxpayers who would otherwise be able to reduce their liability substantially through the use of numerous deductions and other tax breaks.

• **Personal Exemption Phase-Out.** Phased out the value of the personal exemption, the deduction allowed each taxpayer and dependent, as a taxpayer's adjusted gross income exceeded a certain level. The phase-out began at $150,000 for joint returns, $125,000 for heads of households, $100,000 for single filers and $75,000 for married individuals filing separately. The phase-out ended at $122,500 above each of these amounts. The figures would be adjusted each year to offset the effects of inflation. The value of the deduction, $2,050 in 1989, would also be adjusted each year for inflation.

Under the law, the value of the exemption would be reduced by 2 percent (4 percent for married individuals filing separately) for each $2,500 or fraction thereof that a taxpayer's adjusted gross income exceeded the threshold amount. Thus, a single taxpayer with $162,500 in adjusted gross income (halfway through the phase-out range) could deduct half of his or her personal exemption.

The change would expire after the 1995 tax year.

• **Limit on Itemized Deductions.** Limited the value of itemized deductions, other than medical expenses, casualty and theft losses and investment interest, by 3 percent of the amount a taxpayer's adjusted gross income exceeded $100,000. For example, a taxpayer with income of $140,000 would have his or her itemized deductions reduced by $1,200, or 3 percent of $40,000. In no case would a taxpayer's deductions be reduced by more than 80 percent.

The $100,000 threshold amount, which applied to both single and joint filers, was indexed for inflation. The provision was set to expire at the end of 1995.

• **Appreciated Tangible Personal Property.** Repealed for the 1991 tax year a provision requiring the appreciated value of certain property donated to charitable organizations to be included in income subject to the alternative minimum tax. The change generally provided a one-year tax break to upper-income individuals who donated artwork and manuscripts to libraries, universities and museums.

• **Cosmetic Surgery.** Prohibited deductions for expenses paid for unnecessary cosmetic surgery.

• **Earned Income Tax Credit (EITC).** Increased the refundable credit allowed working poor families, from what had been a projected maximum of $994 in 1991 to $1,186 for those with one qualifying child and $1,228 for those with two or more qualifying children. For 1990, the credit was 14 percent of the first $6,810 of earned income and was phased out at a rate of 10 percent of the amount of adjusted gross income or earned income, whichever was greater, that exceeded $10,730. The base income amount and the point at which the phase-out began were adjusted annually for inflation.

The law increased the credit for taxpayers with one qualifying child to 16.7 percent in 1991, 17.6 percent in 1992, 18.5 percent in 1993 and 23 percent in 1994 and after. The phase-out rate for such families was 11.93 percent in 1991, 12.57 percent in 1992, 13.21 percent in 1993 and 16.43 percent in 1994 and after.

The credit for those with two or more qualifying children was 17.3 percent in 1991, 18.4 percent in 1992, 19.5 percent in 1993 and 25 percent in 1994 and after. The phase-out rate was 12.36 percent in 1991, 13.14 percent in 1992, 13.93 percent in 1993 and 17.86 percent in 1994 and after.

The law also stiffened and clarified eligibility requirements for the EITC.

• **Supplemental Young Child Credit.** Provided an additional 5 percent credit, with an increase in the phase-out rate of 3.57 percent, for those with qualifying children under the age of 1. The maximum supplemental credit was expected to be $355 in 1991. Any child for whom the credit was claimed was not considered a qualifying child for the separate dependent care tax credit.

• **Supplemental EITC for Health Insurance.** Allowed an additional credit for premiums paid on health insurance coverage for one or more qualified children. The credit was calculated in a way similar to that used for the EITC, except that the credit percentage was 6 percent and the phase-out rate was 4.285 percent. The maximum credit for 1991 was projected to be $426, although the credit could not exceed the amount paid in health insurance premiums. A taxpayer's medical expenses deduction also would be limited by the amount of any credit claimed.

• **EITC and Means-Tested Programs.** Provided that the EITC and supplemental credits not be considered income or a resource in determining eligibility for Aid to Families with Dependent Children, Supplemental Security Income, Medicaid, food stamps and certain housing programs.

• **Study of Advance Payments.** Required the comptroller general, with the secretary of the Treasury, to conduct a study of the existing system that allowed those eligible for the EITC to request advance payment of the credit. The study was aimed at finding ways to simplify the advance payment system and learning why participation was low. The study had to be submitted to the House Ways and Means and Senate Finance committees within a year of enactment.

• **Public Awareness Program.** Required the secretary of the Treasury to establish a program in 1991 to increase taxpayer awareness of the earned income, dependent care and health insurance credits.

• **Taxpayer Identification Number.** Required taxpayers to provide a taxpayer identification number for any dependent age 1 or older.

• **Effective Date.** Provisions went into effect for the 1991 tax year unless otherwise noted.

Excise Taxes

• **Alcoholic Beverages.** Increased excise taxes on distilled spirits, beer and wine. The tax on distilled spirits was increased from $12.50 per proof gallon to $13.50 per proof gallon. This translated into an increase of 16 cents in the $2 tax on a fifth of 80-proof liquor.

The tax on beer was doubled from $9 per barrel to $18 per barrel. This meant the tax on a six-pack of beer went from 16 cents to 32 cents. The law continued the previous $7 per barrel tax on the first 60,000 barrels of beer produced by domestic breweries with total production of 2 million barrels or less a year.

The tax on still wines with up to 14 percent alcohol content rose from 17 cents per wine gallon to $1.07 per wine gallon; with 14 percent to 21 percent alcohol from 67 cents to $1.57 per wine gallon; and for wine with 21 percent to 24 percent alcohol from $2.25 to $3.15 per wine gallon. The tax on artificially carbonated wines increased from $2.40 to $3.30 per wine gallon. The increase translated into an 18-cent increase in the 3-cent tax on a bottle of table wine.

The law provided a credit of 90 cents per wine gallon on the first 100,000 gallons of wine produced annually for wineries that produced 150,000 gallons or less during the year. The credit was phased out for wineries with total production of between 150,000 and 250,000 gallons during the year. Champagne and sparkling wines were not included in determining the first 100,000 gallons eligible for the credit; however, they were included when determining a winery's total production for phasing out the credit.

• **Tobacco.** Increased excise taxes on tobacco products by 25 percent on Jan. 1, 1991, and the identical dollar amount on Jan. 1, 1993. Thus, the tax on a pack of 20 small cigarettes went from 16 cents to 20 cents in 1991 and to 24 cents two years later.

The tax for small cigars rose from 75 cents per thousand to $0.9375 per thousand in 1991 and $1.125 per thousand in 1993. For large cigars, it rose in 1991 from 8.5 percent of the suggested wholesale price, with a cap of $20 per thousand, to 10.625 percent of the manufacturer's price, with a cap of $25 per thousand. In 1993, it would increase to 12.75 percent of the manufacturer's price, up to $30 per thousand.

The existing tax for small cigarettes, $8 per thousand, went to $10 per thousand in 1991 and $12 per thousand in 1993. For larger cigarettes, $16.80 per thousand, the tax increased to $21 per thousand in 1991 and $25.20 per thousand in 1993. The 25 percent tax increase also applied to cigarette papers, cigarette tubes, chewing tobacco, snuff and pipe tobacco.

• **Ozone-Depleting Chemicals.** Expanded the list of ozone-depleting chemicals subject to tax by including carbon tetrachloride, methyl chloroform, CFC-13, CFC-111, CFC-112, CFC-211, CFC-212, CFC-213, CFC-214, CFC-215, CFC-216 and CFC-217. The base tax rate, multiplied by an ozone-depleting factor assigned to each chemical, was $1.37 per pound for 1991 and 1992, $1.67 per pound for 1993, $3.00 per pound for 1994, $3.10 per pound for 1995 and an additional 45 cents per pound each year after 1995.

• **Motor Fuels.** Raised the excise taxes on highway and motorboat fuels by 5 cents per gallon, effective Dec. 1, 1990. The increase resulted in a 14 cents per gallon tax on gasoline and a 20 cents per gallon tax on diesel fuel. The law also imposed a 2.5 cents per gallon tax on fuel used in rail transportation.

Half of the revenue from the highway fuels tax increase was dedicated to the Highway Trust Fund, and half of the motorboat fuels increase was dedicated to the Aquatic Resources Trust Fund. The other half in each case, as well as all revenue from the tax on fuels used in rail transportation, would be kept in the general fund.

The law also established a wetlands restoration program, generally benefiting Louisiana, within the Sports Fish Restoration Account of the Aquatic Resources Trust Fund and financed it through the taxes on gasoline used in small-engine outdoor power equipment.

• **Aviation.** Increased and extended through 1995 a number of aviation excise taxes, effective Dec. 1, 1990. The law increased the tax on air passenger transportation from 8 percent to 10 percent, the tax on air freight from 5 percent to 6.25 percent, the tax on non-commercial aviation gasoline from 12 cents per gallon to 15 cents per gallon, and the tax on non-commercial aviation jet fuel from 14 cents per gallon to 17.5 cents per gallon.

Revenues from the tax increases would go to the general fund through 1992 and to the Airport and Airway Trust Fund for 1993-95. All revenue from the extension of existing taxes would go to the trust fund.

• **Harbor Maintenance.** Increased from 0.04 percent to 0.125 percent the tax used to fund the Harbor Maintenance Trust Fund. The tax was generally imposed on the commercial value of cargo loaded and unloaded at U.S. ports and on commercial ship passenger fares. The provision limiting expenditures from the trust fund to 40 percent of eligible harbor maintenance and related costs was changed to allow expenditures on up to 100 percent of eligible costs.

• **Leaking Underground Storage Tanks.** Reimposed and extended through 1995 a 0.1-cent per gallon tax on gasoline, diesel fuel, special motor fuels, aviation fuel and fuels used on inland waterways to be deposited in the Leaking Underground Storage Tank Trust Fund. A $500 million revenue ceiling for the trust fund was eliminated.

• **Gas Guzzlers.** Doubled the tax on automobiles that did not meet statutory fuel economy standards. The tax began at $1,000 for vehicles that did not meet the 22.5 miles per gallon standard and rose to $7,700 for those with fuel economy ratings of less than 12.5 miles per gallon. Exemptions for stretch limousines and small manufacturers were repealed.

• **Telephones.** Permanently extended the 3 percent tax on local and toll telephone service.

• **Luxuries.** Imposed a 10 percent excise tax on the portion of the retail price of certain items that exceeded the following: $30,000 for automobiles, $100,000 for boats and yachts, $250,000 for aircraft and $10,000 for jewelry and furs. The tax generally did not apply to boats or automobiles used exclusively in a trade or business. Also exempted were aircraft used at least 80 percent of the time in a trade or business.

The tax was set to expire at the end of 1999 and did not apply to articles purchased pursuant to a contract binding as of Sept. 30, 1990.

• **Effective Date.** Provisions went into effect for the 1991 tax year unless otherwise noted.

Superfund Tax Extension

• **General.** Extended superfund taxes and trust fund for four years, from Dec. 31, 1991, to Dec. 31, 1995. Trust funds were generally available for expenditures incurred in connection with releases or threats of releases of hazardous substances into the environment.

• **Cap.** Increased cap on the aggregate amount of superfund tax revenue that could be collected from $6.65 billion to $11.97 billion.

• **Petroleum Tax.** Extended a tax on petroleum, imposed at a rate of 9.7 cents per barrel, on domestic or imported crude oil or refined products.

• **Hazardous Chemicals Tax.** Extended a tax on listed hazardous chemicals, imposed at a rate that varied from 24 cents to $10.13 per ton.

• **Imported Substances Tax.** Extended a tax on imported substances that contained or used chemical derivatives of one or more of listed hazardous chemicals.

• **Environmental Tax.** Extended an environmental tax equal to 0.12 percent of the amount of modified alternative taxable income of a corporation that exceeded $2 million.

Miscellaneous Revenue

• **Life Insurance.** Required insurance companies to amortize over a 120-month period certain policy acquisition costs that firms had previously been allowed to deduct in one year. These costs were determined as a set percentage of the net premiums on three categories of insurance contracts: annuities (1.75 percent), group life (2.05 percent) and other life (7.70 percent).

To help small companies, a shorter amortization period of 60 months was allowed for the first $5 million of amortizable policy acquisition expenses for the taxable year. This provision was phased out as the total of such expenses for the year increased from $10 million to $15 million. Small firms, those with assets of less than $500 million at the close of the year, also were exempted from certain amortization requirements for acquisition expenses under the corporate alternative minimum tax.

The provision was generally effective Sept. 30, 1990.

• **Property and Casualty Insurance.** Clarified the treatment of salvage and subrogation claims in limiting the deduction firms could take for losses.

• **Compliance.** Made a number of changes to improve tax collections. They included: new penalties on multinational firms that overstated the value of certain property or services resulting in tax underpayments; tighter information reporting requirements and record maintenance rules for foreign corporations that carried on a trade or business in the United States; suspension of the three-year statute of limitations on a tax return while the taxpayer and the Internal Revenue Service were in court litigating over whether the taxpayer had to comply with an IRS summons; an extension from six to 10 years in the statute of limitations for collection of taxes after an IRS assessment; extension for five years of IRS fees to supply written rulings or determinations in response to taxpayer requests; increased penalties for failure to report cash transactions involving more than $10,000.

• **Corporate Taxes.** Included a number of provisions covering corporate transactions. The law required corporations restructuring their debt to pay taxes on the difference between the face value of the original debt instrument and the fair market value of the new debt. The law also attempted to prohibit the use of certain tax-free distributions of subsidiary stock to disguise what was in effect a sale of the subsidiary, a transaction subject to tax. Both provisions generally were effective for transactions after Oct. 9, 1990.

• **Corporate Tax Underpayments.** Increased the interest rate corporations were required to pay on tax underpayments from 3 percentage points above the short-term federal rate to 5 percentage points above, after the corporation had been notified of the deficiency by the IRS. The increased rate did not apply to underpayments of $100,000 or less for any one kind of tax during any one taxable period.

• **Hospital Insurance Payroll Tax.** Increased from $51,300 to $125,000 the amount of employee wages and self-employment income subject to the Medicare hospital insurance payroll tax. The 1.45 percent tax was paid by both the employer and employee; self-employed individuals paid both portions of the tax for a total of 2.9 percent. The wage base would be indexed each year after 1991 to reflect increases in average wages.

• **State and Local Employees.** Extended Social Security and Medicare coverage, and the payroll taxes used to fund the programs, to state and local government employees who did not otherwise participate in a retirement plan. An exception was provided for students employed in public schools, colleges and universities who could be covered at the option of the state. The change was effective for services performed after June 30, 1991.

• **Unemployment Taxes.** Extended through 1995 a 0.2 percent surtax included in the 6.2 percent federal unemployment insurance tax employers paid each year on the first $7,000 of wages paid to an employee. Employers in states with no overdue federal loans and that met certain other requirements were still eligible for a 5.4 percentage point credit on the tax.

• **Tax Deposits.** Required employers to deposit income taxes withheld from employee wages and payroll taxes on the first banking day after the business accumulated an amount to be deposited of $100,000 or more.

• **Grantor Trusts.** Provided that a U.S. citizen who was a beneficiary of a trust be treated as the grantor, or owner, of the trust for income tax purposes to the extent the beneficiary transferred property as a gift to a foreign person who otherwise would have been treated as the owner of the trust.

• **Effective Date.** Provisions went into effect for the 1991 tax year unless otherwise noted.

Extension of Expiring Provisions

• **Allocation of Research Expenditures.** Extended through 1991 rules governing allocation of research and experimental expenditures to U.S. and foreign source income.

• **Research and Experimentation Credit.** Extended through 1991 a 20 percent tax credit allowed for new research expenditures and certain payments to universities for basic research.

• **Employer-Provided Educational Assistance.** Extended through 1991 the exclusion allowed an employee for up to $5,250 a year of certain employer-provided educational assistance. A prohibition against use of the assistance for graduate-level courses was repealed.

• **Group Legal Services.** Extended through 1991 the exclusion for certain employer-provided group legal services. The law also extended the tax-exempt status of organizations that had the exclusive function of providing qualified group legal services.

• **Targeted Jobs.** Extended through 1991 the tax credit available to employers of certain hard-to-place workers, including those who were economically or physically disadvantaged. The credit was generally equal to 40 percent of the first $6,000 of qualified first-year wages and 40 percent of up to $3,000 of wages for a disadvantaged summer youth employee.

• **Business Energy Investments.** Extended through 1991 a 10 percent credit allowed for business investment in solar and geothermal energy. A 15 percent credit allowed for investment in ocean thermal energy was allowed to expire Sept. 30, 1990.

• **Low-Income Rental Housing.** Extended through 1991 a tax credit, allowed in installments over a 10-year period, for certain construction or rehabilitation of existing property to produce low-income rental housing. The bill increased the annual state limit on the credit from $.9375 per resident in 1990 to $1.25 per resident.

• **Mortgage Revenue Bonds.** Extended through 1991 authority for state and local government entities to issue tax-exempt mortgage revenue bonds or mortgage credit certificates to help certain qualified individuals with the purchase, improvement or rehabilitation of single-family, owner-occupied homes.

• **Small-Issue Bonds.** Extended through 1991 authority for small issues of tax-exempt private-activity bonds if at least 95 percent of the net proceeds was used to finance manufacturing facilities or certain land or property for first-time farmers.

• **Health Insurance for Self-Employed.** Extended through 1991 a deduction for 25 percent of the cost of health insurance for a self-employed individual and the individual's spouse and dependents.

• **Orphan Drugs.** Extended through 1991 a 50 percent credit allowed for the costs of human clinical testing of drugs for certain rare diseases and conditions.

Other Tax Incentives

• **Non-Conventional Fuels.** Extended a credit allowed for production of certain non-conventional fuels. The credit, equal to $3 per barrel or Btu oil barrel equivalent, had been available for fuels produced from a well drilled, or a facility placed in service, before Jan. 1, 1991, if the fuel was sold before Jan. 1, 2001. The law extended each of these dates by two years. It also liberalized eligibility requirements for the credit for gas produced from tight formations.

• **Alcohol Fuels.** Allowed a new 10-cent-per-gallon credit for production of up to 15 million gallons a year of ethanol by a small producer, defined as one with a productive capacity not in excess of 30 million gallons of alcohol per year.

The law also reduced from 60 cents per gallon to 54 cents per gallon the credit ethanol blenders were allowed for 190 or greater proof ethanol. The credit for 150 proof to 190 proof ethanol was cut from 45 cents to 40 cents per gallon. The 6-cent-per-gallon exemption from federal motor fuels excise taxes for alcohol fuel mixtures was reduced to 5.4 cents per gallon. Corresponding reductions were made in tariffs on ethanol and ETBE (ethyl tertiary butyl ether), an ethanol blend.

The credit and excise tax exemption generally expired Jan. 1, 2001, and Oct. 1, 2000, respectively.

• **Enhanced Oil Recovery.** Created a new domestic energy tax credit equal to 15 percent of costs for qualified enhanced oil recovery projects, also referred to as tertiary recovery projects. The credit would be reduced when the average price of crude oil exceeded $28 per barrel (adjusted annually for inflation) and would be completely phased out when the price exceeded this amount by $6 or more.

• **Percentage Depletion.** Liberalized the allowance oil and gas producers received for depletion. The deduction had previously been limited to no more than 50 percent of the taxpayer's net taxable income from the property, computed without the deduction. The law increased the limit to 100 percent of net income from the property. A prohibition against claiming the deduction on certain transferred oil and gas properties was repealed, and the percentage depletion rate was increased for certain marginally producing properties when the domestic wellhead price of crude oil dropped.

• **Alternative Minimum Tax Relief.** Reduced the value of certain oil- and gas-related tax preferences used in calculating income subject to the alternative minimum tax. The reductions applied to deductions taken for certain intangible drilling costs and the percentage depletion allowance on marginally producing properties. The tax break would be phased out in taxable years following years in which the price of crude exceeded $28 per barrel (adjusted annually for inflation). It would be completely phased out when the average price of oil exceeded this amount by $6 or more.

• **Estate Freezes.** Revised estate-tax rules governing the transfer of small, family-run businesses from one generation to the next. The law repealed complex and controversial provisions enacted in 1987 that were designed to prevent tax avoidance through the use of so-called estate freezes, which allowed owners to transfer a business to their heirs and avoid estate taxes on any appreciation in the value of the business from the time of the transfer until the original owner's death. The new provisions, effective for transfers of property after Oct. 8, 1990, shifted the focus back onto the value of the stock at the time of the transfer. They included requirements aimed at setting a more accurate value on the property and to prevent transactions designed to avoid transfer taxes.

• **Barrier Removal.** Allowed small businesses a 50 percent income tax credit for expenditures of between $250 and $10,250 in any taxable year to make their businesses more accessible to the disabled. Such expenditures could include amounts spent to remove physical barriers and to provide interpreters, readers or equipment that made materials more available to the hearing or visually impaired and others. To be eligible, a business had to have gross receipts for the preceding taxable year of $1 million or less or have no more than 30 full-time employees in the preceding year. The credit was available for expenditures paid or incurred after the date of enactment.

• **IRS Regulations.** Required the IRS to consider comments by the Small Business Administration on proposed regulations and to discuss them in the preamble of the final regulations.

• **Pie Charts.** Required the IRS to include in individual tax-form instruction booklets two pie charts, one showing where the government gets its revenues and the other showing how they are spent.

• **Technical Corrections.** Included numerous technical corrections (as reported by the House Ways and Means Committee in HR 5822) to the Revenue Reconciliation Act of 1989, the Technical and Miscellaneous Revenue Act of 1988 and other recent tax bills. The law also repealed numerous obsolete provisions in the Internal Revenue Code.

• **Tax Information.** Allowed the release of certain third-party and self-employment tax information to the Department of Veterans Affairs to help the department determine eligibility for certain needs-based pension and other programs. The General Accounting Office was required to do a detailed report on the impact of the provision, which was effective upon enactment and expired after two years.

• **Effective Date.** Provisions went into effect for the 1991 tax year unless otherwise noted.

Public Debt

• **Permanent Limit.** Increased from $3,122,700,000,000 to $4,145,000,000,000 the permanent limit on the public debt, effective upon enactment. The change was expected to accommodate government borrowing needs until sometime in 1993.

• **Federal Funds.** Instructed the secretary of Treasury to credit federal funds, excluding the Civil Service Retirement and Disability Trust Fund and the Thrift Savings Fund of the Federal Employees' Retirement System, for interest income lost due to any disruptions in debt issuance between Oct. 15 and Dec. 31, 1990.

Pensions

• **Treatment of Employer Reversions.** Increased the rate of tax imposed on employers who terminated employee pension plans and reverted excess pension assets to the employer.

The rate, formerly 15 percent, jumped to 20 percent or 50 percent, depending on the circumstances.

The excise tax rate was to be 20 percent if the employer set up a replacement plan and left a "cushion" equal to 25 percent of the surplus, or gave cash payments equaling 20 percent of the surplus to retirees and workers.

Otherwise, the reversion tax would be 50 percent if the company did not maintain a qualified replacement plan or offer the lump-sum payments.

All qualified participants who had a right to an accrued benefit under the terminated plan as of the termination date had to be provided the benefit increases. Those who terminated employment before the termination date and received a lump-sum distribution of their benefits would not be qualified participants.

• **Transfers to Retiree Health Accounts.** Permitted, on a temporary basis, qualified transfers of excess assets from the pension assets in a defined benefit pension plan to the 401(h) retiree health benefit account that was part of such a plan. The assets transferred were not includable in the gross income of the employer and not subject to the excise tax on reversions. Such transfers could only occur once in a taxable year between Dec. 31, 1990, and Jan. 1, 1996.

• **Increase in Pension Benefit Guaranty Premiums.** Raised the flat-rate Pension Benefit Guaranty Corporation (PBGC) premium to $19 from $16, and increased an additional premium of $6 per $1,000 of unfunded vested benefits to $9. Also, the per-participant cap on the additional premium (calculated by dividing the total additional premium by the number of plan participants) was raised from $34 to $53.

The increases were effective for plan years beginning after Dec. 31, 1990.

Discretionary Spending Limits

• **Categories of Discretionary Spending.** Divided discretionary spending in fiscal years 1991-93 into three categories: defense, international and domestic. For fiscal years 1994-95, all discretionary spending was lumped together in a single category.

• **Discretionary Spending Caps.** Mandated the following 1991-93 and 1994-95 caps for discretionary budget authority and outlays (amounts in billions of dollars):

	Fiscal Years				
	1991	**1992**	**1993**	**1994**	**1995**
Defense					
Budget Authority	$288.9	$291.6	$291.8		
Outlays	297.7	295.7	292.7		
International					
Budget Authority	20.1	20.5	21.4		
Outlays	18.6	19.1	19.6		
Domestic					
Budget Authority	182.7	191.3	198.3		
Outlays	198.1	210.1	221.7		
Total Discretionary					
Budget Authority				$510.8	$517.7
Outlays				534.8	540.8

• **CBO, OMB Responsibilities.** Required that, as soon as practicable after Congress completed action on a discretionary appropriation (any of the 13 appropriations bills, a supplemental appropriations bill or a continuing resolution), the Congressional Budget Office (CBO) had to give the Office of Management and Budget (OMB) an estimate of the bill's new discretionary spending authority and outlays for the current year (if any) and for the budget year covered by the bill.

Within five calendar days of enactment of any such bill, OMB was required to send the House and the Senate a report containing the CBO and OMB estimates of budget authority and outlays for the bill, along with an explanation of any differences between the two.

OMB estimates had to be made using existing economic and technical assumptions. OMB and CBO were required to use scorekeeping guidelines agreed to after consultation among CBO, OMB and House and Senate Budget committees.

Under the new law, OMB's role shifted from looking primarily at the overall budget deficit (chiefly through the Oct. 15 sequestration provisions under previous law) to a bill-by-bill evaluation process.

This had the effect of involving the agency even more directly than it already was in congressional lawmaking.

• **General Sequestration.** Required that, if discretionary spending in any category exceeded the annual cap, an across-the-board spending cut — known as sequestration — within that category had to be made to reduce spending in all non-exempt accounts by a pro-rata share of the excess.

Such a sequestration had to take place within 15 days of the end of a session of Congress, except for certain circumstances (see below).

• **Look-Back Sequestration.** Required that, if a supplemental appropriations bill enacted after June 30 for the fiscal year in progress broke a spending cap in any category, the cap for that category for the next fiscal year had to be reduced by the amount of the excess.

• **Within-Session Sequestration.** Required that, if a supplemental appropriations bill that broke the cap in any category was enacted between the time Congress adjourned at the end of one session but before July 1 of the following year, there would be a sequestration 15 days after enactment to reduce the excess in that category.

• **Desert Shield.** Stated that any contributions from other nations to defray the cost of Operation Desert Shield not be counted under any discretionary spending category (and therefore not be used to offset any spending increase). At the same time, any U.S. spending for Desert Shield was to be treated as emergency spending not subject to the defense spending cap.

• **Adjustments to Discretionary Spending Caps.** Required that when the president submitted the budget for fiscal years 1992-95, OMB adjust discretionary spending caps to reflect: (1) changes in concepts and definitions; (2) changes in inflation; (3) re-estimates of the costs of federal credit programs; (4) funding for Internal Revenue Service compliance initiatives, within specified limits; (5) debt forgiveness in calendar years 1990-91 for Egypt and Poland; (6) International Monetary Fund funding; and (7) presidentially designated emergency supplemental appropriations.

• **Special Allowances for New Discretionary Budget Authority and Outlays.** Required the president to increase discretionary budget authority caps in fiscal 1992-93 by a specified formula that varied according to category and fiscal year. Outlay caps also could be increased by specified dollar amounts as long as the budget authority cap for an applicable category was not exceeded.

The special budget authority allowance was designed to add roughly $3 billion a year to discretionary spending in fiscal 1992-93. The special outlay allowance was designed to insulate the legislative process from differences between OMB and CBO cost estimates.

Pay-As-You-Go Limits

• **Sequestration.** Required that any legislation to decrease revenues or increase direct spending (defined as spending for entitlement programs, food stamps and any spending programs not subject to appropriations) that caused a net increase in the deficit trigger an offsetting, across-the-board sequestration in non-exempt entitlement programs.

The sequestration would occur 15 days after Congress adjourned at the end of a session.

• **Exemptions.** Stated that sequestration could not be ordered on the basis of any legislation that continued full funding and the continuation of the deposit insurance commitment, or because of presidentially designated emergency spending.

• **Sequestration Procedure.** Required that the amount to be sequestered come from non-exempt direct spending accounts in the following order: (1) reductions in automatic spending increases for the National Wool Act, the special milk program and vocational rehabilitation basic state grants; (2) the maximum reductions permissible in guaranteed student loans and foster care and adoption assistance; (3) reductions in each remaining non-exempt account.

• **Medicare.** Stated that Medicare could not be reduced by more than 4 percent as part of any sequestration to enforce pay-as-you-go requirements.

• **CBO, OMB Responsibilities.** Required that as soon as practicable after Congress completed action on any direct spending or revenue legislation, CBO provide OMB with an estimate of the change the legislation would make in outlays or revenues. Within five days of enactment of any such legislation, OMB was required to report to Congress on OMB and CBO estimates of the deficit impact of such legislation, along with an explanation of any difference.

Deficit Targets

• **New Deficit Targets.** Established new "maximum deficit amounts" (by fiscal year, in billions of dollars) as follows: for 1991, $327; 1992, $317; 1993, $236; 1994, $102; and 1995, $83.

• **Margins.** Stated that the margin — the amount by which the deficit could exceed the maximum deficit amount in any given year without triggering a sequestration — was zero in fiscal 1992-93. The margin for fiscal 1994-95 was $15 billion.

• **Sequestration.** Required that within 15 days after Congress adjourned at the end of a session, but after any sequestration to enforce discretionary spending caps or pay-as-you-go requirements, a sequestration would be required to eliminate any deficit that still exceeded the margin.

• **Excess Deficit.** Stated that the excess deficit was the amount by which the estimated deficit exceeded the maximum deficit amount, minus: (1) emergency direct spending or revenue legislation; and (2) the re-estimate of deposit insurance costs, if there was not a full adjustment for technical and economic re-estimates in 1994-95.

• **Dividing the Sequestration.** Required that, in implementing a sequestration, half the outlay reductions come from non-exempt defense accounts and half from non-exempt non-defense accounts.

• **Medicare.** Stated that Medicare could not be reduced by more than 2 percent under any sequestration to enforce maximum deficit limits. If Medicare already had been reduced by 2 percent or more under a pay-as-you-go sequestration, it could not be further reduced under a sequestration to enforce the maximum deficit amount.

• **Adjustments to Maximum Deficit Amounts.** Required that when submitting the budget for fiscal years 1992-93, the president adjust the maximum deficit amounts for that year and the remaining fiscal years through 1995 to reflect up-to-date re-estimates of economic and technical assumptions and any changes in concepts and definitions. The president could make similar adjustments for the fiscal 1994 and 1995 budgets.

For the purposes of a sequestration to enforce a maximum deficit, OMB would have to continue to use the economic and technical assumptions submitted with the president's budget.

This meant that, at least through fiscal 1993 (and in fiscal 1994-95 if the president so chose), a sequestration would cover only excess spending legislated by Congress — excesses already subject to sequestration under the procedures to enforce the discretionary caps and pay-as-you-go requirements. A sequestration to enforce a maximum deficit target was unlikely until fiscal 1994 — and not in fiscal years 1994-95 if the president opted to continue adjusting the maximum deficit amounts.

Sequestration Reports and Orders

• **Timetable.** Changed the timetable for sequestration reports and orders as follows:

Jan. 21. President must notify Congress (in 1993 and 1994) whether he will exercise the option to adjust the maximum deficit amounts for fiscal years 1994-95.

5 Days Before President Submits Budget. CBO sequestration preview report.

First Monday in February. President's budget is due; at the same time OMB must provide sequestration preview report.

Aug. 10. President must notify Congress if he intends to exempt military personnel from sequestration or sequester such accounts at a lower percentage rate.

Aug. 20. OMB sequestration update report.

10 Days After End of Session. CBO final sequestration report.

15 Days After End of Session. OMB final sequestration report; presidential order.

30 Days Later. GAO compliance report.

• **Low-Growth Report.** Provided that CBO had to notify Congress if CBO or OMB determined that real economic growth was projected or estimated to be less than zero in any two consecutive quarters within the six-quarter period beginning with the preceding quarter. CBO also was required to notify Congress if the Commerce Department's advance, preliminary or final report of actual real economic growth for each of the most recently reported quarters and the immediately preceding quarter was less than 1 percent.

• **Economic and Technical Assumptions.** Required that in all reports under this section, OMB use the same economic and technical assumptions used in the most recent budget submitted by the president.

• **Exemptions for Social Security and Railroad Retirement.** Exempted from sequestration Social Security benefits and Tier I railroad retirement benefits.

• **Non-Defense Unobligated Balances.** Prohibited sequestration of unobligated balances of non-defense budget authority carried over from prior fiscal years.

• **JOBS Portion of AFDC.** Required that any sequestration order achieve the fully required reduction in the Job Opportunities and Basic Skills Training Program (or JOBS) under Aid to Families with Dependent Children (AFDC) without reducing any federal matching rate. The provision set out formulas for determining amounts available to states in the event of a sequestration.

Budget Agreement Enforcement

• **General.** Set out maximum deficit amounts and discretionary spending caps (see figures above). Provided that it not be in order in the Senate to consider any budget resolution or related legislation for fiscal years 1992-95 or any appropriations bill for fiscal years 1992-93 that would exceed the caps or the suballocations made under the caps. The point of order would not apply if war had been declared or if the low-growth provision had been triggered. The law provided for allocations of the total budget amount to committees and suballocations of discretionary amounts among Appropriations subcommittees.

• **Adoption of President's Budget.** Provided that, if Congress did not adopt a budget resolution by April 15, the chairman of the House Budget Committee would have to make an allocation to the House Appropriations Committee based on the most recent budget submitted by the president. As soon as practicable after that, the Appropriations Committee was required to make suballocations to its subcommittees.

• **Implementing Pay-As-You-Go Requirements in the House.** Provided that, if legislation were enacted that provided for a net reduction in revenues in any fiscal year (not offset in the same measure by cuts in direct spending), the House Budget Committee could report, within 15 legislative days during a Congress, a reconciliation directive in the form of a concurrent resolution that would specify the amount of revenues needed to make up the gap and direct the appropriate committees to make the necessary changes in law.

• **Five-Year Budget Resolutions.** Made temporary changes in the budget act to create five-year budget resolutions that would be enforced by points of order against exceeding committee allocations for both the first year and the five years covered by the budget resolution.

• **Additional Changes in Budget Process.** Allowed for display in the budget resolution of the increase in the national debt as an alternative measure of the deficit, display of federal retirement trust fund balances and the creation in budget resolutions of pay-as-you-go provisions similar to reserve funds established in budget resolutions since 1987. Made a variety of other procedural changes, including codifying the so-called Byrd rule against extraneous matter in reconciliation bills.

• **Clarification of Presidential Authority Absent Appropriations.** Made clear that sequestered funds could not be spent and that ongoing, regular operations of the federal government could not be sustained in the absence of appropriations. This provision was adopted to guard against what the conferees believed might be an overly broad interpretation of a 1981 opinion by the attorney general that addressed the president's authority to continue government operations during a lapse in appropriations.

Credit Reform

• **General.** Recognized that federal credit programs were displayed in the budget on a cash accounting basis, which overstated the real economic cost of direct loans but understated the real costs of loan guarantee programs in the year loans were made. This section in effect reversed that status, so that the real costs of both types of credit would be more accurately reflected in the budget.

• **OMB and CBO Roles.** Provided that the OMB director be responsible for coordinating credit cost estimates for the executive branch. OMB was required to consult with CBO in developing guidelines for credit cost estimates and in reviewing and improving those estimates.

• **Budgetary Treatment.** Required that, beginning with fiscal 1992, the budget cost of credit programs be the net present value of the long-term costs to the government, excluding administrative costs and incidental effects. All other cash flows resulting from credit programs were to be treated as means of financing and included in a non-budgetary financing account.

• **Appropriations Required.** Required the appropriation of new budget authority for new direct loans or loan guarantees for fiscal 1992 and thereafter. The law provided an exception for entitlement credit programs (such as the guaranteed student loan program and the veterans' home loan guaranty program) and for the credit programs of the Commodity Credit Corporation.

Also provided that budget authority must be available for the cost of modifying any outstanding direct loan or loan guarantee. Administrative expenses for credit programs were to continue to be counted on a cash flow basis, but they had to be displayed in a separate subaccount within the account for the credit program.

● **Point of Order.** Provided, as part of the transition provisions, that new credit authority be subject to a point of order (based on violation of allocations) in the Senate during fiscal 1991. This provision was good only until the beginning of fiscal 1992.

● **Exemptions for Deposit Insurance and Other Insurance Programs.** Provided that these credit reforms not apply to the credit or insurance activities of the Federal Deposit Insurance Corporation, the National Credit Union Administration, the Resolution Trust Corporation, the Pension Benefit Guaranty Corporation, national flood insurance, the National Insurance Development Fund, crop insurance or the Tennessee Valley Authority. OMB and CBO were required to study whether the accounting for federal deposit insurance programs should be on a cash basis, on the same basis as loan guarantees or on a different basis.

Each agency was told to report to the president and Congress by May 31, 1991.

President's Budget Submission

● **Date Change.** Provided that the president could delay submitting his budget to Congress from the date required under current law — on or before the first Monday after Jan. 3 of each year — to no later than the first Monday in February.

Status of Social Security Trust Funds

● **Exclusion from All Budgets.** Prohibited counting the receipts or the disbursements of the Old Age and Survivors Insurance trust fund and the Disability Insurance trust fund (collectively: OASDI) in the budget submitted by the president, the congressional budget or for the purposes of the Gramm-Rudman anti-deficit law.

● **'Fire Wall' Protection in the House.** Prohibited consideration in the House of any legislation that would expand Social Security benefits without providing offsetting Social Security tax increases or cut Social Security taxes without providing offsetting cuts in benefits or a corresponding increase in Medicare taxes. The legislation expressed these prohibitions in a complex formula that would bar changes in the actuarial balance of the Social Security trust funds over five years or 75 years.

● **'Fire Wall' Protection in the Senate.** Barred Social Security benefit increases or tax cuts that were not offset with corresponding tax increases or benefit cuts, much as the House fire wall did, but achieved this by expanding certain budget act enforcement procedures, instead of through creating restrictions, as the House did. The Senate provision was confined to changes that would alter the actuarial balance of the Social Security trust funds over five years.

Restoration of Sequestered Funds

● **Undoing Fiscal 1991 Sequestration.** Rescinded the sequestration ordered by the president Aug. 25, 1990, and Oct. 15, 1990, which had been postponed by a series of continuing resolutions while Congress debated the budget issue.

The law required that any sequesterable resource that was reduced or sequestered be restored and that any federal employees who were furloughed during the lapse of appropriations from midnight Oct. 5 until the enactment of a continuing resolution further postponing the sequestration had to be paid for that period.

Government-Sponsored Enterprises

● **Definition.** Defined government-sponsored enterprises (GSEs) as the Farm Credit System (including the Farm Credit Banks, Banks for Cooperatives and the Federal Agricultural Mortgage Corporation), the Federal Home Loan Bank system, the Federal Home Loan Mortgage Corporation, the Federal National Mortgage Association and the Student Loan Marketing Association.

● **Treasury Department Study and Proposed Legislation.** Required the Treasury Department to submit to Congress by April 30, 1991, a study of GSEs and recommended legislation. The study had to include an objective assessment of the financial soundness of GSEs, the adequacy of existing regulations, the financial exposure to the federal government and the effects of GSEs on Treasury borrowing.

● **CBO Study.** Required CBO to submit to Congress by April 30, 1991, a study of GSEs that included an analysis of the financial risks assumed by each GSE, the supervision and regulation of risk management, the financial exposure GSEs posed for the federal government and the effects of GSEs on Treasury borrowing. The study also was to include alternatives for GSE oversight, and the costs and benefits of those alternatives.

● **Requirement to Report Legislation.** Required the committees of jurisdiction in the House to report to the House no later than Sept. 15, 1991, legislation to ensure the financial soundness of GSEs and to minimize the possibility that a GSE might require future assistance from the government. The provision expressed the sense of the Senate that the relevant Senate committees also must report such legislation.

● **President's Budget.** Required that the president's annual budget include an analysis of the financial condition of GSEs and the financial exposure, if any, that they posed to the government.

Appropriations, Fiscal 1991

President Bush on Nov. 5, 1990, signed into law all 13 regular appropriations bills for fiscal 1991. The yearlong budget standoff between the administration and Congress had precipitated the end-of-the-year appropriations logjam. But, in the end, the budget deal forced few changes in the so-called discretionary accounts paid for through the annual spending bills.

Defense spending still took a relatively big cut. Foreign aid was nicked for several million dollars. However, many domestic programs, particularly those involving education, child care, housing, public works and environmental protection, were given modest increases — in spite of the intense pressure to reduce the deficit.

In the Senate, several major showdowns took place on appropriations legislation in 1990. On the bill for the Departments of Labor, Education, and Health and Human

Services (HR 5257 — PL 101-517), abortion opponents narrowly succeeded in adding an amendment to require federally financed clinics to give parents 48 hours' notice before performing an abortion on a minor. It was the first real test of the parental notification question in Congress, and abortion rights supporters tried to table (and thus kill) the amendment, failing on a **key vote of 48-48 (R 8-34; D 40-14)** on Oct. 12. The amendment was attached to another provision that would allow federal financing of abortions in cases of rape or incest. Both were later dropped in conference. *(1990 key votes, p. 1039)*

The defense bill (HR 5803 — PL 101-511) was the scene for two major fights. As the Warsaw Pact disintegrated, and members were annoyed at the paltry troop commitments by allied countries to the Persian Gulf War, the Senate narrowly rejected an amendment to cut U.S. troops in Europe by 80,000. The amendment was defeated Oct. 15 on a **key vote of 46-50 (R 8-34; D 38-16)**, but the administration later acquiesced in that level of troop cuts to avoid being forced to swallow a larger number. And arguments that the B-2 "stealth" bomber was too expensive at a time when relations with the Soviet Union were greatly eased led to an effort to halt production of the plane. The amendment failed Oct. 15 on a **key vote of 44-50 (R 9-32; D 35-18)**.

The foreign aid spending bill (HR 5114 — PL 101-513) also was the battleground for a pair of fights. Congressional critics of human rights abuses in El Salvador succeeded Oct. 19 in cutting in half U.S. aid to that country on a **key vote of 74-25 (R 19-25; D 55-0)**. And populist foreign aid critics tried to strike a provision granting Egypt forgiveness for $6.7 billion in military debts in gratitude for that country's support during the Persian Gulf War. An amendment to remove the debt relief provision failed on an Oct. 19 **key vote of 42-55 (R 10-34; D 32-21)**.

Supplemental Appropriations

Congress in 1990 cleared a $4.3 billion supplemental spending bill (HR 4404 — PL 101-302) for fiscal 1990, partly financed by $2 billion in defense cuts. The bill included $720 million for Nicaragua and Panama, aid urgently sought by the president, plus money for domestic needs. Bush signed the measure May 25.

Bush had sent Congress a supplemental request for $570 million early in the year, most of it to aid the new government of Panama, which had taken office following a U.S. military invasion in December 1989. Bush later asked Congress for $300 million more for the U.S.-backed Nicaraguan president, Violeta Chamorro. *(Panama, p. 223; Nicaragua, p. 219)*

The House passed the bill (H Rept 101-434), 362-59, April 3 with most of Bush's request intact, after adding about $1.5 billion for a variety of domestic programs that were expected to run short of cash, such as food stamps and disaster assistance.

The Senate passed the bill (S Rept 101-272) by voice vote May 1, after adding another $1.3 billion to the price tag. In conference, the amounts added to cover domestic needs grew further, as the estimated cost of the food stamp program, among other things, escalated. The House adopted the conference report (H Rept 101-493), 308-108, May 24. The Senate followed suit, by voice vote, shortly after midnight May 25 (in the session that began May 24), clearing the bill.

Continuing Resolutions

For the third year in a row, Congress managed to clear all 13 spending bills separately, if not on time, and avoided having to roll some or all of them into a massive "must-pass" continuing appropriations resolution.

However, because none of the fiscal 1991 bills had cleared by the Oct. 1 beginning of the fiscal year, Congress had to pass short-term continuing appropriations resolutions — five of which became law and one of which was vetoed — to keep the government running during the prolonged budget fight.

In addition to providing stopgap spending authority, the measures suspended $85.4 billion in automatic spending cuts that would have been triggered Oct. 1 under the 1885 Gramm-Rudman anti-deficit law (PL 99-177), as amended in 1987 (PL 100-119). Failure to adopt a budget or enact a deficit-reducing reconciliation agreement had assured that the anticipated federal deficit would exceed the $74 billion target set by Gramm-Rudman (the target for fiscal 1992 was $64 billion, plus a $10 billion margin of error). All but the first of the continuing resolutions also extended the limit on federal borrowing. *(Budget, p. 53, debt limit increases, box, p. 44, Gramm-Rudman, Congress and the Nation Vol. VII, pp. 44, 67)*

The first continuing resolution (H J Res 655 — PL 101-403) kept the government operating through Oct. 5. It also provided $2 billion in supplemental appropriations for the fall 1990 military operations in the Persian Gulf, called Operation Desert Shield. The House passed the resolution (H Rept 101-754) on a 382-41 vote Sept. 30. The Senate passed the measure by voice vote the same day. Bush signed it Oct. 1. *(Persian Gulf crisis, p. 299)*

On Oct. 6, Bush vetoed the next continuing resolution (H J Res 660), which both chambers had passed the previous day: the House 300-113, the Senate by voice vote. Bush was angry because prior to passing the continuing resolution, the House had rejected a budget resolution (H Con Res 310) drafted to reflect a White House-congressional budget summit agreement. A revolt by House Republicans killed the agreement and forced the administration and congressional budget negotiators back to the summit table. When the House failed by six votes Oct. 6 to override the president's veto of H J Res 660, Bush ordered "non-essential" branches of the government to be shut down over the Columbus Day weekend Oct. 6-8.

Over the holiday, Congress adopted a new version of H Con Res 310, the budget resolution. That in turn led Bush to accept a new stopgap spending bill (H J Res 666 — PL 101-412), which carried the government through Oct. 19. The House passed the joint resolution, 305-105, Oct. 8 (in the session that began Oct. 7) and the Senate followed suit by voice vote the same day, after amending it. The House cleared the measure early Oct. 9, and Bush signed it that day.

With none of the acrimony that had accompanied similar actions since the end of September, the House passed a fourth stopgap spending resolution (H J Res 677 — PL 101-444) on Oct. 18, 379-37, to keep the government functioning through midnight Oct. 24. The Senate passed, and thus cleared, the measure Oct. 19 by voice vote, and Bush signed it the same day. He cooperated because by then, he said, congressional negotiators were making progress on a deficit-reducing reconciliation bill (HR 5835).

With a final deal on HR 5835 in sight — and still none of the 13 regular appropriations bills signed into law — the

House and Senate passed their fifth short-term continuing resolution (H J Res 681 — PL 101-461) on Oct. 24. House action came on a 380-45 roll-call vote; Senate action by voice vote. The measure provided appropriations through Oct. 27. Bush signed it Oct. 25.

The sixth and last short-term spending resolution (H J Res 687 — PL 101-467) for the year was passed by the House, 283-49, and Senate, by voice vote, on Oct. 27 and was good through Nov. 5, giving the president time to consider and sign the 13 regular appropriations bills. Bush signed H J Res 687 on Oct. 28.

Balanced Budget Amendment

After a six-hour debate filled with sharp rhetoric and anguished complaints about Congress' inability to balance the federal budget on its own, the House July 17, 1990, fell seven votes short of approving a constitutional amendment that would have required a balanced federal budget (H J Res 268). The vote was 279-150, less than the two-thirds majority needed to submit the amendment to the states for ratification.

The next day, the House passed Democratic-backed balanced budget legislation (HR 5258 — H Rept 101-603, Part I) that Republicans denounced as a joke. The bill passed the House 282-144, largely along party lines. But the Senate never acted on the measure.

The House vote was the third time in eight years that a balanced budget amendment had been defeated on the floor of either the House or the Senate. Only once has one chamber or the other passed a balanced budget amendment.

President Ronald Reagan threw his weight behind the idea of a constitutional amendment to control the growth in the deficit. The Republican-controlled Senate debated such a proposal for two weeks and, with last-minute lobbying by Reagan, approved it 69-31 on Aug. 4, 1982. The Democratic-controlled House, however, rejected a similar amendment, 236-187 — 46 votes short of the two-thirds majority required. In 1986, a balanced budget amendment again reached the floor of the Senate but failed, 66-34, one vote short of a two-thirds majority. *(1982 amendment, Congress and the Nation Vol. VI, p. 52; 1986 amendment, Congress and the Nation Vol. VII, p. 57)*

The impetus in 1990 was enhanced by the perceived failure of the 1985 Gramm-Rudman anti-deficit law (PL 99-177), as amended in 1987 (PL 100-119), to do its job. *(Gramm-Rudman, Congress and the Nation Vol. VII, pp. 44, 67)*

As passed by the House, H J Res 268 would have:

- Required that the president submit a balanced budget and that Congress and the president agree on an estimate for receipts for the coming year.
- Required, except during a declared war, a three-fifths vote of Congress for spending in excess of that estimate or for any increase in the national debt limit.
- Required a majority vote of the total membership of each chamber by roll-call vote for any tax increase.
- Taken effect beginning in fiscal 1995 or two years after ratification, whichever was later.

The Senate Judiciary Committee approved a similar measure (S J Res 183 — S Rept 101-391) on June 14, but after the House vote it was not brought to the floor for debate.

The statutory alternative to the constitutional amendment was presented by the House Democratic leadership, essentially as political cover for members who voted against the amendment. It would have required the president and the House and Senate Budget committees to offer balanced budgets every year.

1991-92

Budget action in 1991 and 1992 was nothing like the first two years of the Bush presidency, and nothing like most of the prior decade.

While plenty of internal disputes existed among Democrats and between the House and Senate over relatively mundane and typical matters, no high-level budget summitry took place and almost no serious showdowns were evident over spending priorities. Although the deficit continued to grow and set records — it reached $290.2 billion in fiscal 1992 — little pressure was exerted to use the budget and appropriations process to make cuts beyond those put in place by the five-year budget agreement enacted in 1990.

Even in 1992, when Democrats tried to use economic and fiscal matters to draw distinctions between their party and the Republican Party of President Bush in a big election year, the effect was muted.

Chiefly as a result of the 1990 budget deal, the broad outlines for fiscal policy were rigidly set for several years. In 1992, Democrats made a concerted effort to undo a central element of that agreement — chiefly to make a political point. They failed, however, essentially thwarted by disagreements among themselves. At the same time, Republicans and conservative Democrats were no better able to force their will on Congress. Supporters of a constitutional amendment to require a balanced federal budget had their best shot ever in 1992 to send a proposed amendment to the states. They also failed.

Fiscal 1992 Budget

In the view of many analysts, the budget process in 1991 served as tangible proof that Congress and the president intended to stick by their 1990 budget deal.

But it also was seen as more than evidence of the strength of the new budget rules from that 1990 deal, embodied in the fiscal 1991 reconciliation bill (HR 5835 — PL 101-508). The agreement was barely six months old when Congress completed action on its fiscal 1992 budget; little had changed that Congress and the administration had not been able to anticipate in their negotiations. Nevertheless, the quick and relatively painless action in 1991 was a hopeful sign that the budget strife of years past had been laid to rest. *(1990 reconciliation bill, p. 55, budget process changes, box, p. 56)*

Moreover, much of the past pain had come in the nitty-gritty of fights over the specifics of deficit-reducing reconciliation bills. The terms of the 1990 deal made it plain that a reconciliation bill would be unnecessary in 1991, because a specific deficit target did not have to be met each year, at least as long as discretionary spending through appropriations remained under statutory caps. With no mandatory reconciliation bill, Congress could ignore at will presidential proposals to make wholesale changes in spending programs.

President's Proposals

President Bush got the ritual started when he sent Congress a budget requesting $1.445 trillion in fiscal 1992 outlays on Feb. 4, 1991. With revenues projected at $1.165 trillion, the budget anticipated a deficit of $280.1 billion, a record.

By the standards of the past decade, the budget was unusual, almost radical: No attempt was made to hide the enormous deficit; the grim short-term economic outlook was not glossed over; and for the first time in more than 20 years, a request was included for a reduction in defense spending authority.

Left with little room to maneuver, Bush concentrated on reordering priorities, starving some programs to feed others while staying within the limits set in the budget accord. Overall, he sought to increase spending for 250 domestic programs, reduce spending for 109 and eliminate 238 altogether.

Among the biggest winners were research and development, space exploration, highway construction and initiatives aimed at children. Education programs were hit by crosscutting offsets and increases that failed to keep pace with inflation, leading to some cutbacks in real terms. Other targets for cuts included the Community Services Block Grant, the Community Development Block Grant program, urban mass transit and various housing programs.

In line with the 1990 budget deal, Bush showed defense spending on a downward path designed to strip about $180 billion out of the cumulative Pentagon budget by 1995.

Bush also proposed a dramatic revamping of mandatory spending programs, which automatically provided benefits to anyone who met preset eligibility requirements. Insisting that spending for programs such as Medicaid and food stamps was badly out of control, he proposed to scale it back, target it more closely to the truly needy and force middle- and upper-income beneficiaries to pay more for their benefits.

The changes would have generated $6.3 billion in savings in fiscal 1992. That was less than 1 percent of the budget's $707.5 billion in mandatory spending, but the proposed cuts touched everything from Medicare premiums to veterans' benefits and school lunch subsidies, making many of them politically volatile far out of proportion to their financial value.

An important side benefit to downgrading the importance of the deficit was an end to the pressure to find new tax revenues to close the spending gap. The Bush budget contained very little in the way of new revenue initiatives. Treasury Secretary Nicholas F. Brady said the intent was a "still pond, no more movement; let's let people work with the tax code as it is."

Bush only half-heartedly raised in his budget what had been a top tax priority in the first two years of his term: a cut in the rate for capital gains (profits from the sales of stocks, real estate and other assets).

Budget Resolution

Hemmed in by the new budget rules and unwilling to reopen the previous year's battles over big items such as taxes and defense spending, the Democratic-controlled Congress approved a budget blueprint for fiscal 1992 that was in its raw numbers — and that was almost all a budget contained — virtually indistinguishable from the president's.

The conference report on the budget resolution (H Con Res 121 — H Rept 102-69) was adopted with relative ease by both chambers on May 22, 1991 — the second earliest date for final action on a budget since 1981.

H Con Res 121 set expected outlays for the year at $1.448 trillion and revenues at $1.169 trillion; that yielded an anticipated deficit of $278.8 billion. The numbers varied from those in the Bush budget (after it was recalculated using the same economic and technical assumptions) by less than $10 billion — or less than 1 percent of the total.

The budget resolution determined how much budget authority was available to the Appropriations committees, $1.59 trillion in the aggregate. In practical terms, however, that number had already been set for fiscal 1992 in the 1990 budget deal. So by the time the budget resolution was in place, House appropriators had already begun making the real spending decisions. That fueled criticism that the budget resolution, in setting Congress' tax and spending guidelines for the year, was largely irrelevant.

Moreover, with the room for maneuvering constrained by tight discretionary spending caps and pay-as-you-go limits on entitlements and taxes, the Democratic majority was confined to recommending that money be moved from one set of programs to another in the $212 billion domestic discretionary spending category — which accounted for less than 15 percent of all spending.

Democrats touted spending increases for education, health and job training, while Republicans said the Democrats were only tinkering at the margins of Bush's budget.

House Action. The House Budget Committee approved its version of H Con Res 121 by voice vote on April 9, working from a Democratic draft presented by Chairman Leon E. Panetta, D-Calif. The measure was formally reported (H Rept 102-32) on April 12.

Among the biggest changes from Bush's budget was a $2 billion increase over fiscal 1991 spending for education. Bush had requested a $728 million increase for fiscal 1992; a $937 million increase was needed to keep up with inflation. The panel also recommended a deep cut in the 13 percent boost that Bush had proposed for the National Aeronautics and Space Administration, slashing it to a 4.2 percent, inflation-only increase. The difference was critical for big-ticket items such as the proposed space station.

The full House then spent April 16-17 debating the budget resolution and approved it April 17 by a largely party-line vote of 261-163.

The two-day floor debate amplified arguments rehearsed in the Budget Committee. Democrats said that the roughly $13 billion in additions and deletions they made to the Bush domestic spending agenda produced a document that was fairer to working Americans.

But Republicans argued, in the words of Bill Gradison of Ohio, that "the Democrats have merely rearranged a few of the deck chairs," while claiming "that they have steered the entire ship of state on a new course."

The only change approved on the floor was an amendment by William D. Ford, D-Mich., to add $400 million in budget authority and $200 million in outlays for education. The floor change, adopted 261-158 on April 17, was on top of the $2 billion increase approved by the House committee.

Votes on three GOP amendments revealed that House Republicans, who had split badly over budget policy in

1990, remained sharply divided. William E. Dannemeyer, R-Calif., and John R. Kasich, R-Ohio, offered substitutes designed to appeal to Republican sentiment that spending was still too high. Both amendments were variations on a freeze aimed at cutting spending below levels in both the Democratic budget and the Bush proposal, with Dannemeyer's cutting most deeply.

The amendments lost heavily April 17, Dannemeyer's by 79-332 and Kasich's by 114-303; Republicans split on both.

The president's budget, offered as a substitute by Gradison, fared almost as poorly as Dannemeyer's and worse than Kasich's: It lost April 17 in the full House, 89-335, and Republicans abandoned it in large numbers.

Senate Action. The Senate Budget Committee approved its version of H Con Res 121 on an almost strict party-line vote, 11-10. Kent Conrad of North Dakota was the sole Democrat to join the committee's Republicans in opposing the measure. Conrad had unsuccessfully offered an amendment to effectively freeze spending at fiscal 1991 levels, cutting some programs deeply while protecting agriculture, education, health care and veterans' benefits; his amendment failed 10-11.

In lieu of a freeze, the committee voted 15-6 to adopt a sprawling Democratic package, dubbed a Homefront Budget Initiative, that added $4.4 billion to spending in areas such as education, health and children's programs, among others. The amendment boosted spending for education to $3.1 billion and included a $1 billion increase for student aid, which backers said would boost the maximum Pell grant for the neediest students from $2,400 to $2,800. Sponsor Tim Wirth, D-Colo., proposed to finance the spending increase by imposing a 4 percent across-the-board cut in other domestic discretionary spending.

After a low-key, three-day debate, the Senate approved the budget resolution by voice vote on April 25.

The emotional high point in the floor action came when Daniel Patrick Moynihan, D-N.Y., attempted to win approval for a procedural amendment that would have opened the way for a vote later in the year on cutting the Social Security payroll tax. Adoption of Moynihan's amendment would have allowed the Senate to bypass budget rules that required at least 60 votes on the floor to change Social Security, a forbidding prospect.

The Senate voted 60-38 on April 24 to table (and thus kill) Moynihan's amendment, effectively closing the door to a later vote. Senators were clearly worried that constituents would accuse them of tampering with the Social Security system and that cutting the tax would aggravate the deficit and threaten the solvency of the retirement program. *(Social Security, p. 736)*

In considering floor amendments, the Senate turned down every opportunity to save more money than required under the 1990 budget deal, rejecting a spending freeze, proposals to cut defense spending and even a measure that would have eliminated a subsidy for beekeepers. In most cases, leaders warned that tampering with spending levels would violate the budget deal or unravel the fragile consensus that made the 1990 deficit-reduction package possible.

Final Action. Working from similar budget resolutions, House and Senate conferees in most cases made only minor changes, reaching a compromise in private late in the week of May 13. The most controversial item — a Senate Republican proposal adopted in committee that would bar tax increases in fiscal 1992 to pay for expanding entitlements — was killed in conference.

House Republicans had staged a knock-down, drag-out debate on the provision May 9, trying and ultimately failing to instruct House conferees to support the provision in conference. Trading potshots that recalled some of the nastier moments of the protracted debate over taxes in 1990, Republicans accused Democrats of lusting after tax increases on working Americans, while Democrats accused the GOP of shielding wealthy fat cats and raiding benefit programs for cash. The motion to instruct the conferees failed 132-284.

The House adopted the conference report (H Rept 102-69) on May 22 by a vote of 239-181; the Senate followed suit the same day 57-41.

Appropriations, Fiscal 1992

Congress in 1991 had relatively little trouble writing and approving all but one of the 13 regular spending bills needed to keep the federal government in business for fiscal 1992. The job was made easy because lawmakers were working from a script written in the budget deal enacted through the 1990 reconciliation bill (HR 5835 — PL 101-508).

New budget process rules set strict caps for defense, domestic and international spending, and they barred Congress from using savings in one category to exceed the limit in another. *(Budget process changes, box, p. 56, 1990 reconciliation bill, p. 55)*

Moreover, as long as the appropriators stayed within the caps, they did not have to worry about finding additional ways to cut the deficit. Furthermore, the caps allowed discretionary spending authority for domestic programs in fiscal 1992 to grow 5.4 percent from the previous year.

The only bill that was not completed before Congress adjourned would have appropriated money for foreign operations. Action on the bill (HR 2621) was put off until early 1992 to accommodate a request from President Bush that $10 billion in housing loan guarantees for Israel be delayed to allow Middle East peace talks to get under way. In the meantime, a continuing resolution (H J Res 360 — PL 102-145) kept money flowing for foreign operations through March 31, 1992. When an impasse over the loan guarantees persisted, the full-year foreign aid bill was shelved and a second continuing resolution (H J Res 456 — PL 102-266) was cleared April 1, 1992, and signed the same day. It carried foreign operations spending through the balance of fiscal 1992.

Despite the relative ease of enacting the regular spending bills, some trouble spots arose. Budget allocations for each regular appropriations bill, dictated in part by the new discretionary spending caps, were tighter than in recent years.

The most dramatic example was a decision by House appropriators to cut $1.3 billion for the Subcommittee on VA-HUD and Independent Agencies; the cut forced appropriators to choose either to increase housing and veterans' programs or to substantially finance the space station. In a highly controversial move, the subcommittee voted to cut the space station. The full House reversed that decision, but only by cutting housing money and freezing all other National Aeronautics and Space Administration spending at 1991 levels. On a **key vote of 240-173 (R 133-27; D 107-145; I 0-1)**, the House June 6 restored the administration's $2 billion request for the space station. *(1991 key votes, p. 1061)*

Fiscal 1991 'Mini-Sequester'

The Office of Management and Budget (OMB) ordered a tiny across-the-board spending cut on April 25, 1991, to correct overspending by Congress in a fiscal 1991 supplemental appropriations bill (HR 1281 — PL 102-27) cleared in March. The cut was triggered by a single $8 million provision — hardly a ripple in the $5.4 billion ocean of spending in the supplemental.

At stake was an effort by Rep. Dan Rostenkowski, D-Ill., to do a favor for his alma mater, Loyola University of Chicago. Rostenkowski switched the source of $8 million in previously appropriated federal aid for the school.

The money was to have come from a Defense Department account, but Loyola officials reportedly worried that that might require the school to do defense-related research. Rostenkowski managed to have the source of the money shifted to the Department of Education.

But new rules enacted in 1990 as part of the budget-reconciliation bill (HR 5835 — PL 101-508) set strict limits on appropriations for fiscal years 1991-93. The law set specific spending caps for three categories of spending: defense, domestic and international. *(1990 reconciliation bill, p. 55)*

The domestic account was already close to its ceiling for fiscal 1991, and the action of moving the $8 million from a defense account to a domestic account busted the domestic cap by $2.4 million.

This fact had slipped by administration lobbyists who staked out the late-night House-Senate conference on the supplemental spending bill, and the administration initially gave the measure its okay. But when OMB Director Richard G. Darman got a look at the fine print, he fired off a letter to Congress warning that the money would trigger an automatic, offsetting spending cut, known as a sequester, if Congress did not fix the problem.

Darman suggested either doing away with the Rostenkowski transfer or rescinding offsetting appropriations from other domestic accounts. The letter was a call to arms for Rostenkowski and House Appropriations Committee Chairman Jamie L. Whitten, D-Miss., who refused to back down.

But under the rules, Darman's was the only opinion that counted, and OMB ordered a 0.0013 percent "mini-sequester" of fiscal 1991 domestic spending — $13 for every $1 million in appropriations.

It was just one of many important votes that occurred during House and Senate appropriations debates in 1991.

The House rejected an amendment to the energy and water bill (HR 2427 — PL 102-104) that would have halted spending on the superconducting supercollider. The amendment was rejected May 29 on a **key vote of 165-251 (R 58-101; D 106-150; I 1-0)**. The Senate likewise fought off an amendment to halt spending on the big atom smasher. A motion to table (and thus kill) the amendment was agreed to July 10 on a **key vote of 62-37 (R 33-10; D 29-27)**.

On the interior bill (HR 2686 — PL 102-154), the House voted to increase dramatically the fees ranchers paid to graze their livestock on public lands. The amendment was adopted June 25 on a **key vote of 232-192 (R 47-114; D 184-78; I 1-0)**, but the language was dropped in conference with the Senate.

The bill (HR 2707) providing money for the departments of Labor, Education, and Health and Human Services (HHS) was the vehicle for showdowns in both chambers. In the Senate, Labor-HHS Appropriations Subcommittee Chairman Tom Harkin, D-Iowa, tried to end run the new budget rules. Harkin proposed transferring $3.15 billion from defense accounts to accounts under his bill. Although the 1990 budget deal generally prohibited such shifts, they could be accomplished with the concurrence of three-fifths of the House and Senate. Harkin needed 60 votes to waive the budget act prohibition, and his motion to do so failed Sept. 10 on a **key vote of 28-69 (R 3-39; D 25-30)**. Not only did senators stand up for the discipline contained in the new budget rules, but many also were concerned that had Harkin prevailed, the new rules would have still triggered an across-the-board cut in all domestic spending to make up the difference.

In the House, HR 2707 was the scene for a veto override fight with President Bush over abortion. The bill would have repealed an administration order forbidding abortion counseling in federally financed family planning clinics. The House on Nov. 19 failed by 12 votes to get the two-thirds majority it needed to override Bush's veto on a **key vote of 276-156 (R 53-113; D 222-43; I 1-0)**. Ultimately a new Labor-HHS bill (HR 3839 — PL 102-170), without the abortion language, was enacted.

Continuing Resolutions

By Oct. 1, the start of fiscal 1992, Congress had been able to clear three of the 13 regular appropriations bills. (Bush vetoed one of those — for the District of Columbia — over language that would have permitted the District government to pay for abortions with local tax revenues. A revised version with the abortion language removed was cleared before Oct. 1.) As a result, Congress began the process of passing short-term continuing appropriations resolutions to keep the remaining federal departments and programs operating until the 10 outstanding bills had been enacted.

The first stopgap measure (H J Res 332 — PL 102-109), good through Oct. 29, passed the House (H Rept 102-216) Sept. 25 and passed the Senate amended the same day. The House accepted the Senate amendment, changing the bill's expiration date from Oct. 19 to Oct. 29, and cleared the measure on Sept. 26; both chambers acted by voice votes. President Bush signed the resolution on Sept. 30.

A second continuing resolution (H J Res 360 — PL 102-145) kept the government open through Nov. 14. The House passed the measure (H Rept 102-266) 288-126 on Oct. 24; the Senate approved it by voice vote the same day. Bush signed H J Res 360 on Oct. 28. The measure made a special exception for the foreign operations bill (HR 2621), which had passed the House but not the Senate. It extended foreign aid programs at their 1991 levels until March 31, 1992.

A third stopgap measure (H J Res 374 — PL 102-163) extended spending authority for a few departments through Nov. 26. The House passed the resolution by voice vote Nov. 12; the Senate acted 91-4 on Nov. 13, clearing the measure. The president signed it on Nov. 15.

The fourth and final fiscal 1992 continuing resolution (H J Res 456 — PL 102-266) passed the House 275-131 on March 31, 1992, and the Senate 84-16 on April 1. The House accepted the Senate changes the same day.

Supplemental Appropriations

Congress also cleared four supplemental appropriations bills in 1991, three of which provided extra spending authority for fiscal 1991:

Desert Shield/Desert Storm. The first supplemental (HR 1282 — PL 102-28) provided $42.6 billion for Persian Gulf War activities through Operation Desert Shield/Desert Storm. The House passed the bill (H Rept 102-10) on a 380-19 vote March 7, and the Senate passed an amended version (S Rept 102-23) on a 98-1 vote March 19. Both chambers approved the conference report (H Rept 102-30) on March 22 — the House, 379-11; the Senate, by voice vote — and the president signed the bill April 10.

'Dire Emergency.' A $5.4 billion "dire emergency" supplemental (HR 1281 — PL 102-27) paid home-front costs of the Persian Gulf War and provided emergency money for Israel and Turkey. The bill moved in tandem with the Desert Shield/Desert Storm supplemental. The House 365-43 passed HR 1281 (H Rept 102-9) March 7; the Senate 92-8 passed the bill (S Rept 102-24) March 20. Both chambers approved the conference report (H Rept 102-29) on March 22 — the House on a 340-48 vote, the Senate by voice vote. The president signed the bill April 10.

Iraqi Refugees. A $572 million supplemental (HR 2251 — PL 102-55) primarily provided assistance to refugees in Iraq and elsewhere. It passed the House 384-25 and Senate by voice vote May 9. The House 387-33 and the Senate by voice vote adopted the conference report (H Rept 102-71) May 22. The president signed the bill June 13.

Natural Disasters. A $6.9 billion bill (H J Res 157 — PL 102-229) provided extra aid for farmers and communities hit by natural disasters. It also included some mop-up money for Operation Desert Storm. Work on the measure took so long that what was originally a fiscal 1991 measure was not enacted until after the start of fiscal 1992.

H J Res 157 began life as a technical corrections bill for fiscal 1991 measures and was passed by the House Feb. 28. In mid-summer, Bush asked for $3.6 billion in supplemental appropriations, most of which would go to cover extra costs of the Gulf War. The House Appropriations Committee began work on a supplemental bill but, faced with veto threats, did not complete work until October. The committee approved its bill (HR 3543 — H Rept 102-255) on Oct. 17, and the House passed the $7.5 billion measure on Oct. 29 by a vote of 252-162. Meanwhile, the Senate had been at work on its own version of the supplemental and chose to use the earlier measure — H J Res 157 — as its vehicle. The Senate Appropriations Committee approved the joint resolution on Nov. 15 (S Rept 102-216), and the Senate passed the $8 billion measure 75-17 on Nov. 22. The two chambers went to conference on H J Res 157. On Nov. 27, the House adopted a slightly slimmed-down conference report (H Rept 102-394) by a vote of 303-114, and the Senate accepted the measure by voice vote. Bush signed the legislation Dec. 12.

Fiscal 1993 Budget

As Congress in 1992 moved into the third year of the five-year budget deal struck in 1990, the budget peace that had prevailed in 1991 seemed a distant memory.

Democratic leaders were eager to get access to defense savings for use in funding popular domestic programs. But that meant changing the budget rules, enacted as part of the 1990 budget-reconciliation bill (HR 5835 — PL 101-508). That bill erected "walls" between defense, domestic and international programs and barred Congress from taking discretionary money from one to aid another. *(1990 reconciliation bill, p. 55)*

The scramble for money was expected to be particularly intense because the discretionary spending caps enacted as part of the 1990 budget deal were set to become much tighter in fiscal 1993. Moreover, appropriators had set themselves up for a tough year when they decided in 1991 to delay the obligation of more than $4 billion in fiscal 1992 spending authority until fiscal 1993. In the end, however, the process was relatively calm and the walls remained in place.

While the 1990 budget agreement had put strict limits on appropriated spending and required a pay-as-you-go offset for any tax cuts or new or expanded entitlement programs, it had grandfathered existing entitlements. The rapid growth in those programs — particularly Medicaid and Medicare and anti-recession aid such as unemployment benefits and food stamps — contributed to the prodigious growth in the deficit. As a result, fiscal 1992 ended with a deficit of $290.2 billion — far below the $403.8 billion predicted by the Office of Management and Budget in January but still more than the previous record of $268.7 billion chalked up in fiscal 1991.

President's Budget Request

With his popularity badly eroded and the economy struggling to rebound from a recession that began in mid-1990, President Bush combined his annual State of the Union address and the fiscal 1993 budget in a rare one-two punch Jan. 28-29.

Though signs were evident that the economy was on the mend, and economists would later decide that the recession ended in mid-1991, Bush declared war on the residual effects of the recession — and on any Democrat who dared oppose his recovery plan. In his speech, he challenged Congress to meet a 52-day deadline to pass the core of his economic proposals. The budget, issued the morning after the speech, provided details of the anti-recession package and much more.

Bush called for spending $1.52 trillion in fiscal 1993. He projected revenues totaling $1.16 trillion, which resulted in a forecast deficit of $356 billion.

In his budget, Bush proposed a lengthy list of tax cuts, defense cuts and spending shifts that included much to infuriate Democrats and draw a line between the parties nine months before the election. It also virtually guaranteed prolonged warfare on a variety of fronts throughout the year.

Bush's call for tax cuts was countered by passage of two separate Democratic-sponsored bills, both of which died under the president's veto. His call for deep defense cuts partly to finance his proposed tax cut and partly to reduce the deficit was countered by an abortive Democratic leadership plan to tear down budget walls that blocked the use of defense cuts to pay for additional domestic spending. Though Bush did not get his broad economic proposals passed, he did succeed in part with a call for a freeze on discretionary spending. Congressional appropriators ultimately agreed to cuts in spending bills to meet his freeze. *(Middle-class tax cut, p. 100; urban aid tax bill, p. 103; budget walls, box, p. 82; appropriations, p. 81)*

Budget Resolution

The tight limits set by the 1990 budget rules were supposed to make the work of putting together a fiscal 1993 budget resolution relatively easy. But the task was complicated early in 1992 by disputes over how much to cut from defense and how to use the savings — the so-called peace dividend.

Much of the Democratic leadership yearned to celebrate the collapse of the Soviet military threat by shifting billions of dollars from the defense budget to domestic spending projects such as roads, schools, child nutrition and job training. But the White House was deeply opposed.

On May 21, both the House and Senate adopted the conference report on the fiscal 1993 budget resolution (H Con Res 287 — H Rept 102-529), though not without some nail-biting in the House. The final budget called for outlays of $1.5 trillion, revenues of $1.17 trillion and a deficit — the largest ever — of $326.6 billion.

After the president's budget request was re-estimated by the Congressional Budget Office to account for the same economic and technical assumptions as those used for H Con Res 287, the overall totals in the two documents and even the separate function-by-function totals differed little from each other. Nonetheless, Congress did hold defense spending to $11 billion below the spending cap set in the 1990 budget deal. That cut was greater than what Bush had wanted, but it was less than Democratic leaders originally had proposed. All the savings were devoted to deficit reduction.

House Action. The House Budget Committee approved H Con Res 287 by voice vote on Feb. 27 including not one but two sets of budget numbers. Plan A, as it was called, would have used defense savings to pay for a wide variety of domestic spending programs. Plan B — adopted as a concession to conservative Democrats and to reality — abandoned use of defense cuts for anything but deficit reduction and stayed within the spending caps. Both used the same totals for defense spending.

Plan A was to be the operable budget. But, under the budget's provisions, if Congress failed to pass a bill tearing down the budget walls — or if Bush carried through on his threat to veto the bill — the House would automatically switch to Plan B in time for a conference with the Senate.

Democratic budget drafters rejected Bush's proposals to trim entitlements, either piecemeal or with an overall cap. Instead, the committee approved bipartisan language that expressed concern about out-of-control entitlement spending. H Con Res 287 was reported (H Rept 102-450) on March 2.

The House adopted both plans on March 5, though Democratic leaders were barely able to contain a rebellion by conservatives who wanted any peace dividend to go to deficit reduction and by moderates and liberals who worried that deep defense cuts would cost jobs in their districts.

Republicans used House rules to force separate votes on each plan, showcasing the rifts among Democrats. The House first voted 215-201 to adopt Plan A; a total of 44 Democrats voted "nay." The House then voted 224-191 for Plan B; the 39 Democrats voting "nay" included a handful of liberals who wanted increased spending for domestic programs. Plan B became the operative budget at the end of the month when the House rejected a bill to tear down the budget walls.

A majority of House Republicans opted to vote against all proposed budgets, rejecting not only the two Budget Committee plans but also three substitutes: one by the Congressional Black Caucus and the House Progressive Caucus; one by conservative Budget Committee member William E. Dannemeyer, R-Calif.; and one embodying the president's budget request.

The Black Caucus offered a substitute budget that would have cut defense significantly deeper than Plans A and B; the proposal was rejected, 77-342.

Dannemeyer offered the lowest spending levels of any of the five alternative budgets considered. He proposed to freeze all domestic discretionary spending at fiscal 1992 levels, reduce foreign aid by 25 percent and put a strict cap on Medicare and Medicaid. The amendment also assumed savings of $24 billion in 1993 by requiring the Treasury Department to begin refinancing the public debt with low-interest instruments such as gold-backed bonds. Dannemeyer's budget was rejected 60-344.

Bush's own budget was rejected by the widest margin, 42-370, with 119 Republicans voting against it.

Senate Action. The Senate Budget Committee waited until after the fate of the walls bill had been determined before taking up the budget resolution. The committee approved its version of H Con Res 287 by a vote of 11-10 on April 2, after the Senate had failed to cut off a filibuster on the walls bill and the House had rejected the measure.

The size of the cuts in defense was virtually the only substantive item on the committee's agenda. On an 11-10 vote, the committee bowed to heavy White House pressure and upheld the spending levels for defense in Bush's budget. The committee rejected, 9-12, a plan by committee Chairman Jim Sasser, D-Tenn., to more than double the size of Bush's proposed defense cuts.

Republicans united against Sasser, as did some conservative Democrats. Liberal Christopher J. Dodd, D-Conn., said he voted against the Sasser plan for fear that it cut too deeply, too quickly, and might jeopardize Connecticut's defense jobs, including construction of the *Seawolf* submarine in Groton.

By a vote of 54-35, the Senate on April 10 adopted H Con Res 287, again holding the line on defense cuts. The Senate on April 9 rejected, 45-50, an amendment by Jim Exon, D-Neb., to roughly double Bush's proposed defense cuts. A nearly solid bloc of Republicans joined with 13 Democrats to vote "nay."

The Senate also sidestepped efforts to change politically sensitive mandatory spending programs, which made up more than half of federal spending. In its last day of work on the budget, the Senate debated a bitterly controversial amendment by Budget Committee ranking Republican Pete V. Domenici of New Mexico to cap spending for entitlement programs such as Medicare, Medicaid, farm subsidies and food stamps. While virtually all sides agreed that limiting entitlement spending was critical to getting control of the deficit, no consensus existed on how to do it.

The amendment would have imposed a cap on all mandatory spending, except for Social Security and interest on the debt, beginning in 1994. It would have allowed increases to accommodate population growth and inflation starting at 2 percent in 1994 and falling to zero by 1997.

Critics warned that capping entitlements would harm elderly and needy Americans who depended on such programs for survival. They argued that the real problem was rapid growth in Medicare and Medicaid, and the real solution was comprehensive health care reform that constrained costs. Domenici withdrew his amendment after the Senate approved, 66-28, what promised to be the first of a series of amendments exempting veterans and other groups from the cap.

Final Action. House-Senate conferees on the budget resolution met in private and agreed to split the difference between the two chambers on defense spending, to drop a Senate plan to trim domestic appropriations spending authority by about $1 billion, and to go most of the way toward restoring a Senate cut in foreign aid. The trade-offs made the budget — unpopular in the best of times — even less attractive for many members.

In another key area, the compromise budget resolution assumed $2 billion a year in cuts from entitlements — which included such politically sensitive programs as Medicare, Social Security and farm subsidies — but made no specific recommendations for achieving those savings. The budget rejected all Bush's proposed entitlement cuts, however, and the cuts assumed in the resolution were not mandatory.

The House took up the conference report on H Con Res 287 (H Rept 102-529) May 21 and nearly rejected the unpopular measure on a chaotic roll call. As time for the vote expired, the measure was failing and Democratic leaders had to twist arms to get two members to switch their votes to "yea." With the House floor in an uproar, one more member rushed into the chamber to vote against the budget, and Speaker Thomas S. Foley, D-Wash., cast one of his extremely rare floor votes to ensure a 209-207 victory.

Republicans voted without exception against the budget. For Democrats, the budget contained much to dislike: It spent too much on defense for some and too little for others. And it had a deficit in excess of $300 billion.

The Senate later the same day adopted the final version of the budget on a much less dramatic 52-41 vote. That completed action; budget resolutions did not go to the president for signing.

Appropriations, Fiscal 1993

A year that looked at first to be impossible for congressional appropriators turned out to be one of the most efficient, as Congress managed to clear all 13 regular appropriations bills by Oct. 5, 1992, just days after the Oct. 1 start of fiscal 1993. Three years earlier, in 1989, Congress finished all its appropriations work on time. But the completion date in 1992 was still one of the earliest in two decades.

Few predicted such an orderly finish nine months earlier, when Congress began 1992 amid concerns that election-year politics, tightened spending caps, the shaky state of the 1990 budget deal and a shorter-than-usual work year would all combine to make finishing work on every spending bill impossible.

Some legislators predicted they would end the session by wrapping most or all of the bills into a massive continuing resolution. That worried Democrats, however, who feared that such an action would hand President Bush an opportunity to bash the Democratic-led Congress right before the elections for failing to do its most fundamental job.

The Appropriations committees did not know how much money they had to spend until Democrats failed in late March to knock down the budget "walls" between defense and domestic spending to get more money for domestic programs. Then appropriators were distracted by a time-consuming battle with Bush over whether to cancel — rescind — billions in spending they had approved in 1991. That fight ended with an $8.2 billion measure that cut more dollars than Bush proposed but protected some items he wanted to cut and cut some items he wanted to protect. *(Budget walls, box, p. 82)*

Bush and congressional appropriators clashed repeatedly over priorities, but the two sides compromised on most of their differences. Congress was on track for an early finish when lawmakers ran into one final roadblock: Bush threatened to veto any bill that failed to adhere to his call for a freeze in discretionary spending. Bush had outlined the freeze in the fiscal 1993 budget proposed in January but had barely mentioned it since then. While some Democrats talked of confronting the president, leaders reasoned that they could not win a veto fight with the president, and appropriators made last-minute trims in all their bills to meet Bush's cap.

For a time, it looked as if spending might get even tighter. The failed effort in the House June 11 to pass a balanced budget constitutional amendment sparked a budget-cutting fever that seemed to presage a wave of cuts in appropriations programs. *(Balanced budget amendment, p. 84)*

Days after the balanced budget vote, the energy and water appropriations bill (HR 5373 — PL 102-377) came to the floor. In a dramatic act, the House June 17 decided to kill the high-priced superconducting supercollider on a **key vote of 232-181 (R 79-79; D 152-102; I 1-0)**. The budget-cutting fever appeared to fade after that, however. On a **key vote of 181-237 (R 38-127; D 142-110; I 1-0)**, the House July 29 refused for the third time in 13 months to kill the even more expensive space station, which was experiencing huge increases in its expected cost. The vote came on the spending bill for the departments of Veterans Affairs and Housing and Urban Development and several independent agencies (HR 5679 — PL 102-389). *(1992 key votes, p. 1083)*

Budget 'Walls' Survived Battering ...

Hoping to seize political momentum in 1992 by confronting President Bush over a series of economic issues, congressional Democratic leaders decided very early in the year to knock down budget "walls" that prohibited shifting defense money to domestic spending programs. Their efforts failed, however, when they could not even hold members of their own party on the issue, much less win Republican votes.

The walls were erected in the 1990 budget-reconciliation bill (HR 5835 — PL 101-508), which enacted the terms of a sweeping deficit-reduction accord between the administration and Congress. The bill set limits for three years on the total amounts of discretionary spending in three broad areas: domestic, defense and foreign programs. *(1990 reconciliation bill, p. 55)*

In 1992, members who served on the Appropriations Committees were concerned that the caps pinched a bit too tightly, especially on the domestic side. As they began to put together fiscal 1993 appropriations bills, they realized they would have to cut spending in some instances below prior-year levels. It was essentially a one-year problem, because the walls were to expire for fiscal 1994 and after.

In addition, defense spending was expected to be pared considerably, following the collapse of the Soviet Union in late 1991.

By changing the terms of the 1990 law, Democratic leaders hoped to allow a shift of defense savings into cash-short domestic programs, but a political edge existed to their gambit.

Bush and most Republicans were opposed to the idea. First, they were hopeful that the budget walls would deter a wholesale raid on the defense budget; second, they were more supportive of deeper spending cuts to reduce the deficit than were most Democrats.

The White House offered to negotiate, but on terms so odious to Democrats that there was no prospect of compromise. White House budget director Richard G. Darman put two proposals on the table. One would have split defense savings evenly between deficit reduction and a tax cut. And, Darman said, the walls would have to be extended through 1997. The second offer was to allow a defense-to-domestic shift if Congress were to put an enforceable cap on mandatory spending, which went primarily for entitlement programs such as Medicare, Medicaid, food stamps, farm subsidies and the like. Both were rejected.

Bush was virtually certain to veto a bill tearing down the budget walls; and if he did so, the veto would just as certainly be sustained. Many Democrats believed, however, that a veto would sharpen the differences between what they saw as their own invest-in-America policy and what they criticized as the president's outmoded Cold War priorities.

Democratic leaders failed to reckon on dissension in their own ranks, however, both on the deficit question and worries about the depth of defense cuts. In the end, neither chamber was able to pass a bill to tear down the walls. The House overwhelmingly rejected its bill, and a Senate bill never got to a floor vote.

House Action

Trouble surfaced early when conservative Democrats on the House Budget Committee, led by Charles W. Stenholm of Texas, in February forced the panel to retreat partially from its plan to cut defense to pay for domestic initiatives.

The conservatives made the committee adopt an unusual fiscal 1993 budget resolution (H Con Res 287 — H Rept 102-450) that contained two sets of numbers: a walls-down, leadership budget that devoted most defense savings to domestic programs; and a

For most of the rest of the session, the House and Senate contented themselves primarily with amendments that trimmed overhead and administrative accounts in spending bills. Most of the money for the supercollider was eventually restored.

And one arena that had been the scene of members' frustration and desire for spending cuts — foreign aid — was spared in 1992. On a **key vote of 87-12 (R 35-8; D 52-4)** the Senate on Oct. 1 passed a $26.5 billion foreign aid spending bill (HR 5368 — PL 102-391); on Oct. 5 the House adopted the conference report by a **key vote of 312-105 (R 104-58; D 208-46; I 0-1)**.

Continuing Resolution

Congress passed only a single short-term continuing resolution (H J Res 553 — PL 102-376), good through Oct. 5, to allow time to finish work on the regular bills.

The House, 300-104, and Senate, by voice vote, passed H J Res 553 on Sept. 30, and Bush signed it Oct. 1. He signed the last five regular spending bills on Oct. 6, finishing with the foreign aid measure. Although funding for much of the government had run out the previous midnight when the stopgap measure expired, Bush's signal that he would sign the regular bills as soon as he got them made enacting another stopgap measure unnecessary.

Rescissions

After Bush sharply criticized "pork-barrel" spending practices in a tough, partisan speech on March 20, Congress cleared a bill (HR 4990 — PL 102-298) canceling —

... As Spending Shift Bills Faltered

walls-up, conservative budget that would use any defense cuts for deficit reduction. If a bill to tear down the budget walls passed, one set of budget numbers would be put into effect; if the walls bill failed, the others would be used. *(Fiscal 1993 budget, p. 79)*

The House Government Operations Committee on Feb. 20 by voice vote approved a bill (HR 3732) to tear down the walls. By a vote of 13-25, the committee rejected a Republican substitute incorporating one of the administration's counteroffers: to allow defense cuts to finance a tax cut and deficit reduction. HR 3732 was reported from Government Operations (H Rept 102-446, Part I) on Feb. 27. The House Rules Committee reported the bill (H Rept 102-446, Part II) on March 4.

Because House Democratic leaders were worried about support among their rank and file, they repeatedly postponed a floor vote on HR 3732.

The leadership had originally scheduled a vote during the week of March 2, but that was blocked by a storm of opposition from three groups of Democrats: conservatives who wanted all of the peace dividend to go to deficit reduction, conservatives who feared that the defense cuts would be too deep, and a group that included moderates and liberals worried about the loss of defense-related jobs in their districts.

As March progressed with no vote on the bill, Democratic leaders found that they lacked the necessary votes and that members were badly distracted by a check-kiting scandal at the House bank. *(House bank scandal, p. 929)*

Talk was heard of revising the bill to lower the cap on defense and increase the cap on domestic spending, as an appeal to those members most concerned that defense cuts would go too deep. But that move was abandoned.

Democratic leaders appeared consistently to lose ground in their hunt for supporters. When HR 3732 finally came up for a roll call on March 31, the bill was rejected overwhelmingly on a **key vote of 187-238 (R 0-162; D 186-76; I 1-0)**. *(1992 key votes, p. 1083)*

Senate Action

Senate Democrats ran into similar resistance from conservatives on their side. Senate Budget Committee Chairman Jim Sasser, D-Tenn., found support so shaky that he decided not to move his walls bill (S 2399) through his own committee.

At first, key senators disagreed over how to divvy up defense savings. Finance Committee Chairman Lloyd Bentsen, D-Texas, for a time favored spending at least part of any defense savings to finance a tax cut. Appropriations Chairman Robert C. Byrd, D-W.Va., flatly opposed using the money for anything but increased domestic discretionary spending. Byrd disagreed so strongly with Bentsen that he refused to join a high-level task force convened by Majority Leader George J. Mitchell, D-Maine, to thrash out the issue. Bentsen later relented.

Sasser calculated that he could lose no more than one Democratic vote on his committee without losing his majority, and he was uncertain of the positions of at least three Democrats.

He moved the legislation directly to the full Senate, but he was unable to overcome a filibuster against a motion to take up the bill. After weeks of delay and uncertainty over the issue, Senate Democrats on March 26 fell a decisive 10 votes short of the 60 they needed to shut down the GOP-led filibuster. The motion to invoke cloture (and thereby end the filibuster) was rejected on a **key vote of 50-48 (R 3-40; D 47-8)**. That killed the bill in the Senate.

---

or rescinding, in budget parlance — $8.2 billion that had been previously appropriated for fiscal 1992.

Bush unveiled a plan to use procedures from the 1974 Congressional Budget and Impoundment Control Act (PL 93-344) to force repeated, and potentially embarrassing, votes on his call to rescind prior appropriations. *(1974 budget act, Congress and the Nation Vol. IV, p. 71)*

Congressional leaders (including some Republicans) reacted angrily to the threat that Bush would send weekly rescission requests to Capitol Hill, and the president backed off the plan, eventually sending four groups of rescissions worth $7.9 billion. Although Bush highlighted domestic projects when he made his spending-cut proposals, the vast majority — worth $7.1 billion — was to come from defense programs.

Congressional Republicans kept the pressure on the appropriators by threatening to invoke a rule that permitted a minority in the House and Senate to force the rescissions out of the Appropriations committees if the panels had not acted within 25 days of continuous session. Allowing for various recesses, that gave the committees until early May to act.

With broad, bipartisan agreement that Congress should match or exceed Bush's total, the Appropriations committees went to work. House and Senate appropriators assembled two different rescission packages, accepting some of Bush's proposals but rejecting many of the items he wanted to cut and adding others the president wanted to protect.

The key controversy came over funding Bush wanted to eliminate for the *Seawolf* nuclear submarine, which critics said was conceived to meet a Soviet submarine threat that no longer existed. Bush wanted to cut nearly $3 billion for construction of the second and third subs, but House

Appropriations voted to preserve money for one and Senate Appropriations voted to keep the money for both. Democrats and Republicans rallied to protect submarine-building jobs in Connecticut and Rhode Island.

The House passed HR 4990 (H Rept 102-505) on a 412-2 vote May 7. The Senate Appropriations Committee considered a companion measure (S 2403 — S Rept 102-274), which it reported April 30. The full Senate passed an amended HR 4990 by voice vote May 12. A contentious House-Senate conference convened, which reached quick agreement on most items but stalled over the big-ticket defense programs. In the end, the conferees opted to save one of the *Seawolf* subs and insisted on a cut in the space-based anti-missile defense program, the strategic defense initiative (SDI).

By large margins, the House and Senate adopted the conference report on HR 4990 (H Rept 102-530) on May 21; the House voted 404-11, and the Senate voted 90-9. Bush signed the bill June 4.

Supplemental Appropriations

Congress also cleared two supplemental appropriations bills that provided additional fiscal 1992 spending authority.

The first supplemental bill (HR 5132 — PL 102-302) provided $1.1 billion to help rebuild riot-torn Los Angeles, repair Chicago's flooded downtown and finance nationwide summer youth jobs and school programs.

The House, 244-162, passed HR 5132 (H Rept 102-518) on May 14, providing $495 million in urban aid. The Senate followed suit, 61-36, May 21, upping the ante to nearly $2 billion. Despite a veto threat over the amount of money for jobs and school aid, the conference kept the bill at about the Senate's level. But before sending the measure to the floor, congressional leaders agreed informally to modify it without sending the bill back to conference. Both chambers adopted the trimmed-down conference report (H Rept 102-577) on June 18. The House acted 249-168, and the Senate acted by voice vote. The president signed the bill June 22.

A second supplemental bill (HR 5620 — PL 102-368) provided $11.1 billion in aid for storm-stricken Florida, Hawaii and Guam, plus $4.1 billion in unrelated defense spending and $500,000 in urban aid. The bill was passed 297-124 by the House (H Rept 102-672) July 28 as a catch-all defense measure. But after late summer hurricanes and a typhoon ravaged Florida, Louisiana, Guam and Hawaii, the Senate swiftly tacked on disaster aid and passed the bill (S Rept 102-395) on an 84-10 vote Sept. 15. After further negotiations, the bill finally cleared on Sept. 18, and Bush signed it Sept. 23.

Budget-Control Efforts

While no reconciliation bill was required in 1992, Congress nonetheless devoted a great deal of attention to the general subject of deficit reduction — though only one of its legislative initiatives survived a floor vote and none came close to enactment.

Proposals were seriously considered to amend the Constitution to prohibit deficit spending and to grant the president "expedited rescission authority," a sort of watered-down line-item veto for appropriations. The constitutional amendment was rejected, and the expedited rescissions bill passed the House but died in the Senate.

House Budget Committee Chairman Leon E. Panetta, D-Calif., a confirmed deficit-hawk, tried for several months to negotiate a deal with Republicans to produce another update of the 1985 Gramm-Rudman anti-deficit law (PL 99-177). Congress had twice before overhauled Gramm-Rudman, in 1987 (PL 100-119) and as part of the 1990 reconciliation bill (HR 5835 — PL 101-508). *(Gramm-Rudman, Congress and the Nation Vol. VII, pp. 44, 67; 1990 reconciliation bill, p. 55)*

In July, Panetta introduced HR 5676, which would require Congress to balance the budget by fiscal 1998 or endure stiff new enforcement mechanisms, including automatic tax increases and Social Security cuts, as well as the more traditional spending cuts that were embodied in Gramm-Rudman. He began work on the bill to show members the sort of drastic action that would be required if they were to adhere to a balanced budget amendment. Although his Democratic allies on the Budget Committee embraced the effort, including conservatives such as Charles W. Stenholm of Texas, Panetta never picked up a single Republican supporter. Most Democrats viewed his approach as politically unwise, and the bill never made it to the House floor.

Balanced Budget Amendment

For the second time in two years, the House June 11, 1992, narrowly rejected a constitutional amendment to require a balanced budget (H J Res 290).

By a **key vote of 280-153 (R 164-2; D 116-150; I 0-1)** the House fell nine votes short of the two-thirds majority needed to send the measure to the Senate. The margin was roughly the same as in 1990, when the House also fell just short of passing similar legislation. It was the fourth time in a decade that Congress had refused to use the Constitution to enforce fiscal discipline. *(1990 balanced budget amendment, p. 75; 1992 key votes, p. 1083)*

In May, the idea of amending the Constitution had suddenly began gaining converts. Despite the budget agreement hammered out in 1990, deficits had continued to go up; the January estimate from the White House budget office for the fiscal 1992 deficit was roughly $400 billion (it later turned out to be much less, $290.2 billion, still a record). Meanwhile, public regard for Congress and its ability to handle the nation's finances was sinking in a critical election year. Democrats who had long opposed the idea were changing their minds out of sheer desperation.

The growing support was all the more surprising because little of the grass-roots clamor for a balanced budget that had been a hallmark of the late 1970s was heard. The last time a state legislature had passed a resolution calling for a constitutional convention to write a balanced budget amendment was in 1983. Congressional committees had paid only a smattering of attention to the issue, and little up-to-date analysis existed on how an amendment would work — if it would work at all.

Nevertheless, the momentum at first seemed unstoppable. Head counts by proponents and opponents showed the measure probably passing. Somehow, over a matter of a few weeks, Democratic leaders in the House managed to erode enough support to defeat it. Twelve cosponsors of H J Res 290 eventually voted against it.

Stenholm, the sponsor of H J Res 290, modeled it after versions previously defeated on the floor. Once ratified by three-fourths of the states, H J Res 290 would have required Congress and the president to agree on an estimate of total receipts for a given year, which they then had to put into law. Government outlays (actual spending) could not exceed the revenue estimate.

A three-fifths vote of the total membership (not just those present and voting) of each chamber would be necessary to override this requirement. Even then, the deficit could not rise freely: Congress would have to approve a specific amount by which outlays could exceed receipts. No bill to increase revenue could have been enacted unless it were approved by a majority of the total membership of each chamber. And the president would have been required to submit a balanced budget to Congress for each fiscal year.

H J Res 290 also would have required a three-fifths majority in both chambers to pass a bill to increase the limit on the federal debt. The debt limit — a statutory ceiling on the government's total accumulated deficits — had to be increased periodically to accommodate additional borrowing. Under existing law, raising the debt limit required only a simple majority. Those requirements could have been waived if a declaration of war was in effect.

In an effort to draw votes away from Stenholm, House Democratic leaders proposed their own constitutional amendment, requiring a balanced budget but exempting Social Security from spending cuts and revenue estimates. Organized labor also weighed in, launching a national lobbying campaign to head off the amendment. The Children's Defense Fund, Common Cause, the League of Women Voters, Public Citizen and the Religious Action Center of Reform Judaism sent a joint letter to members of Congress warning that the amendment would involve the courts in economic policy and undermine majority rule in Congress by requiring a three-fifths vote for deficit spending.

Perhaps the most important factor was the opposition of Senate Appropriations Chairman Robert C. Byrd, D-W.Va. He gave amendment opponents a crucial lift in late May when he made clear his vehement opposition to the amendment and his plan to devote a great deal of energy to trying to stop it — including a prolonged filibuster, if necessary. Unspoken was the threat that, as Appropriations chairman, Byrd could extract a heavy price from members who crossed him on the issue.

The House began the debate June 9 by rejecting a motion, 199-220, to suspend the rules and pass a bill (HR 5333) to require the president and the House and Senate Budget committees to submit balanced budgets. The House had passed a similar measure in 1990 at the same time it rejected the last balanced budget constitutional amendment.

The House then debated and rejected three alternatives to Stenholm's amendment — the one prepared by the Democratic leadership and two drafted by Republicans. Finally, the House voted on H J Res 290.

Senate Action. A last-ditch attempt to revive the balanced budget amendment in the Senate also failed.

The Senate Judiciary Committee had approved a constitutional amendment (S J Res 18 — S Rept 102-103) in May 1991. Sponsored by Paul Simon, D-Ill., and simpler than Stenholm's measure, it would require that total outlays not exceed the government's total receipts for a given year. A three-fifths majority of the total membership (not just those present and voting) of each chamber would be required to override this requirement. Congress would have to specify the amount of the new deficit.

But thanks to Byrd, the Senate amendment drive fell apart a week before the House vote. "In the final analysis, Congress will not propose this amendment," Byrd predicted June 2, and many of his colleagues concurred. "Once members are really informed on the mischief this amendment could do, the damage it could do . . . I have a feeling that there's enough character to this Senate" to defeat it. Byrd flatly denied using his position as chairman to bludgeon amendment supporters, though he admitted to having called in many of his fellow Democrats for chats.

Immediately after the House voted, Senate Majority Leader George J. Mitchell, D-Maine, said that he would not call up Simon's measure, apparently killing any chance for the amendment in 1992. Simon said that before the House action, his vote count had shown 63 senators for the amendment, four shy of the 67 needed to garner the necessary two-thirds.

Two weeks later, Phil Gramm, R-Texas, and other diehard supporters tried to bring the amendment back to life by attaching it to an unrelated bill regulating government-sponsored enterprises (S 2733). But the partisan tone of the debate splintered what had been a strong, bipartisan coalition in favor of the amendment. In identical 56-39 votes June 30 and July 1, the Senate fell four votes shy of the 60 it would have taken to choke off a Democratic filibuster, finally killing the effort for the year. *(Government-sponsored enterprises, p. 153)*

Expedited Rescissions

Fiscal conservatives, who had tried in vain for years to give the president increased authority to cut individual items out of large appropriations bills, celebrated a partial victory in 1992 with House passage in October of a bill that would have given the president the equivalent of a weak line-item veto.

The bill (HR 2164) would have forced Congress to vote on each of a president's proposals to rescind — or cancel — prior appropriations; if both the House and Senate approved a rescission request by majority votes, the spending would be cut.

The measure, which died when the Senate failed to act on it, fell far short of the full line-item veto of appropriations and tax provisions that some conservatives wanted. In 1985, Senate opponents had filibustered and blocked floor consideration of a bill that was closer to an actual line-item veto by which the president could reject a single provision and force both chambers of Congress to try to muster two-thirds majorities to override his decision. *(Line-item veto, Congress and the Nation Vol. VII, p. 57)*

Instead, the 1992 measure built on authority the president already had to propose that Congress rescind previously appropriated spending. Under the 1974 Congressional Budget and Impoundment Control Act (PL 93-344), the president could request rescissions, but Congress could ignore the requests. If Congress did not act, the requests expired after 45 days. That was where HR 2164 would have made the biggest change in existing law, by requiring Congress to act. *(1974 budget act, Congress and the Nation Vol. IV, p. 71)*

Congressional appropriators bitterly opposed virtually any proposal to increase the president's power to tamper with appropriations bills, and Democratic leaders had generally bowed to the appropriators' wishes to keep such proposals from the floor. But supporters of HR 2164 managed to force the House leadership to schedule a vote by holding hostage a short-term continuing resolution (H J

Res 553 — PL 102-376) that Congress had to pass to keep the government going while the House and Senate finished the final fiscal 1993 appropriations bills. *(Fiscal 1993 appropriations, p. 81)*

The House voted 312-97 on Oct. 3 to suspend the rules and pass the expedited rescissions legislation. But backers knew they were sending the bill to its death in the Senate, where Byrd was prepared to keep it from the floor. When Congress adjourned on Oct. 9, the measure died with other unfinished business.

The House action, however, gave the measure momentum and important backing that promised to make it an issue in 1993 and after. Speaker Thomas S. Foley, D-Wash., endorsed and then voted for the measure — it was a rare event for a Speaker to participate in a roll-call vote. And shortly after Democrat Bill Clinton was elected president in November 1992, he told reporters that he and Foley had discussed the possibility of compromising over Clinton's desire for a true line-item veto — possibly through some form of expedited rescissions measure.

Tax Policy

During his four years in office, Republican President George Bush clashed repeatedly with two Democratic-led Congresses over fundamental issues of tax policy.

Unlike Ronald Reagan, his predecessor in the White House, Bush would leave office without having contributed a significant change to the nation's tax code. And unlike President Reagan, Bush would not survive enactment of a huge tax increase. (Reagan presided over major tax increases in 1982, 1983 and 1984, following the huge tax cut he initiated in 1981; still he was re-elected easily in 1984.) Change eluded those lawmakers who favored it as the two sides fought essentially to a standstill on the biggest matters of principle that divided them. Practical politics, ideological differences between Democrats and Republicans, and the weight of the federal budget deficit all prevented agreement.

Bush and his Republican congressional allies failed in two serious attempts to engineer a deep cut in the tax rate on capital gains — income from the sale of assets that appreciate in value, such as stocks or real estate. Both times, their opponents succeeded by invoking concerns over the cost of such a tax cut and by raising the specter of class differences in arguing that Republican tax proposals unfairly favored the rich.

A few Democrats were prominent among the proponents of a capital gains cut. But the majority of Democrats were unwilling to go along unless projected revenue losses were offset by higher taxes on those wealthy taxpayers, who opponents argued would benefit most from the change.

If Republicans failed to muster majorities on Capitol Hill for their points of view, however, the Democrats found it just as impossible to persuade the occupant of the White House. Democrats in 1992 sent bills to Bush that would have given tax relief to the middle class and to cities, and twice the bills died under Bush's veto.

Nevertheless, the Democrats won both moral and political victories in 1990 when Bush agreed to a five-year, $137 billion tax increase as a significant element of a huge deficit-reduction bill.

For a Republican president to acquiesce in such a big tax increase would have come as a surprise in any event. For Bush, he did not merely acquiesce; he started the ball rolling by asking Democrats to convene a budget summit to attack the deficit. Then, when Democrats balked, he opened the door wider by declaring in a statement of surrender that "tax revenue increases" would be a necessary element of any deficit-reduction package.

But for all of that, the act of signing the tax increase into law directly contradicted Bush's pledge during the 1988 election campaign that he would accept "no new taxes."

The all-too-obvious switch was viewed as treachery by many conservative Republicans, as the ultimate broken campaign promise by many ordinary taxpayers and as a vindication by Democrats who had claimed for years that the only honest way to attack the budget deficit was through spending cuts and tax increases.

Coming as it did as the nation's economy was in the midst of a recession, the tax increase was doubly problematic.

Conservative critics complained that the tax increase exacerbated the downturn by diverting essential investment capital and money that would have been spent on consumption, both keys to economic vitality. Moreover, the combination of the recession and the upfront costs associated with the savings and loan bailout had added significantly to the deficit, masking whatever benefit was provided by the tax increase.

And regardless of its economic effects, the tax increase had the profound political impact of seriously wounding Bush and contributing in an immeasurable but significant way to his defeat at the polls two years later.

The Ideological Divide

Partisan disputes over taxes had deep ideological underpinnings — and, as Bush learned, major political implications — that made compromise extremely difficult.

Republicans have long stressed tax policies that favored savings and investment, arguing that U.S. capital pools were too shallow already and that spurring investment was crucial to sustaining growth and maintaining a competitive position in the world economy.

Thus, during the late 1980s and early 1990s, Republicans showed their preference for tax cuts. And on those

References

Discussion of tax policy for the years 1945-64 may be found in *Congress and the Nation Vol. I*, pp. 397-442; for the years 1965-68, *Congress and the Nation Vol. II*, pp. 141-182; for the years 1969-72, *Congress and the Nation Vol. III*, pp. 77-96; for the years 1973-76, *Congress and the Nation Vol. IV*, pp. 83-106; for the years 1977-80, *Congress and the Nation Vol. V*, pp. 231-251; for the years 1981-84, *Congress and the Nation Vol. VI*, pp. 63-82; for the years 1985-88, *Congress and the Nation Vol. VII*, pp. 75-107.

rare occasions when they discussed tax increases — and they were rare — Republicans generally wanted to tax the sale of consumer goods such as gasoline, alcohol and tobacco. Those sorts of taxes, they argued, did less to hinder economic growth, investment or productivity. But such taxes also were regressive, meaning they would be levied without regard to one's ability to pay and so hit the poor harder than they would the wealthy.

For their part, many Democrats resisted talking about specific taxes — acutely aware that Bush and Reagan had painted Democrats into a corner on tax issues in three consecutive presidential campaigns. Seeking to tailor their message, Democrats stressed their preference for more progressive revenue measures that would place a greater burden on businesses and upper-income taxpayers.

Democrats argued that the tax policies of the 1980s — beginning with the 1981 tax cut — already had done yeoman's work for the investing class. In their view, the tax code was already too regressive, particularly when Social Security taxes were factored in. The end of the decade, Democrats maintained, was the time to reverse the trend.

Favoring Capital Gains

When Bush unveiled his plan for a capital gains cut in 1989, he set in motion a new installment of a debate that went back at least to 1978. The question: Would lower capital gains taxes actually increase government receipts by stimulating investment and other economic activity?

Some academics and other experts argued that lower capital gains rates would spur more revenues in two ways.

First, investors would be induced to sell stocks or other assets that they had held for some time and that had substantially increased in market value. That would allow investors to realize locked-up gains at a more favorable tax rate and, at the same time, generate tax revenue that would not have been collected as long as the assets remained unsold.

Second, investors would direct more capital into business investments that might result in future capital gains in anticipation of a generous after-tax return.

Critics of those arguments conceded a short-term revenue boost when investors unloaded long-held assets. But, they contended, the so-called unlocking effect would be a one-time event, producing additional revenue in only the first year or two that a capital gains cut was in effect.

And, they argued, long-term economic behavior would result in significant revenue losses. First, there would not be a significant increase in total investment because many investors would simply shift money from investments that produced income taxable at ordinary, higher rates to those that resulted in capital gains. Second, whatever increased investment resulted from a reduced capital gains tax would not generate enough broad-scale economic growth to offset the revenue loss from lower taxes on capital gains generally.

Fairness, too, played a part in the debate, and not only in the historical data trumpeted by liberals that capital gains income accrued mostly to the wealthy.

Conservatives — and many liberal economists — said that capital gains taxes were palpably unfair and uneconomic because they were based in large part on inflation and not real increases in asset value. It was that argument that led many to favor not a differential rate for capital gains income, but an indexing provision that would eliminate from tax calculations the amount of an asset's appreciation caused solely by inflation.

Indexing, however, has proved to be difficult to put in place as a practical matter: Would inflation be figured differently for different types of assets — real estate vs. oil industry stock holdings, for instance? And, for which assets would indexing take effect — future acquisitions or those held for some time, or both? Whatever the decision on those questions, it also was plain that indexing would be a huge revenue loser.

In 1989, when Bush began his push for a capital gains cut, the top rate on capital gains was the same as that for all other types of income — 28 percent (or, for some higher-income taxpayers, 33 percent). But that had only been the case since the tax code was overhauled in 1986.

In 1978, a Democratic-controlled Congress, against the wishes of Democratic President Jimmy Carter, had slashed the capital gains rate from 48 percent to 28 percent. The reduction was the centerpiece of a bill aimed at cutting $18.7 billion from taxes in 1979. (Capital gains rates had peaked at 49 percent in 1976 and 1977, the result of a major tax bill in 1969 and subsequent changes.) The next change came in 1981, Reagan's first year in office, when Congress effectively cut the top capital gains rate to 20 percent, where it remained until 1986.

The decision to eliminate the preferential rate was a key element in the 1986 tax deal, which sharply reduced top rates on ordinary income in exchange for elimination of tax shelters and other tax-limiting provisions that chiefly benefited the wealthy. Those opposed to restoring a different capital gains rate in 1989 warned that such a move would unravel the 1986 compromise. "If capital gains gets put back in the code, it's a knife in the back of tax reform," said Sen. Bill Bradley, D-N.J., whose 1982 bill, cosponsored with Rep. Richard A. Gephardt, D-Mo., helped start the reform movement of the 1980s.

But Bush had already indicated that he did not consider the 1986 deal sacrosanct. Even before accepting the Republican nomination in New Orleans, Bush had told *Business Week*: "The [Reagan] administration has been unwilling to open up the tax code for various reasons. Fine, I've been part of this administration. We're going to change in 1989. I will open up the tax code."

So in 1989, Bush proposed a 15 percent top rate for capital gains. A cadre of House Democrats joined with Republicans to propose a top rate of 19.6 percent to be effective for two years; after that, the top rate would be 28 percent and the value of appreciated assets would be indexed for inflation. The House agreed to the capital gains cut, but Senate Democratic leaders forced supporters to overcome a procedural hurdle that required a three-fifths majority — 60 votes — for passage, and there the proposal died.

The following year, Bush refined his proposal to limit the top rate to 19.6 percent, and only for assets held longer than three years. Moreover, the reduced rate would have been available to individuals but not corporations. As budget talks proceeded, the capital gains cut took on an enhanced status, but Democrats insisted that they would consider it only if coupled with an offsetting tax increase on ordinary income received by more wealthy taxpayers. Some Republicans attempted to negotiate such a deal, but in the end the terms of such a compromise could not be reached.

The tax increase enacted in 1990 included a higher top tax rate of 31 percent for most upper-income taxpayers (and a slightly lower rate for those few who had been subject to the prior 33 percent rate), coupled with a top

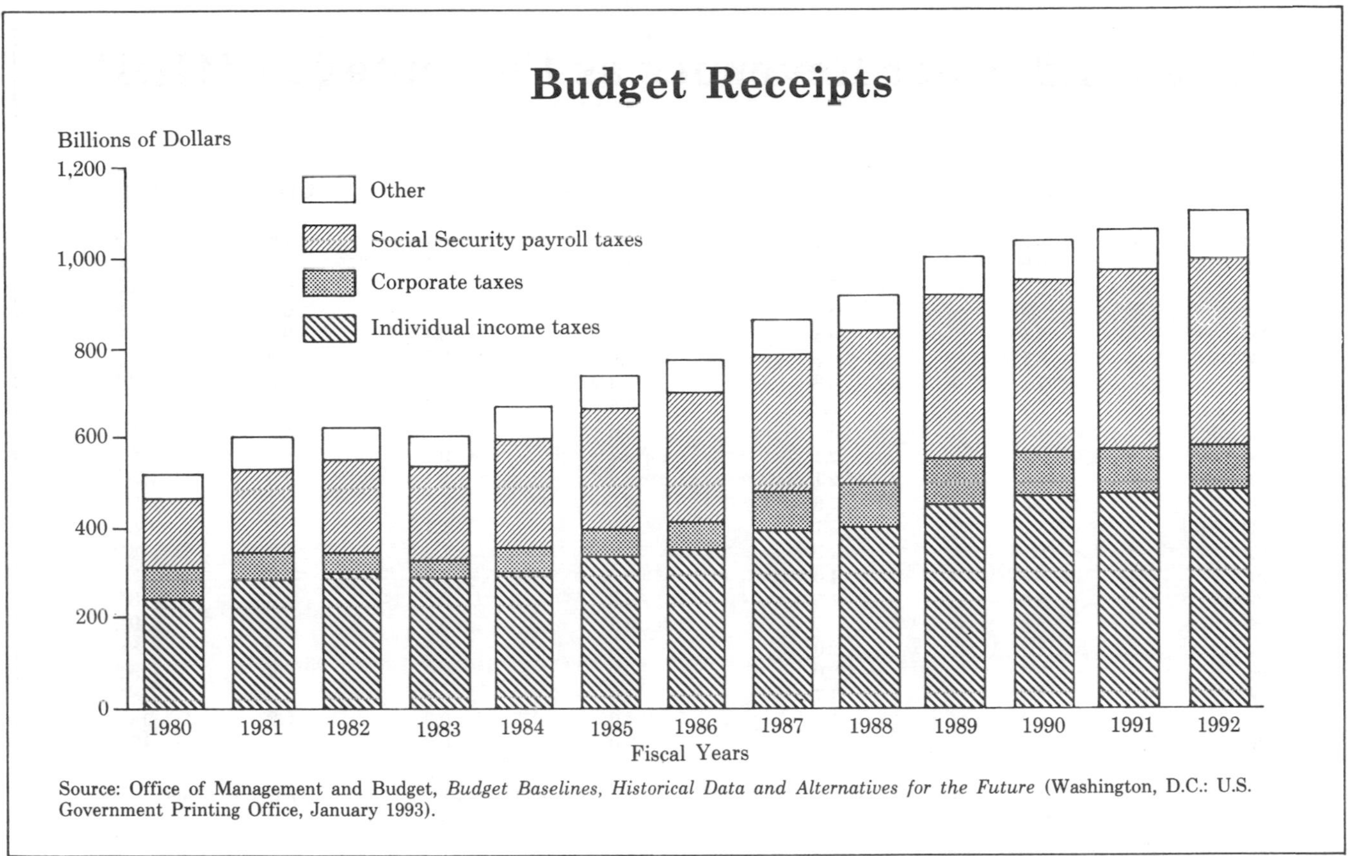

Source: Office of Management and Budget, *Budget Baselines, Historical Data and Alternatives for the Future* (Washington, D.C.: U.S. Government Printing Office, January 1993).

capital gains rate of 28 percent. Most advocates of cutting capital gains taxes scoffed that the differential was too small to yield any economic benefit.

Aiding the Middle Class

Hewing to a strategy intended to prove that Republican tax policies favored the rich, Democrats set out to show they were the protectors of the middle class. Not only did they repeatedly raise class questions during the 1989-90 capital gains fights, they followed up with a series of efforts to reduce the middle-income tax burden in 1991-92.

Democrats did not own the middle-class franchise. In 1992, Bush proposed a series of tax changes that he said would aid middle-income taxpayers — including credits for first-time home buyers and penalty-free withdrawals from individual retirement accounts (IRAs) for certain purchases. And, Republicans tried to claim that a capital gains tax cut would benefit those at the top and bottom of the income scale.

But Bush's veto in early 1992 of a Democratic-drafted, middle-income tax cut bill — paid for by higher taxes on the very wealthy — worked against his assertion that he was a middle-class champion.

It did not seem to matter that most economists viewed middle-class tax cuts as a huge mistake. Such actions were seen as bad fiscal policy because they threatened to increase the deficit if not fully paid for. And they were seen as bad economics generally because savings and investment — not increased consumption — were the driving forces of long-term prosperity. Most believed that there was too little savings already and that money put in the pockets of cash-strapped middle-income individuals had little promise of being saved.

The attempt to help the middle class with a tax cut began in 1990, when Sen. Daniel Patrick Moynihan, D-N.Y., pushed for a cut in Social Security taxes for those at the lower end of the income scale and an increase for those at the top. His plan also would have stopped the buildup of the Social Security trust funds — a curious proposal because Moynihan was a key member of the 1983 commission that proposed big tax increases to be paid into the trust funds.

His two-fold rationale was simple, however. First, the flat Social Security tax was regressive — and for most wage earners becoming a huge portion of their federal tax liability. Second, the federal deficit continued to grow, making it ever more likely that tax increases on everyone would be needed to redeem the federal government bonds in which the trust funds were invested. In essence, he argued, middle-class and lower-class wage earners were financing a disproportionate share of the deficit.

Moynihan's argument had a certain logic and appeal — but it was complicated. Opponents noted that it would yield a rather small windfall to those it sought to benefit — a few dollars a week at most — and threatened the long-term health of the Social Security system and hence the benefits that those same workers expected to receive upon retirement.

His 1990 bill won a majority on the Senate floor but failed when it did not get the 60 votes needed to overcome a parliamentary rule that it violated the Gramm-Rudman anti-deficit law. A similar proposal in 1991, cast as an amendment to the fiscal 1992 budget resolution, was killed easily on a tabling motion.

Taxes and Other Revenues as Percentage of GDP

Year	Individual Income	Corporate Income	Social Insurance	Excise	Other	Total
1935	0.8%	0.8%	—	2.1%	1.6%	5.3%
1940	0.9	1.3	1.9%	2.1	0.7	6.9
1945	8.7	7.5	1.6	3.0	0.5	21.3
1950	5.9	3.9	1.6	2.8	0.5	14.8
1955	7.5	4.6	2.0	2.4	0.5	17.0
1960	8.1	4.3	2.9	2.3	0.8	18.3
1965	7.3	3.8	3.3	2.2	0.9	17.4
1970	9.2	3.3	4.5	1.6	1.0	19.6
1975	8.1	2.7	5.6	1.1	1.0	18.5
1980	9.2	2.4	6.0	0.9	1.0	19.6
1981	9.6	2.1	6.2	1.4	1.0	20.2
1982	9.5	1.6	6.5	1.2	1.1	19.8
1983	8.7	1.1	6.3	1.1	0.9	18.1
1984	8.1	1.5	6.5	1.0	0.9	18.0
1985	8.4	1.5	6.7	0.9	0.9	18.5
1986	8.3	1.5	6.7	0.8	1.0	18.2
1987	8.8	1.9	6.8	0.7	0.9	19.2
1988	8.3	2.0	7.0	0.7	0.9	18.9
1989	8.6	2.0	6.9	0.7	0.9	19.2
1990	8.5	1.7	7.0	0.6	1.0	18.9
1991	8.3	1.7	7.0	0.8	0.9	18.7
1992	8.1	1.7	7.0	0.8	0.9	18.6

Note: The Social Insurance category includes Social Security, Medicare, railroad and other retirement programs, and unemployment insurance. The Other category principally includes estate and gift taxes and customs duties.

Source: Office of Management and Budget.

It was the economy's slow recovery from the recession of 1990-91 that gave the biggest impetus to middle-class tax relief and had politicians of all stripes climbing aboard for a time. The high point of the effort was a Democratic tax bill in early 1992 that earmarked most of its benefits for middle-income taxpayers.

That bill would have given wage-earners an income tax credit for a portion of their Social Security taxes (a provision not different in tax effect from Moynihan's earlier proposals, except that the trust funds would have continued to grow). It would have given a second per-child credit to middle-income taxpayers. And it would have restored full IRA deductibility for all taxpayers. Moreover, the capital gains tax rate would have been reduced for lower- and middle-income taxpayers, but not the wealthiest.

Some of those provisions were not only acceptable to Bush, they came from his own proposals. But they cost money and were to be offset by a new, higher tax bracket for the top 2 percent or so of all taxpayers. That made the proposal completely unacceptable to many Democrats, to most Republicans and most importantly to Bush. He vetoed the bill, and when the House voted on a motion to override the veto, it failed even to win a majority.

That vote spelled the death knell for most efforts to give middle-income earners a tax break. Only the IRA provision — which though targeted to the middle class would have benefited wealthier individuals as well — survived in a second Democratic tax bill later in the year.

The second bill was principally aimed at granting business incentives to locate in inner cities. But Bush vetoed this one as well, the day after he was defeated for reelection. Bush said the benefits were too meager, the giveaways too great and the costs — to small businesses and jobs — too big.

Chronology Of Action On Taxes

1989-90

Congress enacted a few major changes in the income tax code in 1989-90, and many smaller ones. Tax rates were raised for upper-income individuals, who also saw their taxes increase when they lost a portion of their personal exemptions and itemized deductions. Social Security and Medicare taxes also increased for higher-income taxpayers.

These changes all came as a direct result of calls for deficit reduction spawned by budget summits between Congress and the White House. Tax code changes were principally at the margins, however, and did little to alter the basic law, which had been dramatically overhauled in 1986.

More fundamental changes were advocated in 1989-90 — a deep cut in the tax on income from capital gains, for example — but political and fiscal expedience prevented them from gaining sufficient support to win enactment.

1989 Deficit-Reduction Bill

Having ordered itself to produce a relatively small increase in tax revenue as part of a deficit-reducing reconciliation bill, Congress in 1989 settled on a few modest revenue-raisers and at the same time agreed to extend for a few months the lives of a double-handful of favored tax breaks whose authority was expiring.

The net effect was $6.1 billion in new revenues for fiscal 1990 (and $29.6 billion over five years), a bit more than the $5.3 billion that President Bush and congressional leaders had set as their one-year target at an April budget summit. The tax increases and the extensions of expiring provisions were contained in the fiscal 1990 reconciliation bill (HR 3299 — PL 101-239), which won final passage in the early hours of Nov. 22. *(Legislative history, provisions, p. 43)*

Passionate debate over taxes took place for months, and both the House and Senate tax-writing committees had previously approved significantly heftier bills. Much of the fighting involved efforts in both chambers to reduce the tax on capital gains — income from the sale of stocks, real estate and other property that had appreciated in value since acquisition.

A rebellious group of Democrats on the House Ways and Means Committee had teamed with Republicans on Sept. 17 to circumvent Chairman Dan Rostenkowski, D-Ill., and insert a capital gains tax cut into the committee's version of the bill. But a few weeks later, on a 10-10 vote, the Senate Finance Committee refused to approve a capital gains tax cut sponsored by ranking Republican Bob Packwood of Oregon. The Senate committee action came during a middle-of-the-night session Oct. 3-4, during which its version of the reconciliation bill's tax provisions was approved. The Finance Committee's refusal to embrace a capital gains tax cut gave Senate Democratic leaders the necessary ammunition to keep the bill free of that issue — as well as many others — during floor debate. *(Capital gains, p. 96)*

In addition to the proposed capital gains cut, the House committee included about $5.5 billion in miscellaneous revenue increases for fiscal 1990, more than required to meet its deficit-reduction target and enough to offset the cost of extending 10 popular tax breaks for a year.

The Senate committee approved a much larger package of new revenues, totaling $48 billion over five years. But most of the added revenue increases were tied to proposed new spending or to tax changes that would have lost revenue. As the bill progressed, and as these spending programs and revenue-losing provisions were pared from the package, so, too, were the tax increases. Among the losses was a permanent extension of the tax on long-distance telephone calls, which was estimated to raise $10.5 billion over five years, but not until fiscal 1991 (when it was due to expire). Because it contributed nothing to resolving the fiscal 1990 budget problem, it was dropped.

Most of the paring away of riders and provisions that did not contribute to deficit reduction took place in one stroke on Oct. 13, when the Senate decided the reconciliation bill had become too unwieldy and had to be streamlined for passage. Although widely hailed as good governing, the move did not provoke a reciprocal response from the House, which stood by its bulkier bill. Though some of the House provisions had tax implications — and Republicans hoped to preserve the House capital gains provision — most of the fight was over such matters as child care, repeal of the 1988 Medicare Catastrophic Coverage Act and repeal of the "Section 89" rules that required employers to prove they provided all employees with roughly equal health and other benefits.

Ultimately, the Senate succeeded in insisting that the House drop most of its extraneous reconciliation provisions, and the other issues migrated to separate bills.

Social Security Wage Base Increase

One significant revenue-raiser — including employee contributions to tax-deferred savings plans when calculating the Social Security wage base — made it into the final bill with virtually no public debate. Deferred employee compensation — earnings set aside in a 401(k) plan, for instance — previously was not subject to Social Security and Medicare taxes. Nor were such earnings subject to income taxes until withdrawn after retirement. The changes would bring in an estimated $4.8 billion in revenues over five years.

The decision had implications for about 10 million of the nation's more affluent wage earners, not just those whose deferred compensation would be newly taxed. The upper limit on wages subject to Social Security and Medicare taxes increased annually along with the rate of inflation, and the limit above which Social Security taxes were not owed was already scheduled to rise from $48,000 in 1989 to $50,400 in 1990. But the decision to tax deferred compensation required that the wage base be expanded to account for the volume of deferred wages in the economy. That boosted the upper limit on wages subject to tax to $51,300. The effect was not only a Social Security tax increase on those who had deferred compensation, but also a tax increase on all those with wages in excess of $50,400 in 1990. *(Social Security and Medicare taxes, box, p. 92)*

Social Security and Medicare Taxes

The Social Security and Medicare wage bases (income against which the taxes are levied) increase yearly when Social Security recipients receive a cost-of-living increase in their benefits. Periodically, the wage base also is increased by statute. In 1989, for example, Congress voted to subject wage income set aside in 401(k) and other tax-deferred savings plans to Social Security and Medicare taxes. Then in 1990, Congress voted to separate the wage base for Medicare from that for Social Security. The Medicare wage base more than doubled in the process.

Congress also increases the tax rates for Social Security and Medicare periodically. The most recent rate increase was enacted in 1983 as part of a broad Social Security overhaul (PL 98-21). *(Congress and the Nation Vol. VI, p. 659)*

The following table shows selected wage base and tax rate levels for Social Security and Medicare.

	Wage Base		Tax Rate	
Year	Social Security	Medicare	Social Security	Medicare
1937	$ 3,000		1.00%	
1950	3,000		1.50	
1955	4,200		2.00	
1959	4,800		2.50	
1966	6,600	$ 6,600	3.85	0.35%
1970	7,800	7,800	4.20	0.60
1974	13,200	13,200	4.95	0.90
1978	17,700	17,700	5.05	1.00
1979	22,900	22,900	5.08	1.05
1981	29,700	29,700	5.35	1.30
1982	32,400	32,400	5.40	1.30
1984	37,800	37,800	5.70	1.30
1985	39,600	39,600	5.70	1.35
1986	42,000	42,000	5.70	1.45
1987	43,800	43,800	5.70	1.45
1988	45,000	45,000	6.06	1.45
1989	48,000	48,000	6.06	1.45
1990	51,300	51,300	6.20	1.45
1991	53,400	125,000	6.20	1.45
1992	55,500	130,200	6.20	1.45

Source: House Ways and Means Committee.

The deferred-compensation provision had been included in the House bill. It was added to the Senate Finance version, but only as a way to pay for another change, which would have permitted Social Security recipients to keep more of their own earnings after retirement. But the Finance Committee changes were dropped before the full Senate passed the bill. The deferred-compensation portion was kept in the bill by conferees at the last minute because they needed the revenue it generated for deficit reduction. *(Social Security earnings test, p. 717)*

The other revenue provisions that survived the reconciliation process were primarily ideas that had been around since the spring. These included about $2.7 billion in accelerations — the faster collection of taxes that would be paid eventually anyway.

The revenue scoring also claimed credit for recapturing $568 million in revenue losses that would have been incurred through tax benefits to firms purchasing failing financial institutions. Early repeal of the tax breaks had been written into the savings and loan bailout bill (HR 1278 — PL 101-73). *(Savings and loan bailout, p. 117)*

Also included was an extension of the excise tax on airline tickets, which was about to be reduced. That tax alone was worth $895 million in fiscal 1990 ($1.85 billion over five years).

And employee stock ownership plans (ESOPs) used to finance corporate takeovers or to generate new capital were subjected to new tax rules projected to bring in $1.1 billion in revenue in fiscal 1990. The bill repealed the partial exclusion for interest paid on loans for ESOPs where the ESOP owned less than half of the stock.

Other new taxes, on chemicals that depleted the ozone layer and on foreign oil (for an oil-spill liability trust fund), were expected to produce about $600 million in fiscal 1990.

In another revenue-raising accounting change, certain farm workers would see taxes withheld from their pay ($270 million). The remaining revenues resulted from a series of technical and accounting changes primarily affecting foreign taxes and corporations.

Temporary Tax Breaks

The bill also preserved some revenue-losers, including a package of temporary extensions for 10 highly popular tax breaks, such as a credit for hiring hard-to-place workers, tax-free interest on certain bonds and an exclusion from income for employer-paid school costs. These provisions were not a permanent part of the tax code and survived on periodic renewal, usually a year or so at a time. *(Expiring tax provisions, box, p. 94)*

The length of the extensions was tied to the continuing dispute over capital gains. The Senate, at Republicans' insistence, wanted no more than a six-month extension, so that the pending expirations might serve as a vehicle for a capital gains provision in 1990. The House wanted them renewed for a year. In a compromise, the expired or expiring provisions were extended for nine months, through Sept. 30, 1990, at a projected cost of $1.4 billion.

1990 Deficit-Reduction Bill

The tax debate shifted markedly to the Democrats' terrain in 1990.

The year began with President Bush reiterating his 1988 "no new taxes" campaign pledge and again promoting a tax break for capital gains income (profits from the sale of assets, such as stocks, real estate or lumber).

But the congressional session ended with passage of a deficit-reducing reconciliation bill (HR 5835 — PL 101-508) that promised to raise a net of $137 billion in new taxes over five years and increase the top income tax rate on the very wealthiest taxpayers from 28 percent to 31 percent. Republicans suffered a trio of defeats: Congress approved only a cosmetic change in the capital gains tax rate; the GOP took a political drubbing from Democrats on the issue of "tax fairness"; and Bush was pilloried by conservatives for abandoning his anti-tax pledge. *(Legislative history, provisions, p. 55)*

As they scrambled for a compromise that would make the tax system more progressive without imposing a highly visible surcharge on the rich, Congress and the administration added new complexity to a tax system that was supposed to have been simplified once and for all by the 1986 tax overhaul (PL 99-514). Instead of eliminating deductions, lawmakers made calculating them for the wealthy more difficult. And the final tax package included a complicated, last-minute plan to phase out personal exemptions for high-income taxpayers. *(1986 tax bill, Congress and the Nation Vol. VII, p. 79)*

Budget Summit

A number of factors accounted for the way in which Republicans gradually lost control of the tax issue as the parties debated and maneuvered throughout 1990.

Administration officials, concerned that the soaring federal budget deficit could severely damage the economy and hurt Bush's re-election chances in 1992, sought Democrats' help to work out a bipartisan deficit-reduction deal. Democrats entered budget summit talks May 15, but they shrank from discussing taxes and refused to negotiate on reducing the deficit until Bush abandoned his "no new taxes" campaign pledge. On June 26, Bush issued a statement that "tax revenue increases" would have to be part of any package.

With Republicans deeply split over Bush's tax shift and polls revealing a growing public perception that GOP tax policies had favored the rich, Democrats seized on the issue of tax equity and made it the focus of the year's debate. They argued that tax changes made during the 1980s had largely benefited the wealthy and that this trend needed to be reversed. They were emboldened by the summer publication of *The Politics of Rich and Poor*, a book by GOP analyst Kevin Phillips that predicted a backlash against the "ostentatious celebration of wealth" in the 1980s.

Toward the end of the budget summit negotiations, a trade seemed possible between the capital gains tax cut, which many Democrats privately favored, and an increase in tax rates on the rich. But strong opposition from rank-and-file members on both sides blocked such an agreement. When party leaders unveiled the final summit package Sept. 30, both ideas had been dropped. *(Capital gains, p. 96)*

This did not halt the partisan debate, however. Rank-and-file Democrats criticized the package as doing nothing to address their concerns that the tax system was unfair. They said it imposed too much of the burden on low- and middle-income taxpayers and not enough on the rich. Republicans complained that the deal would impede economic growth by calling for too many new taxes and too few breaks for investors. Others said that a limit on deductions for upper-income taxpayers was a thinly disguised attempt to increase the top income tax rate.

Gas, tobacco, alcohol and luxury tax proposals produced partisan and regional splits. Opponents of increasing the deficit objected to other provisions that otherwise had strong cores of support. Proposed tax benefits to businesses that located in economically depressed urban and rural areas would have added $1 billion to the deficit over five years. And tax breaks to oil and ethanol producers would have added $4 billion to the deficit.

And just about everyone thumbed their noses at a last-minute goodie, inserted to attract conservative support, that would have provided generous tax breaks for investors in small businesses. The package of investment benefits would have cost $12.1 billion over five years. Among the incentives proposed were a tax deduction for individuals of 25 percent of the value of stock purchases in qualifying small corporations; indexing to the rate of inflation of the "basis" or purchase price of stock in a small corporation to provide protection against large capital gains taxes on the sale of such stock; and an extra research and development credit for small corporations.

"It's just mucking up the code again," complained House Ways and Means Committee Chairman Dan Rostenkowski, D-Ill., a prime sponsor of the 1986 overhaul bill, which eliminated numerous special interest tax breaks in exchange for lower rates for most taxpayers.

A New Plan

The summit agreement did not survive long following its Sept. 30 unveiling in the White House Rose Garden. Five days later, the House summarily rejected a budget resolution (H Con Res 310) incorporating the summit agreement's outlines on a **key vote of 179-254 (R 71-105; D 108-149)**. Differences over the tax provisions were a major factor in its rejection. *(1990 key votes, p. 1039)*

Conferees on the budget resolution then recast the measure with broad totals that made no specific recommendations about taxes or spending cuts. The House and Senate adopted it on Oct. 8 and Oct. 9, respectively. That set the stage for floor action on a reconciliation bill (HR 5835) and gave Democrats, who controlled both chambers, an opening to fashion a new plan more to their own liking. The administration was forced to go along, with time running out and no substitute in sight.

In the House, Ways and Means Democrats produced a package of tax code changes that not only increased the top income tax rate but also imposed other changes designed to shift the tax burden to the wealthy. Taxpayers with adjusted gross incomes of $200,000 or more were expected to see their tax bills go up 6.3 percent, compared with a 2 percent increase for most other income groups and a tax cut for those with incomes under $20,000, according to the Joint Committee on Taxation. The distribution was dramatically different from that projected for the budget summit package, which would have given the smallest tax increase, 1.7 percent, to those with the highest incomes.

The House agreed to the Ways and Means Democrats' substitute on Oct. 16 by a **key vote of 238-192 (R 10-164; D 228-28)**.

With only a 10-vote majority, Senate Democrats did not have the same advantage in numbers as their House counterparts. And given that not all Senate Democrats could be counted on to support a partisan tax proposal, Senate Democratic leaders knew they could only win passage of a tax bill that had bipartisan support. Thus, they worked with Republicans and the White House to craft a more moderate version of the reconciliation bill. Despite efforts by liberal Democrats to inflict much higher taxes on the wealthy and by conservative Republicans to kill the bill

Expiring Tax Provisions

Congress periodically extended the lives of a dozen popular tax breaks during 1989-92. Some of these provisions had been in the tax code for more than a decade but were rarely renewed for more than a year or two at a time. Occasionally, they were allowed to expire, but they usually were renewed retroactively.

Because of the popularity of the tax breaks, congressional tax-writers often were in the position of needing to move a tax bill just to keep them alive. That, in turn, gave Congress an impetus to enact other tax code changes. Most of the current tax breaks expired at the end of 1989 and were extended that year for nine months, through September 1990. In late 1990, these provisions were extended through 1991. And in late 1991, they were granted a six-month extension, through June 1992. *(1989 deficit-reduction bill, p. 43; 1990 deficit-reduction bill, p. 55; 1991 extenders bill, p. 109)*

At the time of the 1991 extension, House Ways and Means Chairman Dan Rostenkowski, D-Ill., announced that he wanted the tax breaks made permanent or dropped. In 1992, Congress cleared a bill (HR 11) that would have made some of them permanent and allowed others a further temporary extension. That bill was pocket-vetoed by President Bush on Nov. 4, the day after he was defeated for re-election. *(Urban aid tax bill, p. 103)*

Because of the veto, the last extension for most of these tax breaks expired at the end of June 1992. One, which gave businesses a tax credit for some investments in alternative energy sources, was permanently extended by a comprehensive energy bill (HR 776—PL 102-486) enacted Oct. 24, 1992. Congress was expected to renew at least some of the others in 1993, possibly retroactively. *(Energy bill, p. 469)*

Following are descriptions of the 12 tax breaks:

- **Employer-Provided Education Assistance.** Workers could exclude from their taxable income up to $5,250 a year in school costs paid for them by their employers.
- **Group Legal Services.** Workers could exclude from their taxable income certain contributions made by their employers to a qualified group legal services plan. This provision also granted a tax exemption to qualified group legal services organizations.
- **Health Insurance for Self-Employed Individuals.** Self-employed individuals were able to deduct 25 percent of the cost of health premiums for themselves, their spouses and dependents.
- **Mortgage Revenue Bonds.** State and local governments could issue tax-exempt bonds or mortgage credit certificates to help qualified individuals purchase, improve or rehabilitate single-family, owner-occupied homes.
- **Small-Issue Bonds.** Interest on certain small issues of private-activity bonds continued to be tax exempt if at least 95 percent of the proceeds from the bonds were used to finance manufacturing facilities or certain land or property for first-time farmers.
- **Research and Experimentation Credit.** Corporations could claim a 20 percent tax credit for new research expenditures and for certain payments to universities for basic research.
- **Allocation of Research Expenses.** Multinational corporations could continue using existing rules governing the allocation of research and experimentation expenses to offset U.S. and foreign source income.
- **Low-Income Rental Housing.** Individuals who invested in the rehabilitation or construction of qualified low-income housing were eligible for a tax credit in annual installments over 10 years.
- **Targeted Jobs Credit.** Employers of certain hard-to-place workers were eligible for a tax credit of up to $2,400 for each first-year employee. The maximum for disadvantaged summer youth employees was $1,200.
- **Business Energy Credits.** Businesses were eligible for a 10 percent tax credit for investment in solar and geothermal energy. Until 1990, businesses also were eligible for a 15 percent tax credit for investments in ocean thermal properties. That credit was allowed to expire at the end of September 1990, when the other business energy credits were extended until the end of 1991. The solar and geothermal credit was permanently extended in PL 102-486.
- **'Orphan' Drug Credit.** Manufacturers were eligible for a 50 percent credit for the costs of clinically testing drugs to treat rare diseases. This provision was renewed in 1986 through December 1990. It again was renewed with the others, first through 1991 and then through June 1992.
- **Gifts of Appreciated Property.** Donors who gave charitable organizations tangible property, such as artwork, that had gained value were not subject to tax under alternative minimum tax calculations. This was a temporary provision created in 1990 to go through 1991. It was extended through June 1992.

outright, slim majorities of both parties ultimately supported it. The Senate passed its version of the reconciliation measure on Oct. 19 by a **key vote of 54-46 (R 23-22; D 31-24).**

Conferees on HR 5835 eventually accepted parts of both the House and Senate tax packages. From the House bill came a slight tax rate cut for many upper-income taxpayers and a tax rate increase for the wealthiest taxpayers. Also from the House came a slight tax rate reduction for capital gains income. From the Senate bill came a limit on itemized deductions for upper-income taxpayers and an increase in the gasoline tax.

The House bill's millionaire surtax was dropped; in its place conferees inserted a phase-out of the personal exemption for wealthy taxpayers that had been in neither bill, though a similar provision had been part of the tax code since enactment of the 1986 tax-overhaul bill.

Retaining the individual income tax rate increase for the wealthy was perhaps the most difficult fight in conference. Democrats said a rate increase would be the most direct way to make the wealthiest bear a larger share of the tax burden. Privately, they acknowledged that a rate hike also would be the most direct way to remind voters that Bush had to renege on his "no new taxes" campaign pledge to deal with the federal deficit. Republicans argued that such a change would damage both the economy and the principles of tax reform.

In the end, the Democrats had the votes, and time ran out on Republicans looking for alternatives.

Highlights of Tax Changes

The reconciliation bill (HR 5835 — PL 101-508) called for $164.6 billion in new revenues over five years, offset by $27.4 billion in tax breaks. Following were major changes:

Individual Tax Changes. The most notable change in the package was the increase from 28 percent to 31 percent in the top marginal rate paid by the wealthiest taxpayers. Before the law took effect, some upper-income taxpayers paid a top marginal rate of 33 percent. That resulted from the phase-out of the benefit of the 15 percent rate that was assessed on the first several thousand dollars of a taxpayer's income and the phase-out of the personal exemption. Once those benefits were eliminated, a very wealthy taxpayer paid a flat 28 percent rate.

The bill repealed this so-called bubble. Those previously at the 33 percent rate and those with higher incomes were subject to a new 31 percent rate. The 15 percent and 28 percent rates paid by lower-income taxpayers remained. The change was expected to result in a slight tax cut for the almost 4 million taxpayers in the bubble and a tax increase for the 600,000 highest-income taxpayers.

Ironically, the new provision phasing out the value of the personal exemption for upper-income taxpayers (which was somewhat different from the 1986 version of the same idea) created a new tax bubble. The effect was an increase in a taxpayer's top marginal rate by as much as 0.5 percentage point for each personal exemption claimed.

Another provision in the measure effectively increased high-income taxpayers' top tax rate further by limiting itemized deductions. Taxpayers with adjusted gross incomes of $100,000 or more would have their itemized deductions reduced by 3 percent of the amount their income exceeded $100,000. The provision did not apply to deductions for medical expenses, casualty and theft losses, or investment interest. For example, a taxpayer with income of $140,000 would have itemized deductions reduced by $1,200, or 3 percent of $40,000. In no case, however, would a taxpayer's deductions be reduced by more than 80 percent. House Ways and Means Committee Democrat Don J. Pease of Ohio proposed the idea as an alternative to directly raising the top rate or imposing a surtax on the rich, which, he said, would be "the cleanest way to make the tax system more progressive."

One final provision that targeted high-income taxpayers was an increase in the alternative minimum tax rate to 24 percent from 21 percent. The alternative minimum tax was imposed on taxpayers who otherwise would have been able to reduce their tax liability substantially by using numerous deductions and exclusions, including some interest on municipal bond income.

Capital Gains. Although Democrats vehemently rejected Bush's demand for a broad capital gains tax cut, the final package did include a small capital gains cut for those taxpayers who were then in the 33 percent bubble (or who were to be affected by the phase-out of the personal exemption). Before the law took effect, taxpayers paid the same tax rate on capital gains income as they did on ordinary income. The bill set a nominal maximum capital gains tax rate of 28 percent. Thus, those whose top rate was higher on ordinary income would pay less on capital gains.

Business groups that had been pushing for a capital gains cut, however, dismissed the change as too insignificant to have much effect on investment. Bush had wanted the rate on capital gains to be as low as 15 percent.

Help for Low-Income Taxpayers. As part of child care legislation folded into the reconciliation bill, a number of tax changes were made to help lower-income families. *(Child care, p. 611)*

The measure increased the earned-income tax credit (EITC) for working poor families with children. Under existing law, the credit was equal to 14 percent of the first $6,810 of earned income and began to phase out after $10,730 of income. That formula would have set the maximum credit in 1991 at $994. The bill increased the credit in 1991 to a maximum of $1,186 for taxpayers with one child and $1,228 for those with two or more. Taxpayers receiving the EITC were eligible for an additional tax credit for each child under the age of 1. The maximum supplemental credit was expected to be $355 in 1991. An additional refundable credit was allowed for those who purchased health insurance for qualifying children under the EITC. The maximum refundable credit for 1991 was expected to be $426.

Excise Taxes. The bill gained almost half of its revenues through new or increased excise taxes.

The largest increase came from a 5-cents-per-gallon increase in motor fuels taxes, beginning Dec. 1, 1990. This brought the total federal excise tax on gasoline to 14 cents per gallon and on diesel fuel to 20 cents per gallon. Fuel used in rail transportation was subject to a 2.5-cent-per-gallon tax. Previously, railroads were not subject to the fuels tax, and the trucking industry fought hard to have their competitors pay. Half of the increased fuel tax revenue was dedicated to reducing the deficit; the remainder was to go to the Highway Trust Fund, with 20 percent of that amount allocated to mass transit, as under existing law.

The bill also doubled the existing tax — ranging from $500 to $3,850, depending on a vehicle's fuel efficiency — on automobiles that did not meet legal fuel economy standards. Limousines also were subjected to the so-called gas-guzzler tax.

The bill increased excise taxes on wine, beer and distilled spirits. The result was a doubling of the beer tax from 16 cents to 32 cents per six-pack; an increase from 3 cents to 21 cents in the tax on a bottle of table wine; and a distilled spirits tax hike that translated into an increase of 16 cents in the existing $2 tax on a fifth of 80-proof liquor. A reduced tax was imposed on small breweries and domestic wineries.

Taxes on tobacco products were increased 25 percent effective Jan. 1, 1991, and a like amount on Jan. 1, 1993. For example, the 16-cent tax on a pack of cigarettes was to increase 4 cents in 1991 and an additional 4 cents two years later.

As part of the effort to hit the wealthiest taxpayer, the bill imposed a new "luxury" tax on expensive automobiles, boats and yachts, private airplanes, jewelry and furs.

Taxes that financed the Airport and Airway Trust Fund, due to expire Dec. 31, 1990, were extended for five years and increased 25 percent. That meant an increase from 8 percent to 10 percent in the airline ticket tax and increased levies on air freight and fuels used in non-commercial aviation. Increased revenues would go toward deficit reduction in 1991 and 1992 and to the airport trust fund for the three years after that. *(Aviation package, p. 417)*

The existing 3 percent excise tax on local and toll telephone service, set to expire at the end of 1990, was permanently extended.

The bill also expanded the list of ozone-depleting chemicals subject to federal excise taxes; more than tripled the harbor maintenance tax on the value of cargo loaded and unloaded at U.S. ports; and continued a special 0.1-cent-per-gallon fuels tax to be deposited in a trust fund that paid for cleaning up leaking underground storage tanks.

Social Security and Medicare Taxes. Yet another provision inserted to shift more of the tax burden onto upper-income taxpayers was an increase from $51,300 to $125,000 in the wage base subject to the 1.45 percent Medicare payroll tax. The tax was paid by both employer and employee for a total of 2.9 percent.

This was the second year in a row that the wage base for Social Security or Medicare taxes was increased. The argument for increasing the Medicare wage base significantly above that for Social Security was that Medicare benefits were not determined by previous salary history. In contrast, the level of Social Security benefits was partly a function of previous wage income subject to tax. *(Social Security and Medicare taxes, box, p. 92; 1989 tax bill, p. 91; Medicare, p. 573)*

The bill also extended Social Security retirement, disability and hospital insurance coverage to state and local workers not covered by a public employee retirement system. The provision was effective after June 30, 1991, and immediately resulted in higher tax receipts by the Social Security and Medicare trust funds and over the long term created a larger pool of beneficiaries.

Other Revenue-Raisers. The bill also raised revenue through a variety of lesser tax provisions affecting businesses. A 0.2 percent surtax on federal unemployment insurance taxes paid by employers was extended through 1995. The tax had been set to expire after 1990.

Taxes also increased for employers that tapped excess reserves in overfunded pension plans. The bill increased from 15 percent to 20 percent the excise tax on assets that reverted to an employer upon a pension plan's termination. If an employer failed to meet certain requirements, the excise tax was increased to 50 percent. Those who used excess pension funds to pay premiums on retiree health plans were subject to the tax. *(Pension reversions, p. 719)*

The bill also increased premiums that employers with defined benefit pension plans had to pay the Pension Benefit Guaranty Corporation. It increased from $16 to $19 the flat rate, per-participant premium and increased from $6 to $9 the additional premium that had to be paid for each $1,000 of unfunded vested benefits.

The bill made few changes in corporate taxes, although the life insurance industry got an $8 billion hit over five years because of a lengthening in the period over which companies were required to write off certain acquisition costs. The bill also increased the interest rate paid by corporations on tax underpayments following notification by the Internal Revenue Service.

Tax Breaks. Not everyone's taxes were increased by the bill. It provided $2.5 billion over five years in energy-related tax breaks, primarily to benefit oil and gas operations. It also granted $773 million in tax breaks for small businesses.

The bill extended tax credits for the production of non-conventional and alcohol fuels; provided new credits for ethanol production and costs associated with certain difficult oil-recovery projects; expanded percentage depletion deductions allowed independent oil and gas producers; and provided alternative minimum tax relief for oil and gas producers.

Small businesses benefited from revised rules governing taxation of estates and a new tax credit for costs associated with making a facility more accessible to the disabled. The bill, however, reduced from $35,000 to $15,000 the amount that a business could deduct for such expenses.

The bill also extended the lives of 11 popular tax breaks. In 1989, 10 of the 11 had been extended for nine months, through September 1990. They included such disparate benefits as a credit for new research spending by businesses, a tax credit for construction or rehabilitation of low-income rental housing, an exclusion for employer-provided education aid and a deduction for health insurance costs incurred by self-employed persons. *(Expiring tax provisions, box, p. 94)*

In one case, involving a collection of credits for business investment in renewable energy sources, the 15 percent credit for ocean thermal energy was allowed to expire.

The 11th expiring provision granted a 50 percent credit for the costs of testing "orphan" drugs — those with limited commercial application because they were used for certain rare diseases or conditions. This credit had last been extended in the 1986 tax-overhaul bill and was due to expire at the end of December 1990.

Each of these so-called extenders was retained in the code through December 1991, at a five-year cost projected to be $5.9 billion. Some critics noted, however, that these provisions were usually extended each year and that as a result the five-year cost could be much higher.

In addition, the bill created one temporary provision. It repealed for one year, through December 1991, the alternative minimum tax on the appreciated value of tangible personal property such as artworks and manuscripts that were donated to museums, libraries and universities. Prior to 1986, gifts of property that appreciated in value could be deducted at market value. After 1986, the appreciated value of such gifts was treated as a so-called preference item for the alternative minimum tax, which meant it was treated as income subject to that tax. The change made in 1990 did not apply to non-tangible property, such as stocks, or to real estate.

Capital Gains Cut

President Bush's greatest legislative disappointment in 1989-90 was a near-miss each year in his goal of cutting the tax on capital gains — income from the sale of appreciated assets, such as real estate or corporate stock.

In 1989, the issue was effectively settled on Nov. 2, when Bush formally asked Congress to strip a cut in the tax rate on capital gains from a pending deficit-reduction bill (HR 3299 — PL 101-239). That move cleared the way for final action on the legislation, which had been stalled by a deadlock over capital gains. *(1989 deficit-reduction bill, pp. 43, 91)*

In 1990, capital gains taxes threatened to be the spoiler in deficit-reduction negotiations among congressional leaders and the White House. Many issues divided Republican and Democratic budget negotiators, but the dispute over capital gains brought those differences to a head. When the issue appeared to lose momentum, Bush himself brought it back to the fore, leaving no doubt that it remained his top tax priority.

In the end, a sweeping deficit-reduction bill that grew out of those negotiations (HR 5835 — PL 101-508) included a House provision that set the top tax rate on capital gains income at 28 percent. That meant a slightly lower tax rate for capital gains that accrued to high-income taxpayers, whose top marginal tax rate for ordinary income was set at 31 percent in the bill. But the difference was dismissed as negligible by many who had campaigned for a substantial rate cut. *(1990 deficit-reduction bill, pp. 55, 92)*

The tax rate on capital gains historically was set below that for ordinary income, at least in part because of the argument that some element of an asset's appreciated value was the result of inflation, not a true increase in value, and should not be taxed. But in 1986, as part of a plan (HR 3838 — PL 99-514) to cut all tax rates sharply and eliminate many tax breaks from the law, the tax rate on capital gains was made the same as that for ordinary income. That set the top rate on capital gains at 28 percent (except for some upper-income taxpayers who paid a top marginal rate of 33 percent). *(Congress and the Nation Vol. VII, p. 79; capital gains history, box, p. 98)*

1989 Action

In his February 1989 budget request for fiscal 1990, Bush reiterated a proposal made during his 1988 presidential campaign for a top tax rate of 15 percent on capital gains. The idea languished until the summer, when it found friends among six House Ways and Means Committee Democrats, led by Ed Jenkins of Georgia. They joined with committee Republicans to force a version of the cut into the committee's deficit-reduction bill (HR 3299 — H Rept 101-247).

The committee action came over the objections of Ways and Means Chairman Dan Rostenkowski, D-Ill., and strenuous efforts by the House Democratic leadership to defeat the Jenkins plan on the floor failed on a **key vote of 190-239 (R 1-175; D 189-64)**. *(1989 key votes, p. 1021)*

Senate supporters of a capital gains cut were unable to win enough support during Finance Committee debate on the bill. And Majority Leader George J. Mitchell, D-Maine, erected an insurmountable procedural roadblock that prevented passage on the floor. Republicans and Democratic supporters of a capital gains cut ultimately settled for a symbolic roll-call vote. In November, they lost a motion to shut off a Democratic-led filibuster on a **key vote of 51-47 (R 45-0; D 6-47)**; that was nine votes short of the 60 votes needed.

Bush's capital gains proposal was for a permanent top rate of 15 percent, tied to new, longer holding periods. The preferential rates would be limited to corporate securities, land and owner-occupied housing. (Before 1986, assets eligible for special treatment also included property qualifying for depreciation write-offs, such as mineral reserves and commercial real estate, as well as paintings and other "collectibles.")

The Treasury Department estimated that the Bush plan would bring in an additional $4.8 billion in revenue in fiscal 1990, and a total of $15 billion in 1990-93 (although it showed a loss of $20 billion in the subsequent three years). Much of the revenue gain was forecast to come from the "unlocking" of assets held for some time, the sale of which would result in tax payments not otherwise anticipated.

The Joint Committee on Taxation, Congress' official scorekeeper on revenue estimates, concluded that the Bush plan had not solved the problem of turning an immediate revenue increase into a sustained pattern. Its analysis found that the plan would produce $3.3 billion in added revenue in fiscal 1990, but an overall loss of $24.2 billion for fiscal 1989-94.

House Ways and Means Action. After seeming to rule out a capital gains tax cut, Rostenkowski in June indicated that he would be willing to consider Bush's proposal as part of wider bargaining on a tax package for fiscal 1990. But Rostenkowski quickly backed away after failing to overcome strong objections from a majority of committee Democrats. He had created an opening, however, that was quickly seized by backers of a rate cut.

Jenkins put together a coalition of committee Republicans and Southern Democrats ready to back a variant of the Bush proposal that would have set the top marginal rate on capital gains at 19.6 percent for assets (except collectibles) held for more than a year. The new rate would have been effective through 1991, at which time the top rate would increase to 28 percent, but taxpayers would be able to reduce the taxable value of sold assets to account for inflation.

Rostenkowski held off a vote on the Jenkins plan until September, while he worked in vain to sell a Democratic compromise that called for the White House and the six committee Democrats to abandon their proposal in favor of an alternative Democratic plan to index capital gains to inflation. Despite weeks of lobbying, however, Rostenkowski was unable to break Jenkins' coalition. When the committee finally voted on Sept. 14, Jenkins' plan was approved, 19-17.

House Floor Action. The newly elected House leadership — Speaker Thomas S. Foley of Washington, Majority Leader Richard A. Gephardt of Missouri and Majority Whip William H. Gray III of Pennsylvania — chose to make a fight over Jenkins' capital gains proposal. They offered an alternative that would have paired an expansion of individual retirement accounts (IRAs) with an increase in the top rate for ordinary income. The 1986 tax-overhaul bill had greatly restricted the availability of IRAs, which allowed eligible taxpayers to save up to $2,000 a year, tax free. The leadership proposed to restore universal eligibility for IRAs and to permit penalty-free withdrawals for the purchase of a first home or to cover college costs. The intent was to offer a larger tax break to middle-income taxpayers, but one that would ostensibly benefit investment by encouraging saving.

The plan was opposed by some liberal Democrats, such as Budget Committee Chairman Leon E. Panetta, Calif.,

Capital Gains History

The debate over taxing the capital gain from the sale of an appreciated asset dates back to the institution of the individual income tax in 1913 and has rarely abated. At first, capital gains were taxed as regular income. Beginning in 1921, some form of differential was recognized between earned income and profits; a portion of capital gains was "excluded" from income to account for the portion of the gain attributable to inflation, and not to the intrinsic value of the asset.

When the top marginal tax rate climbed above 90 percent during World War II, the excluded amount rose to 69 percent. (In a progressive tax system, the top marginal rate is that charged on the last dollar of income earned.)

As tax rates slowly declined in the postwar era, the exclusion did, too. But that trend stalled in the Vietnam War years, and the top marginal rate on capital gains reached a peak of 49 percent in the early years of the Carter administration.

The rate was then cut in 1978 and again in the Reagan administration's 1981 tax package (PL 97-34). In the 1986 Tax Reform Act (PL 99-514), the exclusion was eliminated altogether in exchange for a dramatic reduction in the top marginal tax rate. (For taxpayers with the highest incomes, the top marginal rate under the 1986 act actually dropped, although the net effect of other changes was not a decrease in their effective tax rate.)

Then, in 1990, in concert with a reduced top marginal rate, the top rate charged on capital gains was capped at 28 percent, the top marginal rate for all but the wealthiest taxpayers.

The following table shows the portion of capital gains income that was not subject to tax, the top marginal tax rate on ordinary income and the top marginal rate on capital gains:

Years	Exclusion	Taxable Capital Gain	Top Marginal Rate for Ordinary Income	Top Marginal Rate for Capital Gains
1954-67	50%	50%	77-87%	25%[a]
1968-71	50	50	70	27-39[b]
1972-75	50	50	70	35-46[b]
1976-77	50	50	70	40-49[b]
1978-80	60	40	70	28
1981-86	60	40	50	20
1987-90	0	100	28-33	28-33
1991-	0	100	31	28[a]

Note: Figures refer to individuals' income tax.

[a] Maximum rate on capital gains capped below the nominal rate derived from the rate on ordinary income applied to the taxable portion of the gain.

[b] Application of special alternative taxing schemes for high-income taxpayers caused the maximum rate on capital gains to exceed the nominal rate derived by applying the rate on ordinary income to the taxable portion of the gain.

Source: Congressional Budget Office.

who objected that the IRA proposal would lose vast amounts of revenue in later years and significantly add to the federal budget deficit. Many other Democrats were simply enamored of Jenkins' plan. On the 190-239 vote by which the House refused on Sept. 28 to substitute the IRA proposal, 64 Democrats broke ranks with their leadership.

Senate Finance Committee Action. Attention turned to the Senate, where Finance Committee Chairman Lloyd Bentsen, D-Texas, also proposed an IRA expansion — though substantively different from the House alternative — as a key element of that chamber's deficit-reduction package. Bentsen narrowly fended off efforts led by ranking Republican Bob Packwood of Oregon to replace his IRA plan with a variant of the capital gains reduction. Packwood's capital gains plan eventually was paired with yet another IRA proposal crafted by William V. Roth Jr., R-Del., that would not have permitted tax-free contributions but would have allowed tax-free withdrawals of principal and interest — at a substantial revenue loss in the future.

The Finance Committee held off marking up its revenue package until Oct. 3-4, after the House battle over capital gains was done. Packwood's capital gains substitute failed on a 10-10 tie, with one Democrat, David L. Boren of Oklahoma, voting in favor with the panel's nine GOP members.

Senate Floor Action. Bentsen's success in keeping the capital gains cut out of the reconciliation bill in committee gave Mitchell an opening to block it on the Senate floor. Mitchell quickly made clear that he would force Republicans to muster 60 votes to overcome a budgetary point of order to a capital gains amendment. (Under the so-called Byrd rule, named for Sen. Robert C. Byrd, D-W.Va., a point of order could be lodged against tacking "extraneous matter" onto reconciliation bills.) Republicans said they had 50 votes; they were not confident they could get 60.

In a surprise move on Oct. 5, Mitchell offered a way around the impasse: a stripped-down reconciliation bill that would exclude capital gains as well as hundreds of other extraneous items, including Democratic initiatives such as federal aid for child care, that did not contribute to deficit reduction.

After a week of negotiations and partisan maneuvering, Senate Republicans accepted Mitchell's offer. At first, they stuck with the White House, which continued to demand a vote on capital gains, apparently insisting it come on the reconciliation bill. But because failure to reach agreement on reconciliation by Oct. 16 would lead to across-the-board budget cuts under the Gramm-Rudman law, GOP leaders seemed to lose patience with their position as middlemen. They accepted the Mitchell plan, giving up their insistence on a promise of a simple majority vote on capital gains. On Oct. 13, the stripped-down reconciliation bill passed the Senate by a vote of 87-7. *(Gramm-Rudman cuts, box, p. 56)*

Final Action. The maneuvering continued for another month, with Republicans unwilling to drop the House capital gains provision in conference until they had secured an agreement from Mitchell for a Senate floor vote on capital gains on another bill.

The stalemate held up not only reconciliation, but also a must-pass debt-limit bill, along with popular provisions to repeal the catastrophic health costs law and the tax code's "Section 89" regulations against discriminatory employee benefit plans. An aid bill for Poland and Hungary also was stalled, as Packwood tried to attach the capital gains provision to it. *(Catastrophic care, p. 565; Section 89, p. 708; debt limit, p. 44; Eastern Europe aid, p. 210)*

Finally on Nov. 2, Bush broke the logjam, calling for the capital gains provision to be stripped from the reconciliation bill. Senate Republicans won agreement for two symbolic votes on the issue. For that purpose, the House on Nov. 9 passed the Jenkins plan as a free-standing bill (HR 3628). Then on Nov. 14, after the Senate debated the Packwood plan as a substitute amendment to HR 3628, supporters of the cut fell nine votes shy of the 60 needed to close debate. The cloture motion failed 51-47; an identical vote was taken the next day.

1990 Action

In 1990, again as part of his budget request for the coming fiscal year, Bush called for a cut in the tax on capital gains. The proposal was somewhat more complex than the 1989 plan and contained a smaller rate cut. In part, the changes were an effort to mitigate the potential for steep revenue losses in the years after the cut took effect. Like his 1989 proposal, Bush's 1990 offer was intended to target longer-term investments in businesses, to make it appear less of a giveaway to wealthy people and more of an inducement to economic growth.

Bush proposed that taxpayers who held assets a year or more be allowed a 10 percent exclusion for each year (up to 30 percent). In effect, the cap on the tax rate would have been 25.2 percent after one year, 22.4 percent after two years and 19.6 percent after three. The reduced rate would have applied only to individuals, not corporations, and would not have been available for collectibles, such as artwork.

The administration projected that the rate cut would yield a $4.9 billion revenue increase in the first year. Beyond that, according to the Treasury Department, the tax cut would continue to contribute net revenue, during the five-year period of official estimates and thereafter. The estimate through fiscal year 1995 was $12.5 billion.

In February, the Joint Tax Committee released its own sharply different estimates, showing that Bush's plan would bring in $3.2 billion in the first year but lose $11.4 billion over five years.

Because of Bush's strong backing, a capital gains cut was expected to be an important component of budget negotiations, which got under way in May. Democrats, however, made clear that they would accept a capital gains cut only if it were offset by higher taxes on ordinary income for the wealthy. That led to an impasse with Republicans who were adamantly opposed to an offsetting tax increase.

By the time budget negotiators recessed for the August congressional break, the deadlock seemed so intractable that some predicted capital gains would fade as an issue. But Bush strongly endorsed it again Sept. 11 in a speech before a joint session of Congress, and the political costs of concession by either side soared.

During 10 days of closed-door deliberations at Andrews Air Force Base outside Washington, D.C., following the August recess, budget negotiators for the two sides were unable to make progress. Republicans proposed offsetting the five-year cost of a capital gains cut with limits on deductions for upper-income taxpayers. Democrats countered with a smaller capital gains cut and an income tax surcharge on high-income taxpayers.

Finally, the negotiators gave up, producing a summit package on Sept. 30 that included neither a capital gains cut nor a rate increase on ordinary income. The plan was rejected in the early hours of Oct. 5 (in the session that began Oct. 4) on a **key vote of 179-254 (R 71-105; D 108-149)**, in part because of fierce disputes over other tax provisions. *(1990 key votes, p. 1039)*

Congressional leaders scrambled to produce a new budget resolution (that was vague on what tax changes would be required to achieve a necessary reduction in the deficit) and a deficit-cutting reconciliation bill (HR 5835).

By then, Democrats had turned GOP support for a capital gains cut into the cornerstone of their argument that Republicans were out to help the rich at the expense of the lower- and middle-class taxpayer. And Republicans were deeply divided, with GOP House members pushing for some trade between a capital gains tax cut and a marginal rate increase in the reconciliation bill, Senate Republicans trying to keep the two contentious issues off the negotiating table and the White House waffling in a highly public manner that contributed to a portrait of a presidency in disarray.

With pressure mounting to finish the reconciliation bill, achieving a significant capital gains cut clearly became undoable. Republicans were willing to accede to Democratic demands to push up the top rate on ordinary income — but only to 31 percent — in exchange for a capital gains cut. Democrats wanted to take the top income tax rate up to 33 percent.

In the end, conferees on HR 5835 included a House provision that set the top rate on capital gains at 28 percent — the same top rate that had been in effect for most taxpayers since 1986 — and the top marginal rate for ordinary income at 31 percent.

1991-92

Despite an enormous expenditure of time and energy, Congress produced no significant tax changes of lasting consequence in the final two years of the Bush presidency.

Very little happened in 1991, except for enactment of a brief extension of 12 popular tax breaks. In 1992, however, continuing concern over the nation's stagnant economy combined with election-year politics to give strong impetus to proposals generating tax relief for some classes of taxpayers.

Democrats in Congress forced passage of one bill, aimed chiefly at reducing taxes on the middle class. And Democrats joined with some Republicans (and even the White House for a time) to craft a second bill, which contained tax incentives to stimulate investment generally, and particularly in urban areas.

Neither bill became law, however; both were vetoed by President Bush. The more partisan middle-class tax relief measure died when the House fell far short of overriding the veto. And the urban aid tax bill died because Bush's veto came after Congress had adjourned for the year and no opportunity was available for an override vote.

Middle-Class Tax Cut Veto

A drive for middle-class tax relief provided the focus for the first major tax bill (HR 4210) cleared by Congress in 1992. The bill died when the House sustained President Bush's veto.

Assembled quickly in February and March, the $77.5 billion measure included a two-year middle-class tax credit, a permanent tax credit for families with children and restoration of individual retirement account (IRA) deductions for middle-class taxpayers. It also incorporated six of seven tax relief proposals made by Bush in January, including a capital gains tax cut and restoration of so-called passive-loss deductions for the real estate industry. The capital gains cut was radically changed from what Bush had proposed, and it was targeted to the middle class. The only item on Bush's list dropped from the final bill was a tax credit for first-time homebuyers.

Under new budget rules adopted in 1990, all tax cuts had to be paid for; Democratic leaders tried to turn that to their advantage by offsetting their tax cuts with increased taxes on the rich — including a higher top income tax bracket and a surtax on millionaires. They hoped to force Bush to choose between denying the middle class a tax break or raising taxes on the well-to-do — something he vowed not to repeat after signing a tax increase in 1990. *(New budget rules, box, p. 56)*

But the strategy fizzled. Democratic leaders found themselves pressing the rank and file to vote for a tax bill that everyone agreed was certain to die on Bush's desk. Bush issued his veto statement on the bill before it even reached the White House, and Democratic leaders could not muster the votes to override him. Bush suffered little or no backlash: The final impression was of a president vetoing a political document, not serious legislation.

The stage had been set for a tax bill in late 1991, when Democrats began raising the banner of tax relief for the middle class, presenting it as a question of fairness as well as a tonic to the slowly recovering economy. Increasingly, however, they concentrated on the fairness argument, perhaps in part because most economists were warning that a tax cut would boost the deficit, drive up interest rates and choke off economic recovery.

Bush resisted, stressing instead his proposal for a capital gains tax cut to stimulate economic growth. But by late December 1991, with his poll ratings slipping and widespread public support for a tax cut, he joined the call for middle-class relief.

In his Jan. 28, 1992, State of the Union address, Bush called on Congress to act by March 20 on a set of economic growth measures from his fiscal 1993 budget request. *(Budget request, p. 79; 1992 State of the Union address, p. 1213)*

Bush's tax plan included a core of seven items, plus a host of others, among them an increase in the personal exemption. Ultimately, Republicans rallied around Bush's seven-point plan and backed away from his broader tax proposals, which as a package lost revenue. Democrats derided the Republicans for that move, particularly because the proposed increase in the personal exemption — the main middle-class tax cut proposal in Bush's budget — was abandoned.

Bush's seven key tax proposals were:

- A cut in the tax rate on capital gains income — profits from the sale of stock, real estate and other assets.
- A credit of up to $5,000 for purchasers of houses during 1992 who had not owned a house during the preceding three years.
- Penalty-free withdrawals from IRAs for first-home purchases and certain medical and education expenses.
- The repeal for real estate professionals only of passive-loss rules, enacted as part of the 1986 tax-overhaul bill (HR 3838 — PL 99-514), that restricted deductions of losses from rental activities. *(PL 99-514, Congress and the Nation Vol. VII, p. 79)*
- A one-year extra depreciation deduction for the cost of newly purchased business equipment.
- A simplification and reduction in the alternative minimum tax on corporations, designed to ensure that no corporation completely escaped taxation.
- New rules allowing real estate investments by pension funds.

Bush also announced several steps that did not require congressional approval, including a reduction in the tax withheld from employees' paychecks. The administration said that, as a result, the average married worker would get a $345 cash boost in 1992 and, presumably, more money would be pumped into the economy. The plan, however, also would mean little or no refund for those taxpayers in 1993, and as much as $15 billion would be added to the fiscal 1992 deficit because the government would collect less in withheld taxes.

Democratic leaders embraced Bush's March 20 deadline (and ultimately met it), saying they did so not because Bush had ordered it but because it was the right thing to do. However, they were clearly concerned that missing the date would give Bush an opportunity to accuse them of failing to act on urgent economic problems.

House Action

Ways and Means Committee. House Democrats wanted a chance to put their own tax agenda up against the overall tax package in Bush's budget, so Ways and Means Committee Chairman Dan Rostenkowski, D-Ill., insisted that Bush's proposal be introduced in its entirety.

House Republicans rejected the idea, however, deciding instead to present a slimmed-down GOP tax bill crafted in cooperation with the White House. That set the stage for an unusual sequence of actions by Ways and Means.

In a closed-door committee markup on Feb. 12, the panel's Democrats voted unanimously to send Bush's full tax package to the floor. The bill (HR 4210 — H Rept 102-432) was introduced not by Republicans but by Democratic Majority Leader Richard A. Gephardt, Mo. Furious, committee Republicans voted against the bill, charging that Gephardt had altered some of Bush's provisions and left

out his spending cuts so that the plan lost half a billion dollars over six years.

The committee then defeated the Republican seven-point plan (HR 4200) on a straight 13-22 party-line vote.

Ways and Means Democrats then turned their attention to crafting their own tax proposal (introduced as HR 4287 but considered on the floor as a substitute amendment to HR 4210), based on a draft prepared by Rostenkowski. The Democratic plan featured higher taxes on the well-to-do to pay for a two-year middle-class tax cut that was tied to Social Security tax payments. The plan also incorporated a fresh approach to cutting the capital gains tax.

Even with higher taxes, the Democrats' plan would have added $30.2 billion to the federal deficit over three years. Enough revenue would have been recouped when the tax cuts expired, however, that the bill would have produced a net gain of $13.9 billion by the end of 1997.

The bill adopted some of Bush's ideas, including accelerated depreciation deductions, changes in the corporate alternative minimum tax, repeal of passive-loss rules as they applied to real estate professionals and new penalty-free IRA withdrawals.

It would have permanently extended several popular tax breaks that were scheduled to expire June 30 and were ordinarily extended for about a year at a time. And it would have repealed excise taxes enacted in 1990 on a portion of the cost of luxury yachts, airplanes, jewelry and furs. The tax on expensive cars would have remained. *(Expiring provisions, box, p. 94; luxury tax, p. 92)*

The bill would have set a uniform depreciation period of 14 years for businesses to write off most intangible assets — such as subscription lists, unique recipes and good will (the value to a company of loyal customers, skilled workers or a well-known brand name). Exceptions were made for software, government licenses, movies and other items, which could be written off over a shorter period. And it would have continued two controversial tax increases enacted in 1990. Limits on itemized deductions and personal exemptions that could be claimed by high-income taxpayers were to expire in 1995, but the bill would preserve them for an additional two years through 1997. The provisions would have raised $11.6 billion, money needed to pay for many tax breaks in the bill.

House Floor. The Democratic tax plan, with $93.5 billion in tax relief for some taxpayers (offset by increases on others) narrowly escaped defeat on the House floor Feb. 27. Party members grudgingly complied with a direct plea from their leadership to support the measure even though many of them considered it deeply flawed. The House adopted the Democratic plan as a substitute amendment to HR 4210 by a **key vote of 221-210 (R 1-164; D 219-46; I 1-0).** *(1992 key votes, p. 1083)*

Some Democrats complained that the bill would add to the federal deficit in the short run; others said that it did not contain generous enough incentives for savings and investment. Most worrisome to many was the inclusion of a permanent increase in taxes on the wealthy, with only a temporary tax cut for the middle class.

Finding themselves short of a majority just hours before the scheduled vote, Democratic leaders fell back on a hard-nosed political appeal. They argued that their party had made tax cuts for the middle class its rallying cry for the year and could not turn back. They cautioned that the House would be pilloried if it ignored Bush's call for quick action on a tax bill. And they warned members that their votes would be remembered when it came time to hand out choice committee seats, many of which would come open the following year.

The lobbying worked. But many members voted for the bill hoping that it would be drastically changed or bog down completely in the Senate.

On a nearly party-line vote earlier the same day, the House easily rejected a Republican substitute that embodied the narrow seven-point tax plan endorsed by Bush. It won only 14 Democratic votes and was defeated, 166-264.

In an empty gesture on Feb. 26, the House voted 1-427 against a Gephardt motion to substitute the full list of tax proposals in Bush's budget. By bringing it to a vote, Democrats had hoped to show how little support Bush's full tax plan had on Capitol Hill. But Republicans refused to vote for the package on the grounds that it was a partisan ploy.

Senate Action

Finance Committee. The Senate Finance Committee approved its version of the tax bill by an 11-9 party-line vote on March 3. By then, the bill clearly was going nowhere. But the consensus in both parties was that it would be best to finish the fight off quickly.

Democrats worked out the details of the bill in private before the public markup. It included a $300-a-child tax credit for families making less than $50,000 a year. It would have imposed higher taxes on the wealthy through higher rates and a millionaire surtax.

Like the House measure, the Senate bill would have reduced the capital gains tax — but only for future investments, a feature that the White House said would prevent any immediate economic stimulus. The Senate bill's capital gains proposal contained a complex new progressive rate structure for taxing gains on assets held at least two years. Like the House measure, the Senate bill would have cut the capital gains tax on the sale of stock newly issued by small companies and held at least five years.

The bill included a proposal championed by Finance Chairman Lloyd Bentsen, D-Texas, to restore the deductibility of IRA contributions for all taxpayers. Under the bill, individuals would have had the option of making non-deductible contributions to a new type of IRA and withdrawing the money tax-free after five years.

The Finance bill also partly restored the deductibility of passive real estate losses. And it included the remaining items from Bush's seven-point list, though in some cases they were altered. And the bill incorporated lengthy health and education sections not in the House version.

Bentsen also peppered the bill with provisions for domestic automakers, oil and gas drillers, small businesses, investors with capital gains and others. And he included numerous provisions intended to win votes in committee and on the floor. Among them were an 18-month extension of a handful of expiring tax provisions; a $1 million cap on the deduction a company could take on an executive's pay; repeal of the luxury tax on yachts, private planes, furs and jewelry; and creation of a deduction or credit for student loan interest.

Senate Floor. The Senate passed its $71 billion version of HR 4210 on March 13 by a vote of 50-47, with four Democrats joining all Republicans to vote "nay." The bill included a $28 billion tax cut for the middle class and nearly $20.7 billion in tax breaks for business and investors.

The partisan vote masked deep unease among many Democrats, who did not relish voting for a controversial tax bill that had almost no chance of becoming law. Many senators appeared to agree with Warren B. Rudman, R-N.H., who denounced both the Democrats and the White House for pandering to the electorate by offering tax cuts that would add to the record deficit, while doing virtually nothing to help the economy.

Democrats said that by 1996 the tax cuts in the bill would be fully paid for through higher taxes and thus not add to the deficit. But their estimates showed the bill losing revenue in 1993 and 1994.

After vowing at the start of the four-day Senate debate to oppose all amendments, Finance Chairman Bentsen was unable to stop the onrush of members who knew the bill was doomed but insisted on seeking tax breaks for senior citizens, American Indians, small business owners and many others.

Facing unanimous Republican opposition, Senate Democratic leaders were forced to scale back slightly the number of families eligible for the $300-per-child tax credit. Democrats modified the credit after learning that the Senate parliamentarian did not intend to accept the assertion that the bill complied with budget rules that barred additions to the deficit. Ranking Budget Committee Republican Pete V. Domenici of New Mexico was prepared — before the bill was amended by Bentsen — to object that the bill violated the budget rules. To proceed with a budget waiver, Democrats would have needed a 60-vote majority, which they did not have.

But the most serious threat to the bill came from the Democratic ranks. An amendment by Carl Levin, D-Mich., and Bob Graham, D-Fla., would have eliminated the child care credit and substituted language urging the Senate to apply the $28 billion that the credit would cost to what sponsors said was better long-term medicine for the economy — reducing the deficit and spending more on federal job training and transportation programs.

Republicans, seeing a chance to cut out the core of the bill, joined in opposing a March 12 leadership motion to table (and thus kill) the amendment. When it looked as if the motion would fail, a visibly angry Majority Leader George J. Mitchell, D-Maine, prolonged the 15-minute roll call for nearly an hour while he twisted arms for votes. Finally, three Democrats — Robert C. Byrd, W.Va.; Charles S. Robb, Va.; and Herb Kohl, Wis. — changed their votes, saving the middle-class credit. After the Democratic switches, many Republicans followed suit; the final tally was 57-38.

It was a bitter defeat for Republicans, who were still angry with Mitchell for blocking an up-or-down vote on Bush's seven-point tax plan the day before. The GOP plan was defeated on a procedural motion.

Final Action

Democratic leaders rammed the final version of HR 4210, a $77.5 billion tax bill, through Congress on March 20, the White House deadline. Even before he had received the bill, Bush gave a speech March 20 to announce his veto, saying that Democrats "could not resist their natural impulse to raise taxes." He used the occasion to launch a broad attack against the Democratic-controlled Congress, saying "it is no longer accountable to individual American citizens and voters, and this must change."

After Democratic leaders hammered out the final bill in a late-night negotiating session March 19, the House adopted the conference report (H Rept 102-461) on March 20 by a vote of 211-189 — far short of the two-thirds majority needed to override a veto. One Republican, Olympia J. Snowe of Maine, supported the measure. The vote was even closer in the Senate, which adopted the conference report, thus clearing the bill, 50-44, later in the day over unanimous Republican opposition.

The bill's dim future helped speed along negotiations on the final provisions, which were conducted in a day's worth of closed meetings between Rostenkowski and Bentsen. To include several expensive tax cuts without adding to the deficit, they had to scale back some items and eliminate others, notably the $5,000 credit for first-time home buyers that was in the Senate-passed bill and was proposed by the Bush administration. Also dropped were provisions on health care reforms, direct education loans, tariff treatment of imported light trucks and welfare work requirements that the Senate had included in its bill.

When the House voted on Bush's veto March 25, the bill failed even to draw a majority — much less the two-thirds support needed to override. The vote was 211-215.

The outcome was never in doubt, and Democratic leaders did not bother to lobby party members to support the override. That may have explained some of the defections; 52 Democrats opposed the bill on the override vote. Republicans demanded the roll call to expose how fragile Democratic support was for the controversial measure. Again, Snowe was the only Republican to vote "yea."

Highlights

As approved by conferees, HR 4210:

Middle-Class Tax Cut. Included a $42.4 billion tax cut over five years — more than twice what was in the Senate bill and slightly less than in the House-passed version. As cleared, the bill offered not one but two tax credits aimed at the middle class.

The first was similar to a provision in the House bill. In 1992 and 1993, workers would have qualified for a 20 percent credit, based on their Social Security taxes, worth up to $150 a year for individuals and $300 for married couples. Only taxpayers with adjusted gross incomes of less than $50,000 for couples and $35,000 for individuals qualified for the full credit. Individuals making more than $50,000 and couples making more than $70,000 were eligible for a partial credit. The credit was to be refundable for families with children, meaning that qualifying poor who did not pay taxes would still receive the credit in cash.

In addition, starting in 1994, families with children under age 16 would have been eligible for a permanent $300-per-child tax credit, like that in the Senate bill. The full credit was to be available to families making less than $50,000 a year; those making more than $70,000 would not have gotten the tax break. The child credit was not refundable.

Higher Taxes on Wealthy. Imposed $64 billion in new taxes on the wealthy over five years. The bill would have created a new top income tax bracket of 36 percent, applied to taxable income of $115,000 for individuals and $140,000 for married couples. Wealthy individuals would have had to pay a 10 percent surtax on income above $1 million. High-income taxpayers would have continued to see their deductions limited through 1996; they would have lost the personal exemption permanently.

IRAs. Restored the full deductibility of IRA contributions of up to $2,000 and created the new type of IRA included in the Senate bill, with non-deductible contributions and tax-free withdrawals after five years. Taxpayers who already had IRAs could convert them to the new type of IRA through Jan. 1, 1994.

The bill also included penalty-free IRA withdrawals for first-time home purchases, for medical and education expenses and for those receiving unemployment compensation for longer than 12 weeks.

Capital Gains. Cut the capital gains tax rate by establishing the progressive rate structure from the Senate bill. Those in the 15 percent income tax bracket would have paid no capital gains tax; those in the 28 percent tax bracket would have paid 14 percent; those in the 31 percent bracket, 21 percent; and those in the new 36 percent bracket, 28 percent.

The new rates would have applied to assets held two years, including those possessed before enactment.

The bill also included a 50 percent exclusion for individual and corporate investors with profits on the sale of stock in qualified companies with less than $100 million in gross assets.

Passive Losses. Allowed real estate professionals, including real estate agents, to deduct losses on rental property (so-called passive losses) against income from non-rental real estate investments. The tax break applied only to existing properties.

Extenders. Extended most expiring provisions through June 30, 1993, including a research and development tax credit, tax-free mortgage revenue bonds, exclusions for employer-provided educational assistance and group legal services, tax-free small-issue bonds, an orphan drug tax credit, a business energy tax credit and a targeted jobs tax credit. A low-income housing tax credit would have been made permanent. A 25 percent deduction for health insurance costs for self-employed workers would have been extended for one year. Lawmakers abandoned efforts to expand the deduction to 100 percent and make it permanent.

Intangibles. Allowed taxpayers to write off newly acquired intangible assets over 14 years and to elect a 17-year write-off period for existing intangible assets.

Investment Allowance. Allowed businesses to depreciate an additional 10 percent of investments in property over the following two years. The bill also would have increased the tax write-offs available to small businesses that bought new equipment from $10,000 to $20,000 for the following two years.

Luxury Tax. Repealed the luxury tax for yachts, airplanes, furs and jewelry, and indexed for inflation the $30,000 threshold above which automobiles were subject to the tax.

Alternative Minimum Tax. Simplified and reduced the alternative minimum tax as it applied to corporations.

Earned-Income Tax Credit. Repealed the portion of the earned-income tax credit available for children under age 1, and used the revenue to expand the benefits available to working families with children.

Urban Aid Tax Bill Veto

The second major tax bill of 1992 (HR 11) started as a response to the riots that tore apart sections of Los Angeles in late April and early May in the wake of the verdict in the first Rodney King trial. But what began as a bipartisan effort by the White House and the Democratic-controlled Congress to provide federal tax benefits to help revitalize inner cities ended with a presidential veto of the $27 billion measure. President Bush acted Nov. 4, the day after his reelection defeat.

Sponsors had won broad support for the bill in Congress by including dozens of popular tax breaks unrelated to urban aid — many of which had been in a tax bill (HR 4210) that Bush vetoed earlier in the year. However, they did not foresee how opposed Bush would become in the midst of an increasingly tough presidential campaign to virtually anything resembling a tax increase.

The House passed a $17 billion tax bill in July, which included a version of a White House proposal to create urban enterprise zones eligible for special tax benefits and other federal assistance aimed at spurring investment and employment. Enterprise zones were the centerpiece of the administration's response to the Los Angeles riots.

The bill ballooned to a $37 billion measure in the Senate, where lawmakers attached numerous expensive provisions, including a restored middle-class tax break for contributions to individual retirement accounts (IRAs), that had to be offset with new revenue.

The final bill — the product of negotiations primarily between House Ways and Means Committee Chairman Dan Rostenkowski, D-Ill., and Senate Finance Committee Chairman Lloyd Bentsen, D-Texas — was a $27 billion compromise that would have created 50 enterprise zones at a cost of $2.6 billion over five years, restored and expanded IRA deductions for middle-class taxpayers and extended a handful of expiring tax breaks.

In addition, the bill would have repealed luxury taxes on yachts, furs, jewelry and airplanes; partially restored the passive-loss deduction for rental property; provided for a 14-year write-off period for most intangible assets, including good will; allowed penalty-free IRA withdrawals for certain uses; authorized pension plans to invest in real estate; and provided tax relief for companies that paid the alternative minimum tax.

To offset the lost revenue, as required under new budget rules adopted in 1990, the bill included $27 billion in revenue-raisers. Most had been either proposed or supported by administration officials during the year. Two revenue-raisers that had rankled the White House — making permanent the limit on itemized deductions and the phaseout of the personal exemption for upper-income taxpayers — were removed in conference. *(Budget rules, box, p. 56)*

But the Bush campaign repeatedly attacked the Democratic nominee for president, Gov. Bill Clinton, for signing into law what it said were 128 tax increases in Arkansas, and Bush could not afford to do the equivalent right before the election.

House Action

Ways and Means Committee. The House Ways and Means Committee on June 25 approved a $14 billion tax bill (H Rept 102-631) aimed at aiding blighted urban neighborhoods, but committee Democrats rejected a White House proposal to include a waiver on capital gains taxes for investors who put money into enterprise zones.

The bill, approved by voice vote, provided for the creation of 50 enterprise zones in economically distressed communities. To attract businesses and revitalize the areas, it would provide tax breaks and other federal aid, costing $2.5 billion over five years.

In addition, the committee approved a collection of revenue-losers, including a permanent extension of the low-income housing tax credit and other expiring provisions, partial restoration of a deduction for passive losses on rental properties and repeal of a controversial luxury tax.

Despite agreement on the basic approach, however, the bill reopened a split between Democrats and the White House over cutting the tax rate on capital gains — the profits from the sale of stocks, real estate and other assets. The bill included a limited proposal, which would have allowed investors in an enterprise zone to defer taxes on capital gains only as long as the profits were reinvested in the zone.

The most significant vote during the two days of markup came on a substitute offered by Bill Archer of Texas, the committee's top Republican. His amendment, which was supported by the Bush administration, would have eliminated capital gains taxes for investors who sold businesses or other assets in an enterprise zone — whether or not they were reinvested there. Democrats unanimously rejected Archer's amendment on a 23-13 party-line vote.

Rostenkowski had included enterprise zones in the bill chiefly at the behest of Charles B. Rangel, D-N.Y., a senior member of the committee who represented Harlem. Rostenkowski also wanted to go along with the administration, which had put the zones at the top of its urban agenda. Few other Democrats liked the idea, however, and even among House Republicans, support for enterprise zones was concentrated among a handful of members. To win backing from members from rural districts, Rostenkowski agreed that only half of the 50 enterprise zones would be in cities. That compromise angered urban members, who pointed out that it was the unrest in the cities that provided the impetus for the tax incentives in the first place.

Another controversial component of the bill was a 14-year write-off period during which businesses could deduct the cost of most intangible assets from their taxable income. The Internal Revenue Service (IRS) had challenged many deductions for intangibles, which included such things as state-of-the-art software, special recipes and good will. Rostenkowski's bill was an attempt to settle the controversy by establishing a uniform write-off period and defining what kinds of intangible assets could be written off and for how long.

The committee adopted an amendment by Byron L. Dorgan, D-N.D., eliminating language that would have allowed companies to deduct intangible assets acquired before the bill was enacted. The 22-11 vote for Dorgan's amendment reflected concern by many members about giving a retroactive tax break to companies that acquired valuable intangible assets during the takeover spree in the 1980s.

House Floor. House leaders and the White House wrapped up two months of negotiations on the bill July 2, compromising on a plan to provide a deep capital gains tax cut and other federal aid to businesses that located in inner-city enterprise zones. The House-passed bill contained $17 billion in tax relief for some taxpayers (offset by $17 billion in additional taxes on others). The changes were cut in high-level negotiations intended to hold Republican support.

As a consequence, the bill passed by a vote of 356-55 — a surprisingly comfortable margin for a measure that had seemed in danger of falling apart just the day before. Even though many rank-and-file lawmakers considered the final aid package inadequate, they voted for it in droves after the leadership argued passionately that the bill was the best that could be produced and that the credibility of Congress was riding on its passage.

For the first time since 1990, the White House and Democratic leaders collaborated on getting a tax bill written. Both Bush and House leaders were desperate for a legislative triumph before the July 4th holiday so they could take to the campaign trail with ammunition to rebut criticism that Washington was paralyzed and riven by partisanship.

To prevent changes that might unravel the deal, the House leadership brought the bill to the floor under special procedures that barred amendments and required a two-thirds majority to pass. On the final tally, there were 82 votes to spare. Little floor debate took place on most provisions — debate was limited to an hour — and critics suggested that a minuscule amount of urban aid was being used as a cover to push through a much larger package of tax breaks, mostly benefiting businesses and investors.

Enterprise zones survived because of some late-night deal-cutting by administration officials and Majority Leader Richard A. Gephardt, D-Mo., who forged the capital gains compromise that was the key to attracting Republican votes.

Led by Housing and Urban Development Secretary Jack F. Kemp and House Minority Whip Newt Gingrich, R-Ga., a handful of House Republicans insisted that capital gains taxes be waived when a business or investment in an enterprise zone was sold. They also wanted assets in the area at the time the zone was created to be eligible for the capital gains cut. But Rostenkowski balked, arguing that forgiving capital gains taxes would encourage investors to use the enterprise zone as a tax shelter and then abandon the inner city after making a quick profit.

Late in the evening of July 1, Gephardt worked out a compromise with Gingrich and the administration: Profits made in an enterprise zone would be taxed at a maximum rate of 14 percent (half the existing top rate of 28 percent). To qualify, an investor would have to maintain his investment in the zone for a minimum of five years. In addition, zone investors would be exempt from the alternative minimum tax.

Republicans eventually backed down on their demand that existing assets qualify for the lower rate. And Democrats secured White House approval for $2.5 billion in additional spending through fiscal 1997 to pay for expanded job training, education, health, housing and law enforcement programs.

Bush then put in a pitch for enterprise zones in a Capitol Hill meeting with Republicans. And in a floor speech urging support for the bill, Gingrich praised Gephardt and hailed the inclusion of the capital gains provisions.

Democratic leaders had to deal with a mini-revolt among lawmakers who tried to bring up an unrelated benefits grievance by "notch baby" Social Security recipients, and organized labor groups were upset about a provision permitting non-unionized airlines to offer their pilots more generous benefit packages than were available to other employees. Those critics were stifled, however, by the leadership strategy that blocked amendments on the floor.

Senate Action

Finance Committee. The Senate Finance Committee on July 29 approved a $31 billion tax bill, considerably larger than the House-passed version but still containing just $2.5 billion in aid to rehabilitate inner-city slums. The bill was approved by voice vote.

The measure contained a wealth of tax breaks for investors, middle-class families and businesses, but it did not include the tax break Bush wanted most — a cut in the capital gains tax rate. The White House, faced with a faltering economic recovery and a difficult re-election campaign, had signaled that it would drop its demand for the capital gains cut if congressional Democrats would deliver a bill that provided other generous tax incentives intended to stimulate the economy.

Finance Committee Chairman Bentsen did just that. To gain White House support for the bill, he included variations of the six other tax incentives that Bush had proposed in January to give the economy a quick jolt — among them a $2,500 tax credit for first-time home buyers and generous additional write-offs for businesses that bought equipment in the coming months. *(Bush seven-point tax plan, middle-class tax cut bill, p. 100)*

The Democrats also agreed to drop one of their priorities — a tax cut for the middle class.

One of the most expensive parts of the Finance Committee bill was a provision to restore and expand the tax deduction for IRA contributions. The provision, authored by Bentsen and William V. Roth Jr., R-Del., gave IRA holders the option of either taking a deduction for their IRA contributions or making after-tax contributions to an IRA from which taxpayers could make tax-free withdrawals after five years.

Bentsen's bill provided for 25 enterprise zones — 15 in urban areas, eight in rural areas and two on Indian reservations. Bentsen insisted that the number be kept small, and he balked at waiving capital gains taxes for zone investors. The capital gains issue was all but ignored in the bipartisan rush to get a bill to the Senate floor. Committee Republicans made no effort to include the administration's proposal in the bill, but Minority Leader Bob Dole, R-Kan., characterized the bill's enterprise zone provisions as "very anemic" and promised that Republicans would offer a floor amendment to substitute the administration's proposal.

Bentsen won support for the measure by including numerous tax incentives that committee members had long sought. The bill would have expanded and made permanent an existing tax break for donations of artwork and manuscripts to universities and other charitable organizations to include all gifts of appreciated property, including stocks, bonds and real estate. And it would have extended for 18 months, though 1993, several other popular tax breaks that expired in June. The Finance Committee had approved these provisions on June 16 in a separate bill (HR 3040 — S Rept 102-300).

Like the House bill, Bentsen's measure also would have repealed luxury taxes on personal airplanes, jewelry, furs and yachts.

While administration officials said they were happy with most of the Senate bill, they were opposed to sections aimed at overhauling federal programs to care for abused and neglected children, including foster care and adoption. The key provision aimed at creating an entitlement program — vehemently opposed by the Bush administration — to help states pay for services designed to keep troubled families together. *(Child welfare, p. 621)*

The $31 billion cost of the bill was offset by provisions raising roughly the same amount over five years. The Senate committee bill contained no income tax increases of the sort that had caused Bush to veto the massive tax bill (HR 4210) sent to him earlier in the year. Administration officials said that as long as that remained the case, Bush was likely to accept whatever tax bill he received.

Yet the White House was unhappy with several provisions aimed at raising income taxes for wealthy taxpayers. The bill would have made permanent a limitation on itemized deductions among high-income taxpayers, raising $6.5 billion. It also would have extended a higher rate on estate taxes through 1997 and maintained a limitation on the personal exemption for high-income taxpayers, for a total of $2.6 billion.

Senate Floor. The Senate got to work on the tax bill Aug. 11-12, but the list of potential amendments was too long to allow senators to finish before Congress broke for the Republican National Convention.

Before the recess, Bentsen appeared confident that he had beaten back the chief floor challenges. Shrewd maneuvering by Bentsen and some bipartisan cooperation seemed to clear the way for passage of the bill. Bentsen pre-empted critics of the enterprise zone and IRA provisions by modifying the committee-reported version of the bill to permit 125 zones (Kemp wanted 300) and denying IRAs to upper-income taxpayers. The expansion of the enterprise zone plan seemed to neutralize efforts to add a capital gains tax break for zone investors.

The only item that appeared to be keeping the administration from supporting the bill was the permanent extension of two tax increases on wealthy persons: the phase-out of the personal exemption and the limitation on itemized deductions. But by the time the Senate resumed action on the legislation in late September, the dynamic had changed considerably, with growing signs of opposition from the White House.

Bush had apologized in his acceptance speech before the Republican National Convention for having agreed to raise taxes as part of the 1990 budget deal, and on the campaign trail he promised he would never do it again, "ever." The two highly visible tax increases on the wealthy were plainly in violation of Bush's new anti-tax pledge.

On Sept. 25, the day the Senate resumed work on HR 11, Dole offered an amendment to change that section of the bill. By a **key vote of 34-59 (R 31-8; D 3-51)**, Dole's amendment was rejected. The vote symbolized the difficulty of producing a bill that had sufficient tax incentives for inner cities and other popular constituencies, yet at the same time did not add to the deficit. *(1992 key votes, p. 1083)*

Dole's big problem was finding a way to offset the $7.7 billion that would have been lost in 1996 and 1997 by eliminating the provisions. Dole would have scaled back the assistance for inner cities, removed provisions to restore tax breaks for IRAs and shortened to 12 months the extension given to a dozen expiring tax breaks.

During five days of debate, the Senate adopted a few significant amendments, including some modest health care reforms, but progress was slow, and many lawmakers remained skeptical of the bill's chances.

The Senate finally voted to pass the tax bill Sept. 29 by a vote of 70-29.

Final Action

The House-Senate conference began on Oct. 1 with conciliatory words from Rostenkowski and Bentsen. Both said their goal was to send Bush a bill he would sign.

With the clock ticking toward final adjournment, the two top congressional tax-writers did most of the negotiating on the final bill, finishing their work the evening of Oct. 5. The $27 billion compromise would have created 50 enterprise zones at a cost of $2.6 billion over five years; special tax benefits included a 50 percent capital gains tax cut for investors who put their money into a zone for five years. The bill also included Bentsen's proposal to restore and expand tax breaks for contributions to IRAs, along with an extension of a handful of expiring tax breaks.

In an effort to make the measure acceptable to Bush, Bentsen and Rostenkowski dropped the two revenue provisions for upper-income taxpayers — the limit on itemized deductions and the phase-out of the personal exemption — that were in the Senate-passed bill and that White House officials repeatedly had said would have to be removed for Bush to sign the bill.

The measure contained four of seven proposals for stimulating the economy put forward by Bush: passive-loss deductions for real estate, penalty-free IRA withdrawals for certain uses, authorization for pension plans to invest in real estate and tax relief for companies that paid the alternative minimum tax. Left out were White House proposals for a first-time home-buyer credit, a cut in the capital gains tax rate and an expanded depreciation allowance for businesses.

The House narrowly voted 208-202 to adopt the conference report (H Rept 102-1034) on the bill early in the morning of Oct. 6, in the session that began Oct. 5. Many House lawmakers who had supported the bill when it passed overwhelmingly in July opposed the final version, believing that a veto was certain.

Republicans voted against the measure in overwhelming numbers, but they were joined by 79 Democrats, many of whom feared being on record for a bill that had become identified with tax increases a month before the election and that was unlikely to become law. Budget Committee Chairman Leon E. Panetta, D-Calif., voted against the bill, describing it as a "budget-buster." He said the tax breaks — in particular the IRA provisions — were not fully financed and would add significantly to the deficit in later years.

In its last major act of the year, the Senate voted 67-22 on Oct. 8 to clear the measure and send it to Bush. While senators from both parties challenged Bush's assertion that revenue provisions in the bill qualified as tax increases, the president clearly was unlikely to sign the measure and invite an attack from Clinton for ostensibly breaking his promise not to raise taxes again.

Final consideration in the Senate was delayed by Alfonse M. D'Amato, R-N.Y., who waged an ultimately unsuccessful all-night filibuster beginning Oct. 5. He was objecting to Bentsen and Rostenkowski's decision to drop from the final bill a provision that would have helped Smith-Corona, a British-owned typewriter company based in New York. Smith-Corona had complained that its chief competitor, Brother Industries, a Japanese-owned company, had established a U.S. assembly plant to dodge extra duties imposed on typewriters "dumped" in the United States at prices below cost.

D'Amato, who was up for re-election, held the floor for 15 hours and 15 minutes — the sixth longest one-man filibuster in the history of the Senate. But he abandoned it once the House effectively adjourned for the year on Oct. 6.

Those backing the tax bill still held out hope that Bush could be persuaded that it was politically beneficial to sign the bill. Lawmakers and lobbyists launched a furious, last-minute blitz, arguing that failing to renew a handful of tax breaks included in the bill would amount to a tax increase for some taxpayers.

Democratic leaders delayed sending the final version of the bill to the White House so that Bush could wait until after the election to make his decision.

But Bush vetoed the bill Nov. 4, saying it "includes numerous tax increases" and "giveaways to special interests" and would "destroy jobs and undermine small business." The veto killed the bill; having adjourned, Congress had no opportunity to override.

Highlights

As approved by conferees, HR 11:

Revenue-Losing Provisions

Enterprise Zones. Created 50 enterprise zones, 25 in urban areas and 25 in rural areas, that qualified for special tax incentives and other federal assistance to attract businesses and help revitalize the areas. Following the House language, lawmakers agreed to offer zone businesses a 15 percent credit on the first $20,000 in wages paid to employees, a deduction of up to $25,000 for purchases of stock in zone businesses, more rapid write-offs for property and a 50 percent cut in the capital gains tax on zone investments that had been held for at least five years.

Altogether, the tax benefits provided for enterprise zones would have been worth $2.6 billion over five years. The bill also would have authorized new direct federal spending targeted to the enterprise zones.

Conferees adopted a Senate provision that would have made Indian reservations eligible for an array of special tax breaks to stimulate economic development.

IRAs. Restored to middle-income taxpayers the tax deduction for contributions of up to $2,000 to individual retirement accounts beginning in 1995. Individual taxpayers making up to $75,000 and married taxpayers earning up to $100,000 would have qualified. Beginning in 1994, the bill would have created a new type of IRA; the holder would not have received an upfront deduction but could have made tax-free withdrawals after five years. Taxpayers who already held IRAs could have converted to the new IRA beginning in 1993.

The bill included penalty-free IRA withdrawals for first-time home purchases, education and medical expenses and income for unemployed workers. People whose houses had been destroyed during recent natural disasters, such as Hurricane Andrew, would have qualified for penalty-free IRA withdrawals.

The IRA provisions would have cost $2.6 billion.

Passive Losses. Permitted people in the real estate industry to deduct against ordinary income losses on rental property (the so-called passive-loss deduction). Conferees rejected a narrower Senate provision allowing the deduction to be taken only against income from real estate. The provision was estimated to cost $2.1 billion over five years.

Other Real Estate Benefits. Given passive-loss relief to owners of small timber lots; given tax relief to real estate investors who were deeply in debt; and allowed homeowners who sold their houses at a loss to roll that loss over until they were able to deduct it against ordinary income.

Extenders. Extended permanently several popular tax breaks that expired in June 1992, including a low-income housing tax credit to encourage the building of rental housing for the poor; a targeted jobs tax credit for businesses that hired disadvantaged workers; and a tax exemption for interest on mortgage revenue bonds and mortgage revenue certificates, which financed subsidized mortgages to encourage home ownership. These provisions would have cost $5.4 billion over five years.

Lawmakers agreed to extend for 12 months several other expired tax breaks, including those for employer-provided educational assistance, research and development, and "orphan" drugs (developed to treat rare diseases). Conferees dropped a Senate provision to allow self-employed persons to deduct 100 percent of the cost of health insurance for their employees; instead they retained an existing 25 percent deduction, extending it for 12 months. *(Expiring tax provisions, box, p. 94)*

Appreciated Property. Exempted from calculations for the alternative minimum tax all charitable gifts of appreciated property, including artwork, real estate and corporate stock. The provision expanded a prior exclusion from the alternative minimum tax that applied only to tangible property and would have been permanent. It would have cost $319 million over five years.

Excise Tax Repeal. Repealed luxury taxes enacted in 1990 on yachts, personal airplanes, jewelry and furs. The $30,000 threshold above which the tax applied to automobiles was to be increased based on inflation. These provisions would have cost $5.4 billion over five years. The bill also would have repealed an excise tax of up to $100 on recreational boats, losing $394 million over five years. *(Luxury tax, p. 92)*

Payroll Tax Credit. Given employers a tax credit equal to the amount of payroll tax they paid on employees' tip income, at a cost of $1.3 billion over five years.

Revenue-Raisers

Securities Tax. Taxed securities dealers on the full value of their inventories, raising $3.7 billion. The accounting change was to be phased in over four years.

Real Estate Depreciation. Lengthened the period over which owners could write off the cost of commercial real estate from 31.5 years to 40 years. By decreasing the yearly tax break, the provision would have raised $3 billion over five years.

Moving Expenses. Capped the existing deduction for moving expenses at $10,000, barred writing off closing costs and other moving expenses, and increased to 60 miles the distance someone had to move to qualify for the deduction. That would have raised $3.2 billion.

Estate Tax. Extended through 1997 the 53 percent and 55 percent tax rates on taxable estates of $2.5 million and larger. The tax rates, which were applied at the time the estate owner died, were scheduled to fall after 1993. Extending them would have raised $1.4 billion over five years.

Quarterly Estimated Payments. Raised nearly $10 billion by increasing the amount that individual and corporate taxpayers who made estimated tax payments had to pay to avoid a penalty for underpayment. Individuals would have had two options — pay 90 percent of what they were estimated to owe in the current year or 120 percent of what they owed the previous year. Corporations would have had to pay the same amount they owed the previous year.

Thrift Purchasers. Barred investors who purchased failed thrifts from the government, principally in 1988, from receiving double tax benefits after March 4, 1991. Under the 1988 thrift deals, some investors were promised tax-free payments for overvalued assets owned by the thrift as well as a tax deduction on losses stemming from those assets. In outlawing such double-dipping, the bill would have raised $421 million over five years.

Miscellaneous Revenue-Raisers. Barred companies from claiming a deduction for club dues ($1.4 billion), denied taxpayers interest on refunds as long as the Treasury sent the refund within 45 days ($195 million), barred business travelers from deducting the cost of bringing their spouses ($120 million) and increased the withholding rate on bonuses to 28 percent ($155 million).

Intangibles. Required most intangible assets — such as a company's work force, subscription lists or good will — acquired after enactment to be written off over a 14-year period. That would have shortened the write-off period for some intangibles and lengthened it for others, raising $425 million over five years. The bill would have denied the write-off for costs associated with mergers and acquisitions. It would have allowed shorter write-off periods for software, movie rights and several other types of intangible assets. Conferees dropped a section of the Senate bill allowing companies to claim retroactive write-offs for intangibles they already owned.

Miscellaneous

Pilot Pension Plans. Allowed non-unionized airlines to offer their pilots more generous pension plans than those given to other employees. Under existing federal pension law, only unionized airlines were permitted to discriminate in favor of their pilots. The provision was controversial because it was sought by Federal Express, the Memphis-based courier company, which was trying to fend off attempts to organize its employees.

Footwear Imports. Reimposed duties on imports of footwear made entirely with U.S. materials from countries that were part of the Caribbean Basin Initiative (CBI). But the bill would have granted exceptions for footwear manufacturers who located in Caribbean countries because of the duty-free treatment such footwear had enjoyed under the CBI. Those manufacturers could have continued to export their existing volume of footwear or the output of any factories under construction to the United States duty-free.

Child Welfare. Included major portions of the Family Preservation Act (S 4, HR 3603), which aimed to keep dysfunctional families together, thus lessening the need for expensive foster care. It also would have increased funding for the Job Opportunities and Basic Skills Training Program (or JOBS), the work-training education program created in the 1988 welfare overhaul (PL 100-485), and established demonstrations of a new workfare program. Together, the child welfare provisions would have cost an estimated $2.8 billion over five years. *(JOBS, Congress and the Nation Vol. VII, p. 616; child welfare, p. 621)*

Medicare. Included a series of mostly minor changes to coverage and reimbursement policies for Medicare, the federal health program for the elderly and disabled. Among them were provisions to cut down on fraud and reduce payment for "durable medical equipment," such as wheelchairs, and to restore separate payments for doctors who interpreted electrocardiograms (EKGs). The separate EKG payments were eliminated in 1990.

The provisions would have extended Medicare coverage of drugs to prevent rejection in organ transplant patients. Dropped was a small-group health insurance reform proposal included in the Senate bill, as well as all provisions regarding Medicaid, the joint federal-state health program for the poor. *(Medicare payment rules, p. 575)*

Customs Service. Included the text of HR 5643 (H Rept 102-728, S Rept 102-430), which would have modernized U.S. customs operations and permitted companies to file electronically much of the information necessary to clear goods through ports of entry.

Energy Taxes

As part of a comprehensive energy policy bill (HR 776 — PL 102-486) enacted in late 1992, Congress made some significant changes in tax policy, in particular providing long-sought benefits for mass transit users, alternative-fuel vehicles and small oil and gas drillers.

The bill was two years in the making, and the tax provisions, while considered important, were not the driving force behind the legislation. *(Energy bill, p. 469)*

Legislative Action

House. Tax provisions were first added to HR 776 by the House Ways and Means Committee. The committee largely ignored the pleas of environmentalists and energy companies when it drafted a tax bill (HR 4210) in early 1992 that mostly benefited the middle class. But after the Energy and Commerce Committee completed action on HR 776 in March 1992, Ways and Means took a different view of the issue.

In April, the committee adopted a package of "green" proposals, including a new tax credit to promote renewable energy sources, conservation and alternative fuels. The most controversial item was creation of a new tax credit for use of biomass (crops grown as a fuel source) and wind energy. Pete Stark, D-Calif., tried to limit the new credit to biomass, saying that wind could compete without the government's help. But his amendment failed 9-21.

Independent oil and gas drillers had been lobbying for years for relief from the Alternative Minimum Tax (AMT), a section of tax law designed to ensure that individuals and corporations paid at least some tax. They complained that application of the AMT through the 1986 Tax Reform Act (PL 99-514) had unfairly reduced their ability to deduct some drilling and exploration costs.

Ranking Committee Republican Bill Archer of Texas offered an amendment during committee markup April 29 to exempt a substantial portion of drilling costs from the AMT, but it was defeated 16-20. The following day, Archer offered a revised version that applied the larger deduction only to independent drillers, not big, integrated oil companies. It was approved 19-16.

To pay for the extensive new tax breaks, the committee approved one significant tax increase on certain ozone-depleting chemicals. And it also approved a series of small adjustments to non-energy parts of the tax code, each of which was expected to produce a small amount of new revenue. Ways and Means approved the entire tax section of HR 776 on April 30 and reported the bill (H Rept 102-474, Part VI) on May 5.

The House passed HR 776 by a vote of 381-37 on May 27, without changing its tax section.

Senate. The Senate had passed, 94-4, a version of the energy bill (S 2166) on Feb. 19, but it contained no tax provisions. Following the House action, the Senate Finance Committee met on June 16 and approved a package of tax provisions that paralleled the House bill, with a few mostly minor variations.

The biggest difference was a benefit package for coal miners that was to be financed by a new tax on all coal companies. The controversial provision was the work of John D. Rockefeller IV, D-W.Va., and had been included in HR 4210, which was vetoed earlier in the year. *(Miners' fund, box, p. 717)*

The committee approved the tax section of HR 776 on June 16 by a 10-8 vote, without issuing a written report. The bill headed for the floor, where the previous Senate-passed energy measure — plus the tax language — was to be substituted for the House version.

Rockefeller's coal tax created a storm of opposition, however, that blocked floor consideration for several days. A compromise was finally reached that dropped the tax, and the Senate proceeded to pass the bill on July 30, by a 93-3 vote.

Final. The House-Senate conference committee charged with resolving the differences between the two energy bills had its hands full with energy provisions. Although the tax provisions were largely the same in the two bills, the tax conferees were entangled in action on a broad urban aid tax bill (HR 11), which was eventually vetoed. *(Urban aid tax bill, p. 103)*

Conferees on the tax provisions finally completed their work Oct. 4, finishing the last piece of the bill. The House adopted the conference report (H Rept 102-1018) on Oct. 5 by a vote of 363-60. The Senate adopted the conference report, thus clearing the bill, by voice vote Oct. 8.

Following are the energy tax provisions and the revenue-raising provisions of HR 776, as enacted.

Energy Tax Provisions

Transportation Benefits. Restructured the tax treatment of employer-provided transportation benefits to encourage more mass transit and carpooling.

The bill allowed employers to provide tax-free mass transit and carpooling subsidies of up to $60 a month, up from $21 a month. At the same time, it capped tax-free parking benefits, which were unlimited, at $155 per month. The new rules applied to transit benefits provided as of Jan. 1, 1993.

Conservation Subsidies. Did not tax the rebates utilities provided residential customers for buying or installing conservation measures, beginning in 1993. When utilities provided such conservation rebates to non-residential customers, they would continue to be fully taxed through 1994. In 1995, 40 percent of those rebates would be tax free, rising to 50 percent in 1996 and 65 percent in 1997.

Alternative-Fuel Vehicles. Provided tax deductions for buying (or converting) vehicles that ran on alternative fuels and for related refueling equipment.

The bill allowed a deduction of up to $2,000 for cars that ran on non-gasoline fuels. In the case of cars able to run on alternative and conventional fuels, the deduction only applied to the marginal expense of creating the alternative-fuel capability.

The deductions were to be set at $5,000 for trucks or vans weighing between 10,000 pounds and 26,000 pounds, and $50,000 for heavier trucks and vans or for buses that seat at least 20 adults. These deductions were to be reduced by 25 percent as of 2002, 50 percent in 2003, 75 percent in 2004 and be removed in 2005.

The bill also provided a deduction for the cost of fueling equipment for alternative-fuel vehicles, to be capped at $100,000. Fuels that qualified for these provisions were natural gas, liquefied natural gas, liquefied petroleum gas, hydrogen, electricity or any other fuel that was at least 85 percent methanol, ethanol or another alcohol, or ether. But the deduction would not be applied to electric vehicles that qualified for a new tax credit provided in the bill.

Electric Vehicle Credit. Provided a 10 percent tax credit for the cost of buying an electric vehicle. The credit would be capped at $4,000 per vehicle and be phased out after 2001, ending entirely in 2005.

Renewable Energy. Created a production credit for energy generated by wind or "closed-loop biomass," crops grown exclusively to produce electricity. Producers were to earn a 1.5-cent credit for every kilowatt hour of electricity produced from these sources, but the credit was to be phased out if the price of electricity from these sources rose above a certain threshold. The credit was to be available for 10 years after a renewable energy facility had been put into service.

Business Energy Credits. Made permanent an existing business energy tax credit for investments in solar and geothermal energy. This provision had been periodically renewed for several years. *(Expiring provisions, box, p. 94)*

Oil and Gas Drillers. Provided tax relief for independent oil and gas drillers under the Alternative Minimum Tax, which was intended to ensure that all corporations paid some tax. The changes, which were to be permanent, were estimated to cost about $1 billion over five years.

Nuclear Decommissioning. Sought to encourage nuclear utilities to put more money into decommissioning funds for eventual cleanup. The bill relaxed certain investment restrictions on money placed in a decommissioning fund. It also reduced the tax rate on earnings in a decommissioning fund to 22 percent beginning in 1994 and 20 percent in 1996.

Ethanol Blending. Broadened existing tax breaks for ethanol-blended gasoline.

State Financing. Made building environmental improvements easier at hydroelectric dams by excluding financing for such projects from federal limits on how many tax-exempt bonds each state can issue.

Non-Conventional Fuels. Enabled facilities that produce gas from biomass or synthetic fuels from coal to qualify for an existing tax credit prior to 1996.

Revenue-Raising Provisions

Chemical Tax. Increased the excise tax on certain ozone-depleting chemicals, such as chlorofluorocarbons. The increase was not to affect halons and other ozone-depleters used in foam insulation. The increases were expected to raise about $1 billion over five years.

Seller-Financed Mortgages. Required reporting the tax identification numbers of all parties to a seller-financed mortgage transaction.

Backup Withholding. Increased from 20 percent to 31 percent the amount of tax withheld from certain payments to taxpayers who failed to provide taxpayer identification numbers or supplied obviously incorrect information.

Gambling Winnings. Increased the withholding rate on gambling winnings from 20 percent to 28 percent, as of 1993. However, the law raised the threshold amount for withholding from $1,000 to $5,000.

Travel Expenses. Denied a tax deduction for travel expenses related to out-of-town employment that lasts more than a year, effective as of 1993.

Other Tax Action

Beyond the two, huge tax cut measures (HR 4210, HR 11) that sunk under President Bush's veto, and the energy bill (HR 776 — PL 102-486), the 102nd Congress acted on scores of smaller tax items, only a few of which were enacted.

A dozen popular tax breaks that expired periodically won a six-month reprieve in a bill that cleared on the final day of the first session of the 102nd Congress. Except for one that was wedged into the energy bill, they were not extended again and expired at the end of June 1992. Congress also approved several other targeted tax changes in 1991, mostly to pay for specific programs. No other major tax bill was considered that year, however. An attempt to cut the Social Security payroll tax never got off the ground. *(Social Security, p. 736)*

In 1992, the House passed more than two dozen narrowly drawn tax bills to change miscellaneous small items in the tax code. None of the bills was considered by the Senate, and they died upon adjournment.

Extending Expiring Provisions

With adjournment approaching in 1991, key lawmakers in the House and Senate pledged not to attach any amendments to a bill that was intended only to keep in the law a dozen popular tax breaks that had been preserved for years on temporary renewals.

That agreement paved the way for quick action on the bill (HR 3909 — PL 102-227) and prevented it from becoming bogged down with other controversial tax proposals, such as a Republican plan for reducing the tax rate on capital gains. *(Expiring tax provisions, box, p. 94)*

On Nov. 25, two days before the end of the session, House Ways and Means Committee Chairman Dan Rostenkowski, D-Ill., held a quickly scheduled markup during which the bill (H Rept 102-377) was approved by voice vote. "Welcome to the season of giving," he told lobbyists, who had been working furiously to get the legislation passed. Rostenkowski held off until Sen. John C. Danforth, R-Mo., sponsor of a companion measure in the Senate, had commitments from 98 senators to keep the bill clean. The Senate Finance Committee approved the companion bill (S 2042), also on Nov. 25.

The House, under suspension of the rules, passed HR 3909 in the early hours of Nov. 27 by a vote of 420-0. Rostenkowski, who wanted to take the extenders off their one-year leash, promised that each of the tax breaks would be brought to a vote in 1992 and either made permanent or eliminated.

The Senate gave its assent a few hours later by voice vote, sending the bill to Bush, who signed it on Dec. 11.

Bob Kasten, R-Wis., delayed action in the Senate in hope of offering an amendment to repeal a 10 percent luxury tax on expensive boats that had been adopted the year before as part of the White House-congressional budget-reconciliation bill (HR 5835 — PL 101-508). But he withdrew the proposal after Majority Leader George J. Mitchell, D-Maine, insisted that any amendments would kill the bill. *(1990 budget deal, p. 55)*

The decision to renew the tax breaks for six months was a compromise, dictated in part by the difficulty in finding the money to pay for a full-year extension. Under the 1990 budget deal, tax changes that lost money had to be paid for by offsetting revenue increases or entitlement cuts.

Renewing the 12 provisions for six months was expected to cost $3.2 billion over five years. The extension was paid for by requiring corporations with taxable income exceeding $1 million to prepay more of their taxes. Instead of paying 90 percent of their estimated tax liability on their quarterly returns, the bill required them to pay 93 percent in 1992. The amount was to rise to 95 percent by 1995 and fall back to 90 percent in 1997.

Paying for Spending Programs

Congress in 1991 took other tax action aimed at raising revenue.

In August, House members balked at a proposal to increase the gasoline tax by a nickel a gallon as a way to finance new spending on highways and mass transit. But Congress later agreed to pay for a major highway bill (HR 2950 — PL 102-240) by continuing, for four years, 2.5 cents of a 5-cent gasoline tax that had been imposed in 1990 and was due to expire Sept. 30, 1995. As a result, the tax, which totaled 14 cents a gallon in 1991, was scheduled to fall to 11.5 cents from 1996 through 1999 — instead of dropping to 9 cents as originally slated. *(Highway bill, p. 437)*

Congress agreed to pay for a bill extending unemployment benefits (HR 3575 — PL 102-164) in part by requiring people who paid quarterly estimated taxes to base their payments on what they owed in the current year, not on what they paid the year before. The change applied to taxpayers whose taxable income jumped by $35,000 in one year. Congress also kept the federal unemployment tax at 0.08 percent in 1996, instead of letting it drop to 0.06 percent. *(Unemployment benefits, p. 721)*

And, after months of battling over a move to repeal the recreational boat tax, Congress cleared a Coast Guard reauthorization bill (HR 1776 — PL 102-241) that included non-binding language calling for such a repeal, but only after a way to offset the cost was found. *(Coast Guard reauthorization, p. 448)*

Miscellaneous Tax Bills

The House in 1992 considered a series of small, mostly non-controversial tax measures aimed at correcting perceived inequities or glitches in the tax code, often to the benefit of some small universe of taxpayers and occasionally to the detriment of others. Although 27 of the measures won House passage, they never came up for a vote in the Senate and died at the end of the 102nd Congress.

The special interest tax bills represented a bipartisan effort initiated by the members of the Ways and Means Committee with the acquiescence — if not full support — of Rostenkowski. In several respects, the process was a throwback to the old days of tax law debates in the House. Before 1980, the Ways and Means Committee commonly sent individual tax changes to the floor under suspension of the rules, a special procedure that prohibited amendments, limited debate and required a supermajority for passage. The measures had to rise or fall on their own merit — a two-thirds majority was seen as a fair barometer of whether some proposal was acceptable enough to warrant passage.

That was also a time when the budget effect of tax changes was less critical. With the advent of budget reconciliation in 1980 — when deficit reduction first became an important consideration — tax bills became omnibus measures, limiting opportunities for individual initiatives. And by 1985, the general rule was that tax bills not intended to reduce the deficit could not add to it either. That broad philosophy was formalized with the 1990 budget agreement, and with accompanying changes in congressional budget rules. As a result, most of the 1992 special interest tax bills included some mechanism to cover the revenue loss. (For some, revenue loss would not be incurred or it was so small as not to be measurable.) *(1990 budget rules changes, box, p. 56)*

Bills Passed. The Ways and Means Committee got the ball rolling July 8-9, approving more than two dozen of the little tax bills. The House then passed almost all of the measures over a three-week period under suspension of the rules.

A number of the proposals were combined into a single bill (HR 2735 — H Rept 102-668), which the House passed by voice vote July 21. Rostenkowski had assembled the bill as a favor to committee members, many of whom were retiring and had been pushing the provisions for years. Sponsors said the measure contained less than $100 million in tax benefits, which were to be paid for by several revenue-raising provisions. The Bush administration, however, said the bill would have lost $26 million in 1993, drawing a veto threat.

As passed by the House, HR 2735 would have:

- Barred employees or shareholders from benefiting — through excessive salaries, for example — from earnings made by a tax-exempt social welfare organization.
- Made several changes to rules governing small business corporations, increasing the maximum number of shareholders from 35 to 50, for example, and treating these corporations as partnerships for the purposes of taxing gains on subdivided property.
- Shortened the period over which the cost of purchasing tuxedos for rental could be written off from nine years to two.
- Expanded the tax deferral available to livestock producers who were forced to sell cattle because of drought or "other weather-related conditions."
- Exempted certain small fishing operations from having to pay Social Security and unemployment taxes for their workers.
- Permitted private foundations to form common investment funds for charitable purposes.
- Exempted commercially reloaded ammunition from excise taxes in cases when the purchaser supplied empty shells of a similar type.
- Made qualifying for an exemption from income tax easier for rural cooperatives if at least 85 percent of their income was derived from members.
- Required taxpayers who rented their homes for even a brief time to pay tax on the rental income.

On July 27, the House passed several more of the mini-bills by voice vote, including measures that would have:

● Allowed a homeowner who sold a principal residence at a profit to subtract losses on sales of previous homes before calculating the capital gain for tax purposes (HR 5638 — H Rept 102-696).

● Allowed old buildings that were moved and then renovated to qualify for the rehabilitation tax credit, overturning a Treasury Department regulation denying the credit to moved buildings (HR 5637 — H Rept 102-695).

● Extended from two to four years the period during which individuals could reinvest insurance proceeds before using the money to rebuild a home damaged in a federally declared disaster. If a home were not replaced in time, capital gains taxes would be owed on any accumulated increase in value in the property (HR 5640 — H Rept 102-698).

● Permitted tax-exempt bonds to be issued to finance new office buildings for the United Nations in New York City. The German government had offered free office space in Bonn to several U.N. agencies; New York was trying to keep the agencies by building new offices. Under existing law, tax-exempt bonds could not be used to finance U.N. buildings (HR 5639 — H Rept 102-697).

On July 28, the House took a roll-call vote on a bill to allow organizers of college football bowl games and other sporting events to continue to qualify for a tax exemption on contributions from corporate sponsors. The bill (HR 5645 — H Rept 102-700) passed 296-123.

The Internal Revenue Service (IRS) had proposed new rules requiring colleges and other charitable organizations to pay taxes on the corporate contributions they received for such events as the Mobil Cotton Bowl and the 1996 Olympic Games in Atlanta. The IRS ruled that the contributions amounted to purchased advertising and should be taxed as unrelated business income. The bill's sponsor disagreed, arguing that taxing the income from corporate sponsorships could mean the end of some of the smaller bowl games and could jeopardize the revenue that the games brought to participating universities.

Finally, the House passed 16 additional bills by voice vote on Aug. 3-4. As passed, the bills:

● Exempted charitable organizations, such as volunteer fire departments, from the unrelated business income tax on proceeds from casino-night fund-raisers and other games of chance. The bill (HR 5660 — H Rept 102-703) raised the lost revenue by increasing the withholding tax on gambling winnings.

● Revised the income reporting standards for very small, rural property and casualty insurance companies that applied under the alternative minimum tax system (HR 5642 — H Rept 102-699).

● Granted special tax deductions to owners of certain freight shipping containers, and provided benefits to certain small property and casualty insurers (HR 5674 — H Rept 102-735).

● Revised the tax consequences of renegotiating corporate debts to prevent forced bankruptcies (HR 5655 — H Rept 102-744).

● Exempted students who worked as summer camp counselors from Social Security taxes and clarified that Indian tribes could establish tax-deferred savings plans that were otherwise available to charitable organizations (HR 5656 — H Rept 102-733).

● Adjusted the tax treatment of certain income by tax-exempt farmer cooperatives and of interest on reserves held by housing cooperatives (HR 5650 — H Rept 102-719).

● Granted Group Health of New York Inc., a non-profit health insurer, the same tax treatment reserved for Blue Cross/Blue Shield insurance providers; corrected a problem that caught some employee stock ownership pension plans in the middle of transactions at the time of a 1989 tax law (HR 3299 — PL 101-239) change; and closed the so-called debt-equity whipsaw that gave tax benefits to both sides in certain securities transactions. The last provision, which was expected to raise $69 million, helped pay for several other tax bills that had revenue losses (HR 5641 — H Rept 102-716).

● Permitted the St. Paul, Minn., Port Authority to restructure several hundred bond issues that were in default while retaining their tax-exempt status (HR 5659 — H Rept 102-734).

● Permitted charitable organizations, in particular the Brown Foundation of Kentucky, to cover obligations under the "superfund" hazardous waste cleanup law without jeopardizing their tax-exempt status (HR 5644 — H Rept 102-717).

● Exempted international ferry service from a per-passenger tax established to control gambling on international passenger ships (HR 5661 — H Rept 102-720).

● Exempted charitable organizations from certain excise taxes on gambling activities (HR 5648 — H Rept 102-718).

● Revised accounting rules as they applied to certain cotton warehouses so that income tax assessments were deferred until the income was actually collected (HR 5643 — H Rept 102-728).

● Clarified that payments to individuals under the Alaska Native Claims Settlement Act were not taxable (HR 5658 — H Rept 102-750).

● Extended the time limit for rolling over gains on the sale of a principal residence in cases where taxpayers' money was frozen in accounts at a failed financial institution (HR 5652 — H Rept 102-731).

● Converted existing agreements made before 1982 by estates that limited their tax liability by choosing to value land at its use (for example, agricultural) value, instead of its development value. Prior to 1982, estates had to agree not to change the use or sell the property for 15 years; after 1982, a 10-year usage agreement was required. The bill cut the 15-year standard to 10 in prior agreements (HR 5647 — H Rept 102-730).

● Clarified that deposits (essentially premiums) paid to certain perpetual property insurance companies were not below-market loans to the companies that constituted taxable income (HR 5657 — H Rept 102-745).

Bills Rejected. During the three weeks of action, the House rejected only two of the small tax measures that had been approved by Ways and Means. Both were defeated because of the provisions used to offset the revenue they would have lost.

The first measure (HR 5653 — H Rept 102-702) would have fully exempted bonds issued to finance high-speed intercity rail systems from state caps on tax-exempt bonds. Under existing law, 75 percent of the bonds' value was not counted against the cap. The bill was defeated 48-369 under suspension of the rules on July 28.

Many lawmakers opposed a provision that would have required state and local governments to tell taxpayers what portion of their property tax payments was deductible on their federal tax returns and what portion consisted of non-deductible user fees. The provision was expected to raise revenue by preventing taxpayers from erroneously deducting user fees. Some Texas lawmakers also opposed the bill because of controversy surrounding a proposal to put a high-speed rail system in their state.

Rostenkowski later criticized his committee for having reported the bill by unanimous consent when a majority of committee members voted against it on the floor.

The other bill that failed (HR 5649 — H Rept 102-743) would have repealed a century-old "occupational" tax on producers and retailers of alcoholic beverages. It was defeated 200-207 under suspension of the rules on Aug. 4, gaining not even a simple majority, much less the two-thirds majority that was needed to pass.

To offset the cost, the bill would have changed the collection point for diesel fuel excise taxes, thereby promising to reduce tax evasion and increase revenues. Refiners, who would have had to pay the tax (and pass it along to wholesalers and retailers), objected strenuously.

Financial Regulation

At the end of the 1980s — a time that came to be identified with high-flying financiers and the consequences of greed — Congress was faced with multiple opportunities to correct excesses and prevent future abuses in the nation's banking and securities markets.

It was a challenge that members mostly accepted — if on occasion grudgingly. And, if Congress did not adopt every change proposed by its various committees or by the administration, it was because of the understandable reluctance of members who had been burned more than once for having made wrong choices in this arena.

Virtually every financial entity subject to federal oversight came in for closer scrutiny during the 101st and 102nd Congresses — banks, savings and loans, securities dealers and futures traders, and even some special purpose financial institutions created by the federal government.

Some problems were holdovers from the final years of the Reagan administration; for example, the long-building crisis in the savings and loan industry finally caught up with Congress and the newly elected Bush administration in early 1989. Other problems were of more recent vintage. The threat that several government-sponsored enterprises might pose a huge liability on the federal government, were they to fail, became a concern only in light of the thrift bailout.

And scandals drove much of the debate.

Charles H. Keating Jr. and the five senators who came to his defense when federal savings and loan regulators tried in 1987 to clamp down on Keating's Lincoln Savings and Loan Association became symbols of the fraud that was an endemic part of the thrift debacle.

Lincoln was ultimately seized by regulators in 1989, and the Keating Five senators were subjected to a public trial of sorts by the Senate Ethics Committee in late 1990 and early 1991. One, Alan Cranston, D-Calif., was reprimanded by the committee. The committee ruled that the other four — Dennis DeConcini, D-Ariz., John Glenn, D-Ohio, John McCain, R-Ariz., and Donald W. Riegle Jr., D-Mich. — did not deserve punishment. But they were all mildly rebuked for their poor judgment — and in DeConcini and Riegle's cases of having engaged in conduct that had the appearance of being improper.

On a smaller scale, a bid-rigging scandal shook the market in federal government bonds in 1991 and brought down the top managers of the Wall Street investment house of Salomon Brothers Inc. The 102nd Congress, typically, only began to think about what would be the most appropriate reaction to Salomon's actions (although the administration moved to prevent a repeat). It was left to the 103rd Congress to devise statutory changes in the $2.6 trillion market in federal government securities.

Another scandal of sorts was the stock market crash of Oct. 19, 1987. Among the most dramatic economic events of the 1980s, the Dow Jones Industrial Average plunged a historic 508 points — representing a paper loss in the stock market of perhaps $500 billion in one day.

The scandal was not that investors could lose so much money. The concern instead was that such an event could happen — that market forces could propel financial trading into a free-fall, devastating the computers and other systems designed to keep track of transactions and ensure that the market remained liquid and functioning.

The October 1987 crash was thoroughly analyzed in the months — and years — afterward. It took nearly three years — and a second mini-crash in October 1989 — for Congress to devise a series of regulatory steps finally enacted in 1990.

Deposit Insurance Dominates

Throughout most of the 1980s, politicians and regulators had insisted — hoped really — that the hemorrhaging from a growing list of failed thrift institutions could be contained. The General Accounting Office had determined that the Federal Savings and Loan Insurance Corporation (FSLIC), which protected thrift depositors, was technically insolvent at the end of December 1986. But in response, Congress passed only a limited measure to recapitalize the fund, which proved to be completely inadequate.

By the time George Bush was sworn in as president, the inevitable taxpayer-financed bailout had to be put on the table.

Then, not two years after the thrift bailout, a similar

References

Discussion of financial regulation legislation for the years 1945-64 may be found in *Congress and the Nation Vol. I*, pp. 337-386; for the years 1965-68, *Congress and the Nation Vol. II*, pp. 253-279; for the years 1969-72, *Congress and the Nation Vol. III*, pp. 135-145; for the years 1973-76, *Congress and the Nation Vol. IV*, pp. 107-117; for the years 1977-80, *Congress and the Nation Vol. V*, pp. 253-265; for the years 1981-84, *Congress and the Nation Vol. VI*, pp. 83-93; for the years 1985-88, *Congress and the Nation Vol. VII*, pp. 109-136.

Musical Chairs for Regulators

The savings and loan and banking crises of the late 1980s not only resulted in wholesale changes in the regulatory environment, they also led to multiple shakeups among top regulators.

Two Reagan administration holdovers — M. Danny Wall, the top thrift regulator, and Robert L. Clarke, the top regulator for federally chartered banks — lost their jobs in somewhat different circumstances. Wall's replacement, T. Timothy Ryan Jr., endured a rigorous confirmation fight, and Clarke was not replaced during George Bush's presidency.

L. William Seidman, the man who led the Federal Deposit Insurance Corporation through much of the turmoil and acquired an outsized reputation in the process, left at the end of his term — not entirely voluntarily. His replacement, William Taylor, died suddenly before serving a year.

Of all the key financial regulators in the Bush administration, only Richard C. Breeden, who headed the Securities and Exchange Commission, was confirmed without difficulty and served throughout the balance of the Bush administration, drawing relatively little controversy to himself. *(Details, box, p. 419)*

Wall Resigns

Perhaps the most visible lightning rod for congressional anger about the nation's financial woes was Wall, who had headed the Federal Home Loan Bank Board in the latter years of the Reagan administration and presided over the collapse of the Federal Savings and Loan Insurance Corporation (FSLIC) and the thrift bailout.

One provision of the 1989 thrift bailout bill set Wall up as director of the Office of Thrift Supervision (OTS), created to replace the bank board as the federal government's thrift regulatory agency.

Wall's credibility was badly marred by his repeated assertions that a taxpayer bailout of FSLIC would not be necessary.

He also was inextricably tied to the scandal involving Charles H. Keating Jr. and his failed Lincoln Savings and Loan Association in Irvine, Calif. The collapse of Lincoln was expected to cost $2 billion, and Wall was blamed for moving too slowly to close the thrift — a charge that was heard repeatedly in hearings on Lincoln conducted during the fall of 1989 by the House Banking Committee.

Critics pressed to have the bailout bill require a hearing for Wall's continuance in office, but Senate conferees refused. Wall had worked for 12 years for Jake Garn of Utah, ranking Republican and former chairman of the Senate Banking Committee. However, the six weeks of hearings into Lincoln's failure conducted by the House committee amounted to confirmation hearings; Wall announced his resignation Dec. 4, 1989.

Ryan Confirmed

Wall's replacement, Timothy Ryan, won Senate confirmation April 4, 1990, despite questions about his experience and background. The Senate's 62-37 vote to confirm Ryan as OTS director came despite objections from Democrats that he was ill-suited for the job, as well as reservations from many Republicans that someone with experience in financial regulation might have been preferable.

Ryan, a Washington labor and pension lawyer, had been solicitor of the Labor Department in 1981-83. The Banking Committee had approved his nomination on an 11-10 vote on March 30.

Seidman Leaves, Replaced by Taylor

In the midst of the 1991 banking overhaul debate, Seidman, a leading proponent of change and the most respected banking regulator in Washington left his job. Seidman had headed the FDIC since 1985, and by virtue of that job, also ran the Resolution Trust Corporation, the agency created to salvage failed thrifts.

He stepped down Oct. 16, 1991, at the end of his term, to a chorus of praise from all but officials of the Bush administration, with whom he had repeatedly and publicly clashed over the cost of the thrift bailout. White House Chief of Staff John H. Sununu tried to get Seidman to step down early, but Seidman refused.

Seidman was replaced by William Taylor, top banking regulator with the Federal Reserve System, where he had spent most of his professional career. The Banking Committee recommended Taylor's confirmation by a 21-0 vote on Oct. 18, 1991; he was confirmed by the Senate by voice vote on Oct. 22. His term was to expire Feb. 28, 1993, but he died unexpectedly in August 1992. No replacement was named immediately.

Clarke Rejected

Clarke, who had run the Office of the Comptroller of the Currency — the agency that charters national banks — through the latter 1980s, was nominated for a second five-year term in December 1990, but Senate Democrats held up action.

Many blamed Clarke for having fostered a lax regulatory climate that allowed more than 1,000 banks to fail. On Nov. 6, 1991, the Banking Committee rejected a motion to confirm Clarke for a second term on a 9-12 vote. He remained in office until February 1992; no replacement was named.

calamity threatened the fund that insured bank depositors. That forced Congress back to the drawing boards to reconfigure the entire deposit insurance system.

Deposit insurance was the lubricant that had made the U.S. banking system work for more than 50 years and had brought it back from the Depression-era disaster.

In 1933, the nation's banking system had collapsed, bankrupted by devastating "runs" that sucked out what little cash was held in vaults, forcing President Franklin D. Roosevelt to order all banks closed on March 6, two days after he was sworn into office. During this "bank holiday," cash and gold withdrawals were prohibited for days, and in some cases weeks or months, as the banking industry struggled. Before the year was over, 4,004 banks had closed, costing depositors $540 million.

Three months after Roosevelt's action, Congress passed a sweeping reform of banking laws that included creation of a system of federal deposit insurance that took effect Jan. 1, 1934. The Federal Deposit Insurance Corporation (FDIC) was created to insure bank accounts up to $2,500, raised within months to $5,000 — a sizable sum in the midst of the Depression. Banks paid premiums to finance the fund.

Roosevelt signed the deposit insurance bill into law reluctantly. He and the American Bankers Association strongly opposed insurance. Roosevelt was concerned that the government would be on the hook for losses, despite assertions that the insurance program would be privately financed. The banks were upset for the opposite reason. They would have to pay for insurance, and they had no promise of government aid.

The Federal Savings and Loan Insurance Corporation was created in 1934 with a $5,000 insurance limit for thrifts, the same as that for banks, and a similar but somewhat more costly premium system. Banks had moved quickly into the insurance system; thrifts did not. The number of insured thrifts did not surpass that of uninsured savings institutions until 1951.

Over the years, Congress made few changes in the growing system of deposit insurance other than to increase the insurance limits periodically. In 1950, the limit was raised to $10,000; in 1966, to $15,000; in 1969, to $20,000; and in 1974, to $40,000.

Then in 1980, with little debate, Congress approved a provision to more than double the limit to $100,000 as part of a broad bank and thrift deregulation law. At the end of the decade, many observers said the change contributed to the thrift-industry collapse in the late 1980s, luring billions of dollars into depositories where it was stolen or squandered, leaving taxpayers responsible for bailing out the insurance fund or risking a 1930s style collapse of the banking system.

The high-flying 1980s wrecked havoc on banks and thrifts alike. Both suffered unprecedented numbers of failures as the 1980s wound to a close; for both, 1988 was a record bad year. *(Deposit insurance calamities, box, p. 116)*

That year, the FDIC closed 200 banks and gave financial assistance to 21 more failing banks to keep them open. It was a post-Depression record that declined only slightly to 206 failed and assisted banks in 1989. As a consequence, FDIC reserves fell by $4 billion over the two years and the bank insurance fund recorded its first losses.

For thrifts, the situation was more devastating — 205 thrifts failed in 1988 and hundreds more of insolvent or potentially insolvent institutions were likely to be shut down over the next several years. But the FSLIC was already insolvent itself and incapable of responding to the crisis.

Giving Banks a Break

The result of this string of failures was enactment of a pair of historic measures, the 1989 thrift bailout bill and the 1991 deposit insurance bill. The 1989 bailout abolished the bankrupt FSLIC and created two new insurance funds — one for banks and one for thrifts — both managed by the FDIC.

For the first time, Congress appropriated taxpayer money for deposit insurance, a decision that was projected to cost taxpayers as much as $500 billion over the next 40 years, when interest on borrowing for the bailout was counted. At the same time, insurance premiums for banks and thrifts were increased in an effort to stem losses in the bank fund and partially defray the thrift bailout cost.

What did not happen in 1991 was a wholesale change in the regulation of banks that many said was needed to ensure the long-term health of the industry.

The Bush administration, on Feb. 5, 1991, unveiled its long-awaited plan to overhaul the nation's financial system by providing new business opportunities for banks that would — the administration hoped — also put much less pressure on the deposit insurance system.

Treasury Secretary Nicholas F. Brady had told Congress the previous summer that the nation's banking laws desperately needed an overhaul. "The result is overcapacity and layers of regulation, concentration in the riskier parts of commercial lending, uneven product diversification with rules and exceptions that sometimes make little sense, and inefficient limitations on geographical distribution," he told the Senate Banking Committee on July 25, 1990.

It had become an article of faith that banking regulation was a patchwork that no longer followed a logical pattern. The 1933 law that created the deposit insurance system also barred banks — not totally, it has turned out — from engaging in the securities business. Other laws imposed restrictions on the ownership of banks and the ability of banks to sell insurance.

At the same time, few restraints were placed on securities or insurance companies from horning in on the traditional bank business of making loans. And mutual funds were becoming indistinguishable in the marketplace from checking accounts as a place for depositors to put cash (except that mutual funds did not have deposit insurance).

Banks were prohibited from opening branch offices across state lines, although banking companies could establish separately regulated, separately capitalized banks in multiple states. There were, however, no such geographic limits on securities or insurance companies.

Creative bankers had persuaded regulators and the courts to blow holes in some of these statutory barriers, but the Bush administration sought a radical rewrite of banking law to put virtually all financial institutions on a fairly level playing field. It was not the first such attempt to rationalize financial regulation. A less-far-reaching, congressionally led effort in 1988 fell flat. So, too, did the Bush plan in 1991, perhaps because it was too far-reaching and perhaps because it was tied too closely to the needed overhaul of the deposit insurance system.

Eventually, every major change proposed in 1991 to put limitations on the way that banks do business was jettisoned. That left regulators and the courts in a position to continue to reinterpret generations-old laws as they saw fit.

Deposit Insurance Calamities

Failures of banks and savings and loan associations skyrocketed in the late 1980s.

The calamity first bankrupted the deposit insurance fund that protected thrift depositors — the Federal Savings and Loan Insurance Corporation (FSLIC) — requiring a massive taxpayer bailout. It then threatened to bankrupt the banking system's deposit insurance fund.

Savings and Loan Bailout

From the bailout's inception through 1992, Congress approved the following money for the Resolution Trust Corporation (RTC), the agency created to salvage failed thrifts. The total was $86.7 billion ($105 billion minus $18.3 billion), not counting interest on the $30 billion borrowed in 1989-90.

$50 Billion: Approved Aug. 9, 1989, as part of the original bailout bill (HR 1278 — PL 101-73).

- $18.8 billion appropriated immediately from the Treasury.
- $1.2 billion required to be contributed immediately by the Federal Home Loan Bank System from retained earnings owned by the thrift industry.
- $30 billion borrowed in 1989-90 by a special federal entity created for that purpose, which issued 30- and 40-year bonds. The principal amount of the bonds was to be repaid by the thrift industry; interest was to be paid partly by the Treasury and partly through annual $300 million assessments on the Federal Home Loan Bank System.

$30 Billion: Approved March 23, 1991 (PL 102-18). The entire amount was appropriated from the Treasury.

$25 Billion: Approved Dec. 12, 1991 (PL 102-233). The amount was appropriated from the Treasury, but the RTC was permitted to draw only such sums as could be spent by April 1, 1992. The RTC used only $6.7 billion, and the balance reverted to the Treasury.

RTC Activities

From Aug. 9, 1989, through the end of 1992, the RTC took control of 727 failed or failing savings and loans. Of those, 653 were liquidated or their deposits and branches were sold to healthy banks and thrifts; another 74 remained under RTC conservatorship. During that process, the RTC managed to dispose of assets worth an amount in excess of $300 billion, but another $100 billion in hard-to-sell assets remained in the RTC's portfolio.

Prior to creation of the RTC, a total of 526 thrifts failed from 1980 to 1988, requiring financial assistance from FSLIC to protect depositors — 205 of them in 1988 alone. The sum of those failures plus the RTC's cleanup activities meant that the thrift industry had contracted by about a third and that little more than 2,000 fairly healthy institutions survived the 1980s.

Bank Failures

A rash of bank failures not unlike the one that wrecked the thrift industry prompted Congress in 1991 (S 543 — PL 102-242) to overhaul the deposit insurance system to reduce risks to the insurance fund. In the same bill, Congress gave the Federal Deposit Insurance Corporation a large line of credit with the federal Treasury to help cover depositor losses in the short-term.

Continued failures had depleted the assets of the insurance fund by 1991, which in theory was to be worth at least 1.25 percent of the total amount of insured deposits — a benchmark that reflected historical averages. The fund had not held reserves of that size since the early 1980s, however. Unlike the thrift bailout, the actions taken in behalf of the Bank Insurance Fund were not expected to cost taxpayers. (Though taxpayer money would be loaned to the FDIC at market rates, the banking industry was expected to repay the loans over time from its insurance premiums.)

Improvements to the nation's economy following the 1990-91 recession — in particular dramatically lower interest rates — prompted a revival in the banking sector and expectations that the insurance fund would rebound in the mid-1990s and reach its minimum reserve level by the latter part of the decade.

Year	Total Bank Failures	Fund as Percentage of Deposits
1980	10	1.18%
1981	10	1.25
1982	42	1.20
1983	48	1.23
1984	79	1.20
1985	120	1.19
1986	145	1.13
1987	203	1.10
1988	221	0.79
1989	207	0.70
1990	203	0.46
1991	186	0.00
1992	122	—

Sources: General Accounting Office; Federal Deposit Insurance Corporation.

Chronology Of Action On Financial Regulation

1989-90

The 101st Congress was responsible for two major financial regulatory achievements.

Led by President Bush, Congress in 1989 swiftly enacted a bill to salvage the savings and loan industry, which had been ravaged by a bad economy, lax regulation and supervision, and fraud. Following years in which the Reagan administration insisted that the savings and loan problem would work itself out without taxpayer assistance, the Bush administration reversed course and within weeks of taking office had proposed an extensive taxpayer bailout of the federal insurance fund that protected thrift depositors. In 1990, when increasing the taxpayer contribution to the bailout appeared necessary, Congress balked, however.

In another example of a new administration accepting regulatory intervention where it had previously been rejected, Congress cleared and Bush signed a series of bills tightening up on the securities markets in the wake of a serious market crash in 1987 and a sizable disruption in trading in 1989.

Savings and Loan Bailout

Acting on a proposal presented by President Bush two-and-a-half weeks after his inauguration, Congress took just six months in 1989 to enact the most sweeping overhaul of laws governing savings and loan institutions in 55 years.

The Financial Institutions Reform, Recovery and Enforcement Act (HR 1278 — PL 101-73) was intended to clean up a $100 billion-plus mess in the thrift industry. The bill cleared in the early hours of Aug. 5, and Bush signed it Aug. 9, promising an end to the thrift crisis and renewed stability for the nation's financial system. Within hours, the stroke of his pen had set in motion machinery designed to put an end to losses at insolvent thrifts amounting to as much as $20 million daily.

The measure dramatically restructured federal regulation of thrifts and provided $50 billion over three years to close down or sell off hundreds of insolvent savings institutions.

It abolished the independent Federal Home Loan Bank Board that had supervised the crisis-ridden thrift industry and dismantled the bankrupt Federal Savings and Loan Insurance Corporation (FSLIC) that had insured thrift deposits. A temporary agency — the Resolution Trust Corporation (RTC) — was created to take over failed thrifts and dispose of their assets. A permanent agency — the Office of Thrift Supervision — was created in the Treasury Department to charter and supervise thrifts, and the task of insuring thrift deposits was given to a new insurance fund established under the Federal Deposit Insurance Corporation (FDIC), the agency that insured bank deposits.

The new law also increased the amount of capital, or net worth, that thrifts were required to maintain. Lawmakers hoped that if investors were forced to put more of their own money at risk, they would be reluctant to make the kind of ill-advised investments that had driven many thrifts into bankruptcy.

Background

The drive to salvage the failing thrift industry began Feb. 6, when Bush unveiled the broad outlines of a plan to borrow $50 billion to close down or sell 350-plus sick savings and loans. Bush coupled the financing scheme with an overhaul of the regulatory system to ensure that "the situation is not repeated again."

The crisis in the industry had become clear by late 1988, but neither President Ronald Reagan nor the 100th Congress had attempted to solve it. M. Danny Wall, chairman of the Federal Home Loan Bank Board, said repeatedly in 1988 that a taxpayer bailout would not be needed and that a $10.8 billion infusion of cash into the FSLIC cleared by Congress in August 1987 (PL 100-86) might be sufficient to solve the problem. *(Congress and the Nation Vol. VII, p. 120)*

But Wall's optimism was not widely shared. A General Accounting Office (GAO) report released in May 1988 said that 505 of the nation's 3,147 thrifts were insolvent at the end of 1987. Of those, 181 were in the Southwest, where the depressed Oil Patch and farm economy had hit the industry hardest. The report said another 435 thrifts were barely solvent in 1987 and risked going into bankruptcy in 1988. Other analysts offered assessments that were even grimmer.

With the money that was available, the bank board tried to keep the problem from spinning out of control in 1988, primarily by selling sick thrifts — an approach the bank board said was cheaper than closing them down and paying off depositors. To entice investors, the bank board provided tens of billions of dollars in promissory notes and tax breaks to purchasers of the failed institutions. Many of the benefits were given out in a flurry of deals signed in December 1988, just before a change in the law limiting some of the special tax breaks was to take effect.

In testimony before the House Budget Committee in January 1989, Wall said the FSLIC had closed 205 thrifts in 1988, 75 of them in December, at a cost estimated to exceed $32 billion in obligations to the FSLIC. In addition, Wall calculated that tax breaks given to thrift purchasers as part of the deals could result in a revenue loss of $5.3 billion.

Virtually all of the $32 billion was in the form of 10-year notes and long-term guarantees of the book value or anticipated yields of questionable loans included in the deals. To cover those notes and guarantees, Wall said the FSLIC had committed nearly all of its anticipated revenue from deposit insurance premiums and asset sales. Without a new infusion of money, the FSLIC would no longer be able to sell off bankrupt thrifts to stanch the growing losses. At least 350 insolvent savings and loans were still operating and waiting to be closed.

While they remained in operation, sick institutions continued taking new FSLIC-insured deposits, increasing the ultimate cost of a government bailout. To attract those deposits, they offered inflated interest rates, forcing healthier thrifts to boost their own rates to compete for depositors.

When Bush unveiled his plan, many speculated that it would be gutted by the thrift industry, which had a history of powerful and successful congressional lobbying. Early complaints from industry trade groups receded, however, as publicity grew about the savings and loan mess and about the fraud and incompetence that had exacerbated it. When the final votes came in August, the industry was virtually invisible on Capitol Hill.

As the thrift bill moved through the legislative process, it grew increasingly tougher on the industry. The two issues that received the most attention were capital standards and financing.

Capital Standards. Under Bush's original proposal, thrifts would have been required to maintain capital standards at least as stringent as those for banks. The Bush proposal set no specific capital requirements, however. Instead, the bill merely tied the thrift standard in a broad way to that for banks. Under rules set to go into effect in 1991, national banks were to be required to have a minimum 6 percent ratio of capital to assets, based on generally accepted accounting standards. By 1993, banks were to have 8 percent capital based on the relative riskiness of their loans and other assets.

The final bill adopted those standards but added that, within 120 days of enactment, thrifts would have to maintain 3 percent "core" capital. Half of that had to be "tangible" capital — cash and assets that could easily be converted to cash.

Thrifts carrying supervisory "good will" on their books as an asset were required to write it off as a component of core capital over five years. Good will could not be counted at all as tangible capital. Several hundred healthy thrifts had been given supervisory good will by federal regulators in the mid-1980s in return for their buying failing thrifts with no financial assistance from the government.

In ordinary accounting terms, good will is the difference between the purchase price of a business and its worth as a going concern — thus a measure of real, if intangible, value. Supervisory good will was essentially the opposite, corresponding to the difference between the book price of a failing thrift's bad assets (worthless loans, for example) and the lower market value of those assets — thus a measure of lost value.

Financing. Bush originally proposed that the $50 billion needed over the subsequent three years to close down insolvent thrifts be borrowed by a new off-budget agency, the Resolution Funding Corporation (RefCorp), and not counted as part of the deficit.

The administration argued that an on-budget financing plan would increase the federal deficit and require a waiver of the Gramm-Rudman anti-deficit law, setting an untenable precedent for future big-ticket spending proposals. It also warned that financial markets would react negatively to an effort to avoid Gramm-Rudman.

Those who favored an on-budget approach rejected both notions, arguing that the administration's plan to keep the financing off the books was simply a less honest Gramm-Rudman dodge and that neither plan was likely to upset the financial markets.

The chief argument in favor of an on-budget plan was that to have the Treasury Department (instead of a new, off-budget agency) sell the necessary bonds would save taxpayers an estimated $150 million a year in interest costs, or $4.5 billion over the 30-year life of the financing plan.

The Senate backed the Bush plan, but the House strongly disagreed. In its version of the bill, the $50 billion would have been borrowed from the Treasury and put on budget; it would not have been counted under Gramm-Rudman. Conferees charged with reconciling the House and Senate versions decided to go with the House approach.

Bush then sent a message to Congress warning that he would veto the on-budget approach. Conferees reconvened and struck a compromise: $20 billion was put on the budget in fiscal 1989 (Gramm-Rudman calculations had already been made for fiscal 1989, so it did not count under the anti-deficit law for that year); $30 billion was to be borrowed off budget in fiscal 1990 and 1991.

Legislative History

The thrift bill began moving through both the Senate (in committee) and House (in subcommittee) in early April.

Senate Committee Action. The Senate Banking Committee, having reached general agreement in a series of closed-door meetings, handed Bush a big victory April 12 when it approved a 550-page thrift bailout bill (S 774) that closely tracked his proposal.

The committee approved the measure by a 21-0 vote and formally reported it the next day (S Rept 101-19).

The committee worked from a draft — a revision of Bush's original plan — that was prepared by Chairman Donald W. Riegle Jr., D-Mich., and the committee staff after three days of intense, private discussions. Those talks, which involved all 21 senators on the panel, succeeded in reconciling most controversies and producing a bill that all members of the panel could support.

Throughout 11 hours of public committee debate, it was clear that the only really important vote would come last, on the question of how to raise the $50 billion needed to close down and sell off insolvent thrifts.

Riegle strongly opposed the administration's on-budget financing plan and proposed an equally complex scheme that would have kept most of the Bush plan's structure intact but had Treasury sell the bonds and funnel the money to RefCorp. To avoid triggering automatic Gramm-Rudman budget cuts in fiscal 1990 and 1991, when most of the bonds would be sold, Riegle's plan incorporated a paper transaction between Treasury and RefCorp to put the entire cost of the borrowing on budget in fiscal 1989, when it would have no effect for Gramm-Rudman purposes. The administration argued fiercely that Riegle's approach would set an unacceptable precedent for avoiding Gramm-Rudman strictures. The committee knocked the Riegle plan out of the bill on an 11-10 vote.

Riegle's revised bill departed from the Bush plan in several other respects. It sought much tighter controls on the activities of state-chartered thrifts. The decision by some states to allow thrifts to invest heavily in direct real estate developments, commercial loans, "junk bonds" and other risky ventures had been blamed by some critics of the industry for the existing financial crisis. It also altered the Bush plan's capital requirements for thrifts, making them somewhat more stringent. And it made a significant structural change in federal regulation of thrifts, separating the chartering functions of the Federal Home Loan Bank Board from the board's oversight of the lending activities of the 12 regional Federal Home Loan Banks. None of those provisions was undone during the markup.

Senate Floor Action. Floor consideration also was swift, with dozens of amendments rolled together at the end and adopted by voice vote. The Senate gave overwhelming approval to S 774 on April 19, passing it by a vote of 91-8.

During three days of debate, the Senate made few changes in the measure. Bush and advocates of tighter controls on thrifts won virtually every major fight. Most of the significant changes — including a decision to increase the amount of capital that thrifts would be required to keep on their books — largely strengthened the bill.

Riegle failed on the floor, as he had in committee, to put the financing on budget. The Senate April 18 voted 48-50 not to grant a waiver of budget rules to permit a vote on his financing amendment; 60 votes were required for the waiver, which was needed because the amendment would have increased the deficit by $50 billion in fiscal 1989, breaching budget targets.

The most significant floor amendments that were agreed to were forced by Howard M. Metzenbaum, D-Ohio, who seemingly stood alone against fierce pressure to conclude work on the bill in time for the Senate to begin an 11-day recess at 4 p.m. April 19.

Metzenbaum wanted more than a half-dozen changes, mostly involving capital requirements and consumer protections. He threatened to keep the Senate in session through April 21 if necessary to debate the amendments. Riegle eventually incorporated two of Metzenbaum's ideas in a 76-page "managers' amendment" offered at the close of debate April 19. With almost no discussion about what it contained, the Senate adopted the amendment by voice vote.

One of the Metzenbaum additions required the RTC to review contracts signed by the FSLIC in 1988 for the sale of more than 200 failed thrifts, in an effort to find ways to make the terms more favorable to the government.

The second change, on capital requirements, was heralded by consumer groups, Treasury lobbyists and others as a major improvement to the bill. It required that all thrifts maintain no less than a 3 percent ratio of capital assets by 1991; at least 1.5 percent would have to be tangible capital — cash, securities or other liquid assets. Thrifts carrying good will, "intangible" capital generally not available to banks, would have to write it off within 25 years.

The bill, as it had come to the floor, would not have established a minimum tangible or core capital requirement. Instead, it followed the administration language tying thrift standards to those for banks and allowing good will to count toward all capital requirements.

House Banking Committee Action. The House Banking Subcommittee on Financial Institutions Supervision, Regulation and Insurance and the full Banking Committee spent four days each on HR 1278, their version of the bill, and considered a long list of amendments. Several other House committees then weighed in before the measure went to the floor.

The Banking subcommittee, the first to take a pen to the bill in public, completed its work April 13 after spending more than 32 hours over four days and disposing of about 200 amendments. By voice vote, the subcommittee approved HR 1278, which tracked the administration's proposal somewhat less closely than did S 774.

By far the most important battle in the subcommittee was over capital standards. Although the issue was complicated, changes approved by the subcommittee, largely at the urging of Chairman Frank Annunzio, D-Ill., were widely seen as weakening Bush's proposal. In some respects, however, the changes went beyond the president's proposal, at least in the level of detail. Annunzio's amendment incorporated requests from as many as 30 members of the panel for changes in the capital requirement, reflecting the degree of lobbying on this issue. It was adopted on a vote of 24-23.

The subcommittee approved, 26-18, another Annunzio amendment to revise the "qualified thrift lender" (QTL) test, which was used to qualify thrifts for special tax treatment and the right to borrow at low rates from the Federal Home Loan Bank system. Existing law required thrifts to have 60 percent of their assets in residential loans and some non-residential assets, such as real estate and other property used by thrifts in the course of their business. Company jets qualified, for instance. The amendment increased the test to 80 percent but broadened the types of loans that would qualify — including, for example, consumer loans and credit card balances.

And the subcommittee approved on a 34-12 vote an amendment by Banking Committee Chairman Henry B. Gonzalez, D-Texas, to give state and local public housing agencies a 90-day right of first refusal to buy residential property seized by the RTC from failed thrifts.

The full Banking Committee voted overwhelmingly May 2 to approve HR 1278, after making a number of significant changes that supporters and opponents alike said resulted in a tougher bill.

The House committee approved the bill by a 49-2 vote minutes before midnight. The committee formally reported the measure (H Rept 101-54, Part I) on May 16. (The committee filed a supplementary report (H Rept 101-54, Part III) on June 1.) Only Jim Leach, R-Iowa, and Joseph P. Kennedy II, D-Mass., voted against it. Leach, one of those pushing the panel to stiffen investment and capital rules for thrifts, was an exception to the consensus that the bill accomplished its aims. He complained that it was "not tough enough." Kennedy said he voted "no" because he had lost on two issues — a short-term, tax-supported financing scheme and new, stiffer anti-discrimination provisions for mortgage lenders.

In one of the most significant changes from the subcommittee version, the full committee stiffened the minimum capital standards the bill would require of thrifts, doubling the requirement for tangible capital.

But capital requirements were not the only place where the bill grew tougher. It also put new limits on the kinds of activities in which state-chartered thrifts could invest. State powers to buy and hold real estate, stocks and other risky investments had been identified as a principal cause of the thrift crisis.

In addition, in light of the thrift industry's historic purpose to finance housing, the committee voted to earmark both money and surplus property to boost the available supply of low- and moderate-income dwellings. Fights over the housing provisions precipitated the only partisan splits on the bill.

The administration viewed the committee measure largely as a victory, although it strongly opposed the housing provisions and was unhappy with some of the structural changes made in Bush's plan.

Other House Committee Action. After House Banking acted, four other committees were granted jurisdiction over parts of the bill.

The Ways and Means Committee met before the legislation had been formally reported, holding a "conceptual"

Congress Refuses to Replenish ...

A year of partisan debate, financial uncertainty and political maneuvering over the spiraling cost of salvaging failed savings and loan institutions ended in the 101st Congress' final hours when a single lawmaker blocked a last-gasp effort to add needed money to the bailout operation.

By early 1990, not long after the thrift bailout law (HR 1278 — PL 101-73) was enacted in August 1989, it became apparent that far more money would be needed than the $50 billion provided by that bill.

Congress began talking about the problem in January, but the scent of scandal and the political costs of asking taxpayers to shoulder a higher burden created an atmosphere in which no one — in Congress or in the Bush administration — wanted to take responsibility for seeking more money.

The bickering turned into public squabbling over the summer and reached a high point in October. The House and Senate Banking committees approved bills (HR 5891, S 3222) that would have provided a new infusion of cash, but the legislation died in the House.

Many members blamed Treasury Secretary Nicholas F. Brady, saying he lacked the political courage to make a forthright request for more money. Democrats in Congress refused to act without an administration request as a cover.

As Congress was nearing adjournment, the House leadership finally agreed to let HR 5891 come to the floor. But the effort was thwarted by Frank Annunzio, D-Ill. The senior Banking Committee member objected to a unanimous consent request that the House act on the measure in the early hours of Oct. 28. Several other lawmakers, however, also were said to have been ready to make the parliamentary objection if Annunzio had not.

After Congress quit for the year, leaving the bailout coffers nearly empty, the administration decided Nov. 1 to exploit a loophole in the 1989 thrift salvage law that raised the limit on temporary borrowing for the bailout by $18.8 billion — enough, it was estimated, to keep the salvage operation in business until March 1991.

Background

The cost of the bailout turned out to be far higher than the administration's 1989 estimate for a number of reasons. Failed thrifts numbered more than 500; interest rates paid on borrowed money were higher than forecast; and the economy was headed into a recession, pushing down the value of assets owned by failed thrifts and making their disposal far more difficult and costly than had been anticipated. The Resolution Trust Corporation (RTC), the salvage agency created by the 1989 law, also suffered management problems.

While it was clear from the start of 1990 that more money was needed, the Bush administration did not try to deal with the issue in its fiscal 1991 budget proposal, waiting instead until the summer to make a specific request.

Congress, which had thought the issue was resolved in the 1989 bailout bill, was angry and embarrassed to be dealing with it again in 1990. Both political parties had trouble finding a solution to the problem because both were afraid of being blamed for it.

Warnings about a shortage of funds came early in 1990 and persisted throughout the year.

On Jan. 24, L. William Seidman, chairman of both the RTC and the Federal Deposit Insurance Corporation (FDIC), which insured deposits in banks and thrifts, told the House Banking Committee that the $50 billion approved in August 1989 to cover thrift losses almost certainly would not be enough. But Seidman declined to put a dollar amount on the shortfall. At the same time, Seidman warned that another $40 billion to $100 billion would have to be borrowed during 1991 by the RTC for short-term working capital (money that would be repaid from the sale of assets seized from failed thrifts).

By May, the news had grown much worse. Brady told the Senate Banking Committee on May 23 that between 722 and 1,037 thrifts were facing closure, with expected losses to the government of $89 billion to $132 billion.

Brady's testimony seemed to strike a raw nerve with the public, which had been reading months of press coverage of fraud and abuse in the thrift industry and the government's failure to stop it. Within weeks, partisan knives had been drawn, and members of Congress and the administration were at each other's throats.

Hearings in the House Banking Committee, followed by federal court actions, generated high-intensity publicity about the costly failure of Lincoln Savings and Loan Association in Irvine, Calif., and the roles played by its owner, Charles H. Keating Jr., and five senators to get federal regulators to leave the thrift alone. *(Keating scandal, p. 979)*

The Banking Committee also had turned its attention to Neil Bush, President Bush's son, who had been an outside director of the Silverado Banking, Savings and Loan Association in Denver, Colo., before it collapsed in 1988 at high cost to taxpayers.

Sensing public outrage, congressional Democrats stepped up their rhetoric in early June, charging President Bush with failing to take charge of what

... Thrift Bailout Agency Coffers

Rep. Charles E. Schumer, D-N.Y., dubbed "the second S&L crisis." The House Democratic Caucus meanwhile encouraged its membership to attack the president in a nine-page list of "talking points" about his administration's "mishandling" of the salvage operation.

The White House responded with a long assault on the Democrats, saying they had been in the pockets of the thrift industry and should not be pointing fingers. White House spokesman Marlin Fitzwater June 19 read off the names of a half-dozen Democrats embroiled in the thrift crisis, among them former House Speaker Jim Wright of Texas and former House majority whip Tony Coelho of California. Both men had close ties to the thrift industry and resigned from Congress in 1989 under ethics questions. *(Wright, Coelho resignations, pp. 917, 918)*

The most visible sign of member concern about voters' reaction to the thrift scandal was the rush to pass new penalties for bank fraud and provide the Justice Department with more resources to investigate thrift crimes. *(Bank fraud penalties, p. 133)*

On July 30, the administration came back to Congress to clarify its need for more money, stressing that if Congress failed to act promptly, the thrift bailout would run out of cash and have to shut down before the end of 1990.

Treasury officials suggested several alternatives, including an appropriation of $5 billion to get the RTC through January 1991 or $10 billion to get the agency through February. That would have allowed Congress and the administration to get past the elections and then decide later how to finance the rest of the bailout.

Legislative History

By the fall, the political tensions between Congress and the administration had turned into a public deadlock.

Although the administration had conceded the need for more bailout money — and had sent Seidman and other mid-level officials to ask for it — members wanted Brady to appear personally and answer questions. In September and October, Brady declined repeated requests to appear, while his aides sought to portray congressional pique as petty.

Late Oct. 10, Brady wrote the committees that Treasury would prefer to have Congress give unlimited spending authority to the RTC, but if Congress wanted to make a finite appropriation, $57 billion would be fine for fiscal 1991.

Senate Committee Action. The Senate Banking Committee acted Oct. 12 in direct response to Brady's letter and essentially in line with its recommendations. The committee went even further on one point, giving the RTC an unlimited appropriation to cover costs of renegotiating the controversial December 1988 thrift deals.

By voice vote, the committee approved a bill (S 3222) providing a $57 billion cash infusion that would have given the RTC $40 billion more to cover losses and effectively provided a $17 billion increase in an existing law cap on borrowing for working capital. The bill was formally reported Oct. 19 (S Rept 101-549).

House Committee Action. The House Banking Committee by voice vote on Oct. 23 approved a bill (HR 5891) that would have provided an additional $10 billion for thrift losses. It also would have clarified the bailout law loophole and allowed the borrowing cap to rise by $18.8 billion.

That action would have freed $7 billion to $10 billion of the original $50 billion, which the RTC was holding in reserve to meet the convoluted terms of the lower borrowing cap. And it would have given the administration the go-ahead to take the action it did Nov. 1. The bill was formally reported Oct. 27 (H Rept 101-974).

Final Action. Opposition to both measures was sufficient, as the session ground to a close, to make House and Senate leaders wary of bringing up the bills.

Congressional aides said the administration was silent in the final days of the session. Other than last-minute letters from Seidman and the Congressional Budget Office, pointing out that a delay in approving additional money for losses would add to the overall cost as sick thrifts continued to operate, no external pressure was exerted on Congress to act.

Moreover, White House and congressional negotiators had already decided not to include the money in must-pass bills, such as the deficit-reducing, budget-reconciliation measure (HR 5835), fearing political opposition to such a maneuver. *(Budget reconciliation, p. 55)*

So, after the Oct. 27 session went past midnight and Congress was less than two hours from adjournment, House Banking Chairman Henry B. Gonzalez, D-Texas, asked for unanimous consent for the House to take up HR 5891.

But with the two words "I object," Annunzio prevented the House from considering the bill, and there it died.

Moments after Annunzio's action on the House floor, the Senate, knowing the House had spiked the bill, took up S 3222, amended it to incorporate the House bill language and passed it by voice vote. That bill never came to a floor vote in the House.

markup May 10, which was ratified May 18 on a 26-10 vote. The committee formally reported the bill May 22 (H Rept 101-54, Part II).

Ways and Means handed Bush his first real defeat on the bill, voting 25-11 in favor of an amendment to count the $50 billion to be borrowed over the following three years as part of the federal budget. To avoid triggering automatic spending cuts, it explicitly exempted the $50 billion from Gramm-Rudman calculations. Only two Republicans — Bill Gradison of Ohio and Raymond J. McGrath of New York — voted for the on-budget amendment.

Immediately after the committee vote, Treasury Secretary Nicholas F. Brady renewed a threat to recommend a veto if the final bill contained an on-budget financing plan. The resulting delay in enactment would cost more in added losses at failing thrifts than the on-budget plan would save in interest expenses, Brady said.

The committee also agreed by voice vote to repeal, effective May 10, three special tax rules enacted in 1981 to entice potential purchasers for failing thrifts.

On May 18, when the committee met to ratify its earlier decision, Sam M. Gibbons, D-Fla., tried several tacks to avoid borrowing the $50 billion by temporarily raising taxes instead. His efforts were soundly rejected by a strong bipartisan majority on the committee, led by Chairman Dan Rostenkowski, D-Ill.

On May 24, the Judiciary Committee met to consider the bill and came within one vote of blowing a wide hole in the capital standards crafted by Banking. Henry J. Hyde, R-Ill., led an effort to weaken the capital standards by giving a break to thrifts that had no tangible capital but did have government-granted supervisory good will. Hyde's amendment would have given these thrifts the opportunity to claim injury caused by the required loss of this good-will capital and would have provided a lengthy appeals process through the FDIC. His amendment was defeated on a 17-17 tie vote. Despite Bush administration opposition to the amendment, Hyde was supported by an overwhelming majority of the panel's Republicans.

The committee then approved the bill on a voice vote and formally reported it (H Rept 101-54, Part V) on June 1.

The Government Operations Committee met June 1 and became yet another battleground for the clash over financing the bailout. Members voted 13-22, almost exactly along party lines, not to strike out the Ways and Means recommendation to put the financing on budget and exempt the financing from Gramm-Rudman. The committee then approved the bill on a voice vote and formally reported it the next day (H Rept 101-54, Part VI).

The Rules Committee also had legislative jurisdiction over the Gramm-Rudman exemption for the financing plan; the committee filed a report June 1 (H Rept 101-54, Part IV) without making any recommendations.

House Floor Action. By overwhelming margins, the House June 15 passed HR 1278 on a 320-97 vote after a long day of balloting on 11 amendments. One key amendment by Hyde, which would have relaxed the bill's new capital requirements for certain thrifts, was defeated on a **key vote of 94-326 (R 56-114; D 38-212)**. Both roll calls were expected to be much closer. *(1989 key votes, p. 1021)*

The House action was a victory for Bush and for those in Congress who had championed tougher capital standards for thrifts. It was a big defeat for elements of the thrift industry and their allies who had fought to preserve the ability to count good will as capital.

The House also voted to put financing of the salvage operation on the federal budget, to ban junk bond investments by thrifts, to impose new anti-discrimination disclosure requirements on mortgage lenders, to retain a new low-income housing program and to strike special interest provisions from the bill.

In every instance, the outcome, or at least the margin of victory, was a surprise. That led many members to comment that the symbolic value of their votes to crack down on high-flying thrift operators was more important in the end than the substance of the issues on which they were voting.

Many members credited media attention on the bill, and Bush's summoning of congressional leaders to the White House, the afternoon before the Hyde vote, and threatening a veto if the capital standards were weakened.

Conference Action. Resolution of differences between the House and Senate bills was expedited when the Senate passed HR 1278 by voice vote on June 21, after amending it to the substitute text of S 774, as previously passed.

A 102-member conference committee — 94 from the House and only eight from the Senate — was hastily convened June 22, but work did not get under way until lawmakers had returned from their July 4th recess.

In an unexpected move, Senate conferees July 13 proposed a comprehensive amendment to resolve more than a dozen key differences between the bills. House Banking Chairman Gonzalez, who had proposed an issue-by-issue approach, was upset by the tradeoffs implicit in the Senate offer. But after reviewing it and talking with Riegle, Gonzalez agreed to proceed.

The Senate proposal offered the House victories on stiffer capital rules and on housing components of the bill and provided the Senate and administration with a win by keeping the $50 billion in borrowing off the federal books. The proposal also followed the Senate bill in guaranteeing that top thrift regulator Wall could retain his position under a newly created regulatory scheme.

Work slipped behind closed doors the week of July 17, after the House had presented a counteroffer. Finally, after two daylong negotiating sessions July 26 and 27, conferees reached agreement on all the outstanding issues. The conference report (H Rept 101-209) was filed Aug. 1.

Getting a deal on financing was by far the most difficult and contentious issue. It also was the only issue on which the five Senate Banking Committee conferees (who made up the entire Senate contingent on 99 percent of the bill) presented other than a united front. Alan Cranston, D-Calif., had joined with the two Republicans, Jake Garn of Utah and John Heinz of Pennsylvania, to oppose the on-budget plan. He persisted in his opposition throughout six hours of conference debate on the issue July 27, until the end when he changed his vote. Throughout that period, Cranston tried to find a compromise plan that would put half the cost on the budget and half off. Although he finally crafted such a hybrid that could win the two Republicans on his side of the table, House members loudly rejected it in a voice vote. Finally Cranston gave in, breaking the impasse.

Two concessions by House conferees the day before seemed to help bring Cranston around. On one, the House agreed to allow Wall to become director of the new Office of Thrift Supervision without being subjected to Senate confirmation. The second House capitulation allowed the new agency to supervise state-chartered thrifts.

Wall, a longtime friend and associate of Garn, was staff director of the Senate Banking Committee during the six years Garn was chairman, 1981-86.

Cranston was reported to have interceded with Wall on behalf of Lincoln Savings and Loan Association, a then-insolvent California thrift. Lincoln's chairman, Charles H. Keating Jr., had close ties to Cranston and at Cranston's request helped secure large political contributions. Cranston's ties to Keating would almost certainly have been an issue in a confirmation battle over Wall. *(Lincoln Savings scandal, p. 975)*

Gonzalez said the House decision to drop its opposition to Wall was not a deal. But, he said, he did believe the switch was necessary to get Cranston to change his position. "That's my understanding from the leadership, from the senators, and from Sen. Cranston," Gonzalez said.

Financing was far from the only element of tension among conferees. On issue after issue, the Senate gave in to the House position, prompting Senate conferees to object that House members did not want to give up on anything. For example, the House prevailed by preserving, largely intact, two major housing provisions and two major consumer provisions that were vigorously opposed by the administration.

The House also prevailed in keeping most so-called special interest provisions out of the bill.

And the issue that dominated House debate — tough new capital standards for thrifts — largely dissipated during the conference. The subject of supervisory good will, over which House members had fought bitterly until the end of floor debate on the bill, never came up in the conference.

Final Action. Despite general administration happiness over the conference agreement, the financing scheme still threatened to derail the bill. Because of it, Bush threatened to veto the measure.

And in the Senate, Phil Gramm, R-Texas, vowed to block the on-budget scheme by invoking the anti-deficit law that bore his name. The Gramm-Rudman waiver in the conference agreement violated a Senate rule, and supporters of the on-budget plan needed 60 votes to prevail.

The veto threat, combined with a general public and congressional distaste for the bailout, drove away Republican supporters of the conference report. The House adopted it Aug. 3 by a slim majority — 221-199.

In the Senate, later the same day, achieving the 60-vote majority needed to overcome a ruling that the financing plan violated Gramm-Rudman proved impossible. The conference report was rejected when Riegle's motion to waive the Gramm-Rudman rule fell six votes short on a **key vote of 54-46 (R 1-44; D 53-2)**.

House and Senate leaders quickly reconvened the conference that evening. With most House Democrats on the conference opposed, a compromise was approved that put two-fifths of the spending on budget in fiscal 1989 — which was nearly over and no longer needed a Gramm-Rudman exemption — and the rest off budget in fiscal 1990-91.

That did not end the tension, however. Democrats' emotions were strained by Bush's intransigence and by the willingness of the House leadership to accept the compromise. It took the better part of a day to persuade a majority of House conferees to sign the new conference report. In the end, only 10 of 34 Democratic House conferees and 19 of 21 Republicans signed on. All five Senate conferees signed the report. The conference report (H Rept 101-222) was filed Aug. 4.

The new conference report went immediately to the Senate floor, but there was a last-minute hitch when the leadership tried to have it adopted on a voice vote. Many senators had departed town for a monthlong August recess. Opponents of the bill demanded a standing vote. And first, with only 11 senators on the floor, that vote went against the bill 4-7. Following objections that no quorum was present, and a delay to round up senators from their hide-away offices off the floor, a second standing vote was taken. This time no one objected to the lack of a quorum, and the conference report was adopted 17-4.

The House took up the bill late on Aug. 4, and Democrat after Democrat denounced the compromise financing provisions. But the conference report was adopted shortly after midnight by a vote of 201-175, clearing the bill for Bush.

Major Provisions

As cleared, HR 1278 (PL 101-73):

Financing

- **Resolution Funding Corporation.** Created an off-budget agency, the Resolution Funding Corporation, to sell to the public $30 billion in 30-year bonds in fiscal 1990 and 1991 to pay part of the cost of closing down or selling off insolvent thrifts. RefCorp was placed under the supervision of an oversight board composed of the head of finance for the Federal Home Loan Bank system and two presidents of regional Federal Home Loan Banks. The $30 billion borrowed by RefCorp was not to be counted as part of the federal budget.

The principal amount borrowed by RefCorp was not guaranteed by the federal government. It was to be repaid through the purchase of low-cost zero-coupon bonds that matured at the same time and in the same amount as the obligations incurred by RefCorp. The cost of the zero-coupon bonds was to be paid by using about $1.3 billion in retained earnings of the regional Federal Home Loan Banks (whose dividend-paying stock was held by the nation's thrifts) and about $2.1 billion in deposit insurance premiums paid by thrifts.

Treasury would guarantee repayment of the interest owed on the RefCorp borrowing and pay a major part of it. But part of the cost was to be paid from earnings of the regional Federal Home Loan Banks and part from the proceeds of assets seized from failed thrifts and sold to the public.

- **Fiscal 1989 Financing.** Authorized the Treasury to pay $18.8 billion immediately to close down insolvent thrifts from the date of enactment through Sept. 30, 1989, the end of the fiscal year. An additional $1.2 billion would be paid immediately by the regional Federal Home Loan Banks and drawn from their retained earnings. The combined $20 billion would count as part of the federal budget when it was spent, thereby increasing the fiscal 1989 deficit by that amount.
- **Resolution Trust Corporation.** Created a new on-budget agency, the Resolution Trust Corporation, to take possession of all thrifts that were insolvent on Jan. 1, 1989, but had not been put into receivership by the FSLIC by that date. The RTC also was to take possession of any

Bank Insurance Premiums Raised ...

Fear of a crisis in the banking industry paralleling the debacle that forced a taxpayer bailout of the deposit insurance system for savings and loan associations sent members of Congress scurrying in 1990. The result was legislation to give the Federal Deposit Insurance Corporation (FDIC) authority to increase the premiums banks and thrifts paid to insure their deposits.

Provisions included in the fiscal 1991 budget-reconciliation bill (HR 5835 — PL 101-508) removed restrictions that blocked the FDIC from increasing insurance premiums. Under existing law, bank premiums could be raised only to 19.5 cents per $100 of deposits, though premiums on thrifts were set somewhat higher. *(Fiscal 1991 budget-reconciliation, provisions, p. 59)*

The bill authorized the FDIC to set deposit insurance premiums for banks (covered by the Bank Insurance Fund) and savings and loan institutions (to be covered by the Savings Association Insurance Fund after 1992) at whatever level was necessary to maintain a minimum reserve in each of the insurance funds to cover potential losses. In addition, the FDIC was authorized to adjust insurance premiums twice a year, instead of annually, as under existing law.

Background

The proposal achieved the double aim of reducing the federal deficit (by increasing receipts by $9 billion over five years) and shoring up a deposit insurance fund severely weakened by continued bank failures — but not facing insolvency.

To maximize the insurance fund's reserves, the FDIC had announced plans to increase the premiums in 1991 to the highest amount then allowed by law. But L. William Seidman, chairman of the FDIC, pleaded with Congress to remove the cap on premium increases. The FDIC said that, if given authority to increase premiums further, it would raise them to 23 cents per $100 in deposits in 1992, matching the rate paid by thrifts.

The action avoided taking a serious look at the overall deposit insurance system, but few thought Congress would tackle the issue head-on in 1990. Election-year jitters and weariness from overhauling the savings and loan industry in 1989 left members without much appetite for such a potentially momentous change.

Moreover, Congress was expected to confront the broader issues in 1991. As part of the 1989 thrift bailout bill (HR 1278 — PL 101-73), Congress had required the Treasury Department to produce by early 1991 a deposit insurance reform plan. It was anticipated that the forthcoming study would prompt action not only on deposit insurance but also on banking regulation generally. *(Thrift bailout, p. 117)*

Nevertheless, the Bank Insurance Fund was in need of cash. In reports to Congress on Sept. 11 and Sept. 12, 1990, the General Accounting Office (GAO) and the Congressional Budget Office (CBO) warned that the fund was being drawn to dangerously low levels by repeated years of 200-plus bank failures. The GAO and CBO reports were the first official confirmations that the fund faced a real threat. The GAO and CBO also warned that a deep recession — and greater bank failures — could wipe out the fund.

CBO Director Robert D. Reischauer told the Senate Banking Committee that as many as 700 banks could fail in the following three years, continuing a trend of nearly 200 annual failures since 1987. That could cost the insurance fund a net loss of $21 billion, Reischauer said, and cash outlays of as much as $40 billion, part of which would be repaid to the fund as failed bank assets were sold back to the public.

The GAO took a narrower look, finding 35 banks out of a sample of 300 that required recapitalization

thrifts that became insolvent and were put into receivership within three years of the date of enactment. The RTC was to manage and dispose of the assets of thrifts in its possession and automatically terminate operations not later than Dec. 31, 1996.

Money for the RTC's operations would come from the $20 billion provided in 1989 by the Treasury and the Federal Home Loan Banks, from the $30 billion in RefCorp bond sales and from proceeds of the sale of assets seized from failed thrifts. In addition, the RTC was given authority to issue promissory notes or other obligations equal to 85 percent of the market value of assets held by RTC, plus available cash and that portion of authorized RefCorp borrowing not yet used. RTC obligations were to be guaranteed by the federal government. Further, the RTC could borrow up to $5 billion from the Treasury. All proceeds from the sale of assets not needed by the RTC to close insolvent thrifts were to be paid to RefCorp.

When the RTC was terminated, its assets and liabilities were to be transferred to a new FSLIC Resolution Fund (also created by the bill). The net proceeds of those remaining assets were to be paid to RefCorp.

The RTC was to be overseen by a board chaired by the secretary of the Treasury. The board would include the chairman of the Federal Reserve Board of Governors, the secretary of housing and urban development and two private citizens with experience in real estate or finance appointed by the president for three-year terms and confirmed by the Senate.

The board of directors of the FDIC was to serve as the board of directors for the RTC, and the FDIC would serve as the RTC's day-to-day manager.

... As Fears Loomed of a Bank Crisis

or regulatory assistance — or that were likely to fail. The cost to the fund could be as much as $6 billion, the GAO reported.

Legislative History

Free-Standing Bill. Less than two weeks after the GAO and CBO reports confirmed that the Bank Insurance Fund was running dangerously low of cash reserves, the House passed a bill (HR 5610) to remove the cap on premium increases. The bill, which was not acted on in committee, passed by voice vote under suspension of the rules on Sept. 17.

Although some House members and senators had expressed a desire to move the free-standing bill, the Senate never acted on it. In part, a reluctance to move HR 5610 persisted because of growing interest in a comprehensive approach to revising the deposit insurance system that could have bogged down the bill. An equally compelling concern was the lateness of the session and the pending effort to craft a broad, deficit-reducing budget deal.

Budget-Reconciliation Bill. The House and Senate Banking committees met Oct. 12 to devise their contributions to a reconciliation bill required as part of a plan to reduce the deficit by almost $500 billion over five years. The committees were charged with finding savings in programs under their jurisdiction by a budget resolution (H Con Res 310) adopted Oct. 8. *(Budget, p. 53)*

Both committees chose to include repeal of the cap on deposit insurance premiums as part of their budget savings.

On Oct. 15, the House Budget Committee assembled recommendations from 12 different committees, including House Banking, into HR 5835 and sent the measure to the floor (H Rept 101-881). The following day, the Senate Budget Committee assembled its reconciliation bill (S 3209) from the recommendations of 10 Senate committees and sent it to the floor without a written report. The insurance premium language in the two bills was essentially the same.

The House passed HR 5835 on Oct. 16, by a 227-203 vote. The deposit premium increase drew no special attention.

The Senate passed HR 5835 on Oct. 19 (in the session that began Oct. 18) by a **key vote of 54-46 (R 23-22; D 31-24)**, after substituting the text of S 3209 for that of the House-passed bill. First, however, the Senate rejected several amendments by Bob Graham, D-Fla., to revise the deposit insurance system. *(1990 key votes, p. 1039)*

Graham wanted to prescribe tougher standards for the FDIC to use when determining whether to provide deposit insurance to an institution. Graham said his amendment was important to fill a gap left by existing law that mandated the FDIC to insure federally chartered banks. Another amendment offered by Graham would have authorized the FDIC to establish a risk-based premium system for bank deposits. Under the proposal, a bank's deposit premiums would have been linked to the riskiness of its financial activities.

In light of an anticipated deposit insurance overhaul the following year, Graham was unable to persuade a majority of senators of the merit of the proposals, and the amendments were rejected on a procedural vote.

House and Senate conferees on HR 5835 completed their work on Oct 26. The House voted 228-200 to adopt the conference report (H Rept 101-964) in the early morning of Oct. 27. The Senate adopted the conference report hours later by a vote of 54-45, clearing the bill for the president. No change was made in the language repealing the cap on insurance premiums.

The RTC was required to consider the conditions of local real estate markets in determining how to sell its holdings. It was required to seek to maximize the return on its holdings. A national advisory board was to be established, and no fewer than six additional advisory boards were to be set up to consult on the disposition of real estate in economically distressed areas.

- **FSLIC Resolution Fund.** Created a separate fund administered by the FDIC, called the FSLIC Resolution Fund, to take possession of all thrifts put into receivership by the FSLIC prior to Jan. 1, 1989; all assets seized from failed thrifts prior to that date; and all obligations of the FSLIC to the acquirers of failed thrifts — including notes and guarantees relating to the value and return of assets sold to the acquirers of failed thrifts. The FSLIC Resolution Fund was charged with liquidating or selling any thrifts in receivership and managing and selling the assets it acquired from the FSLIC or from seized thrifts.

Money for the FSLIC Resolution Fund's operations would come from the proceeds of the sale of bonds by the Financing Corporation, created in 1987 to recapitalize the FSLIC, and proceeds of the sale of its acquired assets. The Treasury would make up any shortfall. The bill specified that the FSLIC Resolution Fund would terminate upon the disposition of all its assets, and any net proceeds would be paid to the Treasury (except for proceeds from assets transferred to the FSLIC Resolution Fund from the RTC, which would be paid to RefCorp).

- **Taxpayer Contributions.** Obligated the Treasury to contribute the first $18.8 billion used to close insolvent thrifts, to pay interest on the money borrowed by RefCorp and to cover obligations that the FSLIC made prior to the date of enactment to the purchasers of failed thrifts. Treasury also was required to contribute at least $16 billion through 1999 to establish reserves in the Savings Association Insurance Fund (SAIF), a new deposit insurance fund to be created to replace the FSLIC. Total taxpayer contributions through 1999 were projected by the Treasury Department to be about $80 billion.

• **Thrift Industry Contributions.** Increased thrift industry deposit insurance premiums for three years, from 1991 to 1993, to generate additional income for the RTC and the SAIF. Retained earnings of the Federal Home Loan Bank system plus thrift premium income were to be given to the RTC and used by RefCorp to purchase zero-coupon bonds. The bill required an additional $300 million a year of Federal Home Loan Bank system earnings paid to RefCorp for 30 years, starting in 1992, to cover some interest expenses.

Total thrift industry contributions through 1999 (including costs associated with bonds sold by the Financing Corporation created in 1987) were projected by the Treasury Department to be about $33 billion.

Thrift Regulation

• **New Insurance Funds.** Abolished the FSLIC, previously under the control of the Federal Home Loan Bank Board, and created the SAIF, a new deposit insurance system for thrifts.

The SAIF was to be controlled by the FDIC. Existing bank insurance operations that were under the FDIC were to be placed under the Bank Insurance Fund (BIF), another new entity created under the FDIC.

Although both the BIF and the SAIF were to be administered by the FDIC, insurance premiums from banks and thrifts would go only into their respective funds, and the funds would be kept separate. Just as thrift insurance premiums would be increased for a time under the bill, bank premiums also would be increased, on Jan. 1, 1990, and again on Jan. 1, 1991. The FDIC was authorized to adjust bank or thrift insurance premiums higher or lower as necessary to build insurance fund reserves until they equaled at least 1.25 percent of total insured deposits and, if the FDIC board deemed it necessary, until the reserves equaled 1.5 percent of total insured deposits.

Whenever the reserves reached the level deemed necessary, the FDIC was required to pay rebates to banks or thrifts.

Thrift industry insurance premiums were to begin decreasing in 1994 and be equalized with those of banks by 1998.

The FDIC would be controlled by a newly created, five-member board of directors. The comptroller of the currency, the director of a new Office of Thrift Supervision created to issue federal thrift charters and three private citizens nominated by the president and confirmed by the Senate were to serve on the board. The private citizens were to serve six-year terms; one was to be designated as chairman for a five-year term, and one designated as vice chairman. The chairman and members of the FDIC on the date of enactment automatically became the chairman and members of the new FDIC board.

• **Risk-Based Premiums.** Required the FDIC to study the idea of basing premiums on the relative riskiness of the activities of depository institutions and to report back to Congress by Jan. 1, 1991, including any recommendations for implementing such a system.

• **FDIC Borrowing.** Allowed the FDIC to borrow up to $5 billion from the Treasury. In addition, the FDIC was authorized to issue promissory notes and other guarantees equal to 90 percent of the net worth of the FDIC insurance funds. Such notes and guarantees were to be expressly backed by the full faith and credit of the U.S. government.

• **Insurance Fund Cross-Guarantees.** Made insured institutions liable to the FDIC for any losses to the insurance funds incurred by their insured affiliates or subsidiaries. This cross-guarantee did not apply for five years after enactment to losses incurred by an institution insured by one insurance fund (either the BIF or the SAIF), if its affiliate or subsidiary was insured by the other fund.

• **Exit Moratorium.** Prohibited thrifts for five years from seeking to change their charters to those of banks (or, in certain instances, savings banks) and moving their deposit insurance coverage from the SAIF to the BIF. However, thrifts were allowed to sell up to 35 percent of their deposits over five years to banks. Entrance and exit fees for allowed conversions were required during and after the moratorium.

Thrifts were allowed to convert to bank charters, provided they continued to be insured by the SAIF during the moratorium period. And banks that were permitted to merge with thrifts during the moratorium were required to pay insurance premiums to the SAIF for that portion of their deposits that originated with the thrifts.

• **Restructuring of the Federal Home Loan Bank Board.** Separated the existing chartering and credit functions of the bank board. The Office of Thrift Supervision was created under the Treasury secretary to charter federal savings and loan associations and federal savings banks, and to set capital standards for federally and state-chartered savings institutions. The new agency was roughly parallel to the Office of the Comptroller of the Currency, which chartered national banks. The Office of Thrift Supervision was made the primary federal regulator for state-chartered thrifts and for thrift holding companies.

The Office of Thrift Supervision was headed by a director. M. Danny Wall, the chairman of the Federal Home Loan Bank Board on the date of enactment, automatically became director of the Office of Thrift Supervision.

Another independent entity, the Federal Housing Finance Board, was created to oversee the credit operations of the 12 regional Federal Home Loan Banks. It was to be headed by a five-member board of directors appointed by the president and confirmed by the Senate to seven-year terms; the secretary of the Department of Housing and Urban Development was automatically a member. The makeup of the 14-member board of directors at each of the Home Loan Banks was altered to require that the eight elected thrift-industry representatives come from well-capitalized thrifts, and two of the six directors appointed by the Federal Housing Finance Agency represent consumer or community groups.

• **'Qualified Thrift Lender' Test.** Tightened the "qualified thrift lender" test used to determine whether a depository institution was eligible for tax benefits and access to low-interest Federal Home Loan Bank advances. The previous requirement that 60 percent of a thrift's loans be generally for home financing was stiffened to 70 percent. Also, thrifts were required to maintain 55 percent of their assets in a pool of loans and investments that was more closely connected to home financing and improvement than previously under the 60 percent test. Consumer loans and some other non-residential investments counted toward the 70 percent limit. Also, the 70 percent test was to be measured against all of a thrift's assets except its premises and furnishings, liquid assets such as reserves required by regulators, and good will. The new test was to take effect July 1, 1991.

A thrift that failed to meet the qualified lender test would have to convert to a more restrictive bank charter or remain a thrift and limit its investments and activities to those of a national bank. In either case, it would remain insured by the SAIF and lose its access to Federal Home Loan Bank advances.

Exemptions from the qualified thrift lender test applied to certain mutual savings banks and thrifts in Puerto Rico. The bill authorized banks and credit unions to borrow from Federal Home Loan Banks for the purpose of originating mortgages. Existing law contained an outright ban on such borrowing by banks and credit unions.

• **Capital Requirements.** Left to the Office of Thrift Supervision determination of capital standards for thrifts, but set some statutory minimums. All thrifts were required to meet stiffer, risk-based capital standards "no less stringent" than the standards regulators required for national banks.

In any event, thrifts were required to maintain not less than a 3 percent ratio of core capital to assets, as defined for national banks (which accounted for some intangible assets). Under the bill, core capital for thrifts also included 90 percent of the market value of a thrift's purchased mortgage-servicing rights. Thrifts also were required to maintain 1.5 percent tangible capital — cash, securities, assets easily converted to cash or 90 percent of the market value of purchased mortgage-servicing rights. Thrifts that had so-called supervisory good will — an intangible asset — on their books as of April 12, 1989, were allowed to count that as core capital for five years and as risk-based capital for 20 years. Supervisory good will was not to be counted as tangible capital.

Under rules for national banks that were to be in effect in 1991, thrifts would have to have a minimum 6 percent ratio of capital to assets, based on generally accepted accounting principles. By 1993, they would have to have 8 percent capital, based on the relative riskiness of their loans. Home mortgages, for instance, were considered low-risk. In computing an institution's asset base for determining the dollar value of required capital, mortgage loans were to be weighted at only half their value.

The new standards were to take effect 120 days after enactment. Thrifts that did not meet the new standards were to have an additional 60 days to submit business plans for meeting the standards.

Prior to Jan. 1, 1991, the Office of Thrift Supervision was authorized to restrict the ability of thrifts that did not meet the capital standards to make new loans, and such thrifts were required to operate under an agency-approved business plan for increasing capital. After 1990, thrifts that did not meet capital standards would not be allowed to make new loans, except that the Office of Thrift Supervision might allow such thrifts to make new, low-risk loans equal to the amount of interest credited on deposits, roughly 5 percent to 7 percent a year. The new loans would have to be fully capitalized.

After 1990, thrifts that did not meet the capital requirements were to be put under supervisory agreements by the Office of Thrift Supervision that might limit the payment of dividends or compensation. Thrifts that were operated in a safe and sound manner and showed profitability might seek an exemption from such supervisory agreements but would have to operate under approved business plans.

• **Capital Rules for Subsidiaries.** Required state-chartered thrifts that operated subsidiaries engaged in activities not permitted to national banks to subtract from their capital base the value of all loans to and other investments in those subsidiaries. Such subsidiaries had to be independently capitalized. Capital committed to existing subsidiary functions not permitted for national banks had to be written off over five years. This rule did not apply to subsidiaries engaged solely in mortgage banking or to certain subsidiary depository institutions. Where a thrift had not subtracted from capital its subsidiary investments, the assets and liabilities of that subsidiary had to be consolidated with those of the thrift itself for purposes of determining the thrift's capital.

• **Accounting Standards.** Required all federal bank and thrift regulatory agencies to develop within a year of enactment uniform accounting standards to be used in assessing whether banks and thrifts were meeting the capital standards required by law and regulation. Such standards did not have to be identical and could vary based on differences in the operations of banks and thrifts. Bank and thrift regulatory agencies were required to report annually to Congress about their accounting standards and where and how they differed.

• **Federally Chartered Thrifts.** Altered, and in most cases reduced, the amount of a thrift's loan portfolio that might be invested in commercial real estate from 40 percent, as under prior law, to four times its capital (allowing, for example, 24 percent of a thrift's loans to be in commercial real estate, if it had 6 percent capital). No thrift would be required to divest commercial real estate loans that exceeded the limit allowed by the bill. Except for limits on junk bonds, other existing limits on the lending activities of federally chartered thrifts were not changed. *(See junk bonds, below)*

• **State-Chartered Thrifts.** Restricted state-chartered thrifts from engaging directly in activities prohibited to federally chartered thrifts or investing in amounts above those allowed to federally chartered thrifts, except in very limited circumstances, such as where the thrift was acting only as agent for its customers.

This prohibition particularly applied to equity investments in real estate or stocks, except for investments in service corporations, and included transactions — in the form of loans, for example — that could be construed as equity investments.

Additional activities beyond those available to federal thrifts would generally be permitted only if the thrift fully met capital standards and the FDIC determined that the activities would not pose a significant risk that the insurance fund would suffer a loss.

Thrifts were required to divest their prohibited equity holdings as quickly as possible and not later than July 1, 1994.

• **Junk Bonds.** Prohibited any thrift, federally or state-chartered, from investing in non-investment grade or junk bonds, directly or through a subsidiary. Junk bonds were those not rated in one of the four highest investment categories by at least one nationally recognized rating service but did not include securities issued by the Federal National Mortgage Association, the Federal Home Loan

Mortgage Corporation and the Government National Mortgage Association.

Separately capitalized affiliates of thrifts were permitted to invest without limit in junk bonds, as were separately capitalized subsidiaries of mutual thrift institutions (which typically were not owned by holding companies and had no affiliates). Thrifts were required to divest their junk bond holdings as quickly as possible and not later than July 1, 1994. Federally chartered thrifts previously were prohibited from holding more than 11 percent of their assets in junk bonds.

• **Brokered Deposits.** Prohibited a bank or thrift that did not meet minimum capital standards from accepting so-called brokered deposits, which typically were large — nearing the $100,000 maximum on insured accounts — and were placed by securities firms or other agents seeking the highest interest rates among insured depository institutions. The FDIC was permitted to waive this rule on a case-by-case basis, upon a finding that the acceptance of brokered deposits would not constitute an "unsafe" or "unsound" practice.

• **Loan Limits.** Applied to thrifts the national bank standard of 15 percent of capital for unsecured loans to a single borrower. The bill made exceptions for loans of up to $500,000 and loans of up to 50 percent of capital to aid the sale of real estate acquired by the thrift through foreclosure.

• **Thrift Lending to Affiliates.** Prohibited thrifts from investing in or making loans to, or for the benefit of, another firm affiliated with the thrift through a holding company to the same extent that banks were restricted from such activities. Generally, loans to a single affiliate would not be allowed to exceed 10 percent of capital, and loans to all affiliates would not be allowed to exceed 20 percent of capital. Also, loans would have to be on terms as favorable to the thrift as would loans to a third party.

Consumer and Housing Issues

• **'Redlining.'** Expanded the Home Mortgage Disclosure Act of 1975 (PL 94-200) to require all mortgage lenders to collect and report information on the race, gender and income level of loan applicants and recipients. The additional data were required beginning Dec. 31, 1989. The Community Reinvestment Act of 1977 (PL 95-128) also was amended to require federal financial regulators to disclose summary evaluations and descriptive ratings of institutions under the act. Such disclosures were required after July 1, 1990. *(1975 law, Congress and the Nation Vol. IV, p. 490; 1977 law, Congress and the Nation Vol. V, p. 431)*

• **Limits on Advances.** Required the Federal Housing Finance Board to adopt regulations within two years limiting an institution's ability to receive Federal Home Loan Bank system advances, based on the institution's compliance with the Community Reinvestment Act, its record of lending to first-time home buyers and its record of lending for low- and moderate-income housing.

• **Low-Income Mortgages.** Required each Federal Home Loan Bank to set aside a portion of its annual earnings to subsidize low-income mortgages. The total from all 12 Home Loan Banks committed to this program had to be 5 percent of earnings or at least $50 million a year in calendar years 1990-93; 6 percent of earnings or at least $75 million in 1994; and 10 percent of earnings or at least $100 million a year thereafter.

Each Home Loan Bank was required to appoint an advisory committee drawn from local community and housing organizations to advise on how best to use these mortgage subsidies. These mortgages were to be used to finance houses purchased by families with incomes of 80 percent or less of the median in a given area or multi-family dwellings where 20 percent of the units were permanently set aside for families with incomes at 50 percent or less of a given area's median.

Each Federal Home Loan Bank also was required to develop a program for making moderate-income mortgage loans to families with incomes equal to 115 percent or less of a given area's median and loans to finance commercial and economic development projects that would benefit low- and moderate-income persons.

• **RTC Right of First Refusal.** Gave state and local government and non-profit housing agencies, and families whose incomes were less than 115 percent of the median in a given area, a 90-day right to purchase certain low-cost single-family residential properties acquired by the RTC from failed thrifts. State and local government and non-profit housing agencies would have a 45-day right to purchase certain low-cost multi-family residential properties, provided that a sufficient number of units were maintained for low-income persons at very low rents for the life of the property.

Single-family residences might be sold at prices below their "net realizable market value," if necessary to expedite the sale or aid a lower-income family. Multi-family properties had to be sold at or above their market value. The RTC might make loans at market rates to qualified purchasers.

• **Bank Fees Study.** Required the Federal Reserve Board to report annually to Congress on the scope of banking services being offered by financial institutions and any change in fees charged consumers for such services. The study was to be based on a representative geographic and size-of-institution sample of banks and thrifts.

Enforcement

• **Early Intervention.** Permitted the FDIC to suspend deposit insurance on new deposits received by a thrift whose tangible capital fell to zero. Such action might be taken without administrative hearings but would be subject to later judicial review. This provision did not apply to a thrift whose tangible capital was deemed to be zero solely because it was capitalized only with supervisory good will. Such thrifts would be subject to enhanced FDIC supervision, however.

• **Civil.** Increased civil penalties in cases where a bank, thrift or credit union (or an individual connected to the institution) violated regulations or engaged in an unsafe or unsound practice to $25,000 per day, or to $1 million per day in the case of knowing and reckless violations.

For lesser violations, where an institution's or individual's practices did not constitute an immediate risk of loss to the deposit insurance system or to the safety and soundness of the institution, the fine would be limited to $5,000 per day.

The bill also increased the authority of bank, thrift and credit union regulators to issue cease-and-desist orders or to take other steps to prevent unsafe and unsound operations. And it provided that an individual barred from working in one type of insured financial institution automatically would be barred from working in an insured financial institution regulated by a different agency, even when the second agency had not taken action against the individual.

Civil penalties for theft, fraud, embezzlement or the like were increased to $1 million per day, the amount embezzled or otherwise "misapplied" or $5 million, whichever was greater. Legal actions to recover such civil penalties had to be initiated by the attorney general.

• **Criminal.** Increased the penalties for an individual convicted of embezzlement, theft, defrauding a federal banking agency or accepting gifts in return for procuring loans to a maximum fine of $1 million (from the previous maximum of $5,000) and a maximum prison sentence of 20 years (previously five years), or both. The statute of limitations on banking fraud was extended from five years to 10 years upon enactment.

A person previously barred from working in a financial institution who violated that order was subject to a maximum fine of $1 million, a maximum prison term of five years, or both.

• **RICO.** Expanded the application of the Racketeer Influenced and Corrupt Organizations Act (RICO) to cover bank fraud. This provision relaxed certain statute-of-limitation requirements, permitted seizures of property deemed to have been involved in the fraud and permitted federal and private civil suits for treble damages in the case of such crimes.

• **Grand Jury Information.** Authorized the disclosure of information developed in grand jury investigations to federal banking regulators in certain narrow circumstances, such as for developing civil damage cases involving financial institution fraud. Courts might order release of such information upon a finding of substantial need.

• **Justice Department Activities.** Authorized $65 million annually for fiscal 1990-92 for the prosecution of financial institution crimes and $10 million annually for those years for prosecution of civil violations, in addition to other sums authorized for the Justice Department.

The Justice Department was required to establish within 120 days of enactment a special fraud prosecution office in northern Texas, to pursue crimes stemming from the thrift crisis in that state through 1992. The bill also authorized $10 million annually for fiscal 1990-92 for court-related expenses caused by increased prosecutions.

Miscellaneous

• **Appraisal Standards.** Required bank and thrift regulatory agencies to establish minimum standards for the performance of real estate appraisals.

• **Government Audits.** Authorized the GAO to audit all banking operations referred to in the bill, including those of the RTC and RefCorp and of private parties that contracted with or received assistance from the government under the auspices of the bill. The Federal Reserve would not be subject to GAO audit to the degree that it was previously exempt.

• **Government-Sponsored Enterprises.** Required the GAO and the Treasury Department to conduct separate studies of the riskiness of various government-sponsored enterprises, such as the Farm Credit System, the Student Loan Marketing Association and several secondary-mortgage market agencies. Both the GAO and Treasury were required to report to Congress in May 1990 and May 1991 about the credit, interest-rate, management and business risks of these enterprises, and their effect on federal borrowing. *(Government-sponsored enterprises, p. 153)*

• **Special Tax Provisions.** Repealed effective May 10, 1989, three special tax breaks available to firms that purchased failing banks and thrifts. The special provisions allowed such firms to exclude from income federal financial assistance received as part of the purchase contract, to engage in tax-free reorganizations that otherwise would not be permitted, and to make use of the net operating losses and built-in losses of a failed bank or thrift. The revenue gains resulting from this tax code change were counted toward the budget savings contained in the 1989 budget-reconciliation bill (HR 3299 — PL 101-239). *(Reconciliation bill, p. 43)*

• **Insurance Fund Logotype.** Required that an entirely new logotype be devised for display by thrifts to indicate that their deposits were "backed by the full faith and credit of the United States Government" up to $100,000. The logotype was not to contain the inscription "FDIC." Banks were allowed to continue using their current FDIC logotype or to switch to the new seal.

• **Thrift Purchases.** Authorized bank holding companies to buy healthy thrift institutions immediately upon enactment. And, with permission of the Fed, a bank holding company might purchase a thrift and merge its assets and liabilities into a larger bank subsidiary.

Thrift holding companies were allowed to acquire up to 5 percent of the voting stock of unaffiliated savings institutions.

• **Deposit Insurance Studies.** Required the Treasury Department in concert with bank and thrift regulatory agencies to conduct a broad review of the system of deposit insurance and report back to Congress 18 months after enactment. The study would review such issues as assessing premiums on and providing insurance for foreign deposits held by U.S. banks; prohibiting bank and thrift certificates of deposit sold through securities brokers; limiting bank and thrift bailouts strictly to the amounts of insured deposits (thereby eliminating the idea of "fail-safe" banks where all deposits and all creditors were protected); and calculating the worth of asset portfolios on the basis of market instead of book value.

The GAO was to conduct a similar study, also due in 18 months.

In addition, the FDIC was to report in six months on the subject of so-called pass-through deposit insurance for large certificates of deposit sold to pension funds, where the certificate was fully insured even though it might exceed the $100,000 limit on insured deposits, because each pensioner was deemed to be insured for the full amount.

• **Credit Unions.** Gave the Credit Union National Association (which regulated and insured credit unions) similar authority to that of bank and thrift regulators to move against institutions whose activities were deemed a risk to the deposit insurance fund.

The bill also required the Treasury Department, as part of its overall deposit insurance study, and the GAO to review the financial condition of credit unions and their deposit insurance fund, and to make recommendations 18 months after enactment as to the need for a change in the regulation of credit unions or their insurance-premium assessments.

• **Freddie Mac and Fannie Mae.** Placed the Federal Home Loan Mortgage Corporation (Freddie Mac) under a new, 18-member board similar to the board that governed its sister secondary-mortgage market institution, the Federal National Mortgage Association (Fannie Mae). Freddie Mac, like Fannie Mae, participated in the secondary market in home mortgages. It had been controlled by the Federal Home Loan Bank Board. Both Freddie Mac and Fannie Mae would be subject to oversight by the secretaries of the Treasury and of housing and urban development to ensure their equal footing and continued competition.

The GAO was charged with auditing Fannie Mae (it already audited Freddie Mac) and with reporting to Congress by May 1, 1990, on the desirability of requiring such enterprises to maintain capital based on the riskiness of their investments.

Securities Market Reforms

Lawmakers took what they hoped would be significant steps in 1990 toward stabilizing securities trading by clearing three bills to give regulators more authority over the stock markets.

One bill (HR 3657 — PL 101-432), cleared on Sept. 28, sought to improve the ability of securities regulators to limit major market disruptions, such as the shock that struck the market in October 1987. President Bush signed the bill Oct. 16.

Lawmakers sent to the president a second measure (S 647 — PL 101-429) to establish new civil penalties for securities law violations. And Congress cleared a third bill (HR 1396 — PL 101-550) to give the Securities and Exchange Commission (SEC) more authority to cooperate more closely with foreign governments in securities fraud investigations. S 647 cleared on Oct. 1 and was signed Oct. 15. HR 1396 cleared Oct. 26 and was signed Nov. 15.

Congress failed, however, to clear a bill to shift regulatory control over stock index futures from the Commodity Futures Trading Commission (CFTC) to the SEC, as urged by the Bush administration. That impasse also killed bills reauthorizing the CFTC (S 1729, HR 2869), which contained some enforcement-enhancement provisions. *(CFTC authorization, p. 550)*

The provisions of the market stabilization bill (HR 3657) — by far the most comprehensive of the three that cleared — were largely drawn from requests to Congress submitted by the SEC. The bill required improved clearance and settlement procedures for stock and related options and futures transactions in an effort to make all financial markets more liquid.

The bill gave the SEC authority to close the nation's stock exchanges in an emergency. Previously, presidential action was required to halt trading. It gave the SEC authority to restrict so-called program trading, a computer-driven trading technique, if it was shown to contribute to wild price swings. And the bill gave the SEC new tools to monitor transactions by large traders — to better guard against market manipulation — and to monitor the financial strength of brokerage houses.

Background

The drive to pass stock market reform bills was largely spurred by the 508-point drop in the Dow Jones Industrial Average — a closely watched market indicator — on Oct. 19, 1987. In all, more than $1 trillion in paper wealth was wiped out in one week that October.

The wild swings led lawmakers and regulators to look for ways to tighten regulations and provide traders more information on the market. But jurisdictional disputes and conflicting views over the cause of market disruptions delayed legislative action for three years.

The market disturbance, as well as the interplay between stocks and their "derivative" instruments traded in the futures markets, was the subject of several government studies and many examinations by the markets themselves.

Most studies warned that without regulatory restructuring, the markets would continue to be volatile. "We are looking down the barrel, and the gun is still loaded," said Nicholas F. Brady in 1988. At the time, Brady was chairman of the Presidential Task Force on Market Mechanisms, which was formed by President Ronald Reagan to study the 1987 disruption. In 1990, when the market regulation bills were enacted, Brady was serving in the Bush administration as secretary of the Treasury.

In 1988, Senate Banking Committee Chairman William Proxmire, D-Wis., and House Energy and Commerce Finance Subcommittee Chairman Edward J. Markey, D-Mass., introduced bills in reaction to several market-reform studies. Neither bill was acted on, in part because of jurisdictional fights over the regulation of stock index futures. *(Congress and the Nation Vol. VII, pp. 28, 128, 130)*

Stock index futures were a hybrid instrument, neither a commodity nor a security. But an agreement between the SEC and CFTC enacted into law in 1982 gave the CFTC jurisdiction over index futures.

Members also were divided on restrictions on program trading — a collection of strategies involving the buying or selling of large blocks of stock, often relying on trades in stock index futures as well. Program trading was blamed as a contributing cause of several severe stock market price fluctuations, including the market drop in October 1987. A 190-point drop in the Dow on Oct. 13, 1989, and an 88-point rise the next trading day renewed interest in curbing wide price swings.

HR 3657

In November 1989, both chambers began to focus on specific proposals on market regulation. In the Senate, Christopher J. Dodd, D-Conn., introduced a bill (S 648) to give the SEC authority to shut down markets for up to 90 days if necessary in an emergency to protect investors and the public interest.

Markey introduced a similar bill in the House (HR 3657), with one major difference. Markey's bill would have authorized the SEC to adopt rules to prevent stock price "manipulation" or "any practice" that had previously resulted in excessive stock swings. The language was intended to allow the SEC to restrict program trading. The Senate bill only called for the SEC to study the issue.

House Action. Markey's Finance Subcommittee approved a pair of market stabilization bills (HR 3656, HR 3657) by voice vote on Nov. 14, 1989.

HR 3657 focused on SEC authority to attack trading practices resulting in "high levels of volatility." The bill also gave the SEC enhanced authority to suspend trading in emergencies, required reporting by large traders about their activities and allowed the SEC to collect data on the financial condition of some companies affiliated with brokerages.

HR 3656 was intended to improve the clearance and settlement of stock trades, which had been jeopardized in the 1987 crash. The relatively non-controversial bill was aimed at closing transactions much more quickly than the five days previously required, so investors would have quicker access to their money and the markets would stay "liquid."

The full Energy and Commerce Committee took up the measures March 13, 1990, and approved both bills by voice vote.

Although the two House bills traveled together through committee, they were considered separately on the House floor. HR 3656 was formally reported May 8 (H Rept 101-477) and passed the House by voice vote without amendment the same day. HR 3657 was formally reported June 5 (H Rept 101-524) and passed the House by voice vote without amendment the same day.

Senate Action. The Senate Banking Committee voted 20-1 on Nov. 16, 1989, to approve S 648. The bill was formally reported May 22, 1990 (S Rept 101-300).

In many respects, the measure was similar to HR 3656 and HR 3657. It authorized the SEC to order trading halts in "major market disturbances" and to collect new information on securities firms making very large trades. It also required the SEC and the CFTC, along with the Federal Reserve and the Treasury, to develop coordinated and expedited methods to settle stock and futures transactions to ease cash-flow problems.

Unsure how to address the issue of program trading, the committee agreed to ask the SEC to report within three months of the bill's enactment on the need for more authority to restrain "any practices that are inconsistent with the statutory mission of the SEC to protect shareholders and investors."

The Senate passed S 648 on Aug. 4 by voice vote. Floor action had been delayed by a fight over the regulation of stock index futures contracts. The administration wanted jurisdiction over index futures transferred to the SEC from the CFTC, but resistance to the proposal bogged down the securities bill.

Final Action. After more than a month of negotiations, a breakthrough on market regulation bills came in September when House, Senate and administration representatives agreed on a compromise. On Sept. 25, the Senate passed HR 3657 by voice vote after agreeing to a comprehensive substitute amendment that included elements from S 648 plus the clearance and settlement provisions that were in HR 3656, the second House bill. (HR 3656 was eventually used on Oct. 27 by the Senate and House as a legislative vehicle to carry amendments to the Public Utility Holding Company Act. It was enacted into law as PL 101-572 but by then had no provisions affecting securities market regulation.) The compromise on HR 3657 centered on revised language regarding program trading. Provisions to increase the SEC's authority to halt trading and to collect information on large trades and the financial health of brokerage houses were kept intact.

The program trading compromise gave the SEC the authority to determine what specific individual program trading practices had caused wide price swings and were likely to do so in the future. In those cases, the SEC could order the practices suspended.

The House agreed to the Senate amendment on Sept. 28, clearing HR 3657 on a voice vote.

Major Provisions of HR 3657

As cleared, the Securities Market Reform Act (HR 3657 — PL 101-432):

- **Trading Halts.** Provided the Securities and Exchange Commission with additional authority to suspend trading in any specific security for up to 10 business days and a national securities exchange for a period not to exceed 90 calendar days. Before taking the action, the SEC was required to notify the president of its decision. The president could block the action by not approving the SEC decision.

Before taking action to halt trading, the SEC was charged with consulting with the Commodity Futures Trading Commission to consider the impact of emergency action on the futures markets.

- **Emergency Powers.** Gave the SEC the authority, in the event of a major market disturbance or excessive fluctuation of securities prices, to take steps to maintain or restore order to the securities markets and ensure prompt and accurate settlement of transactions.

Among the options open to the SEC were the authority to alter, supplement, suspend or impose requirements or restrictions with respect to hours of trading, position limits, and clearance and settlement.

The SEC could keep the emergency orders in effect for 10 business days, including extensions. The president could rescind an order at any time.

- **Large Trader Reporting.** Required brokerage houses to provide information to the SEC when engaging in securities transactions involving a substantial volume. After the Oct. 19, 1987, market crash, the SEC was unable to easily reconstruct trading. To help the SEC monitor the impact of large transactions on the markets, brokers were required to identify the trader and accounts used for the transactions. The requirement applied to large transactions, as identified by the SEC, in publicly traded securities. The SEC was given the authority to issue regulations on the manner in which the transactions and accounts would be reported.

Financial institutions that offered customers trust services, which included the buying and selling of securities for the account of the trustees, would be subject to SEC reporting requirements on large transactions.

- **Record-Keeping Requirements.** Required brokers and dealers to keep records on large securities transactions. The figures used to determine a substantial volume or large transaction would be set by the SEC. The records had to be available for reporting to the SEC on the morning of the day following the transaction. The records also could be examined by the SEC or other regulatory bodies at any time. The SEC was given the authority to exempt persons or transactions from reporting requirements.

- **Risk Assessment Requirements.** Required brokers and dealers to keep records on policies, procedures and systems for monitoring and controlling financial and operational risks. The records were designed to provide information to the SEC regarding the overall financial condition of a firm. The provisions were included to address a growing occurrence of brokers forming holding companies and moving potentially risky activities outside of the broker-dealer and away from direct regulatory supervision.

Firms were required to maintain records on securities activities, sources of capital and funding, and the business activities of any person likely to have an impact on the financial or operational condition of the organization. The SEC was authorized to require the brokers and dealers to provide additional information if needed. The SEC was given the authority to exempt certain individuals and businesses.

Financial institutions that offered trust services would be subject to SEC requirements on risk assessment.

• **Settlement of Transactions.** Provided the SEC with authority to establish a national system for settlement and clearance of securities transactions. The intent of establishing the system was to improve the settlement process, which had been overloaded during times of extraordinary market volatility. The SEC was granted the authority to establish linked or coordinated facilities for clearance and settlement of transactions in securities options, futures contracts and commodity options.

• **Program Trading.** Authorized the SEC to adopt regulations concerning practices that affected or contributed to market volatility. To do this, the SEC would first have to make a finding that a specific practice had contributed to instances of wild price swings.

The language was directed at program trading, which involved large blocks of stocks and related instruments, such as options or futures, and often involved use of a computerized order system to cope with the volume of stocks involved.

The SEC was authorized to seek civil penalties and issue cease-and-desist orders against individuals or firms that continued to employ a practice banned by the SEC.

The SEC was given the authority to take steps to prevent manipulation of stock prices that were reasonably likely to affect market volatility.

• **Securities Subsidiaries.** Required federal banking agencies to report to the SEC any concerns regarding a significant financial or operational risk to a broker or dealer resulting from the activities of a financial institution.

• **Congressional Reports.** Required the secretary of the Treasury, the Federal Reserve Board chairman and chairmen of the SEC and CFTC to report to Congress no later than May 31, 1991, and annually thereafter on efforts to coordinate securities, futures and banking regulatory activities. The reports were to cover agency views on the adequacy of margin levels and efforts to create a mechanism for clearance and settlement. The agencies were to file the reports separately.

S 647

As cleared Oct. 1, 1990, S 647 (PL 101-429) established new civil penalties for securities law violations and new disclosure and trading requirements for issuers and traders in so-called penny stocks, inexpensive securities not traded on national exchanges.

S 647 authorized the SEC to impose an array of civil fines for securities violations. Under existing law, the SEC was allowed to pursue only criminal penalties in many cases involving violations. The SEC had requested the bill to gain more flexibility to prosecute fraud, given that the standard of proof in civil cases was substantially easier to meet.

The measure increased the range of civil penalties that the SEC and courts could impose in securities fraud cases. Fines ranged from $5,000 for individuals and $50,000 for businesses for basic violations of securities laws. Fines for violations involving fraudulent actions and substantial financial loss would be higher. Lesser penalties would apply to securities cases not involving fraud.

In addition, the SEC was given the authority to issue cease-and-desist orders against people or businesses found to be violating securities laws.

Senate Action. The Senate Banking Committee approved S 647 by voice vote on May 24, 1990, after agreeing to a substitute that instituted a three-tier system for the dollar amounts of civil penalties and clarifying who was subject to SEC cease-and-desist orders. The bill was formally reported June 26 (S Rept 101-337).

The Senate passed the measure on July 18 by voice vote.

House Action. The Energy and Commerce Subcommittee on Finance approved a pair of related bills (HR 975, HR 4497) targeting securities fraud. Both bills were approved by voice vote on June 20, 1990.

HR 975 was a companion bill to S 647, similar in scope with a few differences, notably a Senate provision allowing the SEC access to grand jury materials. Such information could be used by the SEC to develop civil fraud cases, even if the grand jury investigation did not result in a criminal prosecution.

HR 4497, which had no Senate counterpart, was designed to bring the penny-stock industry under tighter SEC regulation, by requiring penny-stock dealers to provide buyers with a risk disclosure document explaining that these stocks were often difficult to trade because the market for them was small and less liquid.

The full Energy and Commerce Committee approved both bills by voice vote on June 27. HR 975 was formally reported July 23 (H Rept 101-616). HR 4497 was formally reported the same day (H Rept 101-617).

A new bill (HR 5325) incorporating the text of both committee bills was introduced July 20 and passed the House by voice vote July 23 without amendment. The same day the House also passed S 647, after amending it to include the text of HR 5325.

Final Action. Negotiators spent the next two months hammering out differences between the House and Senate versions. The eventual compromise included House-passed language on the tighter SEC regulation of penny stocks and removed the Senate-passed language giving the SEC access to grand jury information.

The full Senate amended S 647 on Sept. 27 by voice vote to incorporate the details of the compromise, and the House accepted the Senate amendment by voice vote Oct. 1, clearing the bill for the president.

HR 1396

As cleared on Oct. 26, 1990, HR 1396 (PL 101-550) was designed to give the SEC additional authority to cooperate more closely with foreign governments in securities fraud investigations.

According to the SEC, requests for cooperation by foreign countries had more than doubled in recent years and numbered about 85 in 1988. But foreign governments were said to be concerned that documents they shared might be released to the public in the United States.

HR 1396, requested by the administration, explicitly exempted foreign confidential information from disclosure under the Freedom of Information Act and allowed the SEC and U.S. stock exchanges to ban individuals from domestic trading if they had been convicted of securities fraud overseas.

The bill included provisions to overhaul the Trust Indenture Act of 1939, which governed registration of corporate bonds, and to require that mutual funds pass along to their shareholders information from firms in which the funds invested.

The measure also reauthorized the SEC at a level of $178 million for fiscal 1990 and $212.6 million for fiscal 1991.

House Action. The Energy and Commerce Finance Subcommittee approved HR 1396 by voice vote on May 25, 1989. The full Energy and Commerce Committee approved the bill by voice vote June 20. It was formally reported Sept. 12 (H Rept 101-240).

In committee, the provisions exempting certain information from disclosure were narrowed to satisfy complaints by news organizations that they had been originally drawn too broadly. The House passed the bill by voice vote under suspension of the rules Sept. 25.

Senate Action. The Senate Banking Committee approved a draft companion bill that included the SEC authorization, introducing and formally reporting the bill (S 1712 — S Rept 101-155) on Oct. 2.

S 1712 was debated on the Senate floor Nov. 16 and amended to add the Trust Indenture Act language. The Senate then passed HR 1396 the same day by voice vote after amending it to substitute the language of S 1712.

Final Action. After nearly a year of inaction on the measure, the House on Oct. 1 agreed to a conference with the Senate on HR 1396 to resolve a disagreement over a Senate provision to remove the pay cap for SEC employees.

The SEC had complained that the rigid federal pay scale had made attracting and retaining personnel, particularly lawyers, difficult for the agency. Despite SEC complaints, the Senate accepted the House position keeping the SEC within the federal pay structure.

Conferees agreed Oct. 23 and filed their conference report the same day (H Rept 101-924). The Senate adopted the conference report by voice vote on Oct. 25; the House did likewise the following day, clearing the measure for the president.

Bank Fraud Penalties

Under political pressure from the costly savings and loan crisis, Congress in 1990 voted to step up penalties against individuals and financial institutions convicted of fraud and other crimes as part of an omnibus anti-crime bill (S 3266 — PL 101-647).

Public anger turned the taxpayer-financed thrift bailout into a political nightmare for lawmakers and the Bush administration. Congressional Democrats claimed the administration had been slow in pursuing criminal prosecutions of thrift executives. And members of Congress discovered that the thrift crisis was a major topic in many of their re-election campaigns. *(Thrift bailout, p. 117)*

Several high-profile thrift failures drew further attention to the issue: Principally, there was the $2 billion failure of Lincoln Savings and Loan Association of Irvine, Calif., and the political connections of its owner, Charles H. Keating Jr. That case tarred five senators who were suspected of doing favors for Keating in exchange for political contributions. In addition, the failure of Silverado Banking, Savings and Loan Association in Denver, Colo., added to the White House's discomfort. A federal investigation into the 1988 collapse of Silverado led to a conflict-of-interest complaint citing ties between the president's son, Neil Bush, once a Silverado director, and businessmen who had sizable loans from the thrift. *(Keating Five, p. 975)*

Tougher thrift fraud penalties were added in the Senate to a broad crime bill (S 1970) that dealt with such hot-button issues as capital punishment, death row appeals and gun control. Similar provisions made their way onto a House-passed crime bill (HR 5269).

Ironically, conferees on those two bills hit an impasse on those major issues, and the thrift fraud provisions ended as the centerpiece of a stripped-down crime bill (S 3266), which cleared Congress on Oct. 27 and was signed into law Nov. 29. *(Crime bill, p. 764)*

As enacted, the measure increased — in future cases — the civil and criminal penalties for financial fraud, including the maximum sentence of life in prison for defendants who received $5 million or more in gross receipts from a continuing financial enterprise during any two-year period. Those defendants also could face a fine of $10 million — $20 million for organizations.

Federal banking agencies and the Justice Department were given enhanced authority to seize assets fraudulently obtained from banks and savings and loans. A new office of special counsel for financial institutions fraud was established at the Justice Department; and new prosecutors, FBI agents and Secret Service agents were authorized to focus on financial crimes.

The measure also placed a lifetime ban on convicted felons from controlling or participating in the management of a financial institution. It prohibited failing institutions from offering so-called golden parachutes — lucrative buyouts or bonuses — to bank executives. And it made obstructing a bank examination a federal offense with a five-year maximum prison sentence.

Although the bill was praised by Democrats and Republicans alike, the new penalties could not be applied retroactively to crimes uncovered prior to enactment.

Legislative History

Senate Action. Thrift fraud provisions were added as a floor amendment to the Senate's anti-crime bill (S 1970) on July 11 by a 99-1 vote. The bill passed the same day by a vote of 94-6.

House Action. The House Judiciary Committee added similar financial fraud provisions to its anti-crime bill (HR 5269 — H Rept 101-681, Part I) that it began marking up July 17.

The fraud section was a bipartisan compromise adapted from a Republican-sponsored bill (HR 5050) that the House Banking Subcommittee on Financial Institutions had approved June 28.

Despite agreement on the need to spend more to investigate and penalize thrift fraud, the deliberations took on partisan overtones after the provisions were laid out before the committee, in particular one that would have authorized the Justice Department to set up a special counsel to investigate bank fraud. An acrimonious debate ensued over an amendment offered by Chuck Douglas, R-N.H., to authorize the special counsel to investigate past and current members of Congress and their ties to officials of failed thrifts. Douglas linked the amendment to Democrats' call for an independent counsel to investigate Neil Bush.

Douglas' amendment was narrowly defeated, 17-19.

The bill came to the House floor in October, but the bank fraud provisions received scant attention. The House passed HR 5269 by a vote of 368-55 on Oct. 5.

Final Action. Worries over the crime bill's prospects prompted both chambers to act to preserve the financial fraud provisions.

On July 31, the House suspended the rules and passed a stand-alone bank fraud bill (HR 5401) by 424-4. Its provisions were lifted from HR 5269. Senate Judiciary reported HR 5401 and its own free-standing fraud bill (S 3194) on Oct. 12.

The Senate then took up the broad House crime bill (HR 5269) on Oct. 22 and passed it Oct. 23 after amending it to include the text of S 1970. But disputes over a range of provisions prevented a conference agreement on the broad measure.

A new, scaled-back crime bill (S 3266) was introduced Oct. 27 incorporating the financial fraud provisions as a key element, along with other provisions agreed upon by conferees on HR 5269.

Both chambers passed the bill the same day — the Senate by voice vote and the House by 313-1 under suspension of the rules.

Money Laundering

Armed with data showing that the nation's financial institutions were often used by narcotics traffickers to hide their drug profits, lawmakers crafted legislation in 1990 to crack down on banks and bank officers that aided drug dealers in hiding or "laundering" their profits.

But three separate bills (HR 3848, S 3037, HR 5889), burdened by the weight of election politics and unrelated initiatives, failed to clear before the 101st Congress adjourned.

Under the bills, banks, thrifts and credit unions could have received the financial equivalent of the death penalty — revocation of their charters or termination of their federal deposit insurance — if found guilty of laundering money. Bank officials caught engaging in money-laundering schemes could have been permanently barred from working in a financial institution. Reporting requirements for cash transactions also would have been stiffened.

The House passed HR 3848 by a 406-0 vote on April 25, and the Senate passed S 3037 by voice vote Oct. 5. Neither chamber, however, took up the other's bill. When it appeared the issue would die with adjournment, the House passed a new bill (HR 5889) by voice vote on Oct. 26, but the Senate never considered it.

Despite the overwhelming support for money-laundering legislation, the weight of the add-ons was too much for lawmakers to bear.

In addition to money-laundering provisions, for example, S 3037 included language from many other, more controversial bills. Among the other provisions were ones to require a redesign of the back of the nation's circulating coins; to require banks, other depository institutions and mutual funds to use a standardized method of computing the annual yield on savings and investments; and to require mortgage lenders to provide copies of house appraisals to applicants. *(Coin redesign, p. 135)*

Background

Drug dealers frequently used bank deposits to make it appear that their cash transactions came from legitimate businesses. Often, large bank deposits were made through the cooperation of corrupt employees or under the guise of a front company.

To detect laundering schemes in the United States, Congress in 1970 passed the Bank Secrecy Act (PL 91-508), which required banks to file a currency transaction report for every large cash transaction. *(Congress and the Nation Vol. III, p. 145)*

Major anti-drug bills cleared in 1986 (PL 99-570) and 1988 (PL 100-690) strengthened the statute by making money laundering a felony, authorizing "sting" operations and requiring the government to negotiate anti-money-laundering agreements with other countries. *(Congress and the Nation Vol. VII, pp. 723, 748)*

Legislative History

House Action. The House Banking Subcommittee on Financial Institutions approved HR 3848 by voice vote on March 8. The subcommittee agreed to give regulators discretion in determining whether to take control of an institution convicted of money laundering. As originally drafted, the bill would have made the sanctions mandatory.

Other provisions of the bill would have:

- Permanently barred any person convicted of money laundering or structuring transactions to evade reporting requirements from working in a financial institution.
- Provided "safe harbor" civil action protection to people who in good faith reported suspicious transactions.
- Provided state financial institution regulators with access to currency transaction reports, maintained by the Treasury Department on cash transactions of $10,000 or more.
- Required Treasury to report annually to Congress for the following three years on the use of the reports.

The full Banking Committee approved the measure by voice vote March 22. The bill was formally reported April 3 (H Rept 101-446).

Committee debate centered on how to stop narcotics traffickers from using the wire-transfer system to funnel billions of dollars of drug profits in and out of the country. The committee agreed to a compromise giving the Treasury Department discretionary authority to require recordkeeping for large wire transfers.

Wire transfers played a central part of drug trafficking. The Federal Reserve estimated that every day $1 trillion was moved through international wire transfers, making it easy for drug profits to be overlooked in the shuffle.

The House passed HR 3848 on April 25 by a vote of 406-0, after rejecting an amendment to require banks to keep records on wire transfers.

Senate Action. On July 17, the Senate Banking Committee approved a draft money-laundering bill, which was similar to the House measure. The Banking Committee bill was introduced and formally reported on Sept. 12 (S 3037 — S Rept 101-460).

Panel members also agreed to lump provisions from other legislative initiatives into the bill to improve the chances that all the measures would be considered by the Senate.

The other measures included:

- Truth-in-savings requirements that would have stipulated that institutions use a standardized method to calculate the yield on savings accounts and investments (S 307).
- A phased-in redesign of coins in general circulation (S 428).
- Steps to further deter the counterfeiting of U.S. currency (S 2748).
- New requirements on how long an institution could put a hold on deposits from automated teller machines.

The Senate passed S 3037 by voice vote Oct. 5.

Final Action. Though S 3037 passed the Senate, some Republicans objected to provisions unrelated to money laundering as needless burdens on banks. Those objections and others appeared to block the convening of a conference committee on the House- and Senate-passed measures.

Some Democrats charged that the real reason for Republican objections was politics. The Senate bill's principal sponsor, John Kerry, D-Mass., was facing a tough re-election fight and might have been aided by the bill's enactment, Democrats said.

In hope that the Senate might accept a "clean" money-laundering bill, the House passed HR 5889 by voice vote on Oct. 26. The measure had been introduced just four days earlier. The Senate never acted on it, however.

Coin Redesign

Despite multiple efforts that extended into the waning hours of the 101st Congress, proponents of redesigning the nation's circulating coins failed to get their proposal enacted into law.

The prime sponsors of the coin redesign effort, Sen. Alan Cranston, D-Calif., and Rep. Henry B. Gonzalez, D-Texas, championed bills to require the federal Mint to redesign the backs of the five major coins — the penny, nickel, dime, quarter and half dollar. The redesigns were to reflect themes embodied in the Constitution.

When their stand-alone bills (S 428, HR 505) failed to move in 1990, the provisions of S 428 were attached to a handful of other measures. They included several that died upon adjournment, among them a money-laundering bill (HR 3848) and a bill naming a Postal Service building in Cleveland for former Olympic track star Jesse Owens (HR 5235).

Coin-redesign provisions were added to and then stricken from an omnibus housing reauthorization bill (S 566) and the 1990 budget-reconciliation bill (HR 5835), both of which cleared Oct. 27, the last full day of the session. It was on the housing bill that redesign proponents placed their greatest efforts and came closest to achieving their goals. *(Housing, p. 665; reconciliation, p. 55; money laundering, p. 134)*

Gonzalez and Cranston, who had walked over from the Senate, lobbied members on the House floor repeatedly in the final days of the session as they continued to look for vehicles that might carry the coin measure to enactment. "They've stuck it on everything but the Pledge of Allegiance," complained House Rules Committee Chairman Joe Moakley, D-Mass.

Despite their positions as Senate Democratic whip and chairman of the House Banking Committee, respectively, Cranston and Gonzalez were unable to get their way. The Bush administration mounted strong opposition to the redesign idea in the closing days of the Congress. And strong opposition also existed from other key members of Congress.

Background

Except for the years 1976-77, when the reverse sides of the quarter and half dollar were temporarily changed to commemorate the bicentennial of the Declaration of Independence, the last major coin redesign had been in 1964, when the John F. Kennedy half dollar was first minted. Proponents said the time for another redesign had come.

The prime mover behind the effort was Diane Wolf, a prominent Upper East Side New York socialite. A contributor to Republican campaigns, Wolf was appointed to the U.S. Commission on Fine Arts by President Ronald Reagan in 1985. The main task of the seven-member fine arts commission was to oversee the architectural appearance of government buildings in the District of Columbia. But since the term of President Warren G. Harding (1921-23), the commission also was authorized to review coin designs. So, starting in 1987, Wolf used her seat on the commission to press her case.

Through constant visits to members, Wolf signed up a majority of the Senate and nearly half the House on coin redesign bills in 1987. Though a bill passed the Senate twice in 1988, it died in the 100th Congress. Bills were quickly reintroduced in both chambers in 1989. The Senate passed one redesign bill in 1989, but it saw no action in the House. *(Congress and the Nation Vol. VII, p. 136)*

Wolf was aided in her efforts by the nation's numismatists, who wanted new coins to collect and promoted the idea of new designs in their publications. Wolf called the old designs "ordinary and boring" and said the public would be happy to see them replaced.

Critics, though, pointed out that the Mint was authorized to redesign the reverse sides of all coins after they had been in circulation 25 years. Its reluctance to do so before the lobbying efforts of Wolf and the numismatists, they said, reflected serious doubt that the public wanted a change in the coin designs. All five major coins had long passed their 25th anniversaries; the oldest extant design, on the quarter, dated to 1932.

Legislative History

Although a majority in both chambers had cosponsored redesign bills (HR 505, S 428), backing was soft and some opposition was strong.

The House Banking Subcommittee on Consumer Affairs and Coinage held hearings on HR 505 in 1989, but opposition to the legislation from subcommittee members prevented it from being considered by subcommittee or full committee.

The Senate passed S 428 by voice vote on June 23, 1989, without the Banking Committee having considered it. The House never acted on the bill.

On June 19, 1990, the Senate added the text of S 428 to the housing bill (S 566). House and Senate conferees on S 566 agreed to a coin-redesign provision — offering redesign proponents their best shot at enacting their plan. House conferees voted 7-5 on Oct. 15, 1990 — with only Democrats in favor and Republicans opposed — to accept the Senate coin language. The housing bill conference report (H Rept 101-922) was filed Oct. 22.

But a rank-and-file revolt against coin redesign caused an uproar on the housing bill and the budget-reconciliation bill (HR 5835) as the 101st Congress rushed to adjourn. Housing bill supporters became afraid that antagonism to the coin language could sink the first major housing bill in 10 years. So, conferees on S 566 called the measure back and issued a new conference report that did not include the coin provision. The new conference report (H Rept 101-943) was filed Oct. 25. A similar concern caused conferees on the reconciliation bill to strip the coin language from that bill's conference report (H Rept 101-964), which was filed Oct. 27.

1991-92

Just as the 101st Congress was momentous in the enactment of a sweeping overhaul of federal laws governing the savings and loan industry, the 102nd Congress was significant for its reform of the nation's deposit insurance system for banks and thrifts.

Thrift failures had dominated the news in the late 1980s, but the early 1990s were filled with reports of bank failures. Dire predictions were heard that the insurance fund protecting bank depositors was in danger of being bankrupted and might need a taxpayer bailout not unlike that for the thrift industry insurance fund.

At the same time, the cost of the thrift bailout was rising rapidly. And Congress was asked repeatedly to pump additional cash into the salvage operation. It was a task that members abhorred, and with which they did not always comply.

Congress in 1991-92 had a mixed record on other regulatory fronts, succeeding in enacting bills to stiffen oversight of some so-called government-sponsored enterprises but failing to enact a string of measures aimed at curbing abuses in the financial marketplace.

Banking Overhaul

Faced with a rising tide of bank failures and their potential consequence — bankruptcy for the federal fund that protected bank depositors — Congress moved expeditiously in 1991 to overhaul the nation's deposit insurance system and to pump needed cash into the insurance fund.

With just hours to spare, House and Senate conferees reached agreement on a comprehensive deposit insurance bill (S 543 — H Rept 102-407) on Nov. 27, following an all-night session that concluded at dawn on the last day of the session. Congressional aides rushed to prepare legislative language for the 437-page bill, and as soon as they were finished, the House adopted the conference report by voice vote. As almost the last act of the session, the Senate did likewise by a vote of 68-15, clearing the bill. President Bush signed the measure (PL 102-242) on Dec. 19.

As enacted, S 543 gave the Federal Deposit Insurance Corporation (FDIC) authority to borrow up to $30 billion to cover depositor losses in failed banks. An additional amount (roughly $45 billion) could be borrowed to acquire assets from failed banks that would be sold later. All the borrowing costs (including interest) were to be covered by insurance premiums levied on banks and by the proceeds from asset sales. In addition, the FDIC and other bank regulators were given broad new powers to prevent banks from taking risks that would expose them to failure and to close weak banks before their capital was completely exhausted and their failure caused a loss to the insurance fund.

What Congress was unable to do in 1991 was to repeal or otherwise radically revise a half-century's worth of laws restricting the activities of the nation's banks. Bush had asked for such a revision, in addition to the deposit insurance overhaul, to make banks more profitable and less subject to the failures that had plagued the nation's financial system.

Congress came close to agreeing with the president — much closer than in 1988, when a more limited banking law overhaul bill never reached the House floor. *(Congress and the Nation Vol. VII, p. 114)*

The administration's proposal survived markup in the House Banking Committee, and in many respects it also survived in the Senate Banking Committee markup. But key elements never faced floor votes in either chamber. Deal-making intended to expedite passage caused many controversial changes to be dropped without votes.

In the end, the broader administration effort succumbed to institutional doubts, to a serious lack of consensus among lawmakers who wanted some change but could not agree on how much and, most importantly, to pressure from assorted interest groups that opposed wholesale change. Ironically, Democrats helped lead the administration's charge; Republicans provided key opposition.

The House voted on three separate banking bills in 1991, each progressively narrower. The first two — HR 6 and HR 2094 — were rejected by the full House. The third — HR 3768 — was passed and provided the basis for the conference agreement that eventually cleared.

The Senate moved significantly more slowly than the House, deferring markup on its bill (S 543) until a month after the House Banking Committee approved HR 6. Senate floor action on S 543 did not begin until after the House voted to kill HR 6, but it concluded within hours of the House having passed HR 3768.

Background

The Bush administration on Feb. 5 unveiled a long-awaited plan to overhaul the nation's financial system. The proposal was an outgrowth of the savings and loan crisis and was ordained by the 1989 thrift salvage law (HR 1278 — PL 101-73), which required the Treasury Department to study the nation's deposit insurance system. Treasury used the opportunity to propose sweeping changes in banking laws to complement deposit insurance reforms. *(Thrift bailout, p. 117)*

Treasury proposed to sweep clean an array of laws that prevented banks from being owned by large commercial conglomerates, from opening branch offices across state lines and from expanding into securities, insurance and other arenas. At the same time, it proposed putting stiff new limits on deposit insurance coverage and streamlining federal bank regulation.

Few surprises were found in the 700-page administration report, "Modernizing the Financial System," except that Treasury officials at first brushed aside concerns that the FDIC's Bank Insurance Fund was desperately in need of cash. The administration's initial legislative proposal ignored the FDIC's immediate problem, and only weeks later did officials submit a plan for replenishing the fund.

Many members of Congress knew, however, that the money issue would drive the debate. It would be the engine that could pull along a bill making other changes in the banking system.

Reserves in the Bank Insurance Fund had been declining steadily under pressure from more than 1,000 bank failures since 1985. In 1990, Congress had voted to put a temporary patch to the problem by removing a statutory cap on deposit insurance premium increases. That, however, was seen as an inadequate solution. *(Deposit insurance premiums, box, p. 124)*

Every report from the FDIC, the General Accounting Office (GAO), the Congressional Budget Office (CBO) and outside experts was more depressing than the one before.

Credit Card Rate Cap

Like a fleeting comet, the idea of Congress voting to mandate a nationwide cap on credit card interest rates flared brightly for a week in mid-November 1991 and quickly disappeared.

Just days after the Senate voted in favor of such a cap — and House Democratic leaders rushed to sign on — House Speaker Thomas S. Foley, D-Wash., went before television cameras on Nov. 18 to urge restraint. "I suggest that the Banking Committee consider any action on credit card rates very, very carefully," Foley said. He added that a study of competition in rates "would be useful," and he suggested that Congress might vote for one. But that did not happen.

Campaign Rhetoric

The furor was set off by a last-minute insertion in a Nov. 11 campaign fund-raising speech, in which President Bush called for lower credit card rates.

Two days later, the Senate voted 74-19 in favor of a rate cap proposed by Alfonse M. D'Amato, R-N.Y. D'Amato's proposal came as an amendment to a broad banking overhaul bill (S 543). *(Banking bill, p. 136)*

Foley and other Democratic leaders immediately predicted that the House would join the Senate's action. But in the days that followed, banks threatened to pull back credit cards from perhaps half of those who had them, bank stocks tumbled, the obscure but huge market in securities backed by credit card debt was rocked and the Dow Jones industrial average plunged 120 points. The Nov. 15 drop was the fifth-largest numerical decline in the Dow's history, and analysts said weakness in bank stocks was a factor.

Treasury Secretary Nicholas F. Brady appeared on the NBC News program "Meet the Press" on Nov. 17, calling D'Amato's amendment "wacky, senseless legislation."

By the end of the week of Nov. 18, a House Banking subcommittee had scheduled, and then postponed indefinitely, a credit card bill markup. Several members went to work to craft a bill calling for a study of rate caps that would produce results, and not upset financial markets, but no committee action on such a bill occurred.

D'Amato Amendment

The D'Amato cap, which was tied to the interest charged by the Internal Revenue Service on overdue tax payments, would have produced a 14 percent rate cap at the time the amendment was being considered.

But the amendment was quietly dropped in conference on S 543, without ever being discussed publicly by conferees, not even D'Amato.

They all concluded that the insurance fund would be technically insolvent by the end of 1991. A month before the administration released its plan to reform the industry, the problem had made national headlines, with the Jan. 6 failure of the Bank of New England. That failure, expected to cost the FDIC $2.3 billion, brought the problem home to taxpayers who were still reeling from the cost of salvaging the savings and loan industry.

No one wanted to talk about a taxpayer bailout of the banks — such as that enacted in 1989 for the insurance fund protecting savings and loan depositors. And none of the proposals on the table in 1991 called for infusion of taxpayer money. All costs were to be borne by the industry itself. But that was a difficult point to get across, and in the face of the thrift crisis, it carried a hollow ring.

Larger banks immediately praised the administration proposal as a way to consolidate and strengthen the banking industry. At the same time, smaller banks and insurance agents, who stood to lose out to big financial conglomerates, opposed the proposal. Consumer groups also complained, worrying about the costs and dangers associated with banking consolidation.

The securities industry, long opposed to sharing its business with banks, called the Treasury plan "innovative," though in need of changes. That stance reflected the industry's weakened state, after years of riding a Wall Street roller coaster.

But it also grew from a split in the industry's position. Despite the 1933 Glass-Steagall Act, which was supposed to keep banks out of the securities business, bank regulators and the courts in recent years had allowed banks to make inroads into both securities dealing and underwriting. Some securities firms continued to oppose repealing Glass-Steagall, at least unless stiff new rules were imposed on actions between banks and their affiliated securities companies. Others, however, saw an opportunity to benefit from affiliations with banks and were willing to permit the change — but only in the context of full-blown commercial affiliations with banks, because many securities houses had non-financial subsidiaries. *(Glass-Steagall, background, Congress and the Nation Vol. VII, p. 118)*

Before the year was out, however, the split in the securities industry was papered over, thanks to the efforts of John D. Dingell, D-Mich., chairman of the House Energy and Commerce Committee. The most outspoken and powerful opponent of the administration's plan for change, Dingell erected the roadblocks that derailed the broader bill. And, as he did in 1988, Dingell proved to be the most important force preventing change in the banking industry.

On the other side, no such central player came forward. Except for the incipient crisis in the bank deposit insurance fund, no apparent urgency drove the overhaul proposal. Many members believed that they had more to lose than to gain if they granted banks broad new powers and found that a taxpayer bailout of the insurance fund would be required somewhere down the road.

House Action on HR 6

The House spent much of 1991 preparing for, debating and finally rejecting the broad administration proposal.

House Banking Chairman Henry B. Gonzalez, D-Texas, and the panel's ranking Republican, Chalmers P. Wylie of Ohio, each introduced deposit insurance bills on the opening day of the 102nd Congress (HR 6, HR 15). Both were "narrow" by the standard set a month later. Neither addressed the broader issues of banking law that the administration said were so crucial. (HR 6 would later be used to carry the broad administration plan to the House floor.) Along with Senate Banking Committee Chairman Donald W. Riegle Jr., D-Mich., both Gonzalez and Wylie said they thought overhauling the deposit insurance system was crucial before making other changes.

That question — whether to pass a narrow deposit insurance bill first — was to dominate the banking debate all year.

Another major issue was how to provide the necessary cash for the Bank Insurance Fund. Disagreement on that point was one reason that the administration failed to include a financing plan in its initial reform proposal.

The administration finally released the text of its banking bill March 20, complete with an FDIC replenishment plan. The Treasury plan called for the FDIC to borrow up to $25 billion from the Federal Reserve System. But Fed Chairman Alan Greenspan rejected that idea on April 23 in testimony to the Senate Banking Committee. He said the move would send the wrong signal to world markets about the Fed's role and its independence. He added that no economic benefit existed to borrowing from the Fed instead of the Treasury.

Some members had their own plans, but multiple trial balloons over how to finance a replenishment eventually burst, leaving only the idea of a loan from the Treasury. By May, that was the informally agreed upon plan and the only issue on the table not to be debated again all year.

Gonzalez and Wylie agreed to work together on a narrow banking bill that would replenish the insurance fund and make changes in the deposit insurance system in an effort to protect taxpayers and restore public confidence. They said they would shelve for the time being the broader administration package — especially proposals to give banks wide new investment powers and allow commercial enterprises to own banks. In April, Gonzalez introduced a new, narrow FDIC replenishment and deposit insurance overhaul bill (HR 2094) that followed the outlined strategy.

Under pressure from the White House and fellow Republicans, Wylie backed away from the narrow-bill strategy. And some Banking Committee Democrats also expressed a desire not to abandon the administration effort. It was agreed that the committee would pursue a two-bill approach: A narrow bill to replenish the insurance fund and overhaul the deposit insurance system would be crafted and held in reserve, to be sent to the floor only if the committee failed to approve a broader bill by the end of June. The scheduling agreement appeared to satisfy all sides.

Banking Subcommittee Action. Action on both the broad and narrow banking bills got under way May 7 in the Financial Institutions Subcommittee, where HR 2094 — the narrow measure — was approved by a 34-1 vote. (The text of HR 2094 was later to become the first title of the broader bill — HR 6.) The narrow bill, which contained a $30 billion line of credit for the FDIC with the Treasury (actually a $25 billion increase from an existing $5 billion line of credit), also would have made numerous changes in the deposit insurance system. Most of them were not controversial.

In addition to providing money to the FDIC, the bill, as approved in subcommittee, would have required closer supervision of banks and quicker regulatory action against those headed for insolvency. Most significantly, it would have altered dramatically the method used most often by the FDIC to close the books on failed banks and cover their insured deposits. The intent was to save money by ending the practice of granting de facto 100 percent insurance coverage in nearly every case.

The issue of de facto 100 percent insurance was part of a bigger fight over the FDIC's so-called too-big-to-fail policy, under which some banks were deemed to be so critical to the nation's financial system that the FDIC stepped in and covered all deposits, and often all creditors, when the bank failed. The subcommittee did not directly address that issue in marking up HR 2094. It did strike language from the bill that would have restricted lending by the Fed to weak banks to no more than five days in a three-month period. Opponents of too-big-to-fail argued that Fed lending to weak banks was an integral part of that policy.

The tough deposit insurance issues — rolling back coverage and ending too-big-to-fail — were all set aside for the following week, when the subcommittee began work on the broader bill.

The subcommittee approved the broad bill (still in draft form) on May 23, by a vote of 36-0. It was an overwhelming victory for the administration, which lost only one significant battle during five long days of work on the measure. Banking industry lobbyists said they were amazed. Treasury officials beamed. And members of the subcommittee gave Chairman Frank Annunzio, D-Ill., a standing ovation.

As approved by the subcommittee, the bill would have torn away an imperfect statutory barrier to banks engaging in securities activities. It would have opened the door to indirect ownership of banks by non-bank businesses, an even more radical idea that included allowing banks to affiliate indirectly with real estate and insurance companies. It would have allowed banks to open branch offices nearly unfettered across state lines. And it would have preserved existing deposit insurance rules for individuals, effectively allowing multiple accounts at a single institution, each insured up to $100,000.

The latter provision was the only major instance where the subcommittee parted with the administration. The administration wanted to roll back coverage to $100,000 per individual per bank and ultimately to restrict it to $100,000 nationwide.

Banking Committee Action. Action on HR 6 in the full Banking Committee got under way slowly June 19 and 20. But the following week, the committee picked up steam. (HR 2094 remained on the shelf, in compliance with the two-bill strategy.) On June 28, after six days of markup during which 160 amendments were considered, the panel agreed to a broad banking overhaul bill that was little changed from the subcommittee version. Most issues that were left untouched in subcommittee were addressed by the full panel, and some votes were close. But the administration bill survived largely intact.

The committee agreed to send HR 6 to the House floor by a 31-20 vote, after amending HR 6 — Gonzalez's original narrow bill — with the much broader language that won acceptance in committee. The bill was formally reported July 23 (H Rept 102-157, Part I).

The committee showed no hesitation about the need to restructure the financial services industry. Only three years before, the House had failed to act on a comparatively minor effort to repeal restrictions on bank activities. But in 1991, wholesale change was the order of the day in the Banking Committee.

Treasury Department lobbyists, who fought off repeated assaults on the bill, prevailed at almost every turn. An amendment to strike the section permitting commercial ownership of banks failed June 26 on a 20-32 vote.

The issue of rolling back deposit insurance rose again, as in subcommittee only to be knocked down by united bank opposition.

Gonzalez had one major victory, extracting a compromise that the Federal Reserve would not have free rein in the future to pump cash into weak banks. The Fed would be able to do so but only at the risk of incurring a loss that would be passed along to taxpayers. That was intended to give the Fed second thoughts and was a key element in Gonzalez's hope to put an end to the doctrine that some banks were too big to fail.

The committee abandoned an effort to restructure the maze of federal bank and thrift regulatory agencies. The Treasury had halfheartedly backed one reorganization plan, but the subcommittee knocked it out of the bill and substituted nothing in its place. Turf fights and an inability to cut the Gordian knot led the full committee also to abandon the effort.

Following the Banking Committee action, HR 6 was referred to the Agriculture, Energy and Commerce, Judiciary, and Ways and Means committees until Oct. 4, ensuring a rush to complete action before adjournment, then set for mid-October. The multiple referrals were directly related to a developing opposition strategy by insurance agents, securities firms, small banks and consumer groups, all of which were unhappy with the Banking Committee bill.

Energy and Commerce Committee Action. The Energy and Commerce Subcommittee on Finance and the companion Subcommittee on Commerce, Consumer Protection and Competitiveness each met Sept. 16 and rejected major portions of the reform agenda put forth by the administration and bigger banks.

Without adopting a single controversial amendment, the Finance Subcommittee approved draft language put forward by Subcommittee Chairman Edward J. Markey, D-Mass., and full committee Chairman Dingell, focusing chiefly on securities issues. The subcommittee bill would have allowed banks and securities firms to join forces, but only in the most restricted of ways.

The only controversy arose over a Republican amendment intended to preserve a portion of the administration proposal to allow broad ownership of banks. Matthew J. Rinaldo, R-N.J., proposed that non-banking businesses be allowed at least to buy failing banks — to bring new capital to the banking industry and save the deposit insurance fund from paying to close some failed banks.

The amendment was defeated on an essentially party-line vote of 11-15.

The Competitiveness Subcommittee approved language drafted by Chairman Cardiss Collins, D-Ill., that was mostly intended to limit banks' ability to get into the insurance business, in the process rolling back opportunities for banks that were permitted by existing law.

Both subcommittees approved their versions of HR 6 by voice vote.

The full Energy and Commerce Committee met Sept. 25 and on a 29-12 vote ratified nearly all the actions of the two subcommittees. The bill was formally reported Oct. 4 (H Rept 102-157, Part IV), and the committee filed a supplemental report Oct. 7 (H Rept 102-157, Part VI).

Particularly galling to bankers were the high fire walls that Energy and Commerce wanted to erect to restrict financial connections between a bank and its securities affiliate. But Energy and Commerce members agreed to mute one key fire wall provision approved in subcommittee that would have virtually ensured that a securities firm affiliated with a bank would get little business from companies that were customers of the bank.

And Rinaldo's bank ownership amendment was again rejected on a party-line vote, 15-26.

Agriculture Committee Action. The Agriculture Committee also met Sept. 25, in the process handing smaller banks and consumer groups a victory by taking a swipe at the interstate branching provisions of HR 6.

The committee had sought referral of the bill on the basis of narrow but serious concerns about a series of provisions relating to failed banks and their role in the settlement of contracts for future delivery of commodities.

But by the time the panel met, concerns about branching had attracted the attention of committee members, who expressed fears that nationwide branching by large banks might reduce competition in rural areas and shrink the amount of credit available to farmers. The committee adopted an amendment to HR 6 that would have forced federal regulators to review the lending operations of interstate branches under certain conditions, to ensure that deposits were not being siphoned out of rural areas.

The committee approved HR 6 by voice vote Sept. 25 and formally reported the measure Oct. 4 (H Rept 102-157, Part III).

Judiciary Committee Action. Despite pressure from small banks and consumer groups to wade into the branching issue, the Judiciary Committee agreed Oct. 3 to approve two relatively narrow amendments to HR 6. The panel approved the bill by voice vote Oct. 3 and formally reported it Oct. 7 (H Rept 102-157, Part V).

Big-bank critics hoped that Judiciary Chairman Jack Brooks, D-Texas, would use his panel's jurisdiction over antitrust matters to restrain interstate branching. But Brooks did not seem interested.

Ways and Means Committee Action. Ways and Means was the only committee to adopt amendments that would not change the banking regulatory core of the bill. The committee's interest was chiefly in a provision of HR 6 that would allow the FDIC to raise cash by selling bonds to banks — instead of by borrowing from the Treasury.

Ways and Means met Sept. 25 and adopted two non-controversial amendments to HR 6, both by voice vote. The committee approved the bill by voice vote and formally reported it Sept. 26 (H Rept 102-157, Part II).

Seeking a Compromise. As other committees weighed in and pressure mounted against the Banking Committee version of HR 6, Gonzalez repeatedly lashed out at the wide scope of his panel's bill and at the delay that had effectively halted action since his committee acted at the end of June. Gonzalez also complained that Treasury Secretary Nicholas F. Brady had backed away from the pressure he had put on Congress earlier in the year to act to replenish the insurance fund.

After Energy and Commerce had taken steps to thwart the Banking Committee's intent, members of that panel met to decide whether to go forward or to retreat to the narrow-bill approach long advocated by Gonzalez. Banking Committee Democrats informally agreed at a two-hour closed-door caucus Oct. 3 to press forward with HR 6.

Some Democrats on the committee joined Gonzalez in opposition to its broad sweep. Others said they would have preferred a narrow bill to avoid a bloody showdown on the floor and to expedite action on replenishing the insurance fund. But most wanted to move ahead. The action allied a majority of the panel's Democrats with a nearly united phalanx of House Republicans and with the administration in preparation for the upcoming floor fight.

The jockeying for position between supporters and opponents of HR 6 continued well into October, but the die was cast the week of Oct. 21, when Gonzalez struck a deal with Dingell that undermined the position of his committee colleagues. In essence, Gonzalez agreed to a substitute for the key title of the bill governing bank affiliations with securities, insurance and commercial companies. It was based largely on the Energy and Commerce version of the bill.

The compromise would not have permitted commercial companies to own banks; it would have imposed higher and thicker fire walls than those in the Banking Committee version of HR 6; and, in most instances, the insurance sales activities of banks would have been more severely limited than they were in the Banking Committee version or existing law. At the same time, Dingell dropped demands for new regulation of banks by the Securities and Exchange Commission that would have enhanced his panel's jurisdiction over the banking industry.

Floor Action. Concern had been building for weeks that with a pre-Thanksgiving adjournment target looming and no floor action yet on a banking bill, Congress might quit for the year without shoring up the insurance fund. The Gonzalez-Dingell compromise cleared the way for House floor action beginning Oct. 30 — even if it did not please all parties.

In the end, the deal did not come close to helping pass the bill. During four days on the floor, HR 6 barely survived two procedural votes that would have killed it. Then it was overwhelmingly rejected on Nov. 4 by a **key vote of 89-324 (R 6-153; D 83-170; I 0-1)**. *(1991 key votes, p. 1061)*

One other crucial vote on Oct. 31 came on an amendment by Doug Barnard Jr., D-Ga., to strike the Gonzalez-Dingell bank-powers language from the bill. For years, Barnard had been the leading House supporter of allowing new investment and affiliation powers for banking companies. However, the restrictions contained in the compromise persuaded him that the best course would be to have nothing in the bill on that subject. The amendment to strike the Gonzalez-Dingell compromise was defeated 200-216.

The narrow vote and growing concern that no committee consensus existed on such important issues began weighing heavily against the bill. By midafternoon Nov. 4, finding a member who planned to back the bill on final passage was difficult. An effort to whip up support fizzled, and HR 6 was defeated overwhelmingly that evening. Almost all the support came from Democrats, but only 12 of 31 Banking Committee Democrats and 17 of 27 Energy and Commerce Democrats voted for the bill.

House Action on HR 2094, HR 3768

Following the defeat of HR 6, supporters of broad changes in banking law began scrambling to preserve as much of the bill as possible. In the weeks leading up to the floor vote on HR 6, the administration had given up much of its overhaul plan.

Following the overwhelming vote on HR 6, Brady conceded that Congress would not agree in 1991 to allow commercial companies to own banks or to allow banks to affiliate with securities firms. (The Senate bill never included the former provision and the latter was dropped unceremoniously from the Senate bill after the House vote on HR 6.) Interstate branching was the last remaining major piece of the package. It was still in the Senate bill — and Brady was not yet of a mind to give that up, even though most of the banking industry had. The fight in the House then became one over how to preserve interstate branching.

As a result, the House walked the plank on a second banking bill (HR 2094) that was amended on the floor to permit interstate branching. That bill was defeated handily Nov. 14.

Finally, a very narrow bill (HR 3768) aimed solely at overhauling the deposit insurance system and replenishing the insurance fund passed.

Committee Action on HR 2094. On Nov. 6, two days after HR 6 was rejected, the House Banking Committee quickly met to send HR 2094 to the floor. The bill had been held in abeyance since it was marked up in subcommittee the first week of May.

The committee voted somewhat reluctantly to discard almost all that was in the first bill, retaining only those provisions designed to keep the deposit insurance system afloat. An amended version of HR 2094 contained the first of six titles in HR 6. But in that form, the bill was plainly too narrow for anyone's taste and stood no chance of passage. The committee then approved the narrow bill, 37-15. The bill was formally reported the next day (H Rept 102-293).

Floor Action on HR 2094. Following the committee action, it was plain that the interstate branching issue was not dead. So House leaders held lengthy negotiations among members, interest groups and administration officials over how to structure floor amendments to win support for the measure.

Vote-counting, not careful consideration of public policy, drove the backroom discussions, particularly because at least 100 — and maybe many more — of the 267 Democrats in the House likely would vote against anything related to a banking bill.

Administration officials said Nov. 7 that they would insist that any bill allow banks to open branches freely across state lines, but they signaled a willingness to accept some restraints that might be imposed by the states. And the administration negotiated with some bankers and with insurance agents to craft a compromise that would put restrictions on the existing ability of some banks to sell insurance across state lines.

The negotiations eventually yielded two substantive floor amendments, one of which was non-controversial.

The other allowed interstate branching but rolled back some existing bank powers to sell insurance and sealed forever a closed window for banks to operate real estate brokerages. Although insurance and real estate agents often appeared invincible on Capitol Hill, they were able to muster only the barest majority for the amendment. It was adopted 210-208 on Nov. 14.

An odd coalition then formed to kill the measure. Virtually the entire banking industry opposed the bill, joined by many of the banks' sharpest critics, including consumer groups and securities firms that did not want banks invading their turf. At the same time, nearly a third of House Republicans voted "nay," despite a personal appeal by Bush. The bill failed 191-227 on Nov. 14.

Action on HR 3768. With the defeat of a second major banking bill in little more than a week, House leaders clearly saw that only a narrow bill could win support on the floor. Administration officials reluctantly conceded the point.

The Banking Committee met Nov. 19 and approved HR 3768 by a vote of 44-7. The bill was formally reported the same day (H Rept 102-330).

As introduced, HR 3768 was virtually identical to the version of HR 2094 that was rejected — not including the controversial interstate branching amendment. The markup did not go as swiftly as hoped, however, and Gonzalez, in league with Wylie, fought off several amendments.

The Rules Committee met the following day and agreed to allow no amendments on the floor.

Floor debate Nov. 21 was largely desultory and almost entirely in support of the bill — though little of it was enthusiastic. Gerald B. H. Solomon, R-N.Y., an ally of the insurance agents, was the only member to forcefully oppose the bill. Solomon, a member of the Rules Committee, was denied the chance to offer a floor amendment rolling back bank insurance powers.

Before the final vote, the House rejected 74-355 a procedural motion offered by Dick Armey, R-Texas, that would have had the effect of adding a frequently rejected amendment to pare back deposit insurance coverage to a single $100,000 account per person per bank. The House then passed the bill 344-84.

Senate Action

For much of the year, action in the Senate was confined to closed-door negotiations intended to satisfy a majority of the 21 members of the Banking Committee — and the banking, securities, insurance, consumer and administration interests that they represented.

Many of the same battles that were waged publicly in the House also were fought in the Senate — only in private. Formal action in the Senate lagged the House all year long, and as the House moved progressively toward a narrower bill, Senate deliberations did likewise.

Riegle was the leading advocate in the Senate of moving slowly: first replenishing the insurance fund, then overhauling the deposit insurance system generally and only later lifting limits on banking in a significant way. He had introduced a deposit insurance bill in late 1990 that served as an early model for elements of both the administration's bill and HR 6. Riegle's 1990 bill was revised and reintroduced in 1991 as S 543.

However, Riegle abandoned his narrow-bill approach under pressure from members of both parties who wanted to broaden the measure, in particular to permit interstate branching and to repeal Glass-Steagall. Thus he spent much of the spring and early summer in consultation with his committee members, trying to find a combination of provisions that would appeal to a majority in committee and on the floor.

Riegle released a draft bill July 16 without the endorsement of ranking committee Republican Jake Garn of Utah. It was far less bold than the administration or House Banking versions in key areas, and it clearly reflected the pressures that were being placed on the House bill — which was by then awaiting action in the House Energy and Commerce Committee.

Riegle's bill would not have permitted commercial companies to affiliate with banks. However, it would have allowed strong banks the right to affiliate with securities firms. And it would have put stricter limits on banks seeking to branch nationwide.

On some points, the measure was similar to HR 6. Riegle's approach to requiring banking regulators to move quickly to shut down failing banks was little changed from his 1990 bill. While differences in detail were apparent on that point with HR 6, the provisions were compatible in broad terms. Riegle's bill also would have provided the FDIC with a $30 billion line of credit with the Treasury, but with a number of refinements, including a swifter payback schedule and a controversial means of assessing banks for the cost.

Riegle's bill also contained a host of provisions not a part of any companion House measure, many of them controversial. Some would have created new consumer responsibilities for banks; others would have granted so-called lender liability protection to banks stuck with foreclosed real estate that turned out to contain toxic waste sites.

Riegle said his bill was as near to a consensus draft as could be prepared. But the measure drew immediate and antagonistic response from the interests that won biggest in the House Banking Committee and support from those who had lost. Administration officials were privately said to be deeply upset over parts of Riegle's bill, though publicly they were restrained.

Despite the brewing objections, Riegle decided to mark up the bill just before Congress left town for its August recess.

Banking Committee Action. Many accommodations and some tough votes were required as the committee struggled through three long days of markup July 31-Aug. 2.

In the last hours of markup, a contentious dispute over a series of amendments that would have tightened existing restraints on insurance activities by banks threatened to derail the process. Several were adopted, and Garn threatened at one point to walk out and stop the markup if yet another insurance amendment were offered.

In the end, the committee approved S 543 by a fairly close 12-9 vote. Riegle's bill suffered some bruises but remained remarkably intact. However, the final vote reflected the feeling of liberals that the measure went too far toward allowing banks into unchartered waters, and of conservatives that it did not go far enough.

The bill was formally reported Oct. 1 (S Rept 102-167).

Floor Action. Nearly two months after the committee voted, a draft report to the Senate was still circulating among committee members. With the administration eager for progress, Riegle blamed committee Republicans for the delay.

After the committee report was filed, the delay continued. As November approached, some hoped that the Senate could act roughly in tandem with the House. Much hinged on the Gonzalez-Dingell compromise on securities and insurance activities of banks. Members in both chambers believed that if the House were to accept the Gonzalez-Dingell compromise, the two bills would move close enough to each other that a House-Senate conference could quickly reconcile differences, increasing the likelihood that a broad banking bill could be enacted before Congress adjourned.

With the House defeat of HR 6 on Nov. 4, those plans were dashed. Nine days later, on Nov. 13, as the House prepared to take up the second of its three banking bills, S 543 finally came to the floor. The Senate made progress Nov. 13-14, disposing of several issues before the bill was sidetracked for the balance of that week by a protracted debate over extending unemployment benefits, and by the failure of the second bill in the House. *(Unemployment benefits, p. 721)*

The Senate returned to the bill the following week and slogged through nearly two dozen amendments, adopting 17. Riegle worked hard to push his committee's comprehensive bill through, cutting dozens of deals in the process. Many of those deals were accommodated in a 165-page "managers' amendment" adopted without debate by voice vote an hour before the bill finally passed.

On the evening of Nov. 21, in a sudden voice vote with fewer than 10 senators in the chamber, the Senate passed S 543. The action came within two hours of the House having passed HR 3768. The confluence of events appeared to be more than happenstance.

During the first two days of floor action, however, the Senate agreed to several changes that were seen by the bill's advocates as enhancing its chances of passage. The bill's language permitting banks and securities firms to affiliate was dropped, and modifications were made to the interstate branching and banking insurance sales sections.

Alfonse M. D'Amato, R-N.Y., surprised nearly everyone with an amendment to cap credit card interest rates. The amendment was adopted 74-19 on Nov. 13. With credit card rates averaging nearly 19 percent, many senators found the amendment difficult to oppose. *(Credit card cap, box, p. 137)*

Conference, Final Action

A two-day House-Senate conference that ended in a marathon overnight session Nov. 26-27 produced a compromise bill that did what all sides conceded was the bare minimum — and largely avoided controversy.

The conference concluded at 4:57 a.m., and the House adopted the conference agreement (H Rept 102-407) by voice vote six hours later, acting just as soon as congressional staff had finished piecing together the legislative language. The Senate adopted the conference agreement later in the afternoon, by a vote of 68-15, clearing the measure for the president.

Although all sides referred to what was passed as a narrow bill, it was hardly anorexic. The final bill weighed in at 437 pages and was still credited as a sweeping measure. The bill fulfilled the pressing need to replenish the nearly depleted Bank Insurance Fund by granting the FDIC a $30 billion line of credit with the Treasury to cover losses in failed banks. In addition, the bill made key changes in the deposit insurance system in an effort to further reduce losses to the fund.

But members resigned themselves to having done only half the job that they had been asked to do by the Bush administration and that many believed was necessary to prevent major bank failures in the future.

In the days immediately after the House and Senate passed HR 3768 and S 543, it was not clear that there would be a conference — or that differences between the bills could be reconciled before adjournment. On Nov. 25, however, the House finally asked for a conference on S 543, after amending it with the text of the much narrower HR 3768. The slim House bill was still 339 pages long. And the Senate bill, which contained a wealth of provisions with no counterpart in the House measure, was 829 pages.

The biggest outstanding question was how to deal with interstate branching. The House had twice rejected bills that would have allowed branching across state lines. Nevertheless, Riegle decided to try to preserve the provision. In the end, he could not generate a strong administration push for the branching language, and it was abandoned. The Senate also quietly dropped its credit card rate-cap amendment.

Most of what was solely in the Senate measure fell on the floor, including provisions that would have restricted the ability of banks to sell insurance, given banks some immunity from the costs of cleaning up toxic waste sites that they inherited through foreclosures and pressed other countries to grant U.S. banks and securities firms treatment similar to that given to their own firms (the so-called Fair Trade in Financial Services Act, which also was incorporated in other measures). *(Fair Trade in Financial Services, p. 198)*

Ultimately — although it took time to work through the complex bills and to settle differences that seemed more a matter of style than substance — few real fights occurred in conference and very few cases arose in which conferees had to vote to resolve matters.

The House forced the Senate to accept language marginally increasing supervision of credit unions, creating new FDIC programs to promote the disposition of low-income housing, giving incentives to banks that made loans in low-income neighborhoods and including the Truth-in-Savings Act. The Senate forced the House to drop language requiring state-chartered banks, thrifts and credit unions to obtain federal deposit insurance.

Major Provisions

As cleared, S 543 (PL 102-242):

Bank Insurance Fund Replenishment

- **Treasury Line of Credit.** Allowed the Federal Deposit Insurance Corporation to borrow up to $30 billion unsecured from the federal Treasury to cover losses in failed banks — principally to pay off insured depositors. Previously, the FDIC had a $5 billion line of credit with the Treasury, which it never tapped.
- **Working Capital.** Altered the statutory limit on other FDIC borrowing, chiefly used to provide temporary working capital for the purchase of assets from failed banks. Such borrowing was to be repaid from the proceeds of the assets when they were sold to another bank or to the general public. The bill allowed the FDIC to borrow from multiple sources (principally the Federal Financing Bank, an arm of the Treasury) an amount equal to 90 percent of the fair market value of the assets the agency took from

failed banks. Existing law allowed the FDIC to borrow up to nine times its net worth for working capital needs. But as the insurance fund neared insolvency, that limit became meaningless.

• **Borrowing from Banks.** Gave the FDIC the option of borrowing from banks instead of the Treasury to cover insurance fund losses. The borrowing was subject to the $30 billion cap on money borrowed to cover losses; it was subject to the public debt limit that governed general Treasury borrowing; and the bonds had to be priced identically to comparable Treasury issues, to hold down interest rates.

• **Repayment Schedule.** Required the Treasury and the FDIC to agree to a schedule of deposit insurance premium payments by banks to repay any money borrowed to cover FDIC losses plus interest. The FDIC and the Treasury were required to consult with the House and Senate Banking committees on repayment schedules, and the FDIC had to demonstrate that insurance premiums paid by banks were sufficient to meet the schedule. The FDIC also was authorized to adjust premiums at any time during the year and to set them at any level. Under existing law, premiums could only be raised at two specific times each year.

• **Emergency Special Assessments.** Allowed the FDIC to impose special premium assessments on bank deposits in addition to regular assessments to repay loans from the Treasury or from banks.

• **GAO Audit.** Required the General Accounting Office to report quarterly to Congress on the repayment of money borrowed by the FDIC from the Treasury and on the FDIC's success at estimating the market value of assets that it purchased with borrowed working capital.

• **Recapitalization Schedule.** Required the FDIC to devise a schedule of deposit insurance premiums to increase the Bank Insurance Fund's reserves to 1.25 percent of insured deposits within 15 years of enactment. The FDIC could adjust the recapitalization schedule but not in ways that would extend the deadline for meeting the required reserve ratio.

Deposit Insurance System Overhaul

• **Minimum Capital Requirements.** Required all federal banking regulators to review their minimum capital requirements for banks and thrifts every other year to ensure that they were sufficient to minimize losses to the deposit insurance funds. At least two standards were required — a leverage standard of total capital as measured against total assets and a risk-based standard of total capital as measured against assets that had been weighted for their relative riskiness. Similar standards existed previously for banks and thrifts. Regulators were permitted to impose additional standards employing other measures. Within 18 months, banking regulators would have to adjust their risk-based standards to account for the risks associated with fluctuations in interest rates, concentrations of loans and non-traditional activities. The Federal Reserve Board was required to discuss with foreign bank regulators similar changes to international risk-based capital standards.

• **Capital Levels.** Established five levels for measuring the capital of banks and thrifts. Supervision and enforcement actions were specified for an institution based on its capital level.

"Well-capitalized" institutions carried amounts of capital measured in several ways that significantly exceeded mandatory minimums. "Adequately capitalized" institutions met the minimum requirements. "Undercapitalized" institutions did not meet all minimums. "Significantly undercapitalized" institutions fell considerably short of minimums. And "critically undercapitalized" institutions failed to meet a "critical capital level."

Regulators were allowed to establish numerical minimums for each category, but the bill set the critical capital level at no less than 2 percent equity capital (excluding some items frequently included in calculations of total capital) as measured against total assets and at no more than 65 percent of the minimum standard. The critical capital level was to be used to trigger specific regulatory actions leading to closure of banks or thrifts. *(See prompt corrective action, below)*

• **Non-Capital Performance Standards.** Allowed regulators to downgrade the rating of a bank or thrift that was found to be operating in an unsafe and unsound manner. The new rating would have to be one level lower than that for which the bank or thrift would qualify based solely on its capital.

Regulators also could downgrade an institution if it were found to have less than satisfactory assets, management, earnings or liquidity — factors that were used along with capital in routine ratings.

• **Enhanced Supervision.** Required the FDIC and other banking regulators to devise standards to measure the operations and management of banks and thrifts, as well as the appropriate proportion of bad loans to total assets and the amount of earnings needed to offset loan losses.

As a part of these standards, federal regulators were required to determine at what point salaries and benefits to officers, employees, directors or stockholders constituted excessive compensation or could cause a material loss to an institution.

Banks and thrifts that failed to meet these standards were required to submit plans to overcome the shortfall. If they failed to do so, regulators could impose restrictions, including limiting the growth of assets, limiting interest rates paid on deposits and requiring an increase in capital.

In addition, unless a bank or thrift received explicit permission from federal regulators, it could not pay dividends to stockholders if doing so would cause the institution's capital to fall below minimum standards. Also, institutions could not pay management fees if doing so would cause them to become undercapitalized.

• **Prompt Corrective Action.** Required any undercapitalized (or worse) bank or thrift to submit a capital restoration plan showing how it would meet minimum standards without increasing its risk of failure, and prohibited any such institution from paying dividends until it met all minimum capital requirements.

Bank regulators could not approve a capital restoration plan unless any company having control over the bank or thrift (a bank or thrift holding company) guaranteed the bank's or thrift's compliance with the plan. The holding company would be liable for an amount up to 5 percent of the value of the bank or thrift, or the amount that would have been required to recapitalize the institution at the time it was found not to be in compliance, if that amount were less.

Regulators had to sharply limit the growth of undercapitalized banks, making exceptions only where asset growth was consistent with an approved capital restoration plan and equity capital was increasing according to schedule. Acquisitions and branching were permitted only where consistent with the plan, or where the FDIC chose to waive that requirement.

For significantly undercapitalized institutions (or those that failed to submit and act on capital restoration plans), the payment of salary increases and bonuses to officers was prohibited, and regulators were required to take other actions, such as requiring the sale of additional stock, prohibiting the acceptance of deposits from other banks and capping the interest paid on deposits. Additional actions could be ordered, including further restrictions on growth or a reduction in the bank's size; replacement of officers, directors or outside auditors; and sale of the bank or any affiliate that the regulators believed threatened the bank's health.

In addition, critically undercapitalized banks generally could not make interest or principal payments on subordinated debt (a class of bond that was not payable until all other creditors were satisfied and that often counted as capital) issued after July 15, 1991. And the FDIC was generally required to prohibit such institutions from making material changes in their business.

• **Prompt Closure.** Required federal banking regulators to take control of (by appointing a conservator) or seize and close (by appointing a receiver) any bank or thrift that failed to maintain capital in excess of the critical capital level, unless an alternative action was more likely to protect the deposit insurance fund.

Notwithstanding contrary state laws, regulators were required to take action within 90 days after an institution's capital fell below the critical level. Regulators could choose to take less drastic action than closure for 90-day periods if they determined that such action would better protect the deposit insurance fund.

If the institution's capital remained below the critical level for one year, regulators would have to appoint a receiver and close the institution in most cases. Regulators could allow an institution to stay open if they certified it to be viable and if the institution had a positive net worth, was in substantial compliance with its capital restoration plan, had sustained improvement in earnings and was reducing its proportion of non-performing loans. Undercapitalized thrifts that prior to enactment had agreed to capital restoration plans under the 1989 thrift salvage law (PL 101-73) were not subject to the bill's prompt closure provisions until after July 1, 1994.

• **Inspector General Reports.** Required the FDIC inspector general to report to the agency and to the GAO whenever the insurance fund suffered a material loss because it provided unreimbursed assistance to a failing bank or thrift or because it closed a bank or thrift whose assets were worth less than the cost of closing the institution. This provision was to take effect July 1, 1993, and was to be triggered only when the FDIC incurred a loss greater than $25 million or 2 percent of the value of the bank or thrift. Inspector general reports were to be made public upon request.

• **Effective Date.** Required federal regulators to put final regulations for these provisions into effect one year after enactment.

• **Least-Cost Resolution.** Required the FDIC to use the least-costly method of protecting insured depositors when it closed institutions and sold them in whole or in part. The purpose was to limit greatly the circumstances under which uninsured deposits were fully protected by preventing the FDIC from incurring a loss when it protected them. When uninsured depositors were not protected, they had to wait along with unsecured creditors (including the FDIC) for the bank's assets to be sold. Uninsured depositors and other creditors then shared in the proceeds, generally receiving only a fraction of what they were owed.

Under existing practice, most failed banks and many failed thrifts were sold virtually intact through so-called purchase and assumption transactions. The FDIC believed that such deals, which usually provided full protection to insured and uninsured depositors alike, were easier to manage and cost less. The bill specifically permitted the FDIC to continue its practice of selling (and thereby protecting) the uninsured deposits of a failed bank or thrift. But to do so, it had to show that it did not incur a greater loss than it would have had it not sold them.

When making least-cost calculations, the FDIC was required to evaluate the long-term costs of various methods of case resolution. The FDIC had to discount all costs and receipts from sales of assets to "present value," subtracting for the long-term effects of inflation. The cost of forgone tax revenues resulting from the transaction had to be included as if they were revenues forgone by the FDIC. And the FDIC could not consider broad economic effects or the effects of a particular method on overall financial industry stability, unless specific consequences for the insurance fund could be identified.

• **Open-Bank Assistance.** Allowed the FDIC to continue to provide financial assistance to weak banks that were in danger of failing, rather than take control of or close them. However, the FDIC could provide such assistance only if doing so would cost less than closing the bank.

• **'Systemic Risk.'** Permitted the government, under very narrow circumstances, to waive the general rule created by the bill that the FDIC could take no action to protect uninsured depositors that would cause a loss to the insurance fund.

In those cases where a large bank failure posed a "systemic risk" to the nation's financial system, the FDIC could sustain a loss by protecting all deposits and non-deposit liabilities in a failing bank or thrift. Such action had to be approved in advance by a two-thirds vote of the FDIC board of directors, by a two-thirds vote of the Federal Reserve Board of Governors and by the Treasury secretary in consultation with the president. The Treasury secretary had to notify the House and Senate Banking committees of any systemic risk determination and the justification for it.

Any loss to the insurance fund from a systemic risk determination had to be recovered expeditiously through a special premium assessment levied against the total assets held by banks, minus their capital. By specifying total assets, that formula had the effect of requiring that insured banks pay premiums on deposits held in their overseas branches. Such foreign deposits were nominally not insured, even under existing law, but were almost always protected when big banks failed. (Banks always paid insurance premiums on the total amount of their domestic deposits, even those that were in excess of the insured amount.) The effect of the provision was to severely restrict the regulator-devised policy under existing law of fully protecting so-called too-big-to-fail banks. Under existing law, the FDIC could protect fully all bank depositors and creditors, regardless of cost, if the bank was deemed essential to its community.

• **GAO Audit.** Required the GAO to report annually to Congress on the FDIC's compliance with the least-cost provisions and to report on each instance where the government protected all depositors because of a finding of systemic risk.

• **Federal Reserve Assistance.** Prevented the Fed from making loans to banks that failed to meet all capital standards for more than 60 days of a 120-day period, unless a banking regulator (which could be the Fed) certified that the bank had capital above the critical capital level and was not expected to be closed.

The Fed was permitted to make loans to critically undercapitalized institutions (or other undercapitalized institutions that were not certified as viable) for more than five days, but not without risk. If the FDIC was later forced to close the bank, and the cost of resolution was greater than it would have been to liquidate the bank at the time of the loan, the Fed was liable to the FDIC for the excess loss. The Fed would have to pay an amount equal either to the interest it earned on the loan or to the loss the Fed would have taken had its loan to the failed bank been unsecured, whichever was smaller. Losses by the Fed would reduce the central bank's earnings and thereby cut its annual payments to the Treasury. The Fed was required to report to Congress on any loss it incurred under this provision.

Limiting Fed lending to weak banks was an essential element of the bill's effort to constrict the too-big-to-fail policy. The concern was that unrestrained Fed lending to a failing bank gave uninsured depositors time to withdraw their money, imposing a higher cost on the FDIC when the bank eventually failed.

• **Final Settlement Procedure.** Authorized the FDIC at the time it closed an insolvent bank or thrift to make payments to uninsured depositors and unsecured creditors at a rate equal to the FDIC's historic cost of closing failed institutions. Such payments would end all depositor and creditor claims on the bank's assets. In previous years, the FDIC had recovered about 85 percent of the book value of bank assets when they were sold.

• **Effective Date.** Required the FDIC to produce final regulations by Jan. 1, 1994, that would put the least-cost resolution provisions into effect as of Jan. 1, 1995. The restraints on Fed loans were to take effect two years after enactment.

State Bank Powers

• **Restrictions on Activities.** Prohibited, with exceptions, insured state-chartered banks from engaging in activities not permitted for federally chartered banks. As a general rule, national banks could not engage in non-banking activities or take an ownership (equity) interest in a non-banking activity. This provision paralleled restrictions imposed on state-chartered thrifts in the 1989 thrift-industry salvage bill (PL 101-73).

The prohibitions on state banks applied to direct activities of state-chartered banks and to activities of the subsidiaries of state banks (which generally could not engage in activities that were not permitted to subsidiaries of national banks). State banks were given five years after enactment to sell any prohibited equity investment.

A bank or bank subsidiary that met all minimum capital standards would be exempt from the general limits on permissible activities if the FDIC did not object and found that the activity posed no significant risk to the insurance fund, except that the FDIC could not waive the general ban on equity investments of state banks.

• **Stock Ownership Exceptions.** Permitted state banks to hold equity stakes in subsidiaries that they controlled. And state banks could invest as limited partners in projects to build, acquire or rehabilitate low-income housing. State banks that were permitted to own publicly traded stocks on Sept. 30, 1991, and were doing so before Nov. 26, 1991, could continue to do so, provided the aggregate investment by a bank did not exceed its capital. Excess investments had to be divested over three years after enactment. State banks also were permitted to own up to 15 percent of a "bankers' bank" that serviced its investor banks.

• **Insurance Activities.** Prohibited state banks and their subsidiaries from underwriting most insurance, as long as such activities were prohibited for national banks. The bill permitted well-capitalized state banks that existed as of Nov. 21, 1991, to continue underwriting insurance, and it permitted state banks that were required before June 1, 1991, by their charter to underwrite title insurance to continue to do so.

The bill also grandfathered the life insurance underwriting activities of New England savings banks but required the FDIC to study that issue within a year of enactment to determine if it posed a risk to the insurance fund. If the FDIC found a risk to exist, it could require a grandfathered bank to modify or terminate its insurance activities.

The bill did not affect the ability of states to allow the sale of insurance by banks chartered in those states and by the subsidiaries of such banks.

• **Effective Date.** Put the general ban on state-bank activities into effect one year after enactment.

Deposit Insurance Coverage Limits

• **Individual Accounts.** Made no change in existing law on the amount of deposit insurance coverage provided. Individuals could still have multiple accounts at a single institution, each insured to the maximum amount of $100,000.

• **Brokered Deposits.** Prohibited banks and thrifts that did not exceed minimum capital requirements from soliciting deposits by paying significantly higher interest rates than did other institutions in the same market.

On a case-by-case basis, the FDIC could allow well-capitalized institutions (and certain institutions under conservatorship) to accept brokered deposits, which typically were placed through securities dealers seeking the highest rates of interest nationwide. Rates paid on brokered deposits could not significantly exceed rates paid on deposits of similar maturity either in the local market area of the bank or nationwide.

Securities brokers who solicited such deposits had to register with and report periodically to the FDIC.

Undercapitalized institutions not only could not accept brokered deposits but also could not advertise interest rates significantly above those in their local market area.

Regulations to enforce this provision were to take effect 180 days after enactment.

• **Pass-Through Insurance.** Required the FDIC to insure very large deposits placed in well-capitalized banks by pension funds as if each beneficiary of the affected pension plan received coverage totaling $100,000. The same restrictions that applied to accepting brokered deposits limited the types of banks that could accept deposits carrying so-called pass-through insurance coverage.

The bill expressly prohibited pass-through coverage for certain types of negotiated certificates of deposits — called bank investment contracts — for which banks agreed to permit periodic withdrawals without penalty for the purpose of paying benefits.

The bill continued pass-through coverage for bundled real estate escrow accounts and similar trust accounts for which the depositor was acting as agent for a large number of individuals and the total deposit exceeded the $100,000 limit.

The bar on pass-through coverage for banks that were not well capitalized was to take effect one year after enactment.

• **Foreign Deposits.** Except as allowed under provisions permitting the FDIC to cover foreign deposits under least-cost calculations or findings of systemic risk, the bill prohibited the insurance fund from protecting foreign deposits.

• **Deposit Insurance Study.** Required the FDIC to study, in conjunction with the Fed, the feasibility and cost of tracking insured and uninsured deposits, which would be necessary in any effort to establish a systemwide limit on individual deposit insurance. The FDIC was required to report to Congress on this issue, along with recommendations, within 18 months of enactment.

Accounting and Examination Changes

• **Annual Exams.** Required the FDIC and other applicable federal banking regulators (the Federal Reserve System, Office of Comptroller of the Currency or Office of Thrift Supervision) to conduct annual on-site examinations of most banks and thrifts. Regulators could allow 18 months between examinations for those banks with assets of less than $100 million that were well capitalized, well managed, received the highest of five regulatory ratings and had not been purchased within the previous year. Examination reports from state banking regulators could be substituted for federal exams in alternate years.

The requirement for annual examinations was to take effect a year after enactment. However, until Dec. 31, 1993, exams were required only every 18 months, except for institutions that were found in their most recent exam to be in less than satisfactory condition, or those that had been purchased.

The bill also required federal banking regulators to devise coordinated examination improvement programs to increase the quality and objectivity of exams.

• **Charges and Penalties.** Permitted the FDIC to assess charges against banks and their affiliates for annual exams in amounts necessary to cover the cost of the exams. The FDIC could impose a $5,000-per-day civil penalty on any bank or thrift that refused to allow an on-site exam or refused to provide any information required for such an exam.

• **Annual Independent Audits.** Required larger banks and thrifts to undergo annual independent audits of their financial statements after 1992. Such audits had to include the auditor's assessment of a bank's compliance with certain laws and regulations designated by the FDIC. Banks with less than $150 million in assets were exempt from this requirement. Only independent auditors that agreed to provide working papers and received a peer review acceptable to the FDIC were to be permitted to perform audits. The FDIC could bar an accounting firm from such work for good cause.

• **Accounting Standards.** Required federal banking regulators to adopt uniform accounting standards for banks and thrifts that were consistent with, and no less stringent than, generally accepted accounting principles. Differences in accounting treatment among regulators had to be explained to the House and Senate Banking committees.

The bill also required that, within one year of enactment, banks and thrifts disclose so-called off-balance-sheet assets and liabilities in their financial statements and quarterly reports of condition to federal regulators.

And within a year of enactment, federal regulators were required to devise a means of reporting, to the extent feasible, the market value (in addition to the book value) of the assets and liabilities of banks and thrifts.

• **Real Estate Loans.** Required federal bank regulators to adopt, within nine months of enactment, uniform standards for making loans for real estate acquisition, development or construction. Regulations to enforce this provision were to take effect not more than 15 months after enactment.

Other Deposit Insurance Changes

• **Risk-Based Premiums.** Required the FDIC to impose a system of deposit insurance premium assessments for banks and thrifts that varied based on the relative risk that each bank and thrift posed to its insurance fund. Risk-based assessments could be derived from all risks posed by a bank's capital levels, the activities in which it engaged, its mix of assets, its holding of foreign deposits and the balance of rates and maturities between assets and deposits.

Banks and thrifts were to be treated separately, and the FDIC could devise separate assessments for large and small institutions.

Proposed regulations for a risk-based premium system would have to be issued by Dec. 31, 1992, and final regulations would have to be issued by July 1, 1993. Risk-based assessments for banks were to take effect no later than Jan. 1, 1994. For thrifts, the risk-based assessment system was not to take effect until Jan. 1, 1998.

• **Uninsured State-Chartered Institutions.** Required all state-chartered banks, thrifts and credit unions that did not carry federal deposit insurance to prominently disclose that fact to existing and prospective customers, along with the fact that depositors were not guaranteed return of their money if the institution failed. The provision also applied to any other institution that might be mistaken for a bank. (Federally chartered banks were insured as a matter of course, but the bill required them to apply formally to the FDIC for insurance, which could be denied.)

• **FDIC Backup Authority.** Authorized the FDIC to recommend that other federal bank regulators take enforcement action against banks or thrifts that posed a significant risk to the insurance funds. The FDIC could itself take action if the other regulators failed to act within 60 days. And the FDIC could adopt rules for taking expedited action without regard to the 60-day period.

• **Insider Abuse.** Limited and in some cases prohibited preferential treatment in the granting of loans or other services to officers, directors or principal shareholders of banks. Generally, under the bill, loans to insiders had to be made on terms used for outside applicants.

• **Limits on Interbank Liabilities.** Required the Fed to devise limits on the amounts that banks could lend to or place on deposit with other banks. The purpose was to reduce the threat of systemic risk to the nation's financial industry posed by large bank failures.

● **Appraisal Standards.** Deferred from July 1, 1991, to Dec. 31, 1992, the effective date for mandatory state standards for licensed real estate appraisers. This provision also was included in a bill providing additional money for the savings and loan salvage operation (HR 3545) that Congress cleared before adjourning.

Foreign-Owned Banks

● **Deposit-Taking.** Prohibited foreign banks from accepting deposits in amounts less than $100,000 except through subsidiary banks that were chartered and regulated in the United States and insured by the FDIC. Branch offices of foreign banks that were insured by the FDIC and accepted such deposits on the date of enactment could continue to accept such deposits.

● **New Operations.** Required Fed approval before any foreign bank could open a branch office or buy a bank, thrift or commercial lending company in the United States. Existing law rarely gave the Fed jurisdiction in these areas, although it and other federal banking regulators had some control over foreign bank operations.

The Fed was not allowed to approve an application from a foreign company that was not engaged in banking abroad and was not subject to comprehensive supervision in its home country. In addition, the Fed had to consider whether the foreign bank's U.S. operations were approved by foreign regulators, whether its financial and managerial resources were sufficient, whether the foreign bank had violated U.S. laws and whether the foreign bank had agreed to supply information to U.S. regulators.

The bill allowed the Fed to close a state-chartered bank or branch owned by a foreign bank for safety and soundness reasons if the bank or any affiliate had violated U.S. law or if the foreign bank was not subject to comprehensive regulation in its home country. The Fed could recommend such action to the comptroller of the currency for federally chartered banks or branches owned by foreign banks.

In addition, purchase of shares in a U.S. bank with the use of loans from a foreign bank that were secured by such shares had to be disclosed to the Fed.

The Fed was allowed to guarantee confidentiality for information provided about foreign banks by their overseas regulators.

After one year, state-chartered banks or offices owned by a foreign bank were required to phase out any activity that was not permitted for national banks or offices, unless the Fed found that the activity was consistent with sound banking and, in the case of an insured branch, the FDIC also approved.

● **State Offices of Foreign Banks.** Gave the Fed authority to regulate certain non-banking offices of foreign banks, which were generally subject only to state regulation under existing law.

● **Capital Standards.** Required the Fed and the Treasury to study the capital standards applicable to foreign banks operating in the United States and determine if such standards were equivalent to those applied to domestic banks. The Fed and the Treasury were required to report their findings to the House and Senate Banking committees no later than 180 days after enactment and revise their report annually thereafter.

● **Consumer Statutes.** Gave federal regulators explicit authority to apply federal consumer protection laws to foreign banks in the United States.

● **Penalties.** Permitted civil penalties against foreign banks for violations similar to those prohibited under the Bank Holding Company Act for U.S. companies that owned banks.

The bill increased from $1,000 to $10,000 a day the penalty for failure to comply with a Fed or FDIC subpoena. And it created a criminal penalty for intentionally violating the International Banking Act (which governed most foreign bank activities in the United States) with the intent to deceive or cause financial gain or loss to any person. The penalty was up to five years' imprisonment and a fine of up to $1 million a day, or both.

Consumer Issues

● **Incentives for Services in Distressed Communities.** Reduced deposit insurance premiums for banks offering certain services to low-income people or in economically distressed neighborhoods.

Banks that offered special, low-cost checking accounts to poor people were to pay half the usual insurance premium for deposits in such accounts.

Banks that increased their deposits or housing-related loans in specially designated distressed communities would receive a 5 percent credit against their deposit insurance premium payments. Banks that established special Community Development Corporations in distressed neighborhoods would receive a 15 percent credit against their insurance premiums.

● **Low-Income Housing Preferences.** Created within the FDIC a program to give preference to low-income persons and to state and local housing agencies in disposing of low- and moderate-income single-family and multi-family housing. The program, which paralleled one created under the Resolution Trust Corporation for the disposal of houses acquired from failed thrifts, was to take effect six months after enactment and run for three years. Low-income individuals would get a right of first refusal for six months on qualified single-family properties. Housing agencies would get preferences for acquisition of multi-family buildings. The FDIC was authorized to finance purchases at or below market rates. The program was subject to annual appropriations to cover losses caused by disposal of properties at less than market rates.

● **Truth-in-Savings.** Required banks, thrifts and credit unions to disclose clearly the terms and conditions on savings accounts. They were required to calculate the interest paid on such accounts based on the full account balance, but the bill did not specify a particular method of calculation or whether or how interest would be compounded. The bill imposed civil fines on institutions that violated these provisions. The savings account disclosure rules were to take effect within 15 months of enactment.

● **Branch-Closing Notification.** Required banks and thrifts to notify their customers and federal regulators 90 days before the scheduled closing of a branch office. Banks would have to establish specific policies for internal review of branch-closure decisions.

● **Small Business Loan Reporting.** Required banks to provide federal bank regulators annually with details of their loans to small businesses and small farms. In an effort to assess credit availability, regulators could require specific data for aggregate dollar amounts of commercial and mortgage loans to small businesses, charge-offs of bad loans and interest income from such loans. The requirement was to take effect six months after enactment.

• **Deposits in Automatic Teller Machines.** Permitted banks to hold for up to four days deposits made at automatic teller machines not owned by the bank.

• **'Whistleblower' Protections.** Prohibited banks and federal bank regulatory agencies from firing, punishing or discriminating against an employee for providing information to bank regulators or the Justice Department regarding possible violations of law or regulations by the bank, the agency or any official of the bank or agency.

• **Regulatory Burden.** Required the Treasury secretary and federal banking regulators to report to Congress a year after enactment on laws and regulations that unduly limited the profitability of banks and on the need for changes in or repeal of those laws. The report was to consider the degree to which changes might harm the safety and soundness of banks or adversely affect consumer protections.

Miscellaneous Provisions, Studies

• **Savings and Loan Associations.** Permitted thrifts that converted to federal bank charters to continue being treated as savings associations, therefore subject to somewhat different regulation than other banks. They had to meet certain conditions, including the so-called qualified thrift lender test, which was designed to concentrate a thrift's loans and other assets in home mortgages and related loans. The bill revised the test to reduce the total percentage of qualifying loans from 70 percent over two years to 65 percent for nine out of every 12 months. The changes also permitted a larger amount of non-housing loans and other assets to count toward the test and permitted federally chartered thrifts to hold a larger share of consumer loans.

The bill also made acquiring thrifts or thrift branches easier for banks and allowed so-called non-bank banks to acquire thrifts without regard to a statutory cap on annual growth by non-bank banks. The effect of the latter provision was to permit commercial companies that acquired insured banks under a pre-1987 loophole in the Bank Holding Company Act to greatly increase the size of their non-bank banks through thrift acquisitions.

• **Private Deposit Insurance.** Required the FDIC to study and conduct a demonstration project in which the agency would seek to have private companies provide "reinsurance" of up to 10 percent of the liabilities at several banks. Within 18 months of enactment, the FDIC was required to report its analysis of the project and its recommendations on the feasibility of instituting a permanent private program to absorb some of the deposit insurance risk borne by the FDIC.

• **Uninsured Deposit-Taking.** Required the FDIC to study and report to Congress within six months of enactment on the feasibility and risk associated with allowing banks to accept both insured and uninsured deposits.

• **Payment of Imputed Interest on Reserves Study.** Required the Fed, the FDIC and other federal banking regulators to study the effects of paying interest on reserves that depository institutions were required to keep in Federal Reserve banks. The study was to look at the consequences for the Federal Reserve System, the deposit insurance system and depository institutions. It was due to Congress six months after enactment.

• **Federal Reserve Lending to Securities Firms.** Clarified that, in extraordinary circumstances, the Fed could lend from its discount window to anyone, including securities firms, not just to banks. The bill also allowed making such loans somewhat easier for the Fed but retained an existing requirement that borrowers show that they needed the Fed's cash to remain in business, could not borrow elsewhere and had secure collateral to back up the loans.

• **Rhode Island Credit Unions.** Required the Treasury secretary to guarantee repayment of up to $180 million borrowed by the state of Rhode Island to cover deposits in banks and credit unions that were not covered by federal deposit insurance, provided certain conditions were met. To qualify, the loans had to be fully secured by a dedicated sales tax or assets held by the state's deposit insurance corporation. The Treasury could assess a guarantee fee equal to one-half of 1 percent of the outstanding guaranteed principal amount, computed daily.

• **Payments System Protections.** Clarified that a failed bank could not claim money due it through the federal system of interbank payments and at the same time decline to make payments that it owed. Payments to a failed bank through the system were limited to the net amount due in excess of payments that the failed bank owed.

• **Freedom National Bank.** Required the FDIC to fully protect deposits placed in the defunct Freedom National Bank by charitable and religious organizations. Freedom National, based in Harlem, New York City, held millions of dollars in deposits from organizations such as the United Negro College Fund. When the bank failed in November 1990, the FDIC could not find a buyer and was forced to liquidate it. As a result, deposits in excess of $100,000 were not fully protected. The FDIC paid about 50 cents on the dollar for uninsured deposits.

• **Securities Law Statute of Limitations.** Reinstated securities fraud claims that had been dismissed under the terms of a June 1991 Supreme Court decision in *Lampf v. Gilbertson.* The Court established a uniform nationwide statute of limitations for certain securities fraud cases and in so doing foreclosed some pending cases. The bill did not alter the statute of limitations for cases not filed before the decision. *(Case summary, p. 811)*

• **Secrecy Ban.** Prohibited the FDIC from agreeing not to disclose the terms of settlement of an action brought by the FDIC in its capacity as conservator or receiver of a failed bank or thrift.

Thrift Bailout Refinancing

On both sides of Capitol Hill, revulsion against the rising cost of salvaging failed savings and loan institutions repeatedly delayed efforts in 1991 to keep the bailout operation moving. Eventually, in 1992, congressional antipathy allowed the bailout coffers to run dry.

Twice in 1991, Congress passed bills to pump more taxpayer money into the Resolution Trust Corporation (RTC), the agency created in 1989 to manage the bailout. One bill (S 419 — PL 102-18) was enacted in March and provided $30 billion to the RTC. Then, as its last act before adjourning in November 1991, Congress cleared a second RTC bill (HR 3435 — PL 102-233), providing up to $25 billion more. *(1989 thrift bailout, p. 117)*

The second installment, however, expired April 1, 1992, with about $18 billion of the $25 billion appropriation unspent. That money reverted to the Treasury, and Congress was faced with the need to vote for yet another infusion of cash.

The Senate was able in March 1992 to muster a bare majority for a bill (S 2482) that would have provided $43 billion more for the bailout — the unspent $18 billion plus an additional $25 billion. But on April 1, the House overwhelmingly rejected a bill (HR 4704) that would have provided just the unspent $18 billion. A separate House bill providing $43 billion (HR 4241) was approved by the House Banking Committee but went no further, after becoming apparent that it could not pass.

As a result, the RTC essentially was forced to stop closing failed thrifts. The agency said the delay cost taxpayers $6 million a day in additional losses incurred by thrifts being needlessly kept open.

Background

Congress had to vote early and often on the issue for several reasons. Members refused to consider the administration's request for a permanent appropriation for the RTC. Such an action would have given the RTC whatever money it needed to cover depositor losses that were guaranteed by the government. And it would have avoided periodic trips to the congressional well.

But members argued that such a move would have removed their oversight control. House Speaker Thomas S. Foley, D-Wash., who constantly worried that the House was tying itself in knots over the RTC, was the only member to vocally support a permanent appropriation.

Another reason Congress had to act in early 1991 was that it had refused in late 1990 to respond to an administration request for $30 billion for the RTC. That request was left hanging when the 101st Congress adjourned in 1990 and was waiting on the doorstep when the 102nd Congress convened in January 1991. *(1990 bailout financing, box, p. 120)*

The primary reason for the repeated votes was that the cost of the bailout continued to climb. When the RTC was created, Congress gave it $50 billion to close failed and failing thrifts. By mid-1990, the administration had conceded that the $50 billion would not come close to completing the job.

Through Dec. 31, 1990, the RTC had closed 531 thrifts and liquidated or sold two-thirds of those, leaving 179 still under its control. Administration officials estimated that as many as 500 more thrifts could require government action before the RTC's task was complete.

Treasury Secretary Nicholas F. Brady had said in mid-1990 that $90 billion to $130 billion would be needed over the RTC's life. In mid-1991 — after Congress had given the RTC $30 billion on top of the original $50 billion — Brady asked for $80 billion more, upping the total estimate of losses in failed thrifts to $160 billion. (The higher number corresponded to the $130 billion estimate of the previous year, adjusted for inflation, he said.)

Opposition to the bailout came from many corners. And an unusual alliance of liberal and conservative groups, ranging from the populist Financial Democracy Campaign to the National Taxpayers Union, found itself opposing the administration's requests for more money. They wanted both a reduction in taxpayer-financed spending and better management of the hundreds of billions of dollars in loans, real estate and other assets the RTC had acquired from failed thrifts. The opponents did not succeed in forcing a wholesale change in the bailout's financing or winning all the management changes they sought.

S 419

Following the failure of Congress to give the RTC more money in late 1990, the issue was plainly on the table in early 1991. Brady appealed to the Senate Banking Committee on Jan. 23, warning that a delay in giving the RTC more money would require it to shut down after Feb. 28, greatly adding to the cost.

No new issues were raised in early 1991 that had not been debated continually since the bailout got under way in 1989. Despite the seeming urgency, Congress still took two months — until March 21 — to approve $30 billion.

Both chambers had difficulty acting, but the House, in particular, went through agony, rejecting multiple bills in committee and on the floor before finally settling on a package that was acceptable to a majority of the membership.

Senate Action. The Banking Committee met Feb. 5 and by voice vote approved a draft bill to provide the RTC with the $30 billion requested by the administration. The bill (S 419) was introduced and formally reported on Feb. 14 (S Rept 102-13).

Senators were clearly unhappy with the circumstances, reflected in their willingness to send such a significant measure to the floor without a roll-call vote. But they had a relatively easy time at their markup session on the bill, especially in light of what was to happen on the Senate floor and in the House.

By voice vote, the committee agreed to an amendment exempting RTC officials from securities laws regulating the packaging of thrift assets into blocks of securities for sale to the public. Federal Deposit Insurance Corporation (FDIC) Chairman L. William Seidman, who also headed the bailout, had expressed concern that RTC officials could be the subject of lawsuits stemming from the sale of the asset-backed securities. Seidman wanted a blanket liability exemption for the RTC, arguing that the legal question had effectively blocked sales of some assets, slowing down the bailout.

S 419 came to the Senate floor on Feb. 26. But the measure was pulled from consideration two days later after Howard M. Metzenbaum, D-Ohio, an arduous RTC critic, threatened "extended debate" on the measure — a euphemism for a filibuster. The bill also was threatened by a flock of amendments to reduce the amount of money or alter the way the salvage operation was managed.

On March 5, the Senate returned to S 419, passing the bill by a 69-30 vote late March 7. But sponsors had to fend off a half-dozen RTC management accountability amendments that they said would jeopardize enactment.

Metzenbaum's filibuster threats disappeared a day or two after he met Feb. 27 with Seidman. In the end, Metzenbaum offered one of only two amendments accepted, clarifying language already in the law requiring the RTC to find ways to reduce the cost of nearly 200 thrifts closed in 1988 with financial guarantees backed by the government. Metzenbaum had made a cause of these pre-bailout 1988 deals and repeatedly but unsuccessfully called for the government to repudiate them.

House Action. On Feb. 26, as the Senate was being frustrated in its efforts to act on an RTC financing bill, the House Banking Committee addressed the issue on the first of several occasions.

The panel spent 10 hours debating a bill (HR 1103) to provide $30 billion to the RTC before killing it on a 19-31 vote. All the Republicans and a third of the Democrats voted against sending the measure to the House floor, after they loaded it with controversial amendments.

The committee met again two weeks later, on March 7, the same day the Senate was finally able to pass its RTC bill. This second markup session was a comparative cakewalk. And the committee ultimately approved not one but two bills:

- HR 1221, sponsored by Chairman Henry B. Gonzalez, D-Texas. It was a slimmed-down measure providing $30 billion and containing some of the controversial provisions embraced a week earlier by the panel's Democratic majority.
- HR 1315, sponsored by Chalmers P. Wylie of Ohio, ranking Republican on the panel. It was a "clean" bill containing only the requested $30 billion.

The committee first approved HR 1315, on a 37-13 vote, after Gonzalez and Wylie cooperated to keep it free of amendments. The committee then approved HR 1221, on a 38-13 vote. The agreement to allow both bills out of committee was obvious; without the deal, neither might have gotten a majority. Of the committee's 31 Democrats, 21 voted in favor of Wylie's bill. In return, 12 of 20 committee Republicans supported Gonzalez's bill. No written report was filed for either bill.

The Rules Committee then devised a complicated floor procedure designed to give members an opportunity to vote as many as four times for the extra $30 billion for the RTC. Each vote was tied to a different scheme to make the bailout agency more accountable or to finance it through tax increases or spending cuts, instead of through long-term borrowing. At the base was Wylie's bill (HR 1315), which would have simply provided the RTC with $30 billion. Under this "king of the hill" procedure, the last version passed was to be the one approved — regardless of the vote totals.

The House met March 12 and, after about seven hours of debate, all four options — essentially two from Democrats and two from Republicans — were defeated. The final option was Wylie's clean, $30 billion measure. It came closest to winning a majority but was defeated on a **key vote of 201-220: (R 120-42; D 81-177; I 0-1).** *(1991 key votes, p. 1061)*

The eventual passage of an RTC bill took intervention at the highest levels.

After the defeats on March 12, both sides dug in their heels. On the morning of March 13, President Bush called Foley, urging him to find a way to give more money to the RTC. The compromise that finally attracted a majority of the House — but importantly, not a majority of Democrats — was hammered out early that afternoon in Foley's office by the Speaker, Republican leader Robert H. Michel of Illinois and Brady. Gonzalez and Wylie were present, as were RTC officials and aides.

The compromise essentially was to take the rejected Wylie alternative and add language from Gonzalez's bill to expand existing law requirements that the RTC aid in enlarging the supply of affordable housing.

Late March 13, the House took up the Senate-passed measure (S 419) and amended it with the compromise. After two more hours of debate, the House first voted 213-197 to amend the Senate measure with the compromise language. It then passed the amended bill by a 192-181 vote.

Final Action. House and Senate conferees had little difficulty agreeing March 19 on a compromise version of S 419. That was primarily because the Senate version had little language beyond that providing the money, and the House version had been negotiated at the highest levels — by Foley, Michel and Brady.

Conferees met for about 15 minutes and agreed to marry the two versions of the bill almost intact (H Rept 102-27). The Senate called up the bill later the same day and adopted the conference report by voice vote. Two days later, on March 21, the House adopted the conference report by a vote of 225-188, clearing the bill with a minimum of debate. It was the biggest margin mustered in a series of contentious votes over the previous two weeks, but a majority of Democrats was still opposed.

Major Provisions of S 419

As cleared, S 419:

- **Additional Financing.** Provided the RTC with $30 billion from the Treasury to cover losses in failed thrifts.
- **Reporting Requirements.** Required the RTC to submit detailed, quarterly financing plans for the bailout. The first such plan was due 30 days after enactment. The bill also required annual General Accounting Office audits of the RTC. Those audits had to be sent to Congress within six months of the end of the fiscal year.
- **Management Reforms.** Directed the RTC to improve its information systems and management of conservatorships, speed its sale of assets and otherwise address complaints about its efficiency and performance.
- **Employee Immunity.** Clarified that RTC officers and employees were not subject to civil securities-fraud suits resulting from the sale of securities backed by mortgages, "junk bonds" or other assets. The provision did not expand protections for government employees; they were still subject to a suit if there was criminal action.
- **Affordable Housing.** Expanded the scope of provisions in the original salvage bill involving sales of low-income housing to individuals and public and non-profit housing agencies. The program was extended to properties held by thrifts being run by the RTC under conservatorship — not just houses and apartments that had been in the inventories of thrifts closed by the RTC. And the bill removed a requirement that the RTC get a minimum sales price for the property, freeing the RTC to sell for nominal amounts.
- **Minority Contracting.** Required the RTC to report twice a year on its efforts to contract with companies headed by minorities or women.

HR 3435

As its final act before adjourning in 1991, Congress cleared HR 3435, giving the RTC whatever money it needed to stay in business through April 1, 1992, up to a maximum of $25 billion. That was far below the $80 billion Brady had requested in the summer, and it ensured that Congress would visit the issue at least one more time in early 1992.

Tied to that bill was a series of management reforms in part requested by the RTC itself. FDIC and RTC chief Seidman told the Senate Banking Committee on June 21 that the time had come to wean the RTC's salvage operation from the FDIC and give it a new board of directors and management team accountable to the administration and Congress. That recommendation paralleled an increasingly strong view on Capitol Hill that the RTC's complex management scheme was too unwieldy and contributed to the sense that the agency was out of control.

House Committee Action. The House Banking Subcommittee on Financial Institutions began work on HR 3435 the first week of October and spent three days on the bill, disposing of more than 50 amendments concerning the financing and management of the bailout, real estate sales by the RTC, plus issues involving the RTC's dealings with small businesses and those owned by women and minorities.

Just before approving the measure on Oct. 8, the subcommittee voted in favor of financing the bailout with new taxes or spending cuts, despite strong opposition from senior House Democrats and a united bloc of Republicans. The subcommittee then approved the bill 20-16, with most Republicans in opposition.

The subcommittee bill provided $20 billion more for the RTC to cover losses in failed thrift institutions and required the president and congressional leaders to come up with a plan to find another $60 billion without borrowing it.

The full Banking Committee waited six weeks before acting on HR 3435. While tied up trying to pass a broader banking overhaul bill, the committee met Nov. 19-20 and narrowly approved the RTC measure. *(Banking bill, p. 136)*

By a 27-25 vote, with most junior Republicans and key senior Democrats opposed, the committee approved the bill, after voting to alter the financing plan that had been approved in subcommittee. The revised bill would have given the RTC $20 billion and required that any additional money for the agency come from spending cuts elsewhere in the federal budget. Thus, the already controversial pay-as-you-go plan was changed to a "cut as you go" plan that did not specifically allow for tax increases to finance the bailout.

The committee spent two long days marking up the bill and disposed of more than 75 amendments, including two comprehensive substitutes for the bill that contained alternative financing mechanisms.

As soon as the committee acted, it was clear that HR 3435 would not be enacted in that form. But just what might happen remained in doubt until Congress was almost ready to adjourn. In the end, much of the Banking Committee bill, including its financing plan, was discarded. Many of its management changes were kept in a revised form.

The bill was formally reported Nov. 22 (H Rept 102-358). A supplemental report was filed Nov. 25 (H Rept 102-358, Part II).

House Floor, Final Action. With work on the bank overhaul bill done and adjournment only hours away, the House finally passed HR 3435 on Nov. 27 — but not the version approved in committee.

The House passed the bill on a 112-63 division vote, a seldom-used procedure requiring members to stand and be counted. GOP efforts to force a roll-call vote failed. And approval came only after conservative Republicans tried unsuccessfully to get a rule allowing them to offer an "economic growth" tax-cut package as an amendment to the RTC bill.

The House vote came on a proposal that had been crafted by Democratic and Republican leaders in consultation with the Senate and the administration, once the House Banking Committee version was found unacceptable. The key financing element, put together by Wylie and Doug Barnard Jr., D-Ga., provided for "such sums as may be necessary until April 1, 1992, not to exceed $25 billion."

It also included language from a draft Senate bill on restructuring the RTC to consolidate its two boards of directors into one and to appoint a chief executive officer who also would serve on the board. The Barnard-Wylie substitute was adopted by voice vote before the House passed the bill.

Until the House passed HR 3435, the Senate had taken no formal action on a bailout bill since early 1991. On a vote of 44-33, the Senate Nov. 27 passed the House bill unamended, clearing it for the president. It was the last significant act the Senate took before adjourning for the year.

Major Provisions of HR 3435

As cleared, HR 3435:

- **Depositor Loss Coverage.** Provided "such sums" from the Treasury as needed by the Resolution Trust Corporation to cover depositor losses in failed thrifts that were liquidated, sold or otherwise closed.

This open-ended appropriation was capped at $25 billion and could be drawn upon only through April 1, 1992, although money transferred to the RTC would not have to be used by that date.

The RTC previously had been granted $80 billion to cover thrift losses (about $49 billion from taxpayers and $31 billion from the thrift industry). Almost all of that money was spent or earmarked for case resolutions by the time Congress cleared HR 3435.

- **Working Capital.** Made no statutory change in the limit on RTC short-term borrowing. The agency borrowed so-called working capital from the public through the Federal Financing Bank (an arm of the Treasury) to cover its cash needs. Those loans were repaid from the sale of assets taken onto the RTC's books from failed thrifts.

A complex formula in existing law limited working capital borrowing in large part to 85 percent of the value of assets held by the RTC. In 1991, the RTC had determined the cap to be $125 billion. The administration sought a statutory increase to $160 billion.

Under the formula, the increase in loss money provided in the law could be used to increase the working capital borrowing cap, but the RTC had no plans to do so, calculating that the existing $125 billion cap would not hinder the agency's operations before April 1, 1992.

- **Extension of RTC Life.** Required the RTC to resolve thrifts that failed before Oct. 1, 1993. Previously, the RTC was responsible only for thrifts that failed before Aug. 9, 1992. Those that failed after Oct. 1, 1993, would be the obligation of the Federal Deposit Insurance Corporation, unless the RTC previously had been appointed as conservator to manage a weakened institution. Thrifts that were under RTC control and failed after Oct. 1, 1993, would be resolved by the RTC.

The law did not change the Dec. 31, 1996, termination date for the RTC, after which the agency's assets and liabilities were to be transferred to the FSLIC Resolution Fund. That fund was administered by the FDIC to manage the assets and liabilities of thrifts that had failed before the RTC was established and were being managed by the now-defunct Federal Savings and Loan Insurance Corporation (FSLIC).

• **Use of Proceeds.** Clarified that after the RTC is terminated on Dec. 31, 1996, proceeds from the sale of assets are first to be used to pay off working capital debt, before being diverted to pay off the $30 billion borrowed by the thrift industry through the Resolution Funding Corporation during the first year of the bailout.

• **Reports.** Required the RTC to report quarterly on details of assets held by and disposed of by the RTC, including specifics on their book and market value, the amount of the RTC's net recovery from asset sales, specifics about auctions of RTC-held assets, details of working capital loans taken from the Treasury and repaid, updates of the annual budgets for the RTC and its oversight board, plans to phase down the agency's operations after the first quarter of 1994, and details about the number and duties of employees and others hired by the RTC and its oversight board.

The bill also required a semiannual, unaudited financial statement in addition to the annual audited financial statement due after the end of each fiscal year.

The requirement for detailed reporting followed complaints from some lawmakers that obtaining timely and complete information about RTC financing and activities was difficult.

• **Chief Executive.** Created the position of chief executive officer to manage the RTC and removed the FDIC as exclusive manager of the agency. The chief executive was to be appointed by the president and confirmed by the Senate. The RTC oversight board previously had created a chief executive position, appointed by the RTC's operating board of directors (which was the same as the FDIC board of directors).

• **Operating Board of Directors.** Repealed existing law designating the FDIC board of directors as the RTC's operating board, leaving daily management in the hands of the newly created chief executive and further insulating the RTC from the FDIC. This and related changes were made effective Feb. 1, 1992.

• **Oversight Board.** Expanded the RTC oversight board from five to seven members, adding the RTC chief executive, the director of the Office of Thrift Supervision and the chairman of the FDIC to its membership and removing the secretary of housing and urban development.

The board also was renamed the Thrift Depositor Protection Oversight Board. The Treasury secretary remained as chairman of the oversight board, and the chairman of the Federal Reserve Board of Governors and two private citizen members remained on the board.

• **Limits on Oversight Board Authority.** Restricted the oversight board's authority by removing its ability to set policies for the RTC. That authority was given to the RTC chief executive. The board was left with the responsibility of reviewing overall strategies, policies and goals.

The bill also eliminated previous statutory requirements that the oversight board be accountable for the RTC's operations. Its role instead was to monitor the agency's operations.

• **National Housing Advisory Board.** Created a board, chaired by the secretary of housing and urban development, to advise the oversight board on issues related to the availability of affordable housing.

This board, required to meet at least four times a year, complemented a previously created national board to advise the oversight board on issues related to the sale of real estate.

• **Preferences in Contracting.** Required the RTC to give companies owned by blacks, Hispanics, Native Americans, Asians and women additional points for technical merit and cost preference when reviewing bids for contracts with the agency.

Joint ventures, in which businesses owned by minorities or women had at least a 25 percent share, were made eligible for contract preferences.

• **Rent-Free Leasing of Branch Offices.** Permitted the RTC to lease branch offices of failed or failing thrifts in minority neighborhoods rent-free to banks or thrifts owned by blacks, Hispanics, Native Americans, Asians and women. If the RTC chose to lease branches under these terms, the rent-free period could not be less than five years; the leasing institution would be responsible solely for insurance, taxes and utilities; and the lease could include an option to buy.

In addition, a bank or thrift that sold a branch office in a minority neighborhood on favorable terms to an institution owned by minorities or women, or leased a branch on a rent-free basis, would receive credit for any loss connected with the transaction toward meeting its community lending obligations under the Community Reinvestment Act of 1977.

• **Acquisitions by Minority-Owned Institutions.** Permitted and in some cases required the RTC to grant assistance to minority investors, including minority-owned banks and thrifts, who were seeking to buy a failed or failing thrift that was not minority-owned. An existing program, devised by the RTC, that granted low-interest financing to minority acquirers of a non-minority thrift was made part of the law.

The RTC would have to provide such assistance if a minority-owned acquirer submitted a bid asking for assistance and no other acceptable bid to buy the failed or failing thrift had been received. Such financing would have to be granted with a minimum two-year payback rate, and the interest rate charged could not exceed the average cost of borrowing for the RTC at the time of the loan.

In addition, the RTC was allowed to grant other assistance, including the transfer of assets from other thrifts under the RTC's control that were not part of the purchase proposal.

• **Small Businesses.** Required the RTC to set an annual goal for contracting with small businesses, including those owned by socially or economically disadvantaged people.

• **Credit Enhancement.** Granted the RTC broad authority to make loans, share in the risk and provide other credit enhancements for the purpose of selling housing units for low- and moderate-income people. The RTC was permitted to extend credit enhancements for tax-exempt bonds that were sold by non-profit organizations to buy low- and moderate-income housing.

• **Property Eligible for Preferential Treatment.** Broadened an existing RTC affordable housing program (created by the original thrift bailout law — PL 101-73) to include single-family and multi-family housing held by thrifts that were open and operating under an RTC conservatorship. The program made certain property available on a right-of-first-refusal basis to eligible low- and moderate-income people, and state and local housing authorities.

Previously, only property seized by the RTC from failed thrifts was eligible. The bill extended the program to property held by thrifts still in business. Because this change was expected to result in a greater loss to the RTC, the provision regarding multi-family housing was allowed to take effect only to the extent that Congress appropriated money to cover the cost.

- **Time Limit for Sale.** Extended from 90 days (under previous law) to 180 days the right-of-first-refusal period during which single-family residences would be marketed under the affordable housing program. The period for housing agencies to submit qualified bids for multi-family housing also was extended.
- **Veterans Preference.** Clarified that households with members who are veterans were eligible to purchase single-family residences under the affordable housing program.
- **Anti-Speculation Requirements.** Required purchasers of low- and moderate-income housing to certify their intent to occupy the property as a principal residence for one year after the purchase. As a further deterrent to speculation in RTC-held affordable housing, the RTC was required to recapture 75 percent of the profits from the resale of a unit within the first year.
- **Protection for Tenants.** Permitted the RTC to sell single-family residences that fell within the affordable housing program to existing tenants who did not meet income criteria, provided that doing so would prevent unnecessary displacement of those tenants and that they agreed to occupy the residence for one year.
- **Sales Price.** Removed a previous law requirement that the RTC sell single-family properties at the minimum sales price set by the agency, unless a lower price was deemed necessary to expedite the sale. The change would permit below-minimum sales at any time.
- **Appraisal Standards.** Deferred from July 1, 1991, to Dec. 31, 1992, the effective date for mandatory state standards for licensed real estate appraisers. This provision also was included in the big banking bill (S 543) that Congress cleared before adjourning.
- **Capital Leniency for Housing Loans.** Required that mortgage loans for the purchase of single-family and multi-family housing be weighted at 50 percent of their value for computation of minimum capital-to-asset ratios for banks and thrifts. The effect was to cut in half the amount of capital required as a cushion for such loans. Immediately after clearing HR 3435, the Senate passed a second bill (S 2131) to repeal the section on capital leniency.

The House did not act on S 2131, but during Senate floor debate, it was asserted that the House would agree to repeal the provision and that the administration would not put it into effect until the House had an opportunity to act.

S 2482, HR 4704

As April 1, 1992, approached — the date upon which the RTC's unused money was to revert to the Treasury — members of both the House and Senate began working on a new financing bill.

The House Banking Committee got off to a faster start than the Senate but came up short when the full House on April 1 rejected a bill (HR 4704) to give the RTC $18 billion by a **key vote of 125-298 (R 45-117; D 80-180; I 0-1)**. That killed any chance that Congress would provide more money in 1992 to keep the bailout operating. *(1992 key votes, p. 1083)*

House Action. The Banking Subcommittee on Financial Institutions voted 25-11 on Feb. 27 in favor of a bill (HR 4241) to pump another $43 billion into the savings and loan salvage operation. It would have freed up the unspent $18 billion and provided an additional $25 billion through April 1, 1993.

The $25 billion in new money was well shy of what the Treasury Department said was needed to finish the job. Treasury Secretary Brady had asked Congress to provide a $55 billion cash infusion to the RTC, but a Republican-led effort to reduce that amount to $25 billion prevailed.

Approval came after one of the tamer markup sessions on the thrift bailout. Subcommittee Chairman Frank Annunzio, D-Ill., refused to allow consideration of 18 amendments, many of them controversial, sparing the panel most of the partisan rancor that had caused several prior bailout bills to implode in committee or on the floor.

The full Banking Committee approved HR 4241 by a 30-17 vote on March 12, after a debate that was notable for its brevity and lack of divisiveness. At the outset, the committee voted 34-11 to shut off debate before any amendments were considered. The bill was formally reported March 19 (H Rept 102-457).

Although the bill had made it out of committee, floor action was stalled by opposition from a majority of Republicans. When it became clear that the measure would not pass the House, Gonzalez and Wylie introduced a new, radically trimmed-down bill (HR 4704) that would have provided the RTC with $18 billion by lifting the April 1, 1992, deadline by which the agency had to spend the balance of $25 billion appropriated in 1991.

The bill was introduced March 31 and went to the House floor the next day, where it was resoundingly defeated.

Senate Action. The Senate Banking Committee by voice vote March 24 approved a draft bill to give the RTC an additional $43 billion and to make some significant changes in the operation of the bailout. S 2482 was introduced and reported the following day without a written report.

Perhaps the most controversial provision was to earmark nearly $2 billion of the RTC's money to give to weakened thrifts as an inducement to merge with healthier institutions. The proposal, which was opposed by the administration, was intended to prevent some thrifts from failing, and thereby reduce the bailout cost. Administration officials said they doubted it would save money and feared it would be seen as a giveaway to thrift shareholders — not the depositors that the RTC's salvage operation benefited.

The Senate took up S 2482 on March 26 and worked late into the night before a bare majority — 52-42 — voted to pass the bill. The Senate killed an amendment to delete the non-financing provisions and killed another that would have required that the bailout be financed through tax increases or spending cuts. The bill died when the House never took it up.

GSEs

A compromise bill to strengthen federal oversight of the nation's two largest government-sponsored enterprises (GSEs) weaved its way through Congress to become law in 1992, despite grumbling by some members that the legislation was not strong enough.

The measure was tacked onto the conference report of an unrelated bill (HR 5334 — H Rept 102-1017) reauthorizing federal housing programs. HR 5334 cleared Oct. 8, and President Bush signed it into law on Oct. 28 (PL 102-550). *(Housing bill, p. 694)*

Fannie Mae, Freddie Mac. The GSE provisions of HR 5334 created a new regulator within the Department of Housing and Urban Development (HUD) to oversee the Federal National Mortgage Association and the Federal Home Loan Mortgage Corporation, better known as Fannie Mae and Freddie Mac, respectively. The two GSEs — which had combined liabilities of more than $1 trillion — were required to meet new "risk-based" capital standards aimed at ensuring that they could withstand fluctuations in interest rates, recession and other factors that might threaten their financial soundness.

The measure also made some changes in the operation of the Federal Home Loan Bank System, a third large GSE that provided credit to savings and loan institutions and other mortgage lenders. The home loan banks were already under the oversight of the Federal Housing Finance Board, created by the 1989 savings and loan bailout bill (HR 1278 — PL 101-73). The GSE bill called on the Housing Finance Board to ensure the financial solvency of the banks and required a study of capital standards. But it did not impose stringent new regulations, as it did in the case of Fannie Mae and Freddie Mac.

Late-breaking opposition from Fannie Mae almost killed the bill for the year, but after some bad publicity, the huge company changed course and cooperated with the legislative effort.

The final GSE provisions were a compromise between bills (HR 2900, S 2733) that the House and Senate had passed previously. The Senate bill had been considered stricter, particularly on capital standards, which were designed to provide a buffer in the event of financial difficulties. The final version of the bill adopted the Senate's capital requirements. It also dropped unrelated provisions that had been included in the Senate version of the legislation.

Other GSEs. In 1992, Congress also cleared provisions tightening regulation of another GSE, the Student Loan Marketing Association (Sallie Mae). The language was in the final version of S 1150 (PL 102-325), a higher education reauthorization bill that cleared July 8. *(Higher education reauthorization, p. 653)*

And Congress cleared a bill to ensure that the Farm Credit System, a GSE that received a federal bailout in 1987, would repay its loan from the government. That bill (HR 6125 — PL 102-552) cleared Oct. 7. *(Farm credit system, p. 554)*

In addition, on Nov. 23, 1991, the House by voice vote under suspension of the rules passed a bill (HR 3365 — H Rept 102-224) aimed at making it harder for new GSEs to borrow money from the Treasury. The measure would have restricted the Treasury from making loans to newly established GSEs unless the loans had been approved in an appropriations bill. Ways and Means had approved the measure by voice vote on Sept. 25. The Senate did not act on it.

Background

Bush administration officials and some members of Congress began to worry in 1989 about the growing liabilities of five GSEs — Fannie Mae, Freddie Mac, the Federal Home Loan Banks, Sallie Mae and the Farm Credit System.

All were private corporations that benefited from federal government charters and some ability to borrow from the Treasury. All were considered to have an implicit federal guarantee by the financial markets.

Each had a role in increasing capital flows to housing, education and agriculture. All sold bonds to finance their activities, and some — Fannie and Freddie in particular — sold securities backed by their assets, chiefly mortgage loans purchased from lenders.

None of the five corporations was in imminent danger. But in the wake of the savings and loan debacle, lawmakers wanted to make sure they would not one day be pouring billions of dollars into these GSEs. So as part of the 1990 budget-reconciliation act (PL 101-508), they had called for studies by the Treasury Department and the Congressional Budget Office of the financial health of the GSEs. The law required House committees to report regulatory bills to the floor by Sept. 15, 1991, and stated the intent of the Senate that its committees do likewise.

In June 1991, the administration sent Congress draft bills to establish stricter government oversight of each of the five corporations. New regulators were to be created in HUD, the Agriculture Department and the Treasury Department to oversee the GSEs.

Treasury recommended several changes in the government's regulatory oversight, including a plan proposed a year earlier to have private-market securities analysts rate the five GSEs based on the riskiness of their borrowing, without taking into account the implicit government guarantee.

The report recommended enhancing the authority of existing federal regulators for each of the enterprises and allowing them to impose capital requirements tied to the risk associated with the lending activities of each corporation. The capital requirement could be waived for an enterprise that received a Triple-A rating, the highest private-market rating.

Two of the enterprises — the Federal Home Loan Banks and Sallie Mae — received Triple-A ratings in April from Standard & Poor's Corp. in a special assessment done for the Treasury Department. Standard & Poor's gave lower ratings to the other three: an A-plus to Freddie Mac, an A-minus to Fannie Mae and a Double-B to the Farm Credit System, reflecting its continued difficulties and the problems associated with farm lending. (Securities sold by all five carried Triple-A ratings in the marketplace because of their implicit federal guarantee.)

Fannie Mae, Freddie Mac

House Action. The House Banking Subcommittee on Housing and Community Development began work in July 1991 on HR 2900, a bill to tighten regulation of Fannie Mae, Freddie Mac and the Federal Home Loan Banks.

The subcommittee approved the bill on July 24 by voice vote, agreeing to create a new regulator within HUD to oversee Fannie and Freddie. But the subcommittee put off two of the most contentious issues for the full Banking Committee: how much capital Fannie and Freddie should have available to cover unexpected losses and whether they should have to set aside a percentage of their profits for low-income housing.

Treasury and the two corporations were locked in a dispute over the amount of capital — assets in excess of liabilities — that Fannie and Freddie should be required to maintain. Treasury wanted high levels of capital to cover potential emergencies and to minimize the chance that taxpayers would be called on to help the two corporations. It also wanted regulators to be free to determine what those levels ought to be, based on existing economic conditions.

Fannie and Freddie, meanwhile, said the capital levels sought by the Treasury were too high and would restrict them from carrying out the job of buying mortgages from banks and other lenders. They also feared that an unfriendly regulator with too much flexibility could push the standards even higher, so they favored writing the standards into the law.

The full Banking Committee voted 49-1 on July 31 to send the bill to the House floor, despite reservations among members about legislating new rules for Fannie and Freddie at a time when both were flush with profits and yielding high returns to stockholders. The bill was formally reported Sept. 17 (H Rept 102-206).

The committee voted 49-1 to adopt an amendment setting out capital levels and goals for financing low-income housing. The amendment set three capital standards, including a critical level below which the two GSEs would be subject to mandatory conservatorship.

The committee also agreed by voice vote to remove a cap from the Federal Home Loan Bank System, allowing the banks to lend more money to commercial banks and credit unions to originate mortgages.

The House passed the bill Sept. 25 by a vote of 412-8. Floor debate turned fiery when Joseph P. Kennedy II, D-Mass., offered an amendment expressing the sense of the House that Fannie Mae should limit the amount of compensation paid to its top executives. (Fannie's chairman had recently retired with compensation of $27 million.) The non-binding amendment was agreed to by voice vote.

An amendment to increase capital standards was rejected 119-298 on Sept. 25.

Senate Action. The Senate Banking Committee was on the verge of marking up a companion measure in late 1991, but work was halted after Fannie Mae said the legislation prepared by committee staff was too tough.

The committee resurrected its bill on April 8, 1992, approving the measure by voice vote. The bill was introduced May 15 as S 2733 and formally reported the same day (S Rept 102-282).

S 2733, which paralleled but went beyond the House-passed bill, had been the subject of months of negotiations. Most, but not all, of the provisions were broadly acceptable to all sides — the administration, mortgage lenders, consumer and housing advocates, and the two corporations.

Banking Committee Chairman Donald W. Riegle Jr., D-Mich., praised the panel for seeking to regulate the financial health of the two corporations. And he singled out a requirement for increased low- and moderate-income housing loans as an effort to "improve long-standing but mostly ignored ... regulations."

The committee took just 25 minutes to agree to a block of relatively minor amendments and to adopt the draft bill by voice vote. Only Phil Gramm, R-Texas, registered a vocal objection to the measure. Gramm complained that the bill "will not increase capital or enhance the market." And he worried that the housing goals ran counter to the mandate to insulate taxpayers.

At Gramm's request, the Senate bill included language stating that Fannie Mae and Freddie Mac did not enjoy the direct or indirect backing of the government. "I never intend to vote a dollar of taxpayer money to bail out one of these GSEs — period," he said.

Under the bill, the new regulator was to be largely outside the control of the HUD secretary — or that of the Office of Management and Budget. The regulatory office was not to be subject to appropriations (instead financed solely by fees assessed on Fannie Mae and Freddie Mac), and it could issue regulations affecting the safety and soundness of Fannie Mae and Freddie Mac without agency clearance.

Senate sponsors hoped this level of independence would ensure strong regulation and direct congressional oversight. Consumer advocates and the two corporations also favored an independent regulator.

The capital standards in the Senate bill were similar to those in HR 2900 and were patterned after standards that Congress had set for banks and thrifts in a 1991 banking bill (S 543 — PL 102-242). *(Banking bill, p. 136)*

The bill required Fannie Mae and Freddie Mac to develop capital restoration plans, should they fail to meet the minimum requirement. The bill set a "critical capital level" roughly equal to half the minimum level. If either corporation fell below that level, it would have to be placed under government control unless the new regulator, with the concurrence of the Treasury secretary, determined that such a move would not be in the public interest.

The bill also required Fannie Mae and Freddie Mac to meet a risk-based capital standard to be devised by the regulator to ensure that they could survive large swings in interest rates or loan defaults.

If the corporations failed to comply with the capital requirements, they and their officers would be subject to cease-and-desist orders and civil fines. This was one area of concern for Fannie Mae and Freddie Mac when the bill was being drafted. The committee version tightened the standard for imposing fines and included a number of opportunities for hearings to challenge regulatory findings.

A key difference between the Senate and House bills was a new requirement in the Senate version that the two GSEs make special efforts to finance low- and moderate-income housing and housing in central cities, urban areas and other underserved areas. The new regulator was to set the goals, but the bill required that 30 percent of the two GSEs' loans in the first two years after enactment be for houses occupied by owners or renters whose incomes were below the medians in their geographic area.

The two corporations also were required to invest a combined $3.5 billion in houses occupied by owners and renters with incomes below 80 percent of their area's median.

The Senate passed S 2733 on July 1 by a 77-19 vote. Work on the regulatory bill had been essentially completed June 24. But passage was delayed by efforts to attach language proposing a constitutional amendment to require a balanced federal budget. The bill was passed after the Senate rejected two attempts to cut off a filibuster by opponents of the balanced budget amendment. *(Balanced budget amendment, p. 84)*

On the floor, the Senate added unrelated provisions on money laundering, interstate branching by savings and loan associations, the liability of banks and other lenders under the "superfund" hazardous waste cleanup law and the regulation of limited partnerships undergoing "roll-ups," or reorganizations (S 1423). Those provisions complicated prospects for a House-Senate conference. First, several House committees would have had to be involved, resulting in jurisdictional and scheduling problems. And second, Gramm was determined to block the limited partnership roll-up provisions. *(Money laundering, this page; limited partnership roll-ups, p. 158)*

Final Action. Efforts to bring the bill to conference were stymied, in part by a move by Gramm, who objected to the usually routine step of calling up the House bill and inserting the Senate language.

Instead of going to conference, staff members of the Banking committees negotiated informally to iron out the details of the GSE bill and strip out the unrelated Senate provisions. Staffers negotiating the compromise were authorized to discuss only the core GSE bill; non-germane material in the Senate bill was dropped. By the end of September, agreement had been reached.

But Fannie Mae objected on Sept. 25 to one version of the bill, saying that the language was too vague and would have given the new regulator too much discretion to set the risk-based capital standards. That objection killed plans to bring the compromise bill to the House floor on Sept. 29.

Fannie Mae denied that it was trying to kill the legislation, but the episode brought a lot of criticism and eventually the compromise was reached.

The House passed the compromise as a stand-alone bill (HR 6094) by voice vote under suspension of the rules on Oct. 3. But in an effort to boost the bill's chances, the language was included in the conference report on the housing bill (HR 5334 — H Rept 102-1017), filed Oct. 5. The House adopted the conference report the same day by 377-37. The Senate adopted the conference report Oct. 8 by voice vote.

Sallie Mae

The House Education and Labor Committee by voice vote July 30, 1991, approved a bill (HR 3083) to regulate Sallie Mae. The bill was formally reported Sept. 13 (H Rept 102-203).

The Senate Labor and Human Resources Committee approved a similar draft bill by voice vote July 31. The bill was introduced as S 1915 on Nov. 5, 1991, and formally reported the same day (S Rept 102-202).

Sallie Mae provided a secondary market for banks to sell their federally guaranteed student loans. Both bills required Sallie Mae to maintain capital equal to 2 percent of its assets to cover emergencies. Both bills called for creating a regulator at the Treasury Department to oversee the agency.

The House measure allowed the regulator to limit Sallie Mae's activities if its capital level fell below 1.5 percent. The Senate bill set that level at 1 percent.

No further action was taken on the bills in 1991, but in 1992, the language was incorporated into legislation reauthorizing federal higher education programs (HR 3553, S 1150). The Sallie Mae language survived in the final version of S 1150 (H Rept 102-630 — PL 102-325), which cleared July 8.

Money Laundering

Legislation to crack down on money laundering was approved in different forms by both the House and Senate chambers in 1991, but the measures languished through much of the 1992 session. Finally, in October 1992, the legislation got a jump start and rode to enactment after being attached to an unrelated housing bill (HR 5334 — PL 102-550).

The money-laundering measure, which set stiff penalties on banks and bank officers found guilty of money laundering, was a swan song for its principal sponsor, retiring representative Frank Annunzio, D-Ill., second-ranking Democrat on the Banking Committee.

The bill had gotten its start in the wake of the Bank of Credit and Commerce International (BCCI) scandal, in which the Luxembourg-based BCCI had been convicted of laundering millions of dollars in Florida for Colombian drug cartels but had been allowed to remain open and fined $14.8 million.

Agents from the Federal Bureau of Investigation testified that drug dealers had found banks, thrifts and credit unions to be the most reliable means to launder profits because many institutions seldom asked questions about the source of the money. The Treasury Department estimated that international drug profits amounted to about $300 billion annually.

The House voted overwhelmingly for nearly identical money-laundering bills in 1990 and 1991. The non-controversial measure had passed the Senate in various forms as well. However, the bill had been snake-bit by Senate politics and, for the third year in a row, was subject to last-minute maneuvering.

In 1990, both chambers passed money-laundering bills, but the Senate version also included a variety of unrelated banking provisions. An end-of-the-session attempt by the House to move a clean bill failed after Senate Republicans blocked consideration. *(1990 money-laundering bill, p. 134)*

Legislative History

House Action. The House Banking Financial Institutions Subcommittee moved quickly in 1991 to renew the push for a money-laundering bill, approving HR 26 by voice vote on Feb. 27.

The full Banking Committee approved the bill by voice vote on March 7. It was formally reported March 20 (H Rept 102-28, Part I).

Under the bill, banks, thrifts and credit unions faced the financial equivalent of the death penalty — revocation of their charters or deposit insurance coverage — if convicted of money-laundering offenses. Bank officers would face a lifetime ban from working in a financial institution if found guilty of involvement in laundering schemes.

Although the bill provided new tools to regulators to punish banks engaged in laundering schemes, it did not require that they be used. Regulators would have to hold a disciplinary hearing for a convicted bank before deciding on a penalty. They would have to consider the extent to which top bank officials were involved in the crime, whether the institution had policies in place to prevent money laundering and the degree of cooperation regulators received from senior management after an offense was uncovered.

The bill also required the Treasury Department to study the feasibility of withdrawing $50 and $100 bills from circulation. Traffickers operated with such a high cash volume that they needed large-denomination bills.

The language in HR 26 had been refined somewhat since the 1990 debate after the Bush administration argued for a few changes.

The maximum civil penalty against a financial institution for engaging in a pattern of violating currency-reporting requirements was set at $50,000, not $5,000.

The House Foreign Affairs Committee then took up the bill, approving it May 21 by voice vote. Foreign Affairs formally reported the bill May 23 (H Rept 102-28, Part II).

Foreign Affairs reinserted language requiring the administration to negotiate anti-money-laundering agreements with other countries. It gave the administration some discretion over when to apply sanctions to countries that did not respond to the negotiations. The international negotiations language had been dropped by the Banking Committee.

The House passed HR 26 under suspension of the rules by a 406-0 vote on June 11.

Senate, Final Action. Conflicts over unrelated issues led Banking Chairman Donald W. Riegle Jr., D-Mich., to avoid considering a separate money-laundering bill in the 102nd Congress.

Instead, in 1991, he attached money-laundering provisions to the Senate's version of a broad overhaul of banking law (S 543), which was approved by the Banking Committee Aug. 2. But the provisions were dropped in conference in an effort to slim down the bill. *(Banking bill, p. 136)*

Then, in 1992, the Senate added money-laundering language to a bill (S 2733) to tighten federal regulation of two government-sponsored enterprises that helped finance the mortgage market. But that and other extraneous provisions were jettisoned in September to get a deal on just the central regulatory provisions. *(Government-sponsored enterprises, p. 153)*

Finally, in a late-session effort to enact a money-laundering bill, House and Senate negotiators ironed out minor differences between House and Senate language, and the compromise was introduced Sept. 28 as a new bill (HR 6048). The House passed the bill by voice vote under suspension of the rules the following day; the Senate did not act on it before adjournment.

To be safe, the compromise money-laundering provisions also were incorporated into the conference report on the housing bill, filed Oct. 5 (HR 5334 — H Rept 102-1017), and in that form the provisions became law. *(Housing bill, p. 694)*

Other Legislation

Credit Reporting Safeguards

A bill to beef up federal regulation of the nation's credit reporting industry reached the House floor in 1992, but sponsors killed the measure (HR 3596) after suffering a white-knuckle defeat on a key amendment. The Senate Banking Committee did not act on a similar bill (S 2776).

The House bill contained several provisions designed to make it easier for consumers to obtain their own credit reports and correct inaccurate information. Most importantly, if a customer disputed information in his credit report, the credit bureau would have had to reinvestigate within 30 days and delete all information that could not be verified within that time.

But at no stage in the legislative process were the bill's sponsors, Banking Committee Chairman Henry B. Gonzalez, D-Texas, and Esteban E. Torres, D-Calif., able to win language that would have allowed states to preserve credit reporting laws that were more stringent than the federal rules proposed in the bill.

Supporters of the credit reporting and banking industries prevailed, and the bill retained language that would have pre-empted state laws.

After losing a seesaw 203-207 vote on Gonzalez's floor amendment Sept. 24 to strike the pre-emption language, Torres and Gonzalez pulled the bill, killing it.

Background. Except for the pre-emption provision, wide support for the bill existed, as well as a sense among members that something needed to be done to rein in the nation's credit bureaus.

Since the Fair Credit Reporting Act (PL 91-508) became law in 1970, the credit reporting industry had grown enormously. But with that growth and the greater automation of the industry came horror stories about consumers who had errors in their reports and great difficulties in getting them corrected. Bill sponsors said that up to 50 percent of credit reports contained errors, and the Federal Trade Commission fielded about 10,000 complaints about the industry the previous year. *(Congress and the Nation Vol. III, p. 673)*

Consumer groups had made the bill a priority in 1992, saying that inaccurate information in credit reports had led millions of consumers to be turned down for loans, credit cards or jobs. In one high-profile mistake, 1,500 residents of Norwich, Vt., were mistakenly labeled as tax deadbeats. That error led Vermont to enact one of the toughest laws in the nation.

House Committee Action. The Banking Committee's Consumer Affairs Subcommittee approved HR 3596 by voice vote March 5, and credit bureaus, department stores and banks seemed content with it. But consumer advocacy groups complained that it had been "eviscerated."

Torres, who chaired the subcommittee, lost several votes, including a 9-7 roll call to adopt an amendment inserting language to pre-empt state credit reporting laws. On a second 9-7 vote, the subcommittee deleted a section of the bill requiring credit reporting agencies to provide a free copy of their credit reports to consumers each year.

Under the bill, if a customer disputed information in his credit report, the credit bureau would have had to reinvestigate within 30 days and delete all information that could not be verified within that time.

Banks and retailers would have been required to follow procedures aimed at ensuring the accuracy of the information they provided to credit agencies. Businesses would have been barred from negligently providing false information to a credit reporting agency. And the bill would have required reporting agencies to set up toll-free telephone lines for consumers who wanted to correct their reports.

The full Banking Committee approved the bill by voice vote June 18, almost three months after a five-hour markup on March 25 that was adjourned after Gonzalez and Torres lost again on the pre-emption language.

At the March 25 session, several amendments were made to the subcommittee bill, including one that would have given states the authority to enforce the law. And consumers would have been given the right to review their credit history files for a fee of no more than $8. Consumers also could have obtained free of charge any credit report that was the basis for an adverse ruling on a credit application.

The bill was formally reported July 23 (H Rept 102-692).

House Floor Action. The bill came to the floor Sept. 24, but Torres said before debate began that unless he was successful in stripping out the pre-emption language, he would kill the bill.

For several moments during the vote on Gonzalez's pre-emption amendment, it looked as if he would prevail. The vote stood at 204-202 with time expiring. But sitting in the chair was amendment opponent Edward F. Feighan, D-Ohio, whose district was home to one of the nation's largest credit reporting bureaus. Feighan held the vote open long enough for the tide to turn.

Gonzalez and Torres then halted action, and the bill was not brought back to the floor.

Government Securities Dealers

A jurisdictional and procedural fight in 1992 between the House Energy and Commerce and Banking committees scuttled a bill (S 1699) to rein in the largely unregulated $2.6 trillion market in federal government securities.

The bill grew out of a 1991 bid-rigging scandal in which the Wall Street firm of Salomon Brothers Inc. bought larger-than-permitted stakes of government bonds. Energy and Commerce Committee members blamed the scandal on lax oversight by the Treasury Department and the Federal Reserve System.

Even before the Salomon scandal broke, Congress was moving to reauthorize the Government Securities Act of 1986 (PL 99-571), which gave Treasury limited authority to regulate the financial capacity and related activities of firms that traded in government bonds. Treasury also set rules for the purchase of federal bonds at auction. *(1986 law, Congress and the Nation Vol. VII, p. 112)*

Senate Action. Prior to reports that Salomon might have violated Treasury auction rules, the Senate had passed a bill (S 1247) in July 1991 that would have reauthorized the Government Securities Act and given various regulators new authority to impose rules on the sales practices in the government bond market.

The Senate Banking Committee approved the measure by voice vote July 10, 1991. It was formally reported on July 29 (S Rept 102-126). The Senate passed S 1247 by voice vote on July 30.

Then, in the wake of the Salomon scandal, the Senate passed a second narrow bill (S 1699) to clarify that fraudulent bids on Treasury bonds and other false statements involving that market were violations of the Securities Exchange Act of 1934.

Without prior committee action, the Senate passed S 1699 on Sept. 25 by voice vote.

House Committee Action. House Energy and Commerce members chose to pursue a more aggressive stance following detailed hearings into Salomon's activities.

In mid-1992, the committee produced a bill (HR 3927) that contained a variety of provisions aimed at preventing fraud and would have greatly broadened the authority of the Securities and Exchange Commission (SEC) to regulate the government bond market.

The Energy and Commerce Subcommittee on Finance approved HR 3927 on May 7 by voice vote. But the easy approval belied remaining tensions. The bill closely tracked the views of the SEC that the largely unregulated Treasury market needed closer attention, similar to the sort that existed for other securities. But Treasury and Federal Reserve officials complained that it would unduly burden the market in Treasury securities. They argued that the bill would raise costs to bond traders that ultimately would be passed on as higher interest costs to the government — and cause a bigger federal deficit.

The bill contained a variety of provisions intended to prevent trading fraud and to make it easier for the SEC and other regulators to probe alleged violations.

Like S 1247, the bill would have renewed Treasury's general authority to regulate the capital of bond traders. And it would have allowed banking and other regulators to establish sales practice rules. It also would have allowed Treasury to require traders with large holdings of Treasury bonds to make periodic reports on their positions.

The bill would have given the SEC two new grants of authority. The agency would have been permitted to require that bond dealers keep records of their transactions and make them available upon request. The SEC also could have stepped in if it appeared that price information on Treasury bonds in the resale, or secondary, market was not widely distributed or incomplete.

The full committee approved HR 3927 on June 2, acting by voice vote and without debate, amendment or any apparent disagreement. The committee met again June 24 to adopt an amendment similar to S 1699, clarifying that a violation of Treasury auction rules would be a violation of securities law. The bill was formally reported July 24 (H Rept 102-722, Part I).

The House Banking Committee weighed in on Aug. 6, approving by voice vote a version of HR 3927 that would have preserved the role of federal banking regulators in the tightened regulation of the government securities market and rolled back the new grant of authority to the SEC. The committee formally reported the bill Aug. 12 (H Rept 102-722, Part II).

The Banking version also would have changed the procedures governing the auction of government securities, requiring the creation of a fully automated system allowing remote participation for all qualified brokers. The aim was to broaden access beyond the small number of primary dealers that had a near-monopoly in the auctions.

The Ways and Means Committee, which shared jurisdiction over bond auctions, did not formally act on the bill but informally proposed some changes.

House Floor Action. With time running out in the 102nd Congress, and the disagreements over the bill unresolved, the House leadership brought an amended version of S 1699 to the floor — combining language from the Energy and Commerce and Ways and Means committees and cutting out the Banking Committee's contribution.

Over vehement protests from Banking Chairman Henry B. Gonzalez, D-Texas, the bill was brought up under suspension of the rules, a procedure that barred further amendments and required a two-thirds majority for passage.

Gonzalez's complaints of a power grab and concerns by rank-and-file members that the bill must be flawed given the disagreements killed the bill. It failed on a 124-279 vote Sept. 16.

Partnership Roll-Ups

Congressional efforts to move a widely backed bill that would have curbed abuses when limited partnership ventures were reorganized, or "rolled up," were stymied by the vehement opposition of Sen. Phil Gramm, R-Texas.

In late 1991, the House passed a roll-up bill (HR 1885), but it was never considered in the Senate. Gramm used parliamentary tactics to prevent the Senate Banking Committee from considering its own roll-up bill (S 1423) in 1992.

Gramm also prevented an unrelated bill to which the Senate roll-up language had been attached from going to conference. The unrelated bill (S 2733) would have beefed up federal regulation of government-sponsored enterprises (GSEs). Because of Gramm's efforts, language from the GSE bill wound up attached to yet a third bill, where it was enacted. *(Government-sponsored enterprises, p. 153)*

Congressional action on roll-ups came in the wake of a slew of horror stories from investors in limited partnerships who said they were ripped off when the partnerships were restructured.

Limited partnerships were designed as long-term, non-traded entities in which investors pooled their money under the supervision of a general partner, who managed the investment. In a roll-up, several limited partnerships were reorganized into a single publicly traded company. The stocks issued by such companies, and provided to investors in lieu of their partnership interest, had generally fared poorly in securities markets. Losses to original investors were calculated at more than $1 billion.

House and Senate bills would have relaxed federal proxy rules to make fighting a roll-up easier for investors and would have required that limited partners who opposed a roll-up be given alternative compensation, or "dissenter's rights," to the new stock offering. The House measure went somewhat further, requiring a "fairness opinion" prepared by an independent expert with no stake in the proposed roll-up to be distributed to investors.

At the core of Gramm's opposition was the dissenter's rights section. He said at the markup that the provision would have allowed a minority of the limited partners to kill a deal, giving them rights they did not have under the original partnership.

But even as Congress worked to enact legislation on the issue, the Securities and Exchange Commission (SEC) drew up new rules governing proxy voting by shareholders and other measures aimed at stemming abusive roll-ups. At the same time, the practice of rolling up partnerships was declining. In 1990-91, 52 roll-ups or similar transactions were registered at the SEC; only eight were pending in mid-1992.

House Action. The House Energy and Commerce Subcommittee on Finance approved HR 1885 by voice vote on May 22, 1991. The full committee approved it by voice vote July 30 and formally reported the measure Oct. 16 (H Rept 102-254).

The House passed HR 1885 by voice vote under suspension of the rules Nov. 5.

Senate Action. The Senate Banking Committee met May 21, 1992, to mark up S 1423, which had 72 cosponsors and one insistent opponent. Gramm invoked a Senate rule that prohibited committees from meeting when the chamber was in session. Two weeks later, on June 3, Gramm insisted that a quorum be present as the committee prepared to mark up the bill, and acting chairman Christopher J. Dodd, D-Conn., was forced to adjourn the meeting.

Stymied in committee, Dodd looked to attach the roll-up bill to a "must-pass" bill on the Senate floor. The GSE bill, strongly backed by the administration, presented one such opportunity. On June 24, Dodd offered the roll-up language to the GSE bill (S 2733). His amendment was adopted by voice vote after easily surviving a tabling motion on a 10-87 vote.

But Gramm persisted. After the Senate passed S 2733 on July 1, he objected to the usually routine step of calling up the House bill and inserting the Senate language. That added another obstacle to the bill going to conference.

Investment Advisers Regulation

After a four-year effort, separate bills to beef up federal oversight of the booming financial planning industry passed the House and Senate, but the two chambers were unable to reconcile their differences.

Both bills (HR 5726, S 2266) would have imposed annual fees on investment advisers, with the proceeds to be used to pay for additional Securities and Exchange Commission (SEC) inspectors. The SEC was unable to keep up with the booming financial planning industry and had only about 50 staff members to oversee 17,500 investment advisers.

But the House bill would have gone further, requiring advisers to disclose information to clients about their fees and financial expertise and to issue reports to them summarizing charges incurred in the handling of their accounts. It also would have required advisers to determine that each recommended investment was "suitable" after taking into account their clients' financial positions.

The Senate passed S 2266 by voice vote Aug. 12; the House passed its more sweeping bill Sept. 22, also by voice vote. Staff began informal negotiations to iron out the differences in the bills but were unable to reach agreement before the 102nd Congress adjourned.

Senate Action. The Banking Committee approved S 2266 on May 21 by an 18-2 vote. The bill was formally reported July 2 (S Rept 102-312).

To expedite approval, the committee agreed to an amendment by bill opponent Phil Gramm, R-Texas, that deleted a section that would have required financial planners to take into account a client's financial situation and investment experience and offer advice accordingly. But bill sponsor Christopher J. Dodd, D-Conn., expressed optimism that a similar "suitability" provision would be included if the bill went to conference.

Under the bill, advisers would have been charged an annual fee ranging from $300 to $7,000, with the money used to pay for a substantial increase in the number of SEC inspectors.

House Action. The Energy and Commerce Subcommittee on Finance approved a draft bill on July 30 by voice vote. The measure was introduced the same day as HR 5726.

The core of HR 5726 — the annual user fees of $300 to $7,000 — was identical to the Senate bill. But the House bill also would have imposed stricter rules on financial planners.

The full Energy and Commerce Committee approved the bill by voice vote Aug. 4. It was formally reported Sept. 22 (H Rept 102-883).

The bill came to the House floor the same day and was passed by voice vote under suspension of the rules. The following day, the House took up the Senate-passed measure (S 2266), amended it with the text of HR 5726 and passed it in hope of going to conference on S 2266.

Final Action. With the clock running out on the 102nd Congress, staff members negotiated informally in an effort to work out a compromise. But differences between the investment advisers bills were complicated because S 2266, as passed by the House, also included the text of a separate and controversial House bill governing corporate auditors.

The auditor bill had been reported separately as well (HR 4313 — H Rept 102-890). But it had no Senate counterpart. It would have required corporate accountants to report to the SEC when they found fraud as they audited corporate financial reports. HR 4313 essentially would have written into law self-imposed standards followed by most accountants, which required auditors to check the books of firms in a manner that "reasonably detected" fraud and report such illegal acts to the SEC if the company did not. *(Corporate auditor requirements, below)*

Also, Senate Banking Committee members were eager to win enactment of a stalled bill to tighten regulations on the $2.6 billion market in federal government securities (S 1699). The bill had passed the Senate in September 1991, but a companion House measure was hung up over a jurisdictional dispute. Some senators wanted to use the investment advisers bill to carry the language of S 1699. *(Government securities regulation, p. 158)*

These obstacles were not overcome before the end of the session, and the investment advisers bills died.

Corporate Auditor Requirements

A bill to require corporate accountants to blow the whistle on fraud they uncovered in the course of routine audits gained committee approval and passed the House in 1992. But the Senate had no companion measure, and the bill died.

The bill (HR 4313) won voice vote approval from the House Energy and Commerce Subcommittee on Finance on July 9 and from the full committee July 28. It was formally reported Sept. 22 (H Rept 102-890).

HR 4313 would have codified and greatly expanded self-imposed standards of the auditing profession aimed at disclosing fraud. It was an outgrowth of a spate of corporate failures that resulted from fraud, often involving savings and loan associations, that either went undetected or was disguised by accountants hired to certify public financial reports.

Finance Subcommittee Chairman Edward J. Markey, D-Mass., said banking regulators pursuing fraud in failed thrifts had settled 11 lawsuits against accounting companies for $40 million and that 19 other cases seeking $2 billion in damages were pending. But Markey said fraud in financial reporting was widespread beyond the thrift industry and said Congress had to act "to correct the current imbalance in incentives that leads some auditors to shield their clients rather than to protect the public."

Like most financial measures that emerged from Energy and Commerce, the bill was the product of extensive negotiations and had bipartisan support. While accountants did not wholeheartedly embrace an enlarged police role, they did not oppose the bill, which would have given them some protection from lawsuits stemming from their public disclosures.

The measure never came to a vote on the House floor. But when the House took up an unrelated Senate bill (S 2266) concerning investment advisers, it added the text of HR 4313. S 2266 — including the auditor language — passed the House Sept. 23 by voice vote but saw no further action. *(Investment advisers, above)*

Versions of the auditor bill were attached in 1990 to a House-passed crime bill (HR 5269) and in 1991 to the Energy and Commerce Committee version of a sweeping banking overhaul bill (HR 6) but did not survive in either measure. *(Crime bill, p. 764; banking bill, p. 136)*

HR 4313 did not include several controversial provisions from the earlier bills. For example, accountants would not have had to report publicly on the ability of internal corporate controls to detect and prevent fraud. And the SEC would not have been given authority to devise auditing standards, which were essentially the province of review boards established by the accounting profession.

Bank Red Tape Relief

A set of mostly non-controversial "regulatory relief" initiatives aimed at cutting red tape on the nation's banks and thrifts became law in 1992.

Hoping to ease what they saw as a regulatory burden on financial institutions, members of a House and Senate conference committee agreed Oct. 2, 1992, on several low-profile regulatory relief provisions.

The language was added to the conference report on a bill (HR 5334 — H Rept 102-1017) reauthorizing federal housing programs. President Bush signed the measure into law Oct. 28 (PL 102-550). *(Housing bill, p. 694)*

Senate Banking Committee Chairman Donald W. Riegle Jr., D-Mich., promised to add the regulatory provisions to the housing bill in conference after some senators threatened to block the housing bill unless he did so.

Action on the regulatory relief issues presaged a more ambitious effort that bankers promised to pursue in 1993. Supporters of the provisions said that various regulatory requirements enacted in previous years had swamped banks and that many of the rules could have been changed without affecting the ability of regulators to ensure safe banking operations. The banking industry said that the new regulations were forcing banks to curb lending.

The red-tape package, said proponents, represented some of the clearest and least controversial examples of regulatory overkill. The major provisions included those that would:

- Relax a requirement that certified appraisers examine property before banks could make loans. The provision clarified that bank regulators had the authority to allow banks to make real estate loans of up to $100,000 without obtaining a certified appraisal. The banking industry argued that the requirement for such appraisals for smaller loans was too burdensome on small and rural banks and that it was mainly large loans for commercial developments, not individual mortgages, that posed risks to the safety of a bank.
- Allow regulators, on a case-by-case basis, to give savings and loan institutions more time to either sell or fully capitalize their real estate subsidiaries, as required by the 1989 thrift bailout bill (HR 1278 — PL 101-73). Under existing regulations, most thrifts chose to sell their real estate operations, but thrifts argued that the deadlines had hurt them because of a slump in the real estate market. Under the provision, regulators first had to determine that the additional flexibility did not pose a risk to the thrift's financial soundness. The provision was to expire in 1996. *(Thrift bailout, p. 117)*
- Scale back a provision of a broad 1991 banking bill (S 543 — PL 102-242) that let regulators limit executives' pay at weak institutions. The language clarified that pay could be limited only if a clear safety and soundness issue was involved or if an enforcement action was under way. *(Banking bill, p. 136)*

• Relax existing restrictions on loans to bank officers and other insiders. The restrictions would be lifted if the loans were fully secured.

• Delay for three months, from March to June 1993, the implementation of the truth-in-savings provisions of the 1991 bank bill. The law was aimed at making it easier for consumers to understand and shop for interest rates, but banks said that the regulations had only recently been issued and that they needed extra time to comply.

Bank Disaster Assistance

In an effort to speed redevelopment in areas devastated by Hurricanes Andrew and Iniki and the Los Angeles riots, Congress cleared a bill (HR 6050) on Oct. 8, 1992, to ease certain banking regulations in those locales. President Bush signed the measure into law on Oct. 23 (PL 102-485).

The bill eased credit requirements for lenders aiding disaster victims. Supporters said that regulations written for normal times impeded banks from making loans in devastated communities. For example, rules that required banks to make appraisals before issuing real estate loans were difficult to comply with in devastated areas.

The bill gave regulators the authority to lift such appraisal requirements in disaster areas. Such authority would last for up to three years after the disaster.

In addition, the new law allowed banks to exclude big infusions of deposits attributable to insurance payments when calculating their capital requirements. Large and quick accumulations of deposits from such sources could have required banks to increase capital reserves.

The bill was a scaled-back version of a proposal sent to the Hill by the Treasury Department. The administration's original request was far too sweeping for Senate Banking Committee Chairman Donald W. Riegle Jr., D-Mich. He said the administration proposal (HR 5999, S 3242) would have allowed regulators far too much authority to lift regulations, even in areas unaffected by disasters.

HR 6050 was not marked up by either Banking committee. It came directly to the House floor on Oct. 3 and passed by voice vote. The Senate passed it Oct. 8 by voice vote, clearing the measure for the president.

Coin Redesign, Commemoratives

Congress cleared a commemorative coin bill (HR 3337 — PL 102-281) in April 1992 only after the House rejected the conference report on the bill and forced the measure back to conference, where offending provisions requiring a redesign of the nation's circulating coins were removed. Bush signed the bill May 13.

It was yet another defeat for Sen. Alan Cranston, D-Calif., who had made coin redesign a pet project and who retired at the end of the 102nd Congress.

The commemorative coin bill authorized the minting of four coins marking the 200th anniversary of the White House, James Madison and the Bill of Rights, the 500th anniversary of the voyage of Christopher Columbus and the 1994 World Cup soccer games to be played in various sites in the United States. The bill also authorized the minting of silver medals for about 640,000 members of the military who had served in the Persian Gulf War.

Although Cranston lobbied vigorously to preserve the redesign provisions, in the end it was his personal commitment to the issue — he had shepherded bills calling for coin redesign through the Senate 13 times since 1987 — that alienated some lawmakers. Several House members expressed annoyance at Cranston's persistence and at the seeming frivolity of spending so much time on the issue.

Cranston had been trying since 1987 to require the U.S. Mint to redesign the tail sides of the half dollar, quarter, dime, nickel and penny. He came close in 1990, after attaching redesign provisions to a housing reauthorization bill (S 566). Conferees on the bill were forced to delete them, however, when a House floor revolt threatened to sink the housing bill. *(Coin redesign, p. 135)*

House Action. The House suspended the rules and passed HR 3337 by voice vote on Nov. 26, 1991. As introduced, it authorized only the White House coin. But as it came to the floor it included the text of three other bills that had been approved July 25, 1991, by the House Banking Subcommittee on Coinage: HR 500, the Columbus coin; HR 1107, the Gulf War medal; HR 2801, the World Cup coin.

Senate Action. The day after the House floor vote, the Senate took up HR 3337, amended it by voice vote to add the James Madison coin and language requiring a redesign of the major circulating coins, and passed the bill by voice vote.

Final Action. Nov. 27 was the final day of the first session of the 102nd Congress, and when HR 3337 was returned to the House with the Senate amendments attached, all it took was the objection of a single member — Curt Weldon, R-Pa. — to block further action.

The coin redesign language was one problem, but Weldon wanted another commemorative coin minted, honoring Benjamin Franklin as the father of the American fire service.

On Feb. 19, 1992, the House rejected a motion to suspend the rules and concur in the Senate amendments on a vote of 172-241. Although the motion did not get even a simple majority, to succeed it needed a two-thirds majority because suspension of the rules blocked further amendments.

HR 3337 was then sent to conference, where conferees agreed March 12 to require that the back sides of two coins, the quarter and half dollar, be changed within the next two years to commemorate the bicentennials of the Constitution and the Bill of Rights. The conference report was filed March 16 (H Rept 102-454).

On April 1, the House took up the conference report and Al McCandless, R-Calif., moved to send the measure back to conference with instructions to House conferees to insist that the redesign provision be dropped. The motion carried 206-199.

Conferees reconvened April 2 and dropped the redesign, although Cranston tried to persuade House members to accept a scaled-back version. House conferees argued that the four commemoratives, which would raise money for the renovations at the White House and the World Cup soccer tournament, were too important to jeopardize with further design fights.

A new conference report (H Rept 102-485) was filed April 7, and the following day the House adopted it by a vote of 414-0.

Cranston had refused to sign the second conference report, and a threat was made that he would attempt to filibuster it. On April 8, Cranston blocked the Senate Banking Committee's plans to recommend confirmation of David J. Ryder as director of the U.S. Mint.

But despite Cranston's efforts, the Senate adopted the conference report on April 28 by a vote of 75-22, clearing the bill for the president.

3

Trade Policy

Introduction 165
1989-90 Chronology 169
1991-92 Chronology 187

Trade Policy

From the standpoint of both domestic and international concerns, the course of world trade was poised to turn several important corners in the 1990s, in large part because of groundwork laid at the turn of the decade. But while some major trade advances were made during George Bush's one term in the White House, more issues were left unresolved than were settled during the period.

Throughout Bush's presidency, neither those with strong internationalist views nor those who opposed what they considered myopic free-trade policies appeared to gain much of an advantage in policy debates.

Bilateral trade imbalances were beginning to right themselves, holding out the promise of eased political tensions in the United States and elsewhere. But that development had little obvious effect in limiting the antagonism that some in the United States felt toward the Japanese — whose merchantilist success in the 1980s was astounding and the subject of intense debate in the United States and abroad.

Fitful steps were taken in the early years of Bush's term to bring Japan to the negotiating table, but despite assertions of successes in opening corners of Japan's market, few tangible signs of change were evident.

Additionally, negotiations continued on both broad and narrow fronts in an attempt to reduce existing barriers to trade. Still, protectionist impulses remained strong.

At the end of 1992, worldwide talks held under the auspices of the GATT — the General Agreement on Tariffs and Trade — were at an impasse over European objections to reducing agricultural subsidies. And the North American Free Trade Agreement (NAFTA), though signed in December 1992 by the leaders of Canada, Mexico and the United States, faced an uncertain future, as opposition arose from some U.S. manufacturers; most unions, consumer and environmental groups; and many with populist or economic nationalist leanings.

During the 1992 presidential campaign, the trade pact won only a lukewarm endorsement from Bill Clinton — the man who would be Bush's successor as president and whose job it would be in the 103rd Congress to present the agreement to Congress for approval.

Finally, dramatic political upheaval in the Soviet Union and in Eastern Europe opened the door for new U.S. trade relationships with those countries. And the Chinese government's crackdown against a fledgling pro-democracy movement led to several failed attempts to shut off normalized trade with China as a lever of foreign policy.

An Evolving Trade Picture

The mid-1980s were a time of significant turmoil domestically, as the nation's balance of trade hit historic low points.

Imports of merchandise had exceeded exports for years, causing concern among those who believed the nation's economic health was a direct function of how successfully it produced the goods society demanded. But the merchandise trade deficit had usually been relatively small compared with the size it attained in the 1980s. And broader measures of international trade, which previously had almost always registered surpluses, began to mirror the increasing merchandise trade deficit.

The trade deficit bottomed out at $159.6 billion in 1987; that same year, the nation's so-called balance on current account — which factored not only merchandise imports and exports, but also trade in services and investment — hit a record deficit of $163.5 billion.

By the end of the decade, however, the picture was beginning to brighten. The merchandise trade deficit hit an eight-year low of $73.4 billion in 1991, partly because the 1990-91 recession sharply curtailed consumption of expensive imports. And thanks to payments by U.S. allies to support military activities in the Persian Gulf following Iraq's invasion of Kuwait, the current account deficit nearly disappeared in 1991.

A contributing factor to the improved trade balance was the continuing decline of the value of the dollar relative to foreign currencies. In 1985, the dollar peaked in foreign exchange markets. That year U.S. policymakers and their counterparts in the major industrialized countries began a concerted effort to drive the dollar down. As a result, it fell in value by almost 40 percent in three years,

References

Discussion of trade action for the years 1945-64 may be found in *Congress and the Nation Vol. I*, pp. 187-207; for the years 1965-68, *Congress and the Nation Vol. II*, pp. 49-116; for the years 1969-72, *Congress and the Nation Vol. III*, pp. 119-134; for the years 1973-76, *Congress and the Nation Vol. IV*, pp. 125-137; for the years 1977-80, *Congress and the Nation Vol. V*, pp. 267-276; for the years 1981-84, *Congress and the Nation Vol. VI*, pp. 95-112; for the years 1985-88, *Congress and the Nation Vol. VII*, pp. 139-166.

when measured against a trade-weighted index of foreign currencies. From 1988 to 1992, the dollar declined further, though slightly.

A cheaper dollar was viewed as a necessary evil by many analysts concerned about trade imbalances. It purchased fewer goods abroad and permitted cheaper U.S. exports. By 1992, although Japan was still running a trade surplus with the United States, on the whole U.S. trade with Europe was on a fairly even basis.

Downsides to the declining dollar included some higher consumer prices (though Japanese exporters attempted to offset foreign exchange-led price increases by trimming their profits). It also made purchases of U.S. real estate and other corporate assets less expensive for foreign investors.

Foreign investment in the United States was a continuing concern and prompted frequent attempts in Congress to impose limits on foreign ownership. Government statistical analysts worked to dispel the notion that foreign owners were taking over a significant share of U.S. productive capacity, in part by better calculating the market value of foreign assets owned by U.S. citizens. Those assets tended to be older than U.S. assets purchased by foreigners, and thus their book value was understated.

In 1992, the Commerce Department's Bureau of Economic Analysis reported that at market value the so-called net investment position of the United States was a negative $381 billion — meaning that foreign-owned assets in the United States were worth that much more than U.S. owned assets abroad. However, Commerce said that U.S. direct investment abroad — defined as ownership of 10 percent or more of an individual asset — exceeded foreign direct investment in the United States by about $150 billion. And, as has been the case for all of the 20th century, U.S. income from foreign investments continued to surpass earnings on foreign investment in the United States.

Bilateral Trade ...

During the period 1989-92, multiple efforts were made to boost trade — in particular U.S. exports. Those efforts were both large and small.

In March 1989, Treasury Secretary Nicholas F. Brady announced a plan for commercial bank debt relief for Latin American countries. Abetted by guarantees of repayment from the World Bank, the International Monetary Fund and the Inter-American Development Bank, the Brady plan relied on negotiations by individual countries with their creditor banks to reduce debt principal or interest owed or to provide new money at better rates.

A year later, in June 1990, Bush announced plans for the federal government to join in the debt-relief effort and forgive some loans made by the federal government to those countries.

Though U.S. interests in the region were multiple, a principal concern was that the economies of Latin America had deteriorated under a crushing debt burden, depriving the United States of what had been one of its best markets for exports. By restoring Latin economies to health, it was hoped, that export markets might once again take off, benefiting the U.S. economy.

Then, there was NAFTA, an idea born during the Reagan administration and seen as a natural extension of the free-trade accord between the United States and Canada.

Negotiating the U.S.-Canada agreement in 1987 was difficult enough, and the two countries had quite similar economies. To try to reach agreement over how to integrate the Mexican economy with its far more developed northern neighbors required significantly more sensitive negotiations. Nevertheless, Bush, Canadian Prime Minister Brian Mulroney and Mexican President Carlos Salinas de Gortari signed a sweeping deal to implement NAFTA on Dec. 17, 1992, in separate ceremonies in their own countries.

Bush's signature on the pact meant little. He had hoped to gain a political advantage from an August announcement that the deal was essentially complete, but that boost did not materialize. To many U.S. citizens, the idea of free trade with Mexico translated into U.S. businesses heading south of the border to take advantage of low-wage labor.

Moreover, trade agreements were subject to majority approval of both houses of Congress. It was guaranteed that NAFTA would not be submitted for approval before late 1993. First, discussions over side agreements on environmental protection and worker rights had to be concluded. Those talks were begun by the Bush administration following objections to the original deal.

... And Global Interests

For NAFTA to go forward, it had to be blessed in 1991 by votes in the House and Senate to permit an automatic, two-year renewal of the president's authority to negotiate trade agreements.

Since 1935, Congress had routinely granted the president authority to negotiate tariff reductions. In the 1988 trade bill, that authority was broadened to permit talks on a broader array of multilateral and bilateral issues. Central to the grant of negotiating authority was the promise that Congress would vote up or down on agreements, without having the opportunity to amend them. Only such "fast-track" authority would guarantee to foreign negotiators that the president was in a position to make serious offers.

The 1991 fast-track renewal was critical not only to NAFTA, but to ongoing multilateral talks in Geneva aimed at overhauling the GATT, where the United States hoped to win concessions in the contentious area of farm subsidies, intellectual property protection and textiles.

Reducing farm subsidies by European countries was most crucial — particularly if the United States was ever to cut back on its level of price- and income-support payments to farmers, not to mention export subsidies paid to purchasers of U.S. farm products.

In 1955, the United States joined with the Europeans in carving agriculture out of the original GATT accord. Along with textiles, agriculture had remained outside of the world trading rules ever since — usually at the insistence of industrialized countries.

Beginning in 1986, the Reagan administration embarked on what seemed a quixotic effort to eradicate agriculture subsidies worldwide by the year 2000. The Bush administration had since pulled back from that goal, although U.S. officials were still calling for deep cuts in "trade-distorting" subsidies in coming years. For the Bush administration, liberalizing agriculture trade offered tremendous potential gain — and several pitfalls. It offered the chance to compete on a level playing field with the Europeans, who had transformed themselves from food importers to major exporters in two decades, using subsidies a good deal more generous than those offered to U.S. farmers.

But with the growth in world agriculture trade slowing, exporting countries were finding stiffer competition for markets overseas. And given the U.S. budget crunch, the Bush administration was afraid it would be too expensive to try to outsubsidize the Europeans.

At GATT, the United States formed an alliance with a group of 14 agricultural nations that were even more desperate to secure open export markets for their products — and even more vulnerable to a subsidy war. Together, these countries refused to negotiate on issues such as services and intellectual property without a prior agreement for imposing strong "disciplines" on European export subsidies.

The talks repeatedly stalled over which agriculture subsidies should be reduced and by how much. The Europeans restricted their offers to internal subsidies, those that countries worldwide used to prop up the domestic price of farm goods or the payments governments made to farmers to ensure them a minimum income.

The European offers were widely criticized by U.S. officials and others as insufficient. The United States, in particular, wanted deep cuts in subsidies paid to purchasers of agricultural exports. But led by France and Germany, the European Community's largest agricultural producers, European negotiators refused to consider making specific commitments to reduce export subsidies.

Although there were hopes that the GATT impasse might be broken in 1993, a near certainty existed that Congress would need to renew the president's fast-track negotiating authority once more for an agreement to be sealed.

Another issue at stake in the GATT talks was protection for the U.S. textile and apparel industries. Textile-state lawmakers failed on several attempts in the mid-1980s to have Congress impose stiff quotas on textile, apparel and shoe imports. GATT negotiators were discussing proposals to replace an existing international regime that governed much of the world's trade in textiles. That regime, known as the Multi-Fiber Arrangement (MFA), provided the framework under which the United States had negotiated 38 bilateral and multilateral agreements limiting textile imports.

The MFA was to expire in 1991, and U.S. negotiators proposed retaining it but allowing it to phase out over 10 years, a change favored by developing countries that were eager for additional exports. In return, the United States sought other concessions from them.

The U.S textile industry did not like the MFA, arguing that it had not worked and that imports exceeded agreed-upon limits because multiple quotas for individual countries were difficult to enforce. But U.S. textile interests also did not want a world in which all restraints had been eliminated. The votes of textile-state members were likely to be an important bloc whenever — if ever — a GATT agreement came to Congress.

Japan Remained a Special Case

In 1988, Congress had tried to stiffen U.S. trade policy through the enactment of provisions in that year's omnibus trade bill that was known as "Super 301." Essentially a strengthened version of enforcement Section 301 of the 1974 Trade Act — Super 301 was designed to identify, cajole and, ultimately, punish major trade partners that inhibited access to their markets.

Under Super 301, the U.S. trade representative (USTR) was required in 1989 and 1990 to identify specific "priority countries" engaged in "priority practices" that limited market access. The cases were selected from the National Trade Estimate, a catalog of unfair foreign trade practices prepared annually by the USTR. The law gave the administration one year to negotiate removal of the barriers, with an option for a six-month extension. If the talks failed after that, the administration was authorized to raise tariffs on the goods of a priority country by as much as 100 percent.

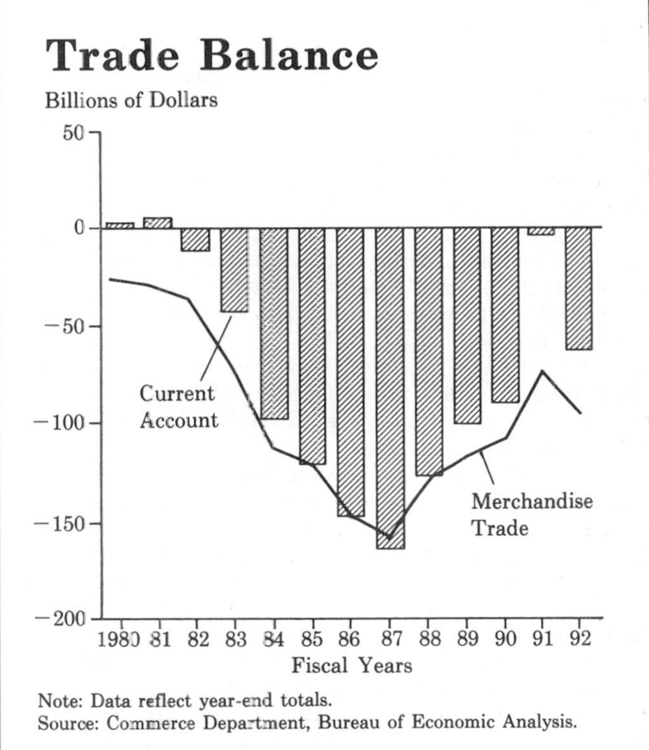

Note: Data reflect year-end totals.
Source: Commerce Department, Bureau of Economic Analysis.

The threat that a country would be placed on the Super 301 "hit list" aided the administration in persuading several countries, including South Korea, to modify their trade policies in 1989. But, while the law's existence proved a useful tool, the administration was not eager to actually name countries for potential retaliation.

In 1989, the Bush administration singled out Japan, India and Brazil for designation under Super 301.

The decision to include Japan on the list was made after a fierce internal debate within the administration. Brady, Secretary of State James A. Baker III, chief economic adviser Michael J. Boskin and budget director Richard G. Darman all reportedly urged more leniency with Japan. Reportedly arguing for a stronger stance were Commerce Secretary Robert A. Mosbacher and U.S. Trade Representative Carla A. Hills.

The three countries were cited for the following:

Brazil. For banning and limiting imports through a complex government licensing system; a prohibition on 1,000 items barred imports of U.S. meat, dairy products, plastics, chemicals and motor vehicles, among other items; and product-specific import quotas that limited sales of electrical machinery, internal combustion engine parts and other goods.

India. For requiring approval by the Indian government of U.S. investments there, frequently requiring that U.S. investors use Indian components in manufactured goods and requiring export of a specified portion of goods produced; for prohibiting private companies from selling insurance in India.

Japan. For prohibiting government purchases of foreign broadcast, communications and other satellites; for effectively barring government and university purchases of foreign supercomputers through government procurement processes; and for discouraging demand for wood products through building codes and product standards that favored other types of building materials.

At the same time, the administration initiated a separate set of high-level talks with Japan that became known as the Structural Impediments Initiative (SII).

The SII talks were conceived to address deep-seated structural practices in Japan that had the effect of excluding imports. These included laws that allowed Japanese corporations to collude in setting prices and allocating sales territory, practices that were forbidden in the United States under antitrust laws.

Other SII targets included keiretsu, the interlocking relationships among Japanese companies; land-use policies; low spending on public works; legal restrictions that forced big retailers to get approval from smaller local competitors before opening an outlet; and pricing mechanisms that forced Japanese consumers to pay as much as 70 percent more than U.S. consumers for the same goods.

The administration said that SII was a way of addressing long-term issues that were not appropriate subjects for Super 301 cases. But many lawmakers saw the initiative, which was not mandated by Congress and had no provision for retaliation, as a way to finesse Super 301.

And when the talks began, Japan succeeded in having them redefined to include U.S. practices that it said hurt U.S. competitiveness. Japan said the United States should cut its budget deficit, increase its savings rate and train its workers to produce better goods at lower cost.

A year later, in 1990, the administration successfully sidestepped pressure to cite Japan again under Super 301 and was able to announce enough progress in the SII talks to blunt congressional criticism.

In early March 1990, the administration turned up the heat in the SII talks, culminating with Bush meeting personally with Prime Minister Toshiki Kaifu and other high-ranking Japanese political figures in Washington on April 2-5. Following four days of intensive negotiations, the administration on April 5 declared a tentative victory in the talks, citing progress on access to large retail stores, ending exclusionary business practices and opening the door for U.S. contractors to bid on large Japanese public works projects.

At the same time, Hills was proclaiming success in negotiations with Japan on 1989 Super 301 cases involving purchases of U.S. satellites and supercomputers.

Appearing before the Senate Finance Committee on April 25, 1990, Hills urged lawmakers not to focus solely on Super 301. She got a vote of confidence from Finance Committee free-traders Bill Bradley, D-N.J., and Bob Packwood of Oregon, the committee's ranking Republican. But others were firm that Japan should be cited again under Super 301. "By definition, Japan has to be on that list," said Donald W. Riegle Jr., D-Mich., a view echoed by John C. Danforth, R-Mo., an original author of Super 301.

Hills came to that meeting with an ace: She was able to announce that, earlier that day in Japan, agreement had been reached on the third and last target issue from the 1989 Super 301 process, the import of forest products such as plywood from the United States. She said the agreement would result in a flow of $1 billion in U.S. products to Japan each year.

Two days later, on April 27, the administration issued its second and final Super 301 list naming a single country: India. And on June 14, 1990, the administration announced that it would not impose sanctions against India, even though that country had failed to negotiate an end to practices that had put it on the Super 301 list in 1989.

Hills said retaliation was inappropriate given the continuing negotiations on some of the same issues at GATT.

The decision drew little congressional response, though there was talk of legislating additional proscriptions on the president's discretion in enforcing trade laws. But no action materialized in the 101st Congress. Late in the 102nd Congress, the House passed a bill to renew Super 301, but the Senate never acted on it.

Chronology Of Action On Trade

1989-90

Congressional action on trade in 1989-90 veered sharply away from the concern of prior years over competition with other industrialized countries — principally Japan — and the protection of U.S. industries. Instead, attention focused more on changes in the communist world and in less-developed countries in the Western Hemisphere.

Dramatic political upheaval in the Soviet Union and in Eastern European countries with close ties to the Soviets caused a wholesale revision of U.S. attitudes toward open trade relationships with communist states — and underscored the often-conflicted link between foreign policy and trade policy.

Increased emphasis continued to be placed on improving the economies of Latin American countries, bolstering these close trading partners in an effort to improve the economy of the United States.

Antagonism toward the trade practices of Japan and some Western European countries — as well as more aggressive developing countries — was muted and resulted in little direct legislative activity.

Soviet, East Bloc Trade

With the ramparts of the Cold War appearing to crumble in Eastern Europe and in the Soviet Union, the United States began taking steps in 1989-90 to revise dramatically its trade policy with Moscow and the former East bloc.

President Bush and Soviet President Mikhail S. Gorbachev signed a broad trade agreement June 1, 1990, to grant the Soviet Union most-favored-nation (MFN) status, which meant normal trade relations would be established with the United States. Bush did not immediately send the pact to Congress for approval, saying that he would wait until the Soviet parliament had codified more open Soviet emigration policies. Although Soviet leaders said many times that an emigration law was about to be completed, the Soviet parliament did not act on it in 1990. *(MFN status, box, p. 172)*

Shortly before adjourning, the 101st Congress approved a trade agreement reached in April 1990 granting temporary normal trade relations with Czechoslovakia. The Senate also ratified a business and economic treaty intended to aid trade and investment between the United States and Poland, and in 1989, Congress passed a pair of bills granting financial aid and some trade assistance to Poland and Hungary. The measures were the first post-Cold War economic agreements with former East bloc countries. The Senate did not act on a House-passed measure to grant a three-year MFN extension for Hungary.

Soviet Union

The signing of the U.S.-Soviet trade agreement was a surprise ending to a dramatic summit meeting in Washington, D.C. In the days before the summit, administration aides had played down the likelihood of a trade deal because of concerns over a Soviet crackdown in the Baltic State of Lithuania. *(Trade agreement highlights, box, p. 170; U.S.-Soviet relations, p. 205)*

But Gorbachev himself reportedly appealed to Bush to sign the agreement, if only as a symbol of further Soviet integration into the world economy. Gorbachev also reportedly tied Soviet approval of a long-term wheat deal to the signing of the trade accord.

According to White House spokesman Marlin Fitzwater, Bush decided to go forward with the trade agreement a half-hour before the two leaders sat down to sign it.

In a news conference at the end of the summit, Bush stressed that his approval was tied to the issue of emigration, nothing more.

Congress, however, would not adopt the trade agreement until the Kremlin also negotiated in good faith with the Lithuanian government and lifted an economic embargo against the breakaway Baltic republic. The Senate went on record with that position, 73-24, on May 1, 1990, in a sense of the Senate amendment to a supplemental appropriations bill (HR 4404); the House followed suit June 6, voting 390-24 to add similar language to an export control bill (HR 4653).

Background. As Bush looked for ways to facilitate the integration of the Soviet Union and Eastern Europe into the world economy, prospects increased in 1989 that he would seek a waiver of the main law blocking U.S.-Soviet trade: the Jackson-Vanik amendment to the 1974 Trade Act (PL 93-618), which restricted grants of MFN status to communist countries that did not permit free emigration of their citizens. (Sen. Henry M. Jackson, D-Wash. (House 1941-53; Senate 1953-83), and Rep. Charles A. Vanik, D-Ohio (1955-81), wrote the amendment.) To get around Jackson-Vanik, the president had to either certify that the communist country was permitting free emigration or grant a one-year waiver of the law, on the ground that the country was making progress in allowing free emigration. Congress was given the power to reject Jackson-Vanik waivers and certifications. *(1974 law, Congress and the Nation Vol. IV, p. 131)*

Bush announced in May 1989 that he was "prepared to work with Congress for a temporary waiver" of Jackson-Vanik for the Soviet Union, once the Soviets had enacted laws to guarantee the rights of their citizens to emigrate freely and had "implemented its new laws faithfully."

By a lopsided margin, the Supreme Soviet approved a statute in November 1989 that would codify liberalized emigration policies already in practice. However, under Soviet procedures, the law had to be approved a second time, which did not happen until 1991.

In the meantime, following a Dec. 2-3, 1989, summit meeting with Gorbachev in Malta, Bush announced plans to begin negotiating a trade agreement with the Soviets. The agreement was expected to be ready when the two leaders met for their next scheduled summit in June 1990.

At Malta, Bush also offered to support Soviet observer status at the talks of the Geneva-based General Agreement on Tariffs and Trade (GATT), the world body that oversaw most trade relationships. Furthermore, he told Gorbachev

U.S.-Soviet Trade Agreement Highlights

Following are key provisions of the trade agreement signed June 1, 1990, by President Bush and Soviet President Mikhail S. Gorbachev:

Most-Favored-Nation Treatment. Each country agreed to grant unconditional most-favored-nation (MFN) treatment to goods produced by the other and imported for domestic consumption. The agreement covered customs duties; rules concerning shipment, warehousing and customs clearance; and payment for imports with hard currency. Generally MFN meant treatment no less favorable than that accorded other countries.

Market Access. Each country agreed to base purchase decisions on customary commercial considerations, such as price, quality and terms of delivery, and not to require or encourage barter or countertrade (the practice of conditioning imports on reciprocal purchases). Each country agreed not to apply technical standards or rules to protect domestic production or imports from a third country (although a side letter to the agreement exempted textile imports into the United States). The Soviet Union agreed, as it moved toward membership in the General Agreement on Tariffs and Trade (GATT) — the organization that governed world commerce — to allow increased "national treatment" for U.S. goods and services.

Business Promotion and Development. Each country agreed to allow companies (including government-owned enterprises) to maintain ordinary business operations in the other. This included the ability to acquire living and office quarters whether or not they were intended for foreigners, to hire nationals of either country and pay them in agreed-upon currency, to advertise in publications designed for that purpose and through the mails, to conduct market studies and to import goods duty-free for trade shows. The Soviet Union agreed to expedite accreditation of U.S. businesses and to pay particular attention to the needs of small businesses.

Financial Conditions. Each country agreed that transactions would be paid for in dollars or other freely convertible currencies, unless otherwise agreed between the parties. (The Soviet ruble was not convertible on world markets and could not be exported.) The Soviet Union agreed that U.S. businesses would be treated as favorably as those of any other country on the question of maintaining bank accounts in rubles and having access to convertible currencies. The Soviet Union agreed to consider requests from U.S. businesses to use rubles to pay for local expenses.

Intellectual Property Protection. Each country agreed to adhere to broad international copyright and patent protection conventions, including the Berne Convention on artistic and literary works; to protect copyrights on sound recordings produced domestically and in the other country; to protect copyrights on computer programs and data bases; and to protect patents on industrial processes, except those used solely in production of nuclear weapons.

Market Disruption. Each country agreed to consult when imports threatened to disrupt domestic markets and to allow for unilateral protections of domestic industries (as allowed under GATT). In such cases, the other country would be free to deny equivalent benefits granted by the trade agreement so as not to be unfairly disadvantaged.

Dispute Settlement. Each country agreed to seek arbitrated settlement of commercial disagreements and to treat businesses from either country alike in its judicial and administrative proceedings.

General. Once approved by Congress, the agreement was to be in effect for three years, renewable for successive three-year periods. The agreement in no way restricted actions deemed necessary for national security reasons, and it permitted adoption of laws and rules, such as those governing health and antitrust, that were otherwise consistent with it. The Soviets also agreed in a side letter to resume repayments on $674 million in World War II lend-lease assistance, conditioned on repeal of U.S. laws that restricted credit to the Soviet Union.

he would talk to Congress about lifting other statutory limits on Soviet trade, including the 1974 Stevenson amendment (named for author Sen. Adlai E. Stevenson III, D-Ill. (1970-81)), which capped Soviet credit from the U.S. Export-Import Bank at $300 million.

Bush promised work on a mutual investment treaty that would enable U.S. businesses to repatriate profits from the Soviet Union and permit the Overseas Private Investment Corporation (OPIC) to insure U.S. capital in the Soviet Union. He also proposed a variety of cooperative economic projects in agriculture, finance and small business development, including a stock exchange and antitrust laws.

All these endeavors depended on a waiver of Jackson-Vanik, which until a short time before had enjoyed such political popularity as to be almost sacrosanct.

Before Jackson-Vanik, the Soviets had hoped to gain MFN status under a trade agreement reached in 1972 with President Richard Nixon. In the wake of Jackson-Vanik's passage, the Soviets withdrew from the agreement and temporarily tightened the emigration limits still further.

But 1989 had brought dramatic change in Soviet emigration policies. Sixty thousand Soviet Jews were expected to emigrate by the end of the year, a post-World War II record. And Bush heard a rising chorus of voices urging him to exercise the waiver power given him under Jackson-

Vanik. As the Malta summit approached, letters circulated by Democrats — including Sens. George J. Mitchell of Maine and Max Baucus of Montana, and Reps. Thomas J. Downey of New York and Robert G. Torricelli of New Jersey — urged Bush to waive the restrictions for a year.

In 1989, American Jewish groups — which had ardently supported the Jackson-Vanik amendment — began openly debating the advantages of reconsidering it in light of Gorbachev's reforms. By year's end, a number of groups backed the idea of a temporary waiver.

Bush's Decision. A legal barrier to completing the trade agreement was temporarily removed Dec. 12, 1990, when Bush announced that he was waiving Jackson-Vanik restrictions against the Soviet Union until July 1991.

Although emigration, particularly of Soviet Jews, had increased dramatically, Bush had expected to await enactment of the new Soviet law before waiving Jackson-Vanik. However, growing instability in the Soviet Union and the prospects of severe winter food shortages led him to grant the waiver, thereby allowing the extension of agricultural credits, even though he was unprepared to forward the broader trade agreement to Congress.

The waiver enabled the Soviets to buy up to $1 billion worth of U.S. agricultural goods. And it also qualified the Soviets to receive credit from the Export-Import Bank (though the separate Stevenson limit of $300 million in Ex-Im credits remained in effect).

In addition to providing agricultural credits, Bush approved sending technical experts to the Soviet Union to help improve the country's troubled food distribution network. The administration also said that financial aid would be given to private groups sending medical equipment and pharmaceutical supplies to Moscow.

At the time of Bush's Jackson-Vanik waiver, Congress had adjourned for the year and thus did not have an immediate opportunity to vote to disapprove it. Congressional sentiment clearly was in favor of the waiver, however.

Fixing Jackson-Vanik. Congress in 1989 amended the 1974 Jackson-Vanik language to correct a probable constitutional defect, based on the 1983 Supreme Court decision in *Immigration and Naturalization Service v. Chadha.* *(Court ruling, Congress and the Nation Vol. VI, pp. 762, 833)*

The 1974 law provided that Congress could reject a Jackson-Vanik waiver or certification if either chamber adopted a simple resolution of disapproval. *Chadha*, however, ruled that such "legislative vetoes" were unconstitutional. Provisions to fix the defect were included in legislation (HR 1594 — PL 101-382) to renew special trade benefits for Caribbean nations. The bill, signed Aug. 20, 1990, changed the 1974 law to require enactment of joint resolutions, which had the force of law, to disapprove Jackson-Vanik waivers and certifications.

Prior law also allowed Congress to approve trade agreements granting MFN status by adopting concurrent resolutions. Though *Chadha* did not address whether such a procedure was constitutionally suspect, Congress played it safe and required enactment of joint resolutions for approval of trade agreements as well. *(Caribbean Basin Initiative, p. 180)*

Czechoslovakia

A trade agreement granting normalized trade relations with Czechoslovakia was approved by Congress on Oct. 24, 1990. The Senate by voice vote passed, and thus cleared for the president, a joint resolution (H J Res 649) that approved the trade agreement and the granting of MFN status to Czechoslovakia for one year. The House had passed the measure Oct. 17 by voice vote.

Once a trade agreement was submitted to Congress, it could not be amended. Bush signed H J Res 649 into law (PL 101-541) on Nov. 8.

The trade agreement signed April 12, 1990, by Czechoslovakian and U.S. trade officials was intended to eliminate or reduce tariffs and other trade barriers, to provide better patent and copyright protections for U.S. companies, to allow immediate repatriation of profits and otherwise to improve economic relations between the two countries.

The agreement also called for the two countries to apply international trading rules established under GATT to their transactions, though Czechoslovakia was not a member of GATT. Czechoslovakia agreed to improve currency exchange provisions for U.S. businesses and legal protections for U.S. patents and other intellectual property rights.

The House Ways and Means Committee reported H J Res 649 (H Rept 101-773) on Oct. 1. The Senate Finance Committee favorably reported an identical companion measure (S J Res 361 — S Rept 101-537) on Oct. 18.

Action on the agreement was preceded by an emotional, personal appeal from Czechoslovakia President Vaclav Havel to a joint meeting of Congress on Feb. 21. Havel, a dissident playwright turned politician, said the United States could best aid the newly freed countries of Eastern Europe by encouraging the Soviet Union's slow march away from communism.

Bush told Havel that he was granting Czechoslovakia a one-year Jackson-Vanik waiver, which opened the door for the trade agreement.

Havel's appearance before Congress was the second within a few months by a major Eastern European political figure. Lech Walesa, leader of Poland's Solidarity labor union, appeared in November 1989.

Poland

In 1989 and 1990, Congress took several steps to ease Poland's transition to a market-based economy and to boost that country's trade with the United States. Poland did not need a grant of MFN, however. It had been given normal trade status in 1960 and therefore was not subject to Jackson-Vanik. Other provisions of federal law, however, prevented the Export-Import Bank from issuing loans and guarantees and other credits to finance U.S. exports to Poland and prevented OPIC from insuring U.S.-owned capital invested in Poland.

Investment Treaty. The Senate on Oct. 28 (in the session that began Oct. 27), 1990, ratified a limited business and economic treaty with Poland that had been signed by Bush and Polish Prime Minister Tadeusz Mazowiecki on March 21.

The treaty allowed for favorable treatment of U.S. investors in Poland and gave U.S. companies free access to the Polish market. "We can now take this treaty to the U.S. business community and say, 'This is why you should invest in Poland,'" Bush said.

Bush and Mazowiecki met twice at the White House during a three-day visit to Washington by the Polish leader, who took office in August 1989 after Solidarity-led forces swept the Communist Party in national elections.

Most-Favored Nations: Nothing Special

Despite its name, most-favored-nation (MFN) trading status was not a special preference for favored nations; it was virtually synonymous with normal or non-discriminatory treatment among trading partners, particularly on the issue of tariffs, or duties, charged on imported goods. The United States extended MFN status to nearly every country in the world.

Who Was Eligible. In general, the nearly 100 members of the General Agreement on Tariffs and Trade (GATT) — the world body that governed most trade agreements — granted MFN to their trading partners. In doing so, they agreed to accept each other's exports at the lowest tariff rates — the rates that each charged its "most-favored nation." Non-MFN tariff rates tended to be about 10 times as high as MFN rates. (Certain developing countries qualified for even lower tariffs on certain products under the Generalized System of Preferences, and bilateral trade agreements often resulted in lower tariffs.)

Communist Countries an Exception. Under the Jackson-Vanik amendment to the 1974 Trade Act (PL 93-618), the president could grant MFN status to a communist country only as part of a congressionally approved commercial trade agreement. (The amendment was authored by Sen. Henry M. Jackson, D-Wash. (House 1941-53; Senate 1953-83), and Rep. Charles A. Vanik, D-Ohio (1955-81).) Such an agreement could be submitted to Congress only if the president certified that the communist country permitted free emigration or if he waived the requirement because the country was improving its emigration policies. A waiver had to be renewed annually. *(Congress and the Nation Vol. IV, p. 131)*

Congress could reject a Jackson-Vanik waiver or certification by passing a joint resolution that had to be signed into law or enacted over the president's veto. That procedure was changed from its original 1974 form, which allowed a single chamber to reject a waiver through adoption of a simple resolution. Such "legislative vetoes" were found by the Supreme Court in *Immigration and Naturalization Service v. Chadha* (1983) to violate the Constitution's separation of powers doctrine. The new procedure was contained in a bill (HR 1594 — PL 101-382) enacted in 1990 to renew special trade concessions for Caribbean nations. *(Caribbean Basin Initiative, p. 180;* Chadha *decision, Congress and the Nation Vol. VI, pp. 762, 833)*

Soviet Union and East Bloc Status. Though written to apply to all "non-market economy countries" that barred free emigration, the Jackson-Vanik amendment was especially aimed at the Soviet Union and its Eastern bloc trading partners. From 1951 until the trade act took effect in 1975, MFN status had been denied to most communist states.

Jackson-Vanik specifically did not apply to Poland or Yugoslavia, which had gained MFN status previously. Romania and Hungary were granted MFN soon after the enactment of Jackson-Vanik. But some in Congress, unhappy with the Romanian government, several times attempted to revoke Romania's Jackson-Vanik waiver. Romania renounced its MFN status in 1988, as Congress was preparing to revoke it as part of a broad trade bill (PL 100-418). *(Congress and the Nation Vol. VI, pp. 103, 107; Congress and the Nation Vol. VII, p. 148)*

With the collapse first of the East bloc alliance and later of the Soviet Union, the United States began granting MFN across the region, beginning with Czechoslovakia in 1990. *(East bloc, Soviet trade status, p. 169)*

China's Status. China first received MFN status from the United States through a commercial trade agreement approved by Congress in 1980. China's Jackson-Vanik waiver was renewed annually thereafter, though repeated efforts were made to revoke China's MFN status following the Chinese government's June 1989 crackdown on pro-democracy demonstrators in Tiananmen Square. *(China action, p. 173; background, Congress and the Nation Vol. V, p. 90)*

Trade Assistance. In 1989, Bush called for several aid packages for Poland in response to its historic break from the Soviet bloc. Congress went further than the administration proposed in passing more ambitious and costly economic aid packages that included $125 million in food aid in fiscal 1990 and a $200 million trade credit insurance program through the Ex-Im Bank.

Bush's moves in 1989 to aid Poland were prompted by an agreement signed April 5, 1989, by the Warsaw government and opposition leaders. The accord called for sweeping political changes, including establishment of a new system of government with a president and a two-chamber parliament, restoration of legal status for the independent trade union Solidarity and the holding of free elections in June. The Polish parliament on April 7 approved six laws putting the major reforms into effect.

Congress responded to Bush's request with a pair of bills to aid both Poland and Hungary. A three-year authorization bill (HR 3402 — PL 101-179) signed into law on Nov. 28, 1989, and a fiscal 1990 foreign aid appropriations bill (HR 3743 — PL 101-167), signed on Nov. 21, contained substantially identical provisions granting food aid, special trade credits and other trade and development assistance. HR 3402, which had passed the House Oct. 19 on a **key vote of 345-47 (R 128-34; D 217-13)**, also lifted Cold War bars to Ex-Im Bank credits for exports to Poland and Hungary and OPIC insurance for investments in those countries. *(Poland, Hungary aid, p. 210; 1989 key votes, p. 1021)*

Hungary

In 1989, Bush had sought trade and development assistance for Hungary at the same time that he asked for aid for Poland. The two 1989 foreign aid bills (HR 3402, HR 3743) that lifted Cold War barriers to Ex-Im Bank and OPIC activities in Poland also applied to Hungary, as did other provisions.

Like Poland, Hungary did not need a Jackson-Vanik waiver or a grant of MFN status. Hungary was first granted normal trade status in 1978, soon after enactment of Jackson-Vanik.

The House, however, in 1989 had passed a bill (HR 1594 — H Rept 101-99) to authorize a three-year extension of MFN trade status for Hungary to improve the climate for U.S. investment in that country. But the Senate used the bill in 1990 as a vehicle for a miscellany of customs and trade provisions, including an extension of the Caribbean Basin Initiative, and stripped the measure of the Hungary provisions.

China Trade

Liberals and conservatives in Congress were angered by the Chinese government's June 3-4, 1989, crackdown on pro-democracy demonstrators who were gathered in Beijing's Tiananmen Square.

As a result, several legislative attempts were made in 1990 to impress upon China official expressions of U.S. indignation, including efforts to withdraw continued most-favored-nation (MFN) trade status for China (H J Res 647) and to impose conditions on China's annual MFN renewal due in July 1991 (HR 4939).

Supporters of congressional action noted that China was becoming one of the largest trading partners of the United States and that it relied heavily on sales of clothing, toys and other goods to support a growing economy. Trade sanctions, they said, which would increase tariffs on imports from China by as much as tenfold (in effect doubling the retail price of some imports), would be such a threat to the Chinese economy that the government would be forced to alter its treatment of dissidents.

Opponents of restricting trade with China as a means to force that country to improve its human rights record were led by President Bush, one-time U.S. envoy to China under President Richard Nixon. Bush was hardly alone, however, in arguing that the tactic would not work and that the Chinese government would not be moved. Opponents argued that pro-democracy factions inside China and U.S. business interests in China and Hong Kong, not to mention U.S. consumers of Chinese-made goods, would suffer the consequences of trade sanctions.

The House passed both China MFN bills in 1990. But they died when the Senate did not act on them. *(U.S.-China relations, p. 250)*

Legislative History

Most communist countries had been denied MFN — also called normal trade status and which included eligibility for the low tariffs assessed on imports from most countries — by the Jackson-Vanik amendment to the 1974 Trade Act (PL 93-618). *(Congress and the Nation Vol. IV, p. 131)*

Under the provisions of Jackson-Vanik, China had been granted MFN in 1980, subject to annual renewal — actually an annual presidential waiver of the Jackson-Vanik requirement, subject to congressional disapproval. Until 1990, China's Jackson-Vanik waiver had been routine. *(Most-favored nations, box, p. 172; 1980 action, Congress and the Nation Vol. V, p. 90)*

H J Res 647 would have disapproved the annual Jackson-Vanik waiver for China that took effect July 4, 1990; HR 4939 would have set new human rights conditions for the president to certify that China had met before he could renew that country's MFN status in 1991.

Action on H J Res 647 was made possible by enactment of a seemingly unrelated bill (HR 1594 — PL 101-382) reauthorizing the Caribbean Basin Initiative. That measure, signed into law Aug. 20, 1990, created a new procedure for expedited consideration of bills rejecting Jackson-Vanik waivers, correcting a constitutional defect. Until that correction was enacted, Congress was not expected to act under the specific terms of the 1974 law to reject a Jackson-Vanik waiver. *(Caribbean Basin Initiative, p. 180)*

House Action. The effort to block renewal of China's MFN status began May 24, 1990 — just shy of a year after the Tiananmen Square massacre — when Bush announced he would waive Jackson-Vanik for another year, as it applied to China. The same day, Rep. Don J. Pease, D-Ohio, introduced HR 4939 to require the president to certify that China had made "significant progress" toward meeting a list of human rights objectives if he wanted to waive Jackson-Vanik again in 1991.

The House Ways and Means Subcommittee on Trade approved the bill by voice vote July 12, after rejecting an amendment that would have stiffened the bill by requiring that the president certify that China had met certain human rights objectives — not merely that it was making progress toward meeting them.

A week later, on July 18, the full committee approved the bill unchanged by voice vote and on July 23 reported it (H Rept 101-620). Ways and Means members rejected an amendment that would have withdrawn China's MFN status immediately, as well as conditioned a future grant of normal trade relations. Pease and his allies argued that his bill imposing conditions was a good middle ground between those arguing for an immediate withdrawal of MFN and those favoring no trade linkage to China's human rights record.

The August enactment of changes to the Jackson-Vanik waiver process, in HR 1594, opened a second avenue for legislative assault on China's trade relationship with the United States. Rep. Gerald B. H. Solomon, R-N.Y., introduced H J Res 647 on Sept. 5, to disapprove China's 1990 Jackson-Vanik waiver. H J Res 647 was subject to an expedited committee and floor process that blocked amendments. The measure was approved for floor action by Ways and Means on Sept. 25 by voice vote and reported without recommendation on Oct. 1 (H Rept 101-772).

Both bills came to the House floor Oct. 18. The House first passed H J Res 647 by a vote of 247-174. The House then adopted several amendments to HR 4939, including a stiffer definition of "significant progress" and a requirement that China release political prisoners detained after Tiananmen Square. The House passed the bill 384-30.

Senate Action. Although Senate Majority Leader George J. Mitchell, D-Maine, favored removing China's MFN status outright or at least restricting its future renewal, he could not muster much support for the idea amongst his fellow senators.

In July, Mitchell introduced a bill (S 2836) to withdraw China's MFN, but it was not subject to the expedited procedures that governed action on H J Res 647. The Senate never acted on Mitchell's measure or on either of the House-passed bills. All died when Congress adjourned at the end of 1990.

Textile Import Quotas

Textile interests failed in 1990, in the face of the third presidential veto in five years, to enact legislation sharply restricting imports of fabrics, clothing and shoes.

By wide majorities in both chambers, Congress cleared a textile quota bill (HR 4328) that would have limited textile and apparel import growth to 1 percent per year and permanently frozen imports of most shoes at 1989 levels.

But President Bush vetoed the measure Oct. 5, calling it "highly protectionist." And the House on Oct. 10 fell 10 votes short of the two-thirds majority needed to override the veto. The House sustained the veto on a **key vote of 275-152 (R 70-103; D 205-49)**. The Senate took no further action on the measure. *(1990 key votes, p. 1039)*

Background

U.S. textile manufacturers claimed that quotas were needed to blunt the effects of low-wage competition from abroad on a vital domestic industry that had lost 500,000 jobs since 1980. Opponents countered that the textile industry was prospering and that quotas would drive up the cost of consumer goods, violate international trade agreements and invite retaliation by U.S. trading partners.

The textile industry was the nation's largest manufacturing sector, employing 2 million people. But during the 1970s and 1980s, it came under increasing pressure from competition from foreign manufacturers. According to textile industry supporters, imports of textiles and textile products tripled from 1980 to 1989, contributing to a textile and clothing trade deficit of $26 billion in 1989.

Furthermore, imports came to dominate the U.S. footwear market. In 1980, imports had claimed 50 percent of the domestic market; in 1989, 80 percent.

Plant closings in the traditional textile centers of the Southeast and Northeast created for many the impression of an industry facing extinction at the hands of low-wage competitors in the Third World. Always a powerful force on Capitol Hill, the industry began in the mid-1980s to push a stringent quota bill as a way of protecting itself from foreign competition.

Opponents, however, maintained that quotas were unnecessary because the industry was adapting to competition from abroad through plant modernization. They also said the industry was adequately protected by existing tariffs and bilateral trade agreements.

Textile imports were governed by the 1973 Multi-Fiber Arrangement, an international trade pact that was aimed at helping fledgling textile and apparel industries in developing countries while providing protection to their domestic competitors though voluntary import limits. The international agreement was enforced through separate bilateral trade agreements with 38 countries.

But textile industry supporters argued that despite the Multi-Fiber Arrangement imports had increased at 10 times the rate of growth of the U.S. market. So their supporters in Congress began pushing for strict country-by-country quotas. Congress cleared such a bill in 1985, but it was vetoed by President Ronald Reagan. His veto was sustained by the House in August 1986, by 276-149, eight votes short of the needed two-thirds majority. *(1985-86 action, Congress and the Nation Vol. VII, p. 141)*

Shortly before the 1986 override vote, the Multi-Fiber Arrangement was renewed for five years through multilateral negotiations. Though the agreement imposed somewhat tougher import limits, industry supporters said it was inadequate.

In 1988, industry supporters modified their proposal to provide overall quotas instead of country-by-country allotments. They also sought to pick up farm-state support by adding a provision that would have allowed for countries to increase their textile quotas by increasing their imports of U.S. agricultural products.

Congress also cleared that bill, but it, too, was vetoed, and the override attempt again failed in the House, 272-152. *(1988 action, Congress and the Nation Vol. VII, p. 164)*

Legislative History

Senate Action. Textile-state senators opened the push for passage of the 1990 bill. On June 21, the Finance Committee allowed proponents to advance a quota bill (S 2411) to the floor, agreeing by voice vote to report it without recommendation (or a written report).

The committee also substituted the text of S 2411 for the language of a minor House trade agencies authorization bill (HR 4328) that it approved without recommendation the same day. The new measure was very similar to the quota bill vetoed in 1988. (The House had passed HR 4328 (H Rept 101-427) on March 27, 424-0, under suspension of the rules.) About half the 20 committee members had indicated support for the quota bill, but several had opposed it vigorously, arguing that it violated the Multi-Fiber Arrangement and the General Agreement on Tariffs and Trade (GATT), an international body that oversaw trade relationships and whose terms generally prohibited protectionist actions by member countries. A new cycle of multilateral trade talks, called the Uruguay Round, was then under way at GATT headquarters in Geneva, where it was hoped that new textile protections might be negotiated.

The full Senate took up HR 4328 July 12. The same day, the White House — as expected — warned that the bill would face a veto.

Opponents of the bill brought six amendments to roll-call votes. All were easily defeated as the bill's sponsors rallied 65 to 70 votes for tabling motions.

Thanks to help from Farm Belt senators, the bill's sponsors scored their best showing ever in passing HR 4328 on July 17 by 68-32, eight votes more than they had in passing the 1985 bill and 11 more than in 1988. The majority would have been sufficient to override a veto if all the votes held firm.

A bare majority of Republicans (23 of 45) stood with Bush in opposing the bill. Some who voted for the measure had big textile industries in their states (Jesse Helms of North Carolina and Strom Thurmond of South Carolina); others had factories that made shoes or clothing (William S. Cohen of Maine and John Heinz and Arlen Specter of Pennsylvania).

Southern Democrats, traditional defenders of the textile industry, backed the bill 16-1. The one exception was Bob Graham of Florida, a major promoter of free trade for the Caribbean Basin, where textile and footwear exporters would have been hobbled by any limit on U.S. import growth.

House Action. House Ways and Means Committee Chairman Dan Rostenkowski, D-Ill., whose committee had jurisdiction over the measure, showed little interest in the bill. And Trade Subcommittee Chairman Sam M. Gibbons, D-Fla., an active opponent of textile quotas, had scheduled no hearings on it.

But after the Senate action, the House leadership asked Rostenkowski to expedite a floor vote on the Senate changes, and he obliged. On July 25, Ways and Means sent the Senate-passed bill to the House floor by voice vote without recommendation and virtually without debate (H Rept 101-649).

HR 4328 came back to the House floor Sept. 18, where the Senate amendments were easily accepted, 271-149, and the bill cleared for Bush. Support for the bill was strongest among Democrats. Southern Democrats showed near unanimity, splitting voting 71-9 for the bill, while Northern Democrats supported it 129-39. A majority of Republicans (71-101), however, opposed it.

Final Action, Veto. Recognizing the likelihood of a veto, supporters of the bill had a secondary reason for pushing it. They wanted to pressure U.S. negotiators at the GATT talks in Geneva to provide protection for the textile industry. U.S. negotiators had proposed phasing out the bilateral agreements under the Multi-Fiber Arrangement over a 10-year period. Developing countries participating in the talks had set removal of existing, negotiated import restrictions as a major goal, and the United States wanted other important concessions from these countries.

A strong vote for the textile bill, supporters reasoned, would warn the negotiating team about the difficulty of winning congressional approval for legislation needed to put a broad GATT agreement into effect.

Bush's anticipated veto came Oct. 5 with a strongly worded message saying the bill "would damage the national economy, increase already artificially high costs to consumers . . . and abrogate our international agreements." He also said it would "eliminate any hope" of successful completion of the GATT talks and added that the measure would particularly hurt two countries, Turkey and Egypt, that were providing important support for U.S. policy in the Persian Gulf. *(Persian Gulf, p. 299)*

When the House debated overriding the veto Oct. 10, the arguments pitted the interests of textile workers against consumers at large. Quota supporters picked up four more votes than they had when the House originally passed the bill, but that was not enough. Solid Democratic support for the bill was offset by relatively strong Republican backing for Bush, leaving quota supporters 10 votes short of the two-thirds majority they needed to override the veto.

Export Controls

Congress cleared a measure in late October 1990 to retain but dramatically overhaul legal controls on the export of high-technology goods. Reluctantly, President Bush pocket-vetoed the bill (HR 4653) because it contained restrictions on foreign aid to countries that used chemical weapons or aided others in manufacturing chemical weapons. The pocket veto, which followed Congress' adjournment, could not be overridden and thus killed the bill.

Although the chemical weapons sanctions drew wide bipartisan backing — 79 senators signed a letter to the president, urging him to sign the bill — Bush said the provisions would "unduly interfere with the president's responsibility for carrying out foreign policy."

HR 4653 would have reauthorized through 1992 the Export Administration Act of 1979, which established the federal government's licensing program for sales of high-technology goods to foreign countries. U.S. licensing of militarily sensitive sales — such as high-grade metal-milling equipment and computers — had been a subject of dispute for years between those who wanted to promote U.S. trade and those who regarded export of some high-tech items as a threat to U.S. national security.

The bill would have sharply reduced the number of items on the Commerce Department's list of controlled exports and eased restrictions on exports to certain Eastern European nations in line with actions taken in June 1990 by the 17-nation Coordinating Committee on Multilateral Export Controls (Cocom).

Despite the veto of HR 4653, the president had authority under other laws, chiefly the International Emergency Economic Powers Act of 1976, to continue export controls. Before announcing the veto, Bush issued an executive order implementing portions of the bill, citing those other laws.

Chemical Weapons

Concern about Iraq's chemical weapons capacity and aid that Iraq reportedly received from other countries prompted inclusion of the contentious sanctions provisions. The provisions, added during Senate floor consideration of the bill, contained the text of legislation that had passed both chambers in various forms (HR 3033, S 195) but had stalled in conference. *(Chemical weapons, box, p. 366)*

The sanctions provisions would have punished foreign companies that helped countries "use, develop, produce, stockpile or otherwise acquire chemical or biological weapons." A company could have faced the loss of U.S. government contracts and been prevented from selling its products in the United States. Governments found to be using chemical weapons would have been subject to a host of penalties, including a cutoff of aid.

The House had passed HR 3033 (H Rept 101-334, Part I; H Rept 101-334, Part II) by voice vote on Nov. 13, 1989. The Senate passed HR 3033 on May 17, 1990, by a vote of 92-0, after substituting the text of S 195 (S Rept 101-166). The Senate then passed an amended HR 4653, the export control bill, which included the text of S 195, by voice vote Sept. 13.

The Bush administration preferred the House chemical weapons bill, because it would have given the president greater discretion in imposing sanctions than would the Senate version. Conferees on HR 3033 essentially came to agreement on the bill in October 1990, though a conference report was not filed. That compromise, which was deemed too restrictive by the administration, was included in the final version of HR 4653, a bill the administration wanted to enact.

Export Controls Background

The 1979 Export Administration Act (PL 96-72) was a continuation of legislative initiatives in place since 1949 to control the flow of U.S. exports to communist countries. *(PL 96-72, Congress and the Nation Vol. V, p. 274)*

In 1969, restrictions were eased on the sale of items to communist countries if they were freely available from such areas as Japan and Western Europe. In 1979, constraints were placed on shipments of militarily sensitive goods, such as sophisticated computer technology, to the Soviet Union, its allies, non-NATO countries and even close U.S. allies.

Congress reauthorized the act in 1985 (PL 99-64), but only after more than two years of negotiations. The act was extended through Sept. 30, 1990, and its procedures were relaxed somewhat as part of the 1988 Omnibus Trade and Competitiveness Act (PL 100-418). *(Congress and the Nation Vol. VII, pp. 144, 148)*

The push for reauthorization in 1990 was driven by concerns about the effects export controls had on U.S. companies' ability to build or hold worldwide markets in the face of stiff competition. In addition, bill sponsors said that simplified licensing procedures would allow enforcement to be focused on the most sensitive high-tech exports.

In June 1990, Cocom (which included most NATO countries, plus Japan and Australia) moved to relax greatly the existing restraints on exports to the former East bloc. HR 4653 embodied in major part the principles Cocom had adopted. Pressure from Japan and Western Europe to ease international export controls paralleled efforts by pro-export forces in Congress to make shipping previously controlled goods to many countries easier.

At the same time, the bill would have tightened controls on a limited number of militarily important items to guard against shipment to the Soviet Union and other countries, notably Iraq. The United States was on the verge of hostilities with Iraq, following that country's invasion of Kuwait on Aug. 2. *(Persian Gulf crisis, p. 299)*

Legislative History

House Action. The House Foreign Affairs Committee approved HR 4653 (H Rept 101-482) by voice vote on May 3, 1990, and formally reported it May 10. The Subcommittee on International Economic Policy and Trade had approved the bill on April 24.

The measure focused on shortening the list of restricted items and clarifying the classifications. It also sought to resolve struggles between executive branch departments, particularly the Commerce and Defense departments, and to otherwise ease the process by which U.S. businesses obtained licenses to export high-tech goods to the Soviet Union and its former satellites.

The committee's action was overshadowed by an announcement May 2 that the Bush administration was willing to ease restrictions on exports to the Soviet Union and Eastern Europe. The plan was to trim immediately the list of restricted product categories from 120 to 90 and narrow the scope of another 13.

White House spokesman Marlin Fitzwater said that by the end of 1990 Bush wanted a "complete overhaul of the control list" leading to a "new core list of goods and technologies that is far shorter and less restrictive." Fitzwater stressed that reducing the list would allow more careful enforcement of the remaining barriers to highly sensitive military technology.

Sam Gejdenson, D-Conn., chairman of the subcommittee and author of the reauthorization bill, called the administration move an improvement but said it "falls short" by not addressing the licensing procedure.

Despite strong administration opposition to many of its key provisions, the House passed HR 4653 on June 6 by a vote of 312-86, with bipartisan majorities in favor.

Gejdenson estimated that between $10 billion and $50 billion a year in export sales was lost because of delays and other difficulties in getting licenses for high-tech exports that other countries were willing to supply. But critics, such as Bill Dickinson, R-Ala., argued that the measure would go too far in making sensitive technologies available to the Soviet Union and other countries. "I share the view of one writer who recently termed HR 4653 the 'Soviet Military Relief Act,' " Dickinson said.

The bill would have eliminated what Gejdenson called a "three-headed monster" composed of the Commerce, Defense and State departments, all of which had a say in export licenses under existing law. Instead, the bill would have made the Commerce Department responsible for all controlled items, except those specifically intended for military use.

Moreover, the lengthy list of restrictions on high-tech exports to countries other than the Soviet Union and its allies would have been wiped out in October 1992. Commerce would have to offer justification for any items put back on the list.

Unlike committee action on the bill, which was swift and relatively uncontroversial, floor debate consumed an entire day and resulted in a dozen roll-call votes on substantive amendments. Three adopted amendments were intended to remove benefits that would have been accorded by the bill to the Soviet Union and China. Many others were turned aside after bill sponsors complained that they were "killers" designed to undo the reforms envisioned in the legislation.

Senate Action. The Senate Banking Committee approved its export control bill (S 2927 — S Rept 101-399) by voice vote on July 17 and reported it July 27. The bill differed in many respects from the House measure, which was drafted and voted on before Cocom voted to relax controls on exports to Eastern Europe.

While both the House and Senate bills would have made exporting high-tech goods to the former East bloc easier, the Senate bill earned administration support because it closely followed the Cocom agreement. For example, unlike the House bill, the measure did not alter the existing relationship between the Commerce, Defense and State departments, all of which had an input into whether export licenses of high-tech goods were granted.

Most committee action on the measure was not contentious, with the exception of an amendment to open the Export-Import Bank's coffers to finance military sales abroad. The Ex-Im Bank had been prohibited for more than 20 years from financing military sales to Third World countries and by policy had refused to finance military sales to developed countries.

The amendment was sponsored by Christopher S. Bond, R-Mo., and Christopher J. Dodd, D-Conn., who argued that defense-based companies in the United States needed to find new outlets for products and that other developed countries provided government financing to military sales. The committee adopted the amendment on a 16-5 vote.

The Senate passed HR 4653 by voice vote on Sept. 13, after amending it with the text of S 2927. Senators by voice vote also added the provisions of S 195, the chemical weapons bill whose provisions were included in HR 3033, which passed the Senate in May.

Senators left intact the language allowing the Ex-Im Bank to finance military sales. And they added other amendments to increase civil and criminal penalties for businesses and individuals who violated the United Nations trade embargo against Iraq and Kuwait; to clarify that the Defense Department could block sales of goods that could be used for chemical, biological or nuclear weapons or missile technology to Iran, Iraq, Libya or Syria; and to reinstate sanctions against sales to Cuba by foreign subsidiaries of U.S. firms.

Final Action, Veto. Using the conference on HR 4653, House and Senate negotiators spent the month of October trying to hammer out agreements on the chemical weapons provisions and other outstanding issues.

In informal meetings, conferees were able to craft a compromise: The chemical weapons provisions were left in the bill, as was language allowing the Defense Department to maintain a role in licensing the sale of high-tech goods abroad. Senate language that would have allowed the Ex-Im Bank to offer loans for military sales was removed.

Conferees on the bill concluded their work Oct. 24 (H Rept 101-944). By voice votes, first the House, and then the Senate, adopted the conference report on Oct. 26, the next to last day of the 101st Congress. The Senate's action cleared the bill for the president, who remained opposed to the chemical weapons sanctions. His pocket veto came on Nov. 16.

Foreign Investment Data

After years of fighting over the notion of collecting information from foreign owners of U.S. businesses and broadly disclosing that data, Congress in 1990 took a new tack, focusing on legislation seeking to better analyze existing data gathered by a variety of federal agencies.

With broad bipartisan support, Congress in late October easily cleared a bill (S 2516 — PL 101-533) requiring the Commerce Department to report on the extent of foreign ownership of U.S. businesses and to compare those companies' employment, investment and other activities with their U.S.-owned counterparts.

It neither required foreign-owned companies to file any new data nor allowed any proprietary information that was confidential to be disclosed publicly. And the bill increased the fines and jail terms that could be imposed for disclosure of confidential information or for failure to provide accurate data to the department's Bureau of Economic Analysis (BEA).

The effort was aided by an administration shift away from opposition to any foreign investment bill to support for the idea of data sharing between the Census Bureau, which maintained confidential plant-by-plant information, and the BEA, charged with analyzing foreign investment in the United States. The two Commerce Department bureaus were given access to each other's information and were to use the shared data to compile detailed annual reports of foreign-owned U.S. businesses.

In addition, employment data from the Labor Department's Bureau of Labor Statistics (BLS) was to be incorporated, and the General Accounting Office (GAO) was to have access to Census Bureau and BEA data so that it could critique the annual Commerce Department report and make recommendations for improvements in data collection and analysis.

Background

The demand for more and better data on foreign ownership stemmed from the rapid rise in overseas capital flowing into the United States in the 1980s. Foreign direct investment — defined as a 10 percent or greater ownership interest in a U.S. business — doubled between 1984 and 1988, according to the BEA.

From 1980 through 1989, total foreign ownership of U.S. assets quadrupled — from $501 billion to just under $2 trillion. Of that, foreign controlling interest in U.S. businesses and real estate increased to $390 billion from $83 billion.

"It matters a great deal who owns businesses, assets and technologies," said Jim Exon, D-Neb., sponsor of the Senate bill and a leading critic of foreign investment. "American economic policy must be concerned about the creation of American wealth and international economic leadership, as well as the creation of American jobs."

With controlling-interest holdings worth $102 billion in 1988, Britain remained the largest single investor, according to the Commerce Department. But it was Japanese investments that seized public attention. The rate of increase in Japanese investments was almost twice that of Britain's. And, in 1988, Japan moved into second place among all countries, with more than $53 billion invested in control of U.S. assets. Japan's economic might frightened many in the United States, at a time when international economic competition appeared to be overtaking national security concerns.

"You can't confuse the meaning of the sale of Rockefeller Center or Columbia Pictures, or . . . Southland Corp. . . . to the Japanese," said Rep. John Bryant, D-Texas, who was among the most outspoken congressional critics of U.S. policy toward foreign investors. "Everybody knows what that means and everybody's immediately uncomfortable about it."

Public opinion polls seemed to reinforce Bryant's views. A *Wall Street Journal*/NBC News poll in January 1990 showed that 58 percent of those surveyed would favor laws restricting foreign investment. A February 1989 Gallup Poll for the *Los Angeles Times* found that 70 percent believed foreign investment was bad for the U.S. economy. And the same month, eight out of 10 respondents to a *Washington Post*/ABC News poll said limits should be placed on Japanese ownership of U.S. businesses.

Strong public sentiment was not necessarily enough, however. Similar support in 1987 and 1988 was sufficient to push foreign investment data-collection bills through the House, but not the Senate, where the measures died.

Although the House twice supported bills sponsored by Bryant in 1987 and 1988, the only foreign investment provisions to become law in that period was language crafted by Exon and others in the 1988 omnibus trade bill (PL 100-418) granting the president authority to restrict takeovers on narrow national security grounds. *(Congress and the Nation Vol. VII, pp. 148, 151)*

Opponents of foreign investment bills, including two successive Republican administrations, argued that they would drive away capital needed both for domestic economic growth and for financing the budget deficit. That, in turn, would push up interest rates. Even collecting data cost money, and the threat of disclosure of confidential information would have a chilling effect, critics said.

During the Reagan administration, the government flatly opposed Bryant's efforts to require more collection and dissemination of data on foreign control of U.S. companies. Bush administration officials, however, finally agreed that policy makers could use better information on foreign ownership. It was that shift that opened the door to action in 1990.

Legislative History

A number of approaches were tried in 1990 on Capitol Hill to get a handle on the growth of foreign investment; the result was a sort of continuous dialogue among various interested members that in the end yielded a compromise bill that was subjected to few formal amendments in committee and essentially none on the floor of either chamber.

The narrowest approach was embodied in administration-drafted legislation, introduced in April in the House (HR 4608) by Norman F. Lent, R-N.Y., and in the Senate (S 2516) by Exon. It sought only to improve the analysis of existing data and formed the core of the measure eventually enacted.

Bryant and Sen. Tom Harkin, D-Iowa, sponsored somewhat broader measures (HR 5, S 289) to impose a new regimen of data collection on foreign ownership. They argued that existing information was insufficient and too scattered.

Rep. Philip R. Sharp, D-Ind., and Sen. Frank H. Murkowski, R-Alaska, argued that existing data in the hands of the BEA and the Census Bureau were more than adequate, except that existing law forbade the two Commerce Department agencies to share their files. Their bills (HR 4060, S 856) aimed to end the ban; that became a key element of the enacted measure.

Sharp, joined by Lee H. Hamilton, D-Ind., and Nancy L. Johnson, R-Conn., also had a bill (HR 4520) to allow broader disclosure of data on foreign investment. Though HR 4520 became the vehicle for House action, the broader disclosure sought by Sharp was largely jettisoned.

Senate Action. The Senate Commerce Committee on Aug. 30 reported S 2516 (S Rept 101-443), the administration-backed bill intended to improve federal data collection on foreign investments.

Before approving the bill by voice vote July 31, the committee adopted watered-down language adapted from S 856, Murkowski's more sweeping measure. It would have given some data on foreign purchases of U.S. firms to the Committee on Foreign Investment in the United States (CFIUS) — an interagency group charged under a provision of the 1988 omnibus trade bill with recommending to the president whether foreign acquisitions of U.S. businesses were a threat to national security. The president was authorized to halt such investments but rarely did so.

Supporters of a stronger federal posture on foreign investments considered the Senate committee action modest at best.

House Action. The Energy and Commerce Subcommittee on Commerce, Consumer Protection and Competitiveness approved HR 4520 by voice vote on Sept. 18, after accepting a bipartisan compromise that focused on the sharing of data with CFIUS and GAO.

Sharp and Lent offered a comprehensive substitute to the bill in an effort to satisfy administration objections. In a move that went further than the Senate committee, the Commerce Subcommittee dropped language altogether on the subject of sharing data.

The companion Senate bill did not allow broad sharing of data with CFIUS, but it did permit the interagency committee to request data from BEA, a provision to which the administration reportedly did not object.

The full House Energy and Commerce Committee approved the subcommittee's version of HR 4520 on Oct. 2 and reported it (H Rept 101-855, Part II) on Oct. 17.

The Foreign Affairs Subcommittee on International Economic Policy and Trade approved HR 4520 by voice vote Oct. 3, after a few further refinements were incorporated. The full committee approved the bill by voice vote Oct. 11 (H Rept 101-855, Part I) and reported it the next day.

Final Action. Action by the two House committees set the stage for final negotiations on a measure acceptable to both the House and Senate and to the administration. In the early morning hours of Oct. 19, the Senate called up S 2516, substituted negotiated compromise language (which closely tracked the House Foreign Affairs version of HR 4520) and passed the bill by voice vote. The House then passed S 2516 by voice vote under suspension of the rules Oct. 23, clearing the measure for the president. Bush signed it Nov. 7.

Major Provisions

As cleared, S 2516:

Commerce Department Reports. Required the Commerce Department to report to Congress within six months of enactment and annually thereafter on the scope, history, economic impact and trends in foreign ownership of U.S. businesses.

The Commerce Department was required to analyze existing data by industry classification and region and to compare foreign businesses with their U.S.-owned counterparts in terms of their employment, market share, productivity, exports and imports, profitability, taxes paid, and investment incentives and services provided by state and local governments.

Data Sharing. Required that information for the annual reports be drawn from existing sources of foreign investment data, including the Commerce Department's BEA and Census Bureau, the BLS, the Agriculture Department, the Internal Revenue Service, the Energy Department, foreign governments and private sources.

The bill specifically authorized the BEA and the Census Bureau to exchange their individually collected confidential information; such sharing was previously prohibited by law.

Confidentiality. Required generally that data shared among agencies be protected so as not to disclose facts about specific foreign or domestic persons or businesses.

Unlawful disclosure of confidential information was subject to fines of between $2,500 and $25,000 and prison terms of up to five years. The same penalties could be imposed on persons who used fraud to obtain confidential data.

The bill also imposed fines of between $2,500 and $25,000 on foreign-owned businesses that failed to file timely or accurate disclosure reports.

GAO Reports. Required the GAO to assess the annual Commerce Department report and to suggest improvements in data collection and analysis. The bill allowed the GAO access to the same data that were used in preparing the report.

Foreign Government Ownership. Required that the BEA's data collection and analysis under existing law be expanded to include information on U.S. businesses and real estate in which foreign governments owned at least a 50 percent share. Existing practices did not require specific data collection or analysis of foreign government ownership — as distinct from ownership by any foreign interest.

Foreign Ownership Controls. Authorized CFIUS, an interagency committee, to request aggregate foreign ownership data from the BEA, including data on foreign government ownership. The requested data had to be provided within 14 days when CFIUS was investigating a particular foreign purchase. Under existing law, CFIUS recommended to the president whether the foreign purchase of a U.S. business should be stopped on national security grounds.

Enterprise for the Americas

A plan to boost economic development in Latin America and the Caribbean — in large part to restore trade between the United States and the region, which had been severely stunted by a continuing debt crisis — was unveiled by President Bush on June 27, 1990. The plan won praise from Congress, but legislative action was slow and none of the elements was enacted into law before the 101st Congress adjourned.

The plan, introduced as the Enterprise for the Americas Initiative (HR 5855, S 3064), aimed to boost economic development as a way to support fledgling democratic and market-based governments in the region.

The three-part program included an offer of trade negotiations designed to lead to a Western Hemisphere free-trade zone; new private investment incentives, including a $300 million program of annual grants; and forgiveness of some loans owed to the U.S. government to bolster an effort to reduce commercial bank debt.

In all cases, the proposal required Latin American countries to continue their march toward market-oriented economies to qualify for aid.

The House passed HR 5855 on Oct. 22, just five days before the 101st Congress adjourned. The measure was never considered in the Senate.

Background

The Bush plan was designed to address several concerns. One was that unless Latin America's debt problem was resolved, the region's newly established democracies would be in danger of falling victim to civil strife and military coups. A second was restoration of trade: Latin American countries had been among the biggest buyers of U.S. goods prior to the debt crisis that hit the region hard in the early 1980s. A third was that the United States might lose control of the process of reducing Latin America's debt to U.S. banks. The Latin debt burden stood in 1990 at about $400 billion, a large part of which was considered uncollectable because the region's economies were weak.

Parts of the plan, such as relief for debts owed the U.S. government, already had congressional proponents. Other ideas — particularly a hemispheric free-trade zone — faced skepticism and some immediate opposition.

Because free-trade negotiations appeared far down the road and the $300 million investment incentive was so modest, the plan's centerpiece was the proposal to relieve part of the Latin American debt to the U.S. government. That proposal was a companion to the so-called Brady plan announced in March 1989 by Treasury Secretary Nicholas F. Brady to encourage commercial banks to reduce the Third World's debt.

The Brady plan relied on negotiations by individual countries with their creditor banks to reduce debt principal or interest owed or to provide new money at better rates. As an incentive, the World Bank and the International Monetary Fund guaranteed repayment of reduced principal or interest.

Many critics said that the Brady plan was flawed because it did not deal with debt owed to governments, particularly the United States. Smaller countries were more burdened by government loans than by debts to commercial banks. And commercial banks had been unwilling to reduce their debt while the U.S. and other governments demanded full repayment.

Brady said that the Enterprise for the America's plan was designed to address Latin American debt owed to the United States. The proposal would have partly reduced $7 billion in Latin American loans from the Agency for International Development (AID) and the Food for Peace (PL 480) program.

Much of that money was lent on concessional terms that probably did not anticipate full repayment. The United States had an additional $5.3 billion in outstanding loans to Latin America that were not covered under the proposal.

Members of Congress who had been eager for government debt relief also had been pushing for more pressure on commercial banks. But that was not a part of Bush's proposal.

Legislative History

The House Foreign Affairs Committee approved HR 5855 by voice vote on Oct. 18 and reported it (H Rept 101-917) on Oct. 22. The measure was not amended.

The bill would have authorized the president to begin negotiating reductions in some nations' long-term, low-interest debt owed to AID. As of the end of fiscal 1989, AID had $5.3 billion in outstanding concessional, or below market-rate, loans.

The measure would have authorized long-term talks on a hemisphere free-trade zone and short-term bilateral negotiations on free-trade agreement "frameworks." It also would have unilaterally cut U.S. tariffs for Latin American countries as part of global trade talks.

A new, five-year $300 million annual multilateral grant program tied to specific market reforms would have been established. Some U.S. development loans would have been written off on a case-by-case basis.

Under the bill, eligible countries could pay the interest on their debts in local currency and put it into a yet-to-be created Environment Fund, which would finance local environmental protection and cleanup activities.

The House passed HR 5855 by voice vote under suspension of the rules on Oct. 22.

Referred to the Senate, the measure died there. The Senate Foreign Relations Committee held hearings on S 3064, the companion measure, but never acted on it.

Caribbean Basin Initiative

After nearly two years of public bargaining and behind-the-scenes negotiations, Congress on Aug. 4, 1990, cleared and sent to the president a trade bill (HR 1594 — PL 101-382) that included permanent trade breaks for countries in the Caribbean Basin. The bill largely extended a series of temporary trade benefits first granted the region in 1983.

The measure incorporated numerous tariff changes and some miscellaneous trade-related provisions, including routine authorizations for several trade agencies. It also contained a permanent ban on unprocessed-timber exports from public lands in the United States. And it included new rules governing congressional approval of negotiated agreements granting normal trade relations — most-favored-nation (MFN) status — to communist countries. *(Most-favored nations, box, p. 172)*

Background

The Caribbean Basin Initiative (CBI) — first approved in 1983 for 12 years as the Caribbean Basin Economic Recovery Act (PL 98-67) — allowed duty-free access to the U.S. market for a variety of Caribbean imports. *(Congress and the Nation Vol. VI, p. 106)*

Although the law was not due to expire until 1995, advocates pressed for an early extension to encourage and support investment in the region. They also sought to extend duty-free or low-tariff treatment to products such as leather goods, textiles, apparel, petroleum and other items important to the Caribbean economies. These goods were left out of the original law because of objections from domestic producers and labor unions.

The beneficiary countries were Antigua and Barbuda, Aruba, the Bahamas, Barbados, Belize, the British Virgin Islands, Costa Rica, Dominica, the Dominican Republic, El Salvador, Grenada, Guatemala, Guyana, Haiti, Honduras, Jamaica, Montserrat, the Netherlands Antilles, Panama (reinstated after the overthrow of Gen. Manuel Antonio Noriega in late December 1989), St. Christopher and Nevis, St. Lucia, St. Vincent and the Grenadines, and Trinidad and Tobago.

Legislative History

Action to broaden and permanently extend the Caribbean Basin Initiative began in the House in 1989. The Ways and Means Committee on June 20 approved by voice vote a Caribbean Basin bill (HR 1233), which it reported (H Rept 101-136) on July 12. The measure was subsequently added to an omnibus budget-reconciliation bill (HR 3299), which passed the House on Oct. 5. *(Reconciliation, p. 43)*

Beyond extending permanently the existing tariff reductions for imports from the Caribbean, the bill would have relaxed other restraints on Caribbean sugar, ethanol, textile and footwear imports.

No matching Caribbean provisions were included in the Senate version of the reconciliation bill, however, and the Senate was unwilling to go to conference on the House-passed language in HR 3299 having not yet developed positions on the controversial issues. The House agreed to drop the Caribbean provisions from HR 3299 if the Senate Finance Committee would report a new bill "as a matter of legislative priority" in the new year and "make every best effort to pass [it] by March 31, 1990."

Provisions to ease restrictions on ethanol imports, which were considered time-sensitive, were included in an unrelated bill that renewed administration authority to enforce steel-import quotas (HR 3275 — PL 101-221). *(Steel VRAs, p. 186)*

House Action. Most House action on the Caribbean Basin Initiative occurred in 1989 on HR 1233. Sponsor Sam M. Gibbons, D-Fla., chairman of the Ways and Means Trade Subcommittee and a leading free-trader, saw the bill through committee and held off colleagues whose districts relied on textiles and apparel and who opposed language expanding duty-free treatment for Caribbean textiles and apparel and reducing tariffs on non-leather shoes and on leather and non-leather luggage and handbags.

To expedite floor consideration of the bill, Gibbons agreed to delete the extension of duty-free treatment to leather footwear and to weaken provisions that would have eased access for textile and apparel imports. By doing so, Gibbons avoided showdowns over footwear with Rules Committee Chairman Joe Moakley, D-Mass., and with the powerful Congressional Textile Caucus on the House floor.

HR 1233 never came to the floor as a free-standing bill. House supporters hoped that by attaching its provisions to HR 3299 they could ensure enactment. When the Senate balked at that approach, the Caribbean measure was left to languish until the Senate acted in 1990.

Senate Action. The Senate Finance Committee on March 1, 1990, approved its Caribbean Basin bill by voice vote. Although the committee was working from a Senate bill (S 504), it ultimately sent to the Senate floor a House measure (HR 1594 — S Rept 101-252) that had been used to grant normal trade status to Hungary for an extended period. The Finance Committee stripped the Hungary language and substituted an amended version of S 504. The House had passed HR 1594 (H Rept 101-99) on a 221-169 vote Sept. 7, 1989.

As approved by committee, HR 1594 would have extended permanently duty-free status for many Caribbean imports, but it did not resolve disagreements over sugar and certain other goods not covered under the 1983 Caribbean Basin Initiative. The committee dropped a controversial provision guaranteeing exporters in the Caribbean a fixed share of the sugar imports allowed into the United States annually. And it rejected several amendments that could have threatened its passage.

Among the amendments considered but rejected on March 1 was an increase in the quota for all sugar imports regardless of source. Also defeated was an amendment to ease the entry of rubber-soled footwear from Caribbean assembly plants.

By voice vote the committee adopted an amendment altering procedures under the Jackson-Vanik amendment to the 1974 Trade Act (PL 93-618) for instituting trade agreements with communist countries or rejecting presidential grants to such countries of most-favored-nation status. The language was intended to fix a constitutional defect in the 1974 law. Jackson-Vanik barred MFN status for communist countries unless the president certified that the nation allowed its citizens free emigration rights or waived the requirement. Congress could disapprove of the certification or waiver by the vote of a single chamber, a procedure that was declared unconstitutional in the 1983 Supreme Court decision in *Immigration and Naturalization Service v. Chadha. (1974 law, Congress and the Nation Vol. IV, p. 131; 1983 Court ruling, Congress and the Nation Vol. VI, pp. 762, 833)*

The Senate bill changed the procedure to require enactment into law of a joint resolution to disapprove a certification or waiver. It also changed procedures for approving trade agreements with communist countries, again requiring enactment of a joint resolution.

By maintaining the constitutionality of Jackson-Vanik, the changes preserved provisions for expedited consideration of resolutions of approval and disapproval. Such procedures were extremely important, especially in the filibuster-prone Senate. The Bush administration supported efforts to preserve the procedures.

After four days of off-the-floor discussion and intermittent floor debate, the Senate on April 24 passed HR 1594 by a vote of 92-0. The Senate firmly rejected efforts to expand the Caribbean Basin program where doing so might have meant lost sales for U.S. manufacturers or lost jobs for American workers.

An attempt to broaden the bill to cover inexpensive footwear was tabled (killed) 63-33 despite support from the Bush administration and a small, bipartisan bloc of free-traders. Amendment sponsor Bob Graham, D-Fla., would have reduced by half the duty on imported Caribbean rubber-soled shoes with fabric uppers. Graham argued unsuccessfully that 97 percent of the shoes in this category sold in the U.S. market were produced in Pacific Rim countries, with the preponderance coming from China.

The only major item added in floor action, 81-17, was an amendment by Bob Packwood of Oregon, ranking Republican on the Finance Committee, to ban the export of unprocessed timber taken from federally owned lands. Besides making permanent an existing ban on selling federal timber abroad, Packwood's proposal tightened restrictions to prevent both direct substitution of federal logs for private logs exported and indirect substitution through third-party arrangements. The amendment was designed to alleviate the shortage of cut timber for mills in the Northwest. After the eruption of Mount St. Helens in 1980, timber surpluses led to increased log exports. With the surplus gone and forest cutting under pressure, domestic mills found themselves competing with foreign buyers for logs.

To expedite adoption, Packwood did not attempt to extend his amendment to timber taken from state lands or private lands (where three-fourths of the logging was done), as many in his home state had urged. He also exempted his neighboring state of Washington, where some logging revenues from public lands were used to support public schools.

Final Action. Virtually all House-Senate conflicts were resolved in the first weeks of the conference, which began May 11. Even the potentially troublesome differences over log exports, a 50 percent cut in the duty on certain goods and a minimum sugar quota had been settled by June 19.

But the conference then nearly foundered in a dispute over ethanol imports, including tax issues that had not been part of the legislation as passed by either chamber. Failure to enact the Caribbean Basin bill in 1989 had led to inclusion of ethanol language in an unrelated measure enacted that year. Conferees agreed to extend the existing arrangement through Dec. 31, 1992.

Two other late-starting issues also held up the conference for a time — one relating to a tax break for investors in Puerto Rico instituted in the 1986 tax overhaul bill (PL 99-514) and another that would have reduced the tariff for an imported ingredient in an ulcer drug manufactured in North Carolina. Both were dropped in exchange for a promise of later consideration.

Most expansions of the original Caribbean Basin Initiative — sought by House sponsor Gibbons but dropped by the Senate — were abandoned in conference. Gibbons was especially interested in providing a higher quota for Caribbean sugar. The region's sugar imports had dropped by more than 70 percent after quotas were imposed in the early 1980s. At one point, after the conferees eliminated his sugar provision, Gibbons said the measure was scarcely worth fighting for in its diluted state.

Conferees concluded their work July 30, and the Senate adopted the conference report (H Rept 101-650) by voice vote the following day. The House adopted it by voice vote Aug. 4, just before the beginning of a monthlong congressional recess. President Bush signed the bill Aug. 20.

Major Provisions

As cleared, HR 1594, the Customs and Trade Act of 1990, included the following major provisions (except for detailed tariff provisions of Title III):

Authorizations, Customs Fees

ITC. Authorized the International Trade Commission to spend $41,170,000 in fiscal 1991 and $44,052,000 in fiscal 1992.

Customs Service. Authorized the U.S. Customs Service to spend $516,217,000 in fiscal 1991 and $542,091,000 in fiscal 1992 for salaries and expenses incurred in noncommercial operations; no less than $672,021,000 in fiscal 1991 and $705,793,000 in fiscal 1992 for salaries and expenses incurred in commercial operations; and $143,047,000 in fiscal 1991 and $150,199,000 in fiscal 1992 for its air interdiction program.

USTR. Authorized the Office of the U.S. Trade Representative (USTR) to spend $23,250,000 in fiscal 1991 and $21,077,000 in fiscal 1992.

Customs Fees. Replaced the existing across-the-board ad valorem customs fee with a new cost-based fee structure intended to bring the United States into conformance with the General Agreement on Tariffs and Trade (GATT), the world body that oversaw most trade relationships.

The new schedule limited fees to the approximate cost of the services rendered and to customs operations related to the processing of imports covered by the fee. It provided for an ad valorem fee but set a minimum of $21 and a maximum of $400. The purpose was to ensure that imports of very high or very low value, which might not have differed substantially in the cost of import processing, did not pay unduly different import fees. The new structure eliminated excess collections on high-value imports and avoided the subsidization of low-value entries.

The bill also set fees for informal entries by air courier facilities and others not covered under the existing merchandise processing fee. It declared that operations identified by GATT as inappropriate (activities associated with passenger processing, export controls and international affairs) were not funded out of the merchandise processing fee.

Israel. Exempted Israeli products from customs user fees if the USTR determined that the government of Israel had made reciprocal concessions.

Customs Forfeiture Fund. Required the Customs Forfeiture Fund to provide annually a complete set of audited financial statements for the previous fiscal year. The bill also required Customs to deposit all forfeited cash into the fund, and it authorized $20 million for discretionary purposes of the fund, of which $14,855,000 was available in fiscal 1991 and $15,598,000 in fiscal 1992 for spending by the Customs Service.

Czechoslovakia, East Germany. Made Czechoslovakia and East Germany eligible for preferential duty rates under the Generalized System of Preferences (GSP). Because East and West Germany achieved economic and monetary union on July 1, the president was authorized to provide tariff treatment for East German products comparable to that of West German products, pending complete political unification.

Jackson-Vanik. Revised the Jackson-Vanik provisions of the 1974 Trade Act. Under Jackson-Vanik, the president could extend most-favored-nation (non-discriminatory) trade status to a communist country as part of a commercial trade agreement, but only if he certified that the country allowed free emigration or waived the requirement. The bill provided that such a bilateral trade agreement could take effect only after adoption of a joint (instead of a concurrent) resolution of approval under special fast-track procedures.

A presidential waiver of Jackson-Vanik or a presidential certification that a country met the freedom-of-emigration criteria was subjected to congressional disapproval by a joint (instead of a single-chamber) resolution approved under fast-track procedures.

Burma (Myanmar). Required economic sanctions on Burma (renamed Myanmar), unless the president certified it had met human rights conditions, including the reinstatement of civilian government, the lifting of martial law and the release of political prisoners.

Census Employees. Stipulated that services performed after April 20, 1990, by temporary employees of the Bureau of the Census relating to the 1990 census constituted "federal service" under the unemployment compensation program. As a result, wages earned by these temporary census workers would be credited to them in determining their eligibility for unemployment compensation.

Caribbean Basin

Permanent Status. Repealed the Sept. 30, 1995, termination date for duty-free treatment of eligible imports from beneficiary countries under the 1983 Caribbean Basin Economic Recovery Act, also called the Caribbean Basin Initiative.

Leather Goods. Authorized the president to reduce tariff rates applicable to leather products — handbags, luggage, flat goods, work gloves and leather wearing apparel — from CBI beneficiary countries by 20 percent, but not more than 2.5 percent ad valorem for any item, to be phased in through five equal annual stages beginning on Jan. 1, 1992. The provision applied to goods that were not eligible for duty-free treatment under GSP.

Workers' Rights. Prohibited the president from designating as a CBI beneficiary any country that was not taking steps to afford internationally recognized workers' rights to workers in the country.

Report. Required the president to submit a complete report on CBI operations to Congress by Oct. 1, 1993, and every three years thereafter. The report would have to review CBI countries based on all the beneficiary criteria, including that on workers' rights.

Puerto Rico. Provided that any article grown, produced or manufactured in Puerto Rico qualified for duty-free treatment otherwise available under the CBI if (1) the article was imported directly from a CBI beneficiary country into the United States, (2) its value was increased in a CBI beneficiary country, and (3) any materials added in a CBI country were products of a beneficiary country or the United States.

Duty-Free Allowance. Increased the duty-free allowance for U.S. residents returning directly or indirectly from a CBI beneficiary country from $400 to $600 and allowed them to bring one additional liter of alcoholic beverages duty and excise-tax free if it was produced in a CBI country. The bill increased the duty-free allowance for U.S. residents returning from U.S. insular possessions from $800 to $1,200.

U.S. Components. Granted duty-free and quota-free treatment for articles (other than textiles, apparel, petroleum and petroleum products) that were assembled wholly from U.S. fabricated components or processed wholly from U.S. ingredients in a CBI beneficiary country. The components and ingredients and the final article could not enter the commerce of a third country.

Rules of Origin. Authorized the president to proclaim, effective Jan. 1, 1991, new rules-of-origin requirements for articles eligible for duty-free treatment under the CBI. Under previous law, the article had to be imported directly from a CBI country; it had to have had at least 35 percent of its value added in a CBI country; and it had to be wholly grown, produced or manufactured — or substantially transformed — in a CBI country. The president would have to first consult with the private sector and report to congressional committees on the new rules.

Cumulation. Allowed CBI imports to be counted separately — not aggregated with non-CBI imports — in antidumping or countervailing duty cases for the purpose of determining whether the CBI imports were causing material injury to a U.S. industry.

Such imports could still be aggregated with imports from other CBI countries under investigation. And imports from CBI countries would continue to be aggregated with those of non-CBI countries under investigation for purposes of determining whether the non-CBI imports were causing injury.

Ethanol. Extended through Dec. 31, 1992, a provision (enacted as part of the 1989 Steel Trade Liberalization Act) easing local feedstock requirements imposed on Caribbean ethanol producers by the 1986 Tax Reform Act.

The 1989 provision granted duty-free treatment for ethanol (and any mixture thereof) that was only dehydrated within a CBI beneficiary country or an insular possession if it met the following annual criteria: (1) No feedstock requirement was imposed on imports up to 60 million gallons or 7 percent of the domestic ethanol market, whichever was greater; (2) a local feedstock requirement of 30 percent by volume applied to the next 35 million gallons of imports; and (3) a local feedstock requirement of 50 percent by volume applied to any additional imports.

The conferees intended to consider later in 1990 the extension of tax preferences enjoyed by the domestic ethanol industry, including a tax credit for blenders of gasohol (gasoline and ethanol) and a partial exemption from the motor-fuel excise tax for sellers of gasohol. The expiration date for the CBI ethanol provision was linked to the expiration of the blenders' tax credit. The conferees expected that this provision would continue in effect as long as the additional tariff or other similar restrictions applied to imports of ethanol.

Ethyl alcohol (or a mixture thereof) that was produced by a process of full fermentation in an insular possession or beneficiary country remained eligible for duty-free treatment in unlimited quantities without regard to feedstock requirements.

These provisions were effective for calendar years 1990 and 1991.

Puerto Rico Investment. Required the government of Puerto Rico to ensure that at least $100 million in new investments that qualified for tax-free treatment under Section 936 of the Internal Revenue Code be made each year in eligible Caribbean Basin countries. Refinancings of existing investments could not constitute "new investments" for this purpose.

Scholarships. Required the Agency for International Development to establish and administer a program of scholarship assistance to enable students from CBI beneficiary countries that also received U.S. foreign assistance to study in the United States.

Tourism. Required the secretary of commerce to complete a study begun in 1986 on tourism development strategies for the Caribbean region. The Customs commissioner was required to carry out a pilot preclearance program during fiscal years 1991 and 1992 at a U.S. Customs Service facility in a Caribbean Basin country to test how such procedures could contribute to increased tourism and to submit a report to Congress.

Nicaragua. Authorized the president to designate Nicaragua as a beneficiary country under the CBI and GSP programs, effective through 1990.

Andean Region. Urged the president to consider the merits of extending CBI benefits to the Andean region, explore additional mechanisms to expand trade opportunities for the Andean region and report to Congress on the results of this review.

Unprocessed Timber

Permanent Ban. Prohibited any person who acquired unprocessed timber originating from federal lands west of the 100th meridian in the contiguous 48 states from exporting, selling, trading, exchanging or otherwise conveying that timber to anyone for the purpose of export.

The bill excepted specific quantities and species of unprocessed timber from federal lands that the secretary of agriculture or the secretary of the interior determined to be in surplus to domestic processing needs.

Direct Substitution. Prohibited any person from purchasing directly from any department or agency of the United States unprocessed timber if such timber was to be substituted for exported timber originating from private lands or the person had during the preceding 24 months exported unprocessed timber originating from private lands.

Contracts for the purchase of federal timber in effect at the time of enactment would be honored.

Indirect Substitution. Prohibited, within 21 days of enactment, indirect substitution of unprocessed timber from federal lands for exported unprocessed timber from private lands. The bill exempted a small number of companies in Oregon and Washington state that were permitted to continue indirectly purchasing western red cedar from federal lands while exporting private logs.

24-Month Rule. Exempted from substitution prohibitions the acquisition of unprocessed timber from federal lands from an area designated by the secretary of the interior or the secretary of agriculture if the acquirer, in the previous 24 months, had not exported such timber from private lands within the designated area. The acquirer, during the period of this approval, could not export unprocessed timber from private lands within the designated area. The 24-month test would not apply to any person who had legally substituted federal timber for exported unprocessed timber originating from private lands under a historical export quota approved by the agriculture or interior secretary.

Denied Applicants. Set rules for people whose sourcing area boundary application was denied. In the event of such a denial, this provision provided an opportunity to phase out federal timber purchases over 15 months and maintain such export operations, or to terminate export of private logs from the area within 15 months and maintain eligibility for federal timber purchases.

Export Ban from State Lands. Prohibited the export from the United States of unprocessed timber harvested from lands owned or administered by a state or any political subdivision of a state, subject to certain conditions.

The effective date was 21 days after enactment for states with annual sales of 400 million board feet or less. For states with annual sales greater than that, the bill set a schedule for the issuance of orders by the secretary of commerce.

Exceptions. Permitted the commerce secretary to increase the amount of unprocessed state timber barred from export (in states with sales greater than 400 million board feet) if the domestic log supply was insufficient to meet the demand of domestic mills.

Equitable Allocations. Required each state to consider the species, grade and geographic origin of its public timber so that restrictions were allocated in a representative and equitable manner — especially with a view to existing state laws. Much of the timber in question was held by states in trust for counties or schools.

State Rules. Provided that each state should develop its own regulations for restricting state exports of unprocessed timber.

GATT Conformity. Authorized the president, after suitable notice and a public comment period, to suspend the log-export provisions if a GATT panel, or a ruling issued under the formal dispute settlement proceeding of any other trade agreement, found that the state export restrictions were in violation of, or inconsistent with, U.S. international obligations.

Presidential Exceptions. Authorized the president to remove or modify any state export restrictions if a state petitioned to do so and the president determined it was in the national economic interests to remove or modify such restrictions.

Previous Commitments. Clarified that no provision of previously enacted federal law that imposed requirements related to the generation of revenue from state timberlands was to affect any action of a state taken pursuant to this act. The state of Washington held a substantial portion of its lands in trust for the benefit of its educational institutions under the 1889 act granting statehood.

Surplus Marketing. Established that the prohibitions on state timber exports should not apply to specific grades and species of unprocessed timber from federal lands that the secretaries of agriculture and the interior determined to be surplus to domestic processing needs.

Review of Restrictions. Provided that, beginning in 1997, the president could suspend the restrictions on the export of unprocessed timber from state lands if they were determined to no longer meet the intent of the bill. The bill did not limit the authority of the president or the USTR to respond to any measure taken by a foreign government in connection with this act.

Enforcement. Anyone who directly or indirectly acquired unprocessed federal timber had to report the receipt and disposition of such timber to the secretaries of agriculture and the interior. The bill provided for civil penalties against violators and provided that they could be barred from entering into a contract for the purchase of unprocessed timber from federal lands.

Effective Date. Provided that, except as otherwise specified, the effective date was the date of enactment.

Ex-Im, IDB, IMF Authorizations

While preparing to adjourn for the year in late 1989, Congress cleared a bill (HR 2494 — PL 101-240) reauthorizing a tied-aid credit program at the Export-Import Bank and authorizing more than $314 million over four years for the Inter-American Development Bank (IDB) and $150 million for a special arm of the International Monetary Fund (IMF).

The bill also required bank regulators to review existing requirements for bank reserves for troubled Third World loans and make adjustments where warranted. That requirement had been weakened repeatedly since the legislation was first drafted.

HR 2494 was the first free-standing authorization bill enacted for multilateral development banks since 1980.

Legislative History

House Action. After significantly watering down controversial Third World debt-reduction provisions, the House Banking Committee's International Development Subcommittee on Sept. 14 approved HR 2494 by voice vote. The full Banking Committee approved the bill on Sept. 26 with only minor changes and reported it (H Rept 101-271) on Oct. 6.

The House bill would have pumped $200 million into the Ex-Im Bank tied-aid fund through 1992, while the administration had sought an extension of $100 million for 1990.

The panel dramatically altered provisions aimed at pressing U.S. commercial banks to cooperate in a debt-reduction plan for Latin America announced by Treasury Secretary Nicholas F. Brady on March 10. Brady sought to get banks to write off some of their tens of billions of dollars in loans to developing countries or to reduce the high interest rates owed on those loans. To encourage cooperation, sponsors of HR 2494 wanted to require banks to set aside large reserves against potential losses from troubled Third World loans. Banks that cooperated in debt-reduction negotiations would have been exempted from the reserve requirement.

But in the face of withering pressure from large banks, strong opposition from Federal Reserve Board Chairman Alan Greenspan and reluctant opposition from the Treasury Department, sponsors Walter E. Fauntroy, D-D.C., and John J. LaFalce, D-N.Y., were forced to soften the reserve requirement in subcommittee.

The House passed the bill on Oct. 18 by a vote of 280-125.

Senate, Final Action. Most Senate action took place on a companion Ex-Im Bank bill (S 1704), which was produced by the Senate Banking Committee. HR 2494 was referred to the Senate Foreign Relations Committee, which never took formal action on it.

The Banking Committee approved S 1704 on Sept. 20 and reported it (S Rept 101-153) on Sept. 29. The measure provided $300 million through 1991 for the Ex-Im tied-aid fund, which was more money than authorized in the House bill and a shorter period for its use. The measure passed the Senate Oct. 3 by voice vote.

After the Foreign Relations Committee was released from considering HR 2494, the Senate took up the bill late Nov. 21. Senators adopted a block of amendments, prepared by staffers from the Senate and House Banking committees and from Senate Foreign Relations, that among other things substituted the Senate-passed version of S 1704 for the House language on Ex-Im Bank reauthorization and further softened the House provision on bank cooperation in Third World debt relief efforts.

The Senate passed HR 2494 by voice vote Nov. 22 (in the session that began Nov. 21). And the House accepted the Senate amendments in the early hours of Nov. 22, the final day of the session, thus clearing the bill for the president. Bush signed the bill into law on Dec. 19.

Major Provisions

As cleared, HR 2494:

Ex-Im Bank 'War Chest.' Reauthorized the tied-aid "war chest" of the Export-Import Bank at $300 million through fiscal 1991. The Ex-Im Bank, which provided low-cost conventional financing for U.S. exports, had set up the fund in 1986 for use in countering tied-aid financing deals from other countries. Typically, tied aid involved giving grants in addition to conventional loans to purchasers of goods from businesses in the donor country. Some members had argued that the fund had been little used and had not reduced tied-aid activity abroad.

The bill also contained a ban on Ex-Im Bank financed trade with China, unless the president certified to Congress that China had made "progress on a program of political reform" or that the financing was in the national interest.

Debt Relief. Required federal bank regulators to take a more active role in reviewing reserve levels of U.S. banks for loans to highly indebted countries and to require "appropriate levels" of reserves to reflect the increased risks of such loans. By pressing for higher reserves on Third World loans, sponsors hoped to encourage commercial banks to cooperate in administration efforts to write off some of those loans.

Inter-American Development Bank. Authorized annual payments from the Treasury of about $78.5 million toward a $26.5 billion capital increase for the IDB, which made development loans and grants in Latin America. The bulk of the U.S. contribution (which amounted to 35 percent of the total to be provided the bank) was not to be paid in; instead, the capital was "callable" in case the bank faced default. The United States had been working for three years to negotiate increased U.S. influence over the IDB's lending program. A new agreement was reached in March 1989, which included an agreement for the capital increase.

International Monetary Fund. Authorized the $150 million U.S. contribution to a special interest-rate subsidy fund within the IMF. The fund, the Enhanced Structural Adjustment Facility, was designed to benefit the very poor nations of sub-Saharan Africa.

Multilateral Lending

Fights over a new bank to aid the emerging democracies of Eastern and Central Europe, debt relief for Poland and Latin America and restrictions on World Bank loans to post-Tiananmen Square China dominated debate in 1990 over U.S. contributions to multilateral lending institutions.

Following a pattern that had become almost routine, Congress was unable to move needed free-standing authorization bills for the multilateral banks in 1990. Instead, provisions allowing for U.S. participation in a handful of lending institutions were added to the fiscal 1991 foreign aid appropriations bill (HR 5114 — PL 101-513). *(Foreign aid appropriations, p. 233)*

European Development Bank

The central focus of multilateral lending efforts in 1990 was a newly proposed bank to aid Eastern and Central European countries in moving toward market-based economies.

Representatives from 42 nations, including the United States, agreed in principle April 9 to form the European Bank for Reconstruction and Development (EBRD). Final terms were adopted May 29, and the bank was to begin its London-based operations in early 1991.

The EBRD was to be capitalized at about $12 billion; the United States was to contribute 10 percent of that amount. Britain, France, Italy, Japan and West Germany were to contribute 8.5 percent apiece. Only 30 percent of the capital was to be paid in. The remainder was to be pledged as collateral for the new bank's borrowing from world financial markets. It would have been "callable" only in case of default.

U.S. participation had to be approved by Congress, which also would have to appropriate the U.S. share of funds.

The Soviet Union was to contribute 6 percent and was entitled to borrow during the first three years only as much as it had paid in. After that, additional Soviet borrowing would have to be approved by 85 percent of the bank's members. The size of the U.S. vote was seen as virtually ensuring that expanded borrowing by the Soviet Union could be blocked, if the White House so desired.

Bank loans were to be concentrated on private companies trying to expand or begin operations in Europe's newly democratic countries, or on the privatization of state-owned enterprises. But 40 percent of the loans could go to government-sponsored activities, including road building and other infrastructure development.

Approval from Congress, however, was uncertain for much of the year. Some lawmakers were wary of the Soviet role, and others wanted a higher percentage of loans earmarked for private enterprise.

Legislative History

House Action. A broad authorization bill (HR 5153) was reported from committee but was never considered on the floor. The measure would have authorized U.S. contributions to the EBRD totaling $1.17 billion over five years. Only about $350 million of that was to be paid directly to the bank.

The bill also would have authorized U.S. payments to the so-called 9th Replenishment of the International Development Association (IDA), the concessional lending arm of the World Bank. Payments to IDA would have totaled $3.18 billion over three years, all of it paid directly to the bank. And it would have permanently authorized U.S. contributions to the African Development Fund, the concessional arm of the African Development Bank, which aided the poorest African countries.

The House Banking Committee approved HR 5153 by voice vote on June 26. The bill was formally reported July 11 (H Rept 101-590).

Committee members fought over only two elements of the bill: provisions promoting debt relief for Third World countries and criticizing China's human rights practices. The China provisions were intended to pressure the administration to hold firm on a policy severely restricting World Bank loans to Beijing.

In the end, most substantive amendments were rejected, and the measure was little changed from a version that had been approved June 20 by the International Development Subcommittee.

The bill would have authorized the Export-Import Bank to make loans for purchases by certain Eastern and Central European countries not then eligible for Ex-Im Bank credits. And it would have increased the Ex-Im Bank's tied-aid "war chest" to combat the practices of countries that combined foreign aid grants with conventional export loans to promote purchases of their products. In 1989, the war chest had been reauthorized through fiscal 1991. HR 5153 would have reauthorized the war chest through fiscal 1992, and its existing $300 million authorization would have been increased to $500 million in fiscal 1991 and 1992. *(Ex-Im authorization, p. 184)*

The bill also called on the secretary of the Treasury to negotiate with other industrialized countries to reduce the government-to-government debt of the poorest Third World nations. It would have directed the Treasury to urge other members of the so-called Paris Club of creditor nations to write off on a case-by-case basis loans that they had made to very poor countries. It also would have authorized the president to write off U.S. loans to poor countries if such write-offs were in the national interest and were used to implement an international debt relief agreement.

Senate Action. A bill (S 2944) that would have authorized $535 million in bilateral aid for Eastern and Central European countries was the vehicle for multilateral bank authorizations in the Senate. Strong GOP opposition to the bilateral aid package kept it off the Senate floor.

The Senate Foreign Relations Committee approved S 2944 on July 19, by a 10-0 vote with Republicans boycotting the markup session. The bill was formally reported July 31 without a written report and was not considered further.

S 2944 was a follow-up to a 1989 bilateral aid measure for Eastern European countries, principally Poland and Hungary, called the Support for Eastern European Democracies (SEED) Act of 1989 (HR 3402 — PL 101-179). The 1990 bill — S 2944, known as SEED II — would have greatly expanded the provisions of the 1989 bill in an effort to boost the business opportunities of U.S. companies in the region. *(Eastern European aid, p. 210)*

Like the House measure, S 2944 would have fully authorized EBRD, IDA and the African Fund.

Final Action. Provisions from HR 5153 authorizing contributions to the EBRD and IDA, permanently authorizing the African Fund, and increasing and extending the Ex-Im Bank's tied-aid program were added in conference to HR 5114, the foreign aid appropriations bill.

Not included were provisions from HR 5153 imposing sanctions against World Bank loans to China and creating Third World and Eastern European debt relief incentives. The House version of the foreign aid bill all along had contained very similar language to that in HR 5153 regarding loans to China. That language was retained in the final version.

The House passed HR 5114 (H Rept 101-553) by 308-117 on June 27. The Senate passed the bill (S Rept 101-519) on Oct. 24 by a 76-23 vote. Conferees reached agreement on Oct. 27 and reported the bill the same day (H Rept 101-968). Also on Oct. 27, the House adopted the conference report, by a 188-162 vote. The Senate adopted the conference report the same day by voice vote, clearing the measure. President Bush signed the bill Nov. 5.

Steel VRAs Extension

In the early hours of Nov. 22, 1989, the Senate passed and the House cleared for the president a bill (HR 3275 — PL 101-221) renewing the administration's authority to enforce agreements limiting steel imports into the United States. The president signed the bill Dec. 12.

Authority for the so-called voluntary restraint agreements (VRAs), which had expired Sept. 30, 1989, was extended through March 31, 1992. The United States had such agreements with 29 steel-producing nations.

U.S. steel users had urged that the import restraints be relaxed after Sept. 30 to give them greater access to foreign steel in periods when domestic manufacturers could not meet their needs. But steel producers and steel union officials argued that the industry, battered by heavily subsidized competition from abroad, needed another five years of quotas to complete its modernization.

On July 25, President Bush took a middle ground, instructing the U.S. trade representative to negotiate extensions of the VRAs for a "transition period" of two-and-a-half years. The restraints limited imports from VRA countries to 18.4 percent of the U.S. market. During the transition, he said, the U.S. trade representative would seek to negotiate an "international consensus" to reduce subsidies and other barriers to international steel trade; the forum would be the Uruguay Round of talks under the General Agreement on Tariffs and Trade.

Bush said the overall ceiling on imports from VRA countries would be increased during that period at an annual rate of 1 percentage point, with the increase allocated to countries that cooperated in reaching an international agreement.

Legislative History

House Action. The House Ways and Means Committee approved HR 3275 (H Rept 101-263) by voice vote on Sept. 27 and reported it the same day. The measure was virtually unchanged from a version negotiated by members of the Congressional Steel Caucus, which represented steel producers and steel users, and administration officials. Committee Chairman Dan Rostenkowski, D-Ill., encouraged members not to press amendments during the markup, noting that the delicate compromise embodied in the bill and approved by the Trade Subcommittee on Sept. 19 would fly apart under the slightest pressure. Rostenkowski extracted an administration promise to oppose all amendments.

The full House passed HR 3275 on Oct. 2 by a vote of 354-10 under suspension of the rules. The bill was unchanged.

Senate Action. The Senate Finance Committee approved the bill by voice vote on Nov. 15, after adding two unrelated amendments that were being stripped from the fiscal 1990 budget-reconciliation bill (HR 3299 — PL 101-239). *(Budget reconciliation, p. 43)*

One concerned Caribbean ethanol imported duty-free into the United States and had originally been included in a stalled measure affecting Caribbean trade (HR 1233, HR 3299). The second concerned a federal excise tax on foreign and domestic crude oil that partly went to the "superfund" hazardous waste cleanup program. *(Caribbean Basin Initiative, p. 180)*

The Senate passed the Finance Committee bill (S Rept 101-206) by voice vote on the last night of the session, Nov. 22, and a nearly deserted House chamber accepted the changes by voice vote just prior to adjournment.

Major Provisions

As cleared, HR 3275:

- Extended until March 31, 1992, presidential authority to limit steel imports, based on the terms of bilateral agreements and a determination that U.S. producers were trying to improve their competitive position through reinvestment, worker training and other actions.
- Authorized the president to renegotiate bilateral steel-import agreements that would be in effect from Oct. 1, 1989, through March 31, 1992.
- Required the president to report by March 1 each year on the status of international talks aimed at reaching a consensus on steel-producer subsidies, market access and enforcement actions. The talks were intended to conclude with agreements by March 31, 1992, that would replace the VRAs.
- Replaced an existing requirement for granting exceptions to import quotas in cases where the secretary of commerce determined that a "short supply" of requested steel products existed, and domestic producers could not meet the demand. The bill provided somewhat relaxed terms for finding evidence of short supply and expedited decisions to within 30 days in most cases and 15 days in circumstances where short supply had been found in prior years.
- Set requirements for the amount of indigenous feedstock required in Caribbean ethanol eligible for duty-free treatment in the United States through Dec. 31, 1991.
- Equalized, at 9.7 cents per barrel, the federal excise tax on foreign and domestic crude oil. The tax was in part for the superfund hazardous waste cleanup program.

Fair Trade in Financial Services

Congress in 1990 tried but failed to enact a new tool to force easier access to foreign markets for U.S. banks and securities firms.

In reaction to a continuing concern that U.S. financial services companies were being frozen out of foreign markets — and that foreign banks were gaining a large share of the U.S. market — a bipartisan group of senators, led by Donald W. Riegle Jr., D-Mich., and Jake Garn, R-Utah, drafted the Fair Trade in Financial Services Act. The measure would have given U.S. banking and securities regulators broad discretion to retaliate against foreign financial companies in cases where U.S. firms were prevented from expanding abroad.

Riegle and Garn, chairman and ranking Republican, respectively, of the Senate Banking Committee, inserted the text of the fair trade measure into an unrelated bill reauthorizing the Defense Production Act of 1950 (HR 486). The conference report on HR 486 (H Rept 101-933), containing the fair trade language, was adopted by the House by voice vote Oct. 25, 1990, but the Senate never acted on it, chiefly because of opposition to provisions in the underlying Defense Production Act reauthorization. The fair trade language was officially opposed by the Bush administration; however, some Treasury Department officials told Congress that it had merit. *(Defense Production Act, p. 368)*

Background

Under existing law, the International Banking Act of 1978 (PL 95-369), foreign banks and financial firms in the United States were given the same rights to expand, open branches and engage in restricted practices as domestic banks and securities firms. This standard, known in trade parlance as "unilateral national treatment," was established even though some other countries imposed tighter controls on U.S. companies than they did on their own nationals. *(Congress and the Nation Vol. V, p. 259)*

The Senate Fair Trade in Financial Services language was designed to create a new standard of "reciprocal national treatment," meaning that the United States would give free rein only to those foreign banks whose home countries granted national treatment to U.S. banks.

The bill would have required the Treasury secretary to report every two years on foreign practices that restricted access to U.S. financial firms. Where a "significant failure" to grant national treatment to U.S. companies was found, the secretary would have had to initiate negotiations to remedy the situation, unless such talks would have been fruitless or run counter to U.S. economic interests.

Retaliatory sanctions could have been imposed only if the Treasury published a formal finding of discrimination by a foreign country. Even then, banking and securities regulators would have had broad discretion to accept or reject applications from companies based in that country to expand operations in the United States. Existing operations could not have been curtailed.

Legislative History

Despite administration opposition to the fair trade provisions, the Senate Banking Committee included them in its version of the Defense Production Act reauthorization (S 1379). The committee approved the bill by voice vote on May 24, 1990, and reported it (S Rept 101-368) on July 13.

The Senate passed HR 486, the House Defense Production Act, by voice vote Oct. 3, after substituting the text of S 1379. No related language was provided in the House bill, but when conferees on HR 486 concluded their work Oct. 22, they retained the Senate fair trade provisions. The House had passed HR 486 on Sept. 24, 295-119, under suspension of the rules.

1991-92

Trade relations among the three countries of North America, and between the United States and the former Soviet bloc, continued to dominate trade policy in the 102nd Congress.

President Bush saw his goal of a North American Free Trade Agreement only partially realized: The trade pact was negotiated and signed by the three countries, but not formally adopted. The demise of the Soviet Union and the overthrow of communist governments across Eastern Europe led Congress to open new avenues for normal trade with many of those countries. And additional steps were taken to ease the debt burden of Latin American countries, in hope of restoring their status as major trading partners of the United States.

Throughout, continued tensions existed with the Japanese, whose success at building the world's largest trade surplus was unchallenged. But legislative efforts aimed at curtailing Japanese surpluses — particularly in the automotive arena — faltered, as they had in the previous Congress.

NAFTA

The most significant trade endeavor of the 102nd Congress — a controversial proposal to link the United States, Canada and Mexico into a continental free-trade bloc — was only partly concluded by the end of 1992. President Bush, Canadian Prime Minister Brian Mulroney and Mexican President Carlos Salinas de Gortari signed a sweeping North American Free Trade Agreement (NAFTA) on Dec. 17, 1992, in separate ceremonies in their own countries.

Bush did not submit the trade agreement to Congress before leaving office Jan. 20, 1993. He left it to the 103rd Congress and a new president, Bill Clinton, to take the final steps to approve or reject NAFTA. Clinton was under no deadline to send the agreement to Congress, and, after taking office in January 1993, he said he would first try to secure additional worker and environmental safeguards by holding negotiations on side agreements to the main pact. *(Trade pact details, box, p. 188)*

Central to Bush's hope of achieving the free-trade pact was persuading Congress in 1991 not to terminate his authority to negotiate such an agreement and presenting it to Congress under so-called fast-track procedures that would expedite its consideration and protect it from amendments. The fast track gave Congress 90 days to act once a trade agreement was submitted, and it required a simple up or

NAFTA Highlights

The North American Free Trade Agreement (NAFTA) was signed by President Bush, Canadian Prime Minister Brian Mulroney and Mexican President Carlos Salinas de Gortari on Dec. 17, 1992, in separate ceremonies held in their own countries. The agreement was intended to join the United States, Canada and Mexico into a single free-trade bloc. (The United States and Canada had put into effect a bilateral free trade agreement in 1989.) About 65 percent of U.S. industrial and agricultural exports to Mexico was to be made eligible for duty-free treatment immediately or within five years. Mexican tariffs averaged 10 percent, more that twice the average U.S. tariff. If approved as signed, NAFTA promised to:

Motor Vehicles and Parts. Cut Mexican tariffs on vehicles and light trucks from 20 percent to 10 percent immediately and eliminate duties on 75 percent of U.S. parts exports to Mexico within five years. Mexican rules requiring a balance in imports and exports of autos and auto parts were to be phased out over 10 years.

Auto Rule of Origin. Require that automobiles and light trucks qualifying for the tariff cuts must derive at least 62.5 percent of their value from North American parts and manufacturing. The level set in the U.S.-Canada Free Trade Agreement was 50 percent. The goal was to prevent companies in other countries from funneling their autos through Mexico to evade U.S. tariffs. *(U.S.-Canada trade agreement, Congress and the Nation Vol. VII, p. 159)*

Telecommunications. Eliminate discriminatory restrictions on U.S. sales to and investment in the Mexican market for telecommunications equipment and services.

Textiles and Apparel. Immediately eliminate barriers to $250 million (more than 20 percent) of U.S. exports to Mexico and eliminate restrictions on another $700 million within six years. All North American trade restrictions were to be eliminated within 10 years, with rules of origin provisions to ensure that the benefits went to North American companies.

Agriculture. Immediately eliminate Mexican import licenses, which covered about 25 percent of U.S. agricultural exports, and within 15 years to phase out all Mexican tariffs, which generally ranged from 10 percent to 20 percent.

Financial Services. Allow U.S. banks and securities firms to establish wholly owned subsidiaries in Mexico. Transitional restrictions were to be phased out by Jan. 1, 2000.

Insurance. Permit U.S. companies with existing joint ventures to obtain 100 percent ownership by 1996; new entrants to the market would be able to obtain a majority stake in Mexican firms by 1998. By the year 2000, all equity and market share restrictions were to be eliminated.

Investment. Eliminate Mexican domestic content rules stating how much of the value of a product must be attributed to local parts and labor, permitting additional use of U.S. parts. U.S. companies operating in Mexico were to receive the same treatment as Mexican-owned firms. Mexico agreed to drop export performance requirements, which forced companies to export as a condition of being allowed to invest.

Land Transportation. Allow U.S. trucking companies to carry international cargo to the Mexican states contiguous to the United States by 1995 and have cross-border access to all of Mexico by the end of 1999.

Intellectual Property Rights. Guarantee U.S. producers of high-tech, entertainment and consumer goods greater protection for their patents, copyrights and trademarks. NAFTA included protection for computer programs, sound recordings and motion pictures.

Environment. Allow the United States to continue to block imports that did not meet U.S. standards, and allow states and cities to enact even tougher standards. The United States could continue to enforce its international treaty obligations, including limits on trade in products such as endangered species and ozone-depleting substances. The parties agreed not to reduce health, safety or environmental standards to attract investment.

down vote in each chamber. The purpose was to give U.S. negotiating partners confidence that the terms they worked out with the administration would not be altered.

In 1991, the House and Senate each rejected a resolution that would have blocked an otherwise automatic two-year renewal of existing fast-track authority through May 1993. In large part, the votes in favor of continuing the fast track were seen as a referendum on NAFTA, because the decision had the effect of allowing the U.S.-Canada-Mexico talks to go forward. But the trade agreement was far from complete at the time, so many members said they would renew the fast track and reserve judgment on NAFTA until the trade pact was before them.

The fast-track renewal also was critical to allowing continued multilateral talks in Geneva aimed at overhauling the General Agreement on Tariffs and Trade (GATT), an international body that oversaw most trade relationships worldwide. The GATT talks repeatedly stalled because of difficult disputes over agricultural subsidies and did not conclude before the end of 1992. A further renewal of fast-track authority in 1993 was likely to be needed, if a GATT agreement was to be reached.

Background

Bush and Mexican President Salinas had first agreed in June 1990 to negotiate a free-trade agreement. That plan was accelerated by a stalemate in the global GATT talks and by Salinas' decision in the spring of 1990 that more open trade with the United States was the best route to economic development for Mexico.

Bush formally notified Congress of his plans to negotiate a free-trade pact with Mexico in September 1990. After months of high-level talks, he announced in February 1991 that Canada — which earlier negotiated a free-trade agreement with the United States — would join the U.S.-Mexico talks. The goal would be a North American Free Trade Agreement. *(Canada free-trade agreement, Congress and the Nation Vol. VII, p. 159)*

Organized labor, led by the AFL-CIO, opposed NAFTA and made defeat of the fast track its legislative priority for 1991. But the Bush administration prevailed, in large part because it issued an "action plan" addressing critics' concerns. The administration pledged to reject any weakening of U.S. environmental laws, to provide for worker adjustment assistance and to allow long transition periods for some industries threatened by the free-trade pact.

Legislative History

The Bush administration won renewal of fast-track authority only after intense White House lobbying overcame concerns by many Democrats and some Republicans that removing trade and investment barriers would take jobs from U.S. workers and that businesses would head south to take advantage of inexpensive labor and lax environmental laws.

Under the terms of the 1988 Trade Act (PL 100-418), the president was granted broad authority through May 1991 to negotiate bilateral and multilateral trade agreements, which would be submitted for congressional approval under the fast track. If the president requested a two-year extension of negotiating authority, it would be automatic, unless either chamber adopted a simple resolution of disapproval. Adoption of such a resolution would terminate the fast-track process. *(1988 trade bill, Congress and the Nation Vol. VII, p. 148)*

Citing the ongoing Mexico and GATT talks, Bush touched off an intense three-month debate on March 1, 1991, in asking for the two-year extension. Congress had until June 1 to block it, and opponents in both the House and Senate tried but failed to win support for resolutions barring the extension.

Dividing more along regional than party lines, the House on May 23 rejected a resolution (H Res 101) blocking the fast-track renewal on a **key vote of 192-231 (R 21-140; D 170-91; I 1-0)**. The Senate followed suit the next day, rejecting its fast-track resolution (S Res 78) on a 36-59 vote. *(1991 key votes, p. 1061)*

Fast-track opponents found devising a common strategy difficult. Some members, particularly those from farm and textile-producing states, wanted to kill the GATT talks. But a larger group, mainly lawmakers from the Rust Belt, wanted to focus on the Mexico talks. No easy way existed to stop one set of negotiations without bringing down the other.

The opposition also lacked leadership from the top. House Majority Leader Richard A. Gephardt, D-Mo., came under intense pressure from labor and environmental groups to lead the charge, turning a procedural issue into a major political confrontation with Bush. But, while he spoke frequently in support of their concerns, Gephardt ultimately backed the extension.

Most of the Democratic leadership cautiously supported extension of the fast track. That included Speaker Thomas S. Foley of Washington and the heads of the two committees that oversaw trade, House Ways and Means Chairman Dan Rostenkowski, D-Ill., and Senate Finance Chairman Lloyd Bentsen, D-Texas. In part, their leanings reflected a traditional free-trade position. But Democrats also feared that if they campaigned against a U.S.-Mexico free-trade pact, Bush would be able to portray them as protectionist.

For its part, the White House saw the fast-track vote as a major test of presidential authority. "I am going to work tirelessly," Bush said April 7, after meeting with Salinas in Houston. "The credibility of the United States as a trading partner is on the line here." By early May, U.S. Trade Representative Carla A. Hills had met individually with about 150 members of Congress, including two-thirds of the Senate.

The administration argued that a free-trade agreement would stimulate Mexican development, lessening pressure on workers to cross the Rio Grande in search of work in the United States. It would lock in reforms by Salinas' government that had transformed Mexico's economy from one of the world's most protected to one of the more open. And it would provide U.S. companies with a vast labor pool and a more stable investment climate.

The turning point came May 1, when the White House released its action plan. Throughout the 80-page document, the administration avoided making ironclad pledges and reiterated its contentions that the agreement would not threaten jobs and would help the environment. But, at virtually every step, it also conceded that the doomsayers had legitimate concerns.

With the action plan, the administration succeeded in driving a wedge between organized labor and some environmental groups that shifted to supporting the negotiations. That gave cover to Democrats, particularly in the House, who could then support the extension.

House Action. With the fight against the fast track unraveling, the Ways and Means Committee met May 14 to consider a resolution (H Res 101 — H Rept 102-63, Part II) to block the extension. Rostenkowski favored renewal but promised opponents a vote in committee and on the floor.

On a 9-27 vote, the committee rejected H Res 101 and by voice vote sent the measure to the floor with an unfavorable recommendation. Then, by voice vote, it approved a second resolution (H Res 146 — H Rept 102-64, Part II) emphasizing that Congress could suspend the fast track if the administration did not keep its promise to include adequate protections for U.S. workers, industries and the environment in the U.S.-Mexico agreement.

The Rules Committee, which shared jurisdiction, reported H Res 101 (H Rept 102-63, Part I) and H Res 146 (H Rept 102-64, Part I) on May 15.

The House on May 23 then rejected H Res 101 and easily adopted H Res 146 by a vote of 329-85.

Senate Action. The Senate Finance Committee met May 14 and voted 15-3 to report its resolution of disapproval (S Res 78) to the floor with an unfavorable recommendation. The full Senate then acted May 24, rejecting S Res 78 overwhelmingly.

Free Trade Agreement

It took another year and a half after Bush won renewal of his negotiating authority, but he and his counterparts in Mexico and Canada finally came to terms on NAFTA, signing the agreement on Dec. 17, 1992.

As signed, NAFTA promised to eliminate tariffs, duties and other trade barriers among the three countries over 15 years, allowing goods produced anywhere in North America to move freely across a continent with more than 360 million people and a combined economic output of more than $6 trillion a year.

The outlines of the agreement began to emerge in August and September. Bush announced that the "historic agreement" had been concluded in a Rose Garden ceremony Aug. 12, just days before the Republican National Convention convened in Houston. Trade officials had completed a feverish two-week round of negotiations in Washington just hours earlier.

U.S. Trade Representative Hills appeared on Capitol Hill in early September to begin explaining the 2,000-page draft agreement. And at a ceremony in San Antonio on Oct. 7, trade negotiators from the United States, Canada and Mexico initialed the final text of the pact.

The terms of the agreement were no less controversial than expected, and the trade pact became an issue in the 1992 presidential campaign — and in not a few congressional races. Independent presidential candidate Ross Perot made opposition to NAFTA a theme of his campaign, and Democratic candidate Clinton did not endorse the agreement until Oct. 4, though he had previously expressed hope for the idea of a free-trade agreement linking the three countries. In endorsing NAFTA, Clinton said that, if elected, he would seek tougher protections than Bush had negotiated for U.S. jobs, the environment, and health and safety standards.

Throughout the negotiation process, opponents — principally Democrats — kept pressure on the White House. In a July 27, 1992, speech, Gephardt accused the administration of ignoring promises made in its action plan. "It is becoming increasingly apparent that environmental controls, worker-adjustment policies, protections for American and Mexican workers, and incentives for American manufacturers to remain in the United States are being omitted from the draft," Gephardt said.

Gephardt outlined a far-reaching series of protections that he said would have to be included in the text of the accord if it was to win congressional approval. He called for turning trade adjustment assistance into an entitlement program; all workers who lost their jobs as a result of "short-term disruptions or long-term decline" attributable to the trade agreement would qualify for payments regardless of the cost. And he called for a dedicated, cross-border transaction tax to pay for programs in worker training, infrastructure development and environmental protection.

On Aug. 6, the House voted unanimously to warn Bush that it would not tolerate any pact that would weaken U.S. health, safety, labor or environmental laws. The vote came on a non-binding, sense of Congress resolution (H Con Res 246 — H Rept 102-635, Parts I and II) sponsored by Gephardt and Henry A. Waxman, D-Calif. The resolution was adopted 362-0, with Republican and Democratic supporters of the trade talks joining with opponents to back a measure that they called "redundant, but not objectionable." H Con Res 246 was referred to the Senate, but that chamber never acted on it.

China Trade

Twice in the 102nd Congress, President Bush vetoed bills that would have restricted normal trade relations between the United States and China. Both times the Senate sustained the vetoes.

Although the House showed overwhelming support for punishing China with trade constraints following the Chinese government's June 1989 crackdown against pro-democracy demonstrators in Tiananmen Square, the Senate was far more reluctant. The Senate did not even act on two House-passed bills in 1990 that would have either withdrawn China's most-favored-nation (MFN) trade status with the United States or put restrictions on future renewals. *(Background, 1990 bills, p. 173; most-favored nations, box, p. 172)*

MFN, essentially a grant of normal trade relations, was available to China only because of an annual presidential waiver of the Jackson-Vanik amendment to the 1974 Trade Act (PL 93-618). Jackson-Vanik denied MFN to most communist countries unless the president certified that they allowed free emigration of their citizens or the president waived the requirement yearly. Congress could reject either a presidential certification or an annual waiver. *(1974 act, Congress and the Nation Vol. IV, p. 131)*

In 1991, the House and Senate passed a bill (HR 2212) that would have limited the president's ability to waive Jackson-Vanik for China in 1992 by requiring him to certify that China was making progress in addressing human rights concerns. Senate passage came July 23 on a **key vote of 55-44 (R 6-37; D 49-7)**. The significance of that vote was the thin margin, which was far short of the two-thirds needed to override a certain presidential veto. *(1991 key votes, p. 1061)*

Although the House adopted the conference agreement for HR 2212 before the end of 1991, the Senate did not act until the following spring. Following the expected veto, the Senate override attempt in March 1992 fell six votes short at 60-38, the high watermark of Senate support for trade sanctions on the Chinese government.

Legislative History — Round 1

House Action. Initially, the House in 1991 seemed likely to pass a more moderate bill than the one anticipated from the Senate, setting the stage for a compromise that some hoped Bush would be able to support. That possibility evaporated when the House Ways and Means Committee took up the issue June 26, producing a version of HR 2212 that was tougher in some respects than a draft Senate bill and that was clearly unacceptable to the White House.

Negotiations among the sponsors of HR 2212 led to an agreement that would have withdrawn China's MFN status in 1992 unless Beijing disclosed the fate of protesters unaccounted for since the 1989 crackdown and released some of those arrested. In addition, the president would have had to certify that China had made "significant overall progress" in ending gross violations of human rights and religious persecution, removing restrictions on the media, ending harassment of Chinese students in the United States, ensuring freedom from torture and inhumane prison conditions, and granting humanitarian groups access to prisons.

Some Ways and Means Republicans argued against making the bill tougher than it already was, as did committee Chairman Dan Rostenkowski, D-Ill., and Trade Subcommittee Chairman Sam M. Gibbons, D-Fla. But their pleas for restraint were ignored. Committee Democrats, joined by several Republicans, won inclusion of amendments attacking China's one-child-per-family policy, its role aiding the nuclear weapons programs of other countries and its alleged use of forced labor to produce goods for export.

The key test of administration clout came on an amendment giving the president wide discretion to decide whether to continue MFN in 1992. All but two of the 13 committee Republicans voted for the amendment, as did Rostenkowski and Gibbons. But it was not enough; the amendment failed by a vote of 15-17.

By voice vote, the committee sent HR 2212 to the floor; the bill was formally reported (H Rept 102-141) on July 9.

The committee also approved by voice vote a resolution (H J Res 263 — H Rept 102-140) disapproving Bush's decision to waive Jackson-Vanik for 1991. That measure, if enacted, would have had the effect of immediately withdrawing China's MFN status. But it was not likely to become law, because it, too, faced a certain veto, much less support in the House and little support in the Senate.

Despite Bush's stiff opposition, the House passed HR 2212 on July 10 by a vote of 313-112, well in excess of the two-thirds majority needed to override a veto, but a slimmer majority than supported a somewhat more restrained bill in 1990 that had the same goals. Amendments were not allowed on the floor; the version of HR 2212 that passed was identical to the committee version.

By a vote of 223-204, the House also on July 10 passed H J Res 263.

Senate Action. Clearly from the outset, the chief fight over extending MFN to China would take place in the Senate, and the White House concentrated its lobbying effort there.

Majority Leader George J. Mitchell, D-Maine, at first proposed cutting off China's MFN status within six months of passage unless that country met a series of stiff conditions. When such a measure seemed unlikely to pass, Mitchell introduced a bill (S 1367) closer in approach to HR 2212.

The Senate Finance Committee took up S 1367 on June 27, the day after the House Ways and Means Committee acted. But White House lobbying was becoming effective. Although several committee Republicans had previously expressed doubts about Bush's position, not one voted for the bill. Several said it would terminate U.S.-China relations, leaving the United States without influence and abandoning reformers within the country.

Mitchell, who served on the committee, did not even get the support of all the Democrats. Panel member Max Baucus, D-Mont., expressed the hope that Congress would forgo placing conditions on MFN if the administration would agree on its own to impose sanctions against China, including retaliation for unfair trading practices. Baucus joined in an 11-9 party-line vote to send Mitchell's bill to the floor, but he and other Democrats balked at giving it a favorable recommendation. The bill was formally reported (S Rept 102-101) on July 9.

The Senate passed HR 2212 on July 23, after first substituting the text of S 1367. The Senate version was similar to the House measure, but following a series of floor amendments it was more detailed in its requirements. The bill passed 55-44, 12 votes shy of the 67 needed to override a veto if all senators vote.

The administration lobbying was aggressive. Farm groups — fearing the loss of the China market, which accounted for more than $500 million in wheat sales in 1990 — lobbied heavily as well.

The administration's success also represented a victory for Baucus, who had taken a prominent role in opposing conditions on MFN status for China. Baucus worked closely with Minority Leader Bob Dole, R-Kan., in urging the White House to take additional punitive steps against China to deflect sentiment in Congress to act.

Bush responded by pledging in a July 19 letter to take several steps to increase pressure on Beijing. He promised, for example, to strengthen multilateral controls on future Chinese weapon sales and to toughen enforcement of U.S. laws prohibiting imports from China made with prison labor.

The Senate never acted on H J Res 263, the disapproval resolution.

Final Action, Veto. Following the Senate action — and the virtual certainty that the bill would not become law over Bush's veto — the measure languished. The House and Senate appointed conferees in late October to produce a compromise version. And without holding a public meeting, conferees did so in late November (H Rept 102-392).

Under the compromise, the president would have been barred from recommending a waiver of Jackson-Vanik in 1992 unless China accounted for and released citizens detained as a result of the Tiananmen Square protests. In addition, China would not receive MFN if it transferred M-9 or M-11 missiles or missile launchers to Syria or Iran or assisted those countries in building nuclear weapons.

Beyond that, most of the other preconditions specified in the House and Senate bills were watered down simply to require that China make "significant progress" in achieving human rights, trade and non-proliferation objectives.

The House adopted the conference report on Nov. 26 by a vote of 409-21. The Senate did not act on the measure before Congress concluded its business for the year on the following day.

When the 102nd Congress reconvened in early 1992, renewed pressure was placed on the Senate to send HR 2212 to the White House. Particular concern arose about news reports that China had sold advanced ballistic missile technology and launchers to Pakistan in the recent past and to other countries previously. China agreed Feb. 21 to abide by an international agreement barring certain missile technology sales.

The Senate voted 59-39 on Feb. 25 to adopt the conference report on HR 2212, clearing the measure for the president. Several senators who opposed the bill in 1991 but voted for the conference agreement cited weapons proliferation as a primary concern.

Bush vetoed the bill, as expected, on March 2. Also as expected, the House easily mustered enough votes March 11 to override him, but the bill obviously would go no further. The House vote was 357-61.

On March 18, the Senate voted 60-38 to override the veto, well short of the necessary two-thirds majority. The veto thus was sustained.

Legislative History — Round 2

When Bush announced on June 2, 1992 — three months after his veto of HR 2212 — that he would again renew China's Jackson-Vanik waiver, extending MFN status to that country for another year, the fight was on again. It played out virtually identically to the prior round, though in a much more timely fashion.

House Action. The House Ways and Means Subcommittee on Trade on June 29 approved a bill (HR 5318) by voice vote to place conditions on a renewal of China's Jackson-Vanik waiver in 1993. The bill was similar to HR 2212 in its requirement that the president certify to Congress that the Chinese government was making significant progress in addressing human rights, trade and weapons proliferation concerns. But it differed in one significant respect. Goods produced by companies that were joint Chinese-foreign ventures, or by Chinese factories that were collectively or privately owned, would automatically have received MFN treatment; only goods produced by state-owned factories were subject to the bill's conditions and threatened with much higher tariffs should China's MFN status be revoked.

The exemption for joint ventures and privately held Chinese businesses was intended to appeal to members who had complained in the past that denying MFN status to China would harm U.S. business interests and hurt reform-minded forces in China. But some congressional critics said the change did not eliminate their objections to using trade sanctions to force a political change. Some doubted that it would be possible to distinguish easily between state-owned enterprises and those not subject to the higher tariffs imposed by the bill.

The full Ways and Means Committee approved HR 5318 by voice vote on July 2; the bill was reported (H Rept 102-658, Part I) on July 8. Previously, on June 24, the committee by voice vote had sent to the floor without recommendation a resolution (H J Res 502 — H Rept 102-632) disapproving Bush's 1992 Jackson-Vanik waiver.

Despite stiff administration opposition, a bipartisan majority of the House July 21 passed HR 5318 by a vote of 339-62. The House also passed H J Res 502, the disapproval resolution, 258-135, on July 21.

Senate Action. The Senate Finance Committee voted 11-9 along party lines Aug. 4 to report an amended version of HR 5318 to the floor without recommendation. The Senate language was nearly identical to the House version.

On Sept. 14, the Senate passed the bill by voice vote, but the lack of a roll-call vote was not an indication of overwhelming support. Instead, it was a recognition that the measure had enough votes to pass but not enough support to override the anticipated veto.

Minority Leader Dole temporarily injected some uncertainty into the debate three days later when he announced that he might reverse his position and vote for the MFN restrictions unless Beijing agreed to resume buying U.S. wheat. China, one of the largest importers of U.S. wheat, had vowed to stop wheat purchases completely to retaliate for a decision announced earlier in the month by Bush to allow the sale of F-16 fighters to Taiwan. Dole, whose home state of Kansas was the leading U.S. wheat producer, had consistently voted against attaching conditions to China's MFN status.

The Senate never acted on the disapproval resolution, H J Res 502, and it died.

Final Action, Veto. With adjournment approaching, the House by voice vote on Sept. 22 accepted the Senate version of HR 5318, thus clearing the bill for the president. The swift action was intended to get the measure to Bush in time to prevent him from killing it with a pocket veto.

Bush vetoed the measure on Sept. 28, saying in his veto message that the bill would have posed "unworkable constraints on our bilateral trade" and that the casualties would have included "the dynamic, market-oriented regions of southern China and Hong Kong, as well as those Chinese who support reform and rely on outside contact for support."

The House voted 345-74 on Sept. 30 to override the veto. But the next day, as it had six months earlier, the Senate upheld Bush's veto by a vote of 59-40. Dole stuck with Bush and voted no, reportedly after receiving assurances from Chinese officials that their wheat purchases would continue.

Soviet, East Bloc Trade

As the Cold War ended and the Soviet Union came apart, Congress and the Bush administration in 1991 and 1992 continued steps begun in 1990 to open trade relations with formerly communist states.

Congress approved most-favored-nation (MFN) status for the Soviet Union, Bulgaria, Mongolia and Albania — allowing for normal trade to be renewed by the president on an annual basis. Congress considered, but did not pass, a bill restoring MFN status to Romania after a four-year hiatus. And, Congress gave the president authority to extend MFN status permanently to Hungary, Czechoslovakia and the Baltic nations. Congress voted to cut off Yugoslavia's MFN status in the wake of trade embargoes adopted to pressure an end to that country's ethnic civil war.

With MFN, a country was eligible for the same low tariff rates available to most other U.S. trading partners. The Jackson-Vanik amendment to the 1974 Trade Act (PL 93-618) had denied MFN to the Soviet Union and most other communist countries, unless the president certified that they allowed free emigration or he waived the restriction. A waiver had to be renewed annually, and Congress could reject it. To receive MFN, a country also was required to have a trade agreement with the United States, which was subject to congressional approval. *(Background, 1990 action, p. 169; most-favored nations, box, p. 172; 1974 law, Congress and the Nation Vol. IV, p. 131)*

Soviet Union/Russia

President Bush and Soviet President Mikhail S. Gorbachev signed a trade agreement between the two countries in June 1990 during a summit meeting in Washington, D.C. But Bush said he would hold off sending the pact to Congress for approval until the Soviet parliament passed a law guaranteeing Soviet citizens the right to emigrate freely. The Soviets adopted such a law on May 20, 1991.

Bush first submitted the pact to Congress on Aug. 2, 1991, shortly after returning from a summit with Gorbachev in Moscow. The chief opposition on Capitol Hill came from members who were disturbed by Moscow's intransigence on the issue of independence for the breakaway Baltic republics — Lithuania, Latvia and Estonia. Some members wanted to grant the Baltics separate MFN status by reinstating trade agreements that were suspended in 1951, when the republics were swept into the Soviet Union. *(See Baltics, below; terms of U.S.-Soviet trade agreement, box, p. 170; U.S.-Soviet relations, p. 205)*

These objections were overtaken by events. A failed coup attempt in late August rocked the Soviet Union and accelerated the drive for independence by many Soviet republics. On Oct. 9, Bush sent Congress a revised version of the U.S.-Soviet trade agreement, crafted to exclude the Baltic nations, which by then were independent countries. And with the Soviet Union coming apart, some lawmakers questioned whether granting that country MFN status was still relevant.

But the administration argued that the trade status would encourage reformers and that the emerging republics had indicated they would abide by the terms of the pact if they won independence from Moscow.

The near-term increase in two-way trade was not expected to be great. Though U.S. trade law set significantly higher tariff rates on goods from the few countries that did not have MFN status, most Soviet exports were raw materials and other goods that already had low tariffs. Moreover, the Soviets had little hard currency to buy U.S. goods and few products attractive enough to export.

In addition to granting MFN, the agreement ensured that U.S. companies could maintain business facilities in the Soviet Union, protected patents and other intellectual property, and established a trade dispute settlement mechanism. Adequate protections for intellectual property were among the last provisions agreed to before the August summit.

Legislative History. The House Ways and Means Committee by voice vote on Nov. 19 approved, and reported, a measure (H J Res 346 — H Rept 102-338) endorsing the trade pact. The bill then easily passed the House the next day, under suspension of the rules, by a vote of 350-78. By voice vote, the Senate then passed the bill unamended on Nov. 25, clearing the measure for the president. Bush signed the bill into law on Dec. 9 (PL 102-197).

As a prelude to gaining approval for the trade agreement, Bush had waived Jackson-Vanik for the Soviet Union on June 3, 1991; Congress did not attempt to reject the waiver, which still had to be renewed annually.

Still on the books at year's end were laws that prevented more than $300 million in export financing by the Export-Import Bank and a separate $300 million cap on loans for the Soviet Union by other government agencies, except the Commodity Credit Corporation, which financed agricultural exports. However, a bill (HR 1724 — PL 102-182) ending a ban on the importing of gold Soviet coins was enacted as the 1991 session came to a close. And a 1992 bill (HR 5739 — PL 102-429) reauthorizing the Ex-Im Bank relaxed restraints on financing exports to the former Soviet Union and other formerly communist states. *(HR 1724, below; Ex-Im reauthorization, p. 199)*

Baltic Republics

The House Ways and Means Trade Subcommittee gave voice vote approval on Sept. 24, 1991, to a bill (HR 3313) exempting the Baltic nations of Lithuania, Latvia and Estonia from Jackson-Vanik restrictions and making them permanently eligible for MFN status. The bill was supported by the Bush administration, which had promised the Baltics that they would be granted MFN status separately from the Soviet Union to emphasize their newly won independence.

The United States had extended MFN treatment to the three nations in the late 1920s when they were independent and had never formally recognized their incorporation into the Soviet Union. On Sept. 2, 1991, the United States established diplomatic relations with the three nations.

The Baltics bill, meanwhile, was one of several trade measures that Ways and Means Chairman Dan Rostenkowski, D-Ill., refused to schedule for full committee action until the Office of Management and Budget (OMB) explained how it planned to account for revenue that would be lost to the Treasury because of the lower duties on imports. The revenue loss was expected to be small, but Rostenkowski said he wanted to avoid the tiny across-the-board cut in spending (a "mini-sequester") that would be triggered if the money were not recouped. OMB Director Richard G. Darman had angered Rostenkowski in April by ordering a tiny sequester because of a favor Rostenkowski did for his alma mater, Loyola University of Chicago. *(Darman's mini-sequester, box, p. 78)*

The full Ways and Means Committee approved HR 3313 on Nov. 19 (H Rept 102-339), after Darman told Rostenkowski that surplus revenue generated by passage of an unemployment compensation bill would cover the tariff losses. The next day, the House folded the Baltics bill (and several others) into another measure granting permanent MFN status to Czechoslovakia and Hungary (HR 1724 — PL 102-182). HR 1724 was eventually enacted.

Hungary, Czechoslovakia

A bill that began as a simple measure to permanently exempt Hungary and Czechoslovakia from Jackson-Vanik restrictions grew in the final days of the 1991 session into a broader trade measure (HR 1724 — PL 102-182) carried to enactment by provisions rejiggering unemployment benefit formulas.

The must-pass unemployment formula changes had been agreed to as part of a deal that had allowed Congress to pass the Emergency Unemployment Compensation Act of 1991 (HR 3575 — PL 102-164). *(Unemployment benefits, p. 721)*

The House Ways and Means Committee had approved HR 1724 as a simple Hungary-Czechoslovakia bill on Sept. 25. The measure, reported (H Rept 102-223) Sept. 26, noted that the two countries had dedicated themselves to respect for fundamental human rights, accorded their citizens the right to emigrate and travel freely, reversed more than 40 years of communist dictatorship, embraced democracy and introduced far-reaching economic reforms.

The House passed the non-controversial measure by voice vote and without amendment, under suspension of the rules, on Oct. 8. The Senate passed the bill by voice vote on Nov. 15, after amending it to include changes in jobless benefit formulas. (The broader unemployment bill, HR 3575, was cleared by the Senate for the president the same day. Congressional leaders believed tucking the formula compromise into the Hungary-Czechoslovakia bill would be simpler than reopening the conference agreement on HR 3575.) On Nov. 20, the House overwhelmingly adopted a resolution (H Res 287) that had the effect of further amending HR 1724. The resolution accepted the Senate's inclusion of the unemployment benefit formula language and then tacked on provisions from several other trade bills. The incorporated bills repealed the prohibition on the importation of gold coins from the Soviet Union (HR 3347 — H Rept 102-336), provided MFN status for the Baltic nations (HR 3313 — H Rept 102-339), provided special benefits for Andean nations (HR 661 — H Rept 102-337) and imposed sanctions for the proliferation of chemical and biological weapons (HR 3409 — H Rept 102-235, Parts I and II). A motion to suspend the rules and adopt H Res 287 was agreed to by a vote of 407-21. *(Baltics, see above; Andean initiative, p. 296; chemical weapons, p. 292)*

The Senate was unhappy about only one piece of the package, the trade benefits for Andean countries. But in conference, the House refused to budge and held the upper hand because it was politically unacceptable to let the unemployment provisions die. The Senate gave in, and conferees on Nov. 25 approved what was essentially the House version of HR 1724.

The House and Senate both adopted the conference report (H Rept 102-391) on Nov. 26, clearing HR 1724 for the president, who signed it Dec. 4.

Mongolia, Bulgaria

On June 25, 1991, the president sent trade agreements to Congress granting MFN status to Mongolia and Bulgaria. Legislation approving those trade agreements moved on parallel tracks to enactment (Mongolia: H J Res 281 — PL 102-157; Bulgaria: H J Res 282 — PL 102-158).

The House Ways and Means Committee approved both measures by voice vote on Oct. 22 (H J Res 281 — H Rept 102-263; H J Res 282 — H Rept 102-264) and reported them the same day. Both passed the House by voice vote without amendment on Oct. 29 and the Senate on Oct. 31. Both were signed by the president on Nov. 13.

Albania

On June 16, 1992, the president sent Congress a trade agreement granting MFN status to Albania. The House Ways and Means Committee by voice vote on July 29 endorsed legislation (H J Res 507) approving the trade agreement. HJ Res 507 was reported (H Rept 102-764) on July 31. The House passed the measure by voice vote under suspension of the rules Aug. 3.

The Senate Finance Committee approved an identical bill (S J Res 317 — S Rept 102-362) by voice vote Aug. 4. On Aug. 11, the Senate passed the House measure by voice vote and without debate. The president signed H J Res 507 on Aug. 26 (PL 102-363).

MFN status was not expected to have a large, immediate impact on trade with Albania because the country was very poor, had few goods that could be sold in the United States and had little money with which to buy U.S. goods.

Romania

On June 22, 1992, Bush sent Congress a trade agreement with Romania. Romania had enjoyed MFN status with the United States from 1975 until 1988, when the Romanian government renounced it. At the time, Congress was about to vote to withdraw Romania's MFN status because of charges of religious persecution and other human rights abuses in that country.

Human rights organizations asked the House Ways and Means Committee to delay action on legislation (H J Res 512) approving the trade agreement until after elections in Romania, which were scheduled for Sept. 27. But the lawmakers went ahead, saying they would monitor developments to make sure that old-line Communists did not return to power. Ways and Means approved H J Res 512 by voice vote on July 29 and reported it on Sept. 16 (H Rept 102-870). The Senate Finance Committee approved its version of the measure (S J Res 320 — S Rept 102-454) on Sept. 22 without debate and reported it Oct. 5.

The House debated the legislation on Sept. 24 but agreed to put off a vote until after the Romanian elections. Rostenkowski urged a prompt vote to make sure enough time was available to complete action before adjournment. He said the Senate would not vote on the measure before Sept. 27. But Rep. Tom Lantos, D-Calif., argued that House passage would be considered a "vote of confidence in a regime that still largely depends on the hated . . . secret police to stay in power." The House Sept. 30 rejected H J Res 512 by a vote of 88-283 under suspension of the rules. Incumbent Romanian president Ion Iliesco, a former high-ranking Communist Party official, had dominated the Sept. 27 election and was expected to win in a runoff.

S J Res 320 saw no further action.

Yugoslavia

Congress moved quickly in late 1992 to suspend Yugoslavia's MFN status, following the outbreak of civil war in that country.

On Sept. 16, the House Ways and Means Committee gave quick voice vote approval to a bill (HR 5258) to suspend Yugoslavia's MFN status — effectively denying low tariff treatment only to imports from Serbia and Montenegro, the remaining republics of that fractured country. HR 5258 was reported (H Rept 102-880) on Sept. 18.

Bill sponsors argued that Yugoslavia "doesn't exist anymore" and said removing its MFN status would send a signal to Serbia and Montenegro that their support of Serbians fighting in Bosnia must stop. The committee rejected, 7-20, an amendment that also would have suspended MFN status for Croatia.

Various ethnic factions in the republic of Bosnia-Herzegovina had been fighting a bloody civil war for months. Reports of atrocities committed on both sides — especially by the Serbs — had outraged the international community and led to calls for action against Serbia by members of Congress. The House and Senate passed non-binding resolutions calling on the president and the United Nations to work to end the bloodshed. *(Yugoslavia, p. 278)*

HR 5258 included a provision to re-establish MFN if the president certified that it would bolster Yugoslavia's compliance with European human rights accords and that Yugoslavia had ended armed conflict with former republics and was respecting their borders.

The House passed HR 5258 by voice vote under suspension of the rules Sept. 22.

The Senate passed a nearly identical version of the bill Sept. 30, amending it to insist that, for Serbia or Montenegro to regain MFN status, they must have ceased all support of Serbian forces inside Bosnia-Herzegovina. On Oct. 6, the House by voice vote accepted the Senate amendments, clearing the bill for the president. Bush signed HR 5258 on Oct. 16 (PL 102-420).

Enterprise for the Americas

The Bush administration saw several key elements of its Enterprise for the Americas Initiative enacted in the 102nd Congress. But efforts to move a comprehensive bill incorporating its chief elements were stymied.

President Bush had proposed in June 1990 that Congress permit some Latin American countries to write off a portion of the debts they owed the U.S. government and to initiate broad trade talks in the region. The House passed a bill in late 1990 to grant some of the requested debt relief, but the Senate never acted on the measure. *(Background, 1990 action, p. 179)*

Several efforts were made to enact portions of the administration proposal in 1991 and 1992, some of them successful.

Foreign Aid Bill. Three subcommittees of the House Foreign Affairs Committee took cracks at the Enterprise for the Americas Initiative in April and May 1991, working on a free-standing bill (HR 964) to authorize reductions in certain foreign aid loans made to Latin American countries.

The full Foreign Affairs Committee rolled those provisions into a broad foreign aid authorization bill, and they survived in the conference report on the bill (HR 2508 — H Rept 102-225). The Senate adopted the conference report on Oct. 8, 1991, but the House rejected it on Oct. 30, killing the bill. *(1991 foreign aid authorization, p. 267)*

Enterprise for the Americas Bill. In October 1992, Congress enacted a big piece of the Enterprise for the Americas debt relief proposal as a free-standing bill that permitted a write-off of up to 40 percent of agricultural loans from the Commodity Credit Corporation (CCC).

The House passed the bill (HR 4059) Oct. 2 by voice vote under suspension of the rules. The Senate passed it Oct. 7 by voice vote, clearing the measure for the president. Bush signed it (PL 102-532) Oct. 27.

According to sponsors, nine countries including Mexico owed about $1.45 billion in agriculture credits to the United States; about $580 million of that could be eliminated through the program. HR 4059 allowed the countries involved in the initiative to reduce their debt burdens by buying back some of the debt they owed the CCC. The countries could repurchase their debt on advantageous terms, but they had to commit 40 percent of the money they saved for environmental restoration and development projects. The remaining debt was to be paid off, with interest, under a renegotiated schedule. Money for the debt relief would be appropriated separately.

The House Agriculture Committee approved the bill by voice vote on June 30 (H Rept 102-667, Part I) and reported it July 16. The House Foreign Affairs Committee approved the bill on Aug. 5 and expanded its scope to make concessional loans from the State Department's Economic Support Fund and Developmental Assistance programs eligible for principal reduction, renegotiation or other debt relief. Those provisions were later dropped and enacted in 1992 as part of a reauthorization bill (HR 4996 — PL 102-549) for the Overseas Private Investment Corporation (OPIC).

OPIC, Ex-Im Bank Bills. The OPIC bill permitted concessional loans — those made at very low interest for extended periods — to be written off to the extent that Congress appropriated money for that purpose. The intent was to grant wholesale relief for some government debt to help ease the overall debt burden for eligible Latin countries.

The House adopted the conference report on HR 4996 (H Rept 102-1026) on Oct. 6 (in the session that began Oct. 5); the Senate followed suit Oct. 8. *(OPIC authorization, p. 199)*

Similar debt relief provisions also were attached to a bill (HR 5739 — PL 102-429) reauthorizing the Export-Import Bank's operations. The conference report on HR 5739 (H Rept 102-1010) authorized the president to forgive, sell or reduce some Ex-Im Bank loans used to finance the sale of U.S.-made goods to Latin American countries.

The House adopted the conference report Oct. 6 (in the session that began Oct. 5), and the Senate did likewise Oct. 8. *(Export-Import bank, p. 199)*

Export Controls

Last-minute delaying tactics in 1992, as Congress prepared to adjourn for the year, doomed a three-year push to update U.S. export control laws. Supporters of a bill (HR 3489) to revise Cold War restrictions on the export of high-technology goods argued that the legislation would boost U.S. trade and allow officials to concentrate enforcement on the most sensitive high-tech exports with military uses.

On its last day in session, Oct. 8, the Senate by voice vote adopted the conference report on the bill (H Rept 102-1025). But the House was unable to bring up the measure before it concluded legislative business on Oct. 6, and the bill died.

Three House Republicans objected to provisions in HR 3489 that would have lessened the authority of the secretary of defense to block exports of high-tech goods that could be used in weapons systems or had other military applications. They threatened to force a series of time-consuming procedural votes that would have prevented action on other bills. So the House leadership abandoned the measure.

For the second Congress in a row, an export control bill died upon adjournment. In 1990, President Bush pocket-vetoed a similar measure (HR 4653), objecting to provisions restricting foreign aid to countries that used chemical weapons or aided others in manufacturing them. He said that it undermined his foreign policy authority. *(Export controls, p. 175)*

Background

The nation's export control law — the Export Administration Act — had expired Sept. 30, 1990, and Bush had invoked his basic national security authority to retain existing restrictions on high-technology sales abroad.

The Export Administration Act, whose origins went back to the 1940s, had been used to keep computers and other sophisticated technology with possible military applications out of the hands of the Soviet Union and other potential U.S. enemies. Congress had been struggling for some time to revise these export restrictions, but the leadership had failed repeatedly to get the legislation enacted.

U.S. law was parallel to and, in some cases, more restrictive than an international system of controls enforced by the Coordinating Committee on Multilateral Export Controls (Cocom), a 17-nation group made up of NATO countries, except Iceland, plus Japan and Australia. With the end of the Cold War, Cocom had moved in 1990 to greatly relax restraints on exports to former countries of the East Bloc. Bipartisan support existed on Capitol Hill for loosening U.S. controls, both to boost U.S. trade and to focus enforcement on the most sensitive high-technology exports.

Legislative History

Action to rewrite the Export Administration Act began in early 1991, when the Senate took up a bill (S 320) that was essentially a duplicate of the measure that Bush pocket-vetoed a few months earlier.

Without sending the bill through committee, the Senate passed S 320 by voice vote on Feb. 20, 1991. The Senate adopted a few relatively minor amendments, but, as passed, S 320 was little changed from the vetoed bill. And despite continued administration opposition, it included the chemical weapons provisions that led to the 1990 pocket veto.

The House, meanwhile, chose to ignore the Senate's effort and late in 1991 started work on a new export control bill almost from scratch. On Oct. 31, the day after the House passed its new bill (HR 3489), it returned S 320 to the Senate as unconstitutional. The chemical weapons provisions would have imposed higher tariffs on countries and companies that contributed to the spread of chemical and biological weapons and of ballistic missiles, raising revenue. The Constitution requires bills that raise revenue to originate in the House.

In the end, the chemical weapons sanctions were passed separately as part of a broad trade bill that among other things granted permanent normal trade status to Czechoslovakia and Hungary (HR 1724 — PL 102-182). *(Czechoslovakia, Hungary, p. 193)*

House Action. The House Foreign Affairs Subcommittee on International Economic Policy started formal work on a new export control bill in late 1991 and approved a draft bill by voice vote on Oct. 1.

The measure, reauthorizing the Export Administration Act for one year, contained several provisions that drew strong objections from the administration. Chief among them was a requirement that the administration propose that Cocom lift export controls on telecommunication equipment to the Soviet Union. Opposition by the United States and Britain had blocked such a move by Cocom, which operated by consensus. The House had passed a similar telecommunications provision as part of the 1990 export control bill, but it had been removed in conference with the Senate.

In addition, the bill required the United States to seek approval from Cocom to remove Poland, Czechoslovakia and Hungary from the list of countries subject to special export restrictions aimed at communist nations. The measure included a provision to speed removal of controls on certain militarily sensitive exports to Lithuania, Latvia and Estonia.

The bill also required that the United States drop controls by the end of 1991 on exports to countries that were members of Cocom.

The subcommittee's draft bill became HR 3489 when it reached the full Foreign Affairs Committee days later. The committee made a few changes to resolve some complaints and approved the measure by voice vote on Oct. 17. HR 3489 was formally reported (H Rept 102-267) on Oct. 23.

The committee voted to extend U.S. export controls through March 1, 1993, instead of Sept. 30, 1992, as approved by the subcommittee. And it refined subcommittee language affecting the sale of telecommunications equipment and the designation of terrorist countries and mandating the imposition of sanctions on countries that spread nuclear weapons technology. All were problems for the administration, and the changes did not seem to satisfy the White House. But remaining roadblocks continued to raise serious doubts about the measure's chances for enactment.

The House passed HR 3489 by voice vote Oct. 30 after rejecting several attempts by conservative Republicans to give the Pentagon more power to block high-technology exports. The administration continued to threaten a veto, if the measure were not substantively changed.

Senate Action. The Senate moved quickly in early 1992, passing HR 3489 by voice vote on Jan. 22 with amendments intended to alleviate administration concerns.

The Senate version won administration support after the removal of provisions mandating sanctions against countries and foreign companies that contributed to the spread of nuclear weapons. Provisions that stiffened sanctions against nuclear proliferation but allowed the president discretion to impose them were left in the bill. *(Nuclear arms proliferation, p. 293)*

Final Action. Conferees on the bill were not named until June, and they made slow progress, producing a conference report for HR 3489 (H Rept 102-1025) on Oct. 5, just days before the session concluded.

The conference agreement would have required the removal of controls on all exports to and from Cocom member countries and set criteria for easing restrictions on exports to countries still subject to Cocom export controls. It would have required the United States to implement Cocom agreements reached in June 1992 on exports of telecommunications equipment for civil uses and urged further liberalization of such controls. The bill would have restricted the sale of dual-use equipment and technology (civilian materials with possible military applications) to terrorist countries and provided stricter sanctions against nuclear proliferation while allowing the president final discretion.

The administration was fairly happy with the result. But on Oct. 6, the last day the House conducted legislative business, three Republicans — Duncan Hunter of California, Jon Kyl of Arizona and John R. Kasich of Ohio — successfully blocked House passage of the conference report. The three disliked provisions that would have given the Commerce Department more control over export licensing decisions, blaming the agency for Iraq's military buildup before the 1990 Gulf War.

The Senate adopted the conference report by voice vote Oct. 8, but the House had already quit work and did not act.

Trade Expansion Act

Defying a Bush administration veto threat, the House in 1992 passed a trade bill (HR 5100) aimed largely at opening Japanese markets to U.S. automobiles, auto parts and rice. The bill included language specifying that cars produced by Japanese-owned U.S. plants should contain 70 percent U.S. parts by 1994.

The Senate, however, never took up the bill, and it died at the end of the Congress.

Background

Dan Rostenkowski, D-Ill., chairman of the House Ways and Means Committee and chief sponsor of HR 5100, assembled the measure at the behest of the Democratic leadership. The bill was above all a political document, designed to draw attention in the middle of an election year to the sponsors' claim that the Bush administration had ignored unfair trade practices by U.S. competitors, particularly Japan. Unveiling the measure May 7, House Majority

Leader Richard A. Gephardt, D-Mo., said the bill represented the Democrats' blueprint for moving toward a more aggressive, retaliatory trade posture.

As introduced, the bill's most controversial provisions would have required the president to negotiate a voluntary restraint agreement with Japan capping sales of Japanese cars in the United States at existing levels and forced the Bush administration to negotiate an agreement with Japan to buy more U.S. automobiles before the cap could be raised.

In addition, the bill would have required the U.S. trade representative (USTR) to begin negotiations to lift Japanese barriers to U.S. automobiles and auto parts and to start separate talks with Japan, Korea and Taiwan on boosting U.S. rice exports.

In drafting the bill, Rostenkowski — a frequent critic of attempts to force the White House hand on trade policy — rejected proposals made the previous year by Gephardt aimed at requiring the president to retaliate against countries that maintained large trade deficits with the United States.

Instead, the bill would have reauthorized for five years the so-called Super 301 section of the 1988 Trade Act (PL 100-418). That provision required the USTR to identify countries with major barriers to U.S. goods and target them for negotiations and possible retaliation. However, it gave the USTR latitude about what countries to name and even more latitude about imposing sanctions. The Super 301 provision lapsed in 1990, and the administration did not want it revived. *(1988 act, Congress and the Nation Vol. VII, p. 148)*

The Democratic bill also included an unprecedented requirement that the USTR initiate Super 301 investigations of Japan on cars and auto parts, and of Japan, Korea and Taiwan on barriers to U.S. rice imports.

Other provisions of the measure would have:

- Established new procedures for annual USTR reviews, upon request by private industry, of foreign compliance with trade agreements, except the U.S.-Canada and U.S.-Israel free trade agreements. The provision was intended to give the U.S. semiconductor industry a way to press Japan to comply with an agreement to buy more U.S. semiconductors.
- Made various changes in customs law, including allowing electronic processing of customs-related transactions.
- Required enforcement of quantitative limits on machine tool imports from Taiwan, under the terms of a lapsed bilateral agreement, until a new agreement could be negotiated.
- Made several changes designed to make it more difficult for foreign producers to evade U.S. anti-dumping laws by importing parts from Third World countries and assembling the product in the United States. Anti-dumping laws prohibited foreign companies from selling goods in the United States at less than their "fair value."
- Made multiple changes in tariffs on U.S. imports. (The changes also were included in a separate tariff bill, HR 4318, which ultimately did not clear.)

Legislative History

The Ways and Means Trade Subcommittee approved HR 5100 by voice vote June 9 after removing the language requiring the administration to cap sales of Japanese cars in the United States. But the change did not satisfy the Bush administration, which made clear its staunch opposition to the bill.

The cap on Japanese auto sales would have applied not only to exports from Japan but also to vehicles produced in U.S. plants owned by Japanese companies. Some Democrats on the subcommittee agreed with Republicans that the provision could have cost workers in foreign-owned U.S. plants their jobs and deterred overseas companies from opening new U.S. plants.

The subcommittee adopted several amendments, including one to require importers of foreign-produced grain and oil seeds, such as soybeans, to specify what the commodities would be used for in the United States.

The full Ways and Means Committee approved the bill by voice vote June 16, after the chief defender of the troubled U.S. auto industry, Sander M. Levin, D-Mich., withdrew an amendment aimed at forcing the Bush administration to open negotiations on placing tighter limits on car imports from Japan.

Levin's amendment, which never came to a vote, would have required the USTR to open negotiations with Japan within 45 days after the bill was enacted. In unusually stringent language, it specified that the talks "shall lead" to an agreement requiring that vehicles assembled at Japanese-owned factories in the United States, known as transplants, contain 70 percent U.S.-made parts and only 30 percent parts from Japan. Several Democrats and most Republicans criticized the language. HR 5100 was formally reported (H Rept 102-607) on June 23.

The House passed the bill July 8 by a vote of 280-145. The margin was not nearly wide enough to override a threatened presidential veto and raised doubts that the measure would go much further.

Before members began debate on the bill, they turned down a parliamentary effort to allow a Republican floor amendment requiring the president to begin negotiations with Japan on a free-trade agreement.

Gephardt and Levin succeeded on the floor in adding their amendment mandating negotiations with the Japanese government over trade in automobiles and auto parts. The auto amendment was adopted July 8 by a 260-166 vote, a surprisingly comfortable margin considering that an earlier version had failed to win majority support in the Ways and Means Committee.

Minivan Tariffs

A measure to raise import tariffs on four-door minivans faltered in 1992. The provision was included by the House Ways and Means Committee in a wide-ranging tariff bill (HR 4318) that passed the House in July. And an attempt in the Senate to add similar language to an urban aid tax bill (HR 11) was defeated.

Backers of the tariff increase said that classifying minivans as passenger vehicles allowed Japanese carmakers to export them to the United States and pay only a 2.5 percent tariff. Arguing that minivans had many of the characteristics of trucks and cargo vehicles, supporters had hoped to reclassify the multi-purpose vehicles as trucks, which would have boosted the U.S. tariff tenfold to 25 percent.

Background

The conflict over the classification began in 1989, when the U.S. Customs Service ruled that minivans were properly considered trucks. Six months later, the

Treasury Department overturned the Customs decision and ruled that any multi-purpose vehicle with two doors could be considered a truck, but that four-door minivans were properly classified as passenger cars for tariff purposes.

Minivans and other multi-purpose vehicles made up a $9 billion market for automobile manufacturers in 1992, with U.S. companies such as Chrysler, General Motors and Ford controlling 88 percent of that market. Minivans, which were treated as trucks by the Environmental Protection Agency and the Transportation Department, had to meet less stringent emissions and fuel economy standards than passenger cars. However, the minivans were widely used as passenger vehicles, serving as the station wagon of the 1990s and widely marketed to families.

The push for changing the Treasury Department decision and forcing four-door minivans to be treated as trucks for tariff purposes mainly came from the Michigan delegation, principally two Democrats: Rep. Sander M. Levin and Sen. Donald W. Riegle Jr.

Opponents characterized the measures as costly for consumers, estimating that the price of minivans would rise between $4,000 and $6,000 per vehicle.

Legislative History

House Action. The provisions to raise the minivan tariff first were provided in an amendment to HR 4318, a bill making nearly 400 modifications to the U.S. tariff schedule, including removing the tariffs on a number of items.

During House Ways and Means Committee markup of HR 4318 on June 24, Levin offered an amendment to reclassify minivans and other multi-purpose vehicles as trucks for tariff purposes. The amendment made exceptions for vehicles imported from countries that sold fewer than 10,000 units, a move to allow minivan imports from Britain and Germany to continue.

Critics, including administration officials, called the amendment protectionist, but members approved it by a vote of 24-12. The committee action came on the same day that the International Trade Commission found that imported minivans sold by Toyota and Mazda did not harm Detroit's Big Three automakers The commission's finding meant that Japanese minivans would not be slapped with anti-dumping duties that could have raised their price by more than $2,000.

Ways and Means reported HR 4318 (H Rept 102-634) on June 30.

On July 31, the House passed the bill by a vote of 273-112, with supporters characterizing the tariff change as protecting U.S. workers' jobs.

Senate Action. The Senate never took action on HR 4318 (most of the tariff provisions, except for the minivan language, also had been included in a broad House-passed trade bill, HR 5100).

The only significant Senate action on the minivan issue came Sept. 26, when Riegle proposed a minivan amendment to HR 11 — the tax bill that Bush later vetoed. *(Urban aid tax bill, p. 103)*

Riegle's amendment was similar to Levin's but was expressed as a sense of the Senate resolution, not a statutory change in the Customs Service rules. The Senate rejected Riegle's amendment, 36-37.

Other Legislation

Fair Trade in Financial Services

Congress failed in 1992, as it had in 1990, to enact new trade restrictions on the operations of foreign banks and securities firms in the United States, where their home countries denied full access to their markets to U.S. financial companies. *(1990 action, p. 187)*

The so-called Fair Trade in Financial Services bill was incorporated by the Senate into a measure reauthorizing the Defense Production Act, which gave the president authority to redirect civilian goods for military use during wartime. The Senate passed the bill (S 347 — PL 102-558) in February 1991; the House passed it in October 1991 without the Senate's financial services language. Conferees did not reach agreement on a compromise until a year later. While some House conferees supported the fair trade language, most did not, and the Senate provision was dropped in the conference agreement (H Rept 102-1028). *(Defense Production Act, p. 412)*

The Senate language would have given authority to the Treasury Department and bank regulators to deny applications by foreign banks and securities firms for licenses in the United States if their home countries did not grant equal market access to U.S. banks and securities firms.

Customs Law Revisions

Efforts to pass legislation modernizing U.S. customs operations and permitting companies to file electronically much of the information necessary to clear goods through ports of entry were unsuccessful in the 102nd Congress.

The customs provisions were included in a major urban aid tax bill (HR 11). The House adopted the conference report (H Rept 102-1034) on Oct. 6, 1992, and the Senate cleared the bill on Oct. 8. But President Bush vetoed HR 11, and the veto was sustained. The House also included customs provisions as part of a broad trade bill (HR 5100), which was never taken up by the Senate and died at the end of the 102nd Congress. *(Urban aid tax bill, p. 103; trade bill, p. 196)*

Under pressure from the U.S. Customs Service and business groups worried that the changes would not be made, the Senate Finance Committee took up an unrelated House-passed bill (HR 5643) and amended it to include the customs provisions. The bill was approved by the committee by voice vote Sept. 22 and reported (S Rept 102-430) Sept. 29.

Electronic filing of customs information was controversial because smaller brokers who handled such duties for importers feared that it would require them to make costly investments in new equipment. Large importers and brokerage companies would be able to employ electronic filing more readily, critics said. In response, the Finance Committee agreed to phase in the new service over seven years and to allow electronic filing only on documents required for entry. Other required documents, such as filings to the Food and Drug Administration, still would have to be submitted by hand.

HR 5643 sought to toughen penalties against importers who failed to submit accurate information, authorize the Customs Service to use private laboratories to test and analyze merchandise, and allow private collection agencies to recover money owed to the federal government under customs laws. The bill would have required customs officials to board a sufficient number of vessels to ensure compliance with U.S. laws.

With the session nearing an end, the bill was held up by a threat of unrelated trade amendments. It eventually died without action on the Senate floor.

The customs provisions also were attached by the House on Oct. 6 to a Senate-passed bill (S 2880) reauthorizing several trade agencies: the Office of the U.S. Trade Representative, the United States International Trade Commission and the Customs Service. No conference committee was convened to reconcile the different versions of S 2880, and it died at the end of the session.

Ex-Im Bank Authorization

Congress in 1992 cleared a five-year reauthorization for the Export-Import Bank — a federal agency that provided market-rate loans and loan guarantees to foreign countries buying U.S.-made goods and services. The bill (HR 5739 — PL 102-429) included a three-year reauthorization of the Ex-Im Bank's tied-aid "war chest," which allowed the agency to provide low-interest credits on the condition that the money be used to buy U.S. products.

President Bush signed the bill Oct. 21.

The bill as cleared also increased the ceiling for total export financing and increased assistance to small and medium-sized export companies. It eased some statutory limits placed on loans used to finance exports to the former Soviet Union and other formerly communist states, and it called for a report on the need for further export financing to the former Soviet republics. The bill authorized the president to write off some Ex-Im Bank loans to Latin American countries, as part of the Enterprise for the Americas Initiative. *(Soviet trade, p. 192; Enterprise for the Americas, p. 194)*

Authorization for the Ex-Im Bank expired on Sept. 30, 1992. The reauthorization extended operations through fiscal 1997. The Ex-Im Bank facilitated about $4 billion in export credits a year and guaranteed another $5 billion in export credits. The tied-aid war chest was created to combat the use of similar financing deals by other countries, in particular Japan and France. Under tied-aid agreements, the United States provided low-interest loans to developing countries on the condition that the money be used to buy U.S. products.

In February 1992, the Organization for Economic Cooperation and Development (OECD), a Paris-based international group, adopted restrictions on the use of tied aid. Members who supported retaining the war chest argued that continued financing would allow Ex-Im Bank authorities to monitor loopholes in the OECD restrictions.

Legislative History. On July 30, the International Development Subcommittee of the House Banking Committee gave voice vote approval to a draft bill granting a five-year extension of the Ex-Im Bank's charter. The bill also extended the bank's tied-aid war chest for another five years at an authorization level of $500 million a year. The House subcommittee agreed by voice vote to nine amendments, including one authorizing forgiveness of some Ex-Im Bank loans as part of the Enterprise for the Americas Initiative.

HR 5739 was introduced the same day, and it went straight to the House floor, where it was passed by voice vote without amendment on Aug. 4.

The Senate Banking Committee approved its Ex-Im reauthorization bill (S 2864) by voice vote on June 18 and reported it (S Rept 102-320) on July 15. The Senate then passed HR 5739 by voice vote on Aug. 12, after substituting the text of S 2864. One key difference between the House and Senate versions was that the Senate restricted the tied-aid war chest reauthorization to three years.

House and Senate conferees reconciled differences between the two bills on Oct. 4 (H Rept 102-1010), retaining the Senate language on the war chest. The House adopted the conference report by a vote of 332-44 on Oct. 6 (in the session that began Oct. 5); the Senate followed suit by voice vote on Oct. 8, clearing the bill for the president.

OPIC Authorization

Congress cleared a bill (HR 4996 — PL 102-549) just prior to adjourning in October 1992 to reauthorize the Overseas Private Investment Corporation (OPIC), an agency that provided insurance, loans and loan guarantees to assist U.S. businesses investing abroad. President Bush signed the bill Oct. 28.

The original House-passed version would have revamped OPIC's charter, but as the session drew to a close conferees on the bill decided to put off their more ambitious goals. OPIC's authorization expired Sept. 30, 1992, and a major sticking point for the bill was whether the reauthorization should be for three years or five years. Ultimately, HR 4996 reauthorized OPIC for only two years.

As cleared, the bill earmarked money for additional export promotion and required companies receiving OPIC assistance to abide by child labor laws and occupational safety and health standards. The bill also authorized spending for the U.S. Trade and Development Program, which promoted export programs to developing countries. In addition, the administration was authorized to write off some loan repayments from countries participating in the Enterprise for the Americas Initiative. *(Enterprise for the Americas, p. 194)*

Legislative History. The House Foreign Affairs Committee approved HR 4996 (H Rept 102-551) on May 28 and reported it June 5. The House began floor debate June 17, but consideration of amendments and the final vote on the bill were delayed until later in the summer. The House passed the bill by voice vote Aug. 5.

With time running out on the 102nd Congress, the Senate bypassed committee action on the bill and opted instead to pursue a short-term extension of OPIC's authorization. On Oct. 1, the Senate passed HR 4996 after first substituting the text of S 3294, a simple, two-year authorization for the agency.

Conferees on the two versions of HR 4996 came to agreement (H Rept 102-1026) fairly quickly on a short-term extension that preserved parts of the House bill without the major overhaul of OPIC's charter. The House adopted the conference report on Oct. 6 (in the session that began Oct. 5) by voice vote; the Senate followed suit on Oct. 8, clearing the bill for the president.

Major Provisions. The bill reauthorized OPIC's programs through Sept. 30, 1994, and included many of the substantive provisions of the House bill that did not directly affect OPIC's charter. The bill required companies receiving OPIC assistance to abide by child labor and worker health and safety laws and dropped language that might have excluded the nations of the former Soviet Union from participating in the export programs. The bill also:

- Authorized $55 million for fiscal 1993 and $65 million for fiscal 1994 for the Trade and Development Agency to provide funds for feasibility studies of development programs.
- Allowed the Department of Commerce to develop commercial centers in the independent states of the former Soviet Union or in the developing countries of Asia, Latin America and Africa. The commercial centers were to provide information on U.S. exporters and to aid U.S. export expansion into these markets.
- Authorized the president to write off a portion of Agency for International Development loans to Latin American countries, as part of the Enterprise for the Americas Initiative.

4

Foreign Policy

Introduction 203
1989-90 Chronology 205
1991-92 Chronology 260
Persian Gulf War 299
End of the Cold War 319

Foreign Policy

The demise of Soviet communism produced the most profound changes in the global landscape in half a century. A series of tumultuous events in 1991 culminated in the breakup of the Soviet Union, sweeping away the superpower rivalry that had shaped U.S. foreign policy since the end of World War II.

President George Bush presided over the transition to a new era, which brought the promise of reduced tensions and dramatic cuts in national security expenditures. Yet it soon became clear that the post-Cold War era would be no less prone to violence and instability than its predecessor. From Europe to Asia, the United States faced new threats and unfamiliar challenges to its interests.

Iraq's invasion of oil-rich Kuwait in August 1990 led to the largest U.S. military engagement since Vietnam. Though the Persian Gulf War achieved its primary objective of reversing the invasion — with far fewer U.S. casualties than had been expected — Iraqi leader Saddam Hussein remained in power and a source of vexation to the Bush administration.

The pace of developments in Eastern Europe was breathtaking. In 1989, the Berlin Wall, once a symbol of a divided Europe, was literally destroyed. Countries that had formed the backbone of the Warsaw Pact, such as Poland, embraced capitalism. But Europe's transformation had a darker side as well. The breakup of Yugoslavia triggered the region's worst bloodbath since World War II, as a new term — "ethnic cleansing" — defined the horrors perpetrated by Serbian forces operating there.

At home, the end of the Cold War necessitated a rethinking of the ideological and partisan disputes over foreign policy that had divided the nation since the Vietnam War. But no consensus emerged on a new foreign policy for the new era. Bush and Secretary of State James A. Baker III reacted cautiously to the upheaval in the former Soviet bloc. The administration offered support to Russian President Boris N. Yeltsin only after it became apparent that the Soviet Union — and as its president, Mikhail S. Gorbachev — would not survive.

Congress generally urged a more activist policy toward the crumbling Soviet empire. As socialist dictatorships began falling in Eastern Europe, Congress prodded the administration to provide large-scale aid programs for the new democracies. After the breakup of the Soviet Union, Congress enacted legislation — which initially received a cool reception from the White House — assisting the former Soviet republics in dismantling their nuclear weapons. But Congress faced problems in defining what Bush termed the "new world order" and new pressures to focus greater attention on the nation's sagging economy and rising budget deficit.

The War and Its Aftermath. The Persian Gulf War represented the crowning achievement of Bush's presidency, but it was a triumph tinged with disappointment.

Iraq's invasion of Kuwait, a close U.S. ally, threw the Middle East into turmoil. Suddenly, Baghdad was in a position to dominate the Persian Gulf, a region that produced nearly one-third of the world's oil. The Bush administration quickly moved to buttress neighboring Saudi Arabia — another key U.S. ally — pouring troops and military equipment into the kingdom. By the fall of 1990, the president had deployed half-a-million troops to the Persian Gulf, setting the stage for a military confrontation with Saddam's forces.

For the president and Congress, the stakes were enormous. For the first time since the Vietnam War, a real possibility existed that large numbers of U.S. troops would fight and die in battle. Backed by U.S. allies, Bush vowed that the Iraqi occupation of Kuwait would not stand. Prodded by the administration, the United Nations Security Council set a deadline of Jan. 15, 1991, for Iraq to withdraw its forces from Kuwait.

Though Congress exhibited no shortage of outrage over Iraq's actions, key Democrats supported tough economic sanctions against Baghdad as an alternative to war. Throughout the fall of 1990, Congress moved fitfully on the issue as the budget crisis and other matters took center stage. With only three days left before the U.N. deadline, lawmakers took up resolutions authorizing the use of military force against Iraq. After a solemn, 20-hour debate, a divided Congress authorized the administration to use "all necessary means" to force Iraq out of Kuwait.

On Jan. 16, 1991, the United States went to war, as part of a multinational force. Allied aircraft pounded away

References

Discussion of foreign policy for the years 1945-64 may be found in *Congress and the Nation Vol. I*, pp. 91-232; for the years 1965-68, *Congress and the Nation Vol. II*, pp. 49-116; for the years 1969-72, *Congress and the Nation Vol. III*, pp. 853-948; for the years 1973-76, *Congress and the Nation Vol. IV*, pp. 847-912; for the years 1977-80, *Congress and the Nation Vol. V*, pp. 31-95; for the years 1981-84, *Congress and the Nation Vol. VI*, pp. 123-197; for the years 1985-88, *Congress and the Nation Vol. VII*, pp. 169-251.

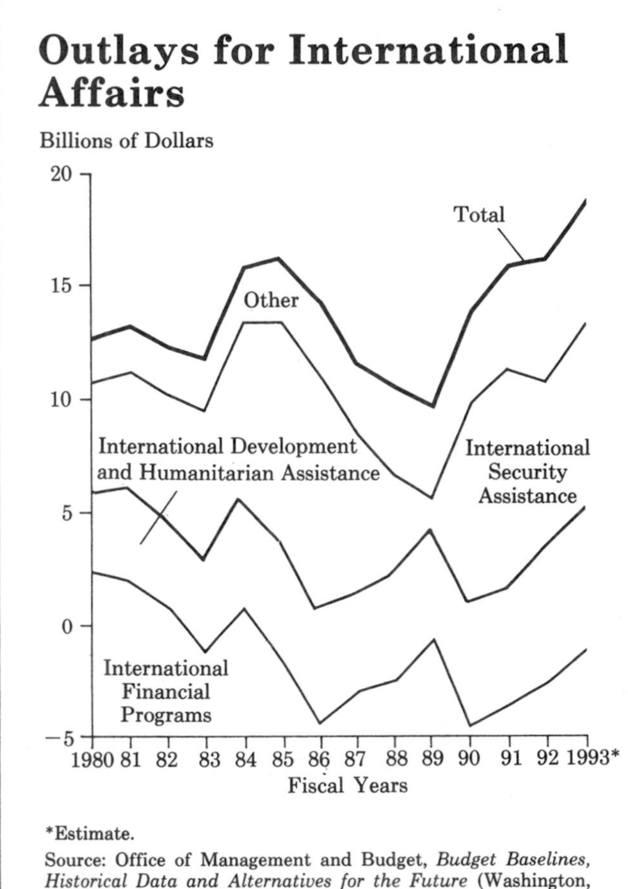

*Estimate.

Source: Office of Management and Budget, *Budget Baselines, Historical Data and Alternatives for the Future* (Washington, D.C.: U.S. Government Printing Office, January 1993).

at targets deep inside Iraq. Within six weeks, following a punishing ground assault by U.S. and allied troops, Iraq's army had been routed and Kuwait was liberated.

For Bush, the euphoria was short-lived. Democrats, who sought to play down their party's opposition to the war, successfully shifted attention to the nation's woeful economy. Equally important, Saddam's stubborn hold on power served as a continuing embarrassment for a president who took considerable pride in his administration's foreign policy record.

As the 1992 election campaign heated up, congressional Democrats found another club to use against the president — the prewar support for Iraq that had been authorized by the Reagan and Bush administrations.

Bush and Congress. Bush's relationship with Congress was a study in contrasts. On several key issues that had provoked bitter battles during the Reagan era — particularly in policies regarding Central America — Bush was far more accommodating than his predecessor. But Bush was unyielding on other matters, and efforts to broach a compromise proved futile.

Just three months into his term, Bush reached an agreement with lawmakers that wound down aid for Nicaragua's contras and paved the way for a return to democracy in that country. By early 1990, the Marxist Sandinistas, whom Reagan had identified as a serious threat to U.S. interests, had been ousted in elections.

Under pressure from congressional Democrats, the administration in 1990 grudgingly accepted the first meaningful constraints on the decade-long U.S. policy of supporting El Salvador's armed forces. Less than two years after Congress approved those restrictions, the government and left-wing guerrillas agreed to a U.N.-sponsored peace pact.

For its part, Congress broadly backed the administration's 1989 decision to invade Panama. While leading Democrats complained that the administration had avoided seeking congressional authorization for the military action, few could object to its results. U.S. forces succeeded in capturing Panamanian leader Gen. Manuel Antonio Noriega and bringing him back to the United States on drug-trafficking charges.

But the administration and Congress were unable to find common ground on issues ranging from preferential trade status for China to loan guarantees for Israel. China's brutal suppression of its pro-democracy movement in 1989 produced a groundswell of congressional support for stiff economic sanctions against Beijing. The president, however, staunchly opposed linking China's performance on human rights and other areas to the annual renewal of its most-favored-nation (MFN) trading status.

In the aftermath of the Persian Gulf War, Bush and Baker made a renewed push to initiate peace negotiations between Israel and its Arab neighbors. But Israeli Prime Minister Yitzhak Shamir adamantly refused to curtail his government's controversial policy of building settlements in territories occupied by Israel since 1967. In the administration's view, such settlements represented an obstacle to regional peace. To pressure Israel into changing its policy, Bush in late 1991 delayed consideration of Israel's request for $10 billion in loan guarantees, which were being sought to help absorb hundreds of thousands of Jewish émigrés from the Soviet Union. Congress, which was traditionally a bastion of support for Israel, loudly protested Bush's decision. But Bush held firm, and Congress avoided a direct confrontation with the White House over the issue.

In June 1992, the political dynamics shifted dramatically when Israel elected a more moderate Labor Party government. The new prime minister, Yitzhak Rabin, promised to slow the growth of settlements in the territories. That eased tensions between Washington and Jerusalem. With Bush on board in favor of the loan guarantees, Congress enacted the program as part of the fiscal 1993 foreign aid appropriations bill.

Unfinished Agenda. In 1989-92, Congress cleared legislation providing billions of dollars in economic and technical assistance for the former Soviet bloc nations. But as Bush prepared to leave office, the United States clearly would be asked to provide even more aid to support their transition to free-market democracy.

The Bush administration and Congress were slow to come to grips with disasters in Somalia and former Yugoslavia. After Somalia's government fell in 1991, the country was beset by factional fighting that destroyed the country's infrastructure and resulted in massive starvation. Moved by televised pictures of the ongoing tragedy, Bush in December 1992 dispatched U.S. troops to protect food shipments to the East African country. The action drew wide congressional backing.

Leading Democrats urged Bush to take a tough stance against attacks by Serbians on Muslims in Bosnia-Herzegovina. Congress enacted legislation urging the president to provide military equipment to the besieged Muslims. But members remained divided on the question of whether to threaten military action to stem Serbian aggression.

Chronology Of Action On Foreign Policy

1989-90

The 101st Congress considered foreign policy legislation against a rapidly changing backdrop. The Soviet Union was taking extraordinary steps toward reforming its economic and political systems. The once-solid Soviet bloc was on the road toward breakup and there would be no turning back. The two Germanies were becoming a single nation once again. The Cold War that had dominated U.S.-Soviet relations since the end of World War II would soon be an anachronism. *(End of the Cold War, p. 319)*

Members of Congress scrambled to take the lead on aiding the East European countries emerging from the Soviet bloc. And with the threat of the Soviet Union receding, more questions were being raised about U.S. covert assistance to rebels in Angola, Cambodia and Afghanistan.

But as the fear of global nuclear war subsided, the United States became preoccupied with the threat of a regional, conventional conflict in the Persian Gulf, following the invasion of Kuwait by Iraq. When the 101st Congress adjourned, the United States was pressuring Iraq with economic sanctions. But by the time the next Congress convened, the United States was on the brink of war. *(Persian Gulf War, p. 299)*

Although breathtaking changes were taking place in the world, some of the old issues and perennial problems had not gone away.

U.S. policy toward Central America continued to be debated in Washington. Aid to El Salvador — an issue that had provoked many a battle between the Reagan White House and Congress in the early 1980s — was again at the forefront as the decade ended. Congress backed the Bush administration's shift from a military to a diplomatic solution to the conflict in Nicaragua. And Congress gave broad support to the reverse policy in Panama. Impatient with the failure of diplomatic and economic pressure to unseat Panamanian strongman Manuel Antonio Noriega, the United States decided to do it militarily.

As had happened so often in recent years, Congress was unable to pass a regular foreign aid authorization bill, and authorizations had to be folded into appropriations bills.

The Iran-contra affair that haunted the Reagan White House in its final years in office continued to capture attention. This was in part because of the ongoing investigation of the affair by a special counsel and the well-publicized trial of former National Security Council aide Oliver L. North. The scandal also was kept alive by congressional attempts to push through legislation to ensure that the scandal would not be repeated. Several of those efforts triggered presidential vetoes.

President Bush was able to deflect attempts on Capitol Hill to force the administration to take a harder line toward China because of Beijing's suppression of pro-democracy movements in mid-1989 and other alleged human rights abuses by the communist regime.

U.S.-Soviet Relations

At the end of 1989, President Bush and Soviet President Mikhail S. Gorbachev took historic steps toward leaving the Cold War behind them and putting relations between the superpowers on a businesslike footing.

Meeting at a Dec. 2-3 shipboard summit off Malta, against a backdrop of political revolutions in Eastern Europe, the two leaders scheduled an ambitious diplomatic agenda to be completed in time for a full-scale summit in June 1990 in the United States. Major items included accelerated negotiations on the entire range of arms control issues and normalizing U.S.-Soviet trade.

At a joint news conference closing the Malta meetings, Bush said: "We stand at the threshold of a brand new era of U.S.-Soviet relations."

Gorbachev declared that the Cold War "epoch" had ended: "We are just at the very beginning of our road, a long road, to a long-lasting peaceful period."

The thaw in relations between the two superpowers continued in 1990. At the June summit meeting in Washington, the two leaders signed a major trade agreement granting the Soviets normal trade status and pledged to wrap up a strategic arms reduction talks (START) treaty by year's end. And in November, Bush, Gorbachev and the leaders of 20 other countries signed a treaty limiting conventional forces in Europe (CFE).

But by the end of 1990, the agreements had stalled. Bush said repeatedly that he would not send the trade pact to Congress for approval until the Soviet parliament had codified more open Soviet emigration policies. Meanwhile, concerns about political retrenchment in Moscow and questions about Soviet compliance with the CFE treaty kept the Bush administration from submitting it to the Senate for approval. U.S. officials were dissatisfied with the Soviets' accounting of forces and weapons covered by the agreement. The Soviet army reportedly was dug in against the treaty, stoking U.S. concerns.

Those fears were exacerbated by continuing political turmoil in the Soviet Union, dramatized in December when Soviet Foreign Minister Eduard A. Shevardnadze resigned abruptly. Shevardnadze, regarded by U.S. officials as a trusted negotiator and an architect of improved relations, denounced the hard-liners who had been attacking Gorbachev but also warned that the Soviet president's drive for increased powers could lead to a "dictatorship."

Progress toward a START agreement, already slowed by a few unsettled technical issues, was eclipsed by more pressing issues. The United States was preoccupied with the Persian Gulf crisis, while Gorbachev struggled with the independence movement in the Baltic States and hard-liners' criticism of his policies. *(Persian Gulf War, p. 299; end of the Cold War, p. 319)*

Another summit meeting had been scheduled for mid-February 1991. But Bush was reluctant to go to Moscow during the Gulf War. In the wake of the Soviets' armed intervention in Lithuania and the other Baltic States in January 1991, the White House announced that the Moscow summit would be indefinitely postponed. Administration officials, however, took pains to state that the crisis in the Baltics had not caused the delay.

Bush Policy

In his first year as president, Bush spent months agonizing about how to deal with Gorbachev's wide-ranging shifts in military and political policy. As a result, he faced complaints from congressional Democrats at home and from allies abroad that he was too cautious in seizing opportunities presented by Moscow's less bellicose posture.

Bush moved to quiet that criticism in a pair of summits, first with North Atlantic Treaty Organization (NATO) leaders in Brussels in May 1989 and then with Gorbachev in December.

NATO Differences. As the NATO leaders gathered in Brussels for the summit marking NATO's 40th anniversary, the United States and European leaders faced the challenge of resolving their significant differences over NATO's arms policy toward the Soviet Union.

Since its foundation in 1949, NATO had relied on the threat of a U.S. nuclear strike against the Soviet Union as its ultimate deterrent against attack by the Warsaw Pact's more numerous conventional forces. In 1967, NATO had codified its reliance on nuclear weaponry as the great equalizer in a strategy of "flexible response," under which it would use nuclear weapons, if necessary, to defeat a non-nuclear attack by the Warsaw Pact.

In the mid-1970s, the problem of fending off a non-nuclear attack from the East took on greater urgency. As a result of new Soviet deployments of manpower and equipment, Soviet forces in Eastern Europe and the western part of the Soviet Union were much better positioned to attack Western Europe without the kind of prolonged mobilization that would cue NATO to begin shipping reinforcements over from the United States.

In that context, short-range (or "battlefield") nuclear weapons took on greater military significance. Because a few of these warheads could devastate a dense concentration of tanks and armored troop carriers, they would provide "tactical deterrence" against the sort of massing of forces by Soviet commanders that would be necessary for an attack.

But in late 1988, Gorbachev made a bold move to put the arms control ball in the Western allies' court. In a Dec. 7 address to the United Nations General Assembly in New York, he belittled the role of military force and ideological struggle in world affairs. And he backed that up with an announcement of Soviet plans to cut 500,000 of the country's 5.1 million troops by 1991. *(Congress and the Nation Vol. VII, p. 345)*

The Soviet plan was intended to make the threat of a surprise Soviet-bloc attack on Western Europe look less plausible. Many of the cuts would be made in tank divisions and other attack units in Eastern Europe.

Gorbachev's proposal left West Germany reluctant to allow the United States to deploy on its territory a new class of short-range nuclear missiles. Chancellor Helmut Kohl insisted that NATO defer any commitment to deploy replacements for the 70-mile-range Lance missiles in Western Europe and begin talks with the Soviets aimed at substantial reductions in the number of short-range nuclear-force (SNF) weapons on the continent.

Kohl's government was under great pressure from opposition groups. As early as 1987, Gorbachev's promise of a military détente in central Europe was feeding the anti-nuclear sentiment in West Germany, as was a more fundamental sense of frustration over Germany's stepchild status among the powers of Europe. The presence of short-range nuclear missiles was seen by opponents as just one more imposition for Germans to tolerate, on top of hosting 400,000 allied troops and 480,000 of their own, frequently engaging in large-scale military exercises and low-level military training flights in a heavily urbanized country the size of Oregon. Opposition groups also objected to any commitment to Lance modernization, partly on grounds that the proposed new missiles would have three times the range of Lance.

But Bush, fearful that formal negotiations would only fuel political pressure to scrap the nuclear weapons, refused Kohl's request. First, he insisted that the conventional arms reduction talks, which began in Geneva in March, had to yield a significant reduction in the Warsaw Pact's superiority in conventional arms, which the nuclear missiles were supposed to offset.

Congressional Criticism. Matters were further complicated by discontent on Capitol Hill. Since the mid-1970s, a swelling chorus of members of Congress from across the political spectrum had complained that West Germany and other U.S. allies — who also were tough trading competitors — were sponging off the American taxpayer. The allies derived military security from U.S. forces deployed abroad at great cost, these critics argued, while spending far less of their national wealth on defense than did the United States.

Demands on Capitol Hill for the allies to bear a greater share of the mutual defense burden drew added force in 1989 from the stringent budgetary limits that stifled popular domestic and defense programs.

Bush Proposals. Bush signaled a more flexible stance during negotiations leading up to the NATO summit.

At the Brussels meeting of NATO leaders, Bush moved to reclaim the arms control initiative and still, for a while, the criticisms that he was too cautious in responding to Gorbachev's policy shifts. He proposed dramatic reductions in conventional armed forces in Europe and engineered a compromise statement that deferred the NATO dispute over short-range nuclear missiles. By declaring that a conventional reduction agreement could be negotiated within a year and carried out by 1992, Bush made the linkage between SNF weapons and conventional forces reductions more palatable to Kohl. The alliance agreed that talks aimed at a "partial" reduction in SNF arsenals could begin once a CFE treaty was concluded and that an SNF cutback could start to take effect once the conventional reduction had been concluded.

Influential congressional Democrats who had criticized Bush's earlier stance as too rigid lauded his Brussels performance. But a few conservatives on Capitol Hill worried that Bush had abandoned well-founded U.S. security policies under political pressure.

1989 Malta Summit

By the December summit in Malta, Bush had decided it was in the interests of the United States to support Gorbachev's uphill efforts to reform the Soviet economic and political systems. Bush offered more than rhetoric by pledging trade concessions and offering to help the Soviet Union fully enter the world economy.

Bush said he made up his mind after watching Gorbachev allow, and even encourage, the breakup of the Soviet empire. As Bush and Gorbachev were meeting, the collapse of communist governments in East Germany and Czechoslovakia accelerated.

Both Bush and Gorbachev had said the Malta summit was not intended to produce major decisions, and the leaders signed no treaty documents and made no significant declarations altering their fundamental policies. But the two leaders agreed to speed up negotiations on arms control and economic issues, in effect trying to keep superpower relations on a par with the pace of political upheavals in Eastern Europe.

They set a schedule calling for:

- An acceleration of negotiations toward a START agreement cutting each superpower's nuclear arsenals by as much as 50 percent. Both sides hoped to lay the groundwork for agreement on the essential details of the treaty in time for the full-scale summit in June 1990 and sign a formal treaty later that year. The leaders also agreed to try to finish work, in time for the summit, on changes to two nuclear-testing treaties signed in the 1970s. *(START treaty, p. 383; nuclear testing treaties, p. 366)*
- Concluding in 1990 the CFE treaty reducing the number of troops, tanks, planes and other non-nuclear forces arrayed by NATO and the Warsaw Pact. The CFE treaty would reduce each alliance's forces to a level roughly 15 percent below NATO's existing deployment, requiring disproportionately greater cuts by the Soviet Union and its allies. *(CFE treaty, p. 383)*
- Hastening work on a U.S.-Soviet treaty cutting each country's stockpile of lethal chemical weapons to a level 20 percent below the U.S. stockpile, as the prelude to a 40-nation treaty intended to ban chemical weapons. *(Chemical weapons accord, box, p. 366)*
- Beginning work immediately toward an overall U.S.-Soviet trade agreement, the first such accord since one was negotiated in the early 1970s but never carried out. Bush said that once the Soviet Parliament enacted laws guaranteeing freedom of emigration, he would waive a 1974 law (PL 93-618) — the Jackson-Vanik amendment — that had prevented Moscow from getting most-favored-nation trade status. *(Congress and the Nation Vol. IV, p. 131)*

Gorbachev sought to add another item to the 1990 agenda: convening a meeting of the 35-nation Conference on Security and Cooperation in Europe to discuss events in Eastern Europe, especially the issue of unifying East and West Germany, which the Soviet Union had staunchly opposed. The conference in 1975 produced an agreement in Helsinki, Finland, calling for greater adherence to human rights standards. *(German unification treaty, p. 214)*

Bush appeared to rebuff the suggestion for a 1990 meeting of the conference, but Gorbachev later won an endorsement of the idea from French President François Mitterrand.

Bush's proposals at Malta changed his past policies in three important respects. In effect, he proposed a deadline to complete a START treaty, something he had previously opposed. He also abandoned his stance — taken as recently as September — that the United States should continue building chemical weapons even after the signing of an international treaty outlawing such weapons. Last, Bush withdrew U.S. opposition to allowing Moscow to participate as an observer at international trade talks.

Reaction to Malta

Two trends had converged to heighten Bush's readiness to take bolder steps to improve the superpower relationship. One was the increasingly harsh criticism by Democrats of his cautious response to world events, particularly the collapse of the Soviet empire in Eastern Europe. The second was Gorbachev's evident hands-off approach as communist regimes in Warsaw, Budapest, Sofia, Prague and East Berlin fell.

Explaining his changed views, Bush said in Brussels on Dec. 3: "As I watched the way in which Mr. Gorbachev has handled the changes in Eastern Europe, it deserves new thinking."

A key element of that new thinking was Bush's revised position on whether the United States had an interest in seeing that Gorbachev's economic and political reforms succeeded. For months, members of Congress and others had argued that Washington should help Gorbachev because his failure might bring hard-line communists back to power. Administration officials had resisted that reasoning.

Bush said after the Malta summit that "there is enormous support in our country for what Chairman Gorbachev is doing." But respect for Gorbachev's reform policies was coupled with concern that the rapid deterioration of the Soviet economy could undermine his position. As a result, Bush said in explaining his willingness to offer economic concessions to Gorbachev: "We want to try to meet him on some of the areas where he needs help."

Secretary of State James A. Baker III was even more explicit in stating a U.S. position favoring Gorbachev's programs of economic reforms. "Whatever we do, we are doing because it is in our best interests to see perestroika [restructuring] succeed, because if it succeeds, we will see a

State Leadership

James A. Baker III, on a 99-0 Senate vote Jan. 25, 1989, was confirmed as Bush's first secretary of state. A longtime confidant of Bush's, Baker had served as White House chief of staff and Treasury secretary during the Reagan administration.

Baker left his post at the State Department on Aug. 23, 1992, to become senior counselor and White House chief of staff, as well as adviser to Bush's sagging re-election effort. By taking the chief of staff position, Baker could keep his hand in foreign policy without violating the Ethics in Government Act, which barred former high-ranking officials from contact with their old agencies for a year after departure.

Republicans generally viewed the move through a political prism and emphasized the assets that Baker would bring to the troubled Bush campaign. Democrats accused the president of placing his own political survival over the need to maintain a stable stewardship of foreign policy. They also were uncharacteristically effusive in their praise of Baker.

Deputy Secretary of State Lawrence S. Eagleburger was tapped in a recess appointment to succeed Baker. No Senate confirmation vote was required. Eagleburger was sworn in Dec. 8. *(Baker, Eagleburger background, p. 1174)*

more stable, open and secure Soviet Union," Baker said Dec. 4.

Most leaders on Capitol Hill seemed ready to embrace the view that the Malta summit was a milestone in superpower relations. Rep. Lee H. Hamilton, D-Ind., said the summit "fundamentally changed the tone and psychology of U.S-Soviet relations. We put aside questions of motives, especially Soviet motives, and the reversibility of glasnost [openness] and made it clear that it's in our interest to help Gorbachev. We now recognize that Soviet policies have changed in ways that justify reciprocal action on our part."

But not everyone agreed. Former Reagan Pentagon official Frank J. Gaffney Jr., for example, said in a Dec. 6 paper that U.S. economic help would not produce a Soviet abandonment of communism but instead would make "the existing Soviet system more efficient and more competitive" — and thus a greater danger to U.S. interests.

Some U.S. defense specialists on the political center and right warned that the deadlines agreed to at Malta might force unwise compromises, while others raised more fundamental objections — among them, the longstanding fear of some conservatives that arms control agreements sap public support for essential defense programs by fostering a false hope for peace.

And conservatives who had been especially active on Central American issues complained about what they said was Bush's failure to demand that Gorbachev stop Soviet support for leftist regimes in Cuba and Nicaragua. "I was disappointed when President Bush did not make the Soviet removal from the American hemisphere a major precondition to economic benefits flowing to the Soviet Union," said Rep. Duncan Hunter, R-Calif.

1990 Troop-Cut Proposal

Scrambling to keep up with developments overseas and to maintain the political initiative at home, Bush for the second time in eight months proposed faster superpower troop cutbacks in Europe. As a centerpiece of his State of the Union speech on Jan. 31, 1990, Bush suggested deeper cuts in U.S. and Soviet troops in Europe than were envisioned in the ongoing arms control talks. *(Troop cuts, box, p. 387)*

Moscow was talking with Czechoslovakia and Hungary about withdrawing its forces; key Polish leaders also demanded a rapid pullout of Soviet troops. In that context, some Western leaders worried that a Soviet retreat from Eastern Europe would create political pressure for a hasty, and possibly destabilizing, U.S. departure from the continent.

Bush's proposal won praise on Capitol Hill, but key Democrats resumed criticizing him for not moving quickly enough to take advantage of the collapse of communism in Eastern Europe. Hoping for Pentagon budget cuts, some Democrats suggested pulling most U.S. troops from Europe. And several members of the Senate Armed Services Committee said on Feb. 1 that Bush's proposal did not go far enough. Democrats challenged Pentagon assertions that the Bush numbers should be a "floor" on U.S. troop strength in Europe as well as the "ceiling."

However, Armed Services Committee Chairman Sam Nunn, D-Ga., said the proposal made "the conventional-arms-control proposal that we now have tabled in Vienna much more relevant both to the changes in Eastern Europe and to the budget reality here at home."

Bush sought, and apparently got, approval of his proposal from key allies in advance of his Jan. 31 speech. Several NATO governments praised the plan. Bush also discussed the proposal by telephone with Gorbachev. A Kremlin spokesman said Feb. 1 that the Soviet Union welcomed the proposal.

Events in Baltics

Events in the Soviet Baltic States throughout 1990 served as a constant reminder of how frail the potential U.S.-Soviet détente was. From the moment the new government of Lithuania declared independence on March 11, a dilemma was created for the United States.

U.S. politicians had demanded freedom for the Baltic States of Lithuania, Latvia and Estonia ever since Soviet leader Josef Stalin absorbed them into the Soviet Union in 1940. Resolutions condemning Soviet occupation of the "captive nations" were rituals in Congress.

Lithuania's bold dash to independence seemed to satisfy those demands, but Lithuania's action also came at an embarrassingly inconvenient time for the Soviets and the West. By insisting on immediate secession before Gorbachev was prepared to deal with it, the Lithuanians exposed anew Gorbachev's domestic difficulties, particularly his political need to court the hard-line constituencies that opposed his economic and political reforms.

From the day that the new government of Lithuania declared independence, most of Washington's policy makers and politicians exercised a rhetorical restraint inconceivable in times past. The Bush administration gathered broad political support for sympathizing with the Soviet Union's situation and pressing for a settlement by negotiation, not by force or capitulation.

Congress seriously debated only one issue: whether to insist that Bush heed the Lithuanian government's appeal for official recognition by Western nations. In their resolutions, both chambers said Bush should do so soon, but they did not demand it or set deadlines.

Sen. Jesse Helms, R-N.C., first sought to force Bush's hand by offering a resolution on March 21 — as an amendment to clean air legislation (S 1630) — demanding recognition of Lithuania's new government and "direct relations" with it. A vehement anti-communist, Helms wanted to slam Bush for not reacting enthusiastically enough to Lithuania's declaration of independence. Caught by surprise, senior Bush administration officials lobbied against Helms' resolution and persuaded the Senate to reject it, 36-59.

The next day, the Senate adopted, 93-0, a much milder resolution (S Con Res 108) urging Bush to "consider" Lithuania's appeal for recognition. The House followed suit on April 4, when it adopted H Con Res 289 by a vote of 416-3 under suspension of the rules, urging the president to "plan for and take those steps, at the earliest possible time," that would create normal diplomatic relations with Lithuania.

In their resolutions, the House and Senate issued identical warnings to Gorbachev that using force against Lithuania would cause "severe repercussions" in U.S.-Soviet relations. But at the administration's request, the resolutions mentioned no specifics.

Little negative reaction emanated from Capitol Hill to the April 5 announcement that Bush and Gorbachev would hold summit meetings in the United States May 31-June 3, despite the Kremlin's confrontation with Lithuania.

Washington Summit

Bush and Gorbachev signed a trade agreement June 1 granting the Soviets most-favored-nation trade status, enabling them to pay lower tariffs on goods imported into the United States. But Bush said he would not send the pact to Congress for approval until the Soviet parliament had codified more open Soviet emigration policies. *(Trade agreement, p. 169)*

Before the summit, Bush had linked his willingness to sign the trade agreement to two actions by Moscow: passage of legislation codifying the right of Soviet citizens to emigrate and a lessening of pressure on Lithuania and the other Baltic States.

Congress in turn served notice to both the Bush administration and the Soviet Union that no U.S.-Soviet trade agreement would be reached unless the Kremlin negotiated in good faith with the Lithuanian government and lifted its economic embargo. The Senate took that position on May 1 with a 73-24 vote (HR 4404); the House followed suit June 6, just five days after Bush and Gorbachev signed the historic trade agreement. The House vote was 390-24 (HR 4653).

At the Washington summit, U.S. and Soviet officials also signed agreements aimed at improving commercial, cultural and other relations. Among them:

Civil Aviation. Baker and Shevardnadze signed an aviation agreement expected to more than triple the allowed number of commercial air flights between the United States and the Soviet Union. The agreement also would allow airlines other than Pan Am and Aeroflot to service U.S.-Soviet routes.

Nuclear Energy. A five-year agreement provided for new U.S.-Soviet cooperation in nuclear energy, including reactor safety, fusion energy and basic nuclear science. This agreement sprang, in part, from international concern about the Soviet Union's lack of safety standards, as demonstrated by the 1986 accident at the Chernobyl plant in the Ukraine. Bush and Gorbachev signed this agreement.

Ocean Studies. Baker and Shevardnadze signed an extension of a 1973 agreement providing for cooperation between the superpowers on oceanographic research. The previous agreement was to expire June 14, 1990.

Maritime. A maritime agreement would allow U.S. ships to call at 42 Soviet ports, and vice versa, with only two days' notice.

Student Exchanges. This agreement established a goal of 1,500 students from each country annually by 1995. Bush and Gorbachev signed it.

Arctic Islands. A maritime boundary treaty would give the Soviets official recognition of their jurisdiction over four Arctic islands. The two nations for years had disputed sovereignty over the islands, the largest of which was Wrangel Island in the East Siberian Sea. Baker and Shevardnadze signed this agreement.

One of the most tangible symbols of eased East-West tensions came later in the year with the signing of the CFE treaty. Calling it "the farthest-reaching arms agreement in history," Bush said at the treaty-signing ceremony in Paris on Nov. 19 that the CFE treaty "signals the new world order that is emerging."

Trade and Aid Issues

Bush appeared with Shevardnadze at the White House on Dec. 12 and announced that, despite continued disagreement over the June trade agreement, he was suspending a 15-year-old ban on extending commercial credits to the Soviets, enabling them to buy up to $1 billion worth of U.S. agricultural goods. Most analysts of Soviet affairs viewed the president's offer of credits as further evidence of the administration's commit-

Moscow Embassy Study

The Bush administration tried to move ahead in 1990 with a plan to tear down and rebuild the bug-riddled U.S. Embassy in Moscow but was blocked by Congress.

Acting in large part because of budget constraints, Congress refused to provide money to raze the building in fiscal 1991 and instead allowed a reprogramming request to begin a design study.

Just to win authority from Congress to reprogram $3.8 million for the study, the administration was forced to agree that the architects also would study and design a separate structure for another site. "In order to avoid further delay, we agreed to do design work on the things we'd prefer not to," said one administration source.

Construction of the embassy began in 1979, but the discovery of listening devices throughout the building halted work in August 1985. After that, the building was in limbo while Congress and the administrations of Ronald Reagan and George Bush debated what to do. *(Congress and the Nation Vol. VII, p. 240)*

Three proposed solutions surfaced: razing the building and rebuilding it from its foundation, replacing only the top four floors or building a secure annex next to the structure and using the current building for non-classified purposes.

Tearing down the building required renegotiation of the 1969 and 1972 agreements under which the United States and the Soviet Union built embassies in each other's capitals. The Soviets could not fully occupy their compound, on Mount Alto in Washington, until the United States occupied its chancery in Moscow.

President Bush in December 1989 opted for razing the structure and rebuilding it, and he requested $270 million in his fiscal 1991 budget to do so. But the high cost of this proposal provoked opposition in Congress far beyond what the State Department had expected, leading to an impasse with no two committees agreeing on how the situation should be handled. Authority to reprogram $3.8 million for a design study was included in the fiscal 1991 State Department spending bill (HR 5021 — PL 101-515) enacted in 1990.

In 1991, Congress turned over to the State Department the burden of deciding what to do with the building. *(Details, p. 263)*

ment to buttress Gorbachev's increasingly shaky leadership.

Members of Congress were generally supportive of the new administration overtures, although some saw the offer of agricultural credits as long overdue. Key Republicans had joined with Democrats in urging the administration to lift the 1974 Jackson-Vanik amendment, which prohibited the extension of credits to the Soviet Union.

Bush waived the law, originally aimed at pressuring communist nations to allow free emigration of their citizens, until June 1991. The president praised the Gorbachev government for its "generally excellent [emigration] practices of the past year."

More substantive criticism came from conservatives who worried that the United States was moving too quickly to assist its old rival. New Jersey Sen. Bill Bradley, a moderate Democrat, voiced similar concerns, calling the economic aid "ill-advised." Bradley said he was especially troubled by reports that the Committee for State Security (KGB), the Soviet security police and intelligence agency, would be overseeing the distribution of foreign assistance and that the Soviet military had denied a request from the mayor of Leningrad to release food stocks.

Sending more direct economic aid to the Soviet Union was not much of an issue for Congress. Few lawmakers saw any value in it or were willing to take the political heat for advocating help to an "enemy."

Congress included $369.7 million in the fiscal 1991 foreign aid appropriations bill to help former East-bloc countries develop market-based economies. But lawmakers and the administration failed to reconcile differences over broader aid programs. And the dispute doomed passage of legislation to authorize U.S. contributions to the lending arm of the World Bank, the International Development Agency. *(Fiscal 1991 foreign aid appropriations bill, p. 233; World Bank bill, p. 185)*

Crackdown in the Baltics

Tensions heightened by year's end as the Persian Gulf crisis heated up and events in Lithuania approached a boiling point.

Shevardnadze's abrupt resignation on Dec. 20 was a precursor of the instability ahead. Shevardnadze shocked Gorbachev by announcing his resignation to the Congress of People's Deputies, and the move stunned U.S. officials as well.

Three weeks later, on Jan. 13, 1991, Soviet tanks rumbled into Lithuania, leading to the deaths of 15 resisters and challenging improved relations with the United States. Democrats and Republicans in both chambers called for the administration to send a strong signal to Gorbachev that continued use of such force would seriously impair future U.S.-Soviet relations.

Both chambers backed away from asking Bush to cancel the program, offered in December, to ease the Soviet Union's food shortage with up to $1 billion in export credit guarantees to buy U.S. grains, oilseeds and meat. Moscow had used more than $750 million of the credit.

Poland, Hungary Aid

Foreign aid rarely is popular on Capitol Hill, but 1989 produced one of the exceptions. Congress showed unusual vigor in pushing for aid to Poland and Hungary, the two East European countries that had gone the furthest to break out of the Soviet bloc.

President Bush proposed several aid packages for those countries, each somewhat more generous than the previous one. But congressional leaders, especially Democrats, went to great lengths to demonstrate that they had more vision than Bush in responding to the historic collapse of the communist empire. The result was a bidding war, in which the two chambers and the two parties vied with each other to take credit for being the most generous in aiding Poland and Hungary. Fiscal reality intervened, however, and the final amounts Congress voted were substantially lower than what many members had wanted.

Congress enacted a three-year authorization bill (HR 3402 — PL 101-179), the nominal value of which was $938 million, more than twice what Bush had proposed. But the figure was misleading because it included an off-budget $200 million trade credit insurance program for Poland that the administration opposed and was unlikely to carry out. The bill also authorized the president to give Poland $125 million in food aid in fiscal 1990, just $25 million more than he had budgeted. Bush signed HR 3402 on Nov. 28.

In a separate foreign aid appropriations bill (HR 3743 — PL 101-167), signed by Bush on Nov. 21, Congress included $532.8 million for aid in fiscal 1990, the first year of the three-year program. *(Fiscal 1990 foreign aid appropriations, p. 228)*

The Bush administration had refused to endorse either measure during congressional consideration of them, largely because Congress added substantially more money than the president wanted. But just as the final version of the authorization bill was about to reach the House and Senate floors, the White House gave in and lent its support.

Bush Proposals

Bush's moves to aid Poland were prompted by an agreement signed April 5 by the Warsaw government and opposition leaders. The result of a series of "roundtable" talks following labor unrest the previous winter, the accord called for sweeping political changes. Among them were establishment of a new system of government to include a president and a two-chamber parliament; restoration of legal status for the independent trade union Solidarity; and the holding of free elections in June. The Polish Parliament on April 7 approved six laws putting the major reforms into effect.

On April 17, Bush announced a trade and investment package keyed to the Polish reforms. However, Bush did not offer an infusion of direct aid for the troubled Polish economy, insisting that the United States and other Western countries instead should offer Poland incentives to discard communism and allow the growth of a free market.

Key members with an interest in Polish affairs backed the Bush proposals. Among them was Dan Rostenkowski, D-Ill., chairman of the House Ways and Means Committee. But some members of Congress called on the administration to consider additional steps to aid the Polish economy.

In the June elections, the Polish people rebuffed the ruling Communist Party. The election victories gave Solidarity a virtual veto over major decisions by the Polish government — a first in the communist bloc.

Hungary's government also was making major concessions to non-communist forces. Party leaders in June signed an accord with opposition groups calling for negotiations toward a multi-party political system.

In a dramatic trip to Eastern Europe on July 9-12, Bush announced new aid proposals that went somewhat beyond the limited trade concessions he had outlined April 17. But he offered little direct new assistance. The president's promised steps to help Poland and Hungary were limited both by budget realities back home and by a recognition that Washington was only a supporting partner in their transformation away from communism.

Bush told leaders in both countries that the long-term solution to their economic problems lay in the evolution toward democracy and capitalism — a process that he acknowledged would take time and involve sacrifice by people who had suffered much since World War II.

His new proposals included $100 million to bolster private enterprise in Poland; $25 million for a similar purpose in Hungary; and $15 million for environmental programs in the ancient Polish capital city of Krakow.

The most immediate help to Poland seemed a relaxed U.S. attitude toward that country's crushing debt. Easing Poland's debt payments would reduce some of the short-term economic pressure and might provide some running room for future expansion, U.S. officials said.

Historic Power Shift

In one of the most startling series of events in modern history, Poland's communist leaders early in August conceded that they lacked public support to form a new government in the wake of June elections that were swept by the Solidarity labor union and other opposition groups.

Solidarity leader Lech Walesa in mid-August negotiated a deal with the communist president, Gen. Wojciech Jaruzelski, for the opposition to take control of the government, although the Communist Party retained control of the powerful Defense and Interior ministries. The new government was the first in the Soviet bloc ever to be led by officials of a non-communist party.

Aside from the obvious difficulties of managing a government composed of such diverse factions, the new regime faced enormous economic problems, starting with labor unrest, triple-digit inflation, food shortages and a massive debt to foreign banks and governments.

Democrats' Plan

Although Bush had proposed $140 million in direct aid to Poland and Hungary, the administration later revealed that it would provide only $18 million of that in fiscal 1990, with the rest to be spread over the following two years.

When Bush formally submitted his aid proposals to Congress, he ran into a buzz saw of criticism from Democrats who thought they were inadequate. These Democrats launched a campaign to portray the president as "timid" in his response to reforms in Eastern Europe and the Soviet Union, and they began moving to extend more U.S. aid than Bush wanted for Poland and Hungary.

Senate Democrats chose the Foreign Relations panel, which they narrowly controlled, as their first major battleground. On a party-line vote boycotted by most Republicans, the committee on Sept. 20 approved a bill (S 1582) authorizing $1.2 billion in aid programs for Poland and Hungary over the next three years — about eight times Bush's request. A third of the money would come from unspent Defense Department funds in fiscal 1990.

Democrats on Foreign Relations displayed uncharacteristic vigor in pushing their plan over Bush's. Foreign Relations had become something of a backwater, rarely taking the lead on significant foreign policy issues and often unable to get its legislation passed in the full Senate. In their eagerness to demonstrate leadership on the Poland issue, however, committee Democrats scheduled a hearing and markup on their bill just one day after they introduced it. Chairman Claiborne Pell, D-R.I., forced a vote on the bill minutes before the committee ran out of time for its meeting under Senate rules. To protest the Democrats' action, all but one committee Republican left just before the voting.

Also on Sept. 20, the full Senate worked on a fiscal 1990 foreign aid appropriations bill (HR 2939) containing increased aid for Poland and Hungary — but far less than the Foreign Relations bill.

New Round of Proposals

In early October, Bush took some of the sting out of the Democrats' attack on his evident reluctance to rush to the aid of reformist governments in Poland and Hungary. He still failed, however, to head off a congressional mandate for a more generous financial response to Polish appeals for Western help.

Responding to an almost daily assault from Democrats, the White House on Oct. 4 announced that Bush would ask Congress to approve a $200 million grant to bolster the Polish economy — but under conditions ensuring that the Solidarity-led government would not get the money until 1990. The grant was in addition to Bush's $140 million proposal in July, as well as $108 million in food aid that the president had ordered.

Bush's announcement followed by one day the unveiling by House and Senate Democrats of a proposal (HR 3402) to provide $837.5 million in aid to Poland and Hungary over three years. The bill was crafted as an alternative to the Foreign Relations Committee's $1.2 billion aid bill in hopes of attracting broader support.

Only a handful of Republicans came to the president's defense. They did so not by praising his proposals but by denouncing the Democrats for seizing on Poland to badger a Republican president.

Other Republicans, however, apparently saw no harm in signing onto the Democratic-drafted aid plan. Among the cosponsors of HR 3402 were House Minority Leader Robert H. Michel, R-Ill., and several of the most senior Republicans on the Foreign Affairs Committee.

House Action

The House in 1989 passed several bills signaling its support for Poland and Hungary.

On June 20, the House passed by voice vote HR 2550, making the two countries eligible for Overseas Private Investment Corporation (OPIC) investment guarantees and making some Polish exports eligible for duty-free treatment under the Generalized System of Preferences (GSP). HR 2550 had been formally reported from Foreign Affairs (H Rept 101-92, Part I) and Ways and Means (H Rept 101-92, Part II) earlier the same day.

The House on Sept. 7 voted 221-169 on HR 1594 (H Rept 101-99) to extend for three years Hungary's most-favored-nation (MFN) status, which it had been granted annually since 1978 (HR 1594 — H Rept 101-99). MFN countries qualified for favorable duty rates on goods shipped to the United States. Later in September, Bush announced that he would extend Hungary's MFN status and make Hungary eligible for GSP trade benefits, but he had opposed HR 1594 as an interference with his legal authority to extend or withdraw MFN status.

And in October, the House took up its Poland-Hungary aid bill (HR 3402). The legislation posed a dilemma for the Bush administration. On the one hand, it was based largely on proposals that Bush had made for U.S. aid and trade benefits to encourage change in Poland and Hungary. House Foreign Affairs leaders also modified several provisions from the original version of HR 3402 to accommodate administration concerns. On the other hand, the bill authorized $837.5 million for several programs over three years, nearly twice as much as Bush requested. Moreover, its adoption would represent a significant political victory for Democrats.

HR 3402 was reported by the Ways and Means Committee (H Rept 101-278, Part I) on Oct. 11 and by the Foreign Affairs (H Rept 101-278, Part II) and the Public Works and Transportation (H Rept 101-278, Part III) committees Oct. 16.

The House on Oct. 19 passed HR 3402 by a **key vote of 345-47 (R 128-34; D 217-13)**, an extraordinarily wide margin for a foreign aid program. *(1989 key votes, p. 1021)*

In fiscal 1989, the House bill would produce only about $50 million more in appropriations than the approximately $230 million that Bush had proposed. Even so, the White House expressed reservations about "excessive funding levels" and refused to endorse the measure. The White House called on the Senate to reverse some of the bill's provisions but did not specify which ones.

During the House debate most members of both parties chose to emphasize the bipartisan nature of support for the bill, and most Democrats said little about Bush's reluctance to back it.

The bipartisan celebration and congratulatory rhetoric was interrupted by a testy argument over whether to exempt Poland from the longstanding cargo preference law, which required three-fourths of bulk shipments of U.S. food aid to be carried on American-flag ships. Cargo preference was championed by the maritime industry and its unions but was opposed by many agricultural interests on the grounds that higher U.S. shipping costs made their products less competitive on the world market. Maritime interests eventually won the argument, when the House Oct. 19 rejected, 170-228, an amendment that would have reduced the U.S.-flag shipping requirement to 50 percent for Poland's food aid in fiscal 1990.

Senate Action

Senators faced a choice between two competing aid plans, which were being offered as substitutes for the $1.2 billion aid bill (S 1582) reported by the Foreign Relations Committee Sept. 20 with no written report.

One proposal, supported by Democrats and a handful of Republicans, would authorize just short of $1 billion for various aid programs to Poland and Hungary over three years. The other plan, which was endorsed only by Republicans, would have authorized about half as much as the Democratic proposal and imposed more restrictions on how the aid could be used. Several of these restrictions were aimed specifically at preventing U.S. funds from benefiting communists.

Action on the aid bill was stalled for a time by a Republican attempt to use it as a vehicle to get a vote on Bush's controversial plan for cutting capital gains taxes. The Democratic leadership, which opposed the capital gains provision, threatened to filibuster — thus forcing the Republicans to try to muster the 60 votes they did not have to cut off debate on the issue. *(Capital gains, p. 96)*

The result was a partisan dispute over who was responsible for delaying aid to Poland and Hungary. Congressional leaders wanted to get the authorization bill enacted quickly so that the money could be included in the follow-up appropriations measure. The leaders also wanted legislation enacted by Nov. 15, when Polish Solidarity leader Walesa would address a joint meeting of Congress — a rare honor for a foreign dignitary who had never held public office.

A Nov. 2 concession by Republicans on the capital gains issue freed the bill of any major hurdles. On Nov. 14, the Senate passed an amended HR 3402 by a 99-0 vote.

The following day, Walesa told an admiring audience that packed the House chamber that Poland "will never be turned back" from its quest for freedom from foreign domination. Recalling the Marshall Plan, which helped Western Europe arise from the ashes of World War II, Walesa asked for a U.S. "investment" in Poland and all of Eastern Europe. Aid to those countries moving toward democracy and freedom, he said "is the best investment in the future and in peace, better than tanks, warships and warplanes, an investment leading to greater security."

Conference Action

The authorization bill had traveled a tortured course, but it was not over yet.

Shortly after the Senate passed its version, an unidentified Senate Republican objected to taking the bill to conference with the House. Staffers of the House Foreign Affairs and Senate Foreign Relations committees negotiated a compromise, which the House quickly accepted.

But at the insistence of Jesse Helms, R-N.C., Senate leaders took the bill to conference. An agreement (H Rept 101-377) hammered out Nov. 17 contained the essentials of the staff-produced compromise.

Just as the final version of the authorization bill was about to reach the House and Senate floors, as Congress was rushing to adjourn, Bush relented and gave his support to it. The House approved the conference bill by voice vote Nov. 17 and the Senate followed suit on Nov. 18.

Appropriations Bill

The fiscal 1990 foreign aid appropriations bill, which contained money for Poland-Hungary aid, also traveled a difficult route.

House-Senate conferees on the appropriations bill approved a $532.8 million aid package for Poland and Hungary in fiscal 1990. Of that amount, only about $293 million would be in hard cash. Another $200 million was for a trade credit program unlikely to get started in fiscal 1990, and an additional $40 million was earmarked for investment guarantees by OPIC.

But the overall appropriations bill (HR 2939) was vetoed by Bush over other issues. After dropping or modifying those provisions, Congress cleared a new version (HR 3743) on Nov. 20, and Bush signed it into law the next day.

Major Provisions of Aid Bills

As signed into law, HR 3402 authorized $938 million in aid to Poland and Hungary in fiscal years 1990-92. HR 3743 appropriated $532.8 million for aid in fiscal 1990.

Major provisions covered:

• **Economic Stabilization.** Both bills approved Bush's request for a $200 million grant in fiscal 1990 to help stabilize the Polish economy. The money was the U.S. contribution to an international fund, which the Poles hoped would reach $1 billion. European nations already had pledged the bulk of the remaining $800 million.

• **Private Enterprise.** The two bills also approved Bush's proposal for "private enterprise funds" intended to help finance the development of private businesses in Poland and Hungary. However, both measures contemplated spending substantially more for those funds than did the president. Bush requested $125 million for the funds ($100 million for Poland and $25 million for Hungary), with fiscal 1990 spending at $15 million.

Congress settled on a $300 million total in the authorization bill, of which $240 million was for Poland and $60 million for Hungary.

The appropriations bill allowed $45 million for the Polish fund and $5 million for the Hungarian fund in fiscal 1990.

• **Food Aid.** The authorization bill called on the administration to give Poland at least $125 million in food aid in fiscal 1990, but it took no position on aid levels for subsequent years. Bush already had ordered about $100 million for fiscal 1989.

• **Trade Credit.** Both measures called for creation of a Trade Credit Insurance Program, which would provide short-term guarantees for U.S. exports to private businesses in Poland. The Export-Import Bank could finance up to $200 million worth of exports each year.

The Bush administration opposed this trade credit program and was considered unlikely to carry it out.

• **Environmental Cleanup.** Both pieces of legislation expanded on Bush's proposals for limited U.S. aid for environmental programs in Poland and Hungary. The president originally suggested a $15 million program, aimed primarily at reducing air and water pollution in the ancient Polish capital city of Krakow.

The authorization bill allowed for $40 million worth of environmental programs over three years. Of that, $10 million was for efforts by the U.S. Environmental Protection Agency to monitor and combat pollution in Krakow and the Hungarian capital, Budapest. The appropriations bill included the fiscal 1990 portion of $3.3 million.

Another $30 million was for Energy Department programs to retrofit a commercial power plant in the Krakow region with "clean coal" technology and to help develop the capability within Poland to manufacture furnaces and other industrial facilities that were environmentally sound.

The appropriations bill included $10 million for these programs in fiscal 1990.

• **Promotion of Democracy.** Each bill allowed continued U.S. funding for "democratic" organizations, such as the Solidarity labor union, in Poland and Hungary. The authorization bill allowed $12 million over three years, without specifying precise amounts for any organization.

The appropriations bill included $2.5 million in fiscal 1990 for democratic organizations generally in Poland and Hungary and $1.5 million for aid to Solidarity, to be provided through the AFL-CIO.

• **Medical Aid.** Poland would get an infusion of medical supplies, hospital equipment and related training under both bills. The authorization bill allowed $4 million over three years, and the appropriations bill included $2 million for fiscal 1990.

• **Peace Corps.** Poland and Hungary would get their first Peace Corps volunteers if the administration carried out provisions in both bills. The authorization bill set a $6 million limit for the three years, and the appropriations bill allocated $2 million in fiscal 1990.

• **Trade and Development.** Both bills allowed funding in Poland and Hungary for the Agency for International Development's trade and development program, which financed economic feasibility studies in developing countries. The authorization bill allowed $6 million over three years, and the appropriations measure allowed $2 million for the first year.

• **Agricultural Programs.** The spending bill provided $10 million in fiscal 1990 to continue a program of training and other aid to farmers in Poland run by the Roman Catholic Church and other non-governmental groups.

• **Labor Reforms.** Both bills authorized new Labor Department programs to help Poland and Hungary adjust their labor laws to meet the needs of free-market systems. The authorization bill allowed $4 million over three years for these programs in Poland and $1 million in Hungary. HR 3743 appropriated $1.5 million for the two countries in fiscal 1990.

• **Technical Training.** Under the authorization bill, up to $10 million over three years was provided for various programs to train farmers, businesspersons, scientists and other professionals in skills needed for a market economy. The appropriations bill included $2 million for these programs, plus $1 million earmarked specifically for the "farmer to farmer" program, under which American farmers and agricultural specialists gave advice to their counterparts in developing countries.

• **Scholarships, Exchanges.** Both bills mandated new programs of scholarships and educational and cultural exchanges to benefit Poland and Hungary. For exchange programs, such as the Fulbright program, the authorization bill allowed $12 million over three years; the appropriations bill allowed $3 million in the first year. For scholarships at American colleges for needy Polish and Hungarian students, the authorization bill provided $10 million over three years, and the appropriations bill included $2 million in fiscal 1990.

• **Science, Technology Exchanges.** The authorization bill allowed the administration to continue funding for science and technology exchange programs with Poland and Hungary. The authorization bill allowed $5.5 million over three years for Poland and $2.5 million for Hungary. No fiscal 1990 appropriations were necessary.

• **Trade Preferences.** Under HR 3402, both countries would be eligible for reduced tariffs on the exports to the United States of some products (particularly raw materials and semifinished goods) under the Generalized System of Preferences, normally used to benefit developing countries.

• **Polish Bonds.** HR 3402 permitted the Warsaw government to sell bonds in the United States at below-market interest rates. Israel was the only other country permitted to sell such bonds, which allowed Americans to make contributions to a foreign country while investing their money.

Internal Revenue Service regulations normally prohibited below-market rate bonds.

- **OPIC.** Both bills made Poland and Hungary eligible for programs of the Overseas Private Investment Corporation, which issued risk insurance for American firms doing business overseas. The appropriations measure allowed the corporation to write up to $40 million worth of insurance for U.S. investments in Poland during fiscal 1990.
- **Ex-Im Bank.** The authorization bill formally allowed the Export-Import Bank to issue loans, guarantees and other credits to help finance exports to Poland and Hungary by American businesses.
- **Suspension.** HR 3402 said the president "should" suspend aid to either Poland or Hungary if he found that it had engaged in international activities "that directly threaten United States national security interests"; imposed martial law or a state of emergency for reasons other than responding to a natural disaster or foreign invasion; or removed any elected member of the parliament through "extra-constitutional processes."
- **Reports.** HR 3402 required several reports to Congress on the progress of the aid programs and on developments in the two countries.

German Unification Treaty

The Senate voted 98-0 on Oct. 10, 1990, to approve the Treaty on the Final Settlement with Respect to Germany to return full sovereignty to a unified Germany, formally ending the division of Germany that followed World War II. The action was a footnote to the merger of East and West Germany that had taken place with international approval on Oct. 3.

The Senate Foreign Relations Committee on Oct. 2 had quickly and unanimously approved the treaty (Treaty Doc 101-20) that marked the close of a 45-year chapter in U.S. foreign policy.

Presenting the treaty on the Senate floor, Foreign Relations Committee Chairman Claiborne Pell, D-R.I., underscored the historic import of the document, which was signed Sept. 12 in Moscow by the two German states and the four World War II allies: the United States, France, Great Britain and the Soviet Union.

"History in our century has been dominated by two overarching events — successive world wars in the first half, and throughout the second half, a great geopolitical rift which has threatened civilization on our planet," Pell said. "The treaty before us today marks an end to both of these major events of the 20th century."

The treaty required Germany to reduce its military from 600,000 to 370,000 troops and to renounce the manufacture and use of nuclear, biological and chemical weapons. Germany would remain in the North Atlantic Treaty Organization (NATO) alliance, a triumph for President Bush and the West, and Soviet troops would have to leave the country by the end of 1994.

Bush signed the treaty's ratification documents Oct. 18.

Background

In October 1989, it had become clear that Soviet President Mikhail S. Gorbachev would not use his troops in East Germany to bolster the government of East German Communist Party leader Erich Honecker against massive public demonstrations in Leipzig and other cities calling for political and economic liberalization. By some accounts, Gorbachev collaborated with some top East German officials to push aside the elderly and ailing Honecker in mid-October.

The East German government's decision on Nov. 9, 1989, to open its borders to the West, followed by the collapse of the communist leadership less than a month later, suddenly revived interest in the possibility of some sort of merger of the two Germanys. West German Chancellor Helmut Kohl seized the initiative on Nov. 28, proposing a 10-point plan leading first to a confederation of East and West Germany and then to a unified nation.

Voicing historic Russian fears of German military power, Gorbachev initially rejected Kohl's plan outright, saying it was "the bidding of history" that there be two German states. Gorbachev subsequently insisted that a unified Germany be neutral.

But the United States opposed transforming West Germany into a neutral state as part of any unification bargain. In a Dec. 4 news conference in Brussels, Bush said it was a major point of U.S. policy that unification occur in the context of West Germany's "continued commitment to NATO."

Under pressure from Bonn, the East German government advanced parliamentary elections in 1990 from May to March. And by early February 1990, the Bonn government was pushing for a rapid monetary and economic union between the two German states.

Finally, amid worldwide attention and excitement, at midnight Oct. 3, 1990, East Germany was absorbed into a unified German state.

El Salvador Aid

Aid to El Salvador re-emerged in 1989 as a major foreign policy issue. Controversy over providing aid to the war-torn Central American country continued in 1990.

The rightist National Republican Alliance (ARENA) party's victory in the March 1989 presidential elections, coupled with human rights abuses by both the right and the left, raised new concerns. Those concerns intensified later in the year with the resurgence of urban warfare and the murder of six Jesuit priests in San Salvador.

Despite controversy over giving military aid to the Salvadoran government, Congress in 1989 approved most of the money President Bush requested. Bush asked for $97 million; the fiscal 1990 foreign aid appropriations bill (HR 3743 — PL 101-167) provided $85 million, the fiscal 1989 amount. In the wake of the renewed violence, congressional liberals tried to withhold some of the aid, but strong majorities in both chambers rebuffed that effort.

However, by 1990, Congress was becoming increasingly frustrated with the slow pace of negotiations to end the conflict and the continuing pattern of human rights violations by the Salvadoran military. A badly flawed investigation into the Jesuit murders was particularly galling to lawmakers.

In approving the fiscal 1991 foreign aid appropriations bill (HR 5114 — PL 101-513), Congress again agreed on an $85 million military assistance program for El Salvador but this time withheld half of it and placed heavy conditions on its release.

In January 1991, reacting to the apparent execution of two U.S. servicemen by leftist guerrillas in El Salvador,

Bush announced that he would release the full allotment of the fiscal 1991 military aid to El Salvador.

Background

In the early 1980s, Congress and the Reagan administration battled constantly over El Salvador. President Ronald Reagan's priority was pumping in hundreds of millions of dollars to prop up a succession of governments that were besieged by leftist guerrillas. Members of Congress, especially Democrats, sought to restrain Reagan and Salvadoran military leaders by limiting the aid and imposing conditions on it.

Washington's political battles over El Salvador halted in 1984, when José Napoleón Duarte was elected president of that nation. A longtime foe of Salvadoran military regimes and an advocate of social reform, Duarte won almost universal respect on Capitol Hill. In subsequent years, Congress voted hundreds of millions of dollars in aid to El Salvador based largely on Duarte's personal appeal. *(Congress and the Nation Vol. VI, p. 186)*

But by 1989 the situation had changed. Renewed reports were heard of human rights abuses, El Salvador's economy was in shambles and political instability surrounded Duarte's government. Duarte was dying of cancer and had lost most of his physical stamina and political clout. With Duarte's term about to expire and an ARENA victory at the polls likely, questions from the early 1980s about how the United States should use its considerable influence to promote peace and democracy in El Salvador were again being raised.

But as Salvadorans prepared to elect Duarte's successor, El Salvador engaged in the most serious talk in years of ending its decade-long guerrilla war. The war had cost an estimated 70,000 lives.

In a surprise move in early 1989, the leftist guerrilla coalition, the Farabundo Marti Front for National Liberation (FMLN), offered to participate in the presidential election — if the March 19 voting day was moved back by six months. That move was a sharp break from the FMLN's longstanding stance of rejecting elections and demanding a share of power with the government.

During subsequent talks, the guerrillas offered an expanded peace plan, saying they would lay down their arms and take part in the country's political system if the government met conditions, primarily reducing the size and influence of the armed forces.

Duarte agreed to a six-week delay in the elections, to be accompanied by a full cease-fire and direct negotiations. The Bush administration aligned itself squarely with Duarte and cast doubt on the guerrillas' true intentions.

The FMLN at first accepted Duarte's call for negotiations but insisted on several strings, most importantly the six-month delay in the elections. However, the guerrillas rejected the military's unilateral cease-fire, saying that the military really was seeking an "underground war." The guerrillas also launched renewed attacks against civilian and military targets.

No agreement was reached, and the elections were held as scheduled.

Wait-and-See Approach

The new elections and the peace prospects left Washington's leaders with a vague policy of supporting diplomacy, but with the details in a holding pattern. The Bush administration adopted a wait-and-see approach, avoiding confrontation. Congressional leaders, too, were unsure about what course to follow.

The Bush administration appeared determined to prove that it was more sensitive than the Reagan administration to Capitol Hill concerns about human rights. During a one-day trip to El Salvador in February, Vice President Dan Quayle reportedly lectured government officials, political leaders and military officers about the need to halt an upsurge in human rights abuses. Quayle pointed in particular to an incident in 1988 in which government troops reportedly murdered 10 civilians in San Sebastion and tried to blame the rebels.

The United States clearly favored the candidate of Duarte's Christian Democrat Party and viewed the prospect of the election of ARENA's presidential candidate, wealthy businessman Alfredo Cristiani, with a mixture of resignation and trepidation.

Cristiani often campaigned in rural areas alongside ARENA's charismatic founder, retired major Roberto d'Aubuisson, alleged by some U.S. and Salvadoran officials to have been a leader of the "death squads" that terrorized El Salvador in the early 1980s. D'Aubuisson heatedly denied the allegations.

ARENA opponents, both in El Salvador and in the United States, insisted that Cristiani was a front man for d'Aubuisson, who they said retained the real power. The unsuccessful ARENA presidential candidate in 1984, d'Aubuisson no longer was the formal head of the party but was the de facto leader of its majority delegation in the National Assembly.

Cristiani won a five-year term as president with 53 percent of the vote in the elections March 19. His victory gave ARENA control over all three branches of government.

Most observers attributed ARENA's surge in popularity to several factors, most having to do with shortcomings of the Duarte government. The government failed to carry through on many of its campaign promises, particularly to end the war with the guerrillas. ARENA also made effective use of corruption allegations against some of Duarte's associates.

Bush administration officials and most Hill leaders agreed to give Cristiani a chance — but warned that Washington would watch his performance closely. At stake for both El Salvador and Washington was the U.S. aid program, the largest on a per capita basis for any country except Israel. The United States provided El Salvador with $373 million in economic, military, development and food aid in fiscal 1989, and the Bush administration requested a $386 million aid program for fiscal 1990.

Cristiani visited Washington the month after his election to ask for a chance to prove that his government deserved continued U.S. assistance. His reception, while cordial, stood in sharp contrast to the treatment accorded Duarte when he made the ritual journey to Washington following his election in 1984. Duarte, the first civilian to win the presidency in an honest election in more than 50 years, got a hero's welcome on Capitol Hill. His election immediately ended three years of divisive debate in Washington over El Salvador and guaranteed a steady flow of U.S. aid dollars.

Cristiani, by contrast, acknowledged that much of official Washington was skeptical about him and even more

U.S. Aid to El Salvador

From 1981 through 1989, the United States provided more than $3.4 billion in economic, development and military aid to El Salvador, making the tiny Central American country one of the biggest recipients of U.S. foreign aid.

The bulk of the aid went to bolster the sagging economy and to fuel the war against leftist guerrillas, who battled a succession of governments for nearly 10 years. About one-fourth of the aid went into development projects, such as schools and health clinics.

President Ronald Reagan stepped up aid to El Salvador shortly after taking office, winning reluctant support for $140 million in fiscal 1981. Congress gradually boosted the aid in subsequent years but showed no enthusiasm for Reagan's policy of backing the Salvadoran government until José Napoleón Duarte won the presidency there in 1984. Throughout the latter part of the 1980s, U.S. aid averaged more than $400 million annually.

Congress imposed conditions on the aid beginning in 1981; they were stringent in the early 1980s, but most were relaxed after Duarte's election.

During fiscal 1982-83, Congress barred military aid unless the president certified every 180 days that the Salvadoran government was moving to end human rights abuses and was making progress toward land reform and free elections.

Congress also linked aid to the successful prosecution of those responsible for the December 1980 murder of four churchwomen in El Salvador. In fiscal 1984, $19.44 million in military aid was withheld pending completion of the case. That money was released after the May 1984 conviction of five former national guardsmen.

Starting in fiscal 1984, Congress ordered the suspension of all aid to El Salvador if the elected civilian government was ousted by a military coup. That provision was later applied to all countries that received U.S. aid.

Beginning in fiscal 1985, $5 million worth of military aid was withheld annually unless the Salvadoran government had "pursued all legal avenues" to prosecute those responsible for the January 1981 murder of one Salvadoran and two American land-reform workers.

skeptical about his political party. But he found most officials ready to accept his message that the ARENA party's victory did not by itself constitute grounds for cutting off aid to El Salvador.

The new president insisted that he was not a mouthpiece for d'Aubuisson.

Cristiani said he wanted a "political solution" to El Salvador's conflict and pledged to try to reopen negotiations with the rebels.

Fiscal 1989-90 Authorization

Aid to El Salvador was a major issue during House committee and floor consideration of the fiscal 1990-91 foreign aid authorization bill (HR 2655).

Democrats on the House Foreign Affairs Committee and administration officials dickered for several weeks over how to restrict military and economic aid to El Salvador. The Democrats demanded what amounted to veto power over spending of the aid money. The administration, in turn, demanded a virtual guarantee that El Salvador would continue to receive U.S. assistance.

The administration particularly objected to a provision that would have required advance approval from four congressional committees before spending semiannual installments of military aid to El Salvador. The bill set an annual limit of $85 million for military aid in fiscal 1990-91.

Democrats and Republicans finally settled on an alternative: Congress could block aid to El Salvador only by enacting a joint resolution — over the president's certain veto. Such a procedure would all but ensure that El Salvador would continue to get aid.

During floor debate on HR 2655, members rebuffed an effort by liberal Democrats to toughen the committee bill. By a vote of 185-233, the House June 28 rejected an amendment that would have suspended military aid to El Salvador early in 1990 unless both houses of Congress passed legislation allowing it to continue.

In another setback for liberal Democrats, the House adopted an amendment allowing the administration to use U.S. military aid to beef up police forces in El Salvador. Foreign Affairs had voted to ban most forms of aid to police forces in El Salvador, Guatemala and Honduras. But the House June 28 voted 220-198 to adopt an amendment allowing military assistance to Salvadoran police forces for training and other equipment except firearms.

The House passed HR 2655 on a 314-101 vote June 29.

The Senate Foreign Relations Committee on July 18 reported its version of the foreign aid bill (S 1347 — S Rept 101-80), but the full chamber never acted on it. During committee consideration, Foreign Relations members elevated the relatively small amount of money for El Salvador — $85 million — into a symbolically important issue.

The fundamental question facing senators was whether to signal broad support for the new government of El Salvador, as Republicans hoped to do. But the panel's Democrats and one Republican joined in defeating a Republican amendment to remove the $85 million military aid cap from the bill. The committee then voted to increase the aid cap to $90 million.

Fiscal 1990 Appropriations

The El Salvador issue resurfaced during congressional action on the fiscal 1990 foreign aid appropriations measure.

House Action. The House Appropriations Subcommittee on Foreign Operations endorsed Foreign Affairs' strict $85 million limit on military aid for El Salvador during markup of the foreign aid bill (HR 2939). But the panel dropped a companion provision, strongly opposed by the administration, that would have divided the aid into two installments so that Congress could have a shot at suspending the aid early in 1990.

The House passed the underlying bill (H Rept 101-165) on July 21, 329-69.

Senate Action. The Senate Appropriations Committee marked up its version HR 2939 (S Rept 101-131) as the first serious Salvadoran peace talks in years were taking place. At the initiation of Cristiani, representatives of the government and of the leftist guerrillas met in Mexico City on Sept. 13-15 and agreed to hold regular meetings.

Administration critics said new restrictions on the military aid would encourage the Salvadoran government to negotiate with the guerrillas in good faith. But administration officials and their Hill supporters insisted that Congress was in danger of undermining the Cristiani government at a politically delicate time.

But the committee went ahead and approved a provision dividing the $85 million in military aid into three equal installments, to be available at four-month intervals. The administration could provide each of the first two installments by reporting to Congress on actions by the Salvadoran government in several areas, such as improving respect for human rights and seeking a negotiated solution to the civil war.

But the administration could send the third aid installment only through "reprogramming." Under that procedure, the administration would send a notice to the appropriate congressional committees of its intent to spend money in a certain way. If none of the committees objected within 15 days, the administration could spend the money. If any committee objected, the administration, for all practical purposes, could not.

The Senate voted to reverse the committee's action during its first full-scale debate on U.S. policy toward El Salvador in years. By a vote of 68-32, the Senate Sept. 20 first rejected an amendment intended to retain the Appropriations Committee-approved aid conditions. Then, by an 82-18 vote, the Senate adopted an amendment raising the limit on El Salvador's military aid to $90 million without conditions. The amendment included non-binding language urging the Salvadoran government and the guerrillas to end their war and negotiate a political settlement.

The vote was a major victory for the administration, which for months had fought a low-key but persistent battle against moves to restrict aid to the new Salvadoran government. The Senate action was doubly important because the House version also contained no crippling conditions on El Salvador aid.

The Senate passed HR 2939 on Sept. 26, 89-11.

Renewed Violence. A resurgence of urban warfare and terrorism in El Salvador threatened to shatter Washington's complacency. After leftist rebels launched widescale attacks in the capital of San Salvador early in November, the army responded with force, including aerial rocket attacks that killed dozens of civilians. By mid-November, more than 700 guerrillas and government soldiers had died and up to 2,000 had been wounded in some of the most intensive fighting in the 10-year civil war.

Armed men on Nov. 16 entered the campus of the Roman Catholic university in San Salvador and tortured and murdered six Jesuit priests. Among them were the well-known rector of the university, Rev. Ignacio Ellacuria, and his deputy, Ignacio Martin-Baro. Two apparent witnesses also were slain. The campus was under the control of government security forces at the time, but the government said it was not involved in the killings.

Those events set off a storm of protest on Capitol Hill. Members were angered by the guerrilla attacks, and many were appalled by the Salvadoran military's willingness to attack poor neighborhoods in hopes of rooting out guerrillas. The killing of the priests further enraged members, some of whom had met Ellacuria and Martin-Baro.

The anger, however, did not move Congress to change its plans for supplying U.S. aid to the Salvadoran government.

Final Aid Bill. House-Senate conferees on the aid appropriations bill (H Rept 101-344) agreed to an $85 million limit on military aid and accepted the thrust of a Senate provision allowing, with certain restrictions, up to $12 million in fiscal 1990 for aid to El Salvador's police forces and criminal justice system. Police aid was to be confined to training in human rights, civil law and investigative techniques and could not be used to provide firearms.

Bush Nov. 19 vetoed the final bill because of two provisions unrelated to El Salvador. Congress then considered a new bill (HR 3743) identical to the vetoed one except for the provisions he cited and another item intended to reflect events in El Salvador. The new provision required the administration to report to Congress on the progress of investigations by the Salvadoran government into the murders of the six Jesuits and two others.

Both chambers passed HR 3743 Nov. 20 after sidelining moves by liberals to withhold 30 percent of the military aid as a protest against the Nov. 16 murders. Bush signed the measure (PL 101-167) on Nov. 21.

The House, on a 194-215 vote Nov. 20, rejected a procedural motion that would have allowed a vote on a Democratic-sponsored amendment delaying release of 30 percent of El Salvador's military aid until after April 1. Although other issues were involved, that vote had the effect of blocking a follow-up vote on the aid question.

The Senate agreed to table a similar amendment later that day on a 58-39 vote.

During the debates in the two chambers, members of all political persuasions condemned the guerrilla offensive as well as the murder of the priests. But a clear difference of emphasis existed: Liberals focused primarily on what happened to the priests, while conservatives tended to stress the violence caused by the rebels.

Instead of withholding aid, both chambers adopted resolutions condemning political violence in El Salvador on all sides. The House adopted its measure (H Con Res 236) by a 409-3 vote on Nov. 20. The Senate followed the next day with S Res 217, adopted 99-0, the chamber's last recorded vote before adjourning for 1989.

Jesuit Murders Aftermath

Lawmakers from both parties agreed that the character of the Salvadoran aid issue changed substantially after the Jesuit murders. The murders caused an international outcry — largely by serving as a reminder of numerous human rights abuses in El Salvador that were never prosecuted. Several of the priests were well known outside El Salvador because of their outspoken criticism of the government and military.

House Speaker Thomas S. Foley, D-Wash., appointed a 19-member task force Dec. 5, 1989, with a mandate to monitor the Salvadoran government's response to the killings.

Salvadoran President Cristiani said on Jan. 7, 1990, that investigators had determined that "some elements of the armed forces" were responsible for the killings. Cristiani also said he had formed a special investigating panel.

Salvadoran authorities indicted nine military personnel in connection with the murders. Those charged included Col. Guillermo Alfredo Benavides, the highest-ranking military officer ever brought to justice in a major human rights case in El Salvador.

The House Democrats task force, headed by Joe Moakley, D-Mass., released its report on April 30. It painted a grim picture of Salvadoran affairs. The group — including supporters and critics of official policy toward El Salvador — found that an investigation there into the brutal murders had come to a "virtual standstill."

In a 56-page report, the task force expressed doubt that the military personnel charged with the crime would be punished and complained that Salvadoran authorities had not seriously investigated the possibility that senior military officials were involved. U.S. and Salvadoran officials said the murders were "committed by individuals, and not an indictment of the armed forces as an institution," the task force noted. "Unfortunately, the task force believes it is both."

Bush administration officials generally praised the task force report, although not all its conclusions. Secretary of State James A. Baker III said on May 1 that the task force had conducted its inquiry "in a balanced and professional manner" and said he would ask Cristiani to respond to it.

Rep. Bud Shuster, R-Pa., head of a counterpart GOP effort to monitor the Jesuits' case, challenged some parts of the Moakley report but said most of it was "fair."

Cristiani acknowledged on May 1 that El Salvador's judicial system "might be a little bit slow" but said that those charged with the murders would be tried. Cristiani insisted that military commanders had supported the inquiry into the case.

Fiscal 1990 Supplemental Authorization

Meeting under United Nations auspices, representatives of the Salvadoran government and the leftist guerrillas agreed April 4, in 1990, in Geneva to negotiate an end to the civil war. The sides signed an accord, along with U.N. Secretary General Javier Pérez de Cuéllar, pledging to "end the armed conflict through political means as speedily as possible" and to "reunify Salvadoran society."

The question in Washington was how to use aid to influence future events in El Salvador.

Congress — wanting to crack down on the government of El Salvador but not yet ready to do it — demonstrated this apparent ambivalence in a set of contradictory actions by the House in late May.

On May 22, during floor action on a fiscal 1990 foreign aid supplemental authorization bill (HR 4636), which included aid to Panama and Nicaragua, the House, by a **key vote of 250-163 (R 31-135; D 219-28),** adopted a proposal backed by the House Democratic leadership to suspend 50 percent of El Salvador's arms aid. The aid would either be resumed or cut off entirely, depending on certain actions by the Salvadoran government or by the leftist guerrillas. The House earlier had rejected, 175-243, a Republican alternative to suspend up to 25 percent of the aid under certain conditions. *(1990 key votes, p. 1039)*

But then, after adopting the Democratic amendment, the House rejected the underlying foreign aid bill 171-244, with 94 Democrats joining all but 16 Republicans in opposing final passage.

Once the House acted, the members disputed the meaning of the vote. Republicans maintained that the final vote — not the one on the Democratic amendment — was the truly important one because it showed that the House was unwilling to take the step of cutting El Salvador's aid in half. Most Democratic leaders, however, insisted that the vote killing the underlying bill was in large part a protest against foreign aid in general — and not just a rejection of the El Salvador aid cut.

After the House rejected HR 4636, some talked of resurrecting an earlier plan to use the Panama-Nicaragua aid package as leverage to encourage concessions on El Salvador by the administration. This plan called for the House to refuse to waive the requirement that the Panama-Nicaragua aid be authorized. Waivers of authorization requirements had become routine provisions on appropriations bills. If the authorizing requirement were not waived, Congress would have to pass two bills before the Nicaragua and Panama money could be spent, doubling the opportunity for El Salvador amendments to be offered and passed.

Foley vetoed that idea, however, reportedly telling his fellow Democrats that they should no longer give Bush grounds to attack Congress for holding up the Nicaragua-Panama aid. With the linkage question cleared away, the House on May 24 passed a new authorization bill (S 2364) without the Salvadoran aid cut.

Fiscal 1991 Appropriations

Further evidence that the congressional mood on El Salvador had changed came during consideration of the fiscal 1991 appropriations bill (HR 5114).

The House on June 27, 1990, passed, 308-117, a $15.6 billion foreign aid bill that would have cut in half the military aid to the Cristiani government. The cut, written into the bill by the Appropriations Committee (H Rept 101-553), was identical to the amendment to HR 4636 the House had adopted in May.

Although Bush vowed to veto the bill if it contained the El Salvador provision, administration allies made no attempt to amend it on the House floor. Administration officials hoped instead to negotiate a compromise that could be incorporated in the conference report on the bill.

But the negotiations on the El Salvador issue never gained momentum, in part because the administration was diverted by the crisis in the Persian Gulf. State Department officials never engaged in serious talks with key members. When the administration finally focused on the issue, a surprising majority in the Senate had already made up their minds.

Personal lobbying by Cristiani in Washington in late September failed to sway members. Skepticism ran strong toward his assertion that his government would improve its poor human rights record.

The Senate Appropriations Committee approved its version of HR 5114 on Oct. 10 (S Rept 101-519). Following the lead of the House, the panel placed heavy conditions on the $85 million military aid program for El Salvador. The Senate committee bill provided that the aid would depend on three major conditions:

- It would be cut in half if the leftists cooperated in peace talks. The full $85 million would be provided if the president determined that the FMLN had rejected a U.N.-drafted peace settlement that the government accepted or if the rebels began a major offensive.

• Aid would be cut off completely if the president determined that El Salvador's government had rejected the peace plan but the FMLN had accepted it.

• It also would be eliminated if the president reported that El Salvador's government "has failed to conduct a thorough and professional" investigation into the November 1989 murders.

The full Senate agreed to the amendment on Oct. 19 by a **key vote of 74-25 (R 19-25; D 55-0).** A milder, administration-backed amendment was rejected 39-58 later the same day. The Senate passed HR 5114, 76-23, on Oct. 24.

In the final shaping of HR 5114, the Bush administration had to accept restrictions on aid to El Salvador to win debt relief for Egypt, a key ally in the Persian Gulf crisis. Politically, the items counterbalanced each other.

Republicans were unable to weaken the Senate-passed restrictions in conference. But Democrats did promise to request special procedures to restore the aid, should the circumstance arise. The compromise also excluded all military aid "in the pipeline" — appropriated but not yet delivered — from the Senate amendment.

The House adopted the conference report (H Rept 101-968) on Oct. 27 on an 188-162 vote — a relatively narrow margin that was blamed on opposition to provisions for forgiving Egyptian debts. The Senate cleared the measure by voice vote the same day.

New Developments. The Bush administration announced Dec. 6 that it was rushing $48.1 million in military aid to El Salvador to help it counter a widening offensive by left-wing guerrillas. The emergency aid included $37.5 million of the $42.5 million that was readily available for El Salvador in fiscal 1991.

Reacting to the apparent execution of two U.S. servicemen by anti-government guerrillas, Bush announced Jan. 15, 1991, that he would release the full allotment of fiscal 1991 U.S. military aid to El Salvador. Bush froze delivery of the funds for 60 days, saying he hoped the pause would encourage peace talks between the Salvadoran government and the FMLN guerrillas.

The FMLN claimed responsibility for downing a helicopter carrying three U.S. servicemen Jan. 2; one died in the crash, and U.S. officials said the other two appeared to have been executed.

The White House said Bush's decision was based on the FMLN's violations of the congressional conditions against attacking civilian targets and receiving military assistance from outside El Salvador.

Nicaragua Policy

More than eight years of partisan conflict over U.S. policy toward Nicaragua all but ended in early 1990 with the upset victory of opposition leader Violeta Chamorro in that country's presidential election.

President Bush and lawmakers in both parties hailed the election of the U.S.-backed Chamorro over leftist President Daniel Ortega. By defeating the Sandinista leader at the ballot box, Chamorro achieved what the United States had been unable to accomplish with $311.7 million in aid from 1982 through 1989 to the anti-government rebels known as the contras. *(Aid to contras, box, p. 221)*

The Reagan administration had clashed repeatedly with Congress over its efforts to topple the Marxist regime. Attempts to circumvent a congressional ban on aid to the contras resulted in the Iran-contra affair, a foreign policy scandal that triggered multiple investigations and curtailed the political effectiveness of the Reagan White House. *(Iran-contra affair, p. 238)*

The Bush administration tried a different approach, crafting a bipartisan policy that emphasized regional peacekeeping efforts and pressure on Ortega to allow a free and fair election.

An intense lobbying campaign early in 1989 by Secretary of State James A. Baker III drained most of the political poison out of debates of U.S. policy toward Central America. A "bipartisan accord" that Baker negotiated with congressional leaders resulted in broad agreement on a diplomatic approach to the region's problems, particularly Nicaragua, in place of the Reagan administration's military emphasis.

As a consequence, Congress in April 1989 approved non-military aid (HR 1750 — PL 101-14) for the Nicaraguan contras, intended to keep the U.S.-backed guerrillas intact as a potential fighting force until after the Nicaraguan elections, scheduled for Feb. 25, 1990.

Congress in October 1989 also approved a rush request by the administration for $9 million for Nicaragua's elections (HR 3385 — PL 101-119). The administration said that the money was needed to help ensure that the elections were free and fair. But the administration also made no effort to disguise the fact that the U.S.-preferred candidate was Chamorro, publisher of the main opposition newspaper.

President Bush's strategy paid off in the February 1990 voting in Nicaragua. In the wake of Chamorro's 55 to 41 percent victory, Bush lifted trade and economic sanctions and proposed $300 million in aid to help her new government. The funds were included in a supplemental appropriations bill (HR 4404 — PL 101-302) signed into law in May, a month after Chamorro's inauguration.

U.S. Policy Shift

Pressure for a shift in U.S. policy toward Nicaragua came early in 1989, when the presidents of the five Central American countries on Feb. 14 signed an accord calling for the rebels to be disarmed in return for new steps toward democracy by the Managua government.

Ortega agreed to release some political prisoners and to give opposition parties greater leeway to participate in the February 1990 national and local elections. Another provision required the Sandinistas to stop supporting anti-government rebels in El Salvador. That requirement reportedly made the accord acceptable to Salvadoran President José Napoleón Duarte, who hosted the meeting.

Bush on Feb. 16 said the accord offered "positive elements," such as Nicaraguan promises for democracy. But it also had "some troublesome elements," he said, such as the prospect that Nicaragua might break its promises once the contras were disbanded. Suggesting that he would ask Congress to extend an existing non-military aid program for the contras, Bush said, "I have every intention of seeing that these people receive humanitarian support."

On Capitol Hill, Democrats voiced cautious optimism, while pro-contra members expressed doubts that the Sandinistas would keep their promises but disagreed about the next U.S. steps.

Consulting with Capitol Hill members in extraordinary secrecy, Secretary of State Baker suggested diplomatic carrots and sticks — "incentives and disincentives" to encourage the Sandinistas to carry out the promised political reforms, including free elections. This would involve for the most part diplomatic and economic steps, such as gradually restoring, or reducing, diplomatic relations and gradually loosening or tightening the economic embargo imposed in 1985.

Baker also stressed the administration's full support of the Central American peace process, as embodied in agreements among the region's presidents since August 1987. The Reagan administration never concealed its unhappiness with the peace agreements, insisting that they did little to force the Sandinistas to make political reforms. But the Bush administration publicly appeared more willing to use the peace agreements to advance U.S. interests in the region.

The Bush administration policy also included pressing the Soviet Union to drop its support of the Sandinistas. Democrats for years called on the Reagan administration to be more aggressive in demanding that Moscow halt its substantial military and economic aid programs to Nicaragua. According to information on the public record, the Reagan administration hesitated, arguing that doing so would give Moscow a diplomatic foothold in the region.

Baker got a generally positive response on Capitol Hill. Congressional and administration sources cited two immediate reasons. Most important, they said, was Baker's conciliatory approach to Capitol Hill. Also crucial was a weariness in Congress of the contra issue; members were eager to embrace almost any administration initiative that did not center on the rebels.

Despite the Reagan administration's statements that it was using the contras merely to "pressure" the Sandinistas into accepting democracy, Reagan clearly had one overriding goal in Nicaragua: ousting the Sandinistas.

Baker privately acknowledged that the Reagan policy failed, for various reasons. As an alternative, he pledged to use diplomatic and economic pressure to isolate the Sandinistas further and persuade them to open up their political system and stop threatening their neighbors.

That left the question of what to do about the several thousand contras.

While insisting that he was not seeking just a contra aid policy, Baker told members of Congress that he wanted to keep the guerrillas intact, in Honduras, at least until after the Nicaraguan elections in February 1990. His plan called for continued "humanitarian" aid to the contras at the existing rate of $4 million per month.

A $27.14 million aid program voted by Congress in September 1988 was to expire on March 31, but the administration had enough money to ship food, clothing and other supplies through April, and possibly May.

On its face, Baker's aid proposal appeared to contradict the Feb. 14 agreement among the Central American presidents. In that accord, the presidents pledged to write a plan within 90 days to disband the contras so they could return to Nicaragua or resettle, either elsewhere in the region or in other countries such as the United States.

However, the presidents' accord did not set a deadline for disbanding the contras. One State Department official said that lack of a date gave the administration "running room" to argue that contra aid should be extended until the Sandinistas had shown that they would keep their promises.

Non-Military Aid

After four weeks of intense negotiations, the administration and top leaders of both parties on Capitol Hill agreed March 24 on continuing non-military aid to the contras until after Nicaragua's elections. Capitol Hill leaders retained a right to block the aid after Nov. 30 if they believed the circumstances warranted it.

In return for the aid, Bush promised his full support for diplomatic efforts by the five Central American presidents to end the region's internal wars.

Although couched as a statement of policy, the accord between Bush and Hill leaders was a political deal designed to end years of partisan and institutional warfare over the contras. A central element of the deal was that Bush had to get the approval of four key committees to continue the aid past Nov. 30. Baker agreed to suspend the program after then if any of four panels — Senate and House Appropriations, House Foreign Affairs or Senate Foreign Relations — objected. The cutoff provision was controversial among conservatives, who maintained that it amounted to an unconstitutional congressional infringement on the president's foreign policy powers. However, House Democrats demanded that provision as the price for their signing the March 24 accord.

The agreement left open the question of whether the contra fighters should be encouraged to leave their Honduran camps, either to return home or move elsewhere in the region. The administration suggested that contra political leaders return to Nicaragua to run for office or to support domestic opposition parties that would contest the Sandinistas in the elections. But the administration did not encourage the thousands of contra fighters in Honduras to return home. The thrust of U.S. policy, a State Department official said, was to keep an option for the contras to stay in Honduras as a unified force until the fighters saw that "appropriate conditions exist for their return and their participation in elections." Some Democrats insisted that the contras should be encouraged to return to Nicaragua as soon as possible because they no longer posed a credible menace to the Sandinistas.

Legislative Action. The House and Senate floor debates on a $49.75 million contra aid bill (HR 1750) were remarkably muted. Most members portrayed it as a modest achievement that took Nicaragua off the political agenda for a while and gave the administration time to experiment with a new policy.

Those members voting "nay" fell into one of two camps: a small number of die-hard contra supporters who decried the bipartisan accord as a sellout of the rebels, and a larger group of liberals who had vowed never to vote for any aid to them.

The House approved the bill on April 13 by a **key vote of 309-110 (R 157-11; D 152-99).** A recommittal motion that would have deleted the potential Nov. 30 aid cutoff and established a procedure for Bush to demand future congressional votes on renewal of military aid to the contras failed on a 94-329 vote. *(1989 key votes, p. 1021)*

HR 1750 had been reported by the House Foreign Affairs Committee (H Rept 101-29, Part I) on April 11 and by the House Appropriations Committee (H Rept 101-29, Part II) the next day.

Senate passage also came April 13. The Senate approved HR 1750 by a **key vote of 89-9 (R 39-5; D 50-**

4), after several conservatives' amendments were rejected by broad margins. The Senate Appropriations Committee had approved the bill April 12.

Major Provisions. As signed into law April 18, HR 1750:

- Authorized $49.75 million for "humanitarian" aid to the contras through Feb. 28, 1990. The aid was defined as food, clothing and shelter; medical services and supplies, and non-military training for health and sanitation; non-military training of the contras with respect to treatment of civilians and other armed forces personnel; payment for the above items; replacement batteries for the contras' existing communications equipment; and support for "voluntary reintegration" and "voluntary regional location" of the contras.
- Authorized a maximum of $5 million for the Agency for International Development (AID) to administer the contra aid. AID ran the existing aid program. The legislation also authorized "such funds as may be necessary" for transportation of the supplies to the contras; the appropriations provided in the bill allowed as much as $7.7 million.
- Authorized $4.166 million for medical aid to civilian victims of the war, to be transported and administered by the Roman Catholic Church in Nicaragua.
- Stipulated that all money authorized and appropriated was to be transferred by the president from Pentagon procurement and research and development accounts. The bill made no new appropriations.
- Barred AID from transporting to the contras military items or any supplies other than those specifically authorized in the bill; this prohibited "mixed loads," shipments containing military and non-military supplies.
- Banned covert actions by any U.S. government agency to provide funds, materiel or other help to the contras "to support military or paramilitary operations in Nicaragua." However, this provision would not affect existing CIA covert aid to contra political operations.
- Prohibited aid to any group that retained in its ranks any individual who had been found to engage in gross violations of internationally recognized human rights, drug smuggling or significant misuse of public and private funds.
- Prohibited any additional aid to the contras unless Congress enacted a law specifically authorizing it.
- Encouraged the president to submit proposals for bilateral and multilateral action for additional economic aid to the democratic countries of Central America.
- Required the secretary of state to consult regularly with Congress on progress toward peace and democracy in Nicaragua.

Aid Continued. Hill leaders in late November agreed to continue the non-military aid for the Nicaraguan contras through February 1990.

Senior leaders sent Baker letters authorizing the administration to continue providing food, clothing, medical supplies and other items to the contras until after the Nicaraguan elections. Democratic leaders urged the administration to give more support to the search for a peaceful end to Nicaragua's war and called on Baker to pressure the contras into participating in the elections.

In a related development, Congress on Nov. 22 (in the session that began Nov. 21) cleared legislation (HR 3696 — PL 101-215) providing aid to victims of "civil strife" in Central America. As part of a non-military aid program in 1988, Congress authorized $17.7 million for children wounded by warfare. But the Sandinista government refused to allow official U.S. aid, and much of the money was not spent.

U.S. Aid to Contras

In fiscal 1982-90, the United States provided $311.7 million in direct aid to the contras. Congressional investigators reported $40.3 million in non-U.S. government aid.

1982. $29 million in CIA covert aid authorized by President Ronald Reagan.

1983. $29 million in CIA covert aid.

1984. $24 million in CIA covert aid.

1986. $27 million in non-military aid administered by the State Department, plus a classified amount for communications equipment.

1987. $100 million in CIA and Defense Department military and non-military aid approved by Congress.

1988. $25.8 million in non-military aid administered by the Agency for International Development (AID). This included $10.3 million in three continuing resolutions (of $3.5 million, $3.2 million and $3.6 million), plus $15.5 million voted after the March 23, 1988, Nicaraguan cease-fire.

1989. $27.14 million in non-military aid administered by AID. This was part of a $47.9 million package that also included up to $1.5 million for communications gear; $17.7 million for aid to Nicaraguan children; $4 million for AID operations; $5 million for medical aid to victims of the civil strife; and $10 million for the Nicaraguan cease-fire verification commission.

1989-90. $49.75 million in non-military aid administered by AID, voted by Congress on April 13, 1989. Congress also authorized $5 million for AID expenses, up to $7.7 million for transportation and $4.166 million for medical aid to civilian victims of the Nicaraguan war.

Other Aid. The House and Senate committees that investigated the Iran-contra affair reported the following non-U.S. government donations to the contras in the mid-1980s: Saudi Arabia, $32 million from June 1984 to March 1985; Iran arms sales diversion, $3.8 million (estimated by the committees); private fund raisers, $4.5 million (includes advertising and lobbying). (Taiwan also donated $2 million; but whether this money reached the contras is uncertain.)

Note: Beginning in 1982, Congress passed a series of "Boland amendments," named for the House Intelligence Committee chairman at that time, Edward P. Boland, D-Mass. These amendments mandated restrictions on and, in fiscal 1985, a cutoff of military aid to the contras. Military aid was resumed in fiscal 1987 but was cut off again the next year.

HR 3696 authorized AID to use $9.6 million in unspent money to provide aid to civilian victims of regional wars. Up to half the money could be spent in

Nicaragua, but none could be channeled through the Sandinista regime.

Election Aid

The five Central American presidents signed another peace accord on Aug. 7, 1989. It was their third major peace pact since Aug. 7, 1987.

Over the opposition of the Bush administration, the five presidents called for the "voluntary demobilization, repatriation or relocation" of the contras by early December — about 11 weeks prior to the scheduled presidential elections in Nicaragua.

The Bush administration had lobbied against any call for dismantling the contras before the Nicaraguan elections. U.S. officials had expressed hope that the continued presence of the guerrillas, along with Nicaragua's desperate need for outside aid to revive its collapsing economy, would pressure the Sandinistas to allow free elections.

To help ensure free elections, the Bush administration proposed an election aid package.

During a series of meetings on Capitol Hill in September, Secretary of State Baker found wide support for the general idea of creating what he called a "level playing field" for the Nicaraguan elections. Baker argued that a coalition of Sandinista opponents led by Chamorro needed automobiles, telephones and money for advertising if it was to have a chance at defeating the ruling Sandinista party, headed by Ortega.

But key liberal Democrats objected to providing direct aid that would appear to be siding with one party over another in a foreign election.

Particularly controversial was the administration's initial proposal to use the National Endowment for Democracy (NED) to funnel cash contributions and other support directly to the opposition. NED was established by Congress in the early 1980s to promote free elections overseas, but its charter specifically prohibited it from siding with any one faction in foreign elections.

In the face of Democratic opposition, the administration dropped this proposal and instead planned to have NED do what it often did overseas: provide technical aid for voter registration, poll-watching and other election-related activities that did not directly benefit one side over another.

After several weeks of behind-the-scenes wrangling over details, Baker sent Congress a request for the transfer of $9 million in unspent money from previous non-military aid programs for the Nicaraguan contras. In a concession to Congress, top administration officials gave private assurances that the CIA would not intervene on behalf of the Chamorro coalition. Congress, in turn, backed away from a confrontation by avoiding legislation that the administration could not support.

The CIA issue had arisen months earlier when State Department officials, testifying on Capitol Hill, refused to rule out the possibility of using the agency during the elections to help parties opposing the Sandinistas. Alarmed by the prospect of renewed CIA intervention in Nicaragua, liberal Democrats in both chambers prepared legislation barring the agency from engaging in any activities to influence the elections.

To head off that legislation, and to ease the way for Bush's request for overt aid to the Nicaraguan elections, Baker and other officials assured congressional leaders that the CIA would not intervene in the elections.

Legislative Action. The House Appropriations Committee marked up the election aid bill on Oct. 3 (HR 3385 — H Rept 101-265, Part I). The bill passed the House easily — 263-156 — the following day, with the backing of Republicans and a coalition consisting mostly of moderate and conservative Democrats. The majority of those voting "nay" were Democrats who always opposed the contra war and who saw the Bush policy as an extension of heavy-handed U.S. intervention.

Liberal Democrats made one try to gut the aid package. But a proposal to delete all of the aid except for $400,000 budgeted for an election-monitoring effort spearheaded by former president Jimmy Carter failed 142-278.

As in the House, Senate leaders gave the bill priority status, rushing it through the Appropriations Committee on Oct. 12 and then onto the floor, for debate only, a little more than an hour later.

The request encountered stronger resistance in the Senate than in the House. Opponents in both parties denounced what they called an attempt by the administration to "buy" the elections. Liberal Democrats were joined by the Senate's premier conservative, Jesse Helms, R-N.C., in harshly criticizing the proposal.

The White House, fearful that Republicans would side with liberal Democrats to defeat the bill, lobbied aggressively for the election aid package. Their campaign paid off.

After invoking cloture by 74-25, the Senate Oct. 17 tabled 59-40 an amendment offered by Tom Harkin, D-Iowa, decreeing that no U.S. aid could be given to the Sandinista government or any of its agencies. Officials had acknowledged that some of the aid, perhaps as much as $2 million, could reach the Sandinista-dominated Supreme Electoral Council because of a Nicaraguan law that imposed a 50 percent tax on foreign contributions to political parties there. The administration called the Harkin proposal a "killer amendment," saying that its adoption could have forced the United States to abandon all direct aid to Chamorro's coalition rather than allow any of the aid to be taxed by the government.

Three other amendments that would have gutted the thrust of Bush's request were rejected, before the Senate passed the bill on Oct. 17 by a 64-35 vote.

Major Provisions. As signed into law Oct. 21, HR 3385:

- Provided $9 million for the Nicaraguan elections. Of this, $5 million was to be funneled through NED to internal groups, such as political organizations, independent elements of the media, independent labor unions, business and civic organizations, to improve election procedures and to help monitor the voting. Another $4 million, part of which would be funneled through NED, was for election support to ensure free, fair and open elections. The law stipulated that this could include contributions through Chamorro's National Opposition Union (UNO) to the Sandinista-dominated Supreme Electoral Council but stated that it was the sense of Congress that the UNO would seek to ensure that such funds were used solely for technical electoral purposes.
- Included in the $4 million were earmarked funds for three organizations promoting voter participation in the Nicaraguan elections: Center for Training and Election Promotion ($400,000), an independent Costa Rican organization; the Council of Freely Elected Heads of Government ($400,000), headed by former president Carter; and the Washington-based Center for Democracy ($250,000).

New Regional Accord

The five Central American presidents on Dec. 12, 1989, signed their fourth agreement since 1987 calling for an end to conflicts in the region.

The presidents demanded that leftist guerrillas halt their war against the rightist government of El Salvador, and they called for demobilization of the contras. The presidents also asked the United States to stop aiding the contras directly and to channel any aid through an international commission appointed by the United Nations and the Organization of American States (OAS).

Both rebel groups rejected the presidents' requests, and the Bush administration appeared to rebuff the call for an end to direct contra aid. Administration spokesmen said they were reviewing the issue but argued that Managua bore the burden of renewing direct talks and creating conditions to encourage the contras to lay down their arms and return home.

Nicaraguan Election

For Nicaragua, the election offered the prospect of ending a conflict that had cost thousands of lives, devastated its economy and produced a desperate longing for peace among Nicaraguans of all stripes.

Moreover, the Sandinistas were being pressed by their primary benefactor — the Soviet Union — to end the confrontation with the United States. Soviet President Mikhail S. Gorbachev cut off direct arms shipments to the Sandinistas, and the Soviets also curtailed their economic subsidies.

Nonetheless, the election process was not easy for anti-Sandinista groups. Accustomed to dominating local politics, the Sandinistas resisted moves that the opposition said were necessary for a free election. Strong outside pressures were needed, for example, to get opposition parties fair access to the major government-owned television station. The government resisted election-law reforms, and it released U.S.-supplied aid to Chamorro's National Opposition Union only after a strong demand by Carter.

The Sandinistas eventually bowed to most outside pressures, however, and satisfied most observers, including many skeptics, that the elections would be untainted.

The balloting was witnessed by thousands of observers and journalists and universally regarded as free and fair. Bush promptly congratulated Chamorro on her victory, promised U.S. help in a "peaceful reconciliation and transition" and called for re-establishment of the cease-fire between the government and the contras.

On Capitol Hill, lawmakers on both sides of the contra debate claimed credit for the outcome. Conservatives stressed the military pressure from the rebels, while liberals discounted the contras' importance and emphasized the Central American leaders' peace process.

General agreement existed, however, on the need for the United States to provide aid to the new government and to move quickly to normalize trade and diplomatic relations with Nicaragua for the first time since 1985.

Aid Package

On March 13, 1990, Bush requested a $300 million aid package and urged Congress to act on it promptly. At the same time, Bush lifted the economic sanctions and trade embargo imposed in 1985 and took other preliminary steps to restore trade with Nicaragua. According to Commerce Department figures, U.S.-Nicaragua trade had dropped from $181 million in 1984 to $7 million in 1988.

Legislative Action. While Congress raised few concerns about Bush's request, final approval came slower than the president had hoped. The funds were added to a previously introduced supplemental appropriations bill (HR 4404) to provide aid to the new government of Panama. *(Aid to Panama, below)*

Parliamentary delays largely unrelated to foreign aid issues held the bill up despite Bush's repeated pleas for speedy action. The measure finally cleared one month after Chamorro had been inaugurated in Managua.

Bills authorizing aid to Nicaragua were reported by House Foreign Affairs (HR 4636 — H Rept 101-470, Part I) on May 1 and Senate Foreign Relations (S 2364) on March 29. By voice votes, the Senate April 5 and the House May 24 passed S 2364. The House May 22 failed to pass HR 4636.

The House Appropriations Committee reported HR 4404 on March 27 (H Rept 101-434), and the House passed it on April 3 by a 362-59 vote.

The Senate Appropriations Committee reported the supplemental appropriations bill on April 24 (S Rept 101-272), and the Senate passed it May 1 by voice vote.

The conference report (H Rept 101-493) was adopted by the House, 308-108, May 24; the Senate followed suit with voice vote approval shortly after midnight May 25 (in the session that began May 24).

Provision. As signed into law on May 25, HR 4404 — a $4.3 billion fiscal 1990 supplemental appropriations bill — appropriated $300 million in aid to Nicaragua.

Panama Invasion, Aid

After nearly two years of legal, diplomatic and finally military action, the United States at the end of 1989 succeeded in ousting from power Panamanian dictator Gen. Manuel Antonio Noriega.

By sending about 13,000 U.S. troops to invade Panama on Dec. 20 and pressuring Noriega until he surrendered, President Bush erased politically harmful doubts about his willingness to act decisively and achieved a goal that had eluded his predecessor. For the first time in his presidency, Bush won nearly unanimous plaudits on Capitol Hill.

With the dictator jailed in Miami on Jan. 3, 1990, facing federal drug-trafficking charges, the Bush administration could boast about a significant foreign policy achievement.

Beyond the dead and wounded from the invasion, the immediate cost of that success was financial. Economic sanctions against Panama since early 1988 had created what administration officials acknowledged was a moral commitment to help that once-friendly country get back on its feet.

Leaders of Panama's new government, headed by President Guillermo Endara, said they needed up to $2 billion in short-term aid to repair the damage from the U.S. invasion and the economic consequences of U.S. sanctions.

But facing a budget crunch, Bush administration officials warned Panamanians to scale back their expectations. On Jan. 25, 1990, Bush proposed an aid package valued at about $1 billion. This included $42 million in humanitarian assistance and an economic recovery plan with $500 million in cash aid, along with off-budget programs that could produce a matching amount.

Congress in 1990 approved a total of $462 million in aid to Panama. While it was weighing Bush's request, Congress on Feb. 7, 1990, rushed through a bill to provide $42 million in emergency aid. That legislation (HR 3952 — PL 101-243) also waived a number of the economic sanctions on Panama.

A supplemental appropriations bill containing the larger amount moved more slowly, however, despite repeated pleas by Bush for Congress to expedite it. The president himself expanded the request to include $300 million in emergency assistance for the new government of President Violeta Chamorro in Nicaragua after the anti-Sandinista leader's election in February 1990. The measure was further delayed by political clashes over foreign aid and unrelated funding provisions added by the administration and lawmakers. *(Nicaragua aid, p. 219)*

Legislation (HR 4404 — PL 101-302) appropriating $420 million finally cleared Congress May 25 (in the session that began May 24).

Background

U.S. pressure on Noriega to step down began in mid-1987, when allegations were made that Noriega had engineered his country's 1984 presidential election and had directed the 1985 slaying of an opposition leader. The sensational charges triggered public demonstrations against Noriega and the military, which led to thousands of arrests and a government crackdown on the opposition. The United States responded by suspending military and economic aid to Panama. *(Congress and the Nation Vol. VII, p. 222)*

On Feb. 4, 1988, Noriega was indicted on drug charges by federal grand juries in Florida. Eric Arturo Delvalle, installed by Noriega as president in 1985, tried to fire Noriega in the wake of the indictments, only to be ousted from office himself. After a clumsy coup attempt and the failure of U.S. rhetorical attacks to remove Noriega, President Ronald Reagan on April 8, 1988, imposed sanctions aimed at depriving the Noriega regime of hard currency.

With Noriega continuing to resist, Washington tried in May 1988 to negotiate with him, offering as an inducement the dropping of the drug charges. But Noriega backed away from an agreement, causing intense embarrassment for the Reagan administration.

Reagan in the summer of 1988 also considered a CIA covert operation against Noriega, but the plan fell victim to Hill opposition and caused a heated dispute between the administration and Congress over classified information "leaks."

The Reagan administration's failure to oust Noriega created a series of headaches for the new Bush administration in the spring of 1989.

Election Nullified. With voters in Panama set to go to the polls on May 7, 1989, to elect a new president, along with members of the Legislative Assembly and local officials, an anti-Noriega coalition held a substantial lead in independent opinion polls.

Free and fair elections presented a major opportunity to ease the crisis in U.S.-Panamanian relations. But the Bush administration and opposition groups in Panama warned that Noriega intended to steal the election by declaring a pro-government coalition the victor.

In the most visible demonstration of U.S. concern, Secretary of State James A. Baker III on April 27 announced plans for former presidents Jimmy Carter and Gerald R. Ford to observe the voting. They would travel to Panama under the auspices of the National Endowment for Democracy, a quasi-governmental agency that promoted free elections worldwide.

Bush reportedly launched a covert operation to aid opposition forces in Panama. Opposition leaders insisted they had received no CIA aid, but the reports about the aid handed Noriega an opportunity to attack U.S. intervention in Panamanian affairs.

The May 7 elections followed the anticipated script. The anti-Noriega coalition claimed victory, and that claim was backed by most observers, including the Panamanian Catholic Church and hundreds of foreign election monitors. Former president Carter angrily accused Noriega of trying to "steal" the elections.

On May 10, the Noriega regime nullified the elections and pro-Noriega paramilitary forces broke up an opposition parade in downtown Panama City, beating presidential candidate Endara and one of his two running mates, Guillermo Ford. Dramatic photographs of a bloodstained Ford trying to fend off his attackers created a sensation in Washington and added to the political pressure on Bush to take action.

Bush responded the next day with several actions, including the ordering of nearly 2,000 additional troops to Panama, ostensibly to help protect thousands of U.S. personnel in the wake of the post-election unrest. Those forces augmented some 10,000 U.S. military personnel regularly stationed there to defend the Panama Canal and to staff the U.S. Southern Command headquarters.

The president's action marked the second time in a month that he had bolstered U.S. military forces in Panama. Responding to reports of harassment of U.S. troops and citizens, Bush in April dispatched 1,300 military police officers and other security personnel.

The limited nature of Bush's move illustrated the dilemma he faced in dealing with Latin Americans sensitive about U.S. intervention, while at the same time appearing in the United States to be strong and decisive.

Bush brushed aside proposals by some members of Congress for more radical moves, such as invading Panama and abrogating the canal treaties. That restraint won plaudits from most congressional leaders. In a highly unusual move, the top five House and Senate leaders issued a joint statement praising Bush's "measured and deliberate steps to assist the Panamanian people in restoring democracy to their people."

Most members of Congress accepted Bush's explanation of the troop move and brushed aside questions about whether the War Powers Resolution should be invoked. That 1973 law barred the president from keeping U.S. forces in hostilities for more than 90 days without the approval of Congress. *(Congress and the Nation Vol. IV, p. 849)*

Bush continued through the remainder of the year to step up diplomatic efforts, unilaterally and through the Organization of American States (OAS), to force Noriega to yield to the election results. But an OAS delegation sent to Panama in August 1989 failed to get Noriega to agree to give up power, and the full OAS refused to follow up with more direct steps — such as multilateral sanctions.

Coup Attempt. A coup attempt in October 1989 was crushed within hours by loyalist troops. U.S. forces blocked two roads but otherwise stood pat.

In the aftermath of the failed attempt, a strong congressional outcry was heard against the administration's passivity. Critics from across the political spectrum protested that Bush had withheld support from exactly the kind of uprising he had publicly urged many times against Noriega. But administration officials insisted that U.S. information about the state of affairs was too uncertain to justify intervention.

Others contended that the administration's freedom to deal with the Panama coup had been hampered by existing laws and policies and by congressional oversight of overseas covert operations. Questions were raised about the effects of a 1976 executive order banning assassinations of foreign leaders.

In a 1988 exchange of letters on the assassinations ban, the White House and the Senate Intelligence Committee had agreed that the CIA would not support a Panamanian coup that would likely result in the killing of Noriega. Bush reportedly cited this issue in complaining to Republican senators that Congress had imposed undue restrictions on the administration.

Although most Bush officials said the 1988 interpretations of the ban played no role in the Bush administration's decision making about the Oct. 3 coup attempt, the issue of whether the administration was hamstrung by the assassinations ban prompted a finger-pointing episode of unusual intensity and duration between Senate Intelligence and the administration. The two sides finally reached agreement that administrative operatives should have some flexibility in interpreting the ban.

Several days after the coup attempt, Sen. Jesse Helms, R-N.C., offered an amendment to an anti-drug strategy bill (S 1711) authorizing the president to use the armed forces to remove Noriega from power. But that proposal drew widespread opposition on grounds that it could reopen the long-simmering controversy over the scope of the president's authority to deploy forces abroad without a congressional declaration of war.

After tabling the Helms amendment 74-25, the Senate Oct. 5 adopted 99-1 an alternative expressing in very general terms the sense of the Senate that the president was entitled to use military force to protect U.S. interests overseas subject to existing legal and constitutional requirements.

U.S. Invasion of Panama

Citing a growing threat to U.S. personnel in Panama, President Bush launched a massive U.S. invasion of Panama on Dec. 20, 1989, that deposed Noriega and crushed most resistance by his military forces.

Bush contended that Noriega's war of words had created a political climate in which the 35,000 U.S. citizens in Panama faced a significant risk of harm. That prospect had been highlighted a few days earlier when Panamanian military personnel killed an off-duty Marine officer and roughed up another U.S. officer and his wife.

In a televised address hours after the invasion, Bush said one aim was to replace Noriega with a government headed by Endara, who had taken the oath of office at a U.S. base in Panama City shortly before the attacks started.

Noriega eluded capture for several weeks. On Christmas Eve, he took refuge in the Vatican Embassy in Panama City, triggering a furious round of diplomatic bargaining over his fate. Told by Vatican officials that he would have to leave, Noriega turned himself over to U.S. authorities on Jan. 3, 1990. He was taken to Miami, where he was arraigned in federal court on drug-trafficking charges.

Reaction. One immediate result of the attack was to shore up Bush against widespread criticism, especially from Democrats, that he had been too cautious, even timid, to act decisively on the world stage.

Acting against Noriega also was important personally for Bush, whom Democratic presidential candidate Michael S. Dukakis criticized as too cozy with Noriega. Bush was CIA director in the mid-1970s when Noriega was on the spy agency's payroll, and he was photographed in 1983 chatting amiably with Noriega during a trip to Panama.

One of the reasons for broad Hill support of Bush's action was that he had tried multilateral diplomacy through the OAS before resorting to a unilateral move.

But the invasion also drew vigorous objections from congressional foes of U.S. intervention abroad, as well as from Latin American nations.

War Powers Act. While U.S. troops were still mopping up in Panama and trying to capture Noriega, Bush sent congressional leaders a letter Dec. 22, refusing to put a time limit on deployment of the U.S. troops.

It is "not possible at this time to predict the scope and duration" of the U.S. operation, Bush said in the letter, which was intended to circumvent a longstanding dispute with Congress over the 1973 War Powers Resolution.

That law, enacted over President Richard Nixon's veto, required a president to submit to Congress a detailed report on any deployment of U.S. forces into combat within 48 hours after the event. It also required withdrawal of those forces within 90 days, unless Congress explicitly authorized their continued deployment.

Nixon and every president since had denounced the act as unconstitutional. But the issue never had been authoritatively adjudicated because, as a rule, whenever U.S. troops had been sent into dangerous situations, presidents salved congressional sensibilities by sending to Capitol Hill within 48 hours a report along the lines required by the statute. To avoid any appearance of conceding that the War Powers act was binding, however, it had become standard practice for presidents to characterize these reports, as Bush did in his letter of Dec. 22, as being "consistent with" the War Powers act, instead of being "pursuant to" the legislation.

Economic Aid. In a step to bolster the new government, Bush ordered top aides to lift economic sanctions that Reagan had imposed starting in March 1988.

Officials from Bush on down acknowledged that the United States had an aid commitment because its economic sanctions helped devastate Panama's economy and because the U.S. invasion resulted in substantial damage to some parts of Panama City and environs.

But, administration officials insisted — because the United States was financially strapped itself — a dose of money from Washington could be only part of the remedy to Panama's economic ills and that Panama should rely on other countries and on international financial institutions for most of its outside financial resources over the next year or two.

Panama was said to owe about $1.6 billion immediately to overseas sources and had a long-term foreign debt of up to $4 billion. Panamanian leaders said they needed up to $2 billion in outside aid to revive the battered economy and repair the physical damage from the U.S. invasion.

While voicing willingness to help, congressional leaders joined the administration in signaling that Panamanians

U.S. Incursions Since 1903

The United States sent military forces into foreign lands 10 times between 1903 and 1983.

1903: Panama. President Theodore Roosevelt ordered warships to protect the isthmus during Panama's successful independence fight against Colombia.

1914-17: Mexican Revolution. U.S. troops invaded Mexico, ousting dictator Gen. Victoriano Huerta. He was replaced by Venustiano Carranza.

1915-34: Haiti. To protect U.S. business interests after two revolutions, U.S. Marines invaded and occupied Haiti. Newly elected president Sudre Dartiquenave signed a treaty with the United States.

1916-24: Dominican Republic. U.S. forces invaded the Dominican Republic and established an internal administration under U.S. naval officers.

1926-33: Nicaragua. U.S. troops invaded and reinstated conservative Adolfo Diaz as president. U.S. forces left in 1933, after the Havana Conference, opened by President Calvin Coolidge in 1928, complained: "No state has the right to intervene in the internal affairs of another."

1954: Guatemala. Threatened by the spread of communist influence under President Jacob Arbenz Guzman, the United States supported an invasion from Honduras by Col. Carlos Castillo Armas. After a promise of $6.4 million in economic help, Castillo Armas, as the new president, signed a U.S. military aid pact.

1958: Lebanon. Amid civil war in Beirut, a U.S. force of 14,000 occupied Lebanon for almost four months, enabling Fuad Shehab to replace Camille Chamoun as president.

1961: Cuba. Cuban exiles with U.S. support launched the Bay of Pigs invasion against Fidel Castro's regime but failed to oust the Cuban leader.

1965: Dominican Republic. After 21,500 U.S. troops invaded, a provisional government was set up under Hector Garcia-Godoy. Congress, alleging a "lack of candor" by the Johnson administration, held closed hearings.

1983: Grenada. U.S. Marines led an invasion of Grenada after its Caribbean neighbors requested help in restoring order and democracy following a Marxist coup. Capitol Hill leaders accepted the action but questioned its legality.

should not expect a total economic bailout from Washington.

In January 1990, Bush submitted to Congress a $500 million aid proposal that included both short-term humanitarian aid and longer-term programs to get the economy moving after years of internal corruption and U.S. sanctions. In addition to this $500 million in direct cash aid, the Bush proposal also called for about $500 million in loans, credits and other off-budget programs. All of the $500 million in hard cash was to be transferred from existing programs so it would not add to the deficit.

Emergency Aid

Hastening to meet Panama's needs and its own recess deadline, Congress on Feb. 7, 1990, cleared $42 million in emergency aid to Panama. Both chambers passed the emergency humanitarian assistance bill (HR 3952 — PL 101-243) by voice vote.

The House Foreign Affairs (H Rept 101-401, Part I) and Ways and Means (H Rept 101-401, Part II) committees reported HR 3952 on Feb. 7. The Senate Foreign Relations Committee approved the proposal on Feb. 6.

The economic aid was to be used for housing, public works, small business loans, and training and equipment for a new Panamanian police force. The bill also lifted numerous U.S. economic and aid sanctions. Removal of those sanctions would speed the $42 million and also enable the administration to begin separate programs of loans and investment credits.

Long-Term Aid

Bush asked Congress to approve the larger aid package in a supplemental appropriations bill (HR 4404) for fiscal 1990. The administration appealed to Congress to move quickly on the proposal, but several factors combined to delay congressional action.

First, Bush expanded the request to include $300 million to assist the new government in Nicaragua. Some lawmakers suggested transferring some of the money for Panama to Nicaragua and others called for providing aid to Eastern Europe with some of the money slated for the two Central American countries. And for a time, some House Democrats wanted to use the bill as a platform to debate U.S. policy toward El Salvador. *(Nicaragua aid, p. 219; El Salvador policy, p. 214)*

Procedural matters also intervened. Bush requested a straightforward supplemental appropriations measure, but the two foreign policy authorizing committees — House Foreign Affairs and Senate Foreign Relations — both insisted on having a role. The upshot was that committees were working on authorization bills at about the same time other panels were working on appropriations — adding substantial complications to the simple process Bush had envisioned.

Finally, the supplemental, as a must-pass bill, attracted a variety of add-ons from both the administration and Congress. The new provisions eventually pushed the total cost of the measure to more than $4 billion, only $885 million of it for foreign affairs items.

The House passed the supplemental appropriations bill (HR 4404) 362-59 on April 3, after the Appropriations Committee on March 27 trimmed the request for Panama to $420 million (H Rept 101-434).

The Senate passed HR 4404, with the House-passed level of funding for Panama, by voice vote May 1. The bill had been reported by Senate Appropriations April 24 (S Rept 101-272). A floor attempt to cut the Panama aid package from $420 million to $300 million was tabled by a vote of 51-48 on April 26.

The House adopted the conference report (H Rept 101-493) 308-108 on May 24; the Senate gave its approval by voice vote shortly after midnight on May 25 (in the session that began May 24).

The final bill withheld 20 percent of the funds until the United States and Panama reached agreement on the issue of Panama's bank secrecy laws, which for years had attracted billions of dollars from drug cartels. Conferees dropped Senate-added conditions for close monitoring of the funds.

The final bill included provisions waiving the requirement for an authorization of the money for Panama and Nicaragua. On March 27, the House Foreign Affairs Committee had endorsed a companion authorization bill (HR 4636 — H Rept 101-470, Part I), which included most of Bush's Panama aid proposal. The Senate Foreign Relations Committee approved a similar measure (S 2364) the next day. The Senate passed it by voice vote April 5. But HR 4636 became entangled in controversy over aid to El Salvador and the House voted 171-244 to reject the bill on May 22. Two days later, the House passed an amended version of S 2364, but there was no further action.

1990-91 Aid Authorization

Congress in 1989 — for the fourth year in a row — failed to enact a foreign aid authorization bill. This failure was the responsibility of the Senate, which considered neither the House-passed aid bill (HR 2655) nor the version produced by the Senate Foreign Relations Committee (S 1347).

But for the second year in a row, Congress enacted a free-standing foreign aid appropriations bill (HR 3743 — PL 101-167). The appropriations bill included provisions making foreign aid authorizations. *(Fiscal 1990 foreign aid appropriations, p. 228)*

Congress was supposed to pass an omnibus foreign aid authorization bill every year or two, but it had not done so since 1985. In theory, the foreign aid bill was the main tool Congress had to put its stamp on foreign policy. In 1989, the House Foreign Affairs Committee got its bill through the House, but the Senate Foreign Relations Committee lacked the political muscle to get its bill to the floor.

The demise of the authorization legislation had little practical effect on the day-to-day conduct of the foreign aid program. But it meant a setback to an attempt by the Foreign Affairs Committee to give the administration more flexibility in handling foreign aid. The committee had included in its bill several provisions reducing the number and extent of congressional restrictions on managing aid programs.

Moreover, Congress' failure once again to pass a foreign aid authorization further diminished the stature of the foreign policy committees, while enhancing the clout of the appropriations panels. *(Setback for committees, box, p. 268)*

Re-Examining Foreign Aid

Early in 1989, proposals for major changes in foreign aid programs were put forward on Capitol Hill and within the administration.

A report by a Foreign Affairs Committee task force proposed scrapping the foreign aid law, along with the main U.S. foreign aid agency, the Agency for International Development (AID), and starting anew.

The task force was chaired by Reps. Lee H. Hamilton, D-Ind., and Benjamin A. Gilman, R-N.Y. Its February report concluded that programs were "hamstrung by too many conflicting objectives, legislative conditions, earmarks and bureaucratic red tape." The task force recommended that the entire foreign aid law be rewritten and that Congress reduce its conditions. In return, Hamilton said, the Bush administration must agree to pay more attention than its predecessors did to legislators' foreign policy views.

The most controversial task force recommendation was the elimination of "earmarks" — congressional requirements that the administration give specific amounts to certain countries or programs. Congress earmarked nearly all of the major foreign aid accounts, a practice that sharply reduced the administration's flexibility to respond to changing circumstances.

In separate appearances before Foreign Affairs, AID administrator Alan Woods and Secretary of State James A. Baker III reacted with enthusiasm to the task force proposal on earmarks. However, committee Chairman Dante B. Fascell, D-Fla., and other Hill leaders pointed out that stopping the earmarking practice would be difficult politically.

The major beneficiary of earmarks was Israel, for which Congress annually set aside $3 billion in aid. Israel and the private lobbies that backed it carried great weight on Capitol Hill and had defeated previous suggestions for eliminating earmarks.

Woods based his criticism of traditional foreign aid programs on AID's own 158-page report, "Development and the National Interest," also released in February. In the report, AID said many of its programs had succeeded in reaching narrow goals, such as feeding starving people or building medical clinics. But overall, the report said, U.S. programs were not helping poor countries dig themselves out of poverty.

Woods said the Bush administration would continue the Reagan administration's approach of reducing aid to government-sponsored development projects and emphasizing instead "private-sector, market-led" policies in foreign countries.

Legislative Action

The House Foreign Affairs Committee was partially successful in its efforts to revamp the foreign aid program. The committee on June 15 reported a bill (HR 2655 — H Rept 101-90) that would have streamlined much of foreign aid law, repealing dozens of obsolete or duplicative provisions.

But the bill disappointed administration officials who wanted the committee to follow the recommendation of Fascell and other leaders that Congress loosen most of the restrictions it had imposed on foreign aid.

The committee agreed to drop some conditions, but in the end it refused to curtail the most important one: earmarking. The committee voted earmarks for the bulk of the military and economic aid programs that the administration used to bolster key foreign allies. It did reduce earmarking of less controversial programs that advanced development in the Third World.

The administration also objected to several other committee provisions.

In an unusual display of bipartisanship and cooperation, the House on June 29 overwhelmingly approved HR

2655. A record number of House members — 314 — voted for the foreign aid authorization bill. The strong vote, with only 101 members dissenting, was the result of hard work to resolve contentious issues by the Foreign Affairs Committee and the Bush administration. Fascell and other House leaders had negotiated compromises on several — although not all — of the items most strongly opposed by the administration. And Fascell headed off dozens of potentially troublesome issues by crafting en bloc amendments containing compromise versions of amendments that members wanted to offer.

The House bill would have authorized $11.6 billion annually in fiscal 1990-91 for foreign development, economic and military aid programs. However, the House added an amendment limiting actual spending under the bill in fiscal 1990 to $11.2 billion, a cut of about $328 million — or 2.8 percent — from the authorizations in the bill, to bring it into compliance with the budget resolution (H Con Res 106) and to head off even deeper cuts.

The Senate Foreign Relations Committee approved a fiscal 1990 foreign aid authorization bill (S 1347 — S Rept 101-80) by an 18-0 vote on July 12 and reported it July 18. The unanimous committee vote appeared to signal not so much universal satisfaction with the bill as relief by committee members to be rid of it. Foreign Relations Chairman Claiborne Pell, D-R.I., had called repeated markup sessions starting on June 9, only to be frustrated by members' refusal to show up or by secret objections to the meetings Republicans lodged under Senate rules.

Publicly venting his frustration at his colleagues' "lack of interest" in the bill, Pell finally refused to schedule committee meetings on any other business, such as pending nominations for top State Department posts, until the aid bill was approved.

Several members also said that they feared the panel would suffer permanent damage to its prestige and clout within the Senate if it did not conclude the legislation that used to be considered its single most important piece of business. Even the ranking Republican, Jesse Helms, N.C., who ridiculed the bill and did not vote on it, said that Foreign Relations should finish its work because "I don't want to see the authority of the committee diminished."

The Foreign Relations-approved bill included $11.4 billion for foreign aid programs in fiscal 1990, a cut of about $100 million from the president's request. Unlike its House counterpart, Foreign Relations made only a modest effort to rewrite the underlying foreign aid law. The Foreign Relations bill would have deleted 20 obsolete provisions from the law — compared with dozens of items in the House bill.

But the bill never made it to the Senate floor. With the August congressional recess approaching, the chamber had time for only one foreign policy bill, and that was the authorization bill for the State Department and related agencies. Pell flirted with the idea of combining the two measures, but Helms opposed such a move. Instead, the State bill was loaded up with foreign policy amendments. *(State Department authorization, p. 247)*

With the bill dead in the Senate, House Foreign Affairs tried — without success — to get parts of its bill enacted in the conference on the State bill. Congress ended up handling foreign aid authorization issues as part of the foreign aid appropriations bill.

1990 Aid Appropriations

Congress in 1989 cleared a $14.6 billion fiscal 1990 foreign aid appropriations bill (HR 3743 — PL 101-167). Final action came after Congress dropped or modified several provisions that had led to President Bush's veto of an earlier version.

In nominal terms, the bill provided a 1.8 percent increase over fiscal 1989 spending. But that represented a real cut after inflation was taken into account, and it was substantially less than Bush wanted, especially for economic and military aid to U.S. allies. The bill also provided $532.8 million for new aid to reformist governments in Poland and Hungary — and some of that money would have to come out of existing aid programs.

Bush's Nov. 19 veto of the earlier version (HR 2939) was the first ever of a free-standing bill making appropriations for foreign aid. Bush had objected to two items: a mandated $15 million contribution to the United Nations Fund for Population Activities (UNFPA, later renamed the United Nations Population Fund), and a clause intended to bar the administration from "leveraging" U.S. aid to get foreign governments to undertake actions that Washington could not legally do itself.

Following Bush's action, the House Appropriations Committee produced a new bill identical to the vetoed one except for the provisions he cited and another item intended to reflect events in El Salvador. The new bill included revised language on the leveraging provision and dropped the U.N. money. The final aid bill also required the administration to report to Congress on the progress of investigations by the Salvadoran government into the Nov. 16 murder of six priests and two others. *(El Salvador, p. 214)*

As in the past, more than a third of all money in the foreign aid bill was to go to just two countries: Israel ($3 billion) and Egypt (slightly more than $2 billion).

New programs funded in the bill included $125 million worth of military and law enforcement aid to Bolivia, Colombia and Peru; and a $160 million U.S. contribution to an international fund to aid the Philippine economy.

House Action

With little of the bipartisan rancor of previous years, the House on July 21 voted 329-69 to pass legislation to appropriate funds for foreign assistance.

The bill (HR 2939 — H Rept 101-165) provided $14.3 billion for foreign development, economic and military aid programs in fiscal 1990, along with export promotion programs such as the Export-Import Bank.

That figure was nearly $400 million less than Bush requested. However, the bill would have made proportionately deeper cuts in the two programs that were the administration's highest priorities: economic and military support for key U.S. allies. Those programs would be cut by about $700 million.

Before approving the package, the House agreed by voice vote to cut about $65 million from the measure reported July 19 by the Appropriations Committee. Funds earmarked for specific countries and various programs, including narcotics control and anti-terrorism assistance, were exempted. With so much of the bill's funding earmarked for Israel, Egypt and other countries, less than half of the bill's total funding was vulnerable to the reductions, according to congressional aides.

By accepting the 1 percent cut, House members avoided a vote on an alternative proposal for an across-the-board cut of 3 percent, or $450 million, in all foreign aid programs except for narcotics control. A vote against the larger cut would have been politically unpopular given the American public's traditionally weak support for foreign aid.

Passage of HR 2939 had been eased by compromises reached earlier between key Democrats and Republicans on the Appropriations Committee and Bush administration officials. The bill had been approved by the Appropriations Subcommittee on Foreign Operations on July 17 and by the full committee two days later.

During negotiations, Foreign Operations Subcommittee Chairman David R. Obey, D-Wis., and administration officials worked to strike a balance between their conflicting priorities. In general, Obey and most of his fellow Democrats put most of their emphasis on economic development programs and contributions to certain international agencies, such as some of the development banks and organs of the United Nations.

The administration, and most Republicans, gave priority to economic and military aid that was used to bolster overseas allies, especially those that hosted U.S. military installations or that were threatened by leftist guerrilla movements.

To get the administration's attention, Obey in late June made public the recommendations of subcommittee Democrats. Chief among them was a cut of nearly $800 million in the programs the administration most favored.

All subsequent negotiations were aimed at narrowing the gap between the two sides. The final agreement effectively gave the administration about $100 million more than Obey had planned for economic and military aid programs. That was much less than the administration wanted, but one senior State Department official called it "the best we can get from this committee."

In a significant departure from past practice, the subcommittee's bill sharply curtailed the number of earmarks, or mandates for the administration to spend specific amounts of money on certain countries or programs. In the past, the subcommittee earmarked the bulk of the foreign aid bill, thus limiting the administration's flexibility to meet emergencies and changing circumstances.

The House Foreign Affairs Committee initiated a move in 1989 to limit the number of earmarks, but members of that panel were unable to resist the urge to nail down spending figures for favored countries. *(Fiscal 1990-91 foreign aid authorization, p. 227)*

Although the Foreign Operations Subcommittee did put in fewer earmarks than in most previous years, it nonetheless earmarked much of its bill simply by setting aside the customary $5 billion-plus just for Israel and Egypt.

As was the case throughout the Reagan years, the House Foreign Operations Subcommittee spent much of its time debating funding levels for the "security assistance" programs that were high priorities for the State and Defense departments. The major beneficiaries of those programs were Egypt and Israel (which together got nearly half of the aid), with several dozen countries sharing the remainder.

Bush requested $8.6 billion for the two major security aid programs: Foreign Military Sales (FMS) grants, which enabled foreign countries to buy U.S. weapons and military services ($5.027 billion), and the Economic Support Fund (ESF), which bolstered the economies of key countries ($3.549 billion). The Obey subcommittee-approved agreement provided $4.664 billion for the FMS program and rejected an administration request to put all aid through that program on a grant basis, instead of the existing mix of grants and loans.

Obey's subcommittee also made what at first glance appeared to be an enormous cut in the ESF program. The subcommittee cut Bush's request to $2.3 billion, a reduction of more than $1.26 billion. However, the bulk of that cut was a $920 million transfer of money from economic aid to the more restrictive development aid accounts.

In doing that, the subcommittee had adopted a highly controversial recommendation of the Foreign Affairs Committee, which had argued that the United States was spending too much to prop up friendly regimes for the short-term and was neglecting long-term economic development overseas. The transfer would have affected primarily Egypt; $500 million of its existing $815 million in economic aid would be shifted to programs under stricter criteria.

In other action, the subcommittee cut by $40 million Bush's request for a $200 million U.S. contribution to an international plan to rescue the Philippine economy.

The Obey subcommittee also endorsed a strict limit of $85 million on military aid for El Salvador recommended by the Foreign Affairs Committee but set no restrictions on the aid.

Despite administration lobbying, Obey stood by his threat throughout the year to allow no U.S. contribution in fiscal 1990 for the main arm of the World Bank. Obey insisted that the World Bank loans were being used to help pay off Third World debts to commercial banks.

Senate Action

The Senate passed its $14.4 billion version of HR 2939 on Sept. 26 by a vote of 89-11. As had the House, the Senate made sharp cuts from the president's request, principally through a $371 million reduction from the $5.5 billion he had asked for overseas military aid.

El Salvador was the most contentious issue during a full day of Senate debate on the measure. In the most significant test of congressional sentiment on El Salvador since the new right-wing government of President Alfredo Cristiani took power in June, the Senate on Sept. 20 voted to give Bush virtually a free hand to continue U.S. support of that government. The impetus for the Senate action was a successful series of meetings in Mexico on Sept. 13-15 between Cristiani's representatives and the leftist guerrillas who had been fighting a succession of Salvadoran governments since 1979.

The Senate, by a 68-32 vote on Sept. 20, agreed to a motion to reject the committee-approved provisions that set an $85 million limit on military aid to El Salvador, divided the aid into three equal installments and enabled Congress to block expenditure of the final third installment. The Senate then adopted, 82-18, an amendment raising the limit on El Salvador's military aid to $90 million without conditions.

The Senate's first test in 1989 on abortion-related issues resulted in a major victory for pro-choice and family planning forces. By 52-48, the Senate Sept. 20 preserved the Appropriations Committee's provision directing the administration to contribute $15 million to the UNFPA.

The Appropriations panel had approved the $15 million contribution to the U.N. agency with a stipulation that the money be put in a separate account and not commingled with any of its funds used in China. But the administration and its anti-abortion allies said that stipulation was not adequate to ensure that no U.S. taxpayer money would be used to support coercive abortion or involuntary sterilization programs in China.

By 57-41, the Senate Sept. 20 killed an attempt to significantly weaken a committee-approved provision intended to prohibit the administration from using foreign aid to promote a foreign policy initiative that was otherwise barred by law. The committee provision was a modified version of an amendment added to the State Department authorization bill earlier in the year by Daniel Patrick Moynihan, D-N.Y. *(State Department authorization, p. 247)*

The Moynihan amendment was aimed at preventing the administration from engaging in some of the activities that were ascribed to the Reagan administration during the Iran-contra affair. Numerous allegations existed that Reagan's aides used the lure of foreign aid to get Honduras and other Central American governments to cooperate with secret U.S. efforts to aid the Nicaraguan contra guerrillas.

In a demonstration of widespread dissatisfaction with Bush's low-key response to rapid political changes in Eastern Europe, the Appropriations Committee included a $45 million economic aid program for Poland. The bill also earmarked $40 million in Overseas Private Investment Corporation (OPIC) risk insurance for Poland. A floor attempt to bar U.S. aid to or risk insurance for enterprises in Poland that were controlled by the Communist Party was tabled (killed), 74-24, on Sept. 20.

Conference Action

The administration objected to the provision mandating a contribution to the UNFPA, as well as to the one prohibiting the administration from using foreign aid money to carry out policies contrary to U.S. law. Despite a veto threat, both provisions were kept in the conference bill.

Conferees dropped House-passed provisions, advanced originally by the Foreign Affairs Committee, to reform the foreign aid process. Among these was a provision that would have transferred nearly $1 billion from the major economic aid program into AID's development programs.

Attempts to reduce the congressional practice of earmarking money for specific countries had mixed results. The practice locked in aid for nations with broad political support but left little for countries that lacked political or lobbying clout. Earmarks for Israel and Egypt were never in question, but House conferees challenged most other Senate earmarks. In the pivotal deal to settle the conference, House conferees agreed in full or part to seven contested Senate earmarks but forced the Senate to retreat on six others.

Conferees worked out an arrangement on three particularly vexing overall security assistance issues. The Senate agreed to drop its provision limiting actual spending, or "outlays," for economic aid in fiscal 1990 to only $1.7 billion, a provision intended to limit the budget impact of the $3 billion-plus economic aid program.

The Senate also was forced to accept a provision in the House bill barring the administration from putting the entire military aid program on an all-grant basis.

Under heavy pressure by the American-Israel Public Affairs Committee (AIPAC), the pro-Israel lobby, House conferees accepted a Senate provision allowing countries such as Israel to refinance their old U.S. military aid loans that carried interest rates of 8 percent or more. Under existing law, only loans of 10 percent or more could be refinanced. Refinancing could save those countries millions of dollars in interest charges, while depriving the U.S. Treasury of the income.

The House also yielded to another Senate provision allowing foreign aid programs to go forward despite the lack of a companion authorization bill, which was required by law.

Central to the conference agreement was a last-minute deal on the contentious question of funding for the World Bank. Conferees settled on a provision that provided a fiscal 1990 U.S. contribution of $50 million to the bank but, in effect, did not allow the bank to spend it. For the bank to use the money, the Bush administration would have to return to Congress the next year with a follow-up request. Obey had complained that the World Bank was channeling contributions from the United States and other donor countries to debtor nations, which then used the money as loan payments to commercial banks. The aim of the provision was to give the administration more time to persuade commercial banks to forgive or reduce the billions of dollars in loans they held from developing countries.

Although they were $60 million short of funds to pay for it, foreign aid conferees approved a $532.8 million aid package for Poland and Hungary in fiscal 1990. That figure was more than twice Bush's request.

Final Action, Veto

The House voted to adopt the conference report (H Rept 101-344) by 324-93 on Nov. 14. But then it became embroiled in the U.N. family planning agency controversy. Staking out diametrically opposing positions, the House on Nov. 14 first voted 244-178 to require Bush to give $15 million to the fund, with the stipulation that the money had to be kept in a separate account that could not be used in China. Then 25 minutes later, the House voted 219-203 to let him withhold the money.

On Nov. 15, the Senate voted 52-44 to stand by its demand for the $15 million contribution. The next day, the House again reversed direction and agreed 207-200 to accept the Senate provision mandating the contribution.

Both chambers agreed to a revised version of the provision barring the administration from leveraging U.S. aid to get foreign governments to do what Washington could not legally do. The compromise limited the ban to traditional foreign aid and arms sales programs — not to covert operations or routine diplomatic missions.

But the Bush administration still objected to the leveraging provision, as well as the mandated contribution to the UNFPA. The president vetoed HR 2939 on Nov. 19.

In his veto message, Bush acknowledged that the leveraging provision might be constitutional. But he said it was "sufficiently ambiguous to present an unacceptable risk that it will chill the conduct of our nation's foreign affairs."

Bush opposed the contribution to the U.N. fund because that agency operated in China, where the government reportedly forced women to have abortions and undergo involuntary sterilizations. Although the bill prohibited use of the U.S. funds in China, Bush said the provision was unacceptable because U.S. policy should be to warn "all family planning organizations that they must refrain from supporting coercive programs" if they wanted to receive American aid.

New Bill Approved

The House Appropriations Committee produced a new bill (HR 3743) that was nearly identical to the original bill but with the changes needed to win Bush's support.

HR 3743 contained a revised leveraging provision declaring that no overseas aid money could be provided to any foreign government or person "in exchange for" that government or person undertaking any action that the U.S. government or any government official was prohibited from doing. The bill also stated what it was not intended to limit.

But administration officials were still not satisfied and said Bush might veto the new aid bill unless further changes were made. Finally Secretary of State James A. Baker III and Obey agreed that Obey would make a "clarifying" statement on the House floor defining what was meant by the "in exchange for" clause. In his floor speech, Obey said that the clause referred to direct verbal or written agreement.

Obey added that the leveraging provision was "in the bill to prohibit the expenditure of foreign aid assistance in a manner that is specifically prohibited by provisions of United States law. It is not an attempt to hamstring government officials in the course of their normal duties or to make them vulnerable to wayward or runaway prosecutors."

Attempts to negotiate a compromise on the $15 million contribution to the population fund went nowhere, and Congress instead deleted the money from the new bill.

The final bill also included a new provision requiring the administration to report to Congress on the progress of investigations by the El Salvador government into the Nov. 16 murder of six Jesuit priests and two others at the university in San Salvador.

The House adopted HR 3743 on Nov. 20 by a 310-107 vote after blocking a move by liberals to offer an amendment delaying release of 30 percent of El Salvador's military aid as a protest against the murders.

The Senate rejected a similar amendment later that day on a 58-39 vote before passing the bill by voice vote, completing congressional action. Bush signed the measure the next day.

Major Provisions

The final version of the foreign aid appropriations bill (HR 3743 — PL 101-167) provided $14.6 billion in fiscal 1990 aid. This included $1.88 billion for multilateral aid, $6.65 billion for bilateral aid, $5.51 billion for military aid and $615 million for the Export-Import Bank direct loan program.

Major provisions of HR 3743:

'Leveraging' Provision. Declared that no overseas aid money could be provided to any foreign government or person "in exchange for" that government or person undertaking any action that, if carried out by the U.S. government or any government official, would be "expressly prohibited" by U.S. law.

The provision also said that it was not intended to limit the ability of the president or any official to make statements or to express views "to any party on any subject"; any official to express the policies of the president; or any official to discuss prohibited actions with a foreign government or official.

Military Aid. Required that $406 million of the military aid program be in low-interest loans, not grants.

- Permitted foreign countries to refinance old U.S. military aid loans that carried interest rates of 8 percent or more.

Middle East. Earmarked $1.8 billion in military aid and $1.2 billion in economic aid for Israel. Of the military aid, $400 million could be spent in Israel; all other countries had to spend all U.S. aid buying U.S. weapons and services. As in previous years, Israel was to receive all its economic aid within 30 days of the bill's enactment.

- Earmarked $1.3 billion in military aid and $815 million in economic aid for Egypt. The bill repealed an annual $115 million limit on the economic aid that Egypt could get as unrestricted cash but retained a requirement that Egypt could get the cash aid each year only if it made "significant economic reforms which are additional to those which were undertaken in previous fiscal years." The cash aid was a major issue in U.S.-Egyptian relations, with the Cairo government struggling to carry out free-market economic reforms demanded by Washington and the International Monetary Fund.
- Earmarked $35 million for economic aid to Jordan.

Poland, Hungary. Provided $532.8 million for Poland and Hungary, including $293 million in hard cash, $200 million for a trade credit program and $40 million for investment guarantees by OPIC. *(Poland, Hungary aid, p. 210)*

El Salvador. Set a limit of $85 million on military aid to El Salvador. The bill allowed $12 million for law enforcement-related aid programs in El Salvador, including training and "non-lethal" supplies for police.

- Required the administration to report to Congress on the progress of investigations by the Salvadoran government into the Nov. 16 murder of six priests and two others.

Persian Gulf Stingers. Barred the sale of Stinger portable anti-aircraft missiles to Persian Gulf countries.

- Allowed Bahrain to keep Stingers it bought from the United States at least through Sept. 30, 1991. Bahrain could keep the missiles after that date if the president reported to Congress that Bahrain needed them for its defense, that no other appropriate air defense system was available from the United States and that Bahrain had agreed to protect the missiles against diversion.

Aid to the Philippines. Provided $160 million of Bush's $200 million request for the U.S. contribution to a new international aid program for the Philippines. Called the multilateral assistance initiative, the program was an outgrowth of congressional moves to bolster the regime of President Corazon C. Aquino. (In December 1989, Aquino — with U.S. air cover — escaped the sixth attempt in four years to overthrow her government.) If any funds over $160 million were provided, the money had to be taken equally from economic aid and the development programs run by the Agency for International Development.

Bush also requested $449 million in other aid programs for the Philippines, all linked to U.S. bases there. Conferees took no position on those programs, allowing the administration to fund as much of them as possible. *(Philippine bases, p. 411)*

U.N. Agencies. Provided $265 million for U.S. contributions to the specialized agencies of the United Nations. The president had sought $209 million. Most of the increase went for agencies with broad support on Capitol

Aid to Pakistan Suspended

The future of the U.S.-Pakistan alliance came into question in 1990 because of that nation's emerging nuclear potential, as well as anti-democratic moves by Pakistan's military rulers. President Bush declined to certify that Pakistan had refrained from developing nuclear weapons, a step that was required under a 1985 law for the continuation of the more than $560 million a year in U.S. assistance to Islamabad.

Suspension of the aid, which took effect Oct. 1, was unpopular in Pakistan, where all political parties had backed a nuclear arms program. Pakistani President Ghulam Ishaq Khan, elected Oct. 24, pledged to resist bowing to U.S. demands to halt the program.

But U.S. Ambassador Robert Oakley responded with a letter to a leading Pakistani newspaper the next month, stating that, for aid to be resumed, Pakistan would have to prove that it had not assembled a nuclear weapon or its components.

By early 1991, however, the Bush administration was indicating that it would seek fiscal 1992 aid for Pakistan. *(Fiscal 1992 foreign aid appropriations, p. 269)*

Background

A 1985 amendment to the Foreign Assistance Act, sponsored by Sen. Larry Pressler, R-S.D., stated that aid must be cut off automatically unless the president certified before the start of each fiscal year that Pakistan "does not possess a nuclear explosive device." *(Congress and the Nation Vol. VII, p. 225)*

In subsequent years, the Reagan and Bush administrations provided the certification despite serious reservations about Pakistan's emerging nuclear potential. In 1989, CIA Director William H. Webster told the Senate Governmental Affairs Committee that "clearly, Pakistan is engaged in developing a nuclear capability." But such concerns were set aside — until 1990 — largely because of Islamabad's activities in support of the U.S.-backed Afghan rebels.

With Soviet troops being withdrawn from Afghanistan, though, Pakistan's role in that conflict became less important. At the same time, experts said that Pakistan had developed the ability to launch a nuclear strike, despite pledges to slow its weapons program. Leonard S. Spector, a senior associate at the Carnegie Endowment for International Peace, said Pakistan was able to deploy 10 to 12 nuclear bombs, probably by aircraft.

1990 Action

The administration lobbied hard for Congress to include a temporary waiver of the Pressler amendment in the fiscal 1991 foreign aid appropriations bill (HR 5114). Even though officials indirectly acknowledged Pakistan's nuclear capability, the administration reportedly wanted the waiver to use as leverage depending on the outcome of the October elections in Pakistan. But the idea of a short-term waiver that would allow aid to continue to flow to Pakistan received a cool response on Capitol Hill.

The administration's stance on aid suspension apparently shifted in response to new intelligence that cast doubt on Pakistan's previous assurances that it was keeping the components of any nuclear bomb separated.

Hill, particularly UNICEF ($65.4 million) and the U.N. Development Program ($109.5 million).

Zaire. Banned economic aid to Zaire and set a $3 million limit on military aid. The administration could breach the $3 million limit only with advance approval of the two appropriations panels.

Ex-Im Bank. Barred Export-Import Bank financing for exports to several countries, including Iraq. Congress had barred U.S. aid to Iraq, but the administration interpreted that ban as not applying to Ex-Im, which had made millions of dollars of loans for exports to that country. The president could waive the prohibition if it would be in the U.S. national interest.

- Approved a limit of $615 million on "direct" subsidized loans by the Export-Import Bank to finance exports of U.S. products. The administration had opposed funding direct loans but eventually relented to congressional pressure.

War Victims. Appropriated $5 million to provide prosthetic devices and other aid for civilian victims of Third World conflicts.

ASHA. Appropriated $35 million for the American Schools and Hospitals Abroad (ASHA) program. The program, which subsidized overseas private institutions that were based in the United States or had American boards of directors, was often controversial because of allegations that members of Congress, particularly senators, exerted undue political pressure on awarding AID grants.

Ireland. Appropriated $20 million for the International Fund for Ireland, established in 1986 to promote economic development in Northern Ireland and the border areas of the Republic of Ireland. The administration had tried to end the program, which was popular on Capitol Hill. But conferees warned that sustaining Hill support for the fund would be difficult unless other countries contributed as well. They noted that the $20 million would put U.S. total contributions to the fund at $150 million — more than 85 percent of the fund's working capital.

Anti-Narcotics. Approved $125 million — transferred from the Pentagon — for military, law enforcement and other aid to Bolivia, Colombia and Peru. That aid was earmarked to help those countries fight cocaine production and trafficking. Narcotics-related aid to those three countries was exempted from a law barring aid for nations that fell more than a year behind in repaying U.S. loans.

- Allowed the president to use money from the State Department's international narcotics program to pay for U.S. participation in an international "anti-narcotics strike force." Michael Manley, prime minister of Jamaica, had proposed an international police force that would help the governments of narcotics-producing countries combat the drug trade.

Afghan Aid. Earmarked $70 million for continued U.S. "humanitarian" aid to Afghan refugees. However, the conferees complained about "drift and uncertainty" in U.S. policy toward Afghanistan since the Soviet withdrawal in February 1989, and they called for better management of the aid by the Afghan resistance groups with headquarters in Pakistan.

This aid was in addition to military assistance the United States provided Moslem rebels in Afghanistan. The companion defense appropriations bill (HR 3072 — PL 101-165) included $280 million for covert CIA aid to the guerrillas.

Pakistan. Extended for another year, until April 1, 1991, Pakistan's exemption from U.S. nuclear non-proliferation laws. Under existing law, the president could not provide aid to Pakistan unless he certified to Congress that it was not pursuing a program to develop nuclear weapons. Pakistan reportedly was trying to develop such weapons, but Congress for years had exempted it, primarily because of Pakistan's crucial role in providing covert military aid to the rebels in neighboring Afghanistan.

Aid Prohibitions. Allowed U.S. aid to Lebanon, Liberia, Somalia, the Sudan, Uganda and Zaire only if the administration sought advance approval from the appropriations committees.

Refugee Aid. Approved $46 million for four programs to aid refugees from Southeast Asia. Another $25 million was earmarked to help Israel handle Soviet, Eastern European and other refugees.

Conferees included a statement in their report calling on the administration to spend $5 million on sanitation, housing and medical supplies for the Kurds, who fled oppression and chemical weapons attacks in their native Iraq.

Refugee Admission. Took steps to make getting into the United States easier for certain categories of foreign nationals with a well-founded fear of persecution. Included would be Soviet Jews, Evangelical Christians and other potential targets of persecution in the Soviet Union. Certain categories of nationals of Vietnam, Laos and Cambodia also would be presumed to be persecuted.

1991 Aid Appropriations

Congress in 1990 cleared a $15.4 billion fiscal 1991 foreign aid appropriations bill (HR 5114 — PL 101-513).

For a brief period earlier in the year, foreign aid had become popular on Capitol Hill. As the Soviet bloc began to break apart, lawmakers scrambled to support new assistance for the fledgling democracies in Eastern Europe.

But that popularity lasted only until the summer budget crunch, which renewed the customary skepticism toward spending abroad the dollars of U.S. taxpayers. Both houses of Congress approved the final bill with a conspicuous lack of enthusiasm.

Kenya Aid Under Scrutiny

Responding to congressional pressure, the Bush administration suspended military aid to Kenya in July 1990 to protest a crackdown on dissent by the one-party government of President Daniel arap Moi. But the administration lifted the freeze in February 1991.

Kenya was one of the largest recipients of U.S. aid in sub-Saharan Africa. Excluding food aid, its total allocation for fiscal 1990 was $10 million in military assistance and $35 million for economic development.

The country's relative stability had made it attractive for investment, and it was one of the largest sub-Saharan importers of U.S. products. Its pro-Western government and its strategic Indian Ocean port of Mombassa added to Kenya's importance to the United States.

But after surviving a coup attempt in 1982, Moi pushed through the National Assembly a ban on rival political parties. U.S. ties to the nation became strained in 1989 and 1990 as Moi stepped up his opposition to multi-party politics, which he claimed would fuel tribal factionalism.

In July 1990, the Bush administration expressed its distress over the detention of political opponents and the violence, and it put a freeze on $5 million in military aid that Kenya had not yet received in fiscal 1990 funds.

After the summer violence, members of Congress working on the fiscal 1991 foreign aid appropriations bill (HR 5114 — PL 101-513) attached a human rights proviso to the $15 million allocation in military aid for Kenya and its share of $800 million in economic aid for sub-Saharan Africa.

The proviso specified that before Kenya could get the money, President Bush had to certify a number of human rights improvements — including that Moi's regime had charged and tried or released all prisoners; stopped physical abuse of prisoners; restored the independence of the judiciary; and permitted freedom of expression.

After Congress adjourned, a three-member Senate delegation visited Kenya in November and warned that Moi's refusal to permit political pluralism was jeopardizing both its military aid and its share of the increased U.S. economic development aid for Africa.

In February 1991, however, the Bush administration lifted the freeze on the $5 million in fiscal 1990 funds. According to newspaper reports, the aid was renewed because of Kenya's support for U.S. policies in the Persian Gulf, its increased anti-terrorist activities and its granting of refuge to Libyan dissidents who had taken part in a failed U.S.-backed effort to destabilize the government of Col. Muammar el-Qaddafi.

As enacted, the spending bill included $369.7 million in aid for Eastern Europe, along with new help for Israel and other favored aid recipients. Most lawmakers welcomed those provisions. But the overall mood was perhaps best expressed by Rep. Clarence E. Miller, R-Ohio, who said during the House floor debate on the bill, "We simply do not have the resources to devote to other nations to the extent we have in the past."

That attitude was reflected in the total amount of aid provided in the bill, which was $129 million less than the administration request for fiscal 1991 and nearly $250 million below the figure approved by the House.

But the real threats to the measure in 1990 were the administration's proposals to secure loan forgiveness for Egypt, a key ally in the Persian Gulf crisis, and to maintain aid for El Salvador despite new concerns about human rights conditions in the Central American country. Heated debate surrounded both proposals.

House Action

The House passed a $15.6 billion foreign assistance appropriations bill, 308-117, on June 27. The House Appropriations Committee had reported a $15.8 billion version of the bill on June 21 (H Rept 101-553).

HR 5114 cut Bush's fiscal 1991 request for military aid to countries outside the Middle East by 13 percent, but the overall appropriation for foreign assistance was more than Bush requested. In effect, the measure shifted more than $400 million that Bush budgeted for security-oriented programs to fund economic development.

Before passage, members debated amendments on two controversial issues: aid for family planning overseas and for non-communist rebels in Cambodia.

Members argued over the White House policy of denying funds for family planning programs from public or private agencies that either promoted abortion or operated in countries with coercive family planning policies. Citing a critical need for large-scale family planning in Romania, critics of the policy offered a floor amendment that would have channeled $3 million for such activity through the United Nations Fund for Population Activities and the International Planned Parenthood Federation.

Both the Reagan and Bush administrations had opposed aid to the U.N. fund because it operated in China, where the government was criticized for allegedly supporting forced abortions and other coercive population control policies. And the White House opposed funding the planned parenthood organization because some of its affiliates offered abortion-related services. *(U.N. fund, box, p. 235)*

President Bush had vetoed a foreign aid bill in 1989, in part because it contained money for the U.N. fund. *(Fiscal 1990 foreign aid appropriations, p. 228)*

The House June 27 wanted to avoid a repeat of that veto in 1990. By a vote of 224-198, the House struck from the proposed amendment the earmarks for the two controversial organizations and voted instead to have other organizations administer the family planning aid. The underlying amendment was then approved by 406-11.

The House also voted to uphold existing administration policy toward Cambodia. Overriding the Appropriations Committee, the House June 27 adopted by 260-163 an amendment by Stephen J. Solarz, D-N.Y., that would allow up to $7 million to be given to the non-communist rebels fighting the government of Cambodia, provided that none of the funds reached the communist Khmer Rouge, which also was fighting the Cambodian government.

Earlier, Solarz and David R. Obey, D-Wis., chairman of the Appropriations Subcommittee on Foreign Operations, had worked out a compromise on providing Cambodian aid, but the Appropriations Committee had added a flat ban on such assistance during markup.

Solarz, chairman of the House Foreign Affairs Subcommittee on Asian and Pacific Affairs, had been the leading political patron since 1985 of aid to the non-communist forces fighting the government set up in Cambodia by Vietnam in 1979. The goal, said Solarz, was to prevent the Khmer Rouge, which had killed more than a million Cambodians when it ruled in 1975-79, from regaining control. *(Background, box, p. 244)*

The House left in the bill a committee-approved challenge to Bush over aid to El Salvador. The bill halved military aid to the government of President Alfredo Cristiani. In part, this reflected Democrats' anger over human rights violations by the Salvadoran military. It also reflected a desire to press Cristiani's government to negotiate a settlement with leftist guerrillas of that country's long and bloody civil war. *(El Salvador aid, p. 214)*

During wrap-up action, the House adopted by voice vote an amendment mandating a 2 percent cut in the bill's appropriations, but many programs were exempted. The amendment was a substitute for a proposal that would have cut by 10 percent all programs in the bill, with few exemptions. This would have reduced funds in the bill by $1.49 billion, as compared with the approximately $140 million reduction that was adopted.

Senate Action

The Senate passed a $15.5 billion foreign aid bill by a 76-23 vote on Oct. 24. The bill had been reported by the Appropriations Committee Oct. 10 (S Rept 101-519).

Senate passage came only after an attempt by two of the Senate's most powerful leaders to send a message of discontent to Israel and after a new clash between the administration and critics of its policy toward El Salvador.

The strained relations between the United States and Israel came under new pressure because of the surprise amendment cosponsored by Minority Leader Bob Dole, R-Kan., and Appropriations Chairman Robert C. Byrd, D-W.Va., and tabled only after a sharp debate. The amendment would have required the president to report to Congress on Israel's policy for housing Soviet immigrants. Aides said the amendment was clearly intended to send a message to Israel.

Byrd said he was "deeply disturbed" by recent events in Israel, including the killing of 21 Palestinian protesters by security forces on Oct. 8. The housing policy also had come under fire because Israeli Foreign Minister David Levy had backed away from a promise not to settle more Soviet immigrants in East Jerusalem. The pledge was made as part of an agreement under which Israel was to receive a $400 million housing loan guarantee.

Senators on Oct. 19 voted by a lopsided 90-8 margin to table the amendment.

In later debate, Byrd tried to strip from the bill an amendment, adopted previously by voice vote, to authorize a defense stock drawdown of $700 million in military equipment for Israel. The attempt was rejected Oct. 22 by a near-unanimous 1-97.

Controversy over U.N. Population Fund

Members of Congress who sparred regularly over abortion and family planning during debate on domestic legislation held similar skirmishes in the foreign policy arena during the Bush administration. *(Abortion, pp. 594, 597)*

Like his predecessor, Ronald Reagan, President Bush opposed federal aid for abortions, at home or abroad. The administration opposed funding the United Nations Fund for Population Activities (UNFPA), which operated in China, where the government was criticized for allegedly supporting forced abortions and other coercive population control policies. And the Bush team opposed funding the private International Planned Parenthood Federation (IPPF) because some of its affiliates offered abortion-related services.

Bush vetoed the fiscal 1990 foreign aid appropriations bill over a provision mandating a $15 million contribution to the U.N. fund. And the administration threatened to do the same in other years if funds for the two agencies were included in foreign aid bills.

Mexico City Policy

UNFPA — which later was renamed the U.N. Population Fund — was the largest multilateral agency aiding family planning. The agency gave assistance to 140 developing nations. The United States had helped set up the UNFPA in 1969 and for a decade was the agency's largest contributor. But in the mid-1980s, Washington shifted gears on international family planning policy.

In a 1984 U.N. population conference in Mexico City, the Reagan administration announced that it would not provide funds to private organizations overseas that offered abortion-related services. This policy effectively cut off funds to the IPPF.

Also at the Mexico City conference, the administration reversed longstanding policy and challenged the assumption that population booms deterred economic development in poor countries. Population expansion was inherently a "neutral" phenomenon, the administration argued. While family planning could contribute to population stability, the White House said, free-market economic policies were the "natural mechanism for slowing population growth."

The Bush administration showed little interest in reversing the Mexico City policy.

China Controversy

The China controversy erupted in January 1985, when media reports revealed that the Beijing government's one-couple, one-child policy included forced sterilizations, abortions and even infanticide. Beijing vehemently denied condoning such actions. The UNFPA denied supporting abortion as a method of family planning. But the Reagan administration withheld $10 million of the $46 million that Congress had appropriated for the agency for fiscal 1985. The $10 million was equal to the U.N. agency's program in China.

Congress subsequently enacted legislation that led to a total funding cutoff. An amendment by then-Rep. Jack F. Kemp, R-N.Y., and Sen. Bob Kasten, R-Wis., to a fiscal 1985 supplemental appropriations bill (PL 99-88) prohibited funding of any organization that supported programs that included forced abortions or involuntary sterilizations. The provision also stated that the determination was up to the president or the secretary of state. *(Congress and the Nation Vol. VII, p. 193)*

In November 1989, abortion rights and family planning groups thought they had scored a victory when the House and the Senate voted to mandate a $15 million contribution to the U.N. agency in the fiscal 1990 foreign aid spending bill. The amendment stipulated that the money had to be kept in a separate account and could not be used in China.

But anti-abortion groups strongly opposed the provision, and Bush vetoed the bill, asserting that U.S. policy should warn "all family planning organizations that they must refrain from supporting coercive programs."

Congress passed a new version of the bill, minus the population provision, and Bush signed it into law. *(1989 action, p. 228)*

Attempts to resurrect the funding in 1990 failed, as did efforts in 1991 and 1992. *(1991 action, p. 269; 1992 action, p. 271)*

The Senate on Oct. 19 also adopted on a **74-25 (R 19-25; D 55-0) key vote** an amendment to require a 50 percent cut in military aid to El Salvador, which was worked out during subcommittee consideration. Senators the same day rejected 39-58 a milder, administration-backed amendment. *(1990 key votes, p. 1039)*

The House had signaled that the congressional mood on El Salvador had changed, when it attached a similar amendment to its foreign aid bill. The administration undertook negotiations with lawmakers from both chambers in an attempt to moderate the House-passed provision. But the negotiations never gained momentum, in part because the administration was diverted by the crisis in the Persian Gulf. *(Persian Gulf War, p. 299)*

The Senate bill also backed an administration plan to forgive Egypt's $6.7 billion military debt, a proposal that the House had deferred after intense criticism. Bush argued that a grant of debt relief was needed to reward

Egypt's President Hosni Mubarak, who was a linchpin of Arab support for the U.S. response to Iraq's invasion of Kuwait.

During floor consideration, the Senate Oct. 19 adopted 94-2 an amendment to delay the forgiveness of Egyptian debt until Dec. 31, 1990, to allow the president time to secure a multilateral agreement on Egypt's international debt crisis. An amendment that would have struck from the bill the provisions on forgiving Egypt's debt and required a restructuring of the debt instead was rejected the same day on a **42-55 (R 10-34; D 32-21) key vote**.

The Senate Oct. 22 adopted 95-3 an amendment by Byrd raising the level of tied-aid credits — funds that, if used, had to be spent on U.S. goods and services — from $50 million to $300 million.

The Appropriations Committee had included in the bill $15 million for the U.N. population agency, but the money was removed during floor consideration.

Conference, Final Action

The House adopted the conference report (H Rept 101-968) by a vote of 188-162 on Oct. 27. The Senate adopted the report the same day without a recorded vote. Bush signed HR 5114 Nov. 5.

The final provisions of the $15.4 billion foreign aid spending bill had been crafted in a grueling all-night session of House and Senate conferees Oct. 25-26.

The conferees approved, with minor modifications, the amendment reducing military aid to El Salvador as well as the administration's plan to forgive Egypt's $6.7 billion military debt. But agreement on both amendments came only after some verbal brawling and several closed-door caucuses.

The White House had underestimated the depth of congressional opposition to generosity abroad when it pressed for an amendment to forgive Egypt's debt. Although the amendment was moderated in conference, many lawmakers said it accounted for the relatively narrow margin by which the House passed the conference report.

Lawmakers, especially in the House, strongly objected to forgiving the debt outright, instead of restructuring payment terms. Obey, who chaired the House-Senate conference on the bill and fought hard to alter the terms of the forgiveness plan, said after the vote, "If this bill had come up any other day than the last day [of the session], it would have been defeated."

In the conference, Obey added language that provided for a six-month payment moratorium, although the president also would get the power he sought to forgive the debt. In addition, Obey won approval for a provision granting similar presidential authority to adjust Poland's debt, which he called the most important provision in the bill.

Rep. Mickey Edwards, Okla., the senior Republican on Obey's subcommittee, also was exercised over the Egyptian debt proposal, especially over its timing. Speaking just hours after the House approved the conference report on the budget-reconciliation bill (HR 5835), he said it was difficult to justify debt forgiveness "when we have just made a substantial increase in the taxes on the American people."

A second controversial provision, requiring the administration to withhold half of the $85 million military aid package for El Salvador in fiscal 1991, triggered broad Republican opposition. That provision also was softened in conference, but conferees retained a provision ensuring that Congress would have final say about resuming the assistance. As part of the compromise, Leahy promised to request expedited procedures for restoring the aid, if the circumstances arose.

The White House, which found the El Salvador aid restrictions onerous, was constrained from making good on a threatened veto because of the crucial importance of the debt relief for Egypt. Congressional opponents of the Egypt provision were likewise limited in fighting the measure because of a range of popular items that were in the bill — including the El Salvador restrictions and important new programs for Israel.

While the foreign aid bill represented a concession to budget realities in the United States, it also was an acknowledgment of the changes in the geopolitical landscape during the year. With the passing of the Cold War, Congress had grown increasingly dubious of the need for foreign military grants, aside from those provided to allies in the Middle East. Excluding the $3.1 billion specified for Israel and Egypt, the bill cut the administration request for grants by nearly 25 percent and replaced some of the grants with low-interest loans.

Perhaps more important, the legislation reduced by $400 million the administration request for Economic Support Fund (ESF) aid. Such aid was widely used, especially by the Reagan and Bush administrations, to bolster the economies of U.S. military allies. Aside from the slightly more than $2 billion in ESF funds earmarked for Israel and Egypt, the State Department was given only about $1 billion to spread among other countries.

Having taken money from security-related accounts such as ESF, Congress redirected the money toward a variety of purposes. The $369.7 million in assistance for Eastern Europe represented a compromise between the House- and Senate-passed figures and a $140 million increase over the administration's original request. The $70 million request for a U.S. contribution for the European Development Bank, which provided loans for Eastern European countries, also was fully funded.

Major Provisions

The final version of the foreign aid appropriations bill (HR 5114 — PL 101-513) provided $15.4 billion in fiscal 1991 aid. This included $1.92 billion in multilateral aid, $7.30 billion in bilateral aid, $5.38 billion in military aid and $750 million for the Export-Import Bank direct loan program.

Major provisions of HR 5114:

Israel. Earmarked $3 billion in military and security-related assistance for Israel. Israel was permitted to use up to $200 million in Economic Support Funds for its own defense purposes. The bill also authorized Israel to receive an accelerated disbursement of $1.7 billion in military financing.

- Authorized the president to transfer up to $700 million of defense supplies to Israel and to preposition another $300 million worth of U.S. defense stockpiles in Israel.

Egypt. Earmarked $2.15 billion in military and security-related assistance for Egypt.

- Provided for a six-month moratorium for payments on Egypt's $6.7 billion military debt but also gave the president authority to forgive the debt.

El Salvador. Withheld half of the $85 million military aid package to El Salvador. The bill barred all military

Disagreement over Notification Issue

One of the most significant issues stemming from the Iran-contra affair concerned the procedure for Congress to be told about CIA covert operations.

A 1980 law had required the president to tell the House and Senate Intelligence committees in advance about all covert operations. Under exceptional circumstances, the president could delay notice until after a covert action had begun — but he must then give notice in a "timely manner." *(Congress and the Nation Vol. V, p. 174)*

In the case of U.S. covert arms sales to Iran, President Ronald Reagan waited 10 months to formally notify Congress and did so only after a Beirut newspaper revealed the sales in November 1986.

In their report, the Iran-contra investigating committees insisted that Congress be told about covert operations — and that advance consultation with Congress might improve administration decision making. The panels recommended legislation putting a limit of 48 hours on the time the president could wait before telling Congress about covert actions. A bill was passed by the Senate in 1988, but the measure died in the House. *(Congress and the Nation Vol. VII, p. 244)*

In 1989, leaders of the Senate Intelligence Committee tried to get Bush to agree to strict guidelines for notifying Congress of covert actions. The panel was blocked for months by legal objections from White House lawyers. That angered the committee leaders, who resurrected the 48-hour bill in October and attached it to their version of the intelligence authorization bill (HR 2748). *(Fiscal 1990 intelligence authorization, p. 239)*

As it was intended to do, that move got the attention of the president, who agreed to some of the guidelines the committee had wanted. In an Oct. 30 letter to the two Intelligence committees, Bush agreed to respect the 1980 law requiring him to tell Congress about covert operations in advance. Under special emergency circumstances, Bush said, he might have to wait for "a few days." Bush also held out the prospect that he might cite his constitutional powers over foreign affairs to delay notice indefinitely.

Senate Intelligence Committee leaders accepted Bush's pledge, but senior Democrats on the counterpart House panel remained dissatisfied. Lee H. Hamilton, D-Ind., who once chaired the House Intelligence Committee as well as the Iran-contra panel, said that the conflict over Congress' right to know about covert operations was likely to continue no matter what legal requirements were imposed on the president because each branch saw its rights and responsibilities at issue.

And continue it did. In 1990, Congress attached to the fiscal 1991 intelligence authorization bill (S 2834) new rules for reporting covert actions to Congress. The bill, which would have repealed the 1980 law, required a written "finding" from the president on covert actions, notification "in timely fashion" and prior notification except "on rare occasions."

It also required that Congress be notified of any request to a foreign government or private citizen to conduct a covert action on behalf of the United States. Bush objected to this and pocket-vetoed the bill. In his memorandum of disapproval, Bush also objected to the conference report's definition of what was a "timely" report. *(1991 intelligence authorization, p. 242)*

A compromise was finally enacted in 1991 as part of a revised fiscal 1991 intelligence authorization measure (HR 1455 — PL 102-88). The administration was required to report all covert activities to Congress and to authorize the actions in advance with a written presidential finding. In the finding, the president had to determine that the covert action was necessary "to support identifiable foreign policy objectives" of the United States. He was not allowed to authorize covert acts that violated the Constitution or any laws.

The revised measure required the president to notify Congress "in a timely fashion" whenever he failed to provide advance notification of a covert operation. But report language accompanying the measure simply took note of an unresolved dispute between Congress and the president as to whether such notification must be given within a few days. *(Revised 1991 intelligence authorization, p. 280)*

aid if the El Salvador government did not fully investigate the 1989 murders of six Jesuit priests and two others or did not participate in talks aimed at ending the country's civil war. *(El Salvador aid, p. 214)*

The conference agreement provided for expedited procedures for restoring the aid, under certain conditions. It also excluded all military assistance already appropriated but not yet delivered.

Cambodia. Appropriated $20 million in overt assistance for the non-communist resistance in Cambodia. Funds were to be subject to congressional oversight.

Eastern Europe. Appropriated $369.7 million in assistance for Eastern Europe.

- Gave the president authority to reduce Poland's $2.85 billion official debt.
- Appropriated $70 million for a U.S. contribution for the European Development Bank, which provided loans for Eastern European countries but conditioned the U.S. contribution on progress in easing Poland's debt.
- Extended the authority of the Export-Import Bank and the Overseas Private Investment Corporation to operate in Eastern Europe.

China. Withheld some contributions to the World Bank's International Development Association if that agency made new loans to China that were not for basic human needs. The president could waive the provision if he certified that it was in the national interest. Fifteen days prior to the release of the funds, the president was to report his finding to the pertinent congressional committees.

Sub-Saharan Africa. Appropriated $800 million for the Development Fund for Africa, more than $230 million above the administration's request.

Zaire. Permitted development aid to Zaire but allowed it to be provided only through non-governmental organizations, private volunteer organizations and universities. The conference provision softened the outright prohibitions on U.S. aid approved by both the House and Senate.

Persian Gulf Crisis. Earmarked $35 million in economic aid for Jordan but dropped a House-passed $50 million military aid earmark for the kingdom. The Senate Appropriations Committee said in its report that it was disturbed by Amman's "unwillingness to comply fully" with the U.N.-approved embargo against Iraq.

- Waived a ban on military sales to Qatar, a small, independent state bordering Saudi Arabia.
- Set aside $10 million to provide health insurance benefits for Americans being detained in Kuwait and Iraq and those being held hostage in Lebanon, and their families. The detainees also could receive a salary from the government, at an annual rate of up to $32,000, for the period of their captivity.
- Granted the president authority to cut off trade with nations not complying with the global embargo against Baghdad.

Anti-Drug Strategy. Appropriated, as part of Bush's Andean Initiative drug strategy, $118 million for military aid to Colombia, Peru and Bolivia. *(Andean Initiative, p. 255)*

- Restricted funding for the State Department's Bureau of International Narcotics until it provided a report detailing steps being taken to correct its "management deficiencies."

Ireland. Provided, over the administration's opposition, $20 million for the International Fund for Ireland.

Iran-Contra Legacy

Congress in 1989 approved three measures to close legal loopholes that became evident during investigations into the Iran-contra affair.

The following year Congress attempted to rewrite the rules for executive branch reporting of covert actions, but President Bush pocket-vetoed the bill. *(Notification issues, box, p. 237)*

The Iran-contra scandal had involved secret U.S. arms sales to Iran — a country many thought to be a hated enemy of the United States — and the diversion of some profits from the sales to aid the contra rebels in Nicaragua — despite a congressional ban on U.S. assistance. The elaborate policy was conducted in secret by the Reagan White House in 1985 and 1986. *(Congress and the Nation Vol. VII, p. 253)*

In the wake of the 1987 investigations into the affair, the Reagan administration feared that Congress would rush to load up the statute books with hastily drafted, ill-considered "reforms" limiting the president's foreign policy powers. But it took Congress two years and much compromising to enact, as a result of the Iran-contra affair, restrictions on arms sales, internal operations of the CIA and foreign aid.

None of the measures was expected to force significant changes in U.S. foreign policy or in routine administration actions. But congressional sponsors said that each of the new provisions would make it more difficult for administrations to repeat the mistakes that got the Reagan White House into such trouble.

Arms Sales

In the closing hours of the session, both chambers gave final approval to legislation (HR 91 — PL 101-222) meant to tighten controls on arms sales to Iran and other countries linked to international terrorism. Similar legislation had died in 1988 as Congress rushed to adjourn before the elections.

The House passed HR 91 (H Rept 101-296) by voice vote on Oct. 23. The Senate passed an amended version by voice vote Nov. 22, and the House cleared the bill later that day.

Bush signed the bill into law Dec. 12, despite complaints from some of his lawyers that it posed an unconstitutional infringement on his powers to conduct foreign affairs.

Major provisions of HR 91:

- Prohibited all foreign aid to countries that were found by the secretary of state to support international terrorism. Countries on the list were Cuba, Iran, Libya, North Korea, South Yemen and Syria.
- Banned government and commercial arms sales to countries on the terrorism list. The president could waive this ban if he reported to Congress, 15 days in advance, that doing so in a particular case was "essential" to U.S. national security. This ban did not apply to covert sales made by the CIA under a presidential order (called a "finding"). However, the president was required by a 1980 law to tell Congress about all covert actions. *(Congress and the Nation Vol. V, p. 174)*
- Imposed criminal penalties of 10 years in prison and a $1 million fine, and civil penalties of up to $500,000, for persons found to have violated the prohibitions. The penalties applied to private individuals or government officials.
- Required quarterly reports to Congress on transfers of U.S. arms from one foreign country to another. For example, such a report would be required if Israel sold U.S.-made weapons to Turkey. These reports also had to cover any transfers of weapons from the Defense Department to other agencies. In the Iran-contra affair, Congress was never told of Israel's sales of U.S.-made missiles to Iran. Nor was Congress told that the Pentagon gave missiles to the CIA, which in turn shipped them to Iran.
- Prohibited the president from using the 1868 Hostage Act to use illegal means to free U.S. citizens held hostage in foreign countries.

CIA Watchdog Provision

In their final report, the Iran-contra investigating committees recommended legislation establishing an office of independent inspector general at the CIA, to be appointed by the president and confirmed by the Senate.

The CIA had had an inspector general for years, but he was appointed by and under the control of the agency director. The Iran-contra committees said that the in-house watchdog did not have "the manpower, resources or tenacity to acquire key facts" about the activities of several CIA officials implicated in the scandal.

The committees' recommendation generated little interest on Capitol Hill until 1989, when the House and Senate Intelligence committees each had run-ins with the CIA over the activities of the existing inspector general. Exercising their clout, the committees attached inspector general provisions to routine legislation authorizing funds in fiscal 1990 for the CIA and other intelligence agencies. Bush signed the bill into law (HR 2748 — PL 101-193) despite CIA objections. *(Details, below)*

'Leveraging' Foreign Aid

Congress in 1989 considered two proposals aimed at preventing administration officials from using indirect means to carry out policies that the U.S. government legally could not conduct itself. Both proposals were in response to the actions of former White House aide Oliver L. North, who directed the Reagan administration's covert campaign of aiding the Nicaraguan contras at a time when Congress barred official U.S. assistance to them.

One proposal, offered by Sen. Daniel Patrick Moynihan, D-N.Y., surfaced in various forms during the year as an amendment to the State Department authorization bill. The essence of Moynihan's proposal was to make it illegal for administration officials to direct money — from any source — to any foreigner who was legally barred from receiving official U.S. aid.

Had the Moynihan language been in effect during the mid-1980s, North's fund-raising efforts in behalf of the contras probably would have been illegal.

The Bush administration objected vehemently to the Moynihan proposal, insisting that it represented an unconstitutional infringement on the president's authority to conduct foreign policy. The administration forced Moynihan to accept numerous changes reducing the potential scope of his amendment.

But even with the changes, Bush vetoed the State Department bill (HR 1487) when it reached his desk. Moynihan agreed to drop his amendment to clear the way for a new State bill (HR 3792 — PL 101-246). *(State Department authorization, p. 247)*

A related, but more limited, proposal did become law at the end of the session. Sponsored primarily by David R. Obey, D-Wis., chairman of the House Appropriations Subcommittee on Foreign Operations, that proposal was widely known as the "leveraging" amendment. It was attached to the fiscal 1990 foreign aid appropriations bill.

In its original form, that amendment had two parts. One barred the use of foreign aid on behalf of "any military or foreign policy activity which is contrary to United States law." The original leveraging amendment also barred the use of foreign aid to solicit funds from anyone (including another government) to support a military or foreign policy that was prohibited by U.S. law. As with the Moynihan amendment, the administration opposed Obey's leveraging language as unconstitutional and demanded numerous changes.

Bush's veto of the original aid bill (HR 2939) — in part because of the Obey language — led to a significantly narrower amendment, barring the administration from providing aid to any foreign government "in exchange for" that government carrying out an action that it legally could not undertake on its own.

At the request of Secretary of State James A. Baker III, Obey also stated on the House floor that the "in exchange for" clause was intended to refer to a "direct verbal or written agreement" between the U.S. government and a foreigner. Bush signed the foreign aid bill (HR 3743 — PL 101-167) on Nov. 21. *(Fiscal 1990 foreign aid appropriations, p. 228)*

1990 Intelligence Authorization

Over the objections of the CIA and some of its closest allies, Congress in 1989 cleared legislation mandating appointment of an independent watchdog at the spy agency — and ensuring that the congressional Intelligence committees could review his or her work.

The inspector general provisions were attached to the fiscal 1990 authorization bill (HR 2748 — PL 101-193) for the civilian and military intelligence agencies.

As signed into law, HR 2748 established an office of CIA inspector general, which would be appointed by the president and confirmed by the Senate. It also required the CIA to give the House and Senate Intelligence committees access to the inspector general's investigative reports.

As in the past, the bill authorized a secret amount of money for the CIA and other agencies, including the National Security Agency, National Reconnaissance Office, Defense Mapping Agency, Defense Intelligence Agency and the intelligence branches of the armed services.

It was estimated in 1989 that U.S. intelligence-gathering operations cost at least $25 billion annually, all of it hidden in the Defense Department budget and most of it used to collect information used by the military. Only a small portion — less than 1 percent by some estimates — was used for controversial "covert" operations, such as funding of guerrillas in Afghanistan, Angola and elsewhere.

House Action

The inspector general became a major institutional issue for both the House and Senate Intelligence committees as they wrote their versions of the usually routine authorization bill.

The House panel drafted its requirement after the CIA refused a request for details on activities of the inspector general, who was assigned to root out mismanagement. The issue had arisen early in 1989 when the Subcommittee on Oversight and Evaluation, chaired by Dave McCurdy, D-Okla., asked the CIA for more information on the activities of the inspector general than was provided by a semiannual report required in 1988 by Congress. McCurdy's panel requested a routine listing of investigative reports by the inspector general, and then for copies of any reports that the subcommittee wanted.

CIA Director William H. Webster refused both subcommittee requests, and after fruitless negotiations, McCurdy's panel suggested an amendment to the authorization bill requiring the CIA to hand over the reports. The full Intelligence Committee agreed, provoking an unusual letter from Webster in which he reportedly complained that the committee was taking a step that was "unnecessary, unwise and not well thought out." The unclassified

North Convicted on Iran-Contra Charges ...

Former White House aide Oliver L. North was convicted in 1989 on charges stemming from the Iran-contra affair. But a federal appeals court overturned his conviction in 1990, ruling that his trial may have been tainted by North's immunized testimony on Capitol Hill.

Independent counsel Lawrence E. Walsh petitioned the Supreme Court to overturn the appeals court's decision, but the Supreme Court in 1991 refused to hear the case. All charges against North subsequently were dropped, after Walsh concluded that it would be nearly impossible to demonstrate that witnesses who testified in North's 1989 trial had not been influenced by North's televised testimony to Congress.

North, a former Marine Corps lieutenant colonel and National Security Council (NSC) aide, was convicted on May 4, 1989, of three felony counts: altering and destroying NSC documents, aiding and abetting the obstruction of a congressional inquiry into the Iran-contra affair and illegally accepting a home security system as a gift. North was sentenced to 1,200 hours of community service and fined $150,000.

North had been fired from the NSC job with the initial disclosure on Nov. 25, 1986, that he helped mastermind the selling of arms to Iran in an effort to win release of U.S. hostages and the funneling of some of the proceeds of the arms sales to the U.S.-backed contras in Nicaragua.

His boss, national security adviser John M. Poindexter, resigned and was ultimately convicted of felony charges for his role in the Iran-contra affair. Poindexter had his conviction overturned on the same grounds as the North reversal.

The Iran-contra scandal and investigations shadowed President Ronald Reagan for most of his last two years in office. Walsh continued his investigation through the four years of the Bush administration. During the final month of his presidency, Bush pardoned top-level officials charged in the scandal. *(Iran-contra pardons, p. 284)*

Immunity Issue

In December 1986, the House and Senate designated members of two special committees to conduct a joint investigation of the affair; the committees were officially constituted when the 100th Congress convened in January 1987.

Also in December, a three-judge panel picked Walsh, a deputy attorney general in the Eisenhower administration and one-time president of the American Bar Association, as independent counsel to investigate the affair and bring any prosecutions.

The investigating committees and Walsh clashed over potential witnesses during congressional hearings. The committees wanted North and other key figures to testify before them, but Walsh strongly objected. In part because of Walsh's arguments, the committees delayed North's testimony for several months and initially questioned Poindexter, a retired rear admiral, in closed session.

While members of Congress publicly voiced little opposition to immunity for North, members of the committees were engaged in a closed-door struggle over the issue. According to accounts that surfaced long after the committees completed their reports in 1987, many Democrats on the House panel had strong reservations about granting North immunity for his testimony. Support for immunity was stronger on the Senate panel, especially among Republicans. In the end, immunity was supported by unanimous votes on the Senate committee and majority votes in the House.

More than 20 witnesses received immunity in the Iran-contra hearings, most of them lower-rung participants whom Walsh also had allowed immunity. At the time, committee members insisted that the witnesses would not necessarily escape prosecution.

The 1970 law (PL 91-452) under which committees were allowed to grant immunity forbade the use of any compelled testimony against a defendant. But it also stated that a witness could be prosecuted for crimes mentioned in his testimony if the evidence used in the prosecution was developed independently of the testimony. This type of "use" immunity was challenged in the 1972 Supreme Court case of *Kastigar v. United States.* The Court upheld the practice so long as the government showed in any subsequent prosecution that it had obtained its evidence from sources independent of the testimony given under a grant of immunity. *(1970 law, Congress and the Nation Vol. III, p. 272;*

letter to individual committee members was leaked to the press in mid-July.

As reported Aug. 3 from the House Intelligence Committee (HR 2748 — H Rept 101-215, Part I), the House bill required the agency to give the panel any investigative report it requested.

In other action, the House committee approved an amendment barring the CIA from spending any money to intervene in the elections in Nicaragua and specifically barring use of the CIA's contingency fund, which normally was used to start covert operations. *(Nicaragua policy, p. 219)*

The House committee joined its Senate counterpart in complaining that "bureaucratic infighting" was hampering efforts to protect overseas U.S. diplomatic missions against espionage and terrorism. Both committees said

... But Appeals Court Overturned Decision

case summary, Congress and the Nation Vol. III, p. 309)

Walsh's staff went to great lengths to shield themselves from the overwhelming media coverage of the congressional hearings. The precautions were designed to refute the anticipated arguments from any convicted defendants that prosecutors had improperly used information gained from the supposedly immunized testimony before the congressional committees.

Conviction Overturned

But the federal appeals court cited the congressional panels' grant of limited immunity in their decision to overturn North's conviction. In a split ruling July 20, 1990, a three-judge panel of the U.S. Court of Appeals for the District of Columbia Circuit set aside all three convictions against North and ordered a lower court to re-examine all the evidence used against him to determine whether any of it was influenced by North's immunized testimony before Congress.

Before North's trial began, U.S. District Judge Gerhard A. Gesell had heard three days of arguments on whether North's congressional testimony had influenced prosecutors and witnesses.

But in the appeals court's opinion, the majority judges strongly criticized Gesell's original hearing on the issue.

"A central problem in this case is that many grand jury and trial witnesses were thoroughly soaked in North's immunized testimony, but no effort was made to determine what effect, if any, this extensive exposure had on their testimony," the court majority wrote.

"Papers filed under seal indicate that officials and attorneys from the Department of Justice, the Central Intelligence Agency, the White House and the Department of State gathered, studied and summarized North's immunized testimony in order to prepare themselves or their superiors and colleagues for their testimony before the investigating committees and the grand jury."

The appeals court said Gesell should not have focused on what the prosecutors might have learned from North's congressional testimony, but on what all witnesses might have picked up from the televised hearings or how their memories might have been refreshed by hearing North.

The judges gave several examples, including the trial testimony of Robert C. McFarlane, Poindexter's predecessor as national security adviser. They said McFarlane had altered his testimony before the congressional committees after listening to North testify and that Gessell made "no effort . . . to determine what use, if any, this government witness made of North's testimony in his trial testimony."

The appeals judges said that Gesell had to review the testimony witness by witness and, if necessary, line by line. The prosecution had to show that no use whatsoever was made of any of the immunized testimony by the independent counsel's staff or by any witness. The rule also held true for grand jury proceedings.

The opinion was signed by Judges David B. Sentelle and Laurence H. Silberman — both Reagan appointees.

In dissent, Judge Patricia M. Wald, an appointee of President Jimmy Carter, argued that North had received a fair trial. "The majority effectively cuts off the trial judge's discretion in choosing the most practical means of ensuring defendant's *Kastigar* rights," she wrote, "and in so doing it makes a subsequent trial of any congressionally immunized witness virtually impossible."

Walsh appealed the decision to the Supreme Court, but on May 28, 1991, the high court refused to hear the case, letting stand the appeals court ruling. On Sept. 16, 1991, Gesell dropped all charges against North at Walsh's request.

Poindexter Case

Poindexter was convicted on April 7, 1990, of five felony counts of conspiracy, obstruction of Congress and lying to Congress. He was sentenced to six months in prison.

On Nov. 15, 1991, the U.S. Court of Appeals overturned Poindexter's conviction on the grounds that his trial may have been tainted by his testimony to Congress. On Dec. 7, 1992, the Supreme Court declined to review the decision, and Walsh said he would move promptly to dismiss the case.

---

that the CIA's Security Evaluation Office — established by Webster to assess security threats to diplomatic posts and to set standards for protecting them — had become embroiled in jurisdictional disputes with the State Department. Battling between the agencies, the House committee said, had "frustrated progress toward security objections which are clearly in the national interest." In diplomatic language, the committee said the State Department should end its refusal to cooperate with the Security Evaluation Office.

The House Armed Services Committee, which shared jurisdiction over the bill, reported it (H Rept 101-215, Part II) on Sept. 13.

The House approved HR 2748 on Oct. 12 by a 369-31 vote. The administration's complaint that the requirement that Congress be given the reports of the CIA inspector general was unconstitutional won no sympathy from members. No one moved to strip the requirement from the bill.

The House adopted only one significant amendment, requiring the CIA director to conduct random tests of drug use among agency employees.

Senate Action

The Senate Intelligence Committee spent several months dueling with the administration before finalizing its version of the intelligence authorization bill.

Moving to close a possible loophole in existing law, the committee included in its initial version of the bill (S 1324 — S Rept 101-78), reported July 14, a provision barring the administration from using the CIA contingency fund to start a covert operation without first telling Congress.

Under a 1980 law, the administration was supposed to tell Congress in advance about covert operations — but it could delay notification in an emergency, so long as it told Congress in a "timely" manner. Many covert operations got their initial funding through the CIA's contingency account, but the 1980 law appeared to give the administration flexibility to avoid telling Congress when it launched such actions.

The committee also warned that it might revive legislation passed by the Senate in 1988 that would have required the president to notify Congress within 48 hours of all covert operations. *(Congress and the Nation Vol. VII, p. 244)*

The panel followed through on its threat in October. When the bill returned to the Intelligence Committee after being reviewed and reported Sept. 29 by the Armed Services Committee (S Rept 101-151), the committee removed the contingency fund provision, put in its place the entire text of the 1988 bill and ordered the bill reported (S Rept 101-174) Oct. 17.

This move got the administration's attention and a round of negotiations ensued. Further incentive to settle their differences was provided by a failed effort to oust Panamanian strongman Manuel Antonio Noriega from power. While the Oct. 3 Panama coup attempt technically was not a U.S. covert operation, it prompted a finger-pointing episode in Washington of unusual intensity and duration. *(Panama policy, p. 223)*

After weeks of negotiating, the two sides on Oct. 25 reached an agreement providing that:

- Consistent with a 1980 law on the question, Bush generally would notify Congress in advance about all covert operations. The 1980 law set a number of procedures for presidents to tell the two Intelligence committees about covert operations.
- In rare cases when time "is of the essence," the president could withhold notice of covert operations until after they had been put into effect. But he had to give the committee "timely" notice, to be interpreted as within a "few days" at most.
- If the president chose to delay notification for more than a few days, or even indefinitely, he had to do so on constitutional grounds and not because he had stretched the interpretation of what "timely" notice meant.

Bush confirmed the agreement in an Oct. 30 letter to the Intelligence committees. In return, Senate Intelligence backed away from the 48-hour reporting requirement. *(Notification issue, box, p. 237)*

In other major action, the Senate panel added a broader inspector general provision than the one in the House bill. The Senate provision made the CIA position a statutory one — to be appointed by the president and confirmed by the Senate.

The committee report blasted the executive branch, particularly the State Department, for allowing "bureaucratic infighting" and other problems to hinder U.S. efforts to counter espionage threats, including those against overseas embassies. In unusually tough words, the panel demanded that the Bush administration embrace a proposal by its predecessor to tear down the unfinished U.S. Embassy building in Moscow. *(Embassy, box, p. 209)*

In a major departure, the Senate legislation authorized funds for two fiscal years, instead of one. Committee officials said the experiment with a two-year budget cycle was in part aimed at allowing the panel to spend more time in off years conducting oversight hearings on non-budget issues.

The Senate passed HR 2748 by voice vote on Nov. 7. The full Senate did not deal directly with the covert operations issue because no one rose to challenge the Intelligence Committee's deal with Bush on the issue.

The main concern during the debate was the requirement for an independent inspector general at the CIA. The Senate Nov. 7 rejected, 64-34, a move to delete the requirement, despite administration opposition.

Final Bill

Conferees reached agreement on a final bill Nov. 16 (H Rept 101-367). The House approved the measure by voice vote Nov. 17. The Senate followed suit Nov. 18.

As signed into law Nov. 30, HR 2748 authorized a secret amount for the CIA and other intelligence agencies in fiscal 1990. The final bill included the Senate provision for an independent CIA inspector general, appointed by the president and confirmed by the Senate.

Conferees modified the House amendment requiring the CIA to make copies of the inspector general's reports available to the committees. Under the final bill, a request for inspector general reports would have to come from the leadership of each committee, not any individual member.

In their conference report, the committees also said the CIA under some circumstances could provide a summary of the report instead of the full document. However, each committee retained the right to demand the report itself if it found the summary inadequate.

Senate conferees agreed to drop from the final bill a long reform of legal procedures to govern covert operations, including the first explicit definition of what they were. Instead of including the reform language in 1989, the committees agreed to make "one more effort" in 1990 to get Bush to accept legislation to set specific standards for his reporting to Congress on covert actions. One option was to ask Bush to agree to put the essence of his Oct. 30 letter into the law, in effect binding him and his successors.

1991 Intelligence Authorization

In a surprise move, President Bush in 1990 pocket-vetoed the fiscal 1991 intelligence authorization bill (S 2834) because of his opposition to a section on executive reporting of covert actions to Congress. The new rules were an outgrowth of the Iran-contra scandal and Congress' attempt to prevent a recurrence.

Bush said he was particularly disturbed by a section requiring that Congress be notified of requests by U.S. government agencies "to a foreign government or a private citizen to conduct a covert action on behalf of the United States."

In his memorandum of disapproval, Bush complained that the provision "purports to regulate diplomacy ... by forbidding the expression of certain views to foreign governments and private citizens."

The authors of the bill insisted that the provision was intended only to curtail unchecked covert operations conducted by third countries at the behest of the United States — of the type that occurred during the Iran-contra affair — and was not an attempt to hamper diplomacy.

In addition, the bill would have placed new restrictions on covert aid to guerrilla forces in Angola and Afghanistan, and it would have terminated secret aid to the Cambodian rebels. The large-scale covert aid programs of the Reagan era had been losing favor with Congress because of the reduction in tensions between the United States and the Soviet Union. The administration had been working toward a diplomatic resolution of conflicts in all three countries. But Congress, impatient with the pace of diplomacy, altered terms of the covert aid programs.

Because of the veto, no specific authorization was provided for about two-thirds of the intelligence community's estimated $30 billion budget for fiscal 1991; under a section of the National Security Act, appropriations for intelligence activities must be authorized.

Administration officials said the bulk of intelligence programs were included in the Defense Department authorization bill (HR 4739 — PL 101-510). Most Democrats on the Intelligence committees apparently disagreed, although few seemed willing to force a confrontation.

A revised fiscal 1991 intelligence authorization bill (HR 1455 — PL 102-88) — with compromise language on the reporting of covert actions to Congress — was enacted in 1991. *(Revised fiscal 1991 intelligence authorization, p. 280)*

Background

Covert action had been used in one form or another since the beginning of warfare, but for the United States, it took on unprecedented importance with the arrival of the Cold War. Successive administrations embraced covert action as a useful tool in fighting Soviet expansionism and other threats to U.S. national security.

Between 1951 and 1975, according to a 1976 Senate Select Intelligence Committee investigation, the Central Intelligence Agency was involved in about 900 major projects in foreign countries, including dozens in Vietnam. Although most of the operations were designed to affect foreign politics at the margin, several were intended to overturn governments. *(Congress and the Nation Vol. IV, p. 182)*

The number of covert operations increased dramatically when President Ronald Reagan took office in 1981 and nominated William J. Casey as the director of central intelligence. Casey had served in the Office of Strategic Services (OSS), the forerunner of the CIA, during World War II. The Reagan administration employed the CIA to assist those seeking to overthrow, or at least harassing, regimes backed by the Soviet Union or its surrogates.

Speaker's Right to Know

Moving to correct what members called an error in its rules, the House on Nov. 14, 1989, approved a resolution to allow the Speaker full access to secret information held by the Intelligence Committee.

By a voice vote, the House adopted H Res 268, making the Speaker eligible to attend all Intelligence Committee meetings and to receive any secret information, including documents, the committee obtains.

The resolution corrected what members said was a flaw in a 1977 House rule that created the Intelligence Committee. The committee's members were appointed by the Speaker, and the Speaker was one of eight congressional leaders entitled to receive notice of covert operations under exceptional circumstances. But under the rule, he was not one of the House members allowed access to classified documents and other secret information.

Technically, every Speaker since Thomas P. O'Neill Jr., D-Mass., had violated the rules by asking for and getting occasional Intelligence Committee briefings. That arrangement proved controversial only once, in mid-1988, when Speaker Jim Wright, D-Texas, alleged that he was aware of secret information that the CIA was attempting to provoke the Nicaraguan government into cracking down on opposition groups. The Reagan administration and House Republicans angrily denounced Wright's statements as false and suggested that he might have violated House rules against disclosure of classified information. *(Congress and the Nation Vol. VII, p. 215)*

According to Gregory F. Treverton, a former staff member on the Senate Intelligence Committee and author of a study of covert action in the postwar era, the number of actions roughly tripled during the Reagan years.

The Iran-contra affair during the Reagan administration triggered great furor over covert operations. Late in 1986, the administration made the startling revelation that it had contradicted its own public policy and secretly sold arms to Iran, whose government it had branded as terrorist. Some of the profits from the arms sales were diverted to secretly supply the Nicaraguan contra guerrillas at a time when Congress had barred U.S. aid to the contras. *(Congress and the Nation Vol. VII, p. 253)*

The Iran-contra affair might have faded into memory as the Reagan era's least praised foreign policy venture, but Congress' Intelligence committees tried for years to enact legislation aimed at preventing a similar scandal from recurring.

Existing law, dating from 1980, required the president to tell the House and Senate Intelligence committees in advance about all covert operations. Under exceptional

With Easing of U.S.-Soviet Tensions ...

With the easing of tensions between the United States and the Soviet Union during 1990, many in Congress had grown increasingly skeptical about the large-scale covert assistance operations that the United States supported in Afghanistan, Angola and Cambodia.

Afghanistan

Less than a month after the Soviet Union invaded Afghanistan in December 1979, President Jimmy Carter declared that the United States had a "moral obligation" to arm the Afghan resistance. Carter reportedly allocated $30 million for covert military assistance in a plan that included sending old Soviet weapons from Egypt.

By the winter of 1982, more than 100,000 Soviet troops had occupied Afghanistan, leaving the resistance comparatively underarmed, and in December, the Senate Foreign Relations Committee called on the administration to provide "effective material assistance."

That same month, Reagan directed the CIA to provide more sophisticated weapons, including mortars and grenade launchers. By September 1986, rebel forces were receiving Stinger anti-aircraft missiles, and total covert military aid to the Afghan resistance had climbed to roughly $300 million.

The Soviet Union withdrew the last of its 100,000-plus troops from Afghanistan in February 1989, but it still provided the Kabul government with an estimated $300 million a month in assistance and left behind a cadre of advisers. The United States, meanwhile, reportedly continued to aid rebel groups fighting the Soviet-backed government. U.S. covert aid for the *Mujahedeen* totaled about $280 million in 1989, according to congressional sources.

In 1990, though, the United States and the Soviet Union appeared close to an agreement to enable both superpowers to exit gracefully. Yet, despite the momentum toward a settlement and the fact that the Afghan program was traditionally popular on Capitol Hill, aid for the rebels drew widespread criticism in 1990. Members of the Senate Intelligence Committee called for a full-scale review of U.S. policy toward Afghanistan.

Others expressed concerns over the Islamic fundamentalist character of the rebels being backed by the United States. "We've been supplying enormous amounts of money to these groups, some of whom have little in common with the United States," said Rep. Lee H. Hamilton, D-Ind.

By the end of 1990, the United States and the Soviet Union still disagreed on what role the existing Soviet-backed Afghan president should play in an interim government before elections could be set up.

Angola

Even in the post-Cold War era, U.S. support for rebels in Angola still managed to evoke some familiar sentiments and raise ideological hackles.

Rep. Ronald V. Dellums, D-Calif., called the military aid "morally indefensible," while an analyst for the conservative Heritage Foundation said continued Soviet support for the government of Angolan President José Eduardo dos Santos was an indication "that Moscow has not yet abandoned the use of military force in pursuit of its global objectives."

The CIA first became involved in Angola in 1975, when it provided money and arms to the pro-Western National Union for the Total Independence of Angola (UNITA) forces in the Angolan civil war. UNITA, led by Jonas Savimbi, lost that battle to the leftist Popular Movement for the Liberation of Angola, which received aid from Cuba and the Soviet Union, but UNITA continued to use its base in southern Angola to fight the new Marxist government.

Because UNITA had relied for years on military and financial support from South Africa, members of Congress were reluctant to support it and, in 1976, approved an amendment to the defense appropriations bill (PL 94-212) by Sen. Dick Clark, D-Iowa, effectively barring CIA intervention in Angola. In June 1980, in light of State Department estimates that about 20,000 Cuban troops remained in Angola at the time, Congress weakened the Clark amendment allowing military support of UNITA if the president openly requested it and Congress approved. In July 1985, after receiving assurances that the Reagan administration had no immediate plans to aid UNITA, Congress repealed the Clark amendment.

Early in 1986, Savimbi visited Washington to appeal for U.S. assistance. Reagan enthusiastically backed Savimbi and in February ordered the CIA to provide up to $15 million worth of arms and ammunition to UNITA.

In spite of regional peace efforts, the United States continued to arm UNITA, providing by some estimates up to $60 million in fiscal 1990.

Congressional opponents questioned whether the administration would be willing to wind down the covert program even if a cease-fire could be negotiated, given Bush's previous statements of support for Savimbi. In January 1989, Bush sent the UNITA leader a letter saying he would continue "all appropriate and effective assistance" until "national reconciliation" was achieved in the country.

"National reconciliation" was usually taken to mean a process leading to multi-party elections, which would include participation by members of UNITA. Thus far, the two sides had been unable to

... Congress Questioned Covert Aid Programs

agree on a formula that would lead to elections, or a cease-fire.

While the administration wanted to see democratization in Angola, many members of Congress apparently would be satisfied with the elimination of all outside military assistance — from the Soviet Union and the United States — to the country.

The administration, however, was concerned about the wide discrepancy in the military stockpiles held by each side. The State Department estimated that the Soviet Union would send the Angolan government $800 million in military aid in 1990 — more than 10 times what the United States would provide for Savimbi forces.

In addition, although the geopolitical situation had changed a great deal since he first burst upon the scene, Savimbi remained an extremely popular figure with American conservatives. For a president concerned about his right flank, it could prove politically risky to endorse any peace settlement for Angola that was perceived as containing less than favorable terms for Savimbi.

Cambodia

Of the three regional conflicts, all sides agreed that the civil war in Cambodia would be the most difficult to resolve.

Vietnamese forces invaded Cambodia in 1979, and in 1982 the United States began trying to force them out, providing covert aid to two small non-communist guerrilla groups allied in a loose coalition with the communist Khmer Rouge against the Vietnamese-backed government.

The United States supported the groups led by former Cambodian leader Prince Norodom Sihanouk and Sonn Sann, a former prime minister. But the two forces were linked to the infamous Khmer Rouge — and that connection formed the basis for congressional opposition to the program. Human rights groups charged that the Khmer Rouge, rulers of Cambodia from 1975 to 1979, killed more than 1 million Cambodians.

By 1990, the United States was reportedly sending the non-communist resistance $10 million a year in covert assistance, although diplomatic sources in the region cited a much higher figure — as much as $24 million annually.

Although foreign aid legislation — including that moving in 1990 — prohibited any assistance for the Khmer Rouge and although the money was only a tiny part of the foreign aid budget, the issue was fraught with controversy. The assistance program also represented the first active U.S. role in the region since the Vietnam War.

For years, concern about Vietnamese expansionism outweighed that of the Khmer Rouge returning to power. But reports in 1990 that the Khmer Rouge was gaining in strength vis-à-vis the non-communist resistance, as well as reports that the Khmer Rouge was indirectly receiving American aid, sparked congressional concern and led to an administration reevaluation of its policy.

Speculating on the likelihood of a Khmer Rouge victory, Secretary of State James A. Baker III said, "It would appear that the risks are greater that that might, in fact, occur." As a result, in July 1990, Baker announced a series of steps he said were aimed at preventing a Khmer Rouge takeover.

The secretary outlined three areas in which U.S. policy would change. The most important shift was the withdrawal of diplomatic support for the anti-government coalition that included the Khmer Rouge and the two U.S.-backed factions. In that regard, Baker said, the United States would no longer back the coalition's claim to a seat in the United Nations.

In addition, Baker said the United States would open a dialogue with Vietnam about Cambodia, although he emphasized that the move "does not constitute a decision to normalize relations with Vietnam."

Finally, Baker said the United States would "enhance our humanitarian assistance to Cambodia."

Baker stressed that the United States would continue to provide aid to the non-communist resistance, despite the Khmer Rouge's presence in the coalition. Significantly, flagging congressional support for the program was given as a key factor behind the decision to withdraw diplomatic — but not financial — support for the coalition.

Most members of Congress welcomed the revisions but said that they would be insufficient to prevent the return to power of the Khmer Rouge. A congressional letter recommending further changes, circulated by Senate Majority Leader George J. Mitchell, D-Maine, attracted 66 signatures.

And to the administration's chagrin, as the House Intelligence Committee deferred consideration of aid measures in mid-1990, undecided members were clearly influenced by reports indicating that the Khmer Rouge had made substantial gains on the battlefield.

The administration, aware of the mood on Capitol Hill, indicated that it might make further policy revisions — including possibly initiating direct talks with the Cambodian government. But the administration said it was committed, in the short run at least, to continuing aid for the non-communist resistance.

In July, a senior administration official said that without the program, "there might be the very real likelihood that they [the resistance] would turn elsewhere for support, and that turn might be to the KR [Khmer Rouge]."

circumstances, the president could delay notice until after a covert action had begun — but he would then have to give notice in a "timely manner."

To head off a Senate bill requiring that the president report a covert action to Congress within 48 hours, the president in 1989 had agreed to new reporting guidelines. *(Iran-contra legacy, p. 238)*

Members of Congress also began to question U.S. support for rebel forces in Afghanistan, Angola and Cambodia. The issue of covert aid to those rebels dominated congressional consideration of S 2834. *(Background, box, p. 244)*

Legislative Action

The Senate approved S 2834 on Aug. 4 by voice vote. The bill had been reported by the Intelligence Committee July 10 (S Rept 101-358) and by the Armed Services Committee July 26 (S Rept 101-394).

The Senate bill contained new rules for executive branch reporting of covert actions to Congress.

The bill reportedly cut off the estimated $10 million in covert U.S. aid to the Cambodian resistance. It also cut approximately $100 million from the $280 million covert aid program for the *Mujahedeen* in Afghanistan but left the Angola program intact.

In response to congressional pressure, Secretary of State James A. Baker III on July 18 announced changes in its Cambodia policy. Baker said the United States would withdraw diplomatic support for the rebel coalition in Cambodia, initiate talks with Vietnam and ease restrictions on humanitarian aid.

The House Intelligence Committee was supposed to take up the covert-assistance question in July as part of its intelligence authorization bill (HR 5422) but voted to defer consideration of the programs for two months. One factor was that members wanted to give the diplomatic process more time to work.

The committee apparently was swayed by those diplomatic efforts. The House Intelligence Committee reportedly voted to continue funding for the three controversial covert assistance programs, before reporting the bill Sept. 19 (H Rept 101-725, Part I). The bill was reported by House Armed Services Sept. 28 (H Rept 101-725, Part II).

The State Department had been able to demonstrate progress toward settlement of the wars in Afghanistan and Cambodia. As a result, the administration apparently was able to persuade the House panel that withdrawing support for the rebels would undercut ongoing negotiations.

But progress toward a peaceful conclusion of the war in Angola was slow. The committee voted to continue funding for the Angola program, but only after a contentious debate, said one source.

That debate continued on the House floor. By a **key vote of 207-206 (R 12-156; D 195-50)**, the House Oct. 17 approved an amendment placing new conditions on military aid to the rebels in Angola. Speaker Thomas S. Foley, D-Wash., cast the deciding vote. *(1990 key votes, p. 1039)*

The amendment, sponsored by Stephen J. Solarz, D-N.Y., chairman of the House Foreign Affairs Subcommittee on Asian and Pacific Affairs, had been narrowly defeated in committee. Under its terms, the lethal portion of the covert aid to the Angolan rebels — which reportedly was close to half of the total aid — would be suspended for three months if the president determined that the Luanda government was engaging in good-faith negotiations and was taking steps toward democratization. If the president did not make such a determination, he could restore the aid.

In other action, the House Oct. 17 rejected 175-246 an amendment that would have required the president to openly request continued aid to the Angolan rebels. An amendment to require prior approval by the Intelligence committees of any type of covert action, except in emergencies, was defeated 70-341.

The House passed HR 5422 by voice vote Oct. 17, then passed S 2834 in lieu.

Conference, Final Action

Conferees accepted most of the Solarz amendment placing conditions on the $25 million to $30 million in lethal aid to the Angola rebels. But they dropped a section that would have allowed Congress to suspend aid through a joint resolution if the president did not make the certification.

For Cambodia, the $13 million covert package for the non-communist resistance would be provided openly beginning early in 1991, along with $7 million in previously approved overt aid. The conference bill reportedly reduced assistance to rebels in Afghanistan from approximately $300 million to $250 million for fiscal 1991.

Conferees also approved Senate language repealing a 1980 law that governed covert action. Under the new legislation, the president would be required to provide a written "finding" reporting a covert action to the Intelligence committees — except in "extraordinary circumstances," when only key leaders would have to be informed.

Most of this was not a marked departure from existing law, said many Democrats. Indeed, one title of the National Security Act of 1947 (50 U.S.C. 413) already required that the president inform the committees of covert operations, at the very least, in a "timely fashion."

The new law would generally require prior notification of such operations but would permit the president to delay informing the committees "on rare occasions." On such occasions, the president would have to report "in timely fashion," just as he was required to do already.

But in language that was a direct response to the Iran-contra affair, the conference report specified that all covert actions would have to be taken to support "identifiable foreign policy objectives of the United States."

The House adopted the conference report (H Rept 101-928) by voice vote Oct. 24, and the Senate followed suit the next day.

Veto

When the Intelligence measure cleared, lawmakers were aware that the White House was less than enthusiastic over the final version of S 2834. Yet lawmakers from both parties generally expected that the president would sign it. So, when Bush announced Nov. 30 that he was pocket-vetoing the bill, the action surprised even opponents of the legislation.

Because the bill did not specify what constituted a covert action request, said Bush, the notification requirement "could have a chilling effect on the ability of our diplomats to conduct highly sensitive discussions."

In his memorandum of disapproval, Bush took the unusual step of criticizing the legislative report, even though it did not have the weight of law. The report's definition of what was timely "would unconstitutionally infringe on the authority of the president and impair any administration's effective implementation of covert actions," he said.

State Department Authorization

Controversy surrounded the fiscal 1990-91 State Department authorization bill, as it traveled a complicated path to enactment — attracting a series of amendments in the Senate, provoking lengthy delays in conference, triggering a presidential veto and suffering a last-minute holdup in the Senate in late 1989 that pushed off final clearance of a revised bill until 1990.

Even when President Bush signed the measure into law (HR 3792 — PL 101-246), the controversy continued. In a sweeping challenge to congressional intervention in foreign policy making, Bush declared that nine provisions represented unconstitutional intrusions into his power to conduct foreign policy and that he was reserving the right to interpret those provisions as he saw fit.

The final bill authorized $4.7 billion in fiscal 1990 and $5 billion in fiscal 1991, including authorizations for the State Department, United States Information Agency, Board for International Broadcasting and U.S. contributions to the United Nations and other international agencies.

HR 3792 put into law several sanctions that the president had imposed on China to protest against the Beijing government's brutal crackdown on dissidents in June 1989. The bill also in effect nullified key provisions of the 1952 McCarran-Walter Act, under which foreigners had been barred from the United States because of their political beliefs.

HR 3792 was the second complete version of the biennial State Department bill. Bush vetoed an earlier version (HR 1487) because it contained a provision, stemming from the Iran-contra affair, that he claimed violated his presidential powers over foreign affairs. *(Iran-contra affair, p. 238)*

House Action

HR 1487 was reported by the Foreign Affairs Committee (H Rept 101-17) April 6, 1989, and passed by the full House April 12 by a 338-87 vote.

The relatively brief floor debate on the bill skirted the kind of foreign policy fights that had made the State Department bill highly contentious two years earlier. A replay of that scenario was avoided in the House in 1989 when the Foreign Affairs Committee struck a bipartisan agreement to restrict the bill to essentially routine issues. *(Congress and the Nation Vol. VII, p. 239)*

Foreign Affairs Committee Chairman Dante B. Fascell, D-Fla., told the House that the bill "represents a rebirth of bipartisanship in the conduct of foreign affairs."

And even on the most hotly contested floor amendment, the party lines were blurred. A proposal to trim the authorization for the National Endowment for Democracy (NED) from the $25 million recommended by the committee to the $15.8 million requested by the administration was rejected April 12, 209-216, with 105 Democrats and 104 Republicans voting for it and 147 Democrats and 69 Republicans voting against. Funds were funneled through the NED to foundations chartered by the Republican and Democratic parties, the U.S. Chamber of Congress and the AFL-CIO to foster democratic values and institutions abroad.

In other action, the House partly reversed the committee's recommendation to resume full funding of U.S. assessments by the United Nations. By voice vote, the House adopted an amendment requiring that 20 percent of such payments be withheld until the president consulted with Congress to show that U.N. budgetary and personnel policies continued to follow Congress' requirements.

Other amendments adopted included one barring the use of funds to carry out the 1988 Namibia peace agreement among South Africa, Cuba and Angola unless the president certified that Cuban troops were being withdrawn from Angola on the prescribed schedule.

Senate Action

Following its biennial practice, the Senate loaded the State Department bill with almost a hundred amendments to steer the nation's foreign policies before passing HR 1487 by voice vote early July 21. One reason for the blizzard of amendments on the State Department bill was the feeling among members that a foreign aid authorization bill might never be enacted, as had been the case since 1985.

Although the administration and managers of the Senate companion bill (S 1160) were able to keep the measure relatively free of baggage that would impose actual restraints on the administration, the Senate ignored a veto threat and attached an amendment stemming from the Iran-contra affair that ultimately killed the legislation.

The State Department bill (S 1160) was reported by the Foreign Relations Committee on June 12 (S Rept 101-46), after some contentious drafting sessions.

Cambodian Aid. The Senate panel resolved the most controversial issue in the bill by dropping a proposal to bar the administration from giving aid to rebels in Cambodia. The proposal was an effort to head off a pending decision by the Bush administration to arm a guerrilla faction represented by former Cambodian leader Prince Norodom Sihanouk.

U.S. officials reportedly argued that providing weapons to Sihanouk's fighters would strengthen them in a battle for control of Cambodia once Vietnam pulled out its occupying forces, as it had promised to do by Sept. 30. Without outside aid, according to this argument, Sihanouk's forces might be overwhelmed by their nominal but militarily stronger ally, the Marxist Khmer Rouge, which ruled Cambodia from 1975 to 1979 and was responsible for killing at least 1 million civilians.

Some opponents of the aid likened the assistance plan to the early days of U.S. involvement in Vietnam. Others argued that no way existed to ensure that the aid — primarily for thousands of rifles — would not fall into the hands of the Khmer Rouge.

The Senate revisited the Cambodian aid issue when S 1160 was taken up on the floor, provoking one of the most heated debates during the six-day floor consideration of the bill. The administration had gone to the House and Senate Intelligence committees to seek approval of the covert CIA aid, but members warned that the proposal should first be debated in public by the full House and Senate.

By a 59-39 vote, the Senate July 20 agreed to allow the president to still seek authority from the Intelligence committees for the covert Cambodian aid.

Iran-Contra Provision. Brushing aside the administration's veto threat, the Senate July 18 approved an amendment intended to prevent a recurrence of some of the alleged abuses of White House power in the Iran-contra affair.

By a **key vote of 57-42 (R 4-41; D 53-1)**, the Senate adopted an amendment by Daniel Patrick Moynihan, D-N.Y., barring U.S. officials from soliciting outside aid, or diverting government money, to support a foreign policy activity for which official U.S. aid was barred by law. *(1989 key votes, p. 1021)*

The amendment, which had the approval of the Foreign Relations Committee, was a direct outgrowth of the Iran-contra affair, during which administration officials (possibly including President Ronald Reagan) solicited funds for the Nicaraguan rebels from other countries, including Saudi Arabia, Taiwan, Israel and Brunei, when Congress had banned official aid to the contras. Evidence — denied by some officials — also was available that the Reagan administration engaged in quid pro quo deals with Central American countries under which those countries would help the contras in return for U.S. aid. *(Congress and the Nation Vol. VII, p. 253)*

Although the provision stated that the amendment could not be construed to "limit the full constitutional powers of the president to conduct the foreign policy of the United States," the Bush administration actively lobbied against the amendment.

Political Appointees. The Senate rejected two attempts to set limits on the percentage of political appointees in top diplomatic posts.

An amendment, sponsored by Al Gore, D-Tenn., prohibiting the president from filling more than 15 percent of all ambassadorial and high-level State Department positions with political appointees was defeated 20-79 on July 18. Another Gore amendment expressing the sense of the Senate that a 30 percent limit should be set was rejected 38-61 the next day.

Sponsors insisted that Bush had placed an excessive number of GOP campaign contributors and other nondiplomats into senior posts at the State Department. But senators of both parties agreed that Congress should not try to limit, by statute, the president's flexibility in appointing his aides, including envoys.

Noriega Dealings. The Senate July 18 rejected, 37-62, an amendment offered by Jesse Helms, R-N.C., that sought to bar any dealings with Panamanian leader Gen. Manuel Antonio Noriega except to ease him out of power. The Helms amendment fell before a bipartisan assault by senators who saw it as an intrusion on the president's powers and a hindrance to efforts to get Noriega out of power. *(Panama invasion, p. 223)*

Middle East Talks. After an intensive lobbying effort by the Bush administration, the Senate brushed aside a move that White House officials said would derail talks crucial to the Middle East peace process.

Members voted 75-23 on July 20 to table an amendment to the State bill that would have prevented administration officials from negotiating with any representatives of the Palestine Liberation Organization (PLO) unless the president certified to Congress that the representative had not been involved in terrorist activities resulting in harm to an American citizen.

In its place, senators then approved, 97-1, a much watered-down provision allowing such discussions unless the president "knows and advises Congress that" the PLO representative had directly planned or carried out terrorist acts resulting in the death or kidnapping of an American.

The initial amendment, proposed by Helms and modified by Charles E. Grassley, R-Iowa, was targeted at the U.S. "dialogue" in Tunis with the PLO and meetings there between U.S. Ambassador Robert Pelletreau and Abu Iyad, who allegedly had headed the PLO's "Black September" terrorist faction. The dialogue was begun late in 1988 by the Reagan administration after PLO leader Yasir Arafat renounced terrorism and recognized Israel's right to exist.

The administration said it still opposed the substitute as an unconstitutional intrusion into presidential authority, but officials said its inclusion would not cause Bush to veto the underlying bill.

The Senate July 20 also approved, 90-8, an amendment expressing the sense of the Senate that the United Nations would be an "inappropriate" forum for an international peace conference to resolve Israeli-Palestinian differences. Israel and its allies in the United States opposed such a conference.

Moscow Embassy. The Senate held another round of debate on what to do about the new U.S. Embassy in Moscow, which was riddled with listening devices, and the new Soviet Embassy, located atop one of the highest points in Washington, D.C. *(Embassy, box, p. 209)*

By a 56-42 vote, the Senate July 20 deleted from the committee bill wording that would have prohibited the Soviets from occupying their new Mount Alto embassy unless the president certified that the new U.S. facility in Moscow was safe and secure and that the espionage threat from the Mount Alto building would not be significantly greater than from any other point in Washington.

Although the administration opposed the committee provision, it considered it more acceptable than language in the 1987 State Department authorization that would make occupation of the embassies considerably more difficult. Under the Senate amendment, that language, which Congress waived for two years, would take effect. The House bill also allowed the 1987 language to take effect. *(Congress and the Nation Vol. VII, p. 240)*

China Sanctions. The Senate voted 81-10 on July 14 to impose economic sanctions against China. Although the amendment largely put into law actions that Bush had already taken, the White House objected to it. *(Details, p. 250)*

Conference, Veto

As the State Department bill was going to conference, House Foreign Affairs Committee leaders considered using it to salvage the moribund foreign aid authorization bill (HR 2655). That bill had died in the Senate for a variety of reasons, including the opposition of some conservatives and an unwillingness by the leadership to devote days of floor time to it.

But Senate leaders reportedly persuaded the House not to attach the foreign aid bill to the State bill, noting that foreign aid opponents might use procedural moves to try to block the State bill.

During conference negotiations, House conferees accepted the less stringent Senate test for lifting sanctions against China in return for an administration pledge not to veto the bill merely because of the sanctions provision.

Conferees also agreed to a watered-down version of the amendment proposed by Sen. Moynihan to prevent a recurrence of some of the activities from the Iran-contra affair. Among the changes made to accommodate administration concerns was the dropping of a provision that barred officials from soliciting money from foreign countries under certain circumstances.

As adopted by conferees, the revised Moynihan amendment would have applied whenever a U.S. law referred to the Moynihan amendment and expressly prohibited all U.S. aid from being provided to any foreign region, country, government, group or individual.

In such a case, the Moynihan amendment would have barred any employee or official of the executive branch from taking three types of actions to assist the foreign country or group for which official U.S. aid was barred. The three actions were:

- Receiving, accepting, spending or otherwise using money or property from a foreign government, a foreign person or a U.S. person;
- Using any U.S. funds or facilities; or
- Providing U.S. assistance to any third party.

Violations of these prohibitions would be punishable by up to five years in prison, a fine or both.

The amendment would have required the president to notify Congress whenever he learned that an administration official had violated one of the prohibitions. However, the amendment stated that the restrictions did not prevent any administration officials from expressing views on any subject, nor did it prevent any official from communicating with a foreign country or group on the subject of the prohibitions.

Despite the compromises that went into the final Moynihan amendment, administration officials were unhappy with it. Administration officials suggested a substitute to give the president substantially more discretion.

But the House approved the conference report (H Rept 101-343) by voice vote on Nov. 15, and the Senate followed suit on Nov. 16, clearing HR 1487 for the president. Hill leaders withheld the bill from Bush while negotiations on the Moynihan provision continued.

By Nov. 21, efforts at a compromise failed, and Congress neared agreement with the administration on a similar provision attached to the foreign aid appropriations bill, an earlier version of which Bush had vetoed. Hill officials then sent the State Department bill to Bush, who vetoed it Nov. 21 over the Moynihan language. *(Foreign aid appropriations bill, p. 228)*

New Bill

The House Foreign Affairs Committee then produced a new version of the bill (HR 3792) without the Moynihan amendment. The House passed it by voice vote under suspension of the rules Nov. 21.

Senate action on the bill was delayed until early in the next session because of a jurisdictional dispute between the Senate Appropriations and Foreign Relations committees. The Senate finally passed the bill Jan. 30, 1990, by a 98-0 vote, completing congressional action.

President Bush signed the bill on Feb. 16. But he declared that nine provisions of the bill represented unconstitutional intrusions into his right, as president, to conduct foreign policy. Bush said he was reserving the right to interpret those provisions as he saw fit — implying that he would ignore several of them. The president said several other parts of the bill were improper and would be enforced according to the views of the executive branch.

Bush several times in the past had challenged the constitutionality of individual legislative provisions that he insisted infringed on his powers. However, he had never before raised constitutional complaints about as many items in one piece of legislation.

Bush said various provisions of the State Department bill violated two of the president's powers under the Constitution: the right to appoint and receive ambassadors, and the right to "make" treaties. The latter power was not spelled out in the Constitution, but presidents generally interpreted it to mean that the executive branch had exclusive control over negotiations with foreign countries.

Because he had those powers under the Constitution, Bush said in a three-page statement, "the president is entrusted with control over the conduct of diplomacy." But several provisions of the State bill "could be read to violate these fundamental constitutional principles by using legislation to direct, in various ways, the conduct of negotiations with foreign nations."

Members of Congress generally acknowledged that the president was responsible for negotiating with other countries. But most members insisted that Congress could use its control over spending to try to influence foreign policy, for example, by determining how much aid the president could give to other countries.

Besides the constitutional issues, Bush complained that the China trade sanctions represented "an unwise constraint" on presidential powers, although he conceded that Congress gave him broad discretion to lift the sanctions.

The most contentious issue was a provision aimed at requiring the administration to accept Hill observers at negotiations on a treaty to reduce conventional military forces in Europe (CFE). Bush said the provision, by specifying the makeup of a diplomatic delegation, "impermissibly intrudes upon my constitutional authority to conduct our foreign relations and to appoint our nation's envoys." As a result, Bush said he would construe the provision as declaring the sense of Congress but not as imposing a "binding legal obligation." *(CFE treaty, p. 383)*

Bush also objected to two provisions that arose out of Hill concerns about the continued dialogue between U.S. diplomats and PLO representatives. One provision was aimed at prohibiting negotiations with any PLO representatives who were known terrorists, and the other required reports to Congress on PLO commitments not to engage in terrorism.

Bush said he would consider as "advisory" rather than mandatory a provision allowing the Soviet Union to open a consulate at the United Nations in New York City only if the secretary of state certified that the United States was able to begin work at its new consulate in the Ukrainian capital of Kiev. The provision was the latest of numerous Hill attempts to enforce equal treatment of U.S. and Soviet diplomatic missions.

Another provision was aimed at curtailing the use of the United Nations as a base for espionage in the United States by the Soviet Union and other countries. The provision said that no one could be admitted as a U.N. representative if he had been found to have engaged in anti-U.S. spying and he could pose a threat to U.S. security. Bush said that provision violated his authority to receive foreign ambassadors, and he warned that he would consider it only as "advisory."

Major Provisions

As signed into law Feb. 16, 1990, HR 3792 (PL 101-246):

Funding Levels. Authorized $4.7 billion in fiscal 1990 and $5 billion in fiscal 1991. The largest share was for the State Department ($2 billion in 1990 and $2.2 billion in 1991). The bill also authorized funding for the United States Information Agency, the Board for International Broadcasting, and contributions to the United Nations and other international agencies.

China Sanctions. Denounced the "unprovoked, brutal and indiscriminate" attack on thousands of protesters in Beijing in June 1989 and put into law a number of sanctions that Bush had imposed under his own authority. *(China sanctions, below)*

Political Exclusions. Eased the ideological exclusions of the 1952 McCarran-Walter Act (PL 82-414) that had kept Nobel laureates and other distinguished foreigners out of the United States. *(Congress and the Nation Vol. I, p. 222)*

The McCarran-Walter Act, enacted over President Harry S. Truman's veto, was aimed primarily at keeping communists from entering the United States. But its broad wording had been used to exclude all sorts of foreigners whom various administrations considered undesirable.

The State Department bill made permanent a temporary provision enacted in 1987 and again in 1988. It said: "No alien may be denied a visa or excluded from admission into the United States ... because of any past, current or expected beliefs, statements or associations which, if engaged in by a United States citizen in the United States, would be protected under the Constitution."

The provision applied only to foreign nationals who were trying to enter the country for short visits, not to people seeking immigrant status.

In addition to excluding communists, the McCarran-Walter Act barred entry into the United States by the mentally retarded, the insane and people afflicted with a "sexual deviation" or with any dangerous contagious disease.

The political exclusions had been used against such noted writers as Gabriel Garcia Marquez and Graham Greene and political figures such as Hortensia Allende, widow of Salvador Allende, the former Chilean president, and Yasir Arafat, chairman of the Palestine Liberation Organization (PLO).

Previous efforts to rewrite the exclusions had failed. *(Congress and the Nation Vol. VII, p. 781; 1991 action, p. 290)*

PLO Talks. Included a lengthy section denouncing "terrorist" actions by the PLO and requiring the administration to submit regular reports to Congress on the status of the U.S. "dialogue" with PLO representatives. Called the PLO Commitments Compliance Act of 1989, this section of the bill listed grievances against the PLO and stated the sense of Congress that the administration should demand that the PLO leadership prevent terrorism by its factions and carry out "concrete steps" to recognize Israel and further the Middle East peace process.

This section also required the secretary of state to submit a report to Congress within 30 days of enactment of the bill, and every 120 days thereafter, describing numerous actions and statements by the PLO. These reports would be mandated as long as the administration continued its informal talks with the PLO.

The bill included language aimed at barring the administration from conducting talks with any PLO representative who was known to have directly planned or carried out terrorist acts resulting in the death or kidnapping of American citizens.

Another provision barred U.S. funding for United Nations agencies that accorded the PLO the same standing as a member state. Since declaring statehood for itself in 1988, the PLO had sought admission to several U.N.-related agencies but had been blocked by the opposition of the United States and other countries.

U.N. and the Middle East. Opposed sponsorship of a Middle East conference by the General Assembly but not by the Security Council or by the U.N. secretary general. The original Senate provision had barred sponsorship by any U.N. agency because of a General Assembly resolution equating Zionism with "racism."

TV Marti. Included the administration's request for a $16 million authorization in fiscal 1990 to begin U.S. government-sponsored television broadcasting to Cuba. The broadcasts, called TV Marti after a famed Cuban nationalist, were to be modeled after Radio Marti, which had been in operation for several years.

Israel Transmitter. Authorized $183.5 million in fiscal 1990 and $23.5 million in fiscal 1991 for construction of a relay station in Israel for Radio Free Europe and Radio Liberty. The administration had requested $207 million in fiscal 1990 and had insisted that costs for the project would be much greater unless Congress assured local contractors that it would be fully funded. But both chambers had trouble squeezing that much money in one year from other programs.

China Policy

Two decades of progress toward improving relations between the United States and China was frozen June 3-4, 1989. The slaughter of hundreds of students and other protesters in Tiananmen Square by the Chinese army appeared aimed at ending seven weeks of peaceful demonstrations in China's main cities.

The protests, calling for steps toward democracy, had captured the world's attention and raised hopes that the communist regime might be goaded into allowing serious political reforms to accompany the country's economic liberalization.

But with Beijing surrounded by a massive military force and with hard-line factions of the government in control, China seemed to be entering a new period of repression. China's senior leaders called on protest leaders to turn themselves in — the latest sign that they were no longer willing to tolerate mass public opposition.

Washington led the international chorus of condemnation of the Chinese massacre, taking steps intended to isolate the government leaders and to express moral support for the opposition. President Bush on June 5 effectively froze relations between the two countries, particularly at the military level. But Bush also said the United States did not want to undermine long-term relations, which had progressed on a step-by-step basis since President Richard Nixon went to China in 1972. Bush had been the official U.S. representative to Communist China in 1974-75.

Members of Congress felt Bush's actions did not go far enough. Both chambers in 1989 passed bills imposing sanctions against China, but it took until early 1990 for one of those measures to be enacted (HR 3792 — PL 101-246).

While Congress was moving to impose the sanctions, the Bush administration tried to patch up relations with Beijing. A new diplomatic overture at the end of 1989 rekindled congressional and public anger at the Chinese government and put Bush on the defensive. Brent L. Scowcroft, Bush's national security adviser, led a high-level U.S. delegation on a surprise trip to China, ostensibly to brief leaders there on the outcome of the U.S.-Soviet summit meeting the week before. Other administration officials later acknowledged that the more important purpose of the trip was to begin repairing U.S. relations with China.

Democrats and Republicans in Congress questioned Bush's judgment in sending senior aides to China. They said that step had the appearance of relaxing the sanctions imposed to punish China for its slaughter of protesters in downtown Beijing and continuing repression of dissent. Members of Congress also were critical of several exemptions the administration granted in late 1989 to some of its sanctions.

Members also blasted Bush for vetoing a bill (HR 2712) that would have allowed all Chinese nationals in the United States on student visas to seek permanent-resident status without first returning to China. Bush promised to use his executive authority to give the students all of the protections offered by the bill. An override attempt failed in the Senate in early 1990.

Congressional efforts to force the administration to take a harder line toward China continued throughout 1990. The main issue that year was trade relations. Some members of Congress wanted to withdraw China's most-favored-nation (MFN) trading status, first granted in 1980. Withdrawal of MFN would have resulted in dramatically higher tariffs on Chinese goods sold in the United States.

Bush defended his decision in May to renew China's trading status as a way of furthering democratic reforms by keeping open channels of commerce and communication. Critics argued that ample evidence was available that the administration's conciliatory approach had failed. But efforts to withdraw MFN status or to put restrictions on a further extension of MFN to China in 1990 failed when the Senate did not act on two House-passed bills or its own measure. The White House had threatened to veto both House-passed bills. *(Details, p. 173)*

Bush vetoed two bills cleared by the 102nd Congress that would have placed restrictions on normal trade relations between the United States and China. The Senate could not muster the votes to override. *(Story, p. 190)*

Sanctions Against China

In the wake of China's repression, broad agreement existed in Washington that the United States had no choice but to suspend normal dealings with the government. But Bush, most congressional leaders and academic experts on China argued against a formal break in relations, saying the United States instead should use its political and moral suasion to promote democracy and respect for human rights.

Bush imposed by executive order several sanctions. They included suspensions of arms sales to China; operations in China by the Overseas Private Investment Corporation (OPIC), writer of political risk insurance for U.S. firms active in foreign countries; a 1988 deal under which China was to use its missiles to launch U.S. commercial satellites; and licenses for exports to China of nuclear power plant supplies and technology.

Bush's actions initially won broad praise on Capitol Hill. Resolutions supporting his approach and harshly condemning the crackdown in China were approved in both chambers. The House had adopted its resolution (H Con Res 136) by voice vote May 24. The Senate passed an amended version 89-0 on May 31. The House agreed to further amend the resolution June 6, 406-0. The Senate acted on a separate measure (S Res 142) on June 6, adopting it 100-0.

But warnings were heard across the political spectrum that members would demand that Bush take tougher measures if the Chinese engaged in further repression. In their resolutions, both chambers called on the president to consider additional steps, especially if the Chinese government refused to lift restrictions on dissent or again used armed force against civilians.

Later in June, Congress' early support began fading as the Beijing government began executing dissidents. Some members of Congress criticized Bush's response as too weak and introduced dozens of pieces of legislation calling for sanctions against China. House leaders also worked on an omnibus package of sanctions to be introduced as a floor amendment to the pending fiscal 1990-91 foreign aid authorization bill (HR 2655).

Asking Congress to refrain from legislating sanctions, Secretary of State James A. Baker III and other officials appealed for a unified position on China. Some leaders — including House Speaker Thomas S. Foley, D-Wash. — said they were heeding that call. But others pressed ahead with criticism of the administration and with plans for legislation, putting political pressure on the administration.

The White House on June 20 announced two steps to protest events in China: a halt to all high-level exchanges between U.S. and Chinese government officials, and a U.S. move to suspend consideration of new loans to China by the World Bank and other international development banks.

Foreign Aid Bill. HR 2655, the foreign aid bill under debate on the House floor, attracted the full range of potential amendments on China. *(Fiscal 1990-91 foreign aid authorization, p. 227)*

Conservative Republicans took the lead in proposing amendments that would have imposed more than a dozen types of China sanctions.

To head off a flurry of votes and the likely passage of even the most extreme amendments, House leaders negotiated an omnibus sanctions package and took it to the floor on June 29. Baker and other administration officials participated in the negotiations but refused to support the package. Recognizing political reality, however, officials made no attempt to stop the package other than to denounce it.

The House on June 29 added the sanctions to the foreign aid bill on a 418-0 vote. The sanctions closely resembled actions Bush already had taken, and the measure commended the president's "clear articulation" of outrage at the repression of peaceful demonstrations.

But the House action demonstrated the widespread view on Capitol Hill that Bush himself had not been outspoken enough about the Chinese government's actions. As a former chief of the U.S. liaison office in China who once boasted of his friendship with the top leaders in Beijing, Bush was restrained in many of his comments about China and allowed his aides to take the lead in denouncing such events as the execution of dissidents.

State Department Bill. The Senate July 14 agreed to a package of sanctions that generally paralleled the provision attached by the House to the foreign aid bill. By an 81-10 vote, the Senate adopted an amendment to the fiscal 1990 State Department authorization bill (S 1160) imposing the sanctions on China. *(Fiscal 1990 State Department authorization, p. 247)*

To show its unhappiness with the Chinese government's repression, the Senate went one step further than the House by calling on the president to reconsider nearly all economic ties with China. It said that the Export-Import Bank should halt its subsidies of exports to China and that the administration should oppose all further loans to China by the World Bank and other international lending institutions. Furthermore, the Senate measure asked the president to reconsider several formal economic links with China, including bilateral trade agreements and China's MFN status.

With the foreign aid authorizations bill moribund in the Senate, the future of the sanctions rested in the House-Senate conference on the State Department bill (HR 1487). Going into that conference, virtually no controversy existed among members about the sanctions. But the administration pushed for flexibility for the president to act on his own to repeal the sanctions.

The House and Senate both had voted to allow the president to lift the sanctions if the human rights situation improved in China. Both chambers also had approved a clause enabling the president to act merely by reporting to Congress. The House said the president could lift the sanctions if he told Congress that doing so was in the U.S. "national security" interest. Lowering that standard somewhat, the Senate bill merely required a presidential determination that the U.S. "national interest" would be served by ending the sanctions.

House conferees agreed to the Senate version in return for a White House pledge not to veto the bill merely because of the sanctions provision.

Congress cleared the underlying bill (H Rept 101-343) on Nov. 16. But the measure included an unrelated restriction on the president's foreign policy powers that prompted Bush to veto it on Nov. 21.

A new bill (HR 3792) without the provision Bush found offensive cleared Congress Jan. 30, 1990.

As signed into law (PL 101-246) on Feb. 16, the State Department bill denounced the Chinese government's "unprovoked, brutal and indiscriminate" attack on the thousands of protesters in Beijing on June 3-4. Adding teeth to the rhetoric, the bill put into law a number of the sanctions that Bush had imposed.

The major sanctions:

- Suspended risk insurance and other financing for private investments in China by OPIC. Aid to China under the U.S. Trade and Development program also was to be suspended.
- Prohibited all exports to China of weapons and military equipment. This did not apply to items intended for civilian use. A similar provision prohibited exports to China of instruments and equipment used for crime control or detection.
- Prohibited exports to China of satellites made in the United States. The main effect of this sanction was to continue a ban on the Chinese launching of a Hughes Aircraft Co. satellite.
- Prohibited exports to China of supplies, equipment and technology used for nuclear power, or of any items that could be used to produce nuclear weapons. This provision had the effect of suspending the July 23, 1985, nuclear-cooperation agreement between the United States and China.
- Required the president to work with U.S. allies to suspend contemplated liberalization of controls on exports of weapons and high-technology goods to China.

The president could lift any or all of the sanctions through the national interest clause, or by reporting to Congress that China had made "progress on a program of political reform," including such items as lifting martial law, halting the executions of dissidents and releasing political prisoners.

By the time the State Department bill was enacted, the White House had already softened the impact of several of Bush's sanctions. In December 1989, the administration allowed the Boeing Corp. to ship to China several airliners that initially had been subject to sanctions on arms sales but, according to the administration, had been found to be commercial in nature. And Bush lifted one of his most visible economic sanctions against China and allowed export to that country of three Hughes communications satellites.

Bush also lifted a sanction that Congress had imposed and allowed the Export-Import Bank to issue loans and other guarantees for U.S. exports to China. Congress on Nov. 22 had cleared legislation, which Bush had signed Dec. 19, barring Ex-Im activities in China. But that bill (HR 2494 — PL 101-240) gave the president discretion to allow the financing if he found that China was making political reforms or if doing so was in the national interest of the United States.

Bush chose the latter course and sent such a report to Congress.

Chinese Students

Congress in 1989 cleared legislation (HR 2712) that would have permitted Chinese students who were in the United States at the time of the Tiananmen Square massacre to remain for an indeterminate period and to seek permanent resident status without returning to China. It also would have waived for four years a requirement that Chinese exchange students on "J" visas return home for at least two years before applying for permanent U.S. residency.

The House passed HR 2712 (H Rept 101-196) by voice vote July 31, and the Senate approved its version by voice vote Aug. 4.

The House adopted the conference report (H Rept 101-370) Nov. 19 by a vote of 403-0, and the Senate followed suit by voice vote the next day. *(Chinese students bill, p. 755)*

Bush vetoed HR 2712 on Nov. 30, saying that he had already used his executive powers to give the Chinese students the protections contained in the bill and that no students would be deported against their will. He insisted that by giving relief to the students through a less formal means he would gain additional leverage to persuade the Chinese government to adopt reforms.

Bush's conciliatory attitude toward China dismayed many in Congress.

The House on Jan. 24, 1990, voted 390-25 to nullify the veto. All those supporting the president were Republican. The following day the Senate narrowly sustained the veto by a **key vote of 62-37 (R 8-37; D 54-0)** — four votes short of the number needed to override the veto. *(1990 key votes, p. 1039)*

Responding to the criticism from lawmakers, Bush on April 11 issued a promised executive order shielding from deportation Chinese students who had been in the United States since the Chinese government crackdown in 1989. The order directed the attorney general to "take any steps necessary to defer until Jan. 1, 1994, the enforced departure of all nationals of the People's Republic of China and their dependents."

Bush had promised he would issue an executive order to accomplish the same goal, but he had not done so until April 11, relying instead on a directive to the Justice Department. His inaction had drawn complaints from many members of Congress.

Congress had one final word on the matter when lawmakers included a non-binding provision in the conference report on legislation (S 358 — PL 101-649) overhauling the U.S. immigration system. The conference report stated that Congress intended that the president's executive order barring the return of Chinese nationals remain in effect as Bush had indicated until 1994. *(Immigration overhaul, p. 752)*

South Africa Policy

The dramatic release by the South African government of imprisoned black leader Nelson Mandela in February 1990 won broad praise around the world, but the United States retained congressionally enacted economic sanctions against the white-minority regime until mid-1991.

Congress and President Bush both hosted Mandela in June 1990 and South African President F. W. de Klerk in September as the two leaders sought to gain support and good will from lawmakers and from the administration.

Mandela, deputy president of the African National Congress (ANC), met with Bush on June 25 and received a warm welcome as he visited Capitol Hill on June 26 to address a joint meeting of Congress — an honor customarily reserved for government leaders. He then continued a 12-city, cross-country tour to raise funds for the ANC.

De Klerk's visit — the first by a South African state leader to the United States since 1945 — was lower key, but his reception at the White House and on Capitol Hill marked an important step in his efforts to regain international standing for his country.

Mandela's release on Feb. 11, 1990, after 27 years in prison, and the legalization of the ANC, the leading black organization in South Africa, were among several moves orchestrated by de Klerk aimed at starting talks with black leaders.

To pressure the Pretoria government to dismantle its system of racial separatism called apartheid and bring the country's majority-black population into the political system, Congress had enacted broad trade sanctions against South Africa in 1986 (PL 99-440). The law, enacted over President Ronald Reagan's veto, demanded a series of steps by the South African government before the sanctions could be lifted.

Mandela's visit helped cement support on Capitol Hill for keeping the U.S. sanctions in place. "We have yet to arrive at the point when we can say that South Africa is set on an irreversible course" toward democracy, Mandela told the lawmakers. Sanctions should continue, he added, because "the purpose for which they were imposed has not yet been achieved."

In his visit, de Klerk did not press to have the sanctions lifted but repeatedly said that the reforms his Nationalist Party government had instituted would not be reversed. "My government's commitment to remove the last pillars of apartheid is final and irreversible," he said in a speech at the National Press Club on Sept. 25.

Some countries were already rewarding de Klerk's government. Portugal and Italy called for a worldwide lifting of sanctions. Britain lifted its ban on new investment in South Africa, and France hinted that it might follow suit. At a June 1990 meeting, the European Community issued a statement promising to relax sanctions if de Klerk's reforms continued.

But Bush made no immediate move to lift sanctions. Speaking with reporters the day after Mandela's release, Bush said, "We can't do that. I am bound by the law."

When he met with de Klerk on Sept. 24, however, Bush indicated the administration would try to persuade Congress to modify or suspend the sanctions if the congressionally established conditions were met.

Echoing de Klerk's assurances, Bush said, "We believe the process of change in South Africa is irreversible, a fact that we'll bear squarely in mind as we consider specific issues in the future."

In July 1991, Bush declared that South Africa had met the requirements of the 1986 law and lifted the sanctions. *(South Africa sanctions lifted, p. 294)*

Background

South Africa's apartheid system, established by the Nationalist Party after a 1948 election victory, was a uniquely pervasive legal system for separating the country's white, black, Asian and mixed-race populations. All South Africans were classified by race, and government facilities and public accommodations were segregated.

The country's 26 million blacks, who outnumbered whites 5-to-1, had no right to vote in local or national elections.

The apartheid system — and the police state measures used to keep it in place — had made South Africa an international pariah, the target of worldwide criticism and economic sanctions voted by the United Nations.

But the country's value to the United States as an anti-communist ally and a source of strategic minerals created a tension between liberal opponents of apartheid in the United States and political conservatives who favored maintaining some ties to the Pretoria regime.

In the 1980s, the Reagan administration sought to bridge that political gap with a policy it called constructive engagement — diplomatic negotiations aimed at bringing about reform in South Africa and settling regional disputes involving South Africa and neighboring Angola, Mozambique and Namibia.

The policy made some progress on the regional issues, but it did not satisfy the increasingly active U.S. anti-apartheid movement or its supporters on Capitol Hill.

The result was the 1986 sanctions law, enacted by Congress over Reagan's veto by votes of 313-83 in the House and 78-21 in the then majority-Republican Senate. Among those instrumental in shaping the legislation was Indiana Republican Richard G. Lugar, then chairman of the Senate Foreign Relations Committee. *(Congress and the Nation Vol. VII, p. 180)*

A study cited in the *Washington Post* Jan. 14, 1990, indicated that the U.S. sanctions, along with those of other countries, had cost South Africa between $32 billion and $40 billion in 1986-90, including $11 billion in net capital outflows and $4 billion in lost export earnings.

The 1986 law said the trade sanctions could be lifted if South Africa freed Mandela and all other political prisoners; repealed the state of emergency and released all people detained under it; legalized democratic political parties and incorporated all South Africans into the political process; repealed the Group Areas Act, which enforced the segregation of neighborhoods, and the Population Registration Act, which classified every South African by race; and agreed to enter into good-faith talks with "truly representative" black leaders.

But the act also permitted the president to suspend sanctions, subject to a congressional veto, if political prisoners were freed and three of the other four conditions were met.

Bush Administration Policy

Breaking with Reagan's confrontational approach, Bush tried to work with Congress in developing a bipartisan policy toward South Africa.

When some lawmakers called for additional sanctions against South Africa in 1989, Bush persuaded leaders to hold off until de Klerk's new government had a chance to deliver on its promise to move the country toward multiracial democracy. De Klerk was elected state president on Sept. 14, 1989, succeeding P. W. Botha, whose 11 years in power had seen only limited moves away from apartheid.

Meeting a requirement in the 1986 sanctions law for the administration to report annually on its policy toward South Africa, Bush told Congress on Oct. 2, 1989, that the South African government had taken no fundamental steps to dismantle apartheid. The administration urged against further economic or political sanctions, instead requesting that de Klerk's government be given "reasonable time to demonstrate" whether it intended to begin abolishing apartheid.

Some advocates of more sanctions complained that the administration was allowing Pretoria too much of a "grace period." Even so, they did not push for more sanctions by legislation.

Change in South Africa

South Africa's announcement the week of Feb. 5, 1990, that it would, among other things, revoke the 30-year ban on the ANC and release Mandela, who had been jailed on treason-related charges since 1962, was greeted warmly on Capitol Hill.

Republicans and Democrats alike commended de Klerk, who in a Feb. 2 speech at the opening of Parliament unveiled the most far-reaching revisions of apartheid since its inception 42 years earlier.

But U.S. lawmakers also called for more change, and most indicated it was premature to suspend the 1986 sanctions. Sanctions had to remain in effect, many said, because de Klerk's announced reforms did not go far enough.

Dramatic as they were, de Klerk's reforms left untouched the basic structure of apartheid. The Population Registration Act and the Group Areas Act remained in place. Also remaining were the national state of emergency laws, except for those curtailing radio and newspaper coverage. Thousands of dissidents had been jailed since the state of emergency was imposed in June 1986.

Rep. Ronald V. Dellums, D-Calif., chair of the Congressional Black Caucus and one of the most vociferous critics of apartheid in Congress, said of the new reforms: "It is imperative to clearly understand that even these measures, laudable as they are, do not constitute the establishment of freedom or true democracy for the black majority."

Dellums and other members dismissed speculation that de Klerk's announced reforms might warrant a review of the U.S. policy of economic sanctions against South Africa.

The reforms, however, deflated efforts for tougher sanctions, and the Bush administration gained more time to negotiate a bipartisan policy with Congress.

Aid Issue

One purpose of Mandela's visit to the United States was to raise money the ANC needed to build a party infrastructure and to repatriate about 20,000 exiled members. After the tour ended, organizers reported raising $7 million.

For its part, Congress had included a $10 million allocation to South African political organizations in the fiscal 1990 supplemental appropriations (HR 4404 — PL 101-302) that Bush signed on May 25. The earmarking provided that the funds go to organizations "committed to a suspension of violence in the context of negotiations to build a democratic system of government in South Africa."

The clause spawned differing views on whether funds could be provided to the ANC. In March 1991, the *Washington Post* reported that the Agency for International Development had formally notified Congress that it intended to allocate $3.7 million to the ANC; $1 million to the rival black political organization Inkatha; and $1.2 million each to Republican and Democratic Party institutes that conducted training programs in emerging democracies. But the *Post* said some conservative lawmakers, including Sen. Jesse Helms, R-N.C., were seeking to block the funds for the ANC.

In addition to the $10 million approved in the supplemental, Congress annually provided $32 million in humanitarian aid to disadvantaged South Africans. This money did not go to political groups.

Chemical Weapons Sanctions

The House in 1989 passed legislation imposing sanctions on countries that used chemical weapons, but no floor action took place in the Senate because of a jurisdictional dispute over a more stringent sanctions bill.

In 1990, Congress attached chemical weapons sanctions to an export controls bill, which President Bush pocket-vetoed on the grounds that the restraints gave him too little discretion. *(Export controls, p. 175)*

Congressional proponents of sanctions legislation finally succeeded in 1991 in winning enactment of a stiff sanctions law. *(1991 action, p. 292)*

1989 Action

The 1989 House bill (HR 3033 — H Rept 101-334, Part I; H Rept 101-334, Part II) would have required the president to impose sanctions on countries that used or were preparing to use chemical or biological weapons and on foreign firms that assisted in developing such weapons. The bill was passed by voice vote under suspension of the rules on Nov. 13.

HR 3033 was the product of months of negotiations between the administration and Congress. The Bush administration had indicated that it would be willing to accept some kind of legislative package so long as it gave the president broad discretion in determining when sanctions should be imposed. Sponsors said the House measure would give the president a "framework" for deciding when and how to act, although some House members complained it would give the president too much discretion.

The Senate sanctions bill (S 195 — S Rept 101-166) was one of the most comprehensive congressional proposals in years to challenge the proliferation of chemical and biological weapons, particularly in the Third World. The bill had broad bipartisan support in the Senate. It was cosponsored by the two senior members of the Foreign Relations Committee, who rarely agreed on anything of substance: Chairman Claiborne Pell, D-R.I., and ranking Republican Jesse Helms, R-N.C.

Even so, the Bush administration opposed the Senate bill, complaining in particular that it did not give the president broad enough discretion to determine when to impose sanctions and when to use other diplomatic means to protest the use or spread of chemical weapons overseas. Some Foreign Relations members also expressed misgivings about the unilateral nature of sanctions mandated by the measure.

The Foreign Relations Committee had approved S 195 on Oct. 6, but the Senate Banking Committee insisted that parts of the bill belonged in its jurisdiction and demanded changes. Aides to the two panels failed to settle the dispute before adjournment in November.

It was the second year in a row that a last-minute dispute in the Senate held up sanctions against countries that used chemical weapons. At the end of the 1988 session, Sen. Helms had blocked action on an omnibus foreign relations bill that included sanctions against Iraq for its use of chemical weapons against its Kurdish minority. Helms' action was over an unrelated foreign policy issue. *(Congress and the Nation Vol. VII, p. 239)*

1990 Action

After resolving the committee turf battle and allaying some concerns expressed by the administration, the Senate in 1990 approved HR 3033. The Senate version, passed May 17 by a 92-0 vote, contained most of the provisions of S 195 that the Foreign Relations Committee had approved the previous year.

The Senate sought to reduce some of the administration's objections to the bill by allowing the president to waive the sanctions against foreign countries for up to a year instead of the nine months in the committee bill. But the Bush administration still opposed the legislation.

The bill also faced objections from the Banking Committee. To resolve those, the Senate May 17 adopted 96-0 an amendment calling for stronger international efforts to restrain trade in supplies and equipment needed to make chemical weapons.

Several months later, the Senate attached the provisions of S 195 to legislation (HR 4653) reauthorizing the Export Administration Act of 1979. Senators agreed by voice vote to add the text of S 195 before passing HR 4653 on Sept. 13. Bush again voiced his opposition to the provisions.

Meanwhile, even after the provisions of S 195 were attached to the export control bill, Congress continued to act on HR 3033. The House on Oct. 22 agreed to the Senate changes with further amendments by voice vote. The bill went back to the Senate, where there was no further action on it.

House-Senate conferees on HR 4653 left the chemical weapons sanctions in the final bill (H Rept 101-944), which both chambers adopted Oct. 26. But Bush stuck by his position that the chemical weapons sanctions language was too restrictive and pocket-vetoed the bill.

"The major flaw with HR 4653 is not the requirement of sanctions, but the rigid way in which they are imposed," Bush said in announcing the veto.

Andean Drug War

President Bush's international drug war strategy stayed the course in 1990, with Congress clearing legislation (HR 5567 — PL 101-623) to authorize funding for military and economic aid to Colombia, Peru and Bolivia.

The strategy, called the Andean Initiative, was aimed at giving those drug-exporting countries funds in return for their promises to crack down on the illicit drug trade in their countries.

Controversy over how much funding the United States should provide for military aid to the countries, though, nearly derailed the bill. The Bush administration had requested about $137 million in foreign military aid for fiscal 1991 for the three countries.

But members of Congress were reluctant to go along with Bush's proposal because of problems in distributing the aid for fiscal 1990 and because of concerns over the amount of aid. Members of the House Foreign Affairs Committee put a $100 million cap on total military aid to the three nations; Bush responded with a threat to veto the bill.

Eventually, the House committee and the administration reached a compromise. Military aid for the Andean countries would be authorized for fiscal 1991 at $118 million with a cap of $250 million in military aid from all U.S. sources.

The House passed the compromise bill by voice vote under suspension of the rules on Oct. 22. The Senate passed an amended version by voice vote on Oct. 26, and the House went along, clearing the measure for the president Oct. 27.

The final bill did not completely please anyone. Democrats disliked the high cap level, while the administration disapproved of the reporting and human rights requirements put on the aid.

Background

Bush's Andean Initiative was based on a rapid infusion of aid to the armed forces in the three major cocaine-producing countries of South America.

Bush first announced his initiative in 1989 and proposed giving the three countries — Colombia, Peru and Bolivia — an additional $129 million in military aid for fiscal 1990. This was on top of the $119.1 million in narcotics-related economic, military and law enforcement aid already authorized for Andean nations in fiscal 1990.

Congress eventually approved $125 million in aid, which was to come from the Pentagon's fiscal 1990 budget.

Bush met with the leaders of the Andean countries in Cartagena, Colombia, on Feb. 15, 1990, and reiterated earlier administration proposals to give the three nations $2.2 billion in unspecified military and economic assistance over five years.

A joint communiqué signed by Bush, Colombian President Virgilio Barco, Bolivian President Jaime Paz Zamora and Peruvian President Alan García also called, in general terms, for more cooperation in interdiction of drug trafficking, greater trade incentives for the Andean region, increased efforts to limit the sale of automatic weapons and chemicals needed for cocaine production, the sharing of drug-related forfeitures and new resolve in seeking alternative work for people employed in growing coca and producing cocaine.

But changes in the region in 1990 led some members of Congress to move to cut back the three nations' military aid for fiscal 1991. The newly elected president of Peru, Alberto Fujimori, refused to accept the fiscal 1990 military aid, and the Bush administration acknowledged that none of the $125 million in aid approved earlier had been distributed to the countries.

House Foreign Affairs Republicans, however, argued that the international war on drugs was progressing well and pleaded with other members of Congress not to cut off the aid precipitously.

Major Provisions

As signed into law Nov. 21, HR 5567:

- Authorized $300 million in economic aid for the Andean countries in fiscal 1991.
- Authorized $118 million in military aid for fiscal 1991. Military aid from all sources was capped at $250 million. A subcap of $175 million was placed on aid to law enforcement agencies and the armed forces.
- Allowed the president to provide such aid only after he had determined that (1) the country had implemented programs to reduce the flow of cocaine to the United States in accordance with a bilateral treaty (to be negotiated) that contained specific quantitative and qualitative performance measures and (2) the armed forces of the country were not engaged in a consistent pattern of human rights violations and the government of that country had made significant progress in protecting internationally recognized human rights. As a part of this requirement, the president would have to notify Congress not less than 15 days before the funds were obligated with details on the aid to be transmitted.

Food for Peace

Congress in 1990 overhauled the nation's principal program for distributing the bounty of its farmland to famine-stricken, less productive regions of the world and insulated it from being used as a foreign policy tool.

Lawmakers made wholesale changes to the so-called Food for Peace program — also called PL 480, after its 1954 public law number — as part of the omnibus farm bill that cleared Congress on Oct. 25 and was signed by President Bush on Nov. 28 (S 2830 — PL 101-624). *(Farm bill, p. 537)*

The PL 480 overhaul trimmed the president's discretion to dole out food. It was expected to result in a modest shift in U.S. food aid dollars away from Central America and the Middle East to the poor countries of sub-Saharan Africa, with the greatest need for food donations, and Asia, with the greatest market potential.

The 1990 action represented the first restructuring of the program since 1966, when Congress replaced the program's original mandate for commodity disposal with more humanitarian and market-development missions. *(Congress and the Nation Vol. I, p. 177; Congress and the Nation Vol. II, p. 567)*

Pressure to streamline PL 480 had come from those who relied on it — farm groups and international relief organizations.

In 1990, less than 5 percent of U.S. agricultural commercial exports were subsidized under PL 480, but farmers and grain traders saw the program as an important mechanism for nurturing the Third World's taste for U.S. farm products. They hoped the cash-poor recipients would eventually "graduate" into full-fledged commercial customers.

World hunger organizations had a different reason for wanting changes to PL 480. Malnutrition and hunger were on the rise. The National Research Council had estimated that the world would need 20 million metric tons of food aid a year from all sources during the 1990s. Only 10 million metric tons were supplied most years, roughly half of which came from the United States.

As enacted, the PL 480 provisions continued to allow the program to be used to advance U.S. foreign policy goals but narrowed the definition of foreign policy to include only improving the food security of recipient nations. A requirement that countries be termed "friendly" before they could receive PL 480 aid was removed.

The overhaul also sought to clarify lines of authority by specifying that the Agriculture Department was to be designated to carry out PL 480 credit sales programs while the Agency for International Development (AID) was to carry out the grants program.

Background

Food for Peace had always had a chameleonlike quality, taking on whatever hue politicians wanted at the time.

Most U.S. food aid was sold to foreign governments on easy credit (loans of up to 40 years at 2 percent to 4 percent interest).

The government also donated food overseas for disaster relief, economic development and feeding programs. By law, at least 1.9 million metric tons of grain (or the equivalent amount of other commodities) had to be donated each year, of which 1.4 million tons had to go to humanitarian feeding organizations.

In 1954, the program had been sold to Congress as a surplus commodity distribution plan. Lawmakers pushing the legislation, including Sen. Hubert H. Humphrey, D-Minn. (1949-64, 1971-78), stressed that the bill — enacted as PL 83-480 — did not call for a "giveaway" program.

Successive administrations had discovered the value of sprinkling PL 480 commodities among strategic allies. Among the first recipients were the war-ravaged countries of Europe — Germany, France, Italy and Poland. Over the years, Congress added restrictions on distribution of food to communist countries.

By 1966, the United States had succeeded in controlling its longstanding problem of farm surpluses, and the foreign policy component of the program became pre-eminent.

The 1966 reauthorization of the program (PL 89-908) reoriented its goals toward combating world hunger and emphasized the need for recipient countries to adopt self-help measures to improve their own agricultural production. The revision, requested by President Lyndon B. Johnson but reshaped by Congress, effectively gave the president more discretion in selecting foodstocks for distribution by eliminating the requirement that commodities used be in surplus.

Despite the stated goal of combating world hunger, aid priorities continued to reflect U.S. foreign policy goals. In the early 1970s, almost half of the aid shipments — more than $400 million a year — went to South Vietnam and Cambodia, while regions of severe famine in Africa received only $61.5 million worth.

Over the years, Congress periodically accused the executive branch of mismanaging food aid and running the program as if it were a private kitty.

The attacks on the program were renewed in 1990, as lawmakers grappled with the scarcity of foreign aid dollars and searched for an economic strategy in the post-Cold War era. When it was needed most, said numerous critics in the Agriculture and foreign affairs committees of Congress, Food for Peace was in disarray.

Washington bureaucrats spent countless hours haggling over shipments to minor markets, many critics said, yet the federal government did not have the cash — and sometimes not even the grain — to send more than a fraction of what was shipped overseas during the heyday of the program.

Determining who ran the program also was difficult. The Agriculture Department bought the commodities, arranged the financing and sometimes the shipping, while AID handled the food after it left the dock.

But the real power — the power to decide which countries received food aid — had been vested in an obscure body called the Development Coordination Committee (DCC), composed of midlevel officials from the Agriculture Department, AID, the State Department, the Treasury Department, the Office of Management and Budget and occasionally the National Security Council. They held weekly meetings to discuss PL 480.

Early in 1990, the Bush administration had to scramble to put together an aid package for the government of Nicaragua after the unexpected victory of Violeta Chamorro in the presidential election that turned the leftist Sandinistas out of power. Initially, the Agriculture Department insisted in DCC meetings that very little wheat was available. Several weeks later, the Agriculture Department revised its estimates and added 800,000 tons of wheat to the docket. Nicaragua subsequently was promised 26,000 tons. Before the Agriculture Department found more wheat, though, the Bush administration found itself in an embarrassing position, unable to assure delivery of an aid package it had already promised to Chamorro.

In Congress, the Nicaraguan case was cited as an example of what was wrong with PL 480. Administration officials countered that the episode showed how important it was for the president to have the flexibility to respond to changing international circumstances.

Legislative Action

House and Senate committees fashioned similar provisions overhauling the PL 480 program that were included in the farm bills the two chambers considered in late July and early August. Neither chamber debated the bulk of the PL 480 overhaul proposals, but the food aid provisions served as the backdrop for several contentious arguments.

Amendments that came to a vote in both chambers on July 27 were aimed at cutting off credit sales to Iraq, whose bellicose policies and use of chemical weapons against its separatist Kurdish population had prompted a number of efforts on Capitol Hill to reverse the Reagan and Bush administrations' policy tilt toward Iraq. By substantial margins, mandated credit cutoffs were added to the food aid provisions in both the House and Senate farm bills. But they became moot after Iraq invaded Kuwait on Aug. 2 and President Bush imposed a total U.S. embargo against Iraq. *(Persian Gulf crisis, p. 299)*

A perennial regional concern also surfaced during the debate: cargo preference provisions to force transport of a specified percentage of PL 480 foodstuffs through dying Great Lakes ports. The final bill allowed Great Lakes states to preserve what they had won in the 1985 farm bill (PL 99-198). Great Lakes ports thus were guaranteed the same percentage of cargo they had had in 1984.

The conference bill provided that, instead of six agencies with veto power over food shipments, the Agriculture Department was to decide which countries to sell to and AID was to determine which countries should receive food donations.

Most food donations were made through humanitarian organizations. The new program would expand donations between the U.S. government and those of nations that could not feed their own people, many of which were in sub-Saharan Africa.

Funding for this program was to be taken out of concessional PL 480 sales. The Senate bill provided that at least 40 percent of the funds appropriated for sales was to be transferred to grants; the House bill put the figure at 33 percent. The final measure set the funds transferred to grants at not less than 40 percent.

Major Provisions

As signed into law, the Food for Peace provisions of the 1990 omnibus farm bill (S 2830 — PL 101-624):

Authorization. Overhauled the Food for Peace program, also known as PL 480, under which U.S. commodities were donated and sold overseas to combat hunger and stimulate export markets. The bill extended the credit sales program (Title I) as well as the grant program (Title II), under which commodities were donated through private voluntary organizations, and established another government-to-government grant program (Title III).

The bill repealed the authorization ceiling on total costs of the concessional sales and government-to-government grant programs. Annual Title II appropriations were limited to no more than $1 billion, unless the president determined that more was necessary to meet urgent humanitarian needs. Not less than 40 percent of the amounts available for Title I could be used to carry out sales programs and not less than 40 percent could be used for the grant program.

Delegation of Authority. Specified that the president should designate the Agriculture Department to carry out the credit sales program and the Agency for International Development to carry out the grant programs. The bill maintained the agriculture secretary's authority to determine commodities available for export; however, such determination would have to be made before the beginning of the fiscal year, and limits were placed on the secretary's authority to change the "docket" during the year.

The bill continued to allow the program to be used to advance U.S. foreign policy goals, but it narrowed the definition of foreign policy to include only improving the food security of recipient nations. It removed a requirement that countries be termed "friendly" before they could receive PL 480 funds.

Eligible Countries. Maintained a requirement that 75 percent of PL 480 funds be programmed to poorer developing countries, as defined by the World Bank. The bill authorized the department to determine which countries were eligible for Title I, but they would have to be countries with a demonstrated potential to become U.S. markets. AID had the authority to determine eligibility for Title III, giving priority to countries with high levels of malnutrition, a daily per capita consumption of less than 2,300 calories, an under-five child mortality rate of more than 100 per 1,000 births and an inability to meet food needs through domestic production or imports.

Shipping Agents. Gave the agriculture secretary or the Commodity Credit Corporation authority to serve as shipping agent for Title I transactions and required full and open competition for the purchase of commodities and ocean transportation.

Cargo Preference. Renewed a requirement that 50 percent of PL 480 shipments be transported on U.S.-flag vessels. Great Lakes ports would have to be assured of the same percentage of such cargo as they had in 1984. Foreign vessels would be exempt from the normal three-year wait for reflagging so that they could qualify to ship PL 480 commodities from Great Lakes ports.

United Nations Funding

Congress in 1990 appropriated $92.7 million — roughly 20 percent of the total requested — to pay the first installment of overdue contributions to the United Nations. The money was included in the fiscal 1991 Commerce, Justice, State and the judiciary spending bill (HR 5021 — PL 101-515).

Since the mid-1980s, Congress had withheld portions of U.S. dues because of congressional objections to various U.N. policies and management practices. But in 1990, President Bush requested $463.6 million to pay the past-due U.S. contributions, called "arrearages," over five years.

As part of a two-year State Department authorization measure enacted in 1985 (PL 99-93), Congress had voted to limit U.S. contributions to the United Nations unless it shifted to a system under which voting strength on budget matters was proportional to each member state's financial contributions. The State Department opposed the provision, and President Ronald Reagan warned in signing the bill that the restriction would create "serious problems" for the United States. *(Congress and the Nation Vol. VII, p. 199)*

Antipathy toward the United Nations began to recede after Secretary General Javier Pérez de Cuéllar negotiated a cease-fire between Iran and Iraq in 1988. Both Bush and his Democratic opponent in the 1988 presidential campaign, Michael S. Dukakis, said they favored resuming payments to the United Nations. On Sept. 13, Reagan announced that he was releasing $188 million in withheld dues.

The United Nations gained further support on Capitol Hill and within the administration in 1990 as it took a high-profile role in putting together the trade embargo against Iraq after its invasion of Kuwait on Aug. 2. *(Persian Gulf War, p. 299)*

Palau Autonomy

Congress in 1989 cleared legislation (H J Res 175 — PL 101-219) giving autonomy to the trust territory of Palau and authorizing $478 million in aid over 15 years — if residents of Palau approved a proposed charter granting autonomy to the sprawling Pacific archipelago while reserving U.S. base rights.

But Palauan voters in early 1990 rejected the Compact of Free Association. It was the seventh time since 1983 that the compact attracted a simple majority but failed to win the 75 percent majority required under the Palauan Constitution.

The vote forced Palauans to rethink their political future and frustrated key players on this side of the Pacific who helped design the compact and pushed it through Congress in 1989.

Made up of more than 200 islands in the western Pacific Ocean, Palau was the last remaining component of the U.N.-sanctioned Trust Territory of the Pacific Islands, administered by the United States since 1947. Other members of the trust territory, such as the Federated States of Micronesia and the Marshall Islands, gained autonomy in 1986 (PL 99-239). *(Congress and the Nation Vol. VII, p. 206)*

Authorizing Legislation

Progress on Palauan independence had traveled a tortuous route on Capitol Hill. "Approval in principle" was provided in PL 99-239, conditional on Palau's ratification of the compact. A second 1986 law (PL 99-658) approved the compact on condition of the enactment of authorizing legislation.

By late 1988, the Senate had approved the authorizing legislation (H J Res 597), but the measure stalled because the House Interior Committee wanted to add provisions that would address a host of social and fiscal problems on the islands. Agreement was finally reached, but too late for enactment in the 100th Congress.

Authorizing legislation cleared Congress in 1989. The House passed H J Res 175 by voice vote under suspension of the rules on June 27, and the Senate passed an amended version (S Rept 101-189) on Nov. 22 (in the session that began Nov. 21). The House accepted the Senate version by voice vote in the early morning hours of Nov. 22, as it rushed to adjourn.

Charter Rejected

In Palau's seventh referendum on the compact, held Feb. 6, 1990, compact supporters fell 15 percentage points short of the required three-fourths majority.

Palauan opponents of the compact objected to the strings it attached to independence. Under the agreement, the United States was to retain responsibility for defense of the archipelago for 50 years. A controversial element of the agreement would have allowed U.S. armed forces to take as much as a third of Palauan land for military bases.

U.S. defense officials had insisted on this clause, arguing that it would enable the United States to maintain a strategic presence in the region, an important factor should the United States lose its rights to key bases in the Philippines — which it did in 1992. *(Philippine base rights, p. 411)*

But Palauans wanted compensation for any land taken from them.

H J Res 175 struck a compromise on the base question. Under the resolution, the U.S. military could take Airai Airfield and Malakai Harbor, but it would have to compensate the owners of any other land it claimed. Levels of compensation would be determined through negotiations between U.S. and Palauan officials. Nonetheless, the base rights issue remained a point of controversy.

The main reason, however, for the compact's defeat was Palau's constitution, which banned all nuclear ships or weapons from their territory unless three-fourths of the voters agreed to overturn that ban. Because the compact provided for a limited presence of U.S. nuclear-equipped aircraft and vessels, a supermajority of 75 percent was needed to ratify the new charter.

That supermajority had eluded compact supporters since 1983. As a spokesman for Palau President Ngiratkel Etpison explained, it was "humanly impossible" to get a supermajority among the many rival Palauan clans.

Torture Treaty

Six years after it was originally passed by the United Nations, the Senate in 1990 approved a treaty that made torture a criminally punishable offense under international law.

Senate passage of the resolution to ratify the Convention Against Torture and Other Cruel, Inhuman or Degrading Treatment or Punishment (Treaty Doc 100-20) came after supporters of the pact and a key critic, Jesse Helms, R-N.C., compromised on reservations to be attached to the resolution.

The General Assembly of the United Nations unanimously approved the torture treaty on Dec. 10, 1984. The pact made torture a criminal offense and required member nations to prosecute those accused of torture or extradite them for prosecution elsewhere. Signatories to the pact also had to include torture as an extraditable offense in their bilateral treaties.

The treaty defined torture as "any act by which severe pain or suffering, whether physical or mental, is intentionally inflicted on a person . . . when such pain or suffering is inflicted by or at the instigation of or with the consent or acquiescence of a public official or other person acting in an official capacity." The definition did not include any action, resulting in pain or suffering, that arose from lawful sanctions.

Another provision of the treaty stated that "no exceptional circumstances," such as war or political instability, were justifications for the use of torture.

The treaty mandated that member states take legislative, administrative or judicial action to prevent torture in any territory under their jurisdiction. To monitor compliance with the treaty's provisions, it created a Committee Against Torture, organized under U.N. auspices, made up of 10 experts in the human rights field. They were to investigate any allegations of the use of torture.

By 1990, the treaty had been ratified by 51 nations and signed by 21 others.

The United States signed the pact April 18, 1988, and President Ronald Reagan submitted it to the Senate for ratification the next month. But Reagan included 19 proposed conditions, many of which concerned treaty supporters, including human rights groups and the American Bar Association.

The Bush administration reconsidered the reservations and agreed to remove most of them. Approval of the measure was then held up by senators concerned that some of the requirements of the treaty would supersede the U.S. Constitution. Somewhat similar concerns had held up for nearly 40 years, until 1986, Senate ratification of a 1948 treaty against genocide. *(Congress and the Nation Vol. VII, p. 205)*

The Senate Foreign Relations Committee on July 19 voted 10-0 to approve the resolution of ratification (S Exec Comm Rept 101-30), after working out, with the administration, a package of reservations to the treaty that addressed Helms' constitutional concerns. The resolution of ratification was passed by division vote of the Senate Oct. 27.

The reservations — expressing the Senate's understanding of how the pact was to be implemented but not amending the treaty itself — did the following:

- Stated that nothing in the treaty required the United States to take any action that would be prohibited by the Constitution. This so-called sovereignty proviso also was adopted during consideration of the genocide treaty.
- Limited the definition of "cruel, inhuman or degrading" treatment to cruel and unusual punishment as defined under the Fifth, Eighth and 14th Amendments to the Constitution.
- Clarified the restrictions on application of the treaty in cases of lawful sanctions.
- Required reciprocity on the part of any nation that filed a complaint with the Committee Against Torture.

Armenian Genocide Resolution

With two failed cloture votes behind him and support waning, Senate Minority Leader Bob Dole, R-Kan., in February 1990 abandoned his effort to break a weeklong filibuster on a joint resolution commemorating the "Armenian genocide of 1915-1923."

A vote of 48-51, down from the 49-49 vote taken Feb. 22, convinced Dole on Feb. 27 that he was not going to get the 60 votes needed to shut off debate on S J Res 212.

The resolution would have marked April 24 as a National Day of Remembrance for the Armenian Genocide for the estimated 1.5 million Armenians killed under the Turkish Ottoman Empire between 1915 and 1923.

The resolution appeared to have widespread support until Turkey, a key NATO ally, raised strong objections. In a letter from its ambassador, the government of Turkey argued the resolution could "inflame nationalist passions and historic grievances and incite further violence."

After Turkey raised its objections, the administration, brushing aside a Bush presidential campaign promise, came out against the resolution and enough senators backed off from their original support for the measure to prevent passage.

But Dole said the idea behind his resolution would not die. Dole had long had a special feeling for Armenia, a kingdom since divided between the Soviet Union, Turkey and Iran. Dole credited an Armenian doctor in Chicago with saving his life after he was severely wounded in World War II.

1991-92

The 102nd Congress began on a somber note as Congress — after a long and moving debate — voted to authorize the use of force to oust Iraqi forces from Kuwait. Although not a formal declaration of war, it was the closest Congress had come to that step since World War II. Four days after the vote, U.S. planes were bombing Iraq. *(Persian Gulf War, p. 299)*

The Persian Gulf conflict ended quickly and Congress turned its attention to other foreign policy issues. At the forefront of these was the Soviet Union. Though a military coup attempt against President Mikhail S. Gorbachev failed in August 1991, the unraveling of the Soviet Union was unstoppable. By the end of the year, the Soviet flag had been lowered at the Kremlin and the Soviet Union was no more.

The dramatic breakup of the Soviet Union triggered numerous calls for aiding the Soviet people and the newly independent republics, but opinions on what type of aid was needed varied widely. In 1991, Congress waited until adjournment day to clear legislation to provide up to $500 million in assistance, $400 million of which was to help dismantle the Soviet nuclear arsenal.

In 1992, Congress approved President Bush's multi-billion-dollar aid plan for the former republics of the Soviet Union. But the aid package was endorsed only after the Bush administration made a number of concessions on domestic programs, which Democratic leaders argued were essential before members could vote for aid to the former Soviet Union in an election year in economically hard times.

The economy also had an impact on a perennial sore subject — foreign aid. In 1991, a foreign aid authorization bill progressed further than it had in recent years — no such measure had become law since 1985 — but in the end it fell victim to an intense backlash. In a strong protest vote against providing foreign aid at a time of economic troubles at home, the House rejected the conference report.

Disagreement between the Bush administration and Israel over Israel's request for $10 billion in loan guarantees prevented passage in 1991 of a regular foreign aid appropriations bill. The foreign aid program instead was funded through continuing resolutions. The United States and Israel resolved their differences in 1992, and a regular foreign aid bill cleared. Putting aside election-year jitters over voting for overseas spending, Congress overwhelmingly approved the spending measure, a bill made more palatable by the Israeli guarantees program.

A major breakthrough in Mideast politics came in 1991, when Bush succeeded in bringing Israel and its Arab neighbors together for peace talks.

The following year two foreign conflicts — in the former Yugoslavia and in Somalia — underlined the uncertainties surrounding the role of the United States in a world no longer dominated by the U.S.-Soviet superpower standoff. Initially, the United States tried to distance itself from the ethnic fighting in the former Yugoslav republics. But the rising death toll and stories of "ethnic cleansing" and concentration camps run by Serbs led to increased calls for action. Congress endorsed the administration's decision to seek U.N. authorization of military force, if necessary, to ensure the delivery of humanitarian relief to besieged Bosnia. Lawmakers later went even further when they authorized the president to provide U.S. military equipment to Bosnia if a U.N. arms embargo in the region was lifted.

In Africa, widespread famine in Somalia gnawed at congressional consciences, but civil warfare there made the administration and its supporters wary of U.S. involvement. Nevertheless, in August, Congress urged the administration to seek deployment of U.N. security forces to ensure the delivery of emergency food. And in December, Bush ordered in U.S. troops to help in the food distribution. Most members of Congress appeared to support Bush's action, although the first official expression of support did not come until February 1993, when the Senate passed a resolution.

Aid to Former USSR

Like others around the world, members of Congress spent much of 1991 transfixed by the extraordinary changes that culminated at year's end in the dissolution of the Union of Soviet Socialist Republics (USSR). But the lawmakers had the added task of debating whether to spend money from the U.S. Treasury to encourage, and perhaps even subsidize, the change from communism and a command economy to democracy and capitalism.

Ultimately, Congress in 1991 voted to give the president authority to spend up to $400 million in Defense Department funds to assist in the dismantling of the Soviet nuclear arsenal and up to $100 million in Pentagon funds to deliver humanitarian aid.

Congress went further in 1992, authorizing $410 million in bilateral humanitarian, economic and other assistance for Russia and 11 other former Soviet republics. (The bill did not include the Baltic States.) Also approved was a $12.3 billion increase in the U.S. contribution to the International Monetary Fund (IMF), which became one of the lead agencies coordinating support for Russia and its neighbors. Congress authorized the use of $800 million from the Pentagon budget, half of which was approved the previous year, to help in the nuclear dismantling.

Enactment of the aid programs did not come easily. Much of 1991 was spent grappling with the questions of whether, when and how to send aid to the United States' longtime adversary. The U.S. economy made a troubling backdrop for the debate. At a time of recession, huge federal deficits and declining foreign aid budgets, how could the United States afford to bail out the Soviet Union?

The White House took a cautious approach, as it continued to support Soviet President Mikhail S. Gorbachev. Congress was torn over whether the Bush administration was doing too little to support historic change in the Soviet Union or too much to coddle a Soviet regime that had stopped short of fundamental economic and political change.

Gorbachev's halting course toward fundamental change, two steps forward and one back, proved not only disconcerting to the West but also unsustainable over the long run. Communist hard-liners, whom the reformist leader had kept in key positions in his government, turned on him and his policies in August 1991. Gorbachev survived but the hard-liners' coup attempt added greater urgency to the debate over U.S. policy. Further fuel was added by the declarations of independence by the Soviet republics, one after another. *(End of the Cold War, p. 319)*

On Capitol Hill in early November 1991, broad opposition forced sponsors to drop an initial aid proposal from the fiscal 1992 defense authorization bill (HR 2100 — PL 102-190).

But Congress dramatically reversed course later that month. Both chambers overwhelmingly approved the $500 million plan (HR 3807 — PL 102-228) that permitted the president to use Pentagon funds to help the Soviet people survive the winter and to dismantle some of their 27,000 nuclear weapons. Funding for the aid was provided by a supplemental appropriations bill (H J Res 157 — PL 102-229).

In December, most of the Soviet republics proclaimed the end of the Soviet Union and the creation of a loose Commonwealth of Independent States. On Dec. 25, Gorbachev bowed to that reality and resigned from office.

Under pressure from foreign policy experts and a bipartisan group of congressional leaders to take advantage of new, friendlier regimes in the former Soviet Union, Bush in 1992 proposed a sweeping plan to help the republics develop free-market economies and democratic forms of government. The plan was part of a $24 billion multilateral aid package proposed by the United States and six other leading industrial nations.

Although the measure was initially well received, House Democratic leaders quickly made clear they would not permit passage of the foreign aid package until the Bush administration made a number of concessions on domestic programs. They argued that, in an election year, lawmakers could not be expected to approve assistance for the former Soviet Union while their constituents were suffering from the effects of a stale economy.

The price exacted for congressional support was extension of jobless benefits and other increased domestic spending, and it was not until the final days of the session that the republics' aid package was cleared (S 2532 — PL 102-511). The foreign aid appropriations bill (HR 5368 — PL 102-391) provided funding for the $12.3 billion IMF increase and for $417 million in economic and technical assistance to the former Soviet republics. *(Fiscal 1993 foreign aid appropriations, p. 271)*

In Search of a Policy

Early in 1991, as Washington remained riveted by the Persian Gulf War, a crackdown in the Baltic States shook Congress' confidence in and enthusiasm for the changes promised by Soviet President Gorbachev. *(Persian Gulf War, p. 299)*

By voice vote on Jan. 16, the Senate approved a nonbinding resolution (S Res 14) that called on the administration to review and possibly cut off economic and other aid to the Soviet Union until it withdrew troops from the Baltic States and undertook good-faith negotiations with the republics of Lithuania, Latvia and Estonia.

On Jan. 23, the House suspended the rules and adopted a concurrent resolution (H Con Res 40), 417-0, condemning the violence and asking Bush to work with allies in Europe toward a "coordinated approach" to sanctions if the Soviets continued to use force to suppress the movements for independence by the Baltic States. The Senate passed a similar resolution (S Con Res 6) on Jan. 24 by a vote of 99-0.

Despite the widespread outrage and disappointment over Gorbachev's turn toward traditional Soviet authoritarianism, some members appeared reluctant to cut short a new era of U.S.-Soviet cooperation. The debate concerned whether it was in the best interest of the United States to support Gorbachev as a wayward but indispensable reformer or attempt to pressure him back toward the path of reform.

Even for the diplomatically attuned Bush administration, the situation required a delicate balancing act: maintaining good relations with the Soviet Union while signaling displeasure with the Soviet army's violent suppression of the democracy movement in the Baltic States.

In late January, the White House announced an indefinite postponement of a U.S.-Soviet summit, originally set to take place in Moscow Feb. 11-13. But administration officials took pains to state that the Baltic crisis had not caused the delay. The Persian Gulf War and slow progress on a strategic arms agreement were cited as the reasons.

During his State of the Union address Jan. 29, Bush announced that Gorbachev's government had provided "representations" that it would "move away from violence" in Lithuania, Latvia and Estonia. Kremlin officials an-

CIA Leadership

On a **key vote of 64-31 (R 42-0; D 22-31)**, the Senate Nov. 5, 1991, confirmed Robert M. Gates as director of central intelligence. Gates, who was President Bush's deputy national security adviser, replaced William H. Webster. *(1991 key votes, p. 1061; Gates background, p. 1177; Webster background, Congress and the Nation Vol. VII, p. 1049)*

Upon the announcement of his retirement, Webster was praised by members of Congress as a man of integrity who restored the CIA's tattered image. Under Webster, sitting and former members of the House and Senate Intelligence committees said, the agency managed to regain some of the stature it lost during the Iran-contra scandal.

Lawmakers were less supportive of the nomination of Gates, whose uncertain role in the Iran-contra affair eventually led him to withdraw his name from consideration as CIA director in 1987. Controversy continued to surround Gates in 1991.

The Senate Intelligence Committee postponed consideration of the nomination while it gathered more information about Gates. And during the hearings, Gates suffered severe criticism about his management style and analytic abilities. Nevertheless, he promised greater CIA cooperation with Congress, and the committee voted 11-4 on Oct. 18 to recommend his nomination.

nounced Jan. 30 that a tentative troop withdrawal had begun in Lithuania.

The reports of a pullout were welcomed by members of Congress, who had been urging that the White House more forcefully oppose Moscow's reversion to hard-line tactics. Some lawmakers had speculated that Bush was restrained in his criticism because of his desire to hold together the anti-Iraq alliance, which included the Soviet Union.

In June, the administration announced that it was extending to the Soviet Union $1.5 billion in U.S. agricultural credits, in addition to the $1 billion extended in December 1990. The Senate had approved a non-binding resolution (S Res 117) on May 15 favoring the agricultural credits. But the 70-28 vote did little to demonstrate a consensus in Congress on Soviet affairs because the farm credits enjoyed strong backing from farm-state lawmakers anxious to secure commodity sales for their constituents.

By summer, Congress was divided over whether the Bush administration was doing too little or too much. But with the Gorbachev government appearing to change its internal and external policies each month — was he a budding democrat or a throwback to a repressive era? — many in Congress were content to let the administration set the diplomatic course.

The White House seemed eager to underscore the prospects for improving U.S.-Soviet business ties by nominating veteran Democratic insider Robert S. Strauss on June 4 to be the U.S. ambassador in Moscow. The appointment of Strauss, who was nearly devoid of experience in Soviet affairs but was a skilled operator in the worlds of politics and commerce, was widely praised. The Senate confirmed Strauss' nomination by voice vote on July 30.

Bush was in Moscow at that time meeting with Gorbachev. The two signed a treaty that called for significant reductions in U.S.-Soviet arsenals of strategic nuclear weapons. They also announced joint U.S.-Soviet sponsorship of a Middle East peace conference, and Bush said he would send to Congress a long-awaited U.S.-Soviet trade agreement. *(Strategic arms treaty, p. 383; Middle East peace talks, p. 277; trade agreement, p. 192)*

The hard-liners' coup attempt came just a few weeks after the Moscow summit. Boris N. Yeltsin, the president of Russia, led a people-power revolt in Moscow that brought about the coup's collapse on Aug. 21.

A still-shaken Gorbachev returned to power and proclaimed the Communist Party dissolved. But his control was uncertain, his judgment in surrounding himself with men who betrayed him was doubted and Yeltsin's more assertive style of leadership was in the ascendant. In the coup's aftermath, more and more of the Soviet republics declared their independence.

With the world turned on end by the political convulsions in the Soviet Union, the aid question gained greater urgency. But there was still no consensus.

Rep. Les Aspin, D-Wis., and Sen. Sam Nunn, D-Ga., chairmen of the House and Senate Armed Services committees, attempted to write an aid plan into the fiscal 1992 defense authorization bill (HR 2100) when the measure was in conference. But mounting pressure to give domestic needs priority over foreign policy doomed their plan to take $1 billion from the defense budget to provide humanitarian aid to the Soviet Union.

Washington was embroiled in a frenzied search for ways to aid the troubled domestic economy. Democrats were accusing Bush of caring more about other countries than about unemployed Americans, and Republicans were determined to show that they, too, cared most about those in the United States. In the face of bipartisan opposition and at best a tepid response from the White House, Aspin and Nunn dropped the plan on Nov. 13.

But just two weeks later Congress reversed itself.

1991 Aid Package

After pondering the breakup of the Soviet Union for most of 1991, lawmakers waited until adjournment day, Nov. 27, to clear authorizing legislation (HR 3807) and a supplemental appropriation (H J Res 157) that made available up to $500 million for Soviet assistance.

The congressional package was only a fraction of the massive direct aid that some outside experts had urged. Nonetheless, it represented a sea change of attitudes from only weeks earlier, when Nunn and Aspin were forced to abandon their aid plan.

The measures that succeeded where Nunn and Aspin had initially failed gave the president the authority to use up to $400 million in defense funding to help the former Soviet Union dismantle its nuclear arsenal. The president also was given authority to use up to $100 million in defense funds to provide U.S. military or commercial transport for emergency food, medical and other humanitarian aid.

Senior senators — concerned that domestic politics were playing havoc with long-term national security interests — pressed hard in the final days of the session to enact the trimmed-down plan. They did it with minimal White House support and against a strong anti-foreign aid tide that was sweeping Congress. In the end, they convinced colleagues that failure to act could prove devastating if instability in the Soviet Union loosened controls over that country's nuclear arsenal.

Some lawmakers said they were fearful that the United States might be duped into providing the aid, only to have the Soviet Union turn around and build newer weapons. But sponsors noted that before the demilitarization assistance could be provided, the president would have to certify to Congress that the recipient was making a "substantial investment" of its own in dismantling weapons and was not undergoing a major military modernization program.

"This is one time when the Congress of the United States should have some faith and confidence in the president of the United States," Nunn said. He and others who worked on the plan were unable to get the administration to take a public position on the proposal, although they said they were privately encouraged to press ahead.

Republicans said the administration kept a low profile to avoid Democratic complaints that Bush devoted too much attention to foreign affairs and not enough to pressing domestic concerns.

Legislative Action. The demilitarization aid was proposed in the Senate on Nov. 25 as an amendment by Nunn and Richard G. Lugar, R-Ind., to legislation (HR 3807), passed by the House Nov. 19, authorizing the transfer to North Atlantic Treaty Organization (NATO) allies of equipment to be disposed of under the conventional forces in Europe (CFE) treaty. The amendment, approved by a **key vote of 86-8 (R 34-8; D 52-0)**, called for up to $500 million to dismantle the Soviet arsenal. *(1991 key votes, p. 1061)*

Another amendment calling for up to $200 million in emergency transport authority for humanitarian assistance was approved Nov. 25, 87-7.

U.S. Embassy in Moscow

After five years of bitter debate, Congress voted in 1991 to shift to the State Department the burden of deciding what to do with the unfinished U.S. Embassy building in Moscow, which was riddled with listening devices.

In mid-1992, the United States signed an agreement with Russia allowing construction of a new U.S. Embassy near the unfinished building.

1991 Action

Congress in 1991 appropriated $100 million for embassy "reconstruction" in Moscow as a part of the appropriations bill for the Departments of Commerce, Justice, State and the federal judiciary (HR 2608 — PL 102-140), which President Bush signed Oct. 28. But the bill did not restrict how the money was to be spent; it required only that the State Department report to Congress on its decision.

Similar language was contained in the law that authorized the activities of the State Department for fiscal 1992-93 (HR 1415 — PL 102-138). *(State Department authorization, p. 290)*

The unfinished building had stood unused since August 1985, when the listening devices were discovered embedded in its walls. Since then, lawmakers and the executive branch had struggled over how to fix the problem. While some wanted to tear down the building and start anew, others wanted to keep it for unclassified purposes or to add new, secure top floors. *(Background, box, p. 209)*

Both the Reagan and Bush administrations advocated tearing down the building and starting over from scratch as the option most likely to produce a secure facility. That decision got the support of Ernest F. Hollings, D-S.C. — chairman of the Senate Appropriations subcommittee in charge of the embassy — the Senate Intelligence Committee and various members of the House.

But for three years, Rep. Neal Smith, D-Iowa, Hollings' counterpart in the House, and members of Smith's House Appropriations Subcommittee on Commerce, Justice, State and the Federal Judiciary successfully blocked attempts to implement the teardown option. Smith and his allies said tearing down the building was a waste of money. Surely, they argued, some use could be found for a nearly completed building.

In 1991, the administration again proposed tearing down the bugged Moscow embassy building and constructing a new one. When that plan ran into immediate problems with Smith, the State Department came up with a new proposal, nicknamed the "Top Hat," which called for knocking down the top two floors of the eight-story building and adding four new, secure floors. The administration estimated that the Top Hat option would cost about $215 million over three or four years, compared with $280 million over five years to tear down and replace the building.

In appeasing Smith, however, the State Department infuriated other members, who accused the department of not pushing hard enough to raze the bug-riddled embassy.

At a June hearing of the Senate Appropriations subcommittee with jurisdiction over the embassy, Secretary of State James A. Baker III implored senators to make a decision — any decision — to push the embarrassing episode to a close. The embassy situation had taken on new urgency after a fire in the old U.S. Embassy in Moscow on March 28 destroyed portions of the building.

During action on the State Department authorization (HR 1415), the House agreed May 15, 223-185, to leave the decision to the State Department. The Senate version did the same.

Both the House and Senate versions of the State Department appropriations bill provided $130 million for the embassy, but only the Senate version specified that the funds were to be used for the teardown option.

In a surprise move, the two Appropriations panels worked out a compromise during the conference on the bill. Both Hollings and Smith agreed to a plan to build a new, small embassy on the compound, near the bug-riddled building. No decision was made as to what to do with the unfinished building.

Members of the House, angry that the plan for a new building was added in conference with no warning and little debate, voted 175-231 on Oct. 3 to reject the compromise. They inserted by voice vote language to give $100 million to the State Department but required that State report back on its plan. The Senate agreed, and HR 2608 was sent on to the president.

1992 Accord

During Russian President Boris N. Yeltsin's June 1992 visit to Washington, Secretary of State Baker and Russian Foreign Minister Andrei V. Kozyrev signed an embassy agreement.

In the accord, the United States agreed to drop a $30 million claim against the Soviet Union for bugging the U.S. Embassy in Moscow. In exchange, the Russians would give the United States a generous long-term lease on the unoccupied building and allow construction of a new facility nearby.

The agreement also allowed the Russians to finally occupy a new embassy complex in Washington that had sat empty for years because of the ongoing dispute. Under earlier agreements, the complex could not be occupied until the United States moved into its new facility in Moscow.

But conferees on a fiscal 1992 supplemental appropriations bill (H J Res 157), which provided the funding for the plan, lowered the maximum amount for demilitarization aid to $400 million and the amount for humanitarian assistance to $100 million.

The House, whose leaders had introduced a broader, $1 billion aid package on Nov. 22, approved the Senate changes early Nov. 27 by voice vote. However, the House amended HR 3807 to lower the aid figures to those provided in the supplemental appropriations bill.

The Senate cleared the amended, $500 million bill by voice vote late in the day.

On Dec. 8, the leaders of Russia, Ukraine and Belarus joined in a new Commonwealth of Independent States and proclaimed that the Soviet Union no longer existed. Russian President Yeltsin gathered support from other republics as Gorbachev threatened to resign.

President Bush signed both HR 3807 (PL 102-228) and H J Res 157 (PL 102-229) on Dec. 12.

In a speech that same day, Secretary of State James A. Baker III said that the administration would make use of the authority the legislation provided. The tone of Baker's speech was one of increased urgency toward U.S. involvement in support of change in the former Soviet Union. Baker invited world leaders to a conference in Washington to coordinate aid, and he announced that the administration would submit a request for technical assistance to support Soviet economic reform.

Calling Baker's speech "a qualitative step forward," House Armed Services Chairman Aspin said, "Until this announcement, the administration's response to the opportunities and dangers of the post-coup former Soviet Union has been tepid and piecemeal."

On Dec. 25, Gorbachev resigned from office, and the Soviet flag was lowered at the Kremlin, marking the end of an empire and sealing the close of the Cold War.

1992 Aid Package

In early 1992, demands built for the Bush administration and Congress to take more aggressive action in providing U.S. assistance to the former Soviet republics.

Bush Proposals. In January, Bush requested $620 million in technical and humanitarian assistance for the former Soviet republics in fiscal 1992 and 1993. This would be in addition to $860 million already available and $3.5 billion in loan guarantees that had been provided for the purchase of U.S. agricultural goods. The administration also had requested a $12 billion increase in the U.S. contribution to the IMF.

On April 1, Bush announced a far more sweeping commitment to aid the former Soviet republics. The plan called for the United States to participate in a $24 billion multilateral initiative, much of it as loans and guarantees, rather than direct assistance. Of that amount, $18 billion was to be in bilateral and multilateral assistance aimed at bolstering Russia's balance of payments. The package included a multilateral fund to stabilize the Russian currency.

Bush also announced that he would increase by $1.1 billion the export credits available for purchase of U.S. agricultural goods by the former republics. The president sought waivers of Cold War-era laws that limited U.S. assistance for, and private business activities in, the former republics.

Lawmakers generally welcomed Bush's proposal. But those promoting the assistance predicted that enactment would require strong guidance from Bush and congressional leaders to avoid potentially disruptive election-year turbulence.

"It will take the best skills of enlightened leadership," said Rep. Henry J. Hyde, R-Ill. "Some people are sure to look at this as money going to St. Petersburg, Russia, rather than St. Petersburg, Florida."

As senior members of Congress had encouraged him to do for months in urging such a package, Bush presented the assistance as insurance for the United States against the re-emergence of an unfriendly regime, not as a handout to the former Soviet people.

"The stakes are as high for us now as any that we have faced in this century," Bush said at a televised White House news conference. "If this democratic revolution is defeated, it could plunge us into a world more dangerous in some respects than the dark years of the Cold War."

While emphasizing that the United States must lead, Bush made clear that the financial effort would be international. The president and White House officials played down the cost to American taxpayers. "It's not a tremendous amount of money," Bush said. "Our commitment is very, very substantial."

Much of the president's package required no legislative action. However, the administration viewed congressional endorsement as crucial, both to provide some of the bilateral aid and to put a bipartisan imprimatur on the overall effort.

Lawmakers repeated their pledge to support the administration's effort — if Bush invested political capital in pushing through the proposals.

The administration appeared ready to take Congress up on the offer. Secretary of State Baker said on April 1 that he was "ready to go up there tomorrow and start fighting for this legislation."

In a letter to Congress on April 3, Bush wrote, "This is an issue that transcends any election.... I urge all members of Congress to set aside partisan and parochial interests."

But early signs of potential resistance existed. House Majority Whip David E. Bonior, D-Mich., threatened to organize a move against assistance to Russia until the administration supported legislation to extend unemployment benefits and to create jobs.

And even the talk of bipartisanship had enough partisan overtones to make lawmakers wary of predicting success for the plan. Democrats applauded Bush for his aid initiatives and then went on to criticize him for offering them too late.

Within minutes of Bush's announcement, Arkansas Gov. Bill Clinton, campaigning for the Democratic presidential nomination, gave a foreign policy speech in New York that largely mirrored the president's proposals for helping the former Soviet empire. But he, too, criticized the president for delay.

"The present administration has been overly cautious on the issue of aid to Russia, not for policy considerations, but out of political calculation," Clinton said. "Now, prodded by Democrats in Congress, rebuked by Nixon and realizing that I have been raising this issue in the campaign since December, the president is finally, even now as we meet here, putting forward a plan of assistance to Russia and the other new republics.... I'd really like it if I could have as much influence on his domestic policy."

In an effort to explain his timing, Bush said that the administration had been pulling together the components of a package for months and had just been able to work out the details with allies. Administration officials also noted that the Russian government of President Yeltsin had only recently implemented credible economic reforms on which the administration had conditioned U.S. assistance.

"This isn't any Johnny-come-lately thing, and this isn't driven by election-year pressures," Bush said. "It's what's right for the United States."

Senate Action. The Senate approved Bush's comprehensive aid initiative on July 2 by a vote of 76-20. The legislation, termed the Freedom Support Act, had been reported by the Senate Foreign Relations Committee on June 2 (S 2532 — S Rept 102-292).

The administration had sought passage of the legislation first in the Senate, where support for the aid appeared greatest. Bush had hoped to have the legislation in hand by mid-June, in time for a scheduled summit meeting in Washington with Yeltsin. But the legislation was still pending in the Senate when the Russian president arrived.

Yeltsin was greeted as a hero and a world-class celebrity. He signed an unprecedented arms control agreement with Bush and talked about mutually beneficial trade, then made sweeping, unqualified promises to cooperate with U.S. officials on such touchstone issues as Vietnam prisoners of war. *(Arms control agreements, p. 383)*

When Yeltsin came to Capitol Hill on June 17 and entered the House chamber, members of Congress greeted him with chants of "Bo-ris, Bo-ris" and hailed him with numerous standing ovations during his speech before a joint meeting of Congress. Yeltsin clearly won over those lawmakers who had been skeptical of his commitment to democratic reforms and his willingness to become an American ally. *(Yeltsin speech, box, p. 327)*

As recently as June 16, the Senate Democratic Caucus had been deeply split over the wisdom of bringing the president's aid proposal to the floor. But Senate Majority Leader George J. Mitchell, D-Maine, told reporters after a leadership luncheon with Yeltsin on June 17 that many members felt that the Russian president had made a "strong and persuasive" case.

The three-day debate on the measure was dominated by expressions of concern over the sagging U.S. economy. Opponents complained during the sometimes rancorous debate that Bush was unwilling to devote similar resources to domestic problems.

Because the measure authorized a combination of new and existing proposals — some of which required no outlays of funds — cost estimates varied widely. The Congressional Budget Office (CBO) estimated the cost of the measure's provisions authorizing aid for the former Soviet republics and Eastern Europe at nearly $1 billion in fiscal 1993, but that figure did not include funds required to back billions of dollars in already approved or proposed agricultural and export credits.

In the mountain of amendments to the measure was a proposal to require the president to match that nearly $1 billion with a similar level of support for domestic programs. The amendment was tabled (killed), 64-32, on July 2.

Perhaps the most serious threat to the aid package came from an amendment that would have barred most U.S. aid for Moscow unless the president certified that Russia was making "significant progress" toward removing its troops still based in the Baltic States. Opponents said the amendment, offered by Dennis DeConcini, D-Ariz., and Larry Pressler, R-S.D., would nullify the act because the president could not make such a certification.

Foreign Relations Committee Chairman Claiborne Pell, D-R.I., proposed to modify the amendment by delaying the certification requirement for a year. Despite Pressler's complaint that Pell's amendment amounted to a "sell-out" of the Baltic people, his motion to table the Pell amendment fell short July 1, in a **key vote of 35-60 (R 11-30; D 24-30).** Pell's amendment was then adopted by voice vote. *(1992 key votes, p. 1083)*

Demonstrating their support for the Baltic States, senators subsequently voted July 2, 96-0, in favor of an amendment to authorize the president to provide shipments of non-lethal military equipment to the Baltics.

Several other efforts were made to attach policy conditions to the aid initiative, but most were blocked. The administration had signaled at the outset that the inclusion of such conditions would kill the bill.

An amendment that could have required U.S. representatives to multilateral banks to oppose loans to the former republics unless they were secured by royalties from commodity exports was tabled 75-21 on July 2. A motion to table an amendment to place tough restrictions on the $12.3 billion increase in the U.S. contribution to the IMF was agreed to July 2, 77-20.

In something of a surprise, the administration did not contest an amendment to bar the use of U.S. aid and credits to repay debts owed by the former republics to international financial institutions. The amendment was approved by voice vote.

Because of uncertainty over how much the aid initiative would actually cost — Senate Republicans put it at about $150 million in fiscal 1992 and $470 million in fiscal 1993 — the Senate adopted by voice vote an amendment to strike the open-ended grant of budget authority sought by the administration and instead set specific funding amounts for many of the categories of direct assistance.

House Action. Setting aside fears that recession-weary constituents would retaliate in November, House members voted overwhelmingly on Aug. 6 for legislation (HR 4547) authorizing approximately $610 million in assistance to the former states of the Soviet Union and the $12.3 billion increase in the U.S. commitment to the IMF. All efforts to amend HR 4547 were blocked by an unusually united leadership, and the measure was approved by a **key vote of 255-164 (R 94-68; D 161-95; I 0-1).** The House then passed by voice vote S 2532, after substituting the text of HR 4547.

Republican and Democratic leaders and the White House rallied behind the aid bill, making passage possible at a time when many politicians were far more concerned about the loss of jobs and urban strife at home than the plight of a former enemy. Sponsors argued that the bill was vital to U.S. self-interest. They warned that failure to support the emerging democracies could prove far more costly in the long run.

The bill was easily approved by the House Foreign Affairs Committee on June 10. The committee reported the measure (H Rept 102-569, Part I) on June 16, then filed a supplemental report (H Rept 102-569, Part II) on June 22. Sharing jurisdiction over the bill, House Armed Services (H Rept 102-569, Part III) and House Agriculture (H Rept 102-569, Part IV) reported HR 4547 on July 2. House Democratic leaders said they would not schedule a floor vote on the aid until the administration agreed to a number of domestic spending initiatives.

The path to House passage was cleared Aug. 5, when administration officials tentatively agreed in a meeting with House leaders to accelerate about $370 million in spending on public works programs and to make new loan guarantees available to local communities, possibly as much as $2 billion.

The agreement to spend more on domestic programs did not alone ensure passage of the bill. A remarkable coalition of current and former public officials, business groups and peace activists also lobbied heavily for the aid legislation.

In an Aug. 3 letter, designed as much to provide political cover for members worried about constituent reaction as to persuade, Bush told members that failure to help the struggling republics "would be a tragic mistake for which history will surely judge us harshly."

Former presidents Ronald Reagan, Jimmy Carter, Gerald R. Ford and Richard Nixon also wrote that the vote could be the most important one members would cast. "The stakes could not be higher," they said, in a letter read on the House floor. "If we fail to seize this historic opportunity now, authoritarianism could return to Moscow and elsewhere, the anticipated peace dividend could evaporate, future markets and jobs for Americans could be lost, and nuclear weapons may again threaten the lives of our children."

Conservatives who were frequently critical of foreign aid spending also joined in the plea for action in this case. One potential stumbling block was strong opposition to a rule providing for floor debate but prohibiting amendments. Sponsors of the bill had argued that the aid could be derailed if it was burdened by conditions or by amendments on extraneous domestic issues.

But an expected confrontation over the rule never materialized. Debate on the rule came to a close and the rule was adopted by voice vote at a time when opponents, who would have called for a recorded vote, were off the House floor.

Conference, Final Action. House and Senate conferees on Sept. 24 quickly resolved their differences over S 2532.

The Senate approved the conference report (H Rept 102-964) by voice vote and with no debate on Oct. 1. More debate and dissent were heard in the House, which adopted the measure on Oct. 3 on a vote of 232-164, completing congressional action.

Still included in S 2532 were conditions on U.S. aid to the republics that the administration had hoped to avoid. However, conferees agreed to soften a Senate provision that would have cut off aid unless the president determined that Russia was withdrawing its troops from the Baltics within 12 months of enactment. The conference report said Russia would be ineligible for aid if it failed to make significant progress in removing troops, but it allowed the president a national interest waiver of the provision.

Administration officials lobbied strongly against any legislative conditions, arguing that the assistance was largely in U.S. — not Russian — interests.

The conference committee on HR 5368, the companion fiscal 1993 foreign aid appropriations bill, also became embroiled in debate over conditions placed on Russian aid. The final version of that bill contained a complicated compromise partially withholding and ultimately cutting off aid if "substantial progress" was not made toward setting a timetable for the withdrawal of Russian troops from the Baltic States. *(Fiscal 1993 foreign aid appropriations, p. 271)*

Major Provisions. As signed into law, S 2532, the Freedom Support Act:

- Authorized $410 million in bilateral assistance to Russia and 11 other republics. (The Baltic States were not included.) The money was made available in fiscal 1993 for a wide range of purposes including humanitarian needs, health care, democratic reforms, the promotion of private enterprise, trade, education, environmental protection, transportation, telecommunications, drug education, refugee assistance, energy efficiency and nuclear reactor safety.

The legislation mostly allowed the administration to decide how funds should be spent. However, the programs were supposed to promote a free-market system in the republics as well as provide opportunities for U.S. businesses.

- Placed several conditions on the aid. Assistance was to be terminated if the president determined that a republic was guilty of gross violations of human rights or international law, or if it failed to meet certain arms control obligations.

In the case of Russia, assistance had to be cut off if the president determined that the country had failed to make "significant progress" in removing its troops from the Baltic States of Estonia, Latvia and Lithuania. However, a more stringent requirement concerning Russian troops in the Baltics was contained in the foreign operations spending bill, which appropriated the aid money.

Most of the conditions in the Freedom Support Act could be waived if the president determined that was in the U.S. interest. However, this did not apply to a prohibition in the bill against any aid to the government of Azerbaijan until the president determined that it was taking "demonstrable steps to cease all blockades and other offensive uses of force against Armenia and Nagorno-Karabakh."

- Authorized a $12.3 billion increase in the U.S. contribution to the International Monetary Fund. The increase was negotiated long before the collapse of the Soviet Union, but it failed to win congressional approval earlier because of lawmakers' reluctance to approve any foreign aid.
- Expressed congressional support for U.S. participation, with sums of up to $3 billion in previously approved funds, in multilateral currency stabilization funds for Russia and the other republics. About half the money was to go toward the U.S. share of a $6 billion fund planned by leading industrial nations to help stabilize the Russian ruble.
- Authorized the use of $800 million from the Pentagon budget to help the former Soviet republics dismantle nuclear and other weapons of mass destruction. The funds, half of which were approved in fiscal 1992, could also be used to assist the former Soviet military establishment to convert to civilian activities and to prevent out-of-work Soviet scientists from selling their knowledge about nuclear weapons to potentially dangerous nations.

The United States had already committed about $190 million of the funds to transport nuclear weapons from other republics to Russia, to build a new storage facility there for radioactive waste from dismantled weapons, and to build science centers in Russia and Ukraine to employ weapons experts.

- Allowed the president to use $100 million in security assistance funds to help dismantle and halt the proliferation of nuclear, biological and chemical weapons worldwide. It allowed another $40 million in defense funds to be used to support international non-proliferation efforts.

• Authorized $12 million for the establishment of American business centers to help U.S. businesses and state development offices pursue joint ventures and other business activities in the republics.

• Allowed the president to establish a Democracy Corps of private U.S. citizens to provide technical and other assistance in setting up local democratic institutions and civic organizations in the republics. It authorized up to $15 million for the program in fiscal 1993.

• Promoted space trade and cooperation between the United States and the republics by expediting approval of U.S. purchases of former Soviet space hardware, technology and services, and by promoting trade missions for the U.S. aerospace industry.

• Made the republics eligible for agricultural credit assistance under the Food for Progress program, which was designed to promote free enterprise in emerging democracies. It also authorized technical assistance for the republics to improve food production and distribution systems.

• Authorized $25 million for the Department of State and the U.S. Information Agency to set up diplomatic posts and other offices in the republics.

• Authorized $71 million for student, business, agricultural and other exchange programs between the United States and the former Soviet republics. Of this amount, $20 million was set aside for short-term visits by secondary school students from the republics to the United States.

• Extended the Support for East European Democracy (SEED) program, already applied in Poland and Hungary, to the rest of Eastern Europe. SEED aid was designed to boost private enterprise in these countries.

• Changed several Cold War-era laws to reflect the collapse of communism. For example, the bill removed the names of the former Soviet republics from the list of communist nations ineligible for aid under the 1961 Foreign Assistance Act.

1992-93 Aid Authorization

In an America-first backlash against foreign aid that transcended partisan and ideological divisions, the House in 1991 defeated the conference report for a foreign assistance authorization measure.

The lawmakers rebuffed a $25 billion measure (HR 2508) for fiscal 1992-93 that had progressed further than any such bill since 1985, the last time a foreign aid authorization bill was enacted.

Despite epochal changes in the world — from the collapse of the Soviet Union to peace talks for the Middle East — Congress ended 1991 without clearing any broad foreign assistance legislation. In addition to spurning the authorization measure, Congress deferred action until 1992 on a foreign operations appropriations bill after President Bush requested a delay in action on Israel's request for $10 billion in loan guarantees. Foreign aid programs were funded through a short-term continuing resolution. *(Short-term appropriation, p. 77)*

The authorization bill's prospects had been fragile even before the House rejection. Bush had vowed to veto it on several grounds, including provisions that would have overturned restrictions on aid to international family planning organizations that promoted abortion as a method of family planning.

Bush had attempted to frame the year's debate on foreign aid by proposing to streamline the foreign aid authorization process — and to give the chief executive the maximum possible leeway in choosing where to channel funds.

Bush's proposed legislation would have significantly streamlined foreign aid by consolidating development assistance in a single account and removing restrictions from many aid programs. The centerpiece of the administration's plan would have been the virtual elimination of earmarks, Congress' mandating of foreign aid funds for particular countries and purposes. In a letter to congressional leaders April 12, Bush said, "The law governing foreign assistance has become so complex, splintered and restrictive that it no longer serves our national interest."

No one on Capitol Hill disputed the idea that the Foreign Assistance Act of 1961 (PL 87-195) that governed foreign aid was an unwieldy vehicle for providing aid abroad in the post-Cold War era. But when lawmakers heard pleas from the administration for greater flexibility, they assumed that it would come at the expense of congressional power. *(1961 law, Congress and the Nation Vol. I, p. 181)*

Indeed, Bush's letter pulled no punches: "The restitution of presidential authorities would extend to all aspects of the proposed legislation."

Once they received the president's plan, members largely ignored it. Lawmakers engaged in their customary practice of asserting a role in foreign policy by earmarking funds or attaching tough conditions to aid.

Despite the measure's ultimate failure, its progress through Congress during 1991 provided significant signposts of lawmakers' attitudes toward foreign aid in particular and toward the historic changes in the world more generally.

Legislative Action

The House approved HR 2508, 274-138, on June 20. The measure would have authorized $12.4 billion for fiscal 1992 and $13 billion for fiscal 1993. HR 2508 had been reported by the Foreign Affairs Committee on June 4 (H Rept 102-96).

During floor debate, the House June 13 voted, 242-141, to prohibit U.S. aid for India if it attempted to increase its nuclear arsenal. By an equally lopsided vote of 151-252, lawmakers June 12 also rejected efforts to lift similar conditions that already had led to a cutoff of aid to Pakistan. *(Aid to Pakistan, box, p. 232)*

The debate over India and Pakistan, while lively at times, had only a fraction of the intensity of the wrangling over abortion and family planning. The House June 12 voted, 234-188, to keep in the bill $20 million for the U.N. Population Fund (formerly the U.N. Fund for Population Activities). The White House and abortion foes opposed this provision because the U.N. fund operated in China, which had a record of forced abortions and sterilizations.

The House then voted 222-200, also on June 12, to keep committee language repealing the so-called Mexico City policy, which imposed restrictions on U.S. aid to family planning organizations abroad. Named for the 1984 conference at which it was unveiled, the Mexico City policy barred aid to organizations that provided or promoted abortion as a method of family planning.

The House June 12 rejected, 175-246, an amendment to strip from the bill a cargo preference requirement that countries that received cash transfers of foreign aid spend an equivalent amount to buy U.S. services and goods; half

Setback for Committees

The defeat of the fiscal 1992-93 foreign aid authorization bill (HR 2508) was a devastating setback for the House Foreign Affairs and Senate Foreign Relations committees. The two panels had seen their influence and prestige diminished in recent decades. Congress' failure to pass a foreign aid authorization had been a contributing factor.

The foreign aid bill, which set overall policy guidelines and spending limits for foreign aid programs, was once one of the most important tools that Congress used to influence U.S. foreign policy. But between 1980 and 1991, a regular foreign aid authorization bill had been passed only twice, in 1981 and 1985.

The foreign affairs committees' loss was the Appropriations committees gain, as the traditional authorization bills were supplanted by appropriations bills. During the House debate on the conference report on HR 2508, Foreign Affairs Committee Chairman Dante B. Fascell, D-Fla., urged his colleagues "not to leave everything up to the appropriators and the administration" in setting foreign assistance policy.

But the sentiment against providing foreign aid at a time of economic troubles at home was too strong. Foreign Affairs members who were known for their foreign policy expertise, such as Lee H. Hamilton, D-Ind., and Stephen J. Solarz, D-N.Y., were silent during the debate on the measure. Instead, the day belonged to lesser-known critics, such as Toby Roth, R-Wis., who quoted from a stack of letters that he said came from people outraged that Congress would vote to fund programs overseas.

Democrats from economically hard-hit regions said they felt loyalty to the Foreign Affairs Committee but that "the committee is in a rut," as Don J. Pease of Ohio put it. Too large a percentage of U.S. foreign aid goes to just a handful of countries, Pease said.

And so the House, which for years had passed authorization measures only to see them die in the Senate, rejected the conference report.

Earlier in 1991, the Senate Foreign Relations Committee had moved to shore up its committee leadership, which had been another factor in its loss of clout. The ideologically diverse panel was recognized more for its failure to gain quorums at meetings than as a force in setting foreign policy.

Frustrated by the panel's weakness, its Democrats persuaded committee Chairman Claiborne Pell, D-R.I., to cede some legislative authority to its subcommittees. For the first time, the subcommittees were to be staffed independently and would mark up bills, a function that had been the exclusive province of the full committee.

of the goods shipped by sea would have to go on U.S. vessels.

The House also adopted, 410-8, on June 19 an amendment cutting off military aid to Jordan unless certain conditions were met. An amendment setting tough conditions on any potential U.S. assistance to the Soviet central government was adopted 374-41 on June 19. *(Soviet aid, p. 260)*

On July 26, the Senate managed a feat that it had not accomplished since Ronald Reagan was just starting his second term as president: passage of a foreign aid authorization bill. Defying predictions from both lawmakers and Bush administration officials that the bill would never pass, the Senate passed, 74-18, an amended HR 2508 authorizing slightly more than $14 billion in foreign aid for each of the following two fiscal years. The Senate companion measure had been reported by the Foreign Relations Committee July 2 (S 1435 — S Rept 102-100).

But the Senate-passed bill, like the House-passed version, included several provisions that appeared nearly certain to trigger a veto. Nonetheless, in action on their amendments, Senate Democrats mounted a strong challenge to Bush administration policies on international family planning and military aid for El Salvador. While the Democrats did not appear capable of overriding a veto, they demonstrated solid majorities on both issues.

In a victory for abortion rights advocates, the Senate July 25 voted, 63-33, to close debate — eliminating the threat of a filibuster — on an amendment to provide $20 million in assistance for the U.N. Population Fund. The amendment was approved by voice vote. The Senate bill also would have overturned the Mexico City policy.

Despite a strong lobbying effort from top administration officials and from El Salvador President Alfredo Cristiani, Republicans July 25 failed by a vote of 43-56 to kill an amendment that would have withheld half of the $85 million military aid package for El Salvador for fiscal 1992, as well as half of the military assistance that had already been approved for that country but not yet delivered. Unlike a fiscal 1991 provision, this amendment would have required Bush to return to Congress for approval to lift the restrictions. The amendment's sponsors, Democratic Sens. Christopher J. Dodd, Conn., and Patrick J. Leahy, Vt., subsequently withdrew their amendment in the face of a Republican filibuster, but they claimed a symbolic victory. *(Fiscal 1991 El Salvador aid, p. 214)*

With the administration involved in negotiations for the convening of a Middle East peace conference, two amendments on Middle East policy were highly controversial. Facing the possibility of filibusters on both amendments, the sponsors heeded the pleas of party leaders and dropped their proposals.

Senators proved to be just as resistant to the notion of providing aid for the Soviet Union as their House counterparts had been. An amendment to bar any U.S. assistance for the Soviet Union unless Moscow cut off its aid to Cuba was approved 98-1 on July 24. The Senate adopted by voice vote a more comprehensive amendment to apply broad conditions to Soviet aid. The provision was similar to one approved by the House.

And the Senate July 25 approved, 99-0, a "Buy American" amendment to reduce the amount of cash assistance provided to foreign governments and raise the amount of credits that would be expended on U.S. projects and equipment. An attempt to strike cargo preference and cash purchase requirements from the committee bill was rejected July 24, 55-42.

Conference Bill Rejected

The prospect of a veto worried members of the Foreign Relations and Foreign Affairs committees, especially senators who had spent most of the year trying to jump-start the foreign aid authorization process.

Those concerns produced on-and-off efforts to reach a compromise on the sensitive issue of family planning funds. But those attempts failed, and the final bill repealed the Mexico City policy restricting aid to family planning organizations and included the $20 million for the U.N. Population Fund.

Conferees weakened a House-passed amendment placing restrictions on aid to Jordan and watered down restrictions in both bills on new U.S. arms sales to the Middle East. The House amendment restricting aid to India was dropped.

The conference committee went along with the Senate bill in allowing an increase of $12.2 billion in the U.S. contribution to the International Monetary Fund.

Conferees retained a Senate provision that, before the conference, nearly everyone was sure would be removed. That provision eliminated authority to provide foreign military assistance in the form of both grants and loans, and instead extended only the grant authority. Maryland Sen. Paul S. Sarbanes, Democratic manager of the bill, refused to bow to repeated entreaties from House conferees and administration officials to drop the provision.

The administration also was dissatisfied by the conferees' effort to water down a "Buy American" provision that had strong backing in both chambers.

The Senate approved the conference report (H Rept 102-225) by a vote of 61-38 on Oct. 8. Senate approval was largely symbolic in light of Bush's vow to veto the bill for its provisions involving family planning and the insufficient support in the Senate for an override.

The House on Oct. 30 rejected the report by a **key vote of 159-262 (R 28-134; D 131-127; I 0-1).** *(1991 key votes, p. 1061)*

The House vote brought together members ranging from hard-line conservatives to the only independent socialist in Congress, Bernard Sanders of Vermont. While the president's veto threat contributed to the defeat of the conference report, lawmakers clearly were not eager to support a $25 billion foreign aid bill during a domestic recession. Sanders echoed sentiments expressed by many Republicans when he urged his colleagues to "take care of some of the problems that we have at home first."

Democrats also had clear political incentives to oppose the bill. Party leaders had sought to portray Bush as more concerned with foreign policy than with the sluggish U.S. economy. The Democrats' message would have been undermined by massive support for a foreign aid bill.

1992 Aid Appropriations

Congress in 1991 did not clear a regular foreign aid appropriations bill for fiscal 1992. Two successive continuing resolutions were enacted to fund the aid programs.

The House passed a $15.2 billion aid appropriations bill (HR 2621) in June 1991. But the Senate deferred action on the measure under an agreement with the administration to delay consideration of a request from Israel for $10 billion in loan guarantees.

In place of the regular appropriations bill, Congress cleared a continuing resolution (H J Res 360 — PL 102-145), which funded foreign aid for six months, through March 1992. The measure provided only $14.3 billion in budget authority — compared with the administration's request for $27.6 billion, which included $15.4 billion for the regular foreign aid programs, plus $12.2 billion for an increased U.S. contribution to the International Monetary Fund (IMF).

In 1992, Congress cleared a second continuing resolution (H J Res 456 — PL 102-266) to fund the aid programs for the nearly six months that remained in fiscal 1992. The resolution provided a total of $14.4 billion, including more than $100 million for an unrelated small business emergency aid program.

Both continuing resolutions generally funded programs at the level enacted in fiscal 1991 or the level in the House-passed bill for fiscal 1992, whichever was lower. They did not include the increased IMF contribution.

House-Passed Bill

The House approved HR 2621 on June 19 by a vote of 301-102. The bill had been reported by the House Appropriations Committee on June 12 (H Rept 102-108).

The 5.2 billion measure included $2.1 billion for multilateral aid, $8.2 billion for bilateral aid, $4.2 billion for military aid and $650 million for the Export-Import Bank.

The bill followed a general pattern of reducing the administration's requests for military assistance, while increasing funds for most development aid, as well as health and child survival programs. The military aid request was reduced by more than $500 million.

David R. Obey, D-Wis., chairman of the House Appropriations Foreign Operations Subcommittee, called the bill the second installment "in a five-year plan to adjust foreign aid spending to the end of the Cold War."

The bill included an ambitious plan to stem the flow of arms to the Middle East, which could have required the administration to temporarily halt weapons sales to the region. While providing $15 million in aid for the Soviet Union's Baltic republics, the legislation also provided guidelines for changes by the Soviet central government that would merit aid from the West.

The bill set aside $135 million to reduce the federal deficit. The bill also appropriated $20 million to the U.N. Population Fund but only if Congress backed the administration's request to grant most-favored-nation (MFN) trade status to China. If MFN was denied, no assistance was to be provided for the fund. President Bush had threatened to veto any bill that included funding for the agency because it operated in China, which had been condemned for its policy of forced abortions. The administration and its congressional supporters refrained from a full-scale battle in the House over the issue, hoping that the provision would be stripped from the aid bill during the House-Senate conference.

Floor action on HR 2621 provided a stark contrast with the deliberations on the foreign aid authorization bill (HR 2508), which were taking place that same week. While lawmakers spent five days on the authorization bill, conducting scores of recorded votes, the appropriations measure breezed through with minimal debate in less than three hours. *(Authorization bill, p. 267)*

HR 2621 saw no further action. At Bush's request, the Senate postponed action on the entire foreign aid appropriations bill to avoid a confrontation on the issue of loan guarantees for Israel.

Loan Guarantee Issue

Bush refused to back the loan guarantees because of Israel's policy at that time of aggressively expanding Jewish settlements in the occupied territories. He said action on the issue could undermine the Middle East peace talks that were to open in October. *(Middle East peace talks, p. 277)*

Israel had previously agreed to postpone its request until September but, despite a request from the Bush administration, refused to delay it again. Israel said the guarantees were needed to help it absorb hundreds of thousands of Jewish immigrants from the former Soviet Union. Israel formally requested the guarantees on Sept. 6.

That day, Bush put his prestige on the line, announcing that he would "ask every single member of Congress to defer for just 120 days consideration" of Israel's request. Highlighting the importance of the issue for his administration, Bush said during a White House photo opportunity, "I know it is in the best interest of world peace to have this deferred."

Meeting with reporters on Sept. 12, Bush raised the stakes by saying he would veto any congressional attempts to provide the guarantees more quickly.

Israel's supporters in the United States sounded just as adamant that the loan guarantees could not wait. "Congress will not take the president's intention to bring this fight lying down," said Rep. Wayne Owens, D-Utah.

The pro-Israel lobby turned up the heat on the issue, deploying 1,200 leaders of major American Jewish organizations to Capitol Hill on Sept. 12. The message they brought was simple but emotional, said Shoshana S. Cardin, chairman of the Conference of Presidents of Major American Jewish Organizations. Referring to the influx of immigrants pouring into Israel, she said, "We must respond to their needs now — not 120 days from now , not six months from now."

Apparently feeling the pressure from the well-coordinated lobbying blitz, Bush tried to portray himself as the underdog in a public political struggle. "I heard today there were something like 1,000 lobbyists on the Hill working the other side of the question," he said. "We've got one lonely little guy down here doing it."

Bush offended many Jewish leaders by adding that he was "up against some powerful political forces." They saw the reference as invoking an age-old prejudice that Jews represented a conspiratorial force. Bush later sent them a letter of apology, saying that his comments "were never meant to be pejorative in any sense." But those on both sides recognized that the potential costs of a long and divisive battle could be steep for backers of Israel, as well as the administration.

Gradually, Israel's supporters on Capitol Hill acknowledged that they could not buck Bush's demand for a delay. Efforts to frame the terms for loan guarantees eventually supplanted the debate over postponing action on them. The issue was finally resolved in 1992. *(Israeli loan guarantees, box, p. 272)*

First Continuing Resolution

Both chambers approved an omnibus continuing resolution Oct. 24 (H J Res 360 — PL 102-145) that included funds for foreign aid through the end of March 1992. The House passed the legislation by a vote of 288-126; and the Senate followed suit by voice vote, completing congressional action.

Congressional Democrats made significant concessions in accepting the delay on the spending bill and agreeing to the continuing resolution. Liberals were reportedly disappointed that they lost the opportunity, for perhaps as long as six months, to place new restrictions on military aid to El Salvador.

Deputy Secretary of State Lawrence S. Eagleburger wrote members of the Appropriations committees assuring them that the administration would abide by existing restrictions on El Salvador, imposed in the 1990 spending bill. Until a 1992 bill was enacted, he said, the administration intended to provide no more than $3.5 million a month in military aid to the Salvadoran government.

Eagleburger said aid could be increased only if there was a "radical change in the military situation in El Salvador." During fiscal 1991, the administration waived conditions on aid, over the objections of some Senate Democrats.

Some lawmakers also were concerned that adoption of the continuing resolution meant that Congress would not have a foreign aid spending bill to use as a vehicle for aid to the Soviet Union. The House bill, approved before the dramatic changes in the Soviet Union, had included $15 million for the Baltic States and democratically elected republics.

Because Congress did not act on a full appropriations bill during 1991, State Department officials had to improvise in allocating military and economic aid for individual countries. Some decisions were easy: Aid levels for the two biggest recipients had been at the same level for several years — $3 billion in military and economic assistance for Israel and $2.1 billion for Egypt on an annual basis — and were not changed. But the situation was murkier for other countries and programs. Several administration officials said funds would be spent slowly while the continuing resolution was in effect — in case congressional priorities changed.

Under the formula for the short-term measure, funding was either at the level in the House-passed measure or the fiscal 1991 foreign operations bill, whichever was lower. The funding was provided under the authority and conditions contained in the fiscal 1991 bill. *(Fiscal 1991 foreign aid appropriations, p. 233)*

The $14.3 billion appropriated for foreign aid by the continuing resolution included $1.87 billion for multilateral aid, $7.51 billion for bilateral aid, $4.24 billion for military aid and $651 million for the Export-Import Bank.

Second Continuing Resolution

Congress had to pass a second continuing resolution (H J Res 456 — PL 102-266) in 1992 because the administration and lawmakers still had not reached agreement on the controversial issue of loan guarantees for Israel. But convincing members to vote for a second resolution was no easy task.

Congressional support for foreign assistance was so weak that some key lawmakers expected most U.S. aid programs to shut down March 31, with the expiration of the continuing resolution enacted in 1991 that funded such programs.

While foreign aid was typically political poison for lawmakers in an election year, an unusual set of circumstances had made the continuing resolution an even tougher sell. House members, tarred by the widening scandal over kited checks, were particularly reluctant to vote to send resources overseas. *(House bank scandal, p. 929)*

Rep. Obey blamed the administration's failure to address the nation's domestic needs for the decline in support for foreign aid. "We are paying the price for that domestic policy vacuum," he said.

House leaders had been seeking to have the unpopular continuing resolution approved quickly and quietly, without a recorded vote. But that strategy met resistance from Republicans, who seemed eager to voice their opposition to the continuing resolution.

As the week of March 23 ended, the House and its Appropriations Committee had failed to take any action on a new stopgap measure. The rush to pass the continuing resolution finally began just hours before the 1991 resolution was to expire. The House approved the $14.6 billion measure, 275-131, on March 31.

When the March 31 deadline passed without Senate action, the Office of Management and Budget prepared an order that would have required the Agency for International Development (AID) effectively to shut down. The order would have forced more than 2,000 furloughs at AID. The Senate approved the measure, 84-16, on April 1, just before the order was to be executed. The House then cleared the measure, accepting without objection an unrelated amendment attached by the Senate that provided $107 million in additional funding for the Small Business Administration's disaster loan program.

The brief hangup in the Senate was caused largely by the continuing dispute over Israel's request for loan guarantees. Supporters of Israel said they intended to amend the measure with loan guarantees despite Bush's pledge to veto any legislation that did not also require Israel to freeze the construction of settlements in its occupied territories. Angered by the administration's tough stance, some supporters of Israel were eager to challenge the president, although there appeared to be no prospect to override a veto. But officials from American Jewish organizations feared another showdown with the White House and persuaded the senators not to attach the loan guarantees to the continuing resolution, according to congressional sources.

In an arrangement negotiated by Senate leaders, the lawmakers settled instead for a vaguely worded, non-binding resolution (S Res 277) that expressed support for "appropriate loan guarantees" for Israel. The resolution was approved 99-1 on April 1. But the vote provided little indication of how the Senate would approach a substantive loan guarantee proposal, because many of those who agreed with the administration's position also voted for the resolution.

The continuing resolution generally retained the spending formula from the previous stopgap bill, funding programs at the level enacted in fiscal 1991 or the level in the House-passed bill for fiscal 1992, whichever was lower. The $14.6 billion measure appropriated $1.86 billion for multilateral aid, $7.65 billion for bilateral aid, $4.24 billion for military aid and $651 million for the Export-Import Bank.

H J Res 456 included $270 million in increased funding for U.N. peacekeeping operations. To help offset this, the resolution reduced all assistance programs — except those going to a few countries for which Congress had usually earmarked aid, such as Israel and Egypt — by an additional 1.48 percent, which saved more than $200 million.

The resolution also permitted expanded efforts to aid the former Soviet Union. While attention was focused on the administration's broad new legislative proposal for the former Soviet republics, the continuing resolution also permitted the administration to provide $150 million in technical and humanitarian assistance in fiscal 1992. *(Soviet aid, p. 260)*

And, although the measure appropriated no new aid, it allowed the administration to more easily shift aid previously allocated for other countries to the former Soviet republics. The continuing resolution also repealed a pair of Cold War-era laws that prevented most Export-Import Bank lending to the Soviet Union.

Members reached a compromise on military aid for El Salvador. The government of El Salvador and left-wing guerrillas had signed a peace agreement in January 1992, ending the country's long-running civil conflict.

H J Res 456 allowed the administration to spend for non-lethal supplies $21.3 million in previously approved assistance to the Salvadoran military. But the legislation transferred the remainder of the administration's request for fiscal 1992, $63.8 million, to a fund to rebuild the country and retrain combatants. The administration had to seek the approval of key congressional committees before spending the remaining aid for fiscal 1992.

1993 Aid Appropriations

Congress in 1992 cleared a $26.3 billion foreign aid appropriations bill (HR 5368 — PL 102-391) for fiscal 1993. A one-time appropriation of $12.3 billion for the International Monetary Fund (IMF) accounted for the dramatic jump in foreign aid appropriations.

HR 5368 was the first foreign aid appropriations bill in nearly two years. Because of disagreement over providing loan guarantees to Israel, foreign aid had been funded through continuing resolutions the previous year instead of a regular appropriations bill. In 1992, the issue was resolved, and HR 5368 authorized $10 billion in loan guarantees for Israel. *(Fiscal 1992 aid appropriations, p. 269; loan guarantees for Israel, box, p. 272)*

In a number of areas, the bill marked a significant departure from foreign aid legislation enacted during the Cold War. A House-Senate conference committee moderated tough restrictions imposed by the Senate on aid to Russia — a program that did not exist the last time such a conference convened.

New controversies, reflecting the evolution of congressional foreign policy interests, replaced old ideological struggles. Over administration objections, the conferees authorized up to $50 million in U.S. military equipment for the besieged republic of Bosnia. That represented the strongest congressional action favoring one side in the former Yugoslavia, although it did not compel President Bush to provide the aid. *(Aid to Yugoslavian republics, p. 278)*

But the changing ideas about foreign assistance did not extend to the Middle East, where most U.S. military and economic aid continued to flow. The bill provided $3 billion in aid for Israel and $2.1 billion for Egypt, the same levels as in recent years.

Congress had long been a wellspring of support for Israel, and the authorization of the five-year program of loan guarantees for that country — on top of the $3 billion in direct aid — made the bill more palatable for many members.

United States, Israel Resolved Differences ...

In August 1992, President Bush and Israeli Prime Minister Yitzhak Rabin agreed on terms for a five-year package of loan guarantees, which Jerusalem had been seeking for more than a year to help the small country absorb hundreds of thousands of Jewish immigrants from the former Soviet Union. The U.S. guarantees for $10 billion in loans were intended to help Israel obtain favorable rates on commercial loans.

The deal easily gained the backing of Congress, long a wellspring of support for Israel. The guarantees were attached to the fiscal 1993 foreign aid appropriations bill (HR 5368 — PL 102-391).

Until the agreement in August, Bush had blocked action on the loan guarantees because Rabin's predecessor, Yitzhak Shamir, insisted on aggressively expanding Jewish settlements in territories that Israel had occupied since the Six-Day War in 1967.

The controversy over the aid had erupted the previous year. In September 1991, Bush asked Congress for a 120-day delay in action on the request. Many members lambasted the president — and then quietly agreed to delay the contentious matter. Bush wanted to put off the issue to avoid undermining Middle East peace talks, which began in Madrid in October 1991. *(Loan guarantees delay, p. 270; Middle East peace talks, p. 277)*

Publicly, U.S. officials referred to the settlements as "obstacles to peace." Privately, Bush was said to view Shamir's hard-line resistance to curtailing new settlement construction as a personal affront.

Pro-Israel members of Congress vowed to spurn Bush's call for delay. But when it became obvious that they lacked the votes to override a veto, they reluctantly went along with the postponement.

With the loan guarantees stalled, Congress failed to enact the fiscal 1992 foreign aid appropriations bill that was to have been the vehicle for the Israel assistance. Instead, foreign aid was funded by two continuing resolutions. *(Fiscal 1992 foreign aid appropriations, p. 269)*

The outlook was equally bleak early in 1992. Although several key members of Congress who controlled legislation on the issue — such as Patrick J. Leahy, D-Vt., chairman of the Senate Appropriations Foreign Operations Subcommittee; David R. Obey, D-Wis., chairman of the House Appropriations Foreign Operations Subcommittee; and Senate Appropriations Committee Chairman Robert C. Byrd, D-W.Va. — echoed the Bush administration's hard line against new settlements, an agreement on the issue remained elusive.

Leahy and the ranking Republican on his subcommittee, Bob Kasten, Wis., led an unsuccessful effort in March to forge a compromise on the loan guarantees. Bush indicated that the proposal contained unacceptable loopholes that would have allowed Israel to continue to expand its settlements.

The stalemate ended after Rabin's Labor Party swept to victory in Israel's parliamentary elections in June. The more conciliatory Rabin pledged to restrain the growth of most settlements. In agreeing to the loan guarantees, Bush also sought to repair relations with the American Jewish community, which had become badly frayed over the issue.

Agreement Terms

Under the terms of the agreement, Israel agreed to pay all costs associated with the program. After the first year's installment of $2 billion, subsequent installments of guarantees were to be reduced by any amount that Israel spent on settlements in its occupied territories. The president could suspend the program, but Congress would be able to reverse that decision with a two-thirds vote by each chamber.

The United States did not provide loans to Israel; it backed loans negotiated by Israel with private commercial lenders. But funds had to be set aside to cover any potential losses, with the amount depending on the estimated risk that Israel would default on the loans and the United States would have to bear the costs. The Office of Management and Budget (OMB) fixed the required set-aside of funds for the first-year installment of $2 billion in guarantees at 4.5 percent.

Because Israel had agreed to pay the $90 million subsidy required by the OMB "scoring" of the risk involved in the first-year guarantees, the administration was able to avoid making a request for an appropriation to cover the guarantees.

But the Congressional Budget Office (CBO), which made independent budget estimates for Congress, reportedly scored the subsidy at about 13 percent. In effect, CBO and OMB differed over the prospects for an Israeli default. Some lawmakers believed that such distinctions were meaningless because it was impossible to accurately assess the risk involved. But the CBO estimate of the loan guarantee subsidy, along with its scoring of other programs, forced the Senate to find reductions elsewhere in the foreign aid bill.

Background

Israel sought the $10 billion in guarantees over five years to help absorb a huge influx of immigrants, most coming from what was the Soviet Union. U.S. Jewish leaders had said that prospects for increasing instability in the former republics of the

... Over $10 Billion Loan Guarantee Package

Soviet Union could lead to the rise of anti-Semitism and a boost in the numbers of Jews wanting to leave.

The Bush administration supported such aid in principle but was strongly opposed to Israel's expansion of settlements on occupied land.

During the Six-Day War with Arab states in 1967, Israel captured the Golan Heights, the Gaza Strip and the West Bank as well as East Jerusalem. The Bush administration considered the settlements — especially those on the West Bank — an obstacle to regional peace and a violation of international law.

Early in 1992, reports grew that the administration might explicitly link the request for guarantees to a settlement freeze in the territories. Critics of Israel's policies insisted that such a connection was logical, that Soviet immigrants would be forced to settle in the occupied territories because that was where much of Israel's new housing was being built.

Israel's request threatened to present Congress with stark and unpalatable alternatives. Politically, it appeared to offer a grim choice in an election year: Alienate Jewish supporters of Israel or fuel the anger of recession-pinched voters who were fed up with foreign aid spending.

As a foreign policy question, the choice appeared equally unsettling: Side with Israel if it demanded assistance with no strings attached or support Bush if he demanded a halt to new Israeli settlements in occupied territories as the price for new U.S. assistance. And either choice could have affected the course, and perhaps even the survival, of the fragile Middle East peace talks.

But all sides had it in their interests to avoid a showdown that would mean a wrenching public debate over U.S. aid to the Jewish state.

History of U.S. Aid

Aid for Israel had taken on aspects of an international entitlement program, seemingly as automatic as Social Security benefits. Year in and year out, usually with no debate, Congress earmarked about one-fifth of the $15 billion foreign aid budget for Israel.

When Egypt was included, the annual level of aid earmarked by Congress for the two countries rose to more than $5 billion by 1992, one-third of all U.S. foreign assistance spending.

A series of extraordinary events, including Iraq's missile attacks on Israel during the Persian Gulf War, pushed grant assistance for Israel to the highest total ever in fiscal 1991, with estimates exceeding $4 billion. This included $650 million in war-related economic assistance that Congress approved in March 1991.

Because Israel received grants and loans from a variety of sources — with aid often provided under defense bills as well as the foreign aid bill — it was difficult to ascertain how much all types of assistance cost the United States.

High levels of aid for Israel did not begin until the 1970s. From 1948 through 1970, the United States provided Israel a total of about $1.6 billion in military and economic aid — most of it in the form of loans. Congress began earmarking specific amounts of assistance for Israel in 1971.

In October 1973, following the surprise attack by Egypt and Syria that began the Yom Kippur War, President Richard Nixon ordered a massive airlift of U.S. military equipment to Israel. Congress then overwhelmingly approved Nixon's request for $2.2 billion in emergency military assistance for the country.

Aid again rose dramatically — in tandem with assistance for Egypt — after those two countries made peace in 1979. With the conclusion of the Camp David Accords, President Jimmy Carter requested a special $4.8 billion package of loans and grants to be shared by Israel and Egypt. The supplemental appropriation was in addition to the regular aid program of nearly $2 billion for Israel and nearly $1 billion for Egypt.

Assistance for the two countries was closely tied through the mid-1980s. In the early 1990s, however, the programs became "delinked." The Bush administration forgave $6.7 billion in Egyptian military debt in 1990. Though Israel was not granted a similar concession, U.S. aid was dramatically increased during the Persian Gulf War.

In the 1980s, members of Congress were successful in securing favorable terms for assistance to Israel, in addition to boosting aid levels. In fiscal 1981, economic aid became an all-grant program. Military aid had been in the form of grants since fiscal 1985.

Also beginning in fiscal 1985, lawmakers had included language in foreign operations bills stating that it was the "policy and intention" of the United States that aid provided under the Economic Support Fund (ESF) be at least equal to Israel's debt repayments to the U.S. government. Israel used most of the $1.2 billion it received annually under the ESF program to pay military debts.

That was one of several unique benefits accorded Israel. Israel also was the only country that received ESF aid in a lump sum at the beginning of the fiscal year, instead of in quarterly installments. The same terms applied to most of the $1.8 billion in Foreign Military Financing aid provided to Israel in fiscal 1991. Investing in U.S. government securities, Israel was able to reap interest income from the military and economic aid.

Excluding the IMF appropriation, the measure provided nearly $1.5 billion less than the fiscal 1991 aid bill, which was the last one to clear Congress. That sharp reduction in spending helped ease anxiety among lawmakers about casting an election-year vote for foreign aid.

Passage of the legislation also represented a qualified success for the Bush administration. The loan guarantees for Israel and the IMF appropriation, which was an essential component of the administration's aid initiative for the former Soviet republics, were regarded as legislative priorities by the White House. In addition, the measure included $417 million in economic and technical assistance for the former Soviet republics and $50 million to restructure debts owed by Latin American governments.

But the final bill also was nearly $1.2 billion less than Bush's request. The administration was forced to swallow major reductions in military aid and in the Economic Support Fund (ESF), a key category of economic assistance.

Military assistance grants for three North Atlantic Treaty Organization (NATO) allies — Turkey, Greece and Portugal — were converted into low-interest loans. The bill provided $3.5 billion in military aid, a $596 million reduction from the fiscal 1992 level. Funding for ESF, a program of cash transfers and other assistance for key U.S. allies, was cut by $498 million from fiscal 1992 to $2.7 billion.

The cutbacks in military aid reflected the views of the two men with the most to say about the foreign aid bill: Rep. David R. Obey, D-Wis., and Sen. Patrick J. Leahy, D-Vt., chairmen of the Foreign Operations subcommittees of the House and Senate Appropriations committees.

Congress had been unable to clear a foreign aid authorization measure — which was supposed to set broad guidelines for providing U.S. foreign assistance — since 1985. In that void, the House and Senate Foreign Operations subcommittees effectively took on the role of authorizers as well as appropriators.

Obey and Leahy clashed, sometimes bitterly, over turf and specific provisions in the bill. But they shared the same overall objective regarding U.S. foreign aid spending. Both supported shifting funds from military aid programs to development and humanitarian assistance.

House Action

The House approved a $13.8 billion version of HR 5368 on June 25 by a vote of 297-124. The bill was reported by the Appropriations Committee on June 18 (H Rept 102-585).

The administration protested that the House bill provided an "inadequate" level of aid funding. The bill sliced about $1.3 billion from the Bush administration's request.

The administration threatened to veto the bill because it included $20 million in aid to the U.N. Population Fund. The White House had long opposed funding for the U.N. agency because it operated in China, which had been condemned for its policy of coerced abortions. The bill revived an Obey proposal from 1991 linking aid for the population fund with the president's extension of favorable trade treatment for China. The bill authorized funding for the U.N. agency, which Bush opposed, only if Congress approved most-favored-nation status for China, which Bush sought. *(China trade, p. 190)*

The administration also protested the bill's fundamental change in the military assistance program for Turkey, Portugal and Greece — countries that had received billions of dollars in U.S. aid largely because they were home to NATO bases. The House-passed bill required that aid for the so-called base rights countries be provided in the form of market-based loans instead of grants and low-interest loans. The bill also reduced the overall amount of military aid provided for the three countries.

In the report accompanying the bill, the Appropriations Committee said "given the end of the Cold War and given the state of the budget deficit" the countries should be "graduated" to a less costly program of loans. But the administration said that the change "could diminish our military readiness in the Persian Gulf, the Mediterranean and the Balkans."

The legislation fully funded the administration's request for $417 million in aid for the former republics of the Soviet Union. But the bill included only $400 million in aid to Eastern Europe — a $50 million cut from the administration request — and imposed new guidelines on how the assistance program should be managed.

The House-passed bill provided no funding to forgive the official debt of Latin American countries under the Enterprise for the Americas initiative, which had been a top legislative priority of the Treasury Department. Subcommittee Chairman Obey opposed the $202 million request for debt relief on the basis that it would do little to address the region's massive debt. But the bill provided $75 million — $25 million less than the administration request — for a regional investment fund that was part of the Latin American initiative. *(Enterprise for the Americas, p. 194)*

The full House left the bill crafted by the Appropriations subcommittee largely intact. In perhaps its most significant action, the House June 25 approved, 219-200, a reduction of $24 million in development assistance, the amount the administration had requested in such aid for India. The amendment, opposed by the administration, was supported by those who wanted to punish India for its harsh military crackdown in the Punjab and Kashmir regions, as well as by members who wanted to cut funding from the bill.

The House approved by voice vote an amendment barring the use of U.S. funds for training Indonesian military officers, a move intended to protest human rights abuses by the Indonesian army, which in 1991 had massacred as many as 100 unarmed civilians on the island of East Timor.

A motion to recommit the bill to the Appropriations Committee with instructions to report back after trimming U.S. financing for the World Bank and the Agency for International Development's (AID) budget was agreed to June 25, 392-28.

Obey decided not to offer his planned amendment to force an additional 1 percent reduction in all foreign assistance programs. That amendment already had been scaled back from the $400 million cut he had proposed during his subcommittee's consideration of the bill. Obey said he had been asked by the administration to drop the proposal. Pro-Israel groups also lobbied intensively against the amendment, which would have forced a rare reduction in aid to Israel.

Senate Action

The Senate passed a $26.4 billion version of HR 5368 on Oct. 1 by a **key vote of 87-12 (R 35-8; D 52-4)**. The bill had been reported by the Senate Appropriations Committee on Sept. 23 (S Rept 102-419). *(1992 key votes, p. 1083)*

The Senate bill granted Israel's request for the United States to guarantee $10 billion in loans over five years, a proposal that was backed by the Bush administration and enjoyed broad support in Congress. In addition, it included the administration's request for $12.3 billion in new financing for the IMF.

Like the House bill, the Senate version of HR 5368 triggered a veto threat because it provided $20 million for the U.N. Population Fund.

The funding in the Senate bill was about $1 billion less than the president's aid request for fiscal 1993. It was about $12.7 billion more than the House-passed version, which did not include the IMF funding.

Other significant differences existed between the Senate- and House-passed bills. The House legislation required the administration to convert about $800 million in military grants and low-interest loans for Turkey, Greece and Portugal to market-based loans. The Senate Foreign Operations Subcommittee had gone along with the House proposal, but the full Senate Appropriations Committee had restored $540 million in funding for grants to the three NATO allies. During floor action, the Senate reaffirmed by voice vote the so-called 7:10 ratio, whereby Congress guaranteed that Greece would receive $7 in military aid for each $10 provided to Turkey.

The Senate bill eliminated $69 million in funding that the House had included for the European Bank for Reconstruction and Development, which provided loans to the former Soviet republics and Eastern Europe. It also included $100 million to restructure some debt owed by Latin American governments, a Treasury Department proposal that had attracted strong House opposition.

Under the Senate bill, the administration could provide deliveries of food and some humanitarian aid to Pakistan. Aid to Islamabad was cut off in 1990 because of its nuclear weapons program. *(Aid to Pakistan, box, p. 232)*

The Senate endorsed tough actions to counter Serbian aggression against Bosnia-Herzegovina in the former Yugoslavia. After a spirited debate, the Senate adopted by voice vote an amendment allowing the president to provide up to $50 million in U.S. defense equipment for Bosnia if the United Nations lifted its arms embargo against that country. The amendment was opposed by the administration but had strong bipartisan support in the Senate.

The Senate went along with the administration's request for $417 million to aid the former Soviet Union but attached several restrictions. The Appropriations Committee had agreed to an amendment offered by Chairman Robert C. Byrd, D-W.Va., barring U.S. assistance to Russia, except for humanitarian aid, until Moscow agreed to withdraw its forces from the three Baltic nations. In addition, the full Senate agreed by voice vote to a floor amendment that conditioned most aid to Russia on a presidential certification that Moscow was not supplying weapons to Iran.

Despite the chronic unpopularity of foreign aid, only a few attempts were made to eliminate funding in the bill. An amendment to cut funding in the bill by 10 percent was rejected on Sept. 30, 38-58.

After rejecting, 40-56 on Sept. 30, a weaker sense of the Senate resolution, the Senate agreed by voice vote to place a ceiling of $52 million on aid to Morocco unless the president certified that the kingdom was cooperating with a U.N. peace plan to end conflict in the Western Sahara.

Conference, Final Action

The House adopted the conference report on HR 5368 (H Rept 102-1011) on Oct. 5 by a **key vote of 312-105 (R 104-58; D 208-46; I 0-1)**. The Senate followed suit by voice vote later that day.

The $26.3 billion spending measure cut about $1.1 billion from the administration's request for fiscal 1993. The final version provided $12.5 billion more than the House-passed bill, which did not include the IMF appropriation, and $162 million less than the Senate bill.

The conference committee faced conflicts over issues including military aid for the NATO allies, debt forgiveness and abortion.

Yet no issue took more time or effort to resolve than the stiff conditions on aid for Russia that had been attached to the Senate bill by Appropriations Chairman Byrd. The amendment would have prohibited aid to Russia until Moscow either withdrew its military forces from Estonia, Latvia and Lithuania or agreed to a timetable for withdrawal. Byrd exempted humanitarian aid from his amendment.

The administration strongly opposed the provision and said that the problem was addressed by conditions in legislation (S 2532) authorizing aid to the former Soviet republics. *(Freedom Support Act, p. 260)*

But Byrd was unyielding. "We have a time bomb ticking on our hands," he told the conferees, arguing that Russia's continued military presence in the Baltics could spur civil unrest.

A complicated compromise was finally reached, under which aid would be partially withheld and eventually cut off unless "substantial progress" was made toward setting a timetable for withdrawal.

It was not clear how much, if any, of the $417 million in the bill for the former republics would be affected by this provision. The administration had not yet allocated the assistance among the newly independent states. Moreover, the definition of "substantial progress" was open to broad interpretation.

With far less controversy, the conference committee eliminated a second Senate amendment barring all but humanitarian aid to Moscow until the president certified that Russia had ceased selling arms to Iran.

Byrd also was at the center of the dispute over military aid for Turkey and the two other countries that hosted NATO bases. The Appropriations chairman had been a tireless supporter of aid for Turkey.

The House and Senate were far apart on the issue. The House cut all military assistance grants for the three NATO allies — replacing them with market-based loans — but the Senate restored $540 million in grants and low-interest loans.

Byrd was the leading proponent of the Senate's position, but it seemed untenable at a time when foreign aid was so unpopular. Even if he had succeeded in conference, intense House opposition would have risen to increasing the funding in the bill by $540 million.

The conference committee essentially split the difference between the two chambers. It eliminated military grants but approved $450 million in low-interest loans for Turkey, $315 million for Greece and $90 million for Portugal. The annual interest rate on such loans was about 5 percent.

The panel attempted to assuage Turkey, an important ally in the Persian Gulf region, by providing $125 million in economic aid. Neither the House nor the Senate had included the earmark in its bill.

The conference bill reduced the administration's request for military assistance to El Salvador from $40 million to $11 billion, as both chambers had done. With a peace agreement in place since January 1992, only non-lethal aid could be provided to the Salvadoran armed forces. The remaining $29 million requested was to be transferred to a fund to help the country recover from the war.

Despite an intense lobbying campaign by the administration and U.S. corporations, the conferees agreed to cut $2.3 million in military training assistance that the administration requested for Indonesia.

Also over administration objections, the conferees went along with the Senate provision authorizing up to $50 million in U.S. military equipment for the republic of Bosnia.

The conference committee dropped abortion-related provisions that had triggered a veto threat. Both chambers had approved $20 million in aid for the U.N. Population Fund.

The conferees easily reached an agreement on $50 million in funding for Latin American debt forgiveness under the administration's Enterprise for the Americas program. The House had provided no funding for debt restructuring, while the Senate had appropriated $100 million.

Because of the cuts in the two main categories of bilateral assistance — Foreign Military Financing (FMF) and ESF — the dominant position of Israel and Egypt among aid recipients had become even more pronounced. Congress earmarked $3.1 billion in FMF for the two allies, leaving only about $350 million for all other recipients of that assistance. Lawmakers earmarked $2 billion in ESF for Israel and Egypt, leaving only $670 million for other countries.

Also for the Middle East, the conference committee earmarked $20 million in economic aid and $40 million in military aid for Morocco, which typically had a strong lobbying presence on Capitol Hill. But the conferees approved a Senate amendment that limited Morocco to $52 million in aid unless the president certified the kingdom was cooperating with the U.N. peace process in the Western Sahara.

Conferees agreed to retain prohibitions on military assistance for Peru. The Senate bill would have allowed the president to provide the aid if President Alberto Fujimori made good on a pledge to restore constitutional democracy in the country.

The final bill included a Senate provision that allowed the president to provide some food aid and humanitarian supplies to Pakistan, if Congress agreed to the shipments.

Conferees endorsed a Senate proposal authorizing the president to provide up to $15 million to support efforts to resolve the fate of U.S. military personnel missing in Southeast Asia since the Vietnam War.

Conferees combined House and Senate language aimed at barring the Agency for International Development from providing any incentives for U.S. companies to relocate abroad. The provisions were in response to a report on the CBS News program "60 Minutes" showing AID officials trying to induce U.S. businesses to move to Central America. Although AID officials denied that the agency had intended to lure U.S. companies overseas, the report had produced a wave of outrage on Capitol Hill.

Major Provisions

The final version of the foreign aid appropriations bill (HR 5368 — PL 102-391) provided $26.3 billion in fiscal 1993 aid. This included $14.21 billion for multilateral aid, $7.71 billion for bilateral aid, $3.52 billion for military aid and $786 million for the Export-Import Bank.

Major provisions of HR 5368:

Israel. Authorized $10 billion in loan guarantees for Israel over a five-year period.

- Earmarked $3 billion in military and economic aid for Israel. Israel was permitted to receive its entire military and economic aid within the first 30 days of the fiscal year, thus enabling Jerusalem to collect interest on the assistance.

Egypt. Earmarked $2.1 billion in military and economic aid to Egypt.

Morocco. Earmarked $20 million in economic aid and $40 million in military aid for Morocco, but set a limit of $52 million on the aid unless the president certified that Morocco was cooperating with the U.N. peace process in the Western Sahara.

IMF. Provided a one-time appropriation of $12.3 billion for the International Monetary Fund.

NATO Allies. Eliminated military assistance grants for Turkey, Greece and Portugal, but provided $450 million in low-interest loans for Turkey, $315 million for Greece and $90 million for Portugal.

- Earmarked $125 million in economic aid for Turkey.

Former USSR. Provided $417 million in aid to the former Soviet republics. The legislation earmarked a substantial portion of this for specific purposes, some of which could benefit domestic interests. It required that $50 million in U.S. agricultural commodities be provided to the former republics. The bill also earmarked $50 million for scholarships and other educational exchange programs.

- Placed conditions on aid to Russia. It stipulated that only half of the assistance for Russia could be provided unless the president certified by June 1993 that "substantial progress" had been made toward establishing a timetable for withdrawal of Russian troops from Estonia, Latvia and Lithuania. If Russia still had not removed its forces by the end of September 1993 — or had not set up a timetable to do so — further assistance would be cut off.

Eastern Europe, Baltic States. Included $400 million to promote private-sector development and provide technical assistance for Eastern Europe and the Baltic States.

Bosnia. Authorized up to $50 million in U.S. military equipment for the republic of Bosnia.

Refugee Aid. Provided about $670 million to aid refugees. It earmarked $35 million to help refugees in Bosnia, Croatia and Slovenia.

El Salvador. Provided $11 million in non-lethal military assistance to El Salvador. An additional $29 million was to be transferred to a fund established to assist the country in recovering from its 12-year civil war.

Latin America. Provided $50 million for Latin American debt forgiveness under the administration's Enterprise for the Americas program.

Africa. Provided $800 million in economic development aid for sub-Saharan Africa, along with $100 million specifically allocated for emergency disaster relief in the region. The legislation earmarked $25 million in aid for war-torn Somalia, where an estimated 1.5 million people were at risk from famine.

Pakistan. Allowed the president to provide some food aid and humanitarian supplies to Pakistan. Such aid had been barred since 1990 because of Islamabad's nuclear weapons program. But the conference report stipulated that Congress must agree to the aid shipments.

Vietnam War MIAs. Authorized the president to provide up to $15 million in U.S. military equipment for Cambodia and Laos to support their efforts to find missing American service personnel from the war in Southeast Asia.

Environment. Provided $650 million for a number of environmental initiatives, reflecting the heightened concern in Congress over problems such as global warming.

- Appropriated $30 million for the World Bank's Global Environmental Facility, which backed efforts to preserve biodiversity and other environmental programs.

Middle East Peace Talks

The Bush administration achieved a historic breakthrough in 1991, when it succeeded in bringing together Israel and its Arab neighbors for the opening of peace talks in Madrid, Spain.

Congress' contribution came in what it did not do. At President Bush's insistence, members delayed into 1992 any action on Israel's request for $10 billion in U.S. loan guarantees to assist in its absorption of immigrants. Bush argued that action on the guarantees could disrupt the peace talks. *(Israeli loan guarantees, box, p. 272)*

Once the Middle East adversaries sat at the same table in Madrid, they quickly lapsed into familiar denunciations of one another. It took 10 months just to resolve niggling disputes over procedural details.

But the June 1992 election of Prime Minister Yitzhak Rabin in Israel — who was more conciliatory than his hard-line predecessor, Yitzhak Shamir — imbued all sides with uncharacteristic flexibility. Subsequent talks were marked by a new sense of purpose.

Prodding Toward Peace

In pushing for the peace talks — arranged through the tireless efforts of Secretary of State James A. Baker III and with the dissolving Soviet Union as cosponsor — the administration sought to take advantage of the scrambled power relations in the Middle East after the Persian Gulf War.

The Palestine Liberation Organization lost influence by backing Saddam Hussein's losing cause, and Iraq was neutralized as a major player. Jordan's King Hussein, who usually attempted to play a kingmaker's role in the region, also lost influence because of his all-but-official support for Saddam.

Meanwhile, Israel had established new credibility with the administration by enduring the Scud missile attacks launched by Iraq. Noted for responding swiftly and massively to any attack, Israel adopted an uncharacteristic posture of restraint at the Bush administration's behest. The United States had immediately rushed Patriot defensive missiles and their crews to Israel. *(Gulf War, p. 299)*

And Syria enjoyed improved relations by joining the anti-Saddam alliance, even though it remained on the State Department's list of nations supporting terrorism.

Baker in March 1991 began pressing for talks in an eight-nation tour of the region. When the secretary of state appeared before the House and Senate Foreign Operations Appropriations subcommittees in May, members promised him a free hand to pursue Arab-Israeli peace talks but expressed frustration with the lack of progress. Baker told members the United States had a "unique obligation" to continue pushing for the peace talks in the aftermath of a war that found Arabs, Israel and the United States on the same side.

By fall, Baker's months of shuttle diplomacy had succeeded in extracting assent from Israel, the Palestinians and Arab states to participate in a Middle East conference that was tentatively set for October.

Peace Conference Convenes

Secretary of State Baker announced in Jerusalem on Oct. 18 that a Middle East peace conference would be convened in Madrid under U.S.-Soviet sponsorship. But Baker, whose prodigious shuttle diplomacy brought about the event, cautioned that the talks were only the beginning of a long process. He said, "Old suspicions will not disappear quickly. . . . So we have no illusions about the hard work that lies ahead."

In Washington, Rep. Lee H. Hamilton, D-Ind., chairman of the House Foreign Affairs Subcommittee on Europe and the Middle East, called the announcement a "significant procedural achievement" for the administration. "We've been trying to get these people to sit down and talk to each other for a long time," he said in an interview.

Bush said the conference was to proceed along a two-track process, with Israel negotiating separately with its Arab neighbors and with Palestinian representatives. The basis for the negotiations, he added, was to be U.N. Security Council Resolutions 242 and 338, which called for Israel to return occupied territories to Arab nations in return for formal Arab recognition of the Jewish state.

Hours before the conference was announced, Israel and the Soviet Union renewed full diplomatic relations, which Moscow had severed after the 1967 Mideast War.

The Middle East peace conference began Oct. 30 with all sides guardedly optimistic that the old hatreds that divided Arabs and Israelis for generations eventually could be overcome. But the ceremonial opening of the conference in Madrid became a forum to rehash those ancient enmities, with only glimmers of compromise or conciliation.

In a blunt speech opening the conference that his administration had engineered, Bush was hopeful but realistic. Merely ending belligerency in the region would not be enough, Bush said. "Rather we seek peace, real peace," he said, calling for treaties, diplomatic exchanges and "territorial compromise." Bush previewed the "painful" process that lay ahead. "There will be disagreement and criticism, setbacks — who knows, possibly interruptions," he said.

In Washington, members of Congress reacted to the diplomatic fits and starts with a mixture of admiration for the Bush administration's achievement in bringing the historical adversaries together and apprehension that the process could fall apart.

Some lawmakers were unabashedly optimistic about the chances for peace. Rep. Wayne Owens, D-Utah, who rose at 4:30 a.m. to watch the opening of the conference on television, said it "will be the dawn of a new age of peace" in the Middle East. Rep. Jim Leach, R-Iowa, said he believed that there were "better prospects of something coming from this than any other single event since the creation of Israel."

Yet a strong undercurrent of concern also existed over Israel's security. Some strong supporters of Israel worried that the administration could prove an insufficiently staunch ally.

Aid to Yugoslavian Republics

Fighting that raged in the former republics of Yugoslavia during 1992 underlined the uncertainty surrounding the role of the United States in a world no longer dominated by the U.S.-Soviet superpower standoff.

After the fall of communism, Yugoslavia broke into feuding republics riven by ancient ethnic rivalries. What remained of Yugoslavia was controlled by Serbia, which fought for territory and dominance with neighboring Croatia and Bosnia-Herzegovina.

While the initial U.S. response was to distance itself from the conflict, calls for action in Congress increased with the rising death toll and with grim stories of "ethnic cleansing" and detention camps run by the Serbian forces that were attacking the Muslim-dominated breakaway state of Bosnia-Herzegovina.

To the outside world, the carnage became most visible in Sarajevo, the capital of Bosnia, where Serbian forces cut off food and medical supplies from the city's more than 300,000 residents. Bosnian President Alija Izetbegovic appealed publicly for U.S. war planes to attack Serbian artillery that were bombarding the city from the hills above Sarajevo with up to 10 shells per minute.

The Senate passed by voice vote on June 12 a resolution (S Res 306), backed by leaders of both parties, calling on President Bush to urge U.N. Secretary General Boutros Boutros-Ghali to draw up a plan and a budget for "such intervention as may be necessary" to enforce a U.N. cease-fire.

But pleas for U.S. involvement were countered by warnings from Pentagon officials that the United States must proceed cautiously lest it find itself mired in an intractable fight that would prove costly in terms of both money and lives.

Nonetheless, the administration decided in August to seek U.N. authorization of military force, if necessary, to ensure the delivery of humanitarian relief to Bosnia-Herzegovina. Both the House and Senate approved resolutions (S Res 330, H Res 554) strongly endorsing the effort, which was intended to send a signal to the warring factions that the international community was willing to act.

The non-binding Senate resolution, adopted 74-22 on Aug. 11, called on the president to seek U.N. authorization to use "all necessary means" to ensure the provision of humanitarian relief in Bosnia-Herzegovina and to gain access for U.N. and International Red Cross personnel to refugee and prisoner of war camps throughout the former Yugoslavia. The resolution also called on the Security Council to review the impact of an arms embargo on Bosnia-Herzegovina.

That same day the House, by voice vote, adopted a similar resolution that largely endorsed the administration's efforts to seek a U.N. resolution on the use of force.

On Aug. 13, the U.N. Security Council approved the U.S.-backed resolution calling for the use of "all measures necessary" to facilitate the delivery of humanitarian relief in Bosnia-Herzegovina.

Two months later, lawmakers went further, earmarking $35 million in the fiscal 1993 foreign operations appropriations bill (HR 5368 — PL 102-391) in refugee assistance for Bosnia, Croatia and Slovenia and $20 million in fuel and construction materials for Bosnia, Croatia and Kosovo. *(Fiscal 1993 foreign aid appropriations, p. 271)*

And in a move that put the United States more squarely on one side of the conflict, Congress also authorized — but did not compel — the president to provide up to $50 million in military equipment to Bosnia. Supporters of the provision, which was added as an amendment on the Senate floor, argued that the ban on arms shipments had left Bosnians almost defenseless against attacks by well-armed Serbians.

The administration was opposed to the amendment but indicated it would not object if the Senate approved it by voice vote. With strong bipartisan support for the amendment, the administration wanted to avoid an embarrassing defeat on a recorded vote.

Bush signed the aid measure on Oct. 6. But no arms shipments or military intervention followed in 1992.

Somalia Relief Effort

In one of the final major decisions of his presidency, George Bush in December 1992 sent almost 28,000 U.S. soldiers to the African country of Somalia to aid workers in their distribution of food to the starving populace.

The problem in Somalia had been growing throughout the year. Relief efforts were at a standstill because of pandemic theft and extortion by gangs of heavily armed gunmen in areas where political structures had disintegrated.

By early December, with the nightly news and daily papers recounting the suffering of the Somali people, Bush decided that action in conjunction with the United Nations was necessary.

Congress had already adjourned for the year when Bush announced the deployment Dec. 4. Although most individual members in both chambers were supportive of the intervention, it was not until Feb. 4, 1993, that the Senate adopted a resolution (S J Res 45) approving the Bush action, which was known as Operation Restore Hope.

Background

For 22 years after Mohammed Siad Barre seized control of Somalia in 1969, he parlayed Somalia's proximity to the oil-rich Arabian peninsula into a cornucopia of superpower arms and aid drawn first from Moscow and then, beginning in 1978, from Washington. But his repressive regime spawned insurgent movements that drove him from power in January 1991.

By the end of that year, the country had disintegrated into warring factions, loosely organized along clan lines and armed to the teeth with the rifles, grenade launchers and larger weapons stockpiled by the Barre regime.

The civil war, coupled with a prolonged drought, triggered famine as food-distribution networks collapsed and hundreds of thousands of refugees assembled in camps.

With an estimated 30 percent of the Somali population facing starvation, the U.N. Security Council approved an emergency airlift of relief supplies in July.

Congressional Concern

With international relief officials warning that a generation of children in Somalia were at risk from war and famine, some members of Congress began to call for a U.N. security force to protect food shipments to the East African country.

Lawmakers said the Somalia crisis could become more devastating than the 1984 famine in Ethiopia, which killed about 1 million people. Relief agency officials had said up to 2 million Somalians were in immediate danger of starvation.

But the Bush administration said it would be premature to deploy U.N. peacekeepers until there was a cease-fire in Somalia. Assistant Secretary of State for International Organization Affairs John R. Bolton told a congressional committee that the United States was the largest single contributor of relief aid for Somalia, providing more than $60 million in emergency assistance since early 1991. But Bolton said that because of the violent instability in the country, the administration was wary about using U.N. peacekeepers. He said one of the country's warlords had boasted that the U.N. observers "would be killed for the boots and berets."

But the Senate on Aug. 3, 1992, approved by voice vote a resolution urging Bush to seek action by the United Nations. The resolution (S Con Res 132) said Bush should urge the United Nations "to deploy a sufficient number of security guards" to protect emergency food shipments to the war-torn country.

On the same day the Senate acted, a Bush administration official reported that up to one-quarter of the children in Somalia under 5 had died because of war and famine, while 1.5 million Somalis faced starvation.

The House approved the resolution one week later on Aug. 10 by voice vote under suspension of the rules.

Troop Deployment

Bush authorized a U.S. relief airlift Aug. 14. Between August and December, the United States, in conjunction with relief agencies, delivered 17,000 tons of supplies.

A 3,500-member multinational military force had been slated for dispatch under U.N. auspices to act as peacekeepers. But only 500 of the U.N.-sponsored troops were allowed in the country by the feuding warlords, and the rules governing their deployment rendered them virtually helpless to stop raids on relief convoys and warehouses by heavily armed and undisciplined gangs of young men and boys.

On Nov. 25, with no public notice, Bush offered U.N. Secretary General Boutros Boutros-Ghali the use of a large U.S. force to pacify Somalia to the point where the stalled relief efforts could resume.

Boutros-Ghali recommended to the Security Council on Nov. 30 that such a U.N.-sponsored force be deployed and that — in contrast to the stringent limitations traditionally placed on U.N. peacekeeping forces — these "peacemaking" forces be authorized to use whatever force was needed to allow the relief effort to resume.

The authorizing resolution adopted Dec. 3 by a unanimous vote of the 15-member council was carefully negotiated to accommodate two sets of demands. The Bush administration insisted that U.S. troops, which would make up the largest share of the force, be under U.S. command. However, several states from Africa and other parts of the developing world insisted that the United Nations not simply give the United States free rein to conduct the operation, as had been the case in the 1991 war against Iraq.

The resolution endorsed, indirectly, Boutros-Ghali's acknowledgment that, as a practical matter, the force would have to be under U.S. command. But it specified that the secretary general would have a hand in designing the command structure for the force. It also gave the Security Council a voice in when to end the operation.

The resolution established a fund through which wealthy U.N. members could subsidize the participation in the Somali operation of military forces from poorer states.

On Dec. 4, Bush announced that he would deploy as many as 28,000 U.S. troops to Somalia to aid in distribution of food to the starving population as the backbone of the multilateral force approved by the Security Council.

"Only the United States has the global reach to place a large security force on the ground in such a distant place, quickly and efficiently, and thus save thousands of innocents from death," Bush said in a brief televised address Dec. 4.

He insisted that the force would have a limited objective. "We will create a secure environment in the hardest-hit parts of Somalia, so that food can move from ships overland to the people in the countryside now devastated by starvation," he said. "Once we have created that secure environment, we will withdraw our troops, handing the security mission back to a regular U.N. peacekeeping force."

President-elect Bill Clinton hailed the Security Council decision as a "historic and welcome step." And he lauded Bush for proposing the U.S. role: "I commend President Bush for taking the lead in this important humanitarian effort."

Congressional Response

Most congressional leaders also backed the deployment, citing the enormity of the Somali tragedy that had been driven home daily to Americans by news accounts picturing starving children.

Yet, even as they endorsed the Somalia deployment, many of them touched on some of the issues that would be ripe for debate when future military missions were weighed.

Indiana Democrat Lee H. Hamilton, in line to take over as chairman of the House Foreign Affairs Committee, insisted that his support was conditioned on a clear delineation of the mission's scope.

Georgia Democrat Sam Nunn, the influential chairman of the Senate Armed Services Committee, questioned whether the decision paved the way for similar deployments to other countries where thousands were threatened by widespread communal violence.

House Defense Appropriations Subcommittee Chairman John P. Murtha, D-Pa., opposed the deployment as not being in the national interest. He worried that it would soak up funds from an already shrinking defense budget and thus erode the Pentagon's readiness to protect more vital U.S. interests.

Concerns over how and when the United States would withdraw from Somalia and whether the Somali operation set a precedent were again raised in a mid-December hearing before the House Foreign Affairs Committee.

War Powers Letter

In a Dec. 10 letter to congressional leaders, Bush said U.S. troops would remain in Somalia "only as long as necessary to establish a secure environment for humanitarian relief operations." The U.S. force was "necessary to address a major humanitarian calamity, avert related threats to international peace and security and protect the safety of Americans and others engaged in relief operations," Bush said.

In the letter, Bush maintained that "we do not intend that U.S. armed forces deployed to Somalia become involved in hostilities" but that they will "have the support of any additional armed forces necessary to ensure their safety and the accomplishment of their mission."

The letter provided Congress all the information the president was required to provide under the War Powers Resolution when U.S. forces were deployed overseas in a situation entailing a significant risk of combat.

But like every other president since the war powers measure was enacted in 1973, Bush contended that it was an unconstitutional infringement on his powers as commander in chief of the armed forces. To avoid appearing to concede the act's validity while also avoiding a showdown on the issue, Bush followed the longstanding practice of providing Congress with the information required by the act but stipulating that the letter was "consistent with" the War Powers act, not pursuant to the disputed legislation.

1993 Action

Bush had hoped to end the U.S. involvement in Somalia before Clinton was inaugurated Jan. 20, 1993, but was unable to do so. While Clinton was taking the oath of office, 850 Marines were beginning their journey home from Somalia. The United States brought part of its troops home in the hope of prodding the United Nations to begin taking over the relief effort. Under an agreement adopted unanimously by the U.N. Security Council on Dec. 3, 1992, the United Nations had pledged to make the Somali relief effort an international undertaking after an initial, U.S.-led deployment.

The Senate on Feb. 4, 1993, approved by voice vote a measure (S J Res 45) authorizing the use of force in support of the U.N.-sponsored operation to establish a "secure environment" for delivery of relief supplies to the war-torn country. The resolution urged Clinton to consult with Boutros-Ghali with the goal of transferring the mission to a U.N.-led force "at the earliest possible date."

The measure skirted thorny questions over the War Powers Resolution by stating that the resolution was "consistent with" the 1973 law, which required that a president seek congressional approval when troops faced "imminent involvement in hostilities."

Revised 1991 Intelligence Bill

Congress in 1991 cleared a revised fiscal 1991 intelligence authorization. An earlier version had been pocket-vetoed in 1990 by President Bush, who objected to provisions rewriting the rules on executive notification of Congress of covert intelligence actions. *(Vetoed bill, p. 242)*

The covert action requirements were recrafted in the new bill (HR 1455 — PL 102-88), although not entirely to everyone's satisfaction. The two sides basically agreed to disagree on the issue of how soon Congress should be notified, and the measure was signed into law.

HR 1455 was designed to replace a combination of statutes, executive orders and informal understandings that had governed covert actions over the prior decade. Existing requirements had failed to prevent the Reagan administration in the mid-1980s from selling arms to Iran and diverting some of the proceeds to anti-government rebels in Nicaragua, without informing Congress and in defiance of a congressional ban against contra aid. Congress had been attempting ever since the Iran-contra affair to enact legislation that would prevent a recurrence. *(Iran-contra legacy, p. 238)*

HR 1455 also reportedly authorized about two-thirds of the estimated $30 billion intelligence operations budget.

Legislative Action

The House passed HR 1455 (H Rept 102-37) by voice vote on May 1. The House bill sidestepped the dispute over reporting covert operations by dropping proposed changes.

House members said they wanted current law tightened. But they argued that existing law, despite its ambiguities and loopholes, was preferable to settling for new reporting requirements that excluded provisions opposed by Bush.

They were wary that Senate negotiators, in trying to specify what should be reported to Congress and when, could end up weakening requirements by failing to mention certain activities, such as operations conducted by other countries or private individuals.

The Senate Intelligence Committee reported a revised intelligence bill (S 1325 — S Rept 102-85) on June 19. The committee's report contained some of the same language that the administration had objected to the previous year, but it also included additional phrases clarifying its intent. The Senate passed an amended HR 1455 by voice vote on June 28.

House and Senate conferees on July 24 reached agreement on a compromise version of the long-delayed bill, including the requirements for reporting of covert activities. With surprisingly little debate, Congress sent the bill to the president on July 31. The House adopted the conference report (H Rept 102-166) by a vote of 419-4. The Senate approved the measure by voice vote later that day.

Final Bill

Although most of HR 1455 was classified, the final bill reportedly authorized about two-thirds of the estimated $30 billion fiscal 1991 budget for the Central Intelligence Agency, the National Security Agency, the Defense Intelligence Agency and other intelligence-related activities.

HR 1455 defined covert action in law for the first time, calling it an action undertaken by the government "to influence political, economic or military conditions abroad, where it is intended that the role of the United States government will not be apparent or acknowledged publicly." Exceptions were provided for what had been generally considered traditional intelligence-gathering, diplomatic, military and law enforcement activities.

The measure required the president to notify Congress "in a timely fashion" whenever he failed to provide advance notification of a covert operation.

The president was required to authorize the actions in advance with a written presidential "finding." If immediate action was required, the president had up to 48 hours to put his decision into a written finding.

In the finding, the president had to determine that the covert action was necessary "to support identifiable foreign policy objectives" of the United States. He was not allowed to authorize covert acts that violated the Constitution or any laws.

For the most part, the findings were to be given to the two congressional Intelligence committees. In extraordinary cases, however, the president could limit notification to the congressional leadership. The president also was required to inform Congress of any significant changes in previously approved covert actions.

The bill expanded to the entire federal government prohibitions against conducting covert actions without both a presidential finding and notification of Congress, which previously had applied only to the CIA. This provision was in response to the Reagan administration's contention that it was not required to tell Congress about the Iran-contra affair because it was managed by the National Security Council.

The bill specifically prohibited covert actions intended to influence domestic politics, public opinion, policies or the media.

The bill included a few important changes from the measure that Bush had vetoed the year before. As in the bill approved by the Senate, the final version required that the president inform Congress if he anticipated that any third party would participate significantly in a covert action, but it did not require that he identify the participant.

In eight months of negotiations, Intelligence Committee leaders and the White House had been unable to resolve their differences over setting a time limit for reporting covert actions. Bush in 1990 had objected to the conference committee report's definition of "in a timely fashion" as "within a few days." Bush argued that, while he intended to meet that standard in most instances, the limit was an unconstitutional infringement on his presidential authority.

The two sides in 1991 in effect agreed to disagree on this point. The new report stated that conferees still believed that notification should be within a few days, but that they realized the president may assert constitutional authority to withhold notice for a longer period.

Conferees wrote that they "recognize that this is a question that neither they nor the Congress itself can resolve," effectively pushing any potential confrontation into the judicial system.

Bush Statement

When the president signed the measure into law on Aug. 14 (PL 102-88), he emphasized that he still opposed efforts to mandate congressional notification of covert activities within a set time. Bush insisted that the Constitution allowed him to wait longer if he thought it necessary to carry out his duties.

His statement also underscored potential differences over what types of covert military activities were covered by the new reporting law. Congressional conferees and administration officials had worked closely together on conference report language to describe which "traditional" military activities would be exempt from reporting requirements.

But when he signed the measure, Bush caught members by surprise by writing in the accompanying statement: "In determining whether particular military activities constitute covert actions, I shall continue to bear in mind the historic missions of the Armed Forces to protect the United States and its interests, influence foreign capabilities and intentions, and conduct activities preparatory to the execution of operations."

Senate Armed Services Committee Chairman Sam Nunn, D-Ga., objected later that Bush's definition was so broad it "would cover everything the CIA has done that I know anything about in covert activity." Nunn called this a "fundamental difference" from what Congress had intended in the new law.

Another lingering area of ambiguity involved a requirement that Congress also be informed of "significant" intelligence activities other than covert operations. Senate Intelligence Committee Chairman David L. Boren, D-Okla., said his committee had made considerable headway in the previous few years working with the administration to clarify just what that meant. But he said a broader definition would become increasingly important if the CIA devoted less time to covert actions and more to other activities.

1992 Intelligence Authorization

Congress in 1991 took the first step toward making public the amount of money spent on the nation's intelligence activities, as part of its fiscal 1992 intelligence authorization (HR 2038 — PL 102-183). The bill included a provision recommending that President Bush reveal the total spent on intelligence activities — believed by experts to be about $30 billion annually.

The provision originally would have required the president to make the number public. But faced with a veto threat, lawmakers backed down and only "recommended" that he do so.

The measure also halted, at least temporarily, a move by the Central Intelligence Agency to relocate some of its workers to Prince William County in Virginia and to Jefferson County, W.Va. Though the bill authorized funds for the move, it also imposed strict reporting requirements on the CIA's method of choosing a new site.

The bill established a new program for U.S. students to learn foreign languages.

Legislative Action

HR 2038 was reported by the House Intelligence Committee on May 15 (H Rept 102-65, Part I) and by the House Armed Services Committee on June 4 (H Rept 102-65, Part II). The House passed the bill by voice vote June 11, after attaching a requirement that all Intelligence Committee members and aides sign an oath of secrecy.

Democratic leaders, who tried unsuccessfully to prevent the secrecy oath amendment from reaching the floor, argued that existing House and committee rules already required secrecy and asserted that most intelligence leaks came from the administration.

Both House and committee rules prohibited members from disclosing any classified information they received while on the panel unless authorized by the committee or the House. Committee aides were required to sign nondisclosure agreements vowing that they would not disclose any secret information unless authorized.

But the committee's ranking Republican and sponsor of the amendment, Bud Shuster, Pa., said the oath was needed to encourage intelligence agencies to be more open with the committee and to emphasize members' commitment to protect government secrets.

By a vote of 169-234, the House June 11 rejected an amendment to require the CIA to conduct random drug testing of all its officers and employees.

CIA Move Put on Hold

A plan to move part of the CIA to West Virginia was put off indefinitely in 1992 after some lawmakers challenged the decision, arguing that the only reason that location had been chosen was the influence of Senate Appropriations Committee Chairman Robert C. Byrd, D-W.Va.

Budgetary constraints gave CIA Director Robert M. Gates a diplomatic way out of a corner, as he put on hold a fiercely disputed plan to relocate 6,000 agency employees to sites in West Virginia and in Virginia's Prince William County.

"In the current budgetary environment," Gates said in a March 31 letter to lawmakers involved in the issue, "high-priority intelligence requirements must take precedence." According to Gates, the move's estimated cost had increased from $1.2 billion to $1.4 billion.

Byrd and Virginia Republican Sen. John W. Warner, who also had supported the move, bowed to Gates' decision. The prospective move had met with criticism from some members of Congress when it was disclosed in 1991. Critics inserted language in the fiscal 1992 intelligence authorization bill requiring a new, public site-selection process and evidence that the consolidation would save money. *(1992 intelligence authorization, p. 281)*

Members of Congress also asked the CIA inspector general to look into the selection process. His Feb. 20 report found no violation of laws or regulations. But it concluded that key members of Congress were given inaccurate information or intentionally kept in the dark during the site selection in 1991 and that the overall process was poorly managed.

According to the report, selection of the West Virginia site was based to a large extent on political considerations. Its detailed account portrayed an agency conscious of its dependence on congressional funding — and well aware of Byrd's quest to obtain more federal facilities for his economically depressed state.

The Senate Intelligence Committee reported its version (S 1539 — S Rept 102-117) on July 24. The bill included a controversial proposal by Sen. Howard M. Metzenbaum, D-Ohio, that the overall budget total for intelligence activities be made public beginning in fiscal 1993.

Many members on the panel believed that disclosure of the number would not harm U.S. security and would satisfy the public's right to know how much it was spending on those activities at a time when pressure was great to cut federal spending. Robert M. Gates, during hearings on his nomination to be director of central intelligence, endorsed the proposal as a way to build public confidence in the intelligence community. *(Gates confirmation, box, p. 261)*

However, the administration insisted that release of the budget total would inevitably force the disclosure of additional details, "which, in turn, could jeopardize U.S. national security." The White House noted that all members of Congress already had access to the information and that the intelligence budget was reviewed by six congressional committees.

The Senate committee bill also sanctioned a plan by the CIA to relocate nearly two dozen of its offices that were scattered throughout the Washington, D.C.-area to two new sites in Virginia and West Virginia. The plan, supported by John W. Warner, R-Va., and Robert C. Byrd, D-W.Va., chairman of the Appropriations Committee, was strongly opposed by Washington-area House members, whose districts would lose jobs in the transfer.

The Senate passed an amended HR 2038 by voice vote on Oct. 16, after rejecting 38-59 a plan to make three additional top CIA posts subject to congressional approval. Although the aim of the amendment was to make the CIA more accountable to Congress, opponents argued that the confirmation process would make the agency more political as potential candidates tried to curry favor with the White House and Congress. Three CIA posts were already subject to Senate confirmation.

Final Bill

Both the House and Senate approved the conference report on HR 2038 (H Rept 102-327) by voice votes on Nov. 20. As signed into law Dec. 4 (PL 102-183), HR 2038 authorized a secret amount in fiscal 1992 for intelligence activities.

Because of a veto threat, the final bill recommended — but did not require — that the administration reveal the overall budget figure for intelligence activities, which was estimated to be about $30 billion.

The conference bill put the brakes on a $1.2 billion plan to move several thousand CIA employees to West Virginia and Prince William County, Va. Instead, the bill required a public re-evaluation of the proposal, which had evolved from secret discussions between CIA officials and Senate leaders, with the considerable influence of Senate Appropriations Committee Chairman Byrd.

House Intelligence Committee members had been especially outraged by the consolidation plan. In a rare public hearing July 30, House panel members had blasted the CIA for not keeping the committee informed.

Conferees decided to approve $10 million for the CIA to purchase property for its relocation effort, but only after the agency had met certain conditions. These included providing a written description of the criteria used in the site selection. Once these conditions were met, an additional $20 million would be made available, subject to the approval of the House and Senate Intelligence and Armed Services committees.

But in 1992, the plan was shelved indefinitely because of budgetary constraints. *(Box, this page)*

Conferees also agreed to authorize $150 million, instead of the $180 million in the Senate version, for a new National Security Education Trust Fund to provide scholarships and grants for foreign language and international studies. Under the conference agreement, $35 million could be obligated in fiscal 1992 from the trust fund: $15 million in scholarships for undergraduate studies abroad, $10 million for graduate fellowships and $10 million for grants to educational institutions. To avoid suspicions that recipients might be working undercover on school campuses, the bill prohibited those receiving the funds from conducting U.S. intelligence activities while participating in the program.

The conference agreement phased out aid for U.S.-backed rebels in Angola before elections were held there in 1992. The bill provided an estimated $20 million in non-military aid, compared with $60 million in fiscal 1991. *(Angola aid, box, p. 244)*

Dropped from the final bill was a House provision requiring members of the House Intelligence Committee to take an oath of secrecy. Instead, the committee passed a rule in October requiring the oaths, which were signed by each member.

1993 Intelligence Authorization

Congress in 1992 cleared a fiscal 1993 intelligence authorization that cut President Bush's request by almost 6 percent. The bill (HR 5095 — PL 102-496) also included plans to streamline U.S. intelligence operations, largely reflecting changes already made by CIA Director Robert M. Gates.

Although the intelligence budget was secret, HR 5095 was believed to authorize slightly more than $19 billion for the CIA, National Security Agency, Defense Intelligence Agency and other activities of what is known as the National Foreign Intelligence Program.

This figure was thought to have been cut further — to an estimated $17.5 billion — in the defense appropriations bill (HR 5504 — PL 102-396). The defense bill also reportedly included a separate budget of $11 billion for tactical intelligence activities of the armed services. Thus, the nation's intelligence spending reportedly totaled $28.5 billion for fiscal 1993, as compared with an estimated $30 billion in recent years.

With the Cold War over and demands growing for the government to do more to address domestic needs, the fiscal 1993 budget was ripe for attack. Leaders of the House and Senate Intelligence committees recognized these pressures early on and started the year with enthusiastic plans to reorganize the nation's web of intelligence programs. *(Intelligence reorganization, box, p. 284)*

Though the plans for a dramatic overhaul did not become law, members did respond to pressure by cutting the secret agencies' budgets.

Legislative Action

The House Intelligence Committee reported HR 5095 (H Rept 102-544, Part I) June 2 and the Armed Services Committee reported the bill (H Rept 102-544, Part II) June 17. With little debate, the full House passed the bill by voice vote on June 25.

The House bill cut 5 percent from the Bush administration's budget request for intelligence activities in fiscal 1993, according to Chairman Dave McCurdy, D-Okla. McCurdy said the legislation did not include his proposals to restructure the nation's multi-agency intelligence apparatus because of extensive efforts by Gates to reorganize the CIA and other intelligence operations administratively.

In House floor debate, members cited the end of the Cold War and the changing global threat both to defend and oppose the spending cuts called for in the authorization bill. McCurdy said the legislation recognized the political reality that a reduced threat from the Soviet Union, the main target of U.S. intelligence efforts for more than 40 years, would require spending cuts. But he said further reductions might seriously harm intelligence efforts as the U.S. military presence around the world was being reduced and intelligence operations were becoming more crucial.

Committee leaders cited growing concerns over nuclear weapons proliferation among Third World nations, increased foreign espionage against U.S. businesses and arms control monitoring as reasons for not trimming further.

The Senate Intelligence Committee reported its version of the legislation (S 2991 — S Rept 102-324) July 21 containing a similar 5 percent — or $1 billion — cut in the intelligence budget. But, unlike the House bill, the Senate legislation also put into law many of the organizational changes for the intelligence community that Gates had announced in April.

The Senate Armed Services Committee reported the bill Sept. 16 (S Rept 102-407), and the full Senate passed an amended HR 5095 by voice vote on Sept. 23. Two days earlier, the chamber had rejected 35-57 an amendment to reduce the intelligence budget by another $1 billion.

Final Bill

The House and Senate adopted the conference version of HR 5095 (H Rept 102-963) on Oct. 2 by voice votes. Despite frequently voiced misgivings about the bill's spending reduction and other provisions, Bush signed the measure (PL 102-496) on Oct. 24.

The final bill cut the administration's request by nearly 6 percent, or more than $1 billion. McCurdy said the spending reduction was larger than the 5 percent cut called for in the House and Senate versions of the bill because of global changes and pressing domestic budget demands.

The measure also included plans to streamline U.S. intelligence operations, largely reflecting changes already made by CIA Director Gates.

One of the major changes was the creation of a central imagery authority within the Department of Defense to coordinate the collection and dissemination of intelligence gathered through satellite and aerial reconnaissance. The Pentagon had created a similar office in May in response to congressional proposals earlier in the year for a separate National Imagery Agency to oversee the activities, which had been spread throughout the sprawling Defense Department. Senate Intelligence Committee Chairman David L. Boren, D-Okla., said the new office was a victory for taxpayers because it would mean greater accountability and less duplication in one of the costliest intelligence-gathering programs.

The final bill also created a more independent National Intelligence Council, made up of senior intelligence analysts and outside experts, to produce national intelligence estimates. These analyses were used by top government officials in making foreign and defense policy decisions.

During Gates' confirmation hearings in 1991, numerous witnesses testified that the estimates had lost much of their value because of political disputes within the agency and the failure of analysts to provide the kind of information policy makers needed. *(Gates confirmation, box, p. 261)*

The legislation also attempted to make it easier for the intelligence director to manage intelligence operations in other agencies by writing into law the budgeting and other powers that the director had under executive orders issued

Changes Made in Intelligence Operations ...

While some members began the 102nd Congress with high hopes for reorganizing the nation's intelligence community, in the end they settled for more moderate changes drawn up by the Bush administration.

CIA Director Robert M. Gates offered a plan that he said would make intelligence operations more efficient and refocus them on possible post-Soviet threats from Third World nations and other sources.

The Intelligence Committee chairmen, Sen. David L. Boren, D-Okla., and Rep. Dave McCurdy, D-Okla., set aside more sweeping overhaul legislation and incorporated provisions in the fiscal 1993 intelligence authorization bill that largely reflected the changes Gates had made. These included a new central imagery office in the Pentagon to oversee intelligence gathered through satellite and aerial reconnaissance and the use of outside experts in preparing certain intelligence analyses. *(Fiscal 1993 intelligence authorization, p. 283)*

Boren-McCurdy Plans

Citing the end of the Cold War and pressures to reduce defense-related spending, Sen. Boren and Rep. McCurdy introduced almost identical bills (HR 4165, S 2198) on Feb. 5, 1992, to reorganize and refocus the nation's intelligence apparatus. The Intelligence chairmen said they were not wedded to their proposals, but they argued that the end of the Cold War and tight budgets required a rethinking of how the United States collected and used intelligence to protect its national security.

The centerpiece of Boren's and McCurdy's plans was the creation of a director of national intelligence and a National Intelligence Center, changes intended to consolidate many of the overlapping intelligence activities then conducted throughout the federal government. The director of national intelligence, a job likely to be filled by Gates, would have had authority over the budget and operations of all U.S. intelligence activities except tactical intelligence gathered for military operations, which would have been consolidated under Pentagon control. Under the existing set-up, the CIA director nominally oversaw the U.S. intelligence community but did not have final say over the budget or allocation of resources.

The bills would have assigned two deputies to assist the director. One would have coordinated intelligence analysis that at the time was conducted by the CIA and analysts throughout the government. A second deputy director would have been appointed to oversee and coordinate intelligence-collection activities conducted by civilian and military agencies, such as the Defense Intelligence Agency and the National Security Agency. Under this jurisdiction, a new National Imagery Agency would have coordinated intelligence gathering with satellites.

Gates Response

Rejecting congressional proposals for legislation to reorganize U.S. intelligence agencies, CIA Director Gates announced April 1 a series of administrative changes.

Testifying before the first hearing ever held jointly by the Senate and House Intelligence committees, Gates warned against locking into law any new structure for the intelligence community in an effort to take account of the collapse of the Soviet Union and the end of the Cold War. "In a world as fast-changing as what we have seen in the last three or four years," he said, "our ability quickly to adjust structurally, as well as reallocate resources, must be preserved and even enhanced."

The organizational changes Gates summarized for the two panels were the product of 14 task forces that he established in November 1991. He had pledged a sweeping reorganization during his 1991 Senate confirmation hearings as director of intelligence. *(Gates confirmation, box, p. 261)*

Gates accepted the recommendations of all but one task force, ordering changes such as a stronger management staff to help him weed out duplication among intelligence agencies and revisions in the production of intelligence estimates to alert policy makers to a wider range of possible interpretations of often ambiguous intelligence data.

over the years, but that in practice were often ignored by agency heads.

As signed into law, HR 5095 expressed the sense of Congress that the annual intelligence budget total should be made public, but it did not force the issue.

One continuing threat addressed by the legislation was the unlawful disclosure of classified information by former employees. The bill allowed the defense secretary to provide financial and other help to unemployed former employees of the Defense Intelligence Agency if he determined that the aid was needed "to maintain the judgment and emotional stability" of such employees and to stop them from releasing government secrets.

Iran-Contra Pardons

On Christmas Eve 1992, President Bush pardoned former defense secretary Caspar W. Weinberger and five others involved in the politically charged Iran-contra scandal.

... More Sweeping Reorganization Set Aside

Boren and McCurdy lauded the scope and speed of Gates' reforms. But they insisted that legislation was needed to give Gates the authority to root out duplication among intelligence agencies. In particular, the two chairmen criticized Gates' decision not to create an agency in charge of all satellite and aerial reconnaissance, most of which currently was controlled by the Defense Department.

One of Gates' task forces had recommended creating an agency in charge of all such intelligence collection by "imagery." But senior Pentagon officials vigorously opposed the idea, and Gates decided to move much more cautiously. As a first step, he and Defense Secretary Dick Cheney agreed that the Pentagon would create a small organization to coordinate the design of tactical photo reconnaissance equipment intended for military use and "national" equipment, such as satellites.

Gates described several of his organizational changes as intended to beef up the director's ability to manage the community efficiently.

The Intelligence Community Staff, which backstopped the director in his role as central coordinator, would be replaced by a new staff charged with establishing a division of labor among agencies and reducing unneeded duplication.

Several of Gates' other moves were intended to insulate from bureaucratic pressures the "national intelligence estimates" that the intelligence community produced for top national decision makers. To underscore its independence from any single agency, the National Intelligence Council, which oversaw drafting of the estimates, would be moved out of the CIA headquarters complex. The council would be given two newly appointed vice chairmen:

- One routinely would perform post-mortems on previously written estimates to assess their accuracy.
- The other would supervise the drafting of estimates, ensuring that they took account of dissenting views among agencies and that they told officials not only what the intelligence experts deemed most likely to happen but also what might occur instead if that "best estimate" turned out to be mistaken. The vice chairman would promote use of the "red team/blue team" technique, using separate teams of analysts to write competing drafts of an estimate, to reduce the risk that important perspectives would be overlooked.

Gates told the committees that he would increase the number of academics and other specialists from outside government on the National Intelligence Council and that the vice chairman for estimates would come from the private sector.

Aside from the thorny issue of who would control imagery systems, with their massive budgets, Gates endorsed as a general principle coordinating the use by different agencies of each type of intelligence-gathering technique.

In the effort to ensure that the CIA placed a higher priority on supporting the military, particularly during crises, Gates created an office of military affairs.

Beyond his steps to reorganize the intelligence community, Gates also announced several changes in the operation of the CIA, including:

- Managers' performance evaluations would take account of any complaints that they politicized subordinates' work, an effort to reduce the risk that analysts would feel pressured to shade their products to back up policies favored by their superiors. Also, an ombudsman was appointed to advise analysts with complaints about such pressure.
- CIA personnel would be trained about their legal obligation to report possible criminal activity they discovered in the course of their work. In addition, each department in the agency would designate an official to funnel such information to the appropriate law enforcement agencies. The agency had come under fire for not passing along information it came across relating to possible criminal activity of the Bank of Credit and Commerce International (BCCI).
- As part of Gates' pledge to be more forthcoming with the public, the agency created an office to review secret documents for possible declassification. The office would review all national intelligence estimates on the former Soviet Union that were 10 years old or older and all documents more than 30 years old, beginning with those relating to President John F. Kennedy and the CIA-sponsored invasion of Cuba at the Bay of Pigs in 1961.

The surprise reprieve brought swift condemnations from several key Democrats in Congress and equally forceful applause from some Republicans.

Bush's action stood as a powerful closing emblem of 12 years of divided government.

Background

The Iran-contra operation involved the sale of weapons to Iran — at least in part in an effort to negotiate the release of U.S. hostages in the Middle East — and the diversion of some of the arms sale profits to aid the contra rebels in Nicaragua despite a congressional ban on U.S. assistance. The elaborate policy was conducted in secret by the Reagan White House in 1985 and 1986. *(Congress and the Nation Vol. VII, p. 253)*

The November 1986 announcement of the operation and the subsequent political fallout were the darkest days of Reagan's presidency.

In December 1986, the Reagan administration, under

political pressure, requested appointment of an independent counsel. Retired federal judge Lawrence E. Walsh, an Oklahoma Republican, was selected.

A presidential commission chaired by former senator John Tower, R-Texas, issued a report in February 1987 sharply critical of Reagan's handling of his staff, which it said mismanaged the Iran-contra policies.

Special House and Senate investigating committees held public hearings on the scandal in the summer of 1987. In their final report, a bipartisan majority of the select committees found that the failures of the affair stemmed from White House "secrecy, deception, and disdain for the rule of law." The committees found a pervasive willingness by administration officials to use any means, legal or illegal, to accomplish the president's policy objectives.

The controversy continued to live on in federal courts and the political arena after Reagan's presidency ended. Two key Reagan administration officials involved in the affair, former national security adviser John M. Poindexter and his deputy, Oliver L. North, were found guilty of lying to Congress, but the convictions were overturned on appeal. *(Details, box, p. 287)*

During Bush's presidential campaign in 1988, the spotlight focused on his involvement as Reagan's vice president. Bush maintained that he was "out of the loop" when Reagan aides decided to divert funds to the contras. The 1987 congressional Iran-contra report said: "The vice president attended several meetings on the Iran initiative, but none of the participants could recall his views."

Weinberger Case

After nearly six years of work and more than $30 million of federal money spent, Walsh's investigation of the Iran-contra scandal came up with its biggest fish in June 1992: Weinberger, the former defense secretary.

Weinberger was indicted June 16 on charges of perjury and making false statements to Iran-contra investigators. The indictment alleged that he concealed the existence of 1,700 pages of personal notes that detailed the Reagan administration's decision to approve arms sales to Iran in 1985 and 1986 in return for the release of American hostages in Lebanon. Investigators found Weinberger's notes at the National Archives.

Among the charges against Weinberger was that he lied under oath to the congressional Iran-contra committees by denying that he had advance knowledge of a 1985 Israeli shipment of U.S.-made missiles to Iran and by testifying that he was unaware of contributions by Saudi Arabia to the Nicaraguan contras. Weinberger, who pleaded not guilty to all of the charges on June 19, called the indictment a "grotesque distortion of prosecutorial power and a moral and legal outrage."

Prosecutors acknowledged that the former defense secretary objected to the arms-for-hostages scheme. The indictment said that Weinberger's notes documented that, after the November 1985 missile transfer, he "informed President Reagan that such arms shipments were illegal."

Democratic and Republican lawmakers rallied to Weinberger's defense. In an April letter to Weinberger's attorney, the leaders of the Senate Iran-contra committee, Daniel K. Inouye, D-Hawaii, and Warren B. Rudman, R-N.H., said that Weinberger's recollection of specific events was less important than the "adamant position that the secretary consistently took with the president in opposing sales to Iran, on which the testimony was incontrovertible."

Rep. Lee H. Hamilton, D-Ind., who chaired the House committee, said on June 17 that he had "high regard for Secretary Weinberger" but added that he had not reviewed the evidence against him.

Some Republican lawmakers charged that Walsh's investigation was politically inspired, had run out of control and should be cut off. Angered by the Weinberger case and rumors that former president Reagan himself could face indictment, GOP members called for abolishing the independent counsel law, which expired Dec. 15, 1992. *(Independent counsel law, p. 795)*

A new stir was caused by a second indictment of Weinberger that was announced on Oct. 30, just days before the presidential election. The charges were dismissed because they were brought past the five-year statute of limitations. But the indictment was explosive because of a passage that suggested that Bush knew more about the Iran-contra affair than he had previously let on.

Senate Republicans claimed the timing was politically motivated and requested the Justice Department to name an independent counsel to investigate whether Bill Clinton's campaign had a hand in it. Attorney General William P. Barr denied the request.

Bush Pardons

On Dec. 24, 1992, Bush brought his strongest weapon to the match: the presidential pardon. In addition to Weinberger, Bush pardoned:

- Robert C. McFarlane, former national security adviser, who pleaded guilty on March 11, 1988, to withholding information from Congress. He was sentenced to two years' probation and 200 hours of community service and fined $20,000.
- Clair E. George, a former top CIA official, who was convicted on Dec. 9, 1992, of lying to Congress. Although George was acquitted on five other counts, the jury found that he gave misleading answers in 1986 to congressional committees looking into the scandal.

"This marks the first time that a senior CIA official was convicted of felony offenses for crimes committed while he was in his position at the CIA," said prosecutor Craig Gillen after George's conviction. It was George's second trial; the first one ended in a mistrial in August when the jury was deadlocked.

- Duane R. Clarridge, a former senior CIA official who was scheduled to go on trial in March 1993 on eight counts of perjury, all involving allegedly false statements he made about the secret missile shipment to Iran.
- Elliott Abrams, former assistant secretary of state for inter-American affairs, who pleaded guilty on Oct. 7, 1991, to four misdemeanor charges of withholding information from Congress. He was sentenced to two years' probation and 100 hours of community service.
- Alan D. Fiers Jr., former head of the CIA Central American Task Force under George, who pleaded guilty on July 9, 1991, to two misdemeanor charges of withholding information from Congress. He was sentenced to one year of probation and 100 hours of community service.

Bush explained the pardons by saying the men were all "patriots" who had given the country years of public service and had not profited from their involvement in the scandal. Bush said the prosecutions of the six men represented not law enforcement, but "the criminalization of policy differences."

Others Indicted in Iran-Contra Affair

In addition to the six people President Bush pardoned for their alleged roles in the Iran-contra affair, there were other key participants who were indicted for their part in the affair:

• **Oliver L. North.** The former National Security Council aide was convicted on May 4, 1989, on three felony counts of obstructing Congress, altering documents and taking an illegal gratuity. North was fined $150,000 and ordered to perform 1,200 hours of community service. But his conviction was overturned and the charges ultimately dismissed. *(Details, box p. 240)*

• **John M. Poindexter.** Robert C. McFarlane's successor as national security adviser and North's boss, Poindexter was convicted on April 7, 1990, on five felony counts of conspiracy, obstruction of Congress and lying to Congress. He was sentenced to six months in prison. His conviction also was overturned and the charges dismissed.

• **Carl R. "Spitz" Channell.** A fund-raiser for conservative causes, Channell pleaded guilty April 29, 1987, to conspiring to defraud the government by soliciting money for the contras while maintaining that the money was for his National Endowment for the Preservation of Liberty, a tax-exempt organization. He was sentenced to two years' probation.

• **Richard R. Miller.** Miller, a public relations executive whom Channell named as a co-conspirator, pleaded guilty to an identical charge May 6, 1987, and promised to assist prosecutors. He was sentenced to two years' probation and 120 hours of community service.

• **Richard V. Secord.** A retired Air Force major general, Secord was recruited by North to run a network of private individuals, companies and bank accounts in the Iran-contra network. Secord pleaded guilty Nov. 8, 1989, to one count of withholding information from Congress and agreed to help prosecutors. Other charges against Secord were dropped. He was sentenced to two years' probation.

• **Albert Hakim.** The Iranian-born businessman who helped build the Iran-contra network pleaded guilty on Nov. 21, 1989, to a misdemeanor count of illegally supplementing North's salary — with a $13,800 security fence at North's home. He was sentenced to two years' probation and a $5,000 fine.

• **Thomas G. Clines.** A former CIA official who was hired by Secord to help supply arms to the contras, was convicted on Sept. 18, 1990, on four felony counts related to his 1985 and 1986 federal tax returns. He was sentenced to 16 months in prison and $40,000 in fines. His conviction was upheld on appeal.

• **Joseph Fernandez.** A former CIA station chief in Costa Rica, Fernandez was indicted April 24, 1989, on four counts of obstructing the Tower Commission and lying to federal investigators, after a 1988 indictment was dismissed. Attorney General Dick Thornburgh refused to release information about CIA operations that Fernandez' lawyer said was essential to his defense. All charges were dismissed on Nov. 24, 1989.

"These differences should be addressed in the political arena, without the Damocles sword of criminality hanging over the heads of some of the combatants," Bush said. *(Text, p. 1221)*

Walsh said Bush's action improperly set some former administration officials above the law and constituted a "cover-up" of misdeeds. He said the pardons were particularly troubling because Bush apparently had withheld notes requested by the independent counsel's office. Bush had become a "subject" of his ongoing investigation, Walsh said.

Senate Majority Leader George J. Mitchell, D-Maine, and House Majority Leader Richard A. Gephardt, D-Mo., were among those criticizing the pardons. But those condemnations were somewhat muted by reports that House Speaker Thomas S. Foley, D-Wash., and Armed Services Committee Chairman Les Aspin, D-Wis., Clinton's nominee for defense secretary, had been contacted by the White House in advance of the announcement and had given tacit approval to a Weinberger pardon.

Several days later, aides to both lawmakers clarified those reports. An aide to Foley said the Speaker had indicated only that he would not criticize a Weinberger pardon and was "shocked" when Bush pardoned the other five men as well. Similarly, Aspin's aide said Aspin had discussed only Weinberger's case and disagreed with Bush's characterization of the offenses as only possible misdeeds or policy differences.

Meanwhile, Senate Minority Leader Bob Dole, R-Kan., called the pardons a "Christmas Eve act of courage and compassion" and reiterated prior criticisms of Walsh.

Congress had no authority to rescind or alter the six Iran-contra pardons. The presidential power to pardon is an absolute one granted by the Constitution. A pardon wipes out guilt and punishment, as if the offense had never been committed.

No further indictments were handed up, and Walsh submitted his final report on the Iran-contra affair to a special three-judge court on Aug. 5, 1993.

'October Surprise' Probe

Two congressional panels found no evidence to support 12-year-old allegations that operatives for the Reagan-Bush presidential campaign had conspired to delay release of American hostages held by Iran.

Proponents of the so-called "October surprise" theory alleged that in the waning days of the 1980 presidential campaign, aides to Ronald Reagan tried to prevent President Jimmy Carter's administration from securing a dramatic hostage release that would boost Carter's sagging popularity. The prospect of such a political coup by Carter became known as the October surprise.

According to the theory, Reagan campaign manager William J. Casey and other officials negotiated a secret arms deal with Iranian officials to induce Tehran to delay the release of the 52 American hostages until after election day.

The Senate Foreign Relations Subcommittee on Near Eastern and South Asian Affairs released a report in November 1992, stating that it could find no conclusive evidence that officials from the 1980 Reagan-Bush campaign negotiated a secret agreement.

In January 1993, a House task force went even further in spiking the allegations. The panel unconditionally rejected the allegations, concluding: "There is no credible evidence supporting any attempt by the Reagan presidential campaign — or persons associated with the campaign — to delay the release of the American hostages in Iran." The report stated that "wholly insufficient evidence" existed that anyone associated with the Reagan-Bush campaign communicated with representatives of the Iranian government.

Background

Allegations of a secret deal to stall the hostages' release had circulated for years. But the scenario gained new attention in April 1991, when a former Carter administration National Security Council aide, Gary Sick, wrote an article discussing possible contacts between the Reagan campaign and the Iranian government.

The hostage crisis, which dragged on from Nov. 4, 1979, to Jan. 20, 1981, consumed Carter's presidency and played a significant role in his defeat for a second term. After negotiations with Iran to secure the hostages' release stalled, Carter ordered a rescue attempt in April 1980, but it failed, and eight soldiers were killed in an accident. *(Congress and the Nation Vol. V, p. 111)*

As talks carried on into the fall of 1980, Reagan campaign officials warned that Carter might try to engineer an October surprise to boost his re-election chances. Sick alleged that the Reagan campaign may have short-circuited such a deal. Former Iranian president Abol Hassan Bani-Sadr told the *New York Times* that a meeting between Republicans and Iranians was held in Paris in October 1980. Richard V. Allen and two other top Reagan-Bush campaign officials acknowledged that they met in Washington with an Iranian emissary in September or October but said they rejected an offer to deliver the hostages in a way advantageous to Reagan.

The charges were explosive because of the suggestion that vice presidential candidate George Bush may have traveled to Europe in the fall of 1980 to negotiate the deal. Bush denied that he was part of any such negotiations and said his travel at the time was well documented.

The secretive Casey, a World War II spymaster who was Reagan's CIA director from 1981 until his death in 1987, was at the center of speculation about a secret agreement. News reports suggested that Casey was in Europe at the time the negotiations supposedly took place.

Congressional Probes

With the 1992 election just nine months away and President Bush a subject of scrutiny, the House conducted a politically charged debate on whether to authorize a special October surprise task force.

On Feb. 5, 1992, by a vote of 217-192, the House adopted H Res 258 to establish a task force of eight Democrats and five Republicans from the House Foreign Affairs Committee to look into the allegations. The vote fell mostly along party lines, but 34 Democrats voted against the resolution, reflecting continuing ambivalence about the wisdom of plunging into the murky allegations.

Republicans lashed out at the investigation, charging that Democrats were listening to "wackos and weirdos." A GOP attempt to require the task force to look into any attempts by the Carter administration to negotiate the release of the hostages prior to the election was defeated Feb. 5 on a party-line vote, 158-249.

In an effort to quell criticism that the investigation was designed to damage Bush before the election, task force chairman Lee H. Hamilton, D-Ind., announced on July 1 that preliminary information indicated that Bush probably did not travel to Europe during the time period alleged by Sick and others.

The House task force released its findings Jan. 13, 1993, rejecting the allegations. Hamilton said the task force found that nearly all of the sources for the October surprise turned out to be "wholesale fabricators or were impeached by documentary evidence." Attorneys for the panel said it had informed the Justice Department of people who might have lied to Congress.

Hamilton praised the 10-month, $1.3 million investigation as a model of bipartisanship. But Republicans bitterly criticized the entire exercise as a Democrat-inspired boondoggle, even as they claimed vindication in the report's exoneration of Reagan and Bush.

The investigation by the Senate Foreign Relations subcommittee found no "sufficient credible evidence" to support allegations that the Reagan-Bush campaign tried to delay the hostages' release. Unlike the House inquiry, the subcommittee never received the approval of the full chamber for its probe. After Democrats were unable on Nov. 22, 1991, to get the 60 votes needed to cut off debate on a resolution (S Res 198) authorizing the probe, Democrats tapped Reid Weingarten to act as special counsel.

In his report, released Nov. 23, 1992, Weingarten said that although the Reagan administration "privately acquiesced in some limited Israeli shipments of American-made weapons to Iran and slightly relaxed" a policy of limiting shipment of weapons to Iran, no credible evidence was available that actions were taken as "a reward to the Khomeini regime in exchange for an agreement relating to hostages."

Weingarten said the failure to obtain Casey's passport and other important documents impeded the investigation. He concluded that Casey conducted "informal, clandestine and potentially dangerous" efforts to collect intelligence on Carter administration negotiations with Iran.

POW/MIA Investigation

A select Senate committee that spent more than 15 months investigating the fates of thousands of servicemen listed as prisoners of war (POWs) or missing in action

(MIA) concluded its investigation in January 1993 saying that it found no "compelling evidence" to suggest that American prisoners were alive in Southeast Asia almost 20 years after the Vietnam War ended.

But in a final report issued Jan. 13, 1993, the Senate Select Committee on POW-MIA Affairs held out the possibility that some U.S. soldiers had languished in enemy hands for at least a period of time after the hostilities ended.

The 1,000-page report capped a $1.9 million investigation that focused primarily on the missing from the Vietnam War but also covered missing military personnel from World War II, the Korean War and the Cold War.

During its short life span, the select committee held 22 days of public hearings, with testimony from 144 witnesses, including former secretaries of defense and state, former North Vietnamese military officials and members of POW families and activist groups.

Committee members also made trips to Vietnam, Laos, Cambodia, Thailand, the Soviet Union and Korea in attempts to track down prisoners or any artifacts that could help determine their fate.

Committee Chairman John Kerry, D-Mass., and other panel members cited the declassification of an immense volume of POW records held by the Defense Department as a singular accomplishment that they said would distinguish the committee's record in congressional history annals. More than 1 million documents relating to POW and MIA cases were declassified and made available to the public at the National Archives.

Background

The Senate adopted a resolution creating the panel (S Res 82) by voice vote on Aug. 2, 1991. National interest in the wrenching, unresolved issue had been renewed by the publication of a grainy photograph purporting to show live American prisoners from the Vietnam War.

The Defense Department disputed the authenticity of such photographs. But Vietnam War activists maintained that American prisoners might still have been alive in Southeast Asia after the U.S. pullout and urged Congress to launch an investigation and to give the issue a full airing.

A dozen or so congressional inquiries into the matter had already been conducted since the end of the war, all of varying degrees of length, sophistication and clout. But one common characteristic they shared were their many inconclusive results concerning what truly happened to thousands of men who vanished in wartime.

The lack of concrete, uncontestable findings led some Vietnam War activist groups to charge that the government was hiding information from the public on unaccounted-for military personnel.

Kerry said the main mission of the select committee was to investigate the matter in public view, so that families of the missing would be able to know as much about a particular POW or MIA file as did the committee, its staff or Pentagon officials who were called to testify.

Investigation

Panel members went on several fact-finding missions to Southeast Asia. During an April trip, they said they were granted unprecedented access to Vietnamese prison camps and foreign intelligence data.

The State Department in April rewarded the increased Vietnamese cooperation on the POW-MIA issue by granting an exception to the economic embargo of Vietnam to permit sales of food, medicine and other items to meet humanitarian needs. The department also lifted restrictions on projects in Vietnam by non-governmental and non-profit organizations.

After another investigative tour in November, Chairman Kerry urged the Bush administration to reward Vietnam for its cooperation by easing the trade embargo on that country. In December, Bush permitted U.S. companies to sign contracts immediately with Hanoi for commercial dealings that would not go into effect until such time as the longstanding economic embargo was lifted.

The panel held a series of hearings throughout the year. During June hearings, panel leaders Kerry and Robert C. Smith, R-N.H., charged that the Pentagon knew that scores of U.S. soldiers had most likely been left behind in enemy hands after the Vietnam War. In questioning witnesses from the Nixon administration, senators repeatedly turned to President Richard Nixon's assurance to the nation in March 1973 that "all of our American POWs are on their way home."

In September, two former defense secretaries — Melvin R. Laird (1969-73) and James R. Schlesinger (1973-75) — told the committee that the Nixon administration had every reason to believe that Americans were left behind in enemy hands as U.S. troops were withdrawn from Vietnam in 1973.

But Nixon's secretary of state, Henry A. Kissinger (1973-77), denounced as a "flat-out lie" any suggestion that Nixon advisers knew of Americans left behind in Vietnam or neighboring Laos. "We did not know of confirmed prisoners, and had we known it, we would have taken the most drastic steps," said Kissinger, defending his reputation as the architect of the accord with North Vietnam that ended the Vietnam War and secured him the Nobel Peace Prize. Kissinger said neither Schlesinger nor Laird ever suggested when they were in office that Americans were left behind in Southeast Asia.

In other testimony that seemed to undercut Kissinger's assertions, Winston Lord, a senior aide to Kissinger in 1970-73, said that Nixon had made a "very tough decision" in proceeding with the withdrawal. "American society would have blown apart" if Nixon had resumed bombing and halted the withdrawal to force the release of any POWs that were still being held, Lord said.

Ross Perot, a billionaire Texas businessman and independent presidential candidate in 1992, testified before the committee that sufficient evidence existed to believe the government left U.S. military personnel in Southeast Asia after the Vietnam War ended. Perot said he had worked for more than 20 years, spending over $3 million of his own money, in trying to win release of any prisoners who might have been left in Indochina.

The committee also heard testimony from retired admiral James B. Stockdale, Perot's running mate in the 1992 election. Stockdale said he fully believed that no living Americans had been left behind in Vietnam after the war. "I would not have come back if they were," said Stockdale, who became a leader of POWs while he was held and tortured in Vietnam after his plane was shot down in September 1965. He said he was not as sure if prisoners were returned from Laos.

The panel devoted several days of hearings — including Nov. 11, Veterans Day — on the missing from World

War II, Korea and the Cold War. But at the end of those hearings, family members of the missing argued that the committee should have sought to have its authorization extended to provide more time to investigate other POW and MIA cases.

Classified Documents

The Senate, in a resolution (S Res 324) adopted 96-0 on July 2, 1992, urged the administration to act "expeditiously" to declassify and make available to the public all files of military personnel listed as POW or MIA. Files could remain classified if they were considered sensitive to national security. Earlier in the day, the select committee approved the resolution, 12-0.

The committee was prepared to release most of the classified files it had obtained from the government if the administration had not acted soon afterward to do so. Under Senate rules, the committee had to first request that the president declassify the files before it could take action to release what it already had accumulated from government agencies.

Release of thousands of files took place on July 23, the same day the committee met to assess the administration's progress in declassifying the files. The release came a day after President Bush signed an executive order requiring all federal agencies to release files and other information relating to POW/MIA cases.

A Pentagon spokesperson said that 30,000 pages of files were declassified and that nearly 1.5 million pages of formerly secret files were expected to be made public after being reviewed.

Committee Findings

In its final report, the committee criticized top U.S. government officials for dismissing the possibility that men might have been left behind but rejected charges that they possessed any "certain knowledge" that prisoners were abandoned.

The report, which was signed by all 12 members of the committee — six Democrats and six Republicans — said, "There is, at this time, no compelling evidence that proves that any American remains alive in captivity in Southeast Asia."

But it also said, "We acknowledge that there is no proof that U.S. POWs survived, but neither is there proof that all of those who did not return had died. There is evidence, moreover, that indicates the possibility of survival, at least for a small number, after Operation Homecoming."

The report rejected outright theories held by some Vietnam POW activists that the government covered up knowledge of prisoners being held against their will. "The isolated bits of information out of which some have constructed whole labyrinths of intrigue and deception have not withstood the test of objective investigation, and the vast archives of secret U.S. documents that some felt contained incriminating evidence have been thoroughly examined by the committee, only to find that the conspiracy cupboard is bare."

The Defense Department listed 2,264 Americans as unaccounted for from the Vietnam War, but the committee said the number of Americans whose fate is "truly unknown is far smaller." Kerry said that, through investigation with the cooperation of the Defense Department, the committee determined that 135 "discrepancy cases" remained in which there was reason to believe that governments in Southeast Asia may have known the fate of the individual.

For the remainder of the 2,264, the committee said the government determined that, in most cases, death was considered almost certain but that it could not be proved because bodies were unrecoverable from crash sites, especially ones at sea or in areas of heavy combat where ground had been lost to the enemy.

After the report was released, Kerry said that more cooperation from Vietnam, Laos and Cambodia was essential to obtaining the fullest possible accounting for missing Americans. "This report does not close the issue," he said. "It is not meant to. This report provides the reality base from which we can now make real judgments about probabilities and possibilities."

Vice Chairman Smith said, "There's evidence that some POWs may have survived to the present, and some information still remains to be investigated. However, at this time, there's no compelling evidence that proves that. And that's a fact, and we all agree to that." Smith had been one of the more aggressive proponents of the possibility that POWs remained alive.

In a footnote in the committee's report, Smith and Charles E. Grassley, R-Iowa, dissented from a majority view that neither "live-sighting" reports nor other sources of intelligence provided any grounds for encouragement that POWs may still be alive. They wrote that they believed there was "evidence that POWs may have survived to the present."

The committee officially dissolved after release of the report. But both Kerry and Smith said the permanent standing committees of the Senate would be able to continue the investigation if events warranted.

State Department Authorization

Congress in 1991 cleared legislation (HR 1415 — PL 102-138) authorizing almost $12 billion for the State Department and related international agencies for fiscal 1992-93.

But the bill's enduring contribution might have been a provision that was removed from the measure in conference and passed as separate legislation: import sanctions against countries that used chemical or biological weapons and against companies that sold the material and technology needed to build them. Because of a legislative turf dispute, the sanctions were attached to a trade bill that also adjusted unemployment benefit formulas (HR 1724 — PL 102-182). *(Chemical weapons sanctions, p. 292)*

The State Department measure authorized funding for the department, the U.S. Information Agency and the Board for International Broadcasting. The measure largely reflected the administration's request, although it authorized $630 million, $140 million more than President Bush requested, in refugee assistance. Sponsors said the additional money was needed for unanticipated expenses related to Soviet, Kurdish, Southeast Asian and African refugees.

The bill authorized $130 million in each of the two fiscal years for a new U.S. Embassy in Moscow but left up to the administration the final decision on how this should be done. Options included razing the existing structure, which was riddled with listening devices, and constructing a new one; adding secure floors on top of the existing structure; or building an entirely new embassy next door. *(Moscow embassy, box, p. 263)*

House Action

The House passed HR 1415 by voice vote on May 15. The bill had been reported by the House Foreign Affairs Committee on May 8 (H Rept 102-53).

Most of the debate on the House floor concerned the longstanding dispute over what to do with the Moscow embassy that was laced with eavesdropping devices. Members turned back an attempt to force the House to vote on a proposal to demolish the partially built, unused embassy chancery. Instead, they voted, 223-185 on May 15, to authorize $130 million in fiscal 1992 for some solution to the embassy quandary. But they left it up to the Bush administration to decide what approach to take.

In other action, the House May 15 rejected, 145-265, a proposal to subject State Department personnel to random drug tests. Also rejected on May 15, 189-224, was a move to slash $14 million from the funds for the National Endowment for Democracy (NED). The Bush administration requested $30 million for NED in fiscal 1992, and the Foreign Affairs Committee had included that amount in HR 1415. But a General Accounting Office report in March criticized NED for its accounting practices, and the panel responded by setting aside $5 million of the funding pending serious efforts to revamp its grant-tracking procedures.

The House May 15 defeated, 155-248, an attempt to cut about $500 million from the overall State Department budget for fiscal 1992-93.

Senate Action

The Senate passed HR 1415 on July 29 by a vote of 86-11. The Senate Foreign Relations Committee had reported its version of the bill on July 2 (S 1433 — S Rept 102-98).

The Senate-passed bill demonstrated the difficulties in developing a consistent approach to global weapons proliferation. Although the legislation sought to impose tough sanctions against foreign governments and companies that engaged in the trade of chemical and biological weapons — provisions that were opposed by the Bush administration but were adopted by voice vote in the Senate — it also authorized a $1 billion loan guarantee program to increase overseas sales by U.S. arms manufacturers. The administration's original loan guarantee proposal was modified to prevent unstable countries in the Middle East and elsewhere from taking advantage of the program.

The administration proposal had run into strong opposition, especially in the House. Critics said the guarantees would encourage arms proliferation abroad at a time when the United States was scaling back its defense budget and seeking international arms controls.

But the program won the approval of the Foreign Relations Committee and remained in the Senate-passed bill. Proponents argued that the guarantees were needed to help domestic military contractors compete with subsidized foreign firms and that involvement in the international arms market would further U.S. clout when it came to seeking multilateral arms control agreements.

The Senate bill also included committee language calling for a moratorium on U.S. weapons sales to the Middle East unless the administration worked to convene a conference of major arms suppliers to the Middle East. But the State Department made that language moot by meeting with other suppliers in Paris in May.

The Senate also touched on the sensitive issue of U.S. servicemen who were declared prisoners of war (POWs) or missing in action (MIA) in the Vietnam War when it modified a provision in the committee bill that called for the lifting of the embargoes against Vietnam and Cambodia. The revision, adopted by voice vote, stated that it was the sense of Congress that the United States move toward normal relations with its wartime enemies — provided that the "pace and scope" of normalization be linked to Vietnam's cooperation in resolving MIA cases and in settling the war in Cambodia. John McCain, R-Ariz., who as a Navy pilot spent six years in a North Vietnamese prisoner-of-war camp after his jet was shot down in 1967, sought the change. *(POW/MIA investigation, p. 288)*

The Senate also tackled the knotty question of whether the United States should provide direct assistance to dissident republics in the Soviet Union and Eastern Europe, when it adopted by voice vote an amendment supporting such aid if the president determined it was in the national interest. *(Soviet aid, p. 260)*

Conference, Final Action

The Senate adopted the conference report (H Rept 102-238) by voice vote on Oct. 4. The House followed suit on Oct. 8, clearing HR 1415.

Final action came after supporters agreed to strip from the bill the provisions imposing trade sanctions on countries and companies deemed to be contributing to the spread of chemical and biological weapons.

The administration had long resisted congressional attempts to legislate mandatory sanctions as an infringement on the president's authority to make foreign policy. Administration officials had warned that Bush would veto the State Department bill if the provisions were not moderated.

After weeks of conflict, a House-Senate conference committee and the White House did work out a compromise giving the president authority to waive the sanctions if he determined it to be in the interest of national security. The president had to notify pertinent members of his plans to waive the sanctions.

But, despite this agreement with the administration, the conference committee was unable to complete work on the bill because the House Ways and Means Committee objected to inclusion of the sanctions on jurisdictional grounds. With Ways and Means backing, the stiff import sanctions were removed from the bill and amended to a bill adjusting unemployment compensation (HR 1724). Some lesser penalties for weapons proliferation remained in the State Department bill. *(Import sanctions, p. 292)*

The conference committee also removed the controversial amendment that would have created a $1 billion loan guarantee program to increase overseas sales by U.S. arms manufacturers. Sen. Paul S. Sarbanes, D-Md., insisted that the United States should not be assisting in the global proliferation of weapons. House members from both parties also opposed the measure. After considerable debate, the Senate conferees agreed by a one-vote margin to eliminate the provision.

Major Provisions

As signed into law Oct. 28, 1991, HR 1415 (PL 102-138):

Funding. Authorized almost $12 billion for fiscal 1992-93 for the State Department and related international agencies.

Chemical Weapons. Called for immediate sanctions against any country found by the president to have used, or prepared to use, chemical or biological weapons. These included a cutoff of U.S. aid and the termination of arms sales and assistance. Additional sanctions were required if the country took no action within three months to end its weapons use.

The only sanction that remained in the State Department bill against companies that sold the material and technology needed to build such weapons was a cutoff of all U.S. government purchases and contracts, which would affect only some foreign concerns. The key provision requiring import sanctions had been removed from the bill.

Political Exclusions. Required the State Department to remove anyone who had been excluded from entering the United States on the basis of political beliefs from its list of those who in the past had been barred entry to the country. The department was given up to three years to excise the names from its list. Legislation (HR 3792 — PL 101-246) barring such ideological exclusions was enacted in 1990. *(State Department authorization, p. 247)*

Moscow Embassy. Authorized $130 million for the U.S. Embassy in Moscow but allowed the administration to decide what to do with it.

Diplomatic Posts. Granted the State Department greater flexibility in closing diplomatic posts.

New Bureau. Established a separate State Department bureau for South Asian affairs, instead of continuing to combine it with Near Eastern Affairs.

China Broadcasts. Established a commission to study the feasibility of instituting government-sponsored broadcasting to China.

'Israel Only' Passports. Banned "Israel only" passports, which were offered by the United States to U.S. citizens traveling to that country. Travelers later could use their regular passports, which had no Israeli stamps, to gain entry into Arab nations.

The practice, necessitated by an Arab boycott of Israel, received widespread attention in 1991 when Sen. Frank R. Lautenberg, D-N.J., was denied entry into Saudi Arabia because of an Israeli stamp on his passport. The legislation also called on the administration to negotiate with Arab nations to end the practice.

Sexual Harassment. Called for the State Department to comply with provisions in its fiscal 1990-91 authorization bill (HR 3792 — PL 101-246) requiring a private study of allegations of sexual harassment within the department.

Congressional Inquiries. Required the State Department to answer questions from members of the Senate Foreign Relations and House Foreign Affairs committees within 21 days of a request.

Vietnamese Students. Created 15 scholarships each year for residents of Vietnam to study at U.S. colleges and universities.

NED. Withheld $5 million of the funds authorized for the National Endowment for Democracy, pending a NED report on efforts to comply with the management recommendations in a March 1991 General Accounting Office report.

Chemical Weapons Sanctions

Congress in 1991 approved import sanctions on countries and companies facilitating the spread of chemical weapons. The sanctions were included in a trade bill that also adjusted employment benefits formulas (HR 1724 — PL 102-182).

The sanctions issue was a volatile one, and the road to enactment was far from smooth. The sanctions originally were included in the fiscal 1992-93 State Department authorization bill (HR 1415 — PL 102-138). The Senate took a hard line on the proliferation of chemical and biological weapons, when it approved by voice vote an amendment by Foreign Relations Committee Chairman Claiborne Pell, D-R.I., to impose tough sanctions on companies and countries that facilitated the transfer of such technology.

Under the amendment, the president would be required to impose sanctions on foreign governments that used chemical or biological weapons. Such countries would face termination of all U.S. assistance and credits, along with restrictions on trade. Companies that "knowingly and materially contribute" to a foreign government's efforts to "use, develop, produce, stockpile or otherwise acquire" chemical and biological weapons would be barred from trade with the United States.

The chemical weapons provisions had wide support in both chambers. In 1990, Congress had attached sanctions to an export controls bill, but President Bush said they were too restrictive and pocket-vetoed the legislation. *(1990 action, p. 175)*

But in 1991, the president had won praise from lawmakers for pledging to destroy U.S. chemical stockpiles and declaring that the United States would not retaliate in kind if attacked by chemical weapons. That position encouraged sponsors of the sanctions provision to hope for a compromise with the administration on their measure.

And, after weeks of conflict, a compromise was reached. Conferees agreed to grant the president authority to waive the sanctions on countries if he determined it to be in the interest of national security. In return, the president was required to notify the chairmen and ranking Republican members of the Senate Foreign Relations Committee and House Foreign Affairs Committee 15 days before waiving the sanctions. Under such notification procedures, the president customarily refrained from taking actions that were strongly opposed by the committee leaders.

But then a jurisdictional dispute erupted.

Ways and Means Objections

Rep. Sam M. Gibbons, D-Fla., chairman of the Ways and Means Subcommittee on Trade, asserted that the legislation's proposed ban on U.S. imports from foreign companies and countries selling chemical or biological weapons came under the jurisdiction of the Ways and Means Committee. Gibbons told the conferees that his panel had not had a chance to consider the provision.

The conference committee tried to address Gibbons' concerns by introducing a new, stand-alone measure (HR 3409) in the House that incorporated the sanctions and the presidential waiver provisions from the State Department bill. The House Foreign Affairs Committee quickly moved to approve the sanctions legislation Sept. 26, referring it to Ways and Means.

Ways and Means Committee Chairman Dan Rostenkowski, D-Ill., said he would not mark up the separate sanctions bill without assurances from the Senate that its members would not attach unrelated revenue provisions, such as a controversial proposal for a capital gains tax cut.

Once Rostenkowski received those assurances, his committee approved the import sanctions on Nov. 19 and sent them to the House floor (HR 3409 — H Rept 102-235, Part II), where they were amended on Nov. 20 into a bill (HR 1724) adjusting unemployment benefit formulas. *(Unemployment benefits, p. 759)*

The administration issued a statement on Nov. 20 saying it had "no objection" to the sanctions language because it allowed the president to waive the penalties.

The House adopted the conference report on HR 1724 (H Rept 102-391) on Nov. 26 by voice vote. The Senate acted likewise later the same day, completing congressional action.

Final Provisions

As signed into law on Dec. 4, HR 1724 (PL 102-182) called for immediate sanctions to be imposed for at least a year on individuals and foreign companies found to be using or stockpiling chemical and biological weapons or their components.

Those identified would be banned from exporting products from the United States and from selling goods or services to the U.S. government.

Foreign governments found to be stockpiling or using these weapons would be subject to several sanctions immediately, including the termination of foreign aid, arms sales, other high-technology exports and financing supplied by the U.S. government.

If the country continued using or building chemical or biological weapons after 90 days, it would be hit with further sanctions, including a ban on its imports to the United States, a prohibition on U.S. bank loans to the country, further restrictions on high-technology exports and downgrading of diplomatic relations.

Nuclear Arms Proliferation

Legislation imposing sanctions on countries that trafficked in technology used for the manufacture of nuclear weapons died in the final hours of the 102nd Congress. The sanctions were included in a bill to reauthorize the 1979 Export Administration Act (HR 3489), but the House was unable to clear the conference report on the measure.

The House passed HR 3489 by voice vote on Oct. 30, 1991. Despite administration objections, the House bill required U.S. sanctions against countries and foreign companies that exported nuclear-related goods. Sponsors added language allowing the president to waive sanctions if he first notified Congress, but the change did not satisfy the White House. *(Export controls, p. 195)*

The Senate version of the export bill did not include the sanctions, but the Senate passed a separate sanctions bill (S 1128) the following year. S 1128 was reported by the Senate Foreign Relations Committee Nov. 22, 1991, without a written report and was passed by the Senate by voice vote on April 9, 1992. Sen. John Glenn, D-Ohio, sponsor of S 1128, called it the most significant such legislation since passage of the Nuclear Non-Proliferation Act of 1978.

The Senate measure would have given the president authority to determine whether transfers of weapons technology had occurred. In a concession to administration objections, the bill was modified so the president could have waived penalties on governments found to be transferring certain design information or components if he certified that sanctions "would have a serious adverse effect on vital U.S. interests." But the president could not have waived sanctions on a foreign government that provided an actual nuclear weapon or components necessary to complete such a device.

House and Senate conferees agreed to include provisions toughening sanctions against nuclear proliferation in the conference version of HR 3489 (H Rept 102-1025) but left with the president the discretion to impose them. To win administration support, conferees dropped House-passed provisions that confined U.S. exports of nuclear and nuclear-related material to countries that maintained full-scale safeguards, as defined by the International Atomic Energy Agency, and signed a nuclear cooperation agreement with the United States.

The Bush administration argued that the House sanctions would have prevented the export of non-military nuclear technology to Eastern Europe and undermined a recently signed accord among the Nuclear Suppliers Group to control the export of nuclear technology with military uses.

Because of disagreement over other provisions of HR 3489, the bill died in the early morning of Oct. 6 as the House rushed toward adjournment.

Controversial Arms Sales

The Bush administration came under attack several times in 1992 for proposing sales of military equipment to foreign nations, including Pakistan and Saudi Arabia. But despite strong talk from some members of Congress, the sales went through without any major problems.

Pakistan

The administration's decision to allow commercial military sales to Pakistan was attacked July 30 by Senate sponsors of a law that they said clearly banned such transactions.

Three senators said in a letter to Secretary of State James A. Baker III that a 1985 law cutting off all U.S. aid and military sales to the Asian nation, if it was found to possess a nuclear weapon, was unambiguous. "We cannot comprehend how our simple and direct language could conceivably be interpreted as permitting commercial sales," said Sens. Larry Pressler, R-S.D., John Glenn, D-Ohio, and Alan Cranston, D-Calif.

They wrote that if the administration did not like the restriction, known as the Pressler amendment, it should "seek a revision of the law, not . . . find some totally baseless legal rationale for evading it."

All U.S. military and economic aid, as well as government-to-government arms sales, were stopped in October 1990 when President Bush was unable to certify that Pakistan did not possess a nuclear device. *(Box, p. 232)*

However, Baker told the Senate Foreign Relations Committee earlier in 1992 that limited commercial sales of military spare parts were being allowed to continue. State Department officials later testified that the administration interpreted the ban in the 1985 Foreign Assistance Act (PL 99-83) to apply only to government activities and that the limited sales gave the United States leverage over Pakistan that could be useful in promoting U.S. non-proliferation policies in South Asia.

Pakistan, once among the top recipients of U.S. aid, had complained that it was being unfairly penalized for a nuclear program that was pursued in response to a similar program in neighboring India.

But Glenn insisted that $4 billion in U.S. aid to Pakistan during the 1980s did little to slow that nation's nuclear program and that "there is considerable evidence that America's aid and high technology probably contributed to Pakistan's nuclear and missile capabilities."

In 1992, Pakistan's foreign secretary said his country had a nuclear capability in 1989.

Saudi Arabia

Merging re-election campaigning with Middle East policy making, President Bush in September agreed to let Saudi Arabia spend up to $9 billion to buy F-15 fighters.

Bush made a quick stop in St. Louis during a campaign swing through Missouri, a pivotal electoral state, to announce that he had approved Saudi Arabia's request to buy 72 additional F-15 fighter jets, built in that city by the economically troubled McDonnell Douglas Corp.

The U.S. Air Force had ordered its final batch of F-15s, so the Saudi sales would prolong for a few more years 7,000 jobs at McDonnell Douglas plants and more than 30,000 jobs at subcontractors.

Congress could have blocked the arms deal, but legislators allowed it to go forward in part because Israel did not appear inclined to seek a confrontation over the sales. The administration tried to assure lawmakers that the sale would not erode Israel's qualitative edge in weaponry in the Middle East.

Saudi Arabia already had "C" and "D" model F-15s, designed to attack other aircraft. No foreign sales had been allowed of the F-15E, the version of the plane equipped with sophisticated electronic gear for precision attacks on ground targets. The 72 planes in the new package, designated F-15XPs, reportedly were to have some ground attack capability, but less than the "E" model. They were not to be equipped with the state-of-the-art avionics of the more advanced F-15Es.

South Africa Policy

President Bush in 1991 lifted congressionally imposed sanctions against South Africa. In contrast to 1986, when a nearly united Congress seized control of U.S. policy toward South Africa and imposed economic sanctions over President Ronald Reagan's veto, Congress in 1991 was divided over Bush's decision and did not challenge it.

Bush declared that South Africa had met all the requirements of the 1986 Comprehensive Anti-Apartheid Act (PL 99-440) and that South African President F. W. de Klerk had led his nation on an unalterable march toward abolishing its policies of discrimination against the black majority. *(1986 law, Congress and the Nation Vol. VII, p. 180)*

"This is a moment in history which many believed would never be attained," Bush said of South Africa's steps toward ending its policy of racial segregation, apartheid. "I really firmly believe that this progress is irreversible."

Bush's July 10 order to lift the sanctions took effect immediately. The president and his supporters predicted that his action would bolster South Africa's economic growth, thereby contributing to an atmosphere for peaceful change.

Supporters of the sanctions had long argued that they were the international community's best method to label South Africa an outlaw state because of its institutionalized racism. But opponents of sanctions had retorted that black South Africans were hit hardest when foreign businesses pulled out.

The South African government's dramatic release of imprisoned black leader Nelson Mandela in 1990, along with other efforts to dismantle its system of racial separation, had won considerable praise. But no efforts were made that year by the United States to lift congressionally enacted economic sanctions against the white-minority regime. *(1990 action, p. 253)*

Some members of Congress insisted that 1991 was too early to ease pressure on the South African government and that Bush had acted illegally and improperly by lifting the sanctions.

Rep. John Conyers Jr., D-Mich., said that Bush had strengthened the political position of the white South African government against the wishes of most of the country's black political leaders, who had sought to sustain the sanctions as they conducted talks on political reform. That view reflected the attitude of African National Congress (ANC) leader Mandela, who spoke to Bush just before the announcement and said he believed the repeal was premature.

Sen. Edward M. Kennedy, D-Mass., decried the sanctions repeal on the Senate floor but afterward said that Congress' hectic schedule would not give critics enough time to challenge Bush's action before Congress adjourned for the year.

The Sanctions

The U.S. sanctions that were lifted included bans on most new corporate investment in South Africa and loans to the Pretoria government, as well as a prohibition on trade between the two countries of products such as uranium ore, iron, steel, textiles and gold coins.

Bush's move also affected a provision that blocked corporations from writing off taxes paid to the South African government — a provision that had been considered an especially potent deterrent to corporate investment in South Africa.

Bush's action solidified an international trend toward easing South Africa's isolation. The European Community in December 1990 lifted its ban on new investment in the country and moved to eliminating other trade sanctions. The International Olympic Committee on July 9, 1991, ended a two-decade ban on South African participation in the Olympic Games.

Administration officials emphasized that some sanctions remained, giving them leverage to push for further progress toward racial equality. The continuing sanctions included bans on arms or intelligence deals with the South African military, on most Export-Import Bank loans and on support for International Monetary Fund loans to South Africa.

But congressional critics said the sanctions contained in the 1986 law were a more powerful tool and that removing them prematurely could be a devastating signal.

Meeting the Conditions

Bush said the South African government had met all the conditions for lifting the sanctions, leaving him no choice but to abide by the 1986 law.

The anti-apartheid law had stated that the sanctions would be lifted once five conditions were met. Those conditions were: The government of South Africa must release from prison all persons, including Mandela, prosecuted for their political beliefs or detained unduly without trial; must repeal the state of emergency in effect and must release all detainees held under such state of emergency; must lift the ban on democratic political parties and permit free exercise by South Africans of all races of the right to form political parties, express political opinions and otherwise participate in the political process; must repeal the Group Areas Act and the Population Registration Act and institute no other measures with the same purpose; and must agree to enter into good-faith negotiations with members of the black majority without precondition.

Critics disputed Bush's determination, with some members questioning whether South Africa had fully met even one of the conditions. For example, they cited reports from international human rights groups that South Africa continued to hold political prisoners, in violation of the law's first, non-negotiable condition.

But administration officials maintained that the only politically motivated prisoners still being held were properly tried for crimes of violence.

Sen. Richard G. Lugar of Indiana, who was a crucial Republican sponsor of the sanctions bill but supported Bush's decision, said the conditions agreed to in 1986 reflected hard-won political compromises. He believed some critics were unfairly seeking to go beyond those original aims. "But the compromise was the law, the law has been met, and our credibility is at stake," Lugar said.

Bush's action met particularly strong opposition from black groups, who had long related South African apartheid to the past enslavement and persistent discrimination faced by blacks in the United States. Several members of the Congressional Black Caucus painted Bush's sanctions decision as part of a broader picture of administration disdain for black concerns.

Although some groups began calling for a new sanctions bill to undo Bush's decision, members were skeptical about re-creating the grass-roots political pressure that spurred Congress to pass the 1986 law.

Cuba Embargo

Language designed to tighten the U.S. economic embargo of Cuba became law in 1992. The provisions were enacted as part of the fiscal 1993 defense authorization bill (HR 5006 — PL 102-484).

Ever since Fidel Castro seized power in Cuba in 1959, the U.S. government fought, both overtly and covertly, to topple the avowed communist from power. One tool in that fight was a U.S. embargo, which prohibited U.S. companies from trading with Cuba and prevented Cuban goods from entering the United States. Travel between the two countries also was restricted.

The collapse of communism in the Soviet Union and Eastern Europe had deprived Castro of his political and economic patrons. Cuba's centrally planned economy was in a tailspin, leading some foreign policy experts to predict the collapse of the Castro government. Many Cuban-American groups had lobbied vigorously for new tough sanctions that they argued would help topple the weakened regime.

The legislation enacted in 1992 prohibited foreign subsidiaries of U.S. companies from engaging in new trade with Cuba, a thriving business that provided an estimated $700 million in annual sales. It also allowed the Treasury Department to apply civil fines of up to $50,000 — in addition to criminal penalties — against U.S. citizens who violated the Trading with the Enemy Act by traveling to Cuba.

In addition, the measure called for barring from U.S. ports for six months any vessel that transported goods or passengers to or from Cuba. The bill allowed the president to impose economic sanctions against nations that provided assistance to Cuba.

While punishing Castro's regime, the bill attempted to support the Cuban people by letting private U.S. groups deliver food and medicine to Cuba. It also permitted the president to open normal phone and mail links to the island nation in the hope that increased communication with the United States would encourage Cubans to change their system of government.

The Bush administration had opposed an earlier version of the measure that would have mandated sanctions against other nations. The White House also had opposed the penalties on corporate subsidiaries, arguing that they would have imposed an undue burden on U.S. companies operating abroad.

But the administration came out in favor of the bill after working out a compromise to give the president discretion to impose the sanctions. More important, when bill supporters agreed to the provision exempting existing contracts, the White House reversed a longstanding policy of opposing penalties against U.S. corporate subsidiaries in third countries. The bill also was supported by Arkansas Gov. Bill Clinton.

The House passed the Cuba Democracy Act (HR 5323) by a 276-135 vote under suspension of the rules on Sept. 24. The bill had been reported by the House Foreign Affairs Committee June 25 (H Rept 102-615, Part I) and by the Merchant Marine Committee July 28 (H Rept 102-615, Part II).

The Senate had approved identical language Sept. 18 by voice vote as an amendment to the fiscal 1993 defense authorization bill (HR 5006). The Senate amendment was proposed by Bob Graham, D-Fla. Two attempts by Christopher J. Dodd, D-Conn., to weaken or kill the embargo amendment were defeated Sept. 18 by votes of 73-12 and 24-61. Among the corporations that would be hardest hit by the ban on indirect trade was Hartford-based United Technologies, whose subsidiaries did an estimated $10 million in business annually with Cuba. Dodd argued that Cuba would make up for any shortfall of imported goods by buying more from Europe and Asia.

Conferees on the defense authorization left the Cuba provision in their version. The political impact of the sanctions was underscored by the locale of the bill signing on Oct. 6. Bush saved the ceremony for a campaign appearance in Miami, where Cuban-American groups had lobbied for the bill. *(1993 defense authorization, p. 395)*

Haitian Refugee Policy

The House and its committees took several actions during 1992 to protest the Bush administration's policy of returning Haitian refugees to their homeland. But none of those measures became law, and the policy was inherited and retained by the Clinton administration in early 1993.

The issue stemmed from a coup in Haiti on Sept. 30, 1991, in which the military ousted Jean-Bertrand Aristide, the island nation's first democratically elected president. Aristide came to the United States, and U.S. policy became a demand for negotiations to bring him back to power, despite qualms among some U.S. officials concerning his militant leftist politics.

Aristide's ouster and the crackdown on dissent that followed produced a flood of Haitians fleeing to the United States on rickety boats. By February 1992, about 15,000 had attempted the trip, and thousands were filling a tent city created at the United States' Guantanamo Naval Base in Cuba.

The Bush administration maintained that the Haitians were fleeing bad economic times in their homeland, not the political repression that would qualify them for asylum, and sent many back after hearings at the Guantanamo base.

But human rights organizations and some members of Congress insisted that the Haitians were fleeing political oppression.

Bush's Directive

The dispute escalated after Bush issued a directive on May 24 that Haitian refugees rescued at sea should be summarily returned — without being taken to the overfilled Guantanamo center and without hearings first to air their claims of political persecution. Critics protested that the administration was violating international law requiring that refugees be given an opportunity to make their case for asylum. But Bush reiterated that most of those fleeing Haiti were economic, not political, refugees who would not qualify for asylum. He said that the Guantanamo base was almost filled to its 12,500-person capacity and that Haitians could apply for asylum to U.S. embassy personnel in Haiti.

During and just after the 1992 presidential campaign, Bill Clinton pledged to give Haitians a hearing before sending them back. But as president-elect, Clinton was forced to revisit that pledge in late 1992 in the face of reports that thousands of Haitians were preparing to set sail for the United States on homemade boats as soon as he took office.

In a Voice of America radio address broadcast to Haitians on Jan. 14, 1993, Clinton announced that he was retaining Bush's policy. The president-elect warned that Haitians would continue to be intercepted and returned by the Coast Guard once he became president. Clinton told reporters that he still believed that summary repatriation was wrong but had come to see the practice as necessary in the short term to help political negotiations advance and to protect the safety of Haitians.

After a flurry of unprecedented diplomatic activity involving Bush and Clinton administration officials, deposed Haitian president Aristide, the Organization of American States and the United Nations, Aristide on Jan. 11 had made a radio address urging Haitians not to flee the country. And Aristide later rescinded an early statement calling on Clinton to halt forced repatriations.

Refugee advocacy groups sharply criticized Clinton's reversal, saying the policy of forced repatriation violated international and U.S. refugee law.

Legislative Action

The House passed legislation (HR 3844) on Feb. 27, 1992, that would have suspended the return of Haitian refugees for six months. The bill, which was approved 217-165, also would have required a study of the conditions of Haitians who had been returned to their homeland. An amendment that would have authorized the federal government to reimburse state and local governments for the increased costs of caring for Haitians was adopted Feb. 27, 241-144.

The measure had been reported by the Judiciary Committee on Feb. 25 (H Rept 102-437).

Three days before the bill reached the House floor, the Supreme Court had ruled, 8-1, that the Bush administration could complete the return of the Haitians.

The House Foreign Affairs Committee on June 18 approved by voice vote a bill to tighten U.S. economic sanctions against Haiti's military government. The legislation (HR 4761) sought to freeze U.S. assets of Haitians who assisted in the military coup in September 1991 that overthrew Aristide. It also would have barred ships that used Haitian ports from entering U.S. ports for 180 days.

The Foreign Affairs Committee on Sept. 30 approved legislation (HR 5360) that would have required the federal government to screen refugees to determine if they should be permitted to enter the United States. The bill would have required the United States to adhere to the 1951 United Nations Refugee Convention and Protocol, which set guidelines for determining if a person was a refugee.

The protocol, which the United States signed in 1968, required signatory nations to determine whether each potential applicant met the criteria for refugee status. A refugee was defined as someone who feared persecution in his own country as a result of his political beliefs, religion or ethnic background.

The administration claimed that passage of the bill would lead to an uncontrollable exodus of Haitians to the United States. But bill supporters argued that a dramatic increase in the number of refugees fleeing Haiti since Aristide's overthrow was evidence that many feared persecution.

Andean Drug War

Congress in 1991 cleared legislation (HR 1724 — PL 102-182) extending duty-free treatment to certain exports from Bolivia, Colombia, Ecuador and Peru.

The trade preferences, part of President Bush's anti-drug effort known as the Andean Initiative, were intended to provide greater access to U.S. markets to encourage peasants in those countries to shift out of coca leaf production (the source of cocaine) and into legal products for export. *(Andean Initiative, p. 255)*

The duty-free treatment was extended to such products as leather handbags, luggage and vegetables. But lawmakers retained duties on a number of important items to shield U.S. producers from greater competition. Excluded from the duty-free list were tuna, petroleum, footwear, apparel and textiles — including llama and alpaca wool, a lucrative export from the region surrounding the Andes mountains.

The House Ways and Means Committee reported an Andean Initiative bill (HR 661 — H Rept 102-337) on Nov. 19. That bill's provisions were incorporated into broader legislation containing other trade provisions and language reworking the existing formula for unemployment benefits (HR 1724). *(Unemployment benefits bill, p. 721)*

The Senate at first refused to approve the Andean Initiative because of its concern that no hearings had been held and that the provisions could harm U.S. businesses. But, because of the must-pass unemployment benefit provisions, the Senate backed down and the provisions were included in the conference version (H Rept 102-391) of the bill. Both chambers agreed to the conference report Nov. 26.

Kurdish Refugee Aid

Congress in 1991 approved $556 million in disaster and refugee relief aid for the waves of Kurdish refugees who fled into the mountains of Iraq and Turkey after Iraqi forces crushed their rebellion in the aftermath of the Persian Gulf War. *(Persian Gulf War, p. 299)*

The money — $235.5 million for State Department activities and $320.5 million to fund the U.S. military's relief efforts — was included in a fiscal 1991 supplemental appropriations bill (HR 2251 — PL 102-55). The State Department money was to come largely from interest accumulating on foreign contributions to the U.S. war effort. Money to fund the military's operations would be drawn from a separate Treasury account established for war costs.

The House passed its version, 384-25, on May 9. The Senate passed its version by voice vote that same day. Both chambers agreed to the conference report (H Rept 102-71) May 22, the House by a vote of 387-33 and the Senate by voice vote. President Bush signed HR 2251 on June 13.

Legislation authorizing emergency aid for displaced Iraqis (HR 2122 — PL 102-45) was passed by voice votes in the House April 30 and the Senate May 9. HR 2122 was signed into law May 17.

Global Warming Treaty

The Senate in 1992 ratified a United Nations treaty that would require signatory countries to limit emissions of heat-trapping "greenhouse gases," including carbon dioxide and methane, that were thought to contribute to global warming. President Bush signed the pact on June 12 at the "Earth Summit" in Rio de Janeiro.

The Senate approved the treaty, entitled the U.N. Framework Convention on Climate Change (Treaty Doc 102-38), by voice vote on Oct. 7. The treaty had been reported by the Senate Foreign Relations Committee on Oct. 1 (S Ex Rept 102-55).

Bush signed the agreement after insisting that specific timetables and levels of emissions be dropped. The president prevailed over U.S. allies such as Germany and Japan, who supported verifiable timetables for reducing their output of such gases.

Claiborne Pell, D-R.I., chairman of the Senate Foreign Relations Committee, and other observers said that specific timetables were the only way to force countries to make the hard decisions needed to reduce such emissions.

Though the treaty contained no timetable, it did call for countries to report on their efforts to reduce such gases with a view toward stabilizing their emissions at 1990 levels.

The treaty was to go into effect after 50 countries ratified it. Some 143 countries signed the draft treaty at the Earth Summit — officially the United Nations Conference on Environment and Development.

Special Report: Persian Gulf War

The invasion and occupation of oil-rich Kuwait by Iraq in August 1990 set in motion a crisis that would remain at the forefront of the international agenda for seven months.

President Bush responded to the invasion by pulling together an international coalition authorized by the United Nations Security Council to oppose Iraq. Nearly 40 nations contributed combat forces, transport assistance, medical teams or financial aid to the coalition effort attempting to force Iraq from Kuwait. The Persian Gulf crisis was the first major test of the effectiveness of the Security Council to confront international aggression in the post-Cold War era. *(Contributions to the Multinational Coalition, p. 316)*

Bush and Secretary of State James A. Baker III directed a major diplomatic initiative aimed at passage by the Security Council of a resolution to authorize the use of force against Iraq if it did not withdraw from Kuwait. The campaign culminated in the Security Council's adoption on Nov. 29 of Resolution 678, which set Jan. 15, 1991, as the deadline for Iraq to pull out of Kuwait. After that, the resolution authorized member states to use "all necessary means" to enforce previous U.N. resolutions demanding the withdrawal.

Congress supported the president's actions from the start of the crisis, but at times the support was wary. Lawmakers generally endorsed Bush's economic embargo against Iraq and his deployment of troops to Saudi Arabia to ward off a possible Iraqi invasion of that country. But many members opposed an early resort to force, hoping instead that the pain of severe economic sanctions would force Iraq to abandon Kuwait.

In early January 1991, last-ditch diplomatic efforts to persuade Iraq to withdraw failed. As the U.S.-led coalition prepared for war, Congress debated whether to authorize the president to use force to expel Iraq from Kuwait. The debate concluded Jan. 12 with the passage of H J Res 77, permitting Bush "to use United States armed forces" to end Iraq's "illegal occupation of, and brutal aggression against, Kuwait."

Once the U.N. deadline had passed, Bush acted swiftly. On Jan. 16, he ordered coalition forces to begin a sustained bombing campaign against Iraq. On Feb. 24, after 38 straight days of bombing, the allies launched a ground offensive into Kuwait and Iraq that overwhelmed Iraqi defenders with surprising ease. On Feb. 27, Bush announced a cease-fire and declared Kuwait liberated. *(Presidential texts regarding the Persian Gulf War, p. 1196)*

Road to Aggression

Iraq's aggression against Kuwait grew out of Iraqi economic problems stemming from the Iran-Iraq War, which lasted from September 1980 until August 1988. The war left Iraq $80 billion in debt. Almost half of this was owed to Saudi Arabia, Kuwait and the other Persian Gulf states. Iraqi leaders believed that debts to Arab nations related to the war with Iran should be forgiven. They reasoned that Iraq has served as a shield against Iran, which threatened all Arab states, especially those on the Persian Gulf. During the eight years of war, Iraq had paid a steep price — hundreds of thousands of Iraqis had been killed or maimed and the country was left with few funds for reconstruction, despite its huge oil reserves.

During the spring and summer of 1990, Kuwait became the focus of Iraqi resentment against its Arab creditors. Not only did Kuwait refuse to write off Iraqi war debts, but it also was exceeding its oil production quota set by the Organization of Petroleum Exporting Countries (OPEC), thereby contributing to low international oil prices. Iraqi reconstruction could only be based upon revenues from its oil resources. But the low price of oil limited the cash Iraq could earn through oil sales. According to Saddam Hussein, Kuwait's overproduction amounted to economic warfare. That Iraq, like most other OPEC members, also had engaged in overproduction made little difference to Saddam.

In a speech in Baghdad on July 17, Saddam Hussein threatened to use force against unnamed Arab oil-producing states if they did not cut back their production. The following day a letter from Iraqi Foreign Minister Tariq Aziz to the Arab League was made public. It named Kuwait and the United Arab Emirates (UAE) as the quota busters. Iraq also charged that Kuwait had pumped $2.4 billion worth of oil that rightfully belonged to Iraq from the Rumaila oilfield, only a small part of which lies under Kuwaiti territory.

In late July, Iraq began massing troops in its southern region near the Kuwaiti border. On July 25, tensions eased somewhat. Egyptian President Hosni Mubarak, who had been the focus of Arab efforts to mediate the dispute, announced that Iraq and Kuwait had agreed to hold talks in Jiddah, Saudi Arabia, on Aug. 1 to discuss their differences. The talks lasted only two hours before they broke down. The following day Iraqi army units invaded Kuwait.

The quick Iraqi resort to military force following a token attempt at direct negotiations with Kuwait appeared premeditated. It is almost certain that Iraq planned before the Jiddah talks to invade Kuwait.

Although Kuwait's oil production policies contributed to the Iraqi regime's aggressive posture toward Kuwait, a possibility exists that even if Kuwait had taken steps to appease Iraq, Saddam Hussein would still have found a pretext to invade his neighbor. The invasion was more than a response to Kuwaiti oil production policies. It was an attempt to provide a quick fix to Iraq's severe economic problems and to obtain funding for continued expansion of Iraqi military capabilities by seizing Kuwait's immense wealth. The invasion also was intended to improve Iraq's access to the Persian Gulf and to redraw colonial borders to which Iraq had long objected.

U.S. Policy Before the War

Bush would receive bipartisan praise for his performance as commander in chief during the Persian Gulf crisis. But after the war, he was criticized for his administration's attempts to carry on a rapprochement with Iraq during 1989 and early 1990.

The administration had opposed the imposition of mandatory economic sanctions against Iraq for its use of chemical weapons against its Kurdish population and other human rights violations. Bush and his advisers believed that Iraq represented a bulwark against a more dangerous Iran, that maintaining a relationship with the Baghdad government could help moderate its behavior, and that American businesses and farmers that exported to Iraq would be the primary losers if sanctions were imposed. Iraq's eventual invasion of Kuwait demonstrated that Iran was not the only threat to the oil-rich Persian Gulf states and that the United States had little success moderating Saddam's government.

Though some members of Congress had loudly denounced Iraq during 1989 and 1990, Iraq was a secondary foreign policy issue. "Looking back, it never seemed terribly difficult to get House and Senate support for pursuing the [U.S.-Iraqi] relationship," recalled Richard W. Murphy, assistant secretary of state for Near Eastern and South Asian affairs during most of the Reagan administration.

Members who fought for tougher action against Iraq blamed their defeat on strong White House opposition. But failure also resulted from members' desires to help constituents tap lucrative Iraqi markets for grain, computers and construction projects. Only six days before Iraq's invasion of Kuwait, for example, the House voted to gut an amendment that would have cut off $1 billion in annual farm credit guarantees for oil-rich Iraq.

The Bush administration also was criticized for sending mixed signals during the summer of 1990 about its willingness to oppose potential Iraqi aggression. On July 24, the administration announced "a short notice" military exercise with the UAE, deploying combat ships and aerial refueling planes to the southern Persian Gulf nation. Officials quoted in news accounts made clear the maneuvers were designed to demonstrate U.S. support for the UAE and Kuwait in their confrontation with Iraq. On the same day, however, State Department spokeswoman Margaret D. Tutwiler told reporters: "We do not have any defense treaties with Kuwait, and there are no special defense or security commitments to Kuwait."

In Baghdad the next day, Saddam summoned the U.S. ambassador, career diplomat April C. Glaspie, for an audience. A purported transcript of the session, disclosed by the Iraqis in September, depicted Glaspie as giving Saddam little reason to expect a strong response if Iraq moved against Kuwait. "We have no opinion on the Arab-Arab conflicts, like your border disagreements with Kuwait," Glaspie was quoted as saying. On July 30, Glaspie left Baghdad, as scheduled, to return to the United States for consultations and home leave. Glaspie contended on March 20, 1991, in a Senate Foreign Relations Committee hearing, that the transcript was "disinformation." She said that she had clearly warned Saddam that the United States would not tolerate aggression against Kuwait.

On July 31, 1990, Assistant Secretary of State John H. Kelly testified before the House Foreign Affairs Mideast Subcommittee that the United States had no treaty obligation to come to the defense of Kuwait. Subcommittee Chairman Lee H. Hamilton, D-Ind., asked Kelly about a statement that Defense Secretary Dick Cheney had made to reporters July 19 promising that the United States would come to Kuwait's defense if attacked.

"We have no defense treaty relationship with any gulf country. That is clear," Kelly responded.

When Hamilton asked specifically what would happen if Iraq charged across the Kuwaiti border, Kelly said: "That, Mr. Chairman, is a hypothetical or a contingency question.... Suffice it to say we would be extremely concerned, but I cannot get into the realm of 'what if' answers."

Iraq Attacks

Before dawn on Aug. 2, Iraqi armored divisions stormed into Kuwait. The well-equipped, battle-hardened Iraqi army, led by elite Republican Guard troops, quickly seized control of the country. At the time of the attack, as many as three-quarters of Kuwaiti military personnel were on leave or away from their military posts. Kuwait's ruler, Sheik Jaber Ahmed al-Sabah, had fled Kuwait by car shortly before Iraqi forces arrived at his palace in Kuwait City. Most members of the al-Sabah family who were in Kuwait at the time of the invasion were able to escape.

Saddam Hussein claimed that his forces were responding to a call for help from Kuwaiti revolutionaries who had overthrown the al-Sabah regime. Iraq's government indicated the day after the invasion that it planned to withdraw from Kuwait by Aug. 5. In actuality, there was no revolution, and Iraq had no intention of withdrawing. On Aug. 8, Baghdad ended the pretense by announcing that it was annexing Kuwait. The northern part of the country would be attached to Iraq's Basra Province, while the southern part would become Iraq's "nineteenth province."

The attack surprised and outraged the international community. This outrage was soon compounded by stories of Iraqi atrocities told by those who had fled Kuwait. The occupation was deliberately bloody, destructive and vindictive; much of the damage done had no strategic or military purpose. Refugees described torture and summary executions of Kuwaiti citizens and widespread looting by Iraqi troops. The invasion force appeared to be systematically stripping Kuwait of everything of value. Throughout its occupation of Kuwait, Iraq refused to allow journalists or Red Cross observers to visit Kuwait to investigate human rights abuses.

While robbing Kuwait of its wealth, Iraq initiated a campaign to depopulate it and replace its citizens with Iraqis. Kuwaitis who were allowed to leave the country had

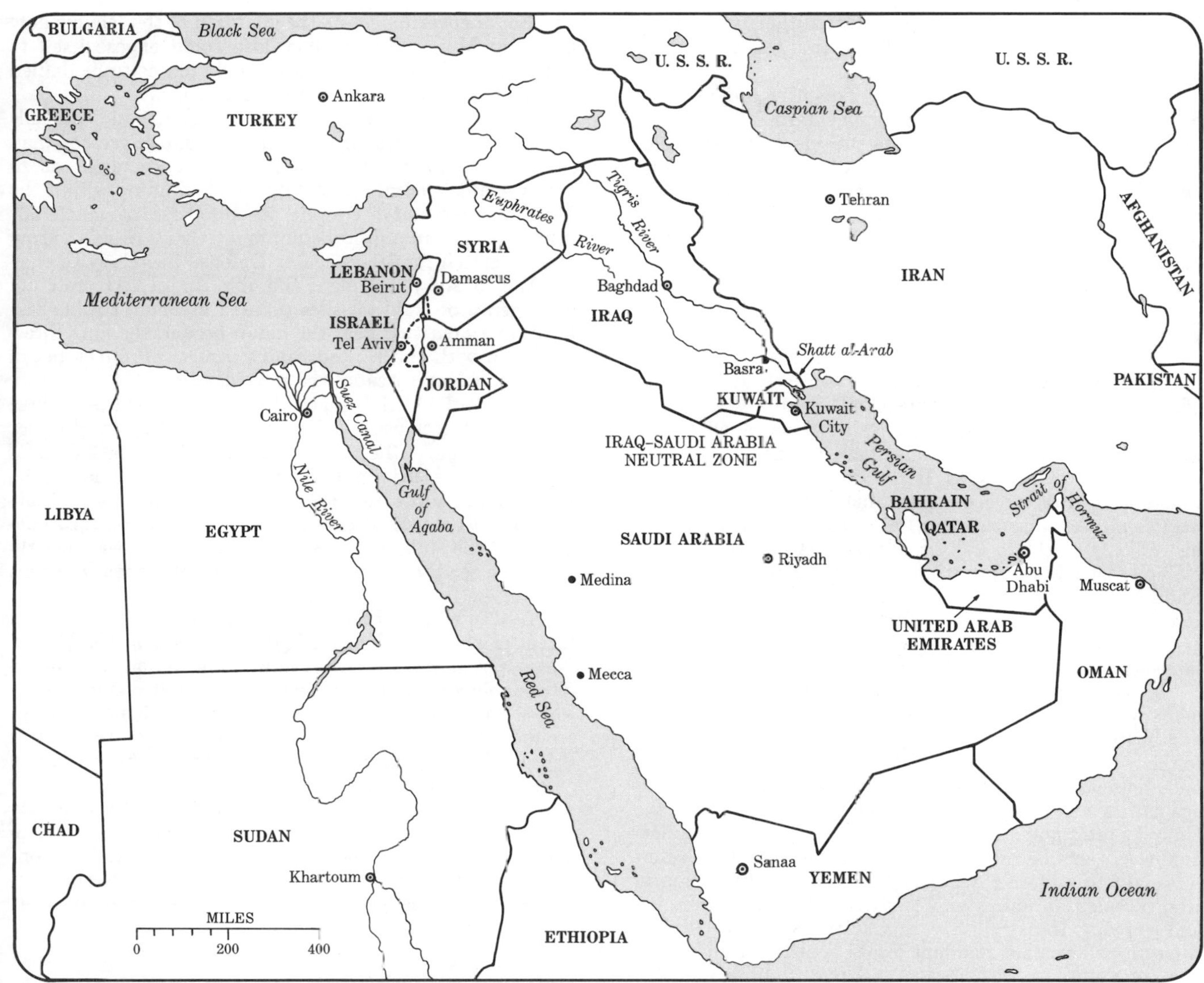

their identity papers and passports confiscated. Kuwaitis out of the country at the time of the invasion were barred from returning. Some Kuwaitis were forcibly deported to Iraq. By October, intelligence reports estimated that only 240,000 of Kuwait's 600,000 citizens remained.

Aside from the immediate threat of a wider regional war, the invasion quickly triggered a sharp rise in the world price of oil. "What [the invasion] means is that OPEC discipline now has been ensured by the point of a gun," said Sen. J. Bennett Johnston, D-La.

American Reaction

Like much of the world, the Bush administration and the U.S. intelligence community were caught off guard by the Iraqi invasion. Although the massing of Iraqi forces on the Kuwait border had caused U.S. leaders concern, few officials or analysts believed that Saddam Hussein was audacious enough to invade Kuwait.

In his first comments on the invasion Aug. 2, Bush indicated that he and his advisers were not discussing the use of military force. After a previously scheduled meeting with British Prime Minister Margaret Thatcher later in the day, however, Bush said, "We're not ruling any options in, but we're not ruling any options out." Bush urged Saudi Arabia and Turkey to close Iraqi oil pipelines, which they soon did. Secretary of State Baker, who was in Moscow, joined with Soviet Foreign Minister Eduard A. Shevardnadze in denouncing the invasion and calling for an embargo on the sale of arms to Iraq.

Presented with a fait accompli in Kuwait and what was perceived as a potential threat to a second key ally and source of imported oil, Bush imposed what amounted to a total ban on economic relations with Iraq. The president's executive order blocked Iraqi access to assets in the United States and prohibited all trade — including oil — with Iraq.

On Capitol Hill, lawmakers scrambled to issue the harshest possible denunciations of Saddam. Several hinted at the possible need to use military force.

"Saddam Hussein is a cancer on the world body politic, and we must excise that cancer now lest it engulf the Middle East," declared Senate Foreign Relations Committee Chairman Claiborne Pell, D-R.I.

On Aug. 2, the House passed an economic sanctions bill (HR 5431) aimed at writing the president's executive order into law. The measure was rushed through two committees and onto the House floor with virtually no debate. The bill passed 416-0; an amendment offered by Sam M.

Gibbons, D-Fla., to grant the president authority to cut off imports from nations that traded with Iraq was adopted by unanimous consent.

The Senate also endorsed the executive order Aug. 2 but chose not to put it in statutory form. The Senate resolution (S Res 318) urged the president to use diplomacy, but it added that a multinational military effort "may be needed to maintain or restore" stability in the region. The measure passed 97-0. On Aug. 5, Bush stiffened the U.S. response, vowing that the invasion "will not stand."

Containing Iraq

The Iraqi occupation of Kuwait was seen by the Bush administration as a serious threat to U.S. interests. Kuwait sits atop one of the largest concentrations of oil in the world. If Saddam Hussein could have permanently added Kuwait's oil resources to Iraq's own huge reserves, he would have directly controlled about one-quarter of the world's oil. Administration officials feared that if he used his military might to bully Saudi Arabia and the smaller Gulf oil states into supporting Iraq's positions in OPEC, he could have dominated oil production and pricing policies. Consequently, uncontested control of Kuwait could have given Saddam dangerous influence over the oil-dependent international economy.

In addition, the attack on Kuwait had unmistakably demonstrated Saddam's propensity for military conquest and brutality. Since 1980, Iraq had invaded Iran, resorted to the use of chemical weapons against Iranian soldiers and ballistic missiles against Iranian cities, and used poison gas against its own Kurdish population. During the 1980s, the United States and the international community had tolerated these acts because Iraq was considered to be a counterweight to a more threatening Iran. But the invasion of Iraq revealed an unmistakable pattern of Iraqi aggression and growing Iraqi military capability. American leaders came to believe that Saddam would continue to use military force until he was checked by greater military power.

Defending Saudi Arabia

Bush's primary concern in the days after the invasion was deterring an Iraqi attack on Saudi Arabia. The Saudi's massive oil reserves were vital to the world's economy. About 15 percent of oil imports to the United States came from Saudi Arabia. An Iraqi move against them would force the United States to take military action, almost regardless of the circumstances or the relative strength of American and Iraqi troops in the region at the time.

Members of Congress generally agreed. Sen. David L. Boren, D-Okla., said an Iraqi attack on Saudi Arabia would represent "a direct threat to the national security of this country."

"We need to tell Hussein that an invasion of Saudi Arabia means war," said Les Aspin, D-Wis., chairman of the House Armed Services Committee.

Bush pressed the Saudi government to accept American soldiers on its territory. Although the Saudis maintained a close relationship with and bought most of their military equipment from the United States, they had never sought or consented to an American military presence in Saudi Arabia. Because of U.S. support for Israel, most Arab countries were wary of accommodating American troops. The Saudi government, as the guardian of the Islamic holy places in Mecca and Medina, also could expose itself to criticism that it was allowing the holy places to be defiled by the presence of a large non-Islamic army.

In the early days of August, however, Saudi officials considered the threat from Iraq to be much greater than the damage an American military presence might do to Saudi Arabia's domestic stability and standing within the Muslim community. Despite its purchase of much advanced American military equipment, Saudi Arabia's army was no match for Iraq's. After Defense Secretary Cheney on Aug. 6 showed King Fahd ibn Abdul Aziz satellite intelligence of Iraqi missiles pointed at Saudi Arabia and Iraqi forces massing near the Saudi border, the king threw his lot in with the United States. American forces began arriving in Saudi Arabia the next day.

During the initial stages of the deployment, American and Saudi forces were badly outnumbered by Iraqi forces in Kuwait and southern Iraq. The Navy had a task force of eight warships in the Persian Gulf at the time of the invasion and subsequently ordered an aircraft carrier battle group to steam to the northern Arabian Sea near the mouth of the Gulf. But U.S. naval forces alone were clearly no match for the enormous contingent of troops Iraq sent into Kuwait.

By the end of the third week in August, however, the threat of an Iraqi offensive had diminished as the United States, Great Britain and several other nations assembled formidable air and naval forces in the Gulf region. Meanwhile, the United States continued its deployment of ground forces. They were joined by troops from Great Britain, France, Egypt, Syria, Morocco, Pakistan and a number of other countries.

On Aug. 22, Bush signed an order calling to active duty nearly 50,000 military reservists to back up U.S. forces in Saudi Arabia. It was the first reserve mobilization in connection with potential hostile action since President Lyndon B. Johnson called up 35,000 reservists during the Vietnam War in January 1968.

Building a Coalition

During August, Bush devoted much of his energy to constructing an international coalition to oppose the Iraqi occupation of Kuwait. Bush hoped that broad international participation would reduce the burden on the United States, increase the effectiveness of sanctions and make the U.S. presence in Saudi Arabia more acceptable to the Arab world. International financial and military support also would strengthen backing for the operation in Congress, which was struggling with the large U.S. budget deficit.

The Bush administration succeeded in building a broad multinational coalition that proved to be enduring and resilient. More than two dozen nations contributed combat forces. Other nations provided medical teams, transport assistance or financial aid to the coalition.

Aside from Saudi Arabia, Egypt and Syria were the most important Arab members of the coalition. By January 1991, Egypt had deployed 30,000 troops in the region. Syria long had denounced U.S. patronage of Israel, and the United States had declared Syria to be a supporter of international terrorists, but both temporarily set aside their differences to pursue their common interest of forcing Iraq out of Kuwait. President Hafez al-Assad sent 19,000 troops to Saudi Arabia. Combat forces from the Arab states of Morocco, Bahrain, Oman, Qatar, the United Arab Emirates and Kuwait also participated in the coalition under Saudi command. The Bush administration placed a high value on the participation of Arab members of the coalition. The presence of troops in Saudi Arabia from a number of Arab countries weakened Iraqi claims that the United States and its Western allies were waging a war of aggression against Arab nations and peoples.

Throughout the Gulf crisis, Great Britain was the staunchest Western ally of the United States, contributing 35,000 troops to the effort. With 17,000 troops committed to the coalition, France also made a sizable contribution. Italy and Canada provided warplanes to the effort, and many other Western nations sent combat ships to the region. Pakistan and Bangladesh each sent several thousand troops to Saudi Arabia, and Turkey maintained an imposing military presence on Iraq's northern border that both guarded against an Iraqi attack and forced Iraq to keep several divisions near its northern border.

Although the Soviet Union declined to send significant forces to the region and sometimes pursued its own agenda during the crisis, Moscow backed the United States in every important vote in the U.N. Security Council, including the votes imposing a total economic embargo against Iraq and authorizing the coalition forces to go to war.

Despite U.S. satisfaction at the participation of many nations, much grumbling was heard in Congress and elsewhere that the U.S. burden in the crisis, particularly if war came, would be disproportionately heavy. Most of the unhappiness was directed at the lack of action by Japan and West Germany.

At a news conference Aug. 30, Bush said that he was asking wealthy U.S. allies — including Japan and West Germany — to step up their contribution to the military deployment in the Gulf and to aid the countries that had been hardest hit as a result of the global trade embargo against Iraq. But some in Congress remained skeptical about how much Japan and other allies would contribute. "They have a reputation for offering things, but when you get beyond the wrapping paper, there's not a lot there," said Rep. David E. Bonior, D-Mich.

The constitutions of both Japan and West Germany contained provisions restricting the deployment of troops in foreign lands. The West German government was prohibited from sending troops outside the territory of members of the North Atlantic Treaty Organization (NATO) alliance, while the Japanese government was prohibited from sending troops to any foreign country. Although observers suggested that it might be possible to get around these provisions, little support was evident in either nation for sending troops to the Gulf. A Japanese government proposal to send non-combat support troops to Saudi Arabia was harshly criticized and defeated in Japan. The German government did send ships to the eastern Mediterranean and 18 warplanes to NATO member Turkey as part of a NATO deployment in January, but Chancellor Helmut Kohl firmly rejected the idea of sending German combat forces to the Gulf.

Yet neither the Japanese nor the Germans wanted to be seen as taking advantage of the crisis by sitting on the sidelines while their major industrial competitors and trade partners committed huge resources to defending Saudi Arabia and liberating Kuwait. Consequently, both nations pledged financial aid instead of troops. The Japanese eventually provided almost $11 billion to the United States for the war effort and an additional $3 billion to Middle East nations. The Germans gave a total of $8 billion with $6.5 billion going to the United States.

The biggest financial contributors to the military effort against Iraq, however, were Saudi Arabia and Kuwait, both of which pledged more than $16 billion. Overall, the United States received more than $53 billion in financial contributions.

United Nations Sanctions

In tandem with the U.S. efforts to create a military coalition to defend Saudi Arabia, the Bush administration launched a diplomatic campaign to create an anti-Iraq consensus within the international community. The U.N. Security Council became the focus of this campaign.

The Security Council is composed of 15 members — five permanent memberships (the United States, Soviet Union (now Russia), China, France and Great Britain) and 10 memberships distributed on a rotating basis between the other members of the United Nations. Because permanent members hold a veto over any Security Council resolution, the body rarely played an effective role in responding to international conflict during the Cold War.

The end of the Cold War between the United States and the Soviet Union, however, invigorated the Security Council. A Soviet veto of a U.S. initiative was no longer a certainty. Because American and European assistance had become critical to Soviet economic revitalization, Soviet leaders were inclined to support Western initiatives, such as confronting Iraq's aggression against Kuwait.

On Aug. 2, the same day as Iraq's invasion, the Security Council met in emergency session and unanimously passed Resolution 660, which condemned the invasion and called for an immediate Iraqi withdrawal. Four days later, the Security Council passed Resolution 661, which established a nearly total embargo on Iraqi commerce. The embargo was to include all imports going to and all exports coming from Iraq, except for humanitarian shipments of medicine and some food. Iraq was particularly vulnerable to an embargo because it depended almost completely on oil exports for foreign earnings and it imported about 75 percent of its food. Iraqi oil could only be exported through the Persian Gulf sea route and through pipelines running across Saudi Arabia to the Red Sea and across Turkey to the Mediterranean. All three avenues of export were quickly cut off by the embargo, depriving Iraq of hard currency earnings.

The embargo was designed to cause economic hardship in Iraq that would compel the Iraqi government to withdraw from Kuwait. It also was intended to weaken Iraq militarily by creating shortages of spare parts, munitions and fuel and by stalling further progress on its chemical weapons and ballistic missile industries and its pursuit of nuclear weapons. Finally, the United States and its allies hoped that the embargo might foment enough discontent within Iraq to cause the ouster of Saddam Hussein's regime. Few strategists, however, believed that this outcome could be accomplished by sanctions alone.

Resolution 661 only called on U.N. member states to observe the embargo. It did not explicitly authorize a military blockade to enforce the sanctions. During the weeks following the passage of Resolution 661, members of the Security Council were split over enforcement of its provisions. The United States insisted that it had the right to use military force to prevent circumvention of the embargo. On Aug. 16, U.S. naval forces in the Persian Gulf began interdicting ships carrying cargoes to or from Iraq. The British concurred in this judgment, but the other three permanent members of the council — the French, Chinese and Soviets — claimed that a new resolution was necessary if military force were to be used to prevent leakage through the embargo.

On Aug. 25, after much lobbying by the United States, the Security Council passed Resolution 665, specifically authorizing the use of force necessary to ensure compliance with the embargo. Any commerce between Iraq and the rest of the world would have to take place over land. While circumvention of the embargo by traders operating out of Jordan (and, to a lesser extent, Turkey and Iran) would help keep Iraq supplied with food and certain other goods, its economy would be crippled by the embargo. The U.N. blockade quickly succeeded in cutting off virtually all of Iraq's exports and, by some estimates, 90 percent of its imports.

Hostages

When it became obvious that the United States and other Western nations were going to oppose the invasion of Kuwait with military deployments and severe economic sanctions, the Iraqi regime moved against the Westerners stranded in Iraq and Kuwait. The State Department estimated that 3,000 Americans were in Kuwait and 500 in Iraq.

On Aug. 9, Iraq announced that it was sealing its borders and allowing only diplomatic personnel to leave. Four days later, Iraqi officials confirmed that foreigners would not be allowed to leave Iraq (or Kuwait) until the crisis was over. Iraq avoided calling the foreigners hostages, referring to them instead as "guests." In late August, the Iraqi government began rounding up Westerners in Iraq and Kuwait for the purpose of holding them at strategic military sites throughout Iraq. The Iraqis primarily used American and British citizens as "human shields," but citizens of a number of European nations and Japan were detained at military sites as well.

Iraq's detention of Westerners was intended to deter a coalition air attack against military targets and stimulate peace movements in Western countries. But by holding hostages, Iraq was taking a big propaganda risk. Only hardcore Iraqi supporters in a few Arab countries would condone the use of innocent civilians as human shields. Western leaders repeatedly pointed to the hostage taking as another example of Saddam's brutality. Bush Aug. 20 declared, "I will hold the government of Iraq responsible for the safety and well-being of American citizens held against their will."

Sensing that holding the hostages could backfire, the Iraqis announced Aug. 28 that they would release foreign women and children. By Sept. 22, all Western and Japanese women and children who wanted to leave Iraq and Kuwait had been flown out on chartered Iraqi flights, for which their governments had to pay Iraq hard currency. The Iraqis, however, continued to house hundreds of adult male hostages at strategic locations.

Finally, on Dec. 6, Saddam informed the Iraqi National Assembly that all foreign hostages would be released. Some observers were surprised that he would give up these potentially valuable pawns. In his statement announcing the impending release of the hostages, Saddam said that during the time foreigners had been held to prevent coalition attacks, Iraq had completed its fortifications of Kuwait. Saddam may have believed that his army, now well dug in in Kuwait, would be able to inflict more than enough coalition casualties to achieve his purpose. In effect, Saddam regarded coalition infantry troops as his ultimate hostages.

Toward War in the Gulf

After U.S. and allied military deployments in Saudi Arabia had ended the possibility that Iraq could launch a successful offensive against Saudi oilfields, the Bush administration had to decide how to deal with Saddam Hussein's occupation of Kuwait.

A broad consensus existed among Americans and members of Congress that Saddam should be opposed and Saudi Arabia should be protected. During the week of Oct. 1, both the House and Senate overwhelmingly backed resolutions offering support for the actions taken by the Bush administration in the first weeks of the crisis. The House approved H J Res 658 by 380-29 on Oct. 1. The following day the Senate passed S Con Res 147 by 96-3.

The public's support for a U.S.-led offensive against Iraq, however, was far more uncertain. Lawmakers had agonized over whether the administration would see the resolutions as a "blank check" for future actions. In a Sept. 24 floor speech, Sen. Daniel Patrick Moynihan, D-N.Y., described the pitfalls created by the resolutions.

"Some [members] are concerned that any resolution on the Persian Gulf crisis would turn into a Tonkin Gulf resolution for the 1990s," he said, referring to the 1964 congressional resolution that President Johnson repeatedly invoked to justify expanded involvement in the Vietnam War.

Sen. Edward M. Kennedy, D-Mass., one of three members to vote against the Senate measure, echoed Moynihan's concern, saying, "It is, in effect, a Tonkin Gulf resolution for the Persian Gulf." But most lawmakers agreed with the assessment of Senate Majority Leader George J. Mitchell, D-Maine, who said, "This resolution is not an authorization for the use of forces, now or in the future."

On Nov. 8, two days after midterm congressional elections, Bush announced that he was reinforcing the 230,000 U.S. troops already in the Gulf participating in what was known as Operation Desert Shield. Bush said more troops were needed to develop an "adequate offensive military option should that be necessary to achieve our common goals." He provided no specific total of how many troops would be sent, but Pentagon sources said that approximately 200,000 more troops would be deployed in the region. Defense Secretary Cheney announced the following day that the United States no longer planned to rotate troops into and out of the Gulf.

The new deployments and the end of the troop rotation plans alarmed critics in Congress, who complained that the administration's policies shortened the time economic sanctions would have to induce Iraq to leave Kuwait. Military experts agreed that the United States could not sustain such a large force in an inhospitable desert environment indefinitely, and the new deployments would force the administration to choose between withdrawing part of the force, which would be perceived as a moral victory for Saddam, or going to war.

During the week of Nov. 12, Bush was caught in what one member of Congress called a "mini-firestorm" of criticism. By midweek, the president managed to quell demands for a special session of Congress by assuring congressional leaders — according to members who recounted a session at the White House on Nov. 14 — that "no Rubicon was crossed" in the movement toward war.

"If there is to be a war in the Persian Gulf or anywhere else," Sen. Mitchell stated repeatedly, "it requires a formal act of Congress to commit to it." The uneasy bipartisanship of summer gave way to increasingly partisan rhetorical skirmishing. "The president's announcement suddenly brought into focus some of the differences that were lying beneath the surface," Rep. Aspin observed.

Senate Democrats, including Kennedy and Colorado's Tim Wirth, were especially sharp in their criticism of the new deployment. Kennedy said the buildup made war "inevitable." In an interview, Wirth said of administration officials: "I am increasingly wondering if they know what they're doing."

After announcing the new deployments, the Bush administration began seeking U.N. Security Council approval for the use of force against Iraq if Saddam did not order a withdrawal from Kuwait. On Nov. 29, the Security Council voted 12-2 (with Yemen and Cuba dissenting) to implicitly authorize coalition nations to use force to expel Iraq from Kuwait. Security Council Resolution 678, however, allowed for a month and a half of diplomacy by authorizing force only after Jan. 15, 1991. Diplomats would have 47 days to persuade Iraq to withdraw from Kuwait peacefully. *(Text of resolution, box, this page)*

China had voted for each of the previous 11 Security Council resolutions related to the Iraqi invasion of Kuwait, but it abstained from the vote to approve military force, saying that the council should avoid "hasty actions" that could lead to war. Nevertheless, the Chinese refrained from vetoing the resolution. Secretary of State Baker, who chaired the Security Council meeting when the vote was taken, declared the vote to be "a watershed in the history of the United Nations." Any U.S.-led military action taken after Jan. 15 to oust Iraq from Kuwait now had international legitimacy.

U.N. Resolution 678

Following is the text of the resolution the United Nations Security Council adopted Nov. 29, 1990.

THE SECURITY COUNCIL, RECALLING, AND REAFFIRMING its resolutions 660 (1990) of 2 August, 661 (1990) of 6 August, 662 (1990) of 9 August, 664 (1990) of 18 August, 665 (1990) of 25 August, 666 (1990) of 13 September, 667 (1990) of 16 September, 669 (1990) of 24 September, 670 (1990) of 25 September, 674 (1990) of 29 October, and 677 (1990) of 28 November,

NOTING THAT, despite all efforts by the United Nations, Iraq refuses to comply with its obligation to implement resolution 660 (1990) and the above-mentioned subsequent relevant resolutions, in flagrant contempt of the Security Council,

MINDFUL of its duties and responsibilities under the Charter of the United Nations for the maintenance and preservation of international peace and security,

DETERMINED to secure full compliance with its decisions,

ACTING under Chapter VII of the Charter,

1. DEMANDS that Iraq comply fully with resolution 660 (1990) and all subsequent relevant resolutions, and decides, while maintaining all its decisions, to allow Iraq one final opportunity, as a pause of good will, to do so;
2. AUTHORIZES Member States cooperating with the Government of Kuwait, unless Iraq on or before 15 January 1991 fully implements, as set forth in paragraph 1 above, the foregoing resolutions, to use all necessary means to uphold and implement resolution 660 (1990) and all subsequent relevant resolutions and to restore international peace and security in the area;
3. REQUESTS all States to provide appropriate support for the actions undertaken in pursuance of paragraph 2 of the present resolution;
4. REQUESTS the States concerned to keep the Security Council regularly informed on the progress of actions undertaken pursuant to paragraphs 2 and 3 of the present resolution;
5. DECIDES to remain seized of the matter.

Bush Administration Strategy

The massive military buildup in Saudi Arabia reflected a change in Bush's strategy. It marked a rejection of the long-term approach of relying on economic sanctions to force Iraq out of Kuwait. Bush believed that his best chance to make Baghdad back down was to confront it with a coalition force capable of inflicting terrible damage on Iraqi forces. Until such a coalition force was in place, Bush did not believe that the threat of attack would be credible. The new buildup, therefore, was a high stakes gamble. It increased the pressure on Saddam to withdraw but greatly heightened the likelihood of war if he did not.

American policy makers viewed Saddam as a ruthless tyrant willing to sacrifice many lives for his purposes, but he also was seen as a leader who could be counted on to act in his self interest. Sanctions might not force Saddam out of Kuwait, but if he could be made to see that his armies were in danger of being destroyed, Bush and his advisers believed that Saddam would find a face-saving way to withdraw from Kuwait.

The Bush administration also took this approach because the perceived fragility of the anti-Iraq coalition created a sense of urgency. It was feared that unrest motivated by support for Iraq within Arab countries supporting the coalition could topple friendly governments or weaken the resolve of these governments to remain in the coalition.

Not everyone agreed, however, that moving toward war was a remedy for the pressures on the cohesiveness of the coalition. These sentiments were expressed by former chairman of the Joint Chiefs of Staff Adm. William Crowe. He said in testimony to the Senate Armed Services Committee on Nov. 28, "I cannot understand why some consider our international alliance strong enough to conduct intense hostilities but too fragile to hold together while we attempt a peaceful solution."

The timing of an offensive, if one became necessary, was an additional consideration. After the middle of March, extreme desert heat would return to the Gulf region, and this would favor the defenders. Also the Muslim holy month of Ramadan would begin in March, complicating Arab participation in the coalition. These factors weighed heavily in favor of resorting to the military option sooner instead of later.

Perhaps the most important factor in the Bush administration's decision, however, was that many officials at the Pentagon and the White House feared an Iraqi withdrawal from Kuwait almost as much as a war. A pullout would have left the formidable Iraqi military (as well as its nuclear research facilities and its chemical and biological weapons industries) intact and capable of threatening its neighbors, including Saudi Arabia and Kuwait. Consequently, Bush stated that if Iraq withdrew, an international peace-keeping force would be needed on the ground and U.S. naval forces in the Persian Gulf would need to be strengthened.

Meanwhile, seeking to prove that his withdrawal from Kuwait was not an act of cowardice or betrayal of the cause of poor Arabs, Saddam Hussein would be tempted to pursue other aggressive policies, particularly against Israel. Such conditions would heighten Arab-Israeli tensions and dramatically increase the possibility of another Arab-Israeli war.

Consequently, the Bush administration regarded peace based on an Iraqi withdrawal as an outcome nearly as dangerous as a war. The official U.S. policy objectives continued to be the ouster of Iraq from Kuwait through economic sanctions and the threat of military force, but implicit in Bush's willingness to make the military threat was an underlying belief that war might be the wise option. The liberation of Kuwait was an important goal of the Bush administration, but it also was seen as the means through which the Iraqi military threat might be destroyed.

American Debate on Going to War

Beginning in September, members of Congress and many Americans questioned if the United States had sufficient interests in Kuwait to do more than contain further Iraqi aggression. Wide agreement existed that Saudi oilfields must be protected from Iraqi seizure, but no consensus developed on whether the United States should attempt to liberate Kuwait by force. Facing a recession and hoping to reap the benefits of a "peace dividend" that would follow the end of the Cold War, Americans worried that expansion of the Gulf mission would undermine the U.S. economy. After witnessing the diminishment of the Soviet military threat, they also had hoped that the world was entering a safer, less confrontational era.

Most Americans backed Bush's initial deployments of troops to Saudi Arabia. As the crisis continued, however, support for Bush's strategy weakened as fears of a recession and a long stalemate in the desert increased. A *New York Times*/CBS News public opinion poll taken Oct. 8-10 showed that 57 percent of Americans supported the president's Gulf policies, as compared with 75 percent in early August.

Perceptions that a war fought to liberate Kuwait would in reality be a war fought for American access to cheap oil created cynicism among some segments of the American public. The rallying cry of many opponents to the military buildup in Saudi Arabia became "no blood for oil." Other Americans accepted the proposition that Saddam Hussein should be stopped but questioned why it was up to U.S. soldiers to do it.

Question of Vital Interests. Many journalists and members of Congress commented that the president had failed to argue persuasively for the need to use force if Iraq did not withdraw from Kuwait. The difficulty the Bush administration was having in explaining its actions stemmed partly from the nature of the Iraqi threat and partly from the administration's haphazard presentation of the motivations behind its policy. The administration had made many arguments why Iraq should be opposed, but it had not outlined a coherent case as to why it was in the vital interests of the United States to go to war over Iraq's invasion of Kuwait.

Saddam Hussein's invasion of Kuwait did not threaten American shores. Instead, it threatened U.S. interests overseas, the international economy and principles of international law. No single reason for going to war with Iraq was entirely compelling by itself. The Iraqi invasion required citizens to weigh a complex balance sheet of variables for and against the use of force, instead of responding to a ringing cry to arms in the interest of national defense. Moreover, for Americans who saw Iraq as a threat but had doubts about the wisdom of going to war, continuing a policy of enforcing severe economic sanctions against Iraq offered a compromise option through which one could oppose both the barbarous acts of Saddam Hussein and the launching of what might be a very bloody war in the desert.

In his Aug. 8 speech announcing the first deployment of U.S. forces in Saudi Arabia, Bush declared: "Four simple principles guide our policy. First, we seek the immediate, unconditional, and complete withdrawal of all Iraqi forces from Kuwait. Second, Kuwait's legitimate government must be restored to replace the puppet regime. And third, my administration, as has been the case with every president from President [Franklin D.] Roosevelt to President [Ronald] Reagan, is committed to the security and stability of the Persian Gulf. And fourth, I am determined to protect the lives of American citizens abroad."

Subsequently, the Bush administration gave several more reasons for the president's strong response to Iraq's invasion of Kuwait and the possible necessity of using military force to reverse it. Often the justifications were moral. Bush announced that the United States would not stand for Iraq's brutal aggression against Kuwait. The administration cited Iraq's duplicity before the invasion; Kuwait's peaceful history; reports of atrocities by Iraqi troops; and Iraqi efforts to depopulate Kuwait, strip it of its valuables and annex it to Iraq. Bush stressed that the Iraqi invasion was an opportunity to establish a "new world order" in which collective action would deter and combat aggression and uphold international law.

As time wore on, the Bush administration cited other factors, depending on what was happening in the crisis and the mood of the American people, as indicated by public opinion polls. In mid-November, growing concerns among Americans about the economy led the Bush administration to emphasize the importance of liberating Kuwait to U.S. economic health.

Iraq's invasion of Kuwait had sent shock waves through international oil markets. During the first two-and-a-half months of the crisis, fear of war and oil shortages created a strong upward trend in oil prices. On July 2, before the crisis began, the price of oil stood at about $17 a barrel. In early October, the price peaked at just under $40 a barrel, before declining gradually to $28 a barrel before the Jan. 15 deadline. Secretary of State Baker said Nov. 13 that the administration's policy in the Gulf was motivated by economic concerns: "If you want to sum it up in one word, it's jobs. Because an economic recession worldwide, caused by the control of one nation — one dictator, if you will — of the West's economic lifeline [oil], will result in the loss of jobs for American citizens."

Similarly, when public opinion polls in late November showed that Americans were more concerned about Iraq's potential for developing nuclear weapons than any other aspect of the Gulf crisis, administration officials noted that Iraq's aggressive nuclear research program could succeed in developing rudimentary nuclear weapons within several years. Some experts disputed that Iraq could build nuclear weapons that quickly, but the prospect of a nuclear-armed Iraq was a potent argument in favor of going to war. Nevertheless, a sizable percentage of Americans and members of Congress continued to have serious doubts that U.S. vital interests were at stake in the Gulf.

Effectiveness of Sanctions. The final decision on whether to go to war depended greatly on estimates of the effectiveness of the economic sanctions being imposed against Iraq by the United Nations. If the sanctions were hurting Iraq, the arguments of those opposed to the war option would be strengthened. In Congress, a significant part of the debate begun Jan. 10, 1991, on a resolution authorizing the president to use force against Iraq focused on estimates of the sanctions' effectiveness. The vast majority of members agreed that Saddam Hussein must not be allowed to keep Kuwait or profit from aggression, but many thought sanctions should be given more time to work and objected to the strategy of going to war shortly after Jan. 15.

Supporters of the sanctions option, including Senate Armed Services Chairman Sam Nunn, D-Ga., cited intelligence reports that claimed that Iraq's economy had been devastated by the U.N. embargo. They emphasized that even though the Bush administration's top intelligence official, CIA Director William H. Webster, had testified that sanctions alone were not guaranteed to produce an Iraqi withdrawal, he also estimated that "more than 90 percent of imports and 97 percent of exports have been shut off."

Many members of Congress argued that even if sanctions failed to cause the downfall of Saddam Hussein or force him to withdraw his army from Kuwait, giving sanctions more time would be wise because they were degrading the Iraqi army's effectiveness with every passing day. Rep. David R. Obey, D-Wis., said of the sanctions, "How long are you willing to wait it out to save lives? My answer is, a fair amount of time."

In response to the argument that delaying war gave the Iraqis more time to build up their defenses in Kuwait, Senate Majority Leader Mitchell said at the beginning of the congressional debate, "Time to fortify Iraq's defenses will do little good if some of Iraq's planes can't fly for lack of spare parts, if some of its tanks can't move for lack of lubricants, if its infrastructure and ability to wage war have been weakened. If it eventually becomes necessary for the United States to wage war, our troops will have benefited from the additional time given the sanctions to degrade Iraq's military capabilities."

Proponents of authorizing military force expressed their doubts that sanctions could squeeze Iraq out of Kuwait within an acceptable time period. They cited the poor record of past international sanctions efforts to force recalcitrant regimes to alter their political behavior. In Iraq's case, evidence showed that while weapons and large industrial equipment were being effectively interdicted, imported consumer goods were reaching stores. Western diplomats and journalists inside Iraq reported that most consumer goods were plentiful, although the price of everything had risen dramatically. Iraqi citizens who were interviewed said they were having no problems buying food, clothing and most household goods. Even beer was readily available in Baghdad shops. The level of deprivation was far from what might be expected to foment unrest in a disciplined, war-hardened society. Given such conditions, starving the Iraqi people into overthrowing their government could take years if it were possible at all.

Advocates of the military force option questioned whether the world community would be willing to deprive the Iraqi people of food over the long run. Even the Security Council resolutions provided for "humanitarian" exceptions to the U.N. embargo. They also observed that Iraq would surely use what supplies it did have to meet the needs of its army in the field first, even if ordinary Iraqis had to go without. Sen. John McCain, R-Ariz., argued, "Who are the ones who would suffer as a result of sanctions? ... [I]t is the innocent civilians and children and others that Saddam Hussein would view as nonessential to his war effort. I don't thing we as a nation are prepared to watch films of children suffering from malnutrition."

The assertion that time was on the side of the international coalition was disputed by advocates of force. They cited the difficulty in holding together for many months or perhaps years a multinational coalition composed of countries with divergent interests. Under pressure of a long stalemate in the desert, allied Arab regimes would be in as much danger from coup attempts and unrest as would the Iraqi regime.

Advocates of force emphasized that the sanctions approach assumed that creating hardships for the Iraqi people could compel Saddam Hussein to order a withdrawal from Kuwait. Most observers, however, believed that Saddam would be neither moved by the economic suffering of the Iraqi people nor easily overthrown. House Armed Services Committee Chairman Aspin, who presided over high-profile hearings on the Gulf crisis, stated, "I am not very bullish on sanctions." He added that while economic measures inflicted pain on the Iraqi people, "that is not the same thing as pain to Saddam Hussein."

Finally, advocates of force observed that the United States had deployed so many troops to the Gulf in preparation for war that adopting a long-term sanctions approach probably would have required a reduction in those forces to allow for troop rotation. A drawing down of U.S. military power in the Gulf, even one that was explained as a strategic decision to allow sanctions time to operate, would have been seen as a retreat from the threat to use military force against Iraq. Such a retreat would have alarmed some allies committed to military force, while confirming Saddam Hussein's suspicions that the United States did not have the stomach for a potentially bloody war. It also would have been a resounding political victory for Saddam within the Arab world that could have emboldened pro-Iraqi opponents of Arab governments supporting the coalition and enhanced Saddam's reputation among many Arabs.

Constitutional Questions. The deployment of large numbers of American forces in Saudi Arabia triggered a constitutional debate on the division of war powers between the executive and legislative branches in the United States. The Constitution states that Congress has the power "to declare war." But it also states that "the executive power shall be vested in a president," and that "the president shall be commander in chief of the Army and Navy." The war power had been debated since the Constitution was written, but the argument had become especially intense since the Vietnam War, when the executive branch was perceived to have pulled the country into a long undeclared conflict. After the Vietnam War, Congress had overridden a veto by President Richard Nixon and enacted the War Powers Act, which attempted to expand and clarify Congress' responsibility for deciding when the nation should go to war and remain at war. Most U.S. military actions since the Vietnam War, including the invasion of Grenada in 1983 and the deployment of troops in Lebanon from 1982 to 1984, brought complaints that the president had not adequately consulted with Congress in accordance with the War Powers Act.

With the increase of U.S. forces in Saudi Arabia, Congress became concerned that a president was again pushing the nation toward war without seeking congressional approval. Most lawmakers, including Senate Majority Leader Mitchell and House Speaker Thomas S. Foley, D-Wash., asserted that because the responsibility to declare war rested with Congress, the president did not have the power to launch a military offensive against Iraq without prior congressional approval — unless Iraq attacked U.S. forces. Mitchell insisted in an Oct. 21 television interview that a decision to go to war required congressional consent.

"Under the American Constitution, the president has no legal authority — none whatsoever — to commit the United States to war," Mitchell declared. "Only Congress can make that grave decision."

Asked what would happen if the administration went to war without congressional approval, he said flatly, "Well, that will not be consistent with the Constitution, and we strongly urge the president to obey the Constitution."

Sen. Kennedy said that going to war without Congress' consent would precipitate a "constitutional crisis." House Majority Leader Richard A. Gephardt, D-Mo., had said that Congress might cut off funding in an undeclared war. Rep. Obey went even further, raising the specter of impeachment if the president ignored Congress.

The administration disputed the assertion that it needed congressional approval, claiming that the president's role as commander in chief empowered him to order offensive actions against Iraq.

The president, however, promised to consult closely with Congress on Persian Gulf policy. On Jan. 8, when war became likely and Bush appeared to have enough votes in Congress to win approval for the war option, he sought to unite the government and the country behind his policies by sending a letter to congressional leaders asking for authorization to attack Iraq if it became necessary in his judgment. It was the first such request by a president since the 1964 Gulf of Tonkin resolution that authorized the use of force in Vietnam. But Bush skirted the question of whether such an authorization was constitutionally required, stating only that it would "greatly enhance the chances for peace if Congress were now to go on record supporting the position adopted by the U.N. Security Council on 12 separate occasions."

Diplomacy Fails

For almost four months, diplomats and leaders of Arab and Western nations had attempted to find a non-military solution to the crisis. The Security Council's Nov. 29 decision to authorize force against Iraq after Jan. 15, 1991, brought new urgency to their endeavors.

On Nov. 30, Bush invited Iraqi Foreign Minister Aziz to visit Washington in mid-December. Secretary of State Baker would then travel to Baghdad sometime before the Jan. 15 deadline. The Iraqis accepted the exchange of foreign ministers in principle Dec. 1 and called for a Dec. 17 meeting in Washington between Bush and Aziz. But they also said that Saddam Hussein's schedule could not accommodate a meeting with Baker in Baghdad until Jan. 12. Bush scoffed at the excuse. On Dec. 14, he declared, "It simply is not credible that he cannot, over a two-week period, make a couple of hours available for the secretary of state, unless, of course, he is seeking to circumvent the United Nations deadline."

The Bush administration considered the proposed Jan. 12 meeting date to be an attempt by Iraq to render the Jan. 15 U.N. deadline meaningless by drawing out diplomatic activity. If the attack were delayed by diplomatic activity past the deadline, Bush and his advisers feared that coalition resolve for an attack could weaken.

During the last half of December, both sides continued their mutual recriminations without any breakthrough on scheduling talks. As the year ended, members of Congress stepped up pressure on the administration to compromise with Iraq on a meeting date, and independent peace initiatives were launched by France and the European Community. On Jan. 3, 1991, in an effort to reassert control over the peace process, Bush proposed a meeting between Baker and Aziz to take place Jan. 7, Jan. 8 or Jan. 9 in Geneva. The following day Iraq accepted Bush's proposal, announcing Aziz would go to Geneva Jan. 9.

The six-and-a-half hour meeting in Geneva produced no movement toward an Iraqi withdrawal. Aziz had refused even to accept a letter written by Bush to Saddam Hussein, saying the letter's language was "not compatible with the language that would be used in correspondence between heads of state." American officials said the letter called upon Saddam to withdraw from Kuwait and described the military capability of the international force arrayed against him. Bush later called Aziz's performance at the meeting "a total stiff-arm, a total rebuff." The Iraqi foreign minister's intransigence at the Geneva meeting had the unintended effect of solidifying support among some members of Congress for the president's threat to use force.

With the failure of the U.S.-Iraqi talks, United Nations Secretary General Javier Perez de Cuellar traveled to Baghdad for talks on Jan. 13 with Saddam Hussein. Perez de Cuellar reportedly offered to guarantee that the coalition would not attack Iraq or its troops if Saddam agreed to an immediate withdrawal from Kuwait. The secretary general also told Saddam that he would work to arrange an international peace conference on the Arab-Israeli conflict at an early date after the Gulf crisis was over. According to Perez de Cuellar, the Iraqi leader was not interested in any formula for peace that involved his unconditional withdrawal from Kuwait. After the meeting, the secretary general said of the chances for a diplomatic solution, "Unfortunately, I don't see any more reasons to be optimistic. I don't see any reason to have real hope."

Resolution Authorizing Use of Force

Following is the Congressional Record *text of the resolution (H J Res 77 — PL 102-1) authorizing the use of U.S. military force again Iraq, cleared by Congress on Jan. 12, 1991, and signed by President Bush on Jan. 14.*

To authorize the use of United States Armed Forces pursuant to United Nations Security Council resolution 678.

Whereas the Government of Iraq without provocation invaded and occupied the territory of Kuwait on August 2, 1990; and

Whereas both the House of Representatives (in H J Res 658 of the 101st Congress) and the Senate (in S Con Res 147 of the 101st Congress) have condemned Iraq's invasion of Kuwait and declared their support for international action to reverse Iraq's aggression; and

Whereas, Iraq's conventional, chemical, biological, and nuclear weapons and ballistic missile programs and its demonstrated willingness to use weapons of mass destruction pose a grave threat to world peace; and

Whereas the international community has demanded that Iraq withdraw unconditionally and immediately from Kuwait and that Kuwait's independence and legitimate government be restored; and

Whereas the U.N. Security Council repeatedly affirmed the inherent right of individual or collective self-defense in response to the armed attack by Iraq against Kuwait in accordance with Article 51 of the U.N. Charter; and

Whereas, in the absence of full compliance by Iraq with its resolutions, the U.N. Security Council in Resolution 678 has authorized member states of the United Nations to use all necessary means, after January 15, 1991, to uphold and implement all relevant Security Council resolutions and to restore international peace and security in the area; and

Whereas Iraq has persisted in its illegal occupation of, and brutal aggression against, Kuwait: Now, therefore be it

Resolved by the Senate and House of Representatives of the United States of America in Congress assembled,

Section 1. Short Title. This joint resolution may be cited as the "Authorization for Use of Military Force Against Iraq Resolution."

Section 2. Authorization for Use of United States Armed Forces

(a) AUTHORIZATION. — The President is authorized, subject to subsection (b), to use United States Armed Forces pursuant to United Nations Security Council Resolution 678 (1990) in order to achieve implementation of Security Council Resolutions 660, 661, 662, 664, 665, 666, 667, 669, 670, 674, and 677.

(b) REQUIREMENT FOR DETERMINATION THAT USE OF MILITARY FORCE IS NECESSARY. — Before exercising the authority granted in subsection (a), the President shall make available to the Speaker of the House of Representatives and the President pro tempore of the Senate his determination that —

(1) the United States has used all appropriate diplomatic and other peaceful means to obtain compliance by Iraq with the United Nations Security Council resolutions cited in subsection (a); and

(2) that those efforts have not been successful in obtaining such compliance.

(c) WAR POWERS RESOLUTION REQUIREMENTS. —

(1) SPECIFIC STATUTORY AUTHORIZATION. — Consistent with section 8(a)(1) of the War Powers Resolution, the Congress declares that this section is intended to constitute specific statutory authorization within the meaning of section 5(b) of the War Powers Resolution.

(2) APPLICABILITY OF OTHER REQUIREMENTS. — Nothing in this resolution supersedes any requirement of the War Powers Resolution.

Section 3. REPORTS TO CONGRESS.

At least once every 60 days, the President shall submit to the Congress a summary on the status of efforts to obtain compliance by Iraq with the resolutions adopted by the United Nations Security Council in response to Iraq's aggression.

Congressional Approval

By the first week in January, five months after the crisis in the Persian Gulf had begun, members had for months been demanding that Bush recognize their authority to declare war. Yet, less than two weeks before American troops could be ordered into combat, Congress had failed to assert its views beyond the language of vague resolutions and the clamor of inconclusive committee hearings.

"To cast the vote to place other Americans in the line of fire is the most humbling, painful decision I can imagine," said Sen. Joseph I. Lieberman, D-Conn. Virtually every lawmaker, in some fashion, echoed Lieberman's concern.

As the Senate fitfully began debate Jan. 4, Iraq accepted Bush's final offer for high-level talks scheduled for Jan. 9. A full-scale debate on a resolution to authorize force was postponed, but speeches on the floor of the Senate focused on the crisis. "We can no longer shun our responsibilities," said Tom Harkin, D-Iowa. "Each senator, each congressman must stand up and be counted."

Whether favoring or opposing the immediate use of force, the vast majority of members agreed on the basic fundamentals — that Saddam was a dangerous enemy of U.S. interests and that strong action had to be taken to counter his invasion of Kuwait. But many Democrats argued that war should be only a last resort. They insisted that sanctions might achieve the goal of removing Iraqi forces from Kuwait without war, if the sanctions were given enough time to work.

Senate Minority Leader Bob Dole, R-Kan., argued Bush's case that only a credible threat of military force would have a chance to cause Saddam to relent. "The best hope for peace is to strengthen the president's hand any way we can," Dole said.

The issue divided political allies. While Sen. Nunn called for delay, Sen. Charles S. Robb, D-Va., a fellow conservative Southern Democrat, supported the use of force. "We are now beyond the point of sanctions taking an indefinite period," he said.

Despite those divisions of opinion, a sense of a common purpose and a shared burden was pervasive as Congress finally began debating the war resolution on Jan. 10. Congressional anger at Saddam had grown after Aziz rebuffed Baker at their meeting in Geneva on Jan. 9. "He stiffed us," complained Rep. John P. Murtha, D-Pa. "We got an excellent illustration of Iraqi intransigence" at the meeting, said Sen. Christopher S. Bond, R-Mo.

During the dignified, often moving, congressional debate, some members offered prayers for the country, the president and the nearly 400,000 U.S. troops arrayed against Iraqi forces in the Persian Gulf region. Gephardt said before the final vote in the House, "Whatever our decision, we will leave this room one again and whole again."

Senate Vote. In the weeks before the vote, a contingent of Senate Democrats supporting Bush had begun to take shape. The administration cobbled together a group of 10 Senate Democrats (three more than needed) to support S J Res 2 — which authorized the use of force against Iraq. These Democrats were: Johnston; Lieberman; Robb; John B. Breaux, La.; Richard H. Bryan, Nev.; Al Gore, Tenn.; Bob Graham, Fla.; Howell Heflin, Ala.; Harry Reid, Nev.; and Richard C. Shelby, Ala. All but two Republican senators — Charles E. Grassley, Iowa; and Mark O. Hatfield, Ore. — voted for the resolution.

Senators Mitchell and Nunn offered a competing resolution (S J Res 1), which called for a continued reliance on economic sanctions. With the exception of Hatfield, who voted against both resolutions, those senators voting for one of the resolutions voted against the other. On Jan. 12, senators rose from their seats one after the other to vocally declare "yea" or "nay." First, S J Res 1 was defeated 46-53. Then S J Res 2 was passed on a **key vote of 52-47 (R 42-2; D 10-45)**, giving Bush the authority to use "all means necessary" to expel Iraq from Kuwait. *(1991 key votes, p. 1061)*

House Vote. In the House, the administration had a much more comfortable margin entering the debate. The opponents of the resolution authorizing force were led by Speaker Foley, but Democrats split sharply on the question of going to war.

With prominent Democrats such as House Armed Services Committee Chairman Aspin and high-ranking Foreign Affairs Committee member Stephen J. Solarz, D-N.Y., strongly in favor of the use of force, rank-and-file Democrats were less concerned about taking a position contrary to the House Democratic leadership. Aspin had gone so far as to predict on Jan. 8 that coalition forces would likely defeat Iraqi forces in less than a month and with relatively few casualties. He predicted 3,000 to 5,000 American casualties, with 500 to 1,000 dead.

Solarz, who cosponsored the resolution authorizing the use of force with Minority Leader Robert H. Michel, R-Ill., worked to bring together disparate Democrats to support the president. Among the 86 Democrats who backed the House resolution authorizing force, H J Res 77, were committee chairmen Dan Rostenkowski, Ill., and John D. Dingell, Mich. The language of H J Res 77 was identical to that of S J Res 2.

Because the issue was deemed "a conscience vote" by the leadership, promises were made of no recriminations against those who voted with the administration. But one supporter of the Solarz-Michel resolution, Howard L. Berman, D-Calif., predicted a party rift that might last for some time. "It won't heal until the crisis is resolved," he said in an interview before the vote.

On Jan. 12, the resolution urging continued reliance on sanctions (H Con Res 33), which was cosponsored by Gephardt, and Hamilton fell on a vote of 183-250. H J Res 77 passed the House that same day on a **250-183 (R 164-3; D 86-179; I 0-1) key vote**. The Senate then passed the joint resolution by voice vote. Bush signed it (PL 102-1) on Jan. 14. *(Text of joint resolution, box, p. 309)*

Most members of Congress who voted against using force said after the votes that given that Congress had expressed its will, they would support the president and U.S. troops.

War in the Gulf

On the morning of Tuesday, Jan. 15, Bush signed an executive order authorizing an aerial offensive against Iraq that would begin the following night unless a diplomatic breakthrough occurred before the deadline passed at midnight EST Jan. 15. Wednesday afternoon, Defense Secretary Cheney ordered the U.S. commander in Saudi Arabia, Gen. H. Norman Schwarzkopf, to launch the attack. The coalition's strategy was to wage an extended air campaign against strategic targets in Iraq and Kuwait. Coalition military leaders were confident that they could quickly establish air supremacy over the badly outmatched Iraqi air force. Coalition warplanes could then methodically destroy Saddam Hussein's military machine and soften Iraqi defenses, so that when a ground offensive was launched, fewer coalition casualties would be suffered.

The Bombing Campaign

The offensive against Iraq — known as Operation Desert Storm — began when the first coalition planes left Saudi airfields at 12:50 a.m. Saudi time Jan. 17 (4:50 p.m. EST Jan. 16 — less than 17 hours after the U.N. deadline passed). At about the same time, U.S. warships in the Persian Gulf launched a barrage of Tomahawk cruise missiles, which fly at subsonic speeds close to the ground toward their targets.

Shortly after 7:00 p.m. EST (3:00 a.m. Iraqi time), White House spokesman Marlin Fitzwater announced, "The liberation of Kuwait has begun." Two hours later, Bush addressed the nation from the Oval Office. He said Saddam Hussein's intransigence left "no choice but to drive Saddam from Kuwait by force. We will not fail."

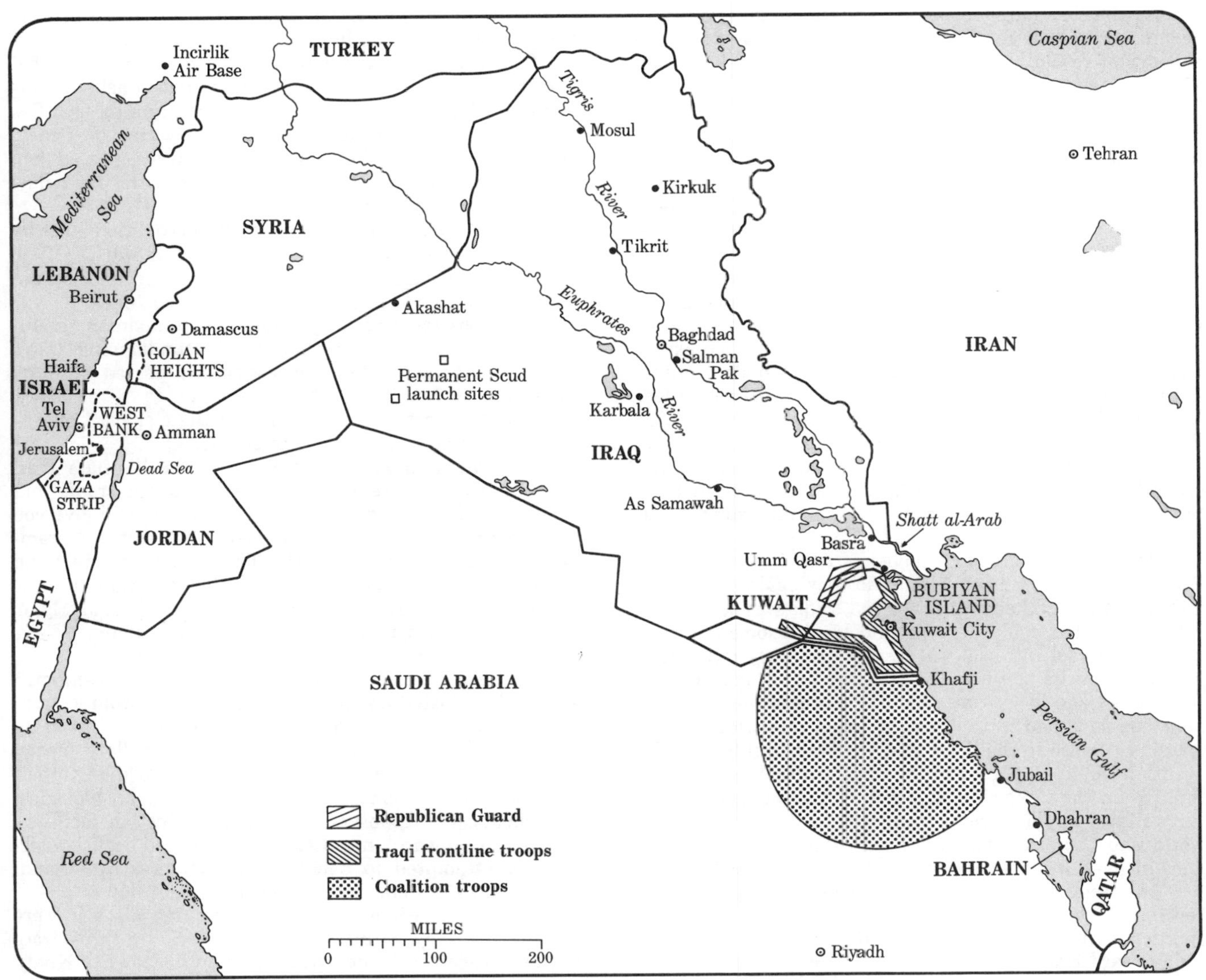

Before the Gulf war began, coalition ground forces were concentrated opposite Iraqi fortifications along the Saudi-Kuwaiti border. Iraqi commanders hoped to bloody the attackers as they tried to breach frontline minefields and obstacles. Republican Guard units were stationed behind Iraqi lines with the mission of responding to coalition breakthroughs. The Iraqis intended to draw Israel into the conflict by firing Scud surface-to-surface missiles at the Jewish state from fixed launch sites and mobile missile launchers positioned in Western Iraq. After the bombing campaign began, the coalition secretly moved much of its attacking ground forces west to positions along the Saudi-Iraqi border, which Iraq had left almost undefended.

American, British, Saudi and Kuwaiti warplanes participated in the first wave of bombing. They were soon joined by French and Italian aircraft. The coalition had assembled more than 2,000 planes in the Persian Gulf theater. Coalition air forces would average about 2,000 sorties (one round-trip mission by one plane) per day during Desert Storm.

The first wave of bombing was highly successful. It disrupted Iraqi command, control and communications abilities; severely damaged Iraq's nuclear, chemical and biological weapons facilities; suppressed many Iraqi anti-aircraft radars and weapons; and grounded most of the Iraqi air force by damaging major air fields. Despite knowing that an attack could be imminent, the Iraqi military appeared to have been surprised.

At a press briefing Jan. 16, Cheney said: "I will simply say that preliminary reports we have received in terms of the success of the operation — and that includes the possibility of casualties — have been very, very encouraging."

On Jan. 17, Congress moved to construct resolutions supporting U.S. forces. Foley and Mitchell wanted to signal the unity of the country during a time of crisis. "I think it's not inappropriate at this time to demonstrate that, regardless of the debate last week, that the Congress stands behind the armed services," said Foley. Democrats were particularly anxious to record their support in light of the divisions that had surfaced in the prewar debate. But many in the party also wanted to stop short of lauding Bush, in part because they sharply disagreed with him on a range of domestic issues. Senate Republicans, however, sought a resolution that would highlight Bush's performance as prominently as possible.

At the last minute, Democrats grudgingly agreed to "commend" Bush for his performance in the war. The concurrent resolution (S Con Res 2), passed 98-0 on Jan. 17, "commends and supports the efforts and leadership of the president as Commander in Chief in the Persian Gulf hostilities," and it "unequivocally supports the men and women of our Armed Forces."

In the House on Jan. 18, differences also were aired over whether to single out Bush for praise. But members approved the resolution 399-6 with six members voting "present."

Scud Attacks. Early on Jan. 18, the Iraqis struck back amid the unrelenting allied bombing campaign by launching toward Israel a salvo of Soviet-made surface-to-surface Scud missiles armed with conventional high-explosive warheads. Eight Scuds struck the Jewish state, injuring more than a dozen people, though no one was killed. Later in the day, the Iraqis launched a Scud missile at Saudi Arabia. A U.S. Patriot anti-missile missile intercepted and destroyed the Scud before it reached the ground. During the coming weeks, Iraq would fire dozens of Scuds at Israel and Saudi Arabia from mobile launchers in Iraq.

Because of their small payloads and inaccuracy, the Scuds could not be used with efficiency against coalition military targets. Their utility for the Iraqis was as a political weapon that could demonstrate Iraqi resolve and perhaps lure Israel into the war. Israel's military reputation was based on its consistent retaliation for attacks against its territory and its citizens. Saddam was counting on Israel behaving as it had in the past. If Israel retaliated against Iraq in response to the Scud attacks, Arab members of the coalition would be placed in the uncomfortable position of fighting on the same side as Israel. Israeli participation in the war also would increase sympathy for Iraq in the Arab world and thereby intensify the domestic political problems of Arab leaders supporting the anti-Iraq effort.

An Israeli entry into the war against Iraq could conceivably have unraveled Bush's careful diplomacy and splintered the anti-Iraq coalition. Regardless of their attitude toward Iraq, Arab states were united in their opposition to and distrust of Israel. No Arab leader would want to be perceived by his people as fighting alongside Israel against an Arab country.

Several members of Congress, including Rep. Hamilton, chairman of the Foreign Affairs Subcommittee on Europe and the Middle East, expressed the belief that an Israeli attack would not unravel the coalition. "The coalition is much firmer than that," said Hamilton. But no one could be certain.

Keeping Israel Out of the War. Consequently, the Bush administration vigorously pressed the Israeli government to stay out of the war. Bush promised Israeli leaders that mobile Scud missile batteries in Iraq would be a top priority target of U.S. pilots. He also dispatched Patriot missile batteries and their U.S. crews to Israel. This deployment represented the first time that U.S. forces had ever been stationed in Israel. The Israeli government declared that the U.S. troops would remain only until Israeli units could be trained to operate the Patriot batteries.

Israeli leaders continued to hint that they might retaliate, but despite frequent Scud attacks, Israel stayed out of the war. Israeli leaders understood that, because Saddam Hussein's purpose in attacking Israel was to draw Israel into the war, an Israeli retaliation would be playing into his hands. In addition, an Israeli attack against Iraq would have had only marginal strategic value, as Iraq was already being pounded by the huge coalition air force.

The House and the Senate weighed in on Israel's behalf, passing resolutions that commended Israel's performance during the crisis. The House resolution (H Con Res 41) "condemns the unprovoked attack by Iraq on Israel" and "commends Israel for its restraint." It was passed Jan. 23 by a vote of 416-0. The Senate acted the next day, approving a similar resolution (S Con Res 4), 99-0.

Allied Prisoners. Iraq angered the coalition allies by producing videotapes of allied prisoners of war (POWs), some of whom appeared battered and dazed as they denounced the U.S. attacks on Iraq in stilted tones.

Congress responded by approving companion resolutions (H Con Res 48, S Con Res 5) condemning Iraq's treatment of the POWs. The resolutions, passed 418-0 by the House on Jan. 23 and 99-0 by the Senate the next day, declared Iraqi actions in violation of the Geneva Conventions governing treatment of prisoners.

Sen. McCain, who was a POW in the Vietnam War, said the resolution sent a clear message to the Iraqis that they would be treated as war criminals: "We will give you the same punishment that was meted out at the Nuremberg trials after World War II." The attacks on Israel and the videotapes of allied prisoners combined to puncture the early giddy optimism in Congress. "Some euphoria early on ... is turning pragmatic now," said Sen. Graham. "We're facing a very large and experienced adversary."

Effects of the Bombing. The bombing campaign against Iraq lasted 38 days. The bombings disrupted Iraqi communications, grounded the Iraqi air force, cut Iraqi supply lines, destroyed many tanks and artillery pieces, caused up to 30 percent of Iraqi troops to desert their positions and obliterated most of Iraq's nuclear, biological and chemical weapons research and production facilities. The few Iraqi warplanes that had challenged coalition aircraft or attempted to penetrate air defenses over Saudi Arabia and the Persian Gulf had been shot down.

Iraqi frustrations with the continuing air war were demonstrated by a futile armored attack by three Iraqi battalions against the deserted Saudi border town of Khafji on Jan. 29. The Iraqis succeeded in occupying Khafji, but after two days of fighting coalition forces recaptured the town along with more than 400 Iraqi prisoners.

In desperation, Iraq also sent dozens of its planes to the safety of airfields in Iran. The Iraqi leadership apparently hoped that the planes could be recovered after the war, or perhaps later in the present conflict. Iran declared that it would not return the planes to Iraq until the war was over. After the war, however, Teheran announced that it would keep the planes.

Despite the destruction experienced by Iraq, the coalition air war had not forced an Iraqi capitulation. Nor had it triggered an internal Iraqi uprising against Saddam Hussein's regime. If coalition forces were going to reclaim Kuwait, they would have to do it on the ground.

Ground War

Military experts predicted that the Iraqi army would be a much more formidable opponent than the Iraqi air force. Saddam Hussein had pinned his hopes of bloodying the attackers on the ground phase of the battle. Iraqi forces in the Kuwait theater were estimated at approximately 540,000 troops (after the war, U.S. military officers with access to revised intelligence reports said that the number

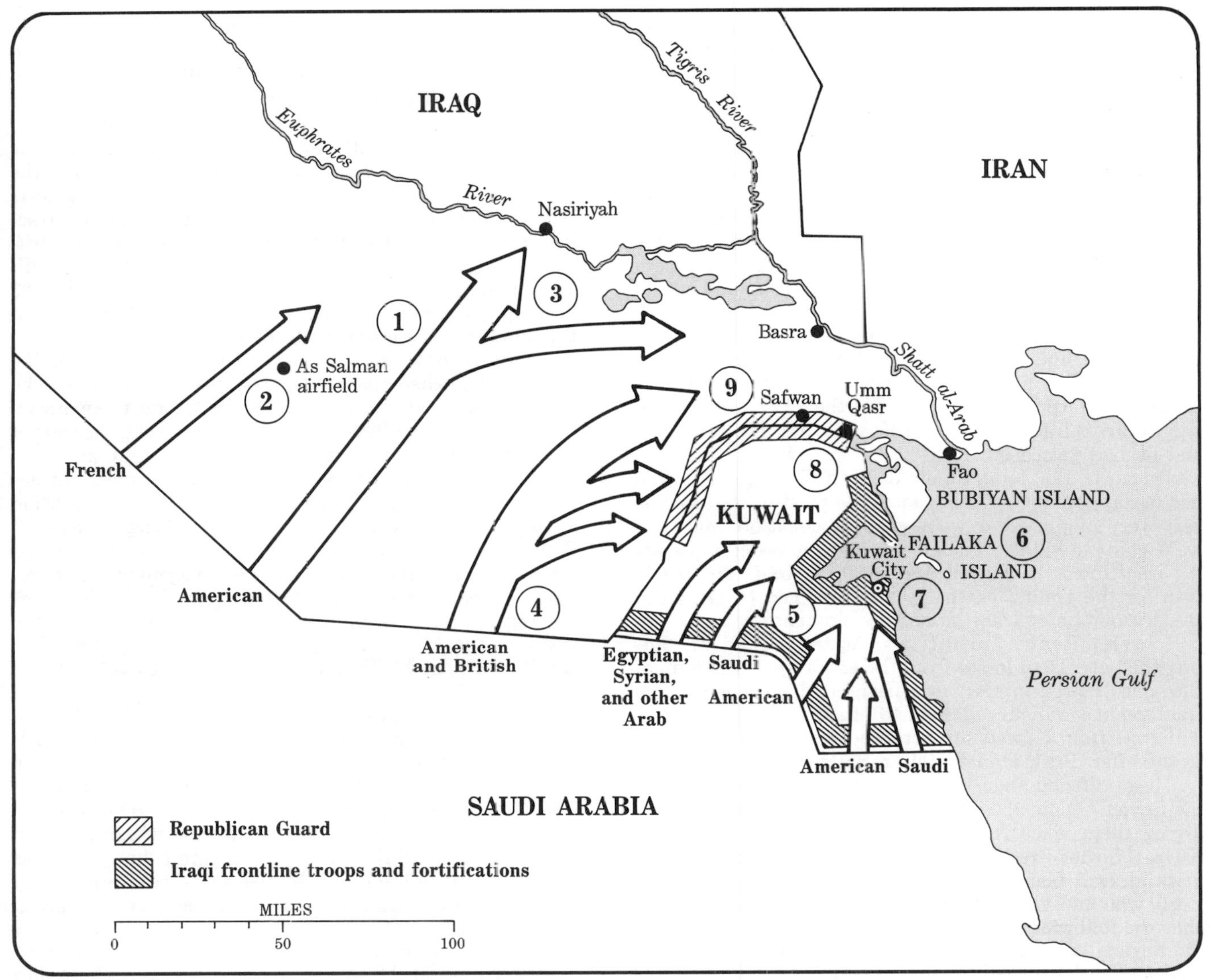

The coalition ground attack that liberated Kuwait began at 4:00 a.m. Saudi time Feb. 24, 1991, and lasted 100 hours until 8:00 a.m. Feb. 28, when the cease-fire declared by President Bush went into effect.

1. American special forces landed deep behind Iraqi lines before the attack was launched to provide strategic reconnaissance.

2. A French division supported by an American brigade destroyed an Iraqi division near As Satman airfield and established defensive positions to guard the western flank of attacking coalition forces.

3. The U.S. Army's 18th Airborne Corps (containing three-and-a-half divisions) launched a lightning attack toward the Euphrates River city of Nasiriyah. By the evening of Feb. 25, American forces had reached the river and severed the main highway leading north to Baghdad, effectively cutting off the Iraqi army in Kuwait and southern Iraq.

4. The U.S. Army's Seventh Corps (containing five divisions) and the First British Armored Division drove into Iraq and turned toward Kuwait and the Basra region.

5. Saudi, Egyptian, Syrian, Kuwait and other Arab forces, along with two U.S. Marine divisions and a U.S. Army brigade, breached Iraqi frontline defenses along the Saudi-Kuwaiti border and converged on Kuwait City.

6. An 18,000-troop U.S. Marine force remained in naval vessels positioned off Kuwait. The Marines feigned a helicopter-borne assault on the Kuwaiti coast to convince Iraqi coastline defenders that an amphibious landing was imminent. Approximately 125,000 Iraqis defending Kuwaiti beaches waited for an attack that would never come.

7. Saudi and Kuwaiti troops supported by U.S. Marines entered Kuwait City on Feb. 27. Most Iraqi troops had abandoned the city the day before. Coalition forces found Kuwaiti resistance fighters already in control of much of the capital.

8. Iraqi troops attempting to flee Kuwait were attacked by coalition pilots who jammed roads by bombing vehicles at the front and rear of Iraqi convoys headed north. Coalition air attacks on Feb. 26 reportedly left more than 1,000 Iraqi vehicles destroyed or disabled on the main highway north of Kuwait City.

9. In the climax to the ground offensive, American and British forces engaged Iraqi Republican Guard units in a might actually have been as few as 350,000). Any force this large had the potential to inflict thousands of coalition casualties, even if it had been bombed for five-and-a-half weeks. The coalition had assembled nearly 700,000 troops in and around Saudi Arabia, but fewer than 400,000 would be directly involved in the attack against the Iraqis. The Iraqis also had the advantage of defending heavily fortified positions. Finally, the Iraqis might use their stocks of chemical weapons against the attackers as they had done effectively during the Iran-Iraq war. Coalition forces were equipped with high-quality protective gear and were very mobile, but chemical attacks were dangerous and would slow the pace of any battle.

The official goal of the coalition offensive against Iraq had been the liberation of Kuwait. But Bush and the other coalition leaders hoped to destroy Hussein's army in the process. The coalition battle plan, therefore, sought not only to drive Iraqi forces from Kuwait, but also to cut off and destroy retreating Iraqi units. In a Jan. 23 briefing, Chairman of the Joint Chiefs of Staff Gen. Colin Powell had declared bluntly, "Our strategy to go after this army is very, very simple. First, we're going to cut it off, and then we're going to kill it." The air war had succeeded in isolating Iraqi forces in Kuwait and southern Iraq. The battle plan for the ground campaign was designed to maximize the destruction of Iraqi military equipment.

Soviet Peace Initiatives. As the ground war approached and Iraqi losses from the air campaign mounted, Baghdad showed interest in a negotiated settlement. The Iraqi regime announced Feb. 15 that it was willing to withdraw from Kuwait but attached numerous conditions to the offer. Bush immediately rejected the proposal.

Iraqi officials then turned for mediation assistance to the Soviet Union, their longtime patron, which had been urging them since August to withdraw peacefully from Kuwait. Soviet President Mikhail S. Gorbachev presented a withdrawal plan to Foreign Minister Aziz on Feb. 18. Bush, who had been informed of its contents, told Gorbachev the following day that it was inadequate. On Feb. 21, the Soviets announced that Iraq had accepted a modified Soviet plan that called for a "full and unconditional Iraqi withdrawal" from Kuwait. The six-point proposal, however, failed to meet a growing list of U.S. conditions for an end to the war, including Iraqi willingness to pay reparations to Kuwait, disclose the location of all mines and abide by all Security Council resolutions related to the Persian Gulf War. The Bush administration also insisted that Iraqi forces withdraw from Kuwait within one week so that they would be unable to take all of their equipment with them. The Soviet plan allowed the Iraqis three weeks to leave.

Many lawmakers viewed the Soviet-Iraqi discussions with suspicion, fearing that they would only lead to a compromise that would allow Saddam to rebuild his military machine after the war. "What the coalition could not stand is Iraq bringing all of its arms back over the border — sitting there, prepared to menace Kuwait and Saudi Arabia in perpetuity as we moved out," said Sen. Richard G. Lugar, R-Ind. Rep. Aspin asserted that the Iraqi army "is on the verge of collapse. This is not the time for us to lose our nerve and compromise ... to allow Saddam to 'save face.' "

Increasingly confident that a coalition ground campaign (which was ready to be launched) would be successful, Bush moved to head off further Iraqi peace proposals that he feared could divide the coalition by offering terms that came close to, but fell short of, meeting all coalition demands. On Feb. 22, he announced that Saddam Hussein had until noon EST Feb. 23 to begin a withdrawal and accept "publicly and authoritatively" all coalition requirements for a cease-fire. The U.S. conditions were designed to allow Saddam no room to save face if he accepted them. They mandated a swift and humiliating retreat that the Bush administration hoped would disgrace Saddam in the eyes of his supporters in Iraq and the Arab world. Reports that Iraqi troops had begun committing systematic atrocities in Kuwait and setting Kuwaiti oil wells ablaze stiffened coalition resolve to launch the ground war immediately if Hussein did not agree to Bush's terms. The Feb. 23 deadline passed without signs of an Iraqi withdrawal, and Bush ordered the offensive to proceed.

100 Hours. At 4:00 a.m. Saudi time Feb. 24, the coalition launched its coordinated ground offensive. The assault would last exactly 100 hours. A huge American, British and French force had been moved far to the west of Iraq's frontline fortifications. With the Iraqi air force grounded by the coalition air forces, Iraqi leaders did not know the redeployment had taken place. The coalition force penetrated deep into Iraq at a blitzkrieg pace. With French forces guarding their left flank, American troops reached the Euphrates River during the evening of Feb. 25. Because coalition bombers had destroyed bridges across the Euphrates, Iraqi units could not escape the coalition envelopment. Meanwhile, American, Saudi, Egyptian, Syrian, Kuwaiti and other Arab forces quickly breached Iraq's supposedly formidable frontline fortifications. These forces pushed toward Kuwait City, taking tens of thousands of Iraqi prisoners along the way. *(Battle plan, map, p. 313)*

With his army collapsing, Saddam Hussein delivered a radio speech on Feb. 26 announcing an Iraqi withdrawal from Kuwait. Saddam maintained a defiant tone, suggesting that the Iraqi retreat was a strategic withdrawal and telling Iraqis that "Kuwait is part of your country and was carved from it in the past." Most Iraqi forces were already engaged in a disorganized retreat by the time the speech was broadcast.

The American and British forces that had penetrated deep into Iraq in the west drove eastward Feb. 26 toward elite Republican Guard divisions trapped below the Euphrates River. In the ensuing battles during the next two days, coalition troops decimated Saddam's best forces, destroying hundreds of tanks, trucks and artillery pieces. American Marines and Arab coalition troops marched into Kuwait City Feb. 27. They found that all but a few stranded Iraqis had fled the capital the previous day. Kuwaiti resistance fighters and citizens welcomed home Kuwaiti troops who led the coalition march into the city.

Throughout the ground campaign, many Iraqi soldiers surrendered as soon as they encountered coalition troops or after giving only token resistance. The bombing campaign had destroyed the equipment and supplies of many units, cut their communications with their military commanders and left them virtually blind to coalition troop movements. Some Iraqi soldiers did not even have water.

The coalition ground attack left the Iraqi army in disarray. Approximately 63,000 Iraqis were taken prisoner and between 25,000 and 100,000 were killed or wounded, according to widely varying unofficial coalition estimates.

Lt. Gen. Sir Peter de la Billiere, the commander of the British forces in Saudi Arabia, called coalition casualties "the smallest number for the size of the campaign in the history of warfare." Only 125 Americans were killed in combat during the war. Another 202 were killed in accidents related to operations in the Middle East between Aug. 2, 1990, and the end of hostilities. In addition, 357 Americans were wounded.

Ending the War

At 9:00 p.m. EST Feb. 27, Bush declared in a televised address, "Kuwait is liberated. Iraq's army is defeated. Our military objectives are met." He announced that coalition forces would cease offensive operations three hours later at midnight EST (8:00 a.m. Feb. 28 in the battle zone). Bush said a permanent cease-fire would require the Iraqis to accept all Security Council resolutions pertaining to the Persian Gulf crisis, release all prisoners of war and Kuwaiti hostages, and disclose the locations of mines. Iraqi commanders also were required to meet with coalition military leaders within 48 hours to work out the military details of the cease-fire.

Earlier on Feb. 27, a letter from Foreign Minister Aziz to the U.N. Security Council had declared Iraq's willingness to observe all Security Council resolutions. On March 3, Gen. Schwarzkopf met with Iraqi military representatives, who agreed to abide by all coalition conditions for the military cease-fire. By March 5, Iraq had released all coalition prisoners of war.

Democrats in Congress, most of whom had voted in January against authorizing Bush to use force against Iraq, joined Republicans in a chorus of congratulations for the president and the troops. Ebullient lawmakers proposed everything from honoring returning troops with a ticker-tape parade in Manhattan to inviting Gen. Schwarzkopf to address a joint session of Congress. All of that happened, and more, to celebrate the victory.

Bush drew some of the most effusive praise. "This man is due every bit of respect this Congress has to offer," said Rep. Bob McEwen, R-Ohio. In an interview, Sen. Patrick J. Leahy, D-Vt., said he "had never seen a president in a stronger position" during his 17 years in Congress. At the invitation of congressional leaders, Bush addressed a joint session of Congress on March 6. He received exuberant ovations from members waving small U.S. flags. "As president," Bush said, "I can report to the nation: Aggression is defeated. The war is over."

As Bush was receiving praise from many lawmakers, the Senate recommended that his counterpart, Saddam Hussein, be the subject of a war crimes tribunal. On March 14, the Senate adopted, 97-0, a resolution (S Res 76) by Arlen Specter, R-Pa., urging the president to consult with other nations to establish a war crimes tribunal that would prosecute Saddam and his deputies.

Aftermath of the War

By most measures, the U.S.-led coalition's war against Iraq was enormously successful. Kuwait was liberated and the legitimate Kuwaiti government was restored to power; coalition forces sustained fewer casualties than almost anyone predicted; Iraq's offensive military potential and nuclear weapons research facilities suffered a serious setback; the wave of terrorism that Saddam Hussein had threatened to loose upon his enemies had not appeared; and the international community had demonstrated that it could collectively respond to aggression.

However, the victory was less complete than it might otherwise have been because Saddam Hussein managed to retain power despite the ravages his leadership had brought to his country. His repression of dissent, frequent purges of the military and his Ba'ath Party, and efforts to prevent anyone from accumulating too much power had blocked the emergence of rival centers of power in Baghdad that could lead a coup against him. Though toppling Saddam had never been a stated purpose of the coalition military effort, his continued belligerence toward his own people and the international community created perceptions that Bush stopped the war too soon.

The Bush administration and the United Nations settled into the task of containing a weakened, but still dangerous, Iraq. In the months after the Gulf War, the United Nations maintained stringent, U.S.-backed economic sanctions against Iraq, and its inspectors engaged in a long-running struggle to force Saddam to reveal and relinquish the elements of his massive effort to develop nuclear, chemical and biological weapons.

Second Guessing. On March 27, newspapers published excerpts from an interview on public television with Gen. Schwarzkopf, who asserted that Bush had called an end to the ground war on Feb. 27 despite the general's recommendation to press ahead with the attack.

"Frankly, my recommendation had been ... [to] continue the march," Schwarzkopf said. "I mean, we had them in a rout, and we could have continued to ... wreak great destruction upon them. We could have completely closed the door and made it in fact a battle of annihilation. And the president ... made the decision that ... we should stop at a given time, at a given place; that did leave some escape routes open for them to get back out."

But Schwarzkopf immediately added, "I think it was a very humane decision and a very courageous decision on his part also because ... it's one of those ones that historians are going to second-guess ... forever."

The administration moved quickly to deny Schwarzkopf's account. Defense Secretary Cheney issued a terse statement indicating that before Bush decided to order an end to combat, "the president and I spoke personally with Gen. Schwarzkopf that evening to congratulate him on the outstanding success of the campaign. He raised no objection to terminating hostilities."

But with Saddam still in power, the president's decision to end the war continued to be questioned by the press and rival politicians. Bush's opponents coupled his decision to end the war early with his administration's failure to oppose Saddam before the Iraqi invasion of Kuwait to take some of the luster off his performance as commander in chief.

Even in defeat, Saddam managed to create headaches for the United States and the international community by refusing to cooperate fully with nuclear weapons inspectors sent to Iraq under the terms of the cease-fire agreement. Iraq's conventional military strength had been sharply reduced by the war, but policy makers worried that if it acquired a nuclear weapon it could again menace the region. Inspectors determined that Iraq's program to develop nuclear bombs was far more extensive and advanced than the Bush administration or independent experts had predicted before the war.

In a public television interview broadcast Jan. 3, 1992, Bush maintained that the United Nations' objective in ousting Iraq from Kuwait had been achieved. He rejected the persistent criticism that the war should have been extended until Saddam had been eliminated.

Bush said that a "march to Baghdad" to overthrow Saddam would have split the U.S.-led coalition and could

Contributions to the Multinational Coalition

Argentina. 100 troops, two transport planes and two warships.
Australia. Two warships and one supply ship.
Bangladesh. 6,000 troops.
Belgium. Two mine sweepers, one supply ship, three other ships and six transport planes.
Bulgaria. Medical personnel.
Canada. Two warships, one supply ship, 18 combat aircraft and 12 other planes.
Czechoslovakia. 200 chemical defense troops and 150 medical personnel.
Denmark. One ship.
Egypt. 30,000 troops and 400 tanks.
France. 17,000 troops, 350 tanks, 38 combat aircraft and 14 ships.
Germany. Five mine sweepers and three other ships in the eastern Mediterranean and 18 warplanes in Turkey as part of a defensive NATO deployment.
Great Britain. 35,000 troops, 120 tanks, 60 combat aircraft and 18 ships.
Greece. One ship.
Gulf Cooperation Council (Saudi Arabia, Bahrain, Oman, United Arab Emirates, Qatar and Kuwait). Combined force of 10,000 frontline troops. Each country also made individual contributions of planes and ships.
Kuwait. 7,000 frontline troops and 34 combat aircraft.
Italy. Four mine sweepers, six other ships and eight combat aircraft.
Morocco. 2,000 troops.
Netherlands. Three warships and 18 combat aircraft.
New Zealand. Two transport planes and medical personnel.
Niger. 480 troops.
Norway. One support ship.
Pakistan. 2,000 troops in Saudi Arabia and 3,000 troops in the United Arab Emirates.
Poland. Medical personnel and one hospital ship.
Portugal. One transport ship.
Saudi Arabia. 66,000 troops (20,000 serving at the frontlines), 550 tanks, 300 planes (about 135 of which were modern combat aircraft) and eight ships.
Senegal. 500 troops.
Soviet Union. Four ships on patrol in the region but not involved in coalition operations.
Spain. Three warships.
Sweden. Medical personnel.
Syria. 19,000 troops deployed in Saudi Arabia, 50,000 deployed along the Iraqi-Syrian border and 270 tanks.
Turkey. 100,000 troops deployed along the Iraqi-Turkish border, two warships stationed in the Persian Gulf and seven ships in the eastern Mediterranean.
United States. 430,000 troops, 2,000 tanks, 1,800 combat aircraft and more than 100 ships (including six aircraft carriers).

Note: Figures are as of Jan. 15, 1991, and include ships stationed in the Red Sea and the eastern Mediterranean.
Sources: Associated Press; Center for Defense Information; *The Economist*; *New York Times*; *Time*; and *Washington Post.*

have bogged down the United States in a lengthy conflict. "I don't want to send young men into a war where I can't see that they're going to prevail and prevail rapidly," he said.

Iraqi Rebellions

Soon after the cease-fire with the U.S.-led coalition forces was declared, Iraq was torn by civil violence. Realizing that much of the Iraqi military's best equipment and some of its best units had been destroyed, Kurdish resistance fighters in northern Iraq and Shi'ite Muslim rebels in southern Iraq began waging open warfare against Iraqi troops loyal to Saddam.

The two rebel movements had divergent goals. The Kurds, an estimated 20 percent of Iraq's population, had fought Baghdad's rulers for decades in pursuit of greater autonomy. The Iraqi Kurdistan Front, a coalition of the two largest Kurdish parties, wanted to establish an independent Kurdish state in northern Iraq. The Shi'ites, who comprise a majority of Iraq's population (Saddam Hussein is a Sunni Muslim), hoped to overthrow Saddam and establish a Shi'ite government in Baghdad. They were less organized than the Kurds, but they were receiving support from Iran's Shi'ite government.

With the war for Kuwait over, Saddam Hussein ordered what was left of his military to put down the rebellions.

During the Persian Gulf War, Bush had repeatedly said he would welcome the overthrow of Saddam. Many commentators noted that his statements may have contributed to the confidence of Iraqi rebels that the United States would come to their aid. But during the postwar insurrections, Bush emphasized that he had never promised to intervene in Iraq's "internal affairs."

"We're not going to get sucked into this by sending precious American lives into this battle," Bush said April 4, 1991. "We have fulfilled our obligations."

But when the Iraqi army brutally turned back the Kurdish and Shi'ite rebellions, large numbers of Kurd and Shi'ite refugees were placed in peril. The Bush administration took limited measures designed to prevent a human disaster.

On April 5, Bush announced that U.S. cargo planes would drop food and other relief supplies to Kurdish refugees thronging the mountains along Iraq's border with Turkey. He also earmarked $11 million in relief funds for victims of the Persian Gulf War and for refugees from the failed uprisings against Saddam. The Bush administration announced April 10 that it had warned Iraq the previous weekend to keep its military forces away from a large section of northern Iraq where relief agencies were trying to aid hundreds of thousands of Kurdish refugees.

Democratic critics in Congress, some of whom had originally opposed going to war, urged Bush to take more effective steps to protect the Kurds, including banning Iraqi armed helicopter flights. The anti-Iraq coalition had prohibited any use of Iraqi combat airplanes since the end of the Gulf War, but flights by armed helicopters had not been banned. Bush remarked on April 11 that those urging him to use force had been among the "severest critics" when he was preparing for war against Saddam. That day the Senate approved by voice vote a resolution (S Res 99) urging "sustained humanitarian" relief for Iraq's refugees.

Bush announced on April 16 that U.S., British and French forces would go back into Iraq to aid the Kurdish refugees. The administration said that U.S. troops, running supply operations out of Turkey, would construct tent cities in dry, relatively low terrain and then would encourage and assist the movement to those sites of hundreds of thousands of Kurds huddled in cold, inaccessible mountain encampments near the Turkish border.

The deployment of an estimated 16,000 U.S., British and French troops in the resettlement operation risked Bush's commitment to avoid interference in Iraq's internal affairs. But Bush justified the deployment saying, "I think the humanitarian concern . . . is so overwhelming that there will be a lot of understanding about this."

Democrats generally backed Bush's decision to aid the Kurds despite the risk of an open-ended entanglement. House Foreign Affairs Committee Chairman Dante B. Fascell, D-Fla., said, "There simply are moments when action must be taken and the consequences sorted out later. With more than 1,000 Kurds dying each day and hundreds of thousands starving on the frigid mountainsides, there is no question that such a moment had arrived."

Iraq denounced the U.S. plan April 18 as an interference in its internal affairs. But the same day, it agreed under pressure to a U.N. plan to conduct relief efforts inside Iraq.

On April 25, the administration sent Congress a letter formally requesting a $150.5 million supplemental appropriation to underwrite Operation Provide Comfort, as the administration's refugee relief effort was called.

In late April, the United States broadened the scope of its relief efforts, providing direct aid for the first time to an estimated 1 million people who had fled from southern Iraq into neighboring Iran. Allied forces also greatly expanded the size of a security zone established for hundreds of thousands of Kurdish refugees. The allies, encountering no resistance from Iraqi forces, created a safe haven for the refugees that encompassed more than 1,800 square miles in northern Iraq.

During the week of April 29, Kurds began to leave their squalid encampments in the mountains, some returning to their villages and others staying in a camp constructed by allied troops. But the slow process was complicated by the Kurds' lingering fear that Saddam still threatened their survival.

On May 22, Congress sent the president a $572 million supplemental appropriations bill for fiscal 1991 (HR 2251) that included $556 million in disaster and refugee relief aid, much of it for the Kurdish aid effort. The conference report (H Rept 102-71) was adopted in the House 387-33. The Senate adopted it by voice vote, completing congressional action. Bush signed the bill (PL 102-55) on June 13.

Special Report: End of the Cold War

Upon the Dec. 25, 1991, resignation of Soviet President Mikhail S. Gorbachev, the Union of Soviet Socialist Republics (USSR) was brought to an end. Minutes after Gorbachev's televised announcement, the red Soviet flag with its hammer and sickle was replaced on the Kremlin flagpole by the Russian tricolored flag. The huge Eurasian nation, which was the wellspring of the international Communist movement and the Western world's main adversary, ceased to exist. It was replaced by 15 nations that had been union republics under the Soviet system.

Eleven of the 15 countries agreed to form an entity that came to be known as the Commonwealth of Independent States (CIS). But it was soon clear that the CIS was not to be a smaller version of the Soviet Union or even an effective confederation. The CIS merely provided a forum for coordinating some policies and resolving some disputes. The 15 nations of the former Soviet Union moved rapidly toward establishing their own national governments and identities.

The largest of the new states was Russia, which had dominated the Soviet Union politically, economically and culturally. In Russia, the first among equals in the CIS, a new leadership under popularly elected president Boris N. Yeltsin advanced a reform program based on the free market and democracy. The Communist Party was banned, and the dismantling of the central economic apparatus was well under way. After 74 years of building communism, Russia had completely abandoned its official ideology and its government embraced what appeared to be very Western economic and political institutions.

The remarkable transformation of the Soviet Union was felt throughout the world. International politics ceased to be dominated by the confrontation between the United States and the Soviet Union. For almost half a century, the foremost objective of American national security policy was containing and countering Soviet aggression and expansion. The presence of a rival superpower devoted to a hostile ideology and possessing a huge nuclear arsenal colored almost every foreign policy and defense decision undertaken by the U.S. government.

With the collapse of communism in the Soviet Union and Eastern Europe, the United States and its allies had won the Cold War. Yet while the revolution in the Soviet Union transformed the international situation for the better, it also opened a new, unpredictable era in world politics. Fears of an instant nuclear holocaust arising out of a superpower confrontation were replaced by fears of nuclear proliferation and the emergence of a vast area of instability and ethnic conflict that would have implications for the security of Europe, the Middle East and East Asia.

Transformation of the USSR

In 1985, when Gorbachev came to power, a prediction that internal forces would cause the demise of the Soviet Union in less than seven years would have been dismissed as unlikely at best and ridiculous at worst. Although the Soviet Union was suffering from numerous economic maladies and scholars long had acknowledged the explosive potential of nationalism among the USSR's 169 ethnic groups, the country also was a model of stability and central government control.

The Communist Party and its bureaucracy dominated virtually every facet of Soviet life. The Committee for State Security (KGB) and other security organs were pervasive in society and had successfully squelched most dissent. The command economy was inefficient, wasteful and overcentralized, but it appeared to be limping along at a pace sufficient to produce jobs and the basic necessities of life for the Soviet people.

The Soviet economy in 1985 was not close to collapse. In foreign affairs, the Soviet Union had established a reputation as a superpower. Its international ambitions were backed up by a huge nuclear arsenal and conventional military force. Despite its troubles, the Soviet system appeared solid and secure.

The Soviet leadership, however, had recognized the need for reforms. Gorbachev had come to power in part because he represented a more energetic younger generation willing to seek innovative solutions to the nagging problems plaguing Soviet society. More than any other factor, the declining state of the economy was the catalyst for reform. Economic growth had declined sharply during the late 1970s and early 1980s, and the USSR suffered from chronic agricultural production shortfalls, a lack of technological sophistication in most industries, unacknowledged inflation, growing environmental problems and labor shortages in regions where most industry was located. Only in military production could the Soviet Union compete with the West, but high rates of defense spending weakened the general state of the economy by siphoning off investment from other areas.

Gorbachev Begins Reforms

Gorbachev took power unwilling to just muddle along. During his first two years as general secretary, he instituted cautious, but significant, reforms. He attempted to improve the economy through greater labor discipline, giving factory managers more autonomy and introducing more sophisticated technology into the workplace.

Along with his mild economic reforms, Gorbachev launched his policy of glasnost (openness). Glasnost had many elements, including more open and honest news coverage by the Soviet media and greater freedom of expression and speech for Soviet artists and common citizens. The policy was designed to put pressure on conservative bureaucrats to accept economic change by allowing the Soviet people and press to criticize abuses of power and unimaginative or timid leadership. Gorbachev apparently believed that his economic reforms could not succeed without glasnost.

But the policy contained inherent risks. Once Soviet citizens felt free to chastise corrupt regional officials and party bureaucrats in the central government, criticisms of the Communist Party and the Soviet leadership could not be far behind. Moreover, moves to make society less repressive risked encouraging dissidents and igniting the ambitions of various ethnic groups.

Beginning in 1987, Gorbachev and his increasingly radical economic advisers responded to the economy's failure to improve by accelerating glasnost, introducing democratic elections and launching farther-reaching economic reforms. The Soviet leadership sanctioned limited private enterprise activities, sought greater Soviet involvement in the international economy and demanded that enterprises and farms become self-financing. Yet these moves were criticized by many experts in the West and liberals in Russia as too cautious to bring real change to the Soviet economy.

Gorbachev's reforms were accompanied by a continuing economic decline that made the Soviet people increasingly restless. Their patience with steps that were seen as threatening their traditional state-provided economic security diminished as their standard of living dropped, lines at stores grew and consumer items became increasingly scarce.

By 1990, the experiment with communism begun in Russia in 1917 appeared to have failed. The Soviet economy was in shambles, and Marxist-Leninist ideology — the basis of Soviet politics, economics and historical interpretation — had been abandoned by all but a few die-hard conservatives.

Responding to angry accusations from conservative party members at the Twenty-Eighth Party Congress in June 1990, Aleksandr Yakovlev, a close Gorbachev adviser, said: "A decision of this congress . . . cannot change the fact that the volume of labor production in South Korea is ten times that of the North, nor the fact that people in West Germany live far better than people in the East." The Communist Party had come to be seen as a cynical anachronism whose actions mainly benefited its elite few, not the Soviet people. Even V. I. Lenin, the revered founder of the Soviet state, was not immune to criticism by Soviet journalists and historians. Gorbachev and his reformist colleagues had hoped to orchestrate a gradual reform of Soviet society from the top, but change had developed its own uncertain momentum that the government could not stop.

Ethnic Unrest

As the Soviet economy collapsed, a parallel collapse of Soviet central authority over its internal empire was occurring. During Soviet rule, the Kremlin leadership advanced the myth that the USSR's myriad nationalities were bonded by communism into a fraternal confederation. The union was imposed on most non-Russian minorities by the Soviet Red Army. Gorbachev's liberalizations had inadvertently opened the way for ethnic groups to pursue their dormant aspirations. Nationalist movements in republics on the Soviet periphery agitated for greater sovereignty or outright independence from Moscow.

Meanwhile, the loosening of coercive controls brought to the surface ethnic rivalries and tensions that had been suppressed under a uniform adherence to Marxism-Leninism. In 1990, Moscow was forced to interpose troops between Armenians and Azeris in the Transcaucasian region. Violence on a smaller scale erupted in Central Asia, the Baltics and within the non-Russian areas of the Russian Federation itself. In March 1990, Lithuania officially declared itself independent of Moscow, setting off a crisis that would last for a year and a half. Gorbachev tried to hold Lithuania and the Baltic states within the union, fearing that a successful secession would encourage an avalanche of demands from independence movements in other republics.

Gorbachev hung his hopes for saving the Soviet Union on a union treaty. This treaty would have redefined the relationship between the republics and the central government, allowing the local governments to exercise autonomy over most affairs while Moscow would play a coordinating role and carry out military and foreign policies.

By the time the treaty was ready to be signed in August 1991, the Soviet Union was in disarray. Gorbachev long had been beset by critics from the left and the right. Liberals saw him as too timid on reform and too willing to continue using repressive measures to hold the country together. Conservatives saw him as someone who was willing to destroy the cherished foundations of Soviet communism. Most Soviet citizens saw him as a leader who had opened up society but failed to deliver on his promises, especially in the economic sphere. The economy was mired in a depression; republic governments, including Yeltsin's Russian government, were openly ignoring the decisions of the central government; ethnic unrest was growing unabated; independence movements in the republics were increasing in strength; and rumors of a coup by conservative Communist Party leaders or the military were commonplace.

The Coup

A day before the union treaty was to be signed, on Aug. 19, 1991, conservative party leaders tried to overthrow the Gorbachev government. Gorbachev was detained at his country home in the Crimea, and some military units were mobilized in support of the coup. The plotters announced over the national media that Gorbachev was ill and that they had formed the "State Committee for the State of Emergency in the USSR" through which they would govern the country. *(Botched coup, box, p. 321)*

Although the coup had many of the trappings of past Communist power plays, it was carried out with little nerve or skill. Yeltsin vigorously rallied the people of Moscow behind his efforts at resistance. As the democratically elected president of the Russian Federation, he quickly became the focal point for popular opposition to the coup. Yeltsin denounced the putsch as a crude and illegitimate attempt by hard-liners to undermine democracy and the rule of law in the Soviet Union. Although he had many well-publicized disagreements with Gorbachev, Yeltsin demanded the Soviet president be restored to power.

A Botched Coup

The conspirators who tried to seize power in the Soviet Union in August 1991 faced open defiance from the Soviet public, which may have brought about the failure of the coup even if it had been skillfully executed. But the poor planning of the conspirators and their incompetent performance during the coup did much to undermine their chances of success. The plotters committed numerous mistakes that virtually doomed the putsch from the start.

First and probably most important, the plotters did not arrest or otherwise silence Boris N. Yeltsin. Yeltsin had flown back to Moscow from Kazakhstan on Aug. 18, the day before the coup. He would have been easy to detain at the airport. The coup leaders also could have orchestrated a quick attack on the Russian "White House" to ensure that Yeltsin would not be able to rally Muscovites against the coup. The opportunity for a quick and simple assault faded on the first day as thousands of citizens went to the Russian White House to form a human barrier against attack and some military units defected to Yeltsin.

Second, although the plotters took some steps to censor the media, they did not completely control it. Western journalists had virtually unimpeded access to Moscow streets and were able to broadcast footage of the coup as it was unfolding. The independent Russian radio station "Ekho Moskvy" circumvented an order to stop broadcasting by setting up an office in the Russian White House. Liberal and independent Russian publications continued to operate in spite of the State Committee for the State of Emergency in the USSR's ban on all but nine national newspapers. All of Leningrad's newspapers but one reportedly appeared on the second day of the coup, and the liberal *Moscow News* distributed news using fax machines located across Moscow. The continued operation of news organizations opposed to the coup reinforced the impression that the plotters were headed for failure.

Third, the plotters overestimated the loyalty of military officers to the Emergency Committee. In Leningrad, for example, the regional military commander ordered 1,000 troops approaching the city in tanks not to enter. In Moscow, Lt. Gen. Pavel Grachev and Yevgeny Shaposhnikov, chief of the air force, defected to Yeltsin's side. These and other mutinies by officers and whole units undermined the coup plotters' confidence and emboldened the resisters.

Fourth, the plotters let three hours elapse between the announcement of the coup and the movement of military vehicles in Moscow. To many observers, this delay was interpreted as a sign that the coup's leaders were indecisive and perhaps locked in disagreement. Some reports suggested that Prime Minister Pavlov's behavior at the Monday Council of Ministers meeting indicated that he had been drinking heavily. The next day, he was hospitalized because of "high blood pressure." Several of his colleagues said that this was Pavlov's way of trying to back out of the coup.

By all accounts, the coup was not the streamlined decisive action typical of previous Soviet intrigues. Mikhail S. Gorbachev's reforms had created a society that would stand up to the use of force and fight to retain its hard-won freedoms. Coupled with the tragicomic behavior of the coup leaders, the putsch could not help but fail.

Tens of thousands of Russians formed a human barrier around the Moscow "White House," the home of the Russian Federation's government and Yeltsin's stronghold. Key Soviet military units and leaders defected to Yeltsin's side. The coup leaders, having failed to move decisively in the hours immediately after seizing the government, backed down in the face of populist opposition. They declined to order an assault on the White House that would have been bloody and was uncertain of success. On Aug. 21, the coup plotters, realizing their position was untenable, tried to save themselves by proposing a deal with Gorbachev, but the Soviet leader angrily refused.

During the failed coup, the United States and the rest of the world held its breath. Alerted by the weakening of Gorbachev's hold on power during the previous year, many analysts had warned that some type of rebellion by reactionary forces in the military or the Communist Party could reverse the process of reform and reinvigorate the Cold War. The quick failure of the coup, however, demonstrated that support for communism had passed. "This is a watershed event for the Soviet Union and perhaps the world," said Rep. Dave McCurdy, D-Okla., chairman of the House Intelligence Committee. The Soviet Union rapidly splintered into 15 independent nations, and Yeltsin advanced his radical reform program in Russia.

With the collapse of the coup, Yeltsin was revered as a hero. He and his democratic and reform-minded supporters assumed a dominant role in Soviet politics. Yeltsin placed many of the functions of the former Soviet Union under the control of the Russian republic. Gorbachev returned to his position as president of the USSR, but power had clearly been transferred to the republic governments, most of which declared their independence soon after the failed coup. Gorbachev was weakened by having had appointed many of the plotters to office.

End of an Era

During the four months between the coup and his resignation, Gorbachev struggled without success to put the union treaty back on track. Yeltsin, meanwhile, asserted the authority of Russia, while exploring possibilities

Gorbachev's Resignation as Soviet President . . .

Following is the translated text of Mikhail S. Gorbachev's Dec. 25, 1991, televised speech, in which he announced his resignation as president of the Soviet Union.

Dear compatriots, fellow citizens: As a result of the newly formed situation, creation of the Commonwealth of Independent States, I cease my activities in the post of USSR president.

I am making this decision out of considerations based on principle. I have firmly stood for independence, self-rule of nations, for the sovereignty of the republics, but at the same time for preservation of the union state, the unity of the country.

Events went a different way. The policy prevailed of dismembering this country and disuniting the state, with which I cannot agree. And after the Alma-Ata meeting and the decisions made there, my position on this matter has not changed. Besides, I am convinced that decisions of such scale should have been made on the basis of a popular expression of will. Yet I will continue to do everything in my power so that agreements signed there should lead to real accord in the society [and] facilitate the escape from the crisis and the reform process.

Addressing you for the last time in the capacity of president of the USSR, I consider it necessary to express my evaluation of the road we have traveled since 1985, especially as there are a lot of contradictory, superficial and subjective judgments on that matter.

Fate had it that when I found myself at the head of the state it was already clear that all was not well in the country. There is plenty of everything: land, oil and gas, other natural riches, and God gave us lots of intelligence and talent, yet we lived much worse than developed countries and keep falling behind them more and more.

The reason could already be seen. The society was suffocating in the vise of the command-bureaucratic system, doomed to serve ideology and bear the terrible burden of the arms race. It had reached the limit of its possibilities. All attempts at partial reform, and there had been many, had suffered defeat, one after another. The country was losing perspective. We could not go on living like that. Everything had to be changed radically.

That is why not once — not once — have I regretted that I did not take advantage of the post of [Communist Party] general secretary to rule as a czar for several years. I considered it irresponsible and amoral. I realized that to start reforms of such scale in a society such as ours was a most difficult and even a risky thing. But even today I am convinced of the historic correctness of the democratic reforms that were started in the spring of 1985.

The process of renovating the country and radical changes in the world community turned out to be far more complicated than could be expected. However, what has been done ought to be given its due. This society acquired freedom, liberated itself politically and spiritually, and this is the foremost achievement — which we have not yet understood completely, because we have not learned to use freedom.

However, work of historic significance has been accomplished. The totalitarian system that deprived the country of an opportunity to become successful and prosperous long ago has been eliminated. A breakthrough has been achieved on the way to democratic changes. Free elections, freedom of the press, religious freedoms, representative organs of power, a multi-party [system] became a reality. Human rights are recognized as the supreme principle.

The movement to a diverse economy has started, equality of all forms of property is becoming established, people who work on the land are coming to life again in the framework of land reform, farmers have

for creating some type of cooperative arrangement among the other republics.

On Dec. 1, the people of Ukraine, the Soviet Union's second most populous and important republic, voted overwhelmingly to endorse independence. The vote removed any hope that the Soviet Union could be salvaged. On Dec. 8, Russia, Ukraine and Belarus proclaimed the Commonwealth of Independent States. Eight other republics joined the CIS on Dec. 21. Lithuania, Latvia, Estonia and Georgia declined (and in the fall of 1992 Azerbaijan withdrew).

On Christmas Day, Dec. 25, Gorbachev resigned as Soviet president, stating that his resignation had been brought on by the creation of the CIS. In a brief farewell address, he hailed the end of the Cold War and stressed that mankind was now living in "a new world." At the same time, he emphasized that he had not changed his position on the necessity of preserving the union but that developments had taken a different course. In a symbolic move, Gorbachev then signed a decree relinquishing his position as commander in chief of the Soviet armed forces and transferring his control of the Soviet nuclear arsenal to Yeltsin. *(Text of Gorbachev address, box, this page)*

During 1992, the CIS failed to accomplish the three most ambitious tasks it might have addressed: constructing a coordinated defense policy, solidifying mechanisms through which the tightly linked economies of the former Soviet Union would continue to support one another and constructing an effective response to ethnic conflicts. Russia's decision in May 1992 to establish its own defense force indicated that a CIS military force had ceased to be a

... Brought End to Soviet Union, Cold War

appeared, millions of acres of land are being given over to people who live in the countryside and in towns.

Economic freedom of the producer has been legalized, and entrepreneurship, shareholding, privatization are gaining momentum. In turning the economy toward a market, it is important to remember that all this is done for the sake of the individual. At this difficult time, all should be done for his social protection, especially for senior citizens and children.

We live in a new world. The Cold War has ended; the arms race has stopped, as has the insane militarization that mutilated our economy, public psyche and morals. The threat of a world war has been removed. Once again I want to stress that on my part everything was done during the transition period to preserve reliable control of nuclear weapons.

We opened ourselves to the world, gave up interference into other people's affairs, the use of troops beyond the borders of the country, and trust, solidarity and respect came in response. We have become one of the main foundations for the transformation of modern civilization on peaceful democratic grounds.

The nations and peoples [of the Soviet Union] gained real freedom of self-determination. The search for a democratic reformation of the multinational state brought us to the threshold of concluding a new union treaty. All these changes demanded immense strain. They were carried out with sharp struggle, with growing resistance from the old, the obsolete forces: for former party-state structures, the economic apparatus, as well as our habits, ideological superstitions, the psychology of sponging and leveling everyone out.

They stumbled on our intolerance, low level of political culture, fear of change. That is why we lost so much time. The old system collapsed before the new one had time to begin working, and the crisis in the society became even more acute. I am aware of the dissatisfaction with the present hard situation, of the sharp criticism of authorities at all levels including my personal activities. But once again I'd like to stress that radical changes in such a vast country, and a country with such a heritage, cannot pass painlessly without difficulties and shake-up.

The August coup brought the general crisis to its ultimate limit. The most damaging thing about this crisis is the breakup of the state. And today I am worried by our people's loss of the citizenship of a great country. The consequences may turn out to be very hard for everyone.

I think it is vitally important to preserve the democratic achievements of the last years. They have been paid for by the suffering of our whole history, our tragic experience. They must not be given up under any circumstances or any pretext, otherwise all our hopes for the better will be buried. I am saying all this straight and honestly. It is my moral duty.

Today, I'd like to express my gratitude to all citizens who supported the policy of renovating the country, got involved in the implementation of democratic reforms. I am grateful to statesmen, public and political figures, millions of people abroad, those who understood our concepts and supported them, turned to us, started sincere cooperation with us.

I am leaving my post with apprehension, but also with hope, with faith in you, your wisdom and force of spirit. We are the heirs of a great civilization, and its rebirth into a new, modern and dignified life now depends on one and all.

I wish to thank you with all my heart all those who have stood together with me all these years for a fair and good cause. Some mistakes could surely have been avoided; many things could have been done better. But I am convinced that sooner or later our common efforts will bear fruit, our nations will live in a prosperous and democratic society.

I wish all the best to all of you.

viable alternative. Currencies and armies became symbols of national sovereignty for the new nations.

International Transformation

Since World War II, international relations had been dominated by the bipolar military balance and ideological competition between the United States and its allies and the Soviet Union and its bloc of Marxist client states. The Soviet Union appeared to most in the West as a blustering, aggressive, imperial colossus that constantly threatened surrounding nations, ignored human rights and pursued an unceasing military buildup.

During Gorbachev's tenure, Soviet foreign policy was realigned according to the principles of "new thinking." This approach aimed at extricating the Soviet Union from costly regional conflicts, cutting foreign aid and defense spending, encouraging foreign trade and investment, concluding major arms agreements and improving the USSR's international image.

In 1987, the Soviet government made major concessions that led to the intermediate-range nuclear force (INF) missiles treaty with the United States. Under this treaty, both sides eliminated all of their intermediate-range nuclear missiles in Europe. In 1988, Gorbachev announced that the USSR would unilaterally cut a half-million troops from its armed forces. In 1989, Moscow withdrew its forces from Afghanistan and began working with the United States to end regional conflicts. Most dramatically, however, the Soviet leadership allowed revolutions to take place in Eastern Europe that effectively broke up the Warsaw Pact military alliance and deprived Moscow of its Eastern European empire.

The Fall of Eastern Europe

The Soviets recognized that Eastern Europe was not a typical empire. Since the 1970s, it had been an economic drain on the Soviet Union. Yet the Soviets felt obliged to continue dominating the region because of its role as a buffer between the Soviet Union and Western Europe.

By the 1980s, Moscow was faced with the breakdown of Communist control in many parts of Eastern Europe. Protests were seen in every country except Bulgaria. Poland in particular seemed on the verge of a collapse. Under the Brezhnev Doctrine, the Soviets had claimed the right to intervene in a fraternal socialist state if that state was threatened by internal instability. In 1956 in Hungary and in 1968 in Czechoslovakia, Soviet tanks had put down movements that threatened to topple Communist rule.

But several factors caused the Soviet leadership in 1989 to reject this approach. A Soviet military intervention would have been the death knell for the improvement of relations with Western Europe and the United States and would have put unbearable strains on an already restless Soviet society.

At the end of Gorbachev's 1988 visit to Yugoslavia, a joint communiqué was issued clearly rejecting the Brezhnev Doctrine. Soviet foreign ministry spokesman Gennady Gerasimov quipped that the "Sinatra Doctrine" was in force in Eastern Europe. Those countries were free to "do it their way."

Despite all of these declarations, most Western observers believed that if Communist regimes were threatened in Eastern Europe, Gorbachev would still take some sort of steps — be they military, economic or diplomatic — to keep Communists in power and the Warsaw Pact intact. Only when the Solidarity government headed by Prime Minister Tadeusz Mazowiecki came to power in Poland in August 1989 did it become evident how serious Gorbachev was.

The changes that took place in Eastern Europe in 1989 followed two different paths, although they headed toward the same results. Hungary and Poland had struggled with reforms for years. Consequently, both countries became early supporters of Gorbachev and perestroika (restructuring). In Bulgaria, Czechoslovakia, East Germany and Romania, however, the hard-line leaders did whatever was necessary to maintain their power as long as possible, giving in to demands for change only after hundreds of thousands had taken to the streets to demand it. All six countries, however, experienced revolutions in 1989 that fundamentally changed the old order. The most climactic moment of the string of revolutions occurred Nov. 9 when the Berlin Wall, which for decades had prevented East Berliners from escaping to the West, was thrown open, symbolically ending the forced separation of East and West Germany.

Along with everyone else, members of Congress watched with awe and wonder as one Eastern European Communist regime after another fell during 1989. The United States could do little to encourage the process, but leaders on Capitol Hill and the administration examined the possibility of extending financial aid to the emerging democracies.

President Bush announced several minor aid packages for Hungary and Poland, but Democrats in Congress pushed for something more generous. After several weeks of negotiations, House leaders of both parties settled on a proposal authorizing $837.5 million in various forms of aid to Poland and Hungary over three years — nearly twice as much as Bush had requested. Despite the administration's refusal to endorse that proposal (HR 3402), the House approved it on Oct. 19, 1989, by 345-47. The Senate passed an amended version, 99-0, on Nov. 14.

The conference report (H Rept 101-377) was approved by voice vote in the House on Nov. 17 and in the Senate on Nov. 18. The final bill contained a three-year authorization total of $938 million. Bush signed HR 3402 (PL 101-179) on Nov. 28. Separate legislation (HR 3743 — PL 101-167) appropriated $532.8 million in fiscal 1990.

A New Foreign Policy

As the USSR turned inward to focus on its domestic troubles, it de-emphasized the international geopolitical struggle with the West and rejected Marxist-Leninist ideology as a significant factor in foreign policy making. Consequently, nations that had looked to the Soviet Union as a source of economic and military aid were forced to repair relations with neighbors or with the West.

The dramatic foreign policy changes could be seen in the Soviet response to the Iraqi invasion of Kuwait in August 1990. Previously, almost any nation or group that threatened the interests of the West would receive Soviet support, encouragement or sympathy. The Soviet Union did not cooperate with the West in combating terrorism and rarely condemned terrorist acts against Western citizens, saying they were regrettable but understandable. Although the West had more to lose than the Soviets from the Iraqi invasion and Moscow was a major Iraqi arms supplier, the Kremlin quickly joined the United States in condemning Baghdad and agreed to impose an arms embargo against the Iraqis.

The breakup of the Soviet Union reduced even further the possibility of conflict between East and West. Soviet and Russian events altered the international landscape in ways that even the most reactionary Russian leader would be unable to change. For example, the credibility of a conventional Russian invasion of Western Europe is beyond restoration. In addition, regardless of who runs Russia, its domestic problems preclude a return to large-scale foreign adventurism in the near term.

Yeltsin stated his intent to pursue not only cooperation, but also active friendship with the Soviet Union's former enemies. The Soviet army contained 4 million troops in 1990. But Yeltsin set about implementing a plan in 1991 under which the Russian military would have no more than 1.5 million troops by 1995.

Russian foreign policy under Yeltsin was aimed at building international support for his domestic reforms, reducing or eliminating costly commitments made during the Soviet era, and advancing Russia as a responsible and important member of the international community.

Relations with the United States

In a historic speech to a joint session of the U.S. Congress on June 17, 1992, Yeltsin declared: "Acting on the will of the people of Russia, I am inviting you, and through you, the people of the United States, to join us in partnership in the quest for freedom and justice in the 21st century." *(Text of speech, box, p. 326)*

Yeltsin's words reflected the remarkable transformation of relations between the former Cold War antagonists. He received numerous standing ovations from Congress, and his speech convinced some skeptics that he was genuinely committed to democratic reform and the construction of a partnership with the United States.

After World War II, the United States and the Soviet Union had developed a hostile rivalry based on their conflicting geopolitical goals, their competing ideologies and their reciprocal military threat. American post-World War II policy aimed at containing Soviet expansionism, building alliance systems to oppose Soviet military power and isolating the Soviet Union diplomatically. The Soviets sought to solidify their domination of Eastern Europe, develop new anti-Western allies around the world and ensure their own security through military might.

In the late 1980s, the superpower relationship began to change. In an effort to repair his country's ailing economy, Gorbachev de-emphasized the USSR's quest for international influence and sought to divert funds from military production to the civilian economy. Competition with the United States was subordinated to a new superpower cooperation that would allow the Soviets to focus on their enormous domestic problems.

Under Gorbachev, U.S.-Soviet relations continued to be based on competition. The new Soviet leader, however, brought a new pragmatism to negotiations and appeared to conduct business with the United States with an eye toward supporting Soviet domestic needs. He also provided a challenge to the U.S. leaders in the area of public relations, as he skillfully lobbied to improve the international image of the Soviet Union.

In 1987, with the conclusion of the INF treaty, superpower relations began to change fundamentally. The Soviets had made several major concessions in agreeing to the treaty, the terms of which were close to a proposal made by President Ronald Reagan in 1981. Meanwhile, the Reagan administration had ceased its harsh anti-Soviet rhetoric and was exploring new areas for superpower cooperation.

Soviet actions in 1989, including withdrawal of forces from Afghanistan and consent to the establishment of democratically elected governments in Eastern Europe, persuaded most U.S. policy makers that the Soviet Union had changed dramatically. Moreover, Soviet society was being transformed. As Marxist-Leninist ideology lost its luster, non-Russian minorities clamored for greater autonomy, the Communist Party leadership introduced democratic processes and Soviet society increasingly became subject to the rule of law. In response to these changes, the United States began trying to support the domestic transformation of the Soviet Union. By the time of the failed August 1991 coup that precipitated the Soviet breakup, superpower relations had already entered a new stage where cooperation had replaced competition.

The United States had grown comfortable with Gorbachev. Although he professed to being a Communist, his genuine efforts to improve relations with the West, advance arms control and open up Soviet society had persuaded many American policy makers that U.S. goals could best be achieved if he remained in power. Critics charged that until the coup Bush and his advisers continued to embrace Gorbachev as the preferred negotiating partner, even though Yeltsin had emerged in 1990 as the leader most likely to advance democracy. Gorbachev had exploited his domestic weakness as a bargaining point, saying that the United States needed to support him to avoid having to deal with someone less conciliatory. Yeltsin's election in May 1990 as president of the largest republic in the USSR, however, signaled that Soviet liberals dedicated to radical reform might be more likely than conservatives to replace Gorbachev if he lost power.

Yeltsin's courageous stand during the coup, and his displays of strength relative to Gorbachev afterward, caused the United States to reorient its policy toward Yeltsin. The Russian leader's accommodating attitude made this reorientation easy. Through flexibility on arms control, an apparent commitment to economic reform, cooperation in resolving a multitude of contentious Cold War issues and his engaging performance at the June 1992 Washington summit, Yeltsin won the admiration of most American policy makers and citizens. All but the hardest-line cold warriors in the United States came to believe that Yeltsin was sincere in his pursuit of a reformed Russia and a highly cooperative American-Russian relationship. A consensus developed that Yeltsin, the best hope for engineering a transformation of Russia into a non-threatening and fully democratic nation, must be supported. Virtually every American policy maker believed that no preferable alternative to Yeltsin existed.

The political, social and economic conditions in the former Soviet Union changed with such speed that U.S. policy had difficulty keeping up. The key Cold War issues of the arms race, the European military balance and competition for influence in the developing world were largely replaced by the questions of how the United States could best aid the domestic transformations of the former Soviet states and how to achieve stability in a vast multi-ethnic empire where weapons of mass destruction were plentiful.

Comparisons were drawn between the former Soviet Union in 1992 and Germany and Japan in 1945. The United States helped its devastated World War II enemies to rebuild their societies and economies. The result was a profound transformation of the defeated nations into thriving democracies and important American political allies and economic partners. Many U.S. policy makers argued that the United States needed to take the same approach with the former Soviet Union.

In a speech at Princeton University on Dec. 12, 1991, Secretary of State James A. Baker III described the importance of helping the former Soviet republics to establish democratic governments and free markets: "If during the Cold War we faced each other as two scorpions in a bottle, now the Western nations and the former Soviet republics stand as awkward climbers on a steep mountain. Held together by a common rope, a fall toward fascism or anarchy in the former Soviet Union will pull the West down, too. Yet equally as important, a strong and steady pull by the West now can help them to gain their footing so that they, too, can climb above to enduring democracy and freedom."

The U.S. debt problem and weak economy, as well as fears that the reform movement in Russia and elsewhere might be reversed, at least for the time being prevented the adoption of a massive aid package on the scope of the Marshall Plan, which helped to rebuild Europe after World War II. But the United States continued to see the outcome of the revolution in the former Soviet Union as the key to stability in Europe and much of Asia and as central to U.S. security. For their part, Russia and the other republics knew that the United States was the most important source of outside aid and political support. Therefore, both parties had much incentive to make partnership a reality.

Yeltsin Was First Russian Leader . . .

Following are excerpts from the Reuter transcript of Russian President Boris N. Yeltsin's speech to a joint session of the U.S. Congress on June 17, 1992, delivered through an interpreter.

Mr. Speaker, Mr. President, members of Congress, ladies and gentlemen:

It is indeed a great honor for me to address the Congress of the great land of freedom as the first-ever, over 1,000 years of history of Russia, popularly elected president, as a citizen of the great country which has made its choice in favor of liberty and democracy.

For many years, our two nations were the two poles, the two opposites. They wanted to make us implacable enemies. . . .

Reason begins to triumph over madness. . . . [It] can be said today, tomorrow will be a day of peace, less of fear and more of hope for the happiness of our children.

The world can sigh in relief. The idol of communism, which spread everywhere social strife, animosity and unparalleled brutality, which instilled fear in humanity, has collapsed. It has collapsed never to rise again. I am here to assure you, we will not let it rise again in our land. . . .

Russia has made its final choice in favor of a civilized way of life, common sense and universal human heritage. I am convinced that our people will reach that goal. There is no people on this earth who could be harmed by the air of freedom. There are no exceptions to that rule. Liberty sets the mind free, fosters independence and unorthodox thinking and ideas. But it does not offer instant prosperity or happiness and wealth to everyone. This is something that politicians in particular must keep in mind. Even the most benevolent intentions will inevitably be abandoned and committed to oblivion if they are not translated into everyday efforts.

Our experience of the recent years has conclusively pointed that out. Liberty will not be fooled. There can be no coexistence between democracy and a totalitarian state system. There can be no coexistence between market economy and powers who control everything and everyone.

There can be no coexistence between a civic society, which is pluralist by definition, and communist intolerance to dissent. The experience of the past decade has taught us: Communism has no human face. Freedom and communism are incompatible.

You will recall August 1991, when for three days Russia was under the dark cloud of dictatorship.

I addressed the Muscovites who were defending the White House of Russia. I addressed all the people of Russia. I addressed them standing on top of the tank whose crew had disobeyed criminal orders. . . .

At that moment, I feared. But I had no fear for myself. I feared for the future of democracy in Russia and throughout the world. Because I was aware what could happen if we failed to win.

Citizens of Russia upheld their freedom and did not allow the continuation of the 75 years of nightmare. From this high rostrum I want to express our sincere thanks and gratitude to President Bush and to the American people for their invaluable moral support for the just cause of the people of Russia.

Last year citizens of Russia passed another difficult test of maturity. We chose to forgo vengeance and the intoxicating craving for summary justice over the fallen colossus known under the name of the CPSU [Communist Party of the Soviet Union].

There was no replay of history. The Communist Party citadel, next to the Kremlin, the Communist Bastille, was not destroyed. There was not a hint of violence against Communists in Russia. People simply brushed off the venomous dust of the past and went about their business.

There were no lynch law trials in Russia. The doings of the Communist Party over many years have been referred to the constitutional court of the Russian Federation. I am confident that its verdict will be fair. . . .

Economic and Political Reforms. . . . [E]conomic and political reforms are the primary tasks for Russia today. We are facing the challenges that no one has ever faced before at any one time.

We must carry through unprecedented reforms in the economy, which over the seven decades has been stripped of all market infrastructure; lay the foundations for democracy; and restore the rule of law in the country that for scores of years was poisoned with political strife and political oppression. . . .

I will not go back on the reforms. And it is practically impossible to topple Yeltsin in Russia. I am in good health, and I will not say "uncle" before I make the reforms irreversible. . . .

New Arms Treaty. Yesterday we concluded an unprecedented agreement on cutting down strategic offensive arsenals. They will be reduced radically in two phases, not by 30 or 40 percent, as negotiated previously over 15 years. They will be slashed to less than one-third of today's strength — from 21,000 nuclear warheads on both sides down to 6,000 to 7,000 by the year 2000. And it has taken us only five months to negotiate. . . .

I am formally announcing that, without waiting for the treaty to be signed, we have begun taking off alert the heavy SS-18 missiles targeted on the United States of America. And the defense minister of Russia is here in this room to confirm that. . . .

An End to Double Standards. . . . Russia . . . once and for all has done away with double standards in foreign policy. We are firmly resolved not to

... To Address Joint Session of Congress

lie any more, either to our negotiating partners, or to the Russian or American or any other people. There will be no more lies — ever.

The same applies to biological weapons experiments and the facts that have been revealed about American prisoners of war, the KAL 007 flight and many other things. That list could be continued.

The archives of the KGB and the Communist Party Central Committee are being opened. Moreover, we are inviting the cooperation of the United States and other nations to investigate these dark pages.

I promise you that each and every document in each and every archive will be examined in order to investigate the fate of every American unaccounted for. As president of Russia, I assure you that even if one American has been detained in my country, and can still be found, I will find him; I will get him back to his family. (Sustained applause.)

... We have made tangible moves to make contact between Russia and foreign business communities much easier. Under the recent legislation, foreign nationals who privatize a facility or a building in Russia are given property rights to the plot of land on which they are located. Legislation on bankruptcy has been recently enacted.

Mandatory sale of foreign currency to the state, at an artificially low rate of exchange, has been ended.

We are ready to bring our legal practice, as much as possible, in line with world standards, of course on the basis of symmetry with each country.

We are inviting the private sector of the United States to invest in the unique and untapped Russian market. And I am saying: Do not be late.

U.S. Policy. Now that the period of global confrontation is behind us, I call upon you to take a fresh look at the current policy of the United States toward Russia, and also to take a fresh look at the longer-term prospects of our relations.... Let us together ... master the art of reconciling differences on the basis of partnership, which is the most efficient and democratic way.

This would come naturally both for the Russians and the Americans. If this is done, many of the problems which are now impeding mutual advantageous cooperation between Russia and the United States will become irrelevant, and I mean legislative frameworks too. It will not be a wasteful endeavor. On the contrary, it will promote a more efficient solution of your problems, as well as of ours. And of course it will create new jobs, in Russia as well as in the United States....

More than 30 years ago, President [John F.] Kennedy addressed these words to humanity: "My fellow citizens of the world, ask not what America can do for you, but what together we can do for the freedom of man." I believe that his inspired call for working together toward a democratic world is addressed above all to our two peoples, to the people of America and to the people of Russia....

Joining the world community, we wish to preserve our identity, our own image and history, promote culture, strengthen moral standards of our people. We find relevant the warning of the great Russian philosopher, Berdyaev, who said to negate Russia in the name of humankind is to rob humankind. At the same time, Russia does not aspire to change the world in its own image. It is the fundamental principle of the new Russia to be generous and to share experience, moral values and emotional warmth, rather than to impose and curse.

It is the tradition of the Russian people to repay kindness with kindness. This is the bedrock of the Russian lifestyle, the underlying truth revealed by the great Russian culture. Free and democratic Russia will remain committed to this tenet. Today, free and democratic Russia is extending its hand of friendship to the people of America. Acting on the will of the people of Russia, I am inviting you, and through you, the people of the United States, to join us in partnership in the quest for freedom and justice in the 21st century.

The Russo-American dialogue has gone through many a dramatic moment. But the peoples of Russia and America have never gone to war against each other. Even in the darkest periods, our affinity prevailed over our hatred.

In this context, I would like to recall something that took place 50 years ago. The unprecedented war, world war, was waging. Russia, which was bleeding white, and all our people were looking forward to the opening of the second front. And it was opened, first and foremost, thanks to the active stance taken by President [Franklin D.] Roosevelt and by the entire American people. Sometimes I think that if today, like during that war, a second but peaceful front could be opened to promote democratic market reforms, their success would be guaranteed early.

The passing by Congress of the Freedom Support Act could become the first step in that direction.

Today legislation promoting reforms is much more important than appropriation of funds.

May I express the hope that the United States Congress, as the staunch advocate of freedom, will remain faithful to its strategic course on this occasion as well. Members of Congress, every man is a man of his own time. No exception is ever made for anyone, whether an ordinary citizen or the president. Much experience has been gained; many things have been reassessed.

I would like now to conclude my statement with the words from a song by Irving Berlin, an American of Russian descent: God bless America, to which I add, and Russia.

End of the Cold War

Arms Control

Throughout the 1960s, 1970s and 1980s, arms control was the central element of negotiations between the United States and the Soviet Union. Both sides stated their desire to conclude agreements that would reduce or otherwise restrict the construction and deployment of nuclear weapons. Some agreements were achieved to limit the size of the superpower arsenals, but mutual fear and distrust continued to fuel an expensive and dangerous arms race.

Beginning in the late 1980s, the fundamental change in Soviet foreign policy under Gorbachev created conditions that led to arms control agreements that significantly reduced the nuclear arsenals of the superpowers. With the breakup in 1991, the dynamics of arms control changed as the United States was faced with four new countries — Russia, Ukraine, Belarus and Kazakhstan — with nuclear weapons on their soil. Arms control initiatives came to depend not only on relations between Washington and Moscow, but also among the nuclear weapons states of the former Soviet Union.

Gorbachev Troop Cuts. On Dec. 7, 1988, Gorbachev delivered an address to the United Nations General Assembly. In the speech, he broke dramatically with traditional Soviet rhetoric, criticizing the role of military force and ideological struggle in world affairs. He announced Soviet plans to cut 500,000 of the country's nearly 5 million troops by 1991. Gorbachev also called for "consistent movement" toward a strategic arms reduction talks (START) agreement, "while preserving the ABM [anti-ballistic missile] treaty."

Gorbachev's troop cut proposal prompted cautious optimism from Western officials. They noted that it seemed to meet the insistence of the North Atlantic Treaty Organization (NATO) that any Soviet troop cut be tailored to hit in particular those Soviet forces in Eastern Europe that Western allies long had claimed were poised to mount a blitzkrieg against West Germany.

Although Gorbachev presented his arms cuts as unilateral, he subsequently told reporters that he hoped the United States and its European allies "will also take some steps."

On March 6, 1989, the conventional forces in Europe (CFE) talks opened in Vienna. These negotiations replaced the Mutual and Balanced Force Reduction talks and included representatives of all NATO and Warsaw Pact countries. The CFE talks sought to reduce the alliances' inventories of conventional weapons such as tanks, aircraft and artillery pieces, as well as the number of military personnel deployed in Europe. In late May, Bush outlined a comprehensive approach to limiting conventional forces at a NATO summit in Brussels.

Malta and Washington Summits. Bush and Gorbachev held a shipboard summit off the Mediterranean island of Malta, Dec. 2-3, 1989. The astonishing events in Eastern Europe tended to upstage the Malta summit. The entire leadership of the East German Communist Party resigned on Dec. 3 as Bush and Gorbachev were winding up their talks. The next day, mass protests in Czechoslovakia forced concessions from that country's teetering Communist leadership.

Bush and Gorbachev agreed to speed up negotiations on arms control and economic issues — in effect keeping superpower relations on a par with the pace of political change in Eastern Europe. Bush and Gorbachev said they hoped a START treaty could be signed during 1990. The two sides also stated their intention to hasten their work on multilateral treaties limiting conventional forces in Europe and banning the use and possession of chemical and biological weapons.

Despite U.S. and Soviet efforts, a START treaty was not ready to sign by the time Gorbachev came to Washington at the beginning of June 1990. The two leaders settled for signing statements outlining the major areas of agreement in the START treaty and setting goals for further reductions.

Bush and Gorbachev also signed a chemical weapons treaty at the Washington summit. It committed both sides to halt production of chemical weapons as soon as the pact was ratified. It mandated that both powers would begin destroying their stocks of chemical weapons in 1992 so that by the year 2000 their arsenals would be half their present size. Two years later, their chemical weapons stocks were to be just 20 percent of their existing levels.

CFE Treaty. On Nov. 19, 1990, the CFE treaty was signed by the United States, the Soviet Union and the 20 other European nations that made up NATO and the Warsaw Pact. The treaty, produced by months of intricate negotiations, committed the signatories to reduce the number of tanks, artillery pieces, helicopters and aircraft deployed between the Atlantic Ocean and the Ural Mountains. These cuts were aimed at reducing the offensive potential of the armies of the two alliance systems. Events in the Soviet Union and Eastern Europe, however, largely superseded the treaty.

Long before the U.S. Senate ratified the treaty in November 1991, the Soviet Union had made additional unilateral cuts in its armed forces deployed in Europe, and on July 1, 1991, the Warsaw Pact was officially dismantled. In the months after the dissolution of the USSR, most of the former republics moved to establish their own militaries. President Yeltsin committed Russia to continue the pullout of forces from Germany, and he announced that Russia's military would be reduced to between 1.0 million and 1.5 million troops by 1995. This compared with a Soviet army that in 1990 still contained 4 million troops. Under budgetary pressure, the United States also might reduce the number of forces in Europe beyond the CFE limits. Nevertheless, the Senate ratified the treaty by a vote of 90-4 on Nov. 25, 1991. The Bush administration urged states of the former Soviet Union to ratify it as a way of formally codifying limitations on military equipment in Europe.

The former Soviet states that had territory west of the Urals agreed in May 1992 on a formula for allocating the cuts in military equipment required by the CFE treaty. Russia was to receive between one-half and two-thirds of the equipment allowed under the treaty, with Ukraine getting the next biggest share.

START Treaty. Just weeks before the failed August 1991 coup, Bush and Gorbachev signed the START treaty in Moscow on July 31. The treaty mandated reductions in the strategic nuclear forces of the two powers. Within seven years of ratification, the START treaty was to reduce the number of Soviet ballistic missile warheads by about 50 percent and the number of U.S. warheads by about 35 percent. This formula would leave the United States with about 8,500 strategic nuclear warheads and the Soviet Union with 6,500.

After the failed coup, however, Bush sought to quickly advance arms control beyond the START limits. On Sept. 27, he announced sweeping unilateral arms reduction measures, including the removal of short-range nuclear weapons from naval vessels and bases in Europe and Asia and the end of the practice of keeping part of the U.S. strategic bomber force on constant alert. Gorbachev responded Oct. 5, by announcing his intention to reduce Soviet strategic warhead levels below the START limits and eliminate all Soviet tactical nuclear warheads.

The end of the Soviet Union and Gorbachev's resignation complicated the ratification and implementation of the START treaty. New arrangements had to be worked out between the United States and newly independent republics. In the meantime, the Bush and Yeltsin administrations attempted to advance strategic arms control beyond the START agreement. Fearing that Yeltsin's hold on power was not completely secure in the unpredictable Russian political climate, Bush sought to quickly conclude arms reduction agreements favorable to the United States in case a less friendly regime came to power.

American negotiators proposed reducing each side's nuclear arsenal to 4,700 warheads and banning multiple-warhead land-based missiles (which were the backbone of the Russian strategic nuclear force). Yeltsin proposed instead to reduce the arsenals to as few as 2,000 to 2,500 warheads. This proposal was designed to force the United States to make cuts in submarine-launched missiles, where it held a significant advantage.

At the June 1992 summit in Washington, Yeltsin and Bush announced an unexpected agreement to cut their arsenals to roughly half the levels envisioned by the START treaty. The Joint Understanding on Nuclear Arms Reductions would reduce current levels of strategic nuclear warheads by two-thirds over the following seven to 10 years. Under the agreement, the United States would be left with about 3,500 warheads and Russia would be left with about 3,000. The agreement represented a compromise between the Russian and American positions. While it would force the Russians to eliminate all of their land-based multiple-warhead missiles, it also would force the United States to cut its submarine-launched missile arsenal in half.

Despite this new agreement, the two sides stated their intention to ratify the START treaty. They planned to convert the Joint Understanding into a treaty that also would be subject to ratification by the U.S. Senate and Russian parliament.

The Senate on Oct. 1 easily approved ratification of the START treaty by a vote of 93-6. Treaty backers said that despite ongoing negotiations on details of the Bush-Yeltsin plan, the START reductions were needed to set the stage for the additional arms cuts and as a hedge against the possible re-emergence of unfriendly governments in the former Soviet Union. Senate Majority Leader George J. Mitchell, D-Maine, declared: "Even as we move toward ratification of START, we look forward to receiving another, more far-reaching strategic arms accord. But each agreement is a step forward."

Before leaving office, Bush concluded a START II agreement with Yeltsin that fleshed out their agreement at the June 1992 summit. The two leaders signed START II on Jan. 3, 1993. It would cut the total number of U.S. warheads to 3,500 and the total number of Russian warheads to 3,000. It also would eliminate all multiple-warhead, land-based missiles. The success of the treaty, however, depended on the cooperation of the other nuclear weapons states that emerged from the Soviet Union — Ukraine, Belarus and Kazakhstan. It also was subject to approval by the conservative Russian parliament. Despite the agreement, therefore, the success of START II was far from assured.

Non-Russian Nuclear States. Although the disintegration of the Soviet Union clearly weakened the direct military threat to the United States, it created new arms control challenges for Washington and the newly independent states. The Soviet Union possessed a staggering 27,000 nuclear warheads. Most of these were deployed or stored in Russia. However, a substantial portion (about 25 percent) were kept in three other republics — Ukraine, Belarus and Kazakhstan. In effect, the breakup of the Soviet Union had yielded four new nuclear powers where previously only one existed.

The three smaller states indicated that they did not want to keep their nuclear weapons. In part, this attitude stemmed from the severe environmental damage in Ukraine and Belarus caused by the 1986 Chernobyl nuclear power plant accident and by decades of Soviet nuclear testing in Kazakhstan. The leaders of the three states, however, sought to use their possession of nuclear weapons as leverage in their relations with Russia and the United States.

In December 1991, when the CIS was created, the non-Russian nuclear states agreed to transfer the tactical nuclear weapons (those having a short range and designed for use on a battlefield) on their territory to the Russian republic, on the condition that all of them would be dismantled. By May 1992, despite a dispute between Ukraine and Russia over monitoring of the dismantlement process, all tactical nuclear weapons from the three nations had been moved safely to Russia, where they were being destroyed.

Dealing with strategic nuclear weapons proved more difficult. As with tactical weapons, the Bush administration promoted the destruction or transfer to Russia of all strategic weapons in the non-Russian states. Both Ukraine and Kazakhstan sought financial aid and security guarantees from the United States in exchange for doing so. The United States did extend some financial aid to the three states and expanded contacts, but it declined to offer security guarantees.

In May 1992, a protocol to START was signed in which all four nuclear nations of the former Soviet Union were named successor states of the USSR with regard to the START treaty. This protocol left the four to decide among themselves how to meet the START limits. The leaders of Ukraine, Belarus and Kazakhstan promised to render their nations nuclear-free by the end of the START treaty's seven-year implementation period. They also committed to signing the Nuclear Non-Proliferation Treaty as non-nuclear states. Nevertheless, the possibility remained that Ukraine, Belarus or Kazakhstan would attempt to keep some of the nuclear weapons on its territory.

Economic Relations

In part because U.S.-Soviet economic ties were not crucial to the American economy and defending against the Soviet military threat was a major concern, commercial interests were almost always subordinated to national security interests. As a result, trade and other forms of economic cooperation were severely restricted by the U.S. government.

With the fall of communism, however, the U.S. approach to economic relations with the former Soviet Union was reversed. Greater economic cooperation with Russia and the other states came to be seen as enhancing the prospects for the success of democracy and free-market principles. Consequently, the United States lifted many restrictions against commerce with the former Soviet Union.

After Gorbachev came to power, U.S.-Soviet trade grew, but it remained minuscule in comparison with U.S. trade with other industrialized nations. Soviet exports to the United States grew from about $600 million in 1986 to about $700 million in 1989. Imports from the United States jumped from $1.2 billion to $4.3 billion in that same time period.

Under Gorbachev, the Soviets sought to use hard currency to purchase high technology and machine tools to modernize Soviet industry. But the bulk of imports from the United States were grain shipments needed to make up for the failure of Soviet agriculture. The Soviets purchased $3.3 billion worth of U.S. grain in 1989. The bulk of Soviet exports to the United States consisted of petroleum products, minerals and chemicals, along with some vodka, caviar and furs.

At the Malta summit, Bush proposed a trade agreement, contingent on the Soviet Union's codifying its new emigration policy in law. The agreement, which would give the Soviet Union most-favored-nation (MFN) status, was signed when Gorbachev came to Washington in June 1990.

Several agreements aimed at improving economic relations were signed by Bush and Yeltsin at the June 1992 summit in Washington. The leaders concluded a bilateral investment treaty and a taxation treaty that encouraged investment by creating procedures for repatriating profits in hard currency, settling disputes and establishing tax arrangements that precluded taxation by both nations of the same profits. Bush and Yeltsin also finalized the trade agreement originally signed by Bush and Gorbachev in 1990. The U.S. Senate had ratified the agreement on Nov. 25, 1991, by voice vote. The House had approved the measure (H J Res 346) on Nov. 20 by 350-78. The Russian parliament ratified the pact just before Yeltsin came to Washington in June 1992.

Under the pact, Russian and American products enjoy MFN status in the other nation. A side letter to the agreement established procedures for Russia's repayment of its World War II lend-lease debt.

The United States attempted to make doing business in the former Soviet Union easier for U.S. firms. Trade restrictions, including the majority of those involving high-technology exports to the former Soviet Union, were lifted. The Overseas Private Investment Corporation (OPIC) was authorized to offer political risk insurance to American firms doing business in the former Soviet Union. In addition, the United States expanded agricultural commodity credit and Export-Import Bank credit guarantee programs targeted at Russia and the independent states.

Many companies, however, discovered that the former Soviet Union remained a difficult place to do business. The goals of American and other foreign firms often differed significantly from those of their Russian partners. Foreign companies were attracted mainly by the untapped Russian market, not by the chance to set up production in Russia or elsewhere in the former Soviet Union. The Russian economy still produced little that Americans wanted to buy, and the ruble was not yet convertible.

Aid to the Former Soviet Union

To accomplish the goal of helping democracy to survive in the former Soviet Union, the United States cooperated with other leading nations, especially Germany, to provide financial aid to Russia and the other former Soviet states.

In late August 1991, Sen. Sam Nunn, D-Ga., and Rep. Les Aspin, D-Wis., the chairmen of the Senate and House Armed Services committees, proposed providing $1 billion in aid to the former Soviet Union. The proposal was withdrawn when lawmakers objected to spending money on a former enemy when so many domestic needs were not being met.

But only days before adjournment, a bipartisan group of senior senators decided to attempt to pass a scaled-back aid bill (HR 3807). These senators — led by Nunn and Richard G. Lugar, R-Ind. — crafted a proposal that targeted funds toward helping the Soviets and the republics collect, protect and dismantle the small nuclear warheads inside their territory. The group argued this aid was a defensive move to reduce the nuclear threat to the United States. The White House refused to support or oppose the bill.

The Senate Nov. 25, 1991, adopted 86-8 an amendment to HR 3807 authorizing up to $500 million in previously appropriated Defense Department funds to address the problem of Soviet nuclear weapons and $200 million to transport humanitarian assistance. The Senate passed HR 3807 by voice vote Nov. 25. Two days later, the House approved an amended version of the aid package by voice vote. It authorized $400 million for demilitarization and $100 million for humanitarian aid transportation. The House originally had passed the bill by voice vote under suspension of the rules Nov. 19. The Senate cleared the amended version by voice vote Nov. 25, and Bush signed HR 3807 into law (PL 102-228) on Dec. 12.

On April 1, 1992, President Bush and Chancellor Helmut Kohl of Germany announced that the Group of Seven (G-7) industrialized nations had agreed to provide the former Soviet Union with $24 billion in financial assistance, conditioned on the progress of its states in reforming their economies. The package was to include $11 billion in bilateral assistance from the individual G-7 nations and a $6 billion ruble stabilization fund. Aid would be delivered in the form of export credits, loans from international financial institutions, education and training assistance, help in establishing political and financial structures, and wide-ranging technical assistance.

The package was seen as an important vote of confidence for Yeltsin from the international community. Faced with domestic opposition to his reforms, Yeltsin could cite this international endorsement of his approach. He also could counter conservatives who criticized his pro-Western stance, by pointing to the tangible benefits of aid that resulted from his policies.

Despite dissatisfaction with foreign aid and public perceptions that he was spending too much time on foreign affairs, Bush supported U.S. participation in the aid program. The United States also favored a major restructuring of the former Soviet Union's $70 billion foreign debt. In a June 17, 1992, joint news conference with Yeltsin during their Washington summit, Bush justified U.S. support for Russia with these words: "Success for Russian democracy will enhance the security of every American. Think for just a moment about what that means — not for presidents, nor for heads of state or historians, but for parents and their children. It means a future free from fear." Proponents of providing financial aid to the Soviet Union supported the president's position by saying that no investment in American national security could be more valuable than helping Russian economic and political reforms succeed.

Congress acted on this principle by passing the Freedom Support Act. The aid bill authorized $410 million in bilateral assistance for the states of the former Soviet Union. It also authorized a $12.3 billion increase in U.S. contributions to the International Monetary Fund. After heated debate, the Senate passed S 2532 by a vote of 76-20 on July 2. The House passed its version (HR 4547) on Aug. 6, 255-164, then passed an amended S 2532 by voice vote the same day. The Senate adopted the conference report (H Rept 102-964) by voice vote on Oct. 1, and the House followed suit on Oct. 3 by a vote of 232-164. The president signed the measure (PL 102-511) on Oct. 24.

Russia Versus Other Republics

Many foreign policy analysts criticized the Bush administration for focusing too much attention on Russia and adjusting slowly to the disintegration of the Soviet Union. Before the breakup, Bush expressed a preference for the Soviet Union's remaining unified. Contributing to his position were a desire to preserve the continuity of an improving U.S.-Soviet relationship, a concern for the arms control agreements that had been previously concluded with the Soviet Union and a fear that the splintering of the Soviet Union would result in ethnic warfare that would destabilize parts of Asia, Europe and the Middle East.

Although the United States recognized all the former Soviet republics as independent states, it was slow to deploy ambassadors or set up embassies in some of the new states. American diplomatic recognition was important to the new republics because it bolstered their legitimacy and was a critical prerequisite to significant foreign investment. U.S. policy on recognizing the various former Soviet republics was to seek assurances of their commitment to the principles of democracy and human rights — particularly protection of minority rights — and transition to a market economy.

Ukraine and Kazakhstan received special American attention. Both President Leonid Kravchuk of Ukraine and President Nursultan Nazarbayev of Kazakhstan visited Washington in mid-1992 to meet with Bush and discuss arms control issues. The two leaders made strong impressions as responsible leaders who wished to expand relations with the United States.

Because the survival of Yeltsin and his reforms was the primary goal of U.S. policy toward the former Soviet Union, the United States was patient with Russian activities in other former Soviet republics. For example, during 1992, the United States avoided demanding that Russia immediately withdraw its troops from the Baltic states, despite strong pressure from Americans of Baltic descent to make such demands. American criticism of the activities of the Russian military in Moldova also was muted. Implicit in the U.S. approach to relations with the former Soviet Union was a belief that Yeltsin, like Gorbachev, was vulnerable to attacks from the right. Because Yeltsin's continuing hold on power was seen as central to the continuation of Russia's relatively benign foreign policy, short-term goals, such as the removal of Russian troops from the Baltics, were subordinated to the goal of bolstering Yeltsin. Some observers in the United States, including high-ranking administration officials, reasoned that the Baltic states and other non-Russian republics would most likely be able to achieve a complete and secure independence if Yeltsin's reforms were allowed to proceed.

A Continuing Revolution

On Jan. 2, 1992, the Yeltsin government implemented a major liberalization of prices — the first step in a radical plan to create a free-market economy. During 1992, the government made progress in implementing the plan, despite some setbacks. But the already weak economy, strained by the shock of the reform measures, fell further into depression. Moreover, Yeltsin had to backtrack in deference to conservative opposition.

The task of reviving the economy was complicated by the severed links between the interdependent states of the former Soviet Union and the ongoing ethnic and political conflicts in those states. Attacks and discrimination against Russians in the non-Russian republics fueled Russian nationalism in Russia. At the same time, seemingly intractable territorial, religious and tribal disputes between ethnic groups — long suppressed under Soviet rule — resulted in open warfare. In Moldova, Russian Communist holdovers in the trans-Dniester region declared their secession, prompting fighting between Moldovan troops and Russian separatists. Violence between Azerbaijan and Armenia over the disputed Nagorno-Karabakh region escalated. In Georgia and Tajikistan, civil wars seriously disrupted travel and trade. These conflicts killed thousands of people, created hundreds of thousands of refugees and raised the specter that outside countries such as China, Iran, Turkey or Romania could become involved.

The future did not seem bright to most Russians. Even in the 14 other republics, where independence was greeted with jubilation by many citizens, optimism deteriorated as the economic depression deepened. The Soviet system, though repressive, undemocratic and anti-nationalist, had at least offered security, predictability and guaranteed employment.

The economy appeared to be in a helpless decline, and the chaos in the former Soviet Union was more widespread than at any time since World War II. Street crime and organized crime became rampant in many cities, and the new states were left to deal with severe environmental degradation without sufficient funds or expertise for cleanup.

Yeltsin and his economic reform program survived in power. But he remained besieged by political troubles. Though he enjoyed the enthusiastic support of liberals and intellectuals, his popularity among the general public was weakened by falling living standards. During the summer of 1992, a public opinion poll showed that fewer Russians trusted Yeltsin than his conservative vice president, Aleksandr Rutskoy, who had sharply denounced Yeltsin's reforms.

In some ways, Yeltsin was less vulnerable to a coup than Gorbachev had been. In particular, he enjoyed the legitimacy of being elected president in a popular vote. After his forthright stand during the August 1991 coup attempt, Yeltsin also came to be regarded by many as a national hero. But in other ways, he was more vulnerable than Gorbachev. A coup could have been undertaken against him in the name of Russian nationalism, a concept enjoying much more popularity in Russia in 1992 than a return to communism enjoyed in the Soviet Union in August 1991.

Like the first Russian revolution, the second Russian revolution progressed in stages. During the late 1980s, Gorbachev instituted far-reaching reforms that propelled Soviet society into a new era. The failed coup ended Gorbachev's efforts to manage change and led to the Soviet breakup. As 1992 ended, the world watched to see if Yeltsin and Russian democracy would survive. The second Russian revolution was an ongoing affair that was not necessarily in its last stage.

5

Defense Policy

Introduction	*335*
1989-90 Chronology	*339*
1991-92 Chronology	*369*

Defense Policy

George Bush's presidential term witnessed the unambiguous — and startlingly abrupt — collapse of the Soviet military threat that had driven U.S. defense policy for nearly five decades. Coming on top of the long-term federal budget crunch that was rooted in tax cuts of the Reagan years, the end of the Cold War accelerated the steady decline of Pentagon budgets (measured in "real" or inflation-adjusted terms) that had begun in 1986. The demise of the Soviet Union also swept from the congressional agenda the nuclear arms and arms control issues that had dominated the defense debate for nearly 20 years.

New cardinal issues — reflecting U.S. security requirements in a new world that was much more turbulent and menacing to important, if not vital, U.S. interests — would take a while to emerge.

In some respects, the determination of how much to spend on defense was a surrogate measure of the priority members of Congress placed on international involvement relative to domestic concerns. But the defense budget was a crude indicator, at best. And it was distorted by members' desire to moderate the pace of defense cuts to protect jobs back home.

A more substantive debate over alternative U.S. strategies for dealing with the post-Cold War world was forestalled in large part by the lack of thought given to the matter by the nation's defense policy establishment, inside government and out. Two generations of diplomatic, military and academic specialists had done their thinking within the parameters of a bipolar world in which the United States faced an expansionist, Marxist superpower. The sudden transformation of that global context resonated in the ideological currents that had made interventionists out of most conservatives and isolationists out of most liberals.

In the late 1940s, conservatives departed from their isolationist roots when confronted by a nuclear-armed Soviet state, which they saw as driven by Marxist dogma into an unconditional struggle against the West. Once the threat was gone, some conservative Republicans, typified by commentator and 1992 presidential candidate Patrick J. Buchanan, moved back toward isolationism.

During the 1960s, the Vietnam War and other Third World conflicts soured mainstream Democrats on the idea of intervention for humanitarian purposes. Too often, ostensibly "pro-Western" forces proved to be brutal and exploitative autocrats mouthing anti-communist slogans to garner U.S. support. With the end of the superpower rivalry, the climate changed.

First, some social conflicts, which had been suppressed, exploded with extraordinary violence, as in the southern republics of the former Soviet Union, the former Yugoslavia and Somalia. Second, a broad international consensus formed for collective action in response to some of these situations. And finally, by the end of Bush's term, some senior Democrats became increasingly insistent that the United States act within this new, multilateral context.

The Old Threat Dies

As early as President Ronald Reagan's second term, Soviet President Mikhail S. Gorbachev had broken the stalemate that had characterized the U.S.-Soviet military standoff since the early 1970s.

In summit meetings at Geneva in 1985 and at Reykjavik, Iceland, in 1986, Gorbachev agreed, at least in principle, on large reductions in long-range nuclear weapons to equal levels — a goal that would require Moscow to give up considerably more warheads on intercontinental ballistic missiles (ICBMs), which were the backbone of the Soviet nuclear force.

But the real earthquake came later, only weeks before Bush replaced Reagan in the Oval Office. In a wide-ranging address to the United Nations General Assembly on Dec. 7, 1988, Gorbachev broke dramatically with traditional Soviet rhetoric to extol individual liberty as the keystone of world peace while belittling the role of military force and ideological struggle in world affairs. And he backed that up by announcing sweeping unilateral cuts in Soviet conventional forces, particularly those deployed in or oriented toward Eastern Europe.

The significance of those cuts was twofold. The most obvious was that the threat of a Soviet-led attack on West-

References

Discussion of defense policy for the years 1945-64 may be found in *Congress and the Nation Vol. I*, pp. 237-334; for the years 1965-68, *Congress and the Nation Vol. II*, pp. 827-890; for the years 1969-72, *Congress and the Nation Vol. III*, pp. 191-252; for the years 1973-76, *Congress and the Nation Vol. IV*, pp. 153-197; for the years 1977-80, *Congress and the Nation Vol. V*, pp. 125-176; for the years 1981-84, *Congress and the Nation Vol. VI*, pp. 201-257; for the years 1985-88, *Congress and the Nation Vol. VII*, pp. 273-340.

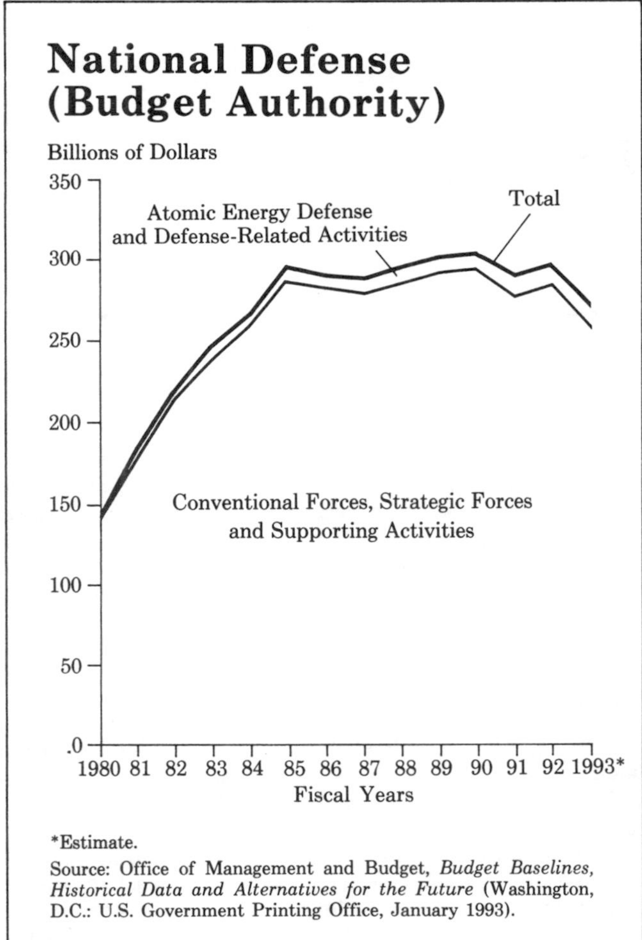

*Estimate.

Source: Office of Management and Budget, *Budget Baselines, Historical Data and Alternatives for the Future* (Washington, D.C.: U.S. Government Printing Office, January 1993).

ern Europe had long been the fundamental consideration driving the size of U.S. conventional forces and the pace at which they were modernized. Beyond that, the conventional standoff in Central Europe between the North Atlantic Treaty Organization (NATO) and the Soviet-led Warsaw Pact was an important factor underpinning U.S. strategic arms policy. Though rarely acknowledged by U.S. officials, one purpose of the size and versatility of the U.S. nuclear arsenal was to plant in the minds of Soviet leaders at least the possibility that, if the numerically superior Warsaw Pact forces began to prevail in a conventional attack, the United States would respond with nuclear weapons.

Thus, a diminution of the Soviet conventional threat in Europe opened up new possibilities for defense cutbacks across the board. That process accelerated rapidly in 1989 as every state in the Warsaw Pact transformed itself — in most cases, peacefully — from an authoritarian Soviet client into a relatively democratic regime intent on shedding Moscow's yoke. It began, early in the year, with Hungary and Poland, where pressures for liberalization had been openly building for some time.

The event that came to symbolize the end of Soviet control in Eastern Europe happened in East Germany. On Nov. 9, the Berlin Wall was opened, and East Germans were allowed freely to travel to the West. The sagging communist system caved in quickly once Gorbachev let it be known that the Soviet troops stationed in the country would not be used to bolster the regime.

By year's end, Moscow-oriented communist rule also had disappeared from Bulgaria, Czechoslovakia and Romania — in the last case, after a brief but brutal civil war, ending in the trial and execution of President Nicolae Ceausescu and his wife.

That left only the Soviet Union, stripped of its satellites and wracked by dissension over Gorbachev's efforts to liberalize the economy, but still armed to the teeth. Over the next two years, Gorbachev and Bush would finalize far-reaching treaties to cut conventional and strategic forces. But on a raft of issues that had long defied resolution, the laborious arms control negotiating process was outstripped by the unraveling of Soviet military power, as Gorbachev orchestrated a process of dramatic retrenchment.

Then, on Aug. 19, 1991, hard-line communists arrested Gorbachev in his Crimean retreat and attempted to seize control of the government. But Russian President Boris N. Yeltsin, backed by tens of thousands of Muscovites, defied the coup forces. Within three days, the putsch collapsed, the hard-liners were arrested and Gorbachev was restored to power. However, the unified Soviet state Gorbachev tried to hold together proved a casualty of the ill-fated takeover.

By the end of December, the Soviet Union was officially dissolved, leaving behind Yeltsin's Russia and 14 other former Soviet republics.

New Dangers

Dealing with the separate independent states was one aspect of the new policy to be devised by U.S. defense planners. All of the former Soviet republics were at least nominally democratic, but many had longstanding grievances, at least against neighboring republics, involving territorial claims or the rights of ethnic minorities. All of the former republics were in critically difficult economic circumstances, and four — Russia, Ukraine, Belarus and Kazakhstan — had inherited significant fractions of the former Soviet nuclear arsenal.

Even before the Soviet Union disintegrated, Iraq's invasion of oil-rich Kuwait on Aug. 2, 1990, defined vividly another dimension of the new military threats the Pentagon would have to anticipate. Shaped by decades of Soviet training and supply, the forces of Iraqi President Saddam Hussein demonstrated that the end of the Soviet Union did not eliminate Soviet-style threats: forces designed for high-speed assaults over long distances, with large forces of tanks, artillery and armored troop carriers.

The Persian Gulf War served to quiet a growing chorus of critics who argued for sharply curtailing Pentagon spending on weapons such as the JSTARS radar plane and the ATACMS long-range bombardment rocket, which were developed to head off massed, mobile ground forces. The war marked the debate over future U.S. defense policy in four other respects:

- It gave added momentum to the longstanding congressional demand that the services spend more money on long-range transport, especially ships. While one program — the C-17 cargo plane, which had a history of cost, technical and management problems — was the subject of debate, no significant public objection was heard to the general proposition that U.S. forces should have the means of intervening in distant trouble spots on a relatively large scale and on relatively short notice.
- Dramatic evidence of the apparent successes of high-tech weaponry — eerie videotape shot at night showed

laser-guided bombs eviscerating buildings and heavily armored airplane shelters — rehabilitated the public standing of a defense establishment that had been bruised by years of criticism for mismanagement and incompetence.

- One particular type of high-tech weaponry — "stealth" aircraft designed to evade enemy detection — got a tremendous boost from the success of the first of the type to enter service: the F-117 Nighthawks. Misleadingly designated as fighters, these small bombers, which carried two laser-guided bombs apiece, destroyed the Iraqi air defense system and thus cleared the way for hundreds of other U.S. and allied planes to pulverize Iraqi targets. The success of the Nighthawks, however, provided little relief to the Air Force's B-2 "stealth" bomber. Congressional skepticism forced Bush to reduce the planned B-2 fleet to a mere 20 planes, after nearly cutting it to 15. The pullback in part was because of a sticker price of several hundred million dollars per plane and because, until far too late in the game, the Air Force insisted on justifying the plane largely in terms of a mission of nuclear retaliation against the Soviet Union.
- Finally, the Gulf War lent political momentum to the anti-missile defense program officially designated the strategic defense initiative (SDI) and unofficially referred to as "star wars." Reagan launched the program in 1983, saying it would free the American people from the threat of Soviet nuclear missiles.

In the course of the war, Iraq launched Soviet-designed Scud missiles at Israel and Saudi Arabia. U.S. Patriot missiles, according to early reports, were highly successful at intercepting the Scuds. SDI critics later complained that the reports were exaggerated.

Also boosting the political fortunes of SDI was the combination of Iraq's willingness to use the Scuds and the widespread fear that Iraq might be able to wed missile technology with the lethal chemical weapons it was trying to develop.

Aspin: A New Role

The most significant change during Bush's term in the way Congress dealt with defense policy was the emergence of House Armed Services Committee Chairman Les Aspin, D-Wis., as the dominant House voice on national security issues.

Consolidating his initially shaky grasp on the position, Aspin pulled the relatively liberal House Democratic Caucus toward his more centrist position on some key issues in 1990-92. Moreover, backstopped by a talented cadre of policy analysts on the committee staff, Aspin cranked out a series of white papers that had a considerable impact on the shape of public debate on defense issues.

With a spate of innovative and expertly promoted arguments, Aspin easily outpaced Bush administration officials (except for Joint Chiefs of Staff Chairman Gen. Colin L. Powell Jr.) in trying to frame public issues. By Bush's last year in office — which proved to be Aspin's last year as chairman, before he became defense secretary to President Bill Clinton — the Wisconsin Democrat's public influence at least rivaled that of Senate Armed Services Committee Chairman Sam Nunn, D-Ga., long the most influential of congressional defense specialists.

Aspin had become Armed Services chair in 1985, with the backing of centrist Democrats concerned that the committee was losing clout under the leadership of its elderly chairman, Mel Price, D-Ill. Although Aspin had long since established himself as an influential defense policy analyst, he took on the job with some important political liabilities.

For one thing, he held some distinctly hawkish positions; for example, he backed deployment of the MX intercontinental ballistic missile. By contrast, many liberals viewed opposition to the MX as an ideal way to highlight what they saw as the undue cost and risk of Reagan's confrontational stance toward the Soviet Union.

Moreover, tension stemming from specific issues was greatly exacerbated by Aspin's indifference to routine political fence-tending and by some members' belief — fairly or not — that Aspin was deceptive in his dealings with them. Early in 1987, the Democratic Caucus ousted Aspin from the chairmanship, though he regained it two weeks later with fervent pledges to be more attentive to his fellow partisans.

In 1989, however, in typically lone-wolf fashion, he decided to back the Bush administration's fiscal 1990 Pentagon budget request as a gesture of support for Defense Secretary Dick Cheney's effort to cut planned defense costs by canceling several major conventional weapons programs. Cheney proposed eliminating some programs with strong congressional support, including the Navy's F-14 fighter and the V-22 Osprey — a hybrid airplane/helicopter intended to transport Marines. Aspin's position was overridden by his own committee and then was swamped on the House floor.

Recovering from that fiasco, Aspin reorganized his committee staff late in 1989, building a new team around a handful of veteran congressional operatives who were both knowledgeable about defense issues and street-smart in the ways of the House. Partly by accommodating committee members' constituent-oriented desires and partly by extensive consultations, Aspin and his aides fostered a strong esprit de corps among the panel's once fractious majority caucus. And he secured the support of fellow Democrats in beginning to reshape U.S. defense policy for the post-Cold War world.

Aspin's efforts to establish himself as the leading Democratic voice on defense issues in the House were strongly supported by Speaker Thomas S. Foley, D-Wash., and other party leaders who were apprehensive that liberals, with their leverage in the Caucus, might draw the party into politically costly positions. While playing a collegial role in prolonged discussions among Democratic leaders over how much to slice from Bush's fiscal 1991 Pentagon request, he persuaded liberal activists in 1990 to drop their insistence on drastic and immediate cuts in defense outlays. He successfully argued that, essentially for technical reasons, deep outlay reductions would have to be phased in over several years.

By January 1991, most Democrats were sufficiently satisfied that Aspin's expertise and newly honed political savvy served their agendas, so no adverse political repercussions were felt when Aspin helped orchestrate the House vote to support Bush's decision to go immediately to war with Iraq. In the end, his detailed prediction of victory — which proved to be one of the more accurate public projections — only boosted his political stock.

Nunn: New Challenges

During the same four years, Nunn remained the most influential single senator on defense questions. That standing was partly rooted in the meticulous care with which he mastered the substance of issues and was partly reflected in the degree to which key defense battles in the Senate often turned on a small group of centrist Democrats who typically voted with Nunn.

Beginning in Reagan's second term, however, Nunn's influence in the Senate came under attack. Key aspects of Reagan's visionary goal for SDI required tests of space-based weapons, which the U.S. government held were banned by the 1972 U.S.-Soviet treaty limiting anti-ballistic missile (ABM) systems. Early in 1987, the Reagan administration announced that a close reading of the treaty and of the negotiating record showed that the pact could be interpreted in a less restrictive way that would allow the disputed tests. In a series of speeches than ran to 98 pages of heavily footnoted text in the *Congressional Record*, Nunn challenged that claim in detail, branding the administration's case as "fundamentally flawed."

Many Republicans complained that Nunn's role in the ABM treaty episode revealed him to be a partisan Democrat. Those arguments became much more forceful in the opening months of Bush's presidency, when Nunn successfully opposed the nomination of former Senate Armed Services Committee chairman John Tower, R-Texas, to become secretary of defense. Nunn argued that Tower had a history of alcohol abuse and of insensitivity to conflict-of-interest problems. But critics contended that Nunn simply feared that, as defense chief, Tower would be sufficiently combative and politically savvy to reduce Nunn's clout.

Allegations of increased partisanship — tied to a possible run for the presidency — also were fueled in 1990, when Nunn eliminated two points of friction with liberal activists. He abandoned his opposition to legalized abortions, and he resigned from Washington's all-male Burning Tree Country Club.

That same year, Nunn lost an important ally in his own party: Appropriations Committee Chairman Robert C. Byrd of West Virginia, one of the centrists who typically had been aligned with Nunn on close votes. Staking out a position he held tenaciously through the remainder of Bush's term, Byrd emerged during budget negotiations with the White House as an unstinting advocate of increased domestic discretionary spending. And he insisted it could be paid for in part by a more rapid reduction in defense spending than Nunn would support.

Through the spring and summer of 1990, Nunn stalled Senate action on a budget resolution that likely would have produced a lower defense spending ceiling than he had called for. Only after Iraq's Aug. 2 invasion of Kuwait reshuffled the political deck did the Senate — and ultimately a conference committee — approve Nunn's defense figure for fiscal 1991.

Many observers insisted that Nunn's prominence in January 1991 as an opponent of immediate war with Iraq was yet another drain on his political leverage, if only because it dented his image of political invincibility. Nunn discounted the argument, contending that his earlier victories had been harder to come by than people had assumed.

In any case, by mid-1991, Nunn demonstrated anew that he still was a key force to be reckoned with in the Senate. In tough negotiations with leading Republicans, he hammered out legislation that refocused the SDI program. The new bipartisan approach emphasized relatively early deployment of ground-based defenses against attacks by a limited number of ballistic missiles of either intercontinental range or shorter "theater" range. In effect, the deal traded Reagan's controversial goal of a global anti-missile shield for bipartisan support — by a narrow margin — of an actual deployment of defenses.

Chronology Of Action On Defense

1989-90

Defense spending was debated in the 101st Congress against a rapidly changing backdrop. Concern over budget deficits continued to mount, as spending for domestic programs tightened. The collapse of the Soviet military threat removed many of the basic tenets underlying the United States' defense policy since World War II and fueled demands for deep cuts in defense spending. But U.S. deployment of troops to the Persian Gulf region when Iraq seized Kuwait cooled some of the defense-cutting fervor. In this unsettled environment, defense experts on Capitol Hill and in the White House debated the course of U.S. policy in the post-Cold War era.

The Bush administration was a bit shaken in its early days, when the Senate rejected its nominee for secretary of defense, former Republican senator John Tower of Texas. But after weeks of bitter partisan wrangling, the issue was put to rest and House Minority Whip Dick Cheney of Wyoming was easily confirmed as the new secretary.

Cheney quickly took charge and marshaled his forces to fight for President Bush's defense proposals. Although overall defense spending was determined in budget agreements negotiated by the administration and Congress, wide disagreement remained over how the money would be spent.

Although Congress approved with relatively minor reductions Bush's request to continue developing two kinds of mobile intercontinental ballistic missiles, deep cuts were made in several of the administration's key strategic arms programs. Congress slowed the production rate of the B-2 "stealth" bomber — a plane designed as a flying wing and built of exotic materials to evade radar — and was deliberately ambiguous about the plane's future.

Congress also slashed requests and placed restrictions on the strategic defense initiative (SDI), the anti-missile defense system launched by President Ronald Reagan. The stage was thus set for future battles over administration plans to deploy a first-phase anti-missile defense, of limited effectiveness, by the end of the 1990s.

In his efforts to cancel major weapons programs to accommodate tight budgets, Cheney confounded many observers in 1989 by winning at least qualified approval for all but one — the V-22 Osprey, a hybrid airplane/helicopter intended for Marine Corps use as a troop carrier. In 1990, Congress again rejected Cheney's plan to terminate the program.

Attempts in 1989 to block military base closings recommended by a blue-ribbon commission the previous year failed. But in 1990, when Cheney came up with a new list of proposed closings, Democrats accused the administration of playing politics and legislation establishing a new commission to make recommendations on base closings was enacted.

Tower Nomination

After a bruising debate with strong partisan overtones, the Senate in 1989 rejected President Bush's nomination of former Texas GOP senator John Tower to be defense secretary. Tower became only the ninth Cabinet nominee turned down by the Senate.

Senate Armed Services Committee Chairman Sam Nunn, Ga., and other Democrats opposed to the nomination cited secret files of interviews conducted by the FBI that alleged that Tower had a long record of alcohol abuse. He would be an unreliable link between the president and the armed forces, the critics contended.

Moreover, they said, Tower's consulting contracts with weapons builders would severely handicap his efforts to restore public confidence in the scandal-wracked Pentagon procurement system.

But Senate Republicans, led by Minority Leader Bob Dole of Kansas, angrily insisted that the vote against Tower was a naked power grab. Given Tower's pugnacious style and his experience as a former Armed Services Committee chairman, his allies contended, Democrats feared he would be too formidable an advocate of Bush's policies.

The day after Tower's nomination was rejected, Bush nominated Rep. Dick Cheney, R-Wyo., to take the defense portfolio. Cheney, the second ranking House Republican, easily won the Senate's approval. *(Box, p. 341)*

Controversial Nominee

The Tower nomination got off to a difficult start when Bush, as president-elect, delayed its widely expected announcement until mid-December 1988.

Tower, who had served in the Senate from 1961 to 1985 and chaired the Armed Services Committee during his final four years of service, had been the front-runner from the start. He had served as chief U.S. negotiator in strategic arms reduction talks (START) with the Soviet Union in 1985-86 and had chaired an investigation of the Iran-contra affair in early 1987. And he was a longtime Bush political ally who had openly hungered for the spot.

But from 1986 to 1988, Tower had served as a consultant for four major defense contractors, as well as for several consulting firms that worked for defense contractors. And the twice-divorced Texan had been plagued by rumors of womanizing and drinking problems.

Bush waited to make his choice official until the FBI had completed an unusually long and thorough investigation of Tower. Announcing Tower's appointment, Bush said he was "totally satisfied" with the results of the inquiry.

But many on Capitol Hill were not.

Committee Action

Questions about Tower's professional and personal life were aired in several days of Armed Services Committee hearings and during committee debate on the nomination.

Concerns about Tower's conflicts of interest centered on his "revolving door" relationship with government and the defense industry. Some committee Democrats argued that Tower faced the perception of a conflict of interest because immediately after leaving his position as an arms control negotiator he signed lucrative consulting contracts with firms whose business would be affected by the results of the arms talks.

According to documents made public by the committee, Tower earned $763,777 for his services for defense contractors from April 1, 1986, to Dec. 1, 1988. Witnesses and committee Democrats voiced concern about how the public would view Tower's contacts in the defense industry and the large fees he received.

In his defense, Tower insisted that he had not disclosed to his clients any confidential information. He told the committee he had terminated all his consulting contracts and would face no conflict of interest as defense secretary. To avoid the appearance of a conflict, Tower said he would turn over to his deputy certain decisions involving firms for which he once had worked.

Democrats on the committee also were concerned about whether Tower had an alcohol problem and had behaved improperly toward women. The panel was said to have conducted an extensive investigation of allegations about Tower's personal life that went beyond the FBI background check provided to the committee. When questioned by the committee, Tower denied having a drinking problem. He said "zero toleration" should be allowed for anyone in a sensitive job in the Pentagon who had a drinking problem. He said discrimination against women or sexual harassment of women likewise should not be tolerated, although he said he opposed combat assignments for women.

When the committee convened to vote on the nomination, the members' views of Tower's fitness for the job had hardened along party lines. The nomination was rejected by an 11-9 party-line vote on Feb. 23, 1989.

Citing the defense secretary's position in the military chain of command, most of the Democrats named as their leading objection to the nomination indications in the FBI reports that Tower had a previous — and potentially existing — drinking problem.

Republicans argued that the Democrats were giving more weight to a handful of anonymous sources than to dozens of distinguished Americans who had served with Tower in the Senate or observed him carrying out official duties, as well as neighbors and waiters in the restaurants he was known to frequent — none of whom recalled an instance when he was inebriated.

Democrats and Republicans also debated the conflict-of-interest and womanizing issues. Republicans cast the issue in broader terms, as a question of whether the Senate would repudiate Bush at the very outset of his administration on a key nomination that had received Bush's unflagging personal support. They vowed to carry the fight to the Senate floor.

Floor Action

In the wake of the committee rejection of Tower, Republicans launched an intense campaign to save the nomination. Bush personally lobbied undecided senators. Tower promised to abstain from alcohol during his tenure as secretary of defense. GOP strategists vowed to go to the mat to win Senate approval.

When the full Senate took up the nomination, the debate over Tower's qualifications and the Senate's right to impose its own standards reprised the debate that had preceded the Armed Services panel vote.

But GOP senators added a new thrust in their defense of the nomination: an attack on the credibility of some of the more lurid allegations that had been leaked to the press and a demand that Tower not be disqualified on the basis of unsworn statements by unidentified individuals who had not been cross-examined. These Republicans said Tower's critics relied on unfounded allegations by anonymous sources that were disproven by senators' personal knowledge of Tower and his solid record of achievement.

But Armed Services Democrats, led by Nunn, contended that the voluminous summaries of FBI interviews indicated that Tower had a record of alcohol abuse that made him a dangerous choice to put next in line to the president in the chain of military command. Moreover, the Democrats argued, Tower's lucrative consulting contracts with weapons builders would gravely impair his ability to restore public trust in the scandal-plagued Pentagon weapons-buying system.

On March 9, the sixth day of debate, the Senate rejected the Tower nomination by a **key vote of 47-53 (R 44-1; D 3-52)**. The last time a Cabinet nominee was rejected was in 1959, when the Senate had voted against Lewis L. Strauss, President Dwight D. Eisenhower's nominee for secretary of commerce. *(1989 key votes, p. 1021)*

Angry Republicans denounced the Senate action. "This has been a pitched partisan battle," Dole said. The Senate had become "a pipeline for gossip ... a partisan hotbed of character assassination."

But Bush struck a more conciliatory tone in a statement shortly after the Senate vote. He regretted that some members had opposed Tower on the basis of "perceptions based on groundless rumor" but added, "Now, however, we owe it to the American people to come together and move forward."

1990 Defense Authorization

In enacting the fiscal 1990 defense authorization bill (HR 2461 — PL 101-189), Congress in 1989 marked a modest but significant transition for the military buildup that began in Jimmy Carter's presidency and ran out of money during Ronald Reagan's.

The bill made the first absolute reduction in funding for the strategic defense initiative (SDI), the anti-missile research program that became the symbolic centerpiece of President Reagan's defense program. Though Congress had slashed the SDI funding request each year beginning in 1986, the 1989 action was the first time members reduced its budget below the current year's amount. *(SDI, box, p. 370)*

HR 2461 also supported the thrust of Defense Secretary Dick Cheney's effort to terminate several major weapons programs, marking the start of a painful triage process among weapons producers as the Pentagon adjusted to tight budgets at home and the reduction in the apparent threat posed by the Soviet Union. Of 10 production lines Cheney wanted to close in fiscal 1990 or 1991, Senate-House conferees on the legislation went along in six cases, delayed two for a year and deferred final judgment for a year on two more. In the two most hotly contested cases, conferees approved one last purchase of F-14D Navy jets and put off until 1990 a decision on whether to kill off production of the Marine Corps' V-22 Osprey aircraft. *(Canceling weapons, box, p. 348)*

The final version authorized a total of $302.96 billion for defense programs of the Pentagon and Energy Department, essentially the amount agreed to by the White House and the bipartisan congressional leadership in a budget summit in April 1989.

Before leaving office in January 1989, Reagan had sent Congress an overall national defense budget for fiscal 1990 that totaled $315.2 billion, with $9.6 billion earmarked for defense-related programs of the Energy Department and other non-Pentagon agencies. This would have amounted to a 2 percent boost over the fiscal 1989 appropriation for defense, on top of inflation costs. But in April, President Bush and Congress agreed to reduce the overall defense figure to $305.2 billion, with $295.6 billion for the Defense Department.

Bush's revised defense budget — $10 billion leaner — followed the broad outlines of Reagan's but held the possibility of fundamental shifts in defense policy. Cuts in the funds requested for procurement and military research accounted for more than 70 percent of the reduction. Bush's most striking break with Reagan's defense posture was his decision to level off the Navy's expansion one ship short of the service's goal of 15 large aircraft carriers.

Defense Leadership

The nomination of House Minority Whip Dick Cheney, R-Wyo., to be secretary of defense won quick and overwhelming support from the Senate. Cheney was tapped by President Bush for the post March 10, 1989, and was confirmed by the Senate March 17 by a 92-0 vote. *(Cabinet profiles, p. 1170)*

The broad, bipartisan support for Cheney was a stark contrast to the bitter six-week-long battle over Bush's first choice for the post, former senator John Tower, R-Texas. Tower's nomination sank in a sea of allegations of excessive drinking and womanizing, and questions about his lobbying activities. *(Tower nomination, p. 339)*

House Committee Action

The House Armed Services Committee reported HR 2461 (H Rept 101-121) on July 1. During markup of its $305.5 billion defense authorization bill, the panel was a kaleidoscope of shifting alliances.

Not surprisingly, when the panel could save from the budget ax two weapons programs — the F-14D fighter plane and the Osprey troop transport — that enjoyed vigorous support from prestigious military leaders and powerful constituency interests, it chose to do so. Armed Services Committee Chairman Les Aspin, D-Wis., had vowed to oppose any changes in the administration's weapons procurement budget, but his hold-the-line stance was overridden by a majority of his fellow Democrats. Seventeen of the committee's 21 Republicans supported the administration.

Across the political spectrum, the committee accepted the premise that defense budgets would be level — at best — for years. And partly for that reason, the costly strategic arms programs that were hallmarks of Reagan's Pentagon buildup faced more skeptical appraisal, even from Republicans.

The B-2 "stealth" bomber program — with a projected price tag of $72 billion for 132 planes — survived a challenge in the committee markup. But the committee's 16-36 vote to reject an amendment to drop the administration's entire request from the bill seemed to reflect at least as much a hesitancy to kill the program abruptly as it did all-out support for the new plane. In the end, the panel cut $800 million from the administration's request and approved production of two planes instead of the three requested. *(B-2 bomber, box, p. 398)*

The panel sliced $1 billion from the $4.9 billion request for SDI. An amendment to restore the administration's funding request failed 12-39. Significantly, while 12 Republicans supported the amendment, nine opposed it. A provision was added to continue the ban enacted in 1987 and 1988 on SDI tests that violated the traditional, restrictive interpretation of the 1972 U.S.-Soviet anti-ballistic missile (ABM) treaty. In effect, this would bar tests in space of SDI weaponry.

The committee approved the amounts the Pentagon requested for two mobile intercontinental ballistic missiles (ICBMs). The bill authorized the Pentagon to buy 12 additional 10-warhead MX missiles ($771 million), to continue development of a rail-mobile basing system for the missile ($789 million) and to buy components that would be used in the projected rail-mobile scheme ($164 million). Also approved without change was the $100 million requested to continue developing a single-warhead weapon nicknamed Midgetman, which was small enough to be launched from a large truck. The panel rejected amendments to kill Midgetman and to delete funding for the rail-mobile version of MX.

The $1.14 billion requested to build the 17th in a class of huge Trident missile-launching submarines was approved, as was the $1.6 billion requested for Trident II missiles.

The administration had requested funding to gear up a production line for converting early, "A" model versions of the Navy's F-14 fighter into F-14Ds by installing new radars and jet engines. But F-14D proponents on the Armed Services panel won approval for the idea of delaying the modification program until fiscal 1991 and including $1 billion for 12 new F-14Ds.

The panel was uneasy about Cheney's plan to end production of the Air Force's F-15 fighter jet in fiscal 1991. It directed the secretary to report on the risk of ending production and on ways the plane might continue to be manufactured without assuming an increase in the size of future budgets.

Administration requests for funds to develop a new fighter plane, designated ATF and scheduled to enter service late in the 1990s as replacement for the F-15 and F-14, and to continue development and begin production of a new ground-attack plane, designated ATA, were approved. Both Armed Services panels had insisted that the Air Force and Navy collaborate on the two new planes.

The 62nd and last sub-hunting submarine of the *Los Angeles* class was approved, as was funding for components that would be used in larger, more heavily armed *Seawolf*-class subs planned in future years.

The panel added $351 million to continue development of the V-22 Osprey airplane/helicopter hybrid and

$157 million for components for Ospreys to be included in the fiscal 1991 budget.

House Floor Action

During three days of debate before passing HR 2461 by 261-162 on July 27, the House substantially changed Bush's defense program. In sharp breaks from administration requests, the House halved the authorization for production of rail-mobile launchers for the 10-warhead MX. It also reduced to $3.1 billion the amount authorized for SDI. It reduced funding for production of the B-2 stealth bomber and barred any purchase of additional copies until Congress formally approved a cheaper B-2 production plan.

Moreover, House Republicans played leading roles in the process. For almost a decade, Republicans could be expected to be sympathetic to Pentagon proposals and Democrats skeptical. While that remained mostly the case, enough members of each party broke ranks during House floor action on HR 2461 to create a more volatile political situation.

The House bill authorized some $226 billion for defense-related programs of the Departments of Defense and Energy. The military payroll, not covered by the original bill, would bring the total defense budget to $305.4 billion.

A tenuous alliance between supporters of the rail-mobile version of the large MX missile and supporters of the smaller, road-mobile Midgetman had been forged when each side realized it could not win the votes for its missile unless it supported the other missile as well. But the two-missile deal and the coalition came undone during the House debate. *(Box, p. 343)*

In a series of votes, the House first rejected amendments to kill the mobile-ICBM programs. But then, to GOP outrage, leading Midgetman backers started piling restraints on the rail-MX. Most importantly, the House July 26 adopted by a vote of 224-197 an amendment to cut funding for the rail-MX program nearly in half, to $600 million, none of which could be used to begin building components. Republican MX-backers growled that so deep a reduction in Bush's MX request undermined the basis for their reluctant support for Midgetman. Anti-Midgetman liberals and Republicans joined forces and by a standing vote of 176-90 deleted the Midgetman funds from the bill.

House liberals allied with several cost-conscious Republicans in an attempt to curtail the expensive and controversial B-2 program. But the House, by a **key vote of 144-279 (R 28-144; D 116-135)** on July 26, rejected their amendment allowing the Air Force to complete a fleet of 13 B-2s already built or under construction and then putting the production line on hold while those 13 were tested. The House earlier had rejected, 176-244, an amendment that reaffirmed the committee bill's authorization of the purchase of two of the planes. House members finally agreed, 257-160, on a third option, an amendment that reduced the committee's B-2 recommendation by $470 million and blocked use of any of the fiscal 1990 B-2 procurement money until the Air Force proposed, and Congress approved, a new, less expensive production plan. *(1989 key votes, p. 1021)*

Several attempts to revise HR 2461's procurement recommendations went down to defeat. One amendment, which would have returned the bill's authorization levels to those in the administration's revised budget and thereby reinstate Cheney's proposed cuts in weapons programs, was rejected 143-278 on July 25. After the vote, Republicans abandoned plans to offer individual amendments to cut the F-14D and Osprey from the bill.

After first rejecting amendments to modestly increase and drastically cut funding for SDI, the House approved a proposal for a $3.1 billion SDI authorization, $1 billion less than Congress authorized in fiscal 1989 and $1.8 billion less than Bush had requested. The amendment was adopted July 25 by a **key vote of 248-175 (R 34-137; D 214-38)**. The House then voted to reallocate the funds for other programs.

The House rejected three amendments by liberal arms control activists seeking to pare nuclear missile programs. Several amendments aimed at nudging the Bush administration toward negotiating arms reduction treaties were adopted, some by impressive margins, but all were non-binding. The highest priority among these for many liberal arms control lobbyists was an amendment urging the president to try to negotiate with the Soviets a verifiable ban on the production of plutonium and enriched uranium, two materials used in nuclear warheads. The amendment was adopted 284-138 on July 27.

Other action included adoption of amendments dealing with wage rates for Pentagon construction projects and pressuring U.S. allies to pay a larger share for mutual defense.

Senate Committee Action

The Senate Armed Services Committee set the stage for a conflict with its House counterpart when it reported its version of the fiscal 1990 defense authorization bill (S 1352 — S Rept 101-81) July 19. The panel endorsed across the board Cheney's decisions to end production of several major weapons — including the Navy's F-14D fighter and the Marine Corps' Osprey transport — and approved production of the costly B-2 bomber.

Senate Armed Services Chairman Sam Nunn, D-Ga., who had strongly criticized past Pentagon budgets for starting up more programs than it could afford over the long run, applauded Cheney for his fiscal realism. And the influential Nunn mounted a forceful defense of the B-2 program, insisting that the new plane was essential if the United States was to continue its policy of keeping bombers as well as ballistic missiles in its nuclear arsenal.

The panel approved $4.1 billion of the $4.4 billion requested to continue developing the B-2 and build three planes. The $300 million reduction reflected fact-of-life changes in the schedule of the program, Nunn said, and would not retard it further. The panel stipulated that production funds could not be spent until certain milestones in the B-2 test program were achieved.

The committee approved a total of $4.5 billion for research by the Defense and Energy departments on SDI. Like its House counterpart, the panel added a provision that would, in effect, extend through fiscal 1990 a prohibition on tests of space-based SDI weapons, which Congress had enacted each year since 1987.

Administration requests for developing the rail-mobile MX missile and the Midgetman missile were approved. The panel also endorsed the purchase of 12 additional MXs and boosted the authorization for research on missile improvements.

The committee approved the request for a 17th Trident missile-launching submarine and increased the funding for Trident missiles to be carried by the big subs on the

Continued Development of Two Mobile Missiles

Congress in 1989 gave the Bush administration the go-ahead to continue developing two kinds of mobile intercontinental ballistic missiles (ICBMs): the rail-launched version of the 10-warhead MX and the smaller, truck-carried, single-warhead Midgetman.

Although the final defense authorization bill (HR 2461) made only minor reductions in President Bush's request, the victory was not easy. Debate had raged within both the administration and Congress over whether to continue with one, both or neither of the two mobile missiles.

Background

Policy makers were well into their second decade of debate over what, if any, scheme should be funded to make American ICBMs mobile to forestall the possibility that a Soviet missile attack could wipe out the U.S. ground-based missile force.

The Air Force and most Republican defense specialists favored putting launchers for the MX on railroad trains that would flee their bases to roam the commercial rail lines at the first sign of a U.S.-Soviet crisis.

But influential defense specialists from the center of the political spectrum — including Senate Armed Services Chairman Sam Nunn, D-Ga., and his House counterpart, Les Aspin, D-Wis. — complained that the MX trains would be too vulnerable to a surprise attack while at their bases. For several years, the two committee chairmen, along with Brent Scowcroft, Bush's national security adviser, had favored developing the Midgetman.

MX backers rejected the small-missile proposal on grounds that a Soviet attack out of the blue, which would catch the MX trains off guard, was too unlikely to warrant the Midgetman price tag, estimated at double or triple the $12 billion cost of deploying 100 rail-mobile MXs.

Congress and the Reagan administration stalemated on the mobile-missile issue, thereby passing along the decision to Reagan's successor. After Bush's election, Aspin and others began advocating a compromise that would fund scaled-down versions of both systems. *(Congress and the Nation Vol. VII, p. 320)*

Liberals discounted the threat to silo-based ICBMs. But by late 1988, many of them backed Midgetman as less strategically provocative.

Bush decided on the two-missile plan. The president insisted that the program to develop both mobile missiles would bolster U.S. deterrence as well as boost America's leverage in the strategic arms reduction talks (START) negotiations.

Legislative Action

Bush requested $100 million for Midgetman and $1.1 billion for the rail MX and to begin buying components and building facilities that would be used to deploy that weapon. Bush decided to deploy on rails the 50 MXs already deployed in armored launch silos in Wyoming.

The requests were approved by the Senate without change, but they faced a bruising battle in the House. The House Armed Services Committee accepted Bush's request, but when the defense authorization bill came to the floor, the shaky, bipartisan coalition that supported the two-missile strategy dissolved.

Liberals who regarded deployment of the rail-MX as a foregone conclusion made a last-ditch effort to win Republican support for a plan to defeat the Midgetman. But Bush mounted strong pressure on Republicans to support the two-missile plan.

The effort seemed to work when the House approved both missile programs by comfortable margins. The House July 26 first rejected by 168-253 an amendment that would have killed the rail MX. It then rejected 168-254 an amendment that would have killed Midgetman. The House also rejected by voice vote an amendment that would have ended both programs.

Had matters rested there, opponents of the Midgetman project would have been routed. But leading Midgetman backers then piled further restraints on the rail MX, eliciting GOP outrage. The House July 26 voted 224-197 to cut rail-MX funding nearly in half, authorizing only $600 million to continue development. The House also adopted by a vote of 259-160 a provision limiting to 50 the number of MX missiles that could be deployed in any fashion.

Irate pro-MX Republicans then teamed up with liberal Democrats to kill funding for Midgetman. A motion that, in effect, was an amendment to kill the small mobile missile was agreed to on a standing vote of 176-90.

House-Senate conferees settled on a total authorization of $1.05 billion, which was to be divided between the two development programs. It also made available for Midgetman an additional $100 million appropriated in fiscal 1989 but not yet spent.

Conferees retained the House-passed cap of 50 deployed MXs. The cap was an important symbol to some arms control lobbyists of their long battle with the Reagan administration, which led to the 1985 agreement that no more than 50 MXs be deployed in fixed silos.

grounds that the Pentagon budget fell short of the minimum amount required for the program by legislation enacted in 1987.

The request for 603 M-1 tanks was approved, but objections were raised to the administration's plan to buy only 516 the following year. Because Congress had directed the Pentagon in 1988 to sign a multi-year contract to buy at least 600 tanks annually, the panel boosted the funding request for components to build 600 M-1s in fiscal 1991.

The committee went along with Cheney's decision to end production of new F-14Ds for the Navy, authorizing the $689 million requested to bring early-model F-14As up to the "D" standard by giving them new engines and radars.

The Air Force's requests for 35 F-15E ground-attack planes and 150 F-16 fighters were approved. But the committee served notice that it would review in 1990 Cheney's plan to end production of the F-15 in fiscal 1991.

The panel ordered the Navy and Marine Corps to shuffle their respective fleets of bombers, with the Marines giving the Navy their five squadrons of A-6Es — big jets packed with electronic gear to find targets at night or in bad weather. This would solve the bomber shortage the Navy was to face because the Pentagon canceled for budgetary reasons a new version of the plane, designated the A-6G. The committee told the Pentagon to replace the Marines' A-6Es with smaller, less expensive F/A-18s.

The committee objected to the administration's plan to end production of the Maverick air-launched anti-tank missiles in 1992 and denied funding for the Air Force program to develop a Maverick replacement, ordering the service to adapt instead a similar Army-developed missile.

The panel cut some from the funding request for the 62nd and last sub-hunting *Los Angeles*-class submarine, saying the money was available from funds appropriated earlier. The request for components for the *Seawolf* submarine was approved.

The committee, endorsing Cheney's position that the V-22 Osprey was too expensive for the Marines to use to haul their landing forces ashore from an amphibious landing fleet, approved the request for 23 CH-53E helicopters to substitute for the planned Ospreys. But the committee insisted that the Osprey flight-test program should be completed, in case the project could drum up other customers in the Pentagon or in the private sector that might drive down the unit cost and thus make it affordable for the Marines.

Senate Floor Action

The Senate on Aug. 2 passed 95-4 an annual defense authorization bill that would result in a $305 billion defense budget in fiscal 1990.

The measure, S 1352, was sharply at odds with the House version over some of the most important strategic arms projects in Bush's defense program. Among the points in disagreement were funds for the B-2 stealth bomber, plans to develop the MX and Midgetman mobile missiles, and the SDI research program.

In general, the House made much larger cuts than did the Senate in the funding requests for those programs and imposed more stringent limits on their management.

The Senate bill generally supported Bush's program, though to some degree that reflected the ability of Armed Services panel leaders Nunn and John Warner, R-Va., to finesse potentially fractious debates by offering amendments through which members could signal concern over such issues as the projected price of the B-2 and how to get U.S. allies to pay more of the cost of mutual defense.

In addition, the relatively high funding levels approved by the Senate for those controversial programs may have been in part a reaction against the relatively deep House reductions. The higher authorizations gave Senate conferees more negotiating room with the House.

In sharp contrast to action the House was taking almost simultaneously, the Senate led off consideration of its version of the defense bill by endorsing two components of the Bush administration's strategic program — the B-2 bomber and SDI.

The Senate made its views clear on the B-2, when members July 25 voted 98-1 to back the administration's plans to continue development of the bomber and to buy three additional planes in fiscal 1990 as well as spare parts and components for the five B-2s scheduled for fiscal 1991. The Senate bill would trim $300 million from the administration's $4.7 billion request, but backers of the B-2 said the decrease would not have a measurable impact on administration plans.

However, senators did attach conditions on the purchase of the B-2 bombers. These included completion of initial tests on the plane's airworthiness and the beginning of additional tests on its ability to avoid radar. The conditions, approved earlier by the Armed Services panel and modified on the floor, were considered essential to winning support of members wary of the $70 billion stealth program. The Senate also adopted 93-7, on Aug. 1, a non-binding sense of the Senate amendment stipulating that the action did not commit the Senate to funding of the entire fleet of 132 bombers planned by the Air Force.

The Senate narrowly turned back a proposal to cut the SDI program by a half-billion dollars. The bill already called for a $366 million reduction in Bush's $4.9 billion request. An amendment to trim an additional $558 million was killed July 27 by a **key vote of 50-47 (R 37-6; D 13-41)**. The Senate Aug. 2 rejected 53-44 an amendment earmarking $100 million of the SDI authorization to begin deploying a limited anti-missile system intended to fend off "accidental" missile launches. Instead, the Senate adopted a non-binding amendment urging the Pentagon to consider an "accidental launch protection system."

An effort to shift $450 million from SDI to programs authorized by the Anti-Drug Abuse Act of 1988 (PL 100-690) was defused by Nunn, who feared erosion of the margin by which the earlier SDI amendment had been defeated. The Senate Aug. 1 accepted 90-9 substitute language offered by Nunn allowing Bush to fund the drug law with up to $1.7 billion of funds appropriated in fiscal 1989 for defense or discretionary domestic programs but not yet legally obligated. *(1988 act, Congress and the Nation Vol. VII, p. 748)*

Further evidence of members' fervor to get tough on drugs came in the Senate's approval of an amendment authorizing Coast Guard, Customs Service and Drug Enforcement Administration aircraft to fire weapons at an aircraft that ignored an order to land. A motion to table (kill) the amendment was rejected 45-55 on Aug. 1.

By 61-39, the Senate Aug. 1 killed an amendment that would have duplicated reductions made by the House in the authorization of the rail-mobile version of the MX missile. The amendment would have removed funding earmarked for buying components for railcar-mounted missile launchers and beginning construction of facilities to deploy the rail-mobile system, but it would have left untouched funds to continue research on the project. The proposal would have reallocated the funds cut to the purchase of conventional weapons. In contrast to the House, no amendment was offered challenging Midgetman funding.

The Senate narrowly turned back a proposal to bar the use of funds to begin construction of the Special Isotope Separation (SIS) plant in Idaho. The $1.2 billion facility was intended to convert spent fuel from nuclear reactors into material that could be used to manufacture nuclear warheads for missiles and bombs. The amendment July 31 was tabled 50-49.

The Armed Services Committee pre-empted a potentially contentious floor debate over how hard to push U.S. allies to begin paying a larger share of the cost of mutual defense efforts. On behalf of the committee, Nunn offered, and the Senate adopted by voice vote, four amendments intended to demonstrate members' frustration with the allies without making any immediate cutbacks in U.S. deployments abroad.

An 84-13 vote Aug. 2 invoking cloture on the debate on S 1352 prevented sponsors from offering their amendment requiring a 10,000-man reduction in the 43,000-man U.S. force in South Korea. The cloture vote also foreclosed the offering of an amendment that would have barred tests of anti-satellite (ASAT) weapons, provided the Soviet Union did likewise.

Among the many other amendments adopted by the Senate were ones changing the service requirements of U.S. military academy graduates, expanding the Pentagon's child care programs, and authorizing the Defense and Energy departments to pay some senior scientists and engineers substantially more than government rates.

The Senate passed an amended HR 2461 by voice vote Aug. 4.

Conference Action

The conference on HR 2461 dragged on for nearly eight weeks. The conferees did not have to deal with the arms control policy provisions that stalled agreement in past years. But as had been usual since early in the Reagan administration, the two houses differed over several controversial strategic arms programs that were very important to the Republican White House.

Compared with the House, the Senate authorized substantially more money for SDI, the B-2 stealth bomber and the rail-mobile version of the MX missile. The Senate also had approved funding for the smaller Midgetman missile, while the House had denied all funds.

Other factors complicated the political equation. For one thing, the House's cuts in the strategic programs were linked in members' minds to the survival of job-rich conventional programs located in states with large and powerful congressional delegations, including New York, Pennsylvania and Texas.

Negotiations were further complicated by uncertainty as to what the House actions on the rail-MX and Midgetman missiles signified. After soundly rejecting separate efforts to kill each program, the House had adopted an amendment drastically reducing funds for the rail-MX. In retaliation, another coalition had engineered the deletion of all funding for Midgetman.

Another complicating factor was House Armed Services Chairman Aspin enraging many influential House Democrats by publicly blasting the House-passed bill as "a [Michael S.] Dukakis defense budget," thus linking the Democratic-led House with the Democratic Party's ill-fated 1988 presidential candidate.

By early October, the conferees had settled one issue: how to meet the April 1989 budget summit agreement, which set both the budget authority and outlays for defense in fiscal 1990. The defense conferees agreed — with Cheney's concurrence — to shift money among the bill's major components. They reduced the budget request for personnel costs and day-to-day operations while increasing the amounts authorized for weapons procurement and military research and development.

That shift ran counter to the conventional wisdom of most defense specialists, who warned that, with the Pentagon's budgets likely to remain level or decline for the foreseeable future, the share of the budget earmarked for military hardware should get smaller, not larger.

But, like many other budgetary exercises that seemed dubious in the long run, this one was driven by the near-term politics of deficit reduction. Because of technical differences between the way outlays were estimated by the Office of Management and Budget (OMB) and the Congressional Budget Office (CBO), the budget Bush sent Congress in April, though consistent with the budget summit by OMB calculations, was nearly $4 billion over the outlay limit according to CBO.

Because Congress had announced that it would follow the CBO rules, the conferees had to shift appropriations from accounts that turned into outlays quickly (personnel and operations) to accounts that were spent slowly (procurement and research and development). Although some of the shifts were cosmetic, the outlay reduction requirement also forced real cuts in the fast-spending accounts. The conferees ordered OMB and CBO to reconcile their chronic dispute over outlay estimations to forestall such problems in the future.

Another month would pass before conferees reached agreement on a final bill. The compromise measure dealt a $1 billion-plus cut to the SDI program but on several other major issues supported Cheney's effort to modernize the strategic force of nuclear-armed missiles and bombers while ending production of some major conventional weapons.

The House approved the conference report (H Rept 101-331) Nov. 9 by a vote of 236-172. Opposition came both from Republicans who insisted that more weapons should have been sacrificed immediately and from liberal Democrats who complained that the final bill would spend too much money on SDI and other strategic weapons.

The Senate adopted the conference report on Nov. 15 by a vote of 91-8, clearing HR 2461. President Bush signed the bill on Nov. 29.

Major Provisions

As signed into law, HR 2461 authorized a total of $302.96 billion for defense programs — $293.15 billion for the Defense Department, $9.66 billion for the Energy Department and $152 million for related agencies.

Included in the Pentagon's total was $78.8 billion for military personnel costs, funding that traditionally had not been included in the defense authorization legislation.

Major provisions of the final bill:

Strategic Arms. Authorized a total of $3.8 billion for SDI research — $3.58 billion for the Pentagon and $220 million for the Department of Energy. The amount authorized was practically an even split between the House-passed authorization of $3.1 billion and the $4.54 billion approved by the Senate. Compared with Bush's $4.9 billion request, the conference report marked a reduction of 22 percent ($1.1 billion).

Not at issue was a provision, approved by both houses, that extended through fiscal 1990 a prohibition on tests of space-based SDI weapons, enacted by Congress annually since 1987. In essence, the provision blocked any effort to put into effect the Reagan administration's contention that, contrary to the prevailing interpretation of the 1972 U.S.-Soviet anti-ballistic missile treaty, tests of space-based ABM weapons would be allowed.

- Authorized $61 million — $25 million more than requested — to develop defenses against short-range, tactical missiles.
- Authorized $86 million of the $95 million requested for an ASAT weapons development program. Conferees approved an additional $2 million, added by the House, to improve methods of verifying a ban on ASAT lasers. They also added $25 million for development of a new type of simplified satellite that could quickly be deployed to replace ASAT-damaged satellites.

The House also had added $20 million to accelerate work on a laser ASAT and $35 million to make U.S. satellites more ASAT-proof. But the conferees provided instead that the Pentagon could divert to those projects funds authorized elsewhere in the bill — up to $20 million for the laser and up to $10 million for satellite "survivability."

They dropped a House provision banning ASAT tests with an experimental laser (designated MIRACL) because Cheney had written that no such tests were planned during fiscal 1990.

- Authorized only $160 million of the $253 million requested for the "air defense initiative" (ADI), intended as an anti-bomber counterpart to the anti-missile SDI program. Echoing the Senate's position, conferees ordered the Pentagon to shift the program's emphasis from coordinating interception of a bomber attack to detecting the attack in the first place.
- To continue deployment of a very long-range bomber-detection radar, provided $200 million, $10 million less than was requested.
- Authorized a total of $1.05 billion to be divided between two programs to develop mobile intercontinental ballistic missiles: a rail-mobile version of the 10-warhead MX and the much smaller, single-warhead Midgetman. This meant the defense secretary would have to slice a total of $150 million from the programs. The Senate had approved the administration's requests for the two mobile missiles, but the House had sharply reduced funding for the rail-MX and eliminated funding for the Midgetman missile.

The conferees also approved Cheney's request to transfer to the Midgetman account $100 million appropriated for fiscal 1989 but never spent. And they accepted a House provision that would limit to 50 the number of MX missiles deployed in any fashion.

- Authorized, despite two test failures of the Trident II submarine-launched missile, $1.3 billion of the $1.6 billion requested to continue production of the weapon — enough, conferees said, to buy the 63 missiles planned. The House had approved the amount requested, and the Senate had increased the funding.

Also approved was $1.04 billion for a Trident missile-launching submarine, which would be the 17th of its type. This was $100 million less than had been requested and approved by both houses.

- Authorized $4.3 billion of the $4.73 billion requested for development, facilities and production of the B-2 stealth bomber.

The authorization included $2.09 billion to buy two planes in fiscal 1990 and components that could be used for five additional planes scheduled for inclusion in the fiscal 1991 budget. The administration had requested $2.52 billion for the purchase of three planes in fiscal 1990 and components for five more. The House had approved $1.78 billion for two planes and components for two more, while the Senate had authorized $2.22 billion for three B-2s and parts for five more.

Funds for the two fiscal 1990 planes could not be spent until the plane met various flight-test requirements and Congress received reports from the defense secretary and certain independent agencies on aspects of the plane's cost and performance.

To underscore their contention that they were not yet committed to full-scale production of the costly plane, the conferees included a provision requiring the Pentagon to submit a report on the cost and national security impact of buying only 60 to 70 of the planes or 90 to 100 of them, instead of the planned 132.

- Put a tight rein on Air Force efforts to bring up to snuff the electronic gear with which its 97 B-1B bombers were supposed to jam enemy radars. They ordered the service to use six of the planes to test the proposed modifications fully before rebuilding any additional planes. And they limited to $527 million the amount that could be spent to upgrade the B-1B fleet without further congressional approval.
- Authorized $182 million to modernize existing B-52 bombers, although both houses had approved the $226 million requested.
- Approved the request for $488 million to put new, more powerful engines on 24 of the tanker planes used to refuel bombers in midair. The Senate had boosted that program to $628 million for 36 planes.
- Authorized $225 million, a $100 million increase over the budget request, to continue development of the so-called National Aerospace Plane, which was designed to fly into orbit at 25 times the speed of sound.
- Authorized, as both chambers had, the requested $209 million for three Titan IVs and $137 million for smaller Atlas and Delta boosters — the Pentagon's principal satellite launch vehicles.

Ground Combat. Approved without change, as both chambers had, the request for 603 M-1 tanks for the Army and Marine Corps ($1.43 billion). The bill also authorized $561 million for 600 Bradley armored troop carriers, a reduction of only $15 million from the request.

- Added $15 million to complete testing of an upgraded version of the M-88 tractor, designed to tow damaged tanks to safety. But conferees concurred in Cheney's decision to cancel the program and barred expenditure of $125 million appropriated in prior years for the project. Cheney complained that even the modified version of the tractor could not safely tow the 70-ton M-1.
- Authorized for 66 Apache anti-tank helicopters $702 million, $50 million less than the budget request. But conferees also codified in the bill Cheney's decision to end Apache purchases after fiscal 1991.
- Added $276 million to install sophisticated AHIP target-finding equipment on an additional 36 "scout" helicop-

ters. But another provision then would end that program, a year after Cheney wished.

• Authorized for continued development of a small armed helicopter, designated LHX, $234 million, only $7 million less than was requested.

• Authorized $259 million for 6,200 laser-guided Hellfire anti-tank missiles, carried by Apaches and some other helicopters. This was an increase of 2,000 missiles ($70 million) over the request.

Conferees approved the request of $125 million for nearly 10,300 of the smaller, more widely distributed TOW anti-tank missiles.

Both houses had approved the $159 million requested to develop a replacement for TOW, designated AAWS-M.

• Approved, as both chambers had, the request for 815 long-range Patriot anti-aircraft missiles ($924 million). For 4,000 short-range, shoulder-fired Stinger anti-aircraft weapons, the bill authorized $188 million, an increase of more than 1,600 missiles ($70 million) over the request.

The procurement requests associated with the Army's new generation of mobile anti-aircraft weapons were approved without significant change. Both houses had approved the $116 million requested to equip 122 jeeps with multiple Stinger launchers and the $32 million requested to gear up for production of a small, television-guided missile intended to hunt down helicopters hovering out of sight up to 10 miles away.

To scale up production of the ADATS, an armored anti-aircraft missile launcher designed to escort tank columns, the bill authorized $139 million. But conferees did not approve the administration's pace of boosting production, and reduced $100 million from the request.

• Authorized double the number of 20-mile-range MLRS artillery rockets, compared with the request — 48,000 instead of 24,000. The $440 million authorization was $129 million more than requested.

The final bill approved the requests for two other long-range missile programs: $87 million to begin building the ATACMS missile, designed to shower dozens of armor-piercing grenades on enemy road convoys up to 100 miles away, and $33 million to develop a longer-range replacement for the 70-mile-range Lance nuclear-armed missile, deployed in Europe. The Army was considering stashing the latter missile in some MLRS launchers. But the conferees ordered it to ensure that the nuclear missile could be distinguished from non-nuclear weapons, for the sake of a possible future arms control agreement.

• Approved $47 million requested to continue production of artillery shells to dispense lethal nerve gas, but the funds could not be spent until the Army assured Congress that various production bottlenecks had been cleared up.

Tactical Air Combat. Authorized $1.45 billion to build 18 additional F-14D carrier-based fighters for the Navy and modernize six older F-14As. Cheney wanted to end production of new F-14Ds and requested only $758 million to modernize the six older planes. The Senate had gone along with Cheney's proposal, but the House had included funds for 12 new F-14Ds.

The conferees also included an extraordinarily detailed provision to ensure that Grumman Corp., builder of the fighter, would not receive funds for the 18 new planes until it signed an ironclad agreement to dismantle its production line as it was finishing work on that batch of aircraft.

• Approved, as both chambers had, the requests for 66 F/A-18 fighters, used by the Navy and Marines ($1.89 billion), and for four E-2Cs, aircraft similar to Airborne Warning and Control System (AWACS) radar planes but built to be used on carriers ($261 million). The House denied Cheney's request to approve multi-year contracts for the planes and instead used the $541 million earmarked for that purpose to offset the cost of the new F-14Ds. The conferees followed suit.

• Authorized the requested $1.34 billion for 36 additional "E" versions of the Air Force's F-15 — a version designed to attack ground targets at night and in bad weather.

But conferees ordered the Pentagon to study the risks entailed in Cheney's decision to end production of the plane in fiscal 1991, years before the initial flight of its planned replacement aircraft, designated the ATA. The two Armed Services panels might try to keep the F-15Es in production if the risks seemed too high, they said.

• Approved the request for 150 of the Air Force's smaller F-16 fighters ($2.51 billion) but with a particularly large string attached: None of the funds could be used until the Air Force conducted to the conferees' satisfaction extensive, comparative tests of how well various aircraft and missiles could carry out bombing missions at the front lines, in direct support of U.S. ground troops.

The Air Force had maintained that a modified version of the F-16 would be best, but some critics insisted that that betrayed the service's intent to shortchange its battlefield mission by concentrating more on attacking targets far behind enemy lines instead of providing close air support for the Army.

The conferees also added a provision requiring the Marine Corps to hand over to the Navy their dozen A-6E bombers. These would be replaced by F/A-18s equipped with more sophisticated radars for locating ground targets.

• Authorized, as both chambers had, the $1.11 billion requested to continue development of a new fighter plane, the ATF, planned to replace both the F-15 and the F-14 in the late 1990s. But the conferees sliced $200 million from the authorization.

Noting that the Navy was considering other planes, including an updated F-14, as potential replacements for the joint-use ATF, the conferees ordered the service to continue to participate in the ATF program.

• Sliced nearly $300 million from the amounts requested for two long-range air-to-air missiles, authorizing $796 million for 965 AMRAAMs, a reduction of 635 missiles ($237 million), and $326 million for 420 of the 100-mile-range Phoenix missiles carried only by the Navy's F-14s.

Naval Warfare. Authorized, as both houses had, the $651 million requested to modernize the carrier *Constellation*, commissioned in 1961, for another 15 years of service.

The conferees ordered the Navy to study the way new technologies might affect the shape of aircraft carriers in the 21st century.

• Authorized $3.53 billion, a reduction of only $67 million, to build five *Arleigh Burke*-class destroyers, equipped with the Aegis anti-missile system to protect carrier task forces.

• Boosted to 960 the number of Standard anti-aircraft missiles authorized for the Navy ($354 million), an increase of 370 missiles ($44 million).

Conferees also added to the bill $15 million to increase from 20 to 25 the number of Phalanx radar-guided machine guns, bought as a last-ditch defense for Navy vessels against cruise missiles.

• Authorized the $817 million requested for components of *Seawolf*-class submarines, scheduled for inclusion

Cancellation of Major Weapons Programs

In his effort to cancel major weapons programs to accommodate tight budgets, Defense Secretary Dick Cheney confounded many observers in 1989 by winning at least qualified approval for all but one.

Under a budget agreement reached in April with Democratic and Republican congressional leaders, President Bush had to trim $9.7 billion from the $305.6 billion requested for the Defense Department in the fiscal 1990 budget President Ronald Reagan had sent Congress in January.

In the revised budget submitted to Congress, Cheney sought to achieve most of the necessary reduction by a few dramatic cuts. Cheney canceled or truncated planned purchases of existing-generation helicopters, submarines and combat aircraft to pay for development and initial production of more sophisticated new weapons of each type. He canceled high-cost programs with narrow or limited military value and slowed production startup of new weapons with technical, budget or schedule problems. He also reduced the size of the Navy's active fleet and reoriented and cut funding for the strategic defense initiative (SDI). *(SDI, box, p. 370)*

Some of Cheney's decisions drew intense fire on Capitol Hill: ending new production of the Navy's F-14 fighter plane and canceling development of the V-22 Osprey, a hybrid airplane/helicopter intended for Marine Corps use as a troop carrier.

Battle over F-14

While most weapons systems that faced cancellation were plagued by cost overruns, doubts about their value or performance problems, the F-14 had seen nothing but success since the Navy began flying it in 1970. Its history included winning missions over Libya and Grenada, aiding in the capture of terrorists and dazzling audiences of the film "Top Gun."

But Cheney hoped to save money by maintaining the existing fleet of F-14s just until the end of the 20th century, when a new generation of fighters — referred to as advanced tactical fighters (ATFs) — was scheduled to replace it.

Reagan's January budget had called for 12 F-14Ds, a new version of the F-14 interceptor. But in April Cheney proposed funding to upgrade six existing F-14s.

Termination of the F-14D production program threatened to end the status of the Grumman Corp., headquartered in Bethpage, N.Y., as the Navy's leading plane builder for half a century. The cancellation came on the heels of other Pentagon cancellations over two years that had hit employment on Long Island very hard. Members of Congress representing the region mounted a full-court press to secure continued funding for F-14 production.

The House granted the F-14D a reprieve in its version of the defense authorization bill (HR 2461), but the Senate went along with Cheney's proposal. House-Senate conferees compromised on a "soft landing" for the F-14D, agreeing to provide $1.45 billion to buy 18 new F-14Ds and to begin the modification of the older planes. But appended to that was a requirement that before receiving any of the money, Grumman agree that it would dismantle the F-14D production line after building the last batch of planes.

Osprey Controversy

Cheney ensured that he would have a major political battle with the Marine Corps' many backers on Capitol Hill by canceling production of the Osprey aircraft. Reagan's January budget had included $1.27 billion to continue development and build the first 12 production-line copies of the airplane/helicopter.

For years, the Marines had cited as one of their highest priorities the purchase of Ospreys to replace the aging transport helicopters they used to haul troops ashore from an amphibious landing fleet. The existing H-46 helicopters were wearing out after more than two decades in service. Moreover, the Osprey would be able to carry troops a greater distance at nearly twice the speed of the H-46, thus giving U.S. commanders more options to outflank enemy defenses, the Marines contended.

Supporters also touted the Osprey's potential civilian applications, saying it could revolutionize the commuter airline business.

But the Osprey had been a perennial target of budgeteers both in the Pentagon and on the Hill. In part, this reflected the aircraft's estimated cost of $23 billion for a fleet of 552 Ospreys. More fundamentally, some critics questioned the feasibility of large-scale amphibious assaults in the face of modern defenses. Arguing that only once since World War II was there an operation in which the Osprey would have had a decisive advantage over conventional troop-hauling helicopters, they said the Osprey was too expensive given the highly specialized mission for which it was intended.

Conferees on the defense authorization bill included $255 million to continue Osprey development and authorized the Pentagon to spend funds that had been appropriated in earlier years to prepare for production. But they warned that, despite Osprey's technical promise, the aircraft might be too expensive, unless the Pentagon came up with more uses for it and a commercial market were developed.

In 1992, Cheney struck a bargain with Congress that permitted continued development of the Osprey aircraft but did not commit to eventual production. *(1992 action, box, p. 406)* in the fiscal 1991 budget. For the last of 62 *Los Angeles*-class subs, the bill authorized $763 million, a $43 million cut.

• Ordered a slowdown in production, because of continued test failures, of the Mark 48 long-range anti-sub torpedo. Authorized only 240 torpedoes ($439 million), a reduction of 80 ($55 million). Both houses had approved the $269 million requested for 200 smaller Mark 50 torpedoes, carried by aircraft and surface ships.

• Authorized the administration's request for three oceangoing mine sweepers ($342 million). But the bill also authorized three smaller coastal mine sweepers ($282 million) instead of the one requested ($120 million).

Conferees also added to the bill $8.5 million to develop a method of using airborne lasers to detect underwater mines.

Air and Sea Transport. Provided $2.14 billion to continue development of the C-17 wide-body cargo jet and build an additional four planes. Both houses had approved without change the $2.9 billion requested for development and for six more planes. Conferees instituted the reduction in funding, contending that the program had fallen behind schedule.

• Authorized $229 million requested for an LSD-type amphibious landing ship. But the conferees increased from nine to 12 the number of air-cushion landing barges (called LCACs) intended to haul heavy combat gear ashore from an amphibious fleet. This boosted the LCAC authorization from $196 million to $250 million.

• Kept alive for at least one more year the V-22 Osprey, a hybrid airplane/helicopter that the Marine Corps wanted to haul troops ashore from distant ships. Cheney wanted to terminate the program.

Conferees included in the bill $255 million — the amount approved by the Senate but about half what the House had authorized — to continue development of the aircraft and authorized the Pentagon to spend funds that had been appropriated in earlier years to prepare for production. But they warned that, despite the Osprey's technical promise, the aircraft might be too expensive, unless the Pentagon came up with more uses for it and a commercial market was developed.

The conference committee also cut back the purchase of Sea Stallion helicopters, which Cheney proposed as a cheaper alternative to the Osprey. The final bill authorized 14 Sea Stallions ($254 million) of the 23 requested ($359 million).

• Added $35 million to begin designing a high-speed cargo ship that could be used to haul combat equipment abroad in case of war.

Personnel Issues. Made only minor changes in the military manpower limits requested by the administration. The bill approved an active-duty force of 2,120,195 — a reduction of 1,305. Reserve forces were boosted by 2,050, to 1,193,200.

But as part of an outlay-reduction effort, the bill cut $461 million from the administration's overall military personnel budget request — a move almost certain to force cuts of upwards of 20,000 men from the active-duty rolls. Though the annual authorization bill traditionally had not covered the military personnel account directly, this time conferees made an exception, including a provision capping the personnel appropriation at $78.8 billion.

• Included provisions extending or increasing bonuses intended to recruit or retain personnel with essential skills, including military aviators and medical personnel.

The House conferees adamantly rejected several Senate-passed provisions intended to let the Defense and Energy departments pay some senior scientists and engineers substantially more than existing government rates.

But the conferees approved a provision that would allow the Energy Department to exempt up to 25 officials from the "revolving door" law, which barred a federal employee for two years after he left the government from taking a job with a contractor with whom he had dealt in his official capacity. The waiver was intended to allow senior scientists from the three "national laboratories" — Los Alamos, Lawrence Livermore and Sandia — to serve in the Energy Department and then return to the labs, which technically were contractors of the department.

Child Care. Required, among other things, that at least $102 million in appropriated funds be available for day-care centers in fiscal 1990. Both houses had added similar provisions intended to codify policy and boost spending for the services' network of child care centers. The centers reflected the high proportion of military personnel who were married with working spouses, a characteristic of the all-volunteer force that evolved after the draft ended in the early 1970s.

Operations and Maintenance. Made several large cuts — as usual — in the operations and maintenance request that conferees said should have little effect on combat effectiveness. The final bill authorized $86.2 billion, compared with Bush's request for $90.2 billion.

The bill boosted by $83 million — to $601 million — the amount earmarked for environmental cleanup on present and former military bases.

Burden-Sharing. To reflect the scrapping of Pershing II and ground-launched cruise missiles (GLCMs) stationed in Europe, as a result of the intermediate-range nuclear-force (INF) treaty, the statutory ceiling on the number of U.S. military personnel in Europe was reduced by 14,559. The new ceiling was 311,855.

• Adopted with modifications four Senate-passed provisions intended to demonstrate members' frustration over U.S. allies' resistance to paying a larger share of the cost of mutual defense efforts. One amendment, setting a ceiling on the ratio of U.S. forces in Europe to non-U.S. forces on the continent, was intended to deter unilateral force reductions by European allies. Another amendment required the president to negotiate with Japan an agreement providing for Japan to pay all the costs of stationing U.S. forces in that country. The bill also required a study of options for reducing the cost of supporting military dependents overseas and a report on the planned deployment of U.S. military personnel in South Korea over the next five years, including a discussion of the feasibility and desirability of partial, gradual reductions in their number.

• Limited to $360 million the amount the United States would pay to build a new air base at Crotone, Italy, to house a wing of 72 U.S. Air Force F-16 fighters. Based at Torrejon, Spain, the unit was being evicted by the Spanish government.

Under the agreement negotiated with other North Atlantic Treaty Organization (NATO) members to cover the cost of the new base, the U.S. share would be $470 million, so the provision was expected to require renegotiation of the deal.

Military Construction. Authorized $4.8 billion for military construction and $3.27 billion for family housing, about the same as the Bush administration request ($4.8 billion and $3.23 billion, respectively). The authorization included funding for both domestic and overseas bases. *(Military construction appropriations, p. 352)*

Conferees approved the $500 million requested to begin closing military bases pursuant to a special procedure enacted in 1988. The Senate had cut the allowance to $300 million.

Drug Wars. Authorized the Pentagon to spend up to $450 million for drug interdiction. A Senate-passed provision that would have allowed military aircraft to shoot down aircraft, identified as drug smugglers, over international waters was dropped.

1990 Defense Appropriations

Congress in 1989 cleared a $286 billion fiscal 1990 defense spending bill (HR 3072 — PL 101-165) that reduced Pentagon purchasing power for the fifth straight year.

Combined with funds in other spending legislation, the total for defense-related appropriations was $302.9 billion. That was in essence the amount President Bush and the bipartisan congressional leadership had agreed to at an April 1989 budget summit, but it was not enough of a boost over the $299 billion appropriated for fiscal 1989 to cover the cost of inflation.

Bush, while maintaining that the bill would meet most of his major priorities, said he was disappointed that Congress had sharply reduced his request for the strategic defense initiative (SDI). The bill earmarked $3.57 billion for the Pentagon's share of research for SDI. Together with funds appropriated in companion bills, this brought total funding for SDI to $3.8 billion, a reduction of $1.1 billion from Bush's request and a reduction of $234 million from the fiscal 1989 appropriation. It was the first time that spending for the space-oriented program had been reduced below the current year's amount since President Ronald Reagan launched it in 1983.

The final version of the defense appropriations bill betrayed misgivings about Defense Secretary Dick Cheney's decision to kill off some weapons programs to make room for others in the Pentagon's declining budget.

Conferees on the legislation flatly repudiated only one of Cheney's proposed terminations — for the Navy's Phoenix air-to-air missile. But they also pressed the defense chief to reconsider several others. And they urged him to defer the planned production wrap-up of two Navy aircraft that had been scheduled before Cheney submitted his budget proposal.

Like the companion defense authorization bill (HR 2461), the appropriations measure continued through fiscal 1990 production of the Navy's F-14D fighter plane and the Army's AHIP helicopter modification program, both of which Cheney wanted to end immediately. *(Fiscal 1990 defense authorization, p. 340)*

But the appropriations conferees also demanded that Cheney reconsider his AHIP decision and his decision that fiscal 1991 would be the last year of funding for the Army's Apache attack helicopter. And they ordered the Pentagon to consider extending the planned production run of the Marine Corps' Harrier jet and the Navy's EA-6B electronic warfare plane.

On most controversial strategic weapons issues, the appropriations bill paralleled the defense authorization measure.

Legislative Action

The House Appropriations Committee reported its version of the spending bill (H Rept 101-208) on Aug. 1. The full House swiftly approved the measure Aug. 4, shortly before recessing for a month. The 312-105 vote followed less than an hour of perfunctory discussion and the adoption of several minor amendments. Passage of HR 3072 seemed almost an afterthought to the House's sharp rejection the previous week of Bush's defense priorities, during floor action on the companion defense authorization bill.

The House-passed appropriations measure would have resulted in a fiscal 1990 defense budget of $304 billion. That was $1 billion less than the amount agreed to in the April budget agreement between the White House and the joint congressional leadership.

In approving HR 3072, the House moved to redirect the Bush administration's defense programs along two broad lines. First, the House legislation rejected Cheney's proposals to end production of several major conventional weapons programs. To continue buying existing types of equipment, House members wanted to shift several billion dollars from programs aimed at developing new weapons. And secondly, the legislation sliced billions of dollars from the new strategic arms programs that Bush and Cheney said were a top priority.

In some cases, the Navy's F-14D fighter and the *Los Angeles*-class submarine, for examples, the difference between the House-passed program and Cheney's was relatively minor. The House appropriated funds for two dozen planes and one more sub, in each case, ostensibly, the last of their kind. But in several other cases, the House Appropriations Committee expressly barred proposals to terminate certain production lines. It thus signaled its intent to continue funding such programs as the Air Force's F-15E fighter plane, the Navy's Phoenix missile and the Army's AHIP helicopter project. Moreover, in the case of the V-22 Osprey aircraft, desired by the Marine Corps as a troop carrier, the House bill envisaged embarking on a long-term production program with a price tag of tens of billions of dollars.

In its report on the bill, the House Appropriations panel said it had "basically continued or 'bought out' various programs in which 'warm' production lines are providing new equipment for our troops in the field, while terminating many classified programs and various programs" in research and development. With three exceptions, however, the programs the House would terminate were relatively minor. The major cuts, each intended to kill off a program with a total cost of tens of billions of dollars, were:

- $1.1 billion requested to continue developing the new advanced tactical fighter (ATF) plane.
- $632 million associated with the Milstar communications satellite.
- A secret amount, likely no less than several hundred million dollars, to continue development of a new long-range bomber missile, the ACM.

The House bill cut nearly $3 billion from the amounts requested for major strategic weapons. HR 3072 incorporated the controversial reductions in fiscal 1990 funding for the B-2 "stealth" bomber, the SDI anti-missile research program and other strategic weapons projects the House had imposed as part of the defense authorization bill.

The White House cited those cuts in strategic programs as one reason that Bush would veto the measure if it reached his desk as the House had passed it. The administration also faulted the bill because the funds it would appropriate, combined with those in other defense-related appropriations bills, were $1 billion less than the defense total set by the budget summit.

The Senate Appropriations Committee approved its version of HR 3072 (S Rept 101-132) on Sept. 14. As was the case with the companion defense authorization bill, the Senate committee's appropriations measure generally supported the two broad themes in Cheney's budget request that the House had repudiated.

For one thing, Senate Appropriations gave the go-ahead to several costly new strategic weapons programs that Bush — like Reagan — had touted as a top priority. It approved essentially the amounts requested to develop new mobile intercontinental ballistic missiles (ICBMs) and to build the new B-2 bomber — programs the House bill would have reined in. It made a hefty slice in Bush's request for SDI, but it still approved $857 million more than the House bill had appropriated.

The Senate panel's sharpest break from the Bush team's strategic arms program was in its denial of production funds for the Trident II submarine-launched missile, which, it said, would need redesign in the wake of two failed test flights.

The second front on which the Senate appropriators basically backed the administration over objections from the House was in their support for Cheney's decisions to end several conventional arms programs, among them production of the F-14D Navy fighter plane, the AHIP Army helicopter and the F-15 Air Force fighter. The House bill had continued those programs.

The Senate passed the defense appropriations bill in the early hours of Sept. 29 (in the session that began Sept. 28) by 96-2.

Passage came after the Senate cast seemingly contradictory votes on how much to spend for SDI. The Senate first, in effect, voted to cut by $600 million the amount it had approved in its authorization bill for SDI but then two days later voted 53-47 to restore the funds. The second vote was taken to shore up the Senate's negotiating position with the House in the conference on the authorization bill.

The Senate Sept. 26 rejected on a **29-71 (R 2-43; D 27-28) key vote** an amendment that would have cut off production of additional B-2s, leaving the Air Force with the 13 planes already built or in construction. The vote was the first direct test of Senate sentiment for a production cutoff. *(1989 key votes, p. 1021)*

In other action Sept. 26, the Senate adopted 65-34 an amendment restating a provision of the Senate's defense authorization bill requiring a Pentagon report reviewing options for reducing the cost of U.S. troop deployments in South Korea. The action in effect killed an amendment that would have required the withdrawal of 3,000 U.S. military personnel from South Korea.

The Senate also rejected, by votes of 23-76 and 25-75 on Sept. 28, two versions of a proposal to cut by 30,000 the 325,000 U.S. military personnel stationed in Europe, unless U.S. allies in the North Atlantic Treaty Organization (NATO) began to pay the cost of stationing the troops in their territories.

An attempt to block the shutdown of a number of military bases, as recommended by a blue-ribbon commission in 1988, was rejected Sept. 26 by an 86-14 vote. *(Base closings, p. 353)*

Conference, Major Provisions

Conferees on the fiscal 1990 defense appropriations bill agreed Nov. 9 on a $286 billion version of the measure (H Rept 101-345).

The House approved the conference report by voice vote on Nov. 15, after deleting several provisions. One of these would have mandated the continued operation of the small fleet of SR-71 reconnaissance planes, which the Pentagon had been trying to put in mothballs for several years. The deleted provision would have required the Air Force to turn over the planes to the Air National Guard.

The Senate agreed to an amended version of the conference report by voice vote late Nov. 17, after rejecting 29-68 an effort to delete $2.4 billion for the B-2 stealth bomber. The House went along with the Senate amendment and cleared the bill on Nov. 19.

The conference bill restored most of the funding requested for two major weapons programs — the ATF fighter plane and the Trident II missile — that earlier versions of the legislation would have killed.

On several controversial strategic weapons programs — SDI, the B-2 bomber, and the Midgetman and rail-mobile MX missiles — the appropriations bill conformed to compromises the conferees struck on the companion defense authorization bill, which the House passed Nov. 9.

Major Provisions. As signed into law Nov. 21, HR 3072 appropriated:

- $4.3 billion to continue developing the B-2 stealth bomber and buy two of them in fiscal 1990, together with spare parts and components that could be used to build five more B-2s in fiscal 1991. This was the amount authorized except for a reduction of $82 million in the allowance for spare parts.
- $3.57 billion for the Pentagon's share of SDI research. Together with funds appropriated in companion bills for military construction and the Energy Department, this brought total funding for the anti-missile research program to $3.8 billion, a reduction of $1.1 billion from the request.
- $1.22 billion — $375 million less than had been requested — to continue producing Trident II submarine-launched missiles. The Senate had denied production funds because of two spectacular flight-test failures. The Navy insisted that the necessary modifications to the missile were in hand, but the conferees provided that no more than $250 million of the appropriation could be spent until the Navy conducted three successful flight tests.
- $1.1 billion to continue developing two mobile intercontinental ballistic missiles, the single-warhead Midgetman and a rail-mobile version of the larger MX. In addition, the conference report made available for the Midgetman $100 million appropriated in fiscal 1989.
- $1.36 billion for 603 M-1 tanks for the Army and the Marine Corps; $549 million for 600 Bradley armored troop carriers; $1.49 billion for 132 missile-armed Apache anti-tank helicopters; $195 million for the AHIP program to equip 36 "scout" helicopters with the new target-locating gear; $227 million to continue developing the smaller LHX attack helicopter; $87 million for the ATACMS long-range artillery missile; $440 million for the shorter-range MLRS artillery rockets; $170 million for the laser-guided ADATS missile, to be carried by an anti-aircraft tank; $161 million requested for a fiber-optic guided missile to hunt down helicopters hovering behind ridges.
- $1.36 billion to build 18 F-14D fighter jets for the Navy and rebuild six older models to the new standard; $2.51

billion for 150 F-16 fighters for the Air Force; $1.89 billion for 66 F/A-18 fighters to be used by the Navy and the Marine Corps; $1.24 billion for 36 Air Force F-15Es; $445 million for 24 Harrier vertical-takeoff jet fighters; $105 million to gear up a production line to modernize the fleet of EA-6B radar-jamming planes; $976 million to develop the ATF fighter plane, intended to supplant the F-14 and F-15 in the late 1990s; $323 million for 420 long-range Phoenix missiles, a program the Pentagon wanted to end; $73 million to develop a replacement for the Phoenix missile (but only two-thirds of this could be spent until the Pentagon decided to either extend production of the Phoenix or accelerate production of the new missile); $796 million for 900 of the smaller AMRAAM air-to-air missiles.

- $3.5 billion for five *Arleigh Burke*-class destroyers; $615 million for components that would be used in *Seawolf*-class submarines slated for inclusion in the fiscal 1991 budget; $753 million for one last copy of the *Los Angeles*-class submarine, built for more than a decade before the first *Seawolf* was funded in fiscal 1989; $198 million for two coastal mine sweepers; $413 million for Coast Guard vessels.
- $885 million for research on the C-17 transport plane and $1.1 billion for procurement of four C-17s; $255 million to complete development of the V-22 Osprey, a hybrid airplane/helicopter, which the Marines wanted as a troop carrier and the administration wanted to cancel; $600 million to build four cargo ships and two tankers to help ship domestically based U.S. troops to distant trouble spots (only $35 million had been authorized to begin designing a high-speed cargo ship).
- $69.6 billion for the cost of about 2 million active-duty military personnel and $85.3 billion for operations and maintenance.
- $450 million for procurement and operations connected with the Pentagon's drug-interdiction mission. Conferees said this was one part of $2.23 billion that the Pentagon would contribute to the war on drugs in fiscal 1990. The largest share, $1.18 billion, was what would come out of the planned Pentagon budget as part of the emergency drug funding package. *(Drug package, p. 768)*

The final bill included a ceiling of 1.2 million on the number of reservists organized into units, an increase of nearly 2,000 over the number requested. More than $1.4 billion for equipment was earmarked for National Guard and reserve units.

Other Action. A fiscal 1990 supplemental appropriations bill (HR 4404 — PL 101-302) was signed into law on May 25, 1990. The measure rescinded $2 billion in previously appropriated defense funds to offset new spending for domestic programs and foreign aid.

1990 Military Construction

Congress in 1989 appropriated $8.49 billion for fiscal 1990 military construction and family housing projects and for military base closings.

The amount in the funding bill (HR 3012 — PL 101-148) was close to the administration's total request of $8.55 billion. Several significant changes, however, were made in how that money was allocated.

For one thing, Congress cut proposed spending on overseas bases by nearly a third, with the legislation providing only about $950 million of President Bush's $1.4 billion request for construction abroad. For projects in South Korea, Panama and the Philippines, the appropriators linked their reductions to uncertainty over how many U.S. troops would remain in those countries and for how long. Hefty cuts in the amounts requested for construction in other countries — particularly European members of the North Atlantic Treaty Organization (NATO) — reflected mounting pressure in Congress for U.S. allies to pay more of the cost of mutual defense efforts.

Underscoring a second Capitol Hill priority, the final bill increased by nearly 50 percent the amount requested for facilities to be used by the reserve elements of the armed services and the National Guard. The $453 million Bush requested for the reserve components was boosted to $662 million by the conference report. Historically, the reserve components had been well-connected on Capitol Hill. In the 1980s, proponents of the reserve forces had gained ammunition from the Pentagon's policy of formally assigning additional missions to the reserves and Guard. As budgets for defense tightened and the Soviet Union under Mikhail S. Gorbachev took a less threatening posture, supporters contended that more resources should be shifted to those units because, as the Senate Appropriations Committee declared, they provided "the biggest bang for the defense buck."

HR 3012 also included $500 million requested by the Pentagon to carry out domestic base closures recommended by a blue-ribbon panel in 1988.

Legislative Action

The House Appropriations Committee reported HR 3012 on July 26 (H Rept 101-176), and the chamber approved it on July 31 by a vote of 382-29. The House-passed bill appropriated $8.7 billion — $143 million more than Bush had requested.

Passage of the House bill meant that a 1988 plan to close 86 military bases had cleared a tough hurdle. Proponents of the closings succeeded in shielding the bill from the parochial interests of members who wanted to save bases in or near their districts by limiting the money needed to begin shutting down bases. As approved by the House, the bill included the $500 million requested to begin the base-closing process. *(Military base closings, p. 353)*

The Senate Appropriations Committee reported its version of HR 3012 on Sept. 14 (S Rept 101-130). The next day, the full Senate passed the $7.7 billion measure by a vote of 93-1.

The Senate version would have cut the Bush administration's request by more $829 million, including about $600 million for construction projects overseas. The bill, however, also provided about $250 million more than had been requested for domestic construction projects, many of them earmarked to service reserve and National Guard units.

Conference, Major Provisions

House-Senate conferees agreed Oct. 24 on an $8.5 billion appropriation (H Rept 101-307). The conference report was adopted by the House Oct. 26 by voice vote. The Senate adopted it the following day, also by voice vote.

The final version of the bill provided $208 million less than the House-passed version but $764 million more than had been appropriated by the Senate.

But the size of the gap was exaggerated by the Senate's shifting of funds for base closings from HR 3012 to the companion Pentagon appropriations measure (HR 3072). In HR 3072, the Senate had included only $300 million of the $500 million requested for base closings. The full $500 million was included in the conference version of HR 3012.

Both houses had rejected the $15 million requested for recreational facilities at Crotone, Italy, that would be part of a new air base, built largely at NATO's expense, to house a U.S. wing of F-16 fighters evicted from Spain. Following a longstanding NATO policy, the alliance agreed to pay for operational facilities at the new base, while leaving the United States to pay for housing and recreational quarters. But Congress had insisted that NATO cover Crotone's entire cost.

Conferees approved only $425 million of the $502 million requested for the annual U.S. contribution to NATO's infrastructure fund, which paid for common-use facilities. But they maintained that the lower amount included funds to cover the U.S. share of Crotone construction in fiscal 1990.

The conferees denied the entire $95 million requested for construction at Clark Air Base and the Subic Bay Naval Base in the Philippines but agreed to a $61 million request for design work on barracks and family housing projects there. Conferees said they wanted the services to be ready to request the funding anew, once another base-rights agreement was concluded to replace the one expiring in 1991. *(Philippine bases, p. 411)*

Major cuts were made in accounts for construction in Japan and South Korea. And both houses denied requests for construction funds for Honduras and Panama. Critics of the Reagan administration's efforts to destabilize the government of Nicaragua were leery of building up a U.S. military presence in neighboring Honduras. Hill resistance to new construction in Panama rested on the fact that U.S. military forces had to leave by the end of the 20th century under the Panama Canal treaties.

Military Base Closings

When Congress enacted legislation in 1988 to set up a blue-ribbon commission that would identify military bases to be closed as a money-saving move, it designed the process to thwart efforts by members to block closure of individual bases. That effort succeeded during 1989, when both chambers voted overwhelmingly not to block or delay the closure process.

Congress opted for the commission route once again in 1990, when controversy erupted over a proposed new round of base closings. The procedure approved by Congress was similar to the one adopted in 1988 but would be used for the next three Congresses instead of on a one-shot basis.

1989 Legislative Action

The 12-member Commission on Base Realignment and Closure, established by PL 100-526, made its recommendations Dec. 29, 1988. The panel targeted 91 bases — 86 for closure and another five for partial closure — and estimated savings at about $700 million annually. *(1988 law, Congress and the Nation Vol. VII, p. 335)*

In a procedure designed to shield the commission's recommendations from congressional meddling, the list could not be amended. The 1988 law gave each chamber 45 working days from March 1, 1989, to vote to kill the list in toto. If Congress did not act, the closings would proceed.

The House Armed Services Committee March 14 voted 43-4 to reject a resolution to block the closures (H J Res 165 — H Rept 101-7). While the House panel's vote was only symbolic — the resolution could be brought up on either floor by any member at any time — it was indicative of how Congress would act.

When the resolution did come to a floor vote April 18, the House easily rejected it 43-381. Thirty-one of the 43 votes for the resolution were from Illinois, California or New Jersey — states that made up 70 percent of the projected annual savings from the closures.

Because the resolution required the approval of both chambers, the Senate did not have to vote on the matter. The Senate Armed Services Committee did hold hearings on the proposed closures.

Because the Pentagon had asked for $500 million in each of fiscal years 1990 and 1991 to start the process of closing bases, opponents of the closures looked to the appropriations process as another possible avenue to thwart the plans. But during House debate in July on the military construction appropriations bill (HR 3012), a point of order killed a committee provision that would have barred funds for the closing of 11 bases if a General Accounting Office (GAO) report found that closing them would not produce savings within six years, as was the mandate of the base-closing commission. *(1990 military construction appropriations, p. 352)*

When the Senate took up the fiscal 1990 defense appropriations bill (HR 3072) in September, senators from four states that would lose jobs under the realignment — Illinois, New Jersey, Indiana and Arizona — made a last-ditch effort to block the proposed shutdowns. They persuaded the Appropriations Committee to add a provision that would block the closure of any base if the GAO found that the resulting savings would not offset the cost of the closure within six years. The full Senate, however, voted 86-14 on Sept. 26 to delete the disputed committee provision. *(1990 defense appropriations, p. 350)*

One detail remained to be resolved, however: the money to start the base-closing process. While the House had approved the Pentagon's $500 million request as part of the military construction appropriations bill, the Senate had approved only $300 million and shifted those funds to the companion defense appropriations bill.

But the Senate yielded to the House in conference, and the full $500 million was appropriated in the military construction bill.

1990 Legislative Action

The debate over the fiscal 1991 defense authorization bill (HR 4739 — PL 101-510) began with raw feelings because of Defense Secretary Dick Cheney's announcement that he would seek to close an additional 47 military bases — 35 domestic and 12 overseas. *(1991 defense authorization, p. 355)*

With 29 of the U.S. bases located in Democratic congressional districts, Democrats accused the Pentagon of drawing up a politically tilted "hit list." Cheney denied the charges, contending that the list was drawn up by the four services and that he neither added nor subtracted bases from it.

Members with hometown bases on Cheney's list did not have to worry about actual closures for at least a couple of years. Cheney had not made his formal announcement to close any new bases and could not by law until he submitted his next budget, a year later. Under a 1977 law, a defense secretary was required to announce all final decisions to close bases during a budget request and at that time also supply Congress with evaluations of the targeted bases' physical, environmental, strategic and operational impact.

The House Armed Services Committee included a ban on closing any additional military bases in fiscal 1991 in its version of the defense authorization bill. As passed by the House, HR 4739 included the committee provision barring closure of any domestic bases until Cheney proposed legislation to establish a non-partisan basis for deciding which bases to close.

The Senate Armed Services version of the defense bill (S 2884) would have made shutting down domestic bases easier for the Pentagon by removing some of the procedural hurdles Congress had created since the mid-1970s to give it leverage to protect constituents' jobs. The bill, for example, would have allowed the Pentagon to act unilaterally to close bases with fewer than 300 civilian employees. During floor consideration Aug. 3, the Senate rejected 43-54 an amendment to nullify Cheney's list, bar domestic base closures through fiscal 1991 and order Cheney to send Congress a report on the size and organization of U.S. forces through fiscal 1996. The Senate also agreed 81-18 to a motion to table (kill) an amendment giving the defense secretary more leeway to shut down domestic bases.

House-Senate conferees agreed on a compromise establishing an eight-member, bipartisan commission for each of the next three Congresses to recommend a list of unneeded military bases that should be closed. The president and Congress each would have to accept or reject a list in toto. Congress, acting under fast-track procedures, could reject a list only by a joint resolution, which could be vetoed.

According to congressional sources, Pentagon officials had objected to the requirement that the commission be subject to Senate confirmation at the start of each Congress; however, that remained in the conference bill.

U.S.-Japan Plane Deal

Congressional opponents of a joint U.S.-Japanese project to develop a new Japanese fighter plane failed in their attempts in 1989 to block or alter the controversial proposal. After the Senate narrowly rejected a move to kill the project, both the Senate and House approved a resolution (S J Res 113) setting stringent conditions on the deal. But President Bush vetoed the measure, and the Senate failed to override the veto by one vote.

Under the deal, firms in the two countries would work together to modify the Air Force's workhorse F-16 fighter to meet special Japanese requirements. The new plane would be designated the FS-X.

The plan became a lightning rod in each chamber of Congress for a bipartisan coalition angry at Japan's alleged exploitation of its commercial and military relations with the United States. The congressional debate embodied that conflict between economic and military interests.

Critics — who ranged across the political spectrum — said the project would give Japanese companies access to the engineering and program management skills of their U.S. counterparts and that the Japanese aerospace industry would use that information to compete more effectively with U.S. aircraft builders for overseas sales. They said Washington should press the Japanese harder to buy U.S.-built fighter planes off the shelf.

Supporters of the sale insisted that the project represented an attempt by Japan to pick up more of the burden of defending allied interests in the northwest Pacific. Japan would develop its commercial aerospace business with or without U.S. cooperation, they argued. And if it chose to develop its own advanced fighter, American firms and workers would be left out in the cold, instead of having a guaranteed share of the business. Moreover, they contended, the United States would learn more about advanced Japanese technology — including radar systems and composite fabrication — than would Japan's aircraft industry benefit from American advances.

In the congressional firestorm surrounding the FS-X deal, however, technical questions were secondary to outrage over other issues in the U.S.-Japanese relationship.

Japan had run up huge trade surpluses, while flooding U.S. and Third World markets with Japanese goods and refusing to open its own market to American supercomputers and cars, computer chips, rice, and other goods and services. Opponents of the FS-X deal knew from the outset they were fighting a losing battle because they did not have the votes needed in each house to override a Bush veto. But, at a minimum, they hoped a stiff fight would demonstrate to Bush and the Japanese government the scope and intensity of bipartisan anger over what critics deemed predatory Japanese trading policies and wimpy U.S. responses that had resulted in a $55 billion U.S. trade deficit with its major Pacific ally.

Members also were unhappy with the relatively minor share of Japan's national wealth channeled into mutual defense efforts — about 1 percent, compared with the U.S. expenditure of about 5 percent of its gross national product.

Background

Under a 1987 agreement negotiated by the Pentagon with the Japanese government, General Dynamics Corp. would help Mitsubishi Heavy Industries modify the U.S. firm's F-16 fighter to produce the FS-X (which stood for "support fighter-experimental") for entry into Japan's arsenal in the late 1990s.

Negotiations of the fine print dragged on for more than a year after the broad outlines of the deal were drawn in October 1987. When the secret deal was finally signed in December 1988, it reportedly assured General Dynamics and its U.S. subcontractors of 35-45 percent of the development work, which had a total budget of $1.2 billion. But it left unsettled how deeply Mitsubishi would allow the U.S. firm to become involved in developing the one-piece composite wing, touted as one of the deal's benefits to the United States.

The agreement included no specific guarantee to U.S. firms of a share in the FS-X production contract, though proponents insisted that it was understood that the United States would get roughly the same share of the production business that it did of the development contract.

As the Bush administration swung into gear, officials of the Japanese government and the Pentagon pressed for early approval of the decision to hand off F-16 production data to Mitsubishi. But objections mounted. Critics on Capitol Hill expressed concern about the project's impact on the long-term health of the U.S. aircraft industry. They called for review of the agreement by agencies other than the Pentagon, including the Commerce Department and the Office of the U.S. Trade Representative. Critics existed even within the administration. Among them initially was Commerce Secretary Robert A. Mosbacher, who won a delay from Bush until the Pentagon and Commerce could review the deal.

To allay objections, the Bush administration in late April 1989 announced that it had negotiated a revised agreement with the Japanese, under which U.S. firms would get approximately 40 percent of the production contracts. It also stipulated that Japanese engineers would be allowed access only to the parts of the software controlling the plane's central computer that were necessary for them to design new parts of the plane.

Legislative Action

Bush submitted formal notice of the FS-X deal to Capitol Hill May 1. Congress had until May 31 — 30 calendar days — to pass a resolution disapproving the deal.

The Senate Foreign Relations Committee May 11 voted to report unfavorably a resolution of disapproval (S J Res 113). On May 16, the Senate in effect rejected the resolution blocking the FS-X project by a **key vote of 47-52 (R 11-34; D 36-18)**. *(1989 key votes, p. 1021)*

The Senate subsequently adopted by voice vote a modified version of the resolution mandating a stiffer U.S. posture in future negotiations over joint production of some 130 FS-X fighters for Japan. It stipulated that any FS-X production deal bar the transfer to Japan of sensitive jet-engine technologies and prohibit Japan from selling or transferring to a third country the FS-X or any major component of the plane resulting from joint development or production.

The revised resolution expressed the sense of Congress that if the plane went into production U.S. companies should be guaranteed 40 percent of the business. (The U.S. and Japanese governments had already agreed that the U.S. share would be "approximately" 40 percent.) It also required the secretary of commerce to review the commercial implications of the FS-X agreement and required the president to take account of the secretary's views. It required the General Accounting Office to monitor Japan's compliance with the existing agreement.

The White House expressed "grave concerns" about the Senate-passed legislation, warning that it intruded on the president's authority to negotiate international arrangements such as the FS-X.

When the House Foreign Affairs Committee met May 23 to mark up its version of S J Res 113 (H Rept 101-71), it voted to water down the Senate resolution by making the limitations on engine technology and third-country sales purely advisory. But the full House reversed that decision June 7, when it voted 262-155 to restore the mandatory restrictions of the Senate resolution. On a procedural vote, the House in effect reaffirmed that version 169-247 and then adopted the resolution by a vote of 241-168.

Bush vetoed S J Res 113 on July 31. In his veto message, he objected that the resolution infringed on his constitutional prerogatives to manage foreign policy. "In the conduct of negotiations with foreign governments, it is imperative that the United States speak with one voice," Bush said. "The Constitution provides that that one voice is the president's."

On Sept. 13, the Senate voted 66-34 to sustain Bush's veto, falling one shy of the two-thirds majority required to override.

1991 Defense Authorization

Facing a budget crunch and remarkable changes abroad in 1990, Congress authorized $288.3 billion in defense spending for fiscal 1991 — $14 billion less than the previous year and $18 billion less than President Bush had requested.

From the beginning of debate over the measure (HR 4739 — PL 101-510), the federal deficit created dollars-and-cents pressures to hold down defense spending. At the same time, the warming of U.S.-Soviet relations and the crumbling of communist regimes in Eastern Europe added a strategic rationale for ending the massive defense buildup that had been a centerpiece of the Reagan administration.

The bill represented a tightening of defense authorizations from the $302.9 billion approved for fiscal 1990. *(Fiscal 1990 authorization, p. 340)*

For fiscal 1991, Bush initially proposed a $307 billion authorization bill, which represented a 2 percent decline in purchasing power, after inflation. Considerable sentiment existed in Congress to cut more deeply. The defense authorization bill (S 2884) passed by the Senate trimmed $18 billion from Bush's request. In the same week, the House Armed Services Committee completed work on a bill reducing Bush's request by $24 billion. As lawmakers left Washington for their August recess, the conventional wisdom was that the deeper cuts sought by the House would prevail.

But the political calculus changed abruptly on Aug. 2, when Iraq invaded neighboring Kuwait. In the weeks that followed, Bush authorized a massive mobilization of U.S. forces to the Persian Gulf to defend Saudi Arabia and confront Iraq President Saddam Hussein. Although U.S. allies, including Saudi Arabia and Kuwait's ousted rulers, were expected to foot much of the direct cost of the Gulf deployment, Saddam's aggression was cited as a vivid example of the enduring threats to world peace that would justify a robust defense in the aftermath of the Cold War. *(Persian Gulf War, p. 299)*

Leaders of the Armed Services committees boasted that the final authorization bill began the reshaping of U.S. defenses for the post-Cold War era, but Congress finessed many of the hard choices.

The Armed Services conferees constrained development of some of the more costly weapons systems but stopped short of eliminating any of them. For the second straight year, for example, Congress rejected Defense Secretary Dick Cheney's efforts to terminate work on the V-22 Osprey, a hybrid airplane/helicopter sought by the Marine Corps as a troop transport.

The authorization measure provided $2.89 billion of Bush's $4.69 billion request for the strategic defense initiative (SDI) and set the stage for battles over plans to deploy a first-phase anti-missile defense, of limited effectiveness, by the end of the 1990s.

Members hammering out the defense authorization bill simply sidestepped the conflict over the future of the B-2 "stealth" bomber. They approved $2.3 billion for B-2 procurement but were deliberately vague about whether the funds could be spent only to pay cost-overruns on the 15 bombers previously authorized (as House members

Pay Deadlock Broken

In mid-1990, the Defense Department and Congress reached an agreement allowing the Pentagon to shift (or "reprogram") $1.4 billion from various parts of the Pentagon budget to cover shortfalls in the accounts for military pay and fringe benefits. The agreement broke a three-month deadlock that had threatened tens of thousands of military personnel with early discharges or delayed promotions and transfers.

The shortfalls were the result of across-the-board budget cuts imposed on all federal agencies for part of fiscal 1990 under the Gramm-Rudman anti-deficit law (PL 99-177, PL 100-119).

The Pentagon's reprogramming request — which required the concurrence of both chambers' Armed Services and Appropriations committees — had been hostage to a power struggle between Defense Secretary Dick Cheney and House Armed Services Committee Chairman Les Aspin, D-Wis.

Aspin insisted that the fiscal 1990 automatic cut (or "sequestration") should be offset by reprogramming some of the money from major weapons programs of interest to the Pentagon, such as the B-2 "stealth" bomber and the strategic defense initiative (SDI).

If the Bush administration could shield the Pentagon against the most painful consequences of sequestration, then Republicans would have the advantage in future budget battles with the Democrats, Aspin maintained.

Cheney, however, hung tough and, while the final agreement would draw $58 million from major weapons, none of it would come from the B-2 or SDI.

asserted) or could be used to buy additional B-2s (as senators maintained). House Armed Services Committee Chairman Les Aspin, D-Wis., who turned from a supporter of the B-2 to its most influential opponent in 1990, called the defense bill's calculated silence "a way to get by this year."

As usual, the defense appropriations bill (HR 5803 — PL 101-511) roughly paralleled the authorization measure in its treatment of most major issues. The spending bill provided $269 billion for fiscal 1991. *(Fiscal 1991 appropriations, p. 363)*

Senate Committee Action

The reshaping of Cheney's defense budget began in earnest in the Senate Armed Services Committee, where members crafted a scaled-down budget with a prophetic price tag of $289 billion, essentially the amount that was eventually enacted. They completed marking up the bill (S 2884 — S Rept 101-384) in the early morning hours of July 13 and formally reported the measure July 20.

The committee agreed to pull the plug on most of the 13 weapons programs that Cheney proposed eliminating. A notable exception was the V-22 Osprey, which was a joint project of contractors in Fort Worth and Philadelphia and, not coincidentally, enjoyed vigorous support in the Texas and Pennsylvania congressional delegations.

The committee also voted to eliminate 15 other weapons to reduce the budget by $2.35 billion in fiscal 1991 and $45 billion over the life of the programs. The panel recommended $3.57 billion of the $4.06 billion Bush requested for the Pentagon's share of SDI research.

The committee agreed to the $4.5 billion request for the B-2 bomber. The administration had originally sought $4.77 billion but scaled back its request in April. At the same time, Cheney cut the number of B-2s to be produced from 132 to 75, trimming the total cost of developing and purchasing the fleet from $72 billion to $61 billion. Because the cost of developing the plane and setting up a manufacturing line to handle its exotic materials would be amortized over fewer planes under Cheney's new plan, the cost per copy was projected to rise from $545 million to about $813 million — which added further heat to the B-2 debate. *(B-2 background, box, p. 398)*

Beyond weaponry, the Senate committee's bill called for a military that would be leaner in personnel. It would have required a reduction of 100,000 active-duty personnel, instead of the 38,000 Cheney had recommended trimming.

Over the longer term, the bill called for reducing active-duty personnel by 385,000 by fiscal 1995. The Army was to take the brunt of the cutbacks because its traditional duty of guarding Western Europe had become less relevant with the fall of the Iron Curtain.

The Senate panel rejected Cheney's call to cut the National Guard and reserves, anticipating a greater reliance on the backup forces.

House Committee Action

The shaping of the House defense bill had begun not in the Armed Services Committee but in the House Democratic Caucus, where members engaged in a series of closed-door debates over the budgetary, military and political implications of cutting Pentagon spending more deeply than the administration wanted.

In sessions in early March, Speaker Thomas S. Foley, D-Wash., sternly warned a group of Budget Committee liberals that the deep cuts they sought were politically unrealistic. Gradually, the caucus moved toward a consensus on how deeply Democrats would seek to cut defense spending and on the practical reality that deep reductions in defense outlays could be achieved only by phasing them in over five or more years.

Equally significant, by summer, Aspin, the influential and relatively hawkish Armed Services Committee chairman, was ready to step forward and offer his own scenario for a scaled-down defense budget. In July, Aspin announced that his panel would come down hard on weapons procurement programs to cut the fiscal 1991 defense budget to $283 billion, $24 billion less than requested by Bush and $6 billion less than the Senate Armed Services Committee had recommended.

Aspin said the committee would make only a minor reduction in Bush's request for military personnel, but he made it clear that something had to give in spending on weapons. The chairman subsequently revealed what he had in mind, when he dropped his longtime support for the B-2 bomber. He announced he would join liberal Democrat Ronald V. Dellums of California and conservative Republican John R. Kasich of Ohio in trying to bar the production of any B-2s beyond the 15 already built or under construction. Aspin said his decision was based on the high cost of the plane in an era of sharply declining defense budgets and the availability of cheaper alternatives for various missions.

The Armed Services Committee followed its chairman's lead. On July 31, the panel voted, 34-20, to cut off production of the B-2. It then adopted the $283 billion defense authorization bill by a vote of 40-12. Despite a warning that Bush would veto the measure in its present form, nine of the panel's 21 Republicans voted "yea."

As approved by the committee, the bill included a ban on closing any additional military bases in fiscal 1991, a $437 million increase for F/A-18 Navy jets and $403 million to move toward production of the V-22 Osprey.

Aspin had supported Cheney's effort to cut the tilt-rotor Osprey the year before. But he argued that he changed his mind because it was well-suited to the new international environment. Noting its capability to move a small number of troops a great distance and land them in small clearings, Aspin reasoned, "You're looking beyond the Soviet threat to other threats — terrorism, drugs, other kinds of things that you're going to call upon your military to do."

The committee version of the bill called for reducing U.S. troops in Europe by 50,000, as part of an overall reduction of 129,500 active-duty personnel. It also called for slowing — but not canceling — development of weapons including the ATF fighter plane and the Army's LH armed helicopter.

It also reduced spending on SDI to $2.9 billion.

Senate Floor Action

The Senate passed a $289 billion defense authorization bill (S 2884) on Aug. 4 by a 79-16 vote. Debate on the bill had begun on Aug. 2, the day Iraq invaded Kuwait.

Conservative defenders of the controversial B-2 bomber, and of large defense budgets more generally, were helped by the coincidental timing of the brutal events in the Persian Gulf. Sentiment had been building against the B-2, as a high-priced weapon and as a symbol of the fading Cold War, but Nunn successfully fended off floor amendments to kill or phase out the program.

The Armed Services chairman argued that the B-2 would enhance nuclear deterrence by confronting Moscow with the threat of a retaliatory strike that could not be stopped. Moreover, Nunn insisted, the plane could carry powerful nuclear weapons to attack targets that could not be reached with other weapons. B-2 proponents also emphasized that the plane's long range would give it great flexibility for striking targets other than the Soviet Union. If the United States had to weigh in against Iraq, Nunn argued, a B-2 squadron would be a far less risky instrument than an aircraft carrier sent into the narrow confines of the Persian Gulf.

An amendment that would have killed the B-2 program outright, after completing six test planes under construction, was rejected 43-56 on Aug. 2. An amendment denying funding for two additional B-2s authorized in the bill was rejected 45-53 the same day. Although the amendments were defeated, the votes showed that opposition to the B-2 had increased over the previous year, when an amendment to kill the B-2 had attracted only 29 votes.

Despite the B-2 victory, the Bush administration's defense policies did not emerge from the Senate unscathed. Splitting almost exactly along party lines, the Democratic-controlled Senate moved to reshape the strategic defense initiative by reining in Pentagon plans to pool resources into a partial anti-missile defense system. Bush had promised to make a decision by late 1992 on deployment of such an initial system. The commitment to begin deploying a first-stage SDI system as soon as possible was an article of faith among some conservatives and a touchstone of their support for Bush.

By a vote of 54-44, the Senate Aug. 4 adopted an amendment to slow development of "brilliant pebbles," the array of tiny heat-seeking guided missiles that was embraced by Bush as the most promising first-stage method to destroy Soviet missiles as they were blasting into space. Imposing spending ceilings on different categories within the wide-ranging SDI program, the amendment called for limiting research on brilliant pebbles to $129 million, the same amount spent in fiscal 1990. At the same time, the amendment called for increasing the emphasis within SDI on developing other kinds of anti-missile defenses. In a letter to Republican senators two days before the vote, Bush had warned that the SDI overhaul was "more serious than a funding cut."

The Senate rejected amendments to make further reductions in SDI funding and to shift funds from SDI to health and drug treatment programs.

The bill approved by the Senate also called for killing several major weapons systems, including the proposed multibillion-dollar system of Milstar communications satellites and a new battlefield anti-aircraft missile for the Army. It also called for slowing development or production of several other costly programs, including the ATF plane, the A-12 ground attack plane, the *Seawolf*-class submarine and the Army LH helicopter.

In other action, the Senate Aug. 3 agreed, 55-44, to a motion to table (kill) an amendment that would have retired one of the Navy's two remaining battleships.

The Senate also agreed Aug. 2 to kill, 51-47, an amendment that would have prohibited U.S. contributions to the construction of a new NATO air base at Crotone, Italy, intended to house a wing of 72 U.S. Air Force F-16s. The base at Crotone had become something of a symbol of congressional resistance to military spending overseas, especially in light of the politically volatile domestic base closings. Language limiting spending on the facility was attached to the annual appropriations bill for military construction. *(Military construction appropriations, p. 365)*

By a vote of 59-40 Aug. 3, the Senate tabled an amendment that would have cut the force of 311,000 Army and Air Force personnel in Europe by 80,000 instead of the 50,000-person reduction written into the measure by the Armed Services Committee. By voice vote, the Senate adopted two amendments that promoted the idea of encouraging the North Atlantic Treaty Organization (NATO) to rent as a training site some domestic U.S. base that otherwise would be closed.

The Senate Aug. 3 rejected 43-54 an amendment that would have nullified Cheney's list of proposed base closings in fiscal 1991, barred domestic base closures through fiscal 1991 and ordered Cheney to send Congress a report on the size and organization of U.S. forces through fiscal 1996. Also rejected was an amendment that would have given the defense secretary more leeway to shut down domestic bases. *(Base closings, p. 353)*

The Senate Aug. 3 tabled 51-48 an amendment earmarking for the treatment of drug-addicted mothers $100 million in unspent funds left over in Pentagon accounts at the end of fiscal 1990. The Senate approved by voice vote several proposals intended to boost the war on drug smuggling.

Also on Aug. 3, an effort to slow the development of an anti-satellite (ASAT) missile was tabled 52-45. Arms control advocates long had pressed for a negotiated ban on anti-satellite weapons given that the United States — which relied on satellite communications more heavily than the Soviet Union — would have more to lose in an ASAT arms race. However, while concurring in the desirability of an ASAT ban, Nunn and other committee members argued for going ahead with the U.S. program pending such an agreement.

The final day of debate on the bill was marked by arguments not about defense policy but about abortions. An amendment that would have overturned the Pentagon's policy banning elective abortions in military hospitals, even when paid for by private funds, was withdrawn after the Senate refused to invoke cloture on the amendment (thereby cutting off debate). The cloture motion would have required 60 votes but was rejected 58-41 on Aug. 3.

House Floor Action

The House passed its $283 billion version of the defense authorization (HR 4739) on Sept. 19 by a 256-155 vote. As the full House had begun debate on the defense authorization bill Sept. 11, Defense Secretary Cheney told House Republicans that he would urge Bush to veto the bill if it were not significantly modified. Cheney's spokesman cited as particularly objectionable the bill's cuts in strategic weapons, its ban on closing domestic military bases and its large reduction in active-duty personnel.

In the weeks after the Armed Services Committee markup, the political climate also had changed because of Iraq's invasion of Kuwait on Aug. 2. Yet, not even conservative Democrats seemed to be having second thoughts about the cutbacks called for by the Armed Services Committee.

Committee chairman Aspin insisted that the Gulf crisis vindicated his strategic premise. "Because the Soviets are being so cooperative [in supporting U.S. policy toward Iraq], the core philosophy of the bill stands," he said. "The guys who want to use it to reverse [cuts in] SDI or B-2 are not finding much resonance."

Champions of the B-2 bomber decided not to try to resuscitate that program on the House floor, biding their time for the Senate-House conference committee.

Much of the House debate concerned burden-sharing, the growing demand that allies pay more of the cost of collective defense. Critics argued that, in effect, the United States was subsidizing the economies of commercial competitors — including Japan and Germany — by spending a substantially larger share of its national income on defenses that provided for their security as well.

This sentiment was reflected in some provisions of the defense bill that came to the House floor from the Armed Services Committee, including a ban on stationing U.S. units at the planned NATO air base at Crotone, Italy. By a largely party-line vote of 174-249, the House Sept. 12 rejected an effort to drop the committee's restrictions on the Crotone base.

Another twist on the burden-sharing theme was a floor amendment that called for reducing the 50,000 U.S. military personnel stationed in Japan by 5,000 a year unless the Japanese government began paying all costs associated with the deployment. In the politically charged atmosphere created by the Iraq crisis, the amendment became a lightning rod for festering congressional anger at Japan. Many lawmakers wanted to send that nation a strong signal, perhaps knowing that the amendment would not make it into the final defense bill. (Ultimately, the version sent to the president called for capping the number of U.S. personnel in Japan at 50,000 but dropped the 5,000-a-year automatic reduction.) The House adopted the amendment, 370-53 on Sept. 12.

The House the same day also approved 287-134 an amendment reaffirming provisions in the committee's bill barring closure of any domestic bases until Cheney proposed legislation to establish a non-partisan basis for deciding which bases to close. Adopted Sept. 11, 230-188, was an amendment blocking closure of a Navy home port on Staten Island, N.Y., until 30 days after the Defense Department sent Congress an overall plan to close and realign Navy installations within the United States.

During debate on the defense bill, Democrats found an opportunity to hone their political message that they were sharpening U.S. defenses for the future. They pushed through an amendment that cut another $600 million from the $2.9 billion that the Armed Services Committee had recommended authorizing for SDI. The House Sept. 18 adopted the amendment by a **key vote of 225-189 (R 20-150; D 205-39)**, after rejecting several amendments to cut SDI more or less deeply. *(1990 key votes, p. 1039)*

Using the money cut from SDI and other funds, Aspin fashioned a $948 million package for equipment and personnel associated with Operation Desert Shield, the deployment against Iraq. The package included new mine sweepers, fast cargo ships and protective clothing to deal with attacks by chemical and biological weapons. It also provided benefits for forces stationed in the Persian Gulf, including "imminent danger pay" of $110 a month. Aspin's Persian Gulf package was adopted, 413-10 on Sept. 19.

Republicans, attempting to portray the Democratic-backed bill as a pork-barrel package, backed an amendment that, in effect, would have deleted $428 million that the committee had added to the budget request for F/A-18 fighter planes and used the money to restore 28,500 of the more than 129,000 personnel the bill would have cut from the Army. The pork-barrel connection was that the F/A-18 was manufactured in St. Louis, hometown of Majority Leader Richard A. Gephardt, D-Mo. The amendment was rejected, 156-254, on Sept. 19.

The House Sept. 18 voted 288-128 to siphon $200 million from the Pentagon budget to help defense workers and communities adjust to the loss of defense contracts. A GOP alternative that would have required the executive branch to provide early warnings to localities of planned defense cuts and also would have authorized $6 million for the Pentagon's economic impact assistance program was rejected, 161-253, the same day.

Some of the great ideological brouhahas of the Reagan years were dealt with in an almost perfunctory way during House debate on HR 4739. For example, opposition to the MX missile was a banner issue for the liberal arms control community during the mid-1980s. In 1990, however, the Armed Services Committee denied funds to begin production of a rail-mobile version of the controversial MX missile and sliced the total amount available for development of both the rail-based MX and the smaller Midgetman mobile missile. While contending that the country could not afford to develop both mobile missiles, the committee left to Bush the choice between the MX and Midgetman. An amendment to cut additional funds from the rail-MX program was rejected, 153-264, on Sept. 18 drawing only nine more "yeas" than "nays" among Democrats.

The House Sept. 18 rejected, by a **key vote of 200-216 (R 35-139; D 165-77)**, an amendment to permit U.S. military personnel or their dependents living overseas to obtain abortions in U.S. military hospitals, provided the costs were privately covered. A similar amendment had been blocked in the Senate by a filibuster.

Aspin's politicization of the defense bill extended even to the decisions about whose amendments would be incorporated into an omnibus package of non-controversial proposals that could be expected to be approved routinely. As adopted 373-45 Sept. 19, the en bloc amendments included 21 provisions. Among the most significant were ones to impose economic sanctions on companies exporting ballistic-missile technology and to sharply reduce, over several years, the amount that the United States would pay toward the salaries of foreign civilians employed at U.S. bases abroad.

Only four of the 21 amendments rolled into the en bloc package came from Republicans, however, and complaints were heard that some GOP proposals had been shelved for no reason. According to other sources, however, some proposals were left out of the package because their sponsors would not promise to vote for passage of the bill. GOP lawmakers split 33-135 against the bill on the final vote.

Conference Action

The Senate passed an amended HR 4739 by voice vote Sept. 25, and the bill then went to conference.

As the House-Senate conference committee went to work Oct. 2, it labored in the shadow of a tentative agreement between the administration and Democratic congressional leaders on the overall federal budget.

Although the agreement would later collapse and have to be pieced together again, the deficit-cutting pact ironically created pressure to spend more for defense. The accord allowed $289 billion in budget authority for defense in fiscal 1991, the higher figure approved by the Senate. Senate Armed Services Chairman Nunn and Defense Secretary Cheney maintained that the deal obliged Congress to appropriate no less than that amount, which brought protests from House liberals.

On Oct. 17, the negotiators reached agreement on a $288.3 billion defense budget. But they arrived at a deal only by remaining calculatedly silent on the touchiest single issue before them — the fate of the B-2 bomber.

They agreed to provide $2.35 billion in additional spending for procurement of the stealth plane but gave no indication whether the money could be used only to pay for cost-overruns on the 15 planes previously authorized or whether some of it could be used to begin work on additional aircraft. Members stepped into the vacuum with conflicting opinions as to what the conferees really had in mind.

"As far as we're concerned, the B-2 is dead," said Dellums. "The B-2 program is alive and well," countered Nunn. Fundamentally, the conference report's B-2 provision was just one more compromise. "The Senate will probably come back with whatever the administration requests [by way of building additional B-2s in fiscal 1992] . . . and we will have another fight," Aspin said.

Aspin and Nunn did their best to portray the defense budget compromise as a significant first step toward a post-Cold War military strategy. But the shift of focus had more impact on the rhetoric than the outcome of the defense debate. In salvaging the big-ticket defense systems initiated in past years, the conferees simply came up with new rationales.

"You'd be surprised," Aspin said wryly, "at how many weapons systems [that] were designed long ago, when we had the threat of the Soviet Union, turned out to be just perfectly suitable for this new situation with Iraq."

After the conferees thought they had completed their grueling work, they received a disconcerting call back to session. Cheney announced he would recommend a veto of their handiwork. In particular, he cited the provision that would have cut 100,000 personnel from the military payroll.

In renewed negotiations between Cheney and the House and Senate Armed Services committees, a provision was added to the bill allowing a more modest troop cut of 80,000, which Cheney deemed tolerable because it could be carried out without forcing thousands of people out of the armed services involuntarily.

Cheney reluctantly accepted the conferees' scaled-down funding of $2.89 billion for the strategic defense initiative, but he demanded more flexibility in allocating SDI funds. Based on a Senate-passed provision, the conferees had divided the SDI funds into five programs, limiting the amount available for each one. The point was to reduce the amount that could be spent on a partially effective, Phase One defense, which proponents said could be deployed by the end of the 1990s. In the revised conference report, the division of SDI's budget into five categories was retained, but Cheney was permitted to increase any one by up to 10 percent, provided that the total SDI budget did not exceed $2.89 billion.

Cheney also was unhappy with the conferees' decision to establish a commission on military base closings. According to congressional sources, Pentagon officials had objected to having the commission be subject to Senate confirmation at the start of each Congress. But the provision remained in the conference report.

The conference report (H Rept 101-923) was filed Oct. 23. It was adopted by the House, 271-156, on Oct. 24 and approved by the Senate, 80-17, on Oct. 26.

In signing the bill Nov. 5, Bush said it reflected "most of the administration's major defense priorities," but he voiced concern about congressional efforts to dictate restrictions on SDI and burden-sharing moves toward U.S. allies.

Major Provisions

As signed into law, HR 4739 authorized $288.3 billion in defense spending for fiscal 1991, $18 billion less than requested. The Senate version had authorized $289 billion and the House version, $283 billion.

Major provisions of the final bill:

Force Cuts. Authorized a reduction of 100,000 active-duty personnel. To meet objections from Cheney, however, the bill permitted the defense secretary to exceed the annual personnel cap by 1 percent, thereby cutting the force by only about 80,000. Prior law gave the defense secretary authority to exceed the annual cap by 0.5 percent.

The House had authorized a reduction of 129,500 in the active-duty force, which had been capped at 1,976,405. The conferees initially had agreed to the reduction of

100,000 authorized by the Senate but revised the bill to meet Pentagon objections that making a cut of that size in one year would force thousands of careerists out of the service, undermining the morale of those who remained and discouraging talented people from signing up. The cut would be particularly disruptive, Cheney contended, when the department had hundreds of thousands of service members deployed in and around Saudi Arabia in response to the Iraqi invasion of Kuwait.

- Required the Pentagon to reduce active-duty manpower by 22 percent by fiscal 1995.

Strategic Arms. Authorized $2.35 billion in additional spending for procurement of the B-2 stealth bomber. But the bill skirted a debate over how many more to build, giving no indication whether the money could be used only to pay for cost-overruns on the 15 planes previously authorized or whether some funds could be used to begin work on additional aircraft.

- Called for spending $2.89 billion on the strategic defense initiative, a reduction of almost $1.7 billion from Bush's budget request. The bill divided the SDI funds into five programs, limiting the amount available to each one but permitting Cheney to increase any category by as much as 10 percent as long as the total SDI budget stayed within the authorized limit.

Based on a Senate-passed provision, the conferees had divided the SDI funds into five programs as a technique to reduce the amount that could be spent on a partially effective, Phase One defense, which proponents said could be deployed by the end of the 1990s.

- Authorized $64 million for components of 100 advanced cruise missiles — bomber-launched nuclear weapons with a range of 2,000 miles and "stealthy" radar-evading design. It specified that an additional $43 million would become available if missile flight tests were successful.

With a minor funding difference, both houses had approved the request for 100 of the high-tech missiles. But conferees tangled over Air Force plans to buy another 250 in fiscal 1992. The Senate approved, as requested, $107 million for enough components for the planned production speedup. The House approved only $64 million to buy enough components to build 100 missiles in fiscal 1992.

- Authorized $10 million to continue slowed-down development of the bomber-launched SRAM II, a short-range attack missile.

Both houses had approved the $156 million requested to continue development of SRAM II and $21 million to gear up for SRAM II production. But the Air Force later informed conferees that technical problems had so slowed the program that only $10 million would be needed to prepare for production; that amount was included in the final version.

- Authorized $35 million for SRAM-T, a "tactical version" of the SRAM II that could be carried by fighter planes.

The Senate had approved $119 million, as requested, to develop SRAM-T. The House had approved only $2 million, contending that the weapon had become superfluous because it had been designed to beef up the European-based U.S. nuclear deterrent against a Soviet-led Warsaw Pact attack on NATO.

- Apportioned $680 million between two projects to develop a new intercontinental ballistic missile (ICBM): one to develop a rail-mobile version of the 10-warhead MX; the other to develop the much smaller, single-warhead Midgetman.

The House had approved $610 million for both programs, while the Senate authorized separate amounts for each, totaling $750 million.

But the conferees also adopted language declaring the sense of Congress that the country would not be able to buy both kinds of mobile missiles, assuming peaceful trends in the Soviet Union permitted declining U.S. defense budgets. The non-binding provision, similar to House-passed language, also declared that the Pentagon should plan to deploy Midgetman in existing missile silos to save money "while preserving a realistic option for subsequent mobile basing."

The provision further declared that the rail-mobile MX program should be directed only toward completing development of key technologies in the expectation that they then would be mothballed. Both houses had rejected the $1.6 billion requested to begin buying rail-mobile MX launchers and building sites for them.

- Authorized $1.34 billion, as requested, for Trident II sub-launched missiles.

The Senate had approved $1.34 billion, as requested, for 52 of the missiles. The House approved $1.14 billion for 42 Trident IIs. The final version authorized the Senate-passed amount but noted that it might buy fewer than 52 missiles because the British government's delay in placing an anticipated order for 14 of the missiles would boost the cost per copy in fiscal 1991.

- Authorized $210 million for a new attack warning satellite for the Air Force as a replacement for its fleet of DSP satellites. The House had approved $230 million; the Senate, $242 million of the administration's original $402 million request for a system known as BSTS, which would have been part of SDI. Subsequently, the project was dropped from SDI and transferred to the Air Force.
- Approved $126 million to develop an anti-satellite (ASAT) missile. The House had authorized $100 million, and the Senate $152 million of the $208 million requested.

The bill also included two House-passed provisions intended to boost the prospects of an arms control agreement limiting ASAT weapons. One banned tests of a ground-based laser designated MIRACL against an object in space; the other added $8 million to develop techniques for verifying a ban on ASAT lasers.

- Authorized $15 million to design a plant to recover plutonium from obsolete bombs, provided that the design work not be oriented toward building the plant at any specific site.

The House had approved the $15 million. But the Senate had rejected the entire $65 million requested to begin designing a plant for construction at Rocky Flats, near Denver, home of a nuclear weapons plant that was contaminated with radioactivity.

Ground Combat. Authorized $747 million to buy some combination of two versions of the M-1 tank. It called for either 225 tanks of the two versions or the larger number of the current "A1" model tanks that could be afforded if the new and untested "A2" model was deemed not yet ready for production.

It also authorized $64 million to begin converting the earliest model M-1s to A2 version tanks and an additional $150 million that could be used either for such modifications or to buy more new A2 model tanks.

Though they differed in detail, both the House and Senate had challenged the Army's plan to buy 163 of the existing model M-1A1 tanks, then 62 of the improved —

but untested — M-1A2 model, after which the two U.S. tank plants would be mothballed.

• Approved $430 million for 300 Bradley armored troop carriers.

The House had approved the Army's plan to buy 1,200 additional Bradley armored troop carriers. To keep the production line running longer, it approved only 300 in fiscal 1991, instead of the 600 requested. The Senate approved the purchase of 600 Bradleys but complained that the Army was cutting off production prematurely.

• Authorized the $176 million requested to develop a "family" of future armored vehicles — including a new tank to replace the M-1, a new troop carrier to replace the Bradley and a new mobile artillery piece — that would share some components, including a chassis.

• Authorized $10 million to help the Army select a relatively lightweight mobile artillery piece for units intended to be flown quickly from U.S. bases to distant trouble spots.

But conferees urged the Army to select one of five weapons that were already available "off the shelf," instead of developing a new one. They complained that the Army was putting too much emphasis on being able to drop the new vehicle by parachute and too little on crew-protecting armor, which might make the weapon too heavy to airdrop.

• Authorized $169 million for the 100-mile-range ATACMS missile and $298 million for the JSTARS airborne radar, intended to steer the missile to its target.

Those were the amounts requested and approved by the Senate for the two systems. The House had proposed canceling both programs, which had been designed with an eye toward stopping a Soviet tank blitz against NATO.

• Approved $77 million for modifications of missile-armed Apache helicopters — including $20 million toward fixing their reliability problems — and $159 million to outfit them with new target-finding radar.

Conferees ordered the Army to draw up a long-term plan to modernize the Apache and make it more reliable. The Army had requested $86 million to modernize Apache helicopters and $159 million to continue developing a new target-finding radar for these aerial tank-hunters. But Congress focused on chronic breakdowns afflicting the Apache. The House approved the radar request but cut modernization funding to $20 million, to be used to make the Apache more reliable. The Senate approved both amounts requested but set aside $30 million of the radar budget to fix the Apache's problems.

• Authorized $291 million to develop a new armed "scout" helicopter under a new name: "scout/attack."

Both houses had cut the $411 million requested to develop a new helicopter designated LH. Both ordered the Army to slow the program and to flight-test some prototypes before making a commitment to buy the new craft. Cheney reorganized the project along these lines and gave it the new name as well.

• Authorized $92 million for trouble-shooting of the ADATS anti-aircraft missile — designed to protect front-line combat units — plus $30 million for the Army to test other mobile anti-aircraft weapons that might replace the ADATS.

Citing test failures of the ADATS, both houses had rejected the $235 million requested to begin production of the weapon. The Senate canceled it outright, arguing that it was too heavily oriented toward the now defunct Warsaw Pact threat; the House approved the $92 million that was later adopted in the final version of the bill for Army researchers to fix the problems.

National Guard Ruling

The Supreme Court on June 11, 1990, unanimously upheld a 1986 law that barred any governor from overriding federal orders to send a state's National Guard units on training exercises outside the United States.

Congress had enacted the law as part of the fiscal 1987 defense authorization act (PL 99-661) after several governors had objected on political grounds to sending state National Guard units to Pentagon-sponsored training exercises in Central America. *(PL 99-661, Congress and the Nation Vol. VII, p. 290)*

The 1986 law was challenged by Minnesota Gov. Rudy Perpich, a Democrat, who objected to members of the Minnesota National Guard being placed in active service and sent to Honduras for joint exercises with that country's military forces. He contended that the law intruded on states' control over the National Guard under the Constitution's so-called militia clauses.

Under Article I, Section 8, Congress had the power to "provide for calling forth the Militia to execute the Laws of the Union, suppress Insurrections and repel Invasions." A second clause gave Congress power to govern the militia while "employed in the Service of the United States, reserving to the States respectively, the Appointment of the Officers, and the Authority of training the Militia according to the discipline prescribed by Congress."

Writing for a unanimous Court in *Perpich v. Department of Defense,* Justice John Paul Stevens said the 1986 law was valid under the National Guard's dual-enlistment system. "[T]he members of the National Guard of Minnesota who are ordered into federal service with the National Guard of the United States lose their status as members of the state militia during their period of active duty," Stevens wrote.

Stevens rejected Perpich's argument that the broad interpretation of Congress' power nullified the states' role under the militia clauses. "It merely recognizes the supremacy of federal power in the area of military affairs," Stevens concluded. *(Case summary, p. 832)*

Tactical Air Combat. Approved $1.54 billion for 36 Air Force F-15Es and $781 million to modernize a dozen existing Navy F-14s.

Both houses essentially had approved the administration requests for the two heavyweights of the Pentagon's fighter plane fleet, and the conferees ironed out minor differences in funding.

• Authorized $1.5 billion for 48 copies of the F/A-18, used by the Navy and Marines as both a fighter and a bomber.

The administration had requested 66 F/A-18s. The House boosted that number to 84, and the Senate cut it to 42.

• Authorized $1.92 billion for 108 Air Force F-16s and an additional $225 million for components to be used in future production runs.

Both houses approved the purchase of 108 Air Force F-16s, instead of the 150 planes requested. Declining defense budgets would require the Air Force to break its existing multi-year contract for F-16 production, conferees on the bill acknowledged.

• Authorized $964 million for development of the advanced tactical fighter (ATF).

Both houses had approved most of the $1.05 billion sought for development of the ATF, intended to replace the F-14 and F-15. But both also had ordered the Air Force to spend more time flight-testing prototype airplanes before committing to production.

• Provided $592 million to permit a resumption of production of the A-12 ground-attack plane if problems with it were eventually solved. (Cheney canceled the plane early in 1991.) Both houses had turned down the $1.21 billion requested for eight A-12s, intended for use by the Navy and Air Force as the next generation of ground-attack plane. The Senate approved no A-12 production money; the House authorized $352 million to keep the production line intact while bugs were worked out. The conferees complained that the futuristic, delta-wing plane was "seriously overweight, far behind schedule, increasingly complex in design and more difficult to manufacture."

• Authorized $815 million to buy 900 AMRAAM air-to-air missiles, the same number as was funded in fiscal 1990.

The House denied the $1.32 billion request for 1,800 AMRAAMs, citing a long history of test failures and production problems. The Senate proposed the amount that was adopted.

• Approved $64 million to upgrade the long-range, half-ton Phoenix missiles carried by the Navy's F-14s. The final version followed the Senate's lead in increasing the funds for modernization from the $4 million requested.

• Authorized the $84 million requested to develop a lightweight replacement for Phoenix, designated AAAM. However, noting that the new missile would not enter service for a decade, the conferees told the Navy to reconsider its plan to end Phoenix production.

• Approved $48 million for continued development of the ASPJ radar jammer to protect combat planes, which began as a joint project with the Air Force but was later supported only by the Navy. Also authorized were $15 million to keep the Air Force involved with ASPJ development, $6.5 million for more testing, $39 million to buy Air Force jammers and $162 million for a consolidated electronic warfare program.

The conferees criticized the Pentagon's weapons managers for allowing the Navy and Air Force to go their separate ways in developing radar jammers. The administration asked for $162 million for the Navy to continue development of the ASPJ jammer and $301 million to buy two other kinds of radar jammers for Air Force planes. The House had slashed the Air Force jammer request, while the Senate had slashed the request for the ASPJ.

Naval Warfare. Authorized $1.46 billion for one *Seawolf*-class submarine and $3.2 billion for four *Arleigh Burke*-class destroyers, equipped with the Aegis anti-aircraft system.

Initially, Cheney had requested another new ship of each type. Early in August 1990, Cheney pared back his fiscal 1991 shipbuilding request, and the final version of the defense bill endorsed the revision.

• Authorized $55 million for the Sea Lance missile, intended to be fired from warships at submerged submarines up to 30 miles away, and $5 million to develop a new version of the existing ASROC anti-sub missile, which had a much shorter range.

The Senate and House Armed Services committees each had challenged the Navy's decision to cancel development of the Sea Lance. The Navy had requested instead $30 million to develop the new version of the ASROC missile.

The House had added $50 million and the Senate $71 million to continue the Sea Lance program, and the House denied all funds for ASROC.

• Approved $398 million for a high-speed supply ship intended to serve as a mid-ocean, one-stop shopping center supplying a fleet with fuel, food and ammunition.

Air and Sea Transport. Authorized the production of two additional C-17 cargo planes but provided only $400 million for procurement.

Because of delays in the production of C-17s, both houses had slashed funding to build additional planes in fiscal 1991, while providing funds to keep the production line intact.

As a practical matter, the Air Force would be unable to build the planes without gaining the approval of the Armed Services and Appropriations committees to reprogram additional funds to the C-17 account from other parts of the defense budget. In addition, the conference report barred the use of any fiscal 1991 C-17 procurement money until after the first plane's initial test flight.

• Authorized $803 million for the V-22 Osprey.

The final version followed the amount approved by the House for the hybrid airplane/helicopter the Marine Corps wanted to use as a troop transport, but which Cheney had tried to kill several times. That total included $238 million to continue development of the plane, $200 million appropriated for procurement in fiscal 1989 but not previously available, and an additional $165 million for procurement.

The conferees emphasized that the procurement funds were to be used only to build enough production-line aircraft for testing.

According to various analyses, the V-22's higher speed made it superior to the conventional helicopters Cheney wanted to buy instead. But before Congress would commit to buying the Osprey, conferees declared, the V-22 would have to demonstrate that it could carry heavy cargo — such as an artillery piece — slung under its belly while flying more than 200 miles per hour.

• Approved $250 million to buy more fast cargo ships to haul tanks and other heavy combat equipment from U.S. ports to trouble spots abroad.

Burden-Sharing. Required a reduction of 50,000 in the number of U.S. personnel stationed in Europe, reducing the number to 261,855.

The conferees also put in the final version several other restrictions intended to reduce the cost of stationing U.S. forces overseas, but they softened initial provisions. One such restriction was intended to force the Pentagon to cut the payroll for foreign civilians employed on U.S. bases abroad by 25 percent. But the final language in the bill permitted the secretary of defense to waive that limit, if the national interest required it, simply by notifying Congress.

• Imposed a cap of 50,000 on the number of U.S. forces stationed in Japan unless the Japanese government shouldered the cost of keeping them there.

The conferees greatly diluted a House provision that not only would have capped the U.S. personnel level at 50,000 but also would have reduced that number by 5,000 annually.

Base Closings. Established an eight-member, bipartisan commission for each of the next three Congresses to recommend a list of unneeded military bases that should be closed. The president and Congress each would have to accept or reject each list in toto. Congress, acting under fast-track procedures, could reject a list only by a joint resolution, which could be vetoed.

Personnel Issues. Provided a 4.1 percent military pay raise, which took effect on Jan. 1, 1991.

• Offered more liberal severance payments to personnel discharged before they qualified for retirement. The measure called for removing the current $30,000 cap on the payment and for making enlisted personnel eligible for the first time.

• Continued eligibility for military medical care for 60 days after discharge (for personnel with less than six years' service) or 120 days (for personnel who had served six years or more).

• Created an option for personnel to buy into contributory veterans' education benefit programs, even if the member previously had elected not to join the program.

• Authorized $1.9 billion for equipment earmarked for use by the National Guard and reserves, $1.4 billion more than requested.

Both houses had rejected Cheney's proposals to reduce the number of personnel in the National Guard and reserves and to disband some Guard and reserve units.

1991 Defense Appropriations

Congress in 1990 cleared a $269 billion defense appropriations bill (HR 5803 — PL 101-511) for fiscal 1991. Combined with funds provided in separate legislation for military construction and for defense-related projects of the Energy Department, the bill brought the total defense-related appropriations for fiscal 1991 to $288.3 billion — the ceiling set by the congressional budget resolution.

As part of the fiscal 1991 budget package, Congress and the White House had agreed to reduce total spending for the Defense Department and defense-related programs to $288 billion from President Bush's initial budget request of $307 billion.

The president's original request had amounted to a 2 percent decline in purchasing power, after allowing for inflation. But the reduced threat of the Soviet conventional military to Western Europe fueled congressional demands for larger cuts.

The political dynamics changed, however, when Iraq marched into Kuwait on Aug. 2, and the administration deployed more than 200,000 U.S. troops to the Persian Gulf. The prospect that U.S. military personnel would wind up engaged in a large-scale combat operation made members more cautious of cutting the defense budget too dramatically. *(Persian Gulf War, p. 299)*

In addition to appropriating $269 billion, HR 5803 authorized the transfer to the Pentagon of $1 billion from contributions made by other countries to defray the cost of U.S. deployments in and around Saudi Arabia.

The big defense issues had already been settled by the time Congress gave its final approval to HR 5803. The vast majority of funding limits set by the bill or described in the conferees' explanatory statement echoed the decisions embodied in the companion defense authorization measure (HR 4739 — PL 101-510), which cleared on the same day as the appropriations bill. *(Fiscal 1991 defense authorization, p. 355)*

Legislative Action

The U.S. military commitment in the Persian Gulf left its imprint on the Pentagon funding bill reported Oct. 9 by the House Appropriations Committee (H Rept 101-822). The measure slowed the cutback of military manpower and provided for the purchase of more high-speed cargo ships.

The Defense Appropriations Subcommittee drafted the Pentagon spending bill at $263 billion, the amount allowed by the House-passed version of the budget resolution. But the final version of the resolution adopted Oct. 9 set a ceiling of $288.3 billion on all defense-related appropriations. Counting defense funds in legislation already passed, that left room for an additional $5.3 billion in the defense appropriations bill, which was added for assorted projects before the measure was reported from committee.

The House passed the $268 billion defense appropriations bill Oct. 12 by a 322-97 vote. While the House bill pared down the Pentagon's money and manpower, it did so by far smaller amounts than had seemed likely prior to Iraq's invasion of Kuwait.

Some provisions responded to problems highlighted by the deployment of U.S. personnel in and around Saudi Arabia, such as the earmarking of nearly $2.5 billion to buy more cargo ships to haul the tanks and other heavy weapons of U.S. combat units to distant trouble spots. More generally, however, the bill's pro-Pentagon tilt reflected members' reluctance to appear soft on defense at a time when U.S. interests faced a challenge from Iraq and U.S. troops were in the field.

But even with the 200,000 U.S. troops deployed against Iraq in October, the House rejected a 2 percent across-the-board cut by only a narrow margin. The Oct. 12 vote was 201-215. Two other budget-reduction amendments also were defeated.

On most contentious issues, the House appropriations bill conformed with positions embodied in the House-passed defense authorization bill. For instance, HR 5803 provided no funds for production of the B-2 "stealth" bomber and sliced $2.4 billion from Bush's request for the strategic defense initiative (SDI).

The Senate Appropriations Committee approved a $268.8 billion defense appropriations bill on Oct. 11 (S 3189 — S Rept 101-521). Committee markup of the defense spending measure had been relatively routine until an amendment was offered to cut $2.75 billion from the B-2 stealth bomber program, which in effect would have killed it outright after the six test planes under construction were completed. The amendment, which triggered a veto threat from Bush, went down to defeat on a narrow 15-14 vote.

The Senate approved a $268.2 billion defense bill, 79-16, on Oct. 15, but only after many members voiced frustration that U.S. allies were not paying more of the defense burden. Complaints that allied governments were sponging off the U.S. defense effort had festered on Capitol Hill since the mid-1970s.

The Senate adopted several amendments reflecting the burden-sharing theme, but it rejected Oct. 15, by a **key vote of 46-50 (R 8-34; D 38-16)**, an amendment that would have sliced the number of U.S. troops stationed in Europe by 80,000 instead of 50,000, as imposed by the bill. The same amendment had been killed on a tabling motion, 59-40, during debate on the defense authorization bill. *(1990 key votes, p. 1039)*

On most issues, the Senate appropriations bill reprised the positions taken by the Senate in the authorization bill. The Senate remained unmoved since early August on the B-2 stealth bomber. It continued to back the controversial and costly plane, although an amendment to cut off B-2 production failed by a narrower margin. The amendment, rejected 43-56 Aug. 2, was rejected Oct. 15 by a **key vote of 44-50 (R 9-32; D 35-18)**.

Conference, Major Provisions

Conferees on the $269 billion defense appropriations bill filed their report Oct. 24 (H Rept 101-938). The report was adopted by the House by voice vote Oct. 25 and by the Senate, 80-17, the following day.

During the conference, the chronic tension between the Armed Services and Appropriations panels flared over several elements of the bill. The appropriations bill, for example, included a provision expressly nullifying language in the authorization bill intended to slow moves toward production of the new Air Force ATF fighter plane. The authorizing committees also objected to a series of "earmarks" in the appropriations bill, which awarded funds to specific colleges and universities, thus bypassing the Pentagon's procedures for awarding university research funds on a competitive basis. Also in dispute was a provision doubling to 360 days the period for which the president could order members of the National Guard and reserves to active duty, except under a declaration of war or in a national emergency.

Senate Armed Services Committee Chairman Sam Nunn, D-Ga., complained that all three elements of the appropriations bill were "invented in a conference committee.... The Senate has never had an opportunity to consider these items."

But these were the exceptions. Most provisions in the appropriations bill reflected the decisions reached in negotiations over the authorization bill and conferees had to settle only relatively minor differences in funding.

Major Provisions. As signed into law Nov. 5, HR 5803 appropriated:

- $2.35 billion for procurement of the B-2 stealth bomber. Conferees did not address the controversy between the Senate and House as to whether the money could be used to begin building additional copies of the controversial plane.
- $2.89 billion for the strategic defense initiative.
- $1.33 billion for an 18th Trident submarine and $1.54 billion for 52 of the Trident II missiles carried by the big submarines.
- $688 million to continue developing two mobile intercontinental ballistic missiles (ICBMs): the rail-launched version of the existing MX missile and the much smaller Midgetman ICBM. Both houses had denied the $1.35 billion requested to begin production of the MX rail launchers.
- $366 million for 100 bomber-launched cruise missiles; $119 million for research and development of a tactical version of the SRAM II nuclear missile; $210 million to develop a new early warning satellite; $126 million for development of a ground-launched anti-satellite (ASAT) missile.
- $1.04 billion for production of 225 M-1 tanks and for modifications on older versions; $688 million for 600 Bradley fighting vehicles; $144 million to develop a new "family" of armored vehicles — including the Block III tank, a new armored troop carrier and several others; $187 million for production of the 100-mile-range ATACMS missile, designed to strike tank columns behind enemy lines, and $226 million to develop an airborne radar, designated Joint STARS (JSTARS), intended to guide ATACMS to its target; $196 million to develop a missile-guidance radar called Longbow, to be added to the Army's Apache anti-tank helicopter; $92 million for continued development of an anti-aircraft missile launcher designated ADATS, intended to protect front-line combat units.
- $2.46 billion for equipment for the National Guard and reserve components.
- $771 million to equip 12 existing Navy F-14s with more powerful engines and radars; $1.54 billion for 36 Air Force F-15s; $1.86 billion for 108 Air Force F-16s; $1.45 billion for 48 F/A-18s, used by the Navy and Marine Corps; $964 million for research and development of a new fighter plane designated the ATF; $592 million for the A-12 ground-attack plane; $162 million to be parceled out to the Navy and Air Force, under a new joint procurement plan, for radar jammers to protect combat planes against guided missiles.
- $401 million to modernize an aircraft carrier launched in 1967, the *John F. Kennedy*; $3.21 billion for four destroyers equipped with the Aegis anti-aircraft system; $1.78 billion for the second *Seawolf*-class submarine and components to be used in future subs of this type; $659 million for 400 Tomahawk cruise missiles; $71 million to continue development of the Sea Lance ship-launched anti-submarine missile — a program the Navy wanted to terminate — and $15 million to develop a short-range alternative; $204 million for two coastal mine sweepers.
- $1 billion for two C-17 wide-body, intercontinental cargo planes and components to be used to build six more in fiscal 1992 and $460 million for C-17 procurement; $900 million to expand the Navy's fleet of fast cargo ships able to haul U.S.-based Army units overseas; $403 million to continue development and slowly begin production of the V-22 Osprey, a hybrid airplane/helicopter, which the Marine Corps wanted as a troop transport but Cheney wanted to terminate.
- $78.1 billion for military personnel and $83.5 billion for operations and maintenance.

The final bill also included several provisions aimed at reducing the cost of U.S. deployments overseas. One capped the number of U.S. personnel stationed in Japan at 50,000 and reduced the cap by 5,000 annually unless the Japanese government paid all direct costs of U.S. deployments in Japan, except for the pay and fringe benefits of service members. The president could waive this provision if he deemed it in the national interest to do so. Cuts also were made in the amounts requested for maintenance of overseas facilities, for foreign nationals employed on U.S. bases and for overseas base operating costs.

The bill included provisions helpful to Israel. One established in Israel a 4.5 million-barrel petroleum reserve "to meet the wartime needs and combined military training requirements of the United States and Israel." Another provision earmarked $15 million of the Navy's operations and maintenance budget to upgrade port facilities in Israel for U.S. use.

Other Action. A fiscal 1991 supplemental appropriations bill to cover the costs of the Persian Gulf War (HR 1282 — PL 102-28) was signed into law on April 10, 1991. The measure provided $42.6 billion for war-related costs. The funds were to be drawn from an account composed of money pledged by foreign governments for the war effort, plus an additional $15 billion in U.S. funds. The $15 billion in U.S. funds was to be used to cover immediate costs pending receipt of foreign contributions, with any portion left over to be returned to the U.S. Treasury. The bulk of the money was returned in a fiscal 1992 supplemental appropriations bill.

Another fiscal 1991 supplemental appropriations bill (HR 1281 — PL 102-27) provided $150 million for Pentagon operations and maintenance, as well as research and development. The bill, also signed into law April 10, 1991, included $623 million for atomic energy defense activities under the Energy Department.

1991 Military Construction

Congress in 1990 appropriated $8.36 billion for fiscal 1991 construction projects and family housing at U.S. military installations and for base-closing costs (HR 5313 — PL 101-519). Because of budget pressures and reduced international tensions, Congress cut $764 million from President Bush's request.

The bill shifted priorities from overseas projects, including cooperative efforts with the North Atlantic Treaty Organization (NATO), to domestic facilities. Lawmakers' refusal to fund a proposed air base at Crotone, Italy, was a key setback for the administration. The new base was slated to house the United States' 401st Tactical Fighter Wing with its 72 F-16 aircraft. The Spanish government had insisted that the unit vacate its base at Torrejon, near Madrid.

Senior defense officials had touted the proposed base at Crotone as a fulcrum for U.S. military leverage in southern Europe and the Mediterranean. While slamming the planned facility as unduly lavish, congressional critics hinted for months that they would consider approving a less elaborate installation at Crotone.

But when the Air Force did not propose a sufficiently austere alternative, the conferees included in the final version of the bill a provision barring the use of any U.S. funds for the project. The ban included funds that made up 28 percent of NATO's infrastructure program — its kitty for construction projects, which would have funded the proposed $800 million Crotone base.

The Pentagon backed away from a recommendation that Bush veto the bill. In signing the legislation, the president said he was "deeply disappointed" with several provisions, including the ban on funding for the Crotone base. He said he would continue to work with Congress on the air base proposal.

As requested by the administration after it had submitted its January budget, the final bill rescinded $286 million in previously appropriated but unspent money for construction overseas. It applied those leftover funds to the fiscal 1991 program, thus reducing by that amount the new budget authority required — to $8.36 billion.

Legislative Action

The House Appropriations Committee reported HR 5313 on July 19 (H Rept 101-608), and the full House passed it on July 30 by a 312-82 vote.

The House-passed bill appropriated $8.3 billion for military construction, after adjustments were made for the $286 million in rescinded funds. The legislation was $815 million less than the January budget request, with overseas projects accounting for the lion's share of the reductions.

The Senate Appropriations Committee reported its version of the military construction bill (S Rept 101-410) on Aug. 1, and the Senate passed the measure by voice vote on Oct. 1.

The Senate bill, after applying the $286 million in leftover funds to the fiscal 1991 program, appropriated $7.98 billion for military construction — $332 million less than the House bill and $1.15 billion less than Bush's January request. Like the House, the Senate targeted overseas projects for most of the cuts. The Senate also used the appropriations bill to take swipes at international terrorists and the government of Iraq.

Conference, Major Provisions

House-Senate conferees compromised on an $8.36 billion measure. The House adopted the conference report on the bill (H Rept 101-888) by voice vote on Oct. 19. The Senate adopted the measure on Oct. 28 — just after midnight in the session of Oct. 27 — by voice vote, clearing HR 5313.

The bill included only one-third of the $955 million Bush had requested for projects in foreign territory. By far the largest single component of the $624 million reduction in foreign-oriented funding came from the annual U.S. contributions to the NATO infrastructure fund. The bill provided $193 million of the $420 million requested. No funds were allowed for the Crotone air base.

Most of the remaining cuts in overseas spending came from five projects planned in five countries: Germany, Britain, South Korea, Japan and Italy. Of a total of $347 million requested for projects in those countries, the bill provided only $20 million.

The hefty cuts in overseas spending reflected some of the thinking behind the widespread, bipartisan opposition in Congress to the proposed air base at Crotone. For one thing, with Soviet military power retrenching on most fronts, members questioned the need for programs oriented toward the threat of a Soviet-led attack on NATO.

That belief, spawned by the collapse of the Soviet-led Warsaw Pact, meshed with longstanding and growing congressional demands that U.S. allies pay a larger share of the cost of mutual defense efforts.

The construction bill also reflected the widespread belief on Capitol Hill that a larger share of the U.S. defense structure could be shifted to the politically potent National Guard and reserve components. With Soviet military retrenchment — the argument went — a large-scale military threat would take so long to develop that ample time would be available to mobilize the reserves. The final bill appropriated $690 million for the National Guard and reserves, more than either the House or Senate version had provided. The administration had requested $280 million.

U.S.-Soviet Advances in Controlling ...

In 1990, the United States and the Soviet Union made important advances in the area of arms control. President Bush and Soviet President Mikhail S. Gorbachev, along with the leaders of 20 other countries, signed a treaty Nov. 19 that would dismantle the massive Soviet army that fostered Europe's Cold War division and militarization for four decades. Bush hailed the pact as "the most far-reaching arms agreement" ever negotiated.

The treaty limiting conventional forces in Europe (CFE) imposed ceilings on military equipment deployed by the North Atlantic Treaty Organization (NATO) states and the former members of the Warsaw Pact in an area between the Atlantic Ocean and the Ural Mountains. The Senate gave the pact its overwhelming endorsement in 1991. *(CFE treaty, p. 383)*

The signing of the CFE treaty marked a high point in relations between Washington and Moscow. Earlier, in summit talks May 31-June 3 in Washington, Bush and Gorbachev moved to codify the transformation of U.S.-Soviet relations in the past year resulting from fundamental changes in the Soviet Union and in the states of Eastern Europe: the easing of the military confrontation, the disintegration of the Warsaw Pact as a military alliance, and the growth of political pluralism and regional separatism in the Soviet Union.

The centerpiece of the Washington summit was the two leaders' agreement on trade. In addition, the two countries reached a host of other, minor agreements. *(Details, p. 169)*

Strategic Arms Reductions

On the arms control front, the two leaders signed one joint statement nailing down the major elements of a strategic arms reduction talks (START) agreement, and a second statement setting goals for further reductions.

Both sides had hoped to produce a final START agreement by the end of 1990, but the pact stalled as a result of a few unsettled technical issues and high-level inattention by both countries' government. Washington was preoccupied with the march toward war in the Persian Gulf while Moscow was grappling with a host of domestic political problems, including independence efforts in the Baltic states and hard-liners' criticisms of Gorbachev's policies. *(Persian Gulf War, p. 299; end of the Cold War, p. 319)*

Agreement on a START pact finally was reached in 1991. Bush and Gorbachev signed the treaty in Moscow only weeks before hard-liners staged a coup attempt that ultimately led to the unraveling of the Soviet superpower. The Senate in 1992 approved the START agreement, along with a subsequent protocol with four nuclear states that were part of the former Soviet Union. *(START agreement, p. 385)*

Testing Treaties

Senate approval of two treaties to limit the size of underground nuclear test explosions was guaranteed by the presidents' approval of protocols intended to tighten up verification procedures. *(Testing treaties, this page)*

Chemical Weapons Accord

Both countries agreed to slash stockpiles of lethal chemical munitions. Throughout the Cold War, the United States and the Soviet Union each stockpiled huge quantities of deadly chemical weapons that — just like nuclear weapons — were supposed to deter an attack. On June 1, during the Washington summit, Bush and Gorbachev signed an agreement to begin a unique cooperation program to destroy those chemical weapons and to persuade other countries to do the same.

In the meantime, the superpowers pledged to press for progress in Geneva, where 40 nations were negotiating for an international treaty banning such weapons.

If an international treaty was signed and ratified, the United States and the Soviet Union would accelerate the destruction of their poison gas supplies. Eight years after the Geneva treaty entered into force, the superpowers pledged to eliminate all

Conferees also accepted the House-passed appropriation of $998 million for closing and cleaning up domestic bases targeted for closure. The Senate bill had included the administration request of $917 million.

Nuclear Testing Treaties

In separate unanimous votes of 98-0, the Senate on Sept. 25, 1990, approved two treaties with the Soviet Union aimed at limiting the power of nuclear test explosions. President Bush signed the document formally ratifying the treaties Dec. 11.

The ease with which the treaties were approved was a sharp contrast to the 14 years of controversy and delay that had surrounded the agreements since they were negotiated during the administrations of Richard Nixon and Gerald R. Ford. Final approval came in 1990 after U.S.-Soviet negotiators tightened the treaties' provisions for verification.

The two treaties barred underground nuclear blasts with an explosive force greater than 150,000 tons of TNT

. . . Conventional, Nuclear, Chemical Arms

but 500 tons of chemical weapons each — equal to 2 percent of the existing U.S. stockpile.

By year's end, the Bush administration had not sent the U.S.-Soviet accord to Capitol Hill. Negotiators were still working on some final protocols, the most difficult of which was how each country would ensure the other's destruction of chemical weapons. And the Kremlin's increasingly hard-line political stance and crackdown on its breakaway Baltic States cast doubt on the accord's future in Congress.

Just how the pact would be ratified also provoked a dispute with implications for both political strategy and congressional prerogatives. Key senators insisted that the Constitution required the agreement to be in "treaty form" and thus subject to approval by a two-thirds vote only of the Senate. But the administration said it planned to submit the accord as an executive agreement, requiring a simple majority vote in each chamber.

Background. In a major step toward U.S.-Soviet action on the issue, Secretary of State James A. Baker III and Soviet Foreign Minister Eduard A. Shevardnadze, at a two-day series of meetings in Wyoming, on Sept. 23, 1989, signed an agreement calling for an exchange of information and on-site inspections of each country's chemical weapons arsenals.

Two days later, Bush told the United Nations that the United States would destroy most of its stocks of chemical weapons within eight years if the Soviet Union did the same. Speaking to the U.N. General Assembly on Sept. 25, Bush also said that the United States would eliminate all its chemical weapons only when every other country possessing them made the same pledge.

Bush did not mention that the Pentagon already was required by law to dismantle 90 percent of its stocks of chemical weapons that were produced before 1969. In its fiscal 1986 defense authorization bill (PL 99-145), Congress agreed to allow production of new "binary" chemical weapons on the condition that the Pentagon dispose of all but 10 percent of its old chemical weapons by Sept. 30, 1994. Congress later changed that deadline to Sept. 30, 1997. The new binary weapons had their chemical agents in two separate containers that would mix, when fired, to create hazardous gas.

In the wake of his pledge, Bush canceled the request for funds in fiscal 1991 for more new chemical weapons. Shevardnadze, addressing the General Assembly the day after Bush, advanced even more radical proposals: that the United States and the Soviet Union halt all chemical weapons production and immediately begin disposing of their existing arsenals.

Each superpower conditioned its proposal on action by the other. In a series of meetings in 1990, Baker and Shevardnadze worked out the essential details of the chemical weapons pact in time for the Washington summit.

Provisions. The accord followed the 1987 intermediate-range nuclear-forces (INF) treaty in calling for destruction of an entire class of weapons, with each superpower monitoring the other's compliance. *(Congress and the Nation Vol. VII, p. 332)*

But the new accord went beyond the INF treaty in providing for active U.S.-Soviet cooperation in developing and using techniques to destroy the weapons. Having built thousands of tons of deadly poison weapons, Washington and Moscow struggled with the question of how to get rid of them. The agreement also allowed for "systematic on-site inspection" of all facilities used for storing and producing chemical weapons.

Under the June 1 agreement, the superpowers were to begin destroying their chemical weapons by the end of 1992. By the end of 1999, each had to destroy at least 50 percent of its declared stockpile and, by the end of 2002, destroy all but 5,000 tons — equal to 20 percent of the existing holdings declared by the United States.

Other Action. Congress also was at work in 1990 on the issue of chemical weapons, clearing legislation imposing sanctions on foreign countries or companies engaged in their manufacture or spread. Bush pocket-vetoed the bill on the grounds that it gave him too little discretion. *(Details, p. 175)*

Legislation was enacted in 1991 imposing import sanctions on countries and companies that contributed to the proliferation of chemical and biological weapons. *(1991 action, p. 195)*

(150 kilotons). The Threshold Test Ban Treaty, signed July 3, 1974, applied to underground nuclear weapons tests.

On May 28, 1976, the companion Peaceful Nuclear Explosions Treaty was signed. This treaty allowed the resumption of limited underground nuclear explosions for peaceful purposes, such as large-scale excavation for dams or canals.

The agreements followed the partial test ban treaty signed in 1963, which banned nuclear test explosions except those that were conducted underground.

Controversy and Delay

Various political factors stalled Senate action. President Jimmy Carter shelved the pacts and sought instead to negotiate a comprehensive test ban treaty with the Soviets. But those negotiations ended without success in late 1980. From 1982 on, the obstacle was President Ronald Reagan's insistence that the networks of seismometers provided for in the treaties could not adequately verify Soviet compliance with the 150-kiloton limits.

Bush requested Senate approval of the two treaties

four weeks after he and Soviet President Mikhail S. Gorbachev signed, at their summit meeting in Washington on June 1, 1990, detailed appendixes (or "protocols") tightening verification procedures. *(Summit meeting, box, p. 366)*

These new agreements would allow each country to use not only seismic measurements but also a U.S.-backed method called CORRTEX to measure the size of any explosion expected to have a force of more than 50 kilotons. This new technique would use instruments located practically adjacent to the explosive device being monitored.

The unanimous votes for the two treaties, and the perfunctory debate preceding them, reflected in part the dramatic decline in U.S.-Soviet tensions as Gorbachev retrenched abroad while grappling at home with economic chaos and ethnic separatism. *(End of the Cold War, p. 319)*

But the Senate's low-key approval of two treaties that dealt, although peripherally, with the U.S. nuclear arsenal also attested to the blandness of the agreements. The U.S. nuclear testing program had lived with the 150-kiloton limit since 1976, when both countries agreed to abide by the ceiling, pending ratification of the two pacts.

Citing seismic measurements, the Reagan administration contended that the Soviet Union had violated that limit many times. But many prominent specialists in seismic measurement sharply contested that claim.

The duel over Soviet compliance was one of many controversies that had kept the two treaties languishing. Proponents of a comprehensive test ban viewed the long duel over new verification methods as just another skirmish within a larger battle over eliminating underground nuclear blasts. Seismic experts aligned with these arms control advocates contended that officials of the Reagan and Bush administrations exaggerated the uncertainties in seismic measurement of nuclear blasts while playing down potential weak spots in CORRTEX.

Policy makers continued to debate whether the United States should maintain an aggressive testing program or press for a comprehensive ban on testing. Both the Senate and House went on record in favor of moving toward a comprehensive test ban treaty while working on the fiscal 1991 Department of Defense authorization bill. The Reagan and Bush administrations had rejected any move toward a total test ban in the near future while insisting that a comprehensive ban remained the ultimate U.S. goal. *(Defense authorization, p. 355)*

The Senate Foreign Relations Committee straddled the controversy by including in the resolution approving ratification of the Threshold Test Ban Treaty two innocuous declarations, one sought by advocates for speedy completion of a comprehensive test ban and another, sought by the administration, intended to forestall such haste. The panel, which had favorably reported the two treaties in 1987, marked up the resolution of ratification Sept. 14 (Exec N 94-2, Treaty Doc 101-19 — Exec Rept 101-31).

Treaty Protocols

The new verification protocols were extremely long, largely because they spelled out in great detail the procedures for using the CORRTEX method. The two-page text of the Threshold Test Ban Treaty was followed by a 107-page protocol.

For each treaty, the protocols provided that:

- When one country planned an explosion with a yield greater than 50 kilotons, the other could monitor its strength using CORRTEX, seismic methods or both.

To monitor such explosions seismically, the verifying country could temporarily install its own equipment at three existing seismic stations in the territory of the testing country. The Soviet Union could use stations at Tulsa, Okla.; Black Hills, S.D.; and Newport, Wash. The United States could use stations at Arti, Novosibirsk and Obninsk in the Soviet Union.

- When one country planned an explosion with a yield of 35 to 50 kilotons, the other could inspect the test site and collect samples of the rock and soil to better interpret its seismic measurements of the blast.
- If one country conducted no explosions larger than 50 kilotons in a year, the other could use CORRTEX to measure two smaller blasts in each of the first five years the treaty was in effect and one blast annually thereafter.
- Explosions could not be conducted in caverns larger than 20,000 cubic meters, because an extremely large hole might muffle the seismic shock of the blast, thus deceiving distant seismic equipment.

Advance estimates of how big a bang to expect from a given nuclear device were inherently uncertain, as were measurements of the actual blast. So the U.S. and Soviet governments agreed that the occurrence of one or two blasts measured as being slightly over the 150-kiloton limit would not be interpreted as a violation of either of the two treaties.

Defense Production Act

Congress in 1990 failed to clear long-term legislation to extend the government's emergency defense preparedness and procurement authority. The bill (HR 486) died when the Senate, faced with administration opposition, did not act on a House-passed conference agreement before adjourning.

HR 486 would have reauthorized the Defense Production Act for three years. That law, which was first passed in 1950, allowed the president to promote the development of strategic materials and technologies, to stockpile critical materials not readily available from domestic sources and to give the military first claim on strategic goods during emergencies.

The conference agreement would have expanded presidential and Defense Department authority to promote development of domestic suppliers of strategic goods and technologies and also to require that certain goods be purchased from U.S. companies. Those provisions drew strong administration fire and an implied veto threat from Defense Secretary Dick Cheney, despite bipartisan support in Congress.

As agreed to in conference, the bill also contained provisions sought by the Senate Banking Committee to give federal regulators authority to deny applications by foreign banks and securities firms to expand their operations in the United States if their home country did not treat foreign and domestic financial businesses alike.

As action on the legislation progressed in 1990, lawmakers cleared three bills (HR 5432 — PL 101-351; HR 5725 — PL 101-407; S 3155 — PL 101-411) temporarily extending the act until Sept. 30, Oct. 5 and Oct. 20, respectively.

The House passed HR 486 (H Rept 101-724) under suspension of the rules on Sept. 24 by a 295-119 vote. The Senate Banking, Housing and Urban Affairs Committee reported its version (S 1379 — S Rept 101-368) on July 13. The Senate passed an amended HR 486 by voice vote Oct. 3. The House adopted the conference report (H Rept 101-933) by voice vote Oct. 25, but the Senate did not act on the measure in the waning days of the 101st Congress and the act expired on Oct. 20, 1990.

Congress approved two short-term extensions of the act in 1991 and cleared a two-year extension in 1992. *(1991-92 action, p. 412)*

1991-92

The collapse of the Soviet Union in 1991 defined defense policy debates in the 102nd Congress, as both the Bush administration and Congress grappled with the difficult task of formulating a post-Cold War strategy.

How quickly could, or should, the United States reduce its defense establishment? How much of the defense budget could be shifted to domestic priorities? What weapons systems were necessary given that the Soviet Union was no longer a military threat? Did a conventional application exist for strategic weapons systems that had been targeted against the Soviet empire? What would the break-up of the Soviet Union mean for carefully negotiated U.S.-Soviet arms agreements?

Despite the collapse of Communist power in the Soviet Union in the fall of 1991, Congress made no significant reduction in the defense budget President Bush had proposed earlier in the year. Defense Secretary Dick Cheney warned that the defense establishment would be damaged if Congress forced a more rapid budget cutback than his program to reduce the size of the force roughly 25 percent by the mid-1990s.

But the more persuasive deterrent against deeper cuts in 1991 seemed to have been members' fear of the political chaos that would result if Congress junked the budget law passed late in 1990. That law limited the allowable deficit each year through fiscal 1995 and limited annual discretional appropriations through fiscal 1993 for defense, international affairs and domestic spending. Funds cut from defense could not be transferred to popular domestic programs without violating the cap on domestic spending.

In 1992, Bush proposed cutting $50 billion over five years from the defense plan he had proposed the previous year. But the immediate savings would be less dramatic — $10 billion lower than what the administration had proposed in 1991. Congress trimmed the defense appropriations bill by another $7 billion, but for the most part demands for cuts in military spending gave way to election-year pressures to save defense-related jobs.

Although the cuts in overall defense budgets were neither deep nor drastic, significant changes were made in major defense programs. Congress, for example, reshaped the strategic defense initiative (SDI) — the anti-missile defense program initiated during the Reagan administration — and went on record for the first time in favor of a rapid deployment of a limited ground-based SDI system.

Already on shaky political ground because of its cost, the B-2 "stealth" bomber program became even more questionable because of the precipitous decline of the Soviet nuclear threat and doubts about whether the plane could evade radar detection as intended. The number of B-2s planned — which had gone from an original goal of 132 to 75 in 1990 — was reduced to 20 in 1992.

Substantial accomplishments were achieved in the arcane but momentous annals of arms control treaties. But the demise of the Soviet Union left the Bush administration without the leader — and, for that matter, without the country — with which it had negotiated those agreements. The administration sought, and generally received, assurances from republics in the new Commonwealth of Independent States that they would honor the arms agreements.

The closing of domestic military bases remained politically painful, but under procedures established in 1990 Congress accepted additional closings of installations.

1992 Defense Authorization

Extraordinary events in the world bolstered and buffeted U.S. defense policy in 1991. In the end, however, Congress cleared a fiscal 1992 defense authorization bill (HR 2100 — PL 102-190) that made no significant reduction in the $291 billion defense budget President Bush had requested.

Nor did members go much beyond the pace set by the Pentagon in restructuring U.S. forces and weaponry to reflect the end of the Cold War and the emergence of what Bush called the "new world order."

Early in the year, the quick and triumphant U.S. victory in the Persian Gulf War bolstered support for the military and the reputation of its high-tech weaponry. *(Persian Gulf War, p. 299)*

Later in the year, the very purposes and dimensions of the military were called into question by the collapse of the Soviet Union, which had been the motivating threat behind U.S. defense policy since World War II. The defense authorization bill cleared Congress more than a month before Soviet President Mikhail S. Gorbachev resigned, making final the dissolution of the Soviet empire. But the members who shaped and approved the defense bill were well aware that they were preparing a budget for the post-Cold War era.

The conflicting tugs and pulls of the year's tumultuous international events were reflected in HR 2100:

- Congress erected a substantial barrier to further production of the controversial B-2 "stealth" bomber.
- Lawmakers went on record in favor of early deployment of a limited version of the equally disputed strategic defense initiative (SDI) anti-missile program.
- Impressed by the performance of the women who served in combat in the Persian Gulf War, Congress removed the statutory ban on women serving in combat as pilots and flight crews in the Navy and Air Force. *(Women in combat, box, p. 374)*
- Members accepted the administration's proposal to reduce military personnel by more than 106,000 (to 1,886,400) but balked at the plan to cut the politically popular National Guard and reserves by more than 107,000 (to 1,068,400). HR 2100 cut the Guard and reserve rolls by 38,000, but the companion appropriations bill gave the defense secretary discretion to cut about 23,000 more personnel. *(Fiscal 1992 defense appropriations, p. 380)*

SDI Underwent Changes in Focus, Funding ...

The strategic defense initiative (SDI) — a controversial anti-missile defense program — had been a cornerstone of President Ronald Reagan's defense policy. Reagan had launched SDI in 1983 with sweeping rhetoric, describing it as a method of rendering nuclear missiles "impotent and obsolete."

But his vision of an impenetrable shield against Soviet attack faced opposition because of its huge cost, disputed technical feasibility and inevitable clash with the U.S.-Soviet anti-ballistic missile (ABM) treaty of 1972, which limited anti-missile defenses to a single ground-based site.

Detractors tagged SDI with the nickname "star wars."

The program was changed significantly during the Bush administration. Budgets were cut and — instead of the global umbrella of defenses against intercontinental missiles envisioned by Reagan — new, more modest goals were proposed both within the White House and on Capitol Hill.

In 1991, Congress reshaped SDI to place much more emphasis on the early deployment of ground-based defenses against limited attacks by both intercontinental and short-range missiles. After reshaping the program, Congress went on record for the first time in favor of a rapid deployment of a limited ground-based SDI system.

Background

Public debate over U.S. strategic policy in the 1970s largely ignored the option of anti-missile defense. The 1972 ABM treaty ruled out militarily significant anti-missile deployments.

Moreover, the ABM systems imagined at the time seemed useless in the face of a Soviet arsenal of multiple-warhead intercontinental ballistic missiles (ICBMs), each of which could dispense several warheads and dozens of decoys.

By the time Reagan took office, foreign policy hard-liners were challenging the conventional wisdom. Missile-defense advocates envisioned armed space satellites that could pick off Soviet missiles in the first few minutes of flight — the "boost phase" — before they spewed out warheads and decoys.

Calls for a revitalized ABM program seemed fruitless until March 23, 1983, when Reagan, after only limited consultation with top aides, launched his SDI. Though Reagan's "dream" of a world free of nuclear missiles seemed unrealistic to most supporters and opponents of anti-missile defense, it dominated congressional debate over SDI for the next few years.

What many conservative backers of the program really had in mind was a defense that would punch holes in the kind of meticulously timed attack with which, they feared, Moscow could use a fraction of its missile force to obliterate the U.S. fleet of ICBMs. An anti-missile system that could so disrupt such an attack would deter it, according to this view.

ABM advocates had tried for years to mobilize public support with the common-sense proposition that it was better to defend the country than leave it undefended. Reagan's clarion call served that purpose by highlighting the threat posed by thousands of unstoppable Soviet warheads.

Most liberals, by contrast, opposed anti-missile research on Reagan's scale. It would be unnecessary, they argued, because the scenario of a Soviet first strike on U.S. missiles was implausible, and it would extend the arms race into a new dimension. They did not challenge Reagan's goal of a world without missiles, but they opposed any program that fell short of that utopian ideal.

Senate Armed Services Committee Chairman Sam Nunn, Ga., and other defense-minded Democrats fit into neither group. They favored a robust program of anti-missile research, partly as a hedge against Soviet ABM developments and partly to put pressure on the Soviets to negotiate arms control agreements. But Nunn in particular complained that the administration had warped the debate over anti-missile costs and benefits by drumming up public support under the false pretense of pursuing Reagan's visionary goal.

Nunn also led the fight against subsequent Reagan administration efforts to reinterpret the ABM treaty to allow development and testing of space-based and air-based anti-missile weapons using lasers and other technologies not available in 1972. Beginning in 1987, the Senate and House repeatedly voted to bar SDI tests in space that would violate the traditional interpretation of the ABM treaty. *(Congress and the Nation Vol. VII, p. 347)*

Phase One and Alternatives

In 1987, SDI took a large step from vision to research program, when the Reagan administration came up with a two-track plan for anti-missile deployments. A so-called Phase One defense, using existing technologies to provide a limited defense, was to be deployed in the 1990s, with more advanced layers to be added later, as they matured.

Phase One reportedly would consist of a network of satellites, each carrying dozens of "space-based interceptors," or SBIs — small heat-seeking missiles intended to home in on Soviet missiles in the first few minutes after their launch — that would be backed up by ground-based ERIS (exo-atmospheric re-entry intercept system) missiles intended to pick off some of the attacking warheads that made it past the initial defenses and were headed toward critical targets.

... With New President and Leaner Budgets

By the time the Bush team was settling into office, the political debate over SDI had focused on the proposed Phase One and on two competing notions of an initial SDI deployment.

Nunn proposed one alternative early in 1988. He called for studying the value of fielding ground-based missiles, which were permitted by the ABM treaty, at the abandoned ABM site at Grand Forks, N.D., to create an "accidental launch protection system" (ALPS). Such a system could ward off a small number of warheads that might be launched toward the United States by accident or by the unauthorized action of a rogue Soviet commander.

The other alternative was called "brilliant pebbles." Developed by scientists at the Energy Department's Lawrence Livermore Laboratory in California, the plan called for orbiting thousands of small interceptor missiles, each equipped with a TV-like optical sensor to home in on Soviet missiles in their boost phase. The premise was that by keeping interceptors simple and cheap, enough of them could be deployed that no need would exist for an elaborate control network to assign each interceptor to a separate Soviet ICBM.

New Focus Under Bush

In submitting its revised Pentagon budget to Congress in 1989, the Bush administration proposed SDI funding that was nearly $1 billion less than Reagan had proposed before leaving office. More important, Bush sought to refocus the program in a technically and politically risky direction, highlighting the brilliant pebbles approach.

The new emphasis drained funds set aside for the earlier SDI approach and, if unsuccessful, would mean no SDI deployment would be possible much before the turn of the century. And, if the brilliant pebbles approach did show promise, a donnybrook with congressional Democrats loomed over whether the United States should withdraw from the ABM treaty.

Funding Cutback

Congress in 1989 cleared a fiscal 1990 defense authorization measure (HR 2461 — PL 101-189) that made even deeper cuts in SDI than Bush proposed. Though Congress had slashed the SDI funding request each year beginning in 1986, this was the first time members reduced the SDI budget below the current year's amount. *(Fiscal 1990 defense authorization, p. 340)*

Reagan's intense personal commitment had given SDI political start-up capital, helping its budget grow even when overall Pentagon funding took a downturn after fiscal 1985. But by 1989, Reagan was gone and a general sense pervaded that Bush did not have that same personal commitment to SDI.

Moreover, with the Pentagon's acute money crunch, some of SDI's longtime conservative supporters saw its relatively large budget as a potential source of funds with which to rescue other programs from the budget ax.

The action in 1989 was a sign of things to come for the program. In 1990, Congress sharply reduced Bush's funding request and imposed — over the president's objections — significant restrictions on how to spend the money. In an effort to impose more control on SDI, Congress divided the funding into categories — and, in the process, limited the Pentagon's flexibility to pour resources into a first-phase anti-missile defense of limited effectiveness.

Before agreeing to accept the defense authorization bill (HR 4739 — PL 101-510), Defense Secretary Dick Cheney demanded that Senate-House conferees loosen the restrictions on SDI. The conferees granted the Pentagon slightly more flexibility to manage the program but retained the new categories of funds. *(Fiscal 1991 defense authorization, p. 355)*

Congress Reshapes SDI

In 1991, Bush redefined SDI's emphasis with a program called GPALS, an acronym for "global protection against limited strikes." It was envisioned as a combination of space-based brilliant pebbles and ground-based missiles. Its goal was to protect U.S. territory, allies or overseas forces against relatively small attacks such as might be launched by a Third World country with short-range (or "tactical") missiles or by a renegade military unit.

The change troubled some of SDI's staunchest conservative backers but mollified some of the program's critics. Among the sticking points, however, was that the modified program still would require renegotiation or repudiation of the ABM treaty.

As part of the fiscal 1992 defense authorization bill (HR 2100 — PL 102-190), Congress negotiated its own compromise between SDI supporters and critics. The congressional agreement excluded brilliant pebbles from the initial anti-missile deployment. Instead, it directed the president to deploy by 1996 a ground-based anti-missile system at a single site near Grand Forks, N.D., which would be consistent with the ABM treaty. But the deal also called on the president to negotiate with the Soviet Union changes in the treaty to allow more extensive tests and deployments. *(Fiscal 1992 defense authorization, p. 369)*

Congress again in 1992 slashed Bush's funding request, but the fragile consensus negotiated in 1991 to press ahead with the SDI program survived. *(Fiscal 1993 defense authorization, p. 395)*

• Changes were made in the measure to reflect a package of unilateral arms reductions that Bush announced on Sept. 27 in light of the eclipse of the Soviet threat. For example, House-Senate conferees eliminated funds that the administration had requested earlier for two supersonic, air-launched missiles and for development of a rail-mobile launcher for the MX intercontinental missile. *(Bush proposals, box, p. 391)*

• And Congress approved separate legislation permitting up to $500 million from the defense budget to be used to demilitarize and deliver humanitarian assistance to the newly independent nations that formerly were part of the Soviet Union. *(Soviet aid, p. 260)*

At least for 1991, Congress stopped short of more fundamental cutbacks in defense. Defense Secretary Dick Cheney warned that the defense establishment would be damaged if Congress forced a speedier budget cutback than his program to reduce the size of the force roughly 25 percent by the end of fiscal 1995. But the more persuasive deterrent against deeper cuts seemed to have been members' fear of the political chaos that would result if Congress junked the budget law passed late in 1990.

That law limited the allowable deficit each year through fiscal 1995 and limited annual discretionary appropriations through fiscal 1993 for defense, international affairs and domestic spending. Funds cut from defense could have gone to deficit reduction but could not have been transferred to popular domestic programs without violating the cap on domestic spending. *(1990 budget law, p. 56)*

Nonetheless, many members made it clear during the 1991 defense debates that they expected the budget law's "walls" to crumble eventually.

Bush Budget Proposal

Congress' task in drafting a fiscal 1992 defense authorization measure was framed by the spending limits set by the 1990 budget deal and by the Bush administration's proposal for a six-year drawdown of defense spending that would shrink the military by one-fourth.

The $290.8 billion budget submitted by the administration in February 1991 was the first increment of a plan to eventually allocate to the Pentagon the smallest share of the gross national product since World War II.

The slimmed-down force was to have a new focus: After four decades of planning to head off on short notice a Soviet invasion of Western Europe, Pentagon planners were to concentrate more heavily on dealing with so-called regional threats to U.S. interests. Iraq — when it seized Kuwait and triggered the Persian Gulf War — had proved to be a particularly timely, if unusually well-armed, example.

The force Bush proposed was not only cheaper but also considerably smaller than the Cold War-oriented force that reached its apogee under President Ronald Reagan. The number of active-duty military personnel was to drop from about 2 million in fiscal 1990 to 1.65 million in fiscal 1995, and the number of combat units also was to decline: active-duty Army divisions from 18 to 12; Navy ships from 545 to 451; active-duty Air Force fighter wings from 24 to 15.

A smaller proportion of personnel would be deployed overseas, but they would be better equipped to be dispatched on short notice to distant trouble spots where no U.S. combat units were regularly stationed. So that the forces could keep their fighting edge, training operations were to continue at a relatively high tempo.

Bush's plan called for reducing by another 4 percent the weapons procurement budget that Congress had slashed in fiscal 1991 by 24 percent (adjusting for inflation), canceling 81 programs large and small. But it would continue to bet heavily — though selectively — on high technology for combat leverage.

House Committee Action

On May 8, a bipartisan majority of the House Armed Services Committee approved, 45-6, an authorization bill (H Rept 102-60) that demonstrated that military prudence can produce some politically advantageous byproducts. HR 2100 was formally reported May 13.

Insisting that the Pentagon hedge its bets on a new generation of high-tech arms, the panel added funds to keep open weapons production lines the Pentagon wanted to shut down. The only new weapon for which the committee made a significant cut for fiscal 1992 was the B-2 stealth bomber — denying the entire $3.2 billion production request.

By contrast, the committee bill backed the billions of dollars requested to develop the F-22 fighter plane for the Air Force, the A-X bomber for the Navy, and the Comanche armed helicopter and several armored combat vehicles for the Army. But in each case, the committee coupled its approval with an admonition: With the decline of the Soviet threat, it said, the Pentagon should pace development programs so that new weapons go into production only after they have been thoroughly tested.

The political payoff came on the other side of the committee's procurement equation: keeping in business several production lines, including those for the M-1 tank, the F-14 and F-16 fighter jets, the Army's scout helicopter, and the Patriot and Stinger anti-aircraft missiles. Pending development of planned new weapons, the committee argued, going for several years with no active production line for certain types of arms would be unwise.

Moreover, in some cases — the M-1 tank, for example — the committee maintained that the Persian Gulf War had demonstrated that thousands of weapons needed extensive upgrading. Each such add-on could save jobs in the district of one or more House members, broadening the bipartisan coalition that Armed Services Chairman Les Aspin, D-Wis., was lining up behind the bill.

In only one case did the committee try to force a major new weapons program on the Pentagon: the V-22 Osprey troop-carrying aircraft, vigorously promoted by the Marine Corps and the congressional delegations from Pennsylvania and Texas, where it would be built. Cheney had tried to kill this program since 1989 on the grounds that it was too expensive.

As had been customary for years in the House, the cost of added conventional arms was to be paid for by stripping funds out of the budget request for strategic weapons — this time, the B-2 and SDI. The bill included the $1.56 billion requested to continue developing the B-2 but none of the $3.2 billion that was sought to buy four planes in fiscal 1992 plus spare parts and components that would be used in the future to build aircraft.

For anti-missile defense research, viewed by many conservative activists as a touchstone of Reagan's defense legacy, the committee sliced the budget request by nearly one-third. Beyond approving only $3.54 billion of the $5.17 billion requested, the panel demanded a substantial shift in the program's focus.

It knocked out the entire $1.61 billion requested for the conservatives' priority within the anti-missile program: developing by the end of the 1990s a so-called Phase One defense. Such a rudimentary space-based defense system would be intended to fend off a few hundred long-range missile warheads, such as might be launched at the United States by a renegade military commander. An effort to restore the cut was rejected on a party-line vote of 18-25.

By contrast, the House panel approved the entire $883 million requested to develop defenses against shorter-range missiles, such as the Scuds fired by Iraq during the Persian Gulf War. But the committee bill put this "anti-tactical missile" program under control of the Army, not the SDI office created by Reagan in 1983 to develop a long-range missile defense.

Three projects absorbed most of the money Aspin cut from the B-2 and SDI: the National Guard and reserve forces, V-22 Osprey development and the rebuilding of 1970s-vintage F-14 Navy fighter planes as F-14Ds, with more powerful engines and radars.

The Armed Services Committee also approved an amendment to remove the statutory ban on female combat pilots in the Air Force and Navy.

House Floor Action

The House passed the $291 billion defense authorization bill May 22 by a vote of 268-161 despite a threatened veto over the bill's cuts in funding for the B-2 bomber and SDI and its failure to reduce funding for the National Guard and reserves as deeply as the administration wanted.

The committee's approach would be more prudent from a military standpoint, said Aspin, complaining that Cheney's budget would strip the country of any capacity to build certain types of weapons for years, pending the development of new designs. Aspin's bill also locked in the support of members whose constituents would keep their jobs because the House bill kept alive the weapons they made. The power of that ironclad political logic was demonstrated May 21, when House GOP leader Robert H. Michel, Ill., offered an amendment that would have wiped out Aspin's changes, restoring Cheney's budget request. Michel's amendment was rejected 127-287, with more than 20 percent of the voting Republicans bucking their leader.

If the House bill underscored the political weakness of those who shared the administration's goals for SDI, an amendment by Ronald V. Dellums, D-Calif., highlighted the weakness of those who opposed any effort to deploy a large-scale anti-missile system. Dellums' amendment, rejected May 20 by a **key vote of 118-266 (R 2-149; D 115-117; I 1-0)**, would have reduced from $2.7 billion to $1.1 billion the authorization for research on defenses against long-range missiles. It also would have limited such research to laboratory efforts and disbanded the SDI program office. It would not have affected the bill's separate authorization of $882 million to develop defenses against tactical missiles. *(1991 key votes, p. 1061)*

Dividing essentially along party lines, the House May 22 also rejected, 161-265, an amendment to require that the anti-tactical missile program develop only weapons that could intercept several types of modern, long-range ballistic missiles in service or under development in various Third World countries. Opponents suspected that the amendment was intended to preserve the more ambitious goals for SDI by de-emphasizing development of defenses against short-range missiles, which were far more numerous.

Laying the groundwork for future efforts to cut Pentagon spending, liberal Democrats offered amendments to the defense bill to make U.S. allies pay a larger share of mutual defense costs. In the short run, their victories were largely symbolic. The most far-reaching of the amendments, adopted 260-163, was purely advisory, calling for a large reduction in U.S. forces in Europe. And the House rejected by large majorities binding proposals to slice $8 billion from the fiscal 1992 defense budget and to reduce deployments in South Korea.

For more than a decade, resentment had festered on Capitol Hill over the belief that the United States shouldered far too much of the cost of collective defense, permitting economic dynamos such as Japan and Germany to pour money instead into extending their competitive edge.

A non-binding amendment urging the president to negotiate a total ban on underground nuclear test explosions was agreed to by voice vote. *(Nuclear test ban, p. 392)*

The House rejected amendments to kill funding for the small intercontinental ballistic Midgetman missile and to mandate drug testing of civilian Pentagon employees. (Military personnel were subject to random drug tests as a matter of Pentagon policy.)

Senate Committee Action

The Senate Armed Services Committee approved its version of the defense authorization bill (S 1507 — S Rept 102-113) on July 17. The unanimous vote belied the fierce and intricate negotiations that were required to develop the committee bill's most significant feature — a long-term plan for the controversial SDI program. S 1507 was formally reported July 19.

The committee's plan for changes in the anti-missile program amounted to a fundamental shift in U.S. policy. The panel included $4.6 billion for SDI and called for deployment by 1996 of an anti-missile defense that would comply with the 1972 U.S.-Soviet treaty that limited anti-ballistic missile (ABM) defenses. The treaty permitted deployment of 100 ground-based interceptor missiles at a single base.

At least as important, the committee backed an effort to liberalize the ABM treaty to allow deployment of a much more extensive anti-missile system that would be aimed at blocking "limited" attacks by a relatively small number of missiles, such as might be launched by a Third World country or a renegade military unit.

Unlike the House, the Senate committee voted to approve Bush's request for $3.2 billion to continue production of the B-2 stealth bomber.

In other provisions of its bill, the Senate committee proposed a 15-member presidential commission to study the question of women in combat, sidestepping the House bill's provision to repeal laws that banned women from serving as combat pilots.

The panel rejected the administration's decision to end production of the MX intercontinental ballistic missile (ICBM) and added funding for a dozen more of the 10-warhead missile. The committee also authorized an increase in the proposed production rate of the Trident II submarine-launched missiles.

The panel said it wanted to prevent the premature dispersal of critical engineering talent. For that reason, it increased the funding requested for several production lines, including those for the Bradley armored troop car-

Congress Debated Role of Women in Military ...

The role of women in the military was the subject of an ongoing debate in the 102nd Congress. Spurred by the performance of women in the armed services who were deployed to the Persian Gulf region during the war with Iraq, Congress in 1991 added to the defense authorization bill (HR 2100 — PL 102-190) a provision repealing the laws that barred the assignment of women to combat aircraft in the Navy and Air Force. The bill, which left the issue to the discretion of the individual services, also established a blue-ribbon panel to study the issue of assigning women to other combat roles.

In November 1992, the panel recommended to President Bush that women be allowed onto warships but kept out of other direct combat roles, including Air Force pilot positions.

Also in 1992, Congress reacted angrily to a tale of military sexual harassment that gained national attention. At least 26 women told of being assaulted during a convention in the summer of 1991 of the Tailhook Association, a private club of naval aviators. In response, Congress barred the organization, which had been closely associated with the Navy, from receiving federal funds.

Background

Prior to the 1991 repeal, women were allowed to fly transport and tanker planes and serve on crews of repair and supply ships — including some that operated in the Persian Gulf region during the war with Iraq. But women were prohibited by law from being assigned to armed aircraft or combat vessels.

The combat prohibition laws, which dated back to 1948, did not apply to the Army, but that service had a policy barring women from direct combat roles.

The 540,000 U.S. personnel stationed in the Gulf region during the war with Iraq included more than 35,000 women, according to the Defense Department.

Since the United States switched to an all-volunteer force in 1973, the percentage of women serving on active duty in the military had increased from 2 percent to 11 percent. Fifteen women died during the U.S. deployment to the Persian Gulf; five of those were killed by enemy fire, although none was officially in combat positions.

The crisis in the Gulf, as well as the invasion of Panama in 1989, highlighted a change in the nature of the modern battlefield: The ubiquity of ground-attack planes, long-range artillery and fast-moving ground forces had eroded the distinction between a dangerous "front" and a safer "rear area," where women in noncombat jobs were once considered relatively immune from attack.

1991 Action

Compared with the usual glacial pace of congressional action, the campaign to clear the way for women to fly combat aircraft rolled through Congress in a political blitzkrieg.

The House Armed Services Committee's decision in 1991 to add to the annual defense authorization bill the provision repealing the "combat exclusion" law for female aircrew members came as a surprise, even to advocates of the move. It was not challenged on the House floor.

The Senate Armed Services Committee included in its defense bill a provision to establish a 15-member presidential commission to study issues involved in assigning women to combat roles and to report its findings and recommendations by Nov. 15, 1992. The president's recommendations was due on Capitol Hill a month later.

The Senate committee bill, however, did not include the repeal of the combat ban for pilots, but the full Senate added it on the floor. An effort by Armed Services Committee leaders to table (kill) the amend-

rier, the launcher for the MLRS artillery rocket and the Patriot anti-aircraft missile.

The panel's bill also authorized nearly $900 million for programs aimed at giving combat commanders readier access to tactical intelligence, a need that became clear during the Persian Gulf War.

The committee dropped $1 billion requested to buy 48 F-16 fighters. But it added roughly the same amount to resume production of the F-117 stealth fighter, which played a prominent role dropping highly accurate "smart" bombs against Iraqi targets.

Senate Floor Action

The Senate passed S 1507 by voice vote on Aug. 2. The bill authorized $213 billion for defense-related programs, essentially the amount requested by Bush. Counting the $78 billion for military personnel costs, which was included in other legislation, the Senate provided for a defense budget in fiscal 1992 totaling $291 billion.

Senate approval of $3.2 billion to build four additional B-2s was a clear win for President Bush, as well as for Armed Services Committee Chairman Sam Nunn, D-Ga., and the panel's senior Republican, John W. Warner of Virginia. Although Bush remained officially committed to his more ambitious version of SDI, administration officials indicated that they were very pleased with the modified, $4.6 billion version of the anti-missile plan that was included in S 1507. The companion bill passed by the House included no funds for B-2 production and only $3.5 billion for a much more restricted SDI program.

... Repealed Ban on Women in Combat Aircraft

ment was rejected July 31 by a **key vote of 30-69 (R 14-29; D 16-40)**. The Senate then adopted the proposal by voice vote. *(1991 key votes, p. 1061)*

The final conference bill included the combat exclusion repeal and the Senate provision establishing the study commission. The repeal of the combat exclusion provision did not force the armed services to open up their combat positions to women. But during an earlier hearing on the subject, both the military chiefs of the Air Force and the Navy said that if the exclusion were repealed, they would find it hard not to offer the combat positions to women. All four men who headed the military branches told members of Congress that they opposed repealing the law.

1992 Action

In its Nov. 15, 1992, report to President Bush, the commission recommended that the ban on assigning women to warships be repealed but that women not be assigned to ground combat units. The commission also recommended, 8-7, that the ban on assigning women to combat aircraft be reinstated in law.

Women at that time were barred by law only from serving on warships, though they served as crew members on supply and repair vessels. They were barred from serving in ground combat units by Pentagon policy.

Instead of reaching a consensus on the role of women in combat, the commission's debates had a fractious tone, with members on each side of the issue contending that their opponents viewed the evidence through ideological blinders.

In the panel's report, five commissioners argued that permitting women in combat "will have a devastating impact on combat readiness, unit cohesion and military effectiveness." They contended that some advocates of wider roles for military women assumed "that the military must pay any price and bear any burden to promote equal opportunities and career progression for an ambitious few."

But the minority case for assigning women to combat cockpits was argued by seven commissioners, including retired Air Force general Robert T. Herres, the former vice chairman of the Joint Chiefs of Staff who chaired the panel. "Laws and policies based on paternalistic notions do not demonstrate the value society places on women," the commissioners said. "They demean women's intelligence and abilities, deny them the respect that they deserve as equal members of society and deny the armed forces the use of the best-qualified individuals."

The debate over the role of women in the military continued on Capitol Hill in 1992. Former and current high-ranking military leaders offered opposing views during congressional hearings.

Sexual harassment of women in the military also became an issue in 1992, as women told of assaults at a 1991 Las Vegas convention of the Tailhook Association, a private club of naval aviators that had worked closely with the Navy hierarchy over the years. A number of high-ranking Navy officials attended the convention but said they witnessed no improper behavior.

In the wake of the scandal, the secretary of the Navy resigned, the Navy's internal inquiry was taken over by the Defense Department's inspector general and the Senate Armed Services Committee delayed Senate consideration of 4,500 promotions of Navy and Marine Corps officers until those officers were cleared of any involvement in the Tailhook meeting. In a provision of the fiscal 1993 defense appropriations bill (HR 5504 — PL 102-396), Congress barred the Tailhook organization from receiving any federal funds.

The committee provisions on deployment of a limited SDI system represented a delicate compromise, which linked Democrats who favored relatively modest, ground-based defenses with Republicans who hoped this would be the first step toward a global network of orbiting anti-missile interceptor rockets.

As most of the critics saw it, their best chance to undermine the Senate panel's SDI package before conference was to drive a wedge into the philosophical crevasse dividing those two groups. During floor action, the critics offered two amendments challenging fundamental elements of the committee compromise. But both were defeated and the compromise held, in another victory for Nunn and Warner.

One amendment would have recast the committee package to emphasize deployment by the mid-1990s of ground-based defenses against short-range missiles such as the Iraqi Scuds. The amendment called for modifying the ABM treaty only as needed to clarify the distinctions between such anti-tactical missile defenses and defensive systems intended to fend off strategic missiles. The amendment was rejected 39-60 on July 31.

A second amendment would have declared that maintenance of "strategic stability" between Washington and Moscow was the overriding goal — and that deployment of a limited ABM defense would be subordinated to it. It also would have deleted all references to the treaty-compliant ABM deployment due by 1996 as an "initial" deployment. Any U.S. anti-missile deployments beyond those allowed by the treaty would be subject to the Soviet government's eventually agreeing on treaty changes. The amendment, offered by Jeff Bingaman, D-N.M., was rejected July 31 by a **key vote of 43-56 (R 2-41; D 41-15).** *(1991 key votes, p. 1061)*

A third amendment, specifying that the bill did not authorize any ABM deployment not allowed by the treaty, was adopted Aug. 1, 99-0, amid conflicting claims about its practical significance. Nunn reasoned that he could live with the amendment because establishing a goal of going beyond the existing treaty did not authorize anything.

The Senate also rejected three other SDI-related amendments. One would have deleted the goal of deploying a treaty-compliant anti-missile system by 1996 and two others would have reduced the SDI authorization.

B-2 opponents coalesced behind an amendment that essentially matched the House position. The amendment, which would have deleted $3.2 billion to build four more bombers but have allowed completion of the 15 planes previously funded, was rejected 42-57 on Aug. 1.

The Senate Armed Services Committee leaders suffered a dramatic defeat, when they tried to stave off an amendment to repeal the statutory ban on assigning women in the Navy and Air Force to fly combat planes. An effort to kill the amendment was rejected July 31 by a **key vote of 30-69 (R 14-29; D 16-40)**. The amendment was then adopted by voice vote.

The Senate Aug. 2 also adopted, 97-2, an amendment supporting the president if he decided to use force to eliminate Iraq's nuclear weapons-making capability.

A threatened filibuster forced withdrawal of an amendment that would have allowed female service members or military dependents stationed abroad to obtain privately funded abortions in local U.S. military hospitals.

In other action, the Senate adopted an amendment to require that closed military bases be turned over to local communities that have suffered severe economic dislocation because of the closure, instead of allowing federal and state agencies priority in claiming the property.

Also adopted was a non-binding expression of the sense of Congress that the Defense Department should begin planning to have no more than 100,000 U.S. military personnel stationed in Europe by the end of 1995.

The Senate Aug. 2 rejected an amendment to terminate production of the short-range, air-launched nuclear missile designated SRAM-T by a vote of 51-47 and an amendment deleting from the bill funds to conclude development of a rail-mobile launcher for the MX missile by a vote of 49-48.

The Senate passed an amended HR 2100 by voice vote Aug. 2.

Conference Action

The House on Sept. 16 turned back an initial effort by liberal Democrats to capitalize on the collapse of communist power in the Soviet Union.

The action came on a procedural question. By a **key vote of 220-145 (R 136-4; D 84-140; I 0-1)**, the House closed debate on a non-binding motion to instruct conferees on the defense authorization bill to permanently extend certain benefits to Persian Gulf veterans. That prevented Massachusetts Democrat Barney Frank from offering an amendment instructing conferees to insist on lower House funding levels for strategic weapons programs such as the B-2 bomber. For conventional weapons programs, Frank's amendment would have urged conferees to back the lower of the amounts authorized by the two chambers, "consistent with emerging national security needs."

Conferees reached tentative agreement on a final version of HR 2100 on Nov. 1. They had spent three months ironing out more than 1,400 items in disagreement, according to Sen. Jim Exon, D-Neb., who later called it the "most difficult" conference he could remember.

The conferees essentially adopted the Senate position on SDI by backing a limited deployment of SDI and authorizing $4.15 billion for it.

They reached a deal on the B-2 stealth bomber that permitted $1.6 billion for additional research and development and $1.8 billion for parts and assembly. But their agreement barred production of any B-2s beyond the 15 previously authorized unless both chambers voted approval of an additional $1 billion to buy a single additional plane. That formulation gave the House an effective veto over its continued production. But it also left open to the Bush administration the opportunity to lobby aggressively to save the high-tech weapon.

And the conferees agreed to drop the statutory ban on assigning women in the Navy and Air Force to fly combat aircraft. A controversial plan, crafted by the Armed Services committee chairmen, Rep. Aspin and Sen. Nunn, to authorize as much as $1 billion from the Pentagon budget to aid the disintegrating Soviet Union was dropped from the conference bill. A stripped-down, $500 million version was later passed as separate legislation. *(Soviet aid, p. 260)*

Once the disputed Soviet proposal was dropped from the defense bill, the conferees agreed to drop the other emotional issue that could have been an obstacle to final approval of the bill or would have prompted a veto: They eliminated a House provision to allow service personnel or their dependents stationed abroad to obtain abortions in U.S. military hospitals, provided the procedure was paid for privately.

The conference agreement provided most of what the administration requested for major weapons programs. But it also provided funds for programs not requested by the Pentagon, including those to convert early-model M-1 tanks to the new M-1A2 model; to equip an additional 24 scout helicopters with sophisticated target-finding equipment; to move toward full-scale production of the V-22 Osprey, the hybrid airplane/helicopter that the Marine Corps wanted to use as a troop carrier; and to resume production of the F-117, a small stealth bomber.

While approving a proposed cut of 106,000 from the services' active-duty rosters, the bill approved a reduction of fewer than 38,000 from the rolls of National Guard and military reserve units. The administration had proposed a Guard and reserve cutback nearly three times that size and strongly criticized Congress' reluctance to cut deeper.

The House adopted the conference report (H Rept 102-311), 329-82, on Nov. 18. The Senate adopted the conference report 79-15, on Nov. 22, clearing HR 2100. The president signed the bill on Dec. 5.

Major Provisions

As signed into law, HR 2100 authorized $291 billion in defense spending for fiscal 1992, essentially the amount requested by the administration and approved by both chambers.

Major provisions of the final bill:

Strategic Arms. Authorized $1.6 billion for additional research and development of the B-2 stealth bomber and $1.8 billion for parts and supplies. No bombers beyond the 15 previously authorized would be permitted unless the

Pentagon certified that the plane's problems had been solved and both chambers of Congress voted approval of an additional $1 billion for a 16th plane.

Bush requested $4.8 billion to continue development and build four more B-2s. The Senate approved the request, but the House opposed any further production.

• Approved spending $4.15 billion on a limited version of the strategic defense initiative. The bill declared a national goal of deploying an ABM system as one way of reducing the threat posed by ballistic missile proliferation. It ordered the Pentagon to install an initial, ground-based defense in Grand Forks, N.D., by 1996 that would comply with the 1972 ABM treaty. Negotiations would be sought to amend the ABM treaty to permit deployment of more than 100 interceptor missiles at more than one site, greater use of space-based detection and control systems, and more flexibility for testing novel ABM weapons. The administration would be permitted to spend $390 million on research into space-based "brilliant pebbles" missile interceptors, with the proviso that Congress did not authorize their inclusion in any ABM system being developed for deployment.

The administration sought $5.2 billion for SDI, including $690 million for brilliant pebbles. The House approved $3.5 billion, with no funds for brilliant pebbles and no support for short-term deployment of anti-missile defenses. The Senate forged the basic outline of the deal accepted by the conferees.

• Authorized $203 million to beef up the B-1 bomber fleet, including $116 million for safety modifications to the 97 planes, $20 million to upgrade their radar-jamming equipment and $67 million for miscellaneous support equipment.

The administration request for B-1 equipment totaled $304 million, and the House more than doubled that to $642 million. The increase included $40 million to equip the planes for conventional bombing missions and $298 million to improve the radar jammers. But the Senate, reflecting the low opinion of the B-1 held by Armed Services Committee Chairman Nunn, approved only the $116 million requested for safety modifications.

• Acted on nuclear weapons cutbacks that Bush announced Sept. 27 by eliminating funds that had been requested earlier in the year for two supersonic, air-launched missiles: $177 million to gear up for production of the SRAM II, to be carried by bombers, and $61 million to develop a tactical version designated SRAM-T, to be carried by smaller planes.

• Authorized $610 million, the amount requested and approved by both chambers, to continue development and production of a stealthy, bomber-launched cruise missile with a range of nearly 2,000 miles. The funds were to buy 120 missiles in fiscal 1992 and components to be used in the 102 missiles slated for inclusion in the fiscal 1993 budget.

• Authorized $587 million to continue equipping with more powerful engines the fleet of KC-135s, 1960s-vintage midair refueling tankers that the Air Force planned to fly for another three decades. The budget request included $465 million; the House approved $630 million, and the Senate, $427 million.

• Eliminated the $260 million requested to develop a rail-mobile launcher for the 10-warhead MX intercontinental ballistic missile because it was another of the programs marked for extinction in Bush's nuclear arms reduction announcement in September. However, the conferees added $252 million to buy five more MX missiles, which were intended for test launches during the years the Air Force expected to keep 50 of the weapons deployed in underground silos. The budget request included $195 million to shut down the MX production line.

• Challenged Bush's decision to cancel development of a road-mobile launcher for the smaller, single-warhead Midgetman missile. Both chambers had approved the $549 million requested for the program, including $115 million earmarked to continue work on the mobile launcher. The conferees appended a provision to bar use of the mobile launcher money until the Pentagon certified to Congress that future requests would include enough funds to retain the option of deploying the missiles on mobile launchers.

• Ordered the defense secretary to report on the cost and feasibility of keeping in service beyond the year 2020 the silo-based Minuteman III missile, which the Midgetman had been slated to replace.

• Authorized $1.3 billion for 49 Trident II submarine-launched missiles. This followed the approach of the Senate instead of the administration and the House, which sought $977 million for 28 missiles.

• Authorized the $65 million requested to develop an anti-satellite missile. Both chambers had supported the request. The conferees added a provision to bar for one year tests of a large experimental laser as an anti-satellite weapon. The House had banned such laser tests for two years.

Ground Combat. Authorized $90 million to build 60 new "A2" versions of the M-1 tank, as well as $225 million to modernize older M-1s. This was intended to keep a tank production line intact for several years.

The conference report provided that, if the Army canceled production of the A2 model, older tanks — which carried a 105mm cannon — would be upgraded to M-1A1s, carrying a 120mm gun. But if A2 production began as planned, the tanks would be converted to that model, carrying both the larger gun and more sophisticated electronic equipment for fighting at night.

Conferees also added to the budget $55 million to complete development of the A2 model.

• Agreed to $161 million of the $183 million requested for heavy-duty trucks to haul tanks long distances at high speeds. The Senate had wanted the Pentagon to fund this from the allied contributions toward U.S. costs of the Persian Gulf War, arguing that hundreds of tank haulers had been worn out in that campaign.

• Authorized the Senate-approved $110 million — $75 million less than requested — to beef up armor on the newest model of Bradley troop carriers. The House had approved the requested funds, plus $150 million to begin upgrading older-model Bradleys.

• Added $21 million to the administration's request, for an authorization of $422 million, to develop a "family" of armored combat vehicles for the 21st century — a tank, troop carrier and other vehicles that would use common automotive components. Of that amount, $62 million was earmarked for a new mobile artillery piece.

Because Iraq and several other countries had mobile guns with longer ranges than U.S. models, both Armed Services committees wanted a new mobile gun developed before work began on a new tank (designated Block III) that the Army had made its top priority within the family of vehicles.

• Authorized $151 million to buy 300 ATACMS bombardment rockets with a range of 60 miles. That was the amount requested and approved by both houses.

• Expanded the administration's plans for 20-mile-range MLRS rockets and launchers. The conferees authorized $196 million to buy them for the Army and an additional $95 million to outfit the Marine Corps. The administration had requested $181 million to buy MLRS launchers for the Army only.

• Backed accelerated production of the JSTARS radar surveillance plane, following the Senate's lead. The plane was designed to locate ground targets more than 100 miles behind enemy lines.

In addition to the $312 million approved by both chambers to continue developing the plane, the conferees wrote into the bill $125 million for components that could be used in two JSTARS to be bought in fiscal 1993. The administration requested components for only one. The conference report also added $25 million to develop a lighter-weight ground terminal to receive JSTARS data.

But the conferees turned down a Senate proposal to buy two JSTARS planes outright with allied contributions from the Gulf War.

• Authorized $120 million to continue developing the Javelin, a one-man anti-tank missile (formerly designated AAWS-M). The administration requested $49 million for development and $71 million to prepare for production, but the House put all the money into development, citing difficulties in perfecting the weapon's infrared guidance system. For the same reason, the Senate approved only the $49 million requested for development.

Conferees ordered the Army to report anticipated increases in the program's cost and to declare a ceiling cost above which the program would not be worthwhile.

• Authorized the $152 million requested — and backed by both the House and Senate — to develop the LOSAT tank-hunting vehicle, armed with large, high-speed, guided rockets intended to punch through the heaviest tank armor with brute force.

• Included $233 million, which had been approved by both the House and Senate, to develop a much improved Longbow model of the Apache anti-tank helicopter, equipped with a target-finding radar and a more powerful engine.

But both chambers had objected to the Army's plan to first modify some Apaches to a modestly improved "B" model. Conferees authorized the $83 million requested to begin the "B" model modifications, including improved navigation equipment and Stinger anti-aircraft missiles. However, they added to the bill $32 million to develop a "C" model that would have all the features of the Longbow model except the radar and the new engine.

• Authorized the $550 million requested to continue to develop the Comanche (formerly LH) missile-armed scout helicopter and the $183 million requested to arm existing Kiowa scout helicopters with missiles. Both requests had been approved by both chambers.

But the conferees added $135 million to modify 24 more armed Kiowas.

• Added $20 million to the $9 million requested to develop equipment to thwart land mines.

Tactical Air Combat. Authorized the $1.6 billion requested to develop the Air Force's F-22 fighter (formerly ATF), which had been approved by both chambers. Conferees added a House-passed provision stipulating that the Air Force should verify that the plane could easily be mass produced.

• Provided for the $1.1 billion requested to buy 48 F-16 fighters for the Air Force.

The administration had planned to close out its F-16 purchases with 24 aircraft in 1993, but the House bill called for buying 48 more planes in each of the succeeding two fiscal years. The plane was built by General Dynamics Corp. in Fort Worth, and members of the Texas House delegation lobbied strongly for the House language.

The Senate, contending that the 1,100 F-16s already funded were adequate for the Air Force's declining size, had approved only $78 million to shut down the production line.

• Authorized $560 million to purchase four new Air Force F-117s, plus $83 million to modify the existing fleet. The F-117 was a small stealth fighter that won popular attention through its performance in the Persian Gulf War.

The administration had not sought to revive F-117 production, which had been shut down in 1989. The House added to the bill $83 million to begin updating the 56 existing F-117s and $140 million to develop further F-117 improvements. But the Senate added $1 billion to resume F-117 production.

Ultimately, renewed production of the F-117 was blocked because no funds for the plane were included in the defense appropriations bill.

• Authorized $173 million, as requested, to shut down the production line for the Navy's F-14 carrier-based fighters.

The conferees rejected House provisions that would have added $680 million to begin converting existing F-14s to an improved "D" model. Also rejected was a separate House provision adding $50 million to adapt the F-14D to attack ground targets.

• Approved $2.1 billion for 48 Navy F/A-18s, which was the amount requested.

• Boosted by $20 million the $452 million authorization requested to develop improvements in the F/A-18, with most of the funds earmarked for new "E" and "F" models, with longer range and larger payloads.

• Backed the start of work on developing a carrier-based bomber designated AX, earmarking $167 million authorized in prior years. Those funds initially had been provided to develop the A-12 naval bomber, which the Pentagon had canceled in January.

• Authorized buying 891 AMRAAM air-to-air missiles for Navy and Air Force fighters but only $740 million for the purchase, $120 million less than requested.

• Dropped a House initiative to continue building an air-launched version of the 60-mile-range Harpoon missile ($175 million) and to develop an improved version of that weapon ($100 million).

Naval Combat. Cut only $55 million from the administration request, authorizing $4.2 billion to buy five *Arleigh Burke*-class destroyers equipped with the Aegis anti-aircraft system.

• Endorsed the $415 million requested to buy 525 Standard anti-aircraft missiles and the $506 million requested to buy 236 new long-range Tomahawk cruise missiles and to modernize 401 Tomahawks. Both chambers had approved those amounts.

• Authorized using $105 million appropriated in fiscal 1991 to begin overhauling the aircraft carrier *John F. Kennedy* at the Philadelphia Naval Shipyard late in 1993. The money originally was set aside for a more extensive reconstruction.

Even with the less ambitious overhaul plans, an additional $386 million was expected to be spent in later years. The carrier renovation was expected to be the last major project at the Philadelphia yard, which was earmarked for closure.

- Authorized $1.8 billion for the third *Seawolf*-class nuclear submarine in addition to $425 million to continue developing the design and $376 million for components that would be used in additional ships.

Members of both chambers had sparred over provisions intended to steer the contract for the new sub to one of two competing shipyards in Connecticut and Virginia. But the conference report was silent on the issue.

- Endorsed the request for $229 million to develop long-range submarine detection equipment. But the conferees added to the bill $20 million to develop a more portable sub detection system that could quickly be deployed to a trouble spot.
- Authorized a naval mine sweeping program nearly half again as large as requested, including $361 million for three *Osprey*-class mine sweepers, as recommended by the Senate, one ship ($130 million) more than requested; $129 million for four mine-sweeping helicopters, the amount requested; $14 million to continue developing the Magic Lantern program — using a helicopter-borne laser to find submerged mines, the budget request included no funds; and $20 million more than the $18 million requested for anti-mine research.
- Subtracted $40 million from the $540 million requested for a high-speed supply ship to replenish a carrier and its escort ships midocean.

Air and Sea Transport. Authorized $1.53 billion for four C-17 wide-body cargo planes, $122 million to buy components for eight planes in fiscal 1993 and the full $377 million requested to continue a testing program. But no more than $400 million of the procurement funds could be spent until the Pentagon sent Congress a report on problems that had delayed tests of the plane.

The administration had requested $2.6 billion for the C-17, which was designed to land tanks and other heavy gear on primitive airstrips. That included $2 billion for six planes, $224 million for components to be used in 12 C-17s slated for inclusion in the fiscal 1993 budget and $377 million to continue developing the aircraft. Both chambers sought to slow the planned production rate because of the plane's problems.

- Authorized the amounts requested and voted by both chambers for the Army's two largest transport helicopter programs: $508 million to continue production of Blackhawk troop carriers; and $257 million to conclude an 11-year program of modernizing 472 Chinooks, used to haul artillery pieces, ammunition and other cargo around the battlefield.
- Authorized an LSD-class amphibious landing ship ($245 million) and a dozen air-cushion landing barges ($289 million), as requested and approved by both chambers.
- Authorized $625 million in new funds, plus $365 million appropriated but not spent in prior years, to build three additional V-22 Ospreys, a hybrid airplane/helicopter designed as a troop carrier for the Marine Corps.

As in each year since 1989, Cheney tried to cancel development of the Osprey. But once again, the effort was thwarted by the Marines, their many congressional supporters and members of Congress from Pennsylvania and Texas, where the program's principal contractors were located. The conferees followed the House's lead in backing the Osprey.

- Authorized 20 large CH-53E helicopters, used by the Navy and Marine Corps to carry cargo and troops.

A-12 Bomber Canceled

In a move that stunned those involved in defense, Defense Secretary Dick Cheney on Jan. 7, 1991, canceled the Navy's bat-winged A-12 attack plane, which was to be the next carrier-based bomber, because of production delays and cost-overruns. It was considered a turning point for reform of the Pentagon.

Cheney spurned the Navy's recommendation to revise contracts for the project so that the government would pick up a larger share of the contractors' escalating costs.

The Navy had planned to spend an estimated $52 billion on a fleet of 620 A-12s to replace aging A-6Es as the roundhouse punch of Navy carriers against surface targets. But the program was plagued with delays and cost increases.

One of the few major weapons to be dropped so far into development, the A-12 would have been considerably costlier than the $39 billion DIVAD anti-aircraft gun canceled in 1985. *(Congress and the Nation Vol. VII, p. 287)*

After Cheney's decision to kill the A-12, members of Congress held hearings to look into charges that the two aerospace companies developing the A-12 — General Dynamics Corp. and McDonnell Douglas Corp. — had misused funds.

The two firms denied Cheney's assertion that they were in default on the A-12's contract and blamed the Navy's insistence in 1988 that they sign a "fixed price" contract. It required them to absorb any cost-overruns in a development program that was "on the cutting edge of technology," in the words of a General Dynamics spokesman.

The Pentagon subsequently abandoned such contracts for development programs that required major technical breakthroughs. Later in the year, Congress earmarked in the defense authorization bill (HR 2100 — PL 102-190) $167 million in funds for the development of another high-performance, high-tech aircraft, the AX, as a replacement for the A-12. These were funds that had already been authorized for the A-12 but had not been spent. The first AX would reach the fleet in 2003.

In the interim, the Pentagon was to buy more F-18 fighter planes and more of an improved, larger version of the F-18. Lawmakers also appropriated funds to equip many of the Navy's A6Es with new, synthetic wings so that they could be flown well into the 21st century.

Military Personnel. Approved the administration's proposal to reduce the ceiling on active-duty military personnel to 1.88 million members, a cut of more than 106,000. Both chambers had backed the cuts.

- Backed the 4.2 percent military pay raise recommended by the administration.

• Endorsed an increase from $110 to $150 in the monthly bonus paid to personnel stationed in places where they were deemed to be in "imminent danger."

• Backed an increase from $60 to $75 in the monthly bonus paid to married personnel assigned to posts where they could not be accompanied by their families.

• Approved two alternative severance packages intended to encourage career-minded members to leave the service in an era of declining military personnel, thereby minimizing the number who would have to be involuntarily dismissed to meet that timetable.

• The conferees agreed on a roster for the National Guard and reserves of 1.15 million, reducing manpower by 37,580 instead of by the more than 105,000 proposed. (The companion appropriations measure later gave the defense secretary discretion to cut about 23,000 more personnel.) Both chambers had trimmed the administration's proposed cutback in National Guard and reserve manpower.

• Approved adding $1.04 billion to the budget for equipment earmarked for Guard and reserve units.

• Established an independent commission to recommend how to distribute missions between active-duty units and their counterparts in the Guard and reserves.

• Repealed 1948 laws that banned the assignment to combat air crews of women in the Navy and Air Force. Both chambers had adopted such language, which did not eliminate the discretion of the armed services to maintain the ban.

In addition, the conferees accepted a Senate provision to establish a presidential commission to study how the assignment of women to additional combat roles might affect combat readiness. The commission was to report to the president by Nov. 15, 1992, and he was to report his recommendations to Congress by Dec. 15.

Construction, Closings. Made minor adjustments in the base-closing review process, which targeted installations in 1991 and was to be repeated in 1993 and 1995. The changes required the president to submit in January 1993 and 1995 a complete list of his nominees to each year's base-closing commission, who would be subject to Senate confirmation; extended by one month the commissions' review of the Pentagon's list of bases recommended for closure; and required the commissions to hold public hearings before adding to their lists any installations not recommended by the Pentagon.

• Opposed any funds for construction at bases slated for closure on the 1991 list.

• Rejected a Senate provision that would have given local communities first crack at taking over closed bases without paying for them.

Existing law gave other federal agencies the right of first refusal and allowed the Pentagon to sell the surplus property.

• Authorized $297 million, $197 million more than the administration's request, to clean up toxic and hazardous waste on bases in the 1991 list of bases to be closed. For hazardous waste cleanup at other bases, the conferees authorized $1.18 billion, $69 million less than requested.

• Backed only $225 million of the $359 million requested for the annual U.S. contribution to the infrastructure fund of the North Atlantic Treaty Organization (NATO), the alliance's kitty for construction projects of mutual benefit. It also included a House provision barring the use of any funds to transfer a U.S. fighter wing or associated activities to a new NATO base at Crotone, Italy.

• Authorized $100 million less than the $2.7 billion requested to pay foreign nationals employed on U.S. bases abroad.

Other Provisions. Accepted a Senate provision to require the Pentagon to open its files on U.S. military personnel counted as prisoners of war or missing in action in the Vietnam War.

• Authorized buying 19 combat planes, 18 M-1 tanks, 300 Patriot anti-aircraft missiles, 14 helicopters and 794 trucks using funds contributed by allied countries to cover the cost of the Persian Gulf War. The purchases were intended to replace equipment lost or used up in the war.

1992 Defense Appropriations

Congress in 1991 cleared a $270 billion fiscal 1992 defense appropriations bill. Combined with funds appropriated separately for military construction and for defense-related nuclear programs conducted by the Energy Department, the defense spending bill (HR 2521 — PL 102-172) brought the total defense budget for fiscal 1992 to $290.5 billion.

As usual, the measure funded without significant change the bulk of President Bush's Pentagon budget request. Also typically, its most significant departures from Bush's defense program echoed changes already incorporated in the companion defense authorization bill. *(Fiscal 1992 defense authorization, p. 369)*

Both bills, for example, trimmed Bush's request for major strategic weapons, including the B-2 "stealth" bomber and the anti-missile strategic defense initiative (SDI) program.

Many of the appropriations bill's significant add-ons to Bush's request also mirrored those previously authorized, including funds to modernize the Army's fleet of M-1 tanks and to continue development of the V-22 Osprey, a hybrid airplane/helicopter designed as a troop carrier for the Marine Corps.

Of the $5 billion in unauthorized funding for procurement and research programs, more than 40 percent was concentrated in a handful of major projects, including fast cargo ships ($600 million), F-15 fighters ($335 million) and air-cushion landing barges ($238 million).

About half of the 170 programs increased were boosted by $10 million or less.

Legislative Action

HR 2521 was reported by the House Appropriations Committee on June 4 (H Rept 102-95). The full House passed the $270.6 billion measure on June 7 by a vote of 273-105.

On two prominent issues — the B-2 and SDI — the appropriations bill mirrored the companion authorization bill passed two weeks earlier.

Despite threats of a veto, the bill appropriated none of the $3.2 billion Bush had requested to continue production of the B-2 stealth bomber, and it slashed $1.6 billion from Bush's funding request for SDI. Both bills approved $1.56 billion to continue B-2 development, $2.66 billion for SDI and an additional $787 million for a separate program to develop defenses against short-range (or "tactical") missiles.

But the appropriations measure also challenged the administration's defense program on two other key fronts:

• It froze the size of the National Guard and reserve components, rejecting out of hand Bush's proposal to slice their number by nearly 108,000 in fiscal 1992. That personnel action plus the addition of unbudgeted equipment for Guard and reserve units added nearly $2 billion to the budget request.

• And the bill provided almost $4 billion, not requested in the budget, for ships and aircraft intended to speed the deployment of U.S.-based forces to distant trouble spots.

During floor action June 7, the House rejected, 155-229, an amendment that would have deleted $260 million earmarked to complete development of a rail-mobile version of the MX intercontinental ballistic missile (ICBM).

The House deleted on procedural grounds a provision that would have allowed women in the service or military dependents stationed abroad to undergo abortions at U.S. military hospitals overseas at their own expense. The House had approved the same provision as an amendment to the defense authorization bill May 22, but it was dropped during conference.

The Senate Appropriations Committee reported HR 2521 on Sept. 20 (S Rept 102-154). The Senate passed a $270.3 billion version on Sept. 26 by voice vote.

Political support for costly strategic arms programs showed heavy erosion during Senate debate on HR 2521. The B-2 bomber and SDI narrowly survived attacks, and the Senate voted to kill the plan to mount MX missiles on rail cars. The debate reflected Congress' increasing doubts about big defense budgets as Democrats sought to protect domestic spending and members of both parties responded to the anti-communist upheaval in the Soviet Union.

The sea change in attitudes toward defense was ratified Sept. 27, when Bush made his boldest proposals to dismantle the nuclear arsenals of the Cold War. *(Details, box, p. 391)*

The controversial B-2 came before the Senate on Sept. 25 with the additional handicap of having failed one test of its ability to evade radar detection — the very rationale for its exotic and costly design and construction. Continued production of the B-2 stealth bomber was upheld by the Senate, 51-48, but opponents rounded up six more votes to kill the program than they had mustered only seven weeks earlier in action on the companion defense authorization bill.

Similarly, a proposal to provide SDI with $3.5 billion, instead of the $4.6 billion in the bill, was tabled (killed) 50-49 on Sept. 25. However, the amendment was supported by three senators who had opposed a similar cut in the authorization bill. In each case, all of the senators who switched positions were Democrats.

But the Senate Sept. 26 swamped, 10-90, a budget-driven attack on another costly weapon: an amendment that would have ended the *Seawolf*-class nuclear submarine program.

The Senate voted 67-33 on Sept. 26 to end development of a rail-based launcher for the MX ICBM. The Pentagon had planned to test the system and then mothball it, but Bush, echoing the Senate action, shelved the rail-MX effort in his Sept. 27 address.

Despite a sense that the Soviet threat had faded and that future defense cuts would relieve long-term restraints on domestic programs, the Senate Sept. 26 agreed to a motion to table, 58-41, an amendment that would have required the Pentagon to submit with its fiscal 1993 budget and long-term spending plan an alternative budget proposal showing how it would accommodate an additional reduction of $80 billion.

Conference, Major Provisions

The House-Senate conference finished its work on HR 2521 on Nov. 15 (H Rept 102-328). The House approved the conference report by voice vote Nov. 20, and the Senate agreed to it by a vote of 66-29 Nov. 23, clearing HR 2521.

Senate action came after another round of the chronic turf fight between the Senate Armed Services and Appropriations committees. Armed Services Committee Chairman Sam Nunn, D-Ga., protested that the bill circumvented the role of the House and Senate authorizing committees by providing more than was authorized.

After a previous round in this perennial battle, leaders of the two committees had signed a formal agreement delineating their respective roles. Among other provisions, it stipulated that Armed Services would not write into its bill "floors," minimum funding levels that had to be appropriated. But it also provided that Appropriations would not appropriate more than the ceiling that was authorized, unless the added funds were made subject to subsequent authorization.

But, as Defense Appropriations Subcommittee Chairman Daniel K. Inouye, D-Hawaii, and his allies pointed out, the agreement did not bind members of the House. It also was unclear whether it applied only to funding levels for large budget accounts or for the specific projects within each account.

However, even considering only the totals for each account, Nunn said, the appropriations bill exceeded authorized limits by more than $3.3 billion.

The final version of HR 2521 echoed the authorization measure by including $1.8 billion to keep alive the production line for the controversial B-2 bomber but approving no funds to begin work on additional planes beyond the 15 previously authorized. Similarly, the bill appropriated $4.15 billion of the $5.2 billion requested to develop anti-missile defenses under SDI.

However, the appropriations conferees rejected a Senate-backed initiative in the authorization bill that would have resumed production of the F-117, a small stealth bomber used successfully in the Persian Gulf War.

On one of the most highly charged issues facing the conferees, they approved a reduction of only 37,000 members in the politically influential National Guard and reserves. This was about one-third as deep a cut as the administration sought. But the conference report did give the Pentagon leeway to cut Guard and reserve manpower by an additional 2 percent, permitting a total cutback in fiscal 1992 of roughly 60,000.

In the face of a veto threat by Bush, the conferees dropped a Senate provision that would have permitted military personnel and dependents stationed overseas to obtain abortions in military hospitals, if they paid for the procedure. Such abortions had been allowed until 1988, when the Reagan administration banned them by administrative order.

Major Provisions. As signed into law Nov. 26, HR 2521 appropriated:

• $1.6 billion for research and development of the B-2 stealth bomber and $1.8 billion for components and spare parts. An additional $1 billion could be used to buy a 16th plane, but only if Congress first passed a bill approving that expenditure.

- $4.15 billion for the strategic defense initiative.
- $434 million for continued development of Midgetman, a small single-warhead intercontinental ballistic missile.
- $1.2 billion for 28 Trident II submarine-launched missiles (plus long lead-time components), and $54 million to continue development of the missile.
- $531 million to continue development and production of a stealth cruise missile. The funds were to buy 120 of the bomber-carried missiles (plus long lead-time items).
- $90 million to buy 60 M-1A2 tanks for the Army and $225 million to upgrade older M-1s to M-1A1s; $301 million for development of a new "family" of armored combat vehicles; $500 million to develop the Comanche (formerly designated LH) helicopter; $254 million to develop the Longbow system; $312 million for development of the JSTARS radar plane.
- $3.3 billion in equipment for the National Guard and reserve units.
- $1.6 billion for continued development of the Air Force F-22 fighter; $1.78 billion for 39 Navy F/A-18s (plus $150 million for long-lead funding); $1.1 billion for 48 Air Force F-16s (plus $78 million for long-lead); $505 million to close out production of the larger Air Force F-15, with six more planes plus support equipment; $173 million to shut down production of the Navy's F-14; $420 million to develop an enlarged version of the F/A-18 fighter; $740 million for AMRAAM radar-guided air-to-air missiles.
- $1.5 billion for the third in the class of *Seawolf* nuclear-powered submarines, with an additional $376 million earmarked for long lead-time components, and $424 million for related development programs; $4.1 billion for five *Arleigh Burke*-class destroyers, plus $16 million for long lead-time items; $341 million for three mine sweepers; $500 million for a giant supply ship.
- $1.5 billion for four C-17 wide-body cargo planes, plus $376 million to continue C-17 development; $448 million for 47 Blackhawk helicopters for the Army and six for the Navy and Air Force; $340 million for 16 of the CH-53E helicopters for the Marine Corps; $494 million for 24 Navy Seahawk helicopters (plus long-lead); $600 million to buy existing cargo ships or build new ones to enlarge the "sealift" fleet intended to haul U.S.-based combat forces to distant trouble spots; $504 million for 24 air-cushion landing barges; $625 million to continue development of the V-22 Osprey, a hybrid airplane/helicopter designed as a troop carrier for the Marine Corps.
- $78.3 billion for military personnel and $83.4 billion for operations and maintenance.

Other Action. A fiscal 1992 supplemental appropriations bill (H J Res 157 — PL 102-229) was signed into law on Dec. 12, 1991. The measure provided $4.1 billion in mop-up costs for Operation Desert Shield/Desert Storm, primarily to replace or repair munitions or equipment expended, destroyed or damaged during the war with Iraq. The bill also authorized the transfer of $400 million in previously appropriated Defense Department funds to help the Soviet Union dismantle its nuclear weapons. Another $100 million could be transferred to defray the cost of using U.S. military equipment and personnel to transport humanitarian aid to the Soviets.

Another fiscal 1992 supplemental appropriations bill (HR 5620 — PL 102-368) was signed into law on Sept. 23, 1992. The defense portion of the bill included $4.1 billion in wrap-up spending for Operation Desert Shield/Desert Storm, almost all of it from funds provided by U.S. allies. The bill also returned to the Treasury nearly $14.7 billion of the $15 billion originally appropriated to pay costs of the Persian Gulf War that were not met by U.S. allies.

1992 Military Construction

Congress in 1991 cleared an $8.56 billion measure to fund construction projects and family housing at U.S. military facilities, as well as military base closings, in fiscal 1992. The bill (HR 2426 — PL 102-136) appropriated $55.7 million less than President Bush had requested.

Congress reduced the funding the administration had sought for overseas bases, shifting more funds to domestic projects and in particular to facilities for the National Guard and reserves.

Like the fiscal 1991 military construction bill, the measure barred U.S. contributions toward a North Atlantic Treaty Organization (NATO) air base being built at Crotone, Italy. Congress was opposed to the project because of its high cost — especially when domestic bases across the country were being closed to save money. *(Fiscal 1991 military construction, p. 365)*

HR 2426 included nearly $759 million to close domestic military bases that had been deemed surplus and to clean up environmental problems at the facilities.

Legislative Action

The House Appropriations Committee reported HR 2426 (H Rept 102-74) May 22, and the House approved the measure May 30 by a vote of 392-18.

The House-passed bill appropriated $8.48 billion. In its most sweeping action to cut U.S. construction costs overseas, the bill reduced by $200 million the $359 million requested for the annual U.S. contribution to NATO's infrastructure fund. U.S. contributions were supposed to account for 28 percent of the fund, which was used to build facilities of benefit to the alliance. Previously, infrastructure spending was earmarked almost exclusively for projects in Europe. But for fiscal 1991, according to the House Appropriations panel, $100 million was programmed for projects in the United States.

The House bill contained no provisions related to the Crotone air base, which was intended to house a wing of U.S. fighter planes being evicted by the Spanish government from a base near Madrid. The House-passed version of the defense authorization bill included a provision to bar using any funds to transfer the U.S. unit.

The Senate Appropriations Committee approved HR 2426 Sept. 12 (S Rept 102-147), and the Senate passed it Sept. 16 by voice vote.

The single deepest cut in the $8.47 billion measure was from funding for the NATO infrastructure account. The Senate bill pared that to $254 million. The savings were redirected to facilities for the popular National Guard and reserve forces.

Conference, Major Provisions

The House approved the conference report (H Rept 102-236) by voice vote Oct. 8, and the Senate followed suit Oct. 16 by a vote of 99-0, completing congressional action on HR 2426.

Fiscal 1992 Defense Rescissions

Congress in 1992 cleared legislation (HR 4990 — PL 102-298) authorizing the cutting of $8.2 billion in previously appropriated fiscal 1992 spending. A big chunk of that — $7.2 billion — came from defense programs.

President Bush had proposed rescissions totaling $7.9 billion. Although Bush highlighted domestic projects when he made his spending-cut proposals, the vast majority — $7.1 billion — also was to come from defense programs.

The key controversy came over funds Bush wanted to cut for the *Seawolf* nuclear submarine, which critics said was conceived to meet a Soviet submarine threat that no longer existed. Bush wanted to cut nearly $3 billion for construction of the second and third subs, but the House voted to preserve money for one and the Senate voted to keep the money for both. House-Senate conferees compromised by cutting $1.3 billion, which left roughly $1.7 billion, more than enough to finish building the second submarine. They set aside $550 million of that on the condition that the secretary of defense use it to start building a third *Seawolf*, restart production of *Los Angeles*-class submarines or otherwise protect the industrial base for submarine construction. (Seawolf *submarine, box, p. 410)*

In looking for substitute rescissions when it opted to continue funding for the two *Seawolf* subs, the Senate slashed funding for the strategic defense initiative (SDI) by $1.3 billion, provoking a veto threat. In the end, conferees said they found the Pentagon had already spent $800 million of that money, leaving only $500 million to cut. Conferees opted to rescind $200 million of that.

The Senate originally proposed to slash $1 billion for construction of a single B-2 bomber. The conferees cut that in half, agreeing to a rescission of $500 million.

The final bill appropriated a total of $8.75 billion for fiscal 1992, including $4.35 billion for military construction, $3.64 billion for family housing and $758.6 million for base realignment and closure. Once various rescissions of prior-year appropriations were taken into account, the new budget authority was set at $8.56 billion.

The bill provided only a portion of the amount Bush wanted for overseas construction projects and for the annual U.S. contribution to NATO's infrastructure account. Savings from these cuts were to go to domestic programs — largely for National Guard and reserve units.

While Bush wanted $359 million for the NATO account, the conference agreed to give him only $225 million. As in previous years, the conference report contained language to prevent any unobligated funds in the NATO account from being spent on the air base in Crotone, Italy.

As for other overseas projects, the conference cut more than a third from the $289 million Bush had requested. The biggest, to build better family housing at Kwajalein Atoll in the Pacific, received $47.4 million of the $77.4 million the Pentagon wanted.

Because of the closure of some overseas bases, the conferees also made across-the-board reductions in worldwide construction projects for the services. Of the $478.9 million Bush wanted for small, unspecified jobs, the conferees approved $362.98 million.

The Defense Department also received less than it wanted to house the B-2 stealth bomber. Bush asked for $49.5 million for weapons storage areas, a survival equipment facility and other support structures for the controversial plane. The conferees provided $29.5 million.

The Senate bill would have provided $971.6 million for base-closing procedures, while the House had approved $758.6 million. The conference took the House-passed figure, which was $25 million more than Bush requested.

Arms Control Agreements

Major advances were made in the area of arms control during the 102nd Congress. But uncertainty existed as to what it all meant and how the agreements would play out in a rapidly changing world.

The Senate in 1991 overwhelmingly approved a treaty on conventional forces in Europe (CFE), which required the destruction of tens of thousands of tanks and other weapons, most of them deployed by the Soviet Union.

The same day the Senate gave its approval to the CFE pact, President Bush submitted to the Senate a strategic arms reduction talks (START) treaty, which was intended to cut by about one-third the arsenals of U.S. and Soviet long-range, nuclear-armed missiles and bombers.

But world events moved so quickly and dramatically during 1991 that such traditional arms control agreements — arrived at through laborious superpower negotiations and loaded down with intricate tradeoffs and safeguards — were effectively eclipsed by the crumbling of the Soviet Union. *(End of the Cold War, p. 319)*

Bush attempted to scramble ahead of the curve of change by announcing an unprecedented decision to scrap thousands of U.S. nuclear weapons — many unilaterally and others if the Soviet Union agreed — and to ease up on the triggers of thousands more. Soviet President Mikhail S. Gorbachev responded by offering to match and exceed the U.S. cuts.

By the end of 1991, the former Soviet republics had declared their independence and the demise of the Soviet Union. On Dec. 25, Gorbachev resigned, and the Soviet flag over the Kremlin was lowered.

That left the Bush administration without the leader — and, for that matter, without the country — with which it had negotiated arms control treaties. The administration sought, and generally received, assurances from republics in the loose-knit new Commonwealth of Independent States that they would honor arms agreements, including the CFE and START treaties.

Members of the Senate indicated that their deliberations on the START agreement would turn in large part on how reliable such commitments would be in the uncertain post-Soviet era. Senators approved the START agreement in 1992 after the four republics that had assumed control of the former Soviet nuclear arsenal agreed in an amendment to the treaty to take on the obligations the treaty would have imposed on the Soviet government. In early 1993, the United States and Russia signed a second START agreement.

With the disintegration of the Soviet Union, nuclear test ban advocates finally won enactment of their long-sought-after goal. In 1992, Congress voted to halt all nuclear test explosions after September 1996. *(Test ban, p. 392)*

So much had changed in the post-Cold War world that a pact to permit reconnaissance overflights of the United States, Russia and other European countries was scarcely noticed when it was signed in 1992. No final Senate action was taken that year.

On another front, Congress in 1991 and 1992 approved legislation providing various types of aid to the former Soviet republics, including assistance to help dismantle nuclear weapons. *(Soviet aid, p. 260)*

Conventional Forces Treaty

Amid unease over the Soviet Union's future, the Senate on Nov. 25, 1991, closed a chapter from the era of superpower military competition by overwhelmingly endorsing the conventional forces in Europe treaty.

The Senate approved, 90-4, a resolution of ratification for the CFE treaty (Treaty Doc 102-8), which had been signed in Paris on Nov. 19, 1990, by President Bush, Soviet President Gorbachev and the leaders of 20 other nations.

The treaty imposed ceilings on military equipment deployed by the North Atlantic Treaty Organization (NATO) states and the former members of the Warsaw Pact in an area between the Atlantic Ocean and the Ural Mountains. *(Treaty effects, box, p. 385)*

Most senators agreed that the pact was "demonstrably and overwhelmingly favorable to the United States and its NATO allies," as Senate Armed Services Committee Chairman Sam Nunn, D-Ga., put it. But a handful of Republicans opposed the resolution, charging that the Soviets had violated the treaty's provisions even before its ratification.

In what Nunn referred to as an "astonishingly asymmetrical outcome," the Soviet Union was required to destroy more than 20,000 pieces of military equipment while the United States was committed to scrap fewer than 3,000.

The goal of the treaty from the outset was sharp reductions in weapons that were seen as particularly useful in a blitzkrieg, which NATO had feared for 20 years from the tank-heavy forces of the Soviet Union and its Warsaw Pact allies.

Background. By early 1988, both alliances had called publicly for an agreement that would set equal ceilings on the conventional forces they deployed in Europe. But wide disparities existed in each side's assessments of the European military balance — how and what weapons would be counted.

The first concrete indication that the two sides might find common ground was Gorbachev's dramatic announcement of unilateral Soviet troop cuts made to the United Nations in late 1988. He said the Soviets would reduce their active-duty military forces by 500,000 men over two years. This would include 50,000 men and 5,000 tanks in six of the 16 Soviet armored divisions deployed in Eastern Europe.

In effect, Gorbachev thus conceded two fundamental premises of NATO's approach to the forthcoming conventional arms reduction talks:

- That the Warsaw Pact enjoyed a substantial numerical superiority over NATO in certain weapons, such as tanks, especially useful in a surprise attack.
- That any conventional arms pact thus would require far larger reductions by the Warsaw Pact than by NATO.

CFE negotiations formally began in Vienna in March 1989. By the time the agreement was signed in November of that year, it essentially ratified an unraveling of Soviet military power that had greatly outstripped the arms control negotiations. Since late 1988, Gorbachev had orchestrated a dramatic military retrenchment in response to political tensions and economic collapse at home. Meanwhile, largely peaceful revolutions in the former Soviet satellites of Eastern Europe supplanted communist regimes with popularly elected governments less pliant to Kremlin wishes and eager to slice their own defense costs.

The contraction had gone so far and so fast that once-major provisions were dropped from the treaty, such as a limit on troop levels in Europe. *(Troop reduction proposals, box, p. 387)*

Provisions. Even though the Warsaw Pact was moribund by the time the CFE treaty was signed, the agreement retained its initial structure. It imposed equal ceilings on weapons that could be deployed in Europe by NATO and by the six countries that formerly made up the Warsaw Pact.

Each group of countries could deploy between the Atlantic Ocean and the Ural Mountains no more than 20,000 tanks, 30,000 armored troop carriers, 20,000 artillery pieces, 6,800 combat airplanes and 2,000 attack helicopters. To further inhibit the concentration of forces for an attack, the treaty also set regional sublimits on the number of tanks, troop carriers and artillery.

The treaty barred either group from deploying more than 740 mobile bridges. A separate agreement attached to the treaty — but not formally part of it — barred either group of countries from deploying more than 430 land-based naval planes.

Any weapons in excess of the treaty limits that were in the area covered by the treaty at the time it was signed had to be destroyed within 40 months. But a certain number of those could be used for other purposes after they had been disarmed under specified procedures.

To verify compliance, the treaty provided for detailed exchanges of data about the organization of each country's military forces and about the number, model and location of its treaty-limited weaponry.

Disputes Resolved. Two disputes between the United States and the Soviet Union threatened final ratification of the treaty. It was not until June 14, seven months after the treaty was signed, that the disagreements were formally settled.

One issue was the Soviet effort to exempt thousands of weapons from the treaty even though it permitted only a few narrow exemptions. The Kremlin insisted that more than 5,400 tanks and other items were exempt because they were assigned to ground combat units of the Soviet navy or to units defending strategic missile bases.

Conventional Forces in Europe

The 1991 treaty limiting conventional forces in Europe (CFE) called for the Soviet Union to destroy or disarm more than 20,000 of the 73,000 tanks, artillery and other heavy weapons that equipped its forces west of the Ural Mountains as of mid-1991.

But that 27 percent reduction was dwarfed by the massive decline in Soviet conventional power in Europe since CFE negotiations began early in 1989. Measured against the Soviet weapons deployed less than three years previously, the arsenal controlled by former republics of the Soviet Union was to be reduced by more than two-thirds under the treaty.

Of the more than 147,000 Soviet weapons covered by the treaty that were deployed early in 1989, nearly 60,000 had been shipped by mid-1991 to Soviet Asia, where they were exempt from CFE limits. Before the Soviet Union crumbled, its leaders assured the Bush administration that 14,500 of those weapons would be destroyed or demilitarized by 1995; the Senate conditioned its approval of the treaty on observance of that side deal.

The rest of the weapons shifted east of the Urals were to remain intact but so far from Europe as to be useless for the kind of surprise attack the CFE treaty was intended to prevent. The remaining Soviet weapons above the CFE limit of 52,975 were slated for destruction or disarmament.

For each of five types of weapons, the treaty imposed equal ceilings on the North Atlantic Treaty Organization (NATO) and what were at the time the six surviving members of the former Warsaw Pact. Each of the two groups of countries, in turn, allocated among themselves national ceilings for each class of weapon.

The following chart describes the effects of the CFE treaty that were expected at the time the Senate considered the pact. It was based on estimates provided by the Institute for Defense and Disarmament Studies.

	U.S.	Other NATO[a]	Soviet Union	Eastern Europe	Comments
Tanks					
Mid-1991	5,904	16,188	20,725	10,988	Category includes wheeled or tracked vehicles carrying a gun of 75mm or larger and weighing at least 16.5 metric tons (excluding the weight of crew, ammunition, fuel and removable armor).
Post-Treaty[b]	4,006	15,136	13,150	6,850	
Armored Combat Vehicles					
Mid-1991	5,747	22,661	29,890	11,941	Of the 30,000 permitted for each group of states, no more than 18,000 could carry a gun of 20mm or larger. Of those 18,000, no more than 1,500 could weigh more than 6 metric tons or more and carry a gun of 75mm or larger.
Post-Treaty[b]	5,372	24,450	20,000	10,000	
Artillery					
Mid-1991	2,601	16,003	13,938	10,818	Category includes both guns and rocket launchers firing projectiles of 100mm caliber or larger.
Post-Treaty[b]	2,492	15,794	13,175	6,825	
Airplanes					
Mid-1991	626	4,690	6,611	1,757	Category includes "combat-capable" aircraft, excluding basic trainers and carrier-based planes. Each alliance would be permitted an additional 430 land-based naval aircraft.
Post-Treaty[b]	784	5,878	5,150	1,650	
Helicopters					
Mid-1991	243	1,300	1,481	181	Category includes armed helicopters but not land-based naval helicopters.
Post-Treaty[b]	518	1,482	1,500	500	

[a] Excludes 10,674 weapons of former East German forces, which would be counted against NATO limits as part of the forces of unified Germany. Virtually all of them would be destroyed.

[b] Projected levels. Based on treaty ceilings or lower levels announced by countries.

Of these, more than 2,600 weapons had been assigned to three Soviet army divisions stationed near the coast, but they were shifted to navy control as the CFE negotiations drew to a close. Most Western observers believed that the sudden reassignment of the army divisions as naval units was intended partly as a ploy to underscore Soviet frustration with the longstanding U.S. refusal to discuss limits on naval forces.

Though none of the other countries that were parties to the treaty supported Moscow's contention that these weapons were exempt, a compromise was struck allowing the Kremlin to keep the disputed equipment in the naval units but requiring the destruction of a corresponding number of weapons within the treaty area. The armored troop carriers assigned to protect missile bases were exempted from the treaty outright. The compromise also stipulated that all other weapons in the treaty zone of the designated types were covered by the treaty limits unless specifically exempted, regardless of the organization to which they were assigned.

The deal was embodied in a unilateral Soviet statement attached to, but separate from, the CFE treaty and having the same binding force in international law.

The second issue settled June 14 involved about 59,000 tanks and other weapons that the Soviet government moved east of the Urals shortly before the treaty was signed, thus exempting them from coverage.

In a statement that was described as "politically binding" but not binding in international law, the Kremlin pledged that the equipment would not be used to create a strategic reserve force and would not be stored in a way that would allow its rapid redeployment into the area covered by the treaty.

The Soviet government also promised to destroy or demilitarize 14,500 of these weapons by 1995.

Senate Committee Action. The Senate Foreign Relations Committee took a step toward formalizing the end of the Cold War on Nov. 19 as it unanimously approved the CFE agreement. A year to the day after the CFE pact was signed in Paris, the committee voted 18-0 to send a resolution of ratification of the treaty to the full Senate (Treaty Doc 102-8).

The committee had attached five conditions and four declarations — essentially sense of the Senate statements — to the resolution of ratification. The administration had originally hoped to win approval of a "clean" resolution of ratification but raised no objections to the committee's conditions.

With the military threat posed by the Soviet central government sharply diminished, members of the Foreign Relations Committee focused on the potential dangers arising from the independence movement sweeping what had been the Soviet empire. The panel attached a condition to the resolution requiring Bush to seek Senate approval for changes in the pact that might arise if any of the breakaway republics refused to abide by provisions of the treaty. The condition was said to be largely directed at the Ukraine, which reportedly intended to maintain a large army as an independent nation.

Two other conditions in the Senate Foreign Relations package were intended to ensure Soviet compliance with the settlements reached in the disputes over the transfer of weapons to navy units not covered by the treaty and to areas east of the Ural Mountains beyond the pact's coverage.

Another condition in the Foreign Relations amendment dealt with the erosion of Soviet control over territory in which Soviet forces were deployed. It stipulated that the United States would count against the Soviet Union's allowance under the treaty any Soviet weapons deployed in the Baltic republics of Estonia, Latvia and Lithuania, which had declared independence from Moscow.

The final condition highlighted a remaining discrepancy in counting the number of Soviet weapons subject to disposal under the treaty. U.S. estimates exceeded the Soviet count by about 800 weapons. The condition provided that, if the higher U.S. estimate turned out to be correct, the United States had to insist that the Soviet Union destroy 800 additional weapons.

The Foreign Relations amendment also included four other provisions intended to stake out the Senate's position in long-running disputes with various adversaries, foreign and domestic. Among these so-called declarations was one stipulating that Senate approval of the CFE treaty was based on the assumption that administration witnesses testifying to Senate committees had provided "authoritative" testimony about the interpretation of the pact. This provision was rooted in the Senate's battle with President Ronald Reagan over his 1985 claim that some provisions of the 1972 anti-ballistic missile (ABM) treaty did not mean what most witnesses from the executive branch had told Senate committees at that time. The Reagan administration said the 1972 testimony had not been "authoritative" and that planned tests of the strategic defense initiative (SDI) anti-missile system would not violate the treaty. But Congress had insisted on adherence to the traditional interpretation of the treaty. *(Congress and the Nation Vol. VII, p. 347)*

The Senate committee, by voice vote, also approved legislation (S 1987) authorizing the president to transfer to NATO allies virtually all of the equipment scheduled to be disposed of under the CFE treaty.

Under the procedure, known as "cascading," the United States could transfer 2,968 tanks, combat armored vehicles and artillery pieces. The NATO allies were required to eliminate a comparable number of older weapons. Turkey was to be the leading recipient, followed by Greece and Spain.

A companion House bill (HR 3807 — PL 102-228) later became the legislative vehicle to authorize aid to the former Soviet republics. *(Soviet aid, p. 260)*

Senate Floor Action. Senate concern over the military dangers associated with the imminent breakup of the old Soviet empire was reflected in the floor debate on the CFE treaty. The Foreign Relations Committee had attached a condition requiring that Bush submit for the Senate's "advice and consent" significant changes in the pact that might be negotiated if a well-armed republic were to spurn the treaty's terms. This was modified by voice vote on the Senate floor to require future presidents to seek a resolution of support under such circumstances. A resolution would require a simple majority for passage, as compared with the two-thirds vote needed for advice and consent.

Before giving its final approval to the treaty, the Senate attached a sixth condition to the resolution of ratification. Conservative Republicans offered an amendment that conditioned U.S. adherence to the treaty on a presidential certification that the Soviet Union was complying with the treaty. The Senate by voice vote modified the amendment to require the president to report on Soviet compliance but not link the report to continued U.S. participation in the treaty.

Strategic Arms Treaty

The Senate on Oct. 1, 1992, approved ratification of a strategic arms treaty, providing for a reduction of about one-third in the arsenals of long-range missiles and bombers of the United States and the former Soviet Union.

The START treaty had taken nine years to complete, with large bureaucracies on each side hashing out details. But by the time the Senate exercised its usual constitutional responsibility to provide advice and consent on treaties, it faced the unusual circumstance of considering a far-reaching arms control pact with a country that no longer existed.

Signed July 31, 1991, by President Bush and Soviet President Gorbachev, the START treaty provided for a reduction in the U.S. inventory of intercontinental nuclear bombs and missile warheads from more than 12,000 to fewer than 9,000. It provided for reducing the Soviet stock of such weapons from about 11,000 to 6,000. *(Major provisions, box, p. 388)*

With the demise of the Soviet Union at the end of 1991, the treaty in some ways seemed to be a Cold War anachronism. However, in a treaty amendment (or "protocol") signed May 23, 1992, the four republics that assumed control of the former Soviet nuclear arsenal agreed to take on the obligations the treaty would have imposed on the Soviet government.

In June testimony before the Senate Foreign Relations Committee, Secretary of State James A. Baker III argued that the START treaty marked an important step toward heading off the emergence of new nuclear-armed states from the debris of the Soviet Union. The key, Baker said, was the protocol signed by the four republics. It provided that all four countries would sign the treaty, but that only Russia would deploy the weapons the treaty would have allowed the Soviet Union to maintain.

The agreement bound the other republics — Ukraine, Belarus and Kazakhstan — to forswear all nuclear weapons by signing the 1968 nuclear non-proliferation treaty. Each also promised in a letter to dispose of all deployed strategic weapons within seven years. Baker said the letters were legally binding on the republics.

Background. START had its roots in Reagan's vehement denunciation of the major U.S.-Soviet strategic arms limitation talks (SALT) agreements of the 1970s — the 1972 SALT I and the unratified 1979 SALT II agreements. *(Congress and the Nation Vol. III, p. 895; Congress and the Nation Vol. V, p. 193)*

Before and during his 1980 presidential campaign, Reagan had denounced the SALT agreements on grounds that they left basically untouched the huge nuclear arsenals the two sides already had, even allowing them to expand in certain ways.

Any further arms agreement would have to impose deep reductions on existing strategic forces, Reagan insisted. In addition, he demanded that future arms pacts concentrate on limiting large, multi-warhead intercontinental ballistic missiles (ICBMs), which were the backbone of the Soviet strategic force. Reagan viewed such weapons as particularly destabilizing because of their potential for wiping out a large part of an enemy's retaliatory force with very little warning.

U.S. and Soviet negotiators began work in 1982 on a treaty shaped in large measure by Reagan's beliefs. Liberal arms control advocates — and some prominent centrists with experience in previous GOP administrations — complained that Reagan's demands were a ploy, intended to block progress toward arms control while mollifying public demands for arms control efforts.

But in 1986, Reagan and Gorbachev confounded critics by agreeing at a summit in Iceland to set a limit of 1,600 on the total number of "strategic nuclear delivery vehicles" — ICBMs, submarine-launched ballistic missiles (SLBMs) and long-range bombers. They also agreed that the total number of nuclear warheads on ICBMs, SLBMs and long-range air-launched cruise missiles (ALCMs) plus the num-

Troop Reduction Proposals

Troop levels had been a key topic in the debate over reductions in conventional forces in Europe (CFE). But by the time the CFE treaty was signed in November 1990, it was a moot issue and had been dropped from the accord.

CFE negotiators had reached a tentative understanding capping the number of U.S. and Soviet troops in Europe at 225,000 for each side, but it became pointless as Moscow concluded a series of agreements to withdraw its forces from the territory of its former satellites.

Soviet leader Mikhail S. Gorbachev had brought the issue of troop cuts to the forefront in a dramatic address before the United Nations General Assembly in New York in December 1988. In a move to make the threat of a surprise Soviet-bloc attack on Western Europe look less plausible, Gorbachev announced Soviet plans to cut 500,000 of the country's 5.1 million troops by 1991.

The North Atlantic Treaty Organization (NATO) initially resisted Warsaw Pact proposals to include in a CFE agreement ceilings on military manpower. But at a May 1989 summit meeting marking NATO's 40th anniversary, President Bush proposed that the CFE agreement include a cap of 275,000 on U.S. and Soviet troop deployments in Europe.

Eight months later, Bush called for even deeper cuts in troop levels in Europe. As a centerpiece of his State of the Union address on Jan. 31, 1990, Bush proposed that each superpower be limited to 195,000 armed forces in the "central zone" of Europe (the two Germanys and most of Eastern Europe).

A senior Bush administration official said the Soviet Union had 565,000 to 570,000 troops in central Europe, including about 355,000 in East Germany.

The United States had about 305,000 troops in Europe, the official said, of which 255,000 to 260,000 were stationed in West Germany. Most of the rest were in Italy, Britain and Turkey. Other NATO nations kept 160,000 foreign troops in West Germany, according to the International Institute for Strategic Studies in London.

Major START Treaty Provisions

Following are the key provisions of the 1991 strategic arms reduction talks (START) treaty between the United States and the former Soviet Union and the 1992 protocol to that treaty:

Overall Ceilings. During the seven years after ratification, each side had to reduce its strategic arsenal to no more than 6,000 aerial bombs and missile warheads (subject to special "counting rules"). These could be carried by no more than 1,600 long-range ballistic missiles and heavy bombers.

Of the 6,000 bombs and warheads, no more than 4,900 could be carried by intercontinental ballistic missiles (ICBMs) or submarine-launched missiles.

Neither country's remaining missile force could have a total throw-weight greater than 54 percent of the size of the Soviet force in 1991. Throw-weight was an indicator of the number and size of nuclear warheads a missile could carry.

Missile Counting Rules. Each type of missile was to be counted as having an agreed number of warheads — 10 apiece for the American MX and the Soviet SS-18, for example. No existing missile could be tested with more than its assigned number of warheads. And no new missile could be tested with more than 10 warheads.

To allow each country to disperse its warheads over a larger number of missiles, up to 1,250 warheads could be "down-loaded" from existing missiles, with that number subtracted from the number attributed to those missiles under the treaty.

Bomber and Cruise Missiles Rules. To encourage a shift from missiles to bombers, certain bomber-launched weapons were not counted against the 6,000-weapon ceiling. That was the major reason that START did not cut arsenals as deeply as the 50 percent reduction described by some of its supporters.

Non-nuclear cruise missiles and nuclear missiles with ranges of less than 600 kilometers were not covered. Unless it was equipped to carry long-range nuclear cruise missiles, a bomber was counted as one delivery vehicle (against the ceiling of 1,600) carrying one warhead (against the ceiling of 6,000), no matter how many gravity bombs and short-range missiles it carried.

Long-range cruise missiles were counted against the 6,000-weapon ceiling under formulas that, in effect, exempted from the limit as many as several hundred missiles for each country.

'Heavy' ICBMs. Neither side could deploy more than 154 ICBMs larger than the Soviet SS-19 and the United States' MX. And such "heavy" missiles could carry no more than 10 warheads apiece. This cut the SS-18 force by 50 percent.

New heavy missiles were barred, and the SS-18 could not be modified to increase its throw-weight.

Mobile ICBMs. No more than 1,100 warheads could be deployed on mobile ICBMs. To aid in verification, several restrictions were placed on how mobile missiles could be based and how they could operate when away from their bases.

Third-Party Weapons. Neither country was permitted to circumvent the START agreement by transferring treaty-limited weapons to a third party, except for "existing patterns of cooperation" — a phrase intended to cover the U.S. sale to Britain of Trident II sub-launched missiles.

Sea-Launched Cruise Missiles. To accommodate Soviet demands for limits on the U.S. Navy's Tomahawk sea-launched cruise missile (SLCM), which was built in both nuclear and conventional versions, each country was required by the terms of the treaty to announce annually its plans for deploying over the following five years any nuclear-armed SLCMs with a range of more than 600 kilometers.

No more than 880 such weapons could be deployed. The U.S. Navy had planned to deploy 637 nuclear Tomahawks. But as part of his nuclear arms reduction initiative in September 1991, President Bush announced that the 350 nuclear Tomahawks then deployed would be mothballed.

Backfire Bomber. The Soviet Union promised to deploy no more than 500 Backfire bombers. For 20 years, U.S. negotiators had insisted that this plane was an intercontinental bomber, while Soviet negotiators denied it.

Post-Soviet Republics. Under an annex (or "protocol") signed at Lisbon in May and made a part of the treaty, the former Soviet republics of Russia, Ukraine, Belarus and Kazakhstan — where all former Soviet strategic weapons were located — accepted the obligations imposed by the START treaty on the Soviet government.

Ukraine, Belarus and Kazakhstan agreed to bar nuclear weapons from their territory by signing the 1968 Nuclear Non-Proliferation Treaty as "non-nuclear weapon states."

In separate letters, those three governments pledged to eliminate all nuclear weapons within seven years.

---

ber of non-ALCM-armed bombers would not exceed 6,000. *(Congress and the Nation Vol. VII, p. 343)*

At a summit in Washington in December 1987, Reagan and Gorbachev nailed down more elements of the START framework. But even as the two sides converged on several of the most fundamental START questions, certain issues remained intractable. These included the fate of mobile ICBMs, how to count ALCM-armed bombers against the warhead limit and how, if at all, to limit nuclear-armed sea-launched cruise missiles.

In addition, the Soviets did not want to conclude START until agreement was reached in the parallel talks on space and defensive weapons. Reagan insisted that any new agreement governing space-based weapons expressly endorse the deployment, after some years, of the strategic defense initiative, his program to develop an anti-ballistic missile defense. But the Soviets insisted that any new agreement reflect their view, shared by most Western analysts, that the 1972 U.S.-Soviet ABM treaty barred SDI deployment. *(SDI, box, p. 370)*

What direction the negotiations would take was unknown when Bush came into office in January 1989 and ordered a full-scale review of strategy and arms control policy. Some arms control advocates suspected that the Bush administration might be fundamentally uncomfortable with START. Brent Scowcroft, Bush White House national security adviser, was only one of many pillars of the national security establishment who had voiced skepticism of Reagan's insistence on "deep cuts" in strategic arms.

One argument of these critics was that, under some circumstances, smaller nuclear forces could make the world riskier, because it might be easier for policy makers to contemplate a first strike that could disarm an adversary — or a strike by an adversary that could disarm their own forces.

START negotiations resumed in June 1989, having been in abeyance since November 1988. At the renewed talks, U.S. negotiators pushed for a controversial new emphasis on procedures to verify each side's compliance with a final treaty.

The new thrust came in for heavy criticism from liberal arms control advocates warning that — intentionally or not — it would delay conclusions of a START agreement. But Bush and several senior aides insisted that the new emphasis was intended partly to capitalize on Soviet willingness to accept highly intrusive verification arrangements.

Moreover, officials insisted that Bush's verification tack was intended to head off obstacles to ultimate Senate approval of the START pact. Doubts over verification procedures had undermined Senate support for the 1979 SALT II agreement and had forced last-minute revisions in the 1988 treaty banning intermediate-range nuclear-force (INF) missiles. *(Congress and the Nation Vol. VII, p. 332)*

Bush also unveiled another potential shift in START negotiating policy, hinting to congressional leaders that he would drop the U.S. proposal to ban mobile ICBMs, if he were convinced Congress would approve the amounts he requested for two mobile ICBM programs. Secretary of State Baker confirmed this position several months later. *(Mobile missiles, box, p. 343)*

Further obstacles to a START agreement were removed during talks between Secretary Baker and Soviet Foreign Minister Eduard A. Shevardnadze, who met in September 1989 to lay the groundwork for a summit meeting in Malta later that year. The Soviets dropped their insistence that START be accompanied by an agreement limiting anti-missile defenses, particularly those based in space. Nonetheless, they vowed to repudiate START if the United States subsequently violated Moscow's understanding of what the ABM treaty had banned.

Shevardnadze also announced that Moscow would dismantle a huge radar station at Krasnoyarsk in western Siberia, which was generally held by non-Soviet experts to violate the ABM treaty's limits on where such powerful radars could be located. Since 1983, conservative critics of the ABM treaty had cited Krasnoyarsk as a violation that justified U.S. withdrawal from the pact. *(Congress and the Nation Vol. VII, p. 351)*

But the Soviets also reiterated complaints about U.S. missile-detection radars in Greenland and Britain. The ABM treaty barred such radars outside U.S. or Soviet territory. But the U.S. government had responded to earlier Soviet complaints by arguing that the two radars were treaty-compliant because they replaced older, much less powerful radars that were "grandfathered in" under the pact. In a joint communiqué, the United States "promised to consider" the Soviet concerns.

The Soviets also agreed to "delink" from START the issue of sea-launched cruise missiles, although they still wanted an agreement limiting the number of SLCMs. The Bush administration, like its predecessor, insisted that limits on the number of nuclear SLCMs were impossible to verify.

At the Malta summit in December 1989, Bush and Gorbachev agreed to accelerate START negotiations in hopes of reaching agreement on the essential details of the treaty in time for a full-scale summit meeting in Washington in June 1990 and the signing of a formal treaty later that year.

Bush's embrace of a fast track for START marked a sharp break from his administration's earlier standoffishness toward the strategic arms treaty. Bush sent Secretary of State Baker to Moscow in the early months of 1990 to meet with Soviet leaders to try to iron out details of the arms pact prior to the June summit.

Although a few relatively technical issues were still to be resolved, agreement was reached on the major elements of an arms treaty. Bush and Gorbachev signed a statement at the Washington summit covering overall ceilings, basic counting rules, "heavy" ICBMs, mobile ICBMs, ALCM counting rules and sea-launched cruise missiles. They also signed a second statement setting goals for further reductions. In their June 1 statement, the two leaders glossed over the remaining problems, expressing "great satisfaction with the great progress that has been made" and saying that the negotiating teams in Geneva had been "instructed . . . to accelerate their work."

Technical disputes continued to dog subsequent negotiations, but both sides were optimistic enough to schedule a summit in Moscow in February 1991. However, by early 1991 the summit had been sidetracked by the Persian Gulf War and the Soviets' crackdown on the breakaway Baltic republics.

Agreement on START was clinched by Bush and Gorbachev at a summit of major economic powers in London in July 1991. In the space of a few hours, U.S. and Soviet negotiators hammered out the last nettlesome details. The mood was as much one of relief as euphoria as almost a decade of negotiation had at last yielded the first treaty to reduce arsenals of strategic nuclear weapons.

Senate Committee Action. The Senate Foreign Relations Committee on July 2 approved, 17-0, a resolution to ratify the START treaty.

The committee added to the resolution of approval several conditions intended to lend greater legal formality to the series of agreements by which Russia and three other former Soviet republics had assumed the former Soviet Union's treaty obligations.

One of the conditions stipulated that the United States regarded the protocol signed on May 23 as tantamount to an integral part of the treaty. In the protocol, Russia, Belarus, Ukraine and Kazakhstan agreed to assume the Soviet obligations.

Other conditions similarly stipulated that U.S. ratification of START was based on compliance by Belarus, Ukraine and Kazakhstan with various commitments that they would dispose of former Soviet strategic weapons and would forswear deployment of any nuclear weapons by signing the 1968 nuclear non-proliferation treaty.

Over the objection of Foreign Relations Republicans, the committee also adopted a condition that directed the president to seek, as part of any future treaty reducing strategic nuclear arms, an agreement for the parties to monitor each others' nuclear stockpiles and nuclear weapons production plants, something U.S. officials had resisted in the past.

The condition bound U.S. negotiators trying to wrap up a follow-on treaty that would implement the much deeper strategic arms cuts, known as START II, agreed to June 17 by Bush and Russian President Boris N. Yeltsin. *(START II, below)*

Senate Floor Action. The Senate on Oct. 1, 1992, easily approved ratification of the START agreement. The somewhat cursory debate and minimal dissent on the Senate floor reflected the changed status of the historic treaty in the wake of the Soviet Union's demise.

After blocking attempts by a few conservatives to amend the treaty (Treaty Doc 102-20), the Senate approved ratification by a vote of 93-6, far more than the two-thirds vote required.

Treaty backers said that despite ongoing negotiations on details of the Bush-Yeltsin plan for a second START agreement, the START I reductions were needed to set the stage for the additional arms cuts and as a hedge against the possible re-emergence of unfriendly governments in the former Soviet Union.

START critics, led by Malcolm Wallop, R-Wyo., argued that the initial treaty did not go far enough and should be delayed and combined with the Bush-Yeltsin pact. Wallop also complained that the historic pact was being rushed through in the final hours of the session, without being given adequate consideration by the Senate. But after he threatened to filibuster, the Senate on Sept. 29 voted 87-6 to limit debate on the measure.

Subsequently, Wallop was defeated in attempts to amend the treaty so that it would not have gone into effect until the president certified that all multiple-warhead ICBMs would be eliminated (16-83), that most non-deployed missiles and launchers would be eliminated (11-88), and that mobile ICBMs and launchers for mobile ICBMs would be eliminated (10-86).

The Senate's resolution of ratification already included a number of conditions and declarations on compliance with the treaty and provisions of the May 23 protocol. The Senate agreed by voice vote to an amendment by John W. Warner, R-Va., strengthening one condition, which would have delayed the treaty from going into effect if the four republics had not reached agreement among themselves on how to implement their side of the arms reduction deal. Warner noted that since the protocol had been signed, some republic officials had indicated that the agreement could be more difficult than originally thought.

The resolution also included the condition directing the president in subsequent pacts to seek agreement on monitoring each others' nuclear stockpiles and production plants.

START II Agreement

On Dec. 30, 1992, President Bush announced that he and Russian President Yeltsin had reached agreement on an arms reduction treaty that called for slashing the number of U.S. and Russian nuclear warheads to no more than 6,500. The treaty thus provided for the removal from service of more than two-thirds of the nearly 24,000 warheads deployed as of 1990 by the United States and the Soviet Union.

The treaty called for eliminating from service all weapons carried by multiple-warhead, land-based (MIRVed) missiles, which U.S. officials long had regarded as the most threatening type in the former Soviet arsenal. And the agreement envisioned the reductions being achieved as early as the year 2000, provided the United States helped Russia bear the cost of demobilizing its large nuclear force.

The second strategic arms reduction talks treaty — START II — was agreed upon in broad terms by Bush and Yeltsin in June 1992, then signed on Jan. 3, 1993. It was sent to the U.S. and Soviet legislatures for approval of ratification.

This second treaty presumed compliance with the first START treaty, signed in July 1991 and approved by the Senate on Oct. 1, 1992. *(Warhead allotments under two treaties, box, p. 392)*

Reconnaissance Overflights Pact

An "Open Skies" treaty binding the United States, Russia and other European countries to allow reciprocal reconnaissance overflights was once considered a radical arms control proposal. But it seemed so unremarkable in the post-Cold War world that its signature March 24, 1992, drew scant notice in the United States.

The Senate failed to take final action on the pact. And only the Foreign Relations Committee held hearings on the subject in 1992.

Background. President Dwight D. Eisenhower proposed a similar agreement in 1955 that would have relied on state-of-the-art aerial photography to deter sudden changes in military deployments that might have ignited crises. But Soviet officials spiked that plan as a crude effort to legitimize U.S. spying.

President Bush resuscitated Eisenhower's Open Skies idea in May 1989, extending the proposed inspections beyond the territory of the United States and the former Soviet Union to cover their allies and former allies.

For more than two years after Bush floated the idea, negotiations had stalled. U.S. negotiators insisted that flights be permitted over any part of a signatory's territory, allowing a country to temporarily block a flight only for safety reasons — if, for instance, the proposed itinerary would take the observation plane dangerously near a scheduled missile test.

Soviet officials rejected such wide-open access and also insisted that overflight rights cover signatories' bases in countries not party to the treaty, such as U.S. bases in South Korea and Japan.

The deadlock appeared to have been broken in late 1990, when Soviet Foreign Minister Shevardnadze dropped the demand for third-country overflights and offered to allow total territorial access, provided the United States

Unilateral U.S. Arms Cutbacks

On Sept. 27, 1991, President Bush went on national television to announce a bold new initiative to reduce strategic arms in recognition of the dramatic changes in the Soviet Union.

"If we and the Soviet leaders take the right steps — some on our own, some on their own, some together — we can dramatically shrink the arsenal of the world's nuclear weapons," Bush said.

The unilateral initiative was a recognition of the dizzying pace of change in the Soviet Union, which pushed the Bush administration to make a radical break from the tradition of mutual arms control agreements crafted in months or years of negotiations.

Bush announced that the United States would scrap more than 3,000 short-range nuclear weapons, pull back 1,275 more from the front lines and remove from alert nearly 2,700 weapons on strategic bombers and missiles. He canceled development of several weapons, including mobile launchers for the MX and Midgetman intercontinental ballistic missiles (ICBMs), which over the years had been the subject of some fierce legislative battles on Capitol Hill. *(Background, box, p. 343)*

He called on Moscow to negotiate a ban on land-based ICBMs with multiple warheads and to ease the 1972 anti-ballistic missile (ABM) treaty. The treaty revision sought by the administration would permit deployment of defenses such as the so-called GPALS (an acronym for "global protection against limited strikes"), which was Bush's version of the strategic defense initiative (SDI). The treaty permitted deployment of no more than 100 ground-based anti-missile rockets at one site and banned anti-missile weapons in space. But GPALS would place several hundred interceptor rockets at up to six U.S. sites in addition to several hundred "brilliant pebbles" interceptors in orbit. *(SDI background, box, p. 370)*

The tactical nuclear weapons that Bush unilaterally scrapped had been a source of political controversy for years in Western Europe, where more than 6,000 such weapons were stationed in the late 1970s.

"When the Soviet Union and its Warsaw Pact allies had the edge in non-nuclear military power, we felt we needed nuclear weapons to compensate," said House Armed Services Committee Chairman Les Aspin, D-Wis. "Now, the United States has the edge in conventional military forces, and we're concerned with such things as terrorist use of nuclear weapons and unauthorized or accidental use."

Congress' Reaction

Bush's arms cutbacks drew enthusiastic support at home and abroad. Responding to Bush's speech on behalf of the Democratic Party, Senate Majority Leader George J. Mitchell of Maine applauded the nuclear reduction moves as steps toward a more secure peace. But he pointedly added that they also were important because "they will enable us to concentrate our efforts and our resources on meeting urgent needs at home."

Most domestic criticism of Bush's proposal came from Democrats unhappy that he still championed the costly B-2 "stealth" bomber and the SDI program. *(B-2 bomber, box, p. 398)*

But some conservative members warned that the package went too far. Senate Armed Services Committee member Malcolm Wallop, R-Wyo., argued that the nuclear cutbacks were risky, in part because they would be difficult to reverse if the Soviet Union's political reforms failed.

Senate Armed Services Chairman Sam Nunn, D-Ga., endorsed the thrust of Bush's package but argued that development of a mobile launcher for the single-warhead Midgetman missile should be continued as a non-threatening hedge against future dangers.

Nunn also objected to taking all U.S. bombers off alert, warning that the crews might lose their edge and that officials would become loath to put bombers back on alert in a crisis for fear of creating a panic. He recommended that the Pentagon routinely put on alert some randomly selected bombers.

Gorbachev's Response

On Oct. 5, Soviet President Mikhail S. Gorbachev matched Bush's initiative with a pledge to scrap unilaterally thousands of short-range (tactical) nuclear weapons.

Gorbachev also upped the diplomatic ante by announcing that he would retire unilaterally 1,000 long-range (strategic) Soviet weapons in addition to those that would have to be scrapped under the strategic arms reduction talks (START) treaty, signed July 31. And he called on Bush to negotiate an additional 50 percent reduction in strategic arms.

"We are decisively advancing the process of disarmament," he said. Gorbachev also renewed arms control measures that the Bush administration already had rejected, such as a one-year ban on underground nuclear testing. Pentagon officials had long insisted that continued testing was essential to ensure the safety and effectiveness of the U.S. nuclear stockpile. But a ban was enacted in 1992. *(Details, p. 392)*

Gorbachev also appeared to temper the Soviet Union's longstanding opposition to SDI. "We are prepared to consider proposals from the United States of America on non-nuclear anti-missile defense systems," he said, suggesting "joint systems for warning against a nuclear missile attack with elements based in space and on land."

Warhead Allotments

	1990	START I	START II
Total Warheads			
United States	12,646	8,556	3,500
Soviet Union	11,012	6,163	3,000
Total Warheads on Land-Based Missiles			
United States	2,450	1,400	500
Russia	6,612	3,153	504
Total Warheads on Multiple-Warhead, Land-Based Missiles			
United States	2,000	1,100	0
Russia	5,958	2,460	0

would let the Soviet Union supply the planes to overfly Soviet territory.

However, Moscow repudiated a tentative agreement on those terms after Shevardnadze, warning of the threat of a right-wing coup, resigned in December 1990. Such a putsch came in August 1991, led by Defense Minister Dmitri T. Yazov and other hard-liners. Although the coup failed, it led to the Soviet Union's collapse.

Open Skies negotiations resumed late that year, and the deal finally struck was along the lines Shevardnadze had proposed.

Provisions. The Open Skies treaty that resulted was signed in Helsinki, Finland, by the United States, the 15 other NATO members, the five surviving members of the Warsaw Pact and four former Soviet republics: Russia, Belarus, Ukraine and Georgia.

The inspection regime in the treaty was not designed to verify compliance with specific arms limitations but was intended to moderate international tensions by making countries' military deployments more "transparent."

Besides conventional cameras, the treaty provided that the inspection planes could carry infrared viewing equipment to permit night operations and radar that could detect ground objects covered by clouds. The radar authorized for use in the treaty could not distinguish between a truck and a tank. To thwart commercial espionage of the detection equipment, the treaty allowed use only of gear already on the commercial market.

The pact assigned each of the 25 countries an annual quota of reconnaissance flights that it must allow other signatories over any part of its territory on 72 hours' notice. The most overflights assigned to any country was 42, the number accepted by the United States and by Russia and Belarus, which shared a quota. The treaty required Ukraine and several large NATO members to accept 12 overflights annually and assigned fewer flights to smaller European countries, with Portugal having the lowest quota, two flights.

For the first three years after the treaty was ratified, however, each country's quota was to be reduced by 25 percent. Each signatory was allowed to conduct the same number of overflights of any other country that it received from that country.

Nuclear Test Ban

After many attempts in previous years, Congress in 1992 acted to ban all nuclear test explosions after Sept. 30, 1996. The final version of a $22 billion energy and water appropriations bill (HR 5373 — PL 102-377) incorporated the provision, initially adopted in the Senate, that banned underground nuclear weapons tests for nine months. Existing treaties banned testing in the air and at sea.

After the nine months, the bill allowed a limited number of tests through 1996 to test safety-related improvements to weapons already deployed. It banned all underground explosive tests after Sept. 30, 1996, unless another country conducted such tests.

Test ban opponents first appended test limitation provisions to the House and Senate versions of the defense authorization bill (HR 5006 — PL 102-484). But the provisions were dropped because the energy and water appropriations measure included the test ban in a package that was too politically appealing for a reluctant Bush administration to veto. Despite his vigorous opposition to the test ban, President Bush accepted the bill, in large part because it included funding for the superconducting supercollider, a huge atom smasher to be built in Texas.

Background

For four decades, a test ban was mostly a distant dream of liberal activists. Every president from Dwight D. Eisenhower to Ronald Reagan proclaimed an end to testing as a national goal, but only Jimmy Carter accorded the goal more than lip service.

In fiscal 1986 through 1988, the House annually had approved an amendment to the defense authorization bill that would have barred tests of nuclear weapons with an explosive punch greater than 1,000 tons of TNT. But those votes were largely symbolic, taken on the assumption the Senate would reject any significant nuclear test limitations. *(Congress and the Nation Vol. VII, p. 352)*

And, indeed, so long as the Soviet nuclear threat was intact, a majority of senators seemed to accept the contention of Pentagon and Energy Department nuclear weapons specialists that continuous testing was required to check on the safety and reliability of weapons already in the U.S. stockpile.

But with the disintegration of the Soviet Union — and with Russian President Boris N. Yeltsin observing a self-imposed nuclear test moratorium — test ban proponents in 1992 stepped up their efforts to terminate the U.S. testing program.

For the first time, they were supported by Senate Armed Services Committee Chairman Sam Nunn, D-Ga., who echoed what had long been one of the liberals' arguments: That a halt to testing might give Washington more diplomatic leverage to dissuade other countries from trying to develop nuclear weapons.

Legislative Action

Reacting to the end of the Cold War and the budget crunch at home, the House broke significant new ground with the $270 billion defense authorization bill for fiscal

1993 that it passed June 5. *(Fiscal 1993 defense authorization, p. 395)*

In particular, the House added to the bill (HR 5006) a one-year moratorium on nuclear weapons tests, a move that had long been vigorously opposed by Republican administrations.

The nuclear test ban amendment, adopted 237-167 on June 4, barred nuclear weapons test explosions during fiscal 1993 unless the president certified to Congress that a former Soviet republic had conducted a nuclear test. All former Soviet states except Russia had renounced nuclear weapons, and Russia announced its own test moratorium in 1991.

Reportedly, the United States conducted six tests annually, which defense officials said were necessary to check the reliability of weapons already in the stockpile and to design warheads with safety features that would make them less likely to explode in case of an accident and harder for a terrorist to detonate.

Test ban advocates contended that computer simulations and other non-explosive experiments could be used instead of test explosions. They also argued that a test ban would give the United States more diplomatic leverage to prevent additional countries from developing nuclear weapons. But critics of a test ban scoffed at that argument, saying that rogue nations would continue developing nuclear weapons whether the United States stopped testing or not.

The Bush administration faced an uphill battle in its attempts to head off the test ban. By early summer, more than half the Senate was already on record as endorsing the ban.

The White House in July announced a new administration policy to limit tests to those essential for safety and reliability but not for modernization. The administration said it expected to conduct no more than six tests per year over the next five years, with no more than three tests per year exceeding 35 kilotons, equal to 35,000 tons of TNT.

But some experts appearing before the Senate Foreign Relations Committee disputed the administration's position. They contended that testing was unnecessary either for safety reasons or as a deterrent to other nations considering developing nuclear weapons. The witnesses argued that, contrary to the administration's claim, the moratorium would encourage other nations to cease testing and would be an important step toward achieving nuclear nonproliferation.

On Aug. 3, the Senate approved 68-26 an amendment to the fiscal 1993 energy and water appropriations bill to impose a nine-month testing halt followed in 1996 by a permanent ban. That vote, however, overstated Senate support for the proposal because several opponents voted for the amendment for tactical reasons.

Armed Services Committee Chairman Nunn had offered a compromise testing proposal during his committee's markup of the defense authorization bill (HR 5006) in July. Nunn's plan would have allowed no more than three tests a year for safety reasons and phased out all testing by 1998. The committee did not agree to the plan.

Proponents of the ban then took their case to the Senate floor. The proposal faced its toughest challenge on Sept. 18, when the Senate, by a **key vote of 55-40 (R 13-29; D 42-11)**, attached to the defense bill a nine-month moratorium on nuclear testing. The provision also would have permanently banned all nuclear testing after fiscal 1996, unless another country was still conducting tests.

Senators rejected a proposal for a shorter initial moratorium followed by a permanent ban at the end of fiscal 1998. That proposal also would have allowed the president to waive the test ban for one year to gain leverage to negotiate a comprehensive test ban.

After Bush signed the energy and water bill, which contained the same provisions as the defense bill, conferees on the defense bill stripped their bill of the test ban language.

Military Base Closings

Congress in 1991 revisited the politically painful process of closing domestic military bases. After four months of deliberation and debate, lawmakers approved a proposal to close 34 military installations — 25 of them major — and realign 37 others. The closings would save an estimated $1.5 billion annually after fiscal 1998.

The fate of the bases on the list was sealed when the House voted against a resolution (H J Res 308) that would have blocked their closing.

The roots of this action dated back to a proposal by Defense Secretary Dick Cheney in January 1990 to close a group of bases. The list he released set off an explosion among Democrats, who said Cheney had unfairly singled out their bases.

That year, in the fiscal 1991 defense authorization measure (HR 4739 — PL 101-510), Congress blocked Cheney's list and included new rules to be used in closing bases. The 1991 base-closing process was the first of three rounds of base closings created in the bill, to be followed by potential closings in both 1993 and 1995. *(1990 action, p. 353)*

Commission Review

Under provisions of PL 101-510, Cheney assembled a new list of bases the Defense Department wanted to close and sent them on April 15 to an eight-member independent commission for review. Cheney proposed closing 31 major domestic military bases and 12 smaller ones and reducing operations at 28 others. The bases were scheduled to close between 1992 and 1997.

The Defense Base Closure and Realignment Commission then took up its assigned task of determining whether Cheney had "deviated substantially" from the published list of eight criteria that the Pentagon had used to decide which bases to close.

To determine the military value of a base, the Pentagon looked at:

- Mission requirements and operational readiness of the total force.
- Availability and condition of land, facilities and associated airspace at both the existing and potential receiving sites.
- Availability to accommodate contingency, mobilization and future total force requirements at both existing and potentially receiving sites.
- Cost and manpower implications.

To determine the impact of a closing, the Pentagon considered:

- The economic impact on communities.
- The ability of the infrastructures in both the existing and potential receiving communities to support forces, missions and personnel.
- The environmental effects.

The Pentagon's final criterion was relative costs —

Bases Slated for Closure or Realignment, 1992-97

Closures

Army

Fort Benjamin Harrison, Ind.
Fort Devens, Mass.
Fort Ord, Calif.
Sacramento Army Depot, Calif.

Navy

Chase Field Naval Air Station, Texas
Construction Battalion Center, Rhode Island
Hunters Point Annex to Treasure Island Naval Station, Calif.
Marine Corps Air Station, Tustin, Calif.
Moffett Field Naval Air Station, Calif.
Long Beach Naval Station, Calif.
Philadelphia Naval Shipyard, Pa.
Philadelphia Naval Station, Pa.
Puget Sound Naval Station, Sand Point, Wash.

Army and Navy labs
8 facilities

Air Force

Bergstrom Air Force Base, Texas
Carswell Air Force Base, Texas
Castle Air Force Base, Calif.
Eaker Air Force Base, Ark.
England Air Force Base, La.
Grissom Air Force Base, Ind.
Loring Air Force Base, Maine
Lowry Air Force Base, Colo.
Myrtle Beach Air Force Base, S.C.
Richards-Gebaur Air Reserve Station, Mo.
Rickenbacker Air Guard Base, Ohio
Williams Air Force Base, Ariz.
Wurtsmith Air Force Base, Mich.

Realignments

Army

Aviation Systems Command/Troop Support Command, St. Louis
Fort Chafee, Ark.
Fort Dix, N.J.
Fort Polk, La.
Letterkenny Army Depot, Pa.
Rock Island Arsenal, Ill.
10 Army RDT&E laboratories
7 Army medical labs

Navy

Midway Island Naval Air Facility
7 Navy RDT&E and Fleet Support Activities

Air Force

Beale Air Force Base, Calif.
Goodfellow Air Force Base, Texas
MacDill Air Force Base, Fla.
March Air Force Base, Calif.
Mather Air Force Base, Calif.
Mountain Home Air Force Base, Idaho

how much it would cost to close and move the base as opposed to keeping it open.

To justify adding or subtracting a base from Cheney's list, the commission had to demonstrate that the Defense Department deviated substantially from the force structure requirements and other criteria established by the department.

After months of hearings and lobbying by members, the commission, in a daylong meeting, voted to accept the vast majority of Cheney's proposals — deleting only four bases of the 31 major facilities from the original list and recommending cutbacks instead of closure of two others. The commission sent the revised list to President Bush July 1, and Bush approved the list July 10, passing it on to Congress.

Legislative Action

Congress had 45 working days in which to accept or reject the list. The House Armed Services Committee voted July 24 to recommend that the House reject the resolution to block the base closings (H J Res 308 — H Rept 102-163). The Armed Services panel could have defeated the resolution outright, but House leaders had promised that the entire membership would have an opportunity to vote on the issue.

The next day the Senate Armed Services Committee voted to reject a resolution (S J Res 175 — S Rept 102-123) that would prevent bases from closing.

In a procedure established by Congress to shackle its own pork-barrel proclivities, members were only able to cast an all-or-nothing vote on whether to reject the entire list. And, over the passionate objections of many members who were going to lose bases in their districts, the House voted 60-364 on July 30 against H J Res 308.

The resolution never made it to the floor of the Senate because the House defeat of the resolution made the Senate bill moot.

Congress, however, did say no to the base-closing commission's recommendation that the U.S. Army Corps of Engineers be reorganized. The reorganization plan, crafted by the corps, would have consolidated many of its administrative and advisory functions. But lawmakers included in the fiscal 1992 defense authorization measure (HR 2100 — PL 102-190) language that retroactively prohibited the commission from taking any action regarding the corps. *(Fiscal 1992 defense authorization, p. 369)*

The corps builds projects such as dams, ports and water control facilities, which are among the most tangible benefits a member of Congress can provide for his or her district. Members were sensitive to any change that might impinge upon their ability to bring home the "pork" of public works projects.

The House also registered its belief that other countries should share the pain of losing U.S. military installations, voting 412-14 on July 30 on a joint resolution (H J Res 313) to include overseas bases in additional rounds of closings in 1993 and 1995.

Members argued that, just as the changing world necessitated closing domestic bases, so should it result in the closure of foreign bases. The Bush administration strongly opposed the resolution, arguing that it would make closing overseas bases more cumbersome, not easier. Shortly before the House took up the issue, the Defense Department announced that the United States planned to close 72 overseas bases in six countries over the next four years.

1993 Defense Authorization

In shaping the fiscal 1993 defense authorization bill, Congress in 1992 made few dramatic cuts in the Pentagon's budget request. Congressional demands to reduce defense spending generally gave way to election-year concerns that defense jobs would be lost.

The final bill (HR 5006 — PL 102-484) authorized $274 billion for defense-related programs, a $7 billion reduction from President Bush's $281 billion request.

However, several provisions in the authorization bill laid the groundwork for potential cuts in manpower and hardware spending by the mid-1990s going far beyond the long-term reductions that Bush had outlined for the post-Soviet world.

In their versions of the bill, the Senate and House each recommended significant cuts in several major weapons programs. But with the economy in disarray and defense industries already squeezed by Bush's cutbacks, the conferees could agree on only a few major reductions. The bill:

- Authorized $4.05 billion — about three-quarters of the amount Bush requested — to continue the anti-missile defense program known as the strategic defense initiative (SDI). Sentiment in the Senate for deeper cuts endangered the overall bill and stalled floor action for more than a month until a compromise was reached. The companion defense appropriations bill (HR 5504 — PL 102-396) funded SDI at the $3.8 billion anticipated in the Senate compromise.
- Included the $2.7 billion sought by the administration to buy four final B-2 "stealth" bombers, bringing the fleet of radar-evading planes to 20. But before more B-2s could be built, Congress required that the Pentagon report back on the plane's cost and capability and that members then cast a vote to proceed.
- Sliced about a fourth from the amounts Bush requested for F/A-18 combat jets and C-17 long-range cargo planes.

But more typically, conferees who shaped the final version of the bill backed whichever chamber approved the larger amount for new fighter planes. They, however, did signal Congress' concern that the Pentagon was committing too much money to develop too many tactical planes in an effort to fulfill the wish lists of each service. The Pentagon had plans under way to spend $350 billion over two decades on a new generation of fighters. The conference bill held back some of the funds for development of the new aircraft until the Pentagon presented a long-term plan to consolidate and pay for them.

- Cushioned the impact of defense cutbacks on military personnel, defense companies and local economies by authorizing $1.5 billion for "economic conversion" programs. This included $694 million for technology programs aimed at helping the defense industry adapt to the commercial marketplace, $132 million to help communities adjust to defense-related changes and $686 million for transition assistance to personnel leaving the services.
- Adopted the administration's request to cut the number of active-duty military personnel to 1,766,500, a reduction of 100,400 from the cap in fiscal 1992. The measure also set a ceiling of 1,095,080 on membership in National Guard and reserve units — a reduction of 40,000 instead of the 116,000-member cutback sought by the administration. The bill also ordered additional cutbacks on U.S. deployments in Europe by the end of fiscal 1996.

In addition to authorizing funds for military programs of the Department of Defense, the defense bill included $11.9 billion for defense-related programs of the Energy Department, most of which involved the development and manufacture of nuclear weapons and nuclear power plants for Navy ships.

Bush Proposals

When Bush presented his fiscal 1993 budget, he offered what he portrayed as a $50 billion defense cut. More precisely, he proposed cutting $50 billion over five years from the $1.7 trillion, six-year defense plan that he had proposed a year earlier for the same period.

Bush's approach to defense budget-cutting produced a gap between long-range reductions and immediate savings. The president offered no significant cuts in the budget for the military payroll — beyond the five-year, 25 percent reduction that was already under way — or for operations and maintenance.

Cutting uniformed manpower more rapidly would have required involuntary discharges on a large scale, which Pentagon officials contended would shatter the morale of personnel. And they argued that the projected budget for operations and maintenance was essential so that the smaller force that was being shaped could retain its fighting edge.

Instead, Bush accelerated his previously planned cutbacks by slicing more deeply into weapons procurement and development. But money for such military hardware was doled out to contractors in installments over several years. Thus, cuts in budget authority for procurement and research yielded much smaller reductions in immediate outlays.

Bush linked his hardware-heavy defense cuts to the demise of the Soviet Union in two ways:

- Because Russian President Boris N. Yeltsin and leaders of the other former Soviet republics had agreed to radical reductions in nuclear weaponry, Bush proposed a sharp cutback in the production of strategic arms, including ending production of the B-2 bomber after 20 planes and canceling outright production of long-range, bomber-launched cruise missiles and of powerful nuclear warheads for Trident II submarine-launched missiles.

- On the assumption that Pentagon planners no longer needed to anticipate a massive Soviet weapons program aimed at nullifying the technical superiority of U.S. conventional arms, the budget request embodied a fundamental shift in the Pentagon's weapons procurement strategy.

Under the new approach, Defense Secretary Dick Cheney announced, the Pentagon would continue to fund the development of new prototypes intended to push back the frontiers of weapons technology. But not all of those new weapons would be rushed to the assembly line.

The new plan's most immediate results would be cancellation of production plans for the *Seawolf*-class nuclear submarine and for the Army's Comanche helicopter. Bush's budget would continue planned production of other high-tech weapons, including Aegis destroyers for the Navy and the Air Force's C-17 cargo plane. Moreover, development of the Air Force's new F-22 fighter would continue, with the expectation of full-scale production beginning in 1996. *(*Seawolf *submarine, p. 410)*

House Committee Action

On May 13, the House Armed Services Committee approved, 47-8, a defense authorization bill (HR 5006 — H Rept 102-527) for fiscal 1993 that would trim Bush's $281 billion budget request to $274 billion, the amount earmarked for defense by the House-passed version of the annual budget resolution. The Senate had passed a budget resolution allowing $6 billion more for defense.

The House Armed Services bill, formally reported May 19, included $1 billion for a yet-to-be drafted program to cushion the economic impact of a long-term cutback in defense spending. Most of the cuts the Armed Services panel made in Bush's request came from certain supply, maintenance and overhead funds. The panel insisted that these funds could be pared without affecting the safety or combat readiness of U.S. forces.

The committee's bill included most of the money Bush requested for major weapons, including the B-2 stealth bomber and SDI. The $2.7 billion recommended by the panel for B-2 bombers was the amount Bush requested for four more planes to fill out the scaled-down fleet of 20 B-2s the Pentagon was seeking. That small force, intended to carry non-nuclear precision-guided "smart" bombs, was similar to what House Armed Services Committee Chairman Les Aspin, D-Wis., and other congressional leaders had been calling for. Earlier Air Force plans had envisioned many more B-2s and put more emphasis on their ability to carry nuclear weapons.

But the committee, which for several years had opposed building more B-2s, was not convinced that the big bat-winged plane would be as difficult for radars to detect as specifications required or that the Air Force had driven a hard enough bargain to buy out the contract at the lowest price. So the panel specified that money could not be spent until the Pentagon reported on the plane's capabilities and cost and Congress voted explicitly to allow expenditure of the $2.7 billion.

The committee bill approved the bulk of Bush's SDI budget — $4.3 billion of the $5.4 billion requested. Bush's request mirrored the policy enacted by Congress in 1991: that the program's top priority should be deployment over several years of a ground-based missile defense that complied with the 1972 U.S.-Soviet treaty limiting anti-ballistic missile (ABM) defenses.

But the committee denied the entire $576 million requested to develop "brilliant pebbles" — space-based anti-missile interceptors, favored by many Republicans but barred by the ABM treaty.

Continuing a three-year feud between Congress and Cheney, the committee added to the bill $755 million to continue development of the V-22 Osprey, a hybrid airplane/helicopter sought by the Marine Corps as a troop carrier. Asserting that the Osprey would be too expensive, Cheney had tried to kill it. But it enjoyed strong support in the large congressional delegations from Texas and Pennsylvania, home to the Osprey's prime contractors. The committee added a provision to cut the office budget of the Pentagon comptroller 5 percent for each month the department refused to spend $790 million that Congress appropriated in fiscal 1992 for the V-22. In July, Cheney reversed his long-held position and agreed to a compromise that included moving ahead with the Osprey's development. *(V-22 Osprey, box, p. 406)*

The panel approved a plan to significantly reorder the Pentagon's plans for a new generation of tactical combat aircraft. Under the committee's approach, the top priority would be fielding the AX, a new carrier-based bomber to replace the Navy's venerable A-6E. The panel's bill increased funding for the AX, while reducing funding for other tactical aircraft.

The committee's tactical aircraft package reflected a new approach to weapons procurement in a period when the Soviet threat had evaporated and Pentagon budgets were headed downward. The committee called for extensive testing of prototypes to wring out problems before signing up for full production of a complex new weapon. In another example of this more cautious approach, the committee slowed production of the C-17 cargo plane.

A second theme of the House Armed Services' procurement approach was the importance it placed on spending to upgrade some weapons and to buy others at a slow rate to keep key contractors in the defense business at a time of cutbacks. The committee, for example, ordered the Pentagon to spend $225 million that was appropriated in fiscal 1992 to upgrade early model M-1 tanks with the larger cannon and night-vision equipment of later versions. The panel added money for other equipment as well.

The committee also ordered the Air Force to plan on buying more F-16 Air Force fighters in fiscal 1994, instead of ending production with the 24 planes authorized for fiscal 1993 ($649 million). The $68 million the Pentagon requested to shut down the line would be used instead to buy components for additional planes in fiscal 1994.

The committee's approach was intended to keep the F-16 production line going as a hedge, in case the F-22 program went sour. It also held open the option of developing an improved F-16 as a lower-cost complement to the F-22. And the promise of continued employment at General Dynamics' F-16 plant in Fort Worth, Texas, did not hurt the political prospects for Aspin's bill in the third-largest state delegation in the House.

The committee sought to retain slightly more National Guard and reserve members than the administration had proposed. This was in part an acknowledgment of the political clout of Guard and reserve units scattered across most congressional districts. But Aspin also insisted that

National Guard ground combat divisions were a good buy, costing a fourth as much to operate as units staffed by full-time Army personnel.

House Floor Action

Reacting to the end of the Cold War and to the budget crunch at home, the House broke significant new ground with the $270 billion defense authorization bill it passed June 5 by a vote of 198-168.

The House added a moratorium on nuclear weapons tests, a move that had long been vigorously opposed by Republican administrations. And the House earmarked $1 billion of Pentagon funding to help defense contractors, their employees and their communities adjust to the long-term defense spending retrenchment.

But the House debate also highlighted an important change in the politics of defense budgeting in the solidly Democratic House. As had become usual in recent years, the bill bore the strong imprint of Armed Services Committee Chairman Aspin. This time, however, on two of the bill's most contentious issues, Aspin prevailed over a majority of fellow Democrats by linking centrist Democrats with a nearly solid Republican bloc. The bipartisan alliance protected Aspin's proposals, embodied in the committee bill, to authorize:

- $4.3 billion for an SDI program aimed at deploying ground-based interceptors within several years.

Aspin's center-right coalition defeated an amendment that would have slowed work on the anti-missile program. The amendment cutting $938 million from the SDI funding recommended by Armed Services was rejected June 5 by a **key vote of 161-211 (R 11-134; D 149-77; I 1-0).** *(1992 key votes, p. 1083)*

The House June 5 also rejected outright, 117-248, an amendment that would have slashed the total for anti-missile development to $2.3 billion, with $1.1 billion earmarked for theater defense work and $1.2 billion for defenses against strategic missiles.

- $2.7 billion to buy four more B-2 bombers, fielding a fleet of 20, provided the Pentagon could convince Congress that the stealth plane could deliver acceptably, even if imperfectly, on its promised invisibility to radar. To hold this position, Aspin beat back an amendment to bar procurement of additional B-2 bombers. The 162-212 vote June 5 by which the House rejected the amendment reflected the same underlying pattern of liberal Democrats being overpowered by a coalition of Republicans with more conservative Democrats.

Aspin and his aides touted the nuclear test ban and economic conversion provisions as new issues for a post-Cold War era in which old left-right labels had lost their meaning. But many of Aspin's Democratic opponents contended that he was ignoring new realities, shoring up political support for costly weapons at a time when the deficit was climbing and domestic needs went unmet.

The relatively close vote to pass the defense bill obscured the strength of the center-right alliance on SDI and the B-2 because most Democrats supported final passage (167-56), while Republicans voted heavily against it (30-112). Republican opposition may have been fueled in part by adoption of two amendments:

- To allow service members stationed abroad and their dependents to obtain privately funded abortions in U.S. military hospitals. The amendment was adopted, 216-193, on June 4.
- To cut $3.5 billion from the amount authorized for overseas base costs. The amendment, adopted 220-185 on June 3, stipulated that U.S. troops could remain but only if allied governments offset the cut in U.S. funding.

This amendment was one of several so-called burden-sharing amendments the House adopted that were aimed at reducing the cost of Pentagon operations overseas. Their adoption reflected a smoldering congressional sentiment that U.S. deployments abroad effectively subsidized allies who also were commercial rivals, permitting them to invest in their economies money that they would otherwise have to spend on defense.

Another amendment, adopted 241-162 on June 3, barred the deployment in Europe of more than 100,000 U.S. military personnel after fiscal 1995. The cap on troops in Europe was 235,000; about 210,000 were deployed there. The Bush administration wanted to retain about 150,000 troops.

The House June 3 also approved, 225-177, an amendment requiring that U.S. military personnel stationed abroad be reduced by 40 percent by the end of fiscal 1995.

The nuclear test ban amendment, adopted 237-167 on June 4, would bar nuclear weapons test explosions during fiscal 1993 unless the president certified to Congress that a former Soviet republic had conducted a nuclear test. The amendment was a forerunner of a test ban that was eventually forced on a reluctant Bush administration as part of the annual energy and water appropriations bill (HR 5373 — PL 102-377). *(Underground testing ban, p. 392)*

The House also adopted an economic conversion package. The congressional budget resolution had earmarked $1 billion of the fiscal 1993 defense budget to help laid-off defense workers and military personnel, weapons contractors and communities adjust to the rapid drop in defense spending brought on by the Soviet collapse. House Democrats assembled a 188-page amendment to parcel out the money among several existing programs, which they argued would not only cushion the shock of cutbacks but also would channel industrial and human resources into new areas that would generate economic growth. The Democratic package was adopted 275-105 on June 4.

The economic conversion amendment required defense contractors to give hiring preference to displaced military personnel and defense workers. The House June 4 rejected, 147-235, a Republican amendment that would have given the Pentagon discretion over whether to apply that requirement and would have deleted various other provisions.

Senate Committee Action

The Senate Armed Services Committee approved a $274.5 billion defense authorization bill (S 3114 — S Rept 102-352) July 24 after debate on issues including the B-2 stealth bomber and SDI.

The Senate committee bill, reported July 31, would authorize:

- $4.3 billion of the $5.4 billion requested for the SDI anti-missile program, the same amount approved by the House.
- $2.7 billion, as requested, to buy four additional B-2s, which would bring to 20 the number approved by Congress.

As happened a year earlier, the fate of these two controversial programs became linked in the end-game bargaining within the committee. To pressure Armed Services Committee Chairman Sam Nunn, D-Ga., and other centrist

Congress, White House Reached Agreement ...

After years of controversy, Congress and the Bush administration in 1992 agreed to end the B-2 "stealth" bomber program. A goal of 20 bombers was set, a far cry from the originally envisioned fleet of 132.

As defense budgets had tightened and domestic programs were cut back, the costly bomber had become increasingly difficult to justify. Questions about the performance and effectiveness of the high-tech aircraft made members more uneasy. And then, with the demise of the Soviet Union, the bomber lost much of its original mission. Although supporters attempted to promote a conventional role for the bomber, it was not an easy sell.

Background

President Jimmy Carter's administration first made public in 1980 what had been a top-secret effort to develop the stealth bomber.

The United States' edge in aerial combat — and billions of dollars of defense spending — was riding on the stealth design as the high-tech premise for a new generation of U.S. warplanes. Stealth was not a single design technique or piece of hardware. Making an airplane stealthy involved masking the many telltale indicators that would allow an enemy to locate and destroy it.

The B-2 bomber was the most costly and controversial of the Pentagon's stealth aircraft. Its manta ray shape and some of its other exotic features were intended to muffle its radar "signature," while its jet engines were designed and placed to mask the heat of their exhaust.

The B-2 was designed mostly of curved surfaces that were sculpted so that probing radio waves would glance off without producing a strong echo. Its wing was thick enough that the plane's engines, bombload and fuel all could be stored inside, instead of being slung underneath on pylons that would stick out like sore thumbs on a radar screen. And its skin and skeleton were made of a synthetic material that absorbed most energy from a radar wave instead of reflecting it as metal would. A skin of wood or conventional plastic would be nearly transparent to radar waves but would expose the B-2's engines, electronic gear and other metal innards.

Heated Debate

For decades, liberal arms control activists had challenged the need for sophisticated bombers able to fly through Soviet air defenses, insisting that the same mission could be performed more cheaply by small, long-range cruise missiles, fired from planes beyond the reach of Soviet defenses.

But in 1989, significant change occurred in the debate over the B-2. Liberals were joined by several GOP defense stalwarts, who insisted that the B-2 fleet of 132 aircraft — with a projected price tag of some $70 billion — was just too expensive given the current circumstances. Rep. Larry J. Hopkins, R-Ky., for instance, citing the large annual appropriations needed when B-2 production got into full swing asked, "Can we afford $8 billion or $9 billion a year for one item?" Rep. John R. Kasich, R-Ohio, strayed even further from strategic orthodoxy, when he suggested during hearings that air-launched cruise missiles could obviate the need for a new manned bomber.

The severity of the budget crunch facing the Pentagon was demonstrated in 1989 by Defense Secretary Dick Cheney's controversial proposals for defense cutbacks. Another factor in the debate was the bad taste left in many members' mouths by the technical shortcomings facing the B-1B bomber fleet. They argued that the sophisticated B-2 had not undergone sufficient testing.

Cheney, Senate Armed Services Committee Chairman Sam Nunn, D-Ga., and other B-2 proponents said the critics' per-plane estimate of $500 million grossly inflated the cost, given that the $23 billion spent by 1989 had yielded a wealth of technical know-how. Excluding money already spent, the average "fly-away" cost of each B-2 would be about $274 million, supporters insisted — about 20 percent more than a new B-1B bomber would cost.

The influential Nunn mounted a forceful defense of the B-2 program. He argued that the B-2 was a crucial deterrent to nuclear confrontation and a more stable one than sea- and land-launched ballistic missiles because the planes could be easily recalled in the event of a mistake. The radar-evading bombers, which could carry up to 20 nuclear weapons each, were designed to penetrate Soviet defenses and retaliate against a first-strike attack upon the United States.

Nunn said the United States would benefit from the B-2 because its development would force the Soviets to spend billions of dollars to upgrade their air-defense system. "That is money that will not go into tanks; that is money that will not go into insurgencies around the world; that is money that will not go into repressing other countries; that is money that will not go into a conventional threat in Europe," he said during Senate debate on the fiscal 1990 defense authorization bill.

In addition, Nunn and other defenders of the bomber argued that the B-2's development was crucial to the U.S. position in the ongoing strategic arms reduction talks (START) in Geneva. This was the case, they said, because of a Soviet agreement not to count any but the first bomb on a B-2 in meeting START totals.

... To End B-2 'Stealth' Bomber Program

In 1990, the Bush administration continued to defend the B-2 as fundamental to U.S. strategic defenses. But the number of B-2s planned was reduced from 132 to 75, trimming the total cost of the fleet from $72 billion to $61 billion.

By the following year, international politics and the strategic equation had changed dramatically. B-2 defenders had always insisted that the bomber was needed to counter the ever-improving strategic forces of the Soviet superpower. But that rationale evaporated in 1991 with the dissolution of the Soviet Union.

Instead, officials at the Pentagon and executives of the Northrop Corp., the prime contractor for the B-2, began to promote it as a weapon for conventional, high-intensity warfare. As a prime selling point, they cited the success in the Persian Gulf War of the smaller F-117 stealth fighter.

But their efforts were set back when the Pentagon announced in September 1991 that an undisclosed flaw had been found in a flight test of the bomber's crucial radar-evading capabilities. Although Defense Department officials declined to provide any information on the classified tests, they insisted that the problem was manageable. Nonetheless, the admission of a problem gave critics new ammunition in the debate over the costly plane.

Additional doubts about the B-2's prospects for survival were created when President Bush in September 1991 proposed a series of unilateral arms reductions to reflect the fading of the Soviet threat. Although the B-2 was spared from cutbacks, the president's move emboldened the plane's critics and troubled some supporters.

"The American people are going to ask the question, 'If there's that much less threat ... why do we need to put that much money into a bomber?' " Senate Armed Services Committee member Trent Lott, R-Miss., said. "I'm a guy who's voted for the B-2 every time, but ... it's getting tougher every time."

In 1992, Bush reduced the goal for the B-2 once again as he presented his fiscal 1993 budget proposal, calling for an end to production after the completion of 20 planes. In addition to the 15 planes already authorized, Bush sought permission to spend funds appropriated the previous year for a 16th plane and requested funding for four more.

In reducing its ambitions for the size of the B-2 fleet, the administration was driven by efforts to cut Pentagon spending and by a new round of weapons cutbacks promised by Bush and Russian President Boris N. Yeltsin.

Legislative Action

Congress in 1989 voted to continue but slow the production rate of the B-2. The fiscal 1990 defense authorization bill (HR 2461 — PL 101-189) authorized funds for two planes in fiscal 1990, as well as components that could be used for five planes in fiscal 1991. Money for the two planes could not be spent until the B-2 met various flight-test requirements and Congress received reports on aspects of the plane's cost and performance. To underscore their contention that they were not yet committed to full-scale production of the costly plane, conferees on the fiscal 1990 bill included a provision requiring the Pentagon to report on the cost and national security impact of buying fewer than the 132 planes planned at that time. *(Fiscal 1990 defense authorization, p. 340)*

Supporters and opponents of the B-2 expected that the fate of the plane would be decided in 1990, but, by year's end, Congress had resolutely sidestepped the issue. During consideration of the fiscal 1991 defense authorization bill, the Senate had supported the B-2; the House had not. The final bill (HR 4739 — PL 101-510) called for continued B-2 procurement. But in the conference report, members were calculatedly vague about whether the funds in the bill could be spent only to pay cost-overruns on the 15 bombers previously authorized (as House members asserted) or used to buy additional B-2s (as senators maintained). *(Fiscal 1991 defense authorization, p. 355)*

In 1991, conferees on the fiscal 1992 defense authorization bill (HR 2100 — PL 102-190) forged a deal that balanced House opposition to the B-2 against continuing Senate support. The agreement authorized funding for continued research and development of the B-2 and for building additional parts and components — keeping the production line intact — but barred construction of additional planes beyond the 15 previously authorized. And it provided money for a 16th plane — but only if Congress subsequently approved it by law. *(Fiscal 1992 defense authorization, p. 369)*

Congress approved Bush's 1992 request for funds to build a final set of four B-2 bombers. But lawmakers provided that the money for those planes and for a fifth, which was previously appropriated, could not be spent until passage of follow-up legislation. The subsequent approval was to be based on reports that Congress demanded from the Pentagon on the stealth plane's cost and its effectiveness in evading radar detection. The provisions were incorporated in the fiscal 1993 defense authorization (HR 5006 — PL 102-484). *(Fiscal 1993 defense authorization, p. 395)*

Supporters of the B-2 boasted of their success in keeping the program alive; opponents declared victory in that construction of the costly aircraft was coming to a close.

Democrats to boost the SDI authorization in the bill, Republicans threatened to block additional procurement of the B-2, a bomber Nunn strongly supported.

At first, Nunn proposed $4 billion for SDI, including $200 million for the space-based interceptor missiles — known as brilliant pebbles — that most Republicans viewed as the key to eventual expansion beyond an initial ground-based deployment that would have only limited capability. Three amendments that would have increased the SDI total — and brilliant pebbles' share of the total — were rejected by narrow margins, with the committee splitting essentially along party lines. Then, with Republican support, the committee voted to drop funding for the additional B-2s. Panel members finally compromised on an SDI authorization of $4.3 billion, including $350 million earmarked for brilliant pebbles. The committee then voted to reinstate funding for the four B-2s.

When the dust had settled, the essential politics of the committee's SDI position seemed unchanged from 1991. Once again, a tenuous alliance of right and center had lined up behind an SDI program aimed at deploying a limited, ground-based system while deferring until the next decade any deployment of space-based anti-missile weapons. *(1991 action, box, p. 370)*

But SDI opponents planned to try, as they did in 1991, to break the pro-deployment coalition when the bill reached the Senate floor. Opponents of the B-2 also planned another effort to block funding.

The Senate committee's bill included the $2.2 billion requested to develop the Air Force's new F-22 fighter. But it ordered the Pentagon to pick and choose among several other proposed new combat planes to eliminate duplication.

The panel approved $944 million of the $1.1 billion requested to develop larger versions of the Navy's F/A-18 fighter. But the panel also ordered the Air Force to buy these "E" and "F" models of the F/A-18 as less expensive complements to the F-22. The Air Force had planned to develop a new plane.

The committee eliminated from the bill $683 million requested to buy the final 24 F-16 fighters that the Air Force had planned to purchase. The House bill authorized funding for those planes and ordered the Air Force to continue F-16 purchases for the next few years.

The committee bill also included provisions to make reducing the size of the military easier by encouraging more military and civilian personnel to retire voluntarily.

Senate Floor Action

The Senate passed its $274 billion version of the defense authorization bill (S 3114) by voice vote in the early hours of Sept. 19 at the end of a marathon session in which it considered more than 60 amendments.

Approval of the bill had been delayed for more than a month after the vote on a floor amendment indicated sentiment in the Senate to slash $2 billion from Bush's $5.3 billion request for SDI. With Bush's threat of a veto to back them up, SDI backers vowed to block final action on any bill that would cut the anti-missile defense program that deeply.

Eventually, Armed Services Chairman Nunn and his allies engineered a compromise authorizing $3.8 billion for SDI research. The Senate bill also included the $2.69 billion the administration sought to build four final B-2 bombers. But it provided for a ban on nuclear testing that the administration opposed.

The movement in the Senate to outdo the House in cutting funding for SDI was a novel twist in the continuing dickering between the chambers. For several years, the Senate had backed higher funding than the House did for the administration's controversial anti-missile defense program. But in 1992, the Senate refused to kill an amendment by Budget Committee Chairman Jim Sasser, D-Tenn., to cut authorized funding for SDI to $3.3 billion, $1 billion less than the amount approved in June by the House. A move to table (kill) the SDI-cutting amendment failed Aug. 7, by a **key vote of 43-49 (R 34-5; D 9-44)**.

Malcolm Wallop, R-Wyo., the Senate's leading advocate of the administration's SDI program, then refused to let the Senate proceed to a final vote on the SDI-cutting amendment. The defense measure was pulled from the floor, and Nunn warned that the bill could die. If that happened, Nunn said, a stopgap appropriations bill would gut key programs and prohibit most of the post-Cold War "defense conversion" initiatives contained in the authorization bill.

Before the SDI dispute bogged down the defense bill, the Senate had adopted, 91-2, a purely symbolic amendment putting members on record in favor of provisions that the Armed Services Committee already had included to cushion the impact of the defense cutback on weapons manufacturers and their communities. The programs were priced at nearly $1.7 billion in fiscal 1993 alone.

Yielding by a narrow margin to threats of a veto, the Senate backed down from the effort to slash SDI funding. After rejecting, 48-50, the amendment Sept. 17 to reduce SDI funding to $3.3 billion, the Senate adopted, 52-46, Nunn's $3.8 billion SDI alternative. That move fit into an emerging pattern on Capitol Hill of Democratic efforts to avert showdowns with Bush that would delay adjournment, interfere with members' re-election campaigning and muddy the duel between Bush and Democratic presidential nominee Bill Clinton.

But another vote on the defense bill lay the groundwork for a major confrontation with Bush on nuclear testing. By a **key vote of 55-40 (R 13-29; D 42-11)**, the Senate Sept. 18 approved an amendment to impose a nine-month halt to nuclear tests. It would be followed by a permanent ban on tests after the end of fiscal 1996 unless another country was still conducting tests.

The test ban amendment was adopted instead of another that would have imposed a shorter initial moratorium followed by a permanent ban at the end of fiscal 1998. The alternative proposal also would have allowed the president to waive the test ban for one year to gain leverage to negotiate a comprehensive test ban.

But many members realized that the issue was likely to be determined — as it ultimately was — on the separate energy and water appropriations bill. Each chamber had included provisions to limit nuclear testing in its version of that bill. The administration had threatened to veto the defense bill if it included a testing ban.

The Senate also defied a veto threat by keeping language that would allow U.S. military personnel and their dependents stationed abroad to obtain abortions in overseas U.S. military hospitals, provided they paid for the procedure. By a vote of 36-55, the Senate Sept. 18 rejected an amendment that would have eliminated the abortion provision.

The Senate Sept. 18 also rejected, 45-53, an amendment to drop from the defense bill $2.69 billion for four additional B-2 stealth bombers.

By voice vote, the Senate agreed to an amendment barring the stationing in Europe of more than 100,000 U.S. personnel after fiscal 1996.

In other action, the Senate adopted by voice vote a number of amendments aimed at aiding the conversion of communities, defense workers and industries to a civilian economy. The most far-reaching of these would require early notification to defense contractor employees of possible layoffs because of canceled contracts. Employees would become eligible for retraining services under the Job Training Partnership Act six months before a scheduled layoff.

Conference Action

The conference committee completed its work on a $274.3 billion version of the defense authorization bill on Oct. 1. Senate-House conferees had found it easier to cut personnel and to cushion the economic impact of cutbacks than to cancel costly weapons.

Conferees embraced House initiatives affecting the politically influential National Guard and to slice the number of U.S. personnel overseas by 40 percent. And they adopted Senate proposals for a wide-ranging review of the division of labor among the armed services and to allow unneeded military personnel to retire after 15 years of service, instead of the 20 years that had been required.

When it came to cutting back on major weapons, however, the conferees agreed on long-range policies but not on specific, immediate reductions. In most cases, they opted for the more generous of the Senate and House alternatives as far as fiscal 1993 funding was concerned. For example, they rejected a House effort to cut more than $500 million from the plan to develop a new version of the Navy 's F/A-18 fighter plane and Senate attempts to terminate production of the Air Force's F-16 fighter and to slow preliminary work on a nuclear-powered aircraft carrier. And they acceded to the House proposal for $225 million to continue upgrading the Army's AHIP scout helicopters and the Senate's decision to add $1.2 billion for a large helicopter carrier.

In each case, proponents of the chosen option cited a post-Cold War need for the particular weapon. Taken collectively, however, the decisions suggested that — in an election year with the economy in trouble and the defense industry contracting rapidly even under Bush's program — it was easier for the conferees to agree on ways to give out money than on ways to cut off money.

Reflecting the Pentagon budget's transition away from the Soviet-oriented programs of the past, the battles over conventional weapons overshadowed disputes about strategic arms that had dominated congressional defense debates through the 1980s.

Conferees dropped from the defense bill two controversial provisions that had been included in other legislation:

- A ban on nuclear testing, which was incorporated into the energy and water appropriations bill (HR 5373). Despite administration opposition to the testing ban, Bush on Oct. 2 signed the energy spending bill, which also included $517 million for the superconducting supercollider, a politically appealing atom smasher in Texas.
- Authorization for military personnel and their dependents stationed abroad to obtain privately funded abortions in U.S. military hospitals. The provision was adopted in a separate bill (S 3144), with members fully aware that Bush would veto that measure.

Congress' reluctance to mandate immediate procurement cuts was vividly illustrated by the conferees' efforts to reshape plans for Navy and Air Force combat aircraft. The administration's budget request included funds to buy a final group of 24 F-16s ($683 million) and 48 "C" and "D" model F/A-18s ($1.66 billion). It also included nearly $3.5 billion as the down payment on a new generation of combat planes, including the Air Force's F-22 fighter, larger "E" and "F" models of the F/A-18 and a small carrier-based stealth bomber, designated AX.

Conferees approved the amount requested to buy the F-16s and begin shutting down the assembly line. The conferees did not mandate its termination, but they barred any expenditure to continue F-16 production beyond fiscal 1993 until the Pentagon submitted to Congress studies on the roles and missions and the funding of future combat aircraft programs.

Conferees cut funding for the F/A-18 by $513 million but authorized nearly the amounts requested for the new generation of development projects.

Although they did not agree on cuts in the three new programs, the conferees did lay the groundwork for subjecting the Navy and Air Force programs to a single set of policy and budget decisions. The conference report provided that:

- No more than 65 percent of the amount authorized for any of the three new programs could be spent until after submission of the reports on roles and missions and long-term funding.
- Both the AX and the F/A-18 E and F programs were required to rely more heavily on prototypes than the Navy had planned. In addition, the enlarged F/A-18 could not cost more than 125 percent of the cost of the current C and D model F/A-18s.

Other highlights of the conference report included:

- A $3 billion cut from the amount requested for spare parts and supplies, linked to various new rules intended to tighten the Pentagon's inventory control.
- $1.51 billion for "economic conversion," including $686 million for transition assistance to personnel leaving the services, $132 million to help communities adjust to defense-related changes in the local economy and $694 million for technology programs aimed at helping the defense industry adapt to the commercial marketplace.

The House approved the conference report (H Rept 102-966), 304-100, in a rare Saturday session on Oct. 3. The Senate voted to adopt the report by voice vote the same day, but paperwork delays held up formal action to clear the bill for the president until Oct. 5. Bush signed HR 5006 on Oct. 23.

Major Provisions

As signed into law, HR 5006 authorized $274.3 billion for defense-related programs of the Pentagon and Energy Department in fiscal 1993, $7.2 billion less than Bush had requested. The final bill was $200 million less than the Senate approved, but $3.2 billion more than was approved by the House.

Major provisions of the final bill:

Strategic Arms. Authorized, as requested, $1.26 billion to continue development of the B-2 stealth bomber and $2.69 billion to buy four additional B-2s so as to complete the scaled-down force of 20 planes sought by the Air Force.

Defense Conversion Programs Approved ...

Congress in 1992 added more than $1.5 billion in defense funds to President Bush's fiscal 1993 budget request to help military personnel, defense contractors and local communities adjust to the downturn in defense spending. The efforts, many of them expanding existing programs, were authorized in the annual defense authorization bill (HR 5006 — PL 102-484) and funded in the companion defense appropriations bill (HR 5504 — PL 102-396).

Philosophically opposed to such federal spending programs, the Bush administration had contended that the most effective ways to help those displaced by the military's downsizing was to improve the overall state of the economy.

But large, bipartisan majorities in Congress favored federal expenditures, drawn from the defense budget, to cushion the impact of the defense spending reductions that followed the end of the Cold War.

The House included $1 billion for defense conversion programs in its defense authorization measure. House Democrats had assembled a 188-page amendment to parcel out the money among several existing programs, which they argued would not only cushion the shock of cutbacks but also would channel industrial and human resources into new areas that would generate economic growth. The amendment was adopted 275-105 on June 4.

The Senate included $1.7 billion for defense conversion programs in its version of the defense authorization bill. The Senate Aug. 7 adopted, 91-2, a symbolic amendment that reprised defense conversion provisions that the Armed Services Committee had included in the bill. The most obvious and immediate payoff of the amendment was political. As several members rose on the Senate floor to laud the conversion package, several Democrats held a news conference nearby to lambaste the Bush administration's own conversion program as inadequate. The final version of the defense authorization bill included $1.5 billion for defense conversion programs.

Following are highlights of the defense conversion programs that were included in the bills:

Retirement Pay

In an initiative championed by Senate Armed Services Committee Chairman Sam Nunn, D-Ga., $254 million went to pay pensions to military personnel who took the option of retiring after 15 years of service instead of the 20 years previously required.

Nunn contended that the early retirement option obviated the need to dismiss service personnel before they were eligible for pensions. The option was to be available only through fiscal 1995 and only to service members in ranks and job specialties deemed overstaffed by Pentagon managers.

Early retirees would receive reduced annuities. But they could increase their military pensions after retirement, collecting credit — up to 20 years' service — by taking a job in some approved category of public service, such as education or law enforcement.

In addition, nearly $200 million was approved for programs intended to tide over displaced military and civilian employees of the Pentagon until they were established in new lines of work.

Worker Retraining

More than $200 million was provided to train former Pentagon and defense industry employees for new jobs. Of this amount, $84 million was for worker relocation and training programs conducted by the Labor Department under the Job Training Partnership Act (JTPA). A provision of the fiscal 1991 defense authorization bill (HR 4739 — PL 101-510) transferred $150 million in Pentagon funds to JTPA retraining and employment-assistance programs specifically aimed at displaced defense workers.

Besides transferring an additional $75 million for the program, the fiscal 1993 authorization bill amended JTPA to increase the number of defense workers who were eligible for its programs because of "substantial" layoffs by their employers. It reduced from 100 to 50 the number of jobs lost for a layoff to qualify as "substantial."

Among the retraining initiatives in the bills were:

- $75 million to reimburse companies that hired former military personnel for part of the cost of retraining them.
- $65 million to help former military personnel, civilian Pentagon employees and defense industry workers become teachers. Participants could receive up to $5,000 to cover the cost of preparing for certification as teachers. For their first two years as teachers, their salaries could be underwritten by the Defense Department up to a total of $50,000.
- $20 million to establish college training programs in environmental restoration and hazardous waste management and to award fellowships in those programs to displaced defense workers.

Community Assistance

The package also provided programs intended to help communities plan for economic development and diversification in the wake of layoffs at local military bases or defense companies.

- $80 million for grants administered by the Commerce Department's Economic Development Administration.
- $80 million for grants administered by the Defense Department's Office of Economic Adjustment.

... To Cushion Impact of Military Cuts

The authorization bill expanded the scope of the program to assist planning efforts by communities that had not yet been hit by the defense downturn but that wanted to avert a future crunch by reducing their dependence on defense dollars.

- $50 million for "impact assistance" to school districts that suffered a sudden drop in enrollment because a military base closed or a defense plant shut down.

Defense Industries

The package included $549 million appropriated — out of $665 million authorized — to help defense contractors become more competitive in the civilian marketplace while retaining the capacity to produce military hardware. Among those efforts were:

'Dual-Use Critical Technologies.' $97 million for the government's contribution to consortia created to develop and foster applications of innovations that had both military and civilian uses.

By law, these partnerships had to include two or more commercial companies and, insofar as "practicable," the federal contribution could cover no more than 50 percent of a consortium's total budget. The Pentagon was to select projects for funding through open competition, based on criteria that included the technical excellence of the proposal and the qualifications of the participants.

'Commercial-Military Integration Partnerships.' $48.5 million for a new program that was to be modeled on established "critical technologies" consortia. It was intended to promote technologies that were more commercially viable and less militarily essential, although still applicable to potential Pentagon needs. Fuel cells and water purification systems were cited as types of technology that might be funded.

These partnerships did not have to include more than a single private company. But they were limited to five years' duration, and the federal contribution could not cover more than 50 percent of the costs in the first year, decreasing to 40 percent in the second year and 30 percent annually thereafter.

Criteria for the competitive selection of these projects included not only the technical excellence of the proposal and the qualifications of the participants but also the likelihood that the partnership could survive without federal funding after five years.

Extension Programs. $97 million to support centers sponsored by the federal government, by state or local governments, or by private organizations to help defense-dependent companies enter the commercial marketplace with dual-use products.

California and New York already sponsored such outreach programs, which were intended to help corporate managers steeped in the Pentagon's procurement practices learn how to find markets, advertise, keep their books and deal with commercial suppliers.

Federal funding could last for no more than five years, starting at a 50 percent cost share and declining to no more than 30 percent in the third year and beyond.

'Regional Technology Alliances.' $97 million for closely situated federal labs, universities and high-tech companies that jointly developed and commercialized critical dual-use technologies.

This program was authorized in fiscal 1992, but no funds were appropriated for it. The fiscal 1993 authorization bill boosted from 30 percent to 50 percent the federal government's allowable share of funding for such a regional alliance.

Manufacturing. $179 million for four programs aimed at developing and disseminating more efficient processes that could be applied to either new or existing technologies. The largest of the four components ($97 million) was earmarked for extension programs in manufacturing to be managed by state governments and regional public agencies.

An additional $29 million was provided for an existing process through which the federal government and participating universities jointly funded programs in manufacturing engineering. Another $29 million was earmarked to disseminate to small- and medium-sized contractors techniques of "agile" manufacturing, which would allow a company to shift more easily from one product to another. And $24 million was to fund government-industry partnerships to develop manufacturing processes that reduced health, safety and environmental hazards.

Synthetic Materials. $29 million for government-industry partnerships to develop new methods to synthesize materials and products.

The authorization bill also doubled a decade-old program that set aside a small percentage of the Pentagon's annual research and development budget to fund research proposals from small businesses. Over the five years, the bill gradually increased, from 1.25 percent to 2.5 percent, the share of the defense research budget earmarked for the small business innovative research (SBIR) program. It also included in the baseline from which the set-aside was calculated more than $11 billion worth of programs that were previously excluded.

The combination of those changes provided the Pentagon's SBIR program with about $426 million in fiscal 1993, compared with the $225 million requested.

Subsequently, the SBIR provisions were incorporated into a broader bill (S 2941 — PL 102-564), which boosted the SBIR set-aside formula in stages to 2.5 percent for all federal agencies. By one estimate, the SBIR total would increase from $484 million in fiscal 1991 to $1.2 billion by 1997.

Both chambers had approved the B-2 funds. But House-Senate conferees specified that only $900 million could be spent unless Congress voted in 1993 to allow completion of those four planes plus a fifth that was funded in the fiscal 1992 budget. That vote was to come after the Pentagon reported to Congress on the B-2's cost and its ability to evade radar detection.

To make the 20-plane force fully operational, the Air Force said it planned to request from Congress a total of $5.7 billion more in fiscal 1994-96.

- Approved $4.05 billion for the strategic defense initiative, splitting the difference between the $4.3 billion agreed to by the House and the $3.8 billion narrowly approved by the Senate. Compared with Bush's $5.4 billion request, both chambers had placed more emphasis on the part of the program aimed at deploying relatively quickly a ground-based defense of U.S. territory against attack by a relatively small number of missiles.

The conference total included only $300 million of the $576 million Bush requested for space-based anti-missile rockets, including those known as brilliant pebbles, which Republicans viewed as essential to eventually expanding SDI's scope.

The conferees repealed the goal set in the fiscal 1992 defense bill of deploying a limited, ground-based defense by 1996. In their report, they endorsed a new Pentagon plan that envisioned deployment by 2002.

They also approved a House-passed provision stipulating that the initial, ground-based defense comply with the 1972 treaty limiting anti-ballistic missile systems. SDI planners had assumed that Russia would agree to ease some of the restrictions in that pact.

The conferees set a $135 million limit on consultants for the SDI program. The Senate version of the bill included a provision to limit consultant fees to $100 million. SDI was said to have spent $165 million for consultants in fiscal 1992.

- Approved the $287 million requested to buy satellites to detect the launch of long-range missiles. In addition, the conferees approved $412 million to develop more sophisticated devices for detecting a missile attack and assessing its target.
- Authorized $409 million of the $446 million requested to modernize B-1 and B-52 bombers that were already in service. Taking a cue from the Senate bill, the conference report also required the Pentagon to conduct realistic tests of B-1s and B-52s in conventional bombing missions against simulated air defenses. The Senate Armed Services Committee had indicated that it would support upgrades for only a portion of the more than 270 B-1s and B-52s.
- Authorized $148 million to wrap up production of a long-range, stealthy cruise missile (designated ACM). After the budget request was submitted in January, the Air Force concluded that it would need the additional funds. Even as they approved the funds, the conferees chastised the Air Force in uncharacteristically blunt terms for seeking a congressional "bailout" from its management "fiasco."
- Authorized $440 million to modify C-135s, with most of the funds earmarked to continue a 10-year-old program of equipping the tanker planes with more powerful jet engines. Both chambers had approved the $527 million requested to upgrade the hundreds of Boeing C-135s — similar to 707 jetliners — that were in use by the Air Force, mostly as midair refueling tankers.
- Incorporated a House provision ordering the Air Force to put new engines on some tankers operated by National Guard and reserve units. But conferees also ordered the Pentagon to analyze in detail whether a reduction in the tanker fleet would obviate the need to upgrade more than 150 other planes in Guard and reserve units.
- Approved the request for 21 Trident II submarine-launched missiles ($764 million) and $223 million for components to be used in additional missiles that were slated for inclusion in the fiscal 1994 request.
- Approved $25 million to develop an anti-satellite weapon, a project the House had rejected. But they dropped from the bill $15 million to develop a target-finding system for anti-satellite missions.
- Ordered a study to review alternative budgets for the Pentagon's program of space satellites and launchers to trim as much as 15 percent from projected requests.

Because of new developments in satellite and launcher technology, the conferees argued, the Pentagon might be able to make do with fewer satellites in orbit, more reliance on commercial satellites and more reliance on less expensive, non-satellite communication systems.

- Authorized the requested amounts for the rockets already being used to loft military satellites into orbit: $525 million for Titan IVs and $269 million for the smaller Atlas-Centaurs.
- Trimmed the amounts requested for two projects to develop space vehicles that were intended largely for civilian missions. Conferees approved $150 million of the $175 million requested for the so-called National Aerospace Plane, intended to take off from a runway and soar into orbit. Arguing that the effort to develop a prototype craft was premature, the conferees approved funding to wrap up that phase of the program while continuing basic research. In future years, they specified, the amount spent for the project in the defense budget could be no more than twice the amount earmarked in the National Aeronautics and Space Administration (NASA) budget.

They approved $85 million of the $125 million requested for a "national launch system" — a family of launch rockets, including one intended to carry much heavier satellites than any already in service. Not more than half the amount authorized could be spent until the Pentagon sent Congress a plan detailing how the Defense Department and NASA would fit the joint program into their long-term budget plans and how the Pentagon would save money by using the new launchers instead of the rockets in service.

Ground Combat. Authorized $148 million to keep intact the production lines for M-1 tanks.

The president's budget requested $25 million to modify M-1s. But the administration subsequently agreed to a much more ambitious, congressionally supported program to modernize the tank fleet with electronic gear for driving and fighting at night. The conferees ordered the Army to start by upgrading the oldest M-1s, installing not only the new electronics but also the larger guns and heavier armor already installed in the most recent models.

- Added $85 million to buy 60 additional Bradley armored troop carriers and $40 million to begin upgrading existing vehicles. The president's budget had included no funds for additional Bradley production, requesting only $104 million to wrap up an existing contract.

After the war with Iraq, Bradley crews complained that they lacked a laser rangefinder for the vehicle's 25mm cannon. The conferees added $5 million to the bill to develop such an improvement.

- Allowed the Pentagon to pay for those tank upgrade

programs with proceeds from the sale to other countries of older tanks and troop carriers.

• Approved the Army's $5 million request to begin buying lightweight tanks to equip its rapid-reaction divisions, intended for aerial deployment. The conferees added $15 million to revive a canceled program to put a tank cannon on a version of the Marine Corps' LAV armored cars.

• Approved $17 million to continue work on potential cannon improvements. Contending that the collapse of the Soviet threat eliminated the need for a new tank more powerful than the M-1, however, neither chamber had approved the $42 million requested to develop a larger tank cannon.

• Approved the $145 million requested to upgrade self-propelled artillery so they could fire more quickly and accurately. Conferees added to the bill $13 million to develop for the Army and Marine Corps large-caliber cannon light enough to be carried by small helicopters.

• Authorized the $188 million requested to continue production of ATACMS artillery rockets, plus a total of $338 million to buy 73 launchers for smaller MLRS artillery rockets and 30,000 of the rockets.

The administration had sought $197 million for 44 mobile launchers for the MLRS rockets and $2 million for miscellaneous related costs but no funds to buy additional rockets.

• Approved the $443 million requested to continue developing the Army's Comanche "scout" helicopter, which the Senate had dropped from the bill.

However, the conferees endorsed the Senate's objections to the Pentagon's plan to build three prototypes and then shelve the program. So they directed the Pentagon to obligate no more than half the funds until it certified that its long-term budget plans included funds to gear up for eventual production of the Comanche.

• Added $225 million to the administration's budget to upgrade 36 older scout helicopters with missiles and target-finding electronics. The proposal followed the lead of the House.

• Granted the administration's request for $49 million for miscellaneous improvements to the Apache anti-tank helicopter and $282 million to develop a Longbow modification with more powerful engines and more sophisticated target-finding electronics. In addition, the conferees authorized $117 million for interim Apache upgrades.

• Approved the $176 million requested to equip 170 pickup trucks with batteries of Stinger anti-aircraft missiles and to buy components for additional systems intended for future budgets.

• Added $9 million to develop an anti-aircraft version of the LAV armored car.

• Authorized $512 million to buy two planes equipped with JSTARS radar, designed to find ground targets far behind enemy lines. The conferees adopted a Senate initiative. The president's budget requested $311 million for one plane.

Tactical Air Combat. Required the Defense Department to send Congress two detailed studies, a process that was intended to impose budgetary discipline on the services' plans for new combat airplanes.

One was an analysis by the chairman of the Joint Chiefs of Staff of the division of labor among the services, known in Pentagon jargon as a "roles and missions" study. Mandated every three years by the 1986 defense reorganization act, such a report was already due by the end of 1992. The conferees ordered that the analysis be a "thorough, everything-on-the-table review," focusing on combat aircraft. In particular, they asked whether one service could take over certain specialized missions — such as radar jamming — that require expensive airplanes. And they asked whether a single type of aircraft could be used by all services to perform similar combat missions.

The second study was an analysis by the secretary of defense of how much of the planned combat airplane programs the Air Force and Navy could afford over the next 20 years. In conducting this study, conferees said, department officials were to consider not only the declining defense budgets that were in prospect but also the portion of its total budget that each branch typically allocated to aircraft procurement. They insisted that the study assume tighter budgets would allow fewer planes to be built overall — and fewer to be built in any one year — than the services planned.

• Approved $683 million, as requested, for 24 Air Force F-16s. But the bill barred any spending to buy additional F-16s pending completion of the two studies.

• Authorized $1.15 billion for 36 of the Navy's F/A-18s, a reduction of 12 planes ($513 million) from the request.

• Specified that, for the following three aircraft development programs, no more than 65 percent of the total authorized could be spent until the two studies were submitted:

The Air Force's F-22 fighter. The conferees authorized $2.2 billion, as requested.

Larger "E" and "F" versions of the F/A 18. The conferees authorized $944 million, about 80 percent of the amount requested.

A stealthy, carrier-based bomber designated AX. The conferees authorized the $166 million that was requested. The conferees also required the Navy to rely more on prototypes than it had planned in the AX and the F/A-18 "E" and "F" projects.

• Provided that the Pentagon must choose between Air Force C-135s and Navy P-3s for electronic eavesdropping missions. Both services had requested funds to modernize their electronic intelligence planes. The conferees approved $57 million, the total requested. But, as proposed by the Senate, they ordered that the defense secretary pick which of the planes would be used by both services and earmark all the money to upgrade that fleet.

• Approved both the $530 million requested for upgrades of the Navy's Prowler and the $68 million requested for work on the Air Force's Ravens.

Responding to the Senate's efforts to try to force the Pentagon to settle on one of those two types of radar jamming planes, the conferees included a provision barring use of more than 65 percent of the Raven money until the Pentagon sent Congress the roles and missions study and the Air Force guaranteed that its long-term budget plans included the Raven.

• Added $24 million for 30 additional copies of a 50-mile-range, Israeli-designed missile to be carried by B-52 bombers.

• Approved only $105 million of the $218 million requested to buy HARM anti-radar missiles. Instead of buying the 846 new missiles requested, the conferees told the Pentagon to upgrade the same number of early model HARMs.

Naval Warfare. Authorized the full $832 million requested for the nuclear power plant and other components of a new aircraft carrier. The Navy said it planned to request the bulk of the ship's cost — probably about $4

V-22 Osprey Deal

Prospects for the V-22 Osprey may not have appeared good in 1992, at least at first glance. The hybrid craft — designed to take off and land like a helicopter but fly like a conventional airplane — had been opposed since 1989 by Defense Secretary Dick Cheney. *(Background, box, p. 348)*

Therefore, the proposed Marine transport plane would have seemed an obvious target in a year of defense budget-cutting. Nor were its prospects enhanced by the untimely crash of a prototype in the Potomac River near Washington, D.C., on July 20, killing four Marines and three civilians. The accident received prominent play on the local television newscasts watched by members of Congress.

But politically, at least, the Osprey proved unsinkable because of its strong base of support in Pennsylvania and Texas, where its prime contractors were located. With President Bush campaigning for re-election, Cheney switched gears on July 2, weeks before the prototype's crash. The defense secretary offered to proceed with development of the V-22 — without committing to eventual production. In return, he asked Congress to approve $10 million to begin designing a conventional helicopter as an alternative. And Bush's Democratic opponent, Bill Clinton, endorsed development of the Osprey, describing it as valuable for the types of missions the military would undertake in the aftermath of the Cold War.

Congress funded Cheney's bargain, including $755 million for the Osprey and $10 million for the alternative helicopter in the fiscal 1993 defense appropriations bill (HR 5504 — PL 102-396). The V-22 was authorized in the companion fiscal 1993 defense authorization bill (HR 5006 — PL 102-484), although the final version of that measure adopted Senate-passed language prohibiting the Pentagon from spending more than half of the $755 million until the Marines reported to Congress on the July crash of the prototype. *(Fiscal 1993 appropriations bill, p. 407)*

billion — in the fiscal 1995 budget. In an effort to delay the major request until fiscal 1996, the Senate had approved only $350 million of the fiscal 1993 request for "long lead-time" items.

- Approved $3.3 billion, all but $50 million of the amount requested, for four *Burke*-class destroyers and the $246 million requested for two mine sweepers.
- Effectively canceled $442 million in shipbuilding projects from the 1992 defense appropriations bill that had not been authorized.

It was a routine skirmish in a continuing turf war between the Armed Services and Appropriations committees. The authorization conferees — who were members of the two chambers' Armed Services panels — added to their bill a provision using those funds instead to cover part of the cost of the fiscal 1993 shipbuilding program.

- Authorized the $404 million requested for 200 Tomahawk cruise missiles.

The Senate had approved $229 million for 100 long-range Tomahawks — half the number requested — arguing that a slower production rate would keep the assembly line open longer, thus preserving the option of buying more weapons than planned.

- Backed $133 million of the $155 million requested to develop a new nuclear-powered submarine designated *Centurion*, intended to be less expensive than the two *Seawolf*-class ships that were being built. *(*Seawolf *submarine, p. 410)*
- Approved the $195 million requested to develop two new types of sub-hunting sonars.

The House had approved only $52 million. In granting the full request, the conferees attached conditions echoing the reasoning behind the House reduction. With Soviet nuclear subs in midocean no longer a major threat, they said, the Navy should reorient its anti-sub investments toward technologies that could be deployed quickly to hunt for small submarines in remote, shallow seas.

- Authorized $27 million, a $9 million increase over the amount requested, to continue development of a helicopter-borne laser called Magic Lantern, intended to detect underwater mines.

Air and Sea Transport. Approved $1.81 billion for six C-17 cargo jets, a reduction of two planes ($703 million) from the request for the long-range, wide-body planes. For components to be used in C-17s slated for the fiscal 1994 budget, the conferees approved $251 million instead of the $206 million requested.

With production of the planes lagging, the conferees added provisions linking the release of new procurement funds to the pace of the assembly line producing previously funded C-17s. They also included a House-passed provision requiring that major components of the C-17 be tested for their resilience to anti-aircraft fire.

- Approved the $300 million requested for eight Hercules cargo planes, and the conferees added $328 million for 12 additional planes earmarked for National Guard and reserve units.
- Adopted a Senate initiative to add $1.2 billion for a large helicopter carrier able to transport 2,000 Marines.
- Included the $755 million that both chambers had added to continue work on the V-22 Osprey tilt-rotor aircraft, intended as a Marine Corps troop carrier.

But the conferees accepted a Senate provision allowing only half that amount to be spent until the Marines reported to Congress on the crash in July 1992 of an Osprey prototype.

- Approved $613 million of the $1.2 billion requested to begin buying additional high-speed cargo ships to haul abroad the combat gear of U.S.-based Army units.

The Navy planned to use the money, together with $1.88 billion previously appropriated, to obtain 20 new ships by some combination of building new vessels and modifying existing commercial ships. No more than five foreign-built ships could be purchased for conversion.

Personnel Issues. Approved the request to cut the number of active-duty personnel to 1,766,500, a reduction of 100,400 from the fiscal 1992 cap.

• Added a provision allowing the defense secretary to exceed the active-duty ceiling if necessary to avoid forcing military careerists out of uniform before they completed the 20 years of service needed to qualify for retirement pay.

• Authorized a ceiling of 1,095,080 on membership in National Guard and reserve units. This was a reduction of nearly 40,000, instead of the 116,000-member cutback the administration proposed.

• Included several elements from a House-passed package intended to make the Army National Guard more combat-ready.

One such provision required the Guard to draw a larger proportion of its new members from former active-duty personnel. Another required an active-duty Army unit to oversee the training of each Guard unit.

Also approved was a provision requiring the Army to assign 3,000 experienced active-duty members to support Guard and reserve units. But the conferees dropped from the House package a requirement for semi-annual physical fitness evaluations and for dismissal or retirement of any Guard member who could not pass screenings within nine months.

• Added, as usual, funds for equipment earmarked for Guard and reserve units. The additions totaled $696 million, more than half for Hercules cargo planes and smaller aircraft.

Burden-Sharing. Approved a Senate provision barring the deployment in Europe of more than 100,000 U.S. troops after fiscal 1996. A House provision had set a 1995 deadline for reaching that ceiling.

The Bush administration planned to keep 150,000 troops in Europe.

• Included a House provision mandating a reduction of 40 percent in the total number of U.S. military personnel stationed overseas. But the conferees set a 1996 deadline, instead of the 1995 date that was approved by the House.

• Reduced $500 million from the amount earmarked for operating costs at overseas bases in the hope of making allied governments pay a larger share of the cost of stationing U.S. troops on their soil. It was a modest gesture compared with the House version of the bill, which would have sliced $3.5 billion on the same rationale.

The conferees also added a non-binding declaration that the budget for overseas base costs should decline significantly in fiscal 1994-96.

Operations, Maintenance. Cut $1.07 billion from the amount requested to purchase additional supplies in an effort to force the Pentagon to draw down its inventories of spare parts and supplies.

• Cut from the budget request $3.11 billion to make various changes in the "defense business operating fund," a revolving fund the Pentagon used to finance operations such as routine overhauls and spare parts purchases.

Other Provisions. Included a provision barring the purchase by a foreign government or foreign-owned company of any of the 36 largest U.S. defense contractors or any contractors supplying the Pentagon with secret technology.

• Authorized $168 million to combat the proliferation of nuclear, chemical and biological weapons.

• Increased to $800 million the amount that could be drawn from Pentagon funds to help former Soviet republics dismantle some of their arsenals.

1993 Defense Appropriations

Congress in 1992 cleared a $254 billion fiscal 1993 defense appropriations bill. Combined with funds appropriated separately for military construction and for defense-related nuclear programs conducted by the Energy Department, the defense spending bill (HR 5504 — PL 102-396) brought the defense budget for fiscal 1993 to $274 billion.

As was typical of defense appropriations bills, HR 5504 conformed to the companion defense authorization bill (HR 5006) so far as most major weapons programs were concerned. *(Fiscal 1993 defense authorization, p. 395)*

The strategic defense initiative (SDI) was one of a few significant instances of the bill earmarking less than was authorized for a major program. The appropriations bill provided only $3.8 billion of the $5.4 billion President Bush requested for the anti-missile defense program, while the final version of the authorization bill called for $4.05 billion.

In a few other prominent cases, the appropriations bill earmarked funds for projects that were not authorized, such as $300 million for an amphibious landing ship. The bill also added to the budget request $1.57 billion for National Guard and reserve equipment. This was more than either chamber had approved in its respective versions of the bill and $872 million more than was authorized.

In political terms, what distinguished the defense appropriations most clearly from the authorization bill was the more widespread — or at least more forthright — earmarking of Pentagon funds for projects that were backed by congressional clout. In some cases, HR 5504 transferred funds from the Pentagon to other departments, in effect circumventing budget limits on Appropriations subcommittees that draft the funding bills for those agencies. In other cases, members of the Senate and House Appropriations committees used the bill to direct the Pentagon to fund projects of interest to constituents.

But the bill included basically the amounts requested and authorized for most major weapons programs, including four B-2 "stealth" bombers, four Navy destroyers and a down payment on a nuclear-powered aircraft carrier.

Tracking the authorization bill, it approved less than Bush requested for several major projects, including the Air Force's new F-22 fighter and the C-17 cargo plane. By the same token, HR 5504 paralleled the authorization measure in adding to Bush's request funds for several projects that the administration opposed — or had come to accept under congressional pressure. Examples included development of the V-22 Osprey, a tilt-rotor aircraft intended as a Marine Corps troop carrier, and upgrading of existing M-1 tanks and Bradley troop carriers, partly to keep alive the production lines for those weapons.

In addition to SDI, the bill appropriated substantially less than was authorized in other cases. The authorization bill provided $1.2 billion for a helicopter carrier, and both chambers included more than $1 billion for it in their appropriations bills. But in an effort to squeeze additional programs into the funding bill, the conferees agreed to include only $305 million — enough to get the ship under contract, thus locking in a price and delivery schedule guaranteed by an option due to expire at the end of 1992. The balance of the ship's cost would have to be included in future funding bills, making this a rare departure from the

Appropriations committees' vigorous opposition to such "incremental funding" of a major program. In general, the committees insisted on "full funding" in a single bill of any major program so members could judge it in light of its full cost.

Legislative Action

HR 5504 was reported by the House Appropriations Committee on June 29 (H Rept 102-627). The House passed a $251 billion defense appropriations bill on July 2 by a vote of 328-94.

Amid much talk about the need to crack down on the deficit, the House had cut nearly $800 million from the defense bill. However, as with most of the other appropriations bills passed after the House's June 11 rejection of a constitutional amendment to balance the budget, the reduction amounted to a fraction of the total amount appropriated, and the specific cuts approved were largely symbolic. *(Balanced budget amendment, p. 84)*

Confounding widespread predictions that members would try to vindicate their votes against the constitutional amendment by voting to kill many big-ticket programs, the House rejected proposals to slash two of the most costly and controversial programs in the bill: the B-2 stealth bomber and SDI.

Critics came much closer to slicing SDI funds than they had come a month earlier, when they tried to make a larger cut in the companion defense authorization bill. An amendment to cut $700 million from the $4.3 billion included in the appropriations bill for SDI lost by only 16 votes on a 201-217 tally July 2. An effort to cut SDI by $1 billion had fallen short by 50 votes during action on the authorization measure.

Opponents of the B-2 lost ground between the two defense debates, even though in that interval both chambers of Congress debated the balanced budget amendment and President Bush and Russian President Boris N. Yeltsin agreed to slash their long-range nuclear arsenals. An amendment to delete funding for four additional B-2 bombers was rejected 173-248, a margin of 75 votes, on July 2. An almost identical anti-bomber amendment had lost by only 50 votes during the authorization debate.

Before reporting the bill to the House, the Appropriations Committee had cut $8.6 billion from Bush's $261 billion request. The amendments adopted on the House floor brought the total reduction to $9.4 billion. However, that net reduction reflected nearly $3 billion that the committee added to the bill for several major weapons the administration did not request — and in most cases vigorously opposed — but which commanded strong congressional backing.

These congressional initiatives included construction of two large amphibious landing ships, additional production of Stinger anti-aircraft missiles, continued upgrades of the Army's Bradley troop carrier and the Navy's F-14 fighter jet, and continued development of the V-22 Osprey aircraft. Taken individually, each of those five programs arguably filled a clear military requirement. But taken together, they underscored the depth of congressional resistance to cutting defense-related jobs in economically tight times.

In the case of the V-22, Congress dug in its heels so deeply over three years that Cheney on July 2 announced a partial capitulation, offering to continue developing the aircraft without promising to eventually buy it. *(Box, p. 406)*

The bill included $1 billion for an "economic conversion" package — also part of the authorization bill — to help laid-off defense workers, military personnel, weapons contractors and communities adjust to the rapid drop in defense spending brought on by the Soviet Union's collapse.

The Senate Appropriations Committee reported its version of HR 5504 on Sept. 17 (S Rept 102-408). The Senate passed a $251 billion Pentagon spending bill on Sept. 23 by an 86-10 vote.

Characteristically, the defense spending bill appropriated essentially the same amounts that had been authorized in the companion bill for major weapons programs: $2.69 billion for B-2 bombers, for instance, and $3.25 billion for four Navy destroyers.

Of three dozen amendments to the bill voted on by the Senate during two days of debate, only one would have significantly changed the amount recommended by the Senate Appropriations Committee for a major program. An amendment by Tom Harkin, D-Iowa, adopted 89-4 on Sept. 22, would have shifted $210 million from SDI to breast cancer research. Immediately after the amendment was approved, however, it was retroactively amended to simply increase cancer research funding, without an offsetting reduction in SDI.

More customary constituent interests were prominent among most of the other amendments, most of which were adopted by voice vote.

The bill included a $2 billion "defense conversion" fund to cushion the impact of Pentagon budget cutbacks on defense contractors, their employees and their communities. The Appropriations Committee had funded the lump sum, in part, by eliminating hundreds of millions of dollars that the administration had requested for various research projects that, the committee argued, were intended to help defense contractors retool for commercial business.

As drafted by the committee, the bill would have given the Defense Department discretion to allocate the $2 billion among conversion-related projects, including those projects for which specific requests had been denied. But the Senate's version of the companion defense authorization bill parceled out money to dozens of specific conversion-related projects. And senators who had hammered out that package were unwilling to see that carefully brokered deal unraveled. By voice vote, the Senate adopted an amendment that earmarked more than half the appropriations bill's conversion fund for projects specified in the authorization measure.

Conference, Major Provisions

The conference version of HR 5504 (H Rept 102-1015) was filed Oct. 5. The House and Senate adopted the conference report by voice votes that same day.

As crafted by conferees, the $254 billion defense appropriations bill for fiscal 1993 accelerated the decline in Pentagon spending. As the post-Soviet drawdown gained momentum, HR 5504 took an ax to operating costs as well as weapons procurement, although hardware programs continued to have the greatest reduction. More than $7 billion was sliced from Bush's request.

Of the major accounts in the Defense Department budget, the bill made the smallest year-to-year change in the military personnel account, which covered pay and fringe benefits for members of the armed services. Congress trimmed $700 million from Bush's $77 billion request.

As requested, the bill reduced the number of active-duty military personnel to 1.77 million, a reduction of nearly 99,000 from the fiscal 1992 ceiling, but the resulting savings were party offset by congressional add-ons to ease the transition of active-duty members to civilian life and to restore large cuts that Bush proposed in National Guard and reserve units.

Congress refused to consider as rapid a reduction in National Guard and reserve personnel as Bush had proposed. The final bill permitted a cut slightly more than one-third as large as Bush called for, setting a ceiling for fiscal 1993 at 1.08 million members. To pay for this larger-than-planned force, the bill added $384 million to the budget request. The bill also added $1.57 billion for equipment earmarked for Guard and reserve units.

For the first time in the era of defense cuts, Congress made significant reductions in the request for operations and maintenance funds, cutting $6 billion from Bush's nearly $84 billion request. For almost two decades, operations and maintenance funding had been politically sacrosanct because it had been treated as the part of the Pentagon budget most directly related to combat readiness. Denying any intention of cutting the tempo of military operations, the conference committee targeted most of the reduction so that the Pentagon would be forced to use some of its massive inventory of spare parts and supplies.

Before the House adopted the conference report, a floor fight occurred over $95 million in unauthorized, science-related university building projects that conferees had inserted into the bill. The same items had been stripped earlier from an energy bill, but this time supporters of the projects prevailed and the funding remained.

Major Provisions. As signed into law Oct. 6, HR 5504 appropriated:

- More than $1.5 billion to help military personnel, defense contractors and local communities adapt to the downturn in defense spending, including $575 million for research and development (R&D) programs expressly designed to help defense-oriented companies retool to produce commercially viable products; $306 million for other R&D programs to develop technologies with civilian and military applications; $254 million to fund a provision of the companion defense authorization act (HR 5006) that temporarily allowed military personnel to retire and begin collecting pensions after 15 years of service, instead of the 20 years normally required; $632 million for other programs, including community planning assistance and job training and transition health insurance for service personnel and defense contractor employees.
- $2.69 billion for four B-2 stealth bombers. (Under terms of the companion defense authorization bill, most of the funds for the planes could be spent only if Congress voted in 1993 to complete their construction.)
- $3.8 billion for the strategic defense initiative.
- $300 million to continue upgrading the fleet of B-1 bombers; $148 million to close out production of a long-range, stealthy, cruise missile intended to be launched from bombers; $764 million for 21 Trident II submarine-launched missiles.
- $161 million (plus $197 million in proceeds from the sale of older tanks to other countries) to upgrade early model M-1 tanks; $125 million to keep the production line for Bradley armored troop carriers "warm" by building new Bradleys and updating older ones; $307 million to modify the Apache anti-tank helicopter, including putting a target-finding radar on the Longbow version; $418 million to continue developing the smaller Comanche armed "scout" helicopter; $225 million to install new target-finding electronics on 36 existing scout helicopters; $512 million for two JSTARS airborne radar planes.
- $615 million for 24 Air Force F-16s and $68 million for components to be used in additional F-16s that would be included in the fiscal 1994 budget; $1.2 billion for 36 Navy F/A-18s; $2 billion to continue development of the Air Force's F-22 fighter; $944 million to develop an enlarged version of the F/A-18; $166 million to develop a new, stealthy bomber, designated AX, to fly from aircraft carriers; $200 million for a long-term program to refurbish the Navy's F-14 long-range fighter planes; $756 million to buy 1,040 radar-guided AMRAAMs.
- $832 million to buy the nuclear power plant and other long lead-time components of an aircraft carrier slated for inclusion in the fiscal 1995 budget request; $3.25 billion for four Aegis destroyers; $404 million for 200 Tomahawk long-range cruise missiles; $361 million for 21 ship-borne, sub-hunting versions of the Army's Blackhawk helicopter; $150 million to continue developing the *Seawolf*-class submarine; $135 million to develop a nuclear-powered sub, dubbed *Centurion*, intended to be less expensive than the *Seawolf*; $236 million for two mine sweepers.
- $1.81 billion for six C-17 wide-body cargo planes; $755 million to continue research and development of the V-22 Osprey tilt-rotor planes, as well as $10 million requested by the administration to begin designing a conventional helicopter that the Marines could use instead of the Osprey; $613 million to expand the Navy's fleet of relatively fast cargo ships, designed to quickly load and unload the tanks and other combat gear of U.S.-based Army units (the new funds, along with $1.9 billion appropriated for sealift in previous years, were to be deposited in a national defense sealift fund, which could be used to build new ships or to buy and modify existing commercial ships); $300 million for an amphibious landing ship; $305 million for a large helicopter carrier designed to carry 2,000 Marines and up to 40 big troop-carrying helicopters.
- $76 billion for military personnel and $69 billion for operations and maintenance.
- $210 million for Army research on breast cancer.
- Funds for various other agencies, including $303 million to be transferred to the Coast Guard; $65 million for emergency assistance to commercial fishermen who suffered uninsured losses in recent hurricanes; $126 million for the Energy Department's Strategic Petroleum Reserve.

The bill also included a provision authorizing payment of an undetermined amount to Turkey as a gesture of regret for the accidental launch from the U.S. aircraft carrier *Saratoga* of a missile that severely damaged an escorting Turkish destroyer and killed several of that ship's crew.

1993 Military Construction

Congress in 1992 cleared an $8.39 billion measure to fund construction projects and family housing at U.S. military installations, as well as military base closings, in fiscal 1993. The bill (HR 5428 — PL 102-380) appropriated $173 million less than President Bush had requested.

The fiscal 1993 bill represented a big shift in Pentagon priorities: less money for new base construction and improvements, and more money to implement two previous rounds of base closures. HR 5428 appropriated about $170 million less than the fiscal 1992 bill but provided $1.28

Survival of the *Seawolf* Submarine

Congress in 1992 confirmed its support for the *Seawolf* submarine by rebuffing President Bush's attempt to cancel all but the first of the projected class of ships.

Bush's effort to rescind previously appropriated *Seawolf* funding was revised to permit a second *Seawolf* to be built, and Congress included $150 million for the submarine's continued development in the fiscal 1993 defense appropriations bill (HR 5504 — PL 102-396).

Congress' position drew political strength from members whose constituents worked in the Connecticut shipyard where the submarine was built, and it gained a military rationale from concern that the United States would lose the "industrial base" needed to make underwater vessels to combat some future threat.

Background

The *Seawolf* (SSN-21) was proposed by the Navy in 1982 as a highly sophisticated replacement for the *Los Angeles*-class submarine (SSN-688), which was scheduled to be phased out by 1997.

The *Seawolf* was designed to be quieter and faster than the *Los Angeles* and to carry twice as many weapons. But the *Seawolf*, with a price tag estimated as high as $2 billion per sub, was criticized as superfluous with the demise of the Soviet threat that it was intended to combat.

As part of the Bush administration's defense cutback in 1991, the Navy had modified its initial plan to buy three *Seawolf* submarines a year. Instead, the plan had been to purchase one *Seawolf* a year through fiscal 1995, and then six more through fiscal 1999. The Navy also wanted to introduce a newer, less expensive submarine, known as the *Centurion*, by fiscal 1998.

Bush's 1992 proposal to complete the single *Seawolf* that won initial funding in 1989 and rescind funds that were appropriated in fiscal 1991 and 1992 for two additional ships sparked an energetic lobbying campaign by the congressional delegations from Connecticut and neighboring Rhode Island.

The submarine was built in Groton, Conn., by the Electric Boat division of General Dynamics. The company, which was the largest employer in Rhode Island and the second largest in Connecticut, said it needed to build one new *Seawolf* a year to stay in operation. Even then, the company planned to let go half of its 21,500 workers by 1997.

Besides costing jobs, advocates for the sub argued, canceling the *Seawolf* would undermine the national defense by forcing the shutdown of one of only two U.S. shipyards that built nuclear-powered submarines.

Rescission Effort

After having fully supported the *Seawolf* in the past, Bush in March sent Congress a rescission package, which included his proposal to rescind $2.77 billion in previously appropriated money for the second and third vessels in this class.

House appropriators insisted on preserving funding for one of the two *Seawolf* subs that Bush had asked Congress to kill. The Defense Appropriations subcommittee opted to preserve $1 billion for that submarine while cutting $1.9 billion that had been appropriated for another.

The Senate Appropriations Committee voted to preserve not just one but both of the *Seawolf* submarines that Bush sought to cancel.

The strong lobbying by New England members of Congress to save jobs in their region was not mentioned by the House and Senate appropriators, who cited instead the arcane economics of defense contracting.

On May 6, the full Senate approved, 61-38, a rescission package (S 2403) that left in place funding for two *Seawolf* submarines. The following day the House adopted, 412-2, a rescission package (HR 4990) that protected funding for one *Seawolf*. Both bills substituted cuts in other programs. *(Rescissions, box, p. 383)*

The House vote on final passage was not a true test of that chamber's sentiment, however. An earlier vote, on May 7, on whether to substitute Bush's rescissions for those approved by the House Appropriations Committee split largely along party lines, 150-266.

House-Senate conferees compromised between the House position calling for money to build one more of the subs and the Senate effort to protect funds for two more. The final legislation cut $1.3 billion. That left roughly $1.7 billion, more than enough to finish building the second submarine.

Conferees agreed to set aside $550 million of the $1.7 billion on the condition that the secretary of defense use it to start building a third *Seawolf*, restart production of *Los Angeles*-class submarines or otherwise protect the industrial base for submarine construction.

Approval of the conference report reconciling House and Senate rescission bills (H Rept 102-530) came May 21 in votes of 404-11 in the House and 90-9 in the Senate. Bush signed HR 4990 (PL 102-298) on June 4.

Congress confirmed its determination to keep the *Seawolf* project alive by adding to the fiscal 1993 defense appropriations bill $150 million for continued development of the submarine.

billion more for base closures. The additional money came out of the military construction account.

The Defense Department estimated that base shutdowns approved by Congress in 1989 and 1991 were to cost $8 billion. Lawmakers were expected to target more bases in 1993. Before many of the bases could be turned over to state and local governments or to private developers, significant environmental hazards needed to be cleaned up. *(Base closings, pp. 353, 393)*

As members of Congress drew up the bill, traditionally the least controversial of the 13 appropriations measures, they discussed repeatedly the difficulty of crafting the fiscal 1993 version.

Legislative Action

The House Appropriations Committee reported HR 5428 (H Rept 102-580) on June 18, and the House passed it on June 23 by a 390-33 vote.

The committee bill emerged relatively unscathed from the House but only after an afternoon filled with unusual procedural votes demanded by Republicans who were upset by the House leadership's intention to restrict amendments to another spending bill, the politically charged legislative appropriations measure. At one point, an archaic "teller" vote was taken, requiring members to file past tellers to have their votes counted.

The committee bill contained about $500 million for 170 construction projects not requested by the Defense Department, many of them in the districts of Appropriations Committee members. An attempt to remove one high-profile project — $19 million for the access road to a National Guard base in Mississippi — was easily defeated on a 143-276 vote June 23.

The sole floor amendment to HR 5428 was a 1 percent across-the-board cut, adopted 266-156. The cut was approved June 23 over the protests of bill sponsors, who said the measure already was bare-bones. The bill's total was reduced from $8.6 billion to $8.5 billion.

The Senate Appropriations Committee reported an $8.2 billion version of the military construction bill (S Rept 102-355) on July 31. The Senate passed it Aug. 5 by voice vote.

Military Construction Subcommittee Chairman Jim Sasser, D-Tenn., said that the bill represented "painful cutting" and that, as a result, the committee declined, in all but a few instances, to sign on to any of the new projects in the House bill, concentrating instead on its own new projects.

The Senate bill provided no money for Bush's request for overseas construction. Appropriators said the tight military construction budget should be directed exclusively to domestic bases.

Although the Senate bill would have fully funded the administration's request to implement two rounds of military base closures, Senate appropriators complained that the Pentagon had underestimated how much it would cost to close the bases and clean up a host of environmental problems on the sites. The Senate bill directed the General Accounting Office to review the base-closing effort before the fiscal 1994 military construction bill was marked up.

Conference, Major Provisions

The House and Senate approved the conference report (H Rept 102-888) by voice votes on Sept. 24 and Sept. 25, respectively. The $8.39 billion compromise bill included $2.4 billion for military construction, $3.9 billion for family housing and $2 billion for military base realignments and closures.

Negotiators dodged some controversy, as members had to grapple with an administration edict that the measure would be vetoed if it exceeded the president's $8.39 billion request. Sasser complained that Bush's veto threat tied the hands of appropriators, who had planned to reallocate money from the separate defense appropriations bill to the military construction funding bill. "To comply with the White House targets, we've had to make some very difficult decisions indeed," Sasser said.

Conferees agreed to pare $150 million from Bush's $2.18 billion request to implement base closures. The Senate bill had fully funded the request.

The conference agreement dropped Bush's $105 million request to build a chemical weapons disposal facility at the Anniston, Ala., Army Depot. The project was a Pentagon priority and was expected to be funded in future years.

To make room for new housing projects, conferees slashed almost $200 million from Bush's request to improve existing housing.

The final bill provided $60 million for the North Atlantic Treaty Organization's infrastructure fund, which was used to build facilities of benefit to the alliance. Bush had requested $221 million. The House had agreed to $121 million, but the Senate bill had included no money for the fund.

Bush had requested only $187 million for National Guard and reserve units' construction projects, but the final bill provided nearly $555 million — more than either chamber had approved in their versions of the bill.

Philippine Base Closings

A series of international and domestic events — ranging from a natural disaster to the breakup of the Soviet Union — made 1991 a turning point in relations between the United States and the Philippines. The culmination came Dec. 27, when the government of President Corazon C. Aquino told U.S. troops to leave the country.

The decision signaled the end of the vast U.S. military presence in the area, a presence that dated back to 1898 when control of the islands was wrested from the Spanish. The Philippines gained independence from the United States in 1946, although the bases continued to play a principal role for U.S. armed forces in the Pacific theater for decades afterward.

In negotiations with the United States throughout 1991, Philippine officials insisted on $825 million in annual U.S. compensation — half in cash and half in trade and other concessions — in return for a seven-year agreement to continue operation of the military bases. U.S. negotiators said they wanted a 10-year pact tied to $360 million in annual aid.

The talks were disrupted by a volcanic eruption of Mount Pinatubo in early June that nearly destroyed Clark Air Base and damaged the Subic Bay Naval Station. Members of Congress who had been skeptical about the need to retain the bases and frustrated by Philippine resistance to the treaty were even more doubtful that the cost of repairing the bases would be worthwhile. U.S. officials in the Philippines were reported to have estimated that Clark's repair bill would have approached $300 million and possibly more.

The future of the bases had been further clouded by geological reports that indicated that the volcano might remain intermittently active for as long as 25 years, potentially disrupting any costly repair of the two remaining U.S. bases. Four other bases had been returned to Philippine control during the year.

While the volcano sealed the fate of the Clark base, U.S. lawmakers and the Bush administration were careful to clarify that they wanted to maintain a strategic relationship with the Philippines and especially to continue to lease the base at Subic Bay. Abandonment of the bases was not the expressed desire of the administration, either before or immediately following the eruption of Mount Pinatubo.

Negotiators finally settled on treaty language that would have provided a 10-year lease for the Subic Bay naval base and $203 million in annual aid for the duration. The operating lease for the naval base expired in September 1991. *(Previous agreement, Congress and the Nation Vol. VII, p. 248)*

But lawmakers in both countries were unhappy with the agreement.

Objections to Treaty

A powerful contingent of Philippine nationalists argued against the base treaty, saying that the presence of the U.S. military amounted to a colonial dominance and an intrusion on Philippine sovereignty. On Sept. 16, the 23-member Philippine Senate voted to reject the base treaty.

U.S. lawmakers, meanwhile, were frustrated by the persistent requests from the Philippines for infusions of aid, especially as a prerequisite for continued U.S. military presence there.

Members of Congress were questioning the strategic importance of the military bases, given the diminished Cold War atmosphere that was accompanying the breakup of the Soviet Union.

A reluctance also existed to pay the Philippines billions of dollars to keep open bases overseas when declining defense budgets were forcing the closing of domestic bases in congressional districts across the United States. *(Base closings, p. 393)*

"This has the Filipinos competing in the U.S. Congress with the Alabama National Guard," said Rep. Jim Leach, R-Iowa. "Everyone in Congress is sympathetic to the Philippines. On the other hand when the tough choices have to be made, the handwriting is on the wall."

Other lawmakers said the Philippine rejection of the treaty could free money that could be redirected as foreign aid in places such as the former Soviet republics.

Salvage Efforts Fail

According to a published report, U.S. officials tried to salvage the Subic Bay lease late in 1991 by proposing a three-year phased withdrawal from the Philippines, in the hope that the lease agreement might be revived and extended following election of a new Philippine government in 1992. But that attempt also foundered, apparently over U.S. reluctance to agree to a firm schedule for removal of troops and equipment under Philippine direction.

Philippine President Aquino, who had strongly supported renewal of the lease agreement, also floated a proposal that a national referendum be held to save the bases. But in the face of widespread political opposition, she backed away from that proposal and later expressed more interest in the U.S. plan for a phased withdrawal.

When all efforts failed, Aquino ordered U.S. troops out of the naval port by the end of 1992. Defense Department officials had told Congress earlier that if the base were closed, the United States would not seek a new naval base in Asia.

Defense Production Act

Congress in 1992 cleared legislation (S 347 — PL 102-558) to extend and expand the Defense Production Act. The expired Korean War-era law granted the president broad authority to redirect domestic goods to military use during times of national emergency.

The reauthorization bill extended the act through September 1994. Provisions aimed at securing the U.S. defense industrial base required the president to undertake a review and take steps to ensure a reliable supply of critical materials. Supporters said the reauthorization was aimed at modernizing the act for the post-Cold War period. One provision promoted the development of "dual-use" technologies that had both defense and non-defense applications.

The bill authorized $200 million for the Pentagon to continue to make loans and purchase guarantees to U.S. companies that agreed to supply the government with militarily significant goods and services during an emergency.

The Defense Production Act had expired and gone without renewal for extended periods several times in the recent past. It expired Oct. 20, 1990, and although Congress did most of the work on a reauthorization in 1990, it failed to clear the bill before the 101st Congress adjourned. As a result, President Bush had to rely on other laws and executive orders to maintain his emergency acquisition powers during the Persian Gulf War. *(1990 action, p. 368)*

In 1991, both chambers passed a multi-year reauthorization of the Defense Production Act. The Senate passed S 347 by voice vote Feb. 21, 1991, and the House approved its version (HR 3039 — H Rept 102-208, Part I; H Rept 102-208, Part II) Oct. 2 by a vote of 419-3. The House passed an amended S 347 by voice vote Oct. 10. But work to reconcile the two versions did not get under way that year. Instead, lawmakers approved two short-term extensions in 1991 (HR 991 — PL 102-99; HR 3919 — PL 102-193).

Conferees on the multi-year reauthorization reached agreement in 1992. A key difference between the House and Senate had been Senate language to enact the Fair Trade in Financial Services bill. That measure would have given the Treasury Department and bank regulators authority to deny applications by foreign banks and securities firms for licenses in the United States if their home countries did not grant equal market access to U.S. banks and securities firms. While some House conferees supported the fair trade language, most did not, and the provision was dropped.

The House adopted the conference report (H Rept 102-1028) Oct. 6 (in the session that began Oct. 5) by voice vote. The Senate adopted the conference report Oct. 8 by voice vote, clearing S 347. Bush signed the measure Oct. 28.

6

Transportation and Commerce

Introduction 415

1989-90 Chronology 417

1991-92 Chronology 436

Transportation and Commerce

During his four years in office, President Bush sometimes compromised with the Democrat-controlled Congress and sometimes adhered to the anti-regulation, anti-big-government philosophy of his Republican predecessor, Ronald Reagan. Bush's actions regarding policy to regulate and fund the transportation and commerce industries were no exception.

Congress and the administration worked out their differences on a six-year, $151 billion highway and mass transit measure. But on another major issue, regulation of the booming cable television industry, Bush fought a losing battle against increased government controls and saw his veto soundly overridden.

Highway and Mass Transit Bill. Bush in early 1991 kicked off the debate on the highway authorization with a major policy initiative, "Moving America into the 21st Century." The Bush plan, which covered railroads and airlines as well as highways and mass transit, called for new user fees, more state and local spending, and a decreased federal commitment to mass transit programs.

The administration proposed a new 155,000-mile National Highway System with an emphasis on upgrading and refurbishing primary and secondary roads. The need for such work was underscored by Transportation Department figures showing that 42 percent of the nation's highway bridges were structurally deficient or obsolete and 65 percent of peak-hour travel on urban Interstate highways was congested in 1987.

Bush did not ask for an increase in the 9-cents-a-gallon federal gasoline tax. His plan, however, did encourage states to raise revenues through their own gasoline tax increases. The final measure extended an existing tax for four years.

In drafting the highway bill, the administration and Congress attempted to stimulate a flagging economy and improve the nation's decaying infrastructure, while reining in federal spending. Lawmakers generally were receptive to the administration's proposal to give states more control over the use of federal highway dollars. But a strong block of urban lawmakers opposed the administration's plan to cut funding for mass transit. The transportation measure that emerged from Congress gave states and cities increased freedom to divert federal highway funds to mass transit projects.

As the legislation progressed, the Bush administration won some concessions from Congress — particularly an agreement to retain the federal role in highways through a new National Highway System made up of the Interstate network and primary arterial roads. The transportation measure departed from other administration goals, but Bush signed it with praise for its potential to create jobs.

Credit for the administration's negotiating success on the transportation bill was given to Transportation Secretary Samuel K. Skinner, a former Chicago transit official who worked well with lawmakers. For example, Skinner negotiated with Robert A. Roe, a New Jersey Democrat who chaired the House Public Works and Transportation Committee, to reduce the number of special highway projects — regarded by many as pork-barrel — included in the legislation.

Other Transportation Legislation. Some members of Congress, worried that the Reagan-era deregulation of the airline industry had reduced, not stimulated, competition, proposed legislation to protect airlines from takeovers and bankruptcies. Congress shied away from a major "re-regulation" of the industry but did approve legislation to increase competition in the airline computer reservation system.

Congress also granted Bush's request for a user fee on airline passengers. The new passenger facility charge added up to $3 to the price of an airline ticket to help pay for airport improvements.

In the area of transportation safety and regulation, Congress produced a new airport noise policy and made permanent a ban on smoking on most commercial flights over the objections of the tobacco lobby and tobacco-state lawmakers.

Passenger cars, beginning in 1996, would be required to have front-seat air bags. New controls were imposed on the transport of hazardous materials. And a long-simmering dispute over drug testing was resolved when Congress

References

Discussion of transportation and commerce policy for the years 1945-64 may be found in *Congress and the Nation Vol. I*, pp. 517-562, 1159-1185; for the years 1965-68, *Congress and the Nation Vol. II*, pp. 227-251, 779-823; for the years 1969-72, *Congress and the Nation Vol. III*, pp. 147-176, 659-700; for the years 1973-76, *Congress and the Nation Vol. IV*, pp. 433-451, 505-555; for the years 1977-80, *Congress and the Nation Vol. V*, pp. 291-362; for the years 1981-84, *Congress and the Nation Vol. VI*, pp. 261-286, 289-329; for the years 1985-88, *Congress and the Nation Vol. VII*, pp. 357-413.

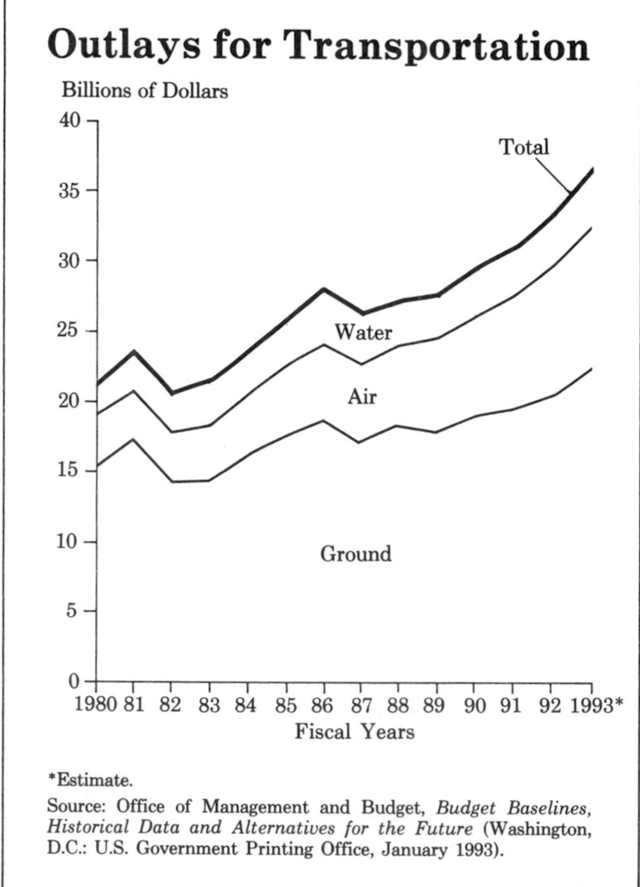

*Estimate.

Source: Office of Management and Budget, *Budget Baselines, Historical Data and Alternatives for the Future* (Washington, D.C.: U.S. Government Printing Office, January 1993).

agreed to require random drug and alcohol testing of all transport workers with safety-sensitive jobs.

Congress stepped in to end two railroad strikes during the Bush administration and continued to fund the Amtrak passenger rail system despite the administration's position that Amtrak should rely on its own revenues.

Cable Television. The spirit of compromise that helped Congress and the administration reach agreement on the transportation measure was lacking during consideration of legislation to impose new federal controls on the booming cable television industry. The measure, the most ambitious re-regulation of an industry during the Reagan-Bush era, was enacted over Bush's veto at the end of the 102nd Congress.

The drawn-out struggle over the cable legislation pitted the cable industry, its congressional defenders and the Bush administration against pro-regulation lawmakers and consumer groups. The supporters also had the backing of the broadcast industry, which stood to benefit from certain provisions added to garner its support.

Defenders of the measure argued that cable rates had outstripped inflation since the industry was freed from regulation at the end of 1986. They said new controls were needed to protect consumers and competitors from price gouging, poor customer service and discriminatory business practices. Opponents said the federal government should not interfere in the cable market and warned that the legislation would increase cable rates, not lower them as supporters claimed.

Bush miscalculated when he made support of his cable bill veto into a test of political loyalty during the final weeks of his uphill battle for re-election in 1992. The strong veto override vote in both houses of Congress may have reflected the waning influence of a president soon to be defeated at the polls. More certainly, the vote demonstrated the members' desire to support legislation popular with many voters back home.

Other Communications Legislation. In another move to restore regulatory controls loosened during the Reagan era, Congress approved limits on the amount of advertising permitted on children's television programs. After debating charges of liberal bias on public television, lawmakers agreed to continue federal funding for public broadcasting with some new restrictions designed to make programming decisions more balanced.

Supporters of the "fairness doctrine" — a requirement that broadcasters present all sides of controversial topics — failed to persuade Congress to reinstate the doctrine in law. The fairness doctrine had been abandoned during the Reagan years, when it was seen as an unnecessary interference in the broadcast business.

Several issues addressed by Congress in 1989-92 reflected rapid changes in the communications industry. Legislation cleared to permit the sale of high-quality digital recording equipment and to regulate the rates and business practices of the new telephone-operator services found in hotels and other public places. Consumer protection legislation was enacted to regulate unsolicited telephone advertising, pornographic material offered over the phone lines and pay-per-call services.

Congress considered but failed to reach agreement on legislation to foster new communications technologies by transferring parts of the radio spectrum from government to commercial use. No agreement was reached on various proposals to govern the business dealings of the seven regional Bell telephone companies created by the 1984 breakup of the American Telephone & Telegraph Co. (AT&T) as they expanded into new communications ventures such as information services.

Consumer Protection. The Consumer Product Safety Commission, a federal agency that had languished during the Reagan years, was strengthened in authorizing legislation approved by Congress during the Bush administration.

Legislation to reform the product liability system under which large damage awards were possible was blocked. The administration and business groups supported the reform legislation as a tonic for competition in the marketplace, but consumer and lawyers' groups said the proposed changes would be unfair to the victims of unsafe products.

Chronology Of Action On Transportation And Commerce

1989-90

The 101st Congress retreated cautiously from the free-market, deregulation philosophy that had dominated transportation and commerce policies during the Reagan years.

Overruling the tobacco industry and its congressional supporters, Congress broadened and made permanent a smoking ban on most commercial flights. Stricter controls were imposed on airplane noise, the transportation of hazardous materials and the practice of "backhauling" — the shipping of food in vehicles previously used to carry garbage or hazardous materials.

An administration proposal for a new user tax on airline passengers was enacted. The tax, a fee added to the cost of airline tickets, was to be used for improvement of airport facilities. However, Congress rejected an administration bid to eliminate federal funding of the Amtrak passenger railroad, authorizing continued funding for Amtrak despite its increasing self-sufficiency.

Consumer advocates applauded in 1990 when the Consumer Product Safety Commission received its first free-standing authorization in almost a decade. The legislation also served to strengthen the agency. Another reversal of the deregulation trend was marked by legislation to reinstate limits on the amount of advertising permitted on children's television programs. The Federal Communications Commission had abolished such limits in 1984. President Bush opposed the bill but allowed it to become law without his signature.

Congress imposed tighter controls on pornographic telephone services and considered legislation to protect consumers from unsolicited telephone calls and facsimile messages. Lawmakers again failed to codify the "fairness doctrine," which required broadcasters to air controversial public issues and to present all sides of such issues. Members also could not reach agreement on legislation designed to reform the system under which the courts awarded damages in product liability suits.

Another controversial issue, the imposition of new regulations on the booming cable television industry, remained unresolved. The House in 1990 passed legislation intended to lower cable rates and spark more competition in the industry. But opposition from the cable industry as well as the Bush administration helped to block the legislation in the Senate.

Aviation Package

President Bush in 1990 achieved some of his transportation policy objectives when Congress approved an aviation package as part of the fiscal 1991 budget-reconciliation bill (HR 5835 — PL 101-508). *(Reconciliation, p. 55)*

The bill allowed new airline ticket fees of up to $3 and provided new guidelines on airplane noise. The aviation package was called "the most significant aviation legislation since deregulation" by Transportation Secretary Samuel K. Skinner on Dec. 10.

Administration Proposal

The Bush administration on March 8 unveiled a major policy initiative for financing the nation's transportation needs. The plan called for new user fees, more state and local spending, and a decreased federal commitment to mass transit programs. The new National Transportation Policy, titled "Moving America into the 21st Century," built on a number of proposals revealed in Bush's fiscal 1991 budget request.

On March 19, Bush sent Congress a $22 billion, five-year plan for commercial aviation programs. The proposal sought to increase fuel and departure taxes for airline passengers and add a new user tax, called a passenger facility charge (PFC), of up to $12 for each round-trip ticket. The money was to be used to improve airport facilities and air traffic control operations.

Critics in Congress objected to the administration's plan, saying the money for aviation programs should come exclusively from a projected $7.6 billion surplus in the Airport and Airway Trust Fund, not from new taxes. The trust fund, created in 1970, was fed by fees on tickets and fuel, although the revenues were not directly earmarked for aviation programs and expenditures from the fund were subject to general appropriations.

The administration's budget proposal called for reducing the surplus in the airport trust fund to $3 billion by 1995 through spending on capital improvement projects and Federal Aviation Administration (FAA) operations. Some critics in Congress argued that the administration plan for reducing the surplus was too gradual, and others objected to using trust fund money for FAA operations.

House Action

The House Public Works and Transportation Committee on June 28 unexpectedly approved Bush's proposal for a PFC imposed directly by airports on each airline ticket. The provision was a key part of broader legislation (HR 5170) authorizing a $22 billion, five-year plan to increase spending from the airport trust fund. The panel approved HR 5170 on a 37-10 vote and formally reported the measure (H Rept 101-581) on July 10.

James L. Oberstar, D-Minn., chairman of the panel's Aviation Subcommittee, called the PFC "a major step forward in improving airport capacity and improving the nation's air-traffic control system." Oberstar, who originally had opposed the PFC idea, estimated that the new fee would raise more than $1 billion a year to supplement spending from the trust fund and suggested the money be spent for airport improvement projects.

Opponents of the fee complained that airline passengers would be taxed twice for the same purpose — once by the existing 8 percent airline ticket tax that went into the trust fund and again by the new fee. They also argued that a new consumer tax was unnecessary in light of the trust fund surplus.

To ensure that federal trust fund spending was not reduced as a result of increased passenger fees, Public Works included language to repeal the fee if federal airport-improvement spending dropped below $3.7 billion over fiscal 1991-92. Backers of the bill assumed that only medium- and large-sized airports would elect to collect the fee. Those airports' share of airport-improvement project money from the trust fund would be reduced by 50 cents for every $1 they collected in passenger fees.

A move to strike the fee provision from the bill was defeated June 27 in the subcommittee by a vote of 25-11, but the matter was not pressed in full committee. Before passing HR 5170 on a vote of 405-15 on Aug. 2, the House rejected 171-252 an amendment offered by Douglas H. Bosco, D-Calif., to kill the PFC provision. As provided in the House-passed bill, the revenue raised from the fees could be used only to pay for facility improvements; small airports would get a portion of the funds received from medium- and large-sized hub airports.

Observers attributed the fee proposal's success to the lobbying efforts of Transportation Secretary Skinner, airport operators from across the country and politically powerful Chicago lawmakers who hoped the fee could help them win a new city airport. Some airlines also decided to support the fees, perhaps hoping the Transportation Department would reward them with desirable route assignments.

Senate Action

The Senate Commerce, Science and Transportation Committee on Oct. 10 approved a package of aviation provisions as part of the panel's fiscal 1991 budget-reconciliation bill. The provisions, sponsored by Aviation Subcommittee Chairman Wendell H. Ford, D-Ky., were agreed to by voice vote despite the protests of some panel members that they were not germane to the budget bill. The controversial passenger fees were included but with a stipulation that they could be imposed only when a federal airport noise policy was adopted and the airport trust fund had dropped below $4 billion. The package also repealed the 1986 buy-sell rule that allowed airlines at four of the nation's busiest airports to purchase or lease takeoff and landing time slots from each other. The provision was supported by smaller carriers who said the rule put them at a competitive disadvantage. A separate bill containing the repeal (S 2851 — S Rept 101-447) was reported by the Senate Commerce panel on Aug. 30.

The Senate Environment and Public Works Committee on Oct. 12 included the same provisions in its reconciliation measure.

Final Action

Ford and Oberstar struck a deal after weeks of negotiation. It included the PFC and the provisions for a tougher airport noise policy but omitted most of the language on airport slots.

During floor consideration of the Senate version of the budget bill (S 3209) on Oct. 18, Ford made additional compromises in the aviation package to diffuse opposition. The compromise, in effect adopted upon agreement 69-31 to a procedural motion, was supported by majorities from both parties. It weakened the airport noise provisions and softened a provision intended to spark competition in the granting of airport slots.

The House and Senate on Oct. 27 adopted the conference report on HR 5835 (H Rept 101-964), which included the aviation package as amended by the Senate. President Bush signed the measure on Nov. 5.

Major Provisions

The following are major aviation provisions included in the 1990 budget-reconciliation act (HR 5835 — PL 101-508):

Passenger Facility Charges. Allowed airports to impose ticket fees of $1, $2 or $3 on passengers to pay for facility improvements. The charges were limited to two boardings per one-way trip and could not be levied on passengers traveling to or from cities receiving subsidized essential air service. Congress in 1992 (HR 5518 — PL 102-388) exempted frequent fliers from the charges.

The fees could be used for any project normally eligible for federal airport improvement funds, noise-abatement projects or airport gates. The charges could be assessed at one airport and used for another airport controlled by the same authority. Proceeds also could be used to pay interest on bonds for eligible projects. The Transportation Department had to approve all passenger facility charges and make a decision within 120 days of application.

No new fees could be put into effect after Sept. 30, 1992, if trust fund spending for airport improvement programs was less than $3.7 billion for fiscal 1991 or 1992, or if essential air service funding was less than $26.6 million in fiscal 1991 or $38.6 million in fiscal 1992. Existing passenger fees were not affected by this provision.

Also, no passenger charges could be imposed until the transportation secretary issued a rulemaking notice on allocation of landing and takeoff slots, as well as a final rule establishing procedures for airports to submit proposed noise restrictions on newer, quieter Stage 3 aircraft.

State and local governments could not regulate the collection of the passenger charges or the use of the revenues, nor could contracts between carriers and airports limit an airport's ability to collect the fees or spend fee revenues.

Large and medium hub airports imposing the passenger fees had their federal airport improvement entitlements reduced by half. Of the half forfeited, 25 percent would go into the trust fund's discretionary program account. The remaining 75 percent would go into a new fund for general aviation and small commercial airports.

Federal Aviation Noise Policy. Required the secretary, by July 1, 1991, to issue regulations establishing a national aviation noise policy that included the phasing out of older, Stage 2 aircraft by Dec. 31, 1999. Carriers that had 85 percent of their fleets complying with Stage 3 noise levels by Jan. 1, 2000, could apply for waivers that would extend the date by which all of their aircraft had to comply with the higher standards to 2003. (The noise guidelines would not apply to aircraft flying solely outside the continental United States.)

Airport Improvement Program. Authorized $1.8 billion for fiscal 1991 and $1.9 billion for fiscal 1992 for the Airport Improvement Program.

FAA Facilities and Equipment Program. Authorized $2.5 billion for fiscal 1991 and $3 billion for fiscal 1992 for the FAA facilities and equipment program.

Airport and Airway Trust Fund. Repealed a law that reduced authorizations for FAA operations from the

Transportation, Commerce Leadership

Andrew H. Card, an engineer and former Massachusetts legislator, was confirmed by voice vote Feb. 21, 1992, to succeed the popular Samuel K. Skinner as transportation secretary. Skinner, unanimously confirmed to the post on Jan. 31, 1989, resigned to become White House chief of staff, succeeding the controversial John H. Sununu. Skinner was viewed as having successfully shepharded much of his legislative agenda through Congress. He had sought to shift more decision-making power — and the fiscal burden — regarding transportation policy from the federal government to the states. *(Skinner, Card, background, Cabinet profiles, p. 1174)*

The Senate by voice vote Feb. 27, 1992, confirmed Barbara Hackman Franklin as secretary of commerce. Franklin headed her own consulting firm and was a member of the Consumer Product Safety Commission (CPSC) in the 1970s. She replaced President Bush's first commerce secretary, Robert A. Mosbacher, who had been confirmed Jan. 31, 1989, on a 100-0 vote. Mosbacher resigned the post to become general campaign chairman of Bush's 1992 campaign. A wealthy Houston oilman, Mosbacher had served as finance chairman to the 1980 and 1988 Bush presidential election campaigns. *(Mosbacher, Franklin, background, Cabinet profiles, p. 1170)*

Richard C. Breeden on Oct. 6, 1989, was designated as chairman of the Securities and Exchange Commission (SEC), succeeding David S. Ruder. Breeden had been confirmed as an SEC member two days earlier by a voice vote in the Senate. Breeden, whose SEC term would expire in June 1993, had been a securities lawyer in New York, staff director of a special task force on financial regulation that Vice President George Bush chaired and chief adviser to Bush on the savings and loan crisis. Bush named three more members of the five-member SEC during his tenure in the Oval Office: in 1989, Mary L. Shapiro; in 1990, Philip R. Lochner Jr. and Richard Y. Roberts.

Anne Graham, a CPSC member since 1985, was named acting chairman upon the 1989 departure of Terrence M. Scanlon. Jacqueline Jones-Smith, who had served as an attorney at the Federal Election Commission, became CPSC head in 1990.

Airport and Airway Trust Fund if amounts for capital programs were not fully funded. Up to 75 percent of the FAA budget could come from the trust fund.

Military Airport Conversion. Earmarked 1.5 percent of airport improvement funds for conversion of up to eight military airports for civilian commercial service by September 1992.

Airport Capacity. Required the transportation secretary by July 1, 1991, to begin a rulemaking proceeding to consider more efficient methods of allocating existing capacity at high-traffic airports.

Airport Noise Abatement

Communities could speed up federally approved airport noise-abatement projects with the help of legislation (HR 968 — PL 101-71) signed by President Bush on Aug. 4, 1989.

The bill allowed communities to start work with their own funds and seek reimbursement from the Federal Aviation Administration (FAA) later. No guarantee of reimbursement was provided, but the measure gave the FAA more flexibility to aid communities that spent their own funds. Previously, airports could not begin projects until they received a grant from the FAA.

The House Public Works and Transportation Committee reported HR 968 (H Rept 101-51) on May 16, and the full House passed the bill by voice vote the same day. The Senate Commerce, Science and Transportation Committee reported the measure (S Rept 101-72) on July 11. The Senate passed HR 968 by voice vote July 24, completing congressional action.

Smoking on Airlines Ban

Against the wishes of the tobacco lobby and its congressional supporters, Congress in 1989 voted to permanently ban smoking on nearly all domestic airline flights. The only exceptions were for flights beginning or ending in Alaska or Hawaii and lasting more than six hours. The ban was included in a fiscal 1990 transportation appropriations bill (HR 3015 — PL 101-164) signed by President Bush on Nov. 21.

In 1987, Congress had imposed a two-year ban on smoking during domestic flights of two hours or less — about 80 percent of domestic flights. That ban, attached to a continuing resolution (H J Res 395 — PL 100-202), was set to expire in April 1990. *(1987 action, Congress and the Nation Vol. VII, p. 387)*

House Action. As introduced by Public Works and Transportation Subcommittee on Aviation Chairman James L. Oberstar, D-Minn., HR 598 called for a permanent end to smoking on all domestic flights. While the subcommittee turned back two efforts to substitute provisions to permanently ban smoking on flights lasting up to four hours, HR 598 was modified to simply extend the two-hour-flight ban for another two years.

In full committee, the bill was subjected to much political maneuvering and a confusing markup. A proposal by Ed Towns, D-N.Y., to replace the two-year extension with a permanent ban on two-hour flights gained the unexpected last-minute support of tobacco-state members. Anti-smoking advocates and tobacco interests came to view the Towns language as having a better chance of passing the House intact, thus forestalling stronger action. It was approved by voice vote. The panel rejected, 23-25, a proposal advocating a simple two-year extension of the two-hour ban.

HR 598 was reported (H Rept 101-212) from Public Works on Aug. 2.

Instead of acting on HR 598, the House included the airline smoking ban in its fiscal 1990 transportation appropriations bill (HR 3015), passed 366-50 on Aug. 3. Barely a word was spoken on the smoking ban during more than five hours of debate on the funding bill, despite the controversy surrounding the issue.

The provision, which made permanent the smoking ban on domestic flights of two hours or less, was offered by Richard J. Durbin, D-Ill., a sponsor of the 1987 ban. Durbin had proposed a total ban on airline smoking, but his amendment was weakened in the House Rules Committee when he sought permission to offer it as a floor amendment. After modifying the amendment to cover only two-hour flights, the Rules panel added it to the spending bill in a way that precluded a separate floor vote on the issue.

Senate Action. The Senate Appropriations Committee Sept. 7 unanimously approved HR 3015 (S Rept 101-121) with an amendment to ban smoking on all domestic flights — not just those of two hours or less.

The panel resisted efforts to weaken the amendment, which was sponsored by Frank R. Lautenberg, D-N.J., chairman of the Appropriations Subcommittee on Transportation. By a vote of 11-18, the committee rejected an amendment by Thad Cochran, R-Miss., to replace Lautenberg's language with the House-approved ban on two-hour flights. A proposal by Ernest F. Hollings, D-S.C., to complicate the issue by adding a ban on the drinking of alcohol on domestic flights was defeated, 8-15.

On the Senate floor, the three main tobacco-state opponents of the airline smoking ban — Hollings, Jesse Helms, R-N.C., and Wendell H. Ford, D-Ky. — conducted a three-day filibuster against the proposal. But the Senate Sept. 14 invoked cloture and thus ended debate on a **77-21 (R 33-11; D 44-10) key vote**, a margin well in excess of the 60 votes needed for that purpose. *(1989 key votes, p. 1021)*

Arguing that the Commerce, Science and Transportation Committee had been unfairly bypassed, Hollings, the committee's chairman, sought to have the smoking ban removed on a jurisdictional point of order. Senators rejected that move by a 34-65 vote on Sept. 14.

None of the amendments threatened by opponents of the ban materialized during floor debate, and the Senate ultimately agreed to the permanent smoking ban on a simple voice vote.

Final Action. When the transportation appropriations conference convened, negotiators faced a choice between the Senate's total ban on all flights and the House's permanent extension of the two-hour flight ban. An initial House offer to accept the Senate version without modifications was rejected when House conferees voted against it, 4-6.

On Oct. 16, the conferees agreed to the Senate's comprehensive ban with only the exception for flights beginning or ending in Alaska or Hawaii and lasting more than six hours. Durbin estimated that the exception would cover 20 to 50 flights out of some 16,000 scheduled each day.

The House adopted the conference report (H Rept 101-315) on Oct. 31 by a vote of 394-21, and the Senate on Nov. 9 by voice vote. After further negotiations, HR 3015 cleared Nov. 14.

Aviation Security

The 101st Congress considered several pieces of legislation aimed at improving aviation security, two of which became law.

Safety Guidelines

The House on July 16, 1990, and the Senate on Aug. 4 by voice votes passed a bill (HR 5131 — PL 101-370) extending a program to allow the Federal Aviation Administration (FAA) to levy civil penalties against airlines and pilots who violated airline safety guidelines. President Bush signed the measure on Aug. 15.

The bill authorized the FAA to continue issuing fines of up to $50,000 for infractions ranging from inadequate X-ray screening to air traffic violations. The enforcement program, started in 1987, was extended for two years retroactive to its expiration on July 31, 1990. Congress agreed to a short extension of the program instead of a permanent authorization because of complaints from the airline industry that the agency's enforcement efforts had been heavy-handed.

The Senate Commerce, Science and Transportation Committee reported HR 5131 (S Rept 101-425) on Aug. 3; the House Public Works and Transportation Committee had reported its version (H Rept 101-602) on July 13.

Security Procedures

A bill (HR 5732 — PL 101-604) designed to strengthen federal aviation security procedures was signed into law on Nov. 16, 1990. The measure passed the House on Oct. 1 and the Senate on Oct. 23 by voice votes.

The legislation established new Department of Transportation positions, including a director of intelligence and security, an assistant administrator for civil aviation security and federal security managers to monitor security activities at selected airports. The bill also called for new personnel standards for airport security employees and an accelerated FAA security research program.

The legislation was primarily the result of a report by a presidential commission that looked into the terrorist bombing of Pan Am Flight 103, which exploded over Lockerbie, Scotland, in 1988. Most of the recommendations contained in the commission's report already had been put into effect by the administration.

HR 5732 was based on HR 5200, which was reported from the House Public Works and Transportation Committee (H Rept 101-845, Part I) on Oct. 10.

Aging Aircraft

The House by voice vote on July 16, 1990, passed HR 3774 to improve inspection requirements for aging commercial aircraft. The measure had been reported the same day by the Public Works and Transportation Committee (H Rept 101-606).

The Senate did not act on the measure, which would have ordered the FAA to require that planes of 15 years or older be inspected for metal fatigue and other effects of aging during their regular heavy-maintenance checks. Because the agency had ordered new inspection procedures for older planes, many senators felt the legislation was unnecessary. The House passed a similar bill in 1991, but again the Senate did not act. *(1991 bill, p. 446)*

Airport Security Funds

After a lengthy tug of war over who should pay for warding off terrorist attacks on airlines — U.S. taxpayers or airline passengers — the House in 1989 passed legislation (HR 1659) authorizing $270 million in federal funds to tighten airport security and install new bomb-detection equipment. The bill was approved on Sept. 20 by a vote of 392-31.

Critics of the legislation, including the Bush administration, argued that the airlines should pay for a $100 million provision in the bill for the purchase of state-of-the-art bomb-detection equipment. Proponents argued that the government should pick up the tab because terrorist attacks were generally aimed at the United States, not the airlines.

The House Public Works and Transportation Committee reported HR 1659 (H Rept 101-59, Part I) on May 18; the House Foreign Affairs Committee reported it (H Rept 101-59, Part II) on May 31.

Aviation Security R&D

The House on Sept. 25, 1989, voted 390-0 to suspend the rules and pass a bill (HR 2365 — H Rept 101-246) authorizing $8 million in fiscal 1990 for research and development (R&D) of technology to detect plastic explosives and other threats to aviation security. Proponents of the bill were concerned that the FAA would focus its efforts on development of Thermal Neutron Analysis (TNA) equipment to the detriment of other security technology.

The Science, Space and Technology Committee reported the measure Sept. 19.

Airline Buyouts

House-passed (HR 3443) and Senate committee-approved (S 1277) legislation to restrict commercial airline leveraged buyouts died upon adjournment of the 101st Congress after the collapse of two attempted takeovers diminished the urgency of the issue on Capitol Hill.

Congressional action had been prompted by a rash of airline takeover bids in the 1980s. The legislation aimed to give the transportation secretary authority to disapprove a takeover if he found that the amount of debt involved in the purchase was likely to threaten an airline's safety, financial fitness or competitiveness.

Bill sponsors said the secretary needed this new authority because existing law allowed him to intervene in a takeover plan only after a takeover had taken place and only by threatening to revoke an airline's operating certificate — a move so heavy-handed it was rarely used.

The Bush administration urged Congress not to intervene in the airline buyout frenzy, arguing that the Transportation Department already had all the power it needed to intervene in unsound deals. President Bush threatened to veto the legislation.

House Action. The Public Works and Transportation Committee approved HR 3443 on a 23-5 vote on Oct. 18, 1989, and formally reported the measure (H Rept 101-303) on Oct. 24.

As approved by the panel, the measure required the transportation secretary to disapprove any acquisition of 15 percent or more of the voting stock of an airline if he found it would give a foreign buyer controlling interest in the airline or that the level of debt involved would result in a deterioration in safety or the sale of a "substantial portion" of aviation-related assets.

Each of the findings alone required disapproval of the buyout plan, although the secretary could make an exception in the case of asset sales if they were "in the public interest." A merger or acquisition automatically would go into effect within 30 days if the secretary took no action, with a possible 20-day extension.

While the committee was able to keep HR 3443 free of controversial amendments, language was added to the bill on the floor that was strongly opposed by the Bush administration. An amendment offered by Douglas H. Bosco, D-Calif., and adopted 283-132 on Oct. 31 required the transportation secretary to prevent an airline buyout if the prospective owner already had taken more than one airline into bankruptcy. The amendment was written specifically to stop Frank Lorenzo, owner of Texas Air, from acquiring more airlines. Lorenzo had bought two airlines — Continental Airlines and Eastern Airlines — that had filed for bankruptcy protection since he acquired them.

Bosco had opposed Lorenzo since 1981, when the airline owner pulled Texas Air's headquarters out of California, taking jobs with him. Many supporters of organized labor backed the Bosco amendment because they believed Lorenzo had used bankruptcy protection to bust unions at Eastern Airlines.

Another labor-backed amendment, offered by Peter A. DeFazio, D-Ore., and adopted 271-147 on Nov. 1, required the transportation secretary to disapprove a transaction if it was likely to lead to a "major reduction in wages, benefits, or number of employees." GOP opponents criticized the provisions as taking away the only option left under the legislation for an airline to cut costs.

The House Nov. 1 rejected two Republican amendments intended to weaken the bill. The first, offered by Ron Packard of California, eliminated as one of the conditions for disapproval of a buyout proposal the finding that the plan was likely to result in sales of a substantial portion of an airline's assets. The second, offered by C. Christopher Cox of California, limited the scope of the secretary's review to airline safety considerations. The Packard amendment was defeated 107-306; Cox, 115-300.

Packard, Cox and others insisted that the open market should determine the financial affairs and management of the airlines. They also argued that many positive buyout proposals — not just the leveraged buyouts the bill intended to inhibit — would not survive the 30- to 50-day waiting period for the transportation secretary to review the plan.

Prospects for the bill dimmed quickly. By late 1989, the financial climate for leveraged buyouts of commercial airlines had chilled. Some Republican supporters of HR 3443 indicated that they might vote to sustain a threatened Bush veto because of the two labor-backed amendments. Also contributing to the legislation's loss of momentum was the collapse of two attempted buyouts — real estate tycoon Donald J. Trump's bid for American Airlines and a union-backed bid for United Airlines.

Senate Action. While the Senate did not consider HR 3443, the Commerce, Science and Transportation Committee did approve a companion measure (S 1277) by voice vote Oct. 5. However, the bill, reported (S Rept 101-169) on Oct. 18, saw no further action.

Blind Airline Passengers

The Senate in 1990 considered legislation (S 341) to end a practice by commercial airlines that prohibited blind passengers from sitting in exit-row seats. On June 12, the Senate voted 56-44 to cut off debate, falling short of the 60 votes needed to invoke cloture and bring the measure to a vote. The bill saw no further congressional action.

The measure had been reported (S Rept 101-45) by the Senate Commerce, Science and Transportation Committee on June 12, 1989.

The Bush administration opposed S 341 on the grounds that the Federal Aviation Administration (FAA) had solved the problem with a regulation that limited the exit-row seats of commercial aircraft to passengers able to perform basic escape functions during emergency evacuations. The FAA argued that the rule did not discriminate against blind people per se, but the National Federation of the Blind disagreed.

In legislation cleared in 1986, Congress explicitly prohibited air carriers from discriminating against the handicapped. The action was taken in response to a Supreme Court decision. *(Congress and the Nation Vol. VII, p. 369)*

During consideration of S 341 on June 6, bill sponsor Ernest F. Hollings, D-S.C., accepted an amendment by Christopher S. Bond, R-Mo., to require commercial airlines to have child-safety systems. Bond argued that children should have the same protection in airplanes as in cars.

Aircraft Liability Insurance

House and Senate committees in 1989 reported legislation (HR 1307, S 640) aimed at cutting the liability insurance costs of small plane manufacturers.

Similar legislation was considered in the 99th and 100th Congresses. *(Congress and the Nation Vol. VII, p. 390)*

Sponsors of HR 1307, approved by voice vote July 20 and formally reported Aug. 4 (H Rept 101-218, Part I) by the House Public Works and Transportation Committee, said high insurance costs had made competing with overseas competitors impossible for domestic manufacturers. The bill set federal standards limiting a manufacturer's liability for an accident to his share of responsibility for damages. In many states, defendants could be required to pay more than their share of damages if victims were unable to recover from other responsible parties.

The Senate Commerce, Science and Transportation Committee on Oct. 5 approved S 640 by voice vote and on Nov. 21 formally reported the measure (S Rept 101-223). The bill, which covered private planes with fewer than 20 seats, restricted the share of a manufacturer's liability for an accident to its share of responsibility for damages. Manufacturers also were shielded from liability for injuries that occurred more than 20 years after an aircraft was delivered. S 640 was adversely reported from Senate Judiciary (S Rept 101-303) on April 5, 1990.

Trial lawyers and consumer groups strongly opposed the legislation, arguing that it limited compensation for victims of small-aircraft accidents and that it reduced industry incentives to improve safety.

FAA Authorization

A fiscal 1991-92 authorization (HR 4986) for the Federal Aviation Administration (FAA) was approved in 1990 by the House Public Works and Transportation Subcommittee on Aviation, but it saw no further action.

The 102nd Congress cleared a three-year FAA authorization in 1992. *(Story, p. 446)*

The subcommittee-approved measure authorized $17.7 billion in fiscal 1991-92 for the improvement and operation of the nation's air traffic system. The bill authorized $5.5 billion for air traffic control modernization — $2.5 billion in fiscal 1991 and $3 billion in 1992 — and allowed increased spending from the Airport and Airway Trust Fund.

The Aviation Subcommittee acted by voice vote June 14.

Hazardous Materials

Legislation (S 2936 — PL 101-615) that strengthened laws governing the transport of hazardous materials cleared in 1990. It was the first major revision of the nation's hazardous materials transportation laws.

The House and Senate had to work out substantial differences among proposals to overhaul the Hazardous Materials Transportation Act (PL 93-633), which was designed to prevent spills of chemicals and other dangerous substances being shipped across the country. The final version of S 2936 required companies involved in the transport of hazardous materials to register and pay fees to help finance enforcement and cleanup efforts.

The bill authorized $30 million over six years for states to develop emergency response plans and $54.8 million for response training and curriculum. States were given some latitude to regulate the transport of hazardous materials, but in most cases they were required to follow federal guidelines.

The bill also:

- Increased civil and criminal penalties for hazardous materials transport violations, setting a maximum of $25,000 and a minimum of $250 per violation per day.
- Provided additional federal inspectors for all transportation modes to enforce the regulations.
- Required the Transportation Department to look for ways to improve the existing system of placard notices on vehicles and to study the idea of a computerized central reporting system.
- Required safety permits for shippers who transported extremely hazardous materials such as explosives, poison gases and radioactive materials.

Background

The Hazardous Materials Transportation Act governed oversight by various federal agencies of the estimated 4 billion tons of hazardous materials that were transported across the country each year in some 500,000 shipments a day. The law was inspired by numerous accidents — many caused by defective railroad tracks — that resulted in release of hazardous materials into the environment. *(PL 93-633, Congress and the Nation Vol. IV, p. 527)*

Supporters of the law criticized the Transportation Department's enforcement of existing regulations and pointed to a lack of coordination among the various agencies that carried out the regulations. To address the problem, the law authorized the secretary of transportation to issue tougher regulations for shipment of hazardous materials and permitted the secretary to require registration of those who transported hazardous materials or manufactured containers for shipping such materials. Civil and criminal penalties were established for violators.

As the number of hazardous materials shipments increased, a consensus emerged that the law needed to be revamped. The original penalties were seen as inadequate deterrents 15 years later. And although the volume of hazardous materials shipments had increased, Transportation Department inspection and enforcement efforts had been cut.

The last previous authorization for the Hazardous Materials Transportation Act expired in 1986 (PL 98-559). *(Congress and the Nation Vol. VI, p. 328)*

Legislative History

By the opening of the second session of the 101st Congress, lawmakers were ready for a major revamping of the hazardous materials act. The Transportation and Hazardous Materials Subcommittee of the House Energy and Commerce Committee approved HR 3520, 11-0, on Jan. 31. The full committee approved the measure on March 13 and reported it (H Rept 101-444, Part I) on April 3. The Surface Transportation Subcommittee of House Public Works and Transportation unveiled its version of the bill on Aug. 2. The full committee approved it on Sept. 26 and reported it (H Rept 101-444, Part II) on Oct. 17.

The Public Works version authorized $25 million in state and local grants in fiscal 1993 for emergency-response planning and training. In contrast, the Energy and Commerce version focused on enforcement, authorizing $13 million to hire 200 new inspectors. Both plans were to be funded through registration and permit fees paid by transport companies.

The Senate Commerce, Science and Transportation Committee, meanwhile, by voice vote had approved its own version (S 2936) on July 31, which it reported (S Rept 101-449) on Aug. 30. The Senate legislation did not contain language included in both House bills to require the Transportation Department to register companies that transport hazardous waste. Instead, the department was to determine within 30 months whether annual registration requirements were necessary.

The Senate bill also included no registration fee requirement; instead, it proposed authorizing $10 million in fiscal 1991 and $25 million in fiscal 1992 for grants to states. The Transportation Department was required to add 10 inspectors above those authorized for fiscal 1990.

All three bills contained the same broad guidelines: Each set up a safety permit program for carriers that hauled extremely hazardous cargo, expanded federal authority to prosecute violators and increased civil and criminal penalties.

Differences remained over whether federal law should pre-empt tougher state laws — a provision avidly sought by industry. The Senate bill did not address the issue. The House Energy and Commerce bill called for federal preemption whenever state regulations differed from federal law, while the Public Works bill outlined more limited preemption standards.

The Senate passed S 2936 by voice vote on Oct. 23, just as sponsors from the House and Senate were working on a compromise. The negotiations that produced the final bill were led by Thomas A. Luken, D-Ohio, chairman of the House Energy and Commerce Subcommittee on Transportation and Hazardous Materials.

The House passed the compromise version of S 2936 on Oct. 25, also by voice vote. The Senate cleared the bill in the session that began Oct. 26. President Bush signed the measure Nov. 16.

The Senate accepted House language to require hazardous cargo haulers to register and pay fees ranging from $250 to $5,000. The fees were to fund grants to states to train state emergency response crews. Under the original Senate bill, the financing would have come through a separate appropriation, not a dedicated funding source.

The Senate also accepted House language aimed at more clearly delineating the federal and state regulatory roles and requiring states in most cases to follow federal guidelines. Haulers, who had feared stricter state regulation, had pushed hard for the language prohibiting states from surpassing federal guidelines with even stricter regulations.

Provisions regarding "backhauling" were stripped from the final bill. Separate legislation, however, was enacted in 1990. *('Backhauling,' below)*

The Bush administration initially opposed the hazardous materials transportation bills, particularly the requirements that companies involved in the transport of hazardous materials register each year and pay fees. But those reservations were not enough to prompt a veto.

'Backhauling' Regulation

The practice of shipping food in trucks or rail cars that earlier had been used to transport garbage or other potentially hazardous materials was more strictly regulated under legislation (HR 3386) enacted in 1990.

The "backhauling" practice was especially common east of the Mississippi River, where trucks hauled trash from the Northeast and returned with food from the Midwest. Backhauling had become more popular as the shortage of landfill space in Eastern states had made interstate garbage transport more frequent and lucrative.

Under the new law, the Transportation Department was required to set standards for what materials could be shipped in trucks and rail cars used to haul food and for decontamination procedures to be required between loads. The law barred food transport by cargo tanks that hauled extremely hazardous materials such as asbestos.

Legislative History

House. The House Public Works and Transportation Committee approved HR 3386 on Nov. 17, 1989, by voice vote and reported it (H Rept 101-390, Part I) on Dec. 1. The bill banned refrigerated trucks from backhauling and prohibited cargo tank trucks from alternating between food and non-food products.

The House Energy and Commerce Committee, which shared jurisdiction over the legislation, approved HR 3386 on March 13, 1990, and reported it (H Rept 101-390, Part II) on March 15. The bill required the Department of Transportation, in consultation with the Environmental Protection Agency and the Department of Health and Human Services, to set standards for what materials could be shipped in trucks and rail cars used to haul food.

The House suspended the rules and passed HR 3386 on March 27 by a vote of 410-15. After resolving a dispute involving an unrelated amendment, the Senate passed an amended HR 3386 by voice vote on Sept. 20. The Senate Commerce, Science and Transportation Committee had reported its measure (S 2393 — S Rept 101-332) on June 13. S 2393 combined two other backhauling proposals: S 1751, by Slade Gorton, R-Wash., and S 1904, by Al Gore, D-Tenn.

The compromise worked out between the House- and Senate-passed versions of HR 3386 dropped Senate provisions to double penalties on drug dealing at truck and rest stops and to exempt from commercial license requirements drivers who delivered agriculture equipment or provided harvesting assistance to farmers. The House accepted the compromise by voice vote in the early hours of Oct. 16; the Senate followed suit Oct. 19, completing congressional action.

President Bush signed HR 3386 (PL 101-500) on Nov. 3.

Amtrak Authorization

Congress and the Bush administration reached agreement in 1990 on legislation (HR 5075 — PL 101-322) to reauthorize the Amtrak national passenger railroad after an earlier measure met with a veto.

President Bush, following in the footsteps of his predecessor Ronald Reagan, proposed in his fiscal 1989 and 1990 budgets to eliminate federal subsidies to the private rail corporation. Ticket revenues covered about three-fourths of Amtrak's costs in 1990, up from about half in 1981. But federal funding of the railroad had remained popular in Congress, particularly among members from the Northeast, where its operations were concentrated.

HR 5075 authorized $684 million for Amtrak in fiscal 1991 and $712 million in fiscal 1992. The bill did not include the provision that prompted the veto of earlier legislation (HR 2364), which would have increased federal regulation of railroad acquisitions. *(Fiscal 1993-94 authorization, p. 447)*

HR 2364. The House Energy and Commerce Committee reported HR 2364 (H Rept 101-207) on Aug. 1, 1989. The House passed the measure on Sept. 25 by a vote of 296-93.

Bush objected to language that broadened the jurisdiction of the Interstate Commerce Commission (ICC) to regulate railroad transactions. Proposed by Dennis E. Eckart, D-Ohio, the provision required the ICC's approval of acquisitions of railroads by companies not involved in the rail business. In 1989, the ICC's authority was confined mainly to mergers between railroads.

Lawmakers were concerned about efforts by various groups of financial investors to acquire CNW Corp., the holding company for the Chicago & North Western railroad. Worried that such a step could prove detrimental for the railroad, they said this and other such potential transactions should be subject to ICC review.

The Senate Commerce, Science and Transportation Committee reported its version of the authorization bill (S 462 — S Rept 101-44) on June 6, 1989. The Senate passed an amended HR 2364 by voice vote Nov. 21.

House and Senate conferees did not reach agreement on HR 2364 until 1990. The House adopted the conference report (H Rept 101-471) on May 9 by a vote of 322-93, and the Senate followed suit the next day by voice vote.

Bush vetoed the bill May 24, citing the House-initiated ICC provision. He said that the agency's existing authority to oversee acquisitions of railroads by other railroads was adequate to protect the public interest and described the acquisition provision in HR 2364 as "an unwarranted regulatory roadblock to financial restructuring of the railroad industry."

The House overrode the veto on June 7 by a comfortable margin of 294-123. But the Senate, voting 64-36 on June 12, fell three votes short of the two-thirds needed to override. The veto thus was sustained.

HR 5075. Identical to the vetoed measure except that it did not include the acquisition provision, HR 5075 passed the House and Senate June 25 by voice votes. Bush signed the bill July 6, despite his earlier request to eliminate Amtrak subsidies.

Amtrak Waste Disposal

Congress in 1990 gave Amtrak, the federally subsidized private rail corporation, six years to stop flushing human waste onto the tracks, thus protecting the rail service from lawsuits filed by several states. The provision was attached to an unrelated bill (S 1430 — PL 101-610) on community service signed by President Bush on Nov. 16. *(Community service, p. 616)*

Up to 500 of Amtrak's long-distance passenger cars built before 1971 had toilets that flushed directly onto the tracks. Cars built since then had 30-gallon retention tanks with a six- or seven-hour capacity. When full, they automatically sprayed liquefied waste from their storage tanks onto the tracks, but only at speeds over 30 miles per hour. In 1990, Amtrak ran 220 routes a day, with 100 of them over short distances where waste disposal was not a problem.

Federal law prohibited the unregulated public dumping of human waste. But, in 1976, Amtrak was granted an exemption. Although the spraying of human waste on railroad beds had not been shown to be a public health hazard, a number of state lawsuits had prompted Amtrak to ask Congress for protection while it upgraded its trains with new waste disposal technology.

In the 1980s, the AIDS (acquired immune deficiency syndrome) epidemic spurred railroad-bed workers in Utah to push Amtrak to change the method of disposing of waste. The waste disposal provision, offered by Orrin G. Hatch, R-Utah, exempted Amtrak from all federal, state and local laws governing waste disposal, while giving the rail service time to retrofit its fleet. Amtrak estimated that the upgrades would cost $50 million to $80 million, but the provision did not explicitly authorize funds.

Local Rail Assistance

Congress on Nov. 19, 1989, cleared a bill (HR 422 — PL 101-213) authorizing $15 million a year in fiscal 1990 and 1991 for a 16-year-old program aimed at helping small towns to retain rail-freight service. President Bush signed the bill Dec. 11.

Funds for the Local Rail Assistance Program were to be used — along with matching funds from private, short-line railroad companies — for the acquisition of rail lines slated for abandonment by major carriers. The funds could be used for rehabilitation of old facilities and construction of new facilities, but not as operating subsidies.

The House Energy and Commerce Committee approved HR 422 on March 22. The House passed the measure on a voice vote under suspension of the rules Nov. 17. The Senate passed it by voice vote Nov. 19.

The Senate by voice vote on May 31 had passed a similar but more generous measure (S 255 — S Rept 101-23) drafted by the Senate Commerce Committee.

Drug Testing Transport Workers

The House and Senate in 1989 passed separate bills (HR 1208, S 561) requiring random drug testing for transport workers.

The House Energy and Commerce Committee reported HR 1208 (H Rept 101-198) on July 28. The House on July 31 passed the bill by voice vote under suspension of the rules; it was almost identical to legislation approved by the House in 1988. HR 1208 required railroad workers in safety-sensitive positions to submit to random drug and alcohol tests. Job applicants and workers involved in accidents or suspected of drug use also would be tested. Rail employees who tested positive could not be fired but would have to be suspended without pay and referred to a rehabilitation program. *(1988 legislation, Congress and the Nation Vol. VII, p. 392)*

The Senate bill was broader, covering employees in the aviation, rail, truck and bus industries. S 561 was approved by the Commerce, Science and Transportation Committee Aug. 1 by voice vote and formally reported (S Rept 101-172) on Oct. 25. The full Senate passed the bill by voice vote Nov. 9. The Senate bill provided no job protections for workers who tested positive, and Senate sponsors of the legislation objected that the House provision protecting employees took away the incentive for workers to voluntarily enter drug or alcohol rehabilitation programs.

In 1990, Congress included in the fiscal 1991 transportation appropriations bill (HR 5229 — PL 101-516) a provision to cut off 5 percent of a state's federal highway money in the first year and 10 percent in later years if that state did not suspend the driver's license for at least six months of anyone convicted of a drug offense *(1991 action, p. 448)*

Truck Stop Drugs

The Senate in 1989 voted to stiffen federal penalties for selling drugs at highway truck stops and roadside rest areas. The bill (S 819), passed by voice vote on Aug. 3, was patterned after a plan to establish "drug-free school zones" contained in a 1988 omnibus anti-drug bill (PL 100-690).

S 819, approved June 20 and reported July 27 by the Senate Commerce, Science and Transportation Committee (S Rept 101-91), set a minimum jail term of one year for a first offense of selling drugs at truck stops and rest areas and a three-year minimum for repeat offenses. Also, it doubled the maximum penalty possible for a first offense of selling drugs and tripled the maximum possible for repeat offenses.

Proponents of the legislation said illegal drugs, a major factor in truck accidents, were widely available at truck stops. The bill was not acted on by the House.

Boat Fees

Conferees from the House Merchant Marine and Fisheries Committee and the Senate Commerce, Science and Transportation Committee agreed in 1990 to impose a user fee on recreational boat owners. A requirement that the owners buy yearly Coast Guard decals was included in the fiscal 1991 budget-reconciliation package (HR 5835 — PL 101-508) cleared by Congress on Oct. 27 and signed by the president on Nov. 5. *(Reconciliation, p. 55)*

The decal provision directed the Coast Guard to set up a system for the collection of $200 million from payments by users of Coast Guard services. The fee system was to take effect immediately and to continue through fiscal 1995. The Coast Guard's authority to collect fees was extended to include direct user fees for inspection and examination of certain vessels and licensing, certification and documentation of personnel.

The Merchant Marine members had proposed, as a way around the fees, raising the duty on tonnage shipped to the United States from Western Hemisphere ports from 2 cents a ton to 27 cents and levies on ships from other foreign ports from 6 cents to 81 cents. Merchant Marine eventually acquiesced on the user fees, but only after modifying the Senate's language by adopting a sliding scale for boats of varying sizes. The proposed tonnage rates also were increased to 9 cents per ton for all ships originating from Western Hemisphere ports and 27 cents for ships from all other foreign ports.

Congress in 1992 cleared legislation to phase out the Coast Guard user fee earlier than stipulated in HR 5835. *(Story, p. 448)*

Coast Guard Authorization

A two-year authorization (HR 2459 — PL 101-225) for the Coast Guard was cleared by Congress in 1989. The bill generally approved the Bush administration's request for up to $3.38 billion in spending authority for fiscal 1990.

HR 2459 authorized $29 million for research and development, including $5 million in new oil-spill cleanup research. The measure included a provision, prompted by the *Exxon Valdez* oil spill, requiring the Coast Guard to check the backgrounds of applicants for merchant seaman's licenses to determine if applicants had abused alcohol. The Coast Guard also was authorized to revoke or suspend a license if a seaman was found to have abused alcohol. The final bill included $244 million requested for a new polar ice-breaker.

HR 2459, reported Sept. 6 by the Merchant Marine and Fisheries Committee (H Rept 101-227), was passed by the House Nov. 7 on a 383-3 vote. The Senate Commerce, Science and Transportation Committee reported its version (S 1512 — S Rept 101-182) on Nov. 2. The Senate passed an amended HR 2459 by voice vote Nov. 18. Each chamber made additional minor changes before the bill was cleared Nov. 21. President Bush signed the measure Dec. 12.

NOAA Authorization

Congress in 1989 reauthorized the ocean and coastal programs of the National Oceanic and Atmospheric Administration (NOAA), providing funding increases for most of the agency's activities. The bill (HR 1668 — PL 101-224) authorized $400.3 million for the agency in fiscal 1990, including $154.9 million for the National Ocean Service and $98.9 million for oceanic and atmospheric research.

The final bill included a Senate floor amendment that extended for two years the Governing International Fishery Agreement with Japan, set to expire at the end of 1989. The agreement allowed Japanese fishermen to operate in U.S. waters. Another Senate amendment required that lobsters imported into the United States meet the same standards as those caught by U.S. fishermen.

The administration's budget request of $323.4 million continued an eight-year trend of proposed cuts in agency programs. HR 1668 was crafted to reverse the decline.

Three House committees shared jurisdiction over HR 1668. Merchant Marine and Fisheries reported the bill (H Rept 101-119, Part I) on June 29; Public Works and Transportation (H Rept 101-119, Part II) and Science, Space and Technology (H Rept 101-119, Part II) on Aug. 3. As passed by the House on Sept. 6 on a vote of 343-44, the bill authorized $539 million. The Senate Commerce, Science and Transportation Committee reported the measure (S Rept 101-187) on Nov. 2. The Senate passed HR 1668 in the session that began Nov. 17 by voice vote, after cutting $138.7 million — mostly in oceanic and atmospheric research funds — and making a few other changes. The House accepted the Senate amendments Nov. 20, clearing the bill. President Bush signed it Dec. 12.

Two other NOAA authorization bills were passed by the House in 1989, but neither saw further congressional action.

HR 1223 authorized $225 million for three years through fiscal 1992 for the agency's marine fisheries programs, which were administered by the National Marine Fisheries Service. The bill on April 25 was reported (H Rept 101-32) from Merchant Marine and Fisheries and was passed by the House by voice vote under suspension of the rules. The Bush administration had proposed a lower authorization level and thus opposed the bill.

HR 2427 authorized $2.6 billion over three years for NOAA's weather, satellite and environmental programs. The National Weather Service would receive a total of $1.3 billion. The bill fulfilled the administration's request for an increase in funds for global-warming research, providing $20 million for such research in fiscal 1990, an increase of $11 million. The Science, Space and Technology Committee reported HR 2427 (H Rept 101-216) on Aug. 3. The full House passed the bill 380-1 on Sept. 6.

An NOAA authorization bill (S 2788 — S Rept 101-463) was reported from Senate Commerce, Science and Transportation on Sept. 14, 1990, but did not advance to the floor.

Maritime Authorization

Congress in 1989 cleared separate fiscal 1990 authorization measures for the Federal Maritime Commission (HR 840 — PL 101-92) and the Maritime Administration (HR 1486 — PL 101-115). The Maritime Commission in 1990 was reauthorized for fiscal 1991 (HR 4009 — PL 101-595), but efforts to enact fiscal 1991 legislation for the Maritime Administration failed. *(102nd Congress action, p. 450)*

Maritime Commission. HR 840 authorized $16.4 million in fiscal 1990 for the Maritime Commission, which regulated the U.S. maritime industry. The amount was equal to the Bush administration request and was nearly $3 million, or 20 percent, more than the fiscal 1989 appropriation. Most of the increase was to establish a computerized system for registering shipping rates.

The House Merchant Marine and Fisheries Committee reported HR 840 (H Rept 101-31) on April 25, 1989. The same day, the House passed the bill by voice vote under suspension of the rules. The Senate Commerce, Science and Transportation Committee reported the measure (S Rept 101-71) on July 11. The Senate Aug. 4 passed an amended version by voice vote. The House agreed to the Senate changes the next day, clearing HR 840. President Bush signed it Aug. 16.

HR 4009 authorized $15.9 million in fiscal 1991 for the Maritime Commission. House Merchant Marine reported the bill (H Rept 101-440) on April 2, 1990. The House passed HR 4009 by voice vote under suspension of the rules the next day. On Aug. 4, the Senate passed an amended HR 4009 by voice vote. The bill finally cleared Oct. 28. The president signed it Nov. 16.

Maritime Administration. HR 1486 authorized fiscal 1990 appropriations for the Maritime Administration, including $3.7 million for research and development activities; $33.2 million for expenses related to manpower, education and training; and $26 million for operating programs. An open-ended authorization was provided for expenses related to national security support capabilities, including the Ready Reserve Force and the National Defense Reserve Fleet.

HR 1486 was reported (H Rept 101-39) from House Merchant Marine on April 25, 1989. The House passed the bill by voice vote May 2. The Senate Commerce Committee reported the measure (S Rept 101-119) on Aug. 30. The Senate passed an amended version Sept. 22 by voice vote, and the House accepted the changes Oct. 2. HR 1486 was signed into law Oct. 13.

In 1990, a fiscal 1991 Maritime Administration authorization (HR 4205) stalled. The House passed the bill by voice vote under suspension of the rules Oct. 1. Merchant Marine and Fisheries had reported it (H Rept 101-487) on May 16.

Marine Fisheries Bills

In addition to its action on various National Oceanic and Atmospheric Administration (NOAA) authorization measures, the House in 1989 passed three other marine fisheries bills. All were reported by the House Merchant Marine and Fisheries Committee and passed by the House by voice vote under suspension of the rules on April 25. *(NOAA bills, p. 425)*

Interjurisdictional Fisheries Authorization. HR 1225 (H Rept 101-34) authorized $23.6 million for three years through fiscal 1992 for Commerce Department programs aimed at conserving stocks of fish in both federal and state waters. Of this amount, $15 million was authorized for federal grants to states for fisheries research projects. The Bush administration opposed the bill, saying that states and industry — not the federal government — should fund such programs.

Panama Canal Authorization. HR 1763 (H Rept 101-35) authorized the Panama Canal Commission to use revenues from tolls and related sources for the maintenance of the canal in fiscal 1990. The bill set limitations on types of expenditures. The administration supported the bill.

Anadromous Fish Conservation Act Authorization. HR 1224 (H Rept 101-33) authorized $24 million through fiscal 1992 for programs under the Anadromous Fish Conservation Act (PL 89-304). The 1965 law was intended to conserve fish such as salmon and shad that swim up rivers from oceans or other large water bodies to spawn. *(Congress and the Nation Vol. II, p. 492)*

The act authorized the Interior and Commerce departments to enter cost-sharing arrangements with states and other non-federal entities. The Bush administration opposed HR 1224, saying that the objectives of the fish act had been met and that states should finance future projects.

Cable Regulation

Legislation to regulate the rates and other business practices of the booming cable television industry was approved in 1990 by the House (HR 5267) but was blocked in the Senate (S 1880) by intense opposition from the industry and the Bush administration.

Both measures authorized the Federal Communications Commission (FCC) to regulate rates for basic cable service. The bills also sought to increase competition in the video marketplace by prohibiting cable programmers with ties to cable operators from discriminating against competing multi-channel video services such as wireless cable, direct broadcast satellite and home satellite dish users.

The Bush administration and the FCC opposed the bills, arguing that deregulation had produced positive results for the cable industry and for consumers and that the legislation would put those gains at risk.

The struggle over cable legislation continued until the end of 1992, when Congress enacted a cable bill over President Bush's veto. *(1992 bill, p. 451)*

Background

The Cable Telecommunications Act (PL 98-549), enacted in 1984, largely deregulated the cable industry. The law eliminated the authority of state and local governments to regulate rates cable operators charged to subscribers as of Dec. 29, 1986, with some exceptions. The act also capped the franchise fee a local government could charge a cable operator at 5 percent of the system's gross revenue. *(1984 law, Congress and the Nation Vol. VI, p. 279)*

Cable operators and their trade association, the National Cable Television Association (NCTA), argued that rate regulation, high franchise fees and other restrictions imposed in the franchising process limited cable's ability to finance investments needed to reach more subscribers and to increase program offerings.

An FCC report issued in July 1990 contended that deregulation had contributed to a growth in cable service. Investment in new and expanded capability, spending on cable programming and the percentage of households with cable service available all increased between 1984 and 1989. At the same time, however, rates for cable services increased faster than the rate of inflation.

Members of Congress, citing individual instances of rates doubling or tripling, charged that cable operators had engaged in monopolistic price gouging. As a result, pressure mounted for legislation to restore some government regulation of cable rates. In addition, some lawmakers wanted to deal with the concerns of broadcasters, wireless cable providers and satellite dish makers that the increasingly integrated cable industry was choking off competitors by keeping cable programming from other multi-channel services, shutting out other program suppliers and disadvantaging broadcasters in their placement on cable systems.

Legislative History

Two sets of companion cable legislation were introduced in 1989. The first — S 1068, sponsored by Al Gore, D-Tenn., and HR 2437, sponsored by Rick Boucher, D-Va. — would have allowed local government regulation of cable rates in areas with only one cable system; barred cable operators and their affiliated program suppliers from discriminatory practices against other cable systems; and allowed telephone companies to offer cable services so long as the funds were not provided by telephone ratepayers. Neither S 1068 nor HR 2437 saw any congressional action.

The second set of bills (S 1880, HR 3826) was introduced by Sen. John C. Danforth, R-Mo., and Rep. Jim Cooper, D-Tenn. The legislation would have allowed local rate regulation in areas with only one cable system; barred programmers with connections to cable operators from discriminating against other cable systems; restored so-called must-carry rules that required cable operators to air local television broadcasts; and limited any multiple cable operator's overall number of subscribers to 15 percent of the national total.

S 1880, HR 3826. The Senate Commerce, Science and Transportation Committee on June 7, 1990, approved 18-1 a substitute version of S 1880. Major provisions of the Senate panel's bill:

- Allowed the FCC to set rates for "basic tier" cable service in most areas where the agency determined that cable systems were not subject to "effective competition."
- Allowed the FCC to regulate rates for ad-supported cable channels such as CNN and the sports channel ESPN based on consumer complaints that rates were "significantly excessive."
- Barred cable programmers with ties to cable operators from discriminating in price and other conditions against the cable company's competitors.
- Forced cable companies to carry local television stations on the same channel number they used over the air or, at the broadcaster's discretion, on the channel used before federal courts struck down the must-carry rules in 1985.
- Directed the FCC, within a year, to limit the number of subscribers a single cable operator could reach and to restrict the number of channels a cable operator could devote to affiliated programming.

NCTA objected to language barring cable operators from "unreasonably" refusing to deal with other multichannel video programming distributors. Angered by the industry's opposition, Gore offered an amendment to strengthen that language. The amendment, adopted by voice vote, also required sale of cable programming carried on satellites to home satellite dish users.

The committee decided not to consider another amendment, opposed by the cable industry, which proposed to allow telephone companies to enter the cable market.

S 1880 was formally reported (S Rept 101-381) on July 19.

Efforts to defuse controversies over S 1880 failed. When Majority Leader George J. Mitchell, D-Maine, sought to bring the measure to the floor under a procedure requiring unanimous consent Sept. 28, opponents Tim Wirth, D-Colo., and Bob Packwood, R-Ore., said they would object. A third senator, Malcolm Wallop, R-Wyo., also voiced opposition to the bill.

Wirth, whose state was home to one of the nation's largest cable companies, said he would support legislation dealing with soaring rates and declining service but criticized provisions in S 1880 that could limit exclusivity agreements and volume discounts. Packwood said cable deregulation had achieved its goal of expanding cable service and programming and called the legislation "an overreaction."

Wirth and Gore made a last-ditch attempt to revive the bill by agreeing Oct. 11 on an amendment to preserve some forms of exclusive agreements between cable operators and programmers. But the Bush administration repeated its opposition to the legislation and the cable industry expressed concerns about a host of potential amendments from Democratic senators to strengthen the bill's regulatory provisions. Sponsors subsequently gave up on S 1880.

HR 3826 saw no congressional action.

HR 5267. A late-drafted bill more to the liking of the cable industry was reported (HR 5267 — H Rept 101-682) on Sept. 6 by the House Energy and Commerce Committee. Drafted by Edward J. Markey, D-Mass., and Matthew J. Rinaldo, R-N.J., chairman and ranking Republican, respectively, of the Telecommunications Subcommittee, HR 5267 contained the explicit protection the cable industry sought for exclusive programming agreements so long as the cable market was deemed competitive. The measure also took a less aggressive approach than S 1880 on limiting monopolistic practices — calling for a study, not new rules, on limiting horizontal and vertical integration in the cable industry.

On rates, the House committee bill required the FCC to cap prices for the "basic tier" of cable programming — local broadcasts and public-access channels — and to reduce rates for other programming deemed "unreasonable or abusive." The bill made it slightly easier to roll back rate increases than did the Senate committee's bill.

HR 5267 included a compromise reached among the cable industry, broadcasters and public television over the must-carry issue. The accord called for cable operators to devote about 25 percent of their channels to local broadcasts and to carry those broadcasts on the same channel number that TV stations used.

As in the Senate, the House panel deferred the controversial issue of letting telephone companies into the cable market.

With most of the controversies removed from HR 5267, House leaders brought it to the floor Sept. 10 under suspension of the rules — with limited debate and no amendments permitted. Despite a threatened veto from the Bush administration, no one opposed the bill on the House floor and it passed by voice vote.

Television Violence

Congress in 1990 exempted industry executives from antitrust law so they could meet to discuss ways to reduce the "negative impact" of TV violence. The exemption was attached to a federal judgeships bill (HR 5316 — PL 101-650). *(Judgeships bill, p. 774)*

Congressional supporters of the exemption, including Sen. Paul Simon, D-Ill., said that violence on television was pervasive and probably had contributed to aggressive behavior, especially among children. They hoped that the networks would agree on guidelines to reduce the level and extent of TV violence.

Some network spokesmen had expressed concern that antitrust laws barred them from jointly considering programming guidelines to reduce violence. But spokesmen for the three major networks said the legislation was not necessary and suggested it would not change their programming decisions.

Both the Senate and House in 1989 passed separate legislation (S 593) containing the exemption. The Senate acted by voice vote on May 31. The House on Aug. 1 first passed its version (HR 1391 — H Rept 101-123) 399-18 under suspension of the rules, then passed by voice vote an amended S 593 with the language of HR 1391.

The Senate-passed version of S 593 permitted program producers to talk about guidelines on the depiction of illegal drug use and explicit sex, as well as violence. The drugs element was added before Senate Judiciary Committee approval of the legislation; the explicit sex provision was an amendment by Jesse Helms, R-N.C., adopted by the Senate 91-0 on May 31.

House Judiciary Committee members objected to adding language beyond the topic of TV violence, arguing that the bill should be as narrow as possible to avoid steps toward censorship. They blocked the appointment of conferees until they could get Helms' guarantee that the explicit sex provision would be dropped. Senate sponsors of the drug language agreed to eliminate it after hearing the House protest.

Helms insisted on his amendment until the last days of the 101st Congress, when it appeared that either the television antitrust exemption would not become law or that inclusion of the sex-on-TV language would kill the judges bill in the House. Helms' GOP colleagues interested in passage of the judgeship legislation eventually persuaded him to back down.

Don Edwards, D-Calif., chairman of the House Judiciary Subcommittee on Civil and Constitutional Rights, opposed S 593 as "indirect censorship," a position supported by the American Civil Liberties Union.

Closed-Captioning

Legislation (S 1974 — PL 101-431) to increase the accessibility of closed-captioned television broadcasts for hearing-impaired viewers was enacted in 1990. Under the bill, television sets had to be equipped with built-in decoder circuitry capable of displaying closed-captioned transmissions.

The bill covered sets with screens 13 inches or larger that were manufactured in or imported to the United States. The requirement was to take effect after July 1, 1993.

Captioning involved converting the spoken parts of TV programs into printed words for display on the television screen, like subtitles in foreign movies. The captions were transmitted as encoded data in video-broadcast signals and seen only by viewers with decoding equipment. In 1990, only about 300,000 TV sets in the United States were equipped with the decoders, which were expensive ($160 to $200 each) and difficult to install.

All prime-time network television programming was closed-captioned, as were many sports events and independent TV and cable programs. But producers of closed-captioned programs expressed concern that, without legislation, the market for decoders would remain limited. By guaranteeing wider access to closed-captioning, sponsors of the bill hoped to help not only the hearing impaired but also children and adults learning to read and immigrants trying to learn English.

The Senate Commerce, Science and Transportation Committee reported S 1974 (S Rept 101-393) on July 25. The Senate passed the bill by voice vote on Aug. 2.

The House Energy and Commerce Committee reported its version of the measure (HR 4267 — H Rept 101-767) on Sept. 27. The House passed HR 4267 by voice vote under suspension of the rules Oct. 1. The measure subsequently was laid on the table, and the House passed S 1974 by voice vote the same day. President Bush signed the bill Oct. 15.

Children's Television

Taking a step to reverse the deregulation trend of the Reagan administration, Congress in 1990 cleared legislation (HR 1677 — PL 101-437) limiting the amount of advertising permitted on children's television shows. Despite objections to the measure, President Bush allowed it to become law at midnight Oct. 17, without his signature.

Bush's predecessor in the White House, Ronald Reagan, had pocket-vetoed a similar bill in 1988, arguing that the government should not interfere in broadcasters' decisions about advertising and programming. *(1988 bill, Congress and the Nation Vol. VII, p. 404)*

In a statement issued on Oct. 17, Bush said that although he supported the goals of HR 1677 "wholeheartedly," he opposed the bill because its methods violated the spirit of the First Amendment by interfering with "free choice." The statement did not explain why the president allowed the measure to become law.

Background. Many supporters of the children's television bill believed that deregulation of broadcasting had led to a sharp decline in the amount and quality of educational programming available to children. Advertising on children's programs was particularly harmful, they argued, because young children often could not distinguish programs from commercials.

Advertisers and some Republicans opposed limits on children's television advertising as a violation of First Amendment protections of commercial speech and a dangerous first step in the direction of more government intrusion.

The National Association of Broadcasters (NAB), however, did not object to the measure and even urged Bush to sign it. The broadcasters had decided not to oppose the popular bill in hopes of gaining congressional support for other industry priorities — particularly a requirement that cable companies carry local television signals. *(Cable bill, p. 427)*

Legislative Action. The House Energy and Commerce Committee approved HR 1677 by voice vote on April 11, 1989, and formally reported the measure (H Rept 101-385) on Nov. 21. As approved by the committee, HR 1677 was identical to the bill pocket-vetoed by Reagan. The measure was the result of extensive negotiations between chief sponsor Edward J. Markey, D-Mass., and the NAB.

The Senate Commerce, Science and Transportation Committee reported its version of the bill (S 1992 — S Rept 101-227) on Nov. 22. The legislation included less stringent limits on children's advertising, but tougher language requiring broadcasters to air shows specifically designed for the educational needs of children.

After months of negotiations intended to mollify opponents, the Senate passed S 1992 by voice vote on July 19, 1990. The House passed its nearly identical version (HR 1677) by voice vote on July 23. The only item that needed to be resolved was a Senate provision to authorize a $10 million National Endowment for Children's Educational Television. The House bill had no such provision.

During the week of Sept. 17, the House and Senate agreed after informal negotiations to lower the amount of the endowment to $2 million in fiscal 1991 and $4 million in fiscal 1992. The Senate by voice vote Sept. 24 passed the compromise version of HR 1677. The House accepted the changes Oct. 1, clearing the bill.

Major Provisions. The bill reinstated limits, abolished by the Federal Communications Commission (FCC) in 1984, on the amount of advertising allowed on children's programs. Beginning in April of 1991, commercials on children's programs were limited to 12 minutes per hour on weekdays and 10½ minutes per hour on weekends.

As a condition of broadcast license renewal, television stations were required to show that their overall programming, as well as children's shows, met the educational needs of children. In a concession to broadcasters, sponsors agreed to this provision instead of a more stringent Senate proposal that would have required stations to air shows specifically designed for the educational needs of children.

On the controversial issue of "program-length commercials" — programs that featured characters drawn from toys — Congress rejected an outright ban and instead required the FCC to report on the programs within 180 days of enactment. In addition, the bill authorized $6 million over two years to develop better programs for children.

Children's TV Grants

The Senate on Aug. 4, 1989, passed a bill (S 797 — S Rept 101-66) authorizing $10 million in fiscal 1990 for federal grants to promote children's educational programming. The grants were to be made by the commerce secretary on the advice of a council to be made up of 10 experts.

Programs produced under the grants would first have to be offered for two years to public television stations and then could be made available at low cost to commercial broadcasters, provided the programs did not include advertising.

Daniel K. Inouye, D-Hawaii, the bill's sponsor, said the amount of money spent on children's educational programs in the United States — about $40 million each year for public TV broadcasts — "pales in comparison to that in other countries."

The bill was reported July 11 from the Senate Commerce, Science and Transportation Committee.

FCC Reauthorization

A two-year reauthorization for the Federal Communications Commission (FCC) was cleared by Congress in 1990. The bill (HR 3265 — PL 101-396) authorized $109.8 million for fiscal 1990 and $119.8 million for fiscal 1991.

The legislation also provided for FCC fee retention by allowing the agency to keep 4 percent of the cost of regulation fees that it collected in fiscal 1990 to defray the costs of collecting such fees; and granted the FCC additional power to prevent willful or malicious interference with radio communications.

HR 3265 was reported by the House Energy and Commerce Committee (H Rept 101-316) on Oct. 27, 1989, and passed the House by voice vote under suspension of the rules on Oct. 30. The Senate passed an amended version by voice vote on July 19, 1990. The House accepted the Senate changes on Sept. 13, clearing the bill.

President Bush signed it on Sept. 28.

An FCC reauthorization measure, providing broadcast user fees, stalled in 1991. *(Story, p. 458)*

Fairness Doctrine

Congressional Democrats, having failed in 1987, tried again without success in 1989 to write into law the "fairness doctrine," a requirement that broadcasters air controversial issues and present all sides of such issues. The doctrine was repealed by the Federal Communications Commission (FCC) in 1987, the same year President Ronald Reagan vetoed a bill to make it law. *(Congress and the Nation Vol. VII, p. 405)*

The 1989 effort to restore the doctrine was sidetracked when the proposal was dropped from a fiscal 1990 deficit-reduction reconciliation bill (HR 3299 — PL 101-239). The fairness doctrine remained on the cutting floor despite a last-minute attempt by House Energy and Commerce Committee Chairman John D. Dingell, D-Mich., to reinsert it. *(Reconciliation bill, p. 43)*

President Bush had indicated he would veto a free-standing bill to codify the fairness doctrine, but Dingell and other sponsors argued that the president would not let the provision stand in the way of approval for a bill that included a capital gains tax cut and other administration priorities.

The House defeated an amendment to strip the fairness doctrine from the reconciliation bill on Oct. 3 by a vote of 162-261. But the provision was dropped from the bill along with several other "extraneous" provisions as part of an agreement between Democrats and the administration to keep the reconciliation bill focused on deficit-reduction issues. *('Dial-a-porn' restrictions, p. 431)*

When the House debated the fairness doctrine in October, arguments for and against were familiar. Opponents said broadcast outlets were no longer scarce, as they were when the FCC first imposed the doctrine. They also argued that the fear of government intervention would inhibit free speech by giving broadcasters a reason to avoid controversial issues altogether. One opponent accused Dingell of reviving the debate primarily because he was angry that the FCC had acted without his panel's approval.

Proponents countered that the doctrine had not prevented broadcasters from covering issues of importance in the 38 years it was law and that covering both sides of issues was part of the public interest responsibility of broadcasters.

Radio Spectrum Allocation

The House in 1990 passed legislation (HR 2965) designed to shift radio spectrum space from defense and other federal uses to the private sector. The Senate did not act on the legislation. The House passed another such bill in 1991, and again the Senate failed to act. *(1991 bill, p. 459)*

Background. Calls for the government to give up some excess frequencies stemmed from the growth in radio spectrum use by cellular telephones, pagers and remote control devices — and from the prospect of new services such as high-definition television and personal-communications networks.

The radio band, part of the broader electromagnetic spectrum, was measured in meters of wavelength and cycles per second, or "hertz." Radio waves ranged from 3 kilohertz (thousands) up to 300 gigahertz (billions), with AM radio at the lower end, television in the middle, and satellites and microwave at the top.

Nearly 200 new radio stations went on the air in the United States in 1926, operating at random and creating interference range wars. Congress subsequently passed the 1927 Radio Act and the 1934 Communications Act to establish rules for allocation and licensing.

By 1990, virtually all of the desirable areas of the spectrum had been taken. Entrepreneurs complained that the congestion was allowing competitors from Europe and Japan to gain an upper hand in the field.

Legislative Action. HR 2965 was approved by the House Energy and Commerce Committee by voice vote on June 19 and reported (H Rept 101-634) on July 27. Committee Chairman and chief sponsor John D. Dingell, D-Mich., called the bill "one of the most important initiatives for our long-term economic prosperity."

The House bill was modified before reaching the floor to accommodate some concerns of the Bush administration. The minimum amount of space to be transferred from public to private use was reduced from 200 megahertz — the equivalent of 30 new TV channels — to 175 megahertz. Also, the range from which the Federal Communications Commission (FCC) could conduct spectrum space transfers was broadened. And federal agencies were given three years, not six months, to vacate the frequencies.

The House passed HR 2965 on July 30 by voice vote under suspension of the rules. Daniel K. Inouye, D-Hawaii, introduced a similar bill (S 2904) in the Senate, but it stalled in the Commerce, Science and Transportation Committee. Pentagon officials and some senators had reservations about the bill, and Congress was preoccupied by a crisis in the Middle East.

Revenue Debate. The spectrum allocation legislation stoked an old debate over whether the government should charge for spectrum space. For decades, economists had recommended that the federal government glean revenue from the airwaves. But Congress had balked, fearing that the wealthy would control the frequencies.

Advocates of charging for spectrum space argued that the private sector already controlled the airwaves with cash. On Aug. 22, 1990, for the first time since Congress in 1981 repealed a law against profiteering from license competitions, a private auction for the right to bid on a license for a new FM radio station was held in Kentucky. *(1981 action, Congress and the Nation Vol. VI, p. 263)*

The administration wanted public auctions to become a part of the FCC license process and had called for auctioning of 6 megahertz of underused spectrum to raise about $3.4 billion over two years. The House Energy and Commerce Committee, responding to the administration's position, removed language in HR 2965 that barred auctioning of the newly available spectrum.

While the National Association of Broadcasters (NAB) saw merit in auctioning licenses of spectrum newcomers such as mobile communications, it argued for years that broadcasters were different and should not be made to pay fees for spectrum. The NAB argued that broadcasters would be hardest hit by spectrum user fees because theirs was a free service to the public, with revenue coming primarily from advertising rates. If those rates went up, the number of ads would go down, making recouping their losses harder for broadcasters. User fees also would deal a fatal blow to many smaller stations on the edge financially, the NAB asserted, and would deteriorate local programming. Finally, NAB maintained that, if fees were imposed, broadcasters would no longer necessarily feel beholden to the concept of operating in the public interest, a keystone of U.S. broadcasting theory. Broadcasters were the only spectrum users who had to provide public service functions, ranging from public service announcements, equal-access rules, commitments to providing local news and an emergency broadcast system.

Critics called broadcasters' arguments ironic, coming from an industry that had worked with the Reagan-era FCC to dismantle public service regulations such as children's television content rules and the "fairness doctrine."

'Dial-A-Porn' Restrictions

A second effort to restrict "dial-a-porn" operations won congressional approval in 1989 as part of a fiscal 1990 spending bill (HR 3566 — PL 101-166) for the departments of Labor, Education, and Health and Human Services (HHS). The amendment partially restored sanctions struck down by the Supreme Court in June 1989.

Congress in 1988 approved an outright ban on obscene and indecent telephone services as part of an education bill (PL 100-279). In *Sable Communications of California Inc. v. Federal Communications Commission*, the Court upheld the ban on obscene dial-a-porn telephone services but overturned the ban on indecent phone services. *(1988 law, Congress and the Nation Vol. VII, p. 658; case summary, p. 838)*

In an effort to circumvent the Court's constitutional concerns, a provision was added to a fiscal 1990 deficit-reduction reconciliation bill (HR 3299), which imposed an outright ban on obscene dial-a-porn and a ban on the use of indecent services unless a person specifically subscribed to the service.

The dial-a-porn provision was included along with a provision to restore the "fairness doctrine," which required broadcasters to air both sides of controversial public issues. Congress failed to override a veto of the fairness doctrine in 1987, and sponsors hoped that pairing it with the dial-a-porn provision sought by conservative Republicans would help get it approved. *(Fairness doctrine, p. 430)*

When "extraneous" items, including the dial-a-porn and fairness provisions, were dropped from the reconciliation bill, the Senate added only the anti-pornography language to the Labor-HHS bill. The House on Nov. 17 turned back a move to reject the Senate dial-a-porn provision by a vote of 98-306 and then agreed to concur in the Senate anti-pornography amendment by a vote of 402-0.

FCC Minority Preference

In a surprising endorsement of affirmative action, the Supreme Court on June 27, 1990, ruled that Congress could mandate preferential treatment of minorities to increase their ownership of broadcast licenses. The Court said "benign race-conscious measures" were constitutional so long as they served important government objectives. The 5-4 decision in *Metro Broadcasting Inc. v. Federal Communications Commission* marked the first time the Court had upheld an affirmative action program not devised to remedy past discrimination.

During the eight years of the Reagan administration, the Federal Communications Commission (FCC) had tried to dismantle two programs designed to help minorities obtain broadcast licenses. One program gave special credit to minorities in proceedings for new licenses, and the other allowed some radio and television stations to be sold only to minority-controlled companies. Beginning in 1987, Congress had blocked the commission from spending any of its appropriated funds to examine or change the two programs.

White-owned broadcasting companies challenged the policies as violating constitutional equal-protection guarantees. Other opponents of the policies, including the Bush administration, contended that the policies were not linked to proof of past discrimination. In his opinion for the Court, Justice William J. Brennan Jr. stressed Congress' determination that race-based preferences were necessary for broadcast diversity and that lawmakers had long dictated protection for minorities. *(Case summary, p. 839)*

Phone Rates

Legislation (HR 971 — PL 101-435) to beef up regulatory oversight of the burgeoning telephone-operator services industry was cleared in 1990. The bill required the Federal Communications Commission (FCC) to review rates charged by companies that operate telephones in hotels, airports, hospitals, gas stations and other public buildings.

The "alternative telephone operators," an industry spawned by the 1984 breakup of the American Telephone & Telegraph Co. (AT&T), leased lines from long-distance carriers and then charged consumers for placing calls. Hotels and other businesses often contracted with such operators because they offered generous commissions. Critics said the costs of the commissions were passed on to unsuspecting phone users, who paid up to 250 percent more for phone services than they would have paid if placing the calls from home.

The bill required the FCC to review rates filed by each operator-service provider. If the rates appeared unreasonable, the agency was to force the provider either to justify the rates or to announce them to consumers at the beginning of calls. As a last resort, the FCC was to regulate the rates.

The House passed its version of the bill by voice vote under suspension of the rules on Sept. 25, 1989; the measure had been reported by the Energy and Commerce Committee on Aug. 3 (H Rept 101-213). The Senate Commerce, Science and Transportation Committee reported a substantially similar bill (S 1660 — S Rept 101-439) on Aug. 30, 1990. After negotiations among lawmakers, the industry and the FCC, the Senate passed a compromise substitute version of HR 971 by voice vote on Oct. 1. The House accepted the changes Oct. 3, clearing the measure for the president, who signed it Oct. 17.

Telemarketing Controls

The House and Senate passed separate bills (HR 2921, S 2494) in 1990 to strengthen regulation of telephone advertising. Differences between the two measures were not resolved, and the legislation died at the end of the 101st Congress. Similar legislation became law in 1991. *(1991 bill, p. 459)*

HR 2921 allowed people and businesses that did not want their phone numbers used for unsolicited advertisements to put their numbers on a nationwide list. Telemarketers would be fined if calls or transmissions were made to any number on the list. The Federal Communications Commission (FCC) was to compile the list and punish offenders.

The measure also made it unlawful for autodialers — computers that dialed large blocks of numbers to deliver prerecorded messages — to place unsolicited sales calls to any emergency phone line of a hospital, law enforcement agency, fire station or physician's office. The FCC was directed to require — as soon as the technology was available — that autodialers disconnect when the called party hung up.

HR 2921 was reported by the House Energy and Commerce Committee (H Rept 101-633) on June 27 and passed the House by voice vote under suspension of the rules on July 30. President Bush said he would veto the measure, arguing that the problems addressed could be solved without legislation.

S 2494 sought to strengthen the authority of the Federal Trade Commission (FTC) to control fraud committed in connection with telephone sales and provided for restrictions on autodialers. S 2494 (S Rept 101-396) was reported July 26 by the Commerce, Science and Transportation Committee and passed the Senate by voice vote Oct. 23.

Related legislation (HR 1354) was approved by the House Energy and Commerce Committee in 1989. The bill would require the FTC to crack down on fraudulent phone sales with new regulations, and it gave states more authority to sue telemarketers across state lines. The House passed a similar bill in 1988, but HR 1354 was more explicit in covering the telemarketing activities of banks that issued credit cards. *(1988 action, Congress and the Nation Vol. VII, p. 411)*

Telephone Monopolies

For the first time since the breakup of the American Telephone & Telegraph Co. (AT&T) in 1984, lawmakers in 1989-90 attempted to loosen court restrictions on the seven regional telephone companies — the so-called Baby Bells. The 102nd Congress would act similarly. *(Story, p. 461)*

The consent decree that led to the breakup of AT&T restricted the Bell companies' activities in the areas of long distance, telecommunications equipment manufacturing and information services. The purpose was to keep the fledgling Baby Bells from committing monopolistic practices and choking off potential competitors. The Bell companies and others argued that the business restrictions hurt U.S. competitiveness by slowing the introduction of new technologies that were available abroad. However, companies — such as the newspaper industry — that saw their interests threatened by allowing the Baby Bells into their business areas countered that keeping the Bell companies from using their monopoly over phone lines to run competitors out of business would be impossible. Consumer groups, meanwhile, were concerned that the phone companies would dip into funds from phone ratepayers to pay for expensive new technologies.

The Senate Commerce, Science and Transportation Committee approved S 1981 by voice vote May 23, 1990. The bill, formally reported (S Rept 101-355) June 29, would allow the Baby Bells to make telephone equipment and would permit the regional phone companies to enter joint manufacturing ventures, so long as they were not with other Bell companies.

A more controversial draft bill was formulated in 1989 and early 1990 by the House Energy and Commerce Subcommittee on Telecommunications. The proposal would allow the Bell companies to research, design and develop telecommunications equipment and, under certain circumstances, to gain Federal Communications Commission approval to fabricate equipment. The draft legislation also would allow the companies to produce telecommunications software and to offer information services, including electronic publishing, in areas outside their own regions where they did not have a monopoly over telephone lines.

The companies' push for legislative relief was blunted April 3, 1990, when a three-judge panel of the U.S. Court of Appeals for the District of Columbia issued a ruling that gave the Baby Bells a second chance on electronic information services. While upholding the earlier decision as it dealt with restrictions on long distance and equipment manufacturing, the court sent the matter of electronic information services back to the lower court with new instructions. A decision was still pending at the end of 1990.

Consumer Product Safety

In a long-sought victory for consumer advocates, Congress in 1990 cleared legislation (S 605 — PL 101-608) to reauthorize the troubled Consumer Product Safety Commission (CPSC). The bill was the first free-standing authorization of the agency since 1981.

S 605 strengthened the agency's rulemaking powers; raised civil penalties for rules violations; and relaxed the commission's quorum requirements, making it easier to do business. Funding for the agency was authorized at $42 million in fiscal 1991 and $45 million in 1992.

Background

Congress created the CPSC in 1972 (PL 92-573) as an independent agency to regulate potentially dangerous consumer products. In its early years, the commission was buffeted by criticism from consumer groups, businesses and Congress for inefficiency and poor management. But the discontent was not intense enough to inspire a major revamp of the agency's structure or mandate. *(1972 act, Congress and the Nation Vol. III, p. 685)*

With the election of Ronald Reagan in 1980, the controversies intensified and the agency became a battleground pitting consumer advocates against a free-market, deregulation-minded Republican administration. The administration failed to abolish the agency as planned but did succeed in reining it in by cutting its budget and staff and by appointing commissioners who subscribed to the deregulation philosophy.

As a result of the continuing political controversies, Congress did not reauthorize the CPSC after 1981. (Funding was provided through appropriations measures.) In the 100th Congress, CPSC reauthorization bills won approval from both the House and Senate Commerce committees. But the Senate measure subsequently was blocked from floor consideration by the two Republican senators from Idaho, James A. McClure and Steve Symms. They objected to efforts by the commission to shut down a small company in their state that manufactured a device designed to assist commercial harvesters of earthworms. The senators believed the device posed no safety threat, contrary to CPSC allegations. Such "product-specific" language had halted reauthorizations in previous years as well. *(100th Congress action, Congress and the Nation Vol. VII, p. 410)*

Legislative Action

Senate. The Senate Commerce, Science and Transportation Committee by voice vote on April 18, 1989, approved a two-year CPSC authorization bill (S 605 — S Rept 101-37), which was formally reported May 25. McClure again held up floor consideration of the measure because of the worm device issue. But when the Idaho worm company went bankrupt, he dropped his objections and the Senate passed S 605 by voice vote on Aug. 3.

The Senate adopted by voice vote an amendment offered by Frank R. Lautenberg, D-N.J., to raise certain civil penalties included in the bill and index the civil penalties to inflation. Richard H. Bryan, D-Nev., chairman of the Commerce panel's Consumer Subcommittee, succeeded in keeping the bill free of the product-specific provisions that had stopped earlier bills.

House. After much debate at the subcommittee level over product-specific provisions, the House Energy and Commerce Committee approved its CPSC authorization bill (HR 4952 — H Rept 101-567) by voice vote on June 19, 1990. The measure was reported June 28. The controversial provisions directed the commission to act on specific products, including reclining chairs, children's toys, amusement park rides, three-wheel all-terrain vehicles (ATVs) and automatic garage-door openers.

Supporters of the product-specific provisions wanted stronger regulatory control of the marketplace, but opponents — most of them Republicans — argued that the commission should be allowed to make its own decisions. Consumer groups backed the provisions, while industry representatives opposed them.

The House passed HR 4952 under suspension of the rules July 16 by voice vote with little debate. The House then passed an amended S 605 by voice vote.

Final Action. The product-specific language remained the biggest difference between the House- and Senate-passed versions of S 605. Also to be resolved was House language requiring manufacturers to report to the CPSC when they were sued over allegedly harmful products. The chambers differed as well on the commission's scope and structure. The House bill called for eased quorum requirements for a five-member CPSC, while the Senate bill would have reduced the number of seats on the panel to three.

On the long-running controversy over product-specific provisions, House conferees acceded to Senate demands to remove language that would have directed the agency to tighten regulation of certain products, such as ATVs, amusement park rides, and children's toys and sleepwear. The deleted House language on ATVs, strongly opposed by the industry, would have permanently banned three-wheeled ATVs and required the development of stability standards for four-wheeled ATVs.

However, the conferees retained other product-specific provisions that were acceptable to the industries involved. The final bill directed the CPSC to develop safety standards for cigarette lighters and automatic garage-door openers. In addition, the agency was required to study the effectiveness of using bittering agents to prevent poisonings and to report on its efforts to reduce indoor air pollution.

On the question of a quorum for doing business, the final bill stipulated that two members would make up a quorum as long as the commission consisted of three members.

The bill responded to criticisms of the CPSC for the practice of suspending rulemaking procedures after manufacturers promised to develop voluntary standards. Under the House language retained in the final bill, promises were not enough; voluntary standards had to be in place before the rulemaking threat could be removed. The conferees also agreed on compromise language that required manufacturers to report to the CPSC when they settled or lost three lawsuits concerning a hazardous product within a two-year period.

The Senate adopted the conference report on S 605 (H Rept 101-914) by voice vote Oct. 23. Two days later, the House 375-41 agreed to suspend the rules and adopt the conference report, thus clearing S 605. President Bush signed the bill Nov. 16.

'Dolphin-Safe' Tuna

Responding to continuing concern about the safety of the world's dolphin population, Congress in 1990 approved stricter labeling requirements for canned tuna. The change, part of a bill (HR 2061 — PL 101-627) reauthorizing the federal fishery conservation program, required that companies labeling their tuna "dolphin safe" be able to prove that their tuna was not caught with methods that killed dolphins.

The tuna-labeling language reflected consumer and congressional concern over the killing of dolphins in the eastern Pacific Ocean. For unknown reasons, dolphins swam with tuna and became entangled in purse seine nets used to harvest tuna. The three largest U.S. tuna processors had pledged to purchase only tuna caught with dolphin-safe methods. But dolphin advocates said that other processors were using the dolphin-safe label dishonestly.

The tuna-labeling provision was added to a bill (HR 2061) reauthorizing the 1976 Magnuson Fishery Conservation and Management Act (PL 94-265), which governed marine life within a 200-mile zone off U.S. shores. The measure was reported from House Merchant Marine and Fisheries (H Rept 101-393) on Dec. 15, 1989. The House passed the bill 396-21 under suspension of the rules Feb. 6, 1990. An amended version passed the Senate on Oct. 11 by a vote of 98-0. After further negotiation, the bill finally cleared on Oct. 27, and the president signed it Nov. 28. *(1976 act, Congress and the Nation Vol. IV, p. 887)*

The dolphin provision was a weaker version of language contained in HR 2926. As introduced, HR 2926 required the labeling of tuna in accordance with the method used to catch it. Tuna caught with methods that did not harm dolphins could be labeled "dolphin safe," while other tuna was to be labeled as caught "with technologies that are known to kill dolphins." During House Merchant Marine and Fisheries Committee markup, the bill (H Rept 101-579, Part I) was amended to ban the import and sale of any dolphin-unsafe tuna. The bill saw no further action.

HR 2061 also imposed a ban on the use of large drift nets in U.S. waters and called on the administration to pursue an international agreement to end use of large-scale drift nets on the high seas. The nets, which stretched for miles and captured fish indiscriminately, were blamed for killing dolphins, birds and other marine life. They were used most often by Taiwan, South Korea and Japan.

The fisheries bill reauthorized the Magnuson Act through fiscal 1993, with increased spending levels for fisheries programs. The measure also quadrupled the maximum penalty for violating U.S. fishing laws and extended the jurisdiction of the U.S. fisheries councils to include tuna, a highly migratory species that had been regulated through international agreements.

Fish Inspection

Legislation (S 2924) that for the first time would have required mandatory federal inspection of fish and shellfish died at the end of the 101st Congress. Both the House and Senate passed S 2924 in 1990, but differences over which federal agencies should have jurisdiction over fish inspection were not resolved before adjournment.

The Senate gave the Agriculture Department (USDA) the job of inspecting and licensing fish processing plants, while the Commerce Department was to prevent fishing in contaminated waters and the Food and Drug Administration (FDA) was to set contaminant standards. The House gave the inspection duties to the FDA and the National Oceanic and Atmospheric Administration (NOAA).

Americans consumed an increasing amount of seafood during the 1980s. By 1990, however, fish sales began to experience a slide that many officials attributed to a crisis of consumer confidence. While the USDA oversaw mandatory meat and poultry inspection, fish was governed only by a voluntary, industry-based program. Fish was the only major flesh food not subject to mandatory federal inspection.

Legislative History

Committee Action. Three House committees and two Senate committees tussled over which agency should be given the duty to inspect fish. Each wanted to give the responsibility to the agency it oversaw.

The House Energy and Commerce Committee's bill (HR 3155 — H Rept 101-875, Part I), reported Oct. 15, converted the government's voluntary seafood inspection program into a mandatory one run by the FDA and required the agency to inspect food processing plants "frequently and randomly." The choice of the FDA was defended by Health and the Environment Subcommittee Chairman Henry A. Waxman, D-Calif., who said only it had the scientific expertise necessary to enforce standards that would be imposed for microbiological contaminants and chemical residues. He also argued that, unlike USDA, the FDA would not be responsible for promoting and helping to market the products it regulates.

Under another bill (HR 3508), approved by the House Agriculture Committee by voice vote July 18, fish inspection duties were divided among three agencies. The Agriculture Department would license and inspect fish processing plants, including processing ships; the Commerce Department would have authority to bar fishing in waters found to be contaminated; and the FDA would be responsible for setting standards governing acceptable levels of contaminants in fish. The bill also would exempt fishing vessels from inspection and would enable states to petition the federal government for the right to set tougher fish safety laws.

A third measure (HR 2511 — H Rept 101-874, Part I), approved by the House Merchant Marine and Fisheries Committee by voice vote on Aug. 1 and reported Oct. 15, called for a two-stage seafood safety progam to be developed by the Commerce Department.

On the Senate side, the Agriculture, Nutrition and Forestry Committee on May 22 approved by voice vote a bill (S 1245 — S Rept 101-335), which it reported June 22, to require the USDA to administer a mandatory fish inspection program — using standards set by the FDA. The Commerce Department would have the authority to prohibit fishing in contaminated waters. The panel agreed 10-9 to an amendment offered by Thad Cochran, R-Miss., to drop a provision that would have protected employees at fish processing plants who reported public health or sanitary violations. Cochran maintained that the provision would duplicate a pending "whistleblowers" protection bill (S 436). *('Whistleblowers' protection, p. 862)*

A second Senate bill (S 2228 — S Rept 101-369) was approved by the Commerce, Science and Transportation Committee by voice vote on June 27 and reported July 13. The measure directed the Commerce Department to carry out periodic inspections of plants and vessels that processed fish, while the FDA was given responsibility for regulating seafood contamination levels and sanitation in processing facilities. The bill prohibited user fees and allowed federal agencies to delegate inspection authority to states that were at least as stringent about inspection as the federal government.

Floor Action. The Senate passed S 2924, a clean version of S 1245, by voice vote on Sept. 12. The measure provided for periodic and unannounced inspections of domestic processing plants by the USDA and required the department to certify foreign processing plants that exported to the United States. The Senate Sept. 12 rejected,

39-59, S 1228, offered as a substitute amendment to S 2924. The Bush administration preferred the substitute, which expanded the existing seafood inspection program at the FDA and Commerce Department.

When the House took up the fish inspection legislation in late October, the bitter debate that ensued pitted the Agriculture panel against the Energy and Commerce and Merchant Marine committees. The Agriculture Committee, led by Chairman E. "Kika" de la Garza, argued that the House should adopt S 2924 with few changes so as to complete action on the legislation before adjournment.

The House, however, on Oct. 24 adopted 277-153 an amendment by Gerry E. Studds, D-Mass., a member of Merchant Marine, and John D. Dingell, D-Mich., chairman of Energy and Commerce, that endorsed mandatory federal inspection but only for shellfish. The program would have been carried out by the FDA and the NOAA, the two agencies that ran a modest, voluntary seafood inspection program.

The House approved its version of S 2924 by a vote of 324-106 on Oct. 24. With little time left in the session, conferees did not meet to resolve differences between the House- and Senate-passed bills.

Product Liability

A scaled-back bill (S 1400) to establish federal standards for product liability suits was approved by the Senate Commerce, Science and Transportation Committee in 1990 but never reached the floor. It was the fourth time since 1984 that the industry coalition pushing measures aimed at reducing payments to consumers injured by dangerous or defective products had won committee approval but failed to get a floor vote. The legislation stalled again in the 102nd Congress. *(Previous action, Congress and the Nation Vol. VI, p. 285; Congress and the Nation Vol. VII, pp. 370, 398; 102nd Congress action, p. 462)*

S 1400 got a small boost early in 1990 when President Bush, in his State of the Union address, included product liability reform on a list of his administration's legislative goals. Vice President Dan Quayle, who had supported previous bills on the subject while in the Senate, lobbied Congress on the issue as head of the President's Council on Competitiveness.

Sen. Bob Kasten, R-Wis., sponsor of S 1400, dropped some of the most controversial language from measures he had sponsored in previous Congresses to gain Democratic support. The bill included provisions to establish a higher burden of proof for consumers bringing product liability suits, to prevent awards to people who were intoxicated or using drugs if that was the primary cause of their injury, and to limit pain and suffering damages to the proportion of a manufacturer's fault.

The bill also established a "collateral source rule" allowing a reduction in damage awards against a defendant for any payment a plaintiff received from another source. The liability of product sellers was limited to cases in which the seller was at fault or the manufacturer could not be sued. The bill imposed a uniform statute of limitations allowing plaintiffs two years to file a suit after discovering an injury and its cause.

Kasten dropped from the bill a cap on punitive damages — the damages ostensibly imposed to punish companies for extreme negligence or wrongdoing. The cap provision had been sought by business interests but opposed by consumer groups and the legal community.

Five Democrats joined eight Republicans to produce the Commerce Committee's 13-7 vote in favor of the bill (S Rept 101-356) on May 22. The bill was formally reported June 19.

S 1400 languished in the Senate Judiciary Committee for two months until the panel discharged it without recommendation after a one-day hearing July 31. Kasten tried but failed late in the session to add product liability provisions to a technology programs bill designed to spur U.S. competitiveness.

A companion product liability bill (HR 2700) was introduced in the House, but the Energy and Commerce Committee did not hold hearings on the measure.

Insurance Antitrust Exemption

Legislation (HR 1663) to limit the freedom of insurance companies to share price information and engage in monopolistic practices narrowly won approval from the House Judiciary Committee in 1990 but received no more attention and died at the end of the 101st Congress.

HR 1663 was approved June 20 by a vote of 19-17, with three Democrats joining 14 Republicans in opposition. The measure, formally reported (H Rept 101-976) on Oct. 27, prohibited monopolization, price-fixing, allocation of territories among competing insurance companies and unlawful "tying," the practice of forcing a consumer to purchase one type of insurance to be eligible to buy another. If enacted, the legislation would have been the first congressional revision of the McCarran-Ferguson Act of 1945 (PL 79-15), which exempted the insurance industry from antitrust laws. *(Congress and the Nation Vol. I, p. 454)*

The bill's chief backer, Judiciary Chairman Jack Brooks, D-Texas, said the legislation was needed to restore competition to the insurance industry. Opponents warned that the measure would call into question the legality of many industry practices and would not make insurance more available or affordable.

Similar legislation had been pushed unsuccessfully in the 99th and 100th Congresses. In 1991, the House Judiciary Committee again reported an insurance antitrust bill, which also died without further action. *(Earlier bills, Congress and the Nation Vol. VII, p. 399; 1991 bill, p. 463)*

SBA Authorization

Congress in 1990 cleared a four-year authorization (HR 4793) of the Small Business Administration (SBA), the agency set up in 1953 to guarantee commercial loans to small business owners who were unable to get credit on their own. The agency also made direct loans to veterans, the disabled, minority businesses and some disaster victims.

President Bush signed the bill (PL 101-574) on Nov. 15, despite lingering concerns about its cost. The bill raised spending for most SBA programs by 5 percent in fiscal 1991-94. It provided $3.55 billion for small business guaranteed loans, $440 million more than Bush requested.

Hoping to address administration and Budget Committee objections to the bill's costs, the Senate insisted on removing a House provision for $42 million over three years for pilot grant programs to help small businesses in rural areas. The final bill instead directed the SBA to hold five regional conferences on rural development. Senators also removed a House provision that would have allowed borrowers to refinance SBA-guaranteed loans with lower penalties than under existing law.

The House Small Business Committee reported HR 4793 (H Rept 101-667) on Aug. 3, and the House passed the measure 398-26 on Sept. 25. The Senate passed an amended version of the bill by voice vote on Oct. 27, and the House cleared it for the president in the early morning hours of Oct. 28 (in the session that began Oct. 27).

Hotel Fire Safety

Congress in 1990 cleared legislation (HR 94 — PL 101-391) designed to encourage hotels and motels to install fire-prevention equipment. The bill prohibited most government employees from staying in hotels that failed to meet new sprinkler and smoke detector guidelines and barred federally funded conferences from being held in such places. Hotels shorter than four stories were exempted from the sprinkler requirement.

States were given two years to compile lists of hotels within their borders that had complied with the guidelines. Within four years, 65 percent of any federal agency's travel funds would have to be spent at hotels with the fire safety equipment. By the seventh year, 90 percent of federal travel funds would have to be spent at such hotels.

According to the American Hotel and Motel Association, of the 3 million hotel rooms in the United States, just under half had sprinklers. Large, high-rise hotels almost all had sprinklers.

The House Science, Space and Technology Committee reported HR 94 (H Rept 101-357) on Nov. 14, 1989. The House passed the bill by voice vote under suspension of the rules on Nov. 17. The Senate Commerce, Science and Transportation Committee reported the measure (S Rept 101-408) on Aug. 1, 1990, and the full Senate passed an amended version by voice vote three days later. The House accepted the Senate changes on Sept. 10, clearing the bill. President Bush signed HR 94 on Sept. 25.

'Fire-Safe' Cigarettes

A cigarette that would not start fires but would appeal to consumers was the goal of legislation (HR 293 — PL 101-352) cleared by Congress in 1990. The measure directed the Consumer Product Safety Commission (CPSC) to supervise a study of cigarette safety, with an eye toward developing safer cigarettes that also were acceptable to smokers.

The House Energy and Commerce Committee on July 26 approved the measure by voice vote. The panel's Consumer Protection Subcommittee had agreed to drop a provision in the original bill that would have required the CPSC to establish a mandatory fire safety standard for cigarettes.

The House and Senate approved the bill by voice votes on July 30, and President Bush signed it Aug. 10.

Fastener Standards

Legislation (HR 3000 — PL 101-592) cleared in 1990 required that high-strength metal fasteners conform to the manufacturing specifications claimed for them. The bill was intended to stop the sale of counterfeit nuts, bolts, screws and washers.

HR 3000 also required that samples from each lot of high-strength fasteners used in critical areas of nuclear power plants, commercial airliners and military vehicles be tested by a laboratory accredited by the National Institutes of Standards and Technology.

The House Science, Space and Technology Committee reported HR 3000 (H Rept 101-211, Part I) on Aug. 2, 1989. The Energy and Commerce Committee, which shared jurisdiction, reported the measure (H Rept 101-211, Part II) on Sept. 12. The House passed the bill by voice vote under suspension of the rules Sept. 19.

The Senate Commerce, Science and Transportation Committee reported HR 3000 (S Rept 101-388) on July 23, 1990. The Senate passed an amended version by voice vote Oct. 26. The House accepted the changes the same day, clearing the bill. Bush signed it Nov. 16.

1991-92

The 102nd Congress produced major legislation authorizing highway and mass transportation programs over six years. After winning some concessions from the Democrat-controlled Congress, President Bush signed the transportation measure and lauded its job-creating potential. The bill gave states and cities new freedom to divert federal highway funds to mass transit projects.

A provision added to the transportation measure ended the long fight over automobile air bags by requiring front-seat air bags on all passenger cars made after Sept. 1, 1996.

Congress also acted twice to end rail strikes and approved more stringent alcohol and drug testing for transit workers.

Some legislators wanted to help economically strapped airlines by imposing new federal protections in the wake of the Reagan-era deregulation of the industry. Congress showed little interest in airline "re-regulation" but did direct the Transportation Department to inject more competition into the airline computer reservation system.

Enactment of a cable regulation measure over Bush's veto culminated four years of debate and intense lobbying on the question of whether the federal government should step in to control the rates and business practices of the booming industry. Public pressure for lower cable rates played a key role in the measure's success; the administration and the cable companies, however, predicted that rates would increase.

Striving to keep up with rapidly changing technologies, Congress cleared legislation to compensate the music industry for home taping with digital audio technology, regulate the pay-per-call telephone industry and protect consumers from unsolicited telephone and facsimile advertising.

Legislation was considered but not enacted to transfer radio frequencies to the private sector and to regulate the business ventures of the seven regional Bell telephone companies created by the 1984 breakup of the American Telephone & Telegraph Co. (AT&T).

Reviving an old issue, Congress debated the question of whether public broadcasting was too liberal. After some heated exchanges, lawmakers agreed to reauthorize the Corporation for Public Broadcasting with adjustments designed to make the non-profit agency more accountable and objective. As in past Congresses, legislation to revise product liability lawsuit rules was considered but not enacted.

Highway Authorization

After months of fighting among lawmakers over the allocation of federal funds, President Bush in 1991 signed into law a sweeping $151 billion measure (HR 2950 — PL 102-240) authorizing highway and mass transit programs for six years, beginning in fiscal 1992. The new law made dramatic changes in the nation's transportation policy, giving states and cities more freedom to divert federal highway funds to mass transit projects.

Bush objected to key components of the bill as it made its way through Congress, but he embraced the final product as the only job-creating legislation of the year. "It moves us closer to our three top domestic priorities: jobs, jobs and jobs," Bush said as he signed the bill on Dec. 18. Sponsors of the legislation said 1.1 million jobs would be created and about a million other jobs preserved.

Congress cleared HR 2950 on Nov. 27 after two weeks of an often rancorous conference that brought together 92 lawmakers from nine House and Senate committees. The bill they produced restructured federal transportation policy at a time when the 44,328-mile Interstate Highway System begun in 1956 was reaching completion and the focus was shifting to mass transit.

"This is the first transportation legislation of the post-Interstate era," said Daniel Patrick Moynihan, D-N.Y., a leading Senate sponsor. "It marks the transition from system building to system performance."

The bill's drafters did retain the federal role in highways, creating a new National Highway System made up of the Interstate network and primary arterial roads. The system was a key component of the Bush administration's transportation proposal. But they allowed state and local officials to transfer more than half of the funds authorized for highways, up to $65 billion, to mass transit programs.

The law consolidated key federal highway programs into one large Surface Transportation Program from which states were free to spend funds on nearly any transportation project. For the first time, urban areas could spend federal transportation funds as they pleased. And metropolitan planning organizations received new powers to negotiate with states for transportation funds.

The dramatic changes in transportation policy proposed in the legislation often were overshadowed by disputes among lawmakers over how to distribute billions of dollars in federal funds. To resolve these disputes, the bill's drafters tossed aside longstanding formulas for distribution of highway funds, resorting instead to lump-sum payments and a record number of special road projects.

Highlights of the Bill

The legislation injected much-needed funds into state highway and mass transit coffers, mostly from gasoline tax revenues paid into the federal Highway Trust Fund. Highway programs were authorized at $119.5 billion over six years, while $31.5 billion was authorized for mass transit for the same period.

Gas Taxes. A House effort to hike gasoline taxes by a nickel failed, but the legislation did impose new gas taxes. The 1990 White House-congressional budget deal included a nickel increase that was set to expire after fiscal 1995; HR 2950 extended half of that five-cent increase through fiscal 1999. That meant federal gas taxes would drop from 14 cents a gallon to 11.5 cents a gallon in October of 1995, not to 9 cents as set out in the budget deal.

Road Construction and Repair. In addition to the funds allocated to states for highway and bridge work, hundreds of local road projects that had been put off by state highway departments received special attention. The authorization included $6.2 billion for 539 priority road projects, most of which were specified by House members.

Mass Transit. Mass transit systems received their biggest funding increases since the federal government began helping out in 1964. Funding was slated to more than double to $31.5 billion over six years. Nearly $5 billion was authorized for 57 new rail and bus systems. And state transit operators were given new flexibility to spend highway funds on mass transit.

Local Control. With construction on the Interstate system nearly complete, lawmakers abandoned federal policies that had left residents powerless to stop freeway construction in their neighborhoods. Urban areas were given much more control over state funding decisions and received money that states could not touch.

Safety. Air bags were required for all passenger cars made after Sept. 1, 1996, on the driver's side and front-seat passenger side. States were given $1.3 billion in grants to improve safety on highways. *(Air bags, p. 444)*

Research. The authorization included $660 million for research on devices such as computer-controlled traffic monitoring and dashboard navigation systems. An additional $700 million was authorized for a prototype "magnetic levitation" train system that would hover at high speeds above an electromagnetic rail.

Administration Proposal

President Bush and Transportation Secretary Samuel K. Skinner unveiled the administration's ambitious five-year, $105 billion transportation bill on Feb. 13, 1991. The plan centered on a 155,000-mile National Highway System designed to integrate the Interstate network with new and existing feeder routes. States would be given more flexibility to spend highway funds on mass transit, but in return they would have to contribute a greater share of funds for road projects.

The administration was less generous with mass transit, calling for just $16.3 billion over five years and a higher local matching share for capital projects. The proposal called for an end to operating assistance for 147 transit systems serving large cities.

Senate Committee Action

The Senate Environment and Public Works Committee approved its own transportation bill (S 965, later renumbered S 1204) by a vote of 15-1 on May 22. The measure was drafted by Moynihan, chairman of the Subcommittee on Water Resources, Transportation and Infrastructure and a long-time critic of federal highway policy. He believed states and cities should have more freedom in their use of federal transportation dollars.

Courthouse Project

Legislation (S 2641 — PL 102-334) cleared in 1992 restored $396 million in fiscal 1992 highway funds cut from the sweeping 1991 highway authorization (HR 2950 — PL 102-240) to help pay to renovate a Brooklyn, N.Y., courthouse.

The measure effectively eliminated funding for the $457 million courthouse project and subjected it to the normal appropriations process.

Sen. Daniel Patrick Moynihan, D-N.Y., had added the courthouse provision to the authorization measure during House-Senate conference negotiations. He had hoped to settle a longstanding dispute about what to do with the overcrowded U.S. District Court building in Brooklyn. A plan to relocate the courthouse to an old post office building across the street was advocated, and Moynihan pressed the General Services Administration (GSA) — which was responsible for courthouse projects — to move forward with it. GSA informed the senator that congressional approval was needed and drafted the provision.

Moynihan insisted that he intended only to authorize the project. But, by attaching it to the highway bill, he effectively skirted the appropriations process. Programs authorized for highway and mass transit programs were considered mandatory spending because they were paid for by dedicated gasoline taxes from the Highway Trust Fund.

The Office of Management and Budget (OMB), having chosen to calculate the courthouse as if it were a highway project with higher upfront costs than public buildings, ruled that $1 billion in fiscal 1992 budget authority was needed to account for it. That put the highway bill over a spending ceiling set by the 1990 budget agreement. So, to offset the courthouse and other smaller cost-overruns, OMB cut the bill's budget authority by $1.2 billion for fiscal 1992. The highway money was to have provided an estimated 50,000 road construction and repair jobs nationwide in 1992.

Moynihan came under immediate pressure from state transportation officials to correct the problem. But his effort became much more difficult when Congress Feb. 4 used $449 million of the money made available by the OMB decision to help pay for the extension of unemployment benefits (HR 4095 — PL 102-244). *(Unemployment benefits, p. 725)*

The Senate March 24 passed Moynihan's initial bill (S 2398) by voice vote. It repealed the courthouse provision, restored the $1 billion and cleared the way for states to receive an immediate 6 percent boost in highway funds. The House Ways and Means Committee buried the bill because the unemployment measure had already used much of the funds.

On April 30, the Senate by voice vote passed a second Moynihan effort (S 2641) to restore only $396 million to highway programs and to repeal the courthouse provision. The bill languished in the House Public Works and Transportation Committee, where it was used as a bargaining chip for other transportation-related concessions the committee members sought from the Senate.

In his third try, Moynihan added S 2641 to the fiscal 1992 supplemental appropriations bill (HR 5132), but the provision was dropped in conference. Moynihan subsequently announced that he had given up on resolving the issue.

Then, in a surprise move, the House July 28 passed S 2641 by voice vote under suspension of the rules, clearing the measure. President Bush signed the bill Aug. 6.

Many viewed the whole episode as a test of wills between Moynihan and the Bush administration. Moynihan accused the White House of abandoning its support for the courthouse, while the administration tried to portray Moynihan's provision as an example of the evils of pork-barreling.

Both the Bush administration proposal and the Moynihan bill covered five years, cost $105 billion and favored road repair over new construction. But while Bush sought to expand the federal role with a new, 155,000-mile National Highway System, Moynihan's proposal gave states complete control over federal transportation funds. That shift of power to the states made the bill popular among urban liberals who wanted more funding for mass transit, as well as among rural conservatives who preferred local to federal control.

The Senate bill proposed to:

- Replace current highway funding programs with a new surface transportation program, from which states could spend $45 billion from fiscal 1992 to 1996 on any surface transportation project.
- Set aside $5 billion for a new congestion and air quality program that would help cities comply with Clean Air Act guidelines by improving transit systems.
- Provide $14 billion to maintain the Interstate Highway System, with an 80-20 federal-state match.
- Provide $7.2 billion to complete the final segments of the Interstate system.
- Require states to coordinate transportation improvement programs with local metropolitan planning organizations in urban areas with populations of more than 50,000 and to update the plans at least every two years.
- Provide $750 million for a magnetic levitation demonstration project.

The mass transit portion of the bill, handled by the Senate Banking, Housing and Urban Affairs Committee, ignored the administration's plan and instead proposed boosting mass transit spending annually by 7 percent. Fiscal 1992 spending would be $3.8 billion, rising to $4.7 billion in fiscal 1996. The banking panel also proposed retaining operating assistance and having equal matching shares for highway and transit programs.

While making no major changes in Moynihan's proposal, the Senate Public Works panel adopted by voice vote an amendment by Frank R. Lautenberg, D-N.J., to ban double and triple trailer trucks from operating outside states that did not then permit them. Another amendment, by John H. Chafee, R-R.I., adopted 12-4, allowed states to repay owners of billboards that violated the 1965 Highway Beautification Act (PL 89-285) by amortizing the owners' costs for the billboards over time. *(1965 act, Congress and the Nation Vol. II, p. 477)*

The committee defeated 4-11 an amendment offered by Bob Graham, D-Fla., to increase the amount of highway funding going to so-called donor states — those that contributed more in gasoline tax revenues to the Highway Trust Fund than they received from the federal government. Opponents argued that some states would always need help from others to maintain the nation's highways.

Before markup, Moynihan agreed to allow the Department of Transportation to study the proposed National Highway System for two years and report back with a detailed map of which existing and new highways would make up the system. The administration, however, was not impressed and vowed to veto the bill if it did not include the new system as well as higher state and local matching shares.

Senate Floor Action

Disagreement over the distribution of federal highway funds continued on the Senate floor for more than a week before a compromise was reached. Before approving S 1204 on June 19 by a vote of 91-7, the Senate agreed to endorse Bush's proposal for a new National Highway System, removing a major reason for a threatened presidential veto.

The allocation of trust fund money became an issue because some states routinely received more from the Highway Trust Fund than they contributed, while others contributed more than they received. The disparity was necessary to build a uniform national system that traversed larger and poorer states. But lawmakers from donor states had become increasingly dissatisfied with the arrangement as the Interstate system neared completion.

Under the committee bill formula for allocating highway funds, a state would receive an average of the difference between what it gave and what it got back over the previous five years. Unhappy with that formula, 35 senators representing 19 donor states called for either a more equitable funding formula or an increase in the 85 percent minimum allocation established by Congress in 1982 (PL 97-424). *(1982 law, Congress and the Nation Vol. VI, p. 301)*

The successful compromise amendment, offered by Robert C. Byrd, D-W.Va., was designed to take advantage of $8.2 billion in extra highway funds made available in the budget resolution after the Senate committee bill was introduced. Originally, the Byrd amendment rewarded states that had gasoline taxes higher than the national average and gave even more help to states with per capita disposable income levels below the national average.

Many donor-state senators were unsatisfied with that formula, however, and the Byrd amendment was modified during backroom negotiations led by Majority Leader George J. Mitchell, D-Maine, and Lloyd Bentsen, D-Texas, author of the 1982 law.

The result was a proposal to divide the $8.2 billion in extra funds into two accounts, with half going to the 33 states that would benefit under the Byrd formula, and half going to donor states in a way that guaranteed each more money than they were getting. Byrd said the amendment would leave only seven states giving more to the Highway Trust Fund than they got back in transportation projects, and that even those states would get back at least 98 percent of what they contributed in gasoline taxes.

Attempting to mollify donor-state senators who remained unsatisfied, Bentsen and John W. Warner, R-Va., offered an amendment, approved on a voice vote, to order the General Accounting Office to study the formula issue. The Senate approved the modified Byrd amendment by a vote of 89-9 on June 18 and later refused further attempts by Republicans to alter it.

Hoping to short-circuit a White House veto threat, the Senate agreed by voice vote to make a nominal commitment to the administration's proposal for a National Highway System to connect the Interstate system and 141,000 additional miles of feeder roads. The amendment, offered by Dave Durenberger, R-Minn., and John B. Breaux, D-La., required states to spend at least 17.5 percent of their funds on the new system and set aside $22 billion over five years to finance it.

The Senate handed a victory to the outdoor advertising industry June 12 when it refused to ban construction of billboards along major federal highways or to make it easier for states to force the removal of existing illegal signs. This change came in an amendment by Harry Reid, D-Nev., adopted 60-39, to delete billboard language in the committee's bill.

The Senate narrowly tabled (killed) another amendment, offered by Trent Lott, R-Miss., that would have changed Moynihan's bill dramatically by continuing to require the government to pick up 90 percent of the cost of Interstate maintenance and bridge projects. Moynihan had long complained that such a high federal share encouraged states to build projects regardless of need. Despite heavy lobbying by state highway officials, the Senate June 19 agreed to a motion to table Lott's amendment on a **53-44 (R 20-23; D 33-21) key vote**. *(1991 key votes, p. 1061)*

Other amendments adopted by voice vote included those offered by:

- Slade Gorton, R-Wash., requiring all newly manufactured passenger cars to have full front air bags by Sept. 1, 1995, and all light trucks to have air bags by 1997. The amendment also required drug and alcohol testing for transportation employees.
- Steven D. Symms, R-Idaho, requiring the attorney general to certify that any new federal regulation did not violate private property rights. An effort to kill the amendment failed June 12, 44-55.
- Symms, eliminating the required distribution of funds and additional planning requirements for urban areas with populations between 50,000 and 250,000 that had exceeded permissible levels of ozone and carbon monoxide.
- Jim Exon, D-Neb., freezing the length limits of trucks with double or triple trailers, as well as weight restrictions.
- Howard M. Metzenbaum, D-Ohio, creating a $31 million highway summer jobs program.

House Committee Action

First Version. The first version of HR 2950 to emerge from the House Public Works and Transportation Committee never made it to the floor because of opposition to a provision increasing the gasoline tax by 5 cents.

The bill, approved by the panel on July 25 by a vote of 49-7 and reported (H Rept 102-171, Part I) the next day, authorized $153.5 billion for transportation programs over five years and included $6.8 billion for 458 special road projects designed to win the support of lawmakers. Except for the special projects, the measure was closer to the Bush administration proposal than the Senate-passed S 1204. For example, HR 2950 wholeheartedly endorsed the concept of a national highway system, an approach strongly favored by Bush.

While not going as far as the Senate measure, HR 2950 gave states and regions more flexibility in deciding whether to spend federal funds on roads or mass transit projects. The House bill was much more kind to the highway lobby, preserving the federal government's traditional emphasis on road building and authorizing $40 billion in spending over five years for the new National Highway System. HR 2950 also authorized $32 billion for mass transit repairs and construction — double the amount proposed by the Bush administration.

The Public Works panel resolved a fight over distribution of trust fund money with a deal struck between donor-state members and committee leaders. The compromise promised that the $6.8 billion in special project funds would be divvied up to guarantee each state a 90 percent return on its dollar.

Among other issues tackled by the panel was a politically charged debate over job quotas that resulted in an unusual defeat for Surface Transportation Subcommittee Chairman Norman Y. Mineta, D-Calif. The panel rejected 24-33 an amendment by Mineta and Gus Savage, D-Ill., to split a minority set-aside program into one for women and another for minorities.

The program required states to award 10 percent of their federal highway dollars to minority contractors and, since 1987, to women. Mineta argued that the program had favored female business owners over minority owners. Opponents, led by Bud Shuster, R-Pa., called the amendment an attempt to impose more job quotas on state highway officials.

Committee Chairman Robert A. Roe, D-N.J., made clear that the special road projects were put in the bill to win support for the gasoline tax hike, which he called "A Nickel for America." Some members complained that the lion's share of the projects went to sponsors' states. Others worried that raising the gas tax to pay for pork-barrel projects would give Bush an opportunity to attack the Democrats in Congress as tax-and-spenders.

Despite growing resistance among the House membership, the Ways and Means Committee approved the financing mechanisms in HR 2950 on July 31 by a vote of 19-17 and reported the measure (H Rept 102-171, Part II) on Aug. 2. As opposition continued to mount, Democratic leaders Aug. 1 pulled the bill from the floor calendar, convinced they did not have enough votes to pass the tax increase.

The delay guaranteed that Congress could not complete action on the legislation by Sept. 30, when authority for states to let highway contracts with federal funds expired. After that date, some states were able to keep road construction projects going by drawing on a surplus of $6.8 billion in the Highway Trust Fund, but other state projects were disrupted.

Revised Version. After weeks behind closed doors, Public Works leaders emerged on Oct. 10 with a scaled-back $151 billion transportation bill (still HR 2950) that stretched funding authority over six years, not five. Instead of the nickel gas tax increase, the bill extended for four additional years half of a 1990 nickel gas tax increase that was set to expire after fiscal 1995.

The Public Works panel approved the revised version of HR 2950 on Oct. 15 by a vote of 52-3. The Ways and Means panel approved the financing mechanism in the bill on Oct. 16.

Sponsors cut funding for most of the special road and bridge projects by 30 percent, while funding levels for the highway formula program were cut to $119 billion from the $122.8 billion in the first version. Spending authority for mass transit remained at $32 billion, but the money was stretched over six years — as with all of the programs authorized by the bill.

Transportation Secretary Skinner renewed the administration's veto threat, saying that states should be required to pay more than the 20 percent share of construction costs as provided in the bill. The administration also opposed the special road projects, which, Skinner said, amounted to "paving America with pork."

House Floor Action

With some disputes settled in advance and a strict rule limiting amendments, HR 2950 passed the House Oct. 23, 343-83.

Despite Republican protests, the Rules Committee limited floor debate to only a dozen amendments and kept about 40 others from being raised. The panel's action also short-circuited Republican attempts to cut road projects and mass transit funding from the bill. In protest, Republicans forced three procedural roll-call votes on the rule, which the House eventually adopted Oct. 23 on a **key vote of 323-102 (R 66-97; D 257-4; I 0-1)**.

Many of the suppressed amendments dealt with potentially explosive issues that had tied up highway bills in the past. Among them were a limit on billboard construction, a repeal of the national speed limit, a weakening of motorcycle helmet laws, a strengthening of drunken-driving laws and a funding cut for some road projects.

Though it accounted for only 3.5 percent of the total authorized in the bill, the $5.4 billion for specific road projects drew the most fire from Republicans on the House floor and from the Bush administration. Along with the highway projects, Skinner criticized the House bill's 2.5-cent gas-tax extension and high federal matching levels. Dick Armey, R-Texas, lambasted the measure as "a Democratic bill" with "a Democratic tax increase in it ... to build pork barrel projects in favored congressional districts."

Under House rules, lawmakers had only one chance to send a bill back to committee for redrafting. Bill Archer, R-Texas, was expected to offer such a motion to kill the gas-tax extension. Republicans on the Public Works Committee foiled that attempt by offering the motion themselves. Bill cosponsor Bud Shuster, R-Pa., won approval of a watered-down motion that had the effect of thwarting Archer's plans.

The House Oct. 23 approved, 400-26, an amendment offered by Anthony C. Beilenson, D-Calif., to permit states to require contractors to guarantee their work, thereby lifting a federal ban on such warranties. The amendment was dropped in conference in exchange for language vowing to study the issue.

The House rejected two other amendments on Oct. 23. One by Del. Eleanor Holmes Norton, D-D.C., felled 133-295, set separate contracting goals for businesses owned by minorities and those owned by women. The amendment was similar to Mineta's proposal, rejected in committee. Another amendment, by Robert S. Walker, R-Pa., rejected 69-348, would have dropped a provision creating a new "Office of Intermodalism."

Conference, Final Action

The Senate passed HR 2950 by voice vote Oct. 31, clearing the way for conference action.

House and Senate conferees met throughout November to reconcile the two different transportation measures. Their task was complicated because of the number of conferees — 66 from the House and 26 from the Senate.

Amid fears of a protracted recession, the Bush administration softened its harsh veto rhetoric and worked closely with congressional negotiators. Skinner on Nov. 26 praised the final version of HR 2950 as "a constructive compromise" and said he would recommend that Bush sign it.

Negotiators agreed to the House bill's six-year, $151 billion scope, boosting mass transit programs by $11 billion and highway funding by $16 billion over the Senate total. The final bill authorized $119.5 billion for highways and $31.5 billion for mass transit through fiscal 1996. It marked a 39 percent average annual increase in highway spending over the previous five-year authorization period. *(1987 highway authorization, Congress and the Nation Vol. VII, p. 378)*

Conferees accepted a House provision that guaranteed states at least a 90 percent return on what they paid into the Highway Trust Fund in annual gasoline taxes. States previously had been guaranteed a return of at least 85 percent.

Another House provision adopted by conferees required the federal government to pay 80 percent of transportation project costs. Under the Senate bill, the government was to pay only 75 percent of the cost of road projects that added new lane capacity for single-occupant vehicles. In exchange, conferees agreed to Senate language giving states and cities much more control over how federal transportation money would be spent.

For the Bush administration, the conferees' agreement to create the National Highway System was a key victory. But the bill focused federal dollars on maintenance instead of new construction of roads and overall improvement of the transportation system, including the development of mass transit.

Two new programs made up the core of the bill, both offering states wide flexibility to shift funds from roads to mass transit. The first was a new National Highway System to replace the old Interstate system. It would receive $38 billion, half of which states could shift to mass transit on their own, and the other half of which they could shift with the approval of the transportation secretary. The second core program was a $23.9 billion Surface Transportation Program to finance roads, mass transit, bridges, bicycle paths and other projects.

Other core programs included $7.2 billion to complete the Interstate system, $16.1 billion for bridges and a new $6 billion program of grants to urban areas that needed help to comply with federal clean air standards.

On the controversial issue of how the funds were to be distributed among the states, conferees blended aspects of both bills. The House measure had distributed funds to states according to highway use factors such as fuel consumption and vehicle miles traveled to ensure the support of members from donor states. The Senate bill took a different approach, basing each state's funding level on an average of its highway receipts over the previous five years.

The conferees decided that the way to satisfy the largest number of states was to allocate most of the funds not as part of any highway program, but in the form of special road projects or lump-sum payments. The House reduced to $4 billion the price tag for the special projects in its bill; Senate conferees tacked on project funding of their own, adding about $2.2 billion. The final bill authorized more than 500 special projects, along with other cash payments designed to mollify particular states.

Negotiators dropped provisions that would have allowed states to require contractors to guarantee their work, begin a tree-planting program along highways and make it more difficult for the government to seize private property when building roads.

Both chambers approved the conference report on HR 2950 (H Rept 102-404) on Nov. 27 — the House by a vote of 372-47 and the Senate by a vote of 79-8. The conferees' work provoked little debate, as lawmakers from trust fund donor states abandoned last-minute plans to extract more money from the bill.

One final glitch put a crimp in the legislation, however. The Office of Management and Budget said across-the-board cuts of $1.2 billion in highway spending for fiscal 1992 would be needed to make the bill comply with domestic spending ceilings under the 1990 budget agreement. Most of the excess spending was attributable to a Moynihan provision to authorize funds for renovation of a federal courthouse in New York City. *(Courthouse, box, p. 438)*

Major Provisions

As cleared, the Surface Transportation Efficiency Act of 1991 (HR 2950 — PL 102-240):

Spending Levels

- **Scope and Cost.** Authorized $151 billion over six years for highway, mass transit, highway safety and other surface transportation programs. Highway and highway safety programs were authorized at $119.5 billion and mass transit at $31.5 billion.
- **Obligation Ceiling.** Recommended that Highway Trust Fund spending be raised from the $14.5 billion fiscal 1991 limit to $16.8 billion in fiscal 1992, $18.3 billion for fiscal 1993, $18.4 billion for fiscal 1994, $18.3 billion for fiscal 1995, $18.4 billion for fiscal 1996 and $18.3 billion for fiscal 1997. (The actual spending limits were established in separate appropriations legislation.)
- **Federal Matching Share.** Required a federal matching share of 80 percent for most programs. States were to put up 20 percent of the authorized federal cost for each road, transit or safety project. A federal share of 90 percent was provided for remaining interstate construction projects.

Financing

● **Motor Fuels Tax.** Maintained a 14-cent-a-gallon gasoline tax through fiscal 1995. Half of the 1990 nickel increase for highways and transit, slated to expire after fiscal 1995, was extended through fiscal 1999. This would keep gasoline taxes at 11.5 cents instead of allowing them to drop to 9 cents a gallon as had been planned.

Most funding for federal transportation programs came out of the Highway Trust Fund, which was fed by taxes on the sale of motor fuels. The 1990 budget-reconciliation law (HR 5835 — PL 101-508) increased gasoline taxes by 5 cents to 14 cents a gallon until the end of fiscal 1995. Only 2.5 cents of that increase was to go toward highways and transit, while the other half was to be used to reduce the budget deficit.

Highway Programs

● **National Highway System.** Authorized $38 billion for a 155,000-mile National Highway System consisting of the Interstate highway network and major primary roads. The amount included $17 billion for maintenance of the Interstate system.

The transportation secretary was to designate segments eligible to be included in the system and submit them to Congress, which would have to approve the system by Sept. 30, 1995.

States could transfer 50 percent of their highway system funds to mass transit, and an additional 50 percent if the secretary certified that such a transfer was in the public interest.

● **Surface Transportation Program.** Consolidated all highway programs other than the Interstate system into one $23.9 billion surface transportation program to provide funds for roads, mass transit and other projects.

Road projects eligible for funding included construction and rehabilitation projects, earthquake-proofing and operational improvements for bridges and highways. Interstate highways and bridges on and off the federal aid system were eligible for additional funds.

Funds also could be used to cover capital costs for mass transit, passenger and high-speed rail and publicly owned bus facilities. In addition, money could be spent on passenger rail or magnetic levitation systems; car pool projects and related parking facilities; bicycle programs; transportation safety; research and planning programs; and transportation control measures required under the 1990 amendments to the Clean Air Act (S 1630 — PL 101-549).

● **Interstate Highway System.** Authorized $7.2 billion to complete the Interstate Highway System, begun in 1956, from fiscal 1993 through fiscal 1996. States were to receive funds based on their share of costs to complete the system, except for Massachusetts, which was authorized $2.55 billion over four years to complete Interstates 90 and 93 in downtown Boston. The bill also authorized $17 billion to maintain the Interstate system as part of the National Highway System.

● **Bridges.** Authorized $16.1 billion to rebuild and replace bridges. Of that amount, $349.5 million was to go into a discretionary program to allow the transportation secretary to direct funds to specific bridges. Timber bridges were guaranteed $50.5 million of the discretionary funds.

● **Urban-Rural Mix of Funds.** Required states to devote 20 percent of their Surface Transportation Program funds to safety and transportation enhancement programs. At least 62.5 percent of the remaining 80 percent of the funds was to be divided among urban areas of at least 200,000 residents and other less populated areas in amounts equal to the proportion of their population. The remaining 37.5 percent of funds could be spent without regard to population.

● **Minimum Allocation.** Authorized $3 billion for the "bonus minimum allocation" program designed to ensure that each state received the highest possible return on its contributions to the Highway Trust Fund. That amount was in addition to the standard minimum allocation program, for which the law authorized $5.2 billion to ensure that each state received a 90 percent return on its gasoline tax contributions.

The bill changed the calculation for the base amount of the minimum apportionment formula to give states more funds. The new base included all payments to states for Interstate construction, substitution and maintenance, bridge and surface transportation programs as well as prior years' discretionary allocations from those programs. Future discretionary road grants and special road project funding were excluded from the minimum allocation formula.

● **Other Apportionment Formulas.** Longstanding formulas would no longer be used to allocate most funds. Instead, states would receive several lump-sum cash payments. States were to divide a total of $4 billion, authorized for fiscal 1996 and 1997, as repayment for segments of the Interstate system that were constructed without federal assistance before the program began in 1956. States standing to benefit most included New York, California, Connecticut, Illinois, Indiana, Maryland, Massachusetts, Michigan, New Jersey, Ohio, Pennsylvania and Texas. Even states with no such roads would get a minimum of $20 million each from this program.

Western states were to receive $1.9 billion for roads that traversed federal lands. Another $1.7 billion was to be divided among states that received fewer funds under the final bill than they would have received under either the House or Senate bills.

● **High-Priority Corridors.** Authorized $2 billion for 21 high-priority corridors that were deemed regionally and nationally important and were to be part of the National Highway System.

● **Special Road Projects.** Authorized $6.2 billion for 539 special road projects, including $4 billion in projects chosen by House members and $2.2 billion chosen by senators to go to states for unspecified projects.

● **Bicycles and Pedestrian Walkways.** Allowed federal transportation funds to be used to build bike and pedestrian paths along federal-aid highways, roads, trails or parkways.

● **Metric System Signs.** Repealed a prohibition on the placement of metric signs along federal-aid highways.

Metropolitan and Statewide Planning

● **Metropolitan Planning.** Required that urban areas of more than 50,000 residents establish metropolitan planning groups to coordinate various transportation modes.

Each group was to work with states to develop a transportation improvement program that encompassed all federal transportation projects within a metropolitan area. The plans were to conform to a long-range transportation plan and state efforts to comply with the Clean Air Act. The program was to be updated every two years. Areas with populations of 200,000 or more were required to meet stricter planning requirements.

• **Statewide Planning.** Required states to develop plans for an intermodal transportation system, to be coordinated with the work of metropolitan transportation planners.

Safety

• **Highway Safety Grant Programs.** Authorized $1.3 billion for National Highway Traffic Safety Administration grant programs from the trust fund.

• **Impaired Driving Enforcement.** Set up a new program of $125 million in grants to states that adopted programs to prevent citizens from driving while under the influence of alcohol or drugs.

• **Other Safety Programs.** Authorized from general funds $291 million through fiscal 1995 for the traffic and motor vehicle safety program and $27.4 million for the motor vehicle information and cost-savings program.

• **Motorcycle Helmet and Safety Belt Use.** Required states that did not have motorcycle helmet and safety belt laws in effect during fiscal 1994 to spend 1.5 percent of their highway funds for highway safety programs. States that failed to enact such laws by fiscal 1995 would have to spend 3 percent of their highway funds on safety programs. The bill also authorized $100 million for incentive grants to states that adopted motorcycle helmet and safety belt laws.

• **Air Bags.** Required that passenger cars made after Sept. 1, 1996, be equipped with driver and front-seat passenger air bags. Trucks, buses and multi-purpose passenger vehicles would have until Sept. 1, 1997, to have driver's side air bags, and until Sept. 1, 1998, for front-seat passenger air bags.

• **Safety Priorities for Passenger Cars.** Directed the secretary to begin writing safety standards by May 31, 1992, to improve the side-impact protection of cars; to reduce the risk of passenger cars, vans and light trucks rolling over; to improve the safety of child booster seats; and to improve safety belt designs and head-impact protection.

• **Rear-Seat Belts.** Directed the secretary to provide consumers, during fiscal 1993, with information about retrofitting their vehicles with rear-seat, lap-and-shoulder belts.

Tolls

• **Toll Facilities.** Provided states up to 35 percent of the cost of building new public toll facilities on roads, bridges and tunnels other than on free segments of the existing Interstate system. Tolls set to expire were allowed to continue. The federal government would pay 80 percent of the cost of converting existing roads and bridges to tolls.

• **Congestion Pricing.** Allowed the federal government to finance, for up to three years, five "congestion-pricing" pilot programs under which states would impose tolls on vehicles traveling on congested routes during peak travel periods.

General Mass Transit

• **Agency Name Change.** Renamed the Urban Mass Transportation Administration to the Federal Transit Administration.

• **Federal Matching Funds.** Increased the federal share of funding for mass transit projects from 75 percent to 80 percent for discretionary programs and retained the 80 percent match for formula grant programs. The federal government would continue to pay up to 50 percent of operating assistance grants. Wheelchair ramps and related equipment required by either the 1990 amendments to the Clean Air Act or the Americans with Disabilities Act (S 933 — PL 101-336) qualified for a 90 percent match.

• **Mix of General Funds, Trust Funds.** Increased the proportion of mass transit funds that came out of the mass transit account of the Highway Trust Fund. Of the $31.5 billion authorized for transit programs, $18.2 billion, or 58 percent, was to come from the trust fund and the rest from the Treasury.

• **Flexibility of Highway and Transit Funds.** Allowed up to $65 billion, or 54 percent, of the federal highway program to be made available for mass transit at the discretion of state and local officials. However, some formula grant funds in urban areas could be used for roads or other transportation programs if requirements of the Americans with Disabilities Act (ADA) were met and a metropolitan planning organization approved. *(ADA, p. 743)*

Discretionary Grants

• **New Rail Projects and Extensions.** Authorized $6.2 billion primarily for new rail and bus projects. Among the 64 new projects designated was authority for $634 million for the New Jersey urban core system and $568.5 million for the rapid rail system in the San Francisco Bay Area.

• **Rail Modernization.** Authorized $4.9 billion for rail and fixed-guideway modernization projects and restructured the way grants were awarded.

• **Buses and Bus Facilities.** Authorized $2.3 billion for the replacement, rehabilitation and purchase of buses and related equipment and the construction of bus facilities.

• **Criteria for New Rail Systems.** The transportation secretary was required to take into account specific criteria in deciding where to spend money for new rail systems. They included cost effectiveness; local financial commitment; and the social, environmental and economic impacts of proposed projects.

Formula Grants

• **Capital and Operating Grants.** Authorized $16.2 billion for capital grants and operating assistance and $941.7 million for rural transit programs.

• **Urban-Rural Funding Proportion.** Increased the amount of formula funds available for rural transit systems to 5.5 percent from 2.9 percent.

• **Operating Assistance.** Retained federal operating assistance for all mass transit systems. The amount of operating assistance available to transit systems was indexed to inflation for all urban transit systems, not just for those in areas with populations under 200,000 as in past practice.

• **Research, Planning and Administration.** Authorized $478.4 million for national and state research, planning and training; and $304.5 million for expenses of the Federal Transit Administration.

• **Programs for the Elderly and Disabled.** Authorized $428.3 million for transit programs to aid the elderly and disabled.

Research

• **Highway Research.** Authorized $240 million for an applied technology program for highway, transit and mixed transportation systems to speed up and deploy advanced highway-building technologies.

• **High-Tech Devices.** Authorized $659 million for a program to use new technology to solve traffic congestion and safety problems on highways. The money was to be used to install high-tech devices such as computer-controlled traffic monitors along highways selected by the transportation secretary. Half of the funds were targeted for areas with high levels of traffic congestion and smog.

• **High-Speed Ground Transportation Program.** Authorized $700 million to design and build magnetically levitated train systems along federal aid highways, including the Interstate system. Another $50 million was authorized for grants to develop all forms of high-speed ground transportation, including steel-wheel rail. An additional $25 million was authorized for general research in the area.

A prototype magnetically levitated train system was slated for testing within three years of enactment, with the federal government paying 75 percent of its cost. The bill also set up a national design program for magnetic levitation trains, to be jointly managed by the Army's civil works department along with state and federal transportation agencies. An initial plan for the prototype was to be submitted to Congress by Jan. 15, 1992, and updated every year.

• **Bureau of Transportation Statistics.** Authorized $90 million to create an office to collect data on the performance of the nation's transportation network and to produce biannual estimates of the productivity and use of the systems.

Trucking

• **Length and Weight Limits on Trucks.** Limited the use of longer-combination vehicles on the Interstate system to states that allowed them before June 1, 1991. Such trucks were defined as having two or more trailers or semi-trailers that weighed more than 80,000 pounds. This included triple-trailer combinations, long double combinations and so-called Rocky Mountain doubles consisting of one long and one short trailer.

Each state was to determine which longer-combination vehicles could use its roads, but the transportation secretary could challenge a state's assessment of its vehicle length and weight laws. States would be allowed to further restrict the use of longer-combination vehicles above and beyond the federal limits.

• **Motor Carrier Safety Assistance.** Authorized $479 million for grants to enforce federal and state trucking regulations and for related programs.

Environmental and Scenic Programs

• **Congestion and Air Pollution.** Authorized $6 billion over five years for a program to reduce congestion and improve air quality in areas that failed to meet requirements of the 1990 amendments to the Clean Air Act.

• **Billboard Removal.** Authorized states to use federal aid highway funds to remove illegal signs and compensate sign owners. In addition, states were permitted to use $3 million in funds authorized for the scenic byways program to remove billboards.

• **Scenic and Historic Byways.** Authorized $30 million over three years for a program to establish national scenic and historic roads. The Federal Highway Administration was to provide technical assistance to state agencies responsible for the roadways and provide grants to those agencies for planning, design and development of the scenic road program.

• **National Recreational Trails Fund.** Set up a trust fund to help states promote the use of recreational trails, using revenues from the excise tax on recreational fuels. Fuel taxes paid into the Highway Trust Fund by commercial users of recreational fuels, such as ski lodge operators, had been refunded through tax credits. Those tax credits were repealed and the revenues instead put into the trust fund.

Miscellaneous

• **Speed Limit Sanctions Repeal.** Repealed a 1987 law requiring federal monitoring of state speed-limit compliance. Instead, states were required to submit data and certify that speed limits were being enforced or risk losing federal highway funds. The bill made permanent the states' authority to raise the speed limit to 65 mph on certain non-interstate highways built to interstate standards and located outside of urban areas.

• **Documentary.** Authorized $2 million for a film documentary examining the health of the nation's infrastructure, with cooperation from a public television station.

• **Driver's License Suspensions.** Required a federal study of state efforts to comply with a 1991 law requiring that convicted drug offenders' driver's licenses be suspended.

• **Office of Intermodalism.** Created an office to coordinate all modes of transportation and oversee research on intermodal transportation.

Air Bags

As part of the fiscal 1992 highway and mass transit authorization bill (HR 2608 — PL 102-140) signed into law Oct. 28, 1991, Congress required auto makers to install air bags in the front seats of all passenger vehicles made after Sept. 1, 1996. *(Highway authorization, p. 437)*

Makers of trucks, buses and multi-purpose vehicles were given an extra year before driver's side air bags would be required and an additional two years before they would have to install front-seat passenger air bags.

Efforts to force domestic automakers to install air bags had bounced between Congress, the Transportation Department and the courts since 1969, when the government first attempted to require them. *(Congress and the Nation Vol. VI, p. 322)*

In a strategy to give the air bag provisions as many legislative vehicles as possible, Sen. Richard H. Byran, D-Nev., a key proponent of boosting motor vehicle safety, introduced two free-standing air bag bills. The Senate Commerce, Science and Transportation Committee reported S 591 (S Rept 102-70) on June 3, 1991, and S 1012 (S Rept 102-83) on June 17. The full Senate passed both bills by voice vote July 9.

Transportation Corrections

Congress in 1992 included "technical corrections" to the 1991 highway and mass transit programs reauthorization bill (HR 2950 — PL 102-240) in the fiscal 1993 transportation appropriation measure (HR 5518 — PL 102-388). The House had passed a separate corrections bill (HR 5753), but it stalled in the Senate. *(Highway authorization, p. 437)*

HR 5753 — reported from House Public Works and Transportation and passed by voice vote under suspension of the rules Aug. 10, 1992 — aimed to correct wording mistakes, describe projects in greater detail and make existing laws consistent with the changes brought in the 1991 law. The bill also authorized $30.9 million for six new road projects, including $7.6 million to build a highway loop around Branson, Mo. Sponsors, however, claimed that no new projects were included in HR 5753. Five of the projects, totaling $23.3 million, were included because sponsors said they were wrongfully omitted from the 1991 bill as a result of clerical errors. The Branson project was funded from money shifted from other Missouri projects authorized in HR 5753.

The House-passed bill also recast road policy by allowing states to defer paying until Aug. 1, 1994, their 20 percent share to match federal grants for mass transit systems. The bill launched a two-year pilot program to use recycled glass and plastic in highway projects.

The Senate opted to include its technical corrections language in the transportation appropriations bill instead of HR 5753. Most of the Senate provisions involved only minor technical changes in PL 102-240, but the scope of some road and transit projects was broadened. For example, Majority Leader George J. Mitchell, D-Maine, won extension of a timber bridge pilot program whether federal aid was received or not. The language allowed Maine to use federal money to repair timber bridges on even the smallest rural roads.

Both the House and Senate adopted the conference report (H Rept 102-924) on HR 5518 on Oct. 1. President Bush signed the bill Oct. 6.

Other enacted provisions of HR 5518 required automakers, beginning in model year 1995, to list on price stickers where each vehicle was built and its percentage of parts and exempted air passengers who used frequent-flier tickets from passenger facility charges — fees of up to $3 per one-way trip levied by airports to pay for improvements. Congress approved new passenger facility charges in 1990. *(Story, p. 417)*

Trucking Bankruptcies

The Senate in 1992 passed legislation (S 1675) aimed at resolving pricing disputes between bankrupt trucking companies and their former customers. The measure was blocked in the House by opposition from the Teamsters union.

The bill settled a controversy over huge discounts offered by truckers during the competitive years after industry deregulation in 1980. Because many of the discounts never were filed with the Interstate Commerce Commission (ICC), estates of bankrupt trucking companies had been pressuring past clients to pay more for the shipments on the grounds that the shippers were undercharged.

S 1675 allowed estates to choose between appealing to the ICC for a ruling or accepting an expedited settlement process for a percentage of the alleged undercharges.

The Senate Commerce, Science and Transportation Committee approved the measure June 16 and reported it (S Rept 102-359) Aug. 4. The full Senate passed it by voice vote Sept. 30. The House Public Works and Transportation Committee did not act on a companion measure (HR 3705).

Airline Reservations

In an attempt to inject more competition into the airline reservation business, Congress in 1992 directed the Transportation Department to write new rules aimed at making the computer reservation systems more equitable. The provision was included in an unrelated foreign aid bill (S 2532 — PL 102-511) signed by President Bush on Oct. 24, 1992. *(Story, p. 260)*

Travel agents and airlines nationwide relied on four major computerized reservation systems. Two companies — owned primarily by American Airlines and United Airlines — controlled about 70 percent of the market. Smaller carriers complained that they were featured less prominently on the systems and that the flight information was structured to encourage agents to favor the two major airlines that owned the systems.

The domestic airline industry, which was deregulated in 1978, had dwindled to just eight major carriers by 1992. Many lawmakers said improving airline competition boiled down to making the computer reservation system fairer to all airlines.

A sweeping House measure (HR 5466 — H Rept 102-724) was reported from the Public Works and Transportation Committee July 27, 1992, and passed 230-160 by the full House Aug. 12. The bill prohibited the air carriers that owned the computerized reservation systems from using "architectural bias," charging other airlines booking fees or using any other arrangements that discriminated against other air carriers and travel agents. American and United said the legislation was unnecessary because they were working to eliminate any bias in the software architecture of their computer systems.

The Senate did not act on HR 5466. However, on July 2, it attached a provision to S 2532 requiring the Transportation Department to complete by Sept. 1, 1992, rules intended to make the reservation systems and the distribution of takeoff and landing time slots at major hub airports fairer.

Aviation Worker Fines

Congress in 1992 cleared a bill (HR 5481 — PL 102-345) requiring the Federal Aviation Administration (FAA) to advise pilots, flight engineers, mechanics or repairmen of the nature and reason for potential civil fines before they were levied. The bill also required that the employees be given a chance to rebut the charges.

HR 5481 allowed the FAA to levy civil penalties against aviation employees for violating such things as safety regulations, bans against civil aircraft flights over security zones and requirements that passengers be notified of the lack of security at certain airports.

Previously, aviation industry employees had been allowed to appeal civil fines only to the FAA administrator's office — which oversaw the officials who issued fines. Supporters of the bill said such an arrangement was a conflict of interest.

The House Public Works and Transportation Committee reported HR 5481 (H Rept 102-671) July 21 and the House passed the measure by voice vote under suspension of the rules on Aug. 3. The Senate passed the bill by voice vote on Aug. 12. President Bush signed HR 5481 on Aug. 26.

Flight Attendants' Workday

The House on Aug. 1, 1991, approved, 228-195, a bill (HR 14) to limit the work hours of airline flight attendants. The measure directed the Transportation Department to issue rules to limit a flight attendant's workday to 14 hours with a minimum of 10 hours of rest between shifts.

Similar work limits were already in place for airline pilots, mechanics and air traffic controllers.

The House Public Works and Transportation Committee reported HR 14 (H Rept 102-128) on June 24.

The Bush administration threatened to veto the bill, saying it would impose financial burdens on the airline industry. A companion measure was introduced in the Senate (S 101), but it saw no action.

In 1992, the House added language similar to HR 14 to its version of the fiscal 1993 transportation appropriations bill (HR 5518 — PL 102-388), but the provision was removed from the final bill because of administration opposition. Another airline labor-related provision was dropped from HR 5518 because of a veto threat; it would have protected airline employees who lost their jobs when international routes were sold.

Aircraft Inspection

A bill (HR 172) tightening inspection requirements for aging aircraft was passed by the House April 23, 1991, by voice vote. The Senate did not act on the bill.

The measure directed the Federal Aviation Administration (FAA) to set up a program to improve inspections of aircraft in service for 15 years or longer. The bill encouraged the FAA to persuade foreign governments to adopt similar standards. The legislation came in response to a 1989 accident in which the roof of an Aloha Airlines jet ripped open in flight, killing one and injuring several others.

HR 172 (H Rept 102-39) was approved by the Public Works and Transportation Committee by voice vote on April 16 and formally reported April 22. Similar legislation passed the House in 1990. *(Aviation security, p. 420)*

FAA Authorization

Congress in 1992 cleared a three-year reauthorization (HR 6168 — PL 102-581) for the Federal Aviation Administration (FAA). The bill renewed most FAA programs for fiscal 1993 through 1995 but extended the airport improvement program for only one year to avoid a controversy over the compensation of victims of air terrorism.

An FAA authorization bill stalled in 1990. *(Story, p. 422)*

Legislative History. The House Public Works and Transportation Committee on April 8 approved an earlier version of the legislation (HR 4691) authorizing FAA funding for two years. The bill was formally reported (H Rept 102-503) on April 28. The Ways and Means Committee on April 29 approved by voice vote the financing portion of the bill, which included continuation of a 10 percent airline ticket tax to finance airport improvements.

The House passed HR 4691 on May 19 by a vote of 410-2. The measure authorized $4.1 billion in fiscal 1993 and fiscal 1994 for the airport improvement program, $9.6 billion over two years for FAA operations and $5.6 billion for air traffic control system modernization.

The bill included provisions permitting local entities to impose noise controls stricter than national guidelines and prohibiting the transportation secretary from approving requests for passenger facility charges until appropriators had provided full funding for general airport improvements and a program that provided subsidies to small rural airports.

The Senate Commerce, Science and Transportation Committee approved a three-year FAA authorization bill (S 2642 — S Rept 102-424) on Aug. 11. That measure, reported Sept. 25, authorized $2 billion for airport improvements grants in fiscal 1993, rising to $2.3 billion by fiscal 1995. FAA facilities and equipment received $2.7 billion in fiscal 1993, rising to $2.9 billion in fiscal 1995. Operations and research received $5 billion in fiscal 1993, rising to $5.9 billion in fiscal 1995.

The bill continued the efforts of Aviation Subcommittee Chairman Wendell H. Ford, D-Ky., to reduce airport noise by setting aside 12.5 percent, up from 10 percent, of airport improvement funds for programs to reduce noise. Legislation enacted in 1990 included stronger airport noise control guidelines advocated by Ford. *(1990 legislation, p. 419)*

S 2642 established a special fund to compensate victims of international airline accidents and their families. Similar compensation requirements were included in the Montreal Protocols on carrier liability, an international accord that the Senate failed to ratify.

The compensation issue was a reaction to the 1988 terrorist bombing of Pan Am Flight 103 over Lockerbie, Scotland. Although many senators supported the compensation provision, aircraft and engine makers raised last-minute concerns that slowed the momentum of the Senate bill.

While S 2642 languished in the Senate, the House on Oct. 6 passed by voice vote a new, trimmed down FAA authorization (HR 6168). It included portions of S 2642 and other House bills (HR 4691, HR 6093) but omitted the compensation provision. The Senate passed HR 6168 on Oct. 8 by voice vote, clearing the measure. President Bush signed it on Oct. 31.

Major Provisions. HR 6168 authorized $2 billion for airport improvement grants for fiscal 1993 from the Airport and Airway Trust Fund, which was fed by a 10 percent tax on all airline tickets. The one-year authorization to upgrade airport terminals and runways cleared the way for federal funds to flow to projects in the works for fiscal 1993, while leaving the compensation issue to be resolved by the next Congress.

Other major provisions of HR 6168:

- Authorized facilities and equipment programs at $8.5 billion over fiscal years 1993-95.
- Allowed airport grants to be used to build new structures and purchase equipment to de-ice aircraft. (This provision was in part a response to a USAir jet crash that

killed 27 people on March 22, 1992, at New York's LaGuardia Airport. A more extensive de-icing program was included in separate legislation (HR 4557 — H Rept 102-511) reported May 4 by the House Science, Space and Technology Committee but not considered by the full House.)

- Allowed the transportation secretary to provide insurance to air carriers through September 1997, so that commercial aircraft could be used for wartime activities. The House Public Works and Transportation Committee had reported the provision as a separate bill (HR 5465 — H Rept 102-723) on July 27.
- Established a research program to be carried out by the FAA and the National Aeronautics and Space Administration to promote the development of a new generation of quieter planes.

FAA Maps

The House in 1992 passed legislation (HR 3243) to require the Federal Aviation Administration (FAA) to publish charts for general aviation pilots detailing safe routes through heavily congested air traffic control areas.

HR 3243 directed the FAA to publish charts showing clearly identifiable corridors through which general aviation pilots could better fly to and from congested airports without interfering with the flight patterns of commercial planes. Use of the charts was optional for pilots.

The House Public Works and Transportation Committee reported the bill (H Rept 102-712) on July 24. The House passed it by voice vote July 30. A companion Senate bill (S 1895) died in the Commerce, Science and Transportation Committee.

Amtrak Authorization

Congress in 1992 cleared a two-year reauthorization (HR 4250 — PL 102-533) for Amtrak, the national passenger railroad.

The measure authorized $381 million for fiscal years 1993 and 1994 for operating expenses, $250 million for each year for capital expenses and $470 million over the two years for high-speed train service along the Northeast corridor. The bill also set aside funds to encourage the establishment of new routes in rural areas. *(Previous authorization, p. 424)*

Federal subsidies for Amtrak were a target of Republican attacks, but HR 4250 won bipartisan support and moved through Congress with little debate. House sponsor Al Swift, D-Wash., called Amtrak "the most efficient passenger rail system in the world" because it covered almost 80 percent of its costs with its own revenues.

The House Energy and Commerce Committee approved HR 4250 on April 7 and formally reported the bill (H Rept 102-513) on May 6. The full House passed the measure by voice vote under suspension of the rules Aug. 11.

The Senate Commerce, Science and Transportation Committee on June 16 gave voice vote approval to its Amtrak authorization bill (S 2608), reporting the measure (S Rept 102-326) on July 21. The Senate passed an amended HR 4250 by voice vote on Aug. 12.

The House agreed to the conference report (H Rept 102-990) by voice vote on Oct. 4, and the Senate followed suit on Oct. 7, thus completing congressional action. President Bush signed the bill Oct. 27.

Railroad Safety

Congress in 1992 cleared the first comprehensive railroad safety bill (HR 2607 — PL 102-365) since 1988.

HR 2607 authorized $54.4 million in fiscal 1992, $68.3 million in fiscal 1993 and $71.7 million in fiscal 1994 to carry out the 1970 Railroad Safety Act (PL 91-458) and $16 million in fiscal 1992, $25 million in fiscal 1993 and $30 million in fiscal 1994 for local rail freight assistance, a formula grant program that helped to maintain railroad right of ways. *(1970 law, Congress and the Nation Vol. III, p. 166)*

The measure also increased fines for safety violations; required the Federal Railroad Administration (FRA) to beef up enforcement of railroad safety regulations; required railroads cited for safety problems to tell the agency what corrective actions they planned to undertake; and mandated that the FRA monitor how well railroads carried out remedial actions.

Controversy arose over language requiring the FRA to issues rules when Congress instructed the agency to do so. The provisions were added to the bill by John D. Dingell, D-Mich., chairman of the House Energy and Commerce Committee. Dingell was upset over the agency's refusal to write rules for some provisions of a 1988 rail safety law (PL 100-342). His change narrowed the agency's authority to interpret the law. The Bush administration responded by threatening to veto the bill. The language, however, remained in the final version. *(1988 bill, Congress and the Nation Vol. VII, p. 395)*

The House Energy and Commerce Committee reported HR 2607 (H Rept 102-205) on Sept. 16, 1991. The House passed the bill by voice vote under suspension of the rules Sept. 23.

The Senate Commerce, Science and Transportation Committee reported its own version of the bill (S 1571 — S Rept 102-219) on Nov. 18. The Senate passed an amended HR 2607 on March 18, 1992, by voice vote. The bill subsequently cleared Congress Aug. 12, and President Bush signed it Sept. 3.

Rail Strikes

The 102nd Congress acted twice to end rail strikes.

The first intervention came on April 17, 1991, when Congress cleared legislation to stop a day-long nationwide rail strike by mandating further mediations between labor and management. The strike by 10 rail unions shut down freight lines nationwide, upset commuter rail service in several cities and threatened to close factories.

The legislation (H J Res 222 — PL 102-29) stated that the strike would end immediately and that the president would promptly appoint a three-member special board which would have 65 days to reach a binding decision on the dispute. The House passed the resolution 400-5; the Senate acted by voice vote. President Bush signed the measure April 18.

Congress was not required to get involved in railway labor disputes but had intervened repeatedly to prevent disruptions in the economy. The round of labor talks that broke down in 1991 began when rail contracts expired in

1988. After two years of unsuccessful negotiations, President Bush formed an emergency board in 1990 to help mediate.

After the board's Jan. 15, 1991, findings were rejected by labor unions, a 30-day cooling-off period went into effect. Both sides agreed to extend the talks for 60 days because of the Persian Gulf War. Two unions reached settlements, but eight others remained at odds with the railroads, forcing the strike on April 17.

Congress acted again on June 25, 1992, ending a two-day shutdown of the nation's rail system and giving labor unions, freight railroads and Amtrak 38 days to resolve their longstanding disputes over wages, work rules and job security.

The measure (H J Res 517) established a bargaining process often used by professional baseball players during salary negotiations. If the parties failed to reach agreement within 25 days, a mediator would settle the dispute within 10 days.

The House approved H J Res 517, 248-140, on June 25. The Senate passed it 87-6 the same day, after agreeing to table (kill), 76-18, an amendment by Paul Wellstone, D-Minn., to scrap the new mediation process and instead impose a 30-day cooling-off period. Bush signed the resolution at 1 a.m. on June 26.

Unlike in April 1991, in 1992 only one union, the International Association of Machinists, went on strike against one company, CSX Transportation Inc., after negotiations ended. Other unions had either reached agreement or delayed strikes as talks continued. However, the entire freight rail system shut down. In a display of management solidarity with CSX, all 40 of the nation's largest rail freight carriers locked out workers.

Drug Testing Transport Workers

A fatal subway crash, believed to have been caused by a drunken motorman, prompted Congress in 1991 to require more stringent rules on random drug and alcohol testing for transport workers.

Appropriators included a provision in the fiscal 1992 transportation spending bill (HR 2942 — PL 102-143) that required new drug and alcohol testing rules for aviation, rail, trucking, bus and mass transit employees performing safety-sensitive jobs. The Transportation Department and the Federal Aviation Administration had one year from the bill's enactment to require the random tests.

Beginning in 1990, the Bush administration had required random drug tests of about 4 million aviation, trucking and bus employees in safety-sensitive positions. Mass transit workers were not covered by the existing rules.

Despite 1989 Supreme Court rulings that upheld mandatory drug testing for workers with public safety and law enforcement duties, efforts to extend such screening to all transit workers whose jobs affected passenger safety continued to meet with resistance. *(101st Congress action, p. 425)*

Attitudes changed after the Aug. 28, 1991, subway crash in New York City, which killed five people and injured 171. The driver of the train, who was charged with murder, was believed to have been drunk and possibly under the influence of cocaine at the time of the accident.

Without the usual fight from key drug testing opponents such as Energy and Commerce Chairman John D. Dingell, D-Mich., the House on Sept. 24 agreed 413-5 to a non-binding motion to instruct conferees on the appropriations measure to accept mass transit drug testing language sponsored by Sen. Alfonse M. D'Amato, R-N.Y. The House conferees went further and adopted the language of a broader bill (S 676) by Ernest F. Hollings, D-S.C., to mandate random drug and alcohol tests on all transportation workers in safety-sensitive positions. Subsequently, House appropriators accepted the D'Amato provision as part of the conference agreement (H Rept 102-243). President Bush signed HR 2942 on Oct. 28.

Boat Fees

Congress in 1992 acted to phase out a controversial tax on the owners of recreational boats, imposed as part of the fiscal 1991 budget-reconciliation measure (HR 5835 — PL 101-508). The tax had raised only $47 million in the two years since its implementation — far short of the anticipated goal of $262 million. The boat tax was to be replaced with a new tax on users of a Federal Maritime Commission data base on tariff information. *(Boat fees imposition, p. 425)*

The phase-out provision was attached to a separate measure (HR 2152 — PL 102-582) restricting the use of fishing nets, which was signed by President Bush on Nov. 2, 1992. *(Fishing nets, p. 528)*

In 1991, Congress included in a fiscal 1992 Coast Guard reauthorization measure (HR 1776 — PL 102-241) a non-binding resolution urging the Bush administration to repeal the fee. The debate over eliminating the boat tax arose again in 1992 — during consideration of the fiscal 1993 Coast Guard reauthorization bill (HR 5055) and a bill regarding foreign shipbuilding subsidies (HR 2056). *(Coast Guard reauthorization, below; foreign ship subsidies, p. 449)*

The House May 13, 1992, passed HR 2056, 339-78, with language calling for repealing the user fees on boats 21 feet or shorter on Oct. 1, 1992; on boats 37 feet or shorter by Oct. 1, 1993; and all other recreational boats by Oct. 1, 1994. The Senate July 31 attached a similar provision to its version of the drift net bill, HR 2152. The House subsequently accepted the Senate action.

Coast Guard Authorization

Legislation (HR 1776) authorizing fiscal 1992 funds for the U.S. Coast Guard cleared in 1991, but a measure (HR 5055) providing a fiscal 1993 authorization stalled in 1992.

HR 1776. HR 1776 called for $2.57 billion for Coast Guard operations and maintenance in fiscal 1992. An additional $466 million was authorized for the purchase of boats and airplanes and to build and renovate facilities. The bill authorized the Coast Guard to take the necessary steps to implement the Oil Pollution Act of 1990, including completion, within a year, of a study of oil tanker safety and the capability of owners to meet legal obligations in the event of a spill.

A controversy over a user fee on owners of recreational boats was resolved by a non-binding provision urging the Bush administration to repeal the fee. Congress in 1992 cleared legislation to phase out the tax. *(Boat fees, above)*

The House Merchant Marine and Fisheries Committee approved HR 1776 on May 2, 1991, by voice vote and reported the bill (H Rept 102-132) on June 26. On June 12, the panel approved a separate bill (HR 534 — H Rept 102-182, Part I) to repeal fees imposed in 1990 on recreational boat owners for use of Coast Guard services. HR 534 imposed a fee on users of a new computer data base that tracked federal shipping tariffs. House Ways and Means reported the measure (H Rept 102-182, Part II) on Oct. 22. It saw no further congressional action.

The House passed HR 1776 on July 18 by voice vote after rejecting amendments that sought to take the teeth out of the recreational boat owners' fee and called for random drug testing of civilian Coast Guard employees. By a vote of 412-6, the House July 18 adopted a non-binding resolution calling for repeal of the recreational boat fee.

The Senate Commerce, Science and Transportation Committee approved its Coast Guard authorization bill (S 1297) by voice vote July 30 and reported the measure (S Rept 102-169) Oct. 3. S 1297 authorized fiscal 1992 and fiscal 1993 funds for the Coast Guard and included a repeal of the boat user fee. On the Senate floor, Ernest F. Hollings, D-S.C., chairman of the Commerce Committee, explained that the repeal provision had to be removed from S 1297 because supporters had not included an alternate source of revenue as required by budget rules.

On Nov. 21, the Senate passed by voice vote an amended version of HR 1776 that included non-binding language calling for repeal of the recreational boat tax once a way was found to offset the cost. On Nov. 25, the bill went back to the House, where it was made a one-year reauthorization bill for fiscal 1992. The Senate cleared HR 1776 on Nov. 27. President Bush signed it (PL 102-241) on Dec. 19.

HR 5055. The House 304-22 on June 22, 1992, passed HR 5055 to authorize $3.6 billion for Coast Guard programs in fiscal 1993 and to stiffen penalties on drunken recreational boat operators.

The House Merchant Marine Committee had approved HR 5055 on June 4 by voice vote and reported the measure (H Rept 102-564) on June 15.

The Senate Commerce, Science and Transportation Committee on June 16 gave voice vote approval to a companion Coast Guard authorization bill (S 2702 — S Rept 102-346). The bill, which included the controversial boat tax repeal, was never considered by the full Senate.

Foreign Ship Subsidies

The House in 1992 passed legislation (HR 2056) to help revive the domestic shipbuilding industry, but the bill died at the end of the 102nd Congress.

HR 2056 required all ships involved in foreign trade to certify that they were not built or repaired with the aid of foreign subsidies. Ships without certificates were to be barred from transporting goods in or out of U.S. ports. The measure also subjected foreign-made vessels to countervailing duties and anti-dumping provisions.

HR 2056 also included a provision gradually repealing a controversial tax on users of recreational boats, imposed in 1990. *(Boat fees, p. 448)*

The House Ways and Means Committee reported HR 2056 (H Rept 102-284, Part I) on Nov. 4, 1991. The House Merchant Marine and Fisheries Committee, which shared jurisdiction, reported it (H Rept 102-284, Part II) on March 6, 1992. Shippers and ship owners objected strongly to the Ways and Means version because it would have taken effect retroactive to October 1991. The Merchant Marine bill would become effective upon enactment.

The House passed HR 2056 May 13, 339-78, after a debate that focused on how the penalties would affect negotiations with other countries over shipbuilding subsidies.

The House May 13 rejected, 179-237, a motion offered by Bill Archer, R-Texas, intended to strip the shipbuilding provisions. Archer argued that they unfairly penalized ship owners and U.S. ports by encouraging subsidized ships to do business in other countries, such as Canada and Mexico.

The House Aug. 10 attached the foreign subsidy measure to a separate bill (HR 2152 — PL 102-582) to ban drift net fishing. The Senate, however, stripped the provisions from the measure before reporting it. *(Drift net fishing, p. 528)*

On Oct. 10, the Senate folded HR 2056 into a companion version of the shipbuilding measure (S 3338). It did not advance.

Congress eliminated U.S. shipbuilding subsidies in 1981. In 1989, the United States entered into discussions to get other countries — primarily Germany, Italy and France — to do the same. The Bush administration threatened to veto HR 2056, saying it would hurt future negotiations.

Ship Inspection

An expansion of the Coast Guard's authority to inspect foreign ships cleared Congress in 1992 as part of a broader maritime bill (HR 5617 — PL 102-587).

Under existing law, the Coast Guard could inspect ships upon their arrival in a U.S. port to ensure compliance with safety laws and regulations. The bill allowed the guard also to inspect foreign-flagged vessels overseas if ship owners agreed and paid the costs of inspection. This right already existed for U.S.-flagged vessels in foreign ports.

Supporters of the provision said ships that undergo reconstruction or repair overseas should be inspected at the dry dock, where it was easier to identify problems and suggest modifications.

The maritime bill also prohibited the abandonment of large barges and empowered the Coast Guard to dispose of the vessels. Previously, barge owners had been allowed to abandon their vessels, but a General Accounting Office study found that abandoned barges often fouled the coastline and became dumping grounds for hazardous materials.

The ship inspection provisions originally were in a bill (HR 4485 — H Rept 102-502) approved April 8 by the House Merchant Marine and Fisheries Committee and reported April 28. The House passed the measure by voice vote under suspension of the rules May 5.

In the Senate, the bill was approved by the Commerce, Science and Transportation Committee on June 16 and reported (S Rept 102-389) on Aug. 12. But in the waning days of Congress, the language of the bill was added to a large package of non-controversial maritime legislation. That measure (HR 5617) cleared Congress on Oct. 7 and was signed by President Bush on Nov. 4.

The same package contained provisions of a separate bill (HR 5397 — H Rept 102-768) prohibiting the abandonment of large barges. HR 5397 had been reported by the Merchant Marine panel on July 31 and passed by the House Aug. 3 by voice vote under suspension of the rules.

Cruise Ship Ownership

To improve the competitiveness of the U.S. maritime industry, the House by voice vote on Sept. 22, 1992, passed legislation (HR 5257) barring foreign-owned ships from engaging in the domestic cruise business. The measure died in the Senate.

The bill, reported Aug. 11 (H Rept 102-835) by the House Merchant Marine and Fisheries Committee, brought so-called voyages to nowhere — which included dinner cruises, whale sightseeing trips and fishing expeditions — under merchant marine laws that required U.S.-flagged ships and U.S. crews.

In 1992, foreign-flagged vessels offering cruises that returned to the same port without having passengers disembark in a foreign country were able to skirt U.S. labor, safety and hiring laws. Under the bill, all ships departing from United States ports to engage in such voyages were required to be built, owned and operated in the United States. The measure phased out the involvement of foreign vessels in the trade, allowing some to continue their business for up to 20 years to recoup their investments before the ban took effect completely.

In other cruise ship action, the House on Nov. 23, 1991, gave voice vote approval to legislation (HR 3282) that allowed gambling on U.S.-flag cruise ships in international waters. The Senate did not act on the bill.

HR 3282 was needed, sponsors said, to correct an inequity in U.S. law that allowed foreign-flag vessels but not U.S.-flag ships to offer gambling at a time when the domestic cruise ship industry was faltering. Ships could provide gambling in international waters only if the gambling activities were not prohibited under the laws of the state from which the ship was operated. The bill, however, did not legalize the operation of ships that engaged solely in gambling.

An effort was turned back during subcommittee markup that would have effectively given U.S. ships a monopoly in the voyages-to-nowhere market.

HR 3282 was reported from House Merchant Marine and Fisheries (H Rept 102-357) on Nov. 22.

Crew Documents

The House by voice vote on Sept. 9, 1992, passed a bill (HR 4394) requiring all crew members of tugs, towboats and barges navigating inland waterways to obtain official documents as seamen. The measure, intended to require the workers to submit to drug testing and background checks, stalled in the Senate.

In 1992, seafarers aboard U.S. merchant vessels of at least 100 gross tons were required to hold merchant mariner documents. The law exempted vessels operating only on inland rivers and lakes. More then 3,000 tugs and towboats operated on inland waterways, many carrying hazardous cargoes.

The House Merchant Marine and Fisheries Committee reported HR 4394 (H Rept 102-669) on July 21.

NOAA Authorization

Legislation (HR 2130 — PL 102-567) cleared in 1992 that reauthorized National Oceanic and Atmospheric Administration (NOAA) weather and coastal research programs for two years.

HR 2130 provided an NOAA authorization of $1.5 billion for fiscal 1992 and $1.7 billion in fiscal 1993. The bill also aimed to slow the pace of closures of national weather stations. The National Weather Service wanted to modernize and consolidate the stations, reducing the number from 250 to 115 uniform offices. The measure banned the closing of weather stations nationwide until 1996 and imposed stricter criteria for closing stations to ensure that levels of service remained acceptably high.

House Merchant Marine and Fisheries reported HR 2130 (H Rept 102-133, Part I) on June 26, 1991. The House Ways and Means Committee reported it (H Rept 102-133, Part II) on July 11. The House passed the bill by voice vote Nov. 20.

The Senate Commerce, Science and Transportation Committee considered a companion measure (S 1405), which it had reported (S Rept 102-198) on Oct. 29. The Senate passed an amended HR 2130 by voice vote Aug. 12, 1992. The measure cleared Oct. 7, and President Bush signed it Oct. 29.

In another NOAA-related matter, the House Merchant Marine Committee on July 1, 1992, approved by voice vote a bill (HR 5324) authorizing $430 million over four years to replace and modernize the NOAA's 22-vessel fleet. The panel rejected an amendment to require that all of the agency's vessels be built or repaired in U.S. shipyards. HR 5324 was formally reported (H Rept 102-896) on Sept. 23. It never went to the floor.

Maritime Authorization

Congress in 1991 cleared legislation (HR 1006 — PL 102-100) authorizing fiscal 1992 funds for the Federal Maritime Commission, but fiscal 1993 measures never progressed beyond committee. No authorization bills were enacted for the Maritime Administration. *(101st Congress action, p. 426)*

Maritime Commission. HR 1006 authorized $18 million in fiscal 1992 for the Maritime Commission. The House Merchant Marine and Fisheries Committee reported the bill (H Rept 102-80) on May 23, 1991. The House passed the measure by voice vote under suspension of the rules June 24. The Senate Commerce, Science and Transportation Committee reported HR 1006 (S Rept 102-134) on Aug. 1. The Senate passed an amended version by voice vote the same day. The House agreed to the Senate changes Aug. 2, completing congressional action. President Bush signed HR 1006 on Aug. 17.

In 1992, House Merchant Marine reported HR 4156 (H Rept 102-495) on April 9 and Senate Commerce reported S 2700 (S Rept 102-384) on Aug. 12; both bills authorized fiscal 1993 funds for the Maritime Commission. Neither measure reached the floor.

Maritime Administration. The 102nd Congress did not clear Maritime Administration authorization legislation. A fiscal 1992 measure was reported from House Merchant Marine on Oct. 21, 1991 (HR 1464 — H Rept 102-260). The House passed a fiscal 1993 authorization (HR 4484) on a 331-48 vote Sept. 9, 1992. Merchant Marine had reported it (H Rept 102-570) on June 16. A Senate companion measure (S 2701 — S Rept 102-360) was reported from the Commerce Committee on Aug. 4.

Cable Regulation

Congress on Oct. 5, 1992, overrode a presidential veto to enact legislation (S 12 — PL 102-385) intended to lower cable television rates and increase competition in the industry.

The drama of the veto override, coming just weeks before the presidential election, overshadowed at least temporarily the significance of the bill itself.

The law, the most ambitious reregulation of an industry during the Reagan-Bush era, was meant to control rates until more competition developed in the booming industry. Since the cable industry was released from local regulation at the end of 1986, it had grown into a $20 billion communications monolith serving 56 million subscribers, or about 60 percent of all homes with television sets.

Along with the boom in cable programming had come complaints of discriminatory business practices, poor customer service and price gouging. By the early 1990s, the rates consumers paid for cable services had more than doubled from their 1987 levels, far outstripping inflation.

Almost all of the nation's approximately 11,000 cable franchises operated without direct competition. Potential competitors, such as the home satellite dish and microwave "wireless" cable industries, complained that cable companies charged them up to 500 percent more than cable operators paid for the same programs, on terms that kept many programs out of competitors' reach.

The bill's enactment was a setback for the cable industry, which warned that the measure would increase, not lower, cable rates. But the legislation was a boon for broadcasters, because it permitted them to earn revenues from cable operators who retransmitted over-the-air local television programs. Representatives of the movie industry sided with the cable industry in opposing the bill, saying that they had a right to share in the broadcasters' new revenues from the cable industry.

The cable legislation required nearly all of the nation's cable operators to follow the mandates of the Federal Communications Commission (FCC) on the pricing of basic cable viewing packages and equipment rentals. Those who produced and sold cable's popular programming, including MTV, Nickelodeon and ESPN, were required to offer their programs to cable's competitors at fair prices, terms and conditions.

Broadcasters, who since 1965 had been required by the FCC to give their programs to local cable systems, were permitted to charge cable operators for the use of their programs. But a station owner who feared being dropped by a local cable company could forfeit that right and instead force the cable operator to transmit the station's signals for free.

Turner Broadcasting System and Daniels Cablevision Inc., two of the most prominent cable programmers and system operators, filed suit against the new law. Among other claims, the suits alleged that cable operators' First Amendment rights were being infringed upon by the law's requirements that they carry broadcast programs. Suits were pending in federal court at the end of 1992.

The House passed a cable television regulation bill (HR 5267) in 1990. A similar measure (S 1880) was blocked in the Senate. *(Cable regulation background, 1989-90 action, p. 427)*

Senate Action

By early 1991, the debate on cable regulation had become more partisan and heated, with the Bush administration stridently opposing any reregulation and the cable industry refusing to cooperate with Congress as it had throughout most of 1990. In a March 13 letter to Congress, the administration said more competition, not more regulation, was needed. Instead of regulating cable rates, the letter said, Congress could increase competition by allowing telephone companies to enter the cable programming business.

S 12, approved on May 14 on a 16-3 vote and reported on June 28 (S Rept 102-92) by the Senate Commerce, Science and Transportation Committee, was similar to the 1990 Senate and House cable bills, but with new language permitting even tighter regulation of the cable industry. The measure was introduced by John C. Danforth, R-Mo., and was cosponsored by Commerce Committee Chairman Ernest F. Hollings, D-S.C., and Communications Subcommittee Chairman Daniel K. Inouye, D-Hawaii.

S 12 required the FCC to regulate basic cable rates in areas with no competition from another multi-channel video provider. Competition was defined as adequate when at least half of an area's households were served by competitors to the primary cable provider — such as satellite systems or cable operators having at least a 15 percent market share.

The bill made it more difficult for cable operators to avert regulation by shifting their most popular programming to another package. It also barred cable programmers from unreasonably refusing to sell programming to competitors. Cable operators, meanwhile, could not discriminate against competitors in pricing or terms. Other new provisions increased local authority to regulate rates and service, encouraged localities to seek second cable franchises and ensured that satellite networks did not favor cable operators over distributors of home satellite dishes in prices and programming access.

Inouye won the support of broadcasters by including a so-called must-carry (also called "retransmission consent") provision allowing local television stations to negotiate their own retransmission deals with cable operators. Stations either could force cable operators to carry their signals free of charge, as smaller stations wanted, or could ask cable operators to compensate them for programs, as larger stations preferred. The legal ramifications of Inouye's language remained in doubt, as must-carry requirements had been thrown out by two federal courts in 1985 and 1987 on grounds that they violated cable programmers' First Amendment rights to carry only programs of their choice.

The committee approved by voice vote an amendment offered by Wendell H. Ford, D-Ky., to include low-power television stations with locally generated programming under the definition of over-the-air broadcasts that cable operators would be forced to carry.

The cable industry objected that S 12 represented a boondoggle for its rivals, especially broadcasters — and the Bush administration threatened a veto.

Senate sponsors of S 12 delayed floor action in anticipation of an announcement by the FCC on new guidelines for cable providers. The agency's ruling, on June 13, 1991, made avoiding regulation more difficult for cable companies, as it boosted the percentage of cable systems subject to local rate regulation from 3 percent to 60 percent. Backers of cable regulation claimed that the FCC ruling would

Cable Lobbying

Legislation (S 12 — PL 102-385) to regulate the cable television industry, cleared by Congress in 1992, provoked intense lobbying by a number of interest groups. Some of the groups supplemented their lobbying efforts with generous campaign contributions. *(Cable regulation, p. 451)*

Cable-Viewing Public. Many cable subscribers had seen their rates double since the industry was deregulated; many also had come to see their local cable company as an unresponsive monopoly. Rural cable viewers had particularly strong feelings about the issue because, for many of them, cable provided their only access to television. Members of Congress visiting their home states and districts heard these views directly from their constituents.

Consumer Groups. The Consumer Federation of America was prominent among consumer groups lobbying for the cable bill on the grounds that it would protect consumers against price gouging and poor service.

Cable Industry. Since deregulation, the cable industry had grown into a communications monolith, yet cable operators did not welcome proposals to regulate them more strictly. Lobbyists for large cable companies and for the industry's trade association, the National Cable Television Association, worked hard to defeat S 12.

After the House and Senate had passed cable bills and conferees were drafting a final version in the fall of 1992, the industry mounted an intense advertising campaign featuring two television spots aired by more than a dozen cable channels nationwide and fliers mailed in the monthly cable bills of 35 million subscribers. The ads claimed that cable rates would rise dramatically if the bill became law.

Movie Industry. Jack Valenti, president of the Motion Picture Association of America, joined other representatives of Hollywood and the cable industry in an attempt to kill the cable bill. Hollywood objected to the "retransmission consent" provision, which permitted broadcasters to seek compensation for cable operators' use of their local signals. Film industry representatives argued that, as the producers of the programs, they deserved a share of the revenues.

The opposition of the film industry put many Democrats, especially those from California, in an awkward position because Hollywood had been a mainstay of financial support for Democrats in congressional and presidential races. At the same time, cable bill supporters advertised their legislation as pro-consumer and hoped to benefit from public dissatisfaction with President Bush shortly before the 1992 presidential election. Asking why he was one of 10 California lawmakers to reverse themselves and vote against the final version, Howard L. Berman, D-Calif., said, "I'm from Los Angeles."

Broadcasters. The broadcast industry joined the fight for cable regulation legislation in 1991 when sponsors of the Senate bill included the retransmission consent provision to recruit a lobby powerful enough to counter the cable industry. Broadcasters had long argued that they deserved a share of the revenues generated when their programs were aired by cable stations.

A memo sent out in the fall of 1992 by board members of the industry's trade group, the National Association of Broadcasters, urged the news departments of member stations across the country to "tell it like it is" on the cable issue and to "generate the news stories." This prompted Sen. Tim Wirth, D-Colo., a leading opponent of the legislation, to accuse broadcasters of manipulating the news for profit.

House Judiciary Committee. Although not an interest group in the traditional sense of the term, some members of the House Judiciary Committee worked hard to protect their turf. About one-third of the panel joined Chairman Jack Brooks, D-Texas, in voting against the conference report and veto override, after voting for passage of the bill, because they believed certain of its provisions encroached on their legislative territory.

The primary focus of this jurisdictional dispute involved the retransmission provision, which allowed broadcasters to charge cable companies for use of their signals. The Judiciary panel members wanted to replace that provision with the language of a bill (HR 4511) authored by William J. Hughes, D-N.J., chairman of the Intellectual Property Subcommittee. The bill would gradually repeal the entire cable copyright system, forcing each cable operator to negotiate directly with each copyright holder for retransmission rights.

The film industry supported the Hughes approach, but critics warned that it would bring higher cable rates and spell the end of free sports on broadcast television. In the end, the House ducked the issue and the retransmission provision survived as part of S 12. Brooks took his troops to the opposition, putting himself in the uncharacteristic position of supporting Bush.

improve, not diminish, support for congressional action.

S 12 did not reach the floor in 1991 because of an end-of-session time crush and the intention of opponents to offer weakening amendments. The Senate moved quickly in 1992, however, approving S 12 by a vote of 73-18 on Jan. 31 after rejecting a substitute measure 35-54.

The substitute, offered by Bob Packwood, R-Ore., Ted Stevens, R-Alaska, and John Kerry, D-Mass., attempted to weaken the regulatory provisions of the bill. It eliminated language aimed at giving cable competitors better access to cable programs and contained no limits on cable system ownership.

Danforth and other supporters of S 12 charged that the cable industry's trade association, the National Cable Television Association, had pushed the substitute as a way to steer votes away from the main bill and not as a legitimate compromise. A Jan. 27 statement from the Bush administration warned of a veto for S 12 but did not endorse the substitute.

Sponsors of S 12 agreed to add two provisions from the rejected substitute to the main bill to encourage administration support. One prohibited local governments from awarding exclusive cable franchises. A second broadened an exemption to a 1984 ban on telephone company entry into the cable business by allowing rural phone companies to offer cable services. (The second provision was dropped during the House-Senate conference.) The Senate Jan. 29 rejected a motion 33-64 to table (kill) an amendment by Bob Graham, D-Fla., to require the FCC to study home shopping broadcast channels; the Graham amendment subsequently was adopted by voice vote. An amendment by Jesse Helms, R-N.C., was adopted 95-0 on Jan. 30, which allowed cable operators to ban pornographic programs and required operators to place such shows on one channel available upon subscriber request. By voice votes, the Senate adopted a Patrick J. Leahy, D-Vt., amendment to ensure that cable systems were compatible with all TV sets and video cassette recorders and a Wyche Fowler, D-Ga., amendment to allow cable operators to ban the use of any public educational channels for programs containing "obscene" material.

House Action

House Energy and Commerce Telecommunications and Finance Subcommittee Chairman Edward J. Markey, D-Mass., introduced his cable bill (HR 4850) on March 25, 1992. Subcommittee action was unusually divisive. Members rejected, 12-14, a weaker alternative proposed by Norman F. Lent of New York, ranking Republican of the full committee. The subcommittee rejected a provision, pushed by consumer organizations, to establish local citizens' groups to monitor local cable operators and franchising authorities. An amendment adopted by voice vote would exclude home-shopping broadcast stations from a provision that would force cable operators to carry local broadcast signals. HR 4850 was approved by the subcommittee 17-7 on April 8.

The subcommittee-approved bill was stronger than the measure passed by the House in 1990 and close to S 12 on most issues. Both HR 4850 and S 12 imposed new federal controls on the price of basic cable service — as well as other rates found to be "unreasonable" — and gave competitors more access to programs controlled by the cable industry.

The full committee scaled back HR 4850 before approving it 31-12 on June 17 and formally reporting it (H Rept 102-628) on June 29. The panel rejected 15-27 a weaker substitute offered by Lent but stripped from the bill two controversial provisions that Energy and Commerce Committee Chairman John D. Dingell, D-Mich., said would cause the measure to become bogged down in a jurisdictional dispute with the Judiciary Committee: the "program access" provision, which aimed to bolster competition by giving satellite distributors and other potential cable competitors lower-priced access to cable programming, and the broadcast retransmission consent proposal. The Judiciary Committee was at work on legislation to phase out a 1976 copyright law (PL 94-553) that allowed cable operators to retransmit the signals of local broadcasters free of charge. Before the full House took up HR 4850, the House Rules Committee ruled that, because the retransmission provision was not in the bill, a floor amendment that incorporated a Judiciary subcommittee bill (HR 4511) to overhaul the copyright royalty payment system was not germane and therefore could not be offered. A floor battle over the issue thus was averted. Later, in conference, the retransmission amendment was reinstated, and it became part of the law. *(1976 law, Congress and the Nation Vol. IV, p. 612)*

The Energy and Commerce Committee amended the cable bill in some ways to be tougher on the industry. One amendment, adopted by voice vote, would allow the FCC to order refunds to consumers for any rate increase collected by a cable company between the time that a complaint about rates was filed and the time that the agency determined price gouging had occurred. Another amendment, adopted by voice vote, would allow local broadcasters to expand the number of cable systems that would be forced to carry their signals under must-carry requirements if they transmitted between two large metropolitan areas.

However, attempts to impose stricter controls on cable — including a provision to set up consumer watchdog groups that would monitor local cable activities — were rejected. Also turned back was an amendment to force cable operators in the markets of the Home Shopping Network's 11 stations to carry the 24-hour advertising channels if they also carried the QVC Shopping Network, a cable industry shopping channel.

Handing the cable industry a significant defeat and setting up a veto confrontation with Bush, the House on July 23 passed HR 4850 by a vote of 340-73. Many of the 98 Republicans who joined 241 Democrats and one independent to pass the bill hailed from rural areas where broadcast signals were weak and television viewers had to rely on cable service or satellite dishes for reception.

A milder substitute amendment, backed by the Bush administration and offered by Lent, was rejected 144-266 on July 23. But Bush had already been given a sign that he was on the losing side of the cable issue — and in danger of having his threatened veto overridden — when a crucial amendment by W. J. "Billy" Tauzin, D-La., was adopted.

Under the Tauzin amendment, which restored the program access provision dropped by Energy and Commerce, programmers affiliated with the cable industry could not discriminate in the price, terms and conditions of programs they sold to cable's competitors — the home satellite dish and "wireless" cable industries. The amendment also barred most exclusive contracts between cable operators and vendors. Despite stiff opposition, the House July 23 adopted the Tauzin amendment on a **key vote of 338-68 (R 116-45; D 221-23; I 1-0)**. *(1992 key votes, p. 1083)*

In an impassioned speech on the House floor, Tauzin contended that competition to cable would never develop unless some controls were put on cable's program pricing policies and increasing market power. Just as the cable television industry relied on free network broadcasts in its infancy, Tauzin said, cable's competitors now needed government help to purchase cable programs at fair prices.

Before approving the Tauzin amendment, the House rejected 162-247 a weaker version offered by Thomas J. Manton, D-N.Y. The Manton amendment had the support of Dingell as well as the cable industry and members of the House Democratic leadership. Manton argued that the Tauzin amendment would unfairly encroach on private business decisions.

The House passed S 12, amended with the language of HR 4850, by voice vote July 23.

Conference, Final Action

House-Senate negotiators included in the final version of S 12 the retransmission provision favored by broadcasters and the program access provision that had been so hard-fought in the House.

Conferees accepted the House bill's guidelines for the FCC to follow in setting a price for basic cable service. However, the House definition of "basic" cable was narrowed. Instead of including long-distance broadcast "superstations" in the basic package, conferees included only local broadcast signals and government access channels. A Dingell compromise also was incorporated that would leave it up to the FCC to determine after nine months whether cable operators should be forced to carry home-shopping broadcast stations on their systems.

The conferees dropped two controversial House provisions addressing future trends in cable television — the migration of sports events from free television to pay television and the foreign ownership of cable systems.

Despite a renewed veto threat by Bush and an intense lobbying campaign waged by the cable and movie industries, the House and Senate adopted the conference report on S 12 by wide margins. The House agreed to the conference report (H Rept 102-862) on Sept. 17 by a vote of 280-128. The Senate acted Sept. 22, 74-25.

Bush vetoed S 12 on Oct. 3, saying that tighter regulation would cause cable television rates to rise, not drop as sponsors claimed. The White House cast the showdown vote on the bill as a test of loyalty to a president fighting an uphill re-election battle, a strategy that backfired as Congress resoundingly rejected the president.

The Senate, on a **key vote of 74-25 (R 24-18; D 50-7)** taken Oct. 5, overrode the veto. The House, voting a few hours later, overrode the veto by a vote of 308-114 — a breakdown that reflected a growth in support for the legislation. With the House action, S 12 became law, and Congress overrode a Bush veto for the first time.

By characterizing the vote as a test of presidential loyalty, White House advisers misjudged Bush's slumping popularity. They also misjudged lawmakers' sensitivity to their constituents' desire for inexpensive television viewing. As Rep. Markey said, "Sometimes 60 million people wielding clickers in their living rooms are more powerful than a president wielding a veto pen."

Major Provisions

As enacted by Congress on Oct. 5, the cable regulation law (S 12 — PL 102-385):

Rate and Service Regulation

- **Basic Rate Regulation.** Required the Federal Communications Commission to ensure that rates for basic cable service, including necessary rental equipment, were reasonable for all cable systems that did not face effective competition.
- **Definition of 'Basic' Cable.** Defined "basic" cable service as the lowest-priced package, or tier, of cable programs. It included retransmission of local over-the-air broadcast signals as well as public, educational and governmental-access programs. Cable operators could add additional programs to their basic packages (such as distant broadcast superstations), but rates for those programs also would be subject to rate regulation.
- **Definition of 'Effective Competition.'** Cable operators were exempted from rate regulation when they were subject to "effective competition." Such competition was defined as franchise areas in which fewer than 30 percent of households subscribed to the cable service. Competition also was considered present in areas served by at least two unaffiliated cable operators or their competitors when either of which reached at least 50 percent of households. Finally, competition was deemed present when the number of households subscribing to a competing programmer exceeded 15 percent of the total households.
- **Reasonable Rates.** Required the FCC to regulate rates by April 3, 1993. Instead of setting a single maximum rate for basic cable service, the FCC was permitted to adopt formulas "or other mechanisms or procedures" to regulate rates.
- **Setting Basic Rates.** Repealed a 5 percent annual rate increase for basic cable television, allowed by the 1984 Cable Telecommunications Act (PL 98-549), and required the FCC to take into account the following factors when setting a basic rate formula: the rates of cable systems that were subject to effective competition; the cost of obtaining, transmitting or providing signals carried as part of the basic viewing package; other company-wide costs related to providing a basic package; advertising revenues received by a cable operator during programming carried on the basic package; any franchise fee, tax or charge imposed by state and local authorities; costs incurred to satisfy franchise requirements to support public, educational or governmental channels; and a "reasonable profit" as defined by the commission.
- **Franchising Authority.** Allowed local cable franchising authorities to exercise regulatory jurisdiction over the cable law's rate provisions. The FCC could deny or revoke any such authority.
- **Premium Channels.** Barred cable operators for 10 years from requiring customers to subscribe to any package other than the basic one to receive so-called premium movie channels (such as HBO or Cinemax) or other per-channel or per-program services. This provision did not apply to cable systems that lacked the technological means to carry it out. The FCC could — at the request of a cable operator — waive the requirement after finding that compliance would lead to higher rates.
- **Cost of Other Cable Offerings.** Allowed cable subscribers to file a complaint with the FCC that a cable system with no effective competition had unreasonably raised rates for any program offering outside the basic viewing package. If the FCC found such rates unreasonable, it could establish reasonable rates and require that subscribers be refunded the unreasonable portion of their fee from the time their complaint was filed.
- **Rate Complaints.** Allowed subscribers and franchising authorities to complain about existing cable rates only during a 180-day period after the effective date of the FCC's new rules. After that period, rate complaints could

be leveled only against future rate increases and had to be filed within a "reasonable period of time" following the increase.

● **Existing Rate Agreements.** Allowed existing agreements between franchise authorities and cable operators lacking effective competition (based on the FCC's pre-July 1, 1990, "three-broadcast-signal" standard) to stay in effect until they expired. Such operators would then be subject to the new rate regulations.

● **Preventing Loopholes.** Required the FCC, by April 3, 1993, to set standards and guidelines to prevent cable operators from evading rate regulation by such methods as shifting more popular programs away from the basic tier.

● **Small Cable Systems.** Required the FCC to write rules in a way that reduced the administrative burdens and costs of compliance for cable systems that had 1,000 or fewer subscribers.

● **Price Reports.** Required the FCC to report annually on the average rates for basic cable service and other programming, as well as for converter boxes, remote controls and other equipment.

● **Price Discrimination.** Permitted federal, state and local officials to set rules barring price discrimination among existing and potential cable customers, other than "reasonable" discounts for senior citizens or other economically disadvantaged groups.

Cable Service Regulations

● **Service Standards.** Required the FCC, by April 3, 1993, to establish customer service standards for cable operators. The standards were to cover office hours, telephone availability, installations, outages, service calls, billings and refunds. States and franchising authorities would be free to enact or enforce stronger consumer protection laws.

● **Customer Equipment.** Directed the FCC, by Oct. 5, 1993, to issue rules governing cable operators' use of converter boxes on subscribers' television sets.

● **Compatibility.** Required the FCC by Oct. 5, 1993, to report to Congress on ways to assure compatibility among cable systems, televisions and video cassette recorders. Within 180 days of submitting the report, the FCC was required to write rules intended to carry out its findings.

● **Scrambling Local Signals.** Required the FCC, by Oct. 5, 1993, to issue rules outlining how cable operators might scramble, or encrypt, a local broadcast signal to protect against signal theft.

● **Home Wiring.** Required the FCC, by Feb. 2, 1993, to establish rules to determine who owned wiring installed by a cable operator within a subscriber's home after service was terminated.

● **Itemized Bills.** Allowed cable operators, beginning Dec. 4, 1993, to identify as a separate line on subscribers' bills the amount of the total bill that was assessed as a franchise fee and the identity of the franchising authority that levied the fee. The operator also would be allowed to identify the amount of the total bill that resulted from requirements imposed on the cable operator by a franchise agreement to support public, educational or government channels.

● **Services and Equipment Not Requested.** Barred a cable operator, after April 3, 1993, from charging for any service or equipment not affirmatively and specifically requested by a subscriber. A subscriber's failure to refuse a cable operator's proposal to provide such service or equipment would not be deemed an affirmative request for that service or equipment.

● **Program Changes.** Allowed franchising authorities, beginning on Dec. 4, 1992, to require cable operators to give subscribers 30 days' notice before changing any channel assignment or video programming service provided on any channel.

● **Technical Standards.** Required the FCC, by Oct. 5, 1993, to establish minimum technical standards to ensure adequate signal quality for all classes of programming provided over a cable system. Franchising authorities could petition to set more stringent technical standards.

Broadcasters

● **Carriage Options.** Required that commercial television stations, by Oct. 5, 1993, and every three years thereafter, choose between the right to negotiate with cable operators for consent to retransmit their broadcast signals and the right to force cable operators to carry their signals for free.

If a station opted for retransmission consent, the requirements of the must-carry provision would not apply, and vice versa. If more than one cable system served the same area, a station's choice would apply to all cable systems serving an area.

● **Retransmission Consent.** Prohibited local cable operators or other video program distributors, as of Oct. 5, 1993, from retransmitting a local broadcast station's originating programs without its express authority. Exceptions included non-commercial broadcast stations; signals retransmitted directly to a home satellite dish of a broadcast station not owned, operated by or affiliated with a network; and signals of superstations that transmitted signals beyond their broadcast area via satellite.

The FCC by Nov. 19, 1992, was required to begin writing rules governing broadcasters' rights to grant retransmission consent. The commission would have to consider the impact of this provision on basic cable rates and ensure that those rates were reasonable.

● **Must-Carry.** Required cable operators to reserve up to one-third of their channel capacity to carry local commercial broadcast stations. Cable systems with 12 or fewer usable activated channels would have to carry the signals of at least three local commercial television stations.

Cable operators were required to carry commercial stations on all cable systems within the station's viewing area, regardless of audience size. The FCC would have to adopt additional requirements when it set standards for high-definition television, an upcoming form of television that required more channel capacity and offered superior picture and sound quality.

A cable system with 300 or fewer subscribers would not be subject to this section as long as it continued to carry any signal of a broadcast television station. Cable operators would not be required to carry the signal of a local commercial television station that substantially duplicated another carried on the system, nor would cable operators be forced to carry the signals of more than one local commercial television station affiliated with a particular broadcast network.

The FCC was required to issue new rules regarding the must-carry provisions by April 3, 1993.

● **Complaints.** Required that whenever a local commercial television station thought that a cable operator had failed to meet its obligations under this section, the station notify the cable operator in writing. The operator would have 30 days to respond. Further complaints would have to be filed with the FCC. The commission would have 120 days from that time to rule on the complaint.

• **Non-Commercial Educational Television.** Required each cable operator, by Dec. 4, 1992, to carry any qualified local non-commercial educational television station that requested to be carried on the system. Cable operators with 12 or fewer usable channels would be required to carry the signal of only one educational station. Operators with channel capacities ranging from 13 to 35 channels would be required to carry one to three non-commercial educational stations. Those with more than 35 usable channels would be required to carry the signals of three educational stations.

• **Low-Power Television Stations.** Cable systems with 35 or fewer channels were required to carry one qualified low-power television station, such as an amateur station that transmitted from a local school or college. Cable systems with 36 or more channels would have to carry two qualified low-power stations. The requirements applied only to areas that had no licensed full-power station and that were outside the nation's top 160 metropolitan areas.

• **Home Shopping Channels.** Cable operators were allowed to choose not to carry any commercial television station or video programming service that was used predominantly for the transmission of sales presentations or program-length commercials, pending the outcome of an FCC study regarding the public interest value of such stations. The study was to be completed by July 2, 1993.

• **Compulsory License.** Declared that nothing in the retransmission consent provision modified the compulsory copyright license provision of the 1976 Copyright Act (PL 94-553) or affected existing or future video-programming licensing agreements between broadcasting stations and video programmers. *(Copyright law, Congress and the Nation Vol. IV, p. 612)*

Access to Cable Programs

• **Program Discrimination.** Required the FCC, by April 3, 1993, to develop safeguards to prevent video program distributors, including satellite broadcast programmers as well as cable operators who had a financial interest in a cable network, from "unduly or improperly influencing" decisions regarding the price, terms or conditions of program sales to non-cable program distributors. Programmers were prohibited from engaging in "unfair methods of competition or unfair or deceptive acts" that deterred or prevented any competitor from providing programs to consumers.

• **Exceptions.** Allowed video programmers to impose reasonable requirements on distributors for creditworthiness, financial stability and ability to offer programs. They also could take into account differences in the cost of creating, selling or transmitting programs, as well as economies of scale or other savings attributable to the number of subscribers served by a distributor.

But vendors were barred from entering into exclusive contracts with cable operators, except where the FCC determined such a contract was in the public interest. The ban on exclusive contracts for satellite cable programs between a cable operator and a cable-affiliated program vendor would expire in 10 years, unless the FCC determined the ban was still needed to preserve diversity and competition.

Exclusive contracts entered into before June 1, 1990, would not be affected. But non-cable distributors in areas not served by a cable operator would be allowed access to programs otherwise off-limits because of exclusive contracts.

• **Remedies.** Any multi-channel video program distributor who was denied fair access to cable programs could complain to the commission. The FCC could order appropriate remedies including setting new prices, terms and conditions of programming sales to the distributor.

• **Coercion and Carriage Agreements.** Required the FCC, by Oct. 5, 1993, to establish rules governing carriage agreements between cable operators and video program distributors. This was intended to prevent a cable operator or other program distributor from requiring a financial interest in a program service as a condition for carrying the program. The agreements also would prohibit cable operators or other video program distributors from coercing a video programmer to provide exclusive rights as a condition of carriage.

• **Cable Competitors' Public Service Requirements.** Required the FCC, by April 3, 1993, to begin considering how to impose public interest or other requirements on any provider of direct-broadcast satellite service that was not regulated as a common carrier. Direct broadcast satellite was an emerging form of video programming for which the FCC had set aside frequencies.

Local Franchising Authorities

• **Local Authorities as Competitors.** Required that nothing in the law prohibit a local or municipal cable franchising authority from operating as a multi-channel video-program distributor within its jurisdiction as of Dec. 4, 1992.

• **Awarding Franchises.** Prohibited franchising authorities, as of Dec. 4, 1992, from granting exclusive franchises and unreasonably refusing to award an additional competitive franchise.

• **Franchise Liability.** Limited the ability of cable operators to collect damages against franchising authorities in lawsuits that alleged First Amendment or other violations because the franchising authority had agreed to build a competing cable system. Damages would be limited to attorneys' fees and legal costs.

• **Franchise Renewal.** Required franchising authorities to begin the renewal process for a cable franchise six months after the cable operator submitted a renewal request. The franchising authority was required to consider whether the operator had substantially complied with the existing franchise contract. A franchise authority could turn down a renewal if it notified a cable operator of problems and had given the operator adequate time to solve them.

Market Control and Cross-Ownership

• **Ownership Limits.** Required the FCC, by Oct. 5, 1993, to set reasonable limits on the number of subscribers that cable system owners were authorized to reach. The FCC also would limit the number of channels that could be occupied by a video programmer financially affiliated with a cable operator. The FCC was required to study whether rules were needed to limit cable program distributors from creating or producing programming.

• **Sales of Cable Systems.** Prohibited cable operators, as of Dec. 4, 1992, from selling or transferring ownership in a cable system within a 36-month period after the acquisition or initial construction of the system. The FCC could waive the provision to permit appropriate transfers in cases of default, foreclosure or other financial distress.

• **Cross-Ownership.** Barred cable systems from owning wireless, or microwave, cable licenses or operating a satellite master antenna service within their cable service areas unless such ownership existed before enactment of the law. The FCC could allow other exceptions to ensure that all households in a franchise area were able to obtain video programs.

Obscene and Violent Programs

• **Notice to Subscribers.** Required cable operators to give subscribers 30 days' notice if they planned to provide a premium channel to non-subscribing customers for free. Premium channels under this provision were defined as any pay service offered on a per-channel or per-program basis that offered movies rated X, NC-17 or R by the Motion Picture Association of America. Subscribers would be allowed to request that the channel be blocked.

• **Protecting Children from Indecent Programs.** Required the FCC, by Feb. 2, 1993, to adopt rules allowing a cable operator to enforce a stated policy of banning programs that the operator reasonably believed described or depicted sexual or excretory activities or organs in a patently offensive manner under contemporary community standards. The FCC would be required to write rules to limit the access of children to such programs. Cable operators were to put indecent programs on a single channel known to subscribers and to block such a channel unless a subscriber requested access in writing. Programmers would be required to inform cable operators of programs considered indecent under FCC rules.

• **Public Channels.** Required the FCC, by April 3, 1993, to establish rules that enabled a cable operator to ban the use of any public, educational or governmental access channel for any program that contained obscene material, sexually explicit conduct or material soliciting or promoting unlawful conduct.

• **Indecent Programs on Leased-Access Channels.** The FCC was to require cable operators to designate one leased-access channel for any "indecent" leased-access program that the operator did not choose to prohibit. The operator would have to block that channel unless a subscriber requested access in writing.

Miscellaneous

• **Equal Employment Opportunity.** Required that the FCC promote equal employment opportunities in each of 15 specified job categories (expanded from nine under previous law) in the cable television industry, to achieve diversity of views in the electronic media. Cable operators also were required, in their annual reports, to identify by race, gender and job title the number of employees within each category. For television broadcast stations, the existing FCC regulations governing the minority hiring requirements of holders of television station licenses would be incorporated into law. The provision also required the FCC, by July 2, 1993, to revise broadcast rules to require a midterm review of a station's hiring practices before a license renewal.

Penalties for violations of equal employment opportunity laws were increased from $200 to $500 a day for each violation. By Oct. 5, 1994, the FCC was required to submit a report to Congress on the effect and operation of the equal employment opportunity provisions.

• **Antitrust Laws.** Required that nothing in the law could alter or restrict the applicability of any federal or state unfair competition laws.

• **Sports Programming.** Required the FCC to conduct an ongoing study of local, regional and national sports programs by broadcast stations, cable programming networks and pay-per-view services. The study was to analyze, on a sport-by-sport basis, trends in the migration of such programming from broadcast stations to cable networks and pay-per-view systems and to examine the economic causes and social consequences of such trends.

• **Theft.** Increased, beginning on Dec. 4, 1992, the punishment imposed on individuals convicted of stealing cable service for commercial advantage or private financial gain, to bring penalties and remedies in line with those imposed on theft of satellite signals. The new penalties, which made commercial theft of cable service a felony, would be $50,000 and two years imprisonment for the first offense; $100,000 and five years imprisonment for any subsequent offense.

Public Broadcasting

Congress in 1992 cleared a three-year authorization (HR 2977 — PL 102-356) for the Corporation for Public Broadcasting (CPB), the non-profit agency responsible for channeling government funds to public television and radio stations. The legislation, passed by the House in 1991, was delayed in the Senate by critics who charged that public broadcasting had a liberal bias and that the CPB was failing its mission to use taxpayer money only for balanced programming.

Senators worked out a compromise that included provisions designed to make the CPB more accountable and objective, while making no sweeping changes in the agency's mandate. The final bill authorized $310 million for the corporation in fiscal 1994, $375 million in fiscal 1995 and $425 million in fiscal 1996. President Bush, who joined in the attacks on the CPB, nevertheless signed the bill on Aug. 26, 1992.

Background. The CPB was created by Congress in 1967 (PL 87-447) to provide grants to public radio and television stations. The goal was to inspire programming with more diversity and educational value than the fare offered by commercial broadcasters. Congress was given control over funding for the CPB, while programming decisions were to be made by the Public Broadcasting Service (PBS), a non-profit corporation that received its funding from the CPB. To further insulate public broadcasting from political pressures, decisions about whether or not to air a particular program were left largely to local public stations. *(Congress and the Nation Vol. II, p. 297)*

Despite the safeguards written into the original law, the CPB came under political attack almost from the beginning. Critics used the CPB authorization bill as an opportunity to make their complaints; they also expressed their views to nominees for seats on the CPB board, who were appointed by the president and confirmed by the Senate.

Liberals had problems with the board, but conservatives usually were its most vocal critics. Conservatives were especially upset during the 1980s by a shift in control over programming from the CPB to PBS, a change they said eroded accountability and made it less likely that programming would be fair and balanced.

During the 1980s, CPB funding levels dropped dramatically, making public broadcasting more reliant on other income sources. In 1980, 27 percent of funding for public broadcasting came from the federal government; 10 percent from corporations; and the rest from state and local governments, colleges and private sources. By 1992, federal funding had dropped to 17 percent, while corporate donations stood at 17 percent and the rest came from other sources. *(Previous authorization, Congress and the Nation Vol. VII, p. 407)*

1991 Action. The House Energy and Commerce Committee approved HR 2977 (H Rept 102-363) by voice vote on July 30, 1991, and reported it Nov. 23. The panel approved an amendment by Don Ritter, R-Pa., to expand reporting requirements for the network's board. The reports were to include data on board funding for programs developed by the Independent Television Service, created by Congress in 1988 to help small independent producers make films.

Ritter was upset because the board had denied local stations satellite access to "The Greenhouse Conspiracy," a documentary critical of global warming theories. He noted that the public network had aired other documentaries contending that global warming posed a serious environmental threat.

The House passed HR 2977 by voice vote under suspension of the rules on Nov. 25. Meanwhile, the Senate Commerce, Science and Transportation Committee reported its version of the bill (S 1504 — S Rept 102-221) on Nov. 19. Like the House bill, it included the provision calling for increased reporting by the CPB board.

1992 Action. By the time the Senate took up the bill in 1992, the attacks on public broadcasting had escalated. Some conservatives called for complete privatization of public broadcasting, particularly in light of new educational viewing choices offered by cable television. Presidential politics added fuel to the fire, as Patrick J. Buchanan, syndicated columnist and former member of the White House staff during the Nixon and Reagan administrations who was challenging Bush in the primaries, attacked the president for not fighting a liberal bias in the arts and media.

The Senate cleared the way for consideration of S 1504 on March 3 with a vote of 87-7 on a motion to invoke cloture. But Republican critics of the corporation blocked floor action for three months until a compromise was fashioned with the help of conservative Ted Stevens, a Republican on the Senate Commerce Subcommittee on Communications. Stevens represented Alaska, a state whose rural population depended heavily on public broadcasting.

The compromise measure (an amended version of HR 2977) passed the Senate June 3 by a vote of 84-11. During two days of deliberation before final passage, the Senate rejected 22-75 an amendment by Trent Lott, R-Miss., to freeze CPB funding at the fiscal 1992 level of $275 million a year. Lott offered the amendment on behalf of Sen. Jesse Helms, R-N.C., who was hospitalized.

Lott described public broadcasting as "an upper-middle-class entitlement program" that produced too many programs with a liberal bias. Sen. Robert Dole, R-Kan., in a lengthy attack on the corporation, described it as a "confusing, clumsy and inefficient bureaucracy with no power at the top and too much funding flowing to a privileged few."

Although Dole and Lott failed to cut the CPB's funding, they and other critics did win a number of concessions from the bill's sponsors. One was language requiring that future grants for documentaries be distributed over a wide geographic range to avoid concentration of funding in New York and California.

Sponsors agreed to two other amendments, approved by voice votes, to mollify the critics. One required the CPB board to gather public comment about the quality, balance and diversity of its programs. The other required the board's annual report to list in greater detail all program grant award amounts, names of recipients and producers, and descriptions of programs.

The Senate also accepted, 93-3, an amendment offered by Robert C. Byrd, D-W.Va., that extended until midnight a 6 a.m.-to-8 p.m. ban on "indecent" programs. Stations that went off the air at or before midnight had the ban extended only until 10 p.m.

The House accepted the Senate changes in HR 2977 by voice vote on Aug. 4, completing congressional action.

Major Provisions

As cleared, HR 2977:

- Authorized $310 million for the CPB in fiscal 1994; $375 million in fiscal 1995; and $425 million in fiscal 1996. The authorization, set two years in advance to maintain program continuity, funded program and administrative expenses for television stations that belonged to the private, non-profit PBS as well as National Public Radio (NPR) member stations.
- Authorized $42 million for each of the three years for capital investments in public television and radio facilities.
- Reduced the number of members on the CPB's board of directors from 10 to nine to avoid tie votes. Board members' terms were staggered so that three terms expired every three years.
- Required the CPB to keep a public file on every organization that received a grant from the corporation, including all programs that were produced with the grants. The board also was required to gather public comment on the quality, balance and diversity of its programs to help in determining the award of grants.
- Set stricter reporting requirements for the Independent Television Service, and directed the service to show that grants were spread out over a broad geographic area.
- Extended until midnight a 6 a.m.-to-8 p.m. ban on "indecent" programs. Stations that went off the air at or before midnight had the ban extended only until 10 p.m.

FCC Reauthorization

The House in 1991 endorsed a Bush administration proposal to levy user fees on holders of broadcast licenses, as part of a two-year reauthorization (HR 1674) of the Federal Communications Commission (FCC).

HR 1674, reported from House Energy and Commerce (H Rept 102-207) on Sept. 17 and passed by voice vote under suspension of the rules in the House on Sept. 24, authorized up to $297 million through fiscal 1993. The user fees were to be imposed on most FCC license holders — radio and television stations, telephone companies, cable television systems and satellite operators. Sponsors estimated that the fees would bring in $65 million a year.

The House bill imposed an annual fee of $2 million on telephone companies and $2,000 on television stations. Fees on other license holders such as cellular telephone companies depended on market size. Public safety entities, amateur radio operators, non-commercial broadcasters and government and non-profit entities were exempted.

The Bush administration had proposed steeper fees that critics said disregarded ability to pay. The National Association of Broadcasters opposed the whole idea of user fees, saying they would be unfair to the many stations already operating at a loss.

The Senate did not act on HR 1674 or on a companion measure (S 1132). *(Fiscal 1990-91 reauthorization, p. 430)*

Radio Spectrum Allocation

The House passed legislation (HR 531) in 1991 to transfer use of a large portion of government-held radio frequencies to the private sector to foster commercial communications technologies. The House passed a radio spectrum allocation bill in 1990. *(Story, p. 430)*

Sponsor Edward J. Markey, D-Mass., chairman of the House Energy and Commerce Subcommittee on Telecommunications and Finance, said the transfer of spectrum would "create much-needed breathing room in which new technologies can make it to market and flourish." The government reserved or had priority access to about 40 percent of the usable electromagnetic spectrum. The Defense Department and the Federal Aviation Administration held about 60 percent of those frequency assignments.

The Bush administration and some Senate Republicans objected to a provision of the legislation authorizing the frequencies to be given away through the traditional system of lotteries instead of by auctioning them off to the highest bidder. Except for routine filing fees, the airwaves always had been free to those who met application standards set by the Federal Communications Commission (FCC).

The increasingly commercial nature of the crowded radio spectrum, however, had inspired the Reagan and Bush administrations to push for the auctioning of FCC licenses. Critics of auctions worried that only the wealthy would have access to the radio spectrum, but advocates said the deepest pockets already had gained control of the airwaves by buying up radio licenses in the private marketplace.

The House Energy and Commerce Committee approved HR 531 by voice vote on May 21, 1991, and reported the measure (H Rept 102-113) on June 18. Despite a veto threat issued by the Bush administration July 8, the full House passed the bill by voice vote under suspension of the rules July 9.

The House-passed bill gave the commerce secretary two years to choose 200 megahertz of government-held radio spectrum — the equivalent of 30 television channels — to be transferred to commercial use during the following 15 years. The measure also required the Commerce Department and the FCC to report to Congress every two years on how best to manage the radio spectrum.

The Senate version of the bill (S 218 — S Rept 102-93) was reported June 28, 1991, by the Commerce, Science and Transportation Committee.

In 1992, members of the Senate Commerce Communications Subcommittee worked out a compromise on the auctions issue, but lawmakers ran out of time before action could be taken on it.

Home Digital Recording

Congress in 1992 cleared legislation (S 1623 — PL 102-563) to compensate the music industry for home taping with digital audio technology, paving the way for the introduction of high-quality recording tapes and equipment into the U.S. market.

Digital audio technology, which first became widely available in the United States in the fall of 1992, offered near-perfect sound quality. But the music industry feared a wave of illicit copying of original recorded works and pushed to keep the technology out of the United States until Congress acted to offset expected financial losses.

The bill applied to digital tape recording technology as well as to any future advances in recordable compact discs. It added a 3 percent royalty fee to the price of blank digital tapes and a 2 percent fee to the price of new digital recording equipment. The fees would go to musicians, recording companies and music publishers as compensation for financial losses from illegal copying.

Makers of digital audio equipment also were required to install an electronic device in all digital recording equipment sold in the United States to prevent consumers from making more than one copy of an original recording.

A limited number of blank digital audio tapes were marketed in the United States more than a decade before the 1992 legislation. But their use was blocked after music industry groups sued Sony Corp., arguing that the company's digital recorders and blank digital cassettes infringed on their copyright protections. The legislation grew out of a compromise reached in July 1991 among the digital audio tape industry, retailers and musicians. It allowed consumers to make home copies of a digital tape without fear of violating copyright laws so long as single copies were made for personal use.

The Senate Judiciary Committee approved a digital recording compensation bill (S 1623 — S Rept 102-294) on Nov. 21, 1991, and formally reported it on Nov. 27. The Senate passed the measure by voice vote on June 17, 1992.

Three House committees considered digital bills in 1992. Energy and Commerce approved HR 4567 (H Rept 102-780, Part I) on June 2 by voice vote and reported it on Aug. 4. The Judiciary Committee approved a similar bill (HR 3204 — H Rept 102-873, Part I) on Aug. 11 by voice vote and reported it on Sept. 17. Finally, the Ways and Means Committee approved HR 3204 (H Rept 102-873, Part II) by voice vote Sept. 16 and reported it Sept. 21.

The House passed HR 3204 by voice vote Sept. 22, then passed S 1623 with the language of HR 3204 by voice vote the same day. The Senate cleared S 1623 on Oct. 7. The president signed the bill Oct. 28.

Telemarketing Controls

The 102nd Congress cleared legislation to protect consumers from unsolicited telephone calls and messages from facsimile machines. As signed by President Bush on Dec. 20, 1991, the bill (S 1462 — PL 102-243) required the Federal Communications Commission (FCC) to prohibit unsolicited calls from automatic dialing devices. The measure also banned "junk faxes" — advertisements transmitted automatically by facsimile machines over telephone lines.

The House passed a bill (HR 2921) on July 30, 1990, that would have allowed people and businesses to have their telephone numbers put on a special list. Telemarketers would have faced fines if calls or transmissions were made to any number on the list. The Bush administration threatened to veto the bill on the grounds that existing regulations were adequate. The Senate passed a related but weaker measure (S 2494) on Oct. 23. *(1990 action, p. 432)*

The House Energy and Commerce Committee on Nov. 15, 1991, reported HR 1304 (H Rept 102-317). The measure, approved by the House Nov. 18 by voice vote under suspension of the rules, covered phone sales pitches made by computer-dialed recorded messages and live operators and through fax machines — but exempted telemarketers with whom callers had an established business relationship.

The Senate Commerce, Science and Transportation Committee on Oct. 8 reported S 1462 (S Rept 102-178), which went further than HR 1304 by imposing a total ban on automatic telephone calls to residences, emergency phone lines, cellular phones and faxes. The Senate passed S 1462 by voice vote Nov. 7.

Also on Nov. 7, the Senate passed by voice vote S 1410, a bill similar to HR 1304. S 1410, reported from Senate Commerce on Oct. 8 (S Rept 102-177), directed the FCC to halt the intrusion of unsolicited marketing calls. Businesses with whom consumers had an established relationship were exempted. The measure also prohibited computer-generated calls to emergency phone lines or pagers used by doctors or health care facilities.

After sponsors from both chambers informally drafted a compromise bill (S 1462, formerly HR 1304), the House passed the measure on Nov. 26 by voice vote under suspension of the rules, and the Senate cleared it for the president Nov. 27.

The final bill required the FCC to find ways to ensure the privacy of phone consumers and emergency phone lines. Businesses with a pre-existing relationship with a telephone subscriber were exempted from the prohibition on solicitations, as were non-profit organizations. Another provision required computer-generated calls to disconnect as soon as the receiver hung up.

In related action, the Senate Nov. 27, 1991, by voice vote passed S 1392, which would require the Federal Trade Commission to set up rules defining and prohibiting deceptive, fraudulent and abusive telemarketing practices. The House passed the bill by voice vote Sept. 29, 1992, after substituting the text of a companion measure (HR 3203 — H Rept 102-688). S 1392 died upon adjournment.

900-Number Regulation

The first federal regulation of the pay-per-call telephone industry was cleared by Congress in 1992. The industry offered information or products over long-distance lines, known as 900 numbers, and charged by the minute for the calls. The legislation (HR 6191 — PL 102-556) sought to protect consumers from unscrupulous 900-number phone services by requiring that callers be warned of the cost and terms of such calls.

The bill required a "preamble" to precede each 900-number call to inform the caller of the price and nature of the service provided. A caller could hang up early without incurring a charge. Services aimed at children under 12 were banned.

Background. The pay-per-call industry mushroomed after the 1984 breakup of the American Telephone & Telegraph Co. (AT&T), offering callers everything from stock quotations and technical help to horoscopes and sex "chat" sessions. But critics soon charged that the industry easily could exploit consumers, who were not always aware of the charges they were incurring by dialing 900 numbers.

In addition, billing for the 900 services was done by long-distance and local phone companies, leaving customers confused about how to challenge unfair charges. Lawmakers soon were inundated with reports of unsavory 900-number schemes, such as a contest that urged callers to redial to win prizes and a $29.95 charge for a call seeking a credit card application available without charge at the bank.

By the early 1990s, negative publicity had slowed the industry's rapid growth. In 1991, two of the four long-distance phone companies that contracted with 900-number providers dropped the service. Many in the industry concluded that federal regulation would help to weed out the dishonest among them and improve consumer confidence in pay-per-call services.

The Federal Communications Commission (FCC) got into the act in September 1991, issuing regulations that included the preamble requirement. The 1992 law strengthened the regulations by codifying them.

Legislative History. S 1579, passed by the Senate by voice vote on Oct. 29, 1991, had been reported Oct. 16 by the Senate Commerce, Science and Transportation Committee (S Rept 102-190). The measure gave the FCC authority to regulate the pay-per-call industry and crack down on unscrupulous services. In addition, the services had to include an introductory message that laid out the costs of the call, during which callers could hang up and not be charged.

The House Energy and Commerce Committee on Oct. 8, 1991, approved a similar bill (HR 3490), which it reported (H Rept 102-430) on Feb. 5, 1992. The House passed HR 3490 by a vote of 381-31 under suspension of the rules on Feb. 25, then passed an amended S 1579 by voice vote later the same day.

The Bush administration argued that the legislation was unnecessary because federal agencies already had taken many of the same steps through regulations. But no veto threat was issued.

The House, in the session that began Oct. 5, by voice vote passed a compromise measure (HR 6191), incorporating changes requested by the industry and the Senate. The changes included more explicit pre-emption of the patchwork of state regulatory requirements for 900 services and a provision excluding pay-per-call services involving data sent to facsimile machines from the bill's consumer protection requirements.

The Senate passed HR 6191 by voice vote on Oct. 7, and the president signed the measure Oct. 28.

Rural Communications

Congress cleared two bills in 1992 aimed at improving communications in rural areas.

Loans. HR 5237 (PL 102-428) amended the Rural Electrification Act (REA) of 1936 to make obtaining federally backed loans easier for small telephone and electric service cooperatives. The measure allowed rural cooperatives to repay federal telephone loans ahead of schedule.

The House Agriculture Committee approved HR 5237 by voice vote June 25 and reported it (H Rept 102-782,

Part I) Aug. 4. The House passed the measure Aug. 5, 359-60, under suspension of the rules.

As reported by the Agriculture panel and passed by the House, HR 5237 included a new grant program along with the loan changes. The three-year, $50 million grant program was to help states bring interactive telephone and computer technologies to rural health care facilities and schools. Grants were limited to $1.5 million each. Some House Republicans objected that the bill increased wasteful spending on REA programs.

The Senate passed HR 5237 by voice vote on Oct. 5, after adopting by voice vote an amendment by Frank R. Lautenberg, D-N.J., to strip the communications provisions from the bill. The House cleared the revised bill Oct. 6, and President Bush signed it Oct. 21.

Grants and Credit. HR 5954 (PL 102-551) was designed to improve rural telecommunications systems to enable rural health care providers to consult more easily with specialists at large urban hospitals. The bill authorized $30 million to help improve communications with rural health care facilities and $20 million to improve them with rural educational institutions.

HR 5954 also included grant provisions — stripped from HR 5237 — to help rural medical and educational institutions purchase advanced communications equipment to quickly transmit medical test results, lab slides and educational material to urban hospitals and schools. Although no set amount was authorized to implement the telecommunications provisions, the bill did set a ceiling of $1.5 million for each communications equipment grant.

The House Agriculture Committee reported HR 5954 (H Rept 102-943) on Sept. 29. The House passed the bill by voice vote under suspension of the rules the same day. The Senate passed an amended version by voice vote Oct. 5, and the House cleared the bill the next day. HR 5954 was signed into law Oct. 28.

Telephone Monopolies

The 102nd Congress wrestled with the question of federal controls on the business dealings of the seven regional Bell telephone companies created by the 1984 breakup of American Telephone & Telegraph Co. (AT&T). The Senate passed a bill in 1991 to give the so-called Baby Bells more freedom, while a measure approved by a House committee in 1992 sought to curb the companies' monopoly powers. Neither measure became law. *(1989-90 action, p. 432)*

Background. The seven regional Bell companies — Ameritech, Bell Atlantic, BellSouth, NYNEX, Pacific Telesis, Southwestern Bell and U.S. West — were spawned by a 1982 court decision ordering the breakup of AT&T. As AT&T ventured into the long-distance arena, the seven Baby Bells continued to provide low-cost, local telephone service across the nation.

The companies were permitted to provide cellular phone services and to engage in some other business activities. But a U.S. District Court barred them from manufacturing telecommunications equipment, competing in the long-distance phone market or offering information services — three areas in which it was thought they would have an unfair competitive advantage.

In addition, a 1984 law (PL 98-549) deregulating cable television barred the companies from offering cable television service. Legislation (S 12 — PL 102-385) to impose new regulations on the cable industry, enacted in 1992, did not alter the legal ban that prevented the Baby Bells from offering cable television services. *(1984 law, Congress and the Nation Vol. VI, p. 279; 1992 cable legislation, p. 451)*

1991 Senate Bill. The Senate signaled its willingness to ease some of the restrictions on the Bells in 1991 by approving legislation (S 173) to lift the ban on manufacturing of telecommunications equipment.

Commerce Chairman Ernest F. Hollings, D-S.C., said the domestic telecommunications industry needed a boost to compete effectively with European and Japanese companies. But AT&T and consumer groups argued that lifting the manufacturing ban would lead to higher phone bills and anti-competitive behavior by the Bell companies.

The Senate Commerce, Science and Transportation Committee on March 19 approved S 173 (S Rept 102-41) by a vote of 18-1 and formally reported the measure April 19. Hollings had successfully deflected a bid by the Judiciary Committee to consider the bill as well.

The measure permitted the Bell companies to design and manufacture telecommunications equipment. It included provisions intended to guard against ratepayer abuses and a labor-backed provision requiring that all manufacturing take place in the United States using some U.S.-made parts.

The Senate passed S 173 by a vote of 71-24 on June 5. An attempt by Phil Gramm, R-Texas, to remove the labor provision failed June 5 when a tabling motion was agreed to, 64-32. The Bush administration, which supported the other provisions of S 173, had threatened a veto because of the labor provision.

Despite grumblings that the consumer protections in the bill were too weak, no amendments were offered to strengthen them. The Senate adopted by voice vote an amendment by Larry Pressler, R-S.D., to require the Bell companies to make the latest software and telecommunications equipment available to other local exchange carriers without discrimination, and to take other actions to protect rural telephone companies.

Court Decisions. The situation of the Bell companies shifted on July 25, 1991, when U.S. District Judge Harold H. Greene ruled that the regional Bell companies could provide information services ranging from home banking and electronic Yellow Pages to video programming. This energized the newspaper and electronic information industries, who feared being trounced by the Bells' potential market power. The U.S. Court of Appeals for the District of Columbia on Oct. 7 cleared the way for phone monopolies to immediately offer information services. But Greene delayed that decision and ordered that it not take effect until appeals were exhausted.

The Supreme Court on Oct. 30 unanimously denied a petition by newspaper publishers to block the seven companies from providing news and information services. The Bells thus were free to own and transmit over their phone lines a wide range of information services such as data base texts and classified ads.

1992 House Bill. In the House, consideration of the Bell issue was complicated by a jurisdictional dispute between two committees with powerful leaders: the Energy and Commerce Committee chaired by John D. Dingell, D-Mich., and the Judiciary Committee chaired by Jack Brooks, D-Texas.

The Judiciary panel was first out of the gate, reporting a bill that amended antitrust laws to impose legal restrictions on the Bells' expansion plans. The Energy and Commerce panel's draft bill, never reported, approached the issue from a regulatory perspective, giving authority to control the Bells' expansion to the Federal Communications Commission (FCC).

The Judiciary Committee approved its bill (HR 5096 — H Rept 102-850) by a vote of 24-9 on July 1, 1992, and reported the measure Aug. 12. The vote was a qualified victory for primary sponsor Brooks, and for those who feared the Bells could use their monopoly power against consumers and competitors. Chief among the bill's supporters were newspaper publishers. Other supporters included consumer groups, business telephone users, long-distance telephone companies, equipment makers and information service providers.

The committee weakened the bill and pleased the Bells when it voted to remove a key provision that would have forced the seven companies to wait three to seven years before seeking to enter the equipment manufacturing and information services markets. As approved by the committee, the bill codified the various court-imposed restrictions on the seven companies, reversed the Court decision allowing the companies to enter the information services market and established a set of legal hurdles the companies would have to overcome before entering a new market.

The Brooks bill did not reach the House floor in 1992, and Congress put off a decision on how to deal with the expansion of the Bell companies.

Caller Identification

Legislation (HR 1305, S 652) to allow telephone users to block technological devices that reveal a caller's telephone number stalled in the 102nd Congress.

Supporters of the legislation argued that the use of caller identification (ID) devices should be restricted to protect the privacy of callers. Opponents contended that regulation of the devices should be left up to the states. More than 20 states allowed the devices in 1992, and four states did not allow them to be blocked.

HR 1305 (H Rept 102-324), approved by the House Energy and Commerce Committee on July 30, 1991, and reported Nov. 18, allowed telephone users to block disclosure of their numbers on a per-call basis. An amendment, offered by Joe L. Barton, R-Texas, and adopted by voice vote, allowed consumers who used Caller ID to buy a device that would "block the blocker." Callers who had blocked their numbers from appearing on Caller ID devices would have their calls automatically rejected.

S 652 (S Rept 102-247), approved by the Senate Judiciary Committee 10-1 on Oct. 31, 1991, and reported Nov. 26, required telephone companies to let customers block the display of their numbers on a per-call basis, free of charge. The measure also allowed receivers of obscene phone calls to refer the caller's number to the police immediately by touching two buttons.

On the Senate floor, S 652 became bogged down May 6, 1992, when Sen. Phil Gramm, R-Texas, attempted to tack on a Republican anti-crime bill amid claims that federal curbs on Caller ID devices were unnecessary. In response, Democrats shelved the telephone legislation and brought up their own anti-crime measure. The full House did not take up the caller ID bill.

Tourism Promotion

Legislation (S 680) cleared in 1992 to promote tourism within the United States.

S 680 reauthorized the Commerce Department's U.S. Travel and Tourism Administration and mandated some organizational changes prompted by criticism of the agency. It also limited the amount of money to be spent on overhead and created a fund to promote tourism in rural areas.

The office had not been authorized for 12 years. House Energy and Commerce Committee Chairman John D. Dingell, D-Mich., had stalled authorization bills in recent past years because of concerns about how the agency was run.

The Senate Commerce, Science and Transportation Committee approved S 680 by voice vote July 30, 1991, and reported the measure (S Rept 102-150) on Sept. 13. The full Senate passed it Oct. 24 by voice vote.

The House Energy and Commerce Committee approved a companion version (HR 3645 — H Rept 102-355) Nov. 7 by voice vote and reported it Nov. 22. The House Nov. 23 passed S 680 by voice vote after stripping its contents and replacing them with the text of HR 3645. Congressional action on S 680 was completed on Sept. 15, 1992. President Bush signed the bill (PL 102-372) on Sept. 30.

Consumer Product Safety

Legislation (HR 4706) to reauthorize the Consumer Product Safety Commission (CPSC) and strengthen certain product safety regulations passed the House in 1992 but was not taken up by the Senate. Even without an authorization bill, Congress appropriated $48.4 million for the agency in fiscal 1993 (HR 5679 — PL 102-389), an increase of more than $8 million from the previous fiscal year.

The CPSC, created by Congress in 1972 (PL 92-573) to protect consumers from unsafe products, quickly became a battleground between consumer advocates who wanted tougher product safety regulations and conservatives who wanted less regulation of business. Consumer advocates won a long-sought victory in 1990, when Congress passed a two-year reauthorization bill for the agency that increased its regulatory powers. *(1972 law, Congress and the Nation Vol. III, p. 685; 1990 bill, p. 432)*

HR 4706, passed by the House by voice vote on Sept. 10, authorized $42.1 million for fiscal 1993 and $43.2 million for fiscal 1994. Additional provisions required manufacturers to label toys with small parts as potential choking hazards and established safety standards for bicycle helmets.

The House Energy and Commerce Committee reported HR 4706 (H Rept 102-649) on July 2.

Although it did not take up HR 4706, the Senate in 1992 by voice vote passed two separate measures to promote the use of bicycle helmets by children. S 3096, reported Sept. 16 by the Senate Commerce, Science and Transportation Committee (S Rept 102-406), was passed Sept. 25; S 2952 passed Oct. 8. The House did not act on either bill.

Product Liability

Congressional efforts to set national standards for personal injury lawsuits that resulted from faulty products, stymied for more than a decade, were blocked once again in

1992. But the Senate came closer than it had in 12 years to passing a product liability bill (S 640) when sponsors fell just two votes short of the 60 needed to invoke cloture.

Background. The push to change the nation's product liability laws, sometimes called tort reform, began in the early 1980s. Proponents argued that excessively large damage awards were driving up liability rates and making it impossible for groups to buy insurance.

In the 1990s, supporters — primarily business interests — emphasized competitiveness. They argued that product litigation was arbitrary, time-consuming and expensive and thus deterred productivity and innovation. In addition, they contended that the patchwork of state product liability laws encouraged plaintiffs to "forum shop" for the most favorable state laws, adding still greater uncertainty to the outcome.

On the other side, working successfully to block the legislation, were trial lawyers and consumer groups. They argued that limits on jury awards unfairly punished the victims of faulty merchandise, and they blamed insurance companies for dramatic increases in manufacturers' liability costs.

A business-backed product liability bill was approved by the House Energy and Commerce Committee in 1988, but it fell by the wayside as had other such bills before it. *(Congress and the Nation Vol. VII, p. 398)*

Legislative Action. The Senate Commerce, Science and Transportation Committee approved S 640 (S Rept 102-215) by a vote of 13-7 on Oct. 3, 1991. The bill was formally reported Nov. 14. A House version of the bill (HR 3030) was not acted on during the 102nd Congress.

The Senate bill, sponsored by Bob Kasten, R-Wis., established uniform national standards for lawsuits based on faulty products, provided incentives to settle lawsuits early and set up an alternative dispute resolution system. The bill also established tougher standards for the awarding of punitive damages — the payments intended to compensate for "pain and suffering" as opposed to compensation based on economic losses. But in an effort to gain support among Democrats, sponsors dropped a provision that put caps on the amounts that could be awarded for punitive damages.

Supporters of S 640 tried a number of maneuvers in 1992 to bring the legislation to a final vote despite the opposition of some Senate Democratic leaders, including Majority Leader George J. Mitchell, D-Maine. To avoid having the bill languish in the Judiciary Committee, a panel dominated by lawyers, Kasten successfully attached S 640 as an amendment to a separate bill (S 250) on voter registration. But the product liability amendment was dropped from S 250 on May 14 when the Senate voted 53-45 to table and thus kill it. *('Motor voter,' p. 893)*

Finally, Mitchell agreed to allow a separate Senate vote on S 640. On Sept. 10, the Senate failed to invoke cloture and thus prevent a filibuster on the bill. The vote was 58-38 in favor of cutting off debate, two votes short of the three-fifths (60) needed. At that point, with little time remaining in the session, sponsors abandoned their effort to take S 640 to the Senate floor.

Insurance Antitrust Exemption

A long-running effort to repeal some of the insurance industry's exemptions to antitrust law continued in the 102nd Congress but did not produce results.

The House Judiciary Committee Nov. 19, 1991, approved HR 9, ending many longstanding insurance industry exemptions from antitrust laws under the 1945 McCarran-Ferguson Act (PL 79-15). Committee Chairman Jack Brooks, D-Texas, had argued for years that the industry had abused its privilege to fix prices and thwart competition. The panel's 19-14 vote was almost entirely partisan, with Democrats favoring the bill and Republicans opposing it. The only Democrat to vote against the bill was Peter Hoagland, whose Nebraska district included Omaha, a major industry center. *(1945 law, Congress and the Nation Vol. I, p. 454)*

HR 9 did not repeal McCarran-Ferguson outright and specifically retained antitrust immunity for some practices. But it sought to end the antitrust exemption for activities that constituted price fixing, monopolization, dividing up insurance markets geographically or forcing consumers to buy a package of insurance policies to receive one type of coverage.

The committee by voice vote accepted a Dan Glickman, D-Kan., amendment that allowed small and mid-size companies to continue sharing statistical data to project the volume of claims — a practice called trending. Companies would qualify for the continued exemption provided they did not have net assets of more than $10 million, or assets of $100 million and did not hold more than 2.5 percent of a state's market share.

Consumer lobbyists complained that the amendment would effectively gut the bill. But Brooks successfully added language specifying that the exemption would not apply if the companies sharing information collectively controlled 20 percent or more of the market.

HR 9 was formally reported (H Rept 102-1036) on Oct. 6, 1992.

A companion bill was introduced in the Senate (S 430), but it was not considered.

Neither the full House nor the Senate acted on HR 9, and it died at the end of the 102nd Congress. A similar measure died upon adjournment of the 101st Congress. *(Story, p. 435)*

Small Business Loans and Capital

In an effort to create jobs and combat the recession, Congress in 1992 cleared legislation (HR 4111 — PL 102-366) to increase funding for loans to small businesses and improve a program aimed at helping small businesses to attract venture capital.

The House Small Business Committee approved the loan part of the legislation March 11 and formally reported HR 4111 (H Rept 102-492) April 9. The House passed the bill May 14 by a vote of 399-2.

The bill increased the authorized funding level of the guaranteed loan offered by the Small Business Administration (SBA) for so-called 7(a) business loans and authorized $5 billion in fiscal 1992, $6 billion in fiscal 1993 and $7 billion in fiscal 1994. Small Business Committee Chairman John J. LaFalce, D-N.Y., said the legislation would allow credit-worthy companies to borrow money, create jobs and get the recession-damaged economy moving.

The House Small Business Committee approved HR 5191, which substantially revised the government program aimed at providing venture capital to small businesses, June 24 on a 39-0 vote and formally reported the measure

(H Rept 102-619) the next day. The House passed HR 5191 on a 356-2 vote July 31.

The small business investment company program was launched in 1958 to help small firms expand and acquire venture capital for start-up costs or research expenses. The program, which helped launch such firms as Apple Computer, Federal Express and Nike, had been hurt by mismanagement and recession. HR 5191 represented an attempt to reverse the downward trend by allowing small business investment companies to delay interest payments on loans owed to the SBA.

The Senate Small Business Committee approved an amended version of HR 5191 on Aug. 6 by a vote of 17-0. The full Senate passed the bill on Aug. 10 by voice vote.

The Senate had passed an amended HR 4111 by voice vote Aug. 6. The House subsequently added the language of HR 5191 to HR 4111. The Senate cleared HR 4111 on Aug. 12, and the president signed it Sept. 4.

High-Tech Small Business

Legislation (S 2941) cleared by Congress in 1992 required federal agencies to earmark a larger portion of their research and development budgets for small, high-technology businesses.

The House Small Business Committee approved an early House version of the bill (HR 4400) May 20 on a 39-0 vote, which was reported (H Rept 102-554, Part I) June 9. The House Science, Space and Technology Committee approved an amended version July 1 on a 7-4 vote and reported it (H Rept 102-554, Part II) July 2. The House Armed Services Committee, which also shared jurisdiction, reported the bill (H Rept 102-554, Part III) July 7. The House passed HR 4400 on Aug. 11 by voice vote under suspension of the rules.

HR 4400 boosted the amount of money 11 major federal agencies spent on research performed by small businesses. It also created a program to ease the way for small businesses to commercialize basic research developed in federal laboratories and universities. An agency with a total research and development budget over $1 billion a year would reserve 0.25 percent of it by 1996 to fund cooperative research projects between small businesses and federal laboratories, universities or non-profit research institutions.

As per existing law, agencies with outside research and development budgets exceeding $100 million were required under the Small Business Innovative Research Program to set aside at least 1.25 percent of their budgets for research projects performed by small businesses. The House-passed HR 4400 called for gradually increasing that requirement, beginning in fiscal 1994, to 2.5 percent by fiscal 1998. In fiscal 1996, when the level was to be set at 2 percent, the bill allowed any agency to block further increases if it determined that the quality of research had declined and that continuing it threatened to harm research activities.

The Senate did not act on HR 4400 but pursued its own version of the legislation (S 2941), which incorporated the House language with minor changes. The Senate passed S 2941 by voice vote Oct. 3. The House passed the bill by voice vote under suspension of the rules Oct. 6, completing congressional action. President Bush signed the measure (PL 102-564) Oct. 28.

Women in Business

Congress in 1991 cleared legislation (HR 2629) aimed at helping women to start and keep their own businesses. President Bush signed the measure (PL 102-191) on Dec. 5. *(Related action, women's employment, p. 732)*

HR 2629 reauthorized two Small Business Administration (SBA) programs for women: a small-loan program and a demonstration program that provided management training and technical assistance to businesses owned by women. The measure authorized $4 million for the programs in fiscal 1992 and $5 million for each of the following three years.

As initially passed by the House on Oct. 8 by voice vote under suspension of the rules, HR 2629 expanded the National Women's Business Council from nine to 11 members and stipulated that the additional seats be filled by an African-American and a Hispanic woman. The Bush administration objected to the requirement, and the House agreed to drop it from the bill.

House and Senate negotiators agreed on a compromise version of the bill, which was passed by the Senate on Nov. 20 and cleared by the House the next day. The House Small Business Committee had reported HR 2629 (H Rept 102-178) on July 31.

7

Energy and Environment

Introduction 467

1989-90 Chronology 473

1991-92 Chronology 500

Energy and Environment

Congress shifted from an adversarial stalemate with the White House during the Reagan administration to substantial achievement in energy and environmental legislation in 1989-92. But the major legislation cleared on President Bush's watch was limited by the politics of practical compromise.

Two of Bush's major legislative initiatives — a clean air bill and a national energy plan — were enacted with many of their original contours still recognizable. This was no small achievement in an era when "gridlock" had become a catch-word to describe relations between the White House and Congress.

Congress and the administration often seemed driven to action by catastrophic events and the media attention they drew. Typical in some ways of the four-year period was the oil-spill prevention, response and liability bill, which had been stuck on legislative shoals for some 15 years. Only the 1989 *Exxon Valdez* oil spill in Alaska's Prince William Sound prodded the various deadlocked interests into compromise and action.

But on other fronts, deadlock and confrontation continued in Congress. Apart from a few truly major legislative accomplishments, the Bush era and the 101st and 102nd Congresses were marked by a new focus on political symbolism and media impact — sometimes to the exclusion of practical legislative substance.

It was the era of the northern spotted owl. Environmental groups made this endangered species, whose habitat centered on old-growth forests in the Pacific Northwest, the symbolic center of a wide-ranging debate over U.S. forest policy. Congress, over decades, had erected structures for deciding the complex economic and ecological questions of timberland management. When the owl was declared a threatened species in 1990, however, environmentalists found a new opportunity to reduce logging — by using the Endangered Species Act of 1973 instead of forest management laws. But the 101st and 102nd Congresses stayed largely on the sidelines as environmentalists and loggers took their fight to the Forest Service planning process, the courts and the media.

It was the era of Earth Day 90 and the Rio Summit. In April 1990, tens of thousands of young demonstrators gathered on the steps of the Capitol's West Front, celebrating the 20th anniversary of Earth Day, which had launched a decade of revolutionary environmental legislation. For many, environmental protection was no longer a political controversy but a moral "given." More movie and rock stars spoke than members of Congress.

Earth Day 90 moved the dialogue over energy and environment beyond the hallways of Congress in more than just a physical sense. It also punctuated the beginning of the "green consumer" and "green marketing" movements. The focus was shifting from controls on corporate and industrial pollution. This new generation was determined to bring about a cleaner planet by changing patterns of consumption. By making environmental and energy decisions a matter of personal choice, they believed policy decisions would be taken out of the hands of government and corporations altogether. Environmentalism was evolving into a "lifestyle." Corporations responded to this new opportunity to make money. Soon the supermarket shelves were filled with cans of tuna labeled "dolphin-safe."

The Rio Summit of June 1992 was a reminder that much of the battle over environment and energy policy had moved beyond U.S. borders. "Globalism" had became a main thrust of the environmental movement, even within the United States. After three decades of steady progress, the U.S. environmental movement was finding its most challenging frontiers elsewhere — from the dwindling rain forests of the Amazon River basin and East Asia, the shanty-towns of South America and the soot-spewing factories of the former Soviet Union, to China's rapidly growing coal-power industry. Congress sparred with Bush over whether he would attend the summit and what his stand would be on issues such as global warming and biodiversity.

The looming of potential global catastrophes such as greenhouse warming of the atmosphere had been evoked in the late 1980s to spur congressional action on air pollution and energy conservation. Scientists were becoming convinced that increasing concentrations of carbon dioxide and other gases in the atmosphere, caused by human activities such as burning coal, would eventually cause warmer

References

Discussion of energy and environmental policy for the years 1945-64 may be found in *Congress and the Nation Vol. I*, pp. 771-1095; for the years 1965-68, *Congress and the Nation Vol. II*, pp. 463-528; for the years 1969-72, *Congress and the Nation Vol. III*, pp. 745-849; for the years 1973-76, *Congress and the Nation Vol. IV*, pp. 201-320; for the years 1977-80, *Congress and the Nation Vol. V*, pp. 451-530, 533-597; for the years 1981-84, *Congress and the Nation Vol. VI*, pp. 333-400, 403-482; for the years 1985-88, *Congress and the Nation Vol. VII*, pp. 417-495.

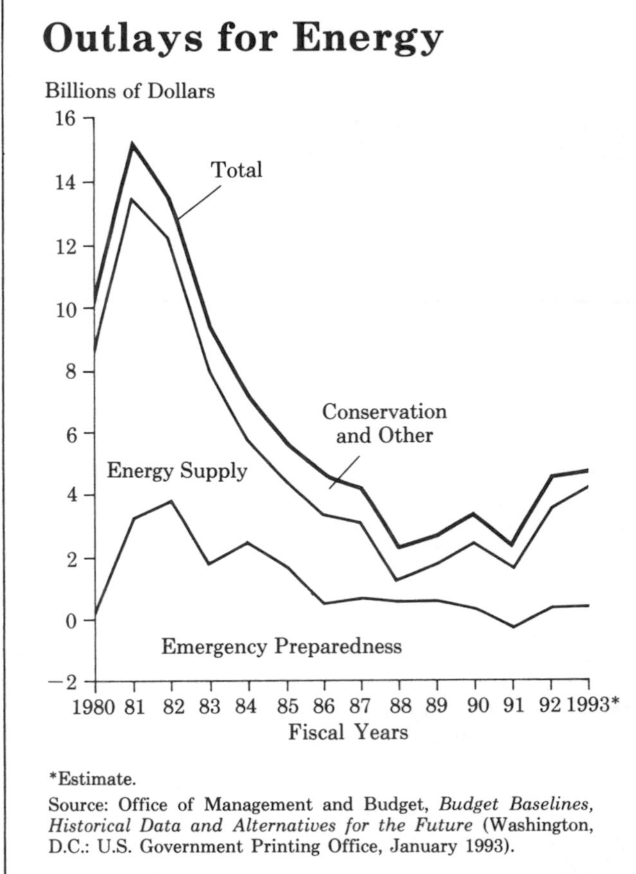

*Estimate.

Source: Office of Management and Budget, *Budget Baselines, Historical Data and Alternatives for the Future* (Washington, D.C.: U.S. Government Printing Office, January 1993).

climate worldwide — a thesis supported by the Intergovernmental Panel on Climate Change in 1990. Neither the clean air bill nor the energy bill addressed global warming in any large-scale or decisive way. But the 101st and 102nd Congresses did make numerous small moves toward conserving energy and cutting greenhouse emissions.

Clean Air Bill

The Clean Air Act amendments enacted in 1990 were an epoch-marking legislative accomplishment.

Congress and the White House actively took control of air pollution control policy — after more than a decade of leaving it to the states, the Environmental Protection Agency and the courts, through deadlock and default. The nation had made huge advances in controlling air pollution over the two decades since the landmark 1970 Clean Air Act. While enjoying persistent economic growth, residents of many cities found their air becoming gradually more breathable. The 1990 legislative upgrade not only updated the law, but also tightened its grip on air pollution problems and extended its reach to new ones.

The clean air bill was a significant accomplishment because the deadlock that had so long prevented legislation was an especially difficult one. The issue of acid rain, much of which was produced by Midwestern electric power plants burning high-sulfur Eastern and Midwestern coal, was an example. The interests of electric utilities in the Midwest were at odds with those of downwind residents of the Northeast and New England whose forests and lakes were sick or dying. The interests of high-sulfur coal miners in West Virginia and Ohio clashed with those of low-sulfur coal miners in Montana and Wyoming.

Other issues in the clean air debate pitted automakers against residents of high-smog cities and chemical refineries against residents of surrounding communities. Air pollution controls affected many kinds of U.S. businesses — from the very smallest, such as gas stations and dry cleaners, to the very largest, such as steelmakers.

Congress had asserted a role for the federal government in air pollution control as early as the mid-1950s merely supplementing the role of the states. It began setting nationwide standards for auto emissions in the mid-1960s. There had been at least four earlier versions of the Clean Air Act and its amendments, but the landmark Clean Air Act Amendments of 1970 first put "teeth" in federal air pollution controls with a complete system of health-based standards, deadlines and sanctions. And the 1970 law left a very strong role for the states and local agencies as front-line regulators.

Congress wrote the original Clean Air Act with the intent of renewing it on a regular five-year cycle. The regulatory requirements of the law did not expire at the end of five years, but by authorizing only five years' worth of funding, lawmakers meant to ensure they would regularly update the law. (In practice, this was only a technicality, which did not stop Congress from continuing to fund the air program on a year-to-year basis.) Congress met the five-year schedule once, when it enacted the Clean Air Act Amendments of 1977. While these amendments tightened many standards, they also extended many of the deadlines in the 1970 law that had gone unmet.

A more important constraint driving lawmakers to act were the sanctions that the 1977 law imposed in areas that had not attained air quality standards by 1982. In these areas, construction of major new pollution sources, such as smokestack factories or power plants, was banned.

House and Senate committees began work on the next reauthorization in 1981, well ahead of schedule. But the Clean Air Act raised so many divisive issues that deadlocks occurred year after year. As the 1980s drew near an end, the lack of fresh legislation was causing real problems in managing the complex program, as legally mandated timetables bore less and less resemblance to reality.

George Bush, who won election promising to be "the environmental president," departed dramatically from Reagan's no-compromise approach. The clean air bill Bush proposed in June 1989 offered something for almost everyone and was hailed even by environmentalists. "We've seen enough of this stalemate," he said as he announced the bill. He called on Congress to "join me in enacting into law a new clean-air act this year."

Acid rain legislation had always been an urgent priority for Sen. George J. Mitchell, D-Maine, as a New Englander; newly installed as Senate majority leader in 1989, he added his weight as an agenda-setter, pressuring the Senate to come to final action on clean air by the end of the 101st Congress.

Chances for a workable compromise took another giant step forward in early October 1989, when two old adversaries on the House Energy and Commerce Committee announced an agreement on auto emissions. Committee Chairman John D. Dingell, D-Mich., from an auto-making district, had for years sparred with Henry A. Waxman, D-Calif., whose Hollywood district was one of the smoggiest. Waxman, who chaired the Energy Subcommittee on

Health and the Environment, negotiated a pact with Dingell behind closed doors, and the rest of the committee fell in place.

Much of the shaping of the final bill was done in such backroom sessions. The Senate bill was pulled from the floor in early February 1990 for a month of such talks, which led to passage. Likewise, the House-Senate conference in the summer and fall of 1990 took place largely in private.

In the end, the 1990 amendments dramatically expanded the boundaries of the Clean Air Act. It established the nation's first program for controlling acid rain — a problem that went beyond human health and comfort to the health of lakes and forests. It set up a tough new program to control emissions of toxic air pollutants, scrapping the non-functioning and unworkable program in the 1977 law. While it made no direct reduction in the carbon dioxide emissions of concern for global warming, it did establish them as a legitimate issue. It brought alternative vehicle fuels and fuel efficiency into the clean air equation. Other new pollutants of concern, such as chlorofluorocarbons (CFCs) and radionuclides, also were brought under the act for the first time.

Energy Bill

The Energy Policy Act of 1992 was the nation's first comprehensive effort to get a grip on its energy problems since the major energy legislation of 1978.

While lobbyists from many competing energy, environmental and consumer groups largely agreed that the bill was a series of concrete steps in the right direction, few believed it would solve the nation's energy problems.

A Wide-Ranging Bill. The bill was a grab-bag, embodying the something-for-everyone approach that had traditionally given omnibus legislation the best chances of enactment by Congress.

It funded global warming research, promoted use of alternative vehicle fuels such as methanol and natural gas, encouraged development of electric vehicles, funded development of renewable energy technologies such as geothermal and photovoltaic power, changed hydroelectric licensing requirements and mandated energy efficiency in federal buildings.

It also made licensing of nuclear power plants for commercial electric generation much easier and subsidized development of more advanced commercial reactors that might be safer than current ones.

The bill privatized the government's multibillion-dollar uranium enrichment plants, allocated costs of cleaning them up and authorized aid to prop up the ailing U.S. uranium mining industry. It eased barriers to import Canadian natural gas and expanded the U.S. Strategic Petroleum Reserve to 1 billion barrels. It authorized a series of tax breaks to encourage energy conservation and use of alternative and renewable energy sources. It expedited preparations for an underground dump site at Yucca Mountain in Nevada to hold commercial and military nuclear waste — over strenuous objections from Nevadans.

The bill also eased restrictions in the 1935 Public Utility Holding Company Act (PUHCA), in an effort to encourage independent power producers to enter the wholesale electric power market. It authorized funds for research on energy independence, petroleum production and a range of conservation, alternative and renewable energy problems. It authorized major funding for research on ways to burn coal more cleanly and created a program to ensure the health benefits of some 120,000 retired union coal miners.

Background. Since the "energy crisis" of the 1970s, efforts to solve the nation's energy problems had repeatedly run aground on profound disagreements among interest groups as to what those problems were.

Environmental Spending

This table lists budget authority and outlays for federal natural resources and environmental programs for fiscal 1989-93 *(in millions)*:

	Budget Authority	Outlays
Water Resources		
1989	$4,312	$4,271
1990	4,332	4,401
1991	4,370	4,366
1992	4,768	4,559
1993 (estimate)	4,703	5,021
Conservation and Land Management		
1989	3,706	3,324
1990	3,783	3,553
1991	3,912	4,047
1992	4,665	4,587
1993 (estimate)	4,500	4,700
Recreational Resources		
1989	1,895	1,817
1990	2,395	1,876
1991	2,482	2,137
1992	2,697	2,378
1993 (estimate)	2,480	2,569
Pollution Control And Abatement		
1989	5,068	4,878
1990	5,545	5,156
1991	6,150	5,853
1992	6,591	6,061
1993 (estimate)	6,835	6,625
Other Natural Resources		
1989	2,005	1,890
1990	2,077	2,080
1991	2,309	2,148
1992	2,580	2,432
1993 (estimate)	2,547	2,548
Totals, Fiscal 1989-93		
1989	$16,987	$16,182
1990	18,132	17,067
1991	19,224	18,552
1992	21,300	20,017
1993 (estimate)	21,064	21,462

Source: Fiscal 1994 budget.

Energy and Environment

After the Arab oil embargo and price shocks of the 1970s, the perceived problem was the growing dependence on unreliable Organization of Petroleum Exporting Countries (OPEC) oil, leaving the nation vulnerable to shortages, price gouging and the sort of geopolitical blackmail that threatened U.S. economic and military security.

Many believed the problem was that oil and gas were drying up or running out, even in the short term. When the immediate panic over foreign embargo and short supplies was relieved by the early 1980s, fewer lawmakers took the view that the problem was not dependence on foreign oil, but dependence on oil itself, undeniably a finite resource in the longer term.

The solutions urged by the U.S. oil, gas and coal industries all focused on raising domestic production — usually through federal tax breaks, subsidies and deregulation. Environmental groups tended to oppose production-raising measures (such as drilling the Arctic National Wildlife Refuge, or ANWR), because they feared damage to natural resources often unrelated to energy. Instead, environmentalists emphasized conservation and efficiency, and a shift to renewable and more environmentally benign sources of energy. They argued that if America's security really rested on domestic oil supplies, then it would be hurt, not helped, in the long term by a strategy of "Drain America First."

Members of Congress, driven inexorably by re-election pressures, could not always afford the luxury of long-term thinking. During the 102nd Congress, only a minority could be heard questioning short-term responses to long-term problems and calling for sustainable national energy policies.

During the 1980s, the House and Senate Energy committees struggled unsuccessfully or inconclusively to enact laws on such major issues as natural gas deregulation, uranium industry restructuring or ANWR drilling. The idea for a National Energy Plan — that is, requiring the president to draw up a big-picture strategy and put his name on it — grew out of such frustrations in the House and Senate committees. All sides were looking for a mechanism to force the unresolved issues.

President Bush and his energy secretary, James D. Watkins, took up the gauntlet Congress had thrown down and delivered a National Energy Strategy on Feb. 20, 1991, only 4 days before the ground invasion of Iraq. The law that finally emerged contained many items in Bush's proposal. Congress rejected other parts of the Bush plan — such as drilling ANWR and new offshore tracts. Congress also added many more energy conservation provisions than Bush had proposed.

The Senate Energy Committee had made several previous efforts to require a national plan. During the 101st Congress, the committee had reported a bill to establish a "least-cost national energy plan" to reduce the threat of global warming. Sponsored by Tim Wirth, D-Colo., the bill set a goal of reducing carbon dioxide emissions by 20 percent, but that goal was dropped before Senate passage, and the House substituted a research-only bill.

Global warming had only been the most recent of looming catastrophes invoked as a rationale for setting a comprehensive energy policy. But even after the string of record-high annual global temperatures posted in the 1980s, it was not enough to force the 101st Congress, much less the administration, to concrete actions such as the imposition of an energy tax.

Iraq's invasion of Kuwait, and the ensuing Persian Gulf War, seemed to offer a newly compelling reason for an energy bill. The air bombing of Iraq in January 1991 provided a dramatic opening drum-roll for the 102nd Congress. Although the war's effect on prices and supply was not as dramatic as many in Congress had feared, it raised awareness of the insecurity of Middle Eastern oil reserves that the nation so heavily relied on. And it put an energy bill on the agenda.

The Gulf War bolstered the arguments of both factions: the one calling for more domestic oil production and the one calling for more conservation and fuel-shifting. The omnibus structure of the bill ultimately allowed each side to get some of what it wanted. If energy security, or the reduction of reliance on Mideast oil imports, was the goal, then the 1992 energy bill took tangible, but quite modest, steps in that direction.

Nonetheless, in forging a bill that could be enacted, both sides had to abandon some of their more ambitious agenda items. As reported by Senate Energy, the bill contained a title opening the Arctic refuge, which oil companies hoped would prove the nation's single largest remaining reservoir, to drilling. But a strong filibuster threat from environmentalists threatened the bill, and Energy Chairman J. Bennett Johnston, D-La., scrapped the ANWR drilling language as the next session started.

But the trade-off was that the conservationists dropped their bid to mandate higher fuel-efficiency standards for automobiles. Cars and trucks consumed a major share of the nation's imported oil, but raising the overall average gas mileage of each carmaker's entire fleet was an idea that met fierce opposition in Detroit — represented by House Energy Chairman Dingell. The proposal lived on in a separate bill, but it did not achieve passage.

Nuclear Benefits. All told, the nuclear industry got many things it wanted in the 1992 energy bill, often costing appreciable amounts of federal money. The industry had sought one-step licensing of commercial nuclear power plants for years. Environmentalists wanted to keep the two-step process, which gave them more opportunities to object to licenses. But because no nuclear power plants had been ordered for more than a decade, they acquiesced. Other parts of the nuclear industry had wanted privatization of the Energy Department's vast uranium enrichment enterprise and aid for the nation's ailing uranium mining industry — and had likewise tried unsuccessfully to obtain them for years. The privatization involved recovery of the government's past costs from private industry; however, strong disagreement existed over how much those costs were. Taxpayer groups claimed privatization would cost the Treasury billions of dollars, while the industry argued that it would bring in billions otherwise forgone.

The energy bill did extract from electric utilities amounts up to $150 million a year for 15 years to help pay for its share of cleaning up the aging uranium processing plants. But it also authorized $310 million in federal funds to clean up private uranium and thorium mill sites.

Much of the bill's subsidy for the nuclear industry came in the area of research and development. It authorized $364 million (out of funds from the privatized enrichment corporation) for development of an advanced enrichment technology known as Atomic Vapor Laser Isotope Separation (AVLIS); $720 million for fusion reactor research in fiscal 1993 and 1994; and $70 million for the Fast Flux test reactor in Hanford, Wash. Most importantly, it authorized federal support for development of a new generation of light-water reactors to be used by the commercial electric power industry. The new type of reactor was expected to be safer than the ones already operating, and utilities pinned on the new design their hopes for a re-opening of the nuclear power option that had been closed for more than a decade.

The final boon for the nuclear industry, both military and commercial, was the Yucca Mountain, Nev., disposal site for high-level radioactive wastes. One indicator of the long-term viability of nuclear power as part of the nation's energy mix was that, more than three decades after commercial nuclear power had gone on-line, neither the industry nor the government had settled the issue of what to do with nuclear power plant wastes. Most of the spent fuel rods and other wastes, which would remain dangerous for thousands of years, were still cooling off in temporary storage at power plant sites. No state wanted to be the permanent repository of all the nation's nuclear waste; but in 1987, Congress voted down a filibuster and imposed the repository on Nevada against the state's strong objections. An elaborate series of health and safety checks would have to be completed first. Nevadans felt these were meaningless, because the Energy Department was restricted by law from considering any other site than Yucca Mountain. The 1992 energy bill expedited the health and safety evaluation — with both Senate and House again voting down Nevada's objections.

Conservation and Renewables. During the 20th century, the federal government had subsidized oil, natural gas, coal and nuclear power as energy sources through tax breaks, direct spending and sales of the resources themselves (for example, the oil beneath government lands). While these policies had ensured abundant energy to drive the U.S. economy, they also had created certain unwanted side effects. Those side effects included market distortions, acid rain, urban smog, potential global warming and dependence on foreign oil.

Congress and the president had attacked these problems once before — with energy bills in 1978 and 1980 following the energy crisis of that era. One prong of that attack was a set of policies on fossil fuels, such as the Synthetic Fuels Corporation and Powerplant and Industrial Fuel Use Act, which proved misguided for various reasons and were repealed by Congress during the 1980s. Another prong of the attack was a wide array of research funding and tax breaks to encourage alternative, renewable and conservation sources of energy.

Most of those Carter-era alternative programs enjoyed only a few years of prosperity before they began to shrink under the steady strokes of the Reagan budget ax and most were eventually dismantled by Congress. Whole industries — such as solar hot water — were created and then destroyed. The free-market rationale for ending the alternative energy incentives, advanced from both the White House and Capitol Hill, was that without subsidies the alternative energy sources were not economically viable. This test was less often applied to the nuclear, coal and petroleum industries, which continued to plead economic hardship and receive federal subsidies.

By the late 1980s, Congress slowly began pushing again for energy alternatives in small ways. An example was the National Appliance Energy Conservation Act of 1987 — which Congress had enacted a second time after Reagan pocket-vetoed it in 1986. It was one sign that the old anti-regulatory approach of Reagan's presidency was giving way.

The 101st Congress took this trend a few steps further. In 1990, it cleared the State Energy Efficiency Programs Improvement Act, which revitalized a longstanding program of federal aid for weatherization of low-income homes, schools and hospitals and tied that aid more closely to development of energy conservation programs at the state level. Another measure cleared in 1990 funded research on hydrogen as an energy storage medium, which held some promise of gains in cleanness and efficiency. A third measure removed limits on the size of wind, solar and geothermal power plants eligible to sell electricity wholesale on the commercial grid. Perhaps the most substantial action of all was the 5-cents-a-gallon increase in the federal tax on gasoline. It was enacted as part of the 1990 deficit-reduction bill as a revenue-raiser, coupled with $2.5 billion in tax breaks for oil companies, to encourage production.

The 1992 energy bill went much further on alternative and conservation energy — although Congress balked at attempts to decrease consumption with further substantive energy tax increases. One main provision required that certain government agencies and private companies with fleets of cars and trucks start switching to alternative fuels such as methanol, ethanol, natural gas, hydrogen or electricity. Another provision set up a federally funded demonstration program to develop electric vehicles. Other research and development (R&D) programs were established to promote a range of renewable energy technologies, such as geothermal, solar thermal (including water heating), photovoltaic, wind, biomass and chemical fuel cells.

The bill added stiff new measures to require energy efficiency and conservation. It mandated minimum efficiency standards for new federal buildings and federally assisted public and private housing. It required states to set efficiency standards in their commercial building codes and encouraged them to do so in residential building codes. It also mandated efficiency standards for manufactured housing. Other federal efficiency standards were mandated for electric motors, electric lights, plumbing fixtures, and commercial heating and air conditioning units. It went further with a range of voluntary approaches to conservation, such as labeling, financial incentives and funds for R&D on energy efficient technologies.

Issues Unaddressed. Ultimately, what was important about the 1992 energy bill was not just what it did, but what it did not do. It was not a global warming bill — it neither set targets for reductions of greenhouse gas emissions nor mandated them. It did not require "least-cost" (energy efficiency) plans for electric utilities, leaving that to state regulators. It did not set stricter CAFE, or fuel-efficiency, standards for automobiles. It did not open up the Arctic refuge to drilling — and largely avoided the perennial congressional controversies over opening particular offshore tracts to drilling, just by remaining mute. It did not impose an oil-import fee — a remedy often proposed for import-dependency. No new or increased tax was provided on fossil fuel consumption — which had been advanced as the most effective way to encourage conservation. And almost nothing (apart from a few tax breaks) was included to stimulate domestic oil and gas production.

The bill did take major steps toward revitalizing the long-ailing nuclear power industry, although whether it was enough to revive the patient remained unclear. The nuclear power industry, in the early 1980s, had helped raise public awareness of potential global warming caused by gases from fossil fuel combustion. Nuclear power emitted no greenhouse gases, and the industry argued that switching to nuclear would help cure the problem. Environmentalists insisted that nuclear power caused more environmental problems than it cured. But by bolstering nuclear energy, the bill did respond to global warming.

Finally, the bill staked out a large new area of consensus with its emphasis on conservation, renewables and alternative energy sources. Most of these provisions were an area of common ground where the long-warring producers and conservationists could agree. Fuels such as natural gas — which had the advantages of both abundant domestic supply and lower greenhouse emissions — got a boost in the process. Senate Energy Committee Chairman Johnston said after final passage: "The theme of this bill is energy made in America."

Although energy security had been the rallying cry originally used to launch the legislation, it did comparatively little to reduce dependency on foreign oil imports. It did raise by another 25 percent — to 1 billion barrels — the size of the Strategic Petroleum Reserve. The Energy Department estimated that the bill could reduce oil imports by about 4.7 million barrels a day by 2010 — but this was out of U.S. consumption that stood at 17 million barrels a day at the start of the 1990s.

The last burning oil well in Kuwait was capped on Nov. 6, 1991, before the energy bill got to the Senate floor. Bush signed the energy bill into law almost a full year later. It was a lesson in how slow Congress could sometimes be to respond to fast-paced world events.

In the last analysis, however, the bill did accomplish much. That was acknowledged even by Sen. Tim Wirth, D-Colo., one of the original advocates of a national energy plan to deal with global warming. "It is a wonderful shift from where we have been going ever since the dawn of the fossil fuel revolution," Wirth said. "We have for the first time the beginning of a balance between environmental and energy policy."

Chronology Of Action On Energy And Environment

1989-90

Arguably the most notable achievement of the 101st Congress was its passage — after a decade-long stalemate — of amendments to the Clean Air Act. In addition to strengthening existing controls on pollutants emitted from motor vehicles and from stationary sources such as factories, the amendments sought to curb the pollutants that cause acid rain.

Congress also cleared two other pieces of legislation that had been considered for years. One decontrolled the wellhead price of natural gas for the first time since 1954. The other put in place a national liability law intended to prevent oil spills and punish those responsible for spills that did occur.

Other initiatives did not fare so well. A move to elevate the Environmental Protection Agency to Cabinet-level status died when Congress and the White House could not reach agreement on provisions that would have strengthened environmental laws. Congress also was unable to overcome opposition to legislation that would eliminate federal irrigation subsidies for large farm operations in the West.

Clean Air

After more than a decade of political stalemate over the nation's clean air laws, Congress in 1990 cleared sweeping legislation (S 1630 — PL 101-549) to impose stricter federal standards on urban smog, automobile exhaust, toxic air pollution and acid rain. The overwhelming approval of the conference report on the bill in the Senate Oct. 27, one day after adoption by an even stronger vote in the House, capped nearly two full years of work by the 101st Congress and the Bush administration to strengthen the main federal law aimed at reducing air pollution.

Previous efforts to revise and extend the 1977 Clean Air Act (PL 95-95) had been bottled up since at least 1981. But President Bush spurred the legislation forward by proposing a clean air package on June 12, 1989 — a marked shift from his predecessor, Ronald Reagan, who had opposed efforts to strengthen the law. The Senate Environment and Public Works Committee had originally approved S 1630 on Nov. 16, 1989, but that version was substantially rewritten on the Senate floor after extensive negotiations with the administration. Senate passage of the modified bill — less pleasing to environmental groups than the original — came on April 3, 1990.

House Energy and Commerce subcommittees had begun work in 1989 on the administration's proposal — introduced as HR 3030 by Energy Committee Chairman John D. Dingell, D-Mich. — but progress stalled at the end of the year because of interregional disputes over how to reduce acid rain and who should pay for doing so. When work resumed in 1990, marathon markup sessions ended with a committee-approved bill on April 5 that went on to win House approval May 23.

House and Senate conferees spent the summer and early fall working out a compromise version. Most of the negotiations were conducted in private at the staff level, with conferees convening formally only to ratify agreements on individual titles of the bill. Conferees completed action on Oct. 22 after yet another in a series of all-night bargaining sessions.

Four Main Titles

Like the original Senate and House bills, the final version was divided into four main titles, dealing with attainment and maintenance of air quality standards (smog), motor vehicles and alternative fuels, toxic air pollutants and acid deposition (acid rain). Other titles outlined permit and enforcement requirements and provisions for phasing out chemicals that contributed to the depletion of the ozone layer. *(Deadlines, box, p. 477)*

As enacted, the bill included the following agreements:

Motor Vehicles and Fuels. The agreement to tighten controls on automobiles and gasoline required automakers to install new pollution controls to reduce emissions of hydrocarbons and nitrogen oxides. The equipment had to last 10 years or 100,000 miles, twice as long as under existing law. The Environmental Protection Agency (EPA) could impose stricter tailpipe standards beginning in 2003.

In cities where high carbon monoxide levels were caused by car exhaust, controls had to be installed to cut the increased carbon monoxide emitted by automobiles in cold weather. In a last-minute concession to the administration and auto lobbyists, conferees knocked the cold-start requirement back one year, to 2001.

To reduce ozone-forming emissions, only reformulated fuel could be sold in the nine smoggiest cities. Areas with high levels of carbon monoxide had to offer fuel blended with the oxygenators methanol, which was made from natural gas, or ethanol, which came from corn. The California pilot program would eventually require auto companies to produce 300,000 clean-fueled vehicles a year. Taxis and other centrally fueled vehicles had to use that new California technology to cut their emissions by 80 percent.

Urban Smog. Language to clean up polluted cities and suburbs established five categories of so-called "ozone non-attainment" areas and set deadlines for them to meet federal air quality standards. That required new anti-smog equipment for a slew of industries ranging from large industrial facilities to gas stations.

Air Toxics. Plants that emitted any of 189 toxic substances had to cut those emissions to the average level of the cleanest 12 percent of similar facilities. Plants would have to shut down if they still posed more than a 1-in-10,000 risk of cancer to nearby residents by 2003, after the best available technology was installed. An extension until 2020 was granted to steel industry coke ovens if they met certain interim conditions.

Acid Rain. This agreement overcame years of stalemate between regions where acid rain-causing pollutants rose from towering smokestacks and those where acid rain fell on trees, mountains and streams. Coal-burning utilities were the main sources of sulfur dioxide and nitrogen oxide emissions, which caused acid rain. Those pollutants reacted in the atmosphere to form tiny acidic particles that could remain airborne for hundreds of miles before being washed out of the atmosphere by rains.

In Congress, compromise had been elusive because any control strategy had to balance the needs of two broad camps. On one side were "clean states" — those with utilities that burned less polluting, low-sulfur coal, or that had installed "scrubbers" or other pollution control devices. On the other side were "dirty states," mostly in the Midwest, that mined and burned high-sulfur coal.

The "cleans" wanted to be given credit for earlier emissions reductions and be able to expand their electric utility capacity, if needed, without violating tight emissions caps. They also did not want to pay for the Midwest's cleanup. The "dirties" wanted to preserve jobs for high-sulfur coal miners in the Midwest and Appalachian states. They also wanted cost-sharing among states to keep the cleanup from further depressing Midwest economies.

Acid rain legislation in previous years had involved such a cost-sharing component, but Bush opposed that approach, calling it a form of taxation. Instead, his bill put forth a market-based system of pollution "allowances" that could be granted to utilities that limited sulfur dioxide emissions. That proposal became the key ingredient in political trade-offs that eventually cemented an acid rain agreement.

Background

A comprehensive reauthorization and overhaul of the Clean Air Act, the nation's most complex and far-reaching pollution-control law, had been overdue since 1982. The law was enacted in 1970 (PL 91-604) and amended significantly in 1977 (PL 95-95). *(1970 law, Congress and the Nation Vol. III, p. 757; 1977 amendments, Congress and the Nation Vol. V, p. 535)*

The law required that states enact pollution controls sufficient to meet federal air-quality standards and protect public health. But by 1990, most urban areas still violated air-quality standards for ozone, which was caused largely by pollutants from industrial facilities, chemical plants and motor vehicles, and carbon monoxide, which came primarily from automobiles.

The EPA had authority to impose sanctions on states, such as bans on the construction of large new pollution sources or cutoffs in federal highway funds, but it rarely used that power.

The Clean Air Act also had largely failed to limit industrial emissions of air toxics — hazardous pollutants such as benzene that caused cancer, neurological disorders or other serious ailments, even when emitted at relatively low concentrations. Since 1970, EPA had brought only seven of some 275 industrial air toxics under federal regulation.

Few argued against the value of clean air, but the potential price in lost jobs and increased costs to industry and consumers left Congress intractably divided for a decade. Although environmentalists had insisted they had the needed votes on the floor, the Reagan administration's lack of interest in new regulation strengthened the hand of key obstructionists in the House and Senate. Chief among them was auto industry ally Dingell, who used his House Energy and Commerce Committee chairmanship to stall any bills that would impose tough new standards on Detroit automakers. In the Senate, Robert C. Byrd of West Virginia, who served as Democratic leader from 1977 to 1989, discouraged action because of fear that acid rain proposals would throw coal miners out of work by destroying the market for high-sulfur coal mined in his home state.

Underlying their opposition were seemingly endless parochial divisions: Midwesterners, for example, opposed acid rain bills year after year because of the heavy cost to coal-burning utilities in their states. California and other states sought controls on emissions from offshore oil drilling, but states bordering the Gulf of Mexico would have none of such proposals. (The conference agreement on S 1630 exempted Texas, Louisiana, Mississippi and Alabama from such controls.) The original Clean Air Act required the EPA to establish safe concentrations for seven major air pollutants and set a 1975 deadline for states to meet those standards. When it appeared most states would not meet the deadline, Congress extended it to 1982 or, for areas with severe auto-related pollution, to 1987.

After legislation again failed to clear in 1987, Congress decided to address the issue in the middle of the 1988 election campaign by extending the deadline when cities would face penalties for failing to meet existing air-quality standards. But even with an election-year deadline, various clean air measures were never brought to the floor of either the House or the Senate. Finally, Sen. George J. Mitchell, D-Maine, the leader of a months-long search for a compromise bill, conceded defeat in October in a charged Senate floor speech. *(Congress and the Nation Vol. VII, p. 462)*

Mitchell's bill was blocked for almost a year by Majority Leader Byrd, who controlled the Senate's floor schedule. In the House, clean air legislation in the Energy and Commerce Committee had been slowed by various members, most notably Chairman Dingell. But even Henry A. Waxman, D-Calif., a longtime advocate for tougher clean air laws, played a role in delaying legislation when it appeared he might get a stricter bill in the next Congress.

New Dynamic in 1989

Clean air legislation got a boost in 1989 when Bush not only supported the rewrite, but also offered his own comprehensive proposal.

Bush's introduction of a clean air bill in June 1989 changed the political dynamic almost overnight. It did not resolve regional conflicts, but it forced key players to sit down and deal. Within a year, members of the House and Senate had struggled through often bitter and prolonged fights to produce bills that had far more similarities than differences.

Another important change was Mitchell's ascension as Senate majority leader, succeeding Byrd, who retired from the leadership post but remained powerful as chairman of the Appropriations Committee. Under pressure from Mitchell, the Senate Environment and Public Works Committee in November agreed to a package (S 1630) of measures to reduce smog, acid rain and toxic air pollution. Mitchell then vowed to make S 1630 the Senate's first order of business when Congress reconvened in 1990.

On the House side, the legislation was able to move forward in large part because two key members showed a willingness to compromise. Long the respective leaders of the Energy Committee's industry and environmentalist blocs, Chairman Dingell and Health and the Environment Subcommittee Chairman Waxman had fought each other to stalemate in previous years.

Although the two men were, by most accounts, soul mates on many of the health issues that came before the Energy Committee, they parted company on clean air. Dingell, whose Detroit district was home to the headquarters of the Ford Motor Co., was the leading proponent of the theory that the dramatic emissions reductions automakers had achieved since the 1970 Clean Air Act had been implemented were about as much as it was reasonable to ask and that the situation would continue to improve as newer, cleaner cars gradually replaced older, dirtier vehicles. Dingell looked at many of the provisions in the clean air legislation and saw fuzzy thinking, a willingness to impose indefinite costs on business and industry, and an indifference to the inevitable erosion of jobs and livelihoods.

Waxman, whose Los Angeles district had some of the worst air in the United States, was the leading voice for the view that motor vehicles, although they were cleaner than they once were, still caused about half the serious air pollution in the nation's cities and should be a large part of the clean air solution. He viewed auto emissions as responsible for many of the cancer deaths and other health problems whose enormous social and financial costs were seldom calculated by those who worried about how much business and industry would have to pay to comply with new air regulations.

But in the fall of 1989, the two men agreed to a surprise deal on automobile tailpipe emissions. With help from other key members, the committee went on to reach several more compromises that resolved arguments on smog, acid rain, air toxics and other matters.

Dingell was said to have given ground because he thought a bill was inevitable and because he calculated that a somewhat pro-environmental House floor would be an unfriendly place for him to try to hold the line on issues dear to him. Observers described Waxman's motivation as uncertainty over just how far he could push tough environmental positions on the floor and a willingness to accommodate members who begged him not to force them to choose between him and Dingell or between environmental lobbyists and the auto industry or autoworkers.

Energy, Environment Leadership

The Senate March 1, 1989, voted 99-0 to confirm retired admiral James D. Watkins as energy secretary. Watkins was one of six Cabinet officers who remained at their posts throughout Bush's four-year tenure. *(Watkins background, Cabinet profiles, p. 1172)*

Manuel Lujan Jr. was confirmed, 100-0, on Feb. 2, 1989, to be secretary of the interior. Lujan, a ten-term (1969-89) Republican representative from New Mexico, also served for Bush's entire term. *(Lujan background, Cabinet profiles, p. 1173)*

By an identical 100-0 vote on Feb. 2, 1989, the Senate confirmed William K. Reilly to be administrator of the Environmental Protection Agency. *(Reilly profile, p. 1175)*

House Committee Action

The House Energy Subcommittee on Health and the Environment was the first to act after Bush announced his support for a rewrite of the 1970 Clean Air Act. The subcommittee spent four weeks marking up clean air legislation (HR 3030) proposed by the president and then approved an amended version on Oct. 11, 1989.

Dingell and the committee's ranking Republican, New York's Norman F. Lent, began the markup with what appeared to be a carefully planned conciliatory move, unveiling a 302-page substitute version of the bill that made a multitude of technical changes and at least 32 substantive alterations — including several designed to satisfy key environmentalist criticisms of HR 3030.

The compromise on auto emission standards that Dingell and Waxman engineered brought unexpected peace to a critical section of the bill that had long been expected to generate fireworks on the House floor. As approved by the subcommittee on a unanimous 22-0 vote, the agreement would begin phasing in strict California emissions standards on all the nation's cars and light trucks beginning in model year 1994. A second stage would impose even tighter standards beginning in 2003, unless the administrator of the EPA ruled such standards impossible to meet or suggested alternative restrictions.

The agreement was a compromise between the speedier timetable and slightly tougher tailpipe standards in Waxman's own bill (HR 2323) and the substantially more moderate approach taken in the White House bill. Waxman won standards tougher than those embodied in the administration bill, along with a probability that emissions restrictions would undergo a second round of tightening after the year 2000. Dingell managed to stretch out compliance dates and won a provision that would give the EPA discretion to find that a less stringent set of second-round standards would be appropriate after 2000. Key to the deal was Waxman and Dingell's agreement to stick with the compromise all the way through a conference with the Senate, resisting any attempts to strengthen or weaken the bill at any stage in the legislative process.

Alternative Fuels Debate. During the final week of the markup, the subcommittee divided sharply over Bush's proposal to mandate a new generation of clean fuels and clean cars. Amid confused and seemingly contradictory signals from the White House, the subcommittee Oct. 11 voted 12-10 to weaken the president's alternative-fuels provisions, which had been touted by the administration in June as "perhaps the most innovative and far-reaching component" of his clean air proposals.

The subcommittee amendment to the Bush bill loosened clean-fuel requirements, expanded the clean-fuel definition to cover more fuels and stripped the bill of the president's proposal to require automakers to build and sell 1 million clean-fuel motor vehicles a year by 1997.

Proponents of the amendment, such as co-author Jack Fields, R-Texas, said it would "level the playing field" for alternative fuels other than methanol, which was widely viewed as the single alternative fuel mandated by the Bush bill. Backers also said the amendment would relieve the auto industry from having to produce large numbers of clean-fuel cars with no assurance that anyone would buy them.

But critics of the amendment, led by Waxman, said it amounted to a "trashing" of one of the most important strategies the White House package offered for reducing air pollution. They vowed to fight the provision all the way to the House floor.

Later that day, the panel voted 21-0 to send the bill to the full Energy and Commerce Committee, where members were expected to grapple with a wide range of issues that the subcommittee left unresolved, including disputes over acid rain and toxic air pollutants.

Cost-Sharing Plan. But the bill then stalled in the Energy Subcommittee on Energy and Power, which had jurisdiction over provisions on acid rain and alternative fuels. That panel's chairman, Philip R. Sharp, D-Ind., delayed markup while he sought a cost-sharing plan to help utilities in his and other Midwestern states pay for complying with the proposed acid rain controls. But with the majority of the panel opposed to cost sharing in any form, Sharp faced an uphill battle.

At year's end, the bill remained in subcommittee with pressure building in the House for the Energy Committee to act.

Senate Committee Action

Senate leaders intent on bringing an overhaul of the Clean Air Act to the floor early in 1990 brushed aside complaints about excessive speed Nov. 16 and moved a massive anti-pollution package through the Environment and Public Works Committee in a single day.

Democrat Max Baucus of Montana, chairman of the Subcommittee on Environmental Protection, had critical backing from panel member and Majority Leader Mitchell in keeping committee members from heading for the doors as the markup extended into the evening.

The committee ultimately approved, on a 15-1 vote, a bill (S 1630) that drew together previously separate measures on acid rain (unnumbered), toxic air pollutants (S 816) and smog (S 1630 originally). Although similar in structure to an administration clean air package moving through the House, the Senate bill went beyond Bush's bill in many areas, calling for more certain pollution reductions, tougher restrictions on industry and tighter controls on motor vehicles.

During its all-day session, the Environment Committee considered at least 40 amendments. Chief among those that won approval was a proposal by John H. Chafee, R-R.I., that would end by the year 2000 the use of chlorofluorocarbons and other chemicals that scientists said were destroying the ozone layer in the upper atmosphere. The committee also put itself on record against taxes and fees to spread the cost of acid rain controls, and it rejected amendments to weaken some of the bill's strongest restrictions on industry and motor vehicles.

The full committee action came after four rapid-fire markup sessions in the Environmental Protection Subcommittee, which approved pieces of the bill in brief, half-day sessions that began in mid-October. The legislative hustle prompted complaints in the full committee, chiefly from Republican Steve Symms of Idaho, who cast the sole vote against the measure. Symms noted that he also had been the lone opponent the three other times the committee reported a clean air measure over the past decade. Symms characterized the bill as a radical assault on business, industry, and state and local authority. "This bill is going to smell like a rotten bag of fish after two months," he said.

But Mitchell said the speedy action was merely an attempt to comply with Bush's criticism on Nov. 7 that Congress was sitting on clean air legislation. Senate leaders had moved the legislation forward in part by deferring resolution of some of the bill's hottest disputes. Baucus said work would continue from then to January on a committee amendment to address some of those issues; others would have to wait for amendments on the Senate floor.

Environment and Public Works formally reported S 1630 (S Rept 101-228) on Dec. 20.

Senate Floor Action

The bill that won overwhelming 89-11 approval on the Senate floor April 3, 1990, was a far cry from the measure that Mitchell had made the first order of Senate business in the second session. The bill was changed markedly, mostly away from environmentalists' positions. But the environmentalist coalition lobbying for the bill pronounced the Senate's action a major step forward and hoped to recover some of the lost ground in the House.

Initial Floor Action. As promised, Mitchell had brought S 1630 to the floor when the Senate reconvened Jan. 23. But the hope that the bill might clear Congress in time for Bush to sign it by Earth Day in April evaporated quickly.

Early skirmishing on the bill centered on disagreements about how much it would cost. Critics insisted it was too expensive; advocates countered that its costs would be more than offset by savings in the costs of health care and other expenses people incurred because of pollution.

Mitchell had vowed to keep the bill on the floor until it was finished. Yet debate abruptly ended by the second week, as key senators and Bush administration officials vanished behind closed doors to seek out compromises on the most contentious sections of the legislation.

The sudden disappearance of the debate's key players from the Senate floor came after several days of sporadic speechmaking that yielded only a single roll-call vote on a relatively minor provision. The big issues that threatened to split the Senate — acid rain cost-sharing, motor vehicle emissions controls and health standards for toxic air pollutants — seemed to be little closer to resolution than they were when the Senate took up the measure.

The bill's managers appeared to be unsure of where the votes lay on those critical provisions, and they also appeared to be fearful of what environmental lobbyists asserted was a filibuster threat orchestrated by the Bush administration. After a day of no substantive floor action Feb. 1, Mitchell emerged from the talks to pronounce them "productive and reassuring of the good faith of all parties to reach agreement." Mitchell then pulled the bill off the floor to allow time for the negotiations.

Negotiated Agreement. Senate and administration negotiators emerged from a month of backroom talks March 1 with a clean air agreement that disappointed environmentalists, heartened industry and appeared to have pacified enough filibuster-prone senators to ensure passage.

The proposed substitute, which substantially moderated the Environment Committee bill, was unveiled at a lunch-hour news conference attended by more than a dozen senators and top Bush administration officials. Senate leaders and White House officials presented a united front in support of the measure, saying it was an aggressive improvement over existing law that also met White House objections to the projected cost of the committee bill.

"The president is extraordinarily pleased with this agreement," said Roger B. Porter, White House assistant for domestic and economic affairs and leader of the Bush negotiating team.

Mitchell said the measure "dramatically expands and strengthens" current clean air law. Minority Leader Bob Dole, R-Kan., called the package "the single most important piece of legislation we'll deal with this year" and pledged to join Mitchell and other backers of the deal in efforts to fight off any significant amendments.

Details of Substitute Bill. Key changes to S 1630:

Motor Vehicles. The substitute moderated the first and second phases of the bill's motor vehicle emissions limits. Instead of imposing first-round limits all at once in 1993, the substitute phased them in, beginning with 40 percent of vehicles sold in 1993, rising to 100 percent of vehicles sold in 1995.

Even stricter second-round restrictions, which were to be imposed unconditionally in 2003, would instead be imposed nationwide (after Oct. 1, 2003) only if at least 12 of the nation's 27 most polluted urban areas continued to violate health standards at the end of 2001.

Air Toxics. The substitute mandated a study of the best way to assess the health risk remaining after first-round, maximum achievable control technology was installed on major sources of toxics such as refineries, chemical plants and coke ovens. A new panel could recommend a different health-risk policy, but Congress would have to vote to agree.

Otherwise, the substitute retained the committee bill's second-round limit on cancer risks posed by emissions from major pollution sources — no more than one additional cancer case per 10,000 population. But the substitute provided a new alternative: Instead of meeting a risk test for a hypothetical "most-exposed individual," a pollution source could subject itself to a site-specific, "actual man" test to assess risk to public health in the vicinity. In addition, coke ovens that installed maximum achievable control technology before 1995 would be given an extension to 2020 to begin meeting the 1-in-10,000 risk test.

Acid Rain. The substitute retained most major features of the committee bill, which focused sulfur dioxide (SO_2) cleanup requirements on the 107 largest coal-fired utilities. The substitute increased the number to 111 but added provisions encouraging them to use scrubbers so they could continue burning high-sulfur coal.

Coal-fired utility plants that used technology such as scrubbers to reduce SO_2 emissions by the Phase I deadline (1995) could either get an extra two years to meet the restrictions or receive bonus pollution allowances for reductions made between 1995 and 1997. As in the committee bill, utilities could sell those allowances to generate cash to defray the cost of installing scrubbers.

Plants using scrubbers would receive 2-ton pollution allowances for every ton of SO_2 reduced during Phase I that went beyond their Phase II (2000) target. Bonus allowances would be given to clean states that had already reduced SO_2 emissions, thus allowing some utility growth.

Alternative Fuels. The substitute added a section to require use of alternative fuels in the nation's nine most polluted urban areas. Phase I required all new cars in those

Clean Air Deadlines

Following are deadlines set by the Clean Air Act amendments (S 1630 — PL 101-549) cleared in 1990.

Cities and Towns

1993: Deadline for "marginal" areas to reach ozone standard (39 cities).

1996: Deadline for "moderate" non-attainment areas (32 cities).

1999: Deadline for "serious" areas (16 cities).

2005-07: Deadline for "severe" areas (8 cities).

2010: Deadline for "extreme" areas (Los Angeles).

Cars, Trucks and Buses

Model Year 1994: 60 percent less nitrogen oxide; 35 percent less hydrocarbons.

Model Year 1998: Cars to be equipped with emission control systems with "useful life" of 10 years or 100,000 miles.

Model Year 2003: Second-round tailpipe standards to go into effect subject to Environmental Protection Agency (EPA) veto.

Motor Fuels

1992: Cities with carbon dioxide (CO_2) non-attainment to use gasoline with 2.7 percent oxygen, unless EPA delayed standard.

1995: Nine smoggiest cities to sell only reformulated gasoline. Volatile organic compounds (VOCs) and toxic emissions to be cut 15 percent.

Utilities

1995: 111 dirtiest coal-fired plants to cut sulfur dioxide (SO_2) emissions.

2000: Annual SO_2 emissions limited to 10 million tons.

Other Industries

1995: EPA to regulate 90 percent of 30 most serious toxic pollutants emitted by dry cleaners, gas stations and other "area" sources. Cancer risks to be reduced 75 percent.

2003: Major sources — including, for example, chemical plants and oil refineries — to apply best available technology to reduce emissions of 189 toxic chemicals by the average of the 12 cleanest similar plants. "Residual" cancer risk to most exposed persons to be reduced to 1-in-10,000.

2020: Extended residual risk deadline for coke ovens to meet tougher interim standards.

areas to meet tight new emissions standards beginning in model year 1995 — most likely by burning reformulated gasoline, instead of methanol, ethanol or other alternatives. Phase II further tightened the emissions standard beginning in model year 1999 and was expected to require changes in the design of the cars themselves.

In addition, a fleet program targeted federally owned fleet vehicles (beginning in 1995) and then privately owned fleets (1997) for even stricter reductions.

Global Warming. The substitute dropped the committee bill's plan to enlist motor vehicles in the fight against global warming. The bill would have set carbon dioxide emission limits roughly equal to 33 miles per gallon (mpg) for the 1996-99 model years and 40 mpg in the year 2000.

Reaction to Substitute. Senate clean air negotiators also came away with a vital no-filibuster pledge from Byrd, long a bitter foe of any acid rain provisions that might force utilities to quit burning the high-sulfur coal mined in his state.

Byrd persuaded other members of the negotiating group to give Midwestern utilities extra compliance time and additional, salable pollution "allowances" for installing scrubbers or other technological controls that helped them meet acid rain restrictions. The Byrd formula would make it more likely that utilities would continue to burn high-sulfur coal and not switch to low-sulfur coal to meet SO_2 limits.

Though not happy enough with the substitute to back it formally, the Senate's senior Democrat uttered the words Mitchell and others long wanted to hear: "I'm not going to be engaged in any filibuster."

Environmentalists, whose expectations had been raised by the comparatively tough bill produced by the Environment Committee, were troubled when the measure disappeared behind closed doors early in February and angry about what emerged March 1. Industry representatives, in contrast, were relieved to see the bill go into closed-door talks and happier with what came out than what went in.

The substitute's Senate defenders preferred not to compare it with the committee bill, but with existing clean air law, which had remained unchanged since 1977. "This bill is a very major improvement over current law," said Baucus, chairman of the Environment Subcommittee on Environmental Protection and the Democratic floor manager of the clean air debate.

Chafee, ranking Republican on Environment and a key player in the agreement, noted that he, like Baucus, would be "in the awkward situation of voting against" amendments to put back provisions that he helped put in the committee bill in the first place — but which he also helped strip out in the backroom talks.

Several senators immediately signaled they would try to amend the compromise on the floor. Tim Wirth, D-Colo., planned to offer one amendment to toughen the bill's motor vehicle provisions, but he conceded that he faced an uphill fight. "They put us in a box," Wirth said of Mitchell's and other Senate environmentalists' agreement to oppose amendments. "It would have been hard to get 51 votes for these [types of amendments] anyway."

Floor Debate Resumes. When the bill finally returned to the Senate floor the week of March 5, Mitchell and others successfully defended the compromise against a series of "deal-buster" amendments that they said would have unraveled the Senate-White House coalition, either by strengthening or weakening the deal worked out with the administration.

Environmentalist senators tried in vain to restore some of the tough restrictions that were stripped out of the bill. First, Richard H. Bryan, D-Nev., agreed to withdraw an amendment to restore a modified version of a carbon dioxide (CO_2) emissions-limits provision stripped out in the negotiations. Bryan's amendment would have set corporate average fuel economy (CAFE) standards of 34 miles per gallon (mpg) by 1995 and 40 mpg by 2001.

Automakers insisted the standards were wildly unrealistic and exorbitantly expensive. But Bryan and backers said the proposal was important both for fuel savings and as a first step toward controlling global warming. Mitchell persuaded Bryan to withdraw the amendment by promising that the Senate would revisit the issue later in the year. *(Fuel efficiency, p. 484)*

Frank R. Lautenberg, D-N.J., tried to restore a motor vehicles provision to a section of the bill that sought to cut cancer deaths by controlling so-called area sources of toxic air pollutants. Lautenberg said motor vehicles had been exempted from controls under this section of the bill at the insistence of White House cost-cutters, who, he said, ignored the fact that motor vehicles were responsible for more than half of all air toxics.

Baucus countered that ample controls were placed on motor vehicles in other sections of the bill. And he added: "The deal will be off, the deal will be busted, and there could very well be no Clean Air Act." The Senate agreed March 8 to table (kill) Lautenberg's amendment on a 65-33 vote.

Holding the Compromise Together. The real challenge to the compromise came the week of March 19, when Senate environmentalists tried but failed to toughen the measure. A motion was made to table (kill) an amendment offered by Wirth and Pete Wilson, R-Calif., that would have added back some of the strict provisions on motor vehicle emissions that Senate negotiators had modified or dropped as part of the February deal with the White House. The motion to table was agreed to March 20 by a **key vote of 52-46 (R 25-19; D 27-27).** *(1990 key votes, p. 1039)*

The outcome appeared to be less a measure of environmentalist vs. industry muscle than of concern that tinkering with the administration-approved deal might kill clean air legislation for years. Mitchell had warned senators that adoption of any of the so-called deal-breaker amendments could destroy the agreement with the administration with dire consequences. "If we do not get a clean air bill this year, we are not going to get a clean air bill in this century," Mitchell said.

The defeat of the Wirth-Wilson amendment was followed the next day by another close vote on an amendment to toughen the urban smog provisions of the Senate-White House compromise. That amendment was tabled, 53-46.

Defeat of the two amendments was an important victory for the administration, which had taken a hard line against any provisions that would have pushed up the bill's cost. Administration officials argued that extra restrictions would clean up little more pollution but would inflate costs enormously for businesses and consumers.

After those two votes, the Senate compromise was able to survive all onslaughts — including an amendment by Appropriations Committee Chairman Byrd that would have authorized $500 million to provide three years of job loss and retraining benefits to coal miners who lost their jobs as a result of the clean air legislation. Senators found it difficult to vote against Byrd, who had 32 years' worth of

IOUs in one vest pocket and countless future chits in the other. But on March 29, the Senate rejected the Byrd amendment on a 49-50 vote.

On April 3, the Senate passed its version of the legislation, moving clean air legislation for the first time since revision efforts began in 1981.

House Committee Action Renewed

At the same time the Senate was preparing to take up the clean air bill on the floor, long-stalled House legislation showed signs of life. HR 3030 had been held up since October 1989 while Philip Sharp, chairman of the Energy Subcommittee on Energy and Power, tried to find a way to spread the costs of complying with the acid rain provisions. Without some sort of cost-sharing plan, Indiana and other Midwestern states were likely to be hard hit by the measure's requirements for reducing the pollutants that cause acid rain.

On Feb. 28, Sharp offered his compromise. Stripped to its essentials, the complex proposal would have levied a fee on industrial emitters of large amounts of sulfur dioxide, a principal precursor of acid rain, and then would have funneled the money to Midwestern utilities to help defray the costs of adding scrubbers to remove SO_2.

After two weeks of negotiations, however, when Sharp appeared no closer to finding agreement on his proposal, committee Chairman Dingell called a halt to the talks and brought the bill before the full committee on March 14.

Almost from the start, committee members and their staffs withdrew behind closed doors to work out the more nettlesome provisions of the wide-ranging bill. On March 22, members emerged to reveal a surprise compromise that incorporated some of the same anti-smog provisions the Senate had just rejected. The agreement took a bitterly divisive issue off the table for the committee and seemed likely to help the panel meet its April 6 deadline to finish work on the bill, which would allow floor action in late April or early May.

The Energy Committee's compromise made an important element of the legislation much clearer. The compromise not only incorporated key parts of the defeated Senate smog amendment, but it also adopted what committee members depicted as strengthening provisions throughout the entire title of the bill that divided the smoggiest cities and nearby rural areas into categories depending on the severity of their pollution and established methods to bring them into compliance with health standards.

The compromise defined the methods for controlling air pollution from stationary sources such as large factories and power plants. The Health and the Environment Subcommittee had reached a similar compromise in October on pollution from mobile sources, such as cars, trucks and buses. Together, the two agreements neutralized disputes over some of the bill's most controversial sections, making floor fights on those provisions unlikely.

Dingell and Waxman both supported the compromise, but the White House was noticeably absent from the closed-door negotiations that produced the arrangement. An administration official who attended the March 22 markup had no comment except to say the administration still preferred Bush's bill and would immediately start a running cost estimate of the committee agreement to see whether it violated the president's limits.

Although the compromise reduced the number of divisive issues left for the committee to work out, the strife was far from over. A week later, the full committee re-fought one of the battles of the 1989 markup in the Health and the Environment Subcommittee. Once again, members disagreed sharply over how aggressive and costly to make alternative-fuels programs for cars, trucks and buses.

The full committee wound up late March 29 by voting narrowly to keep in place a modified version of an alternative-fuels plan that industry officials said they could live with but that environmentalists found unacceptably weak. Both sides indicated that they would keep trying to negotiate a compromise to head off yet another showdown on the issue on the House floor.

The committee began its final week of negotiations with another compromise, this one on air toxics. This had been expected to be a bitterly contested issue, with environmentalists insisting on tough second-round health standards and industry resisting on the ground that those health standards could force plants or even entire industries to shut down.

But in a move that caught many observers off guard, the committee's environmentalist bloc agreed to moderate the second-round health standards significantly. In exchange, they got much more comprehensive first-round technology requirements that covered virtually all major toxics sources and extended controls to many smaller ones, such as gas stations, dry cleaners, print shops and electroplating shops. Motor vehicles, a main toxics source, were specifically exempted because they were covered in a separate section of the bill.

The final issue facing the committee was acid rain, the subject that had stalled the bill in subcommittee. A small group of members from the Midwest continued to insist on some form of cost sharing to help their utilities defray the costs of meeting acid rain controls, while a much larger group of clean-state members did not want to pay.

But the clean-state members had a problem of their own — the bill's stringent cap on emissions meant they would have to buy pollution "allowances," most likely from Midwestern utilities, if they wanted to increase the capacity of their coal-burning utilities in the future. That situation contained the seeds of a compromise and negotiators quickly went to work. After two days, the Midwesterners announced that they had abandoned cash cost sharing in favor of a system that manipulated the allowance trading scheme to give both the Midwest and the clean states extra allowances. The committee then voted, 42-1, to approve the bill.

HR 3030 was formally reported from Energy and Commerce (H Rept 101-490, Part I) on May 17, 1990. House Ways and Means (H Rept 101-490, Part II) and the Public Works and Transportation Committee (H Rept 101-490, Part III), which shared jurisdiction, reported the bill May 21.

House Floor Action

Driven by compromises that cut most of the controversy out of the bill before it reached the floor, the House dispatched a sweeping rewrite of the nation's clean air laws in only two days of floor debate. The House passed HR 3030 May 23 on a **key vote of 401-21 (R 154-16; D 247-5)**. The House then by voice vote passed S 1630, amended with the language of the just passed HR 3030.

Because the Energy and Commerce Committee had produced so many agreements on so many divisive issues, the House had only a handful of decisions to make before final passage. The House made several additions to its core bill during floor debate to bring it close to the Senate measure. In addition to provisions on smog, motor vehicles, acid rain and air toxics that were similar in both the versions, the House added key amendments to complement similar Senate provisions on clean-fueled vehicles, reformulated gasoline, substances that depleted the Earth's stratospheric ozone layer, offshore drilling, visibility in national parks and warranties on automotive pollution-control equipment.

In one of its more controversial votes, the House May 23 shrugged off White House veto warnings and adopted, 274-146, an amendment to authorize a $250 million five-year program for unemployment and retraining benefits to workers who lost their jobs because of the new law.

Bush said the day after the vote that he remained opposed to the amendment and hoped it would be stripped from the bill in conference. Because of the wide margin by which the House amendment passed and the narrow margin by which a more expensive Senate job-benefits amendment was defeated, it seemed likely that some form of the amendment would remain in the final bill despite administration objections. *(Displaced workers, p. 714)*

Conference Action

Although hundreds of differences existed between the House and Senate versions of the clean air legislation, they were so alike in general philosophy and overall structure that participants expected no intractable disputes when negotiators met in conference. But concerns about finishing the bill before the end of the session kept the outcome in suspense for much of the summer and fall.

In the House, Speaker Thomas S. Foley, D-Wash., did not appoint conferees for more than a month after the House acted on the bill. The conference finally convened on July 13, but Senate efforts to accelerate the negotiations ran aground when Dingell refused to be rushed into responding to two early offers from Senate conferees. Environmentalists began to worry in earnest that the dwindling time before adjournment of the 101st Congress would put them at a disadvantage by empowering those who wanted to force concessions by holding the bill hostage to the calendar.

The anxiety level increased as conferees spent weeks making only slow progress on relatively minor differences between the two bills. The pace picked up the week of Sept. 10, when the Senate negotiators agreed to go along with virtually all of the House-passed language relating to smog. The House bill imposed pollution limits further out into the suburbs and rural areas and covered far more industries than the Senate version had — requiring even small emitters such as dry cleaners and bakeries to install anti-smog equipment.

The agreement was a defeat for the administration, which had fought to weaken smog controls in the Senate bill, arguing that the cost could cripple small businesses. The administration declined to commit senators to the deal through conference, leaving conferees free to opt for stricter new controls on industrial pollutants.

Agreement on motor vehicles and clean fuel came next. Negotiators hewed largely to the House-passed language on tailpipe emissions, requiring a 60 percent cut in nitrogen oxides and a 40 percent reduction in hydrocarbons, two primary components of smog, by 1994. More stringent standards would go into effect in 2003, unless the EPA blocked them as not technologically feasible, cost-effective or necessary.

Although the auto industry had lobbied for less strict provisions, it did win some important concessions. Negotiators, for example, stretched out the deadlines for when the nine most-polluted cities would be required to sell only gasoline that was mixed with cleaner-burning fuels. They also linked clean-fueled vehicle programs in California and the rest of the country to ensure that automakers would not have to meet separate standards. And they delayed deadlines for when equipment would have to be installed in cars to capture fuel vapors at the gas pump.

Environmentalists could claim some victories as well. By 1996, automobiles had to be built to meet new tailpipe emissions standards for 10 years or 100,000 miles, meaning that equipment installed in cars had to be twice as durable as was required under existing law. Conferees also adopted the stricter Senate standards requiring controls on the amount of carbon monoxide cars emit in cold weather. Still, environmentalists warned that significantly cleaner cars would not be available for nearly a decade.

In a last-gasp effort to bring a clean air bill to the floor before Congress adjourned, conferees reached a tentative compromise Oct. 17 on the third of four major sections of the bill, agreeing to tough new controls to reduce industrial emissions of airborne toxics. The new proposal, which affected industries ranging from oil refineries to dry cleaners, covered 189 different air toxics, pollutants that posed especially serious health risks such as cancer and birth defects to people who lived near the emissions sources. Most of those toxic emissions had never been regulated by the federal government.

Conferees were clearly relieved that an agreement had been reached. A leadership deadline of Oct. 14 for completion of the entire bill had passed with staff still deadlocked on that one issue, forcing conferees to meet until 3:00 a.m. the morning of Oct. 17 to break the impasse.

The air toxics agreement was aimed at jump-starting what was widely recognized as a failed federal program to control the most hazardous airborne pollutants, such as benzene and asbestos, emitted by industrial facilities. The EPA was required under the 1970 Clean Air Act to identify hazardous pollutants that contributed to death or serious illness and to set emissions standards for those pollutants. The standards were to be set at a level that provided "an ample margin of safety" to protect the public health.

But because of funding shortages, industry pressure and what many viewed as unrealistic standards for reducing health risks, the EPA had listed only eight of the 275 toxic substances known to be emitted by industrial facilities. Standards had been issued for only seven.

Under the new air toxics pact, about 250 major industrial polluters, such as chemical plants and oil refineries, had to install "maximum achievable control technology" — the average emissions limitations of the cleanest 12 percent of similar facilities — to reduce toxic emissions by 2003. The controls were required earlier, in 1995, for 41 of those sources. New plants had to meet higher emissions limits.

If significant risks to public health still remained after those controls were installed, the EPA had to tighten emissions standards further to ensure that nearby residents were not exposed to more than a 1-in-10,000 "residual risk" of cancer. Otherwise, the plants had to shut down.

In addition to regulating major sources of emissions, the agency had to ensure that emissions of the 30 most

Hazardous Air Pollutants

CAS #	Chemical Name
75070	Acetaldehyde
60355	Acetamide
75058	Acetonitrile
98862	Acetophenone
53963	2-Acetylaminofluorene
107028	Acrolein
79061	Acrylamide
79107	Acrylic acid
107131	Acrylonitrile
107051	Allyl chloride
92671	4-Aminobiphenyl
62533	Aniline
90040	o-Anisidine
1332214	Asbestos
71432	Benzene (including from gasoline)
92875	Benzidine
98077	Benzotrichloride
100447	Benzyl chloride
92524	Biphenyl
117817	Bis((2-ethylhexyl)) phthalate (DEHP)
542881	Bis(chloromethyl)ether
75252	Bromoform
106990	1,3-Butadiene
156627	Calcium cyanamide
105602	Caprolactam
133062	Captan
63252	Carbaryl
75150	Carbon disulfide
56235	Carbon tetrachloride
463581	Carbonyl sulfide
120809	Catechol
133904	Chloramben
57749	Chlordane
7782505	Chlorine
79118	Chloroacetic acid
532274	2-Chloroacetophenone
108907	Chlorobenzene
510156	Chlorobenzilate
67663	Chloroform
107302	Chloromethyl methyl ether
126998	Chloroprene
1319773	Cresols/Cresylic acid (isomers and mixture)
95487	o-Cresol
108394	m-Cresol
106445	p-Cresol
98828	Cumene
94757	2,4-D, salts and esters
3547044	DDE
334883	Diazomethane
132649	Dibenzofurans
96128	1,2-Dibromo-3-chloropropane
84742	Dibutylphthalate
106467	1,4-Dichlorobenzene(p)
91941	3,3-Dichlorobenzidene
111444	Dichloroethyl ether (Bis(2-chloroethyl)ether)
542756	1,3-Dichloropropene
62737	Dichlorvos
111422	Diethanolamine
121697	N,N-Diethyl aniline (N,N-Dimethylaniline)
64675	Diethyl sulfate
119904	3,3-Dimethoxybenzidine
60117	Dimethyl aminoazobenzene
119937	3,3'-Dimethyl benzidine
79447	Dimethyl carbamoyl chloride
68122	Dimethyl formamide
57147	1,1-Dimethyl hydrazine
131113	Dimethyl phthalate
77781	Dimethyl sulfate
534521	4,6-Dinitro-o-cresol, and salts
51285	2,4-Dinitrophenol
121142	2,4-Dinitrotoluene
123911	1,4-Dioxane (1,4-Diethyleneoxide)
122667	1,2-Diphenylhydrazine
106898	Epichlorohydrin (1-Chloro-2,3-epoxypropane)
106887	1,2-Epoxybutane
140885	Ethyl acrylate
100414	Ethyl benzene
51796	Ethyl carbamate (Urethane)
75003	Ethyl chloride (Chloroethane)
106934	Ethylene dibromide (Dibromoethane)
107062	Ethylene dichloride (1,2-Dichloroethane)
107211	Ethylene glycol
151564	Ethylene imine (Aziridine)
75218	Ethylene oxide
96457	Ethylene thiourea
75343	Ethylidene dichloride (1,1-Dichloroethane)
50000	Formaldehyde
76448	Heptachlor
118741	Hexachlorobenzene
87683	Hexachlorobutadiene
77474	Hexachlorocyclopentadiene
67721	Hexachloroethane
822060	Hexamethylene-1,6-diisocyanate
680319	Hexamethylphosphoramide
110543	Hexane
302012	Hydrazine
7647010	Hydrochloric acid
7664393	Hydrogen fluoride (hydrofluoric acid)
123319	Hydroquinone
78591	Isophorone
58899	Lindane (all isomers)
108316	Maleic anhydride
67561	Methanol
72435	Methoxychlor
74839	Methyl bromide (Bromomethane)
74873	Methyl chloride (Chloromethane)
71556	Methyl chloroform (1,1,1-Trichloroethane)
78933	Methyl ethyl ketone (2-Butanone)
60344	Methyl hydrazine
74884	Methyl iodide (Iodomethane)
108101	Methyl isobutyl ketone (Hexone)
624839	Methyl isocyanate
80626	Methyl methacrylate
1634044	Methyl tert butyl ether
101144	4,4-Methylene bis(2-chloroaniline)
75092	Methylene chloride (Dichloromethane)
101688	Methylene diphenyl diisocyanate (MDI)
101779	4,4'-Methylenedianiline
91203	Naphthalene
98953	Nitrobenzene
92933	4-Nitrobiphenyl
100027	4-Nitrophenol
79469	2-Nitropropane
684935	N-Nitroso-N-methylurea
62759	N-Nitrosodimethylamine
59892	N-Nitrosomorpholine
56382	Parathion
82688	Pentachloronitrobenzene (Quintobenzene)
87865	Pentachlorophenol
108952	Phenol
106503	p-Phenylenediamine
75445	Phosgene
7803512	Phosphine
7723140	Phosphorus
85449	Phthalic anhydride
1336363	Polychlorinated biphenyls (Aroclors)
1120714	1,3-Propane sultone
57578	beta-Propiolactone
123386	Propionaldehyde
114261	Propoxur (Baygon)
78875	Propylene dichloride (1,2-Dichloropropane)
75569	Propylene oxide
75558	1,2-Propylenimine (2-Methyl aziridine)
91225	Quinoline
106514	Quinone
100425	Styrene
96093	Styrene oxide
1746016	2,3,7,8-Tetrachlorodibenzo-p-dioxin
79345	1,1,2,2-Tetrachloroethane
127184	Tetrachloroethylene (Perchloroethylene)
7550450	Titanium tetrachloride
108883	Toluene
95807	2,4-Toluene diamine
584849	2,4-Toluene diisocyanate
95534	o-Toluidine
8001352	Toxaphene (chlorinated camphene)
120821	1,2,4-Trichlorobenzene
79005	1,1,2-Trichloroethane
79016	Trichloroethylene
95954	2,4,5-Trichlorophenol
88062	2,4,6-Trichlorophenol
121448	Triethylamine
1582098	Trifluralin
540841	2,2,4-Trimethylpentane
108054	Vinyl acetate
593602	Vinyl bromide
75014	Vinyl chloride
75354	Vinylidene chloride (1,1-Dichloroethylene)
1330207	Xylenes (isomers and mixture)
95476	o-Xylenes
108383	m-Xylenes
106423	p-Xylenes
0	Antimony compounds
0	Arsenic compounds (inorganic including arsine)
0	Beryllium compounds
0	Cadmium compounds
0	Chromium compounds
0	Cobalt compounds
0	Coke oven emissions
0	Cyanide compounds [a]
0	Glycol ethers [b]
0	Lead compounds
0	Manganese compounds
0	Mercury compounds
0	Mineral fibers [c]
0	Nickel compounds
0	Polycylic organic matter [d]
0	Radionuclides (including radon) [e]
0	Selenium compounds

Note: For all listings above that contain the word "compounds" and for glycol ethers, the following applies: Unless otherwise specified, these listings are defined as including any unique chemical substance that contains the named chemical (for example, antimony) as part of that chemical's infrastructure.

[a] X'CN where X = H' or any other group where a formal dissociation may occur; for example, KCN or $Ca(CN)_2$.

[b] Includes mono- and diethers of ethylene glycol, diethylene glycol, and triethylene glycol $R\text{-}(OCH_2CH_2)_n\text{-}OR'$ where n = 1, 2 or 3; R = alkyl or aryl groups; R' = R, H or groups that, when removed, yield glycol ethers with the structure $R\text{-}(OCH_2CH_2)_n\text{-}OH$. Polymers are excluded from the glycol category.

[c] Includes glass microfibers, glass wool fibers, rock wool fibers and slag wool fibers, each characterized as "respirable" (fiber diameter less than 3.5 micrometers) and possessing an aspect ratio (fiber length divided by fiber diameter) greater than or equal to 3, as emitted from production of fiber and fiber products.

[d] Includes organic compounds with more than one benzene ring, and that have a boiling point greater than or equal to 100 degrees Celsius.

[e] A type of atom that spontaneously undergoes radioactive decay.

serious air pollutants from smaller "area sources," such as dry cleaners and gas stations, be reduced by 90 percent.

A final marathon negotiating session began late the week of Oct. 15, when conferees worked to resolve their differences on acid rain. The result was an agreement that, with the exception of additional pollution "allowances" granted to Midwest utilities that reduced their sulfur dioxide emissions, followed the Senate bill closely.

After yet another all-night negotiating session, a decade of legislative gridlock came to end when conferees Oct. 22 ratified a final agreement on the bill. The final roadblock was cleared in the wee hours of the morning when the White House gave conferees its approval on a compromise to provide up to $250 million in assistance to workers thrown out of work by the legislation.

Adoption of the conference report (H Rept 101-952) seemed almost anti-climactic. The House voted 401-25 to adopt the conference report on Oct. 26. The Senate acted on an 89-10 vote Oct. 27, clearing S 1630 for the president.

Although the final version was expected to cost the economy $25 billion to $35 billion — substantially more than Bush had said he would tolerate — the cost was no threat to Bush's signing a bill that he had helped nurture for more than 16 months. In the Nov. 15 bill-signing ceremony, Bush took credit for his role in breaking what he called "the logjam that hindered progress on clean air for 13 years." He termed the bill "the most significant air pollution legislation in our nation's history" and ticked off the environmental progress that it promised to accomplish:

- A 56 billion pound reduction in air pollution — "224 pounds for every man, woman, and child in America."
- A 40 percent reduction in smog by the year 2000.
- A 75 percent reduction in dangerous air toxics emissions.
- Reduced dependence on foreign oil "by the next decade" because of the alternative fuel provisions.

In a nod to business concerns, however, Bush stressed that the bill was "balanced" and imposed "reasonable deadlines for those who must comply." And in a written statement, he said he was directing the EPA to implement the act "in the most cost-effective manner possible."

Major Provisions

As enacted, S 1630 (PL 101-549):

Urban Smog

- **State Plans.** Required each state to draw up a plan that included, among other things, enforceable limitations on pollution emissions, provisions for developing air quality data and requirements that stationary sources monitor their emissions. Pollution control plans for non-attainment areas (areas that had not attained the pertinent national smog standard) had to include provisions requiring that existing stationary sources use reasonably available control technology (RACT); that new or modified major stationary sources obtain offsets for their emissions on existing stationary sources; and that contingency measures be automatically implemented when an area failed to meet any applicable milestone, make reasonable further progress or attain the national smog standard by the deadline date. Except under certain conditions, offsets had to be obtained from the same source or other sources in the same non-attainment area.

Ozone Standards

- **Deadlines.** Established five classes of deadlines, beginning with "marginal." Graduated deadlines and minimum control requirements were set for each class — three years for marginal areas, six years for moderate, nine years for serious, 15-17 years for severe and 20 years for extreme.
- **Boundaries of Non-Attainment Areas.** Allowed states to set boundaries of non-attainment areas with approval from the EPA, except that boundaries of serious, severe and extreme ozone and carbon monoxide areas were to be expanded to include the entire metropolitan statistical area or consolidated metropolitan statistical area.
- **Size of Sources Subject to Controls.** Lowered the definition of major source to 50 tons a year of volatile organic compounds (VOCs) in serious ozone areas, 25 tons in severe areas and 10 tons in extreme areas. Thus, states were allowed to impose pollution controls and permit requirements on relatively small sources such as dry cleaners and auto paint shops.
- **Yearly Reductions.** Required all except marginal ozone areas to achieve a 15 percent reduction in VOC emissions within six years and a 3 percent reduction each year thereafter. Reductions in motor vehicle emissions could not be counted. Annual reductions of nitrogen oxides were also required. The EPA was authorized to waive the 3 percent reduction requirement only when all technologically feasible control measures had been used.
- **Federal Implementation Plans.** Required the EPA to issue a federal implementation plan two years after a state failed to submit an adequate state plan. The federal plan could be partial or complete but had to provide for attainment of the air quality standard.

Carbon Monoxide

- **Deadlines.** Set graduated deadlines and minimum control requirements for carbon monoxide emissions — Dec. 31, 1995, for moderate areas and Dec. 31, 2000, for serious areas. In addition, serious areas had to meet specific milestones.

Particulate Matter

- **Deadlines.** Set graduated attainment deadlines and minimum control requirements for emissions of particulate matter (PM-10) — generally, Dec. 31, 1994, for moderate areas and Dec. 31, 2001, for serious areas. In addition, PM-10 areas had to meet specific emissions reductions milestones every three years until the area reached attainment.

Motor Vehicles

- **First-Round Tailpipe Standards.** Set emissions standards for hydrocarbons, carbon monoxide, nitrogen oxides and particulate matter. Forty percent of each automaker's passenger cars and light-duty trucks had to meet those standards by model year 1994, 80 percent by model year 1996 and 100 percent thereafter. By 1998, cars had to contain emission control equipment that would last 10 years or 100,000 miles.
- **Second-Round Tailpipe Standards.** Imposed a second round of tailpipe emission standards — cutting the first-round standards in half — beginning with model year 2003. The EPA administrator could veto the second-

round standards if they were not technologically feasible, cost-effective or necessary.

• **Alternative Fuels.** Required 150,000 clean-fueled vehicles to be sold in California beginning in 1996, with the number rising to 300,000 in later years. Beginning in 1998 in highly polluted cities, fleets of 10 or more motor vehicles would be required to use clean fuels to achieve an 80 percent reduction in emissions for cars and a 50 percent reduction for trucks. The requirement could be delayed for three years, depending on vehicle availability. Rental cars and fleet cars parked at private homes at night were not covered.

• **Reformulated Gasoline.** Required the use of reformulated gasoline in the nine smoggiest cities by 1995. Cities that had not attained carbon monoxide emission standards had to use gasoline containing 2.7 percent oxygen, starting in 1992. The EPA administrator could grant up to a two-year delay if an area's capacity for supplying and distributing the reformulated gasoline was lacking. Volatile organic compounds and toxic emissions had to decrease by 15 percent by 1995; in 2000, emissions had to decrease by 20 percent or more, up to a technologically feasible amount, taking costs into account.

• **Non-Road Vehicles.** Required the EPA to regulate emissions of non-road vehicles within 30 months if study determined it was warranted. Railroad locomotives were not to be included in the study, and state and local governments were pre-empted from regulating new non-road engines smaller than 175 horsepower used in construction or farm equipment.

Air Toxics

• **Emissions Standard.** Set emissions standard for a list of 189 substances and compounds considered to be hazardous air pollutants. Any stationary source that emitted 10 tons a year of any hazardous air pollutant or 25 tons a year of a combination of hazardous air pollutants had to meet the standards. The standards could differentiate among classes, types and sizes of sources so long as there was no delay in compliance. The standards were to require the maximum emissions reduction achievable for new or existing sources, taking into consideration cost, energy requirements and effects on health and the environment not related to air quality. Such reductions could be achieved by any means, including technological pollution controls, process changes, substitution of materials or special training and certification of operators, otherwise known as maximum achievable control technology or MACT.

• **Residual Risk.** Required the EPA administrator to report within six years on the risk to public health remaining, or likely to remain, after sources of hazardous air pollution had applied MACT standards, the available methods and cost of reducing those risks, and the actual health effects on people living in the vicinity of the source. More stringent standards could be applied if the EPA administrator determined them necessary to prevent an adverse environmental effect.

Acid Rain

• **Sulfur Dioxide, Phase I.** Mandated anti-pollution controls to begin Jan. 1, 1995, for 111 plants that emitted sulfur dioxide at a rate above 2.5 pounds per million British thermal units (lbs./mmBtu). Two-year extensions were available to plants that used scrubbers.

• **Sulfur Dioxide, Phase II.** Required a total emissions cap of 8.9 million tons of sulfur dioxide nationwide, beginning Jan. 1, 2000. Utilities were required to reduce their emissions to 1.2 lbs./mmBtu unless they generated less than 75 megawatts and were part of systems with a total capacity less than 250 megawatts. Plants that generated less than 25 megawatts were exempted.

• **Allowance System.** Granted sources one "allowance" for each ton of sulfur dioxide generated in a year. Up to 3.5 million incentive allowances were offered in Phase I to high-sulfur coal plants that made reductions below 1.2 lbs./mmBtu. Allowances could be traded to any unit in the country. Bonus allowances could be offered to "clean" and "growth" states in Phase II, under either a federal or state-option formula. An additional 200,000 annual allowances were allocated to plants in Ohio, Illinois and Indiana during Phase I, and an additional 50,000 allowances to 10 Midwestern plants during Phase II.

• **Nitrogen Oxides.** Mandated controls on nitrogen oxides, to begin Jan. 1, 1995, for 111 plants, with limits of 0.45 lbs./mmBtu for tangentially fired boilers or 0.5 lbs./mmBtu for dry-bottom, wall-fired boilers and cell burners.

Chlorofluorocarbons

• **Production Phaseout.** Phased out production of chlorofluorocarbons (CFCs) that caused or contributed to depletion of stratospheric ozone, a protective layer that protected Earth from the Sun's radiation. Class I CFCs could not be produced after Jan. 1, 2000 (Jan. 1, 2002, in the case of methyl chloroform). Class I CFCs included all fully halogenated CFCs, halons, carbon tetrachloride and methyl chloroform. Class II CFCs could not be produced or used after Jan. 1, 2015, unless they had been used, recovered and recycled; were entirely consumed in the production of other chemicals; or were used to maintain and service appliances manufactured before Jan. 1, 2020. Production of all Class II CFCs was banned after Jan. 1, 2030. Class II covered all transitional substances or partially halogenated chlorine-containing halocarbons.

Global Warming

• **National Goal.** Established a goal of identifying the options for reducing global warming by reducing global methane emissions.

• **Methane Assessment.** Required the EPA administrator to undertake an inventory of methane emissions and to identify those activities, substances and processes that could reduce methane emissions and that were economically justified with or without consideration of environmental benefit.

Job-Loss Benefits

• **Grants.** Authorized $250 million over five years for grants to states to provide needs-based payments, training and employment services to eligible workers laid off or fired as a result of the employer's compliance with the Clean Air Act. Only displaced workers who had used up all of their unemployment benefits and who were enrolled in a job training program at the time the unemployment benefits expired were eligible for these new grants.

Fuel Efficiency

Heavy lobbying by the auto industry and the Bush administration stalled a Senate attempt to raise federal automobile fuel-efficiency standards Sept. 25, 1990, killing the issue for the 101st Congress.

The Senate vote was 57-42, three votes short of the 60 needed to limit debate on the bill. S 1224 (S Rept 101-329) would have forced automakers to increase 1988 corporate average fuel economy (CAFE) levels by 20 percent by 1995 and 40 percent by 2001. The existing standard was 27.5 miles per gallon (mpg).

The legislation, dropped from the clean air package (S 1630 — PL 101-549) in March in exchange for separate floor consideration, got a big boost after Iraq invaded Kuwait on Aug. 2 and set off renewed debate over U.S. dependence on foreign oil. Richard H. Bryan, D-Nev., one of the bill's chief sponsors, said the higher standards would have saved 2.8 million barrels of oil a day and led to 40 mpg fleet averages.

But opposition from the Bush administration offset any momentum Bryan gained from the Persian Gulf crisis. The administration argued that the bill was not economically sound or technically feasible. Energy Secretary James D. Watkins told senators at a Sept. 13 hearing that he and Transportation Secretary Samuel K. Skinner would recommend a veto on those grounds.

Bryan's bill was controversial largely because it would have changed the basic approach of the government's CAFE standards. Under the standards first mandated in 1975, automakers were required to meet across-the-board incremental increases in fuel economy. Bryan's bill would have required percentage increases based on the 1988 fuel-economy averages of each manufacturer's fleet. Thus, Japanese companies that made smaller, more fuel-efficient cars would have had to meet higher standards than U.S. companies, which catered to larger-car markets.

Asian automakers said that the legislation was unfair to those companies that had made the most progress in increasing fuel economy. Domestic manufacturers also opposed the bill, although Chrysler and Ford officials said they would support the Bryan bill if changes in the CAFE standards appeared to be inevitable.

The Senate's failure to cut off debate on the bill came just 11 days after the Senate voted 68-28 to cut off debate on a motion to proceed to consideration of the bill. The intense lobbying campaign paid off for the administration when 11 senators — eight of then Republicans — switched their votes Sept. 25 to vote against the second cloture motion.

In the House, the Energy and Commerce Subcommittee on Energy and Power held a hearing on fuel efficiency standards for the first time in five years, but no further action was taken. Legislation to raise the CAFE standards had been consistently blocked by the full committee's chairman, John D. Dingell, D-Mich., the Big Three's strongest political ally in Congress. Dingell allowed the hearing only after environmental groups made pleas to the House leadership to allow a CAFE bill to bypass him.

Energy Tax Breaks

One of President Bush's only victories on energy policy in 1990 was the enactment of a new set of tax breaks to encourage domestic energy production. The package, which was added to the budget-reconciliation bill (HR 5835 — PL 101-508), included a 5-cents-a-gallon increase in gasoline taxes. But a broad-based energy tax that would have raised taxes on home heating oil did not survive budget summit negotiations. *(Reconciliation bill, p. 55)*

The reconciliation bill provided $2.5 billion in energy-related tax breaks, primarily to benefit oil and gas operations, over five years. The bill extended tax credits for the provision of non-conventional and alcohol fuels; provided new credits for ethanol production and costs associated with certain difficult oil-recovery projects; expanded percentage-depletion deductions allowed independent oil and gas producers; and provided alternative minimum tax relief for oil and gas producers.

The bill also extended through the end of 1991 tax credits for businesses that invested in solar or geothermal energy. A credit for ocean thermal energy was allowed to expire.

Under the legislation, the excise tax on gasoline, diesel and other motor fuels increased by a 5 cents a gallon, which brought the federal tax on gasoline to 14 cents a gallon. The House wanted no increase; the Senate wanted a boost of 9.5 cents a gallon.

Natural Gas Decontrol

Congress in 1989 cleared a measure (HR 1722 — PL 101-60) to lift wellhead price controls from natural gas for the first time since 1954, when the Supreme Court ruled that such governmental controls were legal.

In contrast to previous years, when gas decontrol was one of the most contentious issues on Capitol Hill, the legislation virtually sailed through Congress, as members from gas-producing and gas-consuming states agreed that controls kept very little gas below market prices and had thus become largely irrelevant to consumers.

The measure ended 35 years of wrangling over price controls by decontrolling natural gas as contracts expired or were renegotiated no later than Jan. 1, 1993. Gas not under contract would be decontrolled immediately.

Background

Federal controls on interstate natural gas dated back to 1954, but they touched off bitter controversy in Congress in the mid-1970s when they were blamed for market distortions and gas shortages. Congress cleared the Natural Gas Policy Act (PL 95-621) in 1978 to encourage gas production by allowing higher prices for "new gas" from wells drilled after enactment, but it left controls on pre-1978 "old gas." New gas was totally decontrolled on Jan. 1, 1987, but controls remained in place on old gas. *(Congress and the Nation Vol. V, p. 468)*

Gas price controls were the subject of a lengthy but inconclusive dispute in the 98th Congress. While legislation stalled at the committee level and never reached the full House, the Senate Energy and Natural Resources Committee brought legislation to the Senate floor in November 1983, only to see both pro-control and decontrol amendments fail by overwhelming majorities. *(Congress and the Nation Vol. VI, p. 387)*

House Action

The legislation moved easily through the House. Behind the momentum for decontrol were two factors not in evidence in 1983. First, the partial gas decontrol that began with the Natural Gas Policy Act had ushered in an era of lower gas prices, not the higher ones widely feared. Second, very little gas was still controlled by law at below-market prices — less than 10 percent of domestic production. Although an estimated 35 percent to 40 percent of domestic gas supplies was still subject to controls, most sold at market prices, and some was actually kept at above-market prices by controls.

"Six years ago this bill would have had no chance for enactment," said Philip R. Sharp, D-Ind., chairman of the Energy Subcommittee on Energy and Power and author of HR 1722. Sharp had opposed gas decontrol in the 1970s and early 1980s on the grounds that it would hurt consumers.

For most decontrol proponents, the only apparent sticking point was when to terminate all controls. Major gas producers and trade associations pushed for decontrol upon enactment. But some independent producers, who benefited from above-market, incentive prices for some of their gas, and pipeline companies, some of which feared immediate decontrol could force them to absorb price increases, called for a phase-in period of up to five years. The Jan. 1, 1993, compromise date proposed by Sharp would end all controls about 3½ years after a mid-1989 enactment date.

Energy Committee Chairman John D. Dingell, D-Mich., who had once reportedly vowed that price ceilings would be lifted only "over my dead body," presided over a strife-free markup of the decontrol bill. Panel members who had fought bitterly for years over the issue spent barely half an hour congratulating one another and praising the measure before approving it by voice vote on April 11. HR 1722 (H Rept 101-29) was formally reported April 17.

The measure was then summoned to the House floor under suspension of the rules, an accelerated procedure that prohibited amendments and required a two-thirds vote for passage. The bill breezed through by voice vote, also on April 17.

Senate Action

Gas decontrol momentum picked up in the Senate April 13 when J. Bennett Johnston, D-La., chairman of the Energy and Natural Resources Committee, introduced his own decontrol bill (S 783), which was virtually identical to the House measure.

But gas decontrol ran into some trouble at its debut hearing before the Energy and Natural Resources Committee May 8. Longtime gas decontrol foe Howard M. Metzenbaum, D-Ohio, insisted the legislation before the committee would do "nothing, zero, zip" for consumers faced with higher gas prices, and he told colleagues he was "in no hurry to pass this legislation, now or if it comes to the Senate floor." Metzenbaum said he would probably not raise serious opposition to the legislation in the committee markup but indicated that he might mount a filibuster on the Senate floor.

Witnesses representing the Bush administration, gas producers, gas pipelines and industrial gas users told the committee that lifting remaining price controls would rationalize the gas market, help boost supplies and not boost prices to consumers — at least in the short run.

But other witnesses criticized the bill, claiming that decontrol would eventually shift drilling capital from independent producers to major oil and gas companies, increasing "big-oil" control. Witnesses also predicted shortages and higher prices as the existing gas "bubble" disappeared and warned that, with no control mechanism in place, nothing would protect consumers from escalating prices.

Shrugging off amendments at a May 17 markup, the committee voted 17-2 to substitute Johnston's bill for the text of the House-passed version. Senate Energy reported HR 1722 (S Rept 101-39) on May 31.

When the gas decontrol package reached the floor on June 8, Metzenbaum made good on his threats to try to amend, kill or at least discuss the bill at length. The Ohio Democrat's pile of 31 amendments and his apparent willingness to air fully his misgivings about the measure prompted James A. McClure, R-Idaho, the Energy Committee's ranking minority member, on June 9 to file a petition to shut off debate on the bill.

Metzenbaum's floor attacks on the Energy and Natural Resources Committee and oil-and-gas state senators supporting the bill drew an angry response from Johnston. "I would be severely and personally resentful of the remarks of my distinguished colleague from Ohio had I not heard this story before. It is the same old tired rhetoric," Johnston said.

As a freshman senator in 1977, Metzenbaum had teamed up with James Abourezk, D-S.D. (1973-79), to stage a wrenching, nine-day, post-cloture filibuster against a bill that deregulated some natural gas prices. Although the bill finally passed, the Senate — stung by that experience — overhauled its rules in 1979 to limit post-cloture filibusters to 100 hours of debate. *(Congress and the Nation Vol. V, pp. 468, 915)*

The cloture vote set for June 13 on HR 1722 was never held. Metzenbaum, who lost on two amendments the week of June 5, offered another four the week of June 12, lost on all of them and did not seek to delay the vote on final passage June 14.

Bill Bradley, D-N.J., also attempted to amend the bill, offering a proposal to empower the Federal Energy Regulatory Commission (FERC) to order the nation's principal interstate gas pipelines to act as "open access" carriers. Pipelines had once purchased gas from producers, transported it and then sold it to distribution companies. But by 1989, they were beginning to act as carriers for distribution companies and others who bought gas on their own and wanted it delivered by the pipelines.

Bradley wanted that arrangement codified in law, but Johnston argued that the FERC already had that authority. Furthermore, he said, at least 20 of the nation's 23 major interstate gas pipelines were already certified as open-access carriers by the FERC, and the remainder had applications pending.

Johnston's motion to table (kill) the Bradley amendment was agreed to June 14 by a vote of 55-44.

After brushing aside several other amendments, the Senate passed HR 1722 June 14 by a vote of 82-17.

Conference Action

The bill then went through a short, but contentious, negotiating session June 20, in which House and Senate conferees resolved the single difference between their two versions of the bill. They agreed to create a subcategory of gas from newly "spudded" (begun) wells in existing fields that were subject to existing contracts. Any such well spudded after the bill's enactment date would qualify; gas from such wells would be decontrolled beginning May 15, 1991.

The House wanted that gas decontrolled after March 23, 1989, the date Sharp introduced the original version of the decontrol legislation. But the Senate wanted that gas treated no differently from any other, which would have kept it under controls until Jan. 1, 1993.

The negotiators were handicapped by a lack of authoritative information on how many wells would be affected. Each side claimed the support of gas producers, and each side insisted that its version would enhance prospects for added drilling, while the other would cause wells to go undrilled.

At various points in the negotiations, both sides threatened to pull out and let the issue languish until after the July Fourth recess. But a strong desire to get a bill to Bush before then prevailed, and neither side carried through with its threats. Instead, conferees agreed to the compromise provision to create a new category of gas from newly spudded wells in natural gas fields.

The Senate adopted the conference report (H Rept 101-100) by voice vote on June 22. Final action came on July 12 as the House adopted the conference report by voice vote. President Bush signed HR 1722 on July 26.

Alternative Power

Congress in 1990 cleared legislation (HR 4808 — PL 101-575) that gave regulatory breaks to producers of alternative forms of power. As signed into law Nov. 15, the measure removed limits on the size of wind, solar, geothermal and waste-based power plants that could take advantage of regulatory breaks and exemptions first provided only to small plants in 1978.

A provision by Senate Energy and Natural Resources Committee Chairman J. Bennett Johnston, D-La., eased license requirements for private uranium enrichment facilities, including one planned for northern Louisiana.

Background. Congress in 1978 enacted the Public Utility Regulatory Policies Act (PL 95-617) to attempt to foster the fledgling alternative-energy industry by exempting small producers from state and federal utility regulations and requiring existing local utilities to buy electricity from them. That law was enacted when the nation was looking for ways to maximize domestic power sources as it rebounded from its first major energy crisis and headed into its second. *(Congress and the Nation Vol. V, p. 468)*

To appease utilities worried about unfair competition, Congress limited eligibility to alternative producers with only a small fraction of the capacity of the biggest conventional plants: 30 megawatts to 80 megawatts, depending on the technology involved, compared with 1,100 megawatts for big traditional plants.

The existing law and market forces fostered a growing alternative-energy industry, although it still provided just a small percentage of the nation's electricity needs. A House Energy Committee staff memo in 1990 said that wind and solar energy producers nationwide had grown from "virtually nothing" in 1978 to 1,500 megawatts and 2,500 megawatts, respectively — "enough power each year for the residential needs of a city the size of San Francisco." Likewise, geothermal production (tapping heat from beneath the Earth's surface) increased from 900 megawatts in 1980 to 2,600 in 1989. Nevertheless, only about 2 percent of the generating capacity installed from fiscal 1980 to 1988 came from all renewable sources, according to the Congressional Research Service.

Renewable-energy companies said they needed more room to grow. The law's limits did not bother them in years past because all alternative-energy plants were small; by 1990, bigger plants were technologically feasible.

Legislative Action. Although HR 4808 drew wide support in both the House and Senate, it became entangled in unrelated legislative disputes that almost killed it on several occasions. The House Energy and Commerce Committee reported HR 4808 (H Rept 101-885) on Oct. 16. The House passed the bill by voice vote under suspension of the rules Oct. 23. The Senate Energy and Natural Resources Committee Sept. 21 reported a companion measure (S 2415 — S Rept 101-470). The full Senate passed S 2415 by voice vote Sept. 26. The Senate then passed an amended HR 4808 by voice vote Oct. 27. The House accepted the Senate changes the next day, clearing the measure.

Energy Conservation

Legislation (S 247 — PL 101-440) to redefine national energy conservation goals and to promote state energy efficiency programs was signed into law on Oct. 18, 1990. The measure updated parts of the wide-ranging 1975 Energy Policy and Conservation Act (PL 94-163), which provided states with federal funds for conservation programs such as low-income home weatherization, school energy-saving projects and conservation training. *(Congress and the Nation Vol. IV, p. 235)*

The 1975 measure had been enacted following an energy scare brought on by escalating oil prices during the oil embargo of 1973. Backers of S 247 said it would help make the nation less dependent on foreign oil, a situation made more precarious by the Persian Gulf crisis. *(Persian Gulf War, p. 299)*

S 247 amended the 1975 law by requiring states seeking federal energy conservation funds to set a goal of increasing statewide energy efficiency by 10 percent by the year 2000. In addition, the bill required states to have comprehensive energy emergency policies in place for supply disruptions and to improve integration of state and local energy conservation programs.

The legislation also ordered the Department of Energy to review and revise, if warranted, a formula it used to allocate low-income weatherization funds to the states. The department was told to determine whether the funding formula should be revamped to give more weight to energy assistance for cooling. The existing formula emphasized heating assistance, which meant the warmer states stood to receive fewer funds.

The Senate Energy and Natural Resources Committee reported S 247 (S Rept 101-235) on Jan. 10. The Senate passed the bill by voice vote Jan. 25. The House Energy and Commerce Committee had reported a companion measure (HR 711 — H Rept 101-646) on July 30, 1989. The House passed HR 711 by voice vote under suspension of the rules Oct. 1, 1990, then passed S 247 by voice vote in lieu. The Senate accepted the House amendments Oct. 4, clearing the bill.

Hydrogen Fuel Research

Congress created a hydrogen fuel research program in the Department of Energy in 1990 and named it for the late senator Spark M. Matsunaga, D-Hawaii.

Alternative Fuels

Use of motor fuels other than gasoline had been looked to in the 1970s and 1980s as a way to reduce U.S. dependence on foreign oil. In 1990, faced with diminishing returns from traditional air pollution controls, lawmakers and the administration turned to proposals to mandate a partial shift to alternative-fueled vehicles to ease severe ozone and toxic-air pollution in major cities.

Following are the main alternative fuels that could be used as substitutes for traditional, liquid, oil-derived motor vehicle fuels, such as gasoline or diesel fuels:

Methanol. An alcohol fuel derived from natural gas, coal, wood or municipal wastes and used as a pure fuel (M-100) or as an 85 percent additive to gasoline (M-85). Its potential to reduce air pollutants — particularly the emissions of ozone-forming hydrocarbons — was hotly debated. The Environmental Protection Agency (EPA) said M-85 and M-100 could dramatically reduce hydrocarbons, but the oil industry and Sierra Research, a California consulting company, disputed that contention.

Ethanol. Also an alcohol fuel, derived from fermented agricultural commodities such as corn, wheat and barley; usually blended with gasoline to form gasohol. From 5 percent to 10 percent of motor fuel was sold as gasohol in 1990. Emissions resulted in less ozone-forming hydrocarbons than gasoline.

Compressed Natural Gas. Considered one of the cleanest alternatives because of low hydrocarbon emissions that were relatively non-ozone producing. The EPA also expected a 50 percent reduction in tailpipe emissions of carbon monoxide. However, compressed natural gas did emit a significant quantity of nitrogen oxides, and it required refitting gasoline-powered cars.

Propane and Butane. Components of liquefied petroleum gas, derived by processing natural gas and refining crude oil. It had similar air-quality benefits to natural gas vehicles — that is, less ozone-forming hydrocarbons than gasoline.

Electricity. Electric vehicles powered by rechargeable batteries. They still required considerable research and development — particularly in developing small, long-range battery power — before they could be commercially available.

Hydrogen. Produced from natural gas, petroleum, coal or water. It had low exhaust emissions and, because hydrogen reacts with oxygen to produce water, virtually no hydrocarbon emissions. But hydrogen could not be compressed effectively, creating the problem of finding room to store it on cars.

Reformulated Gasoline. Gasoline whose composition had been changed to achieve more benign emission characteristics, both from the tailpipe and from evaporative emissions. Though some versions were sold in Detroit and Southern California, reformulated gasoline was still in development. It was the favored alternative of the oil and auto industries. The Energy Department expected it to have less reactive hydrocarbon emissions and less benzene emissions than existing gasoline.

Matsunaga, who had died on April 15, had long pressed the government to investigate hydrogen as an alternative energy source.

Hydrogen was considered to have a very important potential role as an energy storage medium, especially for solar energy, which could be produced efficiently only during certain daylight hours — and then only when the sky was clear. By 1990, however, the only widespread use of hydrogen as a fuel occurred in the space program, where no practical alternatives were available. It seemed likely that any new applications for hydrogen would remain infeasible until the cost of producing hydrogen was reduced significantly.

Matsunaga introduced S 639 in 1989 to support a strong federal research, development and demonstration program for low-cost hydrogen production technologies. He had been pushing similar legislation for years, arguing that until the costs of producing hydrogen could be reduced, consumers would be denied the benefits of the alternative fuel, especially its environmental advantages.

As cleared, S 639 (PL 101-566) called for spending $20 million for the new hydrogen research program in fiscal 1992-95. The Senate passed the bill (S Rept 101-385) by voice vote on Oct. 16; the House passed it by voice vote under suspension of the rules on Oct. 23. President Bush signed the measure Nov. 15.

Octane Labeling

After perfunctory debate, the House Oct. 23, 1990, passed by voice vote a measure (HR 5520) to encourage states to crack down on gasoline dealers who sold low-octane fuel at high-octane prices, cheating customers out of millions of dollars a year. The Senate never acted on the legislation, however, and it died at the end of the 101st Congress.

As passed, HR 5520 would have made prosecuting service station owners easier, allowed states to order businesses to stop selling mislabeled gas immediately and broadened the octane-labeling law to include new fuels such as gasohol.

Although no firm national figures existed, a General Accounting Office (GAO) investigation uncovered big problems in states that did not conduct regular octane-testing programs. In some areas tested for GAO, more than half of the gasoline was below octane by as much as six points. According to the GAO report, which was released in April, relatively little mislabeling occurred in 20 states that had active octane-testing programs.

One purpose of the bill seemed to be to raise the consciousness level of the issue. That tack appeared to have some success. After Congress began looking into the matter, several states began testing programs or considered doing so.

HR 5520 (H Rept 101-823) was reported from House Energy and Commerce Oct. 10.

Pipeline Inspections

Prompted by pipeline accidents off the Gulf of Mexico, Congress in 1990 cleared legislation (HR 4888) that required owners of gas pipelines in the gulf to inspect and rebury exposed lines.

Rep. W. J. "Billy" Tauzin, D-La., sponsored the bill after two accidents occurred in which boats slammed into exposed pipelines and set off explosions that claimed 13 lives. A cross section of interest groups in the area, including pipeline owners, the fishing industry and vessel operators who serviced the Gulf's oil platforms, supported the measure.

As enacted, the law applied to pipelines in the Gulf of Mexico in up to 15 feet of water. The law required pipeline owners to inspect each pipeline periodically, to mark exposed pipelines with buoys until buried as required and to tell the government about them so vessel owners and operators could be warned of the dangers.

Three House committees shared jurisdiction over HR 4888. Public Works and Transportation (H Rept 101-814, Part I) reported it Oct. 5, and Energy and Commerce (H Rept 101-814, Part II) and Merchant Marine and Fisheries (H Rept 101-814, Part III) reported it Oct. 10. The House passed the bill by voice vote under suspension of the rules Oct. 15. The Senate accepted the House bill without change, passing it by voice vote Oct. 27. President Bush signed HR 4888 into law (PL 101-599) on Nov. 16.

Strategic Oil Reserves

Backing off from repeated veto threats, President Bush on Sept. 15, 1990, signed a bill (S 2088 — PL 101-383) to expand the nation's rainy-day supply of crude oil and to create a second reserve for refined products such as heating oil. Bush retreated from his veto threats after Iraq's invasion of Kuwait on Aug. 2 heightened concerns over U.S. dependence on foreign oil. *(Persian Gulf War, p. 299)*

On Aug. 10, Bush had signed S 2952 (PL 101-360), a one-month extension of the Strategic Petroleum Reserve (SPR), pending approval of S 2088. The SPR's existing authority expired Aug. 15. The Senate passed the bill by voice vote Aug. 2. The House followed suit Aug. 4, clearing the measure.

Congress failed to clear legislation (HR 5731) aimed at pressuring Bush to sell off 10 million barrels of oil from the SPR to hold down the price of gasoline, which had shot up in the weeks following the invasion and an ensuing worldwide trade embargo against Iraq.

Background

The Energy Department's Strategic Petroleum Reserve was a huge supply of unrefined crude set up in 1975 (PL 94-163) in response to the 1973-74 oil embargo. The reserve, stored in salt domes in Louisiana and Texas, had grown fairly constantly since 1977 and by mid-1990 contained nearly 580 million barrels. But the number of days of protection the SPR provided dropped as energy use and imports increased. The system could have replaced up to 110 days of imports in the mid-1980s, but that figure had dipped to fewer than 80 days in 1990, according to the Senate Energy Committee. *(SPR creation, Congress and the Nation Vol. IV, p. 235)*

Even if the system reached its 750 million-barrel goal within the next several years — it was being filled at a rate of 40,000 barrels a day — that cushion could have dropped to as low as 50 days by 2010, the committee said.

The administration said increasing the reserve to 1 billion barrels would be too expensive. The country already spent about $20 billion on the stockpile, and it was expected to cost several billion dollars more to reach 750 million barrels. It would cost many billions of dollars more to hit 1 billion barrels.

Legislation Action

Energy Department officials told Congress that they would urge Bush to veto any SPR measure that expanded the size of the reserve. They also opposed creation of a reserve for refined products.

The two provisions had wide support in Congress before Iraq's invasion of Kuwait, however, and overwhelming support afterward, making it unlikely that either chamber would have sustained a Bush veto.

The administration's position was weakened by the rhetorical beating that lawmakers from both parties laid on Bush for refusing to draw oil from the 580 million-barrel reserve, which they said would not only have offset the loss of Iraqi and Kuwaiti oil but also would have helped hold down the sharply rising price of gasoline.

For those reasons, Energy Department officials dropped their opposition to both provisions. Deputy Energy Secretary W. Henson Moore told the Senate Energy Committee on Sept. 13 that the administration would not oppose the conference report on S 2088. The decision, Moore said, reflected "political reality," not a change in the administration's philosophical objection: that the multibillion-dollar cost of the provisions was too high.

The Senate Energy and Natural Resources Committee reported S 2088 (S Rept 101-289) on May 15. The Senate passed the bill by voice vote May 22. The House Energy and Commerce Committee reported a companion measure (HR 3193 — H Rept 101-604) on July 16. The same day, the House first passed HR 3193 by voice vote under suspension of the rules, then passed an amended S 2088 in lieu. Both the House, by 391-0, and the Senate, by voice vote, adopted the conference report (H Rept 101-698) on Sept. 13.

As cleared, S 2088:

- Forced the administration to expand its plan to fill the SPR to 1 billion barrels from the existing goal of 750 million.
- Created a reserve for refined petroleum products. In a compromise, the House agreed that the reserve would be undertaken only as a three-year test and would contain many fewer than the 20 million barrels originally envisioned. The president also would be allowed to trade crude oil for imported refined products.

• Expanded the president's authority to sell off oil from the reserve. Previously, he could dip into the reserve only to respond to an emergency caused by an import disruption, a natural disaster or sabotage. The bill allowed him to act any time "a domestic energy supply shortage of significant scope or duration" existed or was imminent.

Sale from the Reserve

Less than two weeks after he signed the SPR bill, Bush announced that he would release 5 million barrels for sale from the reserve. The president was relying in part on a provision in S 2088 that allowed him to draw out that much as a test of the system.

Bush had been under heavy bipartisan pressure to sell off some of the reserve to calm oil markets as prices spiraled toward $40 a barrel in response to the crisis in the Middle East. Democrats wanted Bush to sell off 10 million more barrels. The House on Sept. 28 passed HR 5731 by voice vote under suspension of the rules, and the Senate Energy Committee reported the bill (S Rept 101-548) on Oct. 19.

After peaking in early October, however, oil prices declined significantly, easing pressure on both lawmakers and the president to do something about gasoline prices. By the end of the year, the weekly world average had dropped back to $25 a barrel. The full Senate did not take up HR 5731 before adjournment, and it died with the end of the 101st Congress.

Antarctica Mining Ban

Congress, seeking to avert environmental despoliation of Antarctica, enacted legislation (HR 3977 — PL 101-594) in 1990 to bar U.S. exploration or development of minerals on the ice-covered continent. Lawmakers also cleared a joint resolution (S J Res 206 — PL 101-620) in 1990 calling on President Bush to begin negotiations aimed at tighter international guardianship of the continent. In October 1991, the president signed a treaty barring mineral exploration in Antarctica, but the Senate did not act on ratification by the end of the 102nd Congress. *(Details, p. 529)*

HR 3977 and S J Res 206 reflected a broad agreement in Congress on the importance of protecting Antarctica's environment. The administration professed it shared those goals but originally opposed HR 3977, fearing that it would hamper the administration's ability to conduct foreign policy. Enactment of the ban on U.S. development and exploration came only after supporters of the bill agreed to the administration's insistence that U.S. environmental laws not be applied to government activities in Antarctica.

As cleared, HR 3977 made it illegal for any U.S. citizen to engage in, finance or otherwise assist in any mineral development in Antarctica. The regulation was to stay in effect until the conclusion of an international treaty that indefinitely prohibited any Antarctic mineral activity. Violations would be punished under the regulations of the 1984 Antarctic Marine Living Resources Convention Act.

The measure also stated that it was the sense of Congress that the president should urge the secretary of state to negotiate an international treaty to ban mineral activity in Antarctica indefinitely. The legislation authorized $1 million in fiscal 1991-92 for the under secretary of commerce to carry out the provisions of the bill and $500,000 for the secretary of state in fiscal 1991-92 to carry out the treaty negotiations.

HR 3977 was reported from House Merchant Marine and Fisheries (H Rept 101-692, Part I) on Sept. 10 and passed by voice vote under suspension of the rules in the House Oct. 15. The Senate passed an amended version by voice vote Oct. 25. The House accepted the Senate changes the next day, clearing the measure. Bush signed the bill Nov. 16.

S J Res 206 called on the Bush administration to begin international negotiations concerning the administration of Antarctica. The joint resolution urged the Bush administration to regard Antarctica as a part of the global ecological commons and to push for this classification during the multinational discussions.

The Senate passed S J Res 206 by voice vote Oct. 4. The House passed an amended version by voice vote under suspension of the rules Oct. 23. The Senate accepted the House amendments Oct. 25. The president signed S J Res 206 on Nov. 16.

Uranium Enrichment

Legislation to revise and strengthen the Energy Department's troubled uranium enrichment enterprise failed to win enactment in the 101st Congress. The enterprise sold nuclear fuel to utilities and provided core material for some of the government's deadliest warheads.

The Senate, 73-26, on July 20, 1989, passed S 83 (S Rept 101-60), sponsored by Wendell H. Ford, D-Ky., to spin off the uranium enrichment enterprise into a government corporation designed to operate at a profit. But the House balked. In 1990, Ford succeeded in attaching S 83 to the 1990 budget-reconciliation bill (HR 5835). But the measure was stripped from the final version in conference with the House. *(Reconciliation, p. 55)*

Ford also attached the uranium enrichment language to an alternative energy bill. But again the House refused to act, and Ford ultimately agreed to let the alternative fuels measure clear without his provision. *(Alternative power, p. 486)*

Provisions restructuring the uranium enrichment enterprise were finally cleared as part of the 1992 energy bill. *(Story, p. 500)*

NRC Fees

Congress in 1990 ordered the Nuclear Regulatory Commission (NRC) to collect all of its operating costs for a five-year period from fees imposed on the nuclear power industry. Conferees on the 1990 budget-reconciliation act (HR 5835 — PL 101-508) agreed to impose a projected $287 million a year in new fees on nuclear power producers to reduce the deficit by $1.6 billion over a five-year period. *(Reconciliation, p. 55)*

The NRC had been under a congressional mandate to recover 45 percent of its costs from such fees. The new provision raised that figure to 100 percent through fiscal 1995.

The agreement — by leaders of the Senate Environment Committee and the House Interior and Energy committees — represented a major concession by the Senate, which in the past had resisted House and administration attempts to raise NRC fees substantially. In return, House members accepted a Senate proposal to limit the fee increase to five years.

Oil-Spill Liability

Congressional and public outrage over the March 24, 1989, *Exxon Valdez* oil spill did what years of inconclusive wrangling had never achieved. It erased the key difference between the House and Senate on oil-spill liability legislation, which led to enactment in 1990 of a "get tough" bill (HR 1465 — PL 101-380) intended to prevent oil spills and punish those responsible for spills that did occur.

Environmentalists had been pressing Congress to enact a comprehensive liability bill since the mid-1970s. And the House and the Senate for years had agreed on the rough outlines of oil-spill legislation. Bills envisioned taxing imported and domestic oil to create a huge fund to clean up spills and compensate for damages. A spiller's liability would be capped at a level high enough to take care of most spills, and the fund would pay any further costs. However, spillers found guilty of gross negligence or willful misconduct or who failed to observe federal regulations would be liable for all cleanup and damage costs.

Although other issues occasionally stymied action over the years, the primary obstacle concerned whether a federal liability and compensation law should override, or pre-empt, state laws. The Senate said no, insisting that states with their own oil-spill laws and cleanup funds should be allowed to keep them, even if that meant exposing spillers to unlimited liability. (In 1990, at least 19 states had laws imposing unlimited liabilities on oil spillers.) Proponents of the hands-off approach argued that other federal environmental laws allowed states to keep and enforce their own statutes.

The House insisted on pre-emption, however, arguing that it made little sense to impose a national liability and compensation system that did not replace the patchwork of conflicting state laws. And there matters stood, with neither side willing to give way.

As some lawmakers had predicted would happen, it took a catastrophe to break the legislative stalemate. That occurred when the *Exxon Valdez* ran aground and dumped more than 10 million gallons of oil into Alaska's Prince William Sound; it was the largest spill in U.S. history. Total costs of cleanup, restoration and economic damage were initially estimated at $1 billion or more.

1989 Action

Both chambers once again set to work drafting a national liability law. The Senate Environment and Public Works Committee approved S 686 (S Rept 101-94) on July 27, 1989. The legislation, which was formally reported July 28, set up a $1 billion fund to clean up spills and set liability limits on tankers, barges, onshore and offshore facilities and deepwater ports. It did not pre-empt state liability law.

The Senate passed the measure Aug. 4, 99-0, after amending it to raise the liability limits. Senate Majority Leader George J. Mitchell, D-Maine, a leader of the effort to pass a liability bill, initially opposed the higher liability limits for fear they would scuttle the bill. He gave in when it became clear that a majority in the Senate backed the increases. But he warned that he would not send the bill to conference with the House if that chamber insisted on pre-empting state liability laws.

For a while, it seemed that the House would approve a pre-emption statute as it had repeatedly in the past. Bills reported by the Public Works Committee (HR 3027 — H Rept 101-241, Part I) Sept. 13 and the Merchant Marine Committee (HR 1465 — H Rept 101-242, Part II) Sept. 18 carried pre-emption language and restricted the uses of state cleanup and compensation funds.

But when the legislation came to the floor, the mood in the House was definitely pro-environment and anti-big oil. Critics of pre-emption repeatedly invoked the *Exxon Valdez* disaster, arguing that the House should not reward big oil by setting up national liability limits and junking stricter state laws. The House Nov. 8 reversed more than a decade of tradition and on a **key vote of 279-143 (R 75-99; D 204-44)** adopted a package of amendments to HR 1465 that included provisions to strike the pre-emption language. The House passed the bill on Nov. 9, on a 375-5 vote. *(1989 key votes, p. 1021)*

The Senate passed an amended HR 1465 by voice vote Nov. 19.

1990 Action

The differences between the House and Senate versions were worked out in conference in 1990. The most significant difference was whether to require tankers and barges to have double hulls (double bottoms and sides) or only double bottoms to help prevent spills when vessels ran aground. The House bill required all tankers carrying oil to U.S. ports to have double bottoms within seven years and double hulls within 15 years. But the Senate Aug. 3, 1989, had rejected the double-hull mandate, 51-48.

The House reinforced its position on Feb. 7, 1990, agreeing 376-37 to a motion to instruct its conferees to insist on a double-hull provision. The shipping and oil industries and the Bush administration all preferred the Senate version. Conferees ultimately settled on a provision halfway between the two positions. It would require almost all tankers to have double hulls by the year 2010.

Final action came when the Senate adopted the conference report (H Rept 101-653) Aug. 2 by a vote of 99-0 and the House adopted it Aug. 4 (in the session that began Aug. 3) by a vote of 360-0. President Bush signed HR 1465 on Aug. 18.

Major Provisions

As cleared, HR 1465:

- Increased spillers' liability many times over existing federal limits and imposed stiffer civil and criminal penalties. Liability would top $200 million for big tankers.
- Required spillers to pay for cleaning up oil spills and compensated parties economically injured by them.
- Continued to allow states to impose unlimited liability on shippers.
- Authorized using money from a federal fund, subject to annual appropriations, to pay for cleanup and compensation costs not covered by spillers. The fund, designed eventually to contain $1 billion, was to be financed by a recently enacted 5-cents-a-barrel oil tax.
- Required shippers to draft "worst-case" oil-spill response plans for quick cleanup.
- Enhanced the federal government's oil-spill response capability. District response groups were to be positioned

across the county to aid strike teams, and a national command center was to be established in Elizabeth City, N.C.

- Expanded the president's power to take control of a spiller's cleanup operations.
- Required the government to do an audit of the structural soundness of the Trans-Alaska Pipeline, taking into account safety, health and environmental protection.
- Established a multi-agency oil-pollution panel to coordinate federal research.
- Stiffened anti-drug and anti-alcohol laws for ship operators by requiring testing for certain workers and threatening substance abusers with license revocation.
- Blocked oil or gas drilling off the coast of North Carolina until Oct. 1, 1991.

Offshore Drilling Bans

As it had since 1982, Congress in 1989 and 1990 included bans on offshore oil and gas drilling in the annual appropriations bill for the Interior Department and related agencies.

In 1989, Congress approved one-year moratoriums on leasing and drilling in areas off Alaska, California, Florida, Massachusetts and a broad stretch of the Atlantic Coast from Rhode Island to Maryland. These provisions were part of the fiscal 1990 Interior appropriations bill (HR 2788 — PL 101-121).

In 1990, President Bush sought to forestall legislative action when he announced on June 26 a ban for the rest of the 20th century on drilling in huge areas off the California, Florida and New England coasts. But lawmakers whose regions were left unprotected by the administration lobbied for a more restrictive policy.

The one-year moratorium included in the final version of the fiscal 1991 Interior appropriations bill (HR 5769 — PL 101-512) encompassed all the areas included in the administration's drilling ban as well as Alaska's Bristol Bay, the Florida Panhandle and a portion of the mid-Atlantic region stretching from New Jersey to Maryland.

Senate conferees accepted the House language in exchange for an agreement to drop a provision to raise fees for cattle ranchers who grazed their cattle on public lands. *(Grazing fees, p. 518)*

A similar moratorium on oil and gas drilling was included in the fiscal 1992 Interior appropriations bill (HR 2686 — PL 102-154) in 1991. A move to include offshore oil drilling bans in the 1992 energy bill ultimately went awry in a dispute over whether one of the provisions would violate the terms of the 1990 budget agreement and trigger a sequester. Although both the House and Senate had approved versions of the drilling bans, conferees were unable to resolve the budget problem and decided to drop the entire section on offshore drilling from the final bill. *(Energy bill, p. 500)*

Coastal Zone Management

Congress in 1990 revamped and expanded the 1972 Coastal Zone Management Act (CZMA) as part of the fiscal 1991 budget-reconciliation bill (HR 5835 — PL 101-508).

Differing versions of the rewrite had been approved by the House (HR 4450) and the Senate Commerce Committee (S 2782). The House approved the revamping of the law again as part of the Merchant Marine Committee's contribution to the deficit-reduction bill, leaving it to conferees from Senate Commerce and House Merchant Marine to agree on the final language.

HR 5835 extended the CZMA through fiscal 1995 and gave states more say over federal activities off their shores.

Separately, Congress renewed and expanded a moratorium on federal offshore oil and gas leases as part of the Interior appropriations bill. *(Story, above)*

Background

The CZMA (PL 92-583) used federal grants to entice states into drafting plans for protecting their shore areas from the adverse effects of development. It also promised states that federal coastline activities would be "consistent" with federally approved state plans. *(Congress and the Nation Vol. III, p. 799)*

In 1982, the Supreme Court watered down the consistency provision when it held in *Secretary of the Interior v. California* that the law did not cover federal oil and gas drilling lease sales on the outer continental shelf. In overturning that ruling, HR 5835 stipulated that all federal activities, whether in or outside the coastal zone, were subject to the consistency requirement. The president was authorized to grant a waiver if he found that a specific activity was "in the paramount interest of the United States." *(Case summary, Congress and the Nation Vol. VI, p. 754)*

Many shore-state members of both parties supported the new consistency provision because it gave states more power to try to block or alter federal decisions, including offshore oil or gas drilling, that affected their coastal zones. In many states, most notably California and Florida, offshore drilling was widely unpopular with the voters, so members wanted to help enhance the states' authority in such matters.

Administration officials threatened to veto the original House bill over this issue and lobbied GOP senators hard. Especially concerned were the Interior Department, which oversaw drilling leases, and the Defense Department, which was worried that states might attempt to block shore-area training exercises.

Legislative Action

Despite the veto threat, the House passed HR 4550 (H Rept 101-535) on Sept. 26, 1990, by an overwhelming 391-32 vote. The Senate Commerce Committee had reported a similar version (S 2782 — S Rept 101-445) on Aug. 30. But Republican objections prevented the measure from coming to the Senate floor.

The House Merchant Marine Committee then added the coastal zone management legislation to its piece of the deficit-reduction bill, which the House passed on Oct. 16. Despite some continuing objections from Republicans, Senate conferees on HR 5835 worked out a compromise with the House, which both chambers approved Oct. 27 as part of the conference report on the bill (H Rept 101-964). *(Reconciliation, p. 55)*

Great Lakes Cleanup

Legislation (HR 4323) to strengthen pollution control efforts on the Great Lakes became law during the 101st Congress, after the Senate made substantial changes to the House-passed version of the measure.

The new law (PL 101-596) put more pressure on the Environmental Protection Agency (EPA) and Great Lakes states to improve the water quality of the lakes. It also directed the EPA to redouble U.S. efforts to implement the 1978 U.S.-Canada Great Lakes Water Quality Agreement.

Supporters of HR 4323 said that the EPA and the states had done little to implement the agreement, under which the two nations had pledged to develop cleanup plans for 42 badly polluted areas of the lakes. They said that the measure required the states to develop such plans, which were previously developed under voluntary deadlines.

The House Public Works and Transportation Committee reported HR 4323 (H Rept 101-704) on Sept. 14, 1990. The House passed the bill, 376-37, on Sept. 24 under suspension of the rules. The Senate passed HR 4323 on Oct. 18 by voice vote, after amending it to include broader substitute language concerning the Great Lakes contained in S 1178 (S Rept 101-339). The Senate Environment and Public Works Committee had reported S 1178 on June 27. The House agreed to the Senate changes and cleared HR 4323 on Oct. 27, the final full day of the session. President Bush signed the measure on Nov. 16.

Coastal Waters. Related legislation (HR 2647) to clean up coastal water was reported from two House committees in 1990 but went no further in the 101st Congress. Merchant Marine and Fisheries reported the measure (H Rept 101-605, Part I) on July 16, and Public Works and Transportation reported it (H Rept 101-605, Part II) on Oct. 15. Some Republicans objected to the legislation, saying coastal water pollution should be addressed during the scheduled reauthorization of the Clean Water Act in 1991. The Clean Water Act (PL 92-500) governed both inland and coastal waters. *(Clean Water Act, p. 529)*

Beach Pollution. Congress in 1990 also considered but did not clear legislation aimed at providing the public with better information about beach water pollution. The legislation would have required EPA to develop water-quality criteria for coastal recreation waters within a year.

The House passed HR 4333 on Oct. 23, under suspension of the rules, by a 326-89 vote. The bill had been reported Oct. 10 from Merchant Marine and Fisheries (H Rept 101-844, Part I) and Oct. 18 from Public Works and Transportation (H Rept 101-844, Part II). The House Merchant Marine Committee also attached HR 4333 to the omnibus budget-reconciliation bill (HR 5835). But Senate conferees objected, and the language was dropped in conference. The Senate version of the beach water bill (S 2706 — S Rept 101-550), reported Oct. 22 from Environment and Public Works, never came to the Senate floor.

Tongass National Forest

Compromise legislation (HR 987 — PL 101-626) that withheld more than 1 million additional acres of the Alaskan Tongass National Forest from timber-cutting cleared late in the 101st Congress.

The measure designated 296,000 acres of the forest as wilderness (meaning no logging, mining or road-building) and another 722,000 acres on which some mining and road-building could occur. In addition, the bill repealed a requirement that 4.5 billion board feet of timber be harvested each decade and an automatic appropriation of $40 million that paid for roads and other measures needed to cut and remove the timber.

The legislation also required renegotiation of long-term contracts, under which pulp mills in the region were guaranteed cheap timber, so that the timber sales would be profitable to the government.

Environmentalists had pushed for Tongass legislation for years. But the Alaska delegation had thwarted their efforts, contending that limits on Tongass logging would hurt the Alaskan economy. By 1990, however, the state's lawmakers realized that pressure for a bill was strong and decided to participate in crafting the compromise.

The final bill included most of the Senate version's policy language and essentially split the difference between the House and Senate on the amount of Tongass timber acreage that was set aside.

Background

The Tongass National Forest, a 16.7 million-acre preserve located in southeastern Alaska, was one of the world's last remaining temperate rain forests. The below-cost timber sales dated to a 1947 decision by Congress that allowed the Forest Service to enter into 50-year contracts with companies that agreed to build pulp mills in the Tongass region in exchange for long-term sales of timber.

Under the contracts, the U.S. Forest Service made available 4.5 billion board feet (bbf) per decade to pulp mills in the Tongass region, regardless of market conditions. As a result, the timber had sold for as little as $3 per 1,000 board feet, as opposed to $200 on the open market. As of 1990, two of those contracts remained in effect.

Much of the timber and pulp was exported to the Far East, and one of the affected mills was Japanese-owned — a fact that allowed environmentalist critics to use trade arguments to buttress their case against the practice.

Alaska lawmakers insisted that the timber sales were vital to the southeastern Alaska economy and that cancellation of the arrangement would devastate the region.

After a decade of controversy over the issue, Congress crafted a compromise as part of the 1980 Alaska Lands Conservation Act (PL 96-487). The act, which restricted development on more than 100 million acres of federal lands in Alaska, set aside 5.5 million acres of wilderness in the Tongass. Alaska lawmakers won inclusion of provisions mandating the 4.5 bbf requirement and creating a permanent $40 billion annual appropriation for the Forest Service to facilitate timber harvesting.

The compromise did not satisfy critics, who stepped up pressure through the 1980s to further curtail the timber harvests. "Since 1980, it has become increasingly clear that the Alaska Lands Act failed to establish a reasonable balance between timber harvest and other uses of the resources of the Tongass National Forest," said Rep. George Miller, D-Calif. *(Congress and the Nation Vol. V, p. 577)*

Legislative History

The House Agriculture and Interior committees developed competing versions of HR 987 in 1989. The Interior panel's version (H Rept 101-84, Part I), reported June 13, called for canceling the contracts altogether, while the Agriculture Committee's bill (H Rept 101-84, Part II), reported June 29, would have ordered the agriculture secretary to renegotiate them.

The legislation came to the House floor July 13. Members rejected the substitute offered by the Agriculture Committee by a 144-269 vote and then passed the bill in

Water Resources Act: New Projects

Following are new water resources projects authorized by the Water Resources Development Act (S 2740 — PL 101-640):

Bayou La Batre, Ala. Navigation project; total cost, $16.2 million; federal share, $4.5 million.

Homer Spit, Alaska. Storm damage prevention project; total cost, $4.7 million; federal share, $3.1 million.

San Francisco River, Ariz. Flood control project on the river at Clifton, Ariz.; total cost, $12.5 million; federal share, $9.2 million.

Nogales Wash and tributaries, Ariz. Flood control project; total cost, $11.1 million; federal share, $8.3 million.

Coyote and Berryessa Creeks, Calif. Flood control project; total cost, $53.3 million; federal share, $39 million.

Oceanside Harbor, Calif. Navigation and storm damage reduction project; total cost, $5.1 million; federal share, $3.4 million.

Ventura Harbor, Calif. Navigation project; total cost, $6.5 million; federal share, $5.2 million.

Martin County, Fla. Storm damage reduction project; total cost, $9.4 million; federal share, $3.9 million.

Miami Harbor Channel, Fla. Navigation project; total cost, $67.1 million; federal share, $42.8 million.

McAlpine Lock and Dam, Ind. and Ky. Navigation project; total cost, $219.6 million, half from appropriations, half from Inland Waterways Trust Fund.

Fort Wayne, St. Mary's and Maumee Rivers, Ind. Flood control project; total cost, $35.6 million; federal share, $26.5 million

Aloha-Rigolette, La. Flood control project; total cost, $8.3 million; federal share, $6.2 million.

Boston Harbor, Mass. Navigation project; total cost, $26.2 million; federal share, $16.2 million.

Ecorse Creek, Wayne County, Mich. Flood control project; total cost, $9.3 million; federal share, $6.8 million.

Great Lakes Connecting Channels and Harbors, Mich. and Minn. Navigation project; total cost, $13.1 million; federal share, $8.8 million.

Coldwater Creek, Mo. Flood control project; total cost, $21.3 million; federal share, $15.5 million.

River Des Peres, Mo. Flood control project; total cost, $21.3 million; federal share, $15.8 million.

Passaic River, N.Y. and N.J. Flood control project; total cost, $1.2 billion; federal share, $890 million.

Rio De La Plata, Puerto Rico. Flood control project; total cost, $59 million; federal share, $35.9 million.

Myrtle Beach, S.C. Storm damage reduction project; total cost, $59.7 million; federal share, $38.8 million.

Buffalo Bayou and tributaries, Texas. Flood control project; total cost, $727.4 million; federal share, $403.4 million.

Ray Roberts Lake, Texas. Multiple purpose project; total cost, $8.5 million; federal share, $3.2 million.

Upper Jordan River, Utah. Flood control project; total cost, $7.9 million; federal share, $5.2 million.

Buena Vista Lake, Va. Flood control project; total cost, $55.1 million; federal share, $41.3 million.

Moorefield, W.Va. Flood control project; total cost, $16.3 million; federal share, $11.7 million.

Petersburg, W.Va. Flood control project; total cost, $17.9 million; federal share, $10 million.

Los Angeles County, Calif. Flood control project; subject to favorable review of chief of Army Corps of Engineers; total cost, $327 million; federal share, $163.5 million.

the form of the tougher Interior Committee version by a vote of 356-60. That version offered members an unusual three-for-one opportunity to vote for the environment, fiscal responsibility and a small dose of Japan-bashing.

On June 13, 1990, the Senate passed, 99-0, a softer version of the bill. The Senate Energy and Natural Resources Committee had reported the measure (S Rept 101-261) on March 30. Alaska's Republican senators, Frank H. Murkowski and Ted Stevens, had delayed action on HR 987 but eventually conceded that the pressure for action was too great for them to resist.

Conferees reached an agreement late in the session after breaking a standoff that threatened to kill the bill. In the end, the House eased off its demand that the timber contracts be canceled and agreed that the contracts should be modified to prevent below-cost sales. The two chambers also compromised on the total number of acres that would be designated as wilderness. The Senate adopted the conference report (H Rept 101-931) by voice vote Oct. 24. The House followed suit Oct. 26, clearing HR 987. President Bush signed the bill Nov. 28.

Water Projects

After trimming the measure to meet administration objections, Congress in 1990 cleared a two-year authorization bill for Army Corps of Engineers water projects. The measure (S 2740) authorized 27 new projects with an estimated initial federal cost of $2 billion. Conferees removed from the bill two large lock and dam projects that were slated to cost $750 million. The two projects had not received final corps approval.

By far, the largest new authorization in the legislation was a $1.2 billion flood control project along the Passaic River in New York and New Jersey, with a federal share of $890 million. *(New projects, box, p. 493)*

The measure also authorized 30 modifications to previously authorized projects. The original Senate bill contained 11 proposed project modifications, while the House version would have authorized 46.

Conferees dropped the largest project modification, a $270 million proposal to restore wetlands along the Kissimmee River in Florida that were damaged by a corps navigation project in the 1960s. The Bush administration had threatened to veto the bill over the project because the required environmental impact study had not been completed. However, the conferees approved a feasibility study aimed at accelerated authorization of the project in the 102nd Congress.

The conference agreement was hammered out after staff negotiations. Major sticking points were the Kissimmee project and a disagreement between members from North Carolina and Virginia over a plan of the city of Virginia Beach to take drinking water from Lake Gaston, which straddles the states' borders.

Also dropped in conference were two smaller projects that had not received corps approval. But a $327 million flood control project for Los Angeles County that was sought by House Public Works Chairman Glenn M. Anderson, D-Calif., survived despite not having corps approval.

These disagreements were minor compared with the logjams that had held up water projects bills between 1976 and 1986. Objections from Presidents Jimmy Carter and Ronald Reagan blocked corps authorization bills during those years. *(Congress and the Nation Vol. VII, p. 439)*

Perhaps most noteworthy about S 2740 was how smoothly it cleared. "This bill is a harbinger for regularizing this process," said a Senate aide. "It's a pretty major accomplishment."

The new law was the third biennial authorization since 1986, when Congress began requiring states, localities and project users to contribute a higher share of construction costs. User costs averaged about 25 percent. In addition, authorizations for the projects expired automatically if they did not receive appropriations to begin construction within five years. Before 1986, a huge backlog of projects had accumulated that had never received funding.

The Senate Environment and Public Works Committee reported S 2740 (S Rept 101-333) on June 14. The Senate passed the bill by voice vote on Aug. 2. The House Public Works and Transportation Committee reported a companion measure (HR 5314 — H Rept 101-705) on Sept. 14. The House passed HR 5314 on a 350-55 vote Sept. 26, then passed S 2740 with the language of HR 5314. Both chambers adopted the conference report on S 2740 (H Rept 101-966) by voice vote on Oct. 27, and the president signed the measure into law (PL 101-640) on Nov. 28.

Wetlands Bill

On Nov. 19, 1989, Congress cleared and sent to the president legislation (S 804) to help increase the continent's declining waterfowl population through federal preservation of North American wetlands. President Bush signed the bill (PL 101-233) Dec. 13.

The bill authorized up to $15 million a year for fiscal years 1990-93, plus about $11 million annually from interest earned on the unused portion of a federal trust fund made up of excise taxes on hunters' equipment.

With the money, the Interior Department was to buy wetlands in the United States, Canada and Mexico, in an effort to protect the habitats of migratory birds and to double the waterfowl population by the year 2000. The measure carried out the North American Waterfowl Management Plan, a 1986 treaty between the United States and Canada, and a 1988 tripartite agreement that included Mexico.

The bill also established a nine-member North American Wetlands Conservation Council — composed of officials of the U.S. Fish and Wildlife Service, representatives of state agencies and conservationists — to make recommendations about which wetlands to buy.

The final determination of those purchases, however, would be made by the Migratory Bird Conservation Commission, an existing panel that included Cabinet secretaries and two members each from the House and Senate.

On Oct. 6, the White House issued a statement saying that Bush — who in 1988 had made a campaign pledge of "no net loss of wetlands" — supported the bill. With the administration on board, the measure faced no real test in Congress.

The Senate Environment and Public Works Committee reported S 804 (S Rept 101-161) on Oct. 5. The Senate passed the bill by voice vote Nov. 15. The House, meanwhile, considered a companion measure (HR 2587). The House Merchant Marine and Fisheries Committee reported it (H Rept 101-269) on Oct. 5, and the full House passed it by voice vote under suspension of the rules Oct. 10. The House passed an amended S 804 by voice vote Nov. 17. Two days later, the Senate agreed to the House changes, clearing the bill for the president.

Northern Spotted Owl

An impasse over the fate of the northern spotted owl and timber jobs in the Pacific Northwest remained unbroken when the 101st Congress adjourned.

The dispute between timber interests and environmentalists highlighted longstanding tension over the dual roles of the Department of Agriculture's Forest Service. The agency was expected to keep timber harvest levels high. But since 1960, Congress had repeatedly passed laws that required the Forest Service to consider values in addition to timber in managing the national forests. These included preservation of wilderness and wildlife and recreational use of public lands.

The laws were aimed at correcting what many viewed as the agency's timber bias. But the timber industry and its supporters used their influence to win approval of annual Forest Service budgets that allowed logging at levels higher than what environmentalists said the national forests could sustain.

One of the key environmental laws, the Endangered Species Act of 1973 (PL 93-205) required the Interior Department's Fish and Wildlife Service to determine which land species should be listed as threatened or endangered. Federal agencies were then required to ensure that their actions did not jeopardize listed species or harm their habitats. *(1973 law, Congress and the Nation Vol. IV, p. 289)*

Environmental laws — and the extent to which Congress and the executive branch would go to enforce them — were severely tested by the northern spotted owl, which inhabited "old-growth" forests in the western portions of northern California, Oregon and Washington. Declines in populations of the bird, which had been proposed for listing as a threatened species, had prompted suits by environmentalists that led to court-ordered bans against logging in broad areas of both Oregon and Washington.

When faced with the potential loss of thousands of timber jobs, however, lawmakers repeatedly acted to allow continued limited logging in the owl's habitat by passing riders to appropriations bills limiting judicial review of the federal government's logging practices.

A 1989 amendment to the fiscal 1990 Interior Department appropriations bill (HR 2788 — PL 101-121), for example, temporarily freed timber sales in Washington and Oregon from court-ordered injunctions, while slightly reducing timber harvests and imposing some protections for wildlife habitats. On Sept. 19, 1990, however, a federal appeals court struck down that rider. The 9th U.S. Circuit Court of Appeals in San Francisco said Congress could waive or modify environmental laws but could not prevent the courts from reviewing whether agencies were complying with them.

In the meantime, the Fish and Wildlife Service June 22, 1990, had announced that it was officially designating the spotted owl as a threatened species. That decision required the administration to come up with a plan by Sept. 1 for preserving the owl and its habitat.

The plan the administration finally announced on Sept. 21 was seen as unrealistic even by some of its supporters. It asked Congress to exempt timber sales in the Pacific Northwest from environmental laws and to amend the Endangered Species Act to allow economic factors to play a greater role in decisions about how, or whether, to protect the spotted owl. *(Endangered Species Act reauthorization, p. 521)*

With their options limited and the issue increasingly polarized between environmentalists and logging interests, authorizing committees could come to no agreement in 1990 on a long-term solution. Congress was able to agree on a limited step before adjournment. The fiscal 1991 Interior spending bill (HR 5769 — PL 101-512) allowed enough funding for about 3.2 billion board feet (bbf) to be sold in fiscal 1991 from Washington and Oregon — a 20 percent reduction from the 3.85 bbf in fiscal 1990.

As might have been expected, the move pleased no one. Timber lobbyists said the funding levels were too low, while environmentalists said the harvest levels were too high to allow the spotted owl to be saved. *(1991-92 action, p. 520)*

Global Warming

Congress in 1990 cleared for the president a measure (S 169 — PL 101-606) to provide a national plan to improve scientific understanding of global warming changes. Some scientists said the buildup of carbon dioxide in the atmosphere from burning fossil fuels would lead to a dangerous increase in the Earth's temperature.

Lawmakers, however, failed to clear a more extensive bill (S 324 — S Rept 101-361) designed to to establish a national energy policy to reduce the threat of global warming. The Senate passed S 324 by voice vote on Aug. 4 to stem emissions of carbon dioxide, methane and other greenhouse gases. The House took no action on the measure, however, and it died upon adjournment.

S 169 was reported from Senate Commerce, Science and Transportation (S Rept 101-40) on May 31, 1989, and passed the Senate 100-0 on Feb. 6, 1990. The House passed an amended version of the legislation by voice vote under suspension of the rules on Oct. 26, based largely on legislation (HR 2984) approved by the House Science, Space and Technology Committee earlier in the year. The Senate accepted the House-passed version in the early hours of Oct. 28. It was signed into law Nov. 16.

Environmental Education

Legislation (S 3176 — PL 101-619) setting up an Office of Environmental Education within the Environmental Protection Agency (EPA) was signed into law Nov. 16, 1990. In addition to setting up an office in EPA specifically charged with administering and coordinating the federal government's environmental education programs, the legislation established an Environmental Education Foundation, which would use private donations to support EPA environmental education efforts.

The measure authorized up to $12 million annually in fiscal 1992-93, rising to $14 million annually by fiscal 1996. Of that, about $5 million a year would go for grants to school systems, colleges, environmental agencies or nonprofit organizations.

The final bill was a compromise between similar measures that passed in the Senate on July 18 (S 1076 — S Rept 101-284) and the House on Sept. 28 (HR 3684 — H Rept 101-671). To avoid a conference, proponents introduced the compromise measure, S 3176. The Senate and the House passed S 3176 by voice vote in the session that began Oct. 26.

Irrigation Subsidies

Provisions to eliminate federal irrigation subsidies for large farm operations and for Western farmers who grew surplus crops were approved by the House but killed by an adamant Sen. Pete Wilson, R-Calif., in the final week of the 1990 session.

The dispute concerned millions of dollars in federal irrigation subsidies received by large Western farm operations. Urban and environmentalist-minded lawmakers wanted to tighten enforcement of acreage limitations designed to target the subsidies to small and midsize farms.

The House adopted the water-subsidy limits by solid margins — 316-97 and 338-55 — on June 14, 1990, as amendments to a non-controversial Bureau of Reclamation water and power projects authorization bill (HR 2567 — H Rept 101-336, Part I). The House passed HR 2567 by voice vote under suspension of the rules June 14. When the bill reached the Senate, Wilson, a strong supporter of his state's giant agricultural sector, blocked consideration of the measure unless the restrictions were removed.

Wilson prevailed, and the Senate passed the bill without the subsidy limits by voice vote Oct. 26. But the House sponsor of the amendment, George Miller, D-Calif., responded by trying to reattach the subsidy limits. When neither side gave way in last-minute negotiations, the bill died. In 1992, Miller and his counterpart in the Senate, Bill Bradley, D-N.J., prevailed when Congress cleared a measure that revamped huge water projects all across the West. *(Story, p. 513)*

Grand Canyon Erosion

The House and Senate both acted to protect the Grand Canyon from man-made erosion caused by large volumes of water rushing out of the Colorado River's Glen Canyon Dam. But the effort fell victim in the last week of the 1990 session to unrelated disputes over a water project bill that was carrying the erosion language.

Arizona's congressional delegation and key environmentalist-minded lawmakers had been pushing bills (HR 4498 — H Rept 101-641; S 2807) to control the fluctuating flows from the dam, located 30 miles upriver from the Grand Canyon. The fluctuations, which varied the river level by as much as 13 feet a day, were caused as dam operations were adjusted to meet water supply obligations to several different areas of the Southwest.

Environmentalists and outdoor enthusiasts strongly supported the bills. They were opposed by the Bush administration and by Western power users who feared that the dam's power production would be reduced.

The House passed HR 4498 by voice vote under suspension of the rules on July 30, after revising it to conform with S 2807. In the Senate, S 2807 was folded into another House-passed measured (HR 2567) authorizing a number of water reclamation projects. That bill died, however, in a dispute over a House amendment to limit irrigation subsidies for large agricultural operations. *(Water subsidies, p. 495)*

In 1992, Congress put provisions to protect the Grand Canyon in an omnibus water bill (HR 429 — PL 102-575). *(Story, p. 513)*

Nevada Wilderness

The House Nov. 21, 1989, cleared and sent to President Bush a bill (S 974 — PL 101-195) to create 733,000 acres of wilderness in Nevada. It was the first wilderness land set aside in Nevada since the Wilderness Act of 1964 mandated that federal agencies carve out such areas.

"Every [Western] state has added significant areas to the wilderness system since the 1964 act — except Nevada," said Harry Reid, D-Nev., during Senate debate. The Senate Energy and Natural Resources Committee reported S 974 (S Rept 101-113) on Aug. 30, and the full Senate passed the bill by voice vote on Sept. 20.

The House Interior and Insular Affairs Committee reported S 974 (H Rept 101-339, Part I) on Nov. 9, and the House passed the bill, 323-75, on Nov. 17, after rejecting amendments by Barbara F. Vucanovich, R-Nev. She sought to cut back the wilderness acreage by more than 40 percent to 412,000. She argued that the bill as drafted by committee would put off-limits to development areas known or thought to contain valuable deposits of oil, gas and minerals such as gold, uranium and molybdenum. Her amendment was rejected 126-283 on Nov. 17. Other amendments, rejected 118-285 and 139-261, dealt with language involving water rights.

The Senate agreed to the House-passed version of the bill with a slight change on Nov. 20, and the House agreed to the change the next day, clearing the measure for the president, who signed it into law Dec. 5.

Arizona Wilderness

In the final hours of the 1990 session, Congress cleared legislation reclassifying 1.1 million acres of land in Arizona as wilderness protected from development, mining and motor vehicles. The legislation (HR 2570 — PL 101-628) had passed the House early in the year but was then delayed by disagreements within the Arizona delegation over the exact boundaries of the new wilderness areas.

Opposition also surfaced from legislators from large Western states, who argued that a further expansion of the wilderness system was not needed, and from mining operations and some outdoor enthusiasts, who did not want the areas closed to their activities.

The House Interior and Insular Affairs Committee reported HR 2570 (H Rept 101-405) on Feb. 21. The House passed the bill, 356-45, on Feb. 28. The Senate Energy and Natural Resources Committee reported the bill (S Rept 101-359) on July 10. Senate approval came on Congress' last full day, Oct. 27. The measure cleared only after the Senate acceded to House demands to delete some extraneous amendments senators had added. President Bush signed HR 2570 on Nov. 28.

Among the other wilderness bills Congress cleared in 1990 were:

- HR 5428 (PL 101-633), to designate as wilderness about 26,000 acres of the Shawnee National Forest in Illinois. The House passed the bill (H Rept 101-784, Part I) by voice vote under suspension of the rules Oct. 10. The Senate passed the measure by voice vote Oct. 27, and the president signed it Nov. 28.
- S 2205 (PL 101-401), to designate as wilderness about 12,000 acres in the White Mountain National Forest in Maine. The Senate passed S 2205 (S Rept 101-299) by voice vote June 6. The House Agriculture Committee reported the bill (H Rept 101-714, Part I) on Sept. 17. The House passed it by voice vote under suspension of the rules the same day. President Bush signed the legislation Sept. 28.

Zebra Mussels Control

Congress enacted legislation (HR 5390 — PL 101-646) in 1990 to combat small, tenacious mollusks known as zebra mussels, which were threatening to take over the Great Lakes and other water systems. The measure — the Non-Indigenous Aquatic Nuisance Act of 1990 — set up programs to monitor and eradicate zebra mussels and other foreign organisms that might cause harm to the waterways. President Bush signed it Nov. 29.

The mussels inhabited large swaths of the coastal areas of the Great Lakes, attaching themselves to water intake pipes and grills, power plant water lines and boat motors. By 1986, almost 10,000 square miles of the Great Lakes had been infested. If left unchecked, water ecology experts predicted, the mussels would eventually inhabit two-thirds of the nation's drinking water systems, according to a Senate committee report. The original mussels were thought to have arrived in the ballast discharge of a merchant ship perhaps in the early 1980s.

As enacted, the legislation required the U.S. Coast Guard to issue binding regulations to prevent ships from introducing "aquatic nuisance species" into the United States. The legislation also called for the establishment of an Aquatic Nuisance Species Task Force to coordinate efforts among six federal agencies to halt the introduction of foreign species in U.S. water systems.

The House passed the zebra-mussels bill by voice vote under suspension of the rules on Oct. 1. The Senate Energy and Natural Resources Committee reported a companion measure (S 2254 — S Rept 101-523) on June 8. The Senate passed an amended HR 5390 by voice vote Oct. 26. The next day, the House accepted the Senate changes, thus clearing the bill for the president.

Barrier Islands

Congress on Oct. 27, 1990, cleared legislation (HR 2840 — PL 101-591) that more than doubled the acreage in the coastal barrier island system where federal development aid was prohibited. The barrier island system was established in 1982 to save the fragile environments by limiting federal aid that encouraged their development.

Barrier islands are long, narrow, mostly sand-based land formations or atolls that sit off mainland coasts. They serve as protective buffers for lagoons, wetlands and salt marshes and the marine species that thrive in them. Though unstable and far from permanent, many barrier islands had been developed over the years, and some, such as Atlantic City, N.J., and Miami Beach, Fla., became among the biggest resorts and most densely populated areas of the country.

For decades, the government had financially aided development of barrier islands, directly and indirectly, through flood insurance, flood control and other public works projects; disaster relief; housing subsidies and mortgage insurance; beach restoration and erosion protection efforts; community development grants; wastewater-treatment grants and other forms of assistance.

Environmentalist concerns, buttressed by budgetary considerations, led Congress in 1982 to enact the Coastal Barrier Resources Act (PL 97-348) to slow federal spending and discourage development on the fragile coastal barriers. The law, supported by environmental groups and the Reagan administration, prohibited most federal assistance to a specified list of still-undeveloped coastal barrier lands comprising about 453,000 acres of shoreline from Maine to Texas. Exceptions were made for extracting or transporting energy resources, maintaining existing navigation channels, Coast Guard facilities and expenditures related to national security. The law did not bar people from building on their land but made it quite difficult, because developers almost always needed federal flood insurance to secure mortgages. *(Congress and the Nation Vol. VI, p. 467)*

In 1988, the Interior Department recommended expanding the acreage covered by the law by about 791,000 acres and 423 miles of coastline. Once in office, the Bush administration also supported expanding the law's coverage.

HR 2840 added 700,000 acres to the coastal barrier islands system, most of it along the Atlantic and Gulf coasts. For the first time, however, protection was extended to about 30,000 acres along the shores of the Great Lakes, 48,000 acres in the Florida Keys, 20,000 acres in Puerto Rico and 3,700 acres in the U.S. Virgin Islands.

Some 50,000 acres in the Florida Keys proposed for inclusion were removed in a deal to appease Democratic Rep. Dante B. Fascell, who represented that part of the state and objected to any of the Keys being included in the barrier island system. Separate legislation, sponsored by Fascell, declared the Florida Keys a national marine sanctuary, protected from oil drilling and the passage of certain ships. *(Story, below)*

HR 2840 also established a mechanism for states or localities to bring areas into the system. And it directed the Interior Department to begin mapping undeveloped barriers along the Pacific Coast for possible inclusion in the system.

The House Merchant Marine and Fisheries Committee reported HR 2840 (H Rept 101-657, Part I) on Aug. 2. The Banking, Housing and Urban Affairs Committee, which shared jurisdiction, reported the bill (H Rept 101-657, Part II) on Sept. 19. The House passed the measure by voice vote under suspension of the rules Sept. 28. The Senate passed an amended version by voice vote Oct. 26. The House accepted the Senate changes the next day, and President Bush signed the bill Nov. 16.

Florida Keys

The Florida Keys were declared a national marine sanctuary under legislation (HR 5909 — PL 101-605) signed by President Bush on Nov. 16, 1990. The measure, sponsored by Rep. Dante B. Fascell, D-Fla., protected the Keys from oil drilling and from certain ships that could disrupt marine life and fragile coral reefs that meander through the Keys.

HR 5909 also required the Commerce Department to develop a comprehensive management plan and a water quality program for the Keys. The bill bypassed the usual route — an extensive Commerce Department evaluation — to qualify areas as sanctuaries.

Fascell and Florida's Democratic senator, Bob Graham, introduced parallel bills (HR 3719, S 2247) in late 1989 after three freighter groundings earlier in the year had destroyed more than 5,000 square meters of reefs in the Keys. Fascell and Graham said day-to-day use by tourists and divers also posed a risk for the reefs.

After the House passed HR 3719 (H Rept 101-593, Part I) by voice vote under suspension of the rules on July 23, 1990, Fascell worked out an agreement with concerned senators that was embodied in a new bill, HR 5909. That measure was passed by voice vote in the House on Oct. 26 and the Senate on Oct. 27.

Federal Facilities Cleanup

Measures (HR 1056, S 1140) that would have allowed states to levy fines against federal facilities that failed to comply with hazardous and solid waste laws moved ahead in both chambers but fell short of final passage in the 101st Congress. In 1992, however, Congress cleared similar legislation. *(Story, p. 525)*

The bills considered in the 101st Congress sought to establish the power of the Environmental Protection Agency (EPA) and state governments to enforce compliance with the Resources Conservation and Recovery Act (RCRA) at federal facilities. RCRA was the 1976 law (PL 94-580) that regulated hazardous and solid waste. *(Congress and the Nation Vol. IV, p. 309)*

The House passed HR 1056 on July 19, 1989, by a vote of 380-39. The House Energy and Commerce Committee had reported it (H Rept 101-141) on July 13. After the Senate failed to act, Rep. Dennis E. Eckart, D-Ohio, tried to give the measure new life in 1990 by attaching it to a separate bill (HR 3847) elevating the EPA to Cabinet-level status. The House passed that bill in March 1990, but it stalled after President Bush threatened a veto. *(EPA status, this page)*

On Oct. 24, 1990, the Senate Environment and Public Works Committee reported a companion version of the measure (S 1140 — S Rept 101-553), but objections from several senators prevented the bill from coming to the floor.

Cleanup Plan. In a related development, Energy Secretary James D. Watkins on Aug. 1, 1989, unveiled his promised five-year plan to clean up the nation's troubled nuclear weapons plants, proposing a $19.1 billion down payment on a process that was expected to take 30 years and billions more dollars.

In the plan, which Watkins had promised during congressional appearances in March, the Department of Energy (DOE) was committed to clean up environmental and health hazards within 30 years at 16 nuclear weapons facilities, across the country and at dozens of other sites where nuclear materials had been handled or processed. The plan included a site-by-site identification of environmental and health hazards, together with specific plans and funding proposals to clean them up.

A draft summary of the proposal unveiled by Watkins laid out spending plans for the next six fiscal years, from 1990 through 1995. During the five fiscal years from 1991 to 1995, spending would rise from $3.3 billion to slightly more than $4 billion a year, for a total of $19.09 billion during that period. Estimates of the total cleanup cost had ranged from a previous DOE projection of $81 billion to other projections of $150 billion or more. Watkins called the $150 billion figure too much, predicting that DOE organizational changes coupled with aggressive research and development of improved cleanup technology would substantially reduce the cost.

In remarks at the National Press Club on Aug. 1, Watkins promised that DOE would "do everything scientifically feasible to solve the problems in place and not transfer problems from one hole in the ground to another hole in the ground."

Pesticide Residues

Legislation (S 722) to stiffen regulation of pesticide residues in food advanced in the Senate but died upon adjournment of the 101st Congress.

The Senate Labor and Human Resources Committee approved the measure, but its main sponsor, committee Chairman Edward M. Kennedy, D-Mass., was unable to reach agreement with the Bush administration, which had unveiled its own proposal to overhaul pesticide laws in 1989.

At the heart of the impasse was the issue of state preemption. The Kennedy bill would have allowed states to set tougher food safety standards than the federal government. The administration proposed to set a uniform federal standard, which would have done away with tougher state laws. The Kennedy bill also would have permitted the Environmental Protection Agency (EPA) to consider only health risks when determining what level of pesticide residues could be present in foods. The administration had proposed to allow the EPA also to consider the economic benefits of the pesticide to the food industry.

The Labor Committee approved the legislation June 27 by voice vote, despite protests from Republicans on the committee. Kennedy said he did not want to bring the bill the floor without GOP support. The House took no legislative action on an identical bill (HR 1725).

EPA Cabinet Status

Legislation to elevate the Environmental Protection Agency (EPA) to Cabinet-level status died in 1990 after a standoff between Congress and the White House over provisions in a House-passed bill that would have strengthened environmental laws.

The EPA had been created in 1970 by President Richard Nixon, under his executive reorganization powers. The agency consolidated management of existing environmental programs from the Departments of Interior, Agriculture and Health, Education and Welfare; Atomic Energy Commission; Federal Radiation Council; and Council on Environmental Quality.

By 1990, the EPA had established itself as the lead federal agency on environmental issues, and its administrators had been key figures in environmental policy making in successive administrations. Environmentalists began pushing to raise it to Cabinet-level status. They pointed to benefits such as better interagency communication, more clout with foreign governments, more prestige within domestic government and better efficiency through restructuring.

Members of both chambers had introduced legislation Jan. 23, 1990, to elevate the EPA to a Department of Environment, to establish an office to coordinate and compile environmental statistics and to authorize other restructuring of the agency. President Bush endorsed the idea the next day.

But Bush's support in principal turned to opposition to several provisions of the bill (HR 3847 — H Rept 101-428) reported March 22 by the House Government Operations Committee. In particular, Bush objected to the creation of an independent Bureau of Environmental Statistics. The bureau would have been able to release data on environmental quality and its effect on public health without review by the executive branch, notably the Office of Management and Budget or the new environment secretary. Bush also opposed a provision that would have limited the number of political appointees in the new department.

Despite repeated veto threats, the House passed HR 3847 March 28 on a vote of 371-55. In an unexpected move that further displeased the administration, the House also agreed to attach the contents of another bill (HR 1056), which would have given states the power to prosecute federal agencies for failing to comply with environmental laws at nuclear weapons production plants and other federal facilities. Although states were able to prosecute private firms for violations of federal solid- and hazardous-waste regulations, the federal government claimed "sovereign immunity" for its own facilities. *(Federal facilities, p. 497)*

The Senate Governmental Affairs Committee April 2 reported a bill (S 2006 — S Rept 101-262) to elevate the EPA to Cabinet-level status. The bill never went to the floor, however, because of concerns that an attempt would be made to attach an amendment on federal facilities and because of turf battles between the Governmental Affairs Committee and the Commerce, Energy and Environment panels.

The Senate passed a bill similar to S 2006 in 1991, but the House took no action in the 102nd Congress. *(Story, p. 513)*

Other Legislation

National Park Service Autonomy

Angered by what they viewed as unwarranted political interference in National Park Service decision making, Democrats in 1989 pushed through the House a measure (HR 1484) to insulate the Interior Department agency from administration pressure.

The House Interior and Insular Affairs Committee reported HR 1484 (H Rept 101-133) on July 11. The proposal to make the Park Service a semi-independent agency was passed by the House by voice vote on July 17. Approval came after members July 17 rejected, on a 148-251 vote that largely followed party lines, a Republican substitute that would have stripped out the most controversial provisions.

As passed, HR 1484 would free the Park Service director from having to answer to the interior secretary and would require that all day-to-day functions of the Park Service except for budget and Cabinet liaison be transferred to the director's control. The bill also required that the director be a professional with experience in the field and be appointed by the president and confirmed by the Senate for a five-year term.

The Senate took no action on the measure, which died at the end of the 101st Congress. The House had passed a similar bill in 1988, which also died in the Senate.

Arctic Wildlife Refuge

The massive oil slick that spilled from the tanker *Exxon Valdez* on March 24, 1989, desecrated the once-pristine waters of Alaska's Prince William Sound, but the political damage reached considerably further. Already in some trouble before the Exxon disaster, legislation to open the Arctic National Wildlife Refuge (ANWR) in northern Alaska to oil and gas drilling was clearly dead after the oil spill.

The *Valdez* spill — viewed by some as a tragic aberration but by others as an inevitable consequence of flawed energy policies — seemed to exacerbate congressional divisions over the future of ANWR, an area on Alaska's North Slope that oil companies believed to be the richest remaining U.S. oil field. Environmentalists opposed lifting the federal ban on oil and gas leasing in ANWR, arguing that drilling there would harm caribou and other rare indigenous wildlife.

Debate over drilling within the refuge's 1.5 million coastal plain (about half the size of Connecticut) had raged since 1980, when Congress abandoned efforts to settle the issue by ordering the administration to study the question. *(Congress and the Nation Vol. V, p. 577)*

In response to a 1987 report by the Reagan administration, committees dominated by pro-industry members — House Merchant Marine and Senate Energy — reported out bills during the 100th Congress to open the refuge to oil exploration. Attempts to appease drilling opponents went nowhere, however, and the bill died. *(Congress and the Nation Vol. VII, p. 476)*

The high hopes oil-drilling proponents held going into the 101st Congress were dashed with the *Valdez* disaster, which occurred just eight days after the Senate Energy Committee approved legislation (S 684 — S Rept 101-10) similar to that it had approved in 1988. S 684 was formally reported March 29.

The issue was sidelined indefinitely. But Iraq's invasion of Kuwait in August 1990 renewed concern about U.S. dependence on imported oil and interest in opening the Arctic refuge to oil drilling. Frank H. Murkowski, R-Alaska, wanted the committee to include S 684 in the budget-reconciliation bill. But he backed off after hearing that the move was opposed by Senate and House Democratic leaders.

In the 102nd Congress, a provision to open the Arctic refuge to oil and gas drilling killed a Senate omnibus energy bill in 1991. Congress ultimately passed the energy bill in 1992 but did not take up the drilling issue again. *(Story, p. 512)*

Oil Shale Claims

Congressional attempts to block the "giveaway" of federal oil shale lands inched forward in 1990 but were not ultimately successful. Proponents had been trying to get legislation passed since 1986, when the Department of the Interior transferred 82,000 acres of oil shale land in Colorado at $2.50 an acre to claimants under the Mining Law of 1872. Some of the land was later resold to major oil companies for $2,000 an acre. Oil shale could be made to yield oil through a costly process that was generally not commercially viable in 1990.

Altogether, there was a total of 1,600 longstanding claims to about a quarter of a million acres of oil-shale land in Colorado, Utah and Wyoming. Filed under the 1872 law, these claims had been grandfathered by the 1920 Mineral Leasing Act. With the department's action, the claims, most of them originally filed between 1915 and 1918, could be legally "patented," or converted into private property, for the $2.50 price. *(Congress and the Nation Vol. I, p. 1000)*

A bill to prevent the recurrence of such a windfall was introduced in 1986 but died in a House committee. In 1987, a similar measure passed the House on a 295-93 vote, only to languish in the Senate. *(Congress and the Nation Vol. VII, p. 478)*

In 1989, the House passed a bill (HR 2392 — H Rept 101-65) that would have limited the number of claimants that could buy the land at the $2.50 price. It was passed June 1 on a 301-80 vote.

The Senate Energy and Natural Resources Committee reported a similar measure (S 30 — S Rept 101-259) on March 29, 1990. But after Republican Sen. William L. Armstrong of Colorado held up floor consideration of the Senate bill, the House Interior Committee succeeded in attaching the measure to the budget-reconciliation bill (HR 5835). Conferees were unable to reach a compromise on the issue, however, and the language was dropped.

BLM Reauthorization

The House on July 17, 1989, passed a bill (HR 828 — H Rept 101-132) to reauthorize the Bureau of Land Management (BLM) and reorganize the Interior Department agency to emphasize environmental concerns and break what sponsors characterized as an excessively cozy relationship between the agency and various commercial interests that used public lands. The Senate, however, did not act on the measure, and it died at the end of the 101st Congress.

The BLM managed about 270 million acres of public land in 28 states and also oversaw subsurface mineral development on another 300 million acres where surface rights were owned by other entities. Commercial uses of BLM land included livestock grazing, mining, and oil and gas development.

The bill, which the House passed by voice vote, would have reauthorized BLM activities for another four years and would have amended the 1976 law (PL 95-579) governing the management of public lands, mainly by depoliticizing much of the BLM's top management and by requiring the agency to give more weight to environmental concerns. *(1976 action, Congress and the Nation Vol. IV, p. 314)*

In 1991, a bill to reauthorize the BLM got caught in a debate over grazing fees and died. *(Story, p. 520)*

1991-92

Congress in 1992, with the cooperation of President Bush, cleared an energy bill that represented the first major attempt since the late 1970s to decrease the nation's dependence on foreign oil. The bill streamlined the process for licensing nuclear power plants, required the use of alternative fuels for fleets of cars and made changes in federal regulation of electric utilities to promote competition and efficiency.

On another front, Congress began to respond to pressure to increase the recreational use of public lands, predominantly in the West. This development took shape piecemeal. Bitter battles were fought over increasing grazing fees to strip subsidies for cattle ranchers; revamping the 1872 mining law to make it harder for speculators to lay claim to valuable land; charging Western states substantially more for oil- and gas-royalty collections; and overhauling federal water subsidies.

In the end, no dramatic turn was made away from the deference long shown to rural Westerners. Although Congress agreed to significant changes in the way water was allocated in California's Central Valley, Western legislators were able to block passage of legislation on grazing fees, mining reform and royalty collections. Nonetheless, the battles revealed that Congress was beginning to listen to an increasingly urban and environmentally minded nation.

Compromise eluded lawmakers on yet another issue — protecting the environment at the expense of jobs. The dilemma cropped up in several areas, but nowhere was it more clearly symbolized than in the controversy over extending protection to the northern spotted owl, a threatened species that lived in "old growth" forests in the Pacific Northwest where logging made up a substantial proportion of the rural economy. Although the issue was debated in both the 101st and 102nd Congress, legislators seemed no closer to finding a balance.

Energy Bill

The 102nd Congress opened with fierce debate over the Persian Gulf War and impassioned calls for a national energy policy to wean Americans from their addiction to Middle Eastern oil. It ended with enactment of a sprawling energy bill (HR 776), the first major attempt to decrease U.S. oil dependence since the late 1970s. A non-stop work schedule maintained throughout the 1992 session was needed to produce the conference report that cleared Congress Oct. 8, moments before adjournment. On Oct. 24, President Bush signed the legislation (PL 102-486), which included pieces of his proposed energy strategy.

The legislation sought to make policy advances across the spectrum of energy industries and issues.

Electric utilities were expected to see the most dramatic change under a rewrite of the 1935 Public Utility Holding Company Act. The bill's so-called PUHCA reform allowed established utilities and independent producers to compete freely in the wholesale power market — a change that sought to increase competition and, with it, efficiency. Related provisions provided independent producers with greater access to utility-owned transmission lines.

Tax incentives were enacted to encourage conservation, the use of renewable energy and development of cars that ran on non-gasoline fuels. Tax relief was granted to independent oil and gas drillers. The bill streamlined the licensing process for nuclear power plants and mandated greater energy efficiency for appliances, plumbing equipment and buildings. Federal and state governments were required to start buying cars that ran on alternative fuels, with private companies to follow later. The bill also authorized billions of dollars' worth of research and development projects within the Energy Department and restructured the department's uranium enrichment program into a government-owned corporation that eventually could be privatized.

Yet for all this, the bill failed to resolve some of the most heated energy controversies to emerge in the previous two decades: whether to drill for oil off the U.S. coasts and in Alaska's Arctic National Wildlife Refuge (ANWR), make cars and trucks more fuel-efficient or impose energy taxes to curb consumption. Taken as a whole, the final bill was expected to cap, not reduce, dependence on foreign oil.

That disappointed some lawmakers and policy analysts who believed the Gulf War presented a historic opportunity for a more dramatic rewrite of the nation's energy policy. But the bill also appeared to reflect the limits of the possible where energy policy was concerned — at least in 1992.

For one thing, experts warned that clear, long-term goals were needed to reorient energy practices that went to the heart of the way the country lived and worked — a process some likened to turning a large supertanker. "Great policy shifts come slowly," said Sen. J. Bennett Johnston, D-La., the key Senate author of the energy bill. "They're hard to do, and they're hard to undo."

Political Limitations

Perhaps more daunting were the political limitations on crafting energy policy. The developing legislation continually was tugged between the competing interests of producing states and consuming regions. Lawmakers struggled to bridge the gap between the demands of energy production and environmental protection.

Fuel-Efficiency Mandates

Just as oil companies saw the energy debate as an opportunity to open new areas for drilling, environmental groups perceived it as an opportunity to force automakers to build more fuel-efficient cars.

In an effort to cut oil consumption, Congress in 1975 mandated that automakers' fleets, on average, achieve certain minimum mileage standards known as corporate average fuel economy, or CAFE. Environmentalists and their allies in 1991 set out to raise that above the existing 27.5 miles per gallon standard, noting that transportation fuels accounted for a large portion of oil imports and the gases believed to create global warming.

Their rallying point was a bill (S 279 — S Rept 102-48), sponsored by Sen. Richard H. Bryan, D-Nev., to increase gas mileage mandates 40 percent by 2001. Bryan's bill was easily approved by the Commerce, Science and Transportation Committee, 14-5, on March 19, 1991, and was formally reported April 25. But it went no further, becoming mired in the controversial politics of broader energy legislation. The Energy and Natural Resources Committee in May voted against including specific new mileage mandates in the omnibus energy bill (S 1220).

Bryan's proposal had originally been debated as part of the Clean Air Act (S 1630) reauthorization in the 101st Congress. Dropped from that legislation, it got a political second wind after the Iraqi invasion of Kuwait, as legislators focused on its impact on cutting oil consumption. However, separate fuel-efficiency legislation (S 1224) drew only 57 votes in a Sept. 25, 1990, floor vote, three short of the 60 needed to invoke cloture and end debate on the bill. *(Story, p. 484)*

Bryan returned with his bid to boost gas mileage standards early in the 102nd Congress. The updated version (S 279) had some new features, including indexing existing civil penalties to keep pace with inflation. The penalties had not been adjusted since 1975. It also proposed to give the Department of Transportation some leeway to reduce the mandates beginning in 1996, not 2001 as specified in the earlier versions of the legislation.

In the House, the Energy and Commerce Subcommittee on Energy and Power held hearings on increasing gas mileage standards in connection with its work on energy policy but eventually approved a draft energy bill that did not address the issue.

As the Bryan bill languished on the Senate calendar, it nonetheless generated a furious lobbying campaign. Campaigning in its behalf was a coalition of environmental and consumer groups that helped stall the broader energy bill. That network included the Sierra Club, the Union of Concerned Scientists, the National Wildlife Federation and the U.S. Public Interest Research Group.

Opposing any mandated increase was the Coalition for Vehicle Choice, a lobbying group that was created by the auto industry but that also included such groups as the American Farm Bureau Federation and the National Campground Owners Association. The United Auto Workers also opposed the Bryan measure. Both sides inundated Capitol Hill with an array of brochures, studies and testimony. Each accused the other of distortions. Below are some of the chief arguments presented for and against new fuel-efficiency mandates:

- **Oil Imports.** An estimated 40 percent of oil was consumed by the transportation sector, making automobile fuel economy one of the prime arenas for gaining real cuts in oil consumption. Supporters of the Bryan bill estimated that it would save 2.5 million barrels of oil daily. But opponents said it was impossible to know what oil savings would result, because consumers might react by driving more frequently or longer distances.
- **Emissions.** Automobile tailpipes were a major source of the carbon dioxide emissions believed to help cause global warming. By reducing the amount of gas a car needed to burn, efficiency technologies could cut carbon dioxide emissions. But critics argued that there were trade-offs as well; for example, they said some pollution control devices had added weight to new cars, which cut into fuel efficiency.
- **Safety.** Auto safety was the rallying cry of opponents of the Bryan bill and other proposed CAFE mandates. They argued that to meet Bryan's ambitious targets, manufacturers would have to build smaller, less safe cars. Advocates of the higher efficiency standards disputed these claims, saying smart engineering could yield better mileage without sacrificing safety.
- **Consumer Choice.** Critics said new mileage mandates would force manufacturers to phase out some of their larger cars and light trucks to meet new fleetwide efficiency goals, thus depriving consumers of certain showroom choices and curtailing the best-selling portion of the U.S. fleets. Adding fuel efficiency and safety technologies also would drive up the price of new cars, they said. Consumers had been favoring less efficient cars and light trucks in recent years, but environmentalists maintained that Americans wanted more fuel-efficient cars, provided they were well-designed, and were willing to pay more for them.
- **Big Three.** The failing economic health of the Detroit automakers had prompted some lawmakers to question whether automakers could afford heavy investments in efficiency technologies, especially for cars the public might not want. But supporters said that this view was shortsighted and that prodding Detroit to build better cars would ultimately enhance its competitiveness.

The desire for greater energy independence had to compete with other goals, such as limiting the financial drains on taxpayers and businesses. The public had little stomach, for example, for an energy tax that would encourage conservation. And lawmakers were hesitant to lead where the voting public was unlikely to follow.

That left Congress with an energy bill that many believed offered a balanced foundation for cleaner and more secure energy supplies, but one that did not chart a decisive course away from current reliance on imported oil.

On the Crest of a Crisis

Ambitious legislative proposals on energy have typically followed a crisis, such as the 1973 Arab oil embargo, that frightens lawmakers into activity, if not always into action.

It was the oil embargo and 1979 oil shortfalls that prodded Congress to adopt dramatic new energy policies proposed by President Jimmy Carter. The 1980 Energy Security Act (PL 96-294) established a massive federal synthetic fuels project to encourage production of non-gasoline fuels. *(Congress and the Nation Vol. V, p. 512)*

But the synfuels corporation became a huge pork-barrel program that absorbed billions of dollars before being dismantled in the mid-1980s amid fierce criticisms. Lawmakers also became disillusioned with other pieces of their energy handiwork and spent much of the 1980s undoing previous regulations, such as natural gas controls.

The oil price shocks following Iraq's invasion of Kuwait in August 1990 triggered a new round of congressional concern, as well as the customary disputes over whether to emphasize incentives for production or penalties for consumption. That split affected debate not only on whether to open the Arctic refuge and coastal areas to drilling but also on issues of siting gas and oil pipelines and building hydroelectric plants. Although the war strengthened the case for the pro-production arguments, many lawmakers remained skeptical that it had fundamentally altered the political strength of the pro-environment forces.

Many Democrats joined with environmentalists in blaming the administration for lacking a policy to curb oil imports. But they had trouble uniting behind a new energy proposal. Although some Democrats saw substantive merit in a conservation-based energy policy, its political benefits were less apparent. Such a bill would have come at great cost within Congress, facing a near-certain presidential veto and providing dubious political gain. Environmental groups were unlikely to throw their support to Republican candidates, whose party had produced the policies they so despised.

Nor were Democrats of one mind on energy policy. Some members from oil- and gas-producing states backed tax breaks and other incentives to boost production. And many Democrats appeared unwilling to assume the political risk of advocating major energy taxes to boost prices, a step many experts said was the essential appetite suppressant for America's oil gluttony. For example, although U.S. gas prices remained far below those of Western Europe, members in 1990 fought bitterly over increasing the federal gas tax by 5 cents a gallon. Analysts said it would take a far larger boost to deter consumption significantly. *(1990 gasoline tax, p. 484)*

Nevertheless, the war did provide Congress with a powerful reminder of the geopolitical costs of U.S. oil imports. And even as that crisis receded during 1991, lawmakers fretted about the sustained drag on the nation's balance of trade from imported oil.

Ongoing concern about global warming also argued for new energy policies, giving strength to calls for greater conservation and, in some minds, for more nuclear power. And there were institutional pressures to move: Throughout the years in which Congress did not address energy planning, members had stockpiled energy-related proposals. Many of the energy measures that blossomed early in 1991 had no direct relation to the Gulf crisis but represented a decade of pent-up legislative need.

Administration Proposal

The administration made its opening gambit in the energy policy debate on Feb. 18, 1991, when Energy Secretary James D. Watkins released a 214-page "National Energy Strategy" that had been 18 months in the making. Watkins had promised to base the strategy on extensive public input, and lawmakers and some lobbyists had initially looked forward to its release. But the plan bogged down in the final months when free-market advocates in the administration successfully stripped out some of the proposed mandates and incentives designed to cut oil consumption. When the final version was released, it drew quick and vehement criticism from many quarters.

The administration's plan acknowledged that no hope existed of ending the nation's strong reliance on oil imports. Instead, it laid out measures to contain that dependency. They included proposals to boost domestic energy production, most notably by encouraging oil and gas drilling in Alaska's Arctic National Wildlife Refuge and in some portions of the outer continental shelf. Other production-related proposals included measures to streamline the construction and licensing of nuclear power plants and natural gas pipelines. To boost competition and supply in electricity generation, the administration proposed loosening the 1935 Public Utility Holding Company Act governing utilities.

The administration plan also contained some measures aimed at cutting oil consumption, most notably mandating that private fleets buy increasing numbers of vehicles that ran on non-gasoline fuels such as methanol or natural gas.

But other mandatory conservation and efficiency proposals were watered down or deleted by free-market advocates in the White House. The conservationists' top priority of strengthening gas mileage standards, known as corporate average fuel economy or CAFE, was weeded out early on. Other proposals, such as a tax credit for renewable energy production and a federal fund to pay for energy efficiency improvements by government agencies, were crossed out when the draft reached the Office of Management and Budget.

Bush won credit for producing a major energy initiative, and the proposal was warmly received by some producing groups. But environmental groups and their allies quickly jumped on the administration plan, branding it a "Drain America First" policy.

The administration plan drew criticism from some legislators, who said it did not provide enough incentives, such as tax breaks, for domestic oil and gas drilling.

1991 Action

Johnston took the lead early in 1991, drafting a massive energy bill (S 1220, originally S 341) and guiding it through the Senate Energy and Natural Resources Committee, which he chaired. But that legislation faced strong criticism from environmental groups and their allies and stalled over the summer. S 1220 was formally reported (S Rept 102-72) on June 5.

In the House, Rep. Philip R. Sharp, D-Ind., began marking up a parallel bill (HR 776) in his Energy and Commerce Subcommittee on Energy and Power. The subcommittee reported that bill to the full committee in October 1991, but it moved no further that year.

Johnston made an end-of-session push on his bill, but on Nov. 1 he failed to muster the 60 votes necessary to bring it to the floor on a **key vote of 50-44 (R 32-9; D 18-35).** *(1991 key votes, p. 1061)*

Johnston had relied heavily on Republican support to help advance his energy package. He consulted closely with the administration, and during committee markup, Republican votes often provided the victory margin for key measures such as the Arctic drilling provision. *(Arctic drilling, p. 512)*

But that strategy got Johnston into trouble with Democrats on two fronts: On substance, especially on the Arctic drilling, Johnston appeared to have strayed too far from mainstream thinking within his party. And he also irritated fellow Democratic committee chairmen by writing policy for issues in their jurisdiction, such as nuclear power and electric utility regulation.

Although Johnston got 50 votes, 44 senators, including nine fellow committee chairmen, blocked his energy bill from coming to the Senate floor — largely because it would have allowed oil and gas drilling in the Arctic refuge. The vote represented a stunning defeat for Johnston, who had insisted repeatedly that he had enough votes to bring the bill to the floor for debate. Even his opponents had not expected to win by such a large margin. Johnston left the vote dispirited and unsure how to proceed. Although various Democrats pledged to return with revised energy legislation in 1992, the likely contours or prospects for such a bill were not at all clear.

1992 Senate Action

Action in the new year shifted to the Democratic Caucus, and by the week of Jan. 27, 1992, Johnston had come to an agreement with his former critics. He promised to drop the Arctic drilling provision from his bill and to keep it out. In exchange, the dissident Democrats agreed not to block the bill from the floor or try to append higher fuel-efficiency mandates. *(Fuel-efficiency mandates, box, p. 501)*

That was a minimal sacrifice for proponents of new mileage standards. With the automobile industry in serious economic trouble, lawmakers recognized the timing was not propitious to pass major new mileage requirements.

Johnston also worked to smooth out differences with rival Democratic chairmen while holding on to Republican support. Wyoming Sen. Malcolm Wallop, the ranking Republican on the Energy Committee and cosponsor of S 1220, agreed to cosponsor the new version. And the administration abandoned earlier threats to veto any energy bill that did not allow the Arctic drilling to begin.

Johnston introduced the new, leaner energy bill (S 2166) on Jan. 29. It sought to speed construction of nuclear power plants and natural gas pipelines, mandate the use of non-gasoline fuels and certain energy-efficiency technologies and authorize energy-related research and development projects.

Johnston cleared a key hurdle on Feb. 4, when senators voted 90-5 to begin work on the bill. The final hurdle was cleared on Feb. 19, when the Senate passed the bill 94-4. In the intervening days, several significant amendments were considered.

Nuclear Power. One of the most contentious fights came over the bill's provisions to streamline federal licensing of nuclear power plants. The once-thriving nuclear power industry had fallen on hard times. The accidents at Three Mile Island near Harrisburg, Pa., and at the Chernobyl plant in the former Soviet Union had shaken public confidence in the safety of nuclear power. The problem of how to dispose of radioactive nuclear waste had not been solved, and power plants sometimes were costlier than anticipated. Nonetheless, congressional support for nuclear power was substantial, especially given the new limits on air pollution from other power sources established in the 1990 Clean Air Act amendments. Nuclear power advocates thus were seeking regulatory changes that would advance the industry, and licensing reform was among those changes.

The Nuclear Regulatory Commission (NRC) had used a two-step process that required applicants to obtain a construction license, then an operation license. But industry officials said the system had been used to delay plant operations and increase costs. Industry officials sought a combined construction and operation license that would force regulators to rule early on controversial issues — and thus protect investment in a plant from opposition from nuclear power critics.

The NRC in 1989 issued a rule to create such a combined license, but it had been challenged in court. To override that action, S 2166 included language authorizing the one-step licensing process. Environmentalists opposed the authorization, however, claiming that it would increase the possibility of approving unsafe power plants. On the Senate floor, Bob Graham, D-Fla., offered an alternative that would permit the one-step process but ensure an additional review if critics raised valid safety concerns or new information.

But Johnston undercut Graham's proposal by modifying S 2166 to include additional guarantees of public participation. Johnston moved to table (and thus kill) Graham's proposal; he prevailed Feb. 6 on a **key vote of 52-43 (R 31-11; D 21-32).** Senators then adopted the revised Johnston language by voice vote. *(1992 key votes, p. 1083)*

Alternative Fuels. Senators also wrangled at length over an amendment by James M. Jeffords, R-Vt., to promote non-gasoline motor fuels. The Senate Feb. 5 voted 57-39 to table the proposal.

The amendment sought to ensure that, by the year 2001, 10 percent of motor fuel sold by refiners would be so-called alternative fuels, such as ethanol, methanol, natural gas and electricity. To meet that target, oil refiners would have to make alternative fuels at least 10 percent of their fuel production. The administration had warned that the Jeffords amendment would draw a veto, and the proposal also was a prime target of lobbyists for the oil industry.

PUHCA Reform. One of the biggest items in the bill generated little debate on the Senate floor. This was a provision to loosen federal regulation of the wholesale electric power market. The controversial proposal, known as PUHCA, sought to make it easier for small generators to sell power and for utilities to build plants outside their home bases.

The proposal was popular with the natural gas industry, which was expected to be the fuel of choice for many independent generating plants envisioned under the bill. Renewable energy producers also could benefit, especially if the proposal enhanced their ability to ship power to different wholesale companies.

But sponsors said the biggest beneficiaries would be consumers, who would pay lower electric rates as a result of competition. Consumer and environmental groups initially showed more apprehension than interest, however; they were wary the proposal would open the door to misconduct by the utilities. A coalition of utilities vigorously opposed the reform package.

The issue had been expected to spark huge debate, but Johnston successfully negotiated agreements with some of the biggest skeptics and promised to take up other concerns during conference with the House.

Other Issues. In other action, the Senate agreed to ban new drilling leases off the costs of New England, Oregon and Washington. The bill already called for a moratorium on new drilling off the California and New Jersey coasts. An amendment by Graham to extend the drilling moratorium to the Florida coast was adopted after it was modified to permit drilling leases in the waters off the Florida Panhandle, which were believed to hold large oil and gas reserves.

The Senate also agreed to a package of amendments to strengthen the bill's energy efficiency provisions. Among the most significant were proposals to set national energy efficiency standards for most lamps and for electric motors.

Although Alaska's senators, Republicans Frank H. Murkowski and Ted Stevens, had reserved the right to offer an amendment to allow oil and gas exploration in the ANWR, they ultimately decided not to press for the vote they realized they could not win.

1992 House Action

The spotlight then shifted to the House, where the full Energy and Commerce Committee approved HR 776. The bill was formally reported (H Rept 102-474, Part I) on March 30, 1992.

HR 776 was more to the liking of environmentalists and tilted still further in that direction as eight other committees with rival jurisdiction marked up their pieces of the legislation.

The most significant additions came in the Interior and Insular Affairs and the Merchant Marine and Fisheries committees, each of which added provisions sought by environmentalists, such as offshore drilling bans, and in Ways and Means, which added an entire new section of energy-related tax incentives. The five other committees — Public Works and Transportation; Science, Space and Technology; Foreign Affairs; Judiciary; and Government Operations — made smaller additions or revisions.

Energy Chairman John D. Dingell, D-Mich., initially resisted incorporating the other committees' amendments into his draft. But Speaker Thomas S. Foley, D-Wash., held a meeting with the chairmen on May 12 and urged them to resolve as many disagreements as possible.

In the following days, committee staff did just that, and panels with relatively minor amendments were able to wrap up their negotiations quickly. But other disputes — including differences on uranium enrichment, nuclear power and the Strategic Petroleum Reserve — were left for the Rules Committee to mediate.

In fact, so many disputes were left to the Rules Committee for resolution that the panel had to issue guidelines for floor consideration in two parts. The second half of the rule for floor action was not issued until after the House had debated the bill for a full day.

Still, the Rules Committee took some decisive actions. For example, the panel included sweeping bans on offshore oil and gas drilling that had been approved by the Interior and Merchant Marine committees, and Rules refused to allow a separate floor vote to strike or limit those bans.

The bill also included a sweeping overhaul of the federal law governing electric utilities, tax incentives for renewable energy and cars that ran on non-gasoline fuels, and tax relief for independent oil and gas drillers. None of these provisions was subject to amendment on the floor.

Four House committees had agreed on restructuring the government's uranium enrichment program but disagreed about how to allocate costs for cleaning up the old enrichment plants. At issue was how much nuclear utilities that bought uranium from the plants should pay for the cleanup and how much the federal government should pay. The panels agreed to a compromise — approved by Rules — that would create a 15-year cleanup account, to be funded at $500 million a year. Utilities would pay about 30 percent of that, but no more than $2.5 billion over 15 years.

The Science Committee (H Rept 102-474, Part II) and Public Works (H Rept 102-474, Part III) reported HR 776 on May 1. Foreign Affairs (H Rept 102-474, Part IV), Government Operations (H Rept 102-474, Part V), Ways and Means (H Rept 102-474, Part VI), Judiciary (H Rept 102-474, Part VII), Interior (H Rept 102-474, Part VIII) and Merchant Marine (H Rept 102-474, Part IX) reported the bill May 5.

Floor Debate. Relatively few issues were left for lawmakers to resolve during floor debate. One concerned licensing reform for nuclear power plants. The industry had complained that the provision sent to the House floor would be used to block power plant operations unfairly, and a substitute amendment, with the same language approved by the Senate, was adopted May 20, 254-160.

Over the strenuous objections of the Nevada delegation, members by voice vote agreed to allow the federal government to pre-empt state permitting laws while it studied whether to build a dump to store high-level waste from commercial nuclear power plants at Yucca Mountain, Nev. And over the objections of lawmakers from states that produced natural gas, the House May 20 adopted, 238-169, an amendment to create federal oversight of state limits on producing new gas and prohibit such limits when they were aimed at increasing gas prices. Gas states argued that these so-called pro-rationing limits were necessary to ensure proper management of wells and to protect the rights of multiple drillers drawing from the same gas reservoir.

In other action, the House removed one key difference with the Senate — and the administration — during its final day of floor debate. On a 263-135 vote May 27, members deleted a proposal that would have forced oil importers and refiners to help fill the Strategic Petroleum Reserve, the nation's oil stockpile.

House passage of HR 776 came May 27 on a **381-37 (R 135-23; D 245-14; I 1-0) key vote.** *(1992 key votes, p. 1083)*

Senate Tax Provisions

Before the energy bill could go to conference, the Senate added a package of energy-related tax proposals to HR 776. That package paralleled many of the items included in the House-passed bill, such as providing tax incentives for renewable energy, conservation and cars that run on clean-burning fuels and giving about $1 billion over five years in tax relief to independent oil and gas drillers. To pay for those items, the Senate closed a loophole that allowed taxpayers to deduct some club dues and increased the tax on ozone-depleting chlorofluorocarbons.

The Senate Finance Committee also made some adjustments to the House tax provisions and added a highly controversial tax, sponsored by John D. Rockefeller IV, D-W.Va., to help pay for health benefits for retired miners. Rockefeller's provision drew the opposition of the administration and of Wallop, who vowed to bring down the energy bill he helped write rather than let the tax go through. A motion to invoke cloture (and thus limit debate) on a motion to proceed to floor consideration of HR 776 failed July 23 on a 58-33 vote, two votes shy of the 60 votes needed.

Although Rockefeller said after the cloture vote that he would not yield, he eventually agreed to a compromise that abandoned the notion of a new coal tax and instead sought to bail out the fund that financed the miners' health benefits. A second cloture vote was agreed to July 28 on a 93-3 vote.

Another threatened filibuster had been diffused when Johnston agreed to oppose the House-passed language on Yucca Mountain. Nevada's two senators, Democrats Harry Reid and Richard H. Bryan had said they were prepared to offer more than 100 amendments to delay action on the tax package.

After three days of debate, the Senate adopted the package of tax provisions. Much of the time was devoted to disputes unrelated to the energy bill; in the one significant energy-related discussion, however, the Senate July 29 agreed, 63-32, to table an amendment that would have deleted the provisions granting tax relief to independent oil and gas drillers. The Senate passed HR 776 on a 93-3 vote July 30.

Conference Action

House and Senate negotiators approved the final legislation on Oct. 4. One of the most difficult challenges in conference was PUHCA reform. The House generally placed more restrictions than the Senate had on what utilities could do under the new rules. Senate conferees were particularly critical of House language intended to open utility transmission lines to independent producers. The final compromise retained a modified version of the transmission access language. In exchange, the House moved in the direction of the Senate on other provisions, such as letting utilities buy power from independent affiliates so long as state regulators approved the deals.

The final version retained the Senate provision ensuring health benefits for coal miners. But two issues could not be resolved and were ultimately dropped from the bill. The first concerned offshore oil and gas drilling; the second, natural gas. Conferees also dropped House language that would have limited state power to "pro-ration," or control, gas production. In its place, conferees inserted a statement pledging commitment to free and fair gas markets.

The bill had to cross one final hurdle before final passage — the opposition of the Nevada delegation to the conference agreement on the Yucca Mountain nuclear waste dump. True to his word, Sen. Johnston worked to remove the House language that would have pre-empted Nevada's authority to issue environmental permits for federal studies needed to site the dump. But Johnston agreed with key House negotiators to insert a different proposal regarding the dump.

This one would require the National Academy of Sciences to conduct a study on radiation standards for proper disposal of nuclear waste at the dump. The Environmental Protection Agency (EPA) would then be required to issue new radiation standards for Yucca Mountain consistent with the findings of the study.

The Nevada delegation objected, arguing that the same safety standards should be applied to Yucca Mountain as were applied to other nuclear waste facilities. They also complained that the terms of the proposed study were slanted to produce a weak standard.

In the House, Barbara F. Vucanovich, R-Nev., offered a motion designed to strip the Yucca Mountain language from the final bill. The House rejected that motion on a 102-323 vote on Oct. 5 and then adopted the conference report (H Rept 102-1018) on HR 776, 363-60.

The Senate turned back one last delaying attempt by Reid and Bryan, voting 84-8 on Oct. 8 to invoke cloture and thus move on to consideration of the conference report. The Senate then approved the final version of the bill by voice vote, clearing it for the president.

Major Provisions

As cleared, HR 776 *(Energy tax provisions, p. 108)*:

Global Warming

- **Greenhouse Gases.** Required, within two years, an administration study on the methods and costs of curbing greenhouse gas emissions. The study was to assess the feasibility of stabilizing such emissions by 2005, or of reducing them. The study also was to examine the potential to cut carbon dioxide emissions 20 percent below 1988 levels by 2006.

Within 18 months, the energy secretary was required to submit another study assessing specific policies to cut greenhouse emissions, including caps on emissions and federal efficiency standards for automobile fuel economy and industrial processes.

- **Energy Strategy.** Required the energy secretary to develop a least-cost national energy strategy that promotes energy efficiency and seeks to limit the emission of carbon dioxide and other greenhouse gases. The plan was to take into account the economic, energy, environmental and social costs of various energy technologies. It was to seek to attain a 30 percent increase in efficiency by 2010 and a 75 percent increase in the use of renewable energy by 2005, both based on 1988 levels. The law also set a goal of decreasing oil consumption, from 40 percent of total energy use to 35 percent, by the year 2005.
- **International Initiatives.** Established a technology transfer program to promote the export of domestic energy technologies to cut greenhouse gas emissions through such means as financial aid to projects. The Energy Department was to administer the program working with the Agency for International Development. The law

authorized $100 million for the program in each of fiscal years 1993-98.

The legislation also created a fund to aid global efforts to fight greenhouse warming, authorized at $50 million in fiscal 1994 and unspecified amounts in the next two years. It stipulated that no money could be put into the fund until the United States ratified the U.N. Framework Convention on Climate Change, which committed nations to rolling back their emissions of greenhouse gases. The Senate ratified that treaty Oct. 7. *(Treaty, p. 297)*

Fleets and Fuels

• **Alternative-Fuel Fleets.** Mandated that certain government entities and private businesses with fleets of automobiles or light trucks phase in vehicles that run on non-gasoline or alternative fuels.

• **Eligible Fuels.** Designated as eligible alternative fuels: methanol, ethanol and other alcohols; mixtures of at least 85 percent alcohol with gasoline or other fuels; natural gas; liquefied petroleum gas; coal-derived liquid fuels; electricity, including that derived from solar energy; and any other fuels that are primarily non-petroleum.

An alternative-fuel vehicle could be one that runs solely on these fuels or a so-called dual-fueled vehicle that runs on both conventional and alternative fuels. The bill generally directed fleet operators to run the vehicles purchased under these mandates solely on alternative fuels unless they were not available. That requirement did not apply to fleets owned by private businesses and municipalities to protect them against potential price gouging.

• **Eligible Fleets.** Applied purchase mandates to fleets of 20 or more vehicles that were centrally garaged and operated in a major metropolitan area, provided that the parent companies, government agencies or other entities owned 50 or more vehicles nationwide. In the case of federal fleets, however, individual agencies or federal entities operating 20 or more vehicles in an urban area qualified for the purchase mandates regardless of whether they owned 50 vehicles.

• **Federal Requirements.** Expanded programs directing the government to buy cars and light trucks that run on non-gasoline fuels. The legislation directed the federal government to buy at least 5,000 alternative-fuel vehicles in 1993, at least 7,500 in 1994 and at least 10,000 in 1995. In addition, individual federal fleets were required to phase in alternative-fuel vehicles — at least 25 percent of new vehicle purchases in fiscal 1996, rising to 75 percent by fiscal 1999 and each year thereafter.

The mandates also generally applied to Congress, the administration and the U.S. Postal Service.

• **Alternative-Fuel Providers.** Required that producers of alternative fuels begin phasing in alternative-fuel vehicles for their own fleets, beginning with 30 percent of those purchased in model year 1996 and rising to 90 percent by model year 1999.

The mandate applied to companies whose primary business was producing, processing or distributing alternative fuels for use as an end product — such as ethanol refiners or electric utilities. If a company had affiliates, only those divisions that were significantly engaged in the alternative-fuels business were affected.

The requirement was not to kick in until 1998 for electric utilities that committed to buying electric vehicles.

• **State Fleets.** Required, pursuant to a federal rule-making, that states begin phasing in alternative-fuel vehicles for their government fleets at the following rate: 10 percent of new vehicles in the 1996 model year, rising annually to 75 percent in model year 2000 and thereafter.

States could opt out of these purchase mandates if they submitted a plan, to be approved by the energy secretary, that would result in an equal or greater number of alternative-fuel vehicles by such means as converting conventional-fuel vehicles.

• **Private and Municipal Fleets.** Set a two-stage timetable for forcing private companies and municipalities to phase in alternative-fuel vehicles.

The bill set purchase targets for these fleets of 20 percent in model year 1999, rising to 70 percent in 2006 and thereafter. The bill called on the energy secretary to issue a rule to achieve those targets. The secretary was to have broad discretion to modify or drop the mandates altogether if the program proved unfeasible.

If the early rule-making did not result in a fleet purchase program, the legislation mandated a second, later rule-making to be completed by the year 2000 and required alternative-fuel vehicle purchases beginning at 20 percent in 2002 and rising to 70 percent in 2005.

• **Exemptions.** Exempted from alternative-fuel mandates a number of large fleets, such as rental cars, car dealers' stock, law enforcement or emergency vehicles, certain military vehicles and non-road vehicles, such as farm and construction vehicles. The mandates also were limited to light-duty vehicles weighing less than 8,500 pounds, although some discretion existed to include urban buses.

Electric Vehicles

• **Demonstration Projects.** Created a program to demonstrate the viability of vehicles that run solely or in part on electricity. The bill authorized up to 10 joint demonstration projects, with at least half of the funding to come from non-federal sources. The program was to include subsidizing the cost differential between electric vehicles and conventionally fueled ones, although the federal share of such subsidies was to be capped at $10,000 per vehicle. The program was authorized at $50 million over 10 years.

The federal government also was authorized to help states develop an infrastructure for electric vehicles, and the legislation called for up to 10 cost-shared joint ventures, each capped at $4 million, to promote technologies, facilities and regulations to support electric vehicles. This infrastructure program was authorized at $40 million over five years.

• **Research and Development.** Required the energy secretary to create a five-year research and development program for electric vehicles, in consultation with other agencies, utilities and automakers. It also authorized joint research and development programs with industry in areas such as advanced batteries for electric vehicles, high-efficiency electric power trains and hybrid power trains that draw on electricity and conventional liquid fuels. Project costs were to be split at least equally with the private sector or other non-federal sources, except in the case of a specific effort to develop fuel cell technology.

This program was authorized at $60 million in fiscal 1993, rising yearly to $100 million in fiscal 1998.

Alternative Fuels

• **Goal.** Directed the energy secretary to develop a plan to promote alternative fuels and so-called replacement fuels, motor fuels that can be mixed with conventional gasoline or diesel fuel. The plan was to evaluate a goal of replacing 30 percent of projected petroleum-based motor fuel by the year 2010. At least half of these replacement fuels should be from domestic suppliers.

• **Supply Plan.** Directed the energy secretary to analyze the supply and demand for alternative fuels and obtain voluntary commitments from suppliers to provide these fuels.

Promotion of Renewable Energy

• **Demonstration Programs.** Expanded and adjusted an existing program to promote the commercial development of various renewable energy and energy efficiency technologies, and authorized $50 million in fiscal 1994 for a series of joint ventures. The projects could promote a range of renewable technologies, including high- and low-temperature geothermal energy; solar thermal energy, including solar water heating; photovoltaic and wind energy systems; biomass; and fuel cells. The projects were to include at least one for-profit business, and federal funds generally were to account for no more than half the costs of each joint venture. They had to be selected on a competitive basis and could include measures such as subsidizing loans for renewable energy projects.

The demonstration projects were in addition to a broader Energy Department research program on renewable energy, authorized at $209 million for fiscal 1993 and $275 million for fiscal 1994. Within that authorization, $22 million in fiscal 1993 was allotted to research into superconducting technologies to improve the efficiency and capacity of electric power equipment.

• **Production Incentive.** Authorized the energy secretary to grant incentive payments of up to 1.5 cents per kilowatt hour of energy produced from certain renewable energy sources. The incentive was available for a maximum of 10 years, for facilities that first began producing renewable energy within 10 years of the law's enactment.

The payments were to be made out of available appropriations, casting doubt on the likelihood that they would be implemented.

Hydroelectric Power

• **Licensing.** Allowed third-party contractors to prepare some environmental documents and reviews for proposed hydroelectric power projects, potentially speeding the licensing process for these proposals.

However, the legislation also stiffened existing requirements in several respects.

It barred licensing new hydroelectric dams within areas managed by the National Park Service if they would have an adverse impact on the land.

The law also strengthened the role of several federal agencies vis-à-vis the Federal Energy Regulatory Commission (FERC) in determining federal hydropower licenses. For example, it clarified that a FERC license does not automatically grant the licensee the right to build roads, pipeline or transmission lines to the project over federal lands. Instead, the Bureau of Land Management and the Forest Service must approve rights of way and potentially could set conditions for them.

• **Federal Dams.** Called for a study, within two years, on the potential for boosting hydropower production at existing federal facilities. Another study was to examine the potential for selling more federal hydropower by cutting back on water for reclamation or by boosting conservation, as well as analyzing possibilities for enhancing fish and wildlife through these measures.

Efficiency Standards

• **Federal Building Standards.** Required the energy secretary to set minimum efficiency standards for federal buildings within two years of passage, to take effect one year after that. All new federal buildings would have to meet those standards, which would be developed in consultation with industry groups and relevant federal agencies.

New public housing and new homes receiving federal mortgages through agencies such as the Federal Housing Administration and the Department of Veterans Affairs also were to meet the federal standards.

• **Non-Federal Building Standards.** Required states within two years to update their commercial building codes to meet or exceed model industry standards designed to enhance energy efficiency. The states also were encouraged, but not required, to update their residential building codes to boost energy efficiency. The bill directed the energy secretary to create a technical assistance program to help local officials and others involved with building codes to update and enforce their provisions.

• **Homes.** Directed the energy secretary to issue voluntary guidelines to help states and localities rate the energy efficiency of residential buildings and authorize technical assistance to develop these rating systems.

• **Manufactured Housing.** Required the secretary of housing and urban development to recommend ways to make manufactured housing more energy efficient and to test the energy performance of such housing.

• **Industrial Efficiency.** Authorized grants of up to $250,000 to industry associations to promote energy efficiency in their field. The law directed the energy secretary to report on the benefits of establishing mandatory efficiency reporting and voluntary efficiency targets for industries that were major energy consumers.

The legislation also authorized another grant program to help states promote energy-efficient technologies in the food, lumber, wood, petroleum, coal and other manufacturing industries.

• **Electric Motors.** Established new federal efficiency standards for commercial and industrial electric motors, ranging from 1 horsepower to 200 horsepower. The law also authorized the energy secretary to establish testing requirements and then efficiency standards for small electric motors — those under 1 horsepower — when feasible and economically justifiable.

• **Lights.** Set minimum efficiency standards for certain fluorescent and incandescent reflector lamps. The bill also authorized the energy secretary to set standards for some high-intensity discharge lamps. And it mandated that the Federal Trade Commission (FTC) establish labeling standards for a wide range of lamps.

• **Plumbing Fixtures.** Established federal minimum efficiency standards for showerheads and other plumbing equipment, such as faucets, toilets and urinals. Restricting the water flow of such equipment in turn curbs the amount of energy required to heat or pump the water.

• **Commercial and Industrial Equipment.** Established efficiency standards for commercial heating systems and air conditioners and authorized the energy secretary to create efficiency standards for utility distribution transformers.

The bill directed the energy secretary to help create a voluntary efficiency labeling system for office equipment. Failing that, the bill authorized the FTC to develop a mandatory system.

• **Federal Energy Use.** Established a range of measures to prompt federal agencies to pay more attention to energy efficiency in running their building management and procurement policies.

The law set a January 2005 deadline for federal agencies to install energy and water efficiency improvements that would pay for themselves within 10 years, and it established a federal fund to help pay for such energy-saving projects. That fund was authorized at $10 million in fiscal 1994, $50 million in fiscal 1995 and open-ended amounts thereafter.

• **States.** Amended the existing state energy conservation program to allow the energy secretary to provide states with up to $1 million to help establish state revolving funds to finance energy-efficiency improvements in state and local government buildings. It also permitted states to use the grants for a range of programs, including training building designers and contractors and adopting retrofit standards for buildings to increase efficiency.

The law specified that, to receive federal aid under the conservation program, states must allow vehicles to turn left on a red light after stopping provided they are turning from a one-way street onto a one-way street.

Nuclear Power Licensing

• **One-Step Licensing.** Adopted the Nuclear Regulatory Commission's proposal, currently under review by the federal courts, to issue a combined construction and operation license for nuclear power plants instead of the traditional process of granting two licenses. The commission would have to certify that the terms of the license have been met.

The change eliminated a second public hearing required before a plant could begin to operate, unless critics could show that the plant had failed to follow the specifications of the combined license in a way that could endanger public health or safety.

If the NRC opted for a second hearing, it was to be allowed to permit the reactor to begin operating in the interim so long as it would not jeopardize public health or safety. The bill clarified that the commission's final decision to allow or prohibit plant operation under a combined license was subject to judicial review.

Advanced Reactors

• Authorized a research and development program to commercialize advanced reactor technologies that were meant to be safer and more efficient than existing designs, allotting $213 million for the effort in fiscal 1993.

Within 180 days of the bill's enactment, the energy secretary was to submit a five-year plan for commercializing these reactor designs. The law set October 1996 as the target date for approving a standardized design for an advanced light-water reactor. The Energy Department was to provide technical and financial assistance for companies seeking to develop such reactor designs and could help pay for some of the required research and engineering. The bill also set 1996 as the target date for researching other advanced technologies, such as high-temperature, gas-cooled reactors and liquid-intake reactors, to determine whether the government should select in 1996 one of those technologies for a demonstration project. This portion of the advanced reactor commercialization effort was authorized at $100 million over fiscal 1993-97.

• **Demonstration Project.** Directed the energy secretary to solicit preliminary engineering proposals for an advanced reactor demonstration project and to report to Congress by October 1998 whether the government should build a full-scale prototype reactor. That report was to include cost estimates, based on a requirement that at least half the money come from the private sector.

Uranium Enrichment

• **Enrichment Corporation.** As of July 1, 1993, restructured the Energy Department's uranium enrichment program into a government corporation aimed at processing uranium ore more efficiently and staving off foreign competition, potentially to be sold to private investors. The corporation was to enrich uranium and sell it to the Energy Department and other domestic and foreign customers, such as nuclear power plants. It was to be run by a five-member board of directors, to be appointed by the president with the advice and consent of the Senate.

The new corporation was directed to lease two existing Energy Department enrichment plants, at Paducah, Ky., and Piketon, Ohio, for at least six years. After that, the corporation was to have exclusive rights to lease the facilities for longer periods.

The corporation was directed to charge fees that would generate a profit. It also was authorized to handle the marketing of highly enriched or weapons-grade uranium from former Soviet republics, to be converted into lower-grade uranium for civilian use. The Bush administration in 1992 agreed to purchase weapons-grade uranium from Russia.

The law gave the corporation exclusive rights to develop a promising enrichment technology, known as Atomic Vapor Laser Isotope Separation (AVLIS), although it was to pay the federal government royalties for the privilege. The corporation could take preliminary steps toward moving ahead with AVLIS but would have to set up a private, for-profit business to build a plant using the new technology. The enrichment corporation could make grants of up to $364 million to this private enterprise for work leading up to construction of an AVLIS plant.

• **Privatization.** Directed the corporation to draw up a plan for privatizing the enrichment enterprise, potentially through a stock offering or merger. The corporation then would be authorized to implement the plan subject to presidential approval and a period of congressional review.

• **Debt.** Sought to recover some of the federal government's past investment in the enrichment operation. Strong disagreement existed over the extent of unrecovered costs. Some claimed that the government incurred no such costs, while other critics estimated them as high as $11 billion.

The law did not set a specific debt that must be repaid but seeks to recapture money for the federal Treasury in several ways. The government was to hold stock in the corporation equal to at least $3 billion and receive corporation net profits in the form of dividends. In addition, the Treasury would glean the proceeds from a stock sale if the enterprise was privatized.

• **Price-Anderson Act.** Clarified that the existing uranium enrichment plants were to continue to qualify for financial protections under the Price-Anderson Act, which limited industry liability in the case of a nuclear accident. The law stated that a new AVLIS plant would not qualify for such federal liability protection, however.

• **Cleanup.** Made the federal government and nuclear utilities share the cost of cleaning up the Energy Department's aging enrichment plants. The cleanup and decommissioning work was expected to cost about $20 billion.

The law established a $480-million-a-year fund to clean up the aging enrichment plants, with authorization indexed for inflation. Nuclear utilities were to pay about 31 percent of this (the percentage of enriched uranium that was produced for their use) over 15 years, up to $150 million a year but no more than $2.25 billion total, or a similar sum indexed for inflation. Individual utilities were to pay in proportion to the amount of enriched uranium they had purchased from the program. The federal share was to come from congressional appropriations.

• **Uranium and Thorium Milling.** Authorized $270 million to help clean up uranium mill sites that were used to supply government programs and $40 million for thorium mill site cleanup.

• **Uranium Reserve.** Established a strategic uranium reserve for defense and government research purposes consisting of the amount of U.S. defense-related uranium stockpiles at the time of passage. This provision sought to aid domestic producers by stabilizing the uranium market.

The law also directed the government to study the technological and economic factors involved with converting highly enriched uranium into lower grade uranium suitable for commercial use.

• **Imports.** Required U.S. nuclear power plant owners who imported raw or enriched uranium to report annually on the seller and country of origin of the uranium or enrichment services.

Natural Gas

• Loosened existing restrictions on Canadian natural gas, blocking the need for special import approvals and specifying that neither federal nor state regulators could treat it differently from domestic natural gas once it was in the United States.

• **Pro-Rationing.** Declared congressional support for competitive natural gas markets. This language was a watered-down version of a controversial provision in the House energy bill regarding state regulation of natural gas. That bill would have barred states from imposing natural gas production restrictions that were aimed at boosting prices. States would still have been allowed to impose traditional "pro-rationing" regulations to protect the respective claims of multiple drillers tapping a common reservoir or to prevent waste.

Conferees' report language accompanying the energy legislation stated that the Supreme Court already had established limits on state powers to regulate natural gas production that should effectively preclude efforts to boost prices through unnatural supply controls.

Strategic Petroleum Reserve

• **Expansion.** Directed the administration to expand the Strategic Petroleum Reserve to 1 billion barrels. The law authorized a series of measures to achieve this goal, including transferring oil from the Naval Petroleum Reserve. If the president found that domestic oil production had declined to a level that jeopardized national security, the energy secretary could be directed to buy oil from stripper wells, defined as wells producing 15 or fewer barrels a day on average.

• **Drawdown.** Broadened the conditions under which the president was authorized to sell oil from the reserve to include economic factors, such as a sharp increase in the price of oil, instead of solely in the event of physical shortages or supply disruptions.

Radioactive Waste

• **Nuclear Negotiator.** Extended the term of the federal nuclear waste negotiator two years to January 1995. The position was created by the 1982 Nuclear Waste Policy Act (PL 97-425) to help the government identify host sites for nuclear waste repositories.

• **Yucca Mountain Dump.** Required the Environmental Protection Agency to issue new public health and safety standards for a proposed high-level nuclear waste dump at Yucca Mountain, Nev. The new standards were to be based on a study to be conducted by the National Academy of Sciences, to be completed no later than the end of 1993. According to the legislation, the EPA standards should prescribe a maximum radiation exposure level for individuals — a departure from the previous standard, which dictated exposure levels for the population as a whole.

The law also directed the NRC to modify its licensing criteria for the repository based on the assumption that the Energy Department was to continue to oversee the facility indefinitely after it was closed to guard against intrusion. Previously, the NRC had been directed to assume that active monitoring would continue for only 100 years after closure.

Report language accompanying the bill specified that the National Academy of Sciences study could look at issues not mentioned in the bill, including collective doses of radiation. And it stated that the EPA was not strictly bound by the findings or parameters of the study when it made its final rule.

• **Waste Report.** Directed the Energy Department to prepare a report on whether current nuclear waste programs were sufficient to handle any waste that would be generated by newly licensed nuclear plants. The report was to be prepared in collaboration with the NRC and the EPA and was due within one year of the bill's enactment.

Electric Utilities

• **Wholesale Generators.** Created a category of wholesale power producers that were exempt from the 1935 Public Utility Holding Company Act. The change was to allow utilities to operate independent wholesale plants outside their service territories and encourage independent producers to operate generating plants. Many of the independent plants were expected to be small- to medium-sized facilities, fueled by natural gas or renewable energy.

Power producers would have to apply to the Federal Energy Regulatory Commission for this designation on a case-by-case basis.

Utilities could not win this exempt status for plants that had already been built and their costs all or partially included in a utility's rate base unless all affected state utility commissions determined that it would benefit consumers to do so.

• **Safeguards.** Banned utilities from buying power from an independent affiliate unless state regulators determined that the sale would benefit consumers. The ban was an attempt to prevent so-called self-dealing, whereby a utility built an independent power plan then sold power to itself at inflated rates.

The law allowed "hybrid" power plants, pieces of which were owned by a utility and included in its rate base and other pieces of which were exempted from PUHCA rules under the new classification. However, a utility could not own both the exempt and non-exempt portions of such a hybrid plant, eliminating some risks of taxpayer abuse.

• **State Review.** Allowed state regulators to examine the debt load of an independent generator and impose a specific debt-to-equity ratio if needed. Some utility advocates feared that independent producers would have a financing edge over federally regulated utilities, which were required to maintain a prescribed debt-to-equity ratio.

The law granted state regulators access to the relevant financial records of wholesale power generators that were exempt from the PUHCA law, as well as any affiliated utility. This access applied to all affected state utility commissions.

• **Foreign Investment.** Changed existing law to allow registered utility holding companies covered under the PUHCA law to build or invest in power plants or distribution facilities in foreign countries. The Securities and Exchange Commission would be responsible for regulating those investments to protect the utility's ratepayers. State regulators could offer recommendations for or against such investments but would not be required to approve such a deal.

However, state regulators would oversee foreign electricity investments by utilities that were not owned by registered holding companies and could block them if they determined that the investments would jeopardize ratepayers.

• **Transmission Access.** Allowed wholesale electricity generators to request that the Federal Energy Regulatory Commission order a utility to transmit their power. FERC was authorized to issue this order whenever the transaction was in the public interest.

Wholesale producers would have to pay for this transmission, and those charges would have to cover the utility's transmission costs plus a reasonable return on investment. Mandatory transmission orders would not be allowed when they jeopardized the reliability of established electric systems.

The law banned FERC from issuing a transmission order that would result in a wholesale power producer selling directly to consumers or in "sham transactions" whereby a third party bought electricity wholesale and resold it to disguise what was basically a retail transaction.

The transmission language did not fully apply to the Bonneville Power Administration and the Tennessee Valley Authority.

Octane-Level Posting

• **Enforcement.** Strengthened state authority to enforce octane posting requirements and extend such posting to non-traditional automotive fuels such as diesel fuel, some reformulated gasoline and gasohol. The provisions were meant to deter octane mislabeling, whereby suppliers overrepresented the octane level of gas.

Energy Research

• **Goals.** Outlined goals for federal energy research, including reducing reliance on imported oil, minimizing the health and environmental hazards of energy production and use — including the generation of greenhouse gases — and enhancing U.S. competitiveness.

• **Management.** Required the energy secretary to prepare a management plan for energy-related research and commercialization programs, consistent with the goals above, and submit the first plan to Congress within a year of enactment. The plan would subsequently have to be updated every other year. The law created an advisory board to help the energy secretary prepare this and other reports required by the legislation.

The legislation included other general guidelines and requirements for Energy Department research and development programs. For example, the secretary would have to send Congress a management plan for any major construction project involving $100 million or more and could not spend money on such a project until Congress had had 30 working days to review that report.

Another provision restricted financial aid under the Energy Department's research and development programs to companies that substantially contributed to the U.S. economy, effectively tightening the terms under which foreign-owned companies would qualify.

The law also laid out cost-sharing requirements for most of the energy-related research and development programs. Non-federal sources would have to account for 20 percent of the funding for research programs, and at least 50 percent of demonstration or commercial application projects. However, the energy secretary had discretion to reduce or, in the case of basic research, waive those requirements.

And the legislation directed the energy secretary to account for so-called uncosted obligations, money that had been obligated for programs but not spent.

Some of the specific programs included:

• *Advanced Oil Recovery.* Promoting techniques to get more oil out of wells, particularly existing wells that would otherwise be abandoned.

• *Natural Gas.* Enhancing conventional gas production and helping discover ways to extract natural gas from unconventional sources, such as tight sands and Devonian shales, surface gasification of coal and methane recovery from biofuels.

• *Transportation Energy.* Promoting techniques to reduce oil consumption in the transportation sector through increased efficiency and substitute or alternative fuels. Many of these programs were to take the form of cooperative research agreements or demonstration projects, with costs being shared by the private sector. The law specifically called for research and development on technologies to increase the efficiency of conventional gasoline-burning cars, to improve the capability of vehicles that run on non-gasoline fuels, to promote hydrogen-fueled cars and to reduce dangerous emissions from diesel engines.

• *Efficiency.* Authorizing a large research and development program to promote energy efficiency and the use of renewable energy in the building, industrial and utility sectors.

The specific programs within this effort included natural gas and electric heating and cooling technologies, improving the energy efficiency and reducing the adverse environmental impact of pulp and papermaking industries, creating more efficient heat engines and better construction designs.

• *Nuclear Waste.* Authorizing the energy secretary to design and implement a five-year research and development plan aimed at developing technologies to reduce the hazards of nuclear waste from civilian reactors.

• *Fuel Cells.* Authorizing a five-year program to promote fuel cells, which use an electrochemical process to transform a fuel's chemical energy into electrical energy without combustion — a cleaner and more efficient way to produce power.

• *Electromagnetic Fields.* Increasing and coordinating federal research on the potential health hazards of electromagnetic fields, which were generated by utility transmission lines, computers and other electrical appliances.

Clean Coal Promotion

• **Advanced Technologies.** Authorized $278 million in fiscal 1993 and such sums as needed in fiscal 1994-97 for federal research and development projects designed to promote advanced coal technologies, including efforts to burn coal with fewer acid emissions and to convert coal for use as a transportation fuel. The program would seek to speed development of these technologies for commercial use by 2010 or sooner. Specific program areas included:

• The non-fuel use of coal; for instance, as a component of chemical production.

• Coal-refining technologies to help reduce emissions and facilitate the production of coal-based transportation fuels to displace imported oil.

• Underground coal gasification, to convert coal on site to a cleaner-burning and more easily transported fuel. The programs in this field could include one or more demonstration projects.

• Burning coal in connection with various solid wastes, such as used tires, to produce energy.

• Magnetohydrodynamics, a high-temperature coal-burning process that uses a magnetic field to create electricity.

• **Technology Transfer.** Created a technology transfer program to export "clean coal" energy technologies to other nations. The program was to be developed by the Energy Department, working with the Agency for International Development and a newly created interagency clean coal subgroup of the Trade Promotion Coordinating Committee.

• **Exports.** Required within 180 days of passage the development of an interagency plan to boost U.S. coal exports. The plan had to address trade barriers to U.S. coal and recommendations for alleviating these barriers, as well as an assessment of the environmental implications of coal exports.

• **Small Coal Operators.** Expanded an existing program to help pay the permitting costs of coal operators who produced fewer than 300,000 tons annually.

• **Retiree Health Benefits.** Created a program to ensure the health benefits of about 120,000 retired union coal miners and their dependents who worked for companies that had gone out of business or were no longer paying into the miners' health fund. The law was to bail out the anemic health fund by letting the union shift $210 million over three years from its overstocked pension fund. It was to force many of the original companies, or a related business, to pay for its retirees. The legislation extended the Abandoned Mines Land fund, a reclamation fund gleaned from a fee on coal companies, until 2004 and tapped interest on the fund to help pay for the health benefits. In exchange, the miners' union agreed to certain health care cost containment measures.

The law also established a second fund to protect the health benefits of thousands of additional coal miners whose benefits might have been jeopardized in the future.

• **Coal-Bed Methane.** Sought to promote the recovery of methane gas, found in coal seams, for use as a fuel. The gas was viewed as a hazard and was usually released into the atmosphere, but advocates believed it needed to be recovered to limit greenhouse gas emissions and to utilize its energy potential.

The legislation sought to break the logjam over conflicting ownership rights that could complicate methane recovery. States that did not yet have a mechanism for resolving such conflicts and promoting methane recovery would have up to three years to develop one. If they failed to do so, the interior secretary would be required to implement a program to let methane recovery take place in those areas. Interior could establish "pooling" arrangements under which a designated developer would extract the methane gas and the subsequent profits would be held in escrow until conflicting ownership claims were resolved.

States could block such federal intervention through a governor's petition or by action of the state legislature. Methane drillers would have to get permission from owners of adjacent coal mines, and those coal operators still would be free to vent the methane gas for safety reasons.

The provision applied immediately to West Virginia, Pennsylvania, Kentucky, Ohio, Tennessee, Indiana and Illinois, although that list was subject to revision by the interior secretary. It specifically would not affect Colorado, Montana, New Mexico, Wyoming, Utah, Virginia, Washington, Mississippi, Louisiana and Alabama.

Oil Pipelines

• **Streamlining.** Directed the Federal Energy Regulatory Commission to simplify its method for setting "just and reasonable" rates for interstate oil pipelines. The law allowed rates that were approved at least one year before enactment and that were not subject to challenge to remain in effect.

The legislation also directed the commission to streamline consideration of rate changes.

Federal Onshore Leases

• **Leasing Bids.** Specified that all federal oil and gas leases run for 10-year primary terms, regardless of whether they were issued on a competitive or non-competitive basis. Before, non-competitive leases ran for 10 years while competitive leases lasted only five — a situation some critics said discouraged drillers from bidding competitively for federal leases.

• **Oil Shale Claims.** Designated a settlement for disputed, pre-1920 oil shale claims to about 250,000 acres in Colorado, Utah and Wyoming that were under federal control. The bill specified that claimholders who already had won initial certification of plans to develop oil shale on their holdings could go ahead and buy the federally controlled land for $2.50 an acre. Other claimholders could buy rights to the oil shale, not other minerals or the surface property, or pay fees to maintain their claims.

• **Allegheny National Forest.** Increased environmental safeguards on oil and gas development in the Allegheny National Forest.

• **Stripper Wells.** Allowed certain small oil and gas wells, known as stripper wells, to continue operating on federal lands even after the mineral rights reverted to the federal government.

Indian Energy and Insular Areas

• **Commission.** Established an Indian Energy Resource Commission to promote the development of energy resources on land belonging to American Indians through measures such as tax incentives. The commission was charged with developing a report within one year. The commission was to be disbanded 30 days after the report was submitted to Congress.

• **Federal Aid.** Authorized a federal program of financial aid and technical assistance to promote energy independence for American Indians. The aid was to include grants and low-interest loans for projects that, among other things, would create vertically integrated energy industries within tribal reservations. These programs were authorized at $30 million a year in fiscal 1994 through 1997.

The law authorized an additional $10 million in each of fiscal years 1994 through 1997 to advance tribal regulatory policies that would enhance energy development.

• **Insular Areas.** Authorized up to $2 million annually for federal grants to help insular areas decrease their energy dependence.

• **PCB Cleanup.** Allowed the Marshall Islands and Federated States of Micronesia to be eligible for "superfund" money to clean up contamination by polychlorinated biphenyls (PCBs) that occurred during U.S. trusteeship of the islands.

Arctic Wildlife Refuge

Environmentalists, oil companies and their respective legislative allies during 1991 continued a longstanding battle over whether to open the coastal plain of Alaska's Arctic National Wildlife Refuge to oil and gas drilling. During 1989, the environmentalists gained the upper hand when the *Exxon Valdez* oil spill in Prince William Sound highlighted the environmental risks of the oil business. Two years later, drilling advocates believed the oil shocks accompanying the Persian Gulf War might have tipped the political scales in their favor.

The refuge's coastal plain, a strip 100 miles long and 30 miles wide, represented the last piece of the Arctic shoreline in the United States free of oil development. Congress had long debated the area's fate. In 1980, it prohibited oil development in most of the refuge but directed the Interior Department to study the coastal plain's oil and gas potential. Members subsequently debated proposals to open it to drilling, or place it off-limits for all time. *(101st Congress action, p. 499)*

In 1991, the administration made opening the refuge a centerpiece of its new energy strategy, and Sen. J. Bennett Johnston, D-La., included a similar provision in his energy bill (S 1220).

Although no proof was available of how much oil lay under the Arctic wildlife refuge, some specialists believed its coastal plain might be the nation's last great oil field. The Interior Department estimated that the refuge could yield as much as 9.2 billion barrels of oil, about the amount contained in Prudhoe Bay, 65 miles to the east. With the United States importing almost half its oil, administration officials and other drilling advocates argued that it was absurd not to tap this domestic resource. The oil could displace imports, help control the trade deficit and provide domestic jobs. Alaska officials and the Inupiat Eskimos who owned the coastal plain wanted the economic boost that would accompany drilling and strongly supported opening the refuge.

Drilling advocates minimized the beauty and environmental significance of the refuge and noted that the area was already home to three military radar stations and the small Eskimo village of Kaktovick.

But the drilling proposal enraged environmental groups, who made protecting the refuge their top legislative priority for 1991. These activists, as well as the local Gwich'in Indians who subsisted on caribou in the refuge, were unimpressed by industry claims that drilling would not do significant harm to the caribou and other wildlife.

Johnston's bill sought to protect wildlife habitat at the same time that it would open the area to oil development. It would set aside 5 cents from every barrel of oil to pay for restoring the environment. But environmentalists were skeptical of such efforts, citing a test well in the refuge that remained barren four years after it was abandoned, despite an oil firm's best efforts to reclaim the land.

For both sides, the symbolism of the Alaska drilling debate at times seemed to overpower factual considerations. Drilling proponents saw opening the refuge as a signal that lawmakers were serious about promoting the country's domestic energy supply, while opponents claimed it would send a dangerous "business as usual" message about sacrificing the environment to feed the nation's appetite for oil. These critics said that, even under the most optimistic scenarios, the refuge would not yield enough oil to dent imports significantly.

Sen. Tim Wirth, D-Colo., tried unsuccessfully to strike the Arctic drilling proposal from Johnston's energy bill in the Energy and Natural Resources Committee markup. After the committee approved the bill May 23, 1991, several junior Democrats announced plans to filibuster it because of the provision to open the refuge to oil and gas drilling. That opposition helped dissuade Senate Majority Leader George J. Mitchell, D-Maine, from scheduling floor action on the measure until late fall.

When the energy bill did come up in the closing days of the session, senators refused even to debate it. On a **key vote of 50-44 (R 32-9; D 18-35)**, they rejected Nov. 1 a motion to cut off a filibuster on a motion to take up the bill, 10 votes short of the 60 needed. Although other controversial provisions of the energy bill contributed to the Senate's refusal to proceed with its consideration, the controversial Alaska drilling provision dominated much of the debate. *(1991 key votes, p. 1061)*

The House had been considered even less friendly to the drilling proposal, and leaders there did not even bring the matter up for a vote in committee.

Yucca Mountain Nuclear Dump

Federal efforts to build a high-level nuclear waste dump in Yucca Mountain, Nev., moved forward during the 102nd Congress, despite the strenuous objection of the state's congressional delegation.

The 1982 Nuclear Waste Policy Act (PL 97-425) originally envisioned two nuclear dump sites, one in the East and one in the West. But political pressures led the Reagan administration to suspend its search for a site in the East in 1986, while the search for one in the West soon focused on three potential locations: Deaf Smith County, Texas; Hanford, Wash.; and Yucca Mountain, Nev. *(1982 act, Congress and the Nation Vol. VI, p. 361)*

Although the 1982 law called for the Energy Department to study all three sites before choosing one, politics and budget pressures again intervened in 1987. First the Senate voted to restrict the dump study to one site, with language tilting the selection toward Nevada. Then the House, with direction from its powerful Texas and Washington members, explicitly fingered Yucca Mountain.

The agreement was passed and became known in Nevada as the "Screw Nevada" bill. While some observers said there was scientific cause to choose the Nevada site over the Texas and Washington sites, few disputed the critical role politics played. "We did arbitrarily reach out and pick Yucca Mountain, no question about that," Sen. Larry E. Craig, R-Idaho, said at a Senate hearing. *(1987 action, Congress and the Nation Vol. VII, p. 483)*

State officials called the 1987 law unconstitutional and initially refused to process environmental permits for site work at Yucca Mountain. However, the courts had since ordered Nevada to begin processing permits, and some had been granted.

Despite that progress, Bush administration officials had pushed for legislation, saying they could not trust the state to process the 15 additional permits that were needed. As part of its omnibus energy bill (HR 776), the House in 1992 approved a provision that would let the federal government bypass state environmental permit requirements as it studied the suitability of the proposed dump site. *(Energy bill, p. 500)*

Nevada's senators, Democrats Harry Reid and Richard H. Bryan, successfully used a filibuster threat to force J. Bennett Johnston, D-La., the powerful chairman of the Senate Energy Committee and the primary sponsor of the Senate energy bill, to oppose the House provision in conference. They argued that the provision represented a political end run around state environmental safeguards and threatened to set a dangerous precedent for other controversial projects.

Johnston honored the pledge, but in conference he insisted on a different provision that critics said would lead to unsafe radiation exposure standards for the dump. The House bill had directed the Environmental Protection Agency (EPA) to reinstate the 1985 standards governing disposal of nuclear waste to protect public health, except for those portions that had been struck down by a federal court. Johnston, who was eager to move ahead with the proposed dump, instead wanted the EPA to issue new standards specifically tailored to the Yucca Mountain site. Under his proposal, later adopted by the conference committee, EPA would have to base new standards on a study to be conducted by the National Academy of Sciences.

The Nevada delegation and several environmental groups protested that Johnston was trying to fix the regulatory process in favor of opening the Yucca dump and at the expense of Nevadans' health.

During debate on the conference report, the House rejected an effort to strip Johnston's provision from the final version of the energy bill, and only six senators joined Reid and Bryan in their effort to block the Senate from taking up the conference report.

But the Nevadans were not expected to allow their crusade to die. "I remain confident there will be no nuclear dump at Yucca Mountain," Bryan said.

Irrigation Subsidies

Despite the ardent opposition of California lawmakers with ties to agribusiness, Congress in 1992 cleared a 40-title omnibus bill (HR 429 — PL 102-575) that promised to have a wide-ranging effect on the West's most valuable natural resource: water. The move was part of a reappraisal of traditional notions of how Western water should be used. For much of the West's history, a river's water was considered wasted unless its bounty was spread over farmland or sent crashing through power-generating turbines.

One prime example of traditional Western water policy was California's Central Valley Project, the largest federal irrigation and power project. It controlled about one-fifth of the state's usable water supply — enough for every household in the state. But the project, instead, was devoted to agriculture, with more than 85 percent of its supply in 1992 being sold at heavily discounted rates to 23,000 farming operations in the 500-mile long Central Valley.

The project and others like it had always been blamed for environmental problems such as changed stream flows, declining salmon populations and diminishing wildfowl habitat. Critics in both the East and West also said that federal water policy was slow to recognize the urbanization of the West. The 1992 drought that continued to parch major portions of the West for a sixth year only intensified complaints about urban dwellers being subject to rationing and high rates while nearby farmers had first call on increasingly scarce water and paid less for it.

As a result, the political dynamic in the 102nd Congress was ripe for a change in water policy. And supporters of a change were in position to see that it occurred.

In the House, George Miller, D-Calif., had become chairman of the Interior and Insular Affairs Committee in 1991. As a representative of the urban East Bay area near San Francisco, Miller long had been determined to put an end to special breaks for Western agricultural interests and to divert more water to the valley's decimated wetlands and refuges, as well as to urban families.

In the Senate, Democrat Bill Bradley of New Jersey was chairman of Energy and Natural Resources Subcommittee on Water and Power. He had been a longtime champion of revamping federal water policy and doing away with agricultural subsidies.

Over the protests of rural Western interests, Miller and Bradley managed to insert provisions into a traditional water projects bill that would begin to change water use in the West to reflect urban and environmental values.

In its most significant provisions, the omnibus water bill:

- Reassigned water away from farmers in the Central Valley to environmental and wildlife uses, allowed water contractors to sell their water to buyers outside the valley and established a tiered pricing system to encourage conservation.
- Sought to protect the Grand Canyon by mandating changes in the operation of the Colorado River Storage Project's huge Glen Canyon Dam. Although the dam's hy-

droelectric facility provided power to users throughout the Southwest, the fluctuating levels of water released through its turbines had begun to erode the beaches and shoreline of the river as it passed through the Grand Canyon.

- Authorized $924 million to complete the Central Utah Project, a series of massive water diversion tunnels and pipelines that would bring more Colorado River water to rapidly growing cities in the center of the state. The bill also required the water project to include environmental protections.

Despite the environmental protections in HR 429, most of the projects were intended for irrigation and power generation. The bill also did not substantially raise the price of irrigation water, as some lawmakers had wanted.

Although many California legislators, led by Republican Sen. John Seymour, vigorously opposed the Central Valley provisions, they were unable to carry with them Western lawmakers in states that stood to benefit from the projects in the bill's three dozen other titles. In the midst of his campaign for re-election, President Bush was caught between the need to bow to the concerns of California farmers, a potent force in a critical electoral state, and the equally crucial need to carry the rest of the West.

Bush signed the bill Oct. 30, despite calls from Interior Secretary Manuel Lujan Jr. and Agriculture Secretary Edward R. Madigan that he veto it.

Background

The 1992 omnibus water bill continued a tradition of federal activism in water policy that dated to 1902, when the first irrigation and reclamation laws were passed to encourage the development of the West. Legislation enacted that year subsidized the cost of water to farms of 160 acres for an individual farmer and 320 acres for a couple. As machinery allowed farmers to expand the size of their farms, the acreage limits became outmoded, and some landowners devised elaborate schemes to circumvent them.

The law had been amended several times. The last major revision came in 1982 (PL 97-293), when the acreage limitation was raised to 960 acres for an individual or small corporation. Federal water could be used on leased acreage beyond the limit, but farmers would have to pay higher fees for that water. *(Congress and the Nation Vol. VI, p. 431)*

Despite the revision, which had been pushed through by Miller and other lawmakers, many large agribusinesses continued to get subsidized water by splitting their operations — on paper — into 960-acre pieces. Moreover, some farming operations were "double dipping" by using subsidized water to grow surplus crops whose prices were guaranteed by the government.

Miller's attempt in 1987 to win a broad revision of the reclamation law failed. In 1990, he won a significant victory when the House voted to tighten the law, but the legislation died in the Senate. *(1990 action, p. 495)*

1991 Action

HR 429 was introduced by Craig Thomas, R-Wyo., in January 1991 to authorize funds for the Buffalo Bill Dam in his state. By the time it was approved by the House Interior Committee on May 1, the bill included some 21 other titles for projects across the West. It also included some of the reforms that Miller, now chairman of the committee, had been seeking for years. These included strict limits on which farm operations could receive subsidized water and a prohibition on receiving subsidized water to grow subsidized crops. The committee version, however, did not include a reform of the Central Valley Project. The Interior Committee formally reported HR 429 (H Rept 102-114, Part I) on June 18.

The House passed HR 429 June 20 on a vote of 360-24. But then the bill stalled in the Senate, where it did not get beyond the hearing stage in 1991. Late in the year, Miller tried to win passage of the reform measure by attaching it to a separate bill (HR 355) intended to ease the effects of the drought in the West. But his motion, brought to the House floor Nov. 18 under suspension of the rules, which requires a two-thirds majority vote, was rejected 245-164.

Senate Action

Senate action in 1992 began in the Energy and Natural Resources Committee, where Bradley offered amendments to HR 429 on the Central Valley Project that would have shortened the life of water contracts, permitted water sales to customers outside the project and reserved water for wildlife. Seymour, like his mentor, California Gov. Pete Wilson, was closely allied with Central Valley agricultural interests and opposed the Bradley language. Seymour offered his own Central Valley Project provisions that were more protective of the status quo. On March 19, the full committee rejected Bradley's provisions and adopted Seymour's before approving the bill by voice vote. Bradley, joined by committee Chairman J. Bennett Johnston, D-La., did nothing to stop what was happening. They knew Seymour could bottle up a bill he did not like, and they wanted to keep the bill moving. HR 429 (S Rept 102-267) was formally reported from the Energy Committee on March 31.

The full Senate passed HR 429 by voice vote and with no debate on April 10. By that time, the bill had grown to some 40 titles between the House and Senate versions. That gave Bradley, Johnston and Miller a good deal of political leverage with their Western colleagues during conference negotiations. But first they had to get the version of the Central Valley Project package that they favored into conference.

House Action

That was accomplished when Miller introduced a new measure (HR 5099) that dealt solely with the Central Valley Project. The House Interior Committee approved HR 5099 by voice vote on May 28, 1992, and formally reported it (H Rept 102-576, Part I) on June 16. The full House passed the bill by voice vote on June 18. The House subsequently further amended HR 429 with the language of HR 5099.

Conference, Final Action

After nearly four months of behind-the-scenes negotiations, conferees agreed to strip Seymour's Central Valley Project provisions from HR 429 in favor of a package very much like Bradley's original proposal. Valley farmers and the California legislators who represented them cried foul. But a phalanx of other state interests lined up behind Miller and Bradley: most of the state's urban country governments, the big metropolitan water district of Los Angeles, corporate business groups and environmentalists. Moreover, other Western lawmakers who might have been counted on to support the California lawmakers in the past were unwilling to give up the water projects that HR 429 would authorize in their own states.

In the House, the showdown on the conference report (H Rept 102-1016) came in the early morning hours of Oct. 6, when Rep. Bill Thomas, R, who represented the southern tip of the valley, offered a motion to recommit the bill to committee and to strip out all of the provisions relating to the Central Valley. The House was unmoved; it rejected the motion on a **key vote of 159-244 (R 117-41; D 42-202; I 0-1)**. Members then adopted the conference report by voice vote. *(1992 key votes, p. 1083)*

In the Senate, Seymour fought with all the dilatory weapons afforded him by that chamber. He helped Alfonse M. D'Amato, R-N.Y., to mount an all-night filibuster on a 1992 tax bill (HR 11). And he insisted that the clerk read the entire 396-page bill, a procedure that took hours of precious Senate time in the closing days of the session. But like Thomas in the House, Seymour got little support from his Western colleagues. On Oct. 6, a delegation of stalwart Western Republicans, including Malcolm Wallop of Wyoming, Jake Garn of Utah and John McCain of Arizona, met with White House Chief of Staff James A. Baker III to lobby for Bush's signature. They were looking not at Seymour's lonely stance but at the big projects that would benefit their states and their own political prospects.

When it became clear that he did not have the votes to prevent Senate leaders from invoking cloture, Seymour conceded the fight. He agreed to a deal in which the Senate would approve a symbolic bill (S 3365) that incorporated Seymour's Central Valley provisions, but because that bill moved on the next-to-last day of the session, it died when the House failed to act. The Senate, meanwhile, finally adopted the conference report Oct. 8 on a **key vote of 83-8 (R 30-8; D 53-0)**.

Major Provisions

As cleared, HR 429:

Central Valley Projects

- **Purposes.** Made wildlife and environmental protection, mitigation and restoration official purposes of the Central Valley Project, along with irrigation, flood control and power.
- **Impact.** Required the Interior Department to complete an environmental impact statement analyzing the effects of the bill within three years.
- **Environmental Goals.** Prohibited the Bureau of Reclamation from entering into new water contracts with Central Valley Project users until the following conditions were met:
- A program was developed to double population levels of salmon, steelhead, striped bass, sturgeon, American shad and other anadromous fish over the average level attained form 1967 through 1991.
- A program was developed to reduce damage to the environment caused by the operation of the Central Valley Project's vast array of pumping plants, dams and canals.
- A minimum of 800,000 acre-feet of Central Valley Project water was set aside for fish, wildlife and environmental restoration, including wetlands. An acre-foot is approximately 326,000 gallons of water, enough to cover an acre of land with a foot of water. The U.S. Fish and Wildlife Service continued to have authority to determine how that water would be managed.
- Adoption of changes by the project to reduce the number of migratory fish killed. Among such changes were the installation of a device at Shasta Dam to reduce high water temperatures linked to the deaths of migratory fish and modification of the fish trap at Keswick Dam to reduce the number of fish killed as they passed through the spillway.
- Development of a fish and wildlife restoration plan by the Interior Department for the San Joaquin and Stanislaus rivers by Sept. 30, 1996.
- Allowed for three-year contracts to be drafted in the interim while the environmental impact statement was being completed.
- **Exceptions.** Allowed the Bureau of Reclamation to temporarily reduce water reserves for wildlife and the environment by up to 25 percent if natural conditions such as droughts mandated such a change. Any unneeded water could be used for agricultural purposes.
- **Environmental Studies.** Directed Interior to complete numerous studies within five years, including studies on water conservation, alternative water supplies, temperature control, hatchery operations, salmon migration and water supplies. Within two years, a report on the project's effects on migratory fish and the groups economically dependent upon them was to have been completed.
- **Restoration Fund.** Established a restoration fund of up to $50 million a year to carry out the law's environmental and wildlife mandates. The account would be funded through surcharges on Central Valley water users. For example, agricultural water users were to be levied a charge of up to $6 for each acre-foot of water used, and municipal and industrial water users were each to be assessed a maximum of $12 for each acre-foot. Any state or agency that had not previously been a project customer faced a fee of up to $25 per acre-foot.

Any revenues from the sale of project water to those outside the project would be deposited in the restoration fund. Any revenues from a new tiered-pricing system also would be put in the fund. The bill allowed Interior to aid state governments, Indian tribes and non-profit groups that were assisting in efforts to follow the bill's mandates.

- **Water Sales.** Allowed Central Valley Project users to sell their water allotments at market prices so long as the sales posed no adverse environmental or groundwater effects. Project contractors had to pay full cost for water later sold to agricultural users and higher rates for water sold to municipal and industrial users. The bill allowed conventional Central Valley Project users the right to bid on outside water sales first, so long as they agreed to pay the same price charged outsiders. Any water transfers or sales that would shift more than 20 percent of a water district's water allotment would be subject to review by the Interior Department or the affected water district.
- **Contract Renewals.** Authorized renewal of existing long-term water contracts for a 25-year period; successive renewals also could be for up to 25 years. Before the bill passed, contracts were renewed for 40 years. Contracts renewed after Jan. 1, 1988, were subject to new changes mandated for the restoration fund.
- **Water Prices.** Created a tiered-pricing system to encourage water conservation. Longstanding subsidized water rates applied to the first tier, which covered the first 80 percent of the total amount of water allocated in any contract. The subsidized rate was as low as $3.50 an acre-foot but could be higher depending on the district. A sec-

ond tier applied to the next 10 percent of the water used and the price for that water was halfway between the long-standing contract rate and the government's full cost of delivering the water, which was $15 to $50 an acre-foot, depending on the district and the distance it was from a Central Valley Project storage or pumping facility. The final 10 percent of water allocated under any contract would be subject to a price equal to the full cost of supplying the water.

Any water used to produce a crop that could provide breeding grounds for wildfowl was exempted from the tiered pricing system.

Central Utah Project

• **Authorization.** Authorized $924.2 million over five years for the completion of the Central Utah Project, the last major section of the Colorado River Storage Project. It is a system of reservoirs, pipelines and aqueducts to divert water from the Uintah Basin, a part of the Colorado River Basin east of Salt Lake City, over the Wasatch Mountains to the Bonneville Basin in western Utah. The authorization gave the Central Utah Water Conservancy District the option to use the Bureau of Reclamation as the main contractor to complete construction of the project or to use a private group.

• **Bonneville Unit.** Authorized $242.5 million for the construction of the Bonneville Unit of the Central Utah Project. The bill required local water users to pay 35 percent of the project's construction costs and half the cost of conducting feasibility studies.

The Bonneville section authorized $150 million for a major pipeline that would deliver water to more than 175,000 acres of farmland in rural western-central Utah, $69 million to complete the Diamond Fork System, $10 million for a study of ways to better manage and recharge groundwater supplies, $10 million for construction of water-management demonstration facilities in Wasatch County in northeastern Utah and $1 million to study ways to reduce the salinity of Utah Lake, a prime water resource for central Utah. Another $1 million was authorized to study the impact on the Provo River's salinity levels when the river was diverted to the Central Utah Project.

• **Water Conservation.** Required the Central Utah Water Conservancy District to complete a water conservation plan by Jan. 1, 1995, with the goal of cutting projected water consumption by at least 30,000 acre-feet a year. The bill authorized a study of water-pricing policies to encourage conservation. It also created a conservation advisory board to set minimum conservation targets.

• **Surplus Crops.** Levied a surcharge on project water used to produce government-subsidized surplus crops (wheat, feed grains, cotton, rice). The fee equaled 10 percent of the full cost to the government of delivering the water.

• **Fish, Wildlife and Recreation Protection.** Provided for the conservation and restoration of fish, wildlife and recreation resources affected by past and future Central Utah Project facilities. To carry out these mandates, the bill established a five-member commission appointed by the president. It authorized up to $1 million a year to pay for the commission's expenses and created a $13.75 million trust fund to pay for ongoing conservation activities after the project's completion.

The bill provided $15 million to buy 25,000 acre-feet of water to augment stream levels for fish and wildlife. It also provided funds to lease water necessary to sustain fish and wildlife in the upper Strawberry River, the Uintah Basin and the Diamond Fork River. The measure also authorized $1.3 million to buy big-game winter rangelands, $14 million to preserve wetlands around the Great Salt Lake and $16.7 million to establish a Utah Lakes Wetlands Preserve. It provided protection for the southern half of Provo Bay from commercial development and provided $22 million for various habitat and streambed restoration projects. The measure also authorized $5 million to restore lakes in the Uintah Mountains for fisheries and recreation and $22.8 million to improve existing fish hatcheries and build new ones.

• **Ute Indians.** Set forth a water rights agreement reached among the Ute Indians, the state of Utah and the Central Utah Water Conservancy District in which the Indians were guaranteed $2 million a year for the next 50 years for Indian water diverted by the Bonneville Unit. The bill ratified the 1990 Ute Indian compact, regarding tribal water rights and use of the Central Utah Project water. It authorized $45 million to help the tribe improve farming operations and $125 million over three years for an economic development fund.

The Grand Canyon

• **Glen Canyon Dam.** Directed the Interior Department to operate Glen Canyon Dam, which empties into the Colorado River north of the Grand Canyon, in such a way as to minimize damaging environmental effects on Grand Canyon National Park and the Glen Canyon National Recreation Area.

• **Environmental Impact Statement.** Required the department, within two years after enactment, to complete a final environmental impact statement on the operation of Glen Canyon Dam.

• **Audit.** Required Interior's comptroller general, within two years after enactment, to complete an audit of the costs and benefits of the dam not only to water and power users, but also to natural, recreational and cultural resource users.

• **Fees.** Required local power users to shoulder the full cost of preparing the environmental impact statement. The bill set aside proceeds from electric power sales to pay for the study and credited those revenues against power users' repayment obligations.

• **Power Levels.** Directed the Energy Department to find economically and technically feasible ways to replace any power lost caused by the bill's environmental regulations. The measure directed the Energy Department to study changes in the operation of Hoover Dam to replace lost power or to study adjusting the system's power transmission lines for the same purpose.

Other Reclamation Projects

• **Leadville Mine Drainage Tunnel.** Authorized $10.7 million for the construction of a plant to treat contaminated water flowing from the World War II-era Leadville Mine drainage tunnel in Colorado into the East Fork of the Arkansas River. The bill also authorized new concrete linings for the tunnel and provided for restoration of fish and wildlife resources in the Arkansas River Basin.

• **East Texas' Lake Meredith Salinity Control.** Authorized construction and testing of a series of wells to intercept salt water leaching into Lake Meredith, a Bureau of Reclamation storage reservoir in East Texas. The brine was to be disposed of by deep-well injection. The federal government was to pay no more than 33 percent of the project's cost.

• **Mid-Dakota Rural Water System.** Authorized the Interior Department to make $100 million in grants and loans to the Mid-Dakota Rural Water System Inc., a non-profit corporation, to build a water system providing safe and reliable water to central South Dakota users. The bill also allotted a $100,000 annual grant to restore regional wetlands known as "Prairie Potholes." It also required local water users to put in place a water conservation program.

• **Central Arizona Project.** Provided for the repair or replacement of four siphons along the Hayden-Rhodes Aqueduct at the Salt River, the New River, the Hassayampa River and the Aqua Fria River as well as Jackrabbit Wash and Centennial Wash — all part of the Central Arizona Project.

Research Projects

• **Wastewater and Groundwater Studies.** Directed the interior secretary to enter into cost-shared studies on ways to reuse agricultural, domestic, municipal and industrial waste water in five feasibility studies and four demonstration projects in California, Arizona and Colorado.

• **South Dakota Study.** Authorized a five-year demonstration program to determine whether the soils of the Lake Andes-Wagner area had unsafe levels of selenium, a pollutant that leaches from irrigated farmland and contaminates water supplies. The bill required the Interior Department to certify that any new water project complied with federal water-quality standards and would not produce selenium contamination.

Pending completion of the demonstration project, the bill authorized $175 million to complete the Lake Andes-Wagner Unit, which was to irrigate 45,000 acres of dry-farmed land using water from the North Bay arm of Lake Francis Case. An additional $24 million was allocated for the Marty II Unit, a 3,000-acre irrigation project designed to serve the Yankton Sioux Reservation. The project diverted Missouri River water to the reservation.

• **High Plains Groundwater Program.** Raised the authorization ceiling for the High Plains groundwater program. The bill allotted $31 million for the program, up from $20 million. The project was designed to investigate and build projects to show the potential for artificially recharging aquifers and recharging groundwater supplies.

• **Western Water Policy Review.** Directed the president to review Western water resource problems and issues, including programs administered by the U.S. Geological Survey and the Bureau of Reclamation, and to report findings within three years of enactment. The bill authorized $10 million to create an 18-member advisory commission to study expected Western water resource and storage problems, federal water policy and water resource problems faced by rural communities. The commission also was to review the water-allocation system, flood control and interstate compacts in the West.

• **San Francisco Demonstration Project.** Authorized the Interior Department to work with the city and county of San Francisco to examine the feasibility of "greenhouse-based" water reclamation technologies, especially those that used densely populated marsh and pond ecosystems to purify polluted water for reuse. The bill mandated that the cost of the project would be shared equally by the federal and local governments.

Environmental, Recreation Projects

• **South Dakota's Biological Diversity Trust Fund.** Authorized a federal trust of up to $12 million for projects to protect or restore the best examples of South Dakota's biological diversity, its rare species and ecosystems. The bill authorized up to $7 million over the next five years to establish a wetlands foundation to be operated by the South Dakota Game Fish and Parks Foundation to buy and preserve the state's outstanding wetlands.

• **California's Sonoma Baylands.** Authorized a $15 million wetlands demonstration project in the San Francisco Bay-Sacramento/San Joaquin Delta to use dredged materials to restore and expand the area's Sonoma Baylands by July 1, 1994. The project was to have been carried out by the U.S. Army Corps of Engineers.

Indian Water Rights

• **Standing Rock Indian Reservation.** Made additional water available to the Standing Rock Sioux Indians in South Dakota for irrigation. The provision altered the Garrison Diversion Unit Reformulation Act of 1986 (PL 99-294). A related section required that the Three Affiliated Tribes of the Fort Berthold Reservation and the Standing Rock Sioux Indians be compensated for the taking of reservation lands when the Garrison Dam and reservoir and the Oahe Dam and reservoir were built. The payment was not to exceed $149.2 million for the Three Affiliated Tribes and $90.6 million for the Standing Rock Sioux Indians.

• **San Carlos Apache Indians.** Provided Arizona's San Carlos Apache Indians 152,435 acre-feet of water annually and $38.4 million to start a fund to develop water resources in exchange for the federal government's use of 292-406 acre-feet of the Indian tribe's water.

Miscellaneous

• **Renaming Salt-Gila Aqueduct.** Renamed this section of the Central Arizona Project after former Arizona governor (1959-65) and Republican senator (1965-77) Paul Fannin and former governor (1955-59) and Democratic senator (1941-53) Ernest McFarland.

• **New Mexico's Vermejo Project.** Transferred Lake 13 in New Mexico from the federal government to New Mexico's Vermejo Conservancy District but allowed the U.S. Fish and Wildlife Service to continue to manage the lake as part of the Maxwell National Wildlife Refuge.

• **New Mexico's Rio Grande Floodway.** Modified the Rio Grande Floodway Project, a series of flood control levees along a 55-mile stretch of the Rio Grande River, to reduce New Mexico's contribution to the project. The move came after it was determined that federal projects, such as the Bosque del Apache National Wildlife Refuge, were the main beneficiaries of the $50 million project.

• **Washington's Sunnyside Valley.** Conveyed a small parcel of improved, but no longer used, property in the town of Sunnyside, Wash., to the Sunnyside Valley Irrigation District. The district planned to sell the land and use the proceeds to build a district office building.

• **Colorado's Platoro Reservoir and Dam.** Directed the interior secretary to accept a one-time payment of $450,000 from Colorado's Conejos Water Conservancy District in exchange for transferring the operation and maintenance of the Platoro Dam and Reservoir to the district. The federal government, however, was to retain authority over the recreational and environmental uses of the dam and reservoir.

- **California's Redwood Valley.** Authorized the Interior Department to sell or accept prepayment of two loans totaling $7.3 million made to the Redwood Valley County Water District, in Mendocino County, to build water-pumping facilities to divert water from Lake Mendocino to Redwood Valley. The terms of the prepayment plan were still to be negotiated at time of passage.
- **California's United Water Conservation District.** Authorized the Interior Department to sell or accept prepayment of an $18.7 million loan made to this Ventura County water conservation district. The loan was extended to make improvements to the Freeman Diversion Dam on the Santa Clara River to increase water supplies to the Oxnard Plain for irrigation and domestic purposes and to recharge the ground water. The terms of the prepayment plan were yet to be negotiated at time of passage.
- **Montana Irrigation Project.** Directed the Energy Department to sell low-cost Pick-Sloan Missouri River Basin Project power to the Haidle Irrigation Project in Prairie County, Mont., and to the Hammond Irrigation District in Rosebud County, Mont.
- **California's San Juan Suburban Water District.** Required the Interior Department to credit the San Juan water district for the $300,000 cost of two water pumps purchased by the district for use at the Bureau of Reclamation's Folsom Dam.
- **Oklahoma's Mountain Park.** Authorized the Interior Department to sell or accept prepayment on the Tom Steed Reservoir from the Mountain Park Master Conservancy District in Oklahoma. The reservoir provided a supplemental municipal and industrial water supply to the Oklahoma cities of Altus, Snyder and Frederick.
- **New Mexico's Elephant Butte Irrigation District.** Transferred title to certain easements, ditches, laterals, canals, drains and rights of way from the Interior Department to the Elephant Butte Irrigation District and El Paso County Water Improvement District No. 1. The receptive districts had provided the facilities to the federal government for the project.
- **National Historic Preservation Act.** Amended the 1966 National Historic Preservation Act to clarify and streamline the act to help facilitate the preservation of historical resources.

Oil and Gas Royalties

Congress in 1991 shifted its focus from limiting offshore oil and gas leasing to reducing the administrative costs of the onshore leasing program administered by the Interior Department's Mineral Management Service.

During consideration of the fiscal 1992 Interior spending bill (HR 2686 — PL 102-154), appropriators sought to raise to 50 percent the states' share of the cost of collecting royalties from onshore leasing to reap the government an additional $68 million annually. But they were rebuffed in the House and Senate.

In the House, Nick J. Rahall II, D-W.Va., on June 25 got the fee provision stripped out of the bill on a point of order. He said it amounted to new legislation. In the Senate, Malcolm Wallop, R-Wyo., and other Western lawmakers were able to win approval Sept. 12 of an amendment effectively keeping the state share of costs at the existing 25 percent. In conference, negotiators left the fees unchanged.

Royalties from oil and gas companies operating on federal lands were shared by the states and the federal government. Western states depended on the royalties to fund important programs such as education and were vehemently opposed to any change. In the end, Congress directed the Mineral Management Service, in cooperation with the Bureau of Land Management and the Forest Service, to study revising the way in which royalties were collected and distributed, with an eye to giving more responsibilities to the states.

Grazing Fees

A coalition of lawmakers and environmentalists sought unsuccessfully to force Westerners to pay higher fees for grazing their cattle on public land. Although the House in 1991 attached grazing fee increases to two measures — one reauthorizing the Bureau of the Land Management (BLM) and the other making fiscal 1992 appropriations for the Interior Department — the increases ultimately fell victim to the political strength of Western senators. Efforts to impose an increase in fees also failed in 1992.

The issue encapsulated the growing conflict among users of the country's vast public lands. By almost any measure, the fees ranchers paid to graze their cattle on public land were lower than those paid by ranchers who grazed their cattle on private pastures. The federal grazing fee per animal unit month (AUM) — the amount of forage that a cow and calf typically consumed in that time — was $1.97 in 1991, compared with an average private market rate of $9.22 for Western rangeland.

The inevitable result, argued some lawmakers and environmentalists, was overgrazing of arid Western rangeland and millions of dollars of lost federal revenue every year.

But Western lawmakers had turned the issue into a symbolic lightning rod, portraying themselves as struggling ranchers, the backbone of the Old West. And they noted that the BLM in a 1990 report said that the public rangelands were in better condition than at any time in the 20th century.

For years, Westerners on the House Interior Committee and in the Senate had been able to block any proposals to hike the grazing fees. Then, in 1990, Rep. Mike Synar, D-Okla., was able to bypass the committee and add to the fiscal 1991 Interior appropriations bill (HR 5769 — PL 101-512) language raising the fees. On Oct. 15, the House, 251-155, adopted an amendment to impose gradually a 500 percent increase in the grazing fees. The Senate, however, struck the amendment from its version of the bill, and conferees ultimately sided with the Senate.

Fiscal 1992 Interior Spending Bill

With Western lawmakers protesting every step of the way, the House on June 25, 1991, adopted an amendment to raise grazing fees to $8.70 over four years, more than quadruple the existing rate, on a **key vote of 232-192 (R 47-114; D 184-78; I 1-0)**. The increase was included as part of the fiscal 1992 Interior appropriations bill (HR

2686 — PL 102-154) and replaced a provision adopted by the Appropriations Committee that would have raised the fees by 33 percent. *(1991 key votes, p. 1061)*

Synar's 1991 amendment passed by a smaller margin than his 1990 amendment had. What made the 1991 vote significant was that it emboldened Senate supporters of a fee hike, who for the first time since 1978 pushed for a vote in their chamber. The effort failed, when the Senate voted 60-38 on Sept. 17 to table an amendment by Sen. James M. Jeffords, R-Vt., that would have raised grazing fees to $5.13 by 1996.

Conference negotiators then sealed the victory for Western lawmakers opposed to a fee increase when they agreed to a deal that guaranteed a freeze in federal grazing fees for a truce on arts funding. The "corn for porn" deal, as it was quickly labeled, came after days of deadlock. The trade-off called on House negotiators to drop the grazing fee hike in exchange for Senate abandonment of restrictions on arts funding sought by Sen. Jesse Helms, R-N.C. The House Oct. 24 adopted the conference report (H Rept 102-256) after narrowly rejecting, 205-214, a move to strike the compromise. The Senate Oct. 31 tabled 73-25 an amendment by Helms to add more restrictions on arts funding. HR 2686 eventually cleared Nov. 1. *(Arts funding controversy, p. 865)*

BLM Reauthorization

Synar also succeeded in attaching a grazing fee increase to a House bill (HR 1096) to reauthorize the BLM. The House on July 23, 1991, agreed by voice vote to Synar's amendment increasing the fee to $8.70 per AUM by 1995. It then adopted, 254-156, another amendment that would cap those increases at 33 percent a year, making the top grazing fee in 1995 $4.68 per AUM. In the Senate, however, the BLM reauthorization encountered vigorous resistance and died of inaction. *(BLM reauthorization, p. 520)*

1992 Action

The debate over raising grazing fees was replayed in 1992, but it was not nearly as spirited. The House version of the fiscal 1993 Interior appropriations bill (HR 5503 — PL 102-381) contained a provision that would raise the grazing fee to $2.56 — much less than the original Synar amendment. During floor consideration, the House July 22 rejected, 164-245, an attempt to remove that proposed increase.

In the Senate, a motion to table a Jeffords amendment that would have raised the fees to $2.40 was agreed to 50-44 on Aug. 6; Jeffords had attracted six more votes than he had the year before. In conference, the House agreed to drop its provision increasing grazing fees in return for the Senate agreeing to drop a package of mining reforms. It was the third year in a row that grazing fee increases adopted by the House had been traded away in conference. *(Mining reform, below)*

Mining Law Overhaul

The 102nd Congress came closer than it had in years but ultimately failed to enact a comprehensive rewrite of the nation's 120-year-old mining law. A modest change in the mining law, however, was folded into the fiscal 1993 spending bill for the Interior Department and related agencies (HR 5503 — PL 102-381).

Action began with House lawmakers pushing a bill (HR 918) by Nick J. Rahall II, D-W.Va., that aimed to change the 1872 Mining Law to conform to 20th century realities. Proponents said the original law, passed when the settlement of the West was a national priority, was partly responsible for a litany of ills.

Problems included a continued sell-off of federal land to private use for as little as $2.50 an acre; improper use of mining claims for real estate development; a legacy of abandoned mines left to scar the landscape and pollute water supplies; and the practice of mining companies (often foreign-owned) to extract billions of dollars in minerals without paying royalties to the federal Treasury.

The House took up the bill during the last-minute crush of business Oct. 4, 1992, and voted on several amendments — most notably rejecting an amendment to impose a royalty fee of up to 12.5 percent of gross receipts derived from mining public lands. But the House never finished debating the bill, and it died when Congress adjourned. HR 918 had been reported July 3 by House Interior and Insular Affairs (H Rept 102-711, Part I) and Sept. 11 by House Agriculture (H Rept 102-711, Part II).

A companion Senate bill (S 433) by Dale Bumpers, D-Ark., never made it out of the Energy and Natural Resources Committee. But Senate appropriators sought their own reforms, which were inserted into HR 5503 Aug. 5.

In conference, however, all but minor changes in the mining law were stripped from the Interior appropriations bill. The surviving provision imposed a new annual $100 fee on miners to keep their mining claims active. The change did away with a longstanding requirement that miners perform $100 worth of mining-related work each year to keep a claim active — a mandate that environmentalists said led to the unnecessary scarring of public lands. Both the House and Senate adopted the conference report (H Rept 102-901) Sept. 30 by voice vote. President Bush signed the appropriations bill Oct. 5.

Background

Efforts to reform the 1872 law were nearly as old as the law itself. As early as 1879, a federally appointed public land commission recommended that it be rewritten.

But it was not until 1987 that efforts to overhaul the law began. The Interior Subcommittee on Mining and Natural Resources, chaired by bill sponsor Rahall, reviewed the law, and the effort produced in 1989 a widely read report by the General Accounting Office (GAO) that documented abuses and revealed conflicts with federal land-management policies.

The 1872 Mining Law had made mining one of the most favored uses of Western federal land. Mining superseded anything else the land might be used for, such as grazing, logging or recreation, unless the government specifically withdrew the land from mining purposes.

In 19 states, mostly in the West, the law guaranteed "free and open access to certain public lands to prospect" for minerals, according to the Interior Department's Bureau of Land Management (BLM). The GAO noted that the law gave mining advantages over other uses that ran "counter to other national natural resource policies and legislation." There were 1.2 million active claims in the country; 160,000 new claims were filed in 1988, a 1990 GAO report said.

Aided by the 1872 law, hard-rock mining had become a $9 billion industry that employed about 47,000 people, according to the Congressional Research Service. Many small towns in the West were dependent on mining income.

But critics said the law had turned into a massive giveaway to large, often foreign-owned corporations. Corporations and individuals used the law's provisions to patent or take title to 3.2 million acres of federal land for hard-rock mining for as little as $2.50 an acre. Miners were able to extract minerals such a gold, silver and platinum without paying royalties to the Treasury — unlike oil and gas operations. The scarred landscapes left behind were expected to cost $11 billion to restore.

Speculators also used the law to buy land inexpensively and turn it into developments, resorts and vacation homes. A 1990 GAO study said that, of 59 mining claim sites it visited, "33 had unauthorized residences ranging from small, run-down shacks to permanent, more expensive, year-round dwellings.... All these claim holders live rent-free on public land."

Earlier Action

In 1990, language designed to stop the sale of federal lands claimed for oil shale development — just a fraction of the lands covered under the mining law — was attached to a must-pass budget-reconciliation bill (HR 5835). It was later dropped in conference amid Senate objections. *(Story, p. 499)*

In 1990, the House approved a one-year moratorium on the issuance of mining patents on federal land. The moratorium, attached to the House version of the fiscal 1991 Interior Department appropriations bill (HR 5769 — PL 101-512), was later dropped in conference — again because of Senate resistance.

Members of Congress attempted in 1991 to block the "giveaway" of federal lands, but a one-year moratorium on the patenting of all mining claims included in the House version of the fiscal 1992 Interior appropriations bill (HR 2686 — PL 102-154) was dropped in conference. An agreement, however, had been reached to consider an overhaul of the mining law the following year.

BLM Reauthorization

The House on July 23, 1991, passed by voice vote a reauthorization (HR 1096) of the Bureau of Land Management (BLM) that sought to heighten the agency's environmental consciousness. The effort stalled in the Senate where it encountered vigorous resistance by Western lawmakers. No companion legislation was even introduced.

The four-year authorization bill was intended to improve the natural quality of the bureau's 270 million acres and to give more voice to public land users other than ranchers, loggers and miners. The bill was responding to the increasing demand that public lands also be used for recreation — a trend that generated revenue for both the federal government and the affected states and localities.

Western lawmakers and the Bush administration opposed the bill. Interior Secretary Manuel Lujan Jr. recommended that the president veto it. Among other things, the administration opposed limitations on the number of political appointees at the bureau.

Members of Congress from the West warned that the bill threatened to shatter the bureau's multiple-use mandate and transform the bureau into a conservation agency. Western members were particularly incensed by an amendment that would have made the bureau manage its land with "biological diversity" in mind.

Proponents of the amendment said that long-term productivity of BLM lands depended on the conservation of all plants and animals found on them. But Barbara F. Vucanovich, R-Nev., said the amendment presented "a clear and present danger for crippling environmental lawsuits brought by non-residents of the rural West." Opponents did not attempt to strike the provision, however, and the House strengthened it by accepting by voice vote another amendment directing the BLM to manage its lands to restore their "natural productive capability."

Western lawmakers were further angered when the House accepted an amendment to increase grazing fees on BLM lands. *(Grazing fees, p. 518)*

HR 1096 was reported from House Interior and Insular Affairs (H Rept 102-138) on July 2. The Senate Energy and Natural Resources Committee reported the bill (S Rept 102-460) on Sept. 24.

A similar reauthorization measure had easily passed the House in 1989, but it was strongly opposed by the administration and disappeared without even a hearing in the Senate. *(1989 action, p. 499)*

Northern Spotted Owl

The 102nd Congress failed to achieve any consensus on a plan to protect the northern spotted owl or to manage the "old-growth" forests in the Pacific Northwest that were the home of the threatened bird. The standoff between the timber industry and environmentalists was made all the more bitter by the slumping economy and the prominence of the controversy as a campaign issue in the 1992 presidential and congressional elections. *(1989-90 action, p. 494)*

The stalemate on the issue also doomed a reauthorization of the Endangered Species Act. *(Story, p. 521)*

Scientists said the old-growth forests were the backbone of a unique ecosystem. In addition to the owl, many other species of wildlife lived there, and the forests' streams were the spawning grounds for the Northwest's salmon runs.

But the towering stands of Douglas firs and spruce also were prime sources of timber — a vital part of the region's economy, which sputtered even as the urban parts of the Pacific Northwest boomed. Logging in the region had come to a virtual standstill, as federal courts agreed with environmentalists that the U.S. Forest Service and the Bureau of Land Management had violated federal forest management laws and, in some cases, the Endangered Species Act.

Members in 1991 and 1992 introduced a hodgepodge of bills to deal with the issue, ranging from proposals supported by the timber industry that would circumvent the Endangered Species Act and judicial review of timber policy to measures that would give ironclad protection to whole swaths of the owl's habitat. Congress also failed to act on a series of competing administration proposals.

On May 14, 1992, the seven-member Endangered Species Committee, known as the "God squad," voted to suspend the Endangered Species Act and allow logging on 13 of 44 disputed tracts of federal timberland that were home to the owl. The committee was composed of the secretaries of the Departments of the Interior, Army and Agriculture and the administrators of the Environmental Protection Agency and the National Oceanic and Atmospheric Administration. The chairman of the Council of Economic Advisers and a state representative also sat on the special committee, which was the only panel that had the authority to grant exemptions to the Endangered Species Act.

It was only the second time the committee had voted to override the species protection law. But the timber sales could not go forward unless two federal court injunctions were lifted.

On the same day, Interior Secretary Manuel Lujan Jr. released the government's official recovery plan for the owl, required under the Endangered Species Act. It would set aside some 5.4 million acres of forestland and 2.1 million acres of wilderness and national parks — levels that were projected to help restore the owl's population to a level that would take it off the list of threatened species. The plan, however, would cost up to 32,000 jobs.

Calling that level of job loss unacceptable, Lujan also announced an alternative plan, which would set aside some 2.8 million acres of timberland and 1.5 million acres of parks and wilderness. The patchwork of areas could support an estimated 1,340 pairs of owls — less than half the 3,000 pairs that were known to exist.

HR 4899 (H Rept 102-1039, Part I), reported from House Agriculture Oct. 6, 1992, would have placed 6.8 million acres of old-growth forest off limits to logging. The plan would cost an estimated 22,000 to 27,000 timber jobs and, according to some scientists, give the spotted owl a 50-50 chance of recovery.

A more stringent version of HR 4899 considered by the House Interior Committee — which would have protected 9 million acres — never made it out of committee after disgruntled lawmakers called on House Speaker Thomas S. Foley, D-Wash., to lobby against it.

In the Senate, a bill (S 1156) that was more to the timber industry's liking died when its fate was linked with a measure (HR 2929) to protect millions of acres of California desert. *(Story, p. 522)*

Endangered Species

A bill (HR 4045) to reauthorize the Endangered Species Act went nowhere in the 102nd Congress. The law was originally enacted in 1973 to keep politics and money from deciding the fate of America's threatened animal and plant species. But when the act faced renewal in 1992, its reauthorization became embroiled in the politics of an election year and the economic imponderables of a recession.

The Endangered Species Act (PL 93-205) was among the most popular and well-known laws ever passed by Congress. The recovery of the bald eagle, a symbol of America, and the stabilization of the grizzly bear population were just two examples of protection given species under the act. *(Congress and the Nation Vol. IV, p. 289)*

But, fueled by the dearth of jobs, an anti-environmental backlash had made the act a highly divisive issue in several states — most especially in Oregon and Washington, where protection of the threatened northern spotted owl threatened to cost the timber industry thousands of jobs. In California, builders and landowners were nervously awaiting the outcome of a petition to list the California gnatcatcher — a small bird that nestled in prime developable coastal areas — as a threatened species. California builders said up to 200,000 jobs in the region could be affected. *(Spotted owl controversy, p. 520)*

By congressional intent, the law did not consider economic factors in deciding whether to list a species as endangered. Section 4 of the act stated that listing decisions should be made "solely on the basis of the best scientific and commercial data available."

Conservationists had welcomed the introduction Nov. 26, 1991, of a tough reauthorization bill by Gerry E. Studds, D-Mass., chairman of the Merchant Marine Subcommittee on Fisheries and Wildlife Conservation and the Environment, which had jurisdiction over the Endangered Species Act. Studds' bill sought authorization of $517 million over five years for the Interior and Commerce departments to carry out the act, more than twice what was authorized for 1988 through 1992. *(Previous authorization, Congress and the Nation Vol. VII, p. 465)*

The Interior Department's Fish and Wildlife Service had attracted environmentalists' ire for not developing species recovery plans quickly enough. Studds' proposed reauthorization required that such plans be developed by Dec. 31, 1996, for all 601 species awaiting protection. It also gave the service a two-year deadline to come up with a recovery plan for any species listed after 1993.

A key complaint of business interests was the act's emphasis on saving species on an inefficient, individual basis. This had sometimes forced projects to be halted by the discovery of a small population of endangered or threatened species, even if they were being protected elsewhere.

HR 4045 directed Fish and Wildlife — and the National Marine Fisheries Service, which ran recovery programs for endangered marine animals — to emphasize "integrated multi-species recovery plans" that would maintain and restore discrete habitats. Under such an approach, businesses, local government and federal agencies could call for a promising habitat or watershed to be set aside as the breeding area for an array of species, allowing several species to be saved while also permitting development nearby.

Related Action

Although the 102nd Congress could not agree on an Endangered Species Act reauthorization and could not resolve the issue of the northern spotted owl, it did take steps to protect several other endangered animal species.

Striped Bass Protection. In 1991, Congress extended protection of the striped bass — one of the East Coast's premier game fishes — when it renewed for three years the 1984 Atlantic Striped Bass Conservation Act (PL 98-613). That law required states along the Atlantic seaboard to follow the recommendations of the federal chartered Atlantic States Marine Fisheries Commission or face a moratorium on commercial bass fishing. *(1984 law, Congress and the Nation Vol. VI, p. 481)*

The striped bass, a tasty and sought-after fish whose numbers suddenly declined during the early 1980s, was commonly called the striper in New England and the rockfish in the mid-Atlantic region. An anadromous fish, it spawned in the fresh waters and adjacent estuaries of the Chesapeake and Hudson bays and spent its adult life in the ocean. Since enactment of the 1984 law, the fish had enjoyed a bit of resurgence.

Passage of the extension (HR 2387 — PL 102-130) was uneventful. The House Merchant Marine and Fisheries

Committee reported the measure (H Rept 102-144) on July 9. The same day, the House suspended the rules and passed the bill by voice vote. The Senate Commerce, Science and Transportation Committee reported it (S Rept 102-145) on Sept. 11. The Senate passed it, also by voice vote, on Oct. 2, clearing the measure. The president signed the bill Oct. 17.

Snake River Salmon and Trout. Appropriators in 1991 made saving the Northwest's Snake River salmon stocks and steelhead trout a priority in the fiscal 1992 Interior Department spending bill and allotted $10.8 million to build a dozen hatcheries in Idaho and Oregon. The Bonneville Power Administration had agreed to reimburse the government for hatcheries at the end of fiscal 1992. The appropriations bill (HR 2686 — PL 102-154) was signed into law Nov. 13, 1991.

Despite these and other efforts, prospects for the sockeye salmon species remained so bleak that it officially was declared endangered on Nov. 14, 1991. The announcement by the National Marine Fisheries Service was expected to have far-reaching effects on a regional economy dependent on cheap hydropower. A drawdown of some of the area's reservoirs to allow the salmon to complete their spawning runs more easily could lead to an increase in electric rates and a decrease in navigability, according to regional officials.

Exotic Birds. Congress in 1992 cleared a bill (HR 5013 — PL 102-440) that banned the importation of endangered exotic wild birds. The United States was the world's largest importer of such birds, and much of the international pet trade existed to feed U.S. demand. The measure also reauthorized the African Elephant Conservation Act and established a national biological resources center to inventory the nation's animal and plant species.

HR 5013 was reported from House Merchant Marine and Fisheries (H Rept 102-749, Part I) on July 29 and from Ways and Means (H Rept 102-749, Part II) on July 31. The House passed HR 5013 Aug. 11 by voice vote under suspension of the rules. The Senate passed an amendment version Sept. 30, also by voice vote. The House agreed to those changes Oct. 5, clearing the bill. President Bush signed it Oct. 23.

California Desert Protection

A Democratic bill (HR 2929) to protect vast swaths of desert in Southern California fell victim to politics in the Senate in 1992 and died at the end of the session. The House had passed the measure overwhelmingly in 1991.

On its own, the measure was controversial. Environmentalists considered the California desert, which included the East Mojave and Death Valley, a priceless natural resource. But off-road enthusiasts prized it for its trackless spaces, and miners said a fortune in minerals lay beneath its sands. The desert also was home to several major military bases.

As passed 297-136 by the House on Nov. 26, 1991, the measure sought to turn 4.1 million acres of federal land into 73 national wilderness areas, a designation that would limit activities such as mining and off-road vehicles. It also sought to expand the 3.3 million-acre Death Valley and 800,000-acre Joshua Tree National Monument into similarly protected national parks and to turn 1.5 million acres of the East Mojave Desert into a national monument. Under a compromise approved by the House, at least 114 miles of routes and trails were left open to continued use by off-road vehicles, and current mining and ranching claims were allowed to remain valid for a number of years.

The bill had attracted wide support in California from most newspapers and many cities and counties. It had long been a personal crusade for Sen. Alan Cranston, D-Calif., who had backed similar legislation since 1974 and who earlier in the year had announced that he would not seek re-election in 1992. But opposition, first from former Republican senator Pete Wilson and then his Republican successor, John Seymour, had frustrated Cranston's plans. Wilson and Seymour successfully argued that the measure would displace too many people and cost 20,000 jobs and $3 billion in income. The measure also was opposed by the administration because of its potential effect on the military installations in the area and by off-road vehicle manufacturers and enthusiasts.

HR 2929 had been reported (H Rept 102-283, Part I) from House Interior and Insular Affairs Nov. 4. After House passage, the measure went to the Senate Energy and Natural Resources Committee, which scheduled it for a markup on the same day as markup for another controversial bill, S 1156, to protect "old-growth" forests in the Pacific Northwest. The forests were home to the threatened northern spotted owl.

When the committee took up the timber bill, Tim Wirth, D-Colo., like Cranston, a longtime advocate of the desert protection measure and who also was retiring at the end of the 102nd Congress, asked Seymour whether he would try to block a committee vote on the desert bill. When Seymour indicated that he planned to oppose HR 2929, Wirth moved to fold the desert proposal into the timber bill. He wanted to ensure that any attempt to block the desert bill would also block the timber proposal, which Seymour supported.

Seymour immediately tried to quash the move to link the two measures, but his tabling motion failed on a 9-11 vote. Seymour then invoked a special Senate rule that allowed him to object to the continuation of the markup. The impasse effectively killed both measures; the committee never returned to either one before the 102nd Congress ended. *(Timber controversy, p. 520)*

Pesticide Reauthorization

Efforts to rewrite the Federal Insecticide, Fungicide and Rodenticide Act (FIFRA), which governed the labeling and use of the nation's pesticides, failed to advance in the 102nd Congress, with lawmakers reluctant to take on the complex and politically charged issue in an election year.

Both environmentalists and representatives of the chemical industry had been lobbying for changes in the law since it was reauthorized in 1988.

Environmental and consumer protection groups wanted to allow quicker removal from the market of pesticides if they proved dangerous. Pesticide producers and users wanted to amend the law to prevent local governments from regulating pesticide use. Most agriculture industry offices argued that local regulations made manufacturing and marketing pesticides too expensive.

Caught between the two sides, lawmakers opted not to rewrite the law. Even a federal court decision issued in July, which prohibited any pesticide residues from foods, was unable to break the legislative logjam. Though the Agriculture Subcommittee on Department Operations, Research and Foreign Agriculture did mark up a FIFRA revamp bill (HR 3742) on May 19, the measure died with no further action.

Background

The last major change in pesticide laws came in 1988 (PL 100-532), when Congress rewrote FIFRA and accelerated the timetable for the Environmental Protection Agency (EPA) to review existing pesticide licenses based on new scientific standards and information. *(Congress and the Nation Vol. VII, p. 458)*

Since the early 1970s, the EPA had been working on such a review but had made little headway. The 1988 legislation set a 1997 deadline to complete the review and increased fees charged to chemical producers to pay for it.

The mammoth task, known as "reregistration," was designed to review all pesticides in light of existing scientific standards. It required pesticide manufacturers to update laboratory tests to show whether chemicals or their components caused cancer, birth defects or a variety of other medical problems. About 400 pesticides were undergoing the lengthy review.

Because of the cost associated with the reregistration process, some chemical companies had decided to take their pesticides off the market. That caused problems for fruit and vegetable farmers dependent on those chemicals to grow their crops.

Sorting out all the difficulties became a highly charged issue for Congress as the 1992 election approached. Voters feared their health was being threatened, and farmers and pesticide makers feared their livelihood was at stake. Finding consensus seemed likely to remain difficult. A compromise would have had to satisfy agricultural chemical manufacturers, farmers, environmentalists and consumers — interests with widely divergent views.

A compromise also had eluded Congress because food safety policy involved technical language and complex scientific ideas. In addition, the issue sparked turf battles because eight committees in Congress had jurisdiction over the issue and four federal agencies were involved in administering food safety laws.

Solid Waste

A two-year effort to reauthorize the nation's main solid and hazardous waste law — the Resource Conservation and Recovery Act (RCRA) — came to naught, when the 102nd Congress failed to clear even a slimmed-down compromise bill.

The law (PL 94-580), which governed the disposal of hazardous, industrial and municipal wastes, had expired in 1988. But committees in the House and Senate did not seriously begin to consider a reauthorization until 1991, and then they dealt only with the smallest — but most politically charged — element of the solid waste problem: municipal trash.

The increasing tide of garbage the nation generated and the dwindling number of landfills in which to place it combined to generate bitter conflicts that the 102nd Congress was unable to resolve. Midwestern states complained of being dumping grounds for Eastern garbage; environmentalists were opposed to new increases in incineration; and the Bush administration and industry representatives opposed the effort to rewrite the law as unnecessary.

In the House, Al Swift, D-Wash., chairman of the Energy and Commerce Subcommittee on Transportation and Hazardous Materials, pushed through a bill (HR 3865) that dealt only with municipal waste. Swift had planned eventually to add provisions dealing with industrial and mining waste and recycling used oil and hazardous materials — problems that collectively dwarfed those posed by municipal solid waste. But faced with opposition from industry and the administration, those provisions never got into the bill. HR 3865 (H Rept 102-839) was reported from the full committee on Aug. 11, 1992.

In the Senate, the Environment and Public Works Committee June 19, 1992, had reported a somewhat broader bill (S 976 — S Rept 102-301). Opposition to both the House and Senate measures continued to mount. Major issues concerned the levels of recycling and incineration that should be required and whether state or local governments should have the authority to stop imports of solid waste into landfills.

By July, Senate sponsors had abandoned hope of passing a major rewrite in 1992. So they decided to concentrate on the more limited but politically palatable issue of giving states the power to control imports of out-of-state garbage. States on their own were prevented from doing so under the U.S. Constitution, which restricted them from passing any law interfering with interstate commerce. That fact had been emphasized by two Supreme Court rulings June 1 that struck down two state laws that attempted to control garbage imports — *Chemical Waste Management Inc. v. Hunt* and *Fort Gratiot Landfill Inc. v. Michigan Department of Natural Resources*. *(Case summaries, p. 831)*

The limited Senate bill (S 2877) allowed governors to ban or limit garbage imports, subject to a request by local authorities. A grandfather clause allowed landfills that already received out-of-state garbage to continue to do so. The governors of Indiana, Ohio, Pennsylvania and Virginia, the states that received the most out-of-state garbage, were given additional powers to step garbage imports. The Senate passed S 2877 by a vote of 89-2 on July 23, but the House never took up the measure.

Nuclear Test Ban

Congress in 1992 greeted the end of the Cold War by enacting historic restrictions on nuclear weapons testing, including an immediate nine-month moratorium and a total testing cutoff after Sept. 30, 1996, unless another nation was still conducting tests. A limited number of tests through 1996 would be allowed to test safety-related improvements to weapons already deployed.

The testing restrictions were included in the $22 billion fiscal 1993 energy and water appropriations bill (HR 5373 — PL 102-377). President Bush signed the measure Oct. 2. *(Details, p. 392)*

The Bush administration had maintained that it needed to continue at least some safety-related testing so long as the country had nuclear weapons. Bush did not veto the energy spending bill, despite the test ban language, largely because it included $517 million to keep building the superconducting supercollider, a highly favored White House project. *(Supercollider, p. 901)*

The congressional action marked a dramatic victory for test ban proponents, who began 1992 unsure they could win any testing restrictions.

The nuclear testing debate initially focused on a one-year moratorium that had substantial support in both chambers. The ban was intended to be a response to unilateral testing moratoriums imposed by Russia and France, encouraging them to continue their bans and to work toward a comprehensive test ban agreement for all nations.

The House June 4 adopted 237-167 an amendment to impose the one-year ban. The action came on a fiscal 1993 defense authorization bill (HR 5006). *(Defense authorization, p. 395)*

But as the issue moved to the Senate, some lawmakers began pressing for a more complex provision. Some senators sought to ensure ongoing tests for issues such as safety and reliability, while others pressed not only for an initial testing pause but also for some commitment toward a permanent ban.

The Senate Aug. 3 voted 68-26 for a Mark O. Hatfield, R-Ore., amendment to HR 5373, the energy and water spending bill, imposing a nine-month testing halt followed in 1996 by a permanent ban. Support for the proposal was not as strong as the vote indicated because several opponents voted for the amendment for tactical reasons.

During Senate floor consideration of the defense authorization on Sept. 18, Hatfield offered an amendment calling for a nine-month moratorium and permanently banning all nuclear testing after 1996 unless another country was still conducting tests. In approving the Hatfield amendment, the Senate rejected an attempt by William S. Cohen, R-Maine, to impose a shorter initial moratorium followed by a permanent ban at the end of fiscal 1998. Cohen's proposal also would have allowed the president to waive the test ban for one year to gain leverage to negotiate a comprehensive test ban.

The House Sept. 24 agreed, 224-151, to accept the testing restrictions in the energy bill. After the president signed HR 5373, conferees on the defense authorization dropped the test ban provisions from that bill (HR 5006).

Nuclear Waste Dump

In the final hours of the 102nd Congress, the Senate cleared compromise legislation (S 1671 — PL 102-579) that ended a lengthy battle and paved the way for the Energy Department to begin storing certain defense-related nuclear waste at a facility in New Mexico.

Built in salt caverns 2,000 feet below the desert near Carlsbad, N.M., the Waste Isolation Pilot Plant (WIPP) was designed to store plutonium-tainted waste from the nation's nuclear weapons factories. The dump, which cost $1 billion to build, had been ready, but the Energy Department lacked the necessary congressional approval to beginning storing waste there.

The legislation transferred management of the New Mexico dump site to the Energy Department and set certain requirements that had to be met before testing could begin. These included oversight by the Environmental Protection Agency (EPA), which had to issue standards ensuring safe disposal of the waste before the site could be used. The measure also authorized payment of $20 million a year for 15 years to the state of New Mexico.

The final terms were more restrictive than the Bush administration wanted but represented the minimum some key lawmakers would accept to allow the project to move forward.

Background

Congress authorized the Energy Department to begin construction of the WIPP in 1979 (PL 96-164). It was designed and built as a permanent repository for transuranic nuclear waste, considered low in radiation but high in toxic plutonium. *(Congress and the Nation Vol. V, p. 501)*

The Energy Department intended to open the site in 1988, but in 1987 a federal court struck down the EPA disposal standards for the nuclear waste because they violated other EPA standards for drinking water. In addition, congressional investigators had doubts about the safety and stability of the facility, particularly the stability of the rock within the salt caverns.

Other problems also developed. Before the facility could be tested to determine its suitability for storing the wastes, jurisdiction for managing it had to be transferred from the Interior Department's Bureau of Land Management to the Energy Department. Such a "land withdrawal" could be done either administratively or legislatively, although only a legislative withdrawal would have been permanent.

Frustrated by congressional inaction, the Energy Department on Oct. 3, 1991, attempted to obtain control of the site through the less preferable administrative route. But the state of New Mexico filed suit and prevailed in a decision issued on Nov. 26.

Legislative Action

The attempt to seize the WIPP site by executive fiat, however, prodded Congress into action. The Senate Energy and Natural Resources Committee reported S 1671 (S Rept 102-196) on Oct. 28, 1991. The Senate passed the bill Nov. 5, allowing waste storage to begin in exchange for certain payments to state and local governments and the department's pledge to abide by certain environmental standards.

In the House, three committees with jurisdiction over the issue approved competing versions of a bill (HR 2637) that would have imposed stiffer environmental conditions than the Senate version. As they struggled to produce a compromise that could be taken to the House floor, a federal district court ruled that congressional authorization was necessary before the Energy Department could proceed.

The House July 21, 1992, passed HR 2637, 382-10, which gave the EPA a stronger role in overseeing tests at the dump and allowed much less waste to be buried at the facility during the test phase. The House then passed an amended S 1671 by voice vote.

Although conference negotiators nearly were derailed on other legislation, including the huge energy bill and disputes over a nuclear waste disposal site planned for Yucca Mountain, Nev., a compromise was finally struck. The agreement gave the House most of the safety standards it had sought but sped up the timetable for federal action, which pleased Senate conferees. The agreement specifically stated that the new EPA safety standards would apply only to the New Mexico site and not to the proposed facility at Yucca Mountain. *(Yucca Mountain, p. 512)*

The House adopted the conference report (H Rept 102-1037) by voice vote under suspension of the rules Oct. 6. The Senate adopted the conference report by voice vote

Oct. 8, completing congressional action. S 1671 was signed into law Oct. 30.

Federal Facilities Cleanup

After years of effort, Congress Sept. 23, 1992, cleared a bill (HR 2194 — PL 102-386) that explicitly prohibited federal agencies from claiming sovereign immunity as a shield against prosecution and fines for violating federal solid and hazardous waste laws. According to Senate Majority Leader George J. Mitchell, D-Maine, and other lawmakers, the federal government had long been among the country's worst polluters, with the prime offenders being the nuclear weapons and energy complexes managed by the Energy and Defense departments. *(1989-90 action, p. 497)*

In states such as Ohio, Maine and Washington, hazardous and nuclear wastes had been dumped, had escaped into the air and had contaminated groundwater supplies. Although the Environmental Protection Agency (EPA) and various state legal authorities had attempted to rein in federal pollution through fines and lawsuits, the facilities had claimed sovereign immunity. In effect, they said that, although they were bound by federal and state environmental laws, the facilities could not be punished if they violated those laws.

One of the more notorious examples was an Energy Department facility in Fernald, Ohio, that had spewed at least 393,000 pounds of uranium into the surrounding environment over three decades. When the EPA fined the department $372,000, the department refused to pay, saying that the EPA lacked jurisdiction.

That view was disputed by Congress, which said the solid waste Resource Conservation and Recovery Act (PL 94-580) waived sovereign immunity for federal polluters. Federal courts, however, had not unanimously supported the congressional position, leaving the issue open to further challenge. *(1976 law, Congress and the Nation Vol. IV, p. 309)*

HR 2194, which stripped federal polluters of their shield against punishment easily passed the House by voice vote under suspension of the rules June 24, 1991. The measure had been reported from House Energy and Commerce (H Rept 102-111) on July 13. The Senate companion bill (S 596 — S Rept 102-67) had a rockier path — at one point it attracted an amendment dealing with documents leaked during Clarence Thomas' confirmation hearings as an associate justice of the Supreme Court. The Senate passed an amended HR 2194 by a vote of 94-3 on Oct. 24.

After that, progress slowed as House and Senate negotiators sought to work out differences between the two versions and to deal with objections raised by the Bush administration.

In the final bill, conferees agreed to give federal facilities a three-year grace period to come up with needed technologies to dispose safely of mixed hazardous and nuclear wastes. Conferees also agreed that any hazardous waste generated on a ship would not be subject to the bill's hazardous waste rules unless the material was kept on board for more than 90 days. The time limit was intended to stop ships from becoming floating waste dumps.

The House Sept. 23 voted, 403-3, to adopt the conference report (H Rept 102-886). The Senate acted by voice vote within hours, clearing the measure for the president. HR 2194 was signed into law Oct. 6.

National Park System

The 102nd Congress considered several measures to add specific parcels to the national park system, clearing some but failing to complete action on others.

Niobrara River

Congress in 1991 cleared a measure (S 248 — PL 102-50) to designate parts of the Niobrara River in Nebraska as wild and scenic, ending a decade-long dispute among Nebraska lawmakers over efforts to preserve the waterway.

As enacted, the measure protected a 95-mile stretch of the Niobrara and a 39-mile segment of the Missouri River in Nebraska and South Dakota by placing them in the federal wild and scenic river system.

The measure easily passed the Senate by voice vote on April 17. It had been reported (S Rept 102-19) by Senate Energy and Natural Resources on March 7. The bill ran into a little trouble in the House, where it was opposed by Bill Barrett, R-Neb., through whose district the river flowed. Taking up the fight of his predecessor, Rep. Virginia Smith, a Republican who had ardently fought the designation, Barrett warned that hundreds of landowners would lose control over their property. But S 248 was supported by the other two members of the Nebraska House delegation, and the House sided with them. The Interior and Insular Affairs Committee reported the bill (H Rept 102-51, Part I) on May 7, and the House passed the bill on May 14, 333-71. President Bush signed it May 24.

Bighorn Battlefield

The House on Nov. 25, 1991, cleared a bill (HR 848 — PL 102-201) that authorized a monument to honor American Indians who fought to preserve their way of life at the Battle of Little Bighorn. The measure authorized $1.5 million to build the monument. It was intended to provide visitors with an "improved understanding of the events leading up to and the consequences of the fateful battle" where Gen. George A. Custer made his last stand in 1876.

The bill also changed the name of the battlefield from the Custer Battlefield National Monument to the Little Bighorn Battlefield National Monument.

HR 848 (H Rept 102-126) was reported from House Interior and Insular Affairs June 24. The House passed the bill by voice vote under suspension of the rules later the same day. The Senate Energy and Natural Resources Committee reported it (S Rept 102-173) on Oct. 3. The Senate passed an amended HR 848 by voice vote Nov. 22. The House accepted the Senate changes three days later, and the president signed HR 848 on Dec. 10.

Mark Twain National Forest

Congress in 1991 cleared a bill (HR 3604 — PL 102-220) to authorize the U.S. Forest Service to buy 6,900 acres in Missouri, known as the Dennig Tract, to add to the Mark Twain National Forest. HR 3604 barred mining and logging on about 2,800 acres that ran along a river protected from development under the 1968 Wild and Scenic Rivers Act. The remaining 4,100 acres were designated as a special management area to be used for outdoor recreation.

HR 3604 was reported from House Agriculture (H Rept 102-346, Part I) on Nov. 21 and from House Interior and Insular Affairs (H Rept 102-346, Part II) on Nov. 22. The House passed the bill by voice vote Nov. 22, and the Senate followed suit Nov. 26, completing congressional action. The bill was signed into law Dec. 11.

Scenic Trail

A bill (HR 6184 — PL 102-461) directing the National Park Service and the U.S. Forest Service to study the feasibility of creating a national, coast-to-coast scenic trail cleared Congress in 1992. The trail was to link wilderness areas and historic trails and use existing paths whenever possible. The bill generated little controversy as it passed the House on Oct. 6 and the Senate on Oct. 8 by voice vote. President Bush signed the measure Oct. 23.

National Parks Projects

Provisions of a bill aimed at stemming the tide of pork-barrel projects funded with National Park Service money became law late in 1992. The provisions prohibited funding or spending of appropriated money on National Park Service historic projects that Congress had not formally authorized. The bill was intended to deter spending on unauthorized projects such as the roundly criticized Lawrence Welk birth place in North Dakota.

The full House passed HR 4276 (H Rept 102-480) on April 7, 331-0, under suspension of the rules, and the Senate Energy Committee reported it (S Rept 102-461) on Sept. 24. The major provisions of the bill were then folded into the water reclamation bill that was signed into law on Oct. 30 (HR 429 — PL 102-575). *(Water bill, p. 513)*

Aviation Park

Congress in 1992 cleared legislation (HR 2321 — PL 102-419) creating a national park in Dayton, Ohio, to honor Orville and Wilbur Wright, the founding brothers of flight. The Wright brothers built and flew the world's first airplane and established an aviation school in Dayton.

The bill proposed to add four sites to the national park system, each with existing national historic landmarks associated with the Wright brothers. These included the Wright Cycle Co., the bicycle shop that the Wrights owned and operated while they were doing their airplane experiments, and the home of Laurence Dunbar, the African-American poet who also was a friend and business partner of the Wright brothers.

HR 2321 was reported from House Interior and Insular Affairs (H Rept 102-449) on March 2. The House passed the measure on March 4, by a vote of 278-133, under suspension of the rules. The Senate passed its version (S Rept 102-462) by voice vote Oct. 1, after adding several technical amendments. The House agreed to those amendments on Oct. 4, clearing the bill. It was signed into law Oct. 16.

Montana Wilderness

Legislation (S 1696) that would have demarcated Montana's federally protected wilderness failed to clear in the 102nd Congress, leaving Montana as one of only two states — Idaho was the other — without a statewide federal wilderness plan.

The House and Senate passed significantly different versions of the measure. The Senate bill was a compromise worked out between the state's two senators, Max Baucus, D, and Conrad Burns, R. It would have placed 2.2 million acres in various categories of wilderness and created thousands of acres of special land management and environmental study areas. The Senate Energy and Natural Resources Committee reported S 1696 (S Rept 102-225) on Nov. 26, 1991. It passed the Senate on March 26, 1992, on a 75-22 vote.

The House bill, reported Sept. 30 from House Agriculture (H Rept 102-958, Part I) and Interior and Insular Affairs (H Rept 102-958, Part II) passed Oct. 2 on a 282-123 vote, would have protected 2.57 million acres and shifted many wilderness area boundaries to protect more headwaters and areas such as elk calving grounds.

Faced with time constraints characteristic of the end of a session, Baucus worked out a compromise proposal with the Montana House delegation in an attempt to avoid a formal, time-consuming House-Senate conference. But Burns preferred the original Senate bill, and as a result of his objections, several senators placed a hold on the compromise. Baucus was thus unable to bring it up for consideration before adjournment.

Colorado Wilderness

A dispute over water rights doomed legislation (S 1029) to designate about 700,000 acres in Colorado as wilderness. The Senate version (S Rept 102-129), which passed by voice vote on Aug. 2, 1991, allowed the state of Colorado to retain jurisdiction over water rights in areas that the bill designated as federal wilderness. The House version (H Rept 102-810, Part I), passed by voice vote under suspension of the rules on Sept. 14, 1992, reserved water rights for the federal government.

Landowners upstream from federally protected wilderness areas were concerned that they could lose access to water if a reserved federal water right was claimed to sustain wilderness areas. But key House lawmakers and environmentalists were concerned that giving water rights to the state would reverse existing law and that state water authorities were more likely to rule in favor of the claims of landowners and municipalities to water, possibly to the detriment of the wilderness areas.

After House action, the bill went back to the Senate, which added an amendment prohibiting the construction of new or expanded water projects in areas to be protected by the legislation. But the Senate version explicitly disclaimed any federal water right. House lawmakers never acted on the revised version.

Other Action

After a two-year effort, the 102nd Congress failed to give additional protection to the unique geothermal resources of Yellowstone National Park — home of the famous "Old Faithful" geyser. Increased development around the park, and the plans of a neighboring property owner, the Church Universal and Triumphant, to tap the geothermal power of Corwin Springs, which runs under the park, sparked concerns about the preservation of the park's famous hot springs and geysers.

On Nov. 25, 1991, the House by voice vote under suspension of the rules passed a bill (HR 3359 — H Rept 102-374) that prohibited wells from being drilled to tap the geothermal power. Although the Senate Energy and Natural Resources Committee reported a modified version of that bill (S Rept 102-363) on Aug. 10, 1992, it advanced no further and died at the end of the session.

The House on Oct. 15, 1991, passed 284-121 a bill (HR 2369 — H Rept 102-244) to create an 11,000-acre national park to preserve a tall-grass prairie in the Flint Hills of Kansas. But the measure failed to advance in the Senate. It would have been the first national monument created in Kansas.

The House Interior and Insular Affairs Committee in 1992 also approved legislation (HR 4325, HR 4326 and HR 4327) designed to improve the management of the nation's wilderness areas. But no further action was taken in the 102nd Congress.

Udall Foundation

An effort to honor the 30-year congressional career of Rep. Morris K. Udall, D-Ariz., with a foundation devoted to fostering environmental awareness was realized early in 1992. The bill (S 2184 — PL 102-259) authorized $40 million to create the Morris K. Udall Scholarship and Education Foundation in Tucson to expand awareness of environmental issues and to fund scholarships, fellowships and research in environmental studies. It also established a trust fund to receive private donations. Udall, a popular lawmaker who served in the House from 1961 to 1991, had long championed environmental causes.

The Senate passed the bill by voice vote on Feb. 4. The House passed the measure on March 3 by voice vote under suspension of the rules, clearing the bill. President Bush signed it on March 19.

Congress had cleared an earlier version of the bill (S 1176) on Nov. 25, 1991, but Bush announced that he had pocket-vetoed that measure during the congressional intrasession adjournment. Bush challenged on constitutional grounds a provision of S 1176 that would have given Congress the power to appoint a majority of the 10-member board that was to oversee the foundation.

Instead of pressing for a showdown on whether the president was making proper use of the pocket veto, supporters of the bill chose to introduce a new version of the bill (S 2184) that gave the president more room to appoint members to the foundation's board.

Despite the authorization, supporters of the Udall bill were unable to get funds approved for the center in the fiscal 1992 Interior appropriations bill. The Udall center was one of a slew of projects that conferees jettisoned from the bill in an effort to bring down overall spending levels. Sponsors said they would attempt to find start-up funding for the center in 1993.

Rocky Mountain Arsenal

The Army's huge Rocky Mountain arsenal in Colorado was to be transformed into a de facto wildlife refuge under a bill (HR 1435 — PL 102-402) cleared by Congress on Sept. 25, 1992 — even though parts of the proposed refuge had become so contaminated that they were on the nation's list of its worst hazardous waste sites.

Contamination from years of chemical weapons work at the arsenal by the Army and its prime contractor, Shell Oil Co., was concentrated on about 20 percent of the arsenal. The Army, which had managed the arsenal since 1942, had left the unused portion of the facility in its natural state.

Although the arsenal was only about nine miles north of Denver, an untainted part of it had become a haven for wildlife, with large populations of bald eagles, falcons, prairie dogs and deer. The arsenal had attracted about 50,000 visitors over the previous two years. Transforming the arsenal into a refuge had long been a goal of Rep. Patricia Schroeder, D-Colo., the bill's sponsor.

The Army and Shell Oil were to be responsible for cleanup of the arsenal under the bill, but the Interior Department was charged with operating the refuge. The arsenal was not to become an official wildlife refuge until the cleanup was completed, a process that was expected to take up to 20 years. But it was to be managed as if it were a refuge in the interim.

HR 1435 was reported March 20 from House Armed Services (H Rept 102-462, Part I) and July 7 from House Merchant Marine and Fisheries (H Rept 102-462, Part II). The House passed the bill by voice vote under suspension of the rules July 7. The Senate passed an amended version by voice vote Sept. 18. The House cleared the bill when it accepted the Senate amendments, which aimed to ensure the cleanup of the refuge. President Bush signed the measure Oct. 9.

Pacific Yew

Congress cleared legislation (HR 3836 — PL 102-335) in 1992 to provide a reliable supply of a cancer-fighting substance, called taxol, which is derived from the bark of the Pacific yew tree. The chemical compound had shown significant promise in treating ovarian cancer and possibly breast cancer.

Known as the Taxus brevifolia, the slow-growing Pacific yew grew in the underbrush of ancient forests in the Pacific Northwest. It was considered almost worthless, and the Pacific yews that grew in federal forests were either destroyed during logging operations or sold by the Agriculture Department's Forest Service for use as fence posts and lumber.

Then, in 1990, the National Cancer Institute reported that taxol was effective in treating ovarian cancer, which killed more than 12,000 women a year. Under congressional pressure, the Forest Service announced that it would limit wasteful destruction of the Pacific yew. The Forest Service and the Interior Department's Bureau of Land Management agreed to supply 750,000 pounds of yew bark annually for five years to Bristol-Myers Squibb Co., which used the bark to manufacture the drug Taxol.

Despite that agreement and Forest Service assurances that yew trees on public lands would be sold, with a few exceptions, only to further the production of taxol, lawmakers decided to push through legislation codifying the administration intentions. HR 3836 required that yews be harvested before an area of public land was opened to commercial logging, unless the action threatened loggers' safety. The trees had to be harvested in ways that promoted new growth, and new tress had to be planted.

The measure also authorized research on alternatives to taxol. If a synthetic substitute for the substance was found, loggers would not be required to harvest the yew before cutting commercial timber.

HR 3836 was reported June 9 from House Merchant Marine and Fisheries (H Rept 102-552, Part I) and July 7 from House Interior and Insular Affairs (H Rept 102-552, Part II) and House Agriculture (H Rept 102-552, Part III).

The House passed the bill by voice vote under suspension of the rules July 7. The Senate passed HR 3836 by voice vote July 23, clearing the measure. It was signed into law Aug. 7.

Drift Net Fishing

Congress in 1992 cleared two bills to protect dolphins from being killed during tuna fishing operations.

One measure (HR 2152 — PL 102-582) broadened import sanctions applicable under U.S. law to countries whose ships continued to use drift nets on the high seas. The miles-long nets snared everything in their paths, including dolphins, tortoises and sea birds, although they were used primarily to catch tuna.

The second bill (HR 5419 — PL 102-523) authorized the administration to implement an international agreement to establish a global moratorium on tuna-fishing practices using purse seine nets, which also trapped and killed dolphins.

Action on the bills began in 1991, when the Senate by voice vote Aug. 1 passed a bill (S 884) mandating sanctions on the fish products of countries that used drift nets after June 1992 and the House Merchant Marine and Fisheries Committee reported HR 2152 (H Rept 102-262, Part I) on Oct. 22.

Japan, possessor of the world's largest drift net fishing fleet, announced on Nov. 26, 1991, that it would phase out all drift net fishing by the end of 1992. On the same day, the Senate ratified the Wellington Convention (Treaty Doc 102-7) by standing vote. It declared the South Pacific off limits to drift netters. But other countries besides Japan used drift nets, and signs of drift net fishing had been detected in the Northeast Atlantic and other areas.

The House Ways and Means Committee reported HR 2152 (H Rept 102-262, Part II) on Feb. 19, 1992. The House passed the bill, 412-0, under suspension of the rules Feb. 25. The bill supported two U.N. resolutions (44-225, 46-215) that called for an end to drift net fishing by the beginning of 1993. The legislation barred fishing vessels from any country that practiced drift net fishing from docking at any U.S. port. It also banned imports of shellfish, fish, fish products or sport fishing equipment from such countries.

The Senate passed an amended HR 2152 by voice vote July 31. The bill then bounced back and forth between the two chambers as the Senate and then the House added unrelated provisions to the bill. The final version, accepted by the Senate on Aug. 12 and by the House on Oct. 4, partially repealed a tax on recreational boat owners, in addition to imposing the sanctions on drift net fishing. President Bush signed the bill Nov. 2.

Action on HR 5419 was more straightforward. House Merchant Marine reported the bill (H Rept 102-746, Part I) on July 28, 1992, and Ways and Means reported it (H Rept 102-746, Part II) on July 31. The House passed the bill Sept. 24 on a 389-15 vote under suspension of the rules. The Senate passed it Oct. 8 by voice vote. In addition to authorizing a five-year global moratorium on drift net fishing, the bill authorized funding for research into tuna-fishing methods that did not threaten dolphins. Bush signed HR 5419 on Oct. 26.

Water Projects

Congress in 1992 sent President Bush a biennial reauthorization of water projects built by the U.S. Army Corps of Engineers. The $2.1 billion bill (HR 6167 — PL 102-580) authorized, over five years, a raft of projects for harbors, dredging of waterways and flood control.

The final measure was a scaled-back version of an earlier House-passed bill (HR 5754) that would have authorized about $ 1 billion more for water projects. Lawmakers trimmed the measure after administration officials said the president would veto the bill because it was too costly.

HR 6167 included a $195.8 million project to deepen the Delaware River Channel that runs through Delaware, New Jersey and Pennsylvania and a $144 million flood control project in Las Vegas. In all, new projects were authorized in 17 states and Puerto Rico. State and local contributions, which ranged from 20 percent to 30 percent, came to roughly $600 million.

The final version did not include some of the most costly projects proposed by lawmakers. The House rejected a $698 million project that would have built the country's fifth highest dam, ostensibly to protect 300,000 residents of the Sacramento area from 200-year floods.

The House passed HR 5754 (H Rept 102-842) on a 326-87 vote Sept. 23, 1992, after eliminating the Sacramento project, 273-140, and rejecting an attempt to lower the bill's overall authorization level. With differences over the California project preventing action on the Senate version of HR 5754 and time running out in the session, the House passed a compromise measure, HR 6167, by voice vote under suspension of the rules on Oct. 6. It scaled back some projects that had been approved as part of HR 5754 and eliminated others. The Senate passed HR 6167 Oct. 8 by voice vote, completing congressional action. The legislation was signed into law Oct. 31.

Environment Summit

After months of indecision, President Bush announced May 12, 1992, that he would attend the U.N. Conference of Environment and Development in Rio de Janeiro, Brazil, in June, largely defusing a congressional effort to prod his attendance.

The House March 17 and Senate April 7 had passed varying versions of a non-binding resolution (H Con Res 292) by Rep. Dante B. Fascell, D-Fla., the Foreign Affairs Committee chairman, urging Bush to attend the meeting and show "leadership" there.

Similar resolutions were introduced by Sens. John Kerry, D-Mass. (S Con Res 89), and Al Gore, D-Tenn. (S Con Res 87), and by Reps. Gus Yatron, D-Pa. (H Con Res 266), and Robert G. Torricelli, D-N.J. (H Con Res 263). None of those resolutions was reported from committee.

Such resolutions, which expressed the sense of Congress on a particular issue, required passage in the same form by both chambers but did not require the president's signature.

Still, the resolutions sent a clear election-year message to the administration that Congress disapproved of Bush's initial resistance to commit to attend the conference. For his part, Bush at first was reluctant to attend because he did not want to be forced into signing binding treaties to limit the United States' and other nations' emissions of "greenhouse" gases, such as carbon dioxide. Carbon dioxide was a principal cause of the greenhouse effect that many scientists said produced global warming.

When the administration's negotiators succeeded in softening treaty language so that it contained no specific commitments, Bush pledged to go, saying "environmental problems are global, and every nation must help in solving them." The Senate ratified the global warming treaty on Oct. 7. *(Treaty, p. 297)*

The summit was billed as one of the largest international gatherings of nations in the post-World War II era, with more than 140 nations slated to attend. Its goal was the creation and signing of international treaties to arrest the changes in the global climate caused by pollution and to protect the Earth's forests and the diverse species within them.

Sponsors of the Earth summit also hoped delegates would sign an "Earth Charter," an international statement linking environmental protection with economic development.

The Bush administration had been a cautious, conservative presence at the international negotiating forums leading up to the Earth summit. The negotiations, which moved along several tracks for two years, were working toward agreements on climate change, biological diversity and the Earth Charter and were being readied for signature by the time of the summit.

Japan and the entire European Community had agreed to limit their carbon dioxide emissions to 1990 levels through the end of the 20th century. The United States, which accounted for 20 percent of the world's carbon dioxide emissions, opposed such caps. Instead, the administration maintained that U.S. initiatives already in place, such as a ban on other greenhouse gases (for example, chlorofluorocarbons) and its program to plant a billion trees were enough to stabilize emissions.

The U.S. delegation argued that each country should decide how to go about cutting greenhouse emissions.

Also attracting controversy was developing countries' demand that industrialized nations transfer money and technology to them to help spur development without harming the environment. U.S. negotiators resisted committing such financial resources as part of the summit. The United States was committed to using market mechanisms, instead of aid, to guide countries into making environmentally sound decisions, according to the U.S. State Department's U.N. Conference Coordination Center.

Clean Water Revision

Although both chambers began work on a comprehensive reauthorization of the clean water law, no measure was acted on during the 102nd Congress. The legislation posed the potential for high costs as well as for far-reaching environmental regulation.

The clean water law had last been revised in 1987 (PL 100-4) with amendments to the original Federal Water Pollution Control Act of 1972 (PL 92-500). *(1987 law, Congress and the Nation Vol. VII, p. 454; 1972 law, Congress and the Nation Vol. III, p. 792)*

The key challenge before lawmakers in 1991-92 was to control polluted runoff that drained over fertilized farmland directly into streams. Another issue was how to stem sewer overflows that bypassed treatment plants after heavy rainfall. The Environmental Protection Agency (EPA) said such "non-point source" pollution accounted in 1991 for half the pollution affecting the nation's lakes, streams and costs. Controlling such pollution defied broad-stroke fixes.

Congress considered a range of changes to the clean water law, including imposing new taxes to discourage land management practices, such as cutting down trees, that contributed to non-point source pollution. Another proposal would ban outright commonly used industrial and agricultural chemicals.

Amid tight budget constraints, questions also arose about how much new federal money to authorize to help state and local governments build treatment plants to keep pace with growing populations and developments.

Congress also grappled with wetlands regulations. Under Section 404 of the original clean water law, landowners were required to get permits from the Army Corps of Engineers before dredging or tilling property meeting the definition of a wetland. With the nation losing about 290,000 acres of wetlands a year, the federal government in 1989 tightened those rules and sharply limited development. Landowners who were barred under the new regulations from developing their land were outraged.

Congress, the Bush administration and the EPA struggled to devise a way to loosen the rules while still protecting "ecologically significant" wetlands. Several bills to provide relief to landowners were introduced in the 102nd Congress, but none was acted upon. Sen. J. Bennett Johnston, D-La., did succeed in attaching a provision to the fiscal 1992 energy and water appropriations bill (HR 2427 — PL 102-104) that barred the corps from enforcing its 1989 regulations. Under the bill's language, the corps could not enforce those rules until it submitted them or a revised version to a public approval process.

EPA Cabinet Status

The Senate by voice vote Oct. 1, 1991, passed a bill (S 533) to raise the Environmental Protection Agency to Cabinet-level status, but the House never acted on the matter, and the legislation died at the end of the 102nd Congress.

S 533, which had been reported from Senate Governmental Affairs (S Rept 102-82) on June 13, contained none of the controversial provisions that had derailed a House-passed bill in 1990. S 533 called for a Bureau of Environmental Statistics, but, instead of having independent status as the House had sought, the new bureau was designed to serve as a clearinghouse on environmental data collected by other governments and agencies. The Senate bill also provided for more political appointees in the proposed Department of Environment than the House bill had. *(1990 action, p. 498)*

Although John Conyers Jr., D-Mich., chairman of the House Government Operations Committee, promised to act on a Cabinet-status bill as soon as possible, he apparently saw little reason to hand the Bush administration an environmental plum in an election year. His committee took no action.

Other Legislation

Antarctica

The United States signed a treaty in 1991 to ban the exploration for oil and other minerals in Antarctica, joining with other voting members of the 26-member Antarctica Treaty. The Oct. 4 signing followed House approval April 30 of a resolution (H Con Res 109 — H Rept 102-45, Part I) calling for Bush administration support. The administration had earlier opposed the treaty but reversed itself in July. The action also followed the enactment of a law in the 101st Congress that barred U.S. exploration or development of Antarctica. *(Story, p. 489)*

The administration had initially objected to the treaty because of a provision that would have required unanimous approval by treaty signatories to lift the ban on mining after 50 years. The United States later agreed to sign a compromise version that would have required a vote of two-thirds of the treaty participants to overturn the ban. The House resolution called for an international agreement banning commercial mineral development in Antarctica for 99 years.

By the end of the 102nd Congress, the Senate had not acted on ratification of the treaty. The House Merchant Marine and Fisheries Committee sought to prod some action by reporting legislation Sept. 29, 1992, to implement the treaty, but the bill (HR 5459 — H Rept 102-932, Part I) went no further.

Indian Electric Project

Congress in 1991 cleared a bill (HR 1476 — PL 102-231) to transfer the electric transmission and distributions systems of the San Carlos Indian Irrigation Project in Arizona from the Interior Department to a local water district and two Indian tribes. Customers had complained of mismanagement while the project was run by the Interior Department's Bureau of Indian Affairs.

The House Interior and Insular Affairs Committee reported HR 1476 (H Rept 102-360) on Nov. 23. The House passed the measure by voice vote under suspension of the rules the same day. The Senate passed the bill by voice vote Nov. 25, clearing it. The president signed HR 1476 on Dec. 12.

Lead Use Restrictions

A Senate committee approved legislation in 1991 to protect children from lead poisoning, but no further action was taken in the 102nd Congress. As reported Oct. 8 by the Senate Environment and Public Works Committee, the measure (S 391 — S Rept 102-179) called on the Environmental Protection Agency to restrict the use of lead in a variety of products most likely to result in lead concentrations in the environment and human food chain.

The bill mandated recycling of lead-acid batteries, which contained nearly 75 percent of all lead used in the country. But the committee voted not to ban the sale of leaded gasoline in urban areas.

Service Station Competition

A slew of bills moved in 1992 in response to charges that oil companies were using unfair tactics to protect their retail stations from competition. But none of the measures advanced to the floor.

The House Energy and Commerce Committee (HR 5000 — H Rept 102-1029) Oct. 5 and the Senate Energy and Natural Resources Committee (S 2656 — S Rept 102-325) July 21 reported companion measures to prohibit oil companies from setting unduly stringent franchise terms that would effectively force independent station owners out of business.

The Senate Judiciary Committee Oct. 1 reported a bill (S 790 — S Rept 102-450) that would bar oil producers and refiners from owning their own gas stations. The panel also reported two related bills (S 2041 — S Rept 102-423; S 2043 — S Rept 102-458), Sept. 24 and Oct. 8, respectively, that would limit how much refiners could charge for gas they sold wholesale to service stations.

Meanwhile, the House Energy and Commerce Subcommittee on Energy and Power approved a bill (HR 2966), which also would restrict the wholesale prices refiners could put on their gasoline.

Colorado Oil Shale Reserves

Legislation (HR 3168) to promote drilling for natural gas within the federal naval oil shale reserves in Colorado won approval from three House committees in 1992 but never advanced to the floor. The reserves were established early in the 20th century to give the Navy access to the oil that could be obtained from the oil shale deposits.

Proponents of the legislation said the federal government must drill the gas or lose it to private interests that were drawing down the reservoir from outside the boundaries of the naval reserve. Some members, however, questioned whether the legislation would save or cost the federal Treasury money.

HR 3168 was reported June 23 from Interior and Insular Affairs (H Rept 102-610, Part I) and July 24 from Energy and Commerce (H Rept 102-610, Part II) and Armed Services (H Rept 102-610, Part III).

Radon Abatement

Legislation (S 792) to renew programs established by the 1988 Indoor Radon Abatement Act (PL 100-551) passed both chambers in 1992. But the differences between the versions were not reconciled before adjournment.

The 1988 law set up regional radon centers to help inform the public of the dangers of radon gas. When concentrated, radon gas was considered a factor in lung cancer. The Senate on March 10, 82-6, passed S 792 (S Rept 102-201), which would have reauthorized the federal radon abatement programs through 1994. The legislation also would have required certification of contractors who tested for radon and testing of the devices they use, mandated that schools regularly check for radon, extended a grant program that provides funds to state government to reduce radon in public buildings, and set up a presidential commission to educate the public on the dangers of the gas. *(1988 law, Congress and the Nation Vol. VII, p. 464)*

The House passed S 792 by voice vote on Sept. 29, after amending it to incorporate its own language (HR 3258 — H Rept 102-922). The House version was similar to the Senate language, but it did not require radon testing in federally owned housing.

New England Ground Fish

Congress failed to complete action on legislation to soften a proposed 50 percent cut in the allowable harvest of New England ground fish, such as cod and haddock.

Under a secret September 1991 consent agreement with the Boston-based Conservation Law Foundation, the Commerce Department's National Marine Fisheries Service agreed to direct the New England Fishery Management Council to ensure that ground fish stocks doubled in five years. The agreement required the allowable harvest of ground fish stocks to be cut in half immediately. The regional fishing industry complained that the cut was draconian.

A House bill (HR 2919 — H Rept 102-885, Part I), reported from Merchant Marine and Fisheries on Sept. 22, 1992, sought to override that agreement and phase in the harvest cutback over seven years. In the Senate, a similar bill (S 2849 — S Rept 102-412), reported Sept. 21 by the Commerce, Science and Transportation Committee, received no action on the Senate floor. In an effort to move the legislation forward, Rep. Gerry E. Studds, D-Mass., offered a compromise version (HR 5557), which the House passed by voice vote on Sept. 22. This measure was placed on the Senate calendar two days later but never advanced.

Mining Restrictions

Legislation (S 1187) that sought to protect federal rangelands from being mined without ranchers' approval died at the close of the 102nd Congress.

At issue was a 76-year-old law that allowed both ranchers and miners to use the same federal land. The 1916 Stock Raising Homestead Act allowed miners to explore federal lands for minerals without first gaining permission of ranchers. Only after a miner had decided to extract minerals did he have to give affected ranchers 30 days' notice. The law covered about 70 million acres of land in the West.

The legislation required miners to give 30 days' notice to ranchers before prospecting the land. Miners also were required to restore mined land to its previous condition. Ranchers had complained that miners had disrupted ranching operations and destroyed grazing lands. Miners objected to the legislation because of the high cost entailed in restoring the land to its original condition.

The Senate passed S 1187 (S Rept 102-218) by voice vote on Nov. 26, 1991. The House passed its version of S 1187 by voice vote on Sept. 15, after amending it to contain the language of a House bill (HR 450 — H Rept 102-641) that failed 248-168 on July 28 to win passage under suspension of the rules.

The Senate on Oct. 7 further amended the bill, but the House took no more action.

Marine Die-Off

The House on Aug. 3, 1992, passed by voice vote a bill to set up a coordinated federal response to the occasional and mysterious mass coastal strandings and deaths of marine mammals such as dolphins and whales. The bill (HR 3486 — H Rept 102-758) proposed to create a bank to preserve tissue samples of healthy marine mammals so that when such die-offs occurred, scientists could use the normal tissue to determine the reasons for the unusual events.

The House by voice vote Aug. 3 also passed HR 5350 (H Rept 102-759), to set up a similar bank to store tissue samples of Great Lakes fish. Both bills died when the Senate took no action before the 102nd Congress adjourned.

Undersea Research

Legislation (HR 3247) that would have written into law an undersea research program administered by the National Oceanic and Atmospheric Administration was passed by the House in 1992 but died when the Senate took no action. The program, which was started in 1980 and which had never been formally authorized, channeled funding to new research projects — in such fields as offshore dumping of sewage and dredging — through five centers.

As reported by the House Merchant Marine and Fisheries Committee on March 26, the bill (H Rept 102-469, Part I) would have set the program's authorization level at $20 million in fiscal 1992 and raised it by $5 million each year through fiscal 1996.

On May 6, the House failed to pass the bill under suspension of the rules. The vote was 255-133, short of the two-thirds majority needed for passage under the special procedure. On June 29, under regular rules, the House passed the bill 265-86.

Ocean Dumping

The House by voice vote on Feb. 4, 1992, passed legislation that would have reauthorized an Environmental Protection Agency program that regulated ocean dumping. The measure (HR 3749 — H Rept 102-423) would have authorized $14 million each year through fiscal 1995.

Following House passage, the bill was referred to the Senate Environment and Public Works Committee, which did not act on it.

Beach Pollution

The House on Sept. 22, 1992, passed a bill (HR 12 — H Rept 102-424, Part I) by voice vote to require states to monitor their beaches and coastal waters for pollution. The measure died upon adjournment.

The proposal was a revised version of a similar measure that failed in the closing week of the 101st Congress.

HR 12 directed the Environmental Protection Agency to set uniform standards for beach water quality and required states within three years to begin testing with the standard in mind.

It also required the states to post signs on beaches notifying the public of potential health risks during periods when the water quality did not meet state coastal water recreation standards.

Unlike the 1990 legislation, however, the bill did not require states to shut down beaches that failed to meet EPA standards.

Indoor Air Pollution

The Senate voted overwhelmingly, 88-7, on Nov. 6, 1991, for a bill (S 455) that sought to reduce the exposure of Americans to harmful indoor air pollutants. The House never acted on the measure.

Indoor air pollutants were thought to be responsible for more than 14,000 cancer deaths a year and $4 billion in lost productivity. S 455 would set up a separate office at the Environmental Protection Agency to handle research and regulation of indoor air pollution. It authorized $242.5 million through fiscal 1996 for programs related to indoor air pollution. The Bush administration opposed the bill.

Pipeline Safety

The House on Oct. 6, 1992, cleared a bill (S 1583 — PL 102-508) that aimed to curb environmental damage from natural gas and hazardous liquid pipelines.

Energy and Environment

S 1583 reauthorized pipeline safety laws and required the Transportation Department to consider potential harm to the environment when setting safety requirements for pipelines. Existing rules emphasized the protection of life and property. The bill also required the department to study the use of safety valves to shut off the flow of natural gas whenever a leak occurred.

The Senate Commerce, Science and Transportation Committee reported S 1583 (S Rept 102-152) on Sept. 16, 1991. The Senate passed the bill by voice vote Oct. 7. The House passed an amended version by voice vote Sept. 15. The Senate further amended the bill Oct. 5, and the House accepted the changes the next day. President Bush signed S 1583 on Oct. 24.

Energy Labs

The Senate tried to nudge the Department of Energy's high-technology laboratories into the post-Cold War, business-dominated era, but the House never acted on the Senate-passed measure.

The labs' longstanding task — development of top-secret nuclear weapons development — fell to a 30-year low in activity in 1991, according to the trade publication *Aviation Week and Space Technology*. The labs, including facilities at Los Alamos and Sandia in New Mexico and Lawrence Livermore in California, were searching for new missions. Lawmakers believed their high-technology facilities and professional expertise made the labs ideal for research work in emerging technologies such as superconductivity, fuel cells and environmental cleanup.

The bill (S 2566 — S Rept 102-287), as passed by the Senate on July 1, 1992, on a voice vote, would authorize and encourage the labs to form partnerships with businesses, universities and other federal agencies.

National Map Project

Congress in 1992 directed the U.S. Geological Survey to launch a program to map all of the nation's geologic features, most of which had not been formally documented.

The legislation (HR 2763 — PL 102-285) authorized $37 million in fiscal 1993 for the project, which was to provide detailed maps of the nation's geologic features as well as energy, mineral and water resources. Such maps were considered crucial for the safe siting of toxic and nuclear waste dumps.

The House Interior and Insular Affairs Committee reported HR 2763 (H Rept 102-333) on Nov. 19, 1991. The same day, the House passed the bill by voice vote under suspension of the rules. The Senate passed an amended HR 2763 by voice vote on March 31, 1992. The House accepted the Senate changes and cleared the bill April 30. President Bush signed the measure May 18.

8

Agricultural Policy

Introduction 535
1989-90 Chronology 537
1991-92 Chronology 551

Agricultural Policy

In a mood of fiscal austerity and with prodding from the Bush administration, Congress in 1989-92 cut federal spending on farm programs and continued to move the agriculture economy toward greater reliance on market forces.

Farm policy was not the burning issue it had been during the previous administration of Ronald Reagan, when the nation's farmers suffered one of the worst economic depressions since the 1930s and clamored for help from the federal government. Reagan's calls for the dismantling of many longstanding farm programs met with stiff resistance within Congress, even among Republicans.

By 1990, when Congress again prepared to draft an omnibus five-year farm bill, the farm economy was on the rebound: Debt was down, exports and farm income were up. Even severe droughts in the late 1980s had not prevented the recovery — in fact they helped by reducing government crop surpluses and increasing prices. The Bush administration, although echoing the call for a more market-oriented farm economy, adopted a strategy of negotiation and compromise with Congress in contrast with Reagan's more ideological approach.

Spending Cuts. With the farm crisis of the 1980s behind them and the budget crisis of the 1990s looming, many farm-state lawmakers found themselves caught between their loyalty to farmers and traditional farm programs and their credibility as responsible legislators.

Although the bill agreed upon by Congress and the administration did not make drastic changes in farm policy, it did freeze farm income-support levels at existing rates. Drafters of the farm bill then made about $14 billion in agriculture spending cuts that were included in an omnibus budget reduction bill — a significant bite out of the projected $54 billion authorized in the farm bill.

Congress had balked at Reagan's plan to abolish key farm programs, yet the 1985 farm bill (PL 99-198) did lower price supports and loan rates in an effort to make U.S. farmers more competitive in world agriculture markets. By 1990, after losing ground to European and Asian nations in the mid-1980s, exports were on the rise again and most members of Congress agreed with the Bush administration that keeping crop prices artificially high was counterproductive. Efforts by farm-state populists to impose higher levels failed in the House and Senate in 1990.

The drafters of the 1985 farm bill offset decreases in price-support levels with increases in direct income-support payments, a strategy that had helped return the farm economy to prosperity. But as lawmakers began to write the 1990 bill, the federal government had spent nearly $90 billion on farm programs during the previous five years — more than $60 billion of that in direct income subsidies. By 1990, the federal budget clearly could no longer sustain such a generous policy.

In the belt-tightening atmosphere of the early 1990s, legislators questioned not only the amounts spent on farm programs but also their underlying premises. Critics had always attacked farm subsidies as unwarranted handouts. But few farmers or their congressional defenders had questioned the traditional view that federal spending for agriculture was a necessary intervention in an unstable but essential sector of the economy — a price stabilization policy that benefited all citizens, not a welfare program for farmers.

Whether all recipients were in need thus became an issue. Neither the House nor the Senate in 1990 had enough votes to put through an amendment — offered by a coalition of conservative and urban members and endorsed by the Bush administration — to deny subsidies to farmers who made more than $100,000 a year. But the idea of a "means test" for farm subsidies seemed likely to come up again during the 1990s as Congress struggled to reduce the federal deficit.

The cost-cutting device Congress settled on was flexibility. The government would save an estimated $7 billion a year by reducing the amount of cropland eligible for support payments, while farmers would be given more flexibility to decide what crops to plant. How the flexibility plan would work in practice was unclear, but President Bush said it would allow farmers some freedom from the strictures of the traditional farm program. But fears existed that the reduction in subsidies would hurt farmers who could not rotate crops because of weather and soil conditions or because

References

Discussion of agricultural policy for the years 1945-64 may be found in *Congress and the Nation Vol. I*, pp. 665-767; for the years 1965-68, *Congress and the Nation Vol. II*, pp. 555-597; for the years 1969-72, *Congress and the Nation Vol. III*, pp. 331-352; for the years 1973-76, *Congress and the Nation Vol. IV*, pp. 717-740; for the years 1977-80, *Congress and the Nation Vol. V*, pp. 365-395; for the years 1981-84, *Congress and the Nation Vol. VI*, pp. 485-516; for the years 1985-88, *Congress and the Nation Vol. VII*, pp. 499-539.

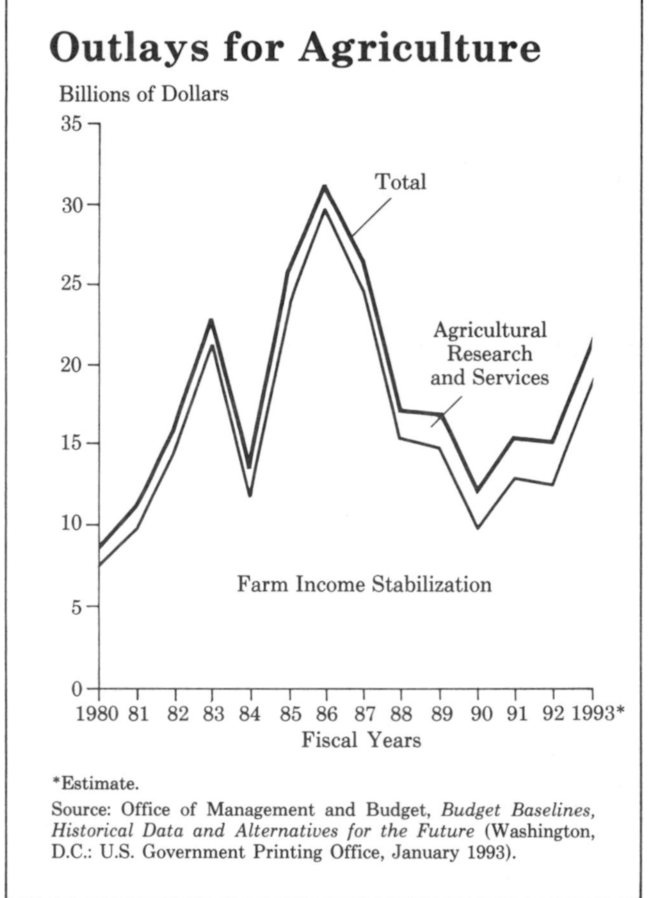

*Estimate.

Source: Office of Management and Budget, *Budget Baselines, Historical Data and Alternatives for the Future* (Washington, D.C.: U.S. Government Printing Office, January 1993).

their operations were not large enough.

Export Subsidies. The nation's long dominance of world agriculture markets was facing new challenges when Bush took office. The U.S. share of the world's major commodity trade had declined during the decade as other nations improved their ability to grow and export crops. An important contributing cause was the willingness of some governments, especially those of European countries, to subsidize agricultural exports heavily.

With at least one-fourth of U.S. agricultural production each year leaving the country, the Bush administration took the position that strength in world markets was crucial to the continuing prosperity of the farm sector. Exports increased during the four years of the Bush administration, and the favorable trade balance in agricultural goods jumped from $5.4 billion in 1986 to $18 billion in 1992.

But the administration failed to achieve one of its chief goals in the agriculture area: to convince other nations, particularly in Europe, to reduce export subsidies. Continuing Reagan's policy, Bush's trade negotiators urged members of the European Economic Community (EC) to reduce export subsidies and change other policies that distorted world agricultural trade in their favor. But the United States and the 12-nation EC had not formalized an agreement on the agriculture question when Bush left office in 1993, passing on to the new Clinton administration the long-running talks on proposed changes in the General Agreement on Tariffs and Trade (GATT).

The Bush administration's strategy at the GATT talks made its position on the 1990 farm bill tricky. While the president called for cuts in farm spending, trade negotiators did not want to leave the impression that the United States would reduce its farm subsidies while other nations continued theirs. Thus the administration did not send a formal legislative proposal to Congress and was willing to compromise with legislators behind the scenes while periodically threatening to veto the bill if it became too expensive.

Congress responded to the trade dilemma by adding a provision to the 1990 budget-reconciliation bill requiring the agriculture secretary to increase spending by $1 billion a year on export promotion programs if a GATT agreement was not reached by mid-1992. Some members raised questions, however, about the value of those programs.

The Export Credit Program, which provided loan guarantees for commodity sales abroad, encountered little resistance. But some influential members questioned the need for the Export Enhancement Program, which, beginning in 1986, provided about $1 billion a year to subsidize agricultural exports. And a third program, aimed at helping companies to market their products abroad, was attacked as a windfall for wealthy producers.

Changing Attitudes. Along with the realization that farm programs could not be funded as generously as they had been in the past, farm-state lawmakers in the early 1990s had to deal with environmentalists determined to influence farm legislation. The 1985 farm bill had for the first time included significant environmental provisions to protect wetlands and other land compromised by crop production.

In 1985, farm and environmental interests were able to reach a compromise on those provisions partly because many farmers needed to get land out of production to reduce surpluses, and the conservation programs did just that. Yet by 1990, the new environmental programs were moving more slowly and doing less for the environment than had been hoped.

Environmentalists won some battles and lost others during the drafting of the 1990 farm bill. Despite setbacks, lobbyists for environmental groups were becoming expert in the complexities of farm policy and gradually were building support within Congress and among the public. Farming had a profound impact on the environment, not only through soil erosion and the destruction of wetlands, but also through the widespread use of pesticides and fertilizers that polluted soil and water. Lawmakers increasingly recognized that farm policies had contributed to the damage and should be revamped to start correcting it.

Another sign of change was the fading from power of Mississippi Democrat Jamie L. Whitten, a staunch defender of traditional farm programs and foe of environmentalists. In 1992, ill health forced Whitten to turn over to a colleague his duties as chairman of the House Appropriations Committee and its Agriculture Subcommittee. For four decades, Whitten had controlled the annual agriculture appropriations legislation and strongly influenced agriculture policy through his detailed knowledge of farm programs.

Whitten had remained loyal throughout his half-century in Congress to agriculture policies framed during the New Deal, when farm programs had much in common with public works projects. His views on most issues were shared by his Senate appropriations subcommittee counterpart, Quentin N. Burdick, a North Dakota Democrat who died in 1992. Their support for traditional programs had meant fewer dollars for new programs and only small changes in the focus of the Agriculture Department.

Whitten in 1993 gave up the chairmanship of House Appropriations and its Agriculture Subcommittee but remained as a member of both.

Chronology Of Action On Agriculture

1989-90

The agriculture agenda during the first two years of the Bush administration was dominated by the drafting of a five-year omnibus farm bill. The final product reflected the sobering reality that, despite the bias of many lawmakers in favor of generous programs for their farm constituents, the federal budget could no longer accommodate increases in farm spending. Even after Congress finished work on the cost-conscious bill, it made additional cuts in farm spending as part of budget-reconciliation legislation.

As the House and Senate Agriculture committees began work on the farm bill in 1990, the farm economy had recovered from its deep depression of the mid-1980s and was generally healthy despite severe droughts in 1988 and 1989. In fact, the droughts and other weather adversities had driven up prices, reduced government surpluses and boosted U.S. exports.

And farmers were gratified that Congress had come to their aid with a $900 million disaster relief bill in August 1989.

President Bush, following the lead of the preceding Republican administration of Ronald Reagan, called for cuts in farm programs and fewer government controls on agriculture.

But administration pressure for changes in farm policies was less intense than it had been in 1985, when the previous farm bill was written. The pressure needed to keep farm programs in check seemed likely to come from within Congress, where the dominant mood favored spending cuts. As one lawmaker said, "In 1990, we have a budget crisis, not a farm crisis."

The Bush administration's relatively low profile on the farm spending question also was a result of its involvement in international trade talks. U.S. trade negotiators hoped to convince other nations, particularly those in Europe, to reduce agricultural subsidies in the interest of free trade. The administration did not want to undercut its bargaining power by going on record in opposition to subsidies for U.S. farmers.

The trade talks dragged on throughout the Bush years with no agreement on agriculture subsidies, but the administration was able to reach agreement with Congress on a farm bill at the end of the 101st Congress. Bush praised a provision of the bill that was intended to reduce federal spending on subsidies and at the same time give farmers more freedom to respond to market forces.

Aside from the farm bill of 1990 and the disaster relief bill cleared in 1989, the 101st Congress worked on but did not complete legislation to reauthorize the Commodity Futures Trading Commission (CFTC). The CFTC bill raised a number of issues that were not resolved until the end of the 102nd Congress.

Omnibus Farm Bill

Under increasing pressure to reduce federal spending, Congress in 1990 hammered out an omnibus farm bill (S 2830 — PL 101-624) that retained the existing framework for farm programs but froze farm price- and income-support rates. In a separate bill, the 1990 budget-reconciliation act (HR 5835 — PL 101-508), Congress included provisions to reduce federal crop subsidies by about $14 billion, cutting the overall price tag for 1990-95 agriculture programs from a projected $54 billion to about $40 billion.

S 2830 was less generous than farm-state lawmakers had hoped when deliberations on the bill began in the spring of 1990. But it passed both chambers by solid majorities in mid-summer. After a delay, while an agreement was reached on spending cuts required by the congressional budget resolution, the bill won final approval in October.

Signing the measure on Nov. 28, 1990, President Bush said he was pleased that it would "continue the market-oriented shift" begun in the 1985 farm bill, which was due to expire at the end of 1990. The Bush administration had threatened to veto earlier versions of the 1990 bill as too costly.

The largest chunk of the $13.6 billion in savings — an estimated $7 billion over five years — was to come from a new "triple base" acreage allotment plan. In place of the existing two-tier system under which farmers either planted a particular subsidized crop or left land idle, the triple base system established a third category of land on which farmers could grow whatever mix of crops they chose, except for fruits and vegetables.

The triple base plan saved money for the government because no subsidies would be paid for crops grown on the third category of land. And, it was hoped, farmers would prosper by selling crops in demand on the open market. In any case, the amount of a farmer's land on which subsidized crops could be grown was reduced by 15 percent.

Bush said the plan would "allow farmers to break out of the traditional farm program straitjacket, which bound them to produce the same crop year after year, regardless of market opportunities." House and Senate conferees on the farm bill chose the plan over other money-saving proposals in part because it reduced federal payments to farmers indirectly, inflicting less pain than an outright cut such as a reduction in target prices.

In addition to the triple base plan added to the budget bill, the farm bill included a provision giving farmers even wider latitude to plant their choice of crops if they agreed to forfeit subsidies. The bill's "flexibility" provision allowed farmers to plant up to 25 percent of their land in any mix of crops, excluding fruits and vegetables. This provision was optional, in contrast to the triple base provision, which mandated a 15 percent cut in the amount of land on which subsidized crops could be grown whether or not a farmer decided to rotate his crops.

The farm bill and the farm provisions of the budget-reconciliation bill amended and added to permanent enabling legislation of 1938 and 1949. The 1990 bills authorized programs through 1995 for commodity price supports, agricultural exports, soil conservation, farm credit, agricultural research and food stamps.

Although conferees weakened or removed some environmental provisions, the final version established a 1 million acre wetlands reserve, required farmers to keep records

Agriculture Terms

Following is a glossary of frequently used agriculture policy terms:

Acreage Reduction Program. A plan established by the Agriculture Department to limit production if necessary to control crop prices and supplies. Producers of program crops agreed to the terms of an acreage reduction program — known as an ARP — as a condition of receiving federal loans and subsidies. An ARP typically directed a farmer to idle a certain percentage of his acreage determined by existing surplus levels.

Base Acreage. The portion of a farmer's land that is eligible for federal subsidies, calculated as a five-year rolling average of the acreage enrolled in a particular crop subsidy program. The base acreage was intended to ensure that farmers were not unfairly penalized for unproductive years or unfairly rewarded in boom years. But because the base acreage determined federal income payments, the program often encouraged farmers to keep planting the same crop each year to guarantee a predictable income at harvest, even though market conditions or other factors made planting some other crop more logical.

Deficiency Payments. Subsidies paid to producers of program crops when domestic market prices dropped below target prices.

Loan Rate. The floor under domestic farm prices. The rate told farmers how much per bushel they could borrow from the federal government at harvest time, using their crop as collateral. If the market price of the crop did not exceed the loan rate during the loan period, producers could leave their crop in the hands of the government and keep the principal.

Marketing Loan. A variation on the traditional non-recourse crop loan, designed to avoid excess government surpluses and help U.S. farmers compete in international markets. As with the traditional loan, the marketing loan provided money to farmers at harvest at a certain rate, to be repaid after the farmer sold the crop. Even if world market prices remained below the loan rate, holders of marketing loans were expected to sell their crops on the world market and keep the difference between the market price and the loan rate. Marketing loans were established for cotton and rice in 1985; the 1990 farm bill (S 2830 — PL 101-624) established a marketing loan for soybeans and other oilseeds.

Non-Recourse Loans. Government loans given to farmers at harvest, with the condition that if market prices dropped below a certain level, the government would have no recourse but to keep the crop and forgive the principal on the loan.

Program Crops. Storable grain and fiber crops for which farmers received subsidies: wheat, corn and other feed grains (oats, barley, sorghum), rice and cotton. In exchange for the subsidies, producers of program crops were required to participate in acreage reduction programs. Different federal subsidy programs applied to dairy products, honey, peanuts, soybeans, sugar, tobacco, wood and mohair.

Target Price. The ideal price for a particular commodity, as set by Congress. When market prices were depressed, the government paid farmers the difference between the target price and either the average domestic market price or the loan rate, whichever was higher. Target prices had a powerful symbolic importance for farmers, but loan rates also were important in determining subsidy levels.

of their use of dangerous chemicals and called for national standards for foods labeled "organically grown."

Other sections of the farm bill consolidated rural development programs in the Department of Agriculture and overhauled the Food for Peace program.

Background

The programs Congress reauthorized and updated in 1990 had their beginnings in President Franklin D. Roosevelt's New Deal, when federal intervention was considered essential to the survival of the farm economy. The Agricultural Adjustment Act of 1938 established a price-support and production control system for non-perishable agricultural commodities: wheat, corn and other feed grains, cotton and rice. These came to be known as "program crops."

The Agricultural Act of 1949 revised the system by giving the agriculture secretary more flexibility to set price-support levels, moving toward a less managed, more market-oriented agriculture policy. But the basic New Deal mechanisms of price supports and production controls remained in place. *(Congress and the Nation Vol. I, p. 665)*

By the late 1960s, political and economic conditions were threatening the survival of the New Deal-era programs. The increased mechanization of U.S. agriculture was driving many small farmers out of business, which in turn led to diminishing political clout for the Farm Belt in Congress. Republican President Richard Nixon, first elected in 1968, initiated a series of steps away from government management of farm prices that continued under Democrat Jimmy Carter and that Republican Ronald Reagan vowed to accelerate in the 1980s.

The Agricultural Act of 1970 (PL 91-524) maintained the system of crop and price controls but added a "set-aside" program that allowed farmers to be compensated for taking a portion of their land out of production and then to raise whatever they wanted on the remaining land. The Agriculture and Consumer Protection Act of 1973 (PL 93-86) replaced the old support prices for the major commodities of cotton, wheat, corn and other feed grains with lower "target prices" that would reimburse farmers only when market prices dropped sharply. *(PL 91-524, Congress and the Nation Vol. III, p. 336; PL 93-86, Congress and the Nation Vol. IV, p. 719)*

Despite his fervent free market rhetoric, Reagan signed the 1981 farm bill (PL 97-98), which maintained price supports and added a new support program for sugar. Outlays under the 1981 bill were projected to be about $11 billion over its four-year duration. But a devastating farm depression forced the government to buy up huge amounts of surplus commodities and support farmers' incomes with artificially high prices — at a final, four-year cost of $54.7 billion. *(1981 farm bill, Congress and the Nation Vol. VI, p. 487)*

In the midst of that depression, Congress in 1985 produced a farm bill (PL 99-198) that lowered artificially high prices but kept a lifeline to struggling farmers through massive income-support payments. The bill helped restore the farm economy to health at a cost to the federal government of $88.6 billion over five years. *(1985 farm bill, Congress and the Nation Vol. VII, p. 501)*

Administration Plan

The Bush administration approached the drafting of the 1990 farm bill with caution. Reagan's 1985 proposal to eliminate or substantially reduce the basic farm price- and income-support programs had provoked intense opposition in Congress and appeared to have contributed to the electoral defeat of three Republican senators from farm states in 1986.

With the farm economy on the mend in 1990, neither the Bush administration nor Congress was in the mood for another brutal battle over the direction of federal farm policy. General agreement was reached that cuts would have to be made in farm subsidies to help curb the mounting federal deficit, but no consensus existed on how those cuts would be made.

Sidestepping the painful issue of how to cut farm subsidies, the Bush administration on Feb. 6, 1990, sent Congress a set of farm policy recommendations. By submitting recommendations instead of the usual formal legislative proposal, the administration, led by Agriculture Secretary Clayton Yeutter, hoped to sustain its leverage in the upcoming farm bill debate and to avoid looking like an enemy of politically popular farm programs.

The administration proposed modest changes in farm policy aimed at increasing farmers' responsiveness to market signals. The centerpiece of the recommendations was a plan to give farmers more flexibility to decide what crops they would plant. To do this, the administration wanted to revamp the "base acreage" system that determined what share of a farmer's land was eligible for federal farm payments. A farmer's base acreage for program crops was calculated as a five-year average of what the farmer had planted. If he planted a crop other than the one for which he had a base, he lost some of his subsidy payments and reduced his base for future payments.

Instead of a base acreage for each crop, the Bush administration proposed to give a farmer one overall base on which he could plant whatever amount he chose of program crops such as corn and wheat — as well as oilseeds such as soybeans and sunflowers, which were not program crops. Regardless of what mix of those crops he planted, the farmer would receive his subsidy just as if he had planted his usual acreage of program crops.

Agriculture Leadership

The Senate voted unanimously, 100-0, on Feb. 8, 1989, to confirm Clayton Yeutter as President Bush's first secretary of agriculture. Yeutter, who had served as U.S. trade representative during the Reagan administration, continued to emphasize trade while in the agriculture post. During his tenure, Yeutter represented the administration in negotiations with Congress on the omnibus 1990 farm bill (S 2830 — PL 101-624). He resigned on March 1, 1991, and was succeeded by Edward R. Madigan, a Republican representative from Illinois.

Madigan was confirmed, 99-0, on March 7, 1991. *(Cabinet profiles, p. 1169)*

"Farmers throughout the country feel that the ability to handle their operations in the most efficient manner is hampered," said Yeutter in defense of the proposal. "They have to plant for the program and not for the market." Although most farm-state legislators liked the idea of increased flexibility, some voiced concerns that removing the link between support payments and production made government assistance for farmers look like welfare instead of a program to ensure a stable food supply. The administration dismissed that characterization.

The issue of environmental problems stemming from agriculture also was raised. The administration argued that by allowing farmers to respond better to market signals, the environment ultimately would benefit. For example, farm operations would become more efficient, synthetic pesticides and fertilizers would be used more sparingly and crop rotation would be practiced more widely. The administration also proposed that new land enrolled in the Conservation Reserve Program (CRP), under which farmers were paid to take environmentally fragile land out of production, meet tougher erosion-control standards if returned to production. The CRP would be reoriented to deal with groundwater contamination problems and wetlands loss.

In other areas, the administration called for setting all loan rates — the price at which the government provided loans to farmers to enable them to hold their crops for later sale — using the same formula; changing the way the government determined how much land to idle to control production and limit budget outlays; scrapping the federally subsidized crop insurance program and relying exclusively on direct disaster payments; broadly restructuring the Farmers Home Administration (FmHA) lending priorities and restricting opportunities for restructuring debt; and reauthorizing the food stamp program to support the existing level of services.

House Action

Committee. After lengthy negotiations, the House Agriculture Committee on June 14 approved an omnibus farm bill (HR 3950 — H Rept 101-569, Part I) that made no sweeping policy changes and froze support levels for major commodities for five years. The most contentious issue was resolved May 24 when the panel rejected, 17-28, a proposal to significantly increase price-support levels.

The defeated proposal, offered by Iowa Democrat Dave Nagle and endorsed by a group of junior Democrats, was intended to increase crop prices to help struggling farmers stay in business. Senior Democrats on the panel joined with all but one Republican to oppose the idea, warning that the plan might return agriculture to its mid-1980s woes, when constantly increasing price supports caused U.S. commodity exports to plunge and forced the government to buy the huge crop surpluses.

The committee voted to retain the thrust of the 1985 farm bill by freezing support rates for crops such as wheat, corn, cotton and rice. It also approved a flexibility provision, more modest than the one proposed by the Bush administration, to encourage farmers to rotate their crops in response to market forces. The bill also established an inexpensive subsidy program for growers of soybeans and other oilseeds.

After protracted negotiations at the subcommittee level, the full committee approved provisions extending subsidy programs for sugar, dairy products and peanuts. The bill also included provisions that represented compromises between farm interests and environmentalists on issues such as pesticide use and wetlands conservation.

The Agriculture Committee formally reported HR 3950 on July 3. Other House committees shared jurisdiction over the measure. The Foreign Affairs Committee reported it (H Rept 101-569, Part II) on July 16, and Education and Labor (H Rept 101-569, Part IV) and Ways and Means (H Rept 101-569, Part V) on July 18. The Agriculture Committee filed a supplemental report (H Rept 101-569, Part III) on July 17.

Floor. Led by Agriculture Committee Chairman E. "Kika" de la Garza, D-Texas, supporters of the committee version of HR 3950 defeated a number of challenges on the House floor aimed at cutting deeper into farm subsidies. The House passed HR 3950 on Aug. 1 by a vote of 327-91, then passed an amended S 2830 in lieu by voice vote on Aug. 4.

The legislation froze existing income subsidy levels for crops such as wheat, corn, cotton and rice. Its cost was estimated by the Agriculture Committee to be about $55 billion. Lawmakers voted for the bill knowing that they would have to reduce farm spending even further later in the year when cuts recommended by the budget resolution had to be made.

The most dramatic challenge to the farm bill came from Charles E. Schumer, a New York Democrat, and Dick Armey, a Texas Republican, leaders of a coalition of urban liberals and Republican conservatives. The liberals wanted to divert money from agriculture to social programs, while the conservatives wanted to make farmers less dependent on government controls and subsidies. The Armey-Schumer amendment would have denied crop subsidies to farmers with gross adjusted incomes of more than $100,000 a year.

Debate on the amendment involved the philosophical underpinnings of federal farm programs. Armey and Schumer argued that their amendment would save the government up to $700 million a year and would correct glaring inequities in the farm program. Farm-state lawmakers responded that wealthy farmers with large operations were central to farm programs because their participation gave the government more control over the nation's largest food producers and thus over prices and supply.

The House rejected the Armey-Schumer amendment July 26 on a **key vote of 159-263 (R 66-109; D 93-154)**. The Bush administration had endorsed the amendment, while organized labor and some environmental groups joined farm interests in opposing it. The Senate rejected a similar proposal during floor debate on its version of the farm bill. *(1990 key votes, p. 1039)*

The House rejected another amendment to reduce the proportion of government benefits going to affluent farmers. In 1986, Congress had put a $50,000 limit on income subsidies and a $250,000 cap on total government benefits paid to individual farmers. As written, however, the law allowed a farmer to collect payments from three different entities: his own farm (subject to the maximum limits) and two other farming operations in which he had up to half-ownership (and for which he was eligible for half the limit). Thus, a farmer could legally double his take — $100,000 in income subsidies and $500,000 in total benefits. Silvio O. Conte, R-Mass., sought to close the loopholes by eliminating the three-entities exemptions. Seeing little support, he attempted to add his language to a Jerry Huckaby, D-La., substitute that would lower the total benefits allowed to $200,000 while permitting the doubling of income subsidies. On Aug. 1, the Conte amendment first was rejected 171-250, and the Huckaby substitute then was adopted 375-45. *(1986 legislation, Congress and the Nation Vol. VII, p. 518)*

The House on July 24 defeated, 150-271, a Thomas J. Downey, D-N.Y., proposal to trim 2 cents off the 18-cent-per-pound sugar price support. Advocates of the cut argued that no other crop program was more blatantly protectionist than sugar and that, although it cost the taxpayer nothing, no other imposed such a burden, both on consumers in higher sugar prices and on U.S. sugar-exporting allies, whose exports to the U.S. market were severely limited. The administration supported the cut but did not push its adoption. Opponents, meanwhile, lobbied hard against the proposal, saying it would cost U.S. jobs. Earlier July 24, the Senate had voted down an amendment similar to Downey's.

The Agriculture Committee's bill remained largely intact, but the House did make some changes in its environmental protection provisions. In one of the closest votes of the debate, the House on Aug. 1 adopted, 234-187, an organic foods amendment, sponsored by Peter A. DeFazio, D-Ore., to replace a hodgepodge of state laws with a national standard governing what foods could be labeled organic. And de la Garza accepted a compromise version of the "circle of poison" amendment restricting the export of pesticides considered too dangerous for use in the United States so that they would not return to the country on imported food.

Senate Action

Committee. The Senate Agriculture, Nutrition and Forestry Committee, 15-4, approved its version of the five-year omnibus farm bill (S 2830 — S Rept 101-357) on June 21, formally reporting it out July 6. The Senate panel made only modest changes in federal crop subsidy programs. Like the House committee-approved bill, the Senate committee bill froze income subsidy levels for crops such as wheat, corn, cotton and rice and for dairy products. The bill's estimated price tag of $54 billion was close to that of the House bill.

As approved by committee, S 2830 also would offer marketing loans — under which farmers, using their crops as collateral, received advances from the government at harvest time — to growers of wheat, feed grains and soybeans. In addition, the bill put new constraints on the agriculture secretary's power to lower the loan rate — the amount the government would lend a farmer on a crop — by up to 20 percent each year for wheat and feed grains. The committee also agreed to bar the agriculture secretary from buying up and slaughtering dairy herds; toughen some elements of "swampbuster" — the federal law that barred the draining of swamps and marshes for farming — and relax others; require farmers to keep records of their use of certain pesticides; encourage the agriculture secretary to enroll wetlands in CRP; curtail the circle of poison and allow the export of some unregistered pesticides as long as the Environmental Protection Agency ruled that they could be present on food below a certain level; authorize new spending to research alternative farming techniques to reduce the use of toxic chemicals; adopt new provisions to improve the quality of U.S. grain; renew a two-tiered price-support system created in 1985 that provided subsidies for peanuts grown under a national domestic sales quota, with a lower support level for "additional" peanuts sold overseas; reauthorize for five years controversial subsidy programs for wool, mohair and honey; and change agricultural trade laws by consolidating most commercial trade authorities under one statute, eliminating redundant and contradictory programs and calling for a long-term trade strategy.

The committee rejected a proposal to increase target prices, as well as amendments to abolish the sugar price-support program and to cut sugar price supports by about 10 percent.

The Senate committee's bill represented a delicate compromise worked out among senior Democrats and the panel's Republicans. As on the House side, a group of farm-state Democrats had tried in vain to increase farm subsidy levels.

Floor. The Senate passed S 2830 on July 27 by a vote of 70-21. The Senate went along with almost all of the compromises hammered out in committee, continuing the basic outlines of farm policy as set out in 1985 farm legislation.

With a veto threat from the Bush administration goading them on, Agriculture Committee Chairman Patrick J. Leahy, a Vermont Democrat, and ranking Republican Richard Lugar of Indiana won voice vote approval of an amendment to cut $3.5 billion from the bill. Administration and congressional negotiators were still at work on an overall budget-cutting agreement, and further reductions in the farm bill were likely before it reached the president's desk.

While senators appeared willing to slash federal farm programs if necessary, they proved more reluctant to deprive affluent farmers of their sizable share of subsidy payments. On July 19, the Senate tabled (killed) a Harry Reid, D-Nev., amendment, 66-30, to bar farmers who made gross sales of more than $500,000 a year from receiving most federal subsidies.

Senators also continued to protect the controversial sugar program. By a **key vote of 54-44 (R 17-26; D 37-18)**, the Senate on July 24 tabled, and thus killed, an amendment offered by Bill Bradley, D-N.J., to cut the 18-cent sugar support price by 2 cents. Supporters of the amendment, including Agriculture Secretary Yeutter, argued that U.S. sugar prices had been kept artificially high, gouging consumers at home and hurting some of America's best and poorest allies abroad. The Bradley amendment was thought likely to succeed, but in the end farm-state lawmakers upheld their tradition of uniting to defeat challenges to specific programs.

Other amendments were defeated that attempted to raise subsidy levels and direct more benefits to smaller farms. For example, a Tom Daschle, D-S.D., amendment to restructure income-support programs for wheat and feed grain producers by offering two target prices was rejected 24-72 on July 24. And a Max Baucus, D-Mont., amendment to provide target price increases to partly offset inflation in years that it exceeded 4.3 percent was rejected 26-72 on July 25.

Also on July 25, the Senate tabled, 57-41, a William V. Roth Jr., R-Del., amendment to repeal the peanut price-support system.

The only crop program touched by the Senate was one with a relatively tiny constituency, some 6,000 beekeepers. With no opposition from the bill's sponsors, the Senate on July 24 rejected, 46-52, a motion to table an amendment, offered by John H. Chafee, R-R.I., that provided a four-year phase-out of honey price supports. The Chafee amendment subsequently was adopted by voice vote.

Conference Action

House and Senate conferees on the 1990 farm bill were delayed for weeks while Congress struggled to reach agreement with the administration on an overall budget reduction plan. After those efforts failed, Congress proceeded with its own budget-cutting plan. In early October, congressional budget writers told the farm bill conferees to come up with $13.6 billion in deficit savings over five years.

Working with Yeutter to avoid a presidential veto, the conferees tried to spread the pain of budget cutting evenly among the various commodities and farm interests under the government subsidy umbrella. Instead of dismantling farm programs, they added new layers of complexity.

For example, under the triple base plan adopted in conference, a farmer's total acreage eligible for crop subsidies would be cut by 15 percent, saving the government an estimated $7 billion over five years. In return, the farmer would have increased freedom to plant crops in response to market conditions. The conferees included the triple base plan and the other farm program cuts in one title of the omnibus budget-reconciliation bill (HR 5835). S 2830, as it emerged from conference, froze farm-price and income-support rates at their current levels.

On another issue, loan rates, the Bush administration abandoned its objections to provisions raising price-support loan rates for wheat and feed grains. The per bushel loan rate, the set amount the government pays farmers for their program crops if market prices are low, acts as a floor on crop prices. The administration had wanted to keep loan rates lower so U.S. crops would remain competitive in world markets.

Farm-state lawmakers gained another concession in conference: a provision requiring the secretary of agriculture to increase spending on export promotion programs if the United States did not achieve a reduction in world agriculture subsidies in negotiations on the international General Agreement on Tariffs and Trade (GATT) by mid-1992.

The bill also was praised by its sponsors as the most environmentally conscious farm measure ever. But conferees dropped the controversial circle of poison provision, included in varying forms in the House and Senate versions of the legislation, that would have banned the export of most pesticides prohibited for use in the United States. The provision was opposed by chemical companies and some farm-state members. The House Oct. 11 had rejected, 162-248, a motion to instruct House conferees to insist on the pesticide provision.

Another environmental protection provision, requiring farmers to keep a record of their pesticide use, was redrafted to cover only the most hazardous chemicals and to restrict access to the records. Environmentalists applauded, however, the conferees' decision to retain, and in some cases strengthen, provisions of the 1985 farm bill intended to conserve wetlands and highly erodible land. *(Wetlands funding, p. 556)*

The House adopted the conference report on S 2830 (H Rept 101-916) on Oct. 23 by a vote of 318-102. The Senate gave its final assent on Oct. 25 on a 60-36 vote, clearing the legislation.

Major Provisions

Following are major provisions of the Food, Agriculture, Conservation and Trade Act (S 2830 — PL 101-624), along with agriculture provisions of the Omnibus Budget Reconciliation Act (HR 5835 — PL 101-508) as signed by Bush on Nov. 5, 1990. *(Food for Peace provisions, story, p. 256; rural development provisions, story, p. 547; food stamps provisions, story, p. 618)*

Wheat and Feed Grains

• **Price and Income Supports.** Maintained the existing system of offering crop loans to farmers at harvest, with farmers using their crops as collateral and having the option of repaying the loans plus interest, or defaulting on the loans, keeping the principal and leaving the government with no recourse except to take possession of the crops.

• **Target Price.** Maintained a system of offering "deficiency" payments to farmers to make up any shortfall between the national weighted average market sale prices received by farmers during the year and certain target prices.

The bill set a floor under target prices for wheat and feed grains, effectively freezing them at 1990 levels — $4 per bushel of wheat and $2.75 per bushel of corn.

The target price for sorghum was set at a level the agriculture secretary determined to be fair and reasonable in relation to corn. The same was true for oats, though the price could not be less than $1.45 per bushel. The price for barley could not be less than 85.8 percent of the target price for corn.

• **Loan Rates.** Changed the formula for setting loan rates. Instead of giving the agriculture secretary discretion to set the basic loan rate at 75 percent to 85 percent of the previous five-year moving average of market prices, excluding the high and low years, the bill mandated that the loan rates be set at 85 percent of the previous five-year average, excluding the high and low years. The decline in the basic loan rate was limited to no more than 5 percent a year.

The agriculture secretary was authorized to reduce the loan rate, based on estimates of surplus levels.

For wheat, if the estimated year-end surplus was at least 30 percent, the secretary could reduce the loan level by up to 10 percent. If the ratio was less than 30 percent but not less than 15 percent, the loan rate could be lowered by up to 5 percent.

For feed grains, if the estimated year-end surplus was at least 25 percent, the loan rate could be reduced up to 10 percent. If the ratio was less than 25 percent but not less than 12.5 percent, the loan rate could be reduced by as much as 5 percent.

The secretary was authorized to reduce the loan rate an additional 10 percent if he determined that it was necessary to keep U.S. wheat and feed grains competitive in the world market. The loan rate could not be lower than $2.44 a bushel for wheat and $1.76 a bushel for corn, except under the basic 85 percent formula.

• **Acreage Reduction Program (ARP).** Set acreage reduction requirements for producers as a condition for receiving price- and crop-support loans. For wheat in 1992-95, if surpluses exceeded 40 percent, producers were required to retire from 10 percent to 20 percent of their land. If surpluses were 40 percent or less, the secretary could provide for an ARP of no greater than 15 percent.

For feed grains in 1991-95, if surpluses were greater than 25 percent, the ARP would have to be at least 10 percent but no more than 20 percent. If surpluses were 25 percent or less, the secretary could set the ARP at 12.5 percent or less.

The agriculture secretary was not required to establish an ARP. For the 1991 crop of wheat, the ARP was set at 15 percent.

• **0/92 Program.** Reauthorized the 0/92 program, under which producers who did not plant wheat and feed grains were eligible for 92 percent of the deficiency payment they collected for these crops. Producers would be allowed to plant oilseeds other than soybeans (including canola, sunflowers, safflower and flaxseed) on 0/92 acres devoted to conservation uses.

The secretary had the option to offer producers an increase or decrease in their acreage reduction program percentages in return for a corresponding increase or decrease in their target price.

For wheat, the allowable increase in the ARP would be 10 percent for 1991 and 15 percent for the following crop years, with a maximum overall ARP of 25 percent.

For feed grains, the allowable ARP adjustment would be 5 percent in 1991 and 10 percent the following years, not to exceed a total ARP of 20 percent.

For every 1 percentage point increase in the ARP, the Agriculture Department would have to increase the producer's target price by 0.5 percent to 1 percent. This option was not supposed to cause additional outlays.

When the secretary determined that domestic oat production would not meet domestic demand, he was authorized to let producers plant oats on their set-aside acreage. If domestic oat production was estimated to exceed domestic demand, the secretary was authorized to limit the amount of oat acreage so that output met demand.

Cotton

• **Target Price.** Set a floor under the upland cotton target price of 73 cents a pound, effectively freezing it at the existing 1990 level for 1991 through 1995. For extra long staple cotton, the target price was set at 120 percent of the loan rate.

• **Loan Rate.** Kept the existing formula for setting the loan rate. For upland cotton, the loan level would have to be either 85 percent of the five-year moving average, dropping the high and low years, or 90 percent of a 15-week average of the five lowest cotton-price quotes for Northern Europe, whichever was lower.

The loan rate could not be reduced by more than 5 percent a year or fall below 50 cents a pound.

For extra long staple cotton, the loan rate would have to be set at 85 percent of the five-year moving average of market prices, dropping the high and low years.

• **Marketing Loan.** Continued the marketing loan for cotton, which permitted producers to repay their government loans at the world market price when it was lower than the loan rate.

The bill established a new procedure for ensuring that the price of U.S. cotton was competitive abroad. Marketing certificates were to be issued to domestic users and exporters when the lowest U.S. price as quoted in Northern Europe exceeded the average of the five cheapest Northern European prices by more than 1.25 cents per pound for four consecutive weeks.

• **Import Quota.** Required a quota on imported cotton if U.S. cotton was uncompetitive in world markets for 10 consecutive weeks. The quota was to be equal to one week's consumption of upland cotton by domestic mills at the average price during the most recent three months.

• **Acreage Reduction Program.** Required the agriculture secretary to announce no later than Jan. 1 the percentage of land that farmers would have to idle in the coming year to qualify for price and income supports.

The secretary was directed to achieve a 30 percent surplus of stocks, but he was barred from imposing an acreage reduction of more than 25 percent. The secretary also was required to use a paid land diversion to achieve the surplus target.

The bill maintained the 50/92 option, which gave producers 92 percent of their annual deficiency payments if they idled at least 50 percent of their acreage.

The secretary had the option of offering producers not participating in 50/92 an increase or decrease in their ARP percentages in return for a corresponding increase or decrease in their target price.

ARPs could be increased a maximum of 10 percent, with a maximum overall ARP of 25 percent. For every percentage point increase or decrease in the ARP, the secretary was required to increase or decrease the producer's target price by 0.5 percent to 1 percent.

Rice

• **Target Price.** Set a floor under the target price for the 1991 through 1995 crops of rice, effectively freezing it at the existing 1990 level of $10.71 per hundredweight.

• **Loan Rate.** Established the loan level at 85 percent of the moving average of market prices, dropping the high and low years. The loan rate could not be reduced more than 5 percent a year and could not drop below $6.50 per hundredweight.

• **Marketing Loan.** Continued the marketing loan for rice.

The bill required payments to rice producers to be made in the form of negotiable marketing certificates, redeemable for cash or government-owned commodities, whenever the world price was below the loan rate.

• **Acreage Reduction Program.** Directed the agriculture secretary to employ an acreage reduction program to achieve an annual surplus equal to 16.5 percent to 20 percent of the average production over the three preceding years. The acreage reduction could not exceed 35 percent.

The bill continued to give producers the 50/92 option to idle at least 50 percent of their land and receive 92 percent of their annual deficiency payments. The secretary had the option to provide 92 percent payment to producers who planted none of their acreage, but he was required to do so for producers who were prevented from planting rice by natural disasters.

The secretary had the option of offering producers not participating in 50/92 an increase or decrease in their ARP percentages in return for a corresponding increase or decrease in their target price. The secretary could offer this option only if the ARP was 20 percent or less.

ARPs could be increased a maximum of 10 percent, with a maximum overall ARP of 25 percent. For every percentage point increase or decrease in the ARP, the secretary was required to increase or decrease the producer's target price by 0.5 percent to 1 percent.

Soybeans

• **Marketing Loan.** Restructured the soybean price-support program by mandating the use of a marketing loan. A marketing loan also was required for other oilseeds, including sunflower, canola, safflower, mustard seed, flaxseed and other crops designated by the Agriculture Department.

• **Loan Rate.** Set the soybean loan rate at $5.02 per bushel for the 1991-95 crop years.

The loan level for sunflower seed, canola seed, rapeseed, safflower seed, flaxseed and mustard seed was 89 cents per pound. For other oilseeds, the agriculture secretary was directed to set a loan level that was "fair and reasonable" in relation to soybeans.

• **Acreage Limitation.** Barred the secretary from requiring producers to participate in production adjustment programs as a condition of eligibility.

Sugar

• **Price Support.** Continued the existing system of giving non-recourse loans to sugar processors who agreed to pay the support price to sugar cane and beet producers. The bill maintained the existing loan rate at 18 cents a pound for raw cane sugar (plus a 3-cent transportation differential) and gave the agriculture secretary authority to increase the loan rate based on the cost of production and other factors. The bill set the beet loan level based on the weighted averages of the most recent five years of producer returns for sugar beets relative to cane.

The secretary was to continue to operate the program at no cost to the federal government. This had the effect of requiring the government to limit sugar imports to maintain domestic prices above the loan rate.

• **Imports.** Set a minimum import level of 1.25 million short tons a year and authorized a tariff rate quota system to replace import quotas.

• **Marketing Controls.** Required the secretary to establish marketing allotments for sugar processors if he estimated that imports would fall below 1.25 million short tons. Processors would be prohibited from marketing, including pledging as loan collateral, any sugar in excess of their marketing allotment. The bill required a proportionate allocation of allotments among producers of sugar cane in states with more than 250 producers. It imposed a marketing control on crystalline fructose equivalent to 200,000 tons of sugar, but none on high fructose corn syrup.

• **Disaster Payments.** Required disaster payments to producers who lost more than 40 percent of their crop in 1990. The payment would have to be at a rate of 50 percent of the loan rate and made on the amount of sugar that was harvested. The payments would be subject to advance appropriation.

Dairy

• **Price Support.** Continued the system of government purchases of milk products (butter, cheese and dry milk) from processors to ensure a minimum price to producers during periods of oversupply. The bill set a floor for the support price at $10.10 per hundredweight through 1995.

The bill mandated an increase of at least 25 cents in the support price if purchases by the Commodity Credit Corporation (CCC) were projected to be less than 3.5 billion pounds in a year. The support price would have to be lowered between 25 cents and 50 cents if purchases were projected to exceed 5 billion pounds. The support price would remain unchanged if purchases were from 3.5 billion pounds to 5 billion pounds.

The bill excluded any increase in imports of dairy products from projections of annual surpluses, allowing greater accumulation of surplus before triggering price-support cuts.

• **Supply Management.** Required the secretary to recommend measures for limiting government purchases of surplus dairy products. The study could not consider such measures as mandatory cattle slaughter or price-support cuts.

The bill directed the secretary to impose assessments on dairy farmers beginning in 1992 if CCC purchases were projected to exceed 7 billion pounds. The assessments could be imposed only if Congress failed to enact legislation to limit production of surplus milk.

The amount of the assessments was intended to cover the cost of the CCC purchasing dairy products above the 7 billion pound level.

• **Make Allowances.** Prohibited the states, effective 12 months after the enactment, from using a greater allowance than provided for in the federal program to establish a Grade A price for milk for manufacturing butter, non-fat milk or cheese.

• **Export Sales.** Continued the existing mandate to make export sales by the CCC of not less than 150,000 metric tons of dairy products (not less than 100,000 metric tons of butter and not less than 20,000 metric tons of cheese) if this did not interfere with regular commercial trade.

Wool and Mohair

• **Price Support.** Extended the existing price-support program, freezing the wool price support at 77.5 percent of an amount formulated from production costs and continuing the support level for pulled wool and mohair in relation to the level for shorn wool.

The bill set an annual per farmer payment limitation of $200,000 in 1991, $175,000 in 1992, $150,000 in 1993 and $125,000 in 1994 and 1995.

Honey

• **Price Support.** Extended the non-recourse loan program for honey, including the marketing loan. A floor was set at the existing support rate of 53.8 cents per pound.

• **Payment Limits.** Set a total per-farmer payment limitation of $200,000 in 1991, $175,000 in 1992, $150,000 in 1993 and $125,000 in 1994.

Peanuts

• **Quota System.** Continued the existing peanut program, in which the government supported the price of peanuts through a quota system. Growers who held marketing quotas for domestic sales would have to comply with those quotas to qualify for price supports. The bill set a national marketing quota floor of 1.35 million tons. When the Agriculture Department made adjustments in the national quota, state quota allocations would have to be based on a state's 1990 share of the national quota.

The bill permitted the distribution of up to 25 percent of all poundage quotas released in the state to farms not having a poundage quota in the previous year. In Texas only, one-third of poundage quota increases would have to be distributed to quota farms producing contract non-quota "additional" peanuts, and two-thirds of additional poundage quota increases would be distributed to other farms in the state.

The bill required a tenant to share equally in any increase in the quota resulting from the tenant's production.

• **Support Level.** Continued non-recourse loans, which were available for all peanuts produced at two support levels. The higher loan rate, available only for quota peanuts, was set at the previous year's support level. The department was authorized to increase the quota price up to 5 percent annually to mitigate the cost of production. Additional peanuts produced in excess of the quotas or by producers without a quota would be supported at a lower rate.

General Commodity

• **Flexibility.** Allowed producers limited flexibility to alter their crop mix without losing base acreage for program crops such as wheat, feed grains, cotton and rice. The goal was to allow producers to respond to market signals instead of producing crops merely to bring in subsidies.

(Base acreage was the average of acres planted to particular crops and considered planted for harvest during the five preceding years. Losing base acreage for specific crops reduced the amount of price-support loans and other benefits available to a producer in the future.)

The bill allowed producers to plant up to 25 percent of their wheat, feed grains, cotton and rice base acreage with other crops, including any program crop, oilseed crop, industrial and experimental crop, except any fruit and vegetable crop, including potatoes and dry edible beans not designated by the secretary as experimental or industrial. No deficiency payments could be made on flexible acres.

If the secretary estimated that the national average soybean price would be less than 105 percent of the loan rate, the quantity of crop acreage that could be planted with soybeans could not exceed 15 percent.

In addition, to make required deficit-reduction savings in agriculture programs, the budget-reconciliation bill made a mandatory reduction of 15 percent in the amount of acreage that was eligible for government subsidy payments from 1991 to 1995.

(The effect of the flexibility provisions in the farm bill and the budget-reconciliation bill was that producers could plant whatever they wanted on up to 25 percent of their acreage usually devoted to program crops. On 15 percent of that, the producer was ineligible for program payments regardless of what he planted. On the remaining 10 percent, the producer had the option of planting something other than program crops, but he would have to forgo payments.)

• **Payment Limitations.** Maintained the existing $50,000 limit on direct payments and deficiency payments, adding a new limit of $75,000 on total marketing loan payments and so-called Findley payments that resulted from lowered loan rates. The effective cap on total payments was lowered from $500,000 to $250,000.

Most farm program payments would be allocated directly to individuals for the purpose of payment limitations, while deficiency and land diversion payments would continue to be attributed to farming entities.

• **Commodity Reserves.** Extended the operation of the long-term Farmer-Owned Reserve, which kept stocks of wheat and feed grains off the market as long as market prices were below designated release levels.

The bill required the Agriculture Department to replenish, within 18 months, the Food Security Wheat Reserve, which was used during periods of tight U.S. wheat supplies to provide international food aid, either by using appropriated funds or drawing on CCC stocks.

The levels stored in the reserve could not be less than 300 million bushels or more than 450 million bushels of wheat, and not less than 600 million bushels or more than 900 million bushels of feed grains.

Crops could be stored in the reserve when the average price for wheat or corn during the previous 90 days exceeded 120 percent of the loan rate, and when the projected surplus-to-use ratio was at least 37.5 percent for wheat and 22.5 percent for corn.

Exports

• **Export Enhancement Program (EEP).** Extended through 1995 the Export Enhancement Program, under which the government subsidized exports of U.S. farm products by paying cash bonuses or giving surplus commodities to exporters. The bill established a minimum funding level of $500 million a year. *(1991 action, p. 554)*

The bill required exporters, users or processors who received EEP bonuses to maintain records of such transactions for five years and permitted the secretary to have complete access. The secretary could require participants to maintain and make available all of their transaction records for the five previous years, even transactions not conducted through EEP.

• **Market Promotion Program.** Reauthorized and broadened the scope of the old Targeted Export Assistance program, which provided funds and commodities to trade organizations for the purpose of promoting U.S. exports, and renamed it the Market Promotion Program. While priority would still be given to markets that were subject to unfair trade practices, the program could be used to help encourage the development and expansion of foreign markets generally.

The bill allowed program funds to be used to advertise specific brands of products in a foreign country under terms and conditions established by the secretary. The bill authorized funding of $200 million a year through fiscal 1995. *(1992 funding, p. 555)*

• **Export Credit Guarantees.** Reauthorized the program providing short-term (up to three years) and intermediate-term (three to 10 years) export credit guarantees. The bill provided at least $5 billion annually for five years in short-term credits and $500 million annually for intermediate credit guarantees. It required that only the export of commodities with U.S. components as defined by the revised 1978 Trade Act could be financed or guaranteed.

The bill prohibited the granting of credit to countries that had a pattern of human rights violations. It authorized the secretary to waive restrictions on loans that would be detrimental to U.S. farmers.

• **High-Value Products.** Required that at least 25 percent of the funds for export subsidy programs be used to promote the export of high-value commodities and value-added products.

• **Emerging Democracies.** Authorized additional short-term export credit guarantees of $1 billion for fiscal years 1991-95 for short- and intermediate-term credit guarantees to emerging democracies.

Research

• **General Research.** Authorized spending ceilings for federal agriculture research of $850 million annually, including funds for several new programs; $310 million for state agricultural experiment stations; $420 million for extension programs; and $50 million for research facilities. The bill also authorized $63 million in fiscal 1991 for food and nutrition education with annual increases to $83 million by fiscal 1995; $60 million for animal health and disease programs; and $50 million for higher education grants and fellowships.

• **Competitive Grants.** Expanded the competitive grant program for high-priority agricultural research, including plant systems; animal systems; nutrition, food quality and health; natural resources and the environment; engineering products and processes; and markets, trade and policy.

The bill authorized $150 million in fiscal 1991, $275 million in fiscal 1992, $350 million in fiscal 1993, $400 million in fiscal 1994 and $500 million in fiscal 1995.

• **Sustainable Agriculture.** Authorized $40 million for research into sustainable agriculture. The bill defined sustainable agriculture as an integrated system of plant and animal production practices having a site-specific application that would, over the long-term, satisfy human food and fiber needs; enhance environmental quality and the natural resource base upon which the agriculture economy depended; make the most efficient use of non-renewable resources and on-farm resources and integrate, where appropriate, natural biological cycles and controls; sustain the economic viability of farm operations; and enhance the quality of life for farmers and society.

The bill authorized matching grants for state programs, cooperative research with colleges and universities, and training for agricultural extension agents, among other programs.

• **Alternative Agriculture.** Established an Applied Agricultural Research Commercialization Center within the Agriculture Department to promote the development of marketable farm products aside from food and other traditional forest or fiber products and to foster economic development in rural areas. The center was authorized to offer low-interest loans and loan guarantees to researchers and consortia, including up to six regional centers created by the bill.

The bill authorized funding of $10 million in fiscal year 1991, increasing to $75 million by 1994.

Conservation

• **'Sodbuster.'** Reauthorized the "sodbuster" program to discourage cultivation of fragile soils. Monetary penalties ranging from $500 to $5,000 could be imposed on producers for inadvertent violations, and they would lose all of their federal benefits if they violated the statute more than once in a five-year period.

The bill expanded the list of federal benefits denied farmers who cultivated such land without an approved conservation plan to include disaster assistance payments for tree planting, conservation program payments, Conservation Reserve Program (CRP) payments, Wetland and Environmental Easement program payments, Natural Resource payments and funds under the Small Watersheds Program.

• **'Swampbuster.'** Reauthorized the "swampbuster" program to deny federal benefits to producers who drained and cultivated wetlands. The bill specified that all three characteristics of a wetland — hydric soils, hydrology and hydropytic vegetation — would have to be present for a wetland to be subject to the swampbuster restrictions. The Agriculture Department would have to exempt farmers from swampbuster when draining of a wetland would have a minimal effect.

Swampbuster was triggered at the time a wetland was drained, not when it was cropped, as existing law provided. The bill allowed the use of penalties ranging from $750 to $10,000 for inadvertent drainings, as long as the producer agreed to restore the wetlands. However, the producer would lose all of his benefits if he violated the statute more than once during a 10-year period. The bill expanded the list of federal benefits denied farmers who cultivated such land without an approved conservation plan to include disaster assistance payments for tree planting, conservation program payments, CRP payments, Wetland and Environmental Easement program payments, Natural Resource payments and funds under the Small Watersheds Program.

The bill exempted producers from loss of benefits if the wetland had been farmed in the past and its conversion was mitigated by the restoration of another drained wetland.

• **Conservation Reserves.** Created an Agricultural Resources Conservation Program (ARC) to protect highly erodible land, wetlands and land susceptible to water pollution caused by farming. Included in the ARC umbrella were three programs: the existing Conservation Reserve Program, under which producers were paid to remove highly erodible land from production for 10 years; a new Wetlands Reserve Program, which paid farmers to place wetlands in easements for 30 years or longer; and a new Water Quality Incentives Program, which gave producers financial assistance to reduce water pollution caused by farming.

Enrollment in the CRP was targeted to reach not less than 40 million acres nor more than 45 million acres by 1995. That could include environmentally sensitive land, shelterbelts, windbreaks and marginal pastureland on which trees had been planted. Up to 1 million acres of wetlands could be enrolled in the wetlands reserve, while a 10 million acre target existed for the water quality program. *(1992 funding, p. 556)*

• **Crop Rotation.** Established a new program to encourage farmers to rotate their crops and plant beneficial resource-conserving crops, without losing eligibility for the same level of crop subsidy payments.

• **Pesticide Recordkeeping.** Required farmers to keep a record of their application of certain hazardous chemicals, known as "restricted use" pesticides. The records would have to be provided to the Agriculture Department and made available to health care professionals who requested information about specific cases. The public could gain access to the pesticide-use information through a Freedom of Information Act request, but the names of producers and the specific locations of their farms could not be released.

Forestry

• **Forest Stewardship.** Reauthorized and created several programs to encourage better stewardship of private forests and offered financial assistance for timber conservation activities.

• **America the Beautiful.** Established a private, nonprofit foundation to promote tree planting and related conservation activities by providing grants. The goal was to plant 1 billion trees. The bill authorized a $25 million grant in fiscal 1991 with future support to come from private sources.

• **Disaster Assistance.** Authorized the Agriculture Department to provide disaster assistance to forestland owners who suffered losses due to damaging weather or wildfire after October 1989. Landowners could be reimbursed for up to 65 percent of the cost of re-establishing tree stands or given sufficient tree seedlings to reforest the areas. Individuals could not receive more than $25,000 a year in assistance, and the bill barred landowners with gross revenues of more than $2 million a year from receiving assistance.

Miscellaneous

• **Disaster Protection.** Required that crops covered by crop insurance in one county of a state be covered throughout the state and that rates be adjusted to achieve actuarial sufficiency. However, rate increases were capped at no more than 20 percent of the previous year's rate. The bill directed the secretary to use the Agricultural Stabilization and Conservation Service to provide crop insurance information and agent lists to farmers. It included a sense of Congress resolution supporting the continuation of crop insurance and the use of funds borrowed from the Commodity Credit Corporation to continue the program. *(Crop insurance, box, p. 549)*

Direct disaster payments were authorized for 1990 crops.

• **Organic Certification.** Required the Agriculture Department to set national minimum standards for the production and labeling of organic foods and permitted states to adopt more restrictive standards.

• **Credit.** Reduced from three years to one year the time during which the FmHA would have to dispose of land in its inventory. People who had leased property acquired by FmHA before Jan. 6, 1988, had the right of first refusal on the sale of the property during a limited period. Beginning farmers and ranchers also had preference to purchase inventory property.

The bill required that the continued viability of farms be maintained when conservation easements were placed on inventory property. Easements placed on drained wetlands could not exceed 10 percent of the existing cropland. Easements placed on frequently cropped wetlands could not exceed 20 percent of the farm. The bill increased the interest rate subsidy on certain guaranteed loans to 4 percent. It also provided for a gradual shift from direct government lending to farmers in favor of government guarantees of private loans.

The bill limited FmHA borrowers to a single write-down for loans made after Jan. 6, 1988. There was a lifetime cap of $300,000 in principal and interest on FmHA borrowers. The Farm Credit Administration was authorized to oversee the financial condition of the Federal Agricultural Mortgage Corporation (Farmer Mac). The bill also created a secondary market for FmHA loans through Farmer Mac.

Deficit Reduction

• **Triple Base.** To comply with the deficit-reduction reconciliation target for agriculture, HR 5835 reduced by 15 percent the amount of program crop acreage on which the government made subsidy payments from 1991 through 1995.

Under the triple base plan, farms receiving subsidies had three categories of land: the annually announced acreage reduction percentage, which took land out of production; the permitted acreage on which the program crop was planted and that was eligible for deficiency payments; and the 15 percent of land that was not eligible for payments.

On the third category, producers could plant any program crop (wheat, corn, cotton and rice), oilseeds (such as soybeans, canola and sunflower) or non-program crops except fruits and vegetables. Crops planted on this land were eligible for loans and marketing loans.

For the 1991 crop of winter wheat only, producers had the option to participate in the 15 percent triple base plan or to have their deficiency payments calculated on a 12-month average.

For other crops of wheat, feed grains and rice, the deficiency payment was to be calculated on a 12-month basis, not the existing five-month basis, in 1994 and 1995. The change would reduce government outlays.

• **Acreage Reduction Program.** Established maximum acreage levels of 20 percent for wheat and feed grains, 25 percent for cotton and 35 percent for rice, based on certain surplus levels. The reconciliation bill set a minimum ARP level for wheat of 6 percent in 1992, 5 percent in 1993, 7 percent in 1994 and 5 percent in 1995, and a minimum ARP level of 7.5 percent for feed grains.

• **Other Commodities.** Authorized loan origination fees and other assessments on other commodities. Dairy producers would have to pay a 5-cent fee in fiscal 1991 and an 11-cent fee for 1992 through 1995. The secretary could refund this fee if a producer could prove his milk production had not increased from the previous year's level. Producers of oilseeds would have to pay a 2 percent loan-origination fee. Peanuts, honey and tobacco were subject to a 1 percent loan fee. Wool and mohair producers would have 1 percent deducted from their incentive payments.

• **Loan Authorizations.** Established loan levels for the Rural Electrification and Telephone Revolving Fund, then reduced the levels to be able to claim the savings, as follows: an $896 million authorization in fiscal 1991 reduced by $224 million; a $932 million authorization in fiscal 1992 reduced by $234 million; a $969 million authorization in fiscal 1993 reduced by $244 million; a $1.01 billion authorization in fiscal 1994 reduced by $256 million; and a $1.05 billion authorization for fiscal 1995 reduced by $267 million.

The reconciliation bill established loan levels for the Farmers Home Administration Agricultural Credit Insurance Fund, then reduced the levels to claim the savings, as follows: a $4.2 billion authorization in fiscal 1991 and a reduction in direct loans of $482 million; a $4.3 billion authorization for fiscal 1992 and a reduction in direct loans of $614 million; a $4.5 billion authorization for fiscal 1993 and a reduction in direct loans of $760 million; a $4.7 billion authorization in fiscal 1994 and a reduction in direct loans of $859 million; and a $4.9 billion authorization for fiscal 1995 and a reduction in direct loans of $907 million.

• **GATT.** Required the secretary, if the United States did not enter into an agreement under the General Agreement on Tariffs and Trade by June 30, 1992, to increase by $1 billion the level of spending in fiscal years 1994 and 1995 on export promotion programs for agricultural goods. The secretary also was authorized to waive minimum levels of acreage that would have to be retired by producers of program crops in 1993, 1994 and 1995. And the secretary could allow producers to repay their crop loans for wheat and feed grains at levels established in the Agricultural Act of 1949.

If no GATT agreement was reached by June 30, 1993, the secretary could waive all cuts in agriculture spending required to meet the deficit-reduction targets, in addition to the other measures.

Rural Development

As part of the omnibus farm bill (S 2830 — PL 101-624) signed by President Bush on Nov. 28, 1990, Congress redesigned and upgraded federal programs for rural economic development. *(Farm bill, p. 537)*

The rural development provisions included in S 2830 were drawn from two bills considered earlier by the 101st Congress: S 1036 and HR 3581. A priority of Senate Agriculture Committee Chairman Patrick J. Leahy, D-Vt., S 1036 established new loan programs to encourage rural development but gave responsibility for administering the programs to existing agencies such as the Farmers Home Administration (FmHA) and the Rural Electrification Administration (REA). HR 3581 took a different approach. It pooled roughly $1 billion in existing rural development funds and decentralized the funding process by allowing states to allocate their share of the funds. S 1036 was reported (S Rept 101-73) from Senate Agriculture, Nutrition and Forestry on July 11, 1989, and passed by the Senate on a voice vote Aug. 2. The House Agriculture Committee reported HR 3581 (H Rept 101-415) on March 7, 1990, and the full House passed the bill, 360-45, on March 22. After substituting the text of S 1036 with HR 3581, the House passed S 1036 by voice vote on March 27.

The rural development provisions inserted in the farm bill represented a blending of the two bills, with modifications. For example, the House plan for a new agency to administer rural development programs was included, but another House provision giving the states more control over the programs was scaled back.

Leahy had been pushing for rural development legislation since 1988 but had found forging a consensus difficult. Little money was available for new agriculture programs and little agreement existed on what was needed. And many of the influential farm lobbying groups, representing farmers who grew particular commodities, had been unenthusiastic about spending on rural development at a time when their constituents were being asked to accept continued cuts in support payments. *(1988 action, Congress and the Nation Vol. VII, p. 538)*

As signed into law, the rural development provisions of the omnibus farm bill:

- Established a new Rural Development Administration within the Agriculture Department and transferred most duties relating to rural development to the agency. New programs were authorized to promote economic development and improve schools, health care and water supply in rural areas.
- Permitted up to five states to set up state rural economic development review panels to rank applications for funds within the state's allocation of federal funds. The secretary retained authority for distributing funds. The bill authorized appropriations to establish revolving loan funds in up to five states, which would provide lines of credit to non-profit corporations and public agencies engaged in rural development.
- Removed the cap on authorization of appropriations for rural water and waste facilities and authorized the secretary to make loans to Rural Electrification Administration borrowers for water and sewer projects. Up to 50 percent of the cost of the projects could be loaned. The bill expanded the authority of the banks for cooperatives of the Farm Credit System to make water and sewer loans to communities with populations of less than 20,000.
- Authorized the FmHA to make up to $25 million in loans to small communities for emergency water and waste facility projects. Another $30 million was authorized for loans to communities facing significant health risks because of a lack of sewer and water treatment facilities.
- Established grants to encourage and improve the use of telecommunications and computer networks. The bill authorized low- and market-rate loans to businesses, local governments or public agencies to fund facilities in which participants shared telecommunications equipment, computers and software. It authorized $15 million annually for fiscal 1991-94.
- Allowed REA borrowers to defer making any loan payments if funds in an amount equal to the deferment of five or 10 years were used for rural development projects, as long as the deferral was not more than half the cost of the project and the borrower made a payment to REA equal to the amount deferred. The bill created a Rural Business Incubator fund and permitted the REA to make grants or low-interest loans (5 percent or less) to its borrowers and other non-profit entities to support the operation of incubators.

Farm Program Cuts

Congress approved a package of belt-tightening changes in farm programs for fiscal 1990 as part of a deficit-reduction bill (HR 3299 — PL 101-239) enacted in 1989. The farm program provisions added up to $1.2 billion in budget cuts. *(Deficit-reduction bill, p. 43)*

The changes were approved Sept. 14 by the Senate Agriculture Committee and subsequently were adopted in a House-Senate conference on HR 3299 (H Rept 101-386).

Congress struggled with meeting deficit-reduction targets without significantly cutting payments to farmers, who made up a formidable lobby. Many of the enacted changes, which essentially were modifications in accounting, qualified as budget savings but did not cut spending. However, the bill did slash $232 million in advanced deficiency payments, the government subsidies paid to farmers before the crop marketing year.

The deficit-reduction bill also included farm provisions that:

- Allowed farm program participants to devote a portion of their base acreage to planting oil seeds, which were not covered by federal income subsidies, saving $116 million.
- Delayed the effective date of a change in the Farm Credit System bailout, saving $420 million.
- Limited export assistance for farm products, saving $143 million.
- Delayed until 1990 any repayments of excess price supports from farmers who suffered natural disasters in 1988 and 1989, saving $54 million.
- Allowed discretionary decreases in the purchase prices for dry milk and butter, saving $27 million. The bill also claimed $25 million in additional price adjustments that were provided in separate legislation (S 553 — PL 101-7) enacted earlier in the year. *(S 553, dairy price supports, below)*

Dairy Price Supports

Congress in 1989 cleared legislation (S 553) making technical changes in the dairy program, which saved an estimated $10 million in fiscal 1989 and $25 million in fiscal 1990. As a result, the amount that had to be cut from agriculture programs to meet deficit-reduction targets was lessened.

The bill mandated the mix of butter and non-fat dry milk purchased by the federal government between April 1 and July 1, 1989.

S 553 was passed, by voice vote, in the Senate on March 9. The House passed an amended version, also by voice vote, on March 15. The Senate agreed to the House amendments March 17, thus clearing the measure. President Bush signed S 553 (PL 101-7) on March 29.

Disaster Relief

Congress in 1989 cleared a $900 million disaster assistance bill (HR 2467) that offered relief to farmers with crops affected by drought, hail, flooding, freezing and a host of other weather and related conditions. The bill was signed into law (PL 101-82) on Aug. 14.

The legislation's price tag was to be covered by savings the government was expected to reap as a result of the poor farm conditions. Commodity prices were expected to rise because of the drought, reducing government outlays for price- and income-support payments. This made the bill acceptable to the Bush administration.

The relief measure began as a response to drought and cold conditions that had decimated at least half of the winter wheat in Kansas, the nation's largest wheat producer. Portions of surrounding states also were suffering, as was California. To broaden the bill's appeal, sponsors extended eligibility to farmers of virtually every crop hit by severe weather conditions.

Not all farmers were equally eligible, however. To keep intact the fragile coalition behind the bill, as well as to keep the cost around $900 million as the Bush administration insisted, lawmakers settled on a complicated formula for determining how much loss a farmer would have to suffer to receive payments.

Farmers who participated in federal crop subsidy programs were eligible for payments if they lost at least 40 percent of their crops. Program crop farmers who had crop insurance only had to lose 35 percent of their crops to get payments. Soybean farmers were eligible if they lost 45 percent of their crops.

Other farmers would be eligible if they lost a minimum of half their crops. That included producers who grew program crops but did not participate in federal subsidy programs and those who grew crops not covered by federal support programs.

All farmers were paid at the same rate: 65 percent of what they would have received from price-support programs or by marketing their crops. Payments were limited to a total of $100,000 per farmer.

Farmers who received benefits under the bill were required to buy crop insurance for 1990 if they suffered more than a 65 percent loss. The insurance program had been unpopular with farmers, who complained that the premiums were too expensive and the coverage inadequate. *(Crop insurance, box, this page)*

Other provisions of the disaster relief bill put limits on payments for damaged fruit and permitted farmers to plant alternative crops, including the oilseed canola, on up to 20 percent of their base acreage.

Final legislative action on HR 2467 took place while Congress was pressing to get out of town for its monthlong August recess. HR 2467 (H Rept 101-91) had been reported June 19 from the House Agriculture Committee. On June 27, the full House passed the bill by voice vote, and the Senate Agriculture, Nutrition and Forestry Committee reported the Senate version of the legislation (S 1429 — S Rept 101-93). The Senate, by voice vote Aug. 2, passed an amended HR 2467. The House agreed to the Senate-passed bill with amendments on Aug. 4. Later that day, the Senate accepted the House changes, thus clearing the measure for the president.

HR 2467 followed on the heels of an emergency relief bill (PL 100-387) enacted in 1988 for farmers who suffered major financial losses from a disastrous summer drought in the Corn Belt. *(Congress and the Nation Vol. VII, p. 533)*

Crop Insurance

Congress in 1980 expanded and revamped the federal crop insurance program (PL 96-365) in the hope that farmers would no longer rely on disaster relief legislation to bail them out when their crops were destroyed. But farmers complained that the insurance was inadequate and costly, and participation in the program remained poor. Congress continued to provide relief funds, clearing five disaster relief bills during the 1980s. *(PL 96-365, Congress and the Nation Vol. V, p. 391; 1983 disaster relief, Congress and the Nation Vol. VI, p. 507; 1986 disaster relief, Congress and the Nation Vol. VII, p. 518; 1987 disaster relief, Congress and the Nation Vol. VII, p. 532; 1988 disaster relief, Congress and the Nation Vol. VII, p. 533; 1989 disaster relief, p. 548)*

Run by the Agriculture Department's Federal Crop Insurance Corporation, the crop insurance program was plagued during the 1980s by financial losses and charges that participating insurers were receiving too much of the government's money. In 1987, the General Accounting Office, an arm of Congress that investigates executive branch spending, reviewed $9.4 million in claims and concluded that about $3 million should not have been paid. For their part, the private insurance agents who marketed the insurance and were reimbursed by the government for losses complained that the paperwork was too complex.

Proposals to redesign the crop insurance program circulated in the 101st Congress, but drafters of the 1990 omnibus farm bill (S 2830 — PL 101-624) avoided the issue. House Appropriations Committee Chairman Jamie L. Whitten, D-Miss., backed by the Bush administration, argued in 1990 that high prices and low farmer participation had made the program unworkable and convinced the House to abolish it during consideration of the fiscal 1991 agriculture appropriations bill (HR 5268). But Whitten reversed himself during the House-Senate conference, and the final bill (PL 101-506) retained the crop insurance program. *(Omnibus farm bill, p. 537)*

As a concession to Whitten, conferees inserted instructions in the conference report (H Rept 101-907) that called for changes to make administration of the program more efficient.

Earthquake Aid

As part of legislation (S 1793 — PL 101-220) making technical and correcting changes in agriculture programs, Congress provided disaster aid to farmers who suffered damage in a Northern California earthquake.

The Senate passed S 1793 by voice vote on Oct. 25, 1989. The House passed an amended version, also by voice vote, on Nov. 9. The Senate agreed to the House changes, with further amendments, Nov. 22. The House accepted the Senate amendments the same day, clearing the measure. President Bush signed S 1793 on Dec. 12.

The House Nov. 13 passed another earthquake aid bill (HR 3589). It had been reported (H Rept 101-347) from House Agriculture also on Nov. 13. HR 3589 would amend the 1989 disaster relief legislation (HR 2467 — PL 101-82) by adding earthquakes to the list of natural disasters under which farmers could apply for relief. The bill also would increase the authorization for guaranteed loans from $200 million to $300 million; make damaged crops of ornamental flowers and shrubs eligible for disaster payments; and provide federal assistance to orchardists whose trees, planted for commercial purposes, were destroyed in earthquakes. *(1989 disaster relief, p. 548)*

HR 3589 saw no further congressional action.

Commodity Futures

Legislation (HR 2869, S 1729) to reauthorize and strengthen the Commodity Futures Trading Commission (CFTC) passed the House and was reported by the Senate Agriculture Committee in 1989 but became bogged down in a dispute over regulation of stock index futures in 1990. Congress subsequently cleared a CFTC bill in 1992. *(102nd Congress action, p. 551)*

Congress established the five-member CFTC in 1974 (PL 93-463) to regulate the commodity futures trading business and oversee commodity exchanges. Since its inception, the commission periodically returned to Congress for reauthorization. *(1974 act, Congress and the Nation Vol. IV, p. 723; 1986 reauthorization, Congress and the Nation Vol. VII, p. 517)*

1989 Action

An unusually fervent debate on futures trading unfolded in 1989, spurred largely by the Aug. 2 announcement that a federal undercover investigation had brought indictments against 46 futures traders. The traders allegedly had skimmed investors' profits in floor trading at the Chicago Board of Trade and the Chicago Mercantile Exchange.

The announcement also helped propel HR 2869 through the House Agriculture Committee, which reported the bill (H Rept 101-236) on Sept. 7. The full House, on a unanimous 420-0 vote Sept. 13, passed HR 2869, designed to toughen federal regulation of the commodity futures markets and to permanently authorize the CFTC to oversee those markets.

As passed, HR 2869 prohibited dual trading — the practice of brokers executing customer orders while also trading on their own accounts — in any market where the average daily trading volume was greater than 7,000 contracts. The practice had been widely criticized because it created opportunities for traders to capitalize on their knowledge of impending customer orders.

The bill also toughened the "audit trail" standards that exchanges must meet. Within a year, an exchange would have to have been able to pinpoint the time a trade took place to the nearest minute; within three years, to 30 seconds. If the standards could not be met, the CFTC would be prohibited from approving new contracts at the exchange. Some flexibility existed in the provision.

S 1729, reported (S Rept 101-191) from Senate Agriculture, Nutrition and Forestry on Nov. 6, would crack down on futures trading abuses and expand the enforcement powers of the CFTC. Like the House-passed bill, S 1729 provided new audit trail standards as well as dual trading provisions. The committee amended the bill to give the CFTC authority to charge futures traders fees totaling $68 million over five years. Supporters argued that the funds were crucial if the CFTC was to transform itself into a rigorous overseer of the markets. The U.S. futures industry bitterly opposed the fees, warning that the large assessments would diminish its competitive position in the world.

1990 Action

The focus of CFTC legislation shifted in 1990 to jurisdiction over stock index futures, and, as a result, progress on the measure came to a grinding halt. Stock index futures were contracts used by specialists to bet on the market's direction and by holders of large stock portfolios as insurance against declines in the value of their holdings. The commodity was a bundle of stocks instead of a bushel of cotton or a carload of pork bellies.

Trading of stock index futures began in 1982 at the Chicago Mercantile Exchange and quickly skyrocketed. Some analysts believed that the October 1987 stock market crash was accelerated by heavy trading of stock index futures. Part of the problem, they said, was the low level set for the margins, the amount of money an investor paid up front for the stock or futures contract. Stock margins were set at 50 percent of the purchase price; futures margins varied but generally were much lower.

A dispute within the Bush administration and Congress about which agency should regulate stock index futures — the CFTC or the Securities and Exchange Commission (SEC) — kept S 1729 from the Senate floor.

The SEC and the Treasury Department advocated transferring regulation of the futures to the SEC. Supporting this position were the New York-based stock markets and retail stock brokerage firms, which wanted to protect small investors from wild market fluctuations. The CFTC, meanwhile, did not want to lose turf to another agency, and the Chicago-based futures industry feared that a jurisdictional change would upset commodity futures markets and farm prices.

In an attempt to end the struggle, Dan Glickman, D-Kan., and Dennis E. Eckart, D-Ohio, introduced legislation (HR 4477) in April to merge the SEC and CFTC. The bill went nowhere. Efforts in the fall to move S 1729 to the Senate floor were blocked, and neither S 1729 nor HR 2869 saw further action in the 101st Congress.

Screwworm Eradication

Congress in 1990 cleared legislation (HR 4010) to stop the spread of screwworms, flesh-eating parasites that had been eradicated in the United States but had become a growing problem in Central and South America and North Africa.

The bill authorized the Agriculture Department to produce sterile screwworms and sell them to foreign countries to eradicate fertile screwworms. The United States and the government of Mexico jointly operated a facility in Mexico where the sterile screwworms were produced.

HR 4010 was reported (H Rept 101-408) by the House Agriculture Committee and passed, by voice vote under suspension of the rules, by the House on Feb. 27, 1990. The Senate passed the bill, also by voice vote, on March 5. President Bush signed the measure (PL 101-255) on March 15.

Crop Yields

The House on June 13, 1989, passed, by voice vote under suspension of the rules, HR 2042, to allow wheat, feed grains, cotton, rice and soybean farmers to report their annual crop yields to the federal government to establish a record of their actual yields. HR 2042 was reported (H Rept 101-80) from House Agriculture on June 9.

HR 2042 also would require the Department of Agriculture to study alternative ways of figuring out what amount of a farmer's crop was eligible for federal agriculture subsidies. Farmers complained that the existing formula for calculating benefits, known as program payment yield, did not reflect true output in any given year. The administration opposed any change.

The bill died at the end of the 101st Congress.

Farmland Acquisition

Both the House and Senate in 1989 passed legislation (HR 2469) to bar anyone who was convicted of fraud from acquiring farmland that the federal government came to possess through foreclosure.

The Agriculture Committee reported HR 2469 (H Rept 101-81) on June 9. The House passed the bill by voice vote, under suspension of the rules, June 13. The Senate passed an amended version by voice vote Nov. 22. The bill saw no further congressional action.

1991-92

In the aftermath of passage of the 1990 farm bill, Congress made no big changes in farm policy during the last two years of the Bush administration.

In 1992, after nearly four years of work, Congress agreed on legislation to reauthorize the Commodities Futures Trading Commission, the agency with authority over the multi-billion-dollar futures trading industry. The bill tightened regulation of futures traders in response to reports of abuses in the nation's trading pits and resolved — at least temporarily — a long-running controversy about how to regulate new instruments such as stock index futures.

Another bill, also cleared in 1992, put new restrictions on farm credit and made getting loans easier for beginning farmers.

As Bush administration trade negotiators continued to push for worldwide reductions in agriculture subsidies, Congress debated a number of programs intended to increase U.S. strength in international agriculture markets. The administration won approval of a provision in a 1991 supplemental spending bill that raised the amount of subsidies U.S. exporters could be offered under the Agriculture Department's Export Enhancement Program. Another program favored by the administration, subsidizing the advertising efforts of U.S. agriculture exporters, survived an attempt by congressional appropriators in 1992 to sharply cut its funding.

Farm-state legislators in 1991 successfully pressured the Bush administration to grant the Soviet Union $2.75 billion in credit guarantees to purchase U.S. grain — a move the members said would significantly boost sales and thus reduce the need for direct subsidy payments to farmers.

Commodity Futures

Ending a long impasse, Congress in 1992 cleared legislation reauthorizing the Commodities Futures Trading Commission (CFTC) for two years and imposing significant new restrictions on futures trading. The bill (HR 707 — PL 102-546) increased the regulatory powers of the agency, which oversaw futures trading on the Chicago Board of Trade and other exchanges.

The long-delayed bill took nearly four years to develop and pass, despite early momentum spurred in 1989 by federal indictments of numerous Chicago futures traders. The legislation addressed problems related to the scandal, such as outdated auditing methods and the practice of dual trading, in which brokers made transactions for clients and for their personal accounts at the same time. *(1989-90 action, p. 550)*

Congress appeared headed for agreement on reforms to address those problems, but passage of the bill was delayed by disagreements on two other issues: the regulation of stock index futures and of exotic financial instruments known as "hybrids" and "swaps." Hybrids combined some of the traits of more traditional financial instruments such as stocks or bonds, while swaps involved futures in debt obligations and currencies.

As cleared, the bill allowed the CFTC to exempt swaps and hybrids from regulations applied to other futures products under the Commodity Futures Act. This provision bought time while the question was studied, and it delayed the search for a long-term regulatory solution until 1994, when the CFTC would again come up for reauthorization.

On the other contested issue, the bill allowed the Federal Reserve Board to set margin limits on stock index futures, a trading instrument used by investors to bet on the direction of the stock market and hedge against declines in the value of other investments. The Bush administration argued that enabling the Fed to coordinate margin requirements for stocks and stock index futures could minimize market plunges such as the October 1987 one that shook the exchanges.

Conferees dropped from the bill a Senate provision, vigorously opposed by the futures industry, to impose a transaction tax to help finance the commission's enforcement efforts.

Legislative Action

Both the House and Senate in 1991 passed HR 707, reauthorizing the CFTC. As in 1990, however, disputes over regulation of stock index futures and other new financial instruments derailed the legislation. The House Agriculture Committee reported HR 707 (H Rept 102-6) on March 1. The House passed the measure, 395-27, under suspension of the rules on March 5. The Senate Agriculture, Nutrition and Forestry Committee reported the Senate version (S 207 — S Rept 102-22) on March 12. The Senate passed HR 707, 90-8, on April 18, after substituting the text of S 207.

Both versions of HR 707 contained provisions cracking down on abuses in the trading pits and establishing new "audit trail" standards. The House-passed bill was silent on stock index futures, while the Senate version incorporated a compromise that would have left the CFTC with jurisdiction over those instruments but given the Securities and Exchange Commission (SEC) new authority to oversee margins. The Senate-passed bill also included provisions creating a formula to determine whether hybrid financial instruments should be regulated by the SEC or CFTC and authorizing the CFTC to exempt certain instruments from regulation under the Commodity Exchange Act. The House made no such provision.

Lack of consensus over stock index futures stalled action on HR 707. Conferees met for an hour on Nov. 6, leaving their differences unresolved until 1992. Serious negotiations on the bill began in late July 1992, and a final compromise was agreed to by the conferees in late September. The House agreed to the conference report (H Rept 102-978) by voice vote on Oct. 2; the Senate followed suit on Oct. 8, clearing HR 707. President Bush signed the measure (PL 102-546) on Oct. 28.

Major Provisions

As cleared, HR 707:

Limitations on Trading Practices

- **Dual Trading.** Prohibited dual trading in any futures market unless the CFTC made a specific exemption. (Dual trading occurred when brokers traded for a client and for themselves or a fellow broker on the same day. Abuse of the practice enabled a broker to capitalize on inside knowledge of a client's order.)

The bill allowed the CFTC to exempt an exchange from the prohibition on dual trading if (1) the exchange had an electronic internal audit system set up to monitor the times and amounts of all trades; (2) the commission found that banning dual trading would harm the public interest; or (3) the contract market was small.

- **Broker Associations.** Made it illegal for brokers knowingly to execute customer orders in cooperation with someone with whom they were associated through a broker association or an employment or other relationship.

Regulatory Enhancement

- **Market Auditing.** Required exchanges to put into place electronic or computerized systems to monitor all floor trades, recording the parties and the exact time of the transaction. Within three years, the auditing methods would have to be sophisticated enough to provide data to the market continuously and to register the time of each transaction and check it against the time entered by the trader. (With accurate auditing of transactions, dual trading would become permissible because trading abuses could be identified.)

The bill gave the CFTC broad authority to inspect and monitor the audit technology and to determine when it met the statutory standards. The commission was required to report within two years of enactment on how the futures exchanges were complying with the audit requirements.

The bill required each futures market in each exchange to maintain and use an audit system that included inspectors for floor trading, electronic records of transactions and appropriate discipline for infractions. The CFTC was to audit exchange systems at least once every two years, following mandatory inspection guidelines.

- **Telemarketing Fraud.** Required futures associations to establish guidelines for telephone solicitation aimed at protecting customers.
- **Undercover Operations.** Directed the CFTC to cooperate with federal agencies in requesting and arranging undercover operations.
- **Board Memberships.** Outlined the requirements for members serving on the oversight boards for each contract market and required that the futures associations refuse membership to individuals who violated trading rules.
- **Floor Trader Registration.** Required all individuals who traded in a contract market for their own accounts to register with the CFTC. The registration could be revoked if a trader violated CFTC regulations. All registered traders would have to attend periodic ethics training seminars.
- **Penalties.** Established a range of felony penalties for individuals who violated trading rules, to be determined by the gravity of the infraction as well as the financial strength of the violator. The penalty for embezzlement was increased to $1 million for corporations and $500,000 for individuals.

The bill also set criteria for establishing the financial liability of brokers who violated trading rules and authorized the CFTC to force violators to pay restitution to clients.

- **Insider Trading.** Made it a felony to trade on the basis of material, non-public information.
- **Commissioner Requirements.** Set guidelines for CFTC commissioners and conflict-of-interest requirements for members of futures market governing boards.
- **Fee Collection and Competitiveness Studies.** Directed the General Accounting Office to study a fee collection system that would help pay for enforcement of the new rules. The CFTC was directed to study the competitiveness of the U.S. futures trading industry in relation to those of other countries.
- **Civil Penalty Guidelines.** Required the CFTC to publish and allow public review of all guidelines governing civil penalties.

Intermarket Coordination

- **Futures Margins.** Allowed the Board of Governors of the Federal Reserve System to set or change margin levels required on stock index futures transactions or on options on stock index futures. This authority could be delegated to the CFTC on a daily basis. (Margins are deposits on futures transactions that ensure the contract will be fulfilled by both parties.)
- **Swaps and Hybrids.** Authorized the CFTC to exempt certain exotic financial instruments from the requirements of the Commodity Exchange Act. The conference report specified that the exemption was to be used "sparingly." The provision applied only to swaps and other derivative products known as hybrids, forwards and deposits, which did not fall within the traditional definition of futures products.
- **Studies of Derivatives.** Directed the CFTC to cooperate with the Securities and Exchange Commission and the Federal Reserve Board to conduct a comprehensive study of swaps and the off-exchange derivatives trading industry. The study was to determine whether a single federal agency should regulate the markets for futures, securities, options, swaps and derivative products.

Other Provisions

- **Assistance to Foreign Exchanges.** Allowed the CFTC to assist foreign futures authorities in investigating possible violations of futures trading laws when the investi-

Dairy Production

Legislation (HR 2837, S 1527) to help dairy farmers by limiting production died in 1991, despite winning approval by the Agriculture committees of both chambers. The story of the derailed dairy bill illustrates some of the complexities and conflicts that arise when lawmakers try to change agriculture policies.

The legislation was offered in response to plummeting milk prices, which in the spring of 1991 hit a 13-year low. The drop was especially hard on dairy farmers in New England and the Great Lakes region, who were more vulnerable to financial losses than were the large dairies of the western states.

Government support for dairy farmers dated back to World War II, when the nation needed to produce more milk. The Agriculture Department set a minimum price for milk by buying all unsold milk at a price set by Congress, the support price. The 1991 dairy legislation would have boosted the income of dairy farmers by increasing the government price support for milk, while placing quotas on the amount of milk farmers could produce.

The legislation provoked a formidable array of opponents. The Bush administration supported a policy of reducing government controls on the agriculture economy, so it objected. The livestock industry protested that the changes would prompt dairy farmers to slaughter more cows, driving down beef prices. And advocates for consumer and nutrition programs warned that the legislation would raise milk prices and cut into programs for the poor, such as food stamps.

The opposition of the consumer and nutrition interests posed a special dilemma for a key supporter of the legislation, Democrat Patrick J. Leahy, chairman of the Senate Agriculture Committee. Dairy farmers in his home state of Vermont were among the hardest hit by the drop in milk prices, but Leahy was a liberal who usually supported the goals of consumer and nutrition groups.

Economic changes added another wrinkle. Although dairy prices were plunging when the legislation first was proposed, they were on the rise when the Senate committee began its consideration in the fall. By then, dairy farmers were getting nearly the same price for milk as they had the year before.

The original legislation had been drafted with the help and support of the National Milk Producers Federation, but the fragile coalition of regional and national dairy groups started collapsing as opposition to the legislation increased.

HR 2837 was approved by the House Agriculture Committee by voice vote July 16; it was reported (H Rept 102-173, Part I) on July 29. House Education and Labor (H Rept 102-173, Part II) and House Ways and Means (H Rept 102-173, Part III) shared jurisdiction over the bill; they both reported it Oct. 17.

S 1527 was approved by the Senate Agriculture Committee by voice vote Oct. 23 and folded into an unrelated House-passed measure (HR 2893) to renew disaster assistance programs. HR 2893 subsequently was passed by the Senate, but it saw no further congressional action. *(Disaster relief, p. 557)*

On Nov. 22, Leahy offered an amendment to the fiscal 1992 supplemental appropriations bill (H J Res 157—PL 102-229) that would increase the amount of money dairy farmers were paid for milk. It was rejected, 47-51. *(H J Res 157, p. 77)*

gation was deemed to be in the "clear interest" of the United States.

- **Fiscal 1993 and 1994 Funding.** Authorized appropriations of $53 million for fiscal 1993 and $60 million for fiscal 1994.

New Farmer Loans

Legislation to help young farmers and make a number of other modifications in the farm credit program cleared Congress in 1992. The bill (HR 6129 — PL 102-554), signed by President Bush on Oct. 28, was designed to attract more young people to farming by easing some of the restrictions for direct and guaranteed loans from the Farmers Home Administration (FmHA), the Agriculture Department agency that acts as a lender of last resort for farmers.

A new farmer who drew up a 10-year plan was eligible for FmHA-approved operating loans for that period, with annual reviews to make sure that the money was being well spent. The bill also established a low-interest loan program to help farmers buy ranches or farmland.

Another provision gave the FmHA something it had wanted for a number of years — a limit on the period during which farmers were eligible for operating loans from the agency. Farmers were restricted to a total of 15 years in the FmHA program, with only 10 years of direct loans and five years of guaranteed loans. House Agriculture Committee Chairman E. "Kika" de la Garza, D-Texas, said that FmHA had been "allowed to stray from its original purpose as a temporary lender of last resort to become a de facto permanent source of credit for far too many borrowers."

The bill nearly died because of a dispute over a new bank loan approval policy for the FmHA. An early version of the bill (HR 4906 — H Rept 102-783), passed by the House under suspension of the rules by voice vote on Aug. 4, 1992, included a provision to make granting FmHA-backed loans easier for commercial lenders. HR 4906 would give the FmHA 14 working days to act on a lender's loan-guarantee application. If the FmHA did not act, the loan would be approved automatically. However, those loans

Food Pyramid

The Agriculture Department (USDA) on April 28, 1992, unveiled a 30-page guide to healthy eating, but the $885,000 spent to redo an accompanying graphic induced indigestion among some lawmakers. The graphic depicted a pyramid that was designed to encourage people to de-emphasize meats and dairy products in their diets in favor of grains, fruits and vegetables.

A version of the graphic had been completed more than a year earlier, but Agriculture Secretary Edward R. Madigan called for additional studies that led to the 1992 revised graphic. Some critics charged that the delay in issuing the eating guide was a result of meat industry opposition to the original graphic. Others complained that the revision was too similar to the original pyramid to justify its cost.

Madigan said that the food guide was delayed to study the graphic's effectiveness as a communication device. "It doesn't matter whether USDA picked a pyramid, a bowl or an upside-down ketchup bottle to show consumers what to eat," said Senate Agriculture Committee Chairman Patrick J. Leahy, D-Vt. "USDA's delay cost nearly $1 million, and the administration ended up right where they started."

would receive only an 80 percent guarantee from the government, instead of the 90 percent guarantee for regular FmHA-approved loans. The Senate modified that provision — requiring a yes or no answer from the FmHA within 14 days of the application — before passing HR 4906 by voice vote on Oct. 7. By then, the House had adjourned for the year and could not act on the Senate change.

House sponsors of the bill, having anticipated the situation, had won House approval on Oct. 4 for another bill (HR 6129) identical to HR 4906 except that it included a compromise version of the bank loan provision. The Senate, also by voice vote, approved HR 6129 on Oct. 8, clearing the measure.

The compromise provision on FmHA-backed commercial loans set up a two-tiered system for expedited loan approval. For banks that had a longstanding and positive relationship with the agency, the FmHA would have 14 days to act on a loan-guarantee application. If the agency did not act, the loan would be approved automatically. In the case of banks that were new to the FmHA, the agency was required to give a yes or no response to a loan-guarantee request within 14 days.

Farm Credit

Congress in 1992 cleared legislation (HR 6125 — PL 102-552) aimed at ensuring that the Farm Credit System paid back the $1.3 billion it borrowed from the federal government in 1987. The bill clarified a plan under which the nation's farm credit banks were required to pay into a fund intended to retire the debt that resulted from the 1987 federal bailout of the system. *(1987 action, Congress and the Nation Vol. VII, p. 522)*

The Farm Credit System was one of five government-sponsored enterprises (GSEs) that received breaks from the government in exchange for boosting lending in different sectors of the economy. HR 6125 was part of an ongoing effort to tighten oversight of the GSEs, which Congress and the Bush administration agreed were insufficiently regulated and might become a risk to taxpayers.

Before taking up HR 6125, the House considered another farm credit bill (HR 3298). Its first attempt to pass HR 3298 (H Rept 102-277) failed on Nov. 6, 1991, on a 221-203 vote, which was well short of the needed two-thirds majority required because the bill was brought up under suspension of the rules. The House voted again on Sept. 23, 1992, passing the measure by voice vote. Before doing so, several unrelated farm bills were attached, including one to encourage people to get into farming and another to refine the sugar cane allotment process. *(New farmer loans, p. 553; sugar cane allotment, p. 557)*

The House on Oct. 4, 1992, passed by voice vote HR 6125, a new version of the legislation that resulted from negotiations between the House and Senate Agriculture committees and that left out the unrelated bills, to be passed separately. The Senate passed HR 6125, also by voice vote, on Oct. 7, clearing the measure. President Bush signed it Oct. 20.

Export Enhancement Program

Congress in 1991 granted a Bush administration request to make more funds available to bolster foreign sales of wheat and other agricultural commodities. The change came in an amendment to a 1991 supplemental spending bill (HR 1281 — PL 102-27), which removed a cap of $425 million on the Agriculture Department's Export Enhancement Program (EEP). President Bush signed the bill April 10, 1991. *(Legislative history, supplemental, p. 77)*

Under the EEP, the Agriculture Department compensated exporters who agreed to discount agricultural sales abroad by giving the exporters government-owned commodities such as wheat, corn and other feed grains. The subsidies were intended to cover the difference between world market prices and U.S. prices, which usually were higher.

The Bush administration had called for the elimination of export subsidies worldwide, but the president wanted added authority to use the export program in the hope that it would spur the European Economic Community (EC) to reduce its use of agriculture subsidies.

The Agriculture Department said that, as a result of the removal of the ceiling, it would spend about $900 million in fiscal 1991 to subsidize exports of wheat and other commodities.

Background

The EEP had been controversial since its creation as part of the 1985 farm bill (PL 99-198). Critics — most notably House Appropriations Committee Chairman Jamie L. Whitten, D-Miss. — argued that the program benefited large grain-exporting companies that did not need government subsidies. Another complaint was that the program favored wheat growers at the expense of farmers who raised other crops. During the 1990 market year, 80 percent of subsidized foreign sales involved wheat and wheat flour, according to the Agriculture Department.

Despite advocating a general policy against government interference in the free market, the Bush administration asked Congress to lift the spending cap on the EEP because administration trade officials wanted to use the additional export funds as leverage in their negotiations on the General Agreement on Tariffs and Trade (GATT). They hoped the increase in funds would show the EC that the United States was ready to enter a subsidy trade war if it refused to lower price supports for its farmers.

Legislative Action

On Feb. 26, the House Agriculture Committee gave voice vote approval to HR 805, which would raise funding for the EEP by $475 million in fiscal 1991 and authorize the Agriculture Department to spend up to $5 billion on the program over the succeeding five years. Controversy arose over whether the bill would violate the new "pay-as-you-go" budget deal and trigger automatic spending cuts in domestic programs.

HR 805 was formally reported (H Rept 102-22, Part I) on March 15.

The House Foreign Affairs Committee, which shared jurisdiction over the bill, approved HR 805 by voice vote March 19. No written report was issued.

The same day, the Senate considered raising subsidies for the EEP as part of the fiscal 1991 supplemental appropriations bill (HR 1281). The Senate proposal would lift the existing $425 million cap for export subsidies. Senate Agriculture Committee Chairman Patrick J. Leahy, D-Vt., also won approval, 60-40, of an amendment to increase the price dairy farmers were paid for their milk through the end of 1991. Leahy won support by adding clauses that would allow rice, cotton and feed grain farmers to skirt restrictions in the 1990 farm bill (S 2830 — PL 101-624) on what could be planted on idle land. *(1990 farm bill, p. 537)*

Leahy's language could not stand up to a veto threat and pressure from Whitten, however, and it was stripped by conferees on HR 1281. The final measure retained repeal of the cap on the export program.

Soviet Credit Guarantees

Responding to pressure from farm-state lawmakers, President Bush in 1991 granted the Soviet Union a total of $2.75 billion in new credit guarantees for agriculture products. The credits were an attempt to prop up the crumbling Soviet state and help American farmers at the same time. The assistance came in two installments: $1.5 billion announced on June 11 and $1.25 billion awarded on Nov. 20.

Under the export credit guarantee program, private lenders extended credit to a foreign country after the United States, through the Agriculture Department, agreed to repay the debt if the country defaulted. The 1990 farm bill (S 2830 — PL 101-624) had specified that credit could not be extended if the agriculture secretary determined that a country could not repay the debt. Before that change, the secretary had been required to "take into consideration" a country's ability to repay. *(1990 farm bill, p. 537)*

Despite concern that the Soviet Union was on the brink of economic disaster, farm-state senators led by Minority Leader Bob Dole, R-Kan., convinced the Senate to pass a non-binding resolution (S Res 117) that urged the president to extend the guarantees. The Senate approved the resolution May 15, 1991, by a vote of 70-28.

Dole said the extension of credits would increase U.S. grain sales to the Soviets, boosting the price of wheat and corn enough to save taxpayers as much as $800 million in farm price-support payments. "Selling agricultural commodities to other countries increases demand and increases prices and income for farmers," agreed Democrat Tom Harkin of Iowa, a major corn-producing state.

Dole in 1986 had convinced the Reagan administration to subsidize 4 million metric tons of Soviet wheat sales despite its opposition to subsidized exports to communist countries. In 1991, the debate over Soviet agricultural credits took place in a more complex and unpredictable context, with the Soviet Union in the midst of economic and political turmoil.

Market Promotion Program

A controversial subsidy program for exporters of U.S. agricultural products survived an attempt by the House to severely slash its budget in 1992. The market promotion program offered matching funds to help companies advertise their products abroad, if the company's product contained something grown in the United States.

President Bush had requested funding for the program of $200 million, but the House Agriculture Committee trimmed that back to $75 million during consideration of the fiscal 1993 agriculture appropriations bill (HR 5487 — H Rept 102-617). The full House went further, agreeing 331-82 to stop any of the program's funds from being used to promote tobacco products overseas. The market promotion program won a reprieve from the Senate Agriculture Committee (S Rept 102-334), which gave the program $174.5 million for fiscal 1993. Program supporters were able to beat back an attempt on the Senate floor to cut about $100 million from the program. House and Senate conferees subsequently agreed to $150 million for the program, $50 million less than in fiscal 1992. The president signed HR 5487 (PL 102-341) on Aug. 14.

Defenders of the market promotion program said it helped establish markets for U.S. goods, increased foreign sales and created new jobs. Detractors, including House Appropriations Committee Chairman Jamie L. Whitten, D-Miss., branded it a subsidy for wealthy companies. Opposition to the program was fueled by press reports that spotlighted some of the program's fiscal 1992 payments to large companies, including $4 million to the Dole Food Company and $9 million to Sunkist Growers.

Farm Bill Changes

A year after clearing the 1990 omnibus farm bill (S 2830 — PL 101-624), which reauthorized most of the government's agriculture and nutrition programs for five years, Congress made hundreds of non-controversial changes in farm programs sought by lawmakers from Kansas to Florida. As required by the Bush administration, the bill (HR 3029) did not authorize new expenditures. *(1990 farm bill, p. 537)*

Streamlining the Agriculture Department

Lawmakers talked about streamlining the huge bureaucracy of the Agriculture Department, but the project did not get beyond the planning stage during the 102nd Congress. The nation's third largest civilian agency, with more than 110,000 workers in 1992, the Agriculture Department maintained a bewildering array of offices throughout the country to administer its various programs.

A General Accounting Office report issued in September 1991, presenting evidence of the inefficiency of the department's field offices, prompted members of Congress to call for a leaner Agriculture Department. Richard G. Lugar of Indiana, ranking Republican on the Senate Agriculture Committee, called on Agriculture Secretary Edward R. Madigan to close 92 county offices that had spent more in overhead than they had handed out in federal benefits to farmers. Patrick J. Leahy, D-Vt., chairman of the Senate committee, called for a plan (S 2752) to establish a review panel to recommend which offices should be shut down.

In the House, Dan Glickman, D-Kan., introduced legislation (HR 4784) to consolidate hundreds of Agriculture Department county offices and reduce the amount of paperwork farmers had to complete each year to qualify for federal subsidy programs.

In response, Madigan began an eight-month study of his department's field offices, which resulted in recommendations to close and consolidate more than 1,000 of them, amounting to about 16 percent of the department's outposts. The new administration of President Bill Clinton swept Madigan out of office in 1993, before he was able to carry out the recommendations, which had brought complaints from farmers throughout the affected areas.

Three Big Agencies

Most of the Agriculture Department cutbacks under discussion in 1992 would have reduced the size of three agencies: the Agriculture Stabilization and Conservation Service, the Farmers Home Administration (FmHA) and the Soil Conservation Service. These agencies administered programs established during the New Deal era. Each had separate offices and served different sets of constituents, making consolidation especially difficult.

The most extensive cutbacks were to come from the Agriculture Stabilization Service, set up in 1933 to help farmers obtain benefits under the new federal crop price-support program. The service helped farmers complete paperwork, processed it and wrote benefit checks. Difficult travel conditions originally required the service to set up offices in most of the nation's counties. But by the 1990s, the agency still had offices in about 85 percent of counties although only about 16 percent of those counties were defined as farming communities.

FmHA, created in 1935 and transferred to the Agriculture Department in 1937, was the farmer's lender of last resort. For farmers who could not get money elsewhere, the FmHA extended a direct loan or backed a private loan with a federal guarantee. In its early years, the agency concentrated on alleviating rural poverty by providing loans to bankrupt farmers in danger of losing their land and to small towns for improvements in living conditions.

The Soil Conservation Service, founded in 1933 and shifted to the Agriculture Department from Interior two years later, offered technological advice to farmers.

The most significant provision made borrowing money easier for the Federal Agricultural Mortgage Corporation (Farmer Mac), a new secondary market for farm loans. It also placed Farmer Mac under the regulatory control of the Farm Credit Administration.

Among the special interest provisions was "the Pizza Hut amendment," added by the House Agriculture Committee. Offered by Charles W. Stenholm, D-Texas, and modified by Dan Glickman, D-Kan., in whose district the company was based, the provision allowed fresh pizza with meat toppings to be part of the government's school lunch program. Existing rules allowed frozen pizza, sausage sandwiches and hot dogs to be offered for school lunches but barred fresh pizza because of fears that meat toppings would require cumbersome and costly inspections.

HR 3029 was reported (H Rept 102-175) by the House Agriculture Committee on July 30, 1991. The House passed the bill, 417-5, under suspension of the rules, the next day. The Senate passed an amended version of HR 3029 on Nov. 22. The House agreed to the Senate version, with further amendments, on Nov. 26. The Senate agreed to the House amendments later the same day, clearing the measure. President Bush signed HR 3029 (PL 102-237) on Dec. 13.

Wetlands Funding

A new farm program designed to preserve wetlands lost its funding in 1992 during congressional deliberations on the fiscal 1993 agriculture appropriations bill. As signed by President Bush on Aug. 14, 1992, the bill (HR 5487 — PL 102-341) did not fund the wetlands reserve program established in the 1990 omnibus farm bill (S 2830 — PL 101-624). *(1990 farm bill, p. 537)*

Supporters of the program, which paid farmers to take wetlands out of production so that their natural vegetation could return, had hoped to preserve 1 million acres of wetlands from the environmental ravages of farming. According to Senate Agriculture Committee Chairman Patrick J. Leahy, D-Vt., the program was the "heart of an historic compromise" struck by farmers and environmentalists during the drafting of the 1990 farm bill.

Despite the Bush administration's request for $161 million for the program in fiscal 1993, the House refused to provide any funds and prohibited the Agriculture Department from expanding the program until a status report was completed. An amendment offered by Jim Jontz, D-Ind., to shift $46 million from flood prevention programs to the wetlands program was defeated by a vote of 109-308. According to Jontz, the $46 million provided in fiscal 1992 had helped to protect about 50,000 acres of wetlands. "I thought the farm bill did a good job of avoiding a collision between environmentalists and farmers," he said. "But these programs will not work if they're not funded."

The Senate agreed by voice vote to divert $54.9 million from farm program administrative expenses to the wetlands program. But Senate conferees agreed to leave the program unfunded in exchange for a House concession on funding of a controversial market promotion program. *(Market program, p. 555)*

Disaster Relief

A bill (HR 2893) authorizing $1.75 billion in fiscal 1991 supplemental disaster relief for farms in areas hit by natural disasters received House and Senate approval but died upon adjournment of the 102nd Congress. The funds, however, were made available through a fiscal 1992 supplemental appropriations bill (H J Res 157 — PL 102-229). *(H J Res 157, p. 77)*

HR 2893 would extend the disaster provisions included in the 1990 farm bill (S 2830 — PL 101-624) to 1991 disasters affecting farmers from Kansas to California. The bill would limit relief payments to $100,000 per person and would prohibit assistance to farmers with gross revenues of more than $2 million a year.

The House Agriculture Committee reported HR 2893 (H Rept 102-158) on July 23, 1991. The House passed the bill, under suspension of the rules, on a 328-67 vote July 25. The Senate Agriculture Committee reported HR 2893 (S Rept 102-195) on Oct. 25. The Senate passed its version by voice vote Oct. 7, 1992.

H J Res 157 provided $1.75 billion in disaster payments to farmers and ranchers to compensate them for losses caused by natural disasters during crop years 1990-92. Of the total, $995 million was available immediately, for losses in either 1990 or 1991. The remaining $755 million was available for losses in 1990-92, but only if the president specifically requested it and designated the money as emergency spending under the budget rules. The $755 million included $100 million for program crops planted in 1991 for harvest in 1992; this provision reportedly was inserted at the request of Senate Minority Leader Bob Dole, R-Kan., to cover winter wheat.

In separate action, Congress provided $1.4 billion in disaster payments for producers who suffered crop losses resulting from Hurricane Hugo, which struck the Carolinas, Puerto Rico and the Virgin Islands in 1989. The funds were included in fiscal 1991 supplemental appropriations legislation (HR 1281 — PL 102-27). *(HR 1281, p. 77)*

Sugar Allotment

Congress in 1992 cleared legislation (HR 5763) revamping part of the sugar allotment process.

Under the federal quota system for sugar cane and beets, farmers each year get an allotment stating how much they are allowed to grow. Sugar farmers complained that they did not get their allotment figure until after they planted their crops. To make sure that farmers were not penalized for harvesting beyond their allotment, HR 5763 made sugar processors responsible for not processing more sugar than allowed under annual quotas.

HR 5763 was reported (H Rept 102-831) from House Agriculture and passed by the House, by voice vote under suspension of the rules, on Aug. 10. The Senate passed the bill by voice vote Oct. 5, clearing it. President Bush signed HR 5763 (PL 102-535) on Oct. 19.

Tobacco Quota

Legislation (S 3327) allowing tobacco farmers who buy an acre of land to grow two minor types of tobacco under the U.S. quota system was signed into law (PL 102-566) on Oct. 20, 1992.

The Senate passed S 3327 by voice vote Oct. 5; the House followed suit the next day, clearing the measure.

9

Health and Human Services

Introduction	*561*
Health	*565*
Human Services	*611*
Veterans' Affairs	*625*

Health and Human Services

When the history of U.S. health policy is written, the years 1989 to 1992 will likely have special significance — but primarily for what Congress failed to accomplish.

While the annual tab for health services continued to spiral virtually out of control — topping $800 billion by 1992 — and the number of Americans with no health insurance continued to swell upwards — estimated to be between 31 million and 37 million — Congress' most notable action during the period was to repeal a major Medicare expansion passed with much fanfare in 1988.

By 1992, America's health care "crisis" had become a major political issue. In November 1991, underdog Democrat Harris Wofford used a call for universal health care as the centerpiece of a pitch to middle-class voters and in the process defeated expected shoo-in and former Bush attorney general Dick Thornburgh in Pennsylvania's special Senate election. In 1992, Arkansas Gov. Bill Clinton campaigned heavily on the need to control health care costs and expand health insurance coverage in his successful effort to oust President George Bush.

But while just about everyone agreed on the severity of the problem, consensus about how to cure what ailed the health system proved elusive. Congressional Democrats blamed President Bush for a lack of leadership on the sensitive issue; Republicans contended that Democrats, with comfortable majorities in both houses, could not get anything passed, either.

Catastrophic Coverage

One of the biggest problems was that many health policy makers were still smarting from the drubbing they took following passage of the 1988 Medicare Catastrophic Coverage Act.

The 1988 law, cleared with bipartisan support, was notable for being the biggest expansion of the federal program for the elderly and disabled since the program's inception in 1965. But what made it landmark was that Medicare recipients themselves would finance 100 percent of the cost of the new benefits, including Medicare's first-ever outpatient drug coverage.

The novel financing, however, was what brought about the law's downfall. A combination of outrage among those who would be hardest hit financially, misunderstanding of the complicated new program and misinformation by groups that sought to raise funds by tapping the unrest produced an unprecedented backlash. Under a virtual deluge of complaints even from those who stood to benefit handsomely under the reconfigured Medicare program, Congress and the new Bush administration caved in to the pressure.

All but a few provisions primarily affecting the Medicaid program for the poor were repealed in November 1989, just 16 months after the legislation was signed by President Ronald Reagan.

Physician Payments

Despite the undoing of the catastrophic coverage law and the inability to pass a major health reform bill, Congress did enact some significant laws that were considered likely to help set the stage for a broader health system overhaul.

References

Discussion of health policy for the years 1945-64 may be found in *Congress and the Nation Vol. I*, pp. 1122-1194; for the years 1965-68, *Congress and the Nation Vol. II*, pp. 665-707; for the years 1969-72, *Congress and the Nation Vol. III*, pp. 551-580; for the years 1973-76, *Congress and the Nation Vol. IV*, pp. 323-375; for the years 1977-80, *Congress and the Nation Vol. V*, pp. 601-653; for the years 1981-84, *Congress and the Nation Vol. VI*, pp. 521-556; for the years 1985-88, *Congress and the Nation Vol. VII*, p. 547-606.

Discussion of human services policy for the years 1945-64 may be found in *Congress and the Nation Vol. I*, pp. 1225-1331; for the years 1965-68, *Congress and the Nation Vol. II*, pp. 745-778; for the years 1969-72, *Congress and the Nation Vol. III*, pp. 605-633; for the years 1973-76, *Congress and the Nation Vol. IV*, pp. 403-432; for the years 1977-80, *Congress and the Nation Vol. V*, pp. 679-712; for the years 1981-84, *Congress and the Nation Vol. VI*, pp. 581-612; for the years 1985-88, *Congress and the Nation Vol. VII*, p. 607-632.

Discussion of veterans' programs for the years 1945-64 may be found in *Congress and the Nation Vol. I*, pp. 1335-1373; for the years 1965-68, *Congress and the Nation Vol. II*, pp. 453-460; for the years 1969-72, *Congress and the Nation Vol. III*, pp. 537-548; for the years 1973-76, *Congress and the Nation Vol. IV*, pp. 158-181; for the years 1977-80, *Congress and the Nation Vol. V*, pp. 177-191; for the years 1981-84, *Congress and the Nation Vol. VI*, pp. 613-625; for the years 1985-88, *Congress and the Nation Vol. VII*, p. 633-644.

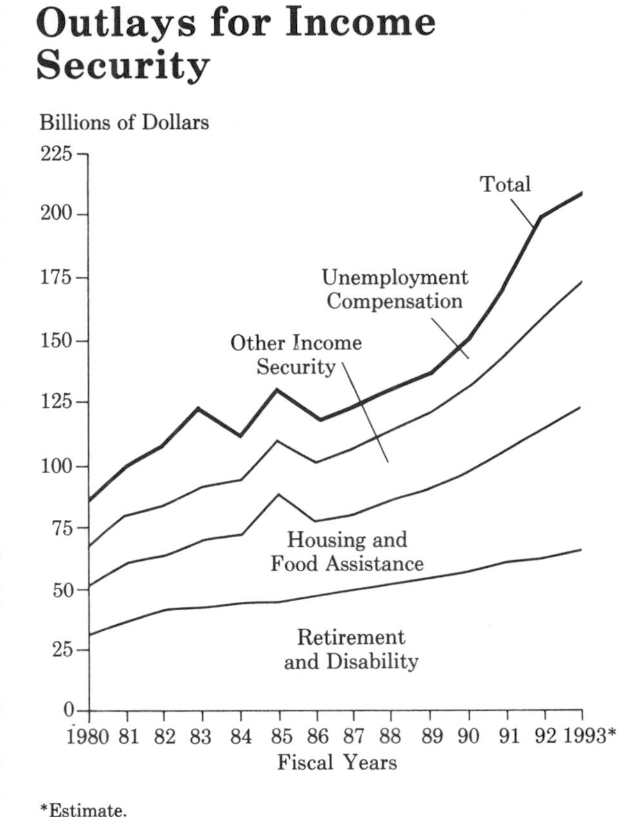

*Estimate.

Source: Office of Management and Budget, *Budget Baselines, Historical Data and Alternatives for the Future* (Washington, D.C.: U.S. Government Printing Office, January 1993).

The biggest was a complete change in the way Medicare paid doctors. Since the program was launched in 1965, Medicare essentially paid physicians based on what they charged. Under the new program, to be phased in gradually over several years, payments for each individual physician service, from office visits to open-heart surgery, were to be set according to a national fee schedule.

The underpinning of that schedule was the resource-based relative value scale, devised by a group of Harvard University researchers who compared the time, training and skill required for a physician to perform a particular service.

The new scheme, provided in the fiscal 1990 budget-reconciliation bill, also took into account the possibility that some physicians would try to make up what they stood to lose in fees by charging patients more, or by increasing the number of services they provided. The law thus limited the amount doctors could charge beneficiaries over and above the fee schedule amount and created annual volume targets, which, if exceeded, would reduce inflation increases in fee schedule amounts for the subsequent year.

Medigap Revisions

In the fiscal 1991 budget-reconciliation bill, Congress took a step toward more direct regulation of the health insurance industry by imposing restrictions on private Medigap policies that were sold to supplement Medicare coverage. The 1990 action built on a series of 1980 voluntary guidelines Congress passed in response to widespread reports of sales and marketing abuses in the Medigap industry.

But a decade later, when abuses continued, Congress moved to put some teeth in the 1980 law. For starters, the revisions required that all policies be approved by either the state or the federal government before being sold to the public. Policies could not duplicate existing Medicare benefits, and the law called for a standardized, and thus more understandable, set of benefits. The insurance industry, fearing a heavier federal hand, opposed many of the changes.

Medicaid Drug Prices

In addition to taking on the powerful insurance industry, Congress in 1990 sought to force the makers of prescription drugs to provide the same discounts to the federal-state Medicaid program that they routinely offered other bulk purchasers such as hospitals, nursing homes and health maintenance organizations.

Drug companies vehemently opposed the action; because Medicaid was a major purchaser of prescription products, they stood to lose significant amounts of profit. By 1992, the companies had managed to circumvent the law by raising prices for other customers instead of lowering them for Medicaid. Particularly hard hit was the Department of Veterans Affairs (VA), which for years had enjoyed some of the deepest drug discounts.

An omnibus veterans bill cleared late in 1992 required drug companies to resume discounts for veterans programs, although Congress would likely have to revisit the issue in 1993 and beyond.

AIDS

The AIDS (acquired immune deficiency syndrome) epidemic did not go completely overlooked by the 101st and 102nd Congresses. An omnibus bill named for Ryan White, the young Indiana hemophiliac whose bout with AIDS helped raise awareness about the disease, cleared in 1990. The new law authorized emergency aid to the cities hardest hit by the epidemic. It also called for grants to states to help create and operate treatment programs, and grants to provide early intervention services for those with AIDS and HIV (human immunodeficiency virus), the AIDS virus.

Congress, however, had difficulty appropriating funds for the AIDS programs. Because of serious budget restraints, the money had to be taken from other health and social service programs, which was the source of much protest.

At about the time the Ryan White bill cleared, more than 143,000 cases of AIDS had been diagnosed in the United States, and more than 87,000 of those people had died. An estimated 1 million were infected with HIV.

Abortion

Congress was unable to change any federal abortion policies from 1989 through 1992, but the issue remained the focus of tremendous debate.

The Supreme Court in its July 1989 decision in *Webster v. Reproductive Health Services* upheld a 1986 Missouri law that required tests for fetal viability and banned the use of public employees and facilities for performing abortions. The ruling, which would allow states to impose new restrictions on abortions, galvanized abortion rights forces.

Congress responded quickly, with the historically anti-abortion House voting for the first time since 1980 to relax a federal abortion restriction against using District of Columbia tax funds to pay for abortions for poor women. But the stalwartly anti-abortion Bush used his veto power in 1989 to block that effort, as well as legislation to allow federal funds to be used to pay for abortions in cases of rape or incest and to provide funding for a United Nations family planning program.

The pattern thus had been set and continued for the duration of Bush's tenure: The abortion rights activists mustered majorities in both houses for relaxations of the restrictions, only to have Bush veto any bills that made it to his desk.

In 1991, two abortion-related issues were resurrected. In May, the Supreme Court ruled in *Rust v. Sullivan* that the federal government could ban abortion counseling and referrals in federally funded family planning clinics. And in a bill to reauthorize portions of the National Institutes of Health, strong majorities in both the House and Senate voted to overturn a provision originally imposed during the Reagan administration that barred federal funding of research using tissue from aborted fetuses.

Fearing the Court would use a Pennsylvania law restricting abortion access to overturn *Roe v. Wade*, the landmark 1973 ruling legalizing the procedure nationwide, abortion rights advocates in 1992 prepared the Freedom of Choice Act, which would codify a woman's right to abortion. The Court, however, surprised both sides of the debate by coming down firmly in the middle with its June decision in *Planned Parenthood of Southeastern Pennsylvania v. Casey*.

The Court upheld key portions of the state law, including requirements that women wait 24 hours before obtaining an abortion and listen to information designed to encourage them not to have the procedure. The Court, however, declined to overturn *Roe*. Furthermore, the Court reiterated a new, albeit somewhat more limited, basic right to abortion. As a result of the *Casey* ruling, the Court effectively took the wind out of the sails of both pro-choice and anti-abortion forces. With no firestorm of protest to carry forward the Freedom of Choice Act, it failed to reach the floor of either house.

The fortunes of abortion rights advocates improved tremendously with the election of Bill Clinton. One of his first acts upon assuming the presidency in 1993 was to reverse several abortion-related policies of his Republican predecessors. For example, Clinton lifted restrictions on abortion counseling in federally funded family planning clinics and eliminated the ban on federal funding of medical research using fetal tissue from elective abortions.

Other Health Legislation

In other health-related matters, Congress in 1989-92 cleared legislation that expanded the Medicaid program to cover more low-income people; required manufacturers to display nutritional information on food packaging; revised the procedures for federal approval of medical equipment; provided compensation for victims of radiation fallout resulting from nuclear tests conducted by the government; reauthorized a program that helped pay for childhood vaccines; extended a grant program to health services to prevent tuberculosis; sought to improve the health status of disadvantaged minorities; revised programs to match organ and bone marrow donors with needy patients; improved emergency care services; promoted research on the prevention and treatment of injuries; reauthorized programs providing medical services to Alzheimer's disease patients; improved cervical and breast cancer screening; protected the rights and promoted the independence of those with developmental disabilities; overhauled federal substance abuse and mental health programs; instituted penalties for abusing the generic drug approval process; put restrictions on infertility clinics; devised new rules designed to prevent lead poisoning; and updated federal programs that assisted in the funding of doctor and nurse training.

A number of other health bills were considered by Congress but were not enacted into law, including measures to publicize the health risks of smoking, require employers to provide health insurance to their employees, reauthorize the Adolescent Family Life Program, increase penalties for health care fraud and establish a disability prevention program.

Bush vetoed legislation providing incentives to companies to develop "orphan" drugs — drugs used to treat relatively rare diseases, as well as a bill reauthorizing programs of the National Institutes of Health.

Child Care

One of Bush's key promises during the 1988 campaign was to help working families cope with the high costs of caring for their children. And while congressional Democrats also were eager to expand federal child care assistance, turning the rhetoric into reality proved much more difficult than anticipated.

The key sticking points were more philosophical than financial: whether aid should be provided to all families or only those in which both parents worked outside the home, whether states or the federal government should set the rules regulating child care providers, and how to provide aid to religious-based child care programs without running afoul of the constitutional separation of church and state.

The issues were resolved as part of the fiscal 1991 budget-reconciliation bill. Congress approved $18.3 billion in tax credits and $4.25 billion for new grant programs over five years to help low- and moderate-income families pay child care costs and to help states improve the quality and availability of such care.

The law capped three years of fractious, sometimes ugly, debate. In the end, the White House backed off threats to veto any major new grant program. And an internal House fight over whether a new grant program should be subject to the regular appropriations process or be an entitlement, with funding guaranteed, was settled in a time-honored way — lawmakers decided to do some of each.

Head Start

One of the few programs that saw its budget increase from 1989 to 1992 was Head Start, the popular health, education and social service program for low-income preschoolers. But Congress and President Bush, who campaigned hard for the program in 1988, disagreed on how best to carry out that expansion.

Congress wanted the first new dollars to go toward improving the quality of existing programs. Administration officials, however, wanted any additional funds to be used to bring more children into Head Start. The omnibus human services reauthorization bill cleared in 1990 allowed for both.

If appropriations were to keep up with the newly authorized level, the program would be able to reach virtually all eligible children by 1994. Chances looked doubtful by 1992, however.

Other Human Services Legislation

The huge federal budget deficit stymied other efforts to bring about major human services initiatives, but Congress was able to enact some significant legislation besides the child care and Head Start measures. For example, Congress authorized grants to establish community service programs; reauthorized the Women, Infants and Children (WIC) supplemental food program; extended the food stamp program; and reauthorized Older American Act programs.

Congress also acted to combat child abuse, fund early intervention services for infants with disabilities, find foster homes for abandoned children, assist abused or neglected children, protect the legal rights of the mentally ill and reimburse homeless shelters for feeding children.

Bush in 1992 vetoed a tax bill that included provisions overhauling child welfare programs.

Veterans' Affairs

The more than 27 million U.S. veterans gained a stronger voice in the fashioning of veterans' policy on March 15, 1989, when the Veterans Administration was upgraded to a Cabinet-level department. The new Department of Veterans Affairs became the 14th Cabinet department and would serve to represent the interests of the estimated 80 million Americans eligible for veterans' benefits — including veterans and their dependents and survivors.

Taking the helm at the new department was Edward J. Derwinski, a veteran of World War II and a former 12-term U.S. representative from Illinois. His tenure as the first veterans secretary proved to be rocky. He was praised for being able to secure substantial increases in funding for veterans' programs despite the federal budget crunch. However, some of his policy positions — including his endorsement of allowing VA hospitals in poor, rural regions of the South to accept patients without access to other health care facilities — caused a firestorm among veterans' organizations. He stepped down in September 1992 to work on Bush's re-election campaign.

The 1991 Persian Gulf War, in which a U.S.-led multinational force responded to Iraq's invasion of oil-rich Kuwait, served as a catalyst for enactment of a number of veterans-related bills.

Congress provided increased combat pay and doubled the death gratuity for Gulf War veterans — as well as provided additional GI education benefits for veterans, reservists and National Guard members — in generous Gulf War benefits legislation.

The war also encouraged settlement of the debate over Agent Orange, the chemical defoliant used during the Vietnam War that some said was responsible for various ailments suffered by veterans. A compromise was struck that required the federal government to compensate veterans exposed to Agent Orange for certain diseases, including non-Hodgkins lymphoma and soft-tissue sarcoma. The agreement freed the way for passage of several other bills, such as those providing a cost-of-living adjustment to disabled veterans and their survivors, increasing the pay of VA doctors and dentists, and stipulating additional financial and civil protections for reservists called to active duty.

A 1992 omnibus veterans bill was a sign of the times; it provided psychological counseling for women who were sexually harassed or abused during military service.

The most significant veterans legislation produced by the 101st Congress was a 1989 omnibus bill that provided health, education and home-loan benefits to veterans, among other things.

Chronology Of Action On Health

1989-90

Action on health legislation in the 101st Congress was overshadowed by the dramatic, and unprecedented, repeal of a major social program — the catastrophic care Medicare law enacted with great fanfare in 1988. In less than a year, members of Congress were on the run in the face of senior citizen outrage over what critics called the "seniors only" tax to pay for the expanded coverage.

While less controversial, action on other health legislation provided significant contributions to efforts to reduce the federal budget deficit. Both in 1989 and 1990, Congress approved cost-saving Medicare changes, by altering the method of paying physicians under the program and by requiring beneficiaries to contribute more to their own care. Other important bills cleared by the 101st Congress included mandates of expanded coverage of poor women and children under the Medicaid program and a new attempt to facilitate the treatment of AIDS (acquired immune deficiency syndrome) patients outside of hospital settings.

Catastrophic Coverage Repeal

In a stunning reversal of social policy, Congress in 1989 repealed a landmark expansion of the Medicare program that it had enacted the year before.

The repeal of the 1988 Medicare Catastrophic Coverage Act (PL 100-360) marked the first time that Congress rescinded major social benefits. The 1988 law provided stop-loss coverage of hospital, doctor and prescription drug costs, and it expanded existing coverage of nursing home, home health and hospice care. *(Congress and the Nation Vol. VII, p. 561)*

Congress cleared the repeal measure (HR 3607) on Nov. 22, 1989, and President Bush signed it (PL 101-234) on Dec. 13.

Lawmakers reversed course because senior citizens — the very people the 1988 law was intended to help with the crushing expense of medical care — angrily protested being forced to pay the entire cost of the new benefits. Particularly outraged were the 40 percent of the 33 million Medicare enrollees who would have to pay an income surtax of up to $800 per person in 1989, climbing to $1,050 in 1993.

As the result of the repeal law, Medicare hospital benefits on Jan. 1, 1990, reverted to their previous levels, under which beneficiaries received full coverage for up to 60 days of hospitalization, after payment of a deductible, and partial coverage for the next three months. They then were left fully responsible for any further costs.

The repeal bill also eliminated premiums in the 1988 law intended to pay for the new benefits: an addition to the flat monthly premium most beneficiaries paid for coverage of outpatient and doctor bills under Part B, and the surtax.

Background

The catastrophic coverage law cleared in 1988 with overwhelming congressional support and the backing of President Ronald Reagan, who said in signing the measure that it would "remove a terrible threat from the lives of elderly and disabled Americans." However, the subsequent reaction to the law was to prove that federal officials had misread the sentiments of the elderly, who mostly did not believe themselves at risk and resented having to pay for a threat they did not perceive.

The major sticking point was that the law required beneficiaries alone, and not federal taxpayers in general, to pay for the program — unlike the rest of Medicare, which was funded in part by a payroll tax on wage earners. Another problem was that the new program's benefits duplicated ones that many people already had through private-sector Medigap policies.

In addition, resentments — and confusion — among the elderly were heightened by fund-raising appeals from such groups as the National Committee to Preserve Social Security and Medicare, which was headed by former Rep. James Roosevelt, D-Calif. (1955-65), the son of President Franklin D. Roosevelt. In mass mailings to the elderly, that and other groups warned of a "seniors-only surtax" that would be imposed under the law. Their rhetoric was so effective that many members of Congress reported receiving complaints about the surtax from low-income elderly people, who would not be affected by it.

House Action

As the 101st Congress convened, rumblings were heard from the public and some members that sentiment had turned strongly against the 1988 law. Although sponsors, such as Senate Finance Committee Chairman Lloyd Bentsen, D-Texas, continued to defend the measure, actions in both chambers showed that members wanted to reconsider the issue.

During House Energy and Commerce Subcommittee on Health and the Environment consideration of HR 1359, a minor bill concerning the Pepper commission, Michael Bilirakis, R-Fla., offered an amendment to repeal the catastrophic coverage law and replace it with a more modest plan. However, on April 11, the subcommittee, on a straight party-line vote, upheld a ruling that the amendment was out of order because it went beyond the scope of the bill. On April 12, the Senate adopted, 97-2, a sense of the Senate amendment that the Senate Finance Committee should hold hearings on the catastrophic law. The amendment was attached to HR 2, which would raise the minimum wage. The House April 18 agreed, 408-0, to a motion to instruct House conferees on HR 2 to accept the Senate's amendment. HR 2 subsequently cleared Congress but was felled by a presidential veto. *(Pepper commission, box, p. 584; minimum wage, p. 705)*

The first major battle came in the House Ways and Means Committee, which in July began considering Medicare provisions of a budget-reconciliation measure (HR 3299). The leaders of the repeal effort, notably Bill Archer, R-Texas, the panel's ranking member, and Brian Donnelly, D-Mass., offered amendments to delay or kill the law. Although the amendments were defeated, committee leaders responded to the growing public outcry by proposing an amendment to cut in half the controversial surtax and allow Medicare beneficiaries to opt out of catastrophic

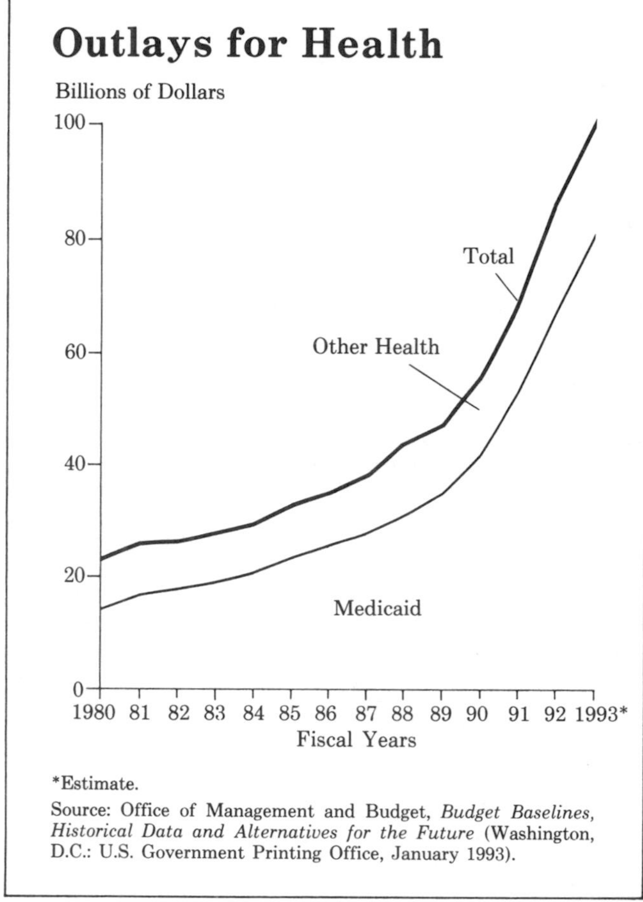

*Estimate.

Source: Office of Management and Budget, *Budget Baselines, Historical Data and Alternatives for the Future* (Washington, D.C.: U.S. Government Printing Office, January 1993).

coverage if they also agreed to drop their Part B physician and outpatient coverage. While those with the highest incomes would still have had to pay the maximum surtax, the proposal would reduce premiums for middle-income beneficiaries. The amendment, offered by the law's original sponsors, Pete Stark, D-Calif., and Bill Gradison, R-Ohio, was adopted on a narrow 19-17 vote.

Unfortunately, the vote came not long before the congressional August recess. Before the full House got a chance to vote on the issue, members returned to their districts to be besieged by an army of angry seniors demanding repeal. In the most dramatic episode, newspaper photographs and television footage showed House Ways and Means Committee Chairman Dan Rostenkowski, D-Ill., trapped in his car in Chicago by a crowd of irate old people.

By the time the issue reached the House floor Oct. 4, repeal leaders held the upper hand. A Donnelly amendment to HR 3299 to repeal the law outright was adopted on a **360-66 (R 164-10; D 196-56) key vote**. *(1989 key votes, p. 1021)*

Senate Action

From the beginning, the Senate Finance Committee fought to preserve the catastrophic coverage law. In the full Senate as well as the House, however, sentiment against the law quickly grew to unstoppable proportions.

Advocates of repeal were led by conservative Republicans voicing the concerns of the affluent elderly, who were to bear the chief burden of the law and who were its most outspoken critics. In addition, a number of liberal Democrats, while favoring the benefits in the law, felt that the surtax was unfair and should be repealed.

The first test in the Senate came June 7, when a floor rebellion against the law was barely beaten back. Leaders managed to push through an amendment calling on the Finance Committee to re-examine the issue, as a way of holding off an amendment by the law's chief critic, John McCain, R-Ariz., calling for a delay in benefits and the surtax. The leadership amendment, offered as part of a fiscal 1989 supplemental appropriations bill (HR 2072), was adopted by voice vote after a tabling motion was defeated 49-51. *(Supplemental, p. 52)*

Bentsen and other Finance members then sought to find a way to defuse the movement for repeal by cutting the surtax. But to do that, they had to find other savings to cover the cost of benefits. After weeks of wrestling with various proposals, the panel was unable to reach an agreement by the end of September. Although committee Democrats tried to work out a compromise with the Bush administration, they were unable to win any Republican support for a deal.

On Oct. 6, McCain brought a bill (S 1726) to the floor calling for repeal of the surtax, while retaining unlimited coverage of hospital bills. The plan would pay for the benefits by keeping the 1988 law's increase in the flat Part B premium that most beneficiaries already paid for optional coverage of doctor bills and outpatient costs. Before the Senate passed S 1726 on a 99-0 vote, backers of the original law placed their hopes for fending off repeal on an amendment offered by Dave Durenberger, R-Minn. The amendment would preserve the core catastrophic benefits, while retaining about one-quarter of the surtax. The amendment was rejected on a **37-62 (R 8-37; D 29-25) key vote**.

How the two chambers would resolve their differences initially was unclear. The agreement governing Senate debate specified that the catastrophic costs language would not be attached to reconciliation, as in the House. And because the Constitution prohibited revenue bills from originating in the Senate, S 1726 could not move to the House on its own.

Final Action

With the Senate seeking a compromise measure and the House intent on repeal, negotiators were unable to reach an agreement in time to include catastrophic provisions as part of a debt limit bill (H J Res 280 — PL 101-140) that cleared Oct. 7.

To create a new vehicle for considering the issue in conference, the House re-passed its repeal provisions as a free-standing bill (HR 3607) by voice vote on Nov. 8. The Senate the same day substituted the text of McCain's proposal and passed the bill, setting up a formal conference.

The conference committee took weeks of difficult negotiations, as House backers of the original law sought to enlarge upon McCain's proposal, while repeal advocates tried to narrow its scope. Adding to the complications was the uncertain position of the Bush administration, which did not make clear whether it wanted to repeal the law or retain a modified version of it.

A majority of the conferees finally decided to sign the conference report on repeal with the understanding that it would be rejected on the floor and that the McCain proposal would again be put up for a vote. The House, however, adopted, 349-57, the conference report (H Rept 101-378) on Nov. 19; the Senate rejected it by voice vote the same day. The House Nov. 21 then agreed, 352-63, to a motion to insist on repeal. In response, the Senate sent the House a slightly modified version of the McCain proposal that would lower the planned increase in the Part B premium by requiring that beneficiaries who need more than one hospitalization during the year pay a second deductible. The House Nov. 21 rejected, 55-346, a motion to concur in the Senate amendment. The Senate receded from its amendment in the early morning hours of Nov. 22, thus clearing HR 3607.

Physician Payments

Six years after moving to gain control of soaring Medicare spending on hospital care, Congress in 1989 completely overhauled the program's system for paying physicians.

The changes were enacted as part of the fiscal 1990 budget-reconciliation bill (HR 3299 — PL 101-239). *(Reconciliation, p. 43)*

The Medicare changes were estimated to save just over $3 billion in fiscal 1990. However, the bill also permitted about $100 million in new Medicare spending on increased coverage for mental health services, higher payments for hospice care and new coverage for Pap smears.

The new physician-payment system was scheduled to be phased in over several years. Its major components included:

- A nationwide fee schedule based on the relative value of medical services and procedures. The goal of the measure was to redress what analysts said was Medicare's existing tendency to pay too much for surgery and diagnostic tests, while underpaying for "primary care" that involved examining and talking with patients.
- Limits on the amounts doctors could bill their patients over and above the Medicare-approved charge. Beginning in 1991, doctors who did not accept Medicare's fee as payment in full could charge patients no more than 125 percent of the Medicare-approved fee, dropping to 120 percent the next year and 115 percent in 1993 and thereafter.
- A mechanism by which the government could try to prevent doctors from making up price cuts by increasing the volume of services they provided. In general, the bill authorized the federal government to set annual targets for how much Medicare should pay doctors, based on inflation, increases in the number and age of beneficiaries, and an allowance for an increase in the volume of services provided.

A related provision created a new office within the Public Health Service to carry out research to evaluate the effectiveness of various medical treatments, with an initial authorization of $50 million.

In addition, HR 3299 contained provisions barring doctors from making referrals to clinical laboratories in which they had an ownership interest. It also required diagnostic imaging centers and other Medicare providers to disclose ownership arrangements involving physicians who referred patients to the facility.

Background

The Medicare provisions of HR 3299 were driven by a concern that run-away spending on the health care program for the elderly and disabled — and in particular its optional Part B program covering physician and outpatient costs — was threatening to bleed the federal Treasury dry. At an estimated cost of $95 billion in fiscal 1990, Medicare was the fifth-largest item in the federal budget and was growing faster than the four larger items. Within Medicare, Part B spending for doctor bills also was growing faster than Part A spending for hospitals, which had been slowed by a flat, per-patient payment system imposed by Congress in 1983. *(Congress and the Nation Vol. VI, p. 538)*

Several reasons existed for the explosive growth in Part B costs. Doctors blamed patients who expected too much care and a legal system that forced them to practice "defensive" medicine against the threat of lawsuits.

Analysts pointed to other factors as well. The fee-for-service payment system imposed by Congress when it created Medicare in 1965, for example, was said to be inherently inflationary, because it gave doctors an incentive not only to raise prices but also to provide more services.

As pressure built for controls on cost increases, experts developed a new system for measuring how much each doctor's service was worth, known as the resource-based relative value scale (RBRVS). A study of the idea ordered by Congress in 1986 found that Medicare paid too much for procedures for surgery and diagnostic tests, and not enough for hands-on primary patient care.

House Action

Action on the physician-payment issue began in the House Ways and Means Committee, which was under orders to pare a total of $2.3 billion from Medicare spending to meet budget targets.

By an 11-3 vote on June 14, the Ways and Means Subcommittee on Health approved a payment package devised by Chairman Pete Stark, D-Calif. The package was then approved as part of a total Medicare proposal, including cost-saving changes in the hospital program, that called for $2.9 billion in cuts in fiscal 1990 and $3 billion in fiscal 1991.

The subcommittee-approved bill created a fee schedule for physician services based on the RBRVS and limited the amounts that doctors could charge patients above the

HHS Leadership

The Senate March 1, 1989, by a 98-1 vote confirmed the nomination of Louis W. Sullivan to be secretary of health and human services (HHS). *(Cabinet profiles, p. 1172)*

After a yearlong search complicated by abortion-related issues, President Bush nominated Bernadine P. Healy to be director of the National Institutes of Health (NIH). The Senate confirmed her nomination by voice vote on March 21, 1991. Healy, who became the first woman to head NIH, succeeded James Wyngaarden, who had resigned in August 1989. *(Controversial nominations, p. 1176)*

Medicare payment. The proposal's most controversial element, however, was its expenditure targets, which were aimed at curbing increases in the volume of services. Although backed by the Bush administration, the provision was vehemently opposed by the American Medical Association (AMA), which warned that the targets represented a health care rationing scheme for the elderly.

The full Ways and Means Committee approved the payment system overhaul on June 28. The only roll call on the plan came on an effort by Nancy L. Johnson, R-Conn., to strike the expenditure targets. Her amendment failed, 11-25. The most significant change made by the full committee involved creating a separate expenditure target for surgical services, which represented about a third of Medicare physician spending.

The Ways and Means package also contained a scaled-back version of legislation (HR 939) to ban outright payment for physician referrals.

The physician-payment section was included in the budget-reconciliation measure approved by the Energy and Commerce Committee, which shared jurisdiction with Ways and Means over Part B of Medicare. The Commerce panel approved its payment-overhaul provisions by a 30-13 vote July 13. The provisions reported by Commerce were similar to the Ways and Means proposal, except that they did not include the controversial expenditure targets. The targets were opposed by Henry A. Waxman, D-Calif., the chairman of the Subcommittee on Health and the Environment, who warned that they would force reductions in pay for all doctors.

The House did not debate or amend the Medicare provisions of the budget-reconciliation bill before passing that massive measure on a 333-91 vote Oct. 5.

Senate Action

The Senate Finance Committee approved Medicare reconciliation provisions on Oct. 3. The proposal sought to save a total of $2.8 billion in 1990, mostly by holding inflation increases for most hospitals and doctors to less than the inflation rate.

The physician-payment provisions of the legislation were similar in a number of respects to the House position. The most important difference centered on the controversial expenditure targets. Instead of the targets, the Senate panel established a system called the Medical Volume Performance Standards (MVPS), under which Congress was to set non-binding volume standards annually.

Although both the expenditure targets and the MVPS set an annual rate of growth for Medicare spending on doctor services, the MVPS was advisory, while the expenditure targets were essentially mandatory. Under the House plan, if Medicare spent more on doctors than the targets allowed, the excess was taken out of the following year's fee increase. The Senate provisions softened the spending limits enough to win the support of the AMA.

The physician-payment provisions were stripped from the Senate budget-reconciliation bill on the floor, however, after Majority Leader George J. Mitchell, D-Maine, proposed to eliminate all provisions that did not directly reduce the deficit in 1990. Although the physician-payment provisions were expected to save substantial amounts in future years, they did not have a significant impact on 1990 spending. Provisions limiting self-referrals by doctors also were dropped by the Senate.

Conference Action

Although the physician-payment plan was a major priority both for congressional health policy leaders and the Bush administration, it almost did not survive in the huge House-Senate conference committee on the budget-reconciliation bill.

During the month of sharp partisan maneuvering over the reconciliation measure, sponsors at several points concluded that the physician-payment provisions would die. But key backers refused to give up, and a compromise package was worked out shortly before a final conference agreement reached the House and Senate floors on Nov. 22.

The final bill included the Senate committee's MVPS provisions on volume limits, which while acceptable to the AMA were viewed by legislative leaders as differing from the House expenditure targets more in semantics than in real effects.

Major Provisions

As enacted, the physician payments, physician referrals and other Medicare Part B provisions of HR 3299 *(Other Medicare and health reconciliation provisions, p. 571)*:

Medicare Part B/Physician Payments

- **Resource-Based Relative Value Scale.** Established a system to pay physicians under Medicare according to a fee schedule based on a resource-based relative value scale (RBRVS). The fee schedule was to be phased in from 1992 to 1996.

The RBRVS was to be based on the combination of the work, overhead and cost of malpractice insurance required to provide a given medical service. The fee schedule would be based on the relative value for a particular service, a conversion factor set by Congress or the secretary of health and human services (HHS) and an adjustment for geographic differences.

- Required current fee schedules for radiology and anesthesiology services to be adjusted to conform to the RBRVS fee schedule and required the HHS secretary to develop a fee schedule based on relative values for pathology services by Jan. 1, 1991.
- Required the HHS secretary to review and adjust the relative value units at least every five years, although such adjustments could not change expenditures by more than $20 million.
- Specified that in 1992, the first year of the phase-in, charges within 85 percent to 115 percent of the fee schedule be paid at the fee schedule rate. Charges outside that range would increase or decrease by 15 percent that year, with the remaining gap between the charge and the fee schedule amount decreasing by 25 percent per year over the ensuing four years. Thus, by 1996, all services would be paid according to the fee schedule.
- Required that in 1992 the conversion factor be set to produce budget neutrality; that is, that the same amount be spent on physician services as would have been spent without the fee schedule.
- Retained the Participating Physician Program, under which physicians received favorable treatment if they agreed to accept Medicare's payment as payment in full for all Medicare beneficiaries all the time. The bill retained the 5 percent differential in fees for participating and non-partici-

pating physicians, providing that non-participating physicians be paid only 95 percent of the fee schedule amount.

• **Medicare Volume Performance Standards.** Provided that annual updates in the conversion factor for the fee schedule be made based on Medicare Volume Performance Standards.

• Required the HHS secretary, after consulting with physician organizations, to recommend a Medicare Volume Performance Standard (MVPS) each April 15 for the next fiscal year. The MVPS was to reflect the rate at which Part B expenditures for the coming fiscal year should grow. It was to be based on the change in the number of beneficiaries, inflation, changes in volume and technology, and other factors.

• Required the Physician Payment Review Commission (PPRC) to comment on the secretary's recommendation and make its own recommendation by May 15. Congress would then set the next year's MVPS. The first recommendation by the HHS secretary was to be made April 15, 1990, for fiscal 1991.

• Should Congress fail to act, required the HHS secretary to set the MVPS, based on specific criteria, including changes in fees, growth in the beneficiary population, a historical five-year average of the rate of growth in volume and intensity, and statutory and regulatory changes, minus a "performance standard factor," which would be 0.5 percentage point in fiscal 1990, 1 point in fiscal 1991, 1.5 points in fiscal 1992 and 2 points thereafter.

• Beginning in 1991, required the HHS secretary to recommend a separate MVPS for surgery and required a study of the feasibility of establishing separate MVPSs by geographic area, by specialty or type of service or both.

• **Update.** Required the HHS secretary, when making the recommendation concerning the MVPS, to make a recommendation for the next year's update in the conversion factor for the fee schedule. The update recommendation was to be based on actual performance compared with the previous year's performance standard, as well as on changes in use and access to services, evidence of physician response to the fee schedule, changes in the quality or appropriateness of care and other factors.

Similarly, the PPRC was required to comment on the secretary's recommendation and make its own recommendation regarding the update by May 15.

• If Congress failed to act, set the "default" update at the predicted inflation increase, plus or minus the difference between actual performance and the year's performance standard. In no case, however, could the update be reduced by more than 2 percentage points in 1992 and 1993, by 2.5 percentage points in 1994 and 1995, and by 3 percentage points thereafter.

• **Bonus Payments for Physicians in Health Manpower Shortage Areas.** Beginning in 1991, provided for a 10 percent bonus for all physician services provided in designated health manpower shortage areas.

• **Limits on Extra Billing by Physicians.** For physicians who did not accept Medicare's payment as payment in full, limited to 125 percent of the amount allowed for non-participating physicians the total they could charge Medicare beneficiaries in 1991. In 1992, that limit would drop to 120 percent and in 1993 to 115 percent.

Beginning April 1, 1990, required physicians to accept assignment (Medicare's payment as payment in full) for beneficiaries with incomes low enough to qualify for Medicaid payment of their Medicare cost-sharing requirements. By 1992, physicians would be required to accept assignment for all beneficiaries with incomes below the federal poverty threshold.

• **Physician Submission of Medicare Claims.** Beginning Sept. 1, 1990, required physicians, suppliers and other entities to submit all Part B claims for beneficiaries, regardless of whether they accepted assignment. Under existing law, only those accepting assignment were required to submit the claims, with beneficiaries having to file themselves for Medicare reimbursement for unassigned claims.

• Required the HHS secretary to develop a system of electronic claims submission and direct deposit to expedite payment of claims.

Medicare Part B/Physician Referrals

• **Prohibited Referrals.** Beginning Jan. 1, 1991, prohibited physicians from referring a patient to a clinical laboratory for a Medicare-covered service if the physician or an immediate family member had an ownership or investment interest or other compensation arrangement with the laboratory.

• Barred the laboratory from submitting bills or claims for reimbursement pursuant to a prohibited referral and stipulated that Medicare payment be denied for any such services.

• Required physicians or laboratories that received any payments from beneficiaries for a prohibited referral to make refunds.

• Set civil penalties for knowing violations of the referral prohibitions at up to $15,000 for each item or service pursuant to a prohibited referral, plus an amount equal to twice the amount billed for the item or service.

• **Exemptions.** Provided for a variety of exceptions to the prohibition, including services provided directly by the physician or his employee or by an employee under the physician's direct supervision, services provided as part of a group practice, services within prepaid health plans and services provided in any rural area or in Puerto Rico. The bill also allowed physician ownership of stock in large publicly held corporations.

• **Reporting Requirements.** Beginning Oct. 1, 1990, imposed a series of reporting requirements, including a requirement that all bills or claims submitted for Medicare Part B payment for services not directly provided by a physician include the name and provider number of the referring physician.

• By one year after enactment, required all Medicare providers to give the HHS secretary information concerning ownership arrangements, including all physicians (and their provider numbers) or members of their immediate families who were investors.

• **GAO Study of Physician Ownership.** Required the General Accounting Office (GAO) to study and report to Congress on the effect that ownership of hospitals or other entities by referring physicians had on utilization, access and quality of services provided to Medicare beneficiaries.

Medicare Part B/Other

• **Part B Premium.** Extended through 1990 a requirement that beneficiary premiums for Part B be set at a rate sufficient to cover 25 percent of the program's costs. For the first time since the 25 percent requirement was imposed in 1982, the provisions would result in a premium lower than would otherwise be the case ($28.60 monthly instead of $29).

• **Extension of Sequester/Payment Update.** Extended through March 31, 1990, the 2.1 percent reductions imposed Oct. 16 under the Gramm-Rudman anti-deficit law (PL 100-119). Otherwise, physician fees were frozen at their 1989 level until March 31, 1990. Beginning April 1, 1990, the bill imposed a new sequester of approximately 1.4 percent and provided for inflation adjustments of 2 percent for most services. Primary-care services were to receive increases of 5.3 percent, while no increases were to be granted for radiology and anesthesiology services and services the conference report (H Rept 101-386) identified as "overvalued."

• **Reduction in Payments for Overvalued Procedures.** Beginning April 1, 1990, imposed reductions of up to 15 percent on overvalued procedures, as well as on procedures closely related to those deemed overvalued.

Overvalued procedures were defined as those with national average allowed charges at least 10 percent higher than would be paid under the RBRVS recommended by the PPRC.

• **Reduction in Payments for Radiology Services.** Beginning April 1, 1990, reduced payments for all radiology services except portable X-ray services by 4 percent.

• **Payments for Anesthesiology Services.** Beginning April 1, 1990, required that payments for anesthesiology services be calculated according to actual time spent, not in 15- and 30-minute time units, as was current practice.

• **Restrictions on Clinical Laboratory Referrals.** Beginning Jan. 1, 1990, prohibited in most cases Medicare payments for clinical laboratory services referred by one laboratory to another. Exceptions were allowed for referring laboratories that were in or part of a rural hospital, that referred less than 30 percent of tests for which they submitted claims, or that were wholly owned subsidiaries of the entities performing the test, or if both labs were owned by the same third party.

• **Durable Medical Equipment.** Froze payments for durable medical equipment (DME) at 1989 levels; limited to 15 months rental payment for enteral and parenteral nutrients, supplies and equipment; and expanded the definition of home health services to include ostomy bags and supplies.

• Required a GAO study of appropriate standards to determine the medical necessity of various items of DME.

• **Overpriced DME.** Effective April 1, 1990, reduced payments for seat-lift chairs and transcutaneous electrical nerve stimulation devices (used primarily for pain relief) by 15 percent.

• **Mental Health Services.** Beginning July 1, 1990, allowed direct reimbursement for services provided by clinical psychologists and clinical social workers. Both would have to accept Medicare payment as payment in full, and clinical social workers would be paid the lesser of their actual charge or 75 percent of the amount allowed for psychologists.

• Beginning in 1990, eliminated the annual cap of $1,100 for coverage of outpatient mental health services.

• **Coverage of Pap Smears.** Beginning July 1, 1990, provided for Medicare coverage of Pap smears every three years to screen for cervical cancer and other diseases in women. Payment for more frequent tests was allowed for women determined to be at high risk of developing cervical cancer.

• **Coverage of Nurse Practitioners in Nursing Facilities.** Authorized reimbursement for nurse-practitioner services provided in nursing homes so long as the nurse practitioner was working in collaboration with a physician. The bill required creation of a mechanism to pay for up to 1.5 routine "team" visits to patients in nursing facilities per month, with a team to consist of a physician and either a nurse practitioner or a physician assistant.

• **Physical and Occupational Therapy Services.** Increased from $500 to $750 the annual limit on Medicare payments for physical and occupational therapy.

• **Medicare Secondary Payer Provisions.** Authorized disclosing information from both the Internal Revenue Service and the Social Security Administration to help identify Medicare beneficiaries who had employer-provided health insurance. (When Medicare beneficiaries were covered by other forms of insurance, Medicare payments were required to be secondary, picking up only the costs the primary insurer did not pay.)

• Required employers of 20 or more workers to reply to requests for information concerning employees' health insurance status within 30 days or be subject to fines of up to $1,000.

• Extended to employers who failed to provide required primary coverage to the working aged or to individuals with end-stage renal disease (ESRD) penalties (an excise tax of 25 percent of the cost of the firm's group health plan) that already applied to employers who failed to provide required primary coverage to Medicare beneficiaries who were disabled and working.

• Established for the HHS secretary a legal right of action to enforce the secondary-payer provisions, with provisions for double damages.

• Prohibited Medicare from requiring companies that administer Medicare benefits to cross-match data files to identify secondary-payer cases as a condition of continuing their contracts with Medicare.

• **End-Stage Renal Disease.** Required maintenance through fiscal 1990 of the composite rate paid to facilities that provided kidney dialysis to Medicare ESRD patients.

• Capped, at 100 percent of the median composite payment level for hospital-based facilities, payments under "Method II," in which beneficiaries who had dialysis at home received supplies from suppliers other than approved ESRD facilities. Written agreements were required between such suppliers and ESRD patients to provide all needed supplies and to provide backup in-facility dialysis services when necessary.

• Required the HHS secretary to report to Congress a methodology and rationale for payment for EPO, a drug used to treat anemia in dialysis patients.

• **Health Maintenance Organizations (HMOs).** Required the HHS secretary to notify HMOs of the methodology and assumptions used to devise the Average Adjusted Per Capita Cost, the figure that determined payments for Medicare beneficiaries enrolled in HMOs.

The bill delayed until April 1, 1991, the prohibition against incentive payments to physicians to reduce or limit services to Medicare or Medicaid beneficiaries enrolled in HMOs or competitive medical plans.

• **Study of Administrative Costs.** Required a GAO study, to be completed by March 31, 1990, of the administrative burden of Medicare regulations on providers of health services and on insurance companies that administer claims.

• **Peer-Review Organization (PRO) Quality Denials.** Required PROs, in cases in which payment was denied for a service because of poor quality of care, to give the service provider an opportunity to request reconsideration of the formal determination before notice was sent to the beneficiary. Such reconsideration would be in lieu of any subsequent reconsideration of the payment denial.

1989 Medicare Reconciliation

In addition to overhauling Medicare's physician payment system and restricting physician referrals, the fiscal 1990 budget-reconciliation act (HR 3299 — PL 101-239) made a number of Medicare Part A and other health-related changes. *(Physician payments, physician referrals, p. 567; reconciliation, p. 43)*

As cleared, HR 3299:

Medicare Part A

• **Medicare Hospital Payments/Extension of Sequester.** Extended through Dec. 31, 1989, reductions of 2.092 percent in Medicare payments to hospitals imposed Oct. 16, 1989, under the Gramm-Rudman anti-deficit law (PL 100-119).

• **Medicare Hospital Payments/Capital Costs.** Beginning Jan. 1, 1990, extended through the rest of fiscal 1990 the 15 percent reduction in payments to hospitals for capital-related costs (including depreciation, leases and rentals, and interest). The bill continued the exemption from the payment reductions for sole community hospitals.

• **Medicare Hospital Payments/Payment Update.** Provided for payment rate increases, beginning Jan. 1, 1990, for hospitals under Medicare's Prospective Payment System (PPS) as follows: Hospitals in large urban areas (population more than 1 million) would receive increases equal to the increase in the "market basket" (a measure of goods and services bought by hospitals) minus 1.1 percentage points; hospitals in other urban areas would receive increases of market basket minus 1.75 percentage points; rural hospitals would receive increases of market basket plus 3 percentage points.

• Beginning with fiscal 1990, required the secretary of health and human services (HHS) to undertake on a budget-neutral basis the annual recalibration of factors determining the payments for each diagnosis-related group (DRG) to reflect changes in treatment patterns, technology and related factors. Thus, aggregate payments could not be increased or reduced, although the recalibration would alter payments for individual DRGs.

• **Medicare Hospital Payments/Disproportionate Share.** Effective April 1, 1990, increased payments for hospitals that served a disproportionate share of poor patients.

• **Rural Referral Centers.** "Grandfathered" through fiscal 1991 rural hospitals designated as Regional Referral Centers. Referral centers were paid at a higher rate than other rural hospitals.

• **Sole Community Providers.** Redefined sole community hospitals (SCHs) as any hospital more than 35 miles from another hospital, as well as other hospitals the HHS secretary so designated. Beginning April 1, 1990, SCHs, at their option, would be paid a target amount based on 1982 costs, a target amount based on 1987 costs or the regular Medicare prospective payment system rates. From April 1, 1990, to March 31, 1993, hospitals that were not SCHs, but that had 100 or fewer beds and depended on Medicare for at least 60 percent of their patient days or discharges, also would be eligible for the SCH payment options.

• Required a study by the Prospective Payment Assessment Commission (ProPAC) on the feasibility of returning small rural hospitals to cost-based reimbursement, developing alternative measures of market share for use in classifying SCHs and the feasibility of applying a volume adjustment to the payments for small rural hospitals.

• **Geographic Classification of Hospitals.** Required establishment of a board within HHS to which hospitals could apply to change their geographic status. The board would be authorized to reclassify an urban county into a large urban area and to classify an urban county into a different wage area, although a change in wage areas could not cause a reduction in the wage index of hospitals in an adjoining area. All such changes would have to be made on a budget-neutral basis, and the HHS secretary would be required, beginning in fiscal 1993, to update the area wage index annually, also on a budget-neutral basis.

• **Essential Access Community Hospitals.** Required the HHS secretary to establish a program in seven states to create rural health networks and authorized spending $50 million from the Medicare Hospital Insurance (Part A) trust fund for the program. Such networks were to include facilities designated as Essential Access Community Hospitals (EACHs) and Rural Primary Care Hospitals (RPCHs).

EACHs were required to have at least 75 beds unless no other hospital were within 35 miles or the HHS secretary granted a waiver. They would have to provide emergency and backup services for the network and throughout the service area, would have to accept transfers from RPCHs in the network and would have to provide staff privileges to physicians in the service area providing care at RCPH hospitals.

RCPHs were required to agree to stop providing acute-care hospital services, instead providing 24-hour emergency care. RPCHs could maintain up to six holding beds to care for patients for up to 72 hours before transfer to another hospital and also could provide long-term care services as part of the swing-bed program.

• **PPS Standardized Amounts.** Required the HHS secretary to submit a legislative proposal by Oct. 1, 1990, to eliminate the urban-rural distinction in the standardized amounts on which PPS rates are based. The proposal had to include a transition to a single rate by fiscal 1995.

• **Cancer Hospitals.** Exempted from the PPS hospitals extensively involved in treatment for and research on cancer.

• **Hospice Payments.** Beginning Jan. 1, 1990, increased rates for hospice services by 20 percent. In future years, increases in hospice payments would be based on the increase in the hospital market basket.

• **Medicare Buy-In for Working Disabled.** Permitted beneficiaries of Social Security Disability Insurance under age 65 to buy Medicare coverage after they had returned to work for a full 48 months, thereby exhausting their entitlement to Medicare coverage. Monthly premiums would be the same as for uninsured individuals.

• **Dentists as Hospital Medical Directors.** If allowed under state law, permitted a doctor of dental medicine or dental surgery to serve as a hospital's medical staff director, a position that formerly had to be filled by a doctor of medicine or osteopathy.

• **Intermediate Sanctions for Psychiatric Hospitals.** Authorized the HHS secretary to impose intermediate sanctions on psychiatric hospitals for quality deficiencies that did not pose an immediate threat to the health and safety of the facility's patients.

• **Information on Accreditation.** Required hospitals deemed to meet conditions of participation in Medicare due to accreditation by the Joint Committee on the Accreditation of Health Organizations (JCAHO) to agree to let JCAHO release accreditation information to the HHS secretary. The secretary was authorized to withdraw Medicare participation status based on information from JCAHO concerning significant deficiencies.

• **Hospital-Based and Free-Standing Skilled Nursing Facilities.** Required a General Accounting Office (GAO) study to assess the differences in costs and case mix between hospital-based and free-standing skilled nursing facilities and to make recommendations on the payment difference between the two types of facilities.

• **Prohibition of Nursing Home Balance Billing.** Barred nursing homes from charging Medicare beneficiaries more than the Medicare-approved payment.

• **Hospital Anti-Dumping Provisions.** Clarified requirements for hospitals that participated in Medicare to treat patients with health emergencies, including women in active labor. Hospitals were required to post "conspicuous" signs informing patients of their right to emergency treatment and whether or not the hospital participated in the Medicaid program.

• Required hospitals to maintain for five years records on individuals transferred to or from the hospital.

• Extended obligations of physicians to treat emergency cases to on-call, attending physicians, and required hospitals to maintain a list of such physicians.

• Provided "whistleblower" protections for physicians who refused to transfer a patient they considered to be medically unstable.

Other Health Provisions

• **Effectiveness and Outcomes Research.** Created within the Public Health Service an Agency for Health Care Policy and Research charged with enhancing the quality, appropriateness and effectiveness of health care services through research and promotion of improvements in clinical practice and the organization, financing and delivery of health care services.

• Authorized the conduct and support of research, demonstration projects, evaluations, training, guideline development and dissemination of information with respect to the effectiveness, efficiency and quality of health care services, the outcomes of health care services and procedures, and other health care topics.

• Authorized $35 million in fiscal 1990, $50 million in fiscal 1991 and $70 million in fiscal 1992 for overall activities of the agency.

• Transferred to the new agency existing functions of the National Center for Health Services Research and Health Care Technology Assessment, which was abolished.

• Created a national program of research on the quality, effectiveness and appropriateness of medical care, to be coordinated by the administrator of the new agency in consultation with the administrator of the Health Care Financing Administration. Authorized for the research program $50 million in fiscal 1990, $75 million in fiscal 1991, $110 million in fiscal 1992, $148 million in fiscal 1993 and $148 million in fiscal 1994. Two-thirds of the amounts authorized for fiscal 1990 and 1991, and 70 percent thereafter, were to come from the Medicare trust funds, with the rest to come from general revenues.

• By Jan. 1, 1991, required establishing a demonstration program to test the practice guidelines and medical review criteria.

• **Extension of Continued Coverage for Disabled Employees.** Provided that workers disabled at the time of job termination were eligible to continue health insurance coverage through their former employer for 29 months (after which they become eligible for Medicare). For months 19-29, employers could charge former workers premiums of up to 150 percent of the group rate, instead of the 102 percent allowed for months 1-18. The fiscal 1986 reconciliation bill (PL 99-272) required that employers with 20 or more workers provide certain workers leaving their jobs the option to buy continuing health insurance coverage at the group rate plus 2 percent for administrative costs for up to 18 months. *(Fiscal 1986 reconciliation, Congress and the Nation Vol. VII, p. 551)*

• **Vaccine Injury Compensation Amendments.** Made certain technical and other changes in the program established in PL 99-606 and PL 100-203 to compensate families of children injured or killed as a result of side effects of required vaccines against childhood diseases. The changes, designed to streamline the no-fault compensation process and ensure that it remains as non-adversarial as possible, were as follows:

The HHS secretary was required to publicize the program. The bill clarified the medical information that must be included in a petition for compensation. It also established in statute the Office of Special Masters, which was to conduct the vaccine-compensation proceedings and provided for up to eight such special masters, who need not be lawyers, to serve four-year terms. The special masters were required to decide within 240 days in most cases and provided for appeals to the U.S. Claims Court under very limited circumstances. The HHS secretary was required to participate in proceedings and be represented by the office of the attorney general.

• **GAO Review of Long-Term Care Insurance Standards.** Required the GAO, by April 1, 1990, to review and report to Congress on standards states might use to regulate private long-term care insurance policies with respect to inflation protection, non-forfeiture of benefits and other provisions.

• **Inner-City Hospital Triage Demonstration.** Required establishing a demonstration project in a public hospital in a large urban area that had established a triage system. The HHS secretary was required to pay up to $500,000 for three years to reimburse the hospital for the reasonable costs of providing trauma and emergency services to patients who might otherwise be denied care.

• **Moratorium on Regulations Reducing the Baseline.** Prohibited, through Oct. 15, 1990, regulations or policy changes estimated to reduce the current services baseline by more than $50,000. Exceptions would be for regulations ordered by law and for certain other situations.

• **Pepper Commission.** Provided that the Bipartisan Commission on Comprehensive Health Care might also be known as the "Claude Pepper Commission" or the "Pepper Commission," in honor of Rep. Claude Pepper, D-Fla., who died May 30, 1989.

The bill required that members of the commission select four vice chairmen. It delayed until March 1, 1990, the commission's deadline to report its recommendations on how to address the needs of those who lacked health insurance and on how to finance long-term care for the chronically ill or disabled. And it authorized congressional mailing privileges and printing and binding costs for the commission. *(Pepper commission, box, p. 688; Pepper profile, box, p. 919)*

• **National Commission on Children.** Extended commissioners' terms until March 31, 1991, authorized for fiscal 1991 "such sums as may be necessary" and authorized the commission to accept donations of money, property or personal services.

• **Nursing Home Reform.** Delayed effective dates and altered certain requirements that were part of an overhaul of federal nursing home regulations included in PL 100-203, the fiscal 1988 budget-reconciliation law, as follows:

• Postponed from Jan. 1, 1990, to Oct. 1, 1990, requirements regarding training or competency evaluation of nurses' aides and directed the HHS secretary to issue proposed regulations within 90 days. (PL 100-203 required those regulations to be issued by Sept. 1, 1988.)

• Allowed states to waive competency evaluation requirements for nurses' aides who could show that they had worked for the same employer in the state for at least 24 months before enactment of PL 100-203. Also stipulated that a nurse's aide would be considered to have completed an approved training and competency-evaluation program if the aide had completed a training course of at least 100 hours and was found competent before July 1, 1989, or had received, as of that date, 60 hours of initial training and at least 15 hours of supervised practical nurse's-aide training or regular in-service education.

• Directed the HHS secretary to issue, within 90 days of enactment, proposed regulations on pre-admission screening programs to prevent mentally ill or mentally retarded people from inappropriate placement in nursing homes. (PL 100-203 required the issuance of such rules by Oct. 1, 1988.)

• Postponed until Oct. 1, 1990, implementation of HHS regulations issued Feb. 2, 1989, altering the "conditions of participation" for nursing homes to receive reimbursement from Medicare or Medicaid.

1990 Medicare Reconciliation

The 1990 budget-reconciliation bill (HR 5835 — PL 101-508) included provisions that cut $44.2 billion over five years from Medicare spending by slashing payments to providers and raising out-of-pocket costs to beneficiaries.

The measure cleared Congress Oct. 27 and was signed by President Bush on Nov. 5. *(Reconciliation, p. 55)*

The 1990 action came on the heels of additional Medicare changes provided in a 1989 reconciliation bill (HR 3299 — PL 102-239). *(Physician payments, p. 567; 1989 Medicare reconciliation, p. 571)*

While significant, the increase in costs to Medicare's 33 million beneficiaries was only a third of that envisioned in the budget summit agreement approved by White House and congressional negotiators on Sept. 30, which had proposed a $30 billion, five-year hit on beneficiaries. Public opposition to the Medicare cutbacks was a major factor in the fatal blow delivered to the budget pact in the early hours of Oct. 5.

The cleared version of HR 5835 included only a modest increase in the costs borne by beneficiaries. The bill raised to $100, from $75, the annual deductible for Medicare's optional Part B program for physician and outpatient costs. The bill also continued requiring that the Part B premium, which was $28.60 a month in 1990, cover 25 percent of the program's costs. Instead of letting the premium amount float with actual costs each year, however, the bill fixed the premiums in advance at what was estimated to be 25 percent of future-year costs, reaching $46.10 in 1995.

The legislation also called for some increased spending. It boosted payments to inner-city and rural hospitals by $1 billion each over five years, in an effort to shield those facilities from the effects of Medicare's shift in the 1980s to a payment system based on each patient's diagnosis.

HR 5835 also contained a number of Medicare and Medicaid provisions not directly related to reconciliation. The legislation provided for a major expansion of Medicare coverage, for example, by allowing the program for the first time to pay for routine screening mammograms every two years for women age 65 and older. Although the change was expected to cost $1.25 billion over five years, backers said it would save lives and money by enabling the early detection of breast cancer.

Another provision responded to controversy over the so-called "right to die" issue by requiring Medicare and Medicaid providers to inform patients about the rights under state law to execute "living wills" or other advance directives about their care should they become unable to communicate their wishes. The provision came in the wake of a 1990 Supreme Court decision in *Cruzan v. Director, Missouri Department of Health* that said a state could require clear and convincing evidence of a comatose patient's wish to be allowed to die under such circumstances before allowing family members to order life-support systems to be removed. *(Case summary, p. 843)*

HR 5835 also clarified provisions enacted by Congress in the 1980s prohibiting doctors and hospitals from refusing to serve uninsured patients needing emergency care. Other provisions tightened regulation of Medigap insurance policies, expanded Medicaid coverage to include more poor children and modified nursing home regulations. *(Medigap, p. 582; Medicaid, p. 578; nursing homes, p. 586)*

Legislative Action

Recognizing that Medicare curbs would be a key part of any budget agreement, the congressional committees with jurisdiction over the program decided to await the results of the months-long budget summit between the Bush administration and congressional leaders.

The budget summit agreement called for a total of $4.6 billion in Medicare savings in 1991 and $60 billion over five years, of which half was to come from higher payments by beneficiaries and half from reduced payments to health care providers.

The increased costs to beneficiaries were expected to save $27.8 billion over five years. The provisions called for increasing the $75 Part B deductible to $150 by 1993; raising to 30 percent, from 25 percent, the share of Part B costs expected to come from premiums; and requiring beneficiaries to pay 20 percent of outpatient laboratory-test costs, which previously had been fully covered. The agreement left to the congressional committees how to allocate the reduced payments to providers.

But unhappiness over the Medicare cuts proved to be a major factor in the House's 179-254 rejection of the budget deal on Oct. 5, in the session that began Oct. 4. Opponents objected to the size of the cuts and to the higher premiums and fees recipients would have to pay to achieve half the cuts. Senior citizen lobbyists noted that many elderly people were already paying higher Medicare costs as a result of health care inflation and congressional cost-cutting steps in previous years.

After the stinging rejection of the budget pact, congressional committees went to work drafting their own cost-cutting changes in the Medicare program. On Oct. 10, the House Ways and Means Committee approved a barebones proposal that sought to pare $4.2 billion in fiscal 1991 and $50 billion over five years. The committee's proposal on reductions to providers was similar to the budget pact, cutting $32.9 billion. The savings produced by increased costs to beneficiaries, however, were reduced to $17.2 billion.

The House on Oct. 16 then approved a Democratic alternative to the Ways and Means plan that reduced the added beneficiary cost-sharing by $7 billion, mainly by imposing a smaller premium increase and raising the Part B deductible to $100 instead of $125.

The Senate Finance Committee, meanwhile, approved a plan that was similar to the House's on provider cuts but called for $17.6 billion in savings from higher payments by beneficiaries, compared with $10 billion passed by the House. The Senate plan called for higher Part B premiums and higher annual deductibles than did the House bill and also required beneficiaries to pay 20 percent of lab costs.

On the Senate floor, Al Gore, D-Tenn., and Barbara A. Mikulski, D-Md., offered an amendment to lower the added Medicare costs while raising taxes on the wealthy. A motion to waive a budget act rule against the amendment was rejected 45-55, 15 votes short of the 60 required, on Oct. 18.

Major Provisions

As enacted, the Medicare provisions of the 1990 reconciliation bill (HR 5835 — PL 101-508):

Medicare Part A

• **Medicare Hospital Payments/Capital Costs.** Continued through fiscal 1991 the 15 percent reduction in payments to hospitals under Medicare's Prospective Payment System (PPS) for capital-related costs (including depreciation, interest and rent). Exempted from the reductions were facilities designated as Rural Primary Care Hospitals, Essential Access Community Hospitals and sole community hospitals. Capital costs still had to be folded into PPS by Oct. 1, 1991.

• **Medicare Hospital Payments/Payment Update.** Provided for payment rate increases, beginning Jan. 1, 1991, for hospitals (other than rural hospitals, listed below) under PPS as follows:

For the remainder of fiscal 1991, hospitals would receive increases equal to the increase in the "market basket" (a measure of goods and services bought by hospitals) less 2 percentage points. (The fiscal 1991 market basket increase was estimated at 5.2 percent, meaning the increase would be 3.2 percent.) For fiscal 1992, the payment update would be market basket less 1.6 percentage points.

For fiscal 1993, market basket less 1.55 percentage points.

In fiscal 1994 and 1995, hospitals would receive the full market basket increase.

• **Medicare Hospital Payments/Disproportionate Share.** Increased and made permanent the so-called disproportionate share adjustment, a special add-on payment for hospitals that served a disproportionately large share (15 percent or more) of poor patients, whose ailments tended to be more expensive to treat.

• **Medicare Hospital Payments/Rural Hospitals.** Provided for payment rate increases for rural hospitals under PPS as follows:

For fiscal 1991, market basket (5.2 percent) less 0.7 percentage points (yielding an increase of 4.5 percent).

For fiscal 1992, market basket less 0.6 percentage points.

For fiscal 1993, market basket.

For fiscal 1994, market basket plus 1.5 percentage points.

For fiscal 1995, market basket plus whatever percentage increase was needed to close the gap between rates paid to rural hospitals and those paid to urban hospitals.

• **Medicare Hospital Payments/Area Wage Index.** Delayed until Jan. 1, 1991, the requirement that the Department of Health and Human Services (HHS) use a new wage index based on 1988 data. (Under PPS, hospital payments were adjusted for labor costs using an index that compared hospital wages in a particular geographic area with those paid nationwide. The existing wage index was based on a 1984 survey of wages and wage-related costs, after adjustments for inflation.)

• **Medicare Hospital Payments/Regional Floor.** Extended through fiscal 1993 a special payment adjustment, known as the regional floor, for hospitals in areas of the country with costs higher than the national average. Required the HHS secretary to collect data on non-labor costs to create a geographic index for non-labor costs.

• **Prospective Payment Assessment Commission.** Expanded the responsibilities of the Prospective Payment Assessment Commission (ProPAC), a 17-member board charged with making recommendations concerning hospital payments under PPS. Charged ProPAC with recommending the development or modification of policies to promote the delivery of efficient, accessible, high-quality health care.

Continued to require ProPAC to recommend the hospital update factor under PPS annually by March 1. In addition, though, every June 1, ProPAC would have to report on trends in health care costs, payment of institutional providers (including hospitals, outpatient departments, nursing homes and ambulatory surgery centers) and new methods of health care cost containment.

(In their report, conferees noted that they intended that ProPAC include in its analysis and recommendations proposals for changes in policies regarding: (1) payment of inner-city hospitals, taking into account the costs of charity care and bad debts; (2) payment of rural hospitals, taking into account appropriate responses to issues affecting access to health care services in rural areas; and (3) ways to help constrain the costs of health care to employers, including the ways in which Medicare payment policies affect other payers.)

Required ProPAC, by Oct. 1, 1991, to analyze Medicaid payment to hospitals and recommend any changes in federal law relating to Medicaid hospital reimbursement.

• **DRG Payment Window.** Under PPS, Medicare payments were made on the basis of a patient's diagnosis, according to what was called a diagnosis-related group, or DRG. The DRG payment was intended to cover all hospital services provided to a Medicare beneficiary during his or her stay. In recent years, however, many hospitals had begun having patients scheduled for a hospital stay come in two or three days in advance for routine tests and then billing them separately for those tests under Medicare's Part B, which covered outpatient costs.

Beginning Jan. 1, 1991, the new rule provided that services related to the admission rendered up to 72 hours before the day of hospital admission were to be considered part of the hospital stay and could not be separately billed to Part B.

• **Hospitals Exempt from PPS.** Required the HHS secretary to develop a prospective payment methodology for hospitals exempt from PPS (including children's hospitals, cancer hospitals, psychiatric hospitals, rehabilitation hospitals and long-term care hospitals) by April 1, 1992.

Further provided that PPS-exempt hospitals, which were paid based on their costs up to a specific target amount, be allowed to receive 50 percent of their costs in excess of that target, up to a limit of 120 percent (thereby making them eligible to receive 110 percent of their target amount).

• **Hospice Care.** Beginning Jan. 1, 1990, allowed Medicare beneficiaries to receive hospice-care services in excess of the existing 210-day limit if the beneficiary was recertified as terminally ill by a physician or hospice medical director. (This provision was part of the 1988 Medicare Catastrophic Coverage Act (PL 100-360) and was repealed along with most of the rest of the law in 1989. *(1988 act, Congress and the Nation Vol. VII, p. 561; 1989 repeal, p. 565)*)

• **Partial Sequester.** Froze all payments under Medicare Part A at fiscal 1990 levels through Dec. 31, 1990.

• **Waiver of Liability for Skilled Nursing Facilities and Hospices.** Extended through Dec. 31, 1995, the so-called waiver of liability for skilled nursing homes and hospices, which allowed them to receive Medicare payment for patients not technically eligible for the services if the agencies involved reasonably thought they were providing covered services.

• **Hospital Anti-Dumping Provisions.** Further clarified provisions of past deficit-reduction bills that required hospitals that participated in Medicare to treat any patients with health emergencies, particularly women in "active" labor, regardless of whether they were covered by Medicare or any other health insurance.

The provisions reduced to $25,000 (from $50,000) the maximum penalty that could be assessed against small hospitals (those with fewer than 100 beds). It also changed the standard for what could be considered "patient dumping" to make assessing civil penalties against hospitals and doctors easier and clarified standards for excluding providers from the program.

Medicare Part B

• **Part B Premium.** Set the Part B premium as follows: For calendar year 1991, the monthly premium would be $29.90. For calendar year 1992, $31.80; for 1993, $36.60; for 1994, $41.10; and for 1995, $46.10. (The calendar year 1990 monthly premium was $28.60.)

• **Part B Deductible.** Increased the annual Part B deductible from $75 to $100 for calendar year 1991 and thereafter.

• **Overpriced Procedures.** Beginning Jan. 1, 1991, cut Medicare payments for 244 procedures that analysts had determined to be overpaid by Medicare. The procedures would be cut by the same amount for which payments were reduced in 1990. Also reduced by 6.5 percent payment for certain other procedures that had been identified as overvalued.

• **Radiology Services.** For 1991, reduced, by up to 9.5 percent, fees for radiology services under Medicare. Exact reductions would vary by the area of the country in which they were performed.

• **Anesthesiology Services.** Beginning Jan., 1, 1991, reduced fees for anesthesiology services by up to 15 percent. Reductions would average about 7 percent and would vary by locality. Also extended, through Dec. 31, 1995, payment reductions imposed in the 1987 deficit-reduction bill (PL 100-203) for anesthesiologists who supervised multiple procedures in which anesthesia was delivered by certified registered nurse anesthetists.

• **Pathology Services.** Beginning Jan. 1, 1991, reduced most fees for pathology services by 7 percent and provided that pathology services be paid according to a fee schedule beginning Jan. 1, 1992, instead of Jan. 1, 1991.

• **Physician Payment Update.** For calendar 1991, froze Medicare fees for all physician services except primary care, which would increase by 2 percent. Reduced fees for 1992 by 0.4 percent below inflation projections (which would produce an estimated fee increase of 2 percent). Set minimum payment for primary care services at 60 percent of the national average. Also, for calendar 1991, increased from 125 percent of the Medicare-approved amount to 140 percent the total amount a physician could charge for so-called evaluation and management services, such as most routine office visits.

• **Medicare Volume Performance Standards.** Required the HHS secretary to set separate volume targets for surgery and all other medical procedures. The volume target, known as the MVPS, in conjunction with the fee schedule, was intended to control increases in both the price and volume of Medicare physician services.

• **New Physicians.** Made permanent the policy of setting fees for physicians in their first year of practice at 80 percent of the amount otherwise payable, and at 85 percent in their second year.

Also provided that fees for physicians in their third year be set at 90 percent, and those in their fourth year 95 percent.

Beginning Jan. 1, 1991, set similar limits for nonphysician health practitioners (including physician assistants, psychologists and nurse midwives).

• **Assistants at Surgery.** Limited payments for doctors who served as assistants during surgical procedures to no more than 16 percent of the primary surgeon's fee. Eliminated payments for assistants at surgery for procedures in which a physician served as an assistant less than 5 percent of the time.

• **Diagnostic Tests.** Limited payments for the technical component of certain diagnostic tests to the national median charge. Also, beginning Jan. 1, 1992, eliminated separate payments for the interpretation of a routine electrocardiogram (EKG) ordered or performed in conjunction with an office visit or consultation.

• **Reciprocal Billing Arrangements.** Specifically allowed payment to a physician who arranged for services to be provided by another physician when the first physician was unavailable on an occasional, reciprocal basis.

• **Practicing Physicians Advisory Council.** Established a 15-member Practicing Physicians Advisory Council whose role would be to consult with the HHS secretary on proposed changes in Medicare's physician payment policies.

• **Study of Regional Variations in the Impact of Medicare Physician Payment Reform.** Required the HHS secretary to conduct a study of regional variations in the impact of Medicare's physician payment reform law (included in the fiscal 1990 reconciliation bill (PL 101-239)). The study would examine:

(1) factors contributing to variations in charges not attributable to variations in practice costs;

(2) the impact on access to care in areas that would experience disproportionately large payment reductions under the new fee schedule (set to begin Jan. 1, 1992); and

(3) appropriate adjustments or modifications in the transition to or determining payments under the fee schedule.

• **Hospital Outpatient Services.** Reduced capital payments for hospital outpatient services by 15 percent in fiscal 1991 and by an additional 10 percent in each of the following four fiscal years.

The same hospitals that were exempt from the Part A capital reductions would be exempt from the outpatient capital reductions.

In addition, payments for hospital outpatient services would be cut by 5.8 percent from fiscal 1991 through 1995, except for hospitals exempt, as noted above.

Directed the HHS secretary to develop, by Sept. 1, 1991, a proposal for paying for hospital outpatient services under a prospective payment system, as was the existing case for most inpatient hospital care.

• **Overpriced Durable Medical Equipment (DME).** Reduced by 15 percent fees paid for transcutaneous electrical nerve stimulation (TENS) devices (used primarily to treat chronic pain). This was in addition to the 15 percent reduction ordered for 1990.

Coverage and payment for seatlift chairs furnished in 1991 and thereafter would be limited to the lift mechanism only and would not include the chair and upholstery.

• **National Limits on DME Fees.** Eliminated the system in which fees were determined on a regional basis in favor of one instituting upper and lower national fee limits for various items of durable medical equipment. Limits for all items except customized equipment would be phased in over a three-year period.

• **Rental Items.** Allowed patients the option to purchase certain rented items of DME (including wheelchairs and hospital beds) following nine months of continuous rental. If the patient exercised the option, rental payments would continue through the 13th month of continuous use, after which ownership of the item would transfer to the patient. Medicare would continue to make payments for servicing and maintenance at rates to be determined by the secretary.

• **Oxygen Retesting.** Required patients who qualified for oxygen therapy to be retested after three months to confirm their continued need for such use.

• **DME Payment Update.** Reduced the inflation increase for DME by 1 percentage point in each of 1991 and 1992. Stipulated that no increases be granted for enteral and parenteral (largely intravenous) nutrients, equipment and supplies, and that payments for orthotics and prosthetics (orthopedic items) be frozen at 1990 levels for calendar year 1991.

• **Medical Necessity Forms.** Before Medicare would pay for certain items of DME, a physician had to certify that the equipment was medically necessary. Beginning Jan. 1, 1991, the provision prohibited DME suppliers from distributing completed or partially completed Medicare medical-necessity forms to physicians or beneficiaries to facilitate purchase of a particular item. Violators would be subject to civil penalties of up to $1,000 for each form distributed.

• **Clinical Laboratory Services.** Limited the annual payment update for clinical laboratory services to 2 percent for each of 1991, 1992 and 1993. Also, beginning Jan. 1, 1991, limited payment for clinical laboratory services to no more than the amount that represented 88 percent of the median fee paid for such services nationwide. The previous national limit was 93 percent.

• **Partial Sequester.** Reduced all payments to Part B providers (except health maintenance organizations (HMOs)) by 2 percent for services furnished between Nov. 1, 1990, and Dec. 31, 1990.

• **Alzheimer's Disease Demonstration Projects.** Reauthorized for one additional year, at $15 million, demonstration projects to provide comprehensive services to Medicare beneficiaries with Alzheimer's disease.

• **Coverage of Nurse Practitioners and Clinical Nurse Specialists in Rural Areas.** Allowed direct reimbursement for services provided by nurse practitioners and clinical nurse specialists in rural areas. Under existing law, reimbursement for both categories of health professionals was generally limited to the physician for whom the service-provider worked.

Payments would be limited to 85 percent of the amount that could be paid to a physician providing the same service, and services would be required to be provided only on an assignment basis (under which the provider agreed to accept the Medicare-approved fee as payment in full).

• **Coverage of Injectable Drugs for Treatment of Osteoporosis.** Beginning Jan. 1, 1991, and ending Dec. 31, 1995, provided for Medicare coverage of injectable drugs used to treat bone fractures related to post-menopausal osteoporosis.

Coverage would include only patients who were otherwise eligible for Medicare home-care coverage and whose physicians certified that they were unable to learn the skills needed to administer the drug themselves or were otherwise physically or mentally incapable of self-administration. Also required the secretary to study the impact of such coverage and report any findings and recommendations to Congress by Oct. 1, 1994.

• **Partial Hospitalization Services Provided by Community Mental Health Centers.** Partial hospitalization services included individual and group therapy, occupational therapy, administration of certain drugs and other services provided by a hospital or hospital-affiliated institution on a less than 24-hour basis. Beginning April 1, 1991, the provision allowed Medicare payment for partial hospitalization services provided by community mental health centers, as well.

• **Certified Registered Nurse Anesthetists.** Altered the payment system for certified registered nurse anesthetists (CRNAs) over six years to conform them to the manner in which physicians who performed anesthesia services would be paid under the new Medicare fee schedule.

By 1995, payments for CRNAs working under the direct supervision of a physician would be approximately 70 percent of the amount that would be paid to a physician performing the same service.

• Mammography Screening. Beginning Jan. 1, 1991, provided coverage for mammograms used to screen for breast cancer. (Medicare already paid for diagnostic mammography, used after breast cancer was suspected.) For Medicare beneficiaries over age 65, Medicare would pay for a screening mammogram every two years.

For those under age 65:

(1) No coverage would be provided for women under age 35.

(2) A baseline screening would be covered for those between ages 35 and 40.

(3) Biennial coverage would be provided for women between ages 40 and 49 who were not determined to be at high risk for breast cancer.

(4) Annual coverage would be provided for all female beneficiaries between ages 50 and 64, as well as for high-risk women between 40 and 49.

Payment would be limited to $55 in 1991, with that amount to be increased for inflation in future years. Providers would be prohibited from charging more than 125 percent of the Medicare-approved price in 1991, 120 percent in 1992 and 115 percent in 1993.

Medicare Parts A and B

• End-Stage Renal Disease (ESRD) Facility Payments. For the remainder of 1990, required that the rate of payment to free-standing and hospital-based kidney dialysis facilities be maintained at the rates in effect on Sept. 30, 1990. Beginning Jan. 1, 1991, increased the per-patient rate by $1.

• Coverage of Erythropoietin (EPO). Beginning July 1, 1991, allowed coverage of EPO, an anti-anemia drug used by kidney dialysis patients. Under existing rules, EPO was covered when administered in a dialysis facility, but only in home-dialysis settings if administered directly by a physician. Also restructured the way Medicare paid for the drug.

• Demonstration for Staff-Assisted Home Dialysis. Required establishment of a three-year demonstration to evaluate the safety and cost-effectiveness of providing professional assistance to up to 800 Medicare ESRD beneficiaries who used dialysis at home and met other conditions. The final report on the demonstration would be due no later than Dec. 31, 1995.

• Secondary Payer Provisions. Extended, through Sept. 30, 1995, authority for Medicare to gain access to records of the Social Security Administration and Internal Revenue Service to identify Medicare beneficiaries who had other forms of health insurance. (Medicare was supposed to be the "secondary" payer for many beneficiaries with other forms of insurance, covering only costs not paid by the primary insurer.)

• Extended, through Oct. 1, 1995, a provision making Medicare the secondary payer for disabled Medicare beneficiaries covered by an employer health plan in a business with more than 100 employees.

• Extended from 12 to 18 months the period during which employer-provided insurance was the primary payer for Medicare ESRD patients. Made it illegal to offer incentives to an individual not to enroll in (or to terminate enrollment from) a health plan that would be a primary payer under Medicare rules unless the same incentives were offered to all individuals covered under the plan, regardless of their Medicare status.

• Patient Self-Determination/Living Wills. Beginning one year after enactment, required hospitals, nursing homes, home health agencies, hospice programs and HMOs that participated in Medicare or Medicaid to provide written information to all adult patients with respect to their rights under state law to make decisions concerning their medical care, including the right to accept or refuse medical or surgical treatment and the right to formulate advance directives.

(Such advance directives included so-called living wills, in which individuals could state in advance whether they wanted life-sustaining treatment continued should they become unable to communicate their wishes, or "durable powers of attorney," in which a patient delegated to another person the right to make decisions regarding medical care if the patient became incapacitated.)

Providers would be required to maintain written policies detailing how those rights would be protected, including documenting in the patient's medical record whether the patient had executed an advance directive. They also would be required to provide education for staff and the community regarding advance directives but could not condition the provision of services or otherwise discriminate against a patient based on whether he or she had executed an advance directive.

This provision left room for states to allow health care providers to object, as a matter of conscience, and refuse to carry out a patient's advance directive.

• Health Maintenance Organizations. Watered down previous efforts to prevent HMOs from cutting costs by offering incentives to doctors not to provide patient care.

The bill also repealed a provision of the fiscal 1987 budget-reconciliation legislation (PL 99-509) that would have prohibited HMOs and Competitive Medical Plans (CMPs) from paying physicians incentives designed to directly or indirectly encourage needed care to be withheld from patients. It replaced that requirement with a provision that physician-incentive plans operated by HMOs and CMPs be operated with certain protections for both physicians and patients.

• Payment Cycles. Made permanent a provision barring the HHS secretary from making policy changes whose primary effect was to slow down or speed up the rate at which Medicare claims were paid.

• Waiver of Liability for Home Health Agencies. Extended through Dec. 31, 1995, the so-called waiver of liability for home health agencies, which allowed them to receive Medicare payment for patients not technically eligible for the services if the agencies involved reasonably thought they were providing covered services.

• Social Health Maintenance Organizations. Extended through Sept. 30, 1995, authority for a series of social health maintenance organizations (SHMOs), which provided not only traditional HMO health care services but also long-term care and other social services. Required the creation of up to four additional SHMOs.

• Case-Management Demonstrations. Required the secretary to reinstate three demonstration projects to test the cost-effectiveness of providing case-management services to Medicare beneficiaries with high-cost illnesses. (Case management involved designating a single person to oversee and coordinate all health services for particular individuals.)

The demonstrations were originally authorized as part of the 1988 Medicare Catastrophic Coverage Act, but the authority was repealed along with most of the rest of that law in 1989. Authorized $2 million for each of fiscal 1991 and 1992 to cover administrative costs.

● **Prospective Payment for Home Health Agencies.** Required the secretary to develop a prospective payment system for home health agencies and submit it to Congress by Sept. 1, 1993.

● **User Fees for Survey and Certification.** Specifically prohibited HHS from imposing, or from requiring states to impose, on hospitals, nursing homes, hospices, kidney dialysis facilities or other health institutions fees to offset the costs of inspections to certify compliance with Medicare rules and regulations. (The prohibition was in response to a similar user-fee proposal included in Bush's fiscal 1990 budget.)

● **Peer Review Organizations.** Made several alterations in the requirements for Medicare Peer Review Organizations (PROs), which reviewed the appropriateness, reasonableness, medical necessity and quality of care provided to Medicare beneficiaries. Among the changes were:

(1) Requiring PROs to notify state licensing boards when a physician was excluded from Medicare.

(2) Requiring coordination in review activities between PROs and insurance company "carriers" that paid Medicare claims.

(3) Allowing podiatrists and optometrists to participate in decisions about payment denials for services provided by those specialists.

Medicaid

Following a recent pattern, the 101st Congress twice used budget-reconciliation bills as vehicles for ordering an expansion of the Medicaid program to cover more low-income people, particularly children.

The 1989 reconciliation measure (HR 3299 — PL 101-239) and its 1990 counterpart (HR 5835 — PL 101-508) both included provisions making more people eligible for the federal-state health care program for the poor. *(HR 3299, p. 43; HR 5835, p. 55)*

Both bills were part of a long-term trend in which Congress sought to move the basis of Medicaid eligibility away from its original link to eligibility for Aid to Families with Dependent Children or Supplemental Security Income. Backers of the expansion argued that society also should ensure adequate health care for children and pregnant women from "working poor" families that held jobs but did not earn enough to pay for their own coverage.

Backers of expanded coverage also contended that the federal government needed to impose more uniformity on the crazy quilt of state Medicaid coverage, which varied widely both in the level of eligible income and in the types of services provided.

The expansions of Medicaid were strongly opposed by the nation's governors, however, who argued that it was wrong for Congress to impose costly new mandates on the states without providing additional funding. On average, the federal government funded 55 percent of Medicaid costs, with the rest left up to the states. One governor who criticized the new mandates was Bill Clinton of Arkansas, who noted that the Medicaid mandates for 1989 had consumed nearly a third of his state's new revenues for the year. Congress "ought to have to live with our budgets," he said, instead of running a huge deficit while also forcing new costs on the balanced budget states.

1989 Action

The reconciliation measure cleared by Congress in 1989 required states to provide Medicaid coverage to pregnant women (for pregnancy-related services) and to children up to age 6 (for all Medicaid services) in families with incomes up to 133 percent of the federal poverty level. The bill also required states to provide early-screening services — such as a physical exam and vision and hearing tests — for Medicaid beneficiaries up to age 12 and to provide treatment for all health problems uncovered by the exams, even if the treatment was not part of the state's regular Medicaid benefits. In addition, the measure expanded state funding of services provided through community health, migrant health and homeless centers, and it directed states to inform Medicaid recipients who were pregnant or the parents of young children of their eligibility for the Supplemental Food Program for Women, Infants and Children (WIC).

The 1989 Medicaid expansion was considerably less than that sought by the program's congressional backers. On June 29, the House Energy and Commerce Subcommittee on Health and the Environment approved a reconciliation measure that included an expansion of Medicaid coverage estimated to cost $6 billion over five years. The proposal sought to require states to extend certain Medicaid services to pregnant women and children up to age 1 in families with incomes up to 185 percent of the federally defined poverty level. Moreover, the bill mandated states to offer full Medicaid coverage to all children in families living below the federal poverty level.

The Health Subcommittee's proposal ran into criticism in the full committee, where it was approved on a 29-14 vote. Committee Republicans and a few Democrats expressed concern about the costs of the proposal, which the Congressional Budget Office estimated at about $4.15 billion over five years.

The Senate Finance Committee, however, called for a less generous expansion when it approved its version of the budget-reconciliation bill on Oct. 3. The Finance proposal would require states to provide Medicaid to pregnant women and to children up to age 6 in families with incomes at or below 133 percent of the poverty level.

Stripped from the Senate bill on the floor along with all other provisions not directly related to saving money, the Medicaid expansion survived in conference in a scaled-back form similar to the Finance Committee's proposal.

1989 Medicaid Provisions

As enacted, the Medicaid and maternal- and child-health provisions of the 1989 reconciliation bill (HR 3299 — PL 101-239):

Medicaid

● **Mandatory Coverage of Pregnant Women and Children.** Required states to provide Medicaid coverage by April 1, 1990, to pregnant women (for pregnancy-related services) and to children up to age 6 (for all Medicaid services) in families with incomes up to 133 percent of the federal poverty threshold ($13,380 for a family of three). This superseded a provision included in the 1988 Medicare Catastrophic Coverage Act (PL 100-360) and preserved in the law's repeal (PL 101-234) requiring states to provide such coverage by July 1, 1990, to pregnant women and to infants up to age 1 in families with incomes at or below the poverty threshold. *(1988 act, Congress and the Nation Vol. VII, p. 561; 1989 repeal, p. 565)*

• **Payment for Obstetric and Pediatric Services.** Required states to reimburse providers of obstetric and pediatric care at levels sufficient to ensure that services were as available to Medicaid beneficiaries as they were to the general population in a particular area. The bill also required states to annually submit to the federal government their payment rates for such services.

• **Early and Periodic Screening, Diagnostic and Treatment Services.** Beginning April 1, 1990, defined in statute the minimum requirements for state coverage of early and periodic screening, diagnostic and treatment (EPSDT) services for Medicaid beneficiaries under age 12. Such requirements included a health and development history, a comprehensive physical exam, vision and hearing testing, appropriate laboratory tests and a dental exam by age 3.

• Required that states treat any physical or mental problem uncovered in such screening if such treatment was allowed by Medicaid, whether or not that treatment was part of the state's regular Medicaid package of benefits. Further required the secretary of health and human services (HHS) to establish EPSDT participation goals for states and required states to report annually on progress toward meeting those goals.

• **Payment for Federally Qualified Health Center Services.** Beginning April 1, 1990, required states to include as Medicaid benefits services provided by federally qualified health centers, defined as community health centers, migrant health centers, programs providing health services for the homeless or clinics meeting standards for the above programs but not actually receiving grant funds. States would have to pay such centers 100 percent of their reasonable costs.

• **Medicaid Coordination with WIC.** Beginning July 1, 1990, required states to notify Medicaid beneficiaries who were pregnant, postpartum or breast-feeding, or who had children under age 5, of the availability of benefits under the Special Supplemental Food Program for Women, Infants and Children, and to refer such people to the state agency administering the WIC program. Included in the reauthorization measure for WIC (HR 24 — PL 101-147) was a provision automatically deeming Medicaid beneficiaries financially eligible for WIC services. *(WIC reauthorization, p. 617)*

• **Nurse Practitioners.** Beginning July 1, 1990, required states to cover services of certified pediatric or family nurse practitioners operating in accordance with state law, regardless of whether they were associated with or under the supervision of a physician.

• **Demonstration Programs for Poor Pregnant Women and Children.** Required the HHS secretary to establish state demonstration projects to test alternative ways to provide health insurance coverage to pregnant women and children under age 20 in families with incomes below 185 percent of poverty who are otherwise ineligible for Medicaid. Projects could not run longer than three years, and federal financial participation would be limited to $10 million annually in fiscal 1991-93.

• **Medicare 'Buy-In' for the Working Disabled.** Required states, beginning July 1, 1990, to pay the Medicare Part A (hospital coverage) premiums for working disabled people with incomes below 200 percent of the federal poverty line and with resources less than twice the maximum allowed under the Supplemental Security Income (SSI) program. States could charge income-related premiums for those with incomes above 150 percent of poverty.

• **State Matching Payments.** Reimposed until Dec. 31, 1990, the moratorium on publishing final regulations to limit states' ability to use funds donated or provided by a dedicated tax to meet their matching requirement under Medicaid. A previous moratorium, included as part of PL 100-647, expired May 1.

• **Minnesota Family Investment Plan Demonstration.** Authorized Minnesota to waive certain Medicaid rules to test an alternative program to help families become self-sufficient.

Medicaid Pay Suits

The Supreme Court in 1990 ruled that health care providers could challenge the adequacy of Medicaid reimbursement rates. In *Wilder v. Virginia Hospital Association*, the Court said that hospitals, nursing homes and other providers could invoke a federal civil rights law, known as Section 1983, to seek higher reimbursement rates from the states.

The federal government paid just over half of Medicaid costs, but states set the reimbursement rates for providers. As a result of the Court ruling, program costs were expected to rise. *(Case summary, p. 834)*

Maternal and Child Health

• **Increase in Authorization.** Increased from $561 million to $686 million the permanent authorization level for the Maternal and Child Health Block Grant, which supported improving the health of mothers and children.

• **Use of Funds and Federal Set-Aside.** Required the HHS secretary to keep 15 percent of the first $600 million appropriated for special projects, including screening of newborns for sickle-cell anemia and other genetic disorders. Of appropriations more than $600 million, the secretary was required to keep 12.75 percent for maternal- and child-health projects and to support providing outpatient and community-based services to children with special health care needs.

• **Application for Block Grant Funds.** Required a new maternal- and child-health grant application procedure for states, including a statewide needs assessment at least every five years. States also were required to dedicate 30 percent of their block grant funds for children with special health care needs and 30 percent for preventive and primary-care services. However, states were required to maintain the level of funds provided solely for maternal- and child-health programs in fiscal 1989.

In their applications, states were required to specify program goals and how they relate to the surgeon general's health-status goals for the year 2000.

• Required that states provide a toll-free telephone

number so parents could get information about health care providers and other health care services.

• **Reports.** Required states to include new information in their annual reports to HHS on various maternal- and child-health indicators and required the HHS secretary to report annually on the program to the House Energy and Commerce and Senate Finance committees.

• **Application for Maternal- and Child-Health Programs.** Required the HHS secretary to develop within a year a model application that could be used to apply simultaneously for benefits under a number of programs, including Medicaid, the maternal- and child-health block grant, migrant and community health centers, WIC, Head Start and health care programs for the homeless.

• **Maternal- and Child-Health Handbook.** Required the HHS secretary to develop and make available to pregnant women and families with young children a maternal- and child-health handbook. The handbook would be distributed through providers of the programs listed above and targeted at women at high risk for health problems for them or their children.

• **Research on Infant Mortality and Medicaid Services.** Required the HHS secretary to develop a national system to link infant mortality data with any record of Medicaid services.

• **Health Insurance for Medically Uninsurable Children.** Authorized establishing up to four three-year demonstration projects to provide health insurance to otherwise uninsurable children under age 19.

1990 Action

The most significant provision of the 1990 Medicaid expansion required states to provide Medicaid coverage to all children born after Sept. 30, 1983, in families with incomes at or below the federal poverty level. Thus, all children up to age 19 would be covered by 2002.

The legislation also expanded coverage for the elderly poor. It required Medicaid to cover more cost-sharing requirements, such as premiums, for poor Medicare beneficiaries who were not quite poor enough to qualify for full Medicare coverage. It also made available $850 million over five years to provide home care for frail elderly people who would otherwise require costly institutional care.

The bill contained cost-saving provisions estimated to trim $2.9 billion from projected Medicaid spending. One provision sought to save $1.9 billion by requiring pharmaceutical companies to give bulk discounts on sales of drugs to Medicaid. Another $1 billion was to be saved by requiring states to pay the premiums of Medicaid beneficiaries eligible for private group health insurance if that would save money.

Following the defeat of the White House-congressional budget summit agreement in early October, the House Energy and Commerce Committee approved a package calling for Medicaid spending cuts of $3.24 billion over five years, largely through the drug discount provision. However, the committee spent all but $337 million of the savings on Medicaid expansions, included requiring states to extend coverage to children up to age 12 in families with incomes below the poverty line.

The bill also included provisions aimed at helping low-income elderly people cope with the increased costs of the Medicare program. An effort by Joe L. Barton, R-Texas., to remove the new help for poor Medicare beneficiaries was rejected by the panel on a 17-26 vote.

The Senate Finance Committee's Medicaid provisions were similar to the House panel's on expansion of child benefits but were less generous on providing new help for Medicare recipients.

In the budget-reconciliation conference, negotiators agreed to provisions expanding child-health programs by about $1.1 billion over five years, mostly by requiring coverage of all children in families living below the federal poverty line.

1990 Medicaid Provisions

As enacted, the Medicaid provisions of the 1990 reconciliation bill (HR 5835 — PL 101-508) *(Nursing home regulations, p. 586; Medigap, p. 582)*:

Prescription Drug Discounts

• **Required Rebate Agreements.** Beginning Jan. 1, 1991, generally prohibited federal Medicaid funds from being spent for prescription drugs made by any drug manufacturer that did not enter into an agreement to provide specified rebates to states on a quarterly basis.

States that elected to offer prescription drug coverage under Medicaid (although such coverage was optional, all 50 states offered it) would be required to cover all drugs sold by a manufacturer who had entered into a rebate agreement, except for vaccines and classes of drugs specifically excluded by statute. To assist states with start-up administrative costs, the federal government would pay 75 cents of each dollar spent on the program in fiscal 1991.

• **Excluded Drugs.** Drugs whose coverage was not required included drugs to treat anorexia or weight gain; fertility drugs; drugs used for cosmetic purposes or hair growth; smoking cessation drugs; cough and cold remedies; prescription vitamins and minerals, except for vitamins and fluoride preparations prescribed for pregnant women; non-prescription drugs; drugs for which the manufacturer required, as a condition of sale, that associated tests or monitoring services be purchased exclusively from the manufacturer or its designee; and barbiturates and minor tranquilizers.

Required the HHS secretary to update the list periodically to add or strike classes of drugs determined to be subject to clinical abuse or inappropriate use.

• **Prior Authorization.** Permitted states to impose "prior authorization" requirements for certain drugs, under which a state official would have to grant specific permission before a prescribed drug could be dispensed to the patient.

However, beginning July 1, 1991, states were required to have an official available to grant such permission 24 hours per day and had to ensure that patients had access to a 72-hour emergency supply of a prescribed drug. New drugs could not be subject to prior authorization requirements until after they had been available for six months.

• **Amount of Rebates.** In calendar 1991 and 1992, required rebates to be the difference between the average manufacturer price (AMP) and the lower of 12.5 percent or the "best price" at which the manufacturer sold the drug to any other customer except the Department of Veterans Affairs.

The average manufacturer price was defined as the average price paid to the manufacturer in the United States by wholesalers for drugs distributed to retail pharmacies. Rebates did not have to be higher than 25 percent of the AMP in calendar 1991 and 50 percent of the AMP in 1992. In calendar 1993 and thereafter, the rebate was the difference between the AMP and lower of 15 percent of the AMP or the manufacturer's "best price."

• **Single-Source Drugs.** Rebates for drugs available from only a single source and the original of a drug for which generic copies were available would include an inflation adjustment.

Prior to 1994, the adjustment would be made on a drug-by-drug basis; in 1994 and thereafter, the inflation adjustment would be made on an aggregate basis for each manufacturer's entire product line, weighted for the volume of sales in the state.

• **Multiple-Source Drugs.** Rebates for generic and over-the-counter drugs would be 10 percent of the AMP in each of calendar 1991 through 1993, and 11 percent of the AMP thereafter.

• **Pricing Information.** Required manufacturers, wholesalers and direct sellers of drugs to provide pricing information, subject to confidentiality restrictions. Violators were subject to fines of up to $100,000 for failure to provide information or for providing false information, and up to $10,000 per day for every day required information was late in being provided.

• **Electronic Point-of-Sale Systems.** Provided for a federal match of 90 percent for each of fiscal 1991 and 1992 to help states create mechanisms to electronically document and manage claims at the point-of-sale.

• **Generics Required.** Beginning July 1, 1991, prohibited federal matching payments for the original version of a drug available in generic form if a less expensive copy could have been dispensed.

• **Pharmacy Reimbursements.** Prohibited states from reducing payments to pharmacists for dispensing drugs to Medicaid patients for four years.

• **Prospective Drug Review.** Before any covered drug was dispensed to the patient, required that a review be performed to screen for potential problems caused by drug interactions, contra-indications, potentially serious interactions with non-prescription medications, incorrect dosage or duration of treatment, allergies, and potential misuse or abuse.

• **Retrospective Drug Review.** Required ongoing review, through a mechanized drug claims processing and information retrieval system, of claims data and other records to identify patterns of fraud, abuse, gross overuse, or inappropriate or medically unnecessary care among physicians, pharmacists and patients or associated with specific drugs or classes of drugs.

• **Education Programs.** Required states to operate outreach programs to educate physicians and pharmacists on common drug therapy problems with the aim of improving prescribing or dispensing practices.

Child Health

• **Phased-In Coverage of Children in Families with Incomes Below Poverty Level.** Beginning July 1, 1991, required states to begin to provide Medicaid coverage to all children born after Sept. 30, 1983, in families with incomes up to 100 percent of the federal poverty level. Thus, by 2002, all children up to age 19 would be covered.

• **Outreach.** Beginning July 1, 1991, required states to receive and process applications from children and pregnant women for Medicaid at locations other than welfare offices. Such alternate locations would have to include hospitals that served large numbers of low-income patients and community and migrant health centers.

• **Continuation of Benefits Throughout Pregnancy and First Year of Life.** Required states to continue to provide Medicaid coverage for low-income women for at least 60 days after they gave birth, even if they would otherwise lose eligibility because of a change in income. States would also have to continue Medicaid coverage for an infant born to a Medicaid-eligible woman throughout the first year of its life, so long as the infant remained in the mother's household and she would remain eligible if she was still pregnant.

Home- and Community-Based Elderly Care

• **Option to Provide Services.** Allowed states, at their option, to use Medicaid funds to provide home- and community-care services to Medicaid beneficiaries over age 65 who were "functionally disabled." Defined functionally disabled as meeting one of the following requirements:

(1) the person was unable to perform without substantial assistance two of the three daily-living activities of eating, moving about or going to the bathroom;

(2) the person had been diagnosed with Alzheimer's disease; and either was unable to perform without assistance or supervision at least two of the five activities of bathing, dressing, going to the bathroom, moving about or eating; or required supervision because he or she engaged in inappropriate behavior that posed serious health or safety hazards to himself or herself or others.

• **Types of Services.** Services provided could include homemaker/home health aide; chores; personal care; nursing care provided by or under the supervision of a registered nurse; respite care to allow family or other unpaid caregivers time off; training for family members in caring for the patient; adult day health; or certain mental health services.

• **Assessments, Care Plans.** Before a person could receive services, states would have to perform a comprehensive assessment to determine if the person was functionally disabled. The assessment would have to be reviewed and revised at least once a year. Care would have to be provided according to an individualized care plan.

• **Spending Limits.** Limited the amount of federal Medicaid funds that could be spent for such services to $40 million in fiscal 1991, $70 million in fiscal 1992, $130 million in fiscal 1993, $160 million in fiscal 1994 and $180 million in fiscal 1995.

Community Living Arrangements

• **Option to Provide Services.** Allowed up to eight states, at their option, to use Medicaid funds to provide "community supported living arrangements services" to individuals with mental retardation or a related condition that would permit them to live in the community instead of an institution.

Eligible states would be selected by the HHS secretary. To be eligible, individuals would have to be otherwise eligible for Medicaid and living with no more than three other individuals receiving services.

• **Types of Services.** Specific services provided could include personal assistance, training and rehabilitation needed to help the individual attain increased independence and productivity, 24-hour emergency assistance, assistive technology or adaptive equipment.

• **Spending Limits.** Limited the amount of federal Medicaid funds that could be spent for such services to $5 million in fiscal 1991, $10 million in fiscal 1992, $20 million in fiscal 1993, $30 million in fiscal 1994 and $35 million in fiscal 1995.

Miscellaneous

• **Required Payment of Premiums for Group Health Plans.** Beginning Jan. 1, 1991, required states to pay premiums and other cost-sharing for group health plans for which Medicaid beneficiaries could be eligible if enrollment in the group plan could save Medicaid money.

Required the HHS secretary to issue guidelines to determine cost-effectiveness. Beneficiaries could not be required to pay more for group coverage than if they were receiving only regular Medicaid benefits, and states would have to provide "wraparound" coverage to ensure that beneficiaries remained eligible for the full range of Medicaid-required services.

• **State Matching Payments.** Extended through Dec. 31, 1991, the moratorium on HHS regulations limiting states' ability to use donated funds to meet their matching requirement under Medicaid. Also provided that states would be able to use provider-specific taxes to help pay the state share of Medicaid costs, with certain restrictions.

• **Minimum Qualifications for Physicians.** Beginning Jan. 1, 1992, prohibited Medicaid payment to physicians for services provided to pregnant women and children under age 21 unless the physician was board-certified in family practice, pediatrics or obstetrics; had admitting privileges at a Medicaid-participating hospital; was a member of the National Health Service Corps; or had a documented consulting relationship with a certified family practitioner, pediatrician or obstetrician for purposes of providing specialized treatment or hospital admission. Physicians not meeting any of the above requirements could apply to the secretary for special certification.

• **Notice to State Medical Boards.** Required state Medicaid agencies to notify state licensing boards when a physician was terminated, suspended or sanctioned by Medicaid.

• **Required Continuation of Health Insurance Coverage.** Allowed state Medicaid programs to pay continuation premiums for people with incomes below 100 percent of the federal poverty level and assets less than twice the limit to qualify for benefits under the Supplemental Security Income program. The provision would apply only to people employed by firms with 75 or more workers, and states would have to determine that anticipated Medicaid savings would be larger than the cost of the premiums.

The fiscal 1986 budget-reconciliation bill (PL 99-272) had required that employers with 20 or more workers who provided group health insurance offer continued coverage for up to 18 months for certain former employees as long as the former employee paid the full premium plus 2 percent in administrative costs. The fiscal 1990 reconciliation bill (PL 101-239) had extended coverage to 29 months in certain cases, with the former employee to pay a premium of up to 150 percent of the employer's cost. *(Fiscal 1986 reconciliation, Congress and the Nation Vol. VII, p. 551; fiscal 1990 reconciliation, p. 43)*

• **German Reparations.** Excluded payments to Holocaust victims made by the Federal Republic of Germany from being counted as income in determining how much income an institutionalized Medicaid beneficiary had to contribute to the cost of his care.

• **Personal Care Services.** Allowed Minnesota, for fiscal 1991 through 1994, to use Medicaid funds to pay for the provision of personal care services (including helping with basic personal hygiene and administering medications) at home or elsewhere as long as they were prescribed by a physician, provided by a qualified person and supervised by a registered nurse. Beginning in fiscal 1995, all states were to be given the option of providing such personal care services.

• **Alcohol and Drug Treatment.** Clarified when states might use Medicaid funds to pay for substance abuse treatment.

• **Reciprocal Billing Arrangements.** Specifically allowed payment to a physician who arranged for services to be provided by another physician when the first physician was unavailable on an occasional, reciprocal basis.

• **Demonstration Projects for Low-Income Families.** Authorized $40 million over three years for up to four states to conduct three-year demonstration projects to test the effect on access to and costs of health care for uninsured families with incomes below 150 percent of poverty who were not otherwise eligible for Medicaid.

• **New Jersey Respite Care Demonstration.** Extended through Sept. 30, 1992, authority for a project in New Jersey that provided "respite" care for people who cared for Medicaid-eligible and other elderly and disabled people.

• **HIV Demonstration.** Authorized up to $30 million for three-year demonstration projects in two states to provide regular Medicaid coverage as well as additional services to people who tested positive for HIV (human immunodeficiency virus), the AIDS (acquired immune deficiency syndrome) virus.

Services in addition to those normally provided by Medicaid would include general and preventive medical care, prescription drugs, counseling and social services, substance abuse treatment, home care, case management, health education, respite care and dental services.

Medigap Regulation

In a move hailed by consumer advocates, Congress in 1990 greatly tightened federal regulation of so-called Medigap insurance, giving new protections to the millions of elderly people who relied on such policies to pay medical bills not fully covered by Medicare.

The provisions were part of the budget-reconciliation measure (HR 5835 — PL 101-508) cleared by Congress Oct. 27. *(Reconciliation, p. 55)*

The new rules required that Medicare beneficiaries be allowed to buy Medigap policies within the first six months they were eligible for Medicare, regardless of their health status. In an attempt to crack down on fraud in the industry, the bill also imposed civil penalties for the sale of duplicative policies and required that insurers pay rebates if policies failed to return specified percentages of each premium dollar in benefits.

Background

The immediate reason for the passage of the new Medigap rules was the elimination of the 1988 catastrophic coverage law, which had set up a new federal system for insuring seniors over and above their Medicare coverage. With the repeal of the law, experts said that new federal standards were needed. *(Catastrophic coverage repeal, p. 565)*

Analysts pointed to several problems with the Medigap industry that needed federal attention. One was the level of premiums, which were expected to rise with the repeal of the catastrophic coverage law. An even greater concern was the evidence of abuse and fraud in some parts of the industry. Consumer advocates argued that unscrupulous companies frequently sold policies to worried seniors that duplicated their existing coverage or, in the case of those eligible for Medicaid, provided coverage that they already could receive for free from the government.

One sign of the extent to which companies were taking advantage of the elderly, advocates said, was that many commercial policies were paying out in benefits less than 60 percent of the amounts they were taking in as premiums. The potential for abuse was particularly strong, the consumer groups said, in light of the widespread confusion among seniors about benefits and coverage. *Consumer Reports* magazine and other organizations also faulted as inadequate state regulation of Medigap policies, which was supposed to have been the bulwark of control ever since Congress passed the first Medigap regulation law in 1980 (PL 96-265). *(Congress and the Nation Vol. V, p. 645)*

Major Provisions

As enacted, the Medigap insurance provisions of the 1990 reconciliation bill (HR 5835 — PL 101-508):

• **Simplification.** Required all Medigap insurers to offer in their policies a core group of benefits. The specific benefits would be determined by the National Association of Insurance Commissioners (NAIC) or, if the association failed to develop such standards within nine months, by the secretary of health and human services (HHS).

Insurers also could sell policies including up to nine other packages of commonly offered benefits in addition to the core package (for a total of 10 different policies) but would have to offer to all individuals purchasing policies the option of buying a policy containing only the core benefits.

New or innovative benefits in addition to the approved packages could be offered but only if they were first approved by the state or the secretary. The secretary would have to review the simplification standards every three years to determine if changes were needed to accommodate new benefits.

The simplification standards generally would apply to new policies (not renewals) sold after the standards had been adopted by the state.

The secretary could waive the simplification requirements for states already operating simplification programs as of the date of enactment (Massachusetts, Minnesota and Wisconsin already had such programs in effect). Violators would be subject to fines of up to $25,000 for each violation.

Required the General Accounting Office to study the effectiveness of the simplification program on consumer protection, health benefit innovation, consumer choice and health care costs.

• **Uniform Policy Description.** Required that insurers provide to prospective customers a summary information sheet describing the policy's benefits and premium. To facilitate comparison of policies, the summary information had to be printed on a standardized form. Violators would be subject to fines of up to $25,000 for each violation.

• **Preventing Duplication.** Made it illegal to sell any Medigap policy without obtaining a written statement from the prospective purchaser detailing other Medigap policies the person owned and whether he or she was eligible for Medicaid. The form including the statement had to include:

(1) a statement to the effect that a Medicare beneficiary did not need more than one Medigap policy;

(2) a statement that individuals age 65 or older could be eligible for Medicaid and that Medicaid beneficiaries usually did not need Medigap policies at all (because Medicaid paid all health costs covered by Medigap policies);

(3) the telephone numbers of the state Medicaid office, a new toll-free number to be established by HHS that would provide information regarding Medicare, Medicaid and Medigap insurance;

(4) the address and any local telephone number of any state agency providing counseling services for health insurance or the telephone number of the state agency on aging.

Made it illegal to sell or issue a policy to any individual whose statement indicated that he or she already owned another Medigap policy or was entitled to Medicaid coverage.

It also would be illegal to sell a Medigap policy to a person who already owned another Medigap policy unless the buyer indicated in writing that the new policy would replace the old policy or the seller certified that, to the best of his or her knowledge, the new policy did not duplicate other coverage. In general, it made it illegal to sell Medigap policies to Medicaid beneficiaries. The law included an exception in cases in which the state Medicaid program paid the premium on the policy for the beneficiary.

Sellers of policies who violated the duplication rules would be liable for fines of up to $15,000 per violation, and companies who issued such policies would be liable for fines of up to $25,000 per violation.

• **Suspension of Policies While Eligible for Medicaid.** Required that at the request of the policyholder, Medigap benefits and premiums be suspended for up to 24 months if the policyholder became eligible for Medicaid. Should Medicaid eligibility be lost, the policy would have to be automatically reinstated.

• **Loss Ratios and Refund of Premium.** Increased to 65 percent from 60 percent the required projected loss ratio (the percentage of each premium dollar returned in benefits) for individual policies, including those sold through the mail or by mass media advertising. The required loss ratio for group policies would remain at 75 percent. Allowed states to require higher loss ratios.

Required companies to submit annually to state regulators (or HHS, in the case of states without an approved program) information on actual loss ratios. To facilitate comparison, the information would have to be compiled using a standardized methodology and be submitted on a standardized form developed by the NAIC.

Companies whose policies failed to meet the required loss ratios would have to provide a proportional refund or a credit against future premiums, including interest, to policyholders to make up the difference between the required and actual loss ratio. Violators would be subject to fines of up to $25,000 for each violation.

Required states to report to HHS annually on Medigap loss ratios of policies sold in the state and the use of sanctions to enforce the requirements. Beginning in 1993, the

Pepper Commission

A bipartisan, 15-member commission in 1990 issued recommendations on providing health insurance coverage for all Americans and on long-term care for the elderly. The proposals, however, had no discernible impact because the commission was sundered by partisan and philosophical divisions.

The commission was established as the U.S. Bipartisan Commission on Comprehensive Health Care in the 1988 catastrophic coverage law (PL 100-360). It was renamed the Pepper Commission upon the death of its first chairman, Rep. Claude Pepper, D-Fla. Sen. John D. Rockefeller, D-W.Va., succeeded Pepper as chairman. Although most of the 1988 law was repealed in 1989, lawmakers preserved the authorization for the commission. *(PL 100-360, Congress and the Nation Vol. VII, p. 561; 1989 repeal, p. 565; Pepper profile, box, p. 919)*

The panel called for creation of a new public health plan to replace the state-federal Medicaid program for basic health care, including hospital treatment, doctor bills and preventive care. The aim was to assist the estimated 31 million to 37 million without health insurance in gaining access to health care. The plan stipulated various tax incentives and subsidies to encourage businesses to provide health insurance to their workers; advocated changes in private insurance to prevent companies from refusing to cover those most likely to need it; and urged expanded federal health coverage of the poorest Americans. If, after five years, at least 80 percent of small business employees still lacked health insurance coverage, a "pay or play" system would kick in, which would require employers either to provide workers with health insurance or to pay into a special fund from which insurance would be provided.

The commission also recommended that a largely federal program be created to provide long-term health care for all Americans, regardless of age. The program would help pay for home care for all severely disabled individuals and would pay for three months of care in a nursing home.

The cost of both proposals to the federal government was estimated at $66.2 billion per year, but the commission members could not reach consensus on how to cover the tab. The Bush administration, meanwhile, was reluctant to support a program that required a large infusion of new revenue.

---

secretary would have to report to Congress annually regarding loss ratios and use of sanctions and provide a list of policies that failed to meet the loss-ratio requirements.

• **Guaranteed Renewability.** Required that Medigap policies be guaranteed renewable and not be canceled solely for reasons of health status or for any other reason except non-payment of premiums or material misrepresentation.

If group policies were canceled by the group and not replaced, required that policyholders be offered individual policies with equivalent benefits. If a group policy was canceled and replaced by a different group policy, required that the new policy not exclude coverage based on any pre-existing condition that would have been covered under the old policy.

Violators would be subject to fines of up to $25,000 for each violation.

• **Pre-Existing Condition Limitations and Limitations on Medical Underwriting.** Required an "open enrollment" period of six months after a person age 65 or older became eligible for Medicare Part B, during which he or she could purchase any individual Medigap policy sold in the state and could not be turned down or be charged higher premiums because of medical or health status.

Such policies could exclude benefits for the first six months based on pre-existing conditions for which the policyholder was diagnosed or received treatment during the six months immediately before the policy became effective. However, policies that replaced similar policies in effect for at least six months could not impose pre-existing condition restrictions, or waiting, elimination or probationary periods. Violators would be subject to fines of up to $25,000 for each violation.

• **Prior Approval of Policies/Enforcement of Standards.** Beginning July 1, 1991, required all Medigap policies to be approved in advance either by the state, if the state had in place a regulatory program approved by HHS, or by HHS in states with no such program. Required the secretary to review periodically state regulatory programs to ensure that they remained in compliance with the required standards.

To be approved by HHS, required states to have in place a process to review proposed premium increases, including the holding of public hearings before approval of premium increases.

• **Medicare 'Select' Policies.** Authorized a three-year demonstration program in up to 15 states in which policies could be sold that otherwise met the requirements except that certain benefits and services would only be available through selected health care providers.

• **Health Insurance Information, Counseling and Assistance Grants.** Required HHS to establish a health insurance advisory service program to assist Medicare beneficiaries with the receipt of services related to Medicare, Medicaid and other health insurance programs.

The program would provide information regarding eligibility, benefits, payment processes, rights and appeals processes, linkages between Medicare and Medicaid, and other information.

The program would have to provide information on private insurance plans regarding federal standards, ways to make informed decisions about purchasing such plans and any other information deemed appropriate by the secretary.

Authorized $10 million for each of fiscal 1991, 1992 and 1993 (to be paid from the Medicare Hospital Insurance Trust Fund) for a series of grant programs to help states create and operate information, counseling and assistance programs to help Medicare beneficiaries obtain appropriate health insurance coverage.

- **Medicare and Medigap Information by Telephone.** Required the secretary to make the program known to those eligible to use it, as well as to set up a toll-free telephone number to provide information and counseling. Also authorized a five-state demonstration project in which statewide toll-free numbers would be set up to provide information regarding Medicare, Medicaid and Medigap policies available in that state.

Food Labeling

Responding to consumer groups' calls for controls on advertising of health claims for food, Congress in 1990 cleared legislation (HR 3562 — PL 101-535) that for the first time ordered manufacturers to display detailed nutritional information on most packaged food items and some seafood.

The measure prohibited manufacturers from making certain nutritional claims about their products on the label — for example, "high fiber" — when other equally important nutritional information, such as cholesterol level, was not mentioned. Manufacturers also were barred from making health claims for food if they were not verified by the Food and Drug Administration. In addition, the Department of Health and Human Services was directed to come up with standards for such terms as "natural" or "low-fat," which then could be used only if the products met the standards.

Under the legislation, most packaged food products would have to provide specific information on the amounts of fat, saturated fat, cholesterol, sodium, fiber, protein and carbohydrates per each serving portion. Retailers were required to provide similar information for 20 types of raw agricultural products and raw fish.

The bill pre-empted a variety of state nutrition labeling laws but allowed states to require their own labeled health warnings.

In 1992, the Bush administration issued regulations concerning food labeling. *(Story, box, p. 604)*

Legislative Action

With the support of the Bush administration and consumer groups, the food labeling measure moved relatively easily through Congress.

Perhaps the most controversial issue concerned the measure's pre-emption of state standards. Manufacturers argued that a single, national set of standards was necessary to prevent the expense of having to provide different information for products sold in different states. But consumer groups opposed pre-emption, contending that states should have the right to impose more stringent standards if they wanted — for example, a tough California law requiring disclosure of carcinogens.

The Senate Labor and Human Resources Committee approved its labeling bill (S 1425) on April 25, with five Republican members voting against it.

The House Energy and Commerce Committee approved HR 3562 by voice vote May 16, formally reporting the measure (H Rept 101-538) June 13. The only roll-call vote came on an amendment offered by Thomas A. Luken, D-Ohio, to exempt fresh fish, fruit and vegetables from the labeling requirement. The amendment was rejected on a 19-24 vote.

The House passed HR 3562 by voice vote July 30, with little debate and no opposition. The bill as passed contained compromise language, worked out with a number of industry groups, slightly broadening the pre-emption of state standards while still leaving states the right to require ingredient warnings.

After informal negotiations, a modified version of the House measure was passed by the Senate on Oct. 24. The House accepted the changes Oct. 26, clearing the bill. President Bush signed HR 3562 on Nov. 8.

'Orphan' Drug Veto

President Bush on Nov. 8, 1990, pocket-vetoed legislation (HR 4638) amending rules governing rights to "orphan" drugs developed to combat rare diseases.

The bill represented a lengthy attempt at compromise between congressional health leaders and the drug industry to amend the Orphan Drug Act (PL 97-414), which granted incentives to companies to develop drugs for diseases that afflicted fewer than 200,000 people. *(Congress and the Nation Vol. VI, p. 536)*

The 1983 law had been passed amid evidence that many promising drugs were not brought to market because potential sales were considered too small to pay back the substantial costs of going through the federal drug-approval process. The law, which granted exclusive marketing rights for seven years to developers of orphan drugs, was generally seen as successful in meeting the goal of expanded availability. However, some analysts argued that companies were taking advantage of the law to gain windfall profits, either by charging high prices with no fear of competition or by seeing the market base expand.

As introduced, HR 4638 would have revoked the exclusive marketing rights to profitable drugs already on the market. After compromises with the drug industry, the final measure would have let market exclusivity be shared in the future, while preserving exclusive rights for drugs already on the market or in development. Exclusive rights also would have been opened if a disease affected more than 200,000 people.

Legislative Action

The House Energy and Commerce Committee approved HR 4638 (H Rept 101-635) on July 17 and reported it July 27. The bill passed the House by voice vote under suspension of the rules July 30.

The Senate Labor and Human Resources Committee approved S 2576, which was identical to HR 4638, on Sept. 26. The full Senate passed HR 4638 by voice vote on Oct. 12, and the House cleared the measure Oct. 23.

Although the administration had expressed doubts about the need for the legislation, Bush's veto was a surprise to many. In his memorandum of disapproval, Bush expressed "serious concerns" that weakening the exclusivity language of the 1983 law would "certainly discourage development of desperately needed new orphan drugs."

Medical Device Regulation

Congress in 1990 overhauled federal regulation of medical devices in legislation (HR 3095 — PL 101-629) requiring the Food and Drug Administration (FDA) to upgrade its procedures for approving all such equipment.

The legislation aimed at streamlining the marketing approval process for new devices, which included everything from tongue depressors to heart-lung machines. It also sought to improve the oversight of equipment already on the market and to make recalling defective products easier.

The House in 1988 passed a similar bill. *(Congress and the Nation Vol. VII, p. 596)*

The basic federal law overseeing medical devices was cleared by Congress in 1976 (PL 94-295). But that measure, which required that devices be classified on the basis of their potential to cause serious injury or death, had inadvertently created a large loophole through which most new products reached the market without undergoing the regular approval process. The loophole was that most risky medical devices, known as Class III devices, could be sold without FDA review if they were deemed to be "substantially equivalent" to a device already on the market at the time the law was enacted. Another problem was that studies had shown that the FDA had inadequate procedures for reporting when problems or injuries were caused by different types of equipment. *(PL 94-295, Congress and the Nation Vol. IV, p. 366)*

HR 3095 required the FDA to review the safety of all Class III devices by 1995 if they had not been previously screened. To tackle the reporting problem, the bill required that users of medical devices report to the FDA or the product manufacturer when a product caused a serious injury or death. The bill provided for civil penalties of up to $15,000, with a $1 million ceiling for all penalties, for violations of the new mandates.

The Senate Labor and Human Resources Committee reported its medical devices bill (S 3006 — S Rept 101-513) on Sept. 26, and the Energy and Commerce Committee approved HR 3095 (H Rept 101-808) the same day.

The House passed HR 3095 by voice vote on Oct. 10. The Senate passed the bill, after substituting the text of S 3006, on Oct. 12.

Conferees had to resolve a difference between the House bill, which called for civil penalties for violations, and the Senate measure, which did not. The compromise agreement (H Rept 101-959) imposed a modified version of the penalty provisions in the House bill.

The House adopted the conference report by voice vote Oct. 26, and the Senate followed suit the following day. President Bush signed the measure Nov. 28.

Congress in 1992 cleared legislation delaying implementation of parts of PL 101-629. *(Story, p. 607)*

Radiation Victims Compensation

Redressing the sufferings of some of the forgotten victims of the Cold War, Congress in 1990 cleared legislation (HR 2372 — PL 101-426) to compensate Americans who developed cancer because they lived downwind from open-air nuclear tests in the 1950s or mined the uranium used in nuclear weapons.

The bill authorized payments of $50,000 per person for fallout victims in three Western states and $100,000 per person for uranium miners in five states who developed cancer or respiratory diseases. Family members could collect compensation for those who had died of radiation-induced illnesses. The money would come from a $100 million special Radiation Exposure Trust Fund authorized under the bill.

The "downwinders" eligible for compensation were persons who lived in certain counties of Nevada, Utah and Arizona for at least two years in the period from Jan. 21, 1951, to Oct. 31, 1958, or during July 1962. That was when the United States conducted above-ground nuclear tests in Nevada without warning the civilian population. Eligible miners were those who worked in uranium mines in Colorado, New Mexico, Arizona, Wyoming or Utah between 1947 and 1971 and were exposed to unsafe levels of radiation. Roughly 1,000 downwinders and 500 miners, many of them Navajo Indians, were estimated to be eligible for compensation under the bill.

Although President Bush signed the legislation, his administration and previous Democratic and Republican administrations had opposed compensation, arguing that no proof existed that illnesses suffered by downwinders and miners were caused by radiation exposure.

The House Judiciary Committee approved HR 2372 on March 28 and reported it (H Rept 101-463) on April 25. The House passed the bill by voice vote June 5.

The Senate Labor and Human Resources Committee reported its version (S 2466 — S Rept 101-264) on April 19. The Senate passed an amended HR 2372 on Aug. 2 by voice vote. The House accepted the Senate changes Sept. 27, clearing the measure. Bush signed the bill Oct. 15.

FDA Consolidation

Legislation (S 845 — PL 101-635) cleared in 1990 that aimed to revitalize the Food and Drug Administration (FDA) by automating some activities and consolidating its 23 offices in the Washington, D.C., area into one facility.

The legislation allowed FDA to centralize its operations at a single campus, similar to one occupied by the National Institutes of Health in Bethesda, Md. To enable the FDA to create such a single administrative and laboratory complex, the bill authorized $100 million in fiscal 1991. The bill also authorized the FDA to pay higher salaries for senior biomedical scientists and to move toward creation of an automated system for handling its huge number of drug applications each year.

Backers of the bill said the agency needed new help to handle its vast workload, which had brought it under fire from members of Congress on issues ranging from approval of new AIDS (acquired immune deficiency syndrome) drugs to enforcement of food labeling regulations.

The Senate Labor and Human Resources Committee approved S 845 on Nov. 1, 1989, and reported it (S Rept 101-242) on Feb. 1, 1990. The Senate passed the bill by voice vote on Oct. 24, and the House followed suit on Oct. 27, clearing the measure. President Bush signed S 845 (PL 101-635) on Nov. 28.

Nursing Home Regulation

Congress in 1990 responded to complaints by states and the nursing home industry about delays in promulgating regulations to implement the 1987 nursing home reform law by limiting financial penalties against states that had made good-faith efforts to comply prior to the issuance of two principal sets of rules in May 1989.

The provisions were included in the fiscal 1991 budget-reconciliation bill (HR 5835 — PL 101-508). *(Reconciliation, p. 55)*

The 1987 provisions, part of an omnibus reconciliation measure (PL 100-203), had tightened regulation of nursing homes certified to participate in the Medicare and Medicaid programs. The law imposed training requirements for nurses' aides, mandated preadmission screening and required preparation of individual treatment plans each year for nursing home residents. *(Congress and the Nation Vol. VII, p. 591)*

However, the Department of Health and Human Services was slow in issuing rules to implement the law. Although Congress in the 1989 reconciliation bill (HR 3299 — PL 101-239) granted a delay on some of the law's deadlines, states continued to complain about the cost of compliance and the uncertainty produced by delays in the regulations. *(1989 action, p. 43)*

As enacted, the nursing home reform amendments in the 1990 reconciliation bill:

- Prohibited the secretary of health and human services (HHS) from taking punitive actions against states that had made a good-faith effort to comply with the nurse's aide training requirements before May 12, 1989, the effective date of the HHS guidelines. The secretary also was prohibited from taking action against states that made good-faith efforts to comply with rules relating to preadmission screening of patients and annual resident reviews before May 26, 1989.
- Prohibited from operating their own nurse's aide training programs nursing homes that, within the previous two years, had been subject to certain sanctions, including civil fines of $5,000 or more or having had payment denied by Medicare or Medicaid or residents transferred because of substandard care.

Also prohibited from operating their own training programs were facilities that had operated under a waiver permitting them to have a licensed nurse on duty less often than 24 hours per day, five days per week.

- Extended until Oct. 1, 1990, authority for enhanced federal matching rates (up to 90 percent) to help states pay the cost of training nurses' aides or assessing the competency of those already working in the field. The authority had expired July 1, 1990, when the federal payment was to revert to a flat 50 percent.
- Modified the definition of mental illness to target preadmission screening rules on patients with serious disorders.
- Extended from four to 14 days the period during which a nursing home would have to complete the initial assessment of a newly admitted resident.
- Clarified conditions under which states could grant nursing homes waivers of the nurse staffing rules, which generally required facilities to have on duty a licensed nurse 24 hours per day, seven days per week. Allowed waivers only to the extent that a facility could not recruit adequate staff and required that notice of any nurse staffing waiver be given to residents, their families and appropriate state agencies.
- Required that results of inspections be made available to the public within 14 days of the time they were made available to the nursing home and that approved plans to correct any deficiencies found also be made available.
- Required the secretary to establish requirements for social workers, dieticians and other "activities" professionals that were at least as strict as those applicable to such professionals before enactment of the nursing home reform law.

Childhood Vaccines

Congress in 1990 cleared legislation (HR 4238 — PL 101-502) to reauthorize the federal program that helped pay for childhood vaccines. The measure also altered a 1986 law (PL 99-660) providing compensation to families of children injured or killed as a result of adverse vaccine reactions. *(1986 law, Congress and the Nation Vol. VII, p. 547)*

The bill provided a $205 million authorization in fiscal 1991, and an open-ended authorization in fiscal 1992-95, for the Centers for Disease Control program that paid for vaccines. The amount was intended to pay for a double dose of measles vaccine and to fund outreach programs to find children who were not being immunized against childhood diseases.

In addition, HR 4238 authorized $5 million in 1991 and open-ended amounts in 1992-95 to maintain a six-month supply of vaccine and $30 million in 1991 for the National Vaccine Program, which coordinated research, licensing and distribution of vaccines.

The bill extended for four months — from Oct. 1, 1990 — the deadline for families of children killed or injured by vaccines before Oct. 1, 1988, to apply for benefits under the vaccine compensation program.

HR 4238 was approved by the House Energy and Commerce Committee on May 15. The House passed the bill under suspension of the rules by voice vote July 23.

A companion measure (S 2629) was approved by the Senate Labor and Human Resources Committee on May 16. The Senate passed a compromise version of HR 4238 by voice vote on Oct. 12, and the House cleared the measure on Oct. 16. President Bush signed it Nov. 3.

TB Prevention

Legislation (HR 4273 — PL 101-368) cleared in 1990 that extended the Centers for Disease Control program of grants to health services to prevent tuberculosis.

The bill authorized $36 million in fiscal 1991 and open-ended funding in fiscal 1992-95 for the program. HR 4273 also established an advisory council to provide advice on eliminating the disease, which health officials said was on the rise in the United States, killing an estimated 2,000 people a year.

The House Energy and Commerce Committee reported HR 4273 (H Rept 101-542) on June 16. The Senate Labor and Human Resources Committee reported a companion bill (S 2630 — S Rept 101-372) on July 17.

The House passed HR 4273 by voice vote under suspension of the rules June 18, and the Senate passed the bill by voice vote Aug. 4. President Bush signed it Aug. 15.

Health Service Corps

A bill (HR 4487 — PL 101-597) reauthorizing the National Health Service Corps (NHSC) through fiscal 1993 cleared in 1990.

The NHSC offered incentives to doctors and other health professionals to practice in medically underserved areas, such as inner-city neighborhoods and Indian reservations. The program provided scholarships to medical students and repaid the loans of health providers who agreed to work in underserved areas.

The bill authorized $63.9 million for the program in 1991 and provided open-ended funding for the next two years.

HR 4487 also increased from $20,000 to $35,000 the annual amount that could be repaid through the loan program. It required that at least 30 percent of the appropriations be used for scholarships, instead of loan repayments, and reserved at least 10 percent of funding for scholarships for nurse practitioners, nurse midwives and physician assistants.

Backers of the legislation said it was needed to revive the NHSC, which they argued had become nearly moribund under the Reagan administration. By the late 1980s, few health professionals were joining the corps as new members.

Legislative Action

The House Energy and Commerce Committee reported HR 4487 (H Rept 101-642) on July 30. Before approving the bill June 28, the panel adopted an amendment by Edward R. Madigan, R-Ill., to substantially scale back the bill. The bill as approved earlier by the Health and the Environment Subcommittee had reauthorized the corps through 2000. But Madigan's amendment extended the program for only three years and set the authorization level at $63.9 million, the amount requested by the Bush administration. Madigan's amendment also lowered the percentage of funds set aside for medical school scholarships. Congressional Democrats favored shifting funds to scholarships, while the administration preferred repaying medical school loans for personnel in the corps.

The House passed HR 4487 by voice vote under suspension of the rules on July 30.

The Senate Labor and Human Resources Committee approved its NHSC bill (S 2617) on May 16 and reported it (S Rept 101-370) on July 16. The Senate by voice vote passed an amended HR 4487 on Aug. 4.

The House adopted the conference report (H Rept 101-945) on Oct. 26. The Senate followed suit the next day, clearing the legislation for President Bush, who signed it Nov. 16.

Minority Health Programs

Spurred by strong evidence that members of minority groups suffered disproportionately high rates of cancer, heart attacks, AIDS (acquired immune deficiency syndrome) and other diseases, Congress in 1990 cleared legislation (HR 5702 — PL 101-527) aimed at improving the health status of disadvantaged members of minority groups and increasing their role in the health professions.

The legislation contained a number of proposals that were part of a minority health initiative developed by the Bush administration, including a provision to give communities federal funding to pay for health training for local residents in exchange for a service commitment.

HR 5702 authorized $112 million in fiscal 1991 for the new programs, including one to make health care more accessible to residents of public housing. It also authorized through fiscal 1994 the Public Health Service's community and migrant health centers. The legislation expanded the funding and responsibilities of the Office of Minority Health within the Department of Health and Human Services.

The Senate Labor and Human Resources Committee reported a minority health bill (S 1606) on Nov. 17, 1989 (S Rept 101-211). The bill, passed by the Senate on a voice vote Nov. 20, authorized $451 million over three years to enlarge and coordinate programs aimed at preventing disease and promoting health among minorities.

The version of the legislation approved by the House Energy and Commerce Committee (HR 5702 — H Rept 101-804) on Sept. 26, 1990, and reported Oct. 5 was considerably smaller in scope. The House passed the bill by voice vote under suspension of the rules on Oct. 10, and the Senate accepted HR 5702 on Oct. 16.

President Bush signed the bill on Nov. 6.

AIDS

Legislation (S 2240 — PL 101-381) cleared in 1990 that authorized $875 million in fiscal 1991 for programs aimed at helping health and social service organizations cope with the mounting costs of the AIDS (acquired immune deficiency syndrome) epidemic.

Although he expressed concerns about the "narrow, disease-specific approach" of the legislation, President Bush signed the measure into law on Aug. 18.

As of July 30, 1990, according to the U.S. Public Health Service, 143,286 cases of AIDS had been recorded in the United States, and 87,644 of those people had died. An estimated 1 million Americans were infected with HIV (human immunodeficiency virus), which causes AIDS.

Backers of the bill said its primary purpose was to increase the availability of non-institutional care for persons with AIDS and related conditions. One reason the disease was taking such a heavy financial toll on many cities was that AIDS patients ended up in hospitals because they had nowhere else to go to get care, even though they frequently did not need the intensive care provided in a hospital.

To help provide options for alternative care, the bill created a series of grant programs, some of which were to go exclusively to areas with the most confirmed cases of AIDS, some to states and others directly to public or private non-profit health care and social service providers.

Although concern over the heavy financial burden of frequently uninsured AIDS patients on urban health facilities spurred broad support for S 2240 in Congress, the legislation faced criticism from conservatives in both the Senate and House. As he had on previous AIDS bills, Sen. Jesse Helms, R-N.C., contended that the crisis was being overstated by a powerful AIDS lobby and funding was being drained from other serious diseases. In the House, consideration of the legislation was dominated by debate over restrictive amendments offered by William E. Dannemeyer, R-Calif., an outspoken opponent of homosexuality.

Senate Action

The Senate Labor and Human Resources Committee approved S 2240 on April 4 and reported it (S Rept 101-273) on April 24. The bill authorized $1.2 billion in fiscal years 1991-92 for grants to hard-hit urban areas and to states.

The Senate passed S 2240 by a 95-4 vote on May 16. Before final passage, sponsors had to overcome determined resistance from a small group of conservative Republicans, who forced a cloture vote before the bill could come to the floor and kept the Senate at work for two full days on the measure. The May 15 cloture vote was 95-3.

The most significant amendment adopted by the Senate directed states to have programs to enable public health officials to notify sexual partners of those testing positive for HIV. The amendment gave states the option of putting such programs into effect, however.

The Senate also approved 98-0 an amendment, offered by Edward M. Kennedy, D-Mass., to bar use of funds to provide clean needles to intravenous drug users, after rejecting on a 28-70 vote a Helms amendment to bar funds for both needles and bleach, which was often used to cleanse needles to prevent transmission of the virus.

Also rejected, 33-65, was an amendment by Malcom Wallop, R-Wyo., to allow states with fewer than 100 reported AIDS cases to use grant funds for other chronic diseases.

House Action

Action in the House Energy and Commerce Committee on the House companion bill (HR 4470) was dominated by debate over restrictive amendments offered by Dannemeyer.

In the Health and the Environment Subcommittee, Dannemeyer successfully offered an amendment to require states to make knowing transmission of HIV a crime. However, the subcommittee rejected a Dannemeyer amendment to require hospitals to offer AIDS tests routinely to patients and require states to encourage testing of marriage license applicants in high-risk areas.

In the full committee, which considered the legislation in the form of a clean bill (HR 4785), Dannemeyer offered an amendment to require states to report to public health authorities the names of those who tested positive for HIV. The amendment was rejected.

As approved by the Energy and Commerce Committee May 15, the bill (H Rept 101-511) authorized more than $1.6 billion for fiscal 1991-92.

On the House floor, Dannemeyer renewed his effort to require reporting to state officials of the names of those testing positive. But members instead approved on a 312-113 vote a substitute amendment, offered by J. Roy Rowland, D-Ga., to give states the option of requiring name reporting. The House subsequently adopted Dannemeyer's amendment, as amended by Rowland, on a 422-1 vote June 13.

Rejected by voice vote was an amendment by Dan Burton, R-Ind., to require universal annual blood testing for AIDS.

The House passed HR 4785 on a 408-14 vote June 13, then passed S 2240 by voice vote after substituting the text of HR 4785.

Conference Action

In the conference committee, House and Senate sponsors had to resolve differences over both money and the basic approach to funding. Conferees easily resolved most of the issues facing them, adopting a compromise that included the Senate block grant program to states and the House initiative to provide funding for early intervention services. However, conferees also had to stand firm against criticisms from the Bush administration, which warned that the measure "sets a dangerous precedent, inviting treatment of other diseases through similar ad hoc arrangements."

Both the House and Senate adopted the conference report (H Rept 101-652) by voice vote on Aug. 4, clearing the measure.

Major Provisions

Following are the major provisions of PL 101-381, the Ryan White Comprehensive AIDS Resources Emergency Act of 1990:

- Provided a new program of emergency relief grants for areas heavily hit by AIDS, defined as metropolitan areas with more than 2,000 reported cases of the disease or with a high percentage of the population affected.
- Authorized $275 million for the program in fiscal 1991-92, and provided open-ended funding through fiscal 1995.
- Required that the funds be distributed to public or private non-profit hospitals and other health care facilities to deliver HIV-related outpatient and ambulatory health and support services.
- Required that patients with incomes above the federal poverty level be required to pay for a portion of the services they received, according to a percentage of their income.
- Authorized $275 million in fiscal 1991-92 and open-ended funding through fiscal 1995 for a program of grants to states to enable them to improve the quality and availability of services to persons with HIV disease.
- Required states that received large grants under the program to provide matching funding from other sources.
- Required that states use at least 15 percent of their funds to provide services to infants, children, women and families with HIV disease.
- Authorized $230 million in fiscal 1991 and open-ended funding through fiscal 1995 for grants to states to provide early intervention services for persons who had AIDS, had tested positive for HIV or were considered at risk for contracting the virus.
- Directed states to use the funding for such services as blood testing for exposure to HIV, testing of the extent of immune system deficiency, referrals to providers of health and social services, and medical evaluations.
- Required states to set up public information programs to inform persons who received blood transfusions between 1978 and 1985 of the availability of early intervention services.
- Required states to establish procedures for notifying sexual partners of those with HIV disease.
- Required states to have laws adequate to provide for the prosecution of anyone who had sexual contact, shared hypodermic needles or donated blood with the specific intention of exposing another person to HIV.
- Authorized $75 million in fiscal 1991, and open-ended funding through fiscal 1995, for grants to public and private non-profit entities for early intervention and outpatient services.
- Required states to ensure the confidentiality of HIV testing information and to establish programs for counseling for those being tested for the virus.
- Authorized $20 million in fiscal 1991 and open-ended funding through fiscal 1995 for demonstration grants to

develop therapeutic drugs and provide services to pediatric AIDS patients.

- Authorized $1.5 million in fiscal 1991 and open-ended funding through fiscal 1995 for materials and information designed to improve the safety of the blood supply.
- Authorized $5 million in each of fiscal years 1991-95 for grants to states to aid in protecting police, fire and other emergency workers against exposure to HIV.

Organ, Bone Marrow Programs

Legislation (S 2946 — PL 101-616) to renew and improve programs to match organ and bone marrow donors with patients in need became law in 1990.

The measure sought to strengthen the National Bone Marrow Donor Registry with new initiatives and money in hopes of building the list to 250,000 potential donors. The registry was a file of potential volunteers whose marrow could be matched with that of a victim of leukemia or other diseases.

S 2946 authorized $15 million in fiscal 1991 for the registry and $8 million in 1991 and open-ended funding in 1992-93 for the Department of Health and Human Services (HHS) Division of Organ Transplantation.

The bill also contained provisions aimed at fostering better coordination between the national bone marrow registry and private registries that met quality standards to be established by HHS.

In addition, the measure called for increasing the number of ethnic and racial minority members in the registries.

Although two earlier laws enacted in 1984 (PL 98-507) and 1988 (PL 100-607) encouraged organ and marrow donations, key lawmakers believed more steps were needed to increase the number of potential donors. *(1984, Congress and the Nation Vol. VI, p. 549; 1988 law, Congress and the Nation Vol. VII, p. 572)*

The House Energy and Commerce Committee approved its bone marrow measure (HR 5146) on June 27 and reported it (H Rept 101-614) on July 23. The House passed the bill by voice vote under suspension of the rules July 23.

The Senate Labor and Human Resources Committee approved S 2946 on Aug. 1 and formally reported the measure (S Rept 101-530) on Oct. 12. The bill as reported contained a provision, not in the House bill, authorizing funds to help transplant patients cover the high costs of anti-rejection immunosuppressive drugs.

House and Senate members worked out a compromise between the two bills without a conference. The final agreement dropped the Senate provision on transplant drugs.

The Senate passed the compromise version of S 2946 by voice vote on Oct. 25, and the House followed suit, clearing the measure, Oct. 26. President Bush signed the legislation on Nov. 16.

Emergency Services

Legislation (HR 1602 — PL 101-590) seeking to beef up emergency care nationwide for the victims of accidents and violent crime was cleared by Congress in 1990.

The legislation authorized $60 million in fiscal 1991 and open-ended funding in fiscal 1992-93 for grants to states to develop and implement regional trauma care and emergency medical networks.

Backers of the legislation said new federal help was needed because, while studies had shown that trauma systems could dramatically reduce the rates of death and disability for injured people, such care was very expensive. Because of financial losses in providing such treatment to injured persons, many of whom were uninsured, many hospitals were withdrawing from existing trauma care systems.

However, the bill barred states from using funds to pay for uninsured trauma care until they had emergency medical systems in place, including in rural areas.

The House Energy and Commerce Committee reported HR 1602 on Nov. 13, 1989 (H Rept 101-346). The House passed the bill by voice vote under suspension of the rules Nov. 14.

The Senate Labor and Human Resources Committee approved its bill (S 15) on Feb. 28, 1990, and reported it (S Rept 101-292) on May 15. The Senate passed S 15 on Oct. 18, then passed HR 1602 the next day, after substituting the text of S 15.

The House adopted the conference report (H Rept 101-956) by voice vote on Oct. 26, and the Senate followed suit the following day, thus clearing the bill. President Bush signed the measure Nov. 16.

NIH Reauthorization

After stripping out all controversial provisions, Congress late in the 1990 session cleared legislation (S 2857 — PL 101-613) to authorize certain programs at the National Institutes of Health (NIH).

The bill as cleared authorized creation of a new, nongovernmental National Foundation for Biomedical Research to support the work of senior scientists at NIH. In addition, the bill established a National Center for Rehabilitation Research within the National Institute on Child Health and Human Development.

However, S 2857 did not contain what had been intended to be its primary provisions — language reauthorizing NIH's largest entities, the National Cancer Institute and the National Heart, Lung and Blood Institute. Sponsors decided to wait until 1991 to pass those provisions, knowing that the work of the institutes could go on through funding in the regular, annual appropriations bill for the Department of Health and Human Services (HHS).

Moreover, S 2857 contained neither controversial House provisions to overturn an NIH ban on certain types of fetal research nor provisions in both chambers' bills authorizing new research on infertility and contraception. The Bush administration had objected to the provisions on the grounds that they might encourage abortion. Also dropped were provisions intended to eliminate sex and race bias in NIH-funded research and to provide new research on women's health.

Efforts to enact a full NIH reauthorization bill in the 102nd Congress failed. *(Story, p. 602)*

Senate Action

During consideration of the NIH legislation, the Senate Labor and Human Resources Committee focused on women's health. Responding to studies showing that women had systematically been excluded from much of the research funded by NIH, the bill included a half-dozen initiatives aimed at increasing scientific attention to women's health needs.

Controversy also was stirred by the addition of the provisions of S 2215, authorizing research into infertility and contraception. The proposal by Tom Harkin, D-Iowa, adopted on a 10-6 vote, was criticized by abortion opponents, who warned that it would open the door to federal funding of research on RU 486, the abortion-inducing drug used in France. The panel rejected, on a 4-12 vote, an amendment by Daniel R. Coats, R-Ind., to bar all research on drugs or devices, including RU 486, known to terminate pregnancy after implantation of a fertilized ovum into a woman's uterus.

The women's health provisions of S 2857 included codification of an existing NIH policy encouraging the use of women and minorities in clinical drug studies. The bill also created an Office of Women's Health Research and Development in NIH, required NIH to establish a research program on gynecology and required the NIH director to submit an annual report on progress on women's health issues.

The committee approved the bill Aug. 1 and reported it (S Rept 101-459) Sept. 12.

On the Senate floor, sponsors faced the possibility that resistance from abortion opponents would block the bill. So they moved to drop the provisions on infertility research. The Senate then passed the bill by voice vote Oct. 19.

House, Final Action

In the House Energy and Commerce Committee, the most controversy surrounded an effort by Henry A. Waxman, D-Calif., to lift the existing ban on research involving transplants of tissue from aborted fetuses.

Scientists had been using fetal tissue for decades. Cell lines derived from fetuses were instrumental in developing vaccines for polio, for example. By 1990, many scientists had hopes that fetal tissue transplants could treat such diseases as juvenile diabetes and Parkinson's. Debate over abortion, however, had virtually halted federal regulation and funding of most types of fetal research. Over the course of more than a decade, Congress and HHS had imposed a variety of funding bans and moratoriums on fetal research.

The most publicized of the fetal research bans was a 1988 moratorium on fetal tissue transplants opposed by HHS, which barred transplantation of fetal tissue from induced abortions. Although an advisory commission subsequently recommended that the ban be lifted, provided safeguards were established against commercial profit from the tissue or the encouraging of abortions, the Bush administration continued to back the ban.

Republicans on the committee were sharply critical of the fetal tissue provision and other parts of the House bill (HR 5661). In addition, HHS Secretary Louis W. Sullivan sent a letter to the committee outlining a lengthy list of Bush administration objections to the legislation. Sullivan warned in particular that the overturning of the fetal tissue ban would "create a demand cycle, dependent upon maintaining the legality of induced abortions."

But Republicans were unable to muster the strength to challenge the bill either in the Health and the Environment Subcommittee or in the full committee. HR 5661 was approved by Energy and Commerce on Sept. 26 and reported (H Rept 101-869) on Oct. 15.

Opposition to the House and Senate measures' controversial provisions and the lateness in the session quickly convinced sponsors that they would be unable to win their proposals in the 101st Congress. So the House approved a bare-bones version of S 2857 by voice vote, under suspension of the rules, on Oct. 27, and the Senate followed suit later the same day, clearing the legislation. President Bush signed S 2857 on Nov. 16.

Anti-Smoking Bills

House and Senate panels in 1990 approved omnibus anti-smoking bills, but neither measure reached the floor.

Although the bills, which were strongly opposed by the tobacco industry, did not become law, the progress they did make boosted the hopes of backers of stronger tobacco restrictions.

The Senate Labor and Human Resources Committee on May 16 approved a bill (S 1883) to authorize $110 million in fiscal 1991 to publicize the health risks of tobacco. The measure would have created a Center for Tobacco Products in the Department of Health and Human Services to administer a $50 million-a-year information program featuring public service and paid advertisements pointing out the dangers of tobacco.

The House Energy and Commerce Subcommittee on Health and the Environment on Sept. 11 approved a bill (HR 5041) imposing new restrictions on cigarette promotion. The bill would have banned most cigarette sales by vending machine, ended public distribution of free tobacco samples and forbidden the sale of candy and gum in packages designed to resemble tobacco products.

An earlier version of the House legislation also would have banned tobacco company sponsorship of sports and entertainment events and permitted print advertisements only in black and white with no photographs or graphics.

A related issue — opening up markets for U.S. tobacco products abroad — came under increasing attack throughout 1990. Legislation (HR 1249) was introduced to require the same health warnings on exported tobacco products as required on cigarettes sold in the United States, but it saw no congressional action.

Congress in 1990 did increase the cigarette excise tax as part of the reconciliation bill (HR 5835 — PL 101-508), but the tax was principally aimed at raising revenue, not decreasing consumption.

Legislation (S 293 — PL 101-352) also was enacted that directed the Consumer Product Safety Commission to supervise a study of cigarette safety and the technical feasibility of devising self-extinguishing, or "fire-safe," cigarettes. *(Reconciliation, tax provisions, p. 92; fire-safe cigarettes, p. 436)*

Injury Research

Legislation (HR 5113 — PL 101-558) cleared by Congress in 1990 reauthorized through fiscal 1993 programs the provided grants for research on the prevention and treatment of injuries.

The bill authorized $30 million in fiscal 1991 and open-ended funding through fiscal 1993 for the grant program of the Centers for Disease Control. The grants were awarded to state and local health departments and to academic institutions.

The House Energy and Commerce Committee approved HR 5113 on June 27 and reported it (H Rept 101-

613) on July 23. The House passed the bill July 23 by voice vote under suspension of the rules. The Senate added minor amendments from an earlier bill (S 2631 — S Rept 101-373) and passed HR 5113 on Oct. 24 by voice vote. House approval of the changes on Oct. 26 cleared the measure for President Bush, who signed it Nov. 15.

Elderly Health, Alzheimer's

Pilot programs providing medical services for individuals with Alzheimer's disease and home health care for low-income people were reauthorized under legislation (HR 5112 — PL 101-557) cleared by Congress in 1990.

The home health care program provided services to low-income people who might otherwise have had to go to an institution or hospital, while the Alzheimer's program provided similar services for those with the disease.

Backers of the legislation urged that expanded federal efforts were needed against Alzheimer's, a degenerative disease primarily affecting the elderly that gradually sapped the memory of its victims, altering their behavior and eventually killing them. They noted that the number of those with the disease was expected to double within a decade and grow to 14 million by the middle of the 21st century, imposing huge health care costs on society. The measure expanded the government's Alzheimer's disease research program to incorporate facilities such as diagnostic and treatment clinics to serve minority and rural populations.

HR 5112 authorized $7.5 million for each program in fiscal 1991 and open-ended funding through fiscal 1993. The legislation reserved at least 25 percent of home health care money for people over age 65, and at least 10 percent of those funds for people over age 85.

The bill also established a task force within the Department of Health and Human Services to coordinate aging research and named a series of federally backed research centers on aging after the late representative Claude Pepper, D-Fla. (House 1963-89; Senate 1936-51). *(Pepper profile, box, p. 919)*

The House Energy and Commerce Committee approved HR 5112 on June 27 and reported it (H Rept 101-612) on July 23. The House passed the bill by voice vote under suspension of the rules July 23.

The Senate companion bill (S 2602) was considerably larger in scope than HR 5112. As approved by the Senate Labor and Human Resources Committee Sept. 26, S 2602 (S Rept 101-512) authorized $80 million in fiscal 1991 for a variety of elderly health care programs, including $40 million for research into Alzheimer's.

The Senate measure never reached the floor. But sponsors in both chambers worked out a compromise version that included House funding levels, while adding some provisions of the Senate measure — for example, expanding authority for Alzheimer's disease centers.

The Senate passed the revised version of HR 5112 on Oct. 23 by voice vote, and the House accepted the changes on Oct. 25. President Bush signed the bill Nov. 15.

Mental Health Projects

Congress in 1990 cleared legislation (S 2628 — PL 101-639) to renew for three years certain demonstration projects within the National Institute of Mental Health.

The bill authorized $40 million in fiscal 1991 and open-ended funding through fiscal 1993 for a variety of services, including those for the seriously mentally ill and for children and adolescents with severe emotional and mental disturbances. The legislation also called for $5 million a year for states to develop comprehensive mental health service plans to provide community-based programs that helped mentally ill people function without being institutionalized.

The Senate Labor and Human Resources Committee reported S 2628 (S Rept 101-389) on July 24. The Senate passed the bill by voice vote on Aug. 4. The House passed an amended version by voice vote under suspension of the rules on Oct. 23, and the Senate cleared the bill Oct. 25.

President Bush signed the measure Nov. 28.

Family Planning

Seesawing votes on abortion combined with unrelated end-of-session disputes in 1990 doomed efforts in the 101st Congress to reauthorize the federal family planning program, Title X of the Public Health Service Act.

A bill (S 110) to reauthorize Title X was pulled from the Senate floor by sponsors after they were unable to muster enough votes to cut off a filibuster.

The House Energy and Commerce Committee approved a Title X bill (HR 5693 — H Rept 101-870) on Sept. 26, but sponsors made no effort to bring the bill to the floor after the Senate measure stalled.

In the absence of a formal authorization, which had expired at the end of fiscal 1985, Title X programs continued to receive funding through the appropriations process.

Controversy over Title X programs focused on their disputed connection to abortion. Although the program since it was established in 1970 had barred the use of federal funds to pay for abortions, critics said it was tainted by its close association with facilities that did perform the procedure.

Family planning reauthorization legislation also failed in the 102nd Congress. *(Story, p. 598)*

Senate Action

The Senate Labor and Human Resources Committee reported S 110 on July 31, 1989 (S Rept 101-95). The bill as approved authorized $547.7 million for family planning programs over three years.

When the bill finally reached the Senate floor, late in the 1990 session, debate centered around a challenge to the Reagan and Bush administrations' policy barring Title X grant recipients from informing pregnant women about abortion as an option. The abortion counseling ban, issued by the Reagan administration in 1988, was strongly criticized by family planning advocates, who called it a "gag rule" that intruded on the relationship between patient and doctor. A legal challenge to the rule reached the Supreme Court in 1990, but no decision had been issued at the time of congressional action.

On the Senate floor, John H. Chafee, R-R.I., offered an amendment to codify rules in effect before the ban. Those rules allowed family planning centers to provide women with unintended pregnancies "non-directive counseling, and referral on request" to alternatives that included childbearing, adoption or abortion. Chafee's amendment was adopted on a 62-36 vote Sept. 25.

Abortion foes won on another issue, however. William L. Armstrong, R-Colo., offered an amendment to require that Title X recipients who also performed abortions to notify parents of minors seeking an abortion 48 hours before the procedure would be performed. Armstrong's amendment was adopted by voice vote after confusing parliamentary maneuvering over an unrelated amendment on the Strategic Petroleum Reserve.

When S 110's chief sponsor, Edward M. Kennedy, D-Mass., moved to cut off debate on the bill Sept. 26, his cloture motion fell 10 votes short, 50-46.

Cancer Screening

Congress in 1990 cleared legislation (HR 4790 — PL 101-354) aimed at preventing cervical and breast cancer deaths by providing grants to states for early-detection programs.

The bill gave low-income women top priority for the cancer screenings and called on states to provide referrals and follow-up care for women who have Pap smears and mammograms. States were authorized to use some of the funds to develop public education materials and improve training of health professionals in detecting and controlling the diseases. States participating in the program were required to provide $1 for every $3 in federal grants — either from public or private funding.

HR 4790 authorized $50 million in fiscal 1991 and open-ended funding through fiscal 1993 for matching grants to states. States with unusually high death rates from breast and cervical cancer were given preferences for the grants, as were those with inadequate services for early detection.

Bill supporters said that 43,000 women died from breast cancer and 6,000 from cervical cancer in 1989.

The House Energy and Commerce Committee approved HR 4790 on May 10 and reported it (H Rept 101-543) on June 18. The bill passed the House by voice vote under suspension of the rules June 18.

The Senate Labor and Human Resources Committee approved its bill (S 2283 — S Rept 101-380) on June 27, formally reporting it July 19. The Senate passed HR 4790 with minor changes by voice vote Aug. 4. The House accepted the Senate amendments and thus cleared the measure the same day.

President Bush signed the bill Aug. 10.

Health Planning Grants

Legislation (S 2056 — PL 101-582) authorizing $10 million in public health planning grants to states cleared Congress in 1990.

The grants were to be used to develop plans to meet health goals set by the secretary of health and human services. Backers said the goal was to help reduce health care costs by encouraging steps to promote health and prevent disease.

The Senate Labor and Human Resources Committee approved the bill on Aug. 3 (S Rept 101-417). The Senate passed it by voice vote Oct. 20.

The House by voice vote passed the bill with amendments Oct. 26, and the Senate cleared the bill the following day.

President Bush signed the measure Nov. 15.

Developmental Disabilities

Congress in 1990 cleared legislation (S 2753 — PL 101-496) to reauthorize programs aimed at protecting the rights and promoting the independence of people with developmental disabilities, such as mental retardation or cerebral palsy.

The legislation authorized the following amounts for fiscal 1991, along with open-ended funding through fiscal 1993:

- $77.4 million for grants to states for developmental disability councils, which planned, monitored and coordinated services to those with developmental disabilities.
- $24 million for protection and advocacy services.
- $16.5 million for university-affiliated programs that provided interdisciplinary training, information and technical assistance.
- $3.65 million for demonstration projects of new technologies and methods of promoting the independence of those with developmental disabilities.

The Senate Labor and Human Resources Committee approved S 2753 on June 27 and reported it (S Rept 101-376) on July 18. The Senate passed the bill by voice vote Aug. 2.

The House Energy and Commerce Committee approved a companion bill (HR 5679 — H Rept 101-803) on Sept. 26, formally reporting it on Oct. 5. The House passed HR 5679 by voice vote Oct. 10, then passed S 2753 amended with the language of HR 5679. The Senate accepted the House changes Oct. 12, clearing the bill for President Bush, who signed it Oct. 31.

Nutrition Monitoring

Congress in 1990 cleared a bill (HR 1608 — PL 101-445) aimed at better coordinating the federal government's nutrition monitoring efforts.

The bill required the Departments of Agriculture and Health and Human Services (HHS) to develop a 10-year plan to determine what kinds of food Americans ate and how nutritious the foods were. The measure directed the administration to establish a National Nutrition Monitoring Advisory Council and publish a comprehensive report every five years called "Dietary Guidelines for Americans."

A key compromise gave opposing sides a voice in challenging the findings in the report.

The secretaries of agriculture and HHS also were charged with making sure that any other nutritional advice issued by any federal agency was consistent with the dietary guidelines report.

Similar legislation to ensure that the government spoke with one voice about the nutritional value of foods was cleared by Congress in 1988 but was vetoed by President Reagan. The Bush administration took no position on the 1990 legislation. *(1988 action, Congress and the Nation Vol. VII, p. 605)*

The Senate passed its nutrition monitoring bill (S 253 — S Rept 101-137) on Nov. 3, 1989.

On Oct. 2, 1990, the House Agriculture Committee reported HR 1608 (H Rept 101-788) and the full House passed the bill by voice vote under suspension of the rules. The Senate passed HR 1608 by voice vote Oct. 5, clearing the bill. President Bush signed it Oct. 22.

Abortion

The ongoing congressional debate over abortion took a significant turn in the 101st Congress. Although abortion rights advocates were unable to win any major changes in federal policy, they were able to show increased strength during debates on the issue. *(1991-92 action, p. 597)*

The key factor in the apparent shift in congressional sentiment was the Supreme Court's ruling in *Webster v. Reproductive Health Services*. On July 3, 1989, the Court handed down a decision that gave states new leeway to restrict access to abortion. *(Case summary, p. 838)*

While the decision was a legal victory for abortion opponents, it paradoxically increased the political strength of abortion rights backers. Unable to count any longer on the federal courts to guarantee access to abortion, many women became more active in pressing their lawmakers to act to protect abortion rights. The result was a fundamental change in the dynamics of the abortion debate.

Pro-choice members of Congress, jolted into action by the decision, rode a wave of support to their strongest legislative showing in a decade. But, in 1989, four vetoes by President Bush prevented them from relaxing longstanding bans on federal funding for abortion and abortion-related activities.

The key change came in the House, which reversed its strict anti-abortion stance on three separate appropriations bills in 1989. Abortion-related language prompted President Bush to veto fiscal 1990 spending bills for the Departments of Labor, Health and Human Services (HHS) and Education; for foreign operations; and twice for the District of Columbia.

The clearest sign of the shift in House opinion came on Oct. 11, when the House took up the conference report (H Rept 101-274) on the Labor-HHS-Education bill (HR 2990). By a **216-206 (R 41-134; D 175-72) key vote**, the House approved a motion by Barbara Boxer, D-Calif., to accept a Senate provision allowing federal funding of abortion in cases of rape or incest "promptly reported" to public health or law enforcement authorities. As originally passed by the House, HR 2990 barred the use of federal funds for abortions; the only exception was when the life of the woman was endangered by the pregnancy. *(1989 key votes, p. 1021)*

Bush Oct. 21 vetoed HR 2990 over its abortion language, however, and an Oct. 25 override attempt in the House fell 51 votes short of the two-thirds majority needed.

The House handed family planning and abortion rights groups a major victory Nov. 14 when it agreed, 244-178, to accept Senate language in the fiscal 1990 foreign aid spending bill (HR 2939) earmarking $15 million for the United Nations Fund for Population Activities (UNFPA), with the stipulation that the money had to be kept in a separate account that could not be used in China. In response, anti-abortion forces offered another amendment to prohibit the contribution unless the president certified to Congress that the fund did not support or help manage programs of coerced abortion and sterilization in China. The amendment, adopted 219-203, was similar to language used by the Reagan and Bush administrations to withdraw the United States from the U.N. family planning fund.

The next day, Nov. 15, the Senate voted 52-44 to stand by its demand for the $15 million contribution. On Nov. 16, the House reversed itself again, voting 207-200 to accept the Senate provision.

Bush vetoed HR 2939 on Nov. 19, objecting to the UNFPA funds. *(Controversy over UNFPA, box, p. 235)*

For the first time in nine years, the House voted 206-219 Aug. 2 to reject an amendment to the District of Columbia appropriations bill (HR 3026) that would bar the city from using locally raised tax funds to pay for abortions. The Senate version of the fiscal 1990 bill contained identical language.

Bush vetoed HR 3026 on Oct. 27 because of the abortion funding provision. Instead of attempting an override, Congress cleared a compromise (HR 3610) that banned the use of federal funds to pay for abortion, except to save the life of the woman. Bush vetoed that bill on Nov. 20.

The story was similar in 1990, with abortion rights advocates showing new strength but still unable to overcome administration resistance and determined action by abortion foes.

A key test of opinion during the year came on an effort in the House to overturn a 1988 Defense Department directive forbidding abortions in overseas military facilities, even if the woman paid for the procedure herself. Vic Fazio, D-Calif., offered an amendment to the defense authorization bill (HR 4739) to allow the procedure. But after opponents portrayed it as providing "abortion on demand," the amendment was rejected on a **200-216 (R 35-139; D 165-77) key vote** Sept. 18. *(1990 key votes, p. 1039)*

Earlier, on Aug. 3, the Senate, during consideration of its version of the defense authorization bill (S 2884), failed to invoke cloture (thus limiting debate) on a Tim Wirth, D-Colo., amendment to overturn the Pentagon's policy banning elective abortions in military hospitals. The motion, which required 60 votes to be successful, was rejected 58-41. The amendment subsequently was withdrawn. *(Defense authorization, p. 355)*

Abortion funding held up action on the fiscal 1991 appropriations bill for the District of Columbia (HR 5311). The House-passed version would allow the District to use its own funds to pay for abortions but would limit the use of federal funds for abortions to cases of rape or incest or to save the life of the woman. The bill drew a veto threat from Bush, who wanted the District to fund abortions only to save a woman's life.

Conferees on HR 5311 retained the abortion language, causing a highly charged debate when the conference report (H Rept 101-935) reached the House floor. The House rejected the conference report twice: on Oct. 20 by a 185-211 vote, then on Oct. 25 on a 195-211 vote. The bill finally cleared, and was signed into law, after the abortion provisions were dropped.

Another key abortion issue focused on the question of the notification of parents of minors seeking abortions. While abortion rights advocates appeared to be picking up added support, polls also showed that a majority of the public, like abortion opponents, favored requiring parental notification. The issue came to a head on Oct. 12, when Sen. William L. Armstrong, R-Colo., offered an amendment to the fiscal 1991 Labor-HHS-Education appropriations bill (HR 5257) requiring that federally supported family planning agencies notify parents of a minor 48 hours before an abortion was to be performed. Abortion rights advocates showed surprising strength when they came close to killing the amendment, with a motion to table Armstrong's amendment failing on a **key vote of 48-48 (R 8-34; D 40-14)**. The amendment was subsequently dropped from the bill.

Parental notification was at issue in two cases before the Supreme Court in 1990. On June 5, the Court ruled in *Hodgson v. Minnesota* that states could require a woman under 18 to tell both parents before obtaining an abortion as long as she had the alternative of seeking permission from a judge. In *Ohio v. Akron Center for Reproductive Health*, the Court upheld an Ohio statute requiring one-parent notification. *(Case summaries, p. 838)*

Congressional action also stalled on legislation (S 110, HR 5693) reauthorizing the federal family planning program in part because of abortion-related provisions. A National Institutes of Health (NIH) reauthorization bill ran into trouble over language overturning a Bush administration ban on funding of research involving transplants of tissue from fetuses obtained through abortion. *(Family planning, p. 592; NIH, p. 590)*

Disabilities Prevention

The House on July 23, 1990, by voice vote passed a bill (HR 4039) to formally authorize a Centers for Disease Control (CDC) program that sought to reduce the incidence of disability in the general population and to prevent further impairment in the disabled. The legislation died upon adjournment of the 101st Congress.

HR 4039 would have authorized funds over three years — $10 million for fiscal 1991, rising to $20 million in fiscal 1993.

A similar bill was introduced in the Senate (S 2153), but it saw no action.

Legislation also was considered in the 102nd Congress. *(Story, p. 610)*

Research Laboratory

Legislation (S 1390) was enacted in 1989 that authorized $25 million for construction of a laboratory to breed specialized, mutant mice needed for biomedical research.

The bill required 25 percent of the laboratory construction costs to be raised from private sources. It also required the lab to give priority to the research needs of the National Institutes of Health.

The Senate Labor and Human Resources Committee reported S 1390 (S Rept 101-101) on Aug. 1. The Senate passed the bill by voice vote Aug. 4. The House passed an amended version by voice vote under suspension of the rules Nov. 13. The Senate accepted the House changes three days later, clearing the measure. President Bush signed S 1390 (PL 101-190) on Nov. 29.

Mandated Benefits

The Senate Labor and Human Resources Committee on July 12, 1989, approved legislation (S 768) on a party-line vote of 9-7 to require virtually all employers to provide a minimum package of health insurance benefits to workers and their dependents. The bill, sponsored by committee Chairman Edward M. Kennedy, D-Mass., would create a new joint state-federal program that would by the year 2000 phase in coverage for the unemployed uninsured not otherwise covered. Formally reported Nov. 20 (S Rept 101-217), the controversial measure went no further in the 101st Congress.

A modified version of the legislation had been approved by the committee in 1988. *(Congress and the Nation Vol. VII, p. 599)*

Before approving S 768, members rejected a James M. Jeffords, R-Vt., substitute amendment, which was essentially the text of S 1274, a bill sponsored by the panel's ranking Republican, Orrin G. Hatch, Utah. The amendment would have authorized $313 million for a variety of activities, including $50 million for state pools to provide coverage for "uninsurable" individuals and $100 million to increase federal research into the effectiveness of various medical treatments.

The federal costs of the first phase of S 768, which included incentives to help small employers meet the mandate and coverage under the public program of children with incomes below 185 percent of the federal poverty threshold, would total $3.3 billion in fiscal 1991. The net cost to business would be about $18 billion per year.

The bill was anathema to business groups, which despised federal mandates, and was vehemently opposed by the Bush administration.

In 1992, Senate Labor again would approve legislation aimed at making health insurance universally available. *(Health reform, p. 596)*

Adolescent Family Life

The Senate Labor and Human Resources Committee on Aug. 3, 1989, reported a bill (S 120 — S Rept 101-103) reauthorizing the Adolescent Family Life Program, which funded demonstration projects that provided education, counseling and health services for pregnant teens and teenage parents. The bill saw no further congressional action.

The measure, as reported, would provide $30 million a year for fiscal 1990-92; allow religious organizations to receive funds; and soften the emphasis on sexual abstinence in preventing teenage pregnancy.

1991-92

The record on health legislation in 1991 and 1992 was dominated by what Congress did not do. Despite increased political interest in the issue of health care costs and insurance coverage, bills to reform the existing system made little progress. And, despite the growing strength of abortion rights forces, efforts to change or overturn the abortion restrictions put in place under the Reagan and Bush administrations were thwarted by the veto pen of President Bush. Abortion-related controversies also extended into other areas — for example, legislation reauthorizing expiring portions of the National Institutes of Health.

Some significant legislation did become law, however. A compromise curbing state tactics designed to increase their federal Medicaid funding was approved, as was a bill overhauling federal drug abuse and mental health programs. Revisions were made in a 1990 law requiring drug discounts for Medicaid cleared Congress, and efforts to tighten the approval process for generic drugs were successful.

Health Reform

Despite nearly a year of frenzied and often partisan jousting over health care, the 102nd Congress adjourned with almost nothing to show on what had become a major electoral issue. No proposed solution could muster more than a few dozen supporters even though nearly everyone agreed that the existing system cost too much and left too many people with no or inadequate insurance coverage.

House and Senate Democrats were unable to coalesce behind any single plan, despite promises by their leaders for action. About all the Democrats could agree on was that the plans put forth separately by House and Senate Republicans and by President Bush were inadequate to either bring down costs or broadly expand insurance coverage.

The Senate twice passed, as part of tax bills, a bipartisan "incremental" proposal aimed at making insurance more available and affordable for small businesses. But House negotiators forced the package out of the final bills.

The health care issue had taken on major political implications following the surprise victory in November 1991 of Democrat Harris Wofford over former Bush attorney general Dick Thornburgh in Pennsylvania's special Senate election. Wofford's campaign made effective use of the health care issue. Another political factor influencing the issue was the success of Bill Clinton, who promised in the 1992 nomination and general election campaigns to make health costs and coverage a major goal of his presidency.

After Congress failed to act on health reform in 1991, a loud cry was heard for action in 1992. But because so many proposals were circulating, boiling them down into an approach that enjoyed a strong consensus of support became almost impossible.

Democrats were split among those favoring three contrasting approaches to a full-scale reform of the system: a national health insurance system similar to Canada's, a "pay or play" system under which businesses would have the choice either to provide their workers with insurance or to pay a tax to have the government do so, or a "market based" system that would rely on better managing the way health was delivered. In addition, some Democrats favored a more limited bill aimed at tackling the most immediate problems, such as the high cost of health insurance for small businesses.

By mid-1992, House Democrats tried to rally behind legislation (HR 5502) that focused on controlling costs by imposing a national health budget. But it went no further than approval by a House subcommittee.

Congressional Republicans and the Bush administration offered proposals that were similar in some respects, including provisions aimed at making insurance more available by outlawing exclusions based on pre-existing medical conditions. But Republicans also disagreed about key issues, including whether or not to limit the tax deduction for employers who provided their workers with health insurance and the exclusion from taxes for the workers who received such benefits.

Following are the key health reform proposals considered in 1992.

'Pay or Play'

The first legislative volley of 1992 was fired in January by the Senate Labor and Human Resources Committee, which approved an unnumbered bill embracing the "pay or play" concept. The bill was approved on a party-line 10-7 vote. It was a modified version of legislation (S 1227) introduced in 1991 by Senate Majority Leader George J. Mitchell, D-Maine, and cosponsored by committee Chairman Edward M. Kennedy, D-Mass.

In addition to imposing a pay or play system, the committee-approved bill sought to slow health care costs with the creation of a Federal Reserve-like health expenditures board that was to set rates for medical care.

The bill was strongly criticized by the Bush administration, which argued that it would "create a massive dislocation of workers and their dependents from their current coverage, create a public plan of an enormous scale and impose unacceptably high costs on employers and the public." Meanwhile, the plan received mild, not passionate, public support. Lawmakers liked pay or play because it was less unacceptable to the health industry than a single-payer national health insurance plan.

Bush Plan

The Bush administration had planned to unveil its health reform proposal during the president's Jan. 28 State of the Union address. However, the plan ran into such sharp criticism from House Republicans that officials were forced to modify it even before it was made public.

The final plan, released a few weeks later, called for expanding low-income families' access to private health insurance by means of a new voucher system based on tax credits. Middle-income earners who paid their own premiums would receive relief through new tax deductions. The vouchers would be used to buy health insurance or offset the cost of insurance plans.

The proposal also included an idea heavily stressed by the administration as a means of controlling health costs — malpractice reform. The Bush plan contained provisions encouraging states to revise their malpractice laws by eliminating joint and several liability for punitive damages, capping punitive damages and promoting pretrial alternatives to going to court.

Missing from the proposal, however, was an idea that had brought strong protests from the House GOP — helping to finance the new tax credits and deductions by taxing high-income workers on a portion of employer-provided health insurance.

The Bush plan left unanswered key questions about what sorts of insurance plans would be available and how the system would be administered. Furthermore, financing of the proposal was discussed only in vague terms: streamlining the insurance market and reducing government red tape to lower health care costs. The plan promised that no new taxes would be needed to pay for the potential new cost to the Treasury, which White House budget officials estimated to be $100 billion over five years.

House Republican leaders on June 4 introduced a bill (HR 5325) with the blessings of the administration. The bill set federal requirements for health insurers aimed at making plans more affordable and available to those who worked for small companies; it saw no congressional action.

Senate Finance Committee

The Senate Finance Committee was the next congressional panel to act, approving a health care proposal as part of a hotly contested tax bill (HR 4210). The core of the proposal sought to reshape, through federal regulation, the private insurance market for small businesses. It would limit the cost of health insurance policies for businesses with 50 or fewer employees and prohibit insurers from denying coverage to employees or their dependents. *(HR 4210, p. 100)*

The proposal, which was a slightly revised version of a bill (S 1872) introduced by Finance Chairman Lloyd Bentsen, D-Texas, in 1991, also would allow self-employed individuals to deduct 100 percent of the costs of their health insurance, instead of the current 25 percent.

The panel included the health provisions in HR 4210, which it approved March 3 on an 11-9 party-line vote. The provisions were accepted by the Senate as part of the tax bill but were dropped in conference.

Later in the year, Finance members offered similar language to a second tax bill (HR 11). The provisions were part of the Senate-passed bill but were dropped in conference. *(HR 11, p. 103)*

House Democrats

Two of the most powerful Democrats on health issues — Reps. John D. Dingell, Mich., and Henry A. Waxman, Calif. — on June 30 introduced a comprehensive bill (HR 5514) that envisioned a full-fledged national health insurance system. The bill would combine a single payer, the federal government, with a delivery system heavily dependent on managed care, which sought to contain costs by providing patients with a single point of entry into the health care system and restricting access to specialists and hospitals. It would have been financed primarily through a new value added tax (VAT), the equivalent of a national sales tax on most goods and services. The bill died upon adjournment of the 102nd Congress.

The only formal action taken on health reform in the House in 1992 was by the Ways and Means Subcommittee on Health, which approved a bill (HR 5502) on June 30 that would impose national limits on health spending and expand access to health insurance for pregnant women, children and those who worked for small businesses.

The heart of the bill was its cost-containment section, which called on Congress to set national limits on health spending that would gradually reduce health care inflation to the growth rate of the overall economy. The key element of the plan would set maximum payment levels for doctors, hospitals and all other providers.

Other Proposals

Sen. Paul Wellstone, D-Minn., in early 1992 unveiled a version of a Canada-like single-payer plan (S 2320) as a companion to a House bill (HR 1300) introduced in 1991 by Rep. Marty Russo, D-Ill.

The single-payer plans would effectively eliminate the private insurance industry, making the federal government responsible for paying all medical bills. They would cover virtually all medical services with no required premiums, deductibles or copayments. Financing would come through a series of tax hikes, including increases in personal and corporate income taxes and taxes on Social Security benefits. Despite the tax increases, sponsors expected a net decrease in most out-of-pocket health costs.

At the other end of the political spectrum, the Conservative Democratic Forum, a group of 60 conservative and moderate Democrats, proposed a "managed competition" system in which consumers would shop for health services on the basis of price and quality. Medicaid would be expanded to cover everyone with incomes at or below the poverty line. The proposal included a plan to eliminate employers' tax deductions for the cost of health insurance over an amount deemed sufficient to provide a "basic" package of services.

Oregon Health Care Plan

After a year of consideration, the Bush administration on Aug. 3, 1992, denied the state of Oregon's request for a waiver of federal requirements needed to allow an Oregon law, widely recognized as an innovative solution to the problem of those lacking health insurance, to take effect.

Under the Oregon Health Plan, more than 120,000 low-income Oregonians without health insurance would have gained coverage under Medicaid, the joint state-federal health program for the poor. In exchange, the services Medicaid covered would have been cut back. Decisions on what to offer — and what to exclude — would have been based on an elaborately designed priorities list that ranked the costs and benefits of 709 ailments and their treatments.

Proponents argued that giving most people some care was preferable to giving a few people everything. Critics charged that the plan amounted to rationing — with those losing out possibly facing death sentences.

On one hand, Bush officials lauded the plan repeatedly as an embodiment of their desire for states to act as laboratories for new policies. On the other hand, the projected cost of more than $100 million in new federal funds was a big problem for an administration seeking to trim spending on entitlement programs. Furthermore, the plan potentially conflicted with another Bush-backed initiative, the 1990 Americans with Disabilities Act (PL 101-336), which prohibited discrimination on the basis of health condition. *(PL 101-336, p. 743)*

Abortion

Lawmakers and the White House remained at a standoff over the abortion issue during the 102nd Congress, as President Bush repeatedly used his veto power to hold off legislation that would have loosened federal restrictions on abortion. The result was a continuation of every anti-abortion policy imposed since Bush's predecessor, Ronald Reagan, took office in 1981. *(101st Congress action, p. 594)*

However, debate over the issue — which found its way into a wide range of legislative measures, from major health programs to foreign aid and federal funding for the District of Columbia — did show a significant shift in favor of abortion rights. The shift was more noticeable in the House, which had long been an anti-abortion stronghold.

In 1991, both chambers voted to jettison five separate abortion-related restrictions. But Bush vetoes and repeated veto threats prevented any policy changes. Bush vetoed two appropriations bills — for the District of Columbia and for the Departments of Labor, Health and Human Services (HHS) and Education — over abortion provisions, and his threats to veto both the fiscal 1992 defense authorization and spending bills helped get abortion provisions in those measures dropped. The president also threatened to veto three bills that did not reach his desk in 1991: a House-passed reauthorization of the National Institutes of Health (NIH) that sought to overturn a ban on research using fetal tissue obtained from abortions, and foreign aid authorization and appropriations bills that would have renewed funding for the United Nations Population Fund (formerly the United Nations Fund for Population Activities).

In 1992, the key development was the Supreme Court's June 29 decision in *Planned Parenthood of Southeast Pennsylvania v. Casey*. Although both supporters and foes of abortion rights had expected the Court to strike down *Roe v. Wade*, the landmark 1973 decision that legalized abortion nationwide, the Court surprised nearly everyone by issuing a split decision. While it upheld several restrictions in the contested Pennsylvania law, including a requirement that women seeking abortions wait 24 hours, a 5-4 majority reaffirmed *Roe*'s core holding of a woman's right to end her pregnancy. The Court's new test was whether a particular restriction imposed an "undue burden" on that right. *(*Casey *summary, p. 839;* Roe v. Wade, *Congress and the Nation Vol. IV, p. 635)*

By leaving abortion rights activists without a rallying point, the *Casey* decision led congressional leaders not to force a fight over the so-called Freedom of Choice Act, which would have codified a woman's right to an abortion. They feared the bill would become the target of amendments imposing the kind of restrictions upheld in *Casey*.

Members, however, did vote on a variety of other abortion-related issues, including the "gag rule" prohibiting abortion counseling in federally funded family planning clinics, proposals to allow U.S. servicewomen and military dependents to obtain abortions in overseas military medical facilities if they paid for the procedure themselves, and efforts to lift an administration ban on research using fetal tissue from elective abortions.

In every case, both the House and Senate voted in 1992 to relax the restrictions but failed to muster the two-thirds majorities needed to override actual or threatened Bush vetoes. Altogether, Bush in 1992 vetoed four bills because of abortion language, while abortion-related language was dropped from the final versions of three other measures to avert threatened vetoes.

Following are summaries of key actions on abortion-related issues in the 102nd Congress:

Abortion Counseling, Parental Notification. A major development in the battle over regulations banning abortion counseling in federally funded family planning clinics came on May 23, 1991, when the Supreme Court, in *Rust v. Sullivan*, upheld the regulations. As a result, opponents of the ban adopted a two-track congressional strategy: pushing appropriations language barring enforcement of the ban and separate legislation overturning the rules. *(Case summary, p. 838)*

During consideration of the fiscal 1992 Labor-HHS-Education appropriations bill (HR 2707), the House Appropriations Committee June 20, 35-20, adopted a John Porter, R-Ill., amendment to bar HHS from spending money to enforce the regulations for a year. Procedural rules precluded any attempt to overturn the regulations outright on an appropriations measure.

Abortion opponents won approval, 28-10, of a Vin Weber, R-Minn., amendment requiring that at least one parent be notified before any facility receiving family planning funds could perform an abortion on a minor. But an effort to append the language to Porter's amendment failed, 24-31. And, on the House floor, the stand-alone Weber amendment was struck from the bill for impermissibly legislating on an appropriation.

The Senate on Sept. 12 adopted, 92-8, a Nancy Landon Kassebaum, R-Kan., amendment requiring notification of, or consent by, at least one parent before a minor could obtain an abortion at a clinic receiving federal family planning funds. The amendment included a long list of exceptions to the general requirement, however, unlike an earlier amendment offered by Don Nickles, R-Okla., that was rejected 45-55. The Kassebaum language did not survive the House-Senate conference on HR 2707.

The House adopted the conference report (H Rept 102-282) on the Labor-HHS-Education spending bill — including the language to block the counseling ban — on Nov. 6 by a 272-156 vote, well short of the two-thirds required to override. The Senate cleared the bill the next day.

On Nov. 8, Bush reiterated his vow to veto the measure over the abortion language. The administration moved to shore up its position by issuing a memo by Bush clarifying that "nothing in these regulations is to prevent a woman from receiving complete medical information about her condition from a physician." Opponents pointed out that the memo did not legally alter the regulations and that, while it permitted physicians freedom of speech, it continued to muzzle nurse-practitioners and other health professionals who did the bulk of the counseling in family planning clinics.

The House on Nov. 19 failed to override the veto on a **276-156 (R 53-113; D 222-43; I 1-0) key vote**, which was 12 votes short of the two-thirds needed. *(1991 key votes, p. 1061)*

The 102nd Congress also considered free-standing bills (S 323, HR 3090) to overturn the counseling ban.

The Senate adopted S 323 (S Rept 102-86) by voice vote on July 17, 1991. Two contradictory amendments regarding parental notification were adopted on the floor. One, offered by Daniel R. Coats, R-Ind., would require that at least one parent be notified in most cases; it was adopted 52-47. The other, sponsored by Senate Majority Leader George J. Mitchell, D-Maine, had numerous exceptions; the vote was 54-45. A House-Senate conference would have to reconcile the conflicting requirements.

On April 30, 1992, the House passed, on a **268-150 (R 55-105; D 212-45; I 1-0) key vote**, HR 3090 (H Rept 102-204), which would overturn the gag rule. The bill called upon clinics to give women with unintended pregnancies "non-directive" counseling about all options, including abortion. HR 3090, unlike S 323, also reauthorized the family planning program, Title X of the Public Health Service Act, for five years, at $180 million in fiscal 1993, rising to $219 million in fiscal 1997. *(1992 key votes, p. 1083; family planning, 101st Congress action, p. 592)*

On the House floor, abortion opponents sought neither a parental notification provision nor elimination of the language overturning the abortion counseling ban. They reportedly did not have enough votes to prevail. Meanwhile, members seeking a middle ground offered amendments, adopted by voice vote, to clarify the counseling requirements. A Ralph Regula, R-Ohio, amendment reiterated that abortion counseling would be provided only if the patient requested it. And a Richard J. Durbin, D-Ill., amendment expanded the "conscience clause" of the Public Health Service Act to allow a counselor or clinic to decline to provide abortion information, as long as a patient seeking it could be referred to a nearby clinic that would provide the counseling.

The House Energy and Commerce Committee had rejected, 20-23, an amendment offered by Thomas J. Bliley Jr., R-Va., to require the notification of at least one parent 48 hours before a girl under 18 could obtain an abortion from an entity that received Title X funds.

The House passed S 323 on April 30, after substituting the text of HR 3090. Conferees agreed on the House-passed version. The House adopted the conference report (H Rept 102-767) on a 251-144 vote Aug. 6; the Senate adopted it by voice vote on Sept. 14, clearing S 323.

Bush vetoed the measure Sept. 25, arguing that the bill would "transform this program into a vehicle for the promotion of abortion."

The Senate on Oct. 1 overrode the veto on a **73-26 (R 20-23; D 53-3) key vote**.

The House, however, sustained the veto the next day, 266-148, 10 votes short of the required supermajority.

On March 20, 1992, the Bush administration issued a directive to regional administrators of the family planning program, which said doctors in federally funded clinics — but not nurses or other health professionals — could discuss abortion with patients in limited circumstances. The directive also said HHS would begin enforcing the gag rule, for the first time since it was issued by the Reagan administration on Feb. 2, 1988.

In response, groups opposed to the counseling ban sued, contending that any significant change made by the memorandum was a violation of the Administrative Procedures Act, which required a public notice and comment period.

On Nov. 3, a three-judge panel in Washington, D.C., barred implementation of the gag rule on grounds that the March directive altering the rule had substantially changed the original 1988 regulation. The panel said the change should have been the subject of a formal rule-making process.

Freedom of Choice Act. A major goal of abortion rights forces in 1992 was enactment of the Freedom of Choice Act (S 25, HR 25), which would codify the Supreme Court's decision in *Roe v. Wade*. The opening shot in that effort came June 18, 1992, when the House Judiciary Subcommittee on Civil and Constitutional Rights approved HR 25 on a party-line vote of 5-3.

Backers of the bill said it was not intended to overrule certain post-*Roe* decisions, such as those allowing states to require parental involvement in a minor's abortion decision. However, critics argued the bill would go much further than *Roe* and impose what Bush called "abortion on demand."

The House Judiciary Committee approved HR 25 by a 20-13 vote June 30, while the Senate Labor and Human Resources Committee backed S 25 (S Rept 102-321) by a 12-5 vote July 1.

However, both actions came after the *Casey* decision, which left abortion rights forces in a state of confusion. No further action was taken on either bill.

Fetal Tissue Research. Provisions reversing the Bush administration's ban on funding research using tissue from aborted fetuses was included in a bill (HR 2507) renewing expiring authorities within the National Institutes of Health. *(NIH bill, p. 602)*

The House Energy and Commerce Subcommittee on Health inserted a provision in HR 2507 overturning the funding moratorium on fetal tissue research. The full committee approved the bill (H Rept 102-136) on a party-line vote of 27-16 on June 4, 1991, after rejecting 16-27 an amendment to strike the language overturning the ban. Although the fetal research issue provoked heated rhetoric, no separate amendment to drop the provision was offered on the floor.

Senate Labor and Human Resources Committee Chairman Edward M. Kennedy, D-Mass., introduced his version of the NIH reauthorization (S 1523) in mid-1991. The bill did not contain fetal tissue language, as Kennedy believed the issue would derail the legislation. However, in October, Kennedy cosponsored a separate bill (S 1902) to overturn the ban. And the committee, 13-4, approved S 1523 with the fetal research provisions of S 1902 attached.

A key moment in action on HR 2507 came on the Senate floor, when senators considered an amendment by Orrin G. Hatch, R-Utah, to allow fetal tissue research to go forward using "banks" to collect tissue from miscarriages and tubal pregnancies. The amendment was rejected on a **23-77 (R 20-23; D 3-54) key vote** on March 31, 1992.

After clearing Congress June 4, HR 2507 was vetoed by Bush on June 23. An override attempt in the House June 24 failed by a 14-vote margin, 271-156.

Military Abortions. Abortion rights supporters in 1991 and 1992 pushed to overturn a 1988 ban on self-paid abortions in overseas military medical facilities.

The House on May 22, 1991, adopted 220-208 a Les AuCoin, D-Ore., amendment to the fiscal 1992 defense authorization bill (HR 2100) providing reproductive health services at military hospitals for service personnel and their dependents while stationed overseas. AuCoin offered language to lift the abortion ban during House Appropriations Committee consideration of the fiscal 1992 defense appropriations bill (HR 2521). The amendment was approved 21-18 on June 4. However, three days later, on the House floor, the provision was dropped on a point of order as impermissibly legislating on an appropriation.

In the Senate, a motion to invoke cloture (and thus limit debate) on a Tim Wirth, D-Colo., amendment to the defense authorization bill (S 1507) overturning the ban was rejected Aug. 2 on a 58-40 vote, two votes shy of the required 60. However, Frank R. Lautenberg, D-N.J., appended military abortions language to the defense appropriations bill in subcommittee, and it remained in the measure through Senate passage.

House and Senate negotiators dropped the language from the authorization bill on Nov. 4, after Bush reiterated his veto threat. Conferees on the appropriations bill deleted the provision on Nov. 14 following a heated debate.

On June 4, 1992, the House adopted, 216-193, an amendment to the fiscal 1993 defense authorization bill (HR 5006) allowing servicewomen and military dependents to obtain abortions in overseas military medical facilities if they paid for the procedure themselves. The House Appropriations Committee June 29 added similar language to the fiscal 1993 defense appropriations bill (HR 5504). The House passed HR 5504 July 2 with the abortion provisions.

Despite veto threats from Bush, the language was retained in the Senate versions of both the authorization and appropriations bills. In the rush to adjourn, however, sponsors convinced abortion rights supporters to agree to a deal stripping the provisions from the defense bills in exchange for sending them to Bush in separate legislation (S 3144), which originally pertained to CHAMPUS, the health program for military dependents. The abortion language was substituted for the other provisions in the bill. The Senate passed S 3144 by voice vote Sept. 19, and the House followed suit Oct. 3. Bush pocket-vetoed the measure Oct. 31.

District of Columbia. President Bush on Aug. 17, 1991, vetoed the fiscal 1992 spending bill for the District of Columbia (HR 2699) and on Sept. 30, 1992, vetoed the fiscal 1993 bill (HR 5517) because they would have allowed the city to use locally raised funds to pay for abortions for poor women. Because the bill sponsors knew they did not have the votes to prevail in the House, no effort was made to override the vetoes.

Foreign Aid. At issue in the fiscal 1992-93 foreign aid authorization bill (HR 2508, S 1435), the fiscal 1992 foreign aid appropriations bill (HR 2621) and the fiscal 1993 foreign aid spending bill (HR 5368) was funding for the U.N. Population Fund. Funding had been barred since 1985, as debate continued over the extent to which the population fund's aid to China bolstered that nation's strict population control programs, which in some cases included coerced abortions. Lawmakers also were divided over the so-called Mexico City policy, which since 1984 had barred funding for international family planning programs that perform or "actively promote" abortion. *(Foreign aid authorization, p. 267; fiscal 1992 foreign aid appropriations, p. 269; fiscal 1993 foreign aid appropriations, p. 271; controversy over U.N. fund, box, p. 235)*

The Senate Foreign Relations Committee on June 12, 1991, rejected, 6-13, a Jesse Helms, R-N.C., amendment to strip from S 1435 the provision overturning the Mexico City policy. On the Senate floor July 25, abortion rights supporters were successful in cutting off debate, 63-33, on a Paul Simon, D-Ill., amendment to authorize $20 million for the population fund. The amendment subsequently was adopted by voice vote.

During House floor consideration of HR 2508 on June 12, an amendment by Peter H. Kostmayer, D-Pa., that effectively blocked a Christopher H. Smith, R-N.J., amendment to strike the U.N. funds, was adopted 234-188. Members also adopted, 222-200, an amendment offered by Howard L. Berman, D-Calif., that blocked another Smith amendment to reinstate the Mexico City policy.

Bush rejected a compromise to leave the Mexico City policy intact and tightly restrict how the population fund could spend its $20 million in U.S. funds. The administration's unhappiness with the defense authorization did not matter in the end, however, because the House killed the bill when it rejected the conference report.

Consideration of HR 2621 was complicated by an amendment, approved 30-19 by the House Appropriations Committee June 12, 1991, that provided $20 million to the U.N. fund (which Bush opposed) if Congress also granted most-favored-nation (MFN) status to China (which Bush supported). If Congress did not grant MFN, no funds would go to the population fund. The matter was not contested on the House floor, but the bill was put on hold until 1992 before the Senate could act. The stopgap measure to fund foreign aid programs in the interim (H J Res 360 — PL 102-145) included no U.N. fund money.

The House-passed version of the fiscal 1993 foreign aid spending bill contained $20 million for the population fund. The Senate also included the appropriation, as well as language to overturn the Mexico City policy. However, eager to adjourn, Congress dropped both provisions from the final version of HR 5368 to avert a veto.

1993 Action. On Jan. 22, 1993, President Bill Clinton redefined the debate over abortion and abortion-related issues when he directed federal agencies to eliminate the 1988 gag rule prohibiting abortion counseling in federally funded family planning clinics; eliminate the 1988 ban on federal funding of medical research using fetal tissue from elective abortions; determine whether the ban on RU-486, the French abortion pill, was justified and, if it was not, to cancel the "import alert" that prevented the drug from being brought into the United States; lift the 1988 directive that barred abortions in overseas military medical facilities, even if the woman paid for the procedure; and overturn the Mexico City policy barring U.S. aid to international organizations that performed or promoted abortions.

Medicaid

As states scrambled to cope with the skyrocketing costs of Medicaid, Congress in 1991 cleared legislation (HR 3595 — PL 102-234) designed to limit the way states could raise funds to pay their share of the joint federal-state health program for the poor.

The legislation was prompted by regulations issued by the Bush administration in September that, beginning Jan. 1, 1992, would have severely curtailed states' ability to obtain federal Medicaid matching money for funds raised by donations from or taxes levied on hospitals, nursing homes and other health care providers.

The House on Nov. 19 passed a version of HR 3595 that would have blocked the regulations through Sept. 30, 1992.

But before the Senate could take up the bill, the Bush administration and the National Governors' Association reached a deal under which contributions would be banned but most provider taxes would be allowed, with a temporary cap on the total amount states could raise using the technique.

The compromise, embodied in HR 3595, "grandfathered" states already over the allowable limits and staggered effective dates of the restrictions, so state legislatures would have adequate time to retool laws to bring their systems into compliance.

A separate part of the deal addressed what the administration saw as a potential budget problem: special payments states made to hospitals that served large numbers of low-income patients.

Background

Action on HR 3595 came amid growing state frustration with the increasing burdens put on their budgets by congressional expansion of the Medicaid program.

In addition to complaining about the heavy cost of expanded coverage for the poor, state officials were pressing Congress and the federal government for more flexibility in Medicaid policy. One of the big fights involved whether states should be able to use voluntary contributions from hospitals and other health care providers to pay the state share of Medicaid costs. In 1990, the Bush administration wanted to disallow such contributions, arguing that letting states use revenue other than from their own treasuries would drive up the matching funds the federal government had to pay without imposing any fiscal restraints on the states.

Congress stepped into the argument in a partial way in the fiscal 1991 budget-reconciliation bill (HR 5835 — PL 101-508), authorizing states to levy specific taxes on health care providers. But the bill delayed a decision on voluntary contributions, ruling that the Bush administration had to wait at least a year before outlawing such contributions by regulation.

The states in 1991 began urging that voluntary contributions be put in the same category as provider taxes.

On Sept. 12, 1991, the Health Care Financing Administration (HCFA) published regulations — scheduled to take effect Jan. 1, 1992 — that severely limited the ways states could raise funds. The regulations sought to ban voluntary contributions outright and to limit severely provider tax programs, in which the state taxed hospitals and nursing homes but not other businesses. The state transferred the revenues to its Medicaid agency, collected the federal match and paid the entire amount back to those providing care to Medicaid patients. "These devices are contrary to the cost-sharing partnership that has been the hallmark of Medicaid," said Health and Human Services Secretary Louis W. Sullivan on Sept. 10.

If left unchecked, HCFA Administrator Gail R. Wilensky said, the funding devices would permit Medicaid spending to rise exponentially.

House Action

Contending that the Sept. 12 regulations broke the deal codified in PL 101-508, Congress set out to block them.

Legislation (HR 3595) to that end was approved 16-6 on Oct. 23 by the House Energy and Commerce Subcommittee on Health and the Environment.

Members acknowledged that the budget bill had allowed the administration to ban voluntary contributions as of Jan. 1, 1992. But by banning most provider taxes, the regulation "violates congressional intent as expressed in" the reconciliation bill, said an Oct. 7 letter to Sullivan signed by the chairmen of the full committees and subcommittees that oversaw Medicaid in the House and Senate, and by Senate Budget Committee Chairman Jim Sasser, D-Tenn.

The House subcommittee's bill permitted states to continue to claim federal matching funds for both voluntary donation and provider tax programs through Sept. 30, 1992. States then were given until Dec. 31, 1992, to make the transition from voluntary donation programs to taxes, although in that last quarter states could not claim more funds than they did in fiscal 1991.

The bill also permanently authorized states to claim federal matching money for payments made on behalf of Medicaid patients by state and local public health agencies.

Republican opponents of the bill said it allowed states to continue putting an unfair drain on the federal Treasury.

The full House Energy and Commerce Committee on Nov. 7 approved, 36-7, the legislation to block the administration regulations, as White House and state officials continued negotiating toward a compromise. HR 3595 (H Rept 102-310) was formally reported Nov. 12.

Before the bill reached the House floor, the White House issued a policy statement that included a veto threat. The administration objected that "state donation and provider-specific tax programs, if unchecked, will undermine a basic premise of the Medicaid program — that states have a stake in the costs of the program."

Nevertheless, the House Nov. 19 passed HR 3595 by 348-71.

Before approving the bill, members rejected, 156-262, an amendment offered by Bill Gradison, R-Ohio, to strike two budget-related provisions of the bill. One required that the Congressional Budget Office, not the White House Office of Management and Budget, estimate the cost of the legislation, while the other exempted the bill from the pay-as-you-go requirements of the 1990 budget act.

The administration and the governors reached a tentative compromise on Nov. 21.

Senate Action

The Senate Finance Committee on Nov. 22 approved two separate measures. The first simply blocked the regulations through March 1992; the other codified the compromise agreement.

The Senate then passed HR 3595 by voice vote Nov. 26.

Under the deal, voluntary donations were banned. States could tax providers, but in most cases those taxes could not account for more than 25 percent of a state's Medicaid costs. The 25 percent cap was to expire after three years.

On another point, the deal permanently capped payments to hospitals that served a "disproportionate share" of Medicaid patients.

The agreement nearly died several times between the time it was reached late Nov. 21 and when it finally passed both chambers.

As the deal took shape, opposition grew. As of Nov. 22, only five states objected to the agreement, but by Nov. 25, after proposed legislative language was drafted, about 10 states were expressing serious concerns about the agreement. Senators and staff members were privately predicting that the Senate would follow the House's lead and approve a simple suspension of the regulations. But administration officials refused to give up, and administration and state officials finally reached an agreement to alleviate state concerns.

House-Senate conferees completed action on the bill Nov. 27, and both chambers approved the conference report (H Rept 102-409) by voice vote the same day. As part of the final deal, the contested regulations, originally scheduled to take effect Jan. 1, were withdrawn.

President Bush signed HR 3595 into law Dec. 12.

Major Provisions

As cleared by Congress, HR 3595:

- Prohibited, beginning Jan. 1, 1992, federal matching payments for funds raised through donations from health care providers.
- Provided for a number of exceptions, including some for states that already had donation programs, which could continue them for certain periods of time.
- Made federal matching money available only to "bona

fide provider-related donations," which were defined as donations that had "no direct or indirect relationship" to Medicaid payments made to that provider.

- Required that to receive federal matching payments, taxes on health care providers had to be broad-based; that is, that they had to be applied uniformly to all providers in a particular class.
- Allowed states to exclude public hospitals and other classes of health care providers from a tax, but required states to tax all services within a class that was being taxed.
- Prohibited states in imposing taxes from including "hold harmless" provisions that had the effect of guaranteeing that the amount of tax paid would be returned to the provider.
- Allowed provider taxes to account for no more than 25 percent of a state's share of Medicaid costs until Sept. 30, 1995, after which the cap was eliminated.
- Limited the total amount of payments states could make to disproportionate share hospitals, generally those that served a higher than average number of low-income patients.
- Barred states from receiving matching funds for disproportionate share payments that exceeded 12 percent of the state's total Medicaid payments.

NIH Reauthorization

Abortion-related controversies prevented the enactment of legislation in the 102nd Congress to reauthorize expiring portions of the National Institutes of Health (NIH) and make other significant changes in the biomedical research establishment.

One bill (HR 2507) cleared Congress in 1992 but was vetoed by President Bush. A scaled-down bill (S 2899) was revived late in the session but did not pass the Senate.

Both bills bogged down partly because of proposals to increase NIH-funded research of diseases primarily affecting women and to require that women and minorities be included as subjects in NIH-funded clinical trials.

Most controversial were provisions to lift a four-year-old ban on funding research using fetal tissue from elective abortions. The abortion language helped prompt Bush's veto, which the House failed to override. Backers of lifting the ban cited research showing that fetal tissue had considerable promise in treating such diseases as juvenile diabetes. But Bush and other critics argued that removing the existing ban would encourage women to have abortions.

The legislation's primary purpose was to reauthorize the National Cancer Institute and the National Heart, Lung and Blood Institute. They were the biggest of NIH's institutes and the only ones requiring periodic reauthorization. HR 2507 would have authorized in fiscal 1993 $2.2 billion for the cancer institute, $1.4 billion for the heart institute and $500 million for the National Institute on Aging.

Controversial provisions, including those pertaining to fetal research, had to be stripped from a 1990 NIH reauthorization bill before winning presidential approval. *(Story, p. 590)*

House Action

The House Energy and Commerce Committee approved HR 2507 on a 27-16 party-line vote on June 4, 1991. The bill, formally reported (H Rept 102-136) June 28, faced strong objections from the Bush administration.

In a detailed letter of criticism, Health and Human Services Secretary Louis W. Sullivan warned that he would recommend a veto of the bill on the grounds that it represented an attempt to micromanage the NIH from Capitol Hill. Sullivan also argued that the authorization levels in the bill were too high.

Republicans on the committee also voiced objections to the provisions requiring that women be included in clinical trials, arguing that the requirements amounted to quotas for scientific experimentation.

The House passed HR 2507 on a 274-144 vote July 25. While a comfortable margin of victory, the vote was short of the two-thirds majority needed to overcome the expected veto.

Senate Action

The Senate Labor and Human Resources Committee approved HR 2507 on a 13-4 vote on Feb. 5, 1992; it was reported (S Rept 102-263) on March 13.

During committee action, Republicans sought unsuccessfully to modify the bill. Orrin G. Hatch, Utah, the panel's ranking Republican, offered an amendment to retain the fetal research ban while calling for a study of the feasibility of using tissue obtained from miscarriages and ectopic pregnancies. The proposal was rejected 4-13.

On the Senate floor, Hatch again offered a fetal tissue amendment, but it was rejected on a **23-77 (R 20-23; D 3-54) key vote.** *(1992 key votes, p. 1083)*

The only other controversial issue to arise during floor debate concerned two proposed surveys to be conducted by HHS examining the sexual behavior of adults and teenagers. As it had done in the past on sensitive issues, the Senate adopted conflicting amendments. First, it adopted a Paul Simon, D-Ill., amendment to allow the surveys, 57-40, then it approved an amendment by Jesse Helms, R-N.C., to prohibit funding for the surveys, 51-46.

The Senate passed HR 2507 on an 87-10 vote April 2.

Final Action

Before the conference report (H Rept 102-525) reached the House floor, the administration and its opponents each waged vigorous lobbying campaigns to sway opinion on the bill, with the President making personal phone calls aimed at shoring up his support.

To reassure members concerned about the fetal tissue ban's effects on research, Bush on May 19 issued an executive order to establish a "human fetal tissue bank" to collect tissue for research on miscarriages and ectopic pregnancies. Critics, however, said that the bank would be unworkable, given that much of the tissue in it would be unusable because of genetic flaws and other problems.

The House on May 28 adopted the conference report on a 260-148 vote, 12 votes short of a two-thirds majority. The Senate acted June 4, voting 85-12 to adopt the conference report and thus clearing the bill.

Citing the reversal of the fetal tissue ban and the bill's funding levels, Bush vetoed HR 2507 June 23.

The next day, the House failed to override the veto on a 271-156 vote.

In the wake of the successful veto, sponsors sought to push a compromise version of the measure. The bills (HR 5495, S 2899) took out some provisions objected to by the administration, left funding levels open-ended and required that researchers first attempt to use the fetal tissue bank proposed by Bush. Language dealing with women's health issues remained in the legislation.

The proposal was unacceptable to the administration, however, and although the Senate voted 85-12 on Oct. 2 to limit debate on S 2899, the measure went no further. HR 5495 saw no congressional action.

Prescription Drug User Fees

Manufacturers of most prescription drugs were required to help underwrite the costs of federal safety and efficacy reviews, under legislation cleared by Congress in 1992.

The measure (HR 6181 — PL 102-571) required makers of prescription drugs to pay both annual "facilities" fees and fees every time they submitted a drug for approval to the Food and Drug Administration (FDA). The facilities fees began at $60,000 and rose to $138,000 in the fifth year, while the application fees started at $100,000 and rose to $233,000 in five years. Drug-makers also had to pay a separate fee for each drug marketed, starting at $5,000 and rising to $14,000. Small and start-up companies were allowed to pay reduced or no fees.

The FDA promised to use the fees — estimated to raise more than $300 million over five years — to speed up the drug review process. Backers of the legislation said the agency's rapidly growing workload had become a bottleneck that was seriously delaying the introduction of new drugs.

The final bill, which was painstakingly negotiated among administration officials, lawmakers and drug company lobbyists, laid to rest a longtime standoff pitting the Reagan and Bush administrations against Congress and pharmaceutical manufacturers.

Presidents Reagan and Bush had been pushing, beginning in the mid-1980s, for the user fees. But the issue stalled because key members of Congress were opposed to the administrations' idea of giving at least some of the revenues to the Treasury, not to the FDA, which would have amounted to a tax on drug innovation to reduce the federal deficit.

As cleared by Congress, HR 6181 made clear that the fees would go directly to the FDA to use to reduce the length of the applications review process. HR 6181 also contained a provision allowing the waiving of user fees for the makers of "orphan" drugs used to treat rare diseases. *(Related action, orphan drugs, this page)*

Legislative Action

After having been negotiated in advance by drug company lobbyists and lawmakers, the original bill (HR 5952) moved quickly through the House. It was approved by the House Energy and Commerce Committee on Sept. 15, reported (H Rept 102-895) Sept. 22 and passed the House by voice vote under suspension of the rules also on Sept. 22.

The bill hit a snag in the Senate, however, threatening its chance for final passage in the waning days of the 102nd Congress. The obstacle was Orrin G. Hatch, Utah, the ranking Republican on the Senate Labor and Human Resources Committee. Although he was a longtime supporter of the user fee concept, Hatch expressed concerns that the fees might rise too much in the future or might not succeed in speeding up the approval process.

In addition, Hatch sought to use the bill to get the FDA to back off plans to limit health claims that could be made by makers of vitamins and other dietary supplements. Utah was a major producer of vitamins.

On Sept. 18, Hatch had won approval, 94-1, of an amendment to the fiscal 1993 Labor, Health and Human Services (HHS) and Education spending bill (HR 5677) placing a one-year moratorium on implementation of nutrition labeling regulations (PL 101-535) as they applied to food supplements such as vitamins and herbs. The amendment was dropped in conference. *(PL 101-535, p. 585)*

HR 5952 eventually was abandoned, and a compromise bill (HR 6181) was introduced. It contained Hatch language delaying regulations on vitamins and minerals until Dec. 15, 1993, and requiring a study of the issue.

The House passed HR 6181 by voice vote Oct. 6; the Senate followed suit the next day, clearing the measure. Bush signed the bill Oct. 29.

Major Provisions

As cleared, HR 6181:

- Authorized the Department of Health and Human Services to collect fees from makers of prescription drugs, beginning in fiscal 1993, with the fees to be credited to FDA funding for salaries and expenses.
- Required companies submitting drugs for FDA approval to pay the following fees: $100,000 in fiscal 1993, $150,000 in fiscal 1994, $208,000 in fiscal 1995, $217,000 in fiscal 1996 and $233,000 in fiscal 1997. Applications for drugs on which clinical data on safety and effectiveness were not required were set at $50,000 in fiscal 1993, $75,000 in fiscal 1994, $104,000 in fiscal 1995, $108,000 in fiscal 1996 and $116,000 in fiscal 1997.
- Required annual fees from makers for prescription drugs for which generic copies were not available of $60,000 in fiscal 1993, $88,000 in fiscal 1994, $126,000 in fiscal 1995, $131,000 in fiscal 1996 and $138,000 in fiscal 1997.
- Required makers of drugs who had new drug applications pending to pay an annual fee for each drug, of $6,000 in fiscal 1993, $9,000 in fiscal 1994, $12,500 in fiscal 1995, $13,000 in fiscal 1996 and $14,000 in fiscal 1997.
- Allowed companies with fewer than 500 employees to pay only half the application fees.
- Allowed HHS to grant fee waivers or exemptions for companies making drugs for rare diseases.
- Prohibited imposing fees unless the FDA's funding for salaries and expenses exceeded the fiscal 1992 level adjusted for inflation.
- Terminated the fee authority at the end of fiscal 1997.
- Prohibited HHS from enforcing provisions of the 1990 Nutrition Labeling and Education Act (PL 101-535) pertaining to dietary supplements until Dec. 15, 1993, and required HHS to develop new regulations on the issue.
- Prohibited until Nov. 8, 1993, the FDA from implementing proposed new regulations to switch from using "recommended daily allowances" in nutrition labeling to "reference daily intakes."

'Orphan' Drugs

A bill (S 2060 — S Rept 102-358) revising the 1983 Orphan Drug Act (PL 97-414) was reported from Senate Labor and Human Resources on Aug. 4, 1992, but received no further congressional attention. The bill was a revival of

Food Labeling

The Bush administration announced Dec. 2, 1992, that most processed foods must include uniform labels that not only showed how much fat each portion contained but also told consumers how that should figure in their diets.

Whether the labels should include recommended daily diet information was a matter of dispute between the Food and Drug Administration (FDA) and the Department of Agriculture. The new regulations, mandated by the Nutrition Labeling and Education Act of 1990 (PL 101-535), represented a win for FDA. *(PL 101-535, p. 585)*

legislation (HR 4638) pocket-vetoed by President Bush in 1990. *(HR 4638, p. 585)*

The purpose of S 2060 was to spur more price competition by reducing or eliminating some of the incentives to develop and manufacture "orphan" drugs. The bill would end the seven-year exclusive marketing rights allowed for highly profitable drugs under the orphan drug law, terminating a company's protected monopoly on a product if sales reached $200 million. Other companies then could seek Food and Drug Administration approval to market the drug.

Critics contended that the effect of the legislation would be that fewer drugs would be produced and, as a result, fewer people would benefit. They also claimed that the sales cap was unfair and arbitrary.

In related action, Congress in 1992 included a provision in a so-called user fee bill (HR 6181), which required manufacturers of most prescription drugs to help underwrite the costs of federal safety and efficacy reviews, to waive fees for manufacturers of orphan drugs. *(Story, p. 603)*

Drug, Mental Health Programs

After several years of regional and partisan strife, a bill (S 1306) to overhaul federal substance abuse and mental health programs, including block grants to states, cleared Congress in 1992.

The legislation reorganized the Alcohol, Drug Abuse and Mental Health Administration (ADAMHA) by essentially disbanding it. Under the measure, the agency's three research branches — the National Institute of Mental Health, the National Institute on Drug Abuse and the National Institute on Alcohol Abuse and Alcoholism — were folded into the National Institutes of Health (NIH), becoming the NIH's 14th, 15th and 16th institutes.

ADAMHA's remaining programs, which administered funds to states to provide treatment and prevention services, were reconstituted as the Substance Abuse and Mental Health Services Administration.

In another major policy change, the existing Alcohol, Drug Abuse and Mental Health block grant program was split into two programs, one for substance abuse and the other for mental health. The combined block grant had been created by Congress in 1981 under pressure from the Reagan administration. But critics led by Rep. Henry A. Waxman, D-Calif., had argued for several years that the block grant should be broken up to make states more accountable for how the money was spent. *(1981 action, Congress and the Nation Vol. VI, p. 523)*

S 1306 authorized $1.5 billion in fiscal 1993 and open-ended funding in fiscal 1994 for the new Substance Abuse Block Grant, and $450 million in fiscal 1993 and open-ended funding in fiscal 1994 for the new Mental Health Block Grants.

During consideration of the legislation, members also debated the issue of tobacco use. The final bill included language requiring states to enforce laws prohibiting the sale of tobacco to anyone under age 18, with states that failed to do so losing up to 40 percent of their federal alcohol and drug abuse treatment funds.

As cleared, S 1306 also contained language banning the use of federal funds for "needle exchange" programs aimed at helping prevent the spread of AIDS (acquired immune deficiency syndrome) by providing drug addicts with clean hypodermic needles.

Senate Action

The Senate Labor and Human Resources Committee by voice vote on July 17, 1991, approved S 1306, which retained the existing block grant structure. The bill, formally reported (S Rept 102-131) on July 30, authorized a total of $3.87 billion for the block grants and some new programs in fiscal 1992. The measure established a new formula for distributing block grant funds, with changes aimed at satisfying members from rural states who complained they were shortchanged under the previous formula. The bill also reorganized the ADAMHA.

The Senate passed S 1306 on Aug. 2 by voice vote.

House Action

House action was marked by controversy over such issues as Waxman's push to divide up the existing block grant.

On Nov. 6, 1991, the House Energy and Commerce Subcommittee on Health and the Environment approved a Waxman-sponsored bill (HR 3698) splitting the block grant in two. During subcommittee consideration, Thomas J. Bliley Jr., R-Va., won approval, 11-10, of an amendment that gutted a provision in the bill cutting off grants to states that did not have laws denying cigarettes to those under age 18. At the time, only three states — Missouri, Montana and New Mexico — had no law on minors and smoking.

Before approving HR 3698 on March 4, 1992, the Commerce Committee adopted a Waxman amendment reviving his anti-smoking provision in a watered-down form, by requiring states to adopt plans to curb purchase of tobacco by minors and cutting up to 40 percent of substance abuse block grant funds to states that failed to do so.

The Commerce Committee reported HR 3698 (H Rept 102-464) on March 24.

The House passed HR 3698 by voice vote March 24, then passed S 1306 with the language of HR 3698 also by voice vote.

Final Action

Conferees on S 1306 were able to put together an agreement that satisfied both chambers and the Bush administration by requiring compromises all around.

The administration and Senate sponsors were most adamant about provisions reorganizing the ADAMHA, an idea that House leaders had resisted. Senators also wanted to change the formula to direct more funding to rural states. Waxman and other House members, meanwhile, wanted to break up the existing block grant, which the administration opposed.

The conference agreement on S 1306 (H Rept 102-522), approved May 12, included the reorganization, the block grant split and the funding formula changes. Nevertheless, the bill faced several obstacles before it could become law. The first was posed by objections from House members whose states, particularly Florida, stood to lose funding under the new formula. In addition, the Bush administration did not like the provision that would lift a ban on federal funding of programs that allowed the distribution of clean hypodermic needles.

A effort to approve the conference report on S 1306 in the House under suspension of the rules failed 264-148 on May 19, short of the two-thirds majority required. On May 28, the House voted 214-157 to recommit the bill to conference.

Conferees approved a new agreement (H Rept 102-546), filed June 3, that restored the ban on needle exchanges.

The Senate approved the new conference agreement on June 9 on an 86-8 vote, after breaking a threatened filibuster by Bob Graham, D-Fla.

The House approved the conference report on July 1 on a 358-60 vote, after voting 266-138 to waive points of order against the conference report.

President Bush signed the bill (PL 102-321) July 10.

Medicaid Drug Discounts

Pummeled by complaints, Congress in 1992 backed away somewhat from an ambitious 1990 law requiring drugmakers to provide discounts to Medicaid.

The 1992 discount drug changes, which were largely inspired by controversy over the 1990 law's impact on Department of Veterans Affairs (VA) health programs, were ultimately included in an omnibus veterans health bill (HR 5193 — PL 102-585). *(Story, legislative history, p. 635)*

The 1990 law, included in a budget-reconciliation measure (HR 5835 — PL 101-508), had required that drugmakers sell their products to state Medicaid programs at the lowest price they offered to other bulk purchasers. Drug companies for years had been offering discounts to hospitals, nursing homes and health maintenance organizations but had generally not included Medicaid programs. Some of the deepest discounts had gone to VA health facilities. *(1990 law, p. 578)*

The problem was that VA programs represented a tiny fraction of all prescription drug sales, while Medicaid programs accounted for 15 percent of the market. As a result, the 1990 law forced manufacturers to offer far more extensive and costly price reductions to Medicaid programs.

Faced with the new requirement, many drugmakers chose to raise prices for the VA and other discount recipients, instead of cutting them for Medicaid. That in turn brought howls of protest from VA officials and veterans groups, who said the change was deeply affecting veterans' health programs.

In response, the 1992 legislation exempted the VA from the program, allowing drugmakers to resume deep discounts for veterans' hospitals without having to offer them to Medicaid. The final version of the measure, which took more than a year to negotiate, also required discounts of at least 24 percent for the VA, mandated discounts for certain other federally funded health facilities and slightly raised the minimum discounts manufacturers had to provide to Medicaid.

Senate Action

Two Senate committees in 1992 approved legislation in response to the discount drug controversy.

The Senate Labor and Human Resources Committee on Feb. 5 approved 17-0 a bill (S 1729 — S Rept 102-259) to require drugmakers to provide discounts to Public Health Service clinics at the larger of either a set discount or the discount provided to the VA. The Senate Veterans' Affairs Committee on Aug. 7 included in a veterans' health bill (S 2575 — S Rept 102-401) a provision requiring drug companies to enter into a "master agreement" to offer discounts to all federal buyers. Under the plan, companies were to enter into agreements to sell drugs at discounted prices to the VA, Public Health Service and other federal agencies. Companies that did not agree to the plan would not be allowed to sell to any agency or receive payment for drugs under Medicaid.

Neither S 1729 nor S 2575 saw further congressional action.

House Action

The House Veterans' Affairs Committee on Nov. 25, 1991, reported a bill (HR 2890 — H Rept 102-384, Part I) to permanently exempt the VA from Medicaid drug pricing calculations. The bill also required drugmakers to roll prices back to their Oct. 1, 1990, levels, plus an increment for inflation.

However, the bill then was sent to the Energy and Commerce Committee, where members were worried that simply exempting the VA would jeopardize the size of Medicaid's discounts. Debate over that and related issues delayed the bill for months. The committee on Sept. 17, 1992, finally reported a version of the bill (H Rept 102-384, Part II) that still exempted the VA from the best price calculation. It also exempted certain public health facilities. To protect Medicaid's interests, the bill increased slightly the minimum discount the 1990 law imposed as an alternative to the best price requirement.

The Energy and Commerce Committee eliminated the requirement to roll back prices to 1990 levels. Instead, it required that the VA receive a discount of at least 24 percent off the average price charged to non-federal buyers.

The House passed HR 2890 on Sept. 22 by voice vote under suspension of the rules.

Final Action

The Senate Finance Committee inserted provisions similar to those in HR 2890 into its version of HR 11, an urban aid tax bill. House negotiators, however, refused to discuss them as part of the tax bill. *(HR 11, p. 103)*

A compromise was worked out to include agreed-upon language — similar to the provisions of HR 2890 — in HR 5193, the House companion to S 2575. Congress cleared HR 5193 on Oct. 8, and President Bush signed it Nov. 4.

Generic Drug Regulation

Congress in 1992 responded to reports of widespread abuses in the approval process for generic drugs by clearing legislation (HR 2454) to increase the authority of the Food and Drug Administration (FDA) to oversee the industry.

HR 2454 authorized the FDA to punish those found to have defrauded or otherwise abused the abbreviated approval process for marketing generic copies of brand-name drugs.

Abuses of the generic drug approval process grew out of 1984 legislation (PL 98-417) that sought to spur drug price competition by making it easier to bring to market generic copies of already approved drugs. Under the law, generic drug makers no longer had to prove that their products were safe and effective; they only had to show that their drug was a "bioequivalent" with the same therapeutic action as a brand-name product whose safety and efficacy had previously been determined. *(1984 law, Congress and the Nation Vol. VI, p. 547)*

The law created a tremendous financial advantage for the first generic copy brought to market after the expiration of a brand-name drug's original patent. As a result, some manufacturers took illegal means to finish first, including bribing FDA officials and substituting samples of actual brand-name drugs for generic copies for the bioequivalence tests.

Hearings by the House Energy and Commerce Oversight Subcommittee in 1989 brought the scandal to light and helped lead to conviction of a number of industry and FDA employees.

The House Energy and Commerce Committee reported HR 2454 (H Rept 102-272) on Oct. 24, 1991. The House passed the bill on a 413-0 vote under suspension of the rules Oct. 31.

The Senate passed an amended version by voice vote April 10, 1992. The House accepted the Senate amendments April 28, clearing the measure for President Bush, who signed it May 13.

The core provisions of HR 2454 as cleared by Congress gave the FDA authority to bar individuals or companies convicted of offenses related to the drug approval process from future dealings with the agency. Specifically, the bill:

- Required the secretary of health and human services (HHS) to prohibit generic drug applications from any company convicted of a felony in connection with the approval process from further submissions for at least one and up to 10 years, and permanently in the case of a second offense.
- Gave the HHS secretary permissive authority to bar further dealings with other individuals and companies, for example in the case of those convicted of felonies before enactment of the law.
- Required HHS to withdraw approval for drugs in cases where approval was obtained through illegal means.
- Imposed civil penalties of up to $250,000 for individuals and $1 million for companies.

Infertility Clinics

Prompted by a growing number of complaints from couples disappointed in expensive artificial insemination procedures, Congress in 1992 cleared legislation (HR 4773 — PL 102-493) establishing new regulations governing infertility clinics.

The bill required clinics to report their rates of successful pregnancies to the Department of Health and Human Services (HHS), which was then to publish the information for couples seeking such services.

The push for government regulation of fertility procedures — in vitro fertilization and a newer procedure called gamete intrafallopian transfer — grew out of complaints that desperate couples were being exploited by relatively uncontrolled clinics. Some of the clinics were accused of exaggerating their pregnancy success rates. According to a congressional study, only about 9 percent of in vitro procedures resulted in live births.

The House Energy and Commerce Committee approved HR 4773 on April 7 and reported the measure (H Rept 102-624) on June 29. In addition to requiring clinics to report and HHS to publish information for consumers, the bill directed the department to establish a model program for inspecting and certifying embryo labs, although states were not required to adopt the model.

The bill did not contain any penalties for clinics that submitted false data.

The House passed HR 4773 by voice vote under suspension of the rules June 29.

The Senate Labor and Human Resources Committee approved the bill Sept. 16 and reported it (S Rept 102-452) Oct. 1. The Senate passed HR 4773 by voice vote Oct. 8. President Bush signed the measure Oct. 24.

Lead Poisoning

After two years of difficult negotiations, Congress in 1992 approved new rules aimed at preventing lead poisoning, especially among children, without overburdening cash-poor cities and industries.

The new rules were included in a housing reauthorization bill (HR 5334 — PL 102-550). *(Story, legislative history, p. 694)*

Lead is a toxic metal found to cause developmental disabilities in children. Although wide agreement existed that children's exposure to lead needed to be reduced, the legislation faced intense lobbying opposition by the real estate industry, which argued that it was too costly and would slow home buying.

The housing bill, which included provisions of a lead poisoning measure (HR 5730), implemented key recommendations of a strategic plan released in 1991 by the federal Centers for Disease Control.

Legislative Action

Panels in both the House and Senate approved lead-control bills in 1991. The Senate Environment and Public Works Committee on Aug. 1 approved S 391, requiring the Environmental Protection Agency (EPA) to restrict the use of lead in products that were the most likely to result in lead entering the environment. S 391 was reported (S Rept 102-179) on Oct. 8. The House Energy and Commerce

Subcommittee on Health and the Environment on Nov. 4 approved a broader bill (HR 2840) tightening federal standards for lead in drinking water and also requiring replacement of lead-contaminated water lines and inspection of apartments for lead.

Concern over the significant costs of a lead-control program blocked further action in 1991. When action resumed in 1992, interest was focused on a more narrow approach to reducing environmental lead.

The House Energy and Commerce Committee on Aug. 5 approved a compromise bill (HR 5730 — H Rept 102-852, Part I) banning some lead uses and requiring labeling of lead products. HR 5730, sponsored by Al Swift, D-Wash., contained some parts of HR 2840, but it dropped some of the more controversial provisions, including a requirement that cities replace lead drinking water pipes. Also eliminated were provisions, strongly opposed by the National Association of Realtors, to require real estate agents to disclose evidence of lead contamination to potential buyers.

HR 5730 as approved required the EPA to inspect schools and day-care centers for lead hazards and authorized $30 million to help schools with lead abatement costs. Arguing that $30 million was not enough to remove lead from thousands of schools and centers, Thomas J. Bliley Jr., R-Va., offered an amendment to allow the poorest schools to receive grants to pay for lead removal and not require federal inspection. The amendment was rejected, 19-24.

The House Education and Labor Committee shared jurisdiction over HR 5730. The bill was reported (H Rept 102-852, Part II) on Sept. 22.

The compromise bill appeared to have only a slight chance for passage as the 102nd Congress drew to a close. As a result, sponsors turned to conferees on the housing bill, who agreed to expand the scope of the lead provisions already in their bill to include numerous provisions of HR 5730.

Major Provisions

As cleared Oct. 8, 1992, the lead provisions of HR 5334:

- Required the disclosure of the risks of lead poisoning before the sale or rental of older homes.
- Required the certification of contractors who provided lead abatement and inspection services.
- Authorized $375 million for inspection and abatement of lead hazards in low-income housing.
- Directed the Environmental Protection Agency and the Occupational Safety and Health Administration to establish training and certification requirements for contractors who used lead products.

Medical Device Regulation

Congress in 1992 agreed to delay for six months implementation of a 1990 law stiffening federal oversight of medical equipment.

The bill (S 2783 — PL 102-300) extended until Nov. 28, 1992, the deadline for the Food and Drug Administration to issue regulations for sections of PL 101-629, which sought to streamline the marketing approval process for new devices, improve the oversight of devices already on the market and make recalling defective products easier. *(PL 101-629, p. 586)*

The extension delayed the requirement for manufacturers to devise tracking systems for certain implanted devices, such as heart pacemakers, and equipment used in patients' homes, such as oxygen tanks.

The Senate passed S 2783 by voice vote May 21, and the House followed suit May 28, clearing the bill. President Bush signed the measure June 16.

Rehabilitation Act

In legislation (HR 5482) cleared in 1992, programs authorized under the Rehabilitation Act of 1973 were extended through 1997.

HR 5482 provided a total fiscal 1993 authorization for the programs of $2.6 billion. *(1986 reauthorization, Congress and the Nation Vol. VII, p. 613)*

The Rehabilitation Act programs — which seek to maximize employment opportunities for the disabled — provide funds to states for independent living centers, rehabilitative training centers, and employment, transportation and technical assistance programs.

While HR 5482 did not make major changes in the existing programs, it made qualifying for rehabilitation services easier for those with disabilities and eliminated all references in the law to "handicaps," a word that advocates for the disabled found objectionable.

The House Education and Labor Committee approved HR 5482 July 8 and reported the bill (H Rept 102-822) Aug. 10. The House passed the measure by voice vote under suspension of the rules Aug. 10.

The Senate Labor and Human Resources Committee approved a companion measure (S 3065) July 29 and reported it (S Rept 102-357) Aug. 3. The Senate passed S 3065 by voice vote Aug. 11. The Senate passed an amended HR 5482 the next day by voice vote.

The House adopted the conference report (H Rept 102-973) on Oct. 2, and the Senate followed suit Oct. 5, clearing HR 5482. President Bush signed the bill (PL 102-569) Oct. 29.

DES Research

Congress in 1992 cleared legislation (HR 4178 — PL 102-409) to authorize research and public education programs on the health effects of DES (diethylstilbestrol), an anti-miscarriage drug found to cause severe health problems in the children of women who took it.

DES, a synthetic estrogen, was prescribed to an estimated 5 million pregnant women between 1938 and 1971. The drug was linked to a rare form of vaginal cancer in the daughters of those women, while other studies suggested links to health problems in the women themselves and in some of their sons.

HR 4178 authorized open-ended funding through fiscal 1996 for the programs, to be operated by the National Institutes of Health.

The House Energy and Commerce Committee reported HR 4178 (H Rept 102-817) Aug. 10. The House passed the bill later that day by voice vote under suspension of the rules. The Senate Labor and Human Resources Committee reported a companion measure (S 2837 — S Rept 102-413) on Sept. 21. The Senate passed HR 4178 by voice vote Sept. 30. President Bush signed the bill Oct. 13.

Breast Cancer Screening

Breast cancer screening facilities were required to meet minimum federal standards, under legislation (HR 6182) cleared by Congress in 1992.

The bill required federal certification for equipment and personnel performing mammography, a special X-ray technique used to detect breast cancer in its early stages.

The Senate Labor and Human Resources Committee approved a breast cancer screening bill (S 1777) on Sept. 16, reporting the measure (S Rept 102-448) on Oct. 1. The House passed its own bill (HR 5938 — H Rept 102-889) under suspension of the rules on Sept. 24, 390-18.

HR 6182, a compromise between the two bills, passed the House Oct. 6 by voice vote under suspension of the rules. The Senate Oct. 7 passed the measure. President Bush signed it (PL 102-539) Oct. 27.

Disease Prevention

After lengthy negotiations between the House and Senate, Congress late in 1992 cleared legislation (HR 3635 — PL 102-531) to renew federal programs aimed at preventing disease and injury.

The final bill boosted to $205 million the authorization for the Preventive Health Services Block Grant. The block grant, created in 1981, provided money for states to use for a wide variety of purposes ranging from rodent control to rape crisis counseling. *(1981 action, Congress and the Nation Vol. VI, p. 523)*

Initiatives in the bill included programs to screen and prevent lead poisoning in children, to screen and prevent infertility arising from sexually transmitted diseases and to establish a non-profit foundation to help fund research on disease prevention.

The Senate Labor and Human Resources Committee approved a disease prevention bill (S 1944) on Nov. 14, 1991, and reported it (S Rept 102-244) on Nov. 25. The House Energy and Commerce Committee approved its version (HR 3635) on Nov. 7 and reported the measure (H Rept 102-318) on Nov. 15. The House passed HR 3635 by voice vote under suspension of the rules Nov. 19. The Senate passed an amended HR 3635 by voice vote Nov. 27.

The House- and Senate-passed bills were far apart on funding levels, with the Senate bill authorizing $275 million for the block grant and the House calling for $135 million, the amount actually appropriated in fiscal 1992.

The bill that emerged from conference (H Rept 102-1019) in 1992 called for a funding level, $205 million, that split the difference between the two chambers' proposals.

The House adopted the conference report by voice vote under suspension of the rules Oct. 6. The Senate adopted the conference report by voice vote Oct. 7, clearing the measure. President Bush signed the bill Oct. 27.

Alzheimer's Disease

Programs designed to increase research into Alzheimer's disease and help families cope with its devastating impact were reauthorized under legislation (S 1577 — PL 102-507) cleared by Congress in 1992.

The bill authorized open-ended funding for a series of Alzheimer's related programs, including a council that coordinated programs and information sharing among the federal agencies that studied the ailment.

The Senate Labor and Human Resources Committee reported S 1577 (S Rept 102-242) on Nov. 25, 1991. The Senate passed the legislation by voice vote Nov. 26.

The House passed its version of the bill (HR 3082 — H Rept 102-623) by voice vote under suspension of the rules on June 29, 1992. The House then passed an amended version of S 1577 by voice vote on Oct. 6.

The Senate Oct. 7 cleared the measure for President Bush, who signed it Oct. 24.

Cancer Registries

Congress in 1992 cleared a bill (S 3312 — PL 102-515) encouraging states to set up registries to keep track of cancer cases.

The bill authorized $30 million for the Department of Health and Human Services to make grants to states to operate registries that tracked cancer cases, with the aim of facilitating research on different forms of the disease.

S 3312 also ordered the National Cancer Institute to study why breast cancer was more common in some states than in others.

Both provisions were originally part of an omnibus bill (HR 2507) reauthorizing portions of the National Institutes of Health, but it was vetoed by President Bush.

The Senate passed S 3312 by voice vote on Oct. 2. The House by voice vote approved the bill with minor changes Oct. 6, and the Senate cleared it Oct. 7. Bush signed the bill Oct. 24.

Drug Licensing

Congress in 1992 gave states an additional two years to meet licensing deadlines imposed under a 1988 law intended to stop the resale of prescription drugs.

The bill (S 3163 — PL 102-353) amended the 1988 Prescription Drug Marketing Act (PL 100-293), which required wholesale distributors of prescription drugs to be licensed in the state in which they conducted business. *(1988 law, Congress and the Nation Vol. VII, p. 601)*

The licensing requirement was supposed to take effect on Sept. 14, 1992. As that deadline approached, however, 23 states had not yet set up the needed licensing mechanisms. Among these states were New Jersey and Pennsylvania, which were home to a significant number of drug manufacturing facilities. Puerto Rico also fell into this category.

Sponsors of S 3163 said more time was needed to prevent potential disruptions of drug distribution. The bill created a two-year program during which distributors in states that had not instituted licensing procedures could register with the Food and Drug Administration.

The Senate passed S 3163 by voice vote Aug. 11, and the House followed suit Aug. 12, clearing the measure. President Bush signed it Aug. 26.

Health Policy Agency

The Agency for Health Care Policy and Research was reauthorized through fiscal 1995, under legislation (HR 5673 — PL 102-410) cleared by Congress in 1992.

The health policy agency, created by the 1989 budget-reconciliation law (PL 101-239), was responsible for reviewing the quality and cost-effectiveness of medical procedures. The agency also published "practice guidelines" for physicians faced with ailments for which myriad treatments were available. *(Reconciliation provisions, p. 571)*

HR 5673, which provided open-ended funding for the agency, was reported (H Rept 102-892) from House Energy and Commerce on Sept. 22. The House passed the bill 397-8 under suspension of the rules Sept. 24. The Senate passed HR 5673 by voice vote Sept. 30, clearing the measure. President Bush signed it Oct. 13.

Medical Training

Congress in 1992 cleared a bill (HR 3508) updating and renewing the federal programs that helped fund the training of doctors, nurses and other health professionals.

The legislation authorized slightly more than $1 billion over four years for the programs. The bill rewrote the existing aid programs so that they focused more specifically on the training of professionals who delivered primary care services, such as pediatrics and family care, and those who planned to practice in rural, inner-city or other medically underserved areas.

HR 3508 reauthorized Titles VII and VIII of the Public Health Service Act, which provided aid to students, in the form of direct loans, loan guarantees and scholarships, and to training institutions, in the form of grants and contracts.

The bill also extended for four years the Health Education Assistance Loan (HEAL) program, which provided federal backing for loans made to students in health professions training. It included provisions aimed at reducing the rate of student defaults under the program.

The House Energy and Commerce Committee approved HR 3508 on Oct. 8, 1991, and reported it (H Rept 102-275) on Oct. 25. The House passed the bill by voice vote under suspension of the rules Nov. 12.

The Senate Labor and Human Resources Committee approved a companion bill (S 1933) on Nov. 13, 1991, and reported it (S Rept 102-227) on Nov. 21. The Senate passed an amended HR 3508 by voice vote Nov. 26.

Differences between the two measures — for example, steps to reduce the default rate in the HEAL program — prevented quick final approval of the bill. After months of staff negotiations, a conference agreement was reached on Sept. 24, 1992. The Senate adopted the conference report (H Rept 102-925) by voice vote Sept. 25, and the House adopted it Sept. 29, clearing HR 3508.

President Bush signed the bill (PL 102-408) Oct. 13.

Malpractice Suits

Legislation (HR 6183 — PL 102-501) to provide federal malpractice protection for doctors and other health professionals who worked in federally backed community health centers was enacted in 1992.

The bill covered clinic workers under the Federal Tort Claims Act and made the federal government the defendant in any malpractice actions. The goal was to help the community and migrant health clinics save the roughly $58 million a year they were spending to purchase private malpractice insurance.

The House passed an initial version of the malpractice immunity bill (HR 3591 — H Rept 102-823, Part I; H Rept 102-823, Part II) on Sept. 15. It then approved a slightly revised bill (HR 6183) by voice vote on Oct. 6. The Senate passed HR 6183 by voice vote Oct. 8, clearing the measure. President Bush signed the bill Oct. 24.

Health Care Fraud

On Oct. 3, 1992, the Senate by voice vote passed a bill (S 2652) to increase penalties for health care fraud, but it died upon adjournment of the 102nd Congress.

S 2652 would have made health care fraud by either patients or providers — such as hospitals and doctors — a federal crime. Convictions of medical fraud would bring a maximum of 10 years in prison and a fine as high as $250,000; if bodily harm had occurred, the maximum prison sentence would rise to 20 years.

The bill would have authorized $20 million to hire 200 FBI agents to investigate medical fraud, $5 million for 50 U.S. attorneys to prosecute cases under the act and $5 million for inspectors at the Department of Health and Human Services to investigate health care fraud.

Medicare Payment Rules

Efforts to reform some of Medicare's administrative procedures, as well as to address areas of waste and fraud in the program, were quashed in 1992.

HR 3837 would have cracked down on unscrupulous sellers of medical equipment by barring Medicare payments for certain items sold by telephone; tightened rules requiring private insurance plans to pay benefits for people who also were covered by Medicare; changed the system for paying overtime to U.S. Customs Service inspectors, which reportedly was vulnerable to abuse; and stopped the payment of benefits to dead people.

The House Ways and Means Committee reported HR 3837 (H Rept 102-486, Part I) on April 7. The House Energy and Commerce Committee, which shared jurisdiction, reported the bill (H Rept 102-486, Part II) on Aug. 3. The House passed HR 3837 by voice vote under suspension of the rules Aug. 3, and the Senate passed an amended version by voice vote Oct. 7.

Many of HR 3837's provisions on Medicare changes subsequently were attached to an urban aid tax bill (HR 11), which was vetoed by President Bush. *(HR 11, p. 103)*

Long-Term Care

The Senate Labor and Human Resources Committee Aug. 12, 1991, reported legislation (S 2141 — S Rept 102-375) that would have subjected sellers of insurance to protect consumers from the cost of long-term health care to new federal regulations. The bill saw no further congressional action.

S 2141, a follow-up to the 1990 law regulating "Medigap" insurance plans, would have established federal standards for coverage, prohibited high-pressure tactics and revised the way insurance agents were paid to change their incentive to sell people more policies than necessary. *(Medigap regulation, p. 582)*

FDA Enforcement

The House Energy and Commerce Committee on Oct. 5, 1992, reported legislation (HR 3642 — H Rept 102-1030) to increase and standardize the enforcement powers of the Food and Drug Administration (FDA).

Sponsors said the legislation was needed because the Food and Drug Act had not been overhauled since its enactment in 1938. Instead, FDA authority had been added in bits and pieces as Congress addressed individual problems in regulated industries. HR 3642 would have standardized enforcement powers across the agency and granted subpoena power the FDA did not have.

Industries regulated by FDA saw the legislation as a threat, and the Bush administration opposed it.

The committee had approved HR 3642 on a straight party-line vote of 27-16 on July 9.

Disabilities Prevention

Legislation to establish a disability prevention program at the Centers for Disease Control was considered by the 102nd Congress but did not clear.

HR 3401, a five-year authorization bill, outlined funding priorities for research, public education and training of health care professionals, demonstration projects and technical assistance.

The House Energy and Commerce Committee reported HR 3401 (H Rept 102-271) on Oct. 24, 1991. The House passed the bill by voice vote under suspension of the rules Oct. 28.

The Senate Labor and Human Resources Committee had approved a companion measure (S 509) on March 13.

Similar legislation had passed the House in 1990. *(Story, p. 596)*

Chronology Of Action On Human Services

1989-90

By far the most important piece of human services legislation produced by the 101st Congress was a massive, $22.5 billion child care bill aimed at making quality day care available to millions of American families. The bill finally cleared in 1990, after several years of intense debate, was seen by many as belated congressional recognition of the social revolution that had occurred in previous decades as a majority of mothers of young children entered the work force.

While efforts to launch other initiatives in the social welfare area continued to be held back by the huge federal deficit, the 101st Congress also approved other significant human services bills, including a major expansion of the Head Start program and a new program aimed at encouraging national, community- and school-based volunteer service projects.

Child Care

Congress in 1990 cleared legislation to give American families billions of dollars in tax credits and other assistance for child care.

The five-year, $22.5 billion package, approved as part of the fiscal 1991 deficit-reduction bill (HR 5835 — PL 101-508), culminated a three-year legislative effort by a coalition of child care advocacy groups, organized labor and educators. The controversy stirred up by the legislation was reflected in the relatively close votes taken Oct. 27 on the conference report (H Rept 101-964) in the House, 228-200, and in the Senate, 54-45.

President Bush signed the reconciliation bill on Nov. 5. *(Reconciliation, p. 55)*

The legislation was the first major child-care measure to emerge from Congress since 1971, when President Richard Nixon vetoed a $2 billion child care bill on the grounds that it would undermine the family by encouraging women to work outside the home. By 1990, however, that issue had become largely moot, with statistics showing that 58 percent of all women with children under age 6 were in the work force. Millions of women worked because they were sole wage earners for their families. Millions of others worked because two incomes were necessary to provide the standard of living formerly achievable on one.

As cleared, HR 5835 included $18.3 billion in tax credits to help low- and moderate-income families cope with the costs of child care, and $4.25 billion for new grant programs to help states improve the quality and availability of such care.

The tax credit package included a $12.4 billion expansion over five years of the earned-income tax credit (EITC) for working low-income families, with an extra credit for infants. It also created a new health insurance credit for families with children, with an estimated five-year cost of $5.2 billion.

The final version of the bill made no change in the existing tax credit for dependent care. Instead, it focused on providing new aid for families whose incomes were too low to benefit from the existing credit.

The grant funding in HR 5835 included $2.5 billion in appropriated funds over three years to help low-income families pay for child care; $1.5 billion for an entitlement program within Title IV of the Social Security Act to help provide care for poor families whose incomes were too high to qualify for welfare; and $200 million in entitlement funds to aid states in improving day-care services.

To partially pay for the new aid and tax credits, the bill made permanent a 3 percent telephone excise tax.

Provisions making changes in the Social Security program, including relaxing the so-called earnings test, were considered as part of the child care legislation, but they were dropped before enactment. *(Social Security, p. 717)*

Background

Child care advocates had made a major push during the 100th Congress to enact legislation popularly known as the ABC (Act for Better Child Care) bill. That $2.5 billion measure had called for allocating federal funds for child care services that met minimum health and safety standards. The measure died in the waning days of the Congress, however, amid partisan discord in the Senate and concern in the House over church-state questions. *(Congress and the Nation Vol. VII, p. 628)*

Child care also became an issue in the 1988 presidential campaign. In August, Vice President Bush, the Republican presidential candidate, outlined a proposal for a tax-credit plan to help poor families retain more of their income so they could pay for child care.

Within two months of his inauguration, President Bush formally outlined his child care proposal. The plan contained two parts, with the first (S 601, HR 1466) calling for altering an existing tax break for poor families and creating a new one. The existing dependent-care tax credit would be made "refundable," meaning that families who were too poor to owe taxes could receive a cash refund. A new credit of up to $1,000 per child up to age 4 also would be provided; it would be available even to families with no child care costs. When fully implemented in 1994, the new credit would have aided an estimated 3.5 million families with incomes below $20,000.

The other part of the Bush plan (S 602, HR 1467) called for an expansion of the Head Start program for disadvantaged 3- and 4-year-olds. The administration estimated that its requested funding increase for the program, to an authorization of nearly $1.5 billion in fiscal 1990, was enough to enroll an additional 95,000 children in Head Start.

1989 Senate Action

The Senate made the first move toward enactment of child care legislation. On March 15, 1989, the Labor and Human Resources Committee, on an 11-5 vote, approved a $1.75 billion version of the ABC bill. S 5 was formally reported (S Rept 101-17) on April 12.

S 5 had been modified in several important ways from the 1988 legislation. After negotiations with Orrin G.

Hatch, Utah, the ranking Republican on the committee, Democratic sponsors agreed to changes in the section on minimum health and safety standards, strengthening the state role in setting the standards and ensuring that any federal standards would not be stiffer than the strictest existing state standard.

Another key change concerned the use of funds for child care services provided by or in religious institutions — an important constitutional issue and a major political problem throughout the debate. The new language, which was endorsed by various religious and education groups, was similar to existing rules governing Head Start. The provisions barred child care programs that received more than 80 percent of their funds from federal or state governments from discriminating on the basis of religion in hiring or admissions. Programs with a smaller share of government funding were allowed to show preference for church members in some cases.

Meanwhile, the Senate Finance Committee June 13 approved a tax-credit plan on a 17-3 vote. The package, attached to legislation (S 1129) making changes in the "Section 89" rules, slightly increased and made refundable the existing dependent-care tax credit; it also created a credit of up to $500 for premiums paid for health insurance coverage by families with children. *('Section 89,' p. 708)*

By the time the child care legislation was ready for floor action, the Labor Committee bill (S 5) clearly did not have enough support to pass. So Majority Leader George J. Mitchell, D-Maine, put together a substitute incorporating a severely amended ABC bill, a Head Start expansion and the Finance Committee's tax credit proposal. Mitchell's bill made two significant retreats from earlier versions of ABC. The first change, pushed by the nation's governors, dropped a requirement that states meet federal health and safety standards to receive funding. The second partially lifted the original bill's ban on funding for sectarian programs.

Senate Minority Leader Robert Dole, R-Kan., countered with a GOP alternative that called for making the existing dependent-care credit refundable, adjusting the existing earned-income tax credit for family size and authorizing a new $400 million program of block grants for child care services.

Floor action on S 5 involved two weeks of sharp partisan skirmishing. In a major setback for the Bush administration, Dole's proposal was rejected June 22 on a **44-56 (R 42-3; D 2-53) key vote**. *(1989 key votes, p. 1021)*

After rejecting the Dole plan, the Senate voted 63-37 to adopt the Mitchell substitute. Then, under pressure from Republicans critical of the bill's health insurance provisions and members of both parties who felt the measure should contain an expansion of the existing earned-income credit, Finance Committee Chairman Lloyd Bentsen, D-Texas, offered an amendment to increase the earned-income credit for families with children under the age of 3 while reducing eligibility for the health insurance credit. It was adopted on a 54-45 vote. Members also scrapped over provisions regarding Section 89.

The Senate passed S 5 by voice vote June 23.

1989 House Action

The House Education and Labor Committee approved its child care bill (HR 3) by a near party-line vote of 23-11 and, on June 27, 1989, formally reported the measure (H Rept 101-190, Part I). Debate on HR 3 was marked by a degree of partisan division unusual for the committee. Peter Smith of Vermont was the only Republican to vote for the bill.

HR 3 authorized $1.78 billion for an ABC grant program, a major Head Start expansion and a new program of school-based child care. Like the compromise Senate bill, the measure no longer mandated federal health and safety standards, instead calling on states to set their own.

On July 19, the Ways and Means Committee approved, 26-10, a package of tax credits and grants to states totaling $16 billion over five years in the fiscal 1990 budget-reconciliation bill (HR 3299). The bill included an increase in the earned-income credit and a $1.5 billion addition to the existing Social Services Block Grant, earmarked for child care.

The jurisdictional battle between the two committees created sharp divisions in those working on the child care issue. The Education and Labor Committee bill was backed by a broad coalition of education and child-advocacy groups, while the Ways and Means bill commanded stronger support among House members. The House leadership worked for months to find a compromise solution to the conflict, which touched off bitter recriminations from child care lobbyists toward Ways and Means Democrats.

Although the jurisdictional battle prevented floor action on HR 3 in 1989, the provisions of both committees' bills were included in HR 3299. When that bill reached the floor, sponsors faced a strong challenge from a bipartisan group led by Charles W. Stenholm, D-Texas. Stenholm's amendment was similar to the Ways and Means plan, but without the requirement that states set standards for child care providers. After an intense and often acrimonious lobbying campaign during which each side accused the other of spreading misinformation, the Stenholm amendment was rejected Oct. 5 on a **195-230 (R 159-16; D 36-214) key vote**.

When the reconciliation measure reached conference committee, members from the House Education and Senate Labor panels initially agreed to a $1.7 billion version of the child care provisions under which a majority of the funds would go to ABC programs. Subsequently, however, negotiators decided to drop all the child care provisions from the bill, leaving the issue to be resolved in 1990.

1990 Action

After months of negotiations, House leaders finally worked out a compromise between the Ways and Means and the Education and Labor committees in March 1990. The agreement dropped the ABC portion of HR 3, while increasing the amount of Social Services Block Grant funding for child care by $2.9 billion over five years. It also included school-based before- and after-school care and an expansion of the EITC, at a total cost of $18.5 billion over five years.

When the measure reached the House floor, sponsors faced a new challenge, this time from a conservative coalition led by Stenholm and E. Clay Shaw Jr., R-Fla. The Stenholm-Shaw alternative differed from the Democratic leadership's plan in that it did not authorize a before- and after-school-care plan and called for saving about $1 billion by barring families with incomes above $90,000 from claiming the dependent-care credit.

The Stenholm-Shaw amendment also required states to provide vouchers that parents could use to buy whatever sort of care they wanted for their children. The voucher proposal was strongly supported by such groups as the National Association of Evangelicals, while it was opposed by education and civil liberties groups. After the Democratic leadership worked furiously to line up votes against the administration-backed proposal, the amendment was rejected March 29 on a 195-225 vote.

The House passed HR 3 by a 265-145 vote March 29.

The Senate passed an amended version of the bill by voice vote April 24.

Conference Action

Even before the conference on HR 3 began, House members demonstrated their opposition to the ABC child care grant program included in the Senate-passed bill. Members voted 411-0 May 9 to instruct conferees to reject the provisions.

The House conference delegation, however, was led by members such as Education Committee Chairman Augustus F. Hawkins, D-Calif., who favored the ABC provisions. After several weeks of negotiations, conferees June 19 agreed on a compromise authorizing $1.9 billion in child care aid, with some of that amount to go for a compromise ABC program. But House members killed that idea the next day by voting 416-0 to reject the proposal.

With funding for the new programs dependent on a resolution of the budget situation, further action on HR 3 was delayed as White House-congressional negotiations dragged on through the summer. The announcement of a budget summit agreement Sept. 30 cleared the way for action on child care.

Soon after, White House officials reached a compromise with members of the Senate Labor Committee: a $2.5 billion authorization over three years in new grants to states to finance child care services for families with incomes below 75 percent of their state's median income. The agreement also called for a limited set of standards for child care providers.

The grant package was further refined Oct. 20 to win the support of Hawkins. Under the final agreement, states were required to use 75 percent of their funds either to provide child care services directly to low-income families or to increase the availability and quality of care. Of their remaining grant money, states were required to spend 75 percent on programs to provide preschool education or before- or after-school care.

On Oct. 26, conferees reached agreement on the tax credit and entitlement provisions of the child care package. The final agreement created a new entitlement program, funded at $1.5 billion over five years, to help pay the child care bills of low-income families not poor enough to qualify for welfare.

The compromise also expanded the earned-income credit and created the child-health credit championed by Senate Finance Committee Chairman Bentsen. In addition, it created a new entitlement program, funded at a total of $200 million over five years, to help states improve the quality of child care.

The package subsequently was folded into the fiscal 1991 reconciliation bill (HR 5835).

Major Provisions

The major child care provisions of HR 5835:

- **Tax Credits.** Increased the earned-income tax credit (EITC), gradually raising the level to 23 percent of an inflation-adjusted base level of income for a family with one qualifying child.
- Provided an additional 5 percent credit for those with qualifying children under age 1.
- Allowed an additional credit for premiums paid on health insurance coverage for qualified children.
- Provided that EITC and supplemental credits not be considered as income for the purpose of calculating welfare eligibility.
- **Grants to States Under Title IV.** Expanded an existing entitlement program of grants to states for child care costs for welfare recipients by adding an additional $300 million for child care help for low-income families not eligible for welfare.
- Allowed states to use the grants either to pay to centers or to give to parents as vouchers for use at the center of their choice.
- Required that to receive federal funds providers be licensed and regulated by the state, and permit parents unlimited access.
- Authorized an additional $50 million a year through 1994 for a program of grants to states to improve child care licensing and monitoring.
- **Child Care Block Grant.** Authorized $750 million in fiscal 1991, $825 million in 1992, $925 million in 1993 and open-ended funding in 1994 and 1995 for a new program of grants to states to help improve and expand child care services.
- Allowed states to use up to 75 percent of funds to pay for care for eligible children from families with incomes below 75 percent of the state median income.
- Required states to use at least 75 percent of funds for programs aimed at improving the quality of child care and encouraging early-childhood development and school-based programs.
- Required states to give parents their choice of programs, to the extent practicable.
- Required that child care providers receiving funds be licensed by the appropriate state and local agencies.
- Required states to develop health and safety standards and to set up procedures to enforce them.
- Prohibited funds from being used for any sectarian purpose, except for care paid through use of vouchers.
- Prohibited funds from being used to provide services during the regular school day for students in grades 1-12, or that duplicated the academic program of any school.
- Affirmed existing federal laws against religious discrimination, except that a sectarian organization may require employees to adhere to the religious tenets and practices of the religion.
- Generally prohibited discrimination against children on the basis of religion in providing child care services, but allowed preference in admitting children to slots not funded by the law to those whose families had a pre-existing affiliation with a religious institution.
- Prohibited any discrimination in hiring or admissions in programs that received 80 percent or more of their budgets from federal or state money.

Head Start

Congress on Oct. 19, 1990, cleared the biggest expansion of the Head Start program for disadvantaged preschoolers since the program was created in 1965.

The action came as part of an omnibus reauthorization of human services programs (HR 4151 — PL 101-501).

Although Health and Human Services Secretary Louis W. Sullivan had expressed "serious concerns" about the bill, President Bush signed the measure on Nov. 3.

The bill increased the funding authorization for the Head Start program, which in 1990 served about 20 percent of eligible children, to be sufficient by 1994 to serve all preschoolers who qualified on the basis of low family income. Budget constraints made it unlikely, however, that appropriations for the program would reach the authorization levels. While HR 4151 authorized $2.4 billion for the program in fiscal 1991, the appropriations bill for that year contained $1.95 billion. HR 4151 also called for $4.27 billion for Head Start in fiscal 1992, $5.92 billion in 1993 and $7.66 billion in 1994. The bill required that 10 percent of the funds be reserved for "quality improvements," such as raising teacher salaries, buying equipment and refurbishing facilities.

The Head Start authorization increases contained in HR 4151 were on top of an earlier funding boost (HR 1300 — PL 101-120) approved by Congress in 1989, that increased the 1990 authorization level from $1.405 billion to $1.552 billion. HR 1300 was reported from House Education and Labor (H Rept 101-12) on March 20 and passed by voice vote under suspension of the rules by the House March 21. The Senate passed the bill, thus clearing it, by voice vote Oct. 5. The president signed the measure Oct. 23.

Legislative Action

Despite Head Start's overwhelming popularity on Capitol Hill, the legislation to increase funding for the program stirred considerable debate. While administration officials and lawmakers agreed that the program should have more money, a dispute erupted over how to spend the added dollars.

On one side was the administration, which thought that the money should be used to enroll more children. In requesting an additional $500 million for the program in 1991, the administration had estimated that as many as 70 percent of eligible children could be served for at least one year.

But Head Start operators and their allies in Congress argued that the increased funding should be used to improve the quality of existing programs. Noting that inflation-adjusted per-child spending in the program had fallen by 13 percent between 1981 and 1989, they warned that the funding decline had reduced the quality of services provided, put financial pressure on program operators and kept salaries for Head Start employees at unacceptably low levels.

HR 4151, which had been approved by the Human Services Subcommittee on April 3, was reported by the full Education and Labor Committee on May 9 (H Rept 101-480).

The bill as approved by committee called for $2.39 billion for Head Start in fiscal 1991, with the authorization rising to $7.66 billion by fiscal 1994. The subcommittee version of the measure had set aside 10 percent of funding for quality improvement efforts, with at least half that amount to go for salary increases for Head Start workers. After bipartisan negotiations, the full committee amended that provision to implement the quality set-aside only when appropriations levels for the program were significantly above the previous year's level.

Before the bill reached the House floor, the Office of Management and Budget released a statement opposing the bill, citing "excessive" funding levels and the quality set-aside provision.

Nevertheless, HR 4151 passed on a 404-14 vote May 16.

The Senate Labor and Human Resources Committee approved HR 4151 unanimously June 27 and reported it (S Rept 101-421) Aug. 3. The full Senate passed the measure by voice vote Sept. 18.

Conferees reached agreement on HR 4151 (H Rept 101-816) Oct. 3. The House approved the conference report by voice vote under suspension of the rules Oct. 10, and the Senate gave final clearance Oct. 19.

Other Programs

As enacted, HR 4151 also increased authorization levels for a number of other social service programs for the poor. They included:

- The Low-Income Home Energy Assistance Program (LIHEAP), which provides grants to states to help poor families pay their heating and cooling bills and improve the energy efficiency of their homes. Funding was set at $2.1 billion in fiscal 1991, $2.3 billion in 1992 and an open-ended authorization in 1993 and 1994.
- The Community Services Block Grant program, which funds efforts to make the poor self-sufficient. The program's funding ceiling would reach $500 million by fiscal 1994.
- Follow Through, which provides Head Start-type services to children in elementary school, received a $20 million funding ceiling in fiscal 1991 and an open-ended authorization through fiscal 1994.
- The Community Food and Nutrition Program, which helps non-profit agencies assist in meeting the nutritional needs of the poor, was authorized at levels that reached $25 million by fiscal 1994.
- State Dependent Care Development Grants, which fund state child care information and referral programs, received a $20 million authorization in fiscal 1991 and open-ended funding through fiscal 1994.
- Comprehensive Child Development Centers, which provide Head Start-type services to a targeted population of mothers and children, was authorized at $50 million a year through fiscal 1994.

Human Services Reconciliation

Both the fiscal 1990 (HR 3299 — PL 101-239) and fiscal 1991 (HR 5835 — PL 101-508) budget-reconciliation bills contained modest changes in human services programs. *(Legislative history, HR 3299, p. 43; HR 5835, p. 55)*

HR 3299

Human Resources

Title XX Social Services Block Grants. Increased by $100 million (to $2.8 billion from $2.7 billion) the entitlement ceiling for the Title XX Social Services Block Grant, which channeled money to states to help provide a wide variety of social services to the poor and disabled.

Child Welfare Authorization. Increased by $59 million, from $266 million to $325 million, the authorization for child welfare services provided under Title IV-B of the Social Security Act.

Authority to Transfer Foster Care Funds. Extended, through fiscal 1992, state authority to transfer unused federal foster care funds to the child welfare services program.

Federal Reimbursement for Foster and Adoptive Parent Training. Increased from 50 percent to 75 percent, for fiscal 1990-92, the federal matching rate for costs of short-term training for foster and adoptive parents or for the staff of licensed or approved child care institutions that provide foster care.

Health and Education Records for Foster Children. Beginning April 1, 1990, required that case plans for foster children include a record of the child's health and educational status, including whether the child received required Early and Periodic Screening, Diagnosis and Treatment examinations under Medicaid, as well as any follow-up treatment. Required that the health and education record be reviewed, updated and provided to the foster family each time the child is placed in a foster home.

Reauthorization, Foster Care Independent Living Program. Extended through fiscal 1992 the Independent Living Initiatives program, which gave states money to help teenage foster children adjust to life on their own. The entitlement was increased from $45 million to $50 million for fiscal 1990, $60 million for fiscal 1991 and $70 million for fiscal 1992. Beginning in fiscal 1991, states would be required to match at 50 percent federal funds of more than $45 million. The bill also required the Department of Health and Human Services (HHS) to evaluate the effectiveness of the program.

Medicaid Transition in Child Support Cases. Permanently extended eligibility for four more months of Medicaid coverage for families who lost their eligibility for Aid to Families with Dependent Children as a result of collections of child support owed.

Minnesota Family Investment Plan. Authorized the HHS secretary to waive certain provisions of current law for the state of Minnesota so it might test an alternative program to help families on welfare become self-sufficient.

Exclusion of Agent Orange Settlements. Effective Jan. 1, 1989, excluded settlements in lawsuits alleging health problems from exposure to Agent Orange from counting in qualifying for federal needs-tested programs, including Medicaid and Supplemental Security Income (SSI).

Supplemental Security Income

Outreach for Disabled and Blind Children. Required HHS to establish a permanent outreach program to inform parents or guardians of disabled and blind children about the potential eligibility of the children for SSI benefits.

Benefits for Disabled Children of Parents Overseas. Beginning in March 1990, allowed paying SSI benefits to disabled children living with a parent in the U.S. armed forces who was assigned to permanent duty ashore outside the United States if the child were receiving SSI disability benefits in the month before the parent's assignment abroad.

Waiver for Severely Disabled Children. Waived certain rules pertaining to the eligibility for SSI benefits of severely disabled children to let them live at home instead of in a medical institution without losing their eligibility for Medicaid if they would have been eligible for such benefits while institutionalized and if the state's Medicaid program covers the home care.

Demonstration Program for Disabled Children. Authorized up to 10 demonstration projects to test using volunteer senior aides to provide basic medical assistance and support to families with disabled or chronically ill children.

Exclusion of Accruals on Burial Spaces. Required excluding interest and other accruals on burial spaces from resource limits used to determine eligibility for SSI benefits.

Exclusion of Value of Income-Producing Property. Required that the value of property used in a person's trade or business not be included in determining the equity value of that person's property (which, in turn, was used to help determine eligibility for SSI).

AFDC Quality Control

Waiver, Pending Sanctions Against States. Permanently waived federal sanctions against states for failing to reduce error rates under the Aid to Families with Dependent Children (AFDC) program to specified levels since fiscal 1981. A congressional moratorium on collecting those payments expired July 1, 1989. The accumulated sanctions were estimated at $2.2 billion through fiscal 1990.

Modification in AFDC Quality Control System. Beginning in fiscal 1991, the Quality Control program would:

- Penalize only those states with error rates above the national average or 4 percent, whichever is higher.
- Require that underpayments as well as overpayments be taken into account in determining error rates.
- Give states financial incentives to improve child support collections for AFDC recipients.
- Establish penalties based on a sliding scale reflecting the degree to which a particular state's error rate exceeded the national threshold.
- Establish a Quality Control Review Board to resolve disputes between states and the federal government as to whether quality control review cases involved errors. The Departmental Appeals Board was kept to resolve other areas of dispute. States could appeal decisions of the Departmental Appeals Board to federal district court.

HR 5835

Child Support Enforcement

Extension of IRS Intercept. Bolstered the authority of the Internal Revenue Service (IRS) to help custodial parents recover overdue child support payments. Previous law gave the IRS permanent authority to deduct from noncustodial parents' federal tax refunds past-due support for children receiving benefits under AFDC.

- Made permanent the IRS' authority to intercept tax refunds for children not getting AFDC benefits.
- Permitted the IRS to intercept refunds to collect overdue payments for non-minor disabled children and payments due to spouses when spousal and child support were included in the same support order.

Extension of Interstate Child Support Commission. Extended through 1992 authority for the Interstate Child Support Commission. The 15-member commission, established under the 1988 Family Support Act (PL

100-485), was to hold one or more national conferences on interstate child support enforcement reform and to submit to Congress recommendations for improving the interstate child support system by May 1, 1991.

Texas Waiver. Waived for Texas certain child support enforcement requirements so Bexar County, including San Antonio, could continue an ongoing demonstration project to monitor child support payments. Required the state to study the cost-effectiveness of the project and report to the federal government.

Unemployment Compensation

Unemployment Compensation. Made permanent the Reed Act of 1954, which allowed excess federal unemployment tax revenues in the Unemployment Trust Fund to be used for administrative purposes or benefits by the states. The law was to expire over a three-year period beginning July 1, 1991. Modified the formula by which states would get any overflow funds so that each state would receive the extra cash based on its share of wages subject to federal unemployment taxes paid in the prior calendar year, instead of the state's total taxable wages.

Supplemental Security Income

Treatment of Victims' Compensation Payments. Exempted amounts paid to crime victims from state victim compensation funds from being counted as income in determining SSI eligibility or benefit amounts. Also excluded from estimation of resources for nine months amounts received for expenses incurred or losses suffered as a result of the crime.

Treatment of State Relocation Assistance. Exempted amounts paid for relocation assistance from being counted as income in determining SSI eligibility or benefit amounts. Such payments would not count toward the resource limit for nine months after being received.

Work Incentives. Eliminated several minor disincentives for disabled SSI recipients who wished to work without losing benefits. Permitted disabled SSI recipients to continue to participate in a special work incentive program after they reached age 65. Expanded situations under which earnings needed to pay for work expenses related to a person's disability were not counted for purposes of reducing benefits. Also treated certain royalties and honoraria as earned income, not unearned income. Unearned income resulted in a dollar-for-dollar reduction in benefits, while earned income amounts were partly disregarded.

Evaluation of Child's Disability by Pediatrician. Required the HHS secretary to make "reasonable efforts" to ensure that a pediatrician or other specialist in a field of medicine appropriate to the disability in question evaluated a child's disability to determine eligibility for SSI.

Reimbursement for Vocational Rehabilitation. Authorized the HHS secretary to pay for the vocational rehabilitation of SSI recipients in months that they were not actually receiving SSI benefits because they were involved in special programs or were eligible only for state benefits.

Presumptive Eligibility. Expanded from three to six months the time during which the Social Security Administration could presume eligibility and pay benefits while a blind or disabled prospective SSI beneficiary's application was being processed.

Continuing Disability and Blindness Reviews. Permitted the Social Security Administration to review no more often than once every 12 months whether certain SSI beneficiaries were still blind or disabled.

Aid to Families with Dependent Children

Treatment of Foster Care Maintenance and Adoption Assistance Payments. Excluded amounts paid by states or localities for foster care from determination of AFDC eligibility or payments. Also excluded federal, state or local adoption assistance payments.

Temporary Assistance. Repealed, for fiscal 1990 and 1991 only, the $1 million limit on the amount of emergency assistance HHS could provide to U.S. citizens and their dependents who had returned or been returned to the United States because of destitution, illness, war, threat of war, invasion or similar crisis. Also permitted HHS to receive gifts from private entities to assist with repatriation costs.

National Commission on Children. Clarified that the final reporting date for the National Commission on Children was March 31, 1991.

Moratorium on Emergency Assistance Regulations. Prohibited HHS, through Oct. 1, 1991, from issuing final regulations altering the AFDC emergency assistance program.

Child Welfare and Foster Care

Administrative Costs. Specifically included "child placement" activities among those for which states were entitled to receive federal reimbursement.

Bar on Payment Reductions. Continued, through Oct. 1, 1991, the ban on HHS reducing payments to states or seeking repayments from states because they failed to meet certain standards regarding child welfare provisions included in the Adoption Assistance and Child Welfare Amendments of 1980 (PL 96-272).

Independent Living Program. Permitted states, at their option, to provide services under the Foster Care Independent Living program to youths up to age 21, instead of the existing cutoff of 18. The program sought to help youths in foster care, beginning at age 16, make the transition to living independently.

Community Service

Legislation (S 1430 — PL 101-610) to authorize grants to establish national, community- and school-based volunteer service programs was enacted in 1990.

Under the bill, grants were to be provided for programs with volunteers of all ages. Colleges and universities could apply for funds to run student community service programs, and community-based groups could seek grants to run programs involving adult volunteers.

As cleared, S 1430 included a three-year national service demonstration program under which people who volunteered for one or two years in a community service program would be eligible to receive up to $5,000 in educational vouchers for each year of service. Backers of the provisions argued that they were necessary to enable young people not from wealthy families to serve their communities.

The bill authorized $62 million in fiscal 1991, $105 million in 1992 and $120 million in 1993.

In the face of administration objections, sponsors agreed to drop the most controversial provision, allowing forgiveness of federal student loans in exchange for service. The bill also did not contain another much-debated proposal, offered by Sen. Sam Nunn, D-Ga., and Rep. Dave McCurdy, D-Okla., to require students to perform community or national service in return for college aid.

In another effort to defer a threatened veto, S 1430 authorized the Points of Light Initiative Foundation, proposed by President Bush, to seek to foster volunteerism and administer service programs.

Legislative Action

In his 1988 Republican presidential nomination acceptance speech, Bush praised eleemosynary organizations as "a thousand points of light" in society. And during his campaign, in which community service was a major theme, Bush outlined a proposal for a "Youth Engaged in Service to America" (YES) program. On June 22, 1989, as president, Bush unveiled a $25 million a year proposal to create a Points of Light Foundation to encourage volunteerism, mostly through outreach efforts. At the time, he repeated his opposition to any financial incentives to volunteers. "You don't need to be bribed with incentives and threatened with penalties to get engaged in community service," he said.

Despite the campaign rhetoric and the fanfare with which the president's proposal was announced, the administration failed to send a formal legislative plan on the subject to Congress in 1989. Congressional Democrats, however, were intent on moving ahead with a plan with financial help for volunteers. Frustrated Senate leaders on July 27 released a proposal combining several different service bills into a single measure (S 1430).

S 1430, a $300 million package of new national and community service programs, was reported by the Senate Labor and Human Resources Committee (S Rept 101-176) on Oct. 27. The bill had been approved Aug. 2 on an 11-4 vote, with Republican opponents complaining that the measure did not include any of Bush's proposals.

Before S 1430 reached the Senate floor, it was substantially modified and scaled back after negotiations between Edward M. Kennedy, D-Mass., the chairman of the Labor Committee, and Orrin G. Hatch, Utah, the ranking Republican member. The compromise reduced funding from $300 million to $125 million and included a $25 million authorization for Bush's Points of Light Initiative Foundation.

Although the compromise agreement reduced some of the controversy over the bill, floor action was still marked by four days of debate, a variety of extraneous amendments and pressure from the White House to cut costs.

The strongest objections were directed against the provision allowing volunteer participants in a national service demonstration program to receive up to $10,000 in educational and housing vouchers in return for two years of work. That brought criticism from John McCain, R-Ariz., who noted that participants would finish the program with a larger voucher than military veterans, who got $9,000 in post-service educational benefits for two years of service. But McCain's amendment to restrict benefits under the program was tabled Feb. 27, 1990, on a 54-41 vote.

The Senate also rejected 48-50 on Feb. 28 an unrelated sense of the Senate amendment by Phil Gramm, R-Texas, to recommend that any savings from the "peace dividend" brought about by the end of the Cold War be used for deficit reduction. However, the Senate adopted 79-19 an alternative by Jim Sasser, D-Tenn., to urge that any savings be used for deficit reduction and "urgent national priorities."

The Senate passed S 1430 on a 78-19 vote March 1.

The House Education and Labor Committee approved its community service bill (HR 4330) on July 19 and reported the bill (H Rept 101-677, Part I) on Aug. 15. As reported, HR 4330 authorized $183 million in fiscal 1991 for volunteerism grants. The bill included a provision to allow college students to have a portion of their student loans forgiven or deferred if they provided volunteer service in such areas as drug counseling and health care.

On the floor, the strongest challenge to the bill came on an amendment offered by Bill Goodling, Pa., the ranking Republican on the Education and Labor Committee. Goodling's amendment to delete the loan forgiveness provision was rejected 200-212 on Sept. 13. Despite the vote, the language continued to face strong opposition from House Republicans and the administration.

The House passed HR 4330 by voice vote Sept. 13, then passed S 1430 after substituting the text of HR 4330.

In conference, the controversial loan forgiveness provision was dropped. The Senate adopted the conference report (H Rept 101-893) by voice vote Oct. 16, and the House followed suit Oct. 24. President Bush signed the bill Nov. 16.

WIC Reauthorization

Congress in 1989 cleared legislation (HR 24 — PL 101-147) reauthorizing the popular Special Supplemental Food Program for Women, Infants and Children (WIC) and other child- and school-nutrition programs for five years.

Although the Congressional Budget Office estimated the measure would result in spending of more than $13 billion in fiscal years 1990-94, the measure sailed through Congress with strong bipartisan backing.

The WIC program provides food and other supplements to nutritionally at-risk pregnant women and young children. Experts and political leaders have given the program wide credit for being successful in preventing expensive health problems associated with inadequate nutrition. Nevertheless, WIC funding levels enabled the program to serve only about half those eligible.

Although the decades-old school lunch program — the cornerstone of federal nutritional efforts for young children — had a permanent authorization, HR 24 extended the authorizations for a number of related programs, including the Summer Food Program, the Commodity Distribution Program and the Nutrition Education and Training Program.

Despite the WIC increases contained in the bill, weather-related price increases in some of the program's chief food commodities soon caused a funding crisis. By the middle of 1990, funding shortfalls were expected to force 27 states to drop an estimated 280,000 women and children from the program.

Lawmakers moved quickly in the face of the funding crisis. On June 29, 1990, Congress cleared a bill (HR 5149 — PL 101-330) allowing states to spend up to 3 percent of their next year's allocation to cover their current shortfalls. The bill, which the president signed July 12, was expected to free an estimated $66 million to meet emergency needs.

Legislative Action

The House Education and Labor Committee reported HR 24 on July 28, 1989 (H Rept 101-194). The House passed the bill by voice vote under suspension of the rules July 31.

Although the Senate Agriculture Committee did not formally report its version of the bill (S 1484), the Senate passed it Aug. 3. The Senate then passed an amended HR 24.

The House- and Senate-passed bills were similar in most respects. One area in which the bills were the same, but at odds with the Bush administration, concerned a provision allowing non-profit groups to sponsor summer feeding programs for low-income children. The administration argued that the non-profit groups, which had been barred from running feeding programs in the early 1980s because of widespread allegations of fraud and abuse, should not be reinstated. But backers of the change contended that excluding non-profit groups had left many children, particularly in rural areas, without access to summer food programs.

The bills also contained provisions aimed at expanding participation in the program by simplifying the application process. After reports that many children were being denied free lunches because some adults in the household could or would not provide their Social Security numbers, the measures limited the reporting requirement to cover only the principal wage earner. Similarly, schools were allowed to get income-eligibility information on children from welfare offices to ensure that the children not be denied eligibility simply because their parents did not fill out an application.

After sponsors informally worked out the minor differences between the two bills, the House passed a compromise version of HR 24 on Oct. 10. The Senate followed suit Oct. 24, clearing the measure. President Bush signed HR 24 on Nov. 10.

Major Provisions

As cleared, HR 24:

- Permitted private, non-profit agencies to sponsor summer feeding programs in areas in which no public sponsor was operating such a program.
- Reauthorized the commodity distribution program through fiscal 1994.
- Required the Agriculture Department to create demonstration programs for providing year-round food service for homeless children in emergency centers, and for allowing for-profit child care centers to participate in the existing child care feeding program if at least 25 percent of their children were from low-income families.
- Required the Agriculture Department to take steps to reduce the amount of paperwork to participate in the program.
- Required the Agriculture and Health and Human Services departments to develop a publication for participants in the program providing guidance on preparing nutritionally appropriate meals for children.
- Authorized $3 million in fiscal 1990 and $5 million a year through 1994 in new entitlement funding for competitive grants to states to aid in covering start-up costs for establishing school breakfast programs.
- Authorized $2.16 billion for WIC in fiscal 1990 and open-ended funding through 1994.
- Provided that mothers and children at nutritional risk who were already eligible for food stamps, Aid to Families with Dependent Children or Medicaid be automatically considered to meet income criteria for WIC.
- Required states to expand WIC coverage to pregnant women and infants in prisons and juvenile detention facilities.
- Required states to use competitive bidding or some other method aimed at controlling costs of purchasing infant formula.
- Required states to promote breast feeding among WIC recipients.
- Authorized the nutrition education program through fiscal 1994, when the funding ceiling would be $25 million.
- Required that upon initial applications for free or reduced-price meals, schools and child care centers collect only the Social Security number of the parent or guardian who was the principal wage earner. Formerly, the Social Security numbers of all adults in the household had to be provided.
- Permitted schools to obtain income-eligibility information on children from local food stamp or welfare offices.

Food Stamps

As part of the 1990 omnibus farm bill (S 2830 — PL 101-624), Congress included provisions extending for five years the authorization of the food stamp program and the commodity donation programs such as the Emergency Food Assistance Program and the Commodity Supplemental Food Program. *(Farm bill, p. 537)*

Unlike the Reagan administration, which fought vigorously to reduce eligibility and costs of the food stamp program, the Bush administration did not push for cuts or major changes in the program.

S 2830, however, provided for a further crackdown on fraud and misuse of food stamps. For example, it increased reporting requirements and imposed fines on stores that accepted loose coupons or food stamps from unauthorized third parties.

Many of the provisions were taken from a separate bill (HR 4100) approved March 22, 1990, by the House Agriculture Subcommittee on Nutrition.

As cleared, the food stamp provisions of S 2830:

- Reauthorized the food stamp program for five years. Basic benefits would be kept at the existing 103 percent of the Thrifty Food Plan (a government estimate of the market-basket value of common foodstuffs). The excess shelter expense ceiling would be kept at the existing $177 a month.

States were authorized to allow approved restaurants to accept food stamps for the purpose of feeding the homeless. Residents of Guam and the Virgin Islands were allowed to use food stamps for meals in senior citizens' centers and private establishments offering meals at reduced prices.

- Excluded from the calculation of income in determining food stamp eligibility education loans, grants and scholarships, clothing allowances provided by state assistance programs, assistance payments for transitional housing and general state welfare payments.
- Authorized online electronic benefit transfer systems replacing coupons with plastic cards as an operational alternative. Required that all checkout lanes in grocery stores where food stamps were used in at least 15 percent of

sales be equipped with special devices at the Agriculture Department's expense.

- Required the existing $410 minimum benefit for one- and two-person households to be adjusted for inflation each October and rounded to the nearest $5.
- Strengthened various reporting requirements and imposed fines on retail and wholesale food operations that accepted loose coupons or food stamps from unauthorized third parties or used food stamps in money-laundering schemes or computer fraud. Retail food stores were permanently disqualified from handling food stamps if firearms or illegal drugs were sold for food stamp coupons. A fine of up to $250,000 and a prison term of up to 20 years would be imposed for laundering coupons or authorization cards worth more than $5,000.
- Reauthorized the Temporary Emergency Food Assistance Program for five years, eliminated the word "temporary" and required the secretary to make surplus commodities from the Commodity Credit Corporation available to feeding organizations. Provided $175 million in fiscal 1991, $190 million in fiscal 1992 and $220 million a year from fiscal 1993 to fiscal 1995.
- Set authorization levels for nutrition block grants to Puerto Rico at $985 million in fiscal 1991, gradually increasing through 1995.
- Reauthorized distribution of commodities to soup kitchens and food banks, with a requirement that $32 million of commodities be purchased annually.
- Reauthorized the Commodity Supplemental Food program, requiring the Commodity Credit Corporation, to the extent inventories existed, to provide 7 million pounds of cheese a year from fiscal 1991 to fiscal 1995.

Child Abuse

Two bills (HR 2087, HR 2088) providing two-year reauthorizations for programs to combat child abuse were enacted in 1989.

HR 2087 authorized $7 million a year in grants to states, and HR 2088 authorized $20 million annually to help provide "respite" aid for those caring for chronically ill children and for "crisis nurseries" for abused or neglected children.

The House Education and Labor Committee reported both HR 2087 (H Rept 101-113) and HR 2088 (H Rept 101-114) on June 27, and the House passed them by voice vote under suspension of the rules July 11.

The Senate versions of the bills (S 1455, S 1454) were approved by the Labor and Human Resources Committee on Aug. 2. After substituting those bills for the House measures, the Senate passed HR 2087 on Sept. 20 and HR 2088 on Sept. 26. The House accepted the Senate changes in both measures Oct. 11. President Bush Oct. 25 signed HR 2087 (PL 101-126) and HR 2088 (PL 101-127).

Volunteer Programs

Legislation (HR 1312) was enacted in 1989 that reauthorized through fiscal 1993 the federal government's principal domestic volunteer program. President Bush signed the bill (PL 101-204) on Dec. 7.

HR 1312, which encountered no serious trouble clearing Congress, reauthorized programs overseen by ACTION, under the Domestic Volunteer Service Act of 1973 (PL 93-113). In addition, the bill sought to stimulate recruitment of more volunteers, especially for VISTA (Volunteers in Service to America). *(1973 law, Congress and the Nation Vol. IV, p. 412; previous reauthorization, Congress and the Nation Vol. VII, p. 611)*

The House Education and Labor Committee June 8 approved two reauthorization measures: HR 1312 (H Rept 101-116) and HR 2421. The House passed HR 1312, which incorporated the provisions of HR 2421, by voice vote under suspension of the rules July 11.

The Senate Labor and Human Resources Committee reported its version (S 1426 — S Rept 101-122) on Sept. 7. The Senate passed HR 1312 by voice vote Sept. 15, after substituting the text of the committee-approved S 1426.

The Senate adopted the conference report (H Rept 101-381) by voice vote Nov. 19, and the House followed suit the next day.

As cleared, HR 1312:

- Authorized for VISTA $30.6 million for fiscal 1990, $39.9 million for 1991, $47.8 million for 1992 and $56 million for 1993.
- Authorized for VISTA Literary Corps $6.05 million for fiscal 1990, $7.5 million for 1991, $9 million for 1992 and $10.5 million for 1993.
- Authorized for the Service Learning Program $1.9 million for fiscal 1990, $2 million for 1991, $2.1 million for 1992 and $2.2 million for 1993.
- Authorized for Special Volunteer Programs $1.1 million for fiscal 1990, $1.15 million for 1991, $1.2 million for 1992 and $1.27 million for 1993.
- Authorized for Drug Abuse Prevention $5.25 million for fiscal 1992 and $5.5 million for 1993.
- Authorized for RSVP (Retired Senior Volunteer Program) $39.9 million for fiscal 1990, $43.9 million for 1991, $48.3 million for 1992 and $53.1 million for 1993.
- Authorized for the Foster Grandparent program $70.8 million for fiscal 1990, $80.9 million for 1991, $91.7 million for 1992 and $98.2 million for 1993.
- Authorized for the Senior Companion Program $36.6 million for fiscal 1990, $39 million for 1991, $44.7 million for 1992 and $48.7 million for 1993.
- Ordered the director of ACTION to set up a placement office at agency headquarters in Washington, D.C., and to maintain a "current and comprehensive" data system that could supply inquiring individuals with information about volunteer openings nationwide and could inform approved programs about the availability of particular candidates.
- Required the director of ACTION to assign at least one ACTION employee in each region of the country to be responsible for recruitment and placement of volunteers.
- Ordered ACTION to recruit at least 2,800 VISTA volunteers in fiscal 1990, rising to 3,400 in 1993.
- Required that, beginning in fiscal 1991, at least 1.5 percent of VISTA's basic appropriation be spent on recruitment and public awareness activities.
- Required that, beginning in fiscal 1991, at least 20 percent of all VISTA volunteers be between 18 and 27 years old.
- Raised the stipend paid to volunteers from the existing $75 per month to $90 per month in fiscal 1991 and $95 per month thereafter. Increased the subsistence allowance to no less than 95 percent of the federal poverty level for an individual, with the average allowance set at 105 percent of the poverty threshold.

1991-92

Tightly constrained by the rules of the 1990 budget summit agreement, the 102nd Congress made only limited changes in human services programs for children, the poor and the elderly. Legislation to expand federal child welfare programs fell victim to a veto of urban aid legislation by President Bush. Even the popular Older Americans Act reauthorization had trouble becoming law, because of controversy over Social Security.

Older Americans Act

Congress in 1992 cleared legislation (HR 2967 — PL 102-375) to reauthorize programs under the 1965 Older Americans Act (PL 89-73) for four years.

The bill authorized a total of $1.7 billion for service, nutrition and preventive health care programs for the poor and minority elderly, including the popular Meals on Wheels program. Nearly 70 percent of the funds were used for grants to states.

The Older Americans Act legislation was not controversial. However, its enactment was delayed by debate over Social Security earnings test provisions. The legislation was finally signed into law a year after the previous authorization had expired, although funding for the programs for the elderly had continued to be provided through the appropriations process. *(1987 reauthorization, Congress and the Nation Vol. VII, p. 629; Social Security, p. 736)*

The goal of the Older Americans Act programs was to foster independence for older people by providing a broad network of social and community services to those in the greatest economic and social need. The assistance included in-home services to help older frail and disabled individuals remain in their homes as long as possible; senior center programs to support group activities for social, physical, educational, recreational and cultural purposes; nutrition programs; and legal assistance and advocacy.

Legislative Action

The House Education and Labor Committee approved HR 2967 on July 30, 1991, and reported the measure (H Rept 102-199) on Sept. 11.

Although the bill enjoyed bipartisan support, the administration threatened a veto over a provision requiring the holding of a National Conference on Aging in 1993 on the grounds that the mandate impinged on executive branch prerogatives. The measure also changed the name from the White House Conference on Aging and gave Congress more authority to set the meeting's agenda and policies.

The dispute over the conference was resolved on the House floor. Matthew G. Martinez, D-Calif., the chairman of the House Education Subcommittee on Human Resources, proposed a compromise changing the name back to the White House Conference and giving the administration more leverage in choosing people to plan the event. His block of amendments was adopted by voice vote.

The House passed HR 2967, 385-0, on Sept. 12.

The Senate Labor and Human Resources Committee approved a companion bill (S 243) on July 17, reporting it (S Rept 102-151) Sept. 13. The most controversial provision considered by the committee was offered by Howard M. Metzenbaum, D-Ohio, to have the Pension Benefit Guaranty Corporation provide $75 for each year of service, up to a total of $1,500, to workers whose companies had defaulted on agreements to provide pensions. The amendment was approved on a vote of 12-5, after Republicans warned that it would cost $500 million to pay workers and their survivors who had lost benefits.

More serious trouble awaited the bill on the Senate floor, however, as John McCain, R-Ariz., offered an amendment to repeal the Social Security earnings test. Adopted by voice vote on Nov. 12, the controversial proposal led to a lengthy delay in enactment of the Older Americans Act provisions.

Before passing HR 2967 by voice vote Nov. 12, the Senate adopted, also by voice vote, an amendment by Thad Cochran, R-Miss., to delete the provision on lost pension benefits. A motion to table (kill) the amendment had failed on a 46-51 vote.

Instead of holding a conference, the House in 1992 moved to counter the Senate stand on the earnings test by adopting a further amendment to HR 2967 that would raise, not repeal, the earnings test. The House first adopted, 269-139, a resolution (H Res 425) permitting consideration under suspension of the rules of another resolution (H Res 433) to agree to the House earnings test amendment to the Senate amendments to HR 2967. That action precluded a challenge that the earnings test provision was in violation of the 1990 budget agreement because it called for new spending without making offsetting cuts or revenue increases. The House then agreed, 340-68 on April 9, to suspend the rules and adopt H Res 433, thus accepting the House provision raising the earnings test.

The Older Americans legislation lay dormant in the Senate for several months. Sponsors were reluctant to bring up the bill because of the controversy over the earnings test. Finally, on Sept. 10, the Senate rejected another McCain earnings test proposal offered as part of the fiscal 1993 Treasury and Postal Service spending bill (HR 5488). With the matter settled, the Senate was free to act on HR 2967, dropping the repeal language.

The Senate Sept. 15 concurred with the House amendment with an amendment; the House accepted the Senate changes Sept. 22, thus clearing HR 2967. President Bush signed the bill Sept. 30.

In addition to extending the authorization of Older Americans Act programs, HR 2967:

- Consolidated and strengthened provisions relating to elder abuse prevention.
- Increased low-income minority participation by requiring state and local agencies on aging to set the goal of reaching more of those in need with supportive and nutrition services.
- Authorized a White House Conference on Aging to be conducted by Dec. 31, 1994, and included congressional appointees with those of the president on the conference policy committee.
- Authorized a new program to provide counseling and training to family care-givers of frail people.
- Authorized several research and demonstration programs, including pension counseling and ombudsmen for older tenants in public housing.
- Reauthorized a 1974 law providing financial assistance to Native American organizations.

• Authorized meals for the elderly in public schools to promote joint activities with troubled students.

Child Welfare Veto

Congress in 1992 cleared a major overhaul of federal child welfare programs. But the $27 billion urban aid tax measure (HR 11), which included the child welfare provisions, was pocket-vetoed by President Bush.

The child welfare changes were aimed at helping abused and neglected children without consigning them to the overburdened foster care system. The provisions rejected by the president would have amended Title IV of the Social Security Act to provide entitlement matching funds to states for family preservation and family support services, substance abuse prevention and treatment and respite care services. The entitlement ceiling was set at $135 million in fiscal 1993, reaching $595 million in 1997.

Background

Reformers argued that new legislation was needed because of the skewed nature of the incentives in the existing child welfare system.

The foster care program under Social Security was an unlimited entitlement, with the federal government paying a set share of whatever it cost to keep in foster care children who would have qualified for welfare if they had remained with their families. The child welfare services program, by contrast, was funded through the regular appropriations process. It had to compete for funds each year with hundreds of other health, social services and education programs. The goal was to put the child welfare services program on the same financial footing as Social Security's foster care program.

Proponents of overhauling the system said that increasing funding for prevention services through the child welfare services program could ultimately reduce costs for foster care, which was much more expensive.

The Bush administration opposed both the increases and making the child welfare program an entitlement. The administration said it favored expanding services for abused and neglected children but wanted funding for an expansion to come from amounts being spent on administrative costs for the foster care program.

In a sharply worded letter sent Sept. 24, 1991, to Thomas J. Downey, D-N.Y., the chief sponsor of the House child welfare measure (HR 3603), Health and Human Services Secretary Louis W. Sullivan raised numerous objections to the bill, "including its excessive cost and highly prescriptive provisions." In addition, he decried the bill's financing scheme as an "egregious" attempt to circumvent the budget agreement and said the "excessive new funding" was "ill advised given current budgetary constraints."

Congressional Republicans agreed with Bush officials that the bill violated the 1990 budget accord.

Legislative Action

The House Ways and Means Subcommittee on Human Resources approved the initial version of the bill (HR 2571) on Sept. 24, 1991, after panel Democrats overrode strong objections from Republican members. The bill, however, lacked a financing mechanism. On July 2, 1992, the full Ways and Means Committee approved a new version (HR 3603) after deciding to provide the money for its $7 billion cost by imposing a 10 percent surtax on people with incomes above $1 million. The increase would have raised $8.2 billion over five years, of which $3.5 billion would have gone for child welfare, $3.5 billion for child nutrition and $1.2 billion for deficit reduction. The Bush administration vehemently opposed the new tax.

The vote in committee was 24-12, with only Nancy L. Johnson, R-Conn., joining the Democrats in backing the bill. HR 3603 was formally reported from Ways and Means (H Rept 102-684, Part I) on July 22. Education and Labor, which shared jurisdiction over the bill, reported the measure (H Rept 102-684, Part II) on July 31.

In the Rules Committee, a modified version of anti-hunger legislation approved by the House and Senate Agriculture committees in 1991 (HR 1202, S 757) was added to HR 3603. The provisions allowed families with children to deduct a larger portion of their housing costs when calculating their income on food stamp applications.

The bill continued to face strong Republican opposition on the House floor. A Republican move to strike the tax surcharge, drop the anti-hunger provisions and scale back the child welfare measure showed considerable strength, failing on a 191-230 vote Aug. 6.

The bill then passed the House by a 256-163 vote later the same day. Because the prospects for a free-standing child welfare bill were bleak, Downey encouraged his colleagues to follow the course set by the Senate.

The Senate companion bill (S 4), which created a similar capped entitlement program to bolster the child welfare program, had languished for months. But Finance Committee Chairman Lloyd Bentsen, D-Texas, had added the measure to HR 11, the urban aid bill, on July 29, 1992.

Most of the child welfare provisions were included in the final version of HR 11 approved by conferees on Oct. 5. The anti-hunger provisions were dropped, however.

The House adopted the conference report (H Rept 102-1034) on HR 11 on Oct. 6, and the Senate adopted it Oct. 8, clearing the legislation. President Bush pocket-vetoed the bill Nov. 4.

Head Start

Congress in 1992 cleared a bill (HR 5630 — PL 102-401) aimed at increasing participation and instituting cost savings in the Head Start program for disadvantaged preschool children.

The bill required Head Start programs to provide literacy and child development training for parents of participating children.

The legislation also allowed local Head Start associations to buy the buildings they used. Previous law had allowed Head Start grant money only to be used for renovations of existing property. Bill supporters, led by Rep. Matthew G. Martinez, D-Calif., argued that the power to buy was necessary because rental facilities were often temporary or were unavailable in such communities as south-central Los Angeles.

HR 5630 also made it easier for a community to win waivers of the requirement that it provide 20 percent matching funds to qualify for grants. Under the measure, federal officials could take into account five elements, including whether the community was located in an area recently hit by a major disaster, when reviewing the community's ability to provide matching funding.

The House Education and Labor Committee approved the bill (H Rept 102-763) on July 30 and reported it the next day. The House passed the bill by voice vote under suspension of the rules Aug. 3, and the Senate passed it by voice vote Sept. 24. President Bush signed the bill Oct. 7.

Children with Disabilities

Congress in 1991 cleared legislation (S 1106 — PL 102-119) reauthorizing funding to states for early intervention services for infants and toddlers with disabilities.

The bill reauthorized the program for three years, with $220 million in fiscal 1992.

The program was created in 1986 (PL 99-457), when the 1975 Individuals with Disabilities Education Act was amended to set up guidelines for states to coordinate education of disabled infants and toddlers. A measure enacted in 1990 (S 1824 — PL 101-476) reauthorized most of the programs under the 1975 law, but the section covering disabled infants was not included because its authorization extended through the end of fiscal 1991. *(1986 law, Congress and the Nation Vol. VII, p. 652; 1990 action, p. 647)*

S 1106 targeted low-income, rural and minority communities. It authorized $15.1 million in 1992 for training centers for parents of disabled children up to age 5.

The Senate Labor and Human Resources Committee approved the bill (S Rept 102-84) on May 22 and formally reported it June 18. The Senate passed S 1106 by voice vote June 24. The House Education and Labor Committee approved a companion measure (HR 3053) on July 30, which it reported (H Rept 102-198) on Sept. 11. The same day, the House passed HR 3053 by voice vote under suspension of the rules, then passed S 1106, also by voice vote, after substituting the text of HR 3053.

The Senate cleared S 1106 Sept. 16. President Bush signed it Oct. 7.

Abandoned Children

Legislation (S 1532 — PL 102-236) reauthorizing for four years programs aimed at finding foster homes for abandoned children was cleared by Congress in 1991.

The measure sought to aid "boarder babies" — children abandoned at hospitals by parents unwilling or unable to care for them.

The legislation bolstered programs included in the 1988 Abandoned Infants Assistance Act (PL 100-505) for boarder babies, who often suffered from AIDS (acquired immune deficiency syndrome), prenatally developed drug addiction or other afflictions.

S 1532 authorized $20 million in fiscal 1992, rising to $35 million by fiscal 1995. The bill authorized funding to 32 agencies and programs that offered early intervention services to prevent the abuse, neglect and abandonment of these children.

The Senate Labor and Human Resources Committee approved S 1532 by voice vote July 31 and reported it (S Rept 102-161) on Sept. 25. The Senate passed the bill by voice vote Oct. 29.

The House considered its companion measure (HR 2722). The House Education and Labor Committee approved the bill by voice vote July 30 and reported it (H Rept 102-209, Part I) Sept. 19. The House Energy and Commerce Committee approved HR 2722 (H Rept 102-209, Part II) by voice vote Oct. 8, formally reporting it Nov. 7.

The House passed HR 2722 by voice vote under suspension of the rules Nov. 19; then it passed an amended S 1532, also by voice vote. The Senate Nov. 26 adopted the House changes with an additional amendment, which the House accepted Nov. 27, clearing the measure. President Bush signed S 1532 on Dec. 12.

Child Abuse

A bill (S 838 — PL 102-295) cleared in 1992 that reauthorized through fiscal 1995 federal programs created to assist the estimated 2.5 million abused or neglected children in the United States.

S 838 authorized $321.7 million for fiscal 1992 for programs under the 1974 Child Abuse Prevention and Treatment Act (PL 93-247). Funding levels for fiscal 1993-95 were unspecified. *(1974 law, Congress and the Nation Vol. IV, p. 333; previous authorization, Congress and the Nation Vol. VII, p. 627)*

For fiscal 1992, almost $186 million was authorized for child abuse treatment and prevention programs, and $93 million for family violence programs.

The Senate Labor and Human Resources Committee approved S 838 on July 31, 1991, and reported it (S Rept 102-164) on Sept. 27. The Senate passed the bill, 96-0, on Nov. 7.

The House passed an amended version by voice vote April 7, 1992. The Senate cleared the bill April 9, and President Bush signed it May 28.

A separate child abuse bill (HR 2720) passed the House July 9, 1991, and the Senate Jan. 24, 1992. The measure, which provided a one-year reauthorization of child abuse prevention programs, did not become law.

Protections for Mentally Ill

President Bush Nov. 27, 1991, signed into law a bill (S 1475 — PL 102-173) authorizing a program to protect the legal rights of the mentally ill.

S 1475 authorized $19.5 million for fiscal 1992 and unspecified amounts through fiscal 1995 for state "protection and advocacy" programs, charged with investigating cases of abuse or neglect, that were first authorized in 1986 (PL 99-319). *(1986 action, Congress and the Nation Vol. VII, p. 614)*

The Senate Labor and Human Resources Committee approved the bill on July 17 and reported it (S Rept 102-114) on July 22. The Senate passed S 1475 by voice vote July 31.

The House Energy and Commerce Committee approved the bill Nov. 7 and reported it (H Rept 102-319) Nov. 15. The House passed S 1475 by voice vote under suspension of the rules Nov. 19, clearing the measure.

Farmers' Markets

Congress in 1992 cleared legislation (HR 3711 — PL 102-314) expanding and reauthorizing a pilot program that promoted the use of fresh fruits and vegetables in the Special Supplemental Food Program for Women, Infants and Children (WIC).

The bill increased authorized funding from $3 million annually to $6.5 million, allowing additional states to participate. The farmers' market project was originally authorized for three years in the 1988 Hunger Protection Act (PL 100-435). *(1988 law, Congress and the Nation Vol. VII, p. 537)*

The House Education and Labor Committee approved HR 3711 on May 20 and reported the measure (H Rept 102-540, Part I) on May 28. The House Agriculture Committee, which shared jurisdiction over the bill, approved and reported HR 3711 (H Rept 102-540, Part II) on June 4.

HR 3711 passed the House by voice vote under suspension of the rules June 22.

The Senate passed the bill by voice vote the next day, clearing the measure. President Bush signed HR 3711 on July 2.

The Senate had passed similar legislation on Sept. 27, 1991 (S 1742), and on May 20, 1992 (S 2761).

Infant Formula Price Fixing

President Bush on Oct. 24, 1992, signed legislation (S 2875 — PL 102-512) that imposed civil penalties on infant formula manufacturers who cheated the Special Supplemental Food Program for Women, Infants and Children (WIC).

S 2875 mandated civil penalties of up to $100 million per year on companies that fixed prices or engaged in related anti-competitive activities that hurt the WIC program. It also barred those manufacturers found guilty from participating in the WIC market for up to two years.

The Senate passed S 2875 by voice vote on Oct. 5; the House followed suit the next day, clearing the legislation.

After a two-year investigation, the Federal Trade Commission on June 11, 1992, had concluded that the three largest manufacturers of infant formula — Mead Johnson & Co., American Home Products Corp. and Abbott Laboratories — had driven up costs to WIC through alleged price fixing.

Meals for Homeless Children

Congress in 1992 cleared legislation (S 2759 — PL 102-342) authorizing $650,000 in fiscal 1993 and $800,000 in 1994 to reimburse homeless shelters for providing meals to children under the age of 6.

The Senate passed S 2759 by voice vote May 20. The House Education and Labor Committee reported the bill (H Rept 102-645) on July 1. The House passed an amended version by voice vote under suspension of the rules. The Senate agreed to the House changes July 30, clearing the measure. President Bush signed S 2759 on Aug. 14.

Welfare Reform

Various welfare-related proposals were included in an urban aid tax bill (HR 11). They did not become law because President Bush pocket-vetoed HR 11 on Nov. 4, 1992. *(Tax bill, p. 103)*

The largest welfare reform item in the package sought to make funding the welfare-to-work programs easier for states. The education, training and work programs, called JOBS (Jobs Opportunity and Basic Skills), were required as part of the 1988 Family Support Act (PL 100-485). The federal government guaranteed about $1 billion per year, but states had to match the funds at varying rates. Because of the recession, however, many states had not claimed their full allotments for JOBS programs. *(1988 law, Congress and the Nation Vol. VII, p. 616)*

HR 11 included a Bush administration proposal allowing welfare recipients to save up to $10,000 in their effort to become self-sufficient through work, training or education without losing their welfare benefits. The tax package also contained the text of HR 3450, which called for a demonstration of "micro-enterprise" programs that enabled welfare recipients to start small businesses.

Welfare Tracking

The Senate on Jan. 29, 1992, gave voice vote approval to a bill (S 1256) designed to identify factors that led to welfare dependency and develop strategies for reducing it. The bill saw no House action.

S 1256, introduced by Daniel Patrick Moynihan, D-N.Y., would have required the secretary of health and human services to collect and analyze information about who received welfare, for what reasons and for how long.

The bill had been approved by the Senate Labor and Human Resources Committee on Oct. 30, 1991, and reported Nov. 5.

Temporary Care

The House Sept. 11, 1991, by voice vote under suspension of the rules passed a bill (HR 3034) extending for three years benefits under a program to provide temporary care for children and infants with disabilities and chronic illnesses.

The bill authorized $20 million in fiscal 1992 for respite care for children. The services in the bill were intended to provide a needed break for families of children who required constant care and supervision.

HR 3034 saw no further congressional action.

A temporary care bill cleared in 1989. *(Story, p. 619)*

Women with AIDS

On Aug. 12, 1992, the House Ways and Means Subcommittee on Social Security gave voice vote approval to legislation (HR 5792) that made qualifying for federal disability benefits easier for women with AIDS-related disorders. AIDS is acquired immune deficiency syndrome.

Under 1992 rules, people whom doctors certified to be suffering from certain HIV-related disorders, such as pneumocystis carinii pneumonia, were assumed to have AIDS and to be disabled, which qualified them for benefits. HIV (human immunodeficiency virus) is the AIDS virus. Those with other HIV-related ailments, however, still had to prove that they were too disabled to work.

In December 1991, the Social Security Administration had expanded its definition of HIV-related disabilities to make qualifying for benefits easier for women and children. Women manifest different symptoms from those of homosexual men, for whom early AIDS definitions were drafted.

Sponsors claimed the new definition did not go far

enough. Under HR 5792, certain ailments often seen in women with HIV, including some forms of cervical cancer and pelvic inflammatory disease, would have automatically qualified for a disability determination.

Subcommittee Republicans opposed the bill, contending it would unnecessarily micromanage eligibility for the two main federal disability programs — Supplemental Security Income and Social Security Disability Insurance.

HR 5792 died upon adjournment of the 102nd Congress.

Chronology Of Action On Veterans' Affairs

1989-90

Action on veterans issues in the 101st Congress was dominated by the emotional and complex issue of the health effects of Agent Orange, a defoliant used during the Vietnam War. Vietnam veterans groups made strenuous efforts to win federal compensation benefits for veterans who claimed that their exposure to Agent Orange had caused cancer. Their efforts were unsuccessful, however, as key legislators argued that no proven causal link existed between the chemical and the disease.

The most significant piece of veterans' legislation cleared was a wide-ranging 1989 measure providing health, education and home-loan benefits to veterans.

Omnibus Veterans' Measure

Setting aside the divisive debate over Agent Orange, Congress late in its 1989 session cleared an omnibus measure (HR 901 — PL 101-237) that combined a number of different bills making changes in veterans programs. *(Agent Orange, box, p. 628)*

Legislative Action

Most of the final provisions of HR 901 were from a raft of separate measures passed by the House by voice vote under suspension of the rules in 1989. They included:

- HR 1335 (H Rept 101-262), passed Oct. 2, giving a cost-of-living adjustment of 4.9 percent in disability benefits.
- The original version of HR 901 (H Rept 101-107), passed June 27, requiring the Department of Veterans Affairs (VA) to provide outpatient medical services to certain veterans.
- HR 1334 (H Rept 101-105), passed June 27, eliminating the existing $60 a month limit on pension benefits to single veterans with no dependents in long-term care.
- HR 3199 (H Rept 101-312), passed Oct. 30, making reservists pursuing degrees in nursing or other health professions eligible to receive increased VA education benefits.
- HR 3390 (H Rept 101-313), passed Oct. 30, expanding the VA work-study program.
- HR 1358 (H Rept 101-68, Part I; H Rept 101-68, Part II), passed Oct. 2, allowing reservists and National Guardsmen to use their Montgomery GI benefits for vocational education or graduate work.
- HR 1415 (H Rept 101-73), passed June 6, requiring recipients of VA-backed loans to pay slightly higher fees to cover the costs of the VA's guaranteed home-loan program.
- HR 1199 (H Rept 101-106), passed June 27, seeking to attract nurses to staff-short veterans' hospitals by allowing local administrators to offer wages that were competitive with the private sector.

The Senate Veterans' Affairs Committee on June 27 approved a bill (S 13) providing special salary rates for nurses and cost-of-living increases for disabled veterans. S 13 was formally reported (S Rept 101-129) on Sept. 13. On Aug. 3, the Senate by voice vote passed a bill (S 1153 — S Rept 101-82) providing compensation to veterans and their survivors who were victims of two diseases linked to Agent Orange. The provisions of S 13 and S 1153 were then combined into the Senate version of HR 901, which was passed by voice vote Oct. 3.

In negotiations between the House and Senate on veterans legislation, both chambers agreed to give up key provisions. The Senate dropped its Agent Orange provisions, while the House lost its competitive-salary provisions for nurses (HR 1199). Also dropped were the original provisions of HR 901 providing outpatient medical services and language providing increased VA education benefits to certain reservists.

HR 1199 would clear Congress (PL 101-366) in 1990. *(Story, p. 627)*

The House adopted the final version of HR 901 on Nov. 20, and the Senate followed suit Nov. 21. President Bush signed the bill Dec. 18.

As cleared, HR 901:

- Provided a 4.7 percent cost-of-living adjustment in rates for disability compensation and dependency and indemnity compensation.
- Provided increased pension benefits for single veterans with no children who were receiving long-term medical care from the Department of Veterans Affairs.
- Reduced from two years to one year the length-of-marriage criteria for certain survivors benefits paid at dependency and indemnity compensation rates.
- Codified a requirement that veterans be furnished notices of decisions and advised of their right to appeal.
- Allowed retired military nurses to keep their military retirement pay if they chose to work as nurses in VA medical centers.
- Allowed VA medical centers to hire certain medical professionals without going through civil service procedures.
- Extended authority for respite- and home-care programs and for a demonstration program of community-based care for homeless and mentally ill veterans.
- Raised the mortgage-indemnity fee for home buyers from 1 percent to 1.25 percent when obtaining a VA home loan with a down payment of less than 5 percent.
- Created a new revolving fund to use mortgage-indemnity fees to help reimburse the VA for paying off guaranteed loans.
- Protected veterans from liability to the VA as a result of foreclosure unless indications of fraud existed.
- Extended eligibility for the VA's work-study program to survivors and dependents.
- Based work-study allowance payments on the higher of the federal or state minimum wage.
- Extended the Veterans Readjustment Appointment authority to Dec. 31, 1993, retaining hiring priority for Vietnam-era disabled veterans.

Veterans Reconciliation

The 101st Congress provided changes in veterans programs in both the 1989 budget-reconciliation bill (HR 3299 — PL 101-239) and the 1990 budget-reduction measure

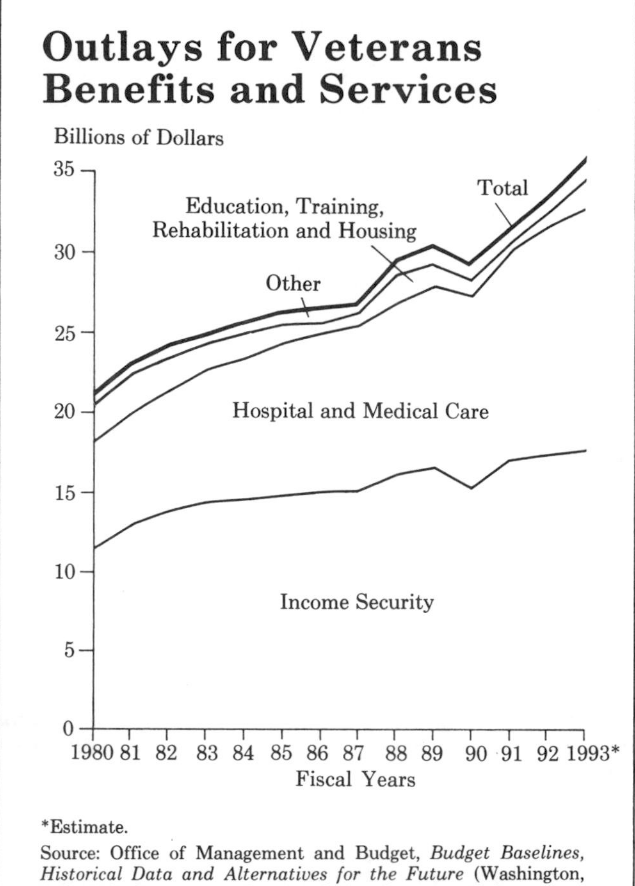

*Estimate.

Source: Office of Management and Budget, *Budget Baselines, Historical Data and Alternatives for the Future* (Washington, D.C.: U.S. Government Printing Office, January 1993).

(HR 5835 — PL 101-508). *(1989 reconciliation, p. 43; 1990 reconciliation, p. 55)*

HR 3299

The veterans programs provisions of HR 3299, as cleared:

- Extended through Sept. 30, 1990, a 1 percent fee on housing loans guaranteed, made or insured by the Department of Veterans Affairs (VA), raising an estimated $169 million in fiscal 1990.
- Continued through Sept. 30, 1990, the VA's ability to sell housing loans with or without recourse, for $496 million in 1990 savings.

HR 5835

The veterans programs provisions of HR 5835, as cleared:

- Suspended compensation for incompetent veterans with no dependents (spouse, child or parent), whose estate (excluding their home) exceeded $25,000, until the estate was reduced to $10,000. If the veteran regained competence for more than 90 days, he or she would receive the money withheld in a lump-sum payment. The provision was expected to save $125 million in fiscal year 1991 and to provide a total savings of $291 million through fiscal 1995.
- Eliminated the presumption of total and permanent disability for veterans 65 or older, and references to age on the presumption for veterans who became unemployable. Under existing law, after age 65, veterans who became unemployable were considered permanently and totally disabled. A veteran who became unemployable at any age as a result of a disability expected to continue throughout his or her life would be considered permanently disabled for purposes of pension eligibility. The provision was expected to save $17 million in fiscal 1991 and $313 million in fiscal years 1991-95.
- Limited monthly pension payments to $90 for some Medicaid-eligible recipients of a VA pension and prohibited any portion of the $90 from being spent on a veteran's nursing home care. Those in state veterans' homes were exempt. The provision was set to take effect the month after enactment and expire Sept. 30, 1992. Veterans would not be liable for overpayment unless they "willfully concealed" information that would lead to a pension reduction.
- Stipulated that remarried spouses of veterans would no longer be able to reinstate their veterans' benefits if the marriage ended in annulment, divorce or death. Under existing law, veterans' spouses who remarried could reinstate veterans' benefits from their spouses if the marriage ended. The provision also applied to married children of veterans.
- Set at 5.4 percent the fiscal 1991 cost-of-living adjustment (COLA) for compensation of veterans with service-connected disabilities and the survivors of veterans who died as a result of such injuries. The figure was based on the COLA for Social Security benefits. The increase that would have been received during December 1990 would be paid at the same time as compensation and DIC payments for January.

  However, because Congress did not pass a bill authorizing the payment of a COLA, a COLA bill had to be enacted before the percentage policy could take effect.
- Authorized the VA to collect from a third-party payer under a health plan contract the "reasonable" cost of a non-service-connected injury to a veteran with a service-connected disability. The authority to make these collections was to expire Oct. 1, 1993.
- Required that funds collected from third-party insurers be credited to a new Medical Recoveries Fund. Existing law required the money to be deposited into the Treasury as miscellaneous receipts. The VA secretary could use the money for expenses for the identification, billing and collection from third-party insurers.
- Required a veteran to pay $2 for each 30-day supply of a medication provided on an outpatient basis. (Veterans with a service-connected disability rated 50 percent or more would be exempt.) The money collected would be credited to the new Medical Recoveries Fund. The provision applied to medications received from Oct. 31, 1990, through Sept. 30, 1991. Copayments were not required for medical supplies.
- Changed health care categories for determining a veteran's eligibility for hospital and nursing home care. The three existing categories (A, B and C according to income) were decreased to two: veterans who were required to pay a copayment and those who were not.
- Required all veterans not entitled to care to pay the copayments for inpatient and nursing home care. Copayments would be: $10 per day for hospital care, $5 per day for nursing home care and the existing copayment for outpatient visits, which was an amount equal to 20 percent

of the estimated cost of a VA outpatient visit. Copayments would also be linked to Consumer Price Index increases.

- Deleted existing caps on the amount veterans could pay in copayments. Required existing copayments for hospital care and other health care to be paid by non-entitled veterans in addition to the copayments for care per day.
- Limited the vocational rehabilitation eligibility to veterans with service-connected disabilities rated at 20 percent or more. This applied only to veterans originally applying for benefits on or after Nov. 1, 1990.
- Allowed the lender to choose between the claim procedure under the current law and submitting the lender's claim when the VA notified the lender of VA's estimated value of the home. The lender would bear any loss or profit on the actual resale.
- Eliminated the headstone allowance for veterans who died after Nov. 1, 1990, and whose families chose to purchase a private marker. Existing law allowed for reimbursement of no more than an $87 stipend. The marker would still be provided for those who chose a veteran's marker. The provision would save $3 million in outlays in fiscal 1991 and $19 million through fiscal years 1991-95.
- Limited the $150 plot allowance for those veterans who were in receipt of veterans' benefits at the time of death or were eligible for compensation. The provision, effective Nov. 1, 1990, would result in savings of $27 million in outlays in 1991 and total savings of $147 million in outlays in fiscal years 1991-95.
- Provided that injuries and diseases occurring during service as "a result of the veteran's own willful misconduct or abuse of alcohol and drugs" would not be compensated by a disability pension. The provision covered illnesses, such as cirrhosis of the liver, found to be the secondary effects of alcohol and drug abuse. Under existing law, veterans received no compensation for such illnesses but did receive disability pensions. The VA estimated that each year 28,000 veterans suffered from such illnesses. The provision covered claims filed after Oct. 31, 1990. The provision was expected to save $10 million in outlays in fiscal 1991 and $334 million in outlays in fiscal years 1991-95.
- Required, upon the VA secretary's request, that compensation and pension claimants disclose their Social Security numbers as well as those of their dependents to receive claims. Benefits would not be paid to those who refused to provide a number, but claimants who did not have a number would not be required to provide one. Also required the VA to verify that recipients of these benefits were not deceased. The provision was expected to save $4 million in fiscal 1991 and $47 million in fiscal years 1991-95.

Veterans' Leadership

With his Sept. 26, 1992, resignation, Edward J. Derwinski ended his controversial tenure as the nation's first secretary of veterans affairs (VA). Derwinski, a Republican representative from Illinois from 1959 to 1983, had been confirmed by the Senate, 94-0, on March 2, 1989. Upon leaving the VA, he became deputy chairman for ethnic coalitions on the 1992 Bush/Quayle campaign. *(Cabinet profiles, p. 1174)*

Throughout his term in office, Derwinski had a series of small run-ins with various veterans organizations, such as when he agreed to a request, later rescinded, from administration POW-MIA negotiators to give Vietnam $250,000 in obsolete VA medical equipment to encourage cooperation. Harsher protest were heard, however, when Derwinski, with Health and Human Services Secretary Louis W. Sullivan, in 1991 proposed that VA hospitals in Southern rural communities accept poor non-veteran patients with no other access to health care. Derwinski also angered veterans when he announced that VA hospitals would no longer sell tobacco products after September 1991 and that VA health facilities were to be smoke-free by the end of 1993. Congress subsequently reversed the smoking ban. *(Story, p. 635)*

Derwinski did score some successes as VA secretary. During his tenure, he won $1 billion in increased funding for VA health care for each year, despite the belt-tightening times. Veterans groups also praised his decision to compensate Vietnam veterans suffering from illnesses that some linked to exposure to the chemical defoliant Agent Orange.

Following Derwinski's departure, Deputy VA Secretary Anthony J. Principi became acting secretary of the department.

In the 101st and 102nd Congresses, Alan Cranston, D-Calif., served as chairman of the Senate Veterans' Affairs Committee, and G. V. "Sonny" Montgomery, D-Miss., served as chairman of the House Veterans' Affairs Committee.

Nurses' Pay

Spurred by concern over shortages of nurses at Department of Veterans Affairs (VA) hospitals, Congress in 1990 cleared a bill (HR 1199 — PL 101-366) making VA nurses' salaries competitive with local labor markets. The bill was the only significant piece of veterans' legislation that became law in 1990.

Sponsored by Rep. Joseph P. Kennedy II, D-Mass., the bill affected the salaries of about 35,000 registered nurses and nurse anesthetists. Backers of the bill said directors of local veterans' medical centers needed to have the ability to offer nurses wages that were competitive with the private sector. Such pay equity was seen as helping fill about 2,400 vacant nursing positions in the VA system.

HR 1199 replaced the existing salary levels paid to VA nurses with four broader pay ranges. Local medical directors then would have the power to hire nurses at salaries anywhere within the ranges without approval by higher-level officials, as long as the salaries could be justified in the next budget process. Kennedy and other sponsors said the provision would give directors the flexibility to respond quickly to changing labor markets.

The Congressional Budget Office estimated that salary increases of $5 million to $10 million annually would result from the plan.

The House Veterans' Affairs Committee reported HR

Agent Orange Controversy

The most contentious veterans' issue facing Congress during the Bush administration focused on the federal government's responsibility to veterans who had been exposed to the defoliant Agent Orange during the Vietnam War.

Although legislation cleared early in the 102nd Congress to provide compensation to veterans exposed to the chemical who contracted certain illnesses, debate over the issue during the preceding years illustrated how strains over the Vietnam War continued to divide members of Congress.

Thousands of Vietnam veterans had sought federal veterans compensation benefits based on claims that their exposure to Agent Orange had resulted in various forms of cancer. Their claims went nowhere under the Reagan administration, which maintained that a causal link between the chemical and cancer could not be established.

From the beginning, the Bush administration appeared more willing to consider Agent Orange. On Nov. 24, 1989, however, Veterans Affairs Secretary Edward J. Derwinski announced that he would delay taking a position on the issue until release of a Centers for Disease Control (CDC) report in February 1990.

Differences over the CDC report showed the continuing scientific uncertainty over the link between Agent Orange and cancer. The CDC report found no relationship between the chemical and the disease. Within a few months, however, a scientific panel backed by a coalition of veterans' groups released a study linking Agent Orange to at least eight disease categories.

Equally significant in determining the fate of Agent Orange legislation, observers said, was a generational split between veterans and between members of Congress. On one side were a number of Vietnam-era veterans in Congress, including Sen. John Kerry, D-Mass., Sen. Bob Kerrey, D-Neb., and Rep. Lane Evans, D-Ill., who argued strongly that many of their peers deserved help from the government for ailments caused by exposure to the toxic chemical.

On the other side, however, were older members of Congress whose interests and personal histories were far more oriented toward veterans from earlier wars. These members, led by House Veterans' Affairs Committee Chairman G. V. "Sonny" Montgomery, D-Miss., expressed doubts about the scientific evidence for Agent Orange-related diseases. These members also were seen as being reluctant to offer what they saw as special treatment to Vietnam-era veterans.

Despite the CDC report, Derwinski announced March 29, 1990, that the VA would compensate Vietnam veterans who were suffering from non-Hodgkins lymphoma and soft-tissue sarcoma. The VA in 1985 had agreed to provide compensation for those afflicted with chloracne, a skin disease.

Before and after Derwinksi's move, Evans and other members pressed hard for legislation on Agent Orange but failed in the 101st Congress because of opposition from Montgomery and his allies.

In 1989, the Senate sought to include Agent Orange provisions in the omnibus veterans' legislation (HR 901), but they were dropped in conference at the insistence of Montgomery. *(HR 901, p. 625)*

A bill sponsored by Evans (HR 3004), which would have expanded the list of diseases eligible for compensation, never made it out of committee in 1990, and controversy over an Agent Orange amendment helped kill a veterans' cost-of-living bill (HR 5326) that same year. Early in 1991, however, legislation (HR 556 — PL 102-4) was cleared by the 102nd Congress providing permanent benefits to veterans with chloracne and two forms of cancer. *(Story, p. 632)*

1199 (H Rept 101-106) on June 22, 1989. The House passed the bill by voice vote under suspension of the rules June 27.

During the House-Senate negotiations on HR 901, the omnibus veterans measure cleared in 1989, the Senate refused to include provisions regarding VA nurses' pay, even though it had passed a bill (S 13) that included similar language to that provided in HR 1199.

The Senate by voice vote Aug. 2, 1990, passed an amended HR 1199. The House cleared the bill the following day, and President Bush signed it Aug. 15.

In separate action, the House provided an increase in salary for VA nurses, as well as VA physicians and dentists, in a bill (HR 4557 — H Rept 101-466) passed by voice vote under suspension of the rules May 1, 1990. Although the bill died upon adjournment, Congress in 1991 cleared legislation (HR 598) providing pay raises to VA doctors and dentists. *(Story, p. 633)*

Other Legislation

Congress considered a number of other veterans-related bills in 1990, but none became law.

Veterans Housing. To deal with veterans' housing needs, the House July 16 passed, by voice vote under suspension of the rules, HR 5002. The bill required the secretary of veterans affairs (VA) to establish a three-year program of transitional housing for participants in the Compensated Work Therapy program, a rehabilitative program for veterans with psychological or physical problems. The VA could provide loans of up to $4,500 to assist nonprofit organizations in leasing housing units for group residences for veterans with substance abuse problems. The measure also authorized mortgage payment assistance up to $10,000 to help veterans avoid foreclosure of their home loans guaranteed by the VA.

During House Veterans' Affairs Committee consideration, an amendment was rejected that would authorize $10 million to forge a "voluntary relationship" between the VA and the Department of Housing and Urban Development to help homeless veterans find affordable housing.

HR 5002 was reported (H Rept 101-592) on July 12.

Personnel Retention. Legislation (HR 5740) to help the VA recruit and retain medical personnel was passed by the House, by voice vote under suspension of the rules, Oct. 15. House Veterans' Affairs reported the bill (H Rept 101-861) on Oct. 13.

HR 5740 would allow part-time medical personnel to accept honoraria for speeches and articles, as long as the payment did not represent a conflict of interest.

Medical Research Grants. By voice vote under suspension of the rules, the House June 12 passed HR 4390, which would create a VA medical research grant program built on existing cooperative research efforts between the VA and the Defense Department.

HR 4390 was reported (H Rept 101-534) from House Veterans' Affairs on June 7.

Recruitment and Hiring. Legislation (HR 4088) establishing a permanent Veterans Recruitment Authority to give preference in federal hiring to veterans, especially disabled ones, passed the House June 12 by voice vote under suspension of the rules. House Veterans' Affairs reported the bill (H Rept 101-533) June 7.

Employment and Training. HR 4087, passed July 10 in the House by voice vote under suspension of the rules, offered VA employment, training and other services to military personnel with no more than 180 days of service remaining. The bill was reported (H Rept 101-562) from House Veterans' Affairs on June 27.

Educational Services. The House passed HR 4089 on July 10 by voice vote under suspension of the rules. The measure extended educational and vocational services to veterans who had been out of the service for less than a year, those still active with 180 days or fewer of duty remaining and some disabled military personnel. House Veterans' Affairs reported HR 4089 (H Rept 101-563) on June 27.

Disability Pay. The Senate Veterans' Affairs Committee on June 28 approved S 190, which would allow disabled veterans to receive both disability and retirement pay. Under existing law, a retiree had to choose between the two. S 190 was reported Sept. 20.

A similar bill (HR 303) was introduced in the House.

Veterans' Rehabilitation. The House Veterans' Affairs Committee May 17 approved legislation (HR 3053) calling for the issuance of rehabilitation certificates, from the Labor Department, to veterans who received dishonorable or general discharges if they proved that their conduct had been exemplary for at least three years. The bill was reported (H Rept 101-561, Part I) June 27.

1991-92

Spurred by patriotic fervor over the Persian Gulf War against Iraq, Congress moved a spate of veterans legislation early in the 102nd Congress. The eagerness of members to display support for U.S. forces engaged in the conflict helped override budgetary concerns and a longstanding deadlock over the issue of the effects of the defoliant Agent Orange on Vietnam War veterans.

In addition to extending benefits to veterans afflicted with diseases caused by Agent Orange, Congress approved generous benefits to Persian Gulf War veterans, provided cost-of-living increases for disabled veterans and offered new health and employment assistance.

Gulf War Benefits

Congress in 1991, while the country was in the midst of the Persian Gulf War against Iraq, moved quickly to approve legislation (S 725 — PL 102-25) to increase combat pay and other benefits for military personnel and to provide additional GI Bill education and other benefits for veterans.

Despite the broad support for increased benefits, congressional proponents had to worry about paying for them without violating spending limits imposed by the 1990 reconciliation law (HR 5835 — PL 101-508). Much of the debate centered on how the benefit package could be crafted to qualify for a provision in the law that exempted spending from the caps. *(Reconciliation, p. 55)*

Leaders from the House and Senate sorted through a grab bag of proposals that included raising combat pay, extending education benefits and providing child care services for Gulf families. Some of the proposals were new, but others had been kicked around for years, and sponsors saw their chance to latch onto a sure-fire piece of legislation. Bush administration officials worked closely with members to try to keep costs down and benefits restricted to those who actually had participated in the Persian Gulf War. *(Gulf War, p. 299)*

Through much of the debate, Democrats faced Republican complaints that their enthusiasm for expanded benefits was largely an effort to win back favor for voting against authorizing the war (H J Res 77 — PL 102-1).

As cleared, the legislation, estimated to cost $655 million, increased imminent danger, or combat, pay from $110 to $150 a month for those who served in the Gulf War. The increase was effective from Aug. 1, 1990, the day before Iraqi troops invaded Kuwait, until 180 days after Bush declared the war ended. The death gratuity for families of those killed in the war was doubled to $6,000, and the group life insurance benefit for service members and veterans doubled to $100,000.

The largest increase for veterans was in GI Bill education benefits. Monthly payments were raised from $300 to $350 a month for those who enlisted for more than three years. Similar increases were provided for two-year enlistees, reservists and National Guard members. The increases became effective Oct. 1, 1991, through Sept. 30, 1993, but the secretaries of defense and veterans affairs had the option of continuing the increased levels. The legislation also provided authorization for $15 billion in supplemental appropriations to cover U.S. Persian Gulf costs and $340 million for defense-related nuclear waste management and environmental restoration activities.

Senate Action

A Senate task force headed by John Glenn, D-Ohio, started early in the 102nd Congress to sift through scores of bills relating to the Persian Gulf War in an effort to shape an omnibus package.

Veterans' Affairs

In its Jan. 30 markup, the Senate Armed Services panel approved five measures that would be rolled into an omnibus bill for floor consideration. One measure (S 237) introduced by Chairman Sam Nunn, D-Ga., would have hiked imminent-danger pay for troops in the Persian Gulf from $110 to $150 per month. The panel also approved a bill (S 232) that would have doubled — from $50,000 to $100,000 — life insurance provided for members of the military. The other measures would have:

- Given members leaving the military the same 26 weeks of unemployment benefits available to civilians who lost their jobs (S 160).
- Allowed retired military personnel recalled to active duty to serve at the highest grade they held while on active duty (S 204).
- Authorized troops serving in the Gulf to invest their pay in a Treasury savings program with an interest rate of up to 10 percent (S 221).

Considered but excluded from the panel's package were provisions giving military personnel serving in the Persian Gulf region more time to repay student loans (S 335); authorizing the Small Business Administration to provide loans to small businesses hurt by the loss of key employees to service in the war (S 360); extending the combat pay tax exclusion to prisoners of war and soldiers missing in action; allowing reservists to deduct expenses associated with the war from their taxes; and extending the earned-income tax credit to qualified military personnel stationed overseas.

As the various pieces of the package were fashioned, Democrats agreed that the fiscal 1991 $311 million price tag should be considered a cost of Operation Desert Storm, exempting it from spending caps set under the 1990 budget agreement.

However, Office of Management and Budget Director Richard G. Darman had already warned that the administration did not consider many of the costs to be directly related to the war. In a Feb. 5 letter to a number of members, he said passage of the legislation could trigger automatic spending cuts under the new budget law.

A more modest set of benefits was recommended March 1 by a Republican Senate task force headed by John McCain, Ariz.

The Armed Services Committee March 5 approved a number of the Democrats' recommendations as part of its authorization (S 578 — S Rept 102-18) of supplemental funding for the war, including the language of S 237, S 204 and S 221.

The Senate package was brought to the floor March 14 as a leadership amendment to S 578. Leaders warned at the start of the debate that approval of amendments to the package could unravel its bipartisan backing, which was crafted after weeks of negotiations.

The Senate voted 58-38 to table (kill) a Dale Bumpers, D-Ark., amendment to provide assistance to Gulf War veterans who owned small businesses. However, a motion to table a Jesse Helms, R-N.C., amendment to prevent the use of any funds authorized in the bill to rebuild Iraq was rejected, 0-98. The Senate then adopted, 98-0, a substitute amendment expressing the sense of the Senate that none of the funds in the bill should be used to rebuild Iraq so long as Saddam Hussein was in power.

The benefits package was then approved by voice vote, followed by a 97-1 vote in favor of the entire bill. The dissenting vote was cast by Oregon Republican Mark O. Hatfield, who had been a strong opponent of going to war.

House Action

As the House bill (HR 1175) authorizing supplemental appropriations for the war took shape in several committees, it included potentially troublesome language designed to avoid tough new budget requirements that such spending be offset by tax increases or cuts in other spending. Republicans had complained about the funding maneuver during a closed-door markup by the House Armed Services Committee on March 6.

HR 1175 tied the veterans' benefits cost to Operation Desert Storm by setting aside $1 billion over the next five years from the appropriations account that was being used to pay for the Persian Gulf War. A number of Republicans objected that such a move would require U.S. allies, whose contributions were largely funding the account, to pay for long-term benefits unrelated to the war.

In addition, the bill included language stating that enactment of the measure would signify congressional designation of the veterans spending as emergency-related, a step required to exempt it from the new budget requirement. That provision caused concern among House budget leaders, who saw it as the first step in the unraveling of the 1990 budget deal.

The language put Bush in an uncomfortable position. If he signed the bill but did not declare the veterans spending an emergency — as he also was required to do — across-the-board cuts would be triggered in veterans and other entitlement programs.

The $1 billion veterans portion of HR 1175 was largely crafted by Veterans' Affairs Committee Chairman G. V. "Sonny" Montgomery, D-Miss., who also was a member of Armed Services. It sought to increase veterans education, health and housing benefits as well as retarget survivors' compensation to provide greater protection for younger families.

In addition, the legislation included numerous changes in military personnel benefits, as approved March 5 by the Armed Services' Military Personnel and Compensation Subcommittee. Among other things, the bill would have raised combat and family-separation pay, increased death gratuity payments and provided transitional medical coverage for reservists after they left active service in Operation Desert Storm.

The bill also sought to protect mothers and single fathers of children under 6 months of age from being called to active duty or reassigned. The fiscal 1991 cost for the provisions approved by the Personnel subcommittee was estimated at $375 million.

HR 1175 was reported from House Armed Services (H Rept 102-16, Part I) on March 7.

The House passed HR 1175 March 13 by an overwhelming vote of 398-25 after a bitter partisan debate over the funding mechanism. Republicans charged that language inserted by House leaders to require a presidential emergency declaration for the benefits to go into effect was a ploy to embarrass Bush and bust the budget at the same time. But House Democrats, who had suffered scathing GOP attacks for their Jan. 12 vote against authorizing the war, were in no mood to cave in. They argued that the price was not too much to pay to show appreciation to U.S. troops.

On March 12, Rules Committee Chairman Joe Moakley, D-Mass., had worked with his panel to craft a rule governing floor debate on the bill that would allow some amendments. The rule was approved on the floor the next day by a largely party-line vote of 247-171. Budget Committee leaders then made a futile attempt to amend the legislation so that the spending would be subject to the "pay-as-you-go" provisions in the 1990 budget law. They argued that if the language declaring the funding emergency-related was successful, it would encourage the use of similar language in other bills to avoid budget restrictions.

The amendment was rejected 175-248. The House also rejected, 165-260, an amendment by Minority Leader Robert H. Michel, R-Ill., that sought to restore a budget law requirement that the Office of Management and Budget, not the Congressional Budget Office, determine the cost of tax and entitlement bills.

Final Action

Differences between the House and Senate bills were resolved through a series of informal meetings among members, aides and administration officials. An official conference was never held.

The biggest difference was cost. The House bill carried a price tag of about $1.4 billion over five years. White House officials had warned that Bush would veto the measure because of its high cost. The House bill also included language that put the onus on Bush to declare all of the spending to be emergency-related before any of the provisions could go into effect.

By contrast, the Senate package targeted most of the benefits to veterans of the Gulf War, at a five-year cost of about $500 million. While it, too, bypassed budget caps, the legislation was drafted with broad bipartisan input and had won White House backing. The package was to be financed largely by foreign contributions to the fund set up to cover U.S. costs of the Persian Gulf War.

In the unofficial conference negotiations, which involved OMB Director Darman, the administration's prime target was the House proposal to greatly expand GI education benefits. The administration said the benefits were 10 ten times greater than similar proposals in the Senate bill. Administration lobbyists encountered strong resistance on the matter from House negotiators, especially Veterans' Affairs Committee Chairman Montgomery.

After a week of negotiations, an agreement acceptable to the White House was reached. The biggest change was a substantial paring back of the new veterans education benefits that had been included in the House package. The administration also refused to declare the spending emergency-related, fearing that it would set a bad precedent for exemptions from budget limits.

The Senate approved the final measure, reintroduced as a new bill (S 725), March 21 by voice vote; the House passed it later that day by a vote of 396-4. President Bush signed the measure April 6.

COLA Increases

Lawmakers acted several times during the 102nd Congress to provide cost-of-living adjustments (COLAs) to disabled veterans and their survivors.

Members in 1991 felt considerable pressure to act on the politically popular increases because 1990 COLA legislation (HR 5326) had stalled when efforts were made to attach provisions ensuring compensation for some veterans suffering from cancer after exposure to Agent Orange during the Vietnam War. It was the first time Congress had failed to clear a veterans COLA in the same year in which it granted such increases to Social Security recipients.

With national attention riveted on U.S. military forces in the Persian Gulf early in 1991, members hastened to break the impasse. Late in January, they overwhelmingly approved a 5.4 percent cost of living increase for disabled veterans in 1991.

A 3.7 percent increase for 1992 followed later in the first session. In 1992, Congress approved a COLA increase for the following year and also revised the system for providing compensation for spouses and children.

1991 Increases

After deadlocking over the Agent Orange issue in 1990, key legislators on veterans issues returned at the start of the 102nd Congress seemingly intent on renewing their battle. On one side was House Veterans' Affairs Committee Chairman G. V. "Sonny" Montgomery, D-Miss., who favored giving just a COLA increase. On the other side were Senate Veterans' Affairs Committee Chairman Alan Cranston, D-Calif., and Rep. Lane Evans, D-Ill., who wanted to tie a COLA increase to a measure compensating veterans for several diseases linked to Agent Orange exposure.

However, on Jan. 17, the day after the start of the Persian Gulf War with Iraq, the two camps settled the issue. Montgomery and Evans agreed to consider the two veterans' proposals in a way that would speed action on both: A COLA bill and Agent Orange legislation would be considered separately, neither with amendments that could complicate enactment. *(Agent Orange, p. 632)*

With the impasse broken, action in both chambers was swift. The House passed HR 3, providing a 5.4 percent COLA, by 421-0 on Jan. 23; the Senate passed the bill 99-0 the next day, completing congressional action. President Bush signed HR 3 (PL 102-3) Feb. 6.

The Senate Veterans' Affairs Committee June 26 opened the bidding on the COLA for 1992, when it approved S 775 (S Rept 102-139) by voice vote. The increase was estimated to cost $486 million in new budget authority, but the actual COLA boost would not be determined until the fall. COLAs for Social Security and veterans' benefits were based on the rate of inflation as measured by the Consumer Price Index, announced in October.

During the panel's markup, Alan K. Simpson, R-Wyo., tried to avert future controversies by amending the bill to make the boosts automatic. He cited the Agent Orange controversy's delay of the 1991 COLA in arguing for automatic benefit adjustments. His amendment failed on a 5-5 tie.

The Senate bill contained provisions that drew opposition from the Bush administration. Cranston included language that would have revised existing law providing for compensation of veterans suffering from diseases related to exposure to radiation during military service.

House members also opposed that approach, and the version (HR 1046 — H Rept 102-164) marked up by the House Veterans' Affairs Committee was a "clean" COLA bill. As approved by the panel July 23, the legislation was to provide disabled veterans and survivors of military personnel who died from service-related illnesses with a 4.8 percent benefits increase, based on an early estimate of what the Consumer Price Index would be. The COLA boost, to be effective Dec. 1, was to show up in January checks.

In writing HR 1046, the Subcommittee on Compensation, Pension and Insurance had provided for a 5.2 percent

COLA. But full committee Chairman Montgomery offered a substitute amendment holding the raise to no more than 4.8 percent, to comply with the 1990 budget agreement between Congress and the White House. The panel approved the amendment by voice vote.

The Department of Veterans Affairs estimated the bill would cost $520.4 million in fiscal 1992 and $3 billion through fiscal 1996.

The House passed the bill authorizing the 4.8 percent increase by voice vote under suspension of the rules on July 29.

Cranston had hoped to get Congress to enact his version that also would compensate veterans suffering from radiation exposure. But the added money remained controversial, and the Department of Veterans Affairs (VA) warned Senate committee members that if the COLA was not enacted by November, the department would not be able to process it in time for money to appear in January checks.

As Congress struggled to wrap up its year's work in October, Cranston opted to heed the VA's admonition and move for floor consideration of the House measure.

The Senate passed HR 1046 on Oct. 28 by voice vote, after amending it to include a 3.7 percent COLA increase based on the Consumer Price Index.

Two days later, the House accepted the Senate changes by voice vote, clearing HR 1046 for President Bush, who signed it Nov. 12 (PL 102-152).

1992 Increase

On July 23, 1992, the House Veterans' Affairs Committee approved a bill (HR 4244) providing for a 3.2 percent COLA increase beginning Dec. 1, 1992. It was formally reported (H Rept 102-752) on July 29.

The Senate Veterans' Affairs Committee reported its version (S 2322 — S Rept 102-322) on July 20. The Senate passed the bill, which tied the COLA adjustment to the increase in Social Security and VA pension benefits, by voice vote July 28.

The House on Aug. 4 incorporated its language into the text of S 2322 and by voice vote passed it with a specified 3.2 percent increase. On Sept. 22, the Senate approved the House changes to the bill, but with no fixed percentage for the COLA increase.

The House cleared S 2322 on Sept. 30 by agreeing to the Senate arrangement, which tied the COLA to the Consumer Price Index or the rate of inflation.

President Bush signed the measure Oct. 24 (PL 102-510).

Dependents' Benefits

In addition, Congress in 1992 cleared a bill (HR 5008 — PL 102-568) that increased benefits to veterans' survivors and dependents, while also reducing benefits for veterans who, based on Internal Revenue Service information, did not need them. The bill extended coverage to widows of veterans who died before Oct. 1, 1992.

On July 8, the House Veterans' Affairs Compensation, Pension and Insurance Subcommittee approved HR 5008, which called for all surviving spouses of service members or veterans who died from a disease or injury related to military service to receive at least $750 a month. The measure also increased the added amount paid for dependents from $71 per month per child to $200 a month per child by fiscal 1995.

The full House Veterans' Affairs Committee approved the bill July 23 and reported it (H Rept 102-753, Part I) July 29.

Before the bill could reach the House floor, however, Veterans' Affairs Committee Chairman Montgomery had to find a way to pay for the benefit increases, which were estimated to cost $1.3 billion through fiscal 1997. To do so, Montgomery won an agreement from the Ways and Means Committee that the Veterans' Affairs Committee could be credited with the savings from extension of an expiring 1990 law requiring reductions in benefits for veterans who did not need them. Thus, the veterans panel was able to comply with the 1990 budget agreement's bar against new spending without other savings or revenue increases. Ways and Means reported HR 5008 (H Rept 102-753, Part II) on Aug. 6.

The House passed HR 5008 by voice vote under suspension of the rules Aug. 10.

The Senate Veterans' Affairs Committee on June 24 approved and on Aug. 12 reported a companion bill (S 2323 — S Rept 102-376) setting basic monthly compensation for surviving spouses at $725. The Senate passed HR 5008 by voice vote Sept. 22 after substituting the text of S 2323.

With time running out in the session, House and Senate aides worked out a compromise under which the basic monthly compensation was set at $750. Surviving spouses received additional compensation of $165 per month if the veteran was totally disabled for at least eight years from a service-connected injury or illness.

The House approved the compromise bill Oct. 3, and the Senate cleared it Oct. 7. President Bush signed the measure Oct. 29.

Agent Orange

Ending a long-running dispute, Congress in 1991 cleared legislation (HR 556 — PL 102-4) to ensure compensation for Vietnam veterans for some diseases linked to Agent Orange and set up a process for determining whether other ailments were caused by exposure to the defoliant.

A bipartisan compromise on the bill, reached in January as the Persian Gulf War got under way, marked the first time in more than a decade that leaders of the House and Senate Veterans' Affairs committees agreed that the government should compensate veterans exposed to Agent Orange for specific illnesses.

The compromise paved the way for Congress to clear legislation (HR 3) to provide a cost-of-living adjustment for disabled veterans and for spouses and children of veterans who died of service-related injuries. *(Story, p. 631)*

HR 556 codified two decisions by Veterans Affairs Secretary Edward J. Derwinski in 1990 to provide benefits to veterans who suffered from either of two forms of cancer, non-Hodgkins lymphoma or soft-tissue sarcoma. The bill also put into statute an earlier department decision to compensate veterans for a skin ailment, chloracne, also linked to Agent Orange.

The legislation also required the National Academy of Sciences (NAS) to analyze existing Agent Orange studies to determine whether scientific evidence linked the disease with other cancers. The NAS would then make recommendations to the secretary.

The Congressional Budget Office estimated the bill would cost $11 million in outlays in 1991 and $17 million in 1992.

The bill also extended through Dec. 31, 1993, veterans' eligibility for free medical care they already received because of Agent Orange or radiation exposure. The eligibility had expired Dec. 30, 1990.

Legislative Action

The Agent Orange issue resurfaced on the first day of the 102nd Congress.

G. V. "Sonny" Montgomery, D-Miss., the chairman of the House Veterans' Affairs Committee, who had long opposed efforts to extend eligibility for benefits based on Agent Orange exposure, reintroduced legislation (HR 3) on Jan. 3 that would provide a 5.4 percent cost-of-living adjustment for disabled veterans and for spouses and children of veterans who died from service-connected injuries. It contained no Agent Orange compensation.

The same day, Lane Evans, D-Ill., the most vocal supporter of expanded federal efforts for Agent Orange victims, reintroduced his competing legislation (HR 321) that would provide the COLA as well as compensate veterans for several diseases linked to Agent Orange exposure.

That set the stage for a repeat of a legislative struggle that could have blocked the veterans' COLA again. But with the nation rallying behind U.S. service personnel in the Persian Gulf, a compromise was worked out among House members, including Montgomery and Evans. Under the agreement, the House would consider the COLA bill (HR 3) without amendments, and a separate Agent Orange bill would be considered without amendments.

The House passed HR 556 by 412-0 under suspension of the rules on Jan. 29. The Senate passed the bill, 99-0, the next day, clearing it. President Bush signed the measure Feb. 6.

Job, Education Aid

Reservists who served on active duty in the Persian Gulf War received a boost in educational benefits and employment assistance under legislation (S 868 — PL 102-127) cleared by Congress in 1991.

Approved by the Senate Veterans' Affairs Committee on June 6 and reported (S Rept 102-124) on July 26, the bill restored education benefits to those who began studies but were not able to complete them because they were called to active duty or were given assignments that prevented them from finishing. The measure also extended eligibility for employment and job training services to reservists who served on active duty by a period of the length of their active duty service plus four months.

Under existing law, reservists who served less than 180 days on active duty did not qualify for school benefits. S 868 expanded eligibility to include reservists with less than 180 days of active duty if the person served in wartime and was honorably discharged.

The Senate passed S 868 by voice vote Aug. 2, and the House followed suit on Sept. 16. President Bush signed the bill Oct. 10.

The Department of Veterans Affairs estimated the bill would cost $3 million a year beginning in 1993.

In other action on job training legislation for veterans, Congress in 1992 cleared legislation on veterans' survivor benefits (HR 5008 — PL 102-568) that included provisions to expand job assistance programs for Vietnam-era veterans. *(HR 5008, p. 631)*

The House Veterans' Affairs Committee on May 28, 1992, approved a bill (HR 5254) to authorize on-the-job training for Persian Gulf and certain other veterans. Although HR 5254 never advanced to the floor, similar provisions were included in HR 5006 (PL 102-484), the Defense Department fiscal 1993 authorization bill.

In addition, the House on Aug. 10 and the Senate on Sept. 25 passed HR 5087 (H Rept 102-751, Part I), which sought to improve vocational rehabilitation programs for veterans with disabilities connected to their service. The Senate had considered a companion measure (S 2647). HR 5087 died upon adjournment of the 102nd Congress.

VA Doctor, Dentist Pay Raise

Congress in 1991 cleared legislation (HR 598 — PL 102-40) to give doctors and dentists at the Department of Veterans Affairs (VA) raises through special rates of pay.

The bill authorized new special pay rates for health care personnel in specialties in which federal salary levels were not competitive with the private sector. The special pay was to supplement regular salary. The measure was designed to help the VA recruit and retain physicians and dentists.

In 1990, the House passed a version of the pay raise bill (HR 4557), but it was one of several veterans measures that stalled over whether to compensate some veterans exposed to the defoliant Agent Orange. With the Persian Gulf War under way in January 1991, Congress compromised on Agent Orange compensation, freeing up the other veterans bills.

The House passed HR 598 on Jan. 30 by 399-0 under suspension of the rules.

But subsequent action was slowed after the Bush administration and some senators raised objections.

The Bush administration opposed a number of the bill's provisions and called the pay boosts "excessive." The main sticking point, however, was a House provision that would have allowed health care workers to accept honoraria for lectures and articles. The Ethics Reform Act of 1989 (PL 101-194) prohibited federal employees, except senators and their staff, from accepting honoraria other than necessary travel expenses. House members wanted to exempt full-time and part-time VA health professionals from that ban. Some senators, among them John Glenn, D-Ohio, chairman of the Governmental Affairs Committee, argued for lifting the ban for all non-appointed federal employees instead of doing it piecemeal. *(Ethics reform, p. 920)*

The Senate passed HR 598 April 17 by voice vote after amending it to exclude the honoraria provision. That put the ball back in the House's court. Veterans' Affairs Committee Chairman G. V. "Sonny" Montgomery, D-Miss., argued that the ban would stifle VA recruiting. But House members decided not to let the honoraria question further stall the bill and approved the Senate's version by voice vote April 23, clearing the measure. President Bush signed the bill May 7.

In addition to increasing pay, HR 598:

- Gave federal medical professionals the same collective bargaining and grievance rights that other VA workers had.
- Allowed VA medical directors the flexibility to set special pay rates, subject to review by the VA secretary, to meet specific needs of their facilities.
- Increased the maximum rates of special pay for those with exceptional qualifications, scarce specialties or long-

time service. Special pay for those with medical specialties in which "extraordinary difficulties" existed in recruitment and retention was set at a maximum of $40,000 a year.

- Authorized the secretary to protect special pay for personnel in non-scarce specialties by creating a new category: "retention pay." The aim was to keep the new law from penalizing those in non-scarce specialties.
- Prevented "unnecessarily high salaries" by requiring a facility director to submit to the VA secretary any agreement that would boost a doctor's total basic pay plus special pay over $134,100 for calendar 1991. The secretary would have 60 days to disapprove.

Veterans Services

After compromising over cost, Congress in 1991 cleared legislation (HR 1047 — PL 102-86) that sought to improve a number of veterans services, among them pension, compensation and life insurance programs. The bill authorized $3 million in fiscal 1992.

Congress had tried to enact many of these benefits in 1990, including them in legislation (HR 5326) that would have provided a cost-of-living adjustment to disabled veterans and survivors of veterans killed in military service. But that measure died after the attachment of controversial provisions to compensate some victims of exposure to the defoliant Agent Orange. Early in 1991, Congress approved separate COLA and Agent Orange bills, clearing the way for quick action on the legislation on veterans services.

As originally introduced, HR 1047 would have authorized $5 million annually for fiscal 1992 through 1996. The House passed the bill on April 11 on a roll-call vote of 399-3 under suspension of the rules. But questions remained over where the money would be found. Under the 1990 budget deal between Congress and the Bush administration, the new spending would have to be offset by cuts in other areas of the veterans budget, causing some members to raise questions about the bill.

The House and Senate Veterans' Affairs committees reached a compromise that would make the bill conform to the budget agreement. They agreed to drop a provision in the House-passed bill that would have increased coverage for the disabled under the Veterans Mortgage Life Insurance Program from $40,000 to $90,000. That provision would have cost $2 million in fiscal 1992, and its removal pared the overall cost of the bill that year to $3 million.

On July 25, the Senate adopted by voice vote the compromise in a substitute amendment, then passed HR 1047 also by voice vote.

On July 29, the House cleared the amended bill by voice vote. President Bush signed it Aug. 14.

As cleared, HR 1047:

- Extending from 30 to 40 years the time during which leukemia had to develop after radiation exposure to be judged service-connected. Some veterans were exposed to radiation during nuclear weapons testing and during the U.S. occupation of the bombed Japanese cities of Hiroshima and Nagasaki. Reservists who had served on active duty or training and were exposed to radiation also would be covered.
- Giving veterans more time to seek Service Disabled Life Insurance, by increasing — from one to two years — the period after veterans had been judged service-connected disabled that they could apply for coverage.
- Authorizing dental care that must be done for medical reasons before the veteran entered a hospital.
- Increasing from $500 to $1,000 the amount the Veterans Affairs Department could spend per year for outpatient dental services for each veteran.

Reservist Protections

With lawmakers eager to show their desire to help U.S. troops in the Persian Gulf, Congress early in 1991 approved legislation (HR 555 — PL 102-12) to increase financial and civil protections for reservists called to active duty.

Members on both sides of the Capitol had tried in 1990 to enact substantially similar legislation (HR 5814, S 3248) to update existing law, under the Soldiers' and Sailors' Civil Relief Act of 1940. But the legislation died at the end of the 101st Congress, one of several veterans bills that were casualties of a dispute over whether to compensate veterans who were disabled by the defoliant Agent Orange.

One of the first actions of the 102nd Congress was to settle the Agent Orange matter, thus clearing the way for the other veterans measures to move.

HR 555 was not controversial, and the House passed it under suspension of the rules by a 414-0 vote Jan. 29.

Action in the Senate was expected to be equally quick. However, the bill ran into a temporary roadblock when John Heinz, R-Pa., sought to offer an amendment asking the Pentagon to ensure that no single parents or couples with children were deployed in the Persian Gulf. Heinz's amendment subsequently was offered to an Export Administration reauthorization bill (HR 320) and rejected. *(Story, p. 195)*

With the Heinz amendment disposed of, the Senate amended and passed HR 555 by voice vote Feb. 21. The House agreed to the Senate amendment on Feb. 27, clearing the bill for President Bush, who signed it March 18.

As cleared, HR 555:

- Made clear that reservists called up to active duty for 90 days or more were guaranteed re-employment rights when they were demobilized. Under existing law, reservists serving longer than 90 days were not protected.
- Prohibited eviction of the families of those serving in the Gulf if their rent was $1,200 per month or less. The previous rent limit — $150 per month — had been set in 1966, during the Vietnam War.
- Guaranteed service personnel the right to resume their individual and family health insurance upon return to civilian life, with no interruptions or coverage exclusions.
- Permitted doctors and other health professionals called to active duty to suspend payment of their malpractice insurance premiums until they returned.
- Required courts, upon request, to suspend civil legal proceedings against those on active duty.

Aid for Homeless Veterans

Congress in 1992 cleared legislation (HR 5400 — PL 102-590) aimed at enhancing existing services for homeless veterans provided by the Labor Department and the Department of Veterans Affairs (VA).

The legislation reflected increased concern about the plight of homeless veterans, who were thought to constitute a significant portion of all homeless people.

HR 5400 would send veterans benefits counselors to 83 VA-run facilities providing readjustment counseling, shelter for homeless veterans and assistance for the mentally ill. Under the bill, the VA was given authority to establish grants for new assistance programs for homeless veterans. The legislation also authorized the VA to lease or donate 10 percent of VA properties repossessed because of loan defaults to non-profit groups and state agencies to provide housing for homeless veterans.

HR 5400 authorized $48 million a year in fiscal years 1993 through 1995. It also gradually expanded the authorization for certain homeless employment programs from $2.2 million in fiscal 1993, reaching $14 million in fiscal 1995.

The House Veterans' Affairs Committee approved HR 5400 July 23 and reported it (H Rept 102-721) the next day. The House passed the bill by voice vote under suspension of the rules July 27.

The Senate Veterans' Affairs Committee on June 24 approved a companion bill (S 2512), which it reported (S Rept 102-361) on Aug. 5. The Senate passed HR 5400 by voice vote Sept. 8 after substituting the text of S 2512.

The House agreed to the Senate amendments with amendments on Oct. 3, and the Senate cleared the measure Oct. 7. President Bush signed HR 5400 on Nov. 10.

Veterans Health

An omnibus veterans health bill (HR 5193 — PL 102-585) that included provisions for psychological counseling for women who were sexually harassed during military service and a health registry for Persian Gulf veterans cleared Congress in 1992.

Perhaps the most controversial issue surrounding the bill concerned smoking in veterans health facilities. Veterans Affairs (VA) Secretary Edward J. Derwinski had announced in August 1991 that VA hospitals would no longer sell tobacco products after Oct. 1, 1991. He also issued a directive in 1992 requiring that VA health facilities be smoke-free by Dec. 31, 1993. After heated debate, lawmakers agreed to reverse the smoking ban and to require the VA to designate smoking rooms for veterans.

HR 5193 also resolved a dispute over discounted drug prices for federal agencies. The bill sought to ensure that VA facilities would continue to receive their traditional deep discounts on prescription drugs. Some manufacturers had raised prices for VA drugs to comply with a new federal law requiring price reductions for the much larger Medicaid program. *(Medicaid drug discounts, p. 605)*

Legislative Action

During House Veterans' Affairs Committee consideration of HR 5192, a bill to expand veterans' health care benefits and services, Harley O. Staggers, D-W.Va., won voice vote approval of an amendment that would allow VA hospitals and facilities to provide an indoor smoking area and would require VA commissaries to sell tobacco products. HR 5192 was reported (H Rept 102-622) from committee on June 26.

On the House floor, Richard J. Durbin, D-Ill., and Timothy J. Penny, D-Minn., sponsored an amendment to strike the smoking provision. In a compromise, Bob Wise, D-W.Va., offered an amendment to the Durbin-Penny amendment that struck the language requiring that cigarettes be sold at VA facilities but kept the provision mandating the smoking areas. The Wise amendment was adopted, 338-71, on Oct. 1, and the amended Durbin-Penny amendment then was adopted by voice vote.

The House passed HR 5192 by voice vote Oct. 1.

The House Veterans' Affairs Committee on May 28 approved HR 5193, which expanded cost-sharing agreements between the VA and the Defense Department, and on July 24 reported it (H Rept 102-714, Part I).

Provisions of HR 5192 subsequently were included in HR 5193, which passed the House by voice vote under suspension of the rules Aug. 4.

The Senate Veterans' Affairs Committee approved a veterans health bill (S 2575) on June 24. Final action was delayed, however, by a dispute over the issue of drug discounts. After further negotiations, the panel reported the bill Sept. 15 (S Rept 102-401).

On Sept. 17, the Senate Veterans' Affairs Committee reported S 2973 (S Rept 102-409), which would improve treatment programs for women veterans who had experienced physical or psychological trauma as a result of sexual assault, harassment or rape while on active duty. The Senate passed S 2973 by voice vote Oct. 1, and its provisions subsequently were incorporated into HR 5193.

The full Senate passed an amended version of HR 5193 on Oct. 1, and the House accepted the Senate changes, with further changes, Oct. 6.

Before the measure could gain final clearance from the Senate, however, several senators placed a "hold" on the bill, expressing concern about the drug-pricing issue and reversal of the smoking ban. Ultimately, a compromise was worked out, and the Senate cleared the bill Oct. 8. President Bush signed HR 5193 on Nov. 4.

Major Provisions

As cleared, HR 5193:

- Reversed a VA ban on smoking in veterans' health care facilities and required the VA to designate smoking rooms for veterans.
- Established a health registry for Persian Gulf War veterans to monitor them for health effects of exposure to burning oil fires and other environmental conditions.
- Expanded cost-sharing agreements between VA and Defense Department medical facilities.
- Provided psychological counseling to women veterans who were sexually harassed or abused during military service.
- Authorized the VA to provide medical services to beneficiaries of the Civilian Health and Medical Program of the Uniformed Services (CHAMPUS), who are dependents of Defense Department personnel and other military retirees.
- Clarified that the VA had the authority to collect on Medicare supplemental insurance policies, for care starting April 7, 1986, for disabilities not connected to a veteran's service.

Loan Guarantees for Reservists

Congress in 1992 cleared legislation (HR 939 — PL 102-547) to expand eligibility for the Department of Veterans Affairs (VA) Home Loan Guaranty Program to members of the National Guard and Reserve.

The measure extended to certain members of the reserve forces eligibility to receive home, farm and business loans through the veterans home loan guarantee program. Reservists who had served at least six years were made eligible for the program, which had previously been open only to active-duty veterans.

The bill provided for a demonstration project on adjustable-rate mortgages. In addition, it allowed veterans to negotiate interest rates directly with lenders during fiscal 1993 and 1994, instead of having the VA secretary determine the permissible interest rates. HR 939 also included provisions from the Senate-passed S 2528 (S Rept 102-378), regarding home loans to American Indians and Alaska natives.

The House Veterans' Affairs Committee approved HR 939 on July 23, 1991, and reported it (H Rept 102-292, Part I) on Nov. 6. The House Ways and Means Committee subsequently amended the bill (H Rept 102-292, Part II) to clarify for tax purposes the determination of veterans' gross income relating to indebtedness for VA home loans. The House then passed the bill by voice vote under suspension of the rules on March 3, 1992.

On Aug. 8, 1992, the Senate Veterans' Affairs Committee approved a companion bill (S 3108), which it reported (S Rept 102-405) Sept. 16. The Senate passed an amended HR 939 by voice vote Oct. 1.

The House agreed to the Senate changes with additional changes Oct. 6, and the Senate cleared the measure Oct. 7. President Bush signed the bill Oct. 28.

Radiation Compensation

Legislation (S 775 — PL 102-578) to expand compensation for veterans exposed to certain kinds of radiation during wartime was cleared by Congress in 1992.

The measure expanded the list of 13 types of cancer-related disease eligible for compensation under the Radiation-Exposed Veterans Compensation Act of 1988 (PL 100-321) to include cancers of the salivary gland and the urinary tract. The bill also removed an eligibility requirement that said the diseases had to appear within 40 years of exposure for the veteran to receive compensation. *(1988 law, Congress and the Nation Vol. VII, p. 643)*

S 775 was approved by the Senate Veterans' Affairs Committee on June 26, 1991, and reported (S Rept 102-139) on Aug. 2. The Senate passed the bill by voice vote on Nov. 20.

The House passed an amended S 775 by voice vote on Sept. 30, 1992, and the Senate on Oct. 7 cleared the bill for President Bush, who signed it Oct. 30.

Post-Traumatic Stress

In 1992, Congress enacted comprehensive veterans health care legislation (S 2344 — PL 102-405) that included provisions to expand treatment of post-traumatic stress disorder, a combat-related psychological problem.

S 2344 allowed thousands of Vietnam War veterans to get treatment without having to prove that the disorder was war-related. Under previous law, veterans who believed they suffered from the ailment had to get approval from the Department of Veterans Affairs (VA) before they could receive treatment.

The bill also improved services to homeless veterans and authorized $10 million a year in fiscal 1993-94 for the VA to provide marriage and family counseling to Persian Gulf War veterans and their families.

A provision that caused some conflict aimed to rein in appropriations panels by banning funding for any major veterans medical projects that had not first been authorized. The provision sought to curb funding of pork-barrel projects in lawmakers' districts.

The House on Nov. 25, 1991, passed by voice vote under suspension of the rules HR 2280 (H Rept 102-130), which required the VA to develop a plan for expanding services to veterans who suffered from post-traumatic stress disorder, authorized funds for marriage and family counseling for veterans returning from the Persian Gulf War, curtailed the power of appropriators to funnel money to projects in their home states and exempted the VA from calculation of drug prices for Medicaid programs.

The Senate passed HR 2280 by voice vote Nov. 20, after substituting the text of S 869, which allowed Vietnam veterans to receive treatment for post-traumatic stress without having to prove it was war-related.

The Senate Nov. 15 passed S 1553 (S Rept 102-159), which made Persian Gulf War veterans and their families eligible for marriage and family counseling. The Bush administration opposed S 1553 and comparable language in HR 2280 as being redundant. It claimed the counseling services already were provided in S 725 (PL 102-25), the Gulf veterans benefits bill. *(Gulf War benefits, p. 629)*

HR 2280 stalled over the appropriations approval provision. On March 11, 1992, the Senate by voice vote passed S 2344, a slightly different version of HR 2280. The House, by voice vote under suspension of the rules, on May 12 passed S 2344, requiring authorization for medical projects of $300,000 or more. The House insisted on a conference, and conferees eventually agreed to the appropriations provision.

The House adopted the conference report (H Rept 102-871) on Sept. 24, and the Senate followed suit the next day. President Bush signed S 2344 on Oct. 9.

Minority Veterans Affairs

One of the existing assistant secretaries of the Department of Veterans Affairs (VA) would be designated as the chief minority affairs officer for the department, under legislation (HR 3327 — PL 102-218) cleared in 1991.

The chief minority affairs officer was to coordinate VA efforts to aid minority veterans and ensure that their concerns were addressed. Backers of the measure, notably Rep. Charles B. Rangel, D-N.Y., argued that minority veterans had a more difficult time readjusting to civilian life because of unemployment and lack of access to counseling and other agency services.

The House Veterans' Affairs Committee approved the bill Nov. 13 and reported it (H Rept 102-347) Nov. 22. The House passed HR 3327 by voice vote under suspension of the rules Nov. 25.

The Senate passed the bill by voice vote on Nov. 27, and President Bush signed it Dec. 11.

Job Discrimination

The 102nd Congress sought to bar employment discrimination against members of the armed services, but legislation (HR 1578) failed to clear.

Veterans had been guaranteed re-employment rights since World War II, but members of Congress said the relevant statute (Chapter 43 of Title 38, *U.S. Code*) had become a confusing and sometimes ambiguous jumble of provisions. An executive branch task force had been studying the problem, and the legislation advanced in the 102nd Congress was based largely on that group's recommendations.

HR 1578 built upon the update (HR 555 — PL 102-12) of the 1940 Soldiers' and Sailors' Civil Relief Act that cleared in 1991. The bill would bar denial of employment, benefits or promotion to people who were applicants or members of the armed forces or who had an obligation to serve. The measure also required employers to re-employ veterans after service and make an effort to accommodate disabled veterans. *(Reservist protections, p. 634)*

The House Veterans' Affairs Committee approved HR 1578 on April 11, 1991. The bill was reported (H Rept 102-56) on May 9. The House passed HR 1578 by voice vote under suspension of the rules May 14.

The Senate Veterans' Affairs Committee approved S 1095 on June 26 and reported it (S Rept 102-203) on Nov. 7. The Senate by voice vote passed HR 1578 on Oct. 1, 1992, after substituting the text of S 1095.

The House and Senate were unable to resolve their differences, and the legislation died upon adjournment.

Hospice Care Pilot Program

The Senate on Oct. 16, 1991, by voice vote passed a bill (S 1358) authorizing the Department of Veterans Affairs (VA) to establish a five-year hospice care pilot program for terminally ill veterans in 15 to 30 VA medical facilities around the country.

The Senate Veterans' Affairs Committee approved S 1358 on June 26 and reported it (S Rept 102-160) on Sept. 24.

10

Education Policy

Introduction 641

1989-90 Chronology 643

1991-92 Chronology 653

Education Policy

During his 1988 campaign, George Bush vowed to be "the education president." Over the next four years as president, he elevated the school reform movement to a national-level discussion from its scattered state and local efforts.

But the administration confronted a wall of opposition in Congress. At the end of Bush's tenure, the state and local attempts at reform were continuing on their own, without much in the way of federal support.

The pressure to fix America's public elementary and secondary schools began in the early 1980s. The federally appointed National Commission on Excellence in Education in April 1983 issued its landmark report, *A Nation at Risk*, which outlined the problems in the schools. Employers were worried about the quality of workers, complaining that the schools were not producing students with the skills necessary to help businesses compete in a global economy. And parents feared that their children were not getting the top-notch instruction and attention they deserved. The quality of education thus became an issue in presidential politics.

Bush made an unprecedented move during his first year in office when he joined with the nation's governors for a summit on education. Together they developed a number of goals for the year 2000: all children in America will start school ready to learn; the high school graduation rate will increase to at least 90 percent; students will leave grades four, eight and 12 having demonstrated competency in English, math, science, history and geography; American students will be first in the world in math and science; every adult American will be literate and will possess the knowledge and skills necessary to compete in a global economy; every school will be free of drugs and violence and will offer a disciplined environment conducive to learning; and every classroom will have a well-qualified teacher, and collectively these teachers will reflect the demographic makeup of the general population.

Enacting legislation to reach those goals proved impossible in the 101st and 102nd Congress, however. Bush's education proposals did not generate the necessary enthusiasm, with even some Republicans withholding support because they philosophically opposed federal involvement in educational issues.

The Federal Role. The notion of what the federal government can do to help educate elementary and secondary school students has evolved dramatically. In the mid-1960s, Congress, the president and the courts focused on large issues such as equal opportunity in education — ensuring the proper assistance for disadvantaged students, minorities, the disabled and those learning to speak English as a second language. By the late 1980s, amid record budget deficits, the legislative and executive branches tended to the reauthorization of a number of programs, which constituted only about 5 percent of all public funds spent on elementary and secondary education.

Because most education money is raised at the state and local level, education has traditionally been a cherished local prerogative, with Washington having little influence over content. However, the attention paid to troubled schools led federal lawmakers to consider what students learn and how they learn it. As a result, they also had to face questions about how much money to spend and how to spend it.

Conservatives said money will not change schools, ideas will. But liberals in Congress, along with teachers unions and education lobbyists, said schools cannot be improved on the cheap. Because of the severe budget constraints, policy leaders were forced to choose between low-cost education reforms and high-cost reforms that would mean tax increases or deep cuts in other government programs. Bush pushed for the low-cost approach, which brought him scorn from congressional Democrats and the education establishment. His agenda included a controversial school choice pilot program, to provide vouchers to families to help pay for private school tuition; national standards, to spell out what is expected of each student in several academic areas; national testing, to find out whether students are meeting those standards; school deregulation, to relax the strings attached to state and federal dollars; and creation of "break the mold" schools, to discover new models of teaching and learning.

Bush was able to implement some of these ideas without congressional action. The Department of Education began awarding grants to develop standards for English, math, science and other academic areas, for example. Many educa-

References

Discussion of education policy for the years 1945-64 may be found in *Congress and the Nation Vol. I*, pp. 1195-1215; for the years 1965-68, *Congress and the Nation Vol. II*, pp. 709-733; for the years 1969-72, *Congress and the Nation Vol. III*, pp. 581-604; for the years 1973-76, *Congress and the Nation Vol. IV*, pp. 377-402; for the years 1977-80, *Congress and the Nation Vol. V*, pp. 655-677; for the years 1981-84, *Congress and the Nation Vol. VI*, pp. 555-580; for the years 1985-88, *Congress and the Nation Vol. VII*, pp. 647-663.

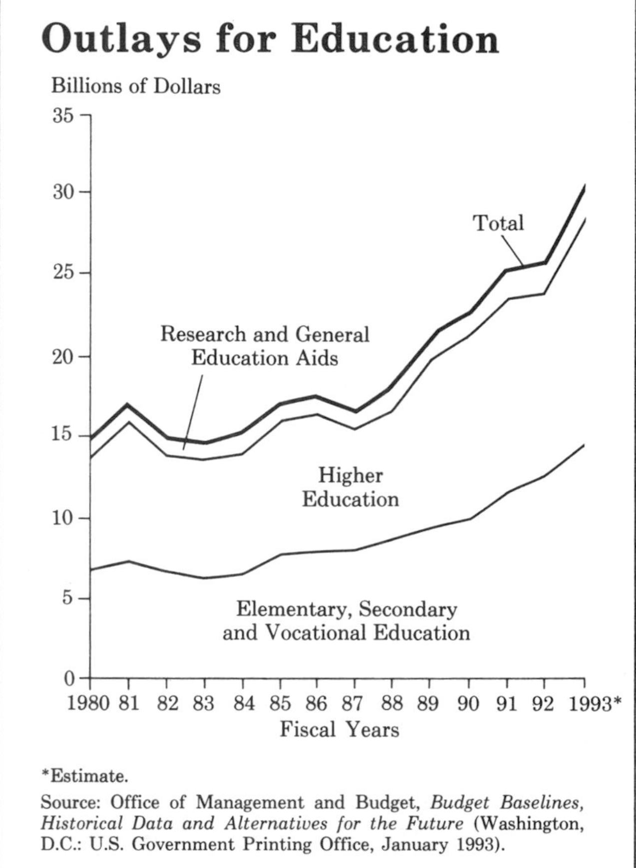

*Estimate.

Source: Office of Management and Budget, *Budget Baselines, Historical Data and Alternatives for the Future* (Washington, D.C.: U.S. Government Printing Office, January 1993).

tion lobbyists and their Democratic allies in Congress, meanwhile, advocated a different approach. They insisted the way to improve education was to increase the federal share and sought full funding for existing programs before establishing new ones.

The federal government had used its dollars to encourage and then require states to educate children — including the gifted, the poverty stricken, and the mentally and physically disabled. But many federal programs were never funded to the extent originally promised, leaving states to either pay the big bills or let some children go unserved.

For example, a 1975 law (PL 94-142) required states to provide a free, adequate education to all their disabled children. The government would pay 40 percent of the cost of educating these students, which typically was twice as much as educating other students and occasionally was as much as $50,000 a year. The Chapter 1 compensatory education for the disadvantaged program, aimed at bolstering basic skills such as reading, does not reach all those who are eligible because the federal government provides funds for only two out of five qualifying children.

Legislative Gridlock. In 1989-92, a clash of political and educational philosophies, intensified by budget constraints and the legislative maneuvering of both Republicans and Democrats, resulted in gridlock in the area of education reform.

Topping the conservative agenda was the concept of "parental choice." Depending upon how drastic, choice plans allowed parents to select among just public schools or, using tuition vouchers or tax credits, public and private schools to send their children. Proponents argued that competition would force bad schools to improve or close. Critics said bad schools would get worse, as they would be left with the poorest and least able students.

Advocates of tuition vouchers to help defray the cost of private school claimed that children sent to private schools were likely to achieve more than they would in public school. Supporters also said that vouchers would give poor families the same choices that wealthy families already had. Opponents countered that a voucher system would undermine public education; would not help the poorest students because the federal government would not cover the total cost of private school tuition; and would violate the separation of church and state by funding private, religious schools.

The subject of school choice set off fireworks in the House and Senate. When Democrats, angered by the idea, would turn a deaf ear, Republicans would accuse them of sticking to business as usual, then frequently would refuse to discuss improvements for existing programs.

Democrats, meanwhile, made unrealistic demands, asking for such large sums for programs that the administration balked.

With Bush's backing, Rep. Bill Goodling, R-Pa., in 1989 introduced a $423 million bill to reward "merit schools" for fighting drugs, preventing dropouts and raising student achievement; to give grants for "magnet schools" that attracted students through special programs; and to hand out $5,000 excellence awards to teachers and $10,000 college scholarships to high school students showing promise in math and science.

Democrats eagerly heaped scorn on the proposal. House Education and Labor Committee Chairman Augustus F. Hawkins, D-Calif., said the bill "just didn't do anything" and refused to hold a markup for close to a year.

Eventually, a compromise was reached that required fuller funding for Chapter 1 before money would be provided for Goodling's bill. As the markup was about to begin, however, the committee's Democrats rejected the deal. Hawkins, abandoning the compromise, decided to test the president's mettle by introducing a $3.7 billion bill to better fund several existing programs.

Republicans were irate. Goodling even canceled a spring-recess trip he and his wife had planned to take with Hawkins to visit preschools in France, Italy and Denmark. Eventually, a $1 billion bill combining Democratic and Republican initiatives passed the House in July 1990. But it never got to the president's desk; Republican senators killed it on the last day the 101st Congress was in session.

In December 1990, Bush asked Education Secretary Lauro F. Cavazos, who was viewed as being ineffectual in what had become a highly charged political arena, to step down. He was replaced by Lamar Alexander, a former governor of Tennessee who had been in the vanguard of governors grappling with school reform issues.

Democrats, who respected Alexander, knew they could not afford to be accused of obstructionism by the new secretary. So instead of blocking the administration, they reluctantly decided to try to work with Alexander. But the relationship wound up being on the Democrats' terms. Alexander spent much of his time threatening presidential vetoes. Ultimately, the second attempt at school reform legislation died at the end of the 102nd Congress at the hands of Senate Republicans.

Chronology Of Action On Education

1989-90

Although he helped stir intensive interest in the education community by his "education summit" with the nation's governors in September 1989, President Bush was unable to win congressional approval of his major education initiative. By the end of the 101st Congress, he remained a long way from fulfilling his 1988 campaign pledge to be "the education president."

Congress, however, did complete action on some significant education legislation. An overhaul of federal vocational education programs was enacted, as was an extension of the landmark law mandating and partially funding the education of the handicapped. In addition, Congress passed a student "right-to-know" bill requiring colleges and universities to provide students with information on graduation rates and campus crime.

Bush Education Initiative

The only education initiative that Bush presented to the 101st Congress died at the end of the 1990 session, a victim of a threatened Senate filibuster by a group of conservative Republicans.

In its final form, the bill (HR 5932) included Bush's proposals to authorize cash awards for excellent schools and teachers, math and science scholarships, and alternative methods for certifying teachers. It also sought to coordinate literacy programs on a regional and local level and included provisions on teacher recruitment and training.

One portion of the legislation, creating new math and science scholarships, did become law as a separate measure (HR 996 — PL 101-589). *(Story, p. 650)*

The death of the larger bill came amid sharp partisan sparring in the Senate. Democrats accused the Republicans who blocked final action of doing so because they philosophically opposed federal involvement in education. But Republican critics said they had legitimate problems with the bill, in particular funding for the National Board for Professional Teaching Standards, a private group that was trying to develop a system for assessing and certifying highly skilled teachers nationwide.

Education Summit

Bush's most dramatic step toward fulfilling his campaign promise to be "the education president" came when he convened a summit meeting with the governors on Sept. 27-28, 1989. The meeting, held in Charlottesville, Va., reached an unprecedented agreement to commit the United States to achieving seven goals in education by the year 2000.

The summit meeting was the first time a president had called the governors together to discuss education, and only the third time a president had ever brought them together to consider a single issue. Bush and the governors agreed that the education goals should be developed to "guarantee an internationally competitive standard" in the following areas:

- "The readiness of all children to start school."
- Student performance on international achievement tests, especially in math and science.
- Reductions in the dropout rate and improvement in the academic performance of "at risk" students.
- Achievement of functional literacy for all adults.
- Providing the training necessary to create a competitive work force.
- Recruitment and retention of qualified teachers.
- Establishment of safe, drug-free schools.

Bush never proposed legislation based on the summit goals during the 101st Congress. Instead, his major education initiative was contained in legislation he had put forward in April 1989 that called for more than $400 million in new funding to reward excellent schools, provide math and science scholarships, and help develop alternative certification methods for teachers.

The legislative history of the proposal would be complex, with several different bills merging and diverging at different points, amid sharp disagreements between the administration and congressional Democrats and most education groups over the direction of education reform and the role of the federal government.

Senate Action

The Bush initiative and related proposals were embodied in the Senate in three bills.

The main portion of the Bush package was contained in S 695, which was reported by the Senate Labor and Human Resources Committee on Sept. 19, 1989 (S Rept 101-136). Before approving the bill July 20, however, the committee made important changes in Bush's proposal, cutting requested funding from more than $400 million to about $300 million and adding significant restrictions on uses of the money. In addition, the panel approved other changes costing about $200 million, mostly by expanding eligibility for federal student aid. The bill also provided for a President's Council on Academic Excellence, to be modeled after the President's Council on Physical Fitness.

On Nov. 1, 1989, the committee approved S 1310, which authorized more than $200 million in new funding to combat adult illiteracy. The measure was reported (S Rept 101-196) on Nov. 9.

A third bill, S 1676, was approved by the committee on June 17, 1990, and reported (S Rept 101-360) on July 10. But that legislation, which authorized new programs to recruit teachers and improve their classroom skills, went no further.

S 1310, the literacy bill, passed the Senate by a 99-0 vote on Feb. 6, 1990. S 695 ran into a heated fight on the Senate floor over a provision authorizing $25 million in federal funding for the National Board for Professional Teaching Standards.

Jesse Helms, R-N.C., led the fight to delete federal funding for the board, which had relied on foundation money since its creation in 1987. Helms argued that the board was dominated by teachers' unions and predicted that the panel's certification guidelines would soon turn into national licensing standards for teachers. "What this board wants is to be the sole standard-bearer on deciding who can and can't teach," Helms said. "And I think that's an outrage. The labor unions want to control education in America."

The Bush administration also opposed the provision, saying federal funds should not be used for a program over which the government had no control.

Defenders of the proposed authorization responded that the two national teachers' unions had only a total of 14 seats on the 63-member board, which also included many other educators and business leaders. Proponents also noted that the board's proposed certification system, which would be only for teachers at the top levels of their profession, was not designed to take the place of state and local standards for teachers.

The Senate Feb. 6 rejected Helms' amendment on a **35-64 (R 35-10; D 0-54) key vote.** *(1990 key votes, p. 1039)*

Helms then offered another amendment, to take $10 million from the grant and give it to an alternate teacher certification program to help retired people and other professionals become teachers without having to obtain teaching degrees. The remaining $15 million would go to states to develop minimum competency standards for teachers. The amendment was tabled (killed) 60-37.

The Senate also rejected a Nancy Landon Kassebaum, R-Kan., amendment to cut the grant from $25 million to $6 million and to force the board to compete for the money. The vote was 40-57.

Among the amendments adopted by voice vote on the Senate floor was one by Bill Bradley, D-N.J., to require colleges and universities that offered athletic scholarships to inform prospective student-athletes of the school's graduation rates. Congress subsequently cleared separate legislation (S 580 — PL 101-542) with this provision. *(Students 'right-to-know,' p. 648)*

S 695 also included a provision earmarking $50 million to extend a dropout prevention program. Separate legislation (HR 2281 — PL 101-150) was enacted in 1990. *(Dropout program, p. 652)*

The Senate passed S 695 on a 92-8 vote Feb. 7.

House Action

House Democrats' response to the House bill (HR 1675) that embodied the president's proposal, which they derided as little more than a vehicle to hand out ribbons and awards, touched off partisan sparring in the Education and Labor Committee.

In a direct challenge to Bush, Education and Labor Committee Chairman Augustus F. Hawkins, D-Calif., introduced a bill (HR 4379) purporting to implement the education goals Bush and the governors had embraced. The bill was patched together from six pending bills, including the administration plan. Each title of the Hawkins bill reflected the national goals and listed programs to achieve them. The measure primarily focused on raising the amount of money that Congress could appropriate for existing, proven programs, such as Head Start; the Women, Infants and Children (WIC) supplemental food program; and the Chapter 1 compensatory education program. Altogether, the bill authorized $3.7 billion in new fiscal 1991 funding.

On June 27, 1990, the Education and Labor Committee approved on a 29-5 vote a scaled-down version of the Hawkins bill, which was combined with elements of the administration plan. A number of committee Republicans who had faulted the earlier bill as a partisan ploy voted for the committee measure (HR 5115 — H Rept 101-570), even while expressing doubt that the $1.1 billion in new funding authority would ever be appropriated.

The committee bill drew a veto threat from the administration, which called it "a complex and costly amalgam" of new programs that were "totally unrealistic" in the existing fiscal environment.

To clear the way for easy action on HR 5115, sponsors worked out a compromise with Republican leaders under which four contentious amendments were dropped, others were watered down and still others were bundled together on a single vote. As a result, the bill — which combined the president's "excellence" initiatives, a literacy bill (HR 3123), and a teacher training and recruitment measure (HR 4130) introduced by Education Committee leaders — passed on a 350-25 vote on July 20.

The House by voice vote July 27 passed S 695, after substituting the text of HR 5115.

Conference Action

After House passage, the education package languished for several months. When members turned to it in the final weeks of the session, the bill got fatally caught up in maneuvering between Democratic sponsors, a group of conservative Republicans in the Senate and the administration.

To set up a conference on the legislation, Senate sponsors needed to get one portion of it, a teacher training bill (S 1676), approved by the Senate. But action was blocked by Helms and a few allies.

With the 1990 session drawing to a close, sponsors turned to the administration to try to mediate a compromise that could become law. With Roger B. Porter, assistant to the president for domestic policy, participating in negotiations, conferees worked out an agreement on a new bill (HR 5932) that passed the House by voice vote Oct. 26.

A final effort to bring up the bill in the Senate was blocked by Helms on Oct. 27, however, and the bill died at adjournment.

Vocational Education

Congress in 1990 cleared a comprehensive overhaul of the federal government's programs of aid for vocational education programs.

The bill (HR 7 — PL 101-392) called for a fresh infusion of funds for vocational education and relaxed federal controls on how the money was used by states and school districts.

Backers of the bill said it was needed to revitalize the decades-old vocational effort, which critics had argued was unfocused and ineffective. Symbolic of the bill's attempt to make the programs better able to help students prepare for an increasingly competitive and technological economy was the change of the law's title to the Vocational and Applied Technology Education Act.

The bill authorized $1.6 billion in fiscal 1991 for the programs, which were intended primarily to serve students unlikely to pursue a traditional college education.

Key provisions of the legislation also sought to remedy what many contended had become major weaknesses in the programs as they evolved over the years. These were a rigid system of "set-asides" mandating that certain percentages of funds be spent on different groups, such as women and the disabled; and a tendency to distribute the limited funding available to so many schools and districts that each one seldom received enough money to make an effective contribution.

Although the final bill did not go as far as some had urged in eliminating set-asides, it boosted to 75 percent the federal aid states would have to direct toward improving programs, while lowering to 25 percent the amount to be carved up for special groups. The measure targeted funds by formula to students who had disabilities, who had limited English proficiency, who were economically disadvantaged or who were studying for occupations that were not traditional for their gender.

HR 7 as cleared also required states to make grants of at least $15,000 to secondary schools and at least $50,000 to postsecondary institutions.

Background

Vocational education had long been the neglected stepchild of the education world. Its slice of the federal education budget had declined significantly between the 1960s and the late 1980s.

Persistent attacks during the Reagan years — culminating in 1988 with an attempt to abolish the Carl D. Perkins Vocational Education Act's grant program (PL 98-524) — left the vocational education budget with nearly one-third less purchasing power than it had in 1980, according to the Congressional Research Service. *(PL 98-524, Congress and the Nation Vol. VI, p. 576)*

The result was a program dominated by small grants — some as little as $100 — that paid primarily for equipment instead of teachers.

Action on the vocational education reauthorization in the 101st Congress also was influenced by the release in November 1988 of a report called "The Forgotten Half," which was produced by the William T. Grant Foundation's Commission on Work, Family and Citizenship.

The report said the U.S. education system unfairly favored college-bound students over those unlikely to attend a traditional postsecondary institution. It concluded that federal, state and local governments and private entities spent $45 billion a year subsidizing college students, but no more than $7 billion annually on postsecondary training for the roughly half of all students who did not go to traditional colleges.

House Committee Action

HR 7 (H Rept 101-41) was approved by the House Education and Labor Committee by voice vote on April 25, 1989.

The bill as reported April 28 called for sharply increased spending, from about $900 million in fiscal 1989 to $1.4 billion in 1990 and an open-ended authorization in fiscal 1991-95.

Most of the increased funds were to go to two new programs:

- A $200 million "tech-prep" program of grants to encourage the creation of four-year vocational education programs — two years in high school and two years in a community college or other postsecondary institution.
- A $100 million program to bolster facilities and equipment for low-income areas.

The most far-reaching and controversial part of the bill was its elimination of most set-asides. Existing law had required that a total of 57 percent of funding be divided among special populations — the handicapped, the disadvantaged, adults, single parents, anti-sex stereotyping programs and jailed criminals. In place of the set-aside system, the bill called for allocating money according to how many poor and handicapped students schools served. It also required states, through which the money was to be funneled, to "provide assurances" that the special populations would be served. In addition, some of the set-asides were preserved, including a 10 percent share for programs for displaced homemakers and against occupational sex stereotyping.

The Bush administration favored keeping intact the 57 percent set-aside for special populations. But it wanted to allow states to split up the money themselves by eliminating the six specific set-asides within that total.

The bill was criticized by advocates for the disabled, who warned that the handicapped would lose access to services. During committee consideration of the measure, Major R. Owens, D-N.Y., sought to win support for an amendment reserving 5 percent of funds for the disabled. He was unable to obtain broad backing for the proposal, however, and so did not formally offer it as an amendment.

Another controversial proposal was settled in committee on a party-line vote. The amendment, offered by Pat Williams, D-Mont., sought to curb the power of the Office of Management and Budget (OMB) to review reports to Congress that HR 7 required from the Department of Education. Backers of the amendment, adopted 18-13, said that OMB had amassed too much power over federal agency reports and regulations. They pointed to a number of reports that they said OMB had delayed because the

Education Leadership

The Senate confirmed former Tennessee governor Lamar Alexander as secretary of education by voice vote on March 14, 1991. That action came one day after the Senate Labor and Human Resources Committee voted 16-0 to recommend the nomination. *(Cabinet profiles, p. 1172)*

Alexander succeeded Lauro F. Cavazos, who assumed the post Sept. 20, 1988, during the Reagan administration, and had been kept on by President Bush. Cavazos' resignation was announced Dec. 12, 1990, after he was asked to step down by the White House.

Although he was credited with reopening lines of communication shut by his combative predecessor, William J. Bennett, Cavazos was viewed as ineffective by members of Congress, administration officials and the education community. *(Cavazos, background, Congress and the Nation Vol. VII, p. 1046)*

findings were at odds with administration policy. But Republican opponents of the amendment warned that it was sure to lead to a presidential veto.

House Floor Action

HR 7 passed the House on a 402-3 vote May 9.

Before approving the bill, however, members moved to delay for three years the full impact of its new funding formula, under which aid would be targeted to needy schools. Members from wealthy areas that stood to lose much of their funding as a result of the change argued that their schools needed more time to prepare for the funding reductions.

The House also removed a major potential stumbling block to the bill by watering down the committee-added provision limiting OMB power. Shortly before the bill reached the House floor, OMB officials had released a statement calling the provision an "unacceptable intrusion upon the prerogatives of the Executive Branch" and making clear the bill was in danger of being vetoed as a result.

In a compromise worked out by Bill Goodling, R-Pa., the ranking member on the Education and Labor Committee, the House adopted by voice vote an amendment removing the restrictions on OMB review authority. Instead, the amendment called for a General Accounting Office study of any delays in reports required under the bill.

In a surprise move that caught bill sponsors unawares, the House adopted a potentially explosive school prayer amendment. Offered by William E. Dannemeyer, R-Calif., the amendment barred school districts from receiving money under the bill if they did not have a policy of allowing voluntary prayer in the schools. The amendment was adopted May 9 on a 269-135 vote. Sponsors did not make a major effort to defeat it, as they were confident that it would be rejected by the Senate in conference committee. Conferees subsequently did agree to drop the provision.

Senate Action

The Senate Labor and Human Resources Committee approved its version of the vocational education reauthorization (S 1109) on Nov. 1, reporting the measure (S Rept 101-221) on Nov. 21.

While much of the debate in the House committee had focused on set-asides, the most controversial issue in the Senate panel concerned the split of funding between secondary and postsecondary schools. The question of the funding was a significant one for vocational education experts because of the wide variation in how states allocated money to the two sectors. While New Mexico gave all its federal vocational grants to postsecondary schools, for example, Mississippi gave 92 percent of its money to secondary schools.

The House bill retained current law, which allowed states to decide how to divide the money. But Claiborne Pell, D-R.I., the chairman of the Senate Labor Committee's Education Subcommittee, argued that the bulk of the bill's funding should go to secondary programs. "That is where the dropout problem has reached tragic proportions," Pell said. "If we do not afford these young people the help they need, they will not even complete secondary school, let alone attend college."

The version of the bill approved by the Education Subcommittee Oct. 26 called for mandating that states give 70 percent of their grants to precollegiate programs, with 30 percent available for postsecondary schools. That division brought complaints, however, from members whose states spent a larger share of their funds on postsecondary programs. So the full committee adopted a compromise permitting states to spend 65 to 75 percent on secondary programs and 25 to 35 percent on the postsecondary sector. Dave Durenberger, R-Minn., proposed several amendments to allow states to spend more on postsecondary programs, but his proposals were rejected.

The Senate passed HR 7 on a 96-0 vote on April 5, 1990.

The only major change approved by the Senate before final passage came on a compromise amendment agreed to by Durenberger and bill sponsors. Arguing that his and other states needed the flexibility to direct funds to the greatest need, Durenberger won approval of an amendment allowing states to seek waivers under which they could direct up to 50 percent of the federal funds to postsecondary and adult education programs.

The compromise also required that up to 15 percent of the money received by postsecondary programs be used only for the neediest students, including high school dropouts and adults without a high school diploma.

Conference Action

The secondary-postsecondary split also proved to be a bone of contention in the conference committee, which approved compromise legislation on July 23 (H Rept 101-660).

House conferees objected to the Senate language specifying the share of funding for secondary and postsecondary schools. They argued that the goal of the program was to train skilled workers for the economy, not to help reduce the dropout rate among high school students.

The House prevailed under the conference agreement, which let states continue to decide where the money was needed most.

On the set-aside issue, both sides agreed to boost to 75 percent the aid states direct toward improving programs, lowering to 25 percent the amounts set aside for special groups.

The Senate approved the conference agreement by voice vote on Aug. 2. The House did so on Sept. 13, clearing HR 7 for the president.

In a statement, President Bush faulted the measure for excluding many of his administration proposals but said that he would sign it because it still represented "progress over current law."

Major Provisions

As signed into law Sept. 25, 1990, the Carl D. Perkins Vocational and Applied Technology Education Act (HR 7 — PL 101-392):

- **Authorization Levels.** Authorized $1.6 billion in fiscal 1991 and such sums as might be necessary through fiscal 1995.
- **Assistance to States.** Limited states to receiving no more than an amount calculated by multiplying the number of individuals in the state counted in the formula for vocational education funds by 150 percent of the national average per student payment.
- Required 10.5 percent of the basic state grants to go to

programs for single parents, displaced homemakers and single pregnant women, and for sex equity programs designed to encourage women to go into traditionally male occupations and vice versa.

• Required any state that wanted to receive federal vocational education funds to submit a three-year plan to the secretary of education.

• Required each state board of vocational education receiving funds to develop and put into effect a statewide system of core standards and measures of performance for vocational education programs.

• Required the state board in its plan to provide assurances that people who were members of special populations, such as those who were disabled or had limited English proficiency, be provided with a full range of services.

• **State Programs.** Required states to conduct a range of programs, including professional development for vocational education teachers, partnership programs between business and the schools, programs aimed at reducing sex bias in vocational education and at providing young women and displaced homemakers with marketable skills, and programs for criminal offenders.

• Required states to distribute vocational education grants to secondary school programs based on the following formula: 70 percent on each school district's share of Chapter 1 basic grants for the disadvantaged; 20 percent on the number of disabled students; and 10 percent on the number of adults enrolled in training programs. Set the minimum grant to local education agencies at $15,000, but allowed districts to enter into consortiums with other districts to receive a minimum grant.

• Directed that states distribute funds for postsecondary and adult programs based on the following formula: 70 percent on the number of students receiving Pell grants or aid from the Bureau of Indian Affairs; 20 percent on vocational rehabilitation enrollment; and 10 percent on general enrollment. Set the minimum grant at $50,000.

• **Special Programs.** Authorized grants aimed at encouraging training partnerships between business, labor and education.

• Authorized $125 million in fiscal 1991, and sums as needed in subsequent years, for tech-prep programs that combined two years of secondary school with two years of higher education or apprenticeship.

• Authorized grants to help in the purchase of training equipment for schools in economically depressed areas, to establish community education employment centers and to create "lighthouse" schools that would serve as models for vocational education programs.

• **National Programs.** Directed the secretary of education to research the development of performance standards and measures for vocational education programs, to set up a national network for curriculum coordination and to conduct a national assessment of vocational education, with a report to Congress by July 1, 1994.

• Authorized creation of a variety of demonstration programs, including instructional telecommunications programs, centers for retraining displaced workers, grants for people entering the vocational education field and awards for high-quality local programs.

• **General Provisions.** Required the secretary of education to conduct regional meetings of vocational educators, including representatives of the disabled and other special groups, to aid in developing proposed regulations to implement the legislation.

Student Religious Groups

On June 4, 1990, the Supreme Court upheld the constitutionality of the 1984 Equal Access Act (PL 98-377), which barred secondary schools that received federal funds and allowed extracurricular student groups to meet on the school grounds before or after classes from discriminating against any group because of the subject it wished to discuss. *(1984 law, Congress and the Nation Vol. VI, p. 572)*

The Court, 8-1 in *Board of Education of Westside Community Schools v. Mergens*, affirmed an appeals court ruling that a student who wanted to start a Bible study group at her high school in Omaha, Neb., should have been permitted to. *(Case summary, p. 835)*

• Replaced the term "vocational education" with "vocational and applied technical education."

• Made the act effective as of July 1, 1991.

Education for the Disabled

Congress in 1990 cleared a bill (S 1824 — PL 101-476) reauthorizing some of the programs under the Education of the Handicapped Act (EHA), the landmark 1975 law that mandated free education for children with disabilities and created a permanent federal grant program to states.

The bill authorized $321 million in fiscal 1991, rising to $409 million in fiscal 1994, for the discretionary programs under EHA (PL 94-142). Included in the funding total was $25 million for programs aimed at enabling disabled youths to make the transition from school to the outside world. *(1975 law, Congress and the Nation Vol. IV, p. 389)*

The legislation also renamed the act the Individuals with Disabilities Act and substituted the word "disabilities" for "handicapped" throughout the law.

In addition, one provision in S 1824 had the effect of reversing a Supreme Court decision. In June 1989, the Court ruled 5-4 in *Dellmuth v. Muth* that children with disabilities who were denied an appropriate, free public education by a state were not entitled to be reimbursed for tuition paid by their parents for their education in an alternative program.

S 1824 made clear that Congress' intention was to allow litigants the right to sue in federal court to enforce their rights. *(Case summary, p. 842)*

The most recent reauthorization, in 1986, focused on programs aimed at disabled infants and preschoolers. *(Congress and the Nation Vol. VII, p. 652)*

Senate Action

As introduced by Tom Harkin, D-Iowa, the chairman of the Senate Subcommittee on Disability Policy, S 1824 focused on "fine-tuning" the existing discretionary programs under the law, which included early education, training for special educators and research.

The Senate Labor and Human Resources Committee approved S 1824 on Nov. 1, 1989, and reported (S Rept 101-204) on Nov. 15. The bill then passed the Senate by voice vote Nov. 16.

As passed, the bill called for $27.5 million for school-to-work transition programs, $19.25 million for historically black colleges and universities to encourage more minority students to become special educators and $6.5 million for research on teaching the emotionally disturbed.

House Action

The House version of the reauthorization (HR 1013) was approved by the Education and Labor Committee on May 16, 1990, after having been approved by the Subcommittee on Select Education on May 3. HR 1013 (H Rept 101-544) was reported June 18.

In subcommittee, Chairman Major R. Owens, D-N.Y., offered an amendment to ban corporal punishment of students with disabilities. Steve Bartlett, R-Texas, then proposed a substitute amendment that would have allowed the teacher and parents of a disabled student to meet before each school year to determine whether corporal punishment should be used. The panel rejected Bartlett's amendment and included the outright ban.

In the full committee, however, Bartlett was able to win adoption, on a 16-12 vote, of an amendment deleting the punishment ban. Critics of the ban argued that the line between punishment and certain types of therapy was not clear.

The House on June 18 passed HR 1013 by voice vote under suspension of the rules, then passed S 1824 by voice vote after substituting the text of HR 1013. As approved, the measure included a new $25 million transition program to help disabled students move from school to the workplace and $17.5 million for historically black colleges and universities to recruit and train students to become special-education teachers.

The mostly technical differences between the Senate- and House-passed versions of the bill were quickly resolved in conference. The Senate adopted the conference report (H Rept 101-787) on Oct. 2. The House adopted it under suspension of the rules Oct. 15. President Bush signed S 1824 on Oct. 30.

Student 'Right-to-Know'

College students and applicants became entitled to detailed information about graduation rates and campus crime statistics under legislation (S 580 — PL 101-542) cleared by the 101st Congress.

The landmark student "right-to-know" bill grew out of public and congressional concern about colleges and universities that recruited star athletes with scholarships but made little effort to see that the students learned enough to earn a degree. "Too many student-athletes sacrifice academic achievement to the fantasy of professional sports. It is a national shame," said the bill's chief sponsor, Sen. Bill Bradley, D-N.J., a Rhodes Scholar as well as a former star collegiate and professional basketball player.

Although the National Collegiate Athletic Association, which regulates college sports, decided in January 1990 to begin reporting graduation rates of athletes after the 1990-91 season, lawmakers said an additional push was needed.

While its initial focus was on athletics, the legislation subsequently was modified to require colleges and universities to disclose graduation rates for all other students and statistics on campus crime.

Specifically, the bill directed colleges and universities that awarded athletic scholarships to disclose annually the graduation rate, broken down by race and sex, of students who had received such aid. The rates were to be reported separately for football, basketball, baseball, cross-country and track, and all other sports combined. Schools were to start collecting the information July 1, 1991, and provide it to prospective student-athletes, their parents and coaches beginning July 1, 1993.

The measure also required institutions to disclose graduation rates of all full-time, degree-seeking students and defined graduation as receiving a degree within 150 percent of the standard length of time for doing so.

In addition, S 580 directed schools to provide an annual security report on all violent crimes against students in the most recent school year, on and off campus. The information was to be collected beginning July 1, 1991, and made available starting Sept. 1, 1992.

The legislation also amended the Family Educational Rights and Privacy Act to allow colleges and universities to tell a student victim of violent crime of the outcome of any disciplinary proceedings taken against an accused assailant.

House, Senate Action

The original version of S 580, which applied only to student-athletes, moved easily through the Senate. The measure was approved by the Senate Labor and Human Resources Committee with only one opposing vote on Nov. 1, 1989. The bill (S Rept 101-209) was formally reported Nov. 16.

The Senate passed S 580 by voice vote on Feb. 22, 1990. The provisions of the bill also had been included in legislation (S 695) embodying President Bush's education initiative. *(Story, p. 643)*

The House version of the legislation (HR 1454) underwent several significant changes that greatly expanded its scope. First came the addition of provisions from two other bills (HR 3344, HR 4570) dealing with reporting of campus crime. The provisions were included in the bill approved by the House Education and Labor Subcommittee on Postsecondary Education on May 15, 1990.

The subcommittee also approved two other important amendments. One, offered by Carl C. Perkins, D-Ky., made schools responsible for reporting graduation data for all students. The second, proposed by Paul B. Henry, R-Mich., required schools to disclose each sport's revenues and spending.

In the full Education and Labor Committee, Chairman William D. Ford, D-Mich., sought to modify the provision requiring reporting of financial data. But his amendment to require separate financial reporting only for football and basketball was rejected on a 16-17 vote.

The Education and Labor Committee then approved HR 1454 by voice vote May 22 and reported it (H Rept 101-518) June 5.

The House June 5 passed HR 1454 by voice vote under suspension of the rules, then passed S 580 after substituting the text of HR 1454.

Conference Action

In the conference on S 580, two key differences had to be resolved between the two versions.

One point at issue was the House provision requiring schools to break down expenditures and revenues by sport. Senate conferees refused to accept the provision, which had barely gotten through the House committee. So House conferees agreed to drop it.

On the second difference, reporting of campus crime, the two chambers compromised. While the House wanted crime rates sent to the Department of Education, the Senate wanted to give them to students. The compromise bill called for distribution of crime information to students and, on request, to the department.

Conferees reached agreement on the bill Oct. 9. The House adopted the conference report (H Rept 101-883) by voice vote under suspension of the rules Oct. 22. The Senate adopted the conference report by voice vote two days later. The president signed S 580 on Nov. 8.

Student Loan Defaults

Spurred by the rapidly climbing losses from defaults on government-insured loans for students, the 101st Congress moved to curb abuses of the programs. Student loan provisions were included in budget-reconciliation bills cleared by Congress in 1989 and 1990.

The 1989 reconciliation measure (HR 3299 — PL 101-239) barred schools that produced high percentages of loan defaulters from accepting funds for the Supplemental Loans for Students (SLS) program, a key source of funds for proprietary trade schools. Another provision curtailed trade schools' ability to enroll high school dropouts by mandating that all SLS borrowers have a diploma or an equivalency degree. *(1989 reconciliation, p. 43)*

The bill passed in 1990 (HR 5835 — PL 101-508) barred participation in the student loan program by colleges or trade schools with default rates of 35 percent or greater. The ban and other cost-cutting provisions were projected to save $1.7 billion over five years. *(1990 reconciliation, p. 15)*

Background

As the cost to the government of defaults on student loans soared — $224 million in 1978, approaching $2 billion in 1987 — pressure grew in Congress to clamp down on the offenders.

Contributing to the high level of defaults were increases in the annual volume of Guaranteed Student Loans and a shift from receiving government grants to borrowing by low-income students, who were a greater financial risk.

The default problem was most acute among trade school students, who were receiving training in such areas as cosmetology and truck driving. Critics of the industry, including William J. Bennett, who served as secretary of education during the Reagan administration, argued that many of the trade schools were diploma mills designed to trick the poor into taking on federally backed debt, milk them for their loan money and then provide inadequate training. But defenders of the schools argued that they were an important way for low-income young people to better their job prospects and that the high rate of default was a function of the students' poverty.

Another part of the problem was the dramatic Reagan-era shift from grants to loans, which turned the SLS program from a last resort to the primary source of funds for many students. Unlike other student loan programs, the SLS program neither provided an interest subsidy nor required that students show a need for the money.

To curb the rising costs, Bennett in 1987 proposed rules that would cut off from federal programs any school that had a higher-than-average default rate. Trade school groups, many of whose members would have been forced to close under the Bennett proposals, mounted a strong lobbying effort to block the changes. In response, Congress in 1988 killed the Bennett plan and adopted relatively mild regulations (PL 100-369) tightening the SLS program instead. *(Congress and the Nation Vol. VII, p. 661)*

1989 Legislation

In the 101st Congress, pressure to do something about the rising costs intensified. Lobbyists and aides pointed to several factors that led to a change in attitude toward trade schools by many members.

First, the fiscal 1990 budget resolution (H Con Res 106) required the authorizing committees — Senate Labor and House Education and Labor — to make substantial cuts in the programs under their jurisdiction. After years of limiting access to student-aid programs generally, the panels had few choices but to consider anti-default measures that would hurt trade schools. In addition, the authorizing panels were under heavy pressure from the Appropriations committees to do something about spiraling costs.

Another factor was a shift in the approach taken by key members, such as House Education and Labor Committee Chairman William D. Ford, D-Mich., who had long fought to protect loans for trade school students. Finally convinced that significant abuses of the program were taking place, these members concluded that accepting some curbs was necessary to preserve the larger loan programs for students in more conventional postsecondary institutions.

To meet their budget-cutting targets, the House and Senate committees took different approaches. The House voted to deny SLS loans to all first-year students, while the Senate panel opted to find most of its required savings in other, non-education programs. In the conference on the reconciliation bill, members approved a final compromise under which an automatic cutoff of SLS funds was imposed on schools with default rates higher than 30 percent.

The student loan provisions of HR 3299, as cleared:

- Barred schools with default rates of 30 percent or more from accepting money from the SLS program.
- Delayed disbursing SLS loans to first-year undergraduate students for 30 days so that if students dropped out before then, they would get no loan money to pay their tuition.
- Established a six-month amnesty program to encourage borrowers who were in default on so-called Stafford loans to repay them.
- Required all SLS borrowers to have a high school diploma or an equivalency certificate. The bill also reduced the SLS borrowing limit for students attending schools with programs of less than one academic year, and it revoked the student-aid eligibility of schools that lost their accreditation and limited their ability to "shop" for substitute accreditation.

Faculty Tenure

The Supreme Court on Jan. 9, 1990, rejected a university's plea on grounds of academic freedom to limit an investigation by the Equal Employment Opportunity Commission (EEOC) of its faculty tenure decisions for possible violations of job-discrimination laws.

The Court's unanimous ruling in *University of Pennsylvania v. EEOC* held that colleges and universities had no special privilege that would require judicial review of EEOC requests for so-called peer review materials used in granting or denying tenure to prospective faculty members. *(Case summary, p. 843)*

- Limited the ability of former medical students to delay repaying Title IV Education Department loans during residency.
- Gave the education secretary power to take short-term emergency action to bar schools and lenders from student-aid programs if they were breaking laws or rules.
- Authorized the education secretary to use information from the proposed National Student Loan Data System to verify the eligibility of borrowers and detailed the information to be collected.
- Restricted the power of schools' financial-aid administrators to waive borrowing requirements for classes of students, forcing them to consider all waivers case by case.

1990 Legislation

In 1990, the budget-reconciliation measure again served as the legislative vehicle for further efforts to tighten the student loan rules.

The centerpiece of the student loan provisions of HR 5835 was a plan to cut off loans for students at schools with default rates of 35 percent or higher (falling to 30 percent in 1993) for the three most recent fiscal years.

The bill allowed schools to appeal a decision to cut off eligibility. In addition, the Education Department was authorized to allow schools to continue to participate in the program if officials determined that errors had been made in calculating the default rate, or if there were mitigating circumstances.

About two dozen colleges controlled by Native American tribes and 117 historically black colleges and universities were exempted from the cutoff until July 1, 1994.

Education Department officials estimated that 268 private trade schools would be affected by the ban, along with 57 two-year colleges and fewer than 20 four-year institutions.

In other efforts to control defaults, schools were prohibited from giving first-year students the first installment of any loan until 30 days after the student enrolled in the institution. To deal with the problem of loans to unqualified students, the bill required that students without high school diplomas pass an independently administered examination before enrollment.

The Bush administration had proposed a plan that included attaching the wages of people who defaulted on student loans. The proposal (S 2029), introduced by Phil Gramm, R-Texas, and Minority Leader Bob Dole, R-Kan., barred schools from employing commissioned sales representatives to recruit students, required lenders to offer graduated repayment plans to borrowers, mandated that schools with default rates higher than 30 percent refund tuition to aid recipients who dropped out early and required that students lacking a high school diploma or its equivalent pass a test before enrolling in post-graduate training. S 2029 died upon adjournment of the 101st Congress.

The student loan provisions of HR 5835, as cleared:

- Reversed the incentive system provided by the government for collection of delinquent student loans by paying collection agencies for their work in getting students to repay loans.
- Prohibited schools from giving first-year students the first installment of any loan until 30 days after the student enrolled in the institution. The loans, however, could be delivered to the school before the end of that 30-day period. This was effective for loans made on or after the date of enactment to cover the cost of instruction beginning on or after Jan. 1, 1991.
- Prohibited institutions whose default rate was equal to or greater than 35 percent in fiscal 1991 and 1992 and 30 percent for fiscal 1993 through 1996 from participating in the student loan program. The default rate had to equal or exceed those rates for each of the three most recent fiscal years in which data were available. The school would be ineligible in the fiscal year in which the determination was made and for the next two fiscal years.

Schools could appeal the ineligibility ruling within 30 days of notification from the secretary of education. The secretary was required to rule on the appeal within 45 days of receiving it.

- Retained eligibility for student loans, until July 1, 1994, of historically black colleges and universities, tribally controlled community colleges and the Navajo Community College in Tsaile, Ariz., even though they had high default rates.
- Authorized schools' financial aid administrators to certify students for loans.
- Required default rate cutoffs and exceptions to begin July 1, 1991.
- Required that people without high school diplomas, who were admitted to schools based on the ability to benefit from the education and offered any grant, loan or work assistance, to pass an independently administered examination approved by the secretary, effective Jan. 1, 1991.
- Extended existing provisions through fiscal 1996. Authorized $4,000 for full-time students; $2,500 for students attending school two-thirds of full time; $1,500 for less than two-thirds but at least one-third of full-time attendance.
- Prohibited accreditation, state licensure and student aid from being considered protected assets during bankruptcy proceedings of a school.
- Terminated the student loan provisions on Oct. 1, 1996.

Math, Science Education

Legislation designed to spur students to study and work in mathematics, science and engineering was signed into law by President Bush on Nov. 16, 1990 (HR 996 — PL 101-589).

The three-year bill authorized $149.1 million in fiscal 1991, but only $26.2 million was new authorization. The remaining funds were carved out of an existing authority in the National Science Foundation (NSF) act (PL 100-570). *(NSF act, Congress and the Nation Vol. VII, p. 860)*

The lion's share of the new money — $23.7 million — was directed toward the Department of Education, with the remaining $2.5 million earmarked for teaching scholarships at the NSF.

The legislation established 10 regional consortia on math, science and engineering education. It also created a clearinghouse at the Department of Education to help disseminate information on teaching methods for math and science.

In addition, the bill provided for a congressional scholarship program to be established at the NSF for undergraduate scholarships in math, science and engineering. The program was aimed at encouraging greater participation in those fields by women, minorities and the disabled.

Background

The impetus for the legislation came from growing concerns about both the tenuous U.S. position in the global technology marketplace and the bleak state of U.S. math and science education.

The nation's schools — already battered for failing to teach students to read and write adequately — were criticized by many experts for turning out "technologically illiterate" students. Many teachers were considered unqualified to teach their subjects, while some experts predicted massive shortages of scientists and engineers in the 21st century.

Several studies underscored the problems in math and science education. "During recent years, a steady stream of international comparisons of elementary and secondary education has painted an increasingly bleak picture of the deficiencies of American mathematics and science education," said a 1988 report by the Office of Technology Assessment.

In addition, "Everybody Counts," a National Research Council report released in January 1989, concluded that most students left school ill-prepared mathematically to perform most jobs.

Behind poor student performance were many apparently unqualified teachers. "Few elementary-school teachers have even a rudimentary education in science and mathematics, and many junior and senior high-school teachers of science and mathematics do not meet reasonable standards of preparation in those fields," said "Science for All Americans," a report by the American Academy for the Advancement of Science (AAAS).

According to an NSF summary of studies of science and math teachers, many states had no science and math course credit requirements for elementary school teachers; 31 states had no such requirements for middle or high school teachers; and about half the states did not require such teachers to take courses on science and math teaching methods.

As a result, other studies warned, the nation faced a potential shortage of trained scientists in the future. The AAAS estimated in a 1989 report that the nation would need about 18,000 new science and engineering Ph.D.-holders a year in the early part of the 21st century but would be producing only about 10,500. Figures from the NSF predicted a cumulative shortfall of 103,000 between 1989 and 2006.

Legislative Action

The House Committee on Science, Space and Technology approved HR 996 (H Rept 101-220) on July 27, 1989.

The bill as reported Aug. 4 created three merit-based congressional scholarship programs. It authorized $13 million in fiscal 1990, rising to $40.75 million in fiscal 1993, for the scholarship programs, all of which were to be administered by the NSF.

The House passed HR 996 by voice vote under suspension of the rules on Sept. 12.

Attention was again directed toward the science and math issue on July 17, 1990, when the House passed, on a 347-19 vote, a bill (HR 4982 — H Rept 101-571) authorizing $250 million for science and math education programs. A component of the legislation called for substantially increasing budget authority for the Dwight D. Eisenhower Mathematics and Science Education Act (PL 98-377), which since 1984 had been the main federal conduit for grants to local education agencies for math and science instruction. *(PL 98-377, Congress and the Nation Vol. VI, p. 571)*

The Bush administration opposed HR 4982, arguing that it cost too much, reduced discretion for local education agencies and duplicated existing activities.

The Senate Labor and Human Resources Committee, meanwhile, had been working on a math-science bill with a substantially smaller authorization, $125 million. The bill (S 2114 — S Rept 101-412), approved July 18 and reported Aug. 1, authorized a scholarship program for women and minority students, a math-science teacher corps, a national science scholars program and a doubling of the NSF graduate fellowship program.

The Senate by voice vote passed HR 996 on Aug. 3, after amending the bill to include the language of S 2114.

The conference committee subsequently met to consider the Senate-passed HR 996, the House Science Committee version of HR 996 and HR 4982. The compromise contained provisions from HR 4982 and the Senate-passed HR 996.

The conference agreement made a number of changes in the Eisenhower program, including provisions to require that funds be focused on training elementary school teachers; to direct the Department of Education to establish a model program for training and instruction in computers; and to establish a National Clearinghouse for Science, Mathematics, and Technology Education.

The bill also included the National Science Scholars Program proposed by President Bush and two other smaller scholarship programs to encourage students to major in the sciences.

The House by voice vote approved the conference report (H Rept 101-937) on Oct. 25, and the Senate followed suit the next day, clearing HR 996.

Taft Institute

With passage of a 1990 authorization bill, Congress gave the Taft Institute, a quasi-governmental institute that conducted seminars on American government for educators, its final four years of federal funding.

The bill (S 1939 — PL 101-638) authorized a total of $1.8 million for the institute through fiscal 1994. After 1994, the bill provided, funding for the institute would have to come from private donations.

The Taft Institute for Two-Party Government had been founded in 1961 under a charter from the New York State Board of Regents. The non-partisan corporation was named in honor of the late Sen. Robert A. Taft, R-Ohio (1939-53). The federal government began giving money to the institute under the Higher Education Act Amendments of 1980. That year, $750,000 was authorized.

The Taft Institute funding was reauthorized at that level through 1988. In that year, however, reauthorizing legislation died because of arguments over the many costly extraneous amendments attached to the bill. *(Congress and the Nation Vol. VII, p. 663)*

Because of the problem in 1988, sponsors of the bill in 1990 worked hard to keep the measure free of amendments. Members also made clear their intention that the new money be the final federal funding for the institute.

Legislative Action

The House Education and Labor Subcommittee on Postsecondary Education approved a three-year version of the bill (HR 3315) on Nov. 14, 1989. Before approving the measure, the panel turned down an amendment offered by ranking Republican E. Thomas Coleman of Missouri that would have cut off federal funding after only two years.

The Education and Labor Committee approved the bill by voice vote on Feb. 6, 1990, and reported it (H Rept 101-406) on Feb. 26. The House passed HR 3315 by voice vote under suspension of the rules Feb. 27.

The Senate, meanwhile, passed its version of the bill (S 1939) on Nov. 20, 1989. Before doing so, however, senators attached a $50 million dropout prevention program.

The House passed S 1939 on June 7, 1990, after inserting the provisions of HR 3315.

Under the compromise worked out in the conference committee, Senate members agreed to drop the unrelated amendments, while House members agreed to give the institute an additional year of funding.

The conference report (H Rept 101-884) provided $750,000 for fiscal 1991, $550,000 for 1992, $325,000 in 1993 and $150,000 for 1994.

The House adopted the conference report on Oct. 22, and the Senate followed suit on Oct. 28. President Bush signed S 1939 on Nov. 28.

Chapter 1 Assessment

Congress in 1990 cleared a bill (HR 3910 — PL 101-305) authorizing a detailed national assessment of the Chapter 1 program of compensatory education for the disadvantaged.

The assessment was intended to provide Congress with a detailed look at Chapter 1, the cornerstone of federal aid to education, before it came up again for reauthorization in 1993.

HR 3910 (H Rept 101-404), authorizing $6 million for the assessment from existing appropriations, was passed by the House by voice vote under suspension of the rules on Feb. 27. The Senate passed the bill by voice vote May 7 with minor changes, most of which were accepted by the House May 10. The Senate then cleared the bill May 14, and President Bush signed it May 30.

Library Aid

Legislation (HR 2742 — PL 101-254) reauthorizing federal support for libraries for five years cleared in 1990.

The bill made few substantive changes in the existing program of federal aid to libraries. Sponsors said they were waiting for an assessment of the nation's libraries from an upcoming White House Conference on Libraries before considering more major changes.

HR 2742 was reported (H Rept 101-237) by the House Education and Labor Committee on Sept. 12, 1989. The same day, the House passed the bill by voice vote under suspension of the rules. The Senate Labor and Human Resources Committee reported its version of the legislation (S 1291 — S Rept 101-125) on Sept. 12. The Senate passed an amended HR 2742 by voice vote Oct. 12.

The House adopted the conference report on the measure (H Rept 101-407) on a 401-4 vote Feb. 27, 1990. The Senate adopted the conference report by voice vote March 1, and President Bush signed HR 2742 March 15.

As cleared, HR 2742 authorized $207.5 million in fiscal 1990, an amount that was well above the $126.3 million appropriated for the program that year.

Conferees on the bill accepted a House proposal authorizing $3 million in 1990 for a family literacy program aimed at encouraging libraries to remain open in the evenings and on weekends. Conferees also accepted a Senate plan authorizing $3 million in fiscal 1991 for a program of grants to create adult literacy centers at libraries.

Conferees specified, however, that no funds could be spent for either of the two new programs until the basic library aid programs received appropriations at least 4 percent above the fiscal 1989 level.

Dropout Program

Legislation (HR 2281 — PL 101-150) to reauthorize a national program of demonstration projects designed to reduce school dropout rates cleared in 1990.

The bill, which authorized $50 million a year for fiscal 1990-91, was signed by President Bush on March 6.

Since the dropout prevention program was created in 1988 (PL 100-297), the federal government had spent more than $45 million on 89 projects affecting 50,000 students in 32 states. Most of the projects targeted disadvantaged students, including pregnant teenagers. *(1988 law, Congress and the Nation Vol. VII, p. 655)*

The House Education and Labor Committee reported HR 2281 on June 13, 1989 (H Rept 101-82). The House passed the measure by voice vote under suspension of the rules June 13.

The Senate had included provisions reauthorizing dropout prevention programs in two other bills — S 1939, a reauthorization of the Taft Institute, and S 695, its version of the Bush education initiative. The Senate passed HR 2281 by a 94-0 vote on Feb. 20, 1990, clearing the measure. *(Taft Institute, p. 651; Bush initiative, p. 643)*

Pepper Program

Legislation (HR 2666) creating a new education program named for Claude Pepper, D-Fla. (Senate 1936-51; House 1963-89), and his wife, Mildred, stalled in

1990. Rep. Pepper died May 30, 1989. *(Profile, box, p. 919)*

As passed by the House by voice vote under suspension of the rules Sept. 12, 1989, the Mildred and Claude Pepper Scholarship Act would have established a $500,000 program to bring the hearing impaired to Washington, D.C., to learn about government. The House Education and Labor Committee had reported HR 2666 (H Rept 101-234) on Sept. 7.

Before passing the bill by voice vote Nov. 16, the Senate added $25.2 million in authorizations for six projects in the states of influential members — including Majority Leader George J. Mitchell, D-Maine, and Minority Leader Bob Dole, R-Kan.

HR 2666 died upon adjournment of the 101st Congress, differences between the House- and Senate-passed versions unresolved.

A 1988 effort to set up the Pepper program, as part of a Taft Institute reauthorization, was thwarted by "pork-barrel" projects. *(Congress and the Nation Vol. VII, p. 663)*

1991-92

Although the 102nd Congress approved a major measure extending federal higher education programs, the two years of legislative action were marked by frustration and sharp conflicts between Capitol Hill Democrats and the Bush administration.

Key Democratic leaders on education issues tried without success to guarantee funding for the Pell grant program, the cornerstone of federal aid to college students, and to radically revise the troubled federal loan program for students. President Bush, meanwhile, tried without success to push through school reform legislation aimed at fulfilling his 1988 campaign pledge to become "the education president."

Higher Education Aid

After rejecting controversial proposals to make federal Pell grants to college students a mandatory entitlement program and make the federal government the direct provider of loans to students, Congress in 1992 cleared a wide-ranging bill (S 1150 — PL 102-325) reauthorizing higher education programs.

As cleared, S 1150 expanded access to federal college aid for the middle class. It created a new program of unsubsidized loans for all students, regardless of income, and removed the value of a family's home or farm from consideration in the process used to determine eligibility for aid.

In addition, the bill created a demonstration program to test the idea of making the federal government the direct lender to students, in hopes of saving the money used to subsidize the banks that made the loans under the existing system.

By making more aid available to students from middle-class families, S 1150 represented a marked change from education policy as carried out since 1981, when a budget-cutting campaign inspired by the Reagan administration spurred Congress to steer aid toward students from the poorest families.

However, the bill earned only mixed reviews from lobbyists for students and higher education institutions, which had argued that Pell grants, the centerpiece of federal grant aid, should be made into entitlements to ensure that students received all the aid to which they were due. The effort to establish a new entitlement ran afoul of budget rules and concern over the increasingly uncontrollable federal budget and massive deficit.

S 1150 as cleared also extended aid to historically black colleges and universities, provided grants to academic libraries and instituted programs to recruit and train elementary and secondary teachers. In addition, it contained provisions aimed at curbing loan defaults and other alleged abuses in the aid programs.

The law was last reauthorized in 1986. *(Congress and the Nation Vol. VII, p. 649)*

Background

Action on higher education legislation in the 102nd Congress was shaped by rising public and congressional frustration with the existing student aid programs.

In the 25 years since passage of the Higher Education Act of 1965 (PL 89-329), federal student aid programs were widely credited with expanding access to postsecondary education, channeling $18 billion a year in aid to 6 million students in the form of grants, loans, work-study aid and fellowships. *(1965 law, Congress and the Nation Vol. II, p. 716)*

Nevertheless, a number of problems existed. Middle-income and working-class students were finding obtaining grant aid or borrowing money harder as eligibility rules tightened. And poor students, who had the most difficulty carrying debt, were receiving fewer direct grants and were being forced to take on more loans.

Meanwhile, Congress and the administration were concerned about the growing number of student loan defaults and the resulting increase in costs to the U.S. Treasury, which guaranteed the loans made by private banks and savings institutions. Between fiscal 1980 and 1990, the volume of loans had almost tripled, to $13 billion in 1990. During that same time, the percentage of students who failed to repay their loans climbed from 12.5 percent in 1980 to 14.9 percent in 1990. The combination of more loans and higher default rates pushed up the cost of the program. Although the cost of loan defaults had been $200 million in 1981, it was expected to reach $2.7 billion in 1991.

Legislation cleared in 1990 to cut off guaranteed loans to students at colleges and trade schools with high default rates. *(Student loan defaults, p. 649)*

House Committee Action

The most radical and controversial ideas for changing student aid programs — to make Pell grants an entitlement program and to switch to direct federal loans to students — were embodied in the draft bill considered by the House Education and Labor Subcommittee on Postsecondary Education on Oct. 8, 1991.

The measure, which carried an estimated price tag of $100 billion, included a number of proposals by both Democrats and Republicans to increase both loans and grants to middle-class students. Although those efforts put the panel at odds with the Bush administration, which sought to focus aid on the neediest students, the suggested changes created the greatest conflicts within the subcommittee itself.

Backers of entitlement status for Pell grants, which was supported by major higher education groups, argued that the change was needed to protect students from the whims of the budget process. While conceding that the estimated $11.7 billion cost of full funding for the program would exceed the 1990 budget agreement between the White House and congressional leaders, Democratic sponsors noted that the move to mandatory status would not take place until 1994, when Congress would be free to cut defense spending to boost domestic programs.

But Republican opponents of the provision contended that creating a new non-controllable spending program was irresponsible at a time when the federal deficit was nearing $350 billion a year. Moreover, they warned, including the provision would shatter the bipartisan harmony that typically prevailed on higher education legislation and put the bill on a collision course with the Bush administration.

During subcommittee consideration, ranking Republican Tom Coleman of Missouri offered an amendment to delete the entitlement provision. His amendment was rejected on a 9-17 vote.

Other parts of the bill expanding Pell grants generated less debate, however. The bill raised the family income threshold for the program to $50,000, from $30,000; excluded a family's house, farm or small business from income eligibility calculations; and increased the maximum grant from $2,400 to $4,500 a year.

The chief backer of the direct loan proposal in subcommittee was Robert E. Andrews, D-N.J., who argued that direct lending could save $1.4 billion a year by eliminating the federal interest subsidy to the 13,000 private lenders that participated in the program. The federal government could finance the loans by selling government securities, he said, and then farm the money out to schools to lend to students. All students could borrow money under the proposed program, but only lower-income students would receive interest subsidies from the government while they attended school.

The direct loan provision was strongly opposed by the Bush administration and an array of interest groups, including those representing banks and guarantee agencies. Critics argued that the plan would create new administrative headaches for the government, add to the federal debt and leave schools with too great a responsibility for managing federal funds.

Differences over the entitlement and direct loan provisions led to two days of partisan squabbling and party-line voting in the full committee, which finally approved the bill (HR 3553) on a 26-14 vote Oct. 23.

Before committee action, Secretary of Education Lamar Alexander sent a letter to the panel's chairman, William D. Ford, D-Mich., warning that he would recommend a presidential veto. In addition, concern about the entitlement provision was voiced by Leon Panetta, D-Calif., the chairman of the Budget Committee.

Efforts by Coleman to change the bill were defeated, however. An amendment to eliminate the entitlement provision fell 15-26, while a substitute proposal to create a pilot direct loan program at 100 schools was rejected 12-27.

In other action, the committee adopted by voice vote an amendment offered by Scott L. Klug, R-Wis., on behalf of the administration to create a new scholarship program providing $500 awards to Pell grant recipients who ranked academically near the top of their high school and college classes.

On a 28-13 vote, members approved a Steve Gunderson, R-Wis., amendment to cut off financial aid to students convicted of possessing or using illegal drugs unless the student enrolled in a drug rehabilitation program.

HR 3553 (H Rept 102-447) was formally reported Feb. 27, 1992.

Senate Committee Action

Although the bill (S 1150) approved by the Senate Labor and Human Resources Subcommittee on Education on Oct. 24, 1991, also sought to steer aid to middle-class students, it was less generous in terms of new spending and more cautious in terms of fundamental changes in existing programs.

Observers attributed the Senate's stance to concern over the 1990 budget agreement. Although the House committee choose to ignore that pact's limits, the Senate panel tried to obey it.

The Senate bill provided a smaller increase in Pell grants, for example, and would not make the program an entitlement until the sixth year of the bill's seven-year authorization. Similarly, although Paul Simon, D-Ill., and Dave Durenberger, R-Minn., endorsed a direct loan program, S 1150 left the existing guaranteed loan structure intact.

The full Labor and Human Resources Committee approved the bill on a 17-0 vote Oct. 30 and reported it (S Rept 102-204) Nov. 12. The unanimous vote concealed sharp partisan divisions and the strong likelihood of a veto over even the more limited entitlement provision in the legislation.

Nancy Landon Kassebaum, R-Kan., the ranking Republican on the Education Subcommittee, offered an amendment to drop the entitlement provision and restrict the bill to a five-year reauthorization. But her amendment was rejected on a 6-11 vote.

The committee did not vote on the Simon and Durenberger direct loan proposal, which also called for loans to be repaid on the basis of a student's income after leaving school, with the Internal Revenue Service to collect loan payments directly.

Senate Floor Action

In the face of the strong concerns over the entitlement provision, Education Subcommittee Chairman Claiborne Pell, D-R.I., and other sponsors of S 1150 decided to drop the idea even before the bill reached the Senate floor. Not only was the entitlement provision in danger of losing in a floor vote, observers noted, but the possibility also existed that the entire bill could be blocked by a point of order, given that the provision committed the government to spending money in a future year without a budget resolution.

In the weeks before the vote on Senate passage of S 1150, Simon, Durenberger and Bill Bradley, D-N.J., brought new attention to the direct loan proposal. They waged an effective public relations campaign calling for a stop to the subsidizing of banks at the expense of students. In the end, however, the trio did not offer their plan as an amendment to S 1150. Instead, they added it to a tax measure (HR 4210), but the loan provision was dropped in conference.

S 1150 passed the Senate on a 93-1 vote Feb. 21, 1992.

House Floor Action

Just as Senate sponsors had been forced to substantially modify their bill before bringing it to the floor, so, too, in the House Ford and other sponsors had to make major retreats on key provisions before HR 3553 could be considered by the full House.

The biggest problem for Ford was the opposition among his fellow Democrats to the provision making Pell grants an entitlement. During the course of several months of negotiations, the House leadership adamantly refused to support a waiver for the provision from the 1990 budget agreement, which had required that any new entitlement spending be offset with tax increases or spending cuts. Particularly after the Senate dropped its delayed entitlement provision, thus leaving the change with little chance of becoming law, Ford had no choice but to jettison the idea.

Even so, the bill continued to face a major problem because it continued to call for increased mandatory spending without compensating tax increases or budget cuts. Although a substitute bill (HR 4471) introduced by Ford in March 1992 shaved $60 billion off the committee bill's new mandatory spending, it still left $2 billion in uncovered costs. And even after Ford moved to cut the special allowance paid to banks when student loan interest rates did not match the market, the bill was $1.2 billion over.

Finally, House leaders forced through a change to save the needed money by imposing a 5 percent loan origination fee on Supplemental Loans for Students and Parent Loans for Undergraduate Students, and by maintaining the existing origination fees on Stafford loans. Origination fees were subtracted from a loan when it was issued, although the borrower had to pay back the full amount.

Once it finally reached the floor, the bill did not undergo major changes. One series of successful amendments aimed at reducing loan defaults among students at trade schools was offered by Marge Roukema, R-N.J., Maxine Waters, D-Calif., and Bart Gordon, D-Tenn. House members March 26 also voted 351-39 for an amendment by Gordon and Coleman to prohibit Pell grants from going to prisoners in federal and state prisons.

The only other major point of controversy on the floor focused on an amendment by Bill Gradison, R-Ohio, and J. J. Pickle, D-Texas, to strengthen oversight of the Student Loan Marketing Association (Sallie Mae), the federally chartered corporation that operated the secondary market for student loans. Gradison and Pickle proposed to move oversight over Sallie Mae from the Department of Education to the Treasury. Their amendment was rejected 181-232 on March 26.

The House passed HR 3553 by a 365-3 vote March 26.

Conference Action

With the demise of the entitlement provision, the House and Senate bills were substantially similar, leaving conferees with relatively non-controversial differences to resolve.

One point at issue concerned the House's demonstration program of direct loans, which was not in the Senate bill. Although Education Secretary Alexander threatened to urge the president to veto the bill if the direct loan program was included, conferees agreed to accept it. Democrats voiced confidence that Bush was unlikely to veto the bill containing popular student aid programs in an election year.

House conferees gave in to the Senate, however, on their provision banning Pell grants to prisoners. The Senate bill prohibited the grants only to prisoners serving life without parole or awaiting the death penalty.

After all differences were resolved, the Senate adopted the conference report on S 1150 (H Rept 102-630) by voice vote June 30. The House approved it on a 419-7 vote July 8, clearing the bill. The president signed S 1150 on July 23.

Scholarships Ban

Secretary of Education Lamar Alexander announced Dec. 4, 1991, that colleges would be barred from issuing scholarships based solely on race, but they could consider race as a factor. Alexander had ordered a review of federal policy on March 20.

In December 1990, Michael Williams, assistant secretary for civil rights, said that minority-only scholarships violated Title VI of the Civil Rights Act, which prohibited discrimination in any program receiving federal funds. Williams had tried to stop Fiesta Bowl officials from donating money for minority scholarships to the two schools playing in the football game. Williams' determination angered black leaders and caused confusion among higher education institutions.

An American Council on Education study found that 4 percent of the 1.3 million minority students in four-year colleges received "race-exclusive" scholarships.

Major Provisions

As cleared, S 1150:

Grant Programs

- Increased the maximum grant available to students under the Pell grant program to $3,700 in academic year 1993-94, rising by $200 a year to $4,500 by 1997-98.
- Repealed the existing formula used for the Pell grant program and provided for a single needs-analysis formula for all student-aid programs.
- Prohibited Pell grants from going to prisoners who were serving life without parole or awaiting a death sentence.
- Authorized a total of $650 million in fiscal 1993 for postsecondary aid programs for students from disadvantaged backgrounds, including the Talent Search, Upward Bound, Student Support Services, Educational Opportunity Centers and Staff Development Activities programs.
- Established a program aimed at encouraging states to set up programs under which low-income students who graduated from high school would be guaranteed financial

aid needed to attend a postsecondary institution. Authorized $200 million for the program in fiscal 1993.

• Established a program of Presidential Access Scholarships to provide aid to students who had taken a rigorous academic program in high school; authorized $200 million for the program in fiscal 1993.

• Authorized the following amounts for programs in fiscal 1993: $35 million for counseling about college opportunities and community partnerships; $20 million for a computerized database on available financial aid; $10 million for a demonstration program to encourage families to save for their children's education; $20 million for programs to aid students from migrant-farmworker families; and $10 million for Robert C. Byrd Scholarships for students in their first year of college.

• Authorized the Department of Education to develop a single financial aid form to help students determine how much aid they are eligible for.

• Authorized $675 million in fiscal 1993 for the Federal Supplemental Educational Opportunity Grant program, which provided matching funds to institutions to distribute to needy students; increased the matching amount required to schools to 25 percent from 15 percent.

• Authorized $105 million in fiscal 1993 for State Student Incentive Grants and increased the maximum grant under the program to $5,000 from $2,500.

Student Loans

• Authorized the Federal Robert T. Stafford Student Loan Program through fiscal 1998.

• Set limits on the amount of loans students could take out, ranging from $2,625 for students who had not completed their first year of college to $8,500 for graduate and professional students.

• Set interest on Stafford loans at the rate for 91-day Treasury bills plus 3.1 percent, with a cap of 9 percent.

• Imposed a 5 percent origination fee on Supplemental Loans for Students and Parent Loans for Undergraduate Students.

• Increased the limit on Parental Loans for Undergraduate Students to the cost of education minus other financial aid.

• Required lenders to offer students the option of repaying their loans according to an income-sensitive repayment schedule.

• Limited the situations in which borrowers could defer repayment to those cases in which students were in school, unemployed or suffering economic hardship.

• Established a program of unsubsidized Stafford loans for students who did not qualify for subsidized loans; unlike the main loan program, borrowers would be required to pay interest while they were still in school.

• Authorized a demonstration program under which Stafford loans would be forgiven for people who entered the teaching or nursing professions or performed national community service.

• Reduced the default rate used to determine institutional eligibility for participation in student loan programs to 25 percent from 30 percent.

• Authorized $800 million in fiscal 1993 for federal work-study programs, and required all schools, beginning in fiscal 1994, to use at least 5 percent of their work-study funds for community service programs.

• Directed the secretary of education to establish a four-year demonstration program of direct loans to students, bypassing banks and other lenders. Under the program, students at selected schools would receive an entitlement to loans on the same basis as existing loan programs. The program would be carried out at schools selected by the secretary with an aggregate loan volume of $500 million for the Stafford, supplemental and parental loan programs.

• Authorized $250 million in fiscal 1993 for Perkins loans, a campus-based program using a revolving fund to provide low-interest loans to students.

• Changed the definition of student need used in calculating eligibility for benefits, by defining need as the cost of school attendance minus the expected family contribution for the student, minus the expected financial aid from non-federal sources.

• Provided that, in determining the family's net worth in aid calculations, the value of the family's principal place of residence or family farm not be included.

• Provided for a simplified needs analysis for students from families with incomes below $50,000, and assumed no required contribution from families with incomes of less than the maximum federal earned income credit, or about $11,300 in 1992.

General Provisions

• Excluded schools that enrolled more than 50 percent of their students in correspondence courses from eligibility for aid programs, and barred aid for correspondence courses unless aimed at a traditional postsecondary degree.

• Barred schools from aid programs if they had filed for bankruptcy or if their owner had been convicted of a crime involving aid programs.

• Required students applying for federal aid to use a form developed by the Education Department, and prohibited schools from charging a fee for processing the forms.

• Barred students without a high school diploma from receiving aid unless they had passed a test showing their ability to benefit from postsecondary instruction.

• Required institutions to collect statistics on serious campus crimes and to develop policies for combatting sexual assault.

• Required schools that provided athletic scholarships to issue annual reports showing the total revenues and expenses for football, men's and women's basketball, and all other men's and women's sports.

• Authorized $75 million in fiscal 1993 for a program of state review of institutional eligibility for federal aid, to examine such issues as default rates and academic programs.

• Authorized funding for a series of grant programs, including efforts to build partnerships between postsecondary institutions and secondary schools, ease the transition for students from two-year to four-year schools, expand telecommunications programs and improve library services.

• Authorized $135 million in fiscal 1993 for aid to institutions with severe financial problems, and $45 million to aid institutions serving significant numbers of Hispanic students.

• Authorized $135 million in fiscal 1993 for historically black colleges and universities.

• Authorized $350 million in fiscal 1993 for aid to state and local education agencies and higher education institutions to improve the skills of classroom teachers.

• Authorized $20 million in fiscal years 1993-97 for the National Board for Professional Teaching Standards, which was working to develop guidelines for voluntary certification of highly skilled teachers.

- Authorized funds for a variety of other programs to improve teaching, including efforts to create "teacher corps," develop alternative routes to teacher certification, improve middle-grades teaching, study the effects of reducing class sizes and recruit minority teachers.
- Authorized funding for programs aimed at improving international education.
- Authorized $350 million in fiscal 1993 for matching grants to states for construction and renovation of academic and library facilities.
- Authorized funds for grants aimed at increasing participation by women and minorities in graduate studies.
- Authorized $20 million in fiscal 1993 for the Fund for the Improvement of Postsecondary Education.

School Reform

The 102nd Congress failed to clear legislation (S 2) aimed at providing federal aid for school improvement efforts.

The measure died because of conflicts between President Bush and congressional Democrats resulting both from political maneuvering for advantage in the 1992 elections and from fundamental philosophical disagreements about the best way to improve the American educational system.

The legislation, known as the Neighborhood Schools Improvement Act, would have provided $800 million in block grants to states and schools, leaving specific reforms up to local education officials.

The conference report on S 2 was approved by the House late in the 1992 session but was blocked in the Senate by a Republican filibuster, against which Senate leaders failed by one vote to invoke cloture.

Although the bill came within a narrow margin of clearing Congress, it evoked little enthusiasm on Capitol Hill. Democrats, many of whom would have rather directed any additional funding to successful existing programs, moved the bill along mostly because they did not want to appear to be obstructing Bush's education efforts.

But the Bush administration and many congressional Republicans objected to S 2 because it included none of the administration's America 2000 program. That program, introduced in 1991, called for such initiatives as national student testing, widespread elimination of federal and state education regulations, and funding for "break the mold" schools.

An even more controversial issue dividing Bush and the congressional majority concerned efforts to expand parental choice in education. Bush's initial support for school choice, as included in America 2000, called for $200 million in federal funding for states and school districts to experiment with allowing parents to pick their children's schools. In 1992, under the pressure of election-year politics, Bush expanded the choice idea to include a $500 million demonstration program under which low- and middle-income parents could have received vouchers of up to $1,000 to send their children to any public or private school.

Advocates of school choice argued that it would spur competition and force bad schools to improve so as to retain and attract students. But critics warned that allowing choice plans to include private schools would drain money from public education and, if the plans included religious schools, violate the constitutional ban on state establishment of religion.

Bush Proposal

The genesis of the school reform legislation in the 102nd Congress lay in Bush's 1988 campaign pledge to be "the education president." That vow led, in turn, to the 1989 education summit, at which Bush and the nation's governors agreed to a set of national education goals. Bush was unsuccessful in the 101st Congress in pushing legislation to begin to implement the goals, however. *(Bush initiative, p. 643)*

In December 1990, stung by charges that he lacked a domestic agenda, the president asked his education secretary, Lauro F. Cavazos, to step down and subsequently replaced him with Lamar Alexander, a former governor of Tennessee with an extensive education reform record.

Within a few months, Alexander had produced America 2000. The plan included voluntary national testing for fourth-, eighth- and 12th-grade students; merit pay for teachers; reduction of regulations; and the creation of 535 innovative "New American Schools" funded by the federal government and private businesses. America 2000 became Bush's education rallying cry, and he and Alexander barnstormed the country to enlist cities and states to join.

Congressional Democrats, meanwhile, pushed legislation to allow local school districts to try some of Bush's ideas, albeit under different names.

1991 Action

Congressional Democrats initially responded to Bush's America 2000 plan in two different ways, with the House pursuing a conciliatory strategy on the much-debated issue of private school choice and the Senate adopting a stance of opposition.

The first move came a day before release of America 2000, when the Senate Labor and Human Resources Committee added to an adult literacy bill (S 2 — S Rept 102-43) a total of $312 million in authority for programs to spur school-based management, reward excellent schools, and improve math and science education. The bill approved on April 17, 1991, also included a controversial provision to monitor the president's education goals.

The adult literacy and other provisions subsequently were enacted separately, leaving the more contentious proposals to wait for several months. On Nov. 13, Senate Labor reconsidered S 2, making a number of changes. As approved, the bill authorized $850 million in fiscal 1992 for block grants to states for school improvement plans. *(Adult literacy, p. 658)*

The Senate bill was much less specific than the Bush proposal on how states should spend the money. More importantly, the Senate measure allowed for experimentation only with parental choice among public schools, leaving out Bush's proposal that private schools potentially be included.

Fearing the strength of support in the House for private school choice, leaders of the House Education and Labor Committee took a less confrontational approach. On Oct. 17, the committee approved a $700 million measure (HR 3320 — H Rept 102-294) that included Bush's school choice plan.

Despite a record of strong opposition to private school choice, committee Chairman William D. Ford, D-Mich., said the provision had to be included because committee leaders had reached an agreement with the White House to back the bill if the full choice program was in it.

Still, Ford had to overcome resistance from other committee Democrats and some Republicans, who vocally raised a number of objections to the private school choice provision. The leading critic was a freshman Democrat from Louisiana, William J. Jefferson, but his amendment to limit choice only to public schools was rejected on a 17-23 vote.

Meanwhile in the Senate, the inability of Democratic leaders and the White House to reach a compromise on the choice issue prevented S 2 from coming to the floor.

1992 Action

The decisive moment in the course of action on the reform legislation came early in 1992, when supporters and opponents of private school choice waged a direct test of strength on the Senate floor. The defeat of private school choice emboldened House sponsors to drop the idea, permitting Democrats to move ahead with the bill but ensuring that it would not become law.

The amendment to add private school choice was offered by Sen. Orrin G. Hatch, R-Utah, to S 2. Hatch's amendment was a sharply scaled-back proposal that would have set up six demonstration projects in which federal school aid could be used to allow low-income students to attend schools of their parents' choice. The amendment called for spending only $30 million on the program, far less than Bush's proposal.

But Senate Democrats, viewing the amendment as an opening wedge for choice plans to drain resources from the public schools, waged an all-out fight against it. The amendment was rejected on a **36-57 (R 33-6; D 3-51) key vote** Jan. 23. *(1992 key votes, p. 1083)*

The only other issue that threatened to delay the bill came when Jesse Helms, R-N.C., offered a non-binding sense of the Senate amendment urging the Supreme Court to allow prayer in schools. Although senators were reluctant at first to vote on the amendment, it was rejected Jan. 23, 38-55. The Senate Jan. 28 voted 55-43 to table (kill) a Don Nickles, R-Okla., amendment to allow states to require welfare recipients to ensure that their children attended schools, and it rejected 45-53 a Tim Wirth, D-Colo., amendment to override the 1990 budget agreement to allow defense savings to be used for domestic programs.

The Senate passed S 2 on a 92-6 vote Jan. 8. As passed, the bill authorized $850 million in fiscal 1992 for block grants, with at least 75 percent of all funds going to schools with the lowest levels of achievement and the highest levels of poverty. In a compromise with the administration, the bill allowed states to spend 25 percent of the money — up from 10 percent in the original bill — on creating New American Schools, but the money could go only to public schools.

Confident that the Senate would never accept private school choice, Rep. Ford moved to drop the bill reported by his committee in 1991 (HR 3320) and replace it with another measure (HR 4323) that made no mention of the issue. As a result of pressure from the National School Boards Association, the new bill also rewrote provisions on the crafting of local school improvement plans to give the local school board final authority.

Ford's actions disrupted the normally bipartisan tone on the Education and Labor Committee, as Republicans complained that Ford had excluded them from decisions and reneged on his earlier agreement. Nevertheless, the committee approved HR 4323 (H Rept 102-691) on a 23-12 vote May 20.

The pattern of partisan confrontation in committee also was evident on the House floor, with the administration and many others denouncing the bill. Moreover, a number of Democrats voiced only lukewarm support, arguing that the money would be better spent on existing programs. After rejecting Republican amendments to add some form of private school choice, the House passed HR 4323 on a 279-124 vote Aug. 12. It then laid HR 4323 on the table and passed an amended S 2 by voice vote.

With Democrats confident that they had the votes on key issues — and that Bush might be reluctant to veto an education reform bill shortly before the election — conferees crafted a bill that offered few compromises to the administration. The conference agreement approved Sept. 25 contained neither funding for private school choice nor a separate authorization for Bush's New American Schools.

In response, Alexander wrote a strongly worded letter denouncing the bill as "a monument to business-as-usual thinking" and said it "evidences the cozy relationship between the majority members of the Education committees and the entrenched education special interests."

The House adopted the conference report (H Rept 102-916) by voice vote Oct. 2. But Senate Republicans were determined to block it, and the measure died the same day after a cloture motion failed 59-40 (60 votes are necessary).

Adult Literacy

Congress in 1991 cleared legislation (HR 751 — PL 102-73) to expand existing adult literacy programs and create new ones in an effort to reach the estimated 30 million functionally illiterate adults in the United States.

The bill created a National Institute for Literacy to coordinate federal literacy programs, as well as State Literacy Resource Centers to coordinate federal, state and local literacy efforts.

HR 751 authorized new funding of $197.5 million in fiscal 1992 and $1.1 billion in adult education and literacy programs through fiscal 1995.

Backers said the new efforts were necessary because existing literacy programs reached only a small portion of those in need. With the number of functionally illiterate workers predicted to grow to 50 million by the year 2000, sponsors said the problem was a burden the U.S. economy could not afford.

Similar legislation (S 1310) had passed the Senate in 1990. However, the bill died amid partisan maneuvering over President Bush's education initiative. *(Story, p. 643)*

HR 751 threatened to get caught up in larger disputes over education policies. Initially, Senate Democrats included adult literacy programs in a comprehensive education reform bill (S 2) they put forward to counter Bush's America 2000 proposal. But Labor and Human Resources Chairman Edward M. Kennedy, D-Mass., subsequently agreed to allow the literacy bill to move ahead on its own with bipartisan support.

Legislative History

The House Education and Labor Committee approved HR 751 on March 12, and it was reported (H Rept 102-23) on March 18. The House passed the measure by voice voice under suspension of the rules March 19.

In the Senate, provisions similar to those in HR 751 originally were included in the Democratic education reform bill (S 2). During consideration of S 2 in the Labor and Human Resources Committee, Nancy Landon Kassebaum, R-Kan., offered an amendment to remove the literacy provisions from the broader bill and put them in separate legislation, arguing that the popular literacy measure should not be held up by partisan disputes. Her amendment was rejected on a 10-7 party-line vote, however, after which S 2 was approved on a 10-7 vote.

When it became clear that S 2 would not move quickly, Paul Simon, D-Ill., convinced Kennedy to allow the literacy provisions to go ahead on their own. The Senate passed HR 751 by voice vote on June 26.

The only significant difference between the two measures concerned a House amendment, offered by Minority Whip Newt Gingrich, R-Ga., to require all prisons to put literacy programs into place within five years if federal funds were available. That provision was dropped, however, by the Senate, where members argued that it was another burdensome mandate on states.

During subsequent consideration of an omnibus crime bill (S 1241), the Senate approved language to give states discretion to create literacy programs in prisons. When that bill ran into trouble, the language was added to HR 751 by the House July 11. The Senate cleared the measure on July 15. President Bush signed it July 22. *(Crime bill, p. 786)*

Major Provisions

As cleared, HR 751:

- Created a National Institute for Literacy, with a fiscal 1992 authorization of $15 million, to coordinate federal literacy programs.
- Authorized $25 million in fiscal 1992 to create State Literacy Resource Centers to provide training and coordination of literacy programs.
- Authorized $5 million in fiscal 1992 for the Department of Labor to help small- and medium-size businesses and labor unions establish literacy programs.
- Authorized $60 million in fiscal 1992 to expand the Workplace Literacy Partnerships program.
- Increased the authorization for Adult Education Act programs to $260 million in fiscal 1992 and required the Department of Education and the states to develop methods of evaluating the effectiveness of literacy programs and award funds on that basis.
- Allowed the Chapter 2 state block grant program for elementary and secondary education to be used to help schools identify students with reading problems.
- Authorized $10 million for state programs to provide literacy programs for prisoners. Required functionally illiterate prisoners to participate in literacy programs and prohibited parole for those who refused to participate.

Longer School Year

Congress in 1991 cleared legislation (S 64 — PL 102-62) to establish a National Commission on a Longer School Year to study proposals to lengthen the school year so that U.S. students could better compete with students in other countries.

The bill authorized $1 million in fiscal 1991 and open-ended funding through fiscal 1994 for the commission, which also was to study the idea of lengthening the school day.

Backers of the bill argued that the current school year, which in most states averaged around 180 days for elementary and secondary school students, was based on an agricultural economy, when young people were needed to help out on the farm over the summer, and was no longer appropriate in an industrial society. Students tended to forget some of what they had learned over the three-month summer break, and so a significant portion of each year needed to be devoted to reviewing the previous year's material.

The bill also authorized national programs aimed at improving students' writing abilities and understanding of the U.S. Constitution. In addition, it authorized grants for programs to help truck drivers with reading and writing skills so they could pass a written test required under a 1986 truck safety law.

The Senate Labor and Human Resources Committee approved S 64 on March 13 and reported it (S Rept 102-26) March 19. The Senate passed the bill by voice vote April 17.

The House amended and passed the bill June 10 by voice vote. The conference report (H Rept 102-110) was adopted by the House June 13, and by the Senate the following day, clearing the measure. President Bush signed the bill June 27.

Dropout Prevention

Congress in 1991 cleared legislation (HR 2313 — PL 102-103) to reauthorize programs aimed at preventing youths from dropping out of school.

The bill authorized $115 million for the programs in fiscal 1992 and open-ended funding in fiscal 1993.

The measure aided mentor programs and other methods aimed at keeping students in school. In addition, it included $50 million for the Star Schools program, which funded distance-learning projects connecting classrooms with teachers via satellite.

The bill also expanded program services to groups of students, including disabled children and adults who were housebound or in hospitals.

The House Education and Labor Committee reported the bill (H Rept 102-77) on May 23, and the House passed it by voice vote under suspension of the rules June 3.

The Senate passed an amended HR 2313 by voice vote July 30. The House accepted the Senate changes Aug. 1, clearing the bill for President Bush, who signed it Aug. 17.

Video Programs

Congress in 1992 cleared legislation (S 3134) that directed the secretary of education to award grants to develop and distribute video programs focused on school readiness for children, parents, child care providers and educators.

The bill, known as the Ready to Learn Act, established a "ready to learn" satellite channel to distribute the programming and authorized $50 million in fiscal 1993.

The Senate passed S 3134 by voice vote Oct. 1. The House passed an amended bill by voice vote under suspension of the rules Oct. 6. The Senate cleared S 3134 the next day, and President Bush signed it (PL 102-545) on Oct. 27.

Education of the Deaf

President Bush on Oct. 16, 1992, signed legislation (HR 5483 — PL 102-421) reauthorizing through fiscal 1997 Gallaudet University, the National Technical Institute for the Deaf and other programs for people with hearing problems.

Gallaudet, in Washington, D.C., and the technical institute, in Rochester, N.Y., received most of their funding from the federal government.

The House Education and Labor Committee reported HR 5483 (H Rept 102-818) on Aug. 10, 1992. The House passed the bill by voice vote Aug. 10. The Senate passed an amended version by voice vote Oct. 5. The House accepted the changes the next day, clearing the measure.

Education Research

The House on Sept. 22, 1992, by voice vote under suspension of the rules passed HR 4014, which reauthorized and restructured the Office of Educational Research and Improvement, the research branch of the Department of Eduation. The bill went no further.

The restructuring aimed to improve education by promoting research, development and dissemination of information. HR 4014 would have created an 18-member board of governors to oversee the office and develop research priorities. The board would consist of education researchers, teachers, parents, school administrators and others to be appointed by the secretary of education.

The House Education and Labor Committee reported HR 4014 (H Rept 102-845) on Aug. 12, 1992.

A related Senate measure (S 1275) did not advance beyond subcommittee consideration.

11

Housing and Urban Aid

Introduction	*663*
1989-90 Chronology	*665*
1991-92 Chronology	*694*

Housing and Urban Aid

Between the revelations of serious wrongdoing at the Department of Housing and Urban Development (HUD) during the Reagan administration, the enactment of the first major overhaul of housing programs since 1974 and the three days of rioting in Los Angeles following the first Rodney King trial, the policy areas of housing and urban aid were in a tumult in 1989-92.

HUD Scandal

In testimony before Congress about the HUD scandal, HUD Secretary Jack F. Kemp stated, "When I said, when I first took the nomination of President Bush, that I wanted to make HUD a high-profile agency, I don't think I had this in mind."

Congressional investigations into influence peddling and political favoritism at HUD during the Reagan era were prompted by an April 1989 inspector general's report. Within a year, the attorney general had appointed an independent counsel to determine whether former HUD secretary Samuel R. Pierce Jr. and other officials had engaged in criminal activity. By mid-1993, former top aides to Pierce, including Deborah Gore Dean, former high-ranking HUD officials and a number of other individuals had been indicted — and some convicted — on HUD-related charges.

The scandal initially centered around the so-called Section 8 Moderate Rehabilitation Program (mod-rehab), which guaranteed developers federal rent subsidies in exchange for making improvements in privately owned substandard housing to be occupied by the poor. Local public housing authorities were supposed to apply for mod-rehab funds and then designate developers to do the construction work. What happened instead, according to the HUD inspector general's report, was that HUD officials in Washington were earmarking funds for specific developers, who in turn would approach local officials about applying for the money. Also implicated in the scandal were former Reagan administration officials and other prominent Republicans who earned millions in consulting fees. Former interior secretary James G. Watt, for example, made hundreds of thousands of dollars as a consultant. The investigations later were expanded to include special projects, technical assistance and Urban Development Action Grant programs.

In 1989, with Kemp's backing, Congress cleared HUD reform legislation that sought to safeguard against fraud and mismanagement. In 1993, the independent counsel's investigation was ongoing and indictments were still being issued.

Housing Policy

As consideration of housing legislation was undertaken with the new Bush presidency, Congress found itself locked into the same stalemate with the White House as during the Reagan years: Should the government subsidize the construction of more housing for low-income families or help the poor pay rent on the private market?

The policy debate turned in part on the issue of housing supply. Administration officials opposed to construction programs contended that many existing dwellings were empty. They pointed to a 7.3 percent vacancy rate for all rental units during the first three quarters of 1989 and a 35 percent vacancy rate for new apartments during much of the 1980s as proof that the federal government should help make the market work better instead of finance expensive construction.

Housing advocates, however, insisted that the national vacancy rate was meaningless. Unlike some commodities, homes could not be moved to satisfy demand. And besides ignoring regional differences, an overall vacancy rate obscured the lack of usable low-cost housing by including vacancies in top-dollar luxury units and in uninhabitable buildings, housing advocates maintained. According to the Joint Center for Housing Studies at Harvard University, vacancy rates for apartments renting for $150 to $300 a month had increased from 4.7 percent in 1981 to 8 percent in 1987, but the overall number of apartments had dropped from 10.1 million in 1974 to 8.5 million in 1985.

Housing advocates emphasized that most people eligible for federal help were not getting it even though the number of people served had increased slowly since cre-

References

Discussion of housing and urban aid action for the years 1945-64 may be found in *Congress and the Nation Vol. I*, pp. 459-515; for the years 1965-68, *Congress and the Nation Vol. II*, pp. 183-226; for the years 1969-72, *Congress and the Nation Vol. III*, pp. 635-657; for the years 1973-76, *Congress and the Nation Vol. IV*, pp. 471-502; for the years 1977-80, *Congress and the Nation Vol. V*, pp. 429-448; for the years 1981-84, *Congress and the Nation Vol. VI*, pp. 629-639; and for the years 1985-88, *Congress and the Nation Vol. VII*, pp. 667-684.

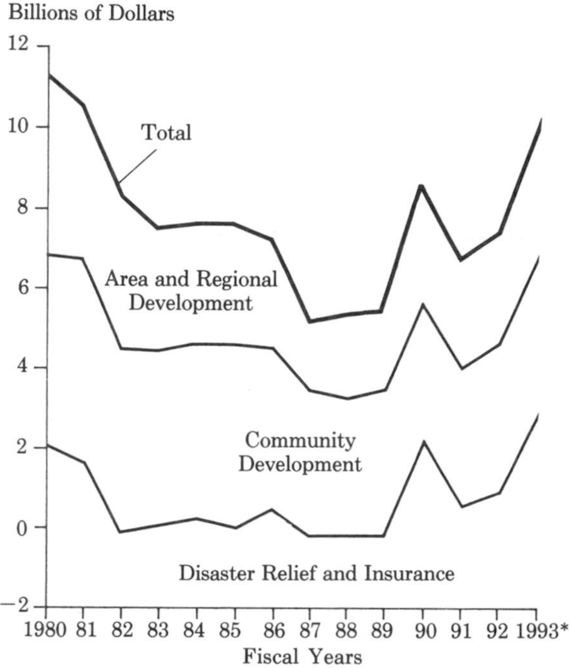

*Estimate.

Source: Office of Management and Budget, *Budget Baselines, Historical Data and Alternatives for the Future* (Washington, D.C.: U.S. Government Printing Office, January 1993).

ation of the rental assistance program. In 1974, 19 percent of poverty-level renters received housing subsidies from the government. In 1980, 23 percent received help, and in 1985, 31 percent did, according to the Joint Center. As of 1988, the Congressional Budget Office said that, depending on the factors considered, the percentage of eligible households receiving assistance varied from a low of 25 percent to a high of 44 percent.

HUD recommended that a household spend no more than 30 percent of its income for a place to live. But housing advocates said the poor often spent much more, indicating that not enough low-cost housing was available. According to the Joint Center, the total number of poverty-level households spending more than 50 percent of their monthly income on rent jumped from 57 percent in 1974 to 70 percent in 1985. A study by the Low Income Housing Information Service showed that 45 percent of all poor renters in 1985 paid more than 70 percent.

The Bush administration, as well as the Reagan administration before it, advocated rent-subsidy vouchers for the poor as the alternative to expensive construction programs for low-income people. Families could choose where they lived as long as they paid the difference between the voucher and the rent. Housing certificates were like vouchers, except that no more than 30 percent of monthly income could be used to make up the difference. Proponents argued that the voucher system would spur private construction because demand for housing would increase. Opponents charged that the market probably would not respond as the proponents suggested because vouchers were not worth enough to guarantee developers a return on their investment.

In the overhaul legislation enacted in 1990, Congress tried to regain ground lost with the Reagan administration's deep cuts in federal housing programs. Existing programs were reauthorized, and new programs were created, including the Democratic-backed HOME (Homeownership Made Easy) Investment Partnerships program providing block grants to state and local governments. Also established was the Homeownership and Opportunity for People Everywhere (HOPE) program, a Bush administration initiative that would allow public housing to be sold to tenants. In addition, the legislation shored up the Federal Housing Administration mortgage insurance fund and attempted to solve the problem of mortgage "prepayments."

Urban Aid

While the 1992 Los Angeles riots were deemed, by most accounts, the worst civil disturbance in the United States in generations, the tragedy did not become the catalyst for bold policy initiatives. Boxed in by a combination of political considerations, budget constraints and lack of a clear consensus on how to address the ills plaguing U.S. cities, neither President Bush nor congressional Democrats rushed forward with radical new agendas.

In the election year of 1992, bringing forth an innovative urban aid plan was fraught with difficulties. For Bush, the risk was that he would not be able to deliver an aid package that he promised for the domestic front — his well-known weak spot. Congress could produce a bill that was too expensive, raised taxes or added to the federal deficit, which might prompt him to veto the measure. For Democrats, the risk was that if they did get a bill enacted, Bush would take the credit and Democrats would lose a major argument in the presidential race — that Bush was incapable of doing anything about the country's economic and social problems.

Most lawmakers agreed, however, that neither policy differences nor strategy would be the main obstacle to creation of a new urban agenda. How to pay for it would be. Under the rules of the 1990 budget summit agreement, all new spending had to be offset by cuts in programs or an increase in revenue. Republicans were adamant that they would not pay for an urban initiative with taxes or by declaring an emergency and adding to the deficit.

Much of the early response to the unrest in Los Angeles was marked by partisan bickering over which party was at fault. Bush spokesman Marlin Fitzwater touched a nerve by suggesting that the failure of Democratic President Lyndon B. Johnson's Great Society anti-poverty programs of the 1960s was responsible for "many of the root problems that have resulted in inner-city difficulties." House Speaker Thomas S. Foley, D-Wash., among others, called the statement "totally absurd." Citing Medicare, aid to education, food stamps, Head Start and college loan programs, he said, "We can go through a long list that has made a very positive contribution to the fairness and justice of our society."

In the face of widespread condemnation, Bush backed off somewhat, with administration officials pointing out that spending for many popular Great Society social programs had increased during Bush's tenure. However, the president did not say that Fitzwater was wrong.

The only substantial urban aid bill cleared by the 102nd Congress was enacted soon after the riots and provided emergency funds to help rebuild Los Angeles.

Chronology Of Action On Housing, Urban Aid

1989-90

Housing Reauthorization

After lengthy negotiations with the Bush administration, Congress in 1990 enacted the first major overhaul of federal housing programs since 1974 with the goals of increasing the nation's stock of affordable housing and helping public housing tenants become homeowners.

Passage of the Cranston-Gonzalez National Affordable Housing Act (S 566 — PL 101-625) was spurred by congressional dissatisfaction with the Reagan administration's deep cuts in federal housing programs and the desire of the Bush administration's activist secretary of housing and urban development (HUD), Jack F. Kemp, to make his imprint on national housing policy.

The legislation authorized $27.5 billion in fiscal 1991 and $29.9 billion in fiscal 1992 to continue existing housing programs — such as rent subsidies, public housing and housing for the elderly and disabled — and to create a number of programs. The authorization sought to provide as many as 360,000 additional units over two years.

The centerpiece of S 566 was the HOME (Homeownership Made Easy) Investment Partnerships, to provide block grants to state and local governments to meet local housing needs. Included in that program was a set-aside for construction of affordable housing — 10 percent the first year and 15 percent the second year.

The measure contained a Bush administration initiative called HOPE (Homeownership and Opportunity for People Everywhere), which was designed to sell off public housing projects to tenants, and a Kemp initiative called Shelter Plus Care, which combined housing assistance with social services. House Banking, Finance and Urban Affairs Committee Chairman Henry B. Gonzalez, D-Texas, offered a new program — National Housing Trust — to help first-time home buyers meet down payment costs and afford mortgage interest rates.

Lawmakers in S 566 also resolved the longstanding problems of the Federal Housing Administration (FHA) mortgage insurance fund losing money and of building owners who wanted to pay off their federally subsidized mortgages. *(FHA insurance fund, p. 690; prepayments, p. 692)*

Background

The major federal role in housing dated to the founding of the FHA in 1934 to insure home mortgages and expanded after World War II with passage of the 1949 National Housing Act (PL 73-479), a broad slum clearance and public housing bill. *(1949 law, Congress and the Nation Vol. I, p. 472)*

Insuring home mortgages, effectively a middle-class subsidy, remained as the most important federal housing program and stirred little controversy. But urban renewal — construction of central city public housing units to replace slums — was very controversial.

Republican President Dwight D. Eisenhower maintained federal support for urban renewal but fought with the Democratic-controlled Congress to reduce the commitment, vetoing two omnibus housing bills in 1959 before an acceptable compromise was worked out (PL 86-372). *(1959 action, Congress and the Nation Vol. I, p. 490)*

President John F. Kennedy won passage of an omnibus act in 1961 (PL 87-70) authorizing new low-interest FHA loans for housing for low- and moderate-income families and increasing federal support for urban renewal. In 1965, President Lyndon B. Johnson, as part of his Great Society program, won enactment of a $7.8 billion housing bill (PL 89-117) that included a controversial rent supplement program. An individual was to pay 25 percent of his or her income for rent in private, non-profit housing and the government would make up the balance. Separate legislation in 1965 (PL 89-174) established HUD, consolidating the variety of federal housing programs into a single, Cabinet-level department. *(1961 act, Congress and the Nation Vol. I, p. 494; 1965 action, Congress and the Nation Vol. II, p. 185)*

A 1968 housing act (PL 90-448) passed with bipartisan support, but in the Nixon administration housing programs again became a focus of partisan debate. In 1973, President Richard Nixon declared a moratorium on new commitments for subsidized housing projects. In 1974, soon after Nixon resigned, President Gerald R. Ford signed housing overhaul legislation (PL 93-383) that supplanted previous home-ownership and rental subsidy programs with a new rental assistance plan providing for public housing authorities to subsidize rents in privately owned leased units. *(1968 law, Congress and the Nation Vol. II, p. 215; 1974 law, Congress and the Nation Vol. IV, p. 477)*

Congress in 1976 ordered HUD to resume spending on new public housing (PL 94-375). In 1977, the first year of the Carter administration, Congress authorized funds for about 373,000 additional subsidized units (PL 95-128). Under budget pressure, that number dipped by a third in 1979 and rose again in 1980 to a total of 282,000 units, half new and half rehabilitated. *(1976 action, Congress and the Nation Vol. IV, p. 498; 1977 action, Congress and the Nation Vol. V, p. 431)*

In the 1980s, President Ronald Reagan directed a fundamental shift in federal housing policies by cutting funds for new construction and pushing vouchers, which poor people could use like cash toward rent for housing they found on their own. Immediately upon taking office, Reagan proposed reducing the number of additional subsidized units for fiscal 1982 to 175,000. The number would drop below 35,000 units — mostly for the elderly and the disabled — in 1988, his last year in office. Spending, which had peaked at $30.1 billion in the last year of the Carter administration, totaled barely more than that — $33.2 billion — for Reagan's entire second term. Administration critics blamed the cuts for the growing problem of homelessness. *(Reagan housing policy, first term, Congress and the Nation Vol. VI, p. 629; Reagan housing policy, second term, Congress and the Nation Vol. VII, p. 667)*

George Bush came to office promising to work with lawmakers in restructuring housing programs. Housing advocates said the need was great. Some 800,000 to 1 million families were on waiting lists for public housing across the country, and another 1 million were waiting for federal vouchers and certificates to subsidize their rents, according to the National Association of Housing and Redevelopment Officials. In many cases, public housing authorities had closed their waiting lists to new names.

But fiscal constraints made increased housing opportunities for the poor difficult. Housing advocates in Congress conceded that so long as pressure was exerted to reduce the deficit and Bush refused to endorse higher taxes, no big-dollar attack on housing problems would be possible.

Legislative Proposals

Congress had three omnibus housing bills to weigh; each took a different approach to reworking federal housing programs.

HR 1180. The Gonzalez bill would boost funding ceilings of existing programs, authorizing spending $27.8 billion in fiscal 1991 — an increase of roughly $11 billion over fiscal 1990 spending — and adding about 183,000 households to the overall assistance rolls in fiscal 1991. HR 1180 also would authorize a new $5 million National Housing Trust, offering a maximum 6 percent interest rate on mortgages for first-time home buyers. To qualify, a home buyer would have to have a total family income that did not exceed 115 percent of the median income for a family of four in the metropolitan area in question.

The bill also provided for a new Community Housing Partnership program that would provide grants to local governments and non-profit sponsors for the production of housing and for assistance to low- and moderate-income families in buying a home. The partnership was designed to encourage non-profit groups to develop and manage housing projects as well as to build and rehabilitate units for sale to low- and moderate-income families.

Additional budget authority would be provided for construction and operating subsidies of public and Indian housing, for construction of housing for the elderly and disabled, for rental certificates, and for Section 8 moderate rehabilitation assistance. The legislation would authorize $300 million in grants for rental housing development.

The bill set aside about $8 billion in fiscal 1991 to extend for five years contracts with owners of low-rent subsidized units covered by the congressional moratorium on mortgage prepayments due to expire on Sept. 30, 1990. Without the extensions, landlords could pay off their mortgages and convert their buildings to condominiums or rent the apartments at market rates.

S 566. The bipartisan efforts of Senate Banking Subcommittee on Housing and Urban Affairs Chairman Alan Cranston, D-Calif., and ranking Republican Alfonse M. D'Amato, N.Y., culminated in S 566, which would reorganize existing programs and create new ones. When introduced in 1989, the Cranston-D'Amato bill proposed spending $15.1 billion in fiscal 1990 and $15.7 billion in fiscal 1991, and it would provide rental assistance to about 30,000 new households in fiscal 1991.

At the heart of S 566 was a new $3 billion-a-year subsidy program — Housing Opportunity Partnerships (HOP) — to encourage development of rental apartments for low-income families. State and local governments would be required to match federal grants by at least 25 percent. They could use the funds to buy, build or rehabilitate housing. And at least 10 percent of a local jurisdiction's funds would have to go to housing developed, sponsored or owned by non-profit community housing groups. The HOP program would be administered by a new agency within HUD, called the HOME Corporation.

For first-time home buyers, the bill would require people to save money in a federally insured institution for at least three years to receive an FHA-insured mortgage. The FHA mortgage could be as much as $125,000 or 90 percent of the median sales price for the state.

The bill would have done away with the certificates and vouchers that tenants received to help pay their rent. Instead, it would have created a "rent credit" program, a new form of assistance that would be either tenant-based or project-based, depending on local need. Rent credits would be used to renew expiring Section 8 assistance contracts, to help tenants displaced by owners who refused to renew project-based contracts and to increase the number of very-low-income families receiving housing aid.

HR 4245, S 2304. The Bush administration's HOPE proposal focused on creating programs to help low-income people buy homes. The president urged $1.2 billion in new budget authority for fiscal 1991, plus $187 million in tax expenditures. Under the HOPE proposal, about 35,900 new households would receive housing assistance in 1991.

The HOPE legislation consisted of four parts. Title I would authorize HUD to distribute grants to public housing tenants to purchase their apartments. HUD also could make grants to low-income people to purchase homes from HUD in multi-family projects with mortgages that were insured by the FHA and later foreclosed upon. And grants could be awarded to non-profit groups to develop programs for the transfer of publicly held, vacant, single-family homes to low-income people.

Title II sought to shield from sudden rent increases low-income tenants of thousands of housing units covered by the moratorium on mortgage prepayments for federally subsidized housing. The moratorium was to expire Sept. 30, 1990.

Title III included a Shelter Plus Care program to provide both rental assistance and support services to homeless people who were seriously mentally ill or had alcohol and drug problems; a demonstration program to test whether combining housing vouchers with support services would help elderly people continue to live independently; and Operation Bootstrap, which would require public housing agencies to develop local programs to help families become economically independent.

Under Title IV, the HUD secretary would designate 50 Housing Opportunity Zones and encourage them to design "barrier removal plans" that scrapped restrictive zoning laws, outdated building codes and other regulations to spur building affordable housing.

Other Developments. In an attempt to rein in and revive what they saw as a runaway, floundering housing bill, D'Amato and Christopher J. Dodd, D-Conn., introduced legislation (S 2504) April 24, 1990, to consolidate nine federal housing programs into a single block grant to states and local governments. S 2504 would circumvent the scandal-scarred HUD and give away $7 billion from public housing, construction programs for the elderly and disabled, rehabilitation programs, Indian housing and Housing Development Action Grants.

Following a barrage of criticism from housing groups and the National Governors' Association and a demonstrative lack of support among their fellow senators, D'Amato and Dodd retreated, conceding that public housing should not be included in a block grant. No congressional action was taken on S 2504.

Senate Committee Action

After scuttling a number of existing programs and cutting back new spending, the Senate Banking, Housing and Urban Affairs Committee on May 2 approved the Cranston-D'Amato bill by 16-4. As approved, S 566 would authorize $17.6 billion for housing programs in fiscal 1991. The bill was formally reported (S Rept 101-316) on June 8.

The compromise, brokered by Christopher S. Bond, R-Mo., would cut the new fiscal 1991 spending authorized in the bill from $3.7 billion to $3.1 billion. The remaining authorization would go to maintain rent subsidies and other programs at their existing levels. HUD had asked for only an $80 million increase in new budget authority in fiscal 1991, about 1 percent more than fiscal 1990 spending.

The 10 small programs earmarked for extinction — worth $551 million — were urban homesteading, Nehemiah grants, home ownership counseling, rental rehabilitation, public housing development, rehabilitation loans, housing development action grants (HoDAG), Section 8 moderate rehabilitation, congregate housing services and public housing sales. The funds would be shifted to the new HOP program; cities and states would split the money 60-40, respectively, instead of 50-50 as the original bill provided.

In addition, the compromise called for eliminating several proposed structural changes to HUD, such as creation of the HOME Corporation, the Office of Affordable Housing Preservation and the post of assistant secretary for supportive housing. The committee bill would extend existing law regarding the FHA mortgage insurance program for two years, instead of increasing ceilings for mortgages for first-time home buyers. Dropped from the original version was a provision to merge rental vouchers and certificates into a new program called rental credits. The existing programs were modified to allow the HUD secretary to approve locally developed fair market rent standards, and tenants were allowed to use HUD certificates, not just vouchers, to rent apartments that cost more than 30 percent of their monthly income.

Most unhappy about the legislation as it emerged from the Senate subcommittee were advocates of public housing, which would lose $369 million of the development funding proposed under the original bill. That money was being used to acquire, rehabilitate and build public housing; to replace demolished housing; and to undertake major reconstruction of public housing.

House Committee Action

After picking through 147 amendments over the course of five days of markup, the House Banking Subcommittee on Housing and Community Development approved HR 1180 by voice vote on May 10, 1990. The full committee approved the bill on June 13, after three days of markup. It was reported (H Rept 101-559) on June 26.

The legislation, which essentially renewed existing programs, reauthorized about $28 billion for federal housing programs for one year. In case the omnibus housing bill bogged down, the committee duplicated provisions to help the homeless under the Stewart B. McKinney Homeless Assistance Act and reported them out in separate legislation (HR 3789). *(Aid for homeless, p. 693)*

Sharp divisions among committee members caused delays in consideration of the bill. Fearing Republicans had the votes to quash a $300 million rental housing production program, proposed by Charles E. Schumer, D-N.Y., Chairman Gonzalez canceled a markup of HR 1180 scheduled for June 6 and introduced a second bill (HR 4971) reordering the titles. His purpose was to force the committee to act on the rental housing program before it decided whether to approve a title incorporating the Bush administration's proposals to spur home ownership. Gonzalez was concerned that some Democrats — particularly with Floyd H. Flake of New York leading the way — might join committee Republicans in opposing the rental housing program.

Flake had challenged the Schumer program in subcommittee, offering an amendment to increase the percentage of low- and lower-income families that would live in the rental projects from 15 percent to 35 percent. The amendment was rejected by voice vote. Also rejected in subcommittee, 15-25, was a Tom Ridge, R-Pa., amendment to kill the entire program.

Schumer's plan would establish a revolving loan fund to provide advances to developers, non-profit groups and public housing agencies to construct or rehabilitate affordable rental housing. Loans could cover up to 50 percent of the cost, and interest rates could not be more than 3 percent. If not enough cash flow was generated to provide a minimum return on the equity, no interest would be paid. If the cash flow was greater than the interest due, HUD would receive 50 percent of the additional money.

The principal and remaining interest would be due 25 years after construction was completed, but if the developer agreed to continue renting to low-income families, the balance would be forgiven at a rate of 6.7 percent a year. During the 25-year period, at least 15 percent of the units would have to be rented to low-income families and another 15 percent to lower-income families. Low-income families were defined as earning 60 percent or less of area median income, and lower-income families as those who earned 80 percent of area median income. Rents would be 30 percent of the family's income.

Flake said that the program would not provide enough units to the very poor and ultimately would subsidize people who were not poor. In addition, he said developers should be required to share the risk by putting their own money into the projects.

Housing Leadership

By a unanimous 100-0 vote on Feb. 2, 1989, the Senate confirmed President Bush's choice of Jack F. Kemp to head the Department of Housing and Urban Development. A well-known conservative, Kemp served nine terms in the House as a GOP representative from New York. *(Background, Cabinet profiles, p. 1173)*

However, after Flake met with Schumer on June 6 and extracted promises from Schumer that the program would be modified, he dropped his opposition and the bill was back on track. According to the agreement reached, the program would require that either 40 percent of a building's tenants would be low-income or 20 percent would be lower-income. In addition, developers would have to put equity into the projects so that the government's loan would not effectively subsidize construction of units going to middle- or upper-income people.

In the meantime, GOP lawmakers and the administration continued to strongly oppose Schumer's program, saying developer subsidies for construction of low-income housing never worked in the past and would only lead to influence peddling and scandals. With Republicans threatening to kill Schumer's plan in the full committee markup, Democrats mobilized to retaliate against the administration's HOPE provisions. But when the committee finally convened June 12, Republican Ridge quietly agreed not to put up a fight. Democrats then promised to leave HOPE alone, and Gonzalez said he would seek an open rule governing the floor debate to give Ridge a chance to offer his amendment there.

The subcommittee also had rejected, 16-23, a Steve Bartlett, R-Texas, amendment to allow people who bought homes through the bill's proposed Community Housing Partnership program to reap a profit if they sold the home after five years. The partnership program, proposed by Joseph P. Kennedy II, D-Mass., was similar to the Senate's proposed HOP program, but smaller grants would be provided to cities, states and non-profit groups to rehabilitate, construct and acquire low- and moderate-income housing. Grants also could be used to buy and manage rental-housing projects, as well as to help families buy their own homes.

Poor people should not have to bear the risks of home ownership without being able to earn the rewards, Bartlett said. But Kennedy responded that sellers could receive the price they paid, plus an adjustment for inflation and improvements to the home. Kennedy said that if the homes were sold at the market rate, they would be lost from the stock of affordable housing for low-income families.

During full committee action, Bartlett proposed an amendment to allow families to retain any increase in value minus the public subsidy after the fifth year of ownership. By the 10th year, the family would keep all the equity in the home. Kennedy offered a substitute amendment that would allow a family to keep 5 percent of the profits for each year the family lived in the home until the 10th year. From then on, the family could keep 50 percent of the profits. The committee adopted the Kennedy amendment 27-20 on a party-line vote.

Contentious debate in subcommittee and committee also surrounded language offered by John Hiler, R-Ind., to relax the National Manufactured Housing Construction and Safety Standards Act of 1974 and give the HUD secretary discretion to set standards for such homes. Gonzalez called the plan "an open invitation for irresponsible manufacturers to turn out sleazy, unsafe products, forcing legitimate companies to the sidelines and placing thousands of homeowners at great risk." Gonzalez objected to removing from the law's statement of purpose the "reduction of deaths and injuries." He also said HUD's power to test homes for safety defects would be sharply curtailed by Hiler's amendment.

Gonzalez repeatedly tried to beat back Hiler's amendment by urging hearings on the subject, but six subcommittee Democrats defected and the amendment was adopted, 24-20.

A replay of the controversy in full committee was averted when a compromise bipartisan leadership amendment was drawn up and accepted. It retained the language that Hiler wanted to strike from existing law and stated that manufactured home standards should meet the highest standards of quality, safety and affordability. Manufacturers would notify purchasers of all serious defects and would correct them for the life of the home.

The committee also adopted, 29-19, a Bartlett amendment to lift the moratorium on mortgage prepayments by landlords with federally subsidized mortgages, while providing incentives to building owners to continue renting to low-income families for the full 40 years of their mortgages instead of paying off the loans at the 20-year mark. And an effort to kill a new provision to authorize $150 million in housing assistance for people with AIDS (acquired immune deficiency syndrome) was thwarted, 17-31.

Senate Floor Action

Senators had begun action on the bill June 18, while staff members for the two prime sponsors, Cranston and D'Amato, started negotiating with administration officials.

The administration said that the bill put too much emphasis on building rental housing, did not target the very poor, did not include the administration's plan to bring the FHA back to financial health and cost too much. In addition, Kemp strenuously objected that his HOPE program, which would help public housing tenants and other low-income people to buy homes, was not fully funded.

After about a week of veto threats and uncertainty, the principals got back together and ironed out the last wrinkles. The Senate passed S 566 on a 96-1 vote June 27. Kemp got almost everything he wanted.

The Senate bill would authorize about $25 billion in spending in fiscal 1991 to add 213,844 subsidized housing units to the market. The bill's goals were to provide housing for the elderly and disabled, to help low-income tenants buy their public housing units, to preserve older subsidized housing projects threatened by condominium conversion and to provide shelter and services to the homeless.

An administration proposal to shore up the FHA Mutual Mortgage Insurance Fund was accepted, calling for higher premiums, two-thirds of closing costs to be paid with the down payment and increased capital requirements for the insurance fund. In addition, the FHA would continue to insure homes up to $124,875, the existing mortgage limit in high-priced areas of the country.

During floor action June 21, the Senate voted 52-45 to table (kill) an amendment by Connie Mack, R-Fla., to refocus the HOP program to allow its funds to be used for rental assistance for a community's poorest residents. Helping tenants pay their rent does nothing to increase affordable housing, the program's intention, Democrats argued.

The administration, however, strongly opposed new construction programs and feared that HOP money would be used primarily for that purpose. And in his compromise with Senate sponsors, Kemp succeeded in curtailing construction under HOP. The agreement would impose criteria for communities to meet to qualify to build housing. HUD would allow new construction if an area had a low vacancy rate, a low turnover of units renting below the existing fair market rent levels and a high ratio of substandard housing. HUD would be required to approve at least

30 percent of all localities in the HOP program for construction.

Before the funds could be used for construction, however, state and local governments also would have to show that a severe shortage existed of buildings that could be renovated and used as rental housing.

The criteria would not have to be met if the construction was intended for large families, people with disabilities, single-room occupancy units or other special housing needs. Also excluded from the restrictions would be neighborhood revitalization efforts.

Despite their protests against the Mack amendment, Democrats agreed to let local governments spend HOP funds on rental assistance. But they included restrictions of their own — for example, requiring local governments to certify that rental assistance was an essential element of their overall housing strategy.

Democrats also gave in to Kemp's insistence that rental and home-ownership programs target very-low-income people. Democrats had wanted to primarily help a mix of moderate-, low- and very-low-income families. Under the agreement, 90 percent of the rental units were to be aimed at very-low-income families and 10 percent allotted for low-income households. For home-ownership programs, the agreement called for 100 percent of the home-ownership programs to be targeted to low-income families.

Negotiators also agreed to provide full authorization for Kemp's brainchild, the HOPE program, at $240 million in fiscal 1991, $650 million in fiscal 1992 and $1 billion in fiscal 1993. The bill originally called for $435 million in authorizations over three years.

Although the administration and lawmakers on both sides of the aisle had glowing words for the compromise, Senate floor proceedings were not without histrionics. Phil Gramm, R-Texas, filibustered for more than four hours on the day S 566 would pass. He offered an amendment to allocate the $3 billion in block grant funds to states by population instead of through the existing formula, which weighted age of the housing, population, poverty and housing overcrowding. The result would be that 36 states, including Texas, would receive more money and 14 states would receive less.

Gramm complained that the existing formula used was designed to favor the Northeast. By concentrating funds to areas with older housing, Gramm argued, the formula ignored areas such as Texas that had inadequate new housing. D'Amato countered that Gramm was thinking solely of parochial interests and that taxpayers in the Northeast were bearing the cost of the savings and loan bailout even though thrift collapses were concentrated in Texas. D'Amato then offered a second-degree amendment to cap the amount of block grant funds a state could receive if that state also received more than a per-capita proportion of savings and loan bailout funds.

The Gramm amendment was killed, 65-35. But, before final passage of S 566, the Senate agreed to instruct HUD to study the formula used to distribute block grant funds.

House Floor Action

The House passed its version of the housing legislation (HR 1180), 378-43, on Aug. 1. The House then passed S 566 by voice vote, after substituting the text of HR 1180. With many contentious issues worked out in advance, the legislation moved swiftly despite an open rule lifting customary restrictions on amendments to complex bills.

Before the measure reached the floor, the Office of Management and Budget (OMB) weighed in with a veto threat contained in a five-page, single-spaced statement spelling out its objections. The OMB statement protested that both the rental production program and the Community Housing Partnership program would "encourage costly, developer-driven new construction in lieu of more efficient tenant-based housing assistance." Banking Chairman Gonzalez said the complaints were nothing new.

Despite the intention of each chamber to craft effective measures to prevent homelessness and expand the supply of affordable housing, both bills faced budget cuts. Chalmers P. Wylie of Ohio, ranking Republican on the Banking Committee, insisted that members of the House recognize that fact by offering an amendment to require the legislation to conform to the House budget resolution. The amendment was agreed to by voice vote after no discussion. William E. Dannemeyer, R-Calif., proposed a more stringent amendment to limit the increase in housing authorizations to 4.8 percent of the fiscal 1990 level. The amendment was rejected 62-354 on Aug. 1.

One controversial item, to create the first housing entitlement program ever, survived House floor action but faced a battle over its cost in conference. Schumer had inserted language to require HUD to provide rental aid to families when their lack of adequate housing caused their children to be placed in foster care. The Congressional Budget Office estimated that the program would require more than $1 billion in budget authority over the following five years.

The administration opposed the entitlement, saying that it would put pressure on local welfare agencies to certify that a family was about to be broken up to get housing assistance for the family. Republicans, not wanting to be seen voting against children just before an election, never mentioned it on the floor.

The most ballyhooed debate on the housing bill was not over providing shelter for those who needed it most, but over how to protect the solvency of the FHA fund used to help middle-income families buy homes. After the Senate had voted to shore up the agency's Mutual Mortgage Insurance Fund by tightening lending conditions, interest groups — including state housing finance agencies, housing industry groups and activist organizations — teamed to back a plan developed by Republican Ridge and Democrat Bruce F. Vento, Minn., that would avoid increased upfront costs for home buyers but charge an annual 0.6 percent premium over the life of the 30-year loan.

The administration opposed the plan, saying that it was not strong enough to revive the fund. Kemp said Bush would veto any legislation that did not include his plan to fix the insurance fund. But Kemp found few allies on the Hill, even among Republicans. Vento-Ridge was adopted by an overwhelming 418-2 vote on July 31.

The House also adopted, 400-12 on July 31, a Democratic-sponsored refinement to the federally subsidized mortgage program containing additional incentives and requirements to persuade owners to continue renting to low-income tenants.

Conference Action

After nearly three weeks of painstaking negotiations to complete the housing bill, Congress Oct. 15 reached an agreement that had something for everyone.

The administration had continued to oppose new construction programs included in both the House- and Senate-passed versions of S 566. While conferring with HUD and OMB officials, the senators backed down, agreeing that block grant money also could be used for rental assistance, duplicating the Section 8 rent subsidy program. Senators also accepted limits on the number of communities that could use the money for construction, and they agreed to structure federal matching funds to make it more expensive for a community to build housing instead of providing rent subsidies.

The House, however, was not so easily swayed. Conferees insisted on retaining public housing construction as well as Schumer's rental construction program. The administration opposed both.

To gain concessions on the Schumer program, the administration held public housing hostage. Backed by Senate Republicans, the administration insisted on killing construction of public housing. The House was unable to roll over the GOP objections because with Democrat Dodd's support, Republican senators had a majority on the issue. For Gonzalez, who had lived and worked in public housing in San Antonio in the 1950s, the program was a must. Senate Democrats had promised public housing advocates that the program would be restored in conference, after they had killed the program to gain votes in the Banking Committee and on the floor.

Public housing advocates were puzzled by Dodd's refusal to discuss his reasons for opposing the program. But Gonzalez said Dodd held out to extract a concession from the Banking chairman on an unrelated matter. Dodd wanted Banking conferees on the Export Administration Act (HR 4653) to support his provision requiring the Export-Import Bank to finance defense sales to NATO and Japan. This would enable Sikorsky helicopters, which were made in Connecticut, to be sold to Turkey, bringing in millions of dollars.

The Ex-Im Bank was not allowed to finance military sales for developing countries and its policy was not to finance them at all. Conferees were divided over that issue. Gonzalez refused to intervene.

Finally, Kemp told Gonzalez that he would free public housing if conferees agreed to limit Schumer's program. That left Dodd out in the cold.

Although Schumer had been negotiating with Cranston all along to combine his program with the Senate's block grant, the administration's action forced some last-minute tinkering. Schumer intended for the program to be run by HUD with exact guidelines on financing loans for developers and non-profit groups. Instead, his program was added to the Senate's block grant, with construction funds making up 10 percent of the total the first year and 15 percent the second year.

Under the bill, communities would have to show HUD that they had low vacancy rates before they could qualify to build. Then they could use the construction money as loans or grants, depending on their preference. Finally, if a community kept its construction money for two years without using it, the money could then be used for other housing activities.

A conference report (H Rept 101-922) was filed in the House Oct. 22. A recommitted conference report (H Rept 101-943) was filed Oct. 25, and the House adopted it by voice vote the same day. The Senate acted, 93-6, Oct. 27, clearing S 566. President Bush signed the bill (PL 101-625) on Nov. 28.

Major Provisions

As enacted, the Cranston-Gonzalez National Affordable Housing Act (S 566 — PL 101-625):

HOME Investment Partnerships Act

• **Funds.** Authorized $1 billion in fiscal 1991 and $2.1 billion in fiscal 1992 for the HOME Investment Partnerships Act. The program would provide federal block grants to state and local governments, which would be responsible for matching the money and fulfilling local housing needs.

• **Eligible Uses.** Stipulated that funds could be used to provide incentives to develop and support affordable rental housing and home-ownership programs through the acquisition, construction and moderate or substantial rehabilitation of affordable housing. Eligible activities also included financing costs, relocation expenses of displaced people and rental assistance.

Jurisdictions would have to give preference to using their federal funds for the rehabilitation of substandard housing unless that was not the most cost-effective way to expand the affordable housing supply.

• **Neighborhood Revitalization.** Authorized jurisdictions to use federal funds for construction if they certified that construction was needed to help a neighborhood revitalization program that emphasized rehabilitation of substandard housing for rent or home ownership by low- and moderate-income families; housing would be built in a low- or moderate-income neighborhood; the number of units to be built did not exceed 20 percent of the total number of units in the neighborhood revitalization program; and the housing would be built by a community housing development organization or by a public agency.

• **Exemptions.** Eliminated the 20 percent cap on units to be built out of the total neighborhood revitalization program when the housing was located in a severely distressed area with large tracts of vacant land and abandoned buildings; the housing was to be in an area with an inadequate supply of existing housing that could economically be rehabilitated to meet the area's housing needs; or the construction was required to finish the neighborhood revitalization program.

• **Special Needs Housing.** Allowed jurisdictions to use funds for construction in certain cases without meeting the criteria for construction. For example, the money could be used to build affordable housing for large families, affordable housing for people with disabilities and single-room occupancy housing.

• **Tenant-Based Rental Assistance.** Authorized jurisdictions to use HOME block grant funds for rental assistance that was provided directly to the tenant to be used for the apartment or home of the tenant's choice under certain circumstances. For example, tenant-based rental assistance could be provided if it was an essential element of the jurisdiction's annual housing strategy to expand the supply of affordable housing. And, it could be used if given to people on waiting lists for Section 8 rental assistance.

• **Model Programs.** Required the secretary to develop a variety of model housing programs designed to address local market conditions and housing problems. Allowed participating jurisdictions discretion to adopt one or more model programs according to their own needs.

• **Income Targeting.** Required jurisdictions to invest federal HOME funds each fiscal year. For rental assistance and rental units, no less than 90 percent of the money invested would have to go to families whose incomes did not exceed 60 percent of the median family income for the area. The remainder of the money invested would have to benefit families that qualified as low-income.

For home-ownership assistance, 100 percent of the funds invested would have to benefit low-income families. All funds invested would have to be used for affordable housing.

• **Participation by State and Local Governments.** Required the secretary to designate a state or local government to be a participating jurisdiction when it complied with procedures set out by the secretary.

Required the secretary to deem a consortium of geographically contiguous units of local government as one local government if the consortium had the ability and authority to carry out the program.

• **Allocation of Resources.** Required the secretary to allocate 60 percent of federal funds to local governments and 40 percent to states. Required the secretary to reserve 1 percent of the total amount appropriated by Congress for Indian tribes.

Required the secretary to establish regulations for an allocation formula reflecting each jurisdiction's share of the total need among eligible jurisdictions for an increased supply of affordable housing for very-low- and low-income families. Required the secretary to apply the formula giving 20 percent weight to measuring states' needs and 80 percent weight to measuring the local governments' needs.

Required that the minimum state allocation be $3 million under the HOME Investment Partnerships program. If no unit of local government within a state received any funds under the program, the state's allocation would be increased by $500,000.

• **Home Investment Trust Funds.** Required the secretary to establish a trust fund for each jurisdiction participating in the HOME Investment Partnerships program. Jurisdictions that drew money from the trust funds would have to invest that money in affordable housing within 15 days. If the money was not used within two years of deposit in the trust fund, the secretary would have to reduce the line of credit and reallocate the money.

• **Matching Requirements.** Required each jurisdiction to contribute money to its affordable housing plans during each fiscal year. For rental assistance and housing rehabilitation, the jurisdiction would have to contribute 25 percent of the total amount of money drawn from its trust fund. For substantial rehabilitation, the state or local government would have to provide 33 percent of the total amount drawn from the trust fund. And for construction, the jurisdiction would have to provide 50 percent of the total amount coming from its trust fund.

Authorized the secretary to reduce the matching requirement if a jurisdiction demonstrated that it was necessary to carry out the program. The matching requirements could be reduced for no more than three years. The reduction could not exceed 75 percent the first year, 50 percent the second year and 25 percent the third year.

• **Private-Public Partnership.** Required each jurisdiction to make all reasonable efforts to involve the private sector, including non-profit and for-profit groups, in carrying out the housing strategy.

• **Tenant and Participant Protections.** Prohibited owners from ending the tenancy or refusing to renew the lease of a tenant in rental housing assisted under the HOME program except for serious or repeated violation of the terms of the lease or for violation of federal, state or local laws. Any termination of a lease would have to be preceded by 30 days' notice.

• **Community Housing Partnership.** Required jurisdictions to reserve no less than 15 percent of their HOME funds for investment in housing to be developed, sponsored or owned by community housing development organizations.

• **Specific Model Programs.** Required the secretary to include model programs for jurisdictions to follow under the HOME Investment Partnerships program.

• **Second Mortgage Assistance for First-Time Buyers.** Required the secretary to design a model program in which local governments provided loans, secured by second mortgages, with deferred payments of interest and principal to first-time home buyers.

The property secured by the second mortgage would have to be a single-family home and the buyer's principal residence. The principal obligation of the deferred payment loan secured by the second mortgage could not exceed 30 percent of the home's cost.

• **Equal Opportunity.** Required each jurisdiction in the HOME program to ensure that minorities, women and companies owned by minorities and women were included in the effort to provide affordable housing.

• **Termination of Existing Housing Programs.** Prohibited new grants or loans after Oct. 1, 1991, under the following programs: housing development action grants (HoDAG), which provided aid to developers to help reduce the cost of building low-income housing; rehabilitation loans, which provided low-interest loans to bring housing and commercial property to local housing code standards; rental rehabilitation, which provided grants to local governments for the rehabilitation of rental property; Nehemiah grants, which provided financing for the construction of single-family homes for moderate-income families; moderate rehabilitation, which provided Section 8 housing aid to finance the modernization of substandard housing; and urban homesteading, which allowed the federal government to transfer ownership of housing to local communities for resale to low-income people whose existing housing is substandard.

National Homeownership Trust

• **Establishment.** Authorized the establishment of a new program called the National Homeownership Trust, within HUD, providing financial aid to first-time home buyers. The trust would be governed by a board of directors, including the HUD and the Treasury secretaries.

• **Assistance for First-Time Home Buyers.** Required the trust to provide interest-rate subsidies and down payment assistance to first-time home buyers. The interest-rate subsidies would ensure that the rate paid by home buyers did not exceed 6 percent.

• **Maximum Mortgage Amount.** Required that the principal obligation of the mortgage not exceed $124,875.

• **Authorization.** Authorized appropriations of $250 million in fiscal 1991 and $521.5 million in fiscal 1992.

• **Termination.** Terminated the trust on Sept. 30, 1993.

FHA and Secondary Mortgage Market

• **Limitation on FHA Insurance Authority.** Required the HUD secretary to insure mortgages with a total principal amount of $76.8 billion in fiscal 1991 and $79.8 billion in fiscal 1992.

• **Increase in Mortgage Limit.** Removed the termination date of fiscal 1990 from the $124,875 FHA mortgage limit.

• **Mortgagor Equity.** Prevented homeowners from borrowing more than the value of their home when other fees were financed into the mortgage.

• **Mortgage Insurance Premiums.** Required the secretary to institute a new premium structure to shore up the financially shaky FHA insurance fund for single-family homes. The plan, which used a risk-based premium based on how much money a buyer put into the down payment, was designed to prevent people who were likely to default on loans from receiving them.

• **Mutual Mortgage Insurance Fund Distributions.** Required the secretary to consider the actuarial status of the fund in determining whether a surplus of funds existed to distribute to mortgagors.

• **Actuarial Soundness of Mutual Mortgage Insurance Fund.** Required the secretary to ensure that the fund attained a capital ratio of no less than 1.25 percent within 24 months after enactment. The capital ratio was the percentage of the amount of cash on hand out of the total amount of outstanding mortgages.

Required the secretary to ensure that the fund attained a capital ratio of no less than 2.0 percent within 10 years of the date of enactment and to ensure that the fund maintained that ratio at all times thereafter.

• **Home Equity Conversion Mortgage Insurance Demonstration.** Extended the termination date to Sept. 30, 1995, from Sept. 30, 1991. Limited the number of mortgages insured under the program to no more than 25,000.

• **Auction of Federally Insured Mortgages.** Required HUD to arrange for the sale of interests in mortgage loans through an auction instead of accepting the multi-family mortgages from the original holders and giving a 10-year market-rate bond.

• **Limitation on Secondary Residences.** Prohibited the secretary from insuring mortgages on second homes, except when a second home was necessary to avoid hardship. For example, seasonal employment in different areas might require a second home.

• **Neighborhood Accountability.** Prohibited banks that provided FHA mortgages from varying mortgage interest rates, the level of discount points, loan origination fees or any other amount charged based on the neighborhood and the loan amount.

• **Property Disposition.** Authorized groups that assisted the homeless to obtain HUD-held property for use under a $1 lease program without a 30-day waiting period.

• **GNMA Guarantees of Mortgage-Backed Securities.** Authorized the Government National Mortgage Association (Ginnie Mae) to guarantee securities issued by private lenders of $85 billion in fiscal 1991 and $88.3 billion in fiscal 1992. GNMA sells securities backed by mortgages insured by the FHA and the Department of Veterans Affairs.

• **Property Improvement Insurance.** Increased the maximum loan available from $17,500 to $25,000 for single-family homes and from $43,750 to $60,000 for multi-family buildings.

HOPE

• **Home Ownership of Public and Indian Housing.** Authorized $68 million in fiscal 1991 and $380 million in fiscal 1992 to be appropriated.

• **Planning Grants.** Authorized the HUD secretary to award planning grants of up to $200,000 to applicants to develop home-ownership programs for public and Indian housing. Applicants could include public housing authorities, cooperative associations, and public or private non-profit groups.

• **Implementation Grants.** Authorized the secretary to award grants to carry out the public and Indian housing ownership program.

Required grant recipients to match 25 percent of the federal funds with money from non-federal sources.

• **Affordability.** Required that home-ownership programs provide sale prices that did not force eligible families to spend more than 30 percent of their income to complete the sale.

• **Home-Ownership Plans.** Required that home-ownership programs include a plan to identify and pick eligible families to participate.

• **Home Ownership of Multi-Family Units.** Authorized the secretary to make planning grants and grants to carry out home-ownership programs for multi-family housing, such as buildings owned or insured by HUD, the Department of Agriculture, the Resolution Trust Corporation (RTC) or a state or local government. Authorized $51 million in fiscal 1991 and $280 million in fiscal 1992 to be appropriated.

• **Home Ownership of Single-Family Homes.** Authorized the secretary to make planning grants and grants to carry out home-ownership programs for single-family homes, such as those owned or held by HUD, Veterans Affairs, Agriculture, RTC, state or local governments and public housing authorities. Authorized $36 million in fiscal 1991 and $195 million in fiscal 1992 to be appropriated.

Public and Indian Housing

• **Public Housing Preferences.** Reduced from 90 percent to 70 percent the amount of public housing that was set aside specifically for "preference" families. Preference families were those that lived in substandard housing, including families that were homeless, that paid more than 50 percent of their monthly income for rent or that were involuntarily displaced from their homes.

• **Public Housing Management Reforms.** Required the HUD secretary to develop and publish indicators to assess the management performance of public housing agencies. Indicators should include the number and percentage of vacancies and the percentage of rents uncollected.

Required the secretary to designate troubled public housing agencies by their failure to perform according to the indicators.

• **Eviction Procedures.** Authorized the public housing agency to establish an expedited grievance procedure concerning an eviction that involved any criminal activity threatening the health, safety or right to peaceful enjoyment of the premises by other tenants.

• **Public Housing Operating Subsidies.** Authorized $2 billion in fiscal 1991 and $2.1 billion in fiscal 1992.

• **Utility Subsidy.** Required the secretary, in determining how much money to give public housing agencies for utility subsidies, to consider extremely hot and extremely cold weather conditions. Under existing law, the secretary considered only extremely cold weather.

• **Modernization.** Required the secretary, in fiscal 1992, to reserve no more than $75 million for modernization needs resulting from natural and other disasters. The money provided for emergencies would be repaid by agencies from future funds.

• **Vacancy Reduction.** Required any public housing agency that had a vacancy rate that twice exceeded the average rate among all agencies or that was designated as a troubled agency to participate in a vacancy-reduction program.

Authorized $105 million in fiscal 1991 and $220 million in fiscal 1992 to be appropriated from modernization funds for large public housing agencies.

• **Income Eligibility.** Authorized public housing agencies to raise from 5 percent to 15 percent the number of units that could be leased to low-income families, not including very-low-income families. The number of low-income families in any project was limited to 25 percent, except for projects that exceeded the limit before enactment.

• **Resident Management.** Authorized up to $5 million out of modernization funds in fiscal 1991 and 1992 to be used for public housing resident management programs.

• **Family Investment Centers.** Provided families living in public housing with better access to educational and employment opportunities to help them become independent. Developed facilities in or near public housing for training and support services such as child care, job training, literacy training and computer training. Authorized the secretary to make grants to public housing agencies to provide family investment centers in or near public housing. Authorized $25 million in fiscal 1991 and $26.1 million in fiscal 1992 to be appropriated.

• **Early Childhood Development Grants.** Authorized $15 million in fiscal 1991 and $15.7 million in fiscal 1992 to be appropriated. Changed the name of "child care services" program to "early childhood development services."

Authorized a set-aside from Indian housing development funds for an Indian public housing early childhood development demonstration program. Authorized $5 million in fiscal 1991 and $5.2 million in fiscal 1992.

• **Rent Waiver for Police.** Authorized the secretary to permit public housing agencies to allow police officers and other security officers to live in public housing units even if they were not otherwise eligible for public housing. Housing agencies could set special rents for the officers.

• **One-Stop Perinatal Services Demonstration.** Required the secretary, in consultation with the secretary of health and human services, to provide grants to public housing agencies so that they could provide space for a one-stop services program for pregnant women living in public housing. Required the secretary to make no more than 10 grants to 10 public housing agencies. Grants could not exceed $15,000 for any one housing project.

Low-Income Rental Assistance

• **Drug-Related Rent Adjustments.** Authorized HUD to approve rent increases of no more than 20 percent in communities in which drug-related criminal activity was prevalent and had caused the housing project's operating expenses to rise.

• **Tenant Rent Contributions.** Authorized families receiving tenant-based rental assistance to pay more than 30 percent of their monthly income toward rent if the family notified its public housing agency and the agency determined that the rent was reasonable and that the family could handle it.

• **Preference Rules.** Required that 70 percent of project-based rental assistance for families go to people living in substandard housing, paying more than 50 percent of their monthly income toward rent or who were involuntarily displaced from their homes.

Required that 90 percent of the rental assistance to families that was not tied to a specific housing project go to people living in substandard housing, paying more than 50 percent of their monthly income toward rent or who were involuntarily displaced from their homes. Required that the remaining spots for housing assistance during any one-year period go to families that qualified under a system of local preferences, determined by local need.

• **Tenant Protections.** Authorized project-based rental assistance to be terminated in response to any criminal activity that threatened the health, safety or right of peaceful enjoyment of the premises by other tenants or any drug-related criminal activity on or near the premises by any tenant or guest of any tenant.

• **Manufactured Home Rentals.** Authorized rental vouchers to be used for people who rented mobile homes.

• **Assistance to Avoid Foster Care.** Authorized an increase in Section 8 rental assistance by $35 million in fiscal 1991 and fiscal 1992 to aid families that were eligible for rental assistance and were on the verge of losing their children to foster care because of inadequate housing.

• **Family Self-Sufficiency.** Authorized a new program to coordinate the use of public housing and rental assistance with other public and private resources to promote economic independence.

Supportive services in the program could include child care, transportation to receive services, remedial education, education to complete high school, job training, drug and alcohol abuse treatment and counseling, parenting training, money-management training and any other services to help families achieve self-sufficiency.

Required the head of any participating family to seek employment during the program.

Prohibited rent increases for any family participating in the program if the family's income increased, unless the income exceeded 50 percent of the area median income. Families with incomes between 50 percent and 80 percent of median income would have rents raised as incomes increased so that families paid 30 percent of their income toward rent.

Authorized $25 million out of the public housing operating subsidies to be used for administrative costs incurred by the family self-sufficiency program.

• **Income Eligibility.** Required that any new housing or housing that had been substantially rehabilitated be reserved for low- and very-low-income families.

• **Low-Income Housing.** Authorized an additional $16.2 billion in fiscal 1991 and $14.7 billion in fiscal 1992 for assisted housing programs. In fiscal 1991 that included $742.1 million for public housing grants, of which no more than $228 million could be spent for Indian housing; $1.88 billion for Section 8 rental vouchers and certificates; $1.2 billion for Section 8 rental assistance for tenants in Section 202 housing for the elderly and disabled; $2.15 billion for public housing modernization, of which no more than $3 million may be used for resident home-ownership financial assistance; $420 million for Section 8 property disposition; $160 million for Section 8 loan management; $7.7 billion to extend expiring Section 8 rental assistance contracts; $1.6

billion to shore up existing Section 8 rental assistance contracts that had run out of money; $207 million for public housing lease adjustments; and $79 million for public housing replacement activities.

• Family. Amended the definition of family to include single people but did not entitle them to housing with two bedrooms or more.

• Adjusted Income. Amended the definition of adjusted income by increasing the allowance for each dependent from $450 to $550 and allowing medical expense deductions for non-elderly people. This change would go into effect if included in future appropriations measures.

• Housing Counseling. Authorized $3.6 million in fiscal 1991 and $3.7 million in fiscal 1992 for housing counseling services. Authorized $6.7 million in fiscal 1991 and $7 million in fiscal 1992 for emergency home ownership counseling, including $2 million each year to set up a toll-free telephone number for information on counseling agencies. Authorized $350,000 in fiscal 1991 and $365,000 in fiscal 1992 to be spent on a foreclosure-prevention demonstration counseling program to reduce defaults and foreclosures on FHA-insured single-family loans.

• Flexible Subsidy Fund. Authorized $50 million in fiscal 1991 and $52.2 million in fiscal 1992 to be spent on the flexible subsidy fund, which was used to make capital improvements to multi-family housing to prevent prepayments of federally subsidized mortgages.

• Public Housing Drug-Elimination Grants. Authorized the secretary to make grants to public housing authorities to help eliminate drug-related crime. Grants could be used to hire security officers, reimburse local law enforcement agencies, make physical improvements to the property to enhance security and to hire people to investigate drug-related crime, among other things.

Authorized $160 million in fiscal 1991 and $166.9 million in fiscal 1992 to be spent on drug-elimination grants.

Preservation of Affordable Rental Housing

• Prepayment of Mortgages. Under the terms of federally subsidized mortgages signed with private building owners in the late 1960s and early 1970s, owners were to be allowed to pay off their loans after 20 years and do whatever they wished with their property. About 350,000 low-income households would have been at risk of eviction because of the resulting increased rents when a congressionally imposed moratorium on prepayments was set to expire in the fall of 1990.

New provisions, called the Low-Income Housing Preservation and Resident Home Ownership Act of 1990, provided owners with incentives to continue renting to low-income tenants for the remaining useful life of the property or with fair-market value to owners who wished to sell their property to others who would continue to rent to low-income families. If no one were willing or able to purchase the property, the owner would be allowed to prepay the mortgage.

• Safeguards. Offered six protections to tenants if an owner was able to prepay the mortgage: (1) Provided Section 8 rental certificates or vouchers to tenants with incomes below 80 percent of the area median income. (2) Required owners who prepaid to continue renting to existing tenants at the existing rent for three years. This applied to housing located in low-vacancy areas. (3) Required owners in all areas who prepaid to continue renting to tenants with special needs, such as the elderly and people with disabilities, for three years. (4) Required owners to pay 50 percent of moving expenses to displaced tenants. State or local laws would apply if they required a higher level of assistance to tenants. (5) Required owners who prepaid but continued renting to accept tenants with rental certificates or vouchers. (6) Required HUD to set aside from appropriations for preservation the amount of money necessary to help tenants displaced from prepaid projects.

• Resident Home-Ownership Program. Required tenants who wished to purchase eligible low-income housing to organize a resident council to develop a resident home-ownership program. Required the resident council to work with a public or private non-profit organization to develop the ability to own and manage the housing.

• Pre-Emption of State and Local Laws. Required that no state or local government could establish, continue or enforce any law that restricted the prepayment of any mortgage on eligible low-income housing, restricted owners from receiving the authorized 8 percent annual return and was not consistent with federal law.

The pre-emption of state and local laws would not apply to building standards, zoning limitations, health or safety standards, rent control or conversion of rental housing to condominiums or cooperatives.

• Funding. Authorized $425 million in fiscal 1991 and $858 million in fiscal 1992, including $100 million in each year for grants in mandatory sales of housing.

Rural Housing

• Funds. Authorized the Farmers Home Administration (FmHA) to insure and guarantee loans during fiscal 1991 and 1992 not to exceed a total of $2.1 billion and $2.2 billion, respectively. That included $1.4 billion in fiscal 1991 and $1.5 billion in fiscal 1992 for the Section 502 single-family loan program; $11.9 million in fiscal 1991 and $12.4 million in fiscal 1992 for Section 504 home repair loans; $12 million in fiscal 1991 and $12.5 million in fiscal 1992 for Section 514 loans to provide housing for farm laborers; $709 million in fiscal 1991 and $739.5 million in fiscal 1992 for Section 515 loans to finance rural rental housing projects; $800,000 in fiscal 1991 and $800,000 in fiscal 1992 for Section 523 self-help loans; $800,000 in fiscal 1991 and $850,000 in fiscal 1992 for Section 524 site loans.

Authorized $1 million in fiscal 1991 and $1.1 million in fiscal 1992 to supplement Section 502 loans in remote rural areas; $20.2 million in fiscal 1991 and $21.1 million in fiscal 1992 in Section 504 home repairs; $550,000 in fiscal 1991 and $600,000 in fiscal 1992 for construction defects; $5 million in fiscal 1991 and $5.3 million in fiscal 1992 for assistance in preparing applications for housing loans in underserved areas; $20.9 million in fiscal 1991 and $21.7 million in fiscal 1992 for Section 516 farm labor housing; $10 million in fiscal 1991 and $10.5 million in fiscal 1992 for Section 516 assistance for rural housing and migrant workers; $13.4 million in fiscal 1991 and $13.9 million in fiscal 1992 for self-help housing; and $29.6 million in fiscal 1991 and $30.8 million in fiscal 1992 for Section 533 housing preservation.

Authorized $397 million in fiscal 1991 and $414.1 million in fiscal 1992 for rural assistance contracts.

Authorized $5.2 million in fiscal 1991 and $5.5 million in fiscal 1992 for supplemental contracts.

• Deferred Mortgage Demonstration. Authorized the agriculture secretary to defer mortgage payments on single-family Section 502 loans. This loan program was the largest housing program operated by the FmHA. It consisted of subsidized and unsubsidized direct loans and unsubsidized guaranteed loans to finance the construction or acquisition of a new or existing home. Up to 25 percent of Section 502 mortgage payments could be deferred at 1 percent interest for very-low-income families or people otherwise unable to afford the regular payment.

Required the secretary to set aside 3.5 percent of the department's appropriations from fiscal 1991 and 5 percent in fiscal 1992 from five of its rural housing programs to be targeted to the designated areas.

In addition to the designated areas, set-aside funds could be used in "colonias," areas within 150 miles of the Mexican border in Arizona, California, New Mexico or Texas that lacked adequate housing, water and sewerage systems.

• **Rural Homeless and Migrant Farm Workers.** Authorized $10 million in fiscal 1991 to provide assistance to groups providing affordable rental housing for migrant farm workers.

Housing for People with Special Needs

• **Supportive Housing for the Elderly.** Changed the Section 202 housing program for the elderly and disabled by creating two separate programs, one for the elderly and one for the disabled. Instead of providing direct loans to build housing, HUD would provide capital advances and rental assistance to build housing for the elderly.

The housing for the elderly would be combined with services to enable the tenants to continue to live independently. Services included meals, housekeeping, transportation, personal care and health services.

Required that all units built with funds from the program be available to very-low-income people for at least 40 years.

Authorized the revised Section 202 program to go into effect in fiscal 1992. Authorized $659 million for capital advances and $363 million for rental assistance in fiscal 1992. Required 20 percent of funds to be allocated to nonmetropolitan areas. Authorized $714.2 million in loans for the existing Section 202 program in fiscal 1991.

• **Congregate Housing Services.** Authorized HUD and the FmHA to administer a revised congregate housing services program providing meals and other services to residents of federally assisted housing. Residents would have to be elderly or disabled. To better accommodate the physical needs of residents, the program would also adapt housing, such as installing grab bars in bathrooms.

Authorized $25 million in fiscal 1991 and $26.1 million in fiscal 1992. Required HUD and the FmHA to split the cost proportionately according to the number of units participating in the program under their jurisdiction.

• **HOPE for Elderly Independence.** Authorized a five-year demonstration program to combine rental certificates and vouchers with supportive services for frail elderly people. The purpose was to enable elderly people to continue to live independently.

Authorized $34 million in fiscal 1991 and $35.5 million in fiscal 1992 for Section 8 rental assistance. Authorized $10 million in fiscal 1991 and $10.4 million in fiscal 1992 for supportive services.

• **ECHO Units.** Authorized a demonstration program expanding the definition of housing in the Section 202 elderly housing program to include elder cottage housing opportunity (ECHO) units. ECHO units were designed to be installed next to existing homes and were typically used for elderly parents.

• **Supportive Housing for People with Disabilities.** Authorized HUD to provide capital advances and project rental assistance to private non-profit groups to finance, acquire, build and rehabilitate buildings for people with disabilities and to provide supportive services to enable them to live independently. Also authorized funds to be used to acquire properties from the RTC.

The program would become effective in fiscal 1992.

Authorized $271 million for capital advances in fiscal 1992 and $246 million for rental assistance in fiscal 1992.

• **Supportive Housing for the Homeless.** Revised the Stewart B. McKinney Homeless Assistance Act (PL 100-77) to combine existing McKinney Act emergency shelter grants program, supportive housing demonstration program and permanent housing for the homeless disabled program. Other existing programs would be considered eligible activities.

• **Funds.** Authorized for fiscal years 1991 and 1992, respectively, $125 million and $138 million for the Emergency Shelter Grants program; $125 million and $150 million for the Supportive Housing Demonstration Program; $30 million and $30 million for the Supplemental Assistance for Facilities to Assist the Homeless (SAFAH) program; $79 million and $82.4 million for the Section 8 Moderate Rehabilitation for Single Room Occupancy (SRO) Dwelling Program; $80.4 million and $167.2 million for the Shelter Plus Care Rental Housing Assistance Program; $24.8 million and $54.2 million for the Shelter Plus Care Single Room Occupancy Dwelling Program; and $18 million and $37.2 million for the Shelter Plus Care Section 202 Program.

• **Shelter Plus Care Program.** Authorized rental housing assistance to be used in conjunction with supportive services paid for by other sources for homeless people with disabilities. In particular, this program was aimed at people who were seriously mentally ill or had chronic problems with alcohol, drugs or both, or had AIDS.

• **Comprehensive Homeless Assistance Plan (CHAP).** Required state and local governments to report to HUD on how they were using their McKinney funds and what their strategy was to address homelessness.

• **Housing Opportunities for People with AIDS.** Required the secretary to make grants to state and local governments to meet the long-term housing needs of people with AIDS. Ninety percent of the funds appropriated were to be allocated on the basis of the incidence of AIDS, with 75 percent going to local governments with populations above 500,000 and more than 1,500 AIDS cases or to states with more than 1,500 AIDS cases. Twenty-five percent would go to local governments with populations over 500,000 and more than 1,500 AIDS cases that had a higher than average per capita incidence of AIDS.

• **Funds.** Authorized $75 million in fiscal 1991 and $156.5 million in fiscal 1992 for housing for people with AIDS.

Community Development, Miscellaneous

• **Funds.** Authorized $3.1 billion in fiscal 1991 and $3.3 billion in fiscal 1992 for Community Development Block Grants (CDBGs). Of those amounts, the HUD secretary was required to provide no less than $3 million in fiscal 1991 and 1992 in grants to institutions of higher education to provide assistance to economically disadvantaged and minority students who participated in community development work-study programs; no less than $6.5 million in fiscal 1991 and $6.5 million in fiscal 1992 in grants to historically black colleges; and no less than $7 million in fiscal 1991 and $7 million in fiscal 1992 for grants in Guam, the Virgin Islands, American Samoa, the Northern Mariana Islands and the Trust Territory of the Pacific Islands.

- **Targeting.** Changed the low- and moderate-income targeting requirement in the block grant program from 60 percent to 70 percent.
- **Urban Homesteading.** Authorized the HUD secretary to acquire single-family homes from the RTC for use in urban homesteading programs.
- **Neighborhood Reinvestment Corporation.** Authorized appropriations of $35 million in fiscal 1991 and $36.5 million in fiscal 1992.
- **Miscellaneous Programs.** Authorized $21.2 million in fiscal 1991 and $22.1 million in fiscal 1992 for HUD policy development and research. Up to $500,000 in fiscal 1991 was to be used for a demonstration project to test affordable housing technologies.

HUD Scandal

The biggest scandal to rock the federal government since the Iran-contra affair of 1986-87 came to light on Capitol Hill in 1989, as lawmakers began looking into charges of alleged influence peddling and political favoritism at the Reagan-era Department of Housing and Urban Development (HUD). In 1990, an independent counsel (special prosecutor) was appointed to investigate whether former HUD secretary Samuel R. Pierce Jr. and other HUD officials had conspired to defraud the United States or committed any other federal crimes during the Reagan administration.

As of mid-1993, the special prosecutor's investigation was ongoing. *(Related court action, box, p. 678)*

Congress in 1989 cleared legislation aimed at addressing the problems uncovered at HUD. *(Story, p. 685)*

Inspector General's Report

Congressional scrutiny of HUD was prompted by an April 26, 1989, report by the department's inspector general (IG), Paul A. Adams. It showed how favoritism in the so-called Section 8 Moderate Rehabilitation Program (mod-rehab) had helped former Reagan administration officials and other prominent Republicans make almost $4 million in consulting fees — a figure eventually upgraded to $6 million.

Designed to fix up privately owned substandard housing and make it available to the poor, the program guaranteed developers 15 years' worth of federal rent subsidies for renovating projects. Mod-rehab was one of the few programs that survived the Reagan-era shift away from construction subsidies aimed at increasing the supply of low-rent housing. Liberal Democrats and urban Republicans struggled to keep it alive as its annual appropriation was slashed from $1.6 billion in fiscal 1980 to $368.5 million in 1989.

Local public housing authorities were supposed to apply for funds from the program and then choose developers. However, the IG report said, many local officials were approached by developers who claimed money had been reserved specifically for them by HUD officials in Washington; all the local officials had to do was apply for the money and they would probably get it. In many cases, awards made by HUD for a specific number of apartments were suspiciously close to the number of apartments owned or controlled by the developers who ultimately got the awards. In addition, the report said, many developers paid well-connected consultants — including former interior secretary James G. Watt, five former HUD officials and several other prominent Republicans — more than $3.9 million for helping them get money from the program. Seventeen well-connected individuals benefited financially from about 55 HUD-subsidized projects, Adams testified. Ten states received 51 percent of all subsidy "units" funded by HUD.

Everyone mentioned in the report either declined to comment or denied wrongdoing upon its release. The IG report, meanwhile, stopped short of alleging criminal misconduct. Adams, who was not a lawyer, said, "The investigation points to nothing that would be a violation of a specific criminal statute." Nonetheless, he said he had forwarded his findings to the Department of Justice's Public Integrity Section and, when pressed, conceded that some crimes might have been committed, including perjury and fraud.

HUD Secretary Jack F. Kemp concluded that, during the Reagan administration, allocation of mod-rehab money "was based on the perception and reality of favoritism." He immediately put the whole program on hold pending further review and reform.

Pierce Testimony

By May, three separate HUD inquiries were under way in Congress — by the House Banking, Finance and Urban Affairs Committee; the Senate Banking, Housing and Urban Affairs Committee; and the House Government Operations Subcommittee on Employment and Housing. The Employment and Housing panel, chaired by Tom Lantos, D-Calif., emerged as the leader of the investigation.

The subcommittee began a heated interrogation of former HUD secretary Pierce on May 25. Responding to questions about the Section 8 program, Pierce denied wrongdoing and attempted to shift part of the blame to Congress and his former underlings. He described what happened to the program under his watch as "funny business." The entire scandal could have been prevented, he said, if members had listened to his repeated advice: "We should have terminated it." Members did not take kindly to his suggestion.

Pierce said he had virtually nothing to do with the program because he had delegated all responsibility for it to others at HUD, including Deborah Gore Dean, his top aide. In the May 25 *Wall Street Journal*, Dean was quoted as saying the program "was set up as a political program" and "run in a political manner."

Former assistant secretary Thomas T. Demery had testified that Pierce, acting through Dean, decided which projects to fund. "It was his decision," Demery said.

In answer, Pierce said, "She did not speak for me."

Christopher Shays, R-Conn., reminding Pierce several times that he was under oath, questioned him closely on this point.

Shays: "Did you ever ask Deborah Gore Dean to fund a particular project?"

Pierce: "Not that I can recall."

Shays: "You never said: 'This is a good project. I think we should fund that'?"

Pierce: "No, I don't believe so."

Pierce also said he did not recall talking about the program to the many prominent Republicans and former HUD officials who were either directly involved in projects subsidized under the program or were paid hefty consulting fees for helping to secure federal money for them. But he did acknowledge telling Watt that his project would get "careful consideration." Pierce denied that that meant it would get special treatment.

Pierce allowed HUD to ignore regulations governing the program's selection process because Congress had waived the provision of law upon which they were based. New regulations were never issued, he said. Pierce implicitly admitted that the department's selection decisions were project-specific. The program was supposed to allow local government officials to award projects competitively after receiving subsidies from headquarters, thereby insulating developers from HUD's Washington office. *(HUD rules, box, p. 682)*

In prepared testimony, Pierce spoke of "the selection of particular projects" by a panel of his staff. Four other times, he said "projects" were selected for funding, not local governments. Questioned on this point, Pierce appeared unaware of its significance.

In the course of the hearing, Pierce said he was "sorry" about the problems at HUD. "Perhaps we should have watched the program better than we did," he said.

In comments to reporters after the hearing, Pierce made several additional observations. He said he felt betrayed by Dean. He hinted that he thought she and others on his staff used the program for political purposes. He said there was "some lying going on," but he did not elaborate. Asked if he agreed there had been influence peddling, he replied: "To some degree, there must have been." Asked why he allowed that to happen, he backed off: "Maybe I better take that back. I retract the statement."

Watt Testimony

Former secretary Watt testified June 9 before the Employment and Housing Subcommittee that the lobbying he did for more than $420,000 worth of consulting fees was "legal, moral, ethical and effective." Watt said he spoke to Pierce and contacted other high-ranking HUD officials to make sure his clients' projects were considered. At least three times, his contacts paid off, he said. Watt also said, however, that "the system is flawed" because it resulted in big fees being paid to well-connected consultants, including himself.

Watt's involvement in the program was surprising to many in Congress because, as secretary of the interior (1981-83), he frequently railed against government-subsidy programs. Lantos said, "While in government, Mr. Watt often belittled federal programs to assist the poor and less fortunate. He spoke of the dangers of being and I'm quoting here 'lured by the crumbs of subsidies, entitlements and giveaways.' One would have thought that when Mr. Watt left the government, he would have devoted all his efforts to the private sector, but he apparently decided to take advantage of the 'crumbs of subsidies, entitlements and giveaways.' " Watt said he still agreed with the words Lantos quoted. He added, "If our desire — which it was — was to create housing, we had to work within the system that exists."

Watt also angered members by insisting that none of his fees were paid from government funds. "We totally disagree with your point," Lantos said.

Questioned by Barney Frank, D-Mass., Watt conceded that fees like those paid to him would increase the long-run cost of government housing programs. Frank's logic went like this: The more developers paid in fees to get government subsidies, the less profit they made. That, as a result, would increase the cost to government to get people to participate in the program.

Watt repeatedly resisted efforts by members to make him admit that he was involved in "influence peddling," calling it a "partisan" term. Pressed by Ted Weiss, D-N.Y., he said, "If I were a Democrat, I would say that Jim Watt engaged in influence peddling."

Members spent much effort trying to nail down exactly how much Watt was paid for consulting work between 1984 and 1986. The IG report identified only one $300,000 fee, of which Watt gave $131,000 to a consulting firm run by Joseph A. Strauss — a former assistant to Pierce — for "technical" assistance. (Watt admitted he was not a housing expert.) Under pressure, Watt told the committee he was paid fees of $100,000 and $20,000 for work on two additional projects. He testified that he was involved in other projects, but not so directly, and was paid for that work, too. He refused to say how much. Eventually, however, Watt said that, for the record, he would supply the information desired, asking that it be kept confidential.

Dean, DeBartolomeis Appearances

Deborah Gore Dean June 13 invoked her Fifth Amendment right against self-incrimination in refusing to testify before Congress. Dean said her lawyers still were trying to obtain HUD records that would enable her "to prepare adequately for testimony that would be complete and truthful." She refused to answer even the most basic of questions, such as when she began work at HUD. Lantos said he would urge Kemp to cooperate with her request for records.

Some members, however, questioned whether Dean was using the Fifth Amendment to delay Congress' investigation. "I see no reason why she should not be able to testify," Shays said. Schumer said some of her requests for documents appeared irrelevant to the issues at hand or too broad to be met. Lantos was more sympathetic: "It remains to be determined whether Ms. Dean was the powerbroker or is unfairly being made the scapegoat."

Silvio DeBartolomeis, former HUD general deputy assistant secretary and acting commissioner of housing, also appeared before the subcommittee June 13. Of the selection process, he testified, "I would have to say that there were political influences involved." He repeatedly declined to elaborate.

DeBartolomeis said he tried to ignore documents relating to the subsidy programs that landed on his desk. He said on a number of occasions he returned from trips to find that other staff, acting for him, had approved subsidy awards. He said he was mostly relieved that someone else had signed the documents, because while he believed that Dean and Pierce strongly backed the highly discretionary selection process, he wanted no part of it. He said he suspected that Dean took advantage of his absences to have other staff approve the documents.

DeBartolomeis said mod-rehab was the only HUD enterprise in which career staff did not review proposals and

Investigation into HUD Scandal...

As of mid-1993, a number of individuals had been ensnared in court action related to the unfolding investigation into wrongdoing at the Department of Housing and Urban Development (HUD) during the Reagan administration.

• Marilyn Louise Harrell, in a plea arrangement, admitted in federal court Jan. 29, 1990, to having embezzled at least \$4.5 million from HUD and to having knowingly under-reported her income. She was sentenced June 22 to a 46-month prison term and to pay \$600,000 in restitution.

Harrell had been dubbed "Robin HUD," after claiming that she gave much of the HUD money to the poor.

• Samuel P. Singletary, a friend of HUD Secretary Samuel R. Pierce Jr., was indicted Dec. 11, 1991, on tax evasion charges. Singletary allegedly received and failed to report large sums of money from the Center for Resource Development, a consulting group, which had gotten a \$350,000 HUD grant in 1985 with Singletary's aid.

On Feb. 20, 1992, Singletary pleaded guilty to one federal felony count of tax evasion, concerning his 1985 tax return. He also agreed to cooperate with the investigation into the HUD scandal. In exchange, charges related to Singletary's 1986 and 1987 tax returns were dropped, and the prosecution recommended that he not be fined or jailed.

As reported Aug. 21, Singletary was sentenced to five years' probation and 300 hours of community service.

• Lance H. Wilson, who had served as executive assistant to Pierce from 1981 to 1984, was indicted Jan. 14, 1992, on 24 counts of fraud, conspiracy and making false statements to HUD. After leaving HUD, Wilson went to PaineWebber, a brokerage firm, as a senior vice president. According to the indictment, he wrote letters in behalf of Leonard E. Briscoe Sr., a Texas developer, falsely stating that PaineWebber would provide financial support for projects under development by Briscoe. In turn, Briscoe allegedly used the letters to get \$8 million in HUD grants. Briscoe was named in the indictment, adding to charges filed against him June 12, 1991, for making false statements to obtain a HUD grant. DuBois R. Gilliam, who was a deputy assistant secretary at HUD, was named as an unindicted co-conspirator. With Wilson and Briscoe, Gilliam allegedly conspired to funnel grants to Briscoe. Gilliam had pleaded guilty to corruption concerning HUD contracts in 1989 and had served a four-month jail term.

Wilson, Briscoe and Nebraska lawyer Maurice Steier were found guilty Jan. 5, 1993, of giving gratuities to a federal official in connection with government contracts; they were acquitted of more serious charges of bribery, mail fraud and conspiracy.

• Victor R. Cruse, real estate developer and co-owner of CFM Development Corp., was indicted March 24, 1992, on perjury and obstruction of justice charges. After CFM was rejected for a bank loan to purchase a Georgia housing project, Cruse allegedly tried to have a federal grant for the project canceled. According to the indictment, an unidentified political consultant at Black, Manafort, Stone & Kelly of Washington, D.C., contacted HUD about

were not significantly involved in awarding subsidy contracts. He added that he did not know what criteria were used in the awards and that he assumed that Dean was operating at Pierce's direction. He said although he continually resisted signing any documents related to the programs, twice Dean ordered him to sign the papers.

New Developments

As the summer wore on, the scandal widened. "Like a case of poison ivy that gets worse when scratched, we've addressed one HUD scandal only to find that two have burgeoned in the meantime," said Rep. Charles E. Schumer, D-N.Y. Authorities uncovered evidence of widespread embezzlement by HUD contractors acting as closing agents in the sale of foreclosed homes. HUD's closing agents were supposed to collect money from home sales and quickly turn it over to the government.

IG Adams told Lantos' subcommittee June 16 that about a dozen HUD contractors were under investigation by the Justice Department for embezzling a total of up to \$20 million. One agent in Texas had been charged with stealing \$2.5 million, and Adams said another in Alabama had pleaded guilty to a crime related to the investigation.

Another closing agent, Marilyn Louise Harrell of Maryland, publicly admitted to stealing about \$5 million from HUD over the course of three-and-a-half years. In interviews with several news organizations and testimony before the House subcommittee, she said she spent the money helping the poor — a claim (which was not supported by the evidence) that won her the sobriquet "Robin HUD."

Although Adams' audits and reports had helped uncover the HUD scandal, lawmakers began criticizing the inspector general for not having been more aggressive. Adams, they said, failed to question some key HUD officials during his investigation; others, including Pierce and Dean, were questioned only briefly. Adams defended his investigation as "very thorough and comprehensive."

Mortgage Insurance Program

On June 29, Kemp said he planned to kill HUD's Title X Land Development Mortgage Insurance Program, because it was "riddled with abuse." Under the program, HUD

. . . Brought Court-Related Action

canceling the grant. Paul J. Manafort also was a co-owner of CFM.

- Deborah Gore Dean, who had been special assistant and then executive assistant to Pierce from 1982 to 1988, was indicted April 28, 1992, for unlawfully accepting $4,000 from a person who had applied for a Section 8 Moderate Rehabilitation Program grant. She also was charged with making a false statement to the Senate when she said in a 1987 written statement that she was not involved in any "potential conflicts of interest."

Dean was indicted July 7 on 13 charges of fraud, perjury and conspiracy to divert HUD funds from housing for the poor to developers who were politically favorable. The indictment included the charges made in April and superseded the earlier indictment. Former attorney general John Mitchell was named an unindicted co-conspirator; he died in 1988.

On July 13, Dean entered a plea of not guilty. If convicted, she could receive 67 years in jail and be fined $250,000.

- Thomas T. Demery, an assistant secretary of HUD from 1986 to 1989, was indicted June 9, 1992, on conspiracy and conflict-of-interest charges. Demery allegedly steered HUD housing subsidies to the PM Group Inc., a real estate management company in Michigan. Phillip McCafferty, a paid representative of the PM Group, in 1986 had bought Demery's Michigan real estate brokerage, according to the indictment, at an inflated price. Demery allegedly received payments from the sale while at HUD. McCafferty was named as a co-defendant in the indictment.

As reported Dec. 7, Demery was indicted on 19 felony counts including fraud, perjury and obstruction of justice. The new charges superseded his June 1992 indictment.

Demery pleaded guilty June 17, 1993, to felony charges of accepting bribes and obstructing justice. He could be sentenced to seven years in prison and charged with a $500,000 fine.

- Silvio J. DeBartolomeis, who was a deputy assistant director of HUD, pleaded guilty Oct. 16, 1992, to making false statements to Congress and regional HUD offices, accepting an illegal loan from a developer and participating in the creation of a false receipt that was offered to investigators as evidence. DeBartolomeis as part of a plea bargain, agreed to cooperate with the HUD investigation.
- Elaine Richardson, an aide to former senator Edward Brooke, R-Mass. (1967-79), pleaded guilty Nov. 20, 1992, to lying to a grand jury and to the FBI during an investigation into Brooke's possible involvement in the HUD scandal. After retiring from the Senate, Brooke became a lobbyist for housing developers; as of mid-1993, he had not been charged.

Richardson, indicted on nine counts Aug. 20, agreed to cooperate with the independent counsel.

On Jan. 3, 1993, she was sentenced to two years' probation and fined $500.

- Philip Winn, who had been an assistant housing secretary and U.S. ambassador to Switzerland, pleaded guilty Feb. 9, 1993, to one count of conspiracy. Winn had a financial interest in two housing projects; he tried to bribe two HUD officials who were involved with them. Winn was fined $980,000 and agreed to cooperate with the investigation.

insured mortgages to finance the development of building sites for residential communities. Of 58 loans insured since 1977, 25 defaulted, with estimated losses of $90 million. Some developments financed by the program, originally intended to foster affordable housing, were luxury projects.

The *New York Times* June 30 said Kemp had decided to preserve the program earlier in the year after being lobbied to save it by Shirley McVay Wiseman, a former HUD official who later became head of the National Association of Home Builders and was listed in HUD documents as a consultant on two Title X projects. The newspaper — which had been investigating the program before Kemp moved to kill it — said that Wiseman wrote to Kemp on Feb. 21, urging him to continue the program. Kemp replied March 21, saying he would consider the request. The next day, Kemp was presented with an option paper, offering him the choice between moving to kill the program and continuing it under tighter supervision. He decided to continue it.

A Kemp spokeswoman told the newspaper that Kemp's March decision was a temporary move meant to give investigators time to see if the program could be improved and, eventually, spared. Later, the aide said, Kemp determined that the program suffered from "systemic problems" that could not be solved, so he decided to terminate it. "She denied that Mr. Kemp acted because of Freedom of Information Act requests [by the *Times*] for documents about his handling of the program," the newspaper said.

A spokesman for Wiseman said her letter had nothing to do with her private consulting work and was merely a statement of a longstanding association position.

On June 30, Lantos' panel expanded its investigation to include HUD's mortgage coinsurance program.

Testimony Clarified

Frederick M. Bush — a longtime aide and fund-raiser for George Bush and his nominee to be ambassador to Luxembourg — came before Lantos' subcommittee June 29 "to make a few clarifying statements" about his May 25 testimony to the panel. Fred Bush, no relation to the president, was one of many consultants who lobbied HUD for mod-rehab funds.

Housing, Urban Aid

In May, Bush had told the panel that he had been in contact with Pierce aide Dean only four or five times during her tenure at HUD. Subsequently, a note to Dean from Bush and his wife found in Dean's HUD files indicated closer ties. Bush said June 29: "I did over time develop a social relationship with Ms. Dean and had lunch or dinner with her on several occasions." He added that he spoke with her "numerous" times. He said 15 to 18 times would be a "good guess." He blamed his previous estimate on faulty memory.

Investigators were interested in Bush's dealings with Dean because he was very successful in lobbying HUD for funds under a number of other programs, including the Urban Development Action Grants Technical Assistance Grants. Altogether, Bush said, he and his firm grossed more than $600,000 from HUD-related business dealings, about $200,000 of which went to subcontractors. Bush denied that he was engaged in selling his influence, even though a promotional letter touting the government-related experience of members of his now-defunct firm, Bush & Company, bragged about their "access to government officials."

Bush subsequently withdrew his nomination as ambassador to Luxembourg.

Kemp Testimony

Secretary Kemp's testimony before the Government Operations Subcommittee on Employment and Housing July 11 and the House Banking Subcommittee on Housing and Community Development July 12 marked his first detailed comments on the HUD scandal. He attempted to keep things upbeat, telling both panels about a saying that was taped to his refrigerator door at home: "Problems are opportunities disguised as insurmountable barriers." But he could not avoid the negative.

Kemp told both panels that more HUD programs were troubled by abuse and mismanagement. Although he did not elaborate, candidates for scrutiny included the popular Community Development Block Grant program; the Loan Management Set Aside program, which provided subsidies to avert foreclosures on financially ailing housing projects; and the Section 202 elderly and handicapped housing loan program.

Earlier, a House Appropriations subcommittee had included no money for mod-rehab in the fiscal 1990 HUD-Veterans Affairs appropriations bill (HR 2916). Kemp did not object to that decision, given that the administration had sought no funds for the program. However, in his appearance before the Banking subcommittee, Kemp chafed at another idea put forth by the Appropriations panel.

A draft copy of the Appropriations report said: "The committee notes that many of the worst program abuses emanated from 'political' appointees who profited from departmental contacts after their services at HUD. In this connection, the committee is recommending language which will provide that all deputy assistant secretaries at the department be reclassified as career [service] positions rather than 'political' positions. This will ensure that 'revolving door' political appointees are not in a position to exercise undue influence over the award of programmatic funds." The effect would be to limit the administration's ability to place political allies in key upper-middle-level positions at HUD.

Another issue brought up before the Housing Subcommittee, which resulted in a less-than-cordial exchange, was Kemp's decision to terminate two HUD programs without Congress' permission. Kemp had temporarily suspended two programs, and no one had questioned his authority to do that. However, his intention to end the Title X Land Development Mortgage Program appeared to some members as a foray onto congressional turf.

In a press release June 29, Kemp said that he would propose a rule to kill the program. Using administration regulations to kill a program clearly would give HUD the upper hand, because Congress would have to pass legislation, subject to presidential veto, to keep the program alive. Challenged on that point, Kemp appeared to back off: "It was suspended, not terminated. I cannot terminate it." However, he warned, "If you want to keep it, you'll have to defend a program that goes to fat-cat developers instead of to the poor."

Members did not belabor the point, apparently because they were not sure the program was worth saving, but they were worried about precedent.

Wiseman, Cushing, Hills

In what became the most significant testimony before Lantos' subcommittee, Shirley McVay Wiseman said July 14 that Pierce told her in 1985 that he wanted a North Carolina mod-rehab project funded. The project was backed by some old friends of Pierce and a consultant who was an adviser to the Reagan-Bush campaigns, according to the *Wall Street Journal.*

Wiseman had been in charge of approving mod-rehab projects at the time. Agency career staffers urged that the North Carolina project be rejected, and Wiseman said she agreed with their assessment. Her decision, she said, did not sit well with Pierce and Dean. First Dean called her and said that "the secretary wanted it funded." Wiseman resisted. And then Pierce called.

"It was a very short conversation," Wiseman testified. "The secretary said, 'I want this project funded. . . .' I believe that's the exact words, and I said, 'I won't fund it, Mr. Secretary,' and he said, 'I want it funded.' " She told him that he could fund it, saying, " 'I will send it upstairs to you.' That was the end of the conversation."

Funds for the project, composed of several subsidies including $11.3 million in mod-rehab money, were later released by Wiseman's successor, Janet Hale, who later joined the Bush administration's Office of Management and Budget. Testifying with Wiseman, she said Dean ordered her to fund the project.

Wiseman contradicted Pierce's May 25 assertion that he had set up a panel of underlings to review mod-rehab requests. Wiseman said she never heard of such a panel.

Chairman Lantos announced July 19 that Pierce had agreed to testify again on Aug. 3 and in September about the contradictions between his May 25 testimony and Wiseman's July 14 statements. But as it turned out, he never did.

On July 17, R. Hunter Cushing took the same route as Dean, becoming the second former HUD official to invoke the Fifth Amendment to avoid testifying about the scandal. Lawmakers wanted to know what Cushing knew about Dean, with whom he was closely associated at HUD.

Cushing's name also had come up a few times in testimony from well-connected Republicans who benefited from HUD programs. Richard Shelby, a former White

House personnel aide, said Cushing was among those he contacted in working on HUD-related projects, for which he shared in hundreds of thousands of dollars in fees. Fred Bush said members of his consulting firm met Dean through Cushing. The GOP consultant later helped Cushing get a job in the new administration as deputy assistant secretary of commerce, but Bush said his aid was minimal.

The *Wall Street Journal* reported that Cushing made a key decision shortly before leaving HUD that might have saved an influential Republican lawyer, Edward Weidenfeld — general counsel to the 1980 Reagan-Bush campaign — a sizable amount of money. HUD's regional staff in Atlanta had determined that Weidenfeld's investment group owed the agency almost $600,000 in "unsupportable and unallowable costs" on a housing project in Georgia. Cushing overruled the decision, cutting the debt by more than $500,000, but the matter remained unresolved.

The same day Cushing refused to testify, U.S. Trade Representative Carla A. Hills, HUD secretary during the Ford administration, defended her role in lobbying HUD on behalf of DRG Funding Corp. of Washington, D.C. She said her representation of DRG was not a case of influence peddling. "We worked as lawyers, and we were paid as lawyers," she said, adding that her work for DRG generated $33,500 in fees over several months in 1984 and 1985.

DRG took part in HUD's coinsurance program. In November 1984, HUD accused the company of "serious breaches" of its rules, including inflating the value of insured properties, which had the effect of increasing DRG's fees. HUD placed the company under severe restrictions, which Hills attempted to persuade mid-level agency officials to lift. Having failed there, she appealed to Pierce, who lifted the harshest restrictions in May 1985. Later, the company's defaults mounted, and by the end of 1989, government losses had topped $300 million, Lantos said. In addition, the company became the subject of a criminal investigation by the Justice Department.

Hills also testified that she helped a South Florida developer, Swezy Realty Inc., get mod-rehab money to fix up units in Broward and Dade counties.

Hills' testimony was well received by some Republican members of the subcommittee. Some Democrats, while not wholly won over, were not too critical and were generally sympathetic.

Criminal Investigation

Toward the end of July, Democrats began pressing the Bush administration to search more aggressively for criminal violations by Republican consultants and former HUD officials involved in the scandal.

"We have a Justice Department that is failing miserably to do its job," Rep. Frank said July 24, shortly before a former HUD official and a prominent Florida Republican testified to Employment and Housing about their lucrative HUD-related business dealings.

The Bush administration was quite aggressive and vocal in investigating cases in which people stole money from HUD. But the people involved in that aspect of the scandal were not the political types who provided most of the grist for congressional hearings. And at this point, HUD Secretary Kemp and the Justice Department still stood behind the HUD inspector general's report, which found no evidence of criminal wrongdoing among the high-profile witnesses. Some Democrats, basing their suspicions on the testimony they had heard, publicly disagreed with that conclusion.

Rep. Frank lambasted the Justice Department after reading a copy of a letter to HUD IG Adams from Justice's Public Integrity Section, which said, "Should you come to obtain information not contained in your report implicating Mr. [Thomas T.] Demery [former HUD assistant secretary] or any other HUD officials in possible criminal violations, we would be happy to review that information." Accusing the Justice Department of using "the minimalist approach to law enforcement," Frank suggested that agency officials were allowing politics to play a role in their decisions.

Attorney General Dick Thornburgh lashed back: "I've been in the business too long to have to put up with that kind of accusation. . . . I will categorically deny that there is any intent not to prosecute anyone on whom we have evidence of wrongdoing. That's absolute nonsense."

Frank called on Thornburgh to investigate possible instances of perjury by witnesses appearing before Congress and of conspiracy to rig bids in awarding HUD subsidies. Thornburgh responded: "Mr. Frank has the luxury of characterizing people's conduct as criminal without having to prove it in court. . . . Anybody who has committed a violation of the federal criminal laws in connection with any of the allegations of wrongdoing at the office of Housing and Urban Development is going to be prosecuted. Make no mistake about it."

At a July 28 hearing, Lantos said Thornburgh had contacted him to assure him that Justice's investigation would be aggressive. Lantos told his colleagues that he felt certain they had nothing to worry about. "We will see to it that people who ought to go to jail in fact go to jail," Lantos said.

Taylor Testimony, N.Y. Cases

Testimony before the subcommittee July 24 provided the scandal's most glaring example of influence peddling.

William M. Taylor, a member of the Republican National Committee (RNC) and former Florida state GOP chairman, described how he was paid more than $500,000 in cash and property interests for successful HUD-related lobbying work in behalf of projects in Florida, Texas and Georgia. He used his GOP office stationery on several occasions to advocate projects to Dean and Pierce. Taylor said he also used the stationery of his consulting firm, Bill Taylor & Associates Inc., but only when the official involved already knew who he was.

Taylor received the largest single fee revealed in the course of the inquiry. For about 100 hours' work landing mod-rehab subsidies for a Texas project, he received an equity interest worth roughly $400,000 and $15,000 cash. Lantos noted that Taylor's hourly rate on that project was $4,150.

In a related development, the *New York Times* July 28 reported that, from 1986 to 1988, two-thirds of the projects from an elderly housing program that went to HUD's New York region, which included New Jersey and Puerto Rico, involved someone who contributed to the campaign of Sen. Alfonse M. D'Amato, R-N.Y. D'Amato "flatly denied" having anything to do with selecting HUD grant recipients, the newspaper said.

The story said that a perception existed among housing industry figures in the New York region that those wishing to do HUD-related business would be wise to contribute to D'Amato's campaigns. Asked about the percep-

Bending the Rules at HUD

As members of Congress left town for the August 1989 recess, three months into their investigation of the Department of Housing and Urban Development (HUD), the scandal's most intriguing mystery remained unsolved: Who decided HUD could ignore rules governing the so-called Section 8 Moderate Rehabilitation Program (mod-rehab) and on what authority?

Until fiscal 1984, Congress required HUD to distribute all housing funds under a needs-based "fair share" formula designed to spread the money nationwide. HUD field offices were given funding to hand out to local housing authorities. In 1984, as HUD's budget was dropping sharply, Congress began waiving the requirement at HUD's request because in some programs it would have spread money too thinly. HUD continued to use the formula for most housing programs, but not for mod-rehab, which was too small.

In consolidating the power to make mod-rehab funding decisions in HUD headquarters, somebody at HUD decided that the agency's own rules for allocating the money could be ignored. That was because the rules were based in part on the fair-share requirement. Top HUD officials gave themselves free rein to allocate funds using an informal, undocumented system apparently having little to do with need.

But who made that decision?

According to the report prepared by Paul A. Adams, the HUD inspector general, the decision was based on a "verbal opinion" on the fair-share waiver's effect by general counsel John J. Knapp, who left HUD in 1986. The report said Knapp was wrong.

Before the House Government Operations Subcommittee on Employment and Housing, Knapp testified May 25, 1989, that his memory was fuzzy, but that based on a conversation he had with a former aide, he believed he had in fact issued that opinion. He explained the reasoning: "If the first step of the process — i.e., the fair-share allocation was removed, then the second step fell as well." Earlier the same day, former HUD secretary Samuel R. Pierce Jr. recounted a similar version of events.

In a letter June 9 and testimony July 31, Knapp recanted, saying he had misunderstood his aide in preparing for the May 25 hearing. He "advised me that the question was never discussed between us," Knapp wrote.

Subcommittee member Christopher Shays, R-Conn., asked him, "If you didn't waive the regs, who did?" Knapp: "I don't believe anybody did." Shays: "Why did HUD function as if they had been waived?"

When pressed to concede that because the rules were ignored, apparently without legal authority, some HUD officials must have decided together to violate them, Knapp said, after offering several caveats, "That may be a criminal conspiracy."

tion, HUD's former regional administrator for New York, Joseph D. Monticciolo, told Employment and Housing Subcommittee members July 28 that "there was no basis [for it] as far as I'm concerned." He also said he could not recall with certainty whether D'Amato — who helped get him his high-ranking HUD position — contacted him in behalf of individuals seeking HUD business.

D'Amato, long known as an aggressive and unabashed advocate of federal housing for New York, used an appearance before the Senate Banking Committee Oct. 31 to lash out against his accusers. He said his "blood boils" when members fighting for constituents were "tarnished with the same brush" used to criticize influence peddlers who got rich off HUD. Later, speaking to reporters, D'Amato denied that he ever attempted to be "involved in the process of selection" of projects to receive HUD funding but said he often advocated proposals brought to his attention that he thought had merit. He promised to continue fighting for money for New York: "Absolutely. . . . My state elected me to go for it."

Senate Banking Committee

On Aug. 2, the Senate Banking Committee returned to the fray. It had held an initial hearing early in the scandal but had since lain low. Staffers had been preparing what appeared to be a more analytic look at the scandal's underlying causes — how the structure of housing programs invited abuse.

Witnesses from three agencies released new studies of projects funded under the mod-rehab program.

Adams, updating earlier estimates, said 20 well-connected consultants lobbied HUD on 51 successful projects for a total of almost $6 million in fees. In all during 1984-88, one in five mod-rehab units involved projects in which consultants were used, and a great many others benefited well-connected developers and mortgage brokers.

Almost all such projects went to states that received more units than they would have if the needs-based fair-share formula had applied. In addition, many projects received excessive subsidies because developers made their rents "artificially high" compared with actual area rents.

John M. Ols Jr. of the General Accounting Office released a study showing how mod-rehab developers were able to layer low-income housing tax credits and other government subsidies onto mod-rehab-funded projects to make profits skyrocket. Per-unit, pretax profit estimates on eight projects ranged from $3,500 to $11,400 on investments with little risk. One developer made almost $2 million from an $8 million project in which he had invested only $46,000. All of the projects studied involved well-connected individuals.

The third witness, housing specialist Morton J. Schussheim from the Congressional Research Service, said at least 13 of 20 projects he studied went to areas with relatively weak rental markets, places where low-rent housing was least needed because of high vacancy rates. He said developers might have sought out soft markets because cheap land and out-of-date HUD rent data allowed them to maximize profits.

Pierce Documents

New disclosures about Pierce's role at HUD came Aug. 4 in newspaper reports about the contents of some 50 boxes of documents from the former HUD secretary's files, which were sent by HUD to congressional investigators. The new revelations were the clearest contradiction of Pierce's May 25 testimony yet.

After HUD approved funding for a project he was advocating, James Watt wrote to Pierce in 1986: "Dear Sam: Thanks! You are a man of your word." Pierce also was thanked in May 1988 by Republican Sen. David K. Karnes for helping obtain housing assistance for Nebraska. Others added to the list of well-connected individuals who got key help from Pierce included Joseph Coors, the Colorado brewer, and Lionel Hampton, the jazz star; both were ardent GOP supporters.

The documents also shed new light on DRG Funding Corp. The firm helped establish a Maryland prep school's minority scholarship that was named for Pierce, an April 1985 letter showed. In May 1985, after lobbying from Carla Hills, Pierce lifted tough curbs that had been placed on the company's HUD work by another top agency official, Maurice Barksdale.

The disclosures about Pierce came when many lawmakers were becoming increasingly vocal in suggesting that crimes had been committed. Soon, calls were made for a formal criminal investigation. Amid still more reports about political favoritism at HUD, Rep. Bruce A. Morrison, D-Conn., said in a letter to Attorney General Thornburgh, "the time has come to convene a grand jury."

The letter was released Aug. 8 as newspaper reports, mostly in the *New York Times*, documented more cases in which well-connected Republicans and former HUD officials benefited financially from the agency's programs, sometimes with Pierce's help. Pierce also apparently used his position in several instances to help his former New York law firm, Battle Fowler, and its clients. The *Times* uncovered an internal memo indicating that HUD officials gave incomplete information in 1988 to Sen. John Heinz, R-Pa., to hide the political nature of funding decisions in the mod-rehab program.

Pierce Takes the Fifth

Pierce, who for weeks had been scheduled to testify before the Employment and Housing Subcommittee on Sept. 15, canceled his appearance at the last minute. In response, Lantos announced that his subcommittee would subpoena Pierce. The House subcommittee unanimously approved three subpoenas for Pierce for Sept. 26, Oct. 27 and Nov. 3.

Pierce called the subpoenas "vindictive." He was considering refusing to testify.

The weekend before the Sept. 26 hearing, Pierce's lawyers — Paul L. Perito, Robert Plotkin and Inez Smith Reid — announced that they would invoke a rarely used House rule that allowed subpoenaed witnesses to demand that radio, television and photographic coverage of their appearances be banned. The proceedings had turned into a media circus.

When hearings began shortly after 9:30 a.m., Pierce was elsewhere in the Rayburn House Office Building. After more than an hour of opening statements, Lantos ordered broadcasters to turn off their equipment. Print reporters were directed to sign statements saying, "under penalty of perjury," that any tape recordings of the hearing would not be broadcast.

After a short recess, Pierce entered the room at 11 a.m. and was sworn in. He read his opening statement in the same monotone he used in many other appearances before Congress over the years. His purpose this time was to complain that he was being treated unfairly because Lantos had refused to give him more time to prepare. Pierce also accused panel members of leaping to conclusions about his role in the HUD affair.

He waited until the last page of his four-page statement to make the announcement many had predicted: "[M]y counsel has advised me and I have agreed to assert my constitutional rights under the Fifth and Sixth Amendments by refusing to answer questions before this subcommittee."

After Pierce finished, Lantos indicated that he was not sure if Pierce had not waived his right to invoke his right to remain mute by testifying on May 25. He requested written arguments from Pierce's attorney on the issue. In response to a complaint by Pierce that HUD had not yet given him all the documents he requested, Lantos promised "total cooperation" in pressuring HUD to hurry up. "You are entitled to nothing less," Lantos said.

Lantos proceeded to ask Pierce a series of eight questions, carefully crafted to reveal new evidence of Pierce's knowledge of political favoritism and influence peddling. The questions were based on two memos to Pierce that had just been discovered. One indicated that President Ronald Reagan ordered HUD funds to a New Jersey project to help a Republican Senate candidate, then-representative Millicent Fenwick; the other, from Deborah Gore Dean, informed Pierce that two projects, identified only by their well-connected Republican consultants' names, "are set" to be selected for funding by a committee that had not yet met to make a decision.

Pierce declined to answer Lantos' questions, thus becoming only the third former or sitting member of the Cabinet to use the Fifth Amendment to avoid testifying before Congress. The other two were figures in the Teapot Dome scandal of the 1920s.

On Oct. 27, Pierce once again invoked the Fifth Amendment in refusing to testify. But he also disavowed any guilt for his activities at HUD for the first time in public: "I believe that I committed no illegal or wrongful acts."

A month earlier, Pierce had cited lack of time for preparation as a major reason behind his refusal to testify, but on this occasion he no longer relied on that argument. Instead he blamed the Employment and Housing Subcommittee for its handling of the investigation: "I will continue to rely upon the advice of my counsel and invoke my constitutional protections ... until such time as I believe the accusatory atmosphere that presently exists has changed," he said. "I have become a target of these hearings and have been unfairly accused of alleged lies and dishonesty."

Members questioned the propriety of Pierce's invoking the Fifth Amendment on such grounds.

Lantos gave Pierce a chance to challenge the July 14 testimony of Shirley Wiseman, but he refused to answer Lantos' questions. Pierce's lawyers attempted to cast doubt on Wiseman's statements. In a report, they said Pierce did not recall ordering her to fund the project. The report revealed that HUD's inspector general had investigated complaints about "undue pressure" involving the project in question and "found no evidence that improper influence or pressure was used." Moreover, when Wiseman was questioned about the project by HUD investigators in 1985, she said nothing about being ordered to fund it by Pierce, even though she mentioned pressure from his top aide, Dean.

The report by Pierce's lawyers also rebutted suggestions that Pierce was to blame for political favoritism at HUD.

Lantos canceled the Nov. 3 hearing, the last of the three for which Pierce had been subpoenaed, after Pierce told Lantos that he would again invoke the Fifth.

Wilson Appearance

On Sept. 27, Lance H. Wilson, who had been an aide to Pierce, became the fourth former HUD official to refuse to testify before the Lantos panel. He also had broadcasters and photographers banned from recording his appearance.

Lantos laid out the case against Wilson in his opening statement. In 1985, he said, Wilson was given a 15 percent interest in a $24 million Florida project from a developer two years after playing a role in a HUD decision to award the developer a $7 million grant. In 1988, Wilson made $325,000 working for PaineWebber, the investment company, partly for being its "ambassador to HUD" — using more than $10,000 of the firm's money "wining and dining HUD officials," with many dinner tabs running upwards of $150.

Although they went unanswered, several questions were asked by Lantos, including why Wilson felt the need to inform Pierce, through a phone message, that Pierce's former law firm had been picked as counsel for HUD bond work PaineWebber was performing.

Mindful of the public relations harm that could come from the case, PaineWebber Chairman and Chief Executive Officer Donald B. Marron came to the hearing to introduce James C. Treadway Jr., a PaineWebber official who outlined the results of an internal investigation of Wilson's affairs. On most matters, Treadway said he found no instances of impropriety or illegality. PaineWebber, however, intended to seek reimbursement of the expense account charges.

Independent Counsel Sought

Under a little-used provision of the Independent Counsel Act (PL 100-191), a majority of members of either party on the House or Senate Judiciary Committee could request the appointment of an independent counsel (special prosecutor) to investigate current or former top government officials. The attorney general had to consider the request and act on it one way or the other. *(PL 100-191, Congress and the Nation Vol. VII, p. 773)*

Schumer and Morrison rounded up 19 of the House Judiciary Committee's 20 Democrats to support the request in a Nov. 2 letter to Thornburgh. Chairman Jack Brooks, D-Texas, was not asked to sign because he was in the hospital with an inflamed pancreas.

The members said the prosecutor should investigate whether Pierce — as well as "other high-ranking officials who may be involved" — "committed serious federal crimes." Political favoritism at HUD, they said, may have been the result of a criminal conspiracy to defraud the government "by ignoring or deliberately circumventing federal statutes and regulations applicable to the selection of HUD grantees." They also said Pierce had possibly committed perjury May 25 when he told the subcommittee that he did not direct HUD subordinates to fund specific projects or make other decisions.

Thornburgh waited until late Feb. 1, 1990 — his 60-day deadline — before asking a panel of the U.S. Court of Appeals for the District of Columbia Circuit to select a special prosecutor. Thornburgh asked that allegations be investigated that Pierce and others engaged in a conspiracy to defraud the U.S. government through HUD's mod-rehab program. But he said the evidence did not warrant investigating Pierce for perjury, as the Judiciary Committee had asked.

A three-judge panel on March 2 chose Arlin M. Adams, a member of the 3rd U.S. Circuit Court of Appeals from 1969 to 1986, as independent counsel in the case.

Gilliam Testimony

Appearing before the Government Operations subcommittee the week of April 30, 1990, DuBois L. Gilliam, who served under Pierce as deputy assistant secretary for program policy development and evaluation, testified that the former HUD secretary funded housing and community development projects based on personal relationships and political favoritism. Gilliam contradicted Pierce's sworn statements from 1989 that he did not make decisions on who got HUD grants.

"I know for a fact that the secretary made decisions," said Gilliam, who was serving an 18-month prison sentence for taking bribes during his HUD tenure from 1984 to 1987. Gilliam said he received about $100,000 in gifts, trips and money from developers and consultants while at HUD. He testified under a court-ordered grant of immunity from prosecution for anything related to his testimony except perjury. Gilliam was up for parole in June and said he was motivated to cooperate with Congress because doing so would help him get out of jail.

While at HUD, Gilliam was responsible for overseeing the Urban Development Action Grant (UDAG) program and the secretary's discretionary fund. Action grants were intended to boost development in blighted areas. Gilliam said Pierce asked him to provide a grant to a project at Hampton University, a predominantly black college in Virginia, before the school had even filled out an application or lined up financing.

And Gilliam said that when Lance Wilson, Pierce's former executive assistant, applied for a grant with a developer for a project in Belle Glade, Fla., the secretary dropped the cutoff line for funding projects to include Belle Glade, which had not qualified. In March 1987, HUD awarded the project a $5.6 million grant.

Gilliam said he, Pierce and Dean decided to transfer David Sowell, a career HUD official who became suspicious of the arrangement. He said they feared Sowell would call HUD's inspector general, who might investigate the deal.

Ultimately, Sowell was placed in Gilliam's office, where Gilliam "kept him traveling."

Pierce not only ordered that certain projects receive funding, he also told Gilliam not to fund a project in San Antonio, Texas, the district of Democrat Henry B. Gonzalez, chairman of the House Banking Committee and its Subcommittee on Housing and Community Development. Pierce had long held a grudge against Gonzalez, said Gilliam, because the representative had once called the HUD secretary a "Stepin Fetchit" for the Reagan administration.

Gilliam also testified that someone in Vice President George Bush's office had urged HUD officials to fund a project that did not qualify for money from Pierce's discretionary fund. After Gilliam told Hector Barreto, president of the U.S. Hispanic Chamber of Congress, that his application for $500,000 to conduct a feasibility study for a Hispanic Trade Center in Kansas City, Mo., was not approved, Gilliam received a phone call from Dean. Gilliam said Dean told him in early 1985 that Bush's office had called to support the funding after Bush met with Barreto. Gilliam said he could not provide the grant directly, so he worked out an arrangement for Kansas City to supply the $500,00 and promised that HUD would approve $500,000 for a housing project the city was seeking.

Other Testimony, Action

In his third appearance before the Lantos subcommittee, former assistant secretary for housing Demery on May 23 told of a January 1987 meeting in which Pierce said he wanted to know which consultants and lawyers were behind each request for mod-rehab grants. "At that time, I realized that political considerations were to be a factor in the award of mod-rehab units as viewed by Secretary Pierce," Demery said.

Demery also testified that during his first couple of months on the job, Dean would hand him scraps of paper listing various public housing authorities, saying, "The secretary wants these requests funded."

In a letter released May 29, Thornburgh asked Adams to broaden his inquiry beyond allegations of wrongdoing in the mod-rehab program. The attorney general called Adams' attention to Gilliam's testimony. The investigation was expanded to scrutinize the special projects, technical assistance and UDAG programs.

Leonard E. Briscoe Sr., a Texas real estate developer who had business dealings with two former HUD officials, was subpoenaed to testify before Lantos' subcommittee. Briscoe exercised his Fifth Amendment right against self-incrimination June 21, saying he had not been given enough time to prepare for his appearance.

On July 24, subcommittee members sent Adams a letter requesting that he expand his investigation into the coinsurance mortgage program and possible perjury by Pierce. A 271-page report released Nov. 1 by the panel concluded that Pierce had directed federal grants to political friends and later misled Congress about his involvement. "At best, Secretary Pierce was less than honest and misled the subcommittee," the report said. "At worst, Secretary Pierce knowingly lied and committed perjury during his testimony."

Perito, Pierce's lawyer, criticized the panel's final report, calling it "a rehash of stale and unfounded allegations."

HUD Reform

Responding to months of revelations about political influence peddling, fraud and mismanagement at the Department of Housing and Urban Development (HUD) during the Reagan administration, Congress Nov. 22, 1989, cleared legislation (HR 1) designed to clean up the mess. *(HUD scandal, p. 676)*

HUD Secretary Jack F. Kemp scored a big victory when Congress accepted most of his plan to reform the scandal-ridden department he had inherited from Samuel R. Pierce Jr., who served as HUD secretary from 1981 to 1989.

Kemp's Proposal

Kemp's plan, unveiled Oct. 3, opened HUD and its profit-making beneficiaries to much greater scrutiny, curtailed the ability of outsiders to influence decisions, imposed new internal monitoring requirements on much of the agency's multibillion-dollar budget, limited HUD-related profits for developers and investors, and increased the agency's power to find abuse and punish perpetrators.

House and Senate members quickly embraced the thrust of Kemp's plan. Senate Majority Whip Alan Cranston, D-Calif., chairman of the Banking, Housing and Urban Affairs Committee's Housing and Urban Affairs Subcommittee, called it "right on target." House Banking, Finance and Urban Affairs Chairman Henry B. Gonzalez, D-Texas, who also headed the Housing Subcommittee, said the proposals would be given "prompt attention."

Some of the proposals had strong support, and a few already were moving toward congressional approval. For example, Kemp proposed requiring lobbyists and consultants to register and disclose fees, a move that Congress was being urged to impose governmentwide by Robert C. Byrd, D-W.Va., chairman of the Senate Appropriations Committee. *(Lobbying reforms, p. 862)*

Other provisions appeared to face little opposition. These required that waivers of rules be approved by assistant secretaries and made public; required that funding decisions be made public; increased the subpoena power of HUD's inspector general (IG); created a "chief financial officer" and a comptroller to watch over HUD's financial affairs more closely; increased funding for monitoring and auditing activities; imposed stricter rules for HUD's troubled coinsurance program, under which private lenders and the Federal Housing Administration (FHA) shared risk; allowed the secretary to impose fines on violators of HUD rules; and stopped FHA from insuring vacation homes and homes owned by investors.

Other parts of the plan faced potential difficulty in getting enacted. For example, local governments opposed the idea of targeting more tightly to anti-poverty efforts funds for the popular, $3 billion-a-year Community Development Block Grant (CDBG) program. A related proposal sought to eliminate almost all of HUD's two main "discretionary" programs — one for CDBG-type efforts, the other for housing projects. The funds were supposed to be used to address emergencies or special cases by allowing HUD to ignore merit and competition requirements. The discretionary funds, however, were a favorite congressional target for earmarks — constituent-pleasers tucked into spending bills directing agencies to fund certain projects.

HUD Ethics

The ethics program at the Department of Housing and Urban Development (HUD) came under harsh criticism in a 1990 study conducted by the General Accounting Office (GAO). Blame for the program's failure was placed squarely on former HUD secretary Samuel R. Pierce Jr.

The study, made at the request of a Senate Governmental Affairs subcommittee, was based on financial disclosure forms for HUD officials and experts or consultants hired by HUD. It found that:

- Of 62 consultants hired from 1986 to 1989, no disclosure statements were filed for 52.
- Of 111 HUD employees required to file a public disclosure statement by May 15, 1989, 44 percent missed the deadline.
- Of the statements filed on time, none had been reviewed more than 100 days later. The Ethics in Government Act required the statements to be reviewed and approved within 60 days of filing.

The report was the third such critical analysis since 1982. In 1986, a scathing review by the Office of Government Ethics concluded, "HUD's ethics program is one of the most ill-managed this team has ever seen in a major department." Furthermore, the 1986 report said, little had been done "to save what appears to be a deteriorating program" since a similar review in 1982.

The 1990 report concluded that "the fact that the problems we are reporting existed for so long demonstrates to us that the HUD secretary did not hold the [designated agency ethics official] and his alternate sufficiently accountable for developing and administering an effective financial disclosure system." And without that system, "HUD was not in a position to address actual or potential conflicts of interest," the report said.

Although GAO found that some of the lapses continued after Jack F. Kemp assumed office in 1989, the new HUD secretary said in a letter to the comptroller general that "under my leadership, ethical conduct is the only way of 'doing business' at, or with, HUD." He cited a number of changes he had made to prevent such problems from recurring, including creating a special office to improve HUD's ethics program.

In addition, Kemp wanted Congress to give the HUD secretary more flexibility in deciding which defaulted projects should receive rent subsidies. But many liberals in Congress fought hard for the law as a way to preserve the supply of housing. Kemp also wanted Congress to relax its oversight of HUD's rulemaking procedures. While the power to implement laws rested with the administration, Congress historically imposed restrictions to make sure its intent was not disregarded in the process.

House Action

Subcommittee. House Democrats initially tried to tie the Bush administration's plan for reforming HUD to big bills aimed at expanding HUD programs and creating costly new ones. Kemp opposed the idea, telling the House Banking Subcommittee on Housing and Community Development Oct. 12 that the reform package was "urgent." He added, "Once that is done, we can go beyond reform and focus on the substance of housing issues."

While some members expressed doubt that congressional action was required immediately, especially because many elements of the plan could be instituted right away administratively, efforts to hold the reform package hostage to a broader housing reauthorization bill were abandoned Nov. 9. The stark about-face came after a frenzy of compromise and conciliation by Democrats and Republicans on the liberal-leaning subcommittee. *(Housing reauthorization, p. 665)*

Ironically, the move came after the hostage strategy showed signs of working. Word had spread Nov. 6 that Bush planned to offer a $4.2 billion, three-year set of housing initiatives, which he formally announced Nov. 10.

Gonzalez, meanwhile, had hinted all along that he might be willing to let reform go separately, but he repeatedly insisted that members continue working on the big bill. Then, after the subcommittee finished work on the measure's reform section, Gonzalez accepted, with minor changes, an amendment by Steve Bartlett, R-Texas, to kill the rest of the bill.

The House subcommittee version of the legislation included most of what Kemp asked for — with some refinements — plus a slew of added provisions crafted by several members. Most of the compromises were worked out behind the scenes by staffers; others were agreed to by voice votes. Only one amendment was contested to the point of a vote, and that had little to do with reform: It was a bid by Rep. Carroll Hubbard Jr., D-Ky., to allow rural areas to get more HUD money. Urban members defeated it handily, 9-30.

Marge Roukema of New Jersey, the subcommittee's top Republican, won voice vote approval of an amendment to give HUD's inspector general a mandatory five-year term of office and to restrict the administration's ability to fire an IG by allowing him or her to "be removed from office by the president only for cause." A move by Joseph P. Kennedy II, D-Mass., to insert a Kemp provision that would have more tightly targeted HUD community development funds to anti-poverty efforts was loudly denounced and withdrawn in the face of defeat. Chalmers P. Wylie of Ohio, the ranking Republican on House Banking, managed to get a refined version of a Kemp proposal to allocate a set amount of certain HUD funds for evaluating and monitoring programs. Kemp wanted 0.5 percent (perhaps $100 million). Wylie cut that by half, and the subcommittee eventually agreed to authorize $25 million for such purposes in fiscal 1991.

The measure also was modified to extend, until Sept. 30, 1990, a two-year-old virtual moratorium Congress had imposed on any efforts by owners of subsidized low-rent projects to convert their holdings to upscale apartments or condos. Kemp supported the amendment.

Wylie and Barney Frank, D-Mass., urged Gonzalez to skip full committee action on the reform bill and bring it to the floor under suspension of the rules, a procedure barring amendments and requiring a two-thirds majority. He accepted their recommendation.

After it left the Housing Subcommittee, HR 1 lost one major provision on its direct route to the House floor. Gonzalez decided to strip from the bill proposals that would have made HUD's IG more powerful and independent than any other agency's. The Government Operations Committee, which had jurisdiction over inspector general laws, insisted that the provisions be stripped so it could study the issue.

Floor. House floor action consisted mainly of members standing up to take credit for their contributions to the measure and the events that led to its passage. No one opposed the bill, but some members expressed trepidation about a few provisions.

Roukema and Doug Bereuter, R-Neb., complained about a provision aimed at targeting more CDBG money to anti-poverty efforts. The provision was the only one of several Kemp CDBG-targeting proposals that made it into the bill. Some feared it would make CDBG money harder to use in rural and better-off areas, but liberal Democrats liked the idea.

Frank and Wylie also noted that private officials who managed and owned HUD-subsidized properties feared they would be the unfair victims of the agency's new power to punish wrongdoers.

The House passed HR 1 by voice vote under suspension of the rules Nov. 14.

Senate Action

Senate Banking Subcommittee on Housing Chairman Cranston did not advocate stripping the reform provisions from expansive housing legislation and enacting them separately. He said any such move would be a disastrous blow to his effort because the more conservative Senate would require the locomotive of reform to pull the rest of any big housing bill. "I believe such a move should be strongly resisted," he told Kemp in a letter Nov. 7. "Since legislative pressures in the Senate will permit passage of only one major housing bill this Congress, that legislation must include both reform measures and needed housing initiatives."

Following House passage of HR 1, however, Cranston and his allies had little choice but to quit holding Kemp's reform package hostage to a huge housing reauthorization bill revamping and expanding federal shelter programs. They were not willing to take the heat alone for delaying something called the Department of Housing and Urban Development Reform Act of 1989.

With adjournment fast approaching, staff members of the House and Senate Banking subcommittees on housing met to negotiate and draft a compromise measure. Key HUD officials also sat in on some talks. Among the touchiest issues was a provision replacing the "secretary's discretionary fund" for special community development projects with a much more narrowly focused fund. Proposed by Kemp, the change was designed to prevent HUD funds from being doled out as political favors.

The language worried House and Senate Appropriations leaders because that account had long been a favorite place for members to stick money for pork-barrel projects — a jealously protected prerogative of appropriators. For a while, a caveat asserting that "Congress would retain the ability to designate projects" for funding was considered. In the end, it was defeated.

Without the caveat, the new provision could make it more difficult — but by no means impossible — for appropriators to force HUD to fund special community development projects, aides said. The bill eliminated "special projects" as an allowable use of the fund's money, so appropriators would not be able to earmark projects simply by directing in spending bill reports that HUD fund them. They probably would have to include them in the bill itself.

Some members worried about another provision that prohibited advance disclosure of information relating to funding decisions. They believed the language would prohibit HUD employees from responding to members checking the status of pending grants. Members were reassured, however, that the provision would not cause concern.

The compromise also killed Kemp's proposals to target community development block grant funds more tightly to anti-poverty efforts and to prohibit the use of federal mortgage insurance for vacation homes; retained House-proposed criminal penalties opposed by some senators; and loosened Senate-proposed requirements that HUD enhance subsidies aimed at preserving privately owned, federally assisted low-rent housing projects, making some enhancements discretionary instead of mandatory.

The Senate passed a compromise version of the House-passed HR 1 by voice vote at 12:50 a.m. on Nov. 22. The House accepted the changes by voice vote at 3:15 a.m., shortly before closing shop for the year. The president signed HR 1 (PL 101-235) on Dec. 15.

Major Provisions

As cleared, HR 1:

Spending Decisions. Required most money for housing programs to be distributed to regions of the country on the basis of a needs-based "fair share" formula and then to communities and projects through open competition.

- Required public announcement of all federal, state and local funding decisions. Required HUD, using the *Federal Register*, to notify potential applicants whenever HUD funds became available and to make public its selection criteria. Prohibited awards when no written application had been made.
- Required that HUD funding decisions by federal, local and state governments be documented and that such information be available to the public. Allowed emergency waivers.
- Prohibited advance disclosure of information on funding decisions, with civil fines of up to $10,000 per violation and criminal penalties. Required certain applicants to disclose names of all parties with financial interests in the project in question, with civil fines of up to $10,000 for each violation. Allowed the secretary to rescind funding decisions when violations occurred and imposed other sanctions.

Discretionary Funds. Greatly restricted the secretary's discretion in allocating money from two funds identified as ripe for political abuse.

- Replaced the 15 percent "headquarters reserve" of housing money, which could be used for broadly defined purposes, with a narrowly focused fund limited to 5 percent of housing funds. Allowable uses: disasters, desegregation, litigation settlements and other emergencies.
- Replaced the broad "secretary's discretionary fund" for community development grants with narrowly focused "special purpose grants." Allowable uses: grants for territo-

ries, trusts and historically black colleges; "technical assistance grants" to states, local governments, Indian tribes and community planning organizations needing money to plan for federal projects; and supplemental grants to correct community development block grants (CDBG) formula errors. Eliminated "special projects" grants, but exempted those referred to in the House-Senate conference report (H Rept 101-297) on HUD's fiscal 1990 spending law (PL 101-144).

• Established a separate CDBG program for Indian tribes and limited spending on it to 1 percent of CDBG's total appropriation.

Regulation Waivers. Prohibited anyone but high-ranking HUD officials from granting regulation waivers. Required approvals to be in writing, justified and made public in the *Federal Register*.

Civil Penalties. Gave HUD the power to impose civil fines — up to $5,000 per violation and $1 million per violator in some cases — on private sector participants in HUD mortgage programs for a wide range of abuses. Established procedures for imposing fines and allowing court appeals. Allowed fines and other penalties against local governments or individuals who abused HUD urban-homesteading programs.

• Provided fines of up to $1 million when loan brokers or any other interested party "knowingly" gave false information in applying for HUD-insured property-improvement loans. HUD said some dealers and brokers, in a self-interested desire to make sales, abused the program by encouraging borrowers to falsify applications and to use money for ineligible purposes, such as swimming pools. Directed fines to HUD programs.

Consultants. Required lobbyists, consultants and lawyers attempting to influence HUD decisions to register if they made more than $10,000 in a single year. Required applicants for HUD money and their lobbyists to disclose fees and other expenditures paid and received. Required lobbyists to disclose previous federal employment. Allowed violators to be fined up to $10,000, or more if they were paid more than that for services related to the violation. Barred violators from doing HUD consulting work for three years and provided criminal penalties for those who violated the prohibition. Prohibited, in almost all cases, lobbying fees based or contingent on the amount of subsidy approved by HUD.

Other Subsidies. Limited HUD assistance to that needed to provide affordable housing after taking into account all public subsidies to the project from all sources. Required certain applicants to disclose all such subsidies.

Evaluation and Monitoring. Established a chief financial officer for HUD and a comptroller for the Federal Housing Administration (FHA), HUD's mortgage insurance agency. Authorized $25 million in fiscal 1991 for evaluation and monitoring of HUD programs. Required annual financial statements and independent audits of FHA. Required HUD to devise a strategy within one year for making sure its information systems were adequate. Allowed HUD to contract with private companies to help manage the FHA.

Coinsurance. Required HUD to review the financial strength of coinsurance lenders twice a year and to adjust accordingly the standards they had to meet to ensure the long-term fiscal stability of the FHA. Required a report to Congress on the program.

Other FHA Provisions. Barred use of FHA insurance for most investor-owned, single-family homes. Required credit cards of anyone who wanted to buy a property covered by FHA mortgage insurance. Repealed the Title X program, which provided mortgage insurance to buy and develop land for new communities.

• Required HUD to notify other government agencies that insured mortgages when it suspended FHA mortgagees from HUD programs.

• Required HUD to review its system for allowing private lending to approve FHA insurance applications and to recommend improvements to reduce fraud and defaults. Required HUD to set appraisal standards for properties with FHA mortgages.

• Required mortgagees to maintain foreclosed FHA properties.

• Required HUD and the Department of Agriculture to study the feasibility of making government-owned foreclosed homes available to low-income victims of the Oct. 17 California earthquake and September's Hurricane Hugo and to report the results to Congress within 90 days of enactment.

• Established a new FHA Advisory Board, with nine HUD-appointed members and six congressionally appointed members.

• Established in law and increased the power of the existing HUD-controlled Mortgage Review Board. Gave the board the power to reprimand, suspend and terminate mortgagees' ability to do business with the FHA but gave alleged abusers the right to a hearing. Allowed the secretary to issue temporary cease-and-desist orders to alleged abusers before the board acts. Allowed appeals of such orders in court. Allowed HUD to go to court to request that such orders be enforced with injunctions.

Expedited Rulemaking. Sped congressional oversight of HUD's rules during the drafting stage by giving Congress up to 30 calendar days to review rules instead of 30 legislative days, which were often interrupted when Congress recessed.

***Rainier View* Case.** Attempted to limit costs stemming from a court challenge to HUD's method for calculating rent-subsidy increases to owners of assisted projects. For several years, HUD used a standard formula to figure rent increases. But HUD reduced or wiped out the increases when comparisons with rent paid for nearby unsubsidized units showed that the formula would have had HUD paying much more than the market rate. The way HUD used such so-called "comparability studies" was successfully challenged in the 9th U.S. Circuit Court of Appeals in a Seattle case. In that case, *Rainier View Associates v. United States*, HUD was ordered to use only the standard formula, sharply increasing government-paid rent subsidies to the plaintiffs. HUD argued that the decision would cost as much as $1 billion in retroactive payments if applied nationwide.

HR 1 provided retroactive payments to project owners whose rent increases were wiped out or reduced by HUD's comparability studies. The formula for establishing the payments limited them significantly, however, resulting in total payments of less than $250 million, HUD estimated. Payments were to be made over a three-year period and subject to amounts appropriated in spending bills.

HR 1 did not affect the judgment awarded plaintiffs in the *Rainier* case. But it called for future rent increases to be calculated by formula and limited by comparability studies — implemented in a way Congress believed would withstand legal challenges.

Foreclosed Properties. Nullified state laws allowing former owners of foreclosed properties to reclaim title by making up overdue mortgage payments when the property was vacant or abandoned and secured with one of HUD's "Section 312" rehabilitation loans. In effect, allowed HUD to dispose of such properties more quickly.

Refinanced High-Interest Loans. Established an incentive program to encourage homeowners to refinance certain HUD-subsidized loans with high interest rates to cut the government's costs.

Moderate Rehabilitation Program. Required that projects fixed up under the mod-rehab program involve expenditures of at least $3,000 a unit and allowed subsidies for no more than 100 units per project.

Farmers Home Administration. Applied to the Department of Agriculture's Farmers Home Administration (FmHA), which administered rural housing programs, some of the same reforms imposed on HUD:

- Required the agriculture secretary to notify potential applicants whenever housing funds became available, to make public his selection criteria and to document his decisions.
- Prohibited awards when no written application had been made. Allowed waivers in emergencies.
- Required certain applicants to disclose the names of all parties with financial interests in the projects in question and other sources of public subsidy. Prohibited payments to lobbyists and consultants based or contingent on amount of subsidy received.
- Required lobbyists and consultants to register. For violations, allowed the secretary to fine violators up to $1 million, rescind subsidies and impose other sanctions. Limited the subsidy to that needed to make housing affordable after taking into account all public assistance.

Prepayment Moratorium. Extended until Sept. 30, 1990, the virtual moratorium Congress imposed on owners of low-rent projects seeking to convert their properties to upscale apartments or condos by prepaying their government-subsidized mortgages. The moratorium was due to expire Feb. 5, 1990. Enhanced somewhat the rent-subsidy incentives in existing law to entice owners to voluntarily continue providing low-rent units.

- Prohibited prepayment of future subsidized rural-housing loans insured or made under programs run by the FmHA. In return, allowed owners of such projects to take out government-guaranteed "equity" loans on their properties 20 years after the original loan was secured.

Reauthorizations and Extensions. Extended through fiscal 1991 the Flexible Subsidy Program, which provided money to financially troubled, subsidized housing projects. Added two years to the three-year limit on a provision that allowed public housing agencies to charge some residents less than 30 percent of their income for rent.

This change was requested by officials attempting to retain a mixture of income levels in their projects by allowing some better-off families to pay a smaller cut of their salaries.

Other Housing Provisions. Allowed non-profit owners of certain projects developed with Housing Development Grants to sell units to lower-income individuals and families.

- Allowed HUD, when providing rehabilitation loans to federally assisted housing projects, to assume that rent subsidies would be extended for the life of the loan.
- Required HUD to issue a study on the physical renovation needs of all federally subsidized projects within one year.
- Required HUD to set a three-month timetable for implementing a demonstration program enacted in 1988 allowing state agencies to take over and manage foreclosed HUD-controlled properties.
- Established a National Commission on Severely Distressed Public Housing to identify such distressed projects, assess strategies to improve them and develop a national plan to eliminate problems by the year 2000. The commission would have 18 members, with HUD appointing six members and leaders of various congressional subcommittees appointing the rest. Authorized $3 million for the commission in fiscal 1991-92.
- Established a 12-member National Commission on American Indian and Alaska Native Housing to study issues related to their housing needs. Three members of the commission would be appointed by HUD; leaders of various congressional panels would appoint the rest. Authorized $1 million for the commission in 1991-92. Both commissions would cease to exist 18 months after their members were appointed.

FHA Mortgage Loans

To raise revenues and help more middle-income families to buy homes, Congress in 1989 increased the ceiling on mortgages that the Federal Housing Administration (FHA) could insure.

The increase, to $124,875 from $101,250 for homes in high-cost areas, was approved as part of the fiscal 1990 appropriations bill for the Departments of Housing and Urban Development (HUD), Veterans Affairs (VA) and various independent agencies (HR 2916 — PL 101-144), which was signed into law Nov. 9.

The increase was expected to prompt thousands more families to take advantage of the low down payments and sometimes lower-than-usual interest rates that came with FHA-insured mortgages. An upsurge in borrowers, in turn, was expected to yield millions of dollars in new revenues from the premiums paid by mortgage applicants.

Background

Proposals to increase the FHA limit had been around for some time as Congress struggled to help would-be first-time home buyers who found themselves shut out of the market in high-cost areas, such as Southern California and the Northeast.

Federal insurance for single-family homes began during the Depression. The idea was to attract capital into the home-mortgage market by providing lenders risk-free investments. If a borrower defaulted, the government paid off the lender and took claim to the home, absorbing losses with revenues from the FHA premiums. That protection allowed lenders to offer low down payments, and sometimes slightly lower interest rates and closing costs. Since the mid-1930s, more than 17 million families had used FHA insurance to buy their homes. About 900,000 families made use of the program annually in the late 1980s.

The program began with a $16,000 mortgage limit and a 20 percent minimum down payment. Over the years, Congress reduced the minimum down payment considerably, to less than 5 percent in 1989, and raised the mortgage limit.

But in the 1980s, the FHA limit in high-cost areas did not keep pace with median home prices — the price at which half of all other homes sold for more and half for less. Different areas had different FHA limits, but for most of the 1980s, none in the continental United States was allowed to top $90,000. In 1988, the cap was raised to $101,250 but still fell short of the mortgage needed for a median-priced home in a dozen areas.

Legislative Action

Desperate for some quick money, the Senate Appropriations Committee (S Rept 101-128) raised the mortgage limit to 95 percent of each state's median home price, except in metropolitan areas that encompassed parts of more than one state — the New York City area, for example. Although the effects of the new limits were unclear, they were expected to exceed $150,000 in some states and areas.

While helping more families buy homes, the measure eventually could have increased the FHA's risk because it involved insuring more mortgages. In the short run, however, it was expected to yield added revenue. The FHA collected premiums from home buyers. The more loans made, the higher the revenues. And the expansion would broaden FHA's portfolio to include mortgages held by richer people, who would be less likely to default on their loans.

When the Senate took up the HUD-VA funding bill Sept. 19, opponents of the FHA increase failed on two roll calls to cut it back sharply, but they succeeded in paring it somewhat on a third. The first vote was on a Don Nickles, R-Okla., amendment to limit FHA insurance to mortgages of $118,125 or less. A motion to table (kill) that amendment was agreed to 50-49. A second motion, to reconsider the first vote, then was rejected, 49-50. Later, Nickles tried again, but with a $124,875 limit. This time he won handily, when a move to kill the amendment was rejected, 43-55.

Proponents had the upper hand from the beginning of the debate, because opponents had to find hefty cuts elsewhere in the bill if they tried to kill the FHA provision outright. By expanding FHA's business by up to $8 billion in mortgage insurance, the original measure would have raised an extra $157 million in revenue from premiums — money easily spent on other popular programs. The Nickles amendment finally adopted saved more than $50 million by refinancing some high interest rate loans held by the government and cutting HUD's management account. The rest was covered by the revised FHA ceiling.

The increase had the backing of most of the housing industry — the Realtors, the home builders and the mortgage bankers. The opponents had their own financially motivated allies: mortgage-insurance firms, which said FHA hurt their business with bargain-basement prices they could not match, and the thrift industry, which shied away from FHA programs. They were backed by some low-income housing activists.

The Senate passed the HUD-VA spending bill on Sept. 28; the House had passed HR 2916 on July 20, without the FHA provision.

Conferees came to agreement on the FHA mortgage loans issue in surprisingly quick order.

During the conference, Sen. J. Bennett Johnston, D-La., proposed raising the FHA limit to $161,000. He was trying to placate investors protesting another provision in the spending bill that would refinance high interest loans subsidized by HUD. The provision would save HUD money and cut the investors' profits. Johnston wanted to raise enough revenues from a higher FHA ceiling to allow conferees to kill the refinancing proposal. The Senate conferees rejected Johnston's proposal, 2-11.

House Banking, Finance and Urban Affairs Committee Chairman Henry B. Gonzalez, D-Texas, was a staunch opponent of the FHA language. The committee's ranking Republican, Chalmers P. Wylie of Ohio, and Gonzalez reminded House conferees that a General Accounting Office (GAO) audit, based on a Price Waterhouse study and released in May, had confirmed that FHA's reserve funds were losing massive amounts of money. They urged members to let the Banking Committee consider the issue after mid-November, when the GAO was expected to issue a report on whether raising the limit would increase or decrease FHA's risk. *(FHA insurance fund, below)*

In the end, the House conferees accepted the Senate FHA provision because it raised money they wanted to use to pay for other programs in the bill. Without the provision, millions of dollars in funding would have to be cut from the legislation. Several Banking Committee members complained that appropriators were usurping their authority and jurisdiction.

The decisive vote on the House floor, which cleared the way for adoption of the FHA ceiling limit, was 325-92, taken Oct. 25.

FHA Insurance Fund

Amid warnings of a repeat — albeit on a much smaller scale — of the nation's savings and loan debacle, Congress took steps in 1990 to shore up the Federal Housing Administration (FHA) mortgage insurance fund.

As part of the Cranston-Gonzalez omnibus housing bill (S 566 — PL 101-625), lawmakers required buyers to pay additional costs up front and annual insurance fees when purchasing a home. *(Housing bill, p. 665; FHA and secondary mortgage market provisions, p. 671)*

Since Congress first authorized the FHA in 1934, the agency's single-family insurance program had backed loans for about 15 million homes worth more than $374 billion. The program was intended to spur home ownership and stimulate the housing industry by encouraging banks to make loans to people who did not have the money for a traditional 10 percent to 20 percent down payment. FHA loans required down payments of 3 percent on the first $25,000 and 5 percent on the remainder.

When lawmakers began work on the housing bill, little was planned for FHA beyond extending the maximum loan amount of $124,875. But on June 6, 1990, the Bush administration released a report from the accounting firm of Price Waterhouse that showed the program was in trouble. The long-awaited independent study confirmed suspicions that the FHA was losing money and could be insolvent by the end of the 20th century. The Price Waterhouse study found that the FHA Mutual Mortgage Insurance (MMI) Fund had a net worth of $2.6 billion (later recalculated at $3.2 billion), down sharply from a high of $8 billion in 1979. The single-family loan program, while still solvent, was losing about $350 million a year.

Administration Recommendations

Housing and Urban Development (HUD) Secretary Jack F. Kemp presented a five-part strategy to improve the FHA's financial standing.

Key elements of those recommendations would require Congress to impose an additional 0.5 percent loan assessment on FHA home buyers who provided less than a 10 percent down payment and would require borrowers to pay at least two-thirds of closing costs in cash. The 0.5 percent mortgage premium for buyers would be financed as part of the overall mortgage. It would be paid over a period of from four to 15 years, depending on the amount of the down payment. Under the existing system, the FHA allowed buyers to finance closing costs, which usually ran to several thousand dollars.

The Bush administration's proposals also would hold the FHA mortgage loan limits at $124,875 to keep high-income families from qualifying for loans. Kemp said he opposed any move to allow FHA mortgages on second homes.

The system of paying distributive shares to buyers at the end of their 30-year loans would be discontinued under the administration's plan. The shares were the excess of premiums paid over losses. HUD, however, would continue to pay the distributive shares for home buyers who purchased their homes prior to 1980.

Kemp said he wanted further reforms in the FHA's administrative and accounting procedures to cut costs. According to the Price Waterhouse study, the FHA was losing 37 cents on the dollar on foreclosures. Kemp said the FHA needed to cut losses in foreclosures by reselling those homes faster. The FHA was spending $500 million a year in carrying costs of 80,000 homes it had foreclosed on, Kemp said.

Legislative Action

Senate. On June 20, Alfonse M. D'Amato of New York, ranking Republican on the Banking Subcommittee on Housing and Urban Affairs, offered an FHA-reform amendment even tougher than the administration's proposal. His amendment would increase FHA down payment requirements to 5 percent of the total purchase price; establish a risk-based premium, requiring higher premiums on smaller down payments; require buyers to pay all closing costs up front in cash; and make the existing mortgage limit permanent at $124,875. Housing industry groups — including the National Association of Realtors, the National Association of Home Builders, the Mortgage Bankers Association and Consumers Union — lined up in opposition to D'Amato's amendment, as well as the administration's proposal.

Subcommittee Chairman Alan Cranston, D-Calif., offered a plan that he said would restore the FHA to full financial health "without placing a draconian burden on millions of middle-income families who are trying to buy a home." His proposal would increase the FHA premium to equal to or higher than the level the administration proposed; require the HUD secretary to set an annual premium to reach goals for actuarial soundness, using a small upfront fee and annual premium payments through the life of the mortgage; end the practice of allowing the mortgage loan to exceed the value of the home; and require the secretary to work with independent actuaries to recommend ways to base the premium on the equity the home buyer invested in his home.

In a compromise worked out among the principals — Kemp, Cranston, D'Amato and the deputy director of OMB — and with the help of staff, the Senate Sept. 27 voted to accept a plan that was largely aligned with the administration's proposal. Home buyers would be allowed to continue to finance a 3.8 percent upfront mortgage insurance premium, but they would have to pay two-thirds of their closing costs in cash. Those who could not come up with at least a 10 percent down payment on the price of the home would be required to pay a 0.5 percent annual premium for up to 15 years. In addition, the FHA could continue to insure homes up to $124,875.

House. When the House took up the FHA issue, three proposals were on the table: the administration plan; a proposal by Bruce F. Vento, D-Minn., and Tom Ridge, R-Pa.; and a compromise put forth by Banking, Finance and Urban Affairs Committee Chairman Henry B. Gonzalez, D-Texas.

The Vento-Ridge proposal would spread out the mortgage insurance premium and leave intact the amount of money people paid up front. It would require a 1.35 percent mortgage insurance premium up front, though it could be financed. In addition, the owner would have to pay a 0.6 percent annual premium over the life of the loan; closing costs could be financed.

The Gonzalez plan would use a 2.6 percent upfront premium, with annual premium levels as necessary, and two-thirds of the closing costs could be financed. The secretary would report to Congress every six months on the soundness of the mortgage insurance fund; and with Congress' approval, the secretary could change the annual premium level.

In an unusual alliance, housing industry as well as advocacy groups backed the Vento-Ridge proposal; Kemp and the administration vehemently opposed it. Critics said the plan was not strong enough to revive the fund and that the number of families defaulting on FHA loans would rise.

In a letter to key housing lawmakers that also was sent to every House member, Kemp said President Bush would veto any legislation that did not include the administration's plan to fix the insurance fund. Subsequently, Kemp met with Gonzalez and offered to accept a modified Gonzalez plan to require buyers to pay 50 percent of closing costs up front. Gonzalez rejected the idea, however, saying it would cost buyers too much.

Support for the Vento-Ridge proposal grew steadily, and a few hours before a scheduled vote on the plan July 31, the Republican Leadership Conference decided to back the plan. Kemp, in response, threatened to resign if Vento-Ridge reached Bush's desk. He later said that he did not mean to be taken literally and that he only wanted others to know how strongly he felt.

The House adopted the Vento-Ridge amendment 418-2. The Kemp plan was not offered as an amendment on the floor and thus was not voted on.

Conference. Kemp reiterated his opposition to the House-passed provisions and said he would recommend a veto if they remained in the omnibus housing reauthorization bill, even if it meant sacrificing the administration's home ownership initiative.

Administration officials said that despite the flaws in the FHA program, they would prefer to retain existing law rather than adopt the Vento-Ridge proposal. The reason, they said, was that defaults would increase under the Vento-Ridge plan. Also, administration officials insisted that a risk-based premium was essential to reduce the default rate.

In the end, what did in the House plan was the congressional-White House budget summit agreement, requiring $2.5 billion in revenues from FHA premiums over the next five years. Conferees agreed on an FHA compromise under which first-time home buyers would have to pay, on average, an additional $833 in cash up front on a $65,000 house. New "risk-based" requirements were adopted to weed out people more likely to default on the mortgages.

Furthermore, buyers would pay an annual premium of 0.5 percent for the life of the loan if their down payment was between 5 percent and 10 percent or for 11 years if their down payment was more than 10 percent. Buyers who put down less than 5 percent of their loan would pay a 0.55 percent annual premium for the 30-year life of the loan.

Members of the real estate industry predicted that as many as 60,000 families each year would be unable to afford a house under the new FHA rules.

Mortgage 'Prepayments'

Congress in 1990 crafted a complex compromise to a conflict between landlords who wanted to pay off their federally subsidized mortgages early and their low-income tenants who faced possible eviction if landlords converted the properties to more profitable use.

The solution — part of omnibus housing authorization legislation (S 566 — PL 101-625) — lifted a moratorium on landlords' paying off the mortgages while imposing procedures that guaranteed landlords an 8 percent return on their investments and also gave tenants the chance to buy the property if the landlord wanted to sell. The Department of Housing and Urban Development (HUD) would be required to offer incentives to owners to continue renting to low-income families or to people who bought the property and promised to continue the affordable rents. Owners would be allowed to receive the fair market value for their property, which would then have to be used for low-income tenants until the building was no longer livable. In limited circumstances, owners could pay off their mortgages and continue to own the property. *(Housing authorization, p. 665; preservation of affordable rental housing provisions, p. 674)*

Background

The prepayment dispute pitted owners' rights against tenants' needs and set congressional liberals against conservatives and the Bush administration.

The mortgages stemmed from the government's decision beginning in 1961 to entice private entrepreneurs and non-profit developers to build housing for low-income tenants by offering mortgage insurance and interest-rate subsidies in return for a commitment to keep the housing available for low-income persons for the life of the mortgage, usually 40 years.

As an additional incentive, the government promised that owners could prepay the mortgages after 20 years. By the 1980s, prepayment offered a financial opportunity to the landlords to convert their properties to more lucrative uses — and thus threatened the tenants' interests and the government's goal.

Congress responded with provisions in the 1987 omnibus housing act (PL 100-242) that came to be viewed as an effective moratorium on prepayments. A provision set to expire in 1990 forbade prepayments unless owners could prove that their tenants' "economic hardship" would not be increased and that any shortage of low-rent housing in the area would not be exacerbated. *(1987 law, Congress and the Nation Vol. VII, p. 672)*

Administration Proposal

As part of the Bush administration's Project HOPE (Homeownership and Opportunity for People Everywhere), HUD Secretary Jack F. Kemp March 13, 1990, proposed lifting the moratorium, but softening the blow somewhat to low-income tenants by shielding them from sudden rent increases.

Building owners would have to file notice of whether they intended to prepay their mortgages. If so, tenants would be given a two-year right of first refusal to purchase their building with grants from HUD. Furthermore, if owners decided to prepay a mortgage and tenants did not buy the building, the owners would have to underwrite moving expenses, security deposits and the cost of six months' housing for each tenant.

HUD could approve a building owner's prepayment plan only if the agency had enough money to provide rent-assistance vouchers or certificates to tenants who had to move.

Legislative Action

Senate. Prepayment did not emerge as a contentious issue in the Senate, which tended to favor tenants. Alan Cranston, D-Calif., chairman of the Banking Subcommittee on Housing and Urban Affairs, easily won approval of his plan to allow owners to prepay their mortgages only if they informed HUD 18 months in advance and the secretary approved a plan of action for the project and its tenants.

If owners decided to continue renting to low-income tenants, they could take advantage of incentives giving them an annual return of 8 percent on their equity in the housing. In addition, some rents could be increased, and owners could finance capital improvements to their buildings through HUD loans.

The Senate passed S 566 on June 27.

House. Landlords relied on Rep. Steve Bartlett, R-Texas, to carry the prepayment issue for them in the House and in conference. Bartlett argued that the government had a moral obligation to honor its contracts with building owners. If it did not, he said, people would not be interested in doing business with the government in the future.

By the time the House Banking, Finance and Urban Affairs Committee approved its version of the housing bill (HR 1180) on June 13, Bartlett had spent days huddling with Massachusetts Democrats Joseph P. Kennedy II and Barney Frank, trying in vain to work out a compromise House proposal.

In the markup, Bartlett scored a coup. His amendment, backed by building owners and the housing industry, was adopted, 29-19, after a lengthy debate with Frank, whose alternative proposal went nowhere despite support by committee Chairman Henry B. Gonzalez, D-Texas. Bartlett's plan sought to provide incentives to building owners to continue renting to low-income families for the full 40 years of their mortgages instead of paying off the loans at the 20-year mark. The incentives included increased rents, project-based Section 8 rental assistance to all tenants earning below 80 percent of the area median income, financing of capital improvements under HUD's Section 201 program and equity take-out loans insured by the Federal Housing Administration (FHA).

The plan would require owners to file a notice with HUD two years before they intended to prepay their mortgages. In low-vacancy areas, tenants could stay in their units at existing rents for three more years. Displaced tenants would receive rental vouchers or certificates. If owners decided to sell their buildings during the two-year notice period, they would have to do so to a non-profit or other group that agreed to maintain the property for low-income tenants. Grant assistance also would be provided to help tenants' groups buy their housing projects. To help displaced tenants, the plan would have authorized $250 million in fiscal 1991 and $250 million in fiscal 1992.

The key difference between the Bartlett and Frank proposals was that owners could prepay their mortgages for any reason under the Bartlett plan, but Frank's amendment would have made the existing moratorium permanent, allowing owners to prepay in only limited cases. In addition, the Frank plan would have required owners to continue renting to low- and moderate-income families for the remaining "useful life of the property," instead of the remainder of the mortgage, as under the Bartlett plan.

The committee also agreed, by voice vote, to an amendment by David E. Price, D-N.C., and Thomas R. Carper, D-Del., to require owners to pay at least 50 percent of a tenant's moving expenses. And it authorized $200 million in fiscal 1991 for HUD to provide grants to non-profit organizations purchasing housing.

On the floor July 31, four Democrats who had backed Bartlett's proposal in committee — Carper, Price, Peter Hoagland of Nebraska and Liz J. Patterson of South Carolina — proposed an amendment to build on that plan. Their amendment, adopted 400-12, offered new incentives and requirements to persuade owners to continue renting to low-income families.

Under the amendment, owners would have to give tenants and HUD a two-year notice that they planned to pay off the mortgage. HUD then would appraise the property and offer incentives to the owner to stay in the program. If the owner still wanted to pay off the mortgage, then any group willing to buy the property and maintain it for low-income tenants would have a right of first refusal. The owner would be required to sell to the group if it offered to pay the appraised value set by HUD. If no one offered to buy the property, the owner could pay off the mortgage and do whatever he wanted with the building.

In areas with very low vacancy rates, owners would have to give tenants an additional three years' notice on top of the two years to find a new place to live. The owner would be required to pay up to half of the tenants' moving expenses, and tenants would receive Section 8 rent-subsidy certificates or vouchers to pay for their next home.

The House passed HR 1180, then S 566 with the language of HR 1180, on Aug. 1.

Conference. Before the prepayment language could be reconciled in conference, Congress had to extend a Sept. 30 deadline on the moratorium. The House passed a temporary extension (HR 5558) by voice vote under suspension of the rules Sept. 10. The Senate passed the measure by voice vote Sept. 27, after complicating it by adding an amendment to require Congress to take a pay cut if automatic spending cuts kicked in for federal civil servants. The Senate asked for a conference with the House, but the House instead passed an identical bill (HR 5747) without the Senate amendment by voice vote under suspension of the rules Sept. 28. The Senate approved HR 5747 by voice vote later the same day. President Bush signed it Oct. 1 (PL 101-402).

A compromise was worked out between Frank, Bartlett and Cranston's staff, and conferees gave their final approval of the plan Oct. 12.

The deal provided that owners would be compensated at fair market values in exchange for preserving the housing for low-income tenants for the remaining useful life of the property, not through the 40-year contract. In some cases, the owners could still pay off their loans if the community had high vacancy rates for affordable housing. The plan also would allow owners to sell their properties to residents or non-profit groups committed to maintaining the buildings for low-income families.

Both sides agreed that the legislation was likely to withstand court challenges. The plan was estimated to cost $30 billion over 20 years.

Homeless Aid

Congress in 1990 cleared a reauthorization (HR 3789 — PL 101-645) of the Stewart B. McKinney Homeless Assistance Act, the principal source of federal aid for the homeless.

The McKinney Act, enacted in 1987 (PL 100-77), authorized grants to local governments to provide emergency food and shelter to the homeless, develop transitional housing to help homeless people move toward permanent homes and convert federal surplus property to shelter the homeless. The measure was named for Rep. Stewart B. McKinney, R-Conn. (1971-87), who died several months before the law was enacted. *(Congress and the Nation Vol. VII, p. 677)*

HR 3789 included an initiative by Sen. Pete V. Domenici, R-N.M., to expand services for homeless people who were mentally ill or substance abusers. It authorized $75 million in grants in fiscal 1991 to underwrite screening and diagnostic services, rehabilitation, mental health counseling, and alcohol and drug treatment. Altogether, the legislation authorized $937 million in fiscal 1991 and $941 million in fiscal 1992.

The House Banking, Finance and Urban Affairs Committee on June 13 approved its version of legislation (HR 1180) to overhaul federal housing programs. The committee subsequently duplicated the bill's provisions to help the homeless, formally reporting them out separately in HR 3789 (H Rept 101-583, Part I) on July 10. The precaution was taken in case the omnibus housing bill bogged down. The McKinney Act had become a popular program that few members opposed. *(Housing reauthorization, p. 665)*

The House Energy and Commerce Committee approved the health care for the homeless provisions on July 27 and reported HR 3789 (H Rept 101-583, Part II) on July 30.

The House passed the bill by voice vote under suspension of the rules Oct. 10.

The Senate Labor and Human Resources Committee approved its reauthorization of the McKinney Act (S 2863) on July 18, 16-0. The measure was reported (S Rept 101-436) on Aug. 30. The Senate passed S 2863 on Sept. 26 by voice vote, then it passed an amended HR 3789 on Oct. 12 by voice vote.

The House agreed to the conference report (H Rept 101-951) by voice vote Oct. 26; the Senate followed suit the next day, clearing HR 3789. President Bush signed the bill Nov. 29.

Flood, Crime Insurance

Legislation (HR 3281 — PL 101-137) reauthorizing the federal flood and crime insurance programs for two years cleared in 1989.

The bill included a one-year reauthorization of several rural housing programs and a 10-month extension of the Defense Production Act (DPA). Authority for all the programs had expired Sept. 30, 1989.

Because property owners must carry flood insurance to apply for disaster relief assistance, swift action to renew the program was necessary to ensure that victims of Hurricane Hugo could qualify for needed aid. The late September hurricane wreaked havoc on the Carolinas, Puerto Rico and the Virgin Islands.

Crime Insurance. Since 1971, the crime insurance program had provided home and business owners in high-crime urban areas protection against losses of up to $10,000 and $15,000, respectively. Proponents said that without it people and businesses would desert those places that needed strong community support.

The Bush administration, like the Reagan administration before it, wanted to kill the crime insurance program. Critics claimed that such insurance could be purchased on the private market. The Federal Emergency Management Agency (FEMA), which ran the crime and flood insurance programs, argued that "for the most part" private insurers provided adequate crime-loss coverage and that states had developed their own programs in the few areas where availability was a problem. According to FEMA, fewer than 26,000 policies remained in force by mid-1989 — about 15,000 in New York City alone — at a cost of $12 million a year. At its peak in 1984, the program provided insurance to fewer than 83,000 individuals and businesses.

FEMA and some House and Senate Republicans argued that the decline in policies was evidence that the program was no longer needed. But proponents countered that FEMA had encouraged states to leave the program without ensuring that they could set up replacement programs and had refused to market its product aggressively, as it did with flood insurance. The House Banking Committee said the potential market for federal crime insurance was much larger than the number of policies in force indicated. The committee added that FEMA could cut costs by increasing the size of its portfolio.

The crime insurance extension was approved after its mostly Republican opponents agreed to a compromise that allowed the administration to raise premiums by up to 15 percent a year, as opposed to the 5 percent cap favored by program proponents.

Legislative History. Enacting the flood and crime insurance reauthorization came following a game of legislative Ping-Pong.

The House passed the flood and crime insurance extensions as HR 2771 by voice vote on Sept. 19 and as its revenue-raising contribution to the fiscal 1990 reconciliation package (HR 3299), 333-91, on Oct. 5. Both bills included caps on premium increases of 10 percent on flood insurance and 5 percent for crime insurance.

The Senate Banking, Housing and Urban Affairs Committee July 13, in its reconciliation package, declined to include the crime insurance extension or the cap on flood insurance premium increases. Its version also required a report on the effects of rising sea levels on the flood program and authorized $36.3 million in fiscal 1990 and "such sums as may be necessary" in 1991 to pay for congressionally mandated studies.

The Senate, by voice vote Sept. 25, passed HR 2771, after substituting its reconciliation version of the flood insurance measure, adding its own 10 percent-a-year premium cap, removing the crime insurance provisions and tacking on extensions for several programs that provided loans and grants for housing in rural areas.

Meanwhile, both chambers had been working on the DPA extension on separate tracks as HR 3281 and S 1672. Slightly different versions of HR 3281 were passed by voice vote by the House on Sept. 19 and the Senate on Sept. 27.

On Sept. 28, the House passed a four-part package (H J Res 412) that included both insurance extensions, the DPA provision and the rural housing reauthorizations (but for one year only). It added a one-year extension for a counseling program aimed at helping home owners avoid foreclosure.

Then, after reaching agreement with the Senate on the crime insurance extension, the House Oct. 5 accepted an expanded HR 3281, which included all four sections: flood and crime insurance (each for two years); DPA; and all the housing programs (each for one year). The flood insurance section also included the study and spending authorization in the Senate version of the reconciliation bill. The Senate accepted the changes to HR 3281 on Oct. 24, clearing the measure. The president signed the bill Nov. 3.

1991-92

Housing Reauthorization

Shortly before the 102nd Congress adjourned in 1992, a $66.5 billion two-year authorization of housing programs (HR 5334 — PL 102-550) cleared. Housing and Urban Development (HUD) Secretary Jack F. Kemp opposed the legislation, saying it abandoned the reforms instituted in 1990 that sought to reduce the number of defaults on the Federal Housing Administration (FHA) mortgage insurance fund. *(1990 housing reauthorization, p. 665; FHA insurance fund, p. 690)*

The legislation began chiefly as a vehicle to fine-tune programs created by the 1990 omnibus housing bill (S 566 — PL 101-625) that were aimed at giving more Americans the chance to own homes. Those programs included the administration's Homeownership and Opportunity for People Everywhere (HOPE) program, which was designed to sell public housing to tenants, and the Democrats' HOME (Homeownership Made Easy) Investment Partnerships Act, which provided federal funds to state and local governments on a matching formula.

As momentum for aiding cities increased, encouraged by the riots that shook Los Angeles in April 1992 following the Rodney King police-beating trial, the legislation grew into an 1,100-page bill that included initiatives to revitalize communities and renovate older public housing units. The final measure also contained a new title that gave uniform marching orders to several federal agencies to gradually eliminate lead-based paint from public and private housing.

In addition, HR 5334 addressed the problem of "mixed housing." Numerous districts experienced outbreaks of violence in public and subsidized housing as an influx of younger disabled residents moved into complexes that once housed only the elderly. Many of them were mentally disabled or drug abusers who qualified for public housing under the broadened definition of disability. The bill struck a compromise that provided safety to the elderly while protecting the rights of the disabled.

House Action

Subcommittee. The House Banking Subcommittee on Housing and Community Development, on a 22-13 party-line vote May 20, 1992, approved a $35.4 billion housing reauthorization bill. Republicans opposed the measure's funding levels, a provision to remove limits on FHA financing and the lack of support for Bush administration initiatives.

The panel spent two days wrangling over nearly 60 amendments and deferred several issues for full committee consideration, including the problem of how to integrate the elderly population in a limited supply of federally assisted housing with younger disabled people.

The subcommittee bill reauthorized housing programs for only one year, evidence of the growing philosophical gap between House Banking, Finance and Urban Affairs Chairman Henry B. Gonzalez, D-Texas, and the equally outspoken Kemp. Gonzalez wanted to maintain his flexibility on the chance that he could gain more of what he wanted in 1993 — when a new Democratic administration might be installed. Both Gonzalez and Kemp, however, viewed the Los Angeles riots as a cry for better housing.

Republican lawmakers used the urban unrest to bring new attention to HOPE, the centerpiece of the administration's housing strategy; Democrats, meanwhile, pushed the HOME program. The strategies collided when the ranking Republican on the subcommittee, Marge Roukema of New Jersey, unsuccessfully proposed to raise the local matching funds requirement under the HOME program from the 10 percent called for in the subcommittee draft bill to 25 percent.

Roukema, revealing early her willingness to depart from the GOP ranks, won approval, 19-16, to increase authorized funding for the HOME program from $1.5 billion to $2.1 billion. The administration had requested $700 million. Another amendment by Roukema, to reduce the measure's funding levels across the board by approximately $5.3 billion, was defeated, 16-19. Immediately after, Sam Johnson, R-Texas, proposed that funding for HOPE be increased by $1 billion over the $290 million in the bill. His effort was rejected, 11-24.

The Republicans were divided on other issues as well. For example, the panel defeated, 10-25, an amendment offered by Roukema and Stephen L. Neal, D-N.C., to retain the existing 57 percent limit on the amount of closing costs that could be financed in single-family mortgages insured by the FHA. The draft bill contained a provision that prohibited the HUD secretary from using his discretionary authority to establish any limit on the amount of closing costs that could be FHA-financed.

The panel agreed, by voice vote, to an amendment by Gerald D. Kleczka, D-Wis., to begin exploring a new approach to mixing populations of the elderly and the mentally disabled in public housing. Kleczka's compromise amendment would designate floors and units in public housing for the elderly but would not evict anyone already in residence. But members felt that more needed to be done to protect the rights of the disabled.

Frank Riggs, R-Calif., offered a 72-page radical restructuring of the public housing system, which triggered the longest and most heated debate. The amendment, rejected by voice vote, called for a greater choice in management and ownership of units, with the goal of providing tenants with greater flexibility to buy their apartments.

Committee. The House Banking Committee June 16 approved HR 5334, authorizing $29.7 billion in fiscal 1993 for housing programs. The panel rebuked nearly all of Kemp's new ideas and cut by more than half the administration's funding request for HOPE. The bill authorized $2.1 billion for the HOME program; the president had requested only $700 million. Kemp told Chairman Gonzalez in a June 15 letter that the House version violated "the spirit of bipartisanship that made the 1990 National Affordable Housing Act possible."

Although the committee approved a largely Democratic bill, Republicans scored one major victory when an amendment, offered by Roukema, to scale back funding by nearly $7 billion was approved on a 27-22 vote. Eight of the 31 Democrats on the panel voted for the lower budget figures.

Barney Frank, D-Mass., was defeated in his bid to force removal of certain regulatory barriers to affordable housing. His amendment, offered with Riggs, would have given HUD the authority to say whether a state or local government was in violation of using zoning or "artificial environmental concerns" to increase housing costs and limit the supply of lower-income housing.

A compromise amendment offered by Doug Bereuter, R-Neb., to delete the section in Frank's amendment that would have allowed HUD to withhold HOME funds or Community Development Block Grants from errant local governments was defeated, 11-37. The panel voted, 31-19, to approve another Frank amendment that would push HUD to implement rules for provisions of the 1990 bill not yet acted on.

Before the markup, the full Banking Committee had resolved a number of thorny issues deferred by the subcommittee, including the problem of how to integrate the elderly population in federally assisted housing with younger disabled people. The committee received testimony suggesting a wide range of options, from complete segregation of the two populations to complete integration, which some believed was the only way to avoid violating fair housing laws. Some middle-range solutions also were offered, including the costly proposal to provide special services and hire service coordinators to help ease the lifestyle differences between the two groups.

The compromise worked out by Frank and Kleczka — and agreed to by voice vote — would give owners of buildings originally designed for the elderly the option of maintaining a preference for older people as long as a set number of units were reserved for other groups, such as non-elderly handicapped. As incentives, the proposal permitted a person denied a unit in an elderly-only building to seek additional rental assistance subsidies. Further, it required that at least 5 percent of the housing money allocated for reconstruction of obsolete housing projects be used to

HOPE, HOME Funding

Congress and the administration in 1991 disagreed over how much money to allocate to two contradictory housing programs — Homeownership and Opportunity for People Everywhere (HOPE) and HOME (Homeownership Made Easy) Investment Partnerships. Both were established in the 1990 omnibus housing authorization bill (S 566 — PL 101-625). *(Housing authorization, p. 665)*

HOPE, developed by Housing and Urban Development (HUD) Secretary Jack F. Kemp, would sell off federally assisted housing to public housing tenants and other poor people. HOME, devised by Senate Democrats, would provide block grants to states and local governments to build and renovate affordable housing as well as provide rental vouchers.

The dispute arose during consideration of the fiscal 1992 appropriations bill (HR 2519 — PL 102-139) for HUD, Veterans Affairs (VA) and independent agencies. Although the programs were authorized in 1990, Congress provided no funds for them in the fiscal 1991 HUD-VA spending bill (HR 5158 — PL 101-507).

The House, going against the wishes of its Appropriations Committee, voted 216-183 on June 6, 1990, to earmark $361 million for the HOPE program. The committee had recommended no money to sell public housing to tenants; many VA-HUD Appropriations Subcommittee members were philosophically opposed to the idea.

Most of the big housing groups were lobbying for money for HOME, not HOPE. The House gave the HOME program $500 million. Public housing advocates, however, did not want more money for HOME to come at the expense of other housing programs.

The Senate passed HR 2519 by voice vote July 18. It provided $215 million for HOPE, with $175 million going to the public housing ownership component, and $2 billion for HOME.

Conferees cut back on the HOPE program appropriation even further, providing $136 million, while the HOME partnerships received $1.5 billion.

Kemp, who had sought $865 million for HOPE, said he would ask for a presidential veto. In a Sept. 25 letter to the conference chairman, Kemp charged that the House-Senate compromise was a "betrayal of low-income families" and amounted to a return "to the failed scandal-prone housing programs of the past." The administration had requested $1 billion for HOME.

President Bush did not veto HR 2519, however, as it fully funded his top priority — the space station *Freedom*.

In 1992, Congress provided $661 million for HOPE and $1 billion for HOME in the fiscal 1993 HUD-VA spending bill (HR 5679 — PL 102-389).

reconfigure public housing as an alternative for single people who were not elderly.

HR 5334 was formally reported (H Rept 102-760) on July 20.

Floor. With the backing of most Republicans, the House Aug. 5 voted 369-54 to pass HR 5334, providing a $28.8 billion reauthorization. The vote sent a strong signal to the Bush administration that members of both parties were willing to negotiate on the most controversial issues, including making it easier for home buyers to finance the cost of an FHA mortgage and for state and local governments to obtain matching federal grants for low-income housing initiatives. A key reason for the bill's overwhelming support was a carefully worded provision, worked out by Frank and Kleczka in committee, that sought to resolve the unsettling problem of how to integrate the disabled — including the mentally ill — with elderly residents in public and subsidized housing units.

On the floor, a group of amendments accepted en bloc by voice vote moved toward some GOP goals. The compromise offered a 4 percent across-the-board cut in funding and increased from 10 percent to 20 percent the flat local matching requirement for HOME. The administration, however, wanted the more rigid three-tiered system of matching payments that was contained in the 1990 housing bill. Appropriators waived that system in fiscal 1992 after local officials said it created budgeting problems. The administration won approval of other initiatives, such as a program to allow poorly managed public housing units to be transferred to another management entity.

Republicans did not get all they wanted, however. Just before final passage the House rejected, 147-277, a GOP motion to recommit the bill to committee and require more funding for HOPE.

Many key housing industry groups were satisfied with the House bill. A veto threat loomed over the House bill mainly because it would eliminate a rule that allowed FHA borrowers to use their loans to finance only up to 57 percent of closing costs associated with taking out a mortgage. This would reverse efforts pushed by the administration in the 1990 bill aimed at bolstering FHA solvency. But the National Association of Realtors and other housing lobbyists had argued that the 1990 rules — if not reversed — threatened to block 60,000 families who could otherwise afford home ownership from purchasing homes.

The administration also objected to House language substantially increasing the limit on FHA single-family home loans — from its existing limit of $124,875 to about $151,725. Administration officials maintained that the provision would move the federal mortgage agency away from its traditional role as a resource for the lower-income, first-time home buyers. The industry insisted that it would increase the opportunity of home ownership for more families.

Senate Action

Committee. After weeks of tense negotiations within Congress and with Kemp, the Senate Banking, Housing and Urban Affairs Committee on June 18 unanimously approved by voice vote a bipartisan bill (S 3031) to authorize $22 billion for fiscal 1993 and $22.8 billion for fiscal 1994. Unlike the House bill, the Senate version endorsed the administration's push toward getting the federal government out of the business of subsidized housing. It also sought to refine and expand the Democrats' partnership concept of giving more money to state and local governments to meet housing needs. S 3031 was reported (S Rept 102-332) on July 23.

The committee left for floor consideration the contentious issues of matching funds for the HOME program and the mixing of the elderly and the disabled in public housing.

S 3031 included six key components: additional support for community-based efforts through HOME, empowerment to low-income youth through the new Youthbuild program to provide construction training jobs, a strengthening of fair housing enforcement efforts, steps to prevent lead poisoning of children, expansion of affordable housing by providing more credit to the Federal Housing Administration and a modified version of Kemp's new agenda. The committee bill included a demonstration of Kemp's "Choice in Management Program" — which sought to give tenants of troubled public housing units the opportunity to switch management — and pieces of another new program called "Take the Boards Off," a proposal to allow public housing that was at least 50 percent vacant to be transferred to non-profit organizations for renovation.

The measure also included a small authorization for a new program that would provide interest-free second mortgages for up to $15,000 on any home built or renovated in a state or federal enterprise zone.

Floor. Two takes were needed to get the housing bill through the full Senate by unanimous consent. The process required the mutual cooperation of all senators; often, it meant a number of deals or tradeoffs.

On Aug. 12, as the countdown to recess pressured senators to move quickly on the measure so that conference action could begin, an unidentified Republican had put a hold on S 3031. Some speculated that the opposition was rooted in the growing Republican dislike for Kemp. The secretary's initiatives for selling public housing would be advanced through the bill, giving him something tangible to tout at the upcoming Republican convention in Houston.

A negotiated bipartisan amendment that was to have been offered on the Senate floor would have given Kemp several programs geared primarily toward getting the federal government out of subsidized housing and giving tenants of troubled public housing units more options to choose their managers. The amendment also would have slightly scaled back a new program designed to prevent lead poisoning of children.

What also loomed between the bipartisan compromise and Senate floor passage was the threat of unwanted amendments. John F. Kerry, D-Mass., threatened to bring up a proposal to overhaul the National Flood Insurance Program by reducing premiums for communities that refrained from building in coastal hazard areas. He subsequently agreed not to offer the amendment. Alfonse M. D'Amato, R-N.Y., meanwhile, said he would not put a hold on the bill if the flood insurance issue were dropped. Republicans Connie Mack of Florida and Malcolm Wallop of Wyoming said they would not introduce technical fixes to the 1991 bank overhaul bill (S 543 — PL 102-242). Democrat Terry Sanford of North Carolina also agreed not to attempt similar fixes to the banking measure. *(Bank overhaul, p. 136)*

When Senate Majority Leader George J. Mitchell, D-Maine, brought up the housing bill Sept. 10, all deals held. After a week of intense conversation between senators and the administration, no one spoke as the Senate by voice vote passed HR 5334, a $22.7 billion measure, with some changes and sent it to a conference with the House.

Conference, Final Action

Conferees completed work Oct. 2 with strong Republican backing and despite a veto threat from the administration.

The compromise bill resolved the difficult issue of mixing the elderly and the disabled in a shrinking supply of public and subsidized housing by allowing landlords to give the elderly preference in some units but requiring them to set aside at least 10 percent for the disabled. The bill also included a major new set of rules to clarify and strengthen the federal role in eliminating lead-based paint from homes; streamlined several existing housing programs; and established new initiatives, including one to provide construction job training skills to youth.

House Banking Committee Chairman Gonzalez said he had made considerable concessions to meet the demands of the administration, especially on Kemp's pet project, HOPE. But Kemp said in an Oct. 2 letter to Gonzalez that the conference agreement fell short on a number of issues, especially on his objective of retaining the limits on FHA closing costs, imposed in 1990. Conferees wanted to strike that law and let borrowers finance up to 100 percent of their closing costs so that home buyers did not have to pay so much money up front. But conferees had little power to effect any changes in the FHA rules because they were lifted in the fiscal 1993 spending bill for HUD (HR 5679 — PL 102-389). Yet Kemp remained adamant that something should be done by the authorizers to protect the FHA loan guarantee fund from possible fiscal collapse.

Much of the conference give-and-take occurred over the fine-tuning of existing programs. Kemp used his leverage on several key points, including funding levels for HOPE: Conferees raised HOPE's authorization to $855 million for fiscal 1993. However, this had little real effect because it far exceeded the fiscal 1993 appropriation.

The administration gained something more tangible when negotiations turned to the HOME program. Conferees devised a new formula for requiring state and local governments to match the federal contribution: 25 percent for tenant assistance and rehabilitation, and 30 percent for new construction. Administration officials still objected because they felt more extensive rehabilitation also should be in the 30 percent category.

Kemp won an agreement to reduce the amount of public debt that state and local governments could use as part of their share. Borrowings could make up only 25 percent of the local share.

A middle course was negotiated to broaden the scope of the lead-based paint abatement provisions to give more specific direction to the Environmental Protection Agency (EPA) and the Occupational Safety and Health Administration (OSHA). Furthermore, language from HR 5730 (H Rept 102-852, Part I; H Rept 102-852, Part II), which called for significant lead reduction, was incorporated into the Senate lead title. According to data collected by the Senate Banking Committee, low-level lead poisoning afflicted as many as 3 million children under age 6 and caused reading and other learning disabilities, and more than 3 million tons of lead in the form of lead-based paint remained in American homes.

As approved by the conferees, the bill increased HUD's competitive grant program to state and local governments for lead-based paint hazard reduction in private, low-income housing. It also authorized a program to evaluate and reduce the problem in federally owned and subsidized pre-1978 low-income housing. Provisions outlined how the "lead-hazard reduction" activities would be performed by certified contractors, including certification rules and penalties for non-compliance.

On other issues, conferees agreed to a number of noncontroversial initiatives aimed at easing regulatory burdens on the nation's banks and thrifts.

The House adopted the conference report on HR 5334 (H Rept 102-1017) on a 377-37 vote Oct. 5. The Senate acted by voice vote three days later. Kemp requested a veto, but President Bush signed the bill on Oct. 28.

Major Provisions

As cleared, HR 5334:

Authorization. Authorized $32.5 billion in fiscal 1993 and $34 billion in fiscal 1994 for federal housing and community development programs, including rural housing.

Mixed Housing for the Elderly and Disabled. Allowed public housing authorities to designate separate federal housing based on age or disability, subject to HUD approval.

Allowed owners of federally subsidized housing designed for the elderly to give preference to the elderly if they set aside 10 percent of the units for the disabled.

Authorized additional funding for service coordinators in public and subsidized housing to deal with the difficulties — including outbreaks of violence — the two groups encounter living side by side.

Lead-Based Paint Hazard Reduction Act. Created ground-breaking rules to reduce and eliminate lead-based paint poisoning hazards in private and federal housing. Home buyers had the opportunity to test for lead paint before purchase. Federal grants were to go to states and localities to reduce hazards in all low-income housing. Requirements for evaluating and reducing paint hazards in federally subsidized housing were to be phased in.

Standardized directives for EPA and OSHA. Strengthened protection for workers facing lead hazards through OSHA and directed EPA to establish or approve state certification programs for lead inspectors. Training and certification requirements were imposed on all lead contractors.

HOME Investment Partnerships Act. Established a two-tiered system that asked localities to match 25 percent for substantial and moderate rehabilitation and 30 percent for new construction. Publicly issued debt could be used for up to 25 percent of the total match. Offered a reduced match for communities with extremely high poverty rates. Eliminated restrictions on new construction and allowed up to 10 percent of HOME funds to be used for administrative costs.

As established in the 1990 housing reauthorization legislation (S 566 — PL 101-625), the program lacked a workable formula that balanced the goals of partnership with the difficulty communities had generating the necessary funds.

Federal Housing Administration. Raised the FHA single-family home loan limits to whichever was less: 95 percent of an area's median home price or 75 percent of the 1992 loan limit set by the Federal Home Loan Mortgage Corporation, which was $151,725. (The 57 percent cap on the financing of FHA closing costs, as provided in PL 101-625, was lifted in the fiscal 1993 spending bill for HUD (HR 5679 — PL 102-389).)

Administration Initiatives. Included up to $40 million for a Youthbuild program as part of an $855 million authorization for HOPE. Youthbuild provided construction job skills to disadvantaged youths through their involvement in building low-income housing.

Established pilot projects for several other programs advocated by HUD Secretary Kemp, including Choice in Management, to allow residents of troubled public housing units to choose alternative management; and Moving to Opportunity, to help families with children move out of high-poverty areas.

Preservation of Federally Assisted Housing. Reauthorized the 1990 preservation provisions with modifications. Eliminated the "windfall profits" test under which HUD had attempted to exempt property owners in many areas from the housing preservation provisions. Established a 40-year loan term for owners and purchasers to qualify for FHA-insured financing on equity loans.

New Towns Demonstration Program. Targeted assistance to two areas in or near Los Angeles that were affected by the April 1992 riots. Called for comprehensive community revitalization.

Homeless Assistance. Reauthorized the programs under the Stewart B. McKinney Homeless Assistance Act with small changes. Created a demonstration program known as Safe Havens for the Homeless to provide shelter and support for people living on the street.

GSE and Banking Provisions. Overhauled the structure for regulating government-sponsored enterprises (GSEs) such as the Federal National Mortgage Association (Fannie Mae).

Included the Annunzio-Wylie Anti-Money-Laundering Act, which strengthened anti-money-laundering requirements on non-bank financial institutions.

Flood Insurance

The House in 1991 passed legislation (HR 1236) to shore up the National Flood Insurance Program. But the administration threatened to veto the measure unless its cost estimates were used, and the Senate never acted on the bill.

HR 1236 (H Rept 102-38), as passed 388-18 on May 1, stipulated that mortgage companies could be fined up to $100,000 if they failed to require businesses or home buyers to purchase flood insurance on all mortgaged structures in areas prone to flooding. The bill required a mortgage lender or servicer already putting money aside for insurance or taxes to establish an escrow account for flood insurance premiums. The Federal National Mortgage Association and the Federal Home Loan Mortgage Corporation, however, were exempted.

The legislation required a community rating system, which would allow communities to reduce their costs of flood insurance if they took steps to protect against flooding. In addition, a flood hazard mitigation fund would be established, providing to states, communities and individuals matching grants to relocate or elevate buildings, and institute flood-proofing measures. It would be financed by a $5 per policy fee. The bill encouraged developers to build away from wetlands, the coasts and the Great Lakes.

According to both the Congressional Budget Office (CBO) and the Office of Management and Budget (OMB), the bill would save the program about $11 million a year. But the measure included the CBO estimate instead of OMB's. Bill Gradison, R-Ohio, objected, saying the bill violated the 1990 budget summit agreement, which Republicans contended required Congress to use OMB estimates. His amendment to strike the CBO language was rejected on a party-line vote, 160-248.

Ben Erdreich, D-Ala., chairman of the House Banking Subcommittee on Policy Research and Insurance, said that out of 11 million households in flood hazard areas, only 1.7 million were insured with flood policies, a rate of 15 percent.

Urban Aid

Three days of violence erupted in Los Angeles in late April 1992 after four white police officers were acquitted on all but one charge in the March 3, 1991, beating of black motorist Rodney King. As the riots inevitably brought attention to the poverty, crime and unemployment of that major urban center, a federal response was sought to end the crisis and help the cities.

Congress negotiated with the Bush administration on a quick-fix emergency urban aid bill (HR 5132) to benefit Los Angeles and Chicago. The package gave $1.1 billion in disaster loans and grants.

Then Congress promised to work out a long-term, far-reaching initiative to help all U.S. cities. It never materialized. What emerged was a small demonstration proposal to try out enterprise zones, which gave tax breaks to businesses willing to locate in blighted urban areas. That plan, however, was attached to a controversial tax bill (HR 11), which President Bush vetoed. Additional urban aid subsequently was provided in a disaster relief supplemental appropriations bill that included funding for unrelated defense programs (HR 5620).

A number of bills intended to provide a cash infusion to city governments to help boost regional economies and create jobs were introduced in the 102nd Congress, but none advanced to the floor.

HR 5132

Seven weeks after the riots, Congress cleared legislation (HR 5132) providing $1.1 billion in supplemental appropriations for direct small business loans and emergency grants to Los Angeles and Chicago, whose downtown was flooded underground after a tunnel collapsed beneath the Chicago River.

The version of HR 5132 (H Rept 102-518) passed 244-162 by the House May 14 was a modest $494.7 million bill. On May 21, however, the Senate 61-36 passed the measure after adding approximately $1.5 billion for a nationwide program of urban aid. For the most part, the funding was designated as "emergency," which meant offsetting cuts were not necessary to comply with the 1990 budget summit agreement.

Although the conferees on HR 5132 found the spending levels acceptable, not enough support for the bill existed in the House. Some members objected to increasing the federal budget deficit; rural and suburban members thought inner cities would get a disproportionate share. The money added by the Senate would have gone to a number of programs, including summer youth jobs; a Head Start summer program for preschool children; and "Weed and Seed," which aimed to "weed" drug dealers and other criminals out of inner-city neighborhoods and "seed" the areas with social programs. The administration threatened to veto the bill if it contained the nearly $2 billion appropriation.

A compromise was worked out, providing $1.1 billion. The conference report (H Rept 102-577) was adopted by the House on June 18 by a **key vote of 249-168 (R 43-117; D 205-51; I 1-0)**. The Senate adopted the conference report by voice vote later the same day, clearing HR 5132. The president signed the bill (PL 102-302) on June 22. *(1992 key votes, p. 1083)*

HR 11, HR 5620

States and cities had operated enterprise zones for years, using state and local tax incentives. Enterprise zones were spread throughout 36 states and the District of Columbia. As of June 1991, 22 states reported creating 258,395 jobs and 18 states reported capital investments in their zones totaling $28 billion.

The idea ran into trouble on the federal level, however, because of differences over the use of capital gains tax breaks to stimulate the economy. Republicans supported the capital gains tax cut, while Democrats were wary that allowing it would lead to lowering the tax rate, which would benefit only the wealthy. Some members also were concerned that tax breaks for businesses in enterprise zones would become an excuse not to spend money on other social programs.

Despite disagreements over how the enterprise zones should be structured and how many should be created, the House and Senate in HR 11 created 50 zones, with 25 in rural areas and 25 in cities. Investors who put their money into a zone for five years were to receive a 50 percent capital gains tax cut — a provision the administration said was imperative. Zone businesses would receive a 15 percent credit on the first $20,000 in wages paid to employees, a deduction of up to $25,000 for purchases of stock in zone businesses and more rapid tax write-offs for property. HR 11 was vetoed Nov. 4. *(HR 11, p. 103)*

Shortly before the riots, Congress cleared another tax bill (HR 4210) that included a $700 million demonstration plan to create 10 urban and rural enterprise zones. Bush vetoed HR 4210 March 20. *(HR 4210, p. 100)*

Lawmakers included in a combined fiscal 1992 supplemental appropriations bill (HR 5620) $500 million in direct spending for urban aid. The funds were pulled from the House-passed HR 11 and put in HR 5620. The money was to go to a variety of agencies, with the largest single chunk — $300 million — earmarked for the Interagency Council as a block grant for eligible programs. HR 5620 was signed into law (PL 102-368) on Sept. 23.

Other Bills

Several other bills to provide urban relief in a time of national recession were considered, but most Republicans and some Democrats opposed them, saying that no money was available and that the recession would end before the projects began.

HR 4073. The Housing and Community Development Subcommittee of House Banking, Finance and Urban Affairs gave voice vote approval March 4 to HR 4073, authorizing $15 billion in fiscal 1992 for state and local governments for such job programs as construction and rehabilitation of public buildings and other public facilities.

Committee Chairman Henry B. Gonzalez, D-Texas, who sponsored HR 4073, said that the emergency aid would create more than 600,000 jobs. But GOP opponents said the bill would increase the federal budget deficit and violate the pay-as-you-go rules of the 1990 budget agreement. The subcommittee adopted an amendment to prohibit use of a tax increase to pay for the bill.

The full committee approved the measure March 9 on a party-line voice vote. HR 4073 was formally reported (H Rept 102-524) on May 14.

HR 3601. Government Operations Committee Chairman John Conyers Jr., D-Mich., offered HR 3601, authorizing $2 billion in fiscal 1993, with funding increasing by $3 billion each year until reaching $14 billion in fiscal 1997. The Subcommittee on Human Resources and Intergovernmental Relations approved the bill on a 6-3 party-line vote Feb. 27. Aid would have been distributed under a complex formula that considered unemployment rates and per capita incomes in urban and semi-urban areas.

Conyers wanted to designate the spending in the measure as "emergency" so it would not have to be offset by cuts in other programs. Committee opponents said they would not support a bill that increased the deficit, however.

HR 5259. Another Conyers-sponsored bill (HR 5259) would authorize $5.4 billion in aid in fiscal 1992 and fiscal 1993. After a series of delays, the measure was rejected, 20-20, by the Government Operations Committee June 3.

HR 5798. By a 31-10 vote Aug. 11, Government Operations approved a third city aid bill written by Conyers (HR 5798). The legislation authorized $3 billion for 18,500 cities and localities in fiscal 1992 and fiscal 1993. It also required appropriators to offset costs with program cuts elsewhere. Members adopted an amendment to require 10 percent of any aid under the bill to be set aside for work by small businesses run by women or minorities.

HR 5798 was reported (H Rept 102-872) on Sept. 17.

12

Labor and Pension Policy

Introduction 703
1989-90 Chronology 705
1991-92 Chronology 720

Labor and Pension Policy

By the early 1990s, the U.S. labor force felt squeezed by federal budget woes, a deep recession and corporate realignments. The unemployment rate was on the rise — particularly for the white-collar middle class. And the standard of living for Americans in general was dropping.

The growing numbers of unemployed put added burdens on government to provide needed social services. Exceedingly high federal budget deficits hamstrung congressional efforts to enact job stimulus legislation. The 1990-91 recession led many businesses, if not to shut down entirely, to cut back severely — which for workers meant layoffs or less pay and for the economy meant more stagnant growth. Furthermore, the fall of communism in Eastern Europe and the breakup of the Soviet Union had tremendous repercussions for U.S. companies working under defense contracts.

Unemployment stood at 5.3 percent in 1989, President Bush's first full year in office. In 1992, his last, the average monthly unemployment rate was 7.4 percent. According to the Labor Department, the average weekly wage in constant 1982 dollars dropped from $275 in 1980 to $256 in 1991.

Organized labor continued to command a diminished power base. Union membership showed a marked decline in the 1980s and into the 1990s. Labor statistics reported that, in 1983, 17.7 million (20.1 percent) of the 88.3 million who were employed wage and salary workers over 16 years of age, excluding the self-employed, were union members; by 1991, 16.6 million (16.1 percent) of 102.8 million were union members.

Labor Legislation

President Bush proved less rigid in his approach to labor policy than his predecessor, Ronald Reagan. However, Bush's conservatism was in evidence as he continued to protect the interests of business.

In a departure from the policies of the Reagan administration, Bush in 1989 signed into law an increase in the minimum wage. The legislation raised the rate from $3.35, which had been set in 1981, to $4.25 an hour over two years. Congressional Democrats had sponsored a bill to increase the minimum wage to $4.55 over three years, but Bush vetoed it. Republicans, however, did not want the president to veto another minimum wage bill, and Democrats were eager for a wage increase. A compromise provided for lower rates of increase as well as a temporary "training wage" for teenage employees. The administration had wanted the subminimum wage available for all newly hired workers.

Provisions of the 1986 tax code overhaul — known as "Section 89," after their place in the tax code — were repealed before they took effect in 1989. The regulations were meant to discourage the business practice of providing the most generous benefits plans to the top-level employees of a company. Small businesses in particular rebelled against the impending regulations, not wanting to deal with the time-consuming record-keeping and complex reporting requirements. Labor interests saw Section 89 as the first step toward government taxation of employee benefits, so did not oppose repeal.

Despite his "pro-family" rhetoric, Bush twice vetoed legislation that would have provided unpaid leave to workers who had a new child or a sick family member to tend. He maintained that the issue was one for labor-management negotiations and objected to the government's giving businesses directives on employment policies. Supporters of parental leave pointed to the changing demographics of American society: About 60 percent of all mothers worked outside the home. They also noted that the United States was the only major industrialized nation in the world, besides South Africa, that did not have a family leave policy. Neither veto was overridden. However, a parental leave bill was quickly cleared by Congress and signed into law by President Bill Clinton in 1993.

The 1990-91 recession took its toll on the U.S. work force, driving increasing numbers of people onto the unemployment rolls for longer periods of time. In 1991 and 1992, legislation was enacted to extend unemployment benefits. A permanent change also was made in the unemployment benefits system, allowing for extended benefits to be more readily available when unemployment was high. Bush, believing the economy was on the mend, was reluctant to support the unemployment benefits legislation. Critics

References

Discussion of labor and pension policy for the years 1945-64 may be found in *Congress and the Nation Vol. I*, pp. 565-657, 1220-1224; for the years 1965-68, *Congress and the Nation Vol. II*, pp. 601-622, 734-743; for the years 1969-72, *Congress and the Nation Vol. III*, pp. 703-742; for the years 1973-76, *Congress and the Nation Vol. IV*, pp. 681-713; for the years 1977-80, *Congress and the Nation Vol. V*, pp. 399-425; for the years 1981-84, *Congress and the Nation Vol. VI*, pp. 643-672; for the years 1985-88, *Congress and the Nation Vol. VII*, pp. 687-709.

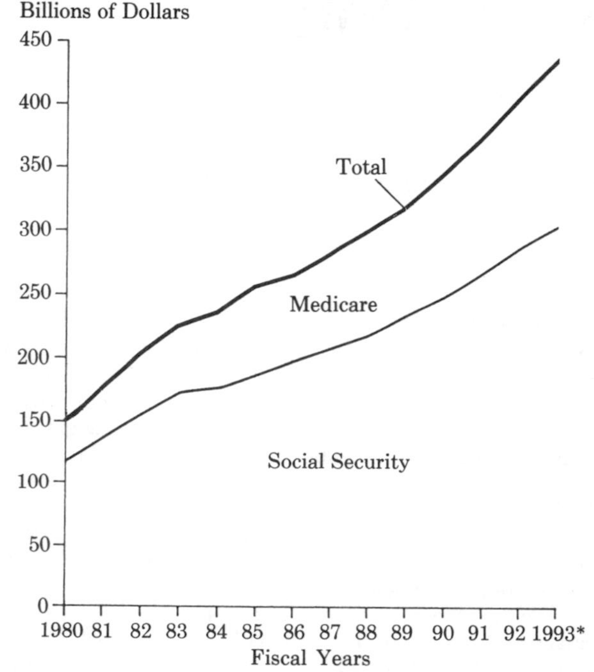

*Estimate.

Source: Office of Management and Budget, *Budget Baselines, Historical Data and Alternatives for the Future* (Washington, D.C.: U.S. Government Printing Office, January 1993).

charged that he did not hesitate to help people in foreign countries while he all but ignored those in trouble at home. Members of Congress, meanwhile, heard directly from constituents about their hardships.

As the unemployment lines continued to grow, the 101st Congress fashioned changes in the 1982 Job Training Partnership Act (JTPA), which sought to aid youths and unskilled adults in entering the job market. JTPA was rededicated to providing help to those who most needed job training while making participants in the program more accountable. Some of the impetus for the legislative reforms, which had been under consideration for several years, stemmed from the April 1992 uprising in Los Angeles following the verdict in the first Rodney King trial.

Pension Policy

Relatively little congressional action took place in the realm of pension policy during 1989-92. The major efforts centered around Social Security reform and pension policy reversions.

No major changes were made in Social Security during Bush's tenure. Controversial proposals to relax the so-called earnings test were considered, however. Under existing law, Social Security recipients aged 65 to 69 who earned more than a stipulated amount each year would have their benefits reduced — $1 for every $3 that exceeded the limit. Senior citizen groups pushed for a higher earnings threshold; some lawmakers advocated eliminating the cap altogether. Budgetary constraints kept a change in the law from taking place.

In other Social Security-related matters, Congress did not increase the benefits of the "notch babies," those born between 1917 and 1921 who were caught between two sets of changes in the Social Security system made in the 1970s; failed to clear legislation to make the Social Security Administration independent from the Department of Health and Human Services; and rejected a plan to cut Social Security taxes.

Congress in 1990 again moved to curtail pension plan reversions — when an employer terminates its pension plan, then uses the surplus cash to engage in activities such as corporate takeovers. Lawmakers included in budget-reconciliation legislation an increase in the excise tax that employers were liable for if they cashed out their pension plans. An excise tax on surplus funds had been instituted as part of the 1986 tax overhaul law, which had served to slow the pace of pension reversions. However, between 1980 and 1989, approximately 2,000 pension plans had been terminated and about $20 billion had reverted to businesses as surplus assets.

Chronology Of Action On Labor And Pension Policy

1989-90

For the first time in almost 10 years, the minimum wage was increased in 1989. President Bush signed the legislation after issuing his first veto on an earlier minimum wage bill. The enacted legislation also provided for a lower "training wage," aimed at new workers.

In response to cries of protest from small businesses, Congress repealed the "Section 89" provisions of the 1986 tax law overhaul, which sought to keep employers from offering more generous benefits to top-level employees than to the rank and file. Small businesses opposed the complex record-keeping and reporting requirements.

Bush in 1990 vetoed the first of two family and medical leave bills that would be put before him during his administration. The second veto would come in 1992. Bush objected to the federal government's dictating policy to businesses, maintaining that the issue was a matter of labor-management negotiations.

Bush also wielded his veto power against legislation requiring the federal government to help settle a strike at Eastern Airlines. Sen. Edward M. Kennedy, D-Mass., said that Bush, by his action, became the first president to dismiss the recommendations of the National Mediation Board.

Efforts to significantly amend the 1982 Job Training Partnership Act failed during the 101st Congress, but changes in the law were made in a bill providing job training to displaced homemakers.

For the first time since the 1970s, Congress in 1990 cleared a bill offering cash payments to workers dislocated by new legislation — in this case, coal miners and others affected by a clean air measure.

Congress also acted to reverse a 1989 Supreme Court ruling that allowed age-based discrimination in employee benefits.

Modest changes were made in Social Security as part of the 1989 and 1990 budget-reconciliation bills. Efforts were made to loosen the so-called earnings test, but they failed. And Congress considered legislation to regulate pension reversions — terminations to make assets available for other purposes.

Minimum Wage

A nearly decade-long stalemate between Republican administrations and Congress ended Nov. 8, 1989, when legislation (HR 2710) cleared that raised the minimum wage from $3.35 an hour to $4.25 an hour over two years and set up a lower "training wage" for teenage employees. President Bush signed the bill (PL 101-157) Nov. 17.

Bush on June 13 had issued his first presidential veto on an earlier Democratic-sponsored bill (HR 2) to raise the minimum wage to $4.55 over three years. The House failed to override the next day.

The nationwide uniform minimum wage was established by the Fair Labor Standards Act in 1938 (PL 75-718), when it was set at 25 cents an hour. The most recent previous increase took place in 1981, when the wage was raised from $3.10. Throughout his two terms of office, President Reagan refused to consider an increase in the minimum wage. Bush thus became the first president in nearly a decade to propose an increase. *(PL 75-718, Congress and the Nation Vol. I, p. 635; 1981 action, Congress and the Nation Vol. V, p. 405)*

The First Bill — HR 2

Labor Secretary Elizabeth H. Dole on March 3 unveiled the administration's proposal to boost the minimum wage to $4.25 over a three-year period and to provide a lower training wage for newly hired workers. Under the administration plan, employers could pay new hires $3.35 an hour for the first six months while they were being trained.

The training wage would help offset some of the job loss that would be caused by raising the minimum, Dole told the Senate Labor and Human Resources Committee. She estimated that 170,000 jobs could be saved. Without the training wage — and with Congress' proposal to raise the wage to $4.65 — 650,000 jobs would be lost, because employers either would cut back on workers or would not create new jobs, Dole testified. Studies pegged job loss anywhere from 175,000 to 882,000.

Congressional Democrats complained that the Bush proposal did not mandate any training and that it did not take six months to learn how to flip a hamburger in a fast-food joint. Nor did the proposal protect employers from firing subminimum wage workers once their six months were up.

"The market would take care of that," Dole said, adding that the cost of training a new worker would exceed the expense of raising the subminimum wage worker's pay.

The Bush administration's proposal was not considered during House Education and Labor Subcommittee on Labor Standards markup of HR 2. Subcommittee aides said they never received a copy of the administration's bill. What they got instead, 15 minutes before markup was scheduled to begin, was a letter from Secretary Dole explaining the administration's proposal and threatening a presidential veto of anything else. Dole had repeatedly refused invitations to testify before the House subcommittee. The panel easily approved HR 2 by a 7-4 vote on March 9.

On March 14, the full House Education and Labor Committee approved HR 2 (H Rept 101-11) on a straight party-line vote of 22-13. The measure, which was reported March 20, did not contain provisions for a training wage. Both the administration's proposal and an amendment offered by Steve Bartlett, R-Texas, to include a new-hire wage were rejected by party-line votes.

The bill increased the minimum wage over three years to $4.65 an hour by Jan. 1, 1992. It exempted small retail and service businesses that grossed less than $500,000 annually and raised the tip credit to 50 percent over two years. At the time, employers could count workers' tips as 40 percent of their minimum wage requirement.

Labor and Pension Policy

The House passed HR 2, 248-171, on March 23. The bipartisan compromise measure — crafted by Austin J. Murphy, D-Pa., Tommy F. Robinson, D-Ark., and Tom Ridge, R-Pa. — was created as a result of the lack of support for the committee-approved bill. The Murphy-Robinson-Ridge alternative was aimed at winning the votes of those most reluctant to support a big wage increase: Southern Democrats whose districts were reeling from an economic slump and Republicans loath to break ranks with the president.

The bill lowered the wage increase to $4.55 and provided for a two-month training wage, equal to 85 percent of the minimum, for first-time workers. The training wage would expire Sept. 30, 1992. The measure also would expand the small business exemption to include most businesses that grossed less than $500,000. Like the committee-approved bill, the compromise increased the tip credit from the current 40 percent to 50 percent; phased in the minimum wage hike for Puerto Rico over seven years; created a review board charged with reporting annually to Congress on the need for a minimum wage increase; and extended coverage to congressional employees.

During House floor debate, Republicans had objected to the rule under which the legislation was to be considered. The Rules Committee had decided that the Bush proposal would be voted on first and then the Murphy alternative. The last one approved would win.

The rule also shut out GOP efforts to offer an alternative to the wage increase: an expansion of the earned-income tax credit (EITC). Pushed by Thomas E. Petri, R-Wis., the EITC — which would give low-wage working families a tax break either by allowing them to pay less taxes throughout the year or by giving them a refund at the end of the year — would be indexed for family size. Supporters argued that an expanded EITC would target aid to those who needed it, while a minimum wage increase would lead to job loss and would help people who were not poor, such as middle-class teenagers living at home. But the Democrats argued that a labor bill was no place to change the tax code and that the House Ways and Means Committee, which had jurisdiction over tax matters, had not approved an EITC.

On a 238-177 party-line vote March 22, the House rejected efforts to block consideration of the rule and open it up for amendment. The rule itself subsequently was adopted by voice vote.

The next day, the administration proposal was defeated 198-218. The Murphy alternative garnered more support and was adopted 240-179.

Before the final version of HR 2 was adopted, the House rejected a George Miller, D-Calif., amendment, 98-321, that would beef up penalties for employers who violated the Fair Labor Standards Act.

S 4, introduced Jan. 25 by Senate Labor and Human Resources Committee Chairman Edward M. Kennedy, D-Mass., would increase the minimum wage to $4.65 over three years and did not provide for a training wage. A similar measure was killed in 1988 when Kennedy, adamantly opposed to a training wage, blocked efforts by Orrin G. Hatch, R-Utah, to allow employers to pay new hires 80 percent of the minimum wage during their first three months at work. *(Congress and the Nation Vol. VI, p. 705)*

Bush scored a victory when the Senate Labor Committee agreed to put the subminimum wage issue on the table for negotiation. The president was unable to keep his troops in line, however, and the administration proposal was rejected, 6-10, on March 8. The committee went on to approve S 4 (S Rept 101-6) the same day, 11-5; it was reported March 13. The bill included provisions to phase in the minimum wage increase for Puerto Rico, gradually increase the tip credit to 50 percent and expand the small business exemption to all companies grossing less than $500,000 a year.

Despite Bush's repeated veto threats, the Senate on April 12 voted 62-37 to pass HR 2 after substituting the text of S 4, boosting the minimum wage from $3.35 an hour to $4.55 over three years and allowing companies to pay employees with little work experience a lower training wage during the first two months on the job. While the Democrats had the votes to pass a minimum wage increase, neither chamber had the two-thirds majority needed to override a presidential veto.

A week before the bill came to the floor, Southern Democrats Bob Graham, Fla., and David Pryor, Ark., announced a package scaling back the increase from $4.65 to $4.55 and including a two-month training wage, equal to 85 percent of the minimum, for people who have never worked more than 60 days. On April 11, the Senate voted 61-39 to adopt the compromise. The Senate then rejected Bush's proposal by a slimmer margin, 41-58. Senators had a second shot at the opposing alternatives the next day when Minority Leader Bob Dole, R-Kan., urged his colleagues to recommit the bill to the Labor Committee and instruct the panel to approve the president's bill instead. But the Senate blocked that move, 43-56, and then promptly passed the $4.55 minimum wage bill.

The Senate also adopted a dozen other amendments, including, on an 86-11 vote, one to raise the cap on the Social Security earnings test limit. In 1989, someone who continued working from ages 65 to 70 lost $1 in benefits for every $2 he earned above $8,880. The amendment lifted the earnings cap to $9,960. *(Social Security, p. 717)*

The House and Senate versions of HR 2 were so similar that conferees found ironing out the differences to take little time. By a 247-172 vote, the House May 11 adopted the conference report (H Rept 101-47) on the bill. The Senate followed suit May 17, voting 63-37.

Although the Senate action cleared HR 2, Democratic leaders waited until June 13 to send the bill to the White House. A coalition of labor, civil rights and women's groups spent tens of thousands of dollars on radio advertising urging Bush to sign HR 2 and coordinated a letter-writing protest by low-wage workers. Senate Majority Leader George J. Mitchell, D-Maine, pointedly contrasted Bush's tough stand on the issue with his support for a cut in the capital gains tax, which was widely viewed as a break for the wealthy. *(Capital gains, p. 96)*

Bush vetoed the bill aboard *Air Force One*, less than one hour after the legislation arrived at the White House. In his veto message, Bush said the bill "would increase the minimum wage by an excessive amount and thus stifle the creation of new job opportunities. It would damage the employment prospects of . . . young people and least advantaged citizens. It would accelerate inflation."

In an interview two weeks before the veto, chief White House lobbyist Frederick D. McClure said that by holding the line on minimum wage, Bush would prove his resolve to thwart other Democratic-sponsored labor initiatives, such as the bid to require companies to give unpaid leave to parents of newborn or sick children. *(Parental leave, p. 710)*

As expected, Congress was unable to override the veto. On a **key vote of 247-178 (R 20-150; D 227-28)**, the House June 14 fell 37 votes shy of the two-thirds majority needed. *(1989 key votes, p. 1021)*

Despite the setback for Democrats, many of them sensed a chance to drive home a message that Bush was insensitive to ordinary working people's needs. Others disagreed, saying Bush had protected his political flank by declaring his willingness to back a more modest increase. Others argued that the issue lacked political punch at a time of general economic prosperity. Whatever the case, this sharply contested fight was not over: Both Democratic and Republican lawmakers were scrambling to plot their next moves.

In the meantime, a band of House Republicans hoped to break the logjam with a fresh proposal of its own. Led by Bill Goodling, Pa., these Republicans on June 14 introduced a bill (HR 2637) to combine a raise in the minimum wage to $4.25 an hour over three years and a compromise training wage with an expansion of the earned-income tax credit. Under the proposal, heads of households with preschool or school-age children and incomes of up to $45,000 would be eligible for expanded credits on a sliding scale. They estimated the cost of the plan at $3 billion.

Rep. Murphy expressed interest in some sort of minimum wage/EITC package as a politically winning compromise. And in his veto message, Bush indicated a willingness to "examine" changes in the EITC if his minimum wage proposal proved unpalatable to Congress. Senate Minority Leader Dole proposed an expansion of the EITC as part of a separate package to help working families with their child care needs. *(Child care, p. 611)*

In a June 14 statement, AFL-CIO leaders said EITC proposals should be handled separately from legislation to raise the minimum wage, which organized labor leaders strongly supported.

HR 2637 saw no congressional action.

Labor Leadership

The Senate on Jan. 25, 1989, voted 99-0 to confirm Elizabeth H. Dole to be secretary of labor. Dole had served as secretary of transportation during the Reagan administration. *(Dole background, Cabinet profiles, p. 1173)*

Dole became the first member of President Bush's original Cabinet to leave when she resigned effective Nov. 23, 1990, to head the American Red Cross. In her nearly two years in the Labor post, Dole was credited with negotiating an agreement to increase the minimum wage, increasing enforcement of job safety and child labor laws, using government contracts to encourage companies to put women and minorities into management positions and moving more women and minorities into policy positions at the Labor Department itself.

Some Democrats, however, questioned her effectiveness. "It cannot have been easy," said Sen. Edward M. Kennedy, D-Mass., "serving as a pro-labor secretary in an anti-labor administration."

The Senate on Feb. 7, 1991, confirmed, 94-0, former representative Lynn Martin, R-Ill., to succeed Dole. Martin had served five terms in the House until she left in 1990 for an unsuccessful run at the Senate. *(Martin background, Cabinet profiles, p. 1173)*

The Second Bill — HR 2710

After Bush vetoed HR 2, Democrats signaled their willingness to compromise. By a party-line vote of 7-4, the House Education and Labor Subcommittee on Labor Standards approved HR 2710 to raise the hourly minimum wage from $3.35 to $4.25 within two years. The measure also permitted employers to pay a subminimum wage to workers with fewer than 60 days of prior job experience. Although the subcommittee-approved version scaled back earlier legislation opposed by the administration, it still did not win Bush's endorsement. Restless Capitol Hill Republicans — uneasy about the president's position and not wanting to back another veto on the minimum wage issue — began prodding Bush to seek a deal that would break the protracted partisan stalemate.

Acting on a voice vote, the full Education and Labor Committee approved HR 2710 (H Rept 101-260) on Sept. 19 and reported it Sept. 26. Although Republicans had strong opposition to the package, they did not insist on a roll-call vote.

Saying committee Democrats had made a significant concession on the wage rate, Education and Labor Chairman Augustus F. Hawkins, D-Calif., declared, "As far as most of us are concerned, we've gone as far as we can possibly go." However, Labor Secretary Dole told the committee's leaders that HR 2710 would trigger a second Bush veto.

Democrats were divided on how to proceed. Although Hawkins wanted to bring his committee's proposal to a floor vote, others said doing so would be a mistake if, as many thought likely, the package failed to win a veto-proof margin of victory.

In the end, U.S. workers may have had Polish Solidarity leader Lech Walesa to thank for the first increase in the minimum wage in nine years. White House Chief of Staff John H. Sununu and AFL-CIO President Lane Kirkland, while meeting Oct. 24 to discuss Walesa's upcoming visit to the United States, agreed to negotiate a solution to the minimum wage standoff.

What followed between Sununu and Kirkland was a series of talks among representatives of the White House, the Labor Department and the AFL-CIO on the remaining obstacles to agreement. Sources in the administration and Congress said the talks focused on the administration's insistence on the training wage, which labor had long opposed. That deadlock was broken when the AFL-CIO suggested, and the administration and congressional leaders accepted, a temporary training wage limited to teenage employees. Bush had hoped to apply the subminimum wage to all new-hire workers, regardless of how old they were or how long they had been employed in the past.

Although a senior Democratic staffer speculated that the political embarrassment of vetoing a minimum wage bill close to Walesa's visit may have helped prompt Bush to break the stalemate with labor, broader pressures existed on both sides to cut a deal. Republicans and conservative

Democrats in Congress — as well as senior members of the administration — were growing increasingly concerned that rejecting substantially modified legislation, which met Bush's primary goal of holding the wage increase to $4.25, could prove politically difficult and unpopular.

The House passed HR 2710 by a vote of 382-37 on Nov. 1.

By voice vote, the Senate Labor and Human Resources Committee on Aug. 2 approved S 1182 (S Rept 101-117) to increase the minimum wage to $4.55. The bill, formally reported Aug. 30, was identical to HR 2. Proponents planned to craft a more modest proposal acceptable to Bush, and they said they had no plans to act on S 1182 as approved by committee.

Organized labor, the Bush administration and House and Senate leaders had already signed off on the compromise by Nov. 1, when the House passed HR 2710. In the final hours of debate in the Senate, which took up the House bill, the only real dissent came from conservative Republicans. Steve Symms, R-Idaho, delayed action on the wage measure by trying to attach a cut in the capital gains tax rate. But Bush and Labor Secretary Dole beseeched senators to keep HR 2710 free of amendments.

On Nov. 8, the Senate, 64-34, tabled (killed) companion amendments by Symms and Hatch that would bar Congress from passing any legislation that would increase the business costs of certain small businesses. The Senate also tabled, 63-35, a proposal by Phil Gramm, R-Texas, to remove a provision to prevent farmers from paying teenage migrant and seasonal workers the lower training wage.

The Senate then passed, 89-8, HR 2710, clearing the measure for the president.

As enacted, HR 2710 raised the minimum wage to $4.25 an hour by April 1, 1991. Under a provision that expired in 1993, teenagers 16 to 19 could be paid a training wage for their first three months of employment. That subminimum wage could be extended another three months if the teenager took a second job and was still being trained.

The administration succeeded in taking out a provision that would have set up a minimum wage review board by 1992 to recommend changes in the minimum wage rate. Republicans saw this board as an attempt at "back-door indexing" of the minimum wage to future inflation increases.

The compromise also retained an exemption from the minimum wage increase for certain small businesses with gross sales under $500,000 a year.

'Section 89'

Lawmakers in 1989 repealed the so-called "Section 89" anti-discrimination employee-benefit provisions of the 1986 tax code overhaul (PL 99-514), which were to take effect Dec. 1. The regulations, named after their place in the tax code, were intended to discourage employers from providing benefit plans for top-level employees that were more generous than those for the rank and file. *(1986 tax law, Congress and the Nation Vol. VII, p. 79)*

For many House members, Section 89 came to symbolize what they saw as the Ways and Means Committee's penchant for tucking innocuous-sounding, but politically ill-conceived, provisions into complex tax bills, which were then closed to amendment on the floor. Anger at the committee and its chairman, Dan Rostenkowski, D-Ill., alone did not explain the revolt against the provisions, however. A grass-roots movement of small businesses, which members could not ignore, mobilized in opposition to the complex record-keeping and reporting requirements. Labor groups, meanwhile, were concerned that Section 89 might become a backdoor way for the government to start taxing employee benefits.

And with virtually no constituents on the other side of the issue demanding non-discrimination protections, adopting a pro-repeal position was politically painless for lawmakers. Democrats could easily demonstrate that they shared business' worries about excessive government regulation; Republicans could show a core constituency that they could accomplish something in Congress even as a minority party.

Background

Throughout the 1980s, various proposals were considered by Congress and debated by the Reagan administration to change the tax treatment of employer-sponsored health plans.

Under previous law, employers could provide benefits to select groups of workers or offer a more generous package to some than to others. Such benefits generally were excluded from the incomes of workers receiving the coverage. Concerns mounted that federal tax policy was encouraging discriminatory health plans and at great expense to the Treasury, which was not collecting revenue on non-taxed benefits. The Joint Committee on Taxation estimated the cost to the government to be $32.6 billion in fiscal 1990, increasing to $50.8 billion in 1994. Section 89 was projected to offset these costs by nearly $1 billion over five years.

The Reagan administration's first effort at tax code overhaul in November 1984 proposed a cap on tax-free health benefits as part of a sweeping package to close tax loopholes and lower rates. A subsequent administration plan, called Treasury II, took an opposite tack: It would impose lengthy rules on employers, requiring them to prove that they were not discriminating on health plans and other benefits. Treasury II also proposed that workers pay taxes on a small amount of fringe payments.

The benefits tax was a political non-starter in Congress, given that both labor and business interests opposed it. But in their core tax-overhaul proposals, Rostenkowski and Senate Finance Chairman Bob Packwood, R-Ore., included versions of the Treasury II non-discrimination rules.

Under the provision that became law, companies could still offer sweeter benefits to their better-paid employees. Workers with "discriminatory" benefits were required to pay income taxes on the value of such perks. However, Section 89 also set up a maze of complicated tests that a company had to pass to prove it was not providing discriminatory benefits to its executives. For example, many employers would have to pass at least three separate tests. One was a 50 percent threshold, under which low-paid workers had to make up at least half of those employees eligible for each benefit offered. Under a 90 percent/50 percent test, at least 90 percent of an employer's low-paid workers had to be eligible for benefits at least half as valuable as those available to top management.

Complaints against Section 89 mounted as the original Jan. 1, 1989, implementation date drew near. Although large employers griped about the rules, it was small businesses least equipped to bear the administrative burden of the new rules that protested the loudest.

Many of the objections first came from local tax attorneys and accountants seeking to advise their clients on the new rules. By all accounts, the early response was genuinely spontaneous, without prompting by Washington business lobbyists. And the complaints often surprised lawmakers, few of whom had ever heard of Section 89.

Groups representing business tried late in the 100th Congress to get Section 89 repealed. But tax lawmakers, fearful that the entire overhaul package might start to unravel, instead responded with Section 89 "technical corrections" in an Oct. 22, 1988, catchall tax bill (PL 100-647). Although aimed at easing compliance burdens, the new provisions left the basic structure of Section 89 intact. *(Congress and the Nation Vol. VII, p. 100)*

That did little to appease employers who already were baffled by the law's complexity. Even the Internal Revenue Service (IRS) had trouble deciphering the law; it was not until March 2 that it issued partial guidelines to help employers comply with Section 89. At that time, Treasury delayed the effective date to July 1 and said that, as long as employers made a good-faith effort to comply with the law, they would not be penalized.

Legislative Action

At the start of the 101st Congress, lobbyists at the National Federation of Independent Business (NFIB), the U.S. Chamber of Commerce and other business groups made repeal or drastic overhaul of Section 89 a top priority. They got a boost from House Small Business Committee Chairman John J. LaFalce, D-N.Y., who agreed to sponsor a repeal bill (HR 634). It was introduced on Jan. 24 with 44 cosponsors. Soon more than half of the House membership had signed on.

Just three months before, Rostenkowski railed against members urging repeal of Section 89. But after LaFalce introduced HR 634, Rostenkowski backed down, introducing a bill (HR 1864) April 13 that would, in effect, repeal Section 89 and start over.

Under HR 1864, which applied only to health insurance, a plan would pass muster if it was not discriminatory "on its face" and if it was available to at least 90 percent of a company's low-paid workers at a weekly cost of no more than $10 for single coverage or $25 for family coverage. That premium, paid by the worker, would be indexed to keep pace with inflation. Highly paid workers would count their benefits as taxable income if the company-paid premium was greater than 133 percent of the same premium paid for most low-paid workers.

In testing their plan for discrimination, employers would not count anyone covered by a collective bargaining agreement or who worked fewer than 25 hours a week. If a benefit plan failed to pass the non-discrimination test, an employer would have to pay a 34 percent excise tax, but it was unclear what amount would be taxed.

Business interests raised a number of concerns regarding HR 1864. They wanted Congress to consider whether a cap on worker-paid premiums should be indexed to general inflation or the faster-rising cost of health care and whether the cap should be varied to take into account regional cost-of-living differences. A suggestion was made that companies with fewer than 10 workers be exempted from the rules. And it was argued that cafeteria plans, under which an employer provided a cash credit and allowed a worker to choose his perquisites, including higher pay, would fail the new non-discrimination test even if they provided the same cash credit to all employees.

During consideration of S 4, a bill to increase the minimum wage, the Senate April 12 adopted 98-0 a Trent Lott, R-Miss., amendment requesting the House to initiate a bill modifying or repealing Section 89. The same day the Senate rejected a Bob Kasten, R-Wis., motion to waive sections of the 1974 Congressional Budget and Impoundment Control Act (PL 93-344) to allow consideration of a Kasten amendment to delay for one year the effective date of Section 89. The 56-42 vote fell short of the three-fifths majority (60) needed to waive the budget act. *(Minimum wage, p. 705)*

Meanwhile, on May 1, Treasury Secretary Nicholas F. Brady announced that the administration would push back the effective date of Section 89 from July 1 to Oct. 1. Brady subsequently would delay the effective date again, until Dec. 1.

Moving on much the same tack as Rostenkowski, Senate Finance Committee Chairman Lloyd Bentsen, D-Texas, in early June introduced a new compromise bill (S 1129) on Section 89, which he crafted with committee member David Pryor, D-Ark. Although Bentsen and Rostenkowski were sympathetic to complaints that the new tax rules were burdensome and overly complicated, they insisted that some sorts of protections were needed to weed discrimination out of employee-benefit plans. But Bentsen-Pryor was viewed by business leaders as a big improvement over Rostenkowski's bill.

For life insurance, both the Bentsen-Pryor and Rostenkowski measures proposed a return to non-discrimination rules in effect before passage of the 1986 tax-overhaul bill. For health insurance, both measures replaced the maze of non-discrimination tests in Section 89 with tests that were intended to be simpler and, in some instances, easier to meet.

Under Bentsen-Pryor, a health insurance plan would pass muster as "non-discriminatory" if it were "affordable" and made available to at least 90 percent of all employees. It would be considered affordable if the worker was not required to pay more than 40 percent of the premiums. By defining "affordable" on a flat percentage basis, instead of as a dollar amount pegged to an inflation index, Bentsen and Pryor sought to remove objections to Rostenkowski's bill. At the same time, they recognized a potential flaw in their approach. An employer could offer employees relatively expensive plans, gambling that few low-wage workers would elect to pay 40 percent. The test against discrimination would be met even if only the most highly paid workers chose the plan. However, the sponsors of S 1129 argued that few employers were likely to pursue such a potentially costly strategy.

S 1129 also delayed the effective date of the Section 89 rules until Jan. 1, 1990.

LaFalce had seen his original repeal bill as merely a prod to force Rostenkowski to revamp the Section 89 language. He believed the goal of Section 89 was legitimate and thought the best outcome would be a compromise amendment.

But several Republicans, including Steve Bartlett of Texas, urged the House GOP leadership to use Section 89 as a test case for a new, more aggressive legislative strategy. Instead of settling for a compromise, the party should stake all on repeal, Bartlett said. Two new members of the GOP leadership team — whip Newt Gingrich of Georgia and chief deputy whip Steve Gunderson of Wisconsin — agreed that Section 89, with its small businesses constituency, was a perfect issue for Republicans.

Their first job was to persuade business lobbyists that repeal was an achievable goal. Groups representing employers, however, had praised HR 1864 when it was introduced, and they feared retaliation from Rostenkowski if they reneged on their vow to work with the Ways and Means Committee to further shape the legislation.

So without much encouragement from business groups, Republicans and supportive Democrats maneuvered for a vote on repeal. On May 24, they tried to defeat a rule for a fiscal 1989 supplemental spending bill (HR 2072) in hopes of clearing the way for a repeal amendment. Over their objections, the House voted 217-203 to order the previous question (thus ending debate and the possibility of amendment) on the rule (H Res 160), effectively preventing George W. Gekas, R-Pa., from offering an amendment to repeal Section 89. *(Supplemental, p. 52)*

In Senate action on the supplemental, Kasten on June 6 offered a motion to table (kill) his amendment to repeal Section 89; it was rejected 99-0. The Senate then adopted, 98-0, an amendment, offered by Senate Majority Leader George J. Mitchell, D-Maine, to the Kasten amendment to express the sense of the Senate that Section 89 rules be delayed for one year and that Congress consider clarifying and revising the law by the time a fiscal 1990 budget-reconciliation bill was taken up. Kasten then went on to offer a motion to waive budget rules against amendments that cost the government, which would have opened the way for an up-or-down vote on the Kasten proposal to repeal Section 89. The Senate rejected the motion, 49-50. (Sixty votes were required to waive the rules.) The Kasten amendment subsequently was blocked on a point of order.

The Senate Finance Committee on June 13 agreed, 17-3, to attach the plan to overhaul the Section 89 rules to legislation to expand child care tax credits for low-income families. Two days later, Senate Majority Leader Mitchell offered on the floor a new proposal that combined the Finance package with a modified version of a bill (S 5 — S Rept 101-17) to fund child care services that was approved earlier in the year by the Labor and Human Resources Committee. *(Child care, p. 611)*

The Section 89 provisions were similar to those contained in S 1129, crafted by Bentsen and Pryor. By voice vote, the Finance panel adopted an amendment by John Heinz, R-Pa., to shrink the pool of employees subject to the 90 percent test to those hired to work at least 30 hours a week.

Before the June 23 passage of the child care measure, the Senate adopted by voice vote a Mitchell amendment to alter the rules for workers covered by certain cafeteria-style plans and an amendment by Kasten and Pryor that modified penalties against employers for non-compliance with the new rules, delayed effective dates in some cases and redefined "highly compensated employees." Members also adopted an amendment by Pete V. Domenici, R-N.M., to exempt from the new rules for one year small businesses with 20 or fewer employees pending a Treasury study of whether the exemption should be made permanent.

At Rostenkowski's urging, the House Ways and Means Committee July 12 agreed to fold a revised version of his original bill, conforming to the Senate's provisions, into a deficit-reduction bill (HR 3299) under consideration by the panel. *(HR 3299, p. 43)*

A crucial moment in the effort to repeal Section 89 came when Republicans on the House Appropriations Committee the week of July 24 proposed a one-year ban on enforcement of the rules. With support from seven Democrats, the Tom DeLay, R-Texas, amendment to a Treasury Department appropriations bill (HR 2989 — PL 101-136) carried by a three-vote margin, 29-26. Some members used the vote to signal their unhappiness with Democratic leaders' practice of not allowing floor amendments to bills reported by Ways and Means.

In a surprise setback for Rostenkowski, the House July 28 approved, 376-26, HR 2989 (H Rept 101-170) with the amendment to delay enforcement of Section 89 rules for one year. And despite Rostenkowski's objections — and against almost all expectations — the Rules Committee had granted appropriators a special waiver from House rules, which otherwise would have allowed Rostenkowski to block inclusion of a tax provision on the appropriations bill.

House debate on the spending bill was largely perfunctory; no effort was made to strike the DeLay provision. After surviving House passage, the provision also was put into the Senate's Treasury spending bill.

Rostenkowski made one last attempt to salvage the matter. On Sept. 12, he called three business groups into his office — including the National Small Business United and the National Association of Wholesaler-Distributors, but not NFIB — and he said he would repeal Section 89. He also said he would reinstate the extension of the 25 percent tax deduction on health insurance costs for self-employed business owners. He added, however, that certain non-discrimination rules should continue to apply to health plans offered to company executives and plans offered by law firms and other "professional service organizations."

The groups praised Rostenkowski, but neither NFIB nor the House Republican leadership was satisfied. They pressed for their long-sought floor vote for flat repeal. The House Sept. 27, in a **390-36 (R 172-2; D 218-34) key vote**, agreed to repeal Section 89 and eliminate from HR 3299 a scaled-back substitute that was crafted by Rostenkowski to accomplish the same purpose as Section 89. *(1989 key votes, p. 1021)*

Following the decisive House vote, Bentsen quickly reassessed the situation. The Senate Finance Committee the week of Oct. 2 agreed to repeal Section 89 and folded the provision into the deficit reduction package.

Section 89 was scheduled to go into effect Dec. 1. But Bush administration sources said the week of Oct. 2 that the Treasury Department was likely to delay the compliance date if Congress, against expectations, had not cleared a repeal measure by Dec. 1. Leaders of the repeal drive said that if unrelated matters bogged down the reconciliation bill, a repeal plan could easily be attached to some other vehicle — which was exactly what happened. All extraneous provisions were stripped from reconciliation, so the Section 89 repeal provision was attached to the measure raising the debt ceiling (H J Res 280 — PL 101-140). *(Debt ceiling, box, p. 44)*

Parental Leave

Congress in 1990 failed to override President Bush's veto of a bill (HR 770) that would have protected jobs for workers in businesses with at least 50 employees who took up to 12 weeks of unpaid leave to care for a newborn, adopted or ill child. It also would have covered time off for personal medical emergencies, including caring for family members.

Bush said he supported the concept of parental and medical leave but believed that such arrangements were the domain of labor-management negotiations. In his veto message, Bush criticized the bill's "rigid, federally imposed requirements."

Background

Supporters of family leave pushed their legislation for years; Rep. Patricia Schroeder, D-Colo., introduced the first parental leave bill in 1985. A bill similar to the 1990 version made it to the Senate floor in 1988 but was killed there after getting mired in election-year politics. *(Congress and the Nation Vol. VII, pp. 695, 706)*

Supporters of a national, mandatory parental leave policy, primarily labor and women's groups, said the country was overdue for federal minimum requirements to bring business in line with the changing demographics of the work place. About 60 percent of mothers worked outside the home, they said, and the United States was the only major industrialized nation other than South Africa that had no family leave policy. In contrast, at least 75 other countries, including all other Western industrialized nations and Japan, required various standard family-related benefits.

A 50-state review by the Women's Legal Defense Fund showed that even within the United States protection for family or medical needs was limited. Twenty-five states had no laws guaranteeing family or medical leave, and no state guaranteed employees the breadth or length of protection HR 770 would have provided.

HR 770 was opposed by the U.S. Chamber of Commerce, the Bush administration and a number of conservative Republicans. They argued that mandated leave would remove employers' flexibility and lead them to cut other benefits workers might prefer. Businesses also were concerned that the bill was merely the next step toward more intrusive legislation that might eventually encompass mandated employee health benefits as well.

Supporters and opponents disagreed over the cost of the bill. Because employers would have had to maintain only health insurance for workers who chose to take unpaid leave, bill sponsors said the cost would be less than $5.30 a year per covered employee.

In addition, according to a 1989 study by the Family Medical Leave Coalition, working women who had no parental leave benefits lost an aggregate of about $607 million a year in earnings. The study also said that it cost $108 million a year in lost taxes and payments for assistance to women who were unemployed or on welfare because they did not get parental leave.

Opponents said the $5.30-a-year estimate of the burden to business was far too low and did not take into account hidden costs, such as litigation and training temporary employees. Estimates by the Chamber on the cost to business, made on the basis of earlier parental leave bills, ranged as high as $23.8 billion a year. But the General Accounting Office, an investigative arm of Congress, said that estimate was based on unrealistic assumptions, including how many employees would take leave and how many would be replaced by temporary workers.

Legislative Action

Three House committees had jurisdiction over HR 770. The Education and Labor Committee voted 23-12 on March 8, 1989, to approve the bill (H Rept 101-28, Part I), after defeating almost two dozen Republican-initiated amendments. The Post Office and Civil Service Committee, which oversaw the title concerning federal workers, approved HR 770 (H Rept 101-28, Part II) by voice vote on April 12. The bill cleared its final House committee hurdle April 26 when House Administration approved the measure (H Rept 101-28, Part III) by voice vote. HR 770 was formally reported from Education and Labor on April 13, from Post Office and Civil Service on April 27 and from House Administration on May 1.

During floor consideration, the House watered down the committee-approved version, which would have tightened the small business exemption after three years to apply to companies with 35 or more employees. Workers also would have qualified for up to 15 weeks a year of medical leave and 10 weeks a year of parental leave. The medical leave would have applied to parents, parents-in-law, stepparents or legal guardians, but not to spouses.

Six weakening amendments had been scheduled for floor debate, but none was offered. Steve Bartlett, R-Texas, said three GOP amendments were withdrawn after discussions with the White House because they might have increased support for the legislation. Bartlett's amendments would have made only full-time employees eligible for leave and would have required workers to give a month's notice before taking the leave and a month's notice before returning to work.

Amendments by Democrats Timothy J. Penny, Minn., and Charles W. Stenholm, Texas, also fell by the wayside, aides said, in part because they did not have the votes. A William L. Clay, D-Mo., amendment also was not offered. Stenholm and Clay had targeted their amendments at conditions under which employees would have resumed work.

Penny had planned to offer his own leave bill (HR 3445) as a substitute amendment. It would have mandated 10 weeks of unpaid leave a year, but only to care for newborns or adopted children. The amendment was withdrawn.

Language in a substitute amendment — sponsored by Bart Gordon, D-Tenn., and Curt Weldon, R-Pa. — was worked out in about a month of negotiations with undecided members. While proponents promoted it as a bipartisan compromise, opponents called it no compromise at all. Business lobbyists said they played no role in the negotiations. Schroeder, meanwhile, said the bill barely resembled the leave policy she pushed in 1985: "I have trouble supporting this compromise because it has been watered down so much."

The House May 10, 1990, adopted the Gordon-Weldon substitute amendment by a 259-157 vote.

With the House certain to approve the bill as amended, nine Republicans and a large bloc of Southern Democrats, who typically were supported by business, for political reasons switched their "yea" votes and opposed it on final passage. The vote, taken May 10, was 237-187, 46 short of the two-thirds needed for an override.

The Senate Labor Committee on April 19, 1989, approved the Senate's version of the bill (S 345 — S Rept 101-77) by a 10-6 vote. The measure, reported July 13, required businesses with 20 or more employees to offer 10 weeks of unpaid leave over two years to workers who had a baby, adopted a child or had a seriously ill child or parent. Workers would receive up to 13 weeks of unpaid leave a year if they became seriously ill themselves. Employees who worked at least 900 hours over the course of a year would be eligible for the leave.

On the floor, the Senate abandoned S 345 and took up the compromise House version. The Senate on June 14 passed HR 770 by voice vote.

Republican opponents conceded that they were uncertain they had the votes to prevent Senate passage of the scaled-back proposal and, with a presidential veto looming, saw little point in putting up a fight. By approving the bill as part of a broader unanimous consent agreement involving several contentious bills, GOP opponents also were able to avoid a recorded vote on an issue that had been widely portrayed as pro-family.

As approved by the House and the Senate, HR 770 would require businesses with 50 or more employees to offer 12 weeks a year of unpaid medical or parental leave. Only one parent could take parental leave at a time. Medical leave, when certified by a doctor, could be used to care for a sick spouse, parent or child. Employees who worked in a job for at least 1,000 hours over the course of a year would be eligible.

The legislation would give federal workers more comprehensive benefits: 18 weeks over two years for parental leave and 26 weeks a year for medical leave. House workers would receive the same protections as private employees; the bill was not amended to include Senate workers.

HR 770 exempted highly paid employees if eligibility for the unpaid leave would cause "substantial and grievous" economic injury to an employer. Such employees were defined as among the highest-paid 10 percent within a 75-mile radius of where they worked. The bill also made violators liable to pay an employee's lost wages, benefits and other compensation and up to three times that amount in damages.

President Bush vetoed HR 770 on June 29. In his veto message, he said, "I want to emphasize my belief that time off for a child's birth or adoption or for family illness is an important benefit for employers to offer employees. I strongly object, however, to the federal government mandating leave policies."

Bush said the bill would place undue burdens on business. "We must ensure that federal policies do not stifle the creation of new jobs, nor result in the elimination of existing jobs," Bush said in his statement. He added, "By substituting a 'one size fits all' government mandate for innovative individual agreements, this bill ignores the differing family needs and preferences of employees and unduly limits the role of labor-management negotiations."

The House on July 25 easily sustained Bush's veto on a **key vote of 232-195 (R 38-138; D 194-57)**, 54 short of the needed two-thirds. *(1990 key votes, p. 1039)*

Democrats immediately moved to capture the political high ground after the failed override attempt. "The president should be ashamed for vetoing this bill and making a mockery of the term 'family values,'" House Majority Leader Richard A. Gephardt, D-Mo., said in a statement.

During the 1988 presidential campaign Bush had opposed the mandatory leave legislation, stating his support even then for encouraging employers to provide parental leave voluntarily. Bush would get another opportunity to record his opposition to the legislation in 1992, when Congress sent him another parental leave bill. *(Story, p. 730)*

Eastern Strike Veto

President Bush in 1989 vetoed legislation that called for government intervention in a labor dispute between Eastern Airlines and its unions, and the House in 1990 voted to sustain the veto.

The strike at Eastern, the nation's seventh-largest air carrier, began March 4, 1989. Five days later, the airline filed for Chapter 11 bankruptcy to gain protection from its creditors.

Leading Democrats, including House Speaker Jim Wright of Texas, called on Bush to follow the advice of federal mediators and establish an emergency panel to recommend a settlement. This procedure, often used in transportation disputes, would send strikers back to work for a 60-day "cooling-off" period. Strikers said they welcomed intervention; management opposed it.

Bush refused to get involved, saying no emergency existed and that it was improper for the government to interfere in the collective bargaining process. He pointed out that negotiations, centering on wage concessions, had already gone on for 17 months. Sen. Edward M. Kennedy, D-Mass., said Bush was the first president to ignore recommendations by the National Mediation Board to set up an emergency commission since the mediation board was established in 1934.

Democrats and their allies in the organized labor movement saw political advantage in trying to tar Bush as an ally of Frank Lorenzo, the chairman of Eastern and its parent, Texas Air Corp. They portrayed Lorenzo as a ruthless buccaneer bent on squeezing profits from his holdings whatever the toll on workers. In 1983, Lorenzo took a second Texas Air subsidiary, Continental Airlines, into bankruptcy, unilaterally abrogated its union contracts and turned the carrier into a low-wage, non-union operation. Partly in response to the Continental episode, Congress in 1984 enacted a law (PL 98-353) to force bankrupt companies to win court approval for such a step. *(Congress and the Nation Vol. VI, p. 702)*

Democrats began targeting Lorenzo with separate legislation to change the bankruptcy code to allow creditors to reach the assets of any bankrupt air carrier's parent holding companies or related entities. Sen. Howard M. Metzenbaum, D-Ohio, March 8 introduced such a bill (S 544); a similar measure (HR 1349) was introduced in the House by Barney Frank, D-Mass. Neither bill saw congressional action. Critics said that, since acquiring Eastern in 1986, Lorenzo had siphoned off assets to other Texas Air operations.

Despite uncertainties posed by Eastern's filing for bankruptcy, Democrats, in light of administration inaction, clamored for government intervention in the strike. The House Public Works and Transportation Committee March 9, 1989, by voice vote approved HR 1231 to create an emergency board to craft a settlement that could be enacted into law. The panel would have at least 14 days to complete its work; the president could extend the investigation by five days. The parties would have seven days to reject or accept the recommendation. During the entire period, workers would return to their jobs at the wages and conditions that existed before the strike.

By a 21-12 vote, dividing generally along party lines, Public Works' Aviation Subcommittee had sent the measure to the full committee on March 7. Republicans on the full committee reiterated their opposition but did not press for a roll-call vote. HR 1231 was reported (H Rept 101-3) on March 13.

The Public Works measure covered not only striking repair and ramp workers, represented by the International Association of Machinists and Aerospace Workers (IAM), but also Eastern pilots represented by the Air Line Pilots Association (ALPA) and flight attendants represented by the Transport Workers Union of America (TWU). Although ALPA and TWU members were not on strike, their contracts with Eastern had expired and their leaders asked to be included in the legislation.

The House March 15 passed HR 1231 on a 252-167 vote. Even though the House vote strongly suggested Congress would be unable to override a threatened White House veto — all but 20 Republicans voted against the measure — Democrats saw political advantage simply in pressing Bush to reject it.

The White House insisted that it was being neutral — not siding with Lorenzo — by opposing intervention. A statement of administration policy, issued before the House vote, declared that Bush's senior advisers would recommend a veto on grounds that it was inappropriate for government to intervene in a labor-management dispute and that Eastern's financial survival was in the hands of bankruptcy court.

Bush's critics, meanwhile, said he was underestimating the threat posed by Eastern's possible demise to the long-term health of the airline industry. They said the loss would further concentrate an already concentrated airline market, putting upward pressure on fares and dampening incentives to offer high-quality service.

While the bill enjoyed favorable prospects in the House, it got bogged down in the Senate. A March 16 bid by Majority Leader George J. Mitchell, D-Maine, to proceed to Senate consideration was blocked by Republicans, and Mitchell on April 4 then postponed floor action on HR 1231 amid intensified efforts by Eastern leaders to sell the bankrupt carrier. At week's end, Lorenzo announced a preliminary agreement to sell Eastern to an investors' group headed by former baseball commissioner Peter V. Ueberroth. But that deal ultimately fell through.

Despite Republican threats of a filibuster, Mitchell said the Senate would return to the bill if private parties failed to resolve the dispute. The Senate finally took up the bill Oct. 26, approving Mitchell's substitute language that only called for establishing a blue-ribbon commission to make recommendations on how to settle the dispute. The Senate first voted 62-38 to end debate on the substitute measure, then voted 65-35 to approve the substitute language. The Senate then passed the bill by voice vote.

On Nov. 7, the House accepted the Senate version, clearing the measure. Bush vetoed the bill Nov. 21.

The House on March 7, 1990, voted to sustain the president's veto. The 261-160 vote was 21 votes short of the two-thirds majority needed to override.

Job Training

The House and the Senate in 1989-90 crafted legislation to refocus and overhaul the federal government's major job-training program for disadvantaged youths, but the effort fell short because of disagreements over funding allocations. Both chambers' bills (HR 2039, S 543) sought to alter the funding formula that determined the amount of money states received for job training.

The 102nd Congress was more successful, clearing a job training bill that President Bush subsequently signed into law. *(1991-92 action, p. 728)*

HR 2039 and S 543 were the first major attempts to amend the 1982 Job Training Partnership Act (JTPA — PL 97-300), which was coauthored by Sen. Edward M. Kennedy, D-Mass., and Vice President Dan Quayle, then a GOP senator from Indiana. Quayle repeatedly cited the JTPA during the 1988 presidential campaign as one of his main legislative accomplishments. JTPA replaced a problem- and abuse-plagued public service employment program known as CETA (the Comprehensive Employment and Training Act). *(JTPA, Congress and the Nation Vol. VI, p. 655)*

Under JTPA, job training funds were allocated according to a formula pegged largely to the number of unemployed individuals in states and local communities. Although many suburban and some rural areas made out well, critics said many of the individuals in most need of training were not formally classified as unemployed. They included young people who had never joined the labor force as well as those who had been out of work for years and were no longer actively seeking a job.

S 543 (S Rept 101-129), crafted by Paul Simon, D-Ill., and approved 15-1 July 26, 1989, and reported Sept. 14 by the Senate Labor and Human Resources Committee, changed the formula, steering funds to people in poverty — and particularly to downtrodden urban communities where poverty was most highly concentrated. To minimize disruption in the existing program — and dampen political opposition from regions threatened by the new formula — the bill provided that each state through fiscal 1992 would receive at least as much money as it already was getting and funding could be shifted at the local level within designated limits.

The measure authorized $2.8 billion in fiscal 1990 for adult and youth training programs — an increase of $300 million over the fiscal 1989 appropriation. Simon's measure also tightened eligibility requirements in response to criticism that the program's administrators tended to focus their efforts on the cream of the training crop — those easiest to serve.

S 543 saw no further action in the 101st Congress, stalling because of opposition from states that would receive less funding under its allocation formula.

The House Education and Labor Committee approved HR 2039 (H Rept 101-747) by voice vote on July 31, 1990. The committee-approved measure, which was reported Sept. 24, included a compromise amendment by Pat Williams, D-Mont., to change the funding formula for youth programs in states to allot 60 percent of funding on the basis of unemployment, 20 percent on the number of Aid to Families with Dependent Children recipients and 20 percent on the number of economically disadvantaged people. Williams described his amendment as a compromise to satisfy those members whose states had previously received the largest funding shares and who may have been afraid of losing funds and those who believed their states were not getting a fair share.

Another amendment that sparked heated debate, offered by Cass Ballenger, R-N.C., would have authorized $15 million to provide emergency employment to disaster victims. The committee agreed to a compromise by Bill Goodling, R-Pa., to limit eligibility to those who both qualified for the JTPA dislocated-worker program and were unemployed because of a disaster.

Voting along party lines, the committee rejected, 14-21, an amendment by Texas Republican Steve Bartlett that would have let participants trained for specific jobs to be placed in related fields.

The House passed HR 2039 on Sept. 27 by an overwhelming vote of 416-1. In addition to accepting the Williams compromise, the House adopted, by voice vote, amendments to revise JTPA eligibility requirements to increase participation of migrant and seasonal farmworkers, to require local grant recipients to keep records to enable the Labor Department to better collect information about the program's effectiveness and to increase the chances for participation for some youths who could not show that they were economically disadvantaged.

Just when it appeared that JTPA legislation was dead, Republicans Oct. 25 appended, 95-1, to the fiscal 1991 Labor, Health and Human Services, and Education appropriations legislation (HR 5257 — PL 101-517) a separate bill to revise the JTPA. The House, however, stripped off the bill early Oct. 26, before sending HR 5257 back to the Senate for clearance.

Congress in 1990 was successful in amending the JTPA in a separate piece of legislation to provide job training to displaced homemakers (HR 3069 — PL 101-554). *(Displaced homemakers, box, p. 715)*

Displaced Workers

After a bruising defeat in the Senate and veto threats aimed at the House, conferees agreed that the government should give income assistance and retraining to coal miners and others who might lose their jobs as a result of clean air legislation (S 1630 — PL 101-549) cleared in 1990. *(Clean air package, p. 473)*

The compromise, while narrower in scope than the original provision by Rep. Bob Wise, D-W.Va., marked the first time since the 1970s that Congress agreed to give cash payments to workers dislocated by new legislation. The Bush administration was adamantly opposed to the original Wise amendment, adopted on a **key vote of 274-146 (R 43-126; D 231-20)** by the House on May 23, which it considered an open-ended entitlement for workers. It would have authorized $250 million over five years to allow workers an additional 26 weeks of unemployment benefits and retraining if they showed the new clean air law was "an important contributing factor" to their job loss. *(1990 key votes, p. 1039)*

The clean air package's acid rain controls were expected to shift jobs from the high-sulfur coal industry in the East to low-sulfur coal workers in Western states. Other provisions could cost jobs in the oil, chemical and auto industries. That prospect prompted a related Senate proposal by Robert C. Byrd, D-W.Va., which was rejected by a **key vote of 49-50 (R 11-34; D 38-16)** on March 29. It would have cost $500 million and was aimed at helping displaced coal miners.

During the House-Senate conference on the clean air bill, the administration sent signals that the Wise provision was a bill-killer. Surprisingly, however, President Bush was willing to deal. The result altered the original provision but left its intent largely intact. Displaced workers could receive cash after their unemployment assistance ran out as long as they remained in a retraining program. The authorization remained at $250 million over five years, but the biggest change involved the source of the funds. Instead of making the plan part of the mandatory unemployment benefits program, which Bush opposed, conferees put all funding under the Economically Dislocated Workers Assistance Act, a part of the larger Job Training Partnership Act (JTPA), which was dependent on yearly appropriations. *(JTPA background, Congress and the Nation Vol. VI, p. 655; Congress and the Nation Vol. VII, p. 695)*

Wise, aware that employment agencies and unions that received JTPA funds rarely used their discretion to give cash to as well as provide retraining for workers, insisted on language ensuring that workers would get both. The payments were to be equal to the unemployment insurance level or enough to keep family income above the poverty level, whichever was higher.

Age-Based Discrimination

Compromise legislation (S 1511) reversing a Supreme Court ruling that allowed age-based discrimination in employee benefits cleared Congress in 1990 and, despite previous reservations from the administration, was signed into law (PL 101-433) by President Bush on Oct. 16.

The Age Discrimination in Employment Act (ADEA — PL 90-202), enacted in 1967, prohibited private and public employers from discriminating on the basis of age against employees age 40 or older in hiring, promotion or compensation. But it contained an exemption for "any bona fide employee benefit plan such as a retirement, pension, or insurance plan, which is not a subterfuge to evade the purposes" of the act. *(PL 90-202, Congress and the Nation Vol. II, p. 620)*

Regulations dating from 1969 interpreted that provision to prohibit age-based differentials in benefits unless they were justified by "significant cost considerations." But the so-called equal cost or equal benefit regulations were invalidated by the Supreme Court in a 7-2 decision handed down on June 23, 1989.

The ruling came in a case, *Public Employees Retirement System of Ohio v. Betts*, brought by a former state of Ohio employee forced to retire at age 61 because of an Alzheimer's-related disease. Under Ohio's pension system, her retirement benefits were less than half what she would have received had she been under age 60 when she retired.

Justice Anthony M. Kennedy, writing for the Court, said that the language of the ADEA did not expressly bar discrimination in employee benefits. The only way to successfully challenge a benefits plan, he said, was to show it was aimed at discriminating in some non-fringe-benefit area, such as hiring or firing. *(Case summary, p. 839)*

Committee Action

Several members of Congress, saying the Court had misconstrued the law, began drafting legislation to overturn the decision within weeks of the ruling. Rep. Edward R. Roybal, D-Calif., chairman of the House Select Committee on Aging, and David Pryor, D-Ark., chairman of the Senate Special Committee on Aging, introduced companion measures (HR 3200, S 1511). Hearings were held on Sept. 21, 1989, by the House Aging Committee and two House Education and Labor subcommittees and on Sept. 27 by the Senate Labor and Human Resources Subcommittee on Labor and the Senate Aging Committee.

The Senate Labor Committee voted 11-5 on Feb. 28, 1990, in favor of a substitute version of S 1511 (S Rept 101-

263) developed by Howard M. Metzenbaum, D-Ohio, and James M. Jeffords, R-Vt. Voting against the measure were five of the panel's seven Republican members. The revised bill picked up support from organized labor, including the United Auto Workers and the AFL-CIO, by sanctioning early-retirement incentives. But it was still opposed by such business groups as the U.S. Chamber of Commerce. The measure was formally reported April 5.

Metzenbaum said the main purpose of the bill was to make clear that the 1967 act covered discrimination against older workers in benefits unless the disparate treatment was justified by "significant cost considerations." The substitute included three major changes urged by the Equal Employment Opportunity Commission (EEOC) and labor unions. It clarified that early retirement incentive programs that were "truly voluntary" would still be legal. It also provided that workers who retired early before they were entitled to a full pension could receive a subsidized pension, even though workers who had reached 65 years of age would not receive such subsidies. Finally, the revised bill also permitted "bridge payments" that were given to some early retirees to subsidize their income until they began collecting Social Security, even though workers who retired at age 65 were not entitled to such payments.

The revised bill also contained a partial concession to employers and unions concerned about the original measure's effect on the practice of "integrating" or coordinating severance pay with pension benefits. In layoffs or plant shutdowns, employers often gave younger workers more in severance pay than they gave older, pension-eligible workers — in recognition that the pensions afforded older workers an income stream that younger workers would not have. The modified bill allowed severance pay for retirement-eligible employees to be offset by the value of any retirement health benefits. In addition, employers offering retirement health benefits could get an additional offset for so-called pension sweeteners — increases beyond the pension an employee would receive based on length of service.

In markup, the committee also approved an amendment by Jeffords to deal with a separate but related issue: the increasing practice among employers of shielding themselves from age-discrimination suits by seeking waivers from affected employees. The amendment set a series of standards to ensure that workers who waived their rights to file age-discrimination claims in exchange for generous early retirement plans knew what they were doing. Specifically, it provided that waivers be in writing and include a recommendation to consult with an attorney, that employees have a period of time after the agreement to change their minds and that in cases affecting groups of employees the employer reimburse any employee for 80 percent of the cost of consulting a lawyer for up to 10 hours of the attorney's time.

One other provision — making the bill retroactively effective to the date of the *Betts* ruling — was particularly troublesome to business groups. Concern arose that some companies might be affected that thought they would not.

The House Labor Committee approved a substantially similar bill (HR 3200 — H Rept 101-664) by a near party-line vote of 20-13 on April 4 after a quarrelsome markup that ended with outvoted Republicans walking out in an effort to deny Democrats the quorum needed to order the bill reported.

Prior to the committee markup, the White House raised the possibility of a veto. In a letter March 27 to the committee's ranking Republican, Bill Goodling, Pa., White House domestic policy adviser Roger Porter listed five areas of concern in the Senate committee's version of the bill: retroactivity; integration or coordination of benefits; waiver of rights; effects on pension plans; and effects on state and local governments. He also criticized as overly restrictive a provision that would permit early-retirement plans as long as they were voluntary and would "further the purposes" of the age-discrimination law.

In markup, GOP members began by attacking the provision on early-retirement plans. "It's vague, it's mysterious, and it's problematic," said Cass Ballenger, R-N.C., echoing the White House stance. But the committee defeated, 12-21, his amendment to substitute language allow-

Displaced Homemakers

Congress in 1990 cleared legislation to provide job training to displaced homemakers. The legislation (HR 3069) amended the 1982 Job Training Partnership Act (JTPA — PL 97-300) by authorizing funding to train the nation's estimated 15.6 million displaced homemakers — women whose long-term roles as homemakers ended because of divorce or the death or disability of their husbands. *(JTPA background, Congress and the Nation Vol. VI, p. 655)*

The number of displaced homemakers had increased an estimated 12 percent between 1980 and 1990. Approximately 60 percent of the women were unemployed.

The language of HR 3069 was contained in House and Senate versions of a broader overhaul of the JTPA (HR 2039, S 543) but was stripped out as a separate measure when those bills stalled. *(JTPA overhaul, p. 713)*

The funding for the homemakers bill would be used to expand and coordinate existing training and support services at the state and local levels. Under the bill, states would have to give special consideration to women 40 and older as well as minority displaced homemakers.

Matthew G. Martinez, D-Calif., chairman of the House Education and Labor Subcommittee on Employment Opportunities, introduced HR 3069 in August 1989. The subcommittee held one hearing, on Sept. 28, 1989. The House passed the bill by voice vote, under suspension of the rules, Oct. 15, 1990.

The Senate gave its approval, by voice vote, to an amended version in the early morning hours of Oct. 20 (during the session that began Oct. 19). As passed by the Senate, the bill provided a $35 million fiscal 1991 authorization. Sen. Strom Thurmond, R-S.C., had objected to the $50 million figure approved by the House.

The House accepted the Senate amendment Oct. 24, clearing the measure. President Bush signed HR 3069 (PL 101-554) on Nov. 15.

ing employers to use age distinctions when offering benefit packages.

The committee also rejected amendments offered by Thomas E. Petri, R-Wis., to shift the burden of proof in lawsuits from the employer to the employee, 11-23; by Goodling, to allow employers to integrate severance with a retiree's pension, 11-22; and by Marge Roukema, R-N.J., to make the legislation effective on the date of enactment, instead of the day of the *Betts* decision, 13-20.

The House panel followed the Senate committee's example in expanding the original legislation to deal with the question of legal waivers in exchange for early-retirement payments. But it adopted a stricter limitation — sponsored by William L. Clay, D-Mo., and Matthew G. Martinez, D-Calif. — barring any waiver unless it was part of a settlement of an allegation of age discrimination made by a worker against an employer.

HR 3200 was reported by House Labor on Aug. 3.

Floor Action

Sen. Orrin G. Hatch, R-Utah, opened floor action on S 1511 by offering an amendment that would have gutted the bill by providing that it would not apply to state or local governments or to private employers unless federal employers also were included. Sponsors of the legislation moved to deflect the attack with an amendment stipulating that the federal government would be covered two years after enactment of the legislation and that the Office of Personnel Management would conduct a study within one year on any changes needed in federal benefit plans to comply. The Senate Sept. 18 voted 80-19 to extend the bill to federal employers and then adopted Hatch's language as amended by voice vote.

Despite the victory over Hatch's amendment, the Democratic managers of the bill recognized that the legislation could not pass as written and overcome a possible presidential veto. As the session was drawing to a close and with the blessing of Majority Leader George J. Mitchell, D-Maine, staff for Metzenbaum and Hatch conducted intricate negotiations aimed at drafting a measure that both senators could endorse. The compromise unveiled Sept. 24 left no one completely happy, but Metzenbaum and Hatch both appealed to colleagues to vote for it.

The compromise preserved the essential features of the original bills, extending the age-discrimination law to employee benefits and codifying the EEOC's equal cost or equal benefit rules that the Supreme Court had invalidated. But it also gave employers "safe harbors" for the two most widely used types of early-retirement incentives — pension subsidies and Social Security bridge payments. Employees participating in those types of incentive programs could sue for age discrimination only if they claimed their participation was coerced.

With other types of early-retirement programs, workers could sue on grounds that their employer's plan was not consistent with the "relevant purposes" of the 1967 age-discrimination law. That language was another compromise between Metzenbaum, who wanted strict adherence to all three specifically stated purposes of the ADEA, and Hatch, who wanted plans to be upheld if an employer could show "legitimate business purposes."

The compromise also allowed employers an offset for plant-shutdown sweeteners even if they did not offer retirement health benefits, omitting a requirement from the committee-passed bill.

On a related issue that had divided the two senators, the compromise allowed employers to offset long-term disability payments with pension benefits when an employee chose to begin receiving a pension or reached normal retirement age.

Metzenbaum had wanted to allow the offset only in case of voluntary retirement; Hatch had wanted a broader offset in every case, based on a worker's accrued pension eligibility.

Employers got further concessions. The burden of proof in employee-benefit claims was placed on workers. Retroactivity was eliminated; instead, the law was to take effect for non-union employees 180 days after enactment and for union employers at the end of existing collective bargaining agreements or by June 1, 1992. And the waiver provision was amended to drop any requirement for employers to pay employees' legal fees.

The provision for covering federal employees also was dropped. State and local governments were given two years to comply with the new law.

Despite the reservations from the authors of the compromise, no senator spoke in opposition to the revised measure. It passed the Senate Sept. 24, 94-1, with James A. McClure, R-Idaho, casting the lone dissenting vote.

The House moved quickly after the Senate action. The bill was brought to the floor Oct. 2 under suspension of the rules — which meant limited debate and no amendments. The roll call was delayed until the next day when the bill passed, 406-17, with Republicans casting all the "nay" votes.

Age-Discrimination Waivers

Legislation (HR 1432, S 54) stipulating that older workers who opted for early retirement in return for generous bonuses could not be forced to waive the right to file age-discrimination claims against their former employers received House and Senate committee approval in 1989 but went no further in the 101st Congress.

The House Education and Labor Committee approved HR 1432 (H Rept 101-221) on June 13 by a vote of 21-13 and formally reported it Aug. 4; S 54 (S Rept 101-79) was approved 11-5 by the Senate Labor and Human Resources Committee June 14 and reported July 18. Championed by Democrats, the measures were opposed by most committee Republicans.

Proponents said workers were being exploited by employers who required them to sign waivers of their rights under the 1967 Age Discrimination in Employment Act in exchange for early-retirement bonuses. Under HR 1432, no waivers were valid except as part of a settlement of an allegation of age discrimination made by a worker against the employer. Less restrictive, S 54 permitted waivers if supervised by the courts or by the Equal Employment Opportunity Commission (EEOC). *(1967 act, Congress and the Nation Vol. II, p. 620)*

As approved June 1 by House Education's Employment Opportunities Subcommittee, HR 1432 permitted court-supervised waivers. However, the full committee adopted by voice vote an amendment by subcommittee Chairman Matthew G. Martinez, D-Calif., to remove this provision, which critics said would hamper already overburdened courts.

Both the House and Senate committee measures scrapped rules issued by the EEOC in 1987 to allow unsupervised waivers. Critics said this approach was likely to backfire by discouraging companies from offering early-retirement packages to workers. They also said it insulted workers by barring them from negotiating such packages on their own.

House Education rejected, 13-20, an amendment by Steve Gunderson, R-Wis., to permit an unsupervised waiver if the employer met certain conditions, such as advising the worker to consult a lawyer before signing the document. A similar plan, offered by Orrin G. Hatch, R-Utah, was rejected 7-9 by Senate Labor.

The General Accounting Office (GAO) found that more and more companies were using generous early-retirement bonus plans to tempt workers into waiving their rights. According to a GAO report released during an April 18 joint hearing by Martinez's subcommittee and the House Select Committee on Aging, the percentage of Fortune 100 companies requiring such waivers as a condition of early retirement rose from about 13 percent in 1983 to nearly 35 percent in 1988.

Some workers told lawmakers horror stories of being forced to sign away their rights or risk being squeezed out of their jobs with very little retirement protection. But others testified that the waivers, coupled with the early-retirement bonus, were the ticket to the good life. And GAO found that most top companies with retirement incentives did not seek waivers often because "the program was voluntary" or to do so would be "insulting to employees."

Housing Benefit Plans

Legislation (S 1949) that for the first time allowed collective bargaining agreements to include provisions for employers to help pay employees' housing costs cleared Congress in 1990.

The measure amended the Taft-Hartley Labor-Management Relations Act of 1947 (PL 80-101) to permit — but not require — employers to establish housing trust funds to give employees money for down payments, closing costs, bank fees and mortgage interest buy-downs to buy homes. The trust fund also could help pay initial rental costs such as security deposits and the first month's rent. Previously, employers were prohibited from making payments into jointly administered trust funds for anything other than a limited number of benefits, including health, life insurance and retirement. *(Taft-Hartley, Congress and the Nation Vol. I, p. 567)*

The Senate passed S 1949 by voice vote on Nov. 22, 1989. The House cleared the bill (S 1949) April 3, 1990, by voice vote, after first approving an identical version (HR 4073 — H Rept 101-441) of its own. President Bush signed the bill on April 18 (PL 101-273).

Unemployment Benefits

A bill (HR 3896) to increase unemployment benefits — and to raise unemployment taxes — was pulled from House Ways and Means Committee consideration July 25, 1990, by its sponsor, Thomas J. Downey, D-N.Y., when it became clear that it lacked the requisite support.

As approved by voice vote March 13 by the Human Resources Subcommittee, HR 3896 sought to extend unemployment benefits by creating a "substate" trigger. This would allow a state's governor to activate extended unemployment benefits in one area of the state, even if the unemployment rate in the state as a whole was not high enough to trigger the extended benefits program.

Jobless people were eligible for 13 weeks of extended benefits after they exhausted the 26-week state plans, but only if the state as a whole had high enough unemployment rates to trigger the program.

Preliminary estimates by the Ways and Means staff showed the bill would cost $3.3 billion over the next three fiscal years and a total of $6.5 billion by fiscal 1995. To pay for these extra benefits, the bill provided for an increase in the federal wage base on which employers paid unemployment taxes. The minimum taxable wage base used to calculate employers' unemployment insurance tax would rise annually from its existing level of $7,000 to $10,000 by fiscal 1993.

The proposed tax increase drew scornful comments from the committee minority — and even some Democrats. Downey defended his proposal, saying that unemployment reserves were inadequate to cover a possible recession and that "this is a preparation for bad times to come." He tried to increase support for the bill with an amendment to authorize a five-year program for dislocated workers who lost their jobs because of action by the federal government, but the proposal also drew opposition.

On June 15, 1989, the Human Resources Subcommittee had voted nearly $3 billion worth of service and benefit increases for the nation's poorest and least influential citizens. The financing mechanism would be an increase in the amount of wages subject to the federal employment compensation tax. The provisions were included in a fiscal 1990 budget-reconciliation package (HR 3299 — PL 101-239). *(Tax policy, p. 91; reconciliation, p. 43)*

The subcommittee also recommended an option for states to pay unemployment compensation to non-professional school employees between academic years or terms and creation of local as well as statewide triggers for the additional 13 weeks of unemployment benefits available through the extended benefits program in areas with high unemployment rates.

The full Ways and Means Committee, the week of June 19, torpedoed the revenue plan by a vote of 18-17. Having lost the financing mechanism, Downey moved to strip the unemployment provisions from the bill.

Unemployment benefits legislation had better luck in the 102nd Congress. *(Stories, pp. 721, 725)*

Social Security

The 101st Congress considered proposals to make major revisions in the Social Security program, notably by relaxing the so-called earnings test.

Although the 1989 and 1990 budget-reconciliation bills (HR 3299 — PL 101-239; HR 5835 — PL 101-508) contained a number of changes in the huge retirement program, members in both years were forced to drop the earnings test provision, citing the substantial additional cost that would be incurred. *(1989 reconciliation provisions, p. 51; 1990 reconciliation provisions, p. 61)*

The Senate, for two days in 1990, debated a bill (S 3167) that would have fundamentally changed the Social Security financing system for the second time in a decade. And the Senate Finance Subcommittee on Social Security in 1989 received the results of a study on the "notch babies."

Efforts by the 102nd Congress in the area of Social Security reform also fell short. *(Story, p. 736)*

Earnings Test

The earnings test reduces the Social Security benefits of persons ages 65-69 who earn more than a certain amount each year. The proposed change would have increased the amount those individuals could earn before benefits began to be reduced.

Senior citizens' groups had been urging a relaxation of the earnings test for years, arguing that it was an unfair disincentive that forced people with the potential to continue working to retire. Lawmakers in both parties — particularly Republicans eager to make happy the small but affluent group of retirees with enough income to be affected by the earnings limit — sought to please the powerful lobbying groups by making the change. But it proved fiscally impossible in light of the massive federal deficit.

Critics of the proposed increase also argued that the earnings test was a minor factor for most people in deciding whether to continue working. Moreover, they said, the change would primarily benefit the wealthiest of the elderly.

The increase considered by the 101st Congress would have been another in a long series of earnings test hikes approved by Congress since passage of the Social Security Act in 1935. The last major change had been in the major overhaul of the program in 1983 (PL 98-21), which provided that benefits be reduced by $1 for every $3 earned, instead of for every $2 of earned income as previously. *(1983 law, Congress and the Nation Vol. VI, p. 659)*

The earnings test did not apply to those age 70 or above, who could draw full Social Security benefits regardless of earnings.

1989 Action. As part of its fiscal 1990 budget-reconciliation proposal, the House Ways and Means Subcommittee on Social Security June 14 approved an earnings test increase to $9,720, from $9,360 in existing law, in 1990, and to $10,440, from $9,840 in existing law, in 1991. To cover the estimated $927 million cost to the Social Security trust fund, the proposal eliminated eligibility for retroactive benefits for certain recipients and froze the earnings test threshold for those aged 62-64.

The subcommittee provisions also granted independent authority to the Social Security Administration (SSA), taking it from the Department of Health and Human Services. The Bush administration vehemently opposed the idea.

The Ways and Means Committee June 19 included the subcommittee language in HR 3299, except for the provision freezing the earnings test threshold for those 62-64. The House approved the Ways and Means proposal when it passed HR 3299 on Oct. 5.

The Senate Finance Committee, meanwhile, approved an earnings test increase — more generous than the Ways and Means version — in its reconciliation recommendations on Oct. 3. In addition to making the SSA an independent agency, the proposal also provided for a 2 percent increase in the wage base subject to Social Security taxes.

On the Senate floor Oct. 13, however, members decided to drop the Social Security provisions along with all other measures that did not contribute to reducing the deficit.

Earnings test provisions were added to two other bills in 1989. During Senate floor action on HR 2, a minimum wage increase bill that President Bush would veto, William L. Armstrong, R-Colo., offered an amendment to raise the cap on the Social Security earnings test limit to $9,960. The amendment, adopted 86-11 on April 12, was dropped from the bill in conference. *(Minimum wage, p. 705)*

Another Armstrong amendment, to exempt from the earnings test wages earned by child care workers aged 65-69, was hotly debated during Senate Finance Committee consideration of a tax credit plan. The amendment was rejected, 9-10. However, the full Senate voted unanimously, 100-0, on June 22 to adopt a Lloyd Bentsen, D-Texas, amendment to increase to $10,560 in 1990 the amount of income that Social Security recipients could earn without a reduction in benefits and to reduce the first $5,000 in earnings above that cap by $1 for every $4 earned instead of every $3. A William V. Roth Jr., R-Del., amendment to exempt child care earnings from the earnings test was similarly adopted. Both the Bentsen and Roth amendments were attached to S 5, child care legislation, which the Senate passed June 23. Further action awaited the issue in 1990.

1990 Action. The Senate on April 24 passed the House companion bill (HR 3), after incorporating the language of S 5. The House did not included earnings test provisions in HR 3 when it had voted to pass the bill March 29. However, the proposal was as popular in that chamber as in the Senate. On June 20, the House voted 384-36 to instruct House conferees on HR 3 to accept the Senate earnings test language. Then, on Aug. 3, the Senate conferees decided to increase the threshold by more than $10,000 to $19,960. To pay for the $1.2 billion additional cost, conferees proposed requiring state and local government employees not participating in a separate retirement plan to participate in Social Security. The provisions subsequently were dropped, and the child care bill was folded into the fiscal 1991 budget-reconciliation bill (HR 5835).

Tax Changes

The Senate in 1990 considered a proposal to cut Social Security taxes for low- and middle-income workers, while increasing them for better-paid workers. The measure (S 3167) was offered by Daniel Patrick Moynihan, D-N.Y., as a largely symbolic protest against the existing financing methods of the system. Moynihan argued that the payroll-deduction tax funding the program was regressive, as it took a considerably higher percentage of the incomes of the working poor and middle class than of the wealthy, whose incomes were not subject to Social Security taxes above a certain point.

Moynihan's proposal to cut the payroll tax rate from 6.2 percent to 5.1 percent by 1996 and to increase the amount of income subject to the tax from $51,300 in 1990 to $85,500 in 1996 would have had the effect of returning the financing of the system to the "pay as you go" method used until 1983. In that year, a commission had proposed, and Congress agreed, to raise taxes to build up a surplus of money to prepare the system for the huge burden it would face when the "baby boom" generation reached retirement age in the 21st century.

Although he had been a prominent member of the commission, Moynihan said he had come to believe the Social Security tax increase was being used to mask the true size of the federal operating deficit. That was because the program's huge surplus was being invested in federal securities, thus helping to pay for current government operations while failing to save money for future retirement costs.

Using the threat of delaying an essential continuing appropriations measure (H J Res 666), Moynihan and his allies forced Senate leaders to bring S 3167 to the floor. Recognizing that the bill was unlikely to pass, members attached a number of major amendments, including elimination of the earnings test and increased benefits for "notch babies" born between 1917 and 1921.

The death of the bill came when Ted Stevens, R-Alaska, made a point of order against it for increasing the federal deficit above the ceiling set by the Gramm-Rudman-Hollings deficit-reduction law. A Moynihan motion to waive the requirement failed Oct. 10 on a 54-44 vote, six votes short of the required 60.

'Notch Babies'

The Senate Finance Committee's Social Security Subcommittee convened Jan. 23, 1989, to receive the results of a National Academy of Social Insurance (NASI) study, commissioned by the subcommittee in March 1988, on the problem of the Social Security "notch babies." While the NASI panel found that the notch phenomenon existed — those born between 1919 and 1921 who retired after age 62 received lower benefits than those born in earlier years who had comparable work histories — it recommended that Congress take no action to correct the inequity. The General Accounting Office reached a similar conclusion in a study it released in March 1988.

The problem began in 1972, when Congress altered the way Social Security benefits were adjusted for inflation (PL 92-336). Because inflation greatly outpaced wage increases in the 1970s, the change resulted in overly generous benefits that threatened to bankrupt the system. Congress acted in 1977 (PL 95-216) to roll back benefits for retirees born after 1921. Recipients born through 1916, some of who had begun retiring, were allowed to continue receiving benefits under the 1972 formula; that is, they received an unintended windfall. Those approximately 7 million born in between — in the notch — were given a choice of the less-generous post-1977 benefit schedule or a phased-down version of the 1972 formula. *(1972 law, Congress and the Nation Vol. III, p. 618; 1977 law, Congress and the Nation Vol. V, p. 235)*

A raft of bills were introduced in the 101st Congress to increase benefits for the notch babies, but none went anywhere.

Pension Reversions

In both 1989 and 1990, Congress considered legislation pertaining to pension plan reversions — the process by which an employer terminated a plan and used the excess funds for other activities, such as financing corporate takeovers. Those efforts stalled, but tax penalty provisions expected to slow the practice were enacted as part of the Omnibus Budget Reconciliation Act of 1990 (HR 5835 — PL 101-508). *(Tax policy, p. 92; reconciliation, p. 55)*

Background

Between 1980 and 1989, nearly 2,000 pension plans were cashed out, according to the Employee Benefit Research Institute. About $20 billion reverted to the companies as surplus assets.

Pension plan raids became popular in 1980 when a West German company bought the A&P Co. supermarket chain, terminated its pension plan and wound up with $273 million in surplus assets. Reversions peaked in 1985 when 584 plans were terminated and companies recovered nearly $7 billion in surplus funds. The pace then began to slow somewhat, in part because Congress slapped penalties on reversions. In the 1986 tax law overhaul (PL 99-514), Congress agreed to levy a 10 percent excise tax on the surplus funds. That tax was upped to 15 percent in 1988 (PL 100-647). *(PL 99-514, Congress and the Nation Vol. VII, p. 79; PL 100-647, Congress and the Nation Vol. VII, p. 100)*

Lawmakers sought a permanent solution to the reversion problem, nearly reaching one late in 1987 during a conference over budget reconciliation, but last-minute disagreements blocked that effort. In response to lawmakers' concerns, the Treasury Department in October 1988 agreed to a temporary moratorium on approvals of reversions. However, a compromise could not be worked out with employers, and since the May 1, 1989, expiration of the moratorium Treasury resumed processing the transactions. *(1987-88 pension legislation, Congress and the Nation Vol. VII, p. 696)*

1989 Action

HR 1661, sponsored by William L. Clay, D-Mo., chairman of the House Education and Labor Subcommittee on Labor-Management Relations, was approved by the subcommittee, 10-4, on April 18, after an abbreviated hearing and almost no debate. As approved, the bill would require companies that cash out their pension plans to set up new plans or be barred from getting any of the surplus assets.

On July 13, the full committee adopted, by voice vote, the subcommittee version of the bill (H Rept 101-169) without amendment; it subsequently was reported July 24. Also on July 13, the committee agreed to fold into its part of a deficit-reduction bill (HR 3299) a plan crafted by Clay that would ban pension reversions, while permitting limited transfers of surplus assets to pay for health benefits of retired workers. Transfers of pension funds in excess of 150 percent of the amount needed to pay current obligations would be permitted. However, employers would have to pay a 15 percent excise tax on the amount of the transfer and would be barred from reducing benefits for retired workers whose health plans were to be funded by transferred assets.

Both HR 1661 and the Clay reconciliation plan were hotly opposed by business interests, who warned, as did the Bush administration, that tight clamps on companies' use of pension funds would backfire by discouraging employers from establishing such plans. Employers insisted they should be free to use surplus cash any way they saw fit, as long as workers received promised benefits. However, tough restrictions were supported by groups representing organized labor and retired workers.

A separate provision tacked on to Clay's plan by Rep. Peter J. Visclosky, D-Ind., was approved by the House Education and Labor Committee on a party-line vote of 22-13. The proposal would require single-employer pension plans to be administered by a joint board of trustees represented equally by management and workers. Proponents, including AFL-CIO lobbyists, said this step was needed to protect against such things as investment of pension assets

Pension Board Ruling

The Supreme Court, in an 8-1 ruling on June 18, 1990, upheld the authority of the Pension Benefit Guaranty Corporation (PBGC) to make financially ailing companies take back responsibility for pension plans.

The decision in *Pension Benefit Guaranty Corp. v. LTV* was an important victory for the government-owned entity created by the 1974 Employee Retirement Income Security Act (ERISA) to ensure private pension plans. It came when the agency faced a possible $1.5 billion deficit of liabilities over assets. *(ERISA background, Congress and the Nation Vol. IV, p. 690)*

The ruling upheld a PBGC order that LTV Corp., a diversified corporation that included one of the nation's largest steel companies, resume responsibility for three pension plans with liabilities totaling $2.3 billion. LTV filed for reorganization under Chapter 11 of the federal bankruptcy code in 1986 and informed the PBGC that it could no longer fund the pension plans.

Writing for the Court, Justice Harry A. Blackmun said the PBGC could restore terminated plans when it found such action "appropriate and consistent with its duties." *(Case summary, p. 846)*

in high-yield "junk bonds" used to finance corporate takeovers. They noted that workers had long been represented on the board of multi-employer plans. Business lobbyists believed the provision threatened to run single-employer plans into the ground through mismanagement.

S 685 (S Rept 101-294), sponsored by Howard M. Metzenbaum, D-Ohio, chairman of the Senate Labor and Human Resources Subcommittee on Labor, was approved by the full committee on July 20. The same day, the committee agreed, on a party-line vote of 8-7, to fold the package into HR 3299.

Like the House, the Senate provided for limited transfers of pension assets to pay for health benefits of retired workers. Neither Clay nor Metzenbaum was enamored of a transfer scheme. They wanted to crack down on employers' use of the surplus. However, such provisions were included to ensure a seat at the bargaining table in the House-Senate conference on the reconciliation measure.

The House Ways and Means Committee the week of July 10 had approved a similar plan, which allowed employers to pay for their retiree health benefits with surplus money that they had set aside for pensions, as long as existing pension obligations and certain other conditions were met. Revenues to the government ensued because companies that used the pension money could not take so many write-offs on their spending for the retiree health care.

Ways and Means did not adopt language to bar reversions, largely because doing so would mean a potentially substantial loss in revenue to the Treasury. The Joint Committee on Taxation estimated that the Ways and Means plan, as adopted, would raise $286 million in fiscal 1990 and $465 million in fiscal 1991.

The Senate Labor Committee's language, based on S 685, would cost the Treasury $200 million in fiscal 1990 and $1.2 billion over five years, according to the Joint Committee on Taxation. Under the Senate plan, these costs would be offset by a "processing" fee to be paid by employers for filing annual reports on pensions and other employee-benefit plans with the Labor Department. The fee would be tied to the size of the company, up to a maximum of $1,000 annually.

Pension language ultimately was dropped from the reconciliation bill along with other "extraneous" provisions. *(HR 3299, p. 43)*

1990 Action

A modified version of S 685 was approved by the Senate Labor and Human Resources Committee on Feb. 28 but saw no further action. The bill would apply 1974 Employee Retirement Income Security Act (ERISA) standards to pension plan terminations only if it was determined to be in the best interest of the plan participants. The measure also included a provision to create a system of "portable pensions" to enable employees to carry their pension funds with them when they changed jobs.

As in 1989, supporters of the legislation tried to use a budget-reconciliation bill as a vehicle for enactment, but this time the effort succeeded.

Title XII (HR 5835 — PL 101-508) increased to 20 percent from 15 percent the excise tax employers would have to pay to cash out their pension plans. The rate would be 50 percent if an employer decided not to set up a new pension plan. An employer, upon terminating a pension plan, then would have to either keep a "cushion" of 25 percent of the surplus in a new pension plan or pay out 20 percent of the surplus in cash to retirees and workers. Employers would not be penalized, however, if they used the excess pension funds to pay premiums on retiree health plans.

The Congressional Budget Office estimated that the pension reversion provision would lose about $388 million in federal revenues over the five years of the budget agreement by discouraging the practice.

1991-92

In both 1991 and 1992, as the economy continued to falter, President Bush signed into law legislation providing extended unemployment benefits. One bill made a permanent change in the unemployment benefits system, allowing extended benefits to be allocated more easily during periods of high unemployment.

After years of trying, Congress in 1992 successfully devised legislation amending the 1982 Job Training Partnership Act.

Bush again vetoed legislation providing unpaid leave to employees with new babies or ill family members. The president had vetoed similar legislation in 1990. A family and medical leave bill finally did become law in 1993, however, soon after Democratic President Bill Clinton assumed office.

The 102nd Congress also considered legislation to revise the 1931 Davis-Bacon Act, to toughen child labor law, to protect striking workers, to make drawing from the Black Lung Disability Trust Fund easier, to amend the Occupational Safety and Health Act, to enact stricter safety guidelines for construction companies and to amend the 1974 Employee Retirement Income Security Act. None of the bills was enacted.

Efforts to make substantial changes in the Social Security program also failed, largely because of long-term fiscal concerns.

1991 Unemployment Benefits

After months of haggling over a temporary extension of unemployment benefits, two measures were crafted in 1991 to finally satisfy the demands of both chambers and the Bush administration. Two previous bills had been blocked by the White House.

Additional action regarding unemployment compensation was taken in 1992. *(Story, p. 725)*

President Bush agreed to sign a $5.3 billion bill (HR 3575 — PL 102-164) to extend unemployment benefits for either six, 13 or 20 weeks, depending on a formula devised by House leaders and the administration. Some of the senators whose states would receive only six weeks argued that they had been left out of the deal making.

To keep HR 3575 on track, Bush agreed to sign a trade bill (HR 1724 — PL 102-182) with new provisions that would raise the six-week states to the 13-week tier and allow workers in all states to qualify for extra benefits if they exhausted their state unemployment benefits after March 1, 1992, and were still unemployed. *(Andean Initiative, pp. 193, 296)*

Bush, by agreeing to give states either 13 or 20 weeks of extended benefits, provided far more than the Democrats had initially asked for. The changes in HR 1724 added $380 million to the original $5.3 billion unemployment measure, according to administration estimates.

The two bills capped a six-month effort to get checks out to the long-term jobless as economic barometers gave off mixed signals on whether the recession was subsiding or getting worse. Bush continued to thwart the efforts of congressional Democrats to get an unemployment measure enacted by citing the more optimistic reports on the number of jobless. The president disagreed that the economic climate warranted triggering emergency spending.

Under the 1990 budget agreement between the White House and Congress, any new programs had to be paid for by cuts in other programs or by tax increases. To add to the deficit, an emergency had to be declared by Congress and seconded by the president in the form of legislation. *(Budget agreement, p. 37)*

In the first round of sparring on the unemployment benefits issue, a bill (HR 3201 — PL 102-107) was enacted, but because Bush refused to designate an unemployment emergency, the money could not be spent. The second round culminated in legislation (S 1722) that was vetoed. Senate Republicans narrowly quashed a major effort to override the veto.

House and Senate leaders seriously considered drafting new legislation — that Bush would sign — only after he agreed that extending unemployment benefits was essential given the upcoming 1992 general election. The president, however, said he would continue to veto any measure that either broke the 1990 budget agreement or would raise taxes.

The hard exercise of getting an unemployment extension passed exposed weaknesses in the entire benefits setup. A major argument in 1991 deliberations was whether the legislation should provide a short-term payout of supplemental benefits or permanently alter the system. Bush's opposition to a long-term change pushed Congress to extend the benefits only into 1992.

Under existing law, states provided unemployed workers with 26 weeks of payments based on their former salary. If a state's insured unemployment rate reached a certain level, then the federal and state government split the cost of providing 13 weeks of extended benefits. Each state, however, had different rules about who qualified for unemployment benefits, making it difficult in many cases to trigger the extended benefits program.

Congress had not voted to extend unemployment benefits for the jobless since 1983, when legislation (PL 98-135) was approved to extend a temporary program of extra benefits through March 31, 1985. *(Congress and the Nation Vol. VI, p. 665)*

Round 1: HR 3201

For the third time in three years, Rep. Thomas J. Downey, D-N.Y., acting chairman of the House Ways and Means Subcommittee on Human Resources, in 1991 attempted to reshape the unemployment compensation system so that it would be more uniform across the country and would more easily trigger extended benefits. *(1989-90 action, p. 717)*

On March 11, Downey introduced HR 1367, which would double the standard 26 weeks of benefits during difficult economic times. To pay for the proposal, the legislation would raise the unemployment insurance taxes on businesses.

Despite the reluctance of the members of the full Ways and Means Committee to raise taxes and a general perception that the economy was starting to pick up, Downey was able to secure subcommittee approval, on a party-line vote June 26, of a scaled-down version of his proposal. His original bill would have cost about $23 billion over six years; the substitute would cost about $9 billion over the same period.

As approved by the subcommittee, HR 1367 would replace the extended benefits program, which provides 13 more weeks of benefits beyond the standard 26 weeks, with a three-tiered program. If a state's unemployment rate reached 6 percent, and that was 120 percent of the average unemployment rate for the past two years, workers would automatically qualify for an additional 10 weeks of benefits on top of the usual 26 weeks; at 7 percent, 15 weeks of benefits would kick in; and at 8 percent, 20 more weeks of compensation would be available. For fiscal 1992, if the national unemployment rate hit 6 percent, all states would qualify for 10 more weeks of benefits for the unemployed. The subcommittee also accepted, by voice vote, a Jim McDermott, D-Wash., amendment to allow workers to collect unemployment benefits for a year if they lost their jobs because of closure of a military base or federal government efforts to protect an endangered species.

Summer Youth Jobs

A fiscal 1992 urban aid supplemental appropriations bill (HR 5132 — PL 102-302) provided $500 million for summer jobs for young people. The measure came in the aftermath of the April 1992 riots in Los Angeles. *(Urban aid supplemental, pp. 81, 699)*

Of the total, $100 million would go to the nation's 75 largest cities. The remaining $400 million would be distributed according to the existing formula for summer youth jobs, which was based on poverty rates and unemployment. The compromise was designed to steer money to smaller urban areas, as many members worried about being short shrifted because the existing formula was seen as tilting toward big cities.

The money was expected to provide an additional 360,000 jobs for youth during the summer.

Senate Finance Committee Chairman Lloyd Bentsen, D-Texas, at the behest of the Democratic Caucus, in mid-July proposed a $6 billion emergency plan to provide additional benefits to unemployed workers. The administration, which insisted that the recession was ending and the economy was looking up, immediately came out against the plan.

Unlike Downey's bill, Bentsen's plan would be temporary and would not raise taxes. Instead, Bentsen would have Congress declare an emergency, allowing it to avoid the 1990 White House-congressional budget law requirement to raise the money to pay for any spending. Bentsen said he was persuaded that the unemployment situation had become an emergency, as he saw benefits expiring in the states while workers still had not found jobs. In June, the national unemployment rate hit 7 percent, up from a low of 5.3 percent the year before, according to the Bureau of Labor Statistics.

As an incentive to senators to support the plan, Bentsen proposed giving every state at least four weeks of extended benefits, paid solely by the federal government. States with a 6 percent total unemployment rate would receive seven weeks of benefits; states with 7 percent unemployment would get 13 weeks; and states with an unemployment rate of 8 percent or more would receive 20 weeks. Those rates would be based on a six-month average of the total unemployment rate. Payments would begin Oct. 1 but would reach back to include people who used up their benefits April 1 or later. The extended benefits would last through June 30, 1992.

Bentsen's plan also would allow veterans who had just left military service — including those who were in the Persian Gulf War — to collect unemployment benefits for 26 weeks. Under existing law, they were entitled to collect only 13 weeks' worth of unemployment compensation. This was the only provision of the plan that would be permanent.

Bentsen said the total cost of the plan would come to $5.8 billion over five years. Of that, $5.4 billion would be spent in fiscal 1992. He also said more than $8 billion already was in the federal unemployment trust fund from federal unemployment taxes paid by employers. But that money was not kept separate from the general Treasury fund, and administration officials said using that money would increase the nation's debt.

During Senate Finance Committee consideration of Bentsen's proposal, designated S 1554, Senate Minority Leader Bob Dole, R-Kan., offered several amendments to limit the program. He proposed using the rate of jobless people who were covered by unemployment insurance, not the total unemployment rate. That would weed out college students and others who should not qualify, he said. For states with more than 5 percent he would give six more weeks of benefits; over 5 percent would bring on 13 more weeks. The panel rejected Dole's amendment, 6-13.

Dole also said giving unemployment benefits to those who had voluntarily left the military was unfair, especially when civilians did not get the same benefits when they quit or retired from a job. The panel, by voice vote, rejected his amendment to modify the provision.

Dole suggested repealing a luxury tax on boats costing more than $100,000, which some members contended cost more to collect than it brought in. But tax bills were required by parliamentary procedure to originate in the House, not the Senate. "The reason to put it on this bill is to kill it," Bentsen said. Bentsen's motion to table (kill) the amendment was approved, 12-6.

Finally, Dole offered an amendment to delete the bill's requirement that Bush declare an emergency to pay for extra jobless benefits. The panel rejected Dole's move by voice vote.

The Senate Finance Committee voted 16-4 on July 25 to approve S 1554; it was reported the next day.

The unemployment benefits issue remained stalled in the House Ways and Means Committee until the Senate Democrats began showing interest in it. House Speaker Thomas S. Foley, D-Wash., urged Ways and Means Chairman Dan Rostenkowski, D-Ill., to join the Democrats' push to highlight the effects of the recession, according to a congressional leadership aide. On the day the Senate Finance Committee approved S 1554, Rostenkowski introduced HR 3040, which would give states with 6 percent total unemployment 10 more weeks of benefits; states with 7 percent unemployment would get 15 more weeks; and states with an 8 percent jobless rate would get 20 extra weeks.

During Ways and Means markup July 30, committee members stripped from the bill (H Rept 102-185) the employer tax provisions, which would have increased the amount of a worker's salary that could be taxed from $7,000 to $69,800. That left two key differences between S 1554 and HR 3040. First, Bentsen's bill was a temporary fix and Rostenkowski's measure would make permanent changes in the benefits program. Second, Bentsen's bill would require Bush to sign it as well as another piece of legislation certifying an emergency for money to be released from the Treasury. The House measure, formally reported Aug. 2, considered the president's signature on the legislation to be a declaration of an emergency.

Some House Democrats feared Bentsen's plan would allow Bush to sign the bill but not sign off on the emergency, letting the issue slip away. However, the House bill could have violated the budget agreement, which required both Congress and Bush to declare an emergency. If Bush vetoed the unemployment bill and Congress overrode that veto, then the law would be enacted without the president declaring an emergency.

On the floor, Dole offered a substitute amendment that would cost $3.2 billion in fiscal 1992 and would provide up to 10 weeks of benefits. His proposal would adhere to the pay-as-you-go rules of the budget agreement, raising $3.4 billion from auctioning frequencies on the electromagnetic spectrum for new communications uses and keeping tax refunds that would have gone to people who had defaulted on student loans.

On Aug. 1, the Senate rejected Dole's amendment by voice vote and adopted the Bentsen bill, also by voice vote.

On Aug. 2, the House Ways and Means Committee agreed to Bentsen's version of the unemployment bill, designated as HR 3201 (H Rept 102-184), sending it quickly to the House floor that same day. Only moments before the House passed the bill, 375-45, Bush reiterated his belief that the economy was recovering. He pointed to a Labor Department report released earlier in the day showing that the rate of unemployment in July had dropped 0.2 percent to 6.8 percent.

The Senate passed HR 3201 later that day by voice vote, clearing the measure for Bush's signature.

In reconciling the House and Senate versions, Democrats gave Bush the option of signing the legislation but not declaring an emergency, and thus not providing for the funds necessary to implement the provisions. Rostenkowski said that Democrats let Bush off the hook by not forcing him to veto the bill.

House Democratic leaders agreed to give up their version of the bill for the Senate's when they heard that Sen. Phil Gramm, R-Texas, had threatened to filibuster the House provisions.

Bush announced Aug. 15 that he would not "bust the budget" by agreeing with Congress that the money was emergency spending. He signed HR 3201 (PL 102-107) on Aug. 17.

Round 2: S 1722

Democrats found during the August recess that the unemployment issue embarrassed Republicans and played well with constituents. The leadership continued to approach it in a partisan fashion, attacking Bush for his willingness to help the people of foreign countries over his own. Bush fought off Democratic attempts to aid unemployed workers by arguing that the economy was on the upswing. But even House Republicans returned from the August break with tales of woe about their districts' economies.

The Center on Budget and Policy Priorities reported that, in July, the largest number of workers in any month since at least 1950 exhausted their state unemployment benefits without being eligible for any additional unemployment money. Almost 350,000 people had exhausted their state benefits, but only 18,000 were receiving extended benefits. Meanwhile, the Office of Management and Budget (OMB), in a statement of administration policy, charged that offering extra weeks of unemployment compensation would encourage people not to work.

Refusing to retreat after the defeat in August, the House on Sept. 17 voted overwhelmingly to pass a $6.3 billion measure (HR 3040) to permanently extend unemployment benefits for up to 20 extra weeks to jobless workers. The bill automatically made the benefits emergency spending and did not require a presidential declaration to be exempt from the spending requirements of the 1990 budget agreement. The **283-125 (R 48-107; D 234-18; I 1-0) key vote** gave Democrats 11 more votes than needed to override a veto. *(1991 key votes, p. 1061)*

During floor debate, the House rejected, 65-341, a Rostenkowski amendment that would have paid for the bill by raising the maximum salary that could be taxed and that would have given Bush the option of declaring an emergency and eliminating the increased taxes.

Minority Whip Newt Gingrich, R-Ga., offered a motion to send the bill back to committee to add an amendment that, among other things, would have killed the existing tax on capital gains and allowed first-time home buyers to use their individual retirement account funds for their down payments. The motion was ruled out of order.

Bill Archer, R-Texas, ranking minority member of Ways and Means, offered a motion, rejected 129-279, to recommit the bill to the committee with instructions to report it back with provisions to allow Bush to have until the end of 1991 to declare an emergency and release the benefits.

Republicans thought they could trip up the bill once it reached the Senate by refusing, 84-324, to take out a provision that raised money from states for unemployed school workers, such as custodians, crossing guards and cafeteria workers. Such a revenue-raiser could have resulted in divisive tax amendments being added to the bill. However, the Senate was working off its own version, making the point moot.

Although the House passed HR 3040 on Sept. 17, members on Sept. 25 voted again, for procedural reasons, on the Senate bill. S 1722 passed 294-127.

A weaker version of S 1722 passed the Senate on Sept. 24 on a 69-30 vote. The $5.8 billion measure, crafted by Bentsen, would require the president to sign a separate declaration of a budget emergency to release the money to pay for the extra weeks of unemployment compensation.

The House-passed bill would permanently change the trigger for additional benefits to the total unemployment rate. Workers could qualify for 10, 15 or 20 more weeks of benefits if their state unemployment rate reached 6, 7 or 8 percent, respectively. All states under 6 percent would get five weeks of benefits for their workers. The Senate bill, meanwhile, would change temporarily the extra benefits trigger during recessionary periods. Workers could receive seven, 13 or 20 more weeks of benefits if their state jobless rate hit 6, 7 or 8 percent, respectively. Workers in all other states would get four more weeks.

On the floor, the Senate on Sept. 24 agreed, 57-42, to a Bentsen motion to table (kill) a Dole amendment to provide up to 10 weeks of additional unemployment benefits and allow the president to finance extended benefits through either declaring the additional spending an emergency or financing the benefits by the auction of frequencies on the electromagnetic spectrum and student loan reform.

The Senate also rejected, 39-60, a Gramm motion to table (kill) a point of order, offered by Minority Leader George J. Mitchell, D-Maine, against the Gramm amendment to index capital gains and cut the capital gains tax from 28 percent to 19.6 percent for assets held more than three years.

An amendment by John McCain, R-Ariz., would have required three-fifths of all senators to vote in favor of any tax increase for them to take effect. The Senate voted 37-62 against waiving the 1974 Congressional

Budget and Impoundment Control Act to consider the amendment.

A House-Senate conference resolved differences between the two versions on Sept. 26, adopting the House requirement that Bush either sign or veto the bill. Unlike the House bill, the conference version was temporary; it would expire July 4, 1992. The House conceded to the Senate on almost every substantive point but the veto language.

The $6.4 billion conference bill gave an additional seven weeks of unemployment benefits to workers in 30 states and the District of Columbia; an additional 13 weeks of compensation to workers in 14 states; and an additional 20 weeks of benefits to workers in six states where unemployment exceeded 8 percent.

The Senate on Oct. 1 voted 65-35 to adopt the conference report (H Rept 102-228); the House followed suit, 300-118, later the same day, clearing the bill.

As expected, Bush, on Oct. 11, vetoed S 1722. In his veto message to Congress, he called the bill "substantively flawed," saying it "would effectively destroy the integrity of the bipartisan budget agreement and put into place a poorly designed, unnecessarily expensive program that would significantly increase the federal deficit."

In the Senate, Democratic leaders held the bill for eight days before sending it to the White House to delay the eventual override vote. Their hope was that constituents would persuade two Republican senators to change their votes during the intervening days. On Oct. 16, Republicans stopped them from overriding Bush's veto of S 1722 on a **key vote of 65-35 (R 8-35; D 57-0)**. The tally was two votes short of the two-thirds necessary for an override. *(1991 key votes, p. 1061)*

Round 3: HR 3575, Amended in HR 1724

Despite the presidential veto and the Senate failure to override, the House Ways and Means Committee took yet another stab at providing benefits to the long-term unemployed. On Oct. 22, the committee voted, 22-14, to approve HR 3575 (H Rept 102-273), which was reported Oct. 24.

The committee-approved bill contained Rostenkowski's provisions that would keep the federal unemployment tax at 0.08 percent instead of allowing it to drop to 0.06 percent, as it was scheduled to do in 1996; that would apply the tax to the first $7,700 of a worker's income instead of the existing $7,000; and that would require the Internal Revenue Service to withhold tax refunds from people who owed money to the federal government. An amendment by Jim Moody, D-Wis., that effectively would have struck the Rostenkowski language from the bill was rejected on a 17-17 tie vote.

Ways and Means also rejected, 13-20, an Archer amendment to substitute a Dole amendment for HR 3575. The Dole language would have cost $3.1 billion and provided either six or 10 weeks of benefits. The panel agreed to an amendment by Benjamin L. Cardin, D-Md., to ensure that the tax provisions expired after five years, in fiscal 1997.

After a White House luncheon Oct. 29 with Republicans who complained about the economy, Bush called House Minority Leader Robert H. Michel, R-Ill., and told him to negotiate a deal with Rostenkowski. Following Bush's phone call and conversations between Michel and Rostenkowski, top Democrats from the House and Senate got together Oct. 30. Democrats, however, became angered by Bush the next day, when he said, during a photo opportunity session, that he had wanted an unemployment bill all along. "I want it to be one that does not bust the budget agreement," Bush said. Democrats remembered when Bush originally said the economy was recovering and a bill was not necessary.

On Nov. 1, the Labor Department announced that the nation's unemployment rate had climbed one-tenth of 1 percent in October to 6.8 percent. That brought the number of jobless workers to 8.6 million. About 300,000 people a month were exhausting their state unemployment benefits without finding work.

Also on Nov. 1, the Ways and Means Committee objected to a Bentsen plan that was in the works. It would require people who paid income taxes quarterly to base their payments on the total income they expected to earn during the tax year, not on the amount of taxes they paid the year before. The stricter restriction would apply to those whose income jumped by at least $30,000 in one year.

Rostenkowski, Michel, Dole, Treasury Secretary Nicholas F. Brady and OMB Director Richard G. Darman subsequently settled down to negotiate a bill. The talks led to a refined Bentsen plan to raise money to pay for up to 20 weeks of benefits by changing the rules for upper-income people who estimated their taxes quarterly.

The Senate, meanwhile, was taking another tack, preferring to let President Bush choose one of three options for paying for an unemployment bill: (1) declaring an emergency, which would eliminate the need for offsetting cuts or a tax increase; (2) cutting foreign aid growth by $3.6 billion over five years, exempting housing loans for Israel and grain sales to the Soviet Union, and collecting $2 billion in delinquent student loans; and (3) requiring certain high-income people to estimate their quarterly tax payments on the total income they expected to earn, collecting student loans and extending the 0.08 percent federal unemployment tax.

Michel, Dole and Foley were not interested in giving Bush a multiple-choice bill, however. Rostenkowski met with Ways and Means Democrats two days in a row behind closed doors to cultivate their support. And Michel brought committee Republicans in for a private meeting Nov. 7.

The Ways and Means Committee approved HR 3575 on Nov. 13. To pay for the $5.3 billion measure, the bill would save approximately $2.6 billion by tightening rules on those paying quarterly taxes. Excluded were income from partnerships or "subchapter S" corporations — companies that resembled specialized limited partnerships — and income received from selling a home. Financing also was made possible by an estimated $1.7 billion to be saved by extending a law that allowed the Internal Revenue Service to collect debts owed the federal government by taking the money out of people's tax returns. Most of these debts came from student loan defaults. The federal unemployment tax would remain at 0.08 percent, saving an estimated $878 million.

Although the bill, according to the Congressional Budget Office, would cost $895 million in fiscal 1992 and thus would violate congressional budget laws, OMB ruled that it would not add to the deficit and therefore would not trigger across-the-board cuts in every other domestic program.

The House passed HR 3575 on a 396-30 vote on Nov. 14.

The momentum slowed in the Senate, however, and Mitchell and Dole were forced to fend off angry senators whose states did not fare well under the deal. The battle shaped up not over the funding mechanisms, which were accepted almost without debate, but over the formula used to determine which states qualified for how many extra weeks of benefits.

The previous bills sent to the president had calculated which state got what according to the total unemployment rate. But Darman strenuously objected to that method, preferring to calculate state need according to an insured unemployment rate, which measured the people who were eligible under state rules to receive compensation, not all people who were unemployed. To save money, many Southern states in particular made qualifying for unemployment benefits extremely difficult for workers. To determine how many weeks of benefits each state would receive, negotiators agreed to a formula that calculated an "adjusted insured unemployment rate" combined with the exhaustion rate of workers using up their state benefits. Complaints were made that Senate Democrats were not represented in the negotiations with the administration to put the unemployment deal together.

Mitchell's repeated attempts to call up the House bill were met with objections from both sides of the aisle until 11 p.m. on Nov. 14. Eventually, he promised to allow four amendments to be offered the next day, although both he and Dole insisted that all four would have to be voted down to preserve the agreement with the House and the White House. The Senate killed, 74-21, the only amendment offered, by Robert C. Smith, R-N.H. It would have cut foreign aid to boost the benefits for five states, including New Hampshire.

The whole bill might have collapsed at the last minute if the administration had not agreed to raise all the six-week states to the 13-week tier. The administration also promised to allow all states to qualify for retroactive benefits, instead of excluding many states. That added $95 million to the cost of the bill, which would be partially paid for by moving the bill's expiration from July 4, 1992, to June 13, 1992.

The Senate on Nov. 15 voted 91-2 to pass HR 3575 in the same form that it came over from the House. Bush signed the measure (PL 102-164) the same day.

The changes were added to a most-favored-nation trade status bill (HR 1724) for Czechoslovakia and Hungary. The House passed the bill (H Rept 102-223) on Oct. 8, 1991. The Senate passed the bill, amended, by voice vote Nov. 15. The House amended and passed, 407-21, HR 1724, under suspension of the rules, on Nov. 20. The Senate asked for a conference. The House adopted the conference report (H Rept 102-391) by voice vote on Nov. 26. The Senate acted similarly the same day, clearing the measure. The president signed the bill (PL 102-182) on Dec. 4.

1992 Unemployment Benefits

Frustrated with the difficulty workers faced in getting extended unemployment benefits from a federal-state program, Congress in 1991 cleared two pieces of legislation that temporarily overrode the program and gave states an extra 13 or 20 weeks of benefits, depending on the number of unemployed people in the state. Then, with 600,000 workers poised to exhaust those benefits in mid-February 1992, Congress cleared another extension (HR 4095 — PL 102-244) on Feb. 4. A second unemployment bill (HR 5260 — PL 102-102) cleared in 1992, on July 2; it included a permanent change to the unemployment benefits system. *(1991 action, p. 721)*

Round 1: HR 4095

By December 1991, according to the Labor Department, approximately 8.9 million Americans were unemployed. The civilian unemployment rate stood at 7.1 percent, up from 6.2 percent at the beginning of 1991. The economy, meanwhile, showed no signs of improvement.

In January 1992, barely two months after winning passage of the second of two 1991 bills (HR 1724 — PL 102-182) extending unemployment benefits, congressional Democrats decided to confront President Bush again with an "emergency" extension. White House reaction at first was not clear.

House Ways and Means Chairman Dan Rostenkowski, D-Ill., proposed giving workers 26 or 33 extra weeks of benefits instead of 13 or 20 weeks as PL 102-182 allowed. That would be on top of the 26 weeks of unemployment compensation provided by the states. Rostenkowski also wanted to extend the expiration date for eligibility from June 13 to Oct. 3.

House Republican leader Robert H. Michel of Illinois showed similar concern about the high unemployment numbers. In separate meetings Jan. 9 with White House Chief of Staff Samuel K. Skinner and budget director Richard G. Darman, Michel said Congress would have to extend the benefits further if the unemployment situation did not turn around.

When Congress and the White House did reach a consensus on the need for another law extending federal unemployment benefits, the snag was how to pay for them. Rostenkowski's proposal would cost $3.5 billion in fiscal 1992 and $1 billion in fiscal 1993. The 1990 budget law allowed such new spending programs only if they were offset by spending cuts or tax increases, or if Congress and the president jointly declared an emergency.

Legislative Action. Ways and Means on Jan. 28 gave voice vote approval to a compromise version of HR 4095 crafted by Rostenkowski and Michel. It cut the cost of Rostenkowski's original proposal to $2.7 billion, mainly by changing the deadline for eligibility from Oct. 3 to July 4. The cost would be offset by $2.2 billion left over from the 1991 bills and $500 million in accelerated collection of estimated taxes from large corporations. The committee reported the bill (H Rept 102-427) on Jan. 29.

The Senate Finance Committee approved its version of the legislation (S 2173) on Jan. 30, also by voice vote, and reported it the next day.

During House and Senate floor debate, few Republicans stood up to voice support for HR 4095. Instead, Democrats mostly decried the tough economic times that required the legislation and jabbed the president for resisting similar measures in 1991.

The funding issue became a matter of dispute on the Senate floor. Hank Brown, R-Colo., cited Congressional Budget Office (CBO) estimates that showed the new bill would cost money and thus add to the deficit. CBO disputed much of the White House estimate on the $2.2 billion pay-as-you-go surplus. A Jan. 13 Office of Management and Budget report said Congress raised a surplus of $1.1 billion in fiscal 1992 and would raise an extra $1.1 billion in fiscal 1993 as a result of legislation enacted in 1991.

Brown raised a point of order against the new jobless benefits bill, citing the CBO estimates and the budget law's pay-as-you-go requirements. But Democrats and Republicans rallied against him, with GOP senators declining to make an issue of deficit spending and Democrats benignly adopting the White House budget estimate even though they previously had stood by CBO.

A motion by Tom Daschle, D-S.D., to waive the budget act prevailed on an 88-8 vote, far more than the 60-vote supermajority needed.

The House voted 404-8, under suspension of the rules, to pass HR 4095 on Feb. 4. The Senate followed suit the same day on a 94-2 vote, clearing the measure. The only "nay" votes in both chambers were cast by conservative Republicans.

Bush signed the bill into law Feb. 7 (PL 102-244).

Provisions. As enacted, HR 4095:

- Offered an additional 13 weeks of compensation for the unemployed who exhausted their 26 weeks of state benefits and then exhausted the 13 to 20 weeks of extended federal benefits. Altogether, jobless workers were to receive either 52 or 59 weeks of benefits, depending upon the severity of the unemployment in their state.

The Labor Department estimated that 1.5 million of the 3.1 million people receiving the 1991 extended benefits would remain unemployed long enough to receive the additional 13 weeks of benefits. The bill also made the extended benefits available through July 4, three weeks longer than allowed in existing law.

- Speeded up the estimated tax payment rules for corporations with $1 million or more in taxable income.
- Provided railroad workers, who were covered by a separate unemployment program, the same benefits as other workers.
- Extended from Jan. 31 to June 30 the deadline for Michigan to repay a $181 million installment on a loan from the federal government. Michigan owed $417 million in loans provided from 1980 to 1985, when the state ran out of money to pay its state unemployment benefits.

Round 2: HR 5260

Permanent law allowed jobless workers to collect extended benefits only when the total number of people collecting benefits in the state reached a certain trigger. Because of disparities between those who were collecting benefits (the "insured" unemployment rate) and those who had exhausted benefits and remained unemployed, some states had to reach total unemployment rates as high as 15 percent for their workers to receive federal compensation.

Without the 1991 emergency legislation to provide extra benefits, only two states would have qualified in 1992 for the federal extended benefits program. Some members wanted to use the total unemployment rate, or a combination of an insured and a total rate, as the trigger for extended benefits.

Congress cleared HR 5260 (PL 102-318) on July 2, just prior to the deadline when workers who had used up their 26 weeks of state benefits would no longer have been eligible for federal emergency benefits. The final measure included a permanent change to the unemployment system — something Bush had vowed he would not accept — that allowed non-emergency extended benefits to kick in more easily during periods of high unemployment.

Background. With federal emergency unemployment benefits set to expire July 4, Congress in late April clashed with the administration over what to do next to help the nation's unemployed workers, whose numbers had grown to 9.2 million. Democrats and Republicans seemed to agree that emergency benefits should be extended. Labor Secretary Lynn Martin suggested extending them until the end of the year. Many Democrats wanted to continue them into 1993. Moreover, House Democrats wanted to overhaul the entire unemployment compensation system, an action the administration opposed. Senate Democrats were interested in permanent changes but fearful of fierce Republican opposition. Lawmakers also disagreed about financing.

In testimony before the Senate Finance Committee on April 29 and the House Ways and Means Subcommittee on Human Resources the next day, Martin repeatedly frustrated members by offering to negotiate an unemployment bill behind closed doors instead of describing the administration's position in public. Martin would not say how many weeks of benefits the administration wanted to provide workers. She did not say how much she was willing to spend. And she would not say how the administration proposed to pay for the program, except to say that tax increases were unacceptable.

Still, her testimony was significant. Congress had been grappling with how to help the long-term jobless for more than a year. Martin's appearances on Capitol Hill represented the first time the secretary of labor testified on the subject. And she expressed support for extended benefits. Republicans were given something to support, even though they opposed Democrats' farther-reaching ideas.

HR 4727. Thomas J. Downey, D-N.Y., who had been pushing for permanent changes in the unemployment system for years, and Rostenkowski proposed a sweeping $7 billion bill (HR 4727) to overhaul the system and eliminate the need for Congress to step in periodically to pass emergency benefits. The bill would extend the emergency benefits program, providing 13 or 20 weeks of benefits through the end of 1992 or until the month after the national unemployment rate's three-month average fell below 6.5 percent.

Downey said his top priority was to permanently change the trigger that released extended unemployment benefits. He wanted to base eligibility on the total unemployment rate — which included people who quit their jobs — to release the benefits more easily. He also would increase the federal share of benefits from 50 percent to 75 percent. The administration and most Ways and Means Republicans opposed Downey's attempt to change the trigger, saying it would release too many benefits costing too much money.

The Ways and Means Subcommittee on Human Resources, chaired by Downey, on May 6 gave voice vote approval to HR 4727, after paring it down to $5.9 billion. Threatening the prospects for the bill, however, was a new plan by Downey to attach another domestic initiative — a Downey-sponsored overhaul of federal child welfare programs (HR 2571) — that would add at least $3.5 billion to the five-year cost of the measure. *(Child welfare, p. 621)*

Meanwhile, House Majority Leader Richard A. Gephardt, D-Mo., also wanted to use the unemployment bill as a vehicle to speed up federal dollars to cities and states for infrastructure — projects such as road and bridge building. Other possible riders, Downey said, included authority to create enterprise zones in inner cities and an extension of temporary tax laws such as the low-income housing tax credit.

In the Senate, Finance Committee Chairman Lloyd Bentsen, D-Texas, was worried that he would not be able to move unemployment legislation through his chamber if members thought they could tack on any pet program.

The subcommittee-approved bill would give workers up to 20 or 26 weeks of extra federal benefits if they had exhausted their state compensation and not yet returned to work — 26 weeks if the state's total unemployment rate averaged at least 9 percent over six months, 20 weeks for all others. HR 4727 would make federal benefits available at least through Jan. 1, 1993, or until the month after the national unemployment rate's three-month average fell below 6.5 percent. Downey had originally proposed giving workers an extra 13 or 20 weeks of benefits, but he was able to increase the number by dropping a proposed change in the way states calculated whether workers were eligible for benefits.

Fred Grandy, R-Iowa, offered an amendment on behalf of the administration to extend benefits by 13 or 20 weeks through Oct. 3; then by seven or 13 weeks through Jan. 2, 1993; then by four or seven weeks through Feb. 13, 1993. The panel rejected it by voice vote.

In another key change to permanent law, Downey's bill would declare the unemployment program "off-budget," an attempt to make the federal unemployment taxes collected from employers solely dedicated to that purpose.

To pay for his bill, Downey would extend a highly controversial tax provision that many Republicans and Democrats opposed. The provision, enacted in the 1990 White House-congressional budget agreement and named for Rep. Don J. Pease, D-Ohio, essentially raised taxes on higher-income taxpayers by limiting their allowable itemized deductions. Joint filers with adjusted gross incomes of $100,000 or more had to reduce their claim by 3 percent of their income over $100,000. If the adjusted gross income was $150,000, the itemized deductions would be reduced by multiplying $50,000 by 3 percent: $1,500. The Pease provision was due to expire at the end of 1995; Downey would extend it through 1997 to raise $7.2 billion over five years.

A second financing mechanism, known as "PEP," the personal exemption phase-outs, would raise $4.5 billion over five years. For every $2,500 increment over $157,900 (joint filers) and $105,250 (individual) in adjusted gross income, each personal exemption would be reduced by 2 percent: $43.

Altogether, the unemployment bill would spend $5.9 billion over five years and would raise a net increase of $8.8 billion in revenue. Downey hoped to use the $2.9 billion left over to pay for his overhaul of child welfare programs.

The bill was scaled back during full committee consideration. Plans to load the legislation with non-germane items were scuttled, when House Democrats decided to move the unemployment bill by itself. As approved by Ways and Means by voice vote May 20 and formally reported May 27, HR 4727 (H Rept 102-536, Part I) provided unemployed workers, who had exhausted their 26 weeks of state benefits, with either 20 or 26 weeks of federal emergency benefits, depending upon the unemployment rate in their state. The extra benefits would be phased out over a three-month period, providing 10 or 13 weeks of benefits during that time to people who had run out of state benefits. Those benefits would begin on Jan. 1, 1993, or on the month after the three-month average national unemployment rate fell below 6.5 percent, whichever came earlier.

After the emergency benefits expired, the unemployment system was to revert back to providing workers with the possibility of receiving an extra 13 weeks of joint federal and state benefits after their first 26 weeks ran out. But the bill also would have permanently changed the trigger that released those 13 weeks of benefits, from a state's insured unemployment rate to its total unemployment rate.

Rostenkowski dropped language that would have taken the unemployment trust fund off-budget. Also eliminated from the refashioned bill was the Pease provision. In its place, the committee called for paying for three financing methods: First, the bill would change the tax rules for people who paid estimated taxes quarterly. Second, businesses would not be allowed to take tax deductions for executive compensation packages — salary and other compensation, such as stock options — over $1 million. And finally, the bill retained the PEP provision.

House Action. After discovering that legislation to extend unemployment benefits would add $140 million to the federal deficit over five years, the House Ways and Means Committee rewrote the financing mechanisms so the measure would instead reduce the deficit by an estimated $249 million. The committee approved the new $5.8 billion bill (HR 5260) by voice vote May 27 and reported it (H Rept 102-543, Part I) June 2. The House Government Operations Committee, which shared jurisdiction, reported the measure (H Rept 102-543, Part II) June 9.

The committee-approved measure would provide 20 to 26 weeks of emergency federal benefits to workers whose 26 weeks of state benefits had run out. It also would:

- Change the effective date for prohibiting businesses from taking tax deductions for executive compensation packages worth more than $1 million.
- Delete the estimated income tax provision for self-employed people who paid on a quarterly basis.
- Delay for one year the rate decrease in the federal unemployment payroll tax that employers paid.

With these provisions, the bill would be paid for over a six-year period. Because the revenues would not come in during the same year as the outlays, a House waiver of the pay-as-you-go provision of the 1990 budget agreement would be required.

The House voted 261-150 on June 9 to pass HR 5260. The emergency program would be phased out over three months, giving eligible workers 10 or 13 weeks of benefits starting either Jan. 1, 1993, or the month after the national unemployment rate's three-month average fell below 6.5 percent, whichever came first.

Republicans tried to defeat a parliamentary vote enabling the House to proceed with its work on the unemployment bill, but it was approved 232-182. Republicans also tried to vote down the rule governing debate of the unemployment bill but failed again, 225-182. And Republicans failed on a motion by Bill Archer, R-Texas, to send the bill back to the Ways and Means Committee, by a vote of 191-219.

Bush threatened to veto the bill, complaining about its cost, the type of taxes used to pay for it and the permanent structural changes that would be made to the system. The bill included a waiver of the 1990 budget agreement's pay-as-you-go rule. It would be paid for by prohibiting businesses from taking tax deductions for executive compensation packages worth more than $1 million; extending the personal exemption phase-out for high-income taxpayers — thereby reducing their deductions — for two years through fiscal 1997; and adjusting the federal unemployment tax rate paid by employers.

Senate Action. The Senate Finance Committee on June 11 approved, by voice vote, a $5.4 billion unemployment bill written by its chairman, Bentsen. It was far more conciliatory toward the White House than the House version, making fewer permanent changes to the unemployment compensation system. Bentsen's bill would extend benefits for 26 or 33 weeks, through March 6, 1993, as long as the national unemployment rate remained at least 7 percent. If the national rate fell below 7 percent for two consecutive months, benefits would drop to 10 and 15 weeks. And if the rate fell below 6.8 percent for two months, benefits would drop to seven and 13 weeks.

The administration supported a more modest extension, at a cost of $2.8 billion, according to a CBO estimate. Under the Bush proposal, workers who exhausted their state benefits by Jan. 2, 1993, would qualify for either 13 or 20 weeks of federal benefits. Those who used up state benefits by March 6 would qualify for seven or 10 weeks.

While the House bill eliminated the existing trigger for determining when benefits would be provided, Bentsen would give states a choice of which trigger to use — the existing insured unemployment rate or a total unemployment rate. Using the former would cost the states less because states had to match federal funds. Under the latter, benefits would be triggered if a state's jobless rate hit 6.5 percent for three months, assuming that figure was 10 percent higher than the jobless rate in the same quarter in either of the previous two years.

The Senate bill, unlike the House bill, would cost $5.4 billion between 1992 and 1997 and would raise an extra $458 million over that five-year period. Like the House bill, it would not be paid for in each individual year. The Senate measure would have been financed by tax provisions included in HR 4210, which Bush vetoed March 20. *(Tax bill, p. 100)*

Those provisions included:

- Allowing any amount from a pension or annuity plan or a tax-sheltered annuity to be rolled over tax-free to an individual retirement account. Remaining money would be taxed at a rate of 20 percent;
- Modifying estimated tax payment rules for large corporations; and
- Requiring most securities dealers to pay tax on their inventories.

With only scant opposition from Republicans, the Senate passed HR 5260 by voice vote June 19. During floor consideration, Minority Leader Bob Dole, R-Kan., offered an $11 billion substitute amendment, which he said the administration supported, to extend unemployment benefits and to, among other things, create federal enterprise zones, extend some expiring tax breaks and repeal the tax on yachts, furs and other luxury goods. The Dole amendment was rejected by voice vote.

The Senate on June 18 agreed, 84-3, to an amendment by Bob Graham, D-Fla., that would continue to exclude the wages of temporary foreign agricultural workers from the unemployment tax.

Although the administration had vowed to veto the House-passed bill, it was relatively silent regarding the Senate measure.

Final Action. The conference version favored the more conservative Senate bill in a bid to win Bush's signature. Several provisions from the House bill were dropped, including the mandatory change to the extended benefits trigger, an increase in the percent of money the federal government paid for extended benefits and an increase in the workers' wage base on which employers paid unemployment taxes.

The final $5.5 billion bill included the Senate trigger, giving states the choice of sticking with the existing system or switching to an easier way of releasing funds. If a state triggered the extended benefits program, workers would receive 13 extra weeks of compensation after using up their state money. The state would have to have a total unemployment rate of 6.5 percent for the most recent three months and the rate had to be at least 10 percent higher than during the same period in either of the two previous years. In states where the total unemployment rate was at least 8 percent, workers would receive an additional seven weeks, for a total of 20.

Before the extended benefits program took over, workers would be relying on the emergency program. In states where the total unemployment rate was at least 9 percent, jobless workers would receive 26 extra weeks of benefits. People in all other states would get 20 extra weeks. As long as the national unemployment rate remained at 7 percent or higher, the number of weeks available would remain at 20 or 26. If, however, the national unemployment rate dropped below 7 percent for two consecutive months, benefits would fall to 10 or 15 weeks. And if the rate fell below 6.8 percent for two months, benefits would fall to seven or 13 weeks.

To pay for the measure, three financing provisions were included. The first changed the rules for large corporations that estimated their tax payments on a quarterly basis. Beginning June 30, 1992, corporations were to base their tax payments on 97 percent of what they owed. After 1996, the payments were to be based on 91 percent. The existing law called for corporations to make those payments based on 93 percent of what they owed. Between 1993 and 1996, the existing law would raise that to 95 percent and drop it to 90 percent in 1997. This change would bring in $800 million, according to the Joint Committee on Taxation.

The conference report also adopted the House's PEP. According to the Joint Committee on Taxation, the provision would raise $2.7 billion.

And finally, the bill made a change to distributions from retirement plans, giving people the option of rolling over money directly to an individual retirement account (IRA). If the money was not rolled into an IRA, it was to be taxed at 20 percent. This would raise $2.1 billion, according to the Joint Committee.

The House on July 2 voted 396-23 to adopt the conference report on HR 5260 (H Rept 102-650). The Senate approved it on a **key vote of 93-3 (R 37-3; D 56-0)** the same day. Bush signed the bill into law (PL 102-318) on July 3. *(1992 key votes, p. 1083)*

Job Training

President Bush's signing of a package of amendments (HR 3033 — PL 102-367) to the 1982 Job Training Partnership Act (JTPA — PL 97-300) on Sept. 7, 1992, culminated nearly four years of work to craft a bill that could both steer clear of changing the formula for sending federal funds to the states and make the locally run programs more accountable to Washington officials.

At the crux of the refurbished JTPA was basic faith in the underlying design of the program: That a partnership between government and industry to train the disadvantaged worked better than depending on public service employment alone. The final push for passage came from two directions: the riots that broke out in Los Angeles the week of April 26 following the not guilty verdict in the criminal trial of police officers who were videotaped using violent physical force against black motorist Rodney King, which heightened members' awareness of the need for jobs and other urban relief, and the desire of both parties and the president to have a major job training initiative to parade out during the 1992 general election campaign.

Background

Since the 1960s, the federal government undertook a series of job training programs, mainly to increase the earnings of participants and reduce their dependence on welfare programs, such as food stamps and Aid to Families with Dependent Children. The first post-World War II program in the early 1960s focused on adults facing potential displacement as a result of automation. By the mid-1960s, that emphasis shifted to minorities and youth.

In 1973, Congress folded a variety of employment and training services — including the War on Poverty's Job Corps — into the Comprehensive Employment and Training Act (CETA). CETA empowered local governments to operate training programs for the unemployed and to offer them public service jobs. Riddled with problems, CETA was amended and reauthorized several times in its nine-year history. Lawmakers let the program expire in 1982. *(CETA, Congress and the Nation Vol. IV, p. 682; Congress and the Nation Vol. V, p. 402; Congress and the Nation Vol. VI, p. 648)*

JTPA took a different approach to federal job training; the private sector was brought in as a full partner, and funds were cut back considerably. Under JTPA, governors divided their states into service delivery areas, known as SDAs, which received funds and provided services. SDAs typically were political jurisdictions, such as cities or counties, or a consortium of small jurisdictions. More than 600 SDAs operated throughout the country in 1992. Federal money was allocated to the service area, which turned it over to a locally appointed Private Industry Council (PIC) that decided what services to provide, planned job training programs and contracted with job training providers. Each PIC consisted primarily of business people, with other members drawn from economic development, education and rehabilitation agencies, organized labor, community-based organizations and public employment services.

Because more income-eligible people existed than did funds to help them, the councils devised point systems based on other barriers to employment and used them to rate candidates. Once chosen, the applicant was assessed to determine appropriate training. Among JTPA activities were occupational classroom training to teach technical skills, basic education to earn a high school equivalency degree, on-the-job training in a specific occupation and job search assistance.

Soon after JTPA's inception, criticism began surfacing. Government reports, for example, showed inadequate oversight and subsequent overcharges by private contractors. Congress considered changes to JTPA as early as 1988. In 1990, efforts to make the program more accountable failed because a proposed rejiggering of funding formulas was opposed by states that potentially would experience a loss of funds. *(JTPA background, Congress and the Nation Vol. VI, p. 655; 1989-90 action, p. 713)*

Legislative Action

Once lawmakers backed off the divisive attempt to change the formula for distributing federal job training funds to the states, the amendments to the 1982 law were largely non-controversial.

The House Education Subcommittee on Employment Opportunity on July 31, 1991, approved, 7-0, HR 3033. The measure, crafted by Carl C. Perkins, D-Ky., was similar to legislation passed by the House in 1990. On Sept. 24, HR 3033 (H Rept 102-240) was approved by voice vote by the House Education and Labor Committee; the measure was reported Oct. 7.

As growing unemployment lines made lawmakers eager to help the jobless, HR 3033 was passed by the House on Oct. 9, 420-6, under suspension of the rules. The goal of the legislation was to focus federal job training aid on those who needed it most. Lawmakers had complained that, to improve success rates, program officials in some communities had provided assistance primarily to people with some skills who could have found a job without federal help. According to a 1989 report by the General Accounting Office (GAO), high school dropouts were underserved by the program, which it said had about an equal number of skilled and unskilled participants. In response, the House-passed measure mandated that at least 60 percent of those enrolled in the adult and youth programs have only limited job skills or face other barriers to employment.

HR 3033 aimed to make program officials, employers and job trainees more accountable by limiting to six months the time that employers could receive training subsidies and provide on-the-job training. The bill also required the Labor Department to ensure that employers who continually failed to retain their participants no longer be eligible to receive the subsidies.

No specific dollar amount for the programs, which had a permanent authorization, was called for in the bill, but a request was made for a funding increase of 10 percent. The fiscal 1991 appropriation for adult and youth programs was $4.08 billion. The measure also authorized $135 million for a number of new initiatives, including a youth program aimed at poverty-stricken communities.

A similar job training measure (S 2055) was introduced in the Senate on Nov. 26 by Paul Simon, D-Ill., chairman of the Labor Subcommittee on Employment and Productivity. However, time ran out in 1991 before the bill could be considered.

The Senate Labor and Human Resources Committee on March 11, 1992, approved S 2055 (S Rept 102-264) by voice vote. The bill, formally reported March 25, required that 65 percent of adults and 70 percent of youths served by the program be economically disadvantaged — living at or below the poverty line — and face other barriers to employment such as homelessness and a lack of basic skills.

S 2055 passed the Senate April 9, also by voice vote. The major task then became reconciling the nearly 300 differences between the House-passed and Senate-passed bills. The conferees, mostly at staff level, worked on the legislation for about four months. Although most differences were minor, some issues required careful, lengthy negotiations.

Among the broader issues settled by the conferees were:

Procurement. The House version, which prevailed, required the labor secretary to prescribe uniform procurement standards, including competitive bidding on buying training services. But governors were permitted some flexibility in establishing the standards to improve accountability, as the Senate bill required.

State Human Resource Investment Councils. The Senate agreed to the House proposal that gave states the option of combining advisory groups into a single council to create better coordination of federal services. Governors were given a voice on who was appointed to the councils.

Jobs for Employable Dependent Individuals. The Senate pushed for and won a slight revision to this program. States would be given bonuses for providing job training to welfare recipients. Added incentives were given for including absent parents in the program.

Out-of-School Youths. The House receded to the Senate version, which called for at least half of the youths in the program to be out of school.

Older Workers. The Senate version prevailed, retaining a state set-aside of 3 percent of the funds for participation by people older than 55. The House had pushed for a larger set-aside after JTPA was criticized for being primarily a youth program.

On-the-Job Training. The negotiated agreement limited training to six months and included some of the House language that barred employers who had shown signs of abusing the program.

The conference agreement (H Rept 102-811) was adopted by the Senate by voice vote on Aug. 7 and by the House by voice vote on Aug. 11, clearing HR 3033 for the president.

The fiscal 1993 appropriations bill for the Labor Department (HR 5677 — PL 102-394) called for about $3 billion in training grants to the states and $1 billion for Jobs Corps.

The signing of the JTPA legislation did not resolve the jobs issue, as the election-year economy waned and the unemployment situation worsened. Sens. Simon and David L. Boren, D-Okla., included $400 million in an urban aid tax bill (HR 11) for a modern-day version of the Works Progress Administration and the Civilian Conservation Corps — jobs programs of the 1930s that built bridges and other infrastructure projects and set inner-city youth to the country to plant trees. HR 11 was vetoed by President Bush. *(Tax bill, p. 103)*

Boren also pushed to get a $50 million provision in the Defense authorization bill (HR 5006 — PL 102-484) that sought to revive the 1930s program as 10 demonstrations of the Youth Civilian Community Corps, a program to provide skills training in exchange for community service. *(Defense authorization, p. 395)*

Meanwhile, Bush Aug. 24 announced, at a campaign stop in Ansonia, Conn., a plan that included a $2 billion-a-year package of new and retooled job training programs. He said the $10 billion cost over five years would be paid by cutting spending for other, unspecified federal programs.

Parental Leave

Saying he objected "to the federal government mandating leave policies for America's employers and work force," President Bush in 1992, for the second time during his administration, vetoed legislation (S 5) requiring unpaid leave for workers with newborn or recently adopted children or with a seriously ill family member. Although the Senate voted to override the veto, the House could not muster the needed votes, and the bill did not become law.

Family leave legislation saw committee action in 1989, but no bill reached the floor in either chamber. In 1990, Congress cleared a parental leave bill, which Bush vetoed. The House voted to sustain the veto. *(101st Congress action, p. 710)*

Senate Action

The Senate Labor and Human Resources Committee voted 12-5 to approve S 5 on April 24, 1991. The bill was formally reported May 30 (S Rept 102-68).

As approved by the committee, S 5 guaranteed employees 12 weeks of unpaid leave to care for a newborn or newly adopted infant or to care for a seriously ill family member. Workers would be eligible for this benefit only after exhausting all other forms of leave, such as vacation or sick time. According to the bill's principal sponsor, Christopher J. Dodd, D-Conn., only about 40 percent of the work force was covered by S 5.

During the Labor Committee markup, Chairman Edward M. Kennedy, D-Mass., proposed an amendment — adopted by voice vote — that applied the measure to senators and Senate staff. Dave Durenberger, R-Minn., proposed an amendment to lower the leave to 10 weeks and change the medical leave provisions, but certain failure caused him to withdraw the proposal.

Kennedy disputed businesses' contention that S 5 would be too expensive, saying April 24 that the costs were greatly exaggerated. He cited a survey commissioned by the Small Business Administration (SBA), which argued that the costs to businesses for permanently replacing a worker were significantly higher than for granting leave. The SBA report — released March 27 — was based on interviews with 1,730 small businesses nationwide.

Trying to pick up votes in the face of a threatened presidential veto, lawmakers on Sept. 18 unveiled a proposal that scaled back the committee bill. Christopher S. Bond, R-Mo., worked out the compromise version with Dodd. Like the committee-approved bill, the new proposal required businesses to give up to 12 weeks of unpaid leave for the birth or adoption of a child or for the serious illness of the worker or an immediate family member. S 5 restricted employee eligibility to employees who had worked 1,000 hours or 19 hours a week over the previous 12 months. The compromise raised the number of hours to 1,250 or 25 hours per week.

The compromise softened potential penalties against businesses that violated the bill. As approved by the Labor Committee, the bill allowed employees to collect quadruple damages including wages, salary, employment benefits and other compensation, plus interest. The new version allowed double the actual losses.

The compromise also allowed employers to deny leave to "key employees," who were defined as those who were the highest paid 10 percent of the company's work force. The new proposal left unresolved the principal objection of Bush and business groups: It still mandated that businesses with 50 or more workers offer family leave.

A Bond substitute amendment, which encompassed the compromise, was adopted on a **65-32 (R 15-28; D 50-4) key vote**, by the Senate on Oct. 2. While the vote was two short of the 67 needed to override a veto, three absent Democrats were on record as supporting the legislation. *(1991 key votes, p. 1061)*

The Senate then rejected, 32-65, a substitute amendment, offered by Orrin G. Hatch, R-Utah, to replace the requirement that employers offer leave with a less stringent requirement that returning workers be given preference in rehiring and resume their seniority and benefits. Under Hatch's plan, workers would have been entitled to take as much as six years of leave to "bond" with a new child and up to two years for medical leave.

Members also rejected, 40-57, a Durenberger amendment to require that disputes over leave between employers and workers be settled by arbitration, not in court. Opponents said the complicated arbitration process would unfairly burden workers who had legitimate complaints.

The Senate passed S 5 by voice vote Oct. 2. The administration did not find the bill acceptable.

House Action

The House Education and Labor Subcommittee on Labor-Management Relations held a hearing Feb. 28 on the House version of the parental leave bill (HR 2). After little more than pro forma debate, the subcommittee voted 16-7 on March 7 to recommend HR 2 for full committee consideration. Only one amendment was offered during the markup. Tom Petri, R-Wis., proposed limiting unpaid leave to six weeks for the birth or adoption of a child and two weeks for serious illness. Employers could have required workers to apply paid vacation or sick leave against the unpaid leave. The amendment was rejected by voice vote.

HR 2 also was referred to the House Post Office and Civil Service Committee, which had jurisdiction over parts of the bill that related to federal employees. The Subcommittee on Compensation and Employee Benefits on March 12 approved the bill, which granted federal workers 18 weeks of unpaid leave over a two-year period and allowed them to take up to 26 weeks of unpaid leave annually if they were ill. The subcommittee also approved an amendment by Gary L. Ackerman, D-N.Y., that granted federal employees leave to care for an ill spouse, a provision that was inadvertently left out of the original bill. The full committee endorsed the subcommittee version on March 13 and reported the bill (H Rept 102-135, Part II) on June 27.

The Education and Labor Committee approved HR 2 by voice vote March 20. As reported (H Rept 102-135, Part I) June 27, the bill provided 12 weeks of leave for all workers except federal employees, who received 18 weeks for family leave and 26 weeks for medical leave.

For weeks before the bill was brought to the floor, the House Democratic leadership lobbied members for votes. Pending was a substitute, sponsored by Bart Gordon, D-Tenn., and Henry J. Hyde, R-Ill., that mirrored the compromise crafted in the Senate by Dodd and Bond. It would have watered down the bill as approved by the House Education and Labor Committee. But in search of the elusive two-thirds support, the leadership floated an alternative offered by Timothy J. Penny, D-Minn., and John J. LaFalce, D-N.Y., which would give 12 weeks of leave for the birth or adoption of a child but limit leave for the care of a seriously ill child, spouse or parent to six weeks.

When the Penny-LaFalce proposal failed to muster two-thirds, the leadership decided to stick with the Gordon-Hyde language, which:

- Raised to 1,250 from 1,000 the number of hours per year an employee must work to be eligible for up to 12 weeks of unpaid leave.
- Required workers to provide 30 days' notice for non-emergency leave.
- Lowered potential penalties against businesses that violated the bill from quadruple damages to double damages.
- Allowed companies to deny leave to "key employees," defined as those who were the highest-paid 10 percent of a company's work force.

The House on Nov. 13 passed the Gordon-Hyde substitute by an overwhelming 287-143. The vote suggested that the House could override a veto, but many who voted for the compromise subsequently voted against final passage of the bill. Members were seen as wanting to be on record for the parental leave legislation, but they did not want the legislation to become law. The House passed HR 2 by a 253-177 vote — well short of the two-thirds needed to override Bush's promised veto. The House subsequently passed S 5 by voice vote, after amending it to contain the provisions of HR 2.

Conference Action

Although family and medical leave legislation received relatively quick action in 1991, lawmakers held over conference consideration of the bill until 1992 to force Bush, who opposed the measure, to veto it in an election year. More than eight months after the bill passed the House and Senate in nearly identical forms, conferees on S 5 finally met Aug. 5, 1992, and swiftly approved a compromise that made only minor changes.

As agreed to by conferees, the measure would require that businesses with 50 or more workers give all but their top employees up to 12 weeks of unpaid leave for the birth or adoption of a child or for the serious illness of the worker or an immediate family member. The only changes made by conferees concerned provisions extending leave rights to congressional employees. The new language included enforcement and grievance provisions that paralleled those in the 1991 civil rights bill (S 1745 — PL 102-166). *(Civil rights, p. 780)*

The bill also extended leave rights to federal civil service employees.

On the eve of the Republican National Convention, the Senate adopted the conference report to S 5 (H Rept 102-816) by voice vote Aug. 11. Dodd had sought a roll-call vote, but Republican leaders told him they would block it, preventing the bill from leaving the chamber before the August recess, which began Aug. 13. Despite the concessions made in the conference agreement, the administration continued to oppose the bill.

The House adopted the conference report on a 241-161 vote Sept. 10, thus clearing the bill for the president.

Veto Action

Bush vetoed S 5 on Sept. 22, saying he objected to mandating how businesses should conduct themselves.

About a week earlier, on Sept. 16, Bush announced an alternative to the mandate for big businesses to provide unpaid leave to their workers. Bush wanted to offer businesses tax credits of up to $1,200 per worker if they gave employees time off for family emergencies. The plan, to be offered to businesses with fewer than 500 employees, would cost about $500 million, according to the White House. Bush's timing, however, ensured that his plan could not become law in 1992.

On Sept. 24, for the first time during the Bush administration, the Senate voted to override the president's veto. The **68-31 (R 14-28; D 54-3) key vote** was two more than the two-thirds necessary. The House, however, was not expected to muster the needed tally. On Sept. 25, House members voted 239-139 to postpone the override vote until Sept. 30. The House fell 27 votes short, sustaining the veto on a 258-169 vote. The Family and Medical Leave Act was dead for the 102nd Congress.

1993 Legislation

During the 1992 presidential election campaign, Democratic presidential nominee Arkansas Gov. Bill Clinton, as well as his running mate, Sen. Al Gore, D-Tenn., spoke often in support of parental leave legislation. When the 103rd Congress convened Jan. 5, 1993, family and medical leave became the top legislative priority for the new White House, which would be ushered in Jan. 20. The House passed HR 1 (H Rept 103-8) on Feb. 3 by 265-163. The Senate passed the bill (S Rept 103-3) Feb. 4 by 71-27, after substituting the text of S 5, as amended. The House cleared HR 1 the same day by agreeing to the Senate language, 247-152. HR 1 was nearly identical to the bill Bush vetoed. President Clinton on Feb. 5 signed the measure (PL 103-3), which:

- Allowed workers to take up to 12 weeks of unpaid leave during any 12-month period because of the birth or adoption of a child; the need to care for a child, spouse or parent with a serious health condition; or the worker's own serious illness.
- Applied to employees who had worked for the same employer for at least one year and for at least 1,250 hours that year.
- Exempted businesses that employed fewer than 50 people.
- Allowed employers to deny leave to a worker who fell among the highest paid 10 percent of workers if that person was considered a key employee whose leave would result in "substantial and grievous economic injury" to the business.
- Became effective in six months, after final regulations were published in the *Federal Register*.

Davis-Bacon Revision

The House Education and Labor Committee on Sept. 23, 1992, gave its voice vote approval to legislation (HR 1987) to revise the 1931 Davis-Bacon Act, which required contractors for federal and public works projects to pay workers the prevailing local wage rate, usually union wages. The act was intended to prevent construction companies offering substandard wages from underbidding local companies.

HR 1987 (H Rept 102-956), reported Sept. 29, aimed to relieve small construction companies, many of them minority-owned, from Davis-Bacon requirements. It raised the size of contracts covered by the act from the existing $2,000 minimum. New construction contracts valued at $100,000 or more and alteration contracts of $15,000 or more would have to comply with Davis-Bacon. Smaller contracts would be exempt. Backers of the change said the existing threshold excluded small and minority-owned construction companies from federal contracts because they could not afford to pay union wages.

Many Republicans opposed the Davis-Bacon Act, saying it hurt businesses and artificially inflated the cost of government contracts.

The bill was approved 5-1 by the Labor Standards Subcommittee on Aug. 4.

Women's Employment

The 102nd Congress considered several measures regarding women in the work place. *(Related action, women in business, p. 464)*

S 367. Congress in 1991 cleared a bill (S 367) aimed at steering more women into non-traditional jobs such as construction and technical work under the Job Training Partnership Act (JTPA — PL 97-300). President Bush signed the measure (PL 102-235) on Dec. 12.

Although the job training program was supposed to help place women in non-traditional jobs, critics complained that women were typically directed to clerical and service jobs with lesser pay and benefits. "Non-traditional" job fields were defined as those in which less than 25 percent of the workers were women. Construction, technical jobs in construction, plumbing and electromechanics fell into this category. A study indicated that less than 9 percent of female participants in the jobs program were assigned non-traditional jobs.

S 367 required agencies receiving the job training funds to set goals for placing women in unconventional fields and to keep records on those placements. The labor secretary was required to report to Congress on progress in this area.

The bill designated $1.5 million a year for four years from the program's regular funds for a grant program to help states promote putting women in non-traditional jobs. Congress appropriated $4.2 billion for the overall JTPA program for the year running from July 1, 1992, through June 30, 1993.

The Senate Labor and Human Resources Committee approved S 367 (S Rept 102-65) by 17-0 on Feb. 20; it was reported May 24. The Senate passed the bill by voice vote Nov. 26. The House, also by voice vote, passed the measure the next day. The Senate passed a similar measure (S 975 — S Rept 101-90) in the 101st Congress, but it died.

A broader bill (HR 3033) to authorize and revise the JTPA was signed into law (PL 102-367) in 1992. *(Story, p. 728)*

HR 3475. Legislation (HR 3475) to help businesses provide women with apprenticeships in non-traditional occupations was signed into law (PL 102-530) Oct. 27, 1992. The House passed the bill by voice vote Sept. 29; the Senate followed suit Oct. 7, clearing the measure.

The bill, introduced by Constance A. Morella, R-Md., directed the Department of Labor to give community-based organizations competitive grants for providing technical assistance to a number of employers and labor unions in preparing the work place to employ women. The bill also required the Labor Department to make labor unions and employers aware that grants would be available.

HR 3476. The House passed legislation (HR 3476) by voice vote, under suspension of the rules, Sept. 29, 1992, to establish a 17-member Commission on the Advancement of Women in the Science and Engineering Work Forces. But the measure went no further.

The commission would have studied barriers in industry, government and academia for women scientists, reporting on its findings in 18 months.

The bill, also introduced by Morella, was approved by the Education and Labor Committee on Sept. 24.

Child Labor

On a 10-7 party-line vote, the Senate Labor and Human Resources Committee March 11, 1992, approved legislation (S 600 — S Rept 102-380) to toughen child labor laws. The bill was reported Aug. 12; the full Senate never took up the measure.

S 600 would remove the existing requirement that an employer could not face criminal penalties until the second conviction. It would prohibit employers who had been convicted from receiving federal grants, loans or contracts for three years. The Labor Department would be required to compile and make available to school districts the names of employers who had violated child labor laws.

Democrats originally wanted employers convicted of willfully violating child labor laws to face up to five years in prison for the injury of a child and up to 10 years in prison for the death of a child. A second conviction would have doubled those penalties. But during committee consideration, Democrats dropped that provision and retained existing law, which included criminal penalties of up to six months in prison.

As approved in committee, the bill also required certificates of employment for minors under the age of 18 who did not have a high school diploma; added to the list of hazardous occupations for 16- and 17-year-olds: poultry processing, fish and seafood processing and pesticide handling; and prohibited employment of children under age 14 as agricultural workers, except for children who worked on their family's farm.

Labor Secretary Lynn Martin sent Labor Committee Chairman Edward M. Kennedy, D-Mass., a letter threatening a presidential veto because the bill would destroy jobs for teenagers and create too much paperwork for the Labor Department.

Striker Replacement

Legislation (HR 5, S 55) that sought to close a loophole in the law and protect the jobs of striking workers died in 1992, despite a heavy lobbying effort by the nation's principal labor lobby, the AFL-CIO.

Existing law barred companies from firing workers solely for going on strike. However, according to supporters of the striker replacement legislation, companies in the 1980s had begun applying a little noticed 1938 Supreme Court decision that allowed employers to temporarily or permanently replace striking workers, unless the employees were protesting unfair or unsafe labor practices. Bill backers argued that every year as many as 10,000 workers were being permanently replaced for participating in lawful strikes.

Labor lobbies, led by the AFL-CIO, had argued strongly for enactment of either the House or Senate version of the bill, saying some companies were using the 1938 Court decision to replace striking union workers with lower-paid, non-union workers. Proponents also said that using permanent replacement workers, or even threatening to use them, undermined the fairness of the collective bargaining process, which guided the contract renewal process between management and organized labor. The striker replacement bill was a particularly difficult test for organized labor, which already was facing declining union membership and waning clout on Capitol Hill.

Opposition was strong and steady in the Republican ranks, especially in the Senate. President Bush and Labor Secretary Lynn Martin were vehemently opposed to the bill, saying it would encourage strikes, damage the economy and tip the balance toward labor's side in contract negotiations.

House Action

Committee. HR 5 was jointly reported to three House committees: Education and Labor, Public Works and Transportation, and Energy and Commerce.

The House Education and Labor Subcommittee on Labor-Management Relations approved HR 5 on March 13, 1991, by a 15-7 vote. The subcommittee rejected, by voice vote, an amendment by the full committee's ranking Republican, Bill Goodling, Pa., that would have allowed companies to hire permanent replacement workers after eight weeks of a strike. The amendment also would have required unions to conduct secret ballot votes on strike motions and would have required a two-thirds majority vote for a strike.

Goodling offered his amendment during full committee markup of the bill; it again was rejected, by voice vote. Education and Labor, however, adopted, 25-14, an amendment by Pat Williams, D-Mont., which stipulated that the protections offered by HR 5 would apply only to union-represented employees. The two other committees approved similar language.

Republicans had objected that the bill as introduced would have led to strikes at non-union companies. But Republicans objected to Williams' amendment as well, saying the language would treat non-union employees as "second-class citizens" because they would not be entitled to the same protections under the law as union members.

Republican amendments to continue to allow hiring permanent replacements in cases of labor violence or to protect public health or safety were rejected by the Education Committee.

The Education and Labor Committee approved HR 5 on April 18 by a party-line 25-14 vote. The bill was reported (H Rept 102-57, Part II) on June 27.

The Public Works and Transportation Committee, which had jurisdiction over those portions of the bill affecting railroads and airlines, had approved the measure April 16 by voice vote. It was formally reported (H Rept 102-57, Part I) on May 9. The Energy and Commerce Committee approved the bill on May 21 and reported it (H Rept 102-57, Part III) on June 3.

Floor. Debate on the bill was generally lackluster, with Democrats talking about their union experiences and Republicans sharing tales of life in the business world.

Goodling tried yet again to strike a middle ground with his amendment, but neither side was interested, and the amendment, offered as a substitute, was rejected, 28-399, on July 17. Rep. Pete Peterson, D-Fla., then offered a substitute designed to attract moderate members. It required that a majority of workers vote to organize at least 30 days before a strike and be certified by the National Labor Relations Board before they could be protected from permanent replacements. Opponents complained that Peterson's provision was just another tool to be used by the unions in gathering members and preparing for a strike.

The House adopted Peterson's amendment, 252-174, before proceeding directly to pass the bill.

The House passed HR 5 on July 17 by a 247-182 vote, 39 shy of the needed 286 to override the threatened presidential veto. All of the 33 Democrats who voted against the bill were from the South, while only 16 Republicans voted in favor of the legislation.

Senate Action

Committee. The Senate Labor and Human Resources Committee approved S 55 on June 19 by a party-line 10-7 vote. The bill (S Rept 102-111) was formally reported July 18.

The Senate committee approved by voice vote an amendment offered by Howard M. Metzenbaum, D-Ohio, and Jeff Bingaman, D-N.M., clarifying that the legislation was intended to apply only to union workers. Committee Chairman Edward M. Kennedy, D-Mass., said he could not understand why business lobbyists continued to oppose the legislation after complaining that it would affect non-union workers. "We changed it, and now they say it will encourage people to join unions. Which is it?" Kennedy asked.

Opponents said the bill would lead to more strikes and upset the balance of power between labor and management that had reigned for 50 years.

Floor. S 55 did not come to the Senate floor until 1992, and once it got there, it did not progress far. To halt work on the measure, Republican opponents used legitimate delaying tactics and Senate procedures that required sponsors to come up with a supermajority to cut off debate by invoking cloture and limit debilitating amendments.

The first attempt on June 11 by sponsors to invoke cloture failed to get the 60-vote minimum needed. That vote was 55-41.

During floor debate before the vote, Metzenbaum argued that workers' main protection and leverage in collective bargaining had been "gutted" in recent years by companies all too willing to replace anyone who went on strike. But opponents said the government should not dictate how businesses deal with labor and added that the bill would have given an unfair advantage to labor negotiators.

On June 9, Labor Secretary Martin renewed the threat of a presidential veto, saying the bill would "create an environment ripe for confrontation, intransigence and an increase in work stoppages."

After the first failed cloture vote, Bob Packwood, R-Ore., inserted substitute language aimed at pulling over more support from the GOP side. It would have allowed employers and unions to submit unresolved contract disputes to a federally appointed fact-finding panel. Under the proposal, if the employer agreed with the panel's recommendations and the union rejected them, the employer could hire permanent replacement workers for the strikers. If, however, the strikers assented to the mediator's proposals, the employer would be barred from hiring permanent replacements.

Robert McGlotten, AFL-CIO director of legislative affairs, said the Packwood substitute drew a reasonable balance between both camps. But Orrin G. Hatch, R-Utah, the ranking member of the Labor and Human Resources Committee, attacked the compromise plan, saying Packwood's fix was worse than the original version and would create an intrusive role for the federal government in the private business sector. The language Packwood inserted into the bill failed to attract any GOP votes.

On June 16, members again failed to invoke cloture, 57-42. Only Al Gore, D-Tenn., and Tim Wirth, D-Colo., added their names to the list of those who wanted to end debate and proceed to the bill. Gore and Wirth had missed the first vote while they were attending the Earth Summit in Brazil.

After the second attempt at cloture failed, the bill was withdrawn from the calendar.

Black Lung Trust Fund

On Oct. 1, 1992, the House passed HR 1637, which would make collecting benefits from the Black Lung Disability Trust Fund, administered by the Labor Department, easier for coal miners and their survivors.

The bill, passed by voice vote, authorized $65 million over five years, beginning in fiscal 1993. It allowed survivors or widows of miners who were receiving black lung benefits to automatically receive survivor benefits without having to prove that the death was a result of black lung. And survivors of miners who were not receiving benefits at death only had to prove that the miner was disabled by black lung at death, without having to prove that the death resulted from black lung.

The bill would greatly restrict the amount of medical evidence a mine owner could produce to refute a miner's claim. Bill supporters contended that owners typically produced reams of medical information that miners could not afford to counter. The bill also would award "reasonable" fees to attorneys representing coal miners, even if the miners lost their case.

The House Education and Labor Committee approved the bill (H Rept 102-882) July 29; it was reported Sept. 21.

The Bush administration was strongly opposed to the legislation because of its cost.

Occupational Safety

The House Education and Labor Committee in 1992 approved a bill (HR 3160) that would have made the first big change in the Occupational Safety and Health Act (PL 91-596) in more than 20 years. The bill died without further action, however.

The 1970 act gave the secretary of labor the authority to set safety and health standards for the protection of workers and required employers to provide a work place free from hazards likely to cause death or serious injury to employees. *(Congress and the Nation Vol. III, p. 713)*

HR 3160, crafted by committee Chairman William D. Ford, D-Mich., would have increased criminal penalties from the six-month maximum to a 10-year maximum for work place safety violations that resulted in a worker's death. The bill also would have applied the penalties to supervisors. Under existing law, only employers could have been held liable.

The bill would have required businesses to establish work place safety and health programs. The programs would have offered education and training to employees to reduce hazards and prevent injuries and illnesses. The bill also would have required the Occupational Safety and Health Administration (OSHA) to issue a standard to control ergonomic — or environmental — hazards such as the repetitive strain injury that could come from using a computer or video display terminal. OSHA would have been

Miners' Fund

A troubled union health care fund covering about 120,000 retired coal miners and their beneficiaries was rescued as part of an energy bill (HR 776 — PL 102-486) cleared in 1992. Many of the unionized coal operators that agreed to provide the benefits had since gone out of business, and the remaining companies said they could not afford to keep up the fund. *(Energy bill, p. 500)*

Championing the cause was Sen. John D. Rockefeller IV, D-W.Va. During Senate Finance Committee consideration of the tax provisions in HR 776, Rockefeller offered a provision to bail out the miners' fund through a tax on all bituminous coal operators — union and non-union. The 10-8 vote was largely partisan. The proposal was identical to one Rockefeller added to an earlier tax bill (HR 4210) that was vetoed. *(HR 4210, p. 100)*

The Bush administration sharply opposed the provision. Minority Leader Bob Dole, R-Kan., and other critics lashed out at the idea of holding companies liable for health benefits they never negotiated. For a time, on the Senate floor, it seemed the provision might derail the entire energy bill.

On July 23, a motion to invoke cloture (thus limit debate) failed 58-33, falling two votes short of the 60 needed. Intense negotiations ensued, with a deal finally set July 28, when a second cloture vote was taken. The motion was agreed to 93-3, clearing the way for floor consideration of HR 776.

The compromise proposal abandoned the notion of a new coal tax and instead sought to bail out the public health fund with a package of measures. The plan called for using a "reach back" formula that would trace as many retired miners as possible back to their previous employers or, if that company had gone out of business, a related company.

The plan would shift $210 million over three years from the union's overstocked pension fund into the health fund. And after 1995, it also would tap interest on the Abandoned Mine Lands fund for up to $70 million a year. The abandoned lands fund, which was filled by a fee on coal companies, was created to reclaim old mining lands.

The plan also would protect the health benefits of as many as 100,000 additional miners, covered under the old contracts, whose companies might go bankrupt. In exchange for these new guarantees for the fund, union lobbyists agreed to impose cost controls on the health fund.

The coal provisions subsequently proved solidly fused enough to survive another test: House Republican conferees and Democratic conferee J. J. Pickle, D-Texas, while negotiating the tax issues during conference action on the energy bill again threatened to remove the Rockefeller position. Pickle eventually agreed to the coal provision so that HR 776 could go forward, but he said it was unfair to make companies with no current connection to the coal business pay for miner benefits. Rockefeller and other proponents stood their ground, and the language eventually passed as part of the overall energy bill.

required to write regulations outlining how businesses should respond to the problem.

In addition, businesses would have been required to establish joint committees for employers and employees to work together to improve job site conditions in companies with 11 or more full-time workers. The committees would have been authorized to review the employer's safety and health program, conduct inspections and make recommendations.

During committee consideration, Paul B. Henry, R-Mich., and ranking Republican Bill Goodling, Pa., offered a less far-reaching substitute that would have required the government to consider a rule's cost-effectiveness and its possible effect on employment when setting health and safety standards. The substitute also would have required employers to consult an "employee participation committee" on health and safety issues — but only for businesses with 50 or more workers. The committee rejected the amendment, 14-25, on party lines.

The committee agreed by voice vote to two amendments: One would allow OSHA citations issued to employers to be dropped if the violations were caused by employees who violated company work rules, and the other would require OSHA to target inspections of work sites to those with a high potential for death, serious injury or exposure to toxic materials.

Republicans had been generally reluctant to overhaul OSHA legislation. They argued that work place safety problems had to do with poor agency enforcement, and they maintained that new rules would have been too costly to small businesses and generally burdensome. Democrats said the legislation needed to be brought up to date. And they said their changes would have saved employers money by reducing injuries and thereby cutting claims for workers' compensation.

In 1970, the Bureau of Labor Statistics reported that of the nation's 80 million workers, 14,500 were killed each year and 2.2 million were injured. As of 1990, the bureau reported that of 92 million workers, 6.4 million were injured each year. It also said that at least 2,900 — and probably more — were killed. The National Safety Council, a non-profit group in Chicago, said that as of 1991 the number of workers killed annually was closer to 10,200.

The committee gave voice vote approval May 28 to HR 3160, which was formally reported (H Rept 102-663, Part I) on July 9. Labor Secretary Lynn Martin said she would have recommended that President Bush veto the legislation.

Construction Safety

The House Education and Labor Committee reported legislation (HR 1063 — H Rept 102-662) on July 9, 1992, to protect construction workers by setting stricter safety guidelines for construction companies.

House Education and Labor Subcommittee on Health and Safety Chairman Joseph M. Gaydos, D-Pa., said he drafted the bill because about 2,500 construction workers were killed and more than 200,000 seriously injured in construction accidents each year. Furthermore, many of the accidents could have been prevented. Although guidelines had been set by the industry, Gaydos said, the plans were voluntary.

The bill covered companies that dealt mainly in construction, not utilities, and required them to produce a written safety and health plan specific to each project. Companies would have to hire or designate a project constructor who would be responsible for the site, oversee the plan and conduct frequent inspections. Builders also would be required to hire a safety coordinator to implement the plan and investigate any serious injuries or deaths at the site.

The bill also sought to address complaints that the method used by the Occupational Safety and Health Administration (OSHA) to target sites for inspections was unfair. Under the measure, a construction site would have to notify OSHA before work began in potentially dangerous work areas. OSHA could then target those sites for inspection.

The bill established within OSHA an Office of Construction Safety, Health, and Education to be headed by a deputy assistant secretary for construction. The office would investigate deaths and injuries "where appropriate" and help develop construction rules. It also would help educate employers and employees on accident prevention.

The subcommittee approved HR 1063 on July 23, 1991, on a 5-3 party-line vote. The full committee approved the measure, 24-14, on Sept. 24.

Critics of the bill said the new reporting requirements would overburden OSHA, impeding its capability to inspect construction sites and probe accidents.

Social Security

The 102nd Congress suffered no shortage of proposals to make major changes in the Social Security program. But none of the efforts to significantly alter the program's financing, benefits or administration was approved.

The most controversial change suggested concerned the Social Security earnings test, which limited the amount older workers could earn before their benefits were curtailed. A campaign led by Sen. John McCain, R-Ariz., to repeal the test, which picked up strong support among congressional Republicans, was unsuccessful, as was a drive by leading Democrats to liberalize the earnings limit.

Sen. Daniel Patrick Moynihan, D-N.Y., renewed his effort to cut the Social Security taxes he had helped raise in 1983, but his proposal was rejected in the Senate.

A House-passed measure seeking to insulate the Social Security Administration from political pressures by breaking it off from the Department of Health and Human Services and giving it independent status died in the Senate.

Finally, the long-running drive for more Social Security benefits for the so-called "notch babies" born between 1917 and 1921 was once again revived but failed to become law.

Attempts to substantially alter the Social Security program in the 101st Congress also proved fruitless. *(Story, p. 717)*

Earnings Test

By 1992, the earnings limit for retirees aged 65 to 69 to receive full Social Security benefits had reached $10,200 a year. Those who earned more had their benefits reduced by $1 for every $3 they earned over that amount. Those aged 62-64 could earn up to $7,440 and collect full benefits, while having their benefits reduced by $1 for every $2 they earned over that amount.

In its fiscal 1992 budget request, the Bush administration proposed increasing the earnings limit by $1,000 over the following two years. But McCain and others argued that a simple liberalization was inadequate. McCain, who counted many older people among his constituents, argued that it would be simpler and fairer to remove the cap altogether.

However, a major stumbling block to repeal was the long-term cost. The Office of Management and Budget estimated that repeal would cost the Social Security trust fund $28 billion over five years, reducing the surplus the fund needed to maintain in preparation for the retirement of the huge "baby boom" generation. Backers of repeal argued that some of the cost would be offset by increased tax revenues from seniors brought back into the work force, although others estimated that the change would not have a major impact on the number of working elderly.

McCain won voice vote approval of a repeal amendment on Nov. 12, 1991, during Senate floor consideration of the Older Americans Act reauthorization (HR 2967). As a result, further action on that otherwise non-controversial legislation was stalled. *(Older Americans Act, p. 620)*

Looking for a middle ground, House Ways and Means Chairman Dan Rostenkowski, D-Ill., and Senate Finance Chairman Lloyd Bentsen, D-Texas, introduced plans to liberalize the rules without repealing them. Determined to abide by the 1990 budget agreement, both lawmakers' proposals included increased taxes to pay for the benefit liberalization. Rostenkowski's bill (HR 2838) would have increased the earnings limit by $3,000 by 1993, with an increase in the Social Security wage base to pay for it. Bentsen's legislation (S 2038), which Senate Finance approved by voice vote June 11, 1992, would have gradually increased the earnings limit to $89,700 by 2001 and raised the wage base to the same level as well.

The House on April 9, 1992, had approved an amended Older Americans Act measure with a more generous version of Rostenkowski's proposal, minus the tax increase. The proposal languished in the Senate, however, and Congress subsequently cleared a clean version of the Older Americans legislation — that is, without the earnings test language.

The key battles for the earnings test proved to be amendments offered by McCain in 1992 to appropriations bills. He sought to attach the provision to the fiscal 1993 agriculture funding bill (HR 5487) on July 28 but had to settle for an amendment, adopted by voice vote, expressing the sense of the Senate that the limit should be repealed or changed.

The watershed event occurred on the fiscal 1993 Treasury Department and Postal Service appropriations bill (HR 5488). McCain on Sept. 10 offered an amendment to raise the earnings limit to $50,000 over five years, but it fell 51-42, nine votes short of the 60 votes needed to suspend the 1990 budget pact.

Tax Changes

Having tried and failed in 1990, Moynihan in 1991 pursued his campaign to reduce the Social Security payroll tax as a way to prevent the government from accumulating surplus revenues in the Social Security trust funds and using them to pay for general government programs.

When Congress enacted a series of automatic payroll tax increases as part of the bailout of the Social Security system in 1983, Moynihan argued, it assumed the federal deficit would be eliminated before the pension system began running a surplus. Because the deficit persisted, he said, the tax increases should be repealed.

By law, the surplus had to be invested in Treasury securities. That meant that most of the surplus was effectively being deposited into the general federal revenue pot. Thus, Moynihan argued, even though Congress removed Social Security from deficit calculations as part of the 1990 budget summit agreement, a regressive tax collected for old-age pensions was still being used to finance deficit spending by the federal government.

The drafters of the 1990 budget pact had sought to prevent Moynihan from offering further payroll tax cuts by including procedural roadblocks requiring a 60-vote majority in the Senate to pass legislation reducing Social Security revenues. But Moynihan found a loophole in the provision, in the form of a little-noticed phrase included in the budget law that ensured that only a simple majority in the Senate would be needed to pass the tax cut.

Moynihan took advantage of the loophole, and when the fiscal 1992 budget resolution (S Con Res 29) came to the Senate floor in April 1991, he offered an amendment to reduce the assumed level of Social Security revenues over the next five years. The amendment would have paved the way for Senate consideration late in the year of an actual bill to cut the payroll tax. Only a majority was needed for passage in both cases.

Democrats were badly divided on the issue. Republicans, by contrast, were mostly united behind President Bush, who opposed Moynihan.

Senators on April 24 voted 60-38 to table Moynihan's initiative. And the loophole subsequently was closed. *(Fiscal 1992 budget, p. 75)*

Social Security Independence

The House in 1992 passed a bill (HR 5429) to give the Social Security Administration independence from HHS, but the measure died in the Senate. A similar scenario played out in 1986 and 1990. *(1986 action, Congress and the Nation Vol. VII, p. 693)*

The bill passed on a 350-8 vote under suspension of the rules June 29 (H Rept 102-621) would have created an independent three-member board to run a free-standing Social Security agency.

In addition, the Senate Finance Committee on June 11 approved a bill (S 33) to create an independent Social Security agency governed by a single commissioner appointed by the president and advised by a seven-member board. S 33 (S Rept 102-304) was formally reported June 26.

Backers of the bills argued that the agency's independence was needed to insulate it from political pressures and protect the Social Security trust fund. But opponents, including the Bush administration, argued that the change would remove a vital service from a department that oversaw companion programs for the elderly.

Neither HR 5429 nor S 33 reached the Senate floor during 1992, and the legislation died at the end of the session.

'Notch Babies'

The continuing battle over the "notch babies" — people born between 1917 and 1921 who claimed they were shortchanged in benefits by falling between the cracks of a pair of fixes made to the Social Security benefit system in the 1970s — flared up again in 1992.

Concerns over the potentially huge cost of aiding those affected, however, prevented any changes in the program from becoming law. Although backers of increasing benefits to notch baby retirees contended the change would cost only $48 billion over 10 years, opponents said the cost could reach $300 billion by 2010 and grow indefinitely.

The first dust-up over the issue in 1992 came when Rep. Barney Frank, D-Mass., led a group of House notch baby supporters in an effort to attach a benefit increase to an urban aid tax bill (HR 11). Although Frank appeared to have the support of a majority of members, he was opposed by House leaders, who ended up moving to forestall a floor vote on the politically explosive issue. *(Tax bill, p. 103)*

In the Senate, Terry Sanford, D-N.C., offered an amendment to the fiscal 1993 Treasury appropriations bill (HR 5488). His Sept. 10 effort to waive the budget act to allow extra benefits failed on a 49-49 vote, well short of the 60 votes required.

ERISA Reforms

The 1974 Employee Retirement Income Security Act (ERISA — PL 93-406), which covered pensions and other employee benefits, was the subject of much discussion in the 102nd Congress but little legislative action. ERISA was under increasing attack because of its complexity and its loopholes. *(PL 93-406, Congress and the Nation Vol. IV, p. 690)*

Administration Plan. The Bush administration sought to encourage small businesses to offer pensions to their employees by easing paperwork demands and relaxing some ERISA restrictions. But small business groups voiced reservations about the proposal, and it saw no congressional action.

Labor Secretary Lynn Martin unveiled the proposal April 30, 1991, saying it could lead to pension coverage for an additional 42 million workers, nearly 45 percent of the nation's work force. A major feature of the proposal would make pensions "portable" by encouraging employees who changed jobs to move their pensions to an individual retirement account (IRA), and penalizing them with higher taxes if they did not.

Martin said the provisions that would lose tax revenues would be offset by others that would increase tax revenues by eliminating retirees' right to spread their tax liability over five to 10 years when they took their pensions in a lump sum. But the Labor Department offered no figures on the tax trade-off, and opinions differed on whether the plan would cost money. Meanwhile, some speculated that the proposal would not end up costing any money because few people would take advantage of it.

The National Federation of Independent Businesses (NFIB), which lobbied Congress on issues affecting small businesses, said proposals that would force employers to pay a minimum contribution per employee were too expensive for most small companies.

Packwood Alternative. Sen. Bob Packwood, R-Ore., ranking member of the Finance Committee, introduced a pension portability bill (S 318) on Jan. 31, 1991.

Packwood's bill was preferred by business interests, including the NFIB, which said it gave employers the option of providing pensions only to workers who requested them. Under the administration's proposal, if an employer chose to establish a pension plan, pensions had to be provided for all workers.

The Joint Tax Committee estimated that Packwood's plan would cost about $100 million over five years. No action was taken on the bill.

HR 1602, HR 2782. ERISA prohibited states from enacting their own laws regulating any employee benefit, including health insurance. In 1987, the Supreme Court ruled, in *Pilot Life Insurance Co. v. Dedeaux*, that ERISA pre-empted state laws on remedies for unfair insurance claims practices. Because ERISA did not permit suits for punitive damages, policyholders who sued their insurers could collect only the costs of their illness. The law also limited lawyers' fees. *(Case summary, Congress and the Nation Vol. VII, p. 826)*

HR 1602 would amend ERISA to clarify how insurance companies and other health care providers should respond to claims from health insurance policyholders. By a bitterly divided, party-line vote of 25-15, the House Education and Labor Committee approved the bill on July 30, 1992. It was formally reported (H Rept 102-1023) on Oct. 5. Supporters said the legislation would make collecting on health care claims easier. But opponents argued that HR 1602 would drastically increase the cost of health insurance.

The bill, known as the Health Insurance Claims Fairness Act, would help people who were seeking payment of health care benefits from their insurance provider. It would amend ERISA to mandate a maximum 30-day period for approval or denial of claims. In cases of a life-threatening illness, the approval time would be limited to three days. To resolve disputes over claims, the bill set out a three-part system. People at odds with their insurance company could choose to settle the matter through binding arbitration or mediation, or they could go to court. People who were successful in court would be awarded attorney's fees. In cases of fraud on the part of the insurance provider, the bill would allow judges to award punitive damages.

HR 2782, which the House Education and Labor Committee approved by voice vote June 10, would give states more latitude to set standards for the employee benefit programs of local contractors. It was formally reported (H Rept 102-644) on July 1.

The committee-approved bill would allow states to require employers to pay their workers the prevailing level of employee benefits in the state when working on state contracts. (The Davis-Bacon federal wage law would prevail if the contracts involved federal funds.) The bill would permit states to establish minimum requirements and certification standards for apprenticeship programs or other training programs. For plans that covered several employers (generally union contracts), it would allow states to provide additional means by which the pensions could be collected if a business did not properly contribute. For example, under some state laws, a pension plan operator could put a lien on a building under construction if the contractor had not fulfilled his obligation.

The bill generated intense opposition from business groups, who feared that it would open the door to 50 new and differing sets of mandated employee benefits. Committee Democrats contended that the legislation was necessary to restore longstanding state laws that federal court decisions had wiped out.

In 1989, the 2nd U.S. Circuit Court of Appeals, in *General Electric Co. v. New York State Department of Labor*, struck down a century-old New York state law that required employers to pay their workers the prevailing level of employee benefits when working on state public works projects. That law dated back to 1894, according to the AFL-CIO, but the court ruled that ERISA pre-empted it. In 1990, the 9th U.S. Circuit Court of Appeals in California, in *Hydrostorage Inc. v. Northern California Boilermakers Local Joint Apprenticeship Committee*, reversed a state administrative order that established minimum standards for apprenticeship programs. The court ruled that such programs were exclusively under federal jurisdiction because of ERISA pre-emption. The courts were split over whether ERISA pre-empted state laws letting pension plans collect unpaid contributions.

During floor consideration of HR 2782, supporters argued that the courts had gone too far in upholding the ERISA pre-emption of state laws. But opponents said any new exemptions would drive employers away from offering benefits.

An amendment by Paul B. Henry, R-Mich., allowed some Republicans to back the measure. It said prevailing state wage laws would apply only to state-funded public works projects. Henry's amendment also would allow state contractors to apply the prevailing wage law in their own way, as long as they offered employees the same dollar value as state-mandated benefits. For example, contractors could have given their employees additional wages instead of a health care plan. Finally, the amendment spelled out what kind of legal remedies states could use to help unions collect benefits.

The House rejected, 140-266, an attempt by Harris W. Fawell, R-Ill., to delete language allowing states to set minimum standards for apprenticeship programs.

The House passed HR 2782 by voice vote on Aug. 4.

Both HR 1602 and HR 2782 drew veto threats from President Bush and died upon congressional adjournment.

13

Law and Justice

Introduction 741

Law and Law Enforcement 743

The Supreme Court 801

Law and Law Enforcement

In the area of law and law enforcement, the Bush presidency often looked like an extension of Ronald Reagan's eight years in office — controversy, contention and frequent stalemates over civil rights, anti-crime proposals and judicial nominations.

The conservative tone Reagan had set in these areas continued with George Bush, but it emanated more from the White House than the Justice Department, which had been so visible under Reagan. Despite the numerous conflicts with Congress, there were moments of consensus, and some important legislation passed. But these successes came only after much public posturing by opposing sides and considerable private negotiation between members, lobbyists and key administration aides.

1989: Court-Driven. While part of 1989 was prologue, laying the groundwork for legislative activity to come in the second session, it also was a year in which the Supreme Court became a major catalyst for legislative controversies in two areas — First Amendment protections and civil rights.

The Court, 5-4, invalidated a state anti-flag desecration law, prompting outcries from the president, members of Congress and veterans groups. Opponents came up with two strategies to overturn the decision; one a federal statute, the other a constitutional amendment.

The legislation cleared Congress, but a constitutional amendment was rejected by the Senate. The issue was not closed, however, because the Supreme Court would speak again on the matter after the new law was challenged as violating the First Amendment.

In a series of decisions that stunned groups representing minorities and women, the Court greatly restricted both the reach and the remedies of civil rights laws. Civil rights advocates and their congressional allies spent the remainder of the year putting together legislation in an effort to overturn the rulings.

Anti-crime legislation had been a regular feature in the Reagan years, and five months into his term, Bush unveiled his plans in this area. But he and congressional Democrats jockeyed for position on the issues — the death penalty, limiting death row inmates' appeals, gun control — and no proposals reached either the House or Senate floor. Similarly, a major immigration bill moved slowly, winning passage in the Senate but going nowhere in the House.

Also in the working stages was a major civil rights bill to protect the rights of the disabled — this one moving through both chambers with Bush's expressed support.

The Senate closed out an extraordinary string of three judicial impeachments in four years. It convicted and removed from office two U.S. district court judges, Alcee L. Hastings of Florida and Walter L. Nixon of Mississippi.

1990: Controversy and Compromise. The Supreme Court reignited the flag controversy when the same five-justice majority struck down the new federal law. This prompted opponents to push for a constitutional amendment again, but the strategy failed. Within two weeks of the decision, a proposed amendment was brought to the House floor, where it failed. The Senate also voted on the proposal even though the vote was meaningless. There, too, the amendment failed to command the required two-thirds majority.

Congress and the Bush administration did find common ground on the disability rights law, which was cleared after months of final negotiations. The bill prohibited discrimination against the disabled in employment, public services and public accommodations and required employers to make "reasonable accommodations" for disabled workers. Changes that would involve "undue hardship" were not required, however.

The business community had expressed reservations about the bill, but the biggest stumbling block to final passage was Congress itself as members struggled to determine whether and how they would be brought under the law. Also required at the last minute was compromise language, prompted by concerns over AIDS (acquired immune deficiency syndrome), that allowed an employer to transfer a worker with an infectious and communicable disease out of a food-handling job.

An important immigration bill also cleared, which increased the number of immigrants who could be admitted to the United States. Special emphasis was given to immigrants who possessed skills needed in the United States and those who had been adversely affected — mostly Euro-

References

Discussion of law enforcement policy for the years 1945-64 may be found in *Congress and the Nation Vol. I*, pp. 1671-1676; for the years 1965-68, *Congress and the Nation Vol. II*, pp. 309-334; for the years 1969-72, *Congress and the Nation Vol. III*, pp. 255-286; for the years 1973-76, *Congress and the Nation Vol. IV*, pp. 559-618; for the years 1977-80, *Congress and the Nation Vol. V*, pp. 715-753; for the years 1981-84, *Congress and the Nation Vol. VI*, pp. 675-709; for the years 1985-89, *Congress and the Nation Vol. VII*, pp. 713-784.

peans — under a 1965 immigration law. The new law allowed legal immigration to climb from about 500,000 each year to about 700,000 during each of the first three years after enactment. After that, a permanent level of 675,000 was to go into effect.

These legislative successes were almost overshadowed by the vituperative fight over a bill to reverse the civil rights decisions from the previous Supreme Court term. Congress had cleared legislation to reverse these decisions, but Bush complained that the legislation would require employers to institute hiring quotas and vetoed it. The Senate failed to override his veto by one vote, the first time in a quarter-century that a major civil rights bill had been defeated.

At the end of the high court term, William J. Brennan Jr., one of the leading liberal voices on the Court, announced his retirement. Bush nominated David Souter, a little-known federal appeals court judge from New Hampshire, to replace him. Though he irritated some Judiciary Committee members by refusing to give his views on some issues, he was recommended for confirmation and eventually confirmed in October.

Though Congress and the Bush administration had struggled over anti-crime legislation throughout the session, a combination of time pressures and irreconcilable differences turned a once-ambitious package into the slender bill that cleared. The key provisions increased penalties for child abuse, provided alternatives to incarceration and provided more money for law enforcement. Stripped from the final version were provisions expanding the death penalty, tougher penalties for illegal firearm use and a Bush-backed provision allowing courts to consider evidence gathered with flawed warrants.

1991: Bitterness and Breakthrough. The bitter spectacle of the Clarence Thomas nomination to the Supreme Court was a central fact of 1991. The charges that he had sexually harassed Anita F. Hill when she worked for him engulfed the Senate, and the televised hearings captured the nation's attention. Thomas, who denied the charges, was ultimately confirmed, though by a slim margin.

The divisive proceedings ended up producing one positive side effect. They broke the logjam over the civil rights legislation that Bush had vetoed in 1990. Republicans and Democrats alike were anxious to defuse the racial tensions that swirled around that bill and that had been a subtext to the Thomas-Hill imbroglio. A compromise that restored a more expansive reading to the disputed laws was worked out between the administration and the Senate and quickly approved by both chambers.

Democrats and their allies in the civil rights community contended the measure varied little from the measure Bush the previous year had a called a "quota bill," but the administration maintained he had won some important alterations.

Bush had returned to the crime issue, challenging Congress at the beginning of the session to pass legislation within 100 days. As he had in the previous Congress, Bush called for authorizing the death penalty for more federal crimes, limiting death row inmates' appeals, making it easier for evidence to come into court despite faulty warrants and stiffening penalties for firearms offenses.

Senate Democrats proposed their own bill, which shared some of the Bush features but also included a ban on assault weapons. In July, well after Bush's 100-day deadline, the Senate did pass a crime bill, but not to the administration's liking. It included a notable feature, however. The Senate adopted an amendment requiring a five-day waiting period before the purchase of a handgun. The House had passed a separate bill requiring a seven-day waiting period, making this the first year that both chambers had approved such language.

After the House passed its crime bill, conferees hammered together a compromise agreement that included a handgun waiting period provision. The bill passed the House just as the session was ending but fell victim to a filibuster in the Senate.

Anti-drug proposals, which once galvanized both parties, had receded on the legislative agenda. A feeling seemed to exist that Congress had done enough, having passed two major drug packages in a five-year period. The first "drug czar," former education secretary William J. Bennett, had come and gone, and the new one, former Florida governor Bob Martinez, had been confirmed in March.

1992: Quiet Conclusion. The last year of the Bush administration was most notable for what did not happen. The Senate failed twice to cut off a threatened filibuster on the crime bill compromise that had passed the House, so no new anti-crime legislation was forthcoming. It demonstrated once again that the National Rifle Association (NRA), which had lobbied hard against the measure, still had some political clout. NRA lobbyists were not the only reason for its failure, though. The bill suffered from opposition over other issues, particularly from those who believed that the proposed limits on prisoners' appeals were too rigid and from those opposed to the death penalty.

Congress also let the major law of the Watergate era, the independent counsel act, lapse. Since its creation in 1978, the statute had survived three presidents and hostile Justice Departments and had been upheld by the Supreme Court. But in the wake of the costly Iran-contra investigation, not enough members were willing to take on the issue and push through another extension. The lack of strong congressional leadership came in part because of the scandals in the House over the bank and the Post Office, and one of the continuing controversy's with the law was how Congress itself should be covered.

Bush Imprint on Judiciary. By the end of his term, Bush had made nearly 190 lifetime appointments to the federal courts, including two Supreme Court justices and nearly one-fourth of the positions on the lower federal bench. Bush kept faith with the politics of Reagan, continuing to appoint conservatives to the bench. But he also made an effort to appoint more women judges, finishing with a record level of female appointments to the district courts.

In addition, Bush appointed 12 black judges to the district and appeals courts, including Clarence Thomas, who was later elevated to the Supreme Court, and eight Hispanic judges, six to district courts and two to the appeals courts.

The Bush years also were noteworthy for the appointments the president could have made but did not. Bush had gotten off to a slow start and never caught up, especially after a 1990 law added 85 seats to the bench. Appointments were further slowed by the tumultuous Thomas hearings, and by the end of the 102nd Congress, Bush had failed to nominate candidates for 45 vacancies. The Judiciary Committee did not vote on another 53 pending nominations, effectively killing them.

Chronology Of Action On Law Enforcement

1989-90

The biggest legislative accomplishment of the 101st Congress in the area of law and law enforcement was enactment of the Americans with Disabilities Act. The new law provided additional civil rights protections to the mentally and physically disabled. The legislation had bipartisan support in Congress as well as the backing of President Bush.

For the first time since 1965, Congress instituted substantial changes in U.S. legal immigration policy. Beginning in October 1991, a significantly larger number of immigrants would be allowed into the country, with particular emphasis on those with skills needed in the United States.

The Senate in 1990 sustained Bush's veto of a major civil rights bill providing employee protections. The legislation was fashioned in response to a series of 1989 Supreme Court decisions that curtailed prohibitions against employment discrimination.

Efforts to add an amendment to the Constitution to outlaw flag desecration fell flat. The movement sought to counteract Supreme Court rulings that claimed flag burning was a form of political expression protected by the First Amendment.

A watered-down crime bill cleared in 1990 as Congress raced toward adjournment. Controversial issues were jettisoned to ensure enactment. No major anti-drug bill was produced either.

Congress was unable to clear measures regarding the admission of refugees into the United States, vertical price fixing and revisions to the federal anti-racketeering law.

The president was given 85 new federal judgeships to fill as a result of 1990 legislation. Judges' workload had increased tremendously, particularly with a notable rise in drug cases.

Two U.S. district court judges — Alcee L. Hastings and Walter L. Nixon Jr. — were impeached by the Senate in 1989. And Clarence Thomas was confirmed as a federal appeals court judge.

Americans with Disabilities

After years of effort and months of final negotiations, Congress in 1990 cleared landmark legislation (S 933 — PL 101-336) to extend broad civil rights protections to an estimated 43 million Americans with mental and physical disabilities. President Bush had supported the measure — known as the Americans with Disabilities Act, or ADA — almost since its inception in 1988.

Passage of S 933 was a major triumph for the coalition of civil rights, disability rights, public health and AIDS (acquired immune deficiency syndrome) support groups that had laid meticulous groundwork for passage of the legislation. The strong, bipartisan support in Congress for the ADA reflected the public's growing endorsement of the goal of helping the disabled have greater access to the activities of daily life. A Gallup Poll released Dec. 20, 1989, found that 81 percent of those queried believed that insufficient attention had been paid to the civil rights of the disabled.

The legislation prohibited discrimination against the disabled in employment, public services and public accommodations, and it required that telecommunications be made accessible to those with speech and hearing impairments through the use of special relay systems. The bill required employers to make "reasonable accommodations" for disabled workers, but not changes that would involve "undue hardship." The employment provisions were to take effect in two years for employers of 25 or more people and in four years for employers of 15 or more.

Although patterned after the 1964 Civil Rights Act, which barred discrimination against racial and ethnic minorities and women, the new law went beyond that statute. Its public accommodations section applied not only to the restaurants, lodgings, places of entertainment and gasoline stations covered by the earlier law, but also to museums and sports stadiums, doctors' offices and hospitals, dry cleaners, pharmacies, grocery stores and all other retail and service establishments. Such places were required to make new and renovated facilities accessible to the disabled and to make whatever "readily achievable" modifications in existing facilities were needed to accommodate the disabled.

The bill also required all new purchased or leased buses and rail cars to be accessible to the disabled but did not require retrofitting of existing vehicles.

The Senate passed S 933 in September 1989, but by the end of the year, the companion House measure (HR 2273) had been approved by only one of the four House committees with jurisdiction over it. Compromise provisions were crafted in 1990 to allay the concerns of the business community, which said the legislation's employment and public accommodations sections would be too costly. The House passed its version in May.

But approval of a conference report on the measure did not come until early July, after floor battles at each end of the Capitol to settle two remaining differences: how Senate employees were to be covered and whether employers should be allowed to transfer workers with AIDS from food-handling jobs. The bill as enacted provided that the ADA would cover Senate employees but that claims of discrimination would be investigated and adjudicated exclusively by either the Senate Ethics Committee or a specially designated Senate panel. The compromise on workers with AIDS required the secretary of health and human services (HHS) to disseminate a list of infectious and communicable diseases that can transmitted through food. Those with such diseases could then be transferred out of food-handling positions.

Background

Discrimination against the disabled was already prohibited in federally funded activities by the 1973 Rehabilitation Act (PL 93-112) and in housing by the 1988 Fair Housing Act amendments (PL 100-430). But the disabled were not among the classes covered by the landmark 1964 Civil Rights Act (PL 88-352). *(1973 law, Congress and the*

Nation Vol. IV, p. 687; 1988 law, Congress and the Nation Vol. VII, p. 681; 1964 act, Congress and the Nation Vol. I, p. 1635)

Senate sponsor Tom Harkin, D-Iowa, noted that if a black man walked into a restaurant and was turned away because of his color, "that man could file a lawsuit and win." But if a person in a wheelchair was turned away from the same restaurant, "it's not against the law."

The drive to extend anti-discrimination provisions to the disabled was not a new one, although it had gained considerable momentum by 1988. S 933 as well as earlier versions stemmed from the work of the National Council on the Handicapped, a 15-member commission appointed by President Ronald Reagan, which determined that no effective law covered the disabled.

The coalition supporting the measure was considerably broader than the groups that traditionally represented the disabled. For instance, the 185 organizations that made up the Leadership Conference on Civil Rights were behind the bill along with health and social organizations that backed comprehensive anti-discrimination protections for AIDS victims and those infected with HIV (human immunodeficiency virus), which causes AIDS. Campaigning for president in 1988, Bush repeatedly endorsed the ADA bill and split from Reagan by endorsing the call from a special AIDS commission for comprehensive legislation to cover those with AIDS and the HIV infection.

Many in the business community viewed the bill as a nightmare of details and definitions that would be a great burden, particularly for small businesses. Business representatives complained that the measure would further erode America's competitiveness, but backers of the legislation said such claims were exaggerated, that many compromises had been made to allay business concerns and that some in the community were bent on obstructionism.

Senate Action

The Senate passed S 933 in late summer 1989 following a daylong debate that featured a sign-language interpreter for hearing-impaired television viewers, a first for the Senate.

The Senate Labor and Human Resources Committee had approved S 933 on Aug. 2. The 16-0 vote came only hours after sponsors reached a compromise with administration officials. Markup of the ADA bill, on the committee's agenda since June, had been delayed for several weeks while negotiations were under way. S 933 (S Rept 101-116) was formally reported Aug. 30.

One of the key issues that needed to be resolved was the matter of remedies to be available to a person who proved discrimination. The compromise measure made the same stipulations as under Title VII of the 1964 act — essentially injunctive relief and back pay — in the case of employment bias. Dropped from the original version were provisions that would have allowed victims of intentional discrimination to seek compensatory and punitive damages.

The compromise also clarified that employers could prohibit the use of alcohol or illegal drugs at the work place by all employees. And it extended several dates for compliance with the various requirements in the bill.

A separate compromise negotiated with administration officials did not require a buildings to have elevators if it was less than three stories high and had fewer than 3,000 square feet per floor unless the building was a shopping mall, shopping center or the professional office of a health care provider. The attorney general could require elevators if they were deemed necessary in other cases.

Despite the changes, the business community still expressed concerns. However, the full Senate vote of 76-8 on Sept. 7 was a foregone conclusion. The bill had 60 cosponsors and the administration's support. All eight "nay" votes were cast by conservative Republicans.

One business lobbyist conceded that fighting the bill was futile. "It's like opposing motherhood," said Stephen F. Owen Jr. of the National Association of Theatre Owners. Indeed, support for the measure was so strong that while many senators sympathized with the business community, the Senate rejected the only major floor amendment aimed at aiding or exempting small businesses. Offered by Orrin G. Hatch, R-Utah, the amendment would have created a refundable tax credit for small businesses to offset the costs of compliance with the public accommodations provisions of the bill. The credit, of up to $5,000, would have been available to businesses with 15 or fewer employees and gross receipts of less than $1 million annually.

Senate Finance Committee Chairman Lloyd Bentsen, D-Texas, called Hatch's proposal a "killer amendment." And he said existing law already permitted a deduction of up to $35,000 for the removal of architectural or transportation barriers that hindered the disabled. He also asserted that the amendment would violate the budget act by reducing revenues an unknown amount below the level envisioned in the fiscal 1990 budget resolution. He lodged a point of order against the amendment on those grounds.

Hatch's motion to waive the budget act — a maneuver that required 60 votes — fell short Sept. 7 by 12 votes, 48-44.

Much of the Senate debate centered on whether drug addicts and alcoholics would be protected under the bill's sweeping definition of disabled. Despite protests from sponsors that such persons would not be covered, conservative Republicans were unconvinced. Members by voice vote adopted three amendments that sought to clarify that current users of illegal drugs were not to be considered disabled solely because of their drug use and that employers could prohibit the use of alcohol or illegal drugs at the work place and require that workers not be under the influence of such substances while at work.

Sponsors also reluctantly accepted, by voice vote, amendments to exempt from the bill's protections persons with certain mental or behavioral disorders.

Finally, members sparred over whether to apply the requirements of the bill to Congress, which was exempt from most civil rights laws. By a standing division vote, senators adopted an amendment offered by Charles E. Grassley, R-Iowa, that included the legislative branch. While no one argued that Congress should be permitted to discriminate against the disabled, some senators, led by Rules Committee Chairman Wendell H. Ford, D-Ky., warned that the amendment could be unconstitutional because it would give the executive branch authority to oversee legislative branch activities.

Although sponsors pressured Grassley to relent on the amendment, he refused to do so. Shortly before final passage, members adopted a "severability" amendment offered by Harkin that would protect the rest of the measure in case any portion was struck down by a court as unconstitutional.

House Action

The House got started on a companion bill (HR 2273) to S 933 in 1989, but progress was slow. One problem was the departure of bill sponsor and leading advocate Tony Coelho, D-Calif., who overcame epilepsy to become a member of Congress and rose to the position of House majority whip. Coelho resigned his seat in June following allegations of questionable financial dealings. Coelho turned the stewardship of his bill over to one of his closest friends in the House, Democratic Caucus Chairman Steny H. Hoyer, D-Md. *(Coelho resignation, p. 918)*

Further complicating matters was that unlike the Senate, where only the Labor Committee considered the legislation, four House Committees — Judiciary, Education and Labor, Energy and Commerce, and Public Works and Transportation — had jurisdiction over parts of HR 2273.

The Energy and Commerce Subcommittee on Telecommunications and Finance in October 1989 became the first House panel to advance HR 2273. The section of the bill approved by the subcommittee required telephone companies to establish a comprehensive network of operators to help hearing-impaired people communicate over the telephone using a typewriter-type device known as a TDD hooked to their telephones. The operator would read what was typed on the TDD and relay it to the hearing person on the other end of the line. The operator also would type the responses of the hearing person on a TDD so that the deaf person could read them.

Currently, deaf persons could communicate via telephone only with callers who also had a TDD. The legislation gave telephone companies three years to comply with the new requirements.

The Education and Labor Committee unanimously approved HR 2273 in November, but backers of the legislation conceded that final passage would have to wait until 1990.

The version of the bill approved by Education and Labor on a 35-0 vote was considerably different from the bill introduced by Coelho. The committee worked from a draft based on the Senate-passed version. In addition to the Senate language, the Education and Labor draft included several "clarifications" negotiated primarily by Hoyer and Steve Bartlett of Texas, ranking Republican on the Education and Labor Subcommittee on Select Education.

A key compromise was language to help determine whether a needed accommodation for a disabled person would be "readily achievable" or pose an "undue hardship" for a business that operated out of more than one location. The compromise called for consideration of both "site specific" factors — the financial resources and structure of the particular facility — and the overall financial success of the business.

Just as the other House committees were beginning to move on ADA legislation in 1990, Bush and administration officials voiced disagreement with Democratic sponsors over a crucial element of a deal struck in 1989. At issue were the proposed remedies for employment discrimination against the disabled. The compromise language negotiated in 1989 specified that remedies under the ADA were to be the same as those provided to women and minorities under Title VII of the 1964 Civil Rights Act. Existing law provided primarily injunctive relief and back pay.

But in response to a series of 1989 Supreme Court rulings, separate legislation (HR 4000, S 2104) was introduced to amend Title VII to permit aggrieved parties to sue for monetary damages. (S 2104 was eventually vetoed by Bush.) *(Civil rights, p. 757)*

The administration opposed expansion of Title VII remedies and wanted to make sure that no monetary damages were possible under the ADA, either. Attorney General Dick Thornburgh on March 12 sent a letter to Hoyer to this effect. But backers of the ADA resisted changing the bill. They maintained that their agreement with the administration was not merely to give the disabled existing Title VII remedies, but to ensure that the disabled had access to the same remedies for employment discrimination that women and minorities had.

On March 13, the Energy and Commerce Committee approved HR 2273 by a vote of 40-3. The committee had primary jurisdiction only over portions of the bill relating to railroads and telecommunications (and therefore did not address the administration's concerns on remedies). Members adopted substitute provisions offered by committee Chairman John D. Dingell, D-Mich., and ranking Republican Norman F. Lent, N.Y. Among other things, the substitute required Amtrak and other commuter rail systems to make at least one car per train accessible to the disabled within five years; all new cars purchased or leased by Amtrak or commuter authorities would have to be accessible from the outset.

The measure required common carriers to provide telecommunications relay services within three years. Such services permitted hearing-impaired people to use telephones. And it required public service announcements on television that were produced with federal funds to be closed-captioned for the hearing-impaired.

Law Leadership

William P. Barr was confirmed by voice vote Nov. 21, 1991, as attorney general. He had been serving as acting attorney general and succeeded Dick Thornburgh. A holdover from the Reagan administration, Thornburgh resigned to run for the Senate. *(Thornburgh, Barr, Cabinet profiles, p. 1170)*

Thornburgh received mixed reviews as attorney general. He was praised for increasing the professionalism of the office, particularly as successor of the embattled Edwin Meese III. Thornburgh, however, drew criticism for a style that was described variously as imperious, cipherlike and secretive.

William J. Bennett, the controversial former education secretary, was confirmed, 97-2, on March 9, 1989, as the first director of the Office of National Drug Control Policy. Bennett served in the "drug czar" position, a Cabinet-level appointment, until his resignation Nov. 30, 1990. He was succeeded by Bob Martinez, former governor of Florida. Martinez was confirmed 88-12 on March 21, 1991. *(Bennett, Martinez background, p. 1176)*

Committee members spent the better part of two hours fending off amendments aimed at narrowing the bill's broad protections by restricting those covered and the types of discrimination to be outlawed. All were rejected by a show of hands.

In April, the Public Works and Transportation Committee became the third panel to give its approval to the ADA, endorsing the measure by a vote of 45-5. Public Works had jurisdiction over transportation provisions, which were considered vital by the groups pressing for enactment of the ADA. Amendments to alter the bill were rejected, with a majority of the committee sticking to compromises worked out in subcommittee. Included in the bill was the request for a special three-year study by the Office of Technology Assessment to determine how intercity buses could best be made accessible to the disabled and a 10-year delay in the requirement that key commuter rail and subway stations be made accessible within 20 years. The subcommittee also had approved an amendment by Dennis Hastert, R-Ill., requiring that only one car per train in commuter rail systems be made accessible, instead of every car.

In May, the Judiciary Committee became the fourth and final House panel to approve HR 2273. The 32-3 vote followed two days of markup during which members rejected a number of amendments to limit the bill and approved a compromise package designed to alleviate the concerns of small businesses.

An anticipated fight over the remedies available to those who suffered illegal job discrimination fizzled, with Republicans not even calling for a recorded vote on an administration-backed amendment that failed. That issue dominated the April markup by the Civil and Constitutional Rights Subcommittee, which had approved the bill 7-1.

The full committee fought most heatedly about whether small businesses would be hurt by the sweeping requirement that public accommodations be made accessible to the disabled. Members rejected 15-20 a proposal by Tom Campbell, R-Calif., that would have delayed the effective dates of the public accommodations provisions for small businesses.

The compromise package, offered by ranking Republican Hamilton Fish Jr., N.Y., had been worked out with the White House; Don Edwards, D-Calif., and F. James Sensenbrenner Jr., Wis., chairman and ranking Republican, respectively, of the subcommittee that considered the bill; and Bill McCollum, R-Fla. It included three amendments sought by small business interests and three sought by lobbyists for the disabled.

The business-backed changes included one to define more specifically the "direct threat" a person with a disabling communicable disease must pose before he or she may be discriminated against. The amendment said direct threat would mean "a significant risk to the health or safety of others that cannot be eliminated by reasonable accommodation." A second change required that consideration be given to an employer's judgment in determining the "essential functions" of a job. The bill barred discrimination against a disabled person if he or she was capable of performing those essential functions. Finally, the changes clarified that a cause of action for "anticipatory" discrimination extended only to situations in which a structure was about to be built or altered in such a way as to render it inaccessible to the disabled.

The changes sought by the disability community included ensuring that alterations made to accessible structures not render them inaccessible, that review courses and examinations necessary for professional licensing and certification be given in accessible locations or that special accommodations be made so that the disabled were not excluded, and that the general prohibition against discrimination in public accommodations cover those who owned, leased or operated such places.

HR 2273 was formally reported from Public Works and Transportation (H Rept 101-485, Part I) on May 14 and from Education and Labor (H Rept 101-485, Part II), Judiciary (H Rept 101-485, Part III) and Energy and Commerce (H Rept 101-485, Part IV) on May 15.

The full House May 22 overwhelmingly passed HR 2273 by a vote of 403-20. The House then passed by voice vote an amended S 933, with the language of HR 2273. Support for the legislation was so strong in both chambers that a House-Senate conference probably would not have been necessary had the House not included a controversial amendment.

By 199-187 on May 17, members adopted an amendment, sponsored by Jim Chapman, D-Texas, that would have permitted employers to transfer workers with contagious diseases out of food-handling jobs, even if the disease could not be transmitted through food. Lawmakers on both sides of the issue said the amendment was aimed at people with AIDS. The bill already specified that its anti-discrimination protections did not apply to workers with contagious diseases that posed a "direct threat" to the health or safety of others, but Chapman was not satisfied.

Supporters of the amendment argued that restaurant owners needed the flexibility to transfer workers with AIDS or HIV, the AIDS virus, out of food-handling positions — not because the virus could be spread via food (AIDS experts said it could not) but because of public perceptions that such workers would present a danger.

Opponents, including most of the bill's key sponsors, said permitting discrimination on the basis of an incorrect perception was exactly what the bill was intended to outlaw. Even representatives of the restaurant industry conceded that the problem they sought to address was not actual risk but the fear of risk.

The White House officially opposed the Chapman amendment in a letter from HHS Secretary Louis W. Sullivan to House Speaker Thomas S. Foley, D-Wash. But the letter did not arrive on Capitol Hill until after debate on the amendment was under way, and ADA supporters complained that it was too little, too late.

The other significant issue left to the conference was the question of congressional coverage. The House-passed bill included Congress under its purview, with enforcement to be handled through the internal grievance procedures set up in 1988 and extended in 1989 to deal with other employee discrimination complaints. Those procedures allowed House employees to seek a formal hearing on their complaints if mediation failed, to obtain a ruling from a hearing examiner and to appeal to a board composed of House members and non-members. Remedies included injunctive relief and back pay.

The Senate-passed version of S 933 also covered Congress but was silent on enforcement, leaving Congress — like private employers — subject to enforcement by the executive branch. Some members said that raised separation of powers problems — an argument that had prevailed in the past when Congress exempted itself from other labor and anti-discrimination laws.

Before passing HR 2273, House members May 22 rejected 192-227 a Bush-backed Sensenbrenner amendment that would have written into the ADA bill the existing remedies available under Title VII of the 1964 Civil Rights Act — injunctive relief, back pay and attorneys' fees.

Conference, Final Action

With only two major items in dispute between the versions of the bill passed by the House and the Senate, conferees were able to reach agreement after only a single two-hour meeting June 25. But those two issues — how Congress should be covered by the new anti-discrimination requirements and whether people with AIDS or other diseases could be transferred out of food-handling jobs — continued to bog down the bill even after they were ostensibly settled by conferees.

While members in both chambers agreed that Congress should be subject to the bill's ban on discrimination in employment and public accommodations, they still disagreed on how the ban should be enforced. The House provided for a wholly internal mechanism both for House employees and those of Congress' "instrumentalities," including the Architect of the Capitol and the General Accounting Office. Complaints would be handled pursuant to the House ruling authorizing that chamber's Office of Fair Employment Practices. The Senate, however, as part of a Grassley amendment, simply made the provisions of the law applicable to the Senate and the instrumentalities.

Conferees agreed that the internal mechanism would apply in the House and to the instrumentalities and that, while the Senate would set up its own internal procedure to handle complaints, those not satisfied with the outcome could still sue in federal court.

Several senators were not satisfied with the proposed resolution of the congressional coverage issue, and others were equally unhappy that conferees dropped the controversial Chapman AIDS amendment.

The food-handling issue took on a new twist when the Senate on June 6 instructed its conferees to accept the AIDS amendment. The instructions technically were not binding on the Senate conferees, but the effect was that they were put in an awkward position. While a majority of both House and Senate conferees voted against the language, both chambers went on record in support of the provision. But Edward M. Kennedy, D-Mass., who chaired the conference, called the instructions "basically meaningless" and announced that Senate conferees proposed to drop the provision.

With the conference completed on June 25, supporters hoped for prompt action on the conference report. But last-minute maneuvering had Democrats in both chambers accusing Republicans of efforts to delay the bill and Republicans hotly denying ill intentions.

The task still ahead was resolving differences over coverage of congressional employees and the Chapman amendment. In effect, the Senate fought its final battle over congressional coverage for the ADA during July 10 consideration of the Civil Rights Act of 1990 (S 2104). After a day of debate, the Senate approved an amendment to that bill offered to codify an existing Senate rule providing civil rights protections for Senate employees. That was a significant change from provisions House and Senate conferees agreed to June 25 on the ADA bill, which would have permitted Senate employees alleging discrimination to sue in federal court if they were dissatisfied with the outcome of the Senate's internal grievance procedure.

S 933 had to go back to conference because of the Senate procedures change, which gave proponents of the Chapman amendment one more chance to get it included in the final version.

Sen. Jesse Helms, R-N.C., tried once more to get the AIDS language into the bill, but he failed. Instead, the Senate approved a compromise that called for the HHS secretary to develop and disseminate a list of infections and communicable diseases that could be transmitted through food. Those with such diseases could then be transferred out of food-handling positions.

The reconvened conference quickly ratified the two changes on July 12, and the House adopted the conference report (H Rept 101-596) on a 377-28 vote the same day. The Senate followed suit July 13 on a **key vote of 91-6 (R 37-6; D 54-0)**, thus completing congressional action. Bush signed the measure into law on July 26. *(1990 key votes, p. 1039)*

Major Provisions

As signed into law July 26, 1990, S 933 (PL 101-336):

Employment Discrimination

• **Discrimination Prohibitions.** Beginning two years after enactment, prohibited a covered entity (defined as an employer, employment agency, labor organization or joint labor-management committee) from discriminating against a qualified individual with a disability in job application procedures; in hiring, advancing, training, compensating and discharging employees; and in other terms, conditions and privileges of employment.

• **Coverage.** Defined "qualified individual with a disability" as a person with a disability who, with or without reasonable accommodation, could perform the essential functions of the job that such individual held or desired. Required that consideration be given to the employer's judgment in determining which functions of a job were essential and that, if an employer had written a job description before advertising or interviewing applicants, such description be considered evidence of the essential functions of the job.

• **Exclusions.** Specifically excluded from that definition any employee or applicant who at that time used illegal drugs, when the employer acted on the basis of such use. Not excluded were people who had been rehabilitated and were no longer using drugs, were participating in a supervised rehabilitation program and were no longer using drugs or who were erroneously regarded as using drugs.

• Provided that homosexuality and bisexuality were not impairments and as such were not disabilities under the act. Specified that for purposes of the act the term "disabled" or "disability" did not apply to an individual solely because that individual was a transvestite. Further excluded from the definition of disability "transvestism, transsexualism, pedophilia, exhibitionism, voyeurism, gender identity disorders not resulting from physical impairments, or other sexual behavior disorders; compulsive gambling, kleptomania, or pyromania; or psychoactive substance use disorders resulting from current illegal use of drugs."

• Permitted as a "qualification standard" a requirement that an individual not pose a direct threat to the health or safety of other individuals in the work place. Defined "direct threat" to mean a significant risk to the health or safety of others that cannot be eliminated by reasonable accommodation.

• **Prohibited Activities.** Defined "discrimination" to include:

(1) Limiting, segregating or classifying a job applicant or employee in a way that adversely affected the opportunities or status of such person because of his or her disability.

(2) Participating in a contractual or other arrangement or relationship that subjected a covered entity's qualified applicant or employee to prohibited discrimination (including arrangements with employment agencies, labor unions, providers of fringe benefits, and training and apprenticeship programs). For example, a company could be found to be discriminatory if its employment agency refused to accept applicants with disabilities.

(3) Using standards, criteria or methods of administration that discriminated on the basis of disability or that perpetuated the discrimination of others who were subject to common administrative control.

(4) Excluding or otherwise denying equal jobs or benefits to a qualified individual because of the disability of a person with whom the qualified individual was known to have had a relationship or association (such as a disabled spouse).

(5) Failing to make "reasonable accommodations" to the known physical or mental limitations of a qualified applicant or employee, unless the employer could demonstrate that the accommodations would impose an "undue hardship" on its operations.

(6) Denying job opportunities to a qualified applicant or employee based on the need to make reasonable accommodation to the person's physical or mental impairment.

(7) Using qualification standards, employment tests or other selection criteria that tended to screen out an individual with a disability or a class of individuals with disabilities unless the tests or other selection criteria were shown to be job-related for the position in question and were "consistent with business necessity."

(8) Failing to select and administer employment tests so that the test results accurately reflected the skills, aptitude or other factors the tests purported to measure of individuals with a disability that impaired sensory, manual or speaking skills (unless those were the skills to be measured).

• Defined "reasonable accommodation" to include making existing facilities used by employees readily accessible to and usable by individuals with disabilities, job-restructuring, part-time or modified work schedules, reassignment to a vacant position, acquisition or modification of equipment or devices, appropriate adjustment or modification of examinations, training materials or policies, the provision of qualified readers or interpreters, and similar accommodations.

• Defined "undue hardship" as an action requiring significant difficulty or expense. Stipulated that factors to be considered in determining whether a specific accommodation would impose an undue hardship included:

(1) The nature and cost of the accommodation needed;

(2) The overall financial resources of the facility or facilities involved in the accommodation, the number of people employed at the facility, and the effect of expenses and resources or other impact of the accommodation on the facility's operation;

(3) The overall financial resources of the covered entity and its size, including number of employees and number, type and location of its facilities; and

(4) The type of operation or operations of the covered entity, including the composition, structure and functions of its work force, geographic separateness, and administrative or fiscal relationship of the facility or facilities to the covered entity.

• **Medical Examinations.** Prohibited employers from requiring medical examinations or asking job applicants whether they had a disability, although employers could make pre-employment inquiries into the ability of an applicant to perform job-related functions and could conduct voluntary medical examinations that were part of an employee health program.

• Permitted employers to require medical examinations after making a job offer but before the applicant began work and allowed them to condition the offer on the examination results, but only if all entering employees were subjected to such examinations and they were job-related and consistent with business necessity.

• Required information collected as a result of such examinations to be kept confidential and separate from other personnel information, except that supervisors and managers could be informed regarding necessary restrictions on the work or duties or necessary accommodations for the employee.

• Stipulated that tests to determine illegal drug use were not considered medical examinations, although it stated that "nothing in this title shall be construed to encourage, prohibit or authorize the conducting of drug testing for the illegal use of drugs by job applicants or employees or making employment decisions based on such test results."

The act also specifically reserved the right of the Department of Transportation to test employees in safety-sensitive positions both for illegal drug use and impairment by alcohol and to remove those who tested positive from such jobs.

• **Coverage Phase-In.** For the first two years following the effective date of the employment section, defined "employer" as a person in an industry affecting commerce who had 25 or more employees for each working day in each of 20 or more calendar weeks in the current or preceding calendar year. After two years, employers with 15 or more employees would be covered.

• **Exempted Employers.** Exempted as "employers" the U.S. government, corporations wholly owned by the U.S. government or by an Indian tribe, and bona fide private membership clubs (other than labor organizations) exempted from federal taxation under Section 501(c) of the Internal Revenue Code of 1986. (Federal agencies and those receiving federal financial assistance were already prohibited from discriminating against those with disabilities by Sections 501 and 504 of the 1973 Rehabilitation Act (PL 93-112). Congressional coverage was addressed in Title V of the act.)

• **Defenses.** Permitted an employer accused of discriminatory qualification standards, tests or other selection criteria to use as a defense that such standards — including the requirement that an individual not pose a direct threat to the health or safety of others in the work place — were job-related and consistent with business necessity and that no reasonable accommodation was possible.

• Specifically permitted a religious corporation, association, educational institution or society to give employment preference to individuals of a particular religion to perform work connected with its activities. Also permitted a religious organization to require that all job applicants and employees conform to its religious tenets.

• Communicable Diseases. Required the HHS secretary, within six months of enactment, to review all infections and communicable diseases that could be transmitted through food handling, publish a list of diseases the secretary determined were transmissible through the food supply and "widely disseminate" the list of diseases and their modes of transmission to the public. The secretary would be required to update the list annually.

• Permitted employers to refuse to assign or continue to assign to a job involving food handling an individual with a disease on the list for which risk of transmission could not be eliminated by reasonable accommodation.

• Stipulated that language relating to food handling not be construed to "pre-empt, modify or amend" any state or local law, ordinance or regulation regarding food handling designed to protect the public health from individuals who posed a significant health or safety risk that could not be eliminated by reasonable accommodation.

• Drug, Alcohol Use. Permitted employers to prohibit the use of alcohol or illegal drugs at the work place by all employees, to require that employees not be under the influence of alcohol or illegal drugs at the work place, and to require that employees conform to the Drug-Free Work Place Act of 1988 (PL 100-690). *(Anti-drug bill, Congress and the Nation Vol. VII, p. 748)*

Public Services

• Definitions. Defined as a "public entity" any state or local government; any department, agency or other instrumentality of a state or states or local government; Amtrak; and any commuter rail authority (as defined in the 1970 Rail Passenger Service Act (PL 91-518)).

Defined "qualified individual with a disability" as one who, with or without reasonable modifications to rules, policies and practices, the removal of architectural, communication and transportation barriers, or the provision of auxiliary aids and services, met the essential eligibility requirements for the receipt of services or participation in programs or activities provided by a public entity.

• Prohibited Activities. Prohibited a qualified person with a disability from being excluded from or denied the benefits of the services, programs or activities of a public entity or from being subjected to discrimination by any such entity.

• New Vehicles. Provided that beginning 30 days after enactment, all new fixed-route buses, rapid- or light-rail vehicles or other vehicles purchased or leased or solicited for public transportation must be "readily accessible to and usable by" individuals with disabilities, including those who used wheelchairs.

• Used Vehicles. Provided that beginning 30 days after enactment, public entities purchasing or leasing used vehicles for public transportation must make "demonstrated good-faith efforts" to purchase vehicles that were readily accessible to and usable by disabled individuals, including those who used wheelchairs.

• Remanufactured Vehicles. Provided that beginning 30 days after enactment, if a public entity remanufactured a vehicle or purchased or leased a remanufactured vehicle for public transportation so as to extend its usable life for five years or more, that vehicle, to the maximum extent feasible, must be readily accessible to and usable by disabled individuals, including those who used wheelchairs.

• Historic Vehicles. Provided an exception for historic vehicles used solely on segments of a fixed-route system included on the National Register of Historic Places, if making such a vehicle accessible would "significantly alter the historic character of such vehicle." In that case, only modifications that did not significantly alter the historic character of the vehicle would be required.

• Paratransit. Provided that, if a public entity operated a fixed-route public transportation system (other than a system providing commuter bus service only), it also had to provide paratransit or other special transportation services to individuals with disabilities, including those using wheelchairs, who otherwise could not use fixed-route systems. (Paratransit was transportation for those unable to board, ride or exit from regular buses. Such service would have to provide a level of services comparable to that of the fixed-route system.) Response time would have to be comparable only to the extent practicable.

• New Facilities. Required that new facilities to provide designated public transportation services be readily accessible to and usable by those with disabilities, including those who used wheelchairs.

• Alterations of Existing Facilities. Provided that facilities or any part thereof used for public transportation that were altered by, on behalf of or for the use of a public entity in a manner that affected or could affect their usability must, to the maximum extent feasible, be made readily accessible to and usable by those with disabilities, including those who used wheelchairs.

• One Car Per Train Rule. Required, as soon as was practicable but no later than five years after enactment, that at least one car on every train with two or more cars in light- and rapid-rail systems be accessible to those with disabilities, including those who use wheelchairs. A special rule applied to historic trains similar to that for historic vehicles.

• Required, as soon as practicable but no later than five years after enactment, that at least one car on every Amtrak train be accessible to those with disabilities, including those who used wheelchairs. The same requirement was applied to commuter rail cars.

• New Intercity Cars. Generally required, as for other categories of train cars, that new Amtrak cars purchased or leased beginning 30 days after enactment be fully accessible. However, special rules applied for different categories of cars.

• Alterations of Existing Facilities. Provided that facilities or any part of them used for public transportation that were altered in a manner that affected or could affect their usability must, to the maximum extent feasible, be made readily accessible to and usable by those with disabilities, including those who used wheelchairs.

Public Accommodations

• Definitions. Defined as "public accommodations" the following: (1) privately operated entities whose operations affected commerce, including inns, hotels, motels or other places of lodging (exempting establishments located within an owner-occupied residence and containing no more than five rooms for rent or hire); (2) restaurants, bars or other establishments serving food or drink; (3) movie theaters, other theaters, concert halls, stadiums or other places of exhibition or entertainment; (4) auditoriums, convention centers, lecture halls or other places of public gathering; (5) retail sales establishments, including bakeries, grocery stores, clothing stores, hardware stores and shopping centers; (6) service establishments, including laundromats, dry cleaners, banks, barber shops, beauty shops, travel services, shoe repair services, funeral parlors, gas stations, accountants' or lawyers' offices, pharmacies, insurance offices, doctors' and other health providers' offices and hospitals; (7) terminals, depots or other stations used for specified public transportation; (8) museums, libraries, galleries and other places of public display or collection; (9) parks, zoos, amusement parks or other places of recreation; (10) schools of all levels; (11) social service centers, including day-care and senior citizen centers, homeless shelters, food banks and adoption agencies; and (12) places of exercise or recreation, including gyms, health spas, bowling alleys and golf courses.

• Defined "specified public transportation" as transportation by bus, rail or any other conveyance (other than airplanes) that provided the public with general or special service (including charter service) on a regular and continuing basis. Stipulated that "vehicle" not include rail passenger cars, locomotives, freight cars, cabooses, or cars otherwise referred to in the Public Services section of the law.

• Defined "readily achievable" to mean easy to accomplish and able to be carried out without much difficulty or expense.

• **General Prohibitions.** Generally forbade discrimination on the basis of disability in the full and equal enjoyment of goods, services, facilities, privileges, advantages and accommodations of any place of public accommodation by any person who owned, leased (or leased to) or operated a place of public accommodation.

• Deemed discriminatory: (1) Direct discrimination against an individual or class of individuals on the basis of disability or through contractual, licensing or other arrangements (although covered entities were only liable in contractual arrangements for discrimination against the entity's own customers and clients and not the contractor's customers and clients); (2) Providing opportunities not equal to those afforded other individuals; and (3) Providing a good, service, facility, privilege, advantage or accommodation that was different or separate from that provided to other individuals, unless such action was necessary to provide an opportunity as effective as that provided to others.

• Required that goods, facilities, privileges, advantages, accommodations and services be provided in the most integrated setting appropriate to the needs of the individual.

• Notwithstanding the existence of separate or different programs or activities, required that individuals with disabilities not be denied the opportunity to participate in programs or activities not separate or different.

• Forbade the use, directly or through contracts or other arrangements, of standards or criteria or methods of administration that discriminated on the basis of disability or that perpetuated the discrimination of others who were subject to common administrative control.

• Also defined as discriminatory the exclusion or other denial of equal goods, services, facilities, privileges, advantages and accommodations or other opportunities to an individual or entity because of the known disability of an individual with whom the individual or entity was known to have had a relationship or association.

• **Transportation.** Beginning 30 days after enactment, defined as discriminatory the failure of a private entity that provided public transportation, but not as a primary business activity (such as a hotel that operated an airport shuttle), to purchase or lease new vehicles with a seating capacity of more than 16 passengers that were not fully accessible to those with disabilities, including those who used wheelchairs. Such an entity could purchase or lease inaccessible vehicles, however, if its overall transportation system provided a level of service to individuals with disabilities equivalent to that provided to persons without disabilities.

• **Health or Safety.** Stipulated that nothing in the act required an entity to permit an individual to participate in or benefit from the goods, services, facilities, privileges, advantages and accommodations of that entity if the individual would pose a direct threat to the health or safety of others. Direct threat was defined as posing "a significant risk to the health or safety of others that cannot be eliminated by a modification of policies, practices, or procedures or by the provisions of auxiliary aids or services."

• **New Construction.** Deemed discriminatory the failure to design or construct facilities for first occupancy later than 30 months following the date of enactment that were not readily accessible to and usable by individuals with disabilities, except where an entity could demonstrate that it was structurally impracticable to meet the requirements of standards set forth in regulations to put the act into effect.

• **Alterations of Existing Facilities.** Required that alterations to a facility or any part of it "to the maximum extent feasible" render the facility readily accessible to and usable by individuals with disabilities, including those who used wheelchairs. Where an entity was altering an area of the facility containing a primary function, such as the ticket counter of a bus terminal, it required the entity to make the alterations so that, to the maximum extent feasible, the path of travel to the altered area and the bathrooms, telephones and drinking fountains serving the remodeled area were readily accessible to and usable by individuals with disabilities.

• **Elevators.** Specified that the bill did not generally require that elevators be installed in facilities of fewer than three stories or less than 3,000 square feet per story. Elevators, however, would be required in buildings to be used as shopping centers, shopping malls or as professional offices of health care providers. The attorney general also could determine that elevators were needed in otherwise excluded buildings based on the type and amount of usage the facility received.

• **Privately Owned Public Transportation Systems.** Generally barred discrimination on the basis of disability in the full and equal enjoyment of public transportation services provided by private entities primarily engaged in the business of transporting people (except by air) and whose operations affected commerce.

• **Exemptions, Private Clubs and Religious Organizations.** Exempted from the requirements of the public accommodations section private clubs or establishments exempt under Title II of the 1964 Civil Rights Act as well as religious organizations or entities controlled by religious organizations.

• **Enforcement.** Provided that the same remedies and procedures set forth in the 1964 Civil Rights Act (preventive relief, including an application for a permanent or temporary injunction; restraining order or other order; and attorneys' fees) were the same remedies and procedures available to any person who was being discriminated against on the basis of disability.

• With respect to violations pertaining to removing barriers in existing facilities, altering existing facilities and undertaking new construction, provided that remedies should include an order to alter facilities to make them readily accessible to and usable by individuals with disabilities.

• **Attorney General's Powers.** Required the attorney general to investigate alleged violations of the public accommodations provisions, including periodically reviewing compliance by covered entities.

• Permitted state and local governments to apply to the attorney general to certify that building codes met or exceeded minimum requirements for accessibility to and usability of covered facilities by persons with disabilities. Specified that such certification could be used as a "rebuttable presumption" that the codes met the requirements of the act at any enforcement proceeding.

• Authorized the attorney general to file a civil suit in U.S. District Court if he "has reasonable cause to believe that any person or group of persons is engaged in a pattern or practice of discrimination under this title" or that any person or group of persons had been discriminated against and that such discrimination raised an issue of general public importance.

• Authorized the court in such civil suits to grant temporary, preliminary or permanent relief, including requiring the provision of an auxiliary aid or service, modification of policy, practice, procedure or alternative method, or that facilities be made readily accessible to and usable by individuals with disabilities.

• Authorized the award of other relief as the court considered appropriate, including monetary damages to aggrieved persons when such damages were requested by the attorney general, as well as civil fines "to vindicate the public interest." Such fines could not exceed $50,000 for a first violation and $100,000 for any subsequent violation.

Stipulated that in "pattern or practice" cases, all violations included in an attorney general suit counted as a single first violation in assessing the maximum civil penalty, and that the $100,000 fine could only be applied in a subsequent case. Also specified that the terms "monetary damages" and "such other relief" did not include punitive damages.

• In determining civil penalties, required the court to give consideration to any good-faith effort or attempt to comply with the requirements of the Public Accommodations section of the law by the entity in question. In evaluating "good faith," required the court to consider, among other factors it deemed relevant, whether the entity could have reasonably anticipated that an appropriate type of auxiliary aid would have been needed to accommodate the unique needs of a particular individual with a disability.

• **Examinations and Courses.** Required that examinations or courses related to applications, licensing, certification or issuing credentials for secondary or postsecondary education, professional or trade purposes be offered in a place and manner accessible to those with disabilities or that alternative accessible arrangements for such individuals be made.

Telecommunications Relays

• **Services Required.** Amended the Communications Act of 1934 to require the Federal Communications Commission to ensure that interstate and intrastate telecommunications relay services were available, "to the extent possible and in the most efficient manner" to hearing- and speech-impaired individuals.

• Required each common carrier providing telephone voice transmission services to provide telecommunications relay services within the area in which it offered service. Such services would have to be provided either individually, through designees, through a competitively selected vendor or with other carriers within three years after enactment.

• **Closed-Captioning of Public Service Announcements.** Required that television public service announcements funded in whole or part by the federal government be closed-captioned for the hearing-impaired.

Miscellaneous

• **Congressional Coverage — Senate.** Reaffirmed the Senate's commitment to Rule XLII, which barred discrimination in employment on the basis of "race, color, religion, sex, national origin, age, or state of physical handicap."

Generally provided that the rights and protections provided pursuant to the ADA, the Civil Rights Act of 1990 (S 2104), the Civil Rights Act of 1964, the Age Discrimination in Employment Act of 1967 (PL 90-202) and the Rehabilitation Act of 1973 should apply to employees of the Senate. Provided, however, that claims of discrimination be investigated and adjudicated exclusively by the Select Committee on Ethics or other entity the Senate designated. *(1967 law, Congress and the Nation Vol. II, p. 620)*

• **Congressional Coverage — House.** Provided that employment protections provided under the act be available to employees of the House of Representatives or any employing authority of the House and that complaints be handled by the Fair Employment Practices Board as approved Jan. 3, 1989, in H Res 15 of the 101st Congress. Provided that the Architect of the Capitol establish remedies and procedures for matters not related to employment (primarily public accommodations).

Such remedies and procedures were to be effective on their approval by the Speaker of the House, after consultation with the House Office Building Commission.

• **Congressional Coverage — Instrumentalities of Congress.** Provided that the ADA applied to each instrumentality of Congress, which included the Architect of the Capitol, Congressional Budget Office, General Accounting Office, Government Printing Office, Library of Congress, Office of Technology Assessment and U.S. Botanic Garden.

• **Opportunity to Decline.** Stipulated that nothing in the act required an individual with a disability to accept an accommodation, aid, service, opportunity or benefit.

• **State Immunity.** Provided that a state was not immune under the 11th Amendment to the Constitution from an action in federal court or a state court of competent jurisdiction for a violation of the act. (The 11th Amendment generally prevented states from being sued in federal courts.) Provided that the same remedies were available for a violation committed by a state as would be available in an action against any other public or private entity.

• **'Whistleblower' Protection.** Prohibited discrimination against any individual because that person had opposed any act or practice outlawed by the act or because that person had made a charge, testified, assisted or participated in any manner in an investigation, proceeding or hearing under the act.

• **Interference or Coercion.** Made it unlawful to coerce, intimidate threaten or interfere with any person "in the exercise and enjoyment of, or on account of his or her having exercised or enjoyed, or on account of his or her having aided or encouraged any other individual in the exercise or enjoyment of, any right granted or protected" by the act.

- **Architectural and Transportation Barriers Compliance Board.** Within nine months of enactment, required that the Architectural and Transportation Barriers Compliance Board issue minimum guidelines to supplement the existing Minimum Guidelines and Requirement for Accessible Design. Required the guidelines to establish additional requirements to ensure that buildings, facilities, vehicles and rail passenger cars were accessible in architecture and design, transportation and communication to individuals with disabilities.
- **Historic Buildings.** Required that, for alterations of buildings or facilities eligible for listing in the National Register of Historic Places or designated as historic under state or local law, the minimum guidelines established procedures at least equivalent to those established by applicable sections of the Uniform Federal Accessibility Standards.
- **Attorneys' Fees.** Authorized the awarding of "a reasonable attorney's fee," including litigation expenses and costs, to the prevailing party (other than the United States) in any action or administrative proceeding under the act.
- **Wilderness Areas.** Required the National Council on Disability to study and report within one year the effect that wilderness designations and wilderness land management practices had on the ability of people with disabilities to use and enjoy the National Wilderness Preservation System.
- Reaffirmed that Congress did not intend that the 1964 Wilderness Act (PL 88-577) be construed as prohibiting the use of a wheelchair in a wilderness area by someone whose disability required its use and that, consistent with the Wilderness Act, no agency was required to provide special treatment or accommodation or to construct facilities or modify conditions of lands within a wilderness area to facilitate such use.
- **Illegal Use of Drugs.** Specified that for both the ADA and the Rehabilitation Act of 1973, the term "individual with a disability" did not include an individual who was currently using illegal drugs if the covered entity acted on the basis of such use.
- Permitted covered entities to adopt or administer "reasonable policies or procedures," including but not limited to drug testing, designed to ensure that a former user of illegal drugs was no longer engaged in such use.
- Required that individuals not be denied health services or services provided in connection with drug rehabilitation on the basis of current illegal use of drugs if the individual was otherwise entitled to such services.
- **Severability Provision.** Stipulated that if any provision of the act was held unconstitutional, it should be severed from the rest of the act and not affect the enforceability of the remaining provisions.

Immigration Reform

Congress in 1990 cleared the most sweeping revision of legal immigration laws in a quarter century, moving to admit more immigrants — especially those with education and skills needed in the United States.

The legislation (S 358 — PL 101-649), several years in the making, comprehensively revised the country's 1965 visa-allotment system, which stressed family reunifications and tended to favor immigrants from Latin America and Asia.

The new law, which took effect Oct. 1, 1991, allowed legal immigration to climb from about 500,000 people to about 700,000 during each of the first three years of the act. After that, a permanent level of 675,000 people was put in place. A category of "diversity" visas was created primarily for Europeans and others adversely affected by the 1965 law. The measure also included an 18-month stay of deportation for people from El Salvador living illegally in the United States. And it made excluding foreigners because of their political beliefs more difficult.

In the two years Congress worked on the legislation, a variety of interests had to be reconciled. While all sides agreed that the system needed an overhaul, opinions differed over how that should be accomplished and how to balance the country's economic needs with its tradition of compassion. The business community wanted flexibility to move personnel in and out of the country with ease; Asian and Hispanic groups were concerned that any change not hamper their efforts to bring relatives to the United States; and the Federation for American Immigration Reform (FAIR) wanted tighter restrictions on all forms of immigration.

The Senate had approved its version of the visa overhaul in July 1989, but the House did not act until 1990, passing a more sweeping measure than the Senate. Sen. Alan K. Simpson, R-Wyo., one of the leading congressional experts on immigration, threatened to kill the legislation unless the House scaled back its generous visa allotment. He also wanted provisions for increased border protections to stem the tide of illegal immigration. Only after extensive negotiations among House and Senate conferees and the White House was a final deal brokered in October.

The key to the compromise was finding a middle ground on the immigration levels. The final bill essentially split the difference between a House-approved level of about 800,000 individuals per year and the Senate's figure of 630,000.

Background

Congress undertook revision of the 1965 legal immigration statutes after spending half a decade in the 1980s transforming the illegal immigration laws. The 1986 Immigration Reform and Control Act (PL 99-603) gave millions of illegal aliens amnesty and instituted sanctions for employers who hire undocumented workers. *(1986 law, Congress and the Nation Vol. VII, p. 717)*

Although members of Congress disagreed over the approach, a consensus existed that the system of legal immigration was too rigid and needed to be more open to immigrants from nations shortchanged by the existing law. Until 1965, immigration policy was based on nationality and reflected narrow attitudes toward race and national origin. Then Congress repealed the country-based quotas and replaced them with a system based primarily on reuniting families and allowing in immigrants with needed skills. The result, however, was a new lopsidedness. In 1965, more than one-third of those admitted were from Europe and only 7 percent were from Asia. By 1990, 85 percent of all immigration came from two areas of the globe, Latin America and Asia.

Under the existing law, only immediate relatives (spouses, minor children and parents) of U.S. citizens were not subject to annual limits on the number of visas. And the visa-allotment system heavily emphasized family unification, reserving most visas for immediate relatives of U.S. citizens and permanent residents.

Many in Congress were frustrated by the system's unintended exclusion of immigrants from "old seed" European countries and by its failure to respond to U.S. labor shortages. Even people who readily qualified for visas spent years on waiting lists, and members of Congress wanted to help clear out backlogs — particularly for spouses and unmarried children of permanent residents, and adult brothers and sisters of U.S. citizens and permanent residents.

And members agreed generally that a new "independent" category of visas was needed for immigrants who had special skills in a particular field, education or knowledge of English.

Sen. Edward M. Kennedy, D-Mass., and Simpson pushed an ambitious legal immigration bill through the Senate in 1988, but it was stymied in the House. Instead, Congress cleared a stopgap measure (PL 100-658) that gave a one-year visa extension to foreign nurses working in the United States and created a means for more Irish citizens to immigrate — a special concern of Kennedy, who had a large Irish-American constituency. *(1988 action, Congress and the Nation Vol. VII, p. 781)*

Senate Action

For the second year in a row, the Senate in 1989 passed legislation overhauling the visa-allocation system to permit more immigration from Europe. The Judiciary Committee approved S 358 by a 12-2 vote June 8 and reported it (S Rept 101-55) on June 19. The bill put the first-ever overall cap on legal immigration to the United States. It was set at 600,000.

The measure created a new category for 54,000 independent immigrants who had skills needed in the United States but did not have employers ready to sponsor them.

The most controversial issue was whether to give points to potential immigrants for their fluency in English. After heated debate during which several senators said members of their own families might not have been able to immigrate because they could not speak English, the committee agreed to drop the provision.

S 358 was passed by the full Senate, 81-17 on July 13, after three days of floor debate and the adoption of several important amendments. Among the biggest changes were a stay of deportation for close family members of illegal aliens granted amnesty under the 1986 immigration law; a halt to direct federal benefits for illegal aliens; and a prohibition against including illegal aliens in the 1990 census figures that would be used for legislative reapportionment.

Also approved were a further increase in visas for professional and skilled workers; a provision ensuring that the number of visas granted to the extended family of U.S. citizens would not drop below the existing level; special sanctuary provisions for Chinese students currently in the United States; and the addition of extra visas for residents of Hong Kong. Concern about the Chinese crackdown in June 1989 against pro-democracy forces was evident throughout the debate.

The Hong Kong amendment, offered by Paul Simon, D-Ill., increased the U.S. quota for immigrants from that offshore colony to 10,000 per year, from 5,000. Even before the Chinese government crushed the student-led protests, Hong Kong residents had been scrambling for safe haven in foreign countries out of fear of what might happen when Beijing assumed control of Hong Kong in 1997. Britain,

AIDS Exclusion Policy

Under authority granted in 1990 immigration reform legislation (S 358 — PL 101-649), Health and Human Services (HHS) Secretary Louis W. Sullivan disclosed Jan. 3, 1991, that HIV (human immunodeficiency virus), which causes AIDS (acquired immune deficiency syndrome), would be removed from the list of sicknesses that could keep someone from entering the United States, effective June 1, 1991. The AIDS exclusion policy had been instituted in 1987, as part of a supplemental appropriations bill (PL 100-71). Sen. Jesse Helms, R-N.C., had undertaken the effort.

The 1952 McCarran-Walter Act (PL 82-414) prohibited the entry into the United States of individuals who fell into 33 categories. Its exclusions based on political ideology had raised protests over the years and brought some revisions of the law. The HHS secretary normally specified by regulation which diseases were grounds for exclusion. HIV infection was the only one set by law.

A person with the HIV virus could apply for a waiver to enter the United States, the same as any individual ineligible under the exclusions of the McCarran-Walter Act. The government sought to ease the procedure to avert potential embarrassment for the United States as San Francisco prepared to host a major worldwide conference on AIDS in June 1990. Some countries and international groups recommended boycotting the meeting to protest the U.S. policy.

In February 1990, the Immigration and Naturalization Service (INS) and the State Department issued guidelines to deal with the large number of foreign HIV-infected visitors expected to attend the conference. If an applicant objected to having the visa and waiver notation placed in his or her passport, consular officers would stamp the visa and note the waiver on a separate sheet that would be attached to the passport. The proposed streamlined process caused a clamor, however. In response, the INS in April announced creation of a special, 10-day visa that could be used to attend the conference. Those applying for the visa would not have to say whether they were HIV-positive.

HR 4506 called for the HHS secretary to review whether HIV should be on the list of excludable diseases. The House Energy and Commerce Health Subcommittee held a hearing on the legislation June 27, but it went no further. The language of HR 4506 subsequently was attached to the immigration reform bill.

which administered the territory, was limiting the number of Hong Kong émigrés it would accept.

The core of S 358 instituted a new overall level of 630,000 visas and a two-tiered system of allocating them: 480,000 visas for family immigration and 150,000 for the new independent category. Within the 480,000 family cap, the legislation, like the existing law, permitted unrestricted admission of immediate family members of U.S. citizens: spouses, minor children and parents.

The bill increased the number of family-preference visas for other relatives to 260,000, from 216,000. Because no limit was set on immediate-family visas, some senators feared that, with a rigid cap, increases in immigration by such people would begin to eat up the visas available for other relatives. Orrin G. Hatch, R-Utah, and Dennis DeConcini, D-Ariz., offered an amendment to ensure that family-preference visas fell no lower than their existing 216,000 level. It was adopted 62-36 on July 12.

Simpson tried to re-insert a provision giving points to potential immigrants for fluency in English, but his amendment was rejected on July 13, 43-56.

The legislation also established up to 4,800 conditional-entry visas for foreign investors who could put up at least $1 million in new capital and generate employment for at least 10 U.S. citizens or legal residents.

House Action

The full House did not act on immigration legislation in 1989, but its Judiciary Subcommittee on Immigration, Refugees and International Law did begin hearings in September with the intention of taking up HR 4300 in 1990. Action was slowed, however, by differences among subcommittee members and by competing demands on the time of the subcommittee chairman, Bruce A. Morrison, D-Conn., who was in a campaign (ultimately unsuccessful) to be elected governor of Connecticut.

The subcommittee finally got to work in the spring and approved a bill in April, sending it to the full committee by a 6-4 vote. The measure increased the number of visas allowed for family members, workers and foreigners who met criteria of a new "diversity" classification. That category was intended to ensure a broader mix of immigrants, increasing, as the Senate bill did, the number of Europeans who could get visas.

Overall, HR 4300 raised the prospect of doubling U.S. visa quotas, because it removed or increased numerical limits on a host of categories. For example, an unlimited number of spouses and minor children of permanent U.S. residents would be admitted, compared with the 70,200 visas being granted annually to those groups.

The subcommittee's bill was such a departure from current law that it looked as though it would be impossible to get full committee approval or to reconcile it with the Senate bill. But Kennedy, the main sponsor of S 358, elicited a promise from House Judiciary Chairman Jack Brooks, D-Texas, that the committee would consider the bill in time for passage in 1990. And Brooks, who wanted a more modest proposal, persuaded Morrison to scale back HR 4300. That paved the way for the full committee to approve the bill on Aug. 1, 1990. The vote was 23-12 and came after two days of debate.

The committee's version, like the Senate's legislation, placed a new emphasis on immigrants' skills and talents. But the House bill called for admitting an estimated 800,000 foreigners a year, in contrast to the 630,000 visas envisioned under the Senate measure and the existing number of about 500,000.

House Judiciary reported HR 4300 (H Rept 101-723, Part I) on Sept. 19. House Ways and Means, which shared jurisdiction, reported the bill (H Rept 101-723, Part II) on Sept. 25.

After turning back efforts to water down or gut the legislation, the House Oct. 3 on a **key vote of 231-192 (R 45-127; D 186-65)** passed HR 4300. The vote followed two days of debate and one major change from the committee-approved bill. *(1990 key votes, p. 1039)*

While a number of amendments were accepted by voice vote on the floor, the most significant change in the committee's bill was the addition of a three-year stay of deportation for illegal immigrants from four war-torn countries — El Salvador, Lebanon, Liberia and Kuwait. The provision was added by the House Rules Committee, whose chairman, Joe Moakley, D-Mass., long had sought to suspend deportation for certain Central Americans. The Rules Committee allowed a vote on an amendment to strike the provision. It was offered by Bill McCollum, R-Fla., Oct. 2 and was defeated, 131-285.

One of the most controversial sections of HR 4300 was deleted by the House Rules Committee, at the request of the Ways and Means Committee: the head tax on employers who brought in foreign workers. Money from the tax would have gone to a training fund for domestic workers.

The Ways and Means panel called the fee a revenue measure that was within its jurisdiction. The Rules Committee concurred.

While the bill was intended to increase the number of trained immigrants, House authors tried to make sure that U.S. workers were not displaced. Employers who wanted to bring in foreigners would have to certify that there was a shortage of domestic workers in the specific field.

An amendment to limit total immigration to 630,000, the same as the Senate bill and favored by the White House, was rejected 143-266 on Oct. 2.

After passing HR 4300 on Oct. 3, the House laid that bill on the table and passed in lieu, by voice vote, S 358, with the language of HR 4300.

Conference Action

House-Senate conferees and the administration reached agreement on the complex S 358 Oct. 24 as lawmakers were struggling toward adjournment. Prior to the agreement, Simpson had presented House and Senate leaders with a list of demands, but he said that, while he had let bills die before, he wanted to see this legislation pass if at all possible. He was most adamant about having some kind of immigration ceiling so U.S. authorities would know each year the number of immigrants the country had to absorb. He also wanted greater efforts to curb illegal immigration. Three of Simpson's Republican colleagues, Hatch, Arlen Specter, Pa., and Rudy Boschwitz, Minn., took the unusual step of writing Senate and House Immigration subcommittee members urging a compromise, specifically to split the difference on the overall immigration level.

Conferees agreed to do just that, setting a cap of 700,000 for the first three years of the act and then reducing it to 675,000. Of the total, 520,000 visas would be reserved in the first three years for people with relatives in the United States. In fiscal 1996, that total would be scaled back to a permanent 480,000 visas.

The other large family category involved visas for siblings of U.S. citizens and for the spouses, parents and minor children of people who were legal permanent residents. Under the existing law, 216,000 visas were being allocated in the so-called family-preference system. The bill called for a guaranteed 226,000 visas annually for these relatives.

The number of visas for immigrant workers also increased, with 40,000 going to workers with "extraordinary abilities," managers and university professors. Another 40,000 were allotted to workers with high abilities and advanced degrees, and 30,000 to skilled workers. The rest of the job visas were set aside for unskilled workers (10,000), foreign investors (10,000) and "special" immigrants, such as ministers (10,000).

A new "independent" or "diversity" visa was created, mainly for people from countries disadvantaged under existing immigration law. To be eligible, an immigrant would have to have a high school diploma or its equivalent, or one year of experience in an occupation that required at least two years of experience or training.

Hong Kong was one of the few homelands that got special treatment under the compromise bill. The provisions were adopted mostly because of fears associated with the Chinese government's planned 1997 takeover of that British colony. Under the existing law, Hong Kong nationals received 5,000 visas. The compromise bill raised that to 10,000 over the first three years of the bill, then increased the quota to 20,000.

One key provision in the bill related to the 1986 illegal-immigration law. It allowed a stay of deportation and work authorization for spouses and minor children of legalized aliens who had been in the United States since May 1988.

And another provision, the 18-month stay of deportation for people living in the United States illegally, was one of the last to be resolved by House and Senate conferees. It pitted Rules Committee Chairman Moakley against lead Senate negotiators Kennedy and Simpson.

Kennedy and Simpson argued against singling out one country for special treatment. Opponents also contended that people who had come to the United States illegally should not be rewarded and that some of the Salvadorans had emigrated for economic, not political, reasons. But Moakley, who had been trying since the 98th Congress to win a stay of deportation for the Salvadorans, noted that he had been willing in other years to back off in the interests of whatever immigration bill was on the table. This year, he said, he was not going to budge. Eventually, Kennedy and Simpson did.

The conferees also approved a new procedure for temporary stays of deportation for people fleeing armed conflict or natural disasters. The attorney general would have discretion to grant such stays.

The Senate adopted the conference report (H Rept 101-955) 89-8 about 10 p.m. Oct. 26. Sponsors thought the measure was headed toward swift approval in the House. But California Democrats Edward R. Roybal and Esteban E. Torres and other Hispanics, unhappy about a Simpson proposal to develop a forgery-proof driver's license, persuaded colleagues to vote against the rule for the bill. They contended that the proposal was a first step toward a national identification card.

House sponsors spent the next several hours scrambling for a way to rescue the bill, finally calling Simpson, who surprised them and agreed to drop the pilot project. He said it had become so diluted in conference negotiations that it was not what he had wanted in the first place.

By voice vote Oct. 27, the Senate and House agreed to drop the license pilot project, and the House then adopted the conference report 264-118.

President Bush signed the bill Nov. 29.

Chinese Student Visas

Congress in 1989 cleared legislation (HR 2712) to allow Chinese students in the United States at the time of the Chinese government's June crackdown on pro-democracy forces to seek permanent residency in the United States without returning home first. But President Bush vetoed the bill, and the Senate sustained his veto early in 1990.

Bush won the veto showdown in the Senate only after intensive personal lobbying that cast the issue as one of presidential power and partisan strength. Democrats accused Bush of "kowtowing" to the Chinese government, which had threatened to cut off all future student exchanges if HR 2712 became law.

Bush said he had already used his executive powers to give the Chinese students all the protections offered by the legislation. None would be deported against his or her will, he said. His veto was a response to threats by the Chinese government that it would permanently pull out of the Fulbright scholarship program and other educational exchanges if HR 2712 became law.

Bush vetoed the measure on Nov. 30, after Congress had adjourned. Although he said his action was a pocket veto, not subject to override, he returned the bill to Capitol Hill. Congress, which did not acknowledge the president's power to pocket-veto legislation between sessions of the same Congress, treated it as an ordinary veto. *(Presidential vetoes, p. 927)*

Although estimates varied, it was generally believed that about 40,000 Chinese students were in the United States when the Chinese government sent its army into Tiananmen Square in Beijing June 3-4, 1989, to crush the pro-democracy movement that had blossomed throughout China during the spring.

Many of those students had participated in demonstrations in the United States supporting their peers back home, who were at the forefront of the democracy forces. After the Beijing government began rounding up and jailing students and other leaders of the peaceful revolt, those in the United States feared for their safety if they were forced to return home when their visas expired.

An estimated 32,000 of the 40,000 Chinese students in the United States were holders of "J" visas, which required them to return home for at least two years before they could seek permanent resident status in the United States. The "J" status was established to alleviate the "brain drain" suffered by other nations when their students gained an education in the United States and then refused to go home.

The House Judiciary Committee reported HR 2712 (H Rept 101-196) on July 28, 1989. The House passed the bill by voice vote under suspension of the rules July 31. The Senate passed the bill by voice vote Aug. 4, but only after adopting an amendment related to China's coercive population control policies that the House refused to accept. But at a conference in November, the chambers reached a compromise that required the Justice Department to give "careful consideration" to all applications by Chinese nationals fearing persecution if they returned home because of the country's "one couple, one child" policy.

The House adopted the conference report (H Rept 101-370) on a 403-0 vote Nov. 19. The Senate acted by voice vote the next day. Bush vetoed the measure Nov. 30.

The House veto override was virtually a foregone conclusion, but in the Senate, where Democrats had only a 10-vote margin, Bush and Secretary of State James A. Baker III worked the phones personally to persuade Republicans to stick with the president. Their efforts paid off in the final vote, which had been cast in partisan terms. Minority Leader Bob Dole, Kan., asserted that the vote was "not about China policy. It's American politics."

The House voted 390-25 on Jan. 24, 1990, to override the veto, but the Senate sustained Bush's action Jan. 25, on a **62-37 (R 8-37; D 54-0) key vote.** That was four votes short of the two-thirds majority needed to override the veto. *(1990 key votes, p. 1039)*

Refugee Asylum

Congress and the Bush administration clashed repeatedly in 1989 over U.S. policy on the admission of refugees and those seeking political asylum. But the disputes remained unresolved.

The year began with thousands of Central Americans flooding across the U.S.-Mexican border and seeking asylum in the United States. It ended with President Bush's veto of a bill (HR 2712) to guarantee Chinese students safe haven in the United States following the June crackdown by their government on pro-democracy demonstrators. *(Chinese students, p. 755)*

In between, there were disputes over the fate of Salvadorans already in the United States illegally and on the admission of Soviet Jews and Evangelicals, previously assumed to be refugees.

Background. As 1989 began, thousands of Central Americans were pouring across the border at Brownsville, in southeast Texas. Several factors contributed to the crush, including continuing deterioration of the Nicaraguan economy, an upswing in violence in El Salvador and policy changes by the Immigration and Naturalization Service (INS). Members of the Texas and Florida congressional delegations soon were pressing the federal government for emergency aid to help their states deal with the new influx.

Half of the newcomers were Nicaraguans. Most made their way to Miami, where more than 100,000 of their countrymen had settled over the preceding decade. Miami officials warned that their area could not absorb another huge influx of foreigners like the Mariel "boatlift" from Cuba in the early 1980s, and Florida lawmakers wanted the administration to give the Nicaraguans work permits and the right to move about the country.

But this suggestion raised questions about the plight of Salvadorans and other Central Americans who made up the other half of new arrivals. Their advocates said all Central Americans should be treated alike.

Legislative Action. The House was first to act on the Central American issue, passing HR 45 (H Rept 101-244, Part I) Oct. 25, after rewriting the bill to include protection for Chinese students. The House-passed measure combined the original HR 45, which provided temporary haven for Salvadorans and Nicaraguans, with HR 2929 (H Rept 101-245), which would allow Chinese students and other foreign nationals to stay in the United States because of special circumstances in their homelands.

The House Judiciary Committee had reported both bills Sept. 19, and they were rolled into one under HR 45 before House consideration. HR 45 passed handily, 258-162.

In the Senate, the bill was referred to the Senate Judiciary Subcommittee on Immigration and Refugees. Ranking minority member Alan K. Simpson of Wyoming, who opposed the legislation, stalled a Senate version (S 458). That measure, which suspended Nicaraguan and Salvadoran deportation for two years, was reported from the full committee (S Rept 101-241) on Feb. 1, 1990.

Neither HR 45 nor S 458 was cleared as a separate measure. However, in 1990, a major immigration bill (S 358 — PL 101-649) was cleared that included a provision granting temporary protected status to El Salvadorans until June 1, 1992. *(Immigration reform, p. 752)*

Soviet Jews and Evangelicals. Swiftly changing events in the Soviet Union and Eastern Europe contributed to tensions between Congress and the administration over refugee admission policy.

Traditionally, nearly all Soviet Jews and Evangelicals who managed to get out of the Soviet Union were regarded by the United States as persecuted and thereby entitled to refugee status. But the Reagan administration changed that policy in late 1988, ordering case-by-case reviews of such applicants and expressing skepticism about the threat faced by Soviet citizens in light of Mikhail S. Gorbachev's liberalized policies.

After months of pressure from Congress, the Bush administration on April 5, 1989, raised the U.S. refugee admissions ceiling for fiscal 1989 by 22,500 to accommodate a large influx of Soviet Jews, Pentecostals and Armenians. That boosted the number of Soviets who could be admitted to the United States during the year to 43,500.

The administration also proposed legislation to provide an additional 30,000 visas annually over the next five years for émigrés whose admission would be in the foreign policy interest of the United States. It was aimed at allowing Soviets who did not qualify for refugee status to apply to come to the United States as immigrants. House Judiciary members criticized the legislation, saying the administration should go back to its earlier presumption that all Jews and Christians in the Soviet Union were entitled to refugee status.

Impatient with the administration's approach, the House Judiciary Immigration Subcommittee April 26 approved legislation (HR 2022) to restore until Sept. 30, 1990, the presumption that Soviet Jews, Evangelicals and certain Indochinese groups were persecuted at home and thus should be treated as refugees.

The measure also required the administration to establish categories for other Soviet citizens and for citizens of Vietnam, Laos and Cambodia "who share common characteristics that identify them as targets of persecution" in their home countries. Those people, too, would qualify as refugees.

Applicants would still be reviewed case by case, but the bill shifted the burden to the INS to show that an applicant in the protected class should *not* be accorded refugee status.

The House Judiciary Committee approved HR 2022 (H Rept 101-122) on June 20 by 30-5. The measure was formally reported on July 6. Despite warnings that members were opening a door that could prove difficult to close, the House passed HR 2022 on July 13 by 358-44.

The Bush administration and Congress went one more round over refugees — the September 1989 consultations on refugee admissions. The administration recommended that 125,000 refugees be allowed into the United States in 1990, with 50,000 for Soviet nationals. Senators generally went along with the administration's plan, but House Judiciary Committee members complained that the Soviet figure was far too low because more than that number already had applied for refugee status and were in various stages of processing. The congressional hearings on refugee admissions were part of annual consultations on refugee limits required by the 1980 Refugee Act (PL 96-212). Congress, however, had no veto power over the limits set by the administration. *(1980 law, Congress and the Nation Vol. V, p. 740)*

Nurse Immigration

Congress in 1989 cleared a bill (HR 3259 — PL 101-238) to allow foreign nurses already working in the United States on temporary visas to apply for permanent residence. The measure was intended to relieve nursing shortages that had developed in many communities. Foreign nurses who had worked in the United States for at least three years were allowed to adjust to permanent resident status without regard to immigration quotas on their country of origin.

The House Judiciary Committee reported HR 3259 (H Rept 101-288) on Oct. 16. The House passed the bill Oct. 17 by voice vote under suspension of the rules. The Senate passed the measure Nov. 21 by voice vote, after amending it by adding provisions to curb illegal immigration. The House accepted the Senate changes the same day, clearing HR 3259. The Bush administration opposed the legislation because it singled out one profession for preferential treatment, but the president signed the bill into law on Dec. 18.

The final version authorized $20 million toward the development of tamper-proof identification and other documentation needed by aliens to gain permanent status in the United States. Many in Congress were disturbed by reports of widespread counterfeiting of documents by aliens eager to qualify for amnesty under the 1986 Immigration Reform and Control Act (PL 99-603). *(1986 act, Congress and the Nation Vol. VII, p. 717)*

Civil Rights

In the first defeat of a major civil rights bill in a quarter-century, the Senate on Oct. 24, 1990, failed by one vote to override President Bush's veto of a bill (S 2104) intended to protect workers against job bias.

The legislation sought to reverse or modify six 1989 Supreme Court decisions that narrowed the scope and reach of laws prohibiting employment discrimination. It also would have permitted monetary damage awards under Title VII of the 1964 Civil Rights Act (PL 88-352), which barred job discrimination based on race, sex, religion or national origin. Bush argued that the bill would lead employers to adopt hiring and promotion quotas for minorities to avoid litigation. *(1964 law, Congress and the Nation Vol. I, p. 1635)*

The bill, introduced after months of bargaining among civil rights activists, was swiftly approved by Senate and House committees. But floor consideration in both chambers was bitter and divisive. For several months, intense but fruitless negotiations were held between the administration and Hill sponsors over how to make sure employers did not turn to quotas.

The sticking point was how to counter the Court's ruling in *Wards Cove Packing Co. v. Atonia*, which shifted from employers to workers the burden of proof in "disparate impact" cases. These involved seemingly neutral employment practices that had an adverse impact on women and minorities. The dispute was over when such practices could be justified on the grounds of "business necessity."

After the failed Senate veto override, the House took no further action. Sponsors vowed to bring the legislation back in the 102nd Congress. *(Story, p. 780)*

Background

In a series of decisions during its 1988-89 term, the Supreme Court significantly restricted both the reach and the remedies of federal civil rights laws. The rulings stunned groups representing minorities and women, prompting calls for legislation to modify the decisions. But by the end of 1989, the civil rights coalition had not yet finished drafting omnibus legislation to counter the rulings. *(Decisions, p. 784)*

Lawyers who handled job-discrimination cases said that because of the tight new standards set by the Court, many legitimate claims simply were not being filed, some complaints were being dismissed and remedies were being limited.

After months of negotiations, a bipartisan coalition of civil rights advocates unveiled the legislation at a large news conference Feb. 7, 1990. In attendance were Coretta Scott King, widow of the Rev. Dr. Martin Luther King Jr., and leaders from various women's, minority and religious organizations.

Companion measures (S 2104, HR 4000) were introduced in Congress by Sen. Edward M. Kennedy, D-Mass., and Rep. Augustus F. Hawkins, D-Calif., with scores of cosponsors. The Kennedy-Hawkins legislation was broad in scope, seeking to overturn the six Supreme Court cases as well as amend other existing rules. The ambitious nature of the legislation set it apart from less controversial civil rights measures of the 1980s that overturned a single high court decision or amended just one title of the *U.S. Code*.

The proposed bills sought to amend Title VII of the 1964 Civil Rights Act to allow financial compensation for pain and suffering and punitive damages in intentional-discrimination cases. Unlike the existing rules, the measures also would have allowed jury trials. And the legislation would have extended the statute of limitations in Title VII job-discrimination cases from six months to two years.

In addition to the Title VII changes, the civil rights measures sought to overturn or modify the following 1989 Supreme Court decisions:

- *Patterson v. McLean Credit Union*, which held that Section 1981 of Title 42 of the *U.S. Code* prohibited racial discrimination only in hiring, not subsequent on-the-job activity. The bill would have made clear that Section 1981 covered all aspects of a job relationship.

The Kennedy-Hawkins legislation stated that Section 1981 outlawed racial discrimination in the "making, performance, modification and termination of contracts and the enjoyment of all benefits, privileges, terms and conditions of the contractual relationship." It would have ensured that the statute covered complaints of racial harassment, and it would have applied the new standards to all legal actions begun after June 15, 1989, the date of the *Patterson* decision, or pending at the time of that ruling.

- *Wards Cove v. Atonio*, which required workers to identify the specific employment practices alleged to have resulted in racial disparities in a work place and shifted to complaining workers the burden of proving that an employer had no business necessity for the challenged practices. The legislation would have returned to the employer the burden of proving that a practice with a "disparate impact" on minorities or women was necessary to the business. It would have allowed employee-plaintiffs to establish that a practice had a disparate impact without pinpointing the specific cause of the discrimination.

Some examples of practices that had been cited as having a disparate impact were aptitude tests that resulted in ethnic minorities being kept out of jobs or physical strength requirements that caused women to lose promotions.

The decision effectively overturned the 18-year-old standard of *Griggs v. Duke Power Co.*, which had required employers to prove a business necessity for practices that adversely affected minorities and women. The bill would have returned the law to the *Griggs* standard and made clear that workers did not have to pinpoint the specific practices that resulted in an adverse impact on women and minorities. *(Case summary, Congress and the Nation Vol. III, p. 314)*

- *Martin v. Wilks*, which allowed court-approved affirmative action plans to be challenged later by individuals affected by a consent decree, even if they did not protest at the time the matter was being negotiated. The legislation would have made consent decrees final, provided that all potentially affected parties were given adequate notice that a court order was being negotiated.
- *Lorance v. AT&T Technologies Inc.*, which required workers who thought a seniority system was discriminatory to file suit soon after the system was adopted. The legislation would have allowed challenges to seniority systems under deadlines that would not begin running until an individual was adversely affected by the plan.
- *Independent Federation of Flight Attendants v. Zipes*, which barred successful plaintiffs from obtaining attorneys' fees for their efforts to defend against intervenors. The legislation would have allowed successful plaintiffs to obtain attorneys' fees from intervenors. It also would have responded to a series of Court decisions since 1985 cutting back on attorneys' fees for prevailing plaintiffs in civil rights cases.
- *Price Waterhouse v. Hopkins*, which allowed an employer to defend a discriminatory employment decision if it could prove the same decision would have been made in the absence of bias. The legislation would have made employers liable for intentional discrimination even if the same decision would have been made for non-discriminatory reasons.

The *Wards Cove* decision became the focal point of the legislative effort. Civil rights activists found the provisions dealing with the case especially important because of their broad effect on the ability of workers to win job-discrimination claims. Employer groups, conservative organizations and the administration came to embrace the decision. They depicted any effort to modify it as all but forcing employers to adopt hiring and promotion quotas in order to avoid lawsuits. But proponents of the legislation insisted that the provisions had nothing to do with quotas and would not encourage them.

After the Kennedy-Hawkins legislation was introduced with its considerable fanfare, the administration countered with its own one-page bill to reverse the *Patterson* and *Lorance* decisions. But while Bush supported bills (S 2166, HR 4081) to overturn *Patterson* — by authorizing monetary damages for the victims of racial discrimination in all phases of a job relationship — the administration opposed provisions of S 2104 and HR 4000 that also would grant such damages to women, religious minorities, ethnic minorities and, indirectly, the disabled. Civil rights lobbyists and their primarily Democratic supporters in Congress insisted that Bush's position was unfair and illogical.

Senate Action

The Senate passed S 2104, 65-34, on July 18 after eight weeks of talks between sponsors and the administration collapsed in mutual recriminations. The Labor and Human Resources Committee had considered the bill in April, approving it after two hours of debate on April 4. The vote was 11-5. Republicans James M. Jeffords, Vt., and Dave Durenberger, Minn., joined all the committee Democrats in supporting the measure. S 2104 was formally reported (S Rept 101-315) on June 8.

Attorney General Dick Thornburgh wrote the committee before the markup that he and "other senior advisers" would recommend that Bush veto the bill.

Only one amendment, offered by Orrin G. Hatch, R-Utah, the bill's most outspoken critic, was adopted. It amended the section relating to practices that had disparate impact on women and minorities, stemming from the *Wards Cove* decision. The amendment provided that employers could bar employees from using or possessing illegal drugs, so long as the no-drug rule was not adopted to discriminate intentionally against minorities.

The committee rejected a Hatch amendment that would have left with complaining workers the burden of proving that an employer had no business necessity for practices that were significantly related to the health or safety of employees, consumers, patients or other persons affected by the business operation. The committee also rejected a Hatch amendment to the *Martin* section that would have allowed adversely affected parties to challenge consent decrees in a discrimination case at a later time.

Senate consideration of S 2104 was an off-and-on affair, punctuated by talks between the administration and sponsors over compromise options and efforts by Majority Leader George J. Mitchell, D-Maine, to pressure the parties to reach an agreement. Twice in early summer, he had filed cloture petitions to cut off debate and amendments but had backed off when compromise seemed near. But on July 17 he persisted, and cloture was invoked 62-38.

The dispute over remedies for women and minorities claiming bias — the *Wards Cove* case — derailed negotiations. As introduced, S 2104 would have required employers to prove that an employment practice that had an adverse impact on women or minorities was "essential to effective job performance." But Kennedy and John C. Danforth, R-Mo., announced on May 17 that they would amend the bill to ensure that it did not lead to quotas.

That proposal brought support for S 2104 from Danforth, John Heinz, R-Pa., and five Southern and Western Democrats. But Hatch said Bush and his advisers were "too smart to be taken in by this new language. The right of employers to hire the most qualified employees ought to be maintained."

Kennedy's amended bill also stated that nothing in the act should be construed to require an employer to adopt hiring or promotion quotas. Hatch called that provision "totally useless." Kennedy's revision on the quota issue was included in an amendment, which was adopted 65-34 on July 18.

Some politically meaningful amendments did not come to a vote. A number of Southern Democrats tried to get the chamber to consider two proposals that would have made the bill more acceptable to business. David Pryor, D-Ark., attempted to ensure that employer practices would not be found discriminatory simply because statistics showed that a plant had a higher percentage of whites than minorities. Another proposal, offered by David L. Boren, D-Okla., would have limited punitive damage awards to $150,000 or to the amount of compensatory damages.

But Minority Leader Bob Dole, R-Kan., objected to Kennedy's effort to get procedure waived and the amendments added. Dole's move effectively guaranteed that the bill would remain unpalatable to Bush. He contended that was fair because, if GOP members' amendments had been choked off, Democratic proposals also should be blocked.

In debate a week before the measure passed the Senate, an amendment offered by Wendell H. Ford, D-Ky., was adopted by voice vote to extend provisions of the bill to Senate workers. Senate aides would not have the right to sue in court but could present their grievances to a Senate panel. Nancy Landon Kassebaum, R-Kan., also tried to draft an entirely new bill that she hoped would draw support from Republicans and conservative Democrats, but her effort died without a vote.

House Action

The House passed its version (HR 4000) in August, after two committees had worked on the measure.

The Education and Labor panel approved HR 4000 on May 8 after four days of consideration. The 23-10 vote saw a single Republican, Peter Smith of Vermont, join a phalanx of Democrats in support of the bill. HR 4000 (H Rept 101-644, Part I) was reported July 30.

When the bill was amended May 2 to soften one of its more controversial provisions, Republican members apparently were caught unaware and said they needed time to reconsider their position and what amendments they would subsequently offer. The committee had voted 33-0 to redefine the test an employer had to meet in defending a job practice shown to have a negative impact on women or minorities. Smith, who sponsored the amendment with Hawkins, said the change in the business-necessity test would improve the bill substantively and politically.

Steve Gunderson, R-Wis., returned to the issue, offering an amendment that would have required an employee charging discrimination to demonstrate which specific practice or practices within a group resulted in the alleged disparate impact. Gunderson said that an employer needed to know what to defend himself against when confronted with a discrimination suit. But Hawkins said the amendment simply restated the *Wards Cove* decision. It was rejected 10-22.

Another Hawkins amendment, adopted 22-11 despite vigorous Republican opposition, broadened one section of the bill. As drafted, it barred an employer-defendant from requiring a plaintiff to waive any claim to payment of attorneys' fees as a condition of a negotiated settlement or consent decree. The amendment extended this ban to negotiated lawsuit dismissals.

Twice during the May 3 markup, angry Republicans walked out of the committee room, once when it appeared no time would be available to debate GOP amendments and another when one Republican contended that a Democrat had improperly questioned another Republican's motive. That imbroglio was settled when Missouri Democrat William L. Clay conceded he had spoken inappropriately about a GOP colleague and asked that his remarks be removed from the record.

The committee's final day of markup on May 8 had a conciliatory tone. Despite the less fiery debate, the committee by voice vote rejected all amendments offered by Republicans.

The House Judiciary Committee did not take up the bill until after the Senate completed work on S 2104. The panel approved HR 4000 July 25 after rejecting several Republican-backed amendments aimed at limiting its scope. The vote was 24-12. Two panel Republicans, ranking GOP member Hamilton Fish Jr. of New York and Tom Campbell of California, joined the 22 Democrats in supporting the measure. The Judiciary Committee reported HR 4000 (H Rept 101-644, Part II) on July 31.

The committee bill closely resembled the Senate measure Bush threatened to veto.

The Judiciary Subcommittee on Civil and Constitutional Rights on July 12 had voted 5-3 to approve the bill.

F. James Sensenbrenner Jr., Wis., ranking Republican on the Civil and Constitutional Rights Subcommittee, sought in full committee to strike the portion of the bill calling for punitive and compensatory damages for intentional discrimination. His amendment, which would have capped potential compensation at $30,000, was defeated, 12-23.

The committee defeated several other amendments, including:

- A proposal by Sensenbrenner, on a 16-20 vote, to make Congress subject to the same anti-discrimination laws as other employers. Opponents, citing constitutional problems, said the bill was the wrong vehicle for such a law.
- A proposal by Henry J. Hyde, R-Ill., 13-23, which, like the underlying bill, would have returned the burden of proof in job-discrimination cases from employees to employers. But it would have imposed a special requirement for workers in job-discrimination suits involving disparate impact. Those plaintiffs would have had to show a link between the statistical disparity and discriminatory work practices.

The full House passed HR 4000, 272-154, on Aug. 3, joining the Senate in a standoff with the Bush administration. The vote was 12 short of the two-thirds voting necessary to override a veto. The Senate had come within two votes of the 67 it would need.

HR 4000 passed only after two politically inspired amendments were adopted that aimed at shoring up the crucial support of conservative Democrats and getting within striking distance of overriding a veto. The two amendments made the bill more palatable by ostensibly softening its impact on business. One gave members a chance to vote against quotas, and the other let them vote against big damage awards.

On the quota issue, Michael A. Andrews, D-Texas, and Stephen L. Neal, D-N.C., proposed language stating that nothing in the bill "shall be construed" to require an employer to adopt hiring or promotional quotas. The amendment also said that a mere statistical imbalance in an employer's shop on account of race, color, religion, sex or national origin could not establish that a boss discriminated. Similar language had been added to the bill during Judiciary Committee action July 25, and committee members chafed at the idea of the superfluous provision. But they acquiesced after the House leadership said a vote against quotas would help Southern Democrats answer worried business constituents. The amendment was adopted Aug. 2, 397-24.

A second amendment that solidified moderates' support of the bill put a cap on punitive damages that could be awarded a victim of intentional discrimination. It was adopted 289-134, also on Aug. 2.

Responding to fears that employers would be saddled with million-dollar damage awards for discrimination, Hawkins and Judiciary Chairman Jack Brooks, D-Texas, proposed a cap on punitive damages for employers with fewer than 100 workers of $150,000 or the amount of compensatory damages. It destroyed in part the equality that bill sponsors were trying to reach for racial, sexual and religious victims of bias because workers who had been subject to racial discrimination on the job could win unlimited damages under Section 1981 of Title 42 of the *U.S. Code*. Other victims, covered by a separate law, would fall under the $150,000 limit.

The administration attacked the cap as a minor change at best, but Brooks said it would apply to more than 97 percent of U.S. businesses. He said the cap was necessary to convince employers that they would not be subject to multimillion-dollar lawsuits because of the bill.

Before passing HR 4000, the House defeated a substitute measure that was partially written by administration officials and initially sponsored by House Small Business Committee Chairman John J. LaFalce, D-N.Y. House leaders denounced the proposal as raising the obstacles and lowering awards for workers who alleged discrimination. It lost 188-238.

The House by voice vote Aug. 3 passed S 2104 with the language of HR 4000.

Conference, Final Action

Conferees reached an initial compromise agreement Sept. 25 to put a cap on punitive damages. The cap was set at $150,000 or compensatory damages plus lost pay, whichever was greater, and applied only to damages under Title VII, the section barring racial, sex, religious and ethnic discrimination on the job. Victims of racial bias could still sue under Section 1981 of Title 42 for unlimited damages.

A White House spokesperson called the new cap "a positive step" but said the bill still faced a veto. In addition to this sobering assessment, sponsors were feeling the effects of a campaign by small business owners arguing that the bill would subject them to increased charges of discrimination,

In the face of these problems, Kennedy continued to try to work out an agreement with the White House. On Oct. 11, conferees reached a new agreement with more compromises intended to address the administration's concerns. One of the key brokers was William T. Coleman Jr., former transportation secretary under President Gerald R. Ford, who said Oct. 11 that the new conference report "takes care of every legitimate concern" of the administration. He predicted incorrectly, as it turned out, that Bush would sign the bill.

Under the new language:

- When an employer tried to defend as a "business necessity" a practice that ended up discriminating disproportionately against women or minorities, its burden of proof would be lower than what the bill originally proposed in most situations, including when employees' use of methadone, alcohol or tobacco was involved. In cases of hiring and promotion, the burden of proof required by the bill would remain higher.
- Workers in disparate impact cases would have to pinpoint specific practices that excluded women, blacks or other minorities. The original bill did not require such precision. The new bill stated, however, that specific practices would not have to be proved when the employer did not produce relevant records.
- The bill said that it should not be interpreted "to encourage" quotas.
- In cases of intentional discrimination, a worker could not win compensatory or punitive damages if an employer could prove that it would have taken the same action even without discrimination.

The Bush administration was not won over by the changes, and, on Oct. 12, the veto threat was renewed.

With proponents of the civil rights bill still short of the two-thirds vote needed to override the expected veto, Congress nevertheless took up the civil rights conference report.

The Senate adopted the conference report (H Rept 101-856), 62-34, on Oct. 16, and the House adopted it Oct. 17 by a **key vote of 273-154 (R 34-139; D 239-15)**. The votes left supporters three Senate votes and 12 House votes shy of the two-thirds needed to override the threatened veto. *(1990 key votes, p. 1039)*

On Oct. 22, Bush followed through with his threat and vetoed the bill, citing once again his concerns that it would lead employers to adopt hiring quotas.

The Senate Oct. 24 failed to override the veto of S 2104 by a **key vote of 66-34 (R 11-34; D 55-0)**, and the measure was dead in the 101st Congress.

During debate before the vote, black House members ringed the Senate floor and watched as the roll was called. Above in the gallery sat David Duke, the unsuccessful senatorial candidate and former Ku Klux Klan leader who had run against affirmative action and programs favoring blacks. Jesse Jackson, a black leader and former Democratic presidential contender, earlier had sat in the gallery watching the debate.

The only senator to switch sides after the vote on the conference report was Minnesota's Rudy Boschwitz, R, who had opposed the bill earlier. Other GOP senators close to switching to vote for the bill said they did not want to abandon Bush during difficult budget negotiations and ongoing trouble in the Persian Gulf.

Flag Desecration

Supporters of a constitutional amendment aimed at preventing flag burning failed for the second year in a row in 1990 to get the measure through Congress, falling well short of the two-thirds majority needed in the House and the Senate.

The flag uproar had begun in June 1989, when the Supreme Court by 5-4 ruled a Texas statute unconstitutional in *Texas v. Johnson*. After months of vocal outrage, public hearings and disagreements over whether to amend the Constitution, pass a statute or do nothing, Congress in October 1989 cleared the Flag Protection Act (PL 101-131). In the same month, the Senate rejected a proposed constitutional amendment to outlaw flag desecration.

But the Supreme Court spoke again on the issue in June 1990. In *United States v. Eichman*, the Court struck down the new statute as unconstitutional, reaffirming its 1989 decision that flag burning was a form of political expression protected by the First Amendment. This prompted renewed calls for a constitutional amendment, but opponents of the proposal (H J Res 350, S J Res 332) were well prepared. They quickly mounted an offensive that framed the battle as a fight over the sanctity of the Constitution in general and the First Amendment in particular. *(Case summaries, p. 778)*

Legal experts who testified before the House and Senate Judiciary committees were divided among those advocating a statute, those believing only a constitutional amendment would suffice and those who wanted no action at all in response to the Court decision. Some supporting a statute said the high court had opened the door to a carefully drawn proposal that punished conduct, not expression. Those supporting a constitutional amendment contended that this was the only remedy that would pass muster with the justices. Opponents of both a statute and an amendment focused their attention on the latter, arguing, as one lawyer put it, that such an amendment "bordered on the reckless." Criticizing the statute approach former solicitor general Charles Fried said it was "an undignified and unworthy way for Congress to play games with a Supreme Court decision."

Even though polls in 1990 had registered strong support for an amendment, supporters could not effectively mobilize outside interest groups. Despite expectations that the issue could figure in the November elections, it faded quickly after the amendment was defeated.

1989 Action

House. Less than a week after the June 21, 1989, Supreme Court decision, President Bush called for a constitutional amendment to reverse the ruling. Proposals were quickly introduced in both chambers. The House stayed in session around the clock June 22 so members could make speeches denouncing the Court and saluting the flag.

House Judiciary Committee Chairman Jack Brooks, D-Texas, and ranking Republican Hamilton Fish Jr., N.Y., agreed that hearings would be held in early July. And by July 27, the committee was ready to move. The committee decided that a statute, not a constitutional amendment, was preferable, and news accounts and opinion polls by late summer showed the public preferred legislation over an amendment. By a vote of 28-6, the committee approved a bill (HR 2978) to outlaw burning, defacing and other physical desecration of the U.S. flag. HR 2978 (H Rept 101-231) was formally reported Sept. 7.

The bill, which was offered by Brooks, was similar to one (S 1338) proposed in the Senate by Judiciary Committee Chairman Joseph R. Biden Jr., D-Del. It stated: "Whoever knowingly mutilates, defaces, burns or tramples upon any flag of the United States shall be fined under this title or imprisoned for not more than one year, or both." The maximum fine was $100,000.

Sponsors said that by eliminating existing-law references to the motivation of flag desecrators, they avoided First Amendment problems. The full House suspended the rules and passed HR 2978 on Sept. 12 by a vote of 380-38. But many members warned that only a constitutional amendment could overturn the Court's June 21 decision.

House Speaker Thomas S. Foley, D-Wash., previously had refused to guarantee floor action on such a proposal. But confronted by the possibility that Republicans could use a discharge petition to force an amendment onto the floor, Foley changed his mind and promised Republican leaders a later floor vote on an amendment.

Senate. Three weeks after the June 21 *Johnson* decision, the Senate agreed that it would consider in October both S 1338, sponsored by Judiciary Chairman Biden, and a constitutional amendment (S J Res 180), proposed by Minority Leader Bob Dole, R-Kan. No flag-related amendments were permitted in the interim on other legislation.

The Senate Judiciary Committee took up the flag issue Sept. 21 and rejected Dole's proposed constitutional amendment, 6-8. Instead, the committee by 9-5 approved S 1338, making it illegal to mutilate, deface, burn, display on the floor or ground, or trample on the flag. S 1338 (S Rept 101-152) was reported Sept. 21.

Over objections from ranking Republican Strom Thurmond, S.C., Biden forced a vote to report the committee's disapproval of S J Res 180. Biden said that after hearing testimony from legal scholars on the best response to the Court's decision, the committee should be able to advise the full Senate on the issue.

The Senate considered the House bill instead of S 1338 and passed HR 2978 by 91-9 on Oct. 5.

But unlike the House, the Senate added language on the floor that critics said could throw the measure into a constitutional quagmire. The bill had been written narrowly to bar physical damage to the flag, avoiding any references to the intent of an individual who would burn or otherwise deface the flag. But Pete Wilson, R-Calif., offered an amendment to punish anyone who physically "defiles" the flag.

Biden tried unsuccessfully to table the amendment, saying that the bill had been crafted to avoid any threat to First Amendment freedoms. "Defile," Biden said, "connotes that there is a communicative, a verbal injury that you can inflict upon someone or something," thus inviting another Supreme Court rejection.

Most of the Senate did not care. Biden's motion to table (kill) the Wilson amendment was rejected 31-69 on Oct. 5, and the amendment was adopted 76-24.

Final Action. The House Oct. 12 accepted the Senate's amendments and sent HR 2978 to the president. The vote was 371-43 and came after little more than an hour of debate.

The bill called for a prison sentence of up to one year or a fine of up to $100,000, or both, for an individual who "knowingly mutilates, defaces, physically defiles, burns, maintains on the floor or ground, or tramples upon" any U.S. flag.

Bush said at an Oct. 13 news conference that he would let the bill become law without his signature "to signal our belief that a constitutional amendment is the best way to provide lasting protection for the flag." HR 2978 (PL 101-131) was enacted Oct. 28.

Constitutional Amendment. On Oct. 19, the Senate rejected the constitutional amendment (S J Res 180) by a **key vote of 51-48 (R 33-11; D 18-37)**. This was 15 votes short of the required two-thirds majority. *(1989 key votes, p. 1021)*

Although much of the early outpouring of dismay over the Court's ruling had come from veterans' organizations, veterans in the Senate spoke out both for and against the flag amendment. Dole, who had lost use of his arm during combat in World War II, said: "It is not too late to listen to the people who sent us here, the real Americans — the members of the American Legion, the members of the Non-Commissioned Officers of America, the farmers, the business people ... who do not read Supreme Court decisions but are willing to fight and die for their country."

But Tom Harkin, D-Iowa, a Vietnam-era Navy pilot, said many veterans he had heard from first wanted a constitutional amendment but, upon reflection, changed their minds. Flag burning, he said, "is a very sick and violent act. It aroused hot passions in me and many other Americans. But there is a difference between America and North Vietnam; there is a difference between America and China, and that difference is freedom."

1990 Action

Two federal district judges — one in Washington, D.C., and the other in Seattle, Wash. — ruled early in 1990 that individuals who burned a flag to challenge the new law were exercising their First Amendment rights. Although the Justice Department argued that the statute had been drafted to protect the physical integrity of the flag, the district judge in Washington, D.C., disagreed. The ruling was a prelude to the decision that came from the Supreme Court June 11. Writing for the majority, Justice William J. Brennan Jr. said that the new statute suffered a "fundamental flaw: it supresses expression out of concern for its likely communicative impact."

House. Two days after the decision, the House Judiciary Subcommittee on Civil and Constitutional Rights voted 5-3 to send a constitutional amendment (H J Res 350) to the full committee with a recommendation to defeat it. The amendment stated: "The Congress and the states shall have the power to prohibit the physical desecration of the flag of the United States."

The subcommittee was dominated by liberal Democrats and did not represent House sentiment, but amendment opponents were encouraged when the full committee June 19 also voted against recommending it. The panel first voted 17-19 to oppose the proposal and then voted 19-17 to send it to the full House without recommendation.

Anxious to prevent amendment supporters from mobilizing their forces, opponents successfully blocked an effort to delay a full House vote on the proposal. The measure was brought to the floor June 21, two days after the Judiciary Committee's action. The seven hours of floor debate appealed to party allegiances and emotions, the latter centered on the sanctity of the Constitution and the importance of the flag as a unique symbol. Rep. Henry J. Hyde, R-Ill., who closed the debate for the amendment proponents, described the flag as "a symbol that unites as a country" and said that "Too many people have paid for it with their blood ... Too many to have this ever demeaned." House Speaker Foley, who followed Hyde's appeal, jabbed at Republicans when he said, "If it is not conservative to protect the Bill of Rights, I don't know what conservatism is today." He warned that "those few people who burn or disrespect the flag" should not "push us, force us into amending for the first time the First Amendment."

By a **key vote of 254-177 (R 159-17; D 95-160),** H J Res 350 was rejected on June 21, 34 votes short of the two-thirds necessary for passage. *(1990 key votes, p. 1039)*

Although the Court rejected the earlier statutory approach to banning flag burning, some House members still wanted an approach other than a constitutional amendment. One bill (HR 5091), drafted somewhat differently from the 1989 measure, was considered and handily defeated 179-236 under suspension of the rules June 21.

Senate. The Senate June 26 followed the House's lead and killed the chances of a constitutional amendment in the 101st Congress. On a **58-42 (R 38-7; D 20-35) key vote**, the Senate failed, nine votes short of the 67 needed, to pass S J Res 332.

Biden had held a hearing on the subject before the Senate session, hoping to draft a narrower amendment than the one rejected by the House. But midway through the day, he said the effort was a "futile exercise." Both he and Dole predicted that the proposal would fail in the Senate, but the matter was brought up anyway.

Before the final vote, the Senate first considered three alternatives to S J Res 332. Dale Bumpers, D-Ark., proposed a statute that would have subjected anyone who knowingly and purposely desecrated the flag to a fine or one year in prison, or both. Bumpers defined desecration as "an act calculated to create a breach of the peace." Bumpers said his was a "narrow legislative remedy," but it was defeated on a procedural vote.

Jesse Helms, R-N.C., then proposed an amendment to the resolution that would have provided for a statute banning the public mutilation, defilement, incineration or other physical abuse of the flag. It also would have removed from the jurisdiction of the federal courts the power to hear any cases involving such acts so that the states would have exclusive jurisdiction over flag burning cases. The amendment failed 10-90.

Biden proposed an amendment that would have given only Congress the power to pass laws against flag desecration. The amendment would have limited the prohibited acts to burning, mutilating or trampling on a flag. His proposal was defeated 7-93.

A tone of fatigue had permeated the June 26 proceedings, and Biden, who managed the floor debate, said he was sorry for "wasting the taxpayers' money in a sense in discussing something that is going nowhere."

Civil Rights Commission

Congress in 1989 cleared a temporary extension (HR 3532 — PL 101-180) of the trouble-plagued U.S. Commission on Civil Rights. As enacted into law, the bill extended the commission's authorization for 22 months, to Sept. 30, 1991.

The commission was established in 1957 to assess the laws and policies of the federal government and to make reports and recommendations to the president and Congress on civil rights. Throughout its history, the commission had often criticized the civil rights record of whatever administration was in office. But none responded as angrily as the Reagan administration. The president sought to dismiss three commissioners and replace them with nominees who shared his opposition to busing and affirmative action quotas.

Rights activists, insisting that the commission was supposed to be independent of the White House, persuaded the Senate Judiciary Committee to hold up action on the three nominees. In 1983, a deal eventually was struck for a new eight-member panel that was to include four members of the old panel who had criticized administration rights policies. But after the compromise bill was cleared, Reagan said no deal had been made on reappointing certain members. Civil rights groups complained that they had been double-crossed.

The commission never regained its independence, its critics said. Made up of four members appointed by the president, two by the Senate and two by the House, the panel had been torn by acrimony. Democrats complained that it had abrogated its fact-finding responsibility.

When the commission came up for reauthorization in 1989, members of both parties seriously considered eliminating it. On Nov. 15, the House passed its version of the measure, 278-135 under suspension of the rules, calling for a six-month extension. Rep. Don Edwards, D-Calif., chairman of the House Judiciary Subcommittee on Civil and Constitutional Rights, asked for the short extension so that his committee could consider several pending bills to overhaul the agency.

The Senate passed HR 3532 by voice vote on Nov. 16, after amending it to extend the commission for 22 months. Final action came Nov. 17, when the House accepted the Senate changes, 389-0. President Bush signed the measure Nov. 28.

In 1991, Congress again extended the Civil Rights Commission, this time for three years. *(Story, p. 785)*

Lucas Nomination

In a major rebuke to President Bush, the Senate Judiciary Committee on Aug. 1, 1989, killed his nomination of William Lucas to be assistant attorney general in charge of civil rights. Most of the nation's major civil rights organizations had opposed the nomination, saying that Lucas lacked the experience necessary for the sensitive Justice Department post.

By a 7-7 vote, the committee rejected a motion to report Lucas' nomination favorably. By another 7-7 vote, members then refused to send the nomination to the floor without a recommendation.

In the end, the vote on the nomination involved far more than the bid of one man to be assistant attorney general. The debate on Lucas was shaped by two facts: first, that he was black, and second, that civil rights activists were defensive after a series of Supreme Court decisions in 1988-89 that they said would make it harder for workers to bring and win discrimination suits. While most Senate Judiciary Committee members said that it was important to have faced and surmounted discrimination — as Lucas had — half of them said that being black was not sufficient qualification for the nation's top civil rights post. *(Civil rights bill, p. 757)*

Lucas was the first black candidate in recent years to have been rejected after a formal nomination. Republicans said he was the victim of racism; Democrats called that allegation cynical and outrageous.

Lucas also was Bush's first nominee to be rejected outright since the March 9 defeat of former senator John Tower for secretary of defense. For Attorney General Dick Thornburgh, who had selected Lucas, the nomination ordeal was the second major loss in as many months. Thornburgh's choice for deputy attorney general, Robert B. Fiske Jr., withdrew from consideration in July after intense criticism from conservative Republicans. Fiske had been chairman of an American Bar Association screening committee that had been critical of some of President Ronald Reagan's judicial nominees and reportedly had passed on to liberal groups the names of some White House choices. *(Tower nomination, p. 339; Fiske, p. 1177)*

Lucas Résumé

Lucas grew up in Harlem and the Bronx. He joined the New York City police force in 1953 and later attended Fordham Law School at night. In 1963, after graduating from Fordham but before passing the bar exam, he worked in the Justice Department's Civil Rights Division.

Lucas eventually joined the FBI, which assigned him to Detroit in 1966. In 1968, Lucas, a Democrat, took a job as under sheriff of Wayne County. The following year, he was appointed sheriff, succeeding incumbent Roman Gribbs, who had been elected mayor of Detroit. In 1970, Lucas was elected sheriff and remained in that post until 1982, when he won the newly created post of county executive. He had been admitted to the Michigan bar in 1971.

Lucas switched to the Republican Party in 1985 and ran for governor the next year. He did not prove to be a strong contender. Incumbent Democratic Gov. James J. Blanchard defeated him overwhelmingly.

Questions about Lucas

Lucas' party-switching left him enemies, and his supporters said it was revenge that motivated the 1989 attacks on his record and character. Questions about Lucas arose immediately after Thornburgh announced his selection. Old controversies from Lucas' days as Wayne County sheriff and county executive resurfaced, as well as new charges. Among the issues that concerned Judiciary Committee members were:

- Instances of brutality and overcrowding at the Wayne County jail when Lucas was sheriff and contempt-of-court citations stemming from his failure to remedy problems there.
- Omissions and exaggerations on job forms, including his statement on résumés in the early 1970s that he had been an assistant U.S. attorney in 1963 instead of the legal assistant he was, and failure to mention in a 1981 application to the New York state bar that he had failed the District of Columbia bar 18 years earlier.
- A 1985 clash with U.S. Customs officers, in which Lucas and his family were fined for failing to declare more than $4,000 in jewelry and other goods purchased on a trip to the Far East.

But the subject that Lucas' critics stressed repeatedly was his lack of courtroom or civil rights background. Lucas had only recently practiced law part time. He had never appeared in court on behalf of a client.

The Judiciary Committee hearings on July 19 and 20 revealed Lucas' uncertainty about civil rights law and, in the words of one Democrat, a lack of "a gut commitment" to the government's role as a watchdog against discrimination. Committee Democrats were particularly appalled when Lucas said he did not think recent Supreme Court decisions in discrimination cases were very significant and conceded, "I'm new to the law."

Committee Votes

Lucas' confused testimony on the Supreme Court cases and other civil rights matters led Chairman Joseph R. Biden Jr., D.-Del., to reverse his initial position that he was "inclined" to vote for Lucas. In the end, all six of the committee's Republicans voted for Lucas, as did Democrat Dennis DeConcini of Arizona. All other Democrats opposed the nomination.

The decisive vote — and the only one in doubt as the meeting began — was cast by Howell Heflin, D-Ala., who on July 27 had sought and won a delay to consider what he described as new information regarding the nominee. Heflin, often a swing vote on the committee, received a phone call from Bush on the morning of the vote, but it failed to change his decision to vote against Lucas.

Ten days after the committee rejected Lucas' nomination, Bush named him to be director of the Justice Department Office of Liaison Services, a post that did not require Senate confirmation. The office worked with local governments and community organizations.

The assistant attorney generalship for civil rights went vacant until January 1990, when Bush nominated former New York state GOP senator John R. Dunne. A graduate of Yale Law school, Dunne was considered a moderate and received the support of both Democratic and Republican officials in New York. Among Dunne's most mentioned accomplishments was his mediation during the 1971 Attica prison riots.

The Senate Judiciary Committee approved Dunne's nomination on March 8 after a two-hour confirmation hearing. The full Senate confirmed Dunne by voice vote on March 9.

Crime Bill

Time pressures and irreconcilable differences over some of the most emotional issues in criminal justice combined at the end of the 101st Congress to dilute a sweeping election-year anti-crime package.

With the clock running out, House-Senate conferees on the legislation (HR 5269, S 1970) abandoned efforts Oct. 26, 1990, to reach agreement on the most controversial provisions before them — a broadened federal death penalty, limits on legal challenges by condemned prisoners and restrictions on semiautomatic assault-type weapons.

Also gone from the final version were provisions sought by the Bush administration that would have allowed courts to consider evidence gathered with flawed warrants, to shorten delays in carrying out executions and to impose tougher penalties for illegal firearm use.

Instead, both chambers approved a stripped-down bill (S 3266 — PL 101-647) that increased penalties for child abuse; provided prison alternatives, such as house arrest; allowed more funding for local law enforcement; and increased authorizations for federal law enforcement agencies such as the FBI.

In a response to the thrift crisis, the measure also set up in the Justice Department an office of special counsel for financial institutions fraud, made it easier for federal banking agencies and the Justice Department to seize the assets of defendants in such cases and limited defendants' ability to use bankruptcy to avoid civil or criminal penalties.

Controversial Senate provisions dealing with the death penalty, habeas corpus, gun control and the exclusionary rule originally had been rolled into a separate bill (S 1970) after they almost derailed anti-drug legislation in 1989. When senators took up the measure in 1990, a surprise vote for restrictions on assault-style weapons almost sank the bill. But surviving a threatened filibuster, the bill passed.

On the House side, the Democratic leadership for months resisted pressure from Bush, GOP members and Democratic moderates for a crime bill. The Judiciary Committee approved a measure (HR 5269), but its safeguards for defendants' rights drew a Bush veto threat. Most were stripped out during floor consideration, and the bill passed by the House was far tougher on criminals than the Judiciary Committee version.

But the House-passed bill included a "racial justice" clause, which would have allowed defendants to get out of a death sentence if they could prove, initially with statistics of racial imbalances, that it was imposed because of racial bias. House conferees would not give up on that provision, which the Senate had rejected. And Senate conferees would not relinquish gun control. Conferees resolved these intractable issues by dumping them altogether in favor of the stripped down legislation that was sent to the White House.

Background

Since 1982, Congress cleared an anti-crime or anti-drug bill every two years, typically in the waning days of the session right before final election campaign swings. Lawmakers broke the biennial rhythm in 1989 by acting on a big anti-drug package in a non-election year. But to ensure speedy passage of that measure, Senate leaders in September agreed to peel off controversial anti-crime provisions and bundle them for later consideration. *(Drug legislation, p. 768)*

Republicans repeatedly used the crime issue as a club against Democrats since Richard Nixon made law and order a major theme of his 1968 presidential campaign. The potency of the subject was demonstrated again 20 years later when 1988 Democratic presidential nominee Michael S. Dukakis failed to counter the impact of Bush campaign commercials that in effect blamed the Massachusetts governor for the rampage of a murderer-rapist, Willie Horton, furloughed from the state's penitentiary. Democrats' efforts to point out that the Massachusetts furlough program had originated under a Republican governor did little to counteract the powerful television image of prisoners' appearing to be let out of prison through a revolving door.

Senate Judiciary Committee Chairman Joseph R. Biden Jr., D-Del., a chief drafter of the crime legislation, wanted to ensure that any Senate bill was written largely by Democrats and that it would be seen as a tough, bold proposal. He conceded that figuratively speaking, "one of my objectives, quite frankly, is to lock Willie Horton up in jail."

But while the debate represented an opportunity for Democrats, it was also a minefield. Some opposed some Republican proposals, such as a broad federal death penalty and a limit on the appeals of prisoners on death row, leaving those Democrats potentially vulnerable to charges that they were soft on crime. The GOP generally spoke with one voice for punishment over rehabilitation, harsher and harsher sentences and no gun control. They also had a valuable platform on the subject, given that Republicans

Gun Control

Gun control proponents made several runs at new weapons restrictions in the 101st and 102nd Congresses, but each time they came up short against the aggressive and well-financed National Rifle Association (NRA) and its congressional allies.

101st Congress Action. In 1990, the gun lobby beat back three separate efforts to enact new federal restrictions on firearms. A ban on assault-style weapons was included in the Senate's version of an omnibus anti-crime bill (S 1970), but it was rejected by the House and stripped from the final measure (S 3266 — PL 101-647). Two other gun control bills languished in the House. *(Crime bill, p. 764)*

On July 24, the House Judiciary Committee reported legislation (HR 4225 — H Rept 101-621) that would have outlawed certain semiautomatic weapons, but the measure was never brought to the floor. The House Rules Committee agreed to let sponsors of the assault weapons ban bring HR 4225 up after the chamber acted on the omnibus crime bill. But backers of HR 4225 did not try for a floor vote because they knew they lacked support — as indicated by a separate House floor vote to water down semiautomatic weapons restrictions already in the crime bill.

On Sept. 10, the Judiciary Committee reported a bill (HR 467 — H Rept 101-691) to require a seven-day waiting period before a person could buy a handgun. But the so-called Brady bill also was never brought to the floor. The bill was named for former White House press secretary James S. Brady — wounded in a 1981 assassination attempt on his boss, President Ronald Reagan. Brady's wife, Sarah, had lobbied relentlessly for the measure.

The Brady bill did not get a rule for floor action because of opposition from Speaker Thomas S. Foley, D-Wash., and other House leaders. Supporters' ability to muster the votes for passage was doubtful anyway.

The NRA had been able to pressure Congress to keep the Brady bill out of a 1988 omnibus crime measure. Instead, that law (PL 100-690) contained a provision to require the attorney general to develop a felon identification system. *(1988 law, Congress and the Nation Vol. VII, p. 748)*

102nd Congress Action. Campaign finance figures for the 1990 congressional campaigns helped explain the NRA's success in the 102nd Congress, even though gun control proponents made some progress. According to the Federal Election Commission, the NRA spent $916,135 on 1990 campaigns, while Handgun Control, one of the leading gun control groups, spent $178,882.

Such financial disparities did not stop gun control advocates in 1991, and they started by pushing the Brady bill once again. Their biggest victory was House passage of the seven-day waiting period (HR 7 — H Rept 102-47) on May 8, by a **239-186 (R 60-102; D 179-83; I 0-1) key vote**. *(1991 key votes, p. 1061)*

Six weeks later, on June 28, the Senate adopted a compromise version of the Brady bill as part of its anti-crime bill (S 1241). This version required a waiting period of five business days and a plan for a nationwide instant background check of buyers. It was adopted on a **67-32 (R 19-24; D 48-8) key vote** and, coupled with the House action, marked the first time both chambers had voted for a waiting period. The bill, which passed the Senate 71-26 on July 11, also included a ban on sales and possession of semiautomatic assault-style guns.

With its own version of the Brady bill already passed, the House took up a broader anti-crime measure (HR 3371) in October. The House passed HR 3371 on a 305-118 vote Oct. 22. The bill had originally included a ban an assault weapons, but the provision was stripped out on the floor Oct. 17 by a vote 247-177. The Senate passed an amended HR 3371 by voice vote Nov. 21.

When the conferees met, they agreed to accept the Senate-passed version of the Brady bill as part of the overall package. The House Nov. 27 barely adopted the conference report on HR 3371 (H Rept 102-405) by a vote of 205-203. But when the Senate then took it up proponents failed Nov. 27 by 11 votes to invoke cloture, and the bill, along with the waiting-period provision, was doomed for the year.

Senate proponents tried again in 1992 to get HR 3371 through the chamber, but they failed twice more to invoke cloture, once on March 19 and again on Oct. 2. Opposition to the waiting-period provisions was a key factor. On Oct. 5, Senate backers of the original Brady bill with the seven-day waiting period tried to bring it up as a separate measure (S 3282). But Republicans in the chamber balked, blocking any consideration for the remainder of the 102nd Congress.

A day later, House Judiciary Chairman Jack Brooks, D-Texas, also tried to revive the bill, but the GOP also blocked his effort.

controlled the White House for all but four years since Nixon was first inaugurated.

1989 Action

President Bush and the Democrats in Congress jockeyed for position in 1989 over crime legislation. Bush unveiled his anti-crime package in May, calling for an expansion of the federal death penalty, more funding for law enforcement, federal prison construction and tougher sentences for criminals. The plan was introduced in the Senate (S 1225) by ranking Judiciary Republican Strom Thurmond, S.C.

Six months later, Biden introduced two broad measures. The first (S 1970) covered six controversial items: a federal death penalty, firearms regulation, revisions in habeas corpus appeals and in the exclusionary rule, a Justice Department reorganization and proposals to combat international money laundering. The death penalty provisions were drawn from a bill (S 32 — S Rept 101-170) that had been approved by the committee and sent to the floor with no recommendation for action. (The Senate Oct. 26 had passed 79-20 a more limited bill (S 1798) applying the death penalty to terrorists who murdered Americans abroad.)

The second Biden bill (S 1972) authorized about $1 billion in law enforcement support, tougher criminal sanctions and firearms penalties, and programs to crack down on gangs and drug trafficking. The bill also carried some of the provisions of S 1970 as well as of S 1711, an anti-drug bill the Senate passed 100-0 on Oct. 5.

Senate Majority Leader George J. Mitchell, D-Maine, said in mid-November that he was prepared to bring up the crime measures later in the month, but Minority Leader Bob Dole, R-Kan., asked him to postpone consideration until 1990.

1990 Action

Senate. After postponing action the previous year, the Senate initially decided to consider crime legislation in February 1990. But that date was put off until April, which in turn was put off until late May. By the time floor consideration began, two major bills were up for debate, S 1970, Biden's bill, and S 1971, an alternative offered by Thurmond incorporating the Bush proposals.

The Senate finally passed S 1970 July 11 by a 94-6 vote after weeks of contentious debate and cloture votes. The measure was largely written on the Senate floor — there was no committee report — and reflected more of Biden's original legislation than Bush's.

The bill banned nine foreign and domestic semiautomatic assault guns; made the death penalty an option for more than 30 crimes — the handiwork of Republicans and a Bush goal; revised the habeas corpus process for death row inmates; and authorized 3,000 federal agents and prosecutors and included a Democratic proposal to authorize $900 million — almost half the nearly $2 billion in the bill — for local law enforcement.

The Senate rejected a provision that would have prohibited a death sentence if a defendant could show that his or the victim's race played a role in sentencing.

While protracted debates were held on several issues, notably habeas corpus and the death penalty, the most serious threat to the bill's passage came from a narrow vote to preserve the committee-approved ban on assault weapons. (The ban had been considered by the Judiciary Committee in 1989 as a separate bill (S 747 — S Rept 101-160).) Opponents threatened to filibuster S 1970 to death and were dissuaded only after senators hammered out a consent agreement providing for debate and votes on some issues and stripping others out of the bill, including efforts to reorganize the Justice Department's crime and dangerous-drug divisions and to relax the so-called exclusionary rule so that evidence seized without a valid search warrant could be introduced in court.

Democrats May 23 unexpectedly mustered enough votes to defeat a motion by Orrin G. Hatch, R-Utah, to delete the ban on making, selling or possessing nine semiautomatic assault-style weapons. Among the weapons to be banned was the AK-47, which had been used in the January 1989 schoolyard massacre in Stockton, Calif. Hatch's motion to delete the weapons ban failed on a **48-52 (R 36-9; D 12-43) key vote** as did an effort to reconsider that vote, which would have allowed a second tally on the issue. *(1990 key votes, p. 1039)*

The vote marked the biggest Senate defeat for the National Rifle Association (NRA), which was known for its lobbying muscle and hefty campaign contributions. But while the vote was a success for Democrats, it cast uncertainty on the entire legislation. The NRA vowed to work to make sure the provisions went no further, and the Bush administration hinted the president would veto a bill with such restrictions. *(Gun control, box, p. 765)*

The NRA struck back after the May 23 vote, writing letters to its members in the districts of senators who had voted to retain the assault weapons provision and charging that those senators had betrayed "honest gun owners." The lobby group's efforts seemed to pay off when, two weeks later, two unsuccessful efforts were made to invoke cloture. Both Majority Leader Mitchell and Biden pointed to opponents of gun control — most of them Republicans — for putting the bill in jeopardy.

Mitchell was ready to give up on the legislation, but he eventually agreed to let Biden and Thurmond search for a way to salvage it. The heart of the pact was an agreement that, when senators finished with S 1970, no motions would be allowed for the rest of the 101st Congress on the death penalty, assault weapons, the exclusionary rule, the availability of firearms for purchase or death row inmates' petitions for writs of habeas corpus.

Despite the agreement, Phil Gramm, R-Texas, took on the assault weapon issue a second time, trying to strike the ban from the legislation. He proposed substituting those provisions for language mandating minimum sentences for firearms violations and for other drug-related and violent crimes. But Dennis DeConcini, D-Ariz., who had originally proposed the assault weapon ban, countered by adding his anti-gun language to the Texan's amendment. Despite the NRA's lobbying and the presence of Vice President Dan Quayle, presiding and ready to break a tie, the DeConcini gun ban prevailed.

Two separate efforts were made to restrict death row inmates' ability to use habeas corpus petitions, the procedure prisoners use to challenge the legality of their detention. The term is Latin for "you have the body" and is a process death row inmates routinely use after their regular appeals fail to reverse their sentences, overturn their convictions or at least delay executions.

Under the existing law, inmates had to exhaust their petitions in state courts before making collateral attacks on their convictions in federal court. A committee appointed by Chief Justice William H. Rehnquist and headed by retired justice Lewis F. Powell Jr. found in a 1989 report that the average time between conviction and execution in capital cases was more than eight years.

Biden and Bob Graham, D-Fla., had authored limited revisions of the habeas corpus process that were included in S 1970 as reported. On the floor, Thurmond and Arlen Specter, R-Pa., offered a substitute with tighter time limits and stricter requirements for second petitions in federal courts. The Thurmond-Specter proposal was rejected, 47-50, on May 23. But the next day, a motion to reconsider was agreed to 52-46, and the amendment was then adopted by voice vote.

The Thurmond-Specter language required inmates to file a federal habeas petition within 60 days of the appointment of counsel and resolution of an appeal to the state's highest court. The Graham-Biden version allowed a year for filings. The Thurmond-Specter plan also set stricter limits on second petitions in federal district court, requiring that an inmate first get permission from a federal appeals court, which would have to follow specific guidelines before granting such permission.

The Senate considered changes to the death penalty on two separate occasions. The bill authorized capital punishment for 30 federal crimes, primarily murder, espionage and treason. Most of these offenses had already carried a death penalty, but the sanction was invalidated in 1972 when the Supreme Court struck down all existing state and federal capital punishment laws in *Furman v. Georgia. (Case summary, Congress and the Nation Vol. III, p. 311)*

The Court later issued guidelines for how to impose the death penalty, outlining a two-stage procedure. Since then, states that allowed capital punishment had set up a process by which a trial was held to determine a defendant's guilt or innocence, and then a second proceeding was conducted to determine the sentence. In 1974, Congress approved capital punishment for airline hijackings that resulted in death (PL 93-366), and in 1988, as part of an omnibus anti-drug law (PL 100-690), it approved capital punishment for certain drug-trafficking murders. *(1974 action, Congress and the Nation Vol. IV, p. 582; 1988 action, Congress and the Nation Vol. VII, p. 748)*

A sizable majority in the Senate supported a broader federal death penalty, but many were unhappy about the provision, incorporated at the behest of Sen. Edward M. Kennedy, D-Mass., that required prosecutors to prove by "clear and convincing evidence" that racial disparities in sentencing were not the result of discrimination but simply reflected pertinent non-racial factors." Several senators saw this provision as an effort to deter capital punishment.

In 1987, the Supreme Court in *McCleskey v. Kemp* rejected challenges to capital punishment based on statistical evidence of racial disparities. The Court said the defendant failed to demonstrate purposeful discrimination. Kennedy, contending that the decision was wrongly decided, had wanted to overturn it with his proposed language. *(Case summary, Congress and the Nation Vol. VII, p. 798)*

But on May 24, the Senate agreed 58-38 to strike the language from the bill. That same day, critics of capital punishment succeeded, however, in preserving two provisions of S 1970 to bar executing anyone who was under 17 at the time a federal crime was committed or who was mentally retarded. This language responded to two recent Supreme Court decisions that refused to impose such limitations as a matter of constitutional law.

The death penalty debate returned June 29, when senators rejected 25-73 an amendment by death penalty opponent Mark O. Hatfield, R-Ore., that would have substituted mandatory life imprisonment for the 30 crimes.

On the last day of debate on S 1970, July 11, the Senate approved a savings and loan fraud amendment. It was a compromise among members of the Judiciary and Banking committees and the Bush administration. The proposal provided $162.5 million to beef up federal investigations of thrift fraud and increase the penalties for defendants, including mandatory life imprisonment for long-term, multimillion-dollar offenders. Violators who acted in concert with at least three other offenders and collected more than $5 million for their crimes over two years would be eligible for life in prison.

With the addition of the savings and loan fraud amendment, the Senate called it quits on the bill. Attention then shifted to the House.

House. Republicans had tried for a year to force consideration of an array of bills containing Bush's anti-crime proposals, only to have them languish in the Judiciary Committee. Meanwhile, Democrats, who had come to expect biennial, election-year crime bills, had been drafting their own proposals.

Judiciary Committee Chairman Jack Brooks, D-Texas, skeptical about the need for crime legislation, eventually changed his tune and scheduled a markup. The committee completed work on its version of the crime bill (HR 5269 — H Rept 101-681, Part I) on July 23. The vote was 19-17. HR 5269 was formally reported by Judiciary Sept. 5. The House Ways and Means Committee, which shared jurisdiction, reported HR 5269 (H Rept 101-681, Part II) on Sept. 10.

Among the Judiciary Committee bill's key elements were provisions that allowed capital punishment for 10 federal offenses, as opposed to 34 in the Senate bill (efforts to expand and reduce the number of offenses were rejected); barred the death penalty for individuals who were mentally retarded or who were under 18 at the time of their crimes; revamped the habeas corpus procedures to set deadlines for inmate petitions; allowed death row inmates to challenge their sentences if they could prove that their race or that of their victims was a factor in imposing the death penalty; and authorized $330 million to improve federal prisons and find alternatives to incarceration.

Concerned about the burgeoning savings and loan scandal, the bill also included language that made it illegal to conceal the assets of a failed thrift and established procedures to seize assets of thrift officials convicted of fraud.

The Bush administration threatened to veto the Judiciary version of the bill, with Attorney General Dick Thornburgh complaining that it would be tougher on law enforcement than on crime.

The House passed HR 5269 Oct. 5, after some procedural jockeying and three days of debate and amendments that allowed members to show some pre-election muscle by making the bill tougher on defendants. The vote was 368-55.

The bill almost did not get to the floor because of a flap over the rule setting the boundaries for the debate. Originally, the Rules Committee sought to preserve the tone of the Judiciary Committee's bill, barring floor amendments to strike the death penalty provisions that Bush opposed. But, in a surprise to both sides of the debate, that effort failed Sept. 25 when the House voted 166-258 against a rule that would have allowed consideration of the bill without the disputed amendments. The Rules Committee returned to the House the following week with a new rule that allowed amendments Republicans had sought, most importantly a proposal by Hyde to tighten further habeas corpus petitions.

Debate on the bill itself began Oct. 3 and was occasionally raucus. Death penalty opponents derisively shouted "Kill! Kill! Kill!" as amendments were adopted to expand the death penalty to about 30 crimes and make imposing and carrying out the sentence easier for states.

Stripped from the bill were provisions aimed at protecting defendants' rights, which in some cases might have resulted in blocking or delaying an execution. New limits on death row inmate appeals also were imposed. The House watered down the committee's language to reduce racial disparities in the imposition of the death penalty. An effort to strike the "racial justice" language entirely was rejected Oct. 5, but only by 12 votes — 204-216.

Although the Judiciary Committee bill had barred use of either imported or domestic gun parts to make assault-type semiautomatic weapons, the House weakened that provision also. Language was adopted making illegal only firearms assembled with foreign parts.

The House bill also increased penalties, mostly for drug crimes; authorized more money for local law enforcement; and required new prison rehabilitation programs and sentencing alternatives.

Final Action. The Senate passed an amended HR 5269 by voice vote on Oct. 23. A large conference — 94 House members and 24 senators — tried to resolve the disputes in time to permit enactment of a bill in some form. Staff members from both chambers worked to settle the less difficult topics, such as new law enforcement programs and child abuse penalties. Saved for the members themselves were subjects related to the death penalty and guns, and on those issues the chambers were far apart: The Senate wanted gun control; the House had voted against it. The House wanted "racial justice" safeguards for the death penalty; the Senate had voted them down. The House had a restrictive proposal for death row appeals, which its Democratic leadership fought in vain; the Senate had a convoluted appeals proposal that many senators were ready to scrap.

The strongest card held by opponents of the death penalty was the House-passed racial justice language, and House Democrats used the provisions as leverage in negotiations to moderate the overall legislation. But when little progress was made on the large, contentious issues, House Judiciary Chairman Brooks suggested a bare-bones approach, stripping out the controversial section. GOP conferees initially resisted and then gave in when a series of votes made it evident that agreement on a broad bill was unlikely.

The much slimmer bill (S 3266), which now included only the savings and loan fraud package, child abuse provisions, law enforcement assistance and stiffened penalties for steroid use — was passed in the Senate by voice vote and in the House 313-1 under suspension of the rules Oct. 27.

House members, while supporting the package, vented their anger about the provisions that were lost. Typical was the jibe tossed by Henry J. Hyde, R-Ill. The bill, he said, left the House "as Arnold Schwarzenegger and came back as Woody Allen."

Bush signed the bill Nov. 29, though he repeated Republicans' complaints about what had been eliminated from the legislation.

Major Provisions

As signed into law Nov. 29, 1990, S 3266 (PL 101-647):

Financial Institutions. Raised the civil and criminal penalties for financial fraud and other wrongdoing. Defendants who received $5 million or more in gross receipts from a continuing financial enterprise during any two-year period could get a fine of $10 million ($20 million for organizations) and a maximum sentence of life in prison.

Prisons. Authorized $220 million for states to develop alternatives to incarcerating inmates in already-crowded prison buildings. It also gave the Bureau of Prisons the authority to set up a shock incarceration program (known as "boot camp") that employed a highly regimented schedule of discipline characteristic of military basic training.

Child Abuse. Provided a statutory option and procedures for children who were witnesses at an abuse trial to testify outside the courtroom through a two-way closed-circuit television and authorized $10 million toward training for judges and prosecutors and child advocates on the abuse issues.

The law also made possession of child pornography a federal offense and required producers to keep a record of the age of people appearing in hard-core pornography.

Steroids. Covered anabolic steroids under federal laws that applied to cocaine and other controlled substances thereby increasing the penalties for trafficking. The penalty for illegal steroids trade increased from three years in prison to a maximum of 20 years.

Law Enforcement, Rural Drug Abuse Funding. Authorized up to $900 million in new federal aid for local law enforcement and called for an increase in federal agents, including 1,000 new Drug Enforcement Administration agents. It also authorized $20 million to help police and prosecutors in rural areas investigate illegal drug-trafficking.

Debt Collection. Put in place a uniform federal system for collection of all debts owed the federal government, replacing a system that relied on differing state laws.

Money Laundering. Required the Treasury secretary to report to Congress every two years during the four years after enactment on international money-laundering activities, investigations and prosecutions; and criminal indictments stemming from information provided by financial institutions. The law also gave the attorney general authority to transfer property forfeited as part of a money-laundering scheme to any foreign country that participated in the seizure of the property, subject to State Department approval.

Drug-Free School Zones. Authorized $15 million to train school personnel on drug-use intervention and counseling and $1.5 million for a model drug-free school zone project.

Drug Legislation

In contrast to several previous Congresses, the 101st passed no major anti-drug packages. Instead, in both 1989 and 1990, smaller measures and provisions in diverse bills covering treatment, education and law enforcement were enacted.

President Bush unveiled two major anti-drug initiatives, one in September 1989 and the other in January 1990, but he won from Congress only part of what he asked for. The rest stalled and died or else were defeated.

Meanwhile, the nation's highest ranking drug official, Director of National Drug Policy William J. Bennett, resigned in November 1990 after a somewhat stormy 20-month tenure as the first so-called drug czar. And it was left to the next Congress to confirm Bush's nominee to replace him, Florida Gov. Bob Martinez, whom critics immediately attacked as lacking adequate credentials for the job. *(Law leadership, box, p. 745)*

1989 Action

Bush won some of the anti-drug legislation he sought in 1989, but the rest fell victim to longstanding congressional disputes over narcotics-related matters.

In the final hours of the session Nov. 22, Congress cleared legislation embodying Bush's proposals to lend drug-fighting assistance to Colombia, Bolivia and Peru (HR 3611) and to require schools to implement programs aimed at preventing illegal substance abuse by students and employees (HR 3614). But two other bills, dealing with alcohol- and drug-abuse treatment programs (HR 3630) and the use of proceeds from assets seized during drug investigations (HR 3550), stalled, dying upon adjournment.

The immediate effect was that $3.18 billion in new anti-drug spending, cleared Nov. 14 as part of a transportation appropriations bill (HR 3015 — PL 101-164), lacked some of the authorizing language the administration wanted to govern how the funds should be spent. About $1 billion in the new funding was allotted to the federal prison system, and $727 million was for substance-abuse treatment and prevention programs. The remainder was earmarked for other law enforcement, education and treatment efforts.

Bush had presented his anti-drug plan in a national television address Sept. 5, laying out a strategy that essentially mirrored existing efforts. He maintained the focus on law enforcement as opposed to drug-abuse prevention and treatment, but he did shift away from the Reagan administration's emphasis on interdiction of drugs at the border. Instead, Bush emphasized apprehension and punishment of drug sellers and users in the United States. One of the main goals of the plan was a 10 percent reduction in two years in the number of people reporting illegal drug use and a 50 percent reduction in 10 years.

While Republicans praised the president, Democrats said the proposal was not bold enough and failed to provide enough resources.

The measure considered the most significant to clear was HR 3611, which paved the way for $125 million in U.S. military and law enforcement aid to the Andean nations that were the main source of cocaine used in the United States. The House Foreign Affairs Committee reported HR 3611 (H Rept 101-342, Part I) on Nov. 9. The House passed the bill by voice vote under suspension of the rules Nov. 13. The Senate passed an amended version by voice vote Nov. 15. The House adopted the conference report (H Rept 101-383) by voice vote Nov. 21. The Senate followed suit the next day, clearing HR 3611.

The funds for Bush's Andean Initiative were provided in a fiscal 1990 foreign aid spending bill (HR 3743 — PL 101-167). HR 3611 granted current-law waivers that were needed before the money could be spent. These included waivers of prohibitions against U.S. aid to foreign police forces and to nations that had fallen behind in debt repayments to the United States, a provision that was applicable to Peru and, possibly, Bolivia. *(Fiscal 1990 foreign aid appropriations, p. 228)*

The other bill that cleared, HR 3614, amended the Drug-Free Schools and Communities Act of 1986. It authorized funding for school-based anti-drug programs and revised some existing funding formulas to provide for emergency grants to areas with high drug use. The House passed HR 3614 Nov. 13 on a 371-0 vote under suspension of the rules. The Senate passed an amended version by voice vote Nov. 15. The conference report (H Rept 101-384) was adopted by voice vote in the House Nov. 21 and in the Senate Nov. 22, completing congressional action.

The administration also had sought legislation requiring states to adopt and implement statewide drug-treatment plans to be eligible for federal substance-abuse treatment grants, which were expected to run about $1.2 billion in fiscal 1990. The provision was part of HR 3630, but it was overwhelmed by a deep-seated dispute between House and Senate members over a proposal to require random drug testing of transportation workers. The House passed HR 3630 by voice vote under suspension of the rules Nov. 13. The Senate passed an amended version by voice vote Nov. 15. The House adopted the conference report (H Rept 101-961) by voice vote Oct. 27. HR 3630 saw no further action.

Negotiations on HR 3550, the asset-forfeiture measure, never even got off the ground. The bill was held up by a dispute between House and Senate members over a provision in the 1988 omnibus drug bill (PL 100-690) that dealt with proceeds from assets seized during drug investigations. The House Judiciary Committee reported HR 3550 (H Rept 101-349, Part I) on Nov. 13. The full House passed the bill 375-0 under suspension of the rules the same day. The Senate passed an amended version by voice vote Nov. 15. *(1988 law, Congress and the Nation Vol. VII, p. 748)*

Major Provisions

International Narcotics Control. As signed into law Dec. 13, 1989, HR 3611 (PL 101-231):

- Authorized the president in fiscal 1990 to provide Bolivia, Colombia and Peru with $125 million in military and law enforcement assistance to control illicit narcotics production and trafficking.
- Limited to $6.5 million the amount of the above funds that could be used for education and training of law enforcement officials.
- Limited to $12.5 million the amount of such assistance that could be used to supply equipment to law enforcement agencies.
- Required the recipient nations, to receive the assistance, to maintain democratic governments and law enforcement agencies that did "not engage in a consistent pattern of gross violations of internationally recognized human rights."
- Required the president to notify Congress, at least 15 days before providing the drug-fighting assistance, of which countries and agencies were receiving the aid, how much and what kind of assistance would be given, and how the aid would be used.
- Authorized the president to waive U.S. debt-repayment obligations for Bolivia, Colombia and Peru, beginning Oct. 1, 1990, if he determined that they were beginning programs to reduce the flow of drugs into the United States, in accordance with a formal agreement.
- Increased from $500,000 to $2 million the maximum award for information concerning acts of terrorism.
- Required nations receiving drug-fighting assistance to bear "an appropriate share" of the costs, instead of the 25 percent contribution currently required.

Drug-Free Schools and Communities. As signed into law Dec. 12, 1989, HR 3614 (PL 101-226):

- Capped at $125 million in fiscal 1990 and $100 million for each year thereafter the amount of funds distributed to governors for use under the anti-substance-abuse education and prevention program established in 1986 (PL 99-570). *(1986 law, Congress and the Nation Vol. VII, p. 723)*
- Distributed remaining funds, in excess of those available in fiscal 1989, to states under a new formula that directed more of the money to disadvantaged areas.

Law Enforcement

- Authorized $25 million a year for emergency grants to areas with high drug use. The grants were to be distributed by governors in fiscal 1990 and by the education secretary in subsequent years.
- Allowed governors to use part of their allocation for random drug testing of students who voluntarily participated in athletic activities in schools that voluntarily participated in such a program.
- Authorized $2 million for the education secretary to begin a demonstration program for creating drug-free school zones.
- Allowed local educational agencies to operate model alternative schools for students with drug problems.
- Authorized use of funds to set up drug-abuse education programs for juveniles in detention facilities.

1990 Action

Bush announced his second national drug-control plan Jan. 25, 1990, and called for a 12 percent increase in federal anti-drug spending, to more than $10 billion in fiscal 1991. The proposal required a substantial increase in federal law enforcement efforts, including hundreds of new Drug Enforcement Administration (DEA) agents, FBI agents and U.S. attorneys.

Critics of the Bush administration's drug policy often focused on its emphasis on law enforcement instead of education and treatment. In 1990, Congress passed a variety of measures that increased both education programs aimed at reducing the demand for illegal drugs and at treating those addicted. Critics, however, still maintained that not enough emphasis or money was given to those programs.

Treatment. Treatment programs received increased funding, an extra $40 million was authorized for a program to reduce the waiting period for addicts needing drug treatment and legislation beefing up treatment and prevention programs was approved by a Senate committee.

- *Increased Appropriations.* The fiscal 1991 spending bill (HR 5257 — PL 101-517) for the Departments of Labor, Health and Human Services, and Education and related agencies provided $2.1 billion for drug treatment.

The National Institute on Drug Abuse received $411 million, the Office for Treatment Improvement got $1.41 billion and the Office for Substance Abuse Prevention was given $272 million. The total amount was $165 million more than in fiscal 1990 and $7.5 million less than the administration requested for fiscal 1991.

- *Reduced Waiting Period.* Bush on Aug. 15 signed into law a bill (S 2461 — PL 101-374) to authorize an extra $40 million for a program to reduce the waiting period for addicts needing drug treatment. The Senate passed the measure (S Rept 101-336) by voice vote on June 29. The House passed an amended version by voice vote under suspension of the rules July 30. The Senate accepted the House changes Aug. 4, clearing the bill.
- *New Prevention Programs.* The Senate Labor and Human Resources Committee on Sept. 12 unanimously approved comprehensive legislation aimed at reducing the demand for illegal drugs by providing more resources to treatment and prevention programs. The bill (S 2649), reported (S Rept 101-476) on Sept. 27, authorized approximately $250 million in new funds for drug treatment and prevention programs in fiscal 1991. The measure died before any further action could be taken.

Education. A number of education measures that included drug-related provisions were considered, but most failed to clear.

- *HR 996.* Legislation (HR 996 — PL 101-589) was signed into law Nov. 16, which established three scholarship programs to provide students with grants in exchange for agreements to work or teach in science, math or engineering and for achieving outstanding work in the fields. The scholarship programs were authorized at $9.2 million in fiscal 1991. The final bill contained a House provision to bar a convicted drug user or distributor from receiving any awards and would require that such a student repay any awards received plus punitive penalties. *(Math, science education, p. 650)*
- *S 695, HR 5115.* The Senate-passed version of S 695 authorized $10 million in fiscal 1991 for a drug-abuse prevention program that involved local law enforcement officials providing classroom instruction and $5 million annually in fiscal 1991-93 for a series of state grants to establish drug-testing programs for secondary school athletes. The House-passed HR 5115 included a provision to halt financial aid to students convicted of drug possession. Neither measure became law. *(Bush education initiative, p. 643)*
- *HR 5064.* The House on July 10 suspended the rules and passed, 388-13, HR 5064 (H Rept 101-572) to establish a $15 million grant program to develop a strategy for teaching elementary school pupils to resist pressures that could lead to drug abuse. An amended version was reported by the Senate Labor and Human Resources Committee July 11. The Bush administration opposed the bill.
- *HR 5124.* The House on July 10 by voice vote under suspension of the rules passed HR 5124 (H Rept 101-573), which was designed to prevent student drug abuse. It included provisions that would establish criteria for drug-free school zones; require the Education Department to reserve $5 million of appropriated funds for grants to replicate successful drug-abuse education programs; and raise the authorization, from $35 million to $50 million, for the existing drug-abuse grant program for training of teachers and antidrug counselors.

The administration opposed the bill, arguing that its provisions were unnecessary, burdensome or redundant.

The Senate Labor and Human Resources Committee reported an amended version of the bill on Sept. 28, but the measure went no further.

Drug Testing and Enforcement. Although separate legislation calling for random drug testing in the transportation industry failed to become law, Congress did address the issue in the fiscal 1991 transportation appropriations bill (HR 5229 — PL 101-516). The House agreed Oct. 19 to a Senate amendment to cut 5 percent of a state's federal highway money in the first year and 10 percent in later years if that state did not suspend the driver's license for at least six months of anyone convicted of a drug offense. *(Drug testing transport workers, 1989-90 action, p. 425)*

A provision expanding the death penalty for drug-related crimes was dropped from 1990 anti-crime legislation. *(Crime bill, p. 764)*

Vertical Price Fixing

Bitterly fought antitrust legislation to prevent manufacturers from fixing the prices dealers could charge for their goods died at the end of the 101st Congress. The

House in 1990 passed a measure (HR 1236) designed to reduce conduct known as resale price maintenance, or vertical price fixing. But a related bill (S 865 — S Rept 101-251) stalled in the Senate, as it had when the House passed similar legislation in 1987. *(Congress and the Nation Vol. VII, p. 776)*

In an effort to get a floor vote on S 865, Sen. Howard M. Metzenbaum, D-Ohio, held up a bill (HR 5316) creating 85 judgeships until the last day of Congress. Metzenbaum finally relented after winning a promise from Senate Judiciary leaders, including bill opponent Strom Thurmond, R-S.C., for a floor vote early in 1991. *(102nd Congress action, p. 791)*

Vertical price fixing occurred when a manufacturer conspired with a retailer to force a rival dealer to charge at least a certain price for the manufacturer's goods.

Typically, the type of case covered by vertical price fixing legislation arose after a distributor decided to sell a particular product at a discount. Then another distributor — usually a bigger and more powerful one that was unwilling to lower its prices to meet the competition — persuaded the manufacturer to terminate the contract with the discounting distributor.

In the Senate, Metzenbaum, chairman of the Judiciary Subcommittee on Antitrust, termed S 865 "the most important, understated bill around, from the consumer standpoint."

Yet many members in both chambers insisted that the legislation was unnecessary and could have exposed businesses to legal actions when no agreement was made to fix prices. They said it could allow ambiguous evidence to be used to establish a conspiracy and in the end could hurt honest manufacturers.

The Justice Department also opposed the proposals, saying they would inhibit legitimate pacts between manufacturers and dealers and spawn endless litigation.

Background. Since a 1911 Supreme Court decision, vertical price fixing had been automatically, or "per se," illegal. But administration policy and two Court decisions had created ambiguity about what was enough evidence to warrant a jury trial. Doubt also existed about whether vertical price fixing would be punished in the courts. The Justice Department had not brought a vertical price fixing case since 1980.

The 1990 legislation originated when it became apparent in the early 1980s that the Reagan administration did not intend to enforce the per se prohibition against resale price maintenance and was in fact supporting its reversal in court cases. The Justice Department's position stemmed from a theory that such price maintenance could enhance rather than inhibit competition.

Effect of Legislation. HR 1236, reported from House Judiciary (H Rept 101-438) on March 29 and passed by the full House 235-157 on April 18, would in effect have reversed two Supreme Court decisions that made it much harder for plaintiffs to win vertical price fixing cases. The first was a 1984 ruling in *Monsanto Co. v. Spray-Rite Service Corp.* that a complaining discounter must provide direct evidence that a manufacturer and another retailer had intended to maintain resale price levels. *(Case summary, Congress and the Nation Vol. VI, p. 743)*

The bill would have allowed a jury trial if the plaintiff could show that a supplier canceled its contract after receiving a communication from a rival dealer about the plaintiff's pricing policies. The plaintiff would have to demonstrate that the supplier's termination or refusal to supply was "substantially caused" by the competitor's communication.

A separate provision would have stated that minimum resale price maintenance was automatically illegal under antitrust law. The provision was intended to override the holding in the 1988 case *Business Electronics Corp. v. Sharp Electronics Corp.* that said no per se violation of antitrust laws had taken place unless the manufacturer and the retailer agreed to set a specific price. The bill would have codified the 1911 Supreme Court holding, in *Dr. Miles Medical Co. v. John D. Park and Sons Co.*, that minimum resale price fixing agreements were illegal per se. *(1988 case, Congress and the Nation Vol. VII, p. 817)*

RICO Limitations

Differing bills (S 438, HR 5111) aimed at cutting back private suits under federal anti-racketeering law won approval from the Senate and House Judiciary committees in 1990, but the industry-dominated coalition behind the bills failed for the third consecutive Congress to push a measure to enactment.

Business groups and others maintained that the 1970 Racketeer Influenced and Corrupt Organizations Act (RICO) had been transformed from a weapon against organized crime into a bludgeon against established businesses, accountants, lawyers and other professionals. They wanted to limit the provisions for bringing triple-damage civil suits under the law and managed to get bills aimed at that goal far along in both the 99th and 100th Congresses.

RICO, enacted as Title IX of the Organized Crime Control Act of 1970 (PL 91-452), was primarily intended to give federal prosecutors stronger weapons against organized crime. A laundry list of so-called predicate offenses could be used to fashion a criminal RICO charge, which carried with it a 20-year prison sentence, a fine of up to $25,000 and the threat of forfeiture of any proceeds from racketeering activities. *(RICO, Congress and the Nation Vol. III, p. 272)*

A less-noticed section also allowed private suits under RICO. A plaintiff could fashion a suit using the law's same broad definitions and, if successful, recover three times any monetary damages suffered from the racketeering activity, plus attorneys' fees.

The law was little used in its first decade, but during the 1980s prosecutors achieved dramatic successes with RICO cases against organized crime groups in several major cities. In addition, prosecutors began to use the law's elastic coverage to go after corrupt politicians, drug dealers, white-collar criminals, labor racketeers, gamblers, terrorists, white supremacists and pornographers.

Civil RICO also went largely unused during the 1970s, but private lawyers began to develop its potential during the 1980s. Plaintiffs ranging from forlorn investors and discontented utility customers to major corporations and fired executives cited RICO in suits against established businesses that included Fortune 500 corporations, major banks and securities dealers, and well-regarded law and accounting firms.

Business groups and others, including the American Civil Liberties Union (ACLU) and the American Bar Association (ABA), complained that civil RICO was being misused in routine commercial disputes that did not warrant enhanced penalties and more properly belonged in state courts.

Law Enforcement

The number of civil RICO cases rose dramatically after a 1985 Supreme Court ruling, *Sedima S.P.R.L. v. Imrex Co. Inc.*, that refused to limit suits to cases in which the defendant had already been convicted under RICO's criminal provisions. From a trickle of cases before 1985, the number tallied by the Administrative Office of the U.S. Courts jumped to 614 in the next nine months and plateaued at about 1,000 a year through 1990. *(1985 case summary, Congress and the Nation Vol. VII, p. 802)*

Lobbying Drive

Three business groups with members often named as RICO defendants — the National Association of Manufacturers, the American Institute of Certified Public Accountants and the Securities Industry Association — had been pressing Congress to change the law since before the *Sedima* ruling. They stepped up their efforts after the Supreme Court decision.

In 1986, the coalition won House passage of a bill to impose the prior criminal conviction requirement on civil RICO suits, but the measure stalled in the Senate. In 1988, a recrafted bill won unanimous approval from the Senate Judiciary Committee but was blocked from the floor.

The ad hoc Business Coalition for RICO Reform got bills introduced early in 1989 and voiced confidence that it would finally bring its drive to success in the 101st Congress. In June 1989, the Supreme Court, in the case of *H. J. Inc. v. Northwestern Bell Telephone Co.*, again rejected pleas for judicial narrowing of the law. Proponents of RICO reform said that decision underlined the need for legislative change. *(Case summary, p. 816)*

But RICO reform had some powerful opponents in Congress, who argued that the legislation could weaken protections for victims of white-collar crimes, including fraud in the savings and loan (S&L) industry. Members were particularly sensitive to the lawsuit filed under RICO against Charles H. Keating Jr., owner of the failed Lincoln Savings and Loan. Five senators, who had accepted more than $1.3 million in political contributions from Keating and his associates, were under Senate investigation for improperly intervening to stave off regulators. *(Keating Five, p. 975)*

The S&L crisis also was the focus of opposition from consumer organizations and state law enforcement organizations. Not only did they cite the S&L crisis as proof of the need for strong legal weapons against sophisticated economic wrongdoing, but they also insisted that the business groups were exaggerating the alleged abuses under the law.

Legislative Action

The Senate Judiciary Committee, which had postponed a markup on the issue in the fall of 1989, moved on Feb. 1, 1990, to approve the coalition-drafted bill (S 438) that would have virtually eliminated triple-damage private RICO suits. S 438 (S Rept 101-269) was reported April 24. The House Judiciary Committee did not act on the companion measure (HR 5111) until Sept. 18, reporting it (H Rept 101-975) on Oct. 27. By that time, proponents were up against the legislative clock.

With only a few weeks left in the session, the business coalition's only hope for enactment depended on getting the legislation onto the House floor under suspension of the rules, a procedure that allowed for no amendments and only 40 minutes of debate. But two opponents, John Conyers Jr., D-Mich., and Banking Committee Chairman Henry B. Gonzalez, D-Texas, raised objections, and HR 5111 never reached the floor. With no House action, supporters of the Senate bill also did not push that measure to the floor.

Antitrust Measures

Shortly before adjournment, the 101st Congress cleared legislation (HR 29 — PL 101-588) that eased the constraints on interlocking corporate directorships and increased penalties in antitrust cases brought by the federal government.

HR 29 updated the Clayton Antitrust Act of 1914 to prohibit individuals from serving on the boards of directors of competing companies if both had $10 million or more in assets. The threshold was indexed to keep pace with economic growth; previously the prohibition applied if either company had $1 million or more in assets or profits. The legislation also extended the restrictions to certain high-level officers.

The measure also contained a Senate amendment that increased tenfold the maximum criminal fines for corporate violations of the Sherman Act — to $10 million from $1 million — and raised the maximum fine against an individual to $350,000 from $100,000. The amendment was essentially the same as the provisions of a bill (HR 3341 — H Rept 101-287) that the House had passed Oct. 17, 1989.

The Senate also added an amendment providing for triple damages in civil suits brought by the United States against antitrust violators. Previously, the U.S. government could win only actual damages.

The House Judiciary Committee reported HR 29 (H Rept 101-483) on May 14, 1990. The House passed the bill by voice vote under suspension of the rules on May 15. The Senate passed it Oct. 27 after adding the two amendments, and the House agreed to the amended version Oct. 28, clearing the bill. President Bush signed the measure Nov. 16.

Joint Ventures. The House on June 5, 1990, passed by voice vote under suspension of the rules a measure (HR 4611) to encourage joint production ventures by U.S. companies, but a similar measure stalled in a Senate subcommittee.

HR 4611 would have limited the antitrust liability of joint manufacturing ventures to single damages, provided that companies notified the government in advance of the venture. The bill was intended to encourage U.S. companies to pool their resources and production efforts, without fear of antitrust liability, so that they could be more competitive in world markets.

HR 4611 (H Rept 101-516) was reported from House Judiciary June 1.

Copyright Legislation

Artists' Rights

In the final hours of the 1990 session, a bill (HR 5316 — PL 101-650) creating additional federal judgeships became the vehicle for a Senate provision regarding artists' rights. At the urging of Edward M. Kennedy, D-Mass., the

Senate adopted an amendment that gave visual artists — painters, sculptors and photographers — a legal right to prevent distortion or modification of their work even after it was sold. *(Federal judgeships, p. 774)*

As approved, the measure made clear that anyone who created a painting, drawing, print, sculpture or still photographic image in a limited number of copies (200 or fewer) had a claim of authorship over the work. The measure did not protect film directors.

Artists would be required to show that the distortion or mutilation prejudiced their honor or reputation. The protections would endure for the life of the artist plus 50 years. The bill also would prevent the use of an artist's name on a work that he or she did not create.

A second Kennedy amendment included in HR 5316 extended copyright protection to architectural designs.

The artists' rights language originally appeared in S 1198, a bill sponsored by Kennedy. It was approved, 5-2, by the Senate Judiciary Subcommittee on Patents, Copyrights and Trademarks on June 28, 1990. The full committee never took up the bill, however. A House companion measure (HR 2690 — H Rept 101-514) was reported from House Judiciary on June 1, 1990, and passed by voice vote under suspension of the rules on June 7. Kennedy attached the provisions to HR 5316 to ensure passage.

Computer Software

The judgeship bill (HR 5316 — PL 101-650), which cleared in 1990, also was the vehicle for an amendment designed to forestall unauthorized copying of computer programs that often required millions of dollars to develop and that typically sold for several hundred dollars. The amendment, offered by Orrin G. Hatch, R-Utah, prohibited commercial leasing or rental of computer software without the permission of the copyright holders.

Computer software producers had long complained of businesses that rented expensive software to clients who then copied the program, obtaining it at a greatly reduced cost. The measure permitted non-profit libraries and educational institutions to lend computer software to faculty, staff and students.

The Senate had passed separate computer software protection legislation (S 198) by voice vote May 1, 1990. The bill had been reported (S Rept 101-265) by Senate Judiciary April 19. The House companion measure (HR 5498 — H Rept 101-735) was reported from House Judiciary Sept. 21. The full House passed the measure by voice vote under suspension of the rules Sept. 27. The House then passed, by voice vote, an amended S 198 with the language of HR 5498. The House-passed version contained only a few minor technical differences in its provisions concerning computer software. However, the legislation also dealt with the rights of artists, architects and video game manufacturers.

On Oct. 20, the Senate stripped a provision from S 198 designed to allow arcade owners to purchase video games from sources other than the manufacturers and authorized distributors. Both chambers subsequently decided to add the House version of S 198 to the judgeships bill.

State, University Coverage

Legislation (HR 3045 — PL 101-553) to allow publishers to collect damages from state governments and universities for infringement of copyrighted material cleared Congress in 1990. The measure responded to federal court rulings since the mid-1980s that held state governments and state-run universities immune from federal copyright infringement suits under the 11th Amendment, unless Congress specifically overrode that immunity.

The legislation allowed copyright owners to sue for actual and statutory damages, attorneys' fees and injunctive relief. The Senate had added a provision to limit attorneys' fees, but it was dropped in conference.

Publishers had sought the legislation, claiming that state universities and colleges were photocopying huge chunks of textbooks and other reference materials without fear of meaningful sanctions.

The House Judiciary Committee reported HR 3045 (H Rept 101-282) on Oct. 13, 1989. The House passed the bill by voice vote under suspension of the rules Oct. 16. The Senate Judiciary Committee reported its version (S Rept 101-305) on June 5, 1990. The Senate passed an amended HR 3045 by voice vote June 26. The House agreed to the conference report (H Rept 101-887) by voice vote Oct. 20. The Senate followed suit Oct. 26, completing congressional action. President Bush signed HR 3045 on Nov. 15.

Copyright Fees

A bill to increase copyright fees (HR 1622 — PL 101-318) cleared Congress in 1990. The legislation changed the fee schedule of the Copyright Office, doubling copyright registration fees to $20 per work, from $10. The bill also provided for the adjustment of copyright fees every five years thereafter to account for inflation.

HR 1622 (H Rept 101-279) was reported from House Judiciary on Oct. 13, 1989, and passed by voice vote under suspension of the rules Oct. 16. The Senate Judiciary Committee reported the measure (S Rept 101-267) on April 19, 1990. The Senate passed HR 1622 by voice vote June 13, clearing the bill. President Bush signed the measure July 3.

Copyright Tribunal

Congress in 1992 also cleared legislation (HR 3046 — PL 101-319) to reduce the number of commissioners on the Copyright Royalty Tribunal from five to three and change the salary classification rates for members of the tribunal and other government offices. The tribunal was responsible for distributing funds collected from transmission of cable and satellite television and from jukebox licenses. The legislation was intended to improve the tribunal's efficiency.

The Judiciary Committee reported the measure (H Rept 101-329) on Nov. 3, 1989. The full House passed HR 3046 by voice vote under suspension of the rules Nov. 13. The Senate Judiciary Committee reported its version (S Rept 101-268) on April 19, 1990. The Senate passed HR 3046 by voice vote June 13. President Bush signed the bill July 3.

Legal Services Corporation

Strife continued to dog the Legal Services Corporation (LSC) during the 101st Congress, despite efforts by President Bush to quiet the controversies surrounding the agency by appointing a new board of directors.

Congress in both 1989 and 1990 attached language to legislation funding the agency to prevent it from putting into effect any new rules or regulations for state and local legal aid programs. Conservative members of the LSC board had sought to put additional limits on the activities of those programs. Congress also rejected a package of restrictions that would have legislatively limited legal aid programs. For the first time since 1981, Congress made an effort to pass an authorization bill for the LSC; a House Judiciary subcommittee approved a reauthorization measure, but it went no further.

Background

Congress created the LSC in 1974 (PL 93-355) as a quasi-independent corporation to dispense federal funds to legal aid programs for the poor free from political pressure by state and local officials. Liberal and conservative lawmakers clashed sharply over the line between legal representation for the poor and political and social advocacy; that ideological battle persisted through both the Carter and Reagan administrations. *(LSC creation, Congress and the Nation Vol. IV, p. 573)*

Congress passed a three-year reauthorization in 1977, but a new reauthorization had to be scuttled in 1980 in the face of opposition from conservative lawmakers. President Ronald Reagan tried to abolish the corporation. Congress refused, but Reagan succeeded in cutting its funds by 25 percent and naming sharp critics of legal aid to the 11-member board of directors.

The Reagan-era LSC boards, created through recess appointments in Reagan's first term, adopted limits on class action suits and lobbying by legal aid lawyers and instituted more critical monitoring of local programs. With Reagan's second term, a compromise of sorts resulted in Senate confirmation of a new board that had some liberal members but was still controlled by conservatives.

In the face of an anticipated Reagan veto, Congress did not try to pass reauthorizing legislation for the LSC after 1985. The corporation was continued through appropriations bills, and lawmakers added several riders limiting the board's power to impose new restrictions on LSC-funded programs. *(Bush appointments, box, p. 776)*

Legislative Action

HR 5271, approved 6-3 by the House Judiciary Subcommittee on Administrative Law on Aug. 3, 1990, would have reauthorized the LSC for three years and set no funding level. It also included provisions to strengthen the authority of local governing boards and to limit LSC monitoring of legal aid programs.

Conservatives suffered a setback when the subcommittee rejected an amendment that would have placed restrictions on legal aid workers who represented farmworkers. A similar amendment had fallen just seven votes short in October 1989 when its sponsors had tried to attach it to the fiscal 1990 funding bill (HR 2991 — PL 101-162) that included the LSC.

HR 5271 was never put on the House Judiciary Committee's calendar. Nor had the Senate begun work on an authorization.

Judgeships Bill

With relatively little controversy, the majority Democratic Congress cleared legislation (HR 5316) in 1990 giving President Bush 85 new federal judgeships to fill — the first increase in the federal judiciary since 1984 (PL 98-353). *(Congress and the Nation Vol. VI, p. 702)*

In a rare formal news conference, Chief Justice William H. Rehnquist in 1989 complained that judges' workload was at an all-time high and morale was at an all-time low. He urged Congress to create more judgeships and raise judicial salaries. Bush subsequently endorsed the judges' pay increase, and judges got a raise as part of Congress' effort to give itself and other federal officials a pay hike. *(Congressional pay, p. 965)*

The request for new judgeships gained new urgency as lawmakers became aware of the caseload implications of the war on drugs. Drug cases increased 15 percent in 1988 and 1989, and judges in many areas said the rising drug caseloads were making it difficult for litigants in civil suits to get their cases to trial.

Attached to HR 5316 was a congressional mandate for judges to adopt special plans to speed up civil litigation. The directive, softened in response to opposition from federal judges, left the details of such plans up to federal judges in most districts but required in 10 districts the adoption of specific guidelines, including an 18-month deadline for bringing cases to trial.

The legislation added 74 new district court judgeships and 11 appellate posts. The Judicial Conference of the United States, the federal judiciary's policy-making body, had requested 96 new judgeships.

Pork-barrel politics shaped the allocation of new seats. Judgeships not recommended by the Judicial Conference were added for Republicans on the Senate Judiciary Committee and for members of both parties on the House Judiciary Subcommittee on Economic and Commercial Law, which handled the legislation. Texas, home state of the Democratic chairman of the House Judiciary Committee, Jack Brooks, got the largest number of new seats — 11.

A separate bill (HR 1620) added to the legislation as it neared passage called for a national commission to consider alternatives to the unwieldy congressional process of impeaching tenured federal judges. HR 1620, which was reported from House Judiciary (H Rept 101-512) on June 1, 1990, was passed by the House by voice vote under suspension of the rules June 5.

Another measure folded into the final bill (HR 5381) put into effect a batch of largely non-controversial recommendations of the congressionally established Federal Courts Study Committee. HR 5381 (H Rept 101-734) was reported from House Judiciary Sept. 21 and passed by the full House by voice vote under suspension of the rules Sept. 27.

The judgeships bill also attracted other late last-minute add-ons not directly related to the court system, including measures to encourage the networks to develop guidelines on TV violence and to give artists copyright protections against modifications of their works. But Sen. Howard M. Metzenbaum, D-Ohio, failed in his bid to attach a bill to tighten rules against manufacturers' fixing prices that dealers could charge for their products. *(TV violence, p. 428; artists' rights, p. 772; vertical price fixing, p. 770)*

The House Judiciary Committee reported HR 5316 (H Rept 101-733) on Sept. 21. The House passed the bill, 387-18, under suspension of the rules Sept. 27. The Senate passed an amended version by voice vote Oct. 27. The House accepted the Senate changes Oct. 28, clearing the measure. Bush signed HR 5316 (PL 101-650) on Dec. 1.

Administrative Law Judges

Legislation (S 594) to establish an independent government agency to handle disputes between federal agencies and private parties won approval from the Senate Judiciary Committee in 1990. But the measure was opposed by the Bush administration and saw no further action.

S 594 would have established an independent corps of administrative law judges (ALJs) to handle legal proceedings at the 29 federal agencies that had in-house ALJs. The Judiciary Committee approved the bill June 27 on a near party-line 9-5 vote and reported it (S Rept 101-467) Sept. 19.

Under the Administrative Procedure Act of 1946, administrative law judges were assigned to a single agency, where they adjudicated disputes between private parties and the federal government on regulations, rulemaking and other matters.

The aim of the bill was to lessen the chances that an administrative law judge would be subject to coercion or improper reward by an agency involved in a dispute. By creating an independent ALJ corps as a separate federal agency and allowing judges to hear cases at different agencies, it was hoped the bill would assure the impartial resolution of administrative law cases.

In opposing the measure, the Bush administration argued that the system was intended to maintain specialist in-house ALJs to resolve arcane disputes.

The administration also stated its belief that the ALJ corps would add unnecessarily to government bureaucracy.

Judicial Impeachments

The Senate in 1989 closed out an extraordinary string of three judicial impeachments in four years, convicting and removing from office two U.S. district court judges — Alcee L. Hastings of Florida and Walter L. Nixon Jr. of Mississippi.

Hastings on Oct. 20 was convicted on eight articles of impeachment and acquitted of three. The Senate chose not to vote on six other articles.

Hastings was the first person to be convicted by the Senate after winning an acquittal from a jury at a criminal trial on related charges. Two weeks later, on Nov. 3, Nixon was convicted on two articles of impeachment and acquitted of one.

Hastings had been appointed to the Southern District of Florida by President Jimmy Carter in 1979. In 1992, he was elected to the House as a Democrat from Florida's 23rd District. Nixon, who had been chief judge for the U.S. District Court for the Southern District of Mississippi, was appointed in 1968 by President Lyndon B. Johnson. In September 1993, he was given clearance by Mississippi authorities to resume the practice of law after passing the state bar.

Hastings and Nixon were the sixth and seventh federal officials (all judges) ever to be removed from office, and both immediately lost their $89,500-a-year salaries.

In 1986, the Senate convicted and removed U.S. District Judge Harry E. Claiborne of Nevada. *(Congress and the Nation Vol. VII, p. 737)*

Hastings Case

Hastings' trouble began in 1981, when the judge was first accused by a grand jury in the Southern District of Florida of plotting to obtain a $150,000 bribe. The bulk of the impeachment articles stemmed from his subsequent 1983 bribery trial.

After Hastings was acquitted in February 1983, a special judicial investigating committee of the 11th U.S. Circuit Court of Appeals, which included Florida, determined that Hastings had lied and had fabricated evidence to secure his acquittal. Using procedures under a 1980 judicial discipline law (PL 96-458), the panel sent its findings to Congress in 1987 and recommended that Hastings be impeached. *(1980 law, Congress and the Nation Vol. V, p. 744)*

Hastings was impeached by the House, 413-3, on Aug. 3, 1988, on charges of conspiracy to accept a bribe, perjury, leaking wiretap information and undermining the judiciary's integrity. He contended that he was singled out for special treatment by law enforcement officers and the federal judiciary because he was an outspoken black. *(1988 action, Congress and the Nation Vol. VII, p. 768)*

Black House members raised concerns about racial discrimination during 1988 proceedings before the Judiciary Criminal Justice Subcommittee, the full committee and the House. But those concerns were defused, largely because the subcommittee chairman, John Conyers Jr., D-Mich., who was black, said that his panel's investigation did not turn up any evidence of racial bias against the judge. Another black Judiciary Committee member, George W. Crockett Jr., D-Mich., also had been concerned about the racism allegation, but in the end, he said he was "convinced that an honest effort was made to put racism aside." Crockett, like Conyers, voted to impeach Hastings.

Following the recommendation of its Rules Committee, the Senate in 1989 approved two resolutions governing the conduct of the trial. The first (S Res 39), passed Feb. 2, provided that the full Senate would hear Hastings' motions to dismiss the impeachment articles. The second resolution (S Res 38), passed March 16, ordered that a committee be appointed by the majority leader to take evidence and report to the Senate, which would then determine whether to remove Hastings from office.

The hearing on the judge's motions to dismiss the impeachment articles took place March 15, with Hastings arguing that a new trial would be unfair. He called on the Senate to give deference to the 1983 jury decision. Managers of the case from the House countered that the Senate had to accept its constitutional role of ensuring the integrity of federal office. The next day, after deliberating in closed session for two hours, the Senate voted not to dismiss any of the charges against Hastings and to set up a 12-member committee to take evidence in the case.

After several weeks of pre-trial jockeying, including denying a Hastings request for public funds for his defense, the committee began taking evidence on July 10.

The House prosecutors, led by Rep. John Bryant, D-Texas, contended that Hastings was part of a conspiracy to obtain a $150,000 bribe from two brothers who were criminal defendants in a racketeering case before him.

William Borders, who was a prominent Washington lawyer and was convicted for his participation in the 1981 scheme, supposedly was the contact between the judge and the defendants, Frank and Thomas Romano. Terence Anderson, the lawyer for Hastings, said Borders was operating on his own. Anderson maintained that any evidence the

Bush Judicial Appointments

During his four-year presidency, George Bush kept faith with the politics of his predecessor, Ronald Reagan, and appointed conservatives to the federal district and appeals courts.

Bush also made an effort to appoint more female judges, finishing with a record level of female appointees to the federal district courts. But he named a smaller percentage of blacks and Hispanics than did President Jimmy Carter.

During his term, Bush appointed 185 district and circuit (appeals) court judges, close to one-fourth of the federal bench. The number of judgeships had grown to 825 in regular district and appeals courts.

Like Reagan, Bush said he wanted judicial conservatives who would not "legislate from the bench." That translated into judges with a comparatively restrictive view of individual rights. These conservative or constructionist judges believed in a relatively narrow reading of the Constitution and federal law, asserting that it is the role of legislators, not the courts, to establish new individual rights and broad social remedies. In certain contexts, their perspective tended to favor the rights of government over those of the individual.

By contrast, "liberal" judges were inclined to construe constitutional and other legal texts more broadly — finding protections for criminal defendants and women seeking abortions, for example, that were not explicit in the Constitution.

Many of Bush's selections for the appeals courts were in fact promotions for Reagan appointees to district courts. For the district courts, Bush often turned to nominees with experience as state judges or federal magistrates.

Several Democrats said the overall quality of Bush's appointments was higher than Reagan's, though some contended he had put forward candidates with marginal credentials. *(Reagan appointments, Congress and the Nation Vol. VII, pp. 770, 909)*

Bush selected 36 female judges during his term, 19.5 percent of all his appointments. That included 29 female appointees to the district bench, a record 19.6 percent. Bush also appointed seven women — or 18.9 percent of his choices — to federal appeals courts. Carter, who appointed more judges than did Bush, named a greater number of women — but a smaller percentage.

Bush appointed 12 black judges to the district and appeals courts, including Clarence Thomas, who was later elevated to the Supreme Court. Bush named eight Hispanic judges, six to district courts and two to circuit courts. By contrast, Carter appointed 37 black judges and 16 Hispanics.

Several observers said Bush officials may have had a hard time finding women and minorities who shared the conservative judicial philosophy or political affiliations Bush sought to promote. Republican senators also bore some responsibility for the percentage of female and minority appointments. Customarily, senators of the president's party suggested names for federal district court openings in their states. Those senators generally offered the names of white men.

In November 1990, Bush wrote to Senate Minority Leader Bob Dole, R-Kan., urging GOP senators to suggest more women and minorities. Momentum subsequently quickened, with the bulk of such appointments coming in the second half of Bush's term.

As striking as the nature of Bush's appointments was the number of appointments he could have made but did not. The president got off to a slow start and never caught up, especially after a 1990 law added 85 seats to the bench. *(Judgeships bill, p. 774)*

Appointments slowed further amid the tumultuous proceedings for the Thomas nomination to the Supreme Court and while the administration and the Senate Judiciary Committee squabbled in late 1991 over how to control access to FBI background checks on nominees.

At the close of the 102nd Congress, Bush had failed to nominate candidates for 46 judicial vacancies. And the Judiciary Committee had failed to vote on another 53 pending nominations, effectively canceling those selections.

Democrats and Republicans alike criticized the administration's slowness in naming nominees and pushing them through the confirmation process. Several said the White House and Justice Department officials had overly rigid screening criteria. "There was a saliva test of purity that was rather unattractive," said Alan K. Simpson, R-Wyo., a senior member of the Judiciary Committee. "While they were waiting for a 100 percenter to show up, they lost the 90 percenter."

When some Republicans criticized committee Democrats for trying to stall nominations, Judiciary staff noted that the committee had approved 124 nominations during the 102nd Congress, 66 of those in 1992 — more than were approved in recent presidential election years.

House had against Hastings in the bribery matter already was rejected by a jury. He claimed Hastings was set up by Borders, whom Anderson called "a big-time rainmaker" who boasted to his criminal friends that he had the power to influence judges.

Borders appeared before the committee under subpoena but refused to answer questions, even with immunity from prosecution. Senate lawyers took the Borders case to a federal district court in Washington, D.C., and on Aug. 22 he was held in contempt and ordered jailed. He was released after the Senate completed its trial Oct. 20.

When the full Senate voted Oct. 20 on the articles of impeachment, it delivered a mixed verdict, convicting Hastings of eight articles of impeachment and acquitting him of three. Senators, as permitted under the rules, declined to vote on six other articles.

The vote on the first article, alleging conspiracy to obtain a bribe, was 69-26, four more than the required two-thirds of those present and voting, and it sealed Hastings' fate. The Senate then adjudged Hastings guilty of falsely stating as a defendant in a criminal case that he had never made any agreement to solicit a bribe from defendants in a case before him, 68-27; that he never agreed to modify the sentences of the defendants in the case against Romano in return for a bribe from those defendants, 69-26; that he never agreed to enter an order returning a substantial amount of property to the defendants in the Romano case, 67-28; that his appearance at a Miami Beach hotel was not part of a plan to show his participation in the bribery scheme, 67-28; his motive for instructing a law clerk to prepare an order returning property, previously ordered forfeited, to defendants in the Romano case, 69-26; that a telephone conversation was about letters of assistance for an acquaintance when in fact it was a coded conversation in furtherance of a bribe, 68-27; and that he had prepared three letters of assistance for an acquaintance and that it was the letters he was referring to in a conversation with Borders, 70-25.

The Senate adjudged Hastings not guilty of falsely stating as a defendant in a criminal trial that he did not expect Borders to appear at his hotel room in Washington, D.C., 48-47; of revealing highly confidential information that he learned as the supervising judge of a wiretap, 0-95; and of undermining confidence in the integrity and impartiality of the judiciary and of betraying the trust of the American people, 60-35.

Hastings immediately lost his judgeship.

Nixon Case

Nixon, who was serving a five-year prison term at the time of his impeachment and trial, was convicted in federal court in Mississippi in 1986 for lying to a grand jury. The perjury charge stemmed from Nixon's denial that he had talked to a state prosecutor about helping the son of a business associate, Wiley Fairchild. Drew Fairchild, Wiley's son, had been indicted on drug charges.

The judge was acquitted of a charge that he accepted an illegal gratuity from Fairchild. Nixon maintained that he was innocent of all charges and that he was convicted on the basis of confusing questions put to him in the grand jury room.

Nixon appealed his conviction to the 5th U.S. Circuit Court of Appeals, which refused to overturn the verdict. The Supreme Court in January 1988 declined to review the conviction, and in December 1988 a federal judge in Mississippi refused to overturn the verdict in a post-trial proceeding. Nixon had said that new evidence casting doubt on witnesses' testimony against him required a new trial.

The House Judiciary Subcommittee on Civil and Constitutional Rights began its impeachment inquiry in the spring of 1988. The panel held six days of hearings in June and July 1988 and then suspended the proceedings pending the decision on Nixon's request for a new trial.

The subcommittee finished its preliminary hearings on March 2, 1989, and on March 21 it voted to charge Nixon with two counts of lying under oath and one count of undermining the integrity of the judiciary.

By 34-0, the full House Judiciary Committee followed suit April 25.

On May 10, the House voted 417-0 to impeach Nixon, making him the third federal judge in four years to be formally charged with "high crimes and misdemeanors." He was the 15th federal official to be impeached since 1798; all but five of the others were district court judges.

The day after the House vote, the Senate appointed a 12-member committee to take testimony in the Nixon trial. On Aug. 17, the 5th U.S. Circuit Court of Appeals rejected a Nixon request to vacate his perjury conviction.

The Senate trial committee began taking evidence in the case on Sept. 7 that covered three articles impeachment. They alleged that Nixon lied to a grand jury in 1984 about talking with the state prosecutor about Drew Fairchild, that he lied to the grand jury about ever trying to influence anyone about the Fairchild case and that he undermined the integrity of the judiciary.

The special committee finished hearings in the Nixon case on Sept. 13, and the trial before the full Senate began Nov. 1.

The chief House prosecutor, Rep. Don Edwards, D-Calif., carefully detailed Nixon's acceptance of a sweetheart deal on oil and gas leases from Fairchild and Fairchild's request to Nixon to help his son, who was indicted on drug-smuggling charges. Edwards said Nixon talked to District Attorney Paul Holmes to win special treatment for the young Fairchild and then lied about trying to influence the matter.

Nixon told the Senate that he was innocent of the original perjury charges stemming from his 1984 testimony before a federal grand jury on the Drew Fairchild matter, and he urged members not to be persuaded by his conviction.

Before voting on the charges against Nixon, the Senate denied the judge's motion that the full Senate try his case. Both Hastings and Nixon had sued in U.S. District Court for the District of Columbia seeking to force a trial by the entire Senate. Their case was dismissed July 5 on the ground that it was premature, because the Senate had not yet voted on the impeachment.

The U.S. Circuit Court of Appeals for the District of Columbia affirmed the dismissal Oct. 18.

In a second preliminary vote, the Senate refused to dismiss the third article of impeachment, which alleged that Nixon undermined confidence in the judiciary.

The Senate Nov. 3 found Nixon guilty of two articles alleging false and misleading statements to the grand jury about the Drew Fairchild case. The vote on the first, which was sufficient to remove Nixon from office, was 89-8. The second vote was 78-19. He was not convicted on a third article, which alleged that by his conduct he had undermined the confidence in the integrity of the judiciary. The vote was 57-40.

Thomas Nomination

After an anticipated fight failed to materialize, the Senate on March 6, 1990, easily approved by voice vote the nomination of Clarence Thomas for one of three vacancies on the U.S. Court of Appeals for the District of Columbia

Circuit, a court often regarded as the second highest in the country and a steppingstone to the Supreme Court.

For the eight years before joining the court, Thomas had been chairman of the Equal Employment Opportunity Commission (EEOC). Some critics complained that Thomas did not understand age-discrimination law and blamed him for botched discrimination claims in 1980s. Other critics complained that Thomas had not been vigilant enough in trying to enforce minority hiring goals and timetables in job-discrimination cases.

Despite these criticisms, Thomas came through the Judiciary Committee without trouble, advancing to the Senate by a 13-1 vote taken Feb. 22. The questions put to him were for the most part congenial, and he appeared to appease skeptical senators by promising to keep his personal views in check on the court.

Thomas had been formally nominated Oct. 30, 1989, by President Bush to replaced Robert H. Bork, who resigned from the court in 1988. A black conservative, Thomas had been mentioned by some Republicans as a potential successor to the only black Supreme Court justice, Thurgood Marshall. A year after Thomas' appeals court confirmation, that speculation would be proved accurate. *(Supreme Court nomination, box, p. 802)*

Starr Nomination

U.S. Court of Appeals Judge Kenneth W. Starr won Senate confirmation as solicitor general by voice vote May 18, 1989. In his new role, he represented the government before the Supreme Court.

Starr's nomination was not controversial, although members of the Senate Judiciary Committee sought to assure themselves that he would not follow in the footsteps of his predecessors in the Reagan administration, Rex Lee and Charles Fried. The two continually urged the Court to narrow its view of individual rights and to restrict the scope of government regulation. They filed a record number of advisory briefs, known as amicus curiae, intended to influence the Court in cases that did not directly involve the federal government.

Starr pledged to stay "true to the rule of law" and said he would not sign a brief on behalf of the administration if it was, in his opinion, legally indefensible. But, he added, "if I felt that a good argument could be made, even if I, as a judge, could not accept that argument . . . it would be my duty to make that argument."

Starr was appointed to the Appeals Court for the District of Columbia by President Ronald Reagan in 1983. He was a protégé of former attorney general William French Smith, whom he served as a counselor from 1981 to 1983. Starr was an associate partner in Smith's law firm, Gibson, Dunn and Crutcher, from 1977 to 1981 and had worked for the firm in 1974 and 1975. He served as a law clerk to Chief Justice Warren E. Burger in 1975-77.

Other Legislation

Hate Crime Statistics

In an effort to document the incidence of prejudice-inspired crimes in the United States, Congress in 1990 cleared legislation (HR 1048 — PL 101-275) requiring the Justice Department to gather and publish "hate crime" statistics for the next five years.

HR 1048 required the attorney general to publish an annual summary showing how many crimes each year manifested evidence of prejudice based on race, religion, sexual orientation or ethnicity. Covered crimes included murder, manslaughter, forcible rape, assault, intimidation, arson and vandalism.

During Senate floor consideration Feb. 8, 1990, of a companion measure (S 419), an amendment sponsored by Orrin G. Hatch, R-Utah, was adopted 96-0 that added language to the bill that said, "American family life is the foundation of American society" and that no funds provided in the legislation could be spent to "promote or encourage homosexuality." The same day, the Senate rejected, 19-77, a Jesse Helms, R-N.C., amendment to add language that said the "homosexual movement threatened the strength and survival of the American family as a basic unit of society" and that "state sodomy laws should be enforced because they are in the best interest of public health."

The House passed HR 1048, 368-47, under suspension of the rules June 27, 1989. The Senate Judiciary Committee reported S 419 (S Rept 101-21) on May 1, 1989. The Senate passed an amended HR 1048, 92-4, on Feb. 8, 1990. The House accepted the Senate changes, 402-18, under suspension of the rules April 4, thus clearing the bill. President Bush signed it April 23.

In 1988, the House passed and Senate Judiciary reported similar language, but it did not become law. *(Congress and the Nation Vol. VII, p. 780)*

Violence Against Women

The Senate Judiciary Committee on Oct. 19, 1990, reported legislation (S 2754 — S Rept 101-545) designed to combat violence against women. Committee Chairman Joseph R. Biden Jr., D-Del., subsequently held the bill from floor action pending a Justice Department review.

S 2754 would have doubled penalties for rape and aggravated assault, imposed new penalties for repeat offenders and provided more restitution for victims; authorized $300 million for new police efforts to identify and combat sex crimes; tripled funding for shelters for battered women; authorized funds for security measures at public transit facilities; created a National Commission on Violent Crime Against Women; created federal penalties for spouse abuse; and required colleges to provide rape prevention programs.

The committee accepted an Orrin G. Hatch, R-Utah, amendment to require a state, on request, to supply rape victims with the results of attackers' AIDS (acquired immune deficiency syndrome) tests.

Law Agents' Liability

Congress in 1989 cleared a measure (HR 972 — PL 101-203) that greatly increased the compensation the government could pay for property damage inflicted on innocent victims by law enforcement agents. The bill raised the maximum damages the attorney general could pay in such cases to $50,000, from $500.

HR 972 was reported from House Judiciary (H Rept 101-46) on May 4. The House passed the bill by voice vote under suspension of the rules May 9.

The Senate Judiciary Committee reported a companion measure (S 604 — S Rept 101-163) on Oct. 12. The

Senate passed S 604 by voice vote Oct. 27, then passed an amended HR 972 by voice vote. The measure cleared Nov. 21. President Bush signed it Dec. 7.

Consolidation of Lawsuits

The House in 1990 passed HR 3406, amending the Federal Rules of Civil Procedure to permit consolidation in a single federal court of suits files by disaster victims or their survivors if at least 25 people were killed or injured and damages sought exceeded $50,000 per person.

The measure applied only to suits arising from single accidents and not to multiple suits involving toxic torts or product liability issues. In most cases, deciding compensatory damages would be returned to the state or federal court in which the individual suit originally had been filed.

HR 3406 was reported from House Judiciary (H Rept 101-515) on June 1 and passed by voice vote under suspension of the rules June 5.

Similar language passed the House in 1991. *(Story, p. 798)*

Whistleblower Rewards

Legislation (S 248 — PL 101-123) to reward individuals who disclosed fraud and abuse — known as "whistleblowers" — by federal contractors was cleared by Congress in 1989. Under the measure, the attorney general would decide who should receive the rewards. The money, up to $250,000, could come from criminal fines imposed in a successful fraud prosecution.

People who tipped off authorities would not be eligible for a reward if it was part of their job to provide such information, if they failed to give the information to their employer before turning it over to law enforcement authorities, if the information was already public or if they had participated in the fraud.

S 248 (S Rept 101-7) was reported from Senate Judiciary on March 13 and passed 82-16 on April 5. House Judiciary reported the measure (H Rept 101-273) Oct. 6. The House passed it by voice vote under suspension of the rules Oct. 10, completing congressional action. President Bush signed the bill Oct. 23.

Earlier in the year, Congress cleared legislation (S 20 — PL 101-12) to strengthen job protections for federal workers who reported government waste, fraud and abuse. *(Story, p. 862)*

Debt Collection

Both the Senate and House passed a bill (S 84) to make it easier for the federal government to collect its debt, but the measure died upon adjournment of the 101st Congress.

S 84 sought to impose uniform procedures nationwide for collecting debt owed the government. Currently, a patchwork of state laws applied. The bill permitted the government to collect civil, criminal and tax judgments through garnishment of wages, attachments of property, liens and sales, and restraining orders.

The Senate passed S 84 by voice vote Nov. 3, 1989. The House Judiciary Committee reported a companion measure (HR 5640 — H Rept 101-736) on Sept. 21, 1990. The House passed HR 5640 by voice vote under suspension of the rules Sept. 27, then passed S 84 by voice vote later the same day.

Included in the crime bill (S 3266 — PL 101-647) enacted in 1990 was a provision establishing a uniform federal debt collection system. *(Crime bill, p. 764)*

Naturalization Process

The House in 1989 passed a bill (HR 1630) streamlining the naturalization process for individuals applying for U.S. citizenship. The measure died upon adjournment of the 101st Congress.

HR 1630 would replace the existing two-tiered system involving the Immigration and Naturalization Service (INS) and the federal courts with a one-stop administration process. The bill did not change any of the requirements for naturalization, however. HR 1630 was developed in response to the massive backlogs in the federal courts in processing citizenship applications.

The House Judiciary Committee reported the measure (H Rept 101-187) on July 27. The House passed it by voice vote under suspension of the rules July 31. *(102nd Congress action, p. 794)*

Philippine War Veterans

The House in 1989 passed legislation (HR 525) to authorize granting U.S. citizenship to natives of the Philippines who served with the U.S. armed forces or in guerrilla forces during World War II.

Congress in 1942 had authorized officers of the Immigration and Naturalization Service (INS) to grant naturalized citizenship outside the United States. Over the next three years, about 7,000 Philippine veterans living outside their homeland (then under Japanese occupation) were made U.S. citizens. In October 1945, the INS officers' authority to travel to the Philippines to perform the naturalizations was revoked. Concerns arose that mass migration of newly naturalized veterans would drain the Philippines of needed manpower. INS regained its authority in August 1946, four months before the law authorizing the naturalizations expired on Dec. 31, 1946. An additional 4,000 veterans were naturalized.

The Supreme Court in 1988 ruled in *Immigration and Naturalization Service v. Pangilinan* that the courts could not order redress to Philippine veterans, many of whom had sued repeatedly over the years. Only Congress could set the terms and conditions of naturalization, the Court said. *(Case summary, Congress and the Nation Vol. VII, p. 836)*

According to the Veterans Affairs Department, about 60,000 Philippine veterans would be eligible to become U.S. citizens under HR 525, but they would have to come to the United States to apply.

The House Judiciary Committee reported HR 525 (H Rept 101-351) on Nov. 13. The House passed the bill by voice vote under suspension of the rules the same day.

The House by voice vote Nov. 13, 1989, passed a related bill (HR 639) to grant permanent resident status to aliens who had enlisted in the U.S. armed services outside of the United States and either had served 12 years of active duty or had served six years and re-enlisted for another six. The Senate Judiciary Committee reported the measure July 26, 1990, but it saw no further action. Congress cleared similar legislation in 1991. *(Story, p. 793)*

Congress in 1990 cleared legislation (HR 150 — PL 101-249) granting posthumous U.S. citizenship to foreigners killed in combat while serving on active duty with the

U.S. armed forces. HR 150 was reported from House Judiciary (H Rept 101-350) and passed by voice vote under suspension of the rules Nov. 13, 1989. The Senate passed the bill by voice vote Feb. 20, 1990, completing congressional action. President Bush signed the measure March 6.

Military Malpractice

The House in 1989, as it had in 1985 and 1988, passed legislation to permit full-time military personnel to sue the federal government for medical malpractice. HR 536 permitted damage claims for injuries or death arising from care furnished at a military facility in the United States. *(Earlier action, Congress and the Nation Vol. VII, pp. 746, 784; 102nd Congress action, p. 798)*

The Supreme Court in a 1950 decision, *Feres v. United States*, said members of the military could not use the Federal Tort Claims Act to sue the government for malpractice. HR 536 aimed to amend that act.

HR 536 was reported from House Judiciary (H Rept 101-87) on June 15 and passed by voice vote under suspension of the rules in the House June 27. The Senate did not act on the bill.

Biological Weapons Ban

The 101st Congress cleared legislation (S 993 — PL 101-298) that made it a federal crime to develop, produce, sell or possess a biological weapon. The measure was designed to implement a 1972 international convention on biological weapons that was unanimously ratified by the Senate in 1974 and had been signed by 111 nations.

The bill authorized the attorney general to seize and destroy any biological agent, toxin or delivery system deemed to have no apparent peaceful purposes. The person whose property was seized would have an opportunity to protest, and the government would have to prove that the biological substance in question was proscribed. Anyone convicted of violating the act would be subject to a sentence of up to life imprisonment or a fine, or both. The act did not restrict research or development for protection or other peaceful uses.

S 993 (S Rept 101-210) was reported from Senate Judiciary Nov. 16, 1989, and passed by voice vote Nov. 21. The House Judiciary Committee reported a companion measure (HR 237 — H Rept 101-476) on May 7, 1990. The next day, the full House suspended the rules and passed HR 237, 408-0. The House then passed S 993 by voice vote. President Bush signed the bill May 22.

1991-92

In an effort to counteract Supreme Court decisions that relaxed federal anti-discrimination laws, Congress in 1991 cleared a civil rights bill aimed at providing additional protections for workers. The bill represented a hard-won compromise between lawmakers and the Bush administration.

Congress was unable to reach agreement on major crime legislation or anti-drug legislation. Congress considered, but did not clear, bills addressing the issues of nonpayment of child support, vertical price fixing and anti-racketeering law restrictions. Reauthorization of the independent counsel law also failed to clear.

However, penalties for "carjacking" were imposed; state sports-based lotteries were limited; and bilingual services for voters were extended.

President Bush suffered his first defeat of a judicial nominee in 1991, when Kenneth L. Ryskamp, tapped to be a district court judge, could not muster the necessary Senate support. Bush did win confirmation of Edward Earl Carnes Jr. as federal appeals court judge. The nomination had been strongly opposed by Democrats and civil rights groups.

Civil Rights

Congress in 1991 cleared a compromise civil rights bill (S 1745 — PL 102-166) that was two years in the making and had become a flash point in President Bush's relationship with black Americans.

S 1745 was Congress' first successful attempt to reverse the conservative Rehnquist Court, which in 1989 had restricted the reach and remedies of federal anti-discrimination laws. Bush vetoed a 1990 version, contending that it would induce employers to hire certain numbers of minorities and women to avoid lawsuits. His warning played to the belief of some whites that race preferences had cost them jobs, and it led to months of often bitter political wrangling. *(1990 action, p. 757)*

Bush, who endorsed the 1991 compromise measure in a deal with Senate leaders in late October, said S 1745 would not lead to quotas. He signed the bill on Nov. 21.

The final legislation countered the effects of nine Supreme Court decisions from 1986 to 1991 that made it harder for workers to bring and win job-discrimination lawsuits. It also amended Title VII of the 1964 Civil Rights Act (PL 88-352) to allow limited money damages for victims of harassment and other intentional discrimination based on sex, religion or disability. Racial minorities already could win unlimited money damages under a Reconstruction-era law. Some members wanted no limits on money damages for women, religious minorities and the disabled. But the ceiling was a key part of the compromise reached by the White House and congressional leaders. *(1964 law, Congress and the Nation Vol. I, p. 1635)*

Although Democrats gave ground on the damages question, most of the compromising was done by Bush. The deal was reached in the wake of the divisive Senate hearings into Anita F. Hill's sexual harassment allegations against Supreme Court nominee Clarence Thomas and the strong Oct. 19 primary election showing of former Ku Klux Klansman David Duke, a Republican, in the Louisiana governor's race. *(Thomas confirmation, box, p. 802)*

Both events caused problems for Bush and the Republicans. In the first, they were accused of insensitivity to sexual harassment, and in the second, of aligning with a former Klansman known for his continued racist statements. Bush clearly did not want to be caught reading from the same script as Duke on the quota issue.

While Republican supporters of the bill insisted that Bush prevailed in the negotiations, Democrats scoffed. "Where did the quotas go? They swam upstream, as red herrings often do," declared Craig Washington, D-Texas, during House floor debate. What made the difference,

Washington suggested, was "David Duke took the sheet off that [quota] argument."

Still in question as the bill became law was how much help workers would actually receive under its provisions, many of which were vaguely worded to ensure passage. Only time was likely to tell who had won on the most troublesome issue, reversal of the Supreme Court's 5-4 June 1989 decision in *Wards Cove Packing Co. v. Atonio*, which made it harder for workers to prove indirect job discrimination. *(Case summary, p. 842)*

Such "disparate impact" cases arose when workers challenged hiring practices, such as physical tests and academic requirements, that were ostensibly neutral but had an adverse impact on women or minorities. *Wards Cove* had shifted the burden of proof in suits alleging indirect discrimination. Instead of employers having to show that a legitimate business necessity existed for challenged practices, workers were required to prove that there was not.

In the administration-Senate deal, both sides agreed to return the burden of proof to employers and to reinstate a requirement from a 1971 Court ruling, *Griggs v. Duke Power Co.*, that hiring and promotion requirements be related to job performance. But S 1745 threw to the federal courts some key issues of interpretations. *(Case summary, Congress and the Nation Vol. III, p. 314)*

S 1745 said that all employment practices had to be "job related for the position in question and consistent with business necessity." However, it did not define "business necessity" beyond stating that the measure's purpose was to reinstate the standard set forth in *Griggs* and subsequent rulings prior to *Wards Cove*.

The courts also were left to decide whether the new law applied to cases pending at the time of its enactment. The bill's language was not clear. Democrats said that it should cover worker-plaintiffs who were engaged in litigation at the time the law took effect. Republicans said the bill applied only to cases brought after enactment. The Equal Employment Opportunity Commission (EEOC), a federal agency that brought lawsuits in behalf of aggrieved workers, issued a statement in December 1991 saying that the law covered only cases begun after enactment.

Background

Bush's 1990 veto of the initial version of the job rights bill marked the first defeat of a major civil rights bill in a quarter-century. The Senate fell one vote short of overriding his veto.

Members of Congress and civil rights activists who were outmaneuvered by the administration in 1990 revived their fight for the job-discrimination bill in early 1991 with a new political strategy: a sales pitch to women. They had been stung by the administration's dismissal of the 1990 legislation as a "quota bill" and decided they would no longer make equal opportunities for minorities the main public relations emphasis of their campaign.

By promoting the bill as a help to working women, advocates hoped to build a broader base of support and defuse charges that the new job protections would lead to quotas. Nonetheless, the debate in early 1991 quickly picked up where the 1990 fight had left off, fueled by the election campaign that had just ended. In November 1990, just a month after Bush's veto of the first bill had been sustained, Sen. Jesse Helms, R-N.C., had narrowly won re-election, in part by accusing his black opponent of supporting racial quotas. GOP strategists said at the time that painting Democrats as supporters of quotas might become part of the 1992 presidential campaign.

Democrats likened such assertions to Bush's successful 1988 use of murderer-rapist Willie Horton's case to suggest that Democrats were soft on crime.

HR 1: A New Vehicle

The main bill on the table through the first half of 1991 was HR 1, which sought to amend two laws — Title VII of the Civil Rights Act of 1964, which barred job discrimination on the basis of race, sex, national origin or religion; and Section 1981 of Title 42 of the *U.S. Code*, an 1866 law prohibiting intentional race discrimination in contracts. The major provisions of HR 1 were as follows:

- In cases in which an employee challenged an ostensibly neutral practice (such as a test or academic requirement) that had an adverse effect on women or minorities, the bill required an employer to prove that the practice was necessary for the conduct of business.

  The bill defined a necessary job practice as one bearing "a significant relationship to successful performance" of the job. The bill said this would codify the meaning of "business necessity" as used in the 1971 Supreme Court case *Griggs v. Duke Power Co.* and overrule the *Wards Cove* use of business necessity as a defense.

- The bill sought to broaden Section 1981 to prohibit racial harassment on the job and other forms of race bias that occurred after a person was hired. The provision reversed *Patterson v. McLean Credit Union*, also from 1989, in which the Court ruled that the law applied only to conduct when a contract was made. Section 1981 prohibited racial discrimination in "making and enforcing" private contracts, and the bill broadened that to cover the modification and termination of contracts and "the enjoyment of all benefits, privileges, terms and conditions of the contractual relationship." *(Case summary, p. 842)*

- To counter the 1989 ruling in *Price Waterhouse v. Hopkins*, the bill made clear that employers were prohibited from considering race, color, religion, sex or national origin as a motivating factor in employment decisions. It forbade decisions that took such factors into account even if they were made primarily for legitimate motives. *(Case summary, p. 842)*

- The bill made it harder for individuals to challenge court settlements called "consent decrees," in which parties to a discrimination lawsuit agreed on a remedy. Typically, these settlements created affirmative action plans for shops that had engaged in past discrimination; white workers said such plans fostered "reverse discrimination."

  Under HR 1, challenges could not be mounted if the potential challenger had been notified of a proposed deal and given an opportunity to object before the case was settled. A person also could be prevented from challenging the order if a court determined that he was adequately represented by another person who challenged the decree. This provision countered the Court's 1989 ruling in *Martin v. Wilks*. *(Case summary, p. 842)*

- The bill broadened the time frame for workers to bring lawsuits against discriminatory employment policies. Intended to reverse *Lorance v. AT&T Technologies*, also from 1989, this tied the deadline for lawsuits to when a worker was harmed, not to when the policy took effect. The bill also made clear that a seniority system in a collective bargaining agreement that was intended to discriminate on the basis of race, color, religion, sex or national origin was illegal. *(Case summary, p. 842)*

- To reverse the 1989 *Independent Federation of Flight Attendants v. Zipes*, the bill stated that parties who prevailed in job-discrimination cases could recover reasonable attorneys' fees if they had to defend their awards in a subsequent challenge. The bill stated that the plaintiff was entitled to recover attorneys' fees from the original defendant, the third party or both. *(Case summary, p. 840)*

Addressing other Supreme Court cases since 1985, the bill also sought to:

- Amend Title VII of the 1964 Civil Rights Act to allow winning plaintiffs in bias cases against the federal government to recover interest for delays in getting relief.
- Make clear that prevailing plaintiffs could recover the reasonable costs of hiring experts to help them in their cases.
- Provide that in certain job-bias cases, plaintiffs could not be required to relinquish claims to attorneys' fees as a condition of settlement. This was intended to keep businesses from pressuring workers to forgo money for their lawyers' fees to get a settlement.
- Dictate that anti-bias protections under Title VII apply to U.S. citizens working overseas for U.S.-owned or controlled companies.

In a key feature not related to court cases, the bill established a new money remedy for victims of intentional job discrimination. HR 1 gave victims the right to recover compensatory and, in egregious cases, punitive damages under Title VII. If such money damages were sought, either a worker or his company could demand a jury trial.

At the time HR 1 was being considered, only injunctive relief, back pay and attorneys' fees were allowed under Title VII. So the provision was intended to make the remedies available for sex, religious and ethnic discrimination the same as the remedies already available under Section 1981 for race discrimination. The bill also extended the new remedies to victims who sued under the 1990 Americans with Disabilities Act. *(Story, p. 743)*

While this new congressional effort was underway, the White House also shifted strategy, retreating from the compromises it had offered in the failed 1990 legislation in favor of a new proposal. Officials admitted it was not as "accommodating" as the earlier one but contended it was nonetheless a good-faith effort.

The administration legislation differed from HR 1 in two key areas — the disparate impact issue and on monetary damages.

Under the administration's bill, an employer could justify a challenged practice, such as a test or academic requirement, by showing that it had "a manifest relationship to the employment" or that the employer's goals were "significantly served" by the practice. HR 1 set a higher test for a discriminatory practice, saying it had to "bear a significant relationship" to an employee's ability to succeed at the job.

The Bush bill also set a stiffer standard, compared with HR 1, for evidence to prove discrimination. It required workers to pinpoint which hiring practices caused the discrimination. The administration abandoned language offered in 1990 that would have allowed workers in certain situations to challenge discrimination caused by a group of practices.

Both proposals said that it should be up to the employer to prove that a practice was necessary for the business. The Supreme Court had ruled in *Wards Cove* that the worker should bear the burden of proving that a test or other screening device was not necessary for the business.

On monetary damages, the Bush bill sought to allow victims of harassment to sue for money damages up to $150,000, provided they had first used an in-house grievance procedure. HR 1 covered all cases of intentional discrimination, not only harassment. It did not require a worker to first use an in-house procedure. And it set no limit on damages.

Civil rights lobbyists met with business interests from December 1990 to April 1991, trying to strike a deal. In the lead was The Business Roundtable, a consortium of chief executive officers from 200 large companies. Working on the assumption that some bill was inevitable, business negotiators said they wanted to try to shape legislation to their liking.

The talks ended when the White House and small and mid-sized businesses banded together to attack both the legislation and the efforts of big corporations. They waged an all-out opposition blitz, including mass mailings to employers, to discredit any deal that might come out of the talks. Those opponents argued that the legislation would increase litigation and costs to businesses, especially small ones that did not have longstanding affirmative action programs in place.

House Action

The House passed HR 1 in June, nearly two months after two committees approved the measure.

The Education and Labor Committee, which approved the bill by voice vote March 12 and formally reported it (H Rept 102-40, Part I) April 24, added provisions to make the legislation more appealing to working women. While some Republicans said this new emphasis was only cosmetic, William D. Ford, D-Mich., who had taken over the Education and Labor chairmanship in 1991, said he believed women would benefit more than minorities from the legislation.

One symbolic change came in the title; the bill became known as the "Civil Rights and Women's Equity in Employment Act of 1991."

Noting in the legislative text that the women were under-represented in executive, management and senior decision-making positions in business, the bill established a 19-member, four-year "Glass Ceiling Commission" to study the representation of women and minorities in executive, management and senior decision-making positions in business. The commission was to make recommendations to help eliminate artificial barriers to the advancement of women and minorities on the job.

The bill set up a program at the Labor Department to study disparities in the wages of men and women and whites and minorities. The idea was to disseminate information on efforts to eliminate wage disparities based on sex, race, national origin or ethnicity. The program was to provide technical assistance to employers to modify wage-setting practices or eliminate such disparities.

The committee rejected two Republican-backed amendments aimed at making it easier for employers to justify practices that disproportionately affected minorities and women. One would have said that an employer's academic requirements for a job were presumed to meet the "business necessity" test. The other lessened the standard for evidence an employer might use to justify a business practice that had a disparate impact on women or minorities.

The administration's bill was offered as a substitute but rejected by voice vote.

The Judiciary Committee approved HR 1, 24-10, on March 19 and formally reported it (H Rept 102-40, Part II) on May 17. The committee defeated six Republican-sponsored amendments, including the administration's bill, which lost on a voice vote.

Before trying to substitute the administration's proposal for HR 1, GOP members attempted to attach various parts of it to the bill. Henry J. Hyde, R-Ill., first tried to substitute the administration's test for whether a disparate-impact practice, such as an aptitude test, could be justified as necessary to business. But his amendment failed 14-20.

F. James Sensenbrenner Jr., R-Wis., tried to strip out the section to allow women and religious minorities who suffered intentional discrimination to win unlimited money damages. The proposal failed on a voice vote. And then Bill McCollum, R-Fla., sought to limit money damages to $150,000 and restrict them to cases involving harassment, instead of all intentional discrimination. The amendment lost, 10-23.

House Democratic leaders, lacking strong support for HR 1, worked after the committees' consideration of the bill to draft a substitute that could draw more support. Their targets were wavering Southern Democrats, and their hope also was to take the air out of business opposition. The goal was to win close to 290 votes — the number needed for a two-thirds majority to override Bush's threatened veto.

Substantively, the Democrats' amendments were not entirely new. For example, their proposed $150,000 cap on money damages for women had been in the 1990 civil rights bill. Another section dealing with "indirect discrimination" allowed employers to justify their hiring practices by showing that they "bear a substantial and manifest relationship to the requirements for effective job performance." This was considered a mid-point between HR 1 and the administration bill.

The bill said that nothing in it was to be construed to "require, encourage, or permit an employer to adopt hiring or promotion quotas on the basis or race, color, religion, sex or national origin, and the use of such quotas shall be deemed to be an unlawful employment practice." Voluntary or court-ordered affirmative action still was allowed.

The bill defined a quota as "a fixed number or percentage of persons of a particular race, color, religion, sex or national origin which must be attained, or which cannot be exceeded, regardless of whether such persons meet necessary qualifications to perform the job."

The Supreme Court had previously ruled that hiring by the numbers was illegal, but HR 1 sought to put that ban into statute. The move was aimed almost exclusively at giving political cover to those who wanted to vote for the job rights bill but faced constituent complaints about "reverse discrimination."

Concerning test adjustments, the substitute said employers, labor organizations and employment agencies could not adjust employment test scores based on the race, color, religion, sex or national origin of individual test-takers. The measure prohibited using tests that did not validly and fairly measure an individual's ability to perform the job.

The substitute said provisions of the bill were to cover only lawsuits filed after the date of enactment, unless a court found that a "manifest injustice" would occur without retroactive application. The original HR 1 would have applied retroactively.

When the House finally took up the substitute bill, House Democratic leaders won no more support than they had in 1990.

The **273-158 (R 22-143; D 250-15; I 1-0) key vote** on final passage came June 5, after a day and a half of debate and the rejection of two alternative proposals — the White House plan (rejected 162-266) and a substitute offered by black and female members with no restrictions on new money damages for victims of intentional discrimination (rejected 152-277). *(1991 key votes, p. 1061)*

Democrats said it was hard to get around Bush's politically potent quota assertion because of latent racial divisions and Americans' fears of joblessness. "It is a shame and a disgrace that in 1991 we are still debating whether or not we should protect our fellow American citizens from discrimination," said John Lewis, D-Ga., who was physically beaten during civil rights struggles of the 1960s and spoke of signs posted to segregate blacks and whites. "The scars and stains of racism are still deeply embedded in the American society."

Republican Hyde countered that the bill would further separate Americans. HR 1 "is about dividing people — tribalizing and balkanizing our society — and in the end . . . it will not have the support of the American people but their resentment and indignation."

Both sides bought advertising, worked key members' districts and lobbied aggressively. Bush was especially visible, driving home the quota charge in speeches before the House vote.

Senate Action

In 1990, an unlikely coalition of senators, led by Edward M. Kennedy, D-Mass., and John C. Danforth, R-Mo., had come close to a winning deal on civil rights before Bush's veto and the one-vote loss on the override. But in early 1991, the senators who were at the core of negotiations a year earlier shifted alliances.

Liberal Kennedy wanted a bill similar to HR 1. Danforth, a middle-of-the-road Republican, tried to interest colleagues in a more conservative version. Southern Democrats who voted for the 1990 bill after winning compromises talked among themselves. All parties said they wanted a bill, but their ideological differences pushed them in different directions.

Danforth introduced a compromise job rights package in the Senate the week of the House vote, and given that the House measure had not secured a veto-proof majority, his proposal became the focus of attention by civil rights activists. The Missouri Republican said he was trying to disentangle the debate from politics and find a bill that would please GOP moderates and Southern Democrats. He split the original legislation into three bills, trying to isolate the most difficult topics so that the less controversial proposals might readily pass.

Under Danforth's plan, one measure (S 1207) addressed five Court rulings in provisions that were relatively non-controversial and attracted some Bush administration interest. A second bill (S 1208) reversed the hotly disputed ruling in *Wards Cove*, which involved standards for indirect bias resulting from tests and other seemingly neutral hiring practices. The third measure (S 1209) gave limited money damages to women, religious minorities and the disabled for deliberate bias.

A major difference between Danforth's offering and Democrats' proposals was that he further limited compensatory damage awards for women and non-racial minorities in intentional bias cases. He also would not have allowed women to win punitive damages.

Throughout the summer, Danforth continued to revise his legislation, talking informally with administration officials and other senators and reintroducing his three-bill package. He said he was trying every avenue to win Bush's support, but it was never forthcoming.

A major breakthrough for the legislation came in the fall, on the heels of the explosive battle over confirmation of Clarence Thomas as associate justice of the Supreme Court.

The administration-Senate agreement averted a brewing confrontation that threatened to divide Senate Republicans and intensify tensions over race and gender issues. "From our Republican standpoint, it's better to be in a position supporting a bill rather than going against Danforth trying to override a veto," said Minority Leader Bob Dole, R-Kan., who acted as a broker between the administration and Danforth to reach the settlement. Dole insisted that the administration could have sustained a veto, but GOP senators John W. Warner, Va., and Ted Stevens, Alaska, told Bush on Oct. 23 that they could not be counted on to support him in an override battle.

The final compromise (S 1745) set caps on compensatory and punitive damages women and minorities could win based on the size of the company. The amount ranged from $50,000 for an employer with 100 or fewer workers to $300,000 for companies with more than 500 workers.

In the section concerning the *Wards Cove* case, the compromise returned the burden of proof to employers to defend job practices challenged as discriminatory. But it left to the courts to decide what constituted a "business necessity."

The bill covered racial harassment and other forms of bias that occurred after a person was hired, reversing the *Patterson v. McLean Credit Union* case.

The measure also spelled out the rules under which third parties could challenge a consent decree in an anti-bias case, ruling out those who had to have been notified beforehand that the agreement might hurt their interests and who could have objected. This reversed the *Martin v. Wilks* decision.

The bill made clear that an employer could not make an employment decision based in any way on race, color, religion sex or national origin, regardless of whether other factors also motived the decision. This overturned the *Price Waterhouse v. Hopkins* decision.

The Senate passed S 1745 on Oct. 30 by a **93-5 (R 38-5; D 55-0) key vote**. All of the opponents were conservative Republicans.

In the end, one of the more hotly disputed questions was whether the Senate would abide by the anti-bias rules imposed by law on private employers. After three days of debate, the Senate voted Oct. 30 to partially apply the bill and other major anti-discrimination laws to Senate employees, allowing them redress through an internal process and a final limited right of appeal in federal court. Senators themselves were made personally liable for damages.

Business groups that had fought the bill for two years pulled back after the White House deal, saying the legislation was inevitable.

S 1745 also prohibited adjusting test scores by race and established a Glass Ceiling Commission to recommend ways to lift barriers to women and minorities seeking job advancement.

Somewhat obscured in the Senate's push to wrap up civil rights legislation was a skirmish over how members tried to dictate court interpretations of the new law, particularly that part dealing with "business necessity." Finessing this disputed section, lawmakers had agreed Oct. 25 to put a three-paragraph memo in the *Congressional Record* as the bill's "exclusive legislative history." Judges commonly looked to floor statements, committee reports and other congressional materials to understand what lawmakers intended, and bill leaders hoped to prevent individual senators from circumventing the hard-won, if vaguely worded, compromise.

In floor speeches during debate over S 1745, senators tried to put their own spin on the bill, hoping to create "legislative history." The result was dueling colloquies, a warning by Dole that the civil rights deal might be off and, finally, an amendment directing courts to pay attention only to the short memo and to recognize that the sponsors did not agree on how to interpret a key element of the bill.

The exclusive legislative history said: "The terms 'business necessity' and 'job related' are intended to reflect the concepts ... of *Griggs v. Duke Power Co.* [1971] and other Supreme Court decisions prior to *Wards Cove Packing Co. v. Atonio.*"

The memo also said that when a challenged practice included several interlocking components measuring the same criterion, such as height and weight requirements to assess strength, the practices could be generally challenged. In other cases, a worker would have to pinpoint the specific employment practice that led to indirect discrimination.

Final Action

The House passed S 1745 on Nov. 7 by a 381-38 vote, completing congressional action. Five Democrats and 33 Republicans opposed the bill. Many of those who voted against S 1745 said it would clog the courts with job-bias lawsuits and hurt small businesses. Most members, however, seemed relieved that a bargain had been struck and the battle was over.

No amendments were allowed because congressional leaders and the White House agreed that amendments would shatter the fragile deal. As a result, floor debate was anti-climactic except for disagreements over the fate of the parties to one of the lawsuits that helped spawn the legislation. Alaskan cannery workers who had sued Wards Cove Packing Co. would not benefit from the new law.

As part of a compromise with the White House and Senate Republicans, the bill specifically exempted ongoing litigation involving the Wards Cove Packing Co. from provisions making it easier to prove indirect job bias. Many House Democrats were outraged that the estimated 2,000 Alaska cannery workers were not covered, but only two Democratic lawmakers, Neil Abercrombie and Patsy T. Mink, both from Hawaii, voted against the bill because of it. Abercrombie called the compromise "extortion," adding: "Do you think for a minute that this would be happening if it involved 2,000 Irish-Americans in Boston? Or 2,000 Jews in New York?"

He and Mink represented large constituencies of Asian and Pacific Americans who shared a heritage with the Alaskans who sued Wards Cove in the early 1970s. But Alaskan Sens. Frank H. Murkowski and Ted Stevens, both Republicans, had won assurances that the law would exempt ongoing litigation affecting the cannery. Murkowski described Wards Cove as a "substantial employer" in Alaska.

During House debate, Speaker Thomas S. Foley, D-Wash., urged concerned House members to support the compromise despite the exemption, promising to move a separate bill to protect the cannery workers.

Bush signed the bill Nov. 21, but even that finale was not without controversy.

In the hours before the signing ceremony, a faction in the White House revealed its smoldering opposition to affirmative action and generated a partial boycott of the signing ceremony by Democrats who had pushed for the legislation. A draft signing statement had directed the government to end the various affirmative action programs it had carried on for decades under executive orders. The draft was prepared under the direction of Counsel to the President C. Boyden Gray.

Disclosure of the preliminary statement reignited political tensions over affirmative action and quotas and prompted Bush at the bill signing to declare that he supported affirmative action. Some congressional Democrats were not so sure and refused to go to the ceremony. But Kennedy, the only Democratic lawmaker to attend the ceremony, said he was willing to give Bush the benefit of the doubt and judge him by his actual remarks instead of "a memorandum that's been prepared by staff."

Major Provisions

As signed into law Nov. 21, 1991, S 1745 (PL 102-166):

- **Money Damages for Intentional Bias.** Set caps on the compensatory and punitive damages women and minorities could win. Employers with 100 or fewer workers were liable for up to $50,000; employers with 101 to 200 workers, $100,000; 201 to 500 workers, $200,000; and employers with more than 500 workers, $300,000. Employers of fewer than 15 workers were exempt from damages.

Title VII of the 1964 Civil Rights Act was amended to allow the new damages and to permit jury trials for victims of bias. Juries were generally thought to be more sympathetic to workers than judges.

- **'Business Necessity.'** Reversed the key *Wards Cove* section, by returning the burden of proof to employers to defend job practices challenged as discriminatory, but basically left it to the courts to decide what constituted a "business necessity."
- **Racial Harassment on the Job.** Reversed *Patterson v. McLean Credit Union*, and barred racial harassment and other forms of bias that occurred after a person was hired. The Court had ruled that Section 1981 of Title 42 of the *U.S. Code*, which prohibited racial discrimination in contracts, applied only to hiring decisions.
- **Consent Decrees.** Reversed the 1989 *Martin v. Wilks*, and spelled out rules under which third parties could challenge a consent decree in an anti-discrimination case. It precluded challenges by those who had to have been notified beforehand that the agreement might hurt their interests and who had opportunity to object. They could not object if their interests had been fairly represented by a direct party to the suit. The settlements in question typically involved affirmative action plans in which employers who had engaged in past discrimination agreed to give preference for some period to minorities or women.
- **Forbidden Considerations.** Made clear that an employer could not make an employment decision based in any way on race, color, religion, sex or national origin, regardless of whether other factors also motivated the decision. This countered the *Price Waterhouse v. Hopkins* decision.
- **Seniority and Filing Deadlines.** Allowed workers challenging a seniority system as discriminatory to wait until the adverse impact of the system was felt to bring a lawsuit. That reversed the Court's 1989 ruling in *Lorance v. AT&T*, which tied the deadline for bringing a lawsuit to a company's adoption of the policy.
- **Other Cases.** Addressed two cases from the 1980s and two from 1991. To overrule the Supreme Court's 1986 decision in *Library of Congress v. Shaw*, the bill amended Title VII to allow winning parties in bias cases against the federal government to recover interest to compensate for delays in obtaining payment. The filing period for actions against the government was increased from 30 to 90 days. In response to parts of the 1987 *Crawford Fitting Co. v. J. T. Gibbons Inc.* and the 1991 *West Virginia University Hospitals v. Casey*, the bill permitted winning parties to recover the costs of hiring experts who assisted them in cases filed under the damages provisions of S 1745, an 1866 racial bias statute and Title VII. *(1987 case summary, Congress and the Nation Vol. VII, p. 835; 1991 case summary, p. 840)*

The bill allowed American workers abroad to sue their U.S.-based employers for discrimination, reversing a 1991 ruling, *Equal Employment Opportunity Commission v. Arabian American Oil Co.* *(Case summary, p. 843)*

- Created a Glass Ceiling Commission to study how business filled management and decision-making positions and required a report and recommendations 15 months after enactment.
- Established a Senate Fair Employment Office to provide for counseling in case of alleged job bias and then a formal complaint and hearing process to handle the allegations. Either side in a dispute could appeal to the U.S. Court of Appeals for the Federal Circuit. (For House employees, the new law left in place procedures adopted in 1988, creating the Office of Fair Employment Practices.)

Civil Rights Commission

After working out a compromise, the House and Senate in 1991 enacted legislation (HR 3350 — PL 102-167) extending the Civil Rights Commission for three years while ensuring that Congress maintained tight control over the agency. Congress had last renewed the troubled commission in 1989. *(1989 action, p. 762)*

For much of the 1980s, the eight-member panel had been deeply divided and had done little to fulfill its mandate, which was to examine discrimination in such areas as employment and housing and report the findings to Congress and the president. Civil rights activists claimed that the problem stemmed from the Reagan administration's efforts to destroy the organization by appointing commissioners who were hostile to programs such as busing and affirmative action.

Lawmakers praised some signs of improvement in the commission's operations since its renewal in 1989 — notably, better internal management and a reopening of some regional offices closed during the 1980s — but were still dissatisfied with the rate of progress. Don Edwards, D-Calif., chairman of the House Judiciary Subcommittee on

Civil Rights, complained that the commission had produced only one report in two years.

Arthur A. Fletcher, chairman of the commission since February 1990, countered that Congress was unwilling to make the financial commitment needed to transform the commission into an effective organization. Fletcher said the commission needed as much as $12 million annually to carry out its mandate.

The Senate by voice vote on Sept. 25 passed a four-year authorization bill (S 1754) with no cap on funding. The House under suspension of the rules on Sept. 30 passed a two-year extension (HR 3350), with an annual budget at $6 million. After members of the House and Senate Judiciary committees worked out a compromise, the Senate passed an amended HR 3550 by voice vote on Oct. 28. The House agreed to the Senate amendment under suspension of the rules on Nov. 6, 420-7, clearing the bill. President Bush signed it Nov. 26.

As enacted, HR 3350 reauthorized the commission for three years, with $7.16 million in fiscal 1992. Funding for the remaining two years was to be determined each year. If no funding was approved during one of those two years, the commission was automatically reauthorized at the 1992 level.

Crime Bill

Despite two years' worth of efforts to craft some kind of tough anti-crime bill, Congress and President Bush failed once again to come up with new legislation that commanded a majority of members and administration support. Although the House narrowly approved a conference report on a crime bill (HR 3371) at the end of the first session of the 102nd Congress, the measure languished in the Senate. It appeared briefly on the floor in March and October 1992, where sponsors tried to forestall a threatened filibuster. But they failed each time when Republicans, reflecting the administration's opposition to the bill, lined up to vote against cloture.

As the Congress came to a close, neither Democrats nor Republicans apparently wanted the sweeping anti-crime bill badly enough to hammer out a compromise in a presidential election year in which crime fell behind the economy and health insurance reform as an issue that could mobilize voters.

The conference report on HR 3371 would have extended the federal death penalty to more than 50 crimes, restricted death row inmates' ability to challenge their sentences and imposed new gun-crime penalties. The bill authorized more than $3 billion for prisons and law enforcement.

The same issues that had surfaced in earlier anti-crime efforts continued to divide the two parties. Democrats did not want tough Republican limits on the ability of death row inmates to ask for federal review of their sentences under habeas corpus provisions. And Republicans objected to handgun control provisions.

HR 3371 included the text of another bill (S 3282) that required a five-day waiting period for potential handgun purchases, allowing time to check a buyer's background. This provision, known as the Brady bill, was named for James S. Brady, former press secretary to President Ronald Reagan, who was wounded in a 1981 assassination attempt on the president. Brady and his wife, Sarah, lobbied hard for the provision.

Early in the year, Republicans unsuccessfully pushed their own crime bill (S 2302), which did not include handgun control.

After the crime legislation died, Senate Republicans blocked efforts to bring S 3282 to the floor. That bill included a seven-day waiting period for handgun purchases. In 1991, the House had passed its own version of the Brady bill (HR 7). *(Gun control, box, p. 765)*

Senate Action

President Bush threw down the gauntlet in early 1991 by challenging Congress to enact a crime bill within 100 days.

Much of what the president wanted had been on the table in 1990, only to get swept away in House-Senate bargaining at the end of the 101st Congress. The 1990 crime bill was gutted by a conference committee on the eve of adjournment. Stripped out were an assault weapons ban, death penalty provisions and limits on death row appeals, among other provisions. Left in the measure that eventually cleared (S 3266 — PL 101-647) were non-controversial items such as new sanctions against thrift fraud and more funding for local law enforcement. *(Crime bill, p. 764)*

The Bush administration's 1991 crime proposal (HR 1400, S 635), which was introduced in the House and Senate on March 12 and March 13, respectively, sought to apply the federal death penalty to about 40 crimes, most of which involved murder. It also limited the ability of death row inmates to challenge the constitutionality of their sentences through so-called habeas corpus petitions. It proposed a "good faith" exception to the exclusionary rule, which barred prosecutors from using illegally obtained evidence against a defendant. And it stiffened penalties for firearms offenses.

Senate Democrats led by Judiciary Chairman Joseph R. Biden Jr., D-Del., countered with S 618, to authorize capital punishment for 44 federal offenses, restrict habeas corpus petitions, loosen the exclusionary rule, ban assault weapons and authorize $1 billion in aid to state and local law enforcement agencies. The measure also included criminal justice safeguards and required that death row prisoners have adequate counsel as a condition to limits on habeas corpus.

On June 6, the provisions of S 618 were incorporated into a new crime bill, S 1241, introduced by Biden. S 1241 became the vehicle for Senate action. Because the measure contained provisions that had been thoroughly debated in 1990, Senate leaders decided to skip the usual public hearings and put the legislation directly on the Senate floor.

Debate began June 20 and culminated July 11, when the Senate passed S 1241 by 71-26.

Bush's 100-day deadline for action on crime legislation was June 14. But when it came time for the Senate to act on the president's bill June 20, Republicans did not want to vote on it. Chief sponsor Strom Thurmond, R-S.C., said he wanted to amend the measure to win more votes.

He added more than $3 billion for state and local law enforcement, patterned after Biden's proposals, and removed two particularly controversial provisions. One would have allowed for closed deportation hearings for foreigners suspected of terrorism, and another would have allowed illegally seized firearms to be used as evidence at trial. Civil libertarians and some editorial writers had denounced the proposals as threats to due process of law.

Even amended, the Bush plan, offered as a substitute amendment, failed to carry, losing 40-56.

The death penalty remained a vexing issue, particularly because of efforts by Democrats to include a "racial justice" provision. The Biden bill allowed death row prisoners to make a prima facie case that their sentence was the result of bias by producing statistical evidence that people of their race in a given jurisdiction were more likely than others to be charged with murder or sentenced to die. A state or federal entity could rebut the showing by "clear and convincing" evidence that factors unrelated to race caused the disproportionate statistics.

Edward M. Kennedy, D-Mass., the sponsor of the provision, cited studies that showed that blacks were more likely to be sentenced to death than whites and that defendants accused of killing whites were more likely subjects for capital punishment than those accused of killing blacks.

But many members in both parties were uneasy about the racial justice language, and when death penalty proponent Bob Graham, D-Fla., offered a motion to strike the section from the bill, he prevailed 55-41 on June 20.

Biden's effort to strike a GOP plan for capital punishment for defendants convicted of operating big-time drug enterprises also failed, 30-68 on June 25. He wanted to substitute life imprisonment unless an intentional killing was involved. The Senate also rejected, 25-73 on June 25, a move by by Paul Simon, D-Ill., to substitute life in prison without parole for all death penalty provisions in the bill.

In a move that had the effect of extending capital punishment to states that did not did authorize it themselves, the Senate, 65-33 on June 26, adopted an amendment by Alfonse M. D'Amato, R-N.Y., to allow federal prosecutors to seek the death penalty for homicides if the gun involved had moved across state or national borders.

On a 60-39 vote June 26, the Senate adopted an amendment by Steve Symms, R-Idaho, to mandate at least a 20-year prison term and to allow the death penalty for drug-related murders in the District of Columbia, which did not have capital punishment for any offenses. That amendment was held up for about 24 hours by a surprise move by Jesse Helms, R-N.C., to outlaw any race preferences in hiring.

Helms proposed that it be illegal for any employer to give anyone "preferential treatment" in hiring, pay or other job conditions based on race, color, religion, sex or national origin. He tried to attach the proposal to an unrelated death penalty amendment. Civil rights activists called Helms' proposal "a full-scale assault" on affirmative action. And Senate Minority Leader Bob Dole, R-Kan., cautioned that what Helms proposed could hurt "good affirmative action programs" and jeopardize any compromise on a job rights bill.

The crime bill managers wanted no quota language in already contentious legislation, and late June 26, Majority Leader George J. Mitchell, D-Maine, successfully moved to table Helms' amendment.

Also on June 26, the Senate adopted an amendment to tightly restrict a prisoner's ability to challenge a conviction in federal court after exhausting direct appeals. The proposal, by Orrin G. Hatch, R-Utah, required prisoners to file habeas corpus petitions within six months of exhausting their state appeals. It restricted the grounds for appeals and it allowed a federal judge to dismiss a petition if the judge decided the prisoner had received a "full and fair hearing" on his claims in a state court.

Senate Democrats held the line on the exclusionary rule, which barred use at trial of illegally seized evidence. Bush and key GOP senators, led by Thurmond, had wanted to allow use of evidence seized without a warrant if the police officer acted in a "good faith" belief that the seizure was constitutional. The Senate retained current case law, which allowed use of evidence seized by an officer relying in good faith on a warrant later found to be defective.

Late on June 28, the Senate adopted a compromise Brady bill provision that required a waiting period for handgun purchases of five business days and a plan for an immediate national background check of buyers that would take effect in two-and-a-half years. The new language, approved 67-32, supplanted a provision for a seven-day wait with no timetable for an instantaneous check.

Before the Senate passed S 1241 July 11, they had to vote twice to cut off debate. The first effort failed by four votes, but the second was successful, despite pressure from the National Rifle Association (NRA), which called the bill "nothing less than an unmitigated attack on the rights of law-abiding gun owners."

House Action

House leaders denounced many provisions of the Senate-passed crime bill as they started work on their measure (HR 3371). The chief criticism of the Senate approach was that it disregarded cost, the effects of stiffened mandatory sentences on prison space and due process for defendants.

The House Judiciary Crime and Criminal Justice Subcommittee approved a draft bill July 31 that cost about one-third as much as the Senate bill but took the same get-tough approach. The same day, the Subcommittee on Civil and Constitutional Rights approved a separate "racial justice" bill (HR 2851) that allowed racial minorities on death row to use statistics in capital sentencing to claim that their sentences were discriminatory. The two measures were later combined.

The $1 billion draft bill approved by the Crime Subcommittee attempted to put more emphasis on prevention through drug-treatment programs and rehabilitation for young criminals. But it also permitted the death penalty for about 50 federal crimes. While it allowed capital punishment for a drug kingpin who headed a large organization, as would the Senate bill, it did not permit the same penalty for smaller-scale drug crimes, manslaughter or obstruction of justice, as did the Senate bill.

The Judiciary Committee approved HR 3371 Sept. 26 and formally reported it (H Rept 102-242, Part I) on Oct. 7. The committee bill, following the lines of the subcommittee measure, differed in key areas from S 1241 and from what the Bush administration wanted.

HR 3371 allowed prisoners to challenge their death sentences as racially motivated — the racial justice provision, knocked out of the Senate bill, prohibited use of coerced confessions at trial and extended other protections to defendants. The House bill also banned certain types of semiautomatic assault-style weapons.

The subcommittee language authorizing the death penalty for about 50 federal crimes, mostly involving murder, remained. The bill also set a one-year deadline for prisoners to file habeas corpus petitions in federal court after exhausting appeals of their state convictions, and it restricted successive petitions. The Senate bill included a six-month deadline.

Law Enforcement

The $1.2 billion for law enforcement and crime prevention was less than half of the more than $3 billion authorized by the Senate bill.

Unlike the Senate, the House committee refused to give federal prosecutors jurisdiction over any murder committed with a firearm that had crossed state lines. Federal judges said that proposal would swamp the federal courts and violate states' rights. Chief Justice William H. Rehnquist on Sept. 19 wrote to the House committee asking members not to adopt it.

During four days of deliberations, the House committee rejected GOP amendments that would have made it easier to impose the death penalty and harder for condemned prisoners to pursue habeas corpus appeals.

Republicans and some Democrats also fought provisions banning the sale of 13 types of assault-style semiautomatic weapons. The NRA sent letters to its members trying to stir up opposition to what it called "a massive attack on your gun rights."

The House bill did not include a waiting period for handgun purchases because the House had already passed the Brady bill (HR 7) in May.

Further departing from the Senate and Bush proposals, the House measure also partially reversed a 1989 Supreme Court decision in *Teague v. Lane* that made it harder for inmates to use favorable court decisions, issued after their own convictions, in their habeas corpus petitions. The Senate bill left the ruling intact. *(Case summary, p. 821)*

The House bill sought to overturn a 1991 Supreme Court ruling that made it easier for prosecutors to use coerced confessions against defendants. In a 5-4 ruling on March 26, the Court held in *Arizona v. Fulminante* that the use of a coerced confession at trial did not automatically invalidate a conviction, provided other evidence of guilt was overwhelming. The Judiciary Committee voted to bar use of a coerced confession under any circumstances. *(Case summary, p. 826)*

Separately, the House panel, like the full Senate, rejected a Bush proposal to allow use at trial of evidence seized without a search warrant, provided the police were acting in "good faith" that their conduct was legal.

The bill had to be considered by the Ways and Means Committee because of four provisions under its jurisdiction. It gave voice vote approval to HR 3371 after deleting three of those four provisions. Ways and Means reported the bill (H Rept 102-242, Part II) on Oct. 9.

At the behest of Chairman Dan Rostenkowski, D-Ill., the panel, by voice vote, eliminated the provisions that could have cut revenues to the Treasury. Two would have extended the statute of limitations for gun registration violations and eliminated a hearing requirement before firearm forfeitures. The Treasury raised money by fining violators of registration requirements and selling forfeited guns. The third provision would have changed U.S. import quotas for opium used in medical drugs such as codeine.

Left intact was a provision to allow the U.S. Customs Service to impose criminal penalties of up to three years in prison for pilots of planes suspected of carrying controlled substances who did not obey an order to land. At the time, only a civil fine of up to $5,000 could be imposed.

The House began work on HR 3371 on Oct. 16 and passed it Oct. 22 by a vote of 305-118.

Republicans assailed the Judiciary Committee's bill as a criminal-coddling measure. With help from some Democrats, they won approval, 247-165 on Oct. 17, of an amendment to allow prosecutors more leeway in using illegally obtained evidence and, 223-191 on Oct. 22, of an amendment to eliminate the "racial justice" provision, which had been stripped from the Senate bill.

Republicans also provided the political heft to squash the bill's ban on certain assault-style weapons and automatic loading devices. Despite emotional references to a gunman's murder of 22 people in a mass shooting in a Killeen, Texas, cafeteria the day before, members voted 247-177 on Oct. 17 to strip out the ban.

But the House narrowly rejected, 208-218 on Oct. 17, another Republican proposal, blocking an amendment that would have greatly restricted appeals by inmates on death row.

Like the Senate bill, the House measure enlarged the list of federal crimes that could draw the death penalty. In one of the tighter floor battles, the House voted 213-206 on Oct. 16 to adopt language that went further still. The amendment, offered by George Gekas, R-Pa., allowed capital punishment of a defendant who showed a reckless disregard for human life, replacing the more stringent "intent to kill" test.

An effort to replace the death penalty in all cases with life imprisonment without parole was rejected 101-322 on Oct. 16.

Conference Action

The Senate passed an amended HR 3371 by voice vote Nov. 21. The way was paved for House and Senate conferees to begin work on the bill after GOP senators dropped their objections to naming conferees. Thurmond, the lead GOP senator on the bill, had protested the Democratic majority's plan to appoint five Democrats and three Republicans as conferees. To help avoid a repeat of 1990's conference, at which most GOP initiatives were dropped, Thurmond wanted more Republicans.

After Democrats accused Republicans of not wanting a crime bill, Thurmond accepted the 5-3 ratio. The House named its conferees on Nov. 21. Meeting in a rare Sunday session, the conferees reached agreement on the final version of HR 3371 on Nov. 24.

Republicans complained they were "steamrollered" on a series of party-line votes that led to the adoption of the weaker provisions of the House or Senate bills on habeas corpus, the exclusionary rule and the death penalty for state gun crimes. Calling the bill a "travesty," Thurmond warned, "I'll take any step I can to stop this bill."

The conferees dropped the ban on semiautomatic assault weapons approved by the Senate but rejected on the House floor. However, they kept the Brady bill provisions calling for a five-day waiting period for the purchase of a handgun.

When House leaders brought the conference report to the floor shortly after dawn Nov. 27, they realized they faced a Senate filibuster and a veto from Bush, who also vehemently opposed the measure. They wanted to leave it to Republicans to be blamed for collapse of the bill.

Amid a flurry of vote switching, Democrats eked out a 205-203 vote on Nov. 27 to adopt the conference report (H Rept 102-405). Members split along party lines, with 199 Democrats and six Republicans supporting it.

Later the same day, the Senate failed, 49-38, to quell a Republican-led filibuster against the bill. The vote was 11 short of the 60 needed to invoke cloture and cut off debate.

The administration had expressed its reservations about the bill strongly and loudly, objecting in particular to the decisions by the Democratic-dominated conferees to discard a Bush proposal for greater restrictions on prisoners' appeals and a plan to allow evidence seized without a warrant to be used at trials.

"I would have to veto this bill because it would weaken our criminal justice system," Bush said.

1992 Action

The focus in 1992 was on the Senate, given that the House had finished its work on HR 3371 at the end of the first session.

In some election-year gamesmanship, Senate Republicans and Democrats fought for control of crime-related issues the week of March 2 and scheduled a political "showdown" for March 10. The eventual outcome, however, left both sides where they started — at an impasse.

The gauntlet was thrown down March 3, this time by GOP leader Dole, Phil Gramm of Texas and other Republicans, who in a news conference vowed to bring to the Senate floor a crime measure backed by Bush. Gramm said he would find a way to raise the issue every week until it passed.

Democrats retorted that it was Republicans who had blocked action in 1991 on HR 3371.

On March 4, Gramm appeared ready to amend an unrelated bill, the reauthorization of the Corporation for Public Broadcasting (S 1504), with the Bush crime bill (S 2305).

But Majority Leader George J. Mitchell, D-Maine, made a pre-emptive strike, calling the conference report on HR 3371 back to the floor. It had been idling on the Senate calendar since the failed cloture vote the previous November. Republicans objected to that move, and senators proceeded to debate the issue for the next two days until Mitchell on March 5 filed another motion to invoke cloture. The two sides agreed to vote on the question March 10, but Democrats remained doubtful that they could muster the 60 votes needed to shut off debate.

The two sides disagreed mainly over how much to restrict death row inmates' petitions to federal courts under the process known as habeas corpus.

Slim chances for enactment of anti-crime legislation in 1992 dwindled to almost nothing March 19 when Senate Democrats failed to stop the Republican filibuster. The 54-43 cloture vote was six short of the votes needed to shut off debate.

Judiciary Chairman Biden said chances for passage of the Bush-backed bill were no better than for HR 3371. Biden blamed Republicans and the NRA, which opposed the Brady waiting-period language, for the demise of the legislation.

The Senate tried once again seven months later, but not enough votes were gathered to cut off the filibuster. Proponents of the measure fell five votes of the needed 60 on Oct. 2, 55-43.

Drug Legislation

Once an issue that galvanized both Republicans and Democrats, the war on drugs had notably subsided a year before the 1992 elections. Little more happened than a quiet changing of the guard at the Office of National Drug Control Policy and a multi-year reauthorization of some of the treatment programs initially passed in a massive 1988 anti-drug bill.

Some questioned the need for new legislation as statistics showed a decline in drug use, and Congress had already passed a raft of laws, including two major drug packages in five years. According to a nationwide household survey by the Department of Health and Human Services' National Institute on Drug Abuse, current drug use was down 11 percent from 1988 levels.

Election-year politics had typically fueled major anti-drug legislation. In 1982, Congress passed crime legislation (HR 3963) that included creating the drug policy office and a Cabinet-level "drug czar." President Ronald Reagan vetoed the bill over the drug czar provisions, which he viewed as unnecessary and likely to produce turf battles. *(Congress and the Nation Vol. VI, p. 689)*

In 1984, just three weeks before the presidential election, Reagan signed into law a sweeping anti-crime package (PL 98-473) that substantially increased penalties for major drug offenses and gave federal prosecutors new authority to seize the assets and profits of drug traffickers. As that campaign wrapped up, Republicans took credit for cracking down on drugs while painting Democrats as soft on crime. *(Congress and the Nation Vol. VI, p. 698)*

In 1988, as the presidential campaigns heated up, the climate changed. The Rev. Jesse Jackson made drugs and drug-related violence a theme of his campaign, and Republicans were on the defensive, focusing on law enforcement. Jackson and other Democrats supported creating a drug czar, additional funding for local law enforcement and treatment on request for drug addicts.

Congress cleared yet another anti-drug bill, a massive $2.8 billion package (PL 100-690). Besides the drug czar, the bill included a provision that would allow the death penalty for major drug traffickers. The drug czar provisions faced little opposition in Congress. Also, an obstacle to GOP support, language establishing Cabinet status for the administrator of the drug policy office, was removed. *(Congress and the Nation Vol. VII, p. 748)*

In 1990, President Bush announced his anti-drug strategy. A drug summit followed in Cartagena, Colombia, with heads of South American countries under siege in the drug war. But with so much legislation already enacted, and no consensus on what to do next, Bush championed no new bill and Congress passed none. *(Story, p. 768)*

Former Florida governor Bob Martinez was sworn in March 28, 1991, as the nation's new drug czar, and the fanfare that accompanied the term of former drug policy chief William J. Bennett was gone. Criticized by some in the Senate for having put too much emphasis on incarceration for drug abusers and not enough on treatment, Martinez promised to boost treatment programs. *(Law leadership, box, p. 745)*

Legislation (HR 3259 — PL 102-132) authorizing drug abuse prevention and education programs for youth gangs and runaways for three years was cleared in 1991.

The first section of the bill, which targeted drug education and prevention programs, authorized $15 million for fiscal 1992, $18 million for fiscal 1993 and $20 million for 1994 for programs under that section. The program had been funded at $14.8 million in fiscal 1991. The second section was aimed a runaway and homeless youths and authorized the same amount for those programs.

The House Education and Labor Committee reported HR 3259 (H Rept 102-222) on Sept. 26. The House passed the bill by voice vote under suspension of the rules Sept. 30. The Senate passed HR 3259 by voice vote Oct. 2, clearing the measure. Bush signed it Oct. 18.

Carjacking Penalties

Congress cleared a bill (HR 4542 — PL 102-519) in 1992 establishing stiff penalties for "carjacking," the armed robbery of a vehicle while the driver is present.

HR 4542 made carjacking a federal crime with a maximum penalty of life in prison when the theft resulted in death. The bill was prompted by a rash of carjackings throughout the United States — particularly in large cities such as New York and Detroit — including some that resulted in the killing of the driver.

The only controversial part of the bill concerned provisions to curb auto thefts by marking major car parts with identification (ID) numbers that would be maintained in a computerized FBI registry. The House Judiciary Committee approved a plan that would require car frames, engines, transmissions and windows to be stamped with the vehicle's ID numbers. The House Energy and Commerce Committee, chaired by John D. Dingell, D-Mich., eliminated those provisions. Dingell, whose congressional district included several automakers, said the labeling was unlikely to be effective and would cost automakers millions of dollars.

The final version of the bill contained a compromise agreed to by both committees, phasing in the labeling over five years and gradually increasing the number of vehicles for which marking was required. The bill allowed the attorney general to determine whether the marking program was effective and exempted from the program certain car lines with auto theft devices.

Three House committees shared jurisdiction over HR 4542. Judiciary reported the measure (H Rept 102-851, Part I) on Aug. 12; Energy and Commerce (H Rept 102-851, Part II) on Sept. 22; and Ways and Means (H Rept 102-851, Part III) on Sept. 23. The House passed HR 4542 by voice vote under suspension of the rules Oct. 6. The Senate acted by voice vote Oct. 8, clearing the bill. President Bush signed it Oct. 25.

Child Support

Congress considered several measures in 1992 to impose stricter penalties on non-custodial parents who failed to uphold their child support obligations.

Courts annually ordered parents to pay about $11 billion in child support, but less than half was ever paid at all, let alone paid on time, according to the Commerce Department. The so-called "deadbeat dad" or "deadbeat parents" situation angered many lawmakers who viewed the delinquency as both willful neglect and, in many cases, another drain on the nation's beleaguered welfare system.

Congress Oct. 7 cleared legislation (S 1002 — PL 102-521) that made it a federal crime for parents who lived in another state from the custodial parent to avoid paying child support. It was signed by the president on Oct. 25.

The measure, which passed the Senate on Sept. 18 and the House Oct. 3 by voice votes, limited criminal liability to those who willfully avoided payments. Those who could not afford child support payments were not covered by the bill. Persons who intentionally avoided payments for six months and owed at least $2,500 could face up to six months in jail and a fine of up to $5,000. Repeat offenders could be sentenced to up to two years in prison and fined as much as $250,000.

The House had passed a companion measure (HR 1241 — H Rept 102-771) by voice vote under suspension of the rules on Aug. 4. The Senate bill, approved by the Judiciary Committee Sept. 17, was similar to HR 1241. Some compromise provisions were worked out to reconcile the two measures prior to final House and Senate.

A bill (HR 6022) requiring consumer credit agencies to include in credit reports information regarding a consumer's failure to meet court-ordered child support payments was signed into law Oct. 27 (PL 102-537). Under the bill, credit bureaus were to record delinquencies of $1,000 or more.

The House passed HR 6022 by voice vote under suspension of the rules Sept. 29. The Senate passed the bill by voice vote Oct. 5, completing congressional action.

The House by voice vote under suspension of the rules passed a bill (HR 5304 — H Rept 102-982) Oct. 3, 1992, aimed at improving the administration of child support payments, but the measure died in the Senate. It would have prohibited a state court from modifying an order of another state court that would affect child support payments.

Sports Lottery Ban

Concerned that state-sponsored gambling could undercut the integrity of professional sports, the leaders of the major sports leagues successfully pushed Congress in 1992 to clear legislation (S 474 — PL 102-559) that would prohibit additional states from sponsoring sports-based lotteries. The measure did not affect betting on horse and dog racing or on the numbers games that were the most common type of lottery. Only betting on professional and collegiate sports such as basketball, football and baseball was prohibited.

"Gambling and sports do not mix," said Arnold "Red" Auerbach, president of the Boston Celtics, before the House Judiciary Subcommittee on Economic and Commercial Law in 1991. Auerbach represented the National Basketball Association.

Either the U.S. attorney general or the sports organization whose games were at stake could seek a federal court injunction to halt any state-sponsored gambling activity based on sports enumerated in the bill. The measure permitted Oregon, Nevada, Delaware and Montana, which had laws on the books allowing sports-based lotteries or casino gambling on sports, to continue their policies. New Jersey, which allowed casino gambling in Atlantic City, was exempted from the bill's prohibitions until January 1994.

Background

The sports leagues feared that cash-starved states would want to emulate Oregon, which in 1989 began a state-sponsored betting operation for pro football and pro basketball games. The state lottery grossed $14.5 million in state receipts in 1989 and 1990 combined, netting $4.9 million in profits. "We do not want our games used as bait to sell gambling," said Paul Tagliabue, commissioner of the National Football League. "Sports gambling should not be used as a cure for the sagging fortunes of

Atlantic City casinos or to boost public interest in state lotteries."

Thirty-two states and the District of Columbia sponsored general lotteries, and opponents of the measure were concerned that several of the states strapped for cash would expand them to include betting on sporting events. "It threatens to undermine public confidence and the integrity of the game themselves," said House cosponsor Hamilton Fish Jr., R-N.Y. "Mere breaks of the game or strategy choices by coaches would become the source of suspicion and cynicism."

Legislative Action

The Senate Judiciary Committee reported S 474 (S Rept 102-248) on Nov. 26, 1991. The Senate passed the bill on an 88-5 vote on June 2, 1992, after a debate over whether the states that already had sport gambling laws should be exempted. House sponsors initially folded their version into an anti-crime bill (HR 3371), but when it became apparent that bill was going nowhere, they took up S 474. After adding an amendment to exempt New Jersey from the bill's prohibitions for a year, the House passed the bill by voice vote under suspension of the rules on Oct. 5. On Oct. 7, the Senate agreed to exempt New Jersey, clearing the bill for the president. The measure was signed into law Oct. 28.

Vertical Price Fixing

Both the House and Senate passed legislation (S 429) in 1991 that sought to block manufacturers from trying to fix product prices in the retail market by cutting off supplies to outlets that sold at discounts. But the measure died in 1992, when the House rejected the conference report. Both the 100th and 101st Congresses had failed to pass similar legislation. *(101st Congress action, p. 770)*

S 429 would have clarified case law by declaring price fixing to be illegal, and it would have set new standards for juries deliberating price-fixing cases. More specifically, the measure would have allowed discount retailers to bring suit against a manufacturer and competing retailers without detailed proof that a price-fixing arrangement had been made.

Supporters of the legislation said it would spur competition and save consumers as much as $20 billion a year. But opponents argued that the bill would be unfair to businesses and would effectively make manufacturers and full-price retailers guilty until proven innocent in court. They also said the legislation would bring on a rash of expensive litigation, the cost of which would be borne by consumers.

The legislation was opposed by President Bush and won only lukewarm support in both chambers. The Senate Judiciary Committee voted to reject the merits of S 429 but agreed to send the bill to the full Senate without a recommendation. It was reported (S Rept 102-42) on April 19, 1991. On the floor, the measure had to overcome two Republican filibusters before it won passage by voice vote on May 9. By a 61-37 vote, the Senate limited debate on a motion to proceed to consideration of the bill, and by a vote of 63-35, the Senate then limited debate on the measure itself. A minimum of 60 votes is needed to limit debate. The two cloture votes indicated that the measure lacked the two-thirds support it would need to surmount a likely veto.

The House Judiciary Committee reported a companion measure (HR 1470 — H Rept 102-237) on Oct. 3. During floor consideration, the House Oct. 10 adopted, 218-195, an amendment to exempt from the price-fixing ban any manufacturer "so small in the relevant market as to lack market power." The amendment's adoption came as a surprise to the bill's supporters, who said it would greatly weaken the effectiveness of the legislation. The House passed HR 1470 by voice vote Oct. 10, then passed S 429 with the language of HR 1470.

When House-Senate conferees deleted the House-added amendment from the compromise version, support for the bill in the House dissipated rapidly. Without the exemption, many lawmakers and the small business lobby argued, the measure would almost certainly inflict staggering legal costs, even bankruptcy, on small businesses to defend against lawsuits from competitors. On June 30, 1992, the House rejected the conference report (H Rept 102-605) on S 429 by a vote of 175-225.

RICO Limitations

Efforts to scale back the civil provisions of the Racketeer Influenced and Corrupt Organizations Act (RICO) won approval from the House Judiciary Committee in 1991, but the measure advanced no further during the 102nd Congress.

Business groups had long complained that RICO provisions intended as a tool against organized crime had been misused against legitimate businesses, lawyers and other professionals. These critics contended that plaintiffs were tempted by the possibility of collecting triple damages in a successful RICO civil action.

During the previous three Congresses, several bills had been introduced to curb the use of the law in civil suits. But a coalition of powerful members and special interest groups consistently opposed these measures, fearing that an important law enforcement tool would be weakened. The savings and loan (S&L) crisis was a case in point. The anti-racketeering law had been used to bring suit against several S&L owners believed guilty of fraud, and Congress was not likely to approve legislation that could appear to spare perpetrators of financial fraud from heavy penalties.

In 1990, the press of other last-minute legislation left little room for negotiation and sealed the fate of RICO bills in both the House and Senate. *(1989-90 action, p. 771)*

The legislation's chief sponsor in the House, William J. Hughes, D-N.J., had hoped that an early start in the 102nd Congress and some compromises designed to satisfy critics would give the bill its best shot yet. But several House committee chairman — among them John D. Dingell, D-Mich., of Energy and Commerce, and John Conyers Jr., D-Mich., of Government Operations — still had reservations about the legislation.

The House Judiciary Committee approved Hughes' bill (HR 1717) by voice vote on July 30, 1991, and formally reported it (H Rept 102-312) on Nov. 13.

Copyright, Patent Legislation

'Fair Use'

Congress in 1992 cleared legislation (HR 4412 — PL 102-492) that allowed writers, scholars and others to use parts of unpublished copyrighted works. The bill upheld

INSLAW

The House Judiciary Committee on Sept. 10, 1992, asked Attorney General William P. Barr to seek an independent counsel to investigate whether a conspiracy existed to steal software from INSLAW Inc., a federal contractor. Barr refused, claiming that his appointment in November 1991 of Judge Nicholas Bua to look into the case was adequate.

In 1982, the Justice Department awarded INSLAW a three-year, $10 million contract to implement a case management software system at 94 department offices. Shortly afterward, according to Democratic congressional investigators, high-level department officials ignored the company's property rights and used the software at locations not covered by the contract.

The committee's request, approved by a party-line vote of 21-13, came after the release of an investigative report in August 1992 that concluded that high-level department officials might have conspired to steal the software and later blocked inquiries into the matter. Republicans argued that the investigation, handled by Democrats, had made accusations without evidence.

the "fair use" principle, which allowed journalists, academics and others who wanted to reproduce parts of a work — without permission from the author — for the purpose of commenting on or critiquing it. The legislation applied the principle to unpublished works, allowing courts to find their use acceptable if fair.

The House Judiciary Committee reported HR 4412 (H Rept 102-836) on Aug. 11. The House passed the bill by voice vote under suspension of the rules the same day. The Senate passed the measure by voice vote Oct. 7, clearing it. President Bush signed HR 4412 on Oct. 24.

Patent and Trademark Infringement

Congress in 1992 cleared two bills that imposed legal penalties on state governments for infringing on patent and trademark protections.

One measure (S 758 — PL 102-560) stripped state governments of their claim of sovereign immunity from legal penalties for infringing on a patent. It specifically amended the 1970 Plant Variety Protection Act, which protected breeders of new varieties of plants, to allow an inventor who believed his patent had been violated by a state government or state-sponsored university to sue the offending institution for damages. The other bill (S 759 — PL 102-542) held state governments similarly liable for trademark infringements.

The legislation came in response to a series of federal court decisions that said states and state-run universities were immune from federal penalties for patent and trademark infringements unless Congress specifically removed that immunity. States were shielded from such penalties under the Constitution's Sovereign Immunity Clause in the 11th Amendment. In 1990, President Bush signed similar legislation making state governments liable for legal penalties for copyright infringement. *(1990 action, p. 773)*

S 758 was reported from Senate Judiciary (S Rept 102-280) on May 21 and passed by voice vote in the Senate June 12. The House passed the measure by voice vote Oct. 3, and Bush signed it Oct. 28.

Congressional action on S 759 coincided with S 758. The president signed S 759 on Oct. 27.

Patent Maintenance Fees

Congress in 1992 cleared a bill (HR 5328 — PL 102-444) to give patent holders more time to pay their maintenance fees, which were used to cover the cost of filing and keeping current records on patents. Under existing law, people holding patents had up to six months to pay their maintenance fees before their patents expired. HR 5328 gave patent owners an additional 24 months to pay if they could prove that their failure to pay was unintentional.

The House Judiciary Committee reported the bill (H Rept 102-993) on Oct. 3. The House passed it by voice vote under suspension of the rules the same day. The Senate passed HR 5328 by voice vote Oct. 7, clearing the measure. The president signed it Oct. 23.

Patent Office Reauthorization

Congress in 1991 renewed the Commerce Department's Patent and Trademark Office for one year and boosted user fees to make the office completely user-supported. HR 3531 (PL 102-204) increased patent and trademark fees across the board, following the mandate of the 1990 budget deal to raise an estimated $95 million from user fees to offset agency costs.

The House Judiciary Committee reported (H Rept 102-382) and the full House by voice vote under suspension of the rules passed the reauthorization measure Nov. 25. The Senate passed HR 3531 by voice vote Nov. 27, completing congressional action. President Bush signed the bill Dec. 10.

On Oct. 5, 1992, the Senate by voice vote passed another one-year extension of the office, but that measure (S 3325) died in the House without action. The office was kept alive by an appropriation for its continued operation in fiscal 1993.

Semiconductor Chips

Congress in 1991 cleared a bill (S 909 — PL 102-64) that allowed the secretary of commerce to continue to grant copyright and patent protection to producers of semiconductor chips. The legislation extended through fiscal 1995 the authority of the 1984 Semiconductor Chip Protection Act (PL 98-620), which granted protection to U.S. companies whose semiconductor chips could not be patented because they did not meet certain criteria, namely, that an invention be novel or not obvious to someone skilled in the art. Differences in semiconductor designs were too subtle to allow for such protection. *(1984 law, Congress and the Nation Vol. VI, p. 706)*

The 1984 law protected the topographies (or masks) that were used to produce the layers of integrated circuits that went into creating a semiconductor chip. The act also allowed the secretary to extend patent protection to chips from countries that offered reciprocal treatment to U.S. producers or were in the process of doing so. Industry advocates estimated that U.S. companies lost billions of dollars every year to foreign companies that pirated designs and made their own chips.

The Bush administration concluded an agreement with Japan on June 11, 1991, that governed trade in semiconductor chips. The agreement was designed to make it easier for the United States to sell chips to Japan and discourage the Japanese from dumping chips on the U.S. market.

The Senate Judiciary Committee reported S 909 (S Rept 102-78) on June 11, and the full Senate passed it by voice vote the next day. The House first considered a companion measure (HR 1998). It was reported (H Rept 102-122) by House Judiciary on June 21. The House passed HR 1998 by voice vote under suspension of the rules June 25, then it passed S 909 by voice vote. The president signed the bill June 28.

Patent Extensions

A bill (HR 5475) that would have tightened up the conditions under which drug companies could receive extensions of their patents at the same time that it granted patent extensions to three drug companies under the old rules passed the House on Aug. 4, 1992, but died when the Senate took no action.

Under the existing rules for consideration of patent extensions, set out in 1984, an individual, to be eligible for a patent extension, had to prove that government action or inaction had resulted in material harm to the patent holder. Under these rules, government delays in approving drugs or other products for sale in the market was enough reason to warrant a patent extension.

Under HR 5475, a person seeking a patent extension would have to show that any material harm caused by government action or inaction was the result of government misconduct, such as dishonest or deceitful behavior or negligence on the part of federal officials.

The three companies that would have been granted patent extensions by HR 5475 were Procter & Gamble Co., maker of the fat substitute Olestra; Upjohn, maker of the anti-inflammatory drug Ansaid; and American Home Products, producer of another anti-inflammatory, Lodine. Critics argued that the three companies should have to meet the tougher standards laid out in the legislation.

House approval of HR 5475 came on a 278-131 vote under suspension of the rules. House Judiciary had reported the measure (H Rept 102-775) on Aug. 3.

Copyright Renewal

Congress in 1992 cleared legislation (S 756 — PL 102-307) regarding copyright renewals. The bill eliminated the requirement for certain authors to make a formal request for a second term of copyright protection for their works. Each term lasted 47 years.

The measure created an automatic renewal system for all works copyrighted before 1978. For works copyrighted in 1978 or later, the law already provided a copyright term of 50 years after the death of the author.

The Senate Judiciary Committee reported S 756 (S Rept 102-194) on Oct. 22, 1991. The Senate passed it by voice vote Nov. 25. The House Judiciary Committee reported a companion measure (HR 2372 — H Rept 102-379, Part I) on Nov. 25. The House passed the bill by voice vote under suspension of the rules the same day. The House by voice vote passed an amended S 756 on June 4, 1992. The Senate accepted the House changes the same day, clearing the measure. President Bush signed it June 26.

Aid for Bilingual Voters

Congress in 1992 cleared legislation (HR 4312 — PL 102-344) that extended and expanded the bilingual assistance provisions of the Voting Rights Act of 1965 (PL 89-110). The provisions required election officials to provide bilingual services in jurisdictions with significant numbers of non-English speaking voters. *(Congress and the Nation Vol. II, p. 356)*

Supporters of the bill used the renewal of the voting act provisions as an opportunity to expand mandated bilingual assistance into areas not previously covered. Bilingual ballots were required to be provided in counties in which at least 5 percent of the population did not speak English. Although Congress in 1982 had extended the enforcement provisions of the 1965 law for 25 years (PL 97-205), the bilingual provisions had been extended only through 1992. *(Congress and the Nation Vol. VI, p. 680)*

HR 4312 extended the bilingual provisions for 15 years, to the year 2007. In addition, it required that bilingual services be provided in jurisdictions with 10,000 or more non-English speakers, even if these people did not make up 5 percent of the total population. House and Senate supporters of the bill justified its expansion by arguing that the old law excluded several heavily populated counties with large numbers of non-English speaking citizens, such as Los Angeles, San Francisco, Chicago and Philadelphia.

The House Judiciary Committee reported the bill (H Rept 102-655) on July 8. The House passed HR 4312 on July 24 by a vote of 237-125, after turning back two amendments. One amendment, rejected 184-186, would have required the federal government to fund the local bilingual assistance programs.

The Senate passed HR 4312 on Aug. 7 by a vote of 75-20, after rejecting amendments that would have required the federal government to pay for the program and that would have extended the program for five years instead of 15. President Bush signed the legislation Aug. 26.

Immigration Legislation

Aliens in the Armed Forces

Congress in 1991 cleared legislation (S 296 — PL 102-110) that gave resident alien status to foreigners who served in the U.S. armed forces. Those who were serving at least a second six-year tour or who had been honorably discharged after 12 or more years of duty were eligible to become resident aliens and U.S. citizens.

The vast majority of the 5,000 people who were immediately eligible for resident alien status were Filipinos, with the remainder from Micronesia, Palau and the Marshall Islands. By treaty, citizens of those nations could enlist in the U.S. armed forces but could not become officers or hold positions that required a security clearance because they were not U.S. residents. Most of these aliens served as support staff on Navy vessels.

The Senate passed S 296 by voice vote Jan. 30. House Judiciary reported the bill (H Rept 102-195) on Aug. 2. The House passed an amended version by voice vote under suspension of the rules Sept. 16. Following negotiations between the two chambers, S 296 cleared Sept. 26. The president signed the bill Oct. 1.

Similar legislation was passed by the House in 1990, but never came to the Senate floor. *(Story, p. 779)*

Naturalization Process

Wrapping two immigration bills together, Congress in 1991 cleared a measure (HR 3049 — PL 102-232) that partially restored the exclusive authority of the courts to naturalize citizens and that eased temporary visa requirements for entertainers and artists.

Until 1991, federal and state courts had exclusive jurisdiction over the process of naturalizing American citizens. Although the Immigration and Naturalization Service (INS) handled all citizenship applications, making recommendations that the courts almost always heeded, the judges usually administered the oath of citizenship.

But after applicants complained about waiting years to become citizens because of court delays, Congress gave people the option to be sworn in by the INS. This option was included in 1990 immigration reform legislation. *(Story, p. 752)*

That in turn brought complaints from some judges who claimed that they had lost a fundamental power. As a result, HR 3049 gave state and federal courts the option of naturalizing citizens. If a court did not request exclusive jurisdiction, or no swearing-in ceremony was scheduled within 45 days, resident aliens could ask the INS to naturalize them. The bill also required the INS to expedite the applications of persons with grave illnesses.

As cleared, HR 3049 also relaxed conditions on foreigners applying in the so-called P and O visa categories — primarily artists and entertainers recognized internationally for their performance or extraordinary ability. The legislation was prompted by provisions of the 1990 immigration law, adopted somewhat inadvertently, that made it more difficult for performers to gain entry into the United States. Those provisions had been temporarily suspended.

The House passed HR 3049 (H Rept 102-287), dealing with the naturalization provisions, by voice vote under suspension of the rules on Nov. 12. On Nov. 25, it passed a separate measure (HR 3048 — H Rept 102-380) containing the visa provisions. The Senate passed HR 3049 on Nov. 26 after first amending it to also contain the provisions of HR 3048. The House accepted the amended version of HR 3049 on Nov. 27, clearing it for the president. The bill was signed into law Dec. 12.

Chinese Nationals

Congress in 1992 cleared legislation (S 1216 — PL 102-404) that allowed about 80,000 Chinese residents who were in the United Sates during the June 1989 massacre of pro-democracy demonstrators in Beijing's Tiananmen Square to apply for permanent residency starting July 1, 1993. An executive order already protected, through Jan. 1, 1994, the Chinese nationals from deportation. Lawmakers said the legislation was designed to provide permanent protection that would ease concerns in the Chinese community.

The Senate passed S 1216 by voice vote May 21. The House Judiciary Committee reported the bill (H Rept 102-826) on Aug. 10. The same day the House suspended the rules and passed an amended S 1216 by voice vote. The Senate accepted the changes and cleared the bill Sept. 23. President Bush signed it Oct. 9.

Soviet Scientists

Congress in 1992 cleared a measure (S 2201 — PL 102-509) that allowed 750 nuclear scientists and their families to emigrate from the former Soviet Union to work in America. Supporters of the measure argued that it would help deter an exodus of Soviet scientific talent to countries such as Iran and Iraq. After the collapse of the Soviet Union in 1991, some scientists, particularly those involved with weapons development — were offered substantial sums of money to work for developing nations bent on creating weapons of mass destruction.

The bill did not increase the 140,000 visa slots available to immigrants with "special skills." But it did amend existing laws to allow the scientists to live and work in the United States for the next four years.

The Senate passed S 2201 by voice vote May 20. On Sept. 21, House Judiciary reported the bill (H Rept 102-881, Part I) and the full House passed an amended version by voice vote under suspension of the rules. The Senate accepted the House amendments Oct. 2. The president signed the bill Oct. 26.

Japanese-American Internees

A federal fund created to compensate Japanese-Americans interned during World War II was expanded under legislation (HR 4551 — PL 102-371) cleared by the 102nd Congress.

The Civil Liberties Act of 1988 (PL 100-383), which had authorized $1.25 billion for the fund to pay each internee $20,000, had been based on an initial estimate of 60,000 claimants. That estimate was later raised to 78,000. As a result, HR 4551 increased the fund's authorization by $400 million to a total of $1.65 billion. The measure also made non-Japanese spouses and parents who were interned with their relatives eligible for compensation. *(1988 law, Congress and the Nation Vol. VII, p. 766)*

On Sept. 14, the House Judiciary Committee reported the bill (H Rept 102-863) and the House passed it by voice vote under suspension of the rules. The Senate Judiciary Committee had reported a companion measure (S 2553 — S Rept 102-394) on Sept. 8. The full Senate passed HR 4551 by voice vote Sept. 16, clearing the bill. It was signed into law Sept. 27.

Visa Exemptions

The House by voice vote under suspension of the rules Sept. 29, 1992, passed legislation (HR 5555) aimed at speeding the entry of foreign visitors into the United States, but the bill went no further during the 102nd Congress.

The measure would have made permanent a pilot project, set to expire in fiscal 1994, that allowed nationals of selected countries to enter the United States without a visa so long as they stayed no longer than 90 days. The 21 nations exempt from the visa requirements were those whose nationals generally did not stay longer than their allotted time. In addition, the Immigration and Naturalization Service would have been required to set up six preinspection stations at foreign airports to help process people with U.S. entry visas.

HR 5555 (H Rept 102-910) was reported from House Judiciary on Sept. 25.

Legal Services Corporation

Several controversial issues stood in the way of the passage in the 102nd Congress of legislation to reauthorize the Legal Services Corporation (LSC). The corporation, which provided legal services to the poor, had long been the subject of ideological wrangling. In 1991-92, battles centered on whether the program's lawyers could work on redistricting or abortion cases. *(Background, earlier action, p. 773)*

The House, 253-154, passed a five-year authorization (HR 2039 — H Rept 102-476) on May 12, 1992. But a related bill (S 2870 — S Rept 102-365) never reached the Senate floor. President Bush had promised to veto the legislation unless it contained provisions prohibiting LSC attorneys from taking abortion cases.

Both the House and Senate bills would have expanded restrictions on the cases LSC lawyers could have handled. Program lawyers would have been barred from involvement in any local, state or federal redistricting cases and from representing convicted drug dealers in public housing eviction cases. They would have been restricted in their representation of undocumented aliens on matters not related to wages and other employment rights, housing and transportation.

Existing law dictated that attorneys could lobby if they were not doing so with federal funds. Both the House and Senate bills would have barred grassroots lobbying altogether, addressing the concern of some lawmakers that program lawyers helped organize and push local efforts on political issues.

With no authorization bill in place, the task of funding the program was once again left in the hands of appropriators. For fiscal 1993, the corporation received $357 million, up slightly from $350 million in fiscal 1992.

Independent Counsel

The 102nd Congress failed to reauthorize the Watergate-era law establishing procedures for appointing an independent counsel to prosecute alleged wrongdoing by federal officials. The law expired Dec. 15, 1992.

House and Senate bills (HR 5840, S 3131) had attempted to reauthorize the law for five years.

The special prosecutor law (PL 95-521) was originally enacted in 1978 in the wake of the Watergate scandal. The law gave the U.S. attorney general the authority to request a special prosecutor to investigate allegations of wrongdoing by high-ranking executive branch officials. The appointment would be made by a special three-judge panel and the person would serve independent of the Justice Department. *(Watergate, Congress and the Nation Vol. IV, p. 931; 1978 law, Congress and the Nation Vol. V, p. 829)*

In October 1973, President Richard Nixon had tried to fire special prosecutor Archibald Cox, who had demanded secret Oval Office tapes. The attorney general and his assistant resigned rather than fire Cox. Finally, the third-ranking person at the Justice Department, Solicitor General Robert H. Bork, got rid of Cox. That episode, known as the "Saturday Night Massacre," made clear the conflict in an administration trying to control an investigation of itself. The incident became a rallying cry, leading to PL 95-521.

The 1978 law was reauthorized (PL 97-409) in 1982 for five years. The special prosecutor was renamed independent counsel in PL 97-409. *(Congress and the Nation Vol. VI, p. 681)*

In the wake of the Iran-contra scandal, President Ronald Reagan grudgingly signed a reauthorization law in 1987 (PL 100-191) following overwhelmingly favorable votes in both houses of Congress. The Iran-contra investigation, led by independent counsel Lawrence E. Walsh, looked into allegations that members of Reagan's administration diverted funds from the sale of weapons to Iran to support the contras in Nicaragua. It took six years and cost taxpayers an estimated $32 million. *(1987 law, Congress and the Nation Vol. VII, p. 773; Iran-contra affair, Congress and the Nation Vol. VII, p. 253; Iran-contra legacy, p. 238; Iran-contra pardons, p. 284)*

At the time of Iran-contra, the independent counsel the law was subject to a court challenge. The Reagan administration argued that the act unconstitutionally denied the president important executive power because it allowed a special three-judge court to appoint the independent counsel and determine the scope of the investigation. But in 1988, the Supreme Court by a 7-1 vote upheld the law's constitutionality. Its ruling in *Morrison v. Olson* said that, for certain kinds of criminal investigations involving potential conflicts of interest, Congress may set the rules for handling the inquiries without infringing on the president's constitutional authority to enforce the law. *(Case summary, Congress and the Nation Vol. VII, p. 834)*

By 1992, the independent counsel law had survived three presidents and relentless opposition from the Justice Department. It had led to 11 independent investigations, three of them resulting in standing convictions.

The 1992 reauthorization bills were clouded by the costly Iran-contra affair, as well as the House bank and Post Office scandals. Republicans felt singled out by the counsel, and Congress' own scandals left the bill without strong leadership backing. A key controversy centered on how Congress should be included under the law. *(House bank, p. 929; Post Office, p. 939)*

The House Judiciary Subcommittee on Administrative Law and Governmental Relations (HR 5840) and the Senate Governmental Affairs Committee (S 3131 — S Rept 102-417) approved legislation the week of Sept. 14 to extend the Independent Counsel Act, leaving supporters hoping that the embattled law might be reauthorized.

But vociferous Republican objections killed last-minute efforts to reauthorize the measure in the 102nd Congress. Republicans, furious about Iran-contra, were especially angry about the 1992 indictment of former defense secretary Caspar W. Weinberger for allegedly withholding information from Congress. And when the Senate tried to bring the bill up for debate Sept. 29, Minority Leader Bob Dole, R-Kan., blocked the move.

Judicial Nominating Process

The tumultuous Senate Judiciary Committee confirmation hearings for Clarence Thomas in 1991 moved the Senate in 1992 to re-examine the judicial nominating process. But few changes were ultimately made, as Senate Democrats focused on shifting the blame for the controversy by stressing the need for the president to consult with them before choosing a candidate.

Thomas' nomination to the Supreme Court embarrassed Senate Judiciary Committee Chairman Joseph R. Biden Jr., D-Del., and other panel members after it was revealed that charges of sexual harassment brought forth against the nominee by former colleague Anita F. Hill had not been adequately investigated. The charges became public only after being leaked to the media. *(Thomas nomination, box, p. 802)*

Calls for change in the judicial nomination process came from both ends of Pennsylvania Ave. This led Senate Majority Leader George J. Mitchell, D-Maine, to appoint a task force to look for ways to make the process better. The group — composed entirely of Democratic committee chairmen — recommended no major changes in the Senate's procedures. Instead, its key proposals focused on the administration and the selection process.

While Mitchell said he did not expect the president "to shrink the scope or exercise of his constitutional powers," he added that the Senate had to exercise its "advice and consent" power under the Constitution. He stressed that, under the Constitution, the president and Senate were to act jointly on nominations.

Not surprisingly, Bush refused all requests for consultation, arguing that the choice of the candidate is the president's prerogative.

The task force, which made its recommendations to the full Senate, also criticized Bush's post-Thomas policy of restricting Senate Judiciary Committee access to FBI background reports on nominees.

But in February 1992, the administration and Judiciary Committee members reached a deal to give senators and key staff access to the background reports under tighter security. And in June, Biden promised all senators access to the FBI files and warned the president that would oppose any nominee if the Senate was not consulted beforehand.

Ryskamp Nomination

President Bush was handed his first defeat of a judicial nominee on April 11, 1991, when a majority of the Senate Judiciary Committee refused to send the nomination of Kenneth L. Ryskamp to the floor. By a party-line vote of 6-8, the committee opposed the elevation of Ryskamp, a district court judge, to the 11th U.S. Circuit Court of Appeals. The panel then failed, on a 7-7 tie, to send the nomination to the floor.

The Ryskamp defeat was not the result of a great ideological battle. Senators opposing Ryskamp said he had failed to dispel criticism that he was unsympathetic to minorities, had too quickly rejected legal precedents and was given to intemperate remarks from the bench.

Each of Bush's previous 77 judicial nominees had passed through the confirmation process with little of the negative publicity that greeted many of President Ronald Reagan's nominees. Indeed, the only Bush nominee rejected by the Judiciary Committee before the Ryskamp nomination was William Lucas to be assistant attorney general in charge of civil rights. *(Lucas nomination, p. 763)*

Ryskamp had been appointed to the Southern District of Florida by Reagan in 1986. Bush nominated him in 1990 to the 11th Circuit appellate court, which covered Florida, Georgia and Alabama and was one of the last appeals courts not dominated by appointees of Republicans Reagan and Bush.

The April 11 action was the second time the Judiciary Committee had blocked Ryskamp's elevation. In the 101st Congress, after allegations arose regarding Ryskamp's record on civil rights and membership in a private club that reportedly had discriminated against blacks and Jews, the Judiciary Committee shelved his nomination. Bush renominated him on Jan. 8, 1991.

Police Brutality Issue

One of the key cases Ryskamp critics cited involved a complaint by blacks who were attacked by city police dogs in West Palm Beach. Not all of these blacks were subsequently found guilty of a crime.

In this case, the jury found the city of West Palm Beach, its former police chief and individual police officers had violated the plaintiffs' civil rights. Ryskamp left alone the verdict against the individual police officers but threw out the verdict against the city and the former police chief. Ryskamp said of the complainants: "It might not be inappropriate to carry around a few scars to remind you of your wrongdoing in the past, assuming the person has done wrong." The 11th Circuit said Ryskamp erred in setting aside the verdict.

When Ryskamp was asked to explain that comment to the Judiciary Committee, he seemed to undermine his nomination further among skeptical Democrats. Under questioning, he said that he was talking only about suspects who were convicted of stealing. "I was thinking for their own welfare ... and the idea of keeping them from committing other crimes, that the painful experience might be a deterrent, whereas, the irony would be if they got a lot of money, it may be a vindication, and they would go on to commit other crimes. That is all I meant by it," he said. Judiciary Committee Joseph R. Biden Jr., D-Del, said he was "astounded" by Ryskamp's remarks on the case.

Graham Opposition

Opposition from one of Ryskamp's home-state senators, Democrat Bob Graham, helped tip the balance against the nominee. Typically, senators of both parties support judicial nominees from their states. But groups representing Cubans, women, Jews and blacks lobbied hard against the nominee, targeting Graham in the hope that if he opposed Ryskamp, so would wavering Judiciary Committee members. After hearing from Ryskamp opponents while making the rounds of dinners and meetings in Florida, Graham wrote an 11th-hour letter to Biden opposing the nomination.

In his letter, Graham said he thought Ryskamp should be rejected because "serious questions have been raised about whether this nominee would be fair and unbiased."

Carnes Nomination

In a decisive victory for President Bush, the Senate voted 62-36 on Sept. 9, 1992, to confirm Bush's nomination of Edward Earl Carnes Jr. to the 11th U.S. Circuit Court of Appeals, over strong objections from key Democrats and the nation's leading civil rights groups.

Carnes was to replace Judge Frank M. Johnson, who retired in October 1991. Johnson was credited with furthering desegregation and racial justice in the South. The 11th Circuit continued to hear a number of the nation's civil rights cases.

The vote brought to a close months of haggling over Carnes, an Alabama assistant attorney general who had headed that state's capital punishment litigation division since 1981. He had been approved by the Judiciary Committee May 7 by a 10-4 vote.

Carnes' supporters and opponents asked senators to choose between two views of the nominee. Some, including a handful of black politicians and lawyers and one prominent Alabama civil rights lawyer, said Carnes had fought for racial fairness. But civil rights groups said Carnes perpetuated racial discrimination in Alabama's criminal justice system.

Although Carnes' role as a national advocate for the death penalty was a deciding factor for a few senators, the vote was far from a referendum on the death penalty. For most senators, the decision was instead a statement on crime and race in a tense election year in which no one could afford to appear soft on crime and candidates were steering clear of racial justice issues.

Most senators who voted against Carnes, primarily liberal Democrats, said they were concerned about his statements before the Senate Judiciary Committee on April 1 about race and capital punishment. "I do not believe that capital punishment is applied in a racially discriminatory manner in Alabama or in the nation," Carnes had said.

Opponents had argued that confirmation would send the wrong message to minorities in the wake of the verdict in the police beating of black motorist Rodney King and ensuing violence in Los Angeles in April.

Other Legislation

'Hate Crimes'

Legislation (HR 4797) to strengthen mandatory sentencing guidelines for federal offenses that involved "hate crimes" passed the House in 1992. But the measure died when the Senate failed to act on it.

HR 4797 would have defined a hate crime as one that was motivated by hatred, bias or prejudice based on race, religion, ethnicity, color, gender or sexual orientation. Under the measure, if a federal crime of any sort were motivated by such hatred or prejudice, the judge would have had to sentence the felon to additional time in prison. Prison terms would have been extended by roughly one-third.

The House Judiciary Committee reported HR 4797 (H Rept 102-981) on Oct. 2. The full House acted Oct. 3 by voice vote under suspension of the rules.

Battered Women

Legislation (HR 1252 — PL 102-527) that promoted the use of expert witnesses in cases in which battered women assaulted or killed their abusers was cleared by Congress in 1992. The bill, which passed the House (H Rept 102-991) on Oct. 3 and the Senate on Oct. 7, authorized $600,000 to the State Justice Institute to provide grants to organizations to collect information on expert testimony about the psychological state of battered women and to help women find expert defense witnesses.

A related measure (S 15 — S Rept 102-197) to curb violence against women was set aside as Congress tried but failed to clear a comprehensive anti-crime bill. The measure, which was reported from the Senate Judiciary Committee on Oct. 29, 1991, would have allowed victims of sexual assault to bring civil rights suits against their attackers and increased penalties for sex crimes. The penalty for rape, for example, would have been doubled, to 10 years. The panel reported a similar measure in 1990. *(Crime bill, p. 786; violence against women, p. 797)*

The Senate Judiciary Committee Aug. 12, 1992, reported another related measure, which would have allowed rape victims and their families to sue hard-core pornographers. However, it got tangled in controversy, met strong opposition and went no further in the 102nd Congress. The bill (S 1521 — S Rept 102-372) would have made those who produced or distributed hard-core pornography liable if victims proved the material incited the offender to commit the crime.

Although the bill's goal of providing more legal recourse to victims of sex crimes was a popular political topic in an election year, First Amendment concerns about free speech dogged the measure, making it difficult for backers to muster support for it. No companion measure was introduced in the House.

Torture Victims

Congress in 1992 cleared a bill (HR 2092 — Pl 102-256) allowing U.S. citizens to file civil lawsuits against foreigners living in the United States who, in an official capacity, engaged in torture or extrajudicial execution outside of the United States. Arlen Specter, R-Pa., the sponsor of the Senate version of the measure (S 313), said that the legislation was needed so that the United States would not become a haven for foreigners who had engaged in torture or other human rights violations.

HR 2092 required lawsuits to be filed within 10 years of the alleged abuse. In addition, the victim had to have exhausted all legal remedies in the country where the torture took place before bringing suit in the United States.

On Nov. 25, 1991, the House Judiciary Committee reported HR 2092 (H Rept 102-367, Part I) and the full House passed the bill by voice vote under suspension of the rules. The Senate Judiciary Committee reported S 313 (S Rept 102-249) on Nov. 26. The Senate passed HR 2092 by voice vote March 3, 1992, clearing the bill. President Bush signed it March 12.

Juvenile Violence

Legislation (HR 5194 — PL 102-586) that aimed to stem juvenile violence cleared Congress in 1992. The bill reauthorized for four years the Office of Juvenile Justice and Delinquency Prevention in the Justice Department. The office is charged with finding ways to prevent children from becoming juvenile delinquents and devising alternatives to detention for juveniles already incarcerated. The measure authorized increased funding for state grants to help deter juvenile violence and financial incentives to encourage states to try alternatives to imprisonment for teens convicted of non-violent offenses.

HR 5194 was reported from House Education and Labor (H Rept 102-756) on July 29. The House passed the bill by voice vote under suspension of the rules Aug. 3. The Senate Judiciary Committee reported a companion measure (S 2792 — S Rept 102-393) on Sept. 8. The Senate passed an amended HR 5194 by voice vote Sept. 25. The bill eventually cleared Oct. 7, and President Bush signed it Nov. 4.

Child Abuse

Congress in 1992 cleared a measure (HR 1253 — PL 102-528) that authorized $600,000 for the State Justice Institute to develop training courses on child custody law to aid courts in identifying those homes at high risk for the abuse of children or their parents.

HR 1253 on Oct. 3 was reported from House Judiciary (H Rept 102-992) and passed by voice vote under suspension of the rules in the House. The Senate passed the measure by voice vote Oct. 7. The president signed it Oct. 27.

DNA Testing

Legislation (HR 3088) that would have promoted the use of DNA technology in solving crimes passed the House in the waning days of the 102nd Congress but was never taken up in the Senate.

DNA carries a genetic code that is unique to each human and has been used to identify the perpetrators of violent crimes. The bill would have authorized $10 million for four years for state and local governments to establish DNA crime labs. It also would have established privacy and quality control guidelines for the labs.

The House passed HR 3088 by voice vote under suspension of the rules Oct. 6.

Customs' Damages

Legislation (HR 2731) that would have held the U.S. Customs Service liable for damages negligently inflicted on private property during searches and seizures passed the House in 1992 but was never taken up in the Senate. President Bush threatened to veto the bill, arguing that it would have exposed the government to too many liability claims.

Under existing law, property owners could sue the Customs Service for no more than $1,000 and the service was prohibited from offering any kind of settlement, even if it acknowledged negligence. The measure would have allowed property owners to sue the service for damages, although punitive damages would continue to be prohibited. Additionally, the measure would have allowed the government to settle claims, with a cap of $50,000.

The House Judiciary Committee reported HR 2731 (H Rept 102-776) on Aug. 3. The House passed the bill by voice vote under suspension of the rules Aug. 11.

Consolidation of Lawsuits

The House on Nov. 25, 1991, passed HR 2450, by voice vote under suspension of the rules, to allow the consolidation of federal lawsuits under certain circumstances. The Senate never took action, and the measure died at the end of the 102nd Congress. A similar bill passed the House in 1990, but it too died when the Senate took no action. *(Story, p. 779)*

The House bill would have authorized federal district courts to consolidate 25 or more lawsuits arising in multiple state courts against the same defendant. The suits could be consolidated only if all the cases arose from the same incident, such as a plane crash; the plaintiffs each sued for more than $50,000 in damages; and the suits were pending in more than one state.

HR 2450 (H Rept 102-373) was reported from House Judiciary on Nov. 25.

Judicial Administration

A measure (S 1569 — PL 102-572) that aimed to improve the operations of the federal court system cleared Congress on Oct. 7, 1992. The bill, which implemented some of the findings of the Federal Courts Study Committee, provided for improvements in the financial administration of the judicial system and revised the judicial survivors' annuity system.

The committee had been created in 1988. Many of its recommendations had already been incorporated in the Judicial Improvements Act of 1990. *(Judicial improvements, p. 774)*

S 1569 also reauthorized the State Justice Institute, which funds studies on improving the operations of state courts and sponsors meetings of judges from different states to discuss issues of common interest.

The Senate Judiciary Committee reported the bill (S Rept 102-342) on July 27. The Senate passed it by voice vote Aug. 3. The House Judiciary Committee reported HR 5933 (H Rept 102-1006, Part I) on Oct. 3. The House passed the measure by voice vote under suspension of the rules the same day. Then, the House passed an amended S 1569 by voice vote in lieu. President Bush signed the bill Oct. 29.

Military Malpractice

The House Judiciary Committee on Oct. 6, 1990, reported legislation (HR 3407 — H Rept 102-1043) to allow members of the U.S. military to sue the federal government for medical malpractice.

Under the Federal Tort Claims Act of 1946, members of the armed forces were prohibited from suing the government in cases of negligence at military medical facilities.

HR 3407 would allow malpractice suits only in cases involving non-combat-related injuries and when treatment occurred in the United States, at permanent medical facilities. Plaintiffs would be able to collect only compensatory damages. No punitive damages could be awarded.

The administration opposed the legislation.

The House passed a similar bill in 1989. *(Story, p. 780)*

Bankruptcy Judges

Congress in 1992 cleared legislation (HR 5688 — PL 102-361) to authorize the appointment of 32 new federal bankruptcy judges in districts that had seen a significant increase in bankruptcy filings.

According to Dennis DeConcini, D-Ariz., in fiscal 1990 there was a 14.2 percent increase in the number of bankruptcy filings nationwide. Much of the boost resulted from a downturn in the real estate market and an increase in the number of failed financial institutions.

In 1991, there were 291 bankruptcy judges. The measure created additional judgeships in Florida, Arizona, Georgia, California, Texas, New Jersey, Pennsylvania, New York, Connecticut, New Hampshire, Massachusetts and South Carolina.

The House Judiciary Committee reported HR 5688 (H Rept 102-825) on Aug. 10. The same day, the full House suspended the rules and passed the bill by voice vote. The Senate passed the measure by voice vote Aug. 12, completing congressional action. President Bush signed the bill Aug. 26.

The Senate also had considered a companion measure (S 646). Senate Judiciary reported it (S Rept 102-156) on Aug. 1, and the full Senate passed the bill by voice vote Aug. 2.

Tobacco Sales Bans

States were required to enforce laws barring the sale of tobacco products to minors under legislation (S 1306 — PL 102-321) cleared by Congress in 1992 to reauthorize the federal mental health, drug and alcohol abuse programs.

All but a handful of states already had laws prohibiting those under a certain age from purchasing cigarettes, chewing tobacco or other tobacco products. But few states made any effort to enforce those laws, anti-smoking advocates said.

Under S 1306, every state was required to ban the sale or distribution of tobacco products to anyone under age 18. The bill also required that states enforce their laws "in a manner that can reasonably be expected to reduce the extent to which tobacco products are available to underage youths."

States were to report annually about their efforts, which were required to include "random, unannounced inspections" of locations where tobacco products were sold. States determined not to be enforcing their laws could lose up to 40 percent of their federal substance abuse funds. *(Reauthorization, p. 604)*

The Supreme Court

During his two-term tenure, President Ronald Reagan created a conservative majority on the Supreme Court through four appointments, including the elevation of William H. Rehnquist to chief justice. President Bush sought to move the Court's center of gravity further to the right with his two nominees: David H. Souter and Clarence Thomas. However, in the Court's final full term of the Reagan-Bush era — from October 1991 to July 1992 — a trio of centrist justices emerged whose rulings served to steady the Court on some of the most volatile issues before it.

Sandra Day O'Connor, Anthony M. Kennedy and Souter formed a triumvirate that provided the critical votes, for example, in a 5-4 ruling that reaffirmed a constitutional right to abortion while giving states greater leeway to regulate abortion procedures. They also joined in a 5-4 decision that rejected a plea by the Bush administration to ease restrictions on religious ceremonies in public schools. The rulings disappointed conservatives, who had looked to Reagan and Bush to appoint justices who would overturn the 1973 abortion rights decision *Roe v. Wade* and narrow or reverse other liberal precedents of the Warren and Burger courts.

The abortion and school prayer decisions underscored the new difficulty in dividing the justices neatly into liberal and conservative camps. The Court's most liberal member was Harry A. Blackmun, and he was usually joined by John Paul Stevens. The other seven justices ranged on a spectrum of conservatism from Rehnquist, Antonin Scalia and Thomas, on the far right; to Byron R. White, a conservative on criminal justice issues but more moderate on some other questions; to O'Connor, Kennedy and Souter, in a loosely formed middle.

When O'Connor, Kennedy and Souter voted together during the 1991-92 term, they were never in the minority. The three justices' moderating influence put a brake on the conservative bloc's desire to abandon earlier rulings.

In the 1990-91 term, the Court had thrown out five precedents, including two decisions easing rules for prisoners to challenge their convictions and a 1987 decision barring use of so-called victim impact statements in death penalty hearings. Thurgood Marshall, in his last dissenting opinion before retiring from the Court in 1991, bitterly criticized the conservative majority for overturning precedent. "The majority today sends a clear signal that scores of established constitutional liberties are ripe for reconsideration," Marshall wrote.

The Court's mixed rulings during the 1991-92 term quieted some of those fears. A conservative tilt could be seen in some of the Court's decisions in criminal law and civil rights. But in other areas, including First Amendment issues, the Court's decisions were harder to classify.

The Court also appeared to be deliberately taking a lower profile. Despite an increasing number of cases brought to the Court, the number of cases reviewed and decided by the justices saw a steady decline. In the 1991-92 term, the number of signed decisions fell to 107 — the lowest total in more than 20 years.

Souter, Thomas Nominations

Bush's two nominations to the Court came against the backdrop of the bitter fight over Reagan's unsuccessful Supreme Court nominee Robert H. Bork in 1987. Unlike Bork, Souter was a little known jurist who had served as a federal appeals court judge from New Hampshire for just four months and had no extensive "paper trail" for skeptics to use against him. Souter was nominated to fill the vacancy caused by the retirement of liberal Justice William J. Brennan Jr. *(Bork nomination, Congress and the Nation Vol. VII, p. 786)*

Souter's testimony before the Senate Judiciary Committee displayed a command of legal scholarship and a cautious approach to many issues. He refused to give his views on abortion, saying that the issue would come before him if he were confirmed. He also passed up an opportunity to criticize judicial activism, a notion conservatives generally did not support.

Some liberals remained distrustful of Souter's stance on abortion and privacy. But Senate Majority Leader George J. Mitchell, D-Maine, a former U.S. district court judge, said he believed Souter had a "reasoned approach and sound understanding" of the Constitution. After four

References

Discussion of the Supreme Court for the years 1945-64 may be found in *Congress and the Nation Vol. I*, pp. 1441-1454; for the years 1965-68, *Congress and the Nation Vol. II*, pp. 335-340; for the years 1969-72, *Congress and the Nation Vol. III*, pp. 289-327; for the years 1973-76, *Congress and the Nation Vol. IV*, pp. 619-659; for the years 1977-80, *Congress and the Nation Vol. V*, pp. 755-791; for the years 1981-84, *Congress and the Nation Vol. VI*, pp. 711-768; for the years 1985-88, *Congress and the Nation Vol. VII*, pp. 735-840.

At Issue in Thomas Confirmation Hearings...

Clarence Thomas, President Bush's choice to succeed Thurgood Marshall on the Supreme Court, was poised to win confirmation in early October 1991. But two days before the Senate vote was scheduled to take place, University of Oklahoma law professor Anita F. Hill made public her accusation that Thomas sexually harassed her while she worked for him at the Department of Education and at the Equal Employment Opportunity Commission (EEOC). An outpouring of anger and protest from women throughout the United States forced the Senate to delay its vote and order an investigation of the charges. What followed were hearings that marked one of the wildest spectacles in modern congressional history, a subject for satire and scorn that rocked the Senate.

The drama, played out before the Senate Judiciary Committee, was larger than Thomas and Hill themselves. At stake was a lifetime appointment to the highest court in the country. In doubt was how the president and Senate screen candidates for the bench. At issue during the nationally televised hearings were sexual harassment and how men and women treat each other on the job.

Hill's Allegations

Anita Hill went public with her allegations of sexual harassment on Oct. 6, 1991. Revealed also was that the members of the Senate Judiciary Committee were aware of the allegations when they sent Thomas' nomination to the floor on a 7-7 vote taken Sept. 27. Majority Leader George J. Mitchell, D-Maine, and Minority Leader Bob Dole, R-Kan., also had known of the charges. Sexual harassment, illegal under federal law, is "unwelcome sexual advances, requests for sexual favors, and other verbal or physical conduct of a sexual nature" when acceptance or rejection of this conduct affects a person's employment.

After public outcry over the seriousness of sexual harassment and whether the Judiciary Committee was right to keep the allegations secret from the full Senate, the Oct. 8 floor vote was postponed. The committee reconvened Oct. 11 in televised hearings that turned into three days of sensational and prurient drama for the Senate and millions of Americans.

The first day began in the Senate Caucus Room with a declaration of innocence by Thomas. For the next seven hours, Hill meticulously recounted her story of how Thomas humiliated her with lewd comments. Hill was an attorney-adviser to Thomas from 1981 to 1982, when he was assistant secretary of education in the civil rights division. She was a special assistant, from 1982 to 1983, to Thomas as EEOC chairman. Hill said that, early on, Thomas asked her out socially. She said she declined because she believed it would corrupt their professional dealings. Under questioning from senators, she detailed the nature of the alleged sexual harassment, which she said occurred mostly in his office and when the two were alone. She said she believed he wanted to have sexual intercourse with her. And she provided embarrassing details of what she said were Thomas' comments to her on the job: talk of women's breasts, the size of penises, accounts of movies of group sex and bestiality. Hill also spoke of the anguish she felt over speaking of the incidents publicly.

Senators asked Hill to explain why, if she was so offended by harassment at the Education Department, she then would move with Thomas to EEOC. "I needed the job," she said, noting that she was 25 years old at the time and perhaps had not made the best judgment. "There was a period prior to the time we went to EEOC, there was a period where the incidents had ceased," she said. "And so after some consideration of the job opportunities in the [civil rights] area, as well as the fact that I was not assured that my job at Education was going to be protected, I made a decision to move to the EEOC."

Thomas' Denials

After nightfall, an angry Thomas was back with his own accusations. "This is a circus, it's a national disgrace, and from my standpoint as a black American," Thomas said, "it's a high-tech lynching for an uppity black who in any way deigns to think for himself." Thomas said the message was "that unless you kowtow to an older order, this is what will happen to you. You will be lynched, destroyed — caricatured by a committee of the U.S. Senate rather than hung from a tree." He categorically denied Hill's claim of sexual impropriety, although he also said he did not listen to any of her testimony. Thomas said he always treated Hill professionally and cordially. He said he never asked her out and never talked in such pornographic terms.

Thomas drew a picture of a man wrongly accused, his reputation in shreds and his family destroyed. "In my 43 years on this Earth, I have been able with the help of others to defy poverty, avoid prison, overcome segregation, bigotry, racism and obtain one of the finest educations available in this country. But I have not been able to overcome this process." Nevertheless, the next day he said he "would rather die" than withdraw from consideration. Witnesses in support of Hill and Thomas testified on the final day of the hearings.

Reaction to Testimony

Hill's poised and unwavering testimony rang true with many who heard it, polls showed, until

. . . Sexual Harassment, Politics of Selection

Thomas returned to testify. Republican senators and the White House then attacked Hill's credibility, portraying her as a deluded, scorned woman. Underneath it all, and despite the fact that Hill also is black, were Republican intimations that Thomas was being attacked out of racism. Thomas was first to introduce the race issue into the hearings, with his charge of a "high-tech lynching," but this was pounded away by committee Republicans during their questioning of subsequent witnesses.

Ironically, Hill's charges raised fundamental questions about Thomas' character — the one attribute that the White House and his Republican Senate supporters had played up. Democrats who opposed Thomas, however, were never able to capitalize on the character issue. Throughout the entire process they lacked a strategy in part because the nomination of a conservative black split their constituency.

In the end, most senators said Hill's charges and Thomas' defense were inconclusive. More of the American public believed Thomas over Hill. (Polls taken a year later would find the reverse, however.) Senators fell back on their previous positions based on Thomas' judicial philosophy or his determined rise from poverty in rural Georgia. Both sides estimated that Thomas lost about 10 votes that he might have had before the allegations emerged — narrowing an outcome that still would have been one of the closest in history.

Hill's charges not only upset Thomas' confirmation but also put under siege the judicial screening process and the Senate as an institution. Senators were barraged with accusations from constituents and the media that they were insensitive to women and out of touch with America. Angry women asked whether the male-dominated institution recognized the seriousness of Hill's charge and why the full Senate had been left in the dark. Senate leaders said that Hill originally sought confidentiality and that they acted properly by keeping her charges within the committee's purview. Hill subsequently went public in an interview with a National Public Radio reporter who obtained a leaked copy of her complaint to the committee.

Larger Issues

Beneath the storm — and in many ways leading to it — was the conservative bent of the Court.

Not since Franklin D. Roosevelt, who completed an unprecedented three full terms, had a president, or a pair of succeeding like-minded presidents, had such sweeping influence over the makeup of the third branch of government and used appointments to further a political agenda. The Court always has been a prize for the White House, and presidents often have attempted to use the Court to execute their priorities. But the politics was tempered, given that the philosophy of successive presidents shifts, that most presidents name an average of three justices and that, with a few exceptions, presidents do not campaign on changing the Court.

Unlike Roosevelt, who was paired with a Congress led by his own Democratic Party, Republican Bush constantly faced off on domestic policy with a Democratic Congress. Factions in Congress struggled with legislation to undo various recent Court rulings, but the needed two-thirds votes to ensure overrides of threatened vetoes proved elusive. The congressional Democratic leadership was foundering, and many members felt that the balance of powers was two against one.

Against this backdrop, the process of confirming justices "has taken on the trappings of a political campaign," said Mitchell. Ronald Reagan and Bush ran on platforms advocating conservative justices, particularly those who oppose abortion, Mitchell observed before the final vote on Thomas. "In the eyes of many Americans, the [confirmation] process has become confused with electoral politics."

But Texas Republican Phil Gramm said, "I submit to my colleagues that the people who voted for George Bush in 1988 had every reason to expect that, if he were elected, he would appoint conservative justices to the Supreme Court. Now what has happened is that the people who lost that election are using the advice-and-consent clause to try to win what they could not win at the ballot box."

Democrats countered by noting that past presidents at times named justices from the other party. William J. Brennan Jr., one of the Court's most liberal activists, was chosen by Republican Dwight D. Eisenhower. "In addition," said Sen. Paul Simon, D-Ill., "presidents have appointed people who have differed very substantially in terms of philosophy. . . . I have suggested that balance is needed."

In the end, the lesson of Thomas' confirmation was that while the Senate Judiciary Committee aspired to be a forum for constitutional debate, it was in reality a political obstacle course for the nominee and the White House to negotiate. The conflict mirrors a larger question: Should the Senate defer to the president once a nominee has been shown to meet minimal qualifications for ability and integrity or should it more independently scrutinize a lifetime appointment to the highest court? Some Democrats remarked that it is almost as if people have come to believe that justices, nominated by the president and owing their confirmation to his political network, serve the executive instead of their separate branch of government.

The Court of 1993

The members of the U.S. Supreme Court in 1993 were:

- Chief Justice William H. Rehnquist, born in 1924, appointed to the Court by President Nixon in 1971; promoted to chief justice by President Reagan in 1986.
- Justice Byron R. White, born in 1917, appointed by President Kennedy in 1962.
- Justice Harry A. Blackmun, born in 1908, appointed by President Nixon in 1970.
- Justice John Paul Stevens, born in 1920, appointed by President Ford in 1975.
- Justice Sandra Day O'Connor, born in 1930, appointed by President Reagan in 1981.
- Justice Antonin Scalia, born in 1936, appointed by President Reagan in 1986.
- Justice Anthony M. Kennedy, born in 1936, appointed by President Reagan in 1987.
- Justice David H. Souter, born in 1939, appointed by President Bush in 1990.
- Justice Clarence Thomas, born in 1948, appointed by President Bush in 1991.

hours of debate, the Senate voted 90-9 on Oct. 2, 1990, to confirm Souter; he was sworn in one week later.

Bush made a more ideologically charged decision in picking Thomas to succeed Marshall, the first black to serve on the Supreme Court. Thomas, also an African-American, had distanced himself from established civil rights groups by aligning with the Reagan administration's opposition to affirmative action as head of the Equal Employment Opportunity Commission (EEOC). He had taken other conservative stands in writings and speeches before being named a federal judge on the U.S. Court of Appeals for the District of Columbia in 1990.

Like Souter, Thomas resisted senators' efforts to pin him down on abortion. He also sidestepped questions on other issues and minimized the significance of his writings before taking the bench — including his apparent endorsement of "natural law," a theory that an individual is endowed with certain inherent rights that cannot be restricted by written law, not even the Constitution. Abortion rights groups led a coalition of liberal forces urging a no vote.

After five days of tense hearings in September 1991, the Senate Judiciary Committee deadlocked 7-7 on the nomination but agreed to send Thomas' name to the full Senate for a vote. On the weekend before the scheduled vote, however, news accounts disclosed that a former Thomas aide, Anita F. Hill, had told Senate and FBI investigators that Thomas had sexually harassed her while she worked for him at the Department of Education and the EEOC.

After a public outcry, the vote on the nomination was postponed and the confirmation hearings reopened. The dramatic hearings were nationally televised and intensely followed, but they failed to resolve the charges. With members sharply split, the Senate voted on Oct. 8 to confirm Thomas. The **52-48 (R 41-2; D 11-46) key vote** was the closest margin on a Supreme Court nominee in more than a century. *(1991 key votes, p. 1061; Thomas hearings, details, box, p. 802)*

Abortion

Abortion rights organizations opposed the Souter and Thomas nominations because they believed the fate of *Roe v. Wade* could depend on each new justice's vote on the issue. The Reagan and Bush administrations had urged the Court to overturn the ruling, and the 1988 Republican Party platform called for appointment of federal judges with "pro-life" views.

In 1989, the Supreme Court heartened anti-abortion forces somewhat with a 5-4 decision upholding a Missouri law setting some new limits on abortion procedures. Kennedy, named to the Court after abortion rights forces helped sink Bork's nomination, joined in calling for a reconsideration of *Roe v. Wade*. But O'Connor, Reagan's first appointee to the Court and the first woman to serve, took a more tentative stand, saying the case did not require a new look at the 1973 precedent.

The Court in 1990 upheld state laws requiring a minor to notify at least one parent before obtaining an abortion. The next year, the Court upheld, 5-4, a Reagan administration policy denying federal aid to family planning clinics if they engage in abortion counseling.

Later in 1991, the Court set the stage for a showdown by agreeing to review a Pennsylvania law with several tough restrictions on abortion procedures. The law imposed a 24-hour waiting period, required doctors to inform women of the risks and alternatives to abortion and required married women to notify their husbands before obtaining an abortion.

The Court's decision was announced in an unusual joint opinion by O'Connor, Kennedy and Souter. Stressing the importance of precedent, the trio reaffirmed what they called the "essential holding" of *Roe v. Wade*. But they also said states could regulate abortion procedures if the restrictions did not put an "undue burden" on a woman seeking an abortion before a fetus was viable. On that standard, the Court struck down the husband notification requirement but upheld the 24-hour waiting period and informed consent provision.

Anti-abortion groups charged that the justices had betrayed them. But abortion rights organizations criticized the ruling, too, saying it invited further restrictions on women's rights. While some states moved to consider new abortion laws, abortion rights groups' fears were allayed somewhat by Bill Clinton's election as president in 1992. During the campaign, Clinton promised to appoint abortion rights supporters to the Court if vacancies arose while he was in office. (Clinton got his first opportunity in 1993; Justice White announced March 19 that he would resign at the end of the 1992-93 term. On June 14, President Clinton announced his nomination of Ruth Bader Ginsburg, a federal judge on the U.S. Circuit Court of Appeals for the District of Columbia. From 1973 to 1976, Ginsburg argued six landmark women's rights cases before the Supreme Court, winning five. Confirmed on Aug. 3 on a 96-3 vote, Ginsburg became the second female member of the Court and the first Jew to serve since Justice Abe Fortas resigned in 1969.)

Criminal Law

The Court showed a more consistent conservative tilt on criminal law issues. The justices were not inclined to expand procedural rights for criminal defendants. And they displayed frequent impatience with challenges to procedures in death penalty cases and prisoners' habeas corpus petitions seeking to set aside convictions already reviewed by state and federal courts.

With the retirements of Brennan and Marshall, none of the sitting justices was consistently opposed to capital punishment on constitutional grounds. The Court frequently rebuffed last-minute pleas to block scheduled executions. Its decisions for the most part upheld death sentences against a variety of specific procedural challenges. And in a pair of 5-4 rulings, the Court in 1989 refused to bar states from executing mentally retarded persons or juveniles aged 16 or over.

Many of the Court's decisions limiting remedies in habeas corpus petitions also came in death penalty cases. In a pair of 6-3 decisions, the Court in 1991 generally limited prisoners to a single habeas corpus petition in federal court and barred habeas corpus petitions when prisoners had failed to comply with state procedural rules. Earlier, in 1989, the Court had refused to require states to appoint counsel for death row inmates challenging their convictions or sentences.

The Court continued to narrow habeas corpus relief somewhat in 1992. But in one closely watched case, the Court sidestepped a Bush administration argument to require federal courts hearing habeas corpus petitions to defer to state court rulings on legal issues.

In other important criminal law rulings, the Court in 1989 upheld tough forfeiture provisions in federal drug law and in 1990 approved the use of police roadblocks to check for drunken drivers. The Court in 1991 also narrowed the use of the Eighth Amendment's Cruel and Unusual Punishment Clause to limit criminal sentences, with a 5-4 decision that upheld a life prison term for a first-time drug offense.

Church and State

The Court's rulings on the separation of church and state reflected division and uncertainty among the justices.

In 1989, a fragmented ruling barred a strictly religious Christmas display in a public courthouse but permitted a display that included a Christmas tree along with a Jewish menorah outside another government building. Kennedy led four justices in voting to permit both displays and urging to lower the barriers to religious activities on public property.

The next year, the Court upheld, 8-1, a federal law that guarantees student religious groups the same right to meet in public high schools granted to other extracurricular activities.

After those decisions, the 1992 decision to bar prayer at public high school graduation ceremonies was a surprise. Kennedy now led a 5-4 majority saying that the inclusion of the prayer carried a risk of indirect coercion of religious belief.

The Court also handed down an unexpected decision in 1990 that narrowed the protection for religious practices that conflict with criminal law. The 6-3 ruling allowed a state to punish the sacramental use of an illegal drug — peyote — by holding that the law's effect on religious freedom was only "incidental."

U.S. Supreme Court Caseload

	1988-1989	1989-1990	1990-1991	1991-1992
Number of Cases on Docket	5,657	5,746	6,316	6,770
Cases Decided Summarily	107	80	109	74
Cases Argued and Decided	173	147	131	130
Cases Disposed of by Signed Opinions	156	143	121	120
Number of Signed Opinions	133	129	112	107

Note: In earlier editions of *Congress and the Nation*, the "Number of Signed Opinions" figures actually reflected the total number of cases disposed of by signed opinions. In some instances, the Supreme Court joins together several related cases and disposes of them in a single opinion. The number of signed opinions thus differs from the number of cases disposed of by signed opinions.

Source: U.S. Supreme Court.

Free Speech, Press

The Court took a broad view of First Amendment protections in several rulings involving freedom of speech and expression. Some of those rulings provoked sharp controversy.

When the Court invalidated, 5-4, a state anti-flag desecration law in 1989, opponents sought to overturn the decision first with a federal statute and then with a constitutional amendment. The same five-justice majority struck down the federal law in 1990, however, and the drive for the constitutional amendment failed in Congress.

In another major First Amendment ruling, the Court in 1992 struck down a local "hate speech" ordinance that prohibited race-, religion-, ethnic- or gender-based epithets. The Court held that the government cannot selectively punish speech on the basis of its subject.

In another groundbreaking ruling, the Court in 1990 said the First Amendment limits the role of political party affiliation in hiring, promotion or transfer policies for most public employees. The 5-4 decision drew a pointed dissent from Scalia.

In other areas, though, the Court rebuffed First Amendment claims. The Court upheld laws banning nude dancing, somewhat narrowed protection for commercial speech and rebuffed efforts to use the "public forum" doctrine to guarantee free speech rights in some public areas.

The Court's free press rulings also were mixed. The Court rejected a privacy claim against a newspaper for publishing the name of a rape victim in violation of state law, but it upheld a damage award against another newspaper for breaking a promise to keep a source's name confidential. In three libel law decisions, the Court favored plaintiffs twice and news organizations once but steered away from expansive, new precedents.

Civil Rights

The Court in 1989 touched off a protracted political battle with several decisions that narrowed remedies in job-discrimination cases. In a separate ruling, the Court overturned a local minority set-aside program for government contracting, casting doubt on similar policies adopted at all levels of government over the previous two decades.

In 1991, however, civil rights forces won enactment of compromise legislation aimed at overturning the job-discrimination rulings. And in 1990, the Court upheld, 5-4, a congressionally mandated minority preference policy for awarding broadcast licenses. Thomas' ascension to the Court, though, was thought likely to tip the balance against affirmative action policies in future cases.

In school desegregation cases, the Court made it easier for local officials to be freed of court-ordered plans to eliminate racial separation. But in 1990, a federal judge's authority to order local taxes raised to pay for a mandated desegregation program was upheld, 5-4. And in 1992, the Court ruled that once-segregated state colleges and universities must do more than adopt race-neutral policies to dismantle a previous dual system.

The Court also extended a 1986 decision barring the use of race-based peremptory challenges by prosecutors during jury selection. The Court imposed the same limit on both sides in civil cases in 1991 and on criminal defendants in 1992.

In an important 1991 sex discrimination ruling, employers were barred from adopting policies that excluded women from jobs that might harm a developing or potential fetus. The Court in 1992 also allowed private damage suits to enforce the federal law prohibiting sex discrimination in federally assisted schools and colleges.

Other Issues

The Court's rulings in other areas gave only limited encouragement to conservatives. The justices took a somewhat narrow view of personal privacy claims but rebuffed efforts to limit damage awards in civil suits or to use property rights to restrict government regulation.

Privacy. The Court rejected broad claims of personal privacy in disputes involving employee drug testing and so-called "right to die" cases. Federal policies mandating drug testing for railroad workers and some law enforcement personnel were upheld in 1989. The next year, in its first ruling on an individual's right to refuse life-sustaining medical treatment, the Court upheld, 5-4, a state law requiring strict evidence of a comatose patient's wishes before ordering medical personnel to withhold treatment.

Civil Suits. The Court in 1991 gave tort reform advocates a mixed ruling by holding that juries have broad discretion to impose punitive damages if the awards are not "extreme." On other civil justice issues, the Court in 1989 refused to limit damage suits under the federal anti-racketeering law and in 1992 opened the door to some product-safety suits against tobacco companies.

Property Rights. The Court encouraged conservatives by accepting four cases in its 1991-92 term challenging government regulation as infringements of property rights. But property rights groups won only one of the cases — a limited ruling in 1992 that property owners are entitled to compensation if government regulations prevent any economically viable use of their land.

Supreme Court Decisions October 1988 — July 1992

Business Law

Antitrust

California v. ARC America Corp. (490 U.S. 93), decided by a 7-0 vote, April 18, 1989. White wrote the opinion; Stevens and O'Connor did not participate.

The rule limiting federal antitrust recoveries to direct purchasers does not prevent indirect purchasers from recovering damages flowing from state antitrust violations. State antitrust statutes are not pre-empted by federal antitrust laws.

Michigan Citizens for an Independent Press v. Thornburgh (493 U.S. 38), affirmed by a 4-4 vote, Nov. 13, 1989. *Per curiam* (unsigned) opinion; White did not participate.

The equally divided Court affirmed a decision by the U.S. Court of Appeals for the District of Columbia that allowed an antitrust exemption given by the Justice Department to Detroit's two major daily newspapers. The exemption permitted a partial merger under the Newspaper Preservation Act of 1970.

Federal Trade Commission v. Superior Court Trial Lawyers Association (493 U.S. 411), decided by a 6-3 vote, Jan. 22, 1990. Stevens wrote the opinion; Brennan, Marshall and Blackmun dissented.

A group of court-appointed criminal lawyers who agreed not to represent indigent clients and went on strike for two weeks to pressure the District of Columbia government to increase their fees engaged in an illegal price-fixing conspiracy.

The Court ruled that the 1983 strike was a violation of antitrust laws even though the rates being protested could be considered unreasonably low. The strike constituted a per se, or automatic, violation of the Sherman Act prohibiting joint efforts in restraint of trade, and the social justification offered for the strike did not make it any less unlawful.

California v. American Stores Co. (495 U.S. 271), decided by a 9-0 vote, April 30, 1990. Stevens wrote the opinion.

States and individuals, not only the federal government, may sue under the Clayton Act to challenge completed mergers that they claim will hurt competition and pricing. The ruling allowed the California attorney general's office to continue to seek divestiture in a case challenging a merger of two grocery store chains.

Atlantic Richfield Co. v. USA Petroleum Co. (495 U.S. 328), decided by a 7-2 vote, May 14, 1990. Brennan wrote the opinion; Stevens and White dissented.

A company that alleges only that it lost sales to a competitor's non-predatory prices under a vertical price-fixing scheme has not established an antitrust injury sufficient for standing. A company must be able to show predatory pricing, the Court said. If prices are not set for competition at below-cost levels, a vertical, maximum-price-fixing scheme is not illegal.

Texaco Inc. v. Hasbrouck (496 U.S. 543), decided by a 9-0 vote, June 14, 1990. Stevens wrote the opinion.

A gasoline supplier selling fuel to wholesalers at a price lower than the supplier charged independent retailers violated the Robinson-Patman Act prohibition against price discrimination because it could not show that the price cut was reimbursement for services. Such discounts may be legitimate in some cases, the Court said, but in this case no evidence existed that the lower price to wholesalers reflected a reasonable reimbursement for the value to the supplier for services.

Kansas v. Utilicorp United Inc. (497 U.S. 199), decided by a 5-4 vote, June 21, 1990. Kennedy wrote the opinion; White, Brennan, Marshall and Blackmun dissented.

When suppliers violate antitrust laws by overcharging a public utility for natural gas, and the utility passes the overcharge on to its customers, only the utility has a cause of action because it alone has suffered antitrust injuries. The Court said that utilities have "an established record of diligent antitrust enforcement" and that the responsibility need not be shared with state or municipal governments.

Norfolk & Western Railway Co. v. American Train Dispatchers Association; CSX Transportation Inc. v. Brotherhood of Railway Carmen (499 U.S. 117), decided by a 7-2 vote, March 19, 1991. Kennedy wrote the opinion; Stevens and Marshall dissented.

Once the Interstate Commerce Commission approves a rail carrier's merger plan, exempting the railway from antitrust and other laws that might hinder the merger, the railway may be released from its legal obligations under a collective bargaining agreement.

City of Columbia v. Omni Outdoor Advertising Inc. (499 U.S. 365), decided by a 6-3 vote, April 1, 1991. Scalia wrote the opinion; Stevens, White and Marshall dissented.

Cities are protected from antitrust liability even when they have conspired with private business to enact regulations favoring one company over another. The Court rejected lower court rulings that recognized a "conspiracy" exception to the long-established state-action immunity doctrine. Localities have wide latitude for regulating domestic commerce, the Court said, and a conspiracy exception would prove to be impractical.

Summit Health Ltd. v. Pinhas (500 U.S. ___), decided by a 5-4 vote, May 28, 1991. Stevens wrote the opinion; Scalia, O'Connor, Kennedy and Souter dissented.

A surgeon who was denied staff privileges at a hospital and claimed he was the target of a conspiracy to drive him out of business was allowed to sue under federal antitrust law. The Court said a sufficient connection, or "nexus," existed between the anti-competitive activity alleged and interstate commerce for the surgeon to invoke the Sherman Act.

Eastman Kodak Co. v. Image Technical Services Inc. (504 U.S. ___), decided by a 6-3 vote, June 8, 1992. Blackmun wrote the opinion; Scalia, O'Connor and Thomas dissented.

A district court should not have granted summary judgment (without a trial) against a claim that Kodak engaged in illegal "tying arrangements" by restricting the sale of equipment parts to buyers who used Kodak's repair service. Tying arrangements violate the Sherman Act if the seller has appreciable economic power in the tying product market. The Court held that the plaintiff, an independent photocopying equipment service firm, had presented sufficient evidence to counter Kodak's argument that its lack of market power in the equipment market entitled it to summary judgment.

Federal Trade Commission v. Ticor Title Insurance Co. (504 U.S. ___), decided by a 6-3 vote, June 12, 1992. Kennedy wrote the opinion; Rehnquist, O'Connor and Thomas dissented.

The ratemaking activities of title insurance companies are not immune from antitrust liability when states have acquiesced in setting uniform rates. The Court said that arrangements in which states allow rates to take effect unless challenged but do not actually scrutinize the rates do not qualify for protection under state-action immunity doctrine.

Aviation

Chan v. Korean Air Lines Ltd. (490 U.S. 122), decided by a 9-0 vote, April 18, 1989. Scalia wrote the opinion.

International air carriers do not lose the benefit of limitations on their liability for passenger injury or death by failing to print a notice of the limitation in a specified size type on passengers' tickets. Such a penalty is not required by the Warsaw Convention, the international treaty that established the limitation on liability, or by the Montreal Agreement, the private accord among airlines that requires notice of the limits to be printed in 10-point type.

Eastern Airlines Inc. v. Floyd (499 U.S. 530), decided by a 9-0 vote, April 17, 1991. Marshall wrote the opinion.

Article 17 of the Warsaw Convention, the international agreement governing airline liability, does not allow recovery for purely mental injuries. Damages are allowed only for "bodily injuries," according to a translation of the French text of Article 17.

Banking

Citibank, N.A. v. Wells Fargo Asia Ltd. (495 U.S. 660), decided by an 8-1 vote, May 29, 1990. Kennedy wrote the opinion; Stevens dissented.

U.S. banks with branch offices overseas are not liable to depositors after foreign governments freeze and seize those accounts. Computerized confirmations used in international banking do not create an agreement to make U.S. banks financially responsible for deposits placed in their overseas branches.

Bankruptcy

United States v. Ron Pair Enterprises Inc. (489 U.S. 235), decided by a 5-4 vote, Feb. 22, 1989. Blackmun wrote the opinion; O'Connor, Brennan, Marshall and Stevens dissented.

A creditor with a secured claim is entitled to receive the amount of his claim plus interest from the date of filing of a bankruptcy petition if the value of the secured property is greater than the amount of its claim.

Granfinanciera S. A. v. Nordberg (492 U.S. 33), decided by a 6-3 vote, June 23, 1989. Brennan wrote the opinion; White, Blackmun and O'Connor dissented.

A person who has not submitted a claim against a bankruptcy estate has a Seventh Amendment right to a jury trial when sued by the trustee in bankruptcy to recover an allegedly fraudulent monetary transfer. That right prevails despite Congress' designation of fraudulent conveyance actions as "core proceedings" to be tried without a jury by non-Article III bankruptcy judges.

Hoffman v. Connecticut Income Maintenance (492 U.S. 96), decided by a 5-4 vote, June 23, 1989. White wrote the opinion; Marshall, Brennan, Blackmun and Stevens dissented.

The 11th Amendment bars a bankruptcy trustee from seeking to recover from a state payments owed to the bankrupt estate or funds obtained from the state after avoidance of preferential transfer. Congress did not completely abrogate the 11th Amendment immunity of the states when it enacted a Bankruptcy Code provision requiring a waiver of sovereign immunity by "governmental units" in certain, limited circumstances.

Pennsylvania Department of Public Welfare v. Davenport (495 U.S. 552), decided by a 7-2 vote, May 29, 1990. Marshall wrote the opinion; Blackmun and O'Connor dissented.

A person ordered by a court to make criminal restitution may be freed of the obligation if he then declares bankruptcy under Chapter 13 of the federal Bankruptcy Code. Restitution obligations are "debts" under that law, the Court said.

United States v. Energy Resources Co. Inc. (495 U.S. 545), decided by an 8-1 vote, May 29, 1990. White wrote the opinion; Blackmun dissented.

A bankruptcy judge has the authority to order the Internal Revenue Service to treat a debtor corporation's tax payments as trust fund taxes withheld from employee paychecks. A bankruptcy court may order such treatment of tax funds in cases where it determines that this designation is necessary for the success of a reorganization plan.

Begier v. Internal Revenue Service (496 U.S. 53), decided by a 9-0 vote, June 4, 1990. Marshall wrote the opinion.

A bankruptcy trustee cannot recover withholding and excise tax payments a debtor placed in a trust fund for the Internal Revenue Service before filing for bankruptcy.

Grogan v. Garner (498 U.S. 279), decided by a 9-0 vote, Jan. 15, 1991. Stevens wrote the opinion.

Under federal bankruptcy law, a defrauded creditor may prove his claim with a "preponderance of the evidence" to ensure that the claim is not discharged in a bankruptcy proceeding. The section of the Bankruptcy Code at issue barred the discharge of debts for money obtained fraudulently. The Court said that the preponderance standard, not the clear and convincing standard, is presumed to apply in civil actions between private parties unless particularly important individual interests or rights are at stake.

Farrey v. Sanderfoot (500 U.S. ___), decided by a 9-0 vote, May 23, 1991. White wrote the opinion.

The homestead exemption of federal bankruptcy law cannot be used by a former spouse to avoid the other spouse's lien on what had been the couple's home.

Owen v. Owen (500 U.S. ___), decided by an 8-1 vote, May 23, 1991. Scalia wrote the opinion; Stevens dissented.

A judicial lien may be avoided under the federal Bankruptcy Code as impairing a debtor's exemption under state law even though the state has defined the exempt property in such a way as to specifically exclude the property encumbered by such liens. The federal law requires courts to determine whether the lien impairs an exemption to which the debtor is entitled or one to which he would have been entitled but for the lien itself.

Johnson v. Home State Bank (501 U.S. ___), decided by a 9-0 vote, June 10, 1991. Marshall wrote the opinion.

A debtor may include a mortgage lien in an approved reorganization plan under Chapter 13 of the Bankruptcy Code even after his personal liability in the mortgage has been discharged in a Chapter 7 liquidation. A mortgage lien securing an obligation for which a debtor's personal liability has been discharged in a Chapter 7 liquidation still is a "claim" under a necessarily broad reading of the Chapter 13 provisions.

Toibb v. Radloff (501 U.S. ___), decided by an 8-1 vote, June 13, 1991. Blackmun wrote the opinion; Stevens dissented.

Individual debtors not engaged in business may file for relief under Chapter 11 of the Bankruptcy Code, which allows reorganization instead of liquidation of assets. Although the structure and legislative history of Chapter 11 demonstrate that it was intended primarily for the use of business debtors, no "ongoing business" requirement exists for Chapter 11 reorganization.

Union Bank v. Wolas (502 U.S. ___), decided by a 9-0 vote, Dec. 11, 1991. Stevens wrote the opinion.

A debtor's prior payments on long-term, as well as short-term, debt may qualify as payments made in "the ordinary course of business" and exempted from a bankruptcy trustee's effort to recover funds for an estate.

Dewsnup v. Timm (502 U.S. ___), decided by a 6-2 vote, Jan. 15, 1992. Blackmun wrote the opinion; Scalia and Souter dissented; Thomas did not participate.

A debtor cannot "strip down" a creditor's lien on real property to the current value of the property when the value has become less than the amount of the claim secured by the lien. The creditor's lien should be what was bargained for at the outset and should stay with the property until foreclosure.

Holywell Corp. v. Smith; United States v. Smith (503 U.S. ___), decided by a 9-0 vote, Feb. 25, 1992. Thomas wrote the opinion.

A bankruptcy trustee appointed to liquidate and distribute property must file income tax returns and pay taxes on the income ascribed to the corporate debtor's property.

United States v. Nordic Village Inc. (503 U.S. ___), decided by a 7-2 vote, Feb. 25, 1992. Scalia wrote the opinion; Stevens and Blackmun dissented.

A bankruptcy trustee trying to recover money that was paid to the Internal Revenue Service without authority cannot sue the government. The bankruptcy law in question does not waive the sovereign immunity of the United States, which exempts the government from lawsuit unless Congress specifically waives immunity.

Connecticut National Bank v. Germain (503 U.S. ___), decided by a 9-0 vote, March 9, 1992. Thomas wrote the opinion.

Federal law allows a party to appeal an interim order issued by a district court sitting as a bankruptcy court of appeals.

Barnhill v. Johnson (503 U.S. ___), decided by a 7-2 vote, March 25, 1992. Rehnquist wrote the opinion; Stevens and Blackmun dissented.

A transfer of funds made by a check occurs on the date the check is honored, not on the date the check was written or dated. The ruling allowed a bankruptcy trustee to use the bankruptcy law provision permitting recovery of property transferred by the debtor within 90 days before the date the bankruptcy petition was filed.

Taylor v. Freeland & Kronz (503 U.S. ___), decided by an 8-1 vote, April 21, 1992. Thomas wrote the opinion; Stevens dissented.

A bankruptcy trustee who missed a deadline for objecting to a debtor's effort to exempt certain funds from the estate waived access to the funds, even if the debtor lacked a good-faith basis for the exemption.

Patterson v. Shumate (504 U.S. ___), decided by a 9-0 vote, June 15, 1992. Blackmun wrote the opinion.

A debtor's pension benefits covered by the Employee Retirement Income Security Act (ERISA) are excluded from the portion of the estate to be divided among creditors. Pensions covered by ERISA fall within the exemption permitted by the federal Bankruptcy Code for a debtor's interest in a trust "that is enforceable under applicable nonbankruptcy law."

Copyright

Community for Creative Non-Violence v. Reid (490 U.S. 730), decided by a 9-0 vote, June 5, 1989. Marshall wrote the opinion.

For purposes of determining ownership of copyright, a commissioned work is "a work made for hire" — with copyright held by the hiring party — only if the creator of the work was an employee, as defined by general common law principles, not an independent contractor. The hiring party does not gain ownership of the copyright through the right of control or actual control of the work.

Stewart v. Abend (495 U.S. 207), decided by a 6-3 vote, April 24, 1990. O'Connor wrote the opinion; Stevens, Rehnquist and Scalia dissented.

The owner of a derivative work infringes on the rights of the owner of the original work by continuing to distribute the derivative work during the copyright's renewal period. On that basis, the owners of the movie "Rear Window" were required to share earnings from the movie's re-

release with the copyright owner of the short story on which the movie was based.

Feist Publications Inc. v. Rural Telephone Service Co. Inc. (499 U.S. 340), decided by a 9-0 vote, March 27, 1991. O'Connor wrote the opinion.

Telephone white pages generally are not entitled to protection under federal copyright law because they lack the "requisite originality" for protection.

Maritime Law

Sisson v. Ruby (497 U.S. 358), decided by a 9-0 vote, June 25, 1990. Marshall wrote the opinion.

Federal maritime law dictates award limits on a liability suit brought in connection with a fire on a boat docked at a marina, because the storage and maintenance of a vessel at a marina on navigable waters are substantially related to traditional maritime activity.

Miles v. Apex Marine Corp. (498 U.S. 19), decided by an 8-0 vote, Nov. 6, 1990. O'Connor wrote the opinion; Souter did not participate.

Families of seamen killed on the job may not win money damages for lost future earnings or "loss of society" under general maritime law. General maritime law allows wrongful-death lawsuits, but damages are limited.

McDermott International Inc. v. Wilander (498 U.S. 337), decided by a 9-0 vote, Feb. 19, 1991. O'Connor wrote the opinion.

A worker on a ship need not aid in the navigation of the vessel to qualify as a "seaman" under the Jones Act. The worker only needs to have employment-related connection to the vessel to be covered by the act.

Exxon Corp. v. Central Gulf Lines Inc. (500 U.S. ___), decided by a 9-0 vote, June 3, 1991. Marshall wrote the opinion.

Admiralty jurisdiction extends to claims arising from contracts between a principal and an agent, the Court held. The decision overruled an 1855 case that had been interpreted as setting an automatic bar to admiralty jurisdiction over agency contracts.

Patents

Bonito Boats Inc. v. Thunder Craft Boats Inc. (489 U.S. 141), decided by a 9-0 vote, Feb. 21, 1989. O'Connor wrote the opinion.

A state law that prohibits use of the direct molding process to duplicate unpatented articles conflicts with federal patent law and is invalid under the Supremacy Clause. The efficient operation of the federal patent system depends upon substantially free trade in publicly known, unpatented designs.

Eli Lilly & Co. v. Medtronic Inc. (496 U.S. 661), decided by a 6-2 vote, June 18, 1990. Scalia wrote the opinion; Kennedy and White dissented; O'Connor did not participate.

Activities that would otherwise constitute patent infringement are acceptable if they are undertaken to develop and submit to the Food and Drug Administration information necessary to obtain marketing approval for medical-device substitutes. The exemption in patent law that allows firms producing generic drugs to develop substitutes for patented drugs applies to patented medical devices as well.

Regulation

Duquesne Light Co. v. Barasch (488 U.S. 299), decided by an 8-1 vote, Jan. 11, 1989. Rehnquist wrote the opinion; Blackmun dissented.

The Court upheld a state law that precluded electric utilities from recovering the cost of construction or expansion of a power plant until the facility is put into operation. States are not required to adopt any single methodology in setting rates for regulated utilities.

Northwest Central Pipeline Corp. v. State Corporation Commission of Kansas (489 U.S. 493), decided by a 9-0 vote, March 6, 1989. Brennan wrote the opinion.

Kansas regulation designed to prevent waste in production of natural gas is not pre-empted by federal law. The federal Natural Gas Act, which establishes federal regulation over the transportation and sale of natural gas in interstate commerce, leaves the regulation of production of natural gas to the states.

Coit Independence Joint Venture v. Federal Savings and Loan Insurance Corp. (489 U.S. 561), decided by a 9-0 vote, March 21, 1989. O'Connor wrote the opinion.

The Federal Savings and Loan Insurance Corporation (FSLIC) has no power to adjudicate creditors' claims against insolvent savings and loan associations placed under FSLIC receivership. The FSLIC's power to "settle, compromise or release claims" does not prevent a creditor from litigating its claim in court. The creditor also need not exhaust administrative remedies through the Federal Home Loan Bank Board before instituting such a suit.

Federal Savings and Loan Insurance Corp. v. Ticktin (490 U.S. 82), decided by a 9-0 vote, April 3, 1989. Stevens wrote the opinion.

The Federal Savings and Loan Insurance Corporation (FSLIC) may bring suit in federal court against former directors of a savings and loan association for breach of fiduciary duty under state law. A statutory provision limiting federal jurisdiction over cases in which the FSLIC appears as a receiver of an insured financial institution does not prevent the FSLIC from exercising the general power of federal agencies to initiate suits in federal court.

Skinner v. Mid-America Pipeline Co. (490 U.S. 212), decided by a 9-0 vote, April 25, 1989. O'Connor wrote the opinion.

A congressional directive that the secretary of transportation establish a system of user fees to cover the costs of administering federal gas pipeline safety programs was not an unconstitutional delegation of the taxing power to the executive branch. Restrictions placed on the secretary's discretion in assessing the fees satisfy the normal requirements of the non-delegation doctrine, and no stricter requirements apply to delegation of taxing powers.

New Orleans Public Service Inc. v. New Orleans City Council (491 U.S. 350), decided by a 9-0 vote, June 19, 1989. Scalia wrote the opinion.

A federal court was not required to abstain from adjudicating a claim that federal law pre-empted a local utility ratemaking body's decision on allocating costs of a nuclear power reactor. Abstention was not mandatory under the doctrine requiring federal courts to refrain from interfering with complex state regulatory schemes where state law questions or policy issues are involved. Abstention also was not required under the doctrine calling for federal courts to refrain from interfering with state court cases, as the ratemaking case was not a judicial proceeding.

Lewis v. Continental Bank Corp. (494 U.S. 472), decided by a 9-0 vote, March 5, 1990. Scalia wrote the opinion.

The Court declared moot a case involving an Illinois bank holding company's challenge to a Florida banking law that allegedly violated the Commerce Clause. The case was rendered moot by 1987 amendments to the federal Bank Holding Company Act, which require that a bank holding company with its principal banking operations in one state may not establish or acquire a bank in another state unless the latter state's statutes specifically authorize it to do so.

Maislin Industries, U.S. Inc. v. Primary Steel Inc. (497 U.S. 116), decided by a 7-2 vote, June 21, 1990. Brennan wrote the opinion; Stevens and Rehnquist dissented.

An Interstate Commerce Commission policy that relieves a shipper of the obligation of paying the filed rate when the shipper and carrier have privately negotiated a lower rate violates the Interstate Commerce Act. The act specifically prohibits a carrier from providing services at any rate other than that filed with the commission.

Arcadia v. Ohio Power Co. (498 U.S. 73), decided by an 8-0 vote, Nov. 27, 1990. Scalia wrote the opinion; Souter did not participate.

A section of the Federal Power Act that governs overlapping jurisdictions of the Securities and Exchange Commission (SEC) and Federal Energy Regulatory Commission (FERC) does not apply to a case in which the SEC authorized a power company to buy coal from an SEC-approved affiliate at a price equal to the affiliate's actual costs and then the FERC declared unreasonable the resulting charges that the power company was to pass on to customers.

The Court sent the case back to the lower court with the suggestion that the FERC's decision might be flawed for reasons other than the Federal Power Act.

Mobil Oil Exploration & Producing Southeast Inc. v. United Distribution Cos.; Federal Energy Regulatory Commission v. United States Distribution Cos. (498 U.S. 211), decided by an 8-0 vote, Jan. 8, 1991. White wrote the opinion; Kennedy did not participate.

The Federal Energy Regulatory Commission had the authority, as part of commission rules adopted in 1986, to set a new single ceiling price for gas from older wells. The Court upheld the government's power to lift price controls on some natural gas and reinstated the federal regulations that allowed gas producers to raise some prices charged to pipeline companies.

Morales v. Trans World Airlines Inc. (504 U.S. ___), decided by a 5-3 vote, June 1, 1992. Scalia wrote the opinion; Stevens, Rehnquist and Blackmun dissented; Souter did not participate.

The federal Airline Deregulation Act of 1978 preempts states from regulating airline advertising to protect consumers from being misled about discount air fares. The state interest in advertising practices is expressly superseded by the act's jurisdiction over laws relating to rates, routes or services of any air carrier.

Securities

Reves v. Ernst & Young (494 U.S. 56), decided by a 5-4 vote, Feb. 21, 1990. Marshall wrote the opinion; Rehnquist, White, O'Connor and Scalia dissented.

An unsecured promissory note, payable on demand by the holder, is a "security" within the meaning of the Securities Exchange Act of 1934.

The Court first ruled unanimously that the notes are presumed to be security for purposes of the federal securities laws. It then ruled 5-4 that even though the notes were payable "on demand," they did not fall under an exception for notes that mature in less than nine months from the date issued because they could mature at a time beyond nine months.

Kamen v. Kemper Financial Services Inc. (500 U.S. ___), decided by a 9-0 vote, May 20, 1991. Marshall wrote the opinion.

State law controls whether a shareholder in a derivative action under the Investment Company Act of 1940 first must make a request to directors to file a lawsuit.

Gollust v. Mendell (501 U.S. ___), decided by a 9-0 vote, June 10, 1991. Souter wrote the opinion.

For standing under an insider trading section of the Securities Exchange Act of 1934, a complaining party only must be the "owner of a security" of the corporation at the time the lawsuit is brought. Any security, including stock, notes, warrants, bonds and debentures, will satisfy the standing requirement. But the person who brings the lawsuit must keep some financial interest in the litigation throughout its duration.

Lampf, Pleva, Lipkind, Prupis & Petigrow v. Gilberston (501 U.S. ___), decided by a 5-4 vote, June 20, 1991. Blackmun wrote the opinion; Stevens, Souter, O'Connor and Kennedy dissented.

Federal securities law, not state statutes, govern the statute of limitations for cases brought under the federal anti-fraud provisions of the 1933 and 1934 securities laws. Litigation based on those provisions must begin within one year after the discovery of the facts constituting the violation and within three years of the violation (or fraud-tainted investment) itself. The limits replace longer deadlines in state laws.

Virginia Bankshares Inc. v. Sandberg (501 U.S. ___), decided by 9-0 and 5-4 votes, June 27, 1991. Souter wrote the opinion.

Proxy statements that contain directors' knowingly false statements of reasons for a recommended corporate transaction may be considered misstatements of material fact under Section 14(a) of the 1934 Securities Exchange Act prohibiting fraudulent proxy materials. The Court unanimously held that the directors' recommendation could be challenged, but only if the statement was factually incorrect or falsely stated the directors' motivations for their recommendations.

In a separate part of the opinion, the Court held 5-4 that shareholders whose votes are not required by law to authorize the transaction cannot recover damages based on the proxy solicitation. The ruling barred a suit by shareholders who had asserted that they were underpaid when a bank bought up their stock. Dissenting from this part of the decision were Marshall, Blackmun, Stevens and Kennedy.

Holmes v. Securities Investor Protection Corporation (503 U.S. ___), decided by a 9-0 vote, March 24, 1992. Souter wrote the opinion.

A plaintiff who sues under the federal Racketeer Influenced and Corrupt Organizations Act — commonly known as RICO — must show that his injury was caused by a specific conspiracy or other violation covered by the law. The ruling barred a suit by a federal agency against a broker-dealer and others seeking to recover money the agency had paid to reimburse the brokerage firms' customers. The Court said an allegedly fraudulent stock manipulation scheme did not directly harm the brokerage customers, but instead affected the investment companies.

Taxation

Shell Oil Co. v. Iowa Department of Revenue (488 U.S. 19), decided by a 9-0 vote, Nov. 8, 1988. Marshall wrote the opinion.

States may include the income earned from oil and gas extracted from the outer continental shelf (OCS) in determining a company's in-state taxable income. The Outer Continental Shelf Lands Act prohibits coastal states from imposing direct taxes on OCS gas and oil but does not preempt otherwise valid state systems for taxing corporate income.

Goldberg v. Sweet; GTE Sprint Communications Corp. v. Sweet (488 U.S. 252), decided by a 9-0 vote, Jan. 10, 1989. Marshall wrote the opinion.

A state may impose an excise tax on the gross charges for interstate telephone calls originated or terminated in the state. Such a tax does not violate the Commerce Clause because it is fairly apportioned, does not discriminate against interstate commerce and is fairly related to services that the state provides to the benefit of taxpayers.

United States v. Stuart (489 U.S. 353), decided by a 9-0 vote, Feb. 28, 1989. Brennan wrote the opinion.

The Internal Revenue Service may issue an administrative summons pursuant to a request by Canadian authorities even if the Canadian tax investigation is directed toward criminal prosecution under Canadian law.

Commissioner of Internal Revenue v. Clark (489 U.S. 726), decided by an 8-1 vote, March 22, 1989. Stevens wrote the opinion; White dissented.

The cash payment — or boot — accompanying a tax-free stock-for-stock exchange was properly treated as capital gain instead of a dividend subject to current taxation as ordinary income. The reorganization was a bona fide arm's length transaction, and the taxpayer's interest in the acquiring company was small. Under those circumstances, the boot is better characterized as part of the proceeds of a sale of stock subject to capital gains treatment than as a proxy for the dividend.

Amerada Hess Corp. v. Director, Division of Taxation, New Jersey Department of the Treasury (490 U.S. 66), decided by an 8-0 vote, April 3, 1989. Blackmun wrote the opinion; O'Connor did not participate.

New Jersey's denial of a state corporate tax deduction for the amount that oil companies paid under the federal "windfall profits" tax does not violate the Commerce Clause. The tax applies to activity having a substantial nexus with the state, does not discriminate against interstate commerce and is fairly related to benefits provided by the state.

Colonial American Life Insurance Co. v. Commissioner of Internal Revenue (491 U.S. 244), decided by a 6-3 vote, June 15, 1989. Kennedy wrote the opinion; Stevens, Blackmun and O'Connor dissented.

The up-front fee, or so-called ceding commission, paid by a reinsurance company to a direct insurer under a contract for indemnity reinsurance is not deductible in the year paid. Instead, the commission must be capitalized and amortized over the anticipated life of the agreement.

United States v. Goodyear Tire & Rubber Co. (493 U.S. 132), decided by a 9-0 vote, Dec. 11, 1989. Marshall wrote the opinion.

"Accumulated profits," defined in the indirect tax credit provision of the Internal Revenue Code of 1954, are to be measured according to U.S. tax principles, not foreign tax principles, when claimed by a multinational corporation's foreign subsidiary.

Commissioner of Internal Revenue v. Indianapolis Power & Light Co. (493 U.S. 203), decided by a 9-0 vote, Jan. 9, 1990. Blackmun wrote the opinion.

The Internal Revenue Service may not tax as income the deposits that utilities charge their customers to ensure payment of future bills. The deposits serve as security, to be returned when an account is closed, not as prepayments of income.

Franchise Tax Board of California v. Alcan Aluminium Ltd. (493 U.S. 331), decided by a 9-0 vote, Jan. 10, 1990. White wrote the opinion.

A foreign company, the sole shareholder of an American subsidiary, lacks standing in federal court to challenge on Foreign Commerce Clause grounds the accounting methods used by a state to determine the locally taxable income of that subsidiary. The Court also held that a federal action for injunctive and declaratory relief is barred by the Tax Injunction Act of 1982.

United States v. Dalm (494 U.S. 596), decided by a 6-3 vote, March 20, 1990. Kennedy wrote the opinion; Stevens, Brennan and Marshall dissented.

The doctrine of equitable recoupment does not apply to a taxpayer who waits too long before filing for a refund of a gift tax paid, in addition to income taxes assessed, on the same transfer of money.

American Trucking Associations Inc. v. Smith (496 U.S. 167), decided by a 5-4 vote, June 4, 1990. O'Connor wrote the opinion; Stevens, Brennan, Marshall and Blackmun dissented.

A state is not required to provide relief for all excessive taxes paid under a state highway-use tax invalidated for discriminating against out-of-state trucking companies.

The Court ruled that a 1987 decision voiding Pennsylvania's unapportioned highway-use taxes could be applied only prospectively and that only taxes imposed by states after that decision could be refunded. At issue was an Arkansas tax similar to Pennsylvania's.

The Court found that state officials could not have anticipated that the tax would be found unconstitutional and that the 1987 decision on which this dispute rested was a sharp departure from precedent. This decision limited the scope of a 1990 companion ruling in *McKesson Corporation v. Division of Alcoholic Beverages and Tobacco, Department of Business Regulation of Florida.*

McKesson Corporation v. Division of Alcoholic Beverages and Tobacco, Department of Business Regulation of Florida (496 U.S. 18), decided by a 9-0 vote, June 4, 1990. Brennan wrote the opinion.

A state must provide "meaningful relief" if it collects taxes under a law later found to be unconstitutional. If a state penalizes a protesting taxpayer for failure to pay taxes on time, requiring him to pay first and obtain review of the tax's validity later, the state must give him sufficient chance to get a refund of taxes paid.

The ruling reversed a state court's decision denying a refund after a taxing scheme was found unconstitutional.

Portland Golf Club v. Commissioner of Internal Revenue (497 U.S. 154), decided by 9-0 and 6-3 votes, June 21, 1990. Blackmun wrote the opinion; Kennedy, O'Connor and Scalia dissented from part of the opinion.

A unanimous Court ruled that a social club, in calculating its liability for federal income taxes, may not offset losses incurred by selling food and drink to nonmembers against income realized from investments unless it had tried to sell the food and drink for profit. By 6-3, the Court then held that in ascertaining whether social clubs' non-member activities are for profit, tax authorities must determine whether clubs have apportioned fixed costs between member and non-member sales according to the same method used to compute profits.

Trinova Corp. v. Michigan Department of Treasury (498 U.S. 358), decided by a 6-2 vote, Feb. 19, 1991. Kennedy wrote the opinion; Stevens and Blackmun dissented; Souter did not participate.

Michigan's single-business tax levied against entities having "business activity" within the state and levied on the value added to merchandise does not violate either the Due Process Clause or the Commerce Clause. The Court ruled that the tax did not unconstitutionally discriminate against interstate commerce because a "rational relationship" existed between the income attributed to the state and the in-state value of the enterprise.

Cottage Savings Association v. Commissioner of Internal Revenue (499 U.S. 554), decided by a 7-2 vote, April 17, 1991. Marshall wrote the opinion; Blackmun and White dissented.

Financial institutions may deduct from their taxes paper losses from "reciprocal sales" of mortgage loans when the properties they exchange are materially different. As long as the property entitlements were not identical, the Court said, their exchange allows the taxpayer the appreciated or depreciated value of the property.

United States v. Centennial Savings Bank FSB (499 U.S. 573), decided by 7-2 and 9-0 votes, April 17, 1991. Marshall wrote the opinion; Blackmun and White dissented from part of the opinion.

A savings and loan association realized tax-deductible losses when it exchanged mortgage interests with another lender, the Court held, 7-2, in a ruling similar to its decision in *Cottage Savings Association v. Commissioner of Internal Revenue.*

The Court also ruled unanimously that penalties collected from depositors who make early withdrawals cannot be excluded from a financial institution's taxable income. The income could be considered as arising from a "discharge of indebtedness" and exempt from taxes only if it comes from the forgiveness of an obligation to repay that is assumed when a transaction originally is made.

United States v. Thompson/Center Arms Co. (504 U.S. ___), decided by a 5-4 vote, June 8, 1992. Souter wrote the opinion; White, Blackmun, Stevens and Kennedy dissented.

When a "Contender" pistol and a conversion kit that would turn it into a rifle are packaged together and sold, it does not constitute the making of a short-barreled rifle, as taxable under federal law. The Court said that the law was ambiguous about how much "making" must take place and at what stage a rifle is produced. It said the statutory ambiguity should be resolved in favor of the gun owner under the rule of lenity.

Trademarks

Two Pesos Inc. v. Taco Cabana Inc. (505 U.S. ___), decided by a 9-0 vote, June 26, 1992. White wrote the opinion.

Federal trademark law protects an inherently distinctive "trade dress" — a product's total image and appearance — even in the absence of evidence that consumers automatically associate a copy of the design with the original. The trade dress also does not have to have acquired a so-called "secondary meaning" — that is, become uniquely associated with the entity that first developed the design.

Courts and Procedure

Appeals

Osterneck v. Ernst & Whinney (489 U.S. 169), decided by a 9-0 vote, Feb. 21, 1989. Kennedy wrote the opinion.

A motion for discretionary prejudgment interest on a jury's award in a civil suit renders ineffective a notice of appeal filed before the motion has been ruled on. Such a motion amounts to a motion to amend or alter a judgment and, under the Federal Rules of Appellate Procedure, must be ruled on before a notice of appeal may be filed.

Lauro Lines s.r.l. v. Chasser (490 U.S. 495), decided by a 9-0 vote, May 22, 1989. Brennan wrote the opinion.

A defendant cannot immediately appeal a ruling denying a motion to dismiss a damages action on the basis of a contractual clause specifying that the action can be brought only in a foreign jurisdiction. Such a ruling is not a final order and also does not fall within the collateral order doctrine that permits review of an interlocutory order if it is effectively unreviewable on appeal from final judgment.

Firstier Mortgage Co. v. Investors Mortgage Insurance Co. (498 U.S. 269), decided by a 9-0 vote, Jan. 15, 1991. Marshall wrote the opinion.

A bench ruling may be considered a "final decision" under federal appellate procedures that dictate the timing for filing notice of appeals after final decisions. Federal rules of appellate procedure allow a notice of appeal filed from a court ruling that was not final to be considered an effective notice of appeal from a subsequently entered final judgment, as long as the bench ruling could have been appealed if immediately followed by the entry of judgment.

Salve Regina College v. Russell (499 U.S. 225), decided by a 6-3 vote, March 20, 1991. Blackmun wrote the opinion; Rehnquist, White and Stevens dissented.

A federal court of appeals may not give a less stringent review to a district court's determination of state law than to a federal law determination. The court of appeals in this case should have reviewed de novo (anew) the district court's determination of the state law at the heart of the case instead of deferring to the district court's determination of state law.

Smith v. Barry (502 U.S. ___), decided by a 9-0 vote, Jan. 14, 1992. O'Connor wrote the opinion.

A document filed as an appellate brief may qualify as the requisite notice of appeal under federal rules of appellate procedure. The key, the Court said, is that the document meet the deadline and content requirements of the federal rule for notice.

Arbitration

Volt Information Sciences Inc. v. Board of Trustees of Leland Stanford Junior University (489 U.S. 468), decided by a 6-2 vote, March 6, 1989. Rehnquist wrote the opinion; Brennan and Marshall dissented; O'Connor did not participate.

The Federal Arbitration Act does not pre-empt a provision of a state law that allows a court to stay arbitration pending resolution of related litigation. The state law provision may be applied where the contract between the parties provides for arbitration but specifies that any dispute shall be decided by that state's law.

Rodriguez de Quijas v. Shearson/American Express Inc. (490 U.S. 477), decided by a 5-4 vote, May 15, 1989. Kennedy wrote the opinion; Stevens, Brennan, Marshall and Blackmun dissented.

A predispute agreement to arbitrate claims under the Securities Act of 1933 is enforceable. The holding in *Wilko v. Swann*, 346 U.S. 427 (1953), that such agreements are void is overruled.

Attorneys

Barnard v. Thorstenn; Virgin Islands Bar Association v. Thorstenn (489 U.S. 546), decided by a 6-3 vote, March 6, 1989. Kennedy wrote the opinion; Rehnquist, White and O'Connor dissented.

A Virgin Islands court rule requiring applicants for admission to the bar to live in the Virgin Islands for one year prior to admission and to state their intention to reside in the Virgin Islands violates the Privileges and Immunities Clause in Article IV of the Constitution. None of the justifications for the rule satisfies the requirement that the discrimination against non-residents be warranted by a substantial governmental objective and bear a close and substantial relation to such an objective.

Mallard v. U.S. District Court for the Southern District of Iowa (490 U.S. 296), decided by a 5-4 vote, May 1, 1989. Brennan wrote the opinion; Stevens, Marshall, Blackmun and O'Connor dissented.

A federal court cannot require an unwilling attorney to represent an indigent in a civil case. A statutory provision authorizing the court to "request" an attorney to handle such a case indicates an intent not to authorize mandatory appointment of counsel.

Keller v. State Bar of California (496 U.S. 1), decided by a 9-0 vote, June 4, 1990. Rehnquist wrote the opinion.

A state bar may not use members' compulsory dues to pay for political activities with which members disagree when the spending is unrelated to the regulation or improvement of the legal profession.

Peel v. Attorney Registration and Disciplinary Commission of Illinois (496 U.S. 91), decided by a 5-4 vote, June 4, 1990. Stevens wrote the opinion; White, O'Connor, Rehnquist and Scalia dissented.

A lawyer who included on his professional letterhead an accurate notation that he was a "certified civil trial specialist by the National Board of Trial Advocacy" should have been protected by the First Amendment against censure by the Illinois Supreme Court. Because nothing was actually or inherently misleading in the lawyer's letterhead, any concern about the possibility of deception in hypothetical cases was insufficient to rebut the constitutional presumption favoring disclosure over concealment.

Gentile v. State Bar of Nevada (501 U.S. ___), decided by separate 5-4 votes, June 27, 1991. Kennedy and Rehnquist wrote for the differing majorities.

The free speech rights of lawyers may be curtailed if their comments present "substantial likelihood of material prejudice" to a judicial proceeding. Rehnquist, joined by White, Scalia, Souter and, in part, O'Connor, said this test — as opposed to a higher "clear and present danger standard" — is a constitutionally permissible balance between the First Amendment rights of attorneys in pending cases and the state's interest in fair trials.

In another part of the ruling, however, the Court found the Nevada rule at issue, as interpreted by the Nevada Supreme Court, to be impermissibly vague. Kennedy, joined by Marshall, Blackmun, Stevens and O'Connor, said a "safe harbor provision" in the law misled a lawyer into thinking that he could hold a press conference without fear of discipline.

Dismissals

Neitzke v. Williams (490 U.S. 319), decided by a 9-0 vote, May 1, 1989. Marshall wrote the opinion.

A federal court may not dismiss as "frivolous" a lawsuit brought by an indigent plaintiff in forma pauperis merely because it fails to state a legal claim on which relief may be granted. Dismissal of a suit as frivolous on the court's own motion, without requiring the defendants to respond, is justified only when the plaintiff cannot make any rational argument in law or fact entitling him to relief.

Denton v. Hernandez (504 U.S. ___), decided by a 7-2 vote, May 4, 1992. O'Connor wrote the opinion; Stevens and Blackmun dissented.

A court can dismiss a complaint filed under a federal law that allows poor people to sue without paying court costs as factually frivolous if the allegations are "clearly baseless." A district court's dismissal on this basis is discretionary and is properly subject only to limited review by an appeals court.

Diversity Jurisdiction

Newman-Green Inc. v. Alfonzo-Larrain (490 U.S. 826), decided by a 7-2 vote, June 12, 1989. Marshall wrote the opinion; Kennedy and Scalia dissented.

A court of appeals may grant a motion to dismiss a party who is not necessary to a suit and whose presence in the suit destroys the statutory basis for diversity jurisdiction. The appeals court need not remand the case to the district court for dismissal in that court's discretion.

Northbrook National Insurance Co. v. Brewer (493 U.S. 6), decided by an 8-1 vote, Nov. 7, 1989. Marshall wrote the opinion; Stevens dissented.

The "direct action" proviso of federal law that says, in a case against a liability insurer, the insurer shall be considered a citizen of the same state as the insured for purposes of diversity jurisdiction does not apply to a workers' compensation lawsuit brought in federal court by insurance companies. The language of the proviso is unambiguously limited to actions brought against insurers and does not apply when the insurance companies are bringing the lawsuit.

Carden v. Arkoma Associates (494 U.S. 185), decided by a 5-4 vote, Feb. 27, 1990. Scalia wrote the opinion; O'Connor, Brennan, Marshall and Blackmun dissented.

The state citizenship of each limited partner must be considered in determining diversity of citizenship among the parties in federal court disputes. The Court rejected arguments that only the citizenship of a limited partnership's general partners need be considered to preserve diversity.

Ferens v. John Deere Co. (494 U.S. 516), decided by a 5-4 vote, March 5, 1990. Kennedy wrote the opinion; Scalia, Brennan, Marshall and Blackmun dissented.

In diversity jurisdiction cases, when a plaintiff seeks to transfer a case from one state to another, the new court must follow the rules of law that prevailed where the case began. The Court had ruled in 1964 that when a defendant initiates the transfer, the rules of law from the transferor jurisdiction apply. In this case, the Court said that no matter who initiates the transfer, the law of the state where the lawsuit began should prevail.

Ankenbrandt v. Richards (504 U.S. ___), decided by a 9-0 vote, June 15, 1992. White wrote the opinion.

A federal court has jurisdiction to hear a civil case stemming from alleged child abuse when the parties are from different states. Generally, federal courts may not accept diversity lawsuits — disputes that go to federal court only because the litigants are from different states — when a domestic relations matter is at issue. But the Court said that the abuse case does not fall into that exclusion.

Due Process

National Collegiate Athletic Association v. Tarkanian (488 U.S. 179), decided by a 5-4 vote, Dec. 12, 1988. Stevens wrote the opinion; White, Brennan, Marshall and O'Connor dissented.

The National Collegiate Athletic Association (NCAA) was not subject to the 14th Amendment's Due Process Clause when it threatened a state university with disciplinary action if it failed to remove a basketball coach for violating NCAA rules. The NCAA's actions did not amount to "state action" as required to invoke the 14th Amendment.

Connecticut v. Doehr (501 U.S. ___), decided by a 9-0 vote, June 6, 1991. White wrote the opinion.

A Connecticut statute that authorizes a person's property to be subject to a lien without prior notice or a hearing, without a showing of extraordinary circumstances and without a requirement that the person seeking to have the property seized post a bond violated the Due Process Clause of the 14th Amendment.

Evidence

Beech Aircraft Corp. v. Rainey; Beech Aerospace Services Inc. v. Rainey (488 U.S. 153), decided by a 7-2 vote, Dec. 12, 1988. Brennan wrote the opinion; Rehnquist and O'Connor dissented in part.

The exception to the hearsay rule established in the Federal Rules of Evidence for "public records and reports" containing "factual findings" permits the use at trial of an investigatory report that also contains conclusions and opinions. The rule provides sufficient safeguards by requiring that reports be based on factual investigation and be shown to be trustworthy.

Green v. Bock Laundry Machine Co. (490 U.S. 504), decided by a 6-3 vote, May 22, 1989. Stevens wrote the opinion; Blackmun, Brennan and Marshall dissented.

The Federal Rules of Evidence require a judge to permit impeachment of a civil witness with evidence of prior felony convictions regardless of any unfair prejudice to the witness or the party offering the testimony. The provision in the rule that requires a judge to weigh the prejudicial effect of such evidence "to the defendant" before permitting its use applies only to criminal defendants.

United States v. Zolin (491 U.S. 554), decided by an 8-0 vote, June 21, 1989. Blackmun wrote the opinion; Brennan did not participate.

A federal district court may conduct, in appropriate circumstances, an in camera (in chambers) review of allegedly privileged attorney-client communications to determine whether the communications fall within the crime-fraud exception to the privilege. The party opposing the privilege must first present evidence sufficient to support a reasonable belief that such review may reveal evidence to establish the applicability of the exception. Any lawfully obtained, relevant evidence that is not privileged may be used to meet the threshold showing for such an in camera review.

Forum Selection

Carnival Cruise Lines Inc. v. Shute (499 U.S. 585), decided by a 7-2 vote, April 17, 1991. Blackmun wrote the opinion; Stevens and Marshall dissented.

A provision of a cruise line's standard passenger ticket requiring any disputes arising from the terms of the ticket to be filed in a Florida court can be enforced. Although the forum-selection clause was not the subject of bargaining, the Court said, it was freely negotiated and passengers likely gain the benefit of reduced fares because a cruise line effectively saves money by limiting where it can be sued.

Burlington Northern Railroad Co. v. Ford (504 U.S. ___), decided by a 9-0 vote, June 12, 1992. Souter wrote the opinion.

A Montana law that allows railroad workers employed by out-of-state companies to sue their employers in any county in the state, but restricts workers suing a railroad that is incorporated in Montana to the county of its principal place of business, does not violate the Equal Protection Clause. The law flows from a legitimate state concern for balancing interests of parties to a lawsuit, the Court said.

Judgments

Kaiser Aluminum & Chemical Corp. v. Bonjorno; Bonjorno v. Kaiser Aluminum & Chemical Corp. (494 U.S. 827), decided by a 5-4 vote, April 17, 1990. O'Connor wrote the opinion; White, Brennan, Marshall and Blackmun dissented.

Postjudgment interest runs from the date of entry of the court's judgment, not the date of the jury verdict.

Jurisdiction

Burnham v. Superior Court (495 U.S. 604), decided by a 9-0 vote, May 29, 1990. Scalia wrote the opinion.

The Due Process Clause of the 14th Amendment does not deny state courts jurisdiction over a non-resident who was personally served with process while temporarily in the state.

American National Red Cross v. S. G. (505 U.S. ___), decided by a 5-4 vote, June 19, 1992. Souter wrote the opinion; Scalia, Rehnquist, O'Connor and Kennedy dissented.

A clause in the charter of the American National Red Cross authorizing the organization "to sue and be sued in courts of law and equity, state or federal, within the jurisdiction of the United States" allows the Red Cross to have all lawsuits against it heard in federal court.

Jury Selection

Edmonson v. Leesville Concrete Co. Inc. (500 U.S. ___), decided by a 6-3 vote, June 3, 1991. Kennedy wrote the opinion; O'Connor, Rehnquist and Scalia dissented.

Potential jurors in civil cases cannot be excluded by lawyers because of the would-be jurors' race. The Court extended to a case involving a negligence claim a 1986 criminal law ruling that barred prosecutors from using so-called peremptory challenges to exclude jurors solely because they were of the same race as the criminal defendant.

Official Immunity

Burns v. Reed (500 U.S. ___), decided by a 6-3 vote, May 30, 1991. White wrote the opinion; Scalia, Blackmun and Marshall dissented in part.

A state prosecuting attorney is absolutely immune from liability for damages under a civil rights law for participating in a warrant hearing at which he withheld information critical to a defendant's rights. But, the Court said, a prosecutor is not immune from lawsuit for the legal advice given to the police on the case.

The key, according to the Court's analysis, is whether the prosecutor's conduct is "intimately associated with the judicial phase of the criminal process."

Wyatt v. Cole (504 U.S. ___), decided by a 6-3 vote, May 18, 1992. O'Connor wrote the opinion; Rehnquist, Souter and Thomas dissented.

Private defendants cannot invoke qualified immunity from lawsuits, as government officials may, when sued for actions they took under a state law later declared invalid. The connection between private parties and the historic purposes of qualified immunity is too attenuated to justify an extension of the doctrine of qualified immunity.

Racketeering

H. J. Inc. v. Northwestern Bell Telephone Co. (492 U.S. 229), decided by a 9-0 vote, June 26, 1989. Brennan wrote the opinion.

To prove a pattern of racketeering activity under the Racketeer Influenced and Corrupt Organizations Act, a plaintiff or prosecutor must show at least two racketeering predicates that are related and that amount to, or threaten the likelihood of, continued criminal activity. It is not necessary to show that the predicate offenses were committed in furtherance of multiple criminal offenses.

Tafflin v. Levitt (493 U.S. 455), decided by a 9-0 vote, Jan. 22, 1990. O'Connor wrote the opinion.

State courts have concurrent jurisdiction over civil actions brought under the federal Racketeer Influenced and Corrupt Organizations Act (RICO). Nothing in the language of RICO or its legislative history suggests that Congress had intended to divest state courts of jurisdiction to hear civil RICO claims.

Removal

Mesa v. California (489 U.S. 121), decided by a 9-0 vote, Feb. 21, 1989. O'Connor wrote the opinion.

An action against a federal officer may be removed from state to federal court only if a federal defense is raised.

International Primate Protection League v. Administrators of Tulane Educational Fund (500 U.S. ___), decided by an 8-0 vote, May 20, 1991. Marshall wrote the opinion; Scalia did not participate.

A lawsuit filed in state court challenging the treatment of monkeys used for medical experiments was improperly removed to federal court by the federal National Institutes of Health (NIH), one of the defendants. The NIH lacked authority to remove the case because the law it asserted applied to "officers," that is, individuals, acting in official capacity, not agencies.

Sanctions

Pavelic & LeFlore v. Marvel Entertainment Group (493 U.S. 120), decided by an 8-1 vote, Dec. 5, 1989. Scalia wrote the opinion; Marshall dissented.

Only the lawyer who signs a court motion or other papers filed in federal district court can be fined under Rule 11 of the Federal Rules of Civil Procedure for violating its prohibitions against meritless filings. The signing attorney's law firm cannot be sanctioned even if the lawyer signed pleadings on behalf of the firm.

Cooter & Gell v. Hartmarx Corp. (496 U.S. 384), decided by an 8-1 vote, June 11, 1990. O'Connor wrote the opinion; Stevens dissented in part.

A plaintiff who files a baseless complaint cannot escape sanctions under Rule 11 of the Federal Rules of Civil Procedure by asking to have the case dismissed at an early stage of the litigation. Despite the voluntary dismissal, jurisdiction to impose Rule 11 sanctions is needed as a means of curbing abuses of the judicial system.

Business Guides Inc. v. Chromatic Communications Enterprises Inc. (498 U.S. 533), decided by a 5-4 vote, Feb. 26, 1991. O'Connor wrote the opinion; Kennedy, Marshall, Stevens and Scalia dissented.

A federal civil procedure rule intended to discourage frivolous court filings applies to clients as well as their attorneys. The Court said that Rule 11 of the Federal Rules of Civil Procedure clearly states that a party who signs a pleading or other paper without first making a "reasonable inquiry" into the merits of the allegations shall be sanctioned. The sanction can be applied even if the represented party did not need to sign the pleading in question.

Willy v. Coastal Corp. (503 U.S. ___), decided by a 9-0 vote, March 3, 1992. Rehnquist wrote the opinion.

A federal district court's sanction of a party for frivolous filings under Rule 11 of the Rules of Federal Civil Procedure should stand even when the court later is found to have lacked subject matter jurisdiction to hear the case. The Court said the sanction is important to keeping "orderly procedure" in the courts without respect to the merits of the case.

Tax Court

Freytag v. Commissioner of Internal Revenue (501 U.S. ___), decided by 9-0 and 5-4 votes, June 27, 1991. Blackmun wrote the opinion; Scalia, O'Connor, Kennedy and Souter dissented from part of the opinion.

Federal law authorizes the Tax Court's chief judge to assign any Tax Court proceeding, regardless of complexity or amount in controversy, to a temporary, special trial judge for a hearing and findings, the Court ruled unanimously. Separately, a five-justice majority held that courts established under Article I of the Constitution, such as the Tax Court, are "Courts of Law" within the meaning of the Appointments Clause.

Writing for the majority, Blackmun said those courts, like life-tenure judges appointed under Article III of the Constitution, exercise the judicial power of the United States. He said the Tax Court is independent of the executive and legislative branches, it exercises judicial power to the exclusion of any other function and its role resembles that of the federal district courts.

Criminal Law

Bail

United States v. Montalvo-Murillo (495 U.S. 711), decided by a 6-3 vote, May 29, 1990. Kennedy wrote the opinion; Stevens, Brennan and Marshall dissented.

The state's failure to comply with a prompt-hearing provision of the Bail Reform Act of 1964 does not require that the prisoner then be released. The safety of society should not be forfeited by accidental non-compliance with the statute's time limits.

Capital Punishment

Hildwin v. Florida (490 U.S. 638), decided by a 7-2 vote, May 30, 1989. *Per curiam* (unsigned) opinion; Brennan and Marshall dissented.

The Sixth Amendment does not require that the specific findings authorizing the imposition of a death sentence be made by a jury instead of a judge. The existence of an aggravating factor is not an element of the offense, but a sentencing factor that comes into play only after a defendant has been found guilty.

Penry v. Lynaugh (492 U.S. 302), decided by a 5-4 vote, June 26, 1989. O'Connor wrote the opinion; Scalia, Rehnquist, White and Kennedy dissented.

The constitutional ban on cruel and unusual punishment does not categorically deny a state the power to execute a mentally retarded person who was found competent to stand trial, whose defense of legal insanity was rejected and who was properly convicted.

Stanford v. Kentucky; Wilkins v. Missouri (492 U.S. 361), decided by a 5-4 vote, June 26, 1989. Scalia wrote the opinion; Brennan, Marshall, Blackmun and Stevens dissented.

Imposition of the death penalty upon a defendant convicted of a capital crime committed when he or she was only 16 or 17 years old does not violate the ban on cruel and unusual punishment simply because of the defendant's youth.

Blystone v. Pennsylvania (494 U.S. 299), decided by a 5-4 vote, Feb. 28, 1990. Rehnquist wrote the opinion; Brennan, Marshall, Blackmun and Stevens dissented.

Due Process, Equal Protection

... Nor shall any state deprive any person of life, liberty, or property, without due process of law; nor deny to any person within its jurisdiction the equal protection of the laws.

14th Amendment, U.S. Constitution

States may make capital punishment the only possible sentence for some murders without violating Supreme Court rulings against a mandatory death penalty, as long as a jury is allowed to consider all relevant mitigating evidence. Upholding a Pennsylvania law, the Court said the death penalty was not automatic but was imposed only after a jury found that whatever aggravating circumstances existed outweighed any mitigating circumstances or that no mitigating circumstances existed.

Boyde v. California (494 U.S. 370), decided by a 5-4 vote, March 5, 1990. Rehnquist wrote the opinion; Marshall, Brennan, Blackmun and Stevens dissented.

A sentencing jury in a capital case may be told that it can consider a list of specific mitigating circumstances and "any other circumstances which extenuate the gravity of the crime." Such an instruction does not stop jurors from weighing mitigating factors such as the defendant's background even if those factors do not lessen the gravity of the crime.

McKoy v. North Carolina (494 U.S. 433), decided by a 6-3 vote, March 5, 1990. Marshall wrote the opinion; Scalia, Rehnquist and O'Connor dissented.

A state death penalty law may not require that jurors be instructed to consider only mitigating circumstances that they unanimously agree exist. The unanimity requirement was unconstitutional because it prevented the jury from considering all mitigating evidence.

Clemons v. Mississippi (494 U.S. 738), decided by a 5-4 vote, March 28, 1990. White wrote the opinion; Blackmun, Brennan, Marshall and Stevens dissented.

An appellate court may reweigh aggravating and mitigating evidence from a murder trial to uphold a death sentence that was based in part on an invalid aggravating circumstance.

Whitmore v. Arkansas (495 U.S. 149), decided by a 7-2 vote, April 24, 1990. Rehnquist wrote the opinion; Marshall and Brennan dissented.

A third party cannot challenge the validity of a death sentence imposed on a defendant who has waived the right to appeal the sentence. The decision barred a challenge by a death row inmate to a fellow inmate's conviction and death sentence.

Walton v. Arizona (497 U.S. 639), decided by a 5-4 vote, June 27, 1990. White wrote the opinion; Brennan, Marshall, Blackmun and Stevens dissented.

An Arizona death sentence law giving a trial judge, instead of a jury, discretion to find aggravating circumstances that justify the death penalty is constitutional. The Constitution does not require that every finding of fact underlying a sentencing decision be made by a jury.

The Court also said that if a murder was committed in an "especially heinous, cruel or depraved" manner, that could be an aggravating factor warranting a death sentence.

Parker v. Dugger (498 U.S. 308), decided by a 5-4 vote, Jan. 22, 1991. O'Connor wrote the opinion; White, Rehnquist, Scalia and Kennedy dissented.

A state supreme court acted arbitrarily when, in considering an appeal of a death sentence, it failed to take into account evidence from the murder defendant that mitigated his crime.

Lankford v. Idaho (500 U.S. ___), decided by a 5-4 vote, May 20, 1991. Stevens wrote the opinion; Scalia, Rehnquist, White and Souter dissented.

A murder defendant's right to due process was violated when a judge sentenced the defendant to death without the defendant's earlier knowing that the death penalty was being considered.

Schad v. Arizona (501 U.S. ___), decided by a 5-4 vote, June 21, 1991. Souter wrote the opinion; White, Marshall, Blackmun and Stevens dissented.

An Arizona law allowing a jury to forgo agreement on the type of first-degree murder that a defendant committed does not violate a defendant's right to due process of law. The decision upheld a death sentence imposed under jury instructions that did not require unanimity on whether the defendant was guilty of premeditated murder or felony murder. Writing for a plurality of four justices, Souter said that a jury may reach one verdict based on any combination of the alternative findings as long as jurors agree the defendant was guilty of first-degree murder. Scalia concurred in the judgment on broader grounds.

Payne v. Tennessee (501 U.S. ___), decided by a 6-3 vote, June 27, 1991. Rehnquist wrote the opinion; Marshall, Blackmun and Stevens dissented.

Evidence of a victim's character and the impact of a crime on a victim's family may be used against a murder defendant in a sentencing hearing for capital punishment. The Eighth Amendment, which bans cruel and unusual punishment, does not bar a capital sentencing jury from considering these factors. The decision overruled two earlier cases that had barred so-called victim impact statements — *Booth v. Maryland*, 482 U.S. 496 (1987), and *South Carolina v. Gathers*, 490 U.S. 805 (1989).

Double Jeopardy

Lockhart v. Nelson (488 U.S. 33), decided by a 6-3 vote, Nov. 14, 1988. Rehnquist wrote the opinion; Marshall, Brennan and Blackmun dissented.

The Double Jeopardy Clause does not prevent the retrial of a defendant after the verdict against the defendant has been set aside because of erroneous admission of evidence. The defendant may be retried if the evidence admitted at trial, including that which was erroneously admitted, would have been sufficient to sustain the original verdict.

United States v. Broce (488 U.S. 563), decided by a 6-3 vote, Jan. 23, 1989. Kennedy wrote the opinion; Blackmun, Brennan and Marshall dissented.

A defendant who has pleaded guilty to two separate conspiracy indictments cannot later attack the convictions by claiming that there was only one conspiracy and that conviction on more than one indictment violated the Double Jeopardy Clause.

United States v. Halper (490 U.S. 435), decided by a 9-0 vote, May 15, 1989. Blackmun wrote the opinion.

A civil penalty may constitute "punishment" for purposes of double jeopardy analysis if it does not bear a rational relationship to the losses suffered by the government. The Double Jeopardy Clause prohibits imposition of such a penalty if a defendant has already been convicted and punished under a criminal statute.

Jones v. Thomas (491 U.S. 376), decided by a 5-4 vote, June 19, 1989. Kennedy wrote the opinion; Scalia, Brennan, Marshall and Stevens dissented.

The double jeopardy rights of a federal habeas corpus petitioner who received improper cumulative sentences for felony murder and the underlying felony were adequately vindicated by a trial court's decision to vacate the shorter sentence and credit the time served on that sentence against the longer sentence. The petitioner's confinement under the single sentence imposed for felony murder with credit for time already served is not double jeopardy.

Dowling v. United States (493 U.S. 342), decided by a 6-3 vote, Jan. 10, 1990. White wrote the opinion; Brennan, Marshall and Stevens dissented.

Neither double jeopardy nor Due Process Clause protections bar the use at trial of testimony that relates to a previous alleged crime for which the defendant was acquitted. The Court said that the jury is free to assess the truthfulness and significance of the testimony.

Grady v. Corbin (495 U.S. 508), decided by a 5-4 vote, May 29, 1990. Brennan wrote the opinion; O'Connor, Scalia, Rehnquist and Kennedy dissented.

The Double Jeopardy Clause of the Fifth Amendment bars a second prosecution for an offense based on conduct for which a defendant already has been prosecuted. The test is whether the alleged offense is based on the same conduct as was the basis of the earlier charge.

United States v. Felix (503 U.S. ___), decided by 9-0 and 7-2 votes, March 25, 1992. Rehnquist wrote the opinion; Stevens and Blackmun dissented in part.

No double jeopardy violation occurs when, in the prosecution of a defendant for a drug conspiracy, a prosecutor uses evidence of overt acts that are based on substantive offenses for which the defendant previously had been convicted. A substantive crime and a conspiracy to commit that crime are not the "same offense" for double jeopardy purposes even if they are based on the same underlying incidents.

Entrapment

Jacobson v. United States (503 U.S. ___), decided by a 5-4 vote, April 6, 1992. White wrote the opinion; O'Connor, Rehnquist, Kennedy and Scalia dissented.

In the case of a Nebraska farmer who was caught ordering child pornography magazines, prosecutors failed to provide evidence that the man was predisposed to buy the pornography and not entrapped by undercover government agents.

After obtaining the defendant's name from a mailing list, the government tried for more than two years to persuade the man to buy child pornography. The Court said the government pressure overstepped the line between setting a trap for the "unwary innocent" and the "unwary criminal."

Evidence

Arizona v. Youngblood (488 U.S. 51), decided by a 6-3 vote, Nov. 29, 1988. Rehnquist wrote the opinion; Blackmun, Brennan and Marshall dissented.

Law enforcement officers' failure to preserve evidence potentially useful to a defendant does not violate the Due Process Clause unless the officers acted in bad faith. Police have no constitutional duty to preserve evidence or to perform any particular tests on evidence.

Double Jeopardy, Self-Incrimination

... Nor shall any person be subject for the same offense to be twice put in jeopardy of life or limb nor shall be compelled in any criminal case to be a witness against himself, nor be deprived of life, liberty, or property, without due process of law....

Fifth Amendment, U.S. Constitution

James v. Illinois (493 U.S. 307), decided by a 5-4 vote, Jan. 10, 1990. Brennan wrote the opinion; Kennedy, Rehnquist, O'Connor and Scalia dissented.

Illegally obtained evidence cannot be used to impeach the credibility of defense witnesses. The exception to the so-called exclusionary rule that permits illegally obtained evidence to be used to contradict testimony in court by the defendant does not extend to the testimony of other defense witnesses.

New York v. Harris (495 U.S. 14), decided by a 5-4 vote, April 18, 1990. White wrote the opinion; Marshall, Brennan, Blackmun and Stevens dissented.

A prosecutor is not barred from using a confession made by a defendant after a warrantless arrest in his home, when the statement is taken outside of the home. The rule against warrantless arrests in a residence was designed to protect the physical integrity of the home, not to protect criminal suspects from statements made outside their premises.

Idaho v. Wright (497 U.S. 805), decided by a 5-4 vote, June 27, 1990. O'Connor wrote the opinion; Kennedy, Rehnquist, White and Blackmun dissented.

Hearsay statements from a child who is unable to testify in an abuse case can be admitted at trial if the child's story is trustworthy. The Court said that the circumstances giving rise to the statements must demonstrate "particularized guarantees of trustworthiness" to be admitted under an exception to the hearsay rule. In such cases, the trial court must look at all the circumstances surrounding the child's account, including how well the child knew the accused and whether the child would make up the story.

Maryland v. Craig (497 U.S. 836), decided by a 5-4 vote, June 27, 1990. O'Connor wrote the opinion; Scalia, Brennan, Marshall and Stevens dissented.

States may shield victims of child abuse by allowing them to testify on closed-circuit television instead of facing the person accused of abusing them. The state interest in protecting child witnesses from the trauma of testifying may justify permitting them to answer questions without a face-to-face confrontation with the defendant. The Court noted that the Maryland procedure preserved other elements of the confrontation right of the Sixth Amendment: that the child had to be competent to testify and testified under oath; that the defendant had an opportunity for contemporaneous cross-examination; and that the judge, jury and defendant were able to view the demeanor of the witness as he or she testified.

Michigan v. Lucas (500 U.S. ___), decided by a 7-2 vote, May 20, 1991. O'Connor wrote the opinion; Stevens and Marshall dissented.

The Confrontation Clause of the Sixth Amendment does not guarantee that an alleged rapist may introduce evidence of a prior romantic relationship with the alleged victim. The Court said a state rule requiring a defendant to notify the prosecutor within 10 days after arraignment that he would seek to introduce such testimony served legitimate interests of protecting rape victims against surprise, harassment and unnecessary invasions of privacy.

Griffin v. United States (502 U.S. ___), decided by an 8-0 vote, Dec. 3, 1991. Scalia wrote the opinion; Thomas did not participate.

A general guilty verdict stemming from a so-called multiple-object conspiracy need not be set aside even if the evidence is inadequate to support conviction on one of two or more objects or purposes. The justices unanimously said the Due Process Clause of the Fifth Amendment and Supreme Court precedents require only that the evidence be enough to support conviction on one of the objects.

Estelle v. McGuire (502 U.S. ___), decided by an 8-0 vote, Dec. 4, 1991. Rehnquist wrote the opinion; O'Connor and Stevens dissented in part; Thomas did not participate.

The due process rights of a father on trial for murder of his child were not violated when evidence of the child's previous injuries was admitted at trial. Even though the earlier injuries were not connected at trial to the father, the Court said that the evidence likely established that the child had been beaten before and that the death was the result of an intentional act.

O'Connor and Stevens dissented in part, saying that a jury instruction about the battered-child evidence was improper.

White v. Illinois (502 U.S. ___), decided by a 9-0 vote, Jan. 15, 1992. Rehnquist wrote the opinion.

The constitutional right of an accused person to face his accuser is not violated when, in a child abuse case, a jury considers out-of-court statements made by an alleged victim, even when the child is available to testify but has been excused.

The child's statements about the alleged incident to her mother, a physician and others were held to qualify for admission under an exception to the hearsay rule for spontaneous declarations or statements made in the course of a medical examination. The Court said that the factor that made the statements reliable could not be recaptured by in-court testimony.

United States v. Williams (503 U.S. ___), decided by a 5-4 vote, May 4, 1992. Scalia wrote the opinion; Stevens, Blackmun, O'Connor and Thomas dissented.

Federal district courts may not dismiss an otherwise valid grand jury indictment because the government failed to disclose to the grand jury evidence that tended to clear the defendant. To require the prosecutor to present exculpatory evidence would alter the grand jury's historical role, transforming it from an accusatory body that sits to assess whether adequate basis exists for bringing a criminal charge into an adjudicatory one that determines guilt or innocence.

United States v. Salerno (505 U.S. ___), decided by an 8-1 vote, June 19, 1992. Thomas wrote the opinion; Stevens dissented.

The Court strictly interpreted one of the hearsay exceptions in the federal rules of evidence so as to limit the ability of a defendant to introduce over the prosecutor's objection the grand jury testimony of witnesses who asserted the Fifth Amendment privilege to avoid testifying at trial. The Court said the defense could introduce the witnesses' grand jury testimony only if it showed, as rule 804(b)(1) requires, that the prosecution had the opportunity and "similar motive" to develop the prior testimony when it was taken.

The decision reversed a ruling by a federal appeals court that had held the evidence should have been allowed in the interest of "adversarial fairness."

Medina v. California (505 U.S. ___), decided by a 7-2 vote, June 22, 1992. Kennedy wrote the opinion; Blackmun and Stevens dissented.

A state may require a defendant who alleges he is mentally incompetent to stand trial to bear the burden of proving his claim by a preponderance of the evidence. The ruling affirmed a California Supreme Court decision that a state statute's presumption of competency and burden of proof on the defendant did not violate a defendant's right to due process.

Grand Juries

Midland Asphalt Corp. v. United States (489 U.S. 794), decided by a 9-0 vote, March 28, 1989. Scalia wrote the opinion.

The denial of a motion to dismiss an indictment because of an alleged violation of grand jury secrecy is not immediately appealable. The action is not a final judgment ending the litigation and does not come within the exceptions for collateral orders reviewable before final judgment.

United States v. R. Enterprises Inc. (498 U.S. 292), decided by a 9-0 vote, Jan. 22, 1991. O'Connor wrote the opinion.

A grand jury may issue a subpoena duces tecum (for specific documents or papers) without having to show that the materials would be relevant to a criminal investigation and admissible at trial. The Court said that the standard for relevancy in its 1974 decision in *United States v. Nixon*, 418 U.S. 683, does not apply in a grand jury proceeding.

Habeas Corpus

Harris v. Reed (489 U.S. 255), decided by an 8-1 vote, Feb. 22, 1989. Blackmun wrote the opinion; Kennedy dissented.

The Court extended to habeas corpus cases a rule permitting it to consider issues of federal law raised in state courts unless the state court plainly stated that its decision was based on independent state grounds. The "plain statement" rule was first adopted in a case, *Michigan v. Long*, 463 U.S. 1032 (1983), that was before the Court on direct review.

Castille v. Peoples (489 U.S. 346), decided by a 9-0 vote, Feb. 22, 1989. Scalia wrote the opinion.

The habeas corpus petitioner did not satisfy the requirement that his claim must first have been "fairly presented" to a state court by raising issues for the first time in a state procedure that permitted discretionary review only for "special and important reasons."

Teague v. Lane (489 U.S. 288), decided by a 7-2 vote, Feb. 22, 1989. O'Connor wrote the opinion; Brennan and Marshall dissented.

The Court rejected a habeas corpus petitioner's effort to set aside his conviction because the prosecutor excused potential jurors on racial grounds. The petitioner's conviction had become final before the Court's ruling in *Batson v. Kentucky*, 476 U.S. 79 (1986), that held racially motivated peremptory challenges by a prosecutor to be a violation of a defendant's equal protection rights, and the petitioner had not raised the claim at trial or on direct appeal.

Dugger v. Adams (489 U.S. 401), decided by a 5-4 vote, Feb. 28, 1989. White wrote the opinion; Blackmun, Brennan, Marshall and Stevens dissented.

The Court refused to consider a habeas corpus petitioner's claim of improper jury instructions because he had failed to object to the instructions during his trial.

Zant v. Moore (489 U.S. 836), decided by an 8-1 vote, March 29, 1989. *Per curiam* (unsigned) opinion; Blackmun dissented.

A federal appeals court decision to permit an inmate to raise a Fifth Amendment claim in a second habeas corpus petition on the ground that the claim was not available at the time of his first habeas corpus petition was vacated. The case was remanded for reconsideration in light of *Teague v. Lane*, 489 U.S. 288 (1989).

Maleng v. Cook (490 U.S. 488), decided by a 9-0 vote, May 15, 1989. *Per curiam* (unsigned) opinion.

A habeas corpus petitioner cannot challenge a conviction for which the sentence has expired even though the conviction was used to increase a sentence imposed under a subsequent conviction.

Murray v. Giarratano (492 U.S. 1), decided by a 5-4 vote, June 23, 1989. Rehnquist wrote the opinion; Stevens, Brennan, Marshall and Blackmun dissented.

Virginia's system of securing representation for indigent death row inmates was not shown to violate the constitutional rights of inmates seeking state habeas corpus relief. The state adequately satisfied the meaningful-access requirement by giving inmates access to a law library or law books, maintaining a staff of "unit attorneys" to assist with incarceration-related litigation and authorizing appointment of counsel after a petition for post-conviction relief is filed.

Butler v. McKellar (494 U.S. 407), decided by a 5-4 vote, March 5, 1990. Rehnquist wrote the opinion; Brennan, Marshall, Blackmun and Stevens dissented.

A defendant may not challenge his conviction by filing a habeas corpus petition in federal court based on a new constitutional decision that a state appellate court could not reasonably have predicted at the time of the defendant's direct appeal. The decision refined the Court's 1989 ruling in *Teague v. Lane*, 489 U.S. 288, which made it harder for a death row inmate to establish an appeal based on a favorable court ruling issued in another case after his own conviction became final.

Saffle v. Parks (494 U.S. 484), decided by a 5-4 vote, March 5, 1990. Kennedy wrote the opinion; Brennan, Marshall, Blackmun and Stevens dissented.

A defendant is not entitled to federal habeas corpus review of his sentence when the grounds he asserts involve a "new rule" of law unless it comes within the narrow — and here inapplicable — exceptions of the Court's ruling in *Teague v. Lane*, 489 U.S. 288 (1989). The petitioner had sought to overturn a conviction and death sentence that became final in 1983 on the basis of a 1987 Supreme Court decision that prohibited a jury instruction — used at his trial — that jurors should avoid any influence of sympathy.

Sawyer v. Smith (497 U.S. 227), decided by a 5-4 vote, June 21, 1990. Kennedy wrote the opinion; Marshall, Brennan, Blackmun and Stevens dissented.

A defendant is not entitled to federal habeas corpus relief based on a new, favorable Court ruling in another case unless the principle of the new case is "fundamental to the integrity of the criminal proceeding." The Court rejected the petitioner's effort to set aside the conviction on the basis of a 1985 ruling that prohibited the death penalty when jurors are misled about their great responsibility in a capital punishment decision.

Lewis v. Jeffers (497 U.S. 764), decided by a 5-4 vote, June 27, 1990. O'Connor wrote the opinion; Blackmun, Brennan, Marshall and Stevens dissented.

When a state court applies an aggravating factor that has been found constitutionally valid, a federal appeals court — considering the case on collateral review — should not conduct a new (de novo) comparison of the facts of the case with other cases to see whether the aggravating factor should have been applied. The Supreme Court said that the appeals court wrongly overturned a state supreme court's finding that a crime was committed in an "especially heinous, cruel or depraved manner."

McCleskey v. Zant (499 U.S. 467), decided by a 6-3 vote, April 16, 1991. Kennedy wrote the opinion; Marshall, Blackmun and Stevens dissented.

Death row prisoners should be allowed one round of federal court review through petitions for habeas corpus, after state court appeals are exhausted, barring extraordinary circumstances. A prisoner may file only one habeas corpus petition in federal court unless good reason exists for not having raised any new constitutional error on the first round. The prisoner also is required to show that he suffered "actual prejudice" from the error he asserts.

Under earlier Court rulings, second and subsequent habeas corpus petitions were dismissed out of hand only if a prisoner deliberately withheld grounds for appeal.

Coleman v. Thompson (501 U.S. ___), decided by a 6-3 vote, June 24, 1991. O'Connor wrote the opinion; Blackmun, Marshall and Stevens dissented.

A death row inmate may not file a habeas corpus petition in federal court if he failed to abide by state court procedural rules. The convicted murderer in this case missed a deadline for filing an appeal at the state level by three days.

The Court said an inmate's petition for habeas corpus review should be barred unless he could show cause for the procedural default and actual prejudice as a result of the alleged violation of federal law or unless he could demonstrate that failure to consider the claims would result in a fundamental miscarriage of justice. The decision reversed an earlier ruling — *Fay v. Noia*, 372 U.S. 391 (1963) — that allowed most prisoners to file habeas corpus petitions in federal court unless they deliberately had bypassed state review.

Ylst v. Nunnemaker (501 U.S. ___), decided by a 6-3 vote, June 24, 1991. Scalia wrote the opinion; Blackmun, Marshall and Stevens dissented.

A state court's failure to explain why it denied a prisoner's petition for habeas corpus is not a sufficient reason to give the prisoner a federal habeas corpus hearing. The Court said that the defendant did not overcome a presumption that the California Supreme Court's last unexplained order considered the merits of his argument.

Stringer v. Black (503 U.S. ___), decided by a 6-3 vote, March 9, 1992. Kennedy wrote the opinion; Souter, Scalia and Thomas dissented.

Supreme Court decisions from 1988 and 1990 that prohibited jurors from voting to impose the death penalty if a murder was "especially heinous, atrocious or cruel" should be given retroactive effect for a defendant challenging the constitutionality of his 1982 death sentence. The Court said the 1988 and 1990 decisions did not embody a new rule of law but were based on a 1980 decision, of which the defendant should have the benefit.

Keeney v. Tamayo-Reyes (504 U.S. ___), decided by a 5-4 vote, May 4, 1992. White wrote the opinion; O'Connor, Stevens, Blackmun and Kennedy dissented.

A new, stricter standard should govern whether state court defendants who challenge their cases through a writ of habeas corpus may obtain evidentiary hearings before federal judges. The Court decided that federal courts no longer are required to hold a hearing to weigh evidence if important facts were not adequately presented in state court.

The Supreme Court said that the petitioner was entitled to an evidentiary hearing if he could show cause for his failure to develop the facts in state court proceedings and actual prejudice resulting from that failure. The appeals court had held a hearing was necessary, under a less rigorous standard requiring a hearing unless the habeas corpus petition constituted a "deliberate bypass" of the orderly procedure of the state courts.

Wright v. West (505 U.S. ___), decided by a 9-0 vote, June 19, 1992. Thomas wrote the opinion.

The Court reinstated the grand larceny conviction of a Virginia man, reversing a federal appeals court decision that the evidence against the defendant was insufficient, under constitutional due process, to support his state court conviction.

The Court's fragmented decision failed, however, to resolve the issue of how much deference a federal court should give to state court findings when the federal court hears an inmate's habeas corpus petition. In this case, all justices agreed that under any standard the evidence was sufficient for conviction.

Sawyer v. Whitley (505 U.S. ___), decided by a 6-3 vote, June 22, 1992. Rehnquist wrote the opinion; Blackmun, Stevens and O'Connor dissented.

A death row prisoner who brings a second or subsequent federal habeas corpus petition alleging he has new information in his case must prove by clear and convincing evidence that if the new information were presented, no reasonable juror would have found him eligible for the death penalty.

Jury Selection

Tompkins v. Texas (490 U.S. 754), affirmed by a 4-4 vote, June 5, 1989. *Per curiam* (unsigned) opinion; O'Connor did not participate.

The decision by the Texas Court of Criminal Appeals that a prosecutor's exclusion of black potential jurors from a black defendant's trial was not motivated by racial discrimination was affirmed by an equally divided Court.

Holland v. Illinois (493 U.S. 474), decided by a 5-4 vote, Jan. 22, 1990. Scalia wrote the opinion; Marshall, Brennan, Blackmun and Stevens dissented.

A defendant's Sixth Amendment right to be "tried by a representative cross section of the community" is not violated when prosecutors exclude prospective jurors because of their race in cases in which the defendant is a different race than those excluded.

Ford v. Georgia (498 U.S. 411), decided by a 9-0 vote, Feb. 19, 1991. Souter wrote the opinion.

A defendant's pretrial motion attacking a pattern of excluding black potential jurors "over a long period of time" adequately raised an equal protection claim even though it did not mention the Equal Protection Clause and even though his new trial motion cited the Sixth Amendment instead of the 14th Amendment.

The ruling overturned a decision by the Georgia Supreme Court that the defendant had not properly raised the argument. The Supreme Court also ruled that the state court erred in barring the claim as untimely under a state procedural rule.

Powers v. Ohio (499 U.S. 400), decided by a 7-2 vote, April 1, 1991. Kennedy wrote the opinion; Scalia and Rehnquist dissented.

A criminal defendant may object to race-based exclusions of jurors through peremptory challenges whether or not the defendant and the excluded jurors share the same race. The decision expanded the right of criminal defendants, stemming from the landmark *Batson v. Kentucky*, 476 U.S. 79 (1986), to object to a prosecutor's use of peremptory challenges to exclude persons because of race.

The Court said that if only blacks were able to challenge prosecutors' exclusion of blacks from juries the process would condone arbitrary exclusion.

Hernandez v. New York (500 U.S. ___), decided by a 6-3 vote, May 28, 1991. Kennedy wrote the opinion; Blackmun, Stevens and Marshall dissented.

A prosecutor who struck from a jury pool bilingual Hispanics did not violate the constitutional guarantee of equal protection of the law, because the trial court found that the potential jurors were not eliminated because of race. The Court said the trial judge acted within his broad discretion in accepting the prosecutor's explanation that Hispanic jurors would not accept an interpreter's English translation of Spanish-language testimony to be offered in the trial.

Mu'min v. Virginia (500 U.S. ___), decided by a 5-4 vote, May 30, 1991. Rehnquist wrote the opinion; Marshall, Blackmun, Stevens and Kennedy dissented.

A criminal defendant does not have a right to ask potential jurors how much they know about a crime as long as they promise to be fair. The Court said a trial court's refusal of a defense request to question prospective jurors about their knowledge of a case and specific contents of news reports did not violate his constitutional right to be tried by an impartial jury.

Morgan v. Illinois (504 U.S. ___), decided by a 6-3 vote, June 15, 1992. White wrote the opinion; Scalia, Rehnquist and Thomas dissented.

A criminal defendant has a constitutional right to ask potential jurors if they automatically would impose the death penalty if they found him guilty of murder. A potential juror answering in the affirmative rightfully can be excluded by the defendant.

Georgia v. McCollum (505 U.S. ___), decided by a 7-2 vote, June 18, 1992. Blackmun wrote the opinion; O'Connor and Scalia dissented.

Lawyers for criminal defendants cannot eliminate prospective jurors based on their race. Any racially motivated approach to choosing a jury violates the constitutional guarantee of equal protection of the laws.

The decision extended an anti-discrimination rule the Court applied in 1986 to prosecutors and in 1991 to parties in civil litigation.

Prisons and Jails

Thornburgh v. Abbott (490 U.S. 401), decided by a 6-3 vote, May 15, 1989. Blackmun wrote the opinion; Stevens, Brennan and Marshall dissented.

Prison regulations limiting prisoners' receipt of publications from outside the prison are valid under the First Amendment if they are reasonably related to legitimate penological interests. Regulations permitting a federal prison warden to reject a publication if it is determined to be detrimental to prison security or if it might facilitate criminal activity are facially valid.

Kentucky Department of Corrections v. Thompson (490 U.S. 454), decided by a 6-3 vote, May 15, 1989. Blackmun wrote the opinion; Marshall, Brennan and Stevens dissented.

Prison regulations that set forth non-binding guidelines for permitting prison visitation do not give inmates a protected liberty interest in receiving visitors. Without explicit mandatory language in the regulations, an inmate is not entitled to due process in enforcing the regulations against prison officials.

Washington v. Harper (494 U.S. 210), decided by a 6-3 vote, Feb. 27, 1990. Kennedy wrote the opinion; Stevens, Brennan and Marshall dissented.

State prison officials may force a mentally ill inmate to take anti-psychotic drugs if the inmate is a danger to himself or others and the treatment is in the inmate's medical interest. The Court said that mentally ill prisoners have a "significant liberty interest" in being free of unwanted medication, but that interest was adequately protected by a hearing before a panel composed of prison staff instead of a judicial-style hearing.

Wilson v. Seiter (501 U.S. ___), decided by a 5-4 vote, June 17, 1991. Scalia wrote the opinion; White, Marshall, Blackmun and Stevens dissented.

A prisoner who claims that the conditions of his confinement violate the Eighth Amendment's prohibition on cruel and unusual punishment must show a culpable state of mind, "deliberate indifference," on the part of prison officials. The decision upheld a lower court test for liability that the prison officials must be shown to have acted "maliciously and sadistically for the very purpose of causing harm."

Hudson v. McMillian (503 U.S. ___), decided by a 7-2 vote, Feb. 25, 1992. O'Connor wrote the opinion; Thomas and Scalia dissented.

The use of excessive physical force against a prison inmate may constitute cruel and unusual punishment under the Eighth Amendment, even if the prisoner does not suffer serious injury. The Court said the test is whether the force was used in a "good-faith effort" to maintain or restore discipline or whether it was "maliciously and sadistically" used to cause harm.

Right to Counsel

Penson v. Ohio (488 U.S. 75), decided by an 8-1 vote, Nov. 29, 1988. Stevens wrote the opinion; Rehnquist dissented.

The Court strictly applied the requirements of *Anders v. California*, 386 U.S. 738 (1967), for permitting a court-appointed attorney to withdraw from an appeal that the attorney considers to be without merit. Under *Anders*, an attorney in such a case must file a brief referring to any possible basis for an appeal and the appellate court must examine the record in the case before acting on the request. In this case, the justices ruled that failure to follow those procedures cannot be excused even if the appellate court finds the denial of counsel did not prejudice the defendant or amounted to harmless error.

Perry v. Leeke (488 U.S. 272), decided by a 6-3 vote, Jan. 10, 1989. Stevens wrote the opinion; Marshall, Brennan and Blackmun dissented.

A criminal defendant has no right under the Sixth Amendment to confer with his attorney during a brief trial recess called while the defendant is on the witness stand.

United States v. Monsanto (491 U.S. 600), decided by a 5-4 vote, June 22, 1989. White wrote the opinion; Blackmun, Brennan, Marshall and Stevens dissented.

The federal drug forfeiture statute authorizes a district court to enter a pretrial order freezing assets in a defendant's possession even if the defendant seeks to use those assets to pay an attorney. For the reasons stated in *Caplin & Drysdale v. United States* (491 U.S. 617), such an order does not violate the defendant's right to counsel of his choice under the Fifth or Sixth Amendment.

Supreme Court

Caplin & Drysdale, Chartered v. United States (491 U.S. 617), decided by a 5-4 vote, June 22, 1989. White wrote the opinion; Blackmun, Brennan, Marshall and Stevens dissented.

The federal drug forfeiture statute, which provides for pretrial freezing and postconviction forfeiture of a defendant's assets, is constitutional even though it contains no exemption for an accused to use assets to pay an attorney. The statute does not impermissibly burden a defendant's Sixth Amendment right to retain counsel of his choice. The statute also does not upset the balance of power between the government and the accused in a manner contrary to the Due Process Clause of the Fifth Amendment.

Powell v. Texas (492 U.S. 680), decided by a 9-0 vote, July 3, 1989. *Per curiam* (unsigned) opinion.

Evidence of future dangerousness was obtained in violation of the defendant's Sixth Amendment's right to the assistance of counsel when neither the defendant nor his counsel was informed prior to a psychiatric examination that he would be examined on the issue. The lower court's holding that the defendant waived his Fifth Amendment privilege against self-incrimination by introducing psychiatric testimony at trial in support of an insanity defense provides no basis for concluding that he waived his Sixth Amendment rights.

Search and Seizure

Florida v. Riley (488 U.S. 445), decided by a 5-4 vote, Jan. 23, 1989. White wrote the opinion; Brennan, Marshall, Blackmun and Stevens dissented.

Police did not violate the defendant's Fourth Amendment rights by observing a partially covered greenhouse on his property from a helicopter circling the property at an altitude of 400 feet. Because the defendant had no reasonable expectation of privacy from such observations, the surveillance did not constitute a "search" that would have required a warrant under the Fourth Amendment.

Brower v. Inyo County (489 U.S. 593), decided by a 9-0 vote, March 21, 1989. Scalia wrote the opinion.

The stopping of a motorist by means of a roadblock established for that purpose is a "seizure" within the meaning of the Fourth Amendment. The Court remanded a federal civil rights suit based on the death of a suspect in a high-speed automobile chase to determine whether the use of a tractor-trailer to block a highway to apprehend the suspect was an "unreasonable" seizure.

United States v. Sokolow (490 U.S. 1), decided by a 7-2 vote, April 3, 1989. Rehnquist wrote the opinion; Marshall and Brennan dissented.

Federal drug agents had sufficient grounds to reasonably suspect that a traveler was transporting illegal drugs and to permit an investigative stop. The grounds included the fact that the traveler paid $2,100 in cash for airline tickets, was traveling under an alias, had taken a short trip to a major source city for drugs, appeared nervous and was carrying unchecked luggage.

Maryland v. Buie (494 U.S. 325), decided by a 7-2 vote, Feb. 28, 1990. White wrote the opinion; Brennan and Marshall dissented.

A police officer without a search warrant may make a protective sweep of a house if, after making an in-home arrest, he reasonably believes he is in danger. The warrantless search must be justified by a "reasonable, articulable suspicion" that someone dangerous is in the house and may extend only to a cursory inspection of places where a person may be hiding.

United States v. Verdugo-Urquidez (494 U.S. 259), decided by a 6-3 vote, Feb. 28, 1990. Rehnquist wrote the opinion; Brennan, Marshall and Blackmun dissented.

U.S. law enforcement agents operating without warrants may search a foreigner's property in a foreign country without violating the Fourth Amendment's prohibition against unreasonable searches and seizures. The decision overturned a federal appeals court ruling that had made no distinction between foreigners and U.S. citizens and had excluded from trial evidence seized in a warrantless search in Mexico.

Florida v. Wells (495 U.S. 1), decided by a 9-0 vote, April 18, 1990. Rehnquist wrote the opinion.

When a state jurisdiction has no highway patrol policy regarding the opening of closed containers found during an inventory search, the opening of any boxes, suitcases or other containers violates the Fourth Amendment's protection against unreasonable searches and seizures.

Minnesota v. Olson (495 U.S. 91), decided by a 7-2 vote, April 18, 1990. White wrote the opinion; Rehnquist and Blackmun dissented.

An overnight house guest has a legitimate expectation of privacy and is entitled to Fourth Amendment protection against police intrusion on the house. The ruling suppressed an incriminating statement made by a suspect after police arrested him without a warrant in the home of an acquaintance.

United States v. Ojeda Rios (495 U.S. 257), decided by a 6-3 vote, April 30, 1990. White wrote the opinion; Stevens, Brennan and Marshall dissented.

A good-faith misunderstanding of the federal law requiring that recordings obtained through court-authorized wiretaps be sealed as soon as the surveillance ends can be a "satisfactory explanation" for delay in sealing. The Court said prosecutors are required to offer such an excuse at a suppression hearing. The case was remanded to determine whether it was.

Search and Seizure

The right of the people to be secure in their persons, houses, papers and effects, against unreasonable searches and seizures, shall not be violated, and no warrants shall issue, but upon probable cause, supported by oath or affirmation and particularly describing the place to be searched, and the persons or things to be seized.

Fourth Amendment, U.S. Constitution

Horton v. California (496 U.S. 128), decided by a 7-2 vote, June 4, 1990. Stevens wrote the opinion; Brennan and Marshall dissented.

Police who have entered a home without a proper search warrant may seize evidence in plain view even if the discovery of the evidence is not inadvertent. Two critical tests are whether the police have a right to be on the premises when the discovery is made and whether police are able to recognize immediately the incriminating nature of the object.

Alabama v. White (496 U.S. 325), decided by a 6-3 vote, June 11, 1990. White wrote the opinion; Stevens, Brennan and Marshall dissented.

Police officers who received and corroborated an anonymous tip had reasonable suspicion to stop a driver whom they discovered carrying illegal drugs. Although the tip alone would not have warranted the stop, the Court said the stop was justified because the tip was sufficiently detailed and matched particulars that the officers themselves observed.

Michigan Department of State Police v. Sitz (496 U.S. 444), decided by a 6-3 vote, June 14, 1990. Rehnquist wrote the opinion; Brennan, Marshall and Stevens dissented.

Police may stop and examine drivers for signs of drunkenness at highway checkpoints.

The Court said that although the practice implicates Fourth Amendment protection, the checkpoints are not unreasonable "seizures" because states have a strong interest in deterring drunken driving, the checkpoints advance that interest and the intrusion on motorists stopped is "slight."

Illinois v. Rodriguez (497 U.S. 177), decided by a 6-3 vote, June 21, 1990. Scalia wrote the opinion; Marshall, Brennan and Stevens dissented.

Police may enter a residence without a warrant based on the consent of a third party who the police, at the time of entry, reasonably believe to possess authority over the premises but who in fact does not. Officers must act responsibly in evaluating the situation, but they need not always be correct. The determination of consent to enter must be objectively made.

California v. Hodari D. (499 U.S. 621), decided by a 7-2 vote, April 23, 1991. Scalia wrote the opinion; Stevens and Marshall dissented.

A youth who was running from police and dropped cocaine as he was being pursued was not "seized" within the meaning of the Fourth Amendment. The Court ruled that to constitute a seizure of the person either physical force or submission to an officer's show of authority must have occurred.

County of Riverside v. McLaughlin (500 U.S. ___), decided by a 5-4 vote, May 13, 1991. O'Connor wrote the opinion; Marshall, Blackmun, Stevens and Scalia dissented.

An individual may be jailed for up to 48 hours without a hearing before a magistrate to determine whether his arrest was proper. Citing the burdens on criminal justice systems, the Court said that local courts need flexibility to combine the probable cause hearing with a bail hearing or arraignment.

Florida v. Jimeno (500 U.S. ___), decided by a 7-2 vote, May 23, 1991. Rehnquist wrote the opinion; Marshall and Stevens dissented.

A criminal suspect's Fourth Amendment right to be free from unreasonable searches is not violated when, after he gives police permission to search his car, officers open a closed container found within the car that might reasonably hold the object of the search. Once a stopped motorist authorizes the search of the car for narcotics, he allows a search of all containers inside the car.

California v. Acevedo (500 U.S. ___), decided by a 6-3 vote, May 30, 1991. Blackmun wrote the opinion; White, Stevens and Marshall dissented.

Police do not need a warrant for a search of a car and all closed containers inside if police have probable cause that a container in the car holds contraband but lack probable cause for the entire vehicle. The Court said the ruling was aimed at ending confusion from conflicting rulings about whether probable cause in a specific case covered the whole car or only particular containers.

Florida v. Bostick (501 U.S. ___), decided by a 6-3 vote, June 20, 1991. O'Connor wrote the opinion; Marshall, Blackmun and Stevens dissented.

Police may approach passengers on buses and ask to search their luggage for illegal drugs without suspicion that the passengers are engaged in wrongdoing. The passengers have the right to refuse.

Self-Incrimination

Pennsylvania v. Bruder (488 U.S. 9), decided by a 7-2 vote, Oct. 31, 1988. *Per curiam* (unsigned) opinion; Stevens and Marshall dissented.

Evidence obtained from a field sobriety test and roadside questioning of a driver after a routine traffic stop was admissible despite failure to give the driver warnings beforehand. Ordinary traffic stops do not involve custody for the purposes of *Miranda*.

Duckworth v. Egan (492 U.S. 195), decided by a 5-4 vote, June 26, 1989. Rehnquist wrote the opinion; Marshall, Brennan, Blackmun and Stevens dissented.

Informing a suspect that an attorney would be appointed for him "if and when you go to court" does not render otherwise adequate *Miranda* warnings inadequate. *Miranda* does not require that attorneys be producible on call, but only that a suspect be informed of his rights and that police not question him unless he waives those rights.

Baltimore City Department of Social Services v. Bouknight (493 U.S. 549), decided by a 7-2 vote, Feb. 20, 1990. O'Connor wrote the opinion; Marshall and Brennan dissented.

A mother who has custody of her child through a court order cannot assert a Fifth Amendment privilege against self-incrimination to defend her refusal to produce the child. The Court said the mother in this case could be jailed until she revealed the whereabouts of her son, who authorities suspected was dead.

Michigan v. Harvey (494 U.S. 344), decided by a 5-4 vote, March 5, 1990. Rehnquist wrote the opinion; Stevens, Brennan, Marshall and Blackmun dissented.

Even when a criminal defendant is illegally interrogated by police, his responses may be used to impeach his testimony at trial. While the prosecution cannot be allowed to build its case against a criminal defendant with illegally obtained evidence, it can use such evidence to rebut the defendant's testimony and impeach his credibility.

Illinois v. Perkins (496 U.S. 292), decided by an 8-1 vote, June 4, 1990. Kennedy wrote the opinion; Marshall dissented.

An undercover police officer posing as an inmate need not give *Miranda* warnings to an incarcerated suspect before asking questions that may elicit an incriminating answer. The *Miranda* doctrine must be enforced only when a coercive atmosphere exists; such warnings are not required when the suspect is unaware that he is speaking to a police officer and volunteers a statement.

Pennsylvania v. Muniz (496 U.S. 582), decided by an 8-1 vote, June 18, 1990. Brennan wrote the opinion; Marshall dissented.

Videotaped sobriety tests showing a suspect's slurred speech in answering routine "booking" questions from police can be used as evidence in a trial even when the person arrested is not given a *Miranda* warning. By an 8-1 vote, the Court said that answers to such questions as a suspect's name, address, height, weight, eye color, date of birth and age constituted physical evidence, not testimonial evidence that would require *Miranda* warnings.

By a separate 5-4 vote, however, the Court held that the suspect's inability to give his birth date was testimonial evidence that should have been excluded because it could have implied a confused mental state. Dissenting from this portion of the decision were Rehnquist, White, Blackmun and Stevens.

Minnick v. Mississippi (498 U.S. 146), decided by a 6-2 vote, Dec. 3, 1990. Kennedy wrote the opinion; Scalia and Rehnquist dissented; Souter did not participate.

Once a suspect has invoked his right to counsel, police may not resume questioning him in custody without the suspect's having his lawyer present, even if he has consulted with counsel in the meantime. The Court extended a rule, established in *Edwards v. Arizona* (1981), requiring the police to stop interrogation after the accused asks for a lawyer.

Arizona v. Fulminante (499 U.S. 279), decided by separate 5-4 votes, March 26, 1991. White first wrote an opinion for five justices saying that a defendant's confession, based on the proper standard of totality of the circumstances, was coerced (Rehnquist, O'Connor, Kennedy and Souter dissented); Rehnquist then wrote for five justices that a coerced confession used at trial does not necessarily taint a conviction (White, Marshall, Blackmun and Stevens dissented); finally, White wrote for a new coalition of five justices that in this case the confession was not "harmless error" (Rehnquist, O'Connor and Scalia dissented; Souter did not sign on to either side for this part of the opinion).

The key legal ruling in the case was that a coerced confession does not automatically destroy a conviction. That decision reversed a 1967 ruling — *Chapman v. California*, 386 U.S. 18 — establishing that it was a denial of due process to use a forced confession against a defendant, regardless of other evidence.

Rehnquist, writing for five justices on the critical part of the case, said that if other evidence was enough to convict the defendant, a compelled confession may be "harmless error" — and thus not dictate a new trial.

McNeil v. Wisconsin (501 U.S. ___), decided by a 6-3 vote, June 13, 1991. Scalia wrote the opinion; Stevens, Marshall and Blackmun dissented.

Police may interrogate a suspect without his lawyer's presence even though the suspect just appeared with a lawyer at a hearing involving another crime. A suspect's invocation of the Sixth Amendment right to counsel during a judicial proceeding does not constitute an invocation of the right to counsel derived from the Fifth Amendment guarantee against self-incrimination in another crime.

Sentencing

Mistretta v. United States (488 U.S. 361), decided by an 8-1 vote, Jan. 18, 1989. Blackmun wrote the opinion; Scalia dissented.

In an important separation of powers ruling, the Court upheld the constitutionality of Congress' creation of the United States Sentencing Commission and the sentencing guidelines issued by the commission.

Congress did not delegate excessive legislative power to the commission, the Court held. Nor did it violate separation of powers principles by placing the commission within the judicial branch or providing for presidential appointment of judges to serve on the commission, as sentencing is a matter uniquely within the knowledge of members of the judiciary.

Alabama v. Smith (490 U.S. 794), decided by an 8-1 vote, June 12, 1989. Rehnquist wrote the opinion; Marshall dissented.

A judge may give a defendant a greater sentence after trial than previously imposed after a guilty plea. The "presumption of vindictiveness" that precludes an unexplained increase in sentence after a defendant wins a reversal of a conviction does not apply in such a case.

South Carolina v. Gathers (490 U.S. 805), decided by a 5-4 vote, June 12, 1989. Brennan wrote the opinion; O'Connor, Rehnquist, Scalia and Kennedy dissented.

A prosecutor's comments about personal characteristics of a murder victim required reversal of the defendant's death sentence. The comments were not relevant to the circumstances of the crime or to the defendant's moral culpability.

Hughey v. United States (495 U.S. 411), decided by a 9-0 vote, May 21, 1990. Marshall wrote the opinion.

A defendant who is told to make restitution under the 1982 Victim and Witness Protection Act may be ordered to make payments only for the loss stemming from his conviction. The decision overturned a lower court order that the defendant pay for losses relating to theft charges other than the single count of which he was convicted.

Taylor v. United States (495 U.S. 575), decided by a 9-0 vote, May 29, 1990. Blackmun wrote the opinion.

An offense constitutes a "burglary" for purposes of federal sentencing law if, regardless of its definition in state codes, it has the basic elements of a "generic" burglary: an unlawful entry into a building or other structure with intent to commit a crime.

Collins v. Youngblood (497 U.S. 37), decided by a 9-0 vote, June 21, 1990. Rehnquist wrote the opinion.

A defendant who was both imprisoned and fined for his crime is not entitled to a new trial when a new statute revises the law under which he was sentenced to remove the fine. A state statute that "reforms" an improper sentence does not violate the Ex Post Facto Clause of Article I of the Constitution.

Gozlon-Peretz v. United States (498 U.S. 395), decided by a 9-0 vote, Feb. 19, 1991. Kennedy wrote the opinion.

All drug offenses specified by the 1986 Anti-Drug Abuse Act fall under the requirements of "supervised release," as defined by the 1987 Sentencing Reform Act's provisions. The Court rejected the defendant's argument that because the sentencing guidelines did not become effective until Nov. 1, 1987, the term "supervised release" as used in the drug act had no significance before that date, and the courts had no power to impose it in cases involving offenses committed before that date.

Braxton v. United States (500 U.S. ___), decided by a 9-0 vote, May 28, 1991. Scalia wrote the opinion.

The Court ruled that a federal district judge had misapplied a provision of the *U.S. Sentencing Commission Guidelines Manual* by sentencing a defendant, who pleaded guilty to assault and firearms charges, as if he had been convicted of an attempt-to-kill count.

Chapman v. United States (500 U.S. ___), decided by a 7-2 vote, May 30, 1991. Rehnquist wrote the opinion; Stevens and Marshall dissented.

When the weight of the hallucinogenic drug LSD is being considered to determine sentencing, federal guidelines require that the blotter paper used to carry the drug be included in the weight. Because the statute at issue refers to a "mixture or substance containing a detectable amount," the entire mixture or substance is to be weighed when calculating the sentence.

Burns v. United States (501 U.S. ___), decided by a 5-4 vote, June 13, 1991. Marshall wrote the opinion; Souter, White, O'Connor and Rehnquist dissented.

A federal judge cannot give a defendant a harsher sentence than the range set by federal sentencing guidelines without providing advance notice to the parties that he is considering a departure from the guidelines and giving the reason for the step.

Harmelin v. Michigan (501 U.S. ___), decided by a 5-4 vote, June 27, 1991. Scalia wrote the opinion; White, Blackmun, Marshall and Stevens dissented.

A state may require life in prison without parole for a first-time drug offense without violating the constitutional ban on cruel and unusual punishment. Consideration of whether an individual deserves the particular statutory penalty is only necessary when a court is considering capital punishment.

Dawson v. Delaware (503 U.S. ___), decided by an 8-1 vote, March 9, 1992. Rehnquist wrote the opinion; Thomas dissented.

A murder defendant's First and 14th Amendment rights were violated when evidence was admitted about the racist activities of the Aryan Brotherhood because the evidence revealed only the defendant's abstract beliefs.

The Court said the sentencing jury wrongly took the membership into account because racial hatred was not an issue in the case and no "good" character evidence on race had been admitted.

Williams v. United States (503 U.S. ___), decided by a 7-2 vote, March 9, 1992. O'Connor wrote the opinion; White and Kennedy dissented.

When a district court relies on an improper ground in sentencing, an appeals court may not affirm a sentence based solely on its independent assessment of the reasonableness of the digression from the federal sentencing guidelines. The appeals court must conduct two separate inquiries: whether the sentence imposed violated the law or was an incorrect application of the guidelines and whether the sentence is an unreasonably high or low departure from the relevant guideline range.

United States v. R. L. C. (503 U.S. ___), decided by a 7-2 vote, March 24, 1992. Souter wrote the opinion; O'Connor and Blackmun dissented.

The Juvenile Delinquency Act requires a prison sentence to be limited to "the maximum term of imprisonment that would be authorized if the juvenile had been tried and convicted as an adult." The Court ruled that the limitation refers to the maximum sentence that could be imposed if the juvenile were being sentenced after application of the U.S. Sentencing Guidelines.

United States v. Wilson (503 U.S. ___), decided by a 7-2 vote, March 24, 1992. Thomas wrote the opinion; Stevens and White dissented.

In a case involving an inmate who wanted credit for the time he spent in jail before he was sentenced, the Court said the attorney general of the United States computes the amount of the credit, not a district court judge. At issue was whether a district court calculates the credit at the time of sentencing, as the defendant argued, or whether the attorney general computes it after the defendant began serving his sentence.

Foucha v. Louisiana (504 U.S. ___), decided by a 5-4 vote, May 18, 1992. White wrote the opinion; Kennedy, Rehnquist, Thomas and Scalia dissented.

A Louisiana statute that allows a defendant once judged to be insane to continue to be institutionalized even when he no longer suffers from mental illness violates constitutional due process. The statute said he could be held until he proved he was not dangerous to himself or to others. The Court said that once an insanity acquitee has recovered his sanity, the basis for confinement no longer exists.

Wade v. United States (504 U.S. ___), decided by a 9-0 vote, May 18, 1992. Souter wrote the opinion.

A federal district court may review the government's refusal to request a lower sentence for a defendant who aided government agents and may grant a remedy but only if the judge finds that the refusal was based on an unconstitutional motive. Neither a claim that a defendant provided substantial assistance nor general allegations of improper motive will entitle a defendant to a remedy, to

> ## Fair Trial
>
> In all criminal prosecutions, the accused shall enjoy the right to a speedy and public trial, by an impartial jury of the state and district wherein the crime shall have been committed . . . and to be informed of the nature and cause of the accusation; to be confronted with the witness against him; to have compulsory process for obtaining witnesses in his favor, and to have the assistance of counsel for his defense.
>
> Sixth Amendment, U.S. Constitution

discovery or to an evidentiary hearing on the issue. A defendant must make a "substantial threshold showing" of a constitutional violation first.

Sochor v. Florida (504 U.S. ___), decided by a 5-4 vote, June 8, 1992. Souter wrote the opinion; Rehnquist, White, Thomas and Scalia dissented.

When a court that is deciding whether a defendant should get the death penalty takes into consideration an invalid aggravating factor, an appeals court must determine whether it was a harmless error.

Speedy Trial

Doggett v. United States (505 U.S. ___), decided by a 5-4 vote, June 24, 1992. Souter wrote the opinion; O'Connor, Thomas, Rehnquist and Scalia dissented.

A delay of eight years between a defendant's indictment and arrest violated his Sixth Amendment right to a speedy trial. The Court said that U.S. officials were negligent in tracking the defendant and noted that the man did not know of his indictment before he left the country eight years earlier.

Miscellaneous Criminal Law Cases

Blanton v. City of North Las Vegas (489 U.S. 538), decided by a 9-0 vote, March 6, 1989. Marshall wrote the opinion.

Defendants charged with driving under the influence of alcohol under a state law providing a maximum prison term of six months are not entitled to a jury trial. Petty crimes or offenses punishable by up to six months are not subject to the Sixth Amendment's jury trial provision. The additional penalties under the law of up to a $1,000 fine and up to a 90-day suspension of driver's license also do not create a right to jury trial.

Schmuck v. United States (489 U.S. 705), decided by a 5-4 vote, March 22, 1989. Blackmun wrote the opinion; Scalia, Brennan, Marshall and O'Connor dissented.

Under the Federal Rules of Criminal Procedure, the use of a jury instruction on a lesser included offense is appropriate only when the elements of the lesser offense form a subset of the elements of the offense charged. Use of the "elements test" was settled doctrine at the time of the promulgation of the Rules. The elements test also is more certain and predictable in its application than the "inherent relationships" test because it involves an objective, textual comparison of criminal statutes and does not depend on inferences that may be drawn from evidence introduced at trial.

Gomez v. United States (490 U.S. 858), decided by a 9-0 vote, June 12, 1989. Stevens wrote the opinion.

A federal magistrate may not preside at the selection of a jury in a felony trial without the consent of the defendant. Presiding over jury selection is not one of the "additional duties" that a district court judge may assign to a magistrate under the Federal Magistrates Act.

Carella v. California (491 U.S. 263), decided by a 9-0 vote, June 15, 1989. *Per curiam* (unsigned) opinion.

Jury instructions establishing mandatory presumptions of theft by fraud or embezzlement after failure to return rented property within specified time periods violated the defendant's due process rights under the 14th Amendment. The presumptions improperly foreclosed independent jury consideration of the facts in the case and relieved the state of its burden of proving every element of the charged offenses beyond a reasonable doubt.

Duro v. Reina (495 U.S. 676), decided by a 7-2 vote, May 29, 1990. Kennedy wrote the opinion; Brennan and Marshall dissented.

An Indian tribe may not assert criminal jurisdiction over a non-member Indian. The sovereignty of a tribe to govern its own affairs does not include the authority to impose criminal sanctions against a citizen who is not a member.

Moskal v. United States (498 U.S. 103), decided by a 5-3 vote, Dec. 3, 1990. Marshall wrote the opinion; Scalia, O'Connor and Kennedy dissented; Souter did not participate.

A person who receives genuine vehicle titles with knowledge that they contain fraudulently tendered odometer readings does so knowing that the titles have been "falsely made" in violation of federal law. The Court rejected an argument by the defendant that the doctrine of lenity required the statute be interpreted to apply to forged or counterfeited securities.

Demarest v. Manspeaker (498 U.S. 184), decided by a 9-0 vote, Jan. 8, 1991. Rehnquist wrote the opinion.

Federal law requires payment of witness fees to a convicted state prisoner who testifies at a federal trial under a writ of habeas corpus ad testificandum (used to order a prisoner to give testimony). The Court said that the statutory witness fee provision makes clear that the fees provision referring to a "witness in attendance at any court of the United States" includes prisoners unless they otherwise are exempted in the statute.

Cheek v. United States (498 U.S. 192), decided by a 6-2 vote, Jan. 8, 1991. White wrote the opinion; Blackmun and Marshall dissented; Souter did not participate.

A taxpayer who asserts a "good faith" belief that he does not have to pay taxes cannot be held criminally liable for willfully violating tax laws. Breaches of tax law require "willfulness," the Court said, to protect the average citizen from prosecution for innocent mistakes made because of the complexity of the tax laws.

Touby v. United States (500 U.S. ___), decided by a 9-0 vote, May 20, 1991. O'Connor wrote the opinion.

A statutory provision giving the U.S. attorney general broad power to classify drugs as illegal substances was not an unconstitutional delegation by Congress of its legislative powers. The decision upheld a 1984 federal law aimed at so-called designer drugs that gave the attorney general emergency power to temporarily designate drugs as illegal substances if the attorney general found it was "necessary to avoid an imminent hazard to the public safety."

Yates v. Evatt (500 U.S. ___), decided by a 9-0 vote, May 28, 1991. Souter wrote the opinion.

The South Carolina Supreme Court failed to apply the proper harmless error standard of a 1967 case — *Chapman v. California*, 386 U.S. 18 — to jury instructions that were found unconstitutional. *Chapman* held that an error is harmless only if it appears beyond a reasonable doubt that the error did not contribute to the verdict obtained.

Peretz v. United States (501 U.S. ___), decided by a 5-4 vote, June 27, 1991. Stevens wrote the opinion; Marshall, White, Blackmun and Scalia dissented.

Magistrates may supervise jury selection in a felony trial if the parties agreed to have magistrates fill in for federal judges. The Court said that the Federal Magistrates Act's "additional duties" clause allows a magistrate to supervise jury selection and that a defendant has no constitutional right to have a judge preside at jury selection if he has raised no objection to the judge's absence.

Riggins v. Nevada (504 U.S. ___), decided by a 7-2 vote, May 18, 1992. O'Connor wrote the opinion; Thomas and Scalia dissented.

Forcing a defendant to take an anti-psychotic drug during his murder trial violated the defendant's rights under the Sixth and 14th Amendments. A state cannot force drugs on a mentally ill defendant without showing that the treatment is medically appropriate and "essential" for the safety of the defendant or others.

Evans v. United States (504 U.S. ___), decided by a 6-3 vote, May 26, 1992. Stevens wrote the opinion; Thomas, Rehnquist and Scalia dissented.

Prosecutors trying to demonstrate that a public official is guilty of extortion need not prove that the official demanded a payoff. An affirmative act of inducement is not an element of extortion "under color of official right" prohibited by the Hobbs Act.

Election Law

Eu v. San Francisco County Democratic Central Committee (489 U.S. 214), decided by an 8-0 vote, Feb. 22, 1989. Marshall wrote the opinion; Rehnquist did not participate.

California laws that prohibit the official governing bodies of political parties from endorsing or opposing candidates in primary elections violate the First Amendment. The laws burden the parties' freedom of speech and association while serving no compelling governmental interest.

The Court also struck down on similar First Amendment grounds other California statutes regulating the size, composition and selection of political parties' official governing bodies.

Board of Estimate of City of New York v. Morris (489 U.S. 688), decided by a 9-0 vote, March 22, 1989. White wrote the opinion.

The structure of New York City's Board of Estimate is inconsistent with the Equal Protection Clause of the 14th Amendment because each of the five boroughs has equal representation on the board despite the boroughs' widely disparate populations. The governmental interests claimed by the city do not suffice to justify a 78 percent deviation from the one-person, one-vote ideal, particularly because the city could be served by alternative ways of constituting the board that would minimize the discrimination in voting power.

Quinn v. Millsap (491 U.S. 95), decided by a 9-0 vote, June 15, 1989. Blackmun wrote the opinion.

A land-ownership requirement for appointment to a local government board of freeholders authorized to propose a reorganization of local government violates the Equal Protection Clause. The fact that the board can only propose a reorganization and cannot enact laws of its own does not immunize it from equal protection scrutiny.

Austin v. Michigan State Chamber of Commerce (494 U.S. 652), decided by a 6-3 vote, March 27, 1990. Marshall wrote the opinion; Kennedy, O'Connor and Scalia dissented.

A Michigan campaign finance law barring corporations from spending money directly from their own treasuries for political campaigns does not infringe the First Amendment. The government has a compelling interest in eliminating from the political process the corrosive effect of political contributions amassed with the aid of the legal advantages given to corporations.

McCormick v. United States (500 U.S. ___), decided by a 6-3 vote, May 23, 1991. White wrote the opinion; Stevens, Blackmun and O'Connor dissented.

An extortion conviction under the federal Hobbs Act arising from an elected official's receipt of a campaign contribution requires a "quid pro quo" — the realization of some benefit to the contributor as a condition that the money be given. Payments are illegal only when they are taken in return for a promise to perform or not to perform a special act.

Renne v. Geary (501 U.S. ___), decided by a 6-3 vote, June 17, 1991. Kennedy wrote the opinion; White, Marshall and Blackmun dissented.

Democratic political activists who sued the state of California over its law prohibiting political parties from endorsing, supporting or opposing candidates for non-partisan offices did not demonstrate a dispute ripe for resolution by the federal courts. The plaintiffs' allegations failed to show any actual threat to a particular individual's or group's free speech rights.

Norman v. Reed; Cook County Officers Electoral Board v. Reed (502 U.S. ___), decided by a 7-1 vote, Jan. 14, 1992. Souter wrote the opinion; Scalia dissented; Thomas did not participate.

An Illinois election law that sought to keep a new party off the ballot in 1990 violated the First Amendment right of political association and the 14th Amendment right of equal protection of the laws.

Provisions of the Illinois statute in question limited access to the ballot by new parties by preventing a "new political party" in Cook County from using the name of a party already established in the city of Chicago and by requiring more than twice as many signatures to qualify the slate in Cook County than were required to field candidates for statewide office.

Department of Commerce v. Montana (503 U.S. ___), decided by a 9-0 vote, March 31, 1992. Stevens wrote the opinion.

Congress acted within its broad discretion over apportionment of members of the House of Representatives when it provided, in a 1941 statute, for using a particular mathematical method — called the "method of equal proportions" — for determining the number of representatives from each state.

The Court said the principle of "one person, one vote" is impossible to achieve precisely in the area of congressional apportionment because the Constitution guarantees each state at least one representative and prohibits House districts that cross state lines. Neither mathematical analysis nor constitutional interpretation can conclusively answer the question of which of several mathematical techniques is best to reduce the inevitable degree of inequality.

Burson v. Freemam (504 U.S. ___), decided by a 5-3 vote, May 26, 1992. Blackmun wrote the opinion; Stevens, O'Connor and Souter dissented; Thomas did not participate.

A Tennessee statute that bars the solicitation of votes and the distribution of campaign materials within 100 feet of the entrance to a polling place potentially encompassing streets and sidewalks does not violate political speech rights. Legislatures should be permitted to protect voters from interference and intimidation, provided the approach is reasonable and does not significantly impinge on free speech rights.

Burdick v. Takushi (504 U.S. ___), decided by a 6-3 vote, June 8, 1992. White wrote the opinion; Kennedy, Blackmun and Stevens dissented.

A Hawaii ban on write-in voting is a limited and permissible infringement of citizens' First and 14th Amendment rights. The state's asserted interest in avoiding "party raiding" during the primaries and unrestrained factionalism at the general election is legitimate and sufficient to outweigh the limited burden that the write-in voting ban imposes.

Franklin v. Massachusetts (505 U.S. ___), decided by a 9-0 vote, June 26, 1992. O'Connor wrote the opinion.

The statement submitted by the president to Congress after the 1990 census showing the number of persons in each state and the number of representatives that would be apportioned to each state was not a "final agency action" subject to judicial review for abuse of discretion under the Administrative Procedure Act (APA). The report submitted by the secretary of commerce to the president also was not subject to review under the APA because it was only a recommendation, not a final action.

The Court also upheld as constitutional the secretary's decision to allocate military personnel living abroad to their home states using "home of record" data in their personnel files. The judgment that many federal employees stationed abroad retained their ties to their states was consonant with the text and history of the U.S. Constitution.

Environmental Law

Robertson v. Methow Valley Citizens Council (490 U.S. 332), decided by a 9-0 vote, May 1, 1989. Stevens wrote the opinion.

The National Environmental Policy Act (NEPA) does not require federal agencies to mitigate adverse environmental effects or to include a fully developed mitigation plan in an environmental impact statement. NEPA also imposes no duty that the agency make a "worst case" analysis in its environmental impact statement if it cannot make a reasoned assessment of the impact of a proposed project.

Marsh v. Oregon Natural Resources Council (490 U.S. 360), decided by a 9-0 vote, May 1, 1989. Stevens wrote the opinion.

A federal appeals court's conclusion that an agency's final environmental impact statement supplement was defective because of failure to include a mitigation plan or "worst case" analysis was erroneous for the reasons stated in *Robertson v. Methow Valley Citizens Council,* 490 U.S. 332 (1989). The agency's decision not to prepare a second supplement after receipt of new information was not arbitrary or capricious and thus should not be set aside.

Pennsylvania v. Union Gas Co. (491 U.S. 1), decided by a 5-4 vote, June 15, 1989. Brennan wrote the opinion; Scalia, Rehnquist, O'Connor and Kennedy dissented.

The Superfund Amendments and Reauthorization Act of 1986 permits a private suit for monetary damages against a state in federal court to recover costs of cleaning up a hazardous waste site. Congress has the authority to create such a cause of action when legislating pursuant to the Commerce Clause despite the 11th Amendment's limits on federal court suits against the states.

Hallstrom v. Tillamook County (493 U.S. 20), decided by a 7-2 vote, Nov. 7, 1989. O'Connor wrote the opinion; Marshall and Brennan dissented.

A provision in the 1976 Resource Conservation and Recovery Act requiring anyone suing under the act to notify the state and Environmental Protection Agency at least 60 days before filing is mandatory and cannot be disregarded by district courts. Failure to comply with the provision requires the district court to dismiss the lawsuit.

General Motors Corp. v. United States (496 U.S. 529), decided by a 9-0 vote, June 14, 1990. Blackmun wrote the opinion.

The Environmental Protection Agency retains the right to penalize a business for air pollution even if the agency has delayed ruling on state-authorized revisions by the companies to remedy the pollution problem. Nothing in federal law limits the agency's authority to enforce antipollution rules solely in those cases in which it has not unreasonably delayed action on state plan revisions for implementing the Clean Air Act.

Lujan v. National Wildlife Federation (497 U.S. 871), decided by a 5-4 vote, June 27, 1990. Scalia wrote the opinion; Blackmun, Brennan, Marshall and Stevens dissented.

The National Wildlife Federation lacked standing to broadly challenge the Department of Interior's reclassification of public lands.

Affidavits filed by the federation from individual members were not specific enough as to who would be hurt by the reclassification.

Arkansas v. Oklahoma; Environmental Protection Agency v. Oklahoma (503 U.S. ___), decided by a 9-0 vote, Feb. 26, 1992. Stevens wrote the opinion.

An Environmental Protection Agency (EPA) decision to issue a permit for an Arkansas sewage treatment plant was within the agency's authority, although the plant's discharge would not meet the water quality standards of a downstream state (Oklahoma).

The Court said that the EPA has the authority to require that downstream state water standards generally prevail. But it also upheld the EPA's determination that the Arkansas discharge would not cause detectable harm to Oklahoma's water quality.

Robertson v. Seattle Audubon Society (503 U.S. ___), decided by a 9-0 vote, March 25, 1992. Thomas wrote the opinion.

Congress' temporary suspension of certain environmental laws that were subject to dispute in pending court cases did not violate constitutional separation of powers. A 1989 mandate temporarily freeing timber sales from most court-ordered bans amounted to a new law instead of an order for specific results under the old law.

Department of Energy v. Ohio; Ohio v. Department of Energy (503 U.S. ___), decided by a 6-3 vote, April 21, 1992. Souter wrote the opinion; White, Blackmun and Stevens dissented.

Congress has not waived the federal government's sovereign immunity from civil penalties sought to be imposed by a state for pollution violations of the Clean Water Act and the Resource Conservation and Recovery Act of 1976. The federal acts did not contain the requisite unequivocal waivers, so the federal government was protected from lawsuits.

Chemical Waste Management Inc. v. Hunt (504 U.S. ___), decided by an 8-1 vote, June 1, 1992. White wrote the opinion; Rehnquist dissented.

States may not discriminate against other states by imposing a special fee on out-of-state hazardous waste discarded at an in-state commercial facility. An Alabama law that set up a two-tier fee system for disposal of wastes generated in and outside the state violated the Commerce Clause.

Fort Gratiot Landfill Inc. v. Michigan Department of Natural Resources (504 U.S. ___), decided by a 7-2 vote, June 1, 1992. Stevens wrote the opinion; Rehnquist and Blackmun dissented.

A Michigan statute that restricts the disposal of out-of-county waste discriminates against interstate commerce. The law barred private landfill operators from accepting solid waste generated in another county, state or country unless officials of the county that would receive the waste explicitly authorized it.

Lujan v. Defenders of Wildlife (504 U.S. ___), decided by a 7-2 vote, June 12, 1992. Scalia wrote the opinion; Blackmun and O'Connor dissented.

An environmental group does not have standing to sue the government over an interpretation of the Endangered Species Act because the group failed to show that it was sufficiently injured by the law. The group, which was challenging an Interior Department interpretation that the law did not apply to federally financed projects overseas, had failed to demonstrate that its members would be hurt by U.S. practices abroad.

Gade v. National Solid Wastes Management Association (505 U.S. ___), decided by a 5-4 vote, June 18, 1992. O'Connor wrote the opinion; Souter, Blackmun, Stevens and Thomas dissented.

States cannot impose licensing and training requirements on hazardous waste site operators that are stricter than federal law.

The Court ruled that regulations under the Occupational Safety and Health Act pre-empt Illinois laws regarding the licensing of workers at certain hazardous waste facilities. The Federal act pre-empts all state laws that directly and substantially regulate workers' health and safety.

New York v. United States (505 U.S. ___), decided by a 6-3 vote, June 19, 1992. O'Connor wrote the opinion; White, Blackmun and Stevens dissented.

A key part of a federal law intended to make states responsible for the low-level radioactive waste they generate unconstitutionally violated state sovereignty as guaranteed by the 10th Amendment.

The provision in question required any state that failed to provide for the disposal of waste generated within its borders to take legal title to the waste and assume liability for any injuries the waste causes.

Family Law

Mansell v. Mansell (490 U.S. 581), decided by a 7-2 vote, May 30, 1989. Marshall wrote the opinion; Blackmun and O'Connor dissented.

A state court has no power to treat, as property divisible upon divorce, military retirement pay that the retiree waived to receive veterans' disability benefits. The Uniformed Services Former Spouses Protection Act plainly allows state courts to treat as community property only a retiree's disposable retirement pay, not the total retirement pay.

Michael H. v. Gerald D. (491 U.S. 110), decided by a 5-4 vote, June 15, 1989. Scalia wrote the opinion; White, Brennan, Marshall and Blackmun dissented.

The Court refused to invalidate a state law that establishes a conclusive presumption, except in certain limited circumstances, that a child born to a married woman living with her husband is a child of the marriage. The statute does not violate the procedural or substantive due process rights of a putative father of the child.

Federal Government

Executive Power

Perpich v. Department of Defense (496 U.S. 334), decided by a 9-0 vote, June 11, 1990. Stevens wrote the opinion.

The president has the power to order National Guard units to training missions outside the United States without the approval of state governors. The Court said a law giving the president such power fell within the power granted to Congress under the Constitution to regulate military affairs.

Federal Employees

Carlucci v. Doe (488 U.S. 93), decided by a 9-0 vote, Dec. 6, 1988. White wrote the opinion.

An employee of the National Security Agency (NSA) may be removed without a hearing under the authority of the 1959 National Security Act. NSA regulations permitting removal with limited procedural rights for the employee are not superseded by other statutory provisions that require a pretermination hearing or a determination that national security prevents such procedures.

Karahalios v. National Federation of Federal Employees, Local 1263 (489 U.S. 527), decided by a 9-0 vote, March 6, 1989. White wrote the opinion.

The 1978 Civil Service Reform Act does not give a federal employee a private cause of action against a union for allegedly breaching its statutory duty of fair representation of the employee. Such claims must be adjudicated administratively before the Federal Labor Relations Authority with a right of appeal by the losing party to a federal court of appeals.

American Foreign Service Association v. Garfinkel (490 U.S. 153), decided by a 9-0 vote, April 18, 1989. *Per curiam* (unsigned) opinion.

A revision of a non-disclosure form that federal employees must sign as a condition of obtaining access to classified information rendered partly moot a lawsuit challenging use of the form. A lower court's decision that a congressional ban on use of the form impermissibly intruded on executive authority to protect national security was vacated. The suit was remanded for consideration of other issues.

Crandon v. United States; Boeing Co. v. United States (494 U.S. 152), decided by a 9-0 vote, Feb. 27, 1990. Stevens wrote the opinion.

A federal law that makes it a crime for a private party to supplement a government worker's salary does not cover funds paid before the individual actually begins federal work. An individual must be on the government payroll before that worker or the private firm involved can be held liable.

Internal Revenue Service v. Federal Labor Relations Authority (494 U.S. 922), decided by a 6-3 vote, April 17, 1990. Scalia wrote the opinion; Brennan, Marshall and Stevens dissented.

The Civil Service Reform Act of 1978 does not compel a federal agency to negotiate with federal employee unions over how to resolve disputes stemming from the government policy of "contracting out," the buying of goods and services from private businesses. The act is not intended to interfere with agency officials' authority to make their own decisions on contracting out.

Fort Stewart Schools v. Federal Labor Relations Authority (495 U.S. 641), decided by a 9-0 vote, May 29, 1990. Scalia wrote the opinion.

The Department of Defense must bargain with unions over wages and fringe benefits paid to civilian teachers at Army-run schools.

Air Courier Conference of America v. American Postal Workers Union (498 U.S. 517), decided by a 9-0 vote, Feb. 26, 1991. Rehnquist wrote the opinion.

Postal employees may not challenge the U.S. Postal Service's use of private courier services known as international remailing. The workers are not within the "zone of interests" of the Private Express Statutes, regulating mail delivery, so they do not have standing to challenge the Postal Service's use of private couriers to handle certain international delivery.

Federal Regulation

Dole v. United Steelworkers of America (494 U.S. 26), decided by a 7-2 vote, Feb. 21, 1990. Brennan wrote the opinion; White and Rehnquist dissented.

The federal Office of Management and Budget (OMB) has no authority under the Paperwork Reduction Act to block another agency's order that businesses disclose health and safety data to their employees or the public. The Court said the paperwork law empowered OMB to review requests for data intended for government use but did not extend to regulations meant to generate information for the benefit of a third party.

Office of Personnel Management v. Richmond (496 U.S. 414), decided by a 7-2 vote; June 11, 1990. Kennedy wrote the opinion; Marshall and Brennan dissented.

The federal government is not prohibited from cutting benefits to a recipient who became ineligible because of a government employee's incorrect answers about eligibility. The government need not pay for its mistakes if the payment would require disbursement of benefits not authorized by law.

Martin v. Occupational Safety and Health Review Commission (499 U.S. 144), decided by a 9-0 vote, March 20, 1991. Marshall wrote the opinion.

Final authority for interpreting ambiguous standards under the 1970 Occupational Safety and Health Act (OSHA) rests with the secretary of labor, not with the Occupational Safety and Health Review Commission. The act gives the labor secretary power to set and enforce workplace health and safety standards while the commission is assigned adjudicatory functions.

The Court said that Congress did not intend to sever the power to interpret OSHA regulations from the secretary's power to promulgate and enforce them. The Court said that federal courts should defer to the secretary when the secretary and the commission give reasonable but conflicting interpretations of regulations under the act.

United States v. Gaubert (499 U.S. 315), decided by a 9-0 vote, March 26, 1991. White wrote the opinion.

The federal government cannot be sued for damages arising from banking regulators' negligent handling of the day-to-day operations of troubled savings and loan institutions. The Court said a regulator is shielded from liability under the Federal Tort Claims Act because his actions presumably flowed from policies at the heart of federal banking statutes.

Board of Governors of the Federal Reserve System v. MCorp Financial Inc.; MCorp v. Board of Governors of the Federal Reserve System (502 U.S. ___), decided by an 8-0 vote, Dec. 3, 1991. Stevens wrote the opinion; Thomas did not participate.

Federal courts lack jurisdiction to hear a challenge to the Federal Reserve Board's "source of strength" regulation — a rule requiring bank holding companies to be responsible for the financial viability of their subsidiary banks — while the board is conducting its own administrative enforcement proceedings under the regulation. The 1966 Financial Institutions Supervisory Act forbids a court from affecting such administrative proceedings by injunction or otherwise.

Freedom of Information

U.S. Department of Justice v. Reporters Committee for Freedom of the Press (489 U.S. 749), decided by a 9-0 vote, March 22, 1989. Stevens wrote the opinion.

Disclosure of the contents of an FBI rap sheet to a third party could reasonably be expected to constitute an unwarranted invasion of personal privacy and therefore is prohibited by Exemption 7(C) of the Freedom of Information Act.

Public Citizen v. Department of Justice; Washington Legal Foundation v. Department of Justice (491 U.S. 440), decided by an 8-0 vote, June 21, 1989. Brennan wrote the opinion; Scalia did not participate.

The public record and open meeting requirements of the Federal Advisory Committee Act do not apply to the Justice Department's solicitation of the views of the American Bar Association's Standing Committee on the Federal Judiciary on prospective judicial nominees. Congress did not intend the act to cover every formal and informal consultation between the president or an executive agency and a group rendering advice.

Department of Justice v. Tax Analysts (492 U.S. 136), decided by an 8-1 vote, June 23, 1989. Marshall wrote the opinion; Blackmun dissented.

The Freedom of Information Act requires the Department of Justice to make available copies of district court decisions that it receives in the course of litigating tax cases. The department improperly "withheld" the decisions when it refused requests for them despite their public availability from the courts that issued the decisions.

John Doe Agency v. John Doe Corp. (493 U.S. 146), decided by a 6-3 vote, Dec. 11, 1989. Blackmun wrote the opinion; Stevens, Scalia and Marshall dissented.

Materials gathered for a law enforcement purpose, but not originally created for such purpose, are exempt from disclosure under the Freedom of Information Act's allowance for "records or information compiled for law enforcement purposes."

Department of State v. Ray (502 U.S. ___), decided by an 8-0 vote, Dec. 16, 1991. Stevens wrote the opinion; Thomas did not participate.

Public disclosure of the names of Haitians who were deported from the United States and later interviewed by the U.S. government to determine whether they were prosecuted in their homeland would be an unwarranted invasion of the returnees' privacy under one of the exceptions in the Freedom of Information Act. The Court said the invasion of privacy from summaries containing personal details about particular returnees, while of little importance when the returnees' identities are unknown, is significant when the information is linked to particular individuals.

Indians

Oklahoma Tax Commission v. Graham (489 U.S. 838), decided by a 9-0 vote, March 29, 1989. *Per curiam* (unsigned) opinion.

An action brought against an Indian tribe seeking to collect unpaid state excise taxes was improperly removed to federal court. The possible existence of a tribal immunity defense under federal law does not provide an independent basis for federal jurisdiction.

Mississippi Band of Choctaw Indians v. Holyfield (490 U.S. 30), decided by a 6-3 vote, April 3, 1989. Brennan wrote the opinion; Stevens, Rehnquist and Kennedy dissented.

Federal law giving Indian tribal courts exclusive jurisdiction over Indian children domiciled on tribal reservations establishes a uniform federal law of domicile. An Indian child is domiciled on the reservation if his or her parents are members of the tribe even if the child is born off the reservation and surrendered for adoption without ever being on the reservation. State courts may not apply a state law definition of "domicile" to determine jurisdiction over Indian children in state adoption proceedings.

Cotton Petroleum Corp. v. New Mexico (490 U.S. 163), decided by a 6-3 vote, April 25, 1989. Stevens wrote the opinion; Blackmun, Brennan and Marshall dissented.

A state may impose severance taxes on the production of oil and gas on Indian reservations even if it also is subject to the Indiana tribe's own severance tax. The state tax is not pre-empted by federal law and does not constitute an unlawful multiple tax burden on interstate commerce.

California v. United States (490 U.S. 920), affirmed by a 4-4 vote, June 12, 1989. *Per curiam* (unsigned) opinion; Marshall did not participate.

A judgment that the United States, by litigating to obtain water rights for an Indian tribe, did not waive its sovereign immunity to any other proceeding that might affect those rights was affirmed by an equally divided Court.

Wyoming v. United States (492 U.S. 406), affirmed by a 4-4 vote, June 26, 1989. *Per curiam* (unsigned) opinion; O'Connor did not participate.

The evenly divided Court affirmed the Wyoming Supreme Court's ruling that the 1868 treaty establishing the Wind River Indian Reservation reserved water for the use of Indians and that reacquired lands on the ceded portion of the reservation are reservation lands subject to the treaty.

Brendale v. Confederated Tribes and Bands of the Yakima Indian Nation; Wilkinson v. Confederated Tribes and Bands of the Yakima Indian Nation; County of Yakima v. Confederated Tribes and Bands of the Yakima Indian Nation (492 U.S. 408), decided by votes of 6-3, 5-4 and 6-3, June 29, 1989. Stevens wrote the opinion; White, Rehnquist, Scalia and Kennedy dissented on one point; Blackmun, Brennan and Marshall dissented on another.

The Yakima Indian tribe did not retain zoning authority with respect to property owned by non-members located in the "open" portion of the reservation in which about half of the land is owned by non-members. The vote on this point was 6-3.

By a 5-4 vote, however, the Court held that the tribe did have exclusive zoning authority with respect to property owned by non-members within the "closed" portion of the tribal reservation in which only a very small percentage of land is owned by non-members.

Powers of Congress

United States v. Munoz-Flores (495 U.S. 385), decided by a 9-0 vote May 21, 1990. Marshall wrote the opinion.

A 1984 act imposing a "special assessment" penalty on persons convicted of a federal misdemeanor was not a "bill for raising revenue" that under the Constitution must originate in the House of Representatives. The Court said the 1984 Victims of Crime Act — first introduced in the Senate — was not a revenue measure within the meaning of the Origination Clause because it supported a special program and not general government operations. The Court also rejected an argument by the Bush administration that the case challenging the law presented a political question that exempted it from judicial scrutiny.

Metropolitan Washington Airports Authority v. Citizens for the Abatement of Aircraft Noise Inc. (501 U.S. ___), decided by a 6-3 vote, June 17, 1991. Stevens wrote the opinion; White, Rehnquist and Marshall dissented.

An interstate airport authority, initiated by Congress to be independent but whose directors were subject to veto power by a review board composed of members of Congress, violated the separation of powers doctrine. The Court said Congress exceeded its powers by dictating in such detail the structure of the airport authority, its membership and powers.

Social Security and Welfare

Bowen v. Georgetown University Hospital (488 U.S. 204), decided by a 9-0 vote, Dec. 12, 1988. Kennedy wrote the opinion.

The secretary of health and human services has no authority under the Medicare Act to issue retroactive rules setting cost limits on reimbursements to health care providers for treating Medicare patients.

Sullivan v. Zebley (493 U.S. 521), decided by a 7-2 vote, Feb. 20, 1990. Blackmun wrote the opinion; White and Rehnquist dissented.

The method used by the secretary of health and human services to decide whether a child is "disabled" and therefore eligible for benefits under the Supplemental Security Income (SSI) program is too restrictive. The Court ruled that the method did not meet the statutory requirement that SSI benefits shall be provided to children with "any ... impairment of comparable severity" to an impairment that would make an adult "unable to engage in any substantial gainful activity."

Sullivan v. Everhart (494 U.S. 83), decided by a 5-4 vote, Feb. 21, 1990. Scalia wrote the opinion; Stevens, Brennan, Marshall and Kennedy dissented.

The secretary of health and human services need not give Social Security or welfare recipients a method by which to appeal when the agency underpays benefits to offset overpayments from years earlier.

Sullivan v. Stroop (496 U.S. 478), decided by a 5-4 vote, June 14, 1990. Rehnquist wrote the opinion; Blackmun, Brennan, Marshall and Stevens dissented.

Insurance benefits paid to children under Title II of the Social Security Act do not constitute "child support" payments subject to be disregarded when determining eligibility under Aid to Families with Dependent Children (AFDC). In upholding the policy — which has the effect of lowering AFDC benefits — the Court said that "child support" is a term of art referring only to payments from absent parents.

Wilder v. Virginia Hospital Association (496 U.S. 498), decided by a 5-4 vote, June 14, 1990. Brennan wrote the opinion; Rehnquist, O'Connor, Scalia and Kennedy dissented.

Hospitals and nursing homes may use a federal civil rights law, Section 1983 of Title 42, to pursue higher Medicaid reimbursement rates from the states. The ruling allowed health care providers to sue to enforce a 1980 amendment to the federal Medicaid act that requires states to reimburse health care providers at rates that are "reasonable and adequate."

Sullivan v. Finkelstein (496 U.S. 617), decided by a 8-1 vote, June 18, 1990. White wrote the opinion; Blackmun dissented.

The secretary of health and human services may immediately appeal a district court order that effectively invalidates a Social Security benefit eligibility requirement. Such an order should be considered a "final decision" under federal statute, qualifying a party to appeal.

First Amendment

Church and State

Frazee v. Illinois Department of Employment Security (489 U.S. 829), decided by a 9-0 vote, March 29, 1989. White wrote the opinion.

The denial of unemployment compensation to an individual who refuses to work on Sunday because of sincerely held religious beliefs violates the First Amendment's free exercise of religion clause. It does not matter that the individual's refusal is not in response to the commands of a particular religious organization or sect.

Hernandez v. Commissioner of Internal Revenue; Graham v. Commissioner of Internal Revenue (490 U.S. 680), decided by a 5-2 vote, June 5, 1989. Marshall wrote the opinion; O'Connor and Scalia dissented; Brennan and Kennedy did not participate.

Payments made to branches of the Church of Scientology for "auditing" and "training" sessions are not deductible charitable contributions. The payments are not "contributions" or "gifts" within the meaning of the Internal Revenue Code. Disallowing a deduction for the payments does not violate the Establishment Clause or the Free Exercise of Religion Clause.

Allegheny County v. American Civil Liberties Union, Greater Pittsburgh Chapter (492 U.S. 573), decided by 5-4 and 6-3 votes, July 3, 1989. Blackmun wrote the opinion; Kennedy, Rehnquist, White and Scalia dissented from one part of the decision; Brennan, Marshall and Stevens dissented from another part.

Allegheny County violated the Establishment Clause when it placed a creche on its courthouse staircase with a banner declaring "Gloria in Excelsis Deo" (which translates "Glory to God in the Highest"). The vote on this point was 5-4. But it was not an unconstitutional establishment of religion for the county to include a menorah as part of a display outside another government building along with a Christmas tree. The vote on this point was 6-3.

Jimmy Swaggart Ministries v. Board of Equalization of California (493 U.S. 378), decided by a 9-0 vote, Jan. 17, 1990. O'Connor wrote the opinion.

The constitutional separation of church and state does not bar a state from taxing religious books, tapes and other materials sold by religious organizations. The Court said the California sales and use taxes in question do not significantly burden religious practices or cause excessive entanglement with religion so as to be in conflict with the Establishment Clause of the First Amendment.

Employment Division, Department of Human Resources of Oregon v. Smith (494 U.S. 872), decided by a 6-3 vote, April 17, 1990. Scalia wrote the opinion; Blackmun, Brennan and Marshall dissented.

A state may outlaw the sacramental use of the drug peyote without having to prove that it has a "compelling interest" in enforcing a statute that infringes on religious freedom. The First Amendment is not breached by an otherwise valid state law that has the incidental effect of prohibiting the exercise of religion.

Davis v. United States (495 U.S. 472), decided by a 9-0 vote, May 21, 1990. O'Connor wrote the opinion.

Parents who gave money to their two sons who were serving as missionaries for the Church of Jesus Christ of Latter-day Saints cannot deduct the funds as charitable contributions because they were not donated for the specific use of the church. The Court said the church never was directly in control of the funds and the sons were able to use the money as they chose.

Board of Education of the Westside Community Schools v. Mergens (496 U.S. 226), decided by an 8-1 vote, June 4, 1990. O'Connor wrote the opinion; Stevens dissented.

A federal law requiring that student religious groups be allowed to meet in public high schools on the same basis as other extracurricular clubs does not violate the constitutional requirement of separation of church and state. Congress did not pass the law to endorse religion, but to achieve a secular purpose of preventing discrimination against religious and other types of speech.

Lee v. Weisman (505 U.S. ___), decided by a 5-4 vote, June 24, 1992. Kennedy wrote the opinion; Scalia, Rehnquist, White and Thomas dissented.

The inclusion of prayers as part of a public high school graduation ceremony compels religious conformance by students and thus violates the First Amendment's Establishment Clause. Prayer exercises in public schools carry a particular risk of indirect coercion of religious belief.

Commercial Speech

Frank v. Minnesota Newspaper Association (490 U.S. 225), decided by a 6-3 vote, April 25, 1989. *Per curiam* (unsigned) opinion; White, Marshall and Stevens dissented.

An appeal of a ruling that held unconstitutional a ban on newspapers' non-commercial publication of lists of lottery winners was declared moot. Because the postmaster general conceded after the ruling that the statutory provision does not apply to non-commercial publication, a live controversy as to its constitutionality no longer existed.

Board of Trustees of State University of New York v. Fox (492 U.S. 469), decided by a 6-3 vote, June 29, 1989. Scalia wrote the opinion; Blackmun, Brennan and Marshall dissented.

A state university's regulation of commercial solicitation in student dormitory rooms is not invalid merely because it goes beyond the least restrictive means to achieve desired ends. The regulation is valid under the First Amendment if it is narrowly tailored to achieve significant government interests in promoting an educational atmosphere, promoting safety and security, preventing commercial exploitation of students and preserving residential tranquility.

Religion, Speech and Press

Congress shall make no law respecting an establishment of religion, or prohibiting the free exercise thereof; or abridging the freedom of speech, or of the press; or the right of the people peaceably to assemble, and to petition the Government for a redress of grievances.

First Amendment, U.S. Constitution

Freedom of Expression

City of Dallas v. Stanglin (490 U.S. 19), decided by a 9-0 vote, April 3, 1989. Rehnquist wrote the opinion.

A municipal ordinance that restricts admission to certain dance halls to persons between the ages of 14 and 18 does not violate the First Amendment or the 14th Amendment's Equal Protection Clause. Recreational dancing does not come within the protection of the First Amendment. The age restriction is rationally related to the city's interest in promoting the welfare of teenagers by reducing the likelihood of their involvement with alcohol, illegal drugs or promiscuous sex.

Texas v. Johnson (491 U.S. 397), decided by a 5-4 vote, June 21, 1989. Brennan wrote the opinion; Rehnquist, White, Stevens and O'Connor dissented.

The First Amendment guarantee of freedom of expression precludes a state from punishing someone for desecrating the American flag in the course of a peaceful political demonstration.

Massachusetts v. Oakes (491 U.S. 576), decided by a 6-3 vote, June 21, 1989. O'Connor wrote the opinion; Brennan, Marshall and Stevens dissented.

The Court remanded to state court a challenge to a conviction under a Massachusetts law prohibiting adults from posing or exhibiting minors "in a state of nudity" for purposes of visual representation or reproduction in any medium. An intervening amendment of the statute rendered the defendant's facial challenge to the law on overbreadth grounds moot. The case was remanded for a determination of whether the statute could be applied to the defendant's photographing of his teen-aged daughter while she posed bare-breasted.

Ward v. Rock Against Racism (491 U.S. 781), decided by a 6-3 vote, June 22, 1989. Kennedy wrote the opinion; Marshall, Brennan and Stevens dissented.

New York City sound amplification guidelines for use of a city-owned outdoor theater, specifying the city will provide sound equipment and sound technicians for all performances, do not violate the First Amendment. The guidelines are a reasonable place and manner regulation, given that they are content-neutral, narrowly tailored to serve significant governmental interests and leave open ample alternative channels of communication. The court of appeals erred in requiring the city to prove the guidelines were the least intrusive means of furthering its interests.

FW/PBS Inc. v. City of Dallas; M. J. R. Inc. v. City of Dallas; Berry v. City of Dallas (493 U.S. 215), decided by a 6-3 vote, Jan. 9, 1990. O'Connor wrote the opinion; Rehnquist, Scalia and White dissented.

A local ordinance regulating "sexually oriented businesses" unconstitutionally constrained free speech by failing to include a deadline for a municipality's decision on a license application and not allowing for prompt judicial review of denial.

Butterworth v. Smith (494 U.S. 624), decided by a 9-0 vote, March 21, 1990. Rehnquist wrote the opinion.

States cannot prohibit grand jury witnesses from disclosing their testimony once the grand jury has completed a case. The Court said the law violated free speech rights.

United States v. Eichman (496 U.S. 310), decided by a 5-4 vote, June 11, 1990. Brennan wrote the opinion; Rehnquist, White, Stevens and O'Connor dissented.

Flag burning in the course of political protest is a right guaranteed by the First Amendment. The decision, invalidating a 1989 law making it a crime to burn, mutilate or otherwise destroy a U.S. flag, followed the Court's 1989 decision in *Texas v. Johnson*, 491 U.S. 397, striking down a similar state law.

Rutan v. Republican Party of Illinois; Frech v. Rutan (497 U.S. 62), decided by a 5-4 vote, June 21, 1990. Brennan wrote the opinion; Scalia, Rehnquist, Kennedy and O'Connor dissented.

Hiring, promotion and transfer policies based on political party affiliation violate the First Amendment rights of public employees unless party membership is "an appropriate requirement" for the job.

United States v. Kokinda (497 U.S. 720), decided by a 5-4 vote, June 27, 1990. O'Connor wrote the opinion; Brennan, Marshall, Stevens and Blackmun dissented.

A U.S. Postal Service regulation that prohibits solicitation of contributions on postal premises does not violate the First Amendment when it is used to bar solicitations by a political group. Government ownership of property does not automatically open that property to the public.

Barnes v. Glen Theatre Inc. (501 U.S. ___), decided by a 5-4 vote, June 21, 1991. Rehnquist wrote the opinion; White, Marshall, Blackmun and Stevens dissented.

States may ban nude dancing as part of public indecency laws without breaching the First Amendment right of expression. A law intended to protect social order and morality may incidentally infringe on nude dancing as a form of expression.

Simon & Schuster Inc. v. Members of New York State Crime Victims Board (502 U.S. ___), decided by an 8-0 vote, Dec. 10, 1991. O'Connor wrote the opinion; Thomas did not participate.

A New York law that prohibited paying criminals to tell their stories violates the First Amendment. The decision struck down the so-called "Son of Sam" law that required any money owed to the convict-writer be paid to a special fund to compensate the criminal's victims.

The Court found the law overly broad because it applied to works on any subject that expressed the author's thoughts about his crime, however tangentially or incidentally, and because it covered authors who admitted to committing a crime, whether or not they were accused or convicted.

Forsyth County v. Nationalist Movement (505 U.S. ___), decided by a 5-4 vote, June 19, 1992. Blackmun wrote the opinion; Rehnquist, White, Scalia and Thomas dissented.

A county ordinance requiring that organizers of a parade pay up to $1,000 for police protection violates the free speech guarantee of the First Amendment.

The ordinance did not provide "narrowly drawn, reasonable and definite standards," as the administrator was free to decide not to assess the fee and was not obligated to provide an explanation for actions taken. The ordinance also was unconstitutionally content-based because the administrator had to evaluate the message or purpose of marchers to determine security for the demonstration or parade.

R. A. V. v. City of St. Paul (505 U.S. ___), decided by a 9-0 vote, June 22, 1992. Scalia wrote the opinion; White, Blackmun, Stevens and O'Connor differed with a key part of the opinion.

Cities may not single out for legal punishment "hate speech" based on race, color, creed, religion or gender. Although some areas of speech, such as obscenity or defamation, can be constitutionally proscribed, the general presumption against content-based regulation prevents the government from prohibiting speech on the basis of the subject addressed in the speech.

Four justices concurring separately joined in striking down the local hate-speech ordinance challenged in the case but disagreed with the Court's holding. They said they would have found the ordinance unconstitutionally overbroad but would have allowed some government regulations based on categorizing different types of speech.

International Society for Krishna Consciousness Inc. v. Lee (505 U.S. ___), decided by a 6-3 vote, June 26, 1992. Rehnquist wrote the opinion; Souter, Blackmun and Stevens dissented.

Government authorities may forbid solicitations for money within airport terminals. The majority held that airports are not traditional forums for public speech and that the ban met the standards for reasonableness applicable to regulations in non-public forums.

A separate majority (Kennedy, O'Connor, Souter, Blackmun and Stevens) ruled in *Lee v. International Society for Krishna Consciousness* that a ban on distributing literature within airport terminals was invalid.

Freedom of the Press

Texas Monthly Inc. v. Bullock (489 U.S. 1), decided by a 6-3 vote, Feb. 21, 1989. Brennan wrote the opinion; Scalia, Rehnquist and Kennedy dissented.

The Court struck down a state statute that exempted religious periodicals but not other publications from sales taxes. The exemption violated the First Amendment's Establishment Clause.

Florida Star v. B. J. F. (491 U.S. 524), decided by a 6-3 vote, June 21, 1989. Marshall wrote the opinion; White, Rehnquist and O'Connor dissented.

The First Amendment precludes punishment of a newspaper for publishing truthful information that it has lawfully obtained unless the punishment is narrowly tailored to a state interest of the highest order. Imposition of civil damages under Florida's rape-victim privacy statute did not further such an interest where a newspaper obtained the victim's identity from a police report mistakenly made available in a press room, where liability was imposed on a per se negligence basis and where the statute was facially underinclusive in applying only to the mass media.

Harte-Hanks Communications Inc. v. Connaughton (491 U.S. 657), decided by a 9-0 vote, June 22, 1989. Stevens wrote the opinion.

A showing of highly unreasonable conduct constituting an extreme departure from journalistic standards does not suffice to support a verdict in favor of a public figure plaintiff in a libel action. A court of appeals correctly applied the actual malice standard despite language that suggested use of the professional standards rule. The court of appeals also correctly found that evidence supported a finding of actual malice, although it should have taken a different approach in reaching that result.

Milkovich v. Lorain Journal Co. (497 U.S. 1), decided by a 9-0 vote, June 21, 1990. Rehnquist wrote the opinion.

Statements of opinion do not enjoy a special privilege under the First Amendment and are within the reach of state libel law.

The First Amendment's guarantee of a free airing of public issues must be balanced by social values that serve as a basis for defamation law and society's interest in preventing attacks on reputation.

Leathers v. Medlock; Medlock v. Leathers (499 U.S. 439), decided by a 7-2 vote, April 16, 1991. O'Connor wrote the opinion; Marshall and Blackmun dissented.

An Arkansas sales tax extended to cable television services, but with an exemption for print media, does not violate the First Amendment unless it is likely to inhibit the free exchange of ideas. At issue was a sales tax on personal property and services. The Court said cable companies could win the discrimination lawsuit only if the Arkansas tax scheme endangered the free expression of ideas.

Masson v. The New Yorker (501 U.S. ___), decided by a 7-2 vote, June 20, 1991. Kennedy wrote the opinion; White and Scalia dissented.

Fabricated quotes may be found libelous if they are published with knowledge of falsity or give a different meaning to what the speaker actually said. A deliberate alteration of a plaintiff's words does not mean knowledge of falsity unless the alteration is a material change in the statement's meaning.

Cohen v. Cowles Media Inc. (501 U.S. ___), decided by a 5-4 vote, June 24, 1991. White wrote the opinion; Blackmun, Marshall, Souter and O'Connor dissented.

The First Amendment does not shield the news media from lawsuits for breaking promises of confidentiality to their sources. The state doctrine of promissory estoppel, which protects people who rely to their detriment on promises from others, applies to all citizens' daily transactions without targeting or singling out the press.

Obscenity

Fort Wayne Books Inc. v. Indiana; Sapenfield v. Indiana (489 U.S. 46), decided by a 6-3 vote, Feb. 21, 1989. White wrote the opinion; Stevens, Brennan and Marshall dissented in part.

A state may include obscenity violations among the predicate offenses of an anti-racketeering law. The statute is not unconstitutionally vague, nor does the Constitution bar the enhanced punishments for obscenity violations under the act.

By a 9-0 vote, however, the Court ruled that the pretrial seizure of an entire bookstore and its contents was improper because no determination had been made that the seized items were obscene or that a racketeering violation had occurred.

Supreme Court

Sable Communications of California Inc. v. Federal Communications Commission; Federal Communications Commission v. Sable Communications of California Inc. (492 U.S. 115), decided by a 6-3 vote, June 23, 1989. White wrote the opinion; Brennan, Marshall and Stevens dissented.

Federal law prohibiting interstate commercial transmission of "dial-a-porn" messages is constitutional insofar as it applies to obscene messages, but unconstitutional insofar as it applies to messages that are merely "indecent." The ban on indecent telephone messages violates the First Amendment because the denial of adult access to such messages goes beyond what is necessary to serve the compelling interest of preventing minors from being exposed to such messages.

Osborne v. Ohio (495 U.S. 103), decided by a 6-3 vote, April 18, 1990. White wrote the opinion; Brennan, Marshall and Stevens dissented.

A state may ban the private possession of pornographic pictures of children. A state's interest in the physical and psychological well-being of a minor is compelling and overrides potential First Amendment concerns.

Immigration Law

McNary v. Haitian Refugee Center (498 U.S. 479), decided by a 7-2 vote, Feb. 20, 1991. Stevens wrote the opinion; Rehnquist and Scalia dissented.

Federal courts have the power to rule on constitutional challenges to the Immigration and Naturalization Service's procedures granting amnesty for certain alien farm workers. Because the immigration law does not clearly preclude federal jurisdiction and because the workers were seeking constitutional relief, a federal court could hear the claims.

Ardestani v. Immigration and Naturalization Service (502 U.S. ___), decided by a 6-2 vote, Dec. 10, 1991. O'Connor wrote the opinion; Stevens and Blackmun dissented; Thomas did not participate.

Administrative deportation proceedings are not adversary adjudications and, as a result, are not covered by a provision of the Equal Access to Justice Act allowing winning parties to receive attorneys' fees and costs. Under the doctrine of sovereign immunity, which generally protects the government from liability for attorneys' fees, any ambiguity in the act's fee recovery provision is construed in favor of the government.

Immigration and Naturalization Service v. National Center for Immigrants' Rights Inc. (502 U.S. ___), decided by a 9-0 vote, Dec. 16, 1991. Stevens wrote the opinion.

The U.S. attorney general has the authority to forbid the employment of foreigners who have been released on bond while awaiting rulings on whether they may remain in the United States. The rule is consistent with the established concern of immigration law to preserve jobs for American workers and thus is squarely within the scope of the attorney general's statutory authority.

Immigration and Naturalization Service v. Doherty (502 U.S. ___), decided by a 5-3 vote, Jan. 15, 1992. Rehnquist wrote the opinion; Scalia, Stevens and Souter dissented in part; Thomas did not participate.

A former leader of the Irish Republican Army must abide by the U.S. attorney general's ruling that he be deported to Great Britain, where he was convicted for the murder of a British officer in Northern Ireland. The Court ruled that Joseph Patrick Doherty exhausted his legal grounds for further hearing and that the attorney general did not abuse his discretion in overturning a decision by the Board of Immigration Appeals that would have allowed Doherty to make new arguments for political asylum in the United States.

Immigration and Naturalization Service v. Elias-Zacarias (503 U.S. ___), decided by a 6-3 vote, Jan. 22, 1992. Scalia wrote the opinion; Stevens, O'Connor and Blackmun dissented.

A Guatemalan guerrilla organization's attempt to coerce a person into joining does not necessarily constitute "persecution on account of . . . political opinion" under federal immigration law for purposes of making the individual eligible for asylum in the United States. The victim's political opinion, not the persecutor's, is at the core of a test for persecution.

Individual and Civil Rights

Abortion

Webster v. Reproductive Health Services (492 U.S. 490), decided by a 5-4 vote, July 3, 1989. Rehnquist wrote the opinion; Blackmun, Brennan, Marshall and Stevens dissented.

Without overturning *Roe v. Wade*, 410 U.S. 113 (1973), the Court upheld Missouri's law barring the use of public facilities or public employees to perform abortions and requiring physicians to test for the viability of any fetus believed to be more than 20 weeks old.

Hodgson v. Minnesota (497 U.S. 417), decided by separate 5-4 votes, June 25, 1990. Stevens wrote the opinion; Scalia, Kennedy, Rehnquist and White dissented.

A provision of a state statute that required an unmarried woman under 18 to notify both biological parents of an abortion decision was held unconstitutional. A separate majority (O'Connor, Scalia, Kennedy, Rehnquist and White) found the remainder of the statute constitutional because it provided the option of a judicial hearing for a pregnant teenager who did not want to tell her parents about her decision.

Ohio v. Akron Center for Reproductive Health (497 U.S. 502), decided by a 6-3 vote, June 25, 1990. Kennedy wrote the opinion; Blackmun, Brennan and Marshall dissented.

A state statute requiring an unmarried woman under 18 to tell at least one parent of an abortion decision or, in the alternative, to appear before a judge is constitutional.

Rust v. Sullivan (500 U.S. ___), decided by a 5-4 vote, May 23, 1991. Rehnquist wrote the opinion; Blackmun, Marshall, Stevens and O'Connor dissented.

An administrative agency may forbid workers at publicly funded clinics from counseling pregnant women on abortion. Title X of the Public Health Service Act of 1970, which prohibits use of federal funds in "programs where abortion is a method of family planning," may be read to bar use of funds not only for abortions but also for abortion counseling. That construction of the law does not violate the constitutional rights of doctors and health clinics who challenged the regulation.

Planned Parenthood of Southeastern Pennsylvania v. Casey; Casey v. Planned Parenthood of Southeastern Pennsylvania (505 U.S. ___), decided by 5-4 and 7-2 votes, June 29, 1992. O'Connor, Kennedy and Souter wrote the opinion; Rehnquist, White, Scalia, and Thomas dissented in part; Blackmun and Stevens dissented in part.

The Court reaffirmed that a woman has a constitutional right to an abortion, upholding the centerpiece of *Roe v. Wade*, 410 U.S. 113 (1973). But the Court changed the legal test for determining whether a state is interfering with an abortion choice by ruling that the standard should be whether a regulation puts an "undue burden" on a woman seeking an abortion before the fetus is viable.

Applying that standard, the Court voted 7-2 to uphold provisions in a Pennsylvania law that required a 24-hour waiting period and informed consent before a woman can obtain an abortion. But by a 5-4 vote, it struck down a provision that said a woman seeking an abortion must sign a statement that she had notified her husband.

Affirmative Action

City of Richmond v. J. A. Croson Co. (488 U.S. 469), decided by a 6-3 vote, Jan. 23, 1989. O'Connor wrote the opinion; Marshall, Brennan and Blackmun dissented.

A minority set-aside plan adopted by Richmond, Va., to ensure that 30 percent of city funds granted for construction projects went to minority-owned firms was too rigid and insufficiently justified by past findings of specific discrimination.

Metro Broadcasting Inc. v. Federal Communications Commission; Astroline Communications Co. Ltd. Partnership v. Shurberg Broadcasting of Hartford Inc. (497 U.S. 547), decided by a 5-4 vote, June 27, 1990. Brennan wrote the opinion; O'Connor, Rehnquist, Scalia and Kennedy dissented.

Congress may order preferential treatment of blacks and other minorities to increase their ownership of broadcast licenses. "Benign race-conscious measures" adopted by Congress, including those that do not compensate victims of past discrimination, are constitutional as long as they further important governmental objectives.

The decision upheld two types of set-aside programs: one gave special credit to minorities applying for new licenses, and the other required some radio and television stations to be sold only to minority-controlled companies. Congress in 1987 had blocked the Federal Communications Commission from dismantling the programs.

Age Discrimination

Public Employees Retirement System of Ohio v. Betts (492 U.S. 158), decided by a 7-2 vote, June 23, 1989. Kennedy wrote the opinion; Marshall and Brennan dissented.

Age-based distinctions in bona fide employee-benefit plans are exempted from the Age Discrimination in Employment Act as long as the plan is not a method of discriminating in other, non-fringe-benefit aspects of the employment relationship. An employee seeking to challenge an employee-benefit plan as a subterfuge to evade the purposes of the act has the burden of proving that the disputed provision was intended to serve a discriminatory purpose.

Stevens v. Department of the Treasury (500 U.S. ___), decided by a 9-0 vote, April 24, 1991. Blackmun wrote the opinion.

A federal employee who intends to bring an age-discrimination complaint directly to federal court must notify the Equal Employment Opportunity Commission (EEOC) of his intent to file the action within 180 days after the alleged incident occurred but need not file suit within 30 days of giving notice. The Court said a lower court misread a federal statute when it said an employee had to notify the EEOC within 30 days before bringing suit.

Gilmer v. Interstate/Johnson Lane Corp. (500 U.S. ___), decided by a 7-2 vote, May 13, 1991. White wrote the opinion; Stevens and Marshall dissented.

A worker's claim under the Age Discrimination in Employment Act of 1967 can be subjected to compulsory arbitration if the worker previously signed an agreement to arbitrate all employment disputes.

Astoria Federal Savings & Loan Association v. Solimino (501 U.S. ___), decided by a 9-0 vote, June 10, 1991. Souter wrote the opinion.

A worker whose age-discrimination claim was reviewed and rejected by a state administrative agency is not precluded from filing a lawsuit in federal court. The law makes clear that collateral estoppel — the legal doctrine that bars further litigation because of a prior judgment in the case — does not apply to state agency findings, as distinguished from court findings.

Gregory v. Ashcroft (501 U.S. ___), decided by a 7-2 vote, June 20, 1991. O'Connor wrote the opinion; Blackmun and Marshall dissented.

Missouri's mandatory retirement requirement for judges does not violate the Age Discrimination in Employment Act of 1967. The authority of a state to determine the qualifications of its governmental officials lies "at the heart of representative government" and is reserved under the 10th Amendment.

Attorneys' Fees

Rhodes v. Stewart (488 U.S. 1), decided by a 6-3 vote, Oct. 17, 1988. *Per curiam* (unsigned) opinion; Blackmun, Brennan and Marshall dissented.

Attorney's fees were improperly awarded in a federal civil rights suit brought by two prison inmates who were no longer in the state's custody when the district court entered a declaratory judgment in their favor. The entry of a declaratory judgment that does not affect the behavior of the defendant toward the plaintiff does not render the plaintiff a prevailing party for purposes of the award of attorney's fees.

Blanchard v. Bergeron (489 U.S. 87), decided by a 9-0 vote, Feb. 21, 1989. White wrote the opinion.

An attorney's fee awarded in a federal civil rights suit is not limited to the amount provided in the plaintiff's contingent fee arrangement with his counsel.

Supreme Court

Texas State Teachers Association v. Garland Independent School District (489 U.S. 782), decided by a 9-0 vote, March 28, 1989. O'Connor wrote the opinion.

A litigant in a federal civil rights suit need not prevail on the central issue in a case to be awarded attorneys' fees as the "prevailing party." Attorneys' fees may be awarded if the litigant succeeds on "any significant issue" that materially alters the legal relationship between the parties.

Sullivan v. Hudson (490 U.S. 877), decided by a 5-4 vote, June 12, 1989. O'Connor wrote the opinion; White, Rehnquist, Scalia and Kennedy dissented.

A federal court may award attorney's fees under the Equal Access to Justice Act to a Social Security claimant for representation during administrative proceedings following a remand from the court. The administrative proceedings are part of the ongoing "civil action" within the meaning of the act.

Missouri v. Jenkins (491 U.S. 274), decided by a 5-3 vote, June 19, 1989. Brennan wrote the opinion; O'Connor, Rehnquist and Scalia dissented; Marshall did not participate.

The 11th Amendment does not prevent a federal court from increasing an award of attorney's fees against a state in a federal civil rights suit to compensate for the state's delay in payment. The work of paralegals and law clerks in such a case may be compensated at market rates instead of the actual cost to the attorneys.

Independent Federation of Flight Attendants v. Zipes (491 U.S. 754), decided by a 6-2 vote, June 22, 1989. Scalia wrote the opinion; Marshall and Brennan dissented; Stevens did not participate.

A federal court may award attorney's fees in an employment discrimination case against an intervening party that is not charged with Title VII violations only if the intervenor's action is frivolous, unreasonable or without foundation. Assessing fees against blameless intervenors is not essential to the central purpose of the attorney's fee provision: to give victims of wrongful discrimination an incentive to file suit.

Venegas v. Mitchell (495 U.S. 82), decided by a 9-0 vote, April 18, 1990. White wrote the opinion.

Lawyers who win civil rights cases in federal court and receive fees from the losing party may still collect a portion of a client's award, pursuant to a contingent fee agreement. The attorneys' fee provision of federal civil rights law was intended to control what a losing defendant must pay, not what a prevailing plaintiff must pay his lawyer.

Commissioner, Immigration and Naturalization Service v. Jean (496 U.S. 154), decided by a 9-0 vote, June 4, 1990. Stevens wrote the opinion.

Under the Equal Access to Justice Act — which provides for the awarding of attorneys' fees and other expenses to a private party in a suit against the government — once a court determines that the government's position was not "substantially justified," a second finding is unnecessary for the awarding of costs in any subsequent related litigation. The initial finding serves as a "one-time threshold" for fee eligibility.

West Virginia University Hospitals Inc. v. Casey (499 U.S. 83), decided by a 6-3 vote, March 19, 1991. Scalia wrote the opinion; Marshall, Stevens and Blackmun dissented.

Winning parties in civil rights litigation cannot recover expert witness fees as part of reasonable attorneys' fees under a 1976 federal law. The provision for award of "a reasonable attorney's fee" — Section 1988 of Title 42 — means only that and was not written by Congress to include fees for experts' services.

Kay v. Ehrler (499 U.S. 432), decided by a 9-0 vote, April 16, 1991. Stevens wrote the opinion.

An attorney who successfully represents himself in a civil rights lawsuit may not be awarded attorneys' fees under Section 1988 of Title 42. The overriding goal of the statute — to ensure that victims of civil rights violations are able to hire lawyers for the effective prosecution of their claims — is served best by a rule that creates an incentive to retain counsel instead of a disincentive to hire a lawyer whenever a party believes himself competent to represent himself.

Chambers v. NASCO Inc. (501 U.S. ___), decided by a 5-4 vote, June 6, 1991. White wrote the opinion; Scalia, Kennedy, Rehnquist and Souter dissented.

A district court judge may require one party to pay the other party's attorneys' fees and expenses as a sanction for the first party's bad-faith conduct. The power to impose sanctions against a party that has abused the court system falls within the court's inherent power to manage its own proceedings and to control the conduct of those who appear before it. And nothing in the Federal Rules of Civil Procedure, including Rule 11 governing lawyers' behavior and allowing sanctions, precludes a court from imposing attorneys' fees as punishment for bad faith.

Melkonyan v. Sullivan (501 U.S. ___), decided by a 9-0 vote, June 10, 1991. O'Connor wrote the opinion.

A decision made by an administrative agency is not a "final judgment" for purposes of triggering the 30-day period in the Equal Access to Justice Act for a winning party in a civil rights action against the United States to apply for an award of attorneys' fees, court costs and other expenses. The law requires a final judgment to be entered by a court, before the 30-day deadline starts to run.

City of Burlington v. Dague (505 U.S. ___), decided by a 6-3 vote, June 24, 1992. Scalia wrote the opinion. Blackmun, Stevens and O'Connor dissented.

The attorneys' fees provisions in two federal environmental laws — the Solid Waste Disposal Act and the Clean Water Act — do not allow fees to be paid beyond what would be a "reasonable rate" for the "reasonable hours" worked, even when an attorney took the case on a contingency basis and expected to earn a percentage of the court award.

Children

DeShaney v. Winnebago County Department of Social Services (489 U.S. 189), decided by a 6-3 vote, Feb. 22, 1989. Rehnquist wrote the opinion; Brennan, Marshall and Blackmun dissented.

A county social services agency that failed to protect a child from severe beatings by his father did not violate the child's rights under the Due Process Clause. The Due Process Clause imposes no duty on the state to provide members of the general public with adequate protective services.

Suter v. Artist M. (503 U.S. ___), decided by a 7-2 vote, March 25, 1992. Rehnquist wrote the opinion; Blackmun and Stevens dissented.

Foster children may not use a federal civil rights law to sue states that fail to make reasonable efforts to prevent the removal of children from homes and to reunite families as required by a 1980 law. The Court said the Adoption Assistance and Child Welfare Act does not give its beneficiaries a private right of action under the civil rights law intended to redress constitutional violations under color of law.

Damage Suits

Owens v. Okure (488 U.S. 227), decided by a 9-0 vote, Jan. 10, 1989. Marshall wrote the opinion.

The time period for filing a federal civil rights suit against state officials under 42 U.S.C. Section 1983 is to be determined by the state's general or residual statute of limitations governing personal injury suits, not the statute of limitations for a specific intentional tort.

City of Canton v. Harris (489 U.S. 378), decided by a 6-3 vote, Feb. 28, 1989. White wrote the opinion; O'Connor, Scalia and Kennedy dissented.

A municipality may, in certain circumstances, be held liable under federal civil rights law for constitutional violations resulting from its failure to train its employees. Inadequate police training may be a basis for liability if the failure to train amounts to deliberate indifference to the constitutional rights of persons with whom the police come into contact.

Graham v. Connor (490 U.S. 386), decided by a 9-0 vote, May 15, 1989. Rehnquist wrote the opinion.

All claims that law enforcement officials have used excessive force in the course of an arrest, investigatory stop or other "seizure" are properly analyzed under the Fourth Amendment's "objective reasonableness" standard. This inquiry asks whether the officers' actions were "objectively reasonable" in light of the facts and circumstances confronting the officials, without regard to their underlying intent or motivation.

Hardin v. Straub (490 U.S. 536), decided by a 9-0 vote, May 22, 1989. Stevens wrote the opinion.

A federal court applying a state statute of limitations to an inmate's federal civil rights action should give effect to the state's provision that extends the time for prisoners to file such suits. Michigan law tolls the limitations period for persons under a legal disability, including prisoners, until one year after the disability has been removed.

Will v. Michigan Department of State Police (491 U.S. 58), decided by a 5-4 vote, June 15, 1989. White wrote the opinion; Brennan, Marshall, Blackmun and Stevens dissented.

Neither states nor state officials acting in their official capacities are "persons" subject to federal suit under 42 U.S.C. Section 1983 for depriving an individual of his or her constitutional rights under color of state law.

Jett v. Dallas Independent School District; Dallas Independent School District v. Jett (491 U.S. 701), decided by a 5-4 vote, June 22, 1989. O'Connor wrote the opinion; Brennan, Marshall, Blackmun and Stevens dissented.

A municipality cannot be held vicariously liable for its employees' violations of the federal civil rights statute — 42 U.S.C. Section 1981 — that guarantees equal rights to make contracts. The express cause of action created by 42 U.S.C. Section 1983 for deprivation of rights under color of law provides the exclusive remedy for rights guaranteed by Section 1981 when the claim is asserted against a state actor.

Zinermon v. Burch (494 U.S. 113), decided by a 5-4 vote, Feb. 27, 1990. Blackmun wrote the opinion; O'Connor, Rehnquist, Scalia and Kennedy dissented.

A man confined against his will at a Florida state mental hospital, without benefit of a hearing, may sue state officials in federal court for money damages under Section 1983 of Title 42. The state has a duty to use procedural safeguards in dealing with patients incompetent to consent to voluntary admission.

Ngiraingas v. Sanchez (495 U.S. 182), decided by a 6-2 vote, April 24, 1990. Blackmun wrote the opinion; Brennan and Marshall dissented; Kennedy did not participate.

Neither the territory of Guam nor territory officials acting in their official capacity can be sued under Section 1983 of Title 42. The 1871 law was mostly concerned with racial unrest in the southern states and was not intended to subject the territories to liability.

Howlett v. Rose (496 U.S. 356), decided by a 9-0 vote, June 11, 1990. Stevens wrote the opinion.

School officials subject to a lawsuit based on Section 1983 cannot invoke a "sovereign immunity" defense applicable to claims raised under state law. States cannot exempt themselves from federal laws.

Dennis v. Higgins (498 U.S. 439), decided by a 7-2 vote, Feb. 20, 1991. White wrote the opinion; Kennedy and Rehnquist dissented.

Lawsuits for violations of the Commerce Clause may be brought under Section 1983 of Title 42, a civil rights law that allows individuals to sue for deprivation of "any rights, privileges, or immunities secured by the Constitution and [federal] laws." The Court said the broad construction of Section 1983 and the idea of "rights" cover state law that might interfere with free interstate trade.

Siegert v. Gilley (500 U.S. ___), decided by a 6-3 vote, May 23, 1991. Rehnquist wrote the opinion; Marshall, Blackmun and Stevens dissented.

A clinical psychologist who claimed that his former employer, a federal hospital, infringed his "liberty" interests by giving him a bad recommendation failed to state a claim for a violation of any constitutional right. An injury to reputation by itself is not a protected liberty interest.

Hafer v. Melo (502 U.S. ___), decided by an 8-0 vote, Nov. 5, 1991. O'Connor wrote the opinion; Thomas did not participate.

The federal law that prohibits depriving a person of his or her civil rights "under color of state law" permits state officials to be held personally liable for actions taken in their official capacity. The decision reinstated a suit by workers who claimed they were fired by a state official without due process and in violation of their First Amendment rights.

The Court said the civil rights law was enacted to enforce due process against those who carry the badge of a state. The capacity in which a person is sued, not the capacity in which he acted, determines the liability.

Collins v. City of Harker Heights (503 U.S. ___), decided by a 9-0 vote, Feb. 26, 1992. Stevens wrote the opinion.

Municipalities have no constitutional obligation to create a safe workplace, even if their failure to warn workers about hazards arises from deliberate indifference. The failure to train or warn employees about known hazards in the workplace does not constitute a violation of the Due Process Clause that would give rise to a claim under the federal civil rights law for depriving a person of his civil rights under color of law.

McCarthy v. Madigan (503 U.S. ___), decided by a 9-0 vote, March 4, 1992. Blackmun wrote the opinion.

A federal inmate need not exhaust a prison's internal grievance procedure before filing a civil rights lawsuit for money damages in federal court. The Court said that, given the nature of the prisoner's claims of abuse and the time-consuming prison grievance process, the inmate's individual interests outweigh concerns favoring exhaustion of the grievance process, such as protecting agency authority and promoting judicial efficiency.

Disabled Persons

Dellmuth v. Muth (491 U.S. 223), decided by a 5-4 vote, June 15, 1989. Kennedy wrote the opinion; Brennan, Marshall, Blackmun and Stevens dissented.

The Education of Handicapped Act does not abrogate states' 11th Amendment immunity from suits in federal court. The amendment therefore bars a suit by the parent of a handicapped child for reimbursement of private school tuition after the state's alleged failure to provide the child a free public education appropriate to his needs.

Housing Discrimination

Town of Huntington v. Huntington Branch, NAACP (488 U.S. 15), decided by a 6-3 vote, Nov. 7, 1988. *Per curiam* (unsigned) opinion; White, Marshall and Stevens dissented.

The record in a housing discrimination complaint brought under Title VIII of the Civil Rights Act of 1968 showed that the town's zoning restriction on location of multi-family housing projects had a disparate racial impact and that the town's justification for the restriction was inadequate. A portion of the court of appeals judgment directing the town to rezone the site of a proposed project will not be reviewed because that portion of the case does not implicate the court's mandatory jurisdiction.

Spallone v. United States; Chema v. United States; Longo v. United States (493 U.S. 265), decided by a 5-4 vote, Jan. 10, 1990. Rehnquist wrote the opinion; Brennan, Marshall, Blackmun and Stevens dissented.

A federal judge abused his power when he imposed contempt fines against city officials in Yonkers, N.Y., who had refused to vote for a court-ordered housing desegregation plan. Traditional equitable principles dictate that federal judges use the least amount of power necessary to win compliance with an order.

The Court upheld fines against the city but said the judge should have waited a "reasonable time" to see if those fines resulted in compliance before sanctioning individual city council members.

Job Discrimination

Price Waterhouse v. Hopkins (490 U.S. 228), decided by a 6-3 vote, May 1, 1989. Brennan wrote the opinion; Kennedy, Rehnquist and Scalia dissented.

An employee who shows that an impermissible motive played a part in an adverse employment decision places the burden on the employer to show that the same decision would have been made in the absence of the unlawful motive. The burden of proof on the employer to avoid a finding of liability in such a case is preponderance of the evidence.

Wards Cove Packing Co. v. Atonio (490 U.S. 642), decided by a 5-4 vote, June 5, 1989. White wrote the opinion; Stevens, Brennan, Marshall and Blackmun dissented.

Making it more difficult for workers to prove racial discrimination against certain ethnic groups by citing statistics that show a particular group is under-represented in a particular workforce, the Court held that a showing that certain employer policies did produce such under-representation can be rebutted by the employer if it can demonstrate that a reasonable business justification exists for its policies.

Martin v. Wilks; Personnel Board of Jefferson County v. Wilks; Arrington v. Wilks (490 U.S. 755), decided by a 5-4 vote, June 12, 1989. Rehnquist wrote the opinion; Stevens, Brennan, Marshall and Blackmun dissented.

Employees adversely affected by a consent decree in an employment discrimination suit are not precluded from challenging the decree later if they were not parties to the suit. Under the Federal Rules of Civil Procedure, the parties to a lawsuit have the burden of joining others who may be affected by it. The employees' failure to intervene in the suit when they became aware of it does not prevent them from subsequently contesting the decree.

Lorance v. AT&T Technologies Inc. (490 U.S. 900), decided by a 5-3 vote, June 12, 1989. Scalia wrote the opinion; Marshall, Brennan and Blackmun dissented; O'Connor did not participate.

The Court upheld the dismissal on statute of limitations grounds of an employment discrimination complaint against a revised seniority system that, although neutral on its face, was allegedly adopted with the intention of adversely affecting female employees' seniority rights. The time period for filing the complaint began with the adoption of the new seniority rules.

Patterson v. McLean Credit Union (491 U.S. 164), decided by a 5-4 vote, June 15, 1989. Kennedy wrote the opinion; Brennan, Marshall, Blackmun and Stevens dissented.

Racial harassment relating to the conditions of employment is not actionable under the federal civil rights law — 42 U.S.C. Section 1981 — that guarantees "all persons" the same right "to make and enforce contracts . . . as is enjoyed by white citizens." That provision does not apply to conduct that occurs after the formation of a contract and that does not interfere with the right to enforce established contract obligations.

Hoffmann-La Roche Inc. v. Sperling (493 U.S. 165), decided by a 7-2 vote, Dec. 11, 1989. Kennedy wrote the opinion; Scalia and Rehnquist dissented.

In an age-discrimination class action, a federal judge may authorize and help in giving notice to potential plaintiffs by allowing the discovery of names and addresses of similarly situated plaintiffs. The Court said such authority would help avoid multiple lawsuits but stressed that the judge must avoid appearing to endorse the merits of the claim.

University of Pennsylvania v. Equal Employment Opportunity Commission (493 U.S. 182), decided by a 9-0 vote, Jan. 9, 1990. Blackmun wrote the opinion.

A university does not enjoy a special privilege, grounded in either the common law or the First Amendment, against disclosure of faculty peer review materials that are relevant to charges of racial or sexual discrimination.

Lytle v. Household Manufacturing Inc. (494 U.S. 545), decided by a 9-0 vote, March 20, 1990. Marshall wrote the opinion.

A district court's resolution of issues raised by a petitioner's equitable claims does not bar relitigation of the same issues before a jury in the context of legal claims. The Seventh Amendment right to a jury trial prevents according collateral estoppel effect to a district court's ruling on issues common to both legal and equitable claims where the court resolved the equitable claims after erroneously dismissing the legal claims.

Yellow Freight System Inc. v. Donnelly (494 U.S. 820), decided by a 9-0 vote, April 17, 1990. Stevens wrote the opinion.

Federal courts do not have exclusive jurisdiction over job-discrimination claims filed under Title VII of the 1964 Civil Rights Act. The absence of language that expressly confines jurisdiction to federal courts or deprives state courts of their jurisdiction is strong evidence that Congress did not intend to divest state courts of concurrent jurisdiction.

Equal Employment Opportunity Commission v. Arabian American Oil Co. (499 U.S. 244), decided by a 6-3 vote, March 26, 1991. Rehnquist wrote the opinion; Marshall, Blackmun and Stevens dissented.

Title VII of the 1964 Civil Rights Act does not cover U.S. workers employed in overseas offices of U.S.-based companies. While it was "plausible" that Congress wanted Title VII to apply to U.S. multinational firms, no persuasive evidence existed to demonstrate such and Congress did not provide guidelines for overseas enforcement.

United States v. Burke (504 U.S. ___), decided by a 7-2 vote, May 26, 1992. Blackmun wrote the opinion; O'Connor and Thomas dissented.

Backpay awards given to settle certain job-discrimination claims are taxable to the recipient as gross income. The Court said the recipients of the money failed to show that recovery under Title VII of the 1964 Civil Rights Act was similar to relief in tort-like injuries and, as such, could be excluded from gross income under Internal Revenue Service law.

Privacy

Cruzan v. Director, Missouri Department of Health (497 U.S. 261), decided by a 5-4 vote, June 25, 1990. Rehnquist wrote the opinion; Brennan, Marshall, Blackmun and Stevens dissented.

A state may require clear and convincing evidence of a comatose patient's previously expressed wish to die before allowing family members to disconnect life-support systems. Although an individual has a constitutionally protected right to refuse lifesaving food and water, a state may legitimately seek to safeguard the personal element of this choice by imposing heightened evidentiary requirements.

School Desegregation

Missouri v. Jenkins (495 U.S. 33), decided by a 5-4 vote, April 18, 1990. White wrote the opinion; Kennedy, Rehnquist, O'Connor and Scalia dissented.

Federal courts may order local governments to raise taxes beyond a limit set by state statute to correct constitutional violations such as segregated schools. State policy must acquiesce when it interferes with vindication of federal constitutional guarantees under the 14th Amendment.

The Court unanimously ruled, however, that the federal judge exceeded his power in raising the property taxes himself instead of ordering Kansas City, Mo., officials to take the step.

Board of Education of Oklahoma City Public Schools v. Dowell (498 U.S. 237), decided by a 5-3 vote, Jan. 15, 1991. Rehnquist wrote the opinion; Marshall, Blackmun and Stevens dissented; Souter did not participate.

Formerly segregated school districts may be freed of school busing orders if they can prove that any elements of past discrimination have been removed to all "practicable" extent. A federal court may lift a desegregation order if the school district has complied with the decree in good faith and eliminated "the vestiges of past discrimination."

Freeman v. Pitts (503 U.S. ___), decided by an 8-0 vote, March 31, 1992. Kennedy wrote the opinion; Thomas did not participate.

While supervising a school desegregation plan, a district court has the authority to give up control of a school district in incremental stages before desegregation has been achieved in every area of school operations. A district court may decide not to order further remedies in areas where the school district is in compliance with the decree while at the same time retaining jurisdiction over the case.

United States v. Fordice; Ayers v. Fordice (505 U.S. ___), decided by an 8-1 vote, June 26, 1992. White wrote the opinion; Scalia dissented.

States that once operated officially segregated university systems must do more than adopt race-neutral admissions policies and allow students freedom of choice to satisfy their duty under the Equal Protection Clause to dismantle the dual system. A court must ask whether the racial identity of a school stems from state policies and must examine a wide range of factors to determine whether the state perpetuated its former segregation in any facet of the system.

Sex Discrimination

International Union, United Automobile, Aerospace & Agricultural Implement Workers of America, UAW v. Johnson Controls Inc. (499 U.S. 187), decided by 9-0 and 5-4 votes, March 20, 1991. Blackmun wrote the opinion; White, Rehnquist, Kennedy and Scalia dissented from a key portion of the opinion.

Title VII of the Civil Rights Act of 1964, as amended by the Pregnancy Discrimination Act, prohibits employers from excluding women from jobs that might harm a developing or potential fetus.

Blackmun, writing for a five-justice majority, said that the federal laws forbid all hiring practices based on a worker's ability to have children. Four justices (White, Rehnquist, Kennedy and Scalia) concurred separately, maintaining that some situations could arise in which an employer, because of personal injury liability and workplace costs, may exclude women based on hazards to the unborn.

Franklin v. Gwinnett County Public Schools (503 U.S. ___), decided by a 9-0 vote, Feb. 26, 1992. White wrote the opinion.

Students who have been sexually harassed may sue for damages under Title IX of the Education Amendments of 1972, which bars sex discrimination in schools and colleges. Although the law did not specify remedies, the general rule is that in the absence of explicit provisions, all appropriate relief is available in an action brought to vindicate a federal right.

Voting Rights

Clark v. Roemer (500 U.S. ___), decided by a 9-0 vote, June 3, 1991. Kennedy wrote the opinion.

A special election for state judgeships should not have been allowed by a federal judge without approval by the U.S. attorney general, as required by the Voting Rights Act. The act bars procedures that cause a "denial or abridgement of the right of any citizen of the United States to vote on account of race or color."

Chisom v. Roemer; United States v. Roemer (501 U.S. ___), decided by a 6-3 vote, June 20, 1991. Stevens wrote the opinion; Scalia, Rehnquist and Kennedy dissented.

The federal Voting Rights Act applies to elections for state Supreme Court justices. The Court rejected an argument that judges are not "representatives" covered by the act, which makes it illegal for states to engage in voting practices or draw district boundaries that cause discrimination on the basis of race.

Houston Lawyers' Association v. Attorney General of Texas; League of United Latin American Citizens v. Attorney General of Texas (501 U.S. ___), decided by a 6-3 vote, June 20, 1991. Stevens wrote the opinion; Scalia, Rehnquist and Kennedy dissented.

The Voting Rights Act applies to elections for state trial judges, the Court ruled in a companion decision to *Chisom v. Roemer*. The case involved the election of trial judges in Texas and a challenge to local law by black and Hispanic citizens.

Presley v. Etowah County Commission (502 U.S. ___), decided by a 6-3 vote, Jan. 27, 1992. Kennedy wrote the opinion; Stevens, White and Blackmun dissented.

State and local governments seeking to change the responsibilities of elected county commissioners do not need federal approval, even when the change adversely affects the political power of black county commissioners. The 1965 Voting Rights Act applies only to modifications that bear a direct relation to voting itself, not to changes in the organization and functioning of government.

Miscellaneous Civil Rights Cases

Irwin v. Veterans Administration (498 U.S. 89), decided by 7-1 and 6-2 votes, Dec. 3, 1990. Rehnquist wrote the opinion; Stevens dissented in one part; White and Marshall dissented in another; Souter did not participate.

Deadlines for filings under Title VII of the 1964 Civil Rights Act that are tied to giving notice to one of the parties may be triggered when the party's attorney is notified. Notice to an attorney's office, which is acknowledged by a representative of that office, qualifies as notice to the client.

White and Marshall dissented from a portion of the Court's opinion holding that the 30-day time period is subject to equitable tolling.

McCarthy v. Bronson (500 U.S. ___), decided by a 9-0 vote, May 20, 1991. Stevens wrote the opinion.

Federal magistrates, not only federal judges, may hear cases involving prison conditions when the inmates have waived a right to a jury trial. A 1976 federal law authorizing magistrates to hear and make findings on prisoner confinement applies to specific complaints from individual inmates as well as to challenges to ongoing prison conditions.

Rufo v. Inmates of the Suffolk County Jail; Rapone v. Inmates of the Suffolk County Jail (502 U.S. ___), decided by a 6-2 vote, Jan. 15, 1992. White wrote the opinion; Stevens and Blackmun dissented; Thomas did not participate.

A consent decree may be modified if one of the parties proves a "significant" change in law or fact since entry of the decree. Citing the "upsurge in institutional reform litigation," the Court said lower courts need the ability to modify a decree in response to changed circumstances. But revising a decree should not be easy, the Court said, and the party seeking the modification bears the burden of establishing that a significant change in circumstances warrants it.

International Law

Argentine Republic v. Amerada Hess Shipping Corp. (488 U.S. 428), decided by a 9-0 vote, Jan. 23, 1989. Rehnquist wrote the opinion.

The Foreign Sovereign Immunities Act prevents federal courts from assuming jurisdiction of a suit against a foreign government for allegedly violating international law by attacking a neutral vessel during time of war.

W. S. Kirkpatrick & Co. Inc. v. Environmental Tectonics Corp. (493 U.S. 401), decided by a 9-0 vote, Jan. 17, 1990. Scalia wrote the opinion.

U.S. courts have jurisdiction over lawsuits involving charges that foreign officials acted unlawfully in carrying out their official duties. The "act of state doctrine" did not apply in this bribery case because nothing in the dispute required a judge to declare invalid the official act of a foreign sovereign. The doctrine concerns the validity of foreign sovereign acts and does not establish an exception for cases that may simply embarrass foreign governments because of the wrongdoing of their representatives.

Republic of Argentina v. Weltover Inc. (504 U.S. ___), decided by a 9-0 vote, June 12, 1992. Scalia wrote the opinion.

A federal district court properly asserted jurisdiction over a suit arising from the Republic of Argentina's default on certain bonds issued as part of a plan to stabilize its currency. The suit met the jurisdictional tests of the Foreign Sovereign Immunities Act of 1976 because the default was "taken in connection with a commercial activity" that had "a direct effect in the United States."

United States v. Alvarez-Machain (504 U.S. ___), decided by a 6-3 vote, June 15, 1992. Rehnquist wrote the opinion; Stevens, Blackmun and O'Connor dissented.

A U.S.-Mexico treaty was not violated when a Mexican citizen implicated in the murder of a U.S. drug agent was abducted in Mexico and flown to Texas, where he was arrested and indicted. Nothing in the Extradition Treaty between the United States and Mexico or its history prohibited abductions, nor could such a prohibition be inferred on the basis of principles of international law.

Labor Law

Black Lung Benefits

Pittston Coal Group v. Sebben; McLaughlin v. Sebben; Director, Office of Workers' Compensation Programs, United States Department of Labor v. Broyles (488 U.S. 105), decided by a 5-4 vote, Dec. 6, 1988. Scalia wrote the opinion; Stevens, Rehnquist, White and O'Connor dissented.

The Court invalidated an interim regulation adopted by the Department of Labor that limited the ability of coal miners with less than 10 years' experience to obtain black lung disability benefits. The regulation, which required short-term miners to present additional evidence of medical disability to obtain the benefits, violated a provision of the Black Lung Benefits Reform Act of 1977.

United States Department of Labor v. Triplett; Committee on Legal Ethics of the West Virginia State Bar v. Triplett (494 U.S. 715), decided by a 9-0 vote, March 27, 1990. Scalia wrote the opinion.

A federal requirement that lawyer fees paid by coal miners seeking relief under the Black Lung Benefits Act of 1972 be approved by the Labor Department does not violate the due process rights of the miners. The Court said the regulation does not deprive claimants of adequate legal assistance.

Pauley v. Bethenergy Mines Inc.; Clinchfield Coal Co. v. Director, Office of Workers' Compensation Programs, Department of Labor; Consolidated Coal Co. v. Director, Office of Workers' Compensation Programs, Department of Labor (501 U.S. ___), decided by a 7-1 vote, June 24, 1991. Blackmun wrote the opinion; Scalia dissented; Kennedy did not participate.

The Court upheld Labor Department regulations that coal companies must have sufficient opportunity to rebut evidence offered by miners seeking benefits for black lung disease. The Court said the interim regulations met a test in federal law that they must not be more restrictive than regulations from the 1960s.

Drug Testing

Skinner v. Railway Labor Executives' Association (489 U.S. 602), decided by a 7-2 vote, March 21, 1989. Kennedy wrote the opinion; Marshall and Brennan dissented.

The Court upheld the Federal Railroad Administration's requirement that railroad workers be subjected to tests for drug and alcohol use after major accidents and other safety violations. Such tests are a search, but they are reasonable in light of the government's compelling interest in protecting public safety, and warrants are not required.

National Treasury Employees Union v. Von Raab (489 U.S. 656), decided by a 5-4 vote, March 21, 1989. Kennedy wrote the opinion; Marshall, Brennan, Stevens and Scalia dissented.

The Court upheld the mandatory drug testing required by the U.S. Customs Service for employees who apply for promotions to positions involving drug-interdiction duties or carrying firearms. In light of the government's interest in the integrity of the law enforcement process, this "search" is reasonable and may be conducted without a warrant and without any particularized suspicion of an employee.

Labor Relations

Trans World Airlines Inc. v. Independent Federation of Flight Attendants (489 U.S. 426), decided by a 6-3 vote, Feb. 28, 1989. O'Connor wrote the opinion; Brennan, Marshall and Blackmun dissented.

An employer is not required by the Railway Labor Act to lay off junior employees who worked during a strike to reinstate more senior full-term strikers at the conclusion of a strike.

Consolidated Rail Corp. v. Railway Labor Executives' Association (491 U.S. 299), decided by a 7-2 vote, June 19, 1989. Blackmun wrote the opinion; Brennan and Marshall dissented.

A labor union's objection to a railroad's decision to add a drug-testing component to routine physical examinations of employees was a "minor dispute" under the Railway Labor Act that was subject to the act's compulsory and binding arbitration provisions. The railroad had an arguable claim under the terms of the collective bargaining agreement to make the change without prior negotiations.

Pittsburgh & Lake Erie Railroad Co. v. Railway Labor Executives' Association (491 U.S. 490), decided by a 5-4 vote, June 21, 1989. White wrote the opinion; Stevens, Brennan, Marshall and Blackmun dissented.

A railroad was not required under the Railway Labor Act (RLA) to notify a union of its decision to sell its assets or to bargain about the effects of the proposed sale. The railroad also was not required to maintain the status quo or postpone the sale after the union filed notices seeking to ameliorate the adverse impacts of the sale. The court of appeals' decision to set aside an injunction against a strike was vacated and remanded for a determination of whether the strike violated the union's duties under the RLA.

Golden State Transit Corp. v. City of Los Angeles (493 U.S. 103), decided by a 6-3 vote, Dec. 5, 1989. Stevens wrote the opinion; Kennedy, Rehnquist and O'Connor dissented.

A city may be held liable for money damages in a federal court action if it illegally interferes in labor negotiations. Federal labor law creates "rights" in labor and management that are protected against government interference and may be the basis for a claim in federal court under Section 1983 of Title 42, which provides a remedy for "deprivation of any rights, privileges, or immunities secured by the Constitution and laws."

National Labor Relations Board v. Curtin Matheson Scientific Inc. (494 U.S. 775), decided by a 5-4 vote, April 17, 1990. Marshall wrote the opinion; Blackmun, Scalia, O'Connor and Kennedy dissented.

The National Labor Relations Board may refuse to presume that strikebreakers oppose the union that represents the striking workers when the board evaluates an employer's claim that the union does not have majority support. The board's refusal to presume the sentiments of replacement workers was rationally directed at protecting the bargaining process.

Groves v. Ring Screw Works (498 U.S. 168), decided by a 9-0 vote, Dec. 10, 1990. Stevens wrote the opinion.

The federal Labor-Management Relations Act gives judges authority to hear labor disputes unless a collective bargaining agreement between a union and management expressly forbids it.

American Hospital Association v. National Labor Relations Board (499 U.S. 606), decided by a 9-0 vote, April 23, 1991. Stevens wrote the opinion.

The Court upheld a National Labor Relations Board industrywide rule that permits separate employee bargaining units for health care workers in acute care hospitals. The Court said that if a disagreement arose about the appropriateness of a bargaining unit, the board still would be able to step in and resolve the dispute.

Litton Financial Printing Division v. National Labor Relations Board (501 U.S. ___), decided by a 5-4 vote, June 13, 1991. Kennedy wrote the opinion; Marshall, Blackmun, Scalia and Stevens dissented.

A union member's grievance that arises after the expiration of a collective bargaining agreement can be arbitrated only if it involves incidents that happened before the agreement expired or the infringement of a right that survived the end of the agreement.

Lechmere Inc. v. National Labor Relations Board (502 U.S. ___), decided by a 6-3 vote, Jan. 27, 1992. Thomas wrote the opinion; White, Blackmun and Stevens dissented.

An employer who bars non-employee union organizers from distributing leaflets on the owner's property does not violate federal labor law. Section 7 of the National Labor Relations Act protects non-employee union organizers only in rare situations, such as logging camps, in which targeted workers cannot be reached by channels other than at the employer's property.

Pensions and Benefits

Firestone Tire & Rubber Co. v. Bruch (489 U.S. 101), decided by a 9-0 vote, Feb. 21, 1989. O'Connor wrote the opinion.

A denial of benefits under a pension plan governed by the Employee Retirement Income Security Act is subject to a new (de novo) review in federal court except in certain circumstances. A more deferential standard of review — upholding a denial of benefits unless the action was arbitrary or capricious — is to be used only if the plan has an independent administrator with discretionary authority to determine benefits or construe the terms of the plan.

Massachusetts v. Morash (490 U.S. 107), decided by a 9-0 vote, April 18, 1989. Stevens wrote the opinion.

A state prosecution of an employer for failing to pay an employee vacation benefits on the date of his discharge is not pre-empted by the federal Employee Retirement Income Security Act (ERISA). An employer's practice of paying employees for their unused vacation time does not constitute an "employee welfare benefit plan" subject to ERISA. The law therefore does not pre-empt state regulation of the practice.

Mead Corp. v. Tilley (490 U.S. 714), decided by an 8-1 vote, June 5, 1989. Marshall wrote the opinion; Stevens dissented.

The administrator of a benefit pension plan covered by the Employee Retirement Income Security Act does not have to pay early retirement benefits upon termination of the plan to employees who failed to satisfy the requirements for such benefits. Those employees were entitled only to the present value of the normal retirement benefits paid under the plan at age 65.

Guidry v. Sheet Metal Workers National Pension Fund (493 U.S. 365), decided by a 9-0 vote, Jan. 17, 1990. Blackmun wrote the opinion.

A union official found guilty of embezzlement may not be forced to repay the union with his pension benefits. The prohibition against transfer of pension benefits contained in the Employee Retirement Income Security Act prevents a district court from imposing a constructive trust on a pension fund.

Pension Benefit Guaranty Corporation v. LTV Corp. (496 U.S. 633), decided by an 8-1 vote, June 18, 1990. Blackmun wrote the opinion; Stevens dissented.

The Pension Benefit Guaranty Corporation does not have to follow federal bankruptcy and labor laws in deciding whether to restore a terminated pension plan under the Employee Retirement Income Security Act.

Ingersoll-Rand Co. v. McClendon (498 U.S. 133), decided by a 9-0 vote, Dec. 3, 1990. O'Connor wrote the opinion.

The federal Employee Retirement Income Security Act (ERISA) pre-empts a state common law claim by workers who assert that they were fired because an employer did not want to pay them benefits under an ERISA-covered pension plan. The Court said that workers must file under the federal law, which does not allow punitive damages as some state laws permit fired workers to win.

Nationwide Mutual Insurance Co. v. Darden (503 U.S. ___), decided by a 9-0 vote, March 24, 1992. Souter wrote the opinion.

The term "employee" as used in the federal Employee Retirement Income Security Act (ERISA) is to be defined on the basis of traditional agency law criteria for identifying master-servant relationships. In distinguishing between an employee, covered by ERISA, and an independent contractor, not covered by the law, a court should use factors from the traditional "common law" test, such as a company's right to control the worker, the location of the employee's work, his skill level, method of payment and the duration of the business relationship.

Union Affairs

Reed v. United Transportation Union (488 U.S. 319), decided by an 8-1 vote, Jan. 11, 1989. Brennan wrote the opinion; White dissented.

The time period for a union member to bring a suit alleging violations of his right of free speech as to union matters is to be determined by borrowing the general or residual statute of limitations of the state where the action is brought. The Court rejected the use of a shorter statute of limitations found in federal labor law for bringing unfair labor practice charges, saying the two causes of action were not analogous.

Sheet Metal Workers v. Lynn (488 U.S. 347), decided by an 8-0 vote, Jan. 18, 1989. Marshall wrote the opinion; Kennedy did not participate.

The removal of a union's elected business agent in retaliation for statements made at a union meeting in opposition to a dues increase sought by the union's trustee violated the free speech provisions of the Labor-Management Reporting and Disclosure Act.

Breininger v. Sheet Metal Workers International Association Local Union No. 6 (493 U.S. 67), decided by 9-0 and 7-2 votes, Dec. 5, 1989. Brennan wrote the opinion; Stevens and Scalia dissented.

The National Labor Relations Board does not have exclusive jurisdiction over a union member's claim that his union both breached its duty of fair representation and engaged in hiring hall discrimination. The Court ruled unanimously that even if a breach of duty of fair representation also might be an unfair labor practice — a matter governed by the board — a federal court still has jurisdiction over the fair-representation claim.

By a 7-2 vote, however, the Court ruled that the union member did not state a claim. He said that the union passed him over for job referrals because he had supported political rivals of union officials. Even if true, the action did not qualify as "discipline" in violation of labor law.

Chauffeurs, Teamsters and Helpers, Local No. 391 v. Terry (494 U.S. 558), decided by a 6-3 vote, March 20, 1990. Marshall wrote the opinion; Kennedy, O'Connor and Scalia dissented.

An employee who sues for back pay as a remedy for a union's alleged denial of fair representation has a right to a jury trial. The remedy of back pay is "legal" in nature, as opposed to an equitable remedy. The Seventh Amendment entitles a plaintiff to a jury trial when a legal right is at stake.

United Steelworkers of America v. Rawson (495 U.S. 362), decided by a 6-3 vote, May 14, 1990; White wrote the opinion; Kennedy, Rehnquist and Scalia dissented.

The Labor-Management Relations Act pre-empts a wrongful-death suit in state court against a miners' union for allegedly failing to meet its collectively bargained duties through negligence in inspection of mine safety conditions.

International Organization for Masters, Mates & Pilots v. Brown (498 U.S. 466), decided by a 9-0 vote, Feb. 20, 1991. Stevens wrote the opinion.

Labor unions must acquiesce to all "reasonable" requests from candidates to distribute campaign literature for union elections, even when a union rule might prohibit such distribution. The test of federal labor law is whether a candidate's distribution request is reasonable.

Air Line Pilots Association v. O'Neill (499 U.S. 65), decided by a 9-0 vote, March 19, 1991. Stevens wrote the opinion.

A pilot union's negotiation of a back-to-work agreement that permitted the airline to discriminate between striking pilots and non-striking pilots in job openings did not breach the union's duty of fair representation. The rule that a union is liable only if its actions are either "arbitrary, discriminatory, or in bad faith" applies to all union activity, including contract negotiation.

Lehnert v. Ferris Faculty Association (500 U.S. ___), decided by 8-1 and 5-4 votes, May 30, 1991. Blackmun wrote the opinion; Marshall dissented in part; Scalia, O'Connor, Kennedy and Souter dissented in part.

Public employee unions cannot use fees collected from non-members covered by an "agency shop" arrangement to pay for political activity or public relations that does not arise from the collective bargaining agreement, without violating the First Amendment. Marshall was the lone dissenter from this part of the decision.

By a 5-4 vote, the Court announced a three-part test for determining the constitutionality of using non-members' funds for various union expenses. Workers who object to the spending can be charged only for union activities that are "germane" to collective bargaining, are justified by the government's interest in labor peace and avoiding "free riders," and do not add significantly to the burden on free speech that is inherent in an agency shop.

Wooddell v. International Brotherhood of Electrical Workers, Local 71 (502 U.S. ___), decided by an 8-0 vote, Dec. 4, 1991. White wrote the opinion; Thomas did not participate.

A union member alleging that the union discriminated against him in job referrals in violation of the union's constitution and by-laws has a federal cause of action against the union. The Court also said the union member is entitled to a jury trial in his effort to obtain money damages as well as injunctive relief under the Labor-Management Relations Act.

Workers' Compensation

Chesapeake & Ohio Railway Co. v. Schwalb; Norfolk & Western Railway Co. v. Goode (493 U.S. 40), decided by a 9-0 vote, Nov. 28, 1989. White wrote the opinion.

Railway workers who were injured while doing work essential to the loading process are covered by the Longshoremen's and Harbor Workers' Compensation Act and are limited to its remedies instead of those provided in the Federal Employers' Liability Act for railroad employees.

Adams Fruit Co. Inc. v. Barrett (494 U.S. 638), decided by a 9-0 vote, March 21, 1990. Marshall wrote the opinion.

Migrant farm workers may sue their employer for violation of the Migrant and Seasonal Agricultural Worker Protection Act even after they have recovered state workers' compensation benefits.

Southwest Marine Inc. v. Gizoni (502 U.S. ___), decided by an 8-0 vote, Dec. 4, 1991. White wrote the opinion; Thomas did not participate.

A maritime worker whose occupation is one of those covered by the Longshoremen's and Harbor Workers' Compensation Act still may be a "seaman" within the meaning of the Jones Act and entitled to damages when he is injured. To be a seaman qualifying for damages under the Jones Act, a maritime worker need only be doing a ship's work, which is not limited to aiding in its navigation.

Hilton v. South Carolina Public Railways Commission (502 U.S. ___), decided by a 6-2 vote, Dec. 16, 1991. Kennedy wrote the opinion; O'Connor and Scalia dissented; Thomas did not participate.

An injured railroad worker may sue a South Carolina public railways agency in state court under the Federal Employers' Liability Act. The Court reaffirmed a 28-year-old precedent that said Congress intended to include state-owned railroads within the phrase "every common carrier railroad" as used in the act.

General Motors Corp. v. Romein (503 U.S. ___), decided by a 9-0 vote, March 9, 1992. O'Connor wrote the opinion.

A Michigan law forcing employers to pay retroactively workers' compensation benefits that they withheld under an old law is constitutional. The Court rejected a contention that the new law violated contractual and due process rights.

Estate of Cowart v. Nicklos Drilling Co. (505 U.S. ___), decided by a 6-3 vote, June 22, 1992. Kennedy wrote the opinion; Blackmun, Stevens and O'Connor dissented.

An injured employee eligible for benefits under the Longshoremen's and Harbor Workers' Compensation Act forfeits all benefits, including medical benefits, if he settles a third-party claim without the written approval of the worker's employer. The act's forfeiture provision applies whether or not the employer was paying compensation to the worker or was subject to an order to pay under the act.

Miscellaneous Labor Law Cases

English v. General Electric Co. (496 U.S. 72), decided by a 9-0 vote, June 4, 1990. Blackmun wrote the opinion.

A laboratory technician at a nuclear plant who complained about safety violations and then was fired may sue the employer under state tort law pertaining to retaliatory discharge. The worker's complaint did not fall within a field pre-empted by the federal Energy Reorganization Act of 1974.

King v. St. Vincent's Hospital (502 U.S. ___), decided by an 8-0 vote, Dec. 16, 1991. Souter wrote the opinion; Thomas did not participate.

Federal law does not limit the time that a civilian employer must leave a job open for a worker going off on military duty.

Property Law

United States v. Sperry Corp. (493 U.S. 52), decided by a 9-0 vote, Nov. 28, 1989. White wrote the opinion.

The U.S. government may collect a small percentage of awards won by U.S. companies against the government of Iran in a special claims tribunal. The deduction was a reasonable "user fee" intended to reimburse the government for its costs in connection with the tribunal.

Preseault v. Interstate Commerce Commission (494 U.S. 1), decided by a 9-0 vote, Feb. 21, 1990. Brennan wrote the opinion.

The federal government's conversion of abandoned railroad rights-of-way into hiking and biking trails does not constitute the taking of private property because landowners claiming a reversionary interest may be compensated for the loss under a separate federal law. The Court also held the National Trails System Act Amendments of 1983 — the so-called rails-to-trails statute — to be a valid exercise of congressional power under the Commerce Clause.

National Railroad Passenger Corporation v. Boston & Maine Corp.; Interstate Commerce Commission v. Boston & Maine Corp. (503 U.S. ___), decided by a 6-3 vote, March 25, 1992. Kennedy wrote the opinion; White, Blackmun and Thomas dissented.

Amtrak — officially, the National Railroad Passenger Corporation — was within its rights under federal law when it forced a private freight railroad to sell portions of its track and then turned the track over to a competitor of the original owner. The Court said federal law includes a strong presumption that Amtrak will make reasonable business judgments in condemning private property and thus the Interstate Commerce Commission acted properly in approving the condemnation.

Yee v. City of Escondido (503 U.S. ___), decided by a 9-0 vote, April 1, 1992. O'Connor wrote the opinion.

The Takings Clause of the Fifth Amendment is not violated by the combination of a city rent control law and state restrictions on mobile home park owners that forces park owners to accept long-term below-market rents. The laws at issue do not amount to a taking, but merely regulate the use of the land by directing the relationship between landlord and tenant.

Lucas v. South Carolina Coastal Council (505 U.S. ___), decided by a 6-3 vote, June 29, 1992. Scalia wrote the opinion; Blackmun, Stevens and Souter dissented.

State regulations that effectively deny a property owner all value of his land constitute a "taking" under the Fifth Amendment and require compensation unless they prevent uses that would not be permitted under prevailing nuisance and property law.

States

Border Disputes

Georgia v. South Carolina (497 U.S. 376), decided by a 9-0 vote, June 25, 1990. Blackmun wrote the opinion.

The Barnwell Islands belong to South Carolina, not Georgia. South Carolina had established sovereignty over the islands through almost two centuries of history, including its continuing practice of taxation, policing and patrolling of the island property.

Illinois v. Kentucky (500 U.S. ___), decided by a 9-0 vote, May 28, 1991. Souter wrote the opinion.

Resolving a dispute between Illinois and Kentucky over their common boundary, the Court said the boundary is the line of the low-water mark of the Ohio River as it was in 1792 instead of the river's northerly low-water mark "as it exists from time to time."

Interstate Compacts

Oklahoma v. New Mexico (501 U.S. ___), decided by a 5-4 vote, June 17, 1991. White wrote the opinion; Rehnquist, O'Connor, Scalia and Kennedy dissented.

Under a 1952 Canadian River water-use agreement among Oklahoma, New Mexico and Texas, New Mexico must count toward its allocation water that spills over the Conchas Dam and is stored in New Mexico's reservoirs downstream.

State Immunity

Port Authority Trans-Hudson Corp. v. Feeney; Port Authority Trans-Hudson Corp. v. Foster (495 U.S. 299), decided by a 9-0 vote, April 30, 1990. O'Connor wrote the opinion.

The 11th Amendment's provision for state immunity does not bar lawsuits in federal court against the Port Authority Trans-Hudson Corporation, which was created in a compact by New York and New Jersey to operate transportation facilities linking the two states. The states clearly agreed to waive any immunity from federal law in legislation that created the agency.

Blatchford v. Native Village of Noatak (501 U.S. ___), decided by a 6-3 vote, June 24, 1991. Scalia wrote the opinion; Blackmun, Marshall and Stevens dissented.

The 11th Amendment, which shields states from being sued in federal courts by individuals seeking money damages, bars Indian tribes from suing state governments for money damages for violations of their constitutional rights.

State Regulation

ASARCO Inc. v. Kadish (490 U.S. 605), decided by a 6-2 vote, May 30, 1989. Kennedy wrote the opinion; Rehnquist and Scalia dissented; O'Connor did not participate.

Arizona law that permits mineral leases on lands granted to the state by the federal government without prior appraisal and public auction for at least the appraised value is invalid. The state law conflicts with federal statutes that impose such requirements for non-hydrocarbon mineral leases.

Healy v. Beer Institute Inc.; Wine and Spirits Wholesalers of Connecticut Inc. v. Beer Institute Inc. (491 U.S. 324), decided by a 6-3 vote, June 19, 1989. Blackmun wrote the opinion; Rehnquist, Stevens and O'Connor dissented.

A state law requiring out-of-state shippers of beer to affirm that their posted prices for products are no higher than prices for the products in bordering states violates the Commerce Clause.

The statute has the impermissible practical effect of controlling activity wholly outside the state. It also violates the Commerce Clause by discriminating against interstate commerce as it does not apply to shippers engaged solely in the state.

North Dakota v. United States (495 U.S. 423), decided by 9-0 and 5-4 votes, May 21, 1990. Stevens wrote the opinion; Brennan, Marshall, Blackmun and Kennedy dissented in part.

States may impose labeling and reporting requirements on distributors that sell liquor at U.S. military posts within their borders. The justices unanimously upheld North Dakota regulations requiring out-of-state shippers to file monthly reports and ruled, by a 5-4 vote, to allow a North Dakota requirement that labels be stuck to each bottle of liquor sold on the federal posts.

California v. Federal Energy Regulatory Commission (495 U.S. 490), decided by a 9-0 vote, May 21, 1990. O'Connor wrote the opinion.

The standards set by the Federal Energy Regulatory Commission for water flows in streams diverted by federally licensed hydraulic projects pre-empt state regulations. The Court said that California requirements for substantially higher stream flows must yield to federal law.

Wisconsin Public Intervenor v. Mortier (501 U.S. ___), decided by a 9-0 vote, June 21, 1991. White wrote the opinion.

The Federal Insecticide, Fungicide and Rodenticide Act does not pre-empt local governments' regulation of residents' pesticide use. The Court said that, while the federal law was intended to be comprehensive to protect the environment from pesticides, it does not prohibit localities from providing more control.

The law said explicitly that states have the power to control pesticide use, but courts had differed in their interpretations of whether localities have similar authority.

Supreme Court

Wyoming v. Oklahoma (502 U.S. ___), decided by a 6-3 vote, Jan. 22, 1992. White wrote the opinion; Scalia, Rehnquist and Thomas dissented.

An Oklahoma state law requiring coal-fired electric utilities to use at least 10 percent Oklahoma-mined coal violates the Commerce Clause. The law invalidly purports to exclude coal mined from other states based solely on its origin.

United States v. Alaska (503 U.S. ___), decided by a 9-0 vote, April 21, 1992. White wrote the opinion.

The secretary of the Army may make approval of a plan to build a port and causeway in Nome conditional on Alaska's waiver of claims to any additional submerged land that might fall within the new port boundary. The Army has broad discretion to grant or deny a permit for construction.

State Taxation

Allegheny Pittsburgh Coal Co. v. County Commission of Webster County; East Kentucky Energy Corp. v. County Commission of Webster County (488 U.S. 336), decided by a 9-0 vote, Jan. 18, 1989. Rehnquist wrote the opinion.

A county violated taxpayers' rights to equal protection under the 14th Amendment by assessing their real property on the basis of its recent purchase price but failing to adjust assessments on other taxpayers' property not recently transferred.

Davis v. Michigan Department of Treasury (489 U.S. 803), decided by an 8-1 vote, March 28, 1989. Kennedy wrote the opinion; Stevens dissented.

A state tax scheme that exempted from taxation retirement benefits paid by the state but not those paid by other employers, including the federal government, was held unconstitutional. The system violated principles of intergovernmental tax immunity by favoring retired state and local government employees over retired federal employees.

California State Board of Equalization v. Sierra Summit Inc. (490 U.S. 844), decided by a 6-3 vote, June 12, 1989. Stevens wrote the opinion; Blackmun, Brennan and Marshall dissented.

A state may impose sales taxes on a bankruptcy liquidation sale. Imposition of state sales taxes does not violate the doctrine of intergovernmental tax immunity or federal bankruptcy law.

Oklahoma Tax Commission v. Citizen Band Potawatomi Indian Tribe of Oklahoma (498 U.S. 505), decided by a 9-0 vote, Feb. 26, 1991. Rehnquist wrote the opinion.

A state may collect taxes on sales of goods to people who are not members of an Indian tribe on land held in trust for the tribe. But under the doctrine of tribal sovereign immunity, a state may not go to court to enforce collection of the taxes. States may, however, sue store managers or seize goods that did not carry tax stamps.

James B. Beam Distilling Co. v. Georgia (501 U.S. ___), decided by a 6-3 vote, June 20, 1991. Souter wrote the opinion; O'Connor, Rehnquist and Kennedy dissented.

A 1984 Supreme Court decision striking down a Hawaii tax on out-of-state liquor as unconstitutional should be applied retroactively. Once the Court has applied a rule of law to parties in one civil case, the rule must be applied to all other litigants bringing similar claims.

County of Yakima v. Confederated Tribes and Bands of the Yakima Indian Nation; Confederated Tribes and Bands of the Yakima Indian Nation v. County of Yakima (502 U.S. ___), decided by an 8-1 vote, Jan. 14, 1992. Scalia wrote the opinion; Blackmun dissented.

Yakima County may impose property taxes on Indian land, but it may not put an excise tax on sales of the land. The Court said the property taxes were allowed under the 1887 Indian General Allotment Act, which permits "taxation of . . . land" conveyed to Indians. The excise tax on land sales was disallowed because it was not a tax on the land itself.

INDOPCO Inc. v. Commissioner of Internal Revenue (503 U.S. ___), decided by a 9-0 vote, Feb. 26, 1992. Blackmun wrote the opinion.

A corporation may not deduct from its income taxes as ordinary business expenses investment banking fees and expenses that it incurred during a friendly takeover. Such expenses, instead of being ordinary business expenses, are like capital expenditures, which generally are amortized over several years.

Barker v. Kansas (503 U.S. ___), decided by a 9-0 vote, April 21, 1992. White wrote the opinion.

The Court unanimously rejected a Kansas scheme that imposed income taxes on military retirement benefits but not on the benefits received by retired state and local government employees.

Quill Corp. v. North Dakota (504 U.S. ___), decided by an 8-1 vote, May 26, 1992. Stevens wrote the opinion; White dissented.

States may not force out-of-state mail order companies to pay taxes. The Court said that while it no longer considered the taxes a violation of the constitutional guarantee of due process, the taxes do infringe on the Commerce Clause. Even though catalog sales companies may have "minimum contacts" with a taxing state as required by the Due Process Clause, they lack the "substantial nexus" with the state required by the Commerce Clause. Commerce Clause conditions may be met only through a company's physical presence in the taxing state.

Allied-Signal Inc. v. Director, Division of Taxation (504 U.S. ___), decided by 9-0 and 5-4 votes, June 15, 1992. Kennedy wrote the opinion; O'Connor, Rehnquist, Blackmun and Thomas dissented in part.

States may not tax out-of-state businesses on the income derived from the sale of stock in separate in-state companies.

The justices unanimously upheld a rule, known as the unitary business principle, that allows a state to tax the investment income of an out-of-state firm doing business in the state only if certain relationships exist between the firm and the in-state entity whose securities produced the income. The unanimous Court said due process and the Commerce Clause generally prevent a state from taxing gains earned outside a state.

The justices then split 5-4 on whether the transaction in question met certain criteria for state taxation. The majority said the relationship between the firms involved was not sufficient and that New Jersey could not tax the capital gain at issue.

Nordlinger v. Hahn (505 U.S. ___), decided by an 8-1 vote, June 18, 1992. Blackmun wrote the opinion; Stevens dissented.

California's Proposition 13 property tax assessment approach, which is based on the value of a home when it was purchased instead of the current market value, does not unconstitutionally discriminate against new home purchasers. By allowing longtime owners to pay less in taxes than newer owners of comparable property, the Court said, the law's assessment scheme rationally furthers at least two legitimate state interests: neighborhood preservation and stability, and the existing owners' protection against higher taxes.

Kraft General Foods Inc. v. Iowa Department of Revenue and Finance (505 U.S. ___), decided by a 7-2 vote, June 18, 1992. Stevens wrote the opinion; Rehnquist and Blackmun dissented.

States may not tax dividends that businesses receive from foreign subsidiaries while exempting dividends from domestic subsidiaries. Such a scheme discriminates against foreign commerce in violation of the Foreign Commerce Clause.

Wisconsin Department of Revenue v. William Wrigley Jr. Co. (505 U.S. ___), decided by a 6-3 vote, June 19, 1992. Scalia wrote the opinion; Kennedy, Rehnquist and Blackmun dissented.

Wisconsin may levy an income tax on an Illinois chewing gum manufacturer that, in addition to seeking orders in Wisconsin, supplies gum for retail display racks, stores gum and requires its sales representatives to replace stale gum in shops. A federal law bars a state from taxing the income of a corporation whose only business in a state is the "solicitation of orders" for tangible goods. But the Court said that Wrigley's activities went beyond mere solicitation of orders and constituted independent business functions.

Torts

Finley v. United States (490 U.S. 545), decided by a 5-4 vote, May 22, 1989. Scalia wrote the opinion; Stevens, Brennan, Marshall and Blackmun dissented.

The Federal Tort Claims Act, which establishes exclusive federal jurisdiction over civil actions against the United States, does not give federal courts "pendent jurisdiction" over related claims against other defendants. Claims against other parties must be tried in separate suits in state or federal courts even if trying such claims together would promote judicial economy and efficiency.

Browning-Ferris Industries of Vermont Inc. v. Kelco Disposal Inc. (492 U.S. 257), decided by a 7-2 vote, June 26, 1989. Blackmun wrote the opinion; O'Connor and Stevens dissented.

The Excessive Fines Clause of the Eighth Amendment does not apply to punitive damages awards in cases between private parties. It does not constrain such an award when the government has not prosecuted the action and has no right to recover a share of the damages awarded.

FMC Corp. v. Holliday (498 U.S. 52), decided by a 7-1 vote, Nov. 27, 1990. O'Connor wrote the opinion; Stevens dissented; Souter did not participate.

State laws that bar insurance companies from going after court awards that an accident victim wins in a tort case are pre-empted by the federal Employee Retirement Income Security Act (ERISA). The court said that Congress had intended ERISA to protect from state insurance laws self-funding insurance plans, such as the one in this case.

Pacific Mutual Life Insurance Co. v. Haslip (499 U.S. 1), decided by a 7-1 vote, March 4, 1991. Blackmun wrote the opinion; O'Connor dissented; Souter did not participate.

Juries have broad discretion to decide punitive damages, even when the awards are greatly disproportionate to the actual damage suffered, as long as the awards are guided by reasonableness and are not "extreme."

United States v. Smith (499 U.S. 160), decided by an 8-1 vote, March 20, 1991. Marshall wrote the opinion; Stevens dissented.

A combination of federal laws protects military doctors practicing at overseas installations from liability lawsuits. The Federal Employees Liability Reform and Tort Compensation Act protects government workers from lawsuits even when an exception in the Federal Tort Claims Act precludes recovery against the government itself.

Molzof v. United States (502 U.S. ___), decided by a 9-0 vote, Jan. 14, 1992. Thomas wrote the opinion.

The Federal Tort Claims Act's prohibition on imposition of punitive damages against the United States does not preclude a veterans hospital patient from recovering money damages for future medical expenses and loss of enjoyment of life.

Although the money for medical expenses and loss of enjoyment of life were not "compensatory," they were not necessarily "punitive" because they did not depend upon any proof that the defendant had engaged in intentional or egregious misconduct.

Cipollone v. Liggett Group Inc. (505 U.S. ___), decided by a 7-2 vote, June 24, 1992. Stevens wrote the opinion; Scalia and Thomas dissented.

Cigarette manufacturers who lie about the dangers of smoking or otherwise misrepresent their products can be sued under state laws and made to pay monetary awards. The Federal Cigarette Labeling and Advertising Act preempts state laws requiring particular warnings on cigarette labels or in cigarette advertising but does not pre-empt state court suits based on allegations that manufacturers breached express warranties, ran fraudulent cigarette advertisements, hid the dangers of smoking from state authorities or conspired to mislead smokers.

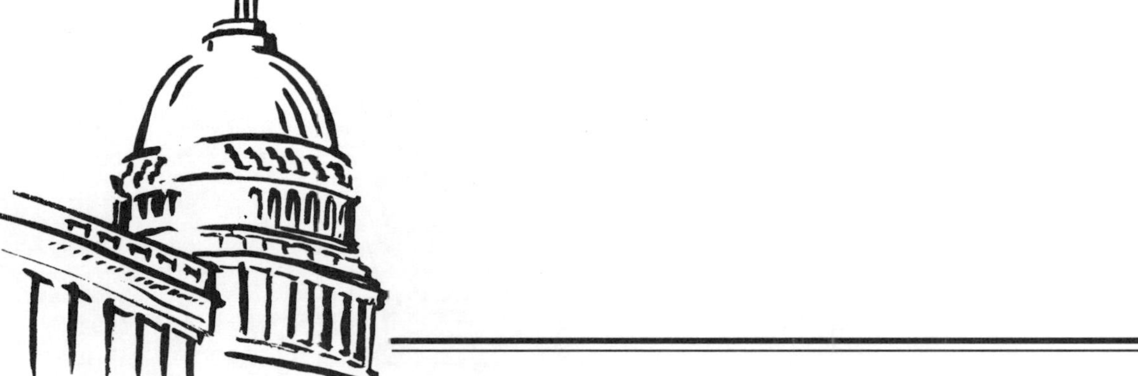

14

General Government

Introduction 855
1989-90 Chronology 857
1991-92 Chronology 886

General Government

Federal employees won some and lost some in 1989-92.

A step toward solving one longstanding problem was made in 1990 when Congress cleared legislation overhauling the federal pay system. To aid in the recruitment and retention of quality personnel, the bill attempted to bring federal salaries in line with private sector salaries. In addition, the president was given less opportunity to restrict pay increases for federal workers. One reason federal salaries had fallen behind was that, from the late 1970s, presidents frequently had chosen to disregard the recommendations of independent pay agents, instead allowing smaller annual salary raises. The legislation also provided higher compensation for federal workers in areas with a high cost of living; previously, all workers at the same level received the same pay, regardless of where they were located.

Congress earlier had lifted a cap on overtime pay to mid- and upper-level federal employees; extended a merit pay program for federal managers and supervisors; and allowed executive agencies to repay the outstanding federal student loans of university graduates who agreed to work for the government for at least three years.

Both the 101st and 102nd Congresses tried and failed to undo provisions of 1989 ethics reform legislation that prohibited federal employees from accepting honoraria, even if the topic of the speech or article was unrelated to their official duties. In 1992, a federal district court judge found the provisions to be an unconstitutional infringement on the freedom of speech. Enforcement of the ruling was suspended, however, pending an appeal.

In a budget-cutting move, Congress eliminated the option for federal employees to receive retirement benefits in a lump sum until 1995. The estimated five-year savings were $8.1 billion. Federal employees, union representatives and government officials, among others, expressed doubt that the payments would again be made available.

President Bush thwarted congressional attempts to revise the Hatch Act, as had President Ronald Reagan before him. The controversial 1939 law, which restricted the partisan political activities of federal workers while off duty, had been the unsuccessful target of reform for decades. In 1990, Bush vetoed a Hatch Act bill, and the Senate sustained the veto. A veto threat was enough to block action on reform legislation in the next Congress.

Added job protections were enacted for federal "whistleblowers" — those who reported on government waste, fraud and abuse and, as a result, found their livelihoods in jeopardy. Congress subsequently provided a permanent authorization for a program to reward whistleblowers.

Legislation also was cleared that aimed to slow the "revolving door" through which former executive branch employees returned to lobby their former colleagues on topics they handled while working for the government. Prohibitions were placed on the kinds of information that could be communicated within certain time frames. The restrictions applied to members of Congress and their staffs as well.

Organization, Procedures. Congress in 1989 used a sleight-of-hand method to reduce the huge budget deficit: The U.S. Postal Service was moved off budget. Because the Postal Service was operating in the red, the change would reduce the size of the deficit on paper. Furthermore, the new classification would shield the quasi-private agency from any across-the-board budget cuts.

A new, centralized financial management system for the federal government was created in 1990 to help combat waste, fraud and abuse. The Office of Federal Financial Management and a new position — deputy director of management — were established at the Office of Management and Budget. In addition, statutory chief financial officers were assigned to the executive departments and a number of federal agencies.

A procedure called regulatory negotiation also won congressional approval. Federal agencies would meet with outside interests, and together they would draw up new regulations. The purpose was to iron out differences and thus avoid delays in the implementation of the regulations. Regulatory negotiation, however, did not replace the existing method of federal rulemaking. A proposed regulation still would be available for public comment, and the agency would issue the final version.

Elections, Census. Proponents saw "motor voter" legislation as a means to open the electoral process by

References

Discussion of general government action for the years 1945-64 may be found in *Congress and the Nation Vol. I*, pp. 1455-1516; for the years 1965-68, *Congress and the Nation Vol. II*, pp. 655-660; for the years 1969-72, *Congress and the Nation Vol. III*, pp. 435-468; for the years 1973-76, *Congress and the Nation Vol. IV*, pp. 795-826; for the years 1977-80, *Congress and the Nation Vol. V*, pp. 817-870; for the years 1981-84, *Congress and the Nation Vol. VI*, pp. 771-79[illegible]; for the years 1985-88, *Congress and the Nation Vol. VII*, pp. 843-867.

Federal Grants to State And Local Governments

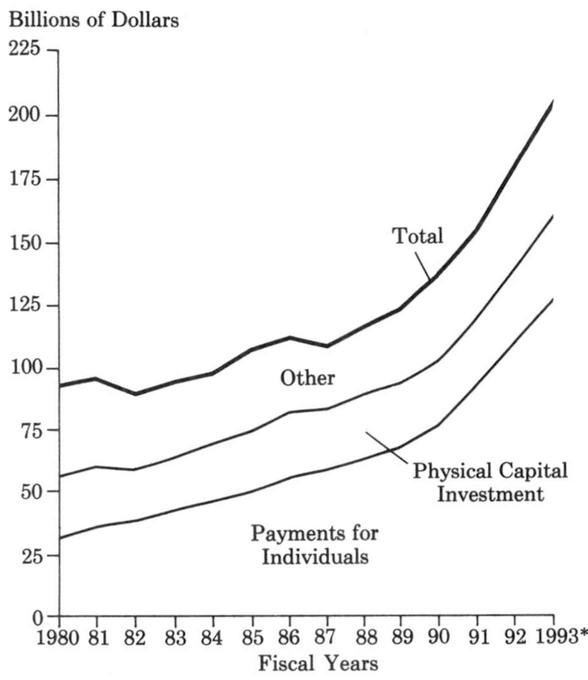

*Estimate.

Source: Office of Management and Budget, *Budget Baselines, Historical Data and Alternatives for the Future* (Washington, D.C.: U.S. Government Printing Office, January 1993).

substantially increasing the number of Americans registered to vote. States would be required to allow voters to register by mail and when applying for a driver's license or other official document. Opponents saw the proposed new procedure as potentially rife with fraud. The Senate was unable to override a Bush veto of the legislation, but Bill Clinton, soon after assuming office in 1993, signed a motor voter bill into law.

District of Columbia voters in November 1990 went to the polls and chose, for the first time, a "shadow" congressional delegation — two senators (including the Rev. Jesse Jackson) and one representative. Prospective states had been provided shadow delegations in the past, including, for example, Tennessee. The D.C. delegation would lobby Congress for statehood for the District.

Administration officials decided not to direct a 1990 census recount, despite an admitted undercount and a bias against minorities. Congress, however, did act to commission a study on census reform, to avoid future problems with the official decennial count.

Space, Science. The National Aeronautics and Space Administration (NASA) was the focus of much contentious debate. Following the 1986 explosion of the space shuttle *Challenger*, NASA struggled to regain its confidence and to determine its long-term goals. The high price tags on the space station *Freedom* and the superconducting supercollider were of primary concern while the federal budget deficit remained uncontrolled. And questions continued to be raised about the wisdom of pursuing manned space flight and about the scientific merits of NASA's big projects.

Increasing the competitiveness of U.S. high-technology companies in world markets was the aim of legislation signed into law in 1992. A top government laboratory in the Commerce Department was provided funds to help industry create and commercialize new technologies. In a separate bill cleared earlier that also was intended to advance U.S. competitiveness, a $2 billion authorization, over five years, was made to develop supercomputers at eight federal agencies and to design a high-speed computer network.

In other science action, Congress made vandalizing animal research laboratories or farms a federal crime.

Indian Programs. Following a two-year investigation, a special Senate committee found incompetence and fraud in the federal agencies responsible for overseeing American Indian programs. The committee recommended that the federal agencies be abolished and that federals funds be given directly to tribal governments. No wholesale action was taken as a result, however.

Congress did clear Indian self-governance legislation, providing authority for 10 additional tribes to participate in a demonstration project, established by a 1988 act, to help tribes manage programs that previously had been administered by the Bureau of Indian Affairs and the Indian Health Service.

Bills seeking to enhance Indian health also were enacted. Immunization services, mental health care, child abuse treatment, health promotion and disease prevention programs were established. Infant mortality-related diseases would be the focus of study and treatment.

In other Indian legislation, Congress provided funds for tribally controlled community colleges, strengthened the authority of Interior Department law enforcement services on Indian lands and set up a grant program to help clean up environmental problems on Indian lands. New protections were installed for Indian grave sites, and provisions were made for the return to the tribes of some Indian remains, long of interest to museums and scientists. Congress also authorized grants and programs to ensure the survival of native Indian languages. The Smithsonian Institution got the go-ahead to build a new museum of Indian culture and history on the mall in Washington, D.C.

Bush vetoed legislation giving preferences to Indian businesses.

Other Action. Outrage was heard from some members of Congress — and particularly conservative Sen. Jesse Helms, R-N.C. — about taxpayer money, in the form of federal grants provided by the National Endowment for the Arts (NEA), being used to finance the creation of art they found objectionable. A major controversy developed, which resulted in 1989 in a ban on NEA against underwriting projects that could be considered obscene, sadomasochistic or homoerotic.

The prohibition did not last long, however. The next year, Congress in essence lifted the ban, leaving it to the courts to determine if a grant recipient's artwork was obscene. If it was found to be so, the artist would be required to return the grant money and would be barred from receiving further grants for three years.

In the art form of motion pictures, a 1991 film acted as a catalyst for 1992 legislation that provided for the reexamination of files accumulated in the course of various government investigations into the Nov. 22, 1963, assassination of President John F. Kennedy.

Chronology Of Action On General Government

1989-90

Federal Pay Overhaul

A sweeping overhaul of the federal pay system was the centerpiece of the $20.9 billion fiscal 1991 spending package for the Treasury Department and U.S. Postal Service. President Bush signed the legislation (HR 5241 — PL 101-509) Nov. 5, 1990.

Under pay revision provisions agreed to the week of Oct. 15 by the administration and House and Senate conferees, federal workers would receive raises equal to the average annual salary increases in the private sector beginning in 1992. Employees were guaranteed salary increases of up to 5 percent annually, based on the Employment Cost Index (ECI), which kept track of changes in the private local labor markets.

The aim of the bill was to close the gap between federal and private sector salaries. According to the president's pay advisers, federal pay had fallen an average of 30 percent behind private sector wages.

Under existing law, all federal workers of the same rank received the same pay, regardless of where they lived. Beginning in fiscal 1994, federal workers in high-cost cities would qualify for extra locality-based pay increases. For nine years, starting in 1995, the remaining gap would be closed by 10 percent.

The agreement marked the end of negotiations between Congress and the administration over how much authority the president would have to limit or deny pay increases. Under the bill, the president could withhold salary increases only in the event of war or negative growth of the gross national product for two consecutive quarters. After 1995, the president would have broader discretion to alter the agreement.

The bill also gave all federal workers a 4.1 percent pay increase effective Jan. 1, 1991. Bush had asked for a 3.5 percent increase.

In other action on federal pay, Congress suspended for five years the option that federal workers had to receive a portion of their pension in a lump-sum payment when they retired. *(Story, p. 858)*

Background

The General Schedule (GS) — a nationwide ranking system for federal workers — was the result of efforts dating back to the mid-19th century striving for uniformity and pay equity for all government employees. A major breakthrough toward that end, the 1923 Classification Act, created a classification system for federal workers in Washington. Legislation mandating a comprehensive nationwide system was enacted in 1949.

Although these systems achieved internal consistency, they did not address the question of parity with private industry. In the 1980s, a number of studies suggested that the federal government could no longer compete with the private sector and had to hire inferior employees or leave positions vacant and often cut back its services.

The principle of pay comparability with the private sector was not enacted until 1970 (PL 91-656). Beginning in 1978, citing economic conditions, successive presidents disregarded the recommendations of their pay agents — a group of federal officials who reported annually to the president and made a pay-adjustment recommendation based on national survey data — and granted smaller annual salary increases than recommended. *(Congress and the Nation Vol. III, p. 454)*

Although it had the power to do so, Congress chose not to override the president's final pay determination or to grant a full pay raise as recommended by the pay agent. Members of Congress blamed the White House for the resulting problems in recruiting and keeping federal workers, but successive administrations argued that economic conditions made it impossible to provide the recommended increases.

As the pay gap grew, the government found attracting and retaining highly skilled workers harder and harder. A number of studies analyzing the problem pointed to the pay disparity as the major cause of the difficulties, including the one done by the National Commission on the Public Service, headed by former Federal Reserve Board chairman Paul A. Volcker, which released its final report in March 1989. *(Volcker Commission, box, p. 859)*

In response to the Volcker Commission, Congress in 1989 considered legislation aimed at making federal government employment more attractive to university graduates. Congress also cleared a measure to make mid- and upper-level federal employees eligible for overtime pay. *(University graduates and overtime pay, p. 858)*

Legislative Action

In early 1989, legislation (HR 3979, S 2274) was introduced in each chamber to make federal salaries competitive with private sector wages. The House Post Office and Civil Service Committee on July 18 voted 19-4 to approve HR 3979. By voice vote July 25, the Senate Governmental Affairs Committee approved S 2274. HR 3979 was formally reported (H Rept 101-730) on Sept. 21, 1990; S 2274 was reported (S Rept 101-457) on Sept. 12, 1990. Neither bill was considered on the floor. Members found the right vehicle for the provision in the fiscal 1991 Treasury appropriations bill (HR 5241).

The pay system was offered as an amendment to HR 5241 by John Glenn, Ohio, and William V. Roth, Del., chairman and ranking Republican, respectively, of Senate Governmental Affairs. The amendment, adopted by voice vote, incorporated the language of S 2274, with some changes. The Senate also gave voice vote approval to an amendment by Dennis DeConcini, D-Ariz., to raise the starting salaries of federal offices by $3,000 a year; grant cost-of-living bonuses to officers assigned to the nation's 13 highest costing cities; and provide relocation, retention and language-skill bonuses. The Senate passed HR 5241 on Sept. 11 by a 93-6 vote. The House had passed the bill, 300-72, on July 13.

House and Senate conferees, after days of negotiation with the Bush administration, reached agreement on the bill Oct. 19. The House approved the conference report (H Rept 101-906) on Oct. 22 by a 343-67 vote. The Senate approved the package Oct. 23 by voice vote, adding two amendments unrelated to the pay increase. The House accepted the amendments Oct. 24, clearing the bill for the president.

Bush had threatened to veto the measure over provisions preventing the Office of Management and Budget from establishing an accounting-standards process for the federal government, but he ended up signing the legislation.

The administration had proposed restructuring the pay system to redirect funds to critical pay categories instead of pumping scarce dollars into a broad program increase. Bush sent Congress a message July 7, 1989, making the proposal, which was the executive branch counterpart to the president's April proposal to increase judicial salaries. Neither the House nor Senate, however, marked up the administration alternatives (HR 4716, S 2547).

Federal Workers

Congress in 1989 acted on several bills related to pay and performance of federal employees.

- HR 215 (PL 101-173) made mid- and upper-level federal employees eligible for extra overtime pay. The bill lifted the cap of $6,565 on "administratively uncontrollable" overtime and permitted employees whose jobs entailed considerable unscheduled overtime hours to receive 10 percent to 25 percent of their own base pay in overtime. In 1989, federal pay for irregular, unscheduled overtime was computed according to the base pay of an entry-level position.

The House Post Office and Civil Service Committee approved HR 215 Oct. 25 and reported it (H Rept 101-325, Part I) Oct. 31. The full House passed the bill by voice vote under suspension of the rules Nov. 13. Later that same day, the Senate passed HR 215 by voice vote, clearing the measure. The president signed it Nov. 27.

- HR 3282 (PL 101-103) extended through March 31, 1991, the Performance Management and Recognition System — a merit-pay program for federal managers and supervisors that was established in 1984.

The House passed HR 3282 on Sept. 19 by voice vote under suspension of the rules. The Senate passed the bill Sept. 27 on a voice vote, adding an amendment that extended until Dec. 31, 1989, a requirement that retiring federal employees could receive only 60 percent of their lump-sum distribution the first year. The House cleared the measure Sept. 28. President Bush signed the bill Sept. 30.

- HR 2544, designed to make jobs in the federal government more attractive to university graduates, allowed agencies to repay outstanding federal student loans of new recruits. Graduates of law schools, medical schools and other institutions of higher education were eligible for assistance. In return for this benefit, the worker was required to agree to stay at the agency for at least three years. If the worker violated the agreement, he or she was required to pay back the agency for any funds paid to the holder of the student loan.

The legislation, approved Oct. 25 by the House Post Office and Civil Service Committee and reported (H Rept 101-402) Feb. 7, 1990, was based on recommendations by the National Commission on the Public Service to improve the quality of the federal work force. In its report, the commission said top college graduates generally perceived public service as a career of last resort. *(Commission, box, p. 859)*

Federal Honoraria Ban

Federal employees mounted a campaign on Capitol Hill and in the courts late in 1990 to nullify a little-noticed provision in the 1989 Ethics Reform Act (PL 101-194) that prohibited even the lowest-grade civil servant from being paid for outside speeches or non-fiction writings. They failed to block the ban, but proposals to modify or repeal it began advancing through congressional committees in early 1991. *(102nd Congress action, p. 886; ethics reform, p. 920)*

The 1989 law, scheduled to take effect Jan. 1, 1991, provided for a congressional pay raise as well as new restrictions on honoraria — reducing the limit for senators and banning speaking fees for House members and federal officials. The extent of the governmentwide honoraria prohibitions went largely unrecognized during congressional consideration of the bill in 1989.

Only as the law was about to go into effect was it widely publicized that the act banned all federal employees in the three branches, except senators and Senate staff, from accepting writing or speaking fees, even if the topic was unrelated to their work and presented to audiences with no knowledge of the employees' official duties. Violators of the law were subject to fines of $10,000 or the amount of the honorarium, whichever was greater.

Previously, federal regulations prohibited receiving payment for speaking or writing if the subject specifically dealt with an employee's agency's "responsibilities, policies and programs" and limited any other honorarium to $2,000 per appearance or speech.

An amendment to an unrelated bill (HR 2431) passed by the Senate on Oct. 27, 1990, might have eased the ban for rank-and-file workers, but House Judiciary Committee Chairman Jack Brooks, D-Texas, refused to consider any bill that did not also lift the ban for higher-level employees.

Interim regulations issued by the Office of Government Ethics Nov. 28 exempted a number of outside activities from the pay ban, including writing fiction or poetry, teaching a course or performing a comedy routine at a dinner theater. Accepting payment for non-fiction articles, however, was expressly forbidden, as was payment for any outside speech or appearance.

The American Federation of Government Employees and the National Treasury Employees Union filed suit in U.S. District Court in Washington in December, seeking a preliminary injunction to block enforcement of the law. The court rejected their plea.

Lump-Sum Pension Payments

In a budget-cutting move, Congress acted in 1990 to take away federal workers' right to receive their retirement benefits in a lump sum upon retirement.

As part of the fiscal 1991 reconciliation bill (HR 5835 — PL 101-508), Congress suspended for five years lump-sum benefits for federal employee retirees. Workers retiring on or before Nov. 30, 1990, or after Sept. 30, 1995, would not be affected. *(Reconciliation, p. 55)*

Volcker Commission

The National Commission on the Public Service, headed by former Federal Reserve Board chairman Paul A. Volcker, conducted a two-year investigation into ways to attract and retain top-notch public servants and to improve the public image of federal bureaucrats. A 64-page final report was released March 29, 1989. The privately held commission was made up of 36 prominent citizens, most of whom had been public officials, including former president Gerald R. Ford and former vice president Walter D. Mondale.

The Volcker Commission recommended:

- An immediate 25 percent increase in executive, judicial and legislative salaries for senior-executive employees, with a second, comparable increase after the 1990 elections. According to the commission, a pay raise of that magnitude would help restore government salaries to 1969-level purchasing power.
- A major overhaul of civil service pay procedures. Labeling the General Schedule (GS) pay system "unworkable," the report proposed a locality-pay system that would raise salaries to reflect real differences in living costs in various parts of the country and also take into account the realities of competitive pay in certain occupations.
- Giving Cabinet officers and agency heads greater flexibility to manage their departments, including more freedom to hire and fire personnel.
- Establishing a Presidential Public Service Scholarship program targeted to 1,000 college or college-bound students annually to encourage service in the public sector.
- Highlighting and improving the role of the Office of Personnel Management as an active recruiting agency for the president.
- Building youngsters' interest in public service through greater emphasis on civic education in the schools and through an expansion of national volunteer service programs such as the Peace Corps and VISTA (Volunteers in Service to America).

The National Treasury Employees Union, while praising the report overall, criticized the commission for not paying enough attention to problems in the current pay system for rank-and-file federal employees and for not putting forth a "systematic program to remedy the pay crisis."

The Office of Management and Budget and the Congressional Budget Office calculated that eliminating the lump-sum option would save $1 billion in fiscal 1991 and $8.1 billion over five years. Many observers — federal employees, union representatives and government officials — doubted that the option would be reinstated in 1995.

Under the lump-sum option, employees would receive two taxable payments, in two calendar years, equal to the amount they had contributed to their pension plan. Acceptance of the payment would reduce a retiree's annual annuity check by 5 percent to 20 percent.

Employees "involuntarily separated" from their jobs would continue to receive a 50/50 lump-sum benefit, as would critically ill employees. U.S. armed forces or Defense Department workers employed because of Operation Desert Shield were given an extra year — until Nov. 30, 1991 — to retire and claim the payment.

Personnel managers in various executive departments reported increases in the number of employees who retired during the later months of 1990, which was attributed in part to the new congressional regulations.

As cleared, HR 5835:

- Suspended lump-sum benefits for retirees for five years. Workers retiring on or before Nov. 30, 1990, or after Sept. 30, 1995, were not affected. Employees "involuntarily separated" from their jobs continued to receive a 50/50 lump-sum benefit. Critically ill employees continued to be eligible for lump-sum benefits. Federal workers employed because of Operation Desert Shield would be required to wait an additional year to be eligible for the lump-sum payment. Workers entitled to the 50/50 lump-sum payments would receive payments in two calendar years.
- Required carriers of the Federal Employees Health Benefits Program (FEHBP) to implement cost-containment measures. It exempted the FEHBP from state premium taxes. It required better coordination between the Office of Personnel Management and the Department of Health and Human Services to ensure correct Medicare payments and limits. The bill also required cash-management controls in administering payments from the Employees Health Benefits Fund.
- Required the U.S. Postal Service to pay premiums for postal employees and survivors of postal workers who retired after June 30, 1971.
- Required the Postal Service to fund Civil Service Retirement Systems cost-of-living adjustments (prorated) for postal retirees and survivors of retirees who retired after reorganization of the Postal Service in 1971. Before fiscal 1991, the adjustments were funded by the government.
- Allowed nearly 200,000 non-appropriated fund (NAF) employees at the Defense Department to change work classifications (for example, from NAF to civil service positions) without a loss in pay, benefits, sick leave and so on. The language had been included in the House-passed HR 3139.

Hatch Act Veto

After intensive lobbying by the White House, the Senate on June 21, 1990, fell two votes short of overriding President Bush's veto of a bipartisan bill (HR 20) to amend the 1939 Hatch Act, which prohibited federal employees from taking part in partisan politics.

As a result, the effort to rewrite the 51-year-old law ended where it began two years earlier, as a wishful goal of federal union leaders and their growing number of allies in Congress. Among those strongly supporting the legislation were the American Federation of Government Employees (AFGE) and the American Postal Workers Union. Groups that lined up against the bill included the U.S. Chamber of Commerce, the American Civil Liberties Union and the independent citizens' lobbying group Common Cause.

Background

The Hatch Act, when passed, was needed to address a growing problem. By the end of 1934, more than 60 new federal agencies had been created and 300,000 new federal jobs had come into being. Lawmakers feared that most were being staffed on the basis of political patronage. In 1938, a Senate panel found that some federal workers had been coerced into contributing to the re-election fund of Sen. Alben W. Barkley, D-Ky. (1927-49, 1955-56). A Senate investigation the next year disclosed that political appointees in the Works Progress Administration (WPA) had coerced workers into making political contributions to protect their jobs.

In response to these developments, Sen. Carl A. Hatch, D-N.M. (1933-49), became an advocate of strict limits on political activity by federal employees as a means of ensuring clean elections. Hatch's bill passed the Senate with no hearings and little debate. Congressional action was so fast that an amendment had to be offered later to exempt the president, the vice president and members of Congress from the restrictions, which would have prevented them from seeking re-election.

Efforts to revise the law, which remained controversial since its passage, were repeatedly blocked. In 1966, Congress established an independent bipartisan commission (PL 89-617), which urged that federal workers be allowed to participate in politics. Similar legislation cleared Congress in 1976, but President Gerald R. Ford vetoed it. Similar efforts again fell short in the 100th Congress but were revived in the 101st Congress. *(Congress and the Nation Vol. II, p. 658; Congress and the Nation Vol. IV, p. 822; Congress and the Nation Vol. VII, p. 857)*

House and Senate Action

The House Post Office and Civil Service Committee approved HR 20 on a 22-1 vote April 12, 1989, and reported the bill (H Rept 101-27) the next day. The measure, which would allow federal and postal employees to campaign, raise funds and run for political office during their off-duty hours, was passed 291-90 by the full House April 17. The legislative procedure used to bring HR 20 to the floor — suspension of the rules — did not allow amendments, a source of criticism from some members.

The Bush administration issued the first of several veto threats against HR 20 following House passage. A statement by the Office of Management and Budget said the bill would "undermine the integrity and independence of the traditionally nonpartisan civil service."

The Senate Governmental Affairs Committee in July 1989 approved S 135, sponsored by committee Chairman John Glenn, D-Ohio. The Senate bill barred a federal worker from raising funds for an individual candidate's campaign or for most political action committees other than the one representing that worker's interests. In addition, such workers could not run for political office, but they could participate in many other political activities, such as organizing voter drives or acting as delegates to the presidential nominating conventions. S 135 was reported (S Rept 101-165) on Oct. 17. A similar bill was approved by the committee in 1988.

Senate Majority Leader George J. Mitchell, D-Maine, forced the bill to the floor May 1, 1990, when he won a 70-28 vote to shut off debate on a motion to proceed to consideration of the bill. Republicans, unwilling to admit defeat, offered amendment after amendment in what Democrats described as a stalling effort. Glenn accused Republicans of attempting to "filibuster" through use of the amendment process. Two substitute amendments offered by Governmental Affairs' ranking Republican, William V. Roth Jr., Del., were turned back May 3 on votes of 67-30 and 66-29 after Glenn complained that they failed to solve the main problem: the federal workers' inability to participate in the political system. Roth, like the Bush administration, argued that the bill's safeguards against coercion were inadequate.

Charles S. Robb, D-Va., and John W. Warner, R-Va., who supported the bill, then offered an amendment to strengthen its anti-coercion provisions. Their amendment, which was adopted voice vote, called for a maximum fine of $5,000 or a prison sentence of up to three years for attempts to coerce an employee into participating in the political process or into making a contribution.

Glenn then mustered his forces to kill, 59-35, an amendment by Pete Wilson, R-Calif., that would require the General Accounting Office to review implementation of the law and to report whether a pattern of illegal political activity existed.

Several GOP amendments were aimed at trying to tie the Hatch Act revisions to the broader issue of campaign finance reform. Republicans failed in a number of efforts to amend sections of the bill that would have allowed federal employees to solicit funds from colleagues for union PACs. Republicans argued that, because the unions were largely Democratic, the provisions would have meant more dollars for Democrats.

On May 9, members rejected an amendment by Mitch McConnell, R-Ky., that would allow federal employees to refuse to pay any part of union dues that was funneled to political campaigns without losing their right to vote on collective bargaining issues. The amendment was killed on a tabling motion, 63-35.

Also on May 9, Minority Leader Bob Dole, R-Kan., offered an amendment that called for federal employees to decide through agency-by-agency referendums every five years whether to exercise their right to participate in political activities. Dole's amendment was tabled, 62-36.

The Senate also voted, 63-35, to table a Roth amendment that would prohibit federal employees from soliciting political contributions from co-workers.

An attempt by Pete V. Domenici, R-N.M., to maintain Hatch Act restrictions on employees of federal agencies such as the Central Intelligence Agency, the Internal Revenue Service and the National Security Council also was killed, 58-39.

On May 10, the Senate voted 67-30 to pass HR 20, after substituting the amended text of S 135. After the vote, White House spokesman Marlin Fitzwater reiterated that the president would veto the bill. "We believe it politicizes the civil service in an inappropriate fashion, makes them vulnerable to political manipulation as well as political solicitation," he said.

The House June 12 adopted, 334-87, without amendment or conference, the Senate changes in HR 20, with 90 Republicans voting for them. Before the vote, Robert S. Walker, R-Pa., read on the House floor a letter stating Attorney General Dick Thornburgh's "grave and unequivocal objections to HR 20." The bill, the letter said, "would permit virtually unbridled partisan activities by federal employees, which, history shows, would in turn inevitably lead to the politicization of public administration."

Veto Action

True to his often-repeated word, Bush vetoed the Hatch Act revisions June 15. He said that "after all the debate, no real need to repeal the existing Hatch Act has been demonstrated."

Five days later, despite the partisan rhetoric from the White House and Senate Republicans, the House voted 327-93 to override Bush's veto. More House Republicans supported the measure than at any other time since legislation to revise the Hatch Act was introduced in 1975. Among the Republicans voting to override was Minority Leader Robert H. Michel of Illinois.

Republican opponents argued that little or no grassroots support existed for the bill, merely union members who wanted to buy influence with PAC dollars. Bush said in his veto message, "The lack of any grassroots clamor for repeal for the Hatch Act . . . testifies to the support this statute has received within the ranks of the federal civil service and among the general public."

The House vote sent the measure back to the Senate where a close, bitter and contentious fight followed. The Senate debate became a partisan contest between Democrats, who argued that the bill was a civil rights issue, and Republican opponents, who countered that Democrats' support was based largely on their desire for PAC dollars.

Meanwhile, Senate aides said the Bush administration, needing at least two votes to sustain the veto, targeted Republicans Arlen Specter of Pennsylvania and Pete V. Domenici of New Mexico for strong arm-twisting. White House Chief of Staff John H. Sununu and Attorney General Thornburgh, a former governor of Pennsylvania, personally lobbied Specter, according to congressional aides and union officials.

In the end, Specter maintained his support for the bill, but Domenici and two other Republicans, Trent Lott of Mississippi and Alfonse M. D'Amato of New York, changed their earlier votes and supported Bush, allowing the president's veto to stand. The June 21 vote was 65-35, two short of the 67 needed to achieve the two-thirds majority to override.

Patronage System

In a rejection of the longstanding tradition of political patronage, the Supreme Court ruled 5-4 June 21, 1990, that hiring, promoting or transferring most public employees based on party affiliation was unconstitutional. The Court said that the patronage system impermissibly infringed on the First Amendment rights of public employees unless party membership was "an appropriate requirement" for the job.

The case of *Rutan v. Republican Party of Illinois* was brought after Illinois Gov. James R. Thompson, a Republican, began a government hiring and promotions freeze in 1980, affecting 60,000 state positions. His executive order allowed no exceptions but those granted by the governor's personnel office. The plaintiffs alleged that the personnel office discriminated against them because they did not support the state's Republican Party. *(Case summary, p. 836)*

In its ruling, the Court expanded the scope of two earlier decisions that prohibited firing public workers because of their party affiliation: *Elrod v. Burns* (1976) and *Branti v. Finkel* (1980). *(1976 case, Congress and the Nation Vol. IV, p. 640; 1980 case, Congress and the Nation Vol. V, p. 776)*

'Revolving Door'

Congress rewrote restrictions on lobbying by former executive branch officials — and, for the first time, applied such limits to its own members and staff — as part of the pay and ethics package (HR 3660 — PL 101-194) cleared Nov. 18, 1989. The provisions were an attempt to clamp down on the "revolving door" problem; that is, officials trading top government positions for high-paying jobs lobbying former colleagues on issues they previously oversaw. *(Ethics rewrite, congressional pay, pp. 920, 965)*

With the new law, members of Congress were prohibited from lobbying in the legislative branch for a year after leaving office. In addition, former government officials were barred for a year from using confidential information concerning trade and treaty negotiations to advise clients. Cabinet secretaries and other top White House officials were banned from lobbying any other senior executive branch officials for a year following their tenure, a broader restriction than one that had prohibited contacts with their former office. The president, meanwhile, remained exempt from lobbying restrictions.

Similar legislation cleared Congress in 1988 but was pocket-vetoed by President Reagan. *(Congress and the Nation Vol. VII, p. 856)*

While the revolving door provisions did tighten some limits, Congress agreed to roll back a 1988 law (PL 100-679) that prohibited former federal employees from working on a procurement contract for two years if they played a role in awarding that contract. *(Congress and the Nation Vol. VII, p. 859)*

Early in 1989, top-level employees at the National Aeronautics and Space Administration, the Defense Department and other agencies began resigning in droves to avoid being covered. Guidelines to implement the law were issued May 11, but Congress, at the Bush administration's request, cleared legislation (S 968 — PL 101-28) May 15 to delay imposing the new rules.

Additional congressional action was taken in 1991 on the revolving door issue during consideration of legislation to scale back the ban on honoraria for all federal workers. *(Federal honoraria ban, p. 886)*

Lobbying Curbs

Using his clout in his first year as the Senate Appropriations Committee chairman, Robert C. Byrd, D-W.Va., in 1989 pushed through Congress the most sweeping changes in lobbying law since 1946, when Congress first required lobbyists to register. *(Congress and the Nation Vol. I, p. 1565)*

The Byrd amendment to the fiscal 1990 spending bill for the Interior Department and related agencies (HR 2788 — PL 101-121) required recipients of federal grants, contracts or loans to file information on the names of, and fees paid to, any lobbyists they hired in pursuit of funds from Congress or the executive branch. It also prohibited recipients of such funds from using federal money to lobby for such contracts, grants or loans. The minimum amount of grant, contract or loan requiring a lobbying report was raised from $50,000 to $100,000, and profits earned on federal contracts would not be considered federal funds.

The measure added to the general body of information about lobbying by (1) forcing the disclosure of information about efforts to court the executive branch as well as Congress and (2) casting a wider net about congressional lobbying so far as appropriations were concerned. For instance, efforts to lobby staff must be disclosed.

Byrd's amendment also put the burden on the client, not the lobbyist, to make public information about lobbyists hired to pursue federal funds in Congress or the executive branch. Byrd's effort came after highly publicized scandals involving influence peddling at the Pentagon, the Department of Housing and Urban Development and savings and loan institutions.

Financial Centralization

Legislation cleared in the final hours of the 101st Congress created a centralized financial management system within the federal government. The aim of the measure was to improve the government's financial management practices and to prevent waste, fraud and abuse.

The House Government Operations Committee approved HR 5687 Oct. 6, 1990, by voice vote and reported it (H Rept 101-818, Part I) the same day. The Government Operations Subcommittee on Legislation and National Security had approved the measure Sept. 25. The bill was jointly referred to the Committee on Post Office and Civil Service, which was discharged Oct. 10. Sen. John Glenn, D-Ohio, introduced companion legislation (S 2840), but the Senate Governmental Affairs Committee never acted upon it.

The House passed HR 5687 by voice vote under suspension of the rules Oct. 15. The Senate passed an amended bill by voice vote Oct. 27. The House accepted the changes in the early hours of Oct. 28, in the session that began Oct. 27. President Bush signed the legislation Nov. 15 (PL 101-576).

The bill's principal sponsor, House Government Operations Committee Chairman John Conyers Jr., D-Mich., said the measure would guard against future cases of mismanagement, such as the scandals involving savings and loan institutions and the Department of Housing and Urban Development, by creating "a means by which Congress can hold agencies more accountable for how their money gets spent — and how it gets wasted." Conyers said that government studies had "identified 78 different problems which potentially pose hundreds of billions of more dollars in liabilities."

As enacted, the bill established a deputy director of management at the Office of Management and Budget (OMB). It split the position of the assistant to the director at OMB into a deputy director for budget and a deputy director for management. The bill also created statutory chief financial officers (CFOs) at 14 executive departments and nine federal agencies as well as the Office of Federal Financial Management (OFFM) at OMB, to be headed by a controller.

The law required that OMB report to Congress annually on the status of financial management along with a five-year plan for improving management operations. By the end of 1991, agencies were to be required to start issuing annual audited financial statements.

The Bush administration preferred comprehensive legislation that would require all agencies to produce financial statements accounting for all their activities. As enacted, the bill authorized agencywide, two-year pilot projects for some agencies and for others a "go-slow approach" requiring financial statements only "where the problems are — in real estate transactions, loans and loan guarantees, trust funds and revolving funds," said Conyers.

Congress was to vote on expanding the program to all agencies after reviewing an OMB cost-analysis report on the program scheduled for 1993.

Whistleblowers Protection

Praising "whistleblowers," President Bush April 10, 1989, signed into law a measure (S 20 — PL 101-12) beefing up job protections for federal workers who report incidents of government waste, fraud and abuse.

President Reagan pocket-vetoed a similar bill in 1988. *(Congress and the Nation Vol. VII, p. 858)*

Background

The Reagan administration opposed a whistleblower protection bill (HR 508), cleared by the 100th Congress, on constitutional grounds, claiming it would have allowed the government to sue itself. The Office of Special Counsel (OSC), a branch of the Merit Systems Protection Board (MSPB), would be charged with protecting whistleblowers, while the MSPB was responsible for settling whistleblower cases. As a result, the special counsel could have challenged MSPB decisions in federal court.

Before leaving office, Reagan Jan. 3, 1989, submitted new whistleblower protection legislation to Congress, where it got a cool reception. The proposal would allow whistleblowers who lost their jobs or suffered other employment problems to seek relief from MSPB and would set up an independent OSC to conduct investigations and protect whistleblowers. However, an aide to Sen. Carl Levin, D-Mich., said the measure limited the independence of the special counsel by requiring that the OSC's actions be reviewed by the Office of Management and Budget. And it would maintain existing law that required federal workers to prove that the "dominant" reason they were fired was because they blew the whistle on federal mismanagement. The vetoed bill required workers to demonstrate that whistleblowing was only a "factor" contributing to their dismissal.

On Jan. 3, Reps. Patricia Schroeder, D-Colo., and Frank Horton, R-N.Y., reintroduced the vetoed bill as HR 25. Levin was the chief sponsor of the Senate version (S 20), which strengthened protections for whistleblowers by making it easier for them to prove they were fired or demoted because they reported government fraud. In addition, the Office of the Special Counsel became an independent agency with more authority to investigate such cases. The bill also was aimed at helping federal workers such as Lynn Bruner, director of the Equal Employment Opportunity Commission (EEOC) office in St. Louis. Bruner, who told a Senate panel in June 1988 that the EEOC was woefully behind in processing age-discrimination cases, alleged that she was demoted because of that testimony and related comments that were critical of the commission. A majority staff report by the Senate Aging Committee (S Rept 100-162) found Bruner had been victimized.

A compromise was announced March 7 between the Senate cosponsors of S 20 and the administration. House cosponsors of HR 25 endorsed the compromise. Attorney General Dick Thornburgh, who recommended the 1988 veto, participated in the negotiations. Most of the administration's concerns centered around the fear that a bill too broadly written would serve not so much to protect "good-faith whistleblowers" but to shield workers against whom managers had legitimate complaints. The compromise:

- Clarified the standard of proof for whistleblowers and employers. Under the compromise, a worker had to prove his whistleblowing was "a contributing factor" in action taken against him. The existing standard required a worker to prove that his whistleblowing was a "significant" or the "predominant" factor; the original S 20 required him to prove it was merely "a factor."

Conversely, an employer had to prove "clear and convincing evidence" that any reprisals or actions taken against an employee would have occurred even without his whistleblowing. This standard contrasted with existing law that required an employer to demonstrate a "preponderance" of the evidence on his side.

- Prevented the special counsel from appealing adverse decisions in federal court or from issuing subpoenas.
- Prohibited the special counsel from opposing a whistleblower in cases before the MSPB.
- Prevented the special counsel from disclosing the name of a whistleblower unless it was necessary to protect the public health and safety.

Senate cosponsors offered the compromise as an amendment when S 20 went to the floor. Supporters hoped to pass the measure with no accompanying legislation, but Minority Leader Bob Dole, R-Kan., sought to offer a nongermane amendment. Dole's amendment broadened the definition of desecration of American flags to include any flag "knowingly displayed on the floor or ground." S 20 sponsors convinced Dole to offer his amendment as a separate bill.

The Senate passed S 20 March 16 on a 97-0 vote. The House passed the bill March 21 on a voice vote.

Major Provisions

As signed into law, S 20 (PL 101-12):

- **Merit Systems Protection Board.** Maintained existing law providing for the Merit Systems Protection Board (MSPB), with the three members appointed by the president and confirmed by the Senate. No more than two members could be from the same political party, and each member was to be appointed for a seven-year term.
- Gave the MSPB authority to protect a witness from harassment during a whistleblower investigation.
- Required the board to issue regulations by which a federal employee, who would be hurt if a colleague refused to cooperate with the investigation by the board, could petition the board to force that colleague to comply with the probe.
- Maintained the existing law, which authorized the MSPB to conduct hearings, appeals cases and special studies, and to review rules and regulations issued by the Office of Personnel Management (OPM) to ensure that they did not result in the unjust demotion or firing of a federal worker.
- **Office of Special Counsel.** Established the Office of Special Counsel (OSC) as an independent federal agency, separate from the MSPB. The counsel continued to be appointed by the president for a five-year term.
- Specified that the special counsel's primary role was to protect federal employees, especially whistleblowers who reported incidents of fraud, waste and mismanagement within their agencies.
- Reiterated the special counsel's responsibilities, such as: investigating allegations of retribution against whistleblowers; filing complaints with the MSPB or recommending disciplinary action; reviewing allegations of waste, fraud and abuse within the federal government and forwarding such complaints to the appropriate federal agency; and reviewing OPM rules and regulations.
- Allowed the special counsel limited authority to intervene in MSPB hearings or appeals, with the consent of the employee who brought the suit. In addition, the special counsel could intervene in cases where the counsel had granted permission to a federal agency to discipline an employee or where a federal employee had been charged with unjustly disciplining one of his workers.
- Protected the identity of any federal employee who exposed government wrongdoing to OSC and ensured that conversations between the special counsel and a complainant remained confidential except in cases where public health or safety might be jeopardized.
- Required the OSC to respond to allegations of "gross mismanagement, a gross waste of funds, an abuse of authority or a substantial and specific danger to public health or safety."
- Maintained existing law that gave the OSC 15 days to determine whether the allegations were valid. If so, the agency involved in the complaint would have to have initiated an investigation into the charges and reported back to the OSC within 60 days.
- Attempted to expedite probes into "prohibited personnel actions" by ensuring that the federal worker filing the complaint was kept up to date about the OSC's actions. The special counsel had to contact the worker within 15 days of receiving the complaint to acknowledge its receipt and provide an OSC contact person. OSC was required to notify that individual of the case's status after 90 days, and then every 60 days. If OSC scrapped the probe, the special counsel had to notify the complainant in writing to explain why the investigation was canceled.
- Allowed a worker to appeal directly to the MSPB only after he had lodged his complaint with OSC and the special counsel had either dropped the case or failed to notify the

worker after 120 days that OSC was seeking corrective action. Certain workers, such as a non-probationary worker who had been fired, could appeal directly to the MSPB without going through OSC.

- Authorized the OSC to request the MSPB to issue a 45-day "stay," prohibiting an agency from demoting or firing a worker who had filed a complaint with the OSC.
- Prohibited the special counsel from opposing whistleblowers in cases brought before the MSPB.
- Allowed the complainant a chance to comment on the case at most stages of the investigation.
- Required the OSC to submit a written report to the MSPB recommending disciplinary action against a federal employee who took unjust personnel action against a colleague, broke the law or refused to cooperate with the probe.

As under existing law, the agency employee under fire from the OSC had the right to respond to the charges, be represented by an attorney, have a hearing before the MSPB or an administrative law judge and request a judicial review of the board's decision. The MSPB could fire, demote or temporarily suspend the employee from federal work for up to five years, reprimand him or fine him up to $1,000 in civil penalties.

In the case of military personnel and those hired by government contractors who were charged with violating personnel laws, the OSC was allowed to recommend disciplinary action to the head of the agency involved in the complaint. The president was in charge of deciding how to discipline employees who hold confidential, policy-making positions.

- Allowed the MSPB to order corrective action, such as the rehiring or promotion of the affected worker, unless the agency proved with "clear and convincing evidence" that it would have taken the same personnel action against the worker had he not brought his complaints of alleged government abuses or negative personnel action to the special counsel.
- Allowed the OSC to give information to Congress without needing the approval or clearance of any other administrative authority.
- Maintained existing law that granted the OSC power to investigate violations of the Hatch Act, which prohibited federal employees from getting involved in most forms of partisan political activities, and other violations of civil service law.
- **Individual Rights.** Allowed any worker who feared his job had been jeopardized since he reported government waste, fraud and abuse to appeal directly to the MSPB once the special counsel had exhausted his responsibilities or scrapped the case.
- Granted a federal employee seeking retribution from the MSPB similar privileges afforded to the special counsel.
- Allowed a whistleblower to appeal MSPB decisions in federal court and to recover lawyer's fees and any other costs within reason.
- **Miscellaneous.** Defined reprisal for whistleblowing as federal employers who "take or fail to take, threaten to take or fail to take, any personnel action against any employee or applicant for employment" because the worker reported incidents of government waste, fraud or mismanagement or the worker complained about the alleged reprisal.
- Gave preference to whistleblowers seeking a job transfer.
- Authorized $20 million annually for fiscal years 1989-93 for the MSPB to carry out its authority under the whistleblower protection law, and authorized $5 million annually for fiscal years 1989-91 for the OSC.

Other Legislation

Other whistleblower legislation was considered by the 101st Congress.

On Oct. 10, 1989, Congress cleared a bill (S 248 — PL 101-123) that provided awards of up to $250,000 to federal whistleblowers. *(Story, p. 837)*

Legislation (S 436, HR 3368) also was considered that sought to protect private sector workers from retaliation if they disclosed federal health and safety violations or refused to participate in an illegal or extremely hazardous activity as long as the employee first tried to correct the violation. The protections would apply to any industry subject to federal health and safety standards.

The Bush administration and GOP lawmakers opposed the legislation, arguing that it was too broad and could encourage malicious disclosures by competitors or disgruntled employees. The National Labor Relations Board also looked unfavorably on the legislation, saying it could be used as an indirect weapon in negotiations on collective-bargaining agreements.

The Senate Labor Subcommittee on Labor held a hearing on S 436 on March 7, 1989. The full Labor Committee on April 25, 1990, approved the bill and on June 28 reported it (S Rept 101-349). S 436 was placed on the Senate calendar but was never considered on the floor.

A House subcommittee held a hearing on HR 3368 in 1989; no further action was taken.

Regulatory Negotiation

A bill was signed into law in 1990 that sought to promote a procedure whereby parties with an interest in a federal regulation could come together in a negotiation session.

The bill (S 303 — PL 101-648) gave explicit authority to a procedure known as regulatory negotiation and established so-called reg-neg guidelines for agencies and affected outside parties when both agreed to work together in drawing up regulations. The measure aimed to limit costly litigation and other delays caused by legal challenges and resistance to regulations.

The bill, while defining conditions under which negotiated rulemaking might be appropriate, did not supersede the practiced method of rulemaking, established by the 1946 Administrative Procedure Act. Under this statute, an agency published in the *Federal Register* a draft of a proposed regulation and provided an opportunity for public comment. After reviewing the responses, the agency made revisions and promulgated a final rule.

S 303 authorized the Administrative Conference of the United States (ACUS) — an agency charged with studying and recommending improvements in federal administration and legal procedures — to serve as an information clearinghouse and adviser to agencies and parties participating in negotiated rulemaking procedures. The bill also authorized $500,000 for the ACUS annually for three years.

The 100th Congress cleared legislation containing reg-neg provisions on an ad hoc basis but deferred enactment of governmentwide negotiated rulemaking legislation to permit individual agencies to experiment with the procedure. In 1988, the Senate passed S 1504, a version of reg-neg legislation, but the measure died in the House.

Sen. Carl Levin, D-Mich., introduced S 303 on Jan. 31, 1989, a revised version of S 1504. The Governmental Affairs Committee approved the measure July 13 and reported it (S Rept 101-97) July 31. The full Senate passed the bill by voice vote Aug. 3.

The House took action on its version (HR 743) in early 1990. The Judiciary Subcommittee on Administrative Law and Governmental Relations Feb. 7 approved the bill after adopting an amendment to provide that a notice of the formation of a negotiated rulemaking committee — composed of representatives of each interested party — be placed in trade and specialty journals in addition to the *Federal Register*. On April 25, the Judiciary Committee formally reported the bill (H Rept 101-461) as approved in subcommittee.

The House passed HR 743 May 1 by a vote of 411-0 under suspension of the rules, then inserted the text of the bill into S 303 and passed it by voice vote.

The Senate Oct. 4 took up the bill as passed by the House, adopting several amendments by Ted Stevens, R-Alaska, aimed at better notifying of residents in rural states. The House concurred with the Senate amendments by voice vote Oct. 22, clearing the bill for the president, who signed it Nov. 29.

In a related matter, Congress in 1990 cleared HR 2497 to authorize federal agencies to use alternative dispute resolution techniques, including settlement negotiations, mediation, "mini-trials" and arbitration, to resolve administrative disputes. Proponents said alternative dispute resolutions could be faster, cheaper and less contentious than court battles. The use of such alternatives to litigation would be voluntary for both parties.

The House Judiciary Committee reported HR 2497 (H Rept 101-573) on June 1. The House passed the bill by voice vote under suspension of the rules June 5. The Senate passed an amended version by voice vote Oct. 25. The House accepted the Senate changes the next day, clearing the measure. President Bush signed HR 2497 (PL 101-552) on Nov. 15.

Fund Transfers

Legislation (HR 4279) designed to eliminate friction between the states and the federal government over the transfers of money to states for funding grant programs cleared in 1990. The new law (PL 101-453) gave the Treasury secretary authority to negotiate state-by-state agreements on how cash would be transferred.

States choosing to receive funds in advance would have to make annual interest payments to the federal government. A state would be owed interest by the federal government if it had to advance funds for a federal grant program.

Federal officials complained that states often withdrew funds before they needed them and put them in interest-bearing accounts. Existing law did not require states to account for the interest earned. Many states, in turn, contended that the federal government was often late in reimbursing states for money advanced for use in federal programs.

The bill was cosponsored by House Government Operations Committee Chairman John Conyers Jr., D-Mich., and ranking Republican Frank Horton, N.Y., and approved by the committee Aug. 2. It was reported (H Rept 101-696) Sept. 13. The House passed the bill, 410-4, under suspension of the rules on Sept. 24. The Senate passed HR 4279 by voice vote Oct. 10, and the president signed it Oct. 24.

NEA Funding

In 1989, lawmakers for the first time prohibited the National Endowment for the Arts (NEA) from underwriting projects that could be considered obscene, sadomasochistic or homoerotic; in 1990, the ban was dropped, when Congress empowered the NEA chairman to ensure that grants were made on "general standards of decency and respect for the diverse beliefs and values of the American public." The controversial issue of obscenity was passed to the courts.

1989 Action

NEA funding for exhibitions of works that members of Congress found pornographic or sacrilegious boiled into a major controversy on Capitol Hill in 1989. Triggering the outcry were two artists: Andres Serrano, creator of "Piss Christ," a photograph of a crucifix in a jar of urine; and the late Robert Mapplethorpe, known for his homoerotic and sadomasochistic photographs.

Despite the debate over the photographs, the House July 12, 1989, decisively rejected attempts to slash or eliminate NEA funding. Dana Rohrabacher, R-Calif., offered an amendment to the fiscal 1990 interior appropriations bill (HR 2788) to zero out both the $144.25 million appropriation for NEA direct grants and a separate line item of $27.15 million that was contingent on matching grants from other sources; it was rejected by voice vote. The main vehicle for members who wanted to punish NEA was a Dick Armey, R-Texas, amendment to cut NEA's primary appropriation by 10 percent, or $14.43 million. But Interior Subcommittee Chairman Sidney R. Yates, D-Ill., and other Appropriations Committee members rallied around a compromise amendment offered by Charles W. Stenholm, D-Texas, which would cut funding only by the amount of the two controversial grants — $45,000. The House adopted the Stenholm language 361-65. It then rejected, 95-328, a proposal by Cliff Stearns, R-Fla., to cut NEA funding by 5 percent and finally approved the Armey amendment as amended by Stenholm, 332-94. The House passed the interior spending bill 374-49 on July 12.

The money bill saw fast action in the Senate. Robert C. Byrd, D-W.Va., chairman of both the full Appropriations Committee and its Interior Subcommittee, convened the subcommittee markup July 24, moved to full committee July 25 and brought the bill to the floor July 26.

The Senate accepted the House's $45,000 cut, but the Appropriations Committee went further, barring for five years NEA funding to the two local groups that made the controversial grants and earmarking $100,000 for a third-party study of NEA grant decisions. The Senate also approved, by voice vote July 26, a far-reaching amendment by Jesse Helms, R-N.C., who led the crusade to impose strict guidelines on federal arts funding. The amendment would ban government arts funding of any material that was "obscene or indecent," "denigrates the objects or beliefs of the adherents of a particular religion or non-religion" or denigrates a "person, group or class of citizens on the basis of race, creed, sex, handicap, age or national origin." On

Sept. 28, Helms attempted to win approval of an amendment to instruct the conferees to insist on the arts funding ban. The Senate voted to table (kill) the amendment to instruct by a **key vote of 62-35 (R 19-25; D 43-10)**, making clear that the language in the funding ban provision was a problem for many senators. The next day, Helms offered a revised version of his instructions that dropped the more troublesome language and called for conferees to insist on the funding ban for "obscene or indecent" works. The amendment was approved by voice vote after the Senate voted 65-31 on a proposal by Wyche Fowler Jr., D-Ga., to delete the word "indecent." The Senate passed the appropriations bill (S Rept 101-85) by voice vote July 26. *(1989 key votes, p. 1021)*

In their modest compromise, conferees on HR 2788 agreed to ban the use of NEA or National Endowment for the Humanities (NEH) funds for works that, in the judgment of the endowments, "may be considered" obscene and that did not have "serious literary, artistic, political or scientific value." The conference also set aside $250,000 for a 12-member commission to review the procedures of the NEA and NEH and recommend possible standards for the awarding of future grants. The panel had to report to Congress four months after enactment of the bill. The final version provided $171.3 million for NEA and $159.1 million for NEH for fiscal 1990.

The House approved the conference report (H Rept 101-264) Oct. 3 on a 381-41 vote. The Senate acted Oct. 7, voting 91-6 to accept the measure. President Bush signed the bill (PL 101-121) on Oct. 23.

1990 Action

As the arts community grappled with the new ban on funding artworks that might be considered obscene, House and Senate committee members in mid-1990 faced a new round of NEA authorization and appropriation bills. The challenge was to craft language that would address the obscenity issue without sparking the ire of either detractors or supporters of the endowment.

Authorization. The Senate Labor and Human Resources Committee on Sept. 12 approved, 15-1, an NEA reauthorization (S 2724), which included a compromise that would pass to the courts the controversial issue of obscenity. The compromise, offered by Orrin Hatch, R-Utah, would not forbid the NEA from funding any art on obscene, homoerotic, sacrilegious or other grounds, but artists or arts organizations would be required to return any federal dollars if a court found that works they created were obscene or violated child pornography laws. In addition, they would be ineligible for NEA grants for at least three years from the date of conviction. If an artist could not repay the grant money, the endowment could require that the state or local arts agency that passed the money along to the artist make the repayment.

The compromise was acceptable to interested groups such as the American Arts Alliance and People for the American Way, but the evangelist right protested, claiming the proposal did not go far enough.

Hatch said the solution was a constitutional method for sanctions against obscenity. Daniel R. Coats, R-Ind., complained that the compromise would do nothing to prevent obscene works from getting federal dollars. He offered his own amendment that would bar grants for obscene projects, for the sexual exploitation of minors and for attacking historically religious tenets, traditions, symbols or figures. Hatch dismissed Coats' proposal as unconstitutional and a prior restraint of freedom of expression. The amendment was defeated, 2-14, with only Strom Thurmond, R-S.C., supporting Coats.

The Senate legislation, formally reported Sept. 25 (S Rept 101-472), also would eliminate the controversial requirement that artists sign a pledge not to create obscene works. Instead, grant recipients would be requested "to note" the sanctions that would be incurred if they created an obscene work. The bill would authorize $195 million in fiscal 1991 and such sums as may be necessary through fiscal 1995 for the NEA; $165 million in fiscal 1991 and such sums through fiscal 1995 for NEH.

Arts advocates were optimistic that the combination of the Hatch plan and an independent commission's report Sept. 11 opposing legislative restrictions on the content of NEA-funded art would protect the endowment from efforts on the House floor to tighten restrictions.

In the House, Interior Subcommittee Chairman Yates and Pat Williams, D-Mont., chairman of the Education and Labor Subcommittee on Postsecondary Education, agreed that the issue concerning what the NEA funds was one of policy and belonged with Williams' authorizing committee. They also agreed that the authorizing legislation would go to the floor first, and the appropriations measure would adopt the language put into that bill. However, neither Williams' subcommittee nor the full Education and Labor Committee could agree on whether or how to write provisions restricting the funding of certain types of work, and a restriction-free bill (HR 4825) went to the floor.

On Oct. 4, Williams and E. Thomas Coleman, Mo., ranking Republican on the Subcommittee on Postsecondary Education, unveiled a compromise version of HR 4825 that would not allow the NEA to fund obscene art but would provide for the courts to judge whether a project was obscene. Following a hearing, the NEA could order grant recipients to return the federal money if they were found guilty of violating obscenity standards. In addition, offending artists would be barred from receiving grants for three years. In an accommodation to fellow subcommittee member Paul B. Henry, R-Mich., the compromise would instruct the NEA chairman to ensure that "artistic excellence and artistic merit" were the criteria used to judge applications, while taking into account "general standards of decency and respect for the diverse beliefs and values of the American public."

The Williams-Coleman compromise followed the approach used by the Senate Labor and Human Resources Committee in the crafting of an acceptable S 2724. HR 4825 was reported from House Education and Labor (H Rept 101-566) on June 28.

During House floor consideration of HR 4825 on Oct. 11, an amendment was offered by Philip M. Crane, R-Ill., to kill the NEA; it was rejected 64-361. Rohrabacher's amendment then was defeated 175-249. It would have restricted the endowment from funding projects that were obscene; that depicted human sexual or excretory activities or organs; that denigrated the beliefs, tenets or objects of a particular religion; or that denigrated a person or group on the basis of race, sex, handicap or national origin.

With little dissent, the House Oct. 11 passed the Williams-Coleman substitute amendment by a **key vote of 382-42 (R 142-31; D 240-11)**. Before the vote, the House accepted by voice vote an amendment to the compromise, offered by Fred Grandy, R-Iowa. It would allow artists to receive grants once they repaid their original grant instead of having to wait three years. The House passed HR 4825 — which authorized $364 million in fiscal 1991 and such sums as necessary through fiscal 1995 for NEA, NEH and the Institute of Museum Services — by a vote of 349-76 the same day. *(1990 key votes, p. 1039)*

Appropriations. While the House was able to pass an NEA authorization bill, the Senate, bogged down with other legislation, did not move so quickly. Furthermore, no supporter appeared willing to bring up S 2724 and face another floor fight with Helms. With the authorization stalled, congressional attention shifted to appropriations. Although the authorization for NEA, NEH and the Institute of Museum Services was due to expire Sept. 30, Congress had the option to not reauthorize the agencies; as long as it appropriated money, the endowments could run for another year.

On July 24, during House Interior Appropriations Subcommittee markup of the fiscal 1991 appropriations bill for the Interior Department and related agencies (HR 5769), Appropriations Committee Chairman Jamie L. Whitten, D-Miss., made a surprise visit and offered a handwritten amendment to bar NEA funds for "filthy pictures." The subcommittee agreed to hold off and debate the issue in committee. By the end of September, that still had not happened because Interior Subcommittee Chairman Yates was continuing to wait for the House to reauthorize the NEA.

During House Appropriations Committee consideration of a continuing resolution (H J Res 655), Whitten inserted language that would bar federal funds from being used to support or finance "any indecent, antireligious or obscene picture, play or writing." Anyone violating the guidelines would have to return the money received. At the appropriations hearings Sept. 25, Yates complained: "This resolution is for 20 days. What is served by proposing to put a standard on art for 20 days?" He also noted that current law allowed the federal government to recapture NEA funds used to create obscene works. Siding with Yates, Silvio O. Conte, R-Mass., said Whitten's language was vague and most likely unconstitutional. Yates' motion to delete the language was approved by voice vote.

Instead of reviving the controversy, the House Oct. 15 agreed 234-171 to insert the text of the House-passed NEA authorization bill (HR 4825) into HR 5769. The text was offered as a Williams amendment to an amendment by Ralph Regula, R-Ohio. Following adoption of the Williams amendment, the House accepted the Regula amendment, as amended, by a vote of 342-58. It required the NEA chairman to take into account, in funding projects, not only artistic excellence and merit but also general standards of decency and respect for the diverse beliefs and values of the American people; changed the NEA grant process; gave states a larger share of NEA funds; and implemented other policy changes. Before being amended by the Williams amendment, it would have established a new definition of artistic excellence to be used by NEA and prohibited the NEA from funding obscene or indecent works. The House passed HR 5769 (H Rept 101-789) on a 327-80 vote on Oct. 15. The bill provided $180 million for fiscal 1991 for NEA and $170.7 million for NEH.

Senate Appropriations Committee Chairman Byrd Oct. 17 placed restrictions on the NEA in the fiscal 1991 spending bill — the same restrictions that were enacted in the fiscal 1990 spending bill. Byrd's move effectively gutted the reauthorization measure (S 2724) approved by the Senate Labor and Human Resources Committee. Under the Byrd language, the endowment would continue to be forbidden to fund projects that "may be considered obscene, including but not limited to, depictions of sadomasochism, homoeroticism, the sexual exploitation of children, or individuals engaged in sex acts and which, when taken as a whole, do not have serious literary, artistic, political or scientific value."

On the floor, however, Hatch was able to supplant Byrd's language with an amendment that reflected the reauthorization compromise. Adopted Oct. 24 by a 73-24 vote, the amendment would leave decisions on obscenity to the courts, require grant recipients who produced works of art that the courts declared obscene to return the money and barred the artists from receiving additional grants for three years. Before the vote, Helms offered an amendment to the Hatch amendment, prohibiting the NEA from using federal funds to promote, distribute, disseminate or produce materials that depict or describe, in a particularly offensive way, sexual or excretory activities or organs. The amendment was rejected 29-70.

Helms also did not succeed in winning adoption of an amendment to prevent grants from being awarded to people whose family income was 1,500 percent of the poverty line; it was rejected by voice vote. However, as the chamber began to empty out in the aftermath of the excitement of adoption of the Hatch amendment, Helms was able to gain voice vote approval of an amendment to ban funding of works that denigrated religion.

The Senate passed HR 5769 (S Rept 101-534) by a vote of 92-6 on Oct. 24. The bill provided $170 million for fiscal 1991 for NEA and $168.3 million for NEH.

Avoiding another series of heated arguments, the Senate conferees accepted the House version, including the Williams-Coleman compromise, without much discussion. As expected, the conferees deleted the Helms provision that would have banned funding works that denigrated religion. The final bill provided $175 million for fiscal 1991 for NEA and $170.9 million for NEH.

The conference report (H Rept 101-971) was agreed to in the House on Oct. 27 by a vote of 298-43. The same day, the Senate accepted the conference report on a voice vote, clearing the bill for the president. Bush signed the measure (PL 101-512) on Nov. 5.

Aftermath. The National Council on the Arts, which advised the NEA chairman, voted on Dec. 14 not to impose standards of decency on panelists who recommended arts grants. Instead, the council instructed panel members that "by virtue of your backgrounds and diversity you represent general standards of decency — you bring that with you."

In January 1991, U.S. District Court Judge John Davies in Los Angeles ruled that the anti-obscenity pledge that grant recipients had been required to sign under the fiscal 1990 provision was unconstitutional. On Feb. 20, the endowment announced that it was dropping the requirement to settle a similar suit brought by the New School of Social Research in New York.

Paperwork Reduction

The 101st Congress failed to clear legislation (S 1742, HR 3695) to reauthorize the 1980 Paperwork Reduction Act (PL 96-511). Efforts fell victim to battles between Congress and the Bush administration over proposed restrictions on the Office of Management and Budget's (OMB) authority to review government regulations.

Regulatory Review

The Supreme Court Feb. 21, 1990, curbed the power of the Office of Management and Budget (OMB) to override health and safety disclosure regulations. The 7-2 decision was hailed by members of Congress who thought OMB exercised too much control over other agencies.

The justices ruled that OMB had no authority under the Paperwork Reduction Act (PL 96-511) to block another agency's directive that businesses disclose health and safety data to their workers or the public. The Court said the law empowered OMB to review requests for data intended for government use but did not extend to regulations meant to generate information for the benefit of a third party. The paperwork law had been a powerful tool in Reagan and Bush administration efforts to rein in the federal regulatory process. OMB used the 1980 law to derail agency rules affecting workplace hazards, wood stoves and food labeling. *(Congress and the Nation Vol. V, p. 849)*

Dole v. United Steelworkers of America involved a regulation from the Labor Department's Occupational Safety and Health Administration (OSHA) that required employers to make sure that their employees were told of potential hazards posed by chemicals at their workplace. When OSHA created the Health Communication Standard in 1983, it was confined to manufacturers, and OMB approved the standard. But unions and consumers sued, and after a federal appellate court in 1987 ordered OSHA to extend the standard's coverage to other employers, OMB rejected OSHA's revised disclosure requirements. It said the requirements were not necessary to protect employees. The Supreme Court affirmed the ruling of the 3rd U.S. Circuit Court of Appeals. *(Case summary, p. 832)*

Gary Bass, executive director of OMB Watch, a private watchdog group, commented that the Court's decision "greatly limits OMB's authority," but that the agency still "has an arsenal of weapons." He cited Reagan-era executive orders that required all agencies to submit proposed regulations to OMB for cost-benefit analysis and for a determination of whether they were consistent with the president's policies.

The Paperwork Reduction Act was scheduled to expire Sept. 30, 1990. *(101st Congress action, p. 867)*

For much of 1990, the administration strongly opposed provisions in both bills that would limit control of OMB's Office of Information and Regulatory Affairs (OIRA) over the regulatory review process. When a compromise finally was reached, too little time remained in the session to overcome delays in the Senate.

OIRA funding was continued, however, within OMB's general appropriations fund.

The Supreme Court in 1990 handed down an important ruling limiting OMB's power under the law. *(Court ruling, box, this page)*

Background

The main goal of the 1980 Paperwork Reduction Act was to reduce, by 25 percent, the public's paperwork burden on such tasks as federal employment guidelines for small businesses, defense procurement contracts and individual income tax forms. OIRA was created to review requests by federal agencies for information and to make sure that the information requested was necessary, that it could not be found elsewhere and that it was being collected efficiently. *(Congress and the Nation Vol. V, p. 849)*

The effect of the 1980 law was to give the executive branch — specifically OIRA — growing control over the form and content of regulations issued by federal departments and agencies. President Ronald Reagan issued a number of executive orders moving OMB toward increased regulatory oversight power.

The legislative and executive branches had fought for years for control of the regulatory process. Because the regulatory review power had accrued to OMB under Republican administrations, it particularly drew the ire of congressional Democrats. Many Democrats resented OMB's OIRA, accusing it of misusing its authority to review agency regulations by delaying proposed rules that the administration disagreed with and changing others to suit administration policy.

From 1983 to 1986, Congress withheld authorization of OIRA. In 1986, leading House Democrats threatened to withhold OIRA's fiscal 1987 funding. OIRA Director Wendy Lee Gramm — wife of Sen. Phil Gramm, R-Texas — agreed to make available to Congress and the public some of its review information, including correspondence between agency heads and OIRA. Congress then renewed OIRA's authorization through fiscal 1989. *(Congress and the Nation Vol. VII, p. 849)*

But members continued to complain about OIRA.

Legislative Action

In early 1990, House Government Operations Committee Chairman John Conyers Jr., D-Mich., and the ranking Republican on the panel, Frank Horton, N.Y., were certain they had reached agreement with OMB Director Richard G. Darman: If Congress approved a simple reauthorization for OIRA, OMB would agree to limit its regulatory power.

Conyers' panel approved HR 3695, a three-year reauthorization of OIRA, March 13 without the limitations on OMB. Instead, the restrictions negotiated by Conyers, Horton and Darman were spelled out in an administrative agreement separate from the legislation, to become effective when the reauthorization became law. The agreement called for OIRA to provide, in writing, a detailed explanation of the reasons for all substantive changes in proposed regulations and would set deadlines for OIRA's review of regulations. The House bill contained provisions requiring OIRA to make available to the public an explanation of any decision to change a regulatory paperwork proposal. It also would limit OIRA's ability to overrule agency decisions on rulemaking.

On April 5, as leaders of the House committee were preparing to take HR 3695 to the floor, White House Chief of Staff John H. Sununu called a meeting with Conyers to raise several questions about the agreement. In a subsequent letter to Conyers, White House legal counsel C. Boyden Gray said the administration would not back the deal.

Meanwhile, the Senate Governmental Affairs Committee was encountering difficulty in marking up S 1742, which contained many restrictions on OIRA. Republicans on the Senate panel objected to the restrictions and boycotted a scheduled April 5 markup.

S 1742, sponsored by Jeff Bingaman, D-N.H., would give OMB 60 days to review proposed regulations and would have given OIRA the right to review regulations only if it found the agency's request for information and consequent paperwork demands unreasonable or incomplete.

The Senate Governmental Affairs Committee June 7 approved S 1742 by a 14-0 vote, after narrowly defeating an amendment that backers said would have gutted the bill. The amendment, defeated on a 7-7 tie, would have eliminated provisions requiring OMB to make information dealing with regulatory reviews available to the public. Republicans, joined by Democrat Sam Nunn, Ga., backed the amendment, claiming that the disclosure requirement would interfere with the president's ability to run the executive branch.

The Senate bill included provisions, insisted upon by Nunn, that were designed to protect small businesses from any increase in paperwork that the legislation might create.

In the last week of the session, the administration and key members of Congress reached another compromise: The administration promised to rein in its own regulatory power if Congress agreed not to write restrictions into law. Senate Governmental Affairs Committee leaders agreed to bring a stripped-down version of S 1742 to the floor. The bill was reported (S Rept 101-487) Oct. 6. Believing that final action was at hand, the House passed HR 3695 by voice vote under suspension of the rules Oct. 23 after about 15 minutes of debate. The bill had been reported from House Government Operations (H Rept 101-927) the same day.

The administration agreement would require some notification when OIRA was considering a new regulation, would require OIRA to explain any changes made in a proposed rule and would set limits on the amount of time the agency had to review regulations.

On Oct. 24, OMB released a statement saying that the administration "strongly supports" the Senate bill containing a straightforward, four-year reauthorization of OIRA. But several Republican senators placed anonymous holds on the measure during the final days of the session and the bill died.

Another casualty of the last-minute holds was the nomination of Vanderbilt University law professor James F. Blumstein to head OIRA. The job was vacant after the Oct. 1, 1989, departure of S. Jay Plager. The Governmental Affairs Committee 5-3 endorsed Blumstein's nomination Oct. 26, but without any great enthusiasm. The nomination was not formally reported to the full Senate before adjournment. Leaders of the panel said that no action on the nomination would be seen unless the legislation cleared.

Acid-Free Paper

Congress in 1990 cleared a measure (S J Res 57 — PL 101-423) providing for the use of acid-free "permanent" paper to preserve federal records, documents and other publications of enduring national value. The joint resolution also urged federal agencies and state and local governments to use acid-free paper for "permanently valuable" records.

When paper mills started using wood pulp in papermaking in the mid-19th century, chemicals and acid solutions were added to strengthen the pulp. While more paper could be produced this way, the average shelf life of the paper product was greatly reduced. Typical acid-based paper had a life expectancy of decades while acid-free paper, if well protected, could last for many centuries.

The resolution first passed the Senate July 31, 1989.

In 1990, the House Government Operations Subcommittee on Government Information May 16 unanimously approved its own resolution (H J Res 226). The full committee approved the measure by voice vote Aug. 2 and reported it (H Rept 101-680, Part I) Aug. 22.

The House passed H J Res 226 Sept. 17 by voice vote under suspension of the rules and then passed S J Res 57 by voice vote in lieu, substituting the text of the just-passed H J Res 226. The Senate Sept. 26 accepted the amended language, completing congressional action. The amendment called for three Library of Congress reports over five years on government use of acid-free paper; the Senate originally wanted annual reports. The library already had begun a program to de-acidify volumes of books that had been printed on acid paper. President Bush signed S J Res 57 on Oct. 12.

Post Office 'Off Budget'

Congress in 1989 removed the U.S. Postal Service (USPS) from the federal budget to shield it from governmentwide spending cuts. The change was approved as part of a 1989 deficit-reduction measure (HR 3299 — PL 101-239). *(Reconciliation, p. 43)*

The House Sept. 12 voted 405-11 to pass a bill (HR 982 — HR 101-177, Parts I and II) to remove the Postal Service from the budget, a step aimed at protecting the quasi-private agency from possible cuts under the Gramm-Rudman anti-deficit law. The Senate never acted on separate off-budget legislation.

Off-budget plans, strongly backed by unions representing postal workers, were projected to reduce the fiscal 1990 deficit for the federal government by $1.8 billion — the amount of the Postal Service's expected shortfall in fiscal 1990. The 1990 budget summit agreement between the White House and Congress called for moving the Postal Service off budget. But the agreement also required $400 million to $500 million in postal "reforms" to reduce taxpayers' subsidies for the Postal Service. The House Post Office Committee balked at that part of the deal. Its leaders said large cuts in subsidies would require a politically unpopular hike in postage stamp rates to make up the difference. Instead, lawmakers found more than $1 billion in additional "savings" with one-time accounting gimmicks: reducing the first year lump-sum payment to federal retirees and expediting Postal Service's workers' compensation payments to the Labor Department.

The Postal Service enjoyed off-budget status from 1973 until 1985, when Office of Management and Budget Director David A. Stockman succeeded in shifting it to on-budget status. Critics saw Stockman's move as a ploy to exploit the service (which was then operating with a surplus) as a source of deficit savings. The 100th Congress tried, but failed, to clear legislation to take the USPS out of the unified federal budget. *(Congress and the Nation Vol. VII, p. 859)*

The Postal Service provisions of HR 3299, as cleared Nov. 22:

- Removed the U.S. Postal Service fund from the federal budget and from provisions of the Gramm-Rudman budget law, reducing on paper the size of the federal deficit.
- Required the Postal Service to cover the cost-of-living adjustments in civil service benefits for postal employees who retired or died on or after Oct. 1, 1986, and for their survivors, resulting in estimated savings to the federal government of $70 million in fiscal 1990.
- Required the Postal Service to pay the health benefits for survivors of employees who died on or after Oct. 1, 1986, saving the government an estimated $190 million in fiscal 1990.
- Accelerated the Postal Service's payments to the Labor Department for workers' compensation so that $330 million more would flow into government coffers in fiscal 1990 instead of fiscal 1991.
- Extended for a year a provision reducing the first installment for federal employees who chose to take their retirement benefits in two annual lump-sum payments, saving the government $700 million in fiscal 1990. The provision continued the 50-50 split set in 1987, which was a change from the law's initial 60-40 division.

Curbs on Deceptive Mail

On Nov. 6, 1990, President Bush signed into law legislation (HR 2331 — PL 101-524) to curb the use of potentially deceptive mailings by advertisers and fund-raisers. The measure, which would become effective within 180 days of enactment, was designed to stop solicitations, especially addressed to the elderly, made to look like federal checks or other correspondence. The U.S. Postal Service could not deliver such "deceptive" mail unless it carried an insignia advising the recipient that the product or service was not endorsed by the federal government.

The bill required commercial mailings that contained any symbols, insignias or seals that could imply a federal government connection to be disposed of by the Postal Service unless it bore a disclaimer such as: "THIS PRODUCT OR SERVICE HAS NOT BEEN APPROVED OR ENDORSED BY THE FEDERAL GOVERNMENT, AND THIS OFFER IS NOT BEING MADE BY AN AGENCY OF THE FEDERAL GOVERNMENT." Envelopes containing such solicitations would be required to carry — also in capital letters — the legend: "THIS IS NOT A GOVERNMENT DOCUMENT."

Lawmakers expected that the bill would apply to such mailings as a "national medical census" sent out in 1988 to raise funds for the National Kidney Foundation and a come-on for vacation homes that came in an envelope bearing "Internal Review Service, Accounting Department" as its return address. One group, the National Committee to Preserve Social Security and Medicare, employed such attention-grabbing phrases as "time-dated legal documents" on envelopes addressed to senior citizens.

HR 2331, sponsored by Frank McCloskey, D-Ind., was approved by the House Post Office Subcommittee on Postal Personnel and Modernization July 11, 1989. The bill was reported from the full committee (H Rept 101-178) July 26. The House passed the measure by voice vote under suspension of the rules July 31. It was similar to a bill the House passed by voice vote in 1988 but which failed to reach the Senate floor. *(Earlier action, Congress and the Nation Vol. VII, p. 860)*

The Senate Governmental Affairs Committee reported its version of the legislation (S 273 — S Rept 101-464) on Sept. 14. The full Senate passed an amended HR 2331 by voice vote Oct. 4. The House accepted the Senate changes Oct. 19, clearing the measure.

Child-Proof Packaging

Congress in 1990 cleared legislation (HR 5209 — PL 101-493) to prevent the mailing of any unsolicited sample of a drug or other hazardous household substances that did not meet child-resistant packaging requirements.

The legislation, effective 180 days after its enactment, authorized the U.S. Postal Service to dispose of improperly packaged samples. Lawmakers said the Postal Service supported the legislation.

The Post Office and Civil Service Committee reported the legislation (H Rept 101-758) Sept. 26; the bill had been approved Sept. 25 by the Subcommittee on Postal Operations and Services. The House passed the measure Oct. 1 by voice vote under suspension of the rules. The Senate passed HR 5209 by voice vote Oct. 16, clearing the bill for the president, who signed it Oct. 31.

Anti-Porn Mail

Unable to untangle the constitutional questions concerning proposed legislation to impose civil fines on mailers of sexually explicit advertisements, the House Post Office and Civil Service Committee June 21, 1990, sent the bill back to subcommittee where it languished and died.

The Subcommittee on Postal Personnel and Modernization had approved the bill (HR 3805) March 27 but deadlocked over language to subject pornographic mailers to civil penalties of $500 to $1,500 for each violation.

Under existing law, companies were prohibited from mailing pornographic materials to households that requested that the U.S. Postal Service place them on a list designed to shield them from unwanted mail. But that law did not specifically call for civil penalties.

Tom Ridge, R-Pa., submitted an amendment that also would impose civil penalties on companies or individuals who mailed unsolicited sexually oriented advertisements, regardless of whether the ads were obscene. The Justice Department told the committee that the amendment was too broad and would be found unconstitutional.

'Motor Voter'

Legislation designed to increase voter registration was unexpectedly stalled in 1990. Dubbed the "motor voter" bill, the measure would require states to allow voters to register by mail and when they apply for driver's licenses or other identification cards issued by motor vehicle authorities.

Following House passage, supporters expressed confidence that the Senate would approve a motor voter bill before the end of the 101st Congress. But growing Republican misgivings, the constant threat of a presidential veto and the increasing pressure on Congress to complete its business and adjourn for the year led to the death of the legislation. Supporters vowed to revive the issue in 1991. *(102nd Congress action, p. 893)*

The House Administration Committee approved HR 2190 (H Rept 101-243) by voice vote May 3, 1989, and reported it Sept. 18. The legislation had been revised from an earlier version (HR 15).

The Democrats described HR 2190 as a bill of "inclusion." Al Swift, D-Wash., chairman of the House Administration Subcommittee on Elections and cosponsor of the bill with Bill Thomas, R-Calif., said a large number of Americans did not vote because too many obstacles existed. Voter turnout in the United States was the lowest of any democracy in the world.

Black House members, including Majority Whip William H. Gray III, D-Pa., and John Conyers Jr., D-Mich., called the bill an extension of the Voting Rights Act of 1965. During floor debate, they recalled the days of the civil rights movement in asking members to support the legislation. Conyers said, "Eliminating the registration barrier is particularly significant for African-Americans for whom registration, along with poll taxes and literacy tests, has historically served as an obstacle to exercising their constitutional right."

Gray noted that supporters of the Voting Rights Act heard the same arguments being used against HR 2190. The bill was a continuation of the struggle for inclusion of all voters, he said. The legislation's provisions were in addition to the Voting Rights Act and would not affect that law.

Although civil rights groups had questioned portions of the bill, Gray said all had come on board, including the National Association for the Advancement of Colored People (NAACP) and the National Urban League. Jesse Jackson endorsed the measure, although he had supported same-day-as-the-election registration — as had a number of House Democrats — instead of the bill's requirement that registration come at least 30 days before an election. The measure also was supported by the League of Women Voters and the AFL-CIO.

The controversy over HR 2190 was aired Jan. 31, 1990, when members took up the rule (H Res 309) for floor consideration of the bill. Republicans objected because the rule would allow only two amendments when the bill reached the floor. The rule was approved on an almost straight party-line vote of 254-166, but not before a heated debate that went far beyond the rule.

Minority Leader Robert H. Michel, R-Ill., charged that the bill, although backed by key Republicans, was not bipartisan because changes had been made without the knowledge of GOP members. Michel went on to say that he had concerns about how the bill was drafted. The bill should have been handled in the same way that campaign reform legislation was handled, he argued. Leadership on both sides should have had an opportunity to look at the bill and negotiate its contents, he believed.

In response, Swift pointed to the wide support the bill had from Republican members. He noted that the agreement had taken months to hammer out and warned that Michel's opposition threatened bipartisanship in the future.

Michel, who also voiced the objections of Illinois Republican Gov. James R. Thompson, argued that states would find complying with the law expensive. Illinois officials estimated that putting the law into effect in that state would cost $38 million. But Conyers told House members that the motor voter procedure was already in effect in Michigan without computers and the price tag was $100,000 annually. The bill would provide $50 million nationwide.

Some states also warned that their constitutions would have to be changed to accommodate the bill. Opponents argued that voter registration was the purview of the states, not the federal government. Critics in the House also said the bill was inviting voter fraud by not requiring notarization of mail-in applications.

To Republicans such as Minority Whip Newt Gingrich, Ga., the bill represented a chance to bring potential GOP voters into the fold. Gingrich tried to ease the concerns of Republicans who feared that the bill could somehow aid the Democrats, saying studies showed that half of the Americans eligible to vote were Democrats and half were Republicans.

Before the vote on final passage, a substitute amendment was offered to strengthen the bill's anti-fraud provisions and make the voter registration procedures voluntary. The amendment also would have provided $120 million in block grants to fund state programs that were designed to encourage voter registration.

Members voted 129-291 to reject the amendment and then voted 156-265 against a motion by Paul E. Gillmor, R-Ohio, to recommit the bill to the House Administration Committee for further study.

The House Feb. 6 passed HR 2190 by a vote of 289-132. Key Democratic Party leaders, including Ronald H. Brown, chairman of the Democratic National Committee, held a news conference the same day to call attention to the bill.

The Senate Rules and Administration Committee Sept. 26, 1989, reported a measure (S 874 — S Rept 101-140) similar to the House committee-approved HR 2190. S 874 made its way to the Senate floor a year later, as Congress was dealing with the budget impasse and a host of other issues that postponed its scheduled adjournment. The Senate debated the issue briefly before voting on a cloture motion Sept. 26, 1990. With only two exceptions — Oregon's Mark O. Hatfield and Bob Packwood — Republicans voted solidly against cutting off debate. Two Democrats — Howell Heflin, Ala., and Max Baucus, Mont. — defected and voted against cloture. The final vote was 55-42, five short of the number required. No further action was taken.

Republicans in the Senate said they opposed the bill because of the potential for fraud and abuse and the costs it would have imposed on states. They also said that elections were state matters and the federal government should not impose uniform regulations.

The Bush administration had threatened to veto the measure, claiming it would have increased the potential for voter fraud and imposed a financial burden on the states.

Uniform Poll-Closing Time

A bill to encourage voter participation in the West by mandating a uniform poll-closing time for presidential elections won House approval in 1989. HR 18 (H Rept 101-15, Part I), reported March 23 from House Administration, required polling places in the 48 contiguous states and the District of Columbia to close at 9 p.m. Eastern Standard Time (EST). The vote on passage, taken April 5, was 238-154.

To allow West Coast polls to stay open until 7 p.m. instead of 6 p.m. — a time election officials said was too early to allow many working voters to participate — the House bill extended daylight-saving time for two weeks in the Pacific time zone during presidential election years only.

The House passed virtually identical bills by narrower margins in 1986 and 1987, but the Senate failed to act because of objections to the extension of daylight-saving time on the West Coast. *(Congress and the Nation Vol. VII, pp. 856, 866)*

The Senate Rules and Administration Committee May 17 approved a uniform poll-closing bill (S 136 — S Rept 101-42) that would create a single poll-closing time of 10 p.m. EST, with no extension of daylight-saving time. Extending daylight-saving time in just one time zone would wreak havoc on airline schedules, argued Sen. Wendell H. Ford, D-Ky. S 136 was formally reported May 31.

Sens. Jesse Helms, R-N.C., and Mitch McConnell, R-Ky., cast the only votes against the poll-closing bill, arguing that the extended hours would impose a hardship on poll workers in the East and Midwest.

East Coast election officials objected to the cost of keeping the polls open late. The Congressional Budget Office estimated the extended hours in the House bill could cost state and local governments up to $3 million in 1992. But the bill would allow states to compensate for the later evening hours by opening polls later in the morning.

The main argument for closing all polls simultaneously was that "exit polling" and television often combined to leave Western voters feeling disenfranchised. In 1980, President Jimmy Carter conceded defeat to Ronald Reagan at 6:50 p.m. Pacific time, long before the polls had closed on the West Coast. Some observers said Carter's concession discouraged Democratic voters who might have made a difference in closer state and local races. Major television networks since had agreed not to broadcast their projections for a given state before the polls closed there. But that did not solve the problem posed when they projected national winners.

D.C. Political Issues

District of Columbia voters in November 1990 elected the District's first "shadow" congressional delegation — two senators and one House representative — which was given the mandate of lobbying Congress for statehood and included as a senator one of statehood's most prominent supporters, Jesse Jackson.

The D.C. City Council in February authorized the election of the shadow delegation but stopped short of appropriating $1.3 million it estimated would be needed to pay the delegation and its staff. The delegation — Jackson, fellow shadow senator Florence Pendleton and shadow representative Charles Moreland — carried no congressional recognition, public budget or salaries.

Tennessee was the first territory to send a shadow delegation to Congress when it acted in 1796. Since then, six prospective states had done the same, though Tennessee's representatives were the only ones allowed on the floor of the Senate during sessions.

Congress had been unwavering in its opposition to D.C. statehood. While a constitutional amendment was approved in 1978 to give the District voting representation in Congress, the effort died in 1985 when the statutory deadline for ratification expired. More recently, in 1989, Congress would not allow the city to spend $150,000 for a statehood lobbying office. *(Congress and the Nation Vol. V, p. 838; Congress and the Nation Vol. VII, p. 855)*

On July 24, 1990, a Senate Appropriations subcommittee gave bipartisan, voice vote approval to an amendment to the District's fiscal 1991 spending bill (HR 5311) prohibiting the city from using federal or locally raised revenues to fund its shadow delegation. The District also could not use its funding to pay for any other attempts to push for statehood. The Senate Oct. 26 cleared the appropriations measure, complete with the amendment. The full Appropriations Committee approved the bill July 27.

Congress had a constitutional right to legislate for the District. It pointedly reserved that prerogative when it passed limited home rule in 1973 (PL 93-198). Residents had since been allowed to elect their own mayor and council members, but District laws were still subject to congressional oversight. *(Congress and the Nation Vol. IV, p. 797)*

Meanwhile, several suggestions were made in 1990 on what to do about the District's disputed political status. On Feb. 25, Maryland Gov. William Donald Schaefer, D, offered to annex the District back into the state. His retrocession offer, he said, would provide residents the opportunity to vote for Maryland's two U.S. senators and an additional voting House member. Jackson immediately blasted Schaefer's proposal, saying it was akin to the South African "Bantustan" concept of segregated black homelands.

On March 6, Ralph Regula, R-Ohio, introduced a retrocession bill (HR 4195) to carry out Schaefer's proposal. Also on March 6, Stan Parris, R-Va., a longtime opponent of statehood who represented Virginia suburbs of the District, announced his "alternative" to statehood. He introduced a bill (HR 4193) to give D.C. residents the right to vote — but only in Maryland. Under Parris' bill, the District would remain autonomous, maintain limited home rule and its mayor and council, and Congress would still approve the city's budget. But D.C. residents would be allowed to vote for a representative and two senators in Maryland. Parris chose Maryland, he said, because in 1790, when Maryland ceded land to form the nation's capital, District residents continued to vote in that state. Congress withdrew those voting rights in 1801.

Sens. Edward M. Kennedy, D-Mass., and Paul Simon, D-Ill., May 17 introduced legislation (S 2647) to make the District the nation's 51st state. The bill would name the state New Columbia and allow District residents to elect two U.S. senators and a House member with full voting rights.

D.C. Del. Walter E. Fauntroy, D, sponsored a similar bill (HR 51) in the House, but the District of Columbia Committee did not act on it.

Some statehood opponents feared that involvement by Jackson could unstick the statehood debate. (Consideration of Puerto Rico plebiscite legislation also prompted discussion of D.C. statehood.) If Democrats in Congress insisted on pressing for statehood, Parris said, his response would be "to increase the stakes by suggesting the alternative to statehood is repeal of home rule." But that argument ignored the reasons Congress granted home rule in the first place. The civil rights movement in the 1960s generated too much political pressure to sustain a system in which the District, a majority-black city, was in effect governed by members of Congress, particularly the white Southerners who dominated the House District of Columbia Committee. Moreover, as the problems of running a city accumulated in the 1960s, Congress simply tired of acting as the District's municipal authority. Neither of those realities had changed. Home rule itself, however, was not in jeopardy, not even when D.C. Mayor Marion S. Barry Jr. went on trial on drug-related charges. Barry was convicted Aug. 10 of one misdemeanor count of drug possession and acquitted of another misdemeanor drug charge. A mistrial was declared on the 12 remaining charges when the jury deadlocked. *(Puerto Rico plebiscite, this page)*

D.C. Police Officers

In an attempt to help contain the skyrocketing crime rate in the nation's capital, Congress in 1989 cleared a bill (HR 1502) to approve the hiring of 700 more police officers for the District of Columbia. The president signed the legislation (PL 101-223) Dec. 12.

As cleared, the bill authorized $127.3 million over five years for the additional hirings, which would expand the District's police force to 5,055 officers. HR 1502 also required the city to institute a "community-oriented" policing system, calling on officers to be assigned to the same areas over time so they could become familiar with neighborhoods and work closely with community leaders.

The bill stipulated that none of the funds could be obligated until 120 days after the District's mayor submitted to Congress a plan to implement such a system. No funds authorized by the bill could be spent after fiscal 1990 unless the mayor certified that such a system was in place.

The administration opposed the bill because of the federal spending it required. White House officials argued that the District government had sufficient budgeting and taxing authority of its own to address the crime problem.

The House passed HR 1502 on a 289-105 vote under suspension of the rules June 13. The Senate Governmental Affairs Committee reported the measure (S Rept 101-123) on Sept. 12. The Senate passed an amended HR 1502 by voice vote Sept. 14. The House adopted further amendments Nov. 2, which the Senate accepted Nov. 20, clearing the bill.

D.C. Metro Assistance

President Bush Nov. 15, 1990, signed into law a bill (HR 1463 — PL 101-551) to authorize $2.1 billion to fund the Washington, D.C.-area Metro rail system to near-completion.

Under pressure from the Bush administration, Congress crafted a compromise to raise the requirement for local contributions to construction from 20 percent — as originally approved by the House — to 37.5 percent. Under the final bill, the federal contribution would be $1.3 billion over eight years. The transportation funding measure (HR 5229 — PL 101-516) appropriated $51.7 million for the Washington rail system in fiscal 1991.

The House District of Columbia Committee reported HR 1463 (H Rept 101-430) March 23. The House voted 260-150 March 28 to authorize $2 billion over 11 years — in annual installments of almost $200 million — to complete the projected 103-mile system. The remaining $675 million needed for the project would come from Washington-area taxpayers. The Senate passed the bill by voice vote Oct. 25, and the House cleared it by voice vote the next day.

Puerto Rico Plebiscite

The House in 1990 passed legislation to give Puerto Ricans the right to determine their future relationship with the United States. It called for a referendum to allow the island voters to choose among statehood, independence or "enhanced" commonwealth status. The legislation, which also saw Senate committee action, died at the end of the 101st Congress, but the issue was revived in the 102nd Congress. *(102nd Congress action, p. 897)*

After four centuries of dominance, Spain ceded control of Puerto Rico in 1898 to the United States. Over the next half-century, Congress extended U.S. citizenship to Puerto Ricans and gave them the power to elect a legislature and a governor. In 1921, the federal government sought to boost the local economy by exempting from federal taxes U.S. corporations doing business in Puerto Rico. The tax credit, later known as Section 936 of the Internal Revenue Code, provided a major incentive for U.S. businesses to operate on the island. Even so, more than 60 percent of the population remained below the United States' official poverty line, putting it below even the poorest of states. As a result, island residents had always been dissatisfied with their relationship to the federal government. In 1951, the island adopted a commonwealth constitution, and Congress approved it a year later, granting full local authority to Puerto Rico's elected officials. The tax credits remained under the commonwealth status. Puerto Ricans also were exempted from the requirement to pay federal income taxes, though they retained basic citizenship rights. In 1967, Puerto Ricans voted in a referendum to continue commonwealth status.

In his first appearance before Congress on Feb. 9, 1989, President Bush, a longtime supporter of statehood for Puerto Rico, made a surprising request that Congress take the necessary steps to allow for the island's self-determination. Spearheading the effort in the Senate, Energy and Natural Resources Committee Chairman J. Bennett Johnston, D-La., and ranking Republican James A. McClure, Idaho, sponsored S 712, which would provide for a self-executing referendum (one whose result would automatically take effect) in Puerto Rico. Several issues provoked contentious debate during committee hearings.

A dispute arose over the cost of statehood or independence to U.S. taxpayers. With data supplied by the Treasury Department, committee leaders projected an $18.7 billion gain to the Treasury during a 1992-2000 transition period if Puerto Ricans opted for independence, and a $13.6 billion net gain during this period under statehood. Don Nickles, R-Okla., however, scoffed at the statehood projection and suggested the real cost of statehood might be more like a net loss of $13 billion. The committee devised "a worst-case scenario" that had the federal government receiving a net gain of $5.2 billion under statehood. But doubters remained. Johnston and McClure, who had attempted to draft language that would be "revenue neutral," emphasized that the financial estimates were based on information provided by the Bush administration — data they said the committee had struggled to extract. Treasury Department officials believed the election should be "unencumbered by finances."

The United States had been spending about $6.2 billion a year in Puerto Rico. Roughly $2.9 billion was in the form of direct payments to individuals and $2.4 billion in grants to the government for nutrition and other programs.

In the final two markup sessions Aug. 1-2, the measure came under increasing fire for favoring the statehood option. The island would be given millions of dollars in special social program benefits if its citizens chose statehood.

Furthermore, controversy surrounded the proposal to provide the island with a non-voting Senate representative. The Johnston-McClure bill allowed the governor to appoint the representative, who could hire a staff made up of official Senate employees. The committee voted 10-9 on Aug. 1 to strike the entire section.

The underlying issue was senators' concern that the provision would propel a similar effort to give the District of Columbia the same staff privileges in the Senate. Saying he was "profoundly opposed" to providing Puerto Rico a non-voting Senate representative, Malcolm Wallop, R-Wyo., warned, "We are setting a precedent the government of the District of Columbia will want and cannot be refused. [It] is irresistible." *(D.C. issues, p. 872)*

A compromise was offered the next day that renamed the Senate representative a "liaison" and, while it would give the staff many of the privileges of Senate employees and provide the same amount of funding as the original bill, explicitly stated that the staff would not be Senate employees. This time, the amendment carried 13-5.

The Senate Energy and Natural Resources Committee approved S 712 Aug. 2 on an 11-8 vote and reported it (S Rept 101-120) on Sept. 6.

The Senate Finance Committee, with jurisdiction over the Social Security, tax and trade provisions, approved the bill Aug. 1, 1990, after making changes in the version reported a year earlier by Energy and Natural Resources. The Finance Committee, which formally reported the measure (S Rept 101-481) Sept. 30, scaled back the benefits section so that the same funding for social programs would be provided under statehood or commonwealth status. The committee also inserted a provision to establish a "transition period" to effectively delay statehood until 1996, if that option were chosen. A gradual phaseout — 25 percent a year — of federal tax credits would be allowed for U.S. corporations that located in Puerto Rico.

The Senate Agriculture Committee, which oversaw food stamp provisions, also had jurisdiction over S 712. The committee failed to act on the bill in the 101st Congress.

The House Interior Subcommittee on Insular Affairs on Aug. 3 approved HR 4765 to grant islanders a referendum on their status. The bill — which, unlike S 712, was not self-executing — would direct House Interior and Senate Energy to draft bills after the referendum to implement the status chosen by a majority of the island's voters. That legislation, if enacted, would become effective in 1992 if approved by another vote of Puerto Rican residents. The full committee on Sept. 19 approved HR 4765 on a 37-1 vote and reported it (H Rept 101-790, Part I) on Oct. 2.

The House Rules Subcommittee on Rules of the House held a hearing and markup on Sept. 27. The panel approved the Interior Committee's version of the legislation and reported it favorably to the full committee. The full Rules Committee approved HR 4765 by voice vote and reported it (H Rept 101-790, Part II) on Oct. 2.

HR 4765 then won quick, voice vote passage in the House under suspension of the rules on Oct. 10.

Following House passage, Johnston announced that fundamental differences between S 712 and HR 4765 could not be reconciled before adjournment, and the legislation died.

Statehood would give Puerto Rico two senators and six or seven voting House members. The island would be eligible for more federal dollars, including full food stamp benefits and other welfare payments. In addition, statehood would allow Puerto Ricans full voting rights of citizenship.

Many people in Puerto Rico feared that the future of their culture and language would be in jeopardy under statehood. At home, admittance of Puerto Rico to the Union threatened to upend the Senate's tenuous balance of power and upset the House. Because the size of the House was set at 435, other states would lose congressional numerical clout. Furthermore, poorer states feared that Puerto Rican statehood might take federal dollars away from them.

If Puerto Rico became the nation's 51st state, an estimated $9.4 billion would be required in additional social program spending during the new state's first four years in the Union, the Congressional Budget Office reported Nov. 14, 1989. Independence would save the federal government a small amount, while continuing the island's status as a commonwealth would cause little change in federal contributions.

Fiscal 1990 NASA Authorization

Both chambers in 1989 passed versions of a fiscal 1990 authorization bill for the National Aeronautics and Space Administration (NASA) but failed to clear the measure before adjourning.

The House Science, Space and Technology Committee technically had jurisdiction over the space program, but the Appropriations Committee wielded considerable influence because it provided funding. Science Committee Chairman Robert A. Roe, D-N.J., in 1989 had special leverage with Appropriations, however, because his committee controlled the fate of the Advanced Solid Rocket Motor (ASRM), which NASA decided to build in the district represented by Appropriations Chairman Jamie L. Whitten, D-Miss. Before the contractors hired to build the ASRM could receive private funding for the project, Congress had to grant authority for the federal government to reimburse the manufacturers should the project be canceled. Whitten wanted the liability authority, and Roe had the power to grant it.

According to Science Committee aides, Whitten and Roe had an agreement that the Science Committee would approve the liability authority as part of the fiscal 1990 authorization bill in return for an appropriation large enough to keep alive the centerpiece of the space program: the space station *Freedom*. The arrangement was not purely political, however. NASA said it needed the added booster thrust the ASRM would give the shuttle to put the space station into orbit. *(Space station, p. 877)*

NASA Leadership

Daniel S. Goldin on March 31, 1992, was confirmed by the Senate, on a voice vote, to be the ninth administrator of the National Aeronautics and Space Administration (NASA). Relatively unknown to federal lawmakers, Goldin had been a NASA engineer and, since 1987, was manager of the space and technology division for TRW, a private aerospace corporation. He had worked on the Pentagon's "brilliant eyes" and "brilliant pebbles" projects, which were part of the strategic defense initiative.

Goldin succeeded Richard H. Truly as NASA head. Truly had been confirmed July 1, 1989, on a voice vote by the Senate. A veteran of two shuttle space flights and NASA's associate administrator for space flight until his appointment, Rear Admiral Truly was the first astronaut and military officer ever nominated for the post. By law, military officers, whether active or retired, are prohibited from heading NASA; Congress waived the requirement for Truly. The day before he was confirmed, Truly retired from the Navy after a career of more than 30 years.

Truly faced a demanding tenure. He took over NASA after the explosion of the space shuttle *Challenger*, helping guide the agency through the attacks and demoralization that followed. He also struggled with ongoing program problems, such as the flawed Hubble Space Telescope. Further, Truly engaged in a longstanding power struggle with the National Space Council, a board of space-related agency heads and other Bush administration officials that Vice President Dan Quayle led. Truly had replaced James C. Fletcher, who retired in April 1989 after his second stint as the space agency chief.

Although the administration praised Truly when it announced his resignation Feb. 12, 1992, Truly said he was asked to step down. Upon Goldin's selection, Sen. Al Gore, D-Tenn., expressed concern that he would become a political pawn of the space council. Lawmakers were reassured, however, after speaking with him and hearing his public testimony, as well as when they witnessed the active and visible role Goldin assumed following confirmation.

The Science Committee's Space Science and Applications Subcommittee, chaired by Bill Nelson, D-Fla., held its markup of the NASA authorization bill July 17. The ASRM liability provision was in the legislation. The subcommittee also agreed to amendments that would gradually move NASA away from using the space shuttle for missions that did not require a manned presence in space; bar the administration from having private industry build two projects — the flight telerobotic servicer, a mechanical arm attached to the space station, and the space station docking module, which would allow vehicles such as the shuttle to dock with the station; bar U.S. satellites from being launched on Chinese- or Soviet-made rockets, thus shielding the U.S. rocket industry from subsidized competition in launching U.S.-made satellites, preventing the Soviets and the Chinese from gaining access to U.S. satellite technology, and, in the case of China, reinforcing Bush administration sanctions imposed on the Chinese government in response to the June 1989 crackdown on the pro-democracy movement; restore $72.3 million for the Advanced Communication Technology Satellite; and authorize $1.6 billion in multi-year budget authority — as opposed to the administration request of $30 million, which was the amount to be spent in fiscal 1990 appropriations — for the Comet Rendezvous Asteroid Flyby (or CRAF, to closely observe an asteroid and a comet) and Cassini (to investigate Saturn and its moons) missions.

The House Science Committee took up HR 1759 on Aug. 3. The committee adopted an amendment, offered by Tim Valentine, D-N.C., that prevented NASA from spending any of its $589 million fiscal 1990 budget for aeronautical and transatmospheric research unless the national aerospace plane (NASP) got an earmark for $127 million — NASA's portion of the project's budget. NASP was expected to achieve low Earth orbit at 25 times the speed of sound. Dave Nagle, D-Iowa, proposed that a series of reports on the cost and need for the ASRM be required. That amendment was adopted by voice vote. Other amendments that were adopted authorized the space station through fiscal 1992; limited fiscal 1990 spending on two components of the space station — the flight telerobotic servicer and the station docking module — to $15 million and $3.7 million, respectively; prohibited the export of U.S.-made satellites for launch on Soviet rockets unless the United States concluded an agreement with the Soviet Union establishing "free and fair" competition for launch services, or unless the president certified that the Soviets were not offering launch services "more than 25 percent below the price of a comparable launch vehicle built in a market-based economy."

HR 1759 was reported from the committee (H Rept 101-226) on Aug. 31.

The House Sept. 21 passed HR 1759 by an overwhelming 398-14, authorizing $12.8 billion for NASA programs in fiscal 1990. It authorized funds for most NASA programs for the next three fiscal years, including $9.3 billion in 1991 and $13.3 billion in 1992.

The Senate Commerce Committee June 20 provided NASA with the entire $13.3 billion requested by the administration in approving S 916, which was reported Oct. 3 (S Rept 101-157). The space station also received the $2 billion requested by the administration. The committee adopted an amendment by John C. Danforth, R-Mo., to fully fund the administration's $127 million request for NASP.

The committee denied an administration request that blanket authority be given to allow NASA to privately finance a variety of projects. The bill included private financing authority for three projects, provided that the space agency could demonstrate that it was cheaper than direct government procurement: the Space Station Processing Facility, the Neutral Buoyancy Laboratory, and the Observational Instrument Laboratory.

The committee-approved bill also required NASA to initiate the so-called Mission to Planet Earth satellite program to study global change; earmarked $25 million to launch a research project to produce a high-speed commercial aircraft; added $62 million for the Advanced Communication Technology Satellite; cut $25 million from NASA's request for the Space Tracking and Data Acquisition budget without specifying where the cuts should be made; and included a sense of Congress amendment by Al Gore, D-Tenn., that called for broadening the current ban on export of U.S. satellites to cover countries that would launch them on Soviet rockets.

The Senate passed S 916 Nov. 9, after making only minor changes to the committee-approved bill. The bill largely was an academic exercise, because Congress already had cleared, and the president signed, a fiscal 1990 spending bill (HR 2916 — PL 101-144) that appropriated $12.4 billion for NASA. Before passing the appropriations bill for the Departments of Veterans Affairs and Housing and Urban Development and assorted independent agencies (including NASA), members stripped out a provision allowing private financing of the Advanced Solid Rocket Motor plant in Mississippi, granting instead $90 million to build the plant.

The House Appropriations Committee approved and reported HR 2916 (H Rept 101-150) on July 17. The House passed the bill by voice vote July 20. The Senate Appropriations Committee reported the legislation (S Rept 101-128) on Sept. 13, and the full Senate passed the bill, 92-8, on Sept. 28. Conferees agreed on a final version (H Rept 101-297) on Oct. 17. The House adopted the conference report Oct. 24, and the Senate followed suit Oct. 27. Further amendments were adopted by both chambers, and the bill finally cleared Oct. 31. Bush signed the measure Nov. 9.

The two chambers engaged in a last-minute volley to produce a compromise authorization bill. The House Nov. 20 passed HR 3729, which would authorize two years' worth of spending for most NASA programs and three years for the space station. The bill also called for a total $1.6 billion for the CRAF and Cassini missions to cover the entire estimated cost of the projects. On the last day of the 1989 session, the Senate stripped the bill of its two-year authorizations but left the space station and deep space probe numbers intact.

Fiscal 1991 NASA Authorization

Congress in 1990 cleared a one-year authorization bill (S 2287) calling for $15 billion in fiscal 1991 for the National Aeronautics and Space Administration (NASA).

President Bush had requested $15.1 billion for NASA for fiscal 1991, including $1.3 billion for space exploration and $2.6 billion for the space station *Freedom.* Although the House and Senate deadlocked on NASA authorization measures at the end of 1989, the new year opened with expectations of an exciting new start for space science. Not since the Kennedy administration did so much enthusiasm exist for exploring the universe.

However, by mid-1990, space agency officials were facing an angry and scrutinizing Congress, following a series of space mishaps and setbacks. NASA revealed, for example, that the main viewing device in the $2 billion-plus Hubble Space Telescope, launched April 24, did not work. NASA announced June 29 that the space shuttle fleet would be grounded until the cause of hydrogen leaks in the *Atlantis* and *Columbia* spacecraft was found. Serious design flaws in the space station also came to light. In response, the White House in July convened a blue-ribbon task force to study NASA's operations and consider its long-term direction. The panel issued a report Dec. 10 recommending that the agency concentrate on science and on building a new launch system for the commercial space program.

The unraveling of these difficulties threatened to cloud future funding prospects, especially as NASA was entering the costly hardware development stage for several big projects, including the space station. Compounding the problem were general budget constraints, accompanied by greater demands for funding in social policy. Furthermore, the same appropriations subcommittees that oversaw NASA determined funding levels for major domestic programs such as housing and veterans' health care.

The Senate Commerce Committee by voice vote approved S 2287 June 27 and reported it (S Rept 101-455) Sept. 11. The measure authorized $14.8 billion for NASA, deleting virtually all of the $188 million the president had asked for the moon-Mars project, which called for returning to the moon by 2000, establishing a lunar base and reaching Mars by 2010. According to Al Gore, D-Tenn., chairman of the Science, Technology and Space Subcommittee, the projected costs of the president's plan would rise from $188 million in fiscal 1991 to $1.1 billion by fiscal 1995.

As approved by the House Science Committee Sept. 19, HR 5649 would authorize $16.9 billion for NASA in fiscal 1991 — including the president's full requests for the space station and the moon-Mars mission — and even more in fiscal 1992-93. Some members believed that a multi-year reauthorization meant more efficient program development. The bill, reported (H Rept 101-763) on Sept. 26, was passed by the House Sept. 28 by voice vote.

A compromise version of S 2287 went first to the Senate, where it was approved by voice vote shortly after midnight on Oct. 25. The House accepted the bill later the same day. The legislation authorized $15 billion in spending for NASA in fiscal 1991, including a $1.6 billion multi-year authorization to develop the CRAF and Cassini missions. The bill limited previously authorized spending on the space station in fiscal 1991 to $2.5 billion; pushed NASA to use more unmanned rockets; helped the commercial space industry by requiring NASA to use outside vendors for some services; attempted to limit the proliferation of man-made debris in outer space; required NASA to spread research money nationwide; and funded a new start on the Earth Observing System (EOS) designed to study the environmental problems that affected Earth.

Bush signed S 2287 (PL 101-611) on Nov. 16.

As approved by the House June 28 on a 355-48 vote, the fiscal 1991 appropriations bill (HR 5158 — H Rept 101-556) for the Departments of Veterans Affairs and Housing and Urban Development and related independent agencies provided $14.3 billion for NASA. The Senate cut the figure to $13.5 billion when it passed the bill (S Rept 101-474) 90-8 on Oct. 3.

Conferees agreed to appropriate $13.9 billion in fiscal 1991 for NASA. The House Oct. 20 adopted the conference report (H Rept 101-900) on a 366-32 vote. The Senate made further amendments in the bill, then agreed to the conference report by voice vote Oct. 25. The House gave final approval by voice vote Oct. 26, clearing the bill for the president. Bush signed it (PL 101-507) on Nov. 5.

Space Station

From the start, the plan devised by the National Aeronautics and Space Administration (NASA) for orbiting a permanently manned space station around Earth by the end of the 20th century had stirred Congress' fascination with the heavens, but not enough to override more pressing concerns on the ground.

The massive project, launched by President Reagan in 1984, limped along for five years — just attractive enough to survive, but too expensive to fund fully. Over that time, Congress provided slightly over $2 billion and work started up in bits and pieces. *(Congress and the Nation Vol. VI, p. 789; Congress and the Nation Vol. VII, pp. 852, 861)*

But in 1989 the proposed space station, *Freedom*, entered a critical stage. Legions of contractors and subcontractors were preparing to move off the drawing board and into production. NASA said it needed $2.1 billion in fiscal 1990, more than double the previous year's appropriation. If the money was not provided, the agency warned, the scheduled 1998 date for when the station could be permanently manned would be missed and costs would enter the stratosphere.

The space station faced formidable hurdles, however. For one thing, the scientific community was deeply divided over its merits. But that was a minor problem compared with the budget deficit.

NASA called the space station the logical next step after the space shuttle. It would be an orbiting laboratory, a launching pad for space missions and a facility for repairing and refueling satellites — all told, the most complex project NASA had ever attempted. The agency offered a host of potential uses — for example, as "a space workshop, laboratory, and viewing platform," as James B. Odom, NASA's associate administrator for the space station, put it, naming just a few. But no one had stated an irrefutable reason why it must be built. In that sense, Bush may have erred, like Reagan, by casting the space station as a goal in itself, instead of a necessary launching pad for some more dazzling venture such as a mission to Mars. The space station lacked the cachet of a moonshot and was often treated more as a glorified construction project than a symbol of the nation's future in space.

Ideological infighting among Reagan administration officials also crippled the effort to win full funding of the station. In 1988, privatization proponents in the Reagan administration won White House endorsement for a plan to have the government lease space on a commercially developed space station until NASA's facility became operational. To many, the administration seemed to be undercutting its own push for full funding for the station.

Many scientists, meanwhile, were not sure that the space station represented the right path into space; many said they would rather see the billions in federal funding spent elsewhere. A report to President Bush by the National Academy of Sciences suggested that "decisions regarding [the station's] final configuration, pace of deployment, and place among competing budgetary priorities are best made in the context of your long-term goals for space." Contractors saw the statement as a thinly veiled assault on the space station.

Despite the budgetary concerns, proponents claimed that the space station had considerable economic potential. NASA originally estimated that the program would provide almost 52,000 jobs across the country by 1994, with California, Alabama, Texas, Virginia and Florida the largest beneficiaries. The agency also maintained that every dollar spent on the space station multiplied throughout the economy seven times. Furthermore, the Reagan administration in 1988 signed agreements with Canada, Japan and the European Space Agency (ESA) under which those nations would produce parts of the station. NASA officials privately conceded they hoped that put pressure on Congress to keep the project on schedule. If that did not happen, the argument went, U.S. allies would be displeased.

The final fiscal 1990 appropriation (HR 2916 — PL 101-144) for the space station was $1.8 billion. It was below the administration's request but considerably above the fiscal 1989 funding level. *(Fiscal 1990 NASA authorization, p. 874)*

In 1990, the space station hit major obstacles when a long-awaited study, conducted by NASA and headed by Dr. William F. Fisher and Charles R. Price of the Johnson Space Center in Houston, found that it could not be built as designed because its vast array of parts would start to break down before the station was complete. The report came amid growing concern about other design aspects of the station. As the scope of the plan developed, for example, the weight kept increasing, which would mean more expensive shuttle flights. Congress also questioned whether the existing spacesuit would be sufficient for astronauts involved in outside construction and maintenance of the orbiting station.

In the bill making fiscal 1991 appropriations for NASA (HR 5158 — PL 101-507), Congress called for a design overhaul of the space station. NASA was ordered to report back to Congress in 90 days with a "new approach" for its massive undertaking. Fiscal 1991 spending for the program was capped at $640 million until the study was completed and Congress was satisfied with the direction of the project. HR 5158 earmarked a total of $1.9 billion in fiscal 1991 funds for the space station, less than the $2.5 billion administration request. The specific cuts included $12 million from the $15 million requested for space station integrated and attached payload activities; $2.3 million from the planning office in Reston, Va.; and $15 million for the neutral buoyancy laboratory. *(Fiscal 1991 NASA authorization, p. 876)*

William Lenoir, NASA's associate administrator for space flight, and Richard Kohrs, director of the space station program, said at a news conference in November that budget cuts would require that the station be built in phases and put into limited use until the next section was completed.

Congress had ordered NASA to base its new approach on an "incremental concept."

The original design envisioned a station made up of four main pressurized modules built by the United States, Japan and the European Space Agency, each to be affixed to a 500-foot-long beam. Solar panels would power the station and a robot arm would function in the space environment. Kohrs said that the redesign effort would look at reducing by 90 feet the length of the beam and eliminating attachment points for scientific experiments outside the station modules.

Space experts in 1990 estimated that the space station as originally designed would cost about $40 billion.

Superconducting Supercollider

The 101st Congress launched a major new science policy initiative that would claim a considerable share of the federal budget for the following decade.

The superconducting supercollider (SSC) was conceived as a 53-mile, underground, racetrack-shaped tunnel in which 10,000 giant magnets would hurl subatomic particles into each other at nearly the speed of light. Scientists planned to use powerful computers to study the resulting subatomic debris to learn about the basic nature of matter and energy. Supporters believed the SSC also would result in tremendous spinoff benefits, such as improved medical techniques and computer technology.

The Energy Department in 1988 decided to build the SSC in President Bush's home state of Texas — in Waxahachie, 25 miles south of Dallas.

Fiscal 1990 Appropriation. On the recommendation of Rep. Tom Bevill, D-Ala., chairman of the Subcommittee on Energy and Water Development, the full House Appropriations Committee June 20, 1989, approved $200 million to fund initial construction for the massive, experimental atom smasher. The appropriation was part of the fiscal 1990 spending bill for energy and water development (HR 2696 — H Rept 101-96). The Bush administration had made it known that anything less than $200 million would have prompted a veto. The seed money represented a breakthrough for project supporters, who fought a hard battle in 1988 to keep the project alive with research and development funds. *(Earlier appropriation, Congress and the Nation Vol. VII, p. 863)*

Initially, Bevill resisted any moves toward breaking ground on the SSC until commitments for financial help were received from foreign governments interested in sharing its scientific fruits. Shortly before the subcommittee marked up the bill, Bevill said, he and ranking Republican John T. Myers, Ind., were called to a meeting with President Bush, Energy Secretary James D. Watkins and budget director Richard G. Darman. Bevill said Watkins was "confident" that countries such as Japan, Italy and India would participate, but only if Congress took the first step. As a result, Bevill was persuaded to proceed with funding.

The House June 28 got a rare opportunity to make a clear choice, and it did so decisively. In its first vote ever on the SSC, the House rejected in a **key vote of 93-330 (R 28-144; D 65-186)** an amendment, offered by Dennis E. Eckart, D-Ohio, to eliminate $110 million in initial SSC construction funds from the $200 million earmarked for research and development. The vote in effect settled the debate over whether to go forward with the project. *(1989 key votes, p. 1021)*

The House passed HR 2696 by voice vote June 28.

To Texans, the SSC was a high-tech Holy Grail that promised to bring thousands of jobs and millions of dollars into the state. To numerous critics, it was a "quark-barrel" project that would drain funds from more important science and domestic priorities. The House decision to begin SSC construction was a significant victory for Bush.

The multibillion-dollar SSC emerged from the Senate not just unscathed, but $25 million better off. The Senate approved, by voice vote, its version of the energy and water spending bill (S Rept 101-83) on July 27. Before passage, the Senate included a provision that would bar the Department of Energy from contracting with foreign governments for in-kind or direct financial contributions to the project until a report on such foreign involvement was made to Congress.

The only serious controversy that arose during Senate floor consideration was on an unrelated matter, when action on the bill was halted for several hours as John McCain, R-Ariz., and Orrin G. Hatch, R-Utah, attempted to attach an amendment to delay implementation of provisions of the 1988 Medicare Catastrophic Coverage Act (PL 100-360). *(Catastrophic care, p. 565)*

Conferees Sept. 7 agreed to the Senate-approved funding level of $225 million, which was a victory for Bush, who had requested $250 million. By settling on the higher sum, Congress would find pulling SSC funding in the future difficult. The House approved the conference report (H Rept 101-235) Sept. 12 on a 392-27 vote. The Senate accepted the conference report, and thus cleared the bill, on a voice vote Sept. 14. Bush signed the legislation (PL 101-101) on Sept. 29.

Fiscal 1991 Appropriation. Congress in 1990 provided $243 million in fiscal 1991 SSC funding — $75 million less than Bush requested, as spiraling cost estimates for the project brought forth renewed efforts in the House to cap spending. Once projected to cost $5.3 billion, the supercollider on July 25, 1990, was officially estimated by the Energy Department's High Energy Physics Advisory Panel, a group of outside experts, to cost $8.6 billion.

The House Science Committee, 32-9, approved an SSC authorization bill (HR 4380) on March 28, 1990, and reported it (H Rept 101-448) on April 12. As originally proposed, the bill would set an overall spending limit for the SSC of $7.5 billion — a federal cap of $5 billion, a $1 billion contribution from Texas and the rest to come from foreign investment. Before approving the bill, however, the panel agreed by voice vote to an amendment by Ralph M. Hall, D-Texas, that removed the $7.5 billion cap. Committee members said the limit would hamper negotiations to secure foreign funding.

During committee consideration, Sherwood Boehlert, R-N.Y., offered an amendment to delay all construction and most design work until the Energy Department certified the prototype magnets needed for the project. Committee Chairman Robert A. Roe, D-N.J., argued that Boehlert's amendment would delay the project by up to 18 months and would cost $1.5 billion to $2 billion more. He offered a substitute to Boehlert's amendment that effectively removed most of its provisions. The Roe amendment was approved, 33-13.

The House May 2 passed HR 4380 on a 309-109 vote, with a cap limiting total federal spending to $5 billion and calling for $2.4 billion in outside contributions. With Roe's endorsement, the cap appeared to be a key compromise that quieted opposition while limiting the government's obligation to the project. The legislation specified that $1 billion of the project's costs would be paid by Texas and 20 percent to 33 percent by foreign sources. Furthermore, spending on the project would proceed in phases only as certain milestones were achieved. For example, the first $1.17 billion could be released only after the Energy Department submitted to Congress plans for the site, magnet development, management, organization and cost estimates. Another $5.98 billion could be released after other goals were met, such as magnet assembly tests.

With Roe's blessing, members adopted by voice vote a Boehlert amendment that aimed to seal the federal obligation at 1990 estimates. Roe and other supercollider boosters, however, failed to stop an amendment by F. James Sensenbrenner Jr., R-Wis., adopted 256-163, deleting a provision that would guarantee Texas a refund of its $1 billion investment if the project was scrapped before Oct. 1, 1995.

The House also adopted, 420-0, a proposal by Howard Wolpe, D-Mich., to require the General Accounting Office to review the various Energy Department reports on the SSC required under the bill. James A. Traficant Jr., D-Ohio, offered an amendment, accepted by voice vote, to prohibit companies based in countries engaged in unfair trading practices against the United States from bidding for supercollider contracts. Also winning voice vote approval was a proposal by Louis Stokes, D-Ohio, calling on the Energy Department to set aside 10 percent of the SSC funds for contracts to businesses or other groups operated by blacks, Hispanics, women and American Indians, and to take steps to ensure participation of such groups in the development, construction and operation of the supercollider.

Senate Energy and Natural Resources Committee Chairman J. Bennett Johnston, D-La., a solid supporter of SSC, had no intention of moving the authorization bill because he could control funding through his other chairmanship — the Appropriations Subcommittee on Energy and Water Development. The bill went no further.

The House Appropriations Subcommittee on Energy and Water Development June 7 approved the fiscal 1991 energy and water appropriations bill (HR 5019), which granted Bush's full request of $318 million for the SSC. The Appropriations Committee June 13 by voice vote approved the bill (H Rept 101-536), which was virtually intact as it came from subcommittee. No anti-collider amendments were offered on the floor, despite the tremendous jump in the project's estimated cost. The House passed HR 5019, with the $318 million figure, by 355-59 on June 19.

The Senate Appropriations Subcommittee on Energy and Water Development July 18 approved HR 5019. The Appropriations Committee followed suit the next day, with $318 million earmarked for the SSC (S Rept 101-378). That figure remained in HR 5019 as passed, by voice vote, by the Senate Aug. 2.

Lawmakers, as a result of the tentative budget agreement outline (H Con Res 310) approved by Congress Oct. 9 (in the session that began Oct. 8), had to trim HR 5019's domestic programs by about $750 million. The SSC proved an easy target, and $75 million was cut. Conferees also rejected a request by Rep. Jim Chapman, D-Texas, to reimburse Texas if it made up the difference on the SSC cuts and if the project subsequently was canceled. The House approved the conference report (H Rept 101-889) on Oct. 19 by a vote of 362-51. The Senate accepted the report Oct. 20 by voice vote, clearing the bill for the president. Bush signed it Nov. 5 (PL 101-514).

Space Inventions Patent

A measure pushed by space industry interests to explicitly extend U.S. patent law protections to inventions developed in space was signed into law by President Bush on Nov. 15, 1990 (S 459 — PL 101-580).

The legislation, aimed at encouraging private investment in space-based research and manufacturing, provided that inventions "made, used or sold in outer space" on U.S. spacecraft would be covered by U.S. patent laws. The House passed similar bills in 1986 and 1988, but they were not acted on by the Senate.

U.S. entrepreneurs had been eyeing the commercial potential of space but were uncertain how existing patent law would apply beyond Earth's surface. International partners in major space endeavors also were concerned about patent rights. The issue gained relevance in 1990 because the proposed space station *Freedom*, an international effort that planned to contain experiments sponsored by different nations, was gaining attention in Congress and moving closer to reality. *(Space station, p. 877)*

Without a new law, patent issues raised by space station inventions would have been left up to the courts to settle — an uncertainty that concerned some international participants in the project. S 459 exempted from U.S. patent law spacecraft or modules of spacecraft that were covered by international agreements dealing with patent rights or that were registered to foreign nations.

With Senate sponsor Al Gore, D-Tenn., pushing the legislation, the Senate Judiciary Committee approved S 459 by voice vote on March 22, 1990, and reported it (S Rept 101-266) on April 19. The full Senate passed the bill by voice vote May 1.

In the House, a similar measure (HR 2946) won approval by the Science Subcommittee on Space Science and Applications on Sept. 21, 1989. Although the full Science Committee never formally acted on the measure, the House Judiciary Committee included the language of HR 2946 as one of five titles in another bill (HR 5598). The Judiciary Committee approved HR 5598 by voice vote on Sept. 18, 1990, and reported it (H Rept 101-960, Part I) Sept. 26.

On Oct. 26, Rep. Robert W. Kastenmeier, D-Wis., chairman of the Judiciary Patents Subcommittee, brought the narrower HR 2946 to the House floor, saying the other titles in HR 5598 would be held until the next Congress. The House passed HR 2946 by voice vote under suspension of the rules and then laid it on the table in lieu of S 459. The House next passed S 459 by voice vote, clearing the measure for the president.

Technology Programs

Despite passing the House and Senate, legislation (S 1191, HR 4329) to reauthorize and expand several Commerce Department programs designed to bolster investment and adoption of new technology by U.S. industry failed to clear in the 101st Congress.

The legislation was largely a response to countries such as Japan that aggressively aided their own industries' high-tech efforts, giving them an edge over American companies. Science-minded lawmakers pushed the bills, but the Bush administration strongly signaled that it did not want the federal government choosing industrial "winners and losers." It preferred that private industry, not the federal government, take the lead in promoting and commercializing new technologies. An urgency was felt in 1990, however, when a Commerce Department study showed that the Japanese and Europeans had made great strides toward carving out market shares in 12 emerging technologies, while the United States had become even less competitive.

The Senate Commerce Committee approved S 1191 (S Rept 101-159) Aug. 1, 1989, and reported it Oct. 3. The committee authorized $320 million in fiscal 1990 funds for the Commerce Department's Technology Administration program, which was created in 1988 and included the National Institute of Standards and Technology (NIST). Committee Chairman Ernest F. Hollings, D-S.C., was particularly interested in getting funding for NIST's Advanced Technology Program (ATP). Adopted in the 1988 trade law (PL 100-418), the ATP was designed to provide seed money for research consortia and small businesses to speed commercialization of new technology in areas such as high-definition television (HDTV), advanced manufacturing and superconductivity. The bill authorized up to $100 million for ATP. It also included $12 million for manufacturing-technology centers, known as Hollings Centers, that were located around the country for research into transferring technology to small and medium-sized businesses. *(Congress and the Nation Vol. VII, p. 148)*

The Senate Oct. 26 passed S 1191 by voice vote.

In late July 1989, the Research and Technology Subcommittee of the House Science Committee approved a three-year authorization bill (HR 3042) for NIST that included $331 million for technology programs in fiscal 1990. The bill also included $150 million under ATP. The bill went no further in 1989.

When the topic was revisited in 1990, the House Science Committee on March 21 approved, 49-0, a bill (HR 4329) to reauthorize NIST and to provide seed money to research consortia to speed commercialization of new technologies; it was reported (H Rept 101-481, Part I) on May 10. Before final passage, the House approved minor, mostly technical changes that had been introduced as a substitute bill (HR 5072). The Judiciary Committee, which also had jurisdiction over HR 4329, voted June 12 to strip a section that would relax antitrust laws for certain joint ventures because the House already had passed a similar antitrust measure (HR 4611) June 5. Judiciary reported HR 4329 (H Rept 101-481, Part II) on June 14. *(Antitrust bills, p. 772)*

The House passed HR 4329 on a 327-93 vote July 11. It would provide $290 million in fiscal 1991 for the technology programs and $468 million in fiscal 1992.

The House set the stage for a conference by inserting its version of the reauthorization package into the Senate bill, passing S 1191 by voice vote July 11. Negotiators then informally crafted a compromise bill. But Sen. Bob Kasten, R-Wis., who won Commerce Committee approval of his product liability bill (S 1400) in May 1990, insisted any technology measure address that issue, too. Hollings, who had fought product liability legislation for a decade, objected, creating an impasse that killed the technology bill.

A last-ditch effort to enact a supercomputer bill separately failed. The Senate approved a three-year, $700 million-plus Commerce-Energy compromise (S 1067) by voice vote Oct. 25, but the House Science Committee declined to bring the measure to the floor.

Although the authorization bills stalled, Congress appropriated $166.2 million in fiscal 1991 for the technology programs, which included $35.9 million for ATP and $11.9 million for the Hollings Centers. Congress had appropriated $9.9 million for ATP in fiscal 1990. The monies were included in the annual appropriations bills (HR 2991 — PL 101-162; HR 5021 — PL 101-515) for the Commerce, Justice and State departments and related agencies.

Legislation to help American high-tech industries compete around the globe was enacted in 1992. *(Story, p. 902)*

Mining Research

Congress in 1990 authorized the creation of a new research institute that was expected to develop new and innovative ways of mining and processing rare minerals critical to U.S. defense and industry. Minerals such as platinum, vanadium, chromium, cobalt and manganese, which were used in a wide variety of consumer products and weapons, were supplied almost entirely from foreign sources.

The Strategic and Critical Minerals Act (HR 4111 — PL 101-498) called for the interior secretary to select the site and authorized a minimum of $1.5 million annually for the center.

Among the criteria for choosing the site, envisioned as a consortium with a leading university and several cooperative affiliates, was that the university not already host a generic mineral technology center. The host site also was to be located west of the 100th meridian and offer advanced degree programs in geology and geological engineering. Once established, the center's research was to be aimed at domestic ore that could not be mined or processed efficiently or economically using existing technologies.

Another major responsibility of the center was to identify new deposits of strategic and critical mineral resources. U.S. Bureau of Mines studies showed that 95 percent of world production of the platinum group metals came from the Soviet Union and southern Africa.

The House Interior Subcommittee on Mining approved HR 4111 by voice vote March 27. The full committee gave voice vote approval to the legislation April 4 and reported it (H Rept 101-465) April 26. The House passed the bill by voice vote under suspension of the rules July 10.

HR 4111 received approval from the Senate Energy Committee Sept. 26 and was reported (S Rept 101-496) Oct. 3. The Senate passed the bill by voice vote Oct. 16, clearing it for President Bush, who signed the measure Nov. 2.

Earthquake Hazards

Congress in 1990 cleared a $363 million three-year authorization for earthquake research and preparedness programs. President Bush signed the measure (S 2789 — PL 101-614) Nov. 16.

The bill reauthorized and expanded the 1977 Earthquake Hazards Reduction Act, providing $102 million in fiscal 1991, $120 million in fiscal 1992 and $141 million in fiscal 1993. Funding for fiscal 1990 was about $73 million. *(Earlier authorization, Congress and the Nation Vol. VII, p. 866)*

Under the legislation, the National Science Foundation would work with the U.S. Geological Survey to identify geographic regions that should be the targets for earthquake research proposals. States also would be eligible to receive earthquake preparedness matching grants from the Federal Emergency Management Agency.

A House companion measure (HR 3533) was reported from Interior and Insular Affairs (H Rept 101-464, Part I) on April 26. The House Science, Space and Technology Committee reported the bill (H Rept 101-464, Part II) July 19. The House passed the bill Sept. 24 by a vote of 283-132 under suspension of the rules.

The Senate Commerce, Science and Transportation Committee reported S 2789 (S Rept 101-446) Aug. 30. The Senate passed the bill by voice vote Oct. 19. The House then passed the Senate measure Oct. 20, clearing it for the president.

Earthquake Research

In the wake of a devastating Northern California temblor, the Senate Oct. 25, 1989, by voice vote passed legislation (S 1062 — S Rept 101-158) designed to expand the federal government's preparedness for earthquakes and promote more research into their causes. But the House did not act on it before Congress adjourned.

The bill, sponsored by Sen. Al Gore, D-Tenn., boosted authorized funding for the National Earthquake Hazards Reduction Act. It called for a state-by-state study of earthquake hazards and for the adoption by June 1, 1993, of seismic design and construction standards for all new and existing federal buildings, and for all buildings funded or insured in whole or in part by the federal government. Many government buildings were not subject to local building codes and therefore were less earthquake resistant.

The Senate Commerce, Science and Transportation Committee reported the bill (S Rept 101-158) on Oct. 3.

Senate passage of S 1062 came the same day that Congress cleared a continuing appropriations resolution (H J Res 423 — PL 101-130) providing $2.85 billion in disaster relief, primarily for victims of the Oct. 17 Loma Prieta quake in California. *(Continuing appropriations, p. 52)*

Animal Research Labs

Legislation to clamp down on animal rights activists who resorted to illegal means to further their agenda won Senate approval in 1989 and saw House committee action in 1990 but died when the 101st Congress adjourned. Revamped legislation was cleared and signed into law in 1992. *(102nd Congress action, p. 904)*

The effort to federalize such crimes was supported by farmers and biomedical researchers but was opposed by animal welfare groups, who denounced it as a public relations effort to brand them as terrorists and stifle whistleblowers who exposed cruelty to animals.

S 727, sponsored by Howell Heflin, D-Ala., was aimed at the more serious acts committed by members of the animal rights movement, such as burglary, but was limited to illegal acts against research labs. The bill won voice vote approval in the Senate on Nov. 20, 1989.

Rep. Charles W. Stenholm, D-Texas, introduced HR 3270 in September 1989. The bill would make trespassing on or committing other illegal acts against farms and animal research labs a federal crime. Supporters viewed the bill as a way to curtail the wave of violence. But some lawmakers had doubts, believing the measure went too far.

The Bush administration's science adviser, D. Allan Bromley, endorsed the bill, as did Health and Human Services Secretary Louis W. Sullivan and former surgeon general C. Everett Koop. But the Justice Department opposed the legislation, arguing that it and similar measures duplicated existing statutes and could raise false hopes that the FBI would jump into every future case.

The Research Subcommittee of House Agriculture held a hearing on HR 3270 on July 17, 1990. Preoccupied with the 1990 farm bill, the full committee did not mark up HR 3270 until Oct. 22. A formal report (H Rept 101-953, Part I) was issued Oct. 26, then the bill was referred to the Judiciary Committee. By that time, however, it was too late for House floor action.

Meanwhile, the Energy and Commerce Subcommittee on Health and the Environment approved a National Institutes of Health (NIH) reauthorization bill (HR 5661) Sept. 18 with provisions aimed at violence against animal research labs. Among other things, the bill, written by subcommittee Chairman Henry A. Waxman, D-Calif., sought to create federal civil and criminal penalties for animal rights activists who broke into federally funded animal research facilities. It included a modified version of a bill (HR 3349) introduced by Waxman earlier in 1990 aimed at deterring break-ins at research facilities by opponents of animal experimentation.

The House Energy and Commerce Committee approved HR 5661 on Sept. 26 and reported it (H Rept 101-869) on Oct. 15. The measure made it a federal offense to knowingly release or injure any research animal in a federally funded facility, to knowingly destroy or alter research records, or to knowingly deter, through intimidation or any degree of physical restraint, people from entering or exiting such facilities. Violators could be subject to jail terms of up to five years and ordered to pay restitution to the facility. The bill also permitted the facility in question to file civil lawsuits.

After a brief debate and adoption of three minor amendments offered by Democrats, the committee approved the bill by voice vote. With time running out in the 101st Congress, however, and the administration opposed to most provisions of the legislation, sponsors decided to strip the NIH bill of all but a couple of non-controversial sections. *(Story, p. 590)*

Indian Programs Investigation

After two years of investigating fraud and mismanagement in federal agencies that were responsible for overseeing Indian programs, a special Senate investigative committee recommended largely abandoning those agencies and giving federal funds directly to tribal governments. A highly publicized, 238-page report was issued by the committee in November 1989.

Dennis DeConcini, D-Ariz., chairman of the Senate Indian Affairs Special Committee on Investigations, said Congress had recommended reorganizing Indian programs at least 42 times in 83 years, to no avail. Despite extensive evidence of major problems in Indian programs, the 101st Congress tampered little with federal Indian policy. Nearly all 1990 congressional legislative activity on Indian issues was limited to fine-tuning existing programs or establishing relatively inexpensive new ones — instead of the major overhaul urged by the special committee.

Many Indians had reason to be skeptical that wholesale changes would be made. In the past, reforms urged by congressional investigators either were not adopted or proved ineffective.

Indians did not have much clout in Congress. Numbers helped explain the lack of influence. Fewer than 1 million Indians lived on U.S. reservations, and most of them never voted in congressional elections. Furthermore, according to the 1990 census, 28 percent of all American Indians lived in poverty. A quarter of all reservation houses lacked complete plumbing such as running hot and cold water, a flush toilet or an indoor bathtub or shower. About 16 percent lacked electric lighting.

Federal Indian Policy

In 1824, the Bureau of Indian Affairs (BIA) was created as an agency within the War Department, and the United States treated Indian tribes like foreign countries, signing treaties and operating on a government-to-government basis. Even in modern times, tribes retained a special brand of sovereignty, subject to federal laws but insulated from most state and local laws.

But soon after BIA was transferred to the Interior Department in 1849, the government started isolating Indians on reservations. By the end of the century, federal policy was aimed at "civilizing" the natives by breaking up tribal life and encouraging Indians to own their own land.

Throughout the 20th century, the federal government see-sawed from one extreme to another, first encouraging tribal life under a law passed in 1934 and then, in 1953, calling for an end to all special federal treatment for Indians. *(Congress and the Nation Vol. I, p. 1096)*

In 1974, the pendulum swung back again when Congress passed the Indian Self-Determination Act (PL 93-638). The law, based on President Richard Nixon's 1970 call for "a new era in which the Indian future is determined by Indian acts and Indian decisions," acknowledged the federal government's role as trustee, but also shifted much of the control of federal programs to the tribes. *(Congress and the Nation Vol. IV, p. 810)*

Passing Indian legislation was not simple, however. It took six years to enact a law regulating tribal gambling. During the 1980s, a number of other relatively minor Indian measures cleared Congress, only to be vetoed by President Ronald Reagan.

Investigation Findings

Sen. Daniel K. Inouye, D-Hawaii, chairman of the Indian Affairs Committee, launched the Senate investigation in February 1988, in response to a 1987 series on Indian problems that appeared in the *Arizona Republic*. Inouye created the three-member investigations panel (DeConcini, John McCain, R-Ariz., and Tom Daschle, D-S.D.) to look into the allegations raised in the articles and to review other federal Indian programs. The investigators sifted through 900,000 pages of documents, issued 270 subpoenas and interviewed more than 600 witnesses. Public hearings were held beginning Jan. 30, 1989.

Day after day, the tales emerging from the Senate hearing room were the stuff of headlines: corruption among Indian tribal leaders, Indian housing scams, sexual abuse in government-run schools for Indian children and the infiltration of organized crime into Indian bingo games. Much of the blame was directed at BIA, even though the responsibility for Indian programs was scattered throughout the federal government. BIA received more than $1 billion annually to oversee a myriad of federal programs affecting Indians and acted as the trustee for Indian lands and interests.

Among the findings were that corruption was rampant in some tribal governments. The panel heard testimony that Navajo leader Peter MacDonald Sr. in 1987 had his tribe pay a vastly inflated price for some land, in an arrangement under which the sellers would kick back to MacDonald up to $750,000. BIA approved the ranch deal even though the bureau's area real estate property management officer estimated that the land's fair market value was about $7 million less. MacDonald also siphoned large amounts of funds from the Navajo government treasury to finance an extravagant lifestyle.

The committee found that a $200 million-a-year minority-preference program set up to aid Indian-owned companies instead was funneling funds to front companies set up by non-Indian contractors. Some Indian witnesses testified that they were forced to go into joint ventures with white men because they could not get financial backing from the banks otherwise.

BIA official Donald Asbra tried to shift blame for the fraud and abuse to the Department of Housing and Urban Development (HUD), which was responsible for Indian housing. Almost 90 percent of the front companies were doing HUD work, he said. Dom Nessi, HUD's director of Indian housing, promised to improve training for HUD officials who review Indian housing contracts and to step up spot checks of construction sites.

BIA also employed teachers who had admitted to child molestation, including one who sexually abused at least 25 Indian students over 14 years, according to the committee report. BIA did not issue child abuse reporting guidelines until 1988, after the investigative committee had held hearings on the subject.

The panel found that organized crime families had infiltrated at least 12 reservation-run bingo games. Gambling was one of the biggest revenue-raisers for Indian tribes. In California alone, tribes grossed about $106 million annually. A former crime family member testified that his company, which managed an Indian bingo operation, skimmed between $600,000 and $700,000 a year from the tribe's profit by running rigged games and paying inflated salaries to company employees. The tribe got less than $100,000.

In 1988, Congress passed a law (PL 100-497) regulating Indian gambling. The law established a five-member National Indian Gaming Commission to oversee such games as bingo, lotto and certain card games. The commission had the authority to enforce tribal gaming ordinances, conduct background investigations of companies running the games and audit gaming operations. But Anthony E. Daniels, deputy assistant director of the FBI's Criminal Investigative Division, told the panel the law only encouraged the mob because it left much of the daily regulation to the tribes themselves. *(Congress and the Nation Vol. VII, p. 864)*

The report also cited examples of neglect and corruption in other federal agencies: The Interior Department's Bureau of Land Management failed to detect millions of dollars in theft of oil and gas on Indian lands; and the Indian Health Service (IHS) diverted $70,000 in federal funds from a juvenile alcohol abuse prevention program to finance a fitness retreat for IHS managers.

Recommendations

The recommendations put forth by the special committee would allow tribes to receive the same share of the federal Indian budget they had been receiving, but as unrestricted block grants. The panel hailed this plan as a "new federalism" for American Indians. Tribal governments would have to follow a written constitution that had been voted on by the tribe's members. They also would be subject to federal laws prohibiting corruption and guaranteeing fair elections. Those requirements were meant to prevent the types of graft by tribal leaders that were publicized during the committee hearings.

The special committee also called for a new agency to be set up to negotiate agreements with tribes that opted to participate in the entitlement program. Other tribal budgets would continue to be managed under a scaled-down BIA.

Some Indian leaders, fiercely protective of their sovereignty, feared that any congressional "solution" to the problems plaguing Indian programs would ultimately work to the detriment of the Indian community. "We have been the victims of so many changing federal policies," Cherokee Chief Wilma P. Mankiller told the panel. "The best solutions to our problems are within our own communities." Indeed, federal policy toward Indians had been capricious, changing every few decades with the whims of Congress and the White House.

Indian Health, Human Services

Congress dealt with a number of Indian health and human service issues in 1990. Measures to prevent child abuse and improve health care were enacted while bills to curb alcohol and substance abuse and to provide greater federal benefits stalled at the committee level.

President Bush signed legislation (HR 3703 — PL 101-360) on Nov. 28 designed to prevent child abuse on Indian reservations. The bill ensured that workers dealing with Indian children had no criminal record and established financial penalties and prison terms for officials who were aware of abuse and did not report it.

The measure stemmed from 1989 hearings that revealed numerous cases of sexual abuse of Indian children by Bureau of Indian Affairs employees. The hearings were held before a special Senate committee created to investigate federal Indian programs. *(Indian programs investigation, p. 881)*

The House Interior and Insular Affairs Committee reported HR 3703 (H Rept 101-687) on Sept. 10. The House by voice vote passed the measure on Oct. 1, and the Senate passed an amended version on Oct. 25. The House accepted the changes the next day, clearing the bill.

The child abuse language was originally introduced in the Senate as S 1783 by John McCain, R-Ariz. S 1783 was reported (S Rept 101-203) on Nov. 13, 1989, by the Senate Indian Affairs Committee and passed by the Senate on Nov. 18 by voice vote. The House Interior and Insular Affairs Committee reported S 1783 (H Rept 101-876) on Oct. 15, 1990, and the House passed it by voice vote under suspension of the rules the next day. S 1783 subsequently was attached to HR 3703, which authorized the Rumsey Indian Rancheria, a small tribe in California, to sell a tract of its land.

HR 3703 also contained the language of S 2645, which aimed at improving the quality and scope of health care available to urban American Indians. The measure, approved by the Senate Select Indian Affairs Committee Sept. 18 and reported (S Rept 101-557) Sept. 26, included funding for immunization services, mental health care, child abuse treatment and a health promotion and disease prevention program. The program was expected to benefit half the off-reservation Native American population.

Meanwhile, a separate measure authorizing up to $30 million annually over five years to develop programs designed to prevent child and family violence passed the Senate by voice vote Aug. 4. Under that bill (S 2340 — S Rept 101-403), counseling and training would be provided, and a caseworker would be assigned to each tribe. The bill stalled in the House Interior and Insular Affairs Committee.

Two other measures made it through the Senate Indian Affairs Committee but went no further. On June 21, the panel by voice vote approved legislation (S 2297) to provide funding for alcohol and substance abuse treatment for American Indian tribes. The bill, introduced by McCain and formally reported (S Rept 101-510) Oct. 8, included a program to treat fetal alcohol syndrome.

The committee Sept. 12 approved a bill (S 2995) to allow American Indians to earn up to $4,000 from reservation lands without the income counting against them in determining eligibility for federal programs. The bill, approved by voice vote, was sponsored by Tom Daschle, D-S.D., who argued that federal benefits, including Supplemental Security Income and food stamps, often were delayed or denied to American Indians because of inaccurate federal estimates of their income from land leases. S 2995 was reported (S Rept 101-509) on Oct. 5.

Indian Education

The House by voice vote Oct. 12, 1990, passed, and thus cleared, legislation to reauthorize funding for tribally controlled community colleges; the Senate had passed the bill by voice vote Oct. 11. Bush signed the measure (S 2167 — PL 101-477) Oct. 30.

The bill increased from $350,000 to $750,000 the federal contribution to the tribally controlled Community College Endowment Program. Indian education programs received $75.8 million in fiscal 1991 through the Interior appropriations bill.

The Senate Select Committee on Indian Affairs approved S 2167 (S Rept 101-371) June 21 and reported it July 16.

Indian Law Enforcement

President Bush Aug. 18, 1990, signed into law a bill (HR 498 — PL 101-379) to strengthen the authority of Interior Department law enforcement services and officers on Indian land.

The measure gave Bureau of Indian Affairs (BIA) law enforcement officials the right to carry guns and arrest people who committed crimes on Indian lands. The U.S. government was responsible for enforcing federal laws on Indian reservations, but that authority had never been put into statutory language that carried the weight of law.

"Law enforcement is on a very shaky basis," said bill sponsor John J. Rhodes III, R-Ariz. "BIA runs the risk of having its authority successfully challenged in court."

BIA officials generally acted as a police force on reservations and aided FBI investigations of major crimes, such as murder and rape, on Indian lands. HR 498 created a criminal inquiry arm within the BIA's law enforcement branch to boost BIA officials' role in such probes.

The House and Senate first passed slightly differing versions of HR 498 in 1989. The House passed the bill on a voice vote under suspension of the rules May 23. The Senate passed the bill with unrelated amendments Nov. 18.

Before HR 498 went to the House floor, sponsors stripped out a provision to make it easier for tribes to investigate criminal cases dropped by federal authorities. The provision, to require the Justice Department to turn over its case files to tribal authorities if the FBI declined to investigate a federal crime committed on Indian lands or scrapped the probe for any reason, would have forced Justice to disclose "information from confidential sources" and "would be burdensome administratively," according to a May 18 Office of Management and Budget statement of administrative policy.

The requirement was added to HR 498 during the Interior and Insular Affairs Committee's May 17 markup. Reportedly at the administration's request, the Judiciary Committee threatened to hold up the bill unless the provision was dropped. HR 498 was formally reported (H Rept 101-60) May 23.

The Senate Indian Affairs Committee approved HR 498 Sept. 15, including a provision authorizing the Justice Department to submit a report to law enforcement officials of an Indian tribe stating the reasons for declining to investigate or prosecute a crime. The provision did not require the FBI to turn over any confidential files, however. The bill was reported (S Rept 101-167) Oct. 18.

The House made further amendments to the legislation Aug. 1, 1990, which the Senate accepted Aug. 4, thus clearing the bill.

Indian Environmental Quality

Congress in 1990 cleared a bill (S 2075) to establish a grant program to help Indian tribes clean up environmental problems. The bill authorized $8 million for each of fiscal 1991-96 for grants to improve the capability of tribal governments to regulate environmental quality on Indian reservations

Bush opposed the bill but never issued a formal veto threat and signed the measure Oct. 4 (PL 101-408).

The Senate Indian Affairs Committee approved the bill May 1 and reported it (S Rept 101-295) May 16, though that version did not authorize a specific funding amount. The Senate passed S 2075 on May 23 by voice vote. The House Interior and Insular Affairs Committee reported the bill (H Rept 101-743) Sept. 24. The House passed it the same day, 316-99, under suspension of the rules, thus clearing the measure.

The Senate Indian Affairs Committee also on May 1 approved a measure (S 2354) that would authorize funds for Community Development Block Grants to Indian tribes. The legislation, reported (S Rept 101-293) May 16, would free $27 million already appropriated for fiscal 1990. The full Senate passed the bill May 22 by voice vote, but it stalled in the House Banking, Finance and Urban Affairs Committee.

Indian Forest Management

The Senate and House in 1990 passed legislation (S 1289) to improve the management of forests and woodlands and the production of forest resources on Indian lands, but the differences were not reconciled before Congress adjourned.

The measure would have required tribes to institute "forest management plans" approved by the tribes and the interior secretary. Special committee investigators in 1989 found that forestry planning and timber marketing in Indian country were grossly inefficient and outdated.

The Senate Indian Affairs Committee reported S 1289 (S Rept 101-402) on July 30. The Senate passed the bill by voice vote on Aug. 4. The House Interior and Insular Affairs Committee reported S 1289 (H Rept 101-835) on Oct. 10. The House passed the measure by voice vote under suspension of the rules the same day.

'Indian Preference'

President Bush Nov. 16, 1990, pocket-vetoed a bill (S 321) to revise provisions of a law that gave a preference to Indian businesses. He called the bill "seriously flawed" and said it "would create more problems than it would solve." In his memorandum of disapproval, Bush said that the bill "would impose new, expensive and often duplicative program responsibilities on the secretary of the Interior that would be difficult to implement." He added, however, that he supported "the goals of S 321."

S 321 would have made the Bureau of Indian Affairs set-aside program for Indian firms more resistant to abuse.

The Senate Indian Affairs Committee reported S 321 (S Rept 101-218) on Nov. 20, 1989. The Senate passed the bill, by voice vote, on Feb. 7, 1990. The House Interior and Insular Affairs Committee reported S 321 (H Rept 101-904) on Oct. 19. The House passed an amended version on Oct. 20. The Senate agreed to the House changes Oct. 23, clearing the measure.

The House first had considered HR 1714, an early Interior Committee companion to S 321 that sought to strengthen the Indian preference in contracting on the reservations. The House in 1990, however, chose to work from the Senate bill.

The Senate passed an Indian preference bill in 1992, but it died upon adjournment. *(Story, p. 907)*

Tribal Remains

Legislation to protect American Indian grave sites and to return remains to the tribes was cleared by the House Oct. 27, 1990. President Bush signed the bill (HR 5237 — PL 101-601) Nov. 16, despite having opposed an earlier version of the measure.

The bill was an attempt to balance the emotional requests of Indian tribes for the return of the remains of their ancestors with the scholarly interests of scientists and museum officials. Under existing law, human remains unearthed on federal lands were considered federal property to be preserved in museums or educational institutions.

Before clearing the measure, the House agreed to some Senate changes, including an amendment that excluded the Smithsonian Institution from the mandates of the bill. The Smithsonian was often criticized by American Indians for holding thousands of Indian skeletons. *(Related action, Indian museum, p. 885)*

The bill protected Indian grave sites on federal and tribal land from looting and established guidelines for museums to return human remains and cultural items. However, the legislation covered only skeletal remains and funeral objects buried with the bodies. In addition, the claimants would have to prove that the remains and objects belonged to their particular tribe.

The House Interior Committee reported the measure (H Rept 101-877) Oct. 15. The House passed the bill by voice vote Oct. 22. The Senate passed an amended version Oct. 26, also by voice vote.

Indian Museum

The Senate Nov. 14, 1989, cleared a bill (S 978) to establish a museum of Indian history and culture at the Smithsonian Institution in Washington, D.C. President Bush signed the measure (PL 101-185) Nov. 28.

The bill transferred to the Smithsonian a renowned collection of Indian artifacts owned by the Heye Foundation in New York City. Sponsors said the private Heye Foundation, at 155th Street and Broadway in upper Manhattan, lacked adequate resources to preserve and display its extensive holdings of Indian art objects and artifacts.

The bill also authorized $10 million in fiscal 1990 to build a museum on the Washington Mall — on the last potential building space, next to the Smithsonian's Air and Space Museum — that would house the collection, as well as Indian artifacts already in the Smithsonian's hands. In keeping with Heye Foundation requirements, the legislation provided for some of the artifacts to continue to be displayed in New York City. The bill authorized $25 million from the federal Building Trust Fund to be used to renovate the Old Customs House in Manhattan to allow for a viewing area.

A clause in the Heye Foundation trust stipulating that the collection must remain in New York, combined with the Smithsonian's demand for total control over the artifacts, stymied initial efforts to rescue the collection. The bill broke through its final logjam Sept. 9 when the Smithsonian and Indian community leaders agreed on a procedure for returning ancestral Indian remains held by the museum. The Smithsonian agreed to turn them over if a "preponderance of the evidence" linked the remains to direct descendants or a particular tribe. The inventory would be overseen by a five-member committee, which would include three Indians. The Smithsonian had an estimated 18,000 Indian remains. *(Related action, tribal remains, p. 884)*

The Senate Select Committee on Indian Affairs approved S 978 by voice vote May 16. The Senate Rules Committee approved S 978 (S Rept 101-143) May 17, also on a voice vote. The bill confirmed an agreement reached May 8 by the Smithsonian Board of Regents and the Heye Foundation: Part of the collection would be displayed in the Customs House, and the Smithsonian would receive legal title to the artifacts and the right to display the collection in Washington. Following the Sept. 9 agreement, the Senate Select Committee on Indians and the Rules Committee again approved the legislation, on Sept. 27. The full Senate then passed the bill on a voice vote Oct. 3.

The Public Buildings Subcommittee of the House Public Works Committee Oct. 3 approved a nearly identical version of S 978 in HR 2668, crafted by the Libraries and Memorials Subcommittee of the House Administration Committee Sept. 12. House Public Works approved the bill (H Rept 101-340, Part I) by voice vote Oct. 12 and reported it Nov. 9; House Administration approved the bill (H Rept 101-340, Part II) by voice vote Oct. 18 and reported it Nov. 13. The House passed HR 2668 Nov. 13 on a voice vote under suspension of the rules, then substituted the text for S 978 and passed that bill. The Senate the next day approved the House's amendments, avoiding a conference and clearing the bill for the president.

Seminole Indians

A bill (S 1096) to distribute about $47 million to Seminole Indians for claims arising over inadequate compensation for lands in the early 1980s was cleared by Congress in 1990.

The bill allocated 75.4 percent of the money to the Seminole Nation of Oklahoma and 24.6 percent to the Seminole Tribe, the Miccousukee Tribe of Indians and the independent Seminole Indians, all of Florida.

The Indian Claims Commission awarded the Seminole Indians $16 million in 1976. The funds were never distributed, however, because of litigation over the distribution method recommended by the Interior Department, which submitted a plan based on population during the period spanning 1906-14.

The legislation essentially adopted the Interior plan.

S 1096 was reported (S Rept 101-212) by Senate Indian Affairs on Nov. 19, 1989. The Senate passed the bill by voice vote Nov. 22. The House Interior and Insular Affairs Committee reported the bill (H Rept 101-399) on Feb. 6, 1990. The House passed the measure by voice vote under suspension of the rules the same day. The House adopted the conference report (H Rept 101-439) under suspension of the rules April 3. The Senate adopted it April 5, clearing the bill. President Bush signed S 1096 on April 30.

Puyallup Settlement

The Senate May 31, 1989, passed on a voice vote, and thus cleared, a bill (HR 932 — PL 101-41) to ratify and implement a settlement under which the Puyallup Tribe gave up its claim to lands in and around Tacoma, Wash. The House passed the bill by voice vote under suspension of the rules May 23. President Bush signed it June 21.

In exchange for ceding all but its fishing rights, the tribe received a cash and in-kind settlement of $77 million from the federal government, plus $85 million from the state of Washington, local government and private concerns. The measure sought to compensate the tribe for the gradual erosion of its 1,900-acre reservation, which was granted under an 1854 treaty.

Micmac Settlement

The House in 1990 failed to pass the Aroostook Band of Micmacs Settlement Act. The bill (S 1413) sought to provide federal recognition of the Aroostook Band of Micmacs as an Indian tribe, making all members of the band eligible to receive all of the federal benefits and services available to recognized Indian tribes. The Congressional Budget Office estimated that if the full amount had been authorized and appropriated, outlays would have been $900,000 in fiscal 1991, and the cost of providing federal benefits and services to the band would have been $1 million annually.

The Senate Indian Affairs Committee reported S 1413 (S Rept 101-291) on May 15. The Senate passed the bill by voice vote May 22. The House Interior and Insular Affairs Committee reported S 1413 (H Rept 101-836) on Oct. 10. The same day, the House rejected the bill 248-172, falling short of the 280 votes (two-thirds of those present and voting) required for passage under suspension of the rules.

Similar legislation cleared in 1992. *(Story, p. 908)*

1991-92

Federal Honoraria Ban

Attempts to reverse the honoraria ban on rank-and-file federal employees stalled in the 102nd Congress. *(Earlier action, p. 858)*

On Jan. 3, 1991, Rep. Barney Frank, D-Mass., introduced legislation (HR 325) to overturn the ban for all federal employees except members of Congress and presidential appointees who required Senate confirmation.

A slightly different bill (S 242) was introduced Jan. 22 by Sens. John Glenn, D-Ohio, and William V. Roth Jr., R-Del., chairman and ranking member, respectively, of the Senate Governmental Affairs Committee. It exempted all workers whose annual rate of basic pay was less than that of a GS-16 — about $60,000 to $70,000.

Both bills stipulated that federal employees could not use government time or resources for outside activities and had to meet certain conditions before honoraria would be permitted. Both also set the maximum for any speaking or writing fee at $2,000 and made repeal of the ban retroactive to Jan. 1, 1991. In addition, both bills prohibited employees from speaking or writing about subjects related to their official duties.

The Senate Governmental Affairs Committee approved S 242 by voice vote on Feb. 27. An hour later, the House Judiciary Administrative Law and Governmental Relations Subcommittee approved an amended version of HR 325 that closely resembled the Senate bill. S 242 was reported (S Rept 102-29) on April 3.

At the markup, Frank offered an amendment to HR 325 to extend the ban to presidential appointees who did not require Senate confirmation (58 positions). Frank suggested that the ethics law was primarily intended to clean up the image of Congress. He termed the ban for non-elected federal officials an "unnecessary and unfair restriction." Judiciary Chairman Jack Brooks, D-Texas, supported Frank's bill.

But the subcommittee's ranking member, George W. Gekas, R-Pa., offered an amendment to maintain the ban for senior executives and other upper-level workers. It would allow employees below the GS-16 level to accept honoraria. The amendment prevailed on a 5-3 vote, but the bill was never sent on to the full committee because of Frank's opposition to the Gekas language.

Instead, with the backing of Brooks, Frank worked out a compromise with Gekas to ban honoraria for non-career employees at a salary level above $101,300. On Sept. 12, the subcommittee, 8-0, approved a clean bill incorporating the compromise. The measure also stipulated that federal workers above the GS-15 level report honoraria to their agency's ethics official before accepting the payment.

After the second subcommittee markup, a clean bill, HR 3341, was introduced on Sept. 16 by Frank and approved by the full committee by voice vote Oct. 29. The committee approved an amendment offered by Frank to change Federal Election Commission regulations requiring campaign workers who temporarily paid incidental expenses to declare such expenses as campaign contributions, even if the worker was reimbursed.

On Nov. 25, with only a handful of members in attendance, the House passed HR 3341 by voice vote under suspension of the rules after less than five minutes of debate. Earlier the same day, the House Judiciary Committee had reported the bill (H Rept 102-385, Part I).

In the Senate, Christopher J. Dodd, D-Conn., put a hold on S 242 to pressure senators into accepting a ban on honoraria for themselves and their staffs. Dodd had introduced a bill (S 469) to bring senators within the scope of the honoraria ban and had announced his intention to attach it to S 242.

Senate Majority Leader George J. Mitchell, D-Maine, while expressing his support for a ban on Senate honoraria, said it "should be at the same time accompanied by a corresponding increase in compensation to offset the loss of income from honoraria." The Senate finally passed an honoraria ban and a pay raise July 17 as part of the fiscal 1991 legislative branch appropriations bill (HR 2506 — PL 102-90), signed by President Bush on Aug. 14.

Dodd then removed his hold on S 242. But the bill still faced opposition from Robert C. Byrd, D-W.Va., the powerful chairman of the Appropriations Committee. Byrd opposed provisions in both the Senate and House measures that would allow all but a small number of higher-level congressional staff to accept honoraria. He did not want to relax the ban for Senate staff so soon after passage of the pay raise and new ethics rules. *(Ethics reform, p. 920)*

As the session entered its final days, another obstacle developed. The Senate Democratic leadership decided it might use S 242 to pressure the administration to accept new presidential campaign finance proposals that the White House opposed. Democratic leaders knew that the administration wanted quick passage of the "revolving door" provisions included in the House bill, but the White House did not want them badly enough to accept Democratic-backed legislation (HR 3750, S 3) that sought to overturn the rules by which presidential campaign matching funds collected through the $1 taxpayer checkoff were to be distributed in 1992. *('Revolving door,' p. 862)*

S 242 saw no further congressional action.

The honoraria ban was declared unconstitutional March 19, 1992, by U.S. District Court Judge Thomas Penfield Jackson. He threw out the portion of the 1989 Ethics Reform Act (PL 101-194) that pertained to federal employees, but restrictions on members of Congress remained in effect. Jackson said the law violated employees' First Amendment right to free speech. However, he barred enforcement of the ruling to allow the Justice Department to appeal the decision. The appeal was argued in November 1992 before the U.S. Court of Appeals, D.C. Circuit. As of January 1993, a decision was still pending.

Hatch Act Revisions

With his veto threat, President Bush effectively blocked consideration of legislation (S 914, HR 20) in the 102nd Congress to revise the 1939 Hatch Act, which governed the political participation of federal and postal employees. Bush vetoed a Hatch Act revision bill in 1990. *(Story, p. 859)*

Bush's two Republican predecessors also did not support changes in the law. President Reagan prevented a Hatch Act bill from reaching his desk in 1988 by threatening a veto. President Ford in 1976 vetoed legislation to ease restrictions on the federal work force. *(Congress and the Nation Vol. IV, p. 822; Congress and the Nation Vol. VII, p. 857)*

The Senate Governmental Affairs Committee approved S 914, sponsored by committee Chairman John Glenn, D-Ohio, on a 7-1 vote March 17, 1992. The bill reported (S Rept 102-278) May 5 would prohibit any partisan politics during working hours. In their spare time, however, federal workers could participate more actively in campaigns. Violators would be subject to a $5,000 fine and up to three years in jail. The panel easily dispatched, all by 4-8 votes, a set of seven amendments offered by ranking Republican William V. Roth Jr., Del., the most vocal opponent to the Hatch Act revision.

Senate Majority Leader George J. Mitchell, D-Maine, unsure of getting the necessary 67 votes to override a presidential veto, never sent S 914 to the floor. HR 20 saw no congressional action because Speaker Thomas S. Foley, D-Wash., said the House would wait until the Senate approved a bill.

Also stalling the legislation were regulations, expected in mid-1991 but not circulated until 1992, by the Office of Personnel Management (OPM) to clarify the rules. Republicans were hopeful they would sway some senators not to support any legislative revision. The regulations did not make wholesale changes in the Hatch Act. Instead, they allowed federal employees greater political freedom, so long as their activities were not part of an organized effort sponsored by a political party. Federal workers were allowed to solicit votes or endorse a candidate for political office only if the worker was acting independently of an organized political group. Hatch Act rules also were changed to allow workers to contribute to candidates running in partisan elections. The Office of Special Counsel, not individual federal agencies, would be charged with investigating and prosecuting allegations of Hatch Act violations.

Officials from federal unions, who had been fighting for years to change the law, called the regulations a political ploy by the administration to deter legislation. Sen. Roth countered that most federal workers did not support easing the Hatch Act. He cited a survey released in March 1991 by the Federal Executive Institute Alumni Association, which indicated that only 18.5 percent of more than 1,100 respondents wanted the law changed so that government employees could be more politically active.

'Revolving Door'

The House Judiciary Subcommittee on Administrative Law and Governmental Relations in 1991 considered an amendment to relax the so-called "revolving door" policy — rules that prohibited former senior government officials from lobbying former coworkers for one year after they left office. The amendment was offered to legislation designed to limit the ban on honoraria for all federal workers. *(Federal honoraria ban, p. 886)*

Republican National Committee (RNC) Chairman Clayton Yeutter brought the issue into the spotlight when he left his job as agriculture secretary in January 1991 to head the RNC, only to find out that he could not lobby most senior White House officials, including the president. Responding to Yeutter's plight, the administration on July 26 asked Congress to exempt former government officials (including former members of Congress and their staff) who lobbied in behalf of political candidates or parties.

Although the proposal originated with the administration, it had broad support in both parties.

President Bill Clinton would set forth new ethics guidelines designed to curb influence peddling by former top government officials in his first executive order issued Jan. 20, 1993. The new standards, affecting approximately 1,100 of the 3,500 presidential appointees, would prohibit officials from lobbying their former agencies for five years and from ever representing foreign governments or foreign parties before the U.S. government.

Lobbying Rules

The Senate Governmental Affairs Committee on July 31, 1992, reported legislation (S 2766 — S Rept 102-354) designed to force lobbyists to comply with stricter reporting and disclosure standards. But the bill never made it to the Senate floor, and the House did not consider a companion measure.

S 2766, sponsored by Sen. Carl Levin, D-Mich., sought to establish more rigorous financial disclosure requirements for lobbyists and to require them to file a semiannual report revealing the income received for lobbying on behalf of a client.

During Governmental Affairs Committee consideration, S 2766 was amended to require those who worked in the executive or legislative branch in the two years before registering as lobbyists to disclose the details of their government service.

As approved by committee, the bill substituted for existing statutes a single, uniform rule, requiring anyone engaged in lobbying the executive or legislative branch to register with a new Office of Lobbying Registration and Public Disclosure, unless these activities were incidental to the job.

Registered lobbyists were to issue a semiannual report revealing the income received for lobbying on behalf of a client or, if representing themselves, provide a good-faith estimate of the amount spent on lobbying activities. Each report also was required to contain a list of issues the lobbyist worked on and the federal agencies and congressional committees contacted.

The Office of Lobbying Registration and Public Disclosure, to be part of the Justice Department, would administer the statute. Its duties included providing interested parties with registration and reporting information as well as investigating and determining non-compliance. The bill established civil penalties for lobbying violations as high as $10,000.

Performance Standards

President Bush March 28, 1991, signed into law legislation (HR 1316 — PL 102-22) that modified the performance system used by the federal government to evaluate and compensate employees.

The bill removed the requirement that federal employees rated "outstanding" were to receive a bonus of at least 2 percent and called for the OPM director to appoint a committee to advise OPM of further improvements needed in the Performance Management and Recognition System (PMRS), the criteria federal supervisors used to grade employees. Authorization of the PMRS system was extended until Sept. 30, 1993; it expired March 31, 1992.

OPM supported the bill, and, according to the Congressional Budget Office, changes did not mean any additional costs to federal agencies over what was appropriated for fiscal 1991.

The House Post Office and Civil Service Committee reported HR 1316 (H Rept 102-20) March 14. The House passed the bill by voice vote under suspension of the rules March 19. The Senate passed the bill by voice vote the same day, clearing the measure for the president.

Waste-Buster Awards

Legislation (HR 2263 — PL 102-487) was enacted in 1992 that permanently authorized a program to reward federal employees who disclosed information on waste, fraud and abuse that led to cost savings for the government. The bill made government contract workers and former federal employees eligible for the awards, which could not exceed $20,000.

HR 2263 on Nov. 22, 1991, was reported (H Rept 102-356) by House Post Office and Civil Service and on Nov. 25 was passed by the House on a voice vote.

The Senate passed HR 2263 on Sept. 24, deleting provisions that would increase the amount a federal agency could pay a worker for finding a better way to do his or her job. The House accepted the amended version of the bill by voice vote on Oct. 4. President Bush signed it Oct. 24.

Ethics Office Funds

Legislation (S 1145) to lift the cap on annual Office of Government Ethics spending cleared in 1992.

The Office of Government Ethics was created in 1978, as part of the post-Watergate government reform. It set guidelines and issued advisory opinions on conflict-of-interest matters, and it monitored each federal agency's ethics program.

Although the ethics office was limited by statute to a yearly authorization of $5 million, $6.3 million was appropriated in fiscal 1992. About $8 million was appropriated for the agency in the fiscal 1993 Treasury spending bill (HR 5488 — PL 102-393).

The Senate Governmental Affairs Committee reported S 1145 (S Rept 102-132) on July 30, 1991. The Senate passed the bill by voice vote on Aug. 2. The House passed an amended version Aug. 4, 1992. The Senate agreed to the House changes Oct. 7, completing congressional action. President Bush signed the bill (PL 102-506) on Oct. 24.

EEOC Revisions

Legislation (HR 3613) to make discrimination or sexual harassment complaints easier and faster to file for federal workers obtained House committee approval but went no further before the 102nd Congress adjourned.

Under the bill, alleged violations of equal employment opportunity laws would be adjudicated by the Equal Employment Opportunity Commission (EEOC), instead of by the agency that employed the complainant as under existing law.

The House Post Office and Civil Service Committee approved HR 3613 on July 1, 1992, by a 17-0 vote.

White House Spending

Legislation (HR 5928) to revamp the way the president and the executive branch accounted for their travel expenses was approved in 1992 by the House Post Office and Civil Service Committee but saw no further action in the 102nd Congress.

A 1978 law (PL 95-570) established a system under which the White House directly paid for only a small portion of its travel expenses, with the executive departments picking up the difference. For example, White House records showed that President Bush spent only $29,000 on travel in fiscal 1991. Meanwhile, the Defense Department calculated that operating *Air Force One* for just one hour of flying time cost $40,243. The Pentagon budget absorbed the costs not paid for by the White House. Under existing law, both the president and the vice president were allowed free travel on government aircraft so long as the trip was not political. The White House paid the cost of a first-class plane ticket plus $1 for political trips, well short of the full cost of flying on government aircraft. *(Congress and the Nation Vol. V, p. 838)*

The Post Office and Civil Service Subcommittee on Human Resources, 3-2, approved HR 5928 on Sept. 17. The full committee followed suit, 20-3, on Sept. 23 and reported the measure (H Rept 102-985) on Oct. 3. The bill would cap the spending allowance at $185 million — a huge increase over the existing level of $100,000. The larger budget reflected what the president already was spending but the White House did not pay for. The bill would require that the president regularly make public how the money was spent and that the White House pay the higher costs of public planes when traveling for political purposes. The president would have to reimburse the Defense Department for use of *Air Force One*, and the $185 million also would be used to pay for personal trips, such as the golf trips taken by Vice President Dan Quayle. The White House budget would have to absorb the costs of salaries of staff who belonged to a federal agency but had been sent to work at the White House, effective after one month, not six months as under current law. The bill also authorized about $83.1 million for the general operation of the White House.

Defense Workers Relief

Legislation (HR 4991) to aid defense workers who lost their jobs as a result of spending cutbacks failed to clear the 102nd Congress, but similar provisions were included in the fiscal 1993 defense authorization (PL 102-484). *(Defense authorization, p. 395)*

Sponsored by William L. Clay, D-Mo., HR 4991 required the Defense Department to give 120 days' notice before laying off employees as a result of cutbacks caused by the dissolution of the Soviet Union and to continue to pay its portion of health insurance for laid-off workers for up to

18 months. The bill also called for other federal agencies to give at least 60 days' notice of impending layoffs. HR 4991 authorized six-month severance packages for eligible Defense Department civilian workers as an incentive for taking early retirement and mandated the temporary continuation of existing health benefits for displaced workers. The legislation required the Office of Personnel Management to expand its job listings to include all vacant positions and to ensure that displaced employees were given full consideration for vacancies at other federal agencies before any candidate from outside the agency was hired.

The House Post Office and Civil Service Committee approved HR 4991 on May 20, 1992.

In a related matter, the House on June 24, 1991, passed by voice vote under suspension of the rules legislation (HR 1341) that federal employees be given 60 days' advance written notice before losing their jobs as a result of military base closings. HR 1341 (H Rept 102-124) had been reported from the House Post Office and Civil Service Committee the same day. *(Base closings, p. 393)*

The Senate Governmental Affairs Committee approved companion legislation (S 1292 — S Rept 102-110) by voice vote on June 27.

The administration opposed the bills, saying the Office of Personnel Management was already in the process of issuing regulations similar to ones that were ordered by the legislation.

Gulf War Compensation

Legislation (HR 3209) died at the end of the 102nd Congress that would compensate federal and U.S. Postal Service employees who were called to active duty during the 1991 Persian Gulf War for the difference between their government salaries and their military pay. The money would come from funds already appropriated to the agencies. *(Gulf war, special report, p. 299)*

The measure allowed the 17,000 federal and postal employees called to active duty to make up back contributions to the Thrift Savings Plan, a federal retirement program. HR 3209 also extended life and health insurance during the service period.

The House Post Office and Civil Service Committee, 22-0, approved HR 3209 on Nov. 13, 1991, and reported it (H Rept 102-426) on Jan. 28, 1992. The House passed the bill, 354-57, under suspension of the rules on March 18. It saw no action in the Senate.

Supercomputers

Congress in 1991 cleared legislation (S 272) authorizing $2 billion over five years to develop supercomputers at eight federal agencies and to design a high-speed computer network. The measure was intended to aid U.S. competitiveness in the field of information technology.

A study by the General Accounting Office found that supercomputers — the fastest computers in operation at any given time — could allow automobile manufacturers, oil producers and aerospace, chemical and pharmaceutical companies to speed up design of new products and decrease costs. The development of supercomputers also was considered crucial to making government research data available to scientists at universities and in private industries nationwide.

A House companion measure (HR 656) was reported by the Science, Space and Technology Committee (H Rept 102-66, Part I) on May 15 and by the Education and Labor Committee (H Rept 102-66, Part II) on May 22. The House passed HR 656 by voice vote under suspension of the rules July 11. The Senate passed the bill Sept. 11.

S 272, written by Al Gore, D-Tenn., was reported from the Senate Commerce Committee (S Rept 102-57) on May 16, and the Senate passed the High-Performance Computing Act by voice vote, with little debate, on Sept. 11.

The differences between the House and Senate bills were largely technical. Both measures conformed to the proposals made by the White House in its fiscal 1992 budget request. But action on the legislation was delayed for months over a provision inserted at the request of House Majority Leader Richard A. Gephardt, D-Mo., and the House Science Committee, which would require Congress to be notified of the purchase of foreign goods or services to carry out the program. The Bush administration opposed the provision. In the end, the notification requirement was dropped. The House passed S 272 by voice vote on Nov. 20. The amended bill mandated that the government report annually to Congress on foreign services and goods purchased for the program. The Senate accepted the House version of the bill on Nov. 22, clearing the measure.

President Bush signed S 272 into law (PL 102-194) on Dec. 9.

Fire Administration

Congress in 1992 cleared legislation (HR 2042) reauthorizing the U.S. Fire Administration, an arm of the Federal Emergency Management Agency, to combat and reduce the risk of fires. The bill directed the federal agency to focus its resources on fire prevention for residential areas and for those most vulnerable: the very young, the elderly, and those living in rural areas and inner cities that were hardest hit by fire.

HR 2042 was reported from the House Science, Space and Technology Committee (H Rept 102-62) on May 15, 1991. The House passed the bill, 326-5, under suspension of the rules on June 3. The Senate passed an amended version by voice vote Sept. 29, 1992. The House accepted the changes Oct. 2, clearing the measure. President Bush signed HR 2042 (PL 102-552) on Oct. 26.

GSA Overhaul

Legislation (HR 3161) to give Congress more oversight of the General Services Administration (GSA) won House approval in 1992 but died upon adjournment of the 102nd Congress.

House Government Operations Committee Chairman John Conyers Jr., D-Mich., sponsor of HR 3161, labeled the GSA a "stealth agency" operating virtually free from accountability. It was responsible in 1991 for more than $10 billion in federal purchases and construction.

HR 3161 put the GSA, which had a permanent authorization, on an annual authorization cycle. It changed the federal procurement process to require the government to emphasize purchasing commercial products instead of items that were custom-made and generally more expensive. The bill also restricted the number of senior officials at the agency who did not have significant federal service experience.

GSA Administrator Richard Austin testified that permanent authorization ensured that the agency's programs retained much-needed continuity.

The House Government Operations Committee reported HR 3161 (H Rept 102-364) on Nov. 23, 1991. The House passed the bill by voice vote under suspension of the rules Oct. 2, 1992.

A Senate companion measure (S 1958), which called for reauthorization every two years, was reported (S Rept 102-348) from Governmental Affairs on July 29, 1992. The bill did not include the provision to require agencies to buy more commercial products.

A separate Senate-passed bill (S 260) encouraged but did not require federal agencies to buy more commercial products. *(Procurement rules, below)*

Procurement Rules

By voice vote Sept. 13, 1991, the Senate passed legislation (S 260) to require federal agencies to buy off-the-shelf, commercially available supplies. The bill saw no further congressional action.

S 260, reported from Senate Governmental Affairs (S Rept 102-137) on Aug. 2, aimed to lower federal procurement costs by eliminating lengthy production start-ups and the need for costly research and development. Supporters said that agencies often had products specially designed and built that were already available on the commercial market at a lower cost.

The bill required government purchasers to order, when possible, commercial or off-the-shelf products, known in the government as non-developmental items or NDIs. Agencies were also required to streamline their product requirements, increasing the possibility that a commercial product could meet their needs.

In related action, HR 5851, to establish a new 19-member commission on Information Technology and Paperwork to study ways to reduce federal paperwork requirements, was derailed in 1992 when the Senate added the language of S 260.

Paperwork Reduction

Congress failed to clear legislation (HR 5851) to set up a new 19-member commission to study ways to reduce federal paperwork requirements.

The House by voice vote passed HR 5851 on Sept. 21, 1992. The Senate Oct. 5 passed the bill by voice vote after adding the provisions of S 260, which streamlined the federal acquisition process for commercial items and off-the-shelf purchases. The House did not act on the amended bill before adjournment. *(Related action, Paperwork Reduction Act reauthorization, p. 867)*

S 260 was reported by Senate Governmental Affairs (S Rept 102-137) on Aug. 2, 1991. The Senate passed the bill by voice vote Sept. 13.

Energy Efficiency

The Senate Governmental Affairs Committee on June 27, 1991, gave easy approval to a bill (S 1040) promoting energy efficiency governmentwide; it was formally reported (S Rept 102-138) on Aug. 2. S 1040 never proceeded to the floor as a separate measure, but some of the provisions were similar to those incorporated in a broader energy bill (S 1220). *(Energy bill, p. 500)*

S 1040 directed the Office of Management and Budget to establish guidelines for monitoring energy consumption at federal facilities. In addition, the General Services Administration was required to identify and promote the use of energy-efficient products and services as well as train employees in energy and conservation planning. Federal agencies and workers were to be offered monetary incentives for significant reductions of energy use at their facilities.

The federal government spent about $13 billion on energy each year. S 1040 would save about $900 million per year in energy costs. However, the bill was estimated to cost as much as $51.5 million, with $40 million of that being directed to promote the use of alternative-fuel vehicles. The remaining $11.5 million was to finance various projects over the next four fiscal years aimed at increasing energy efficiency at the departments and agencies.

Supporters said some of the costs could be absorbed into agency budgets and offset by energy savings. They also viewed the bill as key to carrying out an executive order signed by President Bush in April 1991 requiring the government to achieve a 20 percent reduction in energy usage by the year 2000.

State Aid Disbursement

President Bush Nov. 10, 1992, signed into law a bill (HR 5377 — PL 102-589) that gave states more time to devise plans for disbursement of federal aid. The legislation extended for one year the effective date of a law (PL 101-453) that gave the Treasury secretary the authority to negotiate with each state how its federal aid would be transferred. *(PL 101-453, p. 865)*

The states pushed for the extension because the Treasury Department did not issue the regulations on how the law would work until the week of Sept. 28, 1992.

The House passed HR 5377 by voice vote under suspension of the rules July 21, 1992.

The Senate passed HR 5377 by voice vote Oct. 2, after amending it to include provisions of a related bill (S 2970 — S Rept 102-420), sponsored by Jim Sasser, D-Tenn. The final version offset the projected $75 million cost of delaying enactment by extending for four years a pilot project that allowed private lawyers to go after money owed to the federal government and by codifying an Internal Revenue Service policy called "matching," which checks people who are owed a tax refund against a list of those who owe the government money, thus allowing the government to withhold the refund.

The House cleared the bill Oct. 3.

Joint Ventures

Legislation (S 479, HR 1604) to make conducting joint manufacturing ventures easier for companies died in the 102nd Congress.

The Senate Judiciary Committee reported S 479 (S Rept 102-146) on Sept. 11, 1991. The Senate passed the bill, 96-1 on Feb. 27, 1992, to loosen antitrust restrictions on joint manufacturing after toning down a section that would largely restrict protections to U.S.-based manufacturing. The Bush administration had attacked the section as protectionist.

The proposal encompassed industries across the spectrum but was expected to be most useful in high-technology fields that often required extensive capital investment — for example, the semiconductor industry. Congress already had eased antitrust restrictions on cooperative research and development efforts through the 1984 National Cooperative Research Extension Act. S 479 sought to extend that legal umbrella to joint manufacturing as well.

As passed by the Senate, the bill gave companies relief from antitrust laws in two areas as long as they notified the Justice Department of plans to form a cooperative manufacturing venture. First, the bill required critics seeking to sue the joint venture as anti-competitive to meet a higher standard of proof than had been required. Second, companies found guilty under that higher standard would be subject only to actual damages, not three times that amount as the existing law provided.

Supporters said the bill would encourage companies to enter into joint ventures without fearing penalties under the antitrust statutes and would thus create more jobs.

Howard M. Metzenbaum, D-Ohio, offered the sole dissent, saying current antitrust laws did not deter cooperative production accords. He cited a joint venture by IBM and Apple Computer. Instead, Metzenbaum said, antitrust laws heighten competition and in turn spur advances in American competitiveness.

Floor debate was hampered by an attempt by John McCain, R-Ariz., to offer an amendment to provide the president with a line-item veto on spending bills. McCain eventually was rebuffed but not before he spoke at length and Appropriations Committee Chairman Robert C. Byrd, D-W.Va., delivered a marathon opposition address.

Furthermore, controversy arose over a provision added by Joseph R. Biden Jr., D-Del., during committee markup. It stated that the antitrust exemption would apply only if the joint manufacturing operations were principally located within the United States, and the companies had each made a "substantial commitment" to the U.S. economy. The provision drew protests from the European Economic Community and the Bush administration, which threatened a veto. Administration officials said the language would undermine U.S. efforts to open overseas markets.

The conflict forced sponsors to hold a cloture vote to begin consideration of the bill. The Feb. 25 vote was 98-0. Subsequently, a compromise, amenable to the administration, was worked out. As revised, the bill would apply the antitrust benefits to joint ventures that would bring "substantial" benefit to the U.S. economy and that were located either in the United States or in countries that granted reciprocal legal privileges to U.S. companies.

The House companion measure (HR 1604) set a 30 percent cap on foreign participation in joint ventures that would be eligible for the special antitrust treatment. It was reported from House Judiciary (H Rept 102-972) on Oct. 1, 1992.

Competitiveness Council

Amid escalating charges that the Bush administration was undermining environmental and health protection laws, the 102nd Congress began considering legislation to allow closer scrutiny of the regulatory process. The primary target was the Council on Competitiveness and its chief, Vice President Dan Quayle. Democrats contended that the council, working in concert with powerful business interests, had pressured executive branch agencies to relax regulations meant to enforce laws enacted by Congress.

Administration officials said the council simply issued advice designed to ensure that regulations were imposed with the minimum possible cost to business, but critics likened the panel to a sinister, secret tribunal that had boosted big business at the expense of the nation's safety and environmental laws. President Bush incited further wrath in early 1992 when he proposed a 90-day moratorium on new regulations and called for an intensive regulatory review. On April 29, he extended the moratorium for four months, and at the GOP convention in Houston in August, he promised to continue the moratorium indefinitely.

Several legislative attempts were made to rein in the council, but all proved fruitless.

- The Senate Governmental Affairs Committee reported a "sunshine" bill (S 1942 — S Rept 102-256) on Feb. 25, 1992. The legislation would require the administration to document its review of agency-proposed rules and justify any changes made.
- HR 5702, reported from House Government Operations (H Rept 102-965) on Oct. 1, 1992, would require the council, the Office of Management and Budget and any other administration entity that reviewed regulations to disclose to the public all written and oral communications it received about them. Such entities would have to publicly justify all proposed changes in writing. A 90-day limit for reviewing proposed rules would be imposed.
- Senate Governmental Affairs Committee Chairman John Glenn, D-Ohio, attempted to strip the council's $86,000 budget from the fiscal 1993 Treasury and Postal Service appropriations bill (HR 5488 — PL 102-393), which also funded the White House. However, he ultimately withdrew his amendment after a lengthy floor debate.

The issue became moot on Jan. 22, 1993, when President Bill Clinton disbanded the council and lifted the moratorium on new regulations imposed by Bush.

Competitiveness Bills

Bills (S 1330, HR 5231) aimed at boosting the competitive stance of the United States in world markets by enhancing its technological and manufacturing prowess fell prey to partisan squabbling over the proper government role in technology development.

The legislation sought to reauthorize and expand programs within the Commerce Department to help U.S. industries develop and implement advanced technologies. Those programs included creating more outreach centers to teach advanced manufacturing techniques and government-backed loans for critical technologies.

The House Science Subcommittee on Technology and Competitiveness approved HR 5231 by voice vote on June 24, 1992. The subcommittee bill authorized $1.4 billion in fiscal 1994-97 for grants to promote advanced technologies, create a network of outreach centers to help manufacturers adopt modern production techniques and expand the capital available to develop critical technologies.

Several Republicans on the panel said they preferred their own competitiveness package (HR 5229), drafted by

Robert S. Walker, Pa., ranking Republican on the full Science Committee. Subcommittee Chairman Tim Valentine, D-N.C., however, noted that HR 5229 encompassed tax and antitrust policies that went far beyond the Science Committee's jurisdiction.

Members of the House Science, Space and Technology Committee on July 1 voted 8-2 in support of HR 5231 after lengthy and often heated debate between Democrats and Republicans. The bill sought to coordinate and expand federal efforts to help U.S. businesses compete, such as establishing a network of outreach centers to help manufacturers adopt modern production techniques. Other provisions would let the federal government provide loans to develop critical technologies, authorize $1.4 billion in fiscal 1994-97 for grants for advanced technologies and allow greater access to federal information of potential commercial value.

The Commerce Department threatened to recommend a veto, saying the bill called for unnecessary and duplicative federal programs. Walker attacked the measure as ideologically misguided and absurdly narrow. He again tried unsuccessfully to replace it with HR 5229. Committee Chairman George E. Brown Jr., D-Calif., said the bulk of Walker's proposals fell outside the panel's jurisdiction.

While some committee Republicans backed HR 5231 or parts of it, Walker complained that it ignored fundamental barriers to U.S. economic growth, such as the massive federal debt. He suggested that taxpayers be allowed to voluntarily devote up to 10 percent of their taxes for debt reduction, a proposal touted by President Bush during the 1992 presidential campaign. Participating taxpayers thus would simultaneously authorize dollar-for-dollar spending cuts. The cuts would be in the form of across-the-board reductions in all domestic programs save Social Security, the Federal Deposit Insurance Fund and interest payments on the debt.

Walker said the huge federal debt was the key obstacle for U.S. businesses, because it drove up the cost of capital. He said his plan could eliminate the deficit by 1997 and reduce the debt by two-thirds within 12 years. But Democrats said the blanket cuts were a crude way to reduce spending and could cripple programs that also aided U.S. competitiveness. And they said proposed tax breaks within Walker's bill, estimated to cost $100 billion, flew in the face of his stated dedication to deficit reduction.

The House passed HR 5231 on Sept. 23, 287-122, after rejecting several Walker amendments to delete or weaken portions of the bill. The Senate Commerce, Science and Transportation Committee reported the Senate version (S 1330 — S Rept 102-226) on Nov. 21, 1991. The Senate passed the bill by voice vote June 30, 1992. Like the House bill, the measure sought to expand existing Commerce Department efforts to improve and disseminate advanced manufacturing technologies. It proposed creation of a national quality laboratory to help train industry workers. The bill authorized $55 million in fiscal 1993, jumping to $145 million in fiscal 1994 and $125 million in fiscal 1995.

The House passed S 1330 by voice vote Sept. 23, after substituting the text of HR 5231.

High-Tech Training

Legislation was considered in the 102nd Congress to encourage education, training and employment in high-technology industries to improve the competitive position of U.S. industries.

S 1146, signed into law (PL 102-476) Oct. 23, 1992, authorized $70 million in fiscal 1992-93 for National Science Foundation (NSF) grants to technical or two-year colleges for science and math programs. The grants were intended to provide students at junior or community colleges, especially "non-traditional" students and high school dropouts, with the skills needed in high-technology manufacturing and related fields. Grants also assisted two-year schools in forming partnerships with four-year schools.

The bill was virtually identical to HR 2936, which was reported April 30, 1992, by the House Science, Space and Technology Committee (H Rept 102-508, Part I) and passed Aug. 10 by the House by voice vote under suspension of the rules. The House-passed bill required that community college grant recipients make matching contributions toward the education programs to be eligible for the NSF grants. It also incorporated language from legislation (HR 3606) sponsored by Peter Hoagland, D-Neb., that established a national technology education program for two-year colleges.

The Senate Oct. 2 passed S 1146 by voice vote, after amending the bill with the provisions of HR 2936. The House passed S 1146 on Oct. 3, clearing the measure for the president.

A related piece of legislation (HR 3507) created an apprenticeship program at the Labor Department for high school students to train in manufacturing or technology. It also authorized the Commerce Department to set up programs linking colleges and universities with private industry to train employees. HR 3507 (H Rept 102-418, Part I) was reported Dec. 6, 1991, by the Science, Space and Technology Committee.

Kennedy Documents

Stirred to action by the publicity surrounding a 1991 movie about the Nov. 22, 1963, assassination of President John F. Kennedy, Congress in 1992 cleared legislation (S 3006) creating a special new commission with the authority to review and make public hundreds of thousands of pages of secret government documents, testimony and evidence surrounding the shooting and follow-up investigations into the president's death. Records that would violate privacy or national security concerns would not be released.

The bill's aim was to deflate the many conspiracy theories about the shooting of the president, which were rekindled by the film "JFK," produced by Oliver Stone.

Background

The Warren Commission, headed by then-chief justice Earl Warren, was appointed Nov. 29, 1963. President Lyndon B. Johnson directed the commission to investigate all circumstances relating to the assassination. In its final report issued Sept. 27, 1964, the commission concluded that Lee Harvey Oswald "acted alone" and that only three shots were fired — all from the sixth floor of the Texas School Book Depository in Dallas.

A special House committee, chaired by Louis Stokes, D-Ohio, investigated the assassination in 1976-79. At that time, a majority of the panel members concluded that Kennedy "was probably assassinated as a result of a conspiracy" but declared themselves unable to identify who besides Oswald was involved. The committee agreed with the Warren Commission that Oswald killed Kennedy by firing three shots from the depository but said scientific acoustical evidence indicated a fourth shot was fired, which left open the possibility of a second gunman. The panel cleared the U.S. government and the Soviet Union but said "individual members" either of groups opposed to Cuban leader Fidel Castro or of organized crime "may have been involved." *(Congress and the Nation Vol. V, p. 734)*

"JFK" was based on the premise that Oswald was a bit player in a far-reaching government plot to kill the president. The film popularized the theory that more than one person shot at Kennedy and that Oswald had been recruited by U.S. military leaders as a scapegoat for the shooting. The movie sparked renewed debate over the assassination and served as the major impetus for legislation to make public the government records collected during the various investigations.

Legislative Action

Two House committees worked simultaneously on legislation to reopen the files related to the Kennedy assassination, producing versions with a few significantly different provisions.

The Government Operations Committee approved a measure (H J Res 454) on June 3 that allowed the executive branch to choose the members of the commission that would review the Kennedy documents and to have significant control over the records' release. The committee received a letter April 28 from the Justice Department stressing those provisions.

The House Judiciary Committee, which shared jurisdiction over the legislation, approved a different version July 1 that called for representatives of the U.S. Court of Appeals to name and appoint a document review board. The Judiciary bill also contained provisions, added at the request of the national archivist, to allow the National Archives to exempt certain files and materials from review and permit the agency to charge standard reproduction fees for copies, even those obtained under the Freedom of Information Act.

The administration objected to having the board appointed by the judicial branch, on grounds that the disclosure requirements would unconstitutionally undercut the president's right to protect confidential information and intelligence sources and would violate the executive branch's appointment powers.

Jack Brooks, D-Texas, chairman of the House Judiciary Committee, however, resisted the Government Operations proposal to allow the executive branch to choose commission members. He believed compromising on this point would set a bad precedent, especially because the law that permitted judicial panels to appoint special counsels to investigate wrongdoing in the executive branch soon would be due for reauthorization. Brooks also said that a court-appointed panel would allow its members to avoid "any appearance of conflict of interest."

Government Operations formally reported H J Res 454 (H Rept 102-625, Part I) on June 29, 1992. The Judiciary Committee reported the bill (H Rept 102-625, Part II) on Aug. 11.

On Aug. 12, the House passed H J Res 454 by voice vote under suspension of the rules, preserving the language on having the courts appoint the members of the review board and deleting the provisions sought by the national archivist.

The first Kennedy bill the Senate considered was S J Res 282. It called for judicial branch appointment of the commission. At a hearing of the Governmental Affairs Committee on May 12, 1992, the heads of the CIA and FBI offered their support for releasing most documents. They maintained, however, that their agencies should control the flow.

FBI Director William S. Sessions said his agency wanted to keep the seal on about half the FBI's 499,000 files that he said concerned unrelated organized crime and criminal investigations, and to hold back information that would reveal law enforcement techniques and sources.

A Justice Department official indicated that his department was open to a compromise over control of the board.

The Governmental Affairs Committee on June 25 approved by voice vote draft legislation based on the resolution. The measure, which was later reported out as an original bill and numbered S 3006, required that relevant government offices gather, review and make public documents related to the assassination. All released material was to be transferred to the National Archives. The bill agreed to let the five-member review board be appointed by the president, with the Senate's consent. The committee also approved, by voice vote, language proposed by Chairman John Glenn, D-Ohio, to set strict timetables for reviewing documents.

With little debate, the Senate passed S 3006 by voice vote July 28. The bill set up a procedural maze for preparing the materials for the National Archives, where the public would have access. The process included the following steps:

- Government offices would organize and review their records within 10 months of the law's enactment, recommending what should be withheld. The rest would be released immediately through the Archives.
- A five-member independent board would be created to review the records that had been recommended for continued protection. The board would have up to three years to go through all the materials. The president would appoint the members, subject to Senate confirmation.
- The president could override the board's decision on executive branch files. Congress would have to adopt rules determining eventual release if it wanted records withheld.
- Material withheld would be reviewed periodically for disclosure. All material would be released within 25 years of enactment.

With time running short in the session, Judiciary Chairman Brooks set aside his doubts about executive branch control over the review board, paving the way for the House to pass the Senate version by voice vote on Sept. 30, thus avoiding a House-Senate conference and clearing the bill.

The president signed the bill (PL 102-526) on Oct. 26.

'Motor Voter'

National voter registration legislation (S 250), popularly known as the "motor voter" bill because it sought to link voter registration to applying for a driver's license and other public certificates, was expectedly vetoed by President Bush, on July 2, 1992. The Senate Sept. 22 could not muster the necessary votes to override, thus the veto was sustained.

Bush maintained that while the intent of S 250 was commendable, the bill would have opened the door to election fraud and dumped heavy administrative costs on states. Critics of the legislation also argued that the existing registration process was not complicated and that making registration too easy might dilute the quality of the national electorate by including more people who knew little about the issues or the candidates.

S 250 would have established uniform, nationwide registration procedures and allowed U.S. citizens of voting age to register at most federal and state government offices, such as public libraries and unemployment compensation offices, as well as by mail. Backers, including some black lawmakers, characterized the legislation as an effort to increase not only the size of the electorate but also the voting power of inner-city minorities, comparing it with the Voting Rights Act of 1965.

The House easily passed similar legislation in the 101st Congress, only to see it languish and die in the Senate. *(101st Congress action, p. 871)*

1991 Action

Unlike similar bills in the past, S 250 was cosponsored by a Republican: Mark O. Hatfield, Ore. Hatfield signed on when Senate Majority Whip Wendell H. Ford, D-Ky., chairman of the Senate Rules and Administration Committee and the principal sponsor, agreed to insert tougher anti-fraud language than found in prior legislation.

The most vocal opponent of the bill on the Senate Rules Committee was Mitch McConnell, R-Ky., who said no evidence existed that a motor voter system would lead to higher turnout at the polls. He cited a motor voter analysis completed in February 1990 by the Congressional Research Service (CRS).

CRS studied turnouts in states that had adopted motor voter and found that voter turnout after adoption was generally the same or less than turnout before. But critics charged that the results of the report were inaccurate because researchers included data from states with less sophisticated types of motor voter registrations.

Senate Rules approved the bill, 7-4, on April 24 and reported it (S Rept 102-60) on May 21.

S 250 ran into trouble on the Senate floor in 1991. Two unsuccessful attempts were made July 18 to invoke cloture, thus limit debate, on a motion to proceed to consideration of the bill. The first vote failed 57-41; the second, 59-40. Sixty votes are needed to invoke cloture.

Ted Stevens, R-Alaska, and Minority Leader Bob Dole, R-Kan., had planned to offer a substitute if the bill had been brought up. S 921 would have made motor voter voluntary among the states and would have authorized a $25 million block grant program to assist states that wanted to institute motor voter. It also would have allowed more leeway for federal courts to prosecute voter-fraud cases.

Ford wanted to try for cloture again in late October, but a heavy floor schedule of must-pass legislation took precedence.

1992 Action

S 250 got off to a rocky start on the Senate floor in 1992. On May 7, Ford finally was able to round up enough support to limit initial debate on S 250. The 61-38 vote allowed the Senate to proceed to the bill, but it remained open to debilitating amendments.

Following the cloture vote, Bob Kasten, R-Wis., offered, in the form of an amendment, GOP-backed legislation (S 640) that sought to impose uniform federal standards on state product liability laws. As a result, sponsors pulled S 250 from the floor, planning to return to it when they had the votes to kill the Kasten amendment. *(Product liability, p. 463)*

A May 12 cloture vote to limit amendments failed, 58-40, two votes short of the 60 needed, forcing Majority Leader George J. Mitchell, D-Maine, to pull the bill from floor consideration for a second time.

Then two days later, on May 14, Mitchell returned to the motor voter bill, and the Senate voted, 53-45, on a motion by John D. Rockefeller IV, D-W.Va., to table the Kasten amendment. Also on May 14, members rejected, 37-57, a GOP substitute amendment that would have made the bill's provisions voluntary and authorized $25 million for fiscal 1992-94 to assist states that wanted to implement motor voter systems.

The next obstacle in the bill's path was put forward by Phil Gramm, R-Texas, who offered the GOP anti-crime package as an amendment. This forced Mitchell to again shelve the motor voter bill and retreat for further negotiations. Republicans later agreed to bring the standoff to an end, banking on a presidential veto to thwart the bill.

On May 19, the Senate returned to the bill and rejected a series of Republican amendments, most of which Ford said would have killed his bill. Members voted, 55-40, to table an amendment by John McCain, R-Ariz., that would have banned registration at agencies that provided public benefits to the needy, such as welfare and unemployment offices. McCain argued that the civil rights of the nation's poor might be harmed if they felt pressured into registering to vote before picking up a benefits check. A McConnell amendment, which would have made voting fraud a federal crime punishable by a maximum prison sentence of 10 years and a $10,000 fine, was tabled 57-39. Opponents argued that the amendment would have given federal election officials too much power over states in prosecuting voting fraud cases. Another McConnell amendment was tabled, 61-36; it would have automatically discontinued the bill's requirements in states in which voter turnout in the 1996 election rose less than 2 percent from the 1992 election. Senators also tabled, 55-41, an amendment by Don Nickles, R-Okla., that would have suspended implementation of the bill until Congress provided money to states to pay for it.

On May 20, the Senate passed S 250, 61-38.

The House, after setting aside its companion legislation (HR 4366), passed S 250 on a 268-153 vote June 16, thus completing congressional action. During floor debate, Bill Thomas, R-Calif., had offered a substitute on behalf of Minority Leader Robert H. Michel of Illinois that would have created a $25 million block grant program to help states increase voter registration. The proposal was defeated, 133-290.

Following House passage, Democrats stepped up pressure on Bush to sign the measure into law. "How the president of the United States can make an argument against expanding the opportunities of citizens to participate in their government is beyond me," said House Speaker Thomas S. Foley, D-Wash.

But a June 16 letter from the Office of Management and Budget said the bill was flawed and that White House advisers would recommend a veto.

Bush vetoed S 250 on July 2. In his veto message, the president said, "I cannot . . . accept legislation that imposes an unnecessary and costly Federal regime on the states and that is, in addition, an open invitation to fraud and corruption." He added that despite his veto, he did want to support "legislation that would assist the states in implementing appropriate reforms in order to make voter registration easier for the American public."

The Senate on Sept. 22 sustained the veto. The vote was 62-38, well short of the two-thirds needed.

Similar legislation (HR 2) was introduced in the 103rd Congress. President Bill Clinton, a supporter of motor voter, signed the bill into law (PL 102-31) on May 20, 1993.

Decennial Census Study

Little consensus existed within Congress for legislation forcing an adjustment of the 1990 census, despite an apparent undercount and a bias against minorities. However, Congress in 1991 did mandate a study on ways to improve the nation's future decennial census. *(1990 census, p. 1145)*

HR 3280 authorized the Commerce Department to contract with the National Academy of Sciences for a three-year study on census reform. The study would examine traditional methods of census taking used in the 1990 census, such as questionnaires, and recommend how they could be made more timely and effective. In addition, alternative methods, such as fieldworkers using hand-held computers, would be considered to determine whether they would improve the accuracy of the population count.

Congress included $1.4 million for the study in the fiscal 1992 appropriations bill (HR 2608 — PL 102-140) for the Departments of Commerce, State and Justice and the judiciary. The Bush administration did not oppose HR 3280.

The House Post Office and Civil Service Subcommittee on Census and Population gave quick 4-0 approval of HR 3280 on Sept. 17. The full committee unanimously approved, 22-0, the bill on Sept. 25 and reported it (H Rept 102-227) on Sept. 30. With almost no controversy, and by voice vote, the bill passed the House on Sept. 30 under suspension of the rules and the Senate on Oct. 3 by voice vote.

Before the legislation could be sent to the president, the two chambers had to resolve a minor difference over a provision that called for improving geographic census data. The Senate wanted a more in-depth study of the population — including states, areas, communities and city blocks — than specified in the bill. The House accepted the change by voice vote on Oct. 9, thus clearing the measure. President Bush signed HR 3280 (PL 102-135) on Oct. 24.

Reps. Ronald D. Coleman, D-Texas, and Mervyn M. Dymally, D-Calif., introduced legislation in early 1991 to force some form of undercount adjustment in the 1990 census. House Speaker Thomas S. Foley, D-Wash., on Jan. 16 dismissed the proposals out of hand, saying that nothing of the sort would be signed by the president and that refiguring the count was neither "a partisan issue" nor an issue on which a two-thirds vote could be mustered for a veto override.

Election Day Holiday

Legislation to designate election day an unpaid federal holiday received House committee approval but went no further in the 102nd Congress.

HR 3681, sponsored by Ron Wyden, D-Ore., would make the first Tuesday after the first Monday in November a legal holiday in even-numbered years. "Democracy Day" would be similar in status to Martin Luther King Day, Christmas and the Fourth of July, except it would be purely symbolic. Federal workers would not be urged to take the day off and would not get paid if they did.

The legislation was prompted by low voter turnout. Wyden hoped that extra attention on voting would involve more citizens in the electoral process.

The Justice Department and the Office of Personnel Management (OPM) were opposed to the bill. Justice warned that it would set a precedent and might evolve into a paid day off for federal workers. OPM raised concerns that the legislation would pressure the private sector to add another holiday for employees and could complicate collective bargaining agreements. OPM estimated that giving federal workers a paid federal holiday costs more than $300 million in salaries alone.

The House Post Office and Civil Service Committee on May 4, 1992, reported HR 3681 (H Rept 102-510). Sponsors of a companion Senate bill (S 1901) — Tom Daschle, D-S.D., and Orrin G. Hatch, R-Utah — delayed action until the matter was resolved in the House.

D.C. Legislation

The relationship between Congress and the District of Columbia improved dramatically after Mayor Sharon Pratt Kelly took office in January 1991. Kelly succeeded Marion S. Barry Jr., who on Oct. 26, 1991, began serving a six-month jail sentence on a drug conviction.

(The mayor was elected as Sharon Pratt Dixon, but on Dec. 7, 1991, she married Washington businessman James R. Kelly III and changed her name to Sharon Pratt Kelly.)

Supplemental Appropriation. When lawmakers on March 22, 1991, cleared a $4.1 billion dire emergency supplemental spending bill (HR 1281 — PL 102-27) for fiscal 1991, they included $100 million for the cash-strapped District of Columbia government. *(1991 supplemental, p. 77)*

Mayor Kelly and D.C. Del. Eleanor Holmes Norton, D, steadily lobbied members of both houses for weeks before votes were taken. Their respective predecessors, Barry and Walter E. Fauntroy, although Democrats, were viewed as ineffective in winning significant support for the District from members of Congress.

House District of Columbia Appropriations Subcommittee Chairman Julian C. Dixon, D-Calif., said that before the mayor assumed office, she visited him to discuss the city's financial problems. Dixon said he advised her that she would have no chance of securing needed money unless she demonstrated a good-faith effort to make substantial cuts on her own. After taking office, she developed a budget plan that called for $2 in cuts for every $1 the District would receive from Congress, including $137 million in cuts in fiscal 1991 alone.

The mayor also was invited to the White House for a meeting with President Bush. On Feb. 4, Bush proposed an increase of $53.5 million in the annual federal payment to the District in lieu of taxes for the use of District land. While some said that much of the proposed increase was offset by hidden cuts elsewhere, the gesture was seen as a thaw in relations between the administration and the city government.

Norton visited House Appropriations Committee Chairman Jamie L. Whitten, D-Miss., as did subcommittee Chairman Dixon, in behalf of the District. Dixon said lawmakers noticed that, like members of delegations from the 50 states, Norton and the mayor worked together, another contrast with Barry and Fauntroy.

Senate Appropriations Committee Chairman Robert C. Byrd, D-W.Va., who commended Kelly for her efforts, was instrumental in obtaining $3.5 million to aid law enforcement in the District, which took on added responsibilities stemming from the Persian Gulf War and the threat of terrorist attacks. *(Gulf War, special report, p. 299)*

Funding Formula. A measure (HR 2123) cleared in 1991 that established a formula for determining the annual federal payment to the city. The legislation only authorized a larger federal contribution — it did not guarantee it. City supporters still had to persuade Congress to appropriate the funds. The funding formula bill was expected to help direct future appropriations battles by setting the annual federal payment to the city at 24 percent of locally generated revenue for fiscal 1993-95. HR 2123 authorized a $630 million federal payment for fiscal 1992, a $99.5 million increase over fiscal 1991 and $150 million more than Bush had proposed.

Each year's authorization was to be calculated on revenues raised two years before. The fiscal 1993 authorization, for example, was based on local revenues for fiscal 1991. This was to reduce any temptation on the part of the District government to hike service fees and taxes for a quick fix to fiscal woes on the theory that the more the city raised in taxes, the more it would receive from the federal government.

The House District of Columbia Committee on April 30 approved the measure on a 10-2 bipartisan vote. It was reported (H Rept 102-92) on June 3. The House passed HR 2123 by voice vote June 11. The bill bypassed Senate committee consideration and went directly to the floor. Last-minute confusion over the administration's position on the funding formula measure nearly stalled the bill, but it was passed, and thus cleared, by voice vote Aug. 2. The president signed it (PL 102-102) Aug. 17.

In the meantime, the House District of Columbia Appropriations Subcommittee, during consideration of the fiscal 1992 District of Columbia appropriations bill (HR 3291 — PL 102-111), voted June 13 to increase the federal payment to the city for the first time in five years. By voice vote, the subcommittee approved $695.8 million for the District government, a $44.5 million increase over the fiscal 1991 allocation of $651.3 million. The 1991 figure included the $100 million added in the supplemental appropriations bill (HR 1281) approved by the House on March 22.

In 1990, a bill (HR 5760) containing a provision setting the federal payment to the city at 19.5 percent of local revenues was approved 9-3 by the House District of Columbia Committee but, lacking bipartisan support, was never considered by the full House.

Budget Autonomy. The House District of Columbia Committee on Nov. 19 approved a bill (HR 3581), on a straight party-line vote of 7-4, that would give the District government more budget autonomy. Besides removing locally raised funds from the lengthy appropriations process, HR 3581 proposed to waive the congressional review period for laws passed by the District's City Council and signed by the mayor. The bill was reported (H Rept 102-429) on Feb. 4, 1992.

Assault Weapons Liability. On Nov. 21, 1991, the House District of Columbia Committee again proved its support of local rule when it rejected, 4-7, a measure (HR 3712) that would repeal a 1990 D.C. Council act to make assault weapons manufacturers liable for injuries from the guns. District voters on Nov. 5 had approved, by 77 percent, a referendum endorsing the 1990 council law. The law was in the process of being repealed, under pressure from federal lawmakers, when the referendum was held.

Bill sponsors argued that it was unconstitutional for District residents to approve a law that would affect companies outside of the city's jurisdiction and that the law would make gun manufacturers reluctant to supply weapons to D.C. law enforcement agencies. But those testifying in favor of not overturning the referendum said Congress should not go against residents' wishes.

D.C. Statehood. On May 29, 1991, Norton introduced legislation (HR 2482) to create the "State of New Columbia." The House District of Columbia Committee held hearings on the bill in the fall of 1991, but it went no further.

Another measure (HR 4718) sponsored by Norton, to make the District the 51st state, was approved, 7-4, on April 2, 1992, and reported (H Rept 102-909) on Sept. 25 by the House District of Columbia Committee. The bill had received the Judiciary Subcommittee's approval, 5-3, on March 26. Supporters were unwilling to take up floor time to debate the measure because they knew that they did not have enough votes to override a threatened presidential veto. The bill would have created a new state called New Columbia and would have provided that only buildings in a "federal enclave" would have remained under the exclusive control of Congress. Capitol Hill, the White House, the Supreme Court and all federal buildings surrounding the mall area would have been included in the enclave, an area of approximately 1,400 acres, called the National Capital Service Area.

The push for statehood gained new momentum in 1990 when District residents elected Jesse Jackson as a "shadow" senator to lobby members of Congress on the issue. To garner support for HR 4718, backers had to address several important questions, including whether statehood would be constitutional under Article I, Section 8, Clause 17 of the U.S. Constitution. The Bush administration contended that, absent a constitutional amendment, Congress could not give back control over the lands ceded to it by Maryland more than 200 years ago. (The portion ceded by Virginia had since been returned to that state.) Statehood supporters, meanwhile, argued that District residents had all the burdens of states with none of the benefits. Under existing law, District residents were represented by a D.C. delegate, who could vote in committee but not on the floor, and a shadow delegation of two senators and one representative, who had no voting privileges. *(Shadow delegation, p. 872)*

Health Care Benefits. The House District of Columbia Committee June 10, 1992, rejected 3-6 a resolution (H J Res 480) to overturn a D.C. City Council act expanding health care benefits to non-traditional partners of city workers. The Fiscal Affairs and Health Subcommittee June 4, by voice vote, sent the resolution to the full committee without recommendation.

Congress had 30 legislative days to review all D.C. Council acts under the 1973 Home Rule Act. If a disapproving resolution was not passed by both the House and Senate and signed by the president, the council act would become law. Congress had until June 11 to decide on the health care benefits issue. *(Home rule, Congress and the Nation Vol. IV, p. 797)*

Under the act, members of non-traditional family groups, such as homosexual couples, unmarried couples and their children, could register with the D.C. government as domestic partners, thus qualifying them for family health benefit coverage if one of the partners worked for the D.C. government. City employees would assume the total cost of the additional coverage for their partners.

Resolution sponsor Clyde C. Holloway, R-La., joined several religious leaders in speaking against the act, which Holloway said would undermine traditional family values. He also said that legal experts questioned whether the proposal would be pre-empted by the 1974 Employee Retirement Income Security Act (ERISA), which regulated employee health benefits and superseded state laws. Committee Chairman Ronald V. Dellums, D-Calif., however, said he was satisfied with a letter from the D.C. Corporation Counsel and the D.C. Council's general counsel that the act would not be affected by ERISA. *(ERISA, Congress and the Nation Vol. IV, p. 690)*

Holloway attempted to offer an amendent to the fiscal 1993 District of Columbia appropriations bill (HR 6056 — PL 102-382), prohibiting any of the funding from being used to implement the city law. The amendment was blocked from consideration on a procedural vote. However, in the end, the city was prevented from implementing the act, as the Senate included similar language in its version of the bill. The House on Sept. 24 voted 235-173 to instruct House conferees to keep the Senate provision.

Puerto Rico Plebiscite

Legislation (S 244) to allow residents of Puerto Rico to choose their future relationship with the United States was declared dead when the Senate Energy Committee on Feb. 27, 1991, voted 10-10 against an island referendum sanctioned by Congress.

Failure of the legislation meant that a status referendum would not be held for at least two years. Members of Puerto Rico's three political parties said the plebiscite had to be held in 1991 to avoid disruption of islandwide elections in 1992.

Given the action on S 244, Del. Ron de Lugo, D-Virgin Islands, chairman of the House Interior Subcommittee on Insular and International Affairs, decided not to attempt to push through his legislation (HR 316), which also would allow Puerto Ricans to choose their status.

Both the Senate and House bills would have offered residents three choices: remain a commonwealth, become the 51st state or break off as an independent country. HR 316, however, broadly defined the options, each of which would have left Congress to determine the specifics after the vote, such as what the economic benefits of the chosen option would be. By contrast, S 244 narrowly defined the three options and would have automatically put the result of the plebiscite into effect.

Too many obstacles existed to passage of the island status referendum legislation. Objections were raised about the cost of granting statehood to Puerto Rico, concerns were voiced about the island's lingual and cultural differences from the mainland, worries were heard about the lack of an overwhelming majority of island residents who supported any one option, and questions were asked about whether Congress should be involved with the referendum at all.

Reconciling the House and Senate bills also would be difficult because they sought to do different things. Further complicating the situation was the desire to have legislation cleared before the 1991 Fourth of July recess, which would allow for the referendum to be held in the fall and which would avoid a vote on status in 1992, an islandwide election year.

Before the Senate Energy Committee voted on S 244, it rejected, also on a 10-10 vote, an amendment to leave it up to Puerto Rico to initiate the referendum.

The 101st Congress also failed to clear a status bill. *(Story, p. 873)*

Puerto Rico would remain a commonwealth until a plebescite was held.

1992-94 NASA Authorization

A multi-year reauthorization (HR 1988) for the National Aeronautics and Space Administration (NASA) was signed into law in 1991. But as in past years, the legislation was largely symbolic because, by the time it was enacted, Congress already had appropriated funds for the space agency.

HR 1988 authorized $15.2 billion in fiscal 1992, $15.6 billion in fiscal 1993 and $17 billion in fiscal 1994 for NASA. The fiscal 1992 amount fell $594 million short of the Bush administration request. The bill included full funding of $2.03 billion for the space station. *(Space station, p. 899)*

The legislation also required NASA to estimate the full cost of projects when submitting annual budget requests. This was a significant departure from the way the space agency operated and was designed to give Congress greater ability to oversee major endeavors. Lawmakers had been frustrated by the agency's practice of describing only the first- and second-year costs of new projects. Costs during the planning stages were usually low. But once the projects got off the ground, costs ballooned and Congress was left with the choice of spending much more money than planned or killing a project in progress.

The House Science, Space and Technology Committee departed from past practices (failing to act quickly enough to affect Appropriations Committee decisions) and proposed early in the session to reduce the president's fiscal 1992 NASA budget request by $485 million — the first time in several years that lawmakers attempted to curb the agency's funding authority. Among the cuts were $125 million from the proposed new launch system for the space shuttle, $75 million from a system of satellites to be used to observe Earth for global climate change research and $50 million from a space instrument intended to provide information about the electromagnetic spectrum. The most contentious debate of the markup was over an amendment, sponsored by Dick Zimmer, R-N.J., to request a study on alternative ways to perform scientific work on the space station *Freedom*; it was defeated 23-27.

The Science Committee approved HR 1988, which provided a $15.3 billion authorization, by voice vote on April 24. It was formally reported (H Rept 102-41) from the committee the next day.

The House passed the NASA reauthorization May 2 on a 361-36 vote. The $15.3 billion fiscal 1992 bill was $488 million less than Bush requested. However, it included funding for almost every major program requested, though some at lower levels. Hardest hit was research for the new launch vehicle, the advanced X-ray astrophysics observatory, and planetary probes to observe Saturn and its moon Titan and to conduct a rendezvous with a comet. Zimmer reoffered his amendment on the House floor, where it gained voice vote approval. And the House accepted an amendment by Gerald B. H. Solomon, R-N.Y., that required random drug testing of all NASA employees.

The Senate Commerce, Science and Transportation Committee on May 14 approved a $15.3 billion reauthorization bill, which spared NASA's three largest programs — the space shuttle, the space station and Mission to Planet Earth — but virtually gutted research on manned travel to the moon and Mars. The committee also accepted on a voice vote an amendment offered by Richard H. Bryan, D-Nev., that eliminated all spending for research on extraterrestrial life. HR 1988 was reported (S Rept 102-97) on July 2.

On Sept. 27, the Senate, by voice vote, passed HR 1988, authorizing $15 billion for NASA in fiscal 1992. The bill provided the administration's full request for the space station and for the satellites required for the Mission to Planet Earth project, while prohibiting spending for Bush's proposal to send Americans to explore the moon and Mars and cutting funds for the new launch system.

The House and Senate split the difference on the plan to go to the moon and Mars, agreeing to authorize $41.5 million. While the House provided for drug testing of all NASA employees, the Senate did not. Negotiators compromised by calling for drug testing for a more limited group of NASA employees.

The House on Nov. 7 amended a three-year, $47.8 billion bill renewing the federal space agency and sent it back to the Senate. The Senate cleared the bill by voice vote Nov. 22, and the president signed it (PL 102-195) on Dec. 9.

Fiscal 1992 appropriations for NASA represented a drastic change in fortune for the space agency. NASA funds were provided in the spending bill (HR 2519 — PL 102-139) for Veterans Affairs, Housing and Urban Development, and independent agencies. Conferees on the measure gave NASA a mere 3 percent overall increase in funding, bringing its fiscal 1992 budget to $14.3 billion — a sharp contrast with the 10 to 14 percent annual increases it had received for the past several years. While the bill appropriated $2.03 billion for the space station *Freedom*, the amount requested by the Bush administration, it made deep cuts in other programs. The bill reduced by 80 percent the request for a new national launching system; cut 20 percent from the Earth Observing System, designed to study global climate change; cut 90 percent from the National Aerospace Plane; and reduced by 33 percent the request for the Comet Rendezvous Asteroid Flyby (CRAF) and Cassini missions.

HR 2519 (H Rept 102-94) was approved by and reported from the House Appropriations Committee on June 3. The House passed the measure, 363-39, on June 6. The Senate Appropriations Committee unanimously approved the spending bill (S Rept 102-107) on July 11. The Senate passed it by voice vote on July 18. The House adopted the conference report (H Rept 102-226), 390-30, on Oct. 2. The Senate adopted an amended version by voice vote the same day. The House on Oct. 3 cleared the measure for the president, who signed it Oct. 28.

Fiscal 1993 NASA Authorization

In an era defined more by fears of a deepening recession than by dreams of flights to the galaxies, Congress in 1992 cleared a $14.9 billion fiscal 1993 authorization bill (HR 6135) for the National Aeronautics and Space Administration (NASA).

A multi-year authorization (HR 1988 — PL 102-195) was enacted in 1991, but it did not set specific funding levels for fiscal years 1993-94. *(Story, p. 897)*

HR 6135 emerged as a compromise measure after the House passed and a Senate committee approved widely different versions of earlier multi-year NASA reauthorization legislation (HR 4364). The final bill also incorporated language from HR 3848 (H Rept 102-769, Part I), to spur the development of commercial space activities. *(HR 3848, p. 902)*

The appeal of a multi-year authorization was that lawmakers could set funding priorities for programs that spilled over a period of years. Such an approach gave authorizers leverage to ensure that funding for long-term projects was not sidetracked by appropriators. Estimated costs of space programs inevitably increase as they move from the planning to the building stage, forcing lawmakers to choose between allocating more money than planned or killing a project already under way.

Appropriations for NASA were included in the annual Veterans Affairs, Housing and Urban Development and Independent Agencies spending bill.

House Action

The House Science Subcommittee on Space on April 1, 1992, approved a three-year authorization bill (HR 4364) that laid out two budget menus for the space program: basic and discretionary. Under the bill, NASA's basic spending plan totaled $14.4 billion for fiscal 1993 and included spending for ongoing science and technology programs, the space shuttle and the space station *Freedom*.

Appropriators were to order from the discretionary menu only after basic needs were fully funded. The discretionary menu included a massive program to study global climate and a new solid rocket program. The bill authorized $15.3 billion for fiscal 1993 for basic and discretionary programs combined.

HR 4364 was approved by the House Science, Space and Technology Committee on a voice vote. The bill was formally reported (H Rept 102-500) on April 22.

The full House took up the issue of the space station on April 29, voting 159-254 to reject an amendment that would eliminate the $2.3 billion fiscal 1993 authorization provided in the bill. *(Space station, p. 899)*

The only other point of contention on the floor was the Advanced Solid Rocket Motor, which was being built in the congressional district represented by Appropriations Committee Chairman Jamie L. Whitten, D-Miss. An effort to remove funding in the bill for the project was aborted. Instead, lawmakers by voice vote adopted an amendment that canceled the project if it was not ready in time to help build the space station — specifically by the sixth of a series of shuttle flights designed to lift components of the space station into orbit for assembly. Those flights were scheduled to begin in late 1995.

The bill authorized $260 million to research and develop the project in fiscal 1993. It authorized the additional $180 million only if appropriators gave NASA an overall budget of $15.3 billion or more in fiscal 1993. The administration had left the project out of its budget request.

The House passed HR 4364 by voice vote May 5.

Senate Action

The Senate Commerce, Science and Transportation Committee on June 16 approved a $14.7 billion fiscal 1993 authorization bill for NASA. The committee reported HR 4364 (S Rept 102-364) on Aug. 10.

The bill's price tag was smaller than the House's version because the committee cut funding for almost every space program, including $200 million from the space station, $50 million from space shuttle operations and $95 million from a proposed new launch system to lift heavier loads into space.

The bill was a clear response to the House-passed version, with its two-tiered system of funding. The Senate bill sought to salvage the pet projects of senators that the House bill placed in its discretionary pot — for example, the Earth Observing System and the Advanced Solid Rocket Motor. The Earth Observing System was the centerpiece of Mission to Planet Earth, a large-scale, multi-satellite project to track global atmospheric changes. It was a favorite of Al Gore, D-Tenn., chairman of the Science, Technology and Space Subcommittee and author of the Senate bill.

The committee-approved bill, which unlike the House version provided for only a one-year authorization for the agency, included an amendment to direct NASA to study the Soviet space program for ways to use its space assets in the U.S. space program. The committee deleted $13.5 million for a project to search for extraterrestrial life; the program already had consumed $32 million.

HR 4364 was never considered on the Senate floor.

Final Action

Action on the authorization bill came to a standstill until the end of the session. A compromise measure (HR 6135) was developed with provisions agreed to by both chambers. The House passed HR 6135 by voice vote Oct. 6; the Senate followed suit the next day, clearing the measure. The final $14.9 billion authorization in HR 6135 represented a reduction of $347.4 million from the House-passed version of HR 4364 and $101 million from the president's request for fiscal 1993. The bill provided an authorization for all NASA programs under a single title in contrast to the two-tiered approach initially taken by the House.

As signed into law (PL 102-588) on Nov. 4, HR 6135 authorized $2.1 billion for the space station *Freedom*; $1.3 billion for space shuttle production, of which $315 million was authorized for the Advanced Solid Rocket Motor program; and $838.5 million for earth sciences and applications. Landsat remained fully authorized.

On the day the House passed HR 6135, President Bush signed the fiscal 1993 appropriations bill (HR 5679 — PL 102-389) that included $14.3 billion in funding for NASA. The space station would receive $2.1 billion; the Advanced Solid Rocket Motor, $360 million. To offset the costs of those programs, lawmakers eliminated funding for the National Aerospace Plane, which would have been capable of taking off and flying in a low-level orbit; the Space Exploration Initiative, to send people to the moon and Mars; and the Climsat Earth probe.

The House Appropriations Committee reported HR 5679 (H Rept 102-710) on July 23, 1992. The House passed the bill, 314-92, on July 29. The Senate Appropriations Committee reported the measure (S Rept 102-356) on Aug. 3. The Senate passed an amended version, 92-3, on Sept. 9. The House 286-97 agreed to the conference report (H Rept 102-902) Sept. 25; the Senate adopted it the same day by voice vote, clearing HR 5679.

Space Station

The controversial space station *Freedom* survived serious challenges to its existence in both 1991 and 1992.

Station supporters — including President Bush, members of the House and Senate Science committees, most Republicans and White House lobbyists — argued that killing the project would undermine U.S. leadership in manned space exploration.

Opponents came from two camps: those who believed that Congress should be spending more money on social programs instead of on big science and military projects, and those who feared that big science projects would largely eliminate spending on smaller science programs.

Despite being a target of criticism, the space station continued to attract political appeal, especially among members with hometown companies that had a piece of the project.

The issues raised about *Freedom* in the 102nd Congress were similar to those debated in the 101st. *(Story, p. 877)*

Station Redesign. A 1990 study concluded that the space station would require so much maintenance by spacewalking astronauts that it might not be feasible to build as originally conceived. The National Aeronautics and Space Administration (NASA) in early 1991 released a new, less expensive design. But the Space Studies Board of the National Research Council, a non-partisan group of scientists, concluded the week of March 11 that the redesign "does not meet the basic research requirements of the two principal scientific disciplines for which it is intended: life sciences and microgravity research and applications."

The National Research Council's criticism compounded a growing sense on Capitol Hill and in the scientific community that big science projects spent too much on construction and too little on reaping benefits from research. In response, however, Vice President Dan Quayle, in a letter to NASA Administrator Richard H. Truly, wrote, "Science is but one reason for building a space station." He continued, "The ultimate mission of the Space Station is . . . the reaffirmation of the leadership in space of the United States of America, the world's only superpower."

In June 1993, President Bill Clinton would endorse another redesign of the space station — a simplified and less costly version of earlier plans. And the House, by one vote, would reject an amendment to a NASA authorization bill to kill the proposed orbiting laboratory.

1991 Action. The House Appropriations Committee June 3 eliminated $1.9 billion in funding for the space station in the fiscal 1992 spending bill (HR 2519 — H Rept 102-94) for the Departments of Veterans Affairs (VA) and Housing and Urban Development (HUD), as well as NASA. The House Science, Space and Technology Committee had promoted full funding for the station.

The VA, HUD and Independent Agencies Appropriations Subcommittee on May 15 had recommended the elimination of space station funding, despite the House's May 2 vote, 361-36, on passage of a bill (HR 1988) to keep the space station going as part of NASA's reauthorization. Subcommittee leaders had decided that the only way to meet budget limits was to drop the space station. They insisted that not enough money existed to meet the needs of smaller science projects and social programs in addition to reaching Bush's proposed budget for NASA. *(HR 1988, p. 897)*

The full House reversed the Appropriations Committee's action June 6. On a **240-173 (R 133-27; D 107-145; I 0-1) key vote,** members continued funding of the space station in the fiscal 1992 spending bill by freezing every other space program and cutting public housing money for the poor. Earlier an amendment was rejected, 122-296, to retain the housing money and force NASA to fund the space station entirely from its own budget. *(1991 key votes, p. 1061)*

On the Senate floor, Dale Bumpers, D-Ark., proposed cutting $1.9 billion — of a $2 billion appropriation — from the project in fiscal 1992 and redistributing $600 million to several NASA programs, the National Science Foundation and veterans medical care and prosthetic research. An additional $1.3 billion would be applied to reducing the deficit. Bumpers' amendment was rejected, 35-64, on July 17.

As signed into law (PL 102-139) Oct. 28, HR 2519 provided $2.03 billion for the space station.

1992 Action. The House Appropriations VA-HUD Subcommittee on June 25 approved a fiscal 1993 VA-HUD appropriations bill (HR 5679) that included $1.73 billion for *Freedom.* The full committee sidestepped a fight over NASA's space station, leaving opponents to offer an amendment to strike funding on the House floor.

The House July 29 rejected an attempt by subcommittee Chairman Bob Traxler, D-Mich., to abandon the manned-exploration venture on a **key vote of 181-237 (R 38-127; D 142-110; I 1-0).** As passed by the House, HR 5679 provided $1.73 billion for the space station. *(1992 key votes, p. 1083)*

The Senate Appropriations Committee earmarked $2.1 billion for the station, which the full Senate kept in the spending bill. Bumpers offered an amendment to cut the figure by $1.6 billion, leaving $500 million to close out the space station's contracts and using the rest to fund veterans medical care and research and to reduce the deficit. His amendment was rejected Sept. 9 on a 34-63 vote.

Conferees went with the Senate amount of $2.1 billion. President Bush signed HR 5679 (PL 102-389) on Oct. 6. Congress had provided $2.1 billion in the fiscal 1993 NASA reauthorization bill (HR 6135 — PL 102-588). *(HR 6135, p. 898)*

The space station's survival could be attributed to a number of factors. The manned-space program was wrapped in the national mythology of space as the last frontier, a part of America's manifest destiny. It could fire the imagination unlike, for example, the superconducting supercollider. Proponents also suggested that the research conducted aboard *Freedom* could lead to cures for cancer, AIDS (acquired immune deficiency syndrome), diabetes and other diseases.

Furthermore, the space station's contract dollars were spread among 37 states and the District of Columbia and supported tens of thousands of jobs — not a small consideration in hard economic times. NASA Administrator Daniel S. Goldin spearheaded a serious lobbying effort on Capitol Hill, with NASA officials passing out maps highlighting where the funding went and listing the number of dollars and jobs flowing into congressional districts.

Pulling out of the space station also would have been embarrassing for the United States, because *Freedom* was being built in partnership with Canada, Japan and nine countries in the European Space Agency. Such action also could have jeopardized future international ventures, as foreign interests would be leery of contributing to U.S. projects.

Landsat

Congress in 1992 cleared legislation (HR 6133) shifting management of the Landsat Remote-Sensing Satellite Program to the National Aeronautics and Space Administration (NASA) and the Defense Department. The program had been managed by the Commerce Department's National Oceanic and Atmospheric Administration.

The Landsat program, developed by NASA in 1972, took pictures of Earth that were used for environmental planning, oil and gas development, and military surveillance. The program floundered during the 1980s after an effort to transfer it to the private sector. The resulting problems and insecure funding had jeopardized development of the program's newest remote-sensing satellite, the Landsat 7.

HR 6133 was a compromise version of two bills (S 2297, HR 3614) that had minor differences between them.

The Senate Commerce, Science and Transportation Committee reported S 2297 (S Rept 102-445) on Sept. 30. The measure directed NASA and the Defense Department to jointly manage the satellite program. The bill mandated that federal agencies and affiliated users be able to get images from the current satellite program at cost, and that pictures from a planned new satellite be available to all users on that basis.

The House Science, Space and Technology Committee reported HR 3614 (H Rept 102-539) on May 28. The House passed the bill by voice vote under suspension of the rules June 9.

In keeping with a Bush administration directive issued in February, HR 3614 transferred management of the program from the Commerce Department jointly to NASA and the Defense Department and authorized them to spend federal funds for developing Landsat 7. Specific federal authorizations for Landsat were included in the NASA and Defense authorization bills.

In exchange for federal support, the bill stipulated that government agencies should have access to Landsat images generated by existing satellites at cost instead of at the higher fees that were charged to private users. The administration was expected to establish a uniform, at-cost price policy for pictures generated by the new satellite.

The legislation also set up an advisory council for the satellite program that included representatives from a range of groups that used the images. And it called for a technology demonstration program to help promote a private land remote-sensing industry.

The Senate passed HR 3614 by voice vote Oct. 7.

The compromise bill (HR 6133) watered down a Senate provision to require that federal agencies and affiliated users be able to get images from the existing satellite program at cost, and that pictures from a planned new satellite be available to all users on that basis. The final language would "encourage" one fee.

The House passed HR 6133 by voice vote Oct. 6. The Senate followed suit the next day, completing congressional action. President Bush signed the bill (PL 102-555) on Oct. 28.

Superconducting Supercollider

The 102nd Congress continued to fund the superconducting supercollider (SSC), a massive underground atom smasher, despite growing opposition to the Energy Department project.

By early 1991, the SSC was expected to cost nearly twice as much as advertised when the House voted in June 1989 to break ground in Waxahachie, Texas, 25 miles south of Dallas. Critics complained that the escalating price tag was crowding out many other less expensive, and potentially more fruitful, scientific endeavors. *(101st Congress action, p. 878)*

The administration remained a strong advocate for the SSC.

Fiscal 1992 Appropriation. The House Appropriations Committee included $434 million for SSC in the fiscal 1992 energy and water appropriations bill (HR 2427 — H Rept 102-74) reported May 22, 1991. Bush had requested $534 million, but Appropriations members accepted the recommendation of the Energy and Water Subcommittee to cut the request by $100 million. Even so, the supercollider was one of the few growth items in the bill, jumping from its fiscal 1991 appropriation of $243 million.

During markup, Sidney R. Yates, D-Ill., proposed cutting $43 million from the SSC appropriation to start upgrading a new particle collider ring at the Fermi National Accelerator Laboratory, located outside Chicago, Yates' hometown. Tom Bevill, D-Ala., chairman of the Energy and Water Subcommittee, said funding the new particle injector would unravel the subcommittee's pact not to fund any new construction projects. Yates' motion failed, 11-32.

On May 23, Sherwood Boehlert, R-N.Y., a member of the House Science Committee, sought permission from the House Rules Committee to offer a floor amendment to cap the U.S. investment in SSC at $5 billion. He was denied that request because it involved putting legislative language on an appropriations bill.

The spiraling cost of the supercollider led an increasing number of lawmakers to oppose further funding, but not enough support existed to scrap the project. On the floor May 29, the House rejected an amendment by Jim Slattery, D-Kan., to eliminate SSC funding from HR 2427 on a **165-251 (R 58-101; D 106-150; I 1-0) key vote.** The Slattery amendment would also have transferred $43 million of the funds to upgrade the particle collider ring in Illinois. *(1991 key votes, p. 1061)*

The House, 392-24, passed HR 2427 on May 29.

The Senate Appropriations Subcommittee on Energy and Water Development on June 11 approved by voice vote a fiscal 1992 spending bill that provided a little more than $508 million for the atom smasher. As approved, it restored $75 million of $100 million in cuts made by the House.

The next day, Senate Appropriations Committee members voted, 20-0, to approve the spending bill without any changes to the funding level for the supercollider. The committee reported HR 2427 (S Rept 102-80) on June 12.

On July 10, the Senate for the first time was forced to go on record supporting the controversial project. Dale Bumpers, D-Ark., offered an amendment to eliminate funding for the SSC. Bumpers belittled the necessity of the supercollider, which scientists believed would help them discover the building blocks of matter, and said the project was unlikely to provide commercial spinoff. He argued that the tight economic times overshadowed any scientific merit.

Proponents maintained that the United States could ill afford to turn its back on the scientific and technical promise of the project. Phil Gramm, R-Texas, cast the argument as a choice between investing in future technological competitiveness and spending programs with more immediate political popularity.

On a **62-37 (R 33-10; D 29-27) key vote**, the Senate tabled (killed) the Bumpers amendment. The Senate passed HR 2427 also on July 10, 96-3.

House-Senate conferees agreed to give $484 million to the SSC, $50 million more than the House-passed bill but $24 million less than the Senate had approved for the project. The House adopted the conference report (H Rept 102-177) July 31, 292-32, and the Senate cleared HR 2427 on Aug. 2. President Bush signed the bill (PL 102-104) on Aug. 17.

Fiscal 1993 Appropriation. The administration showed its support for the SSC, recommending $650 million for the project in fiscal 1993. The House Appropriations Subcommittee on Energy and Water slashed $166 million from that request during consideration of HR 5373, the fiscal 1993 energy and water spending bill.

The full committee held SSC funding at $484 million, the subcommittee-approved amount, which also was the fiscal 1992 appropriation. The bill also would set up a trust fund for non-federal contributions to the collider and direct the Treasury to pay interest on money that sat unused. The provision applied chiefly to Texas, which had been paying installments on its overall $1 billion pledge for the program. Richard J. Durbin, D-Ill., offered an amendment to drop the language, but the committee rejected it 13-24. HR 5373 was reported (H Rept 102-555) from House Appropriations on June 11, 1992.

In a surprise move that emerged from a confluence of discontents, the House June 17 cut $450 million of the proposed $484 million appropriation, leaving $34 million to shut down the collider project. The action came on a Dennis E. Eckart, D-Ohio, amendment that was adopted on a **key vote of 232-181 (R 79-79; D 152-102; I 1-0).** *(1992 key votes, p. 1083)*

The vote, which was held about a week after a draining and divisive fight over a proposed constitutional amendment to require a balanced federal budget, reflected a newfound resolve among members to tackle the towering budget deficit at a time of perhaps unparalleled voter dissatisfaction. Pent-up conflict and resentment over spending priorities also was apparent. Members who had fought unsuccessfully to transfer defense spending to domestic needs and win greater urban aid lashed out at what many saw as an esoteric science project chiefly benefiting fiscal conservatives in Texas. Even some members eager to spend money on science balked, fearful the growing costs of the massive project would devour other federal research efforts. Other lawmakers saw the SSC as a huge boondoggle.

Before the vote on the Eckart amendment, the House had adopted, by voice vote, an amendment by Science Committee Chairman George E. Brown Jr., D-Calif., specifying that the administration could not spend money on SSC after May 1993 until it certified at least $650 million in foreign contributions for fiscal years 1993-95.

The House passed HR 5373, 365-51, on June 17.

The sagging fortunes of the SSC were revived July 23 when the Senate Appropriations Committee approved a version of the fiscal 1993 energy and water spending bill that contained $550 million for the project. The committee reported HR 5373 (S Rept 102-344) on July 27.

In a recapitulation of the 1991 Senate floor debate, Bumpers led an unsuccessful effort to halt the SSC. Senators voted 62-32 on Aug. 3 to table (kill) a Bumpers amendment to terminate the project by cutting $516 million of the proposed $550 million appropriation. A second Bumpers amendment was tabled the same day, 62-31; it would have prohibited funding for the project after June 1, 1993, unless the administration secured at least $650 million in foreign contributions.

The Senate passed the bill by voice vote Aug. 3.

House and Senate negotiators agreed to provide $517 million for the supercollider in fiscal 1993. While it was a significant victory for project proponents, given the House vote to virtually eliminate funding, the amount was significantly less than what was sought and could add to the time and cost of building the collider. That, in turn, could increase the SSC's vulnerability to political attacks.

The House adopted the conference report (H Rept 102-866) on a 245-143 vote Sept. 17. The Senate adopted it by voice vote Sept. 24.

Ironically, the last hurdle was the administration. Because the energy and water appropriations bill also included nuclear testing restrictions opposed by President Bush, a chance existed that he would not sign the bill. However, Bush agreed to stomach those restrictions to save the supercollider and signed the legislation into law (PL 102-377) Oct. 2. *(Nuclear test ban, p. 392)*

Commercial Space

The House on Aug. 6, 1992, by voice vote passed legislation (HR 3848) designed to promote the commercial space industry. Although the Senate never acted on the bill, some of the provisions became law in the fiscal 1993 National Aeronautics and Space Administration reauthorization bill (HR 6135 — PL 102-588). *(NASA reauthorization, p. 898)*

HR 3848 sought to encourage the federal government to use private sector equipment for space launches. Sponsors agreed to an Armed Services Committee request to delete a section that would have placed restrictions on using decommissioned missiles for space launches. Armed Services wanted more time to review those provisions.

The House Science, Space and Technology Committee reported HR 3848 (H Rept 102-769, Part I) on Aug. 3, 1992. The House passed the bill by voice vote.

Technology Programs

Congress in 1992 cleared legislation (HR 1989), known as the American Technology Pre-Emption Act, designed to increase the competitiveness of U.S. high-technology companies in world markets.

Attempts to enact similar legislation in the 101st Congress failed. *(Story, p. 879)*

HR 1989 authorized $348 million for fiscal 1992 and $359 million for fiscal 1993 for key technology-related programs within the Commerce Department. Most of the funding was to go to the National Institute of Standards and Technology, a top government laboratory that helped industry develop cutting-edge technologies. In each year, $100 million was earmarked for the institute's advanced technology program to provide grants to businesses and joint ventures to research and develop new technologies. In fiscal 1993, the bill authorized another $35 million to upgrade and renovate institute facilities.

The measure directed the Commerce Department to survey the status of technologies critical to the U.S. economy and develop a plan to support those industries.

Legislative History

The House Science, Space and Technology Committee approved HR 1989 on May 1, 1991, by a 26-5 vote. Committee members debated an amendment that would take $10 million from the Advanced Technology Program, which offered technology grants, and use the money for loans to help companies commercialize specific emerging technologies, such as those in the electronics or computer fields. GOP members opposed the amendment, saying it would lead to a U.S. industrial policy in which Congress would choose which products would get government loans. The amendment was approved 15-13.

HR 1989 was reported (H Rept 102-134) on June 26.

The controversy over the loan program continued on the House floor. Robert S. Walker of Pennsylvania, the ranking Republican on the Science Committee, offered an amendment to strike the provision. The House rejected the amendment 172-246 on July 16. Administration officials had called the loan program a form of industrial policy and argued that by selecting which companies should receive loans, the government would be interfering in the marketplace.

The House by voice vote rejected another Walker effort to attach a non-binding resolution to the bill endorsing a reduction in the capital gains tax to spur U.S. competitiveness.

The House passed HR 1989, 296-122, on July 16.

The Senate Commerce, Science and Transportation Committee approved a companion measure (S 1034) by voice vote on July 30. S 1034, which was formally reported (S Rept 102-157) Sept. 24, did not contain the controversial loan program included in HR 1989.

On the last day Congress was in session in 1991 — Nov. 27 — the Senate by voice vote passed an amended HR 1989. The bill was a compromise. The loan program was dropped, and in exchange, House Republicans agreed to eliminate language to require companies whose research led to the commercialization of successful products to pay back grants.

The House accepted the changes by voice vote under suspension of the rules Jan. 28, 1992, clearing HR 1989. President Bush signed the measure (PL 102-245) on Feb. 14.

Fiscal 1992-93 NSF Funding

The House on July 11, 1991, by voice vote passed legislation (HR 2282) authorizing $5.8 billion for National Science Foundation (NSF) activities and research grants in fiscal 1992-93. The bill also limited the amount of overhead costs that universities could charge to the government when receiving NSF research grants.

Under existing administration regulations, universities that received federal research dollars charged the government for a portion of the costs of maintaining the university's infrastructure and research facilities. Universities charged the government an additional 20 percent to 75 percent of the federal grant to pay for these indirect costs. Rick Boucher, D-Va., offered an amendment, approved on a voice vote by the House Science Committee, to limit the indirect cost reimbursement to 26 percent and require that it be based on items such as salaries and wages, fringe benefits, materials and supplies, services and subcontracts.

The move to limit indirect costs came in response to a government audit showing that Stanford University overbilled the government by as much as $200 million for research-related expenses in the 1980s, using some of the money to pay for such extraneous expenses as a school yacht.

The Science Committee reported HR 2282 (H Rept 102-131) on June 25.

Water Desalination

Congress in 1992 cleared legislation (HR 3673) to advance research on new water desalination techniques. Advocates hoped that the technology would provide a cheaper way to remove the salt from large volumes of ocean water.

The bill would expand and coordinate federal research on removing salt or pollutants from water using membrane filters to produce drinkable water. It also authorized the National Science Foundation to establish a research program on membrane technology and recommended $2.5 million for the program in fiscal 1993.

The Bush administration initially opposed the bill, saying a new program was unnecessary because the Interior Department already funded desalination research. Proponents argued that the membrane research program was of critical importance to drought-stricken regions and the nation as a whole, given that conservation alone was not the answer.

HR 3673 was reported (H Rept 102-566) from House Science, Space and Technology on June 16, 1992. The House passed the bill by voice vote under suspension of the rules June 29. The Senate passed the measure Oct. 7, completing congressional action. President Bush signed HR 3673 (PL 102-490) on Oct. 24.

Metric Packaging

On Aug. 3, 1992, President Bush signed into law a bill (HR 5343 — PL 102-329) amending the labeling provisions of the American Technology Pre-Eminence Act (HR 1989 — PL 102-245) to clarify that manufacturers did not need to convert to metric-size packaging. *(Technology programs, p. 902)*

PL 102-245 had sought to promote metric labeling on some products to make them easier to export. Some packagers worried that that law could be interpreted as requiring them to redesign existing containers and to sell in metric units.

The United States was virtually alone in using the avoirdupois measurement system, based on pounds and ounces.

HR 5343 was reported from House Science, Space and Technology (H Rept 102-581, Part I) on June 18, 1992. The House passed the bill June 29 by voice vote under suspension of the rules. The Senate gave its voice vote approval July 21, clearing the measure.

Biotech Rules

The week of Feb. 24, 1992, President Bush issued new guidelines for manufacturers of genetically altered plants, bacteria and animals that would allow easier access to markets. The new policy sought to closely regulate only products that appeared to carry special risk, such as pharmaceuticals, instead of all new biotechnologies.

The administration did not release new rules, but agencies could use the president's policy statement to assess old rules or write new ones.

Debt-for-Science Swaps

Although both the House and Senate in 1992 passed HR 3215 — to promote scientific cooperation between the United States and Latin America — their differences were not resolved before adjournment and the legislation died.

Among the programs HR 3215 encouraged were so-called debt-for-science swaps, whereby the federal government would pay off part of a nation's foreign debt in exchange for its participation in research and education work.

The administration opposed the bill, saying enough federal programs existed to enhance scientific collaboration with Latin America.

The House Science, Space and Technology Subcommittee on Science approved HR 3215 on May 19, 1992. As approved, the bill established an inter-American scientific cooperation program at the National Science Foundation (NSF) to provide the United States' share of funding for joint research, education exchanges and information transfer. The bill provided a $10 million annual authorization for NSF in fiscal 1992 and 1993.

Members accepted amendments to clarify that the NSF could not put any constraints on countries as a condition for funding a debt-for-science exchange and to ensure that the NSF would not spend more than 25 percent of its budget for international cooperative scientific activities on programs under the measure.

The House Science, Space and Technology Committee reported HR 3215 (H Rept 102-654, Part I) on July 7. The House passed the bill by voice vote under suspension of the rules Aug. 10. The Senate passed an amended version by voice vote Oct. 7.

High-Speed Computer Network

In 1992, legislation (HR 5344) to promote a high-speed national computer network was passed in the House but died in the Senate.

HR 5344 would loosen current law and allow the National Science Foundation (NSF) to carry a broader array of information on its computer network, known as NSFnet, which was used by scientists, schools and research laboratories. The bill would allow the network to carry more commercial information, a move advocates said would lower costs for education and commercial users alike. NSFnet ultimately would serve as the backbone for an ambitious high-speed network for education and research groups.

The House Science, Space and Technology Committee reported HR 5344 (H Rept 102-567) on June 16, 1992. The House passed the bill by voice vote under suspension of the rules June 29.

Fire Safety

The House in 1992 passed a bill (HR 3360) requiring the installation of fire safety equipment in federal office buildings, but the Senate never acted on the measure.

Under existing law, federally owned buildings were exempt from local fire codes. Advocates said HR 3360 was needed because many federal buildings were old and had been neglected. The bill called for most newly constructed and leased federal office buildings for more than 25 employees to be equipped with sprinklers. It also required that federally subsidized housing units have smoke detectors. In some cases, sprinklers would also have been installed, depending on the size of the building.

The House Science, Space and Technology Committee reported HR 3360 (H Rept 102-509, Part I) on April 30, 1992. The House Public Works and Transportation Committee reported the measure (H Rept 102-509, Part II) on Aug. 10. The House passed HR 3360 by voice vote under suspension of the rules Aug. 10.

Electric Vehicles

The House Science, Space and Technology Committee on Sept. 24, 1991, reported legislation (HR 1538 — H Rept 102-217, Part I) that promotes electrically powered vehicles.

HR 1538 would establish a federal research and development program for electric cars and other vehicles aimed at overcoming the barriers that prevented their widespread use. The measure authorized about $570 million over seven years for research, including a joint battery project with the private sector.

The bill saw no further congressional action.

High-Speed Rail

Two bills aimed at promoting transportation research and the development of high-speed train systems were reported from committee during the 102nd Congress.

The Science, Space and Technology Committee on Dec. 6, 1991, reported a bill (HR 2941 — H Rept 102-417, Part I) authorizing $164.5 million in fiscal 1992 for research into such transportation technology as computerized automobile navigation devices; high-speed, steel-rail trains; and trains that levitated on an electromagnetic cushion. It authorized $180 million for research in fiscal 1993 and $200 million in fiscal 1994.

The committee approved the bill largely to show its support for magnetic levitation trains as negotiators hammered out a final surface transportation authorization bill (HR 2950 — PL 102-240). The broad bill authorized $700 million for a prototype train system that would hover at high speeds above an electromagnetic rail. *(Transportation bill, p. 437)*

On Nov. 8, 1991, the House Energy and Commerce panel reported legislation (HR 1087 — H Rept 102-297, Part I) to make high-speed rail projects eligible for loan guarantees under a program for upgrading railroads.

Animal Research Labs

Ending a three-year debate on Capitol Hill, Congress in 1992 cleared legislation (S 544 — PL 102-346) that made it a federal crime to vandalize animal research laboratories or farms. Members had fought over what kinds of animal facilities to include and what kinds of damage to punish. In the end, the bill covered most violent acts against most animal facilities. *(101st Congress action, p. 881)*

S 544, sponsored by Howell Heflin, D-Ala., passed the Senate on a voice vote Oct. 16, 1991. Similar provisions were included in a reauthorization of the National Institutes of Health (NIH — HR 2507) that was passed by the House in July 1991. The measure made it a federal crime to steal, destroy or alter records or property or to steal or injure research animals in any federally funded health facility. Violators would face up to five years in prison. *(NIH reauthorization, p. 602)*

HR 2407 (H Rept 102-498, Part I) was approved by the House Agriculture Committee April 2, 1992, and reported April 9. The bill was narrower than the version that was introduced by Charles W. Stenholm, D-Texas. Stenholm offered the new bill as a substitute amendment, which was approved by voice vote, after the original came under fire for being overly broad. The committee-approved bill was aimed at halting the activities of radical animal rights groups that crossed state lines to commit acts of violence. In such instances, the bill made it a federal crime, punishable by up to 20 years' imprisonment, to steal animals or property or damage anything at an animal research facility. The new bill made clear that current whistleblower protection laws at the state and local level would not be invalidated.

The House Judiciary Subcommittee on Crime and Criminal Justice approved HR 2407 on a narrow 7-6 vote July 8. The full committee approved the bill, 18-16, on July 22 and reported it (H Rept 101-498, Part II) on July 27. The Judiciary bill limited the types of animal facilities protected — to laboratories, farms, zoos and aquariums — and required that damage to a facility had to exceed $25,000 to be covered under the bill (the Agriculture bill had a $5,000 threshold).

The House on Aug. 4 passed S 544 by voice vote after stripping out its language and substituting that of HR 2407, which it had passed by voice vote under suspension of the rules. The bill would apply to virtually all places where animals were held, including research labs, farms, state fairs and dog shows. The bill made it a federal crime to cause $10,000 or more in damage to an animal research facility and increased the possible punishment with each increase in the severity of the crime. In a key difference with the Senate version, the House-passed bill did not make it a crime for intruders to duplicate papers in an animal research lab.

The Senate on Aug. 7 cleared S 544, without the duplication provision. President Bush signed the bill Aug. 26.

Indian Health Services

Congress in 1992 cleared legislation (S 2481) reauthorizing until the year 2000 health services for American Indians and setting goals for Indian health care by improving services and targeting new beneficiaries. The president signed the bill (PL 102-573) on Oct. 29.

Indians had suffered from certain health traumas at a higher rate than other Americans. According to the Indian Health Service (IHS), Indian mortality rates were double those of the rest of the U.S. population, largely because of tuberculosis, alcoholism and diabetes.

During debate on the reauthorization legislation, some members expressed concern that existing programs either had proved inadequate or had not been implemented. They cited a report submitted in 1991 by the inspector general for the Department of Health and Human Services (HHS), questioning the effectiveness of several youth alcohol and substance abuse treatment programs run by IHS.

In response, many new programs were aimed at afflictions primarily affecting Indian women and adolescents. In particular, the measure established a plan to study and treat infant mortality-related illnesses, such as Fetal Alcohol Syndrome (FAS). An Indian child was roughly three times as likely as a non-Indian child to be born with FAS, a condition describing birth defects in children whose mothers drank alcohol during pregnancy.

Legislative Action

The House Energy and Commerce Committee approved the House companion measure (HR 3724) by voice vote April 7, 1992. The bill was formally reported (H Rept 102-643, Part I) on July 1.

The House Interior and Insular Affairs Committee, which shared jurisdiction over the legislation, approved HR 3724 by voice vote April 29. The bill was reported (H Rept 102-643, Part II) on July 28.

Members reached a compromise on the two committee versions before they reached the floor. A new bill was introduced as HR 5752, which members inserted into the text of HR 3724.

During floor consideration of HR 3724, members debated language that exempted tribes that ran their own health care programs from reimbursing the government for medical services. At the time, only the Navajo tribe operated its own health care program. The exemption reportedly was written into the bill to avoid straining the tribe's limited resources and violating its sovereignty.

William E. Dannemeyer, R-Calif., offered an amendment to allow IHS to collect payments from a tribe's insurance plan. Dannemeyer said the exemption would reduce the amount of benefits available to all Indians. The amendment was rejected 165-199 on Sept. 15.

The House adopted by voice vote an amendment to develop a model substance abuse program at the Standing Rock Indian Reservation in North and South Dakota.

The House passed HR 3724, 330-36, on Sept. 15.

During Senate Indian Affairs Committee consideration of S 2481, ranking Republican John McCain, Ariz., won approval of three amendments. The first effectively repealed portions of two anti-drug laws (PL 99-570 and PL 100-690) that fell under the jurisdiction of the IHS. Programs removed under McCain's plan included detoxification and rehabilitation for youths who were alcohol or substance abusers and a treatment program for families of youth substance abusers. *(PL 99-570, Congress and the Nation Vol. VII, p. 723; PL 100-690, Congress and the Nation Vol. VII, p. 748)*

The second McCain amendment made the director of Indian health a presidential appointee subject to Senate confirmation, for a term of up to four years. The director had been appointed by the HHS secretary. According to McCain, the office needed greater accountability to Congress.

The third amendment lowered, from 40 percent to 20 percent, the tribal contribution to a new tribal health scholarship assistance program. It would permit the HHS secretary to tailor the health objectives described in the surgeon general's Healthy People 2000 report for the health needs of American Indians.

Other amendments adopted by the committee included one from Tom Daschle, D-S.D., that increased recruitment of professionals from the areas with the greatest demand, and one from Frank H. Murkowski, R-Alaska, that provided funding for patient travel both to and from medical treatment in remote regions of Alaska where costly commercial air travel was the only means of transportation. Funds previously were provided for the trip to receive medical services but not for the return.

The Senate Indian Affairs Committee reported S 2481 (S Rept 102-392) on Aug. 27. The full Senate passed the bill by voice vote Sept. 18.

Members from both houses and their staff met informally to work out differences between the two bills. In response to administration concerns, members agreed to remove provisions to expand medical coverage and medical provider options for low-income older and disabled Indians by authorizing IHS to pay Medicare Part B premiums for certain Medicare-eligible Indians; to require IHS to contract to administer health programs in tribes and tribal organizations that owned health facilities; and to amend the Social Security Act to allow tribal health care providers to collect Medicare payments for outpatient services offered in tribal clinics.

The House, after reinserting the drug and alcohol provisions removed by McCain's amendment, overwhelmingly passed S 2481 by a vote of 335-74 under suspension of the rules on Oct. 3. Senators agreed to the changes and cleared the measure by voice vote Oct. 7.

Major Provisions

As cleared, S 2481:

- Reauthorized the Indian Health Care Improvement Act of 1976 (PL 94-437) and the Indian Alcohol and Substance Abuse Prevention and Treatment Act, which was included in the 1986 omnibus anti-drug bill (PL 99-570).
- Authorized approximately $940 million for fiscal 1993 for the Indian Health Service, which administered programs first authorized in the 1976 Indian Health Care Improvement Act.
- Established 61 goals aimed at reducing the incidence of such ailments as diabetes, cirrhosis and cancer by the year 2000. The Indian population suffered disproportionately from those afflictions.
- Set more stringent standards by which to measure progress toward the goal of raising the health status of Indians.
- Enhanced professional programs to draw more Native Americans into the IHS. It also provided for comprehensive school health education programs and established an Office of Indian Women's programs.

• Provided financial assistance to tribal governments for safe water and sanitary waste disposal facilities. The bill also exempted payments received by an IHS facility from consideration in determining appropriations for services to Indians.

• Required the IHS to address inhalant abuse in the context of substance abuse. Aside from continuing previously existing drug and alcohol abuse provisions, it authorized several substance abuse and demonstration projects specific to certain tribes.

• Required that the IHS director be subject to confirmation by the Senate. The IHS director had been chosen by the HHS secretary.

Hawaiian Health Care

A reauthorization of federal Native Hawaiian health care programs through fiscal year 2000 became law in 1992 as part of the fiscal 1993 defense appropriations bill (HR 5504 — PL 102-396). *(Defense bill, p. 407)*

HR 5504 aimed to improve the health of Native Hawaiians and set 40 goals for better health to be achieved by the year 2000, including reductions in infant mortality and breast cancer. The bill funded health centers for Native Hawaiians, as well as medical scholarships for Native Hawaiian students.

The measure also expanded and diversified the role of Papa Ola Lokahi, the Native Hawaiian health board, which coordinated health care services provided to Native Hawaiians. Native Hawaiians, who made up 20 percent of the state's population, had a high mortality rate compared with the rest of the country.

The Senate Select Committee on Indian Affairs approved a Hawaiian health care bill (S 2681) by voice vote on May 13, 1992. The legislation was reported (S Rept 102-309) on July 1. The full Senate passed S 2681 by voice vote Aug. 7.

The House Energy and Commerce Committee considered a similar bill (HR 5346), which it reported (H Rept 102-846) on Aug. 12. On the floor, House members took up S 2681. However, a motion to pass the Senate bill under suspension of the rules failed Sept. 30, when the 228-194 fell short of the required two-thirds majority vote.

The Hawaiian health care provisions subsequently were included in the defense spending bill.

Indian Self-Governance

Congress in 1991 cleared legislation (HR 3394) to authorize $700,000 for the addition of 10 tribes to a demonstration project established to help tribes manage programs previously administered by the Bureau of Indian Affairs and the Indian Health Service.

The legislation expanded the authorization under the Indian Self Determination and Education Assistance Act of 1988 (PL 100-472), which set up a demonstration program under which 20 Indian tribes were given the authority to carry out certain tribal services, such as medical and health programs, that otherwise would have been handled by the federal government.

The House Interior Committee reported the bill (H Rept 102-320) on Nov. 18, and the House passed it by voice vote under suspension of the rules the same day. The Senate passed the legislation on Nov. 19, clearing it. President Bush signed the bill Dec. 4.

Another bill (S 668 — S Rept 102-125) that sought to authorize demonstration grants to assist tribes in establishing environmental protection and cleanup programs and apply for related federal grants passed the Senate Aug. 2 on a voice vote. The House Interior Committee approved the bill by voice vote on Nov. 13, but it saw no further action.

Indian Criminal Jurisdiction

President Bush signed legislation (HR 972 — PL 102-137) on Oct. 28, 1991, that reinstated the authority of Indian tribes to exercise limited criminal jurisdiction over all Indians within a tribe's territorial limits. Jurisdiction was limited under the bill to criminal misdemeanors.

Before 1990, a tribe had jurisdiction over all criminal cases on its land involving misdemeanor charges as long as the defendant was an American Indian. But in May 1990, the Supreme Court ruled in *Duro v. Reina* that while a tribe had such jurisdiction over its own members, it had no legal authority over Indians from other tribes. *(Case summary, p. 828)*

Jurisdiction over non-Indians was to remain in the hands of state and federal authorities.

The House Interior and Insular Affairs Committee reported HR 972 (H Rept 102-61) on May 14. The same day, the House passed the bill by voice vote under suspension of the rules. The Senate Indian Affairs Committee reported the measure (S Rept 102-153) on Sept. 19. The Senate passed HR 972 by voice vote Sept. 23. The Senate adopted the conference report (H Rept 102-261) on Oct. 17. The House adopted it Oct. 22, clearing HR 972.

Tribal Courts

Before adjournment of the 102nd Congress, the Senate and House were unable to reconcile their differences over legislation (HR 4004) designed to help Indian tribes retain their sovereignty by shoring up their tribal justice systems.

Under federal law, Indian tribes were accorded authority over any tribal governance that was not specifically divested to Congress. A 1968 Indian civil rights law ensured that Indian tribes had the right to exercise legal jurisdiction over their affairs. Tribal courts, however, had long suffered from a lack of funding and organization. *(1968 law, Congress and the Nation Vol. II, p. 385)*

The Senate Indian Affairs Committee on June 16, 1992, gave voice vote approval to a companion measure, S 1752. The bill was formally reported (S Rept 102-314) July 2.

The House Interior and Insular Affairs Committee on June 17 approved HR 4004 by voice vote. It was reported (H Rept 102-675) on July 21. The House passed the bill by voice vote under suspension of the rules July 27.

The Senate, after inserting the text of S 1752, passed HR 4004 by voice vote Aug. 6.

The main difference between the bills was that the Senate version provided a mechanism for a Tribal Judicial Conference that would help establish a formula for funding tribal courts and intertribal appellate courts. The House version would set up an Office of Tribal Justice Support within the Bureau of Indian Affairs that would have the grant-making authority. The office would provide funds, technical assistance and information to Indian tribes to develop, improve or maintain native tribal justice systems.

Indian Lands Management

The Senate on Oct. 2, 1992, by voice vote passed a bill (S 2977) to create programs within the Bureau of Indian Affairs (BIA) to improve the management of Indian farmlands and ranches that had suffered from a lack of federal investment. In the rush to adjourn, however, the House never took up the legislation.

Bill sponsor Tom Daschle, D-S.D., said that the United States had assumed a trust responsibility to the tribes and to the individual land owners for protection of property. But he said that the United States needed to pay more attention to administration of land management programs, citing a BIA report that showed that more than 1.1 million acres of Indian trust land remained idle nationwide.

Daschle also said that in the 20 years prior to 1992, actual dollar levels for the Indian agriculture program had remained static, and, because of inflation, funding for the programs had been cut to half of their original levels. Over that period, the number of BIA personnel involved in agriculture or natural resources management also had decreased dramatically.

The Senate Select Indian Affairs Committee and the House Interior and Insular Affairs Committee held a joint hearing on S 2977 on Sept. 22. The Department of the Interior met with staff following the hearing to work out bill changes regarding the administration's management role.

The Senate Indian Affairs Committee approved S 2977 by voice vote Sept. 25 and reported it (S Rept 102-442) Sept. 29.

The bill would have required BIA to develop programs in conjunction with Indian tribes to improve productivity and management. It also would have allowed tribes to gain more control over tribal farmlands and provide at least 20 scholarships to Indian students to study land management.

The full Senate adopted an amendment by John McCain, R-Ariz., clarifying that the secretary of the interior would not have to take on any additional land management responsibilities other than those specified in existing law. The bill's purpose was to streamline the administration of the programs and to empower the Indian tribes to assume a greater role in program management.

Indian Job Training

President Bush signed into law on Oct. 23, 1992, legislation (S 1530 — PL 102-477) simplifying the way Indians received federal job training assistance.

S 1530 allowed tribal governments to submit plans to the secretary of the interior to consolidate all job training programs under one administrator. Tribal governments previously had been overwhelmed by the paperwork required by each of the four executive departments — Labor, Education, Interior, and Health and Human Services — that administered Indian job training programs. The bill created a demonstration project within the Interior Department to review plans to combine programs.

The Senate Indian Affairs Committee reported S 1530 (S Rept 102-188) on Oct. 15, 1991. The full Senate approved the measure by voice vote Oct. 30.

The House Interior and Insular Affairs Committee reported the bill (H Rept 102-905) on Sept. 24, 1992. The House passed an amended version by voice vote under suspension of the rules Sept. 29. The Senate accepted the House changes Oct. 7, clearing the bill.

'Indian Preference'

The Senate passed by voice vote Aug. 12, 1992, a measure (S 3118) to revise the Buy Indian Act, which gave preferential treatment to Indian-owned businesses seeking work with the Bureau of Indian Affairs and the Indian Health Service. But the House did not act on the measure.

An earlier attempt at reforming the act had been vetoed by President Bush in 1990, over language that would have required formal certification that companies were owned by Indians. *(Story, p. 884)*

S 3118 represented a compromise that would require spot checks to confirm the eligibility of Indian businesses for preferential contracts. The measure also would set aside for small businesses all Buy Indian contracts below $1 million. The Senate voice vote adopted an amendment to reduce the civil penalties for non-compliance from $50,000 to $1,000.

The Senate Indian Affairs Committee reported S 3118 (S Rept 102-368) on Aug. 10.

Indian Languages

Congress in 1992 cleared legislation (S 2044) that authorized grants and programs to assist Indians and ensure the survival of their native languages. The grants were intended to support community language programs, to train Indians to teach languages and to produce teaching materials.

The measure established a program within the administration for Indians to make grants to Indian groups working to sustain Indian languages. The bill authorized $2 million in fiscal 1993 and unspecified amounts through fiscal 1997.

The Senate Indian Affairs Committee reported the measure (S Rept 102-343) on July 27, 1992. The Senate passed S 2044 by voice vote Aug. 5. The House passed an amended version by voice vote under suspension of the rules Oct. 2. The Senate accepted the House amendments, thus clearing the bill, Oct. 5. President Bush signed the measure (PL 102-524) on Oct. 26.

Alaska Native Languages

Legislation (S 1595) to ensure the survival of Alaska's indigenous languages won voice vote approval in the Senate Nov. 25, 1991.

Of the 20 original native languages that were still being spoken in Alaska, only two were being actively used by children, and many Alaska Native Americans said the loss of the other languages had led to a disintegration of their communities.

The bill would provide grants to villages and eligible Alaska Native groups for language-preservation projects, such as community-sponsored language programs, training courses for teachers and the compilation of oral histories. The grant program would be run by the Administration for

Native Americans within the Department of Health and Human Services.

The Senate Indian Affairs Committee had reported S 1595 (S Rept 102-213) on Nov. 13.

Indian Right-to-Sue

Three bills (HR 5658, HR 1206, HR 4209) were passed by the House in 1992 that would have given Indian tribes the right to sue the federal government over the past seizure or use of tribal lands. The bills saw no Senate action.

HR 5658 would have guaranteed that dividends paid to Alaska natives from certain land sales authorized by the Alaska Native Claims Settlement Act of 1971 would not have been subject to federal, state or local taxes. Members of the corporations in charge of the sales were afraid that the original act was too vague.

The House Ways and Means Committee had reported the measure (H Rept 102-750) on July 29. The House passed it by voice vote under suspension of the rules Aug. 3.

HR 1206 would have allowed the Pueblo of Isleta tribe of New Mexico to file a claim under the Indian Claims Commission Act of 1946 for lands taken by the U.S. government even though the statute of limitations for such actions had run out. Bill supporters said that as a result of poor legal advice from the Bureau of Indian Affairs, the tribe might not have been adequately compensated for land acquired by the government. The legislation would have authorized a U.S. Claims Court to hear the case but would not have granted the tribe any damages.

The bill was reported (H Rept 102-777) by the House Judiciary Committee on Aug. 3. The House passed HR 1206 by voice vote under suspension of the rules the next day.

HR 4209 would have allowed the Cherokee, Choctaw and Chickasaw Indian tribes to sue the U.S. government for having constructed a waterway without their consent. The waterway was built during the 1940s on a part of the Arkansas River owned by the tribes. The bill would have given U.S. courts jurisdiction over the case.

The House Judiciary Committee reported the measure (H Rept 102-773, Part I) Aug. 3. The bill passed the House by voice vote under suspension of the rules Aug. 4.

Unacknowledged Tribes

Legislation (HR 2144) creating a panel to study the problems facing unacknowledged Indian tribes and the financial difficulties of recognized tribes in California became law in 1992. The president signed the bill (PL 102-416) on Oct. 14.

Many Indian tribes lost their lands when the government revoked their federal recognition as part of the 1958 Rancheria Termination Act. These tribes included the United Auburn Indian Community, a 125-member group residing 35 miles from Sacramento, and about 40 other California tribes. Federally recognized tribes had more access to economic aid and other public assistance.

The measure authorized $700,000 to establish the California Indian Policy Council.

The House passed HR 2144 by voice vote under suspension of the rules Aug. 12. The Senate Indian Affairs Committee reported the bill (S Rept 102-441) Sept. 29. The full Senate passed an amended HR 2144 by voice vote Oct. 2. The next day, the House accepted the Senate changes, completing congressional action.

Indian Research

Legislation (S 3155) to establish a non-partisan National Indian Policy Research Institute at George Washington University in Washington, D.C., passed the Senate by voice vote Oct. 2, 1992. The House failed to take up the measure in the rush to adjourn.

S 3155 would have authorized $1 million in fiscal 1994 and unspecified sums through fiscal 1996.

The Senate Indian Affairs Committee reported the bill (S Rept 102-443) on Sept. 29.

Indian Veterans Memorial

The Senate on Oct. 2, 1992, gave voice vote approval to S 3157, to authorize the creation of a memorial to Indian veterans who died in combat. The House did not act on the measure.

The bill would have authorized the federal government to donate a site for the monument but would not have authorized any other federal spending.

The Senate Indian Affairs Committee reported S 3157 (S Rept 102-440) Sept. 29.

Navajo-Hopi Relocation

Congress in 1991 cleared legislation (S 1720) that reauthorized $30 million for the Navajo-Hopi Relocation Housing Program through fiscal 1995.

The program was established to help relocate Indian families displaced by the 1974 congressionally negotiated settlement of land disputes (PL 93-531) between the two tribes in Arizona that dated back to the 1880s when nomadic Navajo herders settled on Hopi lands. Under the mandated settlement, a number of Navajo families were left inside Hopi territory. The program offered relocation services for such families. *(Earlier action, Congress and the Nation Vol. VII, p. 865; 1974 law, Congress and the Nation Vol. IV, p. 809)*

The Senate Indian Affairs Committee reported S 1720 (S Rept 102-176) on Oct. 7. The Senate passed the bill by voice vote Oct. 25. On Nov. 18, the House Interior and Insular Affairs Committee reported S 1720 (H Rept 102-321) and the House passed the bill by voice vote under suspension of the rules. Bush signed it (PL 102-180) on Dec. 2.

Micmac Indians

President Bush on Nov. 26, 1991, signed legislation (S 374 — PL 102-171) that provided federal recognition to the Aroostook Band of Micmac Indians in Aroostook County, Maine, and made them eligible for federal benefits. The bill authorized a $900,000 deposit for a land-acquisition fund for the Micmacs and also authorized them to organize as a government and establish rules for tribal membership.

The Bush administration had threatened to veto the measure, saying it would circumvent the federal government's tribal-recognition procedures, which were handled by the Interior Department. But bill supporters said the legislation was necessary to correct the omission of the Micmacs from the 1980 Maine Indian Claims Settlement Act (PL 96-420), which provided funds for 12.5 million acres of land taken by the federal government. *(Congress and the Nation Vol. V, p. 857)*

S 374 was reported from Senate Indian Affairs (S Rept 102-136) on Aug. 2. The Senate passed the bill by voice vote on Sept. 19. The House passed the legislation on Nov. 12.

Similar legislation failed in the House in 1990. *(Story, p. 885)*

Lumbee Tribe

The House on Sept. 26, 1991, passed legislation (HR 1426) by a 263-154 vote to recognize the Lumbee Tribe of Cheraw Indians of North Carolina, an action necessary to make the tribe eligible for social programs and protection under federal Indian laws.

The measure was designed to get around a decision by the Bush administration that the tribe was ineligible for federal recognition. Members first defeated, 159-251, a Republican-sponsored amendment that would have required the tribe to go through the Interior Department's recognition procedures.

The House Interior and Insular Affairs Committee reported HR 1426 (H Rept 102-215) on Sept. 24. Following full House passage, the bill was referred to the Senate Indian Affairs Committee, which reported it Nov. 26 (S Rept 102-251). A separate companion measure (S 1036) also had been considered by the Senate committee.

The legislation died upon adjournment.

Mimbres Tribe

On Sept. 30, 1992, under suspension of the rules, the House rejected, 179-243, a bill (S 1528) that would have established a national monument in honor of the Mimbres Indian tribe of New Mexico and an archeological protection system for Mimbres historical sites.

Critics of the measure objected to provisions that would have allowed the government to buy land from unwilling landowners to create the monument. They argued that Mimbres culture could be adequately protected by expanding existing federal parks.

The Senate Energy Committee had approved the bill 20-0 on Oct. 30, 1991, and reported it (S Rept 102-222) Nov. 19. The Senate passed the bill by voice vote Nov. 26.

The House Interior and Insular Affairs Committee reported the legislation (H Rept 102-949) on Sept. 29, 1992.

15

Inside Congress

Introduction	*913*
Members and Procedures	*915*
Election Issues	*951*
Pay and Benefits	*965*
The Keating Five	*975*

Inside Congress

The public's opinion of Congress sank lower and lower in 1989-92. Harris surveys found that the percentage of people with a positive view of the job done by Congress dropped from 47 percent in mid-1985 to 40 percent at the end of 1989. By October 1991, according to a *New York Times*/CBS poll, Congress' general approval rating was 27 percent. In a *Wall Street Journal*/NBC News poll released in April 1992, 71 percent thought Congress was contributing to the nation's problems.

Mismanagement and Ethics Troubles

The negative views of Congress could be attributed, at least in part, to a plethora of scandals involving the mismanagement of congressional operations and the misdeeds — alleged and proven — of some members.

When the 101st Congress opened in 1989, House Speaker Jim Wright, D-Texas, was under investigation by the House Committee on Standards of Official Conduct (ethics committee) for a number of questionable financial dealings. The committee subsequently charged him with 69 violations of House rules. In June, Wright became the only Speaker in congressional history to resign his post midterm; then he ended his 34-year career as a U.S. representative by leaving Congress. Majority Leader Thomas S. Foley, D-Wash., succeeded Wright as Speaker.

While the Wright case was coming to a head, another member of the Democratic leadership — Majority Whip Tony Coelho, D-Calif. — was done in by reports of a controversial "junk bond" investment. Coelho, who had proven to be a fund-raising wunderkind for the Democrats, had long been seen as a future Speaker. Unwilling to face an ethics probe, Coelho resigned his seat.

Complaints also were filed in 1989 against House Republican Whip Newt Gingrich, Ga. They centered around the financing of a book he cowrote. The aggressive, conservative Gingrich was something of an upstart, often annoying Democrats and at times alienating even those in his own party. The ethics investigation was dropped in 1990 with no charges filed against Gingrich.

Members of the House rank and file did not fare so well. Barney Frank, D-Mass., for example, was formally reprimanded for improperly using his office to help a male lover, who allegedly ran a prostitution service out of Frank's home. Donald E. "Buz" Lukens, R-Ohio, resigned his seat after being convicted for having sex with an underage girl. He served jail time for his crime. Jim Bates, D-Calif., received a "letter of reproval" from the ethics committee for sexually harassing women on his staff. And the outspoken Gus Savage, D-Ill., was found to have made unwanted sexual advances to a Peace Corps volunteer while on an official trip, but the ethics committee did not take any disciplinary action against him.

The Senate did not escape serious ethics troubles during the 101st Congress. Dave Durenberger, R-Minn., was denounced in July 1990. Among other things, Durenberger took what amounted to honoraria beyond the limit set by Senate rules, accepted reimbursement from the Senate for improper claims and converted campaign funds for personal use. In 1993, Durenberger faced criminal charges stemming from his actions.

The investigation into the so-called Keating Five began in late 1989, and the Senate Ethics Committee opened hearings on the case before television cameras a year later. The focus was on the relationship between thrift executive Charles H. Keating Jr. and five senators — Alan Cranston, D-Calif.; Dennis DeConcini, D-Ariz.; John Glenn, D-Ohio; John McCain, R-Ariz.; and Donald W. Riegle Jr., D-Mich. Cranston, who in the course of the investigation announced his resignation as majority whip, received a reprimand from the committee.

During the 102nd Congress, a major scandal centering on the House bank surfaced in September 1991. Hundreds of sitting and former members of Congress, it was learned, routinely overdrew their accounts. Twenty-two members were found by the ethics committee to have abused the bank system. Many members decided not to run for reelection in 1992 as a result of the scandal, and many others were defeated at the polls. By mid-1993, a Justice Depart-

References

Discussion of congressional affairs for the years 1945-64 may be found in *Congress and the Nation Vol. I*, pp. 1407-1431; for the years 1965-68, *Congress and the Nation Vol. II*, pp. 893-924; for the years 1969-72, *Congress and the Nation Vol. III*, pp. 353-433; for the years 1973-76, *Congress and the Nation Vol. IV*, pp. 743-794; for the years 1977-80, *Congress and the Nation Vol. V*, pp. 873-953; for the years 1981-84, *Congress and the Nation Vol. VI*, pp. 797-840; for the years 1985-88, *Congress and the Nation Vol. VII*, pp. 871-910.

ment investigation into possible criminal wrongdoing was ongoing.

A Justice inquiry also was being conducted into the operations of the House Post Office. Postal clerks were involved in embezzlement and drug dealing, and members were said to have used the post office to convert campaign checks to cash. One member under investigation was Dan Rostenkowski, D-Ill., powerful chairman of the House Ways and Means Committee.

Problems of Leadership

Congress also was taken to task for its seeming inability — some said unwillingness — to get anything done. However, the problems facing the congressional leadership in steering 535 independent and strong-willed legislators went beyond settling partisan differences over legislative and budgetary differences and engaging in a philosophical debate about government's role in society. Several forces in Congress and the country had gathered for years to make the government seem rudderless. They included:

- The decentralization of power in Congress. Before the mid-1970s, leaders could run Congress in consultation with a handful of its titans because power was concentrated and junior members did not expect to share it. Post-Watergate reforms, however, weakened committee chairmen, making them more accountable to their colleagues and forcing them to share power with subcommittee chairmen. Leadership required building consensus across a much broader spectrum.

Leaders were left with few tools of discipline to whip the rank and file into line. "You just have to keep begging and begging and begging," observed House Minority Leader Robert H. Michel, R-Ill., on how difficult it was to get his colleagues to go along with him on some votes.

- The erosion of party identity. Both parties lacked a firm sense of direction in the post-Reagan, post-Cold War era and were riven by divisions over policy and political strategy. Members of Congress were not beholden to the party for their election success to anywhere near the same degree as their predecessors.
- The erosion of public confidence in the government. Politicians fueled hostility toward government by running against Washington, and a groundswell of anti-incumbent sentiment among the American electorate made members of Congress more fearful than ever about enacting policies that demanded sacrifice.

An exasperated Senate Majority Leader George J. Mitchell, D-Maine, asked his colleagues near the end of 1990: "Do we have the minimum level of courage necessary to do something that is difficult, unpleasant, unpopular? Or must we forever say that this institution is incapable of taking any action that meets any of that description?"

Mitchell and Foley

Mitchell and Foley both assumed the No. 1 leadership spot in their respective chambers in 1989. In many ways, their individual styles reflected the changes that had taken place in Congress and the needs that were created as a result.

Senate. Mitchell was a cautious leader, mindful that he owed his election in large part to reform-minded Democrats who had opposed power-hungry autocratic leaders in the past. As a sign to the membership, Mitchell allowed others to assume some of the positions traditionally held by the majority leader. For example, he appointed Daniel K. Inouye, D-Hawaii, to chair the Democratic Steering Committee, which was responsible for assigning Democrats to committees.

Mitchell also was pragmatic. He created good will by living up to his promise to improve senators' working conditions through more predictable hours. Few late-night sessions were held, and no roll-call votes were scheduled after 7 p.m. except on Thursdays. Most roll-call votes were taken in the middle of the week, allowing members to visit their districts and take care of other responsibilities over long weekends. Mitchell continued a popular innovation begun by his predecessor, Robert C. Byrd, D-W.Va.: holding the Senate in session for three weeks, then having a week off for senators to tend to home-state business.

Most senators found Mitchell' s style open and consultative. And he earned good marks for his fairness and serious intent. Mitchell, however, was a devoted partisan. Clashes between the parties became more frequent in election years and when controversial issues came before the chamber. Mitchell would push for roll-call votes that Republicans did not want to take, often inviting a strong partisan response from Minority Leader Bob Dole, R-Kan., and others.

House. In his acceptance speech upon being elected Speaker, Foley said he saw the job as doing more than leading his fellow Democrats and pledged to Republicans "a spirit of cooperation and increased consultation." Known as a conciliator with a low-key, non-confrontational style, Foley received a great deal of credit for restoring stability to the House after the 1989 resignations of Wright and Coelho. Even Republicans who were extremely critical of Wright praised Foley for his civil ways and attempts at bipartisanship.

Foley, however, sometimes was chastised by both ideological wings of his own party. Conservatives and moderates criticized him for being an old-fashioned liberal still championing policies they said most voters had rejected. Liberals occasionally found him too accommodating and lacking the aggression they saw necessary to push their agenda.

Foley seldom played hardball with colleagues and was reluctant to use his influence over committee assignments to reward people who stuck with the leadership and to punish those who did not. He preferred to let the legislative process work, however slowly, rather than impose his own views or push specific legislation. "There is a degree to which you can sort of push, encourage, support, direct," Foley said. "But the Speakership isn't a dictatorship."

The House bank and Post Office scandals put Foley on the defensive and led to speculation about whether he could hang on to his job. Foley struggled to quell the institutional crisis first by pushing in-house reforms: curbing perquisites, overhauling the way the House was administered and endorsing a panel to propose reforms in legislative procedures. He leaned on committee chairmen to get major legislation to the floor, arguing that the best way for the House to put the scandals behind it was to do its legislative business. And Foley began trying to reinforce his personal bond with fellow Democrats by inviting small groups of members to private dinners to discuss the House and its leadership. By the end of 1992, with President-elect Bill Clinton riding high in the polls and Democrats eager for unity, all talk of challenging Foley vanished.

Chronology Of Action On Congress: Members and Procedures

1989-90

The 101st Congress convened Jan. 3, 1989, with a new Senate majority leader — George J. Mitchell, D-Maine — as Vice President George Bush prepared to succeed Ronald Reagan as president on Jan. 20. The old business of ethics troubles, carried over from the 100th Congress, still surrounded House Speaker Jim Wright, D-Texas, however. He made history in June by resigning as Speaker in midterm. The House then got a new Speaker, Thomas S. Foley, D-Wash., who had been majority leader.

Another member of the House leadership, Democratic Whip Tony Coelho of California, resigned when questions were raised about his financial dealings. Among those who stayed and faced ethics committee probes, Sen. Dave Durenberger, R-Minn., was denounced; Rep. Barney Frank, D-Mass., was reprimanded; and Rep. Jim Bates, D-Calif., received a "letter of reproval." An investigation also began into the Keating Five — five senators who were suspected of doing favors for a wealthy campaign contributor. *(Keating Five, p. 975)*

In legislative action, Congress made the most comprehensive changes in the congressional code of conduct since the late 1970s.

Organization

Senators and representatives had to become acclimated to new leaders in the first session of the 101st Congress. Senate Democrats got a new majority leader, and Senate Republicans picked an aggressive, young advocate as their party whip. The House experienced a major shakeup, beginning with the unprecedented midterm resignation of the Speaker. Further turmoil followed shortly after, when the No. 3 spot in the Democratic leadership was vacated.

Senate

Despite the election of a new majority leader, the Senate was a rock of stability compared with the House. Senate Republicans hung onto their 100th Congress leadership.

Majority Leadership. Robert C. Bryd, W.Va., declined to seek re-election as majority leader for the 101st Congress. Democrats Nov. 29, 1988, selected George J. Mitchell of Maine to succeed him. Mitchell's rivals in the election were J. Bennett Johnston of Louisiana and Daniel K. Inouye of Hawaii. Byrd became president pro tempore of the Senate and chairman of the Appropriations Committee.

Alan Cranston, Calif., easily won an unprecedented seventh term as Democratic whip. He survived a challenge from Wendell H. Ford, Ky., a 14-year Senate veteran and a three-time chairman of the Democratic Senatorial Campaign Committee (DSCC). In the weeks prior to the vote, Ford's bid was seen as the most serious threat to an incumbent party leader in the 1980s. However, when the secret ballots were being counted, Cranston's total quickly passed the 28 needed to win. When the tally reached 30-12, Ford moved that Cranston's re-election be made unanimous.

David Pryor of Arkansas won the position of secretary of the Democratic Conference, succeeding Inouye. Pryor was declared winner by acclamation after passing 28 votes in his contest with Patrick J. Leahy of Vermont.

Elected without opposition as chief deputy whip, replacing Spark M. Matsunaga of Hawaii, was Alan J. Dixon of Illinois. In the previous session, Dixon was deputy regional whip for the Midwest.

Mitchell appointed Inouye as chairman of the Democratic Steering Committee and John B. Breaux, La., as DSCC chairman. Mitchell, as majority leader, assumed the traditional mantle of chairman of the Democratic Policy Committee, but he also named Thomas A. Daschle, S.D., as co-chairman.

Minority Leadership. Senate Republicans returned the same leadership team from the 100th Congress. Reelected by acclamation Nov. 29, 1988, were Minority Leader Bob Dole, Kan., and Assistant Minority Leader Alan K. Simpson, Wyo. Without opposition, William L. Armstrong of Colorado was re-elected chairman of the Senate Republican Policy Committee and Thad Cochran of Mississippi was re-elected secretary of the Senate Republican Conference.

John H. Chafee, R.I., retained his position as chairman of the Senate Republican Conference, defeating Frank H. Murkowski, Alaska, 28-17. Don Nickles, Okla., was selected, also by 28-17, over John McCain, Ariz., as chairman of the National Republican Senatorial Committee.

Committees. The chairmanship of the powerful Appropriations Committee opened up in the 101st Congress with the retirement of John C. Stennis, D-Miss. Byrd assumed the post. Jim Sasser, D-Tenn., replaced Lawton Chiles, D-Fla., as Budget Committee chairman, and Donald W. Riegle Jr., D-Mich., assumed the chairmanship of the Banking Committee from William Proxmire, D-Wis. Both Chiles and Proxmire retired at the end of the 100th Congress.

Pryor inherited the post of chairman of the Aging Committee after the electoral defeat of John Melcher, D-Mont.

Among Republicans, Chafee replaced Robert T. Stafford, Vt., as ranking member on Environment and Public Works; McCain replaced Daniel J. Evans, Wash., as vice chairman of Select Indian Affairs; and Rudy Boschwitz, Minn., replaced Lowell P. Weicker Jr., Conn., as ranking member on Small Business.

House

A major reshuffling of majority and minority leadership occurred in the House.

Majority Leadership. The House re-elected Jim Wright of Texas as Speaker on Jan. 3, 1989, by a traditional party-line vote of 253-170. Republicans had talked of recruiting a Democrat to challenge Wright because of his ongoing ethics troubles and partisan method of running the House, but they were not able to find a disaffected Democrat to take on the Speaker.

New Sergeant-at-Arms

The Senate Democratic Caucus Nov. 14, 1990, designated Martha S. Pope to succeed retiring Henry A. Giugni as sergeant-at-arms. Pope became the first woman to be chosen for the Senate's second-ranking position. She was formally elected to the post at the opening of the 102nd Congress.

Pope had served since 1989 as chief of staff to Senate Majority Leader George J. Mitchell, of Maine. As sergeant-at-arms, she would preside over the Senate's chief administrative office, overseeing payroll, Capitol security, computer services, the radio and television recording studio, post office, printing facility and other housekeeping functions.

The House also would get a new sergeant-at-arms, in 1992. Jack Russ would step down from the post amidst allegations of mismanagement of the House bank. *(House bank, p. 929)*

Thomas S. Foley, Wash., returned as minority leader; and Tony Coehlo, Calif., as majority whip.

William H. Gray III, Pa., was named Dec. 5, 1988, as chairman of the Democratic Caucus. Gray, who became the first black to win a top House leadership post, received 146 votes on the first ballot, compared with 80 for Mary Rose Oakar, Ohio, and 33 for Mike Synar, Okla. Gray succeeded Richard A. Gephardt, Mo., who was required to step down after two terms.

Wright made congressional history June 6, 1989, by resigning as Speaker in midterm. Wright stepped down in the wake of an ethics committee determination that he might have broken House rules in as many as 69 instances. He subsequently resigned from the House. *(Wright resignation, p. 917)*

Foley was elected June 6, on a party-line vote of 251-164, as the 49th Speaker of the House. He was challenged by Minority Leader Robert H. Michel, R-Ill. Gephardt was elected June 14 to succeed Foley as majority leader. He easily outdistanced Ed Jenkins, Ga., on a 181-76 tally; one write-in vote went to Lee H. Hamilton, Ind., and one ballot was left blank.

Ethics questions also brought down Coelho, who resigned as majority whip June 15. Gray was elected to succeed him on the first ballot, garnering 134 votes. His rivals, David E. Bonior of Michigan and Beryl Anthony Jr. of Arkansas, received 97 and 30 votes, respectively. Steny H. Hoyer, Md., took Gray's job as chairman of the Democratic Caucus. He beat Barbara B. Kennelly, Conn., by a 165-82 vote on June 21. *(Coelho resignation, p. 918)*

Bonior retained his position as chief deputy whip, and Anthony remained chairman of the Democratic Congressional Campaign Committee.

On Oct. 25, party leaders moved to bolster the role of Southerners and Hispanics by appointing three new deputy whips: Charles W. Stenholm, Texas; Butler Derrick, S.C.; and Esteban E. Torres, Calif.

Minority Leadership. Michel was uncontested for his fifth term as minority leader.

The election of Minority Whip Trent Lott, Miss., to the Senate kicked off a chain reaction of leadership promotions. Dick Cheney, Wyo., ran unopposed to replace Lott. Cheney had been chairman of the House Republican Conference since 1987; he also had served as chairman of the Republican Policy Committee.

Jerry Lewis of California, who was chairman of the Republican Policy Committee, succeeded Cheney as conference chairman. He beat conference Vice Chairman Lynn Martin of Illinois 85-82 on the second ballot. Lewis was ahead by just one vote on the first ballot, with seven votes going to a third candidate, William E. Dannemeyer of California.

Replacing Martin as vice chairman of the conference was Bill McCollum, Fla., who defeated outgoing conference Secretary Robert J. Lagomarsino, Calif. Vin Weber, Minn., successfully challenged Joseph M. McDade, Pa., for secretary of the conference.

Mickey Edwards, Okla., ran unopposed for chairman of the Republican Policy Committee. Guy Vander Jagt, Mich., was unanimously returned to his sixth term as chairman of the National Republican Congressional Committee. For the first time, Vander Jagt was elected to the post; until 1988 the job was assigned by the GOP leader.

Duncan Hunter, Calif., defeated Steve Bartlett, Texas, for the chairmanship of the GOP Research Committee.

House Republicans gambled on a new political strategy in March 1989 by electing a strident political activist — Newt Gingrich, Ga. — to succeed Cheney as GOP whip. Cheney resigned to become secretary of defense. The election was a political wake-up call to incumbent Republican leaders from younger members who wanted a more aggressive, activist role. Gingrich won by a bare 87-85 majority over Edward R. Madigan, Ill.

Rules. New guidelines adoped Dec. 6, 1988, gave the minority leader and the minority whip more power on the Committee on Committees, the panel that decided how members' committee assignments would be doled out. Members' voting strength was proportional to the size of the delegations they represented, except that the minority leader and the minority whip were given 12 and six votes, respectively.

An attempt to disperse power among members failed. Dannemeyer proposed a rules change to limit Republicans to one ranking committee or subcommittee seat. The idea had been rejected twice previously, and it was defeated again by a nearly 2-to-1 margin.

The Republican Conference in 1988 changed its rules to provide for election of the ranking member of the Budget Committee. Until then, the minority leader made the choice. With the new rules, the minority leader named the No. 2 Republican on Budget. The minority leader also was given the power to name the new GOP members of the Rules Committee.

Committees. House Democrats elected four new committee chairmen for the 101st Congress. Jack Brooks, Texas, replaced the retiring Peter W. Rodino Jr., N.J., as Judiciary Committee chairman. John Conyers Jr., Mich., succeeded Brooks as Government Operations chairman. Henry B. Gonzalez, Texas, took over the Banking Committee from Fernand J. St Germain, R.I., who lost his reelection bid. Leon E. Panetta, Calif., succeeded Gray as head of the Budget Committee.

Wright named Anthony C. Beilenson, Calif., as new chairman of the Select Intelligence Committee. Louis Stokes, Ohio, stepped down because he had served the full six-year limit as chairman.

Bill Frenzel, Minn., became ranking Republican on the Budget Committee, replacing Delbert L. Latta, Ohio, who retired. Frenzel gave up his ranking spot on House Administration, which was assumed by Gingrich. Bill Thomas, Calif., became ranking member following Gingrich's election as minority whip.

A number of other committees got new ranking members at the beginning of the 101st Congress: Bill Goodling, Pa., on Education and Labor; Benjamin A. Gilman, N.Y., on Post Office and Civil Service; Robert S. Walker, Pa., on Space, Science and Technology; Thomas J. Bliley Jr., Va., on Select Children, Youth and Families; Lawrence Coughlin, Pa., on Select Narcotics Abuse and Control; John T. Meyers, Ind., on Standards of Official Conduct; and Bob Stump, Ariz., on Veterans' Affairs.

Joe Moakley, D-Mass., took the gavel of the Rules Committee, upon the May 30, 1989, death of Claude Pepper, Fla. Tony P. Hall, Ohio, became chairman of the Select Committee on Hunger after Mickey Leland, Texas, died Aug. 7, 1989.

Wright Resignation

On June 6, 1989, Jim Wright, D-Texas, became the first House Speaker in history to be forced by scandal to leave the office in the middle of his term. Wright brought his 34-year career in Congress to a close June 30.

Wright served only one full term as Speaker, succeeding Thomas P. O'Neill Jr. of Massachusetts in 1987. Wright had been majority leader since 1977. He was succeeded as Speaker by Washington Democrat Thomas S. Foley.

Background

The House Committee on Standards of Official Conduct (ethics committee) opened its investigation on June 9, 1988, after the self-styled non-partisan citizens' lobby Common Cause and Rep. Newt Gingrich, R-Ga., a longtime Wright critic, filed complaints regarding Wright's financial dealings. In September, Republican leaders filed another complaint, alleging that Wright improperly disclosed security secrets about the activities of the CIA in Nicaragua. On Sept. 14, the ethics committee heard testimony from Wright, but it was unable to complete its investigation by the end of the 100th Congress. *(1988 action, Congress and the Nation Vol. VII, pp. 215, 883)*

As the 101st Congress began, few believed Wright's hold on the Speakership was at risk. Democrats remained confident that the ethics committee would clear him. Then, a seemingly unrelated matter started the erosion of his political base. Although many thought a proposal to give members of Congress a 51 percent pay raise was doomed from the start, Wright was blamed by many for its Feb. 7, 1989, demise after he abruptly switched strategies and promised opponents a floor vote on the proposal, which was not required by the procedures in place at the time. *(Pay raise, p. 965)*

The maneuvering unleashed a torrent of public criticism that left members feeling especially vulnerable to political fallout if Wright's ethics troubles did not go away. The next month the political stakes were raised dramatically when the Senate, controlled by Democrats, rejected the nomination of John Tower to be defense secretary. Talk by Republicans of exacting revenge on Wright began immediately. *(Tower nomination, p. 339)*

The most devasting blow came April 13 from the ethics committee itself, when word leaked out that two Democrats had defected and voted against Wright on a key issue. The confidence of Wright and his allies that the committee would bury the accusations was shaken.

Committee Action

On April 17, the ethics committee announced formal charges against Wright. The committee also released a blistering, 279-page investigative report compiled by Richard J. Phelan, the Chicago attorney hired in July 1988 to conduct the investigation. The committee's report, which was milder in tone, ran only 91 pages.

The allegations against Wright were spelled out in a "statement of alleged violations," citing 69 instances in five broad categories:

- Sales of his book *Reflections of a Public Man.* The committee specified seven instances in which Wright made speeches and the sponsoring organizations, in lieu of giving him an honorarium, purchased copies of the book. "The committee has reason to believe that the subject book sales were intended to avoid the limitations of law and House rules [on outside earnings]," the report said.

In another instance, the report said, a Texas real estate developer gave Wright a gift of paying for books that were never delivered to him.

- Use of free housing from Fort Worth developer George Mallick. The report said that Wright's use, in 1979-84, of two Fort Worth apartments owned by Mallick's son amounted to a gift valued at approximately $32,000 from Mallick, who was "an individual the Committee has reason to believe had a direct interest in legislation." House rules prohibited members from accepting gifts worth more than $100 a year from anyone having a direct interest in legislation. According to the *Wall Street Journal*, Mallick was responsible for a $2.2 million loan his son owed a troubled savings and loan.
- Reduced housing costs from Mallick. The report said that while Wright and his wife, Betty, paid Mallick a per diem rate for use of an apartment in Fort Worth for the time they were there in 1985-88, the apartment was devoted solely to their use. That amounted, the report said, to a subsidy of approximately $21,750.
- Salary paid to Betty Wright. From 1981 through 1984, Wright's wife received $72,000 from Mallightco Inc., an investment company the Wrights formed with Mallick and his wife. Betty Wright was vice president and the only salaried employee of the company. "There is no evidence supporting or establishing that the money paid to Mrs. Wright was in return for identifiable services or work" for the company, the committee said. It suggested that the payment could have been a way for Mallick to give money to Wright.
- Free use of a 1979 Cadillac provided by Mallightco to Betty Wright. Use of the automobile was worth $1,416 a year for 1983 through 1988, and maintenance and insurance provided by Mallightco was worth even more.

The committee decided not to pursue half of the 116 possible rule violations identified by Phelan, and it dropped all the charges raised by Gingrich.

One issue left open by the committee centered on a 1988 deal involving an oil well in Lake Sabine, Texas. The investment came under scrutiny because of allegations that the well was overvalued when Mallightco borrowed $440,000 against it in May 1988. That transaction yielded a $350,000 profit to the company and vastly increased the value of Mallightco just before Mallick bought out the Wrights' 50 percent share. Wright said he had no knowledge of the matter because the transaction took place after he had put his personal financial holdings, including his Mallightco stock, into a blind trust.

Resignation

More negative press came Wright's way May 4 when the *Washington Post* ran a story about his top aide, John P. Mack, who, while managing a discount import store in Virginia in 1973, beat and repeatedly stabbed a woman and left her for dead. He served 27 months in a county jail and was paroled to a $9,000-a-year job in Wright's congressional office. At the time, Wright's daughter was married to Mack's brother. The story had appeared earlier in other publications, but the victim allowed her name to used for the first time in the *Washington Post* account. Mack resigned May 11.

On May 17, a group of respected Democrats who had been generally supportive of Wright met and privately discussed the possibility of Wright's resigning. The meeting was described the next day on the front page of the *New York Times* — a clear signal to other Democrats that the end was near.

Wright had one last hope: At a televised hearing May 23, Wright's Houston-based attorney, Stephen D. Susman, argued that the charges should be dismissed. But key committee members made plain that they were not likely to completely exonerate Wright. The next day, Wright's lawyers met with ethics committee representatives and Phelan to discuss a proposal for Wright to step down as Speaker in exchange for the most serious charges against him being dropped. The negotiations, however, snagged.

In seclusion with his wife over Memorial Day weekend, Wright concluded it was time to quit. "It just came to me that I did have peace and happiness by doing what is best for the institution," he later said.

Wright's May 31 farewell speech was an extraordinarily dramatic event. The House chamber was packed, the air charged with tension, because Wright's plans had not been publicly announced. He faced an audience comprised of most of his colleagues, dozens of staff members and a handful of senators. The public galleries overhead were filled to capacity.

Wright began his hourlong speech with an angry, impassioned defense of his wife, describing in detail the work she had done and criticizing ethics investigators for concluding otherwise. He then defended his dealings with Mallick, saying the developer provided him benefits because of their longstanding friendship, not any self-serving interest in legislation. He also said the sales of his book were too meager ever to fit the ethics committee's description of a "scheme" to evade outside income limits. The climax came when Wright began painting in broader political strokes. He portrayed himself as a casualty of a partisan war being fought through attacks on the personal ethics of politicians. He pleaded that revenge not be sought in his behalf. When Wright was through, his colleagues gave him a standing ovation.

With the announcement of Wright's resignation, the House ethics committee postponed a scheduled June 1 meeting to vote on Wright's motion to dismiss the major charges against him. Upon Wright's resignation June 30, the committee's investigation ended.

Coelho Resignation

Democratic Whip Tony Coelho, Calif., resigned from the House June 15, 1989, in the face of intense scrutiny prompted by press reports about a questionable "junk bond" investment. Coelho's decision, announced May 26, caught many members by surprise and increased pressure on beleaguered Speaker Jim Wright, D-Texas, to step down. *(Wright resignation, p. 917)*

Coelho was first elected to Congress in 1978 and became chairman of the Democratic Congressional Campaign Committee in 1981. He transformed the committee from a small, debt-ridden office to a state-of-the-art campaign organization through which millions of dollars in campaign donations were doled out. In 1986, he became his party's first elected whip, a position that previously had been an appointed position. He was succeeded as whip by William H. Gray III, D-Pa.

Long believed to be on a track to the Speakership, Coelho had been expected to run for majority leader to replace Thomas S. Foley, D-Wash., who was seen as the only candidate to succeed Wright. Coelho said he based his decision to resign on his assessment of the ethics-related damage a run for majority leader would cause. He maintained, however, that he had done nothing seriously wrong in his investments.

In response to reports of Coelho's financial dealings, Common Cause, the non-partisan lobbying and government-watchdog group, called for an investigation by the House Committee on Standards of Official Conduct (ethics committee). Coelho tried to put an end to the questions May 14 by issuing a statement and a 16-page analysis of the deal by his attorney. The controversy involved a 1986 transaction that netted Coelho a $6,882 profit from high-risk bonds issued by the investment firm Drexel Burnham Lambert.

According to the lawyer's report, Coelho was advised to invest in the bonds by Thomas Spiegel, head of the Columbia Savings and Loan Association in California and a major Democratic donor. When the deadline for investing approached and Coelho had not yet secured loans for the $100,000 he needed, Speigel bought the bonds for him and held them for a month until Coelho arranged his own financing. After Coelho secured the loans from three California thrifts — including $50,000 from Columbia — he paid Spiegel back, with interest.

When Coelho reported the transaction on his 1986 financial disclosure form, the dates of the purchase and sale of the bonds were misstated. And while Coelho reported two of the loans, the Columbia loan was omitted. The errors were corrected in amendments filed with the ethics committee May 15, 1989.

On his 1986 income tax return, Coelho listed the profits from the bond as a long-term capital gain — the kind from a sale of assets held for more than six months, which, at the time, was taxed at a lower rate than gains from assets held for a shorter period. Coelho's account, however, suggested he did not hold the bond for more than six months.

Rep. Claude Pepper Left Long Legacy

Rep. Claude Pepper died May 30, 1989, at the age of 88. The oldest member of Congress at the time of his death, the Florida Democrat and House Rules Committee chairman also was the last surviving member from the era of his political ascension. No other member of the 101st Congress was in office when Pepper entered Congress in 1936.

After more than two hours of speeches in Pepper's honor May 31, the House voted 397-0 on H Res 163 to allow his body to lie in state in the Capitol Rotunda the next day. Pepper was the first incumbent House member to receive such an honor since Thaddeus Stevens of Pennsylvania (Whig, 1849-53; R, 1859-68).

Pepper was an Alabama farm boy who worked his way through the University of Alabama and Harvard Law School, with government assistance he never forgot. His first elected post — in the Florida state legislature — was limited to one term in 1930 after he voted against a resolution censuring the wife of President Herbert Hoover for inviting the black wife of a member of Congress to a White House tea. Pepper's narrow primary loss in 1934 to incumbent Sen. Park Trammell paved the way for his special election in 1936 to complete the term of Sen. Duncan U. Fletcher, D-Fla., who died in office.

Throughout his 41 years in Congress — 14 years in the Senate (1936-51), 27 in the House (1963-89) — Pepper waged the battle for a bigger federal role in helping the poor, the infirm and the elderly. His first speech on the Senate floor, in defense of a $1.5 billion bill to continue New Deal programs, caught the attention of President Franklin D. Roosevelt. In 1937, Pepper was an active proponent of the first federal legislation to set a minimum hourly wage (25 cents) and a maximum workday (eight hours). The same year, he also cosponsored legislation setting up the National Cancer Institute, the first of 13 National Institutes of Health (NIH) he was instrumental in creating and expanding.

Pepper became increasingly involved in world affairs. As a member of the Senate Foreign Relations Committee in 1938, he traveled to Germany and was alarmed by Adolf Hitler's show of strength at the opening of the Nazi Congress in Nuremberg. He came home convinced that the United States could not remain in isolation. In May 1940, Pepper introduced a resolution that in 1941 became the Lend-Lease Act, through which the United States provided the Allies with U.S. military equipment.

When the war was over, Pepper's political fortunes turned downward. After a visit to Europe in 1945, he described Soviet leader Josef Stalin as "a man Americans can trust," which proved devastating to his Senate career. He also lost a valuable ally with the death of Roosevelt in 1945. The 1950 Senate race in Florida became one of the most sordid in American history. Pepper's remarks about Stalin and photos of the senator standing next to black opera singer and alleged communist Paul Robeson at a 1946 political rally were used to portray him as a communist sympathizer and "nigger-lover." Pepper's opponents, who called him "Red Pepper," reportedly hired blacks to shake the senator's hands at rallies while pictures were taken for distribution. Pepper lost the Democratic primary by 67,000 votes.

In 1958, Pepper unsuccessfully sought the Democratic Senate nomination against incumbent Spessard L. Holland, a conservative. Four years later, however, a new congressional district was created for Dade County, representing a largely Jewish, elderly, black and increasingly Cuban population. Running as a liberal Democrat, Pepper won handily.

In the House, Pepper quickly allied himself with the policies of President John F. Kennedy and later became a strong advocate of Lyndon B. Johnson's Great Society. Pepper was one of a few Southern Democrats to vote for important civil rights legislation, including the Voting Rights Act of 1965. In 1977, he became chairman of the new House Select Committee on Aging, a forum he used to focus attention on problems faced by the elderly. After the 1980 presidential victory of Ronald Reagan, Pepper became the Democratic standard-bearer on Social Security. In late 1981, he was appointed to the National Commission on Social Security Reform, a bipartisan panel charged with keeping the retirement system solvent. *(Reform commission, Congress and the Nation Vol. VI, p. 662)*

Pepper helped shape a 1988 catastrophic health insurance law (PL 100-360). However, to the frustration of some of the bill's sponsors, Pepper was not satisfied with the limited measure. The Pepper Commission, initially designated the U.S. Bipartisan Commission on Comprehensive Health Care, was created to make recommendations on long-term care for the elderly and disabled and on providing comprehensive health care for the uninsured. Lawmakers subsequently repealed most of the 1988 law. *(PL 100-360, Congress and the Nation Vol. VI, p. 561; Pepper Commission, p. 584; 1989 repeal, p. 565)*

Pepper was particularly interested in advancing medical research. His last excursion from Walter Reed Army Medical Center in Washington, D.C., where he spent his final days suffering from stomach cancer, was to the NIH campus in nearby Bethesda, Md., to see a building that on May 10 had been renamed the "Claude Denson Pepper Building." On May 25, President Bush went to Walter Reed to present Pepper with the nation's highest civilian honor, the Medal of Freedom. He was only the fourth member of Congress to receive the award.

Ethics Code Rewrite

Congress in 1989 cleared the most sweeping rewrite of the congressional code of conduct in 12 years. The provisions were part of legislation (HR 3660 — PL 101-194) that also included a congressional pay hike. *(Congressional pay, p. 965)*

The changes in ethics laws and rules contained in the package received little debate on the floor, but they addressed several areas that had brought bad publicity to members in recent years.

The ethics provisions of HR 3660 (PL 101-194), as signed into law Nov. 30, 1989:

Campaign Funds

- Eliminated, by the time the 103rd Congress began in 1993, an exemption in election law (PL 96-187) that allowed House members elected before 1980 to convert campaign funds to personal use when they retired from Congress. *('Grandfather clause,' box, p. 952)*
- Froze the funds members could convert, if they retired before the end of the 102nd Congress, at no more than what they had on hand when HR 3660 was enacted.

Gifts and Travel

- Authorized the Office of Government Ethics to issue rules for receipt of gifts by all federal employees.
- **House.** Amended rules governing House members and employees to bar receiving gifts from any one person, except relatives, more than the ceiling set by the Foreign Gifts Act — $200 as of Jan. 1, 1990, and automatically adjusted for inflation every three years.
- Exempted from the annual gift limit the value of meals and drinks, unless they were part of overnight lodging.
- Raised from $35 to $75 the threshold below which gifts would not count toward the annual ceiling.
- Limited the exemption on gifts of "personal hospitality" to bar receiving more than 30 days of lodging a year from someone other than a relative and to require members, if hospitality extended more than four days, to ensure that it was personal — not corporate-financed or being claimed as a business expense.
- Allowed private sources to pay travel expenses for no more than four days of domestic travel and seven days (excluding travel time) for international trips.
- Allowed travel expenses for one accompanying relative.
- Allowed the Committee on Standards of Official Conduct to waive gift and travel restrictions in exceptional circumstances.
- **Senate.** Amended rules governing senators and Senate employees to prohibit receiving more than $300 a year in gifts from any one source other than relatives and kept the $100 limit on gifts from people with a direct interest in legislation.
- Dropped an exemption allowing unlimited gifts of entertainment.
- Allowed private sources to pay travel expenses for no more than three days of domestic travel and seven days for international trips. Both limits excluded travel time.
- Allowed travel expenses to be paid for one accompanying Senate aide or a spouse.

Ethics Committee

- **House.** Expanded the Committee on Standards of Official Conduct, beginning in the 102nd Congress, from 12 to 14 members and limited each member to no more than three terms during any five successive Congresses. *(Story, p. 947)*
- Required the committee to divide its investigative and adjudicative functions by naming a four- or six-member subcommittee to review allegations whenever a preliminary inquiry was opened. The other members would hold disciplinary hearings when the investigative subcommittee found reason to believe that rules were violated and issued a statement of alleged violation.
- Prohibited the committee from making public a statement of alleged violation until the accused could draft a response, and required that the two documents be released simultaneously.
- Required the committee to issue a report on any investigation, regardless of the case's disposition.
- Allowed the committee to investigate only violations alleged to have occurred in the three most recent Congresses, unless older violations related to more recent ones or unless specifically instructed by the House.
- Allowed members facing ethics sanctions to bring an attorney onto the House floor during consideration of the committee's recommendations.
- Directed the committee to establish an Office on Advice and Education to guide members and employees.

Financial Disclosure

- Brought all three branches of government under the same financial disclosure law, although each would continue to be responsible for administering requirements for its own employees.
- Raised from $100 to $200 the threshold below which income from any source need not be disclosed and raised from $35 to $75 the threshold below which gifts need not be reported.
- Required members of Congress and other federal officials who had charitable contributions made in their behalf in lieu of honoraria to disclose the source and amount of such contributions beginning in 1991. The charities receiving such contributions would not have to be publicly reported but would have to be disclosed in confidential reports to the House Committee on Standards of Official Conduct or other ethics offices.
- Required disclosure of the source and amount of any honoraria spouses of reporting officials earned.
- Required more detailed disclosure of travel reimbursements, including an itinerary and dates of travel.
- Specified that underlying assets of regulated investment companies did not have to be reported if the firm was widely diversified and the reporting official had no control over it.
- Required all federal officials, including members of Congress, to file a final financial disclosure form, known as a "termination report," after they left office.
- Extended the time within which financial disclosure reports must be made available to the public from 15 days to 30 days after they were filed.
- Doubled from $5,000 to $10,000 the maximum civil penalty for violation of financial disclosure law and established a $200 penalty fee for late filing.

Post-Employment Lobbying

- Barred members and officers of Congress from lobbying the legislative branch for a year after they left office.
- Barred former congressional staff members for a year after leaving employment from lobbying the member, office or committee for which they had worked. Leadership staff members were barred from lobbying the members and employees of the leadership for the chamber in which they served.
- Kept a lifetime ban on all former executive branch employees from lobbying on matters in which they were "personally and substantially involved" while in office and kept a two-year ban on matters that were "under their official responsibility within the year preceding termination of government service." No such prohibitions would be applied to the legislative branch, however. *('Revolving door,' p. 861)*
- Barred former Executive Level I officials throughout the government and Level II officials in the White House for a year after leaving office from lobbying any officials at Levels I through V.
- Imposed a one-year ban on lobbying by former executive employees and military officers at the GS-17 pay level or above at the agency they had served. Although the civil service pay scale did not apply to congressional staff, any legislative branch employees paid at the GS-17 level or higher would be barred for a year from lobbying the members who employed them or the committees for which they had worked. Former employees also would be barred from "representing, aiding or advising" foreign governments or foreign political parties for a year.
- Barred executive branch employees who were "personally and substantially involved" in trade or treaty negotiations within a year before leaving office from representing or advising people concerned with such negotiations. The ban would last a year.

Miscellaneous Provisions

- **Conflict of Interest.** Barred House employees from becoming involved with the judiciary or government agencies on non-legislative matters in which they had a significant financial interest.
- Provided civil and misdemeanor penalties, in addition to the existing criminal ones, to impose on federal employees for violating conflict-of-interest law.
- **Procurement Law.** Postponed for one year implementing procurement reform laws that barred former federal employees from working on a procurement contract for two years if they played a role in awarding the contract.
- **Car Rentals.** Relaxed rules barring government officials from using officially leased cars for incidental personal use.
- **Senior Executive Service.** Required members of the executive branch's senior executive service to be recertified in that status every three years beginning in 1991, unless they had been employed as a senior executive for at least 13 years.

Ethics Probes

Besides the two House Democratic leaders who resigned amidst questions of propriety and the five senators who came under scrutiny for their actions in behalf of a prominent political contributor, many other members of the 101st Congress found themselves the target of ethics investigations. *(Wright resignation, p. 917; Coelho resignation, p. 918; Keating Five, p. 975)*

Sen. Dave Durenberger

The Senate on July 25, 1990, denounced Dave Durenberger, R-Minn., for conduct it said was "clearly and unequivocally unethical," was "reprehensible" and had "brought the Senate into dishonor and disrepute."

The denouncement resolution (S Res 311) adopted by the Senate, 96-0, cited Durenberger for:

- Having a book deal with Piranha Press, a Minnesota company, that the Senate Ethics Committee's special counsel, Robert S. Bennett, said amounted to a gimmick to "sanitize" speaking fees that Durenberger otherwise could not have accepted under Senate limits on honoraria.
- Failing to report expense-paid trips he took in connection with the book deal.
- Accepting Senate reimbursement for rent paid on a Minneapolis condominium in which he shared ownership.
- Having improper communications with the blind trust that held his interest in the condominium.
- Accepting free limousine services for personal use.
- Converting campaign funds to personal use when he signed over a $5,000 political donation to Piranha Press.

Along with the denouncement, the Senate ordered Durenberger to pay back the Senate $29,050 plus interest for reimbursements he received for the cost of staying in his Minneapolis condo. That sum was owed on top of the $11,005 Durenberger already had repaid the Senate in early 1990, based on an incomplete calculation by the Rules Committee of the wrongful reimbursements he received. The Senate also required Durenberger to pay approximately $95,000 to charities with which he had no affiliation — the amount of honoraria he allegedly obtained improperly.

Durenberger's case marked the first time the full Senate debated disciplining one of its members since 1982, when it considered expelling Harrison A. Williams Jr., D-N.J., for his role in the Abscam scandal. Williams resigned before the Senate voted. *(Congress and the Nation Vol. VI, p. 804)*

The last time the Senate voted on a disciplinary resolution was in 1979, when Herman E. Talmadge, D-Ga., was accused of financial improprieties. Talmadge was the only previous senator who was denounced. Other senators had been censured or condemned. *(Congress and the Nation Vol. V, p. 924)*

Durenberger's denouncement was the senator's second brush with the Ethics Committee in two years. In 1987-88, the panel investigated allegations that Durenberger, chairman of the Intelligence Committee in 1985-86, inproperly disclosed classified information. Though the panel did not recommend any punishment, it did criticize Durenberger for appearing to disclose "sensitive national security information" about U.S. espionage. *(Congress and the Nation Vol. VII, p. 887)*

Background. Piranha Press, owned by a friend of Durenberger's, published two books by Durenberger: *Neither Madmen Nor Messiahs*, a collection of white papers on defense policy, in 1984; and *Prescriptions for Change*, a collection of speeches about health care, in 1986. Piranha Press paid Durenberger $100,000 in quarterly installments

Capitol Bombing

Three women pleaded guilty in U.S. District Court in Washington, D.C., on Sept. 7, 1990, to bombing the U.S. Capitol in 1983 as a political protest against U.S. military action in Grenada and Lebanon. Marilyn J. Buck, Linda S. Evans and Laura J. Whitehorn also admitted participating in a conspiracy to bomb several other buildings in Washington and New York from 1983 to 1985.

Sentenced Nov. 28, Buck and Whitehorn received 10 years in the Capitol bombing case; Evans, five years. Buck and Evans were given five years on the conspiracy count, to run concurrently with their other sentence. Whitehorn drew a five-year term, to run consecutively.

The Capitol explosion took place Nov. 7, 1983, just outside the Senate chamber. The blast caused minor damage but no injuries. In May 1988, seven people were charged with the bombing, but one remained a fugitive and charges were dropped against three others. *(Details of explosion, Congress and the Nation Vol. VI, p. 813)*

over two years in return for his making 113 appearances to promote the books. The groups he spoke to were asked to write their checks to Piranha Press, which raised questions about whether Durenberger's income from the publisher was redirected honoraria.

Bennett contended that no real intent to promote the books ever existed. He traced the deal to Durenberger's need to replace lost honoraria income. The senator reported $92,750 in honoraria in 1983, the last year the Senate permitted members to collected unlimited speech fees. New Senate rules capped honoraria income at $22,530 in 1985 and $30,000 in 1986, the years of the book deal. In those two years, Durenberger made traditional honoraria speeches until he reached the limit. At that point, speeches were designated as "Piranha Press events," Bennett said. *(Background, honoraria income, Congress and the Nation Vol. VII, p. 897)*

The senator's attorney in 1983 asked the Federal Election Commission (FEC) to rule on the nature of the publishing agreement. The agency said that the payments were not honoraria but stipends — a ruling Durenberger would use as a shield. The request for the opinion, however, did not mention what Bennett said were three crucial facts: Durenberger's contract called for the groups he addressed to pay the publisher a fee; the appearances stemmed from requests for speeches, not book promotions; and the promotional events were identical to traditional honorarium events.

The condominium deal began in 1983, when Durenberger decided he could not afford two residences — a house in McLean, Va., and the one-bedroom condominium. Owning the Minneapolis condo where he stayed also prevented him from being reimbursed by the Senate for living expenses on his frequent trips to Minnesota. Durenberger first changed his legal residence to his parent's address in Avon, Minn., then he sought to change the ownership of the condo.

Initially, Durenberger and Roger Scherer, a friend and political backer who owned another condo in the same building, considered swapping condos. After discovering that idea would have unfavorable tax implications, they settled on a partnership, according to Bennett.

Durenberger stayed in the same condo on his trips home but began billing the Senate for his expenses, paying rent to the partnership. After passage of the 1986 tax overhaul (PL 99-514), which removed the partnership's tax advantages, Scherer decided to dissolve it. Durenberger sold his condo for $52,804 in 1987, but for reasons never fully explained, the sales documents were not forwarded to the purchaser until late 1989. *(Tax law, Congress and the Nation Vol. VII, p. 79)*

From August 1983 until mid-November 1989, Durenberger collected $40,055 from the U.S. Treasury for per diem expenses while staying at the condo. Before seeking reimbursement, Durenberger said, his staff consulted with the Rules and Ethics committees; no objections were raised at the time. Furthermore, he noted that the Senate disbursing office did not question the arrangement, even when the nature of the partnership was clear.

Durenberger asked the Senate Rules Committee to review the rental agreement after it became public knowledge in December 1989. The panel told Durenberger in January that Senate travel regulations prohibited a senator from being reimbursed for "daily expenses incurred while residing at his usual place of residence in his home state" during congressional recesses. Durenberger said he believed that he could be reimbursed because another address was his "official and voting" residence. After receiving the ruling, Durenberger announced he would repay the Senate $11,005 with interest for reimbursements he collected in 1983-87.

Durenberger also asked the Ethics Committee to review whether it was proper for senators to be affiliated with non-profit organizations that raised money from special interest groups. On Dec. 20, 1989, he announced his resignation as chairman of two such organizations — Americans for Generational Equity and the Foundation for Future Choices. The *Minneapolis Star-Tribune* had reported allegations by a former staffer of the first group that Durenberger used the think tank for political purposes during his 1988 re-election campaign. Durenberger said the charges were baseless. The subject did not become part of the committee's investigation.

Committee, Floor Action. The Ethics Committee initiated a preliminary inquiry into Durenberger's arrangement with Piranha Press on March 1, 1989. Bennett was named as outside counsel on July 13. The committee Aug. 3 voted to proceed to an "initial review" and expanded the scope of the case Dec. 21 to include allegations about Durenberger's condominium deal.

On Feb. 7, 1990, the *Minneapolis Star-Tribune* reported that the Commercial State Bank in St. Paul gave Durenberger $927,078 in loans over 10 years, most without collateral and some at low interest rates. Little was made of the bank loan allegation during the committee inquiry, and the Senate did not mention the issue in its resolution of denouncement.

Durenberger appeared before the committee Feb. 8, telling the panel that he had gotten approval from "appropriate, official bodies" before opening the book and real estate deals. Nevertheless, the Ethics Committee on Feb.

22 found "substantial credible evidence" that Durenberger broke federal law and Senate rules.

The committee, however, said it found no evidence to continue examining allegations that Durenberger improperly used his staff to write his books or that he improperly solicited speeches in Boston during 1985 and 1986. The latter allegation stemmed from his supposed desire to have his travel expenses covered for visits to a marriage counselor.

Formal public hearings were held by the Ethics Committee June 12-13. For the first time in its 26-year history, the committee conducted business before television cameras. The hearings were expected to last two weeks, but they abruptly ended after two days. Durenberger successfully petitioned to halt the proceedings to avoid the political cost and financial burden of weeks of trial-like hearings.

When the hearings ended, the committee was left to decide not what to believe, but what to make of it. The dispute boiled down to Bennett's June 12 attack on Durenberger and the senator's June 13 defense of his actions.

A month after the hearing, Bennett completed his final report and submitted it to the Ethics Committee. On July 18, the committee unanimously approved the resolution of denouncement. The committee report on the inquiry was released July 20 and included Bennett's full report. The committee found no criminal wrongdoing but referred the case to the Justice Department and the FEC for further investigation.

The full Senate July 25 conducted a three-hour proceeding on the case and then, without a fight from Durenberger, voted 96-0 to denounce him.

On April 2, 1993, a federal grand jury charged Durenberger, along with two associates, with two felonies — one count of conspiring to make false claims to the Senate and one count of actually making false claims. The indictment came after Durenberger refused to plead guilty to misdemeanor charges. If convicted, Durenberger could face 10 years in prison and $500,000 in fines.

Sen. Alfonse M. D'Amato

The Senate Ethics Committee decided Nov. 17, 1989, to hire an outside counsel to review a complaint against Alfonse M. D'Amato, R-N.Y., alleging that he improperly lobbied the Department of Housing and Urban Development (HUD), which was the subject of a House investigation, in behalf of developers who were political contributors. After a two-year investigation, the committee closed the case against D'Amato, citing lack of evidence to charge him with breaking any rules. *(HUD scandal, p. 676; 1991 D'Amato action, p. 943)*

New York Democrat Mark Green, D'Amato's unsuccessful opponent in 1986, had filed a complaint July 17 with the Ethics Committee asking it to look into a range of allegations based on newspaper reports. The complaint was amended Sept. 26; Henry F. Schuelke III was named outside counsel Nov. 27; and the inquiry was formally opened Dec. 22.

The *New York Times* reported that D'Amato in March 1984 wrote to HUD in support of a Buffalo housing renovation project whose partners included two of his political backers. *Newsday* reported that D'Amato, in a July 1986 letter, urged HUD to finance a project at Sackets Harbor in upstate New York represented by his brother Armand's law firm and developed by a construction firm whose executives were political contributors. D'Amato said his support for the Sackets Harbor project predated the involvement of his political contributors.

D'Amato also was accused of helping Wedtech Corp., a Bronx, N.Y., defense contractor that eventually went bankrupt, in return for $30,000 in illegal campaign contributions and of being the beneficiary of a system under which Unisys, a defense contractor with offices in New York, told executives to donate thousands of dollars to D'Amato's campaign and then to seek reimbursement. D'Amato said he did not know about either contribution scheme.

The *Wall Street Journal* reported that in 1985 D'Amato, while chairman of the Senate Banking, Housing and Urban Affairs Subcommittee on Securities, dropped his backing of legislation restricting high-risk "junk bonds" after receiving $70,000 in donations from Drexel Burnham Lambert. D'Amato said no connection existed between the contribution and his position on the legislation.

Rep. Barney Frank

The House on July 26, 1990, formally reprimanded Barney Frank, D-Mass., for improperly using his office to help a male prostitute. Despite politicians' election-year jitters about ethics issues — heightened in this case because homosexuality was involved — the House quashed efforts to overturn the unanimous recommendation of the Committee on Standards of Official Conduct (ethics committee) and punish Frank more severely.

The last House member to be reprimanded was Austin J. Murphy, D-Pa., in 1987, who diverted government resources to his former law firm, allowed another member to vote for him on the House floor and kept a "no-show" employee on his payroll. *(Murphy, Congress and the Nation Vol. VII, p. 885)*

The *Washington Times* Aug. 25, 1989, reported that Frank in April 1985 bought sex from a man named Steve Gobie and subsequently hired him as a household assistant. Frank, who made his sexual orientation public in 1987, confirmed some details of the report but denied the key suggestion: that he knew Gobie was running a prostitution service from Frank's Washington, D.C., home. *(Frank's homosexuality, Congress and the Nation Vol. VII, p. 890)*

Frank said he knew Gobie was a prostitute but tried to persuade him to get a legitimate job and change his ways. According to Frank's account, Gobie said he could not get a job because he was on probation. After hiring Gobie as his housekeeper and driver — using personal, not congressional, funds — Frank wrote several letters on stationery bearing a congressional letterhead to Alexandria, Va., probation officers to certify that Gobie was employed.

Gobie told the *Washington Times* that he believed Frank was "fully aware" of his activities. Frank disputed that assertion. He said he kicked Gobie out of his apartment in August 1987, after his landlady twice warned him of questionable goings-on in his absence.

On Sept. 7, 1989, the *Washington Times* reported that Frank used his standing as a member of Congress to cancel parking tickets incurred by Gobie while driving Frank's car. Gobie alleged that he got some of the tickets while using Frank's car for his prostitution business. Frank acknowledged that he had requested the waiver of some parking tickets but said he did so only in cases when Gobie was using Frank's care for official business. Frank said he paid for other tickets out of his own pocket.

Members commonly asked the sergeant-at-arms to write off parking tickets. District of Columbia law allowed members of Congress to park in many otherwise illegal spaces if they were on official business.

Three days after the initial newspaper account, Frank requested an ethics committee probe. The panel announced Sept. 12 that it would open an investigation.

In its report (H Rept 101-610) on the inquiry filed July 20, 1990, the committee said no conclusive evidence was found that Frank knew Gobie was running a prostitution service until his landlady mentioned seeing suspicious activity. The panel criticized Frank for a misleading memo written in support of ending Gobie's probation. The memo included assertions that Gobie met Frank through "mutual friends" — when in fact Frank had responded to Gobie's escort service ad in a gay newspaper — and that Gobie was adhering to his probation requirements, when Frank knew Gobie was engaged in prostitution. Frank said candor on those two points would have revealed his own homosexuality. Although the committee concluded that Frank had not improperly pressured probation officials, it said the memo "could be perceived as an attempt to use political influence." The panel also ordered Frank to pay the 33 parking tickets improperly waived because whether they were incurred on official business was not clear.

Many members of the ethics committee sought a light sanction that would avoid action by the full House — a letter of reproval. However, many other members, on and off the committee, thought that, given the extensive publicity that surrounded the case, a letter of reproval would be too mild. On July 19, the committee agreed to the harsher punishment of reprimand.

On the floor July 26, the House rejected, 38-390, a resolution (H Res 442) to expel Frank, the ultimate sanction. Minority Whip Newt Gingrich, R-Ga., then made a motion to recommit the reprimand (H Res 440) to the ethics committee with instructions to report back a recommendation of censure. Censure was considered a greater penalty because, under House rules, the chastised member had to stand in the well of the House when the charges were read and could not hold a chairmanship for the rest of that Congress. The motion was rejected on a **key vote of 141-287 (R 129-46; D 12-241)**. The House adopted the resolution to reprimand Frank 408-18. *(1990 key votes, p. 1039)*

Frank, who did not contest the ethic committee's findings, went to the well of the House near the end of the debate to apologize to his colleagues. Attributing his misconduct to the strain of concealing his homosexuality at the time, Frank said, "I should have known better. I do now."

Rep. Jim Bates

On Oct. 18, 1989, the House ethics committee sent Jim Bates, D-Calif., a "letter of reproval," one of its lightest penalties, for sexually harassing women on his staff.

The controversy surrounding Bates first surfaced in October 1988, when the Capitol Hill publication *Roll Call* made public allegations by former aides that he had asked them for daily hugs, patted their behinds and made other suggestive remarks and gestures. Two former staffers filed a formal complaint with the ethics committee that same month.

The panel said in its letter that Bates violated rules barring discrimination against employees on the basis of sex. It also concluded that he improperly used his congressional office for campaign activity; Bates admitted his campaign staff used official telephones for fund raising. In addition, the committee directed Bates to write a formal apology to the two women who filed the complaint.

Rep. Gus Savage

In a report released Feb. 2, 1990, the House Committee on Standards of Official Conduct concluded that Rep. Gus Savage, D-Ill., made improper sexual advances to a young woman while on an official trip to Africa. The committee, however, did not propose disciplinary action.

The *Washington Post* July 19, 1989, reported allegations that Savage sexually accosted a Peace Corps volunteer during a visit to Zaire. The 28-year-old woman said that Savage had urged her to have sex and fondled her in the back seat of his car despite her repeated demands that he stop. According to the newspaper account, the volunteer had been chosen by the American ambassador to brief Savage on Peace Corps activities and accompany his entourage to some nightspots.

Three Democrats requested an ethics committee investigation into the incident: Barney Frank of Massachusetts, Patricia Schroeder of Colorado, and Matthew F. McHugh of New York. The committee voted Aug. 3 to open a preliminary hearing.

The committee concluded the inquiry without a formal disciplinary hearing. The panel based its conclusions on interviews with Savage and others on the tour, as well as on a sworn deposition from the volunteer. Savage denied any wrongdoing, although he did write a letter to the woman Nov. 20, 1989, saying: "I never intended to offend and was not aware that you felt offended at the time."

In its report, approved Jan. 31, 1990, the ethics panel concluded that "Rep. Savage did, in fact, make sexual advances to the Peace Corps volunteer." The report stated that Savage's actions were contrary to the House rule requiring members' behavior to "reflect creditably" on the House. "The committee clearly disapproves of Rep. Savage's conduct," the report said.

Although it recommended no punishment, the committee said it was putting other House members "on notice" that such conduct in the future would be judged "with the clear possibility that additional action might be pursued."

In an angry floor speech Feb. 1, delivered before the report was released, Savage, an African-American, said he was a victim of racism in politics and the media and launched a broad attack on those questioning his conduct. Savage denounced the *Washington Post* and other news organizations, and he referred to the three Democrats who requested the investigation, but not by name. He said, "Believe it or not, among these self-appointed guardians of personal morality was one who since has admitted keeping and prostituting as a homosexual," alluding to Frank, who in 1987 announced that he was a homosexual and in 1989 acknowledged that he had a relationship with a male prostitute. Savage went on, "As for the other two so-called liberals, I urge them to review their sensitivity to racism and their respect for fairness."

Savage deleted his criticism from the text he submitted for the permanent record of floor proceedings at the suggestion of the House parliamentarian, William H. Brown, who said the presiding officer should have ruled the personal criticism out of order because it impugned the motives of colleagues. Most members of Congress routinely edited their remarks before submitting them for the record, but they typically made minor changes, such as corrections of grammar, instead of wholesale omissions.

In the wake of Savage's criticisms, the House Feb. 7 overwhelmingly approved, 373-30, a resolution (H Res 330) calling for a review by the Committee on House Administration of rules that allowed members to change the text of what they said during floor debate when it was reprinted in the *Congressional Record.* The resolution was introduced by Robert S. Walker, R-Pa., who said the review was needed to maintain the "integrity of the proceedings" of the House.

Savage later drew fire with a campaign speech he made in his Chicago district. At a March 17 rally, he listed what he called "pro-Israel, Jewish" contributors to the campaign of his strongest challenger, Mel Reynolds. Savage said his speech was not anti-Semitic but was distorted by news organizations that he contended were controlled by racist whites.

Rep. Bill Dickinson

In a letter sent in late October 1989 by the House ethics committee, Rep. Bill Dickinson, R-Ala., was asked to explain a transaction involving $300,000 he obtained from Bill Collier, an Alabama friend and defense contractor. According to press accounts, Dickinson turned over the money to an investor for one-third of the profits even though he put up no money of his own.

Dickinson said in a letter to an Alabama newspaper that the business deal, which ultimately failed, was unrelated to — and came long after — his efforts to help Collier's company, the district's largest private employer.

No formal complaint was ever lodged against Dickinson, and the committee did not formally investigate him.

Rep. Donald E. "Buz" Lukens

Amidst sexual misconduct charges, Donald E. "Buz" Lukens, R-Ohio, resigned his House seat on Oct. 24, 1990.

Lukens was convicted May 26, 1989, of a misdemeanor for having sex with an underage girl in Columbus, Ohio. The unidentified girl testified that she and a 19-year-old friend went to Lukens' home on Nov. 6, 1988 — the day before her 17th birthday. Lukens, she said, met them at the door in only his boxer shorts, and the three of them went to bed together.

The case against Lukens unfolded after the girl's mother contacted a Columbus television station. Subsequently, the station surreptitiously videotaped a meeting between the mother and Lukens, at which Lukens appeared to offer to help the unemployed woman get a government job.

Lukens was sentenced June 30 to the maximum: six months in prison and a $1,000 fine. However, all but a month of the jail time and half of the fine were suspended on the condition that Lukens complete a year's probation and participate in a counseling program for sex offenders. On June 21, Lukens' colleagues in the Republican Conference voted to seek an ethics investigation. The House ethics committee opened its investigation on Lukens in August 1989.

Despite pressure from Republicans in Congress and at home, Lukens refused to resign and said he would appeal his conviction. A state appeals court on June 12, 1990, upheld the ruling.

The ethics committee probe was shelved after Lukens lost his bid for re-election in a May 1990 primary. However, the committee Oct. 22 revealed new charges that Lukens made "unwanted and unsolicited sexual advances to a congressional employee." The panel said it was expanding its long-dormant investigation of Lukens to include the new allegations, which centered on reports that he fondled and propositioned an elevator operator in the Capitol.

Lukens did not comment on the allegations but said in his resignation letter that he was leaving "for the good of the Congress and the integrity of the institution."

On Jan. 2, 1991, Lukens gave up his appeals and reported to jail. He was released Jan. 11, after serving nine days.

Rep. Robert Garcia

Robert Garcia, D-N.Y., resigned from the House Jan. 7, 1990, 12 days before he was sentenced to three years in prison for extortion. A three-judge panel of the 2nd U.S. Circuit Court of Appeals June 29 overturned the conviction. U.S. District Judge Leonard Sand, however, Dec. 3 refused to block a new trial.

Garcia and his wife, Jane Lee Garcia, were convicted Oct. 20, 1989, on two counts of extortion and one count of conspiracy. They were accused of taking more than $170,000 in payments and interest-free loans, plus a diamond necklace, from the defunct Wedtech Corp., a South Bronx machine shop that grew into a multimillion-dollar defense corporation. Both were acquitted of four counts of bribery and receipt of illegal gratuities.

In overturning the convictions, the appellate court said the Garcias' actions fell short of extortion.

Before district court, Garcia and his wife argued that a new trial would violate the Double Jeopardy Clause of the Constitution because they would be tried twice for the same offense. Sand, however, ruled that the Constitution did not bar the retrial of a defendant who won a reversal of a conviction on appeal.

Garcia had been indicted Nov. 21, 1988. *(Background, Congress and the Nation Vol. VII, p. 885)*

Rep. Newt Gingrich

The House Committee on Standards of Official Conduct March 7, 1990, dropped its investigation of House Republican Whip Newt Gingrich, Ga.

Interest in the case was high because Gingrich instigated the 1988-89 probe that led to the resignation of Speaker Jim Wright, D-Texas. At a news conference March 8, Gingrich dismissed the accusations against himself as a "political smear."

Rep. Bill Alexander, D-Ark., filed a complaint against Gingrich April 11, 1989, asking for an investigation of the financing behind a 1984 book that Gingrich cowrote with his wife, Marianne, and writer David Drake. The book, entitled *Window of Opportunity*, promoted the vision of the "Conservative Opportunity Society," a group of conservative Republicans that Gingrich helped create.

The questions Alexander posed stemmed from a March 20 *Washington Post* article, which detailed the formation of a limited partnership to promote the book. A total of $105,000 was raised — $5,000 from each of 21 investors who included Republican activists and businesspeople. Gingrich was not a partner, but his wife was; she received about $10,000 for work related to publication of the book. While the book lost money, it still created a tax benefit for the investors.

Alexander's complaint brought up the issue of whether Gingrich devised the arrangement to circumvent House rules on the limits to outside income, the acceptance of gifts, the conversion of campaign funds to personal use and the conversion of government resources to personal use. (A member of Gingrich's congressional staff critiqued chapters of the book.) Gingrich and his wife said they had nothing to hide. She said they checked regularly with the ethics committee in arranging the book deal. He likened the partnership arrangement to the production and promotion of a Broadway play.

The ethics committee in a June memo concluded that the evidence provided by Alexander did not meet the threshold required for opening a preliminary investigation: that the allegations "merit further inquiry."

In early July, Alexander amended his complaint to draw parallels between the book promotion deal and a trip Gingrich took to Europe in 1977 to write a book that he never finished. Gingrich accepted $13,000 from patrons for a novel he did not complete because of his interceding election to the House.

In its July 24 issue, the *Atlanta Business Chronicle* reported that Gingrich allegedly gave large, but temporary, year-end pay raises to his staff members when they returned to his congressional office after taking leave without government pay to work on his campaigns in 1986 and 1988. Federal law and House rules barred members from using public funds to compensate for campaign work. Gingrich denied any wrongdoing and said he was being chastised for a legitimate practice that was widespread on Capitol Hill — members giving their staff year-end bonuses.

The ethics committee announced July 25 that it would retain an independent counsel to look into the allegations made against Gingrich. The panel chose the same Chicago law firm that conducted its investigation into Wright's affairs — Phelan, Pope & John — to help decide whether to open a preliminary inquiry. In a closed meeting Oct. 18, the committee was told by the firm that no reason was found to open a formal investigation.

A week later, Alexander filed a second complaint, claiming that Gingrich misused campaign funds and official resources. Gingrich was accused of failing to report contributions to another candidate and a mortgage for real estate he bought with his daughter; using official stationery to help recruit cruise participants for a Florida travel company and to promote newspaper columns by someone connected to a political contributor; and using his campaign ads to urge defeat of a state constitutional amendment.

After further questioning of Gingrich, the ethics committee voted 11-0 on March 7, 1990, to dismiss all of Alexander's allegations. In its report, the panel said, "The facts alleged in the complaints, even if true, have been generally deemed not to state violations" of House rules or law.

The committee, however, concluded that Gingrich should have reported his participation in his daughter's home purchase. In its letter to him, the committee directed Gingrich to amend his financial disclosure forms to include the real estate transaction. The panel also said that a Gingrich aide violated House rules in sending out the cruise promotion on official stationery under the congressional frank. It told Gingrich he had been "remiss in [his] oversight and administration of [his] congressional office" and directed him to guard against future abuse of mail and office resources.

Rep. Roy Dyson

A complaint against Rep. Roy Dyson, D-Md., filed by a GOP official just before election day 1988, was dismissed by the House Committee on Standards of Official Conduct on Feb. 2, 1990. Dyson allegedly misused official funds for campaign purposes and discriminated against women in hiring.

Dyson's office practices had been thrust into the public eye in mid-1988 when his administrative aide, Tom Pappas, committed suicide after the *Washington Post* reported on his unorthodox personnel practices.

Despite dismissal of the charges, ethics remained a major issue in Dyson's 1990 campaign for re-election. He was defeated at the polls by Republican Wayne T. Gilchrest.

Del. Walter E. Fauntroy

The Justice Department, after deciding not to prosecute Del. Walter E. Fauntroy, D-D.C., on allegations of payroll padding, referred the case to the House Committee on Standards of Official Conduct in 1990. The ethics committee took no action and let the case drop, as Fauntroy planned to leave office at the end of the 101st Congress.

Fauntroy was the subject of a 15-month federal investigation, which concluded in late April 1990, concerning allegations that he improperly kept Thomas John Savage, son of Rep. Gus Savage, D-Ill., on his payroll at the same time the younger Savage was living in Chicago and running for the Illinois legislature. House rules required staff members to work in Washington, D.C., or in the representative's district. Fauntroy said he hired Thomas John Savage to help coordinate the drive for D.C. statehood.

Rep. Gerry Sikorski

The House ethics committee dismissed its investigation of Rep. Gerry Sikorski, D-Minn., on Feb. 2, 1990. The case against Sikorski was filed after articles in several newspapers reported allegations that he had misused staffers by requiring them to do personal chores and campaign work.

Rep. Arlan Stangeland

The Minnesota Democratic Farmer-Labor Party the week of April 2, 1990, filed a complaint with the House Committee on Standards of Official Conduct against Arlan Stangeland, R-Minn., over a series of phone calls Stangeland charged to his House credit card. The ethics committee took no action in 1990 and let the matter drop after Stangeland lost his re-election bid to Colin C. Peterson, D.

The *St. Cloud Times* reported in January 1990 that Stangeland made 341 long-distance calls, at a cost of $762, to or from phones of a Virginia woman who Stangeland said was a friend and lobbyist. Although he initially said that some of the calls might have been personal, Stangeland later said that all were made for business reasons. A former staff aide, he said, stole phone records from his office to try to smear him.

Rep. Harold E. Ford

The trial of Rep. Harold E. Ford, D-Tenn., ended April 27, 1990, with a hung jury. Ford, along with three co-defendants, was indicted April 24, 1987, on 19 counts of conspiracy, bank fraud and mail fraud, based on accusations that they participated in an influence-buying scheme. The trial had been delayed because of a change in venue from Knoxville to Memphis, Ford's hometown.

While under indictment, Ford had to give up his chairmanship of the Ways and Means Subcommittee on Human Resources. He sought to turn his trial to political advantage, repeatedly accusing federal prosecutors of waging a "personal racial vendetta" against him.

Ford was acquitted of 18 charges on April 9, 1993, in a second trial; one count of mail fraud had been thrown out. The jury of 11 whites and one black was selected from the mostly while Jackson area and bused to Memphis.

Rep. Floyd H. Flake

New York Democratic Rep. Floyd H. Flake and his wife, Margarett, were indicted Aug. 2, 1990, on 17 charges of conspiracy, fraud and tax evasion. The charges subsequently were dropped. *(1991 action, p. 945)*

The Flakes allegedly embezzled funds from a senior citizens' housing project run by the Allen African Methodist Episcopal church, where Rep. Flake was pastor, and failed to report the income on their tax returns. Rep. Flake allegedly siphoned off $75,000 in transportation funds from the Allen Senior Citizens Apartments — a $10 million, 300-unit seniors' housing project — and used $66,000 in other church funds for personal purposes.

Pocket-Veto Power

Does a president have the power to pocket-veto legislation by withholding his signature during any adjournment or only after Congress adjourned sine die to end its final session? President George Bush argued that he could exercise the pocket veto whenever Congress adjourned for more than three days. However, many members of Congress contended that a president could pocket veto a bill only after final adjournment. HR 849, which was approved by two House committees in 1990, sought to codify that position.

Article I, Section 7 of the Constitution gave the president the power to sign a measure into law or veto it by returning it to Congress with his objections. Congress then could try to override this veto. If the president did not return the bill within 10 days, excluding Sundays, it became law without his signature, "unless the Congress by their adjournment prevent its return, in which case it shall not be a law." The president pocketed the bill, so to speak, and it died from inaction.

While Congress was on its summer recess in August 1989, Bush pocket-vetoed a minor measure (H J Res 390) to expedite signing of the savings and loan (S&L) bailout bill (HR 1278 — PL 101-73). Lawmakers saw Bush as attempting to set a precedent, because the legislation was otherwise inconsequential. Rep. Butler Derrick, D-S.C., chairman of the House Rules Subcommittee on the Legislative Process, said members considered suing Bush but backed off because the resolution was moot. *(S&L bailout, p. 119)*

Derrick's subcommittee on Nov. 15 approved an early version of HR 849, which would have written into law House and Senate rules designating legislative agents to receive presidential vetoes during lesser adjournments.

On Nov. 30, Bush vetoed legislation (HR 2712) to let Chinese students stay in the United States. He issued a "memorandum of disapproval," the usual vehicle to explain a pocket veto, instead of a "veto message," which is used with returned vetoes. He also returned the bill to Congress, the hallmark of a returned veto, saying he was doing so because of questions arising from recent court decisions.

Bush's actions on HR 2712 were unusual but not unprecedented. President Gerald R. Ford on Oct. 29, 1974, issued a statement declaring a pocket veto of a bill to amend the Vocational Rehabilitation Act. At the same time, he returned the bill to a designated agent of Congress and issued language arguing that his pocket veto was absolute. Congress treated it as a return veto and overrode it the next month. The administration, however, refused to publish the bill as a law. Congress in response passed a new bill identical to the vetoed bill, and Ford signed it into law in December 1974. *(Ford veto, Congress and the Nation Vol. IV, p. 699)*

Sen. Edward M. Kennedy, D-Mass., in March 1975 amended a lawsuit on other pocket vetoes to include the Ford case. A district judge in April 1976 ruled that passing a second version of the law had not made the issue moot and that the original bill should become law because Ford's pocket veto was improper. The Justice Department concluded that the court was correct, and the Ford administration declined to appeal. *(Court ruling, Congress and the Nation Vol. IV, p. 975)*

A federal appeals court ruled Aug. 29, 1984, that President Ronald Reagan acted unconstitutionally when he pocket-vetoed legislation in November 1983, during the Thanksgiving-Christmas recess between the first and second sessions of the 98th Congress, that linked U.S. aid to El Salvador with progress in human rights there. *(Background, Congress and the Nation Vol. VI, p. 817; Congress and the Nation Vol. VII, p. 889)*

In response to Bush's veto, Steven R. Ross, counsel to the House, said, "There is no way he can pocket-veto a bill while at the same time returning it to the clerk. That stands the Constitution on its head and ignores decisions of the court." The issue never came to a direct test, however. The House Jan. 24, 1990, voted to overturn the veto, but the Senate sustained it the next day.

The House Rules Committee on March 7, 1990, approved HR 849 (H Rept 101-417, Part I) by a party-line vote of 7-2. Derrick told the committee the measure was not aimed at Bush so much as it was an attempt to clear muddy waters. Nonetheless, Republicans characterized the bill as inviting a needless fight with the administration.

The bill was approved by the House Judiciary Committee (H Rept 101-417, Part II) on a party-line vote of 23-13 May 22. The committee's Economic and Commercial Law Subcommittee had approved the bill by voice vote May 17. It saw no further action in the 101st Congress.

1991-92

The 102nd Congress, which convened Jan. 3, 1991, was rocked by scandal. Hundreds of sitting and former members of the House were revealed to have overdrawn their

House bank accounts for years, without penalty or rebuke. Mismanagement reigned at the House Post Office, where clerks admitted to embezzlement and drug dealing and members were suspected of illegally converting campaign checks to cash. Members' unpaid bills at the House and Senate restaurants were disclosed; they totaled in the hundreds of thousands of dollars. The Keating Five investigation resulted in a reprimand for Sen. Alan Cranston, D-Calif., who had stepped down in late 1990 as majority whip. And the Senate was damaged by its handling of allegations of sexual harassment lodged against Supreme Court nominee Clarence Thomas. *(Keating Five, p. 975; Thomas confirmation, box, p. 802)*

In answer, the House hired a professional administrator, the Senate conducted a study to determine the source of internal news leaks, and the Joint Committee on the Organization of Congress was created to recommend how to improve congressional operations.

Organization

Political tensions were evident in the selection of party leaders. The House appeared frustrated — seeking young, aggressive types and rejecting challenges by conservative stalwarts to more moderate incumbents. The Senate, meanwhile, advanced conservatives on both the Democratic and Republican sides of the aisle.

Senate

Ethics troubles moved from the House in the 101st Congress to the Senate in the 102nd, helping to down one Democratic leader. And conservatives made inroads into the lower leadership tiers of both parties.

Majority Leadership. While George J. Mitchell, Maine, was unchallenged for another term as majority leader, the second-highest post — majority whip — went unopposed to a conservative Southerner, Wendell H. Ford of Kentucky. Ford succeeded Alan Cranston, who announced Nov. 8, 1990, that he would step down immediately as whip and not seek re-election to the Senate in 1992. Cranston had been diagnosed with prostate cancer and was embroiled in the protracted ethics investigation into the affairs of thrift executive Charles H. Keating Jr. *(Keating Five, p. 975)*

Democrats named Charles S. Robb, Va., to head the Democratic Senatorial Campaign Committee. Other members elected without opposition were David Pryor, Ark., as Democratic Conference secretary; Alan J. Dixon, Ill., as chief deputy whip; and Daniel K. Inouye, Hawaii, as chairman of the Democratic Steering Committee. Tom Daschle, S.D., would continue as co-chairman, with Mitchell, of the Policy Committee.

Robert C. Byrd, W.Va., retained his post as president pro tempore of the Senate.

Minority Leadership. The Senate GOP Conference on Nov. 13, 1990, voted, 22-21, to replace its politically moderate chairman, John H. Chafee of Rhode Island, with the more conservative Thad Cochran of Mississippi. The last time Republican senators bounced a leader was in 1982, when they elected Richard G. Lugar, Ind., as chairman of the National Republican Senatorial Committee (NRSC) over Bob Packwood, Ore.

The conference elected Bob Kasten, Wis., to replace Cochran as conference secretary. Kasten defeated Christopher S. Bond, Mo., 26-17.

Conservatives triumphed in two more positions. Don Nickles, Okla., defeated Pete V. Domenici, N.M., 23-20, for the chairmanship of the Policy Committee. And Phil Gramm, Texas, beat Mitch McConnell, Ky., on a 26-17 vote for NRSC chairman.

Bob Dole, Kan., was re-elected minority leader, and Alan K. Simpson, Wyo., was retained as assistant minority leader.

Committees. The Senate saw little committee leadership turnover among the majority Democrats.

Terry Sanford, N.C., became chairman of the Select Ethics Committee, succeeding Howell Heflin, Ala. John Kerry, Mass., headed the new Select Committee on POW/MIA Affairs; Robert C. Smith, N.H., was ranking Republican.

Malcolm Wallop, Wyo., became ranking Republican on Energy and Natural Resources, succeeding the retiring James A. McClure, Idaho. Kasten replaced Rudy Boschwitz, Minn., in the top GOP slot on Small Business. Boschwitz was defeated for re-election. Because of service limits on Senate Intelligence, Frank H. Murkowski, Alaska, took the ranking Republican spot. Murkowski was replaced as lead Republican on Veterans' Affairs by Arlen Specter, Pa.

William S. Cohen, Maine, became ranking Republican on the Special Aging Committee, succeeding John Heinz, Pa., who died April 4, 1991.

The Sept. 8, 1992, death of Quentin N. Burdick, N.D., opened up the chairmanship of the Environment and Public Works Committee; it was assumed by Daniel Patrick Moynihan, N.Y.

Democrats on the Foreign Relations Committee persuaded Chairman Claiborne Pell, R.I., to cede some legislative authority to its subcommittees. They were to be staffed independently with power to mark up bills — a function that had been the exclusive province of the full committee.

House

House party leadership saw little change in the 102nd Congress, but the Democrats did make a rare move in voting to displace two committee chairmen.

Majority Leadership. During their organizational meetings held the week of Dec. 3, 1990, House Democrats re-elected their party leadership with no change. That left Thomas S. Foley, Wash., as Speaker; Richard A. Gephardt, Mo., as majority leader; William H. Gray III, Pa., as majority whip; and Steny H. Hoyer, Md., as chairman of the Democratic Caucus.

Vic Fazio, Calif., succeeded Beryl Anthony Jr., Ark., as chairman of the Democratic Congressional Campaign Committee.

On July 11, 1991, Democrats voted for David E. Bonior, Mich., to succeed Gray, who had announced his retirement from the House. Bonior defeated Hoyer, 160-109; Hoyer kept his position as caucus chairman.

In an effort to expand the leadership outside a core of white liberal men, Foley on Aug. 2 named a Southerner (Butler Derrick, S.C.), a woman (Barbara B. Kennelly, Conn.) and a black (John Lewis, Ga.) to replace Bonior as chief deputy whip. Foley also appointed Marty Russo, Ill. — a white liberal male — to the newly created post of floor whip.

Minority Leadership. Both Minority Leader Robert H. Michel, Ill., and Minority Whip Newt Gingrich, Ga., were unopposed in their bids for re-election to the leadership when the House GOP Conference met on Dec. 3, 1990. In a more surprising endorsement of the status quo, House Republicans turned back aggressive efforts to sideline two other leaders for the 102nd Congress.

Jerry Lewis, Calif., was re-elected conference chairman, defeating Carl D. Pursell, Mich., 98-64. Pursell had strong support from Gingrich and his allies in the leadership, including GOP Research Committee Chairman Duncan Hunter, Calif., and Republican Conference Secretary Vin Weber, Minn.

Guy Vander Jagt of Michigan held off a challenge for chairman of the National Republican Congressional Committee. Vander Jagt was re-elected over Don Sundquist of Tennessee on a 98-66 vote — a margin considered extraordinary in light of the barrage of criticism leveled by Sundquist about the committee's management and electoral record.

Mickey Edwards, Okla., continued as chairman of the Republican Policy Committee.

Committees. The Democratic Caucus on Dec. 5, 1990, ousted two committee barons: Public Works Chairman Glenn M. Anderson of California and House Administration Chairman Frank Annunzio of Illinois. Both were regarded as weak, ineffectual leaders and were replaced by younger, more aggressive Democrats: Robert A. Roe of New Jersey and Charlie Rose of North Carolina, respectively.

Anderson tried to salvage his position by promising that the 102nd Congress term would be his last as chairman, but the caucus voted against him, 100-152. Annunzio was narrowly rejected, 125-127. Rose, the No. 3 Democrat on House Administration, openly challenged Annunzio. He defeated Joseph M. Gaydos, Pa., who ranked immediately behind Annunzio, by a 158-64 vote.

The last time a chairman had been voted out was in 1985, when the enfeebled Melvin Price, D-Ill., was usurped as Armed Services chairman by the committee's seventh-ranking Democrat, Les Aspin, Wis.

Three other committees got new leaders. William D. Ford, Mich., replaced the retiring Augustus F. Hawkins, Calif., on Education and Labor; William L. Clay, Mo., succeeded Ford on Post Office and Civil Service; and George E. Brown Jr., Calif., defeated Marilyn Lloyd of Tennessee, 166-33, to replace Roe on Science, Space and Technology.

Bruce F. Vento of Minnesota, the seventh-ranking Democrat on House Banking, unsuccessfully challenged Chairman Henry B. Gonzalez of Texas. The vote was 163-89.

Limits on the number of terms a member could serve as chairman caused two vacancies. Louis Stokes, Ohio, inherited the reins of the Committee on Standards of Official Conduct (ethics committee) from Julian C. Dixon, Calif. And Dave McCurdy, Okla., took the gavel from Select Intelligence Committee Chairman Anthony C. Beilenson, Calif. Those panels also got new ranking Republicans: James V. Hansen, Utah, on ethics and Bud Shuster, Pa., on Intelligence.

Bill Gradison, Ohio, succeeded Bill Frenzel, Minn., as ranking Republican of the Budget Committee.

James H. Quillen, Tenn., relinquished the top Republican spot on Rules and was succeeded in the 102nd Congress by Gerald B. H. Solomon, N.Y. Thomas J. Bliley, Va., replaced Stan Parris, Va., as the ranking member of the District of Columbia Committee.

Whitten Service

The House on Nov. 5, 1991, took time out to recognize Rep. Jamie L. Whitten, D-Miss., for a remarkable achievement: 50 years of service. Whitten, 81, was sworn in as a House member on Nov. 4, 1941. His tenure had spanned 10 presidents, starting with Franklin D. Roosevelt, and seven House Speakers.

In January 1992, Whitten broke the record for longest service in the House. Rep. Carl Vinson, D-Ga., served 50 years, 2 months and 13 days. The champion for congressional service was Carl Hayden, D-Ariz., who served a total in the House and Senate of 56 years, 10 months and 28 days, starting in 1912.

The Feb. 8, 1991, death of Silvio O. Conte, Mass., the ranking member of the House Appropriations Committee, elevated Joseph M. McDade, Pa., to that GOP top spot. McDade was replaced as ranking Republican on the Small Business Committee by Andy Ireland, Fla.

The departure of Edward R. Madigan, Ill., on March 8, 1991, to be secretary of agriculture opened the ranking Republican slot on the Agriculture Committee for Tom Coleman, Mo.

With the May 4, 1991, retirement of Morris K. Udall of Arizona, California's George Miller became the permanent chairman of the House Interior Committee. Miller had resigned as chairman of the Select Committee on Children, Youth and Families at the beginning of the 102nd Congress to serve as acting Interior chairman. Patricia Schroeder, Colo., became head of Select Children.

Merchant Marine and Fisheries Chairman Walter B. Jones, N.C., died Sept. 15, 1992; he was succeeded by Gerry E. Studds, Mass.

In 1992, Appropriations Committee Chairman Jamie L. Whitten, D-Miss., was forced by age and illness to give up most of his duties; he did not, however, resign his post. William H. Natcher, Ky., took over the day-to-day leadership. Whitten tried unsuccessfully to reclaim his power for the 103rd Congress. *(Whitten service, box, this page)*

House Bank

The House bank scandal involved more members than any ethics controversy in congressional history. The public learned in 1991 that hundreds of sitting and former House members for years routinely overdrew their House bank accounts without penalty. Infuriated voters, who viewed the practice as further proof that members of Congress refused to play by the rules that governed everybody else, drove scores of representatives to retirement or electoral defeat. While a special counsel exonerated most members from criminal wrongdoing, a Justice Department investigation was ongoing in mid-1993.

Background

The roots of the House bank can be traced to the early 1790s, when one of the first Speakers made an unofficial agreement with the Treasury that money be advanced to him so he could pay members their salaries. Previously, members by law were required to go to the Treasury — an inconvenience to the members and to the Treasury. The new arrangement, however, soon proved cumbersome to the Speaker, who, as a result, called upon his underlings for help. For much of the early 1800s, the sergeant-at-arms did the paperwork, while the assistant doorkeeper fetched the money and paid the members. Around 1830, the system was consolidated under the Office of the Sergeant at Arms. At first merely a disbursing office, it quickly turned into a place members could keep money on deposit, cash checks and, at times, arrange for loans.

Since the early years of the 20th century, the bank was run as a part of the members' payroll system. It operated out of an office off the House floor and was used as a convenient check-cashing service for members and for employees and journalists working in the Capitol (although non-members could not have accounts). For decades it honored personal checks written on members' no-interest accounts even if they did not have funds to cover them. Regular banks would have bounced such checks; by making them good and collecting from the members later, the House bank was in effect giving members interest-free loans.

While the bank was plagued by scandal throughout its history, the one that brought it down erupted swiftly after the General Accounting Office (GAO) disclosed Sept. 18, 1991, that 8,331 bad checks had been written against members' accounts during a 12-month period ending June 30, 1990. The bank made the checks good without penalty or interest by using other members' funds on deposit, the GAO said. During the second six-month period covered by the report, 581 of the bad checks from 134 members' accounts were for $1,000 or more.

Check-floating was a problem at the bank as far back as 1831, although it had never received much public attention. Auditors at the GAO had pressed House bank officials to tighten their check procedures in August 1988 because no rules existed in writing. The GAO reported in 1990 that although rules were drafted, they were not implemented. An audit released that year focused mostly on bad checks written on outside, private bank accounts that were cashed by the House bank and bounced back to it.

In response to criticisms, House Sergeant-at-Arms Jack Russ — who also had bounced checks — promised in December 1989 to stop using the bank himself, and he limited check-cashing privileges to House members, former members and employees. Non-members' check-cashing privileges (such as those for journalists) were to be limited to $75 and cut off the second time a check bounced within a year.

But, the GAO found in its 1991 audit, the member-account problem got worse because no members were penalized. In the six months before the new rules were issued (July to December 1989), 4,006 bad checks were written on members' accounts and made good. In the six months after the rules were issued (January to June 1990), the number increased to 4,325. (The total number of member-accounts for all 8,331 checks was not disclosed.) It took some members weeks to reimburse the bank.

First reported in the Capitol Hill newspaper *Roll Call*, the story was snatched up by other media. Columnists and talk-show hosts weighed in, and the affair took on the dimensions of a scandal. In an attempt to stem the furor, Speaker Thomas S. Foley, D-Wash., and Minority Leader Robert H. Michel, R-Ill., took to the floor Sept. 25 to scold members and announce that the bank would no longer honor their bad checks. Foley said he had instructed officials six months earlier to stop allowing members to float checks without paying interest. He reiterated that directive, then said, as forcefully as he could, "This is now a matter that is over and done with."

The flames continued to be stoked, however. Members of the "Gang of Seven," a group of freshman Republicans, made daily speeches and statements to the media calling for a public airing of the names of those who abused check-writing privileges. William Safire wrote a scathing column in the *New York Times* Sept. 30, suggesting fraud, tax evasion and other crimes were involved in the scandal. By Oct. 1, members were flooding the sergeant-at-arms office with requests for letters declaring them clean, and more than 100 were issued, according to Foley.

Several news organizations began polling members to determine who floated checks. Few fessed up, but those that did included Foley, who initially denied having any; Majority Leader Richard A. Gephardt, D-Mo.; Minority Whip Newt Gingrich, R-Ga.; and Scott L. Klug, one of the freshman Republicans who led the charge for a full accounting. Embarrassed, Klug said he only wanted to target the worst abusers. One member admitted knowingly taking advantage of the float: Charles Hatcher, D-Ga. "It was not infrequent, but it wasn't everyday," Hatcher told the Associated Press. "You could write the check, and they paid it."

Any hopes the leadership had that the scandal would subside were dashed the morning of Oct. 3, when front-page stories focused on unpaid bills at House restaurants, where members could get relatively inexpensive food and sign a chit to be billed later. *(Restaurant bills, p. 942)*

On the floor the same day, a resolution (H Res 236) was offered by Gephardt and Michel with Foley presiding. Adopted 390-8, H Res 236 called for the bank to close by Dec. 31, 1991, and ordered the GAO to turn over its working papers for the past two House bank audits (going back to mid-1988) to the ethics committee, which would conduct an inquiry.

The panel was instructed to review the audits and the operation of the bank to determine whether there was any "potential violation of the rules of the House or any other applicable standards of conduct." The committee was to consider whether members or employees "abused the banking privileges by routinely and repeatedly writing checks for which their accounts did not have, by a substantial amount, sufficient funds on deposit to cover."

Fallout continued Oct. 8, when Louis Stokes, D-Ohio, chairman of the ethics committee, had to back out of the investigation because he had floated checks himself. Matthew F. McHugh, D-N.Y., was named acting chairman of the full committee, as well as acting chairman of a six-member subcommittee established to handle the inquiry.

Ethics Committee Investigation

The ethics subcommittee met twice a week for months, during which GAO officials, outside banking experts and all House bank principals, including Russ, were interviewed. To begin, the subcommittee had the GAO compile a list of accounts that had had any bad checks between July 1, 1988, and Oct. 3, 1991. Officials said the list showed how many bad checks each account had and the total face value of those checks (though not by how much they were short). From that list, the panel requested details on accounts with the most checks and the biggest total face values. That data included every bad check's face value; how much the account was short; and how long it took the member to make the check good. The accounts were coded, so subcommittee members had no idea whose they were.

On March 5, the ethics committee voted 10-4 to recommend that 19 sitting House members and five former members be exposed for abusing their banking privileges. The panel said it would ask the House to approve a resolution authorizing disclosure of the offenders' names and records of their banking transgressions. The investigating subcommittee — which like the full committee was evenly divided between Democrats and Republicans — reached unanimous agreement on its recommendations, which were approved without change by the divided full committee.

McHugh called the inquiry "thorough" and said it was "designed to both ensure the integrity of the House and be fair to individual members." Critics, however, branded the committee's recommendation a whitewash. Plans were made to offer for floor consideration at least one alternative recommendation that would disclose more members' bank records.

The committee's job was complicated by the lack of clear House rules against overdrafts at the bank. The key decision made by the committee was the standard it set to draw a line between abuses that were "routine, repeated and significant" and lesser offenses that would not be disclosed. As a result, the panel singled out members who had been substantially overdrawn in at least 20 percent of the months in which they had an account (eight months for those with an account throughout the 39-month period studied). For each month, the shortfall had to exceed the member's net monthly salary — which McHugh said ranged between about $2,300 and $6,000, depending on deductions.

McHugh acknowledged that no commercial bank would tolerate deficiencies near that magnitude. But he said the committee took account of the House bank's long-standing practice of not notifying members of a deficiency unless an overdraft exceeded the amount of their next paycheck.

Dissenting members of the committee said the standard was too lenient because it overlooked some egregious abuses. For example, some people wrote 800 bad checks but would not be named because the overdrafts did not exceed their monthly salary. And some members overdrew their accounts by far more than their next month's salary but would escape scrutiny because they did so fewer than eight times.

The committee's authority was undermined by its divided vote and by McHugh's acknowledgment that the line drawn was arbitrary.

Russ Resignation

While the ethics committee investigation was under way, many edgy House members tried to blame the overdrafts on sloppy management of the bank. They pointed to Sergeant-at-Arms Russ, but he declined to serve as the fall guy. "If I had created this system, if it had been my system, fine," he said of the bank's policy of routinely honoring members' bad checks. "The perception is that I changed all this to accommodate members, and I really wanted to clarify that I inherited this."

Russ had worked for the House nearly 25 years, starting out on the payroll of his representative and family friend, William M. Colmer, D-Miss. (1933-73), who offered him a low-level staff job. He soon was made a House doorman and five years later, in 1972, was appointed chief page. In 1976, he became deputy doorkeeper. The full House named Russ sergeant-at-arms on Jan. 3, 1983.

Russ insisted that he had little to do with the day-to-day operations of the House bank. He said that before the scandal blew up in 1991 he had attempted to make some changes in the bank's long-established procedures. "We were told flatly: 'It ain't broke; don't fix it,' " he said.

Maintaining to the end that the bank mess was not his fault, Russ ultimately bowed to the political exigencies of the situation and resigned his post March 12. In the meantime, members on both sides were preparing moves to force a vote to fire him.

House Floor Action

Foley confidently predicted March 9 that the House would approve the committee's recommendation for limited disclosure. Democrats reported intense lobbying by the leadership in favor of the plan. Meanwhile, key Republicans, including President Bush, were advocating fuller disclosure.

The ethics committee report on its inquiry was officially released March 11. The report included mitigating circumstances — that some members apparently believed that they were allowed to overdraw their accounts; that no money was lost by recent overdrafts because members eventually covered the checks; that, in the committee's view, other members' money, not public funds, was used to cover overdrafts.

But the report also said, of the panel's abuse standards, "No doubt, many who are unfamiliar with how the House bank operated for many years will find this definition of 'significant amount' generous. It is."

Shortly after the report's release, many Democrats started publicly saying they wanted all names released. At a Democratic whip organization meeting March 12, Foley was verbally pummeled by members who favored full disclosure or saw the fight as a sure loser. Subsequently, leaders of both parties conferred, then the full membership of both parties met. The House recessed in the late afternoon while final details of how to proceed were worked out. During that time, the Senate, in rare comment on the affairs of the other chamber, approved, 95-2, an amendment to a tax bill (HR 4210) declaring that the Senate had nothing to do with the House bank scandal and had no such bank in its chamber. The amendment, sponsored by Jesse Helms, R-N.C., and Minority Leader Bob Dole, R-Kan., also implicitly endorsed full disclosure.

The House reconvened at 8:25 p.m. The first order of business was the reading of Russ' surprise resignation letter. Foley appointed longtime aide Werner W. Brandt acting sergeant-at-arms and swore him in amid funeral-like silence. The debate that followed was livelier, however, reaching its height of partisan animosity when Gingrich took the floor and laid the blame for the scandal at the Democrats' feet, calling it a symptom of the corruption endemic to longtime one-party rule.

At 11 p.m., the House voted 391-36 on H Res 393 (H Rept 102-452), which required the naming of 19 current and five former members deemed by the ethics committee to have "abused their banking privileges." Detailed data

22 Cited for Abuse of Bank

The House Committee on Standards of Official Conduct on April 1, 1992, listed 22 current and former members who, it concluded, had abused their privileges at the House bank.

The committee released official data in accordance with a resolution passed by the House on March 12. Additional information about these accounts was gleaned from a preliminary report on 66 accounts reviewed by the General Accounting Office (GAO).

The unofficial data were taken from the earlier GAO document by matching numbers where they were identical. In five cases the committee's final figures were different; footnotes indicate these changes.

All data were based on the 39-month period from July 1, 1988, to Oct. 3, 1991, that was reviewed by the GAO and the House committee.

Official Data

The following information was released by the ethics committee on April 1:

• **Months Overdrawn:** The number of separate months (of the 39) in which the member's account was overdrawn at any time by more than the member's next monthly net salary deposit.

• **Overdraft Checks:** The number of checks for which the account did not have sufficient funds.

• **Bounced Checks:** The number of overdraft checks that the House bank refused to cover and bounced.

• **Outside Overdrafts:** The number of checks from outside financial institutions that were given to the bank for cashing or deposit and were bounced back to the House bank for lack of funds in the other institution.

Unofficial Data

This information was taken from the earlier GAO chart. Footnotes denote the cases in which the committee's totals differed from the earlier data.

• **Face Value:** The aggregate face value of the overdraft checks. This figure does not reflect the size of the overdrafts — only the size of the checks.

• **Biggest Overdraft:** The highest negative balance — the largest amount the account was overdrawn at any single time.

• **Days in Red:** The number of days (not necessarily continuous) during the study period (1,187 days for the 39 months) that the member's account was overdrawn.

• **Days over $1,000:** The number of days that the member's account was overdrawn by more than $1,000.

	Official Data				Unofficial Data			
	Months Overdrawn	Overdraft Checks	Bounced Checks	Outside Overdrafts	Face Value	Biggest Overdraft	Days in Red	Days over $1,000
Sitting Members								
Charles Hatcher, D-Ga.	35	819	2	0	$273,361	$10,746	1,052	963
Harold E. Ford, D-Tenn.	31	388	11	4	552,447	20,743	1,003	583
Stephen J. Solarz, D-N.Y.	30	743	53	11	594,646	23,019	917	855
Robert J. Mrazek, D-N.Y.	23	920	0	1	351,609[a]	27,398[a]	642[a]	531[a]
Ronald D. Coleman, D-Texas	23	673	6	1	275,849	9,409	927	825
Bill Alexander, D-Ark.	19	487	0	2	208,546[b]	10,957[b]	804[b]	322[b]
Edolphus Towns, D-N.Y.	18	408	0	0	176,503	12,964	560	424
Mary Rose Oakar, D-Ohio	18	213	0	1	227,598[c]	18,515[c]	667[c]	547[c]
Charles A. Hayes, D-Ill.	15	716	0	9	296,681	9,474	1,005	915
Joseph D. Early, D-Mass.	15	140	0	0	182,119	5,449	318	200
Carl C. Perkins, D-Ky.	14	514	25	28	565,651	41,200	506	436
Robert W. Davis, R-Mich.	13	878	0	0	344,450	13,416	756	372
Mickey Edwards, R-Okla.	13	386	0	1	54,299	5,385	409	195
Bill Goodling, R-Pa.	9	430	0	0	188,016[d]	25,078[d]	379[d]	242[d]
William L. Clay, D-Mo.	9	328	0	0	188,136[e]	33,766[e]	519[e]	219[e]
John Conyers Jr., D-Mich.	9	273	0	0	108,386	7,319	489	330
Edward F. Feighan, D-Ohio	8	397	0	0	218,994	13,978	711	533
Former Members								
Tommy F. Robinson, R-Ark.	16 of 33	996	0	0	251,609	28,036	544	499
Doug Walgren, D-Pa.	16 of 31	858	0	0	226,161	14,478	633	560
Douglas H. Bosco, D-Calif.	13 of 32	124	0	4	537,985	75,723	215	126
Tony Coelho, D-Calif.	12 of 18	316	0	0	292,603	60,625	295	226
Jim Bates, D-Calif.	9 of 31	89	0	1	170,686	3,436	492	33

[a] Based on 972 overdraft checks and 23 months in preliminary data.
[b] Based on 499 overdraft checks and 20 months in preliminary data.
[c] Based on 217 overdraft checks and 21 months in preliminary data.
[d] Based on 439 overdraft checks and 11 months in preliminary data.
[e] Based on 329 overdraft checks and 10 months in preliminary data.

also was to be released. In the early hours of March 13, the House then adopted a second resolution (H Res 396), on a **key vote of 426-0 (R 165-0; D 260-0; I 1-0)**, that called for exposure of the other sitting and former members who floated checks during the 39-month period surveyed. Each member's total number of bad checks also was to be disclosed. *(1992 key votes, p. 1083)*

After the second resolution passed, Mickey Edwards, R-Okla., offered a resolution (H Res 397) calling for reconstructing all bank account histories and releasing that information within 20 days, even though ethics leaders insisted that such a task would take months. The first effort to sidetrack the resolution failed, 150-275; the measure then was referred to the ethics committee, effectively burying it, 244-133.

Official List of Abusers

Between the time the House voted on the disclosure resolutions and the ethics committee released the official list of those who abused the House bank, several developments related to the scandal occurred. On March 17, Democrat Charles A. Hayes became the first electoral casualty, when he lost his bid for renomination in the Illinois primary. Hayes was on an unofficial but widely publicized list of the 24 most serious abusers. The same day, three Cabinet officials — Defense Secretary Dick Cheney (R-Wyo., 1979-89), Agriculture Secretary Edward R. Madigan (R-Ill., 1973-91) and Labor Secretary Lynn Martin (R-Ill., 1981-91) — acknowledged having overdrafts when they were in the House. On March 20, Attorney General William P. Barr appointed a retired federal appeals judge, Malcolm R. Wilkey, to conduct a preliminary inquiry into whether the House bank affair involved any federal crimes. Also on March 20, reputed abuser Robert L. Mrazek, D-N.Y., announced he would end his campaign for the U.S. Senate.

Members had until March 27 to file an appeal with the ethics committee before it released their names and overdraft totals. The most frequent complaint was that commercial bank checks deposited into the House bank were held for days before being posted to members' accounts. But bank officials insisted that all deposits were posted the same day or the next business day, depending on how late in the day the deposit was made.

Some members also claimed that their monthly pay was not always deposited on the first of each month; the bank's longstanding policy, however, was to credit accounts the first business day of each month. Any delays beyond that, in either salary or other deposits, were caused by the bank's closing when business was slow before or after holidays or when the computers were down, bank officials said. On such days, they added, neither credits nor debits were posted to members' accounts, so no overdrafts would have occurred.

The ethics committee April 1 named 17 sitting and 5 former members who abused their banking privileges by "routinely and repeatedly" overdrawing their accounts by a "significant amount." Two members who were the unofficial list of 24 abusers — Charles Wilson, D-Texas, and James H. Scheuer, D-N.Y. — were granted reprieves and were not named April 1. Wilson initially was charged with overdrawing his next monthly net salary deposit eight times, which was the committee's threshold for determining abusers. He got the number knocked back to seven by successfully arguing that two of his overdrafts should not have counted because he made deposits to cover them early on the day they arrived. Scheuer proved that wire transfers were not credited to his account on time, apparently because the commercial bank that acted as an intermediary between the House bank and the Treasury, which held members' deposits, failed to notify the House bank of the deposits. *(List of abusers, box, p. 932)*

The subcommittee had close votes on three members' cases — those of Edwards; Joseph D. Early, D-Mass.; and Bill Goodling, R-Pa. Edwards' and Early's cases involved the same basic issue. The panel's overdraft abuse standard was based on the amount of each member's monthly net salary deposit. Early and Edwards had the bank automatically take money from their pay every month to pay bills — a mortgage for Edwards and children's tuition for Early. The money was deducted before their pay was credited. Edwards said that left him with a monthly net deposit as small as $1,600 instead of up to $6,000.

The subcommittee conceded this put them "at some disadvantage for purposes of this inquiry" because it meant that Edwards, for instance, could only get away with writing overdrafts up to $1,600 a month, while members without such automatic deductions could write up to $6,000 or so without breaking the threshold. But the panel, on 3-3 votes, declined to remove Edwards and Early from the list, deciding that the two should have known from their pay stubs and monthly bank statements how much was being put into their account. Early and Edwards tried to appeal to the full committee but were turned down shortly before the list was released. Edwards, Republican Policy Committee chairman, was the only leadership member of either party on the list of top abusers.

Goodling's case involved close calls on when deposits were posted. Though he managed to get nine of 439 overdraft checks and two of 11 months removed from the GAO tallies, he did not persuade the panel to remove the two additional months it would have taken to get off the list.

The Other Overdrafters

The ethics committee April 16 released the names of an additional 252 sitting and 51 former lawmakers who overdrew their checking accounts. The partisan breakdown — 188 Democrats, 114 Republicans and one independent — was nearly proportional to the parties' representation in the House as a whole. In all, including the abusers, 325 members — 269 sitting and 56 former — were caught in the bank scandal. *(Complete list, box, p. 934)*

The Democratic and Republican party leadership did not fare well in the latest revelations. On the April 16 list were Speaker Foley; Majority Leader Gephardt; Majority Whip David E. Bonior, Mich.; Democratic Caucus Chairman Steny H. Hoyer, Md.; Minority Whip Gingrich; GOP Research Chairman Duncan Hunter, Calif.; and Republican Conference Secretary Vin Weber, Minn. Among the leaders who never overdrew their accounts were Democratic Congressional Campaign Committee Chairman Vic Fazio, Calif.; Minority Leader Michel; GOP Conference Chairman Jerry Lewis, Calif.; GOP Conference Vice Chairman Bill McCollum, Fla.; and National Republican Congressional Committee Chairman Guy Vander Jagt, Mich.

The House's Democratic committee chairmen proved more likely than not to have overdrawn their accounts. Fifteen of 22 standing committee chairmen had overdrafts — as did 11 ranking Republicans. Near the top of the list with hundreds of overdrafts were Agriculture Committee Chairman E. "Kika" de la Garza, Texas, and John Paul Hammerschmidt, Ark., ranking Republican on Public

House Ethics Committee Released . . .

Following is a list of 325 102nd Congress and former House members (including non-voting delegates) who were found by the House Committee on Standards of Official Conduct to have had overdrafts at the House bank between July 1, 1988, and Oct. 3, 1991.

It is made up of the committee's April 1, 1992, list of 22 members found to have abused banking privileges — denoted with an asterisk (*) — and the April 16 list of 303 other overdrafters. Former members are listed in *italics.*

Member	Overdrafts
*Tommy F. Robinson, R-Ark.**	996
Robert J. Mrazek, D-N.Y.*	920
Robert W. Davis, R-Mich.*	878
*Doug Walgren, D-Pa.**	858
Ronald V. Dellums, D-Calif.	851
Charles Hatcher, D-Ga.*	819
Stephen J. Solarz, D-N.Y.*	743
Charles A. Hayes, D-Ill.*	716
Gerry Sikorski, D-Minn.	697
Ronald D. Coleman, D-Texas*	673
Louis Stokes, D-Ohio	551
Dennis M. Hertel, D-Mich.	547
Chalmers P. Wylie, R-Ohio	515
Carl C. Perkins, D-Ky.*	514
Bill Alexander, D-Ark.*	487
Henry A. Waxman, D-Calif.	434
Bill Goodling, R-Pa.*	430
Edolphus Towns, D-N.Y.*	408
Duncan Hunter, R-Calif.	399
Edward F. Feighan, D-Ohio*	397
Harold E. Ford, D-Tenn.*	388
Mickey Edwards, R-Okla.*	386
William L. Clay, D-Mo.*	328
*Tony Coelho, D-Calif.**	316
Bill Lowery, R-Calif.	300
E. "Kika" de la Garza, D-Texas	284
John Conyers Jr., D-Mich.*	273
John Paul Hammerschmidt, R-Ark.	224
Mary Rose Oakar, D-Ohio*	213
Bob Traxler, D-Mich.	201
Mike Espy, D-Miss.	191
Bob McEwen, R-Ohio	166
Lawrence J. Smith, D-Fla.	161
Carroll Hubbard Jr., D-Ky.	152
Thomas J. Downey, D-N.Y.	151
Walter E. Fauntroy, D-D.C.	145
Barbara Boxer, D-Calif.	143
Donald E. "Buz" Lukens, R-Ohio	142
Joseph D. Early, D-Mass.*	140
Jim Wright, D-Texas	138
James H. Scheuer, D-N.Y.	133
Morris K. Udall, D-Ariz.	128
Chester G. Atkins, D-Mass.	127
John Lewis, D-Ga.	125
Vin Weber, R-Minn.	125
*Douglas H. Bosco, D-Calif.**	124
Michael A. Andrews, D-Texas	121
Philip R. Sharp, D-Ind.	120
Bill Thomas, R-Calif.	119
Gary L. Ackerman, D-N.Y.	111
Beryl Anthony Jr., D-Ark.	109
John G. Rowland, R-Conn.	108
Ron de Lugo, D-Virgin Islands	106
Bill Grant, R-Fla.	106
Dan Glickman, D-Kan.	105
Jim Ross Lightfoot, R-Iowa	105
Dale E. Kildee, D-Mich.	100
George Miller, D-Calif.	99
Byron L. Dorgan, D-N.D.	98
Bill Paxon, R-N.Y.	96
Edward J. Markey, D-Mass.	92
Joe Moakley, D-Mass.	90
*Jim Bates, D-Calif.**	89
Jerry Huckaby, D-La.	88
Richard E. Neal, D-Mass.	87
Wayne Owens, D-Utah	87
Charles W. Stenholm, D-Texas	86
Alan Wheat, D-Mo.	86
Les AuCoin, D-Ore.	83
Larry J. Hopkins, R-Ky.	83
Charles Wilson, D-Texas	81
Tom Petri, R-Wis.	77
David E. Bonior, D-Mich.	76
Steve Bartlett, R-Texas	73
Brian Donnelly, D-Mass.	70
Howard L. Berman, D-Calif.	67
Pat Williams, D-Mont.	66
Frank McCloskey, D-Ind.	65
David R. Obey, D-Wis.	64
Charles B. Rangel, D-N.Y.	64
Pete Stark, D-Calif.	64
Walter B. Jones, D-N.C.	63
Eni F. H. Faleomavaega, D-Am. Samoa	63
John T. Myers, R-Ind.	61
William H. Gray III, D-Pa.	60
Barbara B. Kennelly, D-Conn.	60
John Miller, R-Wash.	58
David E. Skaggs, D-Colo.	57
Don Young, R-Alaska	57
John Bryant, D-Texas	55
Sam Gejdenson, D-Conn.	51
Peter H. Kostmayer, D-Pa.	50
Jim Slattery, D-Kan.	50
George J. Hochbrueckner, D-N.Y.	49
Edward R. Madigan, R-Ill.	49
John D. Dingell, D-Mich.	48
Major R. Owens, D-N.Y.	48
John M. Spratt Jr., D-S.C.	46
Robert E. Badham, R-Calif.	45
Dennis Hastert, R-Ill.	44
Doug Bereuter, R-Neb.	39
Andy Ireland, R-Fla.	38
Ben Blaz, R-Guam	36
George "Buddy" Darden, D-Ga.	35
James T. Walsh, R-N.Y.	34
Robert A. Borski, D-Pa.	33
Bud Shuster, R-Pa.	32
John J. Rhodes III, R-Ariz.	32
Doug Barnard Jr., D-Ga.	30
Albert G. Bustamante, D-Texas	30
Richard A. Gephardt, D-Mo.	28
Nancy Pelosi, D-Calif.	28
Robert G. Torricelli, D-N.J.	27
George E. Brown Jr., D-Calif.	26
William E. Dannemeyer, R-Calif.	26
Dick Cheney, R-Wyo.	25
Robert T. Matsui, D-Calif.	25
Arlan Stangeland, R-Minn.	25
Jack Fields, R-Texas	22
Newt Gingrich, R-Ga.	22
Steve Gunderson, R-Wis.	22
Eliot L. Engel, D-N.Y.	21
Jill L. Long, D-Ind.	21
Ronald K. Machtley, R-R.I.	21
Peter Smith, R-Vt.	21
Paul B. Henry, R-Mich.	20
Ron Marlenee, R-Mont.	20
Gerald B. H. Solomon, R-N.Y.	20
Dick Armey, R-Texas	19
Robert Garcia, D-N.Y.	19
Kenneth J. Gray, D-Ill.	19
Matthew G. Martinez, D-Calif.	19
Hank Brown, D-Colo.	18
Cardiss Collins, D-Ill.	18
Ralph M. Hall, D-Texas	18
Solomon P. Ortiz, D-Texas	18
Christopher Shays, R-Conn.	18
Denny Smith, R-Ore.	18
Ronnie G. Flippo, D-Ala.	17
Thomas J. Manton, D-N.Y.	17
Carl D. Pursell, R-Mich.	17
Tom Tauke, R-Iowa	17
Lynn Martin, R-Ill.	16
Michael R. McNulty, D-N.Y.	15
Ralph Regula, R-Ohio	14
F. James Sensenbrenner Jr., R-Wis.	14
Gene Taylor, D-Miss.	14
Don Edwards, D-Calif.	13
Mike Parker, D-Miss.	13
Richard J. Durbin, D-Ill.	12
Kweisi Mfume, D-Md.	12
Alan B. Mollohan, D-W.Va.	12

... List of Members with Overdrafts

Member	Overdrafts
Leon E. Panetta, D-Calif.	12
Floyd D. Spence, R-S.C.	12
Wes Watkins, D-Okla.	12
Bud Cramer, D-Ala.	11
Tom DeLay, R-Texas	11
Edward R. Roybal, D-Calif.	11
Mike Synar, D-Okla.	11
Bernard J. Dwyer, D-N.J.	10
Bill Green, R-N.Y.	10
Clyde C. Holloway, R-La.	10
Richard H. Lehman, D-Calif.	10
John P. Murtha, D-Pa.	10
Gerry E. Studds, D-Mass.	10
Sonny Callahan, R-Ala.	9
Larry E. Craig, R-Idaho	9
Mike DeWine, R-Ohio	9
Lane Evans, D-Ill.	9
Robert W. Kastenmeier, D-Wis.	9
Greg Laughlin, D-Texas	9
Claudine Schneider, R-R.I.	9
Ike Skelton, D-Mo.	9
Cliff Stearns, R-Fla.	9
Curt Weldon, R-Pa.	9
William J. Jefferson, D-La.	8
Tom Lewis, R-Fla.	8
Marilyn Lloyd, D-Tenn.	8
David O'B. Martin, R-N.Y.	8
Dave McCurdy, D-Okla.	8
David Price, D-N.C.	8
Matthew J. Rinaldo, R-N.J.	8
Dana Rohrabacher, R-Calif.	8
Richard Stallings, D-Idaho	8
Howard Wolpe, D-Mich.	8
Jack Buechner, R-Mo.	7
Jim Cooper, D-Tenn.	7
Gary Franks, R-Conn.	7
Ben Jones, D-Ga.	7
Paul E. Kanjorski, D-Pa.	7
Stephen L. Neal, D-N.C.	7
Timothy J. Penny, D-Minn.	7
Jose E. Serrano, D-N.Y.	7
D. French Slaughter Jr., R-Va.	7
Les Aspin, D-Wis.	6
Richard H. Baker, R-La.	6
Beverly B. Byron, D-Md.	6
Dave Camp, R-Mich.	6
Bill Emerson, R-Mo.	6
William D. Ford, D-Mich.	6
Bart Gordon, D-Tenn.	6
John Hiler, R-Ind.	6
Austin J. Murphy, D-Pa.	6
Michael G. Oxley, R-Ohio	6
Donald M. Payne, D-N.J.	6
Bill Richardson, D-N.M.	6
Robert A. Roe, D-N.J.	6
Bill Sarpalius, D-Texas	6
Dan Schaefer, R-Colo.	6
Lindsay Thomas, D-Ga.	6
Anthony C. Beilenson, D-Calif.	5
Elton Gallegly, R-Calif.	5
H. Martin Lancaster, D-N.C.	5
Thomas A. Luken, D-Ohio	5
Susan Molinari, R-N.Y.	5
Jim Ramstad, R-Minn.	5
Marge Roukema, R-N.J.	5
Bernard Sanders, I-Vt.	5
Patricia Schroeder, D-Colo.	5
Robert C. Smith, R-N.H.	5
Virginia Smith, R-Neb.	5
W. J. "Billy" Tauzin, D-La.	5
Tim Valentine, D-N.C.	5
Maxine Waters, D-Calif.	5
Charles E. Bennett, D-Fla.	4
Tom Bevill, D-Ala.	4
Tom Campbell, R-Calif.	4
Gary Condit, D-Calif.	4
Jim Jontz, D-Ind.	4
Mike Lowry, D-Wash.	4
Raymond J. McGrath, R-N.Y.	4
Alex McMillan, R-N.C.	4
Dave Nagle, D-Iowa	4
Bill Nichols, D-Fla.	4
Howard C. Nielson, R-Utah	4
Ron Packard, R-Calif.	4
Pat Roberts, R-Kan.	4
Marty Russo, D-Ill.	4
Gus Savage, D-Ill.	4
Dick Schulze, R-Pa.	4
Sidney R. Yates, D-Ill.	4
Glenn M. Anderson, D-Calif.	3
Jim Bacchus, D-Fla.	3
Lindy (Mrs. Hale) Boggs, D-La.	3
Joseph E. Brennen, D-Maine	3
Thomas R. Carper, D-Del.	3
Daniel R. Coats, R-Ind.	3
George W. Crockett Jr., D-Mich.	3
Norm Dicks, D-Wash.	3
Floyd H. Flake, D-N.Y.	3
Jaime B. Fuster, Pop. Dem.-Puerto Rico	3
Joseph M. Gaydos, D-Pa.	3
Pete Geren, D-Texas	3
Joel Hefley, R-Colo.	3
Frank Horton, R-N.Y.	3
Steny H. Hoyer, D-Md.	3
Scott L. Klug, R-Wis.	3
Robert J. Lagomarsino, R-Calif.	3
Norman Y. Mineta, D-Calif.	3
James P. Moran Jr., D-Va.	3
Frank Riggs, R-Calif.	3
John Tanner, D-Tenn.	3
Bruce F. Vento, D-Minn.	3
Craig Washington, D-Texas	3
Ted Weiss, D-N.Y.	3
Edward P. Boland, D-Mass.	2
Bill Brewster, D-Okla.	2
Terry L. Bruce, D-Ill.	2
Thomas S. Foley, D-Wash.	2
Bill Frenzel, R-Minn.	2
Dean A. Gallo, R-N.J.	2
Henry J. Hyde, R-Ill.	2
Nancy L. Johnson, R-Conn.	2
Delbert L. Latta, R-Ohio	2
William O. Lipinski, D-Ill.	2
James L. Oberstar, D-Minn.	2
Charles "Chip" Pashayan Jr., R-Calif.	2
Liz J. Patterson, D-S.C.	2
Tom Ridge, R-Pa.	2
H. James Saxton, R-N.J.	2
Norman D. Shumway, R-Calif.	2
Neal Smith, D-Iowa	2
Don Sundquist, R-Tenn.	2
Robin Tallon, D-S.C.	2
Barbara F. Vucanovich, R-Nev.	2
Bill Archer, R-Texas	1
Sherwood Boehlert, R-N.Y.	1
Rick Boucher, D-Va.	1
Bob Carr, D-Mich.	1
Rod Chandler, R-Wash.	1
Bob Clement, D-Tenn.	1
Jerry F. Costello, D-Ill.	1
Lawrence Coughlin, R-Pa.	1
Randy "Duke" Cunningham, R-Calif.	1
Chuck Douglas, R-N.H.	1
Wayne Dowdy, D-Miss.	1
Mervyn M. Dymally, D-Calif.	1
Glenn English, D-Okla.	1
Dante B. Fascell, D-Fla.	1
Bill Gradison, R-Ohio	1
Joan Kelly Horn, D-Mo.	1
Earl Hutto, D-Fla.	1
Andrew Jacobs Jr., D-Ind.	1
James M. Jeffords, R-Vt.	1
Harry A. Johnston, D-Fla.	1
Jack F. Kemp, R-N.Y.	1
Gerald D. Kleczka, D-Wis.	1
Marvin Leath, D-Texas	1
Nita M. Lowey, D-N.Y.	1
Nicholas Mavroules, D-Mass.	1
Matthew F. McHugh, D-N.Y.	1
Bruce A. Morrison, D-Conn.	1
Jim Olin, D-Va.	1
Owen B. Pickett, D-Va.	1
John Porter, R-Ill.	1
Richard Ray, D-Ga.	1
Steven H. Schiff, R-N.M.	1
Lamar Smith, R-Texas	1
Olympia J. Snowe, R-Maine	1
Fofō I. F. Sunia, D-Am. Samoa	1
Dick Swett, D-N.H.	1
Ray Thornton, D-Ark.	1
Jolene Unsoeld, D-Wash.	1
Fred Upton, R-Mich.	1
Harold L. Volkmer, D-Mo.	1

Works and Transportation. Others cited included Interior and Insular Affairs Chairman George Miller, Calif., and Rules Committee Chairman Joe Moakley, Mass. Among those with no overdrafts were two of the House's most powerful chairmen: Ways and Means Chairman Dan Rostenkowski, Ill., and Appropriations Chairman Jamie L. Whitten, Miss. Also absent was Charlie Rose, D-N.C., chairman of the House Administration Committee, which oversaw the House bank.

Four former House Republican members who were in Bush's Cabinet made the list: Cheney, Martin, Madigan and Housing and Urban Development Secretary Jack F. Kemp (R-N.Y., 1971-89). The panel also cited five senators, all Republicans, who had served in the House: Hank Brown of California (1981-91), Larry E. Craig of Idaho (1981-91), Daniel R. Coats of Indiana (1981-89), James M. Jeffords of Vermont (1975-89) and Robert C. Smith of New Hampshire (1985-91).

The committee made its disclosure during a congressional recess. Speaker Foley, one of the few members remaining in Washington to respond to reporters, moved with uncharacteristic aggressiveness to control the damage by portraying members as victims of sloppy bank practices and misleading news accounts. In an April 17 column he wrote for the *New York Times*, Foley said: "The members named yesterday did not abuse their banking privileges. It would be more accurate to say that most members were abused by the bank." Furthermore, McHugh, acting ethics chairman, said many members had never realized they were overdrawn because the bank did not post negative balances on members' monthly statements.

The banking habits the list exposed varied widely. Thirty-six of the 303 total floated 100 or more checks; 40 members wrote only one overdraft. Because the list gave only the number of checks each member wrote on insufficient funds, distinguishing between members who overdrew by large and small amounts was not possible. Some members on the full list wrote more bad checks than the 22 identified by the ethics committee as abusers of the bank, but they escaped the short list because their overdrafts did not exceed their paycheck often enough to meet the committee's standard of "abuse."

Although more than 200 members had acknowledged writing overdrafts before the committee released all the names, some surprises emerged April 16. Near the top of the new list with 851 checks was Ronald V. Dellums, D-Calif., chairman of the important Armed Services Research and Development Subcommittee and a leading member of the Congressional Black Caucus. Ethics committee Chairman Stokes, it was revealed, overdrew his account 551 times. And Henry A. Waxman, D-Calif., chairman of a powerful Energy and Commerce subcommittee, overdrew his account 434 times.

Special Counsel's Investigation

With the list of overdrafters in the public domain, attention shifted to the special counsel's investigation. On April 21, Wilkey issued a subpoena demanding all the House bank's microfilm records. In a letter to Foley dated the same day, Wilkey said he believed "that the vast majority of House members, if not all, will be found to have committed no crime, but I can only make such a determination by reviewing the bank's records."

At a meeting April 13, the Speaker had told Wilkey and Barr that House leaders from both parties would cooperate with the inquiry only if Wilkey agreed to respect the rights of individual members and the House. "This meant, specifically, that the investigation could not proceed . . . as an open-ended and undefined inquiry into the general financial activities of all members," Foley said.

Foley alerted members about the subpoena in a letter April 24 and indicated that he considered the demand too broad. "The records," Foley wrote, "include all banking transactions over a 39-month period — every single check (whether it caused an overdraft or not), deposit slips and monthly statements of each member or former member of the House, whether he or she had overdrafts or not. The subpoenas also seek every check of every person who used the former bank during that period: employees, members of the press, members' spouses and even some members of the public." Of paramount concern to Democrats was the danger of leaks from the Republican-controlled Justice Department.

Meanwhile, Minority Leader Michel agreed that the subpoena was overly broad, aides said. In a letter to GOP colleagues, he suggested giving Wilkey copies of only those checks that resulted in overdrafts.

Wilkey pressured House members to comply in a combative public letter April 27. In it, he compared the defunct House bank to "a failed S&L or a fraudulently operated BCCI" — referring to the troubled Bank of Credit and Commerce International. Rejecting Foley's protest that his request was too broad, he said investigators decide what is relevant, "not the objects of the inquiry." Wilkey went on to say that the Justice Deparment's "preliminary inquiry has already unearthed evidence that a classic check-kiting scheme may have occurred." Democrats blanched at the suggestion.

The Dictionary of Finance and Investment Terms defined kiting as "depositing and drawing checks between accounts at two or more banks and thereby taking advantage of the float — that is, the time it takes the bank of deposit to collect from the paying bank."

In an interim report to the House in 1991, McHugh said that in some "very limited cases" bad checks on commercial banks were deposited at the House bank "to cover overdrafts the bank was already holding." The ethics panel's final report on the scandal said 60 members cashed or deposited 134 commercial bank checks at the House bank that ultimately bounced.

The Democrats' hope of standing up to Wilkey evaporated April 28 when Michel, facing a revolt in his own ranks, reversed himself and announced support for full compliance. An effort to rally Democrats failed as scores of members bolted in fear, not wanting to appear as stonewalling.

The next day, the House capitulated and voted to give the records to Wilkey. First the House defeated, 131-284, a Democratic proposal (H Res 440) to ask the courts to rule on the matter. Members then voted 347-64 to approve a Republican-sponsored resolution (H Res 441) to turn over the information.

In defeat, Democrats said they feared that Wilkey's appetite for internal House documents would prove insatiable, prompting battles with even higher stakes. As for the long haul, Democratic institutionalists called the measure giving up the records a dangerous precedent that could severely weaken Congress at a crucial moment in its 203-year-old power struggle with the executive branch. As an institution, however, the House decided the public's interest in a scandal-free Congress outweighed concerns over the balance of power and individual rights.

Included in the records subpoenaed were those of 170 members with no overdrafts — the fact that most troubled members from both parties. To appease those with no overdrafts, Wilkey promised to produce a paper copy of the microfilm, segregate the records for the 170 accounts and return them unreviewed.

However, that plan did not satisfy five Democrats — Henry B. Gonzalez, Texas; Sidney R. Yates, Ill.; Jolene Unsoeld, Wash.; Ted Weiss, N.Y.; and Craig Washington, Texas — who decided to ask a federal court to quash the subpoena as being too broad, an invasion of privacy and a violation of the separation-of-powers doctrine. Their lawyer was Alan B. Morrison, director of Ralph Nader's Public Citizen Litigation Group.

U.S. Judge John Garrett Penn ruled against the members May 4, saying he was unwilling to interfere with the House's decision to comply with the subpoena. "The movants do not have a legitimate expectation of privacy in the records," Penn wrote. "The members took the same risk as ordinary depositors in a standard bank when they transacted business" at the House bank. The subpoena was not too broad, Penn ruled, because "the underlying facts certainly establish a basis for the materials subpoenaed."

Shortly after Penn ruled, four House officials — Sergeant-at-Arms Brandt, two lawyers representing both parties' leaders and a Capitol Police officer — set out for an FBI office in Northern Virginia with 41 rolls of House bank microfilm in three boxes. About 3 p.m., Penn denied Gonzalez's and Yates' request for a stay, saying delivery of the microfilm made the matter moot. Lawyers for Gonzalez and Yates appealed to the Court of Appeals and again asked for a stay, but the request was turned down by 5 p.m. On May 6, Chief Justice William H. Rehnquist rejected a request to order the records returned or sealed pending appeal.

The House May 28 adopted, 396-5, H Res 471, which required the chamber to provide the Justice Department with additional documents related to the House bank. The requested information included the bank's balance ledgers; its daily settlement sheets, which listed overdrafts; any lists of members or others whose check privileges had been suspended or restricted; lists of individuals who were allowed to write checks against accounts of members who had overdrafts; computer files showing overdrafts; and records about short-term loans made to members by the National Bank of Washington through the early 1980s. The resolution also authorized the bipartisan leadership of the House to respond to Wilkey's future requests without having to put the matter to a House vote — unless the leaders could not agree among themselves.

Between the beginning of September and mid-October, all but about two dozen of the 325 current and former lawmakers who overdrew their House bank accounts received letters from Wilkey clearing them of criminal wrongdoing. Those left empty-handed had to sweat as election day approached and opponents continued to harp on their overdrafts.

In a statement, the Justice Department stressed that the lack of a clearance letter to a member was "not necessarily indicative of him or her being under criminal investigation." But the statement also stressed that Wilkey's letter dealt only with criminal culpability — "not otherwise addressing the propriety of a member's actions."

Financial Disclosure Reports

The May 15, 1992, deadline for filing financial disclosure forms for 1991 posed a sensitive quandary for the House Committee on Standards of Official Conduct. Members wanted to know whether overdrafts at the House bank for more than $10,000 met the threshold for reporting loans set in the 1978 Ethics in Government Act (PL 95-521).

The law required lawmakers to disclose the approximate value of liabilities that totaled more than $10,000 at any time in the year. Generally, the only exceptions were mortgages on residences, loans from certain relatives and loans secured by a car, furniture or appliances.

The committee on May 7 voted 12-1 not to require members to disclose overdrafts as loans — or as gifts or income. Its rationale was twofold: Complying would be too difficult, and it would not serve the purpose financial disclosure was meant to address — revealing potential conflicts of interest. The decision was significant because the ethics law barred the Justice Department from seeking civil fines against members who filed false financial disclosures if they followed committee advice.

While some members expressed gratitude and others had mixed feelings, the general reaction in Congress to Wilkey's letters was mostly negative. Speaker Foley, who got a letter, said in a statement: "We believe that Judge Wilkey's stated purpose of eliminating public speculation concerning members who used the former House Bank is laudable, but we have never seen the need to buttress what has always been evident to us — that no member has violated any law in this matter."

Some who had not yet received a letter accused the administration of using the probe to defeat Democrats in the upcoming election. The Justice Department denied having political motives.

Electoral Fallout

The House bank proved an effective though by no means perfect weapon for challengers across the country in 1992. Of the 269 sitting members with overdrafts, 77 — more than one in four — retired or were defeated in primary or general election bids for the House or other offices. That was a far higher casualty rate than other members suffered. Only 28 members — about one in six — with clean bank records had their political careers cut short.

The more overdrafts members had, the more likely they were to retire or to be defeated. Only six of the 17 sitting members accused by the ethics committee of having abused their banking privileges were re-elected. Of the 46 members with 100 or more overdrafts, 25 (54 percent) retired or were defeated. Of the 389 with fewer than 100 overdrafts or none at all, 80 (21 percent) retired or were defeated.

On Nov. 3, challengers beat 24 incumbents, far fewer than predicted by many political observers. Most of the damage came in the primary season. All but five of those defeated in the general election had overdrawn their House bank accounts at least once; five had at least 140 overdrafts.

The scandal was a significant, perhaps decisive, issue in many of the incumbent losses. Members with healthy election margins fell: Albert G. Bustamante, D-Texas; Gerry Sikorski, D-Minn.; Thomas J. Downey, D-N.Y.; Mary Rose Oakar, D-Ohio; Bob McEwen, R-Ohio; and Early. Sikorski also was helped along to defeat by changing his position on abortion; Oakar, by her alleged involvement in the House Post Office scandal; and Bustamante, by a federal grand jury investigation and an extravagant lifestyle. Pennsylvania Democrat Peter H. Kostmayer had long been considered vulnerable in his solidly Republican district, so his 50 overdrafts may have been enough to put his challenger over the top.

A handful of overdrafters also were hurt by redistricting, most notably Jerry Huckaby, D-La., who had 88 overdrafts and lost to a fellow incumbent, the GOP's Jim McCrery, in a conservative district.

Even members with few or no checks were hurt by the scandal. Defeated GOP Reps. Don Ritter, Pa., and Tom Coleman, Mo., were nailed for using perks — especially after they showered their district with franked mail to announce that they had no overdrafts. Dave Nagle, D-Iowa, who had four overdrafts, was criticized for trying to persuade House colleagues to resist a federal subpoena of House bank records.

In some races pitting incumbents against each other, the House bank played little or no role because both candidates had overdrafts. In Louisiana, Republican Richard H. Baker (six overdrafts) beat fellow Republican Clyde C. Holloway (10). In Montana, the man with more overdrafts, Democrat Pat Williams (66), beat Republican Ron Marlenee, who had 20.

And some won despite many overdrafts — Jim Ross Lightfoot, R-Iowa (105 overdrafts); Bill Goodling, R-Pa. (430); Ronald D. Coleman, D-Texas (673); Dan Glickman, R-Kan. (105); and Charles Wilson, D-Texas (81).

The House bank also was a factor in several Senate races. Democratic Reps. Barbara Boxer of California and Byron L. Dorgan of North Dakota were both able to win despite their overdrafts. The check scandal helped incumbent GOP Sen. Bob Packwood of Oregon beat back a challenge by Democratic Rep. Les AuCoin, who had 83 overdrafts. Likewise, Democratic Sen. John Glenn of Ohio was able to deflect criticism of his role in the Keating Five affair by pointing to former representative Mike DeWine's nine overdrafts.

Wilkey Report

On Dec. 16, special counsel Wilkey concluded his 8½-month preliminary inquiry of the bank scandal and resigned his post. In his report dated the same day, Wilkey said, "Actual criminal conduct by some members appears to have taken place, but it is quite limited. Where criminal violations were indicated, a full-scale investigation will be undertaken." Although the Justice Department declined to name names or to provide a precise count, approximately 20 sitting members, former members and former House employees were suspected of having committed crimes. Some were expected to be indicted.

The inquiry, Wilkey said, involved examining 611,516 documents from the House bank and entering those dealing with overdrafters into a data base. Each overdrafter's account was reviewed by FBI agents and prosecutors. Some members submitted to interviews or provided prosecutors supplemental information. No leaks occurred, Wilkey said, referring to a major concern of members when he subpoenaed the records.

At times testy and defensive, Wilkey's 49-page report offered a scathing critique of the House bank scandal and members' attempts to explain it away as much ado about nothing. Wilkey defended his decision to clear individual members, which many criticized as a backward approach to prosecution implying that all were guilty until proved innocent.

Several pages were dedicated to supporting Wilkey's conclusion that the bank "dealt exclusively with public funds." Wilkey argued that the bank's assets, though made up of members' salary and other deposits held at the U.S. Treasury, "belonged to the United States until the Sergeant at Arms actually disbursed it." He buttressed his case with numerous court decisions and GAO opinions that reached the same conclusion and the fact that the House three times appropriated public funds to replenish money stolen from its bank. House leaders had long insisted that the bank's money was the sole property of the members. The leaders argued that members' salary and other deposits covered all the overdrafts, which in recent years were all eventually made good, and the Treasury account never had a negative balance overall.

Wilkey belittled other assertions that members offered to minimize the scandal. Of those members who said they were not notified of overdrafts, he said that "this could be true for a limited number of members" with a few small overdrafts, but that "habitual overdrafters were habitually notified." Wilkey also did not agree with those who said no House checks bounced.

Wilkey, however, defended members against arguments that all overdrafters should be prosecuted. He explicitly noted that few if any violated the District of Columbia's bad-check statute because the bank routinely honored overdrafts, shielding members from a law that required knowledge that the check in question would not be honored.

The management and oversight of the bank were sharply criticized. The bank's vault was left open during bank hours, and tellers were allowed to replenish their cash drawers on an honor system. Bad checks were carried on the books "as mutilated money or cash," he said. Check-cashing rules were rarely put on paper, and, when they were, they apparently were never circulated to bank employees or members.

"The credo of the House bank was to serve the House of Representatives and never embarrass a member," Wilkey wrote. "This credo, which underlay the bank's policies, indeed its very existence, ultimately led to its downfall."

Upon conclusion of Wilkey's inquiry, Attorney General Barr set up a special unit of five prosecutors and seven FBI agents in the Criminal Division's Public Integrity Section to conduct an investigation. Wilkey's chief of staff, Thomas J. Eicher, an assistant U.S. attorney from Philadelphia, was put in charge. The Justice Department's criminal investigation was expected to focus on four types of violations: check kiting, conversion of public funds to personal use, misuse of campaign money, and false campaign reports and financial disclosures.

House Post Office

What started in 1991 as a little-noticed inquiry of clerks at the House Post Office suspected of embezzlement and drug dealing soon mushroomed into a full-scale scandal that included allegations that U.S. representatives used the facility to convert campaign checks or House expense vouchers to cash through sham transactions made to look like stamp purchases. By the end of 1992, a Justice Department probe, as well as a House ethics committee investigation, was ongoing.

Investigation Begins

The Capitol Police began the investigation in the spring of 1991 at the request of House Postmaster Robert V. Rota, according to Steven R. Ross, general counsel to the House clerk and the House's top institutional legal adviser. The House Post Office was an independent contractor to the U.S. Postal Service and was overseen by the House Administration Committee.

In the summer, the inquiry was turned over to the U.S. Postal Inspection Service, which was cooperating with the U.S. Attorney's Office for the District of Columbia. The Postal Inspection Service completed an audit in September and briefed Ross on the findings. The inquiry turned up allegations of embezzlement, cocaine dealing, improper loans and check-cashing. More than $33,000 in shortages were discovered; three employees admitted stealing money and one admitted dealing drugs, according to Postal Inspection Service records. The four subsequently were fired. The records also showed more serious but unsubstantiated charges of complicity by supervisors.

No member of the House was implicated directly, but one fired employee told investigators that checks were cashed for members.

Ross informed the office of House Speaker Thomas S. Foley, D-Wash., about the findings, but "not in any great detail." The counsel said he did not tell anyone in the Republican leadership.

Republicans and some Democrats complained that they were not aware of the seriousness of some of the more sensational allegations — especially those involving tolerance of wrongdoing by senior House Post Office officials — until after the *Washington Times* began publishing details on Jan. 22, 1992. (The probe was first made public in two stories that appeared in the summer of 1991 in the twice-weekly Capitol Hill newspaper *Roll Call.*) On Feb. 5, the House adopted, 254-160, a resolution (H Res 340) ordering the House Administration Committee to continue an inquiry into the matter. The House then tabled (killed), 250-161, a Republican alternative (H Res 341) to create a bipartisan select committee to investigate the range of allegations and whether the Democratic leadership sought to cover up the scandal. The floor fight Feb. 5 was one of the most rancorous of the 102nd Congress. Republicans charged Democrats with trying to hush the allegations, while Democrats accused the Republicans of smearing the House in a partisan attempt to take control in future elections.

The *Washington Times*, quoting unidentified sources, on Feb. 7 said that Heather Foley, the Speaker's wife and unpaid chief of staff, was involved in early talks about the post office and ordered Rota to keep it quiet. Speaker Foley confirmed that his wife helped handle the case but vehemently denied that she or anyone else in his office attempted to stifle an investigation. The Speaker again found himself defending his wife March 25, denying that she was being investigated for obstruction of justice in the post office probe. According to the *Washington Times*, a grand jury was weighing whether Heather Foley and House counsel Ross improperly delayed the Capitol Police investigation and whether missing funds were replaced by the time the inquiry was turned over to federal postal inspectors. The previous week, it was disclosed, Heather Foley had testified before the grand jury. House counsel Ross also had testified; in an interview, he subsequently denied any wrongdoing.

New Allegations, Dispute over Leaks

Postmaster Rota resigned March 19, amid new allegations that members had used the post office to cash personal and campaign checks. On March 31, Speaker Foley swore in Michael J. Shinay, a longtime postal executive, as interim House postmaster to replace Rota. Shinay's appointment was a departure for the House, which historically had chosen career House employees for such a position. If a management reform proposal (H Res 423) supported by Foley and other Democrats were accepted by the House, Shinay would oversee the dismantling of the post office. Under the plan, the Postal Service would take over the House complex's five stations, and internal mail would be handled by a new administrator of the House. *(Professional administrator, p. 947)*

The same day Shinay was appointed, Republicans released the results of a surprise General Accounting Office (GAO) audit of the post office's funds, which was conducted March 26-27. The GAO found the post office's internal accounting procedure still lacking. The employees knew little about U.S. Postal Service rules; auditors found open vaults containing money orders; two cash shortages were discovered; personal funds were mixed with public funds at one location; documents that tracked how much money and how many stamps each employee had were improperly handled; an official expense voucher from a member's office was found unprocessed; and an unexplained envelope containing cash was discovered.

Also on March 31, the *Washington Times* reported that House postal employees may have violated federal law by picking up campaign contributions from Postal Service boxes in Northeast Washington and delivering them to members' offices. Solicited campaign contributions may not be received in the Capitol, federal law states. The *Washington Post* the same day paraphrased an unidentified former House member as saying it was "common practice for lawmakers to convert campaign funds to cash by reselling stamps" to the House Post Office.

The House Administration task force running the House's internal investigation of the post office stalled in early April in a dispute over leaks. On April 1, Mary Rose Oakar, D-Ohio, resigned from the task force. In stories based on anonymous sources that began running April 3, the *Cleveland Plain Dealer* reported that she had been pressured to resign after allegations arose that she had placed two "ghost employees" on the House Post Office payroll and that Oakar-connected workers were paid for

Stamp Allowance

For much of the 1970s, Wayne Hays, D-Ohio, solidified his power as House Administration Committee chairman by increasing the size of members' expense accounts, which then were a myriad of different annual "allowances" for various purposes. The panel in 1976 increased the stamp allowance from $910 to $1,140. By law, stamps were to be used for airmail and special delivery, which provided faster service because franked mail traveled overland like other first-class shipments.

Many members, however, traded their airmail and special delivery stamps for first-class stamps, which were used on Christmas cards. Since 1973, franking law barred members from using the frank for holiday greetings because they were not considered official business. Many members, too, traded their stamps for cash at the House Post Office. Rules in effect at the time did not say whether the practice was permissible.

In 1975-76, amidst controversy over members' perquisites of office and misuse of public funds, a House Administration task force was established under the charge of David R. Obey, D-Wis. Hurried by the leadership in the wake of the upcoming general election, Obey's task force fashioned sweeping changes in the allowance system, including abolishment of the postage allowance. The rationale was that the frank covered all official domestic first-class mail; overseas, insured, certified and other special postal services could be paid for with a new consolidated office budget.

In implementing the reforms, no one paid much attention to stamps. Under the leadership of Frank Thompson Jr., D-N.J., the House Administration Committee issued orders ending "cash-outs" — the legal authority to pocket an allowance, regardless of whether the expense was incurred — for the stationery, travel and official expenses outside Washington accounts, which were specifically permitted. The panel remained silent on cashing out stamps, however. When the system of consolidated budgets took effect in 1978, no limit was set on using official funds for stamps. Moreover, at least initially, no regulations limited what members could do with stamps, although a new voucher system required that members certify by signature that the stamps would be used only by the office for official business.

By 1980, a considerable number of members were buying more stamps than ever. Members explained that they were using the stamps for unfrankable mail. Fifteen retiring members reportedly procured stacks of stamps before departing. Shortly thereafter, the House Administration Committee passed a regulation saying that "unused postage stamps shall be forwarded to the clerk of the House prior to the end of a member's service."

By 1985, the committee's regulations prohibited using stamps purchased with official funds "in lieu of the frank." Personal or campaign funds could be used for mail that was ineligible for franking. The only permissible uses for official stamps were foreign, express, certified, registered and insured mail, and self-addressed stamped envelopes. Furthermore, almost all long-distance first-class mail was sent by air, making airmail stamps unnecessary.

overtime hours not worked. Oakar called the allegations of no-show postal workers "damnable lies." She said she quit because she was too busy with other matters and was "tired of leaks" about the probe that she said were designed to damage her reputation. Oakar had been mentioned in connection with the mail pickups off Capitol Hill, and she was named April 1 as one of 22 members who abused the House bank. Oakar subsequently sued the *Plain Dealer* for libel. *(House bank, p. 929)*

On April 4, North Carolina Democrat Charlie Rose, chairman of the House Administration Committee and leader of the task force, boiled over in anger upon reading a front-page story that quoted from a "task force memo obtained by The Plain Dealer." Rose halted the inquiry April 8 until the leaks could be plugged. He ordered the door locks changed to one of the panel's meeting rooms to stop its top Republican, Pat Roberts of Kansas, from deposing witnesses. The task force worked out its differences after determining that "no such memo" as the one quoted in the newspaper existed. Republicans offered a measure (H Res 430) on April 9 that "condemns any attempt to interfere or impede this investigation." After Rose announced that he had "no problem" wth the resolution, it was adopted 417-1.

Republicans also offered H Res 431 on April 9, which would have referred to the House Standards of Official Conduct Committee (ethics committee) the news reports of allegations of ghost employees. It fell by a tabling motion, 231-181. Another resolution (H Res 434), directing House counsel Ross to recuse himself from the Justice Department investigation of the post office, was tabled (killed) on a 239-170 vote.

Subpoenas Issued

The House revealed May 14 that the grand jury probing the post office had subpoenaed voluminous expense account records of three House Democrats: Ways and Means Committee Chairman Dan Rostenkowski of Illinois and Joe Kolter and Austin J. Murphy of Pennsylvania. All three strongly denied wrongdoing. The subpoena was prompted by the testimony of James C. Smith, a supervisor at the post office who was cooperating with federal officials in exchange for immunity. Smith said he helped members of Congress get thousands of dollars in cash through phony transactions disguised as stamp purchases, according to a source involved in the case. Public records showed that, during the period under scrutiny, Rostenkowski, Kolter and Murphy made relatively large purchases of stamps from the post office with office funds. According to quarterly reports of members' expenditures issued by the House clerk, between Jan. 1, 1986, and March 31, 1992, Rostenkowski bought $27,672 worth of stamps (not counting a $2,000 purchase from late 1985 that was included in a 1986 report); Kolter, $17,265; and Murphy, $9,112.

The subpoenas were issued May 6 but remained a tightly held secret among top Democratic officials until Republicans demanded that the House be notified. The House voted 324-3 on May 14 for a GOP-sponsored resolution (H Res 456) ordering Foley to produce the subpoenas and explain the delay. Foley said it took days for House officials to get clarification from the Justice Department on exactly what the subpoenas required. He denied breaking any rules, apologized for not informing Republicans earlier and said the House would comply with the subpoenas.

The subpoenas demanded the following records on the three members — as well as former sergeant-at-arms Jack Russ, who was in charge of the House bank and resigned in the midst of the checking overdraft scandal March 12 — from Jan. 1, 1986, through April 15, 1992:

- All vouchers showing expenses charged to the officials' office accounts or signed by them, "including but not limited to vouchers for postal stamps."
- All records "regarding the status of" or "relating to overdrafts on" the officials' office accounts.
- Documents "regarding the proper use of stamp allotments" for lawmakers' and the sergeant-at-arms' offices.

Inquiry Spreads, Task Force Reports

In late May, the inquiry spread to campaign mail delivery. Griff Williams, son of Rep. Pat Williams, D-Mont., said his bosses at the House Post Office ordered him to fetch five lawmakers' campaign-related mail from postal boxes off Capitol Hill to avoid laws restricting the receipt of political donations in federal office buildings. Federal law, meanwhile, also prohibits paying an employee from public funds to do something unrelated to official duties. The five Democratic members were Oakar; Nicholas Mavroules, Mass.; Edward F. Feighan, Ohio; Jim Moody, Wis.; and Dennis M. Hertel, Mich. Williams, who was subpoenaed May 28 along with two other postal employees, said he complained about the pickups because he thought the practice might be improper and eventually refused to continue making them. He said he did not know whether members were aware of the practice. Several members said they ordered the service stopped when they learned of it.

The House Administration Committee task force completed its inquiry July 22, returning a split verdict. Since the task force's inception, the Democratic and Republican members took different tacks, and, in the end, neither side came out looking like the neutral fact-finders the members claimed to be. Because the task force was unable to agree on a unified report, each party's contingent issued its own. The 93-page Republican report was detailed and harsh and placed much of the blame on Democrats; the 64-page Democratic counterpart was more forgiving and put the responsibility on the post office managers. The Republicans appeared bent on revealing the names of any members — mostly Democrats — who availed themselves of questionable yet relatively minor perks offered by the post office. Democrats seemed most interested in declaring all members innocent of wrongdoing. They asked the ethics committee to investigate only five employees suspected of overtime abuse, excessive absenteeism or embezzlement cover-up. Aside from naming names, the reports differed mostly in their conclusions on whether the initial embezzlement investigation by the Capitol police was improperly impeded by House counsel Ross. The Republicans believed it was; the Democrats said it was not.

Both sides did agree that the post office was badly mismanaged by Rota and blamed the patronage system for producing a bloated, low-quality work force of employees more beholden to their political sponsors than their supervisors and a management team more capable of doling out favors to members and select lobbyists than running an efficient mail room. Both sides also said their reports were incomplete because key post office officials invoked the Fifth Amendment to avoid testifying.

In other issues covered by the task force investigation, the Democrats found "no conclusive evidence" of ghost employees. Republicans, however, said two workers fell into that category. The Democrats conceded that many witnesses said the two frequently were absent. One of the employees was dismissed, and the other was referred by the Democrats to the ethics committee. The most serious allegation, that members got cash from the post office, received relatively scant attention in the two reports. Both said the post office cashed checks for members and others in violation of U.S. Postal Service rules. The Democrats said they could cite no evidence to support allegations that members received cash through phony stamp purchases. However, the source of those allegations — stamp clerk supervisor Smith — invoked the Fifth under questioning that followed his plea bargain. Republicans found that campaign checks may have been cashed, concluding that lax procedures "may have permitted members' personal and campaign offices to convert official funds to personal use by exchanging stamps for cash." Republicans also discovered a service set up in the mid-1970s to help members avoid breaking election laws that prohibit them from soliciting political contributions to be sent to congressional offices. Members' campaigns would rent postal boxes off Capitol Hill; House Post Office couriers would pick up the mail, including donations, and deliver them to members' offices. The Republicans' concern centered on the use of House employees in checking the boxes. The Democrats, while maintaining that scores of members had boxes and violated no law or rule in doing so, recommended that the service be halted "for appearance purposes."

The House adopted 414-0 on July 22 a resolution (H Res 518) to refer the House Post Office matter to the ethics committee and to make the secret files from the task force available to the Justice Department. The House tabled (killed) two Republican proposals to make the files public, H Res 520 by 207-200 on July 22 and H Res 526 by 223-196 on July 23. The ethics committee on Aug. 11 established a special task force to determine whether the panel should open a full inquiry into possible wrongdoing at the post office; it did not conclude its investigation by the end of 1992.

Further Developments

On July 24, it was disclosed that on July 22 Rostenkowski, Kolter and Murphy themselves had been subpoenaed. They defiantly announced that they would plead the

Fifth, calling the ongoing criminal probe a "fishing expedition and political witch hunt." Federal prosecutors sidestepped a public confrontation by agreeing to excuse the members from appearing before a grand jury.

Joanna G. O'Rourke, the former chief of staff of the House post office, was indicted Sept. 10 on two misdemeanor charges of embezzlement and misusing public funds for sending personal items on an official Express Mail account and taking loans from post office money and on one felony charge of conspiring with unidentified others to "defraud the United States" by not running the post office "honestly, impartially and with integrity, free from corruption, conflict of interest, deceit and fraud." O'Rourke pleaded guilty to the two misdemeanors Sept. 17 and agreed to help prosecutors, who in turn agreed to drop the felony charge.

Rostenkowski faced a fresh spate of news stories the week of Dec. 13. The *Chicago Sun-Times* reported that his campaign committee paid him and his sisters more than $73,000 in rent for a campaign office since 1986. The office, which the campaign rented for $1,250 a month, was in a building he owned that was adjacent to his Chicago home. The paper also reported that Rostenkowski's campaign and a political action committee he controlled had reported buying $26,000 worth of stamps from the House Post Office. Those purchases were in addition to the previously disclosed $27,672 spent for stamps.

The post office inquiry continued into 1993 but remained unresolved by mid-year. A federal judge ruled Feb. 12 that government agents were not the source of news leaks regarding the grand jury probe into Rostenkowski, thus rejecting his request that the government be forced to defend itself at a contempt hearing and ordered to stop the leaks. The Clinton administration announced March 23 that it had requested resignations from all Republican U.S. attorneys, including District of Columbia U.S. Attorney Jay B. Stephens, whose office was investigating the House Post Office. On March 31, Gerald R. Weaver III, Kolter's administrative assistant from 1983 to 1987, pleaded guilty to three felonies related to the post office probe and agreed to cooperate with investigators. The grand jury also subpoenaed additional expense records — from Rostenkowski dating back to the late 1970s, from Kolter dating back to 1983 and from the Ways and Means Committee.

On July 19, former House postmaster Rota pleaded guilty to one count of conspiracy, one count of embezzlement of government property and one count of aiding and abetting embezzlement. He admitted helping two members of Congress to obtain cash illegally for personal use, by submitting official House vouchers. Although no names were mentioned in the court papers, other information that was supplied led to the wide belief that the two members were Rostenkowski and Kolter. The court papers also said that other lawmakers took part in similar transactions but were not included in the plea agreement.

Restaurant Bills

The House Administration Committee instituted a new policy regarding the House restaurants: As of Oct. 1, 1991, no free credit would be allowed — only cash or credit cards would be accepted. Public revelations followed that members had not paid a quarter of a million dollars in overdue restaurant bills. A similar problem existed in the Senate.

According to figures released by the House Administration Subcommittee on Personnel and Police, which oversaw the restaurants, about 250 representatives owed a total of $255,000 to Service America Corp., the company that had run the restaurants from 1987 until August 1991. Fifty members and several committees owed $47,000 to the House for bills from before Service America took over. Some of the money was owed by former and deceased members. The numbers had been much higher, approaching $1 million at one point in 1989, with most of the debt more than 30 days old, according to a General Accounting Office (GAO) audit.

Officials familiar with the problem said much of the debt involved events sponsored by members for outside groups. Under the rules, the member who sponsored the event was liable for the bill. House Speaker Thomas S. Foley, D-Wash., announced Oct. 3 that outside groups no longer would be allowed to hold functions on Capitol Hill without paying in advance.

GAO audits for the Senate restaurants, which were overseen by the architect of the Capitol, regularly showed tens of thousands of dollars in debts more than 30 days old. In each of the fiscal years 1988-90, more than $50,000 in debt was more than 90 days old. Just as for the House, most of the problems were attributed to third parties that used the Senate restaurants.

The Capitol and congressional office buildings contain five public restaurants and cafeterias; five restaurants for members, senior staff and their guests; and eight carry-out services. Members may reserve several private dining rooms or arrange banquets and parties in caucus rooms with low-cost food from the House and Senate restaurants. Congress provides the restaurants — free of charge — with space, utilities, janitorial and other services, and the Government Printing Office prints the menus.

Traffic Tickets

House Speaker Thomas S. Foley, D-Wash., announced Oct. 8, 1991, that the House no longer would intervene to fix members' District of Columbia parking tickets.

Under a 60-year-old District law, members on official business were allowed to park in most illegal spots. They were issued special tags to alert police, but sometimes their cars were ticketed anyway. When issued a ticket, members would hand it over to the sergeant-at-arms, who would initiate the process of having it voided by District officials. News reports said about 240 tickets a year were fixed.

Foley said the Senate had earlier "taken similar action, and I thought it was appropriate that the House and the Senate follow the same practice."

Ethics Probes

While Congress as an institution was rocked by the House bank scandal, the House Post Office investigation, the Keating Five case and the Clarence Thomas hearings, a number of individual lawmakers had their own ethics problems in 1991-92. *(House bank, p. 929; post office, p. 939; Keating Five, p. 975; Thomas confirmation, box, p. 802)*

Sen. Mark O. Hatfield

Mark O. Hatfield, R-Ore., was rebuked Aug. 12, 1992, by the Senate Ethics Committee for accepting and failing to report gifts worth nearly $43,000 between 1983 and 1988 as well as three travel reimbursements of unspecified value. The committee, which voted 5-1 on the resolution to rebuke, found that Hatfield had violated the 1978 Ethics in Government Act (PL 95-521) and Senate rules and deemed his actions "improper conduct reflecting upon the Senate." It did not recommend discipline by the full Senate, thus closing the case. *(Ethics act, Congress and the Nation Vol. V, pp. 824, 891)*

In its 15-month investigation, the ethics panel did not find evidence of criminal violations or willful wrongdoing by Hatfield, and no connection was made between Hatfield's official actions and acceptance of the gifts. His shortcomings instead were attributed to "negligence" and "inattention." Nevertheless, the committee said acceptance of and failure to report the gifts were "inappropriate and cannot be condoned."

The Justice Department was conducting its own inquiry into criminal and civil charges against Hatfield, including an FBI probe into his financial disclosure statements. Three times in 1991, Hatfield filed amendments to past financial disclosure statements, bringing to six the number of corrections he had made since 1986.

Most of the gifts cited by the committee were from Dr. James B. Holderman, president of the University of South Carolina during the 1980s. The Ethics Committee and Justice Department inquiries into Hatfield's affairs were prompted in the spring of 1991, when the university released records showing that Holderman had given the senator speech fees, travel expenses and more than $9,000 worth of gifts. Hatfield initially failed to disclose the gifts on forms required by the Ethics in Government Act.

Holderman had lobbied Congress for federal grants during his tenure as president of the university. While Hatfield chaired the Senate Appropriations Committee in 1986, Congress approved a $16.3 million grant to the school.

In a September 1991 financial disclosure form amendment, Hatfield for the first time declared a $17,000 gift, subsequently to be mentioned in the resolution to rebuke, from Dorothy Cook, the wife of the late Charles E. Cook, a California business and banking tycoon. Hatfield's statement accompanying the filing of the amendment said, "Mrs. Cook generously financed the remodeling of a bedroom at the Hatfield's Oregon residence."

The committee also objected to Hatfield's failure to disclose the forgiveness of $4,415 interest due on loans in 1987 and $5,005 in 1988 from former representative John Dellenback, R-Ore. (1967-75). Meanwhile, the committee did not mention — and thus did not object to — the forgiveness of $75,000 in loans from Dellenback, a $58,000 loan from Charles Cook and a $50,000 loan from L. David and James E. Carley. Dellenback, while head of a group of Christian colleges during the 1980s, discussed federal grants for the colleges with Hatfield. Dellenback also lobbied Congress to create the U.S. Institute of Peace, which Hatfield made a reality with a successful amendment. The Carleys were developers who relied heavily on a Housing and Urban Development program Hatfield supported. *(Peace institute, Congress and the Nation Vol. VI, p. 579)*

The committee also found no impropriety in the scholarship to the University of South Carolina, estimated to be worth at least $15,000, that was awarded to Hatfield's son.

Sen. Bob Packwood

The Senate Ethics Committee on Dec. 1, 1992, began a "preliminary inquiry" into allegations that Oregon Republican Bob Packwood had sexually harassed a number of women. It was the first time the panel was publicly known to have undertaken a sexual harassment investigation.

Gloria Allred, a Los Angeles sexual harassment lawyer who headed the Women's Equal Rights Legal Defense and Education Fund, filed a formal complaint with the Ethics Committee in a letter dated Nov. 25 and received Nov. 30. The quick decision to investigate the matter followed pressure by Senate leaders for fast action, reflecting their sensitivity after the 1991 firestorm over the chamber's handling of harassment allegations against Supreme Court justice nominee Clarence Thomas. *(Thomas confirmation, box, p. 802)*

The *Washington Post* Nov. 22 published a long article detailing allegations by 10 women that Packwood made unwanted sexual advances toward them while most were working for the senator. When confronted by *Post* reporters before the November 1992 general election, Packwood denied the allegations and attempted to discredit his accusers. After his electoral victory, Packwood, without admitting to any specific misbehavior, issued an apology. He then entered an alcohol treatment facility on Nov. 30 for an evaluation.

Most of the incidents dated to the late 1970s and early 1980s; frequently, the article said, they occurred when Packwood seemed to have been drinking. Senior women on Packwood's staff reportedly warned some women against working alone with the senator.

Following the appearance of the *Post* story, the Oregon Coalition Against Domestic and Sexual Violence reported receiving calls from five women "with direct, personal experiences of Sen. Packwood's sexually inappropriate behavior."

Several Oregon women's groups and the state Democratic Party called for Packwood to step down, but the senator told a crowded Capitol Hill news conference Dec. 10, "I am not going to resign under any circumstances."

Allegations against Packwood mounted Feb. 7, 1993, when the *Washington Post* reported that 13 more women claimed he made unwanted advances, thus bringing the total to 23. Of the 23 women, 10 agreed to be named in the newspaper, four agreed to be named only to Packwood and nine were not identified.

The irony of the charges against Packwood was that he had long been considered a champion of women's issues, leading the fight for abortion rights. He also won praise from women's groups for hiring and promoting women in his office.

The Senate Rules Committee decided, by voice vote April 29, to hold a public hearing on petitions to deny Packwood his seat. The questions approved for argument focused on whether the Senate could or should exclude someone who lied about "personal, historical facts" to win a seat. On May 20, the committee dismissed the petition by a 16-0 vote. Packwood still faced possible disciplinary action from the Ethics Committee investigation.

Sen. Alfonse M. D'Amato

After a two-year investigation, the Senate Ethics Committee rebuked Alfonse M. D'Amato, R-N.Y., on Aug. 2, 1991, for running his office in an "improper and inappropriate manner" but declared that not enough evidence existed to charge him with breaking any rules. D'Amato had been accused of improperly using his position to help campaign contributors, friends and family. *(Details, p. 923)*

The Ethics Committee investigated 16 charges and found "no evidence" of rules violations in two cases, "no credible evidence" in 12 and "insufficient credible evidence" in two. The case that prompted the committee's rebuke involved the senator's brother, Armand P. D'Amato, who represented a defense contractor — Unisys Corp. — seeking the senator's help in its business with the Defense Department. In response to the brother's requests, D'Amato's office twice sent letters to Defense over the senator's signature, but Sen. D'Amato said his staff acted without telling him, and he denied knowing that his brother worked for Unisys. The Ethics Committee termed the office's help "ordinary and routine." Members declined to say whether they believed D'Amato's denial of knowledge of his brother's work.

In the case involving help provided by D'Amato to campaign contributors in Puerto Rico seeking grants from the Department of Housing and Urban Development, the committee said its inquiry was hampered because "essential witnesses" invoked the Fifth Amendment to avoid testifying. Though some witnesses were compelled to testify under grants of immunity, the committee did not give immunity to the main Puerto Rico witnesses because that would have "put contemplated prosecutions at grave risk." The panel declared the Puerto Rico case closed but said it could be reopened later.

Special counsel Henry F. Schuelke III, in investigating the charges against D'Amato, reviewed about 1 million documents, evidence and testimony before two grand juries, and law enforcement agency wiretaps of "individuals other than Sen. D'Amato." Sixty-eight witnesses were interviewed and 56 were formally deposed, though 25 invoked the Fifth. Ten others told the committee through lawyers that they would invoke the Fifth if called. Seven were forced to testify. The case reportedly cost taxpayers $686,379.

Armand D'Amato was convicted May 7, 1993, on seven counts of mail fraud in connection with the payments he received from Unisys for consulting services he did not perform. He was acquitted on 17 counts.

Sen. Brock Adams

An ethics complaint against Brock Adams, D-Wash., was dismissed May 22, 1992, by the Senate Ethics Committee because the allegations of sexual misconduct were based on anonymous sources and because the alleged incidents occurred before he was a senator. Adams ended his bid for a second Senate term March 1, following a *Seattle Times* account that portrayed him as habitually prone to sexual misconduct. Adams denied the charges.

The *Seattle Times* presented detailed accounts by eight women who said Adams had made unwanted and inappropriate sexual advances toward them. Some women accused him of drugging them. One woman, described as a Democratic activist, said that in the early 1970s Adams drugged and raped her, leaving $200 as he departed.

In a separate allegation that surfaced in 1988, Kari Tupper, a family friend, claimed Adams had drugged and molested her at his Washington, D.C., home. He denied the charges, and the Ethics Committee did not pursue the complaint.

Sen. Daniel K. Inouye

The Senate Ethics Committee announced Dec. 1, 1992, that it had "not yet determined that there is adequate evidence to warrant an inquiry" into Hawaii Democrat Daniel K. Inouye's conduct with women. The panel announced April 7, 1993, that it would not pursue the case.

In campaign advertisements, Republican state senator Rick Reed, Inouye's opponent in the November 1992 Senate race, raised questions about Inouye's behavior toward women. Reed taped Inouye's hairdresser saying the senator had sexually harassed her 17 years before. The hairdresser did not know she was being tape-recorded, it later was disclosed. Democratic state representative Annelle Amaral said nine women with complaints had contacted her, but none was willing to be named.

The formal complaint against Inouye was filed by the Women's Equal Rights Legal Defense and Education Fund, the same group that filed a complaint against Sen. Bob Packwood, R-Ore.

Sen. Charles S. Robb

A federal grand jury on Jan. 12, 1993, voted not to indict Sen. Charles S. Robb, D-Va., on conspiracy and obstruction of justice charges. Robb maintained his innocence throughout the 19-month investigation, but his straight-arrow image was damaged nonetheless.

The case centered on the release of an illegally recorded cellular phone call involving Gov. L. Douglas Wilder, D-Va., a longtime rival. In the tape, recorded in October 1988, Wilder speculated that rumors about Robb's attendance at Virginia Beach parties where cocaine was used would ruin his career. The tape was leaked to the media more than two years later, when rumors about Robb's private life were refueled by a beauty queen's claim that she had had an affair with the senator. Robb's aides apparently believed that the rumors would be discounted if they could be traced to a rival, particularly when they seemed so inconsistent with the image of Robb — a square-jawed former Marine, a son-in-law to President Lyndon B. Johnson and a prospective presidential candidate.

Robb appeared twice before the grand jury, and three aides implicated him in plea agreements they made to criminal charges. Virginia Beach businessman Bruce Thompson, a Robb associate, was indicted on three charges, including witness tampering, related to the case. The Thompson indictment included allegations that Robb declined to listen to the tapes, although he knew their contents, so he could maintain "plausible deniability." Similar allegations were contained in the plea agreements.

Robb was chosen to head the Democratic Senatorial Campaign Committee for the 1992 elections. Instead of being a fund-raising asset, however, he was forced to leave the public work to others.

Rep. Joseph M. McDade

A five-count indictment was handed down May 5, 1992, by a federal grand jury against Rep. Joseph M. McDade, charging the Pennsylvania Republican with running his office as a criminal enterprise by enriching himself over five years with more than $100,000 worth of extorted favors, bribes and illegal gratuities. McDade faced 34 years in prison and $1.25 million in fines if convicted on all counts; he denied wrongdoing.

McDade's troubles were first detailed in a front-page story in the *Wall Street Journal* on Dec. 1, 1988, three months after the Justice Department began its probe. The newspaper reported that the FBI was investigating McDade's ties to United ChemCon Corp. (UCC), a company with headquarters in the southern Pennsylvania city of Lancaster and a factory in McDade's district. Prosecutors said that officials and associates of the bankrupt and then-defunct firm defrauded the government of $12 million. Much of the McDade indictment stemmed from that investigation, which had produced guilty pleas from a dozen UCC associates who were cooperating with the prosecution. McDade helped the once-tiny company get its first big government contract in the mid-1980s to bring jobs to the recession-wracked Allegheny Mountain town of Renovo.

The indictment included allegations related to five other contractors and accused McDade of violating the Racketeer Influenced and Corrupt Organizations (RICO) Act, which originally meant to make convicting mobsters easier. *(RICO, Congress and the Nation Vol. III, p. 272)*

After McDade was charged, some House Republicans pressed him to relinquish his post as ranking Republican on the Appropriations Committee. McDade left the decision up to House Minority Leader Robert H. Michel, R-Ill., who let him keep the position. Despite the indictment, McDade won re-election in 1992 with 90 percent of the vote. When the House GOP members organized in December for the 103rd Congress, the Republican Conference rejected a proposed rule to force any GOP committee leader to give up his post while under indictment.

On Jan. 11, 1993, McDade asked a federal judge to dismiss the indictment against him, claiming it violated the constitutional doctrine of separation of powers. McDade's motion said, "Because many of the allegations in the indictment involve legislative acts and motivations, the Speech or Debate Clause [of the Constitution] prevents the government from forcing Congressman McDade to defend himself on those actions and motivations." On May 6, U.S. District Judge Robert S. Gawthrop III refused to throw out the indictment, saying McDade's interpretation would create "the impression that members of Congress are immune from prosecution merely because they are members of Congress." McDade appealed the ruling, and as of mid-1993, the case was still pending.

Rep. Nicholas Mavroules

Rep. Nicholas Mavroules, D-Mass., was indicted on Aug. 27, 1992, on 17 counts of extortion, racketeering, tax evasion and abuse of office. He initially denied the charges, calling them politically motivated.

While Mavroules acknowledged accepting free use of cars while serving in Congress and failing to report the cars on House financial disclosure forms or annual tax forms, the 25-page indictment stated that Mavroules solicited the use of the cars — valued at $75,000 — and for four years had asked that they be put under a false name. As mayor of Peabody, Mass., Mavroules allegedly extorted $25,000 from the owners of a liquor store for his assistance in securing a license. The indictment also said Mavroules arranged for a job in the store for his brother.

Mavroules was further charged with extorting $12,000 in 1985 in return for arranging a prison transfer for a convicted drug trafficker and soliciting and receiving a discount for the use of a beach house in Gloucester, Mass. The developer who owned the house later allegedly received federal grants and other assistance from Mavroules and his congressional staff.

Upon indictment, Mavroules was required to step down as chairman of the Investigations Subcommittee of the House Armed Services Committee. He lost his reelection bid in 1992.

On April 15, 1993, Mavroules pleaded guilty to 15 counts; on June 29, he received a sentence of 15 months in jail, three years probation after his prison term and a fine of $15,000.

Rep. Bill Alexander

The House ethics committee in 1991 dropped its inquiry into the business ties between Rep. Bill Alexander, D-Ark., and the two managers of a foundation that got federal appropriations with his help, when Alexander severed his connection with the managers.

Alexander had asked the panel June 17 whether his Appropriations Committee work in behalf of the Marine Resources Development Foundation — a non-profit organization in Key Largo, Fla., that specialized in teaching educators about marine life — was a conflict of interest with his business investments with Neil Monney and Ian Koblick, its directors. Three days earlier, the *Wall Street Journal* reported that Alexander had helped direct up to $400,000 a year since fiscal 1988 to the foundation. In 1986, Alexander invested $20,000 in a venture by Monney and Koblick to build a small underwater "hotel" and related facilities in the same lagoon as the foundation's educational programs.

The ethics committee June 27 declined to declare that Alexander had not broken House rules. The committee said it needed more information about his financial dealings. The next day, Alexander's wife, Debra, who had assumed her husband's stock in the venture's two companies, returned the stock for free. Alexander also ended a separate business relationship with Monney. Alexander said Monney had served for free as president of a Key Largo company set up in 1990 to handle what Alexander called a "sizable debt" from a "bad investment" in a Colorado condominium project.

Rep. Floyd H. Flake

Criminal charges of embezzlement and tax evasion against Rep. Floyd H. Flake, D-N.Y., and his wife were dismissed April 3, 1991. The Flakes were indicted in August 1990. *(Details, p. 927)*

The trial opened March 11 in U.S. District Court in Brooklyn, N.Y. Prosecutors said a church fund had been used in funneling income to the Flakes to subsidize a lavish lifestyle. The case fell apart after testimony from 20 witnesses failed to persuade U.S. Judge Eugene H. Nickerson that the fund was anything but an official church account. Prosecutors asked that the charges be dropped after the judge barred them from presenting certain evidence in the case.

Though the Flakes denied evading taxes, their lawyers repeatedly emphasized that the couple would discuss their returns with the Internal Revenue Service. Rep. Flake said the case "probably had something to do with politics. There also could be some racism in it." Prosecutors denied the charges.

Rep. Charlie Rose

U.S. District Judge Thomas Penfield Jackson on April 21, 1992, refused to shield members of Congress who "knowingly and willfully" file false financial disclosure statements from civil suits by the Justice Department and court-imposed fines. The decision came on a motion to dismiss a suit against Rep. Charlie Rose, D-N.C.

The House ethics committee in 1988 reproved Rose for repeatedly breaking House rules by borrowing tens of thousands of dollars from his re-election campaign for personal use, failing to disclose those and other loans (from banks) on financial statements and using campaign funds as collateral on a personal loan. *(Details, Congress and the Nation Vol. VII, p. 886)*

Rose amended his disclosure forms to show the bank loans but did not include the campaign-related loans. The Justice Department pressed Rose to further amend his statements, but the ethics panel told him he did not have to, so he refused. The Justice Department sued Rose in 1989 and requested fines totaling $30,000.

Rose and House leaders contended that even if the Justice Department could prove he had acted "knowingly and willfully," the Constitution's separation-of-powers doctrine protects him from prosecution because the ethics committee had already acted. In a legal brief, the leaders said, if the court "were to allow the Justice Department to follow up congressional ethics proceedings by changing the rules and adding penalties in a second proceeding . . . Congress could not perform the ethics functions consigned to it by the Constitution, and members would not receive their speech-or-debate protection for their participation in ethics committee proceedings."

The Justice Department argued that the House's position would offer special protection to members that was not available to unsuccessful candidates also covered by the ethics law. Its lawyers wrote, "Taking [the House's] argument to its logical conclusion, a congressional investigation of a member of Congress could even be used to immunize a congressman from criminal prosecution. Such a result would be patently unconstitutional."

The case reflected debates over Congress' penchant for exempting itself from laws imposed on the executive branch and private businesses, also on separation-of-powers grounds. It could become an important precedent on how far the executive branch can go in trying to punish members for transgressions already judged by the House or Senate ethics committees.

As of the end of 1992, the case was still pending.

News Leaks Investigation

A four-month investigation, which included interviews with more than 200 witnesses, into internal Senate leaks of information to the media turned up empty-handed in 1992.

The Senate on Oct. 24, 1991, approved, 86-12, a Democratic-sponsored resolution (S Res 202) to authorize an investigation into news leaks that concerned law school Professor Anita F. Hill's allegations that Supreme Court justice nominee Clarence Thomas had sexually harassed her when she worked for him at the Department of Education and the Equal Employment Opportunity Commission and that concerned the Senate Ethics Committee's inquiry into five senators' relationships with thrift executive Charles H. Keating Jr. The resolution called for the Republican and Democratic leaders to appoint a special counsel, who would have subpoena power and assistance from FBI and General Accounting Office (GAO) investigators and who had 120 days to report back. *(Thomas confirmation, box, p. 802; Keating Five, p. 975)*

Republicans had pressed for a stepped-up investigation focused on the Thomas leaks alone. The issue came to a head two days before the vote on S Res 202, on Oct. 22, a week after Thomas was confirmed. During consideration of unrelated legislation (S 596), John Seymour, R-Calif., offered an amendment seeking a 30-day inquiry by the FBI into the Thomas leaks. Majority Leader George J. Mitchell, D-Maine, insisted on a broader investigation using a special counsel. The Seymour amendment was rejected on a 45-55 party-line vote after Mitchell agreed to push his own proposal. S Res 202 was adopted with bipartisan support.

Mitchell and Senate Minority Leader Bob Dole, R-Kan., on Dec. 6 named Peter E. Fleming Jr., a partner in the New York law firm of Curtis, Mallet-Prevost, Colt & Mosle, as special counsel. The investigation began Jan. 1, 1992.

In February, Timothy Phelps, reporter for the Long Island, N.Y., newspaper *Newsday*; Nina Totenberg, reporter for National Public Radio (NPR); and Bill Buzenberg, vice president of news and information at NPR, were subpoenaed with regard to their stories about Hill's allegations. Paul M. Rodriguez of the *Washington Times* was subpoenaed in connection with articles he wrote about the Keating Five investigation. The reporters maintained that they would not reveal their sources on First Amendment grounds.

Thomas was headed for an easy confirmation by the full Senate when *Newsday* and NPR made public Hill's allegations on Oct. 6, 1991. The Senate Judiciary Committee was lambasted for not aggressively investigating the charges; public furor forced the Senate to postpone the vote and open an unusual round of televised hearings. The news accounts quoted Senate sources who had read the FBI report on the matter but made clear that the reporters did not have the report. Only senators and fewer than five staffers had access to it, according to a committee aide. The NPR story also quoted from a copy of a statement Hill sent the committee Sept. 23.

Fleming sought the telephone records of Totenberg and Phelps, saying that the records could point to the person responsible for leaking information. But after lawyers for the two reporters protested, and some senators appeared startled by the maneuver, Fleming backed off, saying that he would wait for a Senate Rules Committee ruling. Rules Committee Chairman Wendell H. Ford, D-Ky., and Ted Stevens, Alaska, the panel's ranking Republican, decided March 25, 1992, to block enforcement of the subpoenas that sought to compel reporters to reveal their sources and the telephone company to turn over the journalists' phone records. The decision ended any possibility that Fleming would learn the source of the Thomas leaks.

The GAO had looked into disclosures of confidential information in October 1990 from the Ethics Committee's Keating Five investigation, but it could not identify the leaker. Fleming, too, failed. In his final report, released May 4, Fleming speculated that several sources of what he dubbed "a sea of leaks" likely were involved in the Keating Five case.

The 171-page report concluded that the FBI report on Hill's allegations had not been leaked to the press. Only Hill's statement to the Judiciary Committee was. The report speculated that Totenberg's source was someone in the Senate, exonerating Hill and various activists who opposed the Thomas nomination. All the report could say about Phelps' source was that it probably was "not a Republican."

The report also confirmed Hill's claim that she was reluctant to go public with her allegations. The Judiciary Committee repeatedly said that it did not initially press the investigation because Hill did not want her name made public, but the Fleming report suggested that staff members were aware that some "misunderstanding" may have existed about Hill's request for confidentiality.

The report also revealed much about individual senators and the mores of the institution. The report noted that Strom Thurmond of South Carolina, the ranking Republican on the Judiciary Committee, never read Hill's statement and did not provide copies of it to fellow GOP committee members.

From the outset, John C. Danforth, R-Mo., Thomas' chief backer, and others focused suspicions for the Thomas leaks on Howard M. Metzenbaum, D-Ohio, a leading Thomas opponent, and his staff. Metzenbaum's aides initiated the talks with Hill that eventually led to an FBI inquiry and subsequent leaks.

Metzenbaum vehemently denied the charges that he was responsible for the leaks, and no evidence was found to support them.

On Oct. 24, 1991, the day the Senate authorized the investigation into the leaks, President Bush, saying that lawmakers could not be trusted, announced that FBI reports would no longer remain on Capitol Hill and that staff would not be permitted to read them. He rescinded that order five months later.

Ethics Reorganization

In compliance with 1989 ethics legislation (PL 101-194), the House Committee on Standards of Official Conduct (ethics committee) reorganized in 1991.

Most members of the House ethics committee resigned after the scandal-plagued 101st Congress. They were replaced largely by institutional loyalists in line with the panel's historically cautious approach. House Speaker Thomas S. Foley, D-Wash., tapped as chairman Louis Stokes, D-Ohio, a veteran troubleshooter for the House leadership with a long record of tackling unpopular tasks. A former defense attorney, Stokes was the panel's chairman from 1981 to 1985. A 10-year veteran of the panel, James V. Hansen of Utah, was named as ranking Republican. The full House approved them Feb. 6.

The other Democrats were Matthew F. McHugh, N.Y.; George "Buddy" Darden, Ga.; Benjamin L. Cardin, Md.; Nancy Pelosi, Calif.; Jim McDermott, Wash.; and Gary L. Ackerman, N.Y.

The Republicans were Fred Grandy, Iowa; Nancy L. Johnson, Conn.; Jim Bunning, Ky.; Jon Kyl, Ariz.; Porter J. Goss, Fla.; and David L. Hobson, Ohio. PL 101-194 expanded the committee, beginning in the 102nd Congress, from 12 to 14 members. *(Ethics legislation, p. 920)*

The committee decided to block anyone from filing official complaints of improper conduct against members during the 60 days before each primary and general election. The prohibition was approved May 29 as part of the reconstituted panel's revised rules, adopted to reflect the 1989 law. It was meant to curb what ethics members said was an increasingly popular tactic among challengers — filing a complaint and then trumpeting the fact that serious charges were being investigated by the ethics committee. The committee retained the right to open an inquiry on its own.

Under the new procedures, the panel was to split on a case-by-case basis into two subcommittees — one investigative and one adjudicatory — if a report of misconduct was deemed worthy of inquiry. If any allegations brought by the investigative subcommittee were found to be proven by the adjudicatory subcommittee, the full committee would recommend sanctions to the House.

In addition, the committee opened a separate Office of Advice and Education to help members and employees understand ethics rules by fielding questions and organizing seminars. Under the new rules, members were shielded from punishment if they followed the committee's written advice — a protection modeled after a Senate rule.

The Senate Ethics Committee also underwent major membership changes in 1991. The two-year investigation of the Keating Five senators prompted the panel's chairman, Howell Heflin, D-Ala., to step down after 12 years as chairman or vice chairman of the committee; he was replaced as chairman by Terry Sanford, D-N.C., a member of the committee. Two other members of the six-person panel resigned as well: Jesse Helms, R-N.C., and David Pryor, D-Ark. The vacancies were filled by Richard H. Bryan, D-Nev.; Slade Gorton, R-Wash.; and Jeff Bingaman, D-N.M. *(Keating Five, p. 975)*

Professional Administrator

Following a rash of scandals involving the management of the House, lawmakers in 1992 approved a resolution (H Res 423) to overhaul the House's internal operations and hire a professional administrator. The House also created the post of inspector general, who was reponsible for auditing the House's administrative functions; eliminated the position of postmaster; and abolished the House Post Office.

The idea for a House administrator had been around since 1977, when it was offered as part of a reform package. A united House Republican Conference opposed it. *(Congress and the Nation Vol. V, p. 886)*

Much like a county executive or town manager, the administrator was to oversee the House buildings, police force and subway system, as well as such services as the House hair salon, car washes and restaurants. The administrator also would supervise the financial and management operations of the House officers: the clerk, doorkeeper and sergeant-at-arms.

The House adopted H Res 423 on April 9 on a 269-81 vote, after a bitter partisan fight. Republicans proclaimed the changes to be cosmetic reform and called for far-reaching modifications in the legislative balance of power — including banning proxy voting and putting more Republicans on the Rules Committee. Democrats countered that the measure represented a major reform that would bring House management into the modern era and allow members to get back to legislative business.

Republicans earlier had offered a substitute bill that was a sweeping agenda of long-sought changes to overhaul committee and floor procedures that Republicans believed put the minority at an unfair disadvantage. Democrats argued that issues of legislative power did not belong in a bill about administrative matters. The substitute was rejected on a 159-254 party-line vote.

H Res 423 provided that the Speaker, the majority leader and the minority leader would choose the administrator. After a six-month search for a candidate all could agree on, the House leaders on Oct. 23 named Leonard P. Wishart III, a retired Army lieutenant general, to be the director of non-legislative and financial services. Wishart would oversee 440 House member offices, 1,100 congressional district offices and 11,000 employees. His term was for two years, and, under the resolution, he could be fired by the Speaker or through a vote of the full House.

One goal of H Res 423 was to end the traditional system of patronage used to fill hundreds of House jobs, which leaders said was at the root of the problem in House operations. But the resolution prohibited patronage only for jobs controlled by the administrator — about 200 of the approximately 600 patronage jobs. In the future, the remaining patronage positions could be put under the administrator's control.

The House Administration Committee was directed to establish in the 103rd Congress a new Subcommittee of Administrative Oversight, with equal numbers of Republican and Democratic members, to oversee the administrator's performance. Tie votes in subcommittee would be referred to the full committee.

Congressional Reform Study

Battered by scandal, scorned by an unforgiving public and abandoned by some of its most talented members, Congress in 1992 created the Joint Committee on the Organization of Congress, which was authorized to review Congress and make recommendations by the end of 1993 on how to improve its operations.

Rep. Lee H. Hamilton, D-Ind., introduced H Con Res 192 in July 1991 to a lukewarm reception. Powerful committee chairmen were suspicious that changes would decrease their clout. Speaker Thomas S. Foley, D-Wash., said he feared that the measure would distract from substantive legislative business. By March 1992, however, Foley changed his mind and actively endorsed the resolution.

The House voted 412-4 on June 18 to adopt H Con Res 192 (H Rept 102-550). The Senate accepted the measure by voice vote July 30 after removing a provision that would allow House members serving on the panel to make interim recommendations before the two parties' caucuses met in December 1992 to organize for the 103rd Congress. Warning that early reporting requirements would enmesh the panel in election-year politics, the Senate inserted language specifying that no official work be conducted before Nov. 15, 1992. The House agreed to the Senate changes by voice vote Aug. 6. The measure did not require the president's signature.

The resolution specified that the panel be made up of 28 members of the House and Senate, equally divided among Democrats and Republicans. The House and Senate majority and minority leaders were the only members specifically assigned to the panel; party leaders would choose the rest. The panel was charged with studying the committee system, the relationship between the House and Senate, the relationship between Congress and the executive branch, and the responsibilities and powers of congressional leadership.

House Voting Privileges

On Dec. 9, 1992, while organizing for the 103rd Congress, Democrats approved a proposal to give delegates from the U.S. territories and the District of Columbia the right to vote when the House considered legislation in the Committee of the Whole — a parliamentary framework under which the entire House met to debate and amend important legislation. The full House accepted the proposal, with some modifications, as part of a package of rules changes (H Res 5) on Jan. 5, 1993. The delegates already had the right to vote in the House's regular committees.

Del. Eleanor Holmes Norton of the District of Columbia persuaded her fellow Democrats that no legal distinction existed between voting in committees and voting on the floor in the Committee of the Whole. She was the chief proponent of statehood for the District and thought to ask for a vote in the Committee of the Whole as an interim step. She sought a Congressional Research Service (CRS) legal opinion on the constitutional or statutory problems that could result from the rule change. In its Nov. 16, 1992, opinion, the CRS American Legal Division concluded: "Since Congress has arguably treated the Committee of the Whole as if it were not the full House for purposes of a quorum, and since Congress has previously allowed delegates to vote in committees, allowing a delegate to vote in the Committee of the Whole is apparently consistent with present congressional interpretation of its constitutional authority."

Most Democrats first got wind of the proposal when it was presented to the Democratic Caucus in December. Skittishness over the idea came principally from allowing delegates who represented thinly populated territories such as American Samoa (population 47,000) to have virtually the same power on many House votes as, for example, the single at-large representative of Montana (population 799,000). Some Democrats wanted to draw a distinction that would allow voting privileges for the District's 607,000 residents, who, unlike residents of the territories, paid federal income taxes, or Puerto Rico's 3.6 million. But few Democrats wanted to go on record against the idea of voting privileges.

David E. Skaggs, D-Colo., offered an amendment to require the House to revisit any issue decided by delegate votes in the Committee of the Whole. He withdrew it after pleas from party leaders, who said they were not sure how a vote would go. The Democratic Caucus approved Norton's proposal by voice vote Dec. 9, but misgivings continued to grow. Later that week, Democratic leaders announced that they had set up a task force to re-examine the issue before the full House considered it in January.

By January, a majority of Democrats had serious reservations about Norton's proposal. Some members feared that it might be unconstitutional, while others expressed concern about fairness. Skaggs revived his amendment, which provided that whenever a question was decided on the strength of delegate votes, regardless of whether it was approved or rejected, the committee would dissolve and the House would immediately vote on the issue without the delegates. The House would then turn itself back into the Committee of the Whole.

The Democratic Caucus held a series of votes on the issue Jan. 5 before the House convened. It first voted 186-16 for the Skaggs amendment and then voted 170-45 for the amended proposal to allow the delegate votes. In addition to the 45 votes against the leadership compromise, 43 Democrats did not vote. The caucus then voted 173-28 to pass the entire package.

The floor fight over the rules was bitter, acrimonious and sharply partisan. In the end, however, the votes were neither close nor surprising. The House voted 224-176 to kill a GOP amendment to set up a task force to study the delegate question. The House subsequently voted 187-238 against a Republican motion to strike the delegate language from the rules package and impose term limits on committee chairmen and ranking members. The House then approved the rules package including the delegate proposal on a largely party-line vote of 221-199.

On Jan. 7, House Minority Leader Robert H. Michel, R-Ill., and a group of fellow Republicans filed suit in U.S. District Court in Washington challenging the new rule. U.S. District Judge Harold H. Greene held a hearing on the suit Feb. 9. On March 8, he ruled that the delegate voting procedure was constitutional because "the votes ... are meaningless." Greene went on to say that, without the provision for a second vote in close calls, the rule plainly would have been unconstitutional.

Closed-Captioned TV

The House and Senate in 1991 initiated closed-captioned television coverage of their floor proceedings.

The House started providing the service, which allowed televisions adapted with decoders to display the printed text of words as they were spoken, on Feb. 19 and the Senate followed suit on Nov. 18.

In providing the service, both chambers were complying with the 1990 Americans with Disabilities Act (S 933 — PL 101-336), which required that those with disabilities have equal access to government proceedings no later than January 1992. *(PL 101-336, p. 743)*

Chronology Of Action On Congress: Election Issues

1989-90

No agreement could be reached — between Democrats and Republicans, the House and the Senate, or Congress and the White House — on campaign finance legislation, even though the desire for change in the existing system reportedly was widespread. Related legislation affecting political advertisements had no better luck; not one bill saw floor consideration.

The idea of congressional term limits began to catch on, however, as public disdain for Congress grew.

Campaign Finance

Despite the professed support of both political parties for the idea, legislation to revise the widely unpopular system of financing congressional campaigns died in 1990, the victim of sharp differences between Republicans and Democrats over the best approach to take, divisions within the majority Democrats and unresolved issues between the two chambers.

The Senate and House passed separate bills (S 137, HR 5400) — both generally backed by Democrats and strongly opposed by Republicans — aimed at reducing campaign spending and limiting the influence of political action committees (PACs). But President Bush threatened to veto any bill setting campaign spending limits, and, with ideological and political differences too wide to bridge so late in the session, conferees on the two bills never met.

Congress in 1992 cleared a campaign finance bill, which Bush vetoed. The Senate sustained the veto. *(102nd Congress action, p. 959)*

1989 Action

The Senate in 1987-88 had taken up the issue of campaign finance but was stalemated. In 1989, momentum again built, as the leaders of both parties in both chambers vowed to press for campaign finance measures. Packages of proposals were offered by Bush and by House Republicans. A House task force could not bridge the yawning partisan gulf on major issues, but it agreed in principle on several lesser changes in federal election law. *(1987-88 action, Congress and the Nation Vol. VII, p. 894)*

Bush Proposal. Bush on June 29 proposed what he called a "sweeping system of reform" for raising and spending money in congressional elections. Bush's plan called for the elimination of business, trade and union PACs, as well as PACs formed by elected officials. It would cut in half, to $2,500, the maximum contribution allowed by the so-called non-connected PACs — those formed to advance causes such as Israel, free trade or children, or by political party leaders.

To replace the loss in financing, Bush wanted to allow more money to come from political parties. The parties could spend 2½ times more than they spent on congressional campaigns through coordinated expenditures. Bush did not support a Republican proposal to raise individual contribution limits to $2,000 per election. He flatly opposed any form of public financing or spending limits, as advocated by some Democrats.

Bush's plan would severely limit the use of one of the major weapons in an incumbent's arsenal, the frank, by banning "unsolicited mass mailings" from congressional offices. It also called for incumbents to donate leftover campaign funds to their party, to the government for debt retirement or to contributors on a pro rata basis. Bush also suggested extending to all members of Congress a law banning the conversion of campaign funds to personal use. Congress did so in a pay and ethics bill enacted near the end of the session. *('Grandfather clause,' box, p. 952)*

The Bush package also raised an issue of paramount importance to Republicans as the 1990 census approached: how the states would draw boundaries in the subsequent congressional redistricting. Bush called for an end to gerrymandering, the practice in which the party in control drew district boundaries to its advantage. Bush called for districts that "adhere to compactness standards and follow established community boundaries."

Democrats assailed the Bush plan as baldly partisan. It would remove the advantage they had gained in recent years raising money from PACs while emphasizing the role of parties, where Republicans outperformed them. Meanwhile, within the GOP, no consensus existed on major items such as curbing the frank and eliminating certain PACs.

Legislation (S 1727) containing Bush's proposals was introduced Oct. 5; it died at the end of the 101st Congress.

House GOP Plan. House Republicans pulled together their own 25-point plan to rewrite election laws. Adopted Sept. 21 by the GOP Conference, the package represented a compromise between the party's senior members and its young turks.

Major proposals in the GOP package would:

- Reduce to $1,000 per election (instead of $5,000 in existing law) the amount a PAC could contribute to a candidate. The amount would rise with inflation.
- Prohibit "bundling" of contributions by corporate, union or trade association PACs.
- Prohibit candidates from forming or controlling PACs. Candidates' committees would be prohibited from giving to other committees except to support the same candidate for another office.
- Restore a tax credit for contributions up to $250 per taxpayer. This would be limited to home-state candidates.
- Require that more than half a candidate's funds be raised locally.
- Remove virtually all limits on parties' contributions and coordinated expenditures, with disclosure to the Federal Election Commission.

House Task Force. The 21-member, bipartisan House Task Force on Campaign Reform, established in early 1989, was unable to reach a compromise on central issues such as the cost of campaigns and the role of special interest money. However, the members did agree to call for:

- Eliminating the "bundling" of individual contributions by intermediaries who often fill in the candidate payee on contributors' checks.

'Grandfather Clause'

A provision in the 1989 ethics and pay law (PL 101-194) closed a loophole in election law that allowed senior House members to pocket leftover campaign funds. Members were forced to choose: leave Congress before the beginning of the 103rd Congress in 1993 or lose their right to take the money. *(Ethics code rewrite, p. 920; congressional pay, p. 965)*

The exemption arose from a 1979 election law (PL 96-187) that barred personal use of excess campaign funds, except by "grandfathered" members — those who were in office on Jan. 8, 1980, even if they left and returned later. Under House rules, they could make personal use of the money after leaving Congress. Once they disclosed its conversion, their reporting obligations ended, although the funds were considered taxable income. Senate rules prohibited personal use by members past or present.

At the beginning of the 101st Congress, 191 House members were eligible to take advantage of what was known as the "grandfather clause."

Cars, Loans, Travel — and Cash

According to a Congressional Quarterly review of federal campaign records, grandfathered ex-members converted to personal use at least $862,000 between 1980 and the beginning of 1989. More than $710,000 of this was in cash. Another $115,000 was either borrowed or used to retire personal loans unconnected to their former campaigns. At least $37,000 went for cars, furniture, travel and other services.

Exempt retirees who had left Congress since 1980 had access to more than $2 million in leftover campaign funds. Most of it — $1.5 million — was controlled by members whose service ended with the 100th Congress.

The loophole-closing provision not only cut off eligibility for exempt members at the beginning of the 103rd Congress but also limited the amount they could convert to what was on hand when the law was enacted.

Major Conversions

Many members took advantage of the grandfather clause:

- William Carney, R-N.Y., resigned from Congress in 1987 after four terms. The Committee to Re-Elect Congressman Carney continued operations until March 31, 1988, when it wrote two final checks: $899.68 to the bookkeeper and $83,695.63 to Carney; he declined to say how he had used the money.
- The will of John J. Duncan, Tenn. (1965-88), the ranking Republican on the House Ways and Means Committee until his 1988 death, divided his campaign funds — $604,521 in four accounts — among his wife and four children. Duncan had raised $175,000 in 1987.
- The largest campaign kitty of the 1989 House retirees belonged to Gene Taylor, R-Mo. Taylor left the House with $457,939, according to his 1988 year-end Federal Election Commission report. In mid-1989, he converted $345,000 of that to his own use.
- Just before the end of 1988, Gene Snyder, R-Mo. (1963-65, 1967-87), pocketed $173,203. Sam Stratton, D-N.Y. (1959-89), gave $198,795 to himself. Ed Jones, D-Tenn. (1969-89), wrote himself a check for $130,686.
- Mendel J. Davis, D-S.C. (1971-81), closed out his campaign committee by forgiving a $20,000 loan made to him, paying $453 to move his furniture and writing checks to himself for the cash balance of $22,047, money he said he used to pay for back surgery.
- In 1981, his first year of retirement, Ray Roberts, D-Texas (1962-81), spent $2,903 to purchase office equipment and to travel. He also wrote himself checks for $13,014.
- Ken Holland, D-S.C. (1975-83), who chose not to run for re-election in 1982, returned $25,435 to contributors and then, in January 1983, lent himself $75,000. No requirement exists that he repay the loan.
- L. H. Fountain, D-N.C. (1953-83), rode into retirement in a Cadillac for which his committee kicked in $13,820, part of the $14,880 it spent on gifts for the L. H. Fountain Appreciation Fund.
- Sam B. Hall Jr., D-Texas (1976-85), who traded his seat for a federal judgeship, added $58,433 in campaign cash to his extensive holdings in oil, real estate and stock.

Some members gave excess funds to charity. Manuel Lujan Jr., R-N.M. (1969-89), who became George Bush's interior secretary, set up a scholarship program for high school students, using $117,243 in campaign funds. Colleges and universities were the beneficiaries of $40,000 from Charles Whitley, D-N.C. (1977-87); $100,000 from Don Fuqua, D-Fla. (1963-87); and $110,000 from Richard H. Ichord, D-Mo. (1961-81).

Among those who formed political action committees were former Speaker Thomas P. O'Neill Jr., D-Mass. (1953-87), the Democratic Candidates Fund, and former Reagan administration budget director David A. Stockman, R-Mich. (1977-81), the Free Enterprise Fund.

Some members returned the leftover cast to contributors. Harley O. Staggers, D-W.Va. (1949-81), returned $59,333; William M. Brodhead, D-Mich. (1975-83), refunded $72,579. Former senator Russell B. Long, D-La. (1948-87), gave back more than $360,000.

- A bar to members converting their campaign funds to personal use after leaving office under the so-called grandfather clause.
- Heightened disclosure requirements to better identify sponsors of independent campaigns run by private groups for or against candidates.
- A prohibition against leadership PACs.
- Restoration of a tax credit to encourage small individual donations.

1990 Action

Both the Senate and House were poised, at the beginning of 1990, to begin the first major overhaul of the campaign finance system since the Watergate era. Flaws in the system were highlighted by the ongoing investigations into the finances of Sen. Dave Durenberger, R-Minn., and the case of the Keating Five. While plans were to move a bill early in the year, partisan bickering and intraparty disagreement kept the House and Senate versions from reaching the floor until the last days before the August recess. *(Durenberger, p. 921; Keating Five, p. 975)*

Senate. Senate leaders in early 1990 set up a bipartisan advisory panel of six outsiders — including academics, lawyers and party operatives — to review proposals and to issue recommendations on campaign finance reform. On March 7, the panel announced a plan that embraced "flexible spending limits" — voluntary, state-by-state limits that would be "reasonably high" and would allow exemptions for party funds and in-state contributions. Candidates who accepted the limits would get lower postal and advertising rates, and their in-state contributors would receive tax credits for modest contributions.

Instead of targeting specific caps, the panel chose to focus on ways to encourage candidates to raise "good money" and discourage their pursuit of "bad money." The panel also called upon Congress to give political parties free broadcast time and more freedom to spend; reduce contributions from PACs once they exceeded an unspecified percentage of a candidate's funds; forbid bundling for corporate, union and trade association PACs; forbid independent expenditures by corporate, union and trade association PACs; and disclose "soft money" donations.

Senate Democrats and Republicans spoke well of the plan.

The Senate Rules and Administration Committee on March 8 approved, on a 7-3 party-line vote, a Democratic bill (S 137 — S Rept 101-253) to reward candidates who obeyed firm state-by-state spending limits with discounted advertising and punish those who did not by compensating their opponents' campaigns with tax dollars.

Republicans huddled at a weekend retreat March 24-25 and, bolstered by advice from GOP consultants, came away renewed in their opposition to spending limits. White House Chief of Staff John H. Sununu reiterated the president's pledge to veto any bill that included spending limits or that otherwise appeared harmful to the GOP.

In April, Senate Democrats spent the weeks leading up to the floor debate negotiating within their 54-member caucus. S 137 was substantially rewritten in caucus, but flexible spending limits remained its centerpiece. Under the Democratic plan, participating candidates would get reduced mail rates, the lowest rate for the broadcast ads they purchased and free television time that would cost the government tens of millions of dollars. Some Democratic strategists said they believed that tax-paid elections could be sold to the public as a way to take special interests out of politics; from the Democratic perspective, such elections represented a much-needed answer to the GOP's plan to kill PACs.

Intraparty fighting among the Democrats had settled on several issues. The most nettlesome was how to make the transition to 1992. Some senators expressed concern that the changes being touted would prevent them from having enough money to gain re-election. David L. Boren, D-Okla., said the issue would be resolved by grandfathering all money raised by candidates as of the law's effective date. Other technical problems nagging Democrats stemmed from the increasing use of campaign accounts by senators for catchall political expenses, such as flying their spouses to campaign events. Senators did not want these expenses to count against the amount they could spend on television ads or the like.

As a result of the meetings among Senate Democrats, Boren — a principal cosponsor of S 137, along with Majority Leader George J. Mitchell, D-Maine — added amendments to the bill providing for tax-paid television advertising and exemptions for in-state fund raising. The government would provide candidates with vouchers equal to 20 percent of their general election spending limit to be used to purchase longer blocks of television time, so that campaigns would rely less on 30-second spots. And candidates could raise and spend an additional amount equal to 25 percent of their spending limit so long as they raised it in small, in-state contributions. The size of a qualifying contribution was not set.

Fearful that spending limits would reduce their chances of regaining the majority in Congress, Senate Republicans tried to re-focus the debate on the sources of money. Republican senators agreed during their own conference April 24 on legislation to eliminate PACs. The measure would halve to $500 the size of contributions candidates could accept from out-of-state donors, a step designed to slow down fund-raising treks to Hollywood and New York City. The measure would place new restrictions on unions and other tax-exempt groups, and parties would be allowed to buy their candidates large blocks of advertising time in addition to the money they could spend in behalf of candidates.

In dueling news conferences held May 1 and May 3, Republicans and Democrats, respectively, announced their new plans. Each party bid for the reformist label in the event that agreement proved impossible.

The Republican proposal to "ax the PACs" sent Democrats, accustomed to the offensive on this issue, scrambling. The Democrats shifted ground substantially; party leaders agreed to take PAC contributions out of Senate campaigns. Under pressure to replace the money, they added public financing to their plan for general election spending limits. Democrats had abandoned this position two years earlier and, in the report accompanying S 137, had "concluded that sufficient support was not there at this time for public financing." The new proposal also maintained a ban against soft money operations used by state parties to pay for voter registration and get-out-the-vote drives.

The Republican measure, S 2595, was introduced on May 9 by Mitch McConnell, R-Ky., and 33 cosponsors. The Democratic substitute had 43 cosponsors.

Senate leaders set up two tracks for campaign finance legislation the week of May 14 — one for airing partisan differences, and the other for resolving them. When no

Presidential 'Checkoff' Fund

The tax-return "checkoff" system, in which taxpayers marked a box on their annual federal income tax returns to earmark one dollar for funding of presidential campaigns, did not fare well during the 1980s. Response to the program became increasingly anemic, and the Federal Election Commission (FEC) warned in 1989 that unless participation increased or additional money was injected, the presidential fund would be bankrupt by 1996.

Public funding of presidential campaigns was established in the Revenue Act of 1971 (PL 92-178), the Federal Election Campaign Act (FECA) of 1971 (PL 92-225) and the 1974 FECA amendments (PL 93-443). Congress sought to curtail severely the role of large private contributions and to broaden the base of financial support for presidential campaigns. Presidential candidates who agreed to abide by primary and general election spending limits would be permitted to share in a pool of public funds; the size of that pool would be determined by the number of taxpayers who designated one dollar — without incurring additional tax liability — for the Presidential Election Campaign Fund. *(PL 92-178, Congress and the Nation Vol. III, p. 410; PL 92-225, Congress and the Nation Vol. III, p. 397; PL 93-443, Congress and the Nation Vol. IV, p. 991)*

Presidential primary candidates who agreed to honor state-by-state spending limits and an overall spending limit were permitted to submit contributions from individuals of up to $250 to be matched with public funds. Because the threshold to become eligible for matching funds was low — raising $5,000 in amounts of $250 from each of at least 20 states — long-shot and third-party candidates found that they could qualify. In the general election, each major party candidate was given a flat grant from the fund of $20 million plus a cost-of-living add-on.

The number of taxpayers who checked off a dollar for the fund steadily declined, from 28.7 percent in 1980 to 19.9 percent in 1991. Meanwhile, because of inflationary adjustments mandated by the law and an increase in the number of private contributions submitted for matching, payouts to candidates increased greatly.

Congress anticipated that a deficit in the fund could occur, but in 1976 it amended the Internal Revenue Code to provide that "moneys shall not be made available from any other source for the purpose of making such payments." Campaign finance experts said that amendment, when read together with provisions of federal election law, established the right of candidates to raise private money to supplement any deficit and — absent additional legislation — prevented the fund from being buttressed with general appropriations. When asked by the Senate Appropriations Committee what it would do if the fund faced a deficit, the FEC said it would be required by law to give priority to financing general election candidates and party conventions. Primary candidates would share leftover funds, if there were any.

The FEC and political scientists were baffled about why a growing number of taxpayers were shunning the checkoff. Some experts said the public did not know enough about the fund; others believed they knew but rejected the idea of government subsidies. The argument also was put forth that voters were disgusted with negative campaigning, and thus looked upon the campaign fund with disfavor. Some scholars believed the declining participation rate stemmed from the same reasons for low voter turnout. Others saw the rise in use of professional tax preparers as the problem.

Supporters of the funds proposed that money be spent on educational and promotional campaigns to increase participation. Another proposal would increase the amount of the checkoff and add a separate tax checkoff for the party of the taxpayer's choice. But opponents said the system should be allowed to collapse of its own weight.

progress was made, both sides agreed that the floor was not the place to work out the differences. Instead, Mitchell and Dole, playing down expectations, each named four-member squads May 16 to conduct off-the-floor negotiations.

During the week of May 21, Senate negotiators began the tedious process of feeling their way through the contentious issues. They quickly found common ground where it was most expected — issues that hit both parties equally: the cost of television advertising, independent expenditures, the use of personal funds in campaigning, and bundling.

Dole on July 25 tested the Democrats' resolve on the contentious issue of spending limits when he told Mitchell that the GOP for the first time was willing to limit spending from money raised through out-of-state contributions, but only those of more than $250. The Republican move apparently was designed to force the Democrats into the position of eschewing compromise on the eve of the floor debate. But with Republicans refusing any limits on money raised in a senator's state, the proposal fell short of the standard Democrats had set. Spending limits had been the heart of every Democratic proposal, and Mitchell indicated that no way existed to resolve the difference short of fighting it out on the floor.

The Senate debate, which stretched over three days and required 16 roll-call votes on amendments, was striking for its lack of rancor, compared with the 100th Congress, when the Senate struggled through eight cloture votes as Republicans filibustered a Democratic campaign finance package.

Each party came to the floor prepared to fight over the merits, not procedure. To this end, Mitchell and Dole cut a deal: The Democrats would not try to shut off debate so long as the Republicans did not delay in presenting amendments.

From the outset, the parties drew the line at spending limits. As the debate opened, Democrats incorporated the GOP ban on PAC contributions. This compromise steered the Senate debate toward four key issues: spending limits; the public funding used to make spending limits possible; the role tax-exempt organizations, in particular labor unions, played in elections; and the advantages enjoyed by incumbents.

S 137 offered candidates incentives to observe spending limits: a voucher equal to 20 percent of the general election spending limit, to be used to purchase television time in blocks of one minute or more; reduced mail costs; and contingent public financing if an opposing candidate exceeded the spending limit. The Congressional Budget Office estimated that the contingency funds would cost $30 million per election. The TV vouchers would add another $21 million and reduced mail costs $5 million, according to McConnell. This added up to $56 million every two years for Senate elections alone.

McConnell sought to strike all such public funds, but his amendment failed on a **46-49 (R 44-0; D 2-49) key vote** taken July 30. An amendment offered by John Kerry, D-Mass., also was rejected, 38-60 on July 31; it would have increased public funding by giving candidates, in addition to the TV vouchers, public funds equal to 70 percent of the general election spending limits. Subsequently, Boren put up a sense of the Senate amendment, which was adopted Aug. 1 on a 55-44 vote, stating that the free TV time and other incentives to comply with spending limits would be paid for with voluntary contributions from tax refunds. Republicans called this a back door to future tax funding and cited the declining participation rate in the Presidential Election Campaign Fund. *(1990 key votes, p. 1039; presidential 'checkoff' fund, box, p. 954)*

Republicans made two runs at reducing the role labor unions played in elections. The first, an amendment by Orrin G. Hatch, R-Utah, sought to let all workers covered by union contracts, including union members, opt out of paying dues or other fees that went for any activity other than bargaining contracts. The second, an amendment offered by McConnell, sought to prohibit tax-exempt status for any organization that supported or opposed candidates. Both measures were vigorously opposed by union lobbyists and defeated on virtually identical, near party-line votes of 41-59 and 41-58, respectively, on July 31.

Not every Republican amendment met defeat. Don Nickles of Oklahoma won, 98-1 on July 31, a move to impose tighter restrictions on the franking privilege, barring the use of the frank for mass mailings in election years, stipulating that senators could not assign their franking budget to other senators, prohibiting franking once the annual appropriation was depleted and requiring House members to join senators in disclosing their spending mail. An amendment by Pete V. Domenici, R-N.M., to limit contributions from individuals who did not live in a candidate's state to $250 per election, passed by voice vote.

The Senate also approved, 73-27 on July 31, an amendment by Lloyd Bentsen, D-Texas, to bar companies with majority foreign ownership from operating a PAC. An amendment by John McCain, R-Ariz., to strike certain provisions allowing incumbent senators to exceed spending limits was rejected 44-55 on Aug. 1. Another McCain amendment had been rejected, 49-49 on July 31, to restrict the use of campaign money to bona fide election activities and to require all surplus funds at the end of a campaign to be turned over to the Treasury to reduce the deficit.

Spurred by election-year ethics turmoil, senators did not stop at campaign finance. On Aug. 1, they voted 77-23, on a Christopher J. Dodd, D-Conn., amendment, to prohibit members from taking speaking fees from lobbying groups and 51-49, on a Daniel Patrick Moynihan, D-N.Y., amendment, to cap all other forms of outside income. The Moynihan provision would have profoundly affected the Senate's many millionaires had the legislation survived. *(Congressional pay, p. 965)*

Before the vote on final passage, the Senate rejected 44-55 a Dole amendment to substitute a GOP package for the Democratic bill, which would ban PACs; cut the limit on individual contributions from $1,000 to $500; limit the amount of money a candidate could spend from personal funds; and limit the amount of money raised from individ-

Corporate Campaign Spending

In a victory for advocates of limiting corporate campaign spending, the Supreme Court on March 27, 1990, upheld the authority of the states or the federal government to bar private corporations from using their funds to run independent political campaigns.

The Court said in its 6-3 decision in *Austin v. Michigan State Chamber of Commerce* that a Michigan law requiring corporations to make their political expenditures through separate political action committees did not violate the First Amendment's protection of free speech. The case grew out of a newspaper advertisement, purchased by the chamber with funds from its own treasury, that endorsed a candidate for the Michigan House of Representatives. *(Case summary, p. 829)*

Federal election law and the laws of 20 other states had similar prohibitions on direct corporate campaign spending.

The ruling limited the Supreme Court's 1986 decision, *Federal Election Commission v. Massachusetts Citizens for Life (MCFL) Inc.*, which held that certain small non-profit corporations could spend directly from their treasuries because they would have difficulty establishing separate funds, creating a disincentive to political speech.

The Court in the *MCFL* case established a three-part test for non-profit corporations that it said the Michigan chamber failed to meet. One of these tests was its independence from the influence of business corporations. *(MCFL case summary, Congress and the Nation Vol. VII, p. 816)*

State Reforms

The Minnesota legislature on April 25, 1990, overwhelmingly adopted partial public financing with voluntary spending limits for congressional campaigns. The law, the first of its kind, applied to congressional candidates running in general or special elections, beginning in 1991.

New Hampshire in 1989 passed a law that created voluntary spending limits for U.S. Senate and House races. Candidates choosing not to abide by the limits had to pay a $5,000 filing fee and submit notarized signatures to appear on the ballot. The Federal Election Commission in 1989 partially voided the law as it applied to parties, arguing that states were pre-empted by federal statutes from regulating federal candidates.

Minnesota went beyond New Hampshire by using public financing as an incentive for the spending limits of $3.4 million for U.S. Senate candidates and $425,000 for House candidates in each election cycle. If both opposing candidates agreed to limit spending, neither would receive public funds. If one candidate agreed to the limits but another did not, the participating candidate not only would receive matching public funds but also would have the spending limits waived.

The public grants could equal 25 percent of the candidate's spending limits. They would be financed with general appropriations, not by the state's voluntary income-tax checkoff that was used to finance state races. Candidates who waged a tough primary battle would be permitted to spend a slightly higher amount of money in the general election.

Meanwhile, New Hampshire lawmakers in 1990 backed away from plans to regulate another area of federal elections. Although both chambers of the legislature passed measures to limit independent expenditures by political action committees in congressional elections, conferees could not agree on a method for enforcing the law before adjournment.

uals living outside a candidate's state, with an exception for money raised in amounts of $250 or less.

The Senate on Aug. 1 passed the Democrats' version of S 137, 59-40, with five of 45 Republicans voting "yea" and only one Democrat voting "nay." The measure would eliminate PACs, limit out-of-state contributions to $250, establish voluntary state-by-state spending limits and, to lure participation by candidates, offer campaigns low-cost mail, free television time and extra funds to fight opponents who exceeded the limits. The Bush administration threatened a veto, citing its opposition to spending limits and public financing at a time of significant fiscal constraints.

House. By early 1990, the Task Force on Campaign Reform had advanced as far as it could without intervention by House leaders. In March, a meeting was held between Speaker Thomas S. Foley of Washington and Minority Leader Robert H. Michel of Illinois. Michel had heightened expectations of a compromise in December 1989 when he said he would consider spending limits for House races if they were set high enough, perhaps at $1 million. Few GOP colleagues rushed to embrace Michel's suggestion, however, and many expressed concern that he had opened a door they had considered firmly shut. Foley's commitment to seek campaign finance reform also spurred some in traditionally Democratic ranks to voice their own opposition. Organized labor expressed concern about measures to regulate political activity within unions. Complaints were heard from Democratic Party leaders about efforts to curb soft money.

Finger-pointing soon began in the House. Talks between Foley and Michel produced nothing but Republican discontent, and the list of reforms agreed on in 1989 began to shrink. In April 1990, for example, Democrats began asserting that they had agreed to give up leadership PACs only if Republicans agreed to prohibit state parties from contributing to candidates across state lines — a trade-off the joint statement never mentioned.

Intraparty squabbles nearly prevented House Democratic leaders from bringing HR 5400 to the floor before the August recess. The leadership was forced to water down the measure just days before its consideration. In closed-door meetings, Democrats yelled about the "what ifs" of their particular circumstances. Democrats from urban areas feared that a $550,000 spending limit would prove too little once depleted by a tough primary fight. As a result, a $165,000 exception to the spending limit was written for candidates who won their primaries with less than 66.7 percent of the vote and faced general election opposition. Exceptions also were made to permit lobbyists to continue serving on members' fund-raising committees and to exempt legal and accounting fees from the spending limit.

A two-tiered system of PACs was created that would diminish the clout of PACs that relied on large contributions from their members. PACs that took donations of more than $240 a year from members would be barred from giving candidates more than $1,000 per election. PACs that took contributions of $240 or less from members would be able to give up to $5,000 — a standard that preserved the clout of labor and trade association PACs that favored Democratic incumbents.

The Democrats did not finish drafting the bill until late in the night of Aug. 2. When it came to the floor the next day, Republicans claimed it was being run through the House in a hurried fashion at a time when members were itching to go home. Republicans lost efforts to keep the bill off the floor, including an attempt to adjourn the House. Illinois Democrat Dan Rostenkowski, chairman of the Ways and Means Committee, joined Republicans in complaining that the Democratic task force that wrote the bill had short-circuited the committee process. His was one of four committees that otherwise would have claimed jurisdiction. No committee report on the bill was issued.

The GOP pushed a Michel alternative that would have limited contributions from PACs to $1,000, would have required candidates to raise at least half their funds within their congressional district and would have imposed no overall spending limits. It was rejected 169-241.

The Democratic leadership, meanwhile, had committed to support the amendment sponsored by David R. Obey, D-Wis., and Mike Synar, D-Okla. The amendment, cast as an attack on "fat cats," sought to commit up to $100,000 in public financing for House campaigns, cut PAC contributions deeper than the underlying bill and reduce the amount an individual could give to House candidates. But Republicans turned the tables on the vote. They knew the Democrats were counting on GOP votes to kill the amendment; the amendment's taxpayer financing, unpopular with Southerners and conservatives, was expected to bring down the entire bill. The Republicans forced the Democrats to ask for a roll call on the amendment and then, with a handful of exceptions, voted present. The result was that even Obey and Synar worked against passage of their amendment. It failed, 122-128, with 153 members voting present.

On Aug. 3, two days after the Senate passed its bill, the House passed HR 5400 on a 255-155 vote. Republicans contributed only 15 "yea" votes. Despite their losses, Republicans argued that voters would hesitate to assign Democrats the reformist label once they learned the cost, estimated at hundreds of millions of dollars. Outside groups such as Common Cause criticized the package for not going far enough on public financing or the reduction in PAC limits. Many insiders questioned the need for action at all, arguing that no public cry had been heard for new election laws.

Conference. The differences between the House and Senate bills showed up most starkly in their treatment of PACs and public financing. The Senate, for example, would ban PACs, but the House would set a limit on PAC contributions that would affect only a fraction of the members. A similar gap existed in their treatment of soft money — the tens of millions of dollars raised off the books to influence federal elections. The Senate would take a big step toward imposing federal rules on state election activities; the House limited itself primarily to abuses that cropped up in the 1988 presidential campaigns.

The House on Sept. 26 named 28 members as conferees. This followed the Senate's Sept. 18 decision also to move to conference. A Republican effort on Sept. 26 to instruct House conferees to accept Senate provisions on franked mail and PACs failed 194-225. Both were issues on which the GOP was unable to get recorded votes on during the floor debate on the bill.

The negotiators never met. The rush to adjournment and the need to handle must-pass legislation left the campaign finance measure unfinished. The likelihood of Congress' being able to reach a compromise that suited both parties, both chambers and the president was not great.

Efforts to pass separate legislation to provide for lower advertising rates for candidates also were stalled. *(Story, below)*

Political Ads

The 101st Congress considered various bills regarding political advertisements, but none progressed beyond committee approval.

Broadcasting Rates. On Sept. 13, 1990, John D. Dingell, D-Mich., chairman of the House Energy and Commerce Committee, introduced HR 5756, which would redefine how broadcasters set the lowest rates offered to those running for office. It was reported Oct. 15 (H Rept 101-871).

Congress since 1972 had required broadcasters, as part of their public trust obligation, to provide political candidates with the lowest advertising rates available. When the law (PL 92-225) was written, finding the lowest rate often was a simple matter of checking a broadcaster's rate card. By 1990, however, the broadcast advertising market had become far more sophisticated, and many considered the "lowest unit charge" obsolete. Instead, negotiations often were based on the season, time of day and ratings points of a particular show. *(PL 92-225, Congress and the Nation Vol. III, p. 397)*

Worst yet for candidates, most buyers agreed up front that their ads could be pre-empted and moved to another time if another buyer was willing to pay more. With timing critical in a campaign, candidates usually would not risk having their ads pulled. So they bought "non-preemptible" time — usually during prime time — at premium rates. A study, released Sept. 7 by the Federal Communications Commission, of 30 radio and television stations in five metropolitan areas found that candidates were paying higher prices than commercial advertisers at most stations.

HR 5756 drew immediate fire from Common Cause, a lobbying group that had been fighting for the campaign finance reform legislation (S 137, HR 5400) that stalled in conference. Both S 137 and HR 5400 contained provisions dealing with advertising rates for candidates. Common Cause's objection was that Dingell's bill would provide incumbents with a major political advantage without attempting to solve the larger problems with campaign finance. *(Campaign finance, p. 951)*

On Nov. 21, 1989, the Senate Commerce, Science and Transportation Committee had reported a measure (S 1009 — S Rept 101-225) that entitled candidates to the lowest cost for any type of advertising while requiring that the spots could not be pre-empted. In 1990, Sens. John C. Danforth, R-Mo., Daniel K. Inouye, D-Hawaii, and Ernest F. Hollings, D-S.C., drew up a substitute for S 1009. The substitute and Dingell's bill would prohibit pre-emption of any class of ads bought by candidates, although they would allow for "circumstances beyond the control of the broadcasting station." The lowest charge available to candidates would be set on a per-show basis. The length of time during which candidates could use the lower rates would be shortened from 45 days to 30 days for a primary and from 60 days to 45 days for a general or special election.

Under the Dingell bill, however, the lowest rate would be calculated over a 60-day period before a primary and a 90-day period before a general or special election. Broadcasters complained that this would unfairly force them to set rates during summer rerun season when rates were lowest, even though most candidates would be buying time for October, when the new fall television lineup and football season sent rates soaring.

In a spirit of bipartisan cooperation, Sens. Harry Reid, D-Nev., and Mitch McConnell, R-Ky., had announced Sept. 21, 1989, that they would introduce S 1655, to cut the cost of campaign advertising on television and radio, as well as discourage certain spending and fund-raising practices and stiffen enforcement measures available to the Federal Election Commission. The measure died.

Negative Advertising. Proposals to combat negative advertising in political campaigns proliferated in 1989, but partisan wrangling and constitutional questions prevented quick action.

Danforth and Hollings introduced S 999, the Clean Campaign Act of 1989. It required that federal candidates personally appear in television ads that "refer directly or indirectly" to their opponents. The bill also required radio and television stations to offer free air time for candidates to respond if they had been attacked in spots paid for by groups independent of a political opponent.

Sens. Bob Graham, D-Fla., and Richard H. Bryan, D-Nev., introduced the Political Broadcasting Disclosure Act (S 1346) on July 18. The bill would stiffen existing requirements for disclosure of who sponsors television and radio ads.

The Communications Subcommittee of the Senate Commerce, Science and Transportation Committee held hearings July 19 on both bills. Despite the bipartisan support for the bills, differences that held up previous campaign law revisions surfaced. John McCain, R-Ariz., decried the Danforth-Hollings measure as making re-election easier for incumbents. Ted Stevens, R-Alaska, said he likely would oppose any political advertising bill that was not part of a comprehensive campaign reform package. McConnell argued that Danforth-Hollings was unconstitutional. The American Civil Liberties Union said the bill violated the freedom of expression.

Term Limitations

The issue of legislative term limitations attracted serious attention in 1990 and was expected to spur debate for years to come. Voters in Colorado approved a ballot initiative in November 1990 to apply a 12-year limit to U.S. senators and House members. Ballot measures to limit the terms of state legislators were approved in California, Colorado and Oklahoma. The constitutionality of term limits on federal lawmakers remained unresolved, however. *(1991-92 action, p. 963)*

The California measure passed only narrowly with 52 percent of the vote, but the Colorado and Oklahoma measures were approved by more than two out of three voters.

The drive for term limits was characterized by some as a bipartisan expression of voters' low esteem for Congress. A Gallup Poll released Jan. 11, 1990, found strong nationwide support for limits: 70 percent of those surveyed were in favor of limiting congressional tenure. A *New York Times*/CBS News poll in October found nearly 60 percent of the respondents favoring limits. In the meantime, however, voters returned to office almost all incumbents who sought re-election in 1990.

Others viewed the push for term limits as a GOP strategem. The Republicans were unable to break the seeming permanence of Democratic control of Congress and many state legislatures. "One should see this movement for what it is: An attempt by the Republican Party . . . to legislate congressional victories," said Rep. Beryl Anthony Jr., D-Ark. "The GOP can't win at the polls, and now they are trying to circumvent the ballot box." Republican Party officials denied the charge, and how much term limits would help Republicans was not clear. However, limiting terms could make recruiting candidates easier for the GOP.

Background

The question of whether members should be allowed unlimited terms first arose at the founding. In 1777, the Continental Congress included a three-year limit on delegates under the Articles of Confederation. But when the Constitution was drafted 12 years later, no cap was imposed either on congressional or presidential tenure. The Constitutional Convention laid aside a proposal to limit congressional service, one of several issues it characterized as "entering too much into detail."

Proposals to limit congressional service were introduced in the First Congress but died, as did similar proposals that followed. Presidents were limited to two four-year terms under the 22nd Amendment, a reaction to Franklin D. Roosevelt's 12-year tenure as president. Congress approved the amendment in 1947, and ratification by the states was completed in 1951. *(Congress and the Nation Vol. I, p. 1434)*

In the late 1980s, proposals to limit congressional terms dovetailed with increasing Republican attacks on the powers of incumbency. In an unprecedented move, the GOP endorsed congressional tenure limits in its 1988 platform.

Constitutional Debate

Did states have the power to limit terms of service in Congress? Argument centered on the first Article of the Constitution.

Article I, Section 5, Clause 1 stated: "Each House shall be the judge of the elections, returns and qualifications of its own members." Lawyers for Congress and academic scholars insisted that a constitutional amendment was the only legal way to limit terms and that state statutes such as Colorado's were unconstitutional. They said the Constitution explicitly gave Congress power to determine the qualifications of its members and to control substantive aspects of congressional elections.

Some experts, however, saw room for debate. They contended that states received the power to limit re-election of members of Congress from Article I, Section 4, Clause 1: "The times, places and manner of holding elections for Senators and Representatives shall be prescribed in each state by the Legislature thereof; but the Congress may at any time by law make or alter such regulations." The Supreme Court and lower federal courts had used this clause, they said, to uphold two types of state election laws affecting who could run for Congress — laws barring a candidate from seeking office as an independent after being defeated in a party primary for the same office, and so-called resign-to-run statutes, which required officials to quit one office to run for another.

The major modern test of the constitutionality of limits on members' qualifications came in 1969, when the Supreme Court ruled in *Powell v. McCormack* that Congress had unlawfully refused to seat a member who met the simple qualifications for office: 25 years of age, seven years of citizenship and residency in the state to be represented. By doing so, the Court found, Congress added to the constitutional qualifications for office.

The case arose after the House voted in 1967 to exclude Adam Clayton Powell Jr., D-N.Y. Powell was a controversial figure, repeatedly prosecuted for tax evasion and other alleged offenses and held in contempt of court. He also was criticized for lavish travel at government expense and for various abuses of his office accounts. *(Background, Congress and the Nation Vol. II, p. 895; Congress and the Nation Vol. III, p. 323)*

After an investigation found Powell misusing Education and Labor Committee funds, the House Democratic Caucus voted Jan. 9, 1967, to remove him from the committee chairmanship. The next day, the House adopted a resolution denying Powell his seat, pending an investigation of his conduct by a select committee. The vote was 363-65, with a majority of both parties in support.

A select committee held hearings in February and recommended that Powell be stripped of his seniority, censured for "gross misconduct" and fined $40,000 (a punishment without precedent in congressional history). The House rejected the recommendations and instead voted 307-116 (with Southern Democrats joining Republicans) to deny Powell his seat for the duration of the 90th Congress (1967-69).

At the hearings, Powell would answer only questions regarding his age, citizenship and residency. He and his lawyers contended that those were the only questions relevant to his being seated as a duly elected member.

After his exclusion, Powell sued (naming Speaker John W. McCormack, D-Mass., among other defendants). His suit eventually was heard by the Supreme Court, which ruled 7-1 on June 16, 1969, that Powell had been improperly excluded because Congress could not add to the basic three qualifications set forth by the Constitution.

The Court's opinion, written by Chief Justice Earl Warren, held that Powell was elected by the voters and "was not ineligible to serve under any provision of the Constitution," referring specifically to the basic three qualifications. So, the Court ruled, "the House was without power to exclude him from its membership."

After the decision, Powell was sworn in and seated, having been re-elected in the interim.

Powell stopped "one step short" of disposing of term limits, according to A. E. Dick Howard, a constitutional law professor at the University of Virginia. "*Powell* clearly limits what the House might do, but it does not necessarily answer the question of what a state might do," said Howard.

Proponents and Opponents

Proponents of limiting congressional terms saw Congress' problems as rooted in the high rate of re-election of House incumbents and warned that Congress was becoming an ossified ruling class. "Entrenchment has turned senators into sovereigns and representatives into royalty," said Trudy Pearce, senior policy analyst for Citizens for Congressional Reform. Proponents also argued that limiting terms would make members bolder about dealing with thorny, long-term policy questions — such as reducing the federal deficit — and less preoccupied with running for re-election.

Promoting the idea nationally in 1990 was Americans to Limit Congressional Terms (ALCT), which was set up by executives of the Eddie Mahe Co., a GOP consulting firm. ALCT was headed by former representative Jim Coyle, a Pennsylvania Republican who lost his re-election bid in 1982 after one term in office. The group's aim was to pass a constitutional amendment, and its members urged state legislatures to pass resolutions calling on Congress to enact such an amendment.

Although most members of its advisory board — state legislators and former members of Congress — were Republican, ALCT said its mission was non-partisan. The issue attracted prominent GOP support throughout 1990. President Bush called congressional term limits "an idea whose time has come," and Vice President Dan Quayle, referring to the 22nd Amendment, said that "what is good for the president is good for the Congress."

Term-limit activists also counted among their number Ralph Nader, the consumer advocate and co-founder of Public Citizen; Free Congress Federation; the National Taxpayers Union; and several conservative think tanks.

Critics of term limits contended that most of the consequences, foreseen or unforeseen, would be bad. Political scientists generally warned that term limits would banish veteran members regardless of their ability or popularity, disenfranchise voters wishing to re-elect those incumbents and ultimately empower people in non-elective jobs: bureaucrats, lobbyists and congressional staff. Some argued that limiting terms would make Congress worse, depriving it of members with historical perspective and established expertise in complex areas of modern government. Moreover, experts argued, a 12-year limit might become, in practice, a 12-year guarantee — as prospective challengers waited for open seats. In the Senate, 12-year limits would make senators lame ducks for half their service.

Opponents of term limits contended that lack of turnover is not a problem in Congress. They dispute the notion of a permanent Congress by noting that two-thirds of all House members in the 101st Congress had served less than 12 years.

1991-92

To counter the drumbeat of negative press coverage of Congress, Democrats mobilized to push through a campaign finance bill in the name of reform. Without bipartisan backing, however, it could not withstand a presidential veto.

The public's view of Congress did not show improvement either. Voters in 14 states brought their displeasure to the polls in 1992, approving term limits for their U.S. representatives and senators.

Campaign Finance

Buffeted by scandal, congressional Democrats moved quickly in 1992 to push through both chambers and send to the White House the farthest-reaching attempt to reform federal election law in two decades. However, the legislation (S 3), which sought to provide public funding and other incentives to congressional candidates who agreed to limit their campaign spending, lacked bipartisan backing. President Bush vetoed the measure, and the Senate fell nine votes short of overriding the veto.

A longstanding threat from Bush that he would veto any bill that included public funding of campaigns and the vast differences between the bills each chamber passed in 1991 seemed to reduce the likelihood of serious consideration. But scandals at the House bank and Post Office sent Democratic leaders on a reform mission and re-ignited the campaign finance issue in 1992. Conferees reconciled differences between the chambers' bills by letting each live by its own rules. The House also went along with the Senate's more restrictive language on "soft money" — money spent by state parties on activities such as voter registration, get-out-the-vote drives and generic advertising that benefited state and federal candidates.

Under the bill, House candidates' spending would have been capped at $600,000 per election cycle; the ceiling for

Senate candidates would have varied between $1.6 million and $8.9 million, depending on state population. House candidates who complied with the spending limits and other restrictions would have gotten up to $200,000 in federal matching funds; Senate candidates would have received taxpayer-financed vouchers to buy discounted TV advertising time worth up to 20 percent of the state spending limit.

Following the veto and the unsuccessful override attempt, Democrats contended that Bush and the Republicans killed the legislation, which would have restricted political action committees (PACs) and curtailed the money marathon congressional candidates were running. Republicans countered that the Democratic proposal was little more than an incumbent-protection plan that would have cost taxpayers millions and denied challengers the ability to compete.

Background

Congress had been examining how to curb the ability of interest groups to dominate the flow of campaign money and attempting to establish a level playing field for all candidates since the first law regulating campaigns was enacted during the Theodore Roosevelt administration. However, major new laws to overhaul the campaign finance system came only after scandals: Teapot Dome in the 1920s, Watergate in the 1970s.

In 1925, the Teapot Dome scandal yielded the Federal Corrupt Practices Act, an extensive statute governing the conduct of federal campaigns. But that law was so riddled with loopholes that it was ineffectual. It took Congress another four decades to adopt two pieces of legislation containing some of the ground rules under which elections were conducted into the 1990s.

President Richard Nixon reluctantly signed the Revenue Act of 1971 (PL 92-178), allowing the $1 tax checkoff for presidential campaign financing to take effect. As a condition for his signature, however, Nixon insisted on postponing the measure until after the 1972 election. *(PL 92-178, Congress and the Nation Vol. III, p. 410)*

On Feb. 7, 1972, Nixon signed the Federal Election Campaign Act (FECA — PL 92-225), which required comprehensive disclosure for contributions and expenditures by candidates for federal office. But FECA ultimately had a limited impact on controlling campaign spending. In the wake of the Watergate scandal, Congress passed the FECA Amendments of 1974 (PL 93-443). The law set limits on contributions and expenditures for congressional and presidential elections, established an independent Federal Election Commission to oversee federal election laws and created a specific framework for providing presidential candidates with public financing. *(FECA, Congress and the Nation Vol. III, p. 397; 1974 amendments, Congress and the Nation Vol. IV, p. 991)*

The Supreme Court ruled in 1976 on a constitutional challenge to FECA in the case of *Buckley v. Valeo*, upholding FECA's disclosure requirements, contribution limitations and public financing of presidential elections. But the Court struck down spending limits for congressional and presidential races, including restraints on using a candidate's personal assets, except for presidential candidates who accepted public financing, as unconstitutional limits on free speech. It also struck down limits on independent expenditures. *(Case summary, Congress and the Nation Vol. IV, pp. 639, 995)*

Subsequent congressional efforts to change the campaign finance system were driven largely by the desire to find a way to limit congressional campaign spending without violating the mandates of the *Buckley* decision. With the ceilings on expenditures removed, campaign costs grew apace during the next decade, and candidates became increasingly dependent on raising money from PACs. In outlawing independent expenditures, the Supreme Court also spurred the rise of non-connected, or ideological, PACs, which often sponsored sharply negative ads.

In 1979, Congress passed a package of FECA amendments (PL 96-187) that, among other things, allowed state and local parties to underwrite voter registration and get-out-the-vote drives in behalf of presidential tickets without regard to financial limits. This provision generated the practice of raising soft money. *(PL 96-187, Congress and the Nation Vol. V, p. 950)*

Although both parties during the Reagan era debated public financing for congressional campaigns, no significant legislation was passed. In 1987, with Democrats back in control of the Senate, Majority Leader Robert C. Byrd of West Virginia decided to make campaign financing a major issue. Democrats brought a public financing bill (S 2) to the floor in June, but it was shelved in early 1988 after a record eight cloture votes failed to break a GOP filibuster. *(1987-88 action, Congress and the Nation Vol. VII, p. 894)*

The House and Senate passed proposals (HR 5400, S 137) to reduce campaign spending and limit the influence of PACs, but the legislation died unresolved at the end of the 101st Congress. *(101st Congress action, p. 951)*

1991 Action

The 102nd Congress felt pressure from several sources to institute reforms in the campaign finance system.

Common Cause, the public interest lobbying group, had for several years made campaign finance a centerpiece of its appeals to members. The Ralph Nader-affiliated group Public Citizen and the labor-affiliated group Citizen Action also pushed for an overhaul of the laws so that tax dollars would replace PAC dollars. Reformers were encouraged when the 33 million-member American Association of Retired Persons joined a coalition in favor of the legislation in 1990 and pushed the issue with its members in 1991.

Common Cause hoped that the Keating Five savings and loan investigation of 1990-91 would provide the impetus for a breakthrough, calling the Keating scandal "the smoking gun" that proved the corruption of the election finance system. The televised Keating Five hearings focused national attention on the influence of money on politics. The hearings showed how Charles H. Keating Jr., the powerful owner of a thrift and real estate empire, used his fund-raising skills to assemble clout in Washington. The testimony left no doubt of the urgency Senate offices attached to raising money. *(Keating Five, p. 975)*

Senate. The Senate Rules and Administration Committee on March 20 set the stage for a floor showdown by approving the Democrats' bill (S 3 — S Rept 102-37), sponsored by David L. Boren of Oklahoma, on a 7-2 vote. Mitch McConnell, R-Ky., offered the only amendment, which sought to strip the taxpayer financing provisions from the measure. The amendment was rejected on a 7-7 vote. The committee also reported a Republican-sponsored measure (S 6), but without a favorable recommendation.

Senate floor debate on S 3 lasted seven days, and more than two dozen amendments were considered. Republicans sought to undercut spending limits, calling them a device that would hamstring challengers who needed to outspend an incumbent to win. Moreover, they argued that the bill's benefits were a hammer held over the heads of candidates to coerce them into giving up the right to spend freely in campaigns. But with Democrats solid on the need for spending limits, the Republicans zeroed in on the more vulnerable target of public financing. They belittled it as "food stamps for politicians" and questioned the willingness of taxpayers to expand the program.

On May 22, the Senate rejected, on a straight party-line vote of 42-56, a McConnell amendment to strip the bill of public financing and spending limits. Both parties made it a test of loyalty. Hank Brown, R-Colo., then offered an amendment to limit any winning Senate candidate who accepted public financing to two terms in office. Boren won agreement, 68-30, to a tabling motion, and the Brown amendment was killed. McConnell then tried to add a disclaimer to television advertisements purchased with public funds that would read: "The preceding political advertisement was paid for with taxpayer funds." The amendment went down when the Senate agreed to table (kill) it, 54-44. *(Term limitations, pp. 958, 963)*

Republicans met with similar outcomes on attempts to kill public financing but leave the spending limits intact; to strip party presidential nominating conventions of public financing; and to strip presidential campaigns of public financing. The latter amendment, which was tabled on a 60-38 vote, came in response to Democratic counterpunching on the public financing issue. Democrats noted that Republican presidential candidates continually accepted taxpayer financing and that Bush accepted more than $60 million in tax funds for his 1980 and 1988 presidential campaigns.

The Democrats were divided on the issue of public financing for broadcast advertising. In the end, they settled for an amendment by Jim Exon, D-Neb., added to the bill May 23, that said broadcasting benefits would be paid for by voluntary tax checkoffs or by eliminating tax breaks that corporations could get for lobbying.

An amendment offered by John Kerry, D-Mass., to extend public financing to cover the cost of 90 percent of a general election campaign went down on a 39-58 vote on May 22. The next day, the Senate tabled, 54-44, an amendment by Don Nickles, R-Okla., to eliminate the 50 percent discount on advertising rates that participating candidates would receive. And by a 79-19 vote, a William V. Roth Jr., R-Del., amendment to strike the spending limits and public financing from the bill and offer candidates free television time during the last 45 days of the campaign was tabled.

The Senate also agreed, 57-40, to table a Bob Dole, R-Kan., amendment to let parties give $250,000 in seed money to candidates who challenged Senate incumbents; accepted, by voice vote, a Paul Wellstone, D-Minn., amendment to prohibit a candidate who agreed to spending limits from spending more than $25,000 of his own money; and accepted, by voice vote, a McConnell amendment providing for a direct appeal to the Supreme Court of cases challenging the constitutionality of the act.

On May 21, senators added to the bill a ban on keeping honoraria payments by a 72-24 vote, but the issue subsequently was settled as part of a Senate pay hike. *(Congressional pay, p. 970)*

Despite Bush's May 22 reiteration of his previous promises to veto any legislation that limited campaign spending, resorted to taxpayer financing of congressional elections or created separate systems for House and Senate candidates, the Senate May 23 passed S 3 on a 56-42 vote. The measure was almost identical to the campaign finance bill passed by the Senate in 1990.

House. The House bill (HR 3750) was written by a House Administration Committee task force chaired by Sam Gejdenson, D-Conn. The task force discussed the bill widely with Democrats before introducing it and gave a full preview at a Democratic Caucus meeting Oct. 9. That meeting renewed reluctance among Democrats to support public financing and led to efforts to change the bill before it went to the floor.

The provision in question would give up to $200,000 in public financing to match the first $200 of each individual contribution. The cost was estimated at $75 million every two years, a figure that would rise with inflation. A group of 46 Democrats led by Glen Browder, D-Ala., under the aegis of the Conservative Democratic Forum, asked the House Administration Committee to kill public financing and instead offer 100 percent tax credits for contributions of $50 or less. Browder acknowledged that tax credits were another form of public financing, but he contended that they were more politically palatable than public matching funds as a way to encourage small contributions.

While public financing was the most controversial feature, objections also were made to the proposed $200,000 limit on PAC contributions. Democratic incumbents from rural and inner-city districts that lacked wealthy Democratic donors said they feared the loss of PACs. Some prominent House Democrats argued that the image of PACs should be less that of favor-seeking special interests than something resembling the political equivalent of the United Way: thousands of small donors giving part of each paycheck to match the clout of the fat cats.

Democratic leaders formally unveiled the task force's handiwork on Nov. 12. To provide political cover for members anxious about public financing, Gejdenson adopted the same approach the Senate used: the bill did not actually raise the money, leaving that to a separate tax bill. Instead, it merely suggested that the money should be raised by limiting the tax deduction organizations took for lobbying, an effort to make special interests bear the cost. The bill received lukewarm but politically essential endorsements from outside lobbies pressing for change, including Common Cause, Public Citizen and the League of Women Voters.

The House Administration Committee approved HR 3750 (H Rept 102-340, Part I) on Nov. 14 on a 14-9 party-line vote. The committee defeated a series of Republican amendments on party-line votes, including one offered by Bill Thomas of California that would have required that a majority of individual contributions come from residents of the congressional district; cut the amount a single PAC could give candidates from $5,000 to $1,000, the same amount individuals were permitted to give; and required that any money spent to influence a federal election be raised under federal law, thus eliminating soft money.

In the days before the measure came to the floor, both House Administration Committee Chairman Charlie Rose, D-N.C., and Gejdenson acknowledged that the opposition to using tax revenues for matching funds was costing Democrats the votes they needed to ensure passage of the bill. The duo cut a deal Nov. 22 with conservatives. While the committee-approved legislation allowed for a future tax bill to raise the necessary funds, the Democratic leaders

Bush's Fund Raising

On April 28, 1992, President Bush raised nearly $11 million for his presidential campaign and other Republican interests; it was a one-day record in fund raising.

An estimated $9 million was collected at an annual gala dubbed the "President's Dinner" at which individual guests contributed as much as $400,000 and corporations delivered bundles of $1,500 contributions from employees. Hours before the dinner, Bush also collected nearly $1.9 million in public funds for presidential campaigns — a system Bush said was anathema for congressional campaigns.

Under existing law, individuals could give up to $25,000 in limited amounts to federal candidates and campaign committees. But no federal limits existed on gifts to state parties for voter contact that indirectly influenced House, Senate and presidential elections. Fundraisers working on the President's Dinner encouraged donors to direct a minimum of $92,000 to various GOP causes.

Altogether it was an embarrassing juxtaposition for a president who had tried to make the campaign finance system a staple of his attacks on Congress.

changed HR 3750 to dodge the issue of where the money would come from. The version that went to the floor provided only for voluntary contributions to an account called the Make Democracy Work Fund.

Conservatives also fought for, and won, language requiring "incentives for individuals to make voluntary contributions to the candidate of their choice" — code wording for tax credits. The rewrite made voting for the bill easier for Southerners, who could claim it did not contain taxpayer financing.

Thomas and Minority Leader Robert H. Michel of Illinois on Nov. 25 offered a substitute to HR 3750, which was rejected 165-265. It would have required candidates to raise at least half of all their campaign money from people living in their districts. It also would have cut the amount a single PAC could give a candidate from $5,000 per election to $1,000.

After nearly five hours of sharply partisan debate, the House passed the bill on a **key vote of 273-156 (R 21-144; D 251-12; I 1-0)** on Nov. 25. *(1991 key votes, p. 1061)*

1992 Action

The House bank and Post Office scandals consumed Congress early in 1992, contributing to a wave of retirements, a fear of defeat and even a threat to the Speakership of Thomas S. Foley, D-Wash. In this environment, House Democratic leaders began grasping for reform measures large and small, and campaign finance was an obvious target. However, while the rush to move the two campaign finance bills through conference at the start of the second session of the 102nd Congress created a whirlwind of activity, it was in the vacuum of a continuing stalemate between the two parties and, to a lesser extent, between the two chambers. Bush, in the meantime, continued to voice his veto threats. *(House bank, p. 929; post office, p. 939)*

Republicans and Democrats disagreed on how to fix the campaign finance system as well as on what was wrong. Their differences were both philosophical and practical. Democrats contended that the campaign finance system operated like an arms race, with candidates engaged in a never-ending quest for a financial edge. Hence, Democrats insisted that any new law had to limit campaign spending. Money they would take away from candidates, by limiting or banning PACs, they would replace with public subsidies. Republicans asserted that the problem lay with tainted sources of money. Instead of capping spending, they proposed curbing specific sources, such as PACs and large out-of-state contributions. They would encourage political parties to spend even more in behalf of their candidates. What Republicans feared most was that locking in spending levels would help lock in a Democratic majority.

While not so deep as the chasm separating the parties, a clear gap existed between senators' visions of reform and the ideas of House members, even of the same party. Some major differences could be difficult to resolve. For example, senators, with their statewide bases and national profiles, were generally less dependent on PAC money than on other sources of funding. Conversely, PACs had become financial pump houses for House incumbents, and thus they were less willing to live with severe limits on PAC activity. Driven by the distinct campaign techniques, fund-raising needs and political pressures facing their members, the two chambers were on separate courses that could produce a bewildering set of federal campaign laws — one for presidential contests, one for the Senate and another for the House.

Conference. The drive to get a conference agreement was partisan from the outset, and the push for the bill clearly came from the House. The conference met in a pro forma session March 31, when Democratic and Republican members gave opening statements reiterating old rhetoric. But it was evident that intense behind-the-scenes negotiating already had taken place. The majority staff distributed recommendations to Democratic members that day. With few modifications, those recommendations were adopted.

Spending limits were at the heart of Democratic proposals for campaign finance reform. The Democrats maintained that the ever-increasing cost of campaigns was the most significant problem with the system. Republicans contended that spending limits unfairly disadvantaged challengers who lacked the benefits of incumbency, such as high name recognition. The GOP also disapproved of the cost of spending limits: public financing.

The House bill included a matching fund system similar to that used in presidential campaigns. The Senate version offered candidates federally funded vouchers to purchase television advertising. House-Senate negotiators agreed early on to let each chamber design its own rules and left these provisions essentially intact.

Neither the House nor the Senate bill said explicitly how to pay for public financing, and the conference agreement was even less precise. Virtually all directions on how tax writers should fund the public financing provisions were stripped by conferees. The conference report also contained a sense of the Congress resolution that funding should not come from general revenues, increase the federal budget deficit or decrease spending on other programs.

Republicans, led by Bush, argued that the major problem with the existing campaign finance system was special interest money funneled through PACs. Republicans had long sought to ban PAC money, a step aimed at diminishing the role of unions that heavily favored Democrats.

Conferees made no effort to reconcile differences between the House and Senate on PACs. The $200,000 aggregate House limit was to remain, and PACs could continue to make $5,000 contributions. Senate Democrats, however, who had supported an outright ban on PAC contributions in their 1991 bill, backed away from that position. The final measure proposed to limit PAC contributions to Senate candidates to an amount equal to 20 percent of the spending limit. This language originally was part of a backup provision that Senate Democrats inserted in case a PAC ban was found unconstitutional. The backup proposal also called for limiting a PAC's contribution to an individual campaign to $1,000, but senators pressed for a higher limit, and the conference upped it to $2,500.

To get Senate Democrats to accelerate consideration of campaign finance legislation, House leaders agreed to language that would sharply restrict the way state parties raised and spent money. While the original House bill essentially codified existing law, the Senate proposal that was included in the final measure placed restrictions on federal candidates in raising soft money and on state party electioneering and required state parties to comply with federal contribution limits.

During House floor consideration of the conference report on S 3 (H Rept 102-487), the cost of the legislation again was debated. The Congressional Budget Office put a biennial price tag of $100 million to $150 million on the measure. Republicans set the figure slightly higher, at $200 million per election cycle. Republicans April 9 attempted to send the bill back to conference with instructions to strip out all public subsidies, but the procedural motion was rejected on a largely party-line vote of 179-243.

Because of a drafting mistake in the initial report, a provision was included that prohibited all members of Congress, not just senators, from using the frank for mass mailings in the calendar year of a re-election campaign. House Democrats sent the bill back to conference to exclude the House from the provision. The House did accept language that barred members from sending franked mail outside their distincts. *(Franking privilege, p. 973)*

The House approved the conference report April 9 on a **259-165 (R 19-145; D 239-20; I 1-0) key vote**, which was 24 votes short of the two-thirds majority needed to override. *(1992 key votes, p. 1083)*

Though no filibuster was threatened and amendments were not permitted to be added to a conference report, the Senate debated S 3 from April 28 through the afternoon of the 30th in part because both parties saw partisan advantage in talking about the measure. The Senate then approved the conference report 58-42.

Veto. As expected, Bush vetoed S 3, without fanfare and scarcely noted in the major media. In the message that accompanied his May 9 veto, the president said, "In addition to perpetuating the corrupting influence of special interests and the imbalance between challengers and incumbents, S 3 would limit political speech protected by the First Amendment and inevitably lead to a raid on the Treasury to pay for the act's elaborate scheme of public subsidies."

While neither House nor Senate Democrats ever had the votes to override, an override attempt was scheduled primarily to draw attention to what was referred to as Bush's stealth veto. The Senate May 13, in a **key vote of 57-42 (R 3-40; D 54-2)** that fell nine votes short of the necessary two-thirds majority to override, sustained the president's veto. In the wake of the legislation's failure, both Democrats and Republicans aggressively argued that the other side stymied their efforts at reform.

Term Limitations

In a backlash against career politicians, voters in 14 states on Nov. 3, 1992, approved initiatives to limit the length of service of their House members and senators. A 15th state, Colorado, had adopted a term-limit measure in 1990. Altogether, 181 House and Senate members entered the 103rd Congress (1993-95) with term limits. *(Colorado action, background, p. 958)*

All 14 states limited Senate service to 12 years. For Arizona, Arkansas, California, Michigan, Montana, Oregon, Washington and Wyoming, House tenure was capped at six years; Florida, Missouri, Nebraska and Ohio, eight years; and North Dakota and South Dakota, 12 years. The legality of such limits under the Constitution had not been tested, however.

Money often was the key to success. U.S. Term Limits, a Washington, D.C.-based group that served as a national clearinghouse for the term-limitation movement, contributed money in 11 of the 14 states, amounting to more than $1.1 million. As a result, questions arose as to whether the voter response was truly a grass-roots effort. Opponents also charged that U.S. Term Limits was being secretly financed by conservative and Libertarian groups, including billionaire brothers Charles and David Koch.

The timing of the spending also proved crucial. In Washington, the state group Legislative Initiative Mandating Incumbent Terms (LIMIT) was unexpectedly thwarted in its efforts to have a term-limit measure (Initiative 553) approved in 1991, when the campaign ran out of money in the final week and a last-minute drive by House Speaker Thomas S. Foley, D-Wash., and other state lawmakers helped turn back the initiative. In 1992, LIMIT spent most of the $190,000 it allocated for media in the last 10 days before the election, when most voters made up their minds. (Foley did not tour the state campaigning against term limits in 1992; instead, he focused on overturning any term-limit initiative in court on the grounds that it was unconstitutional. Supporters also had recrafted the measure so that the limits would not be applied retroactively. If Initiative 553 had been approved, Foley as well as all eight members of Washington's House delegation would have had to retire by the end of the 103rd Congress.)

In related action, the California Supreme Court on Oct. 10, 1991, upheld, 6-1, that state's 1990 election law tightly limiting the length of state legislators' careers. The California ruling held that no constitutional right, federal or state, existed to run for a given office or to vote for a given person. The court said term limits were valid protection "against an entrenched, dynastic legislative bureaucracy."

Only hours after Florida approved a term-limit initiative in 1992, a suit was filed in a U.S. District Court challenging its constitutionality. The year before, Republicans protested a U.S. House counsel's brief that argued that congressional term limits were unconstitutional. The brief was filed with the Florida Supreme Court, which was reviewing the constitutionality of the term-limit measure that would appear on the state's ballot in 1992. The House Nov. 6, 1991, agreed on a near party-line vote of 265-160 to table (kill) a resolution (H Res 268) to declare that Congress had no official opinion on term limits.

In other legislative action, Sen. Hank Brown, R-Colo., offered an amendment to a campaign finance bill (S 3) to impose a two-term limit on senators who used public campaign funding. It was tabled (killed) on a 68-30 vote on May 22, 1991. *(Campaign finance, p. 959)*

Chronology Of Action On Congress: Pay and Benefits

1989-90

The 101st Congress' first attempt to enact a pay increase for itself triggered a public brouhaha, which forced members to strike down the effort. On the second try, Congress was successful, but it ended up with a two-tiered system — one pay scale for representatives, another for senators.

The bill, which also provided changes in the ethics code, banned House members from receiving honoraria beginning in 1991, but senators hung on to the controversial practice.

Meanwhile, with public criticism of Congress on the rise, members moved to place restrictions on one of their most-loved perquisites: the frank.

Congressional Pay

Legislation (HR 3660 — PL 101-194) was enacted in 1989 that provided a two-tiered congressional pay system — with different salaries for senators and representatives — and a substantial change in congressional ethics law. *(Ethics code rewrite, p. 920)*

HR 3660 was unveiled by a bipartisan House task force only three days before it cleared — a contrast with the experience at the beginning of the year, when the public heaped weeks of abuse on Congress for seeking a 51 percent pay raise and forced members to block the hike by wide margins.

Congressional leaders tried to recast the pay issue as part of a drive to wean public officials from private largess by linking the pay raise to new limits on outside income, including a ban on honoraria.

As cleared, the legislation could raise the salaries of House members and top officials of the executive and legislative branches by as much as 40 percent by 1991, depending on the inflation rate. Senators' pay was increased 10 percent in 1990, with cost-of-living raises in later years.

The bill banned honoraria payments for House members in 1991, when the largest pay raise was set to kick in, and established a process for gradually scaling back honoraria levels in the Senate.

In 1990, senators were paid $98,400; representatives, $96,600. In 1991, senators received $101,900; representatives, $125,100. The $27,337 maximum in honoraria that senators could keep in 1990 fell to $23,837 in 1991. *(Pay raise history, box, p. 971)*

The Senate would bring its salary in line with the House and impose a ban on honoraria in 1991. *(Story, p. 970)*

First Pay Raise Attempt

Congressional leaders began laying the groundwork for a pay raise as far back as June 1988, when both the House and Senate voted to exempt themselves from a 4 percent cost-of-living raise provided other federal employees. The decision to forgo the cost-of-living increase was, to some members, further evidence of an ongoing political problem: The fear of voter backlash led members to deny themselves small annual increases, building up pressure for much more controversial raises.

The Commission on Executive, Legislative and Judicial Salaries (also known as the Quadrennial Commission) voted Dec. 13, 1988, to recommend a 51 percent salary increase — from $89,500 for most members to $135,000 — and a ban on honoraria. Shortly after, House Speaker Jim Wright, D-Texas, told reporters he wanted the pay raise to take effect without a vote and he would follow it immediately with a vote on legislation to curb honoraria. *(Congress and the Nation Vol. VII, p. 900)*

The weekend before the 101st Congress convened, cracks in what pay raise advocates had hoped would be a united leadership front began to show. On a Jan. 1, 1989, television talk show, House Minority Leader Robert H. Michel, R-Ill., and Senate Minority Leader Bob Dole, R-Kan., both said that the 51 percent raise was too high. Senate Majority Leader George J. Mitchell, D-Maine, said little about the pay raise except that the issue would be brought to a vote on the Senate floor.

Pay raise proponents got a boost from President Ronald Reagan when he backed the increase in the budget he submitted Jan. 8, which meant the pay hike would take effect on Feb. 8 unless Congress passed a resolution of disapproval. (George Bush, who would be inaugurated president on Jan. 20, also endorsed the pay increase.) The strategy was to keep the issue off the floor until the raise could take effect automatically. As a result, congressional leaders scheduled little legislative business for the first month of the session — an effective tactic in the House, but one that critics immediately portrayed as a strong-arm way to shove through the pay raise.

In the meantime, editorial writers pummeled Congress not only for the size of the pay hike but also for skirting a vote. Mail flooded the Capitol. Some of the most vociferous criticism came from consumer activist Ralph Nader and a network of radio talk-show hosts around the country who gave people a forum for venting their outrage against the raise. One station urged its listeners to send tea bags to their representatives and senators with the slogan, "Read my lips: No pay raise." Thousands did.

By the time the House reconvened after a two-week recess on Jan. 19, Wright was discussing the idea of scaling back the pay raise to 30 percent, which he thought would be more politically acceptable than 51 percent, and which could be portrayed not as a pay hike but as a dollar-for-dollar swap for abolishing honoraria. But he was dissuaded by members who wanted him to hang tough.

Some Democrats were made nervous late in January by a fund-raising letter from Lee Atwater, chairman of the Republican National Committee (RNC), that lambasted Democrats for the pay raise. Although RNC officials said that the criticisms in the letter were included by mistake, the incident made Democrats fear that they were being set up for a major attack on incumbency.

Wright on Jan. 30 sent to each House member a survey asking his or her views on the pay raise. On Feb. 2, Wright, citing the survey, announced a new plan for handling the pay question: He would schedule a vote to scale back the raise to 30 percent on Feb. 9 — the day after the larger hike was to take effect — and to ban honoraria. Wright's last-minute change in strategy infuriated his Democratic allies. It also alienated Michel. Wright had discussed the idea with Michel in a private meeting Feb. 1 but went public with it and suggested Michel would support it before he had a commitment from Michel.

Shortly before announcing the new strategy, Wright held a stormy meeting Feb. 2 with the task force of Democrats that had developed the no-vote strategy. He met with bitter criticism. Hours later, the Senate adopted a resolution (S J Res 7) to kill the pay raise.

By the time House Democrats returned from their Feb. 3 weekend at the Greenbrier resort in West Virginia, the raise was unraveling fast. Pay raise opponents were expected to try to force a vote on the issue during the pro forma session scheduled for Feb. 6. William E. Dannemeyer, R-Calif., offered a resolution, which Democratic leaders blocked by quickly moving to adjourn. Dannemeyer, however, demanded a roll call, portraying it as a vote on the merits of the pay raise. Usually such procedural votes are party-line affairs with Democrats required to support their leaders, but 108 Democrats deserted; the House voted 88-238 against adjourning. Wright immediately went to the floor and announced that a vote on the pay raise would take place the next day.

Debate on H J Res 129 was, somewhat ironically, dominated by warnings about the need for a pay raise — if not for Congress, at least for other federal officials. The keynote was delivered by Ways and Means Chairman Dan Rostenkowski, D-Ill., who gave an emotional defense of the pay raise. "I can't remember a more disheartening or embarrassing debate," he said. "I am proud of what I do and you, my colleagues, should feel the same way."

A Vic Fazio, D-Calif., motion to suspend the rules and pass H J Res 129 to disapprove the recommendation for a pay raise was agreed to 380-48 on Feb. 7. Wright got most of the criticism both for the pay raise strategy and for its ultimate failure. Resentment over how he handled the issue helped erode his position and contributed to his eventual downfall. *(Wright resignation, p. 917)*

The Senate's Feb. 2 vote on S J Res 7 seemed a symbolic gesture because House leaders at the time were vowing to avoid a vote before the raise took effect automatically. S J Res 7, sponsored by Sen. Larry Pressler, R-S.D., would disapprove the recommended raises for members of Congress and senior officials in the legislative and executive branches but preserve them for judges. It would require roll-call votes for all future raises for Congress. The Pressler measure was a substitute for a simple repeal of the pay raise sponsored by Sen. Terry Sanford, D-N.C. Pressler's proposal was approved by a vote of 95-5; the amended measure was then approved by voice vote.

After approving the measure, the Senate adopted another resolution (S Res 40) to bar members from accepting honoraria for speeches and appearances in case the 51 percent raise took effect.

After the House switched its position and voted to block the pay raise Feb. 7, the Senate passed H J Res 129 quickly, with little debate. The vote, clearing the joint resolution, was 94-6. President Bush signed H J Res 129 (PL 101-1) the same day.

Second Pay Raise Attempt

President Bush in April called for a 25 percent increase in judicial salaries, saying the defeat of the larger pay increase left judges far behind what they could earn in the private sector. As soon as he became Speaker June 6, Foley urged a bipartisan task force that had been named by Wright to look at ethics laws to report quickly. The centerpiece of that effort, eliminating honoraria payments, could fly only if members' lost income was offset by a salary increase. Bush on June 29 reiterated his support for the idea of raising congressional salaries and barring lawmakers from accepting speaking fees. On July 7 he proposed a 25 percent increase for top officials of the executive branch. He also outlined a plan for eliminating honoraria but left establishing a specific pay level for lawmakers up to them.

The task force, headed by Fazio and Lynn Martin, R-Ill., quietly began testing the waters with political insiders the week of Nov. 6 to see if the link to tighter ethics standards would make a smaller pay raise politically palatable. The plan met resistance from two directions: from some junior House members fearful of another pay raise vote and from senior members who did not like proposed changes in the ethics code, such as a ban on their freedom to convert campaign funds to personal use after retirement. *('Grandfather clause,' box, p. 952)*

The new measure would be put to a roll-call vote, and a two-stage increase would delay the bigger hike until after the next election, so voters could decide whether incumbents deserved the raise. The Senate would set its own salary and ethics rules.

When a package containing both a pay increase and new ethics rules came to the House floor Nov. 16 as HR 3660, it moved with surprising ease. Its details were a closely held secret until the week it was to go to the floor. Foley and Michel insisted on strong presidential support and did not go public with the task force recommendations until they had a letter of endorsement from Bush. On the floor, few spoke in opposition to the bill, and rhetoric was muted. Foley and Michel put the full weight and prestige of their offices behind the pay raise. The House passed HR 3660 on a **252-174 (R 84-89; D 168-85) key vote**. *(1989 key votes, p. 1021)*

When the Senate took up the bill Nov. 17, members were under pressure to wrap up business and adjourn. At first, momentum seemed to be in favor of the House package; the Senate voted 90-9 to invoke cloture (thus limiting debate) on the bill. But such votes reflected only support for the process, not the substance. Before bringing the bill to the floor, the leaders had persuaded their members to help them defeat procedural moves and keep the bill intact. Thus they could keep their troops in line to block a series of moves by pay raise opponents. But when they counted noses before bringing the pay and honoraria proposal to a final vote, they were four or five votes short.

Assistant Senate GOP leader Alan K. Simpson of Wyoming called his House counterpart, Minority Whip Newt Gingrich of Georgia, seeking lobbying help from House members. In no time, the Senate floor was replete with House members pressuring their colleagues. The leadership, however, was unable to persuade a number of Democrats, including some with national political ambitions — such as Al Gore of Tennessee — and some of the wealthier members.

The House plan never came to a direct vote in the Senate. After several hours of off-the-floor discussions, Senate leaders conceded failure and offered an amendment that left the House's salary structure intact, along with the executive and judicial branch salaries, but raised Senate salaries by 10 percent and provided future cost-of-living raises. The amendment, sponsored by Majority Leader Mitchell, was approved on a **key vote of 56-43 (R 25-20; D 31-23)**, a sign that substantial skittishness still existed about any pay raise. The Senate subsequently passed HR 3660 by voice vote. Along with the pay and honoraria provisions, the Senate also added restrictions on lobbying by former members of Congress after they left government.

The House cleared the bill in the early morning hours of Nov. 18 by accepting the Senate changes.

Major Provisions

The congressional pay provisions of HR 3660 (PL 101-194), as signed into law Nov. 30, 1989:

Pay

- **House, Other Federal Officials.** Provided, in February 1990, a 7.9 percent pay increase to House members, federal judges and top executive branch officials who did not receive cost-of-living increases for 1989 and 1990.
- Provided a 25 percent increase for House members and other top executive and judicial branch officials on Jan. 1, 1991.
- **Senate.** Provided, in February 1990, a 9.9 percent pay increase for senators.
- **Future Increases.** Provided for automatic, annual cost-of-living adjustments (COLAs) for members of Congress and top federal officials of 0.5 percentage point less than the previous year's Economic Cost Index, which measures inflation of private industry salaries. A ceiling on annual COLAs was set at 5 percent.
- Required the House and Senate to take recorded votes on all future congressional pay increases other than annual COLAs.
- Replaced the Quadrennial Commission that met every four years to recommend salary hikes for top federal officials with an 11-member Citizens' Commission on Public Service on Compensation, to include five people chosen by lot from voter registration lists, two by the president, two by congressional leaders and one by the chief justice of the United States.
- Required the commission to meet every four years and report to the president by Dec. 15.
- Specified that the president's pay recommendations, made after receiving the commission's report, would take effect after the next congressional election and only if both the House and the Senate adopted a resolution of approval by recorded vote within 60 days of its submission.

Honoraria

- **House.** Froze at 1989 levels the honoraria and other outside income House members could keep in 1990 — $26,850 for most.
- Barred House members, staff and other federal officials from keeping any honoraria beginning Jan. 1, 1991.
- Allowed House members and others subject to the honoraria ban to request that charitable contributions be made in their name in lieu of honoraria for speeches and appearances.
- Limited such charitable contributions to $2,000 per speech or appearance and prohibited them from being made to any organization that benefited the speaker or his relatives.
- Barred those who had such charitable contributions made in their behalf from getting tax advantages — such as deductions or increases in the amount they could shelter in tax-free Keogh accounts — as a result of those donations.
- **Senate.** Reduced the ceiling on honoraria that senators could keep from 40 percent of salary in 1989 to 27 percent in 1990.
- Provided that any cost-of-living pay increase after Dec. 31, 1990, be accompanied by an equivalent reduction in the ceiling on honoraria until it reached zero.

Other Outside Income

- **House.** Barred House members and senior staff from keeping more than 15 percent of the Executive Level II salary ($96, 600) in outside earned income beginning Jan. 1, 1991.
- Prohibited House members and senior staff from being paid for working or affiliating with a law or other professional firm. They would be allowed to teach for pay if the House Committee on Standards of Official Conduct (ethics committee) approved.
- Prohibited House members and senior staff from being paid for serving on boards of directors.
- Applied the above limits on outside income also to federal, non-career employees at the GS-16 salary level or higher.
- Repealed the House ban on honoraria and other limits on outside income if the 25 percent pay raise in 1991 was repealed.
- Clarified House rules exempting copyright royalties from the cap on outside income to specify that exempt royalties must be paid by an established trade publisher, in line with customary contract terms.

1990 Action

Buoyed by the defeat of the 51 percent pay hike in 1989, opponents of congressional pay increases stayed active in 1990.

Consumer activist Ralph Nader on Aug. 2 announced a stepped-up campaign to repeal the smaller pay raise Congress approved for itself. Nader and a coalition of self-described citizens' groups were joined at a news conference by Hank Brown, R-Colo., who July 31 introduced HR 5416 to roll back congressional salaries to the 1989 level. The measure, which saw no congressional action, was cosponsored by Andrew Jacobs Jr., D-Ind.

During Senate floor consideration of a campaign finance bill (S 137), Christopher J. Dodd, D-Conn., won approval, 77-23, on Aug. 1 of an amendment to bar senators from keeping honoraria. For the first time, the Senate clearly repudiated the speaking fees that critics said were tantamount to legalized bribery. The Dodd amendment also would have barred members from keeping legal fees and other professional income, codifying curbs that had been in Senate rules for years. It would have limited any other form of outside earned income to an amount equal to 15 percent of a senator's salary, which then would have been a cap of about $15,000.

In a surprise move later the same day, the Senate approved an amendment offered by Daniel Patrick Moynihan, D-N.Y., that would have extended the 15 percent cap on earned income to cover unearned income as well. Neither the House nor Senate rules imposed any limit on unearned income, allowing members to continue drawing great wealth from family businesses, stock investments and other sources.

Moynihan introduced his handwritten amendment at a time when few other senators were on the floor. As his colleagues came to the floor for the vote, jocular senators teased each other as they all seemed to vote according to financial need: the wealthiest voted against the amendment and the less wealthy voted for it. As opponents nearly defeated the amendment on a 50-50 tie, Moynihan stood in the center aisle of the chamber, hands outstretched. "One more vote!" he pleaded. Laughing, Alaska Republican Frank H. Murkowski switched his vote to support Moynihan, bringing the final tally to 51-49.

Some members viewed the amendment more as an expression of resentment by the less-wealthy senators than a serious vote to make law. Asked what the vote signified, Texas Democrat Lloyd Bentsen said, "Class warfare." That laid bare some of the divisions within the Senate that typically underlay debate on the subject of compensation.

Neither the Dodd nor Moynihan amendment became law as S 137 died in conference. *(Campaign finance, p. 951)*

Although the Senate did not enact the 1989 House plan to bar members from earning honoraria after 1990, more than one-third of all senators voluntarily refused to supplement their income with speaking fees by mid-1990. A 1989 survey by the independent citizens' lobbying group Common Cause found that 19 senators had refused to keep honoraria in 1988.

Franking Privilege

The franking privilege came under scrutiny in both 1989 and 1990, and Congress imposed new restrictions on the use of congressional mailings in both the House and Senate.

Franking, a cherished perquisite of office, allowed members of Congress to send their constituents mail — including newsletters, press releases, meeting notices and calendars — simply by stamping their signatures on the envelope. Franking had long been criticized as a weapon used unfairly by incumbents to protect their positions. Attempts to rein in the frank were hotly contested by members who said they needed to retain the ability to communicate with their constituents. Mailing costs, meanwhile, increased nearly fourfold from 1972 to 1988; costs were higher still for 1990 because of the elections.

1989 Action

The fiscal 1990 legislative branch appropriations bill (HR 3014 — PL 101-163) for the first time divided mail funding between the two chambers. Proponents of the separate mail accounts said holding each house responsible for its spending would be easier. Under the bill's provisions, if, halfway through a fiscal year, the post office projected that either chamber would overspend its appropriation, that chamber would have to take steps to control costs.

During House floor consideration of HR 3014 (H Rept 101-179), Jerry Lewis, R-Calif., offered an amendment reducing from six to four the number of franked mass mailings that would be permitted. He accepted substitute language from Vic Fazio, D-Calif., to exempt town-hall meeting invitations from the limit, even though Lewis said the practice of blanketing a district with them could be little more than a tax-supported attempt to increase a member's name recognition with voters. The House adopted the amendment 392-10 on July 31.

The House took other steps to exercise more control over its mail. It agreed by voice vote to an amendment by Bill Thomas, R-Calif., to force strict compliance with a law that blocked mass mailings within 60 days of an election. A Timothy J. Penny, D-Minn., amendment was agreed to, 405-8, that trimmed $10.2 million from the House Appropriations Committee-approved $134.7 million mail fund. No new restrictions were included, however, to ensure that those savings would be realized. Bill Frenzel, R-Minn., sought to cut $97 million with a 6.25 percent cut in most programs covered by the bill, but the effort failed 167-246.

The House passed HR 3014 on a 291-123 vote July 31.

As approved by the Senate Appropriations Committee Aug. 3, HR 3014 (S Rept 101-106) provided $80 million for the frank in fiscal 1990. To enforce the spending limit, the Senate bill would require the Postal Service to stop receiving franked mail after the amount appropriated had been spent. The number of mass mailings would be reduced from six to two per year. Each member would be given a specified mail allocation, but senators would continue to be allowed to dip into their office expenses accounts for additional mail money. The House would be required to follow the existing Senate practice of disclosing how much each member spent on mailing. The Senate bill also would set up separate mail accounts for the House and Senate; the House would get $48 million, and the Senate $32 million.

On the floor, an amendment offered by Pete Wilson, R-Calif., was adopted 83-8 on Sept. 7. It would bar the use of the frank for unsolicited mass mailings and transfer the money saved, estimated at $45 million, to the Model Projects for Pregnant and Post Partum Women and Their Infants, an account under the control of the Department of Health and Human Services. The Senate also adopted, by voice vote, three amendments from Gordon J. Humphrey, R-N.H., that would require a disclaimer stating that franked mail was tax-paid; publication in the *Congressional Record* of members' mass mail accounts; and limiting franked mail to no more than the front and back of two legal-sized sheets of paper.

The Senate passed HR 3014 on Sept. 7, 81-9.

The conference committee began its consideration of HR 3014 with a brazen about-face. In the House's case, the turnaround was emphasized by its timing. Less than three hours after the House voted 245-137 on Sept. 25 to instruct its conferees to accept a flat ban on congressional mass mailings financed by tax dollars — as provided in the Senate-passed Wilson amendment — the House conferees took a less restrictive course. They proposed, and the Senate accepted, cutting from six to three the number of newsletters that members could send as franked mail. Fazio said the "emotional content" of the Wilson amendment, combined with the Senate's efforts to skirt a mail ban, made the issue a "straw man." He noted that the Senate rules and spending procedures allowed senators to use funds not available to House members to pay for their mail. Moreover, he added, Wilson had since won funds elsewhere in the budget to help mothers addicted to drugs.

The original conference report provided $115.7 million for mail — $84 million for fiscal 1990 and $31.7 million for fiscal 1989. It established separate mail accounts for the House and Senate, with funds to be drawn from a joint account. If the post office projected that either chamber would overspend its appropriation, the House Franking Commission or the Senate Rules and Administration Committee could issue rules to control costs. The report also included a Senate proposal to limit the length of newsletters.

Conferees dropped two Senate-passed changes considered most important by critics of the frank: First, to require individual House members, like senators, to disclose how much they spent on mass mailings each year; and second, to require the post office to stop accepting franked mail when the annual appropriation ran out.

On the House floor Sept. 28, Frenzel offered a motion to send the bill back to conference; it failed, 137-280. The House then approved the conference report (H Rept 101-254), amended to conform to budget limits, 274-137. The House had cut $15.4 million from the mail account, trimming it to slightly more than $100 million.

During Senate floor consideration of the conference report, Ted Stevens, R-Alaska, offered a motion to table (kill) a Humphrey amendment to force House members to disclose individually how much tax money they spent to underwrite their franking privilege; it was agreed to 64-35 on Nov. 2.

The Senate Nov. 9 also agreed, 66-29, to a Stevens motion to table (kill) an amendment by Wilson to transfer $45 million from congressional mass mailings to anti-drug programs, to bar members from continuing to use the frank after mail appropriations ran out and to close a loophole that allowed senators to use political or personal funds to supplement their office expense accounts, including mailing allowances.

The Senate cleared the conference report by voice vote Nov. 9; the president signed the bill Nov. 21. The measure allocated $31.7 million to make up for a shortfall in fiscal 1989 appropriations, $44.5 million for the House in fiscal 1990 and $24 million for the Senate.

On Nov. 19, the Senate adopted further restrictions (S Res 212) on official mail that applied to the Senate alone. S 212 allocated 90 percent of the $24 million for Senate mail in fiscal 1990 among senators based on the population of their states. Senators from California, the largest state, would receive about $1.2 million for mail. The remaining 10 percent was set aside to make sure no senator received less than $100,000 for mail, to pay for committee mail and to establish a contingency fund should any senator spend all allotted funds and need more to answer incoming mail. These rules tended to favor senators from smaller states.

Senators were still allowed to earmark part of their mail money for colleagues; however, the new rules required any mass mailings to be paid for with tax funds. Senators could no longer use money from their campaign accounts to supplement official spending. The resolution also reinstated allocation and disclosure rules, imposed in 1986, that had been suspended for part of 1989.

1990 Action

The House and Senate in 1990 dealt with a variety of proposals concerning the franking privilege, but again it was the annual legislative branch funding bill that cleared with mailing changes.

Supplemental Appropriations. Rep. Fazio, chairman of the House Appropriations Subcommittee on the Legislative Branch, proposed an amendment to a fiscal 1990 supplemental appropriations bill (HR 4404 — PL 101-302), which would allow the House to use $25 million left over from past years to help cover the deficit in the fiscal 1990 franking budget. The provision won approval in conference May 17 but subsequently was rejected on the House floor. Appropriations Committee Chairman Jamie L. Whitten, D-Miss., offered a motion to concur in the amendment; it was rejected 161-208 on May 24. The vote, however, was mostly symbolic as the Postal Service was required to deliver congressional mail whether or not enough money had been appropriated. *(Supplemental appropriations, p. 73)*

Military Mail. The House Sept. 17 agreed 227-142 to a Tom Ridge, R-Pa., motion to recommit to the Post Office Committee a bill (HR 5611) to extend free mailing services to troops in the Persian Gulf, with instructions to report it back with a provision to fund the mailings through the account for congressional franked mail. The vote was symbolic as HR 5611 was moot. Earlier the same day, the House cleared for the president S 3033 (PL 101-384), which authorized free postage without the franking provision. The House agreed to suspend the rules and pass the bill 368-0; the Senate had passed S 3033 on Sept. 14 by voice vote. *(Persian Gulf War, p. 299)*

Senate Rules Committee Resolution. The Senate Rules and Administration Committee June 13 approved, 9-0, a resolution that would allot every senator mail funds based upon the cost of one mass mailing to each constituent address. To seek parity with House members, the senators representing states with only one congressional district would be allocated enough funds to cover the cost of two mailings. The proposal also would allow senators to stockpile mailings in non-election years and send out up to three mailings in an election year.

Campaign Finance. On July 31, the Senate adopted, 98-1, an amendment to a campaign finance bill (S 137) that would prohibit use of the frank for mass mailings in election years, bar senators from assigning their franking budget to other senators, prohibit franking when the annual appropriation was depleted and require House members to disclose their spending for mail. The campaign finance package eventually died, and the mailing curbs were attached to the legislative operations funding bill. *(Campaign finance, p. 951)*

Legislative Branch Appropriations. The House Appropriations Subcommittee on the Legislative Branch put off handling the divisive issue of curbing congressional mailing privileges in the fiscal 1991 legislative branch appropriations bill (HR 5399 — PL 101-520). Chairman Fazio said he expected the Rules Committee to structure floor debate to allow consideration of one or more plans to change franking. Fazio had been circulating proposals to impose new limits, but he ran into resistance from incumbents of both parties. The subcommittee bill did include provisions that could make it easier for the House to cover future overruns without approving supplemental appropriations. It gave the subcommittee new authority to shift any unused money in other House operating accounts to pay for mail if appropriations for franking fell short.

When HR 5399 was approved July 30 by the Appropriations Committee (H Rept 101-648), the issue of franking was noticeably absent. On the floor, Fazio and Frenzel offered a bipartisan compromise as an amendment, adopted by voice vote Oct. 21, that would give each member an individual mail budget equal to the amount needed to make three first-class mailings to every non-business address in the district; allow members to supplement their mail budget by transferring up to $25,000 a year from other accounts for office expenses; require the amount each member spent to be reported quarterly; and require all mailings to more than 500 recipients to be approved by the House Franking Commission.

The House passed HR 5399 by 292-117 on Oct. 21.

The Senate Appropriations Committee approved its legislative appropriations bill (S 3207 — S Rept 101-533) on Oct. 16. As in the House, amendments on franking were held until floor action. During consideration of HR 5399 on Oct. 25, the Senate, 50-44, adopted a Don Nickles, R-Okla., amendment to prohibit the transfer of funds between different senators' franking accounts. Earlier, the Senate rejected, 42-51, a Wendell H. Ford, D-Ky., substitute amendment to the Nickles amendment to prohibit senators from transferring funds from their franking accounts to other senators' accounts in an election year. The Senate agreed to amendments to allow senators to retain unused mail funds for future use, but only until the next fiscal year; and to allow senators to transfer money from their mail accounts to other accounts in amounts up to $100,000 or 50 percent of their mass mail budget, whichever was less.

The Senate passed HR 5399 by 72-24 on Oct. 25.

During the House-Senate conference, negotiators accepted without major change both the House and Senate proposals to impose new franking restrictions. The House adopted the conference report (H Rept 101-965) 259-129 on Oct. 27. The Senate cleared the measure by voice vote the same day, and President Bush signed it Nov. 5. PL 101-520 provided $122 million to pay for the franking privilege — $59 million for the House, $30 million for the Senate and $33 million to make up for a shortfall in fiscal 1990 appropriations.

1991-92

Unable to live with the disparity in salaries with representatives, the Senate voted to hike its pay, while agreeing to ban honoraria. In other congressional pay-related action, the 27th Amendment to the Constitution was ratified in 1992, prohibiting midterm pay raises. Known as the Madison amendment, it was first submitted to the states in 1789.

Concerns about redistricting led to further changes in the House rules on use of the frank. Members no longer could send mass mailings outside their districts, to voters they expected to represent in the future.

Congressional Pay

The Senate in 1991 gave itself a 23 percent pay raise, which brought senators' salaries in line with representatives', and banned its members from keeping speaking and writing fees. The fiscal 1992 legislative appropriations bill (HR 2506 — PL 102-90) contained the pay and honoraria provisions, as well as changes in rules governing members' acceptance of gifts.

Unlike in 1989, when efforts to implement a pay hike met with public hostility, no widespread furor arose, as congressional leaders acted quickly and quietly. *(1989 action, p. 965)*

Background

Beginning Jan. 1, 1991, representatives received salaries of $125,100, while senators got $101,900. Members of the Senate also could keep $23,068 in honoraria, putting their potential Senate-related income only $132 below House members. Honoraria remained a controversial practice, however, and repeated efforts had been made to end it. The House in 1989 had prohibited its members from keeping honoraria, effective in 1991. *(Pay raise history, box, p. 971)*

Sen. Christopher J. Dodd, D-Conn., twice successfully offered amendments to bar Senate honoraria. The Senate adopted the first one, 77-23, on Aug. 1, 1990, during consideration of S 137; the second gained approval, 72-24, on May 21, 1991, as part of S 3. S 137 and S 3 both were campaign finance legislation, and neither became law. *(S 137, p. 951; S 3, p. 959)*

A ban on honoraria would force a confrontation on the pay issue because most senators supplemented their pay with speaking fees. To accept the prohibition without providing some compensation for the potential loss in income would amount to an 18 percent pay cut.

With rank-and-file senators growing more indignant by the day over House members' higher salaries, a new wrinkle in the 1989 pay legislation (PL 101-194) became apparent. Because the pay of top congressional aides was pegged somewhat below what the members made, the Jan. 1 House pay raise allowed the salaries of scores of its staff members to soar. According to the July 1 issue of *Roll Call*, Capitol Hill's twice-weekly newspaper, 81 House aides — some rather obscure — earned more than senators. The staff director of the House District of Columbia Committee, for example, made $115,092.

Legislative Action

Worried that Senate staff would flee to the House, Senate Appropriations Committee Chairman Robert C. Byrd, D-W.Va., and Ted Stevens, R-Alaska, attached a rider in committee to the legislative appropriations bill, authorizing raises for top Senate aides and barring them from pocketing honoraria. As a result, some Senate employees would make more than their bosses, and senators would be virtually the only federal employees still allowed to keep speaking and writing fees. Byrd's committee reported the spending bill (S Rept 102-81) on June 12. The House had passed its version (H Rept 102-82) 308-110 on June 5.

When Byrd heard that plans were afoot to insert a Senate honoraria ban in HR 2506 on the floor, he began gathering votes for an amendment that would provide a pay raise as well as an end to honoraria. He asked Majority Leader George J. Mitchell, D-Maine, to hold up the legislative appropriations bill until he either got the votes or was sure he could not. Byrd's goal was twofold: a majority of Democrats voting "yea" and an overall margin of victory of more than one. He did not want a pro-raise senator to have to deal with an opponent saying, "If you hadn't voted for it, it wouldn't have passed."

Byrd's count reached 52 on July 17. Mitchell at 7 p.m. pulled the spending bill for veterans, housing and science programs (HR 2519) and called up the legislative branch bill. While an in-depth discussion of HR 2506 went on for about an hour, no official acknowledgment was made that a pay-raise vote was imminent. The issue would not be part of the evening network news. At 8:15 p.m., Byrd offered an amendment to raise Senate salaries, ban honoraria and limit members' outside earned income to 15 percent ($18,765) of their salary. He spoke for 35 minutes, then others in support of his proposal followed. The opponents stayed mostly quiet. At 9:30 p.m., the vote was called. The amendment was adopted on a **key vote of 53-45 (R 25-18; D 28-27)**. *(1991 key votes, p. 1061)*

HR 2506 passed the Senate the same day by voice vote.

The Senate pay raise gave House members considerable leverage over the particulars of the final bill. To pay for House approval of the pay hike, the Senate agreed to a provision barring senators from accepting stipends for hosting radio shows beginning in 1992. According to the Associated Press (AP), two pairs of senators participated in regular staged radio debates: Alan K. Simpson, R-Wyo., and Edward M. Kennedy, D-Mass., were on five days a week, and Richard G. Lugar, R-Ind., and Tom Daschle, D-S.D., were on a program that aired 65 times a year. All but Kennedy, who declined compensation, were paid about $100 per show, the AP said. The Senate Ethics Committee in 1988 had decided that stipends were not honoraria and therefore were not covered by the limit.

Senators also were barred from getting paid for teaching without prior approval from the Senate Ethics Committee, serving on boards of directors, practicing a profession that involved a "fiduciary relationship" or affiliating with any entity that provided such professional services.

The honoraria ban would become effective upon the bill's enactment. However, the negotiators decided that requiring senators to forfeit speaking fees accepted before the bill was signed would be unfair. Senators thus were allowed to keep any such fees already accepted up to the 1991 limit of $23,068. Senaters who kept the maximum would earn $133,797, which would be $8,697 more than House members would make.

House members successfully insisted that the Senate bar its members from deriving any tax benefits from honoraria donated to charity. The tax code already blocked such benefits for House members. Senate Minority Leader Bob Dole, R-Kan., tried to eliminate a $2,000-a-speech limit on honoraria that members could donate to charity in their names, but he relented in the rush to recess.

An effort by Mitchell to raise the pay for the majority and minority leaders in both chambers and for the Senate president pro tempore also was abandoned. All five members' salaries were set at $138,900; Mitchell wanted something closer to the House Speaker's $160,600 but reportedly gave up on the idea after House leaders refused to agree.

The proposal to revise the rules governing gifts arose late in the House-Senate conference, and it received little notice or comment on the floor. Members of both chambers had complained that the rules for accepting gifts and reporting them on annual financial disclosure forms were confusing, particularly because the rules were different for each house.

The new rules allowed members to accept up to $250 worth of gifts annually from anyone (up from $200 in the House and up from $100 from people with legislative interests in the Senate). Members could accept an unlimited number of gifts worth $100 or less (up from $75). All federal officials would have to disclose only who gave them more than $250 in gifts (up from $100) worth more than $100 each (up from $75). A separate category for reporting travel and entertainment-related gifts was eliminated. All of the new thresholds were set to rise automatically every three years to account for inflation.

Pay Raise History

Effective Date	Salary	Percentage Change
March 1789	$ 1,500[a]	
March 1817	2,000[a]	33
December 1855	3,000	50
December 1865	5,000	67
March 1871	7,500	50
January 1874	5,000	−33
March 1907	7,500	50
March 1925	10,000	33
July 1932	9,000	−10
April 1933	8,500	−6
February 1934	9,000	6
July 1934	9,500	6
April 1935	10,000	5
January 1947	12,500	25
March 1955	22,500	80
January 1965	30,000	33
March 1969	42,500	42
October 1975	44,600	5
March 1977	57,500	29
October 1979	60,663	6
December 1982		
Senate	60,663	—
House	69,800	15
July 1983		
Senate	69,800	15
House	69,800	—
January 1984	72,600	4
January 1985	75,100	4
January 1987	77,400	3
March 1987	89,500	16
February 1990		
Senate	98,400	10
House	96,600	8
January 1991		
Senate	101,900	4
House	125,100	29
August 1991		
Senate	125,100	23
House	125,100	—

[a]Per diem rates converted to annual rates, based on full attendance at a 250-day session.

Sources: Congressional Research Service; House sergeant-at-arms; Senate Disbursing Office.

House and Senate negotiators completed work on HR 2506 on July 30. The House approved the conference report (H Rept 102-176) the next day by voice vote. The Senate cleared the bill Aug. 2 also by voice vote. President Bush signed the measure Aug. 14.

Madison Amendment

The 27th Amendment to the Constitution, prohibiting midterm congressional pay raises, was ratified on May 7, 1992 — 203 years after it was proposed.

The Madison amendment, written by James Madison in 1789, said: "No law varying the compensation for the services of the Senators and Representatives shall take effect, until an election of Representatives shall have intervened." The amendment was first sent to the states in September 1789 as part of a package of 12 proposed amendments. Ten became the Bill of Rights, but the pay raise amendment was ratified by only six states between 1789 and 1792, and then languished until 1873, when Ohio affirmed it.

The amendment was revived in the late 1970s, and the latest push began in August 1991 when a House resolution was introduced calling on state legislatures to re-examine the amendment. The results began rolling in May 5, 1992, when Missouri and Alabama ratified the amendment. On May 7, Michigan cast the decisive 38th vote — reaching the necessary three-fourths majority — with New Jersey becoming the 39th state to ratify just a few hours later. Illinois made it 40 during the week of May 11.

The 27th Amendment was officially certified by the United States archivist on May 18, printed in the *Federal Register* on May 19 and became, for all relevant purposes, part of the Constitution.

Background

Once the state legislatures approve a new amendment, statutes require that it be presented to the archivist of the United States. Upon receipt of the Madison amendment, Archivist Don W. Wilson could have either declared the amendment constitutional, delayed issuing a certification pending guidance from Congress or issued a conditional certification of ratification pending congressional action. Upon Wilson's announcement May 13 that he found the measure constitutional, congressional concern about the legality of the drawn-out ratification process melted away.

Most amendments proposed in modern times were sent to the states with a deadline for ratification, usually seven years. But the Madison amendment had no deadline. Therefore, supporters argued, the extensive gaps between state ratifications did not invalidate the proposal. The Supreme Court ruled in earlier cases that the decision on whether the time span between introduction and ratification was too long was up to Congress.

In the days following the Michigan legislature's action, House Speaker Thomas S. Foley, D-Wash., and former Senate majority leader Robert C. Byrd, D-W.Va., suggested hearings in the Judiciary committees to explore whether too much time had lapsed for the amendment to be valid. In the House, Don Edwards, D-Calif., chairman of the Judiciary Subcommittee on Civil and Constitutional Rights, suggested having Congress urge the seven states that acted before 1978 to vote again, removing any doubt of their support. After the archivist's decision, Foley backed away from earlier skepticism about the amendment's validity, and plans for hearings were canceled.

On the Senate side, the move to accept the ratification came from Byrd. However, Byrd, considered a stickler for institutional rectitude, scolded Wilson for not following "historic tradition." When questions arose in the past about the validity of ratification, he said, certification by the archivist or secretary of state was postponed pending congressional discussion and resolution.

In addition to a resolution accepting the language as the 27th Amendment, Byrd asked colleagues to declare four long-outstanding amendments to be invalid. Such language, he maintained, would prevent centuries of delay from becoming precedent. The four amendments were sent to the states without a deadline and remained unratified. They were a proposal to change the apportionment of the House of Representatives (one of the 12 sent to the states in 1789), a stricture forbidding American officials from accepting titles of nobility (1810), language prohibiting federal laws against slavery (1861) and a proposal allowing Congress to regulate child labor (1924).

Two proposals to recognize the 27th Amendment (S Con Res 120, S Res 298) were approved by the Senate on separate 99-0 votes on May 20. The resolution to invalidate the lingering amendments was referred to the Judiciary Committee. On the House side, a somewhat ceremonial debate was held May 19, a day before a resolution (H Con Res 320) similar to Byrd's passed under suspension of the rules, 414-3.

Related Court Action

While the constitutionality of the ratification process did not come under judicial review as a result of the Madison amendment, the courts were asked to determine whether previously approved cost-of-living adjustments (COLAs) were valid under the new amendment. The suit was filed by more than two dozen members of the 102nd and 103rd Congresses and assorted citizens' groups.

They based their challenge on the effective date of the COLA and of a slightly smaller increase (3 percent) in congressional pension benefits. Both took effect Jan. 1, 1993, four days before the 103rd Congress — elected Nov. 3, 1992 — was to convene. Even though "an election of Representatives" had intervened, defeated or retiring members of the outgoing 102nd Congress would benefit from the increases. The effect would be felt primarily in lifetime pension benefits, which were based on the highest three years of pay.

U.S. District Judge Stanley Sporkin on Dec. 16 rejected claims that the 3.2 percent COLA, which raised basic congressional salaries from $129,500 to $133,600 per year, violated the 27th Amendment. Sporkin said that nothing in the constitutional amendment implied that only a new Congress could take advantage of a change in pay. The sole requirement, he said, was for an intervening election between the time Congress approved the raise and the time the increase took effect.

Objections also were raised to the citizens' commission that would review and recommend changes to members' base salaries every four years, as per 1989 congressional pay legislation (PL 101-194). If the Madison amendment was to mean anything, the argument was put forth, it must require a new law and vote each time. But Sporkin ruled that because the commission's recommendations must be voted on by Congress and go into effect only after the next election, the quadrennial review process also complied with the 27th Amendment. *(Congressional pay, p. 965)*

Franking Privilege

Democratic leaders announced July 30, 1992, that the House would no longer allow the franking privilege to be used for mass mailings to constituents outside their current districts. The new rule ended the tradition of House members targeting franked mail at voters in newly drawn districts they expected to represent.

Congress had put other curbs on franking in during the 101st Congress. *(Story, p. 968)*

Just hours before the rule change was announced, the U.S. Appeals Court for the District of Columbia issued a 2-1 decision finding it unconstitutional for members to send "postal patron" mailings — unaddressed mail to every household in a postal zone — to voters outside the existing borders of their districts. That ruling overturned a June 26 lower court decision upholding the practice. The suit was filed by the Coalition to End the Permanent Congress, the National Taxpayers Union and Public Citizen and was joined by five House challengers — three Democrats and two Republicans. The court's decision could not be appealed.

House challengers had agitated for a rule change throughout the redistricting year of 1992, arguing that out-of-district mailings amounted to taxpayer-financed electioneering. Republicans, who stood to gain House seats if the grip of incumbency could be weakened, took up the cause. With the legal victory in hand, Republicans pushed the House beyond the parameters of the court decision. Technically, the federal panel prohibited only out-of-district postal patron mailings, mailings that were sent without an individual name and address.

Bill Thomas of California, ranking Republican on the House Administration Committee, offered a motion July 30 to ban all out-of-district mass mail — which was defined as unsolicited, nearly identical letters of 500 or more, regardless of whether they were individually addressed. He was ruled out of order, which touched off a backroom skirmish. Democratic leaders subsequently relented.

Earlier in the year, the House had voted twice to enact the ban, but neither vote occurred on legislation that was likely to become law in time to affect the 1992 elections.

Complaints about congressional use of franking were emphasized during consideration of campaign finance legislation (S 3) because of a drafting mistake in the conference report (H Rept 102-487). As Democrats were preparing to bring it to the floor, they discovered that a provision barring senators from using the frank for mass mailings in the calendar year of a re-election campaign inadvertently had been applied to all members of Congress. The bill was sent back to conference to exclude the House from the provision. *(Campaign finance, p. 959)*

On a 7-3, party-line vote in the Rules Committee on April 7, Democrats denied a Republican request to offer instructions to conferees to bar members from franking outside their districts. When the matter came to the floor the following day, Republicans threatened an embarrassing showdown, and Democrats backed down. Thomas offered a motion to instruct conferees to include the provisions of HR 4104, a bill he had introduced in January to prohibit congressional funding of franked mail sent outside a member's current district. No Democrat spoke against the Thomas amendment, and the motion was agreed to 408-8 on April 8.

During House floor consideration of the fiscal 1993 legislative branch appropriations bill (HR 5427 — PL 102-392), Thomas won agreement, 417-2 on June 24, to an amendment to prohibit members from sending franked mass mail outside their districts as soon as the bill was signed into law, instead of by Oct. 1, 1992, as originally proposed by the Appropriations Committee. On June 25, he offered a resolution in the House Administration Committee to cut off mailings postmarked after July 15, but it failed 10-12.

PL 102-392 provided the Senate with $20 million to spend on mail in fiscal 1993, compared with $11.7 million it spent in 1991, the last non-election year. House members had $47.7 million at their disposal for franked mail in fiscal 1993, compared with $31.3 million spent in 1991.

The fiscal 1992 legislative branch appropriations measure (HR 2506 — PL 102-90) had allocated $32 million for Senate franked mail, which was slightly below the amount needed to pay for one statewide mailing for each senator and for the mail of committees and Senate officers. The $80 million for House franked mail in fiscal 1992 was much less than that of past election years, reflecting franking limits enacted for fiscal 1991 to check mass mailings. All House members received a mail budget big enough to send three items to each home in their district, and how much they spent was disclosed quarterly. Members were allowed to transfer $25,000 a year from other accounts into their mail account.

Congress was able to cancel $20 million in fiscal 1992 funding for House mail and another $20 million in Senate mail costs in a rescissions package (HR 4990 — PL 102-298) signed by Bush on June 4, 1992. *(Rescissions package, p. 81)*

Nuclear Bunker

Among the congressional perks to come under scrutiny in 1992 was the Greenbrier bunker, part of a plan to relocate and keep the federal government operating during a nuclear war. By the end of the year, Congress had cut its ties to the facility.

The bunker, built for $14 million in the late 1950s during the height of the Cold War, was located beneath a wing of the Greenbrier Hotel, a West Virginia resort famous for its luxurious golf courses and fancy eating spots. The hotel's owner, CSX Corp., was paid between $50,000 and $60,000 a year in rent by the government for maintaining the exclusive space as a potential retreat in case of war. The facility reportedly had its own power plant and was equipped with food, medical supplies, computers and communications equipment. It was not designed to sustain a direct nuclear hit.

First reports of the bunker appeared May 29 in the *Washington Times*, apparently spurred by the scheduled publication May 31 of a feature article on it in the *Washington Post Magazine*. The stories also detailed efforts by House Speaker Thomas S. Foley, D-Wash., and others to keep the bunker's existence secret; only a few top lawmakers and government officials had known about it. In a joint statement, the bipartisan congressional leadership said the usefulness of the facility had been jeopardized by the publicity.

Special Report: The Keating Five

When does the relationship between members' two most time-consuming tasks — helping constituents and raising money — become improper and unethical? That was the fundamental question raised by the case of the so-called Keating Five.

The Senate Ethics Committee in 1989-91 investigated five senators — Alan Cranston, D-Calif.; Dennis DeConcini, D-Ariz.; John Glenn, D-Ohio; John McCain, R-Ariz.; and Donald W. Riegle Jr., D-Mich. — who were suspected of doing favors between 1987 and 1989 for a wealthy campaign contributor, Charles H. Keating Jr. Keating was the head of a California-based thrift, Lincoln Savings and Loan Association, that failed in 1989, costing taxpayers $2 billion. Lincoln became a symbol of one of the largest financial debacles in U.S. history, the near collapse of the savings and loan industry. Keating gave a total of $1.5 million to the campaigns and political causes of the senators.

Never before had the Senate investigated so many of its members at one time. Committee hearings, which began Nov. 15, 1990, and concluded Jan. 16, 1991, examined whether any of the five violated Senate rules against exerting improper influence in return for compensation. Technically, the hearings were only a preliminary inquiry aimed at determining whether the Ethics Committee should proceed to a formal investigation and hearing.

All five senators denied wrongdoing, saying their efforts in behalf of Keating were no more than any member of Congress would do to help a constituent having problems with a federal agency. They denied that they helped Keating for his fund raising and maintained that their actions did not influence the decisions of government regulators with regard to Lincoln.

Establishing the facts of the case proved substantially easier than deciding at what point a senator's conduct crossed ethical boundaries. After more than 33 hours of closed-door deliberations spread over six weeks, the Ethics Committee announced its findings on Feb. 27, 1991. It decided to proceed against Cranston, finding evidence that some of his official actions were "substantially linked" with his fund raising. The other four senators were criticized in written statements for poor judgment, with DeConcini and Riegle also chided for giving the appearance of acting improperly. But the panel decided that existing rules did not warrant further action.

To break an internal stalemate, the Ethics Committee created a new form of punishment for Cranston, which was halfway between a committee rebuke and a full-Senate censure. The unprecedented deal allowed the senator, who was 77 years old and suffering from prostate cancer, to formally accept a reprimand in return for not having to face formal Senate action and a likely divisive floor vote.

The matter was taken to the floor Nov. 20, and, without asking for a vote, Ethics leaders told the assembled Senate that the committee had reprimanded Cranston for "an impermissible pattern of conduct in which fund raising and official activities were substantially linked." It was the Senate's first use of the word "reprimand" in place of "censure," and it was the first time that the Ethics Committee had acted for the full Senate in dispensing a disciplinary action. Normally, formal disciplinary action — censure or explusion — had to be voted by the full Senate.

In response, Cranston apologized for making the chamber look bad and then implied that some of his colleagues looked worse. He expressed sorrow that some people thought he acted improperly but said he had not. He rejected the basis of the Ethics Committee's punishment, saying, "My behavior did not violate established norms. Here, but for the grace of God, stand you."

When Cranston was done, Ethics Committee Vice Chairman Warren B. Rudman, R-N.H., rose in a visible rage to address the chamber. "After accepting this committee's recommendation, what I have heard is a statement I can only describe as arrogant, unrepentant and a smear on this institution. Everybody does not do it." Cranston did not take back his remarks.

Members looking for a lesson from the Keating Five case likely were left unsatisfied. The Senate's ethics watchdogs announced that they could not define improper conduct, but, as with pornography, they knew it when they saw it. "Not all standards offer the opportunity to arrive at easy judgments through the mechanical application of a fixed formula," said Ethics Chairman Howell Heflin, D-Ala., who told members that Supreme Court Justice Potter Stewart's oft-borrowed pornography standard applied to their behavior. In the end, the committee could only advise members to be careful when helping constituents and raising money.

Background

The Keating Five case dated back to the mid-1980s, when Lincoln began a bitter feud with federal regulators. The officials charged that the thrift's rapid, high-risk growth had violated federal regulations. Keating fought back, charging that he was the victim of a "vendetta." Keating successfully lined up well-placed politicians to help him in his fight as things heated up in late 1986 and

Keating and Lincoln Savings

Charles H. Keating Jr. grew to be rich and influential as chairman of American Continental Corp., an Ohio-chartered corporation based in Phoenix, Ariz., that was involved in home construction and land development. Keating formed the company in 1978, with the help of Carl H. Linder, chairman of American Financial Corp. Keating had been vice president and director of American Financial. In 1979, Keating signed a consent decree with the Securities and Exchange Commission, based on allegations that he and Linder had received insider loans. While neither Keating nor Linder admitted to breaking the law, they agreed not to violate securities laws in the future.

American Continental acquired Lincoln Savings and Loan Association of Irvine, Calif., in 1984. Lincoln took aggressive advantage of permissive California state and federal rules to become a high-flying institution that boomed on the strength of relatively risky investments. In response to a new 1985 Federal Home Loan Bank Board regulation to sharply limit direct investments in real estate, Alan Greenspan, then a private financial consultant, wrote to the San Francisco Federal Home Loan Bank seeking permission for Lincoln to exceed the rule's limits. The application was denied. By year's end, San Francisco had informed Lincoln that it had violated bank regulations by its rapid growth.

An examination into Lincoln's activities began in March 1986. The thrift resisted fulfilling the San Francisco examiners' requests for information. A July meeting between the examiners and thrift officials, including Keating, deteriorated into reciprocal allegations of bad faith. From that time on, Lincoln began arguing to Washington bank board officials and in public that the San Francisco office was harassing the thrift. Keating accused Bank Board Chairman Edwin J. Gray of having "a vendetta" against Lincoln. San Francisco completed its examination at the end of 1986 and began meeting with Lincoln officials to discuss the findings. In May 1987, the San Francisco examiners recommended that Lincoln be seized for operating in an unsafe and unsound manner and for dissipating its assets. In October, the deputy director of the Federal Home Loan Bank Board's Office of Regulatory Policy recommended that a consent cease-and-desist order be issued for Lincoln.

The Enforcement Review Committee, a panel of senior bank board officials, met repeatedly with the San Franciso examiners in early 1988. On the committee's recommendation, the bank board voted in May to accept a Lincoln-proposed "memorandum of understanding" that the thrift increase its capital and improve its loan underwriting standards, while supervisory jurisdiction was transferred from San Francisco to Washington. No criminal referrals would be made based on the 1986 examination of Lincoln.

A new examination of Lincoln was begun in July 1988 by officials from several regional home loan banks. Another examination was ordered, in September, of American Continental, because more than $94 million in Lincoln tax payments were made to Continental instead of the Internal Revenue Service as part of a tax-sharing agreement that regulators considered improper. The examinations were completed in December.

On Dec. 20, 1988, American Continental agreed to sell Lincoln, and the California Savings and Loan commissioner issued a cease-and-desist order against Lincoln because Continental bonds were sold to Lincoln customers in Lincoln branches. California state and some federal regulators opposed the sale of Lincoln. Several efforts to sell the thrift fell through.

The bank board concluded in February 1989 that Lincoln was undercapitalized and launched a third examination of the thrift. On April 13, American Continental filed for Chapter 11 bankruptcy. The next day, the bank board, upon concluding that Lincoln was operating in an unsafe and unsound manner, seized control of the thrift and placed it into conservatorship of the Federal Savings and Loan Insurance Corporation (FSLIC). On Aug. 2, the bank board put Lincoln into receivership, ordered its assets liquidated and created a new Lincoln to take over old Lincoln's deposits. *(Thrift bailout, p. 117)*

Keating was convicted Dec. 4, 1991, in Los Angeles on 17 counts of securities fraud under California law. The Superior Court jury acquitted him on one count. Keating was sentenced April 10, 1992, to 10 years in prison and fined $250,000, the maximum financial penalty allowable by state law.

On July 10, 1992, a federal jury in Phoenix ordered Keating and three codefendants to pay a total of $4.5 billion; Keating's part of the bill was $2.1 billion to be paid to more than 20,000 Lincoln investors — $600 million in compensatory damages and $1.5 billion in punitive damages. U.S. District Judge Richard Bilby instructed the jury to set the monetary award after he ruled that the defendants had conspired to defraud investors. After hearing post-trial motions, Bilby decided to reduce the amounts set by the jury, based on legal experts' determination of total damages. On Oct. 22, he set final compensatory damages at $1.15 billion for Keating and two of the three codefendants; Keating alone was ordered to pay $750 million in punitive damages.

Keating was found guilty on 73 counts of fraud and racketeering by a federal jury in Los Angeles on Jan. 6, 1993. He faced a maximum sentence of 525 years in prison.

early 1987. Among them were Cranston, DeConcini, Glenn, McCain and Riegle.

Most of the senators' work in behalf of Keating involved contacting thrift regulators to talk about his case, though some did other favors, large and small, for him. Usually they urged the regulators to quickly make decisions about matters that Keating felt had dragged on for too long. Cranston and DeConcini were the most persistent.

The main events in the affair were two meetings held in April 1987, during which the senators asked top regulators about their lengthy examination of Keating's thrift. (Riegle did not attend the first meeting.) The Keating Five case first came to the attention of the Ethics Committee on Sept. 26, 1989, when the chairman of the Ohio Republican Party filed a complaint against Glenn. Common Cause, a self-styled citizens' lobby, sent a letter Oct. 13 seeking an investigation of all five senators.

On Nov. 17, the committee named Robert S. Bennett — a partner in the Washington office of the New York law firm of Skadden, Arps, Slate, Meagher & Flom — as special counsel to handle the Keating affair. At the time, Bennett was conducting the committee's investigation into the finances of Sen. Dave Durenberger, R-Minn., which would not conclude until July 1990. A preliminary inquiry into the Keating case was announced Dec. 22. The investigation remained out of the public eye for the first part of 1990 as Bennett's staff quietly collected documents and interviewed witnesses, including the five senators. *(Durenberger, p. 921)*

Bennett on Sept. 10, 1990, gave the Ethics Committee a 350-page report and thousands of pages of supporting evidence on the Keating matter. He reportedly recommended dismissing the cases of Glenn and McCain and proceeding with charges against the other three, but the committee did not make his recommendations public.

After studying the report, the committee took testimony from the five senators in early October. In the middle of October, leaks increased the heat on Cranston, DeConcini and Riegle, while Glenn and McCain protested that they should be separated from the case. Reports by the *New York Times*, the *Washington Post* and the Associated Press, among other media organizations, indicated that the three senators were more deeply involved with Keating than previously had been disclosed.

McCain took the Senate floor Oct. 22 to ask for Bennett's report to be released and its recommendation to be acted on quickly. "Justice delayed is justice denied," McCain said. Other senators joined his cause. Senate Democratic leaders denounced the leaks and suggested that Republicans wanted to hurry the case, leaving only Democrats under suspicion as the November elections approached.

On Oct. 23, the Ethics Committee voted unanimously to open a fact-finding hearing. The committee reportedly had split in a vote to follow Bennett's recommendation and excuse Glenn and McCain, who objected strongly to the decision. (The six-member committee was the only one in the Senate divided evenly between the two parties.) By receiving a report from Bennett at the outset and by scheduling public hearings without making preliminary judgments, the committee departed from the typical steps taken in other recent ethics cases, which would have led to a public hearing only after official charges were filed.

Cranston announced, a week before the hearings were scheduled to begin, that he had prostate cancer and would be unable to attend the hearings while he was undergoing treatment in California beginning in late November. He announced at the same time that he would not seek another term as Democratic whip and would not run for reelection in 1992.

Committee Hearings

The hearings opened Nov. 15, 1990, to the glare of television lights in a large wood- and marble-paneled hearing room in the Hart Senate Office Building. Eight long tables were reserved for the press. Each senator was given his own desk, next to one for his attorney.

In his opening remarks, Chairman Heflin provided an evenhanded talk that gave little insight into his own idea of the standard to which the senators would be held. Rudman offered an equally oblique view, noting only that "the committee cannot act on the basis of laws, rules, and standards that some people might like to see." Committee members David Pryor, D-Ark., and Jesse Helms, R-N.C., did not address the standards issue, but Trent Lott, R-Miss., and Terry Sanford, D-N.C., each offered detailed views of what might constitute an ethical violation.

Sanford seemed to challenge the tough standards Bennett laid down for the committee to consider. "In rulemaking and administrative matters, the member may specifically or indirectly ask for favorable action," Sanford said. "The member may complain about the treatment of citizens by investigators or other staff members of the agency." And, he said, "the member may call for reconsideration of a decision."

Sanford also argued, "if indeed there is an appearance of wrongdoing when in fact no wrongdoing is found, the problem is not that of the individual, but of the institution." It would be unfair, he said, "to impose penalties for this appearance on individual senators."

Lott said he could identify a specific point at which intervention with regulators became improper. "The line is crossed, and the action is improper," he said, "if a senator requests that the regulator break the law, if he demands the regulator take a specific action or if he threatens the regulator with reprisal."

On the second day of the hearings, Cranston's attorney, William W. Taylor III, asked Helms to step aside from the deliberations because of remarks Helms had made in a November 1990 campaign appearance drawing connections between Cranston and Keating. Helms refused, and the committee did not press the point.

Bennett's Case

Committee special counsel Bennett, in his opening statement delivered Nov. 15-16, laid out in broad strokes the case he would make over the next two months. Much of what Bennett cited had long been known. But he offered some new information — including affidavits and memorandums — that suggested the possibility of specific connections between Keating's fund raising and some actions by the senators.

Bennett was in an unusual position. Unlike in the Durenberger case, he was not presenting a set of formal charges. Instead, he had to present all relevant facts and gently suggest to the committee members how they might view them. "I'm not suggesting that there is wrongdoing at this stage," he told the committee at the start of his presentation. Nevertheless, he repeatedly said the evidence would

The 'Appearance Standard'

Can a senator's conduct be improper merely because it looks bad? In the Keating Five case, Special Counsel Robert S. Bennett urged the Senate Ethics Committee to conclude that, even absent a finding of actual improper conduct, members could be disciplined just for looking as though they behaved improperly — for violating what he called the "appearance standard."

"Legislators who appear to reasonable persons to do wrong actually do wrong by eroding the trust between citizens and their representatives," Bennett told the panel. He argued that longstanding traditions, Senate and House precedents, previous Ethics Committee pronouncements and common sense supported his position. Such a finding would have been precedent setting. Although Bennett cited several past ethics cases in which appearances came into play, he offered no example of a lawmaker having been punished merely because behavior looked improper.

What Is 'Improper Conduct'?

Senate rules prohibited members from engaging in "improper conduct which may reflect upon the Senate."

Bennett did not build his whole case around the appearance standard; he argued that some of the senators' fund-raising activities and actions to help Keating were clear examples of improper conduct. But if the committee decided that none of the senators' actions by themselves violated Senate rules, Bennett said, it still could hold some of them accountable.

The circumstances, as reflected in many media reports, could look bad. Ethics Committee Chairman Howell Heflin, D-Ala., said that many voters thought the senators were bribed with huge political contributions to come to Keating's aid during his bitter fight with thrift regulators.

Bennett's Standard

Bennett presented his conclusion about the appearance standard in a lengthy legal brief analyzing the history of government ethics. He formulated the standard this way: "A senator should not engage in conduct which would appear to be improper to a reasonable, non-partisan, fully informed person."

Bennett's first principle was not contested: Senators were required to follow written rules and laws as well as to adhere to certain unwritten standards of conduct. He cited numerous precedents going back to the late 1700s to show that senators could be punished, even expelled, for violating unwritten standards. When the Select Committee on Standards and Conduct, forerunner to the Ethics Committee, first proposed a code of conduct in 1968, it stated in a report that "the Senate must not only be free of improper influence but must also be . . . free from the appearance of impropriety."

The committee's 1964 report on its investigation of a top Senate employee — Bobby Baker, who was found to have used his office to promote outside business interests — said that "officials have an obligation to refrain not only from actual wrongdoing but from conduct leaving the appearance of wrongdoing." *(Congress and the Nation Vol. I, p. 1773)*

In its 1978 report on the Korean influence scandal, the Ethics Committee said "a key element" of previous conduct-related Senate resolutions "is that a senator must avoid the appearance of impropriety, as well as impropriety itself." *(Congress and the Nation Vol. V, p. 904)*

Bennett said that the standard had been invoked most recently in the 1989-90 case against Dave Durenberger, R-Minn. Before the Senate unanimously voted to denounce Durenberger for unethical financial dealings, Warren B. Rudman, R-N.H., vice chairman of the Ethics Committee, said his colleague "failed his obligation of protecting both the appearance and reality of propriety." *(Durenberger, p. 921)*

Bennett cited three House cases as well: Robert L. F. Sikes, D-Fla., in 1976; Raymond F. Lederer, D-Pa., in 1981; and Mario Biaggi, D-N.Y., in 1988. *(Sikes, Congress and the Nation Vol. IV, p. 782; Lederer, Congress and the Nation Vol. VI, p. 806; Biaggi, Congress and the Nation Vol. VII, p. 884)*

Bennett's precedents involved more than just appearances, however. The committee found that Durenberger violated rules on speech fees, financial disclosure, gifts and campaign contributions. Lederer and Biaggi were charged with violating criminal bribery statutes, while Sikes was found to have violated House disclosure requirements.

show actions that could be interpreted by the committee as violations.

Bennett noted that he and his staff interviewed 140 people, took affidavits from 44 of them and deposed 16 witnesses. That did not count the seven — among them Keating — who refused to testify, citing their constitutional prerogatives. (No thought was given to forcing Keating to testify by granting limited immunity from prosecution — largely because of the chance that doing so would make prosecuting him in court difficult. Bennett remarked in his opening statement, "One could ask the question: If Mr. Keating was here, would you believe what he said anyway?") Bennett said his most important witness would not be a person. "The most important witnesses are the product of the examination of the pieces of paper," he said. "Ernest Hemingway once said that paper doesn't bleed, and what I think he meant by that is that paper isn't subject to the normal human frailty." The paper he would introduce, Bennett said, had special credibility because it "never thought it would be here."

Bennett said the evidence pointed to a strategy by Keating to pressure regulators by seeking assistance from members of Congress. And to do so, Bennett said, Keating engineered "substantial sums for political contributions."

"It is clear," Bennett said, "that Senators Cranston and DeConcini were important players in Mr. Keating's strategy." He added, "I must reluctantly state that there is substantial evidence that Senator Riegle played a much greater role than he now recalls. The evidence shows that Senator Riegle played an important role at the early stages."

Bennett confirmed that he had found little evidence that Glenn or McCain had stepped across the line of propriety. "Was there anything improper about Senator McCain's conduct? The evidence discovered by special counsel suggests not," Bennett told the committee. Later he said, "We know of no evidence linking [political] contributions to any action on the part of Senator Glenn."

Keating began to seek help from members of both the House and Senate in 1984-86, when he and other thrift executives from around the country wanted Congress to stop the Federal Home Loan Bank Board from putting in force a regulation limiting direct ownership by thrifts of real estate and other assets. More than 200 House members cosponsored legislation in 1985 to delay the direct investment rule, and numerous senators denounced it. But efforts to nullify the rule went nowhere. Bennett said he looked for but could not find any evidence to suggest that the five senators lobbied on the rule as a result of Keating's contributions.

The key events of Bennett's investigation were two meetings held in April 1987. In the first, on April 2, four of the senators (all but Riegle) met privately in DeConcini's office with Edwin J. Gray, chairman of the Federal Home Loan Bank Board, which was responsible for regulating the thrift industry. Gray contended that the senators pressured him to withdraw the direct investment rule, which would rein in Lincoln's ability to pursue its high-flying investment strategy. In his opening, Bennett homed in on an unusual aspect of the first meeting — that Gray was told to bring no aides with him. "While in fairness to the senator, Senator DeConcini, he denies that it was his instruction, the overwhelming evidence suggests that the no-aides instruction came from Senator DeConcini's office. Under all of the circumstances, including the articulated purpose of the meeting, it is at best strange that there was a purposeful effort made to exclude staff."

Detailed notes of the second meeting taken by one of the regulators seemed to be unusually accurate, Bennett said, and they indicated that DeConcini seemed to be negotiating for Lincoln.

Bennett made clear that he viewed Cranston's efforts in Keating's behalf to be the most questionable. He received the most money from Keating, he allowed his fund-raisers to serve as an important link with Keating, he remained active in helping Keating after others had stopped and he seemed the most ideologically incompatible with Keating. "The evidence will show," Bennett said, "that on approximately four separate occasions Senator Cranston accepted or solicited several hundred thousand dollars from Mr. Keating for Senator Cranston's voting registration groups and that each of these four occasions was linked by time and circumstance to a request by Mr. Keating for assistance with the bank board." Those events, from early 1987 to early 1989, were documented by extensive memorandums from Cranston's fund-raiser, Joy Jacobson, Bennett said.

"One is forced to ask, didn't the thought ever occur to Senator Cranston — and I suppose I can say this — he's known as a liberal Democrat — why would Mr. Keating, the antipornographer, the well-known Republican — why would he be giving hundreds and hundreds of thousands of dollars" to Cranston's pet political causes, Bennett asked.

In his opening statement, Bennett also set forth "objective" standards by which he thought a senator should be judged:

- A senator should not take contributions from an individual he or she knows or should know is attempting to procure the senator's services to intervene in a specific matter pending before a federal agency.
- A senator should not take unusual or aggressive action with regard to a specific matter before a federal agency in behalf of a contributor when he or she knows or has reason to know the contributor has sought to procure the senator's services.
- A senator should not conduct fund-raising efforts or engage in office practices that lead contributors to conclude that they can buy access to the senator.
- A senator should not engage in conduct that would appear to be improper to a reasonable, non-partisan, fully informed person.

Of those standards, the fourth or "appearance standard" was the most controversial. Bennett argued that a senator could be disciplined for violating that standard even if his or her specific actions did not, in themselves, directly violate a Senate rule. *(Appearance standard, box, p. 978)*

Senators' Presentations

After Bennett finished his overview of the case, the senators responded in person — some claiming that Bennett's presentation exonerated them, others protesting that Bennett gave a one-sided case that ignored exculpatory evidence and drew too-neat connections between Keating's fund-raising efforts and their actions. Four of the senators gave their statements on Nov. 16, immediately after Bennett had finished his; DeConcini waited until the hearing resumed on Nov. 19 after a weekend break.

For Riegle, it was his first detailed comment on the Keating affair, and he held forth for an hour, focusing particularly on Bennett's suspicion that Keating's fund raising might have influenced the senator's actions. "I would never dishonor my family name or the public trust for any reason or purpose. You couldn't make me do it," Riegle said. "The idea that I would do it for a campaign fund raiser is sheer nonsense."

Glenn emphasized that he had received no contributions from Keating since a year before the 1987 meetings and that he stopped helping Lincoln after learning of its legal troubles. He went on to defend the practice of questioning regulators about their actions. "I believe that a crucial part of my job as a U.S. senator is to ensure that federal regulators and bureaucrats are treating people fairly and carrying out their regulatory activities responsibly," he said.

McCain said he, too, ended his involvement with Lincoln once he heard the federal regulators' side of the story on April 9, 1987. He acknowledged that he and Keating had been friends when he was in the House (1983-87), taking his family on several vacations at Keating's private resort in the Bahamas, but he insisted he had exerted no improper pressure for Keating. "When he came to see me in March of 1987 and asked me to do something I thought was improper, I said no," McCain told the committee. "When he asked me to get Ed Gray off his back, I said no. When he asked me to negotiate for him, I said no. The only thing I said I could do was to inquire whether American Continental Corp. [an Ohio-chartered corporation based in Phoenix, which purchased Lincoln in 1984] and Lincoln Savings were being treated fairly."

Cranston made his only appearance during the hearings a dramatic one Nov. 16 as he displayed a long list of aides, including some in every senator's office, who were designated under Senate rules to accept campaign donations. "It is absurd to suggest that fund raising and substantive issues are separated in Senate offices by some kind of wall," Cranston said. "The notion that it violates Senate rules and established ethical standards if the fund raiser participated in a meeting in which substantive issues were discussed is sheer hypocrisy. I submit that if you decide that it's improper to take a lawful and proper action at any time in behalf of someone who has contributed legally and properly, then every senator, including every member of this committee, had better run for cover — because every senator has done it; every senator must do it."

Cranston, known as a master fund-raiser among Democrats, said that laws and rules governing campaign finance should be reformed. "But they haven't been changed yet," he concluded. "Until they are, the Senate and every senator and candidate will be in dire jeopardy."

DeConcini was particularly aggressive toward the special counsel's tactics, accusing Bennett of behaving like a prosecutor bent on improving his courtroom record. "Bennett says that the facts tilt," DeConcini said. "No, the facts don't tilt. He tilts them, and why does he do that? He wants the victory. He wants to nail somebody."

DeConcini insisted that Keating's complaints of harassment by federal regulators seemed to have merit in 1987. Moreover, he said, he did not always do Keating's bidding. When Keating asked him to push through a sale of Lincoln in early 1989, the senator said, "I said no. I did not push for the approval of that sale." DeConcini acknowledged, however, that he asked regulators about the sale and asked them to give it close consideration.

Senate Aides' Testimony

The first witnesses were aides to the senators. They sought to differentiate the actions of their bosses from those of the other senators, with much testimony focusing on who had taken the initiative in setting up the first meeting with bank board Chairman Gray.

Gwendolyn van Paasschen, McCain's legislative assistant, appeared Nov. 19-20 and testified that she called an independent auditor to check out Keating's claims of unfair treatment by regulators, and that she was convinced they had merit. But, she said, she had an uneasy feeling about Keating and warned McCain not to do too much for him.

Van Paasschen said it was her recollection that Riegle had initiated the meeting, even though he did not attend, and that DeConcini had kept staff away. She also said she heard DeConcini tell McCain in March 1987 that he "wanted to get the regulators off of Mr. Keating's back."

Laurie Sedlmayr, an aide to DeConcini, testified Nov. 26 that she believed the April 2 meeting had been the "brainchild" of Riegle. But under cross-examination by Riegle attorney Thomas C. Green, she said that she had no facts to support her belief.

McCain's attorney, John M. Dowd, attempted to show that McCain had nothing to do with a letter written by Sedlmayr and signed by DeConcini, inviting Riegle to the April 9 meeting. The letter said the invitation was from DeConcini and McCain; Sedlmayr said that had been her belief, but she had mistakenly forgotten to send a copy to McCain's office.

Sedlmayr also testified that she advised DeConcini to avoid helping Keating. "She let me know she didn't think it was a good idea," DeConcini said Nov. 26.

Meeting with Gray

For the equivalent of three days in the week of Nov. 26, the panel heard from the best-known accuser of the Keating senators, Edwin Gray. The meeting that four of the senators — all but Riegle — attended with the nation's top savings and loan regulator on April 2, 1987, was in many ways the beginning of the case against them.

Gray had testified at length before the House Banking Committee in 1989 that the four senators present at the meeting had acted improperly. Gray had been upset by the session and had complained to his aides about it immediately afterward. Gray testified that he had first publicly mentioned the meeting when a reporter called him in May 1989.

He told the committee that he was improperly pressured at the meeting to withdraw a bank board regulation adopted Feb. 27, 1987, limiting certain thrift investments in real estate and other enterprises, that was being strongly opposed by Lincoln. He also alleged that DeConcini offered him a quid pro quo that Lincoln would change some of its controversial practices if the rule was abandoned. While Riegle did not attend the meeting, Gray testified that the senator had told him to "expect a call" to set it up. Attorneys for the senators challenged Gray's suitability for the job of bank board chairman, his memory of dates and other facts, and, most of all, his broad assertions that the senators had acted improperly.

Some members of the Ethics panel had trouble with Gray's assertions. Lott acknowledged "shaking my head in disgust" at some statements, and Sanford said to Gray: "I think probably your explanation of all of this as being politicians chasing money is perhaps not quite accurate."

Gray conceded that he had been the one to suggest that the senators hold a second meeting, on April 9, with the regulators who were in charge of the Lincoln case. He said he had been shocked that Riegle had attended that meeting. But he told Green that he had no recollection of meeting with Riegle on April 21, 1987, less than two weeks later, to ask for help in getting a job on Wall Street. His term as bank board chairman was about to expire.

Meeting with Regulators

All five senators attended the meeting a week later in DeConcini's office with examiners from the San Francisco Federal Home Loan Bank and the Washington office of the bank board. Two of the regulators who attended the April 9, 1987, meeting testified at the hearings: William Black, then deputy director of the Federal Savings and Loan Insurance Corporation (FSLIC), and Michael Patriarca, head of the San Francisco regional office.

A memorandum summarizing notes that Black took during the meeting was submitted by Bennett as a reliable account of what went on. "It is a fairly remarkable document," Bennett said. "Everyone who has seen that memo says that this transcript-like memo is accurate in all essential respects." Bennett went on, "A fair reading of that memo reveals clearly that Senator DeConcini was negotiating or trying to strike a deal for Lincoln."

Black, who at the time of the hearings was chief counsel of the western region of the Office of Thrift Supervision (OTS), testified that he and other regulators were improperly pressured by the senators in the controversial meeting. But, he said, he and his colleagues did nothing in response to the meeting.

Black provided the committee with a picture of Lincoln's deep financial problems and the "scam," as he termed it, that the thrift used to stay solvent. He testified that the thrift was basically a Ponzi scheme that used fraudulent accounting of prohibited ownership investments in real estate to generate income that could be paid to the parent corporation, American Continental. When the bank board in 1986 began to crack down on Lincoln's real estate investments, the thrift was put in the position of potential insolvency, Black said.

As had Gray before him, Black drew few distinctions on his own among the senators who met with him on April 9. He noted repeatedly that DeConcini at the meeting had used the word "we" to refer to the senators' concerns about Lincoln and said he assumed DeConcini was speaking for everyone.

Black asserted that, by poisoning the atmosphere involving Lincoln, the actions of the senators may have led to a two-year delay in closing the thrift at tremendous additional cost to the taxpayers. Regulators first formally recommended in May 1987 that Lincoln be closed; it finally happened in April 1989. No corroborating evidence existed for Black's assertion, however, and members of the Ethics Committee and Bennett did not seem to accept it. None of the regulators present at the April meetings, nor any who came later, testified that they were prevented from doing their jobs because of political pressure from the senators.

Patriarca confirmed details of Black's memo and agreed with Gray and Black that DeConcini had made the most strenuous efforts in Keating's behalf. He testified that DeConcini had "negotiated" with him for special treatment for Lincoln during the April 9 meeting, which he considered improper. Patriarca described Glenn as "blunt," McCain as "uncomfortable" and Riegle as having conducted a "cross-examination" of the regulators. Cranston made a "cameo appearance," he said. The senators' tone changed markedly, Patriarca said, after the regulators informed them that a criminal referral would be made to the Justice Department because of some of Lincoln's practices.

M. Danny Wall, who succeeded Gray as chairman of the Federal Home Loan Bank Board in July 1987, testified Dec. 4 that he had been approached by both DeConcini and Cranston in Lincoln's behalf and that neither had done anything wrong. Wall, former staff director of the Senate Banking Committee, took sharp issue with Black's testimony that political pressure had led to a delay in closing Lincoln.

Cranston Fund Raising

The committee focused in the week of Dec. 3 largely on the possibility of a connection between Cranston's fund raising and his concern for Lincoln.

In his opening remarks, Bennett had used Cranston's candor against him, particularly his admission that campaign contributions result in favored treatment. Bennett cited Cranston's sworn deposition: "A person who makes a contribution has a better chance to get access than someone who does not."

Memorandums to Cranston from a key aide, Joy Jacobson, released by the committee Dec. 3, showed the possibility that Keating expected help in return for his financial contributions.

Jacobson was chief fund-raiser for Cranston's 1986 reelection campaign. She testified that after 1986 she worked regularly out of Cranston's majority whip office to raise money for a variety of voter registration and get-out-the-vote drives and for the Democratic Senatorial Campaign Committee. In those efforts, she said, she helped to collect hundreds of thousands of dollars from Lincoln and American Continental.

Jacobson's strongest testimony was contained in a series of memos to Cranston in 1987 and 1988. A Jan. 2, 1987, summary of her fund-raising plans noted that, because the Democrats again had a majority in the Senate, "there are a number of individuals who have been very helpful to you who have cases or legislative matters pending with our office who will rightfully expect some kind of resolution." Among them she listed Keating, who, she said, "is continuing to have problems with the Bank Board and Ed Gray."

In a Sept. 6, 1987, memo, Jacobson noted that Keating should be pleased with the appointment of Wall to succeed Gray at the bank board. Noting that Cranston had an upcoming Sept. 24 meeting with Keating, Jacobson said he should ask for $250,000 for one of the voter registration committees Cranston supported.

Furthermore, in a memo Jan. 18, 1988, she noted that Cranston and Keating had recently had dinner and reminded him that Keating wanted him to call Wall about Lincoln's continuing troubles with the bank board. Less than a month later, Keating gave $500,000 to two of Cranston's voter drives. Jacobson testified under questioning by Cranston's attorney, Taylor, that the senator never said he was taking action because of the money. But she conceded to Bennett that "in retrospect" a link probably existed in Keating's mind.

As evidence of Cranston's continuing help for Keating and the degree to which Keating apparently counted on the California Democrat, Bennett cited an urgent message to the senator from Keating in April 1989. The message asked for Cranston's help to persuade Wall to approve the sale of Lincoln to a group of employees and other investors. Such a sale would have preserved some or all of Keating's investment in the thrift. "The consequences of not doing the above are a political disaster for anybody and everybody connected with Lincoln's past," Keating wrote.

Testimony Dec. 11 from another Cranston aide, Carolyn Jordan, appeared to provide some cover for her boss. She testified that although she regularly inquired about Lincoln with regulators, she had no knowledge that Keating had contributed large sums to Cranston or to his various political causes. Although Jordan said she had no knowledge of Keating's contributions at the time she and Cranston were meeting with Lincoln officials, she conceded that Cranston fund-raiser Jacobson was also sometimes present.

Jordan testified that on her own, or with the cooperation of others in Cranston's office — but without Cranston's knowledge — she regularly inserted into the *Congressional Record* statements that passed for comments seemingly made during floor debates by Cranston himself. On one such occasion in 1987, she inserted comments contradicting a floor statement by Banking Committee Chairman William Proxmire, D-Wis., on a subject of direct interest to Lincoln. The thrift later cited those comments, attributed to Cranston, as "legislative history" in a lawsuit against federal regulators. Jordan testified that Lincoln officials had not asked for the action. "It may have inadvertently assisted them, but it was certainly not the purpose of the statement," she said.

DeConcini Defense

Of the five senators, DeConcini tried hardest to mount a vigorous defense — largely by calling a phalanx of character witnesses. He called Sen. Daniel K. Inouye, D-Hawaii, and Arizona's governor, Democrat Rose Mofford, to testify for him.

Inouye had experience in dealing with politically sensitive inquiries: He served on the Senate Watergate Committee investigating the Nixon administration in 1973; in 1987 he was chairman of the Senate special committee probing the Iran-contra affair. Linking DeConcini's actions to the normal duties of a senator, Inouye reminded the Ethics Committee members that they all went to bat for constituents who had battles with government agencies. "I think Sen. DeConcini's conduct was spotless," Inouye said. By implication, the same was true of the rest. If what DeConcini did was improper, "I think all of us at one time or another have done that," he said. "I believe that what is on trial here are not the five colleagues of mine but the United States Senate."

On Dec. 10, DeConcini called former U.S. customs commissioner William Von Raab and three Arizona residents: the head of a drug rehabilitation center, a sheriff and a disabled World War II veteran, all of whom had sought and received assistance from DeConcini. DeConcini also introduced statements and affidavits from three colleagues and one former senator, all attesting to his character and taking issue with the contention that his actions in the Lincoln case were out of the ordinary. The statements and affidavits were provided by Ernest F. Hollings, D-S.C.; Paul Simon, D-Ill.; Strom Thurmond, R-S.C.; and former senator Robert Morgan, D-N.C.

Von Raab testified that during the eight years he ran the Customs Service, beginning in 1981, DeConcini intervened with him repeatedly, particularly in behalf of importers when the senator believed the agency had overreacted. He said that DeConcini was "always firm, resolute, but always fair." And he said DeConcini's behavior was no different from that of any other member of Congress.

DeConcini's aggressive defense backfired somewhat on Dec. 10, when former American Continental tax accountant David Stevens testified that DeConcini had tried to use him to discredit McCain. Stevens had written to the Ethics Committee in October, saying that he believed McCain had never intended to repay American Continental for travel provided members of McCain's family in 1984-86.

Failing to receive a response from the Ethics Committee, Stevens wrote to DeConcini and sent him a copy of the original letter. Stevens testified that DeConcini then called him and asked him to sign an affidavit for use in the hearings. He testified that DeConcini also asked if he could release the letter to the news media. The letter was leaked to several newspapers in late November. Under examination by McCain attorney Dowd, Stevens retracted his assertion that McCain had not intended to reimburse American Continental for the trips.

The issue of DeConcini's request to release the Stevens letter to the media raised a sore point because numerous documents in the case had been leaked and Lincoln had previously complained that federal regulators leaked damaging information about the institution. Committee member Pryor had gone so far in his opening remarks at the hearings to say that staff caught leaking information should be fired, senators who were caught expelled and lawyers who were caught disbarred.

DeConcini's office asserted that the letter from Stevens was not Ethics Committee property. But Stevens' appearance was plainly damaging to DeConcini.

Keating Lobbyist

The hearings got a surprise in December when the committee announced that it would make a grant of immunity from future criminal prosecution to obtain the testimony of a new witness.

James J. Grogan was vice president and chief counsel of Lincoln, corporate counsel for American Continental and Keating's point man on Capitol Hill. When Keating went to visit a member, Grogan usually went along; when members visited American Continental's Phoenix headquarters, Grogan went too. He talked to all five senators about Lincoln's problems with regulators, and he delivered some of the $1.5 million in contributions made by Keating and his associates to the senators' campaigns and political causes.

Grogan had previously cited constitutional protections against self-incrimination in declining to testify. He faced no criminal charges at the time, but a federal grand jury in Los Angeles was looking broadly into the Lincoln affair.

In a carefully worded statement Dec. 5, the committee said that "it cannot fulfill its obligations to these members [the five senators] and to the Senate without obtaining [Grogan's] testimony." To obtain it, the committee had to grant Grogan limited immunity from prosecution — meaning that he could not be prosecuted for what he told the committee and that prosecutors could not use what he told the committee to develop new evidence against him. He would be subject to prosecution for perjury, however, if he lied under oath.

The committee first questioned Grogan in closed sessions and then put him on the stand publicly on Dec. 14-15. Grogan raised serious questions about the depth of Riegle's involvement with Keating, and he made a direct link between legislative actions that Keating sought from Cranston and financial assistance that Cranston sought from Keating.

He testified that, in early 1987, he and Riegle had discussed Lincoln's problems with the Federal Home Loan Bank Board, which Keating thought was harassing Lincoln. Grogan testified that Riegle told him he knew the bank board chairman, Gray. "He had done favors for Ed Gray. He thought that he could set up a meeting," Grogan testified. He said Riegle further suggested that Grogan ask DeConcini and McCain to set up the meeting and have them invite Riegle, apparently to provide Riegle with cover.

"It was apparent to me that Senator Riegle knew, as a shrewd politician, that this was a potentially politically explosive situation," Grogan said. As evidence that Riegle had arranged the April 2 meeting, Grogan testified that the senator had mentioned the idea of a meeting to him in early March 1987 when Riegle was visiting Keating and American Continental headquarters in Phoenix. A few days later, Grogan said, Keating told him that Riegle had called and had spoken with Gray.

Other evidence that appeared to corroborate Grogan's testimony was a page from Cranston's calendar for April 2, which noted a meeting in DeConcini's office with Gray, Riegle and McCain. It did not mention Glenn. Grogan said the other senators were "miffed" because they had expected Riegle to attend the April 2 meeting. Grogan said the first meeting had gone so badly that he was unsure the second meeting would come off. So, he said, he flew to Washington during the interim "to keep the team together."

He also testified that the original purpose of the meetings — as he had promoted them — was to inquire about the status of a long-running examination of Lincoln by the regulators. Keating wanted more, he said. According to notes of the second meeting, talking points for the meetings drafted by Lincoln employees and memorandums prepared by DeConcini's staff, the subject expanded to a request that the regulators grant "forbearance" to Lincoln on some of its investments that regulators said violated bank board regulations. And the regulators were asked to reappraise Lincoln's real estate holdings that the thrift said were being undervalued.

Grogan also testified extensively about Cranston's fund raising. He said that within days of meeting Cranston in 1984 at a Democratic Party event, he was called by Cranston fund-raiser Jacobson, who asked him to help raise money for the senator. At that time, Grogan said, Cranston said to him: "I've been very good to savings and loans. I worked hard for California savings and loans. You all should really support me."

In late 1986, Grogan testified, he asked Jacobson for help in killing a Senate floor amendment that would have hurt Lincoln's business. According to Grogan, Jacobson called him back to report that she had tried just that. In that same conversation, Grogan testified, Jacobson said she had another matter to discuss. Grogan quoted Jacobson as saying, "I want to switch gears, and I want you to know this is totally unrelated." Grogan testified that Jacobson then asked for help in securing a personal loan for Cranston's reelection campaign. A short time later, Lincoln granted Cranston a personal line of credit for $300,000, though the senator never used it. Grogan recalled that Cranston greeted Keating at a dinner in Los Angeles in January 1988 by saying, "Ah, the mutual aid society." (Cranston later said he did not recall making the comment.) Grogan said he had few contacts with DeConcini, Glenn and McCain, despite having once worked for Glenn. DeConcini, Grogan testified, had a personal relationship with Keating. He said the two men had repeated contacts to which Grogan was not a party. He said he was not always privy to Keating's thinking. And, he said, on numerous occasions he misread Keating's intentions. Ultimately, he said, he and Keating had a falling out over Grogan's handling of bankruptcy proceedings involving American Continental. They had not spoken since June 1990, he said, when Grogan left the company.

Grogan testified that Keating had decided after the April 1987 meetings not to continue to use the senators to pressure the regulators further. Keating believed the meetings were a "horrible disaster," Grogan said. "It was a mistake. It intensified the wrath of San Francisco."

Grogan was a cooperative witness, answering questions directly. He cast his, Keating's and Lincoln's actions in the most positive light, insisting — as Keating did — that Lincoln was a profitable firm hounded out of business by zealous regulators. Soliciting help from members of Congress to counter those regulators, he said, was only proper. According to Grogan, Keating did not use political contributions as a means to enlist the senators' help. "It never bothered me because I never, either from the senators — any of them — or from Mr. Keating, I never got even a hint that the money was being given in exchange for anything," Grogan said.

As evidence that contributions do not buy influence, Grogan testified that Cranston, DeConcini and Glenn had not always done Keating's bidding. He said that when Riegle announced in early 1988 that he was returning more than $75,000 that Keating had raised for him a year earlier, Keating was angry and offended.

Nevertheless, Grogan said he believed contributions helped to open congressional doors. He also acknowledged the appearance of a conflict of interest when members acted in behalf of large contributors. Grogan contradicted Jordan's recollections of the genesis of the statement she inserted in the *Congressional Record* to offset comments by Sen. Proxmire. Grogan said that he had specifically alerted her to problems in the Proxmire statement and had asked her to insert a statement to neutralize it.

Other Witnesses

The committee on Dec. 2 heard another side to the story of why federal regulators moved slowly to close down Lincoln. According to Rosemary Stewart, former head of enforcement at the Federal Home Loan Bank Board and its successor agency, the Office of Thrift Supervision, the delay had nothing to do with the senators.

Stewart had participated in the 1988 decision to remove the San Francisco regulators from their role in supervising Lincoln, a year after they had recommended that the thrift be seized. Stewart said she believed that the San Francisco regulators had a vendetta against the thrift, as Lincoln was charging at the time. And, she said, the San Francisco regulators had not made their case. "It would have been unprecedented" to have taken control of an institution that had not yet failed, as the San Francisco regulators were urging, Stewart testified.

Stewart was called as a witness by Cranston's attorney, Taylor. Although her testimony was a strong counterpoint to that of the San Francisco regulators, questioning from Ethics Committee Vice Chairman Rudman showed that he was not convinced Stewart had acted in the government's best interests.

The panel heard Jan. 10, 1991, from a Keating lobbyist, Washington lawyer Margery Waxman, who had written to Keating in May 1988 that he had the regulators "right where you want them." Waxman testified that Keating had hired another attorney and that she had used hyperbole to get Keating to notice her letter. She said she had no contacts with the five senators.

Rebuttal: Glenn, McCain

The senators and their attorneys got a chance to make their cases after the committee took a Christmas and New

Year's recess. Glenn and McCain took a low-key approach when they appeared on Jan. 4, 1991, reflecting the fact that little had appeared in the hearings to damage them. During a day of testimony, the committee heard Glenn and McCain argue that they did nothing inappropriate by attending two April 1987 meetings with federal regulators.

Glenn's attorney, Charles F. C. Ruff, urged the committee to judge Glenn "by the sternest ethical standard that you can apply to the conduct of all of your colleagues in the Senate." Even in that light, he said, Glenn emerged unscathed.

Glenn emphasized that he ended virtually all contacts with Keating after the second April 1987 meeting, at which regulators informed the senators that criminal charges might be filed. "I came to the conclusion that Lincoln was in deep trouble," Glenn said. His only action after that time was to set up a lunch meeting in January 1988 between Keating and Speaker Jim Wright, D-Texas. In the summer of 1987, Glenn testified, he turned down Keating's offer to raise campaign contributions because of Keating's battles with the regulators.

McCain testified that he broke off his friendship with Keating just before the April meetings, when Keating asked him to negotiate. "I told him that he was trying to do something that was inappropriate," he said. "I would not do it."

Committee Chairman Heflin questioned McCain closely about vacations he took with Keating between 1983 and 1986, while McCain was still a member of the House. McCain reimbursed American Continental for some of the flights at the time they were taken. In 1989, however, American Continental accountants informed McCain that about $13,400 in flights had not been reimbursed. In May and June of that year, McCain paid the company.

The House Committee on Standards of Official Conduct (ethics committee) took up the case and ruled that his repayment ended the matter. The Senate panel had previously concluded that the House should have final say, because McCain had been a representative at the time.

McCain, who became somewhat defensive during the questioning, insisted that he would have paid for the flights if American Continental had told him sooner that the payments had not been made.

There was little suggestion that McCain had done anything wrong beyond not checking on the payments. "You owe John McCain something," argued his attorney, Dowd. "You owe him a straight, crisp, clear finding, based on the overwhelming, undisputed evidence in the record that his actions, at all times, were honest and ethical." At the conclusion of McCain's testimony, committee member Lott said, "I am compelled to say that you have shown repeatedly that you did nothing improper."

Rebuttal: Riegle, DeConcini

The appearances of Riegle on Jan. 7-8 and DeConcini on Jan. 9-10 concluded the major testimony.

Riegle's attorney blamed "whimsical circumstances" for the close scheduling between a March 23, 1987, Keating-sponsored fund-raiser that netted $78,250 and the controversial April 9 meeting that Riegle attended. He also denied that Riegle had had any intention of misleading the committee, particularly with reference to setting up the April 2 meeting with Gray.

Riegle took pains to say that more than $10,000 collected for his campaign from American Continental employees days before the trip to Phoenix was unrelated to his discussions with Keating. Riegle testified that the money was intended to be given as part of a Keating-sponsored fund-raiser scheduled for Riegle in Detroit a few weeks later.

Riegle insisted that he had not discussed fund raising during the trip. Rudman zeroed in on Riegle's inability to recall events and conversations. Rudman said he found Riegle's testimony "remarkably inconsistent." In particular, he seemed incredulous at Riegle's description of the trip to Phoenix, when Riegle met with Keating, toured American Continental Corp. and — according to other testimony — discussed Keating's problems with federal regulators and proposed a meeting with the senators and Gray. Rudman said he was confused about why Riegle had visited American Continental but told his aides not to deal with issues involving Lincoln. Riegle said he kept his aides out of the issue because the California-based thrift was not a direct constituent. But he said he visited American Continental because the company was investing in Detroit.

Bennett made clear in his cross-examination of Riegle that he did not believe the protests of several of the senators that they were concerned in the meetings not only about Lincoln but also about the entire thrift industry. "I don't see in a year and a half of investigation," Bennett said, "a single piece of paper that suggests you or any of the other senators in connection with this matter were concerned or had an issue about a systematic problem that might be affecting the industry."

DeConcini argued in his own defense that a senator could not be punished for the appearance of improper conduct unless improper conduct existed. His attorney, James Hamilton, argued that DeConcini had not tried to negotiate for Keating, and even if he had, there would have been nothing wrong with it. Hamilton contested Bennett's contention that senators could be punished merely for violating an "appearance standard." But he also argued that adopting such a standard should not condemn DeConcini because he was only doing what many senators did. "Even under special counsel's standard, Senator DeConcini's conduct is wholly proper. No appearance standard can be used to condemn conduct that is commonplace and generally accepted."

The committee voted Jan. 8 not to call Cranston, who was undergoing medical treatment in California. Members decided that the record on Cranston was complete enough to make a decision, and the senator did not ask to speak further. On Cranston's behalf, however, his attorney, Taylor, said senators had a duty to act to help constituents — whether or not they were big contributors. "This duty may create an appearance of mutual dependence," he said. But "there is nothing improper, nor is there an appearance that there is anything improper, about that mutuality."

Closing Remarks

Bennett took more than three hours on Jan. 15-16 to sum up his view of the facts and the standards that should apply to the case. He distinguished carefully among the five senators and, without actually making recommendations, urged the committee to find that Cranston, DeConcini and Riegle had acted improperly. He again called upon the committee to find that Glenn and McCain had acted properly at all times. Bennett distinguished them from the others by arguing that their acceptance of contributions was far removed in time from their actions, eliminating any taint from their fund raising.

Bennett argued that DeConcini had gone beyond the bounds of proper behavior to negotiate for Keating with the regulators in 1987, and he noted that DeConcini weighed in with them again in 1989 on the pending sale of Lincoln, despite knowledge that the regulators had referred evidence of possible criminal conduct at Lincoln to the Justice Department.

Bennett argued that Cranston's case provided the closest connections between money and action. He cited four separate occasions in which Cranston took actions for Keating after soliciting or receiving large amounts of cash for his own campaign or for voter registration groups with which he was affiliated.

Of Riegle, Bennett also drew a connection between fund raising and action, all of which occurred in a three-month period in 1987. And he made a damning accusation that Riegle had misled the committee, perhaps intentionally, about his role in the Keating affair.

As for the senators' contention that their meetings with and repeated phone calls to regulators were merely "status inquiries" to find out whether the Lincoln case was being handled properly, Bennett was derisive. "If I'm sitting on a park bench, and an eight-hundred-pound gorilla comes along and says, 'Excuse me, I'm just making a status inquiry if there are any seats available,' you say, 'You're damn right, there's a seat available.' And there's a lot of eight-hundred-pound gorillas around this place."

Bennett reiterated his position that the senators' actions had been wrong and that they should have known how wrong they would appear to the public. "For this body to conclude that there is no appearance standard requires you to disregard what you have written before, what you have said before, what you have decided before."

The comments of Ethics Committee members clearly revealed that the panel was not going to reach a ruling quickly in the case. "I would dare say that there are six visions — six visions — of this case and what it means or what it doesn't mean, what is relevant, what is not relevant," Pryor said in his closing comments on Jan. 16. A few days earlier, Helms referred to the senators as "Keystone Cops" and to Keating as "Daddy Warbucks." He told Riegle, "I don't believe you would have gone out to Phoenix — I don't believe anybody would have been involved with Mr. Keating, if he didn't have the ability to give away other people's money." Helms added that he was unhappy with the way the senators under investigation seemed to feel that there was nothing in the slightest wrong with anything they had done. "If I'm disturbed about one thing — and I'm disturbed about many things — it's that not once have I heard anything remotely resembling a mea culpa about this," he remarked. Lott, who seemed uncomfortable with the image problems the whole proceeding was creating for the Senate, told reporters on Jan. 8 that he expected the committee to find some significant violations. "I would be amazed if at least one case did not go to the Senate floor" for punishment, he said.

Preliminary Decision

The Ethics Committee Feb. 27 announced its preliminary findings and issued a 12-page summary. The panel rebuked DeConcini, Glenn, McCain and Riegle for poor judgment. DeConcini and Riegle also were criticized for creating improper appearances, and DeConcini's conduct with the regulators was found to be inappropriately aggressive. The committee, however, decided that existing Senate rules did not warrant punishment for any of the four. As far as the panel was concerned, the case against them was closed.

The committee, in effect, indicted Cranston, finding "substantial credible evidence . . . that Sen. Cranston engaged in an impermissible pattern of conduct in which fundraising and official activities were substantially linked." It did not accuse him of breaking a specific rule, charging instead that he violated the Senate's catchall admonition that members shall not engage in "improper conduct which may reflect upon the Senate." The committee had not yet decided to recommend that the full Senate punish Cranston, but it was expected to do so.

In its statement explaining its findings, the committee found nothing intrinsically wrong with the intervention by the five senators with federal regulators in behalf of Keating. It stated explicitly that the senators' actions had nothing to do with Lincoln's collapse. Furthermore, it said, each had ample information to justify contacting regulators about the fairness of the regulatory treatment Lincoln was receiving. But because of the size and frequency of Keating's contributions to Cranston, and the proximity of the contributions to the actions he took in Keating's behalf, the committee found the possibility of wrongdoing on Cranston's part.

With DeConcini and Riegle, the panel found an appearance of improper conduct that it chose to rebuke but not to punish because the rules on appearances of impropriety were unclear. To take further action against the two would have amounted to "setting standards after the fact," according to Lott. The idea that the Senate can punish members for the mere appearance of impropriety was central to Bennett's arguments that DeConcini and Riegle might have gone too far. Heflin and Rudman said they neither accepted nor rejected Bennett's appearance standard. In the cases of Glenn and McCain, even the appearance of impropriety was lacking, the committee said.

Delays and Deadlock

The members of the Ethics Committee were worn out by the Keating Five case. Helms quit the committee Feb. 28 and was replaced by Slade Gorton, R-Wash., although Helms remained on for the duration of the Cranston case. Pryor said March 7 that he would leave once the Cranston matter was settled. Heflin said he, too, wanted to depart, and on May 22 Senate Majority Leader George J. Mitchell, D-Maine, announced that he would be allowed to do so — with Sanford taking over as chairman — although Heflin would remain to wrap up the Cranston case.

The matter was not easily resolved, however. Cranston took two months drafting a response and decided not to demand another hearing. Pryor had a heart attack April 16 and soon after resigned from the committee. His replacement — Jeff Bingaman, D-N.M. — was not named until May 22. He took several weeks learning details of the case and on June 18 joined the panel's deliberations for the first time.

Deliberations intensified in July, but then Bingaman suddenly recused himself after declaring that he had a conflict: His wife's law firm was owed money for representing some of Cranston's principal associates in the case, and

Cranston had promised to make sure the bills were paid. Bingaman said he learned of the potential conflict of interest on July 23, and he immediately disqualified himself. He was not obliged to do so; committee rules left such judgments to members' discretion. The panel, however, unanimously concurred in his decision. Pryor, upon his recovery, was renamed to the panel on Aug. 21.

Long frustrated by the delays, Helms dropped a bomb the weekend of Aug. 3, just after the Senate broke for its summer recess. He released a report demanding that the full Senate censure Cranston for "reprehensible" conduct that "was clearly and unequivocally unethical." The 247-page report, with 936 footnotes, was based on a document submitted to the committee in late June by Bennett, who proposed that his draft be used as a basis for action by the full Senate to sanction Cranston and to justify the panel's Feb. 27 decision to close the cases against the other four Keating senators.

Helms' unilateral action was an unprecedented break with the Ethics Committee's penchant for secrecy. Committee leaders fired back at Helms, suggesting in a terse statement Aug. 5 that he violated committee confidentiality rules by releasing what it called Bennett's draft report. "I did not release any information that had been designated as 'committee sensitive,'" Helms said in an Aug. 6 statement. "I properly used the special counsel's generally excellent draft report as a basis for preparing my own report bearing my own name and signature."

Helms had signaled his frustration to the committee leaders in a July 15 letter. He told Heflin and Rudman that he saw "no adequate resolution of the case in sight." Especially disturbing to Helms was the prospect that the committee might issue only a brief report or no report at all.

The committee met several times after Congress returned in September, but Helms' report had not changed the impasse. Lott openly floated a proposal in late September to declare a deadlock and abandon the case, but more delays followed. The committee's two leaders were sidetracked for weeks: Heflin by the Judiciary Committee's consideration of Clarence Thomas' nomination to the Supreme Court and Rudman by the Intelligence Committee's work on Robert M. Gates' nomination as director of central intelligence. *(Thomas, box, p. 802; Gates, p. 261)*

The uproar over the Senate's handling of the Thomas nomination — and the pummeling its reputation took as a result — prompted Lott to drop his proposal. At a meeting Oct. 17, the committee renewed its effort. A compromise finally began to take shape after Lott suggested a middle ground: a committee rebuke that the Senate would vote to accept — sort of an indirect censure. The panel's Democrats balked at that, wanting to avoid a painful floor fight. Harry Reid, D-Nev., who had been secretly acting as Cranston's liaison to the committee for months, told the panel that Cranston would not accept a vote.

A final concession by the Republicans sealed the deal: no floor vote, but the committee reprimand would contain harsh language and would be delivered in person in full view of Cranston's colleagues. Helms refused to sign on, but he was persuaded not to fight. He abstained, and the rest of the Ethics Committee approved the compromise by 5-0 on Nov. 19 and presented it to the Senate the next day — two years, one month, three weeks and five days after the first public complaint on the case was received.

Committee Report

The Ethics Committee released a 79-page report, along with a copy of Helms' 247-page report as a harsh dissent. Cranston issued a 66-page response to the committee's resolution that argued in detail against almost all of the committee's conclusions.

After reviewing the voluminous evidence presented at the hearings, the committee found no evidence of a corrupt bargain — an illegal exchange of contributions for official action. The committee, however, decided that Cranston's conduct veered too close to a quid pro quo. In summary, the evidence seemed to show that it was not just that Cranston solicited and accepted much more money than the other four senators — $100,000 and more at a clip — and repeatedly did so at times when Keating was successfully seeking his assistance. No one episode sealed Cranston's fate; instead, Heflin said, it was "the totality of the circumstances."

Keating's fund raising for Cranston dated back to 1984. The early help was of comparatively little significance. In 1984-86, he raised $134,000 for Cranston's presidential and Senate campaigns and for the California Democratic Party at Cranston's request. Later donations to voter groups associated with Cranston were most troubling to the Ethics Committee. Keating donated $850,000 in 1987-88 and discussed giving another $100,000 in 1989. The committee found that during the same period Cranston talked to regulators or took other actions in Keating's behalf more than a dozen times.

The panel walked a fine line in attempting to articulate what was wrong with Cranston's conduct. Its leaders insisted they had not relied on the controversial appearance standard. But they were careful not to disavow it and reaffirmed their rebuke of DeConcini and Riegle for giving "the appearance of being improper." In saying that Cranston's actions were linked to Keating's donations in more than appearance, the committee insisted that he had not struck a corrupt bargain. If it had found such evidence, Rudman said on the floor, "this committee would recommend expulsion."

Thus, Cranston's behavior was found to fall somewhere between actually being dishonest and merely looking dishonest. Fund raising and official actions were linked, Heflin explained, but not "causally connected." Rudman offered a clue as to where he thought his colleague's conduct fell in the continuum when he said Keating's $850,000 in contributions to voter groups associated with Cranston were "the major motivation for his actions."

The committee's report offered little new guidance to senators on how to avoid "linkage." The "cardinal principle," the report said, was to make decisions "without regard to whether the individual has contributed or promised to contribute." It cautioned members to consider the following: the merits of the constituent's request; how much money the constituent had contributed; whether the type of official action to be taken in behalf of the constituent deviated from the senator's usual conduct; and "the proximity of money and action." The report, however, did not say how to evaluate these considerations.

Cranston Reprimand

Key to the final compromise was the desire by all concerned to avoid a full-scale floor fight. For that, the committee needed Cranston to accept its decision. Cranston's bottom line: "If the committee had called for any action by the full Senate against me, I would have fought it tooth and nail." Perhaps for this reason, the question of whether there would be a floor vote was a tightly held secret. It became clear by the morning of Nov. 20 that the committee would not ask members to vote. When speculation arose that someone might try to force a vote, President Pro Tempore Robert C. Byrd, D-W.Va., quashed the notion when he took the presiding officer's chair shortly after 2 p.m. and said, "The order does not provide for the taking of any votes by the Senate."

The order did require all senators to go to the floor. The only absent members were four Democrats — Bill Bradley, N.J.; Kent Conrad, N.D.; Bob Kerrey, Neb.; and Tom Harkin, Iowa. Twenty-six aides and lawyers were granted floor privileges, but Byrd sternly warned them: "Only senators will be given the privilege to speak." Byrd's warning seemed aimed at Alan M. Dershowitz, the outspoken criminal defense lawyer whom Cranston persuaded to represent him for free.

Heflin read the panel's resolution and a lengthy statement slowly and deliberately. It was his last act as an Ethics Committee member after 12 years as chairman or vice chairman. He took 35 minutes. A couple of members appeared to doze, some busied themselves with what appeared to be unrelated reading tasks, a few wandered off the floor and back again, but the chamber filled with a wave of turning pages as the members followed Heflin's reading of the text.

Rudman was next, reading his own lengthy statement much faster. While Heflin's statement had focused on standards, Rudman gave a more detailed accounting of Cranston's conduct.

Cranston, frail but resolute, began on a contrite note as his colleagues turned their chairs to face him: "I rise with deep remorse in my heart to accept the reprimand of the committee. I deeply regret the pain all this has caused my family, my friends and my supporters," he said. He choked once as he spoke of how proud he was of his work during the past 23 years in the Senate, 14 as whip.

Then came the defense: He rejected many of the committee's findings and attempted to reinterpret the panel's reasoning, saying he was being reprimanded only because "there appeared to be a proximity in time" between donations and actions. "That is what we're talking about — appearances," he said. "I now realize that what I did looked improper. But I differ, and I differ very, very deeply, with the committee's statement in the resolution that my conduct violated established norms of behavior in the Senate."

He compared the Ethics Committee with a "tyrant king" for deciding ex post facto that any such norms existed. He said he could and had been prepared to produce "example after example of comparable" conduct to show "that my behavior did not violate any established norms." He spoke of contributions as large as $750,000. "You are in jeopardy," he told his colleagues.

During his speech, many members (especially on the Republican side) appeared to grow tense. Some grumbled to each other. Steve Symms, R-Idaho, said he remarked to Wallop, "I heard the same speech 20 years ago when Spiro Agnew resigned." Rudman followed Cranston's remarks with an angry outburst. He called Cranston's statement "poppycock," later telling reporters, "I wanted to call it something else that begins with a 'B.' "

After the floor session, a few Republicans quickly began talking about forcing the issue to a vote. Some censure language was circulated, but it was not offered. Nancy Landon Kassebaum, R-Kan., said, "Rudman took care of it pretty effectively. Maybe it's best to let sleeping dogs lie."

Ethics Committee Findings

Following are excerpts from the text of the Senate Ethics Committee's resolution of reprimand against Alan Cranston, D-Calif., as adopted Nov. 19, 1991.

The committee finds that in connection with his conduct relating to Charles H. Keating Jr. and Lincoln Savings and Loan Association, Sen. Alan Cranston of California engaged in an impermissible pattern of conduct in which fundraising and official activities were substantially linked. It is further resolved:

1) That Sen. Cranston's impermissible pattern of conduct violated established norms of behavior in the Senate, and was improper conduct that reflects upon the Senate.

2) That Sen. Cranston's conduct was improper and repugnant.

3) In reviewing the evidence available to it, the committee finds that Sen. Cranston: violated no law or specific Senate rule; acted without corrupt intent; and did not receive nor intend to receive personal financial benefit from any of the funds raised through Mr. Keating.

4) Further, the committee finds that extenuating circumstances exist, including the following:

a) That Sen. Cranston is in poor health.

b) That Sen. Cranston has announced his intention not to seek re-election to the Senate.

5) Sen. Cranston's improper conduct deserves the fullest, strongest, and most severe sanction which the committee has the authority to impose.

Therefore, the Senate Select Committee on Ethics, on behalf of and in the name of the Senate, does hereby strongly and severely reprimand Sen. Alan Cranston.

Keating Six?

The Ethics Committee on Feb. 26, 1992, revealed that it had secretly reopened its inquiry to see if a sixth senator was involved but concluded after three months of investigation that no basis existed to think so.

The inquiry centered on a two-year-old memo delivered to the panel on Nov. 20, 1991. The memo, from Keating's secretary to him, suggested that someone named "Dickson" — perhaps Sen. Alan J. Dixon, D-Ill. — had taken steps to help Keating and that Riegle had been assisting Keating long after the time he said he quit doing so.

The committee said it had tried to get Keating and his

secretary to talk about the memo, but they invoked the Fifth Amendment and refused. The committee took testimony from the senators named in the memo, key Keating underlings and federal regulators. All the senators, including Dixon, denied knowing anything about the circumstances described in the memo.

The panel concluded the memo was "incorrect and inaccurate" and declined to proceed further.

1992 Legislative Action

The Senate tied up a loose end from the Keating Five investigation July 2, 1992, when it adopted by voice vote a resolution (S Res 273) to spell out when a senator could properly intervene with federal agencies in behalf of constituents. Senate Majority Leader Mitchell had appointed a task force in April 1991 to review Senate rules governing "constituent service."

The measure was criticized by the government watchdog group Common Cause as flawed, partly because it did not attempt to define what was improper use of influence. The resolution said only that "the decision to provide assistance to petitioners may not be made on the basis of contributions or services, or promises of contributions or services, to the member's political campaigns or to other organizations in which the member has a political, personal or financial interest."

16

The Bush Presidency

The Bush Presidency

While the comparison has not often been made, the career of George Bush had parallels with the career of John F. Kennedy. Both men were Ivy League graduates, reputed war heroes and sons of political families. Both could boast strategic triumphs as president — Kennedy in Cuba over Soviet warheads, Bush in Kuwait against Iraq. And both served with towering figures in American politics.

After Kennedy was assassinated, a British journalist predicted that he would go down in history as a footnote to the succeeding presidency of Lyndon B. Johnson. Some might say that Bush will be a footnote in the presidency of Ronald Reagan, with whom Bush had served as vice president.

Besides the obvious ones — Kennedy a Democrat and liberal, Bush a Republican and moderate conservative — differences existed between the two men and their situations. As president, Kennedy had youth and charisma. When Bush took office, he was 64; had he been re-elected, he would have surpassed Reagan as the oldest president. And young or old, Bush was never charismatic. Furthermore, Kennedy was a rich man and comfortable with it. Bush was less rich but self-conscious about his wealth. He reportedly shunned button-down shirts as a badge of his Eastern establishment heritage.

The biggest deviation is that Kennedy came to power before Johnson; Bush, after Reagan. While Kennedy did have problems getting the programs he wanted through Congress — problems the skillful legislative strategist Johnson was largely able to overcome — Kennedy's tenure was cut short, and what he could have done with more time remained a matter of speculation. Bush had a tough act to follow, but he had the opportunity to enhance Reagan's accomplishments while correcting his mistakes. History surely will record that Bush muffed it, however.

At the beginning, it appeared that he might try harder than he eventually did. When he told the 1988 GOP convention that he wanted a "kinder, gentler" nation, it was an unfinished comparison but an obvious poke at his predecessor, who hobnobbed with the rich for eight years while his policies too often exacerbated the social, racial and sexual tensions in American society.

Although his domestic and economic policies remained basically the same as Reagan's, Bush signed into law some social and environmental legislation that Reagan would not have supported. And, according to Douglas Besharov of the American Enterprise Institute, "Bush presided over a veritable explosion of spending. . . . not from defense but from across-the-board increases in domestic spending."

Reagan was not a major player or coach in the Bush presidency. A coolness appeared to exist between the two men. This may have stemmed from the days of the Reagan administration, during which the Reagans reportedly never once invited the Bushes to the White House for purely social purposes. A rumor even circulated in 1992 that Reagan voted for Bill Clinton, which Reagan denied.

Reagan, who chafed at the two-term limit for presidents, may have resented that Bush reaped the harvest of seeds he had sown. The Soviet "evil empire" that Reagan railed at tumbled after he left office, as did the Berlin Wall. While Bush had little to do with those events, he did not shy away from taking some responsibility for them. But how much of the collapse of Soviet communism was the result of Reagan-Bush "peace through strength" policies and how much was caused by global changes that were leading to an inevitable conclusion is unclear. The Soviet communists had been under pressure — from Boris N. Yeltsin's defection, from a repressed populace yearning for the democracy they could now read and hear about thanks to Mikhail S. Gorbachev's perestroika (restructuring) and glasnost (openness), from discontented consumers fed up with their inability to obtain the shiny goods taken for granted in western market economies and from a people weary of the rhetoric and financial burden of the Cold War. A persuasive argument could be made that communism could not have held on much longer, with or without the Reagan-Bush arms buildup.

Whatever credit Bush may have gotten for foreign policy achievements, by the time of his 1992 re-election campaign, domestic concerns — particularly the sorry state of the economy — were foremost on American minds. With his popularity sagging, Bush likened himself to a Democratic hero, not Kennedy but the plain-speaking Harry S. Truman, who staged one of the most memorable electoral comebacks in American political history. Many bristled at the comparison, however; even Truman's daughter, Margaret, went on national television to air her complaints.

The Bush Persona

If not Jack Kennedy or Harry Truman or Ronald Reagan, then who was President George Bush? Above all, he was uniquely George Bush. By all accounts, Bush was, and remains, an amiable, decent man who carried to the White House traits he had exhibited for years as the son of a senator, Navy pilot, husband, father, businessman, politician and public servant. Always patrician, despite his efforts

George Herbert Walker Bush

Republican of Houston, Texas
41st President of the United States

Born: Milton, Mass., June 12, 1924.

Education: Phillips Academy, Andover, Mass., 1942; Yale University, B.A., 1948, Phi Beta Kappa.

Occupation: Oil drilling businessman, Bush-Overbey Development Co., 1951-53; Zapata Petroleum Corp., 1953; president and co-founder, Zapata Off-Shore Co., 1954-66.

Military Service: Lieutenant (jg), U.S. Navy, 1942-45. Torpedo bomber pilot shot down over South Pacific Sept. 22, 1944. Awarded Distinguished Flying Cross.

Religion: Episcopalian.

Family: Son of Sen. Prescott Bush, R-Conn. (1952-63). Married 1945 to the former Barbara Pierce. Five children: George Walker, John Ellis (Jeb), Neil Mallon, Marvin Pierce and Dorothy (Doro). Another daughter, Pauline Robinson (Robin), died of leukemia just before her fourth birthday.

Political Career: U.S. House of Representatives, R-Texas, 1967-71; Republican nominee for U.S. Senate, Texas, 1964 and 1970; chairman, Republican National Committee, 1973-74; sought GOP presidential nomination, 1980; U.S. vice president, 1981-89: U.S. president, 1989-93.

Professional Career: U.S. ambassador to United Nations, 1971-73; liaison to People's Republic of China, 1974-75; director of central intelligence, 1976-77.

to hide it, he was thoughtful in little ways: Holding doors for people with their hands full. Rushing to help push cars stalled in the snows of New Hampshire. Personally typing hundreds of thank-you notes throughout his adult life. (In the White House, he converted from electric typewriter to computer, to demonstrate that he was not too old to learn.)

Mindful of being a New Englander staking his political future on acceptance by his adopted Texas and a nation suspicious of Easterners, he worked at being a good ol' boy — chawing pork rinds, buying socks at J. C. Penney's and using words such as "gonna," "gotta" and "guy." Some of it seemed contrived and at least once on a shopping foray from the White House it backfired. His surprise at discovering that supermarket checkouts were automated only confirmed suspicions that he was no Joe Sixpack.

Yet there were times in his life when a self-proclaimed "Oyster Bay kind of guy" was truly a "Joe Sixpack kind of guy." In the late 1940s and early 1950s, George and Barbara Bush exchanged the shade trees and civility of New England for the live oaks and hardscrabble life of West Texas, taking up a family friend's offer to teach George the oil business. For a time, they and the baby, George Jr., shared a so-called shotgun house (because it looked like a box shotgun shells came in) and a bathroom with a mother-daughter prostitute team who lived on the other side of a partition. But before long, the Bushes added more family and moved on, and on, and on — living in 28 houses before the White House. They became well off and socialized comfortably in the oil drilling business (Zapata), Congress (two terms in the House), a variety of political (GOP chairman) and public service jobs (U.N. ambassador, liaison to China, CIA director) and finally the vice presidency and presidency. *(Bush profile, Congress and the Nation Vol. VI, p. 854; Bush résumé, box, this page)*

As a white-haired first lady, Barbara Bush complemented her husband's studied down-to-earthiness in ways that seemed easy and natural. She was popular throughout their four years in the White House, playing a behind-the-scenes role instead of taking the activist approach of Eleanor Roosevelt. (Like Eleanor Roosevelt, though, Barbara Bush made more money than her husband. Her book about their dog Millie reportedly earned more in one year than the president's $200,000 salary. The book royalties went to her favorite charity, fighting illiteracy.)

Unlike his wife, Bush sometimes seemed to become a different person. He had a tendency toward the petulant, especially after shifting into what he called his "campaign mode." During the 1992 re-election campaign, he sneered at "crazy talk shows" and "crazy polls" that showed widespread discontent with his leadership and the listless economy. He put down Bill Clinton as "the failed governor of a small state" and Al Gore as "Mr. Ozone." He dismissed the search for a better America as "the vision thing." At one point in the campaign, he blurted out for no apparent reason, "Don't cry for me Argentina."

As the *New York Times* noted, "He had a goofy way of speaking but his résumé was dandy." His choppy delivery style often consisted of single words instead of complete sentences. "Message: I care," he told voters in one of the more coherent examples of his unusual speech pattern. (In his 1988 acceptance speech to the GOP convention, Bush acknowledged his awkward style. Over the next four years, however, careers were made by imitating him.)

The *Times'* "On Language" columnist, William Safire, a former Nixon speech writer, said that he saw the Bush persona change four times since the 1970s. Safire described Bush as (1) loose, funny and friendly as head of the CIA and as the GOP chairman; (2) tightened and guarded as Reagan's vice president, afraid to show any sign of disloyalty; (3) assertive at the 1988 convention and self-assured after he assumed Reagan's mantle; and (4) dispirited in 1992 as his ratings dropped and the election loomed.

Age may have been a factor in Bush's behavior during the campaign. Seemingly fit and vigorous, he nevertheless appeared tired and distracted to aides and reporters traveling with him. Several times, he had to confront rumors that he was sick. Earlier in the year, in Japan, he suffered the indignity of throwing up on the prime minister before toppling over in a faint. The next day, he blamed the spell on the 24-hour flu. When a reporter asked if he was worried that his younger Democratic challengers might make "a subtle issue" out of the incident, Bush rejoined: "Do you think only old people get the flu . . .? . . . I think Democrats get the flu from time to time." (In May 1991, Bush had been diagnosed with atrial fibrillation, caused by Graves' disease, a mild hyperthyroid condition. In February 1992, the White House announced that Bush had ceased taking the controversial sleeping pill Halcion. Some had speculated that Bush's tangled syntax and his sudden illness in Japan may have been linked to the drug. Bush's physician denied the charge.) At 46, Bill Clinton was 22 years and 2 months younger than the president, which represented the biggest age difference between the two major party nominees since the Civil War era. It also was more than double the average age discrepancy — nine years — in the previous 34 presidential elections. Clinton's running mate, Al Gore, was 44 at the time of the election.

Bush Appointments

To paraphrase the adage, you can tell a president by the company he keeps — in his Cabinet, his staff, his advisers and his appointments to important posts. In Bush's case, the people he chose to surround himself with, to a certain extent, reflected his personality and his political interests.

Throughout his career, as a political appointee and as a politician, Bush could be relied upon to be intensely loyal — to his constituency, his party, his president. Skepticism had greeted him upon being chosen vice president, in large part because he had been a contender for the presidential nomination and had publicly criticized some of Ronald Reagan's ideas. But he quickly became the leading cheerleader for the Reagan administration and proved himself a trusted White House team player. His appreciation for loyalty could be seen in some of his appointments once he came to occupy the Oval Office.

Of all Bush's advisers, James A. Baker III was his closest. A longtime hunting, fishing and tennis buddy from Houston, Baker chaired Bush's 1980 and 1988 presidential campaigns. When Bush was vice president, Baker served first as Reagan's White House chief of staff, then as Treasury secretary. Upon Bush's elevation to the presidency, Baker became secretary of state. He reluctantly left that post in August 1992 because his friend, the president, was in electoral trouble. Back in the White House as chief of staff, Baker took charge of the failing campaign. While Baker had gained a reputation as something of a political wizard, he was unable to turn the tide running against Bush and the Republicans. The outcome of the election did not sever the relationship between the two men, however. As a lame duck, Bush took his old pal fishing.

Other Bush appointees who had strong ties to him through the oil business, party politics or campaign activities included Robert A. Mosbacher, who was Bush's first secretary of commerce, then left to join the re-election effort; Samuel K. Skinner, who served as chief of staff after a stint as transportation secretary; and Lynn M. Martin, who succeeded Elizabeth H. Dole as labor secretary. Bush also named his longtime political ally John G. Tower, a former GOP senator from Texas, as defense secretary. Tower's reputation as a heavy drinker and womanizer proved his undoing, however. Despite the controversy over the nomination, Bush did not abandon Tower. The Senate ultimately voted not to confirm Tower on recommendation of the Armed Services Committee that he once chaired, and Bush, as a result, became the first president in U.S. history to have a Cabinet nominee rejected at the beginning of his term.

Two notable individuals were rewarded by Bush for their contributions to getting him elected in 1988: John H. Sununu and Lee Atwater. Sununu, a former three-term governor of New Hampshire, became Bush's first chief of staff. He had been instrumental in helping Bush to win his state's primary and go on to lock up the nomination. Sununu was seen as smart, but his style was abrasive and overbearing. When a series of scandals and missteps threatened his position, he found he had very little good will in reserve around Washington. Sununu never fully recovered from a 1990 flap over his use of taxpayer-paid government transportation for personal trips, but what led to his 1991 resignation was his failure to do what he had always done best: catching flak for the president. Instead of accepting blame for Bush's remarks calling for lower credit card interest rates, which indirectly sent the stock market into a dive, Sununu said that the president had ad-libbed the line. In a letter to Bush, he said he feared he was becoming "a drag on your success" and quit as chief of staff. Bush accepted the resignation, praising him for intercepting "many of the 'arrows' aimed my way." Sununu did not leave the administration, however. Bush assigned him "counselor to the president with Cabinet rank." And Sununu was a member of the entourage that accompanied Bush to Kuwait in a celebratory visit in 1993.

Atwater was manager of Bush's 1988 campaign and, upon his appointment by Bush to head the Republican National Committee, was the first career political consultant to hold a major party chairmanship. Atwater was a close adviser to Bush and used tactics against 1988 Democratic nominee Michael S. Dukakis that, to some, set a new low in modern presidential politics. Television commercials featuring furloughed murderer Willie Horton, a polluted Boston harbor and the American flag sought to portray Dukakis as soft on crime, weak on environmental protection and unpatriotic. To critics Atwater was as a below-the-belt street fighter; to admirers he was the GOP's most insightful campaign strategist. Before dying of a brain tumor in March 1991, Atwater expressed regret for his attacks on Dukakis and apologized for some of his aggressive statements. Despite Atwater's legacy, negative campaigning was the hallmark of Bush's re-election effort against Clinton. Under Baker's stewardship, the rhetoric was toned down a bit after the gay-, feminist- and liberal-bashing at the Republican convention produced a backlash.

While the likes of Sununu or Atwater may have ruffled some feathers, Bush was a political pragmatist. Running a negative campaign, for example, was a winning formula for him in 1988. A case can be made that, when Bush became president, the times would not allow a Cabinet filled exclusively with white, Anglo-Saxon males. Although Bush's inner circle had been and remained the domain of those similar to him in cultural background, the Bush Cabinet, at least on the surface, was diverse in its makeup. Louis W. Sullivan, a physician who also was black, was named secretary of health and human services. Bush retained Lauro F. Cavazos, the first Hispanic Cabinet member, from the Reagan administration as education secretary. Another Hispanic, former House member Manuel Lujan, R-N.M., became secretary of the interior. Three women served in the Cabinet during Bush's tenure: Dole, Martin and Commerce Secretary Barbara Hackman Franklin. A fourth, Carla A. Hills, was U.S. trade representative, a post with Cabinet-level status.

Unifying the various individuals who joined the Bush team was conservative-leaning politics. Sullivan, for exam-

Summing Up the "Halfway Man"

As George Bush prepared to leave the presidency, both the *Washington Post* and the *New York Times* took stock of his stewardship. Both found much to commend while agreeing that he had failed in some important respects, particularly in leadership and dealing with the economy.

In an editorial entitled "Summing Up Mr. Bush," the *Washington Post* on Jan. 20, 1993, said, "His presidency may ultimately be judged in terms of pitfalls avoided. Such things are not just negative accomplishments. It is often harder to steer through narrow straits than to make great progress in an open sea." For example, concerning the collapse of the Soviet Union and the transition to the post-Cold War era, the *Post* said that Bush seemed "to have navigated this most difficult of passages without a major mishap and to have left the right predicate for future policy."

In domestic affairs, during his first two years, Bush asserted himself against the Republican Party's conservatives on certain issues "and prospered at it." He was responsible for a major increase in federal aid to the poor, a comprehensive child care program, an extension of civil rights for the disabled, a stronger Clean Air Act "and an election-year budget agreement (including a tax increase), which was the most responsible fiscal action the government had taken in 10 years." His last two years in office, however, proved less ambitious.

According to the *Post*, "Mr. Bush, who never found all that much wrong with the state of the union anyway, produced a cautious and limited presidency." Defenders said that under the confining circumstances — huge deficits, lagging economy — he had little choice and the cautious policies were wise. The circumstances would have to be considered when assessing Bush's tenure. "These are the questions around which the future judgments of his presidency will revolve," the *Post* said.

The Jan. 19 *New York Times* editorial, "The Halfway Man," noted that Bush would almost certainly be the last of the World War II presidents and the last to reach voting age at the start of the Cold War.

The *Times* concluded that the end of the Cold War, which took place on Bush's watch, worked to both his advantage and disadvantage. It gave him "probably the strongest hand in foreign affairs ever awarded a new President, and for the most part he played it prudently although not always imaginatively." However, dissipation of the superpower rivalry took away the Republicans' advantage of casting themselves as the party best able to tame the Soviet bear. Without that edge, "Mr. Bush, with no domestic policy to speak of, came up empty when an America in spiritual disarray asked him to deal with drift."

ple, purportedly shared Bush's stated anti-abortion views. The standout conservative Cabinet member, however, was the secretary of housing and urban development, former N.Y. representative Jack F. Kemp. A darling of the right wing of the Republican Party, Kemp had gained a reputation as a stalwart supporter of Reaganomics. Kemp briefly had tried to contest Bush for the 1988 GOP presidential nomination.

Supreme Court

Bush's interest in furthering the conservative cause extended to his Supreme Court appointments. Two dyed-in-the-wool liberals, William J. Brennan Jr. and Thurgood Marshall, stepped down from the high bench during Bush's tenure, and he took advantage of the opportunity to appoint conservative justices and shift the Court majority more to the right. Abortion foes hoped that eventually the balance would be tipped in favor of overturning *Roe v. Wade*, the 1973 decision that legalized abortion.

Bush's first appointment, of David H. Souter to replace Brennan, caused little commotion. Souter, a New Hampshire judge, had been placed on the federal bench by Bush at the urging of Sununu, then serving as White House chief of staff. At Senate Judiciary Committee hearings on his nomination in 1990, Souter avoided specifics about his judicial philosophy and was easily confirmed.

The story was far different in 1991 with the nomination of black federal judge Clarence Thomas to succeed Marshall, the first black ever to sit on the Supreme Court. Liberals were outraged that Bush or any president would dare to fill Marshall's seat with a fellow black who shared so little in common with Marshall except color. Marshall had been a lifelong crusader for civil rights and racial desegregation. He had argued the government's case in *Brown v. Board of Education,* the 1954 and 1955 cases that outlawed segregation in schools. Thomas held a completely different view of the government's role in erasing racial discrimination. Even though he had experienced the difficulties of growing up poor and black in the South, Thomas as head of the Equal Employment Opportunity Commission (EEOC) had placed more emphasis on individual effort than on government assistance to overcome the ills of prejudice.

But sex, not race, inflamed the Thomas hearings and nearly scuttled the nomination. A black woman law professor, Anita F. Hill, testified that Thomas had harassed her with gross sexual speech when she was his subordinate at the Department of Education and then at the EEOC. Thomas flatly denied the charges, and the hearings boiled down to her word against his. The all-white-male committee's handling of the situation further split the nation and the Senate, which in the end confirmed Thomas by the closest margin in nearly a century. As he had with Tower,

Bush stood by his embattled appointee and refused to withdraw the nomination.

In filling vacancies on lower federal courts, Bush continued Reagan's efforts to build a federal judiciary system compatible with their conservative beliefs. *(Bush judicial appointments, box, p. 776)*

The Economy

Political scientists Robert J. Thompson and Carmine Scavo expounded the widely shared view that Bush "had the most limited domestic agenda of any president since [Herbert] Hoover." During the 1992 campaign, Bush was severely criticized for his seeming lack of action and lack of ideas as president. But the effects of the economic policies of his predecessor would have hamstrung any far-reaching initiatives he may have suggested.

Bush had inherited the dried-up fruits of Reaganomics, which in 1980 he had labeled "voodoo economics." The notion behind this economic theory was that deep cuts in taxes would fuel investment and generate enough income to offset the rising costs of government. It did not work out. Although the nation recovered from the recession of Reagan's first months in the White House, the combination of tax cuts and increased defense spending led to a whopping increase in the deficit. When Reagan took office in 1981, the deficit was $79 billion. When he left office in 1989, he bequeathed Bush a deficit of $155 billion.

However, instead of disavowing Reagan's policies, Bush tried to out-Reagan Reagan. He pledged, "Read my lips. No new taxes." His rhetoric was viewed as a means to appease conservatives, whose support he needed. When Bush left office, the projected deficit for fiscal 1994 had ballooned to $292.4 billion and the accumulated national debt soared to $4 trillion.

While the effects of Reaganomics would be felt for some time beyond the Bush years, a budget summit agreement worked out in 1990 between the Bush administration and Congress helped loosen the constraints somewhat. The agreement — which called for spending increases to be offset by new revenues or cuts elsewhere — helped to bring the congressional budget process back under a semblance of control. The budget agreement cost Bush considerable political capital because as part of the deal he was required to backslide on his "no new taxes" pledge, a move the far right and some Reagan Democrats found unpardonable. Ironically, the rational and responsible, albeit modest, plan served mostly to help Bush's 1992 Democratic opponent, and later president, Bill Clinton.

Besides the woeful state of the federal budget, when Bush assumed office, he confronted the hemorrhaging of funds from failed savings and loan institutions (S&Ls) at the rate of $20 million a day. He proposed, and Congress approved, a bailout of the thrift industry that far exceeded its original expected cost of $100 billion. Most of the deposits at insolvent S&Ls had been insured by the federal government. Congressional action was needed to stop the drain and save the insurance fund. The bailout legislation also marked the most sweeping overhaul of the thrift industry in more than 55 years. Bush's son Neil was an officer of one of the affected S&Ls, the Silverado Banking, Savings and Loan Association of Denver, which failed at a cost of $1 billion to the taxpayers.

Bush's pet issue in economic affairs was the capital gains tax. He, like Reagan, pushed repeatedly for cutting it as a way to stimulate investment in the means of production and thus create more jobs and higher tax revenues. In 1989, he came close to getting a capital gains tax cut, but Democrats succeeded in defeating it as another Republican "trickle-down" gimmick that would benefit mostly the rich.

To help offset a $106 billion annual trade imbalance with the rest of the world, Bush entered into the North American Free Trade Agreement (NAFTA) with Canada and Mexico. The agreement would permit the free movement of goods and currency in a market of 360 million people with an economic output of $6 trillion a year. The battle to overcome strong objections from labor unions and their allies in Congress fell to Bush's successor, who embraced NAFTA and set out to win congressional approval.

Bush's problems with the economy accounted in large part for the sharp drop in his public approval rating, from 91 percent just after the Persian Gulf War (the highest for any president) to 37 percent four months before the 1992 election. Unemployment then was almost 8 percent, up from 5.5 percent in 1988. Political analysts said Bush's biggest failing was in not perceiving or appreciating the economic hardship being suffered by many Americans. During the campaign, many loyal Republicans — traditional supporters and Reagan Democrats — voiced complaints that Bush seemed to be isolated and out of touch. Bush acknowledged that the polls showed most Americans thought the economy was getting worse. Nevertheless, he continued to tell audiences that a "lot of people are hurting, but the overall national economy is growing."

It was growing, but more slowly than expected. The gross domestic product expanded 2.7 percent in the first quarter of 1992, the highest since the final quarter of 1988, when Bush was elected. It had shown negative growth in late 1990 and early 1991.

Foreign Policy

World events in 1989-92 were tailor-made for a president whose strong suit was foreign affairs. As he said of himself in his 1988 acceptance speech at the GOP convention, George Bush was that man.

Momentous events of this period included the fall of the Berlin Wall and reunification of Germany, the unsuccessful coup against Soviet President Gorbachev, the dissolution of the Soviet Union, Iraq's invasion of Kuwait, the capture and conviction of Panamanian dictator Manuel Antonio Noriega, a peace treaty in El Salvador and the cessation of hostilities in Nicaragua — whose civil war figured in the Iran-contra scandal of the Reagan presidency and left unanswered questions about Bush's own involvement in the arms-for-hostages deal.

With each historic change came adjustments in U.S. policy. Bush, with Secretary of State Baker and national security adviser Brent Scowcroft, was credited in most instances with fashioning correct, but cautious, responses.

As president, Bush indulged his passion for foreign travel, logging more miles per month in office than any other president. His peripateticness may have stemmed from his vice presidency, when he attended so many foreign leaders' funerals he quipped, "You die, I fly." Another theory was that he followed the path of least resistance. In dealings with other countries he could negotiate one-on-one with his peers and get things accomplished. At home, he had to deal with a Congress not of his party. He had little luck there.

A Punching Bag Who Punched Back

Plucked from relative obscurity by George Bush, Dan Quayle at 41 became the youngest vice president since Richard Nixon assumed that office in 1953 at the age of 39.

Assured of his party's presidential nomination, Bush surprised the 1988 Republican National Convention in New Orleans by announcing that the senator from Indiana was his choice. The delegates dutifully obliged, despite questions about Quayle's background and suitability for the office. Above all else was the question of whether family connections had enabled him to avoid the Vietnam War draft in 1969. He had served instead in an Indiana National Guard unit at a time when most Guard enlistments were closed because so many men were trying to join to evade Vietnam combat.

Quayle's own efforts to head off the fitness issue by comparing himself with former president John F. Kennedy produced one of the highlights of the 1988 campaign. Debating his Democratic opponent, Sen. Lloyd Bentsen of Texas, Quayle said, "I have as much experience in the Congress as Jack Kennedy did when he sought the presidency." Bentsen responded in measured terms, "Senator, I served with Jack Kennedy. I knew Jack Kennedy. Jack Kennedy was a friend of mine. Senator, you're no Jack Kennedy."

Throughout his four-year term, Quayle was ridiculed by comedians who joked about his youth, good looks, perceived shallowness and occasional gaffes in speaking. The derision reached its peak in 1992 when he wrongly coached a New Jersey spelling bee contestant to add an "e" to "potato," and after a California speech in which he attacked a fictional TV sitcom character, Murphy Brown, for having a baby out of wedlock. He said Hollywood and "cultural elites" were undermining traditional family values.

Newspaper Family

As the grandson of the Eugene Pulliam, conservative publisher of the *Indianapolis News,* Quayle was born with ties to Indiana's political and media establishment. Quayle had a stake in the family trust that made him a millionaire many times over. The trust operated major newspapers in Phoenix, Ariz., along with several in Indiana. His family separately owned and operated the small daily *Herald-Press* in his hometown of Huntington. Quayle was the paper's associate publisher and a political unknown when he entered and unexpectedly won a congressional seat in 1976. He served two terms in the House and was twice elected to the Senate.

Political analysts saw in Bush's choice of Quayle an attempt to appeal to the political right and to use Quayle's obscurity as a foil to enhance his own stature. Teamed with Quayle, Bush created an impression very different from the one when he was at Reagan's side. After years as an overshadowed second in command, Bush came across as seasoned and authoritative, at least by comparison with Quayle.

No doubts existed about Quayle's conservative credentials. Quayle was one of the Reagan administration's strongest supporters. According to a Congressional Quarterly vote study, he supported Reagan's position 85 percent of the time. Quayle echoed the Reagan administration's "peace through strength" line, supporting the strategic defense initiative (SDI), production of the MX missile and spending hikes for the Pentagon. On domestic issues, he voted for school prayer and Reagan's judicial nominees, including the defeated nomination of Robert H. Bork for Supreme Court justice.

A Bum Rap?

As a senator, Quayle chalked up some legislative achievements, notably the Job Training Partnership Act of 1982, which he put together with his political opposite, Sen. Edward M. Kennedy, D-Mass. The act emphasized private businesses in job training and replaced the maligned Comprehensive Employment and Training Act (CETA) public employment programs. Quayle also was respected for his expertise in defense issues.

As vice president, Quayle assembled a bright and savvy team headed by conservative scholar William Kristol as chief of staff. "It is noteworthy that somebody [such as Quayle] who is thought not to be an intellectual is not at all afraid to surround himself with intellectuals," said political scientist Richard F. Fenno Jr.

Quayle drew praise from conservatives for his performance as head of the Council on Competitiveness, which targeted bureaucratic red tape and regulations that could slow economic growth. But critics argued this was often accomplished at the expense of environmental and consumer protection.

In one of his first acts as president, Bill Clinton abolished Quayle's competitiveness council and lifted Bush's moratorium on new federal regulations.

Qu yle's chairmanship of the National Space Council also sparked controversy. The council, charged with developing and monitoring U.S. space policy, clashed repeatedly with the head of the National Aeronautics and Space Administration (NASA), Richard A. Truly. In 1992, Truly resigned and was replaced by Daniel S. Goldin, an engineer who soon overcame speculation that he would be Quayle's pawn as the head of NASA.

As president of the Senate, Quayle was the first vice president since Lyndon B. Johnson who never got a chance to vote to break a tie.

In his final year in office, Bush traveled to the former Soviet Union and negotiated with Russian President Yeltsin what may prove to be Bush's (and perhaps Yeltsin's) most lasting legacy — the START II treaty for reduction of nuclear weapons. The Bush administration also wrapped up a chemical weapons treaty that had been years in the making.

Foreign affairs clearly engaged Bush more than domestic affairs. Midway through his presidency, Iraq's invasion of Kuwait gave Bush his biggest triumph. Marshaling congressional and allied support for driving Saddam Hussein out of Kuwait, Bush shed the "wimp" label that nagged him as Reagan's selflessly loyal vice president.

The overwhelming rout of the Iraqis was accomplished with comparatively few American casualties, and Bush's prestige as a world leader rose dramatically. Though Saddam remained in power, the stated mission of getting Iraqi forces out of Kuwait had been accomplished. The U.N. mandate did not call for Saddam's removal.

In December 1992, with bipartisan support in Congress, Bush sent 28,000 American troops to Somalia where famine and disease fostered by drought and political anarchy had killed some 300,000 people. It was the first large-scale use of U.S. forces for humanitarian, not military, purposes. The Americans were the backbone of a multinational United Nations force dispatched to the African nation to guarantee delivery of food shipments that rival warlords and clans had been diverting from the starving Somalis. The mission later turned sour as Somalis killed and captured American soldiers. As a result, a major military and foreign policy dilemma was created for the Clinton administration: whether to pull out and let the starvation and killing return, or stay and try to build a democratic nation that could deal with its own problems.

Still a mystery months after Bush left office was the extent of his knowledge about Iran-contra while he was vice president. As late as October 1993, legal appeals were blocking release of independent counsel Lawrence E. Walsh's final report of his investigation, which was largely foiled on Christmas Eve 1992 by Bush's pardon of former defense secretary Caspar W. Weinberger and others awaiting trial in the case. Weinberger's indictment contained a previously unreleased note that indicated Vice President Bush had not been "out of the loop," as he insisted, on the decisions to sell arms to Iran and use the proceeds to skirt Congress' ban on aid to the rightist guerrillas (contras) in Nicaragua.

In other foreign policy matters, Bush also drew criticism for proposing special trade treatment for China while its human rights abuses continued, and for not doing more to halt the bloodshed in Bosnia and other areas of the former Yugoslavia.

Nevertheless, James Baker's successor as secretary of state, Lawrence S. Eagleburger, predicted in a farewell speech that Bush would be remembered "as one of our nation's great diplomatists." History would judge Bush, he said, "by the results of his efforts — by his mastery of timing and substance, particularly against the many alternative scenarios that might have come to pass."

Domestic Policy

Bush's scorecard on domestic issues was not entirely blank. Early in his term, he achieved some notable legislative victories, mostly by jumping on bills already moving through Congress and working for their passage.

One piece of significant legislation in which Bush seemed to take genuine interest and pride was the Americans with Disabilities Act (ADA) of 1990, which outlawed discrimination against the handicapped and required public and some private facilities to be made accessible. As a candidate, Bush had supported ADA, saying, "I am going to do whatever it takes to make sure the disabled are included in the mainstream. For too long they've been left out. But they're not going to be left out anymore." Persons close to the president said his empathy with the disabled was longstanding — possibly because his daughter Robin died of leukemia and his son Neil had the reading disorder dyslexia.

But in the fight against AIDS (acquired immune deficiency syndrome), Bush was accused of "dropping the ball." The criticism came from former basketball star Earvin "Magic" Johnson as he resigned in 1992 from the National Commission on AIDS. Bush replaced Johnson with another victim of the AIDS virus, Mary Fisher, who had spoken about her plight at the 1992 GOP convention.

On another health issue, Bush continued to oppose abortion on demand but to support a woman's right to choose in cases such as rape or incest. Yet he claimed to support — without having read — the no-exceptions ban on abortion adopted in Houston at the Republican convention.

As the self-proclaimed "environmental president," Bush could take credit for extending and improving the Clean Air Act of 1970. Reagan had fought renewal, but Bush worked with Congress to enact a new and tougher bill in 1990. Environmentalists later complained, however, that the administration watered down some provisions when translating them into regulations.

Bush only reluctantly attended the Earth Summit of 178 nations at Rio de Janeiro in June 1992, and then mainly to defend his decision not to sign the "biodiversity treaty" to protect rain forests and other Third World resources. Critics maintained that U.S. manufacturers of pharmaceuticals wanted to ensure continued access to the resources.

The president fared less well in his determination to also be "the education president." He convened a governors' conference headed by Lamar Alexander of Tennessee and incorporated some of the suggestions in his proposed Education Excellence Act of 1989. The bill offering awards, grants and other incentives for teachers and students was shot down largely by Republicans opposed to federal intervention in education. Bush later made Alexander his second secretary of education.

Bush and Congress

Bush's relations with the Democratic Congress reached their lowest point in the highly partisan election year of 1992. As measured by Congressional Quarterly's limited but revealing annual study of voting in Congress, Bush's support level fell to 43 percent, the lowest for any president since CQ began keeping the score 39 years earlier.

Throughout the year, Bush bashed Congress — and Congress bashed back — each blaming the other for "gridlock" (a term formerly applied to traffic engineering) that stalled legislative movement. None of the three legislative requests that Bush made in his State of the Union

James Danforth Quayle III

Republican of Huntington, Indiana
44th Vice President of the United States

Born: Indianapolis, Ind., Feb. 4, 1947.

Education: Huntington High School, 1965; DePauw University, B.A., 1969; Indiana School of Law, J.D., 1974.

Occupation: Lawyer, newspaper executive.

Military Service: Indiana National Guard, 1969-75.

Religion: Presbyterian.

Family: Married 1972 to the former Marilyn Tucker. Three children: Tucker Danforth, Benjamin Eugene and Mary Corinne.

Political Career: U.S. House of Representatives, R-Ind., 1977-81; U.S. Senate, 1981-89; U.S. vice president, 1989-93.

Professional Career: Associate publisher of Huntington *Herald-Press*, 1974-76.

address — an economic stimulus package, public-private school choice and a health care plan — became law.

Bush highly successfully used his veto power to kill a wide range of social, regulatory, tax and spending bills during his term. Among the victims of his veto pen were a minimum wage increase in 1988 (although he later signed the first such increase in 10 years), family and medical leave bills, family planning, a civil rights bill, extension of unemployment benefits, campaign finance reform and "motor voter" registration.

While Congress was able to deny Bush his legislative priorities, his nearly perfect record of successful vetoes — only one overridden in four years — pointed up the reality of the Democrats' majority in both the House and Senate. The numerical edge did not necessarily guarantee political or philosophical solidarity when it came to rounding up the two-thirds majority needed to override a veto.

Electoral Defeat

Less than a month before the 1992 election, columnist William Safire wrote in the *New York Times Magazine*: "I was a Bush-watcher long before I thought it would be useful and may be able to pinpoint the time he was seized by his inordinate fear of running without solid support from the far right."

It was in 1970, Safire wrote, when Bush rejected help from the Nixon White House in his campaign for the Senate against another House member, Democrat Lloyd M. Bentsen Jr. Nixon aide Bryce Harlow told the White House speech writers, including Safire and 1992 Bush opponent Patrick J. Buchanan, "Scrub Texas from the schedule. Our senatorial candidate, George Bush, thinks he can do better without the red meat you fellows have been throwing in the cage."

Bush lost to Bentsen, and in Safire's view it was a lesson the Republican candidate never forgot. Whether more help from the right would have meant victory in 1970 is a moot question; the important point is that Bush apparently believed that he had made a serious mistake, and he was not about to repeat it in 1992 when the stakes were higher.

He practically turned over his re-election effort to the hard right, though he seemed uncomfortable with much of the rhetoric, including some of the words coming out of his own mouth. His overcompensation for 1970 may have contributed to the debacle of 1992. Certainly the sneering invective coming from the GOP national convention turned off many moderates and yearners for a "kinder, gentler" presidential campaign.

Having resigned as secretary of state to rescue Bush's foundering campaign after it was well under way, Baker ordered no sharp turns. He went along with Bush's strategy of wooing the far right. The Houston convention went off as planned, heavy on liberal bashing and assumptions that God was on the conservatives' side. The tamer "family values" speeches got lost in the polemics. Bush's own appearance before the convention was notable mostly for his apology for having reneged on his "no new taxes" pledge in the 1990 budget agreement.

The 1992 presidential campaign became a referendum on change. Americans were hurting, and they wanted something different, something better. Both Bush and Clinton presented themselves as the agents to bring it about. Commenting on Bush's campaign tactics, Safire referred to his "quadrennial metamorphosis from compromising Jekyll to partisan Hyde. He is not the candidate of change; he is the candidate who changes." In the end, Bush could not persuade the American people that he genuinely understood their suffering and that he would improve their circumstances if they re-elected him. The Democrats, meanwhile, never forgot that, in the words of Clinton strategist James Carville, "It's the economy, stupid." That was the voters' foremost concern as the race came down to the wire.

In 1988, Bush carried 40 states and took 53.4 percent of the popular vote in defeating Massachusetts Gov. Dukakis. Bush was the first sitting vice president since Martin Van Buren to win the presidency.

In 1992, Bush, also like Van Buren, was unseated after a single term. Bill Clinton won with 43.0 percent of the vote to 37.4 percent for Bush and 18.9 percent for independent Ross Perot. The difference between Bush's 1988 and 1992 vote tallies was the worst falloff in history for any president seeking re-election, with the exceptions of Hoover in 1932 and William Howard Taft in 1912 (who, like Bush, lost in a three-way contest).

Twelve years of Republican hegemony had ended. History would decide whether the presidency of George Bush would be a footnote in the presidency of the man who dominated that era, Ronald Reagan.

Appendix

Glossary of Terms	*1001*
The Legislative Process	*1013*
Key Votes, 1989-92	*1019*
Membership Lists	*1107*
Members of Congress	*1115*
Congressional Committees	*1125*
Post-Election Sessions	*1137*
Senate Cloture Votes	*1139*
Reapportionment	*1143*
Bush Appointments	*1169*
Presidential Vetoes	*1181*
Presidential Texts	*1183*
Political Charts	*1223*

Glossary of Congressional Terms

Act—The term for legislation once it has passed both houses of Congress and has been signed by the president or passed over his veto, thus becoming law. Also used in parliamentary terminology for a bill that has been passed by one house and engrossed. *(See Engrossed Bill, Pocket Veto.)*

Adjournment Sine Die—Adjournment without definitely fixing a day for reconvening; literally "adjournment without a day." Usually used to connote the final adjournment of a session of Congress. A session can continue until noon, Jan. 3, of the following year, when, under the 20th Amendment to the Constitution, it automatically terminates. Both houses must agree to a concurrent resolution for either house to adjourn for more than three days.

Adjournment to a Day Certain—Adjournment under a motion or resolution that fixes the next time of meeting. Under the Constitution, neither house can adjourn for more than three days without the concurrence of the other. A session of Congress is not ended by adjournment to a day certain.

Amendment—A proposal of a member of Congress to alter the language, provisions or stipulations in a bill or in another amendment. An amendment usually is printed, debated and voted upon in the same manner as a bill.

Amendment in the Nature of a Substitute—Usually an amendment that seeks to replace the entire text of a bill. Passage of this type of amendment strikes out everything after the enacting clause and inserts a new version of the bill. An amendment in the nature of a substitute also can refer to an amendment that replaces a large portion of the text of a bill.

Appeal—A member's challenge of a ruling or decision made by the presiding officer of the chamber. In the Senate, the senator appeals to members of the chamber to override the decision. If carried by a majority vote, the appeal nullifies the chair's ruling. In the House, the decision of the Speaker traditionally has been final; seldom are there appeals to the members to reverse the Speaker's stand. To appeal a ruling is considered an attack on the Speaker.

Appropriations Bill—A bill that gives legal authority to spend or obligate money from the Treasury. The Constitution disallows money to be drawn from the Treasury "but in Consequence of Appropriations made by Law."

By congressional custom, an appropriations bill originates in the House, and it is not supposed to be considered by the full House or Senate until a related measure authorizing the funding is enacted. An appropriations bill grants the actual money approved by authorization bills, but not necessarily the full amount permissible under the authorization. For decades, appropriations often have not been final until well after the fiscal year begins, requiring a succession of stopgap bills to continue the government's functions. In addition, much federal spending — about half of all budget authority, notably that for Social Security and interest on the federal debt — does not require annual appropriations; those programs exist under permanent appropriations. *(See also Authorization, Budget Process, Backdoor Spending Authority, Entitlement Program.)*

In addition to general appropriations bills, there are two specialized types. *(See Continuing Resolution, Supplemental Appropriations Bill.)*

Authorization—Basic, substantive legislation that establishes or continues the legal operation of a federal program or agency, either indefinitely or for a specific period of time, or which sanctions a particular type of obligation or expenditure. An authorization normally is a prerequisite for an appropriation or other kind of budget authority. Under the rules of both houses, the appropriation for a program or agency may not be considered until its authorization has been considered. An authorization also may limit the amount of budget authority to be provided or may authorize the appropriation of "such sums as may be necessary." *(See also Backdoor Spending Authority.)*

Backdoor Spending Authority—Budget authority provided in legislation outside the normal appropriations process. The most common forms of backdoor spending are borrowing authority, contract authority, entitlements and loan guarantees that commit the government to payments of principal and interest on loans — such as Guaranteed Student Loans — made by banks or other private lenders. Loan guarantees only result in actual outlays when there is a default by the borrower.

In some cases, such as interest on the public debt, a permanent appropriation is provided that becomes available without further action by Congress.

Bills—Most legislative proposals before Congress are in the form of bills and are designated by HR in the House of Representatives or S in the Senate, according to the house in which they originate, and by a number assigned in the order in which they are introduced during the two-year period of a congressional term. "Public bills" deal with general questions and become public laws if approved by Congress and signed by the president. "Private bills" deal with individual matters such as claims against the government, immigration and naturalization cases or land titles, and become private laws if approved and signed. *(See also Concurrent Resolution, Joint Resolution, Resolution.)*

Bills Introduced—In both the House and Senate, any number of members may join in introducing a single bill or resolution. The first member listed is the sponsor of the bill, and all subsequent members listed are the bill's cosponsors.

Many bills are committee bills and are introduced under the name of the chairman of the committee or subcommittee. All appropriations bills fall into this category. A committee frequently holds hearings on a number of related bills and may agree to one of them or to an entirely new bill. *(See also Report, Clean Bill, By Request.)*

Bills Referred—When introduced, a bill is referred to the committee or committees that have jurisdiction over the subject with which the bill is concerned. Under the standing rules of the House and Senate, bills are referred by the Speaker in the House and by the presiding officer in the Senate. In practice, the House and Senate parliamentarians act for these officials and refer the vast majority of bills.

Borrowing Authority—Statutory authority that permits a federal agency to incur obligations and make payments for specified purposes with borrowed money.

Budget—The document sent to Congress by the president early each year estimating government revenue and expenditures for the ensuing fiscal year.

Budget Act—The common name for the Congressional Budget and Impoundment Control Act of 1974, which established the current budget process and created the Congressional Budget Office. The act also put limits on presidential authority to spend appropriated money. *(See Impoundments, Budget Process.)*

Budget Authority—Authority to enter into obligations that will result in immediate or future outlays involving federal funds. The basic forms of budget authority are appropriations, contract authority and borrowing authority. Budget authority may be classified by (1) the period of availability (one-year, multiple-year or without a time limitation), (2) the timing of congressional action (current or permanent) or (3) the manner of determining the amount available (definite or indefinite).

Budget Process—Congress in 1990 overhauled its budget procedures for the third time since enactment of the 1974 Congressional Budget and Impoundment Control Act. If the deficit increased because of recession, war or specifically exempted programs, across-the-board spending cuts ("sequestration") threatened by the Gramm-Rudman-Hollings anti-deficit law, enacted in 1985 and amended in 1987, no longer would be triggered. The new rules, however, required that spending programs be subject to a sequester if Congress exceeded pre-agreed caps on discretionary spending (appropriations bills) or violated new "pay-as-you-go" rules for mandatory spending (entitlement programs such as Medicare) or tax cuts. *(See Sequestration.)*

The president had until the first Monday in February to submit his proposed budget. Congressional budget resolutions were due by April 15; reconciliation bills, by June 15. *(See Budget Resolution, Reconciliation.)*

Budget Resolution—A concurrent resolution passed by both houses of Congress, but not requiring the president's signature, setting forth or revising the congressional budget for each of three fiscal years. The budget resolution sets forth various budget totals and functional allocations and may include reconciliation instructions. *(See Functions, Reconciliation.)*

By Request—A phrase used when a senator or representative introduces a bill at the request of an executive agency or private organization but does not necessarily endorse the legislation.

Calendar—An agenda or list of business awaiting possible action by each chamber. The House uses five legislative calendars. *(See Consent, Discharge, House, Private and Union Calendar.)*

In the Senate, all legislative matters reported from committee go on one calendar. They are listed there in the order in which committees report them or the Senate places them on the calendar, but they may be called up out of order by the majority leader, either by obtaining unanimous consent of the Senate or by a motion to call up a bill. The Senate also uses one non-legislative calendar; this is used for treaties and nominations. *(See Executive Calendar.)*

Calendar Wednesday—In the House, committees, on Wednesdays, may be called in the order in which they appear in Rule X of the House, for the purpose of bringing up any of their bills from either the House or the Union Calendar, except bills that are privileged. General debate is limited to two hours. Bills called up from the Union Calendar are considered in Committee of the Whole. Calendar Wednesday is not observed during the last two weeks of a session and may be dispensed with at other times by a two-thirds vote. This procedure is rarely used and routinely is dispensed with by unanimous consent.

Call of the Calendar—Senate bills that are not brought up for debate by a motion, unanimous consent or a unanimous consent agreement are brought before the Senate for action when the calendar listing them is "called." Bills must be called in the order listed. Measures considered by this method usually are non-controversial, and debate on the bill and any proposed amendments is limited to a total of five minutes for each senator.

Chamber—The meeting place for the membership of either the House or the Senate; also the membership of the House or Senate meeting as such.

Clean Bill—Frequently after a committee has finished a major revision of a bill, one of the committee members, usually the chairman, will assemble the changes and what is left of the original bill into a new measure and introduce it as a "clean bill." The revised measure, which is given a new number, then is referred back to the committee, which reports it to the floor for consideration. This often is a timesaver, as committee-recommended changes in a clean bill do not have to be considered and voted on by the chamber. Reporting a clean bill also protects committee amendments that could be subject to points of order concerning germaneness.

Clerk of the House—Chief administrative officer of the House of Representatives, with duties corresponding to those of the secretary of the Senate. *(See also Secretary of the Senate.)*

Cloture—The process by which a filibuster can be ended in the Senate other than by unanimous consent. A motion for cloture can apply to any measure before the Senate, including a proposal to change the chamber's rules. A cloture motion requires the signatures of 16 senators to be introduced. To end a filibuster, the cloture motion must obtain the votes of three-fifths of the entire Senate membership (60 if there are no vacancies), except when the filibuster is against a proposal to amend the standing rules of the Senate and a two-thirds vote of senators present and voting is required. The cloture request is put to a roll-call vote one hour after the Senate meets on the second day following introduction of the motion. If approved, cloture limits each senator to one hour of debate. The bill or amendment in question comes to a final vote after 30 hours of consideration (including debate time and the time it takes to conduct roll calls, quorum calls and other procedural motions). *(See Filibuster.)*

Committee—A division of the House or Senate that prepares legislation for action by the parent chamber or makes investigations as directed by the parent chamber. There are several types of committees. Most standing committees are divided into subcommittees, which study legislation, hold hearings and report bills, with or without amendments, to the full committee. Only the full committee can report legislation for action by the House or Senate. *(See Standing and Select or Special Committees.)*

Committee of the Whole—The working title of what is formally "The Committee of the Whole House [of Representatives] on the State of the Union." The membership is comprised of all House members sitting as a committee. Any 100 members who are present on the floor of the chamber to consider legislation comprise a quorum of the committee. Any legislation taken up by the Committee of the Whole, however, must first have passed through the regular legislative or Appropriations committee and have been placed on the calendar.

Technically, the Committee of the Whole considers only bills directly or indirectly appropriating money, authorizing appropriations or involving taxes or charges on the public. Because the Committee of the Whole need number only 100 representatives, a quorum is more readily attained, and legislative business is expedited. Before 1971, members' positions were not individually recorded on votes taken in Committee of the Whole. *(See Teller Vote.)*

When the full House resolves itself into the Committee of the Whole, it supplants the Speaker with a "chairman." A measure is debated and amendments may be proposed, with votes on amendments as needed. The committee, however, cannot pass a bill. When the committee completes its work on the measure, it dissolves itself by "rising." The Speaker returns, and the chairman of the Committee of the Whole reports to the House that the committee's work has been completed. At this time members may demand a roll-call vote on any amendment adopted in the Committee of the Whole. The final vote is on passage of the legislation. *(See Five-Minute Rule.)*

Committee Veto—A requirement added to a few statutes directing that certain policy directives by an executive department or agency be reviewed by certain congressional committees before they are implemented. Under common practice, the government department or agency and the committees involved are expected to reach a consensus before the directives are carried out. *(See also Legislative Veto.)*

Concurrent Resolution—A concurrent resolution, designated H Con Res or S Con Res, must be adopted by both houses, but it is not sent to the president for approval and therefore does not have the force of law. A concurrent resolution, for example, is used to fix the time for adjournment of a Congress. It also is used as the vehicle for expressing the sense of Congress on various foreign policy and domestic issues, and it serves as the vehicle for coordinated decisions on the federal budget under the 1974 Congressional Budget and Impoundment Control Act. *(See also Bills, Joint Resolution, Resolution.)*

Conference—A meeting between the representatives of the House and the Senate to reconcile differences between the two houses on provisions of a bill passed by both chambers. Members of the conference committee are appointed by the Speaker and the presiding officer of the Senate and are called "managers" for their respective chambers. A majority of the managers for each house must reach agreement on the provisions of the bill (often a compromise between the versions of the two chambers) before it can be considered by either chamber in the form of a "conference report." When the conference report goes to the floor, it cannot be amended, and, if it is not approved by both chambers, the bill may go back to conference under certain situations, or a new conference must be convened. Many rules and informal practices govern the conduct of conference committees.

Bills that are passed by both houses with only minor differences need not be sent to conference. Either chamber may "concur" in the other's amendments, completing action on the legislation. Sometimes leaders of the committees of jurisdiction work out an informal compromise instead of having a formal conference. *(See Custody of the Papers.)*

Confirmations—*(See Nominations.)*

Congressional Record—The daily, printed account of proceedings in both the House and Senate chambers, showing substantially verbatim debate, statements and a record of floor action. Highlights of legislative and committee action are embodied in a Daily Digest section of the *Record*, and members are entitled to have their extraneous remarks printed in an appendix known as "Extension of Remarks." Members may edit and revise remarks made on the floor during debate, and quotations from debate reported by the press are not always found in the *Record*.

The *Congressional Record* provides a way to distinguish remarks spoken on the floor of the House and Senate from undelivered speeches. In the Senate, all speeches, articles and other matter that members insert in the *Record* without actually reading them on the floor are set off by large black dots, or bullets. However, a loophole allows a member to avoid the bulleting if he delivers any portion of the speech in person. In the House, undelivered speeches and other material are printed in a distinctive typeface. *(See also* Journal.*)*

Congressional Terms of Office—Normally begin on Jan. 3 of the year following a general election and are two years for representatives and six years for senators. Representatives elected in special elections are sworn in for the remainder of a term. A person may be appointed to fill a Senate vacancy and serves until a successor is elected; the successor serves until the end of the term applying to the vacant seat.

Consent Calendar—Members of the House may place on this calendar most bills on the Union or House Calendar that are considered to be non-controversial. Bills on the Consent Calendar normally are called on the first and third Mondays of each month. On the first occasion that a bill is called in this manner, consideration may be blocked by the objection of any member. The second time, if there are three objections, the bill is stricken from the Consent Calendar. If less than three members object, the bill is given immediate consideration.

A bill on the Consent Calendar may be postponed in another way. A member may ask that the measure be passed over "without prejudice." In that case, no objection is recorded against the bill, and its status on the Consent Calendar remains unchanged. A bill stricken from the Consent Calendar remains on the Union or House Calendar.

Continuing Resolution—A joint resolution, cleared by Congress and signed by the president (when the new fiscal year is about to begin or has begun), to provide new budget authority for federal agencies and programs to continue in operation until the regular appropriations acts are enacted. *(See Appropriations Bill.)*

The continuing resolution usually specifies a maximum rate at which an agency may incur obligations, based on the rate of the prior year, the president's budget request or an appropriations bill passed by either or both houses of Congress but not yet enacted. In recent years, most regular appropriations bills have not cleared and a full-year continuing resolution has taken their place. For fiscal 1987 and 1988, Congress intentionally rolled all 13 regular appropriations bills into one continuing resolution.

Continuing resolutions also are called "CRs" or continuing appropriations.

Contract Authority—Budget authority contained in an authorization bill that permits the federal government to enter into contracts or other obligations for future payments from funds not yet appropriated by Congress. The assumption is that funds will be available for payment in a subsequent appropriation act.

Controllable Budget Items—In federal budgeting this refers to programs for which the budget authority or outlays during a fiscal year can be controlled without changing existing, substantive law. The concept "relatively uncontrollable under current law" includes outlays for open-ended programs and fixed costs such as interest on the public debt, Social Security benefits, veterans' benefits and outlays to liquidate prior-year obligations. More and more spending for federal programs has become uncontrollable or relatively uncontrollable.

Correcting Recorded Votes—Rules prohibit members from changing their votes after the result has been announced. But, occasionally hours, days or months after a vote has been taken, a member may announce that he was "incorrectly recorded." In the Senate, a request to change one's vote almost always receives unanimous consent. In the House, members are prohibited from changing their votes if tallied by the electronic voting system. If the vote was taken by roll call, a change is permissible if consent is granted.

Cosponsor—*(See Bills Introduced.)*

Current Services Estimates—Estimated budget authority and outlays for federal programs and operations for the forthcoming fiscal year based on continuation of existing levels of service without policy changes. These estimates of budget authority and outlays, accompanied by the underlying economic and policy assumptions upon which they are based, are transmitted by the president to Congress when the budget is submitted.

Custody of the Papers—To reconcile differences between the House and Senate versions of a bill, a conference may be arranged. The chamber with "custody of the papers" — the engrossed bill, engrossed amendments, messages of transmittal — is the only body empowered to request the conference. By custom, the chamber that asks for a conference is the last to act on the conference report once agreement has been reached on the bill by the conferees.

Custody of the papers sometimes is manipulated to ensure that a particular chamber acts either first or last on the conference report.

Deferral—Executive branch action to defer, or delay, the spending of appropriated money. The 1974 Congressional Budget and Impoundment Control Act requires a special message from the president to Congress reporting a proposed deferral of spending. Deferrals may not extend beyond the end of the fiscal year in which the message is transmitted. A federal district court in 1986 struck down the president's authority to defer spending for policy reasons; the ruling was upheld by a federal appeals court in 1987. Congress can and has prohibited proposed deferrals by enacting a law doing so; most often cancellations of proposed deferrals are included in appropriations bills. *(See also Rescission.)*

Dilatory Motion—A motion made for the purpose of killing time and preventing action on a bill or amendment. House rules outlaw dilatory motions, but enforcement is largely within the discretion of the Speaker or chairman of the Committee of the Whole. The Senate does not have a rule banning dilatory motions, except under cloture.

Discharge a Committee—Occasionally, attempts are made to relieve a committee from jurisdiction over a measure before it. This is attempted more often in the House than in the Senate, and the procedure rarely is successful.

In the House, if a committee does not report a bill within 30 days after the measure is referred to it, any member may file a discharge motion. Once offered, the motion is treated as a petition needing the signatures of 218 members (a majority of the House). After the required signatures have been obtained, there is a delay of seven days. Thereafter, on the second and fourth Mondays of each month, except during the last six days of a session, any member who has signed the petition must be recognized, if he so desires, to move that the committee be discharged. Debate on the motion to discharge is limited to 20 minutes, and, if the motion is carried, consideration of the bill becomes a matter of high privilege.

If a resolution to consider a bill is held up in the Rules Committee for more than seven legislative days, any member may enter a motion to discharge the committee. The motion is handled like any other discharge petition in the House. Occasionally, to expedite non-controversial legislative business, a committee is discharged by unanimous consent of the House, and a petition is not required. *(Senate procedure, see Discharge Resolution.)*

Discharge Calendar—The House calendar to which motions to discharge committees are referred when they have the required number of signatures (218) and are awaiting floor action.

Discharge Petition—*(See Discharge a Committee.)*

Discharge Resolution—In the Senate, a special motion that any senator may introduce to relieve a committee from consideration of a bill before it. The resolution can be called up for Senate approval or disapproval in the same manner as any other Senate business. *(House procedure, see Discharge a Committee.)*

Division of a Question for Voting—A practice that is more common in the Senate but also used in the House, a member may demand a division of an amendment or a motion for purposes of voting. Where an amendment or motion can be divided, the individual parts are voted on separately when a member demands a division. This procedure occurs most often during the consideration of conference reports.

Division Vote—*(See Standing Vote.)*

Enacting Clause—Key phrase in bills beginning, "Be it enacted by the Senate and House of Representatives . . . ." A successful motion to strike it from legislation kills the measure.

Engrossed Bill—The final copy of a bill as passed by one chamber, with the text as amended by floor action and certified by the clerk of the House or the secretary of the Senate.

Enrolled Bill—The final copy of a bill that has been passed in identical form by both chambers. It is certified by an officer of the house of origin (clerk of the House or secretary of the Senate) and then sent on for the signatures of the House Speaker, the Senate president pro tempore and the president of the United States. An enrolled bill is printed on parchment.

Entitlement Program—A federal program that guarantees a certain level of benefits to persons or other entities who meet requirements set by law, such as Social Security, farm price supports or unemployment benefits. It thus leaves no discretion with Congress on how much money to appropriate, and some entitlements carry permanent appropriations.

Executive Calendar—This is a non-legislative calendar in the Senate on which presidential documents such as treaties and nominations are listed.

Executive Document—A document, usually a treaty, sent to the Senate by the president for consideration or approval. Executive documents are identified for each session of Congress according to the following pattern: Executive A, 97th Congress, 1st Session; Executive B, and so on. They are referred to committee in the same manner as other measures. Unlike legislative documents, however, treaties do not die at the end of a Congress but remain "live" proposals until acted on by the Senate or withdrawn by the president.

Executive Session—A meeting of a Senate or House committee (or occasionally of either chamber) that only its members may attend. Witnesses regularly appear at committee meetings in executive session — for example, Defense Department officials during presentations of classified defense information. Other members of Congress may be invited, but the public and press are not allowed to attend.

Expenditures—The actual spending of money as distinguished from the appropriation of funds. Expenditures are made by the disbursing officers of the administration; appropriations are made only by Congress. The two are rarely identical in any fiscal year. In addition to some current budget authority, expenditures may represent budget authority made available one, two or more years earlier.

Federal Debt—The federal debt consists of public debt, which occurs when the Treasury or the Federal Financing Bank (FFB) borrows money directly from the public or another fund or account, and agency debt, which is incurred when a federal agency other than Treasury or the FFB is authorized by law to borrow money from the public or another fund or account. The public debt comprises about 99 percent of the gross federal debt.

Filibuster—A time-delaying tactic associated with the Senate and used by a minority in an effort to prevent a vote on a bill or amendment that probably would pass if voted upon directly. The most common method is to take advantage of the Senate's rules permitting unlimited debate, but other forms of parliamentary maneuvering may be used. The stricter rules of the House make filibusters more difficult, but delaying tactics are employed occasionally through various procedural devices allowed by House rules. *(Senate filibusters, see Cloture.)*

Fiscal Year—Financial operations of the government are carried out in a 12-month fiscal year, beginning on Oct. 1 and ending on Sept. 30. The fiscal year carries the date of the calendar year in which it ends. (From fiscal year 1844 to fiscal year 1976, the fiscal year began July 1 and ended the following June 30.)

Five-Minute Rule—A debate-limiting rule of the House that is invoked when the House sits as the Committee of the Whole. Under the rule, a member offering an amendment is allowed to speak five minutes in its favor, and an opponent of the amendment is allowed to speak five minutes in opposition. Debate is then closed. In practice, amendments regularly are debated more than 10 minutes, with members gaining the floor by offering pro forma amendments or obtaining unanimous consent to speak longer than five minutes. *(See Strike Out the Last Word.)*

Floor Manager—A member who has the task of steering legislation through floor debate and the amendment process to a final vote in the House or the Senate. Floor managers usually are chairmen or ranking members of the committee that reported the bill. Managers are responsible for apportioning the debate time granted supporters of the bill. The ranking minority member of the committee normally apportions time for the minority party's participation in the debate.

Frank—A member's facsimile signature, which is used on envelopes in lieu of stamps, for the member's official outgoing mail. The "franking privilege" is the right to send mail postage-free.

Functions (Functional Classifications)—Categories of spending established for accounting purposes to keep track of specific expenditures. Each account is placed in the single function (such as national defense, agriculture, health) that best represents its major purpose, regardless of the agency administering the program. The functions do not correspond directly with appropriations or with the budgets of individual agencies. *(See also Budget Resolution.)*

Germane—Pertaining to the subject matter of the measure at hand. All House amendments must be germane to the bill being considered. The Senate requires that amendments be germane when they are proposed to general appropriation bills, bills being considered once cloture has been adopted or, frequently, when proceeding under a unanimous consent agreement placing a time limit on consideration of a bill. The 1974 budget act also requires that amendments to concurrent budget resolutions be germane. In the House, floor debate must be germane, and the first three hours of debate each day in the Senate must be germane to the pending business.

Gramm-Rudman-Hollings Deficit Reduction Act—*(See Budget Process, Sequestration.)*

Grandfather Clause—A provision exempting persons or other entities already engaged in an activity from rules or legislation affecting that activity. Grandfather clauses sometimes are added to legislation in order to avoid antagonizing groups with established interests in the activities affected.

Grants-in-Aid—Payments by the federal government to states, local governments or individuals in support of specified programs, services or activities.

Hearings—Committee sessions for taking testimony from witnesses. At hearings on legislation, witnesses usually include specialists, government officials and spokespersons for individuals or entities affected by the bill or bills under study. Hearings related to special investigations bring forth a variety of witnesses. Committees sometimes use their subpoena power to summon reluctant witnesses. The public and press may attend open hearings but are barred from closed, or "executive," hearings. The vast majority of hearings are open to the public. *(See Executive Session.)*

Hold-Harmless Clause—A provision added to legislation to ensure that recipients of federal funds do not receive less in a future year than they did in the current year if a new formula for allocating funds authorized in the legislation would result in a reduction to the recipients. This clause has been used most frequently to soften the impact of sudden reductions in federal grants.

Hopper—Box on House clerk's desk where members deposit bills and resolutions to introduce them. *(See also Bills Introduced.)*

Hour Rule—A provision in the rules of the House that permits one hour of debate time for each member on amendments debated in the House of Representatives sitting as the House. Therefore, the House normally amends bills while sitting as the Committee of the Whole, where the five-minute rule on amendments operates. *(See Committee of the Whole, Five-Minute Rule.)*

House—The House of Representatives, as distinct from the Senate, although each body is a "house" of Congress.

House as in Committee of the Whole—A procedure that can be used to expedite consideration of certain measures such as continuing resolutions and, when there is debate, private bills. The procedure only can be invoked with the unanimous consent of the House or a rule from the Rules Committee and has procedural elements of both the House sitting as the House of Representatives, such as the Speaker presiding and the previous question motion being in order, and the House sitting as the Committee of the Whole, such as the five-minute rule pertaining.

House Calendar—A listing for action by the House of public bills that do not directly or indirectly appropriate money or raise revenue.

Immunity—The constitutional privilege of members of Congress to make verbal statements on the floor and in committee for which they cannot be sued or arrested for slander or libel. Also, freedom from arrest while traveling to or from sessions of Congress or on official business. Members in this status may be arrested only for treason, felonies or a breach of the peace, as defined by congressional manuals.

Impoundments—Any action taken by the executive branch that delays or precludes the obligation or expenditure of budget authority previously approved by Congress. The Congressional Budget and Impoundment Control Act of 1974 was enacted after frequent use of impoundments by President Richard Nixon. In addition to creating the budget process currently used, the 1974 law established procedures for congressional approval or disapproval of temporary or permanent impoundments, which are called deferrals and rescissions.

Joint Committee—A committee composed of a specified number of members of both the House and Senate. A joint committee may be investigative or research-oriented, an example of the latter being the Joint Economic Committee. Others have housekeeping duties such as the joint committees on Printing and on the Library of Congress.

Joint Resolution—A joint resolution, designated H J Res or S J Res, requires the approval of both houses and the signature of the president, just as a bill does, and has the force of law if approved. There is no practical difference between a bill and a joint resolution. A joint resolution generally is used to deal with a limited matter such as a single appropriation.

Joint resolutions also are used to propose amendments to the Constitution. They do not require a presidential signature but become a part of the Constitution when three-fourths of the states have ratified them.

Journal—The official record of the proceedings of the House and Senate. The *Journal* records the actions taken in each chamber, but, unlike the *Congressional Record*, it does not include the substantially verbatim report of speeches, debates, statements and the like.

Law—An act of Congress that has been signed by the president or passed over his veto by Congress. Public bills, when signed, become public laws, and are cited by the letters PL and a hyphenated number. The two digits before the hyphen correspond to the Congress, and the one or more digits after the hyphen refer to the numerical sequence in which the bills were signed by the president during that Congress. Private bills, when signed, become private laws. *(See also Pocket Veto, Slip Laws,* Statutes at Large, U.S. Code.*)*

Legislative Day—The "day" extending from the time either house meets after an adjournment until the time it next adjourns. Because the House normally adjourns from day to day, legislative days and calendar days usually coincide. But in the Senate, a legislative day may, and frequently does, extend over several calendar days. *(See Recess.)*

Legislative Veto—A procedure, no longer allowed, permitting either the House or Senate, or both chambers, to review proposed executive branch regulations or actions and to block or modify those with which they disagreed.

The specifics of the procedure varied, but Congress generally provided for a legislative veto by including in a bill a provision that administrative rules or action taken to implement the law were to go into effect at the end of a designated period of time unless blocked by either or both houses of Congress. Another version of the veto provided for congressional reconsideration and rejection of regulations already in effect.

The Supreme Court June 23, 1983, struck down the legislative veto as an unconstitutional violation of the law-making procedure provided in the Constitution.

Loan Guarantees—Loans to third parties for which the federal government in the event of default guarantees, in whole or in part, the repayment of principal or interest to a lender or holder of a security.

Lobby—A group seeking to influence the passage or defeat of legislation. Originally the term referred to persons frequenting the lobbies or corridors of legislative chambers in order to speak to lawmakers.

The definition of a lobby and the activity of lobbying is a matter of differing interpretation. By some definitions, lobbying is limited to direct attempts to influence lawmakers through personal interviews and persuasion. Under other definitions, lobbying includes attempts at indirect, or "grass-roots," influence, such as persuading members of a group to write or visit their district's representative and state's senators or attempting to create a climate of opinion favorable to a desired legislative goal.

The right to attempt to influence legislation is based on the First Amendment to the Constitution, which says Congress shall make no law abridging the right of the people "to petition the government for a redress of grievances."

Majority Leader—The majority leader is elected by his party colleagues. In the Senate, in consultation with the minority leader and his colleagues, the majority leader directs the legislative schedule for the chamber. He also is his party's spokesperson and chief strategist. In the House, the majority leader is second to the Speaker in the majority party's leadership and serves as his party's legislative strategist.

Majority Whip—In effect, the assistant majority leader, in either the House or Senate. His job is to help marshal majority forces in support of party strategy and legislation.

Manual—The official handbook in each house prescribing in detail its organization, procedures and operations.

Marking Up a Bill—Going through the contents of a piece of legislation in committee or subcommittee to, for example, consider its provisions in large and small portions, act on amendments to provisions and proposed revisions to the language, and insert new sections and phraseology. If the bill is extensively amended, the committee's version may be introduced as a separate bill, with a new number, before being considered by the full House or Senate. *(See Clean Bill.)*

Minority Leader—Floor leader for the minority party in each chamber. *(See also Majority Leader.)*

Minority Whip—Performs duties of whip for the minority party. *(See also Majority Whip.)*

Morning Hour—The time set aside at the beginning of each legislative day for the consideration of regular, routine business. The "hour" is of indefinite duration in the House, where it is rarely used.

In the Senate it is the first two hours of a session following an adjournment, as distinguished from a recess. The morning hour can be terminated earlier if the morning business has been completed. Business includes such matters as messages from the president, communications from the heads of departments, messages from the House, the presentation of petitions, reports of standing and select committees and the introduction of bills and resolutions. During the first hour of the morning hour in the Senate, no motion to proceed to the consideration of any bill on the calendar is in order except by unanimous consent. During the second hour, motions can be made but must be decided without debate. Senate committees may meet while the Senate conducts morning hour.

Motion—In the House or Senate chamber, a request by a member to institute any one of a wide array of parliamentary actions. He "moves" for a certain procedure, such as the consideration of a measure. The precedence of motions, and whether they are debatable, is set forth in the House and Senate manuals.

Nominations—Presidential appointments to office subject to Senate confirmation. Although most nominations win quick Senate approval, some are controversial and become the topic of hearings and debate. Sometimes senators object to appointees for patronage reasons — for example, when a nomination to a local federal job is made without consulting the senators of the state concerned. In some situations a senator may object that the nominee is "personally obnoxious" to him. Usually other senators join in blocking such appointments out of courtesy to their colleagues. *(See Senatorial Courtesy.)*

Obligations—Orders placed, contracts awarded, services received and similar transactions during a given period that will require payments during the same or future period. Such amounts include outlays for which obligations had not been previously recorded and reflect adjustments for differences between obligations previously recorded and actual outlays to liquidate those obligations.

One-Minute Speeches—Addresses by House members at the beginning of a legislative day. The speeches may cover any subject but are limited to one minute's duration.

Outlays—Payments made (generally through the issuance of checks or disbursement of cash) to liquidate obligations. Outlays during a fiscal year may be for the payment of obligations incurred in prior years or in the same year.

Override a Veto—If the president disapproves a bill and sends it back to Congress with his objections, Congress may try to override his veto and enact the bill into law. Neither house is required to attempt to override a veto. The override of a veto requires a recorded vote with a two-thirds majority in each chamber. The question put to each house is: "Shall the bill pass, the objections of the president to the contrary notwithstanding?" *(See also Pocket Veto, Veto.)*

Oversight Committee—A congressional committee, or designated subcommittee of a committee, that is charged with general oversight of one or more federal agencies' programs and activities. Usually, the oversight panel for a particular agency also is the authorizing committee for that agency's programs and operations.

Pair—A voluntary, informal arrangement that two lawmakers, usually on opposite sides of an issue, make on recorded votes. In many cases the result is to subtract a vote from each side, with no effect on the outcome. Pairs are not authorized in the rules of either house, are not counted in tabulating the final result and have no official standing. However, members pairing are identified in the *Congressional Record,* along with their positions on such votes, if known. A member who expects to be absent for a vote can pair with a member who plans to vote, with the latter agreeing to withhold his vote.

There are three types of pairs: (1) A live pair involves a member who is present for a vote and another who is absent. The member in attendance votes and then withdraws the vote, announcing that he has a live pair with colleague "X" and stating how the two members would have voted, one in favor, the other opposed. A live pair may affect the outcome of a closely contested vote, since it subtracts one "yea" or one "nay" from the final tally. A live pair may cover one or several specific issues. (2) A general pair, widely used in the House, does not entail any arrangement between two members and does not affect the vote. Members who expect to be absent notify the clerk that they wish to make a general pair. Each member then is paired with another desiring a pair, and their names are listed in the *Congressional Record.* The member may or may not be paired with another taking the opposite position, and no indication of how the members would have voted is given. (3) A specific pair is similar to a general pair, except that the opposing stands of the two members are identified and printed in the *Record.*

Petition—A request or plea sent to one or both chambers from an organization or private citizens' group asking support of particular legislation or favorable consideration of a matter not yet receiving congressional attention. Petitions are referred to appropriate committees.

Pocket Veto—The act of the president in withholding his approval of a bill after Congress has adjourned. When Congress is in session, a bill becomes law without the president's signature if he does not act upon it within 10 days, excluding Sundays, from the time he gets it. But if Congress adjourns *sine die* within that 10-day period, the bill will die even if the president does not formally veto it.

The Supreme Court in 1986 agreed to decide whether the president can pocket veto a bill during recesses and between sessions of the same Congress or only between Congresses. The justices in 1987 declared the case moot, however, because the bill in question was invalid once the case reached the Court. *(See also Veto.)*

Point of Order—An objection raised by a member that the chamber is departing from rules governing its conduct of business. The objector cites the rule violated, the chair sustaining his objection if correctly made. Order is restored by the chair's suspending proceedings of the chamber until it conforms to the prescribed "order of business."

President of the Senate—Under the Constitution, the vice president of the United States presides over the Senate. In his absence, the president pro tempore, or a senator designated by the president pro tempore, presides over the chamber.

President Pro Tempore—The chief officer of the Senate in the absence of the vice president; literally, but loosely, the president for a time. The president pro tempore is elected by his fellow senators, and the recent practice has been to elect the senator of the majority party with the longest period of continuous service.

Previous Question—A motion for the previous question, when carried, has the effect of cutting off all debate, preventing the offering of further amendments and forcing a vote on the pending matter. In the House, the previous question is not permitted in the Committee of the Whole. The motion for the previous question is a debate-limiting device and is not in order in the Senate.

Printed Amendment—A House rule guarantees five minutes of floor debate in support and five minutes in opposition, and no other debate time, on amendments printed in the *Congressional Record* at least one day prior to the amendment's consideration in the Committee of the Whole. In the Senate, while amendments may be submitted for printing, they have no parliamentary standing or status. An amendment submitted for printing in the Senate, however, may be called up by any senator.

Private Calendar—In the House, private bills dealing with individual matters such as claims against the government, immigration or land titles are put on this calendar. The private calendar must be called on the first Tuesday of each month, and the Speaker may call it on the third Tuesday of each month as well.

When a private bill is before the chamber, two members may block its consideration, which recommits the bill to committee. Backers of a recommitted private bill have recourse. The measure can be put into an "omnibus claims bill" — several private bills rolled into one. As with any bill, no part of an omnibus claims bill may be deleted without a vote. When the private bill goes back to the House floor in this form, it can be deleted from the omnibus bill only by majority vote.

Privilege—Relates to the rights of members of Congress and to the relative priority of the motions and actions they may make in their respective chambers. The two are distinct. "Privileged questions" deal with legislative business. "Questions of privilege" concern legislators themselves.

Privileged Questions—The order in which bills, motions and other legislative measures are considered by Congress is governed by strict priorities. A motion to table, for instance, is more privileged than a motion to recommit. Thus, a motion to recommit can be superseded by a motion to table, and a vote would be forced on the latter motion only. A motion to adjourn, however, takes precedence over a tabling motion and thus is considered of the "highest privilege." *(See also Questions of Privilege.)*

Pro Forma Amendment—*(See Strike Out the Last Word.)*

Public Laws—*(See Law.)*

Questions of Privilege—These are matters affecting members of Congress individually or collectively. Matters affecting the rights, safety, dignity and integrity of proceedings of the House or Senate as a whole are questions of privilege in both chambers.

Questions involving individual members are called questions of "personal privilege." A member rising to ask a question of personal privilege is given precedence over almost all other proceedings. An annotation in the House rules points out that the privilege rests primarily on the Constitution, which gives him a conditional immunity from arrest and an unconditional freedom to speak in the House. *(See also Privileged Questions.)*

Quorum—The number of members whose presence is necessary for the transaction of business. In the Senate and House, it is a majority of the membership. A quorum is 100 in the Committee of the Whole House. If a point of order is made that a quorum is not present, the only business that is in order is either a motion to adjourn or a motion to direct the sergeant-at-arms to request the attendance of absentees.

Readings of Bills—Traditional parliamentary procedure required bills to be read three times before they were passed. This custom is of little modern significance. Normally a bill is considered to have its first reading when it is introduced and printed, by title, in the *Congressional Record*. In the House, its second reading comes when floor consideration begins. (This is the most likely point at which there is an actual reading of the bill, if there is any.) The second reading in the Senate is supposed to occur on the legislative day after the measure is introduced, but before it is referred to committee. The third reading (again, usually by title) takes place when floor action has been completed on amendments.

Recess—Distinguished from adjournment in that a recess does not end a legislative day and therefore does not interrupt unfinished business. The rules in each house set forth certain matters to be taken up and disposed of at the beginning of each legislative day. The House usually adjourns from day to day. The Senate often recesses, thus meeting on the same legislative day for several calendar days or even weeks at a time.

Recognition—The power of recognition of a member is lodged in the Speaker of the House and the presiding officer of the Senate. The presiding officer names the member who will speak first when two or more members simultaneously request recognition.

Recommit to Committee—A motion, made on the floor after a bill has been debated, to return it to the committee that reported it. If approved, recommittal usually is considered a death blow to the bill. In the House, a motion to recommit can be made only by a member opposed to the bill, and, in recognizing a member to make the motion, the Speaker gives preference to members of the minority party over majority party members.

A motion to recommit may include instructions to the committee to report the bill again with specific amendments or by a certain date. Or, the instructions may direct that a particular study be made, with no definite deadline for further action. If the recommittal motion includes instructions to "report the bill back forthwith" and the motion is adopted, floor action on the bill continues; the committee does not actually reconsider the legislation.

Reconciliation—The 1974 budget act provides for a "reconciliation" procedure for bringing existing tax and spending laws into conformity with ceilings enacted in the congressional budget resolution. Under the procedure, Congress instructs designated legislative committees to approve measures adjusting revenues and expenditures by a certain amount. The committees have a deadline by which they must report the legislation, but they have the discretion of deciding what changes are to be made. The recommendations of the various committees are consolidated without change by the Budget committees into an omnibus reconciliation bill, which then must be considered and approved by both houses of Congress. The orders to congressional committees to report recommendations for reconciliation bills are called reconciliation instructions, and they are contained in the budget resolution. Reconciliation instructions are not binding, but Congress must meet annual

Gramm-Rudman deficit targets to avoid the automatic spending cuts of sequestration, which means it must also meet the goal of reconciliation. *(See also Budget Resolution, Sequestration.)*

Reconsider a Vote—A motion to reconsider the vote by which an action was taken has, until it is disposed of, the effect of putting the action in abeyance. In the Senate, the motion can be made only by a member who voted on the prevailing side of the original question or by a member who did not vote at all. In the House, it can be made only by a member on the prevailing side.

A common practice in the Senate after close votes on an issue is a motion to reconsider, followed by a motion to table the motion to reconsider. On this motion to table, senators vote as they voted on the original question, which allows the motion to table to prevail, assuming there are no switches. The matter then is finally closed and further motions to reconsider are not entertained. In the House, as a routine precaution, a motion to reconsider usually is made every time a measure is passed. Such a motion almost always is tabled immediately, thus shutting off the possibility of future reconsideration, except by unanimous consent.

Motions to reconsider must be entered in the Senate within the next two days of actual session after the original vote has been taken. In the House they must be entered either on the same day or on the next succeeding day the House is in session.

Recorded Vote—A vote upon which each member's stand is individually made known. In the Senate, this is accomplished through a roll call of the entire membership, to which each senator on the floor must answer "yea," "nay" or, if he does not wish to vote, "present." Since January 1973, the House has used an electronic voting system for recorded votes, including yea-and-nay votes formerly taken by roll calls.

When not required by the Constitution, a recorded vote can be obtained on questions in the House on the demand of one-fifth (44 members) of a quorum or one-fourth (25) of a quorum in the Committee of the Whole. *(See Yeas and Nays.)*

Report—Both a verb and a noun as a congressional term. A committee that has been examining a bill referred to it by the parent chamber "reports" its findings and recommendations to the chamber when it completes consideration and returns the measure. The process is called "reporting" a bill.

A "report" is the document setting forth the committee's explanation of its action. Senate and House reports are numbered separately and are designated S Rept or H Rept. When a committee report is not unanimous, the dissenting committee members may file a statement of their views, called minority or dissenting views and referred to as a minority report. Members in disagreement with some provisions of a bill may file additional or supplementary views. Sometimes a bill is reported without a committee recommendation.

Adverse reports occasionally are submitted by legislative committees. However, when a committee is opposed to a bill, it usually fails to report the bill at all. Some laws require that committee reports — favorable or adverse — be made.

Rescission—An item in an appropriations bill rescinding or canceling budget authority previously appropriated but not spent. Also, the repeal of a previous appropriation by Congress at the request of the president to cut spending or because the budget authority no longer is needed. Under the 1974 budget act, however, unless Congress approves a rescission within 45 days of continuous session after receipt of the proposal, the funds must be made available for obligation. *(See also Deferral.)*

Resolution—A "simple" resolution, designated H Res or S Res, deals with matters entirely within the prerogatives of one house or the other. It requires neither passage by the other chamber nor approval by the president, and it does not have the force of law. Most resolutions deal with the rules or procedures of one house. They also are used to express the sentiments of a single house such as condolences to the family of a deceased member or to comment on foreign policy or executive business. A simple resolution is the vehicle for a "rule" from the House Rules Committee. *(See also Concurrent and Joint Resolutions, Rules.)*

Rider—An amendment, usually not germane, that its sponsor hopes to get through more easily by including it in other legislation. Riders become law if the bills embodying them are enacted. Amendments providing legislative directives in appropriations bills are outstanding examples of riders, though technically legislation is banned from appropriations bills. The House, unlike the Senate, has a strict germaneness rule; thus, riders usually are Senate devices to get legislation enacted quickly or to bypass lengthy House consideration and, possibly, opposition.

Rules—The term has two specific congressional meanings. A rule may be a standing order governing the conduct of House or Senate business and listed among the permanent rules of either chamber. The rules deal with issues such as duties of officers, the order of business, admission to the floor, parliamentary procedures on handling amendments and voting and jurisdictions of committees.

In the House, a rule also may be a resolution reported by its Rules Committee to govern the handling of a particular bill on the floor. The committee may report a "rule," also called a "special order," in the form of a simple resolution. If the resolution is adopted by the House, the temporary rule becomes as valid as any standing rule and lapses only after action has been completed on the measure to which it pertains. A rule sets the time limit on general debate. It also may waive points of order against provisions of the bill in question such as non-germane language or against certain amendments intended to be proposed to the bill from the floor. It may even forbid all amendments or all amendments except those proposed by the legislative committee that handled the bill. In this instance, it is known as a "closed" or "gag" rule as opposed to an "open" rule, which puts no limitation on floor amendments, thus leaving the bill completely open to alteration by the adoption of germane amendments.

Secretary of the Senate—Chief administrative officer of the Senate, responsible for overseeing the duties of Senate employees, educating Senate pages, administering oaths, handling the registration of lobbyists and handling other tasks necessary for the continuing operation of the Senate. *(See also Clerk of the House.)*

Select or Special Committee—A committee set up for a special purpose and, usually, for a limited time by resolution of either the House or Senate. Most special committees are investigative and lack legislative authority — legislation is not referred to them and they cannot report bills to their parent chamber. *(See also Standing Committees.)*

Senatorial Courtesy—Sometimes referred to as "the courtesy of the Senate," it is a general practice — with no written rule — applied to consideration of executive nominations. Generally, it means that nominations from a state are not to be confirmed unless they have been approved by the senators of the president's party of that state, with other senators following their colleagues' lead in the attitude they take toward consideration of such nominations. *(See Nominations.)*

Sequestration—Under procedures put in place by the Gramm-Rudman-Hollings anti-deficit law, year-end, across-the-board spending cuts would be imposed if the deficit exceeded a pre-set maximum. The Budget Enforcement Act of 1990 did away with that form of sequester for fiscal years 1991-93, replacing it with a series of targeted "mini-sequesters." *(See Budget Process.)*

Discretionary spending, provided in the 13 regular appropriations bills, was divided into three categories — domestic, defense and international — for fiscal 1991-93. Each category had a spending cap, and money could not be taken from one category to increase another. For fiscal 1994-95, the three categories were to be collapsed into one, with a single cap. If a cap was exceeded, a sequester would take place 15 days after adjournment.

The "pay-as-you-go" plan required that new entitlement spending or tax cuts be deficit-neutral. If Congress cut taxes, created a new entitlement program or expended eligibility or benefits for an existing program, it had to offset the cost. If no offset was provided, a sequester of all non-exempt entitlement programs would take place 15 days after adjournment.

A supplemental that exceeded discretionary spending limits and was enacted before July 1 would trigger a "within-session" sequester within 15 days of enactment, requiring a cutback in the offending category during the current fiscal year. A supplemental that exceeded the caps and was enacted after June 30 would trigger a "look-back" sequester, requiring a cutback in the offending category for the next fiscal year.

Sine Die—*(See Adjournment Sine Die.)*

Slip Laws—The first official publication of a bill that has been enacted and signed into law. Each is published separately in unbound single-sheet or pamphlet form. *(See also Law,* Statutes at Large, U.S. Code.*)*

Speaker—The presiding officer of the House of Representatives, selected by the caucus of the party to which he belongs and formally elected by the whole House.

Special Session—A session of Congress after it has adjourned *sine die,* completing its regular session. Special sessions are convened by the president.

Spending Authority—The 1974 budget act defines spending authority as borrowing authority, contract authority and entitlement authority for which budget authority is not provided in advance by appropriation acts.

Sponsor—*(See Bills Introduced.)*

Standing Committees—Committees permanently established by House and Senate rules. The standing committees of the House were last reorganized by the committee reorganization of 1974. The last major realignment of Senate committees was in the committee system reorganization of 1977. The standing committees are legislative committees — legislation may be referred to them and they may report bills and resolutions to their parent chambers. *(See also Select or Special Committee.)*

Standing Vote—A non-recorded vote used in both the House and Senate. (A standing vote also is called a division vote.) Members in favor of a proposal stand and are counted by the presiding officer. Then members opposed stand and are counted. There is no record of how individual members voted.

Statutes at Large—A chronological arrangement of the laws enacted in each session of Congress. Though indexed, the laws are not arranged by subject matter, and there is not an indication of how they changed previously enacted laws. *(See also Law, Slip Laws,* U.S. Code.*)*

Strike from the Record—Remarks made on the House floor may offend some member, who moves that the offending words be "taken down" for the Speaker's cognizance, and then expunged from the debate as published in the *Congressional Record.*

Strike Out the Last Word—A motion whereby a House member is entitled to speak for five minutes on an amendment then being debated by the chamber. A member gains recognition from the chair by moving to "strike out the last word" of the amendment or section of the bill under consideration. The motion is pro forma, requires no vote and does not change the amendment being debated.

Substitute—A motion, amendment or entire bill introduced in place of the pending legislative business. Passage of a substitute measure kills the original measure by supplanting it. The substitute also may be amended. *(See also Amendment in the Nature of a Substitute.)*

Supplemental Appropriations Bill—Legislation appropriating funds after the regular annual appropriations bill for a federal department or agency has been enacted. A supplemental appropriation provides additional budget authority beyond original estimates for programs or activities, including new programs authorized after the enactment of the regular appropriation act, for which the need for funds is too urgent to be postponed until enactment of the next year's regular appropriation bill.

Suspend the Rules—Often a time-saving procedure for passing bills in the House. The wording of the motion, which may be made by any member recognized by the Speaker, is: "I move to suspend the rules and pass the bill. . . ." A favorable vote by two-thirds of those present is required for passage. Debate is limited to 40 minutes and no amendments from the floor are permitted. If a two-thirds favorable vote is not attained, the bill may be considered later under regular procedures. The suspension procedure is in order every Monday and Tuesday and is intended to be reserved for non-controversial bills.

Table a Bill—Motions to table, or to "lay on the table," are used to block or kill amendments or other parliamentary questions. When approved, a tabling motion is considered the final disposition of that issue. One of the most widely used parliamentary procedures, the motion to table is not debatable, and adoption requires a simple majority vote.

In the Senate, however, different language sometimes is used. The motion may be worded to let a bill "lie on the table," perhaps for subsequent "picking up." This motion is more flexible, keeping the bill pending for later action, if desired. Tabling motions on amendments are effective debate-ending devices in the Senate.

Teller Vote—This is a largely moribund House procedure in the Committee of the Whole. Members file past tellers and are counted as for or against a measure, but they are not recorded individually. In the House, tellers are ordered upon demand of one-fifth of a quorum. This is 44 in the House, 20 in the Committee of the Whole.

The House also has a recorded teller vote, now largely supplanted by the electronic voting procedure, under which the votes of each member are made public just as they would be on a recorded vote.

Treaties—Executive proposals — in the form of resolutions of ratification — which must be submitted to the Senate for approval by two-thirds of the senators present. Treaties are normally sent to the Foreign Relations Committee for scrutiny before the Senate takes action. Foreign Relations has jurisdiction over all treaties, regardless of the subject matter. Treaties are read three times and debated on the floor in much the same manner as legislative proposals. After approval by the Senate, treaties are formally ratified by the president.

Trust Funds—Funds collected and used by the federal government for carrying out specific purposes and programs according to terms of a trust agreement or statute such as the Social Security and unemployment compensation trust funds. Such funds are administered by the government in a fiduciary capacity and are not available for the general purposes of the government.

Unanimous Consent—Proceedings of the House or Senate and action on legislation often take place upon the unanimous consent of the chamber, whether or not a rule of the chamber is being violated. Unanimous consent is used to expedite floor action and frequently is used in a routine fashion such as by a senator requesting the unanimous consent of the Senate to have specified members of his staff present on the floor during debate on a specific amendment.

Unanimous Consent Agreement—A device used in the Senate to expedite legislation. Much of the Senate's legislative business, dealing with both minor and controversial issues, is conducted through unanimous consent or unanimous consent agreements. On major legislation, such agreements usually are printed and transmitted to all senators in advance of floor debate. Once agreed to, they are binding on all members unless the Senate, by unanimous consent, agrees to modify them. An agreement may list the order in which various bills are to be considered, specify the length of time bills and contested amendments are to be debated and when they are to be voted upon and, frequently, require that all amendments introduced be germane to the bill under consideration. In this regard, unanimous consent agreements are similar to the "rules" issued by the House Rules Committee for bills pending in the House.

Union Calendar—Bills that directly or indirectly appropriate money or raise revenue are placed on this House calendar according to the date they are reported from committee.

U.S. Code—A consolidation and codification of the general and permanent laws of the United States arranged by subject under 50 titles, the first six dealing with general or political subjects, and the other 44 alphabetically arranged from agriculture to war. The *U.S. Code* is updated annually, and a new set of bound volumes is published every six years. *(See also Law, Slip Laws,* Statutes at Large.*)*

Veto—Disapproval by the president of a bill or joint resolution (other than one proposing an amendment to the Constitution). When Congress is in session, the president must veto a bill within 10 days, excluding Sundays, after he has received it; otherwise, it becomes law without his signature. When the president vetoes a bill, he returns it to the house of origin along with a message stating his objections. *(See also Pocket Veto, Override a Veto.)*

Voice Vote—In either the House or Senate, members answer "aye" or "no" in chorus, and the presiding officer decides the result. The term also is used loosely to indicate action by unanimous consent or without objection.

Whip—*(See Majority and Minority Whip.)*

Without Objection—Used in lieu of a vote on non-controversial motions, amendments or bills that may be passed in either the House or Senate if no member voices an objection.

Yeas and Nays—The Constitution requires that yea-and-nay votes be taken and recorded when requested by one-fifth of the members present. In the House, the Speaker determines whether one-fifth of the members present requested a vote. In the Senate, practice requires only 11 members. The Constitution requires the yeas and nays on a veto override attempt. *(See Recorded Vote.)*

Yielding—When a member has been recognized to speak, no other member may speak unless he obtains permission from the member recognized. This permission is called yielding and usually is requested in the form, "Will the gentleman yield to me?" While this activity occasionally is seen in the Senate, the Senate has no rule or practice to parcel out time.

The Legislative Process in Brief

Note: Parliamentary terms used below are defined in the glossary.

Introduction of Bills

A House member (including the resident commissioner of Puerto Rico and non-voting delegates of the District of Columbia, Guam, the Virgin Islands and American Samoa) may introduce any one of several types of bills and resolutions by handing it to the clerk of the House or placing it in a box called the hopper. A senator must first gain recognition of the presiding officer to announce the introduction of a bill. If objection is offered by any senator, the introduction of the bill is postponed until the following day.

As the next step in either the House or Senate, the bill is numbered, referred to committee, labeled with the sponsor's name and sent to the Government Printing Office so that copies can be made for subsequent study and action. All bills may be jointly sponsored and carry several members' names. Until 1978, the House limited the number of members who could cosponsor any one bill; the ceiling was eliminated at the beginning of the 96th Congress. A bill written in the executive branch and proposed as an administration measure usually is introduced by the chairman of the congressional committee that has jurisdiction.

Bills—Prefixed with HR in the House, S in the Senate, followed by a number. Used as the form for most legislation, whether general or special, public or private.

Joint Resolutions—Designated H J Res or S J Res. Subject to the same procedure as bills, with the exception of a joint resolution proposing an amendment to the Constitution. The latter must be approved by two-thirds of both houses and is thereupon sent directly to the administrator of general services for submission to the states for ratification instead of being presented to the president for his approval.

Concurrent Resolutions—Designated H Con Res or S Con Res. Used for matters affecting the operations of both houses. These resolutions do not become law.

Resolutions—Designated H Res or S Res. Used for a matter concerning the operation of either house alone and adopted only by the chamber in which it originates.

Committee Action

With few exceptions, bills are referred to the appropriate standing committees. The job of referral formally is the responsibility of the Speaker of the House and the presiding officer of the Senate, but this task usually is carried out on their behalf by the parliamentarians of the House and Senate. Precedent, statute and the jurisdictional mandates of the committees as set forth in the rules of the House and Senate determine which committees receive what kinds of bills. An exception is the referral of private bills, which are sent to whatever committee is designated by their sponsors. Bills are technically considered "read for the first time" when referred to House committees.

When a bill reaches a committee, it is placed on the committee's calendar. At that time, the bill comes under the sharpest congressional focus. Its chances for passage are quickly determined — and the great majority of bills fall by the legislative roadside. Failure of a committee to act on a bill is equivalent to killing it; the measure can be withdrawn from the committee's purview only by a discharge petition signed by a majority of the House membership on House bills, or by adoption of a special resolution in the Senate. Discharge attempts rarely succeed.

The first committee action taken on a bill usually is a request for comment on it by interested agencies of the government. The committee chairman may assign the bill to a subcommittee for study and hearings, or it may be considered by the full committee. Hearings may be public, closed (executive session) or both. A subcommittee, after considering a bill, reports to the full committee its recommendations for action and any proposed amendments.

The full committee then votes on its recommendation to the House or Senate. This procedure is called "ordering a bill reported." Occasionally, a committee orders a bill reported unfavorably. Usually, a report, submitted by the committee chairman to the House or Senate, calls for favorable action on the measure because the committee can effectively "kill" a bill by simply not taking any action.

After the bill is reported, the committee chairman instructs the staff to prepare a written report. The report describes the purposes and scope of the bill, explains the committee revisions, notes proposed changes in existing law and, usually, includes the views of the executive branch agencies consulted. Often committee members opposing a bill include dissenting minority statements in the report.

Normally, the committee "marks up" or proposes amendments to the bill. If they are substantial and the measure is complicated, the committee may order a "clean bill" introduced, which will embody the proposed amendments. The original bill then is put aside and the clean bill, with a new number, is reported to the floor.

The chamber must approve, alter or reject the committee amendments before the bill itself can be put to a vote.

Floor Action

After a bill is reported back to the chamber where it originated, it is placed on the calendar.

There are five legislative calendars in the House, issued in one cumulative calendar titled *Calendars of the United States House of Representatives and History of Legislation*. The House calendars are:

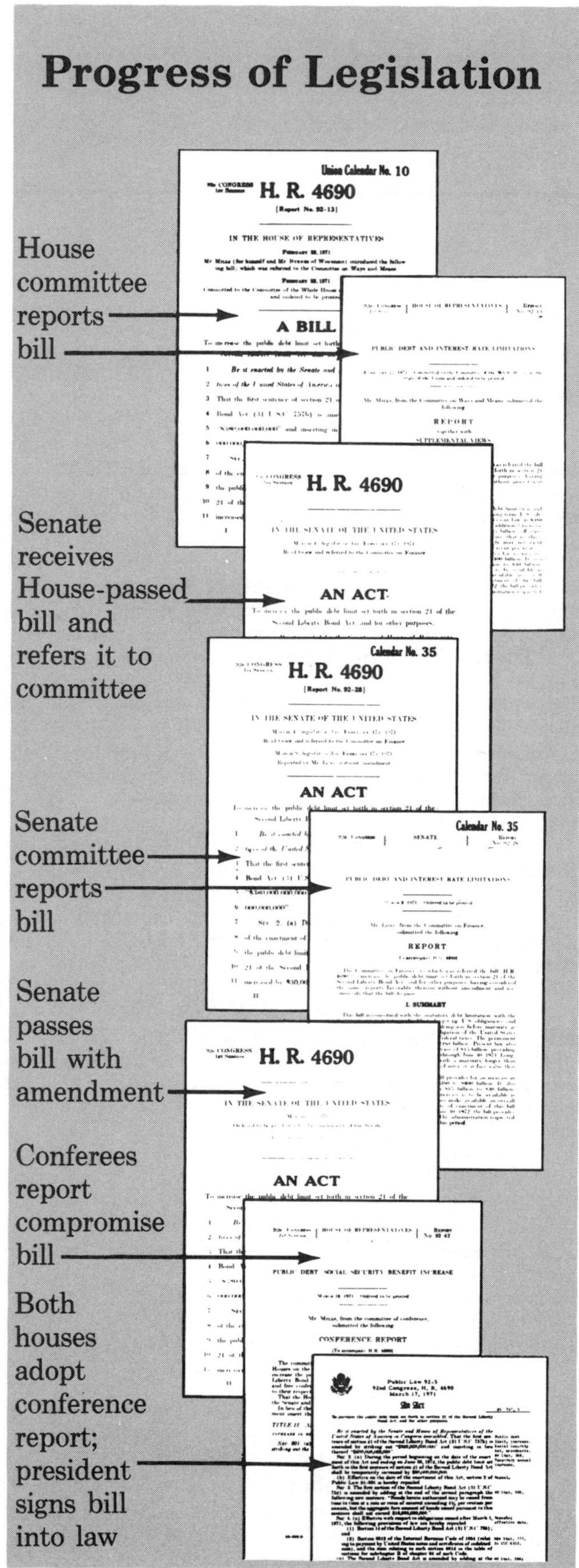

The Union Calendar to which are referred bills raising revenues, general appropriations bills and any measures directly or indirectly appropriating money or property. It is the Calendar of the Committee of the Whole House on the State of the Union.

The House Calendar to which are referred bills of public character not raising revenue or appropriating money or property.

The Consent Calendar to which are referred bills of a non-controversial nature that are passed without debate when the Consent Calendar is called on the first and third Mondays of each month.

The Private Calendar to which are referred bills for relief in the nature of claims against the United States or private immigration bills that are passed without debate when the Private Calendar is called the first and third Tuesdays of each month.

The Discharge Calendar to which are referred motions to discharge committees when the necessary signatures are signed to a discharge petition.

There is only one legislative calendar in the Senate and one "executive calendar" for treaties and nominations submitted to the Senate. When the Senate Calendar is called, each senator is limited to five minutes' debate on each bill.

Debate. A bill is brought to debate by varying procedures. If a routine measure, it may await the call of the calendar. If urgent or important, it can be taken up in the Senate either by unanimous consent or by a majority vote. The majority leader, in consultation with the minority leader and others, schedules the bills that will be taken up for debate.

In the House, precedence is granted if a special rule is obtained from the Rules Committee. A request for a special rule usually is made by the chairman of the committee that favorably reported the bill, supported by the bill's sponsor and other committee members. The request, considered by the Rules Committee in the same way that other committees consider legislative measures, is in the form of a resolution providing for immediate consideration of the bill. The Rules Committee reports the resolution to the House, where it is debated and voted upon in the same fashion as regular bills. If the Rules Committee should fail to report a rule requested by a committee, there are three ways to bring the bill to the House floor — under suspension of the rules, on Calendar Wednesday or by a discharge motion.

The resolutions providing special rules are important because they specify how long the bill may be debated and whether it may be amended from the floor. If floor amendments are banned, the bill is considered under a "closed rule," which permits only members of the committee that first reported the measure to the House to alter its language, subject to chamber acceptance.

When a bill is debated under an "open rule," amendments may be offered from the floor. Committee amendments always are taken up first but may be changed, like all amendments up to the second degree; that is, an amendment to an amendment to an amendment is not in order.

Duration of debate in the House depends on whether the bill is under discussion by the House proper or before the House when it is sitting as the Committee of the Whole House on the State of the Union. In the former, the amount of time for debate either is determined by special rule or is allocated with an hour for each member if the measure is under consideration without a rule. In the Committee of the Whole, the amount of time agreed on for general debate is equally divided between proponents and opponents. At the end of general discussion, the bill is read section by section for amendment. Debate on an amendment is limited to five minutes for each side; this is called the "five-minute rule." In practice, amendments regularly are debated more than ten minutes, with members gaining the floor by offering pro forma amendments or obtaining unanimous consent to speak longer than five minutes.

Senate debate usually is unlimited. It can be halted only by unanimous consent by "cloture," which requires a three-fifths majority of the entire Senate except for proposed changes in the Senate rules. The latter requires a two-thirds vote.

The House considers almost all important bills within a parliamentary framework known as the Committee of the Whole. It is not a committee as the word usually is understood; it is the full House meeting under another name for the purpose of speeding action on legislation. Technically, the House sits as the Committee of the Whole when it considers any tax measure or bill dealing with public appropriations. It also can resolve itself into the Committee of the Whole if a member moves to do so and the motion is carried. The Speaker appoints a member to serve as the chairman. The rules of the House permit the Committee of the Whole to meet when a quorum of 100 members is present on the floor and to amend and act on bills, within certain time limitations. When the Committee of the Whole has acted, it "rises," the Speaker returns as the presiding officer of the House and the member appointed chairman of the Committee of the Whole reports the action of the committee and its recommendations. The Committee of the Whole cannot pass a bill; instead it reports the measure to the full House with whatever changes it has approved. The full House then may pass or reject the bill — or, on occasion, recommit the bill to committee. Amendments adopted in the Committee of the Whole may be put to a second vote in the full House.

Votes. Voting on bills may occur repeatedly before they are finally approved or rejected. The House votes on the rule for the bill and on various amendments to the bill. Voting on amendments often is a more illuminating test of a bill's support than is the final tally. Sometimes members approve final passage of bills after vigorously supporting amendments that, if adopted, would scuttle the legislation.

The Senate has three different methods of voting: an untabulated voice vote, a standing vote (called a division) and a recorded roll call to which members answer "yea" or "nay" when their names are called. The House also employs voice and standing votes, but since January 1973 yeas and nays have been recorded by an electronic voting device, eliminating the need for time-consuming roll calls.

Another method of voting, used in the House only, is the teller vote. Traditionally, members filed up the center aisle past counters; only vote totals were announced. Since 1971, one-fifth of a quorum can demand that the votes of individual members be recorded, thereby forcing them to take a public position on amendments to key bills. Electronic voting now is commonly used for this purpose.

After amendments to a bill have been voted upon, a vote may be taken on a motion to recommit the bill to committee. If carried, this vote removes the bill from the chamber's calendar and is usually a death blow to the bill. If the motion is unsuccessful, the bill then is "read for the third time." An actual reading usually is dispensed with. Until 1965, an opponent of a bill could delay this move by objecting and asking for a full reading of an engrossed

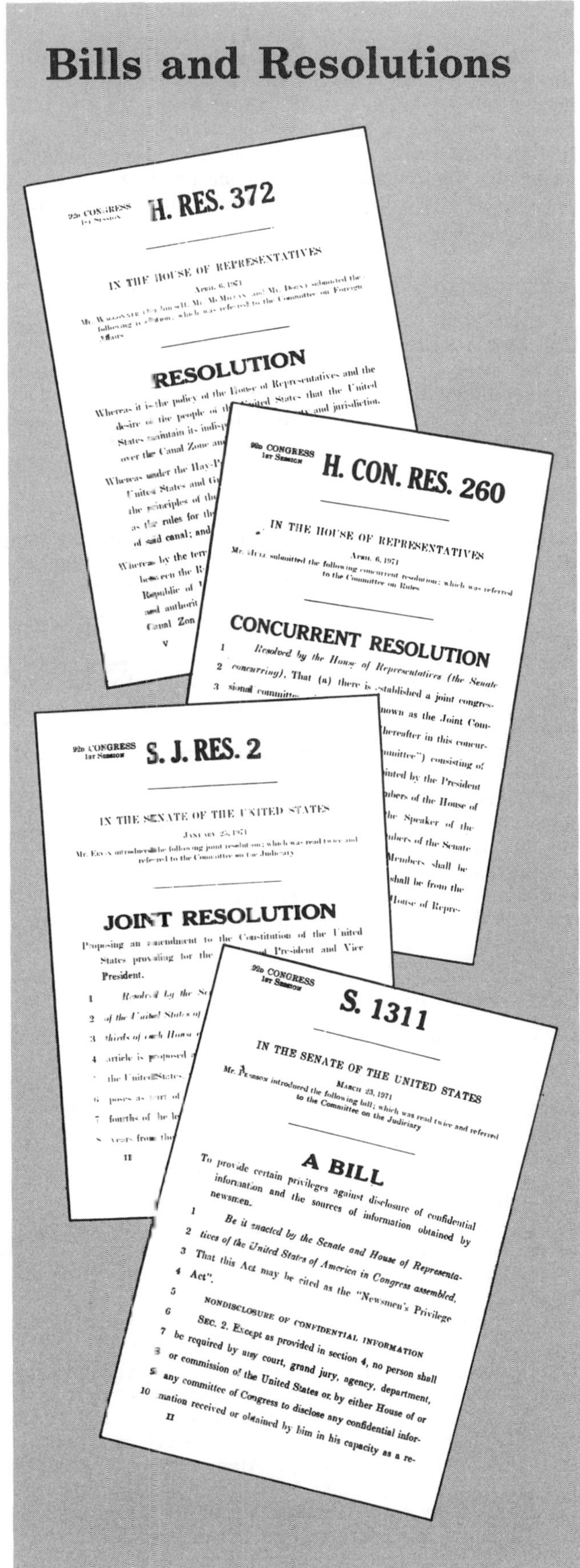

(certified in final form) copy of the bill. After the "third reading," the vote on final passage is taken.

The final vote may be followed by a motion to reconsider, and this motion may be followed by a move to lay the motion on the table. Usually, those voting for the bill's passage vote for the tabling motion, thus safeguarding the final passage action. With that, the bill has been formally passed by the chamber. While a motion to reconsider a Senate vote is pending on a bill, the measure cannot be sent to the House.

Action in the Second House

After a bill is passed, it is sent to the other chamber. This body may then take one of several steps. It may pass the bill as is — accepting the other chamber's language. It may send the bill to committee for scrutiny or alteration, or reject the entire bill, advising the other house of its actions. Or it simply may ignore the bill submitted while it continues work on its own version of the proposed legislation. Frequently, one chamber may approve a version of a bill that is greatly at variance with the version passed by the other house, and then substitute its contents for the language of the other, retaining only the latter's bill number.

A provision of the Legislative Reorganization Act of 1970 permits a separate House vote on any non-germane amendment added by the Senate to a House-passed bill and requires a majority vote to retain the amendment. Previously the House was forced to act on the bill as a whole; the only way to defeat the non-germane amendment was to reject the entire bill.

Often the second chamber makes only minor changes. If these are readily agreed to by the other house, the bill then is routed to the president. However, if the opposite chamber significantly alters the bill submitted to it, the measure usually is "sent to conference." The chamber that has possession of the "papers" (engrossed bill, engrossed amendments, messages of transmittal) requests a conference and the other chamber must agree to it. If the second house does not agree, the bill dies.

Conference, Final Action

Conference. A conference works out conflicting House and Senate versions of a legislative bill. The conferees usually are senior members appointed by the presiding officers of the two houses, from the committees that managed the bills. Under this arrangement, the conferees of one house have the duty of trying to maintain their chamber's position in the face of amending actions by the conferees (also referred to as "managers") of the other house.

The number of conferees from each chamber may vary, the range usually being from three to nine members in each group, depending upon the length or complexity of the bill involved. There may be five representatives and three senators on the conference committee, or the reverse. But a majority vote controls the action of each group so that a large representation does not give one chamber a voting advantage over the other chamber's conferees.

Theoretically, conferees are not allowed to write new legislation in reconciling the two versions before them, but this curb sometimes is bypassed. Many bills have been put into acceptable compromise form only after new language was provided by the conferees. The 1970 Reorganization Act attempted to tighten restrictions on conferees by forbidding them to introduce any language on a topic that neither chamber sent to conference or to modify any topic beyond the scope of the differing versions of the bill.

Frequently the ironing out of difficulties takes days or even weeks. Conferences on involved appropriations bills sometimes are particularly drawn out.

As a conference proceeds, conferees reconcile differences between the versions, but generally they grant concessions only insofar as they remain sure that the chamber they represent will accept the compromises. Occasionally, uncertainty over how either house will react, or the positive refusal of a chamber to back down on a disputed amendment, results in an impasse, and the bills die in conference even though each was approved by its sponsoring chamber.

Conferees sometimes go back to their respective chambers for further instructions, when they report certain portions in disagreement. Then the chamber concerned can either "recede and concur" in the amendment of the other house or "insist on its amendment."

When the conferees have reached agreement, they prepare a conference report embodying their recommendations (compromises). The report, in document form, must be submitted to each house.

The conference report must be approved by each house. Consequently, approval of the report is approval of the compromise bill. In the order of voting on conference reports, the chamber that asked for a conference yields to the other chamber the opportunity to vote first.

Final Steps. After a bill has been passed by both the House and Senate in identical form, all of the original papers are sent to the enrolling clerk of the chamber in which the bill originated. He then prepares an enrolled bill, which is printed on parchment paper. When this bill has been certified as correct by the secretary of the Senate or the clerk of the House, depending on which chamber originated the bill, it is signed first (no matter whether it originated in the Senate or House) by the Speaker of the House and then by the president of the Senate. It is next sent to the White House to await action.

If the president approves the bill, he signs it, dates it and usually writes the word "approved" on the document. If he does not sign it within 10 days (Sundays excepted) and Congress is in session, the bill becomes law without his signature. Should Congress adjourn before the 10 days expire, and the president fails to sign the measure, it does not become law. This procedure is called the pocket veto.

A president vetoes a bill by refusing to sign it and, before the 10-day period expires, returning it to Congress with a message stating his reasons. The message is sent to the chamber that originated the bill. If no action is taken on the message, the bill dies. Congress, however, can attempt to override the veto and enact the bill, "the objections of the president to the contrary notwithstanding." Overriding a veto requires a two-thirds vote of those present, who must number a quorum and vote by roll call.

Debate can precede this vote, with motions permitted to lay the message on the table, postpone action on it or refer it to committee. If the president's veto is overridden in both houses, the bill becomes law. Otherwise it is dead.

When bills are passed finally and signed, or passed over a veto, they are given law numbers in numerical order as they become law. There are two series of numbers, one for public and one for private laws, starting at the number "1" for each two-year term of Congress. They are then identified by law number and by Congress — for example, Private Law 21, 101st Congress; Public Law 250, 101st Congress (or PL 101-250).

How a Bill Becomes Law

This graphic shows the most typical way in which proposed legislation is enacted into law. There are more complicated, as well as simpler, routes, and most bills never become law. The process is illustrated with two hypothetical bills, House bill No. 1 (HR 1) and Senate bill No. 2 (S 2). Bills must be passed by both houses in identical form before they can be sent to the president. The path of HR 1 is traced by a solid line, that of S 2 by a broken line. In practice most bills begins as similar proposals in both houses.

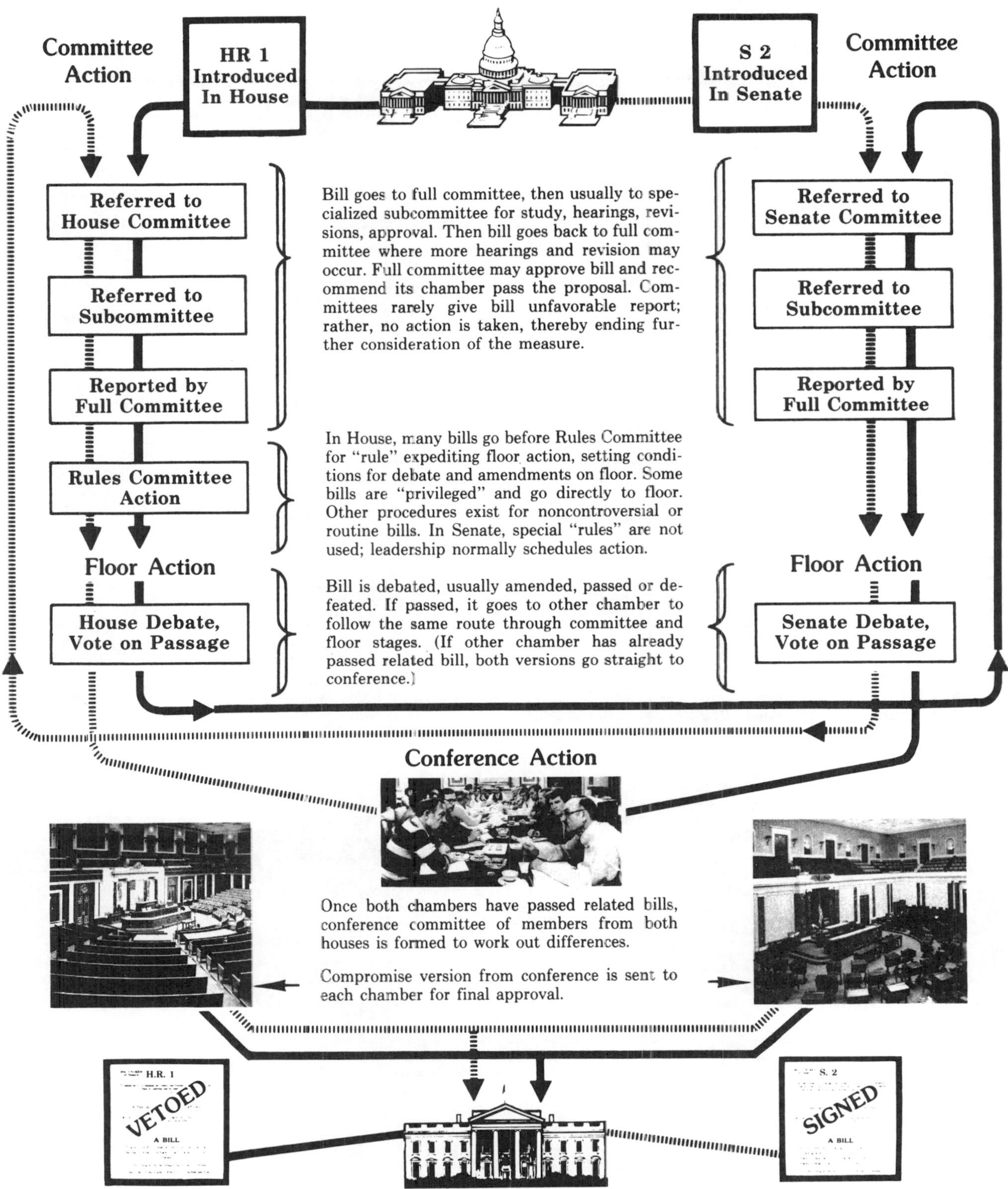

Committee Action
HR 1 Introduced In House
S 2 Introduced In Senate
Committee Action
Referred to House Committee
Referred to Subcommittee
Reported by Full Committee
Rules Committee Action
Floor Action
House Debate, Vote on Passage
Referred to Senate Committee
Referred to Subcommittee
Reported by Full Committee
Floor Action
Senate Debate, Vote on Passage
Bill goes to full committee, then usually to specialized subcommittee for study, hearings, revisions, approval. Then bill goes back to full committee where more hearings and revision may occur. Full committee may approve bill and recommend its chamber pass the proposal. Committees rarely give bill unfavorable report; rather, no action is taken, thereby ending further consideration of the measure.
In House, many bills go before Rules Committee for "rule" expediting floor action, setting conditions for debate and amendments on floor. Some bills are "privileged" and go directly to floor. Other procedures exist for noncontroversial or routine bills. In Senate, special "rules" are not used; leadership normally schedules action.
Bill is debated, usually amended, passed or defeated. If passed, it goes to other chamber to follow the same route through committee and floor stages. (If other chamber has already passed related bill, both versions go straight to conference.)
Conference Action
Once both chambers have passed related bills, conference committee of members from both houses is formed to work out differences.
Compromise version from conference is sent to each chamber for final approval.
H.R. 1
VETOED
A BILL
S. 2
SIGNED
A BILL

Compromise bill approved by both houses is sent to the president, who can sign it into law or veto it and return it to Congress. Congress may override veto by a two-thirds majority vote in both houses; bill then becomes law without president's signature.

Key Votes, 1989-92

Congressional Quarterly each year selects a series of key votes on major issues.

Selection of Issues. An issue is judged by the extent it represents one or more of the following:

- A matter of major controversy.
- A test of presidential or political power.
- A decision of potentially great impact on the nation and lives of Americans.

Selection of Votes. For each series of related votes on an issue, only one key vote usually is chosen. This vote is the roll call in the House or Senate that in the opinion of Congressional Quarterly was the most important in determining the outcome.

In the description of the key votes, the designation ND denotes Northern Democrats, and the designation SD denotes Southern Democrats.

1989 Key Votes

Senate

1. Tower Nomination

After a lengthy and bitter battle largely along partisan lines, the Senate on March 9 rejected President Bush's nomination of former Senate Armed Services Committee Chairman John Tower, R-Texas, to be secretary of defense.

Critics of the nomination, led by the Armed Services panel's current chairman, Sam Nunn, D-Ga., insisted that their opposition was based on concerns about Tower's personal fitness. Citing hundreds of interviews conducted by the FBI, Nunn and others said Tower had a record of alcohol abuse that would make him an unreliable link in the military chain of command. Moreover, they said, Tower's service as a paid consultant to several defense contractors since his retirement from the Senate would impair his efforts to restore confidence in the scandal-plagued weapons procurement system.

But Tower's supporters, led by Senate Minority Leader Bob Dole, R-Kan., insisted that the personal questions about Tower were merely a screen for a Democratic power grab. According to this argument, the Democrats used unsworn statements by unidentified sources in the FBI files to defeat a nominee whose political savvy and grasp of the issues would have made him too powerful an advocate of Bush's policies.

The nomination was rejected by a vote of 47-53: R 44-1; D 3-52 (ND 1-37, SD 2-15).

2. Contra Aid

One of the Bush administration's first priorities was to lance the political wound called contra aid. The administration succeeded, largely because of Secretary of State James A. Baker III's negotiating skills. A "bipartisan accord" that Baker hammered out with congressional leaders in March ended a years-long debate about whether the United States should use military force to oust Nicaragua's leftist Sandinista regime. Instead, Congress and the administration agreed to rely on diplomacy as the principal means of ending conflict in Nicaragua and elsewhere in Central America.

The accord settled on a middle course about the U.S.-backed contras. Instead of resuming military aid to the contras, as many conservatives wanted, or disbanding the guerrillas, as most liberals wanted, the political leadership in Washington decided to keep the contras intact. They did so by agreeing to continue "non-military" aid until after Nicaragua's elections, set for Feb. 25.

Both chambers ratified that agreement by approving legislation (HR 1750) authorizing the use of unspent Pentagon funds to provide food, medicine and other supplies to the contras. The Senate approved the package April 13 on an 89-9 vote — R 39-5; D 50-4 (ND 34-4, SD 16-0) — with opponents including conservatives and liberals who refused to reconcile themselves to the compromise.

Step 2 of the bipartisan accord came in October when the chambers approved another White House request to spend $9 million to promote free and fair elections in Nicaragua. The administration contended it wanted the money to establish a "level playing field" for the elections. But officials made no secret of the fact that the administration supported, and was hoping to provide, as much indirect aid as Congress would allow to an opposition coalition headed by newspaper publisher Violeta Chamorro. The Senate approved the election aid (HR 3385) on Oct. 17. *(House key vote 1)*

3. FS-X Fighter Plane

By a narrow margin, the Senate declined to block outright a joint U.S.-Japan project to develop a new Japanese fighter plane, designated the FS-X. But critics, determined to vent frustration over what they saw as Japan's exploitation of its commercial and military links with the United States, pushed through the Senate a modified version of the resolution (S J Res 113) hedging the deal with conditions.

Warning that the Senate-passed conditions would kill the sale, President Bush vetoed the resolution and, with strong GOP support, the Senate sustained the veto.

Under terms of the FS-X program, U.S. and Japanese companies would modify the U.S. Air Force's workhorse F-16 fighter plane to meet Japan's requirements.

Critics said that this "co-development" would give Japanese companies access to the engineering and program management skills of their U.S. counterparts. The Japanese aerospace industry would use that information to compete more effectively with U.S. aircraft builders for overseas sales, the critics warned.

Supporters of the sale insisted that the project represented an attempt by Japan to pick up more of the burden of defending allied interests in the northwest Pacific. Japan would develop its commercial aerospace business with or without U.S. cooperation, they argued.

But the critics countered that Washington should press the Japanese harder to buy U.S.-built fighter planes off the shelf.

A resolution to block U.S. participation in the joint program in effect was rejected on May 16 by a vote of 47-52: R 11-34; D 36-18 (ND 25-12, SD 11-6). But the Senate adopted a modified version of the resolution that would have barred the transfer to Japan of sensitive jet-engine technologies and expressed the sense of Congress that if the plane went into production, U.S. companies should be guaranteed 40 percent of the business.

An effort to override Bush's veto of the resolution fell one vote short of the constitutionally required two-thirds majority. The vote to override was 66-34.

4. Fiscal 1989 Supplemental

Showing little of the appetite House Democrats had for challenging President Bush on anti-drug funding, Senate Appropriations leaders on June 1 easily fended off efforts to put new drug money into a $3.3 billion midyear appropriations bill (HR 2072 — PL 101-45).

Robert C. Byrd, D-W.Va., the new chairman of the Senate Appropriations Committee, was able to steer the bill through the committee in quick order May 31 after insisting that any attempts to add new funding would draw a certain presidential veto. The Senate measure knocked out the most controversial House provision — $822 million in new anti-drug law enforcement spending — which Bush vehemently opposed unless it was accompanied by equivalent cutbacks in other programs.

Byrd then prevailed on the Senate floor against several drug-related amendments that would have required waivers from budget restrictions against new spending.

The Senate's overwhelming support for Byrd's hard-line stance against new anti-drug funding gave him considerable leverage in a subsequent conference with the House, where he refused to compromise.

House Democrats hoped to step up the pressure on Byrd, who had stocked his version of the bill with a number of pet projects for his home state (as well as for states of other key Senate committee members). Byrd had won administration approval for the Senate bill, but he was coming under increasing pressure from his own Democratic Caucus to take political advantage of the drug issue.

The final compromise — $75 million for anti-drug law enforcement efforts, with offsetting cuts in some pet programs — was worked out by bipartisan leaders of the House and Senate Appropriations committees, under the auspices of House Speaker Thomas S. Foley, D-Wash., and Senate Majority Leader George J. Mitchell, D-Maine. White House budget director Richard G. Darman — who repeatedly threatened to urge a presidential veto if the anti-drug money was left in the bill — participated in the negotiations and was satisfied with the outcome.

Byrd's ability to forge a bill acceptable to the administration hinged on his ability to keep anti-drug amendments off the Senate measure. Indeed, the first such amendment reflected both the mood of some senators for confrontation with the administration over anti-drug funding, and Byrd's power to stave it: It was Pennsylvania Republican Arlen Specter's attempt for a budget waiver to shift $70 million from Pentagon funds to new prison construction. Although three more drug-related amendments would surface afterward, the votes would be similarly lopsided. Byrd turned back Specter's proposal with a motion to table (kill) the waiver request, prevailing on a vote of 77-18: R 30-11; D 47-7 (ND 31-6, SD 16-1). *(House key vote 2)*

5. Child Care

The 1989 debate over increasing federal assistance for child care saw virtually every member of Congress in agreement that some action was warranted, but there was no consensus on what that action should be. At times, it seemed the most vigorous debate was not over what should be done, but whether Democrats or Republicans would ultimately get the credit.

The Senate spent nearly two weeks in June debating a Democratic-backed measure combining very different plans approved by the Labor and Human Resources and Finance committees. The proposals were joined in a shotgun marriage by Majority Leader George J. Mitchell, D-Maine, when it became clear that the Labor Committee's plan to authorize grants to the states for child care subsidies, the so-called ABC bill (S 5), could not pass without the addition of a tax-credit proposal.

The inclusion in the Democratic leadership bill of tax-credit provisions favored by President Bush and most Republicans left the outnumbered Republicans in an awkward position. Bush's proposal, offered in March, had little support on Capitol Hill; most congressional Republicans instead had put forward their own plans. But faced with a relatively united Democratic front, Minority Leader Bob Dole, R-Kan., knew he had to devise an attractive alternative or face defeat in an early test of Bush's domestic agenda.

Dole patched together elements of both the original Bush plan and a bill drafted primarily by House Republicans. His proposal featured an expanded earned-income tax credit (also part of the Democratic plan) and an increase in existing block grants to the states. He spent most of a week making changes in an attempt to lure wavering Democrats, but in the end he could garner only two — Sam Nunn, Ga., and Kent Conrad, N.D. — while losing three Republicans who were cosponsors of the ABC bill.

Dole's substitute amendment was rejected June 22 by 44-56: R 42-3; D 2-53 (ND 1-37, SD 1-16). *(House key vote 12)*

6. Prohibited Foreign Activities

Two years after the Iran-contra hearings, Congress and the administration continued to struggle over the political lessons that were learned. The conflict in 1989 involved several pieces of legislation intended to check what many on Capitol Hill viewed as excessive administration power over foreign affairs.

One such proposal, originally authored by Sen. Daniel Patrick Moynihan, D-N.Y., called for the imposition of criminal penalties on any administration official found guilty of undertaking foreign policy actions that Congress had otherwise barred by law. The Moynihan proposal was aimed at preventing a repetition of the actions of former White House aide Oliver L. North, who supervised a secret supply network for the Nicaraguan contras at a time when U.S. law prohibited official aid.

Despite objections from the White House, the Senate on July 18 approved the Moynihan language, 57-42: R 4-41; D 53-1 (ND 37-0, SD 16-1), as an amendment to the fiscal 1990 authorization bill vote for the State Department and related agencies. That amendment was watered down substantially to try to meet administration objections. Even so, Bush vetoed HR 1487 because of the Moynihan amendment. The House then passed a new version of the State Department bill (HR 3792) without the Moynihan amendment, but that bill was blocked in the Senate at the end of the session because of an unrelated committee jurisdictional dispute.

7. Strategic Defense Initiative

Following what had become a pattern, the Senate narrowly rejected a proposal to slice funding for the strategic defense initiative (SDI) to a level that — in light of larger cuts already made by the House — would have ensured an even larger reduction in President Bush's funding request than the $1.1 billion cut that Congress eventually made.

But there were aspects of the 1989 SDI debate that suggested that the anti-missile defense program faced a grim political future.

The messianic rhetoric with which President Ronald Reagan inaugurated the program in 1983 — to make nuclear missiles "impotent and obsolete" — had long since given way to a more modest goal of shoring up the U.S. nuclear deterrent by ruling out a disarming Soviet first strike.

Moreover, led by conservative Democratic Sen. Sam Nunn of Georgia, Congress had made clear that it would block any early deployment (or realistic, space-based testing) of SDI that would violate the generally held understanding of the 1972 U.S.-Soviet treaty limiting anti-ballistic missile (ABM) systems.

Nevertheless, despite the concerns of many liberal Democrats that SDI was, at best, technically dubious and, at worst, a threat to arms control, Congress had been unwilling to challenge Reagan's commitment to the program.

In 1989, Reagan was gone. And despite Bush's insistence that he supported SDI, there was a general sense on Capitol Hill that he had not given the project the same personal commitment. Moreover, with the Pentagon's acute money crunch, even conservatives who had backed SDI saw its relatively large budget as a potential source of funds with which to salvage other programs from the budgetary ax.

Bush requested $4.9 billion to continue the anti-missile defense research program and the House-passed version of the defense authorization bill approved $3.1 billion.

In its version of the authorization bill, the Senate Armed Services Committee recommended $4.5 billion — a reduction of $366 million from Bush's request — for the program that some called "star wars."

When the Senate took up the bill, J. Bennett Johnston, D-La., who had been at the forefront of opposition to SDI in the Senate, offered an amendment that would have sliced the program's authorization by an additional $558 million, to $4 billion. Johnston had intended to incorporate in his amendment provisions that, in effect, would have transferred the funds cut from SDI to other programs, but that was blocked by an objection on procedural grounds.

Armed Services Committee members argued that they needed the Senate to approve a higher SDI authorization so they would have bargaining leverage with House conferees to produce a final SDI authorization of about the amount Johnston was proposing.

Johnston's amendment was tabled (thus killed) on July 27 by a key vote of 50-47: R 37-6; D 13-41 (ND 5-32, SD 8-9).

Before the House-Senate conferees on the defense authorization bill resolved their disagreement on SDI funding, Johnston prevailed on the Senate Appropriations Committee to cut SDI funding to $4 billion in the companion defense appropriations bill.

But on the Senate floor, Armed Services Chairman Nunn and others argued that their bargaining position in the authorization conference would be undermined if the Senate backed a lower amount in the appropriation bill. So the Senate voted 53-47 to increase the appropriation for SDI up to the level it had authorized. *(House key vote 7)*

8. Savings and Loan Restructuring

As the Senate considered President Bush's plan to salvage the nation's savings and loan industry (HR 1278 — PL 101-73), only one issue rose to prominence — how to borrow the $50 billion needed to close insolvent thrifts.

First in the Banking Committee and later on the Senate floor, Republicans and a few Democrats banded together to oppose a Democratic plan to borrow the money from the Treasury and count the cost as part of the federal budget. Bush's plan — favored by Republicans — was to borrow the money privately and keep it off the federal books, except for those interest costs paid by taxpayers.

Bush argued that because the $50 billion principal would be repaid by the industry, not by taxpayers, there was no justification for counting it as part of the budget. Most Democrats, including Banking Chairman Donald W. Riegle Jr., D-Mich., countered that it was a government expense that should not be hidden, and that borrowing from the Treasury — with its lower costs — would save taxpayers as much as $4.5 billion in interest payments over 30 years.

The central problem for those supporting the on-budget, Treasury-financed approach was that it would greatly increase the federal budget deficit during the three years when the $50 billion was borrowed. So supporters favored an exemption from the Gramm-Rudman anti-deficit law for the amount borrowed. Without such an exemption, other programs would have had to be cut or taxes increased to offset the larger deficit.

The House, led by the Ways and Means Committee, had approved an on-budget financing scheme, and Senate conferees reluctantly accepted that position as their final big decision in conference on the bill. But when the conference report was returned to the Senate, Bush went to the mat. The chief administration argument was that a Gramm-Rudman exemption would set the wrong precedent and destabilize world financial markets.

Bush's objection carried the day. Under Senate rules, adopting the Gramm-Rudman exemption required 60 votes. Riegle's motion to do so (by waiving a point of order that the exemption itself violated Gramm-Rudman) failed by six votes, and the Senate thereby rejected the conference report. The Aug. 3 vote was 54-46: R 1-44; D 53-2 (ND 36-2, SD 17-0).

Conferees then reconvened, adopting a compromise that put $20 billion of the money on budget for fiscal 1989, which was nearly over and would not require a Gramm-Rudman exemption. The remaining $30 billion was put off budget for fiscal 1990 and 1991. And the bill passed. *(House key vote 5)*

9. Airline Smoking Ban

A harsh signal was sent to the tobacco lobby Sept. 14 when the Senate voted to shut off debate on a proposal to ban smoking on all airline flights within the United States. That vote paved the way for perhaps the most far-reaching anti-smoking legislation ever passed by Congress.

Even tobacco-state members leading the filibuster conceded from the start that they were fighting a losing battle. The motion to end debate was approved by a vote of 77-21, well above the 60 votes needed. The Senate then approved the ban Sept. 27 as part of an $11.9 billion fiscal 1990 spending bill (HR 3015 — PL 101-164) for the Department of Transportation and related agencies.

The ban was only slightly weakened in conference with the House, to exempt flights to and from Alaska and Hawaii that lasted six hours or more. That compromise was viewed as a face-saving concession to tobacco interests, which both sides preferred to a messy floor fight.

Both the House and Senate sponsors of the smoking ban circumvented their authorizing committees and attached the legislation to the transportation spending bill. An earlier two-year ban on smoking on flights of two hours or less was to expire on April 23, 1990.

Richard J. Durbin, D-Ill., lacking support for the ban on the House Appropriations Committee, went directly to the Rules Committee, where he persuaded members to include a permanent extension of the ban on two-hour flights in the spending bill.

Frank R. Lautenberg, D-N.J., chairman of the Senate Appropriations Subcommittee on Transportation, attached a stronger, permanent ban on smoking on all flights during his subcommittee's markup.

Lautenberg had no chance of pushing the legislation through the Senate outside the appropriations process. The normal committee of jurisdiction, Commerce, Science and Transportation, included Democratic Chairman Ernest F. Hollings of South Carolina and Aviation Subcommittee Chairman Wendell H. Ford of Kentucky — both staunch tobacco-state members and leaders of the Senate filibuster.

On Oct. 16, conferees agreed to the smoking-ban compromise, and Congress completed final action on the transportation spending bill Nov. 14.

While tobacco interests continued to command a number of loyal allies in Congress, senators ignored the industry's heavy lobbying against the ban extension, with only 21 senators backing the filibuster attempt. Among those voting to end debate were tobacco-state Democrats Al Gore of Tennessee and Sam Nunn of Georgia. Even Republican Pete V. Domenici, a notoriously heavy smoker, supported ban sponsors even though it would prohibit smoking on cross-country flights back to his home state of New Mexico. In a roll call to invoke cloture, the Senate voted 77-21: R 33-11; D 44-10 (ND 35-2, SD 9-8).

10. 'Stealth' Bomber

Cost was the main theme of the first large-scale attack in the Senate on the B-2 "stealth" bomber. The Senate rejected an amendment to the fiscal 1990 defense appropriations bill by Patrick J. Leahy, D-Vt., that would have barred production of additional planes beyond the 13 B-2s built or under construction.

Noting that the predicted total program cost of roughly $70 billion amounted to an average of $532 million for each of the planned 132 planes, Leahy contended that was just too much. Moreover, he argued, the plane's expensive stealth qualities, intended to help it fly through the Soviet Union's extensive anti-bomber defenses, were not necessary. The same missions could be performed more cheaply by long-range cruise missiles fired from existing bombers flying far beyond the reach of Soviet defenses, he said.

But B-2 supporters said that Leahy's math inflated the B-2's unit cost by ignoring the many useful technological spinoffs produced by the $22.5 billion (out of the $70 billion total) already spent on B-2 research.

Moreover, the B-2 backers contended, a manned penetrating bomber offered uniquely valuable military assets not duplicated by cruise missiles. For instance, they said, it would require the Soviets to completely revamp their anti-bomber defenses at huge cost.

Leahy's amendment was rejected on Sept. 26 by a vote of 29-71: R 2-43; D 27-28 (ND 23-15, SD 4-13).

When the Senate took up the conference report on the defense appropriations measure, Alan Cranston, D-Calif., offered an amendment to it that essentially duplicated Leahy's earlier effort. Cranston's amendment was rejected 29-68. *(House key vote 8)*

11. NEA Funding

North Carolina Republican Sen. Jesse Helms' amendment to bar federal funding of "obscene or indecent" artwork touched off a firestorm of debate across the country, pitting the arts community and its defenders against fundamentalist Christians and their allies in an argument that many members warned threatened the existence of federal arts agencies such as the National Endowment for the Arts (NEA).

Helms' amendment to a fiscal 1990 spending bill (HR 2788 — PL 101-121) for the Interior Department and related agencies was prompted by revelations that NEA grants had helped fund exhibitions of controversial photographs many members found obscene or sacrilegious. During floor debate on HR 2788, Helms used copies of the photographs to persuade bill managers Robert C. Byrd, D-W.Va., and James A. McClure, R-Idaho, to accept his amendment on a voice vote. With the issue reduced by Helms to a simple question of whether tax dollars should be spent on obscene art, it was widely assumed the Senate would avoid a roll call at all costs.

But then the Senate went to conference on the interior bill with the House, which had no similar language in its version. NEA defenders from both chambers managed to substantially water down the conference language, granting broad discretion to the NEA and the National Endowment of the Humanities to bar funding only for work that — in the opinion of the endowments — "may be considered" obscene and without "serious literary, artistic, political or scientific value."

That struck Helms as a "loophole so wide you can drive 12 Mack trucks through it abreast," and as the conference was winding up its work, Helms sought to block the language by forcing the Senate, during debate on a fiscal 1990 defense spending bill (HR 3072 — PL 101-165), to vote on a resolution instructing the Senate interior conferees to insist on the original Helms amendment.

Despite some senators' public concern that anyone opposing Helms would be targeted for supporting obscenity, several senators took the floor to speak against the amendment. Tim Wirth, D-Colo., voiced the frustration of many of his colleagues with Helms' efforts to hold their feet to the fire.

"I, for one, am really fed up with it," Wirth said, insisting the Senate had reached the "end of the rope" on the matter, which he argued was censorship and "an egregious violation of the First Amendment." He called on colleagues to "belly up and be serious about the defense of the Constitution of the United States."

In what appeared to be a turning point of the debate, John C. Danforth, R-Mo., a conservative and an ordained Episcopalian minister, took the floor to say that while he found the controversial photos to be "gross" and "totally indefensible," he could not support the Helms amendment. Danforth argued that Helms' broad language barring denigration of any "religion or nonreligion" or any "person, group or class of citizens" could have a dangerously chilling effect on a wide variety of works. He urged colleagues not to try to define appropriate art on the Senate floor.

The Senate agreed, voting to table the Helms amendment 62-35: R 19-25; D 43-10 (ND 33-5, SD 10-5).

12. Catastrophic-Illness Insurance

The congressional about-face on a program to expand Medicare to cover the costs of catastrophic illness was remarkable both for its swiftness and for its sweep. The decision to repeal the 1988 Medicare Catastrophic Coverage law came less than 17 months after the measure was enacted and marked the first time that Congress had voted to take away significant new benefits it had created.

Members who wrote the 1988 law knew that its financing mechanism would be controversial — particularly an income-related surtax that required affluent senior citizens to pay more for their benefits than their less well-off brethren. But they badly underestimated the size of the backlash, the extent to which Medicare's 33 million beneficiaries did not understand the program and the number of outside groups that would seek to exploit the confusion.

Sponsors of the 1988 law fought throughout the year to quell the complaints, but the Bush administration was lukewarm in its support, and by fall the battle was virtually over. On Oct. 4, the House voted 360-66 to repeal both the new benefits and the premiums to finance them.

On Oct. 6, the Senate took up a free-standing bill (S 1726) sponsored by Arizona Republican John McCain, the principal antagonist of the surtax in that chamber. Although several amendments were debated, advocates of the 1988 program pinned their hopes for its survival on a plan crafted by Dave Durenberger, Minn., ranking Republican on the Finance Committee's Medicare subcommittee.

Durenberger's proposal would have preserved the core catastrophic benefits — stop-loss coverage of hospital and doctor bills. But to pay for them, the plan also would have retained about one-quarter of the surtax that had touched off the political firestorm in the first place.

The Durenberger amendment had the support of Majority Leader George J. Mitchell, D-Maine, Minority Leader Bob Dole, R-Kan., and Finance Committee Chairman Lloyd Bentsen, D-Texas. It also was endorsed by Health and Human Services Secretary Louis W. Sullivan, although the White House disavowed that statement. None of the high-level backing mattered in the end; the plan was resoundingly defeated, 37-62: R 8-37; D 29-25 (ND 21-16, SD 8-9).

Members subsequently approved, 99-0, McCain's plan to abolish the surtax but keep the hospital coverage and some smaller benefits. In the end, however, both chambers approved a House measure (HR 3607) repealing the entire program. *(House key vote 11)*

13. Deficit Reduction

The Senate in effect put a stop to President Bush's 1989 drive for a lower capital gains tax rate, and perhaps set a precedent for more streamlined deficit-reduction bills, with its passage Oct. 13 of a $14.1 billion budget "reconciliation" bill (HR 3299). The vote, a bipartisan ending to a most divisive episode, was 87-7: R 40-2; D 47-5 (ND 34-2, SD 13-3).

The outcome ended a week of wrangling over a Democratic offer from Senate Majority Leader George J. Mitchell, D-Maine, to strip the comprehensive budget-cutting bill of the usual array of unrelated and sometimes costly provisions that often hitch a ride on the critical legislation.

Democrats described their strategy in "good government" rhetoric, but their purpose was to block a GOP bid to add another amendment — for the capital gains tax cut, a 1988 Bush campaign priority.

The administration resisted Democrats' overture, demanding a vote on the tax issue, but Republican senators were losing enthusiasm for the apparently futile fight. Convinced they could not overcome a Democratic filibuster of a capital gains amendment, the Republicans finally accepted Mitchell's offer in terms that made it sound like their own.

Republicans reserved their right to offer a capital gains amendment on other legislation, specifically a pending measure to raise the government's debt limit. But within weeks Bush would concede what had become all but certain with the reconciliation bill vote — that the tax-cut effort was dead for the year.

After the reconciliation vote, the Senate still had a hard time in a conference committee persuading House members to go along with a stripped-down bill. House Democrats were eager to drop the capital gains amendment that had made its way into their version, but many opposed forfeiting provisions on priorities such as child care.

They ultimately did so in late November, as part of a $14.7 billion compromise intended to meet Bush's demand for a bill providing at least $14 billion in 1990 savings, without the extraneous add-ons, thus freeing Congress to adjourn for the year before Thanksgiving.

14. Flag Desecration Amendment

Although President Bush insisted that a constitutional amendment was the only way to reverse a June 21 Supreme Court decision striking down laws against flag desecration, the Senate Oct. 19 rejected a proposed amendment (S J Res 180) sponsored by Minority Leader Bob Dole, R-Kan.

The vote was 51-48: R 33-11; D 18-37 (ND 8-30, SD 10-7). That was 15 short of the required two-thirds of those present and voting.

The outcome could not have been predicted in the immediate aftermath of the 5-4 court decision in *Texas v. Johnson.* That ruling, which held that flag burning and similar activities were forms of expression protected by the First Amendment, prompted an outcry by the public and politicians across the country.

With Bush demanding a constitutional amendment to reverse the court's ruling, Democrats worried that the issue would become a test of patriotism, similar to the Pledge of Allegiance requirement that Bush had used so effectively against Democrat Michael S. Dukakis in the 1988 presidential election campaign.

But as each month passed, passions cooled. Public interest and outrage waned, and members began to have second thoughts about amending the Bill of Rights for the first time in the nation's history. A majority of legal scholars and other experts testifying at public hearings opposed a constitutional amendment, and some of them said Congress probably could achieve the same objective with a carefully phrased statute.

On Oct. 12 Congress cleared a bill to prohibit physical defacement of the flag. The measure became law without Bush's signature Oct. 28. Bush and a few Republicans continued urging passage of a constitutional amendment, but the White House made no effort to lobby for the proposal. The House did not vote on its version of the amendment in 1989.

15. Capital Gains Tax Cut

Congress managed only the second pre-Thanksgiving adjournment in a non-election year since 1965 largely because the Senate shelved the session's most contentious issue: cutting the capital gains tax.

In a vote on Nov. 14, echoed in an identical vote the next day, supporters of President Bush's cut in the tax fell nine votes shy of the 60 needed to close debate. Thus the Democrats' threat of a filibuster successfully postponed the day of reckoning. The vote by which the motion for cloture failed was 51-47: R 45-0; D 6-47 (ND 2-34, SD 4-13).

Despite the opposition of Democratic leaders, the House on Sept. 28 had voted to include in its budget-reconciliation bill (HR 3299 — PL 101-239) a cut in the tax on capital gains (profits from the sale of assets). The House approved the bill on Oct. 5. By then, Democratic leaders in the Senate had erected emergency barriers to passage of a similar cut in that chamber.

In a marathon session the night of Oct. 3-4, Senate Finance Chairman Lloyd Bentsen, D-Texas, succeeded in keeping the cut out of his committee's revenue package for reconciliation.

Sen. Bob Packwood, R-Ore., the panel's ranking GOP member, offered a plan that would have excluded from taxation 5 percent of a capital gain for each year the asset had been held. (Packwood initially capped the exclusion at 30 percent but later raised this to 35 percent.) Packwood would have paid for his plan's revenue losses with a revision of Individual Retirement Accounts (IRAs) designed to capture new revenue in the short run. Bentsen (who had an IRA plan of his own) beat back Packwood's amendment on a 10-10 tie vote.

Supporters of the capital gains cut then needed a floor amendment to add it to the reconciliation bill, a move that was subject to special Senate rules requiring 60 votes. Given that procedural advantage, Majority Leader George J. Mitchell, D-Maine, forged a winning minority coalition of those who opposed the cut on substance and those who opposed waiving the usual procedures on its behalf.

Frustrated, Senate GOP leaders on Oct. 13 gave up on the reconciliation bill and began looking for other vehicles. For a time, the cut was a pending amendment on legislation authorizing emergency aid to Poland and Hungary (S 1582). At another stage, supporters threatened to attach it to legislation raising the limit on the national debt (H J Res 280 — PL 101-140).

As Thanksgiving neared, a compromise was reached. The House agreed to drop its capital gains provision in HR 3299, then reapproved it Nov. 9 as a free-standing bill (HR 3628). The following week, the new bill was brought to the Senate floor, where Packwood's plan was substituted for the substance of the House version. After three hours of debate, a vote was held not on the substance of Packwood's plan or on the concept of a capital gains cut but on the procedural question of closing off debate.

The Democrats who wanted the tax cut badly enough to vote for cloture were primarily Southerners with moderate-to-conservative voting records.

Among them was Sen. David L. Boren of Oklahoma, the only Democrat who had voted with Packwood and against Bentsen in Finance. Boren was expected to return in 1990 with a capital gains plan that more Democrats would support. *(House key vote 10)*

16. Pay and Ethics Package

The Senate broke with tradition and established a two-tier congressional salary system, when it refused to take a big salary increase the House had approved for its members. As part of a bill that revamped congressional ethics rules (HR 3660 — PL 101-194), the Senate Nov. 17 voted to take a 10 percent pay raise in 1990, while allowing House members and other federal officials increases of as much as 40 percent over 1990-91.

The vote was a measure of lawmakers' continuing skittishness about the politically explosive job of setting their own pay — a task that blew up in their faces nine months earlier.

In February, Congress bowed to heavy public criticism and killed a proposal to raise the salaries of lawmakers and other top federal officials by 51 percent. Despite promises that the raise's approval would be followed by action on legislation barring members from keeping honoraria and other outside income, the public was outraged by the magnitude of the proposed raise and the fact it was to take effect without Congress voting on it.

The House revived the issue in the closing weeks of the 1989 session, exacerbating longstanding institutional tensions between the Senate and House over members' compensation. Senators had always been more satisfied with the status quo because they were, on average, wealthier and collected more in honoraria than House members. The drive to ban honoraria in exchange for the politically risky pay raise thus came primarily from the House.

Senate leaders endorsed the House's pay plan, which included cost-of-living raises in 1990 and a 25 percent increase in 1991 in conjunction with a ban on honoraria and other tightening of ethics rules. Despite initial victories on procedural votes, the leaders could not garner a majority for the House pay plan and pulled it before bringing it to a vote. Instead, the leaders brought up an alternative providing the smaller increase for the Senate, billed as compensation for cost-of-living adjustments foregone in the previous three years. The key vote approving that alternative was 56-43: R 25-20; D 31-23 (ND 21-16 SD 10-75).

The discrepancy between the chambers' pay and honoraria rules all but guaranteed that the compensation issue would resurface after the 1990 election year began. The only question was whether the House would buckle to pressure to roll back its pay or whether the Senate would raise its salary and drop honoraria, in line with the House. *(House key vote 16)*

House

1. Contra Aid

Ending years of bitter political debate over whether the United States should use military force to oust the leftist government of Nicaragua, the Bush administration reached a "bipartisan accord" with Congress. Under the accord, which Secretary of State James A. Baker III hammered out with congressional leaders in March, Congress and the administration agreed to rely on diplomacy as the principal means to end conflict in Nicaragua and elsewhere in Central America.

Congress and the administration settled on a middle course on the U.S.-backed contras. Instead of resuming military aid, as many conservatives wanted, or disbanding the guerrillas, as most liberals wanted, the political leadership in Washington decided to keep the contras intact — at least temporarily — and continue to provide "non-military" aid to the guerrillas until after Nicaragua's elections Feb. 25, 1990.

Both chambers of Congress ratified the agreement April 13 by approving legislation (HR 1750) authorizing using unspent Pentagon funds to send the contras food, medicine and other supplies. The House approved that package 309-110 — R 157-11; D 152-99 (ND 84-87, SD 68-12) — with opponents including both conservatives and liberals who refused to reconcile themselves to the political compromise.

A follow-up move in the bipartisan accord came in October, when the two chambers approved another Bush request for permission to spend $9 million to promote free and fair elections in Nicaragua. The administration said it wanted the money to establish a "level playing field," but officials made no secret that the administration supported, and hoped to provide as much indirect aid as Congress would allow, to an opposition coalition headed by newspaper publisher Violeta Chamorro.

The House approved the elections aid (HR 3385) on Oct. 4. *(Senate key vote 2)*

2. Fiscal 1989 Supplemental

House Republicans on April 26 found a way to exploit some abiding divisions among their Democratic counterparts and, as a result, help President Bush avert an early showdown with Congress on spending policy. A $4.74 billion supplemental spending bill (HR 2402 — PL 101-45) for fiscal 1989, though laced with politically popular plums such as anti-drug funding, was abruptly pulled from the House floor after members decisively rejected an effort by Democratic leaders to pay for the bill with midyear cuts in federal programs.

The April vote was the first sign that Bush would be no pushover on fiscal policy, as liberal and conservative Democrats alike defected from the party leadership. A proposal to impose across-the-board cuts to pay for the congressional add-ons to Bush's original $2.2 billion request — though amounting to little more than half a percent from each appropriations account — would have sliced deeply into programs ranging from child nutrition and cancer research to military enlistment bonuses. House Majority Leader Thomas S. Foley, D-Wash., had offered the hurriedly prepared amendment to mend fences between the party's Appropriations and Budget committee leaders and to co-opt a similar, but even more stringent, GOP plan to impose offsetting cuts on domestic programs alone.

Silvio O. Conte of Massachusetts, ranking Republican on the Appropriations Committee, had indicated that he would try to impose across-the-board cuts on domestic appropriations to cover increases for anti-drug initiatives and forest firefighting reimbursements opposed by the Bush administration. But even though Democratic leaders pushed through a "king of the hill" rule for floor debate — designed to make Foley's amendment pre-eminent even if the House first approved Conte's — they did not anticipate Conte's countermove (or lack of one), which exposed the flaws in Foley's scheme.

Democrats had tried to cast Foley's amendment as a test of Bush's vows to wage a war on drugs and provide a "kinder, gentler" domestic policy. The Bush administration tried to keep the supplemental in line with a 1987 White House-congressional budget summit, which stipulated that spending cuts must offset any supplemental spending requests that did not fit the description of a "dire emergency."

Before the Democrats' floor-vote scenario got under way, however, Conte backed off, preferring to force an all-or-nothing vote on Foley's plan. Suddenly, Foley's plan was transformed from the less painful alternative to the sole source of widely unappealing spending cuts.

Ninety-two Democrats crossed over to vote with Republicans against Foley's amendment. It was rejected, 172-252: R 9-160; D 163-92 (ND 129-44, SD 34-48).

In the end, Bush's $2.2 billion request would be increased to $3.3 billion. House Appropriations leaders found a way to keep an $822 million funding proposal for anti-drug programs in the House bill, but only by avoiding a direct vote (and thus another fiscal showdown with the administration). When the Senate refused to put extra anti-drug funding in its version of the bill, the increasingly weakened negotiators for House Appropriations were forced to find a face-saving compromise, which in effect kept the supplemental appropriations bill at a funding level agreeable to Bush. *(Senate key vote 4)*

3. Budget Resolution

The House easily endorsed the first budget negotiated in the Bush years (as the Senate would the same week), but while the atmosphere was more conciliatory, the action merely continued the cease-fire in the partisan deadlock over spending and tax policy that had marked the Reagan years.

The $1.17 trillion budget resolution for fiscal 1990 (H Con Res 106) was the product of a bipartisan budget pact that President Bush and congressional leaders sealed April 14 in a Rose Garden ceremony. But the House's lopsided approval May 4, by a vote of 263-157 — R 106-61; D 157-96 (ND 102-71, SD 55-25) — masked the widespread disgruntlement and dashed expectations in both parties over the limited terms of the deal.

The budget resolution called for $28 billion in savings to bring the projected 1990 deficit within the $100 billion target set in the Gramm-Rudman anti-deficit law. But lawmakers knew the full amount would never be realized and that what savings were likely to be implemented in a so-called budget-reconciliation bill would be heavy on accounting gimmicks and one-time windfalls.

The budget resolution, which is an annual outline for fiscal action in the appropriations, tax-writing and authorizing committees, proposed no major cuts in federal programs and required just $5.3 billion in new but unspecified revenues.

That reflected the same standoff between Democrats opposed to significant cuts in social programs and Republicans opposed to higher taxes and defense cuts that had divided the government under Ronald Reagan.

Both sides agreed that they would try, as early as fall, to improve on the modest 1990 budget by negotiating a bold deficit-cutting plan for fiscal 1991. But that promise was soon lost in acrimony, along with the spirit of good will that the leaders had cited in the spring as their chief accomplishment. Congress and the administration fought nearly to Thanksgiving just to implement the 1990 agreement and enact what turned out to be a $14.7 billion reconciliation bill.

4. Minimum Wage Increase

After more than two years of trying — and largely failing — to tarnish Ronald Reagan and George Bush with the minimum wage issue, labor leaders and top congressional Democrats began seeking a face-saving compromise after failing June 14 to override a veto of their bill to raise the hourly minimum wage from $3.35 to $4.55.

Bush's whiplike veto of their bill (HR 2) — and House Democrats' inability to override it — convinced senior strategists in Congress and organized labor that pressing the point for mere political advantage would be futile.

Restless congressional Republicans then began prodding Bush to seek a compromise with Democrats that might finally break the long partisan deadlock. White House Chief of Staff John H. Sununu and AFL-CIO President Lane Kirkland, meeting Oct. 24 to discuss the imminent arrival in the United States of Polish Solidarity leader Lech Walesa, finally agreed to negotiate a solution.

That talk broke the ground for rapid negotiations that resulted Nov. 1 in the House's approving, by a resounding vote of 382-37, legislation (HR 2710 — PL 101-157) to raise the minimum hourly wage to $4.25 over two years. It also provided, for the first time, for a subminimum "training wage," a key request of Bush that organized labor had long opposed.

The Senate followed suit Nov. 8, clearing the bill on an 89-8 vote. Bush signed HR 2710 into law Nov. 17.

Bush had promised to veto the original Democratic proposal in HR 2 almost from the day he entered the White House. Indeed, his opposition to HR 2 became the cornerstone of a White House strategy to show that Bush would be willing to deal on some issues, but on others (such as the minimum wage) he would "lay down a mark" and fight to hold it, if only to show Congress that he was no pushover.

Bush vetoed HR 2 almost before he received it June 13, issuing a statement even as the official papers were being delivered from Capitol Hill. House Democratic leaders scheduled an override the next day, hoping to capitalize on the publicity and put pressure on wavering Republicans.

It was not enough. Proponents fell 37 votes shy of the two-thirds (284 in this case) needed to thwart Bush. The tally was 247-178: R 20-150: D 227-28 (ND 171-3, SD 56-25).

5. Capital Standards for Thrifts

The nation's savings and loan industry had in the past wielded considerable clout on Capitol Hill. It was, after all, the presumed source of money for the American dream of home ownership. So, as Congress began working through President Bush's request (HR 1278 — PL 101-73) for hundreds of billions of dollars from taxpayers to salvage the industry, there was sure to be a showdown.

It came on the issue of "capital" or "net worth" requirements for surviving thrifts. Critics of the industry and its regulators had charged that the financial crisis was caused at least in part by not requiring thrift owners to put their own money into the businesses. Without a sufficient cushion of capital, thrift owners had no incentive to make careful, responsible investments. The only money at risk was that of depositors, and it was insured by the federal government.

Congress had previously yielded to industry requests for exemptions from capital standards. And when the bailout bill reached the House Banking Committee, several members tried to continue the forbearance.

The chief issue was "supervisory good will," in essence an accounting gimmick to offset the difference between the value of a thrift's weak assets and its liabilities. Buyers of hundreds of failed thrifts in the mid-1980s had been allowed to carry this "phantom" capital on their books for up to 40 years.

In April markup sessions, some members of the Banking Committee tried to allow thrifts with good will to continue to count it so they could meet the stiff capital standards being crafted, but they were rebuffed, often by close votes.

The bill was also referred to the Judiciary Committee, where Henry J. Hyde, R-Ill., argued May 24 that preventing the future use of good will was in effect a denial of due process. Hyde offered an amendment in committee to give thrifts that would lose the ability to count good will as capital the right to administrative and judicial appeals. His amendment lost on a 17-17 tie vote.

Hyde took his cause to the floor.

Throughout the Banking and Judiciary committee debate, it had been mostly Democrats who argued against counting good will and Republicans who favored it. Just two days before the floor vote, it appeared that Hyde might prevail on the floor.

But when the issue reached the floor June 15, Bush decided that it would be embarrassing if his party were soft on the thrift industry. Bush lobbied hard, threatening a veto if the capital standards were weakened. And he changed the vote of Minority Leader Robert H. Michel, R-Ill., sealing the amendment's fate.

Hyde's amendment lost by an overwhelming vote of 94-326: R 56-114; D 38-212 (ND 30-144, SD 8-68).

Observers saw the outcome as a clear signal of the end of the thrift industry's clout in Congress. Later votes the same day to ban "junk bond" investments by thrifts and to strike several perceived "special interest" provisions from the bill merely reinforced that view. *(Senate key vote 8)*

6. Superconducting Supercollider

The overwhelming House vote June 28 to begin building the world's largest atom smasher in Waxahachie, Texas, put to rest a simmering controversy over the wisdom of spending billions on this "big science" project, handed President Bush a significant legislative victory and charted a new direction for federal science policy.

The House vote was the first ever on the superconducting supercollider (SSC), and the margin stunned friends and foes alike. An amendment to eliminate the $110 million in initial construction funds from a $200 million earmark for research and development was rejected. It meant that, barring an unusual retreat in 1990, the controversial project would enter the construction phase and cost as much as $900 million a year until it was finished in five to seven years.

The House action thus embarked the federal government on a new science policy initiative that would put an increasingly heavy burden on the budget over the next decade. It also was a revealing case study in how a project of such magnitude and controversy — yet such limited geographical interest — found necessary support in Congress.

The money was included in the fiscal 1990 energy and water development appropriations bill (HR 2696 — PL 101-101). Ultimately, in conference with the Senate, appropriators agreed to provide the SSC $225 million.

Even that did not end the budget and technical problems that have plagued the SSC since its inception. Facing cost overruns of $2 billion, federal officials recommended scaling back the project because it was unlikely its $5.9 billion construction budget would be increased.

Defenders argued that the SSC, one of the largest and most complicated public works projects ever undertaken, would let scientists delve further into the basic nature of matter and energy. Opponents questioned spending so much on a project with comparatively narrow scientific interest.

Intense lobbying by the Texas congressional delegation, the Bush administration and key science budget defenders in the House helped swing the vote in favor of the SSC. The vote on an amendment by Democrat Dennis E. Eckart of Ohio to scale back the construction funds was rejected 93-330: R 28-144; D 65-186 (ND 57-112, SD 8-74).

7. Strategic Defense Initiative

As it has done each year since 1986, the House made a hefty slash in funding for the strategic defense initiative (SDI). By a July 25 vote of 248-175, which broke largely along party lines, the House adopted an amendment to the fiscal 1990 defense authorization bill (HR 2461) approving $3.1 billion for SDI research in fiscal 1990 instead of the $4.9 billion President Bush had requested.

Reflecting the lowered political expectations for the anti-missile program that had been a cornerstone of President Ronald Reagan's program, the Bush administration had scaled back its request. In his revised fiscal 1990 defense budget, Bush sought $4.9 billion for SDI, $1.1 billion less than Reagan had requested before leaving office in January. Even so, the program remained a target for its longtime opponents as well as conservative supporters who saw its relatively large budget as a potential source of money with which to rescue other programs from the budget ax.

The House Armed Services Committee cut the project to $4 billion. And when the House took up the defense authorization bill, even SDI's strongest backers hoped for nothing better than boosting the figure to $4.1 billion. That proposal was rejected 117-299. The House then rejected a second amendment that would have cut SDI funding to $1.3 billion.

Then it approved an amendment setting SDI funding at $3.1 billion by a key vote of 248-175: R 34-137; D 214-38 (ND 163-7, SD 51-31). *(Senate key vote 7)*

8. 'Stealth' Bomber

Against the backdrop of acute budgetary limits and a receding Soviet military threat, the projected $70 billion cost of a planned fleet of 132 B-2 bombers fostered intense Hill skepticism toward the program in 1989.

Built of exotic materials in the shape of a "flying wing," the plane was intended to penetrate Soviet air defenses that would be too lethal for the newly built B-1Bs by the late 1990s. For decades, liberals have challenged the need for sophisticated bombers able to fly through Soviet defense, insisting that the same mission could be performed more cheaply by small, long-range cruise missiles, fired from planes beyond the reach of Soviet defenses.

This year, several prominent Republicans took up that argument, insisting that the B-2 was simply too expensive in the current circumstances.

Bush requested money to buy three of the big bombers in fiscal 1990 and components that could be used to build five more B-2s in fiscal 1991. The House Armed Services Committee, in its version of the defense authorization bill, trimmed the authorization to two planes with components for two more.

By a key vote of 144-279 — R 28-144; D 116-135 (ND 102-68, SD 14-67) — on July 26, the House rejected an amendment to end B-2 production after completing 13 planes already flying or under construction. But it then rejected, 176-244, another amendment to reaffirm the committee position.

The House later voted by 257-160 to adopt an amendment that reduced the committee's B-2 authorization by $470 million and provided that none of the procurement funds could be spent until Congress approved a new, less expensive long-term production plan for the plane. *(Senate key vote 10)*

9. 'Section 89'

Sandwiched in the landmark 1986 tax-overhaul bill between hundreds of other provisions, the so-called "Section 89" rules against discrimination in employee benefit plans at first escaped the watch of many businesses and many in Congress.

But complaints mounted as the implementation date, Jan. 1, 1989, drew near. And while large employers griped about the rules, small businesses least equipped to bear the administrative burden protested the loudest. The complaints often surprised lawmakers, few of whom had ever heard of Section 89.

By the end of the year, sentiment against the rules had grown so intense in the House that opponents overran all efforts to find a compromise. An overwhelming House vote on Sept. 27 to repeal the tax rules forced the Senate to back off its own compromise measure. The repeal provision was finally attached to a bill (H J Res 280 — PL 101-140) raising the federal debt limit, which President Bush signed Nov. 8.

At the start of 1989, the National Federation of Independent Business and the U.S. Chamber of Commerce made repeal or drastic overhaul of Section 89 a top priority. They got a huge boost when House Small Business Chairman John J. LaFalce, D-N.Y., agreed to sponsor a repeal bill, which attracted more than half of the House members as cosponsors.

Meanwhile, Ways and Means Committee leaders and staff, who had drafted the Section 89 provisions, were having second thoughts of their own. Chairman Dan Rostenkowski, D-Ill., agreed to craft a compromise that would revamp the rules. That compromise was folded into the deficit-reduction reconciliation bill (HR 3299 — PL 101-239) moving through the House.

But several of LaFalce's Republican counterparts had other ideas. They urged the House GOP to use Section 89 as a test case for a new, more aggressive legislative strategy and stake everything on repeal. Even Democrats found repeal an easy way to demonstrate that they shared business' worries about excessive government regulation.

But when a bipartisan majority of the Appropriations Committee on July 25 narrowly approved a one-year delay in enforcing the Section 89 rules, Rostenkowski fought back. He lost a key battle in the Rules Committee, however, prompting him to seek further compromise.

Emboldened Section 89 opponents would have none of that, however, preparing the way for a tense vote on outright repeal.

On Sept. 27, the mutiny against Rostenkowski's authority over tax issues turned into a rout. Ways and Means Democrat Byron L. Dorgan of North Dakota offered an amendment to strike Rostenkowski's scaled-backed substitute from the reconciliation bill and repeal the Section 89 tax rules altogether. Lawmakers on both sides of the aisle rushed to support the amendment, which was approved on a vote of 390-36: R 172-2; D 218-34 (ND 140-31, SD 78-3).

10. Capital Gains Tax Cut

President Bush tasted perhaps the sweetest triumph of his first year in office on Sept. 28, when 239 House members voted to cut the tax on capital gains. The plan at issue that day was far from the substance of Bush's own proposal (he had called for a 15 percent top rate for gains on securities and residential real estate, instead of the existing top rate of 28 percent or 33 percent), and it was soon to come to grief in the Senate. But on the House floor, Bush won the support of 64 Democrats who defied their leadership to join Republicans in backing the central feature of the president's tax policy.

The Ways and Means Committee had wrangled over the issue for months, delaying consideration of the fiscal 1990 budget-reconciliation bill (HR 3299 — PL 101-239). Chairman Dan Rostenkowski, D-Ill., whose leanings on capital gains had seemed uncertain through the spring, finally announced against a cut.

Nevertheless, on Sept. 14, a bare majority of the committee supported a two-year plan that would have capped the tax rate at 19.6 percent for a wider range of capital assets, including timber. Rostenkowski, Speaker Thomas S. Foley of Washington and the rest of the Democratic leadership denounced the cut as a tax break for the wealthy and vowed to expunge it from the bill on the floor.

As an alternative, they pushed an amendment restoring universal eligibility for individual retirement accounts (IRAs). To pay for the IRAs, the leadership amendment would have eliminated the "bubble" the 1986 tax overhaul set in the tax rates. In effect, this would have raised the marginal rate from 28 percent to 33 percent on the highest taxpayers' incomes (more than $200,120 for a family of four).

As this amounted to a tax increase, it virtually assured a presidential veto. Moreover, it alienated some members who were otherwise ambivalent about cutting capital gains taxes. In the end, only one House Republican (Doug Bereuter of Nebraska) opposed the president, while a majority of Democrats from the South and from timber-growing districts voted for the cut. The leadership amendment was rejected 190-239: R 1-175; D 189-64 (ND 152-20, SD 37-44). *(Senate key vote 15)*

11. Catastrophic-Illness Insurance

Nothing Congress has done in the 1980s created more aggravation for members than the 1988 Medicare Catastrophic Coverage Act. Hailed at enactment as a shield for senior citizens, it turned into a sword against its authors. By the August recess, Ways and Means Chairman Dan Rostenkowski, D-Ill., who helped write the law, found his car blocked by angry, sign-waving senior citizens when he was leaving a speaking engagement in Chicago.

What happened to Rostenkowski differed only in degree from what confronted virtually every other member of Congress on trips home during the year — a continuing backlash from seniors outraged at being required to pay for the largest expansion of Medicare since it began in 1965.

The Ways and Means Committee agreed just before the August recess to restructure the program's financing. But it was quickly apparent that its action was too little, too late. By the time the issue reached the House floor Oct. 4, members were fed up.

The result was overwhelming approval of an amendment to the fiscal 1990 budget-reconciliation bill (HR 3299 — PL 101-239) that would repeal the program outright. The amendment, offered by one of the 1988 law's authors, Ways and Means member Brian Donnelly, D-Mass., was adopted 360-66: R 164-10; D 196-56 (ND 124-47, SD 72-9).

Two days later, the Senate voted 99-0 to preserve the program's expanded hospital coverage and certain smaller benefits.

But the House position eventually prevailed. Lawmakers cleared a separate repeal measure, HR 3607, only hours before Congress adjourned for the year Nov. 22. *(Senate key vote 12)*

12. Child Care

The new House Democratic leadership team, battered by losses on a capital gains tax cut and several other issues, prevailed Oct. 5 in a floor fight over child care proposals.

Unable to force a compromise between competing plans from the Ways and Means and Education and Labor committees, the leadership reluctantly decided to let both plans stay in the fiscal 1990 budget-reconciliation bill (HR 3299) and resolve the issue in conference. But just as with the capital gains issue, the disagreement left an opening for Republicans to move in and assert themselves.

The leadership was confident that it could turn back the official GOP plan, which would have replaced both Democratic proposals with a simple expansion of the earned-income tax credit (also part of the Ways and Means package). But Democratic leaders feared trouble over an ostensibly bipartisan plan that was cosponsored by Charles W. Stenholm, D-Texas, and E. Clay Shaw Jr., R-Fla., but was drafted by Republican Ways and Means staffers. That plan offered scaled-back elements from both the Education and Labor and Ways and Means proposals.

The leadership pulled out all the stops to defeat Stenholm's plan, which failed Oct. 5 by 195-230: R 159-16; D 36-214 (ND 6-163, SD 30-51).

While a temporary truce between Education and Labor and Ways and Means members to save their proposals certainly helped Democratic leaders, members on both sides said a more decisive factor was rank-and-file Democrats — particularly those who voted against their leaders on the capital gains tax — who wanted to prevent another embarrassing loss for their new top team. Indeed, only 36

Democrats defected from the party line, compared with 64 who broke ranks on the capital gains tax vote the previous week.

The disagreements over how to produce a child care bill proved impossible to resolve in the context of the reconciliation bill, and the issue was put off until 1990. *(Senate key vote 5)*

13. Abortion Funding

The July 3 Supreme Court decision in *Webster v. Reproductive Health Services*, which gave states a green light for stiff new restrictions on abortion, may have been a Pyrrhic victory for abortion opponents. The ruling galvanized abortion rights advocates, who wasted no time putting the heat on their elected representatives. Virtually overnight, abortion became the dominant political issue of the year.

Nowhere was the shift in political momentum more obvious than in the House, where abortion rights forces had not prevailed on a single vote since 1980.

The first sign of change came Aug. 2, when the House rejected, 206-219, an amendment offered by Robert K. Dornan, R-Calif., to the fiscal 1990 spending bill for the District of Columbia that sought to bar the city from using its own tax dollars (as well as federal funds) to pay for abortions for poor women. The year before, the House had approved a similar ban by 222-186.

No one was quite sure how to read the D.C. vote, though; it was muddied by issues relating to the city's home rule rights and by an odd parliamentary situation that prohibited Dornan from offering language that would allow funding for abortions necessary to save the life of a woman.

No such doubts existed Oct. 11, when the House took up the conference report for the $156.7 billion fiscal 1990 appropriation for the departments of Labor, Health and Human Services (HHS), and Education and related agencies. As had been true several times in the 1980s, the original House version barred federal funding of all abortions except in cases in which a woman's life was in danger, while the Senate version also allowed funding of abortions in cases of rape or incest "promptly reported" to public health or law enforcement authorities.

Thirteen months earlier, in dealing with the conference report on the fiscal 1989 Labor-HHS bill, the House had voted 216-166 to insist on its position, and the Senate gave in. But this time, the outcome was different. In a stunning turnabout that saw a swing of 50 votes from the year before, the House agreed to a motion offered by Barbara Boxer, D-Calif., that the House recede from its position. The vote was 216-206: R 41-134; D 175-72 (ND 124-44, SD 51-28).

In a second vote moments later, the House voted 212-207 to concur in the Senate's rape and incest amendment.

President Bush vetoed the Labor-HHS bill over its abortion language, and the House on Oct. 25 fell 51 votes short in an attempt to override. Members did not try to override vetoes of two other spending bills Bush had rejected for abortion related reasons — those for D.C. and foreign operations. But, even though abortion rights advocates gave in for 1989, they vowed to continue the battle in 1990 and to make abortion a central issue in that year's elections.

14. Aid to Poland and Hungary

Along with everyone else, members of Congress watched with awe and wonder as one Eastern European communist regime after another fell during 1989. There was little the United States could do to encourage the process, but Washington's political leaders were determined to help ensure that the new reformist regimes, in what used to be called the Soviet bloc, would not fail.

Poland and Hungary were the first two countries to escape Moscow's clutches, and they were the ones most in need of Western financial assistance. President Bush announced several aid packages for the two countries, each package somewhat more generous than its predecessors. Sensing political opportunity in Bush's characteristic caution, Democrats in Congress began a campaign to denounce his "timidity" and sought to prove that they were more eager to help the reform governments in Warsaw and Budapest.

After several weeks of negotiations, House leaders of both parties settled on a proposal authorizing $837.5 million in various forms of aid to Poland and Hungary over three years — nearly twice as much as Bush had requested. Despite the administration's refusal to endorse that proposal (HR 3402), the House approved it on Oct. 19 by 345-47 — R 128-34; D 217-13 (ND 152-4, SD 65-9) — an unusually lopsided vote for a foreign aid program.

More negotiations involving the Senate and the administration produced a three-year authorization total of $938 million, with $532.8 million appropriated in fiscal 1990. However, both totals were inflated by a $200 million trade credit program that was considered unlikely to get off the ground. Those figures also included a suggested $125 million donation of food aid for Poland in fiscal 1990 — most of which Bush had already provided.

15. Oil-Spill Liability

Congressional outrage over the March 24 *Exxon Valdez* oil spill did what 14 years of inconclusive wrangling had never achieved: It erased the key difference between the House and the Senate on oil-spill liability legislation, bringing passage of a bill nearer than it has been since Congress began debating the issue in 1975.

The crucial roll call came Nov. 8, when the House reversed more than a decade of tradition and voted for an amendment to prohibit federal liability provisions from taking precedence over stricter state oil-spill laws.

The House passed the bill (HR 1465) on a 375-5 vote, clearing the way for a conference with the Senate in 1990.

The House and the Senate had long ago roughly agreed on the shape of oil-spill legislation. Bills on both sides of the Hill envisioned taxing imported and domestic oil to create a huge spill-cleanup and damage-compensation fund. A spiller's liability would be limited at a level to take care of most spills, and the fund would pay any further costs. However, if the spill was caused by gross negligence or willful misconduct, or if it involved failing to observe federal regulations, the spiller would be liable for all costs.

But the House and the Senate diverged sharply over whether the federal liability and compensation regime should override state laws. The Senate said no, insisting that states with their own oil-spill laws and cleanup funds should be allowed to keep them, even if that meant exposing spillers to unlimited liability, as at least 17 state laws do. Proponents of the hands-off approach argued that other federal environmental laws allowed states to keep and enforce their own statutes. The Senate passed a non-pre-emption bill (S 686) by 99-0 on Aug. 4. Majority Leader George J. Mitchell, D-Maine, had threatened early in the year not to go to conference at all if the House passed a measure that pre-empted state laws, as it had done repeatedly in previous years.

For a while, it seemed that the House would approve a pre-emption statute again. Bills reported by both the Merchant Marine and the Public Works committees carried language that pre-empted state liability laws and restricted the uses of state cleanup and compensation funds. Authors of HR 1465 argued that it made little sense to impose a national liability and compensation system that did not replace the patchwork of conflicting state laws.

But as when the Senate passed its bill, the mood in the House when the issue came to the floor in November was decidedly pro-environmental and anti-big oil, and many members were looking for ways to strike back at spillers. Critics of pre-emption repeatedly invoked the *Exxon Valdez* disaster, arguing that the House should not reward big oil by setting up national liability limits and junking stricter state laws. A package of amendments offered by George Miller, D-Calif., and Gerry E. Studds, D-Mass., included provisions to strike pre-emption language, and the House agreed to do so, voting 279-143: R 75-99; D 204-44 (ND 155-14, SD 49-30).

16. Pay and Ethics Package

Nine months after Congress bowed to a storm of public criticism and rejected a 51 percent pay raise, House leaders transformed the dynamics of the issue and won approval of legislation (HR 3660 — PL 101-194) combining a hike of nearly 40 percent over two years with the first overhaul of House ethics rules in 12 years.

The key vote came when House members swallowed political qualms and approved the pay and ethics package by a margin of 252-174 — R 84-89; D 168-85 (ND 121-52, SD 47-33).

Although the Senate balked and took a smaller increase of 10 percent for itself, it let stand the larger raise for House members and other government officials.

The raise was a coup for Thomas S. Foley of Washington, who became Speaker at midyear after Jim Wright resigned under an ethics cloud.

In February, Congress blocked the 51 percent pay raise in the face of virulent opposition from the public, which was unappeased by promises that Congress would ban honoraria after the pay raise took effect. Although many thought the pay plan was doomed from the start, some Democrats blamed Wright for its defeat.

Foley succeeded where Wright had failed in part because the pay raise proposal he pushed at year's end had many features to make it more palatable than the earlier proposal: It was a smaller hike, with the biggest part taking effect only after an election, and the proposal was subject to open debate and a recorded vote.

Moreover, it was conspicuously linked to ethics rules changes a bipartisan task force had drafted. And to allay concerns about political fallout, top political operatives in both parties signed a letter pledging to oppose publicly using the pay raise vote as a campaign issue.

In testament to widespread skepticism that the promise was the end of pay as a political issue, the rolls of those who voted against the bill were dominated by politically vulnerable junior members and House members with higher political ambitions. *(Senate key vote 16)*

KEY

Y Voted for (yea).
Paired for.
+ Announced for.
N Voted against (nay).
X Paired against.
- Announced against.
P Voted "present."
C Voted "present" to avoid possible conflict of interest.
? Did not vote or otherwise make a position known.

Democrats *Republicans*

	1	2	3	4	5	6	7	8
ALABAMA								
Heflin	Y	Y	Y	Y	N	N	Y	Y
Shelby	N	Y	Y	Y	N	Y	Y	Y
ALASKA								
Murkowski	Y	Y	N	?	Y	N	Y	N
Stevens	Y	Y	N	Y	Y	N	Y	N
ARIZONA								
DeConcini	N	Y	N	N	N	Y	N	Y
McCain	Y	Y	N	Y	Y	N	Y	N
ARKANSAS								
Bumpers	N	Y	Y	Y	N	Y	N	Y
Pryor	N	Y	Y	Y	N	Y	N	Y
CALIFORNIA								
Cranston	N	N	N	Y	N	Y	N	Y
Wilson	Y	Y	Y	N	Y	N	Y	N
COLORADO								
Wirth	N	Y	N	Y	N	Y	N	Y
Armstrong	Y	Y	N	Y	Y	N	Y	N
CONNECTICUT								
Dodd	Y	Y	Y	Y	N	Y	N	Y
Lieberman	N	Y	Y	N	N	Y	N	Y
DELAWARE								
Biden	N	Y	Y	N	N	Y	N	Y
Roth	Y	Y	N	Y	Y	N	Y	N
FLORIDA								
Graham	N	Y	Y	Y	N	Y	Y	Y
Mack	Y	Y	N	Y	Y	N	Y	N
GEORGIA								
Fowler	N	Y	N	Y	N	Y	N	Y
Nunn	N	Y	Y	Y	Y	Y	Y	Y
HAWAII								
Inouye	N	Y	N	Y	N	Y	N	Y
Matsunaga	N	Y	N	Y	N	?	?	Y
IDAHO								
McClure	Y	Y	N	Y	Y	N	?	N
Symms	Y	Y	N	?	Y	N	Y	N
ILLINOIS								
Dixon	N	Y	Y	Y	N	Y	Y	N
Simon	N	Y	Y	Y	N	Y	N	Y
INDIANA								
Coats	Y	N	Y	N	Y	N	Y	N
Lugar	Y	Y	N	?	Y	N	Y	N
IOWA								
Harkin	N	N	Y	?	N	Y	N	Y
Grassley	Y	N	Y	Y	Y	N	N	N
KANSAS								
Dole	Y	Y	N	Y	Y	N	Y	N
Kassebaum	N	Y	N	Y	Y	N	Y	N
KENTUCKY								
Ford	N	Y	Y	Y	N	Y	N	Y
McConnell	Y	Y	Y	N	Y	N	Y	N
LOUISIANA								
Breaux	N	Y	Y	Y	N	Y	N	Y
Johnston	N	Y	N	Y	N	Y	N	Y
MAINE								
Mitchell	N	Y	Y	Y	N	Y	N	Y
Cohen	Y	Y	N	N	Y	Y	Y	N
MARYLAND								
Mikulski	N	Y	Y	Y	N	Y	N	Y
Sarbanes	N	Y	Y	Y	N	Y	N	Y
MASSACHUSETTS								
Kennedy	N	Y	N	Y	N	Y	N	Y
Kerry	N	Y	Y	N	N	Y	N	Y
MICHIGAN								
Levin	N	Y	Y	Y	N	Y	N	Y
Riegle	N	Y	Y	N	N	Y	N	Y
MINNESOTA								
Boschwitz	Y	Y	N	N	Y	N	Y	N
Durenberger	Y	+	N	Y	Y	Y	Y	N
MISSISSIPPI								
Cochran	Y	Y	N	Y	Y	N	Y	N
Lott	Y	Y	N	Y	Y	N	Y	N
MISSOURI								
Bond	Y	Y	N	Y	Y	N	Y	N
Danforth	Y	Y	N	Y	Y	N	Y	N
MONTANA								
Baucus	N	Y	Y	Y	N	Y	N	Y
Burns	Y	Y	N	Y	Y	N	Y	N
NEBRASKA								
Exon	N	Y	Y	Y	N	Y	Y	Y
Kerrey	N	Y	Y	Y	N	Y	N	Y
NEVADA								
Bryan	N	Y	Y	Y	N	Y	Y	Y
Reid	N	Y	Y	Y	N	Y	N	Y
NEW HAMPSHIRE								
Humphrey	Y	Y	N	N	Y	N	Y	N
Rudman	Y	Y	Y	Y	Y	Y	Y	N
NEW JERSEY								
Bradley	N	N	N	N	N	Y	N	Y
Lautenberg	N	Y	N	Y	N	Y	N	Y
NEW MEXICO								
Bingaman	N	Y	N	Y	N	Y	Y	Y
Domenici	Y	Y	Y	Y	Y	N	Y	N
NEW YORK								
Moynihan	N	Y	?	Y	N	Y	N	Y
D'Amato	Y	Y	Y	N	Y	N	Y	N
NORTH CAROLINA								
Sanford	N	Y	Y	Y	N	Y	N	Y
Helms	Y	N	Y	Y	Y	N	Y	N
NORTH DAKOTA								
Burdick	N	Y	Y	Y	N	Y	N	Y
Conrad	N	Y	Y	Y	Y	Y	N	N
OHIO								
Glenn	N	Y	Y	Y	N	Y	N	Y
Metzenbaum	N	Y	Y	Y	N	Y	N	Y
OKLAHOMA								
Boren	N	Y	Y	Y	N	Y	Y	Y
Nickles	Y	Y	N	Y	Y	N	Y	N
OREGON								
Hatfield	Y	Y	N	Y	Y	N	N	N
Packwood	Y	Y	N	Y	Y	N	Y	N
PENNSYLVANIA								
Heinz	Y	Y	Y	N	Y	N	N	N
Specter	Y	N	N	N	Y	Y	N	N
RHODE ISLAND								
Pell	N	Y	N	Y	N	Y	N	Y
Chafee	Y	Y	N	Y	N	N	N	N
SOUTH CAROLINA								
Hollings	N	Y	N	Y	N	Y	Y	Y
Thurmond	Y	Y	N	Y	Y	N	Y	N
SOUTH DAKOTA								
Daschle	N	Y	N	Y	N	Y	N	Y
Pressler	Y	Y	Y	Y	Y	N	N	Y
TENNESSEE								
Gore	N	?	N	Y	N	Y	Y	Y
Sasser	N	Y	Y	Y	N	Y	N	Y
TEXAS								
Bentsen	Y	Y	N	Y	N	Y	N	Y
Gramm	Y	Y	N	Y	Y	N	Y	N
UTAH								
Garn	Y	Y	N	Y	Y	N	Y	N
Hatch	Y	Y	N	N	N	N	Y	N
VERMONT								
Leahy	N	Y	Y	Y	N	Y	N	Y
Jeffords	Y	Y	N	Y	N	N	?	N
VIRGINIA								
Robb	N	Y	N	N	N	Y	Y	Y
Warner	Y	Y	N	Y	Y	N	Y	N
WASHINGTON								
Adams	N	N	Y	Y	N	Y	N	Y
Gorton	Y	Y	N	Y	Y	N	Y	N
WEST VIRGINIA								
Byrd	N	Y	Y	Y	N	Y	Y	Y
Rockefeller	N	Y	N	Y	N	Y	N	Y
WISCONSIN								
Kohl	N	Y	Y	Y	N	Y	N	Y
Kasten	Y	Y	Y	Y	Y	N	Y	N
WYOMING								
Simpson	Y	Y	N	?	Y	N	Y	N
Wallop	Y	N	N	N	Y	N	Y	N

ND Northern Democrats SD Southern Democrats Southern states - Ala., Ark., Fla., Ga., Ky., La., Miss., N.C., Okla., S.C., Tenn., Texas, Va.

1. Tower Nomination. Confirmation of President Bush's nomination of John Tower of Texas to be secretary of defense. Rejected 47-53: R 44-1; D 3-52 (ND 1-37, SD 2-15), March 9, 1989. A "yea" was a vote supporting the president's position.

2. HR 1750. Contra Aid/Passage. Passage of the bill to provide $49.75 million in non-military aid to the contras. The bill also includes $5 million for administration of the Agency for International Development, an unspecified amount for transportation of the aid, and $4.2 million for medical aid to victims of the war in Nicaragua. Passed 89-9: R 39-5; D 50-4 (ND 34-4, SD 16-0), April 13, 1989. A "yea" was a vote supporting the president's position.

3. S J Res 113. FS-X Plane Development/Disapproval. Dixon, D-Ill., amendment to the Byrd, D-W.Va., amendment to the resolution, to bar the proposed transfer to Japanese firms of design data on the F-16 fighter plane that would be used for the joint development by U.S. and Japanese firms of a modified version of a plane, designated the FS-X, for Japan's use. Rejected 47-52: R 11-34; D 36-18 (ND 25-12, SD 11-6), May 16, 1989. (In effect, the vote on this amendment was a vote on the underlying resolution to block the deal.) A "nay" was a vote supporting the president's position.

4. HR 2072. Fiscal 1989 Supplemental Appropriations/Budget Act Waiver. Byrd, D-W.Va., motion to table (kill) the Specter, R-Pa., motion to waive the Congressional Budget Act of 1974 to permit consideration of the Specter amendment to transfer $70 million from defense appropriations to prison construction. Motion agreed to 77-18: R 30-11; D 47-7 (ND 31-6, SD 16-1), June 1, 1989. A "yea" was a vote supporting the president's position. (The amendment subsequently fell on a point of order.)

5. S 5. Child Care/Dole Substitute. Dole, R-Kan., amendment to the Mitchell, D-Maine, substitute, to make the dependent-care tax credit refundable, to expand the earned-income tax credit by adjusting it for family size for children aged 4 or under, and to increase block grants to the states by $400 million to increase the availability of child care. Rejected 44-56: R 42-3; D 2-53 (ND 1-37, SD 1-16), June 22, 1989. A "yea" was a vote supporting the president's position.

6. S 1160. Fiscal 1990 State Department Authorization/Prohibited Activities. Moynihan, D-N.Y., amendment to prohibit the solicitation or diversion of funds to carry out activities for which U.S. foreign assistance is prohibited. Adopted 57-42: R 4-41; D 53-1 (ND 37-0, SD 16-1), July 18, 1989. A "nay" was a vote supporting the president's position.

7. S 1352. Fiscal 1990-91 Defense Department Authorization/SDI Funding. Nunn, D-Ga., motion to table (kill) the Johnston, D-La., amendment to reduce to $3.95 billion appropriations for the strategic defense initiative (SDI) program. Motion agreed to 50-47: R 37-6; D 13-41 (ND 5-32, SD 8-9), July 27, 1989. A "yea" was a vote supporting the president's position.

8. HR 1278. Savings and Loan Restructuring/Budget Act Waiver. Riegle, D-Mich., motion to waive Titles III and IV (which, among other things, prohibit breaching deficit ceilings established by the current budget resolution) of the Congressional Budget Act of 1974 with respect to the conference report on the bill to salvage the nation's savings and loan industry and overhaul federal thrift regulation. Motion rejected 54-46: R 1-44; D 53-2 (ND 36-2, SD 17-0), Aug. 3, 1989. A three-fifths majority vote (60) of the total Senate is required to waive the Budget Act. A "nay" was a vote supporting the president's position.

1. HR 1750. Contra Aid/Passage. Passage of the bill to provide $49.75 million in non-military aid to the Nicaraguan contras, including $5 million for administration of the Agency for International Development, an unspecified amount for aid transportation, and $4.2 million for medical aid to victims of the war. Passed 309-110: R 157-11; D 152-99 (ND 84-87, SD 68-12), April 13, 1989. A "yea" was a vote supporting the president's position.

2. HR 2072. Fiscal 1989 Supplemental Appropriations/Offsetting Cuts. Foley, D-Wash., amendment to offset new discretionary outlays provided in the bill with across-the-board percentage cuts in budget authority of 0.57 percent in all discretionary accounts of the government, including defense, foreign affairs and domestic programs, except those programs funded in the bill. Rejected 172-252: R 9-160; D 163-92 (ND 129-44, SD 34-48), April 26, 1989. A "nay" was a vote supporting the president's position. (The bill was later withdrawn from floor consideration.)

3. H Con Res 106. Fiscal 1990 Budget Resolution/Adoption. Adoption of the concurrent resolution to set forth the congressional budget for the U.S. government for fiscal 1990-92. It sets fiscal 1990 ceilings of $1.351 trillion in budget authority and $1.165 trillion in outlays; establishes a revenue floor of $1.066 trillion, with an expected deficit of $99.7 billion; and recommends general spending levels for the various functions of government conforming to the bipartisan budget agreement with the White House for defense and non-defense discretionary spending levels. Adopted 263-157: R 106-61; D 157-96 (ND 102-71, SD 55-25), May 4, 1989.

4. HR 2. Minimum Wage Increase/Veto Override. Passage, over President Bush's June 13 veto, of the bill to raise the minimum wage from $3.35 an hour to $4.55 over three years, and to provide for a 60-day training wage — equal to 85 percent of the minimum — for workers who have not worked a total of 60 days. Rejected 247-178: R 20-150; D 227-28 (ND 171-3, SD 56-25), June 14, 1989. A two-thirds majority of those present and voting (284 in this case) of both houses is required to override a veto. A "nay" was a vote supporting the president's position.

5. HR 1278. Savings and Loan Restructuring/Capital Standards. Hyde, R-Ill., amendment to give savings and loan associations with supervisory "good will" on their books as capital the ability to seek formal hearings — subject to court review — on whether that good will was granted through an enforceable contract that should be upheld, allowing it to continue to count as capital, despite provisions in the bill to the contrary. Rejected 94-326: R 56-114; D 38-212 (ND 30-144, SD 8-68), June 15, 1989. A "nay" was a vote supporting the president's position.

6. HR 2696. Energy and Water Appropriations/Supercollider. Eckart, D-Ohio, amendment to delete $110 million for initial construction of the superconducting supercollider, leaving $90 million for continued research on the project. Rejected 93-330: R 28-144; D 65-186 (ND 57-112, SD 8-74), June 28, 1989. A "nay" was a vote supporting the president's position.

7. HR 2461. Fiscal 1990-91 Defense Department Authorization/SDI Funding. Bennett, D-Fla., amendment to decrease the authorization in the bill for the strategic defense initiative (SDI) to $3.1 billion for the Defense and Energy departments. Adopted 248-175: R 34-137; D 214-38 (ND 163-7, SD 51-31), July 25, 1989. A "nay" was a vote supporting the president's position.

8. HR 2461. Fiscal 1990-91 Defense Department Authorization/'Stealth.' Kasich, R-Ohio, substitute for the Synar, D-Okla., amendment, to allow the Air Force to complete a fleet of 13 B-2s already built or under construction and then to put the production line on hold while those 13 are used to test the new plane's exotic design. Rejected 144-279: R 28-144; D 116-135 (ND 102-68, SD 14-67), July 26, 1989. A "nay" was a vote supporting the president's position.

KEY

Y	Voted for (yea).
#	Paired for.
+	Announced for.
N	Voted against (nay).
X	Paired against.
-	Announced against.
P	Voted "present."
C	Voted "present" to avoid possible conflict of interest.
?	Did not vote or otherwise make a position known.

Democrats ***Republicans***
Independent

ND Northern Democrats
SD Southern Democrats

Southern states - Ala., Ark., Fla., Ga., Ky., La., Miss., N.C., Okla., S.C., Tenn., Texas, Va.

	1	2	3	4	5	6	7	8
ALABAMA								
1 ***Callahan***	Y	N	Y	N	N	N	N	N
2 ***Dickinson***	Y	N	Y	N	N	N	N	N
3 Browder [1]		N	Y	Y	N	N	N	N
4 Bevill	Y	N	Y	Y	N	N	N	N
5 Flippo	Y	N	Y	Y	N	N	N	N
6 Erdreich	Y	N	Y	Y	N	N	N	N
7 Harris	Y	N	Y	Y	N	N	N	N
ALASKA								
AL ***Young***	Y	N	Y	N	Y	N	N	N
ARIZONA								
1 ***Rhodes***	Y	N	Y	N	N	N	N	N
2 Udall	Y	Y	Y	Y	N	N	Y	Y
3 ***Stump***	N	N	Y	N	Y	N	N	N
4 ***Kyl***	Y	N	N	N	Y	N	N	N
5 ***Kolbe***	Y	N	Y	N	N	N	N	Y
ARKANSAS								
1 Alexander	Y	N	N	N	Y	Y	Y	Y
2 Robinson	Y	N	N	Y	N	Y	N	N
3 ***Hammerschmidt***	Y	N	Y	N	Y	N	N	N
4 Anthony	Y	Y	Y	Y	N	N	Y	N
CALIFORNIA								
1 Bosco	N	Y	Y	Y	N	N	Y	N
2 ***Herger***	Y	N	N	N	N	N	N	N
3 Matsui	N	Y	Y	Y	N	N	Y	N
4 Fazio	Y	Y	Y	Y	N	N	Y	N
5 Pelosi	N	Y	Y	Y	N	N	Y	Y
6 Boxer	N	Y	Y	Y	N	N	Y	Y
7 Miller	N	Y	Y	Y	N	Y	Y	Y
8 Dellums	N	Y	N	Y	N	Y	Y	Y
9 Stark	N	Y	N	Y	N	Y	Y	Y
10 Edwards	N	Y	Y	Y	N	N	Y	Y
11 Lantos	Y	Y	Y	Y	N	Y	Y	N
12 ***Campbell***	Y	N	Y	N	N	Y	Y	N
13 Mineta	N	Y	Y	Y	N	N	Y	Y
14 ***Shumway***	Y	N	N	N	Y	N	N	N
15 Coelho[2]	Y	Y	Y	Y	N			
15 Panetta	N	Y	Y	Y	N	N	Y	Y
17 ***Pashayan***	Y	N	Y	N	N	N	N	N
18 Lehman	N	Y	Y	Y	N	N	Y	Y
19 ***Lagomarsino***	Y	N	N	N	N	N	N	N
20 ***Thomas***	Y	N	Y	N	N	N	N	N
21 ***Gallegly***	Y	N	Y	N	N	N	N	N
22 ***Moorhead***	Y	N	N	N	Y	N	N	N
23 Beilenson	Y	Y	N	Y	N	Y	Y	Y
24 Waxman	Y	Y	Y	Y	N	N	Y	Y
25 Roybal	N	Y	#	Y	N	N	Y	Y
26 Berman	Y	Y	Y	Y	N	Y	Y	Y
27 Levine	Y	Y	N	Y	N	N	Y	Y
28 Dixon	Y	Y	Y	Y	N	N	Y	N
29 Hawkins	N	N	Y	Y	N	N	Y	Y
30 Martinez	N	?	Y	Y	N	Y	Y	Y
31 Dymally	N	Y	N	Y	N	N	Y	N
32 Anderson	Y	N	Y	Y	N	N	Y	N
33 ***Dreier***	Y	N	N	N	Y	N	N	N
34 Torres	N	Y	Y	Y	N	N	Y	N
35 ***Lewis***	Y	N	?	N	N	N	N	N
36 Brown	N	N	Y	Y	N	N	Y	N
37 ***McCandless***	Y	N	N	N	Y	N	N	N
38 ***Dornan***	N	N	N	?	Y	N	N	N
39 ***Dannemeyer***	Y	N	N	N	Y	N	N	X
40 ***Cox***	Y	N	N	N	N	N	N	N
41 ***Lowery***	Y	N	Y	N	Y	N	N	N
42 ***Rohrabacher***	Y	N	Y	N	N	Y	N	N
43 ***Packard***	Y	N	Y	N	Y	N	N	N
44 Bates	N	Y	N	Y	N	Y	Y	Y
45 ***Hunter***	N	N	Y	N	N	N	N	N
COLORADO								
1 Schroeder	N	Y	N	Y	N	Y	Y	Y
2 Skaggs	Y	Y	N	Y	N	N	Y	Y
3 Campbell	N	Y	N	N	N	N	Y	N
4 ***Brown***	Y	Y	N	N	N	N	N	N
5 ***Hefley***	?	N	N	N	Y	Y	N	N
6 ***Schaefer***	Y	N	N	N	N	N	N	N
CONNECTICUT								
1 Kennelly	N	Y	Y	Y	N	N	Y	N
2 Gejdenson	Y	Y	Y	Y	N	N	Y	Y
3 Morrison	N	Y	N	Y	N	Y	Y	Y
4 ***Shays***	Y	Y	N	Y	N	Y	Y	Y
5 ***Rowland***	Y	N	Y	Y	N	N	N	Y
6 ***Johnson***	Y	N	Y	Y	N	N	N	N
DELAWARE								
AL Carper	Y	Y	N	Y	N	Y	Y	Y
FLORIDA								
1 Hutto	Y	N	Y	N	N	N	N	N
2 ***Grant***	Y	N	Y	N	N	N	Y	N
3 Bennett	Y	N	Y	Y	N	N	Y	Y
4 ***James***	Y	N	Y	N	Y	N	N	N
5 ***McCollum***	Y	N	Y	N	N	N	N	N
6 ***Stearns***	Y	N	N	N	N	N	N	N
7 Gibbons	Y	Y	Y	Y	N	N	Y	Y
8 ***Young***	Y	?	N	N	N	N	N	N
9 ***Bilirakis***	Y	?	N	N	N	N	N	N
10 ***Ireland***	Y	N	Y	N	N	N	N	Y
11 Nelson	Y	N	N	Y	N	N	N	N
12 ***Lewis***	Y	N	N	N	N	N	N	N
13 ***Goss***	Y	N	N	N	N	N	N	N
14 Johnston	Y	Y	Y	Y	N	Y	Y	Y
15 ***Shaw***	Y	N	N	N	N	N	N	Y
16 Smith	Y	Y	Y	Y	N	N	Y	N
17 Lehman	?	Y	N	Y	-	N	Y	Y
18 Pepper[3]	?	?	?					
19 Fascell	Y	Y	Y	Y	N	N	Y	N
GEORGIA								
1 Thomas	Y	N	N	N	N	N	N	N
2 Hatcher	Y	N	Y	Y	N	N	N	N
3 Ray	Y	N	N	N	N	N	Y	N
4 Jones	Y	N	N	Y	N	N	Y	N
5 Lewis	N	Y	N	Y	N	N	Y	Y
6 ***Gingrich***	Y	N	Y	N	N	N	N	N
7 Darden	Y	N	Y	Y	N	N	N	N
8 Rowland	Y	N	Y	N	N	N	N	N
9 Jenkins	Y	N	Y	Y	N	N	N	N
10 Barnard	Y	N	Y	N	N	N	N	N
HAWAII								
1 ***Saiki***	Y	Y	Y	N	Y	N	Y	N
2 Akaka	Y	Y	Y	Y	N	N	Y	N
IDAHO								
1 ***Craig***	Y	N	N	N	Y	Y	N	N
2 Stallings	Y	Y	Y	Y	N	N	Y	N
ILLINOIS								
1 Hayes	N	Y	N	Y	N	Y	Y	Y
2 Savage	N	Y	N	Y	N	N	Y	Y
3 Russo	N	Y	Y	Y	Y	N	Y	Y
4 Sangmeister	Y	Y	Y	Y	N	Y	Y	Y
5 Lipinski	Y	Y	Y	Y	Y	N	?	N
6 ***Hyde***	Y	N	Y	N	Y	N	?	?
7 Collins	N	Y	N	?	?	X	?	?
8 Rostenkowski	Y	Y	Y	Y	N	N	Y	N
9 Yates	N	N	N	Y	N	N	Y	Y
10 ***Porter***	Y	N	N	N	Y	N	Y	Y
11 Annunzio	+	Y	Y	Y	Y	N	Y	N
12 ***Crane***	Y	N	N	N	Y	N	N	N
13 ***Fawell***	Y	N	N	N	Y	N	N	N
14 ***Hastert***	Y	N	Y	N	Y	Y	N	N
15 ***Madigan***	Y	N	Y	N	C	N	N	Y
16 ***Martin***	Y	N	Y	Y	N	N	N	N
17 Evans	N	Y	Y	Y	N	Y	Y	Y
18 ***Michel***	Y	N	?	N	N	N	N	N
19 Bruce	N	Y	Y	Y	Y	N	Y	Y
20 Durbin	N	N	Y	Y	Y	N	Y	Y
21 Costello	N	Y	N	Y	N	N	Y	N
22 Poshard	N	Y	N	Y	N	N	Y	Y
INDIANA								
1 Visclosky	Y	N	N	Y	N	Y	Y	Y
2 Sharp	Y	Y	N	Y	N	Y	Y	Y
3 ***Hiler***	Y	N	Y	N	Y	N	N	N

[1] *Rep. Glen Browder, D-Ala., was sworn in April 18, 1989, to succeed Bill Nichols, D, who died Dec. 13, 1988.*
[2] *Rep. Tony Coelho, D-Calif., resigned June 15, 1989.*
[3] *Rep. Claude Pepper, D-Fla., died May 30, 1989.*
[4] *Jim Wright, D-Texas, resigned as Speaker, who votes at his own discretion, June 6, 1989. He resigned from the House June 30.*
[5] *Rep. Thomas S. Foley, D-Wash., was elected Speaker June 6, 1989. Speaker votes at his own discretion.*
[6] *Rep. Craig Thomas, R-Wyo., was sworn in May 2, 1989, to succeed Dick Cheney,*

Member	1	2	3	4	5	6	7	8
4 Long	Y	Y	N	Y	N	Y	Y	N
5 Jontz	N	Y	N	Y	N	Y	Y	Y
6 ***Burton***	Y	N	N	N	Y	N	N	N
7 ***Myers***	Y	N	Y	N	N	N	N	N
8 McCloskey	N	Y	Y	Y	N	N	Y	N
9 Hamilton	Y	Y	N	Y	N	Y	Y	N
10 Jacobs	N	Y	N	Y	Y	Y	Y	Y
IOWA								
1 ***Leach***	Y	Y	Y	Y	N	Y	Y	Y
2 ***Tauke***	Y	N	Y	N	N	N	Y	Y
3 Nagle	Y	Y	N	Y	N	N	Y	N
4 Smith	N	Y	N	Y	Y	?	Y	N
5 ***Lightfoot***	Y	N	N	N	N	N	Y	N
6 ***Grandy***	Y	N	Y	N	N	N	Y	Y
KANSAS								
1 ***Roberts***	Y	N	N	N	Y	N	N	N
2 Slattery	Y	Y	Y	Y	Y	N	Y	N
3 ***Meyers***	Y	N	Y	N	N	N	Y	N
4 Glickman	Y	N	Y	Y	N	#	Y	N
5 ***Whittaker***	Y	N	Y	N	Y	N	N	N
KENTUCKY								
1 Hubbard	Y	N	Y	+	N	N	Y	N
2 Natcher	N	N	Y	Y	N	N	Y	N
3 Mazzoli	Y	Y	Y	N	N	N	Y	N
4 ***Bunning***	N	N	N	N	N	N	N	N
5 ***Rogers***	Y	N	N	N	N	N	N	N
6 ***Hopkins***	Y	N	N	N	N	N	N	Y
7 Perkins	N	N	N	Y	N	N	Y	Y
LOUISIANA								
1 ***Livingston***	Y	N	Y	N	Y	N	N	N
2 Boggs	Y	N	Y	Y	Y	N	Y	N
3 Tauzin	Y	Y	N	N	Y	N	Y	N
4 ***McCrery***	Y	N	Y	N	N	N	N	N
5 Huckaby	Y	Y	Y	N	N	N	Y	N
6 ***Baker***	Y	N	N	N	Y	N	N	N
7 Hayes	Y	Y	Y	Y	C	N	N	N
8 ***Holloway***	N	Y	N	N	Y	N	N	N
MAINE								
1 Brennan	N	Y	Y	Y	N	Y	Y	Y
2 ***Snowe***	Y	N	Y	N	N	Y	Y	N
MARYLAND								
1 Dyson	Y	N	Y	Y	N	N	N	N
2 ***Bentley***	Y	N	N	N	N	?	N	N
3 Cardin	Y	Y	N	Y	N	N	Y	Y
4 McMillen	Y	N	Y	Y	N	N	N	N
5 Hoyer	Y	Y	Y	Y	N	N	Y	N
6 Byron	Y	N	Y	N	Y	N	N	N
7 Mfume	Y	Y	N	Y	N	N	Y	Y
8 ***Morella***	Y	Y	Y	Y	N	N	Y	Y
MASSACHUSETTS								
1 ***Conte***	N	N	Y	Y	N	N	Y	Y
2 Neal	Y	Y	N	Y	N	Y	Y	Y
3 Early	N	N	N	Y	Y	Y	Y	Y
4 Frank	N	Y	N	Y	N	Y	Y	Y
5 Atkins	Y	Y	Y	Y	N	N	Y	Y
6 Mavroules	Y	N	Y	Y	N	N	Y	N
7 Markey	N	Y	N	Y	N	Y	Y	Y
8 Kennedy	N	N	N	Y	N	Y	Y	Y
9 Moakley	Y	Y	Y	Y	N	N	Y	Y
10 Studds	N	N	N	Y	N	Y	Y	Y
11 Donnelly	Y	Y	Y	Y	N	N	Y	N
MICHIGAN								
1 Conyers	N	Y	Y	Y	N	Y	Y	?
2 ***Pursell***	Y	N	Y	N	N	N	Y	N
3 Wolpe	Y	Y	Y	Y	N	Y	Y	Y
4 ***Upton***	Y	N	Y	N	N	N	N	N
5 ***Henry***	Y	N	N	N	N	N	Y	N
6 Carr	N	N	N	Y	Y	N	Y	N
7 Kildee	Y	Y	Y	Y	N	Y	Y	Y
8 Traxler	?	Y	N	Y	N	N	Y	Y
9 ***Vander Jagt***	Y	N	Y	N	N	N	N	N
10 ***Schuette***	Y	Y	N	N	N	N	?	N
11 ***Davis***	?	?	Y	Y	Y	N	N	N
12 Bonior	Y	Y	Y	Y	N	N	Y	Y
13 Crockett	N	Y	Y	Y	N	Y	Y	Y
14 Hertel	Y	N	Y	Y	N	Y	Y	Y
15 Ford	N	Y	Y	Y	N	Y	Y	?
16 Dingell	Y	Y	Y	Y	N	Y	Y	Y
17 Levin	Y	Y	Y	Y	N	Y	Y	N
18 ***Broomfield***	Y	N	Y	N	N	Y	N	N
MINNESOTA								
1 Penny	Y	Y	N	N	N	Y	Y	Y
2 ***Weber***	N	N	Y	N	N	N	N	N
3 ***Frenzel***	Y	N	Y	N	N	N	N	Y
4 Vento	N	Y	Y	Y	N	Y	Y	Y
5 Sabo	Y	Y	N	Y	N	Y	Y	N
6 Sikorski	N	Y	N	Y	N	Y	Y	Y
7 ***Stangeland***	Y	N	Y	N	N	N	N	N
8 Oberstar	N	Y	Y	Y	N	Y	Y	Y
MISSISSIPPI								
1 Whitten	Y	Y	Y	N	?	N	N	N
2 Espy	Y	Y	Y	Y	Y	N	Y	Y
3 Montgomery	Y	N	Y	N	N	N	N	N
4 Parker	Y	N	#	N	N	N	N	N
5 Smith	Y	N	Y	N	Y	N	N	N
MISSOURI								
1 Clay	N	?	N	Y	N	N	Y	Y
2 ***Buechner***	Y	N	Y	?	#	Y	N	N
3 Gephardt	N	Y	Y	Y	N	N	Y	N
4 Skelton	Y	N	Y	Y	N	N	N	N
5 Wheat	N	Y	N	Y	N	Y	Y	Y
6 ***Coleman***	Y	N	Y	N	Y	N	N	N
7 ***Hancock***	Y	N	N	N	N	Y	N	N
8 ***Emerson***	Y	N	Y	N	Y	N	N	N
9 Volkmer	Y	Y	Y	Y	N	N	Y	N
MONTANA								
1 Williams	N	N	N	Y	N	Y	Y	N
2 ***Marlenee***	Y	N	X	N	Y	N	N	N
NEBRASKA								
1 ***Bereuter***	+	N	N	N	N	Y	Y	N
2 Hoagland	Y	Y	N	Y	N	N	Y	N
3 ***Smith***	Y	N	#	N	N	N	N	N
NEVADA								
1 Bilbray	Y	N	Y	Y	N	N	Y	N
2 ***Vucanovich***	Y	N	Y	N	N	N	N	N
NEW HAMPSHIRE								
1 ***Smith***	N	N	N	N	N	Y	N	N
2 ***Douglas***	N	N	N	N	Y	Y	N	N
NEW JERSEY								
1 Florio	N	N	X	Y	N	?	?	?
2 Hughes	Y	Y	N	Y	N	N	Y	Y
3 Pallone	Y	Y	N	Y	N	N	Y	Y
4 ***Smith***	Y	N	Y	Y	Y	N	Y	N
5 ***Roukema***	Y	Y	N	N	N	Y	Y	Y
6 Dwyer	Y	Y	N	Y	N	N	Y	N
7 ***Rinaldo***	?	N	Y	Y	N	N	N	N
8 Roe	Y	N	?	Y	N	N	Y	N
9 Torricelli	Y	N	N	Y	N	N	Y	N
10 Payne	N	N	N	Y	N	N	Y	Y
11 ***Gallo***	Y	N	Y	N	N	N	N	N
12 ***Courter***	?	-	N	?	?	?	?	?
13 ***Saxton***	Y	N	N	N	N	N	N	N
14 Guarini	Y	N	Y	Y	N	N	Y	N
NEW MEXICO								
1 ***Schiff***	Y	N	Y	N	N	N	N	N
2 ***Skeen***	Y	N	Y	N	N	N	N	N
3 Richardson	Y	N	Y	Y	N	N	N	N
NEW YORK								
1 Hochbrueckner	Y	N	Y	Y	Y	N	Y	N
2 Downey	N	Y	Y	Y	N	N	Y	Y
3 Mrazek	Y	Y	N	Y	N	N	Y	Y
4 ***Lent***	Y	N	Y	N	N	N	N	N
5 ***McGrath***	Y	N	Y	N	Y	N	N	N
6 Flake	N	Y	Y	Y	Y	N	Y	Y
7 Ackerman	Y	Y	Y	Y	Y	N	Y	Y
8 Scheuer	Y	Y	N	Y	N	N	Y	Y
9 Manton	Y	Y	Y	Y	Y	N	Y	N
10 Schumer	N	Y	Y	Y	N	Y	Y	Y
11 Towns	X	Y	N	Y	N	N	Y	Y
12 Owens	N	Y	N	Y	N	Y	Y	Y
13 Solarz	Y	Y	Y	Y	N	N	Y	N
14 ***Molinari***	Y	N	Y	N	Y	N	?	N
15 ***Green***	N	N	Y	N	N	N	Y	Y
16 Rangel	N	Y	Y	Y	N	N	?	Y
17 Weiss	N	N	N	Y	N	Y	Y	Y
18 Garcia	N	Y	N	Y	N	N	Y	Y
19 Engel	Y	N	Y	Y	N	N	Y	Y
20 Lowey	Y	Y	N	Y	N	N	Y	Y
21 ***Fish***	Y	N	Y	N	Y	N	Y	N
22 ***Gilman***	Y	N	Y	Y	N	N	N	N
23 McNulty	Y	N	Y	Y	N	N	Y	N
24 ***Solomon***	Y	N	Y	Y	Y	N	N	N
25 ***Boehlert***	Y	N	Y	Y	N	Y	N	N
26 ***Martin***	Y	N	Y	N	C	Y	N	N
27 ***Walsh***	Y	N	Y	Y	N	N	N	N
28 McHugh	Y	Y	N	Y	N	N	Y	N
29 ***Horton***	Y	N	?	Y	Y	N	Y	Y
30 Slaughter	N	Y	Y	Y	N	Y	Y	Y
31 ***Paxon***	Y	N	N	N	Y	N	N	N
32 LaFalce	#	Y	N	Y	Y	Y	Y	Y
33 Nowak	Y	Y	N	Y	Y	N	Y	N
34 ***Houghton***	Y	N	Y	N	N	N	N	N
NORTH CAROLINA								
1 Jones	N	Y	Y	Y	N	N	Y	Y
2 Valentine	N	N	Y	N	N	N	Y	N
3 Lancaster	Y	N	N	N	N	Y	Y	N
4 Price	Y	Y	Y	Y	N	N	Y	Y
5 Neal	N	Y	Y	Y	N	Y	Y	N
6 ***Coble***	Y	N	Y	N	N	Y	Y	N
7 Rose	Y	Y	Y	Y	N	N	Y	N
8 Hefner	Y	N	Y	Y	N	?	Y	N
9 ***McMillan***	Y	N	Y	N	N	N	N	N
10 ***Ballenger***	Y	N	Y	N	N	N	N	N
11 Clarke	Y	Y	Y	Y	N	Y	Y	N
NORTH DAKOTA								
AL Dorgan	N	N	N	Y	N	N	Y	N
OHIO								
1 Luken	+	Y	Y	Y	Y	Y	Y	N
2 ***Gradison***	Y	N	Y	N	N	Y	N	N
3 Hall	N	?	Y	Y	Y	?	Y	N
4 ***Oxley***	Y	N	Y	N	N	N	N	N
5 ***Gillmor***	Y	N	Y	N	N	N	N	N
6 ***McEwen***	Y	N	Y	N	Y	N	N	N
7 ***DeWine***	Y	N	Y	N	Y	N	N	Y
8 ***Lukens***	Y	N	N	N	Y	N	N	N
9 Kaptur	Y	Y	Y	Y	N	N	Y	Y
10 ***Miller***	Y	N	N	N	N	N	N	N
11 Eckart	N	Y	Y	Y	N	Y	Y	Y
12 ***Kasich***	Y	N	N	N	N	Y	N	Y
13 Pease	N	Y	N	Y	N	N	Y	Y
14 Sawyer	Y	Y	Y	Y	N	N	Y	Y
15 ***Wylie***	Y	N	Y	N	N	N	N	N
16 ***Regula***	Y	N	Y	N	N	N	Y	N
17 Traficant	N	Y	Y	Y	N	N	Y	Y
18 Applegate	N	Y	N	Y	N	N	Y	Y
19 Feighan	N	Y	Y	Y	N	Y	Y	Y
20 Oakar	N	N	Y	Y	N	N	Y	Y
21 Stokes	N	N	Y	Y	N	N	Y	Y
OKLAHOMA								
1 ***Inhofe***	Y	N	Y	N	Y	N	N	N
2 Synar	Y	Y	N	Y	N	Y	Y	N
3 Watkins	Y	N	N	Y	Y	N	Y	N
4 McCurdy	Y	N	?	N	N	N	Y	N
5 ***Edwards***	Y	N	Y	N	N	N	N	N
6 English	Y	Y	N	N	Y	N	N	N
OREGON								
1 AuCoin	N	N	Y	Y	Y	N	Y	N
2 ***Smith, R.***	Y	N	Y	N	Y	N	N	N
3 Wyden	N	N	Y	Y	N	N	Y	N
4 DeFazio	N	Y	N	Y	Y	Y	Y	Y
5 ***Smith, D.***	?	N	N	N	Y	N	N	N
PENNSYLVANIA								
1 Foglietta	N	N	Y	Y	N	N	Y	Y
2 Gray	Y	Y	Y	Y	N	N	Y	Y
3 Borski	Y	Y	Y	Y	N	N	Y	N
4 Kolter	Y	N	N	Y	Y	N	Y	N
5 ***Schulze***	Y	N	?	N	N	Y	Y	Y
6 Yatron	Y	N	Y	Y	Y	N	Y	Y
7 ***Weldon***	Y	N	Y	?	Y	Y	N	N
8 Kostmayer	N	N	Y	Y	N	N	Y	Y
9 ***Shuster***	Y	N	Y	N	N	N	N	N
10 ***McDade***	Y	N	Y	Y	N	N	N	N
11 Kanjorski	Y	Y	N	Y	Y	N	Y	Y
12 Murtha	Y	N	Y	Y	Y	N	N	N
13 ***Coughlin***	Y	N	Y	N	X	Y	Y	N
14 Coyne	Y	Y	Y	Y	N	N	Y	Y
15 ***Ritter***	Y	N	N	N	N	Y	N	N
16 ***Walker***	Y	N	N	N	N	N	N	N
17 ***Gekas***	Y	N	Y	N	Y	N	N	N
18 Walgren	Y	Y	N	Y	Y	N	Y	N
19 ***Goodling***	Y	N	Y	N	Y	?	Y	N
20 Gaydos	N	N	Y	Y	Y	N	Y	N
21 ***Ridge***	Y	N	Y	Y	Y	Y	Y	Y
22 Murphy	N	Y	N	Y	Y	N	Y	N
23 ***Clinger***	Y	N	Y	N	N	N	N	N
RHODE ISLAND								
1 ***Machtley***	Y	N	Y	Y	N	N	Y	Y
2 ***Schneider***	Y	N	Y	Y	N	Y	Y	Y
SOUTH CAROLINA								
1 ***Ravenel***	Y	N	Y	N	N	N	N	Y
2 ***Spence***	Y	N	N	N	N	N	N	N
3 Derrick	N	N	N	N	N	Y	Y	N
4 Patterson	Y	N	N	N	N	Y	N	N
5 Spratt	Y	N	N	N	N	N	Y	N
6 Tallon	Y	N	N	Y	N	N	Y	Y
SOUTH DAKOTA								
AL Johnson	N	N	N	Y	N	N	Y	Y
TENNESSEE								
1 ***Quillen***	Y	N	Y	N	Y	N	N	N
2 ***Duncan***	Y	N	N	N	N	N	Y	N
3 Lloyd	Y	N	Y	Y	N	N	N	N
4 Cooper	Y	Y	Y	N	N	N	Y	N
5 Clement	Y	N	Y	Y	N	Y	Y	Y
6 Gordon	Y	Y	Y	Y	N	N	Y	N
7 ***Sundquist***	Y	N	Y	N	N	N	N	N
8 Tanner	Y	Y	Y	Y	N	N	Y	N
9 Ford	N	Y	Y	Y	?	N	Y	Y
TEXAS								
1 Chapman	Y	Y	Y	N	N	N	Y	N
2 Wilson	Y	N	N	Y	N	N	N	N
3 ***Bartlett***	Y	N	Y	N	Y	N	N	N
4 Hall	Y	N	N	N	Y	N	N	N
5 Bryant	Y	Y	Y	Y	N	N	Y	N
6 ***Barton***	Y	N	Y	N	N	N	N	Y
7 ***Archer***	Y	N	Y	N	N	N	N	N
8 ***Fields***	Y	N	N	N	N	N	N	N
9 Brooks	Y	Y	Y	Y	C	N	Y	Y
10 Pickle	Y	Y	Y	Y	N	N	N	N
11 Leath	Y	N	N	N	N	N	N	N
12 Wright[4]				Y	?	N		
13 Sarpolius	Y	N	N	N	N	N	N	N
14 Laughlin	Y	N	Y	?	N	N	N	N
15 de la Garza	Y	N	Y	Y	N	N	Y	N
16 Coleman	Y	Y	N	Y	N	N	N	N
17 Stenholm	Y	N	N	N	N	N	Y	N
18 Leland	N	Y	Y	Y	N	Y	Y	#
19 ***Combest***	Y	N	N	N	N	N	N	N
20 Gonzalez	N	N	Y	Y	N	N	Y	N
21 ***Smith***	Y	N	Y	N	N	N	N	N
22 ***DeLay***	Y	N	N	N	Y	N	N	N
23 Bustamante	Y	N	Y	Y	N	N	Y	N
24 Frost	Y	Y	Y	Y	N	N	Y	N
25 Andrews	Y	N	Y	Y	N	N	N	N
26 ***Armey***	N	N	N	N	Y	N	N	N
27 Ortiz	Y	N	Y	Y	N	N	Y	N
UTAH								
1 ***Hansen***	Y	N	N	N	N	N	N	N
2 Owens	Y	Y	N	Y	N	N	Y	Y
3 ***Nielson***	Y	N	N	N	N	N	N	N
VERMONT								
AL ***Smith***	Y	N	Y	Y	N	N	Y	Y
VIRGINIA								
1 ***Bateman***	Y	?	?	N	N	N	N	N
2 Pickett	Y	N	Y	Y	N	N	N	N
3 ***Bliley***	Y	N	Y	N	N	N	N	N
4 Sisisky	Y	N	Y	Y	C	N	N	N
5 Payne	Y	N	Y	N	N	N	Y	N
6 Olin	Y	Y	N	Y	N	N	Y	N
7 ***Slaughter***	Y	N	N	N	N	N	N	N
8 ***Parris***	Y	N	N	?	N	N	N	N
9 Boucher	N	Y	Y	Y	Y	N	Y	Y
10 ***Wolf***	Y	N	Y	N	N	N	N	N
WASHINGTON								
1 ***Miller***	Y	N	N	N	N	N	N	N
2 Swift	N	Y	Y	Y	N	Y	Y	N
3 Unsoeld	N	Y	Y	Y	N	Y	Y	Y
4 ***Morrison***	Y	N	Y	N	Y	N	N	N
5 Foley[5]	Y	Y	Y					
6 Dicks	Y	N	Y	Y	N	N	Y	N
7 McDermott	N	Y	Y	Y	N	Y	Y	N
8 ***Chandler***	Y	N	Y	N	N	N	Y	N
WEST VIRGINIA								
1 Mollohan	Y	N	Y	Y	Y	N	N	N
2 Staggers	N	Y	N	Y	Y	N	Y	N
3 Wise	Y	Y	Y	Y	N	N	Y	N
4 Rahall	Y	Y	Y	Y	N	N	Y	Y
WISCONSIN								
1 Aspin	Y	N	Y	Y	N	N	Y	N
2 Kastenmeier	N	Y	N	Y	N	Y	Y	Y
3 ***Gunderson***	Y	N	Y	N	N	Y	N	N
4 Kleczka	N	Y	Y	Y	N	N	Y	Y
5 Moody	N	Y	N	Y	N	Y	Y	Y
6 ***Petri***	Y	N	Y	N	N	Y	Y	N
7 Obey	Y	Y	N	Y	N	Y	Y	Y
8 ***Roth***	Y	N	N	N	N	N	N	Y
9 ***Sensenbrenner***	Y	Y	X	N	N	N	Y	Y
WYOMING								
AL ***Thomas***[6]			Y	N	N	N	N	N

9. HR 3299. Fiscal 1990 Budget Reconciliation/Section 89. Dorgan, D-N.D., amendment to repeal Section 89 of the 1986 tax code overhaul, which requires employers to prove their health benefit plans are non-discriminatory, and to delete the provision in the reconciliation bill that would deny favorable tax treatment to certain employee health benefit plans that discriminate in favor of owners and executives. Adopted 390-36: R 172-2; D 218-34 (ND 140-31, SD 78-3), Sept. 27, 1989.

10. HR 3299. Fiscal 1990 Budget Reconciliation/Alternative Revenue Package. Rostenkowski, D-Ill., amendment to strike the Jenkins-Archer capital gains tax cut included in the reconciliation bill and substitute restored deductibility for individual retirement accounts, a deficit-reduction trust fund and an increase to 33 percent from 28 percent in the marginal tax rates for the highest incomes. Rejected 190-239: R 1-175; D 189-64 (ND 152-20, SD 37-44), Sept. 28, 1989. A "nay" was a vote supporting the president's position.

11. HR 3299. Fiscal 1990 Budget Reconciliation/Catastrophic Repeal. Donnelly, D-Mass., amendment to repeal nearly all of the 1988 Medicare Catastrophic Coverage Act (PL 100-360), retaining only the non-Medicare provisions — primarily selected Medicaid expansions. Adopted 360-66: R 164-10; D 196-56 (ND 124-47, SD 72-9), Oct. 4, 1989.

12. HR 3299. Fiscal 1990 Budget Reconciliation/Child-Care Substitute. Stenholm, D-Texas, substitute amendment to strike the child-care provisions in the bill and replace them with an expanded earned-income tax credit and increased authorizations for Head Start. Rejected 195-230: R 159-16; D 36-214 (ND 6-163, SD 30-51), Oct. 5, 1989.

13. HR 2990. Fiscal 1990 Labor, HHS and Education Appropriations/Abortion Funding. Boxer, D-Calif., motion that the House recede from its disagreement to the Senate amendment to permit the use of federal funds to pay for abortions in cases of "promptly reported" rape or incest. Motion agreed to 216-206: R 41-134; D 175-72 (ND 124-44, SD 51-28), Oct. 11, 1989. A "nay" was a vote supporting the president's position.

14. HR 3402. Aid to Poland and Hungary/Passage. Passage of the bill to authorize $837.5 million in U.S. aid programs to Poland and Hungary during fiscal years 1990-92. Passed 345-47: R 128-34; D 217-13 (ND 152-4, SD 65-9), Oct. 19, 1989.

15. HR 1465. Oil-Spill Liability/State Pre-emption. Miller, D-Calif., en bloc amendments to prevent federal law from pre-empting state laws on oil-spill liability, compensation and cleanup. Adopted 279-143: R 75-99; D 204-44 (ND 155-14, SD 49-30), Nov. 8, 1989. A "nay" was a vote supporting the president's position.

16. HR 3660. Government Pay and Ethics Package/Passage. Passage of the bill to phase out honoraria, revise ethics rules and raise salaries for members of the House of Representatives and high officials of the executive and judicial branches. Passed 252-174: R 84-89; D 168-85 (ND 121-52, SD 47-33), Nov. 16, 1989.

[1] *Rep. Tommy Robinson, R-Ark., switched from the Democratic to the Republican Party on July 28, 1989.*

[2] *Rep. Gary Condit, D-Calif., was sworn in Sept. 20, 1989, to succeed Tony Coelho, D, who resigned June 15, 1989.*

[3] *Rep. Ileana Ros-Lehtinen, R-Fla., was sworn in Sept. 6, 1989, to succeed Claude Pepper, D, who died May 30, 1989.*

[4] *Rep. Gene Taylor, D-Miss., was sworn in Oct. 24, 1989, to succeed Larkin Smith, R, who died Aug. 13, 1989.*

[5] *Rep. Pete Geren, D-Texas, was sworn in Sept. 20, 1989, to succeed Jim Wright, D, who resigned June 30, 1989.*

[6] *Rep. Mickey Leland, D-Texas, died Aug. 7, 1989.*

KEY

- Y Voted for (yea).
- # Paired for.
- \+ Announced for.
- N Voted against (nay).
- X Paired against.
- \- Announced against.
- P Voted "present."
- C Voted "present" to avoid possible conflict of interest.
- ? Did not vote or otherwise make a position known.

Democrats ***Republicans***
Independent

ND Northern Democrats
SD Southern Democrats

Southern states - Ala., Ark., Fla., Ga., Ky., La., Miss., N.C., Okla., S.C., Tenn., Texas, Va.

	9	10	11	12	13	14	15	16
ALABAMA								
1 ***Callahan***	Y	N	Y	Y	N	N	N	N
2 ***Dickinson***	Y	N	Y	Y	Y	Y	N	N
3 Browder	Y	N	Y	Y	Y	Y	Y	N
4 Bevill	Y	Y	Y	Y	N	?	Y	N
5 Flippo	Y	N	Y	Y	Y	Y	Y	X
6 Erdreich	Y	N	Y	Y	Y	N	Y	N
7 Harris	Y	N	Y	Y	Y	N	Y	N
ALASKA								
AL ***Young***	Y	N	?	Y	N	N	Y	Y
ARIZONA								
1 ***Rhodes***	Y	N	Y	Y	N	Y	N	Y
2 Udall	Y	Y	N	N	Y	?	Y	Y
3 ***Stump***	Y	N	Y	Y	N	N	N	N
4 ***Kyl***	Y	N	Y	Y	N	Y	N	Y
5 ***Kolbe***	Y	N	Y	Y	Y	Y	N	Y
ARKANSAS								
1 Alexander	Y	N	N	N	Y	Y	Y	Y
2 ***Robinson*** [1]	Y	N	N	Y	N	Y	N	N
3 ***Hammerschmidt***	Y	N	Y	Y	N	Y	N	Y
4 Anthony	Y	N	N	N	Y	Y	Y	Y
CALIFORNIA								
1 Bosco	Y	N	Y	N	Y	?	Y	Y
2 ***Herger***	Y	N	Y	Y	N	N	N	N
3 Matsui	N	Y	Y	N	Y	Y	Y	Y
4 Fazio	Y	Y	Y	N	Y	Y	Y	Y
5 Pelosi	Y	Y	Y	N	Y	+	Y	Y
6 Boxer	Y	Y	Y	N	Y	?	Y	Y
7 Miller	N	Y	N	N	Y	?	Y	Y
8 Dellums	N	Y	Y	N	Y	#	Y	Y
9 Stark	N	Y	N	N	Y	?	Y	Y
10 Edwards	Y	Y	N	N	Y	Y	Y	Y
11 Lantos	Y	Y	Y	N	Y	?	Y	Y
12 ***Campbell***	Y	N	Y	Y	Y	?	Y	Y
13 Mineta	Y	N	Y	N	Y	?	Y	Y
14 ***Shumway***	Y	N	Y	Y	N	N	N	N
15 Condit[2]	Y	Y	Y	N	Y	Y	Y	N
16 Panetta	Y	Y	N	N	Y	?	Y	Y
17 ***Pashayan***	Y	N	Y	Y	N	Y	Y	N
18 Lehman	Y	Y	Y	N	Y	?	Y	Y
19 ***Lagomarsino***	Y	N	Y	Y	N	Y	Y	N
20 ***Thomas***	Y	N	Y	Y	Y	Y	N	Y
21 ***Gallegly***	Y	N	Y	Y	N	?	Y	Y
22 ***Moorhead***	Y	N	Y	Y	N	Y	Y	Y
23 Beilenson	Y	Y	Y	N	Y	Y	Y	Y
24 Waxman	Y	Y	N	N	Y	Y	Y	Y
25 Roybal	Y	Y	N	N	Y	Y	Y	Y
26 Berman	Y	Y	N	N	Y	Y	Y	#
27 Levine	Y	Y	Y	N	Y	Y	Y	Y
28 Dixon	Y	Y	Y	N	Y	Y	Y	Y
29 Hawkins	?	Y	N	N	Y	Y	Y	Y
30 Martinez	Y	N	Y	N	Y	Y	Y	Y
31 Dymally	N	Y	Y	N	Y	Y	?	Y
32 Anderson	Y	N	N	N	Y	Y	Y	N
33 ***Dreier***	Y	N	Y	Y	N	?	Y	N
34 Torres	Y	Y	Y	N	Y	Y	Y	Y
35 ***Lewis***	Y	N	Y	Y	N	Y	Y	Y
36 Brown	Y	Y	Y	N	Y	Y	Y	Y
37 ***McCandless***	?	N	Y	Y	Y	N	N	N
38 ***Dornan***	Y	N	Y	Y	N	N	N	N
39 ***Dannemeyer***	Y	N	Y	Y	N	N	N	N
40 ***Cox***	Y	N	Y	Y	N	Y	Y	N
41 ***Lowery***	Y	N	Y	Y	N	Y	Y	Y
42 ***Rohrabacher***	Y	N	Y	Y	N	Y	Y	N
43 ***Packard***	Y	N	Y	Y	N	?	Y	Y
44 Bates	Y	Y	Y	N	Y	Y	Y	Y
45 ***Hunter***	Y	N	Y	Y	N	Y	N	Y
COLORADO								
1 Schroeder	Y	Y	Y	N	Y	Y	Y	N
2 Skaggs	Y	Y	Y	N	Y	Y	Y	Y
3 Campbell	Y	N	Y	N	Y	Y	N	N
4 ***Brown***	Y	N	Y	Y	Y	N	Y	N
5 ***Hefley***	Y	N	Y	Y	N	N	Y	N
6 ***Schaefer***	Y	N	Y	Y	N	N	N	N
CONNECTICUT								
1 Kennelly	N	Y	Y	N	Y	Y	Y	Y
2 Gejdenson	Y	Y	Y	N	Y	Y	Y	Y
3 Morrison	Y	Y	Y	N	Y	Y	Y	N
4 ***Shays***	Y	N	Y	N	Y	Y	Y	Y
5 ***Rowland***	Y	N	Y	Y	Y	Y	Y	N
6 ***Johnson***	Y	N	Y	Y	Y	Y	Y	Y
DELAWARE								
AL Carper	Y	Y	Y	N	Y	Y	N	Y
FLORIDA								
1 Hutto	Y	N	Y	Y	N	Y	Y	N
2 ***Grant***	Y	N	Y	Y	N	Y	Y	N
3 Bennett	Y	Y	Y	Y	Y	Y	Y	N
4 ***James***	Y	N	Y	Y	N	Y	Y	N
5 ***McCollum***	Y	N	Y	Y	N	Y	Y	Y
6 ***Stearns***	Y	N	Y	Y	N	Y	Y	N
7 Gibbons	Y	Y	Y	N	N	Y	Y	Y
8 ***Young***	Y	N	Y	Y	N	Y	Y	Y
9 ***Bilirakis***	Y	N	Y	Y	N	Y	Y	Y
10 ***Ireland***	Y	N	Y	Y	N	Y	Y	Y
11 Nelson	Y	Y	Y	N	Y	?	Y	N
12 ***Lewis***	Y	N	Y	Y	N	Y	Y	N
13 ***Goss***	Y	N	Y	Y	Y	Y	Y	N
14 Johnston	Y	Y	Y	N	Y	Y	Y	N
15 ***Shaw***	Y	N	Y	Y	N	Y	Y	Y
16 Smith	Y	Y	Y	N	Y	Y	Y	Y
17 Lehman	Y	Y	Y	N	Y	?	Y	Y
18 ***Ros-Lehtinen***[3]	Y	N	Y	Y	N	Y	Y	N
19 Fascell	Y	Y	Y	N	Y	Y	Y	Y
GEORGIA								
1 Thomas	Y	N	Y	Y	Y	Y	Y	Y
2 Hatcher	Y	N	Y	Y	Y	?	N	Y
3 Ray	Y	N	Y	Y	N	N	N	Y
4 Jones	Y	N	Y	N	Y	Y	Y	Y
5 Lewis	Y	Y	Y	N	Y	Y	Y	Y
6 ***Gingrich***	Y	N	Y	Y	N	Y	Y	Y
7 Darden	Y	N	Y	Y	N	Y	Y	Y
8 Rowland	Y	N	Y	Y	Y	Y	Y	Y
9 Jenkins	Y	N	Y	N	N	Y	?	Y
10 Barnard	Y	N	Y	Y	N	Y	N	Y
HAWAII								
1 ***Saiki***	Y	N	Y	N	Y	Y	Y	Y
2 Akaka	Y	Y	Y	N	Y	Y	Y	Y
IDAHO								
1 ***Craig***	Y	N	Y	Y	N	N	N	N
2 Stallings	Y	N	Y	Y	N	Y	Y	N
ILLINOIS								
1 Hayes	N	Y	N	N	Y	Y	Y	Y
2 Savage	N	Y	N	N	Y	Y	Y	Y
3 Russo	Y	Y	Y	N	N	Y	Y	Y
4 Sangmeister	Y	Y	Y	N	Y	Y	Y	N
5 Lipinski	Y	Y	Y	N	N	Y	Y	Y
6 ***Hyde***	Y	N	Y	Y	N	Y	N	N
7 Collins	Y	Y	N	N	?	Y	Y	Y
8 Rostenkowski	N	Y	N	N	N	Y	Y	Y
9 Yates	Y	Y	Y	N	Y	Y	Y	N
10 ***Porter***	Y	N	Y	Y	N	Y	N	Y
11 Annunzio	Y	Y	Y	N	N	Y	Y	Y
12 ***Crane***	Y	N	Y	Y	N	N	Y	N
13 ***Fawell***	Y	N	Y	Y	Y	Y	Y	N
14 ***Hastert***	Y	N	Y	Y	N	Y	N	N
15 ***Madigan***	Y	N	Y	Y	N	Y	N	Y
16 ***Martin***	Y	N	Y	Y	Y	Y	Y	P
17 Evans	Y	Y	N	N	Y	Y	Y	N
18 ***Michel***	Y	N	Y	Y	N	Y	N	Y
19 Bruce	Y	Y	Y	N	N	Y	Y	N
20 Durbin	Y	Y	Y	N	Y	Y	Y	Y
21 Costello	Y	Y	Y	N	N	Y	Y	N
22 Poshard	Y	Y	Y	N	N	Y	Y	N
INDIANA								
1 Visclosky	Y	Y	Y	N	Y	Y	Y	N
2 Sharp	Y	Y	Y	N	Y	Y	Y	N
3 ***Hiler***	Y	N	Y	Y	N	Y	N	N

	9	10	11	12	13	14	15	16
4 Long	Y	N	N	N	Y	Y	Y	N
5 Jontz	N	Y	N	N	Y	Y	Y	N
6 ***Burton***	Y	N	Y	Y	N	N	N	Y
7 ***Myers***	Y	N	N	Y	N	N	N	Y
8 McCloskey	Y	Y	Y	N	Y	Y	Y	Y
9 Hamilton	Y	Y	N	N	N	Y	Y	N
10 Jacobs	Y	N	Y	N	Y	N	Y	N
IOWA								
1 ***Leach***	Y	N	Y	N	Y	Y	Y	N
2 ***Tauke***	Y	N	Y	Y	N	Y	N	N
3 Nagle	Y	Y	N	N	Y	Y	Y	Y
4 Smith	Y	N	N	N	Y	Y	?	Y
5 ***Lightfoot***	Y	N	Y	Y	N	Y	N	N
6 ***Grandy***	Y	N	Y	Y	N	Y	N	N
KANSAS								
1 ***Roberts***	Y	N	Y	Y	N	Y	N	Y
2 Slattery	Y	Y	Y	N	Y	Y	Y	N
3 ***Meyers***	Y	N	Y	Y	Y	Y	N	N
4 Glickman	Y	Y	Y	N	Y	Y	Y	Y
5 ***Whittaker***	Y	N	N	Y	Y	Y	N	Y
KENTUCKY								
1 Hubbard	Y	N	N	Y	Y	Y	N	Y
2 Natcher	Y	N	Y	N	N	Y	N	Y
3 Mazzoli	Y	N	Y	N	N	Y	Y	Y
4 ***Bunning***	Y	N	Y	Y	N	N	N	N
5 ***Rogers***	Y	N	Y	Y	N	Y	N	N
6 ***Hopkins***	Y	N	N	Y	N	N	N	N
7 Perkins	Y	N	N	N	N	Y	N	Y
LOUISIANA								
1 ***Livingston***	Y	N	Y	Y	N	Y	N	Y
2 Boggs	Y	Y	N	N	N	Y	N	Y
3 Tauzin	Y	N	Y	Y	N	Y	N	N
4 ***McCrery***	Y	N	Y	Y	N	Y	N	Y
5 Huckaby	Y	N	Y	Y	N	Y	N	N
6 ***Baker***	Y	N	Y	Y	Y	Y	N	Y
7 Hayes	Y	N	Y	N	N	N	N	Y
8 ***Holloway***	Y	N	Y	Y	N	N	N	N
MAINE								
1 Brennan	Y	Y	N	N	Y	Y	Y	N
2 ***Snowe***	Y	N	Y	N	Y	Y	Y	N
MARYLAND								
1 Dyson	Y	N	Y	N	N	?	Y	N
2 ***Bentley***	Y	N	Y	Y	Y	Y	N	N
3 Cardin	Y	Y	N	N	Y	Y	Y	Y
4 McMillen	Y	N	Y	N	Y	Y	Y	Y
5 Hoyer	Y	Y	Y	N	Y	Y	Y	Y
6 Byron	Y	N	Y	Y	N	Y	Y	Y
7 Mfume	Y	Y	N	N	Y	Y	Y	Y
8 ***Morella***	Y	N	Y	N	Y	Y	Y	Y
MASSACHUSETTS								
1 ***Conte***	Y	N	N	N	N	Y	Y	Y
2 Neal	Y	Y	Y	N	N	Y	Y	N
3 Early	Y	N	N	N	N	Y	Y	N
4 Frank	Y	Y	Y	N	Y	Y	Y	N
5 Atkins	Y	Y	Y	N	Y	Y	Y	Y
6 Mavroules	Y	Y	Y	N	N	Y	Y	Y
7 Markey	Y	Y	Y	N	Y	Y	Y	Y
8 Kennedy	Y	Y	N	N	Y	Y	Y	Y
9 Moakley	Y	Y	Y	N	N	Y	Y	Y
10 Studds	Y	Y	Y	N	Y	Y	Y	Y
11 Donnelly	Y	Y	Y	N	N	Y	Y	Y
MICHIGAN								
1 Conyers	N	Y	N	N	Y	Y	Y	N
2 ***Pursell***	Y	N	Y	Y	Y	Y	Y	Y
3 Wolpe	Y	Y	Y	N	Y	Y	Y	Y
4 ***Upton***	Y	N	Y	Y	Y	Y	N	Y
5 ***Henry***	Y	N	Y	Y	N	Y	Y	Y
6 Carr	Y	N	Y	N	Y	Y	N	N
7 Kildee	N	Y	Y	N	N	Y	Y	N
8 Traxler	Y	Y	Y	?	N	Y	Y	Y
9 ***Vander Jagt***	Y	N	Y	Y	N	Y	N	Y
10 ***Schuette***	Y	N	Y	Y	N	Y	N	N
11 ***Davis***	Y	N	Y	N	N	Y	Y	Y
12 Bonior	Y	Y	Y	N	N	Y	Y	Y
13 Crockett	N	Y	N	N	Y	N	Y	Y
14 Hertel	Y	Y	Y	N	N	Y	Y	N
15 Ford	Y	Y	Y	N	Y	?	Y	Y
16 Dingell	N	Y	Y	N	Y	Y	N	Y
17 Levin	N	Y	N	N	Y	Y	Y	Y
18 ***Broomfield***	Y	N	Y	Y	N	Y	Y	Y
MINNESOTA								
1 Penny	Y	Y	Y	Y	N	Y	Y	N
2 ***Weber***	Y	N	Y	Y	Y	Y	Y	N
3 ***Frenzel***	Y	N	Y	Y	Y	N	N	Y
4 Vento	N	Y	N	N	N	Y	Y	Y
5 Sabo	N	Y	N	N	Y	Y	Y	Y
6 Sikorski	Y	Y	Y	N	Y	Y	Y	Y
7 ***Stangeland***	Y	N	Y	Y	N	?	N	N
8 Oberstar	N	Y	N	N	N	Y	Y	Y
MISSISSIPPI								
1 Whitten	Y	N	Y	N	N	Y	Y	Y
2 Espy	Y	Y	Y	N	Y	Y	N	N
3 Montgomery	Y	N	Y	Y	N	Y	N	Y
4 Parker	Y	N	Y	Y	N	Y	N	N
5 Taylor[4]							Y	N
MISSOURI								
1 Clay	N	Y	N	N	Y	Y	Y	Y
2 ***Buechner***	Y	N	Y	Y	N	N	N	Y
3 Gephardt	Y	Y	N	N	Y	Y	Y	Y
4 Skelton	Y	N	Y	Y	N	Y	N	Y
5 Wheat	Y	Y	Y	N	Y	Y	Y	Y
6 ***Coleman***	Y	N	Y	Y	N	Y	N	Y
7 ***Hancock***	Y	N	Y	Y	N	N	N	N
8 ***Emerson***	Y	N	Y	Y	N	Y	N	N
9 Volkmer	Y	Y	Y	N	N	Y	Y	Y
MONTANA								
1 Williams	Y	Y	Y	N	Y	Y	Y	N
2 ***Marlenee***	Y	N	Y	Y	N	X	N	N
NEBRASKA								
1 ***Bereuter***	Y	Y	Y	Y	N	Y	N	N
2 Hoagland	Y	Y	Y	N	Y	Y	Y	N
3 ***Smith***	Y	N	Y	Y	N	N	N	N
NEVADA								
1 Bilbray	Y	Y	Y	N	Y	Y	Y	Y
2 ***Vucanovich***	Y	N	Y	Y	N	Y	Y	Y
NEW HAMPSHIRE								
1 ***Smith***	Y	N	Y	Y	N	N	Y	N
2 ***Douglas***	Y	N	Y	Y	N	Y	Y	N
NEW JERSEY								
1 Florio	?	?	#	?	?	?	?	?
2 Hughes	Y	Y	Y	Y	Y	Y	Y	Y
3 Pallone	Y	Y	Y	N	N	Y	Y	N
4 ***Smith***	Y	N	N	Y	N	Y	Y	Y
5 ***Roukema***	Y	N	Y	N	Y	?	Y	Y
6 Dwyer	Y	Y	Y	N	Y	Y	Y	Y
7 ***Rinaldo***	Y	N	Y	N	N	Y	Y	Y
8 Roe	Y	N	Y	N	?	Y	?	Y
9 Torricelli	Y	Y	Y	N	Y	Y	Y	Y
10 Payne	N	Y	N	N	Y	Y	Y	Y
11 ***Gallo***	Y	N	Y	Y	Y	Y	Y	Y
12 ***Courter***	?	N	?	?	?	?	?	?
13 ***Saxton***	Y	N	Y	Y	N	Y	Y	Y
14 Guarini	Y	Y	Y	N	Y	Y	Y	Y
NEW MEXICO								
1 ***Schiff***	Y	N	Y	Y	N	Y	Y	N
2 ***Skeen***	Y	N	Y	Y	N	Y	N	N
3 Richardson	Y	Y	Y	N	Y	Y	Y	N
NEW YORK								
1 Hochbrueckner	Y	Y	Y	N	Y	Y	Y	N
2 Downey	N	Y	N	N	Y	Y	Y	Y
3 Mrazek	Y	N	Y	N	Y	Y	Y	Y
4 ***Lent***	Y	N	Y	Y	N	Y	N	Y
5 ***McGrath***	N	N	Y	Y	N	Y	Y	Y
6 Flake	N	Y	Y	N	Y	Y	Y	Y
7 Ackerman	Y	Y	Y	N	Y	#	Y	Y
8 Scheuer	Y	Y	N	?	Y	Y	Y	Y
9 Manton	Y	Y	Y	N	N	Y	N	Y
10 Schumer	Y	Y	Y	N	Y	Y	Y	Y
11 Towns	N	Y	N	N	Y	?	Y	Y
12 Owens	N	Y	Y	N	Y	Y	Y	Y
13 Solarz	Y	Y	Y	N	Y	Y	Y	Y
14 ***Molinari***	Y	N	Y	Y	N	?	?	?
15 ***Green***	Y	N	Y	Y	Y	Y	N	Y
16 Rangel	N	Y	Y	N	Y	Y	Y	Y
17 Weiss	N	Y	Y	N	Y	?	Y	Y
18 Garcia	-	?	+	-	?	?	?	?
19 Engel	Y	Y	Y	N	Y	Y	Y	N
20 Lowey	Y	Y	Y	N	Y	Y	Y	N
21 ***Fish***	Y	N	Y	N	N	Y	Y	Y
22 ***Gilman***	Y	N	N	N	Y	Y	Y	Y
23 McNulty	Y	Y	Y	N	Y	Y	Y	Y
24 ***Solomon***	Y	N	Y	Y	N	N	N	Y
25 ***Boehlert***	Y	N	N	N	Y	Y	Y	Y
26 ***Martin***	Y	N	Y	Y	N	Y	Y	Y
27 ***Walsh***	Y	N	Y	Y	N	Y	Y	Y
28 McHugh	Y	Y	N	N	N	Y	Y	Y
29 ***Horton***	Y	N	N	N	Y	Y	Y	Y
30 Slaughter	Y	Y	Y	N	Y	Y	Y	Y
31 ***Paxon***	Y	N	Y	Y	N	Y	Y	N
32 LaFalce	Y	Y	Y	N	N	Y	Y	Y
33 Nowak	Y	Y	Y	N	N	Y	Y	Y
34 ***Houghton***	Y	N	N	Y	Y	Y	N	Y
NORTH CAROLINA								
1 Jones	Y	Y	Y	N	?	Y	N	Y
2 Valentine	Y	Y	Y	N	Y	Y	Y	Y
3 Lancaster	Y	Y	Y	Y	Y	Y	Y	Y
4 Price	Y	Y	Y	N	Y	Y	Y	Y
5 Neal	Y	Y	Y	N	Y	Y	Y	N
6 ***Coble***	Y	N	Y	Y	N	Y	N	N
7 Rose	Y	Y	Y	N	Y	Y	Y	N
8 Hefner	Y	Y	Y	N	Y	Y	N	Y
9 ***McMillan***	Y	N	Y	Y	N	Y	N	Y
10 ***Ballenger***	Y	N	Y	Y	Y	Y	N	Y
11 Clarke	Y	N	Y	N	N	Y	Y	N
NORTH DAKOTA								
AL Dorgan	Y	Y	N	N	Y	Y	Y	N
OHIO								
1 Luken	Y	N	Y	N	N	Y	N	Y
2 ***Gradison***	N	N	N	Y	N	Y	Y	Y
3 Hall	Y	Y	Y	N	N	Y	Y	Y
4 ***Oxley***	Y	N	Y	Y	N	Y	Y	Y
5 ***Gillmor***	Y	N	Y	Y	N	Y	N	N
6 ***McEwen***	Y	N	Y	Y	N	Y	N	Y
7 ***DeWine***	Y	N	Y	Y	N	Y	Y	N
8 ***Lukens***	Y	N	Y	Y	N	N	N	N
9 Kaptur	Y	Y	N	P	N	Y	Y	N
10 ***Miller***	Y	N	Y	Y	N	N	N	N
11 Eckart	Y	Y	Y	N	Y	Y	Y	N
12 ***Kasich***	Y	N	Y	Y	N	Y	Y	N
13 Pease	N	Y	Y	N	Y	Y	Y	Y
14 Sawyer	Y	Y	Y	N	Y	Y	Y	Y
15 ***Wylie***	Y	N	Y	Y	N	Y	N	N
16 ***Regula***	Y	N	Y	Y	N	Y	N	Y
17 Traficant	Y	Y	Y	N	Y	Y	N	N
18 Applegate	Y	Y	Y	N	Y	Y	N	N
19 Feighan	Y	Y	Y	N	Y	Y	Y	N
20 Oakar	Y	Y	Y	N	N	Y	Y	Y
21 Stokes	N	Y	Y	N	Y	Y	Y	Y
OKLAHOMA								
1 ***Inhofe***	Y	N	Y	Y	N	Y	N	N
2 Synar	Y	Y	Y	N	Y	Y	Y	N
3 Watkins	Y	N	Y	Y	Y	Y	Y	N
4 McCurdy	Y	Y	Y	Y	Y	Y	Y	Y
5 ***Edwards***	Y	N	Y	Y	N	Y	N	Y
6 English	Y	N	Y	Y	N	N	Y	N
OREGON								
1 AuCoin	Y	Y	Y	N	Y	Y	Y	Y
2 ***Smith, R.***	Y	N	Y	Y	N	Y	N	N
3 Wyden	Y	N	Y	N	Y	Y	Y	N
4 DeFazio	Y	Y	Y	N	Y	Y	Y	N
5 ***Smith, D.***	Y	N	Y	Y	N	N	N	N
PENNSYLVANIA								
1 Foglietta	Y	Y	Y	N	?	Y	Y	Y
2 Gray	Y	Y	Y	N	Y	Y	Y	Y
3 Borski	Y	Y	Y	N	N	Y	Y	Y
4 Kolter	Y	Y	Y	N	N	Y	N	N
5 ***Schulze***	Y	N	Y	Y	N	Y	N	Y
6 Yatron	?	?	?	?	?	?	Y	N
7 ***Weldon***	Y	N	Y	Y	N	?	N	Y
8 Kostmayer	Y	Y	N	N	Y	Y	Y	N
9 ***Shuster***	Y	N	Y	Y	N	Y	N	N
10 ***McDade***	Y	N	Y	Y	N	Y	Y	Y
11 Kanjorski	Y	Y	Y	N	N	Y	Y	Y
12 Murtha	Y	Y	N	N	N	Y	Y	Y
13 ***Coughlin***	Y	N	Y	Y	Y	Y	N	Y
14 Coyne	N	Y	N	N	Y	Y	Y	Y
15 ***Ritter***	Y	N	Y	Y	N	Y	N	N
16 ***Walker***	Y	N	Y	Y	N	Y	N	N
17 ***Gekas***	Y	N	Y	Y	N	N	N	N
18 Walgren	Y	Y	Y	N	Y	Y	Y	Y
19 ***Goodling***	Y	N	Y	Y	N	Y	N	N
20 Gaydos	Y	Y	Y	N	N	Y	Y	Y
21 ***Ridge***	Y	N	Y	Y	Y	Y	Y	N
22 Murphy	Y	Y	Y	N	N	Y	Y	N
23 ***Clinger***	Y	N	Y	Y	N	Y	N	N
RHODE ISLAND								
1 ***Machtley***	Y	N	Y	N	Y	Y	Y	N
2 ***Schneider***	Y	N	Y	N	Y	Y	Y	N
SOUTH CAROLINA								
1 ***Ravenel***	Y	N	Y	Y	Y	Y	Y	N
2 ***Spence***	Y	N	Y	Y	N	Y	Y	N
3 Derrick	Y	N	Y	Y	Y	Y	Y	N
4 Patterson	Y	N	Y	Y	Y	Y	Y	N
5 Spratt	Y	Y	Y	N	Y	Y	Y	N
6 Tallon	Y	N	Y	N	N	N	N	N
SOUTH DAKOTA								
AL Johnson	Y	Y	Y	N	Y	Y	Y	N
TENNESSEE								
1 ***Quillen***	Y	N	Y	Y	N	Y	N	Y
2 ***Duncan***	Y	N	Y	Y	N	?	Y	N
3 Lloyd	Y	N	Y	Y	N	Y	Y	Y
4 Cooper	Y	Y	Y	N	Y	Y	Y	Y
5 Clement	Y	Y	Y	N	N	Y	N	N
6 Gordon	Y	Y	Y	N	Y	Y	Y	Y
7 ***Sundquist***	Y	N	Y	Y	N	Y	N	Y
8 Tanner	Y	N	Y	N	Y	Y	Y	N
9 Ford	N	Y	N	N	Y	Y	Y	Y
TEXAS								
1 Chapman	Y	Y	Y	N	Y	N	N	N
2 Wilson	Y	N	Y	N	Y	Y	N	Y
3 ***Bartlett***	Y	N	Y	Y	N	Y	N	Y
4 Hall	Y	N	Y	Y	N	N	N	N
5 Bryant	Y	Y	Y	N	?	Y	?	Y
6 ***Barton***	Y	N	Y	Y	N	Y	N	Y
7 ***Archer***	Y	N	Y	Y	N	N	N	Y
8 ***Fields***	Y	N	Y	Y	N	N	N	N
9 Brooks	Y	N	Y	N	Y	?	?	?
10 Pickle	N	N	N	N	Y	Y	Y	Y
11 Leath	Y	N	Y	Y	N	Y	N	Y
12 Geren[5]	Y	N	Y	N	Y	Y	N	N
13 Sarpalius	Y	Y	Y	Y	N	Y	N	N
14 Laughlin	Y	N	Y	N	N	N	N	N
15 de la Garza	Y	Y	Y	N	N	Y	Y	Y
16 Coleman	Y	Y	Y	N	Y	Y	Y	N
17 Stenholm	Y	Y	Y	Y	N	Y	N	Y
18 Vacancy[6]								
19 ***Combest***	Y	N	Y	Y	N	N	N	N
20 Gonzalez	N	Y	N	N	Y	Y	Y	Y
21 ***Smith***	Y	N	Y	Y	N	Y	N	Y
22 ***DeLay***	Y	N	Y	Y	N	N	N	Y
23 Bustamante	Y	Y	Y	N	Y	Y	Y	Y
24 Frost	Y	Y	Y	N	Y	Y	Y	Y
25 Andrews	Y	N	Y	N	Y	?	N	Y
26 ***Armey***	Y	N	Y	Y	N	N	N	N
27 Ortiz	Y	N	Y	N	Y	Y	N	Y
UTAH								
1 ***Hansen***	Y	N	Y	Y	N	?	N	N
2 Owens	Y	N	N	N	Y	Y	Y	Y
3 ***Nielson***	Y	N	Y	Y	N	Y	N	N
VERMONT								
AL ***Smith***	Y	N	Y	N	Y	Y	Y	N
VIRGINIA								
1 ***Bateman***	Y	N	Y	Y	N	?	N	Y
2 Pickett	Y	N	Y	N	Y	Y	N	N
3 ***Bliley***	Y	N	Y	Y	N	Y	N	N
4 Sisisky	Y	Y	Y	N	Y	Y	N	Y
5 Payne	Y	N	Y	Y	Y	?	N	N
6 Olin	Y	Y	Y	N	Y	Y	Y	N
7 ***Slaughter***	Y	N	Y	Y	N	Y	N	N
8 ***Parris***	Y	N	Y	Y	N	Y	N	Y
9 Boucher	Y	Y	N	N	Y	Y	Y	Y
10 ***Wolf***	Y	N	Y	Y	N	Y	N	Y
WASHINGTON								
1 ***Miller***	Y	N	Y	Y	Y	Y	Y	N
2 Swift	Y	Y	Y	N	Y	Y	Y	Y
3 Unsoeld	Y	Y	Y	N	Y	Y	Y	N
4 ***Morrison***	Y	N	Y	Y	Y	Y	Y	Y
5 Foley								Y
6 Dicks	Y	Y	Y	N	Y	N	Y	Y
7 McDermott	N	Y	N	N	Y	Y	Y	Y
8 ***Chandler***	Y	N	Y	Y	Y	Y	Y	Y
WEST VIRGINIA								
1 Mollohan	Y	Y	Y	N	N	Y	N	Y
2 Staggers	N	Y	Y	N	N	N	N	N
3 Wise	Y	Y	X	N	Y	Y	N	N
4 Rahall	Y	Y	Y	N	N	Y	N	Y
WISCONSIN								
1 Aspin	Y	Y	Y	N	?	Y	?	Y
2 Kastenmeier	Y	Y	Y	N	Y	Y	Y	Y
3 ***Gunderson***	Y	N	Y	Y	N	Y	N	Y
4 Kleczka	Y	Y	Y	N	Y	Y	Y	Y
5 Moody	Y	Y	N	N	Y	Y	Y	Y
6 ***Petri***	Y	N	Y	Y	N	Y	Y	N
7 Obey	Y	Y	N	N	Y	Y	Y	Y
8 ***Roth***	Y	N	Y	Y	N	X	Y	N
9 ***Sensenbrenner***	Y	N	Y	Y	N	N	N	N
WYOMING								
AL ***Thomas***	Y	N	Y	Y	Y	Y	N	N

	9	10	11	12	13	14	15	16
ALABAMA								
Heflin	N	N	N	N	N	Y	Y	N
Shelby	Y	N	N	N	N	Y	Y	N
ALASKA								
Murkowski	Y	N	N	N	Y	Y	Y	N
Stevens	Y	N	N	N	Y	Y	Y	Y
ARIZONA								
DeConcini	Y	N	N	N	+	Y	Y	N
McCain	Y	N	N	N	Y	Y	Y	N
ARKANSAS								
Bumpers	Y	Y	Y	Y	Y	N	N	Y
Pryor	Y	Y	Y	Y	Y	N	N	N
CALIFORNIA								
Cranston	Y	N	Y	Y	Y	N	N	Y
Wilson	Y	N	N	N	?	?	Y	N
COLORADO								
Wirth	Y	Y	Y	Y	?	N	N	N
Armstrong	Y	N	N	Y	Y	Y	Y	N
CONNECTICUT								
Dodd	Y	N	Y	N	Y	N	N	Y
Lieberman	Y	Y	Y	N	Y	N	Y	Y
DELAWARE								
Biden	Y	Y	Y	N	Y	N	N	Y
Roth	Y	N	Y	N	Y	Y	Y	Y
FLORIDA								
Graham	Y	N	Y	N	Y	N	N	Y
Mack	Y	N	N	N	Y	Y	Y	N
GEORGIA								
Fowler	N	N	Y	Y	Y	Y	N	Y
Nunn	Y	N	?	N	Y	Y	N	N
HAWAII								
Inouye	N	N	Y	Y	Y	N	N	Y
Matsunaga	Y	Y	Y	?	Y	N	X	?
IDAHO								
McClure	N	N	N	N	Y	Y	Y	N
Symms	N	N	N	N	Y	Y	Y	Y
ILLINOIS								
Dixon	Y	N	Y	N	N	Y	N	Y
Simon	Y	Y	Y	N	N	N	N	N
INDIANA								
Coats	Y	N	N	N	Y	Y	Y	N
Lugar	Y	N	Y	Y	Y	Y	Y	Y
IOWA								
Harkin	Y	Y	Y	N	Y	N	N	N
Grassley	N	N	N	N	Y	Y	Y	N
KANSAS								
Dole	Y	N	N	Y	Y	Y	Y	Y
Kassebaum	Y	N	Y	N	Y	Y	Y	N
KENTUCKY								
Ford	N	N	N	N	Y	Y	N	Y
McConnell	N	N	N	N	N	Y	Y	N
LOUISIANA								
Breaux	N	N	N	N	Y	Y	N	Y
Johnston	N	N	Y	N	Y	Y	Y	N
MAINE								
Mitchell	Y	Y	Y	Y	Y	N	N	Y
Cohen	Y	Y	Y	Y	Y	N	Y	N
MARYLAND								
Mikulski	Y	Y	Y	Y	Y	N	N	Y
Sarbanes	Y	Y	Y	Y	Y	N	N	Y
MASSACHUSETTS								
Kennedy	Y	Y	Y	Y	Y	N	N	Y
Kerry	Y	Y	Y	Y	Y	N	N	N
MICHIGAN								
Levin	Y	N	Y	N	Y	N	N	N
Riegle	Y	Y	Y	Y	Y	N	N	Y
MINNESOTA								
Boschwitz	Y	N	Y	N	Y	Y	Y	Y
Durenberger	Y	N	Y	Y	Y	N	Y	Y
MISSISSIPPI								
Cochran	Y	N	N	N	Y	Y	Y	Y
Lott	?	N	N	N	Y	Y	Y	Y
MISSOURI								
Bond	N	N	Y	N	Y	Y	Y	Y
Danforth	Y	N	Y	N	Y	N	Y	N
MONTANA								
Baucus	Y	Y	Y	N	Y	N	N	N
Burns	N	N	N	N	Y	Y	Y	N
NEBRASKA								
Exon	Y	N	N	N	Y	Y	N	N
Kerrey	Y	Y	Y	Y	Y	N	N	N
NEVADA								
Bryan	Y	N	N	N	Y	Y	N	N
Reid	Y	N	Y	N	Y	Y	N	N
NEW HAMPSHIRE								
Humphrey	Y	N	N	N	Y	N	Y	Y
Rudman	Y	N	Y	N	Y	N	Y	Y
NEW JERSEY								
Bradley	Y	Y	Y	Y	Y	N	N	N
Lautenberg	Y	N	Y	Y	Y	N	N	N
NEW MEXICO								
Bingaman	Y	N	Y	N	Y	N	N	Y
Domenici	Y	N	Y	N	Y	Y	Y	Y
NEW YORK								
Moynihan	Y	N	Y	Y	Y	N	N	Y
D'Amato	Y	N	Y	N	Y	Y	Y	Y
NORTH CAROLINA								
Sanford	N	N	Y	Y	Y	N	N	N
Helms	N	N	N	N	N	Y	Y	N
NORTH DAKOTA								
Burdick	Y	Y	Y	Y	Y	Y	N	N
Conrad	Y	N	N	Y	Y	N	N	Y
OHIO								
Glenn	Y	N	Y	Y	Y	N	N	Y
Metzenbaum	Y	Y	Y	Y	Y	N	N	Y
OKLAHOMA								
Boren	Y	N	Y	Y	?	N	Y	N
Nickles	Y	N	N	N	Y	Y	Y	N
OREGON								
Hatfield	Y	Y	Y	N	+	N	Y	Y
Packwood	Y	N	Y	N	Y	N	Y	Y
PENNSYLVANIA								
Heinz	Y	N	Y	N	Y	Y	Y	Y
Specter	Y	N	Y	N	Y	N	Y	Y
RHODE ISLAND								
Pell	Y	Y	Y	N	Y	N	#	N
Chafee	Y	N	Y	Y	Y	N	Y	Y
SOUTH CAROLINA								
Hollings	N	Y	N	N	N	Y	N	Y
Thurmond	Y	N	N	N	Y	Y	Y	N
SOUTH DAKOTA								
Daschle	Y	Y	Y	Y	Y	N	N	Y
Pressler	Y	N	N	N	Y	Y	Y	N
TENNESSEE								
Gore	Y	N	Y	N	Y	N	N	Y
Sasser	N	Y	Y	Y	Y	N	N	Y
TEXAS								
Bentsen	Y	N	?	Y	Y	Y	N	Y
Gramm	N	N	N	N	Y	Y	Y	N
UTAH								
Garn	Y	N	N	N	Y	Y	Y	Y
Hatch	Y	N	N	N	Y	Y	Y	Y
VERMONT								
Leahy	?	Y	Y	Y	Y	N	N	Y
Jeffords	Y	N	?	Y	Y	N	Y	Y
VIRGINIA								
Robb	Y	N	Y	Y	Y	Y	N	Y
Warner	N	N	Y	N	Y	Y	Y	N
WASHINGTON								
Adams	Y	Y	Y	N	Y	N	N	Y
Gorton	Y	N	Y	N	Y	N	Y	Y
WEST VIRGINIA								
Byrd	N	N	N	Y	Y	Y	N	Y
Rockefeller	Y	Y	Y	Y	Y	Y	N	N
WISCONSIN								
Kohl	Y	Y	Y	N	Y	N	N	Y
Kasten	N	N	N	N	Y	Y	Y	N
WYOMING								
Simpson	Y	N	Y	Y	Y	Y	Y	Y
Wallop	N	N	N	N	+	Y	Y	Y

KEY

Y	Voted for (yea).
#	Paired for.
+	Announced for.
N	Voted against (nay).
X	Paired against.
-	Announced against.
P	Voted "present."
C	Voted "present" to avoid possible conflict of interest.
?	Did not vote or otherwise make a position known.

Democrats ***Republicans***

ND Northern Democrats SD Southern Democrats

Southern states - Ala., Ark., Fla., Ga., Ky., La., Miss., N.C., Okla., S.C., Tenn., Texas, Va.

9. HR 3015. Fiscal 1990 Transportation Appropriations/Cloture. Mitchell, D-Maine, motion to invoke cloture (thus limiting debate) on the Lautenberg, D-N.J., amendment to permanently ban smoking on all airline flights within the United States. Motion agreed to 77-21: R 33-11; D 44-10 (ND 35-2, SD 9-8), Sept. 14, 1989.

10. HR 3072. Fiscal 1990 Defense Appropriations/B-2 Funding. Leahy, D-Vt., amendment to delete all funds for procurement of additional B-2 bombers. Rejected 29-71: R 2-43; D 27-28 (ND 23-15, SD 4-13), Sept. 26, 1989. A "nay" was a vote supporting the president's position.

11. HR 3072. Fiscal 1990 Defense Appropriations/National Endowment for the Arts Obscenity. Mitchell, D-Maine, motion to table (kill) the Helms, R-N.C., amendment to instruct the Senate conferees on the fiscal 1990 Interior Department appropriations bill (HR 2788) to insist on a Senate-passed provision barring the use of federal funds for artworks deemed "obscene or indecent." Motion agreed to 62-35: R 19-25; D 43-10 (ND 33-5, SD 10-5), Sept. 28, 1989.

12. S 1726. Catastrophic Revision/Durenberger Substitute. Durenberger, R-Minn., substitute amendment to preserve stop-loss coverage of hospital and doctor bills, plus most other benefits in the 1988 Medicare Catastrophic Coverage Act except prescription drug coverage, and to cut the maximum surtax to $200 in fiscal 1990. Rejected 37-62: R 8-37; D 29-25 (ND 21-16, SD 8-9), Oct. 6, 1989.

13. HR 3299. Fiscal 1990 Budget Reconciliation/Passage. Passage of the bill to reduce the fiscal 1990 budget deficit by $13.5 billion. Passed 87-7: R 40-2; D 47-5 (ND 34-2, SD 13-3), Oct. 13, 1989.

14. S J Res 180. Anti-Flag Desecration/Passage. Passage of the joint resolution to propose a constitutional amendment to grant Congress and the states the power to prohibit the physical desecration of the U.S. flag. Rejected 51-48: R 33-11; D 18-37 (ND 8-30, SD 10-7), Oct. 19, 1989. A two-thirds majority of those present and voting (66 in this case) of both houses is required for passage of a constitutional amendment. A "yea" was a vote supporting the president's position.

15. HR 3628. Capital Gains Tax Cut/Cloture. Mitchell, D-Maine, motion to invoke cloture (thus limiting debate) on the Packwood, R-Ore., substitute amendment to exclude capital gains from taxable income in the amount of 5 percent for each full year an asset is held (to a maximum of 35 percent) and to make Individual Retirement Accounts available to all taxpayers with varying tax benefits. Motion rejected 51-47: R 45-0; D 6-47 (ND 2-34, SD 4-13), Nov. 14, 1989. A three-fifths majority vote (60) of the total Senate is required to invoke cloture. A "yea" was a vote supporting the president's position.

16. HR 3660. Government Pay and Ethics Package/Pay Raise. Mitchell, D-Maine, substitute amendment to give senators a cost-of-living adjustment different from House pay levels and to reduce the ceiling on honoraria senators may keep. Adopted 56-43: R 25-20; D 31-23 (ND 21-16, SD 10-7), Nov. 17, 1989.

1990 Key Votes

Senate

1. Chinese Students Veto

The first vote of the year was set up as a test of the strength of President Bush's veto. Bush had prevailed on all nine previous vetoes, and Democratic leaders thought they would have a breakthrough with a bill to allow Chinese students to remain in the United States instead of returning home to face possible reprisals by the repressive Chinese government. The bill (HR 2712) had cleared near the end of the first session without a dissenting vote in either chamber. When the House took up the veto override, only 25 Republicans stuck by the president.

In the Senate, Bush marshaled a strong display of GOP solidarity. Only eight Republicans went with the Democrats, and the 62-37 vote, taken Jan. 25, fell four short of the two-thirds majority needed to override the veto: R 8-37; D 54-0 (ND 38-0, SD 16-0). The Republican senators who provided the margin of victory expressed their positions in partisan terms as support for the chief executive, not as support for Bush's China policy.

It was a theme that played out for the rest of the year; Bush ended the Congress without having any of his vetoes overridden, and a credible veto threat was one of the few bargaining chips that the Republican minority had on numerous pieces of legislation.

The bill would have permitted Chinese students who were in the United States at the time of the Tiananmen Square massacre in June 1989 to remain for an indeterminate period and to seek permanent resident status without returning to China. It also would have waived for four years a requirement that Chinese exchange students on "J" visas return home for at least two years before applying for permanent U.S. residency.

Bush vetoed the legislation Nov. 30, while Congress was in recess. The action was part of the administration's effort to restore cordial relations with China despite that country's repression of pro-democracy forces. The Chinese government had threatened to permanently pull out of the Fulbright scholarship program and other education exchanges if HR 2712 became law. Bush originally said he considered his veto to be a pocket veto not subject to override by Congress, but did not press the issue when congressional leaders moved ahead with override votes; they argued that a pocket veto could occur only after the adjournment of a full Congress.

Administration officials said they were trying privately to persuade the government in Beijing to ease oppression. Bush had taken other steps to lessen U.S.-Chinese tensions, including sending U.S. officials to Beijing — a secret delegation in July 1989 and a public visit in December 1989 by national security adviser Brent Scowcroft.

Administration officials pointed to Beijing's lifting of martial law as a sign of human rights progress. But members of Congress were skeptical. Rep. Nancy Pelosi, D-Calif., sponsor of HR 2712, said: "Beijing can lift martial law because it does not need martial law to crush dissent. . . . I am confident the Congress will see through these feeble attempts by Chinese leaders to mislead Western governments."

Members who voted to uphold the veto denounced Chinese oppression but said they believed Bush's behind-the-scenes efforts would do more to help democracy than congressional action.

The House vote to override, 390-25, came a day before the Senate vote.

2. Education Programs

Two weeks after the Senate reconvened in 1990, Jesse Helms, R-N.C., tied up President Bush's education initiative for two days with complaints about a $25 million grant tacked on to the legislation (S 695) by Democrats. Though his amendment to delete the provision was defeated on Feb. 6, 35-64: R 35-10; D 0-54 (ND 0-37, SD 0-17), the same issue came back to kill the package on the last day of the 101st Congress.

The grant was to go to the National Board for Professional Teaching Standards, headed by former North Carolina Gov. James B. Hunt Jr., who had challenged Helms in 1984 for his Senate seat in a rancorous campaign.

The board, which was created in 1987 with funding from the Carnegie Corporation of New York and a number of other foundations, was drawing up guidelines for voluntary certification of teachers nationwide.

Helms charged that the board was dominated by teachers' unions, and he predicted that its voluntary certification guidelines would soon turn into mandatory licensing standards for teachers.

"The labor unions want to control education in America. No one else need apply," he said.

Proponents of the plan stressed that certification was not designed to take the place of state and local standards for teachers. "All we are trying to do is to retain the good teachers, attract new ones and provide some recognition for their accomplishments in what they are doing," said Christopher J. Dodd, D-Conn. Despite administration opposition to the grant, 10 Republicans joined Democrats to defeat the Helms amendment.

But at the end of the session, Helms had another chance. S 695 came back to the Senate in the form of HR 5932. The new bill included the president's education proposals plus literacy and teacher training provisions, and had been worked out with the House in an informal conference.

When Majority Leader George J. Mitchell, D-Maine, tried to call the bill up for a vote on Oct. 27, the last full day of the session, Helms and a number of other conservative Republicans objected. The group kept a rolling hold on the bill, with some objecting to a smaller, $10 million grant to the National Board, and with others objecting to different provisions.

In the end, Helms won his battle to kill the grant as well as the entire bill. In a campaign appearance in North Carolina, Helms boasted that he had saved taxpayers $800 million — the cost of the entire education package.

3. Clean Air

The environment lobby had been waiting years for a vote like this one — yes or no on a get-tough amendment to the most important anti-pollution bill (S 1630) in a decade. It seemed that such a vote would separate the black hats from the white hats, prove the movement's true strength in the Senate and provide campaign fodder for years to come.

For all the frantic lobbying beforehand, however, the outcome the week of March 19 was far from a definitive indication of the new environmental politics. Instead, it proved to be a pivotal show of strength for an unusual alliance: the Republican White House, which had introduced and backed clean air legislation for the first time in a decade, and Senate leaders of both parties, who had fashioned a compromise off the floor in the hope of winning passage for the first time since the Clean Air Act was last amended in 1977.

At stake was an amendment by Sens. Tim Wirth, D-Colo., and Pete Wilson, R-Calif. They wanted to make the bill's auto-emissions controls and clean-fuel provisions substantially tougher than the White House-leadership compromise.

Wirth and Wilson wanted to require an automatic, second round of tailpipe emissions reductions in 2002 — not a conditional review based on how much progress had been made, as called for in the White House compromise. They also wanted to require the use of cleaner burning gasoline mixes by 1993 in all smog-heavy areas — 60 to 70 in all — not just in the nine worst cities, as the compromise stipulated.

The Senate killed Wirth-Wilson 52-46, on a motion to table: R 25-19; D 27-27 (ND 14-23, SD 13-4), March 20.

The result, however, appeared to be less a measure of environmentalist vs. industry muscle than of the unusual political alliances that formed around the Senate bill.

Farm-state members liked the Wirth-Wilson amendment because they believed it favored grain-based ethanol as an alternative clean fuel. Others went for it thinking it would help small businesses by shifting more of the pain of cleaning the air to big oil companies and car manufacturers.

Meanwhile, usually pro-environment senators voted against the amendment, fearing that it would scuttle the still-tenuous compromise with the Bush administration. Majority Leader George J. Mitchell, D-Maine, and his Republican counterpart, Bob Dole of Kansas, made the vote a test of the compromise's survival.

Much of the debate over Wirth-Wilson focused on whether it would indeed doom the bill's chances for yet another year. The environment lobby, dominated by purists, had made it clear that it did not think much of the Mitchell-Dole-White House compromise.

The Wirth-Wilson amendment was the group's main shot at shoring up the bill, so the lobby fought hard to counter the argument that it would harm its chances.

But many of their traditional allies remained swayed by Mitchell and voted with him to table the amendment. Voting to table were senators who usually voted the environmentalist position, including Democrats Christopher J. Dodd of Connecticut, Paul S. Sarbanes of Maryland and Howard M. Metzenbaum of Ohio, and Republican Gordon J. Humphrey of New Hampshire.

Then again, some usually pro-industry senators voted for the Wirth-Wilson amendment — at least one hoping that it would indeed become a "dealbuster."

Voting for Wirth-Wilson were Republicans who rarely toed the environment lobby's line, including Jesse Helms of North Carolina, James A. McClure and Steve Symms of Idaho, Jake Garn and Orrin G. Hatch of Utah, and Malcolm Wallop of Wyoming.

The defeat of Wirth-Wilson was followed the next day by another close vote on an amendment by Bob Kerrey, D-Neb., to toughen the urban smog provisions of the deal. It was killed on a 53-46 tabling vote.

After those votes, the Senate compromise was able to survive all onslaughts — including another test in the attempt by Robert C. Byrd, D-W.Va., to ensure job-loss benefits for coal miners. *(House key vote 3)*

4. Job-Loss Benefits

Ostensibly, the two-week fight over Robert C. Byrd's amendment to the Senate clean air bill (S 1630) was over job-loss benefits for coal miners. The narrow defeat of the West Virginia Democrat's proposal, however, said little about the Senate's sympathy for miners thrown out of work by the bill: The chamber later approved a less ambitious House-crafted package as part of the final bill.

What the episode did show was the complex nature of power within the Senate. When the roll call was taken March 29, traditional liberal-conservative divisions broke down, and members were driven more by loyalty, fear and trickery.

The debate pitted Byrd's formidable force as chairman of the Appropriations Committee against Majority Leader George J. Mitchell of Maine, who had become inextricably linked in an alliance of convenience with the White House. The fight was the climax to Byrd's long struggle against a new clean air law. As the Democrats' leader before Mitchell, Byrd for years helped block such bills, knowing well that reducing acid rain would involve weaning the nation from West Virginia's high-sulfur coal.

Once Byrd stepped down from that post, he lost much of his power over the issue. President Bush was committed to signing a clear air bill so that he could become the "environmental president," and Mitchell had long advocated such legislation.

So Byrd made the best of the situation: He tried to extract a price from the bill's supporters in the form of hundreds of millions of dollars for his constituents.

A master of debate, Byrd spent hours on the floor pleading for support. "Have we looked into the eyes of a hungry coal miner's child?" he asked at one point. For days, few would publicly oppose him; he joked that he had been forced into negotiations with himself.

But the White House remained adamantly opposed, pointedly hinting that President Bush would veto the entire bill over Byrd's amendment. Mitchell fought it hard, but only to preserve a broad clean air deal with the White House; his sympathies clearly rested with Byrd on the need for unemployment benefits.

Byrd took advantage of Mitchell's dilemma. During a photo session the day before the vote, Byrd put his arm around a coal miner's son and said: "Sen. Mitchell is fighting for what he believes in, and I'm fighting for what I believe in."

Byrd had more than symbolic strength, however. His pockets were full of IOUs from 32 years in the Senate, and as the new chairman of the Appropriations Committee, he had plenty of future chits to hand out.

His office-to-office campaign served as a not-so-subtle reminder to his colleagues of what each had at stake in the fight. A large majority of his Democratic colleagues were too loyal or too afraid to vote against him, as were many Republicans. "Had I offered an amendment like this, I would not get five votes," said Republican leader Bob Dole of Kansas.

Minutes before the vote, it looked like Byrd might just win. Said Mitchell: "None of us like the choice we now face."

The White House, however, stole two of Byrd's votes, and thus victory, with a last-minute bit of apparent double-dealing.

During the roll call, Bush's chief of staff, John H. Sununu, assured Joseph R. Biden Jr., D-Del., that the president would veto the bill if Byrd won. Not wanting to scuttle the bill, Biden voted no. Earlier Sununu had told Steve Symms, R-Idaho, just the opposite — that Bush would not veto the whole bill just because he opposed the Byrd amendment.

Symms, convinced that the clean air bill was too expensive already, had been looking for a way to derail it. Assured that the Byrd amendment would not do the trick, he voted against making what he thought was a bad bill worse.

Byrd's amendment fell short by one vote, 49-50: R 11-34; D 38-16 (ND 29-9, SD 9-7). *(House key vote 2)*

5. Assault Weapons

Senate Democrats surprised themselves May 23 by gathering enough votes to preserve in an anti-crime bill (S 1970) a ban on semiautomatic assault-style weapons. The vote temporarily snagged the bill in the Senate, and ultimately, Congress backed away from the controversial topics of gun control and the death penalty as it settled for a much less sweeping anti-crime bill than it had planned.

The provision would have outlawed the manufacture, sale or possession of nine semiautomatic weapons, including the AK-47, used in a January 1989 schoolyard massacre in Stockton, Calif., that sparked an outcry over criminal use of semiautomatics. The gun control provision squeaked by the Senate Judiciary Committee in July 1989 on a 7-6 vote, largely because two usual opponents of gun control did not contest it.

The crime bill made it to the floor 10 months later, with President Bush on numerous occasions criticizing Congress for inaction. Gun control opponents tried to delete the assault weapons ban, but their motion failed 48-52: R 36-9; D 12-43 (ND 5-33, SD 7-10). Two hours later, gun control advocates prevailed again as a motion to reconsider fell short, 49-50. Dennis DeConcini, D-Ariz., whose sponsorship of the gun ban had touched off a brief recall effort in Arizona, brought off the one-vote victory.

The Senate gun vote marked that chamber's biggest defeat for the National Rifle Association (NRA), which was known for its lobbying muscle and hefty campaign contributions. The NRA had been able to dissuade both chambers from voting for restrictions on handguns. But assault weapons were a different story, since they had come to be a symbol of the drug trade.

DeConcini was supported by a handful of Southern Democrats who had generally opposed gun control, including Lloyd Bentsen of Texas, David L. Boren of Oklahoma, Sam Nunn of Georgia and Al Gore of Tennessee. He also won the vote of Majority Leader George J. Mitchell of Maine, who came from a big sporting state and who had been quoted in the past as saying he did not believe in gun control.

The Senate did, however, reject an amendment by Howard M. Metzenbaum, D-Ohio, that would have permanently banned 12 more types of semiautomatic rifles and pistols and limited ammunition magazines to 15 rounds.

Gun control, opposed by most Republicans and the Bush administration, was one of the disputed items that hung up passage of a comprehensive anti-crime bill. House conferees would not give up on racial protections for death penalty defendants, which the Senate had rejected. Senate conferees would not relinquish gun control. Both subjects were stripped from the final bill, paving the way for passage.

6. Flag Burning

Closing out a chapter that began a year earlier, the Senate on June 26 defeated a resolution (S J Res 332) for a constitutional amendment to protect the flag. The 58-42 vote was nine short of the two-thirds needed to pass the amendment: R 38-7; D 20-35 (ND 10-28, SD 10-7).

The resolution stated: "The Congress and the states shall have the power to prohibit the physical desecration of the flag of the United States."

It was a loss for President Bush, who had been pushing for an amendment to the Constitution since the Supreme Court first ruled on June 21, 1989, that a Texas law against flag burning infringed on First Amendment guarantees of free expression. A second Supreme Court ruling, on June 11, 1990, striking down a federal flag law, touched off the second round of political rhetoric on whether the flag needed special protection. But the second ruling sparked much less public outcry than the first, and that gave opponents of a constitutional amendment an edge.

Members against the amendment asserted that it was politically inspired and too radical a solution to the few flag-burning incidents that occurred. Some members thought defeat of the amendment would be used in the fall elections, since it had been mostly Republicans championing the constitutional amendment. But hardly a peep on the flag was heard.

The Senate had rejected a constitutional amendment to protect the Stars and Stripes a year earlier, after the first court ruling. As an alternative, Congress on Oct. 12, 1989, cleared the statute (HR 2978 — PL 101-131) to safeguard the flag from physical desecration; that was the law struck down by the high court in June.

The Senate's June 26 vote was superfluous because a week earlier the House had failed by 34 votes to gain the necessary two-thirds to pass the amendment. Approval by both chambers was needed to send an amendment to the states for ratification. *(House key vote 4)*

7. Americans with Disabilities Act

In contrast to the high-profile debates in 1990 over flag burning, pornographic art and the budget, Congress passed the Americans with Disabilities Act (ADA) with comparatively little fanfare. But while it was barely noticed by most of the general public, the sweeping civil rights measure would affect the lives of far more Americans than the 43 million with physical or mental disabilities.

The ADA guaranteed to those with disabilities protections against discrimination in employment, public transit, public accommodations and telecommunications. It required employers to make "reasonable accommodations" needed by workers with disabilities, and business owners to make "readily achievable" changes to make facilities accessible to and usable by those with disabilities. It also required telecommunications companies to operate relay systems that allowed those with speech or hearing impairments to use the telephone.

Backed by candidate George Bush on the campaign trail in 1988 and by a bipartisan corps in Congress that included leaders of both parties from both chambers, there was never much doubt that the ADA would become law during the 101st Congress. But there were some tense moments for backers of the bill when progress was stalled temporarily over two relatively minor issues: how to include Congress as a covered entity, and whether or not people with AIDS could be transferred out of food handling jobs.

Both issues were ultimately resolved by mid-July, with the House approving a second conference report on the measure by a vote of 377-28 on July 12. A day later, after a brief but emotional debate during which Orrin G. Hatch, R-Utah, broke down as he spoke of the courage with which his late brother-in-law battled polio, the Senate overwhelmingly cleared the measure by a vote of 91-6: R 37-6; D 54-0 (ND 37-0, SD 17-0).

President Bush signed the bill (PL 101-336) on July 26 at a huge outdoor ceremony on the White House grounds.

8. Farm Price Supports

In the weeks leading up to Senate floor action on the 1990 farm bill in July, there was plenty of fierce politicking on the issue of farm price supports. Much of the action centered on supports for one crop, sugar. Sugar seemed to be emerging as a sacrificial lamb, the one crop subsidy program among the multitude that Congress might dare to cut — not so much to save money as to save face: Politically the sugar program had become almost indefensible.

The opportunity came on an amendment by Bill Bradley, D-N.J., to the farm bill (S 2830) to cut the 18-cent sugar support price by 2 cents.

Candy makers and soda companies had directed a steady barrage of invective at the program that guaranteed prices for sugar that were far above world market levels. They charged that it was protectionist and gouged consumers at home and some of our best and poorest allies abroad. Though by law it cost taxpayers nothing, it hurt consumers by artificially bolstering the price of sugar and hurt the nation's sugar-producing allies by preventing them from selling their main product in the United States.

The sugar industry countered that cutting the support price would be devastating, from the cane fields of Hawaii, Louisiana and Florida to the sugar beet and corn fields of the Midwest, all the way to the processing plants in New York, California and elsewhere.

For several months, the Bush administration had been flip-flopping, caught between its support for lifting "trade-distorting" subsidies around the world and the need to bolster the fortunes of Republican Senate candidates in states where the need for a high sugar price verged on gospel.

But before the vote on the Bradley amendment, all the signs suggested that it had a good chance of passing. Agriculture Secretary Clayton Yeutter had unequivocally endorsed it. So had Cargill, the giant Midwestern agribusiness company. That raised the possibility that farm-state lawmakers, who usually banded together to defeat assaults on individual programs, might split their votes.

In fact, the vote proved that the farm coalition remained powerful and mostly unified. The 2-cent cut was tabled, or killed, on July 24 by a vote of 54-44: R 17-26; D 37-18 (ND 22-16, SD 15-2).

Later that day, during debate on its version of the farm bill, the House also rebuffed a similar amendment, 150-271.

The Senate sugar vote foreshadowed what would occur throughout floor action on the farm bill. Amendments cutting or eliminating specific crop programs were repeatedly rejected, often by wide margins. Many lawmakers said they realized that the budget would require deep cuts in farm programs, but they preferred to leave that responsibility in the hands of the budget summit negotiators.

9. Campaign Finance

Perhaps the most surprising thing about the Senate's July 30 vote on taxpayer financing of congressional campaigns was that it took place at all.

It was one of 17 roll call votes on amendments that, taken together, showed how far campaign finance legislation had come since the 100th Congress, when the action never advanced beyond a Republican filibuster. But the results also showed how far there was to go before there was substantive change in the law.

The bill put before the Senate by the Democrats (S 137) sought to impose state-by-state spending limits on Senate races and eliminate political action committees (an idea borrowed from the GOP). But because spending limits had to be voluntary, the bill called for wide-ranging use of public monies to lure participation.

The incentives offered to participants included: discounts on campaign mail; a voucher worth 20 percent of the spending limit for the state, to be used to purchase television time in blocks of one minute or more; and contingent public financing if an opposing candidate exceeded the spending limits. The cost to the Treasury was estimated at more than $56 million a year. While proponents argued that this was a small price to pay for their vision of reform, opponents ridiculed the idea of asking taxpayers to pay for congressional elections in an era of $300 billion federal deficits.

Republicans opposed both spending limits and public financing. Kentucky Sen. Mitch McConnell, the Republican floor manager, argued that because the U.S. election system equated spending with free speech — an opinion expressed by the Supreme Court in its 1976 *Buckley v. Valeo* decision — the government would in effect punish candidates who chose to exercise their First Amendment rights, by giving money to their opponents. Republicans, moreover, were convinced that rigid spending limits would deter their efforts to retake the Senate.

McConnell moved to strip all forms of taxpayer financing from the bill. It was rejected 46-49: R 44-0; D 2-49 (ND 1-34, SD 1-15). The narrow, basically party-line defeat signaled that the Democrats would be in firm control of the debate. But that partisan cast brought a firm veto threat from President Bush, and while the House also passed a bill, the two chambers never attempted to resolve the considerable differences between Democrats at different ends of the Capitol.

10. Abortion/Parental Notification

For several years, the conventional wisdom about the abortion debate held that while it was difficult to tell from opinion surveys how available most Americans thought the procedure should be, two issues regularly claimed large majorities. One was the question of abortion in cases of rape and incest, which both sides conceded was supported by a substantial majority of the public. The other was whether minors should have to notify or obtain consent from their parents before an abortion could be performed. On that question, too, supporters of abortion rights as well as abortion opponents agreed that the public favored some sort of parental notification. Thus, while rape and incest came to be viewed as the weakest issue for abortion opponents, parental notification was considered the Achilles' heel for abortion rights supporters.

Congress had voted often on providing federal funding in cases of rape and incest, and the House's shift in 1989 from a position opposing such funding to support signaled abortion rights gains in the backlash from the Supreme Court's decision in *Webster v. Reproductive Health Services*. That July 1989 decision gave states broader authority to restrict abortion than at any time since the court struck down state abortion bans in the 1973 *Roe v. Wade* decision.

By contrast, Congress had almost no track record on parental notification, an issue generally debated at the state level. Sen. William L. Armstrong, R-Colo., a leader of anti-abortion forces, made a first attempt to force votes on the issue Sept. 26 when he offered an amendment to a family planning reauthorization bill (S 110) that would require federally supported family planning agencies to notify a parent of a minor 48 hours before an abortion could be performed. But a roll call was muddied by the fact that it was tied to an unrelated amendment urging President Bush to tap the Strategic Petroleum Reserve. The amendment was eventually added to the bill by voice vote, but S 110 died the next day when it failed to achieve cloture to limit debate.

But the question was more clear-cut on Oct. 12, when Armstrong sought to append a similar amendment to the fiscal 1991 appropriations bill for the Departments of Labor, Health and Human Services (HHS), and Education (HR 5257). In contrast to the earlier vote, this time abortion rights supporters worked to defeat the amendment, and, to their surprise, they almost succeeded. It was added to the bill only after a motion by Labor-HHS Subcommittee Chairman Tom Harkin, D-Iowa, to table it failed on a 48-48 tie: R 8-34; D 40-14 (ND 31-6, SD 9-8).

In the end, the parental notification language and an amendment permitting abortion funding in cases of rape or incest, to which the notification amendment had been added, were both dropped to clear the bill.

Still, abortion rights supporters were buoyed by the strength of the vote on their weakest issue. And Congress might have been influenced further by the defeat Nov. 6 of a parental notification ballot proposal in Oregon. Even abortion rights supporters, who vehemently opposed the proposal, expected it to pass.

11. U.S. Troops in Europe

The budget crunch and the dramatic improvement in U.S.-Soviet relations added high-octane fuel to the long-simmering congressional unhappiness over the cost of stationing U.S. forces overseas.

Since the mid-1970s, a growing coalition in Congress has argued that high Pentagon budgets are, in effect, subsidies for the United States' strongest commercial competitors, particularly Japan and Germany. The critics argued that countries protected by the U.S. shield could spend a smaller share of their national wealth on defense programs, making available more money for productive investments. Presidents of both parties had countered that overseas deployments directly serve U.S. security interests. But they also had pressed the major allies to begin picking up a larger share of the cost of alliance defense efforts.

In 1990, with the Soviet-led Warsaw Pact disintegrating and a treaty slashing the size of conventional forces in Europe (CFE) nearing completion, demands to bring home some of the 311,000 Army and Air Force personnel in Europe rose to a crescendo. The House and Senate each approved a provision in the fiscal 1991 defense authorization bill (HR 4739) to cut the overseas deployment by 50,000.

By the time the Senate took up the companion defense appropriations bill (S 3189) on Oct. 15, critics had another grievance: the allies' paltry commitments to the U.S.-led deployments to the Persian Gulf to confront Iraq. An amendment to the appropriations measure by Kent Conrad, D-N.D., would have sliced U.S. manpower in Europe by 80,000 — a reduction of 30,000 more than each chamber had approved. It was only narrowly rejected, 46-50: R 8-34; D 38-16 (ND 31-6, SD 7-10).

Days later, in negotiations over the authorization measure, the 80,000-troop-cut was accepted by the administration for fear that even deeper cuts would win out. The final version of the appropriations bill settled on a cut of 78,600 personnel.

12. 'Stealth' Bomber

The B-2 "stealth" bomber, designed to penetrate Soviet air defenses but controversial because of its cost, ran into more congressional flak in 1990 because of the declining Pentagon budget and the receding Soviet threat.

The plane's exotic materials and complex shape were intended to prevent an enemy from locating it with sufficient precision to shoot it down. But those factors also produced a price tag that was all too visible on the political battlefield — between $450 million and $850 million per copy, according to competing estimates.

For decades, liberals had challenged the need for bombers with sophisticated equipment designed to slip through Soviet defenses. The same missions could be performed more cheaply by small, long-range cruise missiles launched from planes flying beyond the reach of Soviet defenses, the critics argued.

Air Force leaders and congressional backers of the program contended that the B-2's hard-to-detect design would give U.S. forces a revolutionary advantage in conventional conflicts, as well as in a nuclear war. To get control of the program's soaring cost, the Pentagon in April cut the planned B-2 fleet from 132 planes to 75. But the argument that the plane simply cost too much, particularly in light of eased U.S.-Soviet relations, made significant headway, even among Senate and House Republicans.

In 1990, a bipartisan coalition persuaded the House to oppose building any more B-2s beyond the 15 planes funded in previous budgets. The Senate approved funds for two additional planes in fiscal 1991, and the two bodies wrestled the issue to an intentionally ambiguous draw: authorizing and appropriating more B-2 procurement money, but not specifying whether it could be used for anything more than unanticipated cost increases on the previously funded bombers. Even in the Senate, where support for the B-2 had been stronger, critics made a creditable showing, reaching their high-water mark on an amendment to the fiscal 1991 defense appropriations bill that would have halted B-2 production. The amendment, by Patrick J. Leahy, D-Vt., was rejected 44-50: R 9-32; D 35-18 (ND 30-7, SD 5-11).

13. Tax and Spending-Cut Package

The House vote to defeat the budget summit deal Oct. 5 deprived the Senate of a chance to weigh in on the most controversial aspect of the budget debate — not that many senators complained. Only two weeks later — after both chambers had given their committees the responsibility for ironing out the specifics of how to raise taxes and cut spending — did the Senate face a tough vote. *(House key vote 11)*

The action came on a budget-reconciliation bill rolled together by the Senate Budget Committee after other committees had filled in the details of a bare-bones budget resolution. Again, the House had acted first. Armed with their 83-vote majority, House Democrats ignored GOP complaints and passed a partisan Democratic alternative reconciliation bill that skewed tax increases heavily toward the wealthiest taxpayers.

The narrower 10-vote Democratic margin in the Senate forced party leaders to temper their reconciliation bill from the start. After lengthy negotiations with GOP leaders and White House officials over the measure's tax and entitlement program components, Democratic leaders agreed to back a more moderate reconciliation measure.

That put Senate Majority Leader George J. Mitchell, D-Maine, and other top Democrats on the defensive during floor debate — primarily against attacks from liberals in their own party. Democratic senators made repeated attempts to amend the reconciliation bill to make it more like the one the House had passed, but Mitchell and Senate Budget Committee Chairman Jim Sasser, D-Tenn., had to fight each amendment on the grounds that it would violate their deal with Republican leaders and the White House, and thereby kill the bill. They killed proposals that appealed to Democrats, such as a proposal by Al Gore, D-Tenn., and Barbara A. Mikulski, D-Md., to raise taxes on the wealthy in order to cut back a proposed increase in the gasoline tax and eliminate proposed increases in payments by Medicare beneficiaries.

The debate stretched over three days, Oct. 17-19. When it came time for a vote on final passage shortly after 1 a.m. on Oct. 19, liberal Democrats had been unable to change it, and conservative Republicans, who were bitterly opposed to the package's broad new taxes, had been unable to kill it. Leaders had agreed that both parties would provide a majority of their members in support of the package, and that took some doing. Some senators with tough re-election races wanted desperately to vote against the measure. The measure went over the top only when GOP leaders persuaded two Republican senators to switch their "nay" votes to "yeas"; others then followed. In the end, the Senate approved the bill 54-46: R 23-22; D 31-24 (ND 20-18, SD 11-6). The final package that President Bush signed looked more like the Senate bill than the House version. *(House key vote 14)*

14. El Salvador Aid

Few foreign policy issues had been more contentious during the 1980s than military aid for El Salvador. Conservatives had argued that the support was essential to prevent left-wing guerrillas from taking over; liberals objected to the assistance because of the poor human rights record of the government in San Salvador.

Although the issue caused fierce ideological divisions, the Reagan and Bush administrations managed to win continued military assistance during the 1980s, thanks to backing in the Senate from Republicans and centrist Democrats. But that loose coalition eventually fell apart in 1990, primarily because of the military's alleged role in yet another atrocity.

Senators from both parties agreed that the character of the issue changed substantially on Nov. 16, 1989, when six Jesuit priests and their two housekeepers were murdered. Eight soldiers were arrested after the execution-style slayings, and there were suspicions that high-ranking officers — including the head of military forces — had prior knowledge of the murders. A House task force concluded that the government botched its investigation of the case, and the House voted in May to cut U.S. aid by half.

The murders and charges of a coverup resulted in a backlash against the Salvadoran military. That sentiment was bolstered by Congress' waning interest in Third World conflicts that had served as proxies for superpower rivalry during the Cold War.

The Senate followed the House in slashing aid Oct. 19, approving an immediate 50 percent cut in the $85 million military aid package for El Salvador by a vote of 74-25: R 19-25; D 55-0 (ND 38-0, SD 17-0).

The measure, an amendment to the foreign aid appropriations bill (HR 5114), was sponsored by Democratic Sens. Christopher J. Dodd, Conn., and Patrick J. Leahy, Vt. Support for the amendment crossed partisan and ideological lines. Dodd said senators were "fed up" with El Salvador's continuing human rights abuses.

An administration-backed amendment aimed at weakening the Dodd-Leahy provision, offered by Bob Graham, D-Fla., was subsequently defeated, also by a wide margin (39-58). President Bush initially had vowed to veto the foreign aid bill if it included restrictions on military aid, but the threat was eventually withdrawn, and he signed the bill. *(House key vote 1)*

15. Egyptian Debt

After Iraq's invasion of Kuwait on Aug. 2, the White House assiduously cultivated Arab backing for the U.N. embargo against the regime of Saddam Hussein and for the U.S. military buildup in the Persian Gulf.

Egypt was considered particularly crucial to the alliance. As a reward for its help and to relieve its economic burden, the White House decided to forgive $6.7 billion in military debts the Egyptian government owed.

The action triggered far more congressional criticism than the initial dispatch of 200,000 troops to the region. Lawmakers from both parties, while recognizing the unique contributions of President Hosni Mubarak's government to the multilateral coalition against Iraq, were concerned that it could set a precedent for debt forgiveness that would lead to new problems. Sen. Patrick J. Leahy, D-Vt., said, "If we grant relief to all of the nations that request it, the total cost could be $60 billion, $61 billion."

But Leahy, chairman of the Senate Appropriations Subcommittee on Foreign Operations, eventually supported the debt relief offer. He led successful opposition to an amendment by Sen. Tom Harkin, D-Iowa, that would have stricken the debt-relief provision from the foreign aid appropriations bill (HR 5114). On Oct. 19, the Harkin amendment was defeated 42-55: R 10-34; D 32-21 (ND 20-16, SD 12-5).

There was no up-or-down vote on the provision in the House because work on the foreign aid appropriations bill had been completed well before the Iraqi invasion of Kuwait. But intense opposition to the provision contributed to the narrow margin (188-162) by which the conference report on the final aid bill was passed by the House on Oct. 27.

16. Civil Rights

By a single vote, the Senate on Oct. 24 failed to override President Bush's veto of a sweeping civil rights bill (S 2104 — H Rept 101-856). The result was the first defeat of a major civil rights bill in the last 25 years.

The vote was 66-34: R 11-34; D 55-0 (ND 38-0, SD 17-0). Democratic sponsors complained that the administration was not honest in its months-long negotiations on the legislation and that Bush likely never intended to sign the measure, which would have made it easier to prove job discrimination.

The administration rejoined that the Hill sponsors wanted too much too fast and were unwilling to compromise. On the day of the override vote, black House members ringed the Senate floor, and in the gallery sat Jesse Jackson and, separately, David Duke, a failed Louisiana senatorial candidate and former Ku Klux Klan leader who had run against affirmative action.

The bill would have countered six 1989 Supreme Court rulings that narrowed the rights and remedies of victims of job discrimination. It also would have responded to four other court decisions from the 1980s by making it easier for lawyers for prevailing plaintiffs to recover costs and fees.

Unrelated to high court action, the bill would have amended Title VII of the 1964 Civil Rights Act to allow victims of intentional discrimination to recover compensatory damages and, in egregious cases, punitive damages. Title VII forbade racial, sex, religious and ethnic bias in the workplace. Title VII remedies were limited to back pay and benefits, attorneys' fees and court orders to correct discriminatory practices. The bill also would have allowed jury trials.

The arguments against the bill could be stated in one word: quotas. Bush and business groups contended that the bill would cause companies to adopt hiring quotas for women and minorities so that they would not be subject to frivolous lawsuits based on the presence of a higher percentage of male or white workers.

That argument arose primarily from the centerpiece of the legislation, intended to reverse the court's June 1989 ruling in *Wards Cove Packing Co. v. Atonio*. The bill would have made it more difficult for an employer to justify in court job practices that were fair in form but that had an adverse impact on minorities or women. Examples of such practices were skill tests or physical requirements. *(House key vote 15)*

House

1. El Salvador Aid

For Rep. Joe Moakley, D-Mass., chairman of the powerful Rules Committee and head of a House task force on El Salvador, tolerance for rights abuses perpetrated by the Salvadoran military reached a breaking point in 1990. "Enough is enough," said Moakley during the House debate on the fiscal 1990 foreign aid supplemental authorization bill (HR 4636).

His colleagues agreed and on May 22 approved a 50 percent cut in military aid to the government in San Salvador by adopting a Moakley amendment 250-163: R 31-135; D 219-28 (ND 166-4, SD 53-24). It was the first of several defeats for the administration on the issue, culminating in Senate passage Oct. 19 of an amendment to the fiscal 1991 foreign aid appropriations bill that also required a 50 percent aid cut.

In a pattern later repeated in the Senate, liberal House opponents of the aid to El Salvador were able to enlist more moderate members — such as John P. Murtha, D-Pa., chairman of the Defense Appropriations Subcommittee — who in the past had been strong backers of the Salvadoran military. Murtha, a member of the Moakley task force, which traveled to El Salvador to investigate the 1989 murders of six Jesuit priests, cosponsored the measure to reduce the aid.

Still, it took some time for a consistent House position on the issue to jell. On May 24, with the El Salvador aid as only one of the issues in dispute, the House voted down the foreign aid bill to which the language sponsored by Moakley and Murtha was attached. But by June, when the House considered the fiscal 1991 foreign aid appropriations bill (HR 5114), support for a 50 percent aid cut had solidified. The bill including the aid cut passed the House, and eventually the Senate, by a wide margin.

As it turned out, David R. Obey, D-Wis., chairman of the Appropriations Subcommittee on Foreign Operations, was prescient in characterizing the May 22 action. "That's the position of the House," said Obey; it was essentially the position that later became law. *(Senate key vote 14)*

2. Job-Loss Benefits

Most of the battles on the clean air package in 1990 were fought along regional rather than partisan lines. But one debate sent the parties scrambling back to their corners: Whether to provide job-loss relief for workers displaced by the new law.

House Democrats, spurning White House veto threats, approved such a measure by a wide margin May 23. In doing so, West Virginia Democrat Bob Wise achieved what his powerful Senate counterpart, Robert C. Byrd, could not.

Wise, along with cosponsors Tom Ridge, R-Pa., and Thomas J. Downey, D-N.Y., patterned his amendment after similar relief available to U.S. workers under the Trade Adjustment Assistance Act. The amendment offered 26 additional weeks of unemployment and retraining benefits to workers who could show that the clean air law was "an important contributing factor" to their job loss. It authorized $250 million in funding over five years.

The Senate barely rejected a similar but more expensive program on a 49-50 vote March 29, marking a rare defeat for Appropriations Chairman Byrd, who — like Wise — was trying to help coal miners in his state.

But part of the appeal of the Wise amendment was its application to workers in all fields and geographic regions, while Byrd's $500 million plan offered aid only to coal miners.

House Democrats pushed the amendment through on a vote of 274-146: R 43-126; D 231-20 (ND 169-2, SD 62-18).

Still, administration threats to veto the entire bill over the provision remained. President Bush argued that it would become an open-ended entitlement that would cost far more than $250 million. And though it was unclear whether Senate conferees would abandon their previous pact with the White House and go along with a compromise job-loss provision, Wise never took the veto threat seriously: "I can't believe the president's going to veto the environmental bill of the decade over $50 million a year."

Wise was right. The amendment was modified in conference — with help from the administration — to address Bush's concerns. Instead of continuing mandatory benefits, conferees agreed to a $250 million needs-based program that would be administered through the Job Training Partnership Act. Qualified displaced workers would be guaranteed cash supplemental payments after their unemployment assistance ran out as long as they remained in a job-retraining program. *(Senate key vote 4)*

3. Clean Air

For a decade, clean air bills were stalled in Congress. But when a package (HR 3030) finally made it to the House floor May 23, members approved the sweeping rewrite of the anti-pollution law by an overwhelming 401-21 vote: R 154-16; D 247-5 (ND 169-4, SD 78-1). The vote, which followed only two days of largely non-partisan debate, demonstrated what environmentalists had long maintained: They had the support they needed on the floor, if only a bill could be navigated through key committee obstructionists — in particular, auto industry ally John D. Dingell, D-Mich. As chairman of the House Energy and Commerce Committee, Dingell for years had blocked a series of earlier bills that would have placed new controls on automobiles and smokestacks.

This time, however, the Energy Committee had produced so many agreements on so many divisive issues that the rest of the House was given only a handful of choices to make before final passage. The long-awaited floor showdown that some lobbyists had promoted as the environmental vote of the decade looked at times like a bipartisan love-in, with members clamoring to take credit for a series of compromise amendments, most of which passed on overwhelming votes.

In the end, the vote on final passage locked in the legislation's major components as the bill entered the next stage — grueling conference negotiations with the Senate — which ended barely in time for a bill to be sent to President Bush's desk before Congress adjourned. Dingell, Henry A. Waxman, D-Calif., the main House advocate of clean air legislation, and Norman F. Lent, N.Y., the ranking Republican on Energy and Commerce, were committed to standing by many parts of the House bill through conference with the Senate, unless all three could agree on a compromise.

House conferees did spend much of their time renegotiating parts of their bill to make it less burdensome on businesses; although pro-environment conferees had the leverage of a strong floor vote, pro-industry conferees had the clock on their side.

Oddly, the soundness of House floor support may have done more to bolster the position of Senate conferees, most of whom supported a stronger clean air rewrite than the bill (S 1630) that passed their chamber. Senate conferees, led by Majority Leader George J. Mitchell, D-Maine, had been forced to strike a deal with the White House, watering down the legislation to get it past strident Senate opposition.

Once in conference, however, Senate negotiators felt free to abandon the White House deal and give in to House-passed language in important areas, opting, for example, to recede entirely to the House's tougher anti-smog provisions. *(Senate key vote 3)*

4. Flag Burning

An early-strike strategy by House opponents of a constitutional amedment to protect the U.S. flag led to a June 21 defeat of the proposed amendment (H J Res 350). The opponents had contended in this politically charged debate that the First Amendment and the Bill of Rights needed more protection than the flag.

The 254-177 vote fell 34 short of the two-thirds necessary for passage: R 159-17; D 95-160 (ND 43-130, SD 52-30).

The resolution stated: "The Congress and the states shall have the power to prohibit the physical desecration of the flag of the United States."

The amendment was proposed after the Supreme Court on June 11 struck down a federal statute that made it illegal to burn, mutilate or otherwise desecrate the flag. As the court had ruled in 1989 on a Texas flag-burning statute, the majority said protesters who burned the U.S. flag were protected by the First Amendment right to free speech.

Supporters of an amendment to reverse the court believed that public sentiment was on their side. But they failed to organize outside interest groups, such as veterans, to write and call members of Congress. At the same time, foes of a flag amendment had spent months putting in place an opposition strategy, anticipating the court's decision to strike down the statute.

Democrats suggested that Republicans were trying to stir up pre-election defensiveness, just as George Bush had challenged Democratic nominee Michael S. Dukakis' patriotism during the 1988 presidential campaign. They used the Bill of Rights as both a legal argument and a symbol, trying to defuse those who argued that support for the flag was a test of patriotism. House Speaker Thomas S. Foley of Washington, who had led opposition to the constitutional amendment, made a rare floor appearance to close debate. In the end, the House vote on the amendment was not close to the two-thirds necessary, and the issue was not a major factor in the fall elections. *(Senate key vote 6)*

5. Family and Medical Leave

"We shall override, someday," vowed Patricia Schroeder, D-Colo., of legislation vetoed by President Bush that would have required employers to grant unpaid leave to workers caring for newborn children or sick relatives.

That day was not July 25, when the House by a wide, 54-vote margin failed to revive the family and medical leave bill (HR 770). Indeed, Schroeder's wistful pledge seemed aimed not only at family leave — it also spoke of Democrats' frustration at being unable to override any of the Bush presidency's vetoes.

The legislation would have protected jobs for workers who took up to 12 weeks of unpaid leave to care for a newborn, adopted or ill child at no cost to the employee. It also would have covered time off for personal medical emergencies, including caring for family members. The bill would have applied only to businesses with 50 or more employees.

Sponsors argued that federal minimum requirements were needed to bring U.S. businesses in line with the changing workplace, with about 60 percent of mothers working outside the home. They also said the United States was virtually alone among industrialized nations in lacking a national family and medical leave policy, though opponents said employees were forced to pay into mandatory leave benefit plans in many other countries.

Bush, in vetoing the bill June 29, said he supported the concept of parental and medical leave but believed such arrangements should be decided in labor-management negotiations.

Despite heavy lobbying, Democrats found the goal of getting a two-thirds vote in the House insurmountable. In fact, sponsors lost eight votes from when the bill was passed by the chamber May 10. The override attempt was rejected 232-195: R 38-138; D 194-57 (ND 156-14, SD 38-43).

Democrats howled that Bush was falling short on a campaign promise to support families. But with 57 Democrats sustaining the veto, Bush could not be held solely accountable. Election-year pressure by business groups opposing the bill swayed more than a few votes.

But Bush's seeming invincibility and popularity over the summer also helped him trounce Democrats resoundingly in their own back yard.

6. Farm Programs

If there was an underlying theme to the 1990 farm bill, it was class warfare. Rich, successful farmers found themselves scorned as "fat cats" who were milking the taxpayer for millions of dollars. Pitted against them were the poorer farmers who produced less of the nation's food and received less of its subsidy bounty. Conflict was inevitable because the budget crisis meant that for the first time in years, farmers would be getting less, not more, government aid. The matter came to a head July 25, when the House debated an amendment to the farm bill (HR 3950) that would have denied crop subsidies to farmers with gross adjusted incomes of more than $100,000 a year. The four-hour debate on the amendment cut to the philosophical underpinnings of farm programs.

The amendment was the handiwork of Charles E. Schumer, D-N.Y., and Dick Armey, R-Texas, the leaders of a coalition of urban liberals who disliked farm subsidies going to a few farmers while programs for the poor had been under pressure, and of Republican conservatives, who clung to a hope of a free market farm sector.

Farm-state lawmakers saw the amendment as a strike at the heart of the program. Having wealthy farmers with large operations in the program was desirable, they argued, because it gave the government more control over those who produced most of the nation's food, and thus over prices and supply. Kick out those affluent farmers, they argued, and the government would have a tougher time keeping food prices stable.

Critics had long contended that the farm program was inequitable, but they had little success in changing it. With the budget crisis, however, 1990 seemed different. Armey and Schumer argued that, in addition to correcting the inequities of the farm program, their amendment would save the government money. In effect, their proposal would convert farm subsidies into a more explicit welfare program for needy farmers.

However, farm-state lawmakers had an alternative: Instead of soaking the rich, they proposed reducing every farmer's subsidy check. In the end, the alternative proved more acceptable. The amendment was defeated 159-263: R 66-109; D 93-154 (ND 85-82, SD 8-72).

7. Ethics Reprimand

Buffeted by a yearlong string of scandals, the House navigated unusually partisan, emotional waters when it debated how harshly to punish Barney Frank, D-Mass., for improperly using his office to help a male prostitute.

The debate came at a time when many politicians were evincing election-year jitters about Congress' scandal-scarred image. The drama of floor debate centered on whether nervous incumbents would go along with the recommendation of the House ethics committee to reprimand Frank or impose the stiffer sanction of censuring him.

The key vote came when the House on July 26 rejected a Republican motion to censure Frank 141-287: R 129-46; D 12-241 (ND 1-171, SD 11-70); clearing the way for overwhelming approval of a reprimand.

Frank's case was the most publicized of several congressional sex scandals of 1990. After investigating allegations that first surfaced in the *Washington Times* in August 1989, the ethics committee concluded that Frank "reflected discredit upon the House" by writing a misleading memorandum in behalf of Steve Gobie, a male prostitute with whom Frank associated in 1985-87, and by improperly using his status as a member of Congress to fix 33 parking tickets. However, the committee found no conclusive evidence to back up allegations that Frank knew Gobie was running a prostitution service out of Frank's apartment.

Frank did not contest the committee's recommendation that he be reprimanded. The motion to increase the punishment to censure was offered by House GOP Whip Newt Gingrich of Georgia, who had instigated the 1989 ethics inquiry that led to the resignation of House Speaker Jim Wright of Texas.

The voting breakdown on the censure motion showed how partisan the ethics issue had become, especially in Frank's case. Disciplinary votes usually did not break down along party lines. But the ethics committee itself, before deciding to recommend a reprimand, had been riven by unusually deep partisan divisions over how far to go. Although the committee's recommendation had been approved unanimously, three Republican committee members voted for censure on the floor.

Solid Democratic opposition to the censure motion was, in part, a measure of Democrats' deep hostility toward Gingrich. Many resented his role in the Wright affair and were irritated that he was criticizing the same ethics committee that he had praised earlier in the year for clearing his own name.

In the end, ethics committee Chairman Julian C. Dixon, D-Calif., depicted the censure vote as a referendum on the ethics panel itself. He portrayed it as a choice between a unanimous, bipartisan committee that had studied the case for almost a year and GOP demagogues who would throw their colleagues to the wolves. Said Dixon, "This case boils down to, really, who do you trust?"

8. Strategic Defense Initiative

Congress continued its persistent effort to reorient and reduce long-term funding for the strategic defense initiative (SDI), the anti-missile defense program launched in 1983 by President Ronald Reagan.

The sweeping rhetoric Reagan used in promoting the program — offering the potential to make nuclear missiles "impotent and obsolete" — had long since been supplanted by the more modest goal of deploying by the end of the 1990s a network of space-based missiles that could protect the U.S. nuclear deterrent against a Soviet first strike.

But in 1990, both the revised goal and President Bush's $4.7 billion SDI funding request for fiscal 1991 were wanting in congressional support.

Following the Senate's lead, the final defense authorization bill included provisions intended to reduce funding for the planned network of space-based missiles while increasing funding for two other kinds of missile defenses: ground-based anti-missile interceptors that could head off a small attack or a few accidentally launched missiles; and lasers and other futuristic weapons that might in the 21st century begin to realize Reagan's grander vision.

Congress also slashed the SDI funding request to $2.89 billion — a compromise between the $3.57 billion authorized by the Senate and the $2.3 billion authorized by the House. The House accepted that figure in an amendment sponsored by Charles E. Bennett, D-Fla., and Tom Ridge, R-Pa., which was adopted by 225-189: R 20-150; D 205-39 (ND 157-7, SD 48-32).

9. Abortion at Military Facilities

The Supreme Court's 1989 decision in *Webster v. Reproductive Health Services*, which gave states new latitude to restrict access to abortion, galvanized abortion rights forces in the country and on Capitol Hill. But abortion rights supporters, while enjoying considerable success in Congress that year on abortion-related issues, were unable to alter policy because they could not muster majorities large enough to override four Bush vetoes.

By 1990, abortion rights backers were looking for new issues on which they might be able to roll back some of the myriad federal restrictions that had cropped up in the years since abortion was legalized nationwide by the Supreme Court's 1973 *Roe v. Wade* decision.

The one they ultimately set out to overturn was a 1988 Defense Department directive forbidding abortions in overseas military facilities, even if the woman paid for the procedure herself.

The first test came in the Senate on Aug. 3, where Tim Wirth, D-Colo., tried to add the amendment overturning the ban to the defense authorization bill (S 2884). Sponsors mustered a majority but fell two votes short of the 60 needed to stop a filibuster.

By the time the issue got to the House, debate had sharpened.

Supporters painted the issue as a vote on simply ensuring access to abortion services for members of the military and their dependents. But opponents portrayed it as a vote for "abortion on demand," which they said would lead to abortions of fetuses potentially able to live outside the womb or for sex selection.

That argument carried the day; an amendment similar to the Senate proposal, offered by Vic Fazio, D-Calif., could not even muster a majority, failing Sept. 18 by 200-216: R 35-139; D 165-77 (ND 113-50, SD 52-27).

10. Immigration

The House on Oct. 3 voted to increase immigration by more than 60 percent and offer amnesty, under certain conditions, to thousands of people living in the United States illegally.

The generous House bill (HR 4300) set the stage for negotiations with the Senate, which had passed a less-sweeping bill (S 358) in July 1989. The compromise that was cleared for the president did not open the door as wide as the House bill would have. But the House's position forced the Senate to broaden its approach toward the numbers and types of immigrants allowed in.

The House legislation passed 231-192: R 45-127; D 186-65 (ND 159-13, SD 27-52). The administration had opposed the measure largely because of its country-specific amnesty and huge increases in visa levels.

The broad purpose of the legislation — and that of the bill that cleared — was to bring in more specially trained workers and increase immigration from countries adversely affected under the existing visa allotment system that favored Latin Americans and Asians. The House bill differed from the Senate legislation beyond sheer numbers. It would have allowed a stay of deportation for illegal immigrants from El Salvador, Lebanon, Liberia and Kuwait. It would have granted more visas to spouses and unmarried minor children of lawful permanent residents under the terms similar to those for immediate relatives of U.S. citizens.

It also would have been more generous in barring deportation of children and spouses of foreigners who were legalized under the 1986 Immigration Reform and Control Act. The children and spouses did not have visas.

During House floor debate, members beat back several attempts to decrease the number of new visas in the bill. The issue divided members who argued that a generous immigration policy was a good thing for reuniting families, adding diversity to the population and building the talent pool, and those who said the government should discourage foreigners and concentrate its money on essential services for U.S.-born.

John Bryant, D-Texas, protested, "We have a shortage of jobs and training, not a shortage of people."

His point of view did not prevail on the House floor or in conference. Under the measure cleared Oct. 27, legal immigration was raised from about 500,000 annually to about 700,000 during each of the first three years of the act. After that, a permanent level of 675,000 would be set. The only country-specific amnesty that remained in the bill was an 18-month stay of deportation for people from El Salvador living in the United States illegally.

11. Budget Summit Agreement

In one of 1990's most dramatic congressional votes, House leaders unsure of their vote counts rolled the dice at 1 a.m. Oct. 5 in a last-ditch attempt to save a budget deal produced by nearly five months of increasingly desperate negotiations between Congress and the Bush administration. When White House and congressional leaders announced the package Sept. 30, they hoped that the pressure of automatic budget cuts threatened by the Gramm-Rudman deficit-reduction law would bring members into line. But five days later, with the House in open rebellion and support for the budget package fading by the minute, leaders felt they had little choice but to gamble. They lost. In a stunning rebuke of President Bush and House leaders of both parties, the House refused to adopt the conference report on the budget resolution 179-254: R 71-105; D 108-149 (ND 63-111, SD 45-38).

The defeat of the budget deal meant that Congress was held hostage in Washington for another three weeks of negotiations — the longest election-year session since World War II — before Congress adopted a final budget-reconciliation package Oct. 27.

By the time of the Oct. 5 vote, many House members felt they had already been prisoners of the budget wars since the talks began in mid-May. Some blamed the defeat on the package's most politically odious components: new taxes and cuts in safety net programs such as Medicare. But others said it was at least in part an angry backlash by members frustrated at having been left out as an elite corps of congressional and White House officials negotiated behind closed doors, only to hand the rank and file a tough, take-it-or-leave-it package just weeks before the fall elections.

The process began in early May when President Bush, driven by fear that the economy would collapse on his watch, agreed to convene a no-preconditions budget summit with congressional leaders. When the talks threatened to stall in June, he abandoned his "no new taxes" pledge to get the negotiations started again.

That shifted the terms of the debate from whether to tax to whom to tax, and how much. Democrats who had been on the defensive over taxes for the decade since Ronald Reagan became president suddenly found themselves making political headway with the "fairness" issue. When Republicans demanded a cut in the capital gains tax to stimulate a dangerously weakening economy, Democrats countered that the cut would be a sop to rich taxpayers that would have little or no effect on the nation's economic health. Instead, they insisted on a hike in the top tax rate for the wealthiest taxpayers.

When it became clear that the budget summit deal would include substantial new taxes, negotiator and House Minority Whip Newt Gingrich of Georgia jumped ship and declared war on the process. When the deal itself was announced Sept. 30, Gingrich refused to attend the Rose Garden ceremony where Bush and congressional leaders said they would support it despite disliking it. Gingrich's defection was an omen.

Backers of the budget deal spent the week furiously lobbying Congress. Early indications were that the Senate would go along but that the package was in trouble in the House. Bush himself went on television to ask for national support, but that only appeared to generate more phone calls to congressional offices against the package. With a stopgap spending bill set to run out at midnight Oct. 5, the House had to vote on the deal less than a week after it was unveiled.

There had long been an understanding that both parties would have to produce a majority of their members to support the package on the floor, but a significant bloc of conservative Republicans had solidified around Gingrich in opposition, and when it became clear that the GOP would not produce its votes, Democrats deserted in droves as well. Ultimately, the deal was done in by a rare alliance between conservative Republicans and liberal Democrats. The Republicans hated the taxes, and the Democrats hated the cuts in Medicare and other programs.

After three more weeks of negotiations, the final budget deal still had both taxes and safety-net cuts, but each in either smaller quantities or more politically palatable forms.

12. Textile Quotas

It had become routine for Congress to send bills to the president mandating stiff new quotas on textile, apparel and shoe imports in an effort to shore up domestic producers. It was just as routine for him to veto those bills and for the House to fail to override the veto by a narrow margin.

It happened in 1986, in 1988 and again in 1990. The show of support for the nation's textile industry had barely wavered on Capitol Hill. But that fact, quota supporters said, was important for the long-term survival of the domestic industry.

Textile quota bills also had been altered somewhat over time in an effort to pick up votes; the 1990 version would have allowed textile and apparel imports to grow by 1 percent annually, and shoe imports would have been frozen permanently at 1989 levels. It also would have given incentives to countries that purchased U.S. farm goods.

Critics said stiff quotas were needed to preserve a shrinking domestic manufacturing base, while opponents argued that a constricted supply would drive up prices for consumers. Besides, they said, the domestic textile industry had never been healthier. Apparel makers, but not their unions, opposed the quota measure.

Although the House had come up a few votes short of overriding the president's veto each time, 1990 was the first time either chamber summoned more than a two-thirds majority for a textile quota bill. In July, the Senate had passed the measure (HR 4328) by 68-32, and opponents feared for the first time that there might be enough congressional support for the measure to ram it through.

But Oct. 10, when the vetoed bill was returned to the House floor for an override attempt, history repeated itself. Supporters could not quite muster the required two-thirds majority — falling 10 votes short — and the override effort failed 275-152: R 70-103; D 205-49 (ND 131-41, SD 74-8).

Quota supporter Ed Jenkins, D-Ga., said he was not surprised at the outcome. But neither was he completely disheartened. He and others said it was important that congressional support for quotas remained strong because international trade negotiators meeting in Geneva and Brussels, Belgium, were hoping to make major changes in the General Agreement on Tariffs and Trade before the end of 1990. A central element of those talks was the proposal to phase out an existing scheme of negotiated bilateral textile and apparel quotas. Third World suppliers of textiles in particular wanted an end to restrictions on textile trade.

Any such trade agreement would have to be submitted to Congress for approval before it could take effect. And Jenkins said after the override attempt failed that if a new trade agreement was reached that would put an end to the existing quota regime, it was clear that Congress would refuse to support it.

13. Obscenity Debate

A year after Congress restricted the National Endowment for the Arts (NEA) from funding works that could be considered obscene, sadomasochistic or homoerotic, lawmakers pulled back. The House on Oct. 11 chose to drop the restrictions in favor of a substitute by Pat Williams, D-Mont., and E. Thomas Coleman, R-Mo., by a vote of 382-42: R 142-31; D 240-11 (ND 160-11, SD 80-0).

The House's lopsided vote marked a turning of the tide in favor of artistic freedom over the concerns of the religious right.

Approval of the Williams-Coleman language, as an amendment to a bill to reauthorize the NEA (HR 4825), followed months of stalemate among arts advocates who wanted to preserve the endowment without any restrictions, moderate Republicans who wanted to include language opposing obscenity and conservatives who wanted to abolish the agency.

The impetus for the compromise between Williams and Coleman was a 15-1 vote in the Senate Labor and Human Resources Committee to reauthorize the arts endowment while leaving the courts to decide what was obscene. Similar to the Senate language, the Williams-Coleman substitute dropped the existing restrictions and placed the onus on courts to determine questions of obscenity.

If an artist was convicted of violating obscenity standards, the NEA could order him or her to return the federal money. In a nod to the right, the substitute included language drafted by Paul B. Henry, R-Mich., stating that although artistic excellence was the standard by which grant applications were judged, "general standards of decency and respect for the diverse beliefs and values of the American public" should be taken into account.

The only serious opposition to the amendment came from Dana Rohrabacher, R-Calif., and a few other conservatives. Rohrabacher offered an amendment containing a series of restrictions aimed at curbing obscenity, blasphemy, flag desecration and racism in NEA-funded projects.

But Amo Houghton, R-N.Y., called Rohrabacher's effort to further restrict the NEA "a ruse" designed to gut federal arts spending. The House agreed, rejecting Rohrabacher's amendment, 175-249, before approving the Williams-Coleman language.

Ultimately, the House plan was adopted in conference on the fiscal 1991 Interior appropriations bill (HR 5769 — PL 101-512), which funded the NEA.

14. Tax and Spending-Cut Package

For much of the year, Democratic congressional leaders worked with their Republican counterparts and White House officials to craft a budget deal that could win majority support from both sides of the aisle. But after the House on Oct. 5 overwhelmingly rejected the best compromise leaders could strike, Democrats decided it was time to take a more partisan tack.

Bowing to pressure from rank-and-file members — most of whom had been shut out of the high-level budget deliberations — House leaders agreed to allow a largely political Democratic alternative to be offered as a floor amendment to the fiscal 1991 reconciliation bill (HR 5835). The alternative did what many Democrats had clamored for throughout the year but which leaders had discouraged because of the ongoing negotiations with the White House.

The package, drafted by Ways and Means Committee Democrats, shifted a much larger share of the tax burden onto the wealthy and made smaller spending cuts in Medicare and other social programs. In short, it did everything President Bush opposed in the budget talks. It raised the top rate for the wealthiest taxpayers from 28 percent to 33 percent and imposed a 10 percent surtax on millionaires. It called for a capital gains tax break but only for the middle class, and it reduced proposed Medicare savings from $60 billion to $43 billion.

As expected, support for the Democratic alternative split along party lines. The amendment was adopted Oct. 16 by a vote of 238-192: R 10-164; D 228-28 (ND 157-16, SD 71-12). The package helped refocus the tax debate from one concerning how much revenue should be raised to one concerning who should pay, and its passage in the House forced conferees to shape a final reconciliation bill much more to Democrats' liking. *(Senate key vote 13)*

15. Civil Rights

The House voted Oct. 16 to accept the final version of a comprehensive civil rights measure, but the vote was 12 short of what would have been needed to override a veto. And, ultimately, it was a veto by President Bush that killed the bill aimed at making it easier for workers to sue and win awards for discrimination.

The House adopted the conference report (S 2104 — H Rept 101-755) by a vote of 273-154: R 34-139; D 239-15 (ND 169-3, SD 70-12). The veto override attempt failed in the Senate by a single vote, so it never came back to the House.

The bill would have countered six 1989 Supreme Court rulings that narrowed the rights and remedies of victims of job discrimination. In response to four other court decisions from the 1980s, it would have given lawyers a greater chance to obtain costs and fees.

The legislation also would have amended Title VII of the 1964 Civil Rights Act to allow victims of intentional discrimination to recover compensatory damages and, in egregious cases, punitive damages. Under existing law, Title VII remedies were limited to back pay and benefits, attorneys' fees and court orders to stop discriminatory practices. The bill also would have allowed jury trials for discrimination victims.

Civil rights advocates and labor groups said the legislation was needed to protect workers from bias. The administration and business argued, however, that its pro-employee slant would have opened the door for frivolous lawsuits and led to quota hiring by employers trying to protect themselves. *(Senate key vote 16)*

16. Aid to Angolan Rebels

President Ronald Reagan had terrific problems persuading Congress to view the Nicaraguan contras as "freedom fighters," but he had a far easier time obtaining support for covert assistance to anti-government rebels in Angola.

For years, a broad coalition of lawmakers, including a substantial number of Democrats, backed secret military assistance for the rebels, who were led by the public-relations savvy Jonas Savimbi.

But the argument in favor of such programs was far more convincing for many lawmakers when the Soviet Union was aggressively funding communist regimes in the Third World. With the Cold War ending and the Soviets less interested in fueling regional conflicts, support for anti-communist movements such as Savimbi's waned.

In October, the House approved tough new restrictions on aid for the National Union for the Total Independence of Angola (UNITA) rebels as part of its fiscal 1991 intelligence authorization bill (HR 5422). While the complicated conditions ultimately were eased somewhat by a House-Senate conference committee, the House vote demonstrated growing congressional skepticism toward large-scale secret programs.

The Angola restrictions, sponsored by Stephen J. Solarz, D-N.Y., a member of the Intelligence Committee, passed Oct. 17 by one vote: Speaker Thomas S. Foley, D-Wash., was called on to cast the deciding vote to approve the Solarz amendment 207-206: R 12-156; D 195-50 (ND 158-10, SD 37-40). Given the razor-thin margin of passage, the administration was confident that the provision would be dropped in conference.

The Senate, in its consideration of the intelligence bill, attached only minor conditions on aid for UNITA. But the conference committee approved language by Solarz withholding half of the military aid for UNITA until congressional intelligence committees approved its release. Solarz termed that a "remarkable victory." The rebels reportedly received about $60 million a year from the United States, about half in military aid.

	1	2	3	4	5	6	7	8
ALABAMA								
Heflin	Y	N	Y	Y	Y	Y	Y	Y
Shelby	Y	N	Y	Y	Y	Y	Y	Y
ALASKA								
Murkowski	N	Y	Y	N	Y	Y	Y	N
Stevens	N	Y	?	Y	Y	Y	Y	Y
ARIZONA								
DeConcini	Y	N	N	Y	N	Y	Y	Y
McCain	N	Y	N	N	Y	Y	Y	N
ARKANSAS								
Bumpers	Y	N	Y	Y	N	N	Y	Y
Pryor	Y	N	Y	N	N	N	Y	Y
CALIFORNIA								
Cranston	Y	N	N	Y	N	N	Y	Y
Wilson	Y	Y	N	N	Y	Y	Y	Y
COLORADO								
Wirth	Y	N	N	Y	N	N	Y	Y
Armstrong	Y	Y	N	N	Y	Y	Y	N
CONNECTICUT								
Dodd	Y	N	Y	N	N	N	Y	Y
Lieberman	Y	N	N	Y	N	N	Y	N
DELAWARE								
Biden	Y	N	Y	N	N	N	Y	N
Roth	N	N	N	N	Y	Y	Y	N
FLORIDA								
Graham	Y	N	N	N	N	Y	Y	Y
Mack	N	Y	Y	N	Y	Y	Y	Y
GEORGIA								
Fowler	Y	N	N	N	N	Y	Y	Y
Nunn	Y	N	N	N	N	Y	Y	N
HAWAII								
Inouye	Y	N	Y	Y	N	N	Y	Y
Akaka [1]					N	N	Y	Y
IDAHO								
McClure	N	Y	N	Y	Y	Y	?	Y
Symms	N	Y	N	N	Y	Y	N	Y
ILLINOIS								
Dixon	Y	N	Y	Y	N	Y	Y	Y
Simon	Y	N	N	Y	N	N	Y	Y
INDIANA								
Coats	N	Y	Y	Y	Y	Y	Y	N
Lugar	N	Y	Y	N	Y	Y	Y	N

	1	2	3	4	5	6	7	8
IOWA								
Harkin	Y	N	N	Y	N	N	Y	Y
Grassley	N	Y	Y	Y	Y	Y	Y	N
KANSAS								
Dole	N	Y	Y	N	N	Y	Y	N
Kassebaum	N	Y	N	N	N	Y	Y	N
KENTUCKY								
Ford	Y	N	Y	Y	Y	Y	Y	Y
McConnell	N	Y	Y	Y	Y	Y	Y	N
LOUISIANA								
Breaux	?	N	Y	N	Y	Y	Y	Y
Johnston	Y	N	Y	+	Y	Y	Y	Y
MAINE								
Mitchell	Y	N	Y	N	N	N	Y	N
Cohen	Y	N	N	N	Y	Y	Y	N
MARYLAND								
Mikulski	Y	N	N	Y	N	N	Y	Y
Sarbanes	Y	N	Y	N	N	N	Y	N
MASSACHUSETTS								
Kennedy	Y	N	N	Y	N	N	Y	N
Kerry	Y	N	N	Y	N	N	Y	N
MICHIGAN								
Levin	Y	N	Y	N	N	N	Y	Y
Riegle	Y	N	Y	N	N	N	Y	Y
MINNESOTA								
Boschwitz	Y	Y	N	N	Y	Y	Y	Y
Durenberger	N	N	Y	N	Y	N	Y	Y
MISSISSIPPI								
Cochran	N	N	Y	Y	Y	Y	Y	Y
Lott	N	Y	Y	N	Y	Y	Y	Y
MISSOURI								
Bond	N	Y	Y	Y	Y	Y	N	N
Danforth	N	Y	Y	Y	Y	N	Y	N
MONTANA								
Baucus	Y	N	Y	N	Y	Y	Y	Y
Burns	N	Y	N	N	Y	Y	Y	Y
NEBRASKA								
Exon	Y	N	Y	Y	Y	Y	Y	Y
Kerrey	Y	N	Y	Y	N	N	Y	Y
NEVADA								
Bryan	Y	N	N	Y	Y	Y	Y	N
Reid	Y	-	N	Y	Y	Y	Y	N

	1	2	3	4	5	6	7	8
NEW HAMPSHIRE								
Humphrey	N	Y	Y	N	Y	N	N	N
Rudman	N	Y	Y	N	Y	N	Y	N
NEW JERSEY								
Bradley	Y	N	N	Y	N	N	Y	N
Lautenberg	Y	N	N	Y	N	N	Y	N
NEW MEXICO								
Bingaman	Y	N	N	Y	Y	N	Y	N
Domenici	N	Y	Y	N	Y	Y	Y	N
NEW YORK								
Moynihan	Y	N	N	Y	N	N	Y	N
D'Amato	N	Y	N	N	N	Y	Y	Y
NORTH CAROLINA								
Sanford	Y	N	Y	Y	Y	N	Y	Y
Helms	Y	Y	N	N	Y	Y	N	Y
NORTH DAKOTA								
Burdick	Y	N	Y	Y	N	Y	Y	Y
Conrad	Y	N	N	Y	N	Y	Y	Y
OHIO								
Glenn	Y	N	Y	Y	N	N	Y	N
Metzenbaum	Y	N	Y	Y	N	N	Y	N
OKLAHOMA								
Boren	Y	N	Y	N	N	N	Y	Y
Nickles	N	Y	Y	N	Y	Y	Y	N
OREGON								
Hatfield	N	N	N	Y	N	Y	Y	N
Packwood	N	Y	N	N	N	N	Y	N
PENNSYLVANIA								
Heinz	N	N	Y	Y	Y	Y	Y	N
Specter	N	N	Y	Y	Y	Y	Y	N
RHODE ISLAND								
Pell	Y	N	N	Y	N	N	Y	N
Chafee	N	N	Y	N	N	N	Y	N
SOUTH CAROLINA								
Hollings	Y	N	Y	Y	Y	Y	Y	Y
Thurmond	N	Y	Y	N	Y	Y	Y	Y
SOUTH DAKOTA								
Daschle	Y	N	N	N	N	N	Y	Y
Pressler	Y	Y	N	N	Y	Y	Y	?
TENNESSEE								
Gore	Y	N	N	Y	N	N	Y	Y
Sasser	Y	N	Y	Y	N	N	Y	Y

KEY

- Y Voted for (yea).
- # Paired for.
- + Announced for.
- N Voted against (nay).
- X Paired against.
- - Announced against.
- P Voted "present."
- C Voted "present" to avoid possible conflict of interest.
- ? Did not vote or otherwise make a position known.

Democrats *Republicans*

	1	2	3	4	5	6	7	8
TEXAS								
Bentsen	Y	N	Y	Y	N	Y	Y	Y
Gramm	N	Y	Y	N	Y	Y	Y	Y
UTAH								
Garn	N	Y	N	N	Y	Y	N	?
Hatch	N	N	N	N	Y	Y	Y	Y
VERMONT								
Leahy	Y	N	N	N	N	N	Y	Y
Jeffords	N	N	Y	N	N	N	Y	N
VIRGINIA								
Robb	Y	N	Y	N	N	N	Y	N
Warner	N	Y	Y	N	N	Y	Y	N
WASHINGTON								
Adams	Y	N	N	Y	N	N	Y	Y
Gorton	Y	Y	N	N	Y	Y	Y	N
WEST VIRGINIA								
Byrd	Y	N	N	Y	N	Y	Y	Y
Rockefeller	Y	N	N	Y	N	Y	?	Y
WISCONSIN								
Kohl	Y	N	N	Y	N	N	Y	N
Kasten	Y	Y	Y	N	Y	Y	Y	N
WYOMING								
Simpson	N	Y	Y	N	Y	Y	+	Y
Wallop	N	Y	N	N	Y	Y	N	Y

ND Northern Democrats SD Southern Democrats Southern states - Ala., Ark., Fla., Ga., Ky., La., Miss., N.C., Okla., S.C., Tenn., Texas, Va.

[1] *Sen. Daniel K. Akaka, D-Hawaii, was sworn in May 16, 1990, to succeed Spark Matsunaga, D, who died April 15, 1990. Matsunaga voted "yea" on key vote 1, "nay" on key vote 2, "?" on key vote 3 and "yea" on key vote 4.*

1. HR 2712. Chinese Students/Veto Override. Passage, over President Bush's Nov. 30 veto, of the bill to defer indefinitely the deportation of Chinese students whose visas expire and waive a requirement that students on "J" visas return to their home country for two years before applying for permanent residence in the United States. Rejected 62-37: R 8-37; D 54-0 (ND 38-0, SD 16-0), Jan. 25, 1990. A two-thirds majority of those present and voting (66 in this case) of both houses is required to override a veto. A "nay" was a vote supporting the president's position.

2. S 695. Education Programs/National Standards. Helms, R-N.C., amendment to delete $25 million in federal matching funds for the National Board for Professional Teaching Standards, which is developing guidelines for voluntary certification of teachers. Rejected 35-64: R 35-10; D 0-54 (ND 0-37, SD 0-17), Feb. 6, 1990. A "yea" was a vote supporting the president's position.

3. S 1630. Clean Air Act Reauthorization/Motor Vehicles. Mitchell, D-Maine, motion to table (kill) the Wirth, D-Colo., amendment to provide for a second round of tailpipe emissions reductions in the year 2003; to require cleaner-burning reformulated gasoline in all ozone non-attainment areas; to require light-duty vehicles to meet new-car emission standards for 100,000 miles; and to provide for use of clean fuels and clean-fuel vehicles in the nation's smoggiest cities. Motion agreed to 52-46: R 25-19; D 27-27 (ND 14-23, SD 13-4), March 20, 1990. A "yea" was a vote supporting the president's position.

4. S 1630. Clean Air Act Reauthorization/Coal Miner Benefits. Byrd, D-W.Va., amendment to provide severance pay and retraining benefits to coal miners who lose their jobs as a result of provisions to control acid rain. Rejected 49-50: R 11-34; D 38-16 (ND 29-9, SD 9-7), March 29, 1990. A "nay" was a vote supporting the president's position.

5. S 1970. Omnibus Crime Package/Assault-Style Weapons. Hatch, R-Utah, amendment to strike provisions that would prohibit for three years making, selling and possessing nine types of semiautomatic assault-style weapons. Rejected 48-52: R 36-9; D 12-43 (ND 5-33, SD 7-10), May 23, 1990. A "yea" was a vote supporting the president's position.

6. S J Res 332. Constitutional Amendment on the Flag/Passage. Passage of the joint resolution to propose an amendment to the Constitution to prohibit the physical desecration of the U.S. flag. Rejected 58-42: R 38-7; D 20-35 (ND 10-28, SD 10-7), June 26, 1990. A two-thirds majority of those present and voting (67 in this case) of both houses is required for passage of a joint resolution proposing an amendment to the Constitution. A "yea" was a vote supporting the president's position.

7. S 933. Americans with Disabilities Act/Conference Report. Adoption of the conference report on the bill to prohibit discrimination against the disabled in public facilities and employment and guarantee access to mass transit and telecommunications services. Adopted 91-6: R 37-6; D 54-0 (ND 37-0, SD 17-0), July 13, 1990. A "yea" was a vote supporting the president's position.

8. S 2830. Farm Programs Reauthorization/Sugar Price Supports. Akaka, D-Hawaii, motion to table (kill) the Bradley, D-N.J., amendment to extend the current sugar program for five years and lower the sugar price-support program loan rate from 18 cents per pound to 16 cents per pound. Motion agreed to 54-44: R 17-26; D 37-18 (ND 22-16, SD 15-2), July 24, 1990.

	9	10	11	12	13	14	15	16
ALABAMA								
Heflin	?	N	N	N	N	Y	Y	Y
Shelby	N	N	Y	N	N	Y	Y	Y
ALASKA								
Murkowski	Y	N	N	N	Y	Y	N	N
Stevens	Y	Y	N	N	Y	Y	N	N
ARIZONA								
DeConcini	-	N	Y	Y	N	Y	N	Y
McCain	Y	N	N	Y	N	N	N	N
ARKANSAS								
Bumpers	N	Y	Y	Y	Y	Y	Y	Y
Pryor	N	Y	Y	Y	Y	Y	Y	Y
CALIFORNIA								
Cranston	N	Y	Y	Y	Y	Y	N	Y
Wilson	Y	?	?	?	N	N	N	N
COLORADO								
Wirth	N	Y	Y	Y	Y	Y	N	Y
Armstrong	?	N	N	N	N	N	N	N
CONNECTICUT								
Dodd	N	Y	Y	N	Y	Y	Y	Y
Lieberman	N	Y	N	Y	N	Y	N	Y
DELAWARE								
Biden	N	Y	Y	Y	N	Y	Y	Y
Roth	Y	N	N	Y	N	Y	N	N
FLORIDA								
Graham	N	Y	N	Y	N	Y	Y	Y
Mack	Y	N	N	N	N	N	N	N
GEORGIA								
Fowler	N	Y	Y	N	Y	Y	N	Y
Nunn	N	N	N	N	Y	Y	Y	Y
HAWAII								
Inouye	N	Y	N	N	Y	Y	N	Y
Akaka	N	Y	N	Y	N	Y	Y	Y
IDAHO								
McClure	Y	N	N	Y	Y	N	N	N
Symms	Y	N	N	N	N	N	N	N
ILLINOIS								
Dixon	N	N	Y	N	Y	Y	Y	Y
Simon	N	Y	Y	Y	N	Y	Y	Y
INDIANA								
Coats	Y	N	N	N	N	N	Y	N
Lugar	Y	N	N	N	Y	N	N	N
IOWA								
Harkin	N	Y	Y	Y	N	Y	Y	Y
Grassley	Y	N	N	Y	N	Y	Y	N
KANSAS								
Dole	Y	N	N	N	Y	N	N	N
Kassebaum	Y	N	?	?	Y	Y	Y	N
KENTUCKY								
Ford	N	N	N	N	Y	Y	Y	Y
McConnell	Y	N	N	N	N	N	N	N
LOUISIANA								
Breaux	N	N	N	N	Y	Y	Y	Y
Johnston	N	N	N	N	N	Y	Y	Y
MAINE								
Mitchell	N	Y	Y	Y	Y	Y	N	Y
Cohen	Y	Y	Y	Y	N	Y	Y	Y
MARYLAND								
Mikulski	?	Y	Y	Y	Y	Y	Y	Y
Sarbanes	N	Y	Y	Y	Y	Y	N	Y
MASSACHUSETTS								
Kennedy	N	Y	Y	Y	Y	Y	N	Y
Kerry	N	Y	+	#	N	Y	Y	Y
MICHIGAN								
Levin	N	Y	Y	N	N	Y	Y	Y
Riegle	N	Y	Y	Y	N	Y	?	Y
MINNESOTA								
Boschwitz	Y	N	N	N	Y	Y	Y	Y
Durenberger	Y	N	N	N	Y	Y	N	Y
MISSISSIPPI								
Cochran	Y	N	N	N	Y	N	N	N
Lott	Y	N	N	N	N	N	Y	N
MISSOURI								
Bond	Y	N	N	N	Y	N	N	N
Danforth	Y	N	N	N	Y	Y	N	Y
MONTANA								
Baucus	N	Y	Y	Y	N	Y	Y	Y
Burns	Y	N	N	N	N	N	N	N
NEBRASKA								
Exon	Y	N	Y	N	N	Y	Y	Y
Kerrey	N	Y	Y	Y	N	Y	Y	Y
NEVADA								
Bryan	N	Y	Y	N	Y	Y	Y	Y
Reid	N	N	Y	Y	Y	Y	Y	Y
NEW HAMPSHIRE								
Humphrey	Y	N	Y	Y	N	N	Y	N
Rudman	Y	Y	N	N	Y	N	N	N
NEW JERSEY								
Bradley	N	Y	Y	Y	N	Y	N	Y
Lautenberg	N	Y	Y	Y	N	Y	N	Y
NEW MEXICO								
Bingaman	N	Y	Y	N	Y	Y	N	Y
Domenici	Y	?	N	N	Y	Y	N	Y
NEW YORK								
Moynihan	N	Y	Y	Y	Y	Y	N	Y
D'Amato	Y	N	Y	N	N	Y	N	N
NORTH CAROLINA								
Sanford	N	Y	Y	X	N	Y	Y	Y
Helms	Y	N	Y	N	N	N	Y	N
NORTH DAKOTA								
Burdick	N	Y	Y	Y	Y	Y	Y	Y
Conrad	N	N	Y	Y	N	Y	Y	Y
OHIO								
Glenn	N	Y	N	Y	Y	Y	N	Y
Metzenbaum	N	?	Y	Y	N	Y	N	Y
OKLAHOMA								
Boren	N	N	Y	N	Y	Y	N	Y
Nickles	Y	N	Y	N	N	N	N	N
OREGON								
Hatfield	Y	?	+	#	N	Y	Y	Y
Packwood	Y	Y	Y	Y	Y	Y	N	Y
PENNSYLVANIA								
Heinz	Y	Y	N	Y	Y	Y	N	Y
Specter	Y	Y	N	N	Y	Y	N	Y
RHODE ISLAND								
Pell	-	Y	Y	Y	N	Y	Y	Y
Chafee	Y	Y	N	N	Y	Y	N	Y
SOUTH CAROLINA								
Hollings	Y	Y	N	Y	N	Y	Y	Y
Thurmond	Y	N	N	N	Y	N	N	N
SOUTH DAKOTA								
Daschle	N	Y	Y	Y	Y	Y	+	Y
Pressler	Y	N	Y	Y	N	Y	Y	N
TENNESSEE								
Gore	N	Y	N	N	Y	Y	N	Y
Sasser	N	Y	Y	Y	Y	Y	Y	Y
TEXAS								
Bentsen	N	N	N	N	Y	Y	N	Y
Gramm	Y	N	N	N	N	?	?	N
UTAH								
Garn	Y	N	N	N	Y	N	N	N
Hatch	Y	N	N	N	Y	N	N	N
VERMONT								
Leahy	N	Y	N	Y	Y	Y	N	Y
Jeffords	Y	Y	N	X	Y	Y	N	Y
VIRGINIA								
Robb	N	Y	N	N	Y	Y	N	Y
Warner	Y	N	N	N	Y	Y	N	N
WASHINGTON								
Adams	N	Y	Y	Y	N	Y	N	Y
Gorton	Y	N	N	N	N	N	N	N
WEST VIRGINIA								
Byrd	N	N	N	Y	Y	Y	Y	Y
Rockefeller	N	Y	Y	Y	Y	Y	Y	Y
WISCONSIN								
Kohl	N	Y	Y	Y	Y	Y	Y	Y
Kasten	Y	N	Y	N	N	N	N	N
WYOMING								
Simpson	Y	N	N	N	Y	N	N	N
Wallop	Y	N	N	N	N	N	N	N

KEY

- Y Voted for (yea).
- \# Paired for.
- \+ Announced for.
- N Voted against (nay).
- X Paired against.
- \- Announced against.
- P Voted "present."
- C Voted "present" to avoid possible conflict of interest.
- ? Did not vote or otherwise make a position known.

Democrats *Republicans*

ND Northern Democrats SD Southern Democrats

Southern states - Ala., Ark., Fla., Ga., Ky., La., Miss., N.C., Okla., S.C., Tenn., Texas, Va.

9. S 137. Campaign Finance Overhaul/Taxpayer Funding. McConnell, R-Ky., amendment to the Boren, D-Okla., substitute amendment to eliminate all taxpayer funding of Senate campaigns. Rejected 46-49: R 44-0; D 2-49 (ND 1-34, SD 1-15), July 30, 1990.

10. HR 5257. Fiscal 1991 Labor, HHS and Education Appropriations/Abortion. Harkin, D-Iowa, motion to table (kill) the Armstrong, R-Colo., amendment to the committee amendment to permit federal funding of abortion in cases of rape or incest. The Armstrong amendment would require organizations receiving funds to notify a parent or legal guardian 48 hours before performing an abortion for a minor, unless there is a medical emergency. Motion rejected 48-48: R 8-34; D 40-14 (ND 31-6, SD 9-8), Oct. 12, 1990. (Subsequently, the Armstrong amendment was adopted by voice vote.)

11. S 3189. Fiscal 1991 Defense Appropriations/Troop Cuts. Conrad, D-N.D., amendment to reduce U.S. forces in NATO by 30,000 troops below the Senate-passed authorization level and reduce the Department of Defense military personnel level by a corresponding 30,000 below the authorized level. Rejected 46-50: R 8-34; D 38-16 (ND 31-6, SD 7-10), Oct. 15, 1990. A "nay" was a vote supporting the president's position.

12. S 3189. Fiscal 1991 Defense Appropriations/B-2 Bomber. Leahy, D-Vt., amendment to cut funds for the two additional B-2 bombers in the bill, thereby terminating the expansion of the program with the 15 bombers being produced and tested. Rejected 44-50: R 9-32; D 35-18 (ND 30-7, SD 5-11), Oct. 15, 1990. A "nay" was a vote supporting the president's position.

13. HR 5835. Fiscal 1991 Budget Reconciliation Act/Passage. Passage of the bill to cut spending and raise revenues as required by the reconciliation instructions in the budget resolution and make changes in the budget process. Passed 54-46: R 23-22; D 31-24 (ND 20-18, SD 11-6), in the session that began, and the *Congressional Record* dated, Oct. 18, 1990.

14. HR 5114. Fiscal 1991 Foreign Operations Appropriations/El Salvador. Leahy, D-Vt., amendment to the committee amendment, to reduce military aid to the government of El Salvador by 50 percent and link future military aid to improvements in human rights and progress toward a negotiated peace settlement. Adopted 74-25: R 19-25; D 55-0 (ND 38-0, SD 17-0), Oct. 19, 1990. A "nay" was a vote supporting the president's position.

15. HR 5114. Fiscal 1991 Foreign Operations Appropriations/Egyptian Debt. Harkin, D-Iowa, amendment to the committee amendment, to strike provisions canceling Egypt's debt to the United States and to require the president to develop in cooperation with Congress a proposal to restructure that debt and convene an international conference to develop a comprehensive and multilateral solution to Egypt's international debt problem. Rejected 42-55: R 10-34; D 32-21 (ND 20-16, SD 12-5), Oct. 19, 1990. A "nay" was a vote supporting the president's position.

16. S 2104. Civil Rights Act of 1990/Veto Override. Passage, over President Bush's Oct. 22 veto, of the bill to reverse or modify six recent Supreme Court decisions that narrowed the reach and remedies of job discrimination law and to authorize monetary damages under Title VII of the 1964 Civil Rights Act. Rejected 66-34: R 11-34; D 55-0 (ND 38-0, SD 17-0), Oct. 24, 1990. A two-thirds majority of those present and voting (67 in this case) of both houses is required to override a veto. A "nay" was a vote supporting the president's position.

1. HR 4636. Fiscal 1990 Foreign Aid Supplemental Authorizations/Military Aid. Moakley, D-Mass., amendment to suspend 50 percent of El Salvador's military aid planned for fiscal years 1990 and 1991, depending on actions by the Salvadoran government or by the leftist guerrillas. Adopted 250-163: R 31-135; D 219-28 (ND 166-4, SD 53-24), May 22, 1990. A "nay" was a vote supporting the president's position.

2. HR 3030. Clean Air Act Reauthorization/Transition Aid. Wise, D-W.Va., amendment to authorize $250 million over a five-year period for a Clean Air Employment Transition Assistance program to provide workers who lose their jobs or have their wages reduced as a result of the bill with retraining assistance and up to six months of additional unemployment benefits. Adopted 274-146: R 43-126; D 231-20 (ND 169-2, SD 62-18), May 23, 1990. A "nay" was a vote supporting the president's position.

3. HR 3030. Clean Air Act Reauthorization/Passage. Passage of the bill (thus clearing for the president) to amend the Clean Air Act to attain and maintain national ambient air quality standards, require reductions of emissions in motor vehicles, control toxic air pollutants, reduce acid rain, establish a system of federal permits and enforcement, and otherwise improve the quality of the nation's air. Passed 401-21: R 154-16; D 247-5 (ND 169-4, SD 78-1), May 23, 1990.

4. H J Res 350. Constitutional Amendment on the Flag/Passage. Brooks, D-Texas, motion to suspend the rules and pass the joint resolution to propose an amendment to the Constitution to prohibit the physical desecration of the U.S. flag. Rejected 254-177: R 159-17; D 95-160 (ND 43-130, SD 52-30), June 21, 1990. A two-thirds majority of those present and voting (288 in this case) of both houses is required for passage of a joint resolution proposing an amendment to the Constitution. A "yea" was a vote supporting the president's position.

5. HR 770. Family and Medical Leave Act/Veto Override. Passage, over President Bush's June 29 veto, of the bill to require public and private employers to give unpaid leave to care for a newborn child or a seriously ill child, parent or spouse, or to use as medical leave due to a serious health condition. Rejected 232-195: R 38-138; D 194-57 (ND 156-14, SD 38-43), July 25, 1990. A two-thirds majority or those present and voting (285 in this case) of both houses is required to override a veto. A "nay" was a vote supporting the president's position.

6. HR 3950. Farm Programs Reauthorization/High-Income Farmers. Schumer, D-N.Y., amendment to prohibit all payments, purchases and loans under the wheat, feed grains, cotton, honey, rice, oil seeds, and wool and mohair programs for any person with an adjusted gross income of $100,000 or more. Rejected 159-263: R 66-109; D 93-154 (ND 85-82, SD 8-72), July 25, 1990.

7. H Res 440. Frank Reprimand/Censure. Gingrich, R-Ga., motion to recommit the resolution reprimanding Barney Frank, D-Mass., to the Committee on Standards of Official Conduct with instructions to report back a recommendation of censure instead of reprimand. Motion rejected 141-287: R 129-46; D 12-241 (ND 1-171, SD 11-70), July 26, 1990.

8. HR 4739. Fiscal 1991 Defense Authorization/SDI Funding. Bennett, D-Fla., amendment to reduce spending for the strategic defense initiative by $600 million to a new level of $2.3 billion. Adopted 225-189: R 20-150; D 205-39 (ND 157-7, SD 48-32), Sept. 18, 1990. A "nay" was a vote supporting the president's position.

[1] *Rep. Daviel K. Akaka, D-Havaii, resigned May 16, 1990.*

[2] *Rep. James J. Florio, D-N.J., resigned Jan. 16, 1990.*

[3] *Rep. Susan Molinari, R-N.Y., was sworn in March 27, 1990, to succeed Guy V. Molinari, R, who resigned Jan. 1, 1990.*

[4] *Rep. José E. Serrano, D-N.Y., was sworn in March 28, 1990, to succeed Robert Garcia, D, who resigned Jan. 7, 1990.*

[5] *Rep. Craig Washington, D-Texas, was sworn in Jan. 23, 1990, to succeed Mickey Leland, D, who died Aug. 7, 1989.*

KEY

Y Voted for (yea).
\# Paired for.
\+ Announced for.
N Voted against (nay).
X Paired against.
\- Announced against.
P Voted "present."
C Voted "present" to avoid possible conflict of interest.
? Did not vote or otherwise make a position known.

Democrats ***Republicans***
Independent

ND Northern Democrats
SD Southern Democrats

Southern states - Ala., Ark., Fla., Ga., Ky., La., Miss., N.C., Okla., S.C., Tenn., Texas, Va.

	1	2	3	4	5	6	7	8
ALABAMA								
1 ***Callahan***	Y	N	Y	Y	N	N	N	N
2 ***Dickinson***	N	N	Y	Y	N	Y	Y	N
3 Browder	Y	Y	Y	Y	N	N	N	N
4 Bevill	Y	Y	Y	Y	N	N	N	N
5 Flippo	?	?	?	Y	Y	N	N	N
6 Erdreich	Y	Y	Y	Y	Y	N	N	N
7 Harris	Y	Y	Y	Y	N	N	N	N
ALASKA								
AL ***Young***	N	N	Y	Y	Y	N	N	N
ARIZONA								
1 ***Rhodes***	N	N	Y	Y	N	N	Y	N
2 Udall	Y	Y	Y	N	Y	N	N	Y
3 ***Stump***	N	N	N	Y	N	C	Y	N
4 ***Kyl***	N	N	Y	Y	N	N	Y	N
5 ***Kolbe***	X	N	Y	N	N	N	Y	N
ARKANSAS								
1 Alexander	?	?	?	Y	Y	N	N	Y
2 ***Robinson***	?	?	?	Y	N	N	Y	N
3 ***Hammerschmidt***	?	N	Y	Y	N	N	Y	N
4 Anthony	Y	Y	Y	N	Y	N	N	Y
CALIFORNIA								
1 Bosco	Y	Y	Y	N	Y	N	N	Y
2 ***Herger***	N	Y	Y	Y	N	N	Y	?
3 Matsui	Y	Y	Y	N	Y	N	N	Y
4 Fazio	Y	Y	Y	N	Y	N	N	Y
5 Pelosi	Y	Y	Y	N	Y	Y	N	Y
6 Boxer	Y	Y	Y	N	Y	N	N	Y
7 Miller	Y	Y	Y	N	Y	Y	N	Y
8 Dellums	Y	Y	Y	N	Y	Y	N	Y
9 Stark	Y	Y	Y	N	Y	Y	N	Y
10 Edwards	Y	Y	Y	N	Y	N	N	Y
11 Lantos	Y	Y	Y	N	Y	Y	N	Y
12 ***Campbell***	Y	N	Y	Y	Y	Y	N	Y
13 Mineta	Y	Y	Y	N	Y	N	N	Y
14 ***Shumway***	N	N	Y	Y	N	N	Y	N
15 Condit	Y	Y	Y	Y	Y	N	N	Y
16 Panetta	Y	Y	Y	N	Y	Y	N	Y
17 ***Pashayan***	Y	Y	Y	Y	N	N	N	N
18 Lehman	Y	Y	Y	N	Y	N	N	Y
19 ***Lagomarsino***	N	N	Y	Y	N	Y	Y	N
20 ***Thomas***	X	X	?	Y	N	N	Y	N
21 ***Gallegly***	N	N	Y	Y	N	N	Y	N
22 ***Moorhead***	N	N	Y	Y	N	N	Y	N
23 Beilenson	Y	N	Y	N	Y	Y	N	Y
24 Waxman	Y	Y	Y	N	Y	Y	N	Y
25 Roybal	Y	Y	Y	N	Y	N	N	Y
26 Berman	Y	Y	Y	N	Y	Y	N	Y
27 Levine	Y	Y	Y	N	Y	Y	N	Y
28 Dixon	Y	Y	Y	N	Y	N	N	Y
29 Hawkins	#	Y	Y	N	Y	N	N	?
30 Martinez	Y	Y	Y	Y	Y	?	N	Y
31 Dymally	Y	Y	Y	N	Y	N	N	Y
32 Anderson	Y	Y	Y	N	Y	N	N	Y
33 ***Dreier***	N	N	Y	Y	N	Y	Y	N
34 Torres	Y	Y	Y	N	Y	N	N	Y
35 ***Lewis***	N	N	Y	Y	N	N	N	N
36 Brown	?	Y	Y	N	Y	N	N	Y
37 ***McCandless***	N	N	Y	Y	N	N	Y	N
38 ***Dornan***	N	N	Y	Y	N	N	Y	N
39 ***Dannemeyer***	N	N	N	Y	N	Y	Y	N
40 ***Cox***	N	N	Y	Y	N	Y	Y	N
41 ***Lowery***	N	N	Y	Y	N	N	N	N
42 ***Rohrabacher***	N	N	Y	Y	N	Y	Y	N
43 ***Packard***	N	N	Y	Y	N	N	Y	N
44 Bates	Y	Y	Y	N	Y	Y	N	Y
45 ***Hunter***	N	N	Y	Y	N	N	Y	N
COLORADO								
1 Schroeder	Y	Y	Y	N	Y	Y	N	Y
2 Skaggs	Y	Y	Y	N	Y	N	N	Y
3 Campbell	Y	Y	Y	Y	N	N	N	Y
4 ***Brown***	N	N	Y	Y	N	Y	Y	N
5 ***Hefley***	N	N	Y	Y	N	N	Y	N
6 ***Schaefer***	N	Y	Y	Y	N	N	Y	N
CONNECTICUT								
1 Kennelly	Y	Y	Y	N	Y	Y	N	Y
2 Gejdenson	Y	Y	Y	N	Y	Y	N	Y
3 Morrison	Y	Y	Y	N	Y	Y	N	Y
4 ***Shays***	Y	N	Y	N	Y	Y	Y	Y
5 ***Rowland***	N	N	Y	Y	Y	Y	Y	N
6 ***Johnson***	N	Y	Y	N	Y	Y	Y	N
DELAWARE								
AL Carper	Y	Y	Y	N	Y	Y	N	Y
FLORIDA								
1 Hutto	N	N	Y	Y	N	N	Y	N
2 ***Grant***	N	N	Y	Y	N	N	Y	Y
3 Bennett	Y	Y	Y	Y	Y	Y	N	Y
4 ***James***	N	N	Y	Y	N	N	Y	N
5 ***McCollum***	N	N	Y	Y	N	Y	Y	N
6 ***Stearns***	N	N	Y	Y	N	Y	Y	N
7 Gibbons	Y	Y	Y	N	Y	Y	N	Y
8 ***Young***	N	N	Y	Y	N	Y	Y	N
9 ***Bilirakis***	N	N	Y	Y	N	N	Y	?
10 ***Ireland***	N	N	Y	Y	N	N	Y	N
11 Nelson	#	#	+	Y	+	-	-	N
12 ***Lewis***	N	N	Y	Y	N	N	Y	N
13 ***Goss***	N	N	Y	Y	N	Y	Y	N
14 Johnston	Y	Y	Y	N	Y	Y	N	Y
15 ***Shaw***	N	N	Y	Y	N	Y	Y	N
16 Smith	Y	Y	Y	N	Y	N	N	Y
17 Lehman	Y	Y	Y	N	Y	Y	N	Y
18 ***Ros-Lehtinen***	N	N	Y	Y	Y	Y	Y	N
19 Fascell	Y	Y	Y	N	Y	N	N	Y
GEORGIA								
1 Thomas	N	Y	Y	Y	N	N	Y	Y
2 Hatcher	N	Y	Y	Y	N	N	N	Y
3 Ray	N	N	Y	Y	N	N	Y	Y
4 Jones	Y	Y	Y	N	N	N	N	Y
5 Lewis	Y	Y	Y	N	Y	N	N	Y
6 ***Gingrich***	N	N	Y	Y	N	N	Y	N
7 Darden	N	Y	Y	Y	N	N	N	N
8 Rowland	Y	Y	Y	Y	N	N	Y	Y
9 Jenkins	N	N	Y	Y	Y	N	N	Y
10 Barnard	#	Y	Y	Y	N	N	Y	?
HAWAII								
1 ***Saiki***	N	N	Y	Y	Y	N	Y	N
2 Vacancy [1]								
IDAHO								
1 ***Craig***	X	X	Y	Y	N	N	Y	N
2 Stallings	Y	?	Y	Y	N	N	N	Y
ILLINOIS								
1 Hayes	Y	Y	Y	N	Y	N	N	Y
2 Savage	Y	Y	Y	N	Y	Y	P	Y
3 Russo	Y	Y	Y	N	Y	Y	N	Y
4 Sangmeister	Y	Y	Y	Y	Y	N	N	Y
5 Lipinski	N	Y	Y	Y	Y	Y	N	N
6 ***Hyde***	N	N	Y	Y	Y	N	Y	N
7 Collins	Y	Y	Y	N	Y	N	N	Y
8 Rostenkowski	Y	Y	Y	N	Y	Y	N	Y
9 Yates	Y	Y	Y	N	Y	Y	N	Y
10 ***Porter***	N	N	Y	N	N	Y	Y	N
11 Annunzio	Y	Y	Y	Y	Y	Y	N	Y
12 ***Crane***	N	N	N	Y	N	Y	Y	N
13 ***Fawell***	N	N	Y	Y	N	Y	Y	N
14 ***Hastert***	N	N	Y	Y	N	N	Y	N
15 ***Madigan***	N	N	Y	Y	N	N	Y	N
16 ***Martin***	N	Y	Y	Y	Y	N	N	N
17 Evans	Y	Y	Y	N	Y	N	N	Y
18 ***Michel***	N	N	Y	Y	N	N	Y	N
19 Bruce	Y	Y	Y	N	Y	N	N	Y
20 Durbin	Y	Y	Y	N	Y	N	N	Y
21 Costello	Y	Y	N	Y	Y	N	N	Y
22 Poshard	Y	Y	N	N	Y	N	Y	Y
INDIANA								
1 Visclosky	Y	Y	Y	N	Y	Y	N	Y
2 Sharp	Y	Y	Y	Y	Y	N	N	?
3 ***Hiler***	N	N	Y	Y	N	N	Y	N

	1	2	3	4	5	6	7	8
4 Long	Y	Y	Y	Y	Y	N	N	Y
5 Jontz	Y	Y	Y	N	Y	N	N	Y
6 ***Burton***	N	N	N	Y	N	N	Y	N
7 ***Myers***	N	N	N	Y	N	N	N	N
8 McCloskey	Y	Y	Y	N	Y	N	N	Y
9 Hamilton	Y	Y	Y	N	N	N	N	Y
10 Jacobs	Y	Y	Y	Y	Y	Y	N	Y
IOWA								
1 ***Leach***	Y	N	Y	N	N	N	N	Y
2 ***Tauke***	Y	N	Y	Y	N	N	N	N
3 Nagle	Y	Y	Y	N	N	N	N	Y
4 Smith	Y	Y	Y	N	Y	N	N	N
5 ***Lightfoot***	N	N	N	Y	N	N	Y	N
6 ***Grandy***	Y	N	Y	N	N	N	N	Y
KANSAS								
1 ***Roberts***	N	N	Y	Y	N	N	Y	N
2 Slattery	Y	Y	Y	N	N	N	N	Y
3 ***Meyers***	N	N	Y	Y	N	N	Y	N
4 Glickman	Y	Y	Y	N	N	N	N	Y
5 ***Whittaker***	N	N	Y	Y	N	N	N	N
KENTUCKY								
1 Hubbard	Y	Y	N	Y	N	N	N	Y
2 Natcher	Y	Y	Y	Y	Y	N	N	Y
3 Mazzoli	Y	Y	Y	Y	Y	Y	N	Y
4 ***Bunning***	N	Y	Y	Y	N	N	Y	N
5 ***Rogers***	N	Y	Y	Y	N	N	Y	N
6 ***Hopkins***	N	Y	Y	Y	N	N	Y	N
7 Perkins	Y	Y	Y	Y	Y	N	N	Y
LOUISIANA								
1 ***Livingston***	N	N	Y	Y	N	Y	Y	N
2 Boggs	Y	Y	Y	N	Y	N	N	N
3 Tauzin	N	N	Y	Y	N	N	N	N
4 ***McCrery***	N	N	Y	Y	N	N	Y	N
5 Huckaby	N	N	Y	Y	N	N	N	N
6 ***Baker***	N	N	Y	Y	N	N	Y	N
7 Hayes	Y	Y	Y	Y	N	N	N	N
8 ***Holloway***	N	?	?	Y	N	N	Y	N
MAINE								
1 Brennan	Y	Y	Y	N	Y	Y	N	Y
2 ***Snowe***	N	N	Y	Y	Y	Y	N	Y
MARYLAND								
1 Dyson	Y	Y	Y	Y	Y	N	N	N
2 ***Bentley***	N	Y	Y	Y	N	N	Y	N
3 Cardin	Y	Y	Y	N	Y	Y	N	Y
4 McMillen	Y	Y	Y	Y	Y	Y	N	Y
5 Hoyer	Y	Y	Y	N	Y	N	N	Y
6 Byron	N	Y	Y	Y	N	N	N	N
7 Mfume	Y	Y	Y	N	Y	Y	N	Y
8 ***Morella***	Y	N	Y	N	Y	Y	N	Y
MASSACHUSETTS								
1 ***Conte***	Y	N	Y	N	Y	Y	N	Y
2 Neal	Y	Y	Y	Y	Y	Y	N	+
3 Early	Y	N	Y	N	Y	?	N	Y
4 Frank	Y	Y	Y	N	Y	Y	C	Y
5 Atkins	Y	Y	Y	N	Y	Y	N	Y
6 Mavroules	Y	Y	Y	N	Y	Y	N	Y
7 Markey	Y	Y	Y	N	Y	Y	N	Y
8 Kennedy	Y	Y	Y	N	Y	Y	N	Y
9 Moakley	Y	Y	Y	Y	Y	N	N	Y
10 Studds	Y	Y	Y	N	Y	Y	N	Y
11 Donnelly	Y	Y	Y	Y	N	Y	N	Y
MICHIGAN								
1 Conyers	Y	Y	Y	N	Y	N	N	Y
2 ***Pursell***	Y	Y	Y	Y	N	N	Y	Y
3 Wolpe	Y	Y	Y	N	Y	N	N	Y
4 ***Upton***	Y	Y	Y	Y	N	N	Y	N
5 ***Henry***	Y	Y	Y	N	N	N	Y	N
6 Carr	Y	Y	Y	N	N	N	N	Y
7 Kildee	Y	Y	Y	N	Y	N	N	Y
8 Traxler	Y	Y	Y	Y	Y	N	N	Y
9 ***Vander Jagt***	N	N	Y	Y	N	N	Y	N
10 ***Schuette***	N	Y	Y	Y	N	N	Y	N
11 ***Davis***	N	Y	Y	Y	Y	N	N	?
12 Bonior	Y	Y	Y	N	Y	Y	N	Y
13 Crockett	Y	Y	Y	N	Y	?	N	?
14 Hertel	Y	Y	Y	N	Y	Y	N	Y
15 Ford	Y	Y	Y	N	Y	N	N	Y
16 Dingell	Y	Y	Y	N	Y	N	N	Y
17 Levin	Y	Y	Y	N	Y	Y	N	Y
18 ***Broomfield***	N	Y	Y	Y	N	Y	Y	N
MINNESOTA								
1 Penny	Y	Y	Y	N	N	N	N	Y
2 ***Weber***	N	N	Y	Y	N	N	Y	N
3 ***Frenzel***	N	N	?	Y	N	Y	N	N
4 Vento	Y	Y	Y	N	Y	Y	N	Y
5 Sabo	Y	Y	Y	N	Y	Y	N	Y
6 Sikorski	Y	Y	Y	N	Y	N	N	Y
7 ***Stangeland***	N	Y	Y	Y	N	N	N	N
8 Oberstar	Y	Y	Y	N	Y	N	N	Y
MISSISSIPPI								
1 Whitten	Y	Y	Y	Y	Y	N	N	N
2 Espy	Y	Y	Y	N	Y	N	N	Y
3 Montgomery	N	N	Y	Y	N	N	N	N
4 Parker	N	N	Y	Y	N	N	N	N
5 Taylor	Y	Y	Y	Y	N	N	Y	N
MISSOURI								
1 Clay	Y	Y	Y	N	Y	N	N	Y
2 ***Buechner***	N	N	Y	Y	N	Y	Y	N
3 Gephardt	Y	Y	Y	N	Y	N	N	Y
4 Skelton	N	Y	Y	Y	N	N	N	N
5 Wheat	Y	Y	Y	N	Y	N	N	Y
6 ***Coleman***	N	N	Y	N	N	N	N	N
7 ***Hancock***	N	N	N	Y	N	Y	Y	N
8 ***Emerson***	N	Y	Y	Y	N	N	Y	N
9 Volkmer	Y	Y	Y	Y	Y	N	N	Y
MONTANA								
1 Williams	Y	#	Y	N	Y	N	N	Y
2 ***Marlenee***	X	N	N	Y	N	N	N	N
NEBRASKA								
1 ***Bereuter***	Y	N	Y	Y	N	N	N	N
2 Hoagland	N	Y	Y	N	N	N	N	Y
3 ***Smith***	N	N	Y	Y	N	N	Y	N
NEVADA								
1 Bilbray	Y	Y	Y	Y	Y	Y	N	Y
2 ***Vucanovich***	N	N	Y	Y	N	N	Y	N
NEW HAMPSHIRE								
1 ***Smith***	N	N	Y	Y	N	Y	Y	N
2 ***Douglas***	N	N	Y	Y	N	Y	Y	N
NEW JERSEY								
1 Vacancy [2]								
2 Hughes	Y	Y	Y	N	?	Y	N	Y
3 Pallone	Y	Y	Y	Y	Y	Y	N	Y
4 ***Smith***	N	Y	Y	Y	Y	Y	Y	N
5 ***Roukema***	Y	N	Y	Y	Y	Y	Y	Y
6 Dwyer	Y	Y	Y	N	Y	Y	N	Y
7 ***Rinaldo***	Y	Y	Y	Y	Y	Y	Y	N
8 Roe	Y	Y	Y	Y	Y	?	N	Y
9 Torricelli	Y	Y	Y	N	Y	Y	N	?
10 Payne	Y	Y	Y	N	Y	Y	N	Y
11 ***Gallo***	N	N	Y	Y	N	Y	Y	N
12 ***Courter***	N	N	Y	Y	N	Y	Y	N
13 ***Saxton***	N	N	Y	Y	N	Y	Y	Y
14 Guarini	Y	Y	Y	Y	Y	Y	N	Y
NEW MEXICO								
1 ***Schiff***	N	Y	Y	Y	N	N	N	N
2 ***Skeen***	N	N	Y	Y	N	N	Y	N
3 Richardson	Y	Y	Y	Y	Y	N	N	N
NEW YORK								
1 Hochbrueckner	Y	Y	Y	Y	Y	Y	N	Y
2 Downey	Y	Y	Y	N	Y	Y	N	Y
3 Mrazek	Y	Y	Y	N	Y	Y	N	Y
4 ***Lent***	N	N	Y	Y	N	Y	N	N
5 ***McGrath***	Y	Y	Y	Y	Y	Y	N	N
6 Flake	Y	Y	Y	N	?	?	N	Y
7 Ackerman	Y	Y	Y	N	Y	N	N	Y
8 Scheuer	Y	Y	Y	N	Y	Y	N	Y
9 Manton	Y	Y	Y	Y	Y	Y	N	Y
10 Schumer	Y	Y	Y	N	Y	Y	N	Y
11 Towns	Y	Y	Y	N	Y	N	N	Y
12 Owens	Y	Y	Y	N	Y	Y	N	Y
13 Solarz	Y	Y	Y	N	Y	Y	N	Y
14 ***Molinari*** [3]	N	N	Y	Y	Y	Y	N	N
15 ***Green***	Y	N	Y	N	Y	Y	N	Y
16 Rangel	Y	Y	Y	?	Y	Y	N	Y
17 Weiss	Y	Y	Y	N	Y	Y	N	Y
18 Serrano [4]	Y	Y	Y	N	Y	Y	N	Y
19 Engel	Y	Y	Y	N	Y	Y	N	Y
20 Lowey	Y	Y	Y	N	Y	Y	N	Y
21 ***Fish***	?	Y	Y	Y	Y	N	N	N
22 ***Gilman***	Y	Y	Y	Y	Y	N	N	N
23 McNulty	Y	Y	Y	Y	Y	Y	N	N
24 ***Solomon***	N	Y	Y	Y	Y	N	Y	N
25 ***Boehlert***	Y	N	Y	Y	Y	N	N	N
26 ***Martin***	N	Y	Y	Y	Y	N	N	N
27 ***Walsh***	Y	Y	Y	Y	N	N	Y	N
28 McHugh	Y	Y	Y	N	Y	N	N	Y
29 ***Horton***	Y	Y	Y	Y	Y	N	N	Y
30 Slaughter	Y	Y	Y	N	Y	N	N	Y
31 ***Paxon***	N	N	Y	Y	N	N	Y	N
32 LaFalce	Y	Y	Y	N	N	Y	N	Y
33 Nowak	Y	Y	Y	N	Y	Y	N	Y
34 ***Houghton***	N	Y	Y	N	N	N	N	N
NORTH CAROLINA								
1 Jones	Y	Y	Y	Y	N	N	N	Y
2 Valentine	Y	N	Y	N	N	N	N	Y
3 Lancaster	N	Y	Y	Y	N	N	N	N
4 Price	Y	Y	Y	N	Y	Y	N	Y
5 Neal	Y	N	Y	N	N	N	N	Y
6 ***Coble***	N	N	Y	Y	N	Y	Y	Y
7 Rose	Y	Y	Y	N	Y	N	N	Y
8 Hefner	Y	Y	Y	Y	N	N	N	Y
9 ***McMillan***	N	N	Y	Y	N	Y	Y	N
10 ***Ballenger***	N	N	Y	Y	N	Y	Y	N
11 Clarke	Y	N	Y	Y	N	Y	N	Y
NORTH DAKOTA								
AL Dorgan	Y	Y	Y	N	Y	N	N	Y
OHIO								
1 Luken	Y	Y	Y	Y	Y	N	N	Y
2 ***Gradison***	N	N	Y	Y	N	Y	Y	N
3 Hall	Y	Y	Y	N	Y	N	N	Y
4 ***Oxley***	N	Y	Y	Y	N	N	Y	N
5 ***Gillmor***	N	N	Y	Y	Y	N	Y	N
6 ***McEwen***	N	Y	N	Y	N	N	Y	N
7 ***DeWine***	N	Y	N	Y	Y	N	Y	N
8 ***Lukens***	?	?	?	Y	N	N	P	N
9 Kaptur	Y	Y	Y	N	?	N	N	Y
10 ***Miller***	N	Y	N	Y	N	Y	Y	?
11 Eckart	Y	Y	Y	Y	Y	Y	N	Y
12 ***Kasich***	N	Y	N	Y	N	N	Y	N
13 Pease	Y	Y	Y	N	Y	Y	N	Y
14 Sawyer	Y	Y	Y	N	Y	N	N	Y
15 ***Wylie***	N	N	Y	Y	N	Y	Y	N
16 ***Regula***	Y	Y	Y	Y	Y	Y	Y	N
17 Traficant	Y	Y	Y	Y	Y	N	N	Y
18 Applegate	Y	Y	N	Y	Y	N	N	Y
19 Feighan	Y	Y	Y	N	Y	Y	N	?
20 Oakar	Y	Y	Y	N	Y	Y	N	Y
21 Stokes	#	Y	Y	N	Y	N	N	Y
OKLAHOMA								
1 ***Inhofe***	N	N	Y	Y	N	N	Y	N
2 Synar	Y	Y	Y	N	Y	N	N	Y
3 Watkins	?	Y	Y	Y	N	N	Y	?
4 McCurdy	N	N	Y	N	Y	N	N	Y
5 ***Edwards***	N	N	Y	Y	N	N	Y	N
6 English	N	Y	Y	Y	Y	N	N	N
OREGON								
1 AuCoin	Y	Y	Y	N	Y	N	N	?
2 ***Smith, B.***	N	Y	Y	Y	N	N	Y	N
3 Wyden	Y	Y	Y	N	Y	Y	N	Y
4 DeFazio	Y	Y	Y	N	Y	N	N	Y
5 ***Smith, D.***	-	N	Y	Y	N	N	Y	N
PENNSYLVANIA								
1 Foglietta	Y	Y	Y	N	Y	Y	N	Y
2 Gray	Y	Y	Y	N	Y	Y	N	Y
3 Borski	Y	Y	Y	N	Y	Y	N	Y
4 Kolter	Y	Y	Y	Y	Y	?	N	Y
5 ***Schulze***	N	Y	Y	Y	N	Y	Y	N
6 Yatron	Y	Y	Y	Y	Y	Y	N	Y
7 ***Weldon***	Y	Y	Y	Y	Y	Y	N	N
8 Kostmayer	Y	Y	Y	N	Y	Y	N	Y
9 ***Shuster***	N	N	N	Y	N	Y	Y	N
10 ***McDade***	N	Y	Y	Y	Y	N	N	?
11 Kanjorski	Y	Y	Y	Y	Y	Y	N	Y
12 Murtha	Y	Y	Y	Y	Y	N	N	?
13 ***Coughlin***	Y	N	Y	Y	Y	Y	N	Y
14 Coyne	Y	Y	Y	N	Y	Y	N	Y
15 ***Ritter***	N	Y	Y	Y	N	N	N	N
16 ***Walker***	N	N	Y	Y	N	Y	Y	N
17 ***Gekas***	N	N	Y	Y	N	N	Y	?
18 Walgren	Y	Y	Y	N	Y	Y	N	Y
19 ***Goodling***	N	Y	Y	Y	N	Y	Y	N
20 Gaydos	Y	Y	Y	Y	Y	Y	N	Y
21 ***Ridge***	Y	Y	Y	Y	N	N	N	Y
22 Murphy	Y	Y	Y	Y	Y	Y	N	Y
23 ***Clinger***	N	+	+	N	N	N	N	N
RHODE ISLAND								
1 ***Machtley***	Y	N	Y	Y	Y	Y	N	Y
2 ***Schneider***	Y	N	Y	N	Y	Y	N	Y
SOUTH CAROLINA								
1 ***Ravenel***	N	N	Y	Y	Y	N	N	N
2 ***Spence***	N	N	Y	Y	N	N	N	N
3 Derrick	Y	Y	Y	Y	N	N	N	Y
4 Patterson	Y	Y	Y	Y	N	N	Y	N
5 Spratt	Y	Y	Y	N	N	N	N	N
6 Tallon	N	Y	Y	N	N	N	N	N
SOUTH DAKOTA								
AL Johnson	Y	Y	Y	Y	Y	N	N	Y
TENNESSEE								
1 ***Quillen***	N	Y	Y	Y	N	N	Y	N
2 ***Duncan***	N	Y	Y	Y	N	Y	Y	N
3 Lloyd	N	Y	Y	Y	N	N	N	N
4 Cooper	N	N	Y	N	N	C	N	Y
5 Clement	Y	Y	Y	Y	Y	N	N	Y
6 Gordon	Y	Y	Y	N	Y	N	N	Y
7 ***Sundquist***	N	N	Y	Y	N	N	Y	N
8 Tanner	Y	Y	Y	N	N	N	N	Y
9 Ford	Y	Y	Y	N	Y	?	N	Y
TEXAS								
1 Chapman	Y	Y	Y	Y	Y	N	?	Y
2 Wilson	N	Y	Y	Y	Y	N	N	N
3 ***Bartlett***	N	N	Y	Y	N	N	Y	N
4 Hall	N	N	Y	?	N	N	Y	N
5 Bryant	Y	Y	Y	N	Y	N	N	Y
6 ***Barton***	?	?	Y	Y	N	N	Y	N
7 ***Archer***	N	N	Y	Y	N	Y	Y	N
8 ***Fields***	N	N	Y	Y	N	N	Y	N
9 Brooks	Y	Y	Y	Y	Y	N	N	Y
10 Pickle	Y	N	Y	N	N	N	N	N
11 Leath	?	Y	?	Y	N	N	N	?
12 Geren	N	Y	Y	Y	N	N	N	N
13 Sarpalius	N	Y	Y	Y	N	N	Y	N
14 Laughlin	N	Y	Y	Y	N	N	Y	Y
15 de la Garza	Y	Y	Y	Y	Y	N	N	Y
16 Coleman	Y	Y	Y	N	Y	N	N	N
17 Stenholm	N	N	Y	N	N	N	N	N
18 Washington [5]	Y	Y	Y	N	?	N	N	Y
19 ***Combest***	N	N	N	Y	N	N	Y	N
20 Gonzalez	Y	Y	Y	N	Y	N	N	Y
21 ***Smith***	N	N	Y	Y	Y	N	Y	N
22 ***DeLay***	N	N	N	Y	N	N	Y	N
23 Bustamante	Y	Y	Y	Y	Y	N	N	Y
24 Frost	Y	Y	Y	N	Y	N	N	Y
25 Andrews	Y	N	Y	Y	Y	N	N	Y
26 ***Armey***	N	N	N	Y	N	Y	Y	N
27 Ortiz	Y	Y	Y	Y	Y	N	N	Y
UTAH								
1 ***Hansen***	N	N	Y	Y	N	Y	Y	N
2 Owens	Y	Y	Y	N	Y	Y	N	Y
3 ***Nielson***	N	N	Y	Y	N	Y	Y	N
VERMONT								
AL ***Smith***	Y	N	Y	N	Y	N	Y	Y
VIRGINIA								
1 ***Bateman***	N	N	Y	Y	N	N	Y	N
2 Pickett	N	N	Y	Y	N	N	N	N
3 ***Bliley***	N	N	Y	Y	N	Y	Y	N
4 Sisisky	N	N	Y	Y	N	N	N	N
5 Payne	Y	Y	Y	Y	N	N	N	N
6 Olin	Y	Y	Y	Y	N	N	N	Y
7 ***Slaughter***	N	N	Y	Y	N	N	Y	N
8 ***Parris***	N	N	Y	Y	N	N	Y	N
9 Boucher	Y	Y	Y	N	Y	Y	N	Y
10 ***Wolf***	N	N	Y	Y	N	Y	Y	N
WASHINGTON								
1 ***Miller***	Y	N	Y	Y	Y	Y	N	N
2 Swift	Y	Y	Y	N	Y	N	N	Y
3 Unsoeld	Y	Y	Y	N	Y	N	N	+
4 ***Morrison***	Y	N	Y	Y	Y	N	N	N
5 Foley				N			N	
6 Dicks	Y	Y	Y	N	Y	N	N	Y
7 McDermott	Y	Y	Y	N	Y	N	N	Y
8 ***Chandler***	Y	N	Y	N	N	N	N	Y
WEST VIRGINIA								
1 Mollohan	Y	Y	N	Y	Y	N	N	Y
2 Staggers	Y	Y	Y	Y	Y	N	N	Y
3 Wise	Y	Y	Y	Y	Y	Y	N	Y
4 Rahall	Y	Y	Y	Y	Y	N	N	Y
WISCONSIN								
1 Aspin	Y	Y	Y	N	N	Y	N	Y
2 Kastenmeier	Y	Y	Y	N	Y	N	N	Y
3 ***Gunderson***	N	N	Y	Y	N	N	N	N
4 Kleczka	Y	Y	Y	N	Y	Y	N	Y
5 Moody	Y	Y	Y	N	Y	Y	N	Y
6 ***Petri***	N	N	Y	N	N	Y	Y	N
7 Obey	Y	Y	Y	N	Y	Y	N	Y
8 ***Roth***	N	N	Y	Y	N	Y	Y	N
9 ***Sensenbrenner***	N	N	Y	Y	N	Y	Y	N
WYOMING								
AL ***Thomas***	N	N	Y	Y	N	N	Y	N

9. HR 4739. Fiscal 1991 Defense Authorization/Abortion Services. Fazio, D-Calif., amendment to provide military personnel and their dependents stationed overseas with reproductive health services, including privately paid abortions, at military hospitals. Rejected 200-216: R 35-139; D 165-77 (ND 113-50, SD 52-27), Sept. 18, 1990. A "nay" was a vote supporting the president's position.

10. HR 4300. Legal Immigration Revision/Passage. Passage of the bill to increase the number of visas for relatives and people coming to the United States to work; suspend deportation for the spouses and children of newly legalized aliens; establish diversity visas for immigrants from countries that currently account for a low number of immigrants to the United States; and reform and revise other immigration procedures. Passed 231-192: R 45-127; D 186-65 (ND 159-13, SD 27-52), Oct. 3, 1990. A "nay" was a vote supporting the president's position.

11. H Con Res 310. Fiscal 1991 Budget Resolution/Conference Report. Adoption of the conference report to set binding budget levels for fiscal 1991: budget authority, $1.49 trillion; outlays, $1.24 trillion; revenues, $1.173 trillion; deficit, $64 billion, by incorporating the spending and revenue targets announced Sept. 30 at the budget summit. The agreement contains reconciliation instructions providing cost-saving changes in entitlement programs, increases in various user fees and taxes, and caps on annual appropriations for defense, international affairs and domestic programs to reduce the deficit by $40.1 billion in fiscal 1991 and $500 billion in fiscal 1991 through 1995. Rejected 179-254: R 71-105; D 108-149 (ND 63-111, SD 45-38), in the session that began, and the *Congressional Record* dated, Oct. 4, 1990. A "yea" was a vote supporting the president's position.

12. HR 4328. Textile Trade Act/Veto Override. Passage, over President Bush's Oct. 5 veto, of the bill to limit the growth of imports of textiles and apparel to 1 percent annually, establish permanent quotas for most non-rubber footwear imports at 1989 levels, authorize the special allocation of textile quotas for countries increasing their purchases of U.S. agricultural goods, and for other purposes. Rejected 275-152: R 70-103; D 205-49 (ND 131-41, SD 74-8), Oct. 10, 1990. A two-thirds majority of those present and voting (285 in this case) of both chambers is required to override a veto. A "nay" was a vote supporting the president's position.

[1] *Rep. Patsy T. Mink, D-Hawaii, was sworn in Sept. 27, 1990, to succeed Daniel K. Akaka, D, who resigned May 16, 1990.*
[2] *Rep. James J. Florio, D-N.J., resigned Jan. 16, 1990.*

KEY

Y	Voted for (yea).
#	Paired for.
+	Announced for.
N	Voted against (nay).
X	Paired against.
-	Announced against.
P	Voted "present."
C	Voted "present" to avoid possible conflict of interest.
?	Did not vote or otherwise make a position known.

Democrats ***Republicans***
Independent

ND	Northern Democrats
SD	Southern Democrats

Southern states - Ala., Ark., Fla., Ga., Ky., La., Miss., N.C., Okla., S.C., Tenn., Texas, Va.

	9	10	11	12
ALABAMA				
1 ***Callahan***	N	N	N	Y
2 ***Dickinson***	N	N	Y	Y
3 Browder	N	N	N	Y
4 Bevill	N	N	Y	Y
5 Flippo	N	?	Y	Y
6 Erdreich	Y	N	Y	Y
7 Harris	N	N	N	Y
ALASKA				
AL ***Young***	N	Y	Y	Y
ARIZONA				
1 ***Rhodes***	N	N	Y	N
2 Udall	Y	Y	Y	N
3 ***Stump***	N	N	N	N
4 ***Kyl***	N	N	N	N
5 ***Kolbe***	Y	N	Y	N
ARKANSAS				
1 Alexander	Y	Y	N	Y
2 ***Robinson***	N	N	Y	N
3 ***Hammerschmidt***	N	N	Y	Y
4 Anthony	Y	Y	N	Y
CALIFORNIA				
1 Bosco	Y	Y	Y	Y
2 ***Herger***	N	N	N	N
3 Matsui	Y	Y	Y	N
4 Fazio	Y	Y	Y	Y
5 Pelosi	Y	Y	N	N
6 Boxer	Y	Y	N	N
7 Miller	Y	Y	N	N
8 Dellums	Y	Y	N	Y
9 Stark	Y	Y	N	N
10 Edwards	Y	Y	N	Y
11 Lantos	Y	Y	Y	Y
12 ***Campbell***	Y	?	N	N
13 Mineta	Y	Y	Y	Y
14 ***Shumway***	N	N	Y	N
15 Condit	Y	Y	N	Y
16 Panetta	Y	Y	Y	N
17 ***Pashayan***	N	Y	N	Y
18 Lehman	Y	Y	N	Y
19 ***Lagomarsino***	N	N	N	N
20 ***Thomas***	Y	Y	N	Y
21 ***Gallegly***	N	N	N	N
22 ***Moorhead***	N	N	N	N
23 Beilenson	Y	N	Y	N
24 Waxman	Y	Y	N	N
25 Roybal	Y	Y	N	Y
26 Berman	Y	Y	N	N
27 Levine	Y	Y	N	N
28 Dixon	Y	Y	N	Y
29 Hawkins	?	Y	N	Y
30 Martinez	Y	Y	N	Y
31 Dymally	Y	Y	N	Y
32 Anderson	Y	Y	Y	N
33 ***Dreier***	N	N	N	N
34 Torres	Y	Y	Y	Y
35 ***Lewis***	N	N	Y	N
36 Brown	Y	Y	N	Y
37 ***McCandless***	Y	N	N	N
38 ***Dornan***	N	Y	N	Y
39 ***Dannemeyer***	N	N	N	N
40 ***Cox***	N	N	N	N
41 ***Lowery***	N	N	Y	N
42 ***Rohrabacher***	N	Y	N	N
43 ***Packard***	N	N	N	N
44 Bates	Y	Y	N	Y
45 ***Hunter***	N	Y	N	Y
COLORADO				
1 Schroeder	Y	Y	N	N
2 Skaggs	Y	Y	Y	N
3 Campbell	Y	Y	N	Y
4 ***Brown***	Y	N	N	N
5 ***Hefley***	N	N	N	N
6 ***Schaefer***	N	N	N	Y
CONNECTICUT				
1 Kennelly	Y	Y	Y	N
2 Gejdenson	Y	Y	Y	Y
3 Morrison	Y	Y	N	Y
4 ***Shays***	Y	Y	Y	Y
5 ***Rowland***	Y	?	N	X
6 ***Johnson***	Y	Y	Y	N
DELAWARE				
AL Carper	Y	Y	Y	Y
FLORIDA				
1 Hutto	N	N	N	Y
2 ***Grant***	N	N	N	Y
3 Bennett	Y	N	Y	Y
4 ***James***	N	N	N	N
5 ***McCollum***	N	N	N	N
6 ***Stearns***	N	N	N	N
7 Gibbons	Y	Y	Y	N
8 ***Young***	N	N	Y	N
9 ***Bilirakis***	?	N	N	N
10 ***Ireland***	N	N	Y	N
11 Nelson	Y	N	Y	N
12 ***Lewis***	N	N	N	N
13 ***Goss***	N	N	N	N
14 Johnston	Y	N	N	Y
15 ***Shaw***	N	N	Y	N
16 Smith	Y	Y	N	Y
17 Lehman	Y	Y	Y	Y
18 ***Ros-Lehtinen***	N	Y	N	N
19 Fascell	Y	Y	Y	Y
GEORGIA				
1 Thomas	Y	N	Y	Y
2 Hatcher	Y	N	Y	Y
3 Ray	N	N	Y	Y
4 Jones	Y	?	N	Y
5 Lewis	Y	Y	N	Y
6 ***Gingrich***	N	Y	N	Y
7 Darden	Y	Y	Y	Y
8 Rowland	Y	N	Y	Y
9 Jenkins	N	N	N	Y
10 Barnard	N	N	N	Y
HAWAII				
1 ***Saiki***	Y	Y	N	N
2 Mink [1]		Y	N	Y
IDAHO				
1 ***Craig***	N	N	N	N
2 Stallings	N	N	N	N
ILLINOIS				
1 Hayes	Y	Y	N	Y
2 Savage	Y	N	N	Y
3 Russo	N	Y	N	Y
4 Sangmeister	N	Y	N	N
5 Lipinski	N	Y	N	Y
6 ***Hyde***	N	Y	N	N
7 Collins	Y	Y	N	Y
8 Rostenkowski	N	Y	Y	N
9 Yates	Y	Y	N	Y
10 ***Porter***	Y	Y	Y	N
11 Annunzio	N	Y	N	Y
12 ***Crane***	N	N	N	N
13 ***Fawell***	Y	N	N	N
14 ***Hastert***	N	N	Y	N
15 ***Madigan***	N	Y	Y	N
16 ***Martin***	Y	Y	N	N
17 Evans	Y	Y	N	Y
18 ***Michel***	N	N	Y	N
19 Bruce	N	Y	N	Y
20 Durbin	N	Y	N	Y
21 Costello	N	Y	N	Y
22 Poshard	N	Y	N	Y
INDIANA				
1 Visclosky	Y	Y	Y	Y
2 Sharp	Y	Y	N	Y
3 ***Hiler***	N	N	N	N

	9	10	11	12
4 Long	Y	N	N	Y
5 Jontz	Y	Y	N	Y
6 ***Burton***	N	N	N	Y
7 ***Myers***	N	N	N	N
8 McCloskey	Y	Y	N	Y
9 Hamilton	Y	Y	Y	N
10 Jacobs	Y	Y	N	Y
IOWA				
1 ***Leach***	Y	Y	Y	N
2 ***Tauke***	N	Y	N	N
3 Nagle	Y	Y	Y	Y
4 Smith	Y	Y	Y	N
5 ***Lightfoot***	N	N	N	N
6 ***Grandy***	N	N	Y	N
KANSAS				
1 ***Roberts***	N	N	Y	N
2 Slattery	Y	Y	Y	N
3 ***Meyers***	Y	N	Y	N
4 Glickman	Y	Y	Y	N
5 ***Whittaker***	N	N	Y	N
KENTUCKY				
1 Hubbard	Y	N	N	Y
2 Natcher	N	N	N	Y
3 Mazzoli	N	N	N	N
4 ***Bunning***	N	N	N	N
5 ***Rogers***	N	N	N	Y
6 ***Hopkins***	N	N	N	Y
7 Perkins	N	N	N	Y
LOUISIANA				
1 ***Livingston***	N	N	Y	N
2 Boggs	?	?	Y	?
3 Tauzin	N	N	N	Y
4 ***McCrery***	N	N	N	Y
5 Huckaby	N	N	N	Y
6 ***Baker***	N	N	Y	Y
7 Hayes	N	N	N	Y
8 ***Holloway***	N	N	N	Y
MAINE				
1 Brennan	Y	Y	N	Y
2 ***Snowe***	Y	Y	N	Y
MARYLAND				
1 Dyson	N	N	N	Y
2 ***Bentley***	N	N	N	Y
3 Cardin	Y	Y	Y	Y
4 McMillen	Y	Y	Y	Y
5 Hoyer	Y	Y	Y	Y
6 Byron	N	N	Y	Y
7 Mfume	Y	Y	N	Y
8 ***Morella***	Y	Y	Y	N
MASSACHUSETTS				
1 ***Conte***	N	Y	Y	Y
2 Neal	+	Y	N	#
3 Early	N	N	N	Y
4 Frank	Y	Y	N	Y
5 Atkins	Y	Y	N	Y
6 Mavroules	N	Y	N	Y
7 Markey	Y	Y	N	Y
8 Kennedy	Y	Y	N	Y
9 Moakley	N	Y	Y	Y
10 Studds	Y	Y	N	Y
11 Donnelly	N	Y	N	Y
MICHIGAN				
1 Conyers	Y	Y	Y	Y
2 ***Pursell***	N	N	N	N
3 Wolpe	Y	Y	N	Y
4 ***Upton***	N	N	N	N
5 ***Henry***	N	N	N	?
6 Carr	Y	Y	N	Y
7 Kildee	N	Y	N	Y
8 Traxler	N	Y	Y	Y
9 ***Vander Jagt***	N	N	Y	N
10 ***Schuette***	N	N	N	?
11 ***Davis***	N	N	N	Y
12 Bonior	N	Y	N	Y
13 Crockett	?	?	?	N
14 Hertel	N	Y	N	Y
15 Ford	?	Y	N	Y
16 Dingell	Y	Y	Y	Y
17 Levin	Y	Y	Y	Y
18 ***Broomfield***	N	N	N	N
MINNESOTA				
1 Penny	N	Y	Y	N
2 ***Weber***	N	Y	N	N
3 ***Frenzel***	Y	N	Y	N
4 Vento	Y	Y	N	Y
5 Sabo	Y	Y	Y	Y
6 Sikorski	N	Y	Y	Y
7 ***Stangeland***	N	Y	N	N
8 Oberstar	N	Y	Y	Y
MISSISSIPPI				
1 Whitten	N	?	N	Y
2 Espy	Y	Y	N	Y
3 Montgomery	N	N	Y	Y
4 Parker	N	N	Y	Y
5 Taylor	N	N	N	Y
MISSOURI				
1 Clay	Y	Y	N	Y
2 ***Buechner***	N	N	Y	N
3 Gephardt	?	Y	Y	Y
4 Skelton	N	N	Y	Y
5 Wheat	Y	Y	N	Y
6 ***Coleman***	N	N	Y	Y
7 ***Hancock***	N	N	N	N
8 ***Emerson***	N	N	N	Y
9 Volkmer	N	N	N	Y
MONTANA				
1 Williams	Y	Y	N	Y
2 ***Marlenee***	N	N	N	N
NEBRASKA				
1 ***Bereuter***	N	N	N	N
2 Hoagland	Y	N	N	Y
3 ***Smith***	N	N	Y	N
NEVADA				
1 Bilbray	N	Y	Y	Y
2 ***Vucanovich***	N	?	Y	Y
NEW HAMPSHIRE				
1 ***Smith***	N	N	N	Y
2 ***Douglas***	N	N	N	Y
NEW JERSEY				
1 Vacancy [2]				
2 Hughes	Y	Y	Y	N
3 Pallone	Y	N	Y	Y
4 ***Smith***	N	Y	N	Y
5 ***Roukema***	Y	N	N	Y
6 Dwyer	Y	Y	N	Y
7 ***Rinaldo***	N	Y	N	Y
8 Roe	N	Y	N	Y
9 Torricelli	?	Y	N	Y
10 Payne	Y	Y	N	Y
11 ***Gallo***	Y	N	Y	N
12 ***Courter***	Y	Y	Y	N
13 ***Saxton***	N	N	N	N
14 Guarini	Y	Y	N	Y
NEW MEXICO				
1 ***Schiff***	Y	Y	Y	Y
2 ***Skeen***	N	Y	Y	Y
3 Richardson	?	Y	Y	Y
NEW YORK				
1 Hochbrueckner	N	Y	N	Y
2 Downey	Y	Y	N	N
3 Mrazek	Y	Y	N	Y
4 ***Lent***	N	Y	Y	N
5 ***McGrath***	N	Y	N	Y
6 Flake	Y	Y	N	Y
7 Ackerman	Y	Y	Y	Y
8 Scheuer	Y	Y	Y	Y
9 Manton	N	Y	Y	Y
10 Schumer	Y	Y	N	N
11 Towns	Y	Y	N	Y
12 Owens	Y	Y	N	#
13 Solarz	Y	Y	Y	N
14 ***Molinari***	Y	Y	Y	N
15 ***Green***	Y	Y	Y	N
16 Rangel	Y	Y	N	Y
17 Weiss	Y	Y	N	Y
18 Serrano	Y	Y	Y	Y
19 Engel	Y	+	N	Y
20 Lowey	Y	Y	N	Y
21 ***Fish***	N	Y	Y	Y
22 ***Gilman***	Y	Y	N	Y
23 McNulty	N	Y	Y	Y
24 ***Solomon***	N	N	N	Y
25 ***Boehlert***	Y	Y	Y	Y
26 ***Martin***	N	N	Y	Y
27 ***Walsh***	N	Y	N	N
28 McHugh	Y	Y	Y	N
29 ***Horton***	Y	Y	Y	Y
30 Slaughter	Y	Y	N	Y
31 ***Paxon***	N	N	N	N
32 LaFalce	N	Y	Y	N
33 Nowak	N	Y	N	Y
34 ***Houghton***	Y	N	Y	Y
NORTH CAROLINA				
1 Jones	Y	Y	N	Y
2 Valentine	Y	N	Y	Y
3 Lancaster	Y	N	Y	Y
4 Price	Y	Y	Y	Y
5 Neal	Y	N	N	Y
6 ***Coble***	N	N	N	Y
7 Rose	Y	Y	Y	Y
8 Hefner	Y	N	N	Y
9 ***McMillan***	N	N	Y	Y
10 ***Ballenger***	N	N	N	Y
11 Clarke	Y	Y	N	Y
NORTH DAKOTA				
AL Dorgan	N	Y	N	N
OHIO				
1 Luken	N	Y	Y	Y
2 ***Gradison***	N	Y	Y	N
3 Hall	N	Y	Y	Y
4 ***Oxley***	N	N	Y	N
5 ***Gillmor***	N	N	Y	N
6 ***McEwen***	N	N	N	N
7 ***DeWine***	N	Y	Y	N
8 ***Lukens***	N	N	Y	Y
9 Kaptur	N	Y	Y	Y
10 ***Miller***	N	N	Y	Y
11 Eckart	Y	Y	N	Y
12 ***Kasich***	N	N	N	N
13 Pease	Y	Y	Y	N
14 Sawyer	Y	Y	Y	N
15 ***Wylie***	N	N	Y	N
16 ***Regula***	N	N	N	Y
17 Traficant	Y	N	N	Y
18 Applegate	N	N	N	Y
19 Feighan	?	Y	N	Y
20 Oakar	N	Y	N	Y
21 Stokes	Y	Y	N	Y
OKLAHOMA				
1 ***Inhofe***	N	N	N	N
2 Synar	Y	Y	N	N
3 Watkins	?	N	Y	Y
4 McCurdy	Y	N	Y	N
5 ***Edwards***	N	N	N	N
6 English	N	N	N	N
OREGON				
1 AuCoin	?	Y	Y	N
2 ***Smith, B.***	N	N	N	N
3 Wyden	Y	Y	N	N
4 DeFazio	Y	Y	N	N
5 ***Smith, D.***	N	N	N	Y
PENNSYLVANIA				
1 Foglietta	N	Y	Y	Y
2 Gray	Y	Y	Y	Y
3 Borski	N	Y	N	Y
4 Kolter	N	Y	N	Y
5 ***Schulze***	N	N	N	Y
6 Yatron	N	Y	N	Y
7 ***Weldon***	N	+	N	Y
8 Kostmayer	Y	Y	Y	Y
9 ***Shuster***	N	N	N	Y
10 ***McDade***	?	Y	Y	Y
11 Kanjorski	N	Y	N	Y
12 Murtha	N	Y	Y	Y
13 ***Coughlin***	Y	N	Y	N
14 Coyne	Y	Y	N	Y
15 ***Ritter***	N	N	N	Y
16 ***Walker***	N	N	N	N
17 ***Gekas***	N	N	Y	Y
18 Walgren	Y	Y	N	Y
19 ***Goodling***	N	N	Y	Y
20 Gaydos	N	Y	N	Y
21 ***Ridge***	Y	N	Y	Y
22 Murphy	N	Y	N	Y
23 ***Clinger***	N	N	Y	Y
RHODE ISLAND				
1 ***Machtley***	Y	Y	N	Y
2 ***Schneider***	Y	Y	N	Y
SOUTH CAROLINA				
1 ***Ravenel***	N	N	N	Y
2 ***Spence***	N	N	N	Y
3 Derrick	Y	N	Y	Y
4 Patterson	Y	N	N	Y
5 Spratt	Y	N	Y	Y
6 Tallon	N	N	Y	Y
SOUTH DAKOTA				
AL Johnson	Y	Y	N	Y
TENNESSEE				
1 ***Quillen***	N	N	Y	Y
2 ***Duncan***	N	N	N	Y
3 Lloyd	N	N	Y	Y
4 Cooper	Y	N	Y	Y
5 Clement	Y	N	Y	Y
6 Gordon	Y	N	Y	Y
7 ***Sundquist***	N	N	Y	N
8 Tanner	Y	N	Y	Y
9 Ford	Y	Y	N	Y
TEXAS				
1 Chapman	Y	N	Y	Y
2 Wilson	Y	Y	Y	Y
3 ***Bartlett***	N	N	Y	N
4 Hall	N	N	Y	Y
5 Bryant	Y	N	N	Y
6 ***Barton***	N	N	N	N
7 ***Archer***	N	N	Y	N
8 ***Fields***	N	N	N	N
9 Brooks	Y	Y	N	Y
10 Pickle	Y	Y	Y	N
11 Leath	?	N	Y	Y
12 Geren	Y	N	N	N
13 Sarpalius	N	N	N	Y
14 Laughlin	N	N	N	Y
15 de la Garza	N	Y	Y	Y
16 Coleman	Y	Y	Y	Y
17 Stenholm	N	N	Y	Y
18 Washington	Y	Y	N	Y
19 ***Combest***	N	N	Y	Y
20 Gonzalez	Y	Y	N	Y
21 ***Smith***	N	N	N	Y
22 ***DeLay***	N	N	N	N
23 Bustamante	?	Y	Y	Y
24 Frost	Y	Y	Y	Y
25 Andrews	Y	N	Y	Y
26 ***Armey***	N	N	N	N
27 Ortiz	N	Y	Y	Y
UTAH				
1 ***Hansen***	N	N	Y	N
2 Owens	Y	Y	Y	N
3 ***Nielson***	N	N	N	N
VERMONT				
AL ***Smith***	Y	Y	Y	Y
VIRGINIA				
1 ***Bateman***	N	N	Y	N
2 Pickett	Y	Y	N	Y
3 ***Bliley***	N	N	N	Y
4 Sisisky	Y	N	Y	Y
5 Payne	Y	N	Y	Y
6 Olin	Y	N	Y	Y
7 ***Slaughter***	N	N	N	Y
8 ***Parris***	N	N	N	Y
9 Boucher	Y	Y	N	Y
10 ***Wolf***	N	N	Y	N
WASHINGTON				
1 ***Miller***	Y	Y	Y	N
2 Swift	Y	Y	Y	N
3 Unsoeld	+	Y	N	N
4 ***Morrison***	Y	Y	Y	N
5 Foley			Y	
6 Dicks	Y	Y	Y	N
7 McDermott	Y	Y	Y	N
8 ***Chandler***	Y	N	Y	N
WEST VIRGINIA				
1 Mollohan	N	Y	Y	Y
2 Staggers	N	Y	N	Y
3 Wise	Y	Y	N	Y
4 Rahall	N	Y	N	Y
WISCONSIN				
1 Aspin	Y	Y	Y	Y
2 Kastenmeier	Y	Y	N	Y
3 ***Gunderson***	N	Y	N	Y
4 Kleczka	N	Y	N	N
5 Moody	Y	Y	N	Y
6 ***Petri***	N	N	N	N
7 Obey	Y	Y	N	Y
8 ***Roth***	N	N	N	Y
9 ***Sensenbrenner***	N	N	N	N
WYOMING				
AL ***Thomas***	N	N	N	N

13. HR 4825. Fiscal 1991-95 NEA Authorization/NEA Funding Standards. Williams, D-Mont., substitute amendment to require the chairman of the National Endowment for the Arts (NEA) in funding projects to take into account not only artistic excellence and merit but general standards of decency and respect for the diverse beliefs and values of Americans. The amendment also gives states a larger share of NEA funds and leaves the courts to decide what constitutes obscenity; requires artists convicted of obscenity to repay their grants; and makes changes in the grant application process. Adopted 382-42: R 142-31; D 240-11 (ND 160-11, SD 80-0), Oct. 11, 1990.

14. HR 5835. Fiscal 1991 Omnibus Reconciliation Act/ Democratic Alternative. Rostenkowski, D-Ill., en bloc amendment to provide smaller increases in the Medicare premium and deductible; delete revenue provisions, including the gas tax, the petroleum fuels tax, the extension of the Medicare tax to additional state and local employees, and the limit on itemized deductions; eliminate the "bubble" and lift the top marginal tax rate to 33 percent; create a 10 percent surtax on income above $1 million; increase the minimum tax rate; delay indexing for one year; provide a limited tax break for capital gains; and for other purposes. Adopted 238-192: R 10-164; D 228-28 (ND 157-16, SD 71-12), Oct. 16, 1990. A "nay" was a vote supporting the president's position.

15. S 2104. Civil Rights Act of 1990/Conference Report. Adoption of the conference report on the bill to reverse or modify six recent Supreme Court decisions that narrowed the reach and remedies of job-discrimination laws and to authorize monetary damages under Title VII of the 1964 Civil Rights Act. Adopted 273-154: R 34-139; D 239-15 (ND 169-3, SD 70-12), Oct. 17, 1990. A "nay" was a vote supporting the president's position.

16. HR 5422. Fiscal 1991 Intelligence Appropriations/Aid to UNITA. Separate vote at the request of Hyde, R-Ill., on the Solarz, D-N.Y., amendment to suspend military aid to the National Union for the Total Independence of Angola (UNITA) — a rebel group fighting the Angolan government — if the government of Angola agrees to accept a cease-fire and a political settlement for the conflict in Angola; receives no military aid from the Soviet Union; and offers free and fair multi-party elections in which UNITA is free to participate. Adopted 207-206: R 12-156; D 195-50 (ND 158-10, SD 37-40), Oct. 17, 1990. A "nay" was a vote supporting the president's position.

---

[1] *Rep. James J. Florio, D-N.J., resigned Jan. 16, 1990.*

KEY

Y	Voted for (yea).
#	Paired for.
+	Announced for.
N	Voted against (nay).
X	Paired against.
-	Announced against.
P	Voted "present."
C	Voted "present" to avoid possible conflict of interest.
?	Did not vote or otherwise make a position known.

Democrats ***Republicans***
Independent

ND	Northern Democrats
SD	Southern Democrats

Southern states - Ala., Ark., Fla., Ga., Ky., La., Miss., N.C., Okla., S.C., Tenn., Texas, Va.

	13	14	15	16
ALABAMA				
1 ***Callahan***	Y	N	N	N
2 ***Dickinson***	Y	N	N	N
3 Browder	Y	Y	Y	N
4 Bevill	Y	Y	Y	N
5 Flippo	Y	Y	Y	Y
6 Erdreich	Y	Y	Y	N
7 Harris	Y	Y	Y	N
ALASKA				
AL ***Young***	Y	N	N	N
ARIZONA				
1 ***Rhodes***	Y	N	N	N
2 Udall	Y	Y	Y	Y
3 ***Stump***	N	N	N	N
4 ***Kyl***	N	N	N	N
5 ***Kolbe***	Y	N	N	N
ARKANSAS				
1 Alexander	Y	Y	Y	Y
2 ***Robinson***	N	N	N	N
3 ***Hammerschmidt***	Y	N	N	N
4 Anthony	Y	Y	Y	Y
CALIFORNIA				
1 Bosco	Y	N	Y	Y
2 ***Herger***	N	N	N	N
3 Matsui	Y	Y	Y	Y
4 Fazio	Y	Y	Y	Y
5 Pelosi	Y	Y	Y	Y
6 Boxer	N	Y	Y	Y
7 Miller	Y	Y	Y	Y
8 Dellums	N	Y	Y	Y
9 Stark	Y	Y	Y	Y
10 Edwards	Y	Y	Y	Y
11 Lantos	Y	Y	Y	N
12 ***Campbell***	N	N	Y	N
13 Mineta	Y	Y	Y	Y
14 ***Shumway***	N	N	N	N
15 Condit	Y	N	Y	Y
16 Panetta	Y	Y	Y	Y
17 ***Pashayan***	Y	N	N	N
18 Lehman	Y	Y	Y	Y
19 ***Lagomarsino***	Y	N	N	N
20 ***Thomas***	Y	?	N	N
21 ***Gallegly***	Y	N	N	N
22 ***Moorhead***	Y	N	N	N
23 Beilenson	Y	Y	Y	Y
24 Waxman	N	Y	Y	Y
25 Roybal	Y	Y	Y	Y
26 Berman	N	Y	Y	Y
27 Levine	N	Y	Y	Y
28 Dixon	Y	Y	Y	Y
29 Hawkins	Y	Y	Y	?
30 Martinez	Y	Y	Y	Y
31 Dymally	Y	Y	Y	Y
32 Anderson	Y	Y	Y	Y
33 ***Dreier***	N	N	N	N
34 Torres	Y	Y	Y	Y
35 ***Lewis***	Y	N	N	N
36 Brown	Y	Y	Y	Y
37 ***McCandless***	Y	N	N	N
38 ***Dornan***	N	N	N	N
39 ***Dannemeyer***	Y	N	N	N
40 ***Cox***	N	N	N	N
41 ***Lowery***	Y	N	N	N
42 ***Rohrabacher***	N	N	N	N
43 ***Packard***	Y	N	N	N
44 Bates	Y	Y	Y	Y
45 ***Hunter***	N	N	N	N
COLORADO				
1 Schroeder	Y	Y	Y	Y
2 Skaggs	Y	Y	Y	Y
3 Campbell	Y	N	Y	N
4 ***Brown***	Y	N	N	N
5 ***Hefley***	Y	N	N	N
6 ***Schaefer***	Y	N	N	N
CONNECTICUT				
1 Kennelly	Y	Y	Y	Y
2 Gejdenson	Y	Y	Y	Y
3 Morrison	+	Y	+	+
4 ***Shays***	Y	N	Y	Y
5 ***Rowland***	?	?	?	?
6 ***Johnson***	Y	N	Y	N
DELAWARE				
AL Carper	Y	Y	Y	Y
FLORIDA				
1 Hutto	Y	Y	N	N
2 ***Grant***	Y	N	Y	N
3 Bennett	Y	Y	Y	Y
4 ***James***	Y	N	Y	N
5 ***McCollum***	Y	N	N	N
6 ***Stearns***	Y	N	N	N
7 Gibbons	Y	Y	Y	Y
8 ***Young***	Y	N	N	N
9 ***Bilirakis***	Y	N	N	N
10 ***Ireland***	Y	N	N	N
11 Nelson	Y	Y	Y	N
12 ***Lewis***	Y	N	N	N
13 ***Goss***	Y	N	N	N
14 Johnston	Y	Y	Y	Y
15 ***Shaw***	Y	N	N	N
16 Smith	Y	Y	Y	N
17 Lehman	Y	Y	Y	Y
18 ***Ros-Lehtinen***	Y	N	Y	N
19 Fascell	Y	Y	Y	N
GEORGIA				
1 Thomas	Y	Y	Y	N
2 Hatcher	Y	Y	Y	N
3 Ray	Y	Y	Y	N
4 Jones	Y	N	Y	N
5 Lewis	Y	Y	Y	Y
6 ***Gingrich***	Y	N	N	N
7 Darden	Y	Y	N	N
8 Rowland	Y	Y	Y	N
9 Jenkins	Y	Y	N	N
10 Barnard	Y	N	N	N
HAWAII				
1 ***Saiki***	Y	N	Y	N
2 Mink	Y	Y	Y	Y
IDAHO				
1 ***Craig***	N	N	N	N
2 Stallings	Y	N	Y	N
ILLINOIS				
1 Hayes	?	Y	Y	Y
2 Savage	Y	N	Y	Y
3 Russo	Y	Y	N	Y
4 Sangmeister	Y	N	Y	Y
5 Lipinski	Y	Y	N	Y
6 ***Hyde***	Y	N	N	N
7 Collins	Y	Y	Y	Y
8 Rostenkowski	Y	Y	Y	Y
9 Yates	Y	Y	Y	Y
10 ***Porter***	Y	N	N	N
11 Annunzio	Y	N	N	Y
12 ***Crane***	N	N	N	N
13 ***Fawell***	Y	N	N	N
14 ***Hastert***	Y	N	N	N
15 ***Madigan***	Y	N	N	N
16 ***Martin***	Y	N	?	?
17 Evans	Y	Y	Y	Y
18 ***Michel***	Y	N	N	N
19 Bruce	Y	Y	Y	Y
20 Durbin	Y	Y	Y	Y
21 Costello	Y	Y	Y	Y
22 Poshard	Y	Y	Y	Y
INDIANA				
1 Visclosky	Y	Y	Y	Y
2 Sharp	Y	Y	Y	Y
3 ***Hiler***	Y	N	N	N

	13	14	15	16
4 Long	Y	N	Y	Y
5 Jontz	Y	Y	Y	Y
6 **Burton**	Y	N	N	N
7 **Myers**	Y	N	N	N
8 McCloskey	Y	Y	Y	Y
9 Hamilton	Y	Y	Y	Y
10 Jacobs	Y	Y	Y	Y
IOWA				
1 **Leach**	Y	Y	Y	Y
2 **Tauke**	Y	N	N	Y
3 Nagle	Y	Y	Y	Y
4 Smith	Y	Y	Y	Y
5 **Lightfoot**	N	N	N	N
6 **Grandy**	Y	N	N	Y
KANSAS				
1 **Roberts**	Y	N	N	N
2 Slattery	Y	Y	Y	Y
3 **Meyers**	Y	N	Y	N
4 Glickman	Y	Y	Y	Y
5 **Whittaker**	Y	N	N	N
KENTUCKY				
1 Hubbard	Y	N	Y	N
2 Natcher	Y	Y	Y	Y
3 Mazzoli	Y	Y	Y	Y
4 **Bunning**	Y	N	N	N
5 **Rogers**	Y	N	N	N
6 **Hopkins**	Y	N	N	N
7 Perkins	Y	Y	Y	Y
LOUISIANA				
1 **Livingston**	N	N	N	N
2 Boggs	?	Y	Y	Y
3 Tauzin	Y	N	Y	N
4 **McCrery**	Y	N	N	N
5 Huckaby	Y	Y	N	N
6 **Baker**	Y	N	N	N
7 Hayes	Y	N	Y	?
8 **Holloway**	N	N	N	N
MAINE				
1 Brennan	Y	?	?	?
2 **Snowe**	Y	N	Y	N
MARYLAND				
1 Dyson	Y	N	Y	Y
2 **Bentley**	Y	N	N	N
3 Cardin	Y	Y	Y	Y
4 McMillen	Y	Y	Y	Y
5 Hoyer	Y	Y	Y	Y
6 Byron	Y	Y	Y	N
7 Mfume	Y	Y	Y	Y
8 **Morella**	Y	Y	Y	Y
MASSACHUSETTS				
1 **Conte**	Y	Y	Y	N
2 Neal	Y	Y	Y	Y
3 Early	Y	Y	Y	Y
4 Frank	Y	Y	Y	Y
5 Atkins	Y	Y	Y	Y
6 Mavroules	Y	Y	Y	Y
7 Markey	Y	Y	Y	Y
8 Kennedy	Y	Y	Y	Y
9 Moakley	Y	Y	Y	Y
10 Studds	N	Y	Y	Y
11 Donnelly	Y	Y	Y	N
MICHIGAN				
1 Conyers	Y	Y	Y	Y
2 **Pursell**	Y	N	Y	N
3 Wolpe	Y	Y	Y	Y
4 **Upton**	Y	N	N	N
5 **Henry**	Y	N	Y	N
6 Carr	Y	Y	Y	Y
7 Kildee	Y	Y	Y	Y
8 Traxler	Y	Y	Y	Y
9 **Vander Jagt**	N	N	N	N
10 **Schuette**	?	N	?	?
11 **Davis**	Y	Y	Y	N
12 Bonior	Y	Y	Y	Y
13 Crockett	Y	Y	Y	?
14 Hertel	Y	Y	Y	Y
15 Ford	Y	Y	Y	?
16 Dingell	Y	Y	Y	Y
17 Levin	Y	Y	Y	Y
18 **Broomfield**	Y	N	N	N
MINNESOTA				
1 Penny	Y	Y	Y	Y
2 **Weber**	N	N	N	N
3 **Frenzel**	Y	N	N	?
4 Vento	Y	Y	Y	Y

	13	14	15	16
5 Sabo	Y	Y	Y	Y
6 Sikorski	Y	Y	Y	Y
7 **Stangeland**	Y	N	N	N
8 Oberstar	Y	Y	Y	Y
MISSISSIPPI				
1 Whitten	Y	Y	Y	N
2 Espy	Y	Y	Y	Y
3 Montgomery	Y	Y	N	N
4 Parker	Y	Y	N	N
5 Taylor	Y	N	N	N
MISSOURI				
1 Clay	Y	Y	Y	Y
2 **Buechner**	Y	N	N	N
3 Gephardt	Y	Y	Y	Y
4 Skelton	Y	Y	Y	N
5 Wheat	Y	Y	Y	Y
6 **Coleman**	Y	N	N	?
7 **Hancock**	N	N	N	N
8 **Emerson**	Y	N	N	N
9 Volkmer	Y	Y	Y	Y
MONTANA				
1 Williams	Y	Y	Y	?
2 **Marlenee**	Y	N	N	N
NEBRASKA				
1 **Bereuter**	Y	N	N	N
2 Hoagland	Y	Y	Y	Y
3 **Smith**	Y	N	N	N
NEVADA				
1 Bilbray	Y	N	Y	Y
2 **Vucanovich**	N	N	N	N
NEW HAMPSHIRE				
1 **Smith**	N	N	N	N
2 **Douglas**	Y	N	N	N
NEW JERSEY				
1 Vacancy [1]				
2 Hughes	Y	Y	Y	N
3 Pallone	Y	N	Y	Y
4 **Smith**	Y	N	N	N
5 **Roukema**	Y	N	Y	N
6 Dwyer	Y	Y	Y	Y
7 **Rinaldo**	Y	N	Y	N
8 Roe	Y	Y	Y	N
9 Torricelli	Y	Y	Y	Y
10 Payne	Y	Y	Y	Y
11 **Gallo**	Y	N	N	N
12 **Courter**	Y	N	N	?
13 **Saxton**	Y	N	N	N
14 Guarini	Y	Y	Y	Y
NEW MEXICO				
1 **Schiff**	Y	N	Y	N
2 **Skeen**	Y	N	N	N
3 Richardson	Y	Y	Y	Y
NEW YORK				
1 Hochbrueckner	Y	Y	Y	Y
2 Downey	Y	Y	Y	Y
3 Mrazek	N	Y	Y	Y
4 **Lent**	Y	N	N	N
5 **McGrath**	Y	N	N	N
6 Flake	Y	Y	Y	Y
7 Ackerman	N	Y	Y	?
8 Scheuer	Y	Y	Y	Y
9 Manton	Y	Y	Y	Y
10 Schumer	Y	Y	Y	Y
11 Towns	Y	Y	Y	Y
12 Owens	Y	Y	Y	Y
13 Solarz	Y	Y	Y	Y
14 **Molinari**	Y	Y	N	N
15 **Green**	Y	N	Y	Y
16 Rangel	Y	Y	Y	Y
17 Weiss	N	Y	Y	Y
18 Serrano	Y	Y	Y	Y
19 Engel	Y	Y	Y	Y
20 Lowey	Y	Y	Y	Y
21 **Fish**	Y	Y	Y	?
22 **Gilman**	Y	N	Y	Y
23 McNulty	Y	Y	Y	Y
24 **Solomon**	Y	N	N	N
25 **Boehlert**	Y	Y	Y	N
26 **Martin**	Y	N	N	N
27 **Walsh**	Y	N	Y	N
28 McHugh	Y	Y	Y	Y
29 **Horton**	Y	Y	Y	N
30 Slaughter	Y	Y	Y	Y
31 **Paxon**	Y	N	N	N

	13	14	15	16
32 LaFalce	Y	Y	Y	Y
33 Nowak	Y	Y	Y	Y
34 **Houghton**	Y	N	Y	Y
NORTH CAROLINA				
1 Jones	Y	Y	Y	N
2 Valentine	Y	Y	Y	N
3 Lancaster	Y	Y	Y	N
4 Price	Y	Y	Y	Y
5 Neal	Y	Y	Y	?
6 **Coble**	Y	N	N	N
7 Rose	?	Y	?	Y
8 Hefner	Y	Y	Y	Y
9 **McMillan**	Y	N	N	N
10 **Ballenger**	Y	N	N	N
11 Clarke	Y	Y	Y	Y
NORTH DAKOTA				
AL Dorgan	Y	Y	Y	Y
OHIO				
1 Luken	Y	Y	Y	Y
2 **Gradison**	Y	N	N	N
3 Hall	?	Y	Y	Y
4 **Oxley**	Y	N	N	N
5 **Gillmor**	Y	N	N	N
6 **McEwen**	Y	N	N	N
7 **DeWine**	Y	N	Y	N
8 **Lukens** [2]	Y	N	N	N
9 Kaptur	Y	Y	Y	Y
10 **Miller**	Y	N	N	N
11 Eckart	Y	Y	Y	Y
12 **Kasich**	Y	N	N	N
13 Pease	Y	Y	Y	Y
14 Sawyer	Y	Y	Y	Y
15 **Wylie**	?	N	N	N
16 **Regula**	Y	N	Y	N
17 Traficant	Y	N	Y	Y
18 Applegate	Y	N	Y	Y
19 Feighan	Y	Y	Y	Y
20 Oakar	Y	Y	Y	Y
21 Stokes	Y	Y	Y	Y
OKLAHOMA				
1 **Inhofe**	Y	N	N	N
2 Synar	Y	Y	Y	Y
3 Watkins	Y	Y	Y	N
4 McCurdy	Y	Y	Y	N
5 **Edwards**	Y	N	N	N
6 English	Y	Y	Y	N
OREGON				
1 AuCoin	Y	Y	Y	Y
2 **Smith, B.**	N	N	N	N
3 Wyden	Y	Y	Y	Y
4 DeFazio	Y	Y	Y	Y
5 **Smith, D.**	Y	N	N	N
PENNSYLVANIA				
1 Foglietta	Y	Y	Y	Y
2 Gray	Y	Y	Y	Y
3 Borski	Y	Y	Y	Y
4 Kolter	Y	N	Y	Y
5 **Schulze**	Y	N	Y	N
6 Yatron	Y	N	Y	Y
7 **Weldon**	Y	N	N	N
8 Kostmayer	N	Y	Y	Y
9 **Shuster**	Y	N	N	N
10 **McDade**	Y	N	N	N
11 Kanjorski	Y	Y	Y	Y
12 Murtha	Y	Y	Y	N
13 **Coughlin**	Y	N	Y	N
14 Coyne	Y	Y	Y	Y
15 **Ritter**	Y	N	N	N
16 **Walker**	N	N	N	N
17 **Gekas**	Y	N	N	N
18 Walgren	Y	Y	Y	Y
19 **Goodling**	Y	N	N	N
20 Gaydos	Y	N	Y	Y
21 **Ridge**	Y	N	N	N
22 Murphy	Y	Y	N	Y
23 **Clinger**	Y	N	N	N
RHODE ISLAND				
1 **Machtley**	Y	N	Y	Y
2 **Schneider**	Y	N	Y	Y
SOUTH CAROLINA				
1 **Ravenel**	Y	N	N	N
2 **Spence**	Y	N	N	N
3 Derrick	Y	Y	Y	Y
4 Patterson	Y	N	Y	Y
5 Spratt	Y	Y	Y	Y
6 Tallon	Y	Y	Y	N

	13	14	15	16
SOUTH DAKOTA				
AL Johnson	Y	Y	Y	Y
TENNESSEE				
1 **Quillen**	Y	N	N	N
2 **Duncan**	Y	N	N	N
3 Lloyd	Y	Y	Y	N
4 Cooper	Y	Y	Y	N
5 Clement	Y	Y	Y	Y
6 Gordon	Y	Y	Y	Y
7 **Sundquist**	Y	N	N	N
8 Tanner	Y	Y	Y	N
9 Ford	Y	Y	Y	?
TEXAS				
1 Chapman	Y	Y	Y	Y
2 Wilson	?	Y	Y	?
3 **Bartlett**	N	N	N	N
4 Hall	Y	N	N	Y
5 Bryant	Y	Y	Y	Y
6 **Barton**	N	N	Y	N
7 **Archer**	Y	N	N	N
8 **Fields**	Y	N	N	N
9 Brooks	Y	Y	Y	?
10 Pickle	Y	Y	Y	N
11 Leath	Y	N	N	Y
12 Geren	Y	N	Y	N
13 Sarpalius	Y	N	N	N
14 Laughlin	Y	N	Y	N
15 de la Garza	Y	Y	Y	?
16 Coleman	Y	Y	Y	Y
17 Stenholm	Y	Y	N	N
18 Washington	Y	Y	Y	Y
19 **Combest**	N	N	N	N
20 Gonzalez	Y	Y	Y	Y
21 **Smith**	Y	N	N	N
22 **DeLay**	N	N	N	N
23 Bustamante	Y	Y	Y	Y
24 Frost	Y	Y	Y	Y
25 Andrews	Y	Y	Y	Y
26 **Armey**	N	N	N	N
27 Ortiz	Y	Y	Y	Y
UTAH				
1 **Hansen**	N	N	N	N
2 Owens	Y	Y	Y	Y
3 **Nielson**	Y	N	N	N
VERMONT				
AL **Smith**	Y	Y	Y	?
VIRGINIA				
1 **Bateman**	Y	N	N	N
2 Pickett	Y	Y	Y	Y
3 **Bliley**	Y	N	Y	N
4 Sisisky	Y	Y	Y	N
5 Payne	Y	Y	Y	Y
6 Olin	Y	Y	Y	N
7 **Slaughter**	Y	N	N	N
8 **Parris**	Y	N	N	N
9 Boucher	Y	Y	Y	Y
10 **Wolf**	Y	N	N	N
WASHINGTON				
1 **Miller**	Y	N	N	Y
2 Swift	Y	Y	Y	Y
3 Unsoeld	Y	Y	Y	Y
4 **Morrison**	Y	N	N	Y
5 Foley				Y
6 Dicks	Y	Y	Y	Y
7 McDermott	N	Y	Y	Y
8 **Chandler**	Y	N	N	N
WEST VIRGINIA				
1 Mollohan	Y	Y	Y	N
2 Staggers	Y	Y	Y	Y
3 Wise	Y	Y	Y	Y
4 Rahall	Y	Y	Y	Y
WISCONSIN				
1 Aspin	Y	Y	Y	Y
2 Kastenmeier	Y	Y	Y	Y
3 **Gunderson**	Y	N	N	N
4 Kleczka	Y	Y	Y	Y
5 Moody	Y	Y	Y	Y
6 **Petri**	N	N	N	N
7 Obey	Y	Y	Y	Y
8 **Roth**	Y	N	N	N
9 **Sensenbrenner**	N	N	N	N
WYOMING				
AL **Thomas**	Y	N	N	N

1991 Key Votes

Senate

1. Persian Gulf War

It was one of the rare instances when the mood of the Senate was as grave as the momentous matter being considered.

One by one, senators rose from their chairs to vote on S J Res 2, authorizing the president to use "all necessary means" to reverse Iraq's occupation of Kuwait. When the "yeas" and "nays" were called on Saturday afternoon Jan. 12, the resolution was approved 52-47: R 42-2; D 10-45 (ND 3-35, SD 7-10).

President Bush, after refusing for months to acknowledge that Congress had a formal role in the ultimate decision of whether to go to war, on Jan. 8 finally requested a congressional resolution authorizing force.

It marked the first such request by a president since the 1964 Gulf of Tonkin resolution, which had authorized U.S. military action during the Vietnam War.

But the administration was forced to scramble for votes even after the president made his request. An early projection by Minority Leader Bob Dole, R-Kan., that the resolution would receive 60 votes proved optimistic. By Jan. 10, Sen. Charles S. Robb, Va., a Democratic supporter of the measure, said the resolution stood only a "50-50 chance" of passing the Senate.

The issue was so much in doubt that the administration's allies delayed the introduction of the war resolution until Jan. 11 — the second day of the Senate debate on the issue.

The opposition was led by Senate Majority Leader George J. Mitchell, D-Maine. In opening the debate on the measure, Mitchell had pleaded with his colleagues to allow economic sanctions — imposed on Iraq after its invasion of Kuwait — more time to work.

Mitchell noted that hundreds of thousands of Americans were then preparing for battle in the gulf. "And the truly haunting question," he said, "which no one will ever be able to answer, will be: Did they die unnecessarily? For if we go to war now, no one will ever know if sanctions would have worked if given a full and fair chance."

Proponents of continued reliance on sanctions received important backing from Sam Nunn, D-Ga., the conservative chairman of the Armed Services Committee. Nunn's panel had held a series of hearings on the gulf that had featured the testimony of former generals and admirals, most of whom cautioned against a precipitous rush to war.

But in the end, a slim majority of senators agreed that the authorization of war represented, in the words of the president, "the last best chance for peace." Joseph I. Lieberman of Connecticut, who emerged as the leading Senate Democrat in support of the president's position, quoted the Greek historian Herodotus: "To have peace, you must prepare for war."

After the vote and the war's successful conclusion, Mitchell and other Democratic opponents of the resolution tried to minimize their differences with the administration. They emphasized that they would have been willing to ultimately support the use of force, provided that economic sanctions had been given more of a chance first.

But Sen. Phil Gramm, Texas, the combative chairman of the National Republican Senatorial Committee, predicted that voters would recall Democratic opposition to the war in 1992. "They are going to pay for that vote," Gramm said. *(House key vote 1)*

2. Highway Funding

To Trent Lott, R-Miss., the amendment was simple: Keep the federal government's share for Interstate maintenance and bridge projects at 90 percent and 80 percent, respectively. That way, states would continue to have funds and incentives to repair those roads.

But to New York Democrat Daniel Patrick Moynihan, principal author of the then-$124 billion surface transportation authorization (S 1204), the Lott amendment meant a relapse of a "public sector disease" — an ailment that caused public funds to be wasted when awarded with too few strings attached.

Despite intense lobbying pressure from state highway officials, the Senate on June 19 narrowly agreed, 53-44, to a Moynihan motion to table the Lott amendment: R 20-23; D 33-21 (ND 30-9, SD 3-12).

The vote on the amendment marked the end of the Interstate highway era, which was launched in 1956 based on a federal promise to pay 90 percent of all road-building costs. By rejecting it, senators showed they were prepared to abandon a 35-year-old policy of channeling highway funds to states at little or no cost. It also set the stage for Congress to clear for the president the sweeping final highway and transit bill on Nov. 26.

Along with lower federal shares, the legislation would force states and urban areas to compete for funds by tying the money to metropolitan planning requirements, giving urban areas more power and giving states flexibility to spend money on roads or transit.

Competition and productivity were central tenets of Moynihan's bill. He viewed his measure as his only chance to make good on a 31-year mission to stop states from blindly pouring concrete and ruining urban neighborhoods.

"The demand for 90-10 highway funds is so great that there is almost nothing, however sensible, that local governments would not do to get their share," Moynihan wrote in a 1960 essay.

Under the new bill, the federal government was to pay 80 percent for most road and mass transit projects. The government would shoulder 75 percent of the cost of building roads and bridges that added lanes for single-occupancy vehicles. The Bush administration wanted a 60-percent federal share for most road programs, but Moynihan refused to go that far because of the fiscal constraints facing states.

Lott had argued that current federal shares should be continued because states could not afford to pay more for road and bridge projects. "It is very important that we not shift more of the burden for these Interstate highways back to the states," Lott said.

After the vote, Moynihan said at least 15 senators told him that state transportation officials had urged them to vote for the crippling amendment. "Of course they did.... How can you say no to free money?" Moynihan asked. "Has no one heard anything we've said?"

3. Gun Control

After weeks of negotiations among Senate leaders, a compromise on the Brady bill was offered late June 28 and won a decisive 67-32 vote. It was the first time the Senate had approved a provision for a waiting period for handgun purchases, and adoption of it into an omnibus crime bill (S 1241) came amid constituent fears of escalating street violence.

Phil Gramm, R-Texas, one of the strongest opponents of the provision, said at the time, "Our bleeding nation cries out for us to do something about crime." The provision required a five-business-day waiting period for handgun purchases and a plan for an immediate national background check of buyers that would take effect in two-and-a-half years. It superseded a House-passed measure (HR 7) for a seven-day wait with no timetable for an instantaneous check.

The proposal was named for former presidential press secretary James S. Brady, who was wounded in a 1981 assassination attempt on Ronald Reagan. Like many other elements of the Senate crime bill, it was folded into a conference committee crime bill (HR 3371) in November. That legislation stalled at the end of the first session of the 102nd Congress because of partisan differences largely unrelated to gun control.

Senate adoption of the gun control measure came after opponents of the waiting period backed away from filibuster threats. Recognition that they could not gather the votes to defeat the bill came early June 28, when senators defeated, 44-54, an attempt to strip the Brady provision from the crime bill.

In addition to local crime concerns, the insertion of a timetable for an instantaneous check appeared to be a key factor in winning strong support for the compromise measure. Although the 67-32 vote was bipartisan, it was mostly Republicans who were fighting the Brady bill: R 19-24; D 48-8 (ND 37-3, SD 11-5).

Existing law made it illegal for felons and people who have been adjudged mentally ill to buy guns. But there was no nationwide system in place to ensure that people who completed firearm purchase forms were not lying. For four years, a handful of lawmakers had been pushing for a waiting period.

They gained momentum in May when the House approved a related bill (HR 7) by a resounding 53 votes. *(House key vote 3)*

That put the spotlight on the Senate, and Majority Leader George J. Mitchell, D-Maine, played a major role in the drive for a Senate version that shortened the waiting period from seven days to five business days and required a police background check.

Having the credibility that comes from representing a big sporting state, Mitchell worked on fellow Democrats to support the Brady bill. At the same time, Brady and his wife, Sarah, kept up their emotional pressure on wavering members.

Senate Minority Leader Bob Dole, R-Kan., helped craft the final compromise to help speed action on the crime bill, as did Howard M. Metzenbaum, D-Ohio, who had proposed the original seven-day waiting period in the Senate.

4. Superconducting Supercollider

For the first time, the Senate went on record in support of the superconducting supercollider — the giant atom smasher under construction in Waxahachie, Texas, and a symbol of government investment in "big science" projects.

Senate supporters July 10 handily rallied to back the project, which could take until the end of the 20th century and cost at least $8 billion to complete. But it was clear that the 1991 battle, sparked by an effort to kill the smasher, would be the first of many such attempts to derail it.

The Senate vote came during debate on the fiscal 1992 energy and water development appropriations bill (PL 102-104). J. Bennett Johnston, D-La., a strong collider supporter, moved to kill on a tabling motion an amendment offered by Dale Bumpers, D-Ark., that would have eliminated $509 million in funding for the atom smasher. Bumpers' attempt failed July 10 when the motion carried, 62-37: R 33-10; D 29-27 (ND 19-21, SD 10-6).

The vote was critical not only because it put the Senate on record for the first time in support of the project but also because it set the stage for what was likely to become an annual debate about the project's cost and scope. The vote also cleared the way to begin construction on the project.

The supercollider was to use powerful magnets to hurl protons — particles of matter smaller than atoms — through a 54-mile underground tunnel. Scientists planned to use powerful computers to analyze the debris in an effort to unlock the secrets of the building blocks of matter.

Bumpers argued that the scientific knowledge likely to be yielded by the project was too uncertain given the nation's tight economic times. In addition, he said, supporters had overstated the potential commercial spinoffs to flow from research on the atom smasher. "It would be nice to know the origin of matter," said Bumpers. "It would also be nice to have a balanced budget."

Johnston, who wielded considerable political clout because of his chairmanship of the Energy and Water Development Appropriations Subcommittee, jumped to the project's defense along with both Texas senators. They argued that the project would provide a crucial step in the nation's search for knowledge and would augment U.S. competitiveness.

Perhaps as important to the success of those who quashed the Bumpers amendment was the promise of lucrative research projects linked to the atom smasher and expected to be spread over 43 states. Supporters asserted that a total of 60,000 jobs nationwide were on the line. The White House also lobbied hard for the project.

Though unsuccessful, the attack on the project's funding signaled an end to an era of uncritical support for big science projects. Opponents several weeks later launched a similar attack on funding for the space station *Freedom.* In the end, the Senate backed the space station by a two-thirds margin, but the vote was the first time the Senate had questioned space station funding.

Although just 37 senators voted against Johnston's motion regarding the supercollider, the group included some prominent Republicans, suggesting that the pro-collider lobbying effort launched by the White House lacked full Republican support. Among Republicans voting against Johnston's motion were Republican Whip Alan K. Simpson of Wyoming and Richard G. Lugar of Indiana. Among Democrats, support for Bumpers' effort to eliminate funding came largely from states in the northern Midwest, Great Plains and East, where the project was not expected to generate contract dollars. *(House key vote 6)*

5. Honoraria Ban

Historians will mark July 17, 1991, as the day the Senate finally outlawed what critics called a legally sanctioned form of bribery: the acceptance by lawmakers of whopping fees for throw-away speeches from favor-seeking interest groups. "There is nothing honorable about honoraria," said Robert C. Byrd, D-W.Va., the Senate patriarch and a converted one-time defender of the system.

Senators had twice previously approved the outright ban on all honoraria, but only on purely symbolic votes void of effect. To make it stick required an incentive, a quid pro quo, in fact — a $23,200 pay raise to compensate members for the forgone honoraria income.

The Senate was the last institution in the federal government that continued to allow officials to accept the speaking fees. For years, ethics purists had been complaining about the practice, which defenders argued had ancient traditions. The critics made some headway in the 1970s, persuading Congress to limit the size of the fees and the total amount that could be pocketed each year. But tales of $2,000 breakfast appearances kept the issue alive for years.

After vacillating on the matter for more than a decade, Congress in 1989 barred every employee but those in the Senate from accepting the fees as of Jan. 1, 1991. The Senate balked because leaders could not persuade a majority to accept a House-passed, 40 percent pay raise. Instead, senators took a much smaller pay raise and voted to phase out honoraria slowly as their government salaries grew with future automatic annual increases.

That decision created the pressure that eventually killed the practice. Senators resented being paid less than House members; as of Jan. 1, their annual salary was $101,900, compared with $125,100 for House members. The vagaries of the rules under which congressional aides were paid provided an additional slap: Some top House staffers were being paid more than senators.

As the annual legislative branch spending bill (HR 2506) began making its way toward the floor, Sen. Christopher J. Dodd, D-Conn., and Patrick J. Leahy, D-Vt., publicly mulled offering the honoraria ban amendment to that must-pass measure. That prompted Byrd to act.

Byrd had laid the groundwork earlier — though he denied a connection — by inserting a provision in the bill to bar Senate staff from accepting honoraria and to allow top aides to earn more than their bosses. The effect was more than symbolic: Senators would be almost totally isolated as virtually the only 100 employees among millions in the federal government still allowed to accept speaking fees.

The former majority leader methodically gathered votes in favor of an honoraria ban/pay raise amendment. He gave members up for re-election in 1992 a pass, and in the end, only seven of those 33 voted for the amendment. To compensate, Byrd pressed the chamber's richest members the hardest, persuading a few to reverse their long-standing opposition to pay raises.

Floor consideration of the spending bill was delayed until Byrd had a majority of both parties ready to vote yea. As dusk approached July 17, he confirmed he had the votes by double-checking each at an invitation-only kaffeeklatsch in his office.

A pending bill was abruptly pulled from the floor at 7 p.m., and the legislative branch spending bill was brought up without notice to the press or the public. Debate was perfunctory on Byrd's amendment.

The amendment passed, 53-45: R 25-18; D 28-27 (ND 22-18, SD 6-9). The House later accepted the provision but not before insisting that the Senate tighten its definition on what constituted honoraria and agreed to loosen congressional gift-acceptance rules.

6. China MFN

Majority Leader George J. Mitchell, D-Maine, won Senate approval for a bill requiring China's communist regime to make deep reforms in order to qualify for a renewal of its low-tariff, most-favored-nation (MFN) trade status in 1992.

But while a majority of senators favored the bill, the July 23 vote fell short of the two-thirds necessary to overcome a promised veto, signaling the failure of Mitchell's effort to retaliate for the Chinese government's brutal attack on pro-democracy protesters in Tiananmen Square two years before.

President Bush had made it clear that he would reject any interference from Congress in his handling of Beijing and its octogenarian communist leaders.

Two weeks earlier, the House had voted by a wide margin to set stiff conditions on an MFN renewal. But there was never any question about the bill's fate in the House, which had shown strong support for conditions in 1990. As a result, the White House largely ignored the House and concentrated its efforts on the Senate. Since there was no chance of the bill being defeated in that chamber, the administration opted from the beginning for a veto strategy — getting enough votes to prevent the president from being overridden and holding on to them at all costs.

Mitchell's bill would have required China to account for and release demonstrators arrested during the Tiananmen Square protests as well as to make progress toward lowering its trade deficit with the United States, improving the treatment of dissidents and religious groups and ending exports of missiles and other weapons. The bill contained a variety of other conditions as well.

Before and during floor consideration, Mitchell accepted numerous modifications in an effort to get enough votes to override a veto. By the end, the bill had become a lengthy laundry list, tying MFN renewal to, among other things, China ending assistance for the Khmer Rouge in Cambodia, providing better protection for U.S. patents, reducing assistance to Cuba and ending forced abortions.

Despite the amendment fest, Mitchell could not overcome two factors: First, Bush, a former U.S. envoy to Beijing, enjoyed a deep well of loyalty among Republicans, who were inclined to give his China policy the benefit of the doubt. Second, farm-state Democrats feared that withdrawing China's MFN status would mean the loss of the lucrative Chinese market, which accounted for more than $500 million in U.S. wheat sales in 1990.

Imitating a strategy that had been successful during the fight over U.S.-Mexico free trade negotiations, the White House pledged to take a series of steps to bring pressure on China — and thus lessen the pressure on Congress to act.

It worked better than the White House might have expected.

After the Senate acted in July, the bill languished until November, when a House-Senate conference was convened to negotiate a final version of the bill.

Only the House voted on the conference report. With no hope of overriding a veto, the Senate did not act on the bill.

In the July vote, a bloc of six conservative Republicans joined 49 Democrats in voting for Mitchell's bill. The vote was 55-44: R 6-37; D 49-7 (ND 36-4, SD 13-3).

7. Women in Combat

Inspired by the prominent role women played in the armed services during the Persian Gulf War, critics of the law that barred assignment of women to certain combat roles began to chip away at that barrier. The law prohibited the assignment of women to Navy warships or to combat aircraft in the Navy, Marine Corps or Air Force. No law prohibited the assignment of Army women to combat jobs, but such assignments were ruled out as a matter of policy.

Female officers long had argued that their career prospects were limited by their inability to serve in combat units that were at the core of their services' missions. Their cause gained clout from the generally glowing reviews of the job performance of women deployed to the gulf region — including women who flew airplanes and helicopters behind enemy lines on ostensibly non-combat missions.

By highlighting the threat posed by ballistic missiles and chemical weapons to warriors far behind the traditional "front lines," the gulf war also called into question the assumption that women assigned to traditionally noncombatant military jobs would be safe.

When the House Armed Services Committee marked up the fiscal 1992 defense authorization bill in May, critics of the combat exclusion law proposed a repeal of the ban on assigning women to combat aircraft. Since all military aviators were volunteers, proposing the change for that group finessed the argument that dropping the law might have forced women into combat against their will.

The committee accepted the provision, and no effort was made on the House floor to delete it before the authorization bill was passed.

But a majority of the Senate Armed Services Committee, led by John Glenn, D-Ohio, and John McCain, R-Ariz., opposed immediate repeal of the combat exclusion law for pilots. As an alternative, the panel included in its version of the authorization bill a provision establishing a blue-ribbon presidential commission to study issues that would be raised by assigning women to combat roles.

When the Senate took up the bill, Glenn and McCain sweetened their alternative by offering an amendment allowing the Pentagon to waive the combat exclusion laws on a trial basis so women would be assigned to any kind of combat unit to provide data for the commission's study. But after accepting that amendment 96-3, the Senate on July 31 also adopted an amendment by Edward M. Kennedy, D-Mass., and William V. Roth Jr., R-Del., waiving the combat exclusion law for women on aircrews in the Navy, Marine Corps and Air Force. A motion to table (kill) the Kennedy-Roth amendment was rejected 30-69: R 14-29; D 16-40 (ND 6-34, SD 10-6).

Although President Bush signed into law the defense authorization measure (HR 2100 — PL 102-190), a Pentagon spokesman said the Defense Department was not likely to make any move to revise its policies banning women from combat until the commission created by the bill completed its work late in 1992.

8. Strategic Defense Initiative

Even before President Reagan launched the strategic defense initiative (SDI) in 1983, Sen. Malcolm Wallop, R-Wyo., and other proponents contended that missile defense would be a winning political issue if it ever got onto the national agenda.

The congressional debate on SDI did not get under way in earnest until 1986. Despite critics who ridiculed the idea as a costly and dangerous "Star Wars" fantasy, Wallop's judgment appeared vindicated by Congress' repeated votes to fund the program. Although Congress annually sliced by one-third or more the amounts requested by Reagan and Bush for anti-missile research, lawmakers repeatedly rejected proposals to make more far-reaching cuts that would have restricted SDI to laboratory-based research.

Reagan presented SDI as a revolutionary improvement in national security that would supplant the balance of nuclear terror as the central influence in the U.S.-Soviet military rivalry. SDI officials and conservative missile defense advocates such as Wallop envisioned a network of space-based weapons intended to intercept Soviet missiles in the first few minutes of flight, before they dispensed multiple warheads and swarms of decoys.

But that approach alienated a cadre of key Democrats, including Senate Armed Services Committee Chairman Sam Nunn, Ga., and his House counterpart, Les Aspin, Wis. These centrist critics deemed Reagan's vision of SDI technically infeasible. Moreover, they warned that a U.S. effort to defend against all-out Soviet attack would foster a more vigorous Soviet effort to develop new strategic weapons intended to circumvent SDI.

As an alternative, Nunn and Aspin promoted a more modest anti-missile program: Designed to avoid the appearance of threatening Moscow's retaliatory capacity, this defense would be intended to protect U.S. territory, overseas forces and allies against "limited" attacks, which might be launched by a Third World country or by a renegade military unit. In 1991, the war with Iraq underscored the potential threat of radical Third World regimes armed with ballistic missiles and nuclear or chemical warheads. And the political disintegration of the Soviet Union highlighted the possibility that Moscow's tight rein on its nuclear weapons might slacken.

President Bush's fiscal 1992 budget request recast SDI toward that kind of mission. But he retained the controversial space-based weapons as a key part of the program.

In shaping the annual defense authorization bill (HR 2100 — PL 102-190), Senate Armed Services Republicans led by John W. Warner, Va., hammered out a compromise SDI package with conservative and centrist Democrats: The new approach put aside plans to deploy space-based weapons while providing funds to continue research on them. It directed the president to deploy by 1996 a ground-based anti-missile system at a single site that would comply with the 1972 treaty limiting anti-ballistic missiles (ABMs). And it called on the president to negotiate with the Soviet Union changes in the ABM Treaty that would allow more extensive ABM testing and deployment.

The compromise provision contained a strong implication that the United States should abrogate the ABM Treaty if the Soviet Union did not agree to amend the pact. On the Senate floor, Jeff Bingaman, D-N.M., offered an amendment intended to dilute that threat by declaring that the maintenance of strategic stability between the U.S. and Soviet arsenals was the overriding goal and by deleting references to the deployment of ground-based weapons at a single site as an "initial" deployment. But Bingaman's amendment was rejected July 31 by a vote of 43-56: R 2-41; D 41-15 (ND 33-7, SD 8-8). *(House key vote 4)*

9. Domestic Spending

When Congress returned from its August recess, the world had been transformed. Plotters in the Soviet Union had tried to mount a coup and failed; the collapse of the Soviet empire appeared assured. The Soviet military threat that the United States had been girding to fight for 50 years had evaporated, and if ever there were a time to cut back on defense spending, this seemed to be it.

It certainly looked that way to Sen. Tom Harkin, D-Iowa, who had started before the recess to push an amendment to the fiscal 1992 Labor-HHS appropriations bill taking $3.15 billion out of defense to beef up spending for 10 domestic programs that he insisted had been underfunded.

As chairman of the Senate Labor-HHS Appropriations Subcommittee, Harkin said an inadequate allocation at the beginning of the year had forced him to give short shrift to such line items as the National Cancer Institute, child immunization programs, Pell student aid grants and Head Start, the widely acclaimed program for low-income preschool children.

Now was the time to right that wrong, Harkin argued. He proposed to rescind sufficient 1992 defense outlays and prior-year unobligated defense balances to pay for the domestic spending increases. "Do we start investing in solutions to our nation's critical problems?" Harkin asked. "Or, in the aftermath of the events of the past month, do we continue to pour billions of dollars into the subsidy of Europe's defense against a now-nonexistent Soviet Union?"

Harkin had a problem, however. Under the terms of the 1990 budget summit agreement, any reduction in defense spending could be used only for deficit reduction — it could not be used to increase spending for domestic programs, as he was proposing. So, before he could get a straight, up-or-down vote on his amendment, he first had to convince three-fifths of the Senate — 60 senators — to agree to waive the Budget Act.

That brought defenders of the budget agreement to the floor, warning that while they might agree with Harkin's desire to increase spending for important programs, it would be far too dangerous to break the budget deal.

"I have a great deal of sympathy" for the amendment, said Budget Committee Chairman Jim Sasser, D-Tenn. But "if we can breach the budget summit agreement for this particular appropriations bill, then clearly we can breach it for a whole host of appropriations bills to follow. [That] is a short-term ticket for fiscal chaos in this body."

Harkin received an even more direct rebuke from Appropriations Committee Chairman Robert C. Byrd, D-W.Va., who spent the better part of an hour warning that the amendment could put all domestic appropriations spending at risk of an across-the-board spending cut. "The amendment would destroy the budget agreement," Byrd said. "I ask all senators not to go down this road of chaos."

In the end, the politically attractive trade-off in Harkin's package could not overcome the Senate's reluctance to break the budget deal they had agreed to less than two years before. The motion was rejected, 28-69: R 3-39; D 25-30 (ND 24-14, SD 1-16), Sept. 10.

The budget agreement's defenders had mounted a major effort to convincingly defeat Harkin so that others with similar ideas would think twice. This turned out to be the clearest test of the strength of the budget deal, which remained intact through the end of 1991.

10. Unemployment Benefits

Throughout the long debate over providing extra weeks of unemployment benefits to the long-term jobless, the Senate took a more conservative approach than the House. Congress first passed an unemployment bill in August but was blocked by President Bush. During Congress' second attempt to enact a bill, the House wanted to require Bush to pay for the measure through deficit spending. Simply signing the bill would have been the equivalent of declaring a budget emergency, and the money would have flowed to the long-term unemployed.

The Senate, on the other hand, said Bush should decide whether there was an emergency and whether the money should be spent. Senators voted 69-30 on Sept. 24 in favor of that approach.

But Congress had already tried that in August. Bush had refused to declare an emergency, and most unemployed workers were receiving no more than 26 weeks of state benefits. Few federal benefits were finding their way into the hands of the unemployed through the standard extended benefits program.

In a House-Senate conference, House Democrats insisted on forcing Bush to sign or veto the measure without any wiggle room. That way, at least, Congress would have a chance to override a veto. The conference report was sent back to the Senate, where many Republicans were angry with the change from the bill they had just passed. Congress' ability to override an expected veto rested with 13 Republican senators who had initially supported the measure. If just four Republicans changed their votes, the Senate would not have the 67 votes needed to override, and Bush's veto would prevail.

The $6.4 billion bill that came back from conference would have given an additional seven weeks of unemployment benefits to workers in 30 states and the District of Columbia, an additional 13 weeks to workers in 14 states and an additional 20 weeks to workers in six states where unemployment exceeded 8 percent.

The vote was a test of loyalty to the president, but the White House was confident of GOP senators' support and barely lifted a finger to lobby them. Rather, the Senate minority leader, Bob Dole of Kansas, worked the issue extensively. Ultimately, the House language on emergency spending was the reason that five Republicans who had voted for the earlier Democratic bill changed their votes on the conference report. They were: John C. Danforth and Christopher S. Bond of Missouri; John Seymour of California; Conrad Burns of Montana; and David Durenberger of Minnesota. The conference report was adopted 65-35 on Oct. 1, two votes short of the number needed to override a veto: R 8-35; D 57-0 (ND 40-0, SD 17-0).

It was a key vote because it finally convinced Senate Democrats that it was time to negotiate with the administration — particularly over finding a way to pay for the measure.

By Nov. 15, Congress sent Bush a $5.4 billion bill to extend unemployment benefits for nearly 3 million people. Bush signed the bill the same day he received it. *(House key vote 11)*

11. Family and Medical Leave

It was the second go-round for legislation to require businesses to allow their workers to take unpaid leave for the birth or adoption of a child or for their own serious illness or that of an immediate family member. Democrats had promoted the issue as their own kinder, gentler vision for the country's middle class. But businesses had responded with stiff opposition to being told what to do.

The legislation had already failed to be enacted in 1990; senators had never gone on record voting for or against the measure; and House and Senate leaders knew they did not have the votes in 1991 to override a promised veto. Enter Christopher S. Bond, R-Mo., and bill sponsor Christopher J. Dodd, D-Conn. The pair forged a slightly modified compromise to attract the votes needed for a two-thirds majority — 67 votes.

The Bond-Dodd compromise raised the number of hours an employee had to work from 1,000 hours to 1,250 hours per year in order to qualify for the unpaid leave. It also allowed employers to deny leave to "key employees," defined as those who were the highest paid 10 percent of the company's work force. That provision was included in the House bill (HR 2) but not in the Senate version.

The bill itself would mandate that businesses with more than 50 workers give workers up to 12 weeks of unpaid leave for the birth or adoption of a child or for the serious illness of the worker or an immediate family member.

The compromise came before the Senate Oct. 2 amid intensive lobbying — by women's groups and unions for the measure and by business organizations against it. In 1990, the Senate approved a family and medical leave bill by voice vote. When Bush vetoed the bill, the House sustained him, and senators were never subject to a recorded vote. In 1991, members voted 65-32 for the compromise language: R 15-28; D 50-4 (ND 38-0, SD 12-4). It was two short of the 67 needed for the two-thirds majority that could override a veto. But both supporters and opponents assumed that all three absent Democrats — David Pryor, Ark., and presidential candidates Tom Harkin, Iowa, and Bob Kerrey, Neb. — would have voted for the substitute.

Despite the big vote, senators were not sanguine that they could force the bill into law over Bush's objections. The House had not been able to attract as much support for the compromise language, and many Republicans who had voted for the measure might have buckled on an override vote. "People understand the loyalty factor" and do not punish those who switch votes to support their party's president, said Orrin G. Hatch, R-Utah. In 1992, the House and Senate were to reconcile their two bills and send them back to their chambers for approval before shipping the final version to the president.

12. Thomas Confirmation

Politics and increasing conflicts between the Court and Congress converged to give Clarence Thomas, President Bush's second high court nominee, the closest Supreme Court confirmation vote in more than a century.

After two sets of divisive hearings before the Senate Judiciary Committee, the full Senate voted on Oct. 15 to confirm Thomas, 52-48: R 41-2; D 11-46 (ND 3-37, SD 8-9).

While Thomas, 43, became only the second black justice on the Court, his confirmation was likely to be remembered more for the upheaval over sexual harassment allegations. Senators were to vote on Thomas' nomination Oct. 8. But two days before that scheduled vote, University of Oklahoma law professor Anita F. Hill went public with allegations that Thomas had sexually harassed her when she worked for him at the Department of Education and Equal Employment Opportunity Commission (EEOC).

The Senate Judiciary Committee reconvened to produce three days of nationally televised hearings that, because of their explicit subject matter and window into Senate discord, became the talk of the country.

Both sides estimated that Thomas lost about 10 votes that he might have had before the Hill allegations emerged — narrowing an outcome that still would have been one of the closest in history. But only three senators publicly shifted positions. Democrats Richard H. Bryan, Nev., Joseph I. Lieberman, Conn., and Harry Reid, Nev., withdrew their support. They said they were influenced by Hill's testimony.

The vote ended up being largely partisan, although 11 Democrats, mostly Southerners, made up the margin of difference needed to seat Thomas, a federal appeals court judge who had worked in the Bush and Ronald Reagan administrations for eight years.

Most opponents said Thomas was too conservative and lacked the qualifications for the high court. They also accused Bush of nominating Thomas more for his color than for his credentials. As a black conservative, Thomas' nomination effectively split the minority community and made it difficult for the liberal groups that traditionally opposed conservative nominees to drum up support.

Sen. John C. Danforth, R-Mo., for whom Thomas had twice worked, was credited with keeping the nomination on track.

In many ways, the Court's conservative tilt raised the stakes on the nomination and led to the storm over Thomas. Before Thomas was nominated to fill the seat of retiring Justice Thurgood Marshall, Bush and Reagan had named a total of six conservative jurists, including the 1986 elevation of William H. Rehnquist to chief justice. A majority on the high court was lining up with the administration in favor of law enforcement over defendants' rights and on many questions involving whether state authority should supersede individual protections, such as on free speech and abortion.

The Democratic majority in Congress was increasingly finding itself on the other side of battles against the administration and the Court, and Senate Democrats said they were not inclined to give another conservative nominee the benefit of the doubt.

13. Civil Rights

The Senate's overwhelming vote on a compromise job-rights bill was not as dramatic as what had come before: a week of sudden and intense negotiations between the White House and senators to produce a compromise on the hard-fought legislation. The bill was approved by the Senate Oct. 30 by a vote of 93-5: R 38-5; D 55-0 (ND 38-0, SD 17-0).

The deal ended a two-year struggle to reinstate protections for victims of job bias that had been narrowed by the Supreme Court. It also closed a chapter of racial politicking in Congress and the White House that earlier in the year had seemed so divisive as to preclude agreement on a bill. President Bush had vetoed a related bill in 1990.

What changed was the political dynamic. The issue of sexual harassment had been elevated on the national agenda by the Clarence Thomas-Anita F. Hill hearings. The Republican White House also was concerned about fallout from the primary success of Louisiana gubernatorial candidate David Duke, a Republican and former Ku Klux Klansman. (Duke eventually lost but declared his candidacy for president.)

The confluence of those October events intensified gender and racial politics and shifted the atmosphere. Sensing that Bush could no longer count enough GOP senators to sustain another veto, the White House cut a deal with Senate proponents the week of Oct. 21.

The final pact involved the liberal Democrats who began the push for the legislation in 1989 (led by Edward M. Kennedy, D-Mass.) and key moderate Republicans who kept negotiations going with the White House while warnings of quota hiring swirled (led by John C. Danforth, R-Mo.). Bush had charged that earlier versions of the bill would have forced businesses to hire set numbers of minorities and women to avoid lawsuits.

Both Democrats and Republicans tried to claim that they had won the better deal. Indeed, each side made concessions. But the bottom line was that overall, most of the original plan to reverse the Court and to give victims of harassment and other intentional discrimination money damages prevailed.

Although workers were likely to be better off under the bill, to what degree was still uncertain because the final agreement left some of the toughest issues to be resolved in the federal courts. The new law, signed by Bush on Nov. 21, countered the effects of nine Supreme Court decisions and made it easier for victims of bias to bring lawsuits to enforce protections already on the books. A key to the compromise was an open-ended provision on how businesses might justify the discriminatory effects of seemingly fair hiring practices, such as tests and academic requirements. Those practices would have to be job-related and necessary to a business' operation. It would be up to the courts to interpret the new standard.

The law also allowed, for the first time, limited money damages for victims of harassment and other intentional discrimination based on sex, religion or disability. Racial minorities already could win money damages under a Reconstruction-era law.

The compromise set caps on damages for intentional bias, ranging from $50,000 for companies with 100 or fewer workers to $300,000 for employers with more than 500 workers.

Democrats in both chambers said that in 1992 they would push legislation to lift such limits. *(House key vote 7)*

14. Energy Policy

The oil concerns of the Persian Gulf War created a legislative push for new energy policy early in 1991. But a massive Senate energy bill was eventually slowed by controversy and, when it finally went to the floor late in the year, lawmakers voted to kill the measure — at least temporarily.

The energy bill (S 1220) was crafted by Louisiana Democrat J. Bennett Johnston, and it sped through the Energy and Natural Resources Committee he chaired. The bill would have touched almost every sector of energy policy. But it became best known for proposing to open Alaska's Arctic National Wildlife Refuge to drilling and for failing to mandate specific increases in federal gas mileage standards. Other provisions would have streamlined the licensing of nuclear power plants, eased federal regulation of the electric industry and mandated certain conservation measures and the use of non-gasoline transportation fuels.

Johnston and other advocates said the bill was politically balanced and would have made a critical move toward reducing U.S. dependence on oil imports. But environmental groups and their congressional allies put the bill at the top of their hit list, saying it would have encouraged environmentally damaging production measures and done little to promote energy efficiency and conservation. Many Democrats in particular were cool to the bill, which they saw as kin to a controversial Bush administration policy unveiled early in 1991.

Johnston fought hard to get the bill to the floor, despite a filibuster led by a group of junior Democrats opposed to the Alaska drilling provision. On Nov. 1, the Senate voted 50-44 to shut off debate, 10 votes short of the 60 needed to invoke cloture: R 32-9; D 18-35 (ND 9-28, SD 9-7).

The vote was a powerful setback in the push to enact new energy legislation. It also represented a stunning defeat for Johnston and the administration, which had endorsed the measure. While acknowledging that the bill included many controversial provisions, Johnston had repeatedly insisted he had enough votes to bring it up for debate. Even opponents had not expected to win by such a large margin.

Environmental groups seized upon the outcome as a mandate for a new approach to energy legislation that would stress efficiency, conservation and environmental protection. Opposition to Alaska drilling did provide the fervor behind the filibuster effort and many of the votes against cloture. Opponents promised to return with a new, more progressive energy bill.

However, the message behind the final tally was considerably more muddled. The filibuster also won support from utilities opposed to the bill's electric industry restructuring and from some auto interests who feared it would become a vehicle for boosting federal fuel-efficiency mandates. Johnston had ignited some turf battles by refusing to refer the bill to several committees that shared jurisdiction on certain energy issues, and nine committee chairmen were among those voting against cloture.

Some of the bill's proponents criticized the vote as proof that Congress, absent an imminent oil crisis, did not have the courage to enact energy policy. However, both

Johnston and some of his critics said they would try to move some energy bill early in 1992.

15. Gates Confirmation

When Robert M. Gates was nominated in May to be director of central intelligence, administration officials bargained that lawmakers would be so weary of investigating the involvement of Gates and others in the Iran-contra affair that he would quickly be confirmed.

They might have been right, had a former CIA official not pleaded guilty on July 9 to unlawfully withholding from Congress information about the agency's role in the 1986 scandal. That plea rekindled a question that had forced Gates to withdraw his name from consideration for the No. 1 job in 1987: As the No. 2 man at the CIA, just how much had he known about the illegal diversion of funds from Iranian arms sales to help the contra rebels in Nicaragua?

The Senate Intelligence Committee delayed Gates' confirmation hearings, initially set to begin July 15, for two months to try to determine what role the CIA had played in the diversion. When the hearings opened, the panel had compiled an exhaustive record revealing numerous inconsistencies between Gates' account of events and the accounts of others.

But it quickly became clear from Gates' testimony and that of other witnesses that it would come down to a question of his word against theirs. The same was true of allegations from former and current subordinates of Gates at the CIA that he had forced agency analysts to slant their reports to bolster administration policy objectives.

In the end, the nominee had a lot going for him. He had solid support from Republicans who vowed to stick with the president's nominee unless convinced otherwise. He also had the strong backing of Chairman David L. Boren, D-Okla., who had worked closely with Gates and had found him extremely candid with Congress.

Gates promised that as the nation's chief intelligence official he would work closely with Congress in its oversight role as he put in place massive changes in the way the intelligence community conducted business in the post-Cold War era. Gates' supporters argued that while he may have made some past errors in judgment, he was the best man for the job because of his intellect, lengthy government service and close ties with President Bush.

Some Democrats, led by New Jersey's Bill Bradley, tried to attack Gates' credibility and questioned how the agency could attain an image of openness and honesty with a leader whose record was tainted. But the arguments fell on deaf ears.

A crucial factor was the timing of the Gates vote, just three weeks after the tumultuous debate over Bush's nomination of Clarence Thomas to the Supreme Court. Few members had any desire to take on another key nomination so soon, especially when there was no clear-cut proof that Gates had behaved illegally or unethically. Gates was confirmed on Nov. 5 by a vote of 64-31: R 42-0; D 22-31 (ND 11-25, SD 11-6).

16. Soviet Aid

In a remarkable reversal, Congress agreed in the last hours of its session to give the president the authority to spend up to $500 million in defense funds to help the transformation of the former Soviet Union.

The action was remarkable because just two weeks earlier the chairmen of the Armed Services committees — Rep. Les Aspin, D-Wis., and Sen. Sam Nunn, D-Ga. — had to withdraw a $1 billion aid proposal because of lawmakers' reluctance to spend money on a former enemy when so many domestic needs were not being met. And President Bush, under attack from Democrats for devoting too much attention to foreign policy, refused to endorse the proposal.

But only days before adjournment, a bipartisan group of senior senators decided to give it one last try. These senators — led by Nunn and Richard G. Lugar, R-Ind. — crafted a scaled-back proposal that targeted the funds toward helping the Soviets and the republics dismantle some of the 27,000 nuclear weapons inside their territories. The group argued that the assistance was not "foreign aid" but a defensive move to reduce the nuclear threat against the United States. The senators cited a Harvard study that detailed the potential disaster that could result if the weapons fell into the wrong hands.

Repeated attempts by the senators to elicit White House support for the plan failed, although sponsors said they had been encouraged privately by administration officials. On the Senate floor, however, the proposal received an unusually warm welcome, a tribute to the high regard in which Nunn, Lugar and other sponsors were held by their colleagues, not to mention to their success in repackaging what had been an unpopular proposal. The proposal was adopted on Nov. 25 by a vote of 86-8: R 34-8; D 52-0 (ND 36-0, SD 16-0).

A subsequent amendment to allow another $200 million in aid to help the Soviets transport food and medical supplies to survive the winter was also approved, 87-7.

With the overwhelming backing of the Senate, the proposal had little trouble in the House. The proposal, modified to provide a total of $500 million for both the demilitarization and humanitarian aid, was approved by voice vote in the early morning hours of Nov. 27.

The Senate cleared the legislation later that day by voice vote.

Eleven days later the administration endorsed it.

House

1. Persian Gulf War

After one of its longest and most moving debates in recent memory, Congress on Jan. 12 approved a resolution (H J Res 77) authorizing President Bush to use military force to reverse Iraq's occupation of Kuwait. Four days later, Bush did just that, ordering the aerial bombardment of Iraq.

On Feb. 27, following six weeks of devastating air strikes and a brief but bloody ground campaign, Bush announced: "Our military objectives are met." Kuwait was liberated and Iraq had been defeated, Bush said.

In the House, opponents of the war resolution, led by Speaker Thomas S. Foley, D-Wash., knew going into the debate that they were facing an uphill struggle.

For several months, Foley and other Democratic leaders had urged the president to stay the course with economic sanctions that had been imposed on Iraq after it invaded Kuwait on Aug. 2, 1990. But in the weeks leading up to the climactic vote, some key members of the party expressed skepticism that sanctions alone would ever force

Iraqi leader Saddam Hussein to withdraw his forces from the tiny, oil-rich emirate.

Armed Services Committee Chairman Les Aspin, D-Wis., had predicted that the United States and it allies could achieve victory over Iraq without sustaining heavy casualties. Stephen J. Solarz, D-N.Y., typified a small group of Northern liberals — most of whom were strong supporters of Israel — who also supported an early resort to force against Saddam.

But the likelihood that the resolution would be approved did little to diminish the tension and emotion that permeated the three-day debate on the issue.

In a rare speech from the well, Foley told his colleagues, "In 26 years in the House of Representatives, I have never seen this House more serious nor determined to speak its heart and mind on a question than they are at this time on this day."

The Senate voted first to approve its war resolution. Minutes later, the House voted 250-183 for H J Res 77, an identical resolution that authorized the president to use military force pursuant to U.N. Security Council Resolution 678. The U.N. resolution, approved in November 1990, had authorized member states "to use all necessary means" to force Iraq out of Kuwait by Jan. 15. *(Senate key vote 1)*

While congressional leaders had urged members to vote their consciences, the vote was split largely along partisan lines: R 164-3; D 86-179 (ND 33-147, SD 53-32); I 0-1.

Pro-defense Democrats from the South joined with Republicans and a handful of liberals to provide the margin of victory. Key committee chairmen — such as Aspin, John D. Dingell, D-Mich., of Energy and Commerce, and Dan Rostenkowski, D-Ill., of Ways and Means — supported H J Res 77.

After the vote, most House members put aside partisan differences and closed ranks in support of the president and hundreds of thousands of U.S. military personnel who were poised for battle in the Persian Gulf.

During the dramatic debate on the measure, Majority Leader Richard A. Gephardt, D-Mo., had said, "Whatever our decision, we will leave this room one again and whole again."

2. Thrift Bailout

Paying for past mistakes is never fun, and the savings and loan debacle was about the biggest mess in Congress' back yard. So it was not surprising that when it came time to ante up the taxpayers' money to cover insured deposits in failed thrifts, members did so reluctantly.

That was never demonstrated more aptly than in March, when the House defeated a succession of plans to give money to the Resolution Trust Corporation (RTC), the thrift bailout agency created in August 1989.

The March votes were required because a bill to give the RTC additional money had failed in the final hours of the 101st Congress. The agency had gotten $50 billion when it was created, a sum that the Bush administration persisted in claiming would be enough. By the summer of 1990, however, administration officials said the cost would range from $89 billion to $132 billion.

So, at the beginning of the 102nd Congress, the House and Senate Banking committees began work on bills to give the RTC another $30 billion — enough, it was plain by then, to last only through 1991, not to finish the job.

In February, the House Banking Committee marked up a bill and then could not summon up the votes to send the measure to the floor. On March 7, it voted to send not one but two bills to the floor.

Eventually, the House voted four times on the two committee options — and variations on their themes — rejecting all four. The final vote, on March 12, was on a "clean" bill (HR 1315) sponsored by ranking committee Republican Chalmers P. Wylie of Ohio, which did little more than provide the needed $30 billion. But even that measure failed on a vote of 201-220: R 120-42; D 81-177 (ND 44-132, SD 37-45); I 0-1.

The clean bill did get more votes than any of the three alternatives, which contained a variety of low-income housing, management reform and so-called pay-as-you-go provisions. These bells and whistles were intended to pick up the votes of disaffected members, but they also generated opposition.

The day after Wylie's bill was rejected, House Democratic and Republican leaders cut a deal with Treasury Secretary Nicholas F. Brady to call up a Senate-passed bill (S 419) that was similarly devoid of controversial amendments and add a few low-income housing provisions to it. The compromise managed to hold the line on Republican support and picked up enough Democratic votes to pass. A conference committee reconciled the two similarly stripped-down versions in about 15 minutes, and both chambers adopted the conference agreement without difficulty.

That did not mean the story was over, however. By the summer of 1991, the administration was asking for $80 billion more. And in the final hours of the 1991 session, almost as its last act, Congress cleared a bill (HR 3435) providing another $25 billion for the RTC and restructuring the agency. It was not at all certain until the end that the second thrift bailout bill of the year would pass either chamber. And with the limited amount of money it contained, Congress set itself up for yet another showdown on the issue in 1992.

3. Gun Control

A May vote on the Brady bill revealed a significant shift in attitudes on gun control in the House and handed the National Rifle Association a rare defeat. Legislation for a waiting period on handgun purchases (HR 7) passed the House on May 8 by a surprising 53-vote margin, 239-186: R 60-102; D 179-83 (ND 138-41, SD 41-42); I 0-1.

Although Democrats were more inclined to back the legislation, the vote was bipartisan. Three years earlier, the powerful gun lobby had blocked a similar measure by 46 votes.

The handgun proposal, which also passed the Senate in 1991, was on hold at the end of the session after having been modified and rolled into an omnibus crime bill (HR 3371), which was held up over partisan differences. Nonetheless, because of the strong votes for the Brady bill in both chambers, many members expected the provision to become law in 1992.

HR 7 would have required a seven-day waiting period on the purchase of handguns for a background check. The compromise version that became part of the crime bill was for a five-business-day wait.

Its supporters chalked up the win in the House to constituent pressure on members in the face of increasing violent crime. Polls had been showing resounding support for firearms restrictions, and swing voters said they were persuaded to back down on their no-gun-control positions by local police and worried constituents.

The waiting period language was named for former presidential press secretary James S. Brady, who was wounded in a 1981 assassination attempt on Ronald Reagan.

Brady made several appearances on Capitol Hill in his wheelchair, with his determined wife, Sarah. They were ubiquitous at the Capitol in the days leading up to the vote and had a strong influence on the legislation.

The Bradys became a poignant contrast to the powerful NRA, which boasted among its members several House leaders, including Speaker Thomas S. Foley, D-Wash.

Under existing law, a gun buyer had to sign a statement that he was not a felon, fugitive, drug addict or mentally ill. But because the form never left the dealer's shop, buyers acted on their honor. Under the Brady bill, gun dealers would have to send that form to the police, who would check the buyer's background to make sure the purchase was legal. HR 7 did not require the police to make the background check, but the new version in the crime bill did.

Before the House passed the Brady bill, it rejected an alternative offered by Harley O. Staggers Jr., D-W.Va., that would have ordered states to set up an instant check system within six months, under which a gun dealer could find out by telephone whether a would-be buyer had a criminal record. The amendment was devised largely to block the Brady bill. Opponents of the Staggers plan pointed to studies showing that because state criminal justice records are not fully computerized, it would take years to put the telephone-check system in place. The House defeated the Staggers substitute, also on May 8, by a strong 193-234.

Overwhelming passage of HR 7, which was offered by Edward F. Feighan, D-Ohio, put pressure on the Senate to develop a similar measure.

The bipartisan compromise was endorsed by the Bradys and adopted in that chamber June 28 by a secure, 67-32 vote as part of a Senate crime bill (S 1241). *(Senate key vote 3)*

4. Strategic Defense Initiative

Since 1985, Congress had routinely slashed the annual funding request for the anti-missile research program called the strategic defense initiative (SDI). And since 1987, it had consistently opposed deployment of space-based anti-missile weapons that would violate the 1972 U.S.-Soviet treaty limiting anti-ballistic missile (ABM) systems.

Despite those hotly contested annual fights over funding and treaty compliance, however, Congress had approved spending at least a few billion dollars annually on a program of anti-missile defense research that was strongly oriented toward eventual deployment of ABM weapons.

President Ronald Reagan launched SDI in 1983, arguing that an array of anti-missile devices could render nuclear weapons obsolete and end the superpower arms race. But many leading arms control advocates had opposed the program on the grounds that missile defenses could stimulate escalating deployments of offensive weapons intended to nullify such defenses.

In past years, some liberals, led by Ronald V. Dellums, D-Calif., had proposed deep reductions in SDI funds that essentially would have limited the program to laboratory research. But most arms control activists had thrown more of their energy into a pragmatic effort to win more modest cuts in SDI. On the other side, conservatives had pushed for rapid deployment of a nationwide anti-missile defense regardless of the 1972 ABM Treaty.

In 1991, the House Armed Services Committee sliced Bush's $5.2 billion request for anti-missile work to $3.5 billion in its version of the fiscal 1992 defense authorization bill. When the House took up the measure in May, no middle-ground amendment was offered to make a relatively moderate additional SDI reduction. However, Dellums offered an amendment that would have sliced the total to $1.1 billion while disbanding the SDI program office and limiting the project to laboratory work.

Dellums' amendment was an effort to draw the line against the kind of ground-based defense against limited missile attacks that had been endorsed by prominent Democratic centrists, including House Armed Services Committee Chairman Les Aspin, Wis. Demonstrating the weakness of the outright opponents of SDI, the amendment was rejected 118-266: R 2-149; D 115-117 (ND 104-55, SD 11-62); I 1-0, on May 20.

By final passage of the defense authorization bill (HR 2100 — PL 102-190) in November, the House acquiesced in a Senate-forged deal that gave a congressional endorsement to a limited SDI deployment. It provided for rapid deployment of a ground-based anti-missile defense at one site and for negotiations with leaders of the former Soviet Union to revise the ABM Treaty in order to permit a more extensive SDI system. *(Senate key vote 8)*

5. Fast-Track Trade Procedures

Democrats in Congress complained regularly that President Bush's trade policy was ineffective and unsound, but they passed up a rare chance to do more of the job themselves. Influential Democrats decided it was wiser to remain in the back seat shouting directions than to take the wheel.

In what had become a referendum on Bush's controversial decision to begin negotiations with Mexico to create a North American free-trade zone, the House agreed May 23 to continue so-called fast-track procedures that bar lawmakers from amending trade pacts submitted for congressional approval. The Senate followed suit a day later.

During weeks of intensive lobbying, the Bush administration had argued that the two-year extension was imperative not only to begin the U.S.-Mexico talks but also to revive negotiations on strengthening the General Agreement on Tariffs and Trade (GATT), the multilateral accord governing most world trade. No country would negotiate with the United States, officials said, if Congress reserved the right to alter the resulting accord.

The vote was a bitter disappointment to organized labor. The AFL-CIO had campaigned hard to convince members that removing trade and investment barriers with Mexico would cause U.S. workers to lose their jobs as companies headed south to take advantage of cheaper labor and lax environmental laws. Defeat of the extension was the organization's top legislative priority, and it was counting on its close ties with Democrats to produce the votes.

In the end, a majority of House Democrats voted against the extension. Midwestern lawmakers were strongly opposed, arguing that a U.S.-Mexico pact would hurt industries such as automobiles, electronics and glassware. Also voting against the extension were members from states with industries such as agriculture and textiles, which feared that a GATT accord would eliminate U.S. laws that had long shielded them from foreign competition.

But key party members — including Majority Leader Richard A. Gephardt, D-Mo., to whom opponents had looked for leadership, and Ways and Means Committee Chairman Dan Rostenkowski, D-Ill. — voted with the president. They did so after the White House issued an "action plan" promising to uphold U.S. environmental laws, phase in changes affecting farmers and industries worried about being swamped by Mexican imports, and assist workers who lost their jobs as a result of the pact.

Gephardt, the Democrats' leading trade warrior, defended his vote, saying he reserved the right to oppose the final agreement with Mexico if it was not protective enough of U.S. workers and industries. Even with the fast track, Gephardt insisted, lawmakers could amend the terms of any trade deal Bush sent them if they wanted.

The defeat of a resolution that would have terminated the fast track was a victory for Bush, who won endorsement from the Democratic controlled Congress for his free-trade agenda in the middle of a recession.

Equally important, Bush persuaded Congress to leave the negotiating to him, knowing that, if he succeeded, he also would get the credit.

The House defeated the resolution 192-231: R 21-140; D 170-91 (ND 128-50, SD 42-41); I 1-0, on May 23.

6. Superconducting Supercollider

Despite increased opposition and resistance from respected members of the Science and Budget committees, the $8 billion atom smasher being built in Waxahachie, Texas, continued to attract substantial House support.

Enthusiasm for the project was evident May 29 when supporters soundly defeated an attempt to drop federal funding for the project. The vote came during debate on the fiscal 1992 energy and water appropriations bill when the House rejected, 165-251, an amendment by Jim Slattery, D-Kan., that would have eliminated funding for the project: R 58-101; D 106-150 (ND 86-87, SD 20-63); I 1-0.

Still, the vote revealed that the project's popularity had eroded considerably since 1989 — when there were 93 votes to cut funding for the collider — and it suggested that in future years opponents might be able to muster the votes necessary to kill it.

The House version called for allotting $434 million for the atom smasher in fiscal 1992, about $100 million less than the Bush administration's budget request. The supercollider was designed to hurl subatomic particles through a 54-mile underground tunnel; scientists hoped that studying particle collisions would help them trace the origins of matter and yield scientific discoveries.

Opposition to the collider was growing in the House among science supporters who feared that its high price tag could cannibalize other science projects and among Budget Committee members who considered it too costly. Joining Slattery's attack were Howard Wolpe, D-Mich., who headed the Science Investigation and Oversight Subcommittee, and Sherwood Boehlert, R-N.Y., ranking member on the subcommittee. Boehlert called the collider a "Texas gila monster" and said support for it came from "Texas and Texas and Texas and Texas."

Boehlert might have added to his short list another 42 states and 1600 Pennsylvania Ave. President Bush had long been an advocate for the project and met personally last year with Tom Bevill, D-Ala., who headed the Appropriations panel with jurisdiction over the project. Bevill, originally a skeptic, had become a strong supporter. Since that meeting with Bush, the White House had been less inclined to oppose additional water projects in the appropriations bill Bevill shepherded through the House. Additional political ballast for the project came from about 8,500 contracts worth hundreds of millions of dollars that had been doled out to 43 states. The contracts had sparked support for the atom smasher from members who otherwise would have had little interest in the project.

In the 1991 debate, supporters of the project were led by the good-natured Joe L. Barton, R-Texas, whose home is just a couple of miles from the collider site. They argued that the atom smasher was likely to produce many lucrative spinoffs and that it was already too far along to stop. The latter was an argument often used by supporters of big, multi-year weapons or science projects.

The 1991 vote was significant because it marked the resurrection of opposition to the project, which had dissipated in 1990. In the tight budget climate that was likely to dominate the decade, high-cost projects had become the target of budget cutters. Supporters also said the vote was key because it provided funds meant to begin construction of the project's tunnel. *(Senate key vote 4)*

7. Civil Rights

An initial blow to civil rights legislation came in late spring when the House failed to gather a two-thirds majority for a bill President Bush was threatening to veto. Bush, who asserted that HR 1 would lead to quota hiring of minorities and women, had vetoed a similar bill in 1990.

The June 5 House vote was the first test of a reconstituted anti-discrimination bill. The vote was largely partisan: 273-158: R 22-143; D 250-15 (ND 177-4, SD 73-11); I 1-0. The 273 votes were 15 short of the two-thirds needed to override a veto; the 1990 House tally on the job rights conference report was 12 short.

The failure to reach two-thirds effectively stalled HR 1 but paved the way for more intense negotiations among Senate moderates on a separate bill. In the end, a compromise was brokered in the wake of the Senate's Supreme Court nomination hearings involving Clarence Thomas and Anita F. Hill. Workplace protections, similar to those proposed in HR 1, had since become law.

The bill was intended to offer workers more protection against bias, largely by reversing a series of Supreme Court decisions that narrowed the reach of anti-bias laws. It would have for the first time allowed limited money damages for victims of harassment and other intentional discrimination based on sex, religion or disability. Minorities already could win unlimited money damages for racial discrimination under a separate post-Civil War law. HR 1 would have reversed more court cases and been more generous to workers than the legislation eventually enacted.

The House vote came at a time when the political and substantive problems with the job rights bill were near their height. Republicans had been pounding away on the message that the measure would force employers to use quotas to avoid costly lawsuits. They struck a nerve with white constituents worried about holding onto their jobs in a frail economy.

Democrats, meanwhile, struggled with how to convey the importance of workplace protections. They had tried to appeal to women by adding a study of pay equity and other items designed to appeal to working women. They also tried to defuse the quota issue by inserting language for an outright ban on quotas. Because the Supreme Court had ruled that hiring by the numbers is illegal, the move appeared to be motivated by attempts to give political cover to members who wanted to vote for the bill but faced constituent complaints about "reverse discrimination."

Before the vote on HR 1, the House rejected two other civil rights proposals — a White House plan and a hard-line effort from liberal Democrats that included unlimited money damages in intentional bias suits.

Only one House member who voted against the 1990 bill switched to support the 1991 version. He was Democrat Bill Sarpalius of Texas.

Sarpalius' switch was more than offset by the one Democrat (Jimmy Hayes of Louisiana) and nine Republicans who voted for the 1990 rights bill but opposed HR 1. *(Senate key vote 13)*

8. Space Station

Bob Traxler, D-Mich., knew he was going out on a limb when he persuaded the House Appropriations Committee to eliminate fiscal 1992 funding for NASA's premier space enterprise, the orbiting space station *Freedom*. He was afraid the massive construction project would take too big a bite out of the $64 billion in discretionary spending allocated to the Subcommittee on Veterans Affairs (VA), Housing and Urban Development (HUD) and Independent Agencies, which oversaw the space agency's funding. At risk were other, smaller space and science projects as well as the many low-income housing, veterans' medical care and environmental programs under the panel's jurisdiction.

Meeting privately, the subcommittee on May 15 informally voted 6-3 against President Bush's $2.03 billion request for the space station in the fiscal 1992 spending bill (HR 2519). The full committee, at Traxler's request, deferred debate until the House floor, where Traxler believed all members should be put to the test. "We simply can no longer afford huge new projects with huge price tags while trying to maintain services that the American people expect to be provided," he said.

The subcommittee action touched off a lobbying firestorm. Low-income housing groups and environmentalists, in particular, began urging representatives to ratify the subcommittee's bill. They feared that if money was put back in, it would come out of their appropriations.

Also lobbying members were NASA officials, aerospace contractors and members of the House Science Committee. The agency passed out maps showing each House member how many jobs and how many dollars flowed into the districts from space station contracts and subcontracts. *Freedom*'s proponents, including Bush, also painted the project as having the potential for scientific breakthroughs with research in space. "It clearly caught the imagination of our colleagues," said Bill Lowery, R-Calif.

But others viewed the space station, estimated to cost a total of $40 billion, as a boondoggle. "If we fund this, it's clearly not for scientific reasons, it's for the contractors who work on the project," said Richard J. Durbin, D-Ill.

The key vote came June 6 on an amendment to restore nearly $2 billion in space station funding. The amendment was drafted by the White House Office of Management and Budget and offered by Jim Chapman, D-Texas, and Lowery, two VA-HUD subcommittee members.

In order to avoid the appearance that the space station would be taking money away from the poor, the amendment primarily cannibalized every other NASA program, including the environmental satellite project, Mission to Planet Earth. But it also proposed cutting $217 million, or nearly 10 percent, of the funds used to maintain public housing.

The House agreed to restore the space station's funding nearly to the level Bush requested by a vote of 240-173: R 133-27; D 107-145 (ND 55-114, SD 52-31); I 0-1.

Sending the bill on to the Senate, *Freedom* proponents knew their project would be protected by Barbara A. Mikulski, D-Md., chairman of the Senate VA-HUD Subcommittee.

Yet in a roundabout way the vote was a victory for Traxler, who may have succeeded in isolating NASA's budget from non-space programs. Space station proponents were so frightened of being cast as foes of the poor that they primarily took from other NASA programs to pay for *Freedom*'s appropriation.

9. Grazing Fees

If any issue encapsulated the growing conflict among users of the country's vast public lands, it was grazing fees, a subject that produced much heated debate on public lands policy in 1991.

By almost any measure, the fees ranchers paid to graze their cattle on public land were lower than those paid by ranchers who grazed their cattle on private pastures. The inevitable result, argued some lawmakers and environmentalists, was overgrazing of arid Western rangeland and millions of dollars in lost revenue yearly.

But Western lawmakers had turned the issue into a symbolic lightning rod, imbuing it with images of another kind of endangered species: struggling ranchers, said to be the backbone of the old West. And they noted that the Bureau of Land Management in its 1990 "State of the Public Rangelands" report said the nation's rangelands were in better shape than at any time in the 20th century.

The rhetoric and lobbying by environmentalists reached a new emotional pitch on June 25 when Mike Synar, D-Okla., proposed an amendment to raise grazing fees from $1.97 to $8.70 per animal unit month by 1995. (Studies from the General Accounting Office had determined that the average private market rate for Western rangeland is $9.22.) The House voted 232-192 to add the amendment to the fiscal 1992 Interior appropriations bill: R 47-114; D 184-78 (ND 140-38, SD 44-40); I 1-0.

Synar's amendment actually passed by a smaller margin than had a similar Synar amendment a year before. On Oct. 15, 1990, the House voted 251-155 to increase grazing fees.

What made the 1991 vote key was that it emboldened Senate supporters of a fee hike, who for the first time since 1978 pushed for a vote in their chamber. The Senate effort, led by James M. Jeffords, R-Vt., ultimately failed, showing that there is a solid phalanx of Western conservatives determined to block a hike in grazing fees. And when the matter reached conference, it became clear that even the House was not willing to place a high enough priority on higher fees to make them stick.

The Senate voted on Sept. 17, 60-38, to table (kill) the Jeffords amendment, which would have raised grazing fees to $5.13 by 1996.

And in conference the House amendment capsized

under a deal that became known as "corn for porn." It preserved low grazing fees in exchange for no new restrictions on federal arts funding.

10. Defense Budget Cuts

The 1990 deficit-reduction act proved a formidable obstacle to those members — mostly liberal Democrats — who wanted to cut President Bush's $291 billion defense budget request. The law limited the allowable deficit each year through fiscal 1995. And it limited through fiscal 1993 annual discretionary spending for defense, international affairs and domestic programs. Funds cut from defense could not be transferred to popular domestic programs without violating the cap on domestic spending.

When the House returned from its August recess, some Pentagon critics, led by Barney Frank, D-Mass., calculated that events might have shifted the political equation in their favor. The unsuccessful mid-August coup attempt in Moscow by hard-line communists had been followed by a total collapse of communist power in the Soviet Union and a powerful surge of separatist sentiment in most of the republics that made up the U.S.S.R. The communist superpower's military might had been the motivating threat behind U.S. defense plans for more than 40 years. Therefore, Frank and his allies contended, the passing of that threat called for a fundamental revision of the budget deal.

But Defense Secretary Dick Cheney warned that the defense establishment would suffer far-reaching damage if Congress forced a more rapid cutback than his program to reduce the force by roughly 25 percent by fiscal 1995.

And many House Democratic leaders were aligned with Cheney in opposing any effort to depart significantly from the existing budget deal, although some were willing to renegotiate the budget deal in 1992. House Budget Committee Chairman Leon E. Panetta, D-Calif., and others expressed fear that the political pressures for an array of domestic programs were so powerful that any effort to tamper with the existing arrangement would risk a bidding war that would torpedo the budget deal, endanger the economy and subject the Democrats to taunts that they were addicted to big spending.

When the House appointed conferees on the defense authorization bill (HR 2100 — PL 102-190) Sept. 16, Frank intended to propose a motion instructing them to back the lower of the amounts authorized by the two chambers for any conventional weapons program, "consistent with emerging national security needs." But he was blocked from offering that defense-cutting motion by a procedural vote, which he lost 220-145: R 136-4; D 84-140 (ND 30-124, SD 54-16); I 0-1.

11. Unemployment Benefits

For the first part of 1991, congressional Democrats and President Bush sparred over whether the country needed a bill to provide extended unemployment benefits for the long-term jobless. But as the economy worsened and unemployment hovered near 6.8 percent during the summer and fall, Bush stopped talking about whether a bill would be prudent. Instead, he criticized Congress for trying to pay for a multibillion-dollar bill through deficit spending. Congress, Bush maintained, wanted to "bust the budget agreement."

Bush had already blocked one bill in August that would have declared unemployment an emergency and therefore not subject to the budget agreement's pay-as-you-go rules. Bush signed that legislation but not an accompanying emergency designation that would have released the funds.

Democrats vowed to try again. They pointed to the $8 billion surplus in revenues from unemployment taxes paid by employers, which they maintained was being used to help mask the overall federal deficit.

They insisted that the budget agreement allowed Congress to spend money without offsetting tax increases or spending cuts if both Congress and the president declared an emergency. So Democrats pushed through a second bill (HR 3040), which would have automatically triggered spending of $6.3 billion in extended benefits if Bush had signed it into law.

The second time, on Sept. 17, the House voted 283-125: R 48-107; D 234-18 (ND 172-2, SD 62-16); I 1-0. The vote gave Democrats 11 more ayes than necessary to exceed the two-thirds margin needed to override Bush. Despite Bush's opposition, 48 Republicans supported the bill, eight more than Democrats had predicted.

The vote was a key one because it signaled to the administration that Democrats had momentum on their side. More and more members were complaining about the economy — Republicans as well as Democrats. With the override strength apparent, the administration began to accept that negotiations would be necessary in order to reach a compromise and get the unemployment issue off the domestic agenda.

Ultimately, after a four-month political standoff, Congress sent Bush a $5.3 billion bill to extend unemployment benefits for nearly 3 million people. Bush signed the measure the same day he received it, Nov. 15. The bill was paid for by tightening a loophole on those paying quarterly taxes; extending a law allowing Internal Revenue Service collection of debts owed the federal government; extending the federal unemployment tax at 0.08 percent; and garnisheeing the wages of those who defaulted on student loans. *(Senate key vote 10)*

12. Surface Transportation

Congress' biggest legislative achievement of the session, a six-year, $151 billion highway and mass transit bill, began the year mired in controversy. But when the final bill came to the House floor on Oct. 23, it passed swiftly after only a single day of debate.

The smooth sailing was aided by the tight rein the Democrat-dominated Rules Committee kept on items open to floor consideration. Despite Republican protests, the committee limited debate to only a dozen amendments and squelched 41 others. On the floor, Republicans forced three procedural roll call votes in protest. In the end, the House adopted the rule, 323-102, with significant help from Republicans: R 66-97; D 257-4 (ND 174-4, SD 83-0); I 0-1.

Votes on rules typically are procedural matters. But this vote was significant because Democrats succeeded in crafting a "stealth" bill that evaded all controversial issues. Despite the small group of dissenting Republicans, most lawmakers went along because the bill included authority for hundreds of local projects.

The roads and transit measure first faced trouble when House sponsors proposed hiking gasoline taxes by a nickel. The plan met with staunch opposition from both parties, and an early version of the bill was pulled from the floor calendar in August. Leaders of the Public Works and Transportation Committee dropped the nickel increase, opting instead to extend 2.5 cents of a 1990 nickel increase that was set to expire after fiscal 1995.

With that issue out of the way, other potential floor fights loomed: Some lawmakers, particularly from states that paid more in gas taxes than they received in highway funds, were upset that much of the $5.4 billion for 489 special road projects ended up in the states and districts of bill sponsors. Others objected to the new gas-tax plan.

But the Public Works panel, with help from the Rules Committee, managed to keep every controversial issue from coming to a floor vote. Almost every amendment blocked by the Rules panel dealt with potentially explosive issues that had tied up highway bills in the past, including a limit on billboard construction, a repeal of the national speed limit, a weakening of motorcycle helmet laws and a strengthening of drunken driving laws.

Republicans, including Rules Committee member Bob McEwen of Ohio, Robert S. Walker of Pennsylvania and Dan Burton of Indiana, opened their assault on the bill by attacking the rule. The Rules Committee had denied Burton's attempts to cut seven special road projects expected to cost $67.1 million.

But the Republican effort to overturn the rule failed in large part because lawmakers feared retaliation from bill sponsors, and they were not eager to lose funding for their hometown road projects.

The Public Works and Transportation Committee's hold over the bill's amendments continued as the bill went to conference with the Senate. The only amendment to pass was one by Anthony C. Beilenson, D-Calif., that would have allowed states to include a warranty clause in highway contracts. Despite the overwhelming approval of the amendment, 400-26, Public Works leaders opposed it, and it was dropped in conference.

13. Foreign Aid

When House members rejected the foreign aid bill on Oct. 30, they were signaling their clear displeasure with helping other nations during a period of economic crisis in the United States.

The key vote came when the House defeated the conference report on the bill (HR 2508 — H Rept 102-225), 159-262: R 28-134; D 131-127 (ND 105-73, SD 26-54); I 0-1.

It was a dramatic mood change from June, when the House had approved the original foreign aid authorization bill by 136 votes (274-138).

President Bush had vowed to veto the bill on several grounds. He objected that the measure would have repealed abortion-related restrictions on aid to international family planning organizations and would have included a "cargo preference" provision requiring that a certain percentage of exports be transported on U.S.-flagged vessels.

But those red flag provisions had also been part of the original bill that won House approval.

House Foreign Affairs Committee Chairman Dante B. Fascell, D-Fla., the manager of the bill, described what had changed since the June vote: "The big difference is the change in attitude toward domestic issues."

Moreover, there was virtually no downside for members who wanted to cast an anti-foreign aid vote. Foreign aid funding for the first six months had been ensured with the passage of a continuing resolution Oct. 24.

Democrats had political incentives to oppose the bill. Party leaders had been hammering away at Bush as being more concerned with foreign policy than the domestic economy. With an eye on the 1992 campaign, Democrats did not want to muddle that message with strong backing for a foreign aid bill.

In an unlikely combination, socialist Bernard Sanders, I-Vt., and bedrock conservative Gerald B. H. Solomon, R-N.Y., attacked a provision — supported by the administration — that would have increased the U.S. contribution in the International Monetary Fund by $12.2 billion.

The failure to enact an authorization bill was hardly unprecedented; no such measure had become law since 1985. But several lawmakers said the vote could be a harbinger of congressional opposition to more significant legislation.

One of the first items on the agenda for 1992 would be the fiscal 1992 foreign aid appropriations bill, which was delayed over the controversy surrounding Israel's request for $10 billion in loan guarantees.

14. Banking Overhaul

On Nov. 4, the House overwhelmingly rejected a comprehensive banking bill that had been debated, amended and negotiated for nine months. The vote marked the beginning of the end for the Bush administration's hopes to overhaul the banking industry in 1991.

The bill (HR 6) had survived hundreds of amendments and two extensive markup sessions in the House Banking Committee, yet emerged much as the administration had wanted. It had been attacked in the Energy and Commerce Committee because of provisions involving the ownership of banks and bank affiliations with securities firms. So those major controversial elements were dropped or revised in post-markup negotiations between Banking Chairman Henry B. Gonzalez, D-Texas, and Energy and Commerce Chairman John D. Dingell, D-Mich.

On the floor a third controversial element — allowing banks to move freely across state lines — was curtailed by giving states power to limit interstate branching.

Yet, in the end, after all the changes and negotiations, members were still far from satisfied. Some regarded the measure as too restrictive; others thought it still too expansive. The bill was rejected by a vote of 89-324: R 6-153; D 83-170 (ND 69-105, SD 14-65); I 0-1.

The bill was nearly sidetracked when the rule permitting floor debate was adopted on a 210-208 vote. The rule came close to defeat, but the vote was turned around by the personal lobbying of Speaker Thomas S. Foley, D-Wash., who had promised Treasury Secretary Nicholas F. Brady that he would keep the bill on track. However, after it became clear that the bill would not be changed on the floor to its liking, the administration joined big banks in working to kill the measure outright.

It took two more tries on the floor before the House finally approved a banking bill.

The second failed attempt was on a bill (HR 2094) that began as a stripped-down measure to replenish the Federal Deposit Insurance Corporation's Bank Insurance Fund and overhaul the deposit insurance system. But at the administration's insistence, provisions allowing interstate branching were added back on the floor. Beyond providing the nearly insolvent insurance fund with a line of credit at the Treasury so it could stay in business closing failed banks, the administration's top priority was to improve bank profitability. Allowing nationwide interstate branching was seen as the best way to improve bank efficiency, spead risk and increase profits.

The third bill (HR 3768), which finally passed the House, was limited to refinancing and overhauling the deposit insurance system.

The Senate went through much the same torment, though mostly in behind-the-scenes negotiations. As the progression of House bills got narrower, so did a parallel Senate measure (S 543), which in a series of floor amendments was pared of its language permitting bank affiliations with securities firms and other contentious provisions. The Senate did manage to pass a bill that would have permitted interstate branching. But in conference, the House's overwhelming rejection of anything but the narrowest bill that focused on the deposit insurance system remained the controlling factor.

House and Senate conferees produced a compromise version of S 543 on the final day of the session, Nov. 27, that was essentially the same as HR 3768.

The conference agreement was adopted easily and sent to the president.

15. Abortion 'Gag Rule'

Abortion rights advocates thought the Supreme Court's May 23 ruling in *Rust v. Sullivan* could be a blessing in disguise. Although they strenuously disagreed with the Court's ruling — that controversial regulations issued in 1988 banning abortion counseling in federally funded family planning clinics did not violate the Constitution — they thought they finally had an issue that could transcend the traditional pro-choice and anti-abortion debates. Indeed, shortly after the Court ruling, many abortion opponents in Congress declared that what opponents dubbed the "gag rule" in their view violated free speech rights by limiting discussion between patients and doctors and other health care providers.

Opponents of the rules adopted a two-track strategy. One track consisted of legislation that would permanently overturn the rules and write into law the counseling and referral guidelines in effect between 1981 and 1988. The Senate in July passed a free-standing bill (S 323) to do just that, while the House Energy and Commerce Committee in August approved legislation to reauthorize the family planning program (HR 3090) that included provisions to overturn the rules.

Proponents knew their best chance of success lay in the other half of the strategy: inserting language to block enforcement of the rules for one year into the popular spending bill (HR 2707) for the Departments of Labor, Health and Human Services, and Education. Procedural rules governing appropriations measures prevented inclusion of language to overturn the regulations outright.

But while abortion rights advocates were telling colleagues that the issue was not abortion but free speech, abortion opponents were stressing exactly the opposite. Together many of the groups formed the "Abortion is Not Family Planning Coalition," which bought newspaper ads to, in their words, clear up misconceptions about the rules and the effect they would have on federally funded family planning clinics.

The preliminary test on the issue came when the House Nov. 9 approved the conference report on the bill by a vote of 272-156, well short of the two-thirds needed to override Bush's promised veto. But the matter was complicated by a budget issue. Several Republicans who had already come out against the counseling ban said they could not vote for the bill because it pushed more than $4 billion worth of spending into fiscal 1993, thus threatening the viability of the 1990 budget agreement between the White House and Congress.

In his Nov. 19 veto message, Bush mentioned the budget issue but made it clear that the veto was primarily if not exclusively because of the abortion language.

The House Democratic leadership, including anti-abortion Majority Whip David E. Bonior, Mich., worked the issue hard, and a day before the vote Speaker Thomas S. Foley, Wash., predicted that the veto would be overridden. But the votes that were picked up with the elimination of the budget issue did not offset votes lost by abortion opponents, particularly 43 anti-abortion Democrats.

Members ultimately fell 12 votes short of the 288 they would have needed to override in the 276-156 tally: R 53-113; D 222-43 (ND 155-26, SD 67-17); I 1-0.

16. Campaign Finance

For the second straight year, House Democratic leaders pushed for legislation to limit campaign spending. But the 1991 version (HR 3750 — H Rept 102-340) contained something the 1990 bill avoided: direct public subsidies of campaigns.

The bill would set a $600,000 optional spending limit for House races in primary and general elections. Candidates who agreed to obey the limit would get benefits, including cut-rate postage and up to $200,000 in public financing doled out to match the first $200 of each individual contribution. The measure would also place a $200,000 aggregate cap on how much a candidate could accept from political action committees and a $200,000 aggregate cap on individual contributions of more than $200.

Given the partisan nature of the issue, the Democratic leadership did not want to risk bringing the measure to the floor without enough Democratic votes to assure its passage. So when conservative Democrats began raising objections to the public financing provisions, Sam Gejdenson, D-Conn., the chairman of a special task force on campaign finance, began giving ground.

Public financing had become the touchstone of opposition to the Senate bill earlier in the year when Republicans ridiculed a Democratic measure (S 3) as "food stamps for politicians." Democrats in both chambers countered that public financing was a small price to pay to control campaign costs and diminish the clout of special interests. But Southern Democrats in the House feared that they could not justify launching a new spending program for campaigns at an estimated cost of $75 million every two years.

Gejdenson sought to meet the objections even before introducing the measure Nov. 12. He rewrote draft language to keep the mechanism for raising the revenue vague, leaving that detail to a future tax bill. Instead, the bill as introduced said the money should be raised by limiting the tax deductions that organizations take for lobbying, an effort to make special interests bear the costs.

That still went too far for some, as it designated tax revenues for campaigns. So Gejdenson bent again. Before floor consideration, the bill was stripped of any meaningful way to pay for public financing of campaigns.

The change ensured widespread Democratic backing for the bill, and on Nov. 26 it easily passed, 273-156: R 21-144; D 251-12 (ND 176-4, SD 75-8); I 1-0.

Appendix

	1	2	3	4	5	6	7	8
ALABAMA								
Heflin	Y	N	N	Y	N	Y	Y	N
Shelby	Y	N	N	Y	N	N	Y	N
ALASKA								
Murkowski	Y	Y	N	Y	Y	N	N	N
Stevens	Y	Y	N	Y	Y	N	N	N
ARIZONA								
DeConcini	N	?	N	N	N	Y	N	Y
McCain	Y	N	N	Y	N	N	Y	N
ARKANSAS								
Bumpers	N	N	Y	N	N	Y	Y	Y
Pryor	N	?	?	?	#	?	?	?
CALIFORNIA								
Cranston	-	Y	Y	N	Y	Y	N	Y
Seymour [1]	Y	N	Y	Y	N	N	N	N
COLORADO								
Wirth	N	Y	Y	N	Y	Y	N	Y
Brown	Y	Y	N	Y	N	N	N	N
CONNECTICUT								
Dodd	N	Y	Y	Y	N	Y	N	Y
Lieberman	Y	Y	Y	Y	Y	Y	N	Y
DELAWARE								
Biden	N	Y	Y	N	Y	Y	N	Y
Roth	Y	Y	Y	Y	Y	N	N	N
FLORIDA								
Graham	Y	N	Y	Y	N	Y	N	Y
Mack	Y	N	N	Y	N	Y	N	N
GEORGIA								
Fowler	N	Y	Y	N	N	Y	Y	Y
Nunn	N	?	Y	Y	Y	Y	Y	N
HAWAII								
Akaka	N	Y	Y	Y	Y	Y	N	N
Inouye	N	Y	Y	Y	Y	Y	Y	N
IDAHO								
Craig	Y	Y	N	Y	Y	N	Y	N
Symms	Y	Y	N	Y	Y	N	Y	N
ILLINOIS								
Dixon	N	Y	Y	Y	N	Y	N	N
Simon	N	Y	Y	Y	Y	Y	N	Y
INDIANA								
Coats	Y	N	Y	N	N	N	N	N
Lugar	Y	N	Y	N	Y	N	N	N
IOWA								
Harkin	N	Y	Y	N	Y	Y	N	Y
Grassley	N	N	N	Y	N	N	N	N
KANSAS								
Dole	Y	N	Y	Y	Y	N	N	N
Kassebaum	Y	N	Y	N	Y	N	N	N
KENTUCKY								
Ford	N	N	Y	Y	X	Y	N	N
McConnell	Y	N	N	Y	N	N	N	N
LOUISIANA								
Breaux	Y	N	N	Y	Y	N	Y	Y
Johnston	Y	N	N	Y	Y	N	Y	Y
MAINE								
Mitchell	N	Y	Y	N	Y	Y	N	Y
Cohen	Y	N	Y	N	N	N	N	N
MARYLAND								
Mikulski	N	Y	Y	Y	N	Y	N	Y
Sarbanes	N	Y	Y	Y	Y	Y	N	Y
MASSACHUSETTS								
Kennedy	N	Y	Y	N	Y	Y	N	Y
Kerry	N	Y	Y	N	N	Y	N	Y
MICHIGAN								
Levin	N	N	Y	N	N	Y	N	Y
Riegle	N	N	Y	N	N	Y	N	Y
MINNESOTA								
Wellstone	N	Y	Y	N	N	Y	N	Y
Durenberger	Y	Y	Y	Y	Y	N	N	N
MISSISSIPPI								
Cochran	Y	N	N	Y	Y	N	N	N
Lott	Y	N	N	Y	Y	N	Y	N
MISSOURI								
Bond	Y	N	N	N	N	N	Y	N
Danforth	Y	N	N	Y	Y	N	N	N
MONTANA								
Baucus	N	Y	N	Y	Y	N	N	Y
Burns	Y	N	N	N	Y	N	Y	N
NEBRASKA								
Exon	N	Y	Y	N	Y	N	N	N
Kerrey	N	Y	Y	N	Y	Y	N	Y
NEVADA								
Bryan	Y	N	Y	N	N	Y	Y	Y
Reid	Y	Y	Y	Y	N	Y	N	Y
NEW HAMPSHIRE								
Rudman	Y	Y	Y	Y	Y	N	Y	N
Smith	Y	Y	N	N	Y	Y	Y	N
NEW JERSEY								
Bradley	N	Y	Y	N	N	Y	N	Y
Lautenberg	N	Y	Y	N	N	Y	N	Y
NEW MEXICO								
Bingaman	N	N	Y	Y	Y	Y	N	Y
Domenici	Y	Y	Y	Y	Y	N	N	N
NEW YORK								
Moynihan	N	Y	Y	Y	Y	Y	Y	Y
D'Amato	Y	Y	Y	Y	N	Y	N	N
NORTH CAROLINA								
Sanford	N	Y	Y	N	N	Y	Y	Y
Helms	Y	N	N	Y	N	Y	Y	N
NORTH DAKOTA								
Burdick	N	Y	Y	Y	Y	N	N	Y
Conrad	N	N	Y	N	N	N	Y	Y
OHIO								
Glenn	N	N	Y	Y	N	Y	Y	N
Metzenbaum	N	N	Y	N	Y	Y	N	Y
OKLAHOMA								
Boren	N	N	Y	Y	Y	Y	Y	N
Nickles	Y	Y	N	Y	N	N	N	N
OREGON								
Hatfield	N	N	Y	Y	Y	N	N	N
Packwood	Y	N	Y	Y	N	N	N	N
PENNSYLVANIA								
Wofford [2]		N	Y	Y	N	Y	N	Y
Specter	Y	N	N	Y	N	N	N	N
RHODE ISLAND								
Pell	N	Y	Y	Y	Y	Y	N	Y
Chafee	Y	Y	Y	N	Y	N	N	Y
SOUTH CAROLINA								
Hollings	N	N	N	N	N	Y	Y	N
Thurmond	Y	N	Y	Y	Y	N	Y	N
SOUTH DAKOTA								
Daschle	N	N	Y	Y	N	Y	N	Y
Pressler	Y	Y	N	Y	N	N	N	N
TENNESSEE								
Gore	Y	N	Y	N	N	Y	N	Y
Sasser	N	N	Y	N	N	Y	N	Y
TEXAS								
Bentsen	N	Y	Y	Y	Y	Y	N	N
Gramm	Y	Y	N	Y	N	N	Y	N
UTAH								
Garn	Y	Y	N	Y	Y	Y	Y	N
Hatch	Y	N	N	Y	N	N	N	N
VERMONT								
Leahy	N	Y	N	N	Y	Y	N	N
Jeffords	Y	Y	Y	N	Y	N	N	Y
VIRGINIA								
Robb	Y	N	Y	Y	Y	Y	N	N
Warner	Y	N	Y	Y	Y	N	Y	N
WASHINGTON								
Adams	N	Y	Y	N	N	Y	N	Y
Gorton	Y	Y	Y	Y	Y	N	N	N
WEST VIRGINIA								
Byrd	N	Y	Y	Y	Y	Y	Y	N
Rockefeller	N	Y	Y	Y	Y	Y	N	Y
WISCONSIN								
Kohl	N	Y	Y	N	N	Y	N	Y
Kasten	Y	N	Y	Y	N	N	N	N
WYOMING								
Simpson	Y	Y	N	N	Y	N	N	N
Wallop	Y	Y	N	Y	Y	Y	Y	N

KEY

Y	Voted for (yea).
#	Paired for.
+	Announced for.
N	Voted against (nay).
X	Paired against.
-	Announced against.
P	Voted "present."
C	Voted "present" to avoid possible conflict of interest.
?	Did not vote or otherwise make a position known.

Democrats ***Republicans***

ND Northern Democrats SD Southern Democrats Southern states - Ala., Ark., Fla., Ga., Ky., La., Miss., N.C., Okla., S.C., Tenn., Texas, Va.

[1] *Sen. John Seymour, R-Calif., was sworn in Jan. 10, 1991, to succeed Pete Wilson, R, who resigned Jan. 7, 1991.*

[2] *Sen. Harris Wofford, D-Pa., was sworn in May 9, 1991, to succeed John Heinz, R, who died April 4, 1991. Heinz voted "yea" on key vote 1.*

1. S J Res 2. Use of Force Against Iraq/Passage. Passage of the joint resolution to authorize military force if Iraq has not withdrawn from Kuwait and complied with U.N. Security Council resolutions by Jan. 15. The resolution authorizes using force and expending funds under the War Powers Act. Passed 52-47: R 42-2; D 10-45 (ND 3-35, SD 7-10), Jan. 12, 1991. A "yea" was a vote supporting the president's position.

2. S 1204. Surface Transportation Reauthorization/Interstate Maintenance. Moynihan, D-N.Y., motion to table (kill) the Lott, R-Miss., amendment to retain the current 90 percent federal share for Interstate maintenance and 80 percent for bridge projects. Motion agreed to 53-44: R 20-23; D 33-21 (ND 30-9, SD 3-12), June 19, 1991.

3. S 1241. Crime Bill/Handgun Waiting Period. Dole, R-Kan., amendment to require a waiting period of five business days before handgun purchases, during which time a mandatory background check of the prospective handgun buyers would be conducted, and to require the attorney general within six months of enactment to select a system and computer software for a National Instant Check system that within five years would be able to provide a record of criminal activity. Adopted 67-32: R 19-24; D 48-8 (ND 37-3, SD 11-5), June 28, 1991.

4. HR 2427. Fiscal 1992 Energy and Water Appropriations/Superconducting Supercollider. Johnston, D-La., motion to table (kill) the Bumpers, D-Ark., amendment to eliminate all funding for the superconducting supercollider by reducing the bill's funding level for the General Science and Research Activities account by $508,700,000. Motion agreed to 62-37: R 33-10; D 29-27 (ND 19-21, SD 10-6), July 10, 1991. A "yea" was a vote supporting the president's position.

5. HR 2506. Fiscal 1992 Legislative Branch Appropriations/Pay Raise. Byrd, D-W.Va., amendment to raise senators' pay from $101,900 to $125,100, ban senators' honoraria and limit outside earned income to 15 percent of a senator's base pay. Adopted 53-45: R 25-18; D 28-27 (ND 22-18, SD 6-9), July 17, 1991.

6. HR 2212. Conditional MFN for China in 1992/Passage. Passage of the bill to prohibit the president from granting China most-favored-nation status for the 12-month period beginning July 3, 1992, unless he reports that China has accounted for and released all political prisoners and made progress in human rights, among other conditions. Passed 55-44: R 6-37; D 49-7 (ND 36-4, SD 13-3), July 23, 1991. A "nay" was a vote supporting the president's position.

7. S 1507. Fiscal 1992-93 Defense Authorization/Women in Combat Pilot Positions. Glenn, D-Ohio, motion to table (kill) the Roth, R-Del., amendment to repeal the 1948 law that prohibits women from flying in combat pilot positions. Motion rejected 30-69: R 14-29; D 16-40 (ND 6-34, SD 10-6), July 31, 1991. (The Roth amendment was subsequently adopted by voice vote.)

8. S 1507. Fiscal 1992-93 Defense Authorization/Strategic Stability. Bingaman, D-N.M., amendment to state that it is the United States' goal to maintain strategic stability with the Soviet Union while deploying an anti-ballistic missile system with one or more ground-based sites and space-based sensors. The amendment would clarify that current actions undertaken by the United States are treaty compliant. Rejected 43-56: R 2-41; D 41-15 (ND 33-7, SD 8-8), July 31, 1991. A "nay" was a vote supporting the president's position.

	9	10	11	12	13	14	15	16
ALABAMA								
Heflin	N	Y	N	N	Y	Y	Y	Y
Shelby	N	Y	N	Y	Y	Y	Y	Y
ALASKA								
Murkowski	N	N	Y	Y	Y	Y	Y	Y
Stevens	N	N	Y	Y	Y	Y	Y	Y
ARIZONA								
DeConcini	?	Y	Y	Y	Y	Y	N	Y
McCain	N	N	Y	Y	Y	Y	Y	Y
ARKANSAS								
Bumpers	N	Y	Y	N	Y	Y	N	Y
Pryor	N	Y	?	N	Y	Y	N	?
CALIFORNIA								
Cranston	?	Y	Y	N	Y	N	?	Y
Seymour	N	N	N	Y	Y	Y	Y	N
COLORADO								
Wirth	Y	Y	Y	N	Y	N	+	Y
Brown	N	N	N	Y	Y	Y	Y	N
CONNECTICUT								
Dodd	N	Y	Y	N	Y	Y	N	Y
Lieberman	N	Y	Y	N	Y	N	Y	Y
DELAWARE								
Biden	Y	Y	Y	N	Y	N	N	Y
Roth	?	N	Y	Y	Y	N	Y	Y
FLORIDA								
Graham	N	Y	Y	N	Y	N	Y	Y
Mack	N	N	N	Y	Y	N	Y	Y
GEORGIA								
Fowler	N	Y	Y	Y	Y	N	N	Y
Nunn	N	Y	Y	Y	Y	Y	Y	Y
HAWAII								
Akaka	Y	Y	Y	N	Y	Y	Y	+
Inouye	N	Y	Y	N	Y	Y	Y	Y
IDAHO								
Craig	N	N	N	Y	Y	Y	Y	N
Symms	N	N	N	Y	N	Y	Y	N
ILLINOIS								
Dixon	N	Y	Y	Y	Y	N	N	?
Simon	Y	Y	Y	N	Y	N	N	Y
INDIANA								
Coats	N	N	Y	Y	N	Y	Y	Y
Lugar	N	N	N	Y	Y	Y	Y	Y
IOWA								
Harkin	Y	Y	?	N	Y	N	N	?
Grassley	N	N	N	Y	Y	N	Y	Y
KANSAS								
Dole	N	N	N	Y	Y	Y	Y	Y
Kassebaum	N	N	N	Y	Y	Y	Y	Y
KENTUCKY								
Ford	N	Y	Y	N	Y	Y	Y	Y
McConnell	N	N	N	Y	Y	Y	Y	Y
LOUISIANA								
Breaux	N	Y	Y	Y	Y	Y	Y	Y
Johnston	N	Y	Y	Y	Y	Y	Y	Y
MAINE								
Mitchell	Y	Y	Y	N	Y	Y	N	Y
Cohen	N	Y	Y	Y	Y	N	Y	Y
MARYLAND								
Mikulski	N	Y	Y	N	Y	N	Y	Y
Sarbanes	Y	Y	Y	N	Y	N	N	Y
MASSACHUSETTS								
Kennedy	Y	Y	Y	N	Y	N	N	Y
Kerry	Y	Y	Y	N	Y	N	N	Y
MICHIGAN								
Levin	N	Y	Y	N	Y	N	N	Y
Riegle	Y	Y	Y	N	Y	N	N	Y
MINNESOTA								
Wellstone	Y	Y	Y	N	Y	N	N	Y
Durenberger	N	N	Y	Y	Y	N	Y	Y
MISSISSIPPI								
Cochran	N	N	N	Y	Y	Y	Y	Y
Lott	N	N	N	Y	Y	N	Y	Y
MISSOURI								
Bond	N	N	Y	Y	Y	N	Y	Y
Danforth	N	N	Y	Y	Y	Y	Y	Y
MONTANA								
Baucus	Y	Y	Y	N	Y	N	N	Y
Burns	N	N	N	Y	Y	Y	Y	Y
NEBRASKA								
Exon	N	Y	Y	Y	Y	N	N	Y
Kerrey	N	Y	?	N	?	X	?	?
NEVADA								
Bryan	N	Y	Y	N	Y	N	Y	Y
Reid	N	Y	Y	N	Y	N	Y	Y
NEW HAMPSHIRE								
Rudman	N	N	N	Y	Y	Y	Y	Y
Smith	N	N	N	Y	N	N	Y	N
NEW JERSEY								
Bradley	Y	Y	Y	N	Y	N	N	Y
Lautenberg	Y	Y	Y	N	Y	N	N	Y
NEW MEXICO								
Bingaman	N	Y	Y	N	Y	Y	N	Y
Domenici	N	N	N	Y	Y	Y	Y	Y
NEW YORK								
Moynihan	N	Y	Y	N	Y	N	N	Y
D'Amato	N	Y	Y	Y	Y	Y	Y	Y
NORTH CAROLINA								
Sanford	N	Y	Y	N	Y	N	Y	Y
Helms	N	N	N	Y	N	Y	Y	?
NORTH DAKOTA								
Burdick	Y	Y	Y	N	Y	N	N	Y
Conrad	Y	Y	Y	N	Y	Y	N	Y
OHIO								
Glenn	N	Y	Y	N	Y	N	Y	Y
Metzenbaum	Y	Y	Y	N	Y	N	N	Y
OKLAHOMA								
Boren	N	Y	N	Y	Y	?	Y	Y
Nickles	N	N	N	Y	Y	Y	Y	N
OREGON								
Hatfield	Y	Y	Y	Y	Y	Y	Y	Y
Packwood	Y	Y	Y	N	Y	Y	Y	Y
PENNSYLVANIA								
Wofford	Y	Y	Y	N	?	?	?	Y
Specter	Y	Y	Y	Y	Y	Y	Y	Y
RHODE ISLAND								
Pell	Y	Y	Y	N	Y	#	Y	Y
Chafee	N	Y	Y	Y	Y	N	Y	Y
SOUTH CAROLINA								
Hollings	Y	Y	N	Y	Y	N	N	Y
Thurmond	N	N	N	Y	Y	Y	Y	Y
SOUTH DAKOTA								
Daschle	Y	Y	Y	N	Y	Y	N	Y
Pressler	N	N	N	Y	Y	Y	Y	N
TENNESSEE								
Gore	N	Y	Y	N	Y	N	N	Y
Sasser	N	Y	Y	N	Y	N	N	Y
TEXAS								
Bentsen	N	Y	Y	N	Y	Y	Y	Y
Gramm	N	N	N	Y	Y	?	Y	Y
UTAH								
Garn	N	N	N	Y	Y	Y	Y	Y
Hatch	N	N	N	Y	Y	Y	+	Y
VERMONT								
Leahy	Y	Y	Y	N	Y	N	Y	Y
Jeffords	N	Y	Y	N	Y	?	Y	Y
VIRGINIA								
Robb	N	Y	Y	Y	Y	N	Y	Y
Warner	N	N	N	Y	Y	Y	Y	Y
WASHINGTON								
Adams	Y	Y	Y	N	Y	N	N	Y
Gorton	N	N	N	Y	Y	Y	Y	Y
WEST VIRGINIA								
Byrd	N	Y	Y	N	Y	Y	Y	Y
Rockefeller	Y	Y	Y	N	Y	N	N	Y
WISCONSIN								
Kohl	Y	Y	Y	N	Y	N	Y	Y
Kasten	N	Y	N	Y	Y	Y	Y	Y
WYOMING								
Simpson	N	N	N	Y	Y	Y	Y	Y
Wallop	N	N	N	Y	N	Y	Y	N

KEY

Y	Voted for (yea).
#	Paired for.
+	Announced for.
N	Voted against (nay).
X	Paired against.
-	Announced against.
P	Voted "present."
C	Voted "present" to avoid possible conflict of interest.
?	Did not vote or otherwise make a position known.

Democrats *Republicans*

ND Northern Democrats SD Southern Democrats

Southern states - Ala.. Ark., Fla., Ga., Ky., La., Miss., N.C., Okla., S.C., Tenn., Texas, Va.

9. HR 2707. Fiscal 1992 Labor, HHS, and Education Appropriations/Budget Waiver. Harkin, D-Iowa, motion to waive the Budget Act with respect to the Harkin amendment to the committee amendment, to rescind $3.148 billion in budget authority from unobligated balances in Defense Department accounts from fiscal 1988-91, and transfer the $3.148 billion in budget authority to domestic programs. Motion rejected 28-69: R 3-39; D 25-30 (ND 24-14, SD 1-16), Sept. 10, 1991. A "nay" was a vote supporting the president's position.

10. S 1722. Unemployment Benefits Extension/Conference Report. Adoption of the conference report to provide an estimated $6.4 billion for up to 20 additional weeks of unemployment benefits based on a state's unemployment rate. The conference report designates the spending as an emergency and would not require a presidential declaration to be exempt from budget agreement limits. Adopted 65-35: R 8-35; 57-0 (ND 40-0, SD 17-0), Oct. 1, 1991. A "nay" was a vote supporting the president's position.

11. S 5. Family and Medical Leave Act/Substitute. Bond, R-Mo., substitute amendment to raise the number of hours an employee must work in order to be eligible for up to 12 weeks of unpaid leave for the birth or adoption of a child or for the serious illness of the worker or an immediate family member. Adopted 65-32: R 15-28; D 50-4 (ND 38-0, SD 12-4), Oct. 2, 1991. A "nay" was a vote supporting the president's position.

12. Thomas Nomination/Confirmation. Confirmation of President Bush's nomination of Clarence Thomas of Georgia to be an associate justice of the U.S. Supreme Court. Confirmed 52-48: R 41-2; D 11-46 (ND 3-37, SD 8-9), Oct. 15, 1991. A "yea" was a vote supporting the president's position.

13. S 1745. Civil Rights Act of 1991/Passage. Passage of the bill to make it easier to sue for employment discrimination and permit women, religious minorities and the disabled to win compensatory and punitive damages for intentional discrimination, mainly by reversing several recent Supreme Court decisions and by expanding Title VII of the 1964 Civil Rights Act. Passed 93-5: R 38-5; D 55-0 (ND 38-0, SD 17-0), Oct. 30, 1991. A "yea" was a vote supporting the president's position.

14. S 1220. National Energy Policy/Cloture. Mitchell, D-Maine, motion to invoke cloture (thus limiting debate) on the Johnston, D-La., motion to proceed to the bill to allow drilling in the Arctic National Wildlife Refuge, mandate that federal and private vehicle fleets use alternative fuels and direct the secretary of Transportation to adopt new corporate average fuel economy (CAFE) standards, and enact other programs related to energy production and consumption. Motion rejected 50-44: R 32-9; D 18-35 (ND 9-28, SD 9-7), Nov. 1, 1991. A three-fifths majority (60) of the total Senate is required to invoke cloture.

15. Gates Nomination/Confirmation. Confirmation of President Bush's nomination of Robert M. Gates of Virginia to be director of central intelligence. Confirmed 64-31: R 42-0; D 22-31 (ND 11-25, SD 11-6), Nov. 5, 1991. A "yea" was a vote supporting the president's position.

16. HR 3807. CFE Treaty Implementation/Dismantlement of Soviet Weapons. Nunn, D-Ga., amendment to authorize $500 million in defense funds to assist the Soviet Union and its republics with the dismantlement of Soviet nuclear, chemical and other weapons. Adopted 86-8: R 34-8; D 52-0 (ND 36-0, SD 16-0), Nov. 25, 1991.

1. H J Res 77. Use of Force Against Iraq/Passage. Passage of the joint resolution to authorize the use of military force if Iraq has not withdrawn from Kuwait and complied with U.N. Security Council resolutions by Jan. 15. The resolution authorizes the use of force and expenditure of funds under the War Powers Act. Passed 250-183: R 164-3; D 86-179 (ND 33-147, SD 53-32); I 0-1, Jan. 12, 1991. A "yea" was a vote supporting the president's position.

2. HR 1315. RTC Financing/Passage. Passage of the bill to provide $30 billion to the Resolution Trust Corporation to cover fiscal 1991 losses of failed thrifts; also requires that requests for more money for the RTC be accompanied by a spending plan. Rejected 201-220: R 120-42; D 81-177 (ND 44-132, SD 37-45); I 0-1, March 12, 1991. A "yea" was a vote supporting the president's position.

3. HR 7. Handgun Waiting Period/Passage. Passage of the bill to require a seven-day waiting period for handgun purchases, allowing local law enforcement authorities to check whether prospective buyers have a criminal record. The waiting period requirement would end when a national computer system for instant checks became operational. Passed 239-186: R 60-102; D 179-83 (ND 138-41, SD 41-42); I 0-1, May 8, 1991.

4. HR 2100. Fiscal 1992 Defense Authorization/SDI. Dellums, D-Calif., amendment to terminate the strategic defense initiative program and permit only a basic SDI research program funded at $1.1 billion. Rejected 118-266: R 2-149; D 115-117 (ND 104-55, SD 11-62); I 1-0, May 20, 1991. A "nay" was a vote supporting the president's position.

5. H Res 101. Disapproval of Fast-Track Procedures/Adoption. Adoption of the resolution to disapprove the president's request to extend for two more years fast-track procedures that would require legislation implementing trade agreements to be considered within 60 days of introduction under limited debate and with no amendments permitted. Rejected 192-231: R 21-140; D 170-91 (ND 128-50, SD 42-41); I 1-0, May 23, 1991. A "nay" was a vote supporting the president's position.

6. HR 2427. Fiscal 1992 Energy and Water Appropriations/Superconducting Supercollider. Slattery, D-Kan., amendment to eliminate all funding for the superconducting super collider, $434 million, primarily by reducing the bill's funding level for general science and research activities. Rejected 165-251: R 58-101; D 106-150 (ND 86-87, SD 20-63); I 1-0, May 29, 1991. A "nay" was a vote supporting the president's position.

7. HR 1. Civil Rights Act of 1991/Passage. Passage of the bill to reverse or modify a series of Supreme Court rulings that narrowed the reach and remedies of job discrimination laws and to authorize compensatory and punitive damages for victims of discrimination based on sex, religion or disability. Passed 273-158: R 22-143; D 250-15 (ND 177-4, SD 73-11); I 1-0, June 5, 1991. A "nay" was a vote supporting the president's position.

8. HR 2519. Fiscal 1992 VA and HUD Appropriations/Restore Space Station Funding. Chapman, D-Texas, en bloc amendments to provide $1.9 billion for the space station *Freedom*, restoring its funding to the fiscal 1991 level, and to offset the increase by holding all NASA programs to fiscal 1991 levels — a decrease of $1.7 billion — and by cutting $217 million from public housing operating subsidies. Adopted 240-173: R 133-27; D 107-145 (ND 55-114, SD 52-31); I 0-1, June 6, 1991. A "yea" was a vote supporting the president's position.

KEY

Y	Voted for (yea).
#	Paired for.
+	Announced for.
N	Voted against (nay).
X	Paired against.
-	Announced against.
P	Voted "present."
C	Voted "present" to avoid possible conflict of interest.
?	Did not vote or otherwise make a position known.

Democrats ***Republicans***
Independent

ND	Northern Democrats
SD	Southern Democrats

Southern states - Ala., Ark., Fla., Ga., Ky., La., Miss., N.C., Okla., S.C., Tenn., Texas, Va.

	1	2	3	4	5	6	7	8
ALABAMA								
1 ***Callahan***	Y	Y	N	N	N	N	N	Y
2 ***Dickinson***	Y	Y	N	N	N	Y	N	Y
3 Browder	Y	N	N	N	#	N	Y	Y
4 Bevill	Y	N	N	N	Y	N	Y	Y
5 Cramer	Y	N	N	N	Y	N	Y	Y
6 Erdreich	Y	Y	N	N	Y	N	Y	Y
7 Harris	Y	N	N	N	Y	N	Y	Y
ALASKA								
AL ***Young***	Y	Y	N	N	N	N	N	Y
ARIZONA								
1 ***Rhodes***	Y	Y	N	N	N	N	N	Y
2 Udall [1]	?	?						
3 ***Stump***	Y	Y	N	N	N	N	N	Y
4 ***Kyl***	Y	Y	N	N	N	N	N	Y
5 ***Kolbe***	Y	Y	N	N	N	Y	N	N
ARKANSAS								
1 Alexander	N	Y	N	?	Y	N	Y	N
2 Thornton	Y	N	N	N	N	N	Y	Y
3 ***Hammerschmidt***	Y	?	N	N	N	N	N	Y
4 Anthony	N	Y	Y	?	N	N	Y	N
CALIFORNIA								
1 ***Riggs***	N	Y	Y	N	N	N	N	Y
2 ***Herger***	Y	N	N	N	N	Y	N	Y
3 Matsui	N	?	Y	Y	N	N	Y	Y
4 Fazio	N	Y	Y	N	N	N	Y	Y
5 Pelosi	N	N	Y	Y	N	N	Y	N
6 Boxer	N	N	Y	Y	Y	Y	Y	N
7 Miller	N	N	Y	Y	Y	Y	Y	N
8 Dellums	N	N	Y	Y	Y	N	Y	N
9 Stark	N	N	Y	Y	Y	Y	Y	N
10 Edwards	N	Y	Y	Y	Y	N	Y	Y
11 Lantos	Y	N	Y	N	Y	Y	Y	Y
12 ***Campbell***	Y	Y	Y	+	N	Y	Y	Y
13 Mineta	N	Y	Y	Y	Y	N	Y	Y
14 ***Doolittle***	Y	Y	N	X	N	N	N	Y
15 Condit	Y	N	N	Y	Y	N	Y	N
16 Panetta	N	Y	Y	Y	N	N	Y	N
17 Dooley	N	N	Y	N	N	Y	Y	Y
18 Lehman	Y	Y	Y	?	Y	N	Y	Y
19 ***Lagomarsino***	Y	Y	Y	N	N	N	N	Y
20 ***Thomas***	Y	Y	Y	N	N	N	N	Y
21 ***Gallegly***	Y	Y	Y	N	N	N	N	Y
22 ***Moorhead***	Y	Y	N	N	N	Y	N	Y
23 Beilenson	N	Y	Y	Y	N	Y	Y	N
24 Waxman	N	Y	Y	Y	Y	N	Y	N
25 Roybal	N	N	?	?	N	N	Y	N
26 Berman	Y	Y	Y	Y	N	N	Y	N
27 Levine	Y	Y	Y	Y	?	N	Y	Y
28 Dixon	N	N	Y	?	Y	N	Y	Y
29 Waters	N	N	Y	Y	Y	Y	Y	N
30 Martinez	N	N	Y	?	Y	N	Y	?
31 Dymally	-	N	Y	Y	Y	N	Y	#
32 Anderson	Y	Y	Y	?	N	N	Y	Y
33 ***Dreier***	Y	Y	N	N	N	N	N	Y
34 Torres	N	N	Y	+	Y	N	Y	Y
35 ***Lewis***	Y	Y	N	N	N	N	N	Y
36 Brown	N	N	Y	N	Y	N	Y	Y
37 ***McCandless***	Y	Y	N	N	N	N	N	Y
38 ***Dornan***	Y	Y	Y	N	X	N	N	Y
39 ***Dannemeyer***	Y	Y	N	N	N	N	N	Y
40 ***Cox***	Y	N	N	N	N	N	N	Y
41 ***Lowery***	Y	Y	Y	N	N	N	N	Y
42 ***Rohrabacher***	Y	N	N	N	N	Y	N	Y
43 ***Packard***	Y	N	Y	N	N	N	N	Y
44 ***Cunningham***	Y	N	N	N	N	N	N	Y
45 ***Hunter***	Y	Y	N	N	Y	N	N	Y
COLORADO								
1 Schroeder	N	N	Y	Y	N	Y	Y	N
2 Skaggs	N	Y	Y	Y	N	N	Y	N
3 Campbell	Y	N	N	?	Y	Y	Y	?
4 ***Allard***	Y	N	N	N	N	N	N	Y
5 ***Hefley***	Y	N	N	N	N	Y	N	Y
6 ***Schaefer***	Y	N	N	N	N	Y	N	Y
CONNECTICUT								
1 Kennelly	N	N	Y	N	N	N	Y	Y
2 Gejdenson	N	N	Y	Y	Y	Y	Y	Y
3 DeLauro	N	N	Y	Y	Y	N	Y	N
4 ***Shays***	Y	Y	Y	Y	N	Y	Y	N
5 ***Franks***	Y	Y	N	N	N	N	N	Y
6 ***Johnson***	Y	Y	Y	N	N	Y	N	Y
DELAWARE								
AL Carper	Y	Y	Y	Y	N	N	Y	N
FLORIDA								
1 Hutto	Y	N	Y	N	N	N	N	Y
2 Peterson	N	N	N	N	Y	Y	Y	Y
3 Bennett	N	N	Y	N	N	Y	Y	Y
4 ***James***	Y	N	Y	N	N	Y	N	Y
5 ***McCollum***	Y	Y	N	N	X	N	N	Y
6 ***Stearns***	Y	N	Y	N	Y	N	N	Y
7 Gibbons	N	N	Y	N	N	N	Y	Y
8 ***Young***	Y	N	Y	N	N	N	N	Y
9 ***Bilirakis***	Y	Y	Y	N	N	Y	N	Y
10 ***Ireland***	Y	Y	N	N	N	N	N	Y
11 Bacchus	Y	N	Y	N	N	?	Y	Y
12 ***Lewis***	Y	N	N	N	N	N	N	Y
13 ***Goss***	Y	Y	Y	N	N	N	N	Y
14 Johnston	N	Y	Y	Y	Y	Y	Y	N
15 ***Shaw***	Y	Y	N	N	N	N	N	Y
16 Smith	N	Y	Y	Y	Y	N	Y	N
17 Lehman	N	Y	?	#	?	N	Y	N
18 ***Ros-Lehtinen***	Y	Y	Y	N	N	Y	Y	N
19 Fascell	Y	Y	Y	N	N	N	Y	Y
GEORGIA								
1 Thomas	Y	Y	N	N	Y	N	Y	Y
2 Hatcher	Y	Y	Y	N	Y	N	Y	N
3 Ray	Y	Y	N	N	Y	N	Y	N
4 Jones	Y	N	Y	N	Y	Y	Y	N
5 Lewis	N	N	Y	?	Y	Y	Y	N
6 ***Gingrich***	Y	Y	N	N	N	N	N	Y
7 Darden	Y	Y	Y	N	Y	N	N	Y
8 Rowland	Y	Y	Y	N	Y	N	Y	N
9 Jenkins	N	Y	N	N	Y	N	N	Y
10 Barnard	Y	Y	N	N	Y	N	N	Y
HAWAII								
1 Abercrombie	N	N	Y	Y	Y	N	Y	N
2 Mink	N	N	Y	Y	Y	N	Y	N
IDAHO								
1 LaRocco	N	N	N	?	N	N	Y	Y
2 Stallings	N	N	N	N	Y	N	Y	Y
ILLINOIS								
1 Hayes	N	N	Y	Y	Y	Y	Y	N
2 Savage	N	N	Y	Y	Y	N	Y	N
3 Russo	N	N	Y	Y	Y	Y	N	N
4 Sangmeister	N	N	Y	Y	Y	Y	Y	N
5 Lipinski	N	N	Y	N	Y	Y	N	Y
6 ***Hyde***	Y	Y	Y	N	N	N	N	Y
7 Collins	N	N	Y	Y	Y	Y	Y	N
8 Rostenkowski	Y	Y	Y	N	N	Y	Y	N
9 Yates	N	N	Y	Y	Y	N	Y	N
10 ***Porter***	Y	Y	Y	N	N	Y	N	Y
11 Annunzio	N	N	Y	N	Y	N	N	Y
12 ***Crane***	Y	N	N	?	N	?	N	Y
13 ***Fawell***	Y	Y	Y	N	N	N	N	Y
14 ***Hastert***	Y	Y	N	N	N	N	N	Y
15 Madigan [2]	Y							
16 Cox	N	Y	Y	Y	N	Y	Y	N
17 Evans	N	N	Y	Y	Y	Y	Y	N
18 ***Michel***	Y	Y	?	N	N	N	N	Y
19 Bruce	N	N	N	Y	Y	N	Y	N
20 Durbin	N	Y	Y	Y	Y	Y	Y	N
21 Costello	N	N	N	N	Y	N	Y	N
22 Poshard	N	N	N	Y	Y	Y	Y	N
INDIANA								
1 Visclosky	N	N	Y	N	Y	Y	Y	N
2 Sharp	N	N	Y	-	N	Y	Y	N
3 Roemer	N	N	Y	N	Y	N	Y	N

[1] *Rep. Morris K. Udall, D-Ariz., resigned May 4, 1991.*
[2] *Rep. Edward R. Madigan, R-Ill., resigned March 8, 1991.*
[3] *Rep. Silvio O. Conte, R-Mass., died Feb. 8, 1991.*
[4] *Rep. Sam Johnson, R-Texas, was sworn in May 22, 1991, to succeed Steve Bartlett, R, who resigned March 11, 1991. Bartlett voted "yea" on key vote 1.*

	1	2	3	4	5	6	7	8
4 Long	N	N	N	Y	Y	Y	Y	Y
5 Jontz	N	N	N	Y	Y	Y	Y	N
6 ***Burton***	Y	Y	N	N	N	Y	N	Y
7 ***Myers***	Y	Y	N	N	N	N	N	Y
8 McCloskey	N	N	Y	N	Y	N	Y	N
9 Hamilton	N	Y	Y	N	N	Y	Y	N
10 Jacobs	N	N	Y	Y	Y	Y	Y	N
IOWA								
1 ***Leach***	Y	Y	Y	Y	N	Y	Y	N
2 ***Nussle***	Y	N	N	N	N	N	N	N
3 Nagle	N	N	N	?	Y	N	Y	N
4 Smith	N	Y	N	N	N	N	Y	N
5 ***Lightfoot***	Y	Y	N	N	N	N	N	Y
6 ***Grandy***	Y	Y	N	N	N	Y	N	N
KANSAS								
1 ***Roberts***	Y	Y	N	N	N	N	N	Y
2 Slattery	Y	N	N	N	N	Y	Y	Y
3 ***Meyers***	Y	Y	Y	N	Y	Y	N	Y
4 Glickman	Y	N	Y	N	Y	Y	Y	Y
5 ***Nichols***	Y	Y	N	N	N	N	N	Y
KENTUCKY								
1 Hubbard	Y	Y	Y	?	N	N	Y	Y
2 Natcher	N	N	N	N	Y	N	Y	N
3 Mazzoli	N	N	Y	N	N	N	Y	N
4 ***Bunning***	Y	Y	N	N	N	Y	N	N
5 ***Rogers***	Y	N	N	-	N	N	N	Y
6 ***Hopkins***	Y	N	N	?	?	?	N	Y
7 Perkins	N	N	N	Y	Y	N	Y	Y
LOUISIANA								
1 ***Livingston***	Y	Y	N	N	N	N	N	Y
2 Jefferson	N	N	Y	Y	N	N	Y	Y
3 Tauzin	Y	N	N	N	N	N	Y	Y
4 ***McCrery***	Y	Y	N	N	N	N	N	Y
5 Huckaby	Y	Y	N	N	N	N	N	?
6 ***Baker***	Y	Y	N	N	N	N	N	Y
7 Hayes	Y	P	N	N	Y	N	N	Y
8 ***Holloway***	Y	Y	N	N	Y	N	N	Y
MAINE								
1 Andrews	N	N	Y	Y	Y	Y	Y	N
2 ***Snowe***	Y	Y	N	N	Y	Y	Y	Y
MARYLAND								
1 ***Gilchrest***	Y	Y	Y	N	N	N	N	Y
2 ***Bentley***	Y	N	Y	N	Y	N	N	Y
3 Cardin	N	Y	Y	N	N	N	Y	Y
4 McMillen	Y	N	Y	N	N	N	Y	Y
5 Hoyer	N	Y	Y	N	N	N	Y	N
6 Byron	Y	Y	N	N	N	N	Y	Y
7 Mfume	N	N	Y	Y	Y	Y	Y	N
8 ***Morella***	N	Y	Y	N	N	Y	Y	Y
MASSACHUSETTS								
1 Conte [3]	N							
2 Neal	N	N	Y	Y	Y	Y	Y	Y
3 Early	N	N	Y	Y	Y	Y	Y	N
4 Frank	N	N	Y	Y	Y	Y	Y	N
5 Atkins	N	N	Y	Y	N	Y	Y	N
6 Mavroules	N	N	Y	Y	Y	N	Y	N
7 Markey	N	N	Y	Y	Y	Y	Y	N
8 Kennedy	N	N	Y	Y	Y	N	Y	N
9 Moakley	N	N	Y	Y	Y	N	Y	N
10 Studds	N	N	Y	?	Y	Y	Y	N
11 Donnelly	N	N	Y	Y	N	Y	Y	N
MICHIGAN								
1 Conyers	N	N	Y	?	Y	Y	Y	N
2 ***Pursell***	Y	N	Y	N	N	N	N	N
3 Wolpe	N	N	Y	Y	Y	Y	Y	N
4 ***Upton***	Y	N	Y	N	N	Y	N	N
5 ***Henry***	Y	N	Y	N	N	Y	Y	N
6 Carr	N	N	N	N	Y	N	Y	N
7 Kildee	N	N	Y	Y	Y	N	Y	N
8 Traxler	N	Y	N	Y	Y	Y	Y	N
9 ***Vander Jagt***	Y	Y	N	N	N	Y	N	Y
10 ***Camp***	Y	N	N	N	N	Y	N	N
11 ***Davis***	Y	Y	N	N	N	Y	Y	Y
12 Bonior	N	Y	Y	Y	Y	?	Y	N
13 Collins	N	N	Y	Y	Y	Y	Y	N
14 Hertel	N	N	Y	Y	Y	Y	Y	N
15 Ford	N	N	Y	Y	Y	Y	Y	N
16 Dingell	Y	Y	N	N	Y	Y	Y	N
17 Levin	N	Y	Y	Y	Y	Y	Y	N
18 ***Broomfield***	Y	Y	Y	N	N	Y	N	Y
MINNESOTA								
1 Penny	N	N	N	N	N	Y	Y	N
2 ***Weber***	Y	Y	N	N	N	N	N	Y
3 ***Ramstad***	Y	N	N	N	N	#	N	N
4 Vento	N	Y	Y	Y	Y	Y	Y	X
5 Sabo	N	Y	Y	Y	Y	Y	Y	N
6 Sikorski	N	N	Y	Y	Y	Y	Y	N
7 Peterson	N	N	N	Y	Y	Y	Y	N
8 Oberstar	N	N	N	Y	Y	Y	Y	N
MISSISSIPPI								
1 Whitten	Y	N	?	?	Y	N	Y	N
2 Espy	N	N	N	Y	N	Y	Y	N
3 Montgomery	Y	Y	N	N	N	N	N	N
4 Parker	Y	Y	N	?	N	Y	N	N
5 Taylor	N	N	N	N	Y	N	N	Y
MISSOURI								
1 Clay	N	N	Y	Y	Y	N	Y	N
2 Horn	N	N	Y	N	Y	Y	Y	Y
3 Gephardt	N	Y	Y	Y	N	N	Y	Y
4 Skelton	Y	N	N	N	N	N	Y	N
5 Wheat	N	N	Y	Y	Y	N	Y	N
6 ***Coleman***	Y	Y	Y	?	N	N	N	Y
7 ***Hancock***	Y	Y	N	N	N	Y	N	Y
8 ***Emerson***	Y	Y	N	N	N	N	N	Y
9 Volkmer	Y	N	N	N	Y	N	Y	Y
MONTANA								
1 Williams	N	N	N	Y	#	Y	Y	?
2 ***Marlenee***	Y	N	N	N	Y	?	N	Y
NEBRASKA								
1 ***Bereuter***	Y	Y	N	N	N	Y	N	N
2 Hoagland	Y	Y	Y	N	Y	Y	Y	N
3 ***Barrett***	Y	Y	N	N	N	N	N	Y
NEVADA								
1 Bilbray	Y	N	N	N	Y	Y	Y	?
2 ***Vucanovich***	Y	Y	N	N	-	N	N	Y
NEW HAMPSHIRE								
1 ***Zeliff***	Y	Y	N	N	N	Y	N	Y
2 Swett	Y	Y	Y	N	Y	Y	Y	Y
NEW JERSEY								
1 Andrews	N	N	Y	N	Y	N	Y	Y
2 Hughes	Y	Y	Y	N	N	N	Y	N
3 Pallone	Y	N	Y	N	Y	Y	Y	Y
4 ***Smith***	Y	Y	Y	N	Y	N	N	Y
5 ***Roukema***	Y	Y	Y	N	N	Y	N	N
6 Dwyer	N	Y	Y	N	Y	N	Y	N
7 ***Rinaldo***	Y	N	Y	N	N	N	Y	Y
8 Roe	N	N	Y	N	Y	N	Y	Y
9 Torricelli	Y	N	Y	N	N	N	Y	Y
10 Payne	N	N	Y	?	Y	Y	Y	N
11 ***Gallo***	Y	Y	Y	N	N	N	N	?
12 ***Zimmer***	Y	Y	N	N	N	Y	Y	N
13 ***Saxton***	Y	Y	Y	N	N	N	N	Y
14 Guarini	N	N	Y	N	N	N	Y	N
NEW MEXICO								
1 ***Schiff***	Y	Y	N	N	N	N	Y	Y
2 ***Skeen***	Y	Y	N	N	N	N	N	Y
3 Richardson	N	N	N	N	N	N	Y	Y
NEW YORK								
1 Hochbrueckner	N	N	Y	N	Y	N	Y	Y
2 Downey	N	N	Y	Y	N	N	Y	Y
3 Mrazek	N	?	Y	Y	N	?	Y	?
4 ***Lent***	Y	Y	Y	?	N	N	N	Y
5 ***McGrath***	Y	N	Y	N	N	N	N	Y
6 Flake	N	?	Y	Y	Y	Y	Y	N
7 Ackerman	Y	N	Y	Y	Y	?	Y	X
8 Scheuer	N	N	Y	Y	Y	Y	Y	N
9 Manton	N	N	Y	N	Y	N	Y	N
10 Schumer	N	Y	Y	Y	N	N	Y	N
11 Towns	N	N	Y	Y	Y	N	Y	N
12 Owens	N	N	Y	Y	Y	Y	Y	N
13 Solarz	Y	N	Y	Y	N	Y	Y	N
14 ***Molinari***	Y	Y	Y	N	N	N	N	N
15 ***Green***	Y	Y	Y	N	N	N	Y	N
16 Rangel	N	N	Y	#	Y	N	Y	N
17 Weiss	N	N	Y	Y	Y	Y	Y	N
18 Serrano	N	N	Y	Y	Y	N	Y	N
19 Engel	Y	N	Y	Y	Y	?	Y	N
20 Lowey	N	N	Y	Y	Y	Y	Y	N
21 ***Fish***	Y	Y	Y	N	N	Y	Y	N
22 ***Gilman***	Y	Y	Y	N	Y	Y	Y	N
23 McNulty	Y	N	Y	N	Y	N	Y	N
24 ***Solomon***	Y	Y	N	N	Y	Y	N	#
25 ***Boehlert***	Y	Y	Y	N	N	Y	Y	Y
26 ***Martin***	Y	Y	?	N	N	Y	N	?
27 ***Walsh***	Y	Y	Y	N	N	N	Y	Y
28 McHugh	N	Y	Y	Y	N	N	Y	N
29 ***Horton***	Y	Y	N	N	N	?	Y	Y
30 Slaughter	N	N	Y	Y	Y	Y	Y	-
31 ***Paxon***	Y	Y	N	N	N	Y	N	N
32 LaFalce	N	N	Y	Y	Y	Y	Y	N
33 Nowak	N	N	Y	N	Y	Y	Y	N
34 ***Houghton***	Y	Y	N	N	N	N	Y	Y
NORTH CAROLINA								
1 Jones	Y	N	Y	N	Y	N	Y	Y
2 Valentine	Y	N	Y	N	Y	Y	Y	Y
3 Lancaster	Y	N	Y	N	Y	Y	Y	N
4 Price	N	Y	Y	N	N	N	Y	N
5 Neal	N	N	Y	?	Y	Y	Y	N
6 ***Coble***	Y	N	N	N	Y	Y	N	N
7 Rose	N	Y	Y	Y	Y	N	Y	N
8 Hefner	N	N	Y	N	Y	N	Y	N
9 ***McMillan***	Y	Y	Y	N	N	N	N	N
10 ***Ballenger***	Y	Y	N	N	Y	N	N	Y
11 ***Taylor***	Y	Y	N	N	Y	N	N	Y
NORTH DAKOTA								
AL Dorgan	N	N	N	Y	Y	Y	Y	N
OHIO								
1 Luken	Y	N	Y	N	N	N	Y	N
2 ***Gradison***	Y	Y	Y	N	N	Y	N	Y
3 Hall	N	?	Y	Y	N	Y	Y	Y
4 ***Oxley***	Y	Y	Y	N	N	N	N	Y
5 ***Gillmor***	Y	Y	N	N	N	Y	N	Y
6 ***McEwen***	Y	Y	N	N	N	N	N	Y
7 ***Hobson***	Y	Y	N	N	N	N	Y	Y
8 ***Boehner***	Y	Y	N	N	N	N	N	Y
9 Kaptur	N	N	Y	N	Y	N	Y	N
10 ***Miller***	Y	?	N	N	Y	N	N	Y
11 Eckart	N	N	Y	Y	Y	Y	Y	Y
12 ***Kasich***	Y	N	N	N	N	N	N	Y
13 Pease	N	Y	Y	Y	Y	N	Y	Y
14 Sawyer	N	N	Y	Y	N	Y	Y	Y
15 ***Wylie***	Y	Y	Y	N	N	N	N	Y
16 ***Regula***	Y	Y	Y	N	N	Y	N	Y
17 Traficant	N	N	Y	Y	Y	N	Y	Y
18 Applegate	N	N	N	?	Y	N	Y	Y
19 Feighan	N	N	Y	Y	Y	Y	Y	Y
20 Oakar	N	N	Y	Y	Y	N	Y	Y
21 Stokes	N	N	Y	Y	Y	N	Y	N
OKLAHOMA								
1 ***Inhofe***	Y	N	N	N	N	N	N	Y
2 Synar	N	N	Y	Y	N	Y	Y	N
3 Brewster	Y	N	N	?	Y	N	Y	Y
4 McCurdy	Y	N	Y	N	N	Y	Y	Y
5 ***Edwards***	Y	Y	N	N	N	N	N	Y
6 English	N	N	N	N	Y	N	Y	Y
OREGON								
1 AuCoin	N	Y	Y	Y	Y	?	Y	N
2 ***Smith***	Y	N	N	N	N	N	N	Y
3 Wyden	N	N	Y	Y	N	Y	Y	N
4 DeFazio	N	N	N	Y	Y	Y	Y	Y
5 Kopetski	N	Y	N	Y	N	N	Y	Y
PENNSYLVANIA								
1 Foglietta	N	N	Y	Y	Y	N	Y	N
2 Gray	N	N	Y	?	Y	N	Y	N
3 Borski	Y	N	Y	N	Y	N	Y	?
4 Kolter	N	N	N	?	Y	N	Y	Y
5 ***Schulze***	Y	N	N	N	N	Y	Y	Y
6 Yatron	N	N	N	?	Y	N	Y	Y
7 ***Weldon***	Y	N	Y	N	N	Y	N	N
8 Kostmayer	N	Y	Y	Y	N	Y	Y	?
9 ***Shuster***	Y	N	N	N	Y	Y	N	?
10 ***McDade***	Y	Y	Y	N	Y	N	N	Y
11 Kanjorski	N	N	N	N	Y	Y	Y	N
12 Murtha	Y	Y	N	N	Y	N	Y	N
13 ***Coughlin***	Y	Y	Y	N	N	Y	N	N
14 Coyne	N	N	Y	?	N	N	Y	N
15 ***Ritter***	Y	Y	N	N	N	Y	N	Y
16 ***Walker***	Y	Y	N	N	N	N	N	Y
17 ***Gekas***	Y	Y	N	N	N	N	N	Y
18 ***Santorum***	Y	N	N	N	N	Y	N	Y
19 ***Goodling***	Y	Y	Y	N	Y	Y	N	Y
20 Gaydos	N	N	Y	N	Y	N	Y	Y
21 ***Ridge***	Y	N	N	?	N	Y	N	Y
22 Murphy	N	N	N	?	Y	Y	Y	N
23 ***Clinger***	Y	Y	N	N	N	N	N	Y
RHODE ISLAND								
1 ***Machtley***	Y	N	Y	N	N	Y	Y	Y
2 Reed	N	N	Y	Y	Y	Y	Y	N
SOUTH CAROLINA								
1 ***Ravenel***	Y	N	N	N	Y	Y	N	N
2 ***Spence***	Y	N	N	N	Y	N	N	Y
3 Derrick	Y	Y	Y	N	Y	Y	Y	N
4 Patterson	Y	N	N	N	Y	Y	Y	N
5 Spratt	Y	Y	Y	N	Y	Y	Y	N
6 Tallon	Y	N	N	N	Y	Y	Y	Y
SOUTH DAKOTA								
AL Johnson	N	N	N	N	Y	Y	Y	N
TENNESSEE								
1 ***Quillen***	Y	N	N	N	Y	N	N	Y
2 ***Duncan***	Y	N	N	?	Y	Y	N	N
3 Lloyd	Y	N	Y	N	Y	N	Y	Y
4 Cooper	Y	Y	Y	N	N	N	Y	Y
5 Clement	Y	N	Y	N	N	Y	Y	N
6 Gordon	Y	N	Y	N	N	Y	Y	Y
7 ***Sundquist***	Y	Y	N	?	N	Y	N	Y
8 Tanner	Y	N	N	N	N	N	Y	Y
9 Ford	N	N	Y	Y	Y	N	Y	N
TEXAS								
1 Chapman	Y	Y	Y	?	N	N	Y	Y
2 Wilson	Y	?	N	?	N	N	Y	Y
3 ***Johnson*** [4]	M	M	M	M	N	N	N	Y
4 Hall	Y	?	N	N	N	N	N	Y
5 Bryant	N	N	Y	Y	N	N	Y	Y
6 ***Barton***	Y	Y	N	X	N	N	N	Y
7 ***Archer***	Y	Y	N	N	N	N	N	Y
8 ***Fields***	Y	Y	N	N	N	N	N	Y
9 Brooks	Y	Y	N	N	Y	N	Y	Y
10 Pickle	N	Y	Y	N	N	N	Y	Y
11 Edwards	Y	Y	N	N	N	N	Y	Y
12 Geren	Y	Y	N	N	N	N	Y	Y
13 Sarpalius	Y	Y	N	N	N	N	Y	Y
14 Laughlin	Y	N	N	N	N	N	Y	Y
15 de la Garza	Y	N	N	N	N	?	Y	Y
16 Coleman	N	N	N	N	N	N	Y	Y
17 Stenholm	Y	Y	Y	N	N	N	N	Y
18 Washington	N	N	Y	?	Y	N	Y	N
19 ***Combest***	Y	Y	N	N	N	N	N	Y
20 Gonzalez	N	N	Y	Y	Y	N	Y	N
21 ***Smith***	Y	Y	N	N	N	N	N	Y
22 ***DeLay***	Y	Y	N	N	N	N	N	Y
23 Bustamante	N	N	N	N	N	N	Y	Y
24 Frost	Y	Y	Y	N	Y	N	Y	Y
25 Andrews	Y	N	Y	N	N	N	Y	Y
26 ***Armey***	Y	Y	N	N	N	N	N	Y
27 Ortiz	Y	N	N	N	N	N	Y	Y
UTAH								
1 ***Hansen***	Y	Y	N	N	N	N	N	Y
2 Owens	N	Y	Y	?	N	N	Y	N
3 Orton	Y	Y	N	N	N	N	N	N
VERMONT								
AL *Sanders*	N	N	N	Y	Y	Y	Y	N
VIRGINIA								
1 ***Bateman***	Y	Y	Y	N	N	N	N	Y
2 Pickett	Y	Y	N	N	N	N	Y	Y
3 ***Bliley***	Y	Y	N	N	N	N	N	Y
4 Sisisky	Y	Y	N	N	Y	Y	?	?
5 Payne	Y	Y	N	N	Y	N	Y	N
6 Olin	N	Y	N	N	N	N	Y	N
7 ***Slaughter***	Y	Y	Y	N	Y	N	N	Y
8 Moran	N	Y	Y	N	N	Y	Y	Y
9 Boucher	N	Y	N	Y	N	N	Y	Y
10 ***Wolf***	Y	Y	Y	N	N	N	N	Y
WASHINGTON								
1 ***Miller***	Y	Y	Y	N	N	N	N	+
2 Swift	N	Y	Y	Y	N	Y	Y	Y
3 Unsoeld	N	Y	N	Y	Y	Y	Y	N
4 ***Morrison***	Y	Y	Y	N	N	N	N	Y
5 Foley	N						Y	
6 Dicks	N	Y	Y	N	N	N	Y	Y
7 McDermott	N	Y	Y	Y	N	Y	Y	N
8 ***Chandler***	Y	Y	Y	N	N	X	N	Y
WEST VIRGINIA								
1 Mollohan	Y	N	N	N	Y	N	Y	Y
2 Staggers	N	N	N	N	Y	?	Y	N
3 Wise	N	N	N	N	Y	Y	Y	Y
4 Rahall	Y	N	N	Y	Y	N	Y	Y
WISCONSIN								
1 Aspin	Y	N	Y	N	Y	?	Y	Y
2 ***Klug***	Y	Y	Y	?	N	N	Y	Y
3 ***Gunderson***	Y	Y	N	N	N	N	N	Y
4 Kleczka	N	N	Y	Y	Y	Y	Y	N
5 Moody	N	N	Y	Y	Y	Y	Y	N
6 ***Petri***	Y	N	N	N	N	Y	N	Y
7 Obey	N	N	N	Y	Y	Y	Y	N
8 ***Roth***	Y	N	N	N	N	Y	N	N
9 ***Sensenbrenner***	Y	N	Y	N	N	Y	N	Y
WYOMING								
AL ***Thomas***	Y	Y	N	?	N	Y	N	Y

9. HR 2686. Fiscal 1992 Interior Appropriations/Grazing Fees. Synar, D-Okla., amendment to increase over four years the domestic livestock grazing fee on public lands administered by the Bureau of Land Management from $1.97 to $8.70 per animal unit month or to fair market value, whichever is higher. Adopted 232-192: R 47-114; D 184-78 (ND 140-38, SD 44-40); I 1-0, June 25, 1991. A "nay" was a vote supporting the president's position.

10. HR 2100. Fiscal 1992 Defense Authorization. Dickinson, R-Ala., motion to order the previous question (thus ending debate and amendment) on the Dickinson motion to instruct the House conferees on the fiscal 1992 defense authorization bill to insist on the House position to make permanent certain changes in benefits for military personnel from Operation Desert Shield/Storm. Motion agreed to 220-145: R 136-4; D 84-140 (ND 30-124, SD 54-16); I 0-1, Sept. 16, 1991.

11. HR 3040. Unemployment Benefits Extension/Passage. Passage of the bill to permanently extend unemployment benefits to long-term unemployed workers for up to 20 additional weeks, at an estimated cost of $6.3 billion through fiscal 1996. The bill automatically declares the benefits to be emergency spending and would not require a presidential declaration to be exempt from the spending requirements of 1990's budget agreement. Passed 283-125: R 48-107; D 234-18 (ND 172-2, SD 62-16); I 1-0, Sept. 17, 1991. A "nay" was a vote supporting the president's position.

12. HR 3566. Surface Transportation Reauthorization/Rule. Adoption of the rule (H Res 252) to provide for House floor consideration of the bill to authorize $151 billion for highway and mass transit programs in fiscal 1992-97 and extend through fiscal 1999 half of the nickel added to the federal gasoline tax in 1990. Adopted 323-102: R 66-97; D 257-4 (ND 174-4, SD 83-0); I 0-1, Oct. 23, 1991.

13. HR 2508. Fiscal 1992-93 Foreign Aid Authorization/Conference Report. Adoption of the conference report to authorize $25 billion in fiscal 1992-93 for foreign economic and military assistance. Rejected 159-262: R 28-134; D 131-127 (ND 105-73, SD 26-54); I 0-1, Oct. 30, 1991. A "nay" was a vote supporting the president's position.

14. HR 6. Banking Reform/Passage. Passage of the bill to restructure the banking industry, overhaul the federal bank deposit insurance system and allow the FDIC to borrow $30 billion to cover losses in failed banks. Rejected 89-324: R 6-153; D 83-170 (ND 69-105, SD 14-65); I 0-1, Nov. 4, 1991. A "nay" was a vote supporting the president's position.

15. HR 2707. Fiscal 1992 Labor, HHS, and Education Appropriations/Passage. Passage, over President Bush's Nov. 19 veto, of the appropriations bill for the Departments of Labor, Health and Human Services, and Education. The measure would block enforcement of the administration rule, known as the "gag rule," barring abortion counseling in federally funded family planning clinics. Rejected 276-156: R 53-113; D 222-43 (ND 155-26, SD 67-17); I 1-0, Nov. 19, 1991. A two-thirds majority of those present and voting (288 in this case) of both chambers is required to override a veto. A "nay" was a vote supporting the president's position.

16. HR 3750. Campaign Finance/Passage. Passage of the bill to provide lower mail costs and up to $200,000 in public matching funds for the first $200 of individual contributions for House candidates who have raised more than $60,000 in individual contributions of less than $200 and agreed to a voluntary spending limit of $600,000. All House candidates would be limited to $200,000 in contributions from political action committees. Passed 273-156: R 21-144; D 251-12 (ND 176-4, SD 75-8); I 1-0, Nov. 25, 1991. A "nay" was a vote supporting the president's position.

KEY

Y	Voted for (yea).
#	Paired for.
+	Announced for.
N	Voted against (nay).
X	Paired against.
-	Announced against.
P	Voted "present."
C	Voted "present" to avoid possible conflict of interest.
?	Did not vote or otherwise make a position known.

Democrats ***Republicans***
Independent

ND	Northern Democrats
SD	Southern Democrats

Southern states - Ala., Ark., Fla., Ga., Ky., La., Miss., N.C., Okla., S.C., Tenn., Texas, Va.

	9	10	11	12	13	14	15	16
ALABAMA								
1 ***Callahan***	N	Y	N	Y	N	N	N	N
2 ***Dickinson***	N	Y	N	Y	N	N	N	N
3 Browder	N	Y	Y	Y	N	N	Y	Y
4 Bevill	N	Y	Y	Y	N	N	Y	Y
5 Cramer	N	Y	Y	Y	N	N	Y	Y
6 Erdreich	Y	Y	Y	Y	N	N	Y	Y
7 Harris	N	Y	Y	Y	N	N	Y	Y
ALASKA								
AL ***Young***	N	Y	Y	Y	Y	N	N	N
ARIZONA								
1 ***Rhodes***	-	?	N	N	N	N	N	N
2 Pastor [1]				Y	Y	N	Y	Y
3 ***Stump***	N	Y	N	N	N	N	N	N
4 ***Kyl***	N	Y	N	N	N	N	N	N
5 ***Kolbe***	N	Y	N	N	Y	N	Y	N
ARKANSAS								
1 Alexander	N	N	?	Y	N	N	Y	N
2 Thornton	?	N	Y	Y	N	N	Y	Y
3 ***Hammerschmidt***	N	Y	N	Y	N	N	N	N
4 Anthony	N	N	Y	Y	N	N	Y	N
CALIFORNIA								
1 ***Riggs***	N	?	N	Y	Y	N	Y	N
2 ***Herger***	N	?	?	N	N	N	N	N
3 Matsui	Y	N	Y	Y	?	Y	Y	Y
4 Fazio	Y	?	Y	Y	Y	Y	Y	Y
5 Pelosi	Y	N	Y	Y	Y	Y	Y	Y
6 Boxer	Y	N	Y	Y	?	N	Y	Y
7 Miller	Y	?	Y	Y	N	N	Y	Y
8 Dellums	Y	N	Y	Y	Y	N	Y	Y
9 Stark	Y	N	Y	Y	N	N	Y	Y
10 Edwards	Y	N	Y	Y	Y	Y	Y	Y
11 Lantos	Y	?	#	Y	Y	N	Y	Y
12 ***Campbell***	Y	?	N	N	Y	N	Y	N
13 Mineta	Y	N	Y	Y	Y	N	Y	Y
14 ***Doolittle***	N	?	X	N	N	N	N	N
15 Condit	N	N	Y	Y	N	N	Y	Y
16 Panetta	N	N	Y	Y	Y	Y	Y	Y
17 Dooley	N	Y	Y	Y	N	N	Y	Y
18 Lehman	N	N	Y	Y	N	Y	Y	Y
19 ***Lagomarsino***	N	Y	N	N	N	N	N	N
20 ***Thomas***	N	?	X	Y	N	?	Y	N
21 ***Gallegly***	N	Y	N	N	N	N	N	N
22 ***Moorhead***	N	Y	N	N	N	N	N	N
23 Beilenson	Y	N	Y	Y	Y	Y	Y	Y
24 Waxman	Y	N	Y	Y	Y	Y	Y	Y
25 Roybal	Y	?	Y	Y	Y	Y	Y	Y
26 Berman	Y	?	?	Y	Y	Y	Y	Y
27 Levine	?	?	?	Y	Y	N	?	Y
28 Dixon	Y	N	Y	Y	Y	?	Y	Y
29 Waters	Y	N	Y	?	N	N	Y	Y
30 Martinez	N	?	Y	N	Y	N	Y	Y
31 Dymally	N	?	?	Y	Y	Y	Y	Y
32 Anderson	Y	Y	Y	Y	N	N	Y	Y
33 ***Dreier***	Y	Y	N	N	N	N	N	N
34 Torres	Y	N	Y	?	Y	Y	Y	Y
35 ***Lewis***	N	?	X	Y	N	N	N	N
36 Brown	Y	N	Y	Y	Y	N	Y	Y
37 ***McCandless***	N	Y	N	Y	N	N	N	N
38 ***Dornan***	N	Y	N	N	N	N	N	N
39 ***Dannemeyer***	N	Y	N	N	N	-	N	N
40 ***Cox***	Y	Y	N	N	N	N	N	N
41 ***Lowery***	N	?	N	Y	N	N	N	N
42 ***Rohrabacher***	Y	Y	N	N	N	N	N	N
43 ***Packard***	N	?	N	Y	N	N	N	N
44 ***Cunningham***	N	Y	N	N	N	N	N	N
45 ***Hunter***	N	?	?	N	N	N	N	N
COLORADO								
1 Schroeder	Y	N	Y	N	Y	Y	Y	Y
2 Skaggs	Y	N	Y	Y	Y	N	Y	Y
3 Campbell	N	Y	Y	Y	N	?	Y	N
4 ***Allard***	N	Y	N	N	N	N	N	N
5 ***Hefley***	N	Y	N	N	N	N	N	N
6 ***Schaefer***	N	Y	N	N	N	N	N	N
CONNECTICUT								
1 Kennelly	Y	Y	Y	Y	Y	Y	Y	Y
2 Gejdenson	Y	N	Y	Y	Y	N	Y	Y
3 DeLauro	Y	Y	Y	Y	Y	Y	Y	Y
4 ***Shays***	Y	N	N	N	Y	N	Y	Y
5 ***Franks***	N	Y	Y	N	N	N	Y	N
6 ***Johnson***	Y	Y	Y	Y	Y	N	Y	N
DELAWARE								
AL Carper	Y	Y	Y	Y	Y	N	Y	Y
FLORIDA								
1 Hutto	N	?	N	Y	N	N	N	Y
2 Peterson	N	Y	Y	Y	Y	N	Y	Y
3 Bennett	Y	Y	Y	Y	N	N	N	N
4 ***James***	Y	Y	N	N	N	N	N	Y
5 ***McCollum***	N	?	N	N	N	N	N	N
6 ***Stearns***	N	Y	Y	N	N	N	N	N
7 Gibbons	Y	N	Y	Y	Y	Y	Y	Y
8 ***Young***	?	Y	Y	N	N	N	N	Y
9 ***Bilirakis***	N	Y	N	N	N	N	N	Y
10 ***Ireland***	Y	Y	N	N	N	N	N	N
11 Bacchus	Y	Y	Y	Y	Y	N	Y	Y
12 ***Lewis***	N	Y	Y	Y	N	N	N	N
13 ***Goss***	Y	Y	N	N	N	N	N	N
14 Johnston	Y	N	?	Y	Y	Y	Y	Y
15 ***Shaw***	N	Y	N	Y	N	N	N	N
16 Smith	Y	N	Y	Y	Y	#	Y	Y
17 Lehman	Y	?	?	Y	Y	Y	Y	Y
18 ***Ros-Lehtinen***	Y	Y	Y	N	N	N	N	N
19 Fascell	Y	Y	Y	Y	Y	Y	Y	Y
GEORGIA								
1 Thomas	N	Y	Y	Y	N	N	Y	Y
2 Hatcher	N	?	Y	Y	N	N	?	Y
3 Ray	N	Y	N	Y	N	N	N	?
4 Jones	Y	N	Y	Y	Y	Y	Y	Y
5 Lewis	Y	N	Y	Y	Y	Y	Y	Y
6 ***Gingrich***	N	Y	N	N	N	N	N	N
7 Darden	Y	Y	Y	Y	N	N	Y	Y
8 Rowland	Y	?	#	Y	?	N	Y	Y
9 Jenkins	Y	?	Y	Y	N	N	Y	Y
10 Barnard	Y	Y	N	Y	N	N	N	Y
HAWAII								
1 Abercrombie	Y	N	Y	Y	Y	Y	Y	Y
2 Mink	Y	N	Y	Y	Y	Y	Y	Y
IDAHO								
1 LaRocco	N	N	Y	Y	N	N	+	Y
2 Stallings	N	?	Y	Y	N	N	N	Y
ILLINOIS								
1 Hayes	Y	N	Y	Y	N	Y	Y	Y
2 Savage	Y	N	Y	Y	N	N	Y	Y
3 Russo	Y	N	Y	Y	N	N	Y	Y
4 Sangmeister	Y	N	Y	Y	N	?	Y	Y
5 Lipinski	Y	Y	Y	Y	N	N	N	Y
6 ***Hyde***	N	Y	N	Y	N	N	N	N
7 Collins	Y	N	Y	Y	N	Y	Y	Y
8 Rostenkowski	Y	N	Y	Y	Y	N	Y	Y
9 Yates	Y	N	Y	Y	Y	Y	Y	Y
10 ***Porter***	?	Y	N	N	Y	N	Y	N
11 Annunzio	Y	N	Y	Y	N	Y	N	Y
12 ***Crane***	Y	Y	N	N	N	N	N	N
13 ***Fawell***	Y	Y	N	N	N	N	Y	N
14 ***Hastert***	N	Y	N	Y	N	N	N	N
15 ***Ewing*** [2]		Y	N	Y	N	N	N	N
16 Cox	Y	N	Y	Y	Y	N	Y	Y
17 Evans	Y	N	Y	N	Y	N	Y	Y
18 ***Michel***	N	Y	N	?	N	?	N	N
19 Bruce	Y	N	Y	Y	N	Y	Y	Y
20 Durbin	Y	N	Y	Y	N	N	Y	Y
21 Costello	Y	Y	Y	Y	N	N	N	Y
22 Poshard	Y	N	Y	Y	N	N	N	Y
INDIANA								
1 Visclosky	Y	N	Y	Y	Y	N	Y	Y
2 Sharp	Y	?	Y	Y	N	N	Y	Y
3 Roemer	Y	Y	Y	Y	N	N	Y	Y

[1] *Rep. Ed Pastor, D-Ariz. was sworn in Sept. 24, 1991, to succeed Morris K. Udall, D, who resigned May 4, 1991.*

[2] *Rep. Thomas W. Ewing, R-Ill., was sworn in July 2, 1991, to succeed Edward R. Madigan, R, who resigned March 8, 1991.*

[3] *Rep. John W. Olver, D-Mass., was sworn in June 4, 1991, to succeed Silvio O. Conte, R, who died Feb. 8, 1991.*

[4] *Rep. Lucien F. Blackwell, D-Pa., was sworn in May 5, 1991, to succeed William H. Gray III, D, who resigned Sept. 11, 1991.*

[5] *Rep. George F. Allen, R-Va., was sworn in Nov. 12, 1991, to succeed D. French Slaughter Jr., who resigned Sept. 5, 1991. Slaughter voted "nay" on key vote 9 and "yea" on key vote 10.*

	9	10	11	12	13	14	15	16
4 Long	N	N	Y	Y	N	N	Y	Y
5 Jontz	Y	N	Y	Y	N	N	Y	Y
6 ***Burton***	N	Y	N	N	N	N	N	N
7 ***Myers***	N	Y	N	Y	N	N	Y	N
8 McCloskey	Y	N	Y	Y	N	N	Y	Y
9 Hamilton	Y	N	Y	Y	Y	N	Y	Y
10 Jacobs	Y	N	Y	N	N	Y	Y	Y
IOWA								
1 ***Leach***	N	Y	Y	Y	N	Y	Y	Y
2 ***Nussle***	N	Y	N	Y	N	N	N	N
3 Nagle	N	N	Y	Y	Y	N	Y	N
4 Smith	N	N	Y	Y	Y	N	Y	Y
5 ***Lightfoot***	N	Y	N	N	N	N	N	N
6 ***Grandy***	N	Y	N	Y	N	N	Y	N
KANSAS								
1 ***Roberts***	N	Y	N	N	N	N	N	N
2 Slattery	Y	N	Y	Y	N	Y	Y	Y
3 ***Meyers***	Y	Y	N	N	Y	Y	Y	N
4 Glickman	Y	N	Y	Y	#	Y	Y	Y
5 ***Nichols***	N	Y	N	Y	N	N	N	N
KENTUCKY								
1 Hubbard	N	Y	Y	Y	N	N	Y	Y
2 Natcher	N	Y	Y	Y	N	N	Y	Y
3 Mazzoli	Y	Y	Y	Y	N	N	N	Y
4 ***Bunning***	N	Y	N	N	N	N	N	N
5 ***Rogers***	N	Y	Y	Y	N	N	N	N
6 ***Hopkins***	N	?	?	?	?	?	N	N
7 Perkins	N	N	Y	Y	N	N	Y	N
LOUISIANA								
1 ***Livingston***	N	Y	N	N	N	N	N	N
2 Jefferson	Y	Y	Y	Y	#	N	Y	Y
3 Tauzin	Y	Y	Y	Y	N	N	N	Y
4 ***McCrery***	Y	?	N	Y	N	N	N	N
5 Huckaby	Y	Y	Y	Y	N	N	N	Y
6 ***Baker***	N	Y	N	N	N	N	N	N
7 Hayes	Y	Y	N	Y	N	N	N	Y
8 ***Holloway***	N	?	?	N	N	N	N	N
MAINE								
1 Andrews	Y	N	Y	Y	Y	N	Y	Y
2 ***Snowe***	Y	Y	Y	N	Y	N	Y	Y
MARYLAND								
1 ***Gilchrest***	N	Y	Y	N	Y	N	Y	N
2 ***Bentley***	N	Y	Y	Y	N	N	Y	N
3 Cardin	Y	N	Y	Y	Y	N	Y	Y
4 McMillen	Y	Y	Y	Y	Y	N	Y	Y
5 Hoyer	Y	N	Y	Y	Y	Y	Y	Y
6 Byron	Y	Y	Y	Y	N	N	Y	Y
7 Mfume	Y	N	Y	Y	Y	N	Y	Y
8 ***Morella***	Y	N	Y	Y	Y	N	Y	Y
MASSACHUSETTS								
1 Olver [3]	Y	N	Y	Y	Y	Y	Y	Y
2 Neal	Y	N	Y	Y	N	Y	Y	Y
3 Early	Y	N	Y	Y	N	Y	Y	Y
4 Frank	Y	N	Y	Y	Y	N	Y	Y
5 Atkins	Y	N	Y	Y	Y	Y	Y	Y
6 Mavroules	Y	?	Y	Y	N	Y	N	Y
7 Markey	Y	N	Y	Y	Y	Y	Y	Y
8 Kennedy	Y	N	Y	Y	Y	N	Y	Y
9 Moakley	Y	N	Y	Y	N	Y	Y	Y
10 Studds	Y	N	Y	Y	Y	Y	Y	Y
11 Donnelly	Y	N	Y	Y	N	Y	N	Y
MICHIGAN								
1 Conyers	Y	?	Y	Y	N	N	Y	Y
2 ***Pursell***	?	?	Y	Y	N	N	Y	N
3 Wolpe	Y	N	Y	Y	Y	Y	Y	Y
4 ***Upton***	Y	Y	Y	Y	N	N	Y	N
5 ***Henry***	Y	Y	Y	Y	N	N	N	N
6 Carr	N	?	Y	Y	Y	N	Y	N
7 Kildee	Y	N	Y	Y	N	Y	N	Y
8 Traxler	Y	N	Y	Y	N	Y	Y	Y
9 ***Vander Jagt***	N	Y	N	Y	N	N	N	N
10 ***Camp***	N	Y	Y	N	N	N	N	N
11 ***Davis***	N	Y	Y	Y	N	N	N	N
12 Bonior	Y	N	Y	Y	Y	Y	Y	Y
13 Collins	N	N	Y	N	Y	N	Y	Y
14 Hertel	Y	Y	Y	Y	Y	Y	Y	Y
15 Ford	Y	?	Y	Y	N	N	Y	Y
16 Dingell	Y	N	Y	Y	Y	Y	Y	Y
17 Levin	Y	N	Y	Y	Y	Y	Y	Y
18 ***Broomfield***	N	Y	N	N	N	N	N	N
MINNESOTA								
1 Penny	N	?	N	Y	Y	Y	Y	Y
2 ***Weber***	N	Y	N	N	N	N	N	N
3 ***Ramstad***	Y	Y	N	N	N	N	Y	N
4 Vento	Y	N	Y	Y	Y	Y	Y	Y

	9	10	11	12	13	14	15	16
5 Sabo	Y	?	Y	Y	Y	Y	Y	Y
6 Sikorski	Y	N	Y	Y	Y	Y	Y	Y
7 Peterson	N	N	Y	Y	N	N	N	Y
8 Oberstar	N	N	Y	Y	N	N	N	Y
MISSISSIPPI								
1 Whitten	N	?	Y	Y	N	N	Y	Y
2 Espy	N	N	Y	Y	N	N	Y	Y
3 Montgomery	N	Y	N	Y	N	N	N	Y
4 Parker	N	Y	N	Y	N	N	N	Y
5 Taylor	N	Y	N	Y	N	N	N	Y
MISSOURI								
1 Clay	Y	?	Y	Y	N	N	Y	Y
2 Horn	Y	N	Y	Y	N	N	Y	Y
3 Gephardt	Y	N	Y	Y	Y	Y	Y	Y
4 Skelton	N	Y	Y	Y	N	N	Y	Y
5 Wheat	Y	N	Y	Y	Y	N	Y	Y
6 ***Coleman***	N	Y	N	N	N	N	Y	N
7 ***Hancock***	N	Y	N	N	N	N	N	N
8 ***Emerson***	N	Y	Y	Y	N	N	N	N
9 Volkmer	N	Y	Y	Y	N	N	N	Y
MONTANA								
1 Williams	N	?	Y	Y	N	N	Y	Y
2 ***Marlenee***	N	?	?	N	N	N	N	Y
NEBRASKA								
1 ***Bereuter***	N	Y	N	Y	N	N	Y	N
2 Hoagland	Y	N	Y	Y	Y	N	Y	Y
3 ***Barrett***	N	Y	N	N	N	N	N	N
NEVADA								
1 Bilbray	N	Y	Y	Y	N	N	Y	Y
2 ***Vucanovich***	N	Y	N	N	N	N	N	N
NEW HAMPSHIRE								
1 ***Zeliff***	Y	Y	N	N	N	N	Y	N
2 Swett	Y	Y	Y	Y	Y	N	Y	Y
NEW JERSEY								
1 Andrews	N	Y	Y	Y	Y	N	Y	Y
2 Hughes	Y	N	Y	Y	N	N	Y	Y
3 Pallone	Y	Y	Y	Y	N	Y	Y	Y
4 ***Smith***	Y	?	Y	Y	N	N	N	Y
5 ***Roukema***	Y	N	Y	Y	Y	Y	Y	N
6 Dwyer	Y	N	Y	Y	Y	?	Y	Y
7 ***Rinaldo***	Y	Y	Y	Y	N	N	N	Y
8 Roe	N	N	Y	Y	N	N	N	Y
9 Torricelli	Y	N	Y	Y	Y	N	Y	Y
10 Payne	Y	N	Y	Y	N	Y	Y	Y
11 ***Gallo***	Y	Y	Y	Y	Y	N	Y	N
12 ***Zimmer***	Y	Y	Y	N	Y	N	Y	N
13 ***Saxton***	Y	?	?	N	Y	N	N	N
14 Guarini	Y	N	Y	Y	N	N	Y	Y
NEW MEXICO								
1 ***Schiff***	N	Y	N	N	Y	N	Y	N
2 ***Skeen***	N	Y	N	N	Y	N	Y	N
3 Richardson	N	Y	Y	Y	Y	N	Y	Y
NEW YORK								
1 Hochbrueckner	Y	Y	Y	Y	Y	Y	Y	Y
2 Downey	Y	N	Y	?	Y	Y	Y	Y
3 Mrazek	Y	?	Y	Y	Y	?	Y	?
4 ***Lent***	N	Y	N	Y	N	N	N	N
5 ***McGrath***	Y	?	Y	Y	?	N	N	N
6 Flake	Y	N	Y	Y	N	Y	Y	Y
7 Ackerman	Y	?	Y	Y	Y	Y	Y	Y
8 Scheuer	Y	N	Y	Y	Y	Y	Y	Y
9 Manton	Y	N	Y	Y	N	Y	N	Y
10 Schumer	Y	N	Y	Y	Y	Y	Y	Y
11 Towns	Y	N	Y	Y	Y	Y	Y	Y
12 Owens	Y	N	Y	Y	Y	N	Y	Y
13 Solarz	Y	Y	Y	Y	Y	Y	Y	Y
14 ***Molinari***	N	Y	Y	Y	Y	N	Y	N
15 ***Green***	Y	N	N	Y	Y	?	Y	Y
16 Rangel	Y	N	Y	Y	Y	N	Y	Y
17 Weiss	Y	N	Y	Y	Y	Y	Y	Y
18 Serrano	Y	N	Y	Y	Y	N	Y	Y
19 Engel	Y	N	Y	Y	Y	N	Y	Y
20 Lowey	Y	N	Y	Y	Y	Y	Y	Y
21 ***Fish***	Y	Y	Y	Y	Y	N	Y	Y
22 ***Gilman***	Y	Y	Y	Y	Y	N	Y	Y
23 McNulty	Y	Y	Y	Y	Y	N	Y	Y
24 ***Solomon***	Y	Y	N	N	N	N	N	N
25 ***Boehlert***	Y	Y	Y	Y	Y	N	Y	Y
26 ***Martin***	N	?	Y	N	N	N	Y	N
27 ***Walsh***	Y	Y	Y	N	N	Y	N	N
28 McHugh	Y	N	Y	Y	Y	N	Y	Y
29 ***Horton***	N	Y	Y	Y	N	N	Y	N
30 Slaughter	Y	N	Y	Y	N	N	Y	Y
31 ***Paxon***	N	Y	Y	N	N	N	N	N

	9	10	11	12	13	14	15	16
32 LaFalce	Y	N	Y	Y	N	N	N	Y
33 Nowak	Y	N	Y	Y	N	N	N	Y
34 ***Houghton***	N	?	Y	Y	Y	N	Y	N
NORTH CAROLINA								
1 Jones	N	?	?	Y	N	N	Y	Y
2 Valentine	Y	Y	N	Y	N	N	Y	Y
3 Lancaster	Y	Y	Y	Y	Y	Y	Y	Y
4 Price	Y	N	Y	Y	Y	N	Y	Y
5 Neal	Y	Y	Y	?	N	N	Y	Y
6 ***Coble***	N	Y	N	N	N	N	N	N
7 Rose	N	N	Y	Y	Y	N	Y	Y
8 Hefner	Y	Y	Y	Y	N	N	Y	Y
9 ***McMillan***	N	Y	N	N	N	N	N	N
10 ***Ballenger***	N	Y	N	N	N	N	N	N
11 ***Taylor***	N	Y	N	N	N	N	N	N
NORTH DAKOTA								
AL Dorgan	N	N	Y	Y	N	N	Y	Y
OHIO								
1 Luken	Y	Y	Y	Y	N	Y	N	Y
2 ***Gradison***	Y	?	N	N	N	N	Y	N
3 Hall	Y	Y	Y	Y	Y	N	N	Y
4 ***Oxley***	N	Y	N	Y	N	N	N	N
5 ***Gillmor***	N	Y	Y	Y	N	N	N	N
6 ***McEwen***	N	?	N	N	N	?	N	N
7 ***Hobson***	N	Y	N	Y	N	N	Y	N
8 ***Boehner***	N	Y	N	N	N	N	N	N
9 Kaptur	Y	N	Y	Y	N	N	Y	Y
10 ***Miller***	Y	Y	N	N	N	N	N	N
11 Eckart	Y	N	Y	Y	Y	Y	Y	Y
12 ***Kasich***	Y	Y	N	Y	N	N	N	N
13 Pease	Y	N	Y	Y	N	Y	Y	Y
14 Sawyer	Y	N	Y	Y	Y	Y	Y	Y
15 ***Wylie***	N	Y	N	Y	N	N	N	N
16 ***Regula***	N	Y	Y	Y	N	N	Y	N
17 Traficant	N	N	Y	Y	N	N	Y	Y
18 Applegate	Y	N	Y	Y	N	N	N	Y
19 Feighan	Y	N	Y	Y	Y	N	Y	Y
20 Oakar	Y	N	Y	Y	Y	Y	Y	Y
21 Stokes	Y	N	Y	Y	Y	N	Y	Y
OKLAHOMA								
1 ***Inhofe***	N	Y	N	Y	N	N	N	N
2 Synar	Y	N	Y	Y	Y	Y	Y	Y
3 Brewster	N	Y	N	Y	Y	N	Y	Y
4 McCurdy	Y	Y	Y	Y	Y	N	Y	Y
5 ***Edwards***	N	Y	?	N	?	N	N	N
6 English	N	Y	Y	Y	N	N	Y	Y
OREGON								
1 AuCoin	N	N	Y	Y	Y	N	Y	Y
2 ***Smith***	N	Y	Y	N	N	N	N	N
3 Wyden	Y	N	Y	Y	Y	Y	Y	Y
4 DeFazio	N	N	Y	Y	N	N	Y	Y
5 Kopetski	N	+	Y	Y	Y	N	Y	Y
PENNSYLVANIA								
1 Foglietta	Y	Y	Y	Y	Y	?	Y	Y
2 Blackwell [4]							Y	Y
3 Borski	Y	N	Y	Y	Y	Y	N	Y
4 Kolter	?	N	Y	Y	N	N	N	Y
5 ***Schulze***	N	?	N	Y	N	N	N	N
6 Yatron	Y	?	?	Y	Y	N	N	Y
7 ***Weldon***	Y	Y	Y	N	N	N	N	Y
8 Kostmayer	Y	N	Y	Y	Y	Y	Y	Y
9 ***Shuster***	N	Y	Y	Y	N	N	N	?
10 ***McDade***	N	?	Y	Y	N	N	N	N
11 Kanjorski	Y	N	Y	Y	N	N	N	Y
12 Murtha	Y	Y	Y	Y	N	N	Y	Y
13 ***Coughlin***	N	Y	Y	Y	N	N	Y	N
14 Coyne	Y	N	Y	Y	Y	Y	Y	Y
15 ***Ritter***	Y	Y	Y	Y	N	N	N	N
16 ***Walker***	Y	Y	N	N	N	N	N	N
17 ***Gekas***	N	Y	Y	Y	N	Y	Y	N
18 ***Santorum***	N	Y	N	Y	N	N	N	N
19 ***Goodling***	N	Y	N	Y	N	N	Y	N
20 Gaydos	N	?	Y	Y	N	N	Y	N
21 ***Ridge***	N	Y	Y	Y	N	N	Y	N
22 Murphy	N	Y	Y	Y	N	X	N	Y
23 ***Clinger***	Y	Y	Y	Y	N	N	Y	N
RHODE ISLAND								
1 ***Machtley***	Y	Y	Y	Y	Y	Y	Y	N
2 Reed	N	N	Y	Y	Y	Y	Y	Y
SOUTH CAROLINA								
1 ***Ravenel***	Y	Y	Y	N	Y	N	Y	Y
2 ***Spence***	N	Y	N	N	N	N	N	N
3 Derrick	Y	?	Y	Y	N	N	Y	Y
4 Patterson	Y	Y	Y	Y	N	N	Y	Y
5 Spratt	Y	Y	Y	Y	N	N	Y	Y
6 Tallon	N	Y	Y	Y	N	N	N	Y

	9	10	11	12	13	14	15	16
SOUTH DAKOTA								
AL Johnson	N	N	Y	Y	Y	N	Y	Y
TENNESSEE								
1 ***Quillen***	N	Y	N	Y	N	N	N	N
2 ***Duncan***	N	Y	N	N	N	N	N	Y
3 Lloyd	Y	Y	?	Y	X	N	Y	Y
4 Cooper	Y	Y	N	Y	N	C	Y	Y
5 Clement	Y	Y	Y	Y	N	N	Y	Y
6 Gordon	Y	Y	Y	Y	Y	N	Y	Y
7 ***Sundquist***	N	Y	N	N	N	N	N	N
8 Tanner	Y	Y	N	Y	X	N	Y	Y
9 Ford	Y	N	Y	Y	N	?	Y	?
TEXAS								
1 Chapman	N	Y	Y	Y	N	?	Y	Y
2 Wilson	Y	?	Y	Y	N	N	Y	Y
3 ***Johnson***	N	Y	N	N	N	N	N	N
4 Hall	N	Y	N	Y	?	N	N	N
5 Bryant	Y	?	Y	Y	N	?	Y	Y
6 ***Barton***	N	Y	N	N	N	N	N	N
7 ***Archer***	Y	Y	N	N	N	N	N	N
8 ***Fields***	N	Y	N	N	N	N	N	N
9 Brooks	Y	N	Y	Y	N	P	Y	Y
10 Pickle	N	?	?	Y	Y	Y	Y	Y
11 Edwards	N	Y	Y	Y	N	N	Y	Y
12 Geren	N	Y	Y	Y	N	N	Y	Y
13 Sarpalius	N	Y	N	Y	N	N	N	N
14 Laughlin	N	Y	N	Y	N	N	Y	Y
15 de la Garza	N	?	Y	Y	Y	N	N	Y
16 Coleman	N	Y	Y	Y	N	N	Y	Y
17 Stenholm	N	Y	N	Y	N	N	N	Y
18 Washington	Y	?	Y	?	N	N	Y	Y
19 ***Combest***	N	Y	N	N	N	N	N	N
20 Gonzalez	N	Y	Y	Y	Y	Y	Y	Y
21 ***Smith***	Y	Y	N	N	Y	N	N	N
22 ***DeLay***	Y	?	N	N	N	N	N	N
23 Bustamante	N	?	Y	Y	Y	N	Y	Y
24 Frost	N	Y	Y	Y	Y	Y	Y	Y
25 Andrews	Y	Y	Y	Y	Y	N	Y	Y
26 ***Armey***	N	Y	N	N	N	N	N	N
27 Ortiz	N	Y	Y	Y	N	Y	N	Y
UTAH								
1 ***Hansen***	N	Y	N	N	N	N	N	N
2 Owens	N	N	Y	Y	Y	N	Y	Y
3 Orton	N	Y	N	Y	N	N	N	Y
VERMONT								
AL *Sanders*	Y	N	Y	N	N	N	Y	Y
VIRGINIA								
1 ***Bateman***	N	Y	N	Y	N	N	N	N
2 Pickett	Y	Y	Y	Y	N	N	Y	N
3 ***Bliley***	N	Y	N	N	N	N	N	N
4 Sisisky	Y	Y	Y	Y	Y	N	Y	N
5 Payne	Y	Y	Y	Y	Y	N	Y	Y
6 Olin	N	Y	N	Y	Y	N	Y	Y
7 ***Allen*** [5]							Y	N
8 Moran	N	N	Y	Y	Y	Y	Y	Y
9 Boucher	Y	?	Y	Y	N	Y	Y	Y
10 ***Wolf***	N	Y	N	N	N	N	N	N
WASHINGTON								
1 ***Miller***	Y	Y	N	N	Y	N	Y	Y
2 Swift	N	N	Y	Y	Y	N	Y	Y
3 Unsoeld	Y	N	Y	Y	Y	N	Y	Y
4 ***Morrison***	N	Y	N	N	N	N	Y	Y
5 Foley							Y	
6 Dicks	Y	Y	Y	Y	Y	N	Y	Y
7 McDermott	Y	N	Y	Y	Y	N	Y	Y
8 ***Chandler***	N	Y	N	N	Y	N	Y	N
WEST VIRGINIA								
1 Mollohan	N	Y	Y	Y	N	N	N	Y
2 Staggers	N	N	Y	Y	N	N	N	Y
3 Wise	Y	N	Y	Y	Y	N	Y	Y
4 Rahall	Y	?	#	Y	N	N	Y	Y
WISCONSIN								
1 Aspin	Y	N	Y	Y	Y	N	Y	Y
2 ***Klug***	N	Y	N	N	N	N	Y	Y
3 ***Gunderson***	N	Y	Y	N	N	N	Y	N
4 Kleczka	Y	?	Y	N	N	Y	Y	Y
5 Moody	Y	?	Y	Y	Y	Y	Y	-
6 ***Petri***	Y	Y	N	Y	N	N	N	Y
7 Obey	Y	N	Y	Y	N	N	Y	Y
8 ***Roth***	N	Y	N	N	N	N	N	N
9 ***Sensenbrenner***	Y	Y	N	N	N	N	N	N
WYOMING								
AL ***Thomas***	N	Y	N	N	N	N	N	N

1992 Key Votes

Senate

1. School Choice

Despite talk of improving public schools with national goals, standards and testing, along with new "break the mold" schools, the 1992 debate over elementary and secondary education hinged on one inflammatory issue: school choice. It would have sent public funds to some private schools.

Although Congress traditionally worked on a bipartisan basis to pass education legislation, the Democratic school improvement bill (S 2) became a political battleground in election year 1992, with President Bush trying to assert his "education president" label and Democrats striving to prove otherwise. The school choice issue was the main point of friction.

Bush and Education Secretary Lamar Alexander argued that all children should be able to vote with their feet, leaving bad schools for better schools, which would in turn spur schools to improve through the competition for students. But opponents said that using federal funds for private schools would undermine public schools and the students left in them.

Choice opponents won a decisive victory Jan. 23 when the Senate declined to support even the smallest demonstration program of private school choice.

After a generally partisan debate over the basic philosophy of public education, the Senate rejected a sharply scaled-back amendment to set up six demonstration projects in which federal school aid could be used to allow low-income students to attend the schools of their parents' choice. Despite the administration's backing, the amendment failed, 36-57: R 33-6; D 3-51 (ND 2-35, SD 1-16).

Offered by Sen. Orrin G. Hatch, R-Utah, the amendment proposed spending $30 million on the program, far less than the nationwide choice plan outlined in Bush's America 2000 program for elementary and secondary education. Hatch and other choice proponents had hoped that by limiting the amendment to a small demonstration program, Democratic senators might be willing to try it.

But Senate Democrats said from the outset that they would not allow the administration to get a foot in the "choice" door. Only three Democrats voted for Hatch's amendment: Bill Bradley, N.J., John B. Breaux, La., and Joseph I. Lieberman, Conn. Six of the Senate's 43 Republicans voted against it.

The Senate vote had larger consequences for school choice advocates. The lack of support for even the scaled-back Hatch proposal prompted House Education and Labor Chairman William D. Ford, D-Mich., to dump unilaterally a compromise school choice provision that he had previously agreed to in committee. Ford said that if the Senate bill did not have public money for private school choice, then the House would not either.

A House-Senate conference report on S 2 — minus any school choice language — eventually died in the Senate in the face of a Republican filibuster threat.

2. Nuclear Energy

Congress administered a political booster shot to the beleaguered nuclear power industry in 1992 by approving a streamlined federal licensing process that could make it easier to build new nuclear power plants.

The Senate was the first chamber to approve the new licensing rules, adopting them by voice vote after rejecting an alternative by Sen. Bob Graham, D-Fla., that was opposed by the industry.

The once-thriving U.S. nuclear industry saw its fortunes wane in recent years. Highly publicized accidents at Three Mile Island, near Harrisburg, Pa., and at the former Soviet Union's Chernobyl nuclear plant shook public confidence in the safety of nuclear power. Nuclear power sometimes proved costlier than anticipated, and experts struggled to determine the best way to dispose of radioactive nuclear waste.

But substantial congressional support for nuclear power still existed, especially in light of the 1990 amendments to the Clean Air Act, which set new limits on air pollution from other power sources such as coal-fired plants.

Nuclear power advocates sought regulatory changes they said would advance the industry. Among them was licensing reform.

In the past, the Nuclear Regulatory Commission (NRC) used a two-step process that required applicants first to win a construction license, then an operation license.

But industry officials complained this system was abused by nuclear critics to delay plant operations and drive up costs. Industry officials sought a combined construction and operation license that would force regulators to rule on controversial issues up front — and presumably protect investment in a plant from eleventh-hour opposition.

The NRC in 1989 issued a rule to create such a combined license, but it was challenged in court. While that case advanced, the administration and congressional supporters sought legislation to authorize the new one-step licensing process.

Senate Energy Committee Chairman J. Bennett Johnston, D-La., included the proposal in his committee's omnibus energy bill (S 2166), over the strong opposition of environmental groups. The new process generally would cut out a second full public hearing that was required before a plant was allowed to operate. Environmentalists and other critics argued that the change could increase the possibility of approving unsafe nuclear plants and undermine public confidence in the licensing system.

During floor debate on the energy bill in February, Graham challenged the licensing proposal and offered an alternative. His proposal also would have created a one-step licensing process, but with greater guarantees for a second public hearing if critics raised valid safety concerns or new information.

But Johnston undercut support for Graham's proposal by slightly modifying his original bill to include some additional guarantees of public participation. In the key vote, Johnston moved to table (and thus kill) Graham's proposal. He prevailed 52-43: R 31-11; D 21-32 (ND 9-27, SD 12-5), on Feb. 6.

Senators then adopted the revised Johnston language by voice vote.

The Senate vote paved the way for similar action in the House, where the nuclear industry traditionally has enjoyed solid support. The House passed identical licensing language, virtually ensuring victory for the proposal if the energy bill passed. The energy bill, with the new one-step licensing provisions, cleared Congress and was signed into law in October.

The licensing change had little practical effect, as no new plants were on order. But the change stood to increase investor confidence in nuclear plants and provide an important symbolic win for industry.

3. Budget 'Walls'

Senate Democratic leaders were confident early in 1992 that they would mount an effective election-year challenge to President Bush by passing economic measures with a Democratic stamp and forcing Bush to veto them.

A key to that strategy was a bill to knock down the budget "walls" between defense and domestic appropriations, allowing a shift of defense savings into cash-short domestic programs. They calculated that while a Bush veto of such a bill was virtually certain, it would sharpen the differences between what they saw as their invest-in-America policy and Bush's outmoded Cold War priorities.

But like their House counterparts, Senate leaders failed to reckon on trouble in their ranks. Before they could confront Bush, they had to unite Senate Democrats to overcome strong GOP opposition, and in the end they could not do it.

When Senate leaders tried to stop a filibuster against the measure March 26, they were defeated by virtually unanimous Republican opposition combined with the same Democratic coalition that would undo House Democratic leaders' plans to pass a walls bill five days later — conservative defense and deficit hawks joined with moderate and liberal Democrats worried about losing hometown defense jobs.

The bill (S 2399), drawn up by Budget Committee Chairman Jim Sasser, D-Tenn., would have changed the terms of the 1990 budget agreement to allow defense savings to be used for purposes other than deficit reduction. Senate appropriators, limited by increasingly tight spending caps, wanted the extra money to help keep domestic programs even with inflation or give them a boost.

Proponents argued that the Soviet threat that had justified the level of defense spending agreed to in the 1990 budget deal no longer existed. The money, they said, should go to other needs. "Are we going to move decisively to invest a portion of our peace dividend?" asked Sasser. "Or are we going to maintain Cold War policy and Cold War sacrifices after the Cold War is over?"

"What peace dividend?" retorted John C. Danforth, R-Mo., who noted that the fiscal 1992 deficit was estimated to be as high as $400 billion or more. "How can we talk about an election-year gift to the American people when we're broke?"

Sasser argued that the bill would simply authorize a shift of money that could have been spent anyway from one spending category to another, with no net impact on the deficit.

But even fellow Democrats disputed him. "There's only one guaranteed result to a change in the budget deal, and that's to increase the deficit," said Senate Armed Services Committee Chairman Sam Nunn, D-Ga. "If we pass this amendment . . . the defense budget will become the equivalent of the House bank."

In the end, Senate Majority Leader George J. Mitchell, D-Maine, was unable to shut down a filibuster against the measure. Mitchell and Sasser came up 10 votes short of the 60 they needed to move the bill forward. The motion to invoke cloture (and thereby end the filibuster) was rejected, 50-48: R 3-40; D 47-8 (ND 35-3, SD 12-5). *(House key vote 3)*

4. Fetal Tissue Research

Of all the abortion-related issues the 102nd Congress grappled with, none hit as close to home as whether to lift the Bush administration's ban on research using tissue from aborted fetuses.

Abortion opponents, including Bush, supported the ban because they feared the research, if successful, could encourage women to have abortions. But that was by no means a universal view among those who opposed abortion. Even some of the Congress's strongest abortion foes — such as Sens. Strom Thurmond, R-S.C., and Mark O. Hatfield, R-Ore. — opposed the ban. They argued that it was wrong to refuse to fund research that scientists said had the potential to provide treatments or even cures for such ailments as diabetes, Parkinson's disease and Alzheimer's disease. And they hammered their message home by citing the plights of friends and relatives who were waiting for a miracle; people such as Thurmond's daughter, Julie, who suffered from diabetes, and former Rep. Morris K. Udall, D-Ariz., who was forced to retire due to Parkinson's disease.

By early 1992, it became clear to abortion foes who supported the ban that they needed to provide an alternative if they were to avert legislative defeat. That alternative, provided during Senate floor consideration in late March of legislation to reauthorize the National Institutes of Health (which contained language to overturn the ban), came in the form of an amendment offered by Sen. Orrin G. Hatch, R-Utah. Hatch's amendment would have allowed the research to go forward, but instead of using remains from elective abortions, it would have created a series of "banks" to collect tissue from miscarriages and tubal pregnancies. Hatch was backed by experts who said such remains could provide enough tissue to allow the research effort to proceed.

Advocates of unfettered fetal tissue research produced experts of their own who said that tissue from miscarriages and tubal pregnancies is often diseased and unusable for research, and that it was not possible to harvest tissue fast enough from such unplanned events as miscarriages. Their argument prevailed overwhelmingly in the Senate, which rejected Hatch's amendment March 31 on a vote of 23-77: R 20-23; D 3-54 (ND 1-39, SD 2-15).

But while opponents of the ban won the battle, the staunch abortion foes temporarily won the war. Bush created the tissue banks by executive order in May and vetoed the NIH bill (HR 2507) in June, and the House failed to override. The Senate in October tried to take up yet another NIH bill that would have required researchers first to seek samples from the tissue banks but, if tissue was not readily available, would then allow them to use samples from abortions. That bill died in an end-of-session filibuster. However, upon assuming office, Bill Clinton on Jan. 22, 1993, by executive order, overturned the 'gag rule.'

5. Campaign Finance

Passing a campaign finance bill was nothing new for the Senate; it had done so in each of the previous two Congresses. But sending a bill to the White House, as the Senate did April 30, was a new experience for many. Only 10 of the senators who voted for the bill (S 3) had been in the chamber in 1974, when the last campaign finance overhaul was enacted.

The 1992 experience, however, was academic. A veto had been guaranteed since Day One.

The Senate had passed S 3 in May 1991. The only question in 1992 was whether House and Senate conferees would try to somehow bridge the chasms that separated the chambers' bills and the gulf separating the parties to produce a bill that the president might sign. In the end, they did not. Instead, Democrats in both chambers found common ground by letting each chamber write its own rules. But that plan left out Republican views, and President Bush vetoed the bill May 9.

The Democrats believed the way to reform the congressional system was to limit campaign spending. To accomplish this within the framework of the 1976 Supreme Court decision in *Buckley v. Valeo*, the bill would have provided federal funds to candidates who agreed to comply with the spending limits and other restrictions.

The bill would have established a complex formula for determining spending ceilings depending on state population. The highest would have been $8.9 million for a candidate from a large state with a contested primary and general election; the low, $636,500, for a candidate from a small state with a primary but no general election opponent.

Candidates who agreed to obey the limit would get benefits, including cut-rate postage and up to 20 percent of the spending cap in broadcast vouchers.

Most Republicans opposed the tenets of the bill. They believed spending limits would put challengers at a disadvantage, and they strongly objected to public funding.

One key Senate provision that changed significantly between 1991 and 1992 concerned contributions from political action committees (PACs).

The 1991 version of S 3 contained a prohibition on PAC participation in Senate campaigns. It was one provision that appealed to Republicans, who had grown tired of watching PAC contributions flow to the party that controlled Congress. Democrats went along with the proposal; it was accepted without a vote or even much debate.

But in 1992, when it was evident that the bill would clear Congress, Senate Democrats looked to their conferees to quietly dilute the ban. While not as dependent on PAC money as their House counterparts, Democratic senators who felt they could do without the politically risky special interest money had already kicked the habit. The others apparently felt they could not do without it.

So, without fuss, the conference changed the Senate provision to allow some contributions, limiting them to $2,500 per PAC per election (half the existing cap). PAC contributions could not total more than 20 percent of the limit for a particular state.

The Senate approved the conference report April 30 on a 58-42 vote, with two Republicans switching their votes from 1991 to oppose the bill because of the PAC provision. Three Democrats changed their positions to support the measure.

When the bill came back with a veto message, only one senator switched his vote: John McCain, R-Ariz., had voted for the conference report but supported the veto. The override on May 13 was 57-42: R 3-40; D 54-2 (ND 39-0, SD 15-2).

That was nine votes short of overriding the veto. "We'll be back again and again until we get it passed into law," vowed David L. Boren, D-Okla., chief Senate sponsor of the measure. *(House key vote 5)*

6. Ex-Soviet Aid

While support for U.S. aid to the former Soviet republics was stronger in the Senate than in the House, there was still a great deal of reluctance among Senators to help the former superpower. A number of Senators felt strongly that the United States should use the opportunity to impose stringent conditions on any such assistance. They argued that U.S. taxpayers should not be asked to send their money to nations that still posed a military threat or acted in other ways contrary to U.S. interests.

But the administration and other proponents of the legislation countered that any conditions would slow the distribution of the urgently needed assistance and possibly undermine the reform governments that it was intended to help. These fledgling regimes, while not perfect, were described as far friendlier to the United States than any replacement regime would be if they failed.

Perhaps the biggest obstacle to Senate approval of aid was the continued presence of about 100,000 former Soviet troops in the Baltic states of Lithuania, Latvia and Estonia. While Russian President Boris N. Yeltsin said it was the intention of the Commonwealth of Independent States to remove the troops eventually, the gradual withdrawal was not fast enough for Baltic supporters in Congress. They argued that these countries had never been part of the Soviet Union and that the troops represented an occupation force. The Russians countered that they could not withdraw the troops more quickly because they lacked housing and jobs for the soldiers and because the country needed first to get its economy in order.

When the ex-Soviet aid package came to the Senate floor July 1, Dennis DeConcini, D-Ariz., and Larry Pressler, R-S.D., offered an amendment to prohibit the United States from giving economic aid to Russia until the president certified that Moscow was making "significant progress" in withdrawing forces from the Baltics.

Backers of the bill said the amendment, if approved, would nullify the commitment of aid to Russia because the president would not be able to make such a certification. Foreign Relations Committee Chairman Claiborne Pell, D-

R.I., tried to modify the amendment by proposing a one-year delay in the certification requirement.

Pressler then made a motion to table (or kill) Pell's amendment for a grace period on the aid restriction. On this key vote, the motion was rejected 35-60: R 11-30; D 24-30 (ND 14-24, SD 10-6). Pell's amendment was then adopted by voice vote.

It was a turning point toward passage of aid with few strings attached. Most subsequent attempts to place conditions on the aid were blocked, and the bill (S 2532) was subsequently passed by a vote of 76-20. *(House key vote 14)*

7. Unemployment Compensation

For months, the House and the Senate had tried to persuade President Bush to extend emergency unemployment benefits for the long-term jobless. Existing authorization of extended benefits was due to expire July 4, 1992, and people exhausting state benefits after that date would not be eligible for federal benefits.

President Bush repeatedly complained about the price of continuing the emergency program, which had cost $2.7 billion. But when the national unemployment rate leaped three-tenths of a percent in June — to 7.8 percent, the highest rate in eight years — Bush softened his opposition considerably. Congress promptly moved on a $5.5 billion bill (HR 5260 — PL 102-318) extending benefits for the long-term jobless.

It may have been the final unemployment bill Congress would have to consider: Besides the emergency benefits, HR 5260 included a permanent change in the compensation system that was expected to make further extension bills unnecessary.

Because the usual mechanism releasing extended unemployment compensation was relatively restrictive, Congress had stepped in twice during the past year to override the regular extension system with emergency benefits. Under the regular system, jobless workers became eligible for state-federal extended benefits after they used up 26 weeks of state benefits, but only when statewide unemployment rates reached a certain trigger level. The bill changed the state-federal trigger, allowing the extended benefits to flow more quickly without intervention by Congress.

When the June unemployment rate was announced July 2, Bush's first reaction was that it was "not good news," but that he might still veto an unemployment bill if it cost too much. By the end of the day, however, Bush referred to HR 5260 as "an important safeguard for workers who still can't find jobs as the economy continues to grow."

The House-Senate conference report to HR 5260 had been written largely by Senate Finance Chairman Lloyd Bentsen, D-Texas, and represented a compromise between Bush and the original $5.8 billion House version.

Bentsen's bill also contained fewer permanent changes to the unemployment system. Bentsen's version provided unemployed workers in 15 states with 26 extra weeks of benefits and workers in all other states and the District of Columbia with 20 extra weeks until March 6, 1993. Those benefits went into effect when workers exhausted their state compensation without finding a job.

The change in the trigger for non-emergency extended benefits also went into effect: It would kick in March 7, 1993, the day after the emergency program expired.

The permanent change in the unemployment system was something Bush had vowed that he would not accept, but the higher unemployment numbers forced him to cave. The Senate on July 2 promptly cleared the conference report, 93-3: R 37-3; D 56-0 (ND 40-0, SD 16-0). Bush signed the bill the next day.

8. Strategic Defense Initiative

The Senate ratified the basic stand it had taken in 1991, funding a version of the strategic defense initiative (SDI) that was aimed at deploying a ground-based, anti-missile defense system. However, with the budget tight and the Soviet threat defunct, a majority of senators voted to rein in SDI spending.

On Aug. 7, the Senate in effect supported an amendment that would have sliced $1 billion in SDI funding from the defense authorization bill (S 3114). The key vote was on a motion to table (and thus kill) the amendment. The motion failed 43-49: R 34-5; D 9-44 (ND 4-33, SD 5-11).

The strong show of sentiment to reduce SDI funding even below the $4.3 billion proposed by the Armed Services Committee blocked action on the overall defense bill for more than a month. SDI opponents refused to back down; SDI supporters, backed by a veto threat from President Bush, refused to permit the Senate to proceed to the next procedural step — a vote on the amendment to cut the funding.

Senate leaders warned that the stalemate could kill the entire defense measure, leaving the Pentagon to rely on a stopgap appropriations bill. On Sept. 17, the Senate backed away from the SDI confrontation, settling on a $3.8 billion SDI research compromise engineered by Armed Services Committee Chairman Sam Nunn, D-Ga. The final version of the bill (HR 5006 — PL 102-484), as crafted by a House-Senate conference committee, included $4.05 billion for SDI. The compromise defense appropriations bill (HR 5504) incorporated the $3.8 billion compromise on SDI funding.

The Aug. 7 vote to slash SDI may have marked the start of a third phase in SDI's contentious political history in the Senate.

President Ronald Reagan launched the program in 1983, offering it as a revolutionary program to liberate the nation from the Soviet nuclear missile threat. In the first phase of the SDI debate, through 1986, Congress routinely reduced the SDI budget from Reagan's request but rejected proposals for deeper cuts that would have restricted the program to laboratory research.

In the second phase, between 1987 and 1992, the SDI debate turned on the role of space-based weapons. Republican conservatives, led by Sen. Malcolm Wallop, R-Wyo., sought an extensive system of space-based interceptors that could destroy Soviet missiles in the first few minutes of flight, before they could swamp the defense with multiple warheads and swarms of decoys. But that goal was challenged as provocative and technically questionable by centrist Democrats, including Nunn and House Armed Services Committee Chairman Les Aspin, Wis.

Nunn and Aspin instead promoted a more modest anti-missile defense intended to protect U.S. territory, overseas forces and allies against "limited" attacks by a Third World country or by a renegade military unit.

In a series of votes between 1987 and 1991, Congress essentially endorsed the Nunn-Aspin approach: It repeatedly forced unwilling Republican administrations to respect the prohibition on space-based weapons tests included in the 1972 U.S.-Soviet treaty limiting anti-ballistic missile defenses. And in 1991, the Senate recast Bush's SDI program to focus on near-term, ground-based defenses and to defer the space-based weapons.

In 1992, liberal Democrats still opposed to such a limited defense conceded that they had lost that fight. So when the Senate took up the Armed Services Committee's $4.3 billion recommendation for SDI — compared with the the $5.4 billion requested by Bush — Jim Sasser, D-Tenn., and Dale Bumpers, D-Ark., proposed the $1 billion cut to $3.3 billion. *(House key vote 8)*

9. Nuclear Test Ban

Symbolically closing the books on the Cold War, the Senate voted to end nuclear weapons testing. The more significant of two votes on the subject came Sept. 18, when the Senate approved, 55-40, an amendment to the fiscal 1993 defense authorization bill (S 3114) that would have imposed a nine-month halt to nuclear testing, to be followed by a permanent test ban after the end of fiscal 1996.

For four decades, a test ban was largely a distant dream of liberal activists. Every president from Dwight D. Eisenhower to Ronald Reagan proclaimed an eventual end to testing as a national goal, but only Jimmy Carter accorded the goal more than lip service.

In fiscal 1986 through 1988, the House annually had approved an amendment to the defense authorization bill that would have barred tests of nuclear weapons with an explosive punch greater than 1,000 tons of TNT. But those votes were largely symbolic, taken on the assumption the Senate would reject any significant nuclear test limitations.

And, indeed, so long as the Soviet nuclear threat was intact, a majority of senators seemed to accept the contention of Pentagon and Energy Department nuclear weapons specialists: that continuous testing was required to check on the safety and reliability of weapons already in the U.S. stockpile.

But with the disintegration of the Soviet Union — and with Russian President Boris N. Yeltsin observing a self-imposed nuclear test moratorium — test ban proponents in 1992 stepped up their efforts to terminate the U.S. testing program.

For the first time, they were supported by Senate Armed Services Committee Chairman Sam Nunn, D-Ga., who echoed what had long been one of the liberals' arguments: That a halt to testing might give Washington more diplomatic leverage to dissuade other countries from trying to develop nuclear weapons.

On Aug. 3, the Senate approved 68-26 an amendment by Mark O. Hatfield, R-Ore., to the fiscal 1993 energy and water appropriations bill (HR 5373) to impose a nine-month testing halt followed in 1996 by a permanent ban. But that vote overstated Senate support for the proposal because several opponents voted for the amendment for tactical reasons.

On Sept. 18, Hatfield offered a similar amendment to the defense authorization bill. It was approved 55-40: R 13-29; D 42-11 (ND 35-3, SD 7-8).

In the end, a halt to nuclear testing was enacted as part of the energy and water spending bill, and the sensitive provision then was dropped from the defense bill.

Despite the administration's vocal opposition to the test ban, President Bush signed the energy and water measure (PL 102-377), which also included funds for the politically appealing superconducting supercollider, an atom smasher being built in Texas that was eagerly sought by the administration.

10. Family and Medical Leave

With two votes more than necessary, the Senate on Sept. 24 overrode President Bush's veto of the Family and Medical Leave Act (S 5), a bill to require large companies to grant unpaid leave to employees for family and medical emergencies. It was the first time in four years the Senate had mustered a two-thirds override majority.

Although the House later sustained the family leave veto, the Senate vote presaged the decline of Bush's power in Congress. And it showed the bipartisan political appeal of an issue that directly targeted middle-age, middle-class families. The measure would have granted unpaid leave of up to 12 weeks to workers for the birth or adoption of a child or the illness of a close family member. Democrats and a number of Republicans generally supported it because of this "pro-family" bent.

And while most Republicans opposed the legislation because of its mandates on business, the override vote demonstrated the frustration of many within GOP ranks over Bush's refusal to negotiate a compromise with Democrats.

Just one year earlier, the Senate had approved with 65 votes — two short of what it took to override a veto — a compromise bill worked out by Democrat Christopher J. Dodd of Connecticut and Republican Christopher S. Bond of Missouri. At that time, two Democratic senators were off campaigning for president, and one was out sick. They all said they supported the bill, however, so it appeared that they would prevail if the president maintained his veto stance.

For the next year, Dodd and Bond tried to pull the administration on board. Seeking to take business interests into account, they agreed to exempt the highest-paid 10 percent of an employer's work force and to restrict eligibility for leave to employees who had worked at least 25 hours a week for the previous 12 months.

As it was, the bill would apply only to those businesses with more than 50 workers, exempting more than 95 percent of all employers (the largest 5 percent of businesses employ 60 percent of all workers).

But White House officials refused to budge. "They were not willing to deal," Bond complained. As the election neared, and as Democratic nominee Bill Clinton stepped up his campaign references to the family leave bill, Senate Democrats decided to make their push on the eve of the Republican convention in August. But GOP leaders threatened to block Dodd's effort to force a roll-call vote. Instead, senators adopted the House-Senate conference report by voice vote, delaying the showdown until after the promised veto.

And as expected, Bush vetoed the bill Sept. 22, sending it back to Capitol Hill. Although Dodd and Bond appeared to have the votes, they worried about Bush peeling away important conservatives, such as Daniel R. Coats, R-Ind., who had come on board in support of a "family values" bill.

But unlike nine previous Senate override votes, Bush could not sway the one or two votes he needed. With 99 senators voting on Sept. 24, the family leave sponsors prevailed on a vote of 68-31: R 14-28; D 54-3 (ND 40-0, SD 14-3).

As expected, three senators who were absent for the 1991 vote voted to override: Tom Harkin, D-Iowa, Bob Kerrey, D-Neb., and David Pryor, D-Ark. The lone Republican to switch over to the president's side — Ted Stevens of Alaska — was offset by a Democratic switch, David L. Boren of Oklahoma.

The House on Sept. 30 voted to sustain the veto, 258-169, killing the bill for the year. In that chamber, Republican opponents were able to convince conservative Democrats that the measure would burden businesses with unnecessary mandates.

In 1993, however, the bill became law. Upholding his promise to sign a family leave bill during his first 100 days in office, President Bill Clinton on Jan. 25 signed the legislation (HR 1 — PL 103-3). The bill was nearly identical to the one vetoed by Bush in 1992.

11. Taxes/Urban Aid

It was the second tax bill of the year — and the second one that appeared predestined for a veto. In came Senate Majority Leader Bob Dole, R-Kan., late on Sept. 25 with an amendment to shed several tax increases in the $32 billion bill (HR 11) in hopes of pleasing President Bush and maybe saving the measure.

But Dole's amendment failed 34-59: R 31-8; D 3-51 (ND 1-38, SD 2-13). If it was not clear before, it was clear then that the bill was doomed.

The demise of the Dole amendment offered a microcosmic glimpse into why Congress and Bush — despite mutual agreement about the need to stimulate the economy and to give tax incentives to blighted inner cities — could not overcome deep divisions that killed this bill and stunted tax policy making throughout much of the Bush administration.

Dole's amendment would have eliminated two tax raising provisions — a limit on itemized deductions and a phaseout of the personal exemption for upper-income taxpayers — that the White House had said it opposed.

To offset the $7.7 billion revenue loss caused by removing the provisions, the amendment also would have scaled back assistance for inner cities, removed a tax break for contributions to individual retirement accounts (IRAs) and shortened to 12 months from 15 months the extension provided for a dozen expiring tax provisions.

The basic problem that Dole was trying to address was one that lay below the surface as the bill progressed through Congress throughout the late summer and early fall.

After trying to tag Bill Clinton as a tax-and-spender because of his support for a slew of mostly minor revenue provisions during his tenure as Arkansas governor, Bush was refusing to open himself to the same charge by supporting anything resembling a tax increase. So Dole was trying to get the two most obvious tax increases out of the bill. "The president of the United States is not going to sign a tax increase 30 days before the election," he told the Senate.

But in cutting the tax increases, Dole also had to cut back on the tax breaks in the bill. And Senate Finance Committee Chairman Lloyd Bentsen, D-Texas, the architect of the IRA provisions, did not appreciate that — Bentsen's opinion carried a lot of weight among fellow Democrats. The vote against Dole's amendment went largely along party lines.

Dole's amendment had an additional problem. It would have lowered from 125 to 30 the number of enterprise zones created by the bill, severely cutting back on the tax assistance for inner cities that had been the original justification for doing the bill.

In short, the Senate discovered that it was impossible to do all it wanted in the bill without tax increases. But it also proved impossible to win Bush's support for a bill with new taxes, regardless of what else it contained. With the failure of the Dole amendment, it became clear there was no overcoming that basic impediment.

12. Abortion Counseling

By the time the Senate finally took its first roll-call vote on a bill to overturn the "gag rule" prohibiting abortion counseling in federally funded family planning clinics, the ultimate fate of the bill was no longer in doubt. Repeated votes in the House had made clear that, while a majority of members opposed the counseling ban, a two-thirds supermajority was not attainable to override a certain Bush veto.

Still, there was more than the usual amount of interest when the Senate on Oct. 1 cast its override vote on a bill (S 323) to overturn the ban and reauthorize the federal family planning program. It was the first time the Senate had taken a roll-call vote on the measure. Both the original bill, approved in July 1991, and the conference report on the measure, approved Sept. 14, had passed on voice votes. Congress watchers also were interested in whether the Senate would, for only the second time in the Bush presidency, muster the two-thirds override margin. (The first time came only a week earlier, when the chamber voted to override Bush's veto of a bill to require employers to provide unpaid family and medical leave.)

It appeared that the Senate would have little difficulty attaining the two-thirds majority to override. Ever since abortion became a major congressional issue in the 1970s, the Senate had traditionally been more sympathetic to abortion rights forces, while the House had generally leaned toward abortion foes. But the Supreme Court's 1989 decision in *Webster v. Reproductive Health Services*, which gave states some leeway in restricting abortions, rejuvenated abortion rights forces in both chambers. As a result, the House shifted to a more abortion rights stance and the Senate moved even further into that camp.

But supporters of the bill to overturn the gag rule remained worried. Bush aides had been amazingly successful over the previous four years in getting Senate Republicans to stand by the president even when they did not agree with his veto. And it was not entirely clear how many Democrats with mixed abortion voting records would go for the override.

But the Senate vote on Oct. 1 left few doubts about where senators stood. The vote was 73-26: R 20-23; D 53-3 (ND 40-0, SD 13-3) — seven more than needed to override. A day later, however, the House surprised no one when members voted to sustain Bush's veto. *(House key vote 6)*

13. Foreign Aid

After President Bush and Israeli Prime Minister Yitzhak Rabin agreed in August on a package of loan guarantees for Jerusalem, Senate approval of the fiscal 1993 foreign aid appropriations bill (HR 5368 — PL 102-391) was virtually assured.

The Senate has long been a wellspring of support for Israel, and the authorization of the five-year program of loan guarantees — on top of the $3 billion usually provided Israel in the foreign aid bill — made the measure palatable for senators even during an election year focused on domestic concerns.

In the key vote Oct. 1, the Senate passed the $26.4 billion foreign aid appropriations bill, 87-12: R 35-8; D 52-4 (ND 39-1, SD 13-3).

It marked the first time in two years that the Senate had approved an aid bill. The fiscal 1992 measure became embroiled in a bitter battle between the Bush administration and Israeli government over loan guarantees.

Despite the chronic unpopularity of foreign aid, there were only a few attempts to cut the funding. Sen. Jesse Helms, R-N.C., failed in a bid to cut funding by 10 percent.

Nor was there opposition to the loan guarantees or to the bill's other major initiative, $12.3 billion in new financing for the International Monetary Fund.

But the measure addressed a host of issues arising from the breakup of the former Soviet Union and the bitter ethnic conflicts exploding in many parts of the world.

The legislation put the Senate squarely on the side of Bosnia-Herzegovina in the Yugoslav civil war by authorizing the president to provide up to $50 million in U.S. defense equipment for the country. Sen. Joseph R. Biden Jr., D-Del., who sponsored the amendment, said that 100,000 Bosnians might be "frozen while under Serbian seige" during the coming winter if Western nations ignored their plight. "Are we truly to adjourn, having done nothing?" he asked his colleagues.

The measure did not require the president to take action, and the United Nations would have to lift its arms embargo on former Yugoslavia for any arms to be provided. Still, Bush administration officials expressed concern that the introduction of more weapons into the region would only fuel the Yugoslav conflict, although they did not actively oppose Biden's amendment.

The legislation also earmarked $55 million in refugee aid and other assistance for victims of the fighting in former Yugoslavia.

Although the Senate fully funded the Bush administration request for $417 million in aid for the former Soviet Union, it imposed restrictions on the assistance program. The measure stipulated that no U.S. aid could be provided to Russia — except for humanitarian assistance — unless Moscow either removed its troops from the three Baltic States or negotiated an agreement for withdrawing its forces.

The bill also barred most assistance to Russia unless the president certified that Moscow had ceased military exports to Iran. The amendment, offered by Helms, came in response to reports that Russia had sold Iran submarines over the objections of the United States. The restrictions were relaxed significantly by House-Senate conferees in the final version of the bill. *(House key vote 15)*

14. Cable Reregulation

Never had the Bush administration worked so hard to whip up support to sustain a veto — only to get whipped so badly.

When the Senate on Oct. 5 voted to override President Bush's veto of a bill to reregulate the cable television industry, followed by similar House action hours later, the president lost his first veto confrontation with Congress. The Senate vote was 74-25: R 24-18; D 50-7 (ND 36-4, SD 14-3), more than the two-thirds majority needed to override the veto.

By casting the showdown as a critical test of presidential loyalty, White House advisers misjudged more than Bush's slumping popularity. They also misread members' awareness of the American public's desire for inexpensive television viewing.

Bush viewed the legislation as an unfair encroachment on the business prerogatives of a successful private industry. He also agreed with cable industry arguments that the bill had become laden with special interest provisions to help broadcasters and the home satellite dish industry, and that those provisions would make cable rates rise, not fall.

But lawmakers from both parties saw cable television as an unregulated monopoly, and their votes responded to heavy lobbying by broadcasters and consumer groups who complained of a 61 percent average increase in cable rates since the industry was deregulated in 1987.

The legislation (S 12 — PL 102-385) required the Federal Communications Commission to regulate rates for the lowest-priced package of programming subscribed to by the nation's 56 million cable viewers. It also took steps to help competitors such as home satellite dish programmers compete with the $20 billion cable industry.

Bush, his Chief of Staff James A. Baker III and Senate Republican leader Bob Dole of Kansas worked hard to persuade enough senators to abandon their support for the legislation. The Senate had adopted the conference report Sept. 22 on a 74-25 vote.

In fact, the administration came close to winning the 34 senators needed to sustain the veto, falling just one or two votes short at one point. When it became apparent that the votes could not be mustered, senators who agreed to switch were released from their commitments. As a result, the override vote was unchanged from the Sept. 22 vote on the conference report.

That the Democratic-controlled Congress denied Bush a perfect veto record — a rarity in modern times — took on heightened importance at a time when the president was struggling to gain ground against Democratic presidential challenger Bill Clinton.

"On this particular bill, [Bush] had very little to trade with, other than loyalty to the party and loyalty to him. And he didn't get it," said James A. Thurber, director of the Center for Congressional and Presidential Studies at American University. *(House key vote 12)*

15. Western Water Bill

The usually solid wall of unanimity among Western senators cracked a bit in the 102nd Congress under the powerful force of water.

In the waning days of the session, Congress approved, and President Bush signed, a huge omnibus water bill (HR 429 — PL 102-575) that had provisions affecting every Western state. The 40-title bill garnered interest from every Western quarter but, in the end, the battle came down to one title.

Title 34, long pushed by Sen. Bill Bradley, D-N.J., sought to revamp the operations of the Central Valley Project (CVP) in California, the federal government's largest irrigation and power project. Environmentalists and urban interests maintained that some way had to be found to reallocate the CVP's water, 85 percent of which was being sold at heavily discounted rates to 23,000 farming operations.

The CVP had always been blamed for environmental problems: changed stream flows, declining salmon populations and diminishing wildfowl habitat. Then a six-year drought in California started to pinch urban families and businesses that complained of being subject to rationing and high rates while nearby farmers got water for much less.

Along with George Miller, D-Calif., chairman of the House Interior and Insular Affairs Committee, and J. Bennett Johnston, D-La., chairman of the Senate Energy and Natural Resources Committee, Bradley fashioned a CVP title that would transfer more water to fish and wildlife purposes; allow urban users to buy project water from willing sellers; and shorten long-term water contracts to enhance flexibility in water distribution.

But Bradley had an implacable opponent on the measure: California Republican John Seymour, who argued that Bradley's proposal would hurt his supporters among the state's powerful farming interests.

In most situations, Seymour could have counted on aid from his fellow Western conservatives, but this time he received scant help. For example, Jake Garn, the retiring Republican from Utah, was consumed with getting the long-sought authorization to complete the massive Central Utah Irrigation Project, a measure also in the bill. Garn was not about to let a lone senator kill off the entire bill, and he said so on a number of occasions.

Seymour's main ally was Republican Gov. Pete Wilson, who once held Seymour's seat and who as governor had appointed Seymour as his replacement in the Senate.

When the conference report came to the Senate floor Oct. 8, Seymour fought with all the dilatory weapons afforded him by the Senate.

He helped Alfonse M. D'Amato, R-N.Y., who mounted an all-night filibuster on another, unrelated bill. And he insisted that the clerk read the entire 396-page bill, a procedure that took hours of precious Senate time in the closing days of the session.

But again Seymour got little support from his Western brethren. Even as the bill was making its way to the floor, word got out that Garn and other senators had met with White House Chief of Staff James A. Baker III to lobby against a veto.

When it became clear that he did not have the votes to prevent Senate leaders from invoking cloture, Seymour caved. He agreed to a deal in which the Senate would approve a symbolic bill that incorporated the California farm community's wish list. But because that bill moved on the next-to-last day of the session, it died when the House failed to act.

The Senate, meanwhile, finally adopted the conference report on HR 429 on Oct. 8. The vote was 83-8: R 30-8; D 53-0 (ND 38-0, SD 15-0). Only two other Westerners joined Seymour in opposing the bill: Republicans Hank Brown of Colorado and Larry E. Craig of Idaho.

President Bush signed the measure Oct. 30 in the midst of his unsuccessful campaign for re-election. The move was widely seen as an attempt to win favor in Utah and other Western states, even at the sacrifice of California. *(House key vote 16)*

House

1. Taxes

When the House passed the first tax bill of the year (HR 4210) on Feb. 27, it was more of an election-year manifesto for the Democratic Party than serious legislation. Even so, party leaders clearly underestimated the difficulty they would have persuading their own rank and file to go along with a measure that promised higher taxes on the rich to finance a tax cut for the middle class.

Finding themselves short of a majority hours before the scheduled vote, House Democratic leaders resorted to a hard-nosed appeal, arguing that their party had made tax cuts for the middle class its rallying cry and could not turn back.

It worked — but just barely. A Democratic substitute amendment by Ways and Means Chairman Dan Rostenkowski, Ill., carried 221-210: R 1-164; D 219-46 (ND 156-27, SD 63-19); I 1-0. The bill (HR 4210) subsequently passed 221-209.

Many members said the bill was inadequate, either because the tax cut was too meager, or because it was the wrong policy in an era of massive deficits. Another contingent of Democrats feared voting for the higher taxes on upper-income earners that their leaders contended would bring greater fairness to the tax code, but which would have kicked in for individuals with taxable incomes as low as $85,000.

Democrats were divided from the start about whether the central feature of their bill should have been middle-class tax relief or help for the economy. Trying to accomplish both, Rostenkowski included provisions to help the real estate industry and other sectors of the economy.

But Democratic leaders, in particular Majority Leader Richard A. Gephardt, Mo., saw the vote and the bill as an opportunity to put President Bush in a political bind: They hoped he would have to choose between opposing the middle-class tax cut or raising taxes — something he vowed never to repeat after signing a tax increase in 1990.

In a heated speech during floor debate on the bill, Gephardt said, "The question in this bill is: Where does the money go? Who do you stand for? Who do you fight for?"

Before the vote, the White House and House Republicans did their best to parry any political advantage for the Democrats, arguing that the bill was a straightforward tax increase that would do little to help the economy and would probably even hurt it. In solidarity with Bush, every House Republican but one voted against the Democratic package.

The Democrat's slim victory underscored the feeling that the bill was doomed to result in an election-year standoff with Bush, who was promising to veto any bill raising taxes. A month later, presented with the final version of the tax bill, Bush did just as he promised. And the Democrats' manifesto, endorsing higher taxes on the rich to pay for lower taxes on the middle class, was done for the year.

2. House Bank Overdrafts

On the surface, the House was in unanimous agreement. In the early morning hours of March 13 it voted 426-0 — R 165-0; D 260-0 (ND 178-0, SD 82-0); I 1-0 — to reveal the names of all who overdrew their House bank accounts.

In fact, members could not have been more divided over an issue that paralyzed the House for weeks, embarrassed hundreds of members and several Cabinet members, increased public disdain for Congress, gave the executive branch unprecedented access to intimate details of members' personal finances, prompted the House to reform its internal operations and eventually helped end the careers of many members from both parties.

The issue was divisive from its inception on Sept. 18, 1991, when the General Accounting Office revealed that despite past reform attempts, the members-only House bank allowed members to routinely overdraw their checking accounts.

Activist Republicans, especially a group of freshmen known as the Gang of Seven, drove the process from the beginning. Both parties' leaders tried to end the matter by scolding members for continuing to overdraw their accounts. But the activists said that was not enough, and in October successfully pushed for the bank to be closed and for the Committee on Standards of Official Conduct to open an ethics inquiry.

After a five-month investigation, the ethics committee on March 5 proposed revealing the names of only the 24 worst offenders — those the panel decided had "abused their banking privileges" by routinely overdrawing their accounts by significant amounts during 3¼ years studied by the panel.

Again the Republicans, who with fewer members in office had less to lose, balked. Under the committee's proposal, more than 300 members who overdrew their accounts, including some with hundreds of overdrafts, could have remained anonymous. Although a bipartisan subcommittee of the ethics panel had approved the proposal unanimously, four GOP members of the full committee dissented, calling the proposal a whitewash.

Democratic leaders tried to rally their members behind the committee's proposal as the week of March 9 opened. They received no help from Republican Leader Robert H. Michel, Ill., who after a GOP leadership meeting March 10 broke his silence to endorse "full disclosure" — publicizing the names and overdraft totals of each current and former member who overdrew. President Bush backed full disclosure March 11.

Rank-and-file Democrats quickly began distancing themselves from the ethics committee's proposal. At a whip organization meeting March 12, Speaker Thomas S. Foley, D-Wash., was pummeled by members who either favored full disclosure or saw the fight as a sure loser. The leadership relented.

Closed-door meetings to work out the details and explain the ramifications of full disclosure to members went into the evening. The final debate did not begin until 8:25 p.m., when Sergeant-at-Arms Jack Russ, who ran the House bank and cashed some of his own bad checks there, resigned.

There was no longer any question what would happen, although members made speeches into the night about what they were doing. The ethics committee proposal to name the abusers (H Res 393) was taken up first, and it was approved 391-36 at 11 p.m., assuring those with fewer overdrafts that the most serious cases would be spotlighted. The full disclosure resolution (H Res 396) was not approved until 1:15 a.m. the next day.

Throughout the night, the mood was somber. "As of today," ethics member Fred Grandy, R-Iowa, told his colleagues, "your talk show hosts have a topic; as of today, your opponent has an issue and your constituents have a reason to support term limitations." Members opposed to full disclosure voiced doubts, but voted "yea" anyway. "I hope it will be clear to the country that we are not hiding any information, embarrassing as it may be, misleading as it may be, in many cases unjust to members as it may be; we are going to release it," Foley said.

After an arduous appeals process, the committee on April 1 cited 17 current and five former members for abusing their banking privileges and on April 16 revealed the names of 252 current members and 51 former members who overdrew their accounts. A week after all the names came out, the Justice Department's special counsel investigating the scandal for criminal wrongdoing, Malcolm R. Wilkey, subpoenaed the bank's records, prompting another weeklong fight over how much to disclose. Again, the Republicans won under the aegis of full disclosure, 347-64, on April 29.

In September, Wilkey resuscitated the issue for fall campaigns when he began sending members letters telling them their records were no longer under scrutiny. Controversy over checks helped account for perhaps a third of the 96 members who retired or were denied re-election in 1992.

On. Dec. 16, Wilkey issued a report calling for a criminal investigation of a few unspecified members and former members, and the Justice Department announced that it had opened such an inquiry.

3. Budget 'Walls'

After President Bush challenged Congress to pass his economic agenda in a combative State of the Union address Jan. 28, House Democratic leaders decided to try to retake the political momentum by confronting him over a series of economic issues. In addition to a tax bill and a budget resolution that would spell out their — not his — priorities, leaders planned to move quickly to knock down the budget "walls" that prohibited shifting defense money to domestic spending programs.

The 1990 budget summit agreement walled off defense, domestic and international appropriations into separate, inviolable categories. While nothing barred Congress from further reducing defense, the savings could only be used for deficit reduction, a psychological barrier that White House negotiators hoped would safeguard defense funds from a Congress that might want to raid defense for domestic projects.

But the disintegration of the Soviet Union and the collapse of the once-potent Soviet military strengthened a conviction among Democratic leaders that the priorities set by the 1990 summit were obsolete. Democratic strategists believed that shifting defense funds to cash-short domestic programs would draw a clear distinction between Democrats and Republicans during the presidential election year — demonstrating that Democrats were committed to investing in critical home-front programs, while the Bush White House and congressional Republicans were still locked in outmoded Cold War thinking. Bush had threatened to veto any bill to knock down the walls, but Democratic leaders figured a veto would draw the political distinctions that much more sharply.

But the leadership failed to reckon on dissension in the ranks. Trouble surfaced early when conservative Democrats on the House Budget Committee forced the panel to produce two budgets: a walls-down, leadership budget that devoted most defense savings to domestic programs; and a walls-up, conservative budget that would use any defense cuts for deficit reduction. The leadership budget would prevail only if the House passed a separate bill to knock down the walls.

Worried about support among their rank and file, Democratic leaders repeatedly postponed a scheduled vote on a bill (HR 3732), drawn up by Government Operations Committee Chairman John Conyers Jr., D-Mich., to eliminate the budget walls. When they finally brought the bill to a vote March 31, members rejected it overwhelmingly, 187-238: R 0-162; D 186-76 (ND 151-28, SD 35-48); I 1-0.

The anatomy of the Democratic coalition against the walls bill was a study in strange bedfellows. On one side were mostly conservative deficit hawks worried about budget discipline and defense hawks concerned about opening the floodgates between defense and domestic spending categories. On the other were members, including moderates and liberals, who worried that a cut in defense funds would mean a loss of hometown defense jobs.

The vote was one of several occasions during the year when House Democratic leaders miscalculated the strength of conservative "boll weevil" Democrats, led by Charles W. Stenholm of Texas. On this and other key issues, conservative Democrats were able to briefly form a working majority with unified House Republicans to push the House in a more fiscally conservative direction than Democratic leaders wanted it to go. *(Senate key vote 3)*

4. RTC Financing

Three years into the government's cleanup of hundreds of failed savings and loan institutions, Congress allowed the salvage operation to grind to a halt in April 1992.

Leary of angry voters and worried about the ever-rising cost, the House overwhelmingly refused to pump any more taxpayer money into the effort — though it was obvious to all that the refusal was nothing more than a costly postponement.

Multiple factors contributed to the House decision — including partisanship, gamesmanship and outright fear. From the beginnings of the thrift bailout in 1989 through the fall of 1991, Congress had pumped $80 billion into the Resolution Trust Corporation (RTC). More than half of that sum had come from taxpayers; a bit over $30 billion was ponied up by the thrift industry itself.

In November 1991, the first $80 billion was gone and hundreds of dead and dying thrifts remained to be shut down. So Congress reluctantly voted to give the RTC an additional $25 billion, with the stipulation that any amount that remained unspent on April 1, 1992, would revert to the Treasury. When April came, about $18 billion was returned, and the RTC's ability to close institutions and pay off depositors (or pay other banks or thrifts to take over failed thrifts) effectively came to an end.

Many members had hoped that agreement could be reached on a package of management and policy reforms for the RTC — a huge agency that created controversy with nearly every decision it made. Some critics thought it moved too slowly to reduce its huge inventory of loans and securities taken from failed thrifts; others accused it of dumping real estate on an already weakened market, or of cutting special deals with a privileged few investors.

Still others complained that other government policies — not decisions by the RTC — were causing some weak thrifts to be needlessly closed. House Republicans, led by Bill McCollum of Florida, rallied to that cause, refusing to support additional money for the RTC unless banking laws were changed to allow some weakened thrifts to be kept open.

Most Democrats saw the GOP plan as yet another instance of forbearance — the sort of policy that contributed to the crisis in the first place — and refused. (House Republican Whip Newt Gingrich of Georgia had his own gambit: He wanted to use the RTC bill to force a vote on a GOP economic stimulus package.) The result was a stalemate in the House.

On March 26, the Senate voted 52-42 in favor of a bill (S 2482) that incorporated a Bush administration request for $25 billion more for the RTC, plus restoration of the unused appropriation from the previous November. That amount would be enough, administration officials assured Congress, to conclude the cleanup. Two weeks earlier, the House Banking Committee approved a similar measure (HR 4241), but it proved impossible to line up enough votes for it to pass on the floor.

House leaders then decided to bring up a very narrow bill (HR 4704) that merely would have restored the unused $18 billion. McCollum was not allowed to offer an amendment, and Republicans decided to abandon the bill — despite administration pleas for support. With little GOP backing for spending taxpayer money on such an unpopular cause, Democrats also voted "nay." The bill went down overwhelmingly on April 1, 125-298: R 45-117; D 80-180 (ND 47-130, SD 33-50); I 0-1.

The stalemate continued for the balance of the year. The House did not try to bring the bill up again, and the administration did not press the matter with any noticeable vigor.

5. Campaign Finance

Context was everything for the 1992 campaign finance bill. For House Democrats, under siege all spring for a series of scandals, the bill became a centerpiece of their efforts to claim the mantle of reform. On April 9, the chamber resuscitated a bill to overhaul campaign law for the first time in 18 years. Just hours later, the House voted to turn the chamber's internal operations over to a professional administrator and voted three times on resolutions to keep the heat on an internal investigation of problems at the House Post Office.

The broader context, however, was decades of wrangling between Democrats and Republicans over which party would be advantaged by a new system. Here Republicans had the last say, because President Bush made good on his oft-repeated veto threats in May, and the bill died.

At the beginning of the year, it was not clear that there would be any campaign finance bill for the House to vote on. In the first session, both chambers had passed legislation to change the financing practices for congressional campaigns. But the Senate and House bills were incompatible — the Senate provided publicly funded broadcast vouchers to candidates, while the House proposed matching funds for its candidates — and Democrats in the two chambers had wide differences in sensitive areas such as political action committee (PAC) contributions. Both bills were veto bait for Bush.

In that environment, there was little incentive to make the tough choices required to reach a conference accord and send it to the House floor. But with the House bank scandal generating headlines and public esteem for the House falling precipitously, the climate changed and Democrats rushed to the conference table.

House negotiators gave up any hope that the House and Senate would agree on one public funding formula, which made drafting a conference report a simple task of essentially stapling the two bills together.

The final bill would have set a $600,000 optional spending limit for House races in primary and general elections. Candidates who agreed to obey the limit would get benefits, including cut-rate postage and up to $200,000 in public funds doled out to match the first $200 of each individual contribution.

Republicans dubbed the measure another congressional perk. They said a spending limit would benefit incumbents, most of whom were Democrats, at the expense of challengers who have to compete against the taxpayer-financed communications network that House members enjoy. Republicans also objected to the public funding, which Minority Whip Newt Gingrich, R-Ga., called "a new House bank with a new line of credit."

Republicans and outside reform advocates found common ground on the PAC issue. For different reasons, both would have preferred that PACs, which traditionally favored incumbents, be locked out of participation in congressional campaigns. Democrats wanted no part of that. For House campaigns, the bill left intact the existing $5,000 limit on individual PAC campaign donations, although it would have placed a $200,000 aggregate cap on how much a candidate could accept from PACs.

When the conference report made it to the House floor on April 9, party positions were already staked out. The bill's promise that public financing provisions would have to be worked out later gave Southern Democrats the cover they needed, and few members crossed party lines. The House adopted the conference report 259-165: R 19-145; D 239-20 (ND 171-6, SD 68-14); I 1-0.

Subsequent action was equally predictable: the Senate passed the bill April 30 and the president vetoed the bill May 9. The Senate override attempt failed. *(Senate key vote 5)*

6. Abortion Counseling

Though ultimately unsuccessful, congressional efforts in 1992 to overturn the "gag rule" prohibiting abortion counseling in federally funded family planning clinics aptly illustrated both how far abortion rights supporters had come and how far they still had to go.

For more than a decade, the House was a stronghold for abortion opponents. In the late 1970s and early 1980s, House members took the lead in imposing a series of restrictions on the procedure, mostly on funding matters.

But the Supreme Court's 1989 decision in *Webster v. Reproductive Health Services* changed all that. Just as 1973's *Roe v. Wade*, which created a nationwide right to abortion, galvanized forces opposed to the procedure, so *Webster*, which gave states more latitude to restrict abortion access, helped rejuvenate abortion rights activists. Since the decision, however, House abortion rights forces could manage to muster only a majority to overturn a variety of abortion-related restrictions, never the two-thirds needed to override repeated vetoes by anti-abortion stalwart President Bush.

The key abortion counseling vote of the year came April 30 on final passage of legislation to reauthorize the federal family planning program, Title X of the Public Health Service Act. It showed the progress abortion rights backers had made. Approval of the measure (HR 3090) marked the first time since 1984 that the chamber had voted to reauthorize the program. The last time sponsors tried to do so, in 1985, the bill received only 214 votes, less than a majority and far less than the two-thirds needed for passage under the fast-track procedure sponsors used at the time. This time the vote for passage was a strong 268-150: R 55-105; D 212-45 (ND 146-28, SD 66-17); I 1-0.

But the vote also signaled that, while abortion rights forces might have turned things around in the House, even on their strongest issues they remained unable to overturn any of the federal government's existing anti-abortion policies — as long as Bush stood by his veto promise. Many abortion foes in both parties opposed the abortion counseling rules, upheld by the Supreme Court in 1991, on the grounds that they violated free speech guarantees and medical ethics. But even with those added votes, the total was 11 short of the number needed to override Bush's promised veto.

And, in fact, the House on Oct. 2 subsequently sustained Bush's veto on a 266-148 vote. *(Senate key vote 12)*

7. National Energy Strategy

There was little drama about the outcome of the May 27 House vote on a massive energy bill even before members passed the legislation 381-37: R 135-23; D 245-14 (ND 173-2, SD 72-12); I 1-0.

But the vote on the House bill (HR 776) was among the most important of 1992, virtually ensuring that Congress would make its first major attempt in more than a decade to curb U.S. dependence on foreign oil.

The 102nd Congress convened in the midst of the Persian Gulf crisis, which highlighted the economic and human cost of the nation's enormous thirst for oil. Not surprisingly, energy policy quickly shot to the top of the political agenda with scores of politicians clamoring for new measures to reduce oil imports.

The Bush administration outlined its policy prescriptions in a massive "National Energy Strategy" almost two years in the making. Many lawmakers peddled their own proposals, attacking the Bush plan as overly generous to oil and gas producers and the nuclear industry while slighting conservation and renewable energy.

Sen. J. Bennett Johnston, D-La., who chaired the Senate Energy Committee, quickly moved a sweeping energy bill through his committee. Environmentalists and other critics blocked it from coming to the floor late in 1991, but Johnston returned early in 1992 with a revised version. That bill, which did not include controversial proposals to allow drilling in Alaska's Arctic National Wildlife Refuge or mandate greater automobile fuel economy, easily passed the Senate in February. The legislation included measures to promote conservation and renewable energy, spur competition in the electricity industry, make it easier to build natural gas pipelines and nuclear power plants, and promote cars that run on non-gasoline fuels

House leaders then stepped up efforts to deliver a parallel energy bill. Although Rep. Philip R. Sharp, D-Ind., already had steered such a bill through the Energy and Commerce subcommittee he chairs, it was no simple matter to get the bill to the floor.

After the full Energy and Commerce Committee approved the legislation, it was referred to eight additional House panels. Critics complained that delays would kill the bill or that the result would be an incoherent or politically doomed patchwork, particularly as committees such as Interior and Merchant Marine and Fisheries added large and controversial restrictions on production sought by environmentalists. The Ways and Means Committee added a package of energy-related tax measures that included tax breaks for independent oil and gas drillers as well as renewable energy and some non-gasoline fuels.

But House Speaker Thomas S. Foley, D-Wash., set a deadline for the panels, and the Rules Committee subsequently trimmed some of the controversial additions. Other conflicts were resolved after key floor votes, and the finished product, while more pleasing to environmentalists, was very similar to the Senate bill.

Once the House acted, the political pressure for the Democratic-led Congress to send a finished product to the White House helped propel the massive bills through a difficult conference committee.

Lopsided votes in both chambers for energy legislation reflect policy weaknesses as well as strengths: The final version was expected to cap instead of decrease the country's growing oil imports, and many lawmakers say it did not go far enough either in aiding domestic production or, alternately, in curbing consumption. However, the legislation was considered a balanced effort bound to reverse the laissez-faire attitude on energy policy that dominated the 1980s and set the groundwork for additional efforts to cut oil imports.

8. Strategic Defense Initiative

In its first clear test of sentiment on the issue, the House on June 5 in effect backed deployment of a ground-based anti-missile defense.

The key vote came when the House rejected an amendment to the fiscal 1993 defense authorization bill (HR 5006 — PL 102-484) that would have reduced funding for the strategic defense initiative (SDI) by almost $1 billion, to $3.3 billion. The vote was 161-211: R 11-134; D 149-77 (ND 125-31, SD 24-46); I 1-0.

Through 1991, the annual House action on SDI basically consisted of members staking out the lowest possible funding figure, anticipating that the Senate would approve a larger budget for the program and that a compromise sum would be hammered out in conference.

Liberal arms control activists, led by California Democrats Ronald V. Dellums and Barbara Boxer, repeatedly had proposed substantial cuts in SDI spending that were designed to limit the program to laboratory research. But the House routinely had rejected their initiatives by substantial margins. Instead, the House annually approved more modest reductions in SDI spending that would not have fundamentally reshaped the program.

In 1991, the Senate recast SDI to focus on the relatively early deployment of a ground-based anti-missile defense, consistent with the 1972 U.S.-Soviet treaty limiting anti-ballistic missile systems. The Senate action was essentially incorporated into the conference report on the fiscal 1992 defense authorization bill. SDI critics objected that the procedure had deprived House members of any opportunity to debate the revamped SDI mission.

In 1992, the House Armed Services Committee brought to the House floor a fiscal 1993 authorization bill that backed $4.3 billion for the revised version of SDI, compared with the $5.4 billion requested. Illinois Democrat Richard J. Durbin offered the amendment to trim $938 million from the committee's recommendation. But members rejected this first opportunity to dissent from the SDI compromise favored by Armed Services Chairman Les Aspin, D-Wis.

During House debate July 2 on the companion defense appropriations bill (HR 5504), a Durbin amendment that would have cut $700 million from SDI was rejected by a much closer vote of 201-217. In the interval between the two votes, the House had narrowly voted to reject a constitutional amendment to require a balanced federal budget. That contentious debate had boosted the pressure on members to demonstrate their willingness to cut spending, a factor that may have motivated some of the 26 members who voted against Durbin's SDI amendment on June 5 but then supported him on July 2. *(Senate key vote 8)*

9. Balanced Budget Amendment

For a decade, advocates of a constitutional amendment requiring a balanced budget had failed to convince their colleagues that such a move was just the sort of strong medicine Congress and the White House needed to bring the federal deficit under control. The high-water mark for advocates had come in 1982, when the Senate passed an amendment by slightly more than the two-thirds majority needed for passage. The House tried in 1982 and again in 1986 but defeated the measure both times.

In May 1992, however, amendment supporters seemed to be gaining converts. Despite the budget agreement hammered out in 1990, deficits had continued to grow; the White House budget office was estimating a fiscal 1992 deficit of roughly $400 billion. Meanwhile, public regard for Congress and its ability to handle the nation's finances was sinking during a critical election year. Democrats who had long opposed the idea were changing their minds out of sheer desperation, and longtime deficit hawk Charles W. Stenholm, D-Texas, had no trouble collecting the 218 signatures he needed on a petititon that allowed the amendment (H J Res 290) to bypass the committee bottleneck that had often stopped it from coming to the House floor.

But just when it looked like backers were sure to rally the support they needed in the House and the Senate, opponents began to fight back.

A psychological turning point came when Senate Appropriations Chairman Robert C. Byrd, D-W.Va., announced his adamant opposition and his intent to filibuster the measure in the Senate. Byrd argued that the amendment would shift fiscal power from Congress to the White House and to the federal courts, which could wind up ordering Congress to make specific spending cuts or tax increases. Byrd's stature and success record in the Senate were such that his announcement alone seemed to turn the tide. Opponents in the House then set about to sow doubt and fear among backers who might not have thought through all the implications of the amendment.

House Budget Chairman Leon E. Panetta, D-Calif., unveiled detailed spending-cut and tax-increase scenarios designed to show just how painful it would be to implement a balanced budget amendment by 1997, when most thought an amendment would take effect. House Democratic leaders took a different tack, offering a substitute amendment that would require a balanced budget but exempt Social Security. Organized labor launched a nationwide campaign, warning that the "balanced-budget hoax would hurt all of us" by raising taxes and cutting government benefits.

Still, passage seemed likely barely a week before the June 11 House vote. In the end, though, the lobbying by Democratic leaders and outside interest groups, plus a creeping uneasiness about tinkering with the Constitution, gave opponents a nine-vote victory margin. The amendment was rejected, 280-153: R 164-2; D 116-150 (ND 52-130, SD 64-20); I 0-1.

10. Superconducting Supercollider

Growing opposition to the costly superconducting supercollider reached a critical mass in June, when the House voted to kill the massive science project that was expected to cost at least $8.3 billion. The June 17 vote was 232-181: R 79-79; D 152-102 (ND 126-49, SD 26-53); I 1-0.

Although the House eventually reversed the decision and agreed to continue funding the project in fiscal 1993, the vote was a shocking blow to project supporters and left the endeavor on precarious political ground.

The supercollider was a giant atom smasher being built underground in Waxahachie, Texas, by the Energy Department. It was designed to produce high-speed particle collisions that scientists said could unlock the fundamental secrets of matter, as well as provide valuable technological spinoffs.

But some critics were skeptical of these claims, while others said the project was simply too expensive at a time when lawmakers were struggling to find money to pay for human services and other pressing needs, including smaller science projects.

Before the June vote, Congress had already appropriated roughly $1 billion for the project.

Opponents had been gaining ground in the House and had predicted a particularly close vote on the project in 1992, when House appropriators earmarked $484 million to keep building the collider. But even sponsors of the amendment to kill the project did not expect their June 17 victory.

Timing played an important role. It was the first key spending vote after the House narrowly defeated a proposed constitutional amendment to require a balanced budget, and many lawmakers found it hard to justify approving hundreds of millions for the supercollider so soon after speechifying against the deficit. The project also drew the ire of urban liberals, who had lost an earlier fight to transfer defense dollars to domestic needs and urban aid.

The atom smasher became a particularly tempting target because some of the Texas lawmakers arguing for the costly project had also been prominent advocates of balanced budget proposals, and the delegation had mostly opposed increased spending for urban aid.

That mood faded, accounting for part of the reason the House later reversed itself, agreeing to provide an additional $517 million for the collider, after the Senate restored funding in its version of the energy and water spending bill. That was less than the $650 million President Bush had requested for fiscal 1993, but more than the $484 million initially approved by House appropriators.

While Texas received the most direct benefits from the supercollider, managers had broadened support for the project by spreading research and procurement contracts across a wide array of states. Moreover, President-elect Bill Clinton had said he supported the project.

Nevertheless, the House vote continued to cast a shadow on the supercollider's prospects. The flip-flop hurt the Energy Department's chances of attracting Japanese or other foreign support for the project, which in turn could erode congressional support. And even some supporters warned that they might not be able to continue backing the project in light of budget constraints.

11. Urban Aid

Congress' first concrete response to the devastating April riots in Los Angeles came when the House passed a $494.7 million supplemental appropriations bill May 14. The measure was designed to direct small business loans and emergency grants to L.A. and to Chicago, where the collapse of a tunnel beneath the Chicago River had flooded the city's downtown.

The House bill turned out to be just the opening bid, however. One week later, the Senate quadrupled the size of the measure to nearly $2 billion by adding money for a nationwide program of urban aid. The extra money was to go for summer youth jobs, a Head Start summer program for preschool children, a summer school program for disadvantaged neighborhoods and the administration-backed "Weed and Seed" program, which aimed to "weed" drug dealers and and other criminals out of inner-city neighborhoods and "seed" the areas with social programs.

Senate backers, including some Republicans, fought off attempts to strip out the nearly $1.5 billion they added to the House bill and defeated a move to force Congress to cut other spending to pay for the programs. Virtually all of the money was to be provided on an "emergency" basis, exempt from spending caps set in the 1990 budget agreement.

Despite a White House veto threat over the size of the bill, House-Senate conferees June 5 decided to keep all the Senate add-ons and leave the bill's price tag at $2 billion. Participants in negotiations between the White House and key members of Congress said last-minute insistence on the full amount by Senate Majority Leader George J. Mitchell, D-Maine, blocked a compromise on a smaller amount, but Mitchell flatly denied the account.

In the end, it was not the veto threat from President Bush that forced the bill to slim down, it was strong GOP opposition and intransigence among rank-and-file Democrats in the House. Some Democratic leaders wanted to send Bush the $2 billion conference report and force him to issue what they assumed would be a politically embarrassing veto. But when House vote-counters ran a whip check, they found that many members objected to the size of the bill, either because it would have added $2 billion to the deficit or because rural and suburban members thought it sent too much to the inner cities.

Bowing to reality, leaders accepted a White House compromise that cut the bill to $1.1 billion. The conference report was adopted by the House on June 18, seven weeks after the riots by a vote of 249-168: R 43-117; D 205-51 (ND 158-17, SD 47-34); I 1-0. The Senate cleared the measure by voice vote later the same day.

While the supplemental was intended as part of a broader urban aid initiative, in the end it contained the only money that Congress would provide to inner cities in 1992 as a response to the L.A. riots. The other big urban aid proposal that grew out of the riots — a plan to set up dozens of "enterprise zones" where investors and businesses would get special tax breaks and other federal assistance — was finally incorporated in the tax bill (HR 11) Congress cleared just before adjournment. Bush vetoed that bill on Nov. 4.

12. Cable Reregulation

The House and Senate votes to override a bill (S 12) to reregulate cable television prices and services represented a stunning defeat for the cable industry and the Bush administration. But the first confirmation that Bush was on the losing side of the issue — and headed toward his first override — came July 23 on a crucial amendment by Rep. W. J. "Billy" Tauzin, D-La.

To Tauzin, along with cable bill sponsor Edward J. Markey, D-Mass., the amendment was the difference between making a serious attempt to improve cable industry competition and passing a halfhearted rate regulation bill.

Would-be competitors to the $20 billion cable industry, such as the home satellite and "wireless" cable systems, had long complained of being effectively locked out of access to cable programs through high prices and exclusive deals. Tauzin's amendment to the House bill (HR 4850) sought to ban cable programmers from discriminating against cable competitors in the price, terms and conditions of sales of their product. It also barred most exclusive contracts between cable operators and vendors.

The House approved the Tauzin amendment, 338-68: R 116-45; D 221-23 (ND 152-18, SD 69-5); I 1-0. The bill as amended by Tauzin subsequently passed the House, 340-73.

Most remarkable about the overwhelming House approval for the amendment was the political clout of the opposition. Urging defeat of the amendment was the Bush administration, the cable lobby, Energy and Commerce Chairman John D. Dingell, D-Mich., and various members of the House leadership.

Dingell supported the cable industry position that Tauzin would unfairly encroach on private business decisions, and during full committee markup of the bill he had the wording struck from the version approved by Markey's subcommittee. Dingell also argued that the provision would cause the bill to be referred to the Judiciary Committee, thus slowing down and possibly killing the entire measure.

The floor vote to replace the Tauzin language took place in the early evening hours of July 23. With little else to do but hear the discussion on the two amendments, members packed the House chamber for the debate between Tauzin and his opponent, Thomas J. Manton, D-N.Y.

Manton had offered a weaker substitute to the Tauzin amendment that was favored by the cable industry. He called Tauzin's amendment "far-reaching and radical" because it would set a government-mandated price for programming and cause program creators to lose control over their product.

Apart from the formidable opposition from Manton, Dingell and House leaders, Tauzin was saddled with the task of selling distinctions between his and Manton's amendments that were complex and difficult to discern.

Tauzin instead launched into an impassioned speech about the future of television, arguing that competition to cable would never arrive unless some controls were put on cable's program pricing policies and increasing market power.

Just as the cable television industry relied on free network broadcasts when it was in its infancy, Tauzin said, cable's competitors now need government help to purchase cable programs at fairer prices.

The House rejected Manton's substitute, 162-247, and subsequently voted to adopt the Tauzin amendment. The surprisingly large margin for Tauzin's amendment made it clear that the cable industry was heading for a big defeat — and that Bush's perfect veto record was in peril. *(Senate key vote 14)*

13. Space Station *Freedom*

In what may have been its last major vote on whether to keep the NASA space station *Freedom*, the House on July 29 turned back an attempt by a key Appropriations subcommittee chairman to abandon the manned-exploration venture.

The House had voted three times in 13 months to preserve the controversial space station, expected to cost from $30 billion to $40 billion by the year 2000. The latest vote came July 29 on the fiscal 1993 appropriations bill (HR 5679) for the departments of Veterans Affairs and Housing and Urban Development and independent agencies (VA-HUD). The $86.8 billion bill, as reported out of the Appropriations Committee, provided $1.73 billion for the space station, $305 million less than its fiscal 1992 appropriation. President Bush, a strong and vocal supporter of the project, had sought $2.25 billion for fiscal 1993.

But Congress had been struggling in the past two years to control high-cost science projects, pare the federal budget deficit and keep its spending bills within limits set by the 1990 budget agreement with the White House. Those budget problems only heightened lawmakers' awareness of big-ticket science projects — the space station and the superconducting supercollider being the biggest — whose missions and eventual paybacks were not easy to justify.

Cost concerns forced NASA to scale back the space station in 1991, and it came under fire from many scientists who felt it was poorly designed and incapable of serious scientific research.

According to NASA officials, the *Freedom* project would allow scientists to study how humans react to long periods in the weightless environment of outer space, thus providing the United States with a steppingstone for planetary exploration.

But members of Congress supported the project largely because of the jobs it generated across the country and in their districts. Before the House vote, NASA officials played that angle hard, passing out maps of the country that showed exactly where the space station contract money and jobs would go.

Bob Traxler, D-Mich., chairman of the VA-HUD Appropriations Subcommittee that oversaw NASA funding, tried to kill the space station in 1991 by leaving it out of the committee recommendation. But at the urging of Bush, NASA officials and space industry lobbyists, the full House subsequently voted 240-173 to restore the money.

In 1992, Traxler waited until the bill went to the floor to make his move to cut *Freedom's* congressional lifeline. He fared no better. Again, under intense lobbying from the White House, industry officials and NASA Director Daniel Goldin, the House rejected Traxler's motion to strike, 181-237: R 38-127; D 142-110 (ND 115-59, SD 27-51); I 1-0.

Space station advocates said they doubted that the project would be subjected in the future to such a thorough going over.

If the budget "walls" separating domestic and defense spending come down in 1993, as scheduled, there could be less of a pinch on space and science funding from other domestic programs. And the two leading House critics of space station funding, Traxler and New York's Bill Green, the ranking Republican on the VA-HUD panel, were not returning to Congress.

Traxler's successor as VA-HUD chairman was Louis Stokes, D-Ohio, whose state benefited greatly from the space station, receiving $101 million in contracts and 253 jobs. Although Stokes supported Traxler's amendment to kill *Freedom*, his opposition appeared to be far less entrenched.

14. Ex-Soviet Aid

In an election year when foreign policy was shunned by both parties, one piece of international legislation stood out. After months of wrangling, Congress approved a massive package authorizing technical, financial and other assistance to the former republics of the Soviet Union.

What made the measure remarkable was that passage came against the backdrop of an extremely partisan session in which the recession-plagued U.S. economy was the main focus. Both Democrats and Republicans were reluctant to devote too much attention to foreign issues when constituents were hurting back home. This was especially true in the House, where most of the 435 members were running for re-election.

In addition, Democrats were eager to blame Republican economic policies of the previous 12 years for many of the nation's domestic troubles. They argued that President Bush's proclivity toward foreign affairs was further evidence of his detachment from the problems of average Americans.

Given these conditions, it was no surprise that Bush's plan to join several other western industrial nations to aid the former republics, in the wake of the Soviet Union's collapse, was not warmly embraced even though some congressional leaders had previously urged him to take such action.

House Democrats, led by Majority Whip David E. Bonior, D-Mich., insisted that agreement be reached on a number of domestic fronts — including extension of jobless benefits, increased urban aid and job-creation legislation — before they would vote on the ex-Soviet aid package. That package, which Bush called his No. 1 foreign policy initiative, called for a $12.3 billion increase in the U.S. commitment to the International Monetary Fund, $410 million in bilateral humanitarian, economic and other assistance, and about $800 million to help dismantle the former Soviet nuclear arsenal.

Squabbling over domestic issues delayed House consideration of the aid bill long past the mid-June deadline for passage that Bush had requested. The president had hoped to get the aid in place before a visit by Russian President Boris N. Yeltsin to Washington on June 16-17.

It was not until early August that House leaders finally agreed to bring to the floor the legislation (HR 4547) that had been marked up by the Foreign Affairs Committee two months earlier. Paving the way for consideration was an extension of jobless benefits, as well as a tentative administration agreement with Bonior to speed up public works spending and to support loan guarantees for urban areas.

While these assurances were enough to win leadership backing, there was still great reluctance among rank-and-file members to vote for such a large foreign aid package before the election. In an unusually united effort, Democratic and Republican House leaders took to the floor to persuade members that the United States would be the long-term beneficiary of secure successor states to the former Soviet Union. They argued that a collapse of reform efforts in the republics could mean a return to totalitarianism and perhaps greater threats to U.S. security and a greater need for more defense spending. Conversely, sponsors argued, successful new free-market economies would mean more business opportunities for U.S. companies.

Leaders drew on a formidable group of aid proponents — including former presidents Ronald Reagan, Jimmy Carter, Gerald R. Ford and Richard Nixon, as well as a coalition of business, farm and disarmament groups — to help win passage of the bill. The legislation passed Aug. 6 by a vote of 255-164: R 94-68; D 161-95 (ND 115-63, SD 46-32); I 0-1. *(Senate key vote 6)*

15. Foreign Aid

A year after the House appeared to sour on foreign assistance, it voted to send President Bush a $26.3 billion foreign aid appropriations bill for fiscal 1993. In addition to continuing funding for foreign aid programs, the measure included $12.3 billion in new financing for the International Monetary Fund and guarantees for $10 billion in commercial loans for Israel (HR 5368 — PL 102-391).

In the key vote Oct. 5, the House voted overwhelmingly to adopt the conference report (H Rept 102-585) for the $26.3 billion spending bill, 312-105: R 104-58; D 208-46 (ND 152-20, SD 56-26); I 0-1.

In October 1991, with lawmakers caught up in an "America first" mood, the House had overwhelmingly rejected a two-year foreign aid authorization bill. With the domestic economy slumping and congressional elections on the horizon, the Bush administration feared that foreign aid would become an even harder sell in 1992.

Congress also failed to complete action on a companion foreign aid appropriations measure in 1991, forcing lawmakers to approve continuing resolutions to fund the program. The fiscal 1992 bill had become tangled in a dispute between the White House and the government of Israel over Jerusalem's request for loan guarantees.

The turnabout came in part because the fiscal 1993 bill slashed actual foreign aid spending, even though it included new programs for Israel and the IMF. The bill cut $1.1 billion from the administration request, largely by eliminating military assistance grants for Turkey, Greece and Portugal and replacing them with low-interest loans.

The conference report also afforded House members their first opportunity to vote for loan guarantees for Israel, a popular program with members of both parties.

The five-year program for Israel provided U.S. guarantees — not loans or direct aid — intended to help Jerusalem secure favorable rates on commercial loans. U.S. taxpayers would not be asked to provide any funding for the program unless Israel defaulted on the loans. Similarly, the $12.3 billion in new financing for the IMF entailed no budgetary outlays.

Rep. David R. Obey, D-Wis., chairman of the House Appropriations Subcommittee on Foreign Operations, said that any foreign aid bill not viewed as fiscally prudent would have drawn intense opposition from anxious lawmakers.

"It's a very tight bill and we gave people some arguments to take home and defend," Obey said after the House vote. In June, the House had voted 297-124 for the underlying appropriations bill. That measure, which did not include the loan guarantees, had reduced the administration request by $1.3 billion.

The legislation continued a long-term downward spiral in foreign aid funding. Excluding the one-time appropriation for the International Monetary Fund, the final version provided $1.4 billion less than the fiscal 1991 bill — the last one to clear Congress. *(Senate key vote 13)*

16. Western Water Bill

Nowhere were the conflicts in the way the West used its water more starkly illustrated than in the House's battle over a single key provision of the 1992 omnibus Western water projects bill (HR 429 — PL 102-575). As crafted by Interior Committee Chairman George Miller, D-Calif., the proposal was an attempt to redirect the purpose of the Central Valley Project (CVP) in California to reflect urban and environmental values.

The CVP is the largest irrigation project run by the Interior Department's Bureau of Reclamation. It controlled one-fifth of the state's usable water supply.

Criticism of the half-century-old project had been building for years and was exacerbated by the ongoing California drought. The CVP historically supplied its water mainly to some 23,000 Central Valley farming operations, which used the water to grow much of California's fabled produce in otherwise arid land. Farmers got the water at rates far below those paid by the other 85 percent of the state's economy — because of subsidies from federal taxpayers.

The result, environmentalists charged, was wasteful farming practices that led to polluted runoff and water diverted from other valuable uses, such as the state's now-decimated salmon fishery.

Miller, from urbanized Contra Costa County just north of the valley, used the omnibus Western water bill to transform the Central Valley Project. His proposal sought to make the CVP protect fish and wildlife and make more water available to outside users. Contracts to farmers would remain short term until the ecological health of the region improved.

The valley's farmers cried foul. They said disrupting their decades-old system of cheap water would cost jobs, make their farms more risky investments and hurt consumers with higher food prices.

They were supported by Republican California Gov. Pete Wilson and by rural lawmakers such as Republican Bill Thomas, who represented the southern tip of the valley, and Democrat Calvin Dooley, whose family had been farming in the valley for four generations.

But a phalanx of other state interests lined up behind Miller: most of the state's urban county governments, the big metropolitan water district of Los Angeles, corporate business groups and environmentalists.

Thomas, Dooley and others complained that the Miller provisions would have had no chance of approval if they were not tied to the 40-title omnibus measure, a must-pass bill for other Western states. But Miller said that was the point: The huge package had widespread support, containing as it did grandiose water projects such as the Central Utah Project and smaller but locally popular provisions dishing out largess to every Western state. Few wanted to see the whole thing sink on the opposition of a handful of California Farm Belt lawmakers.

The showdown came in the early morning hours of Oct. 6, when the House-Senate conference report came before the House. Thomas offered a motion to kick the bill back to committee and strip out all the Central Valley provisions. "If you vote yes ... the hostages will be set free," Thomas said, referring to the other titles of the bill.

But the House was unmoved, rejecting Thomas' motion to recommit the bill to committee, 159-244: R 117-41; D 42-202 (ND 15-152, SD 27-50); I 0-1. Members then adopted the conference report by voice vote. *(Senate key vote 15)*

	1	2	3	4	5	6	7	8
ALABAMA								
Heflin	N	Y	N	N	Y	Y	Y	Y
Shelby	N	Y	N	N	N	Y	Y	Y
ALASKA								
Murkowski	Y	Y	N	N	N	N	Y	Y
Stevens	Y	?	N	N	N	N	Y	Y
ARIZONA								
DeConcini	?	Y	Y	N	Y	Y	Y	N
McCain	Y	Y	N	Y	Y	N	Y	Y
ARKANSAS								
Bumpers	N	Y	Y	N	Y	Y	Y	N
Pryor	N	Y	Y	N	Y	Y	Y	N
CALIFORNIA								
Cranston	N	N	Y	N	Y	N	Y	N
Seymour	Y	N	N	N	N	Y	Y	Y
COLORADO								
Wirth	N	Y	Y	N	Y	N	Y	?
Brown	Y	Y	N	N	N	N	N	Y
CONNECTICUT								
Dodd	N	Y	N	N	Y	Y	Y	N
Lieberman	Y	N	N	N	Y	Y	Y	N
DELAWARE								
Biden	N	N	Y	N	Y	N	Y	N
Roth	Y	Y	N	N	N	?	?	Y
FLORIDA								
Graham	N	N	Y	N	Y	Y	Y	N
Mack	Y	Y	N	N	N	N	Y	Y
GEORGIA								
Fowler	N	N	Y	N	Y	Y	Y	N
Nunn	N	Y	N	N	Y	N	Y	Y
HAWAII								
Akaka	N	N	Y	N	Y	N	Y	N
Inouye	N	#	Y	N	Y	N	Y	Y
IDAHO								
Craig	Y	Y	N	Y	N	Y	N	Y
Symms	Y	Y	N	Y	N	Y	N	Y
ILLINOIS								
Dixon	N	N	?	N	Y	Y	Y	Y
Simon	N	N	Y	N	Y	N	Y	N
INDIANA								
Coats	Y	Y	N	Y	N	N	Y	Y
Lugar	Y	N	N	Y	N	N	Y	Y
IOWA								
Harkin	?	X	+	N	Y	N	Y	N
Grassley	Y	N	N	Y	N	N	Y	N
KANSAS								
Dole	Y	Y	N	N	N	N	Y	Y
Kassebaum	Y	Y	N	N	N	N	Y	N
KENTUCKY								
Ford	N	Y	Y	Y	Y	Y	Y	N
McConnell	Y	Y	N	N	N	N	Y	Y
LOUISIANA								
Breaux	Y	Y	Y	N	Y	Y	Y	N
Johnston	N	Y	Y	Y	Y	N	Y	N
MAINE								
Mitchell	N	N	Y	N	Y	N	Y	N
Cohen	N	N	N	N	N	N	Y	Y
MARYLAND								
Mikulski	N	N	Y	N	Y	Y	Y	N
Sarbanes	N	N	Y	N	Y	Y	Y	N
MASSACHUSETTS								
Kennedy	N	N	Y	N	Y	N	Y	N
Kerry	N	N	Y	N	Y	N	Y	N
MICHIGAN								
Levin	N	N	Y	N	Y	N	Y	N
Riegle	N	?	Y	N	Y	Y	Y	N
MINNESOTA								
Wellstone	N	N	Y	N	Y	N	Y	-
Durenberger	Y	N	N	Y	Y	N	Y	Y
MISSISSIPPI								
Cochran	Y	Y	N	Y	N	N	Y	Y
Lott	Y	Y	N	Y	N	N	Y	Y
MISSOURI								
Bond	?	Y	N	Y	N	N	Y	Y
Danforth	Y	Y	N	N	N	N	Y	Y
MONTANA								
Baucus	N	N	Y	N	Y	N	Y	N
Burns	N	Y	N	Y	N	N	Y	Y
NEBRASKA								
Exon	N	Y	N	Y	Y	N	Y	Y
Kerrey	?	?	Y	N	Y	N	Y	N
NEVADA								
Bryan	N	N	Y	N	Y	N	Y	N
Reid	N	N	Y	N	Y	Y	Y	N
NEW HAMPSHIRE								
Rudman	Y	Y	N	N	N	N	Y	Y
Smith	Y	Y	N	Y	N	Y	Y	Y
NEW JERSEY								
Bradley	Y	Y	Y	N	Y	?	Y	N
Lautenberg	N	N	Y	N	Y	Y	Y	N
NEW MEXICO								
Bingaman	N	Y	Y	N	Y	N	Y	Y
Domenici	Y	Y	N	N	N	N	Y	Y
NEW YORK								
Moynihan	N	N	Y	N	Y	N	Y	N
D'Amato	+	N	N	Y	N	Y	Y	Y
NORTH CAROLINA								
Sanford	N	Y	Y	N	Y	?	?	N
Helms	Y	Y	N	Y	N	+	?	+
NORTH DAKOTA								
Burdick	N	Y	Y	N	Y	N	Y	?
Conrad	N	Y	Y	N	Y	N	Y	N
OHIO								
Glenn	N	N	Y	N	Y	Y	Y	N
Metzenbaum	N	N	Y	N	?	?	Y	N
OKLAHOMA								
Boren	N	N	Y	N	Y	N	Y	N
Nickles	Y	Y	N	Y	N	Y	Y	Y
OREGON								
Hatfield	N	N	Y	N	N	N	Y	N
Packwood	Y	N	Y	N	N	N	Y	Y
PENNSYLVANIA								
Wofford	N	Y	Y	N	Y	Y	Y	N
Specter	N	Y	Y	N	N	Y	Y	Y
RHODE ISLAND								
Pell	N	N	Y	N	Y	N	Y	N
Chafee	N	N	N	N	N	N	Y	N
SOUTH CAROLINA								
Hollings	N	Y	N	N	N	Y	Y	Y
Thurmond	Y	Y	N	N	N	N	Y	Y
SOUTH DAKOTA								
Daschle	N	N	Y	N	Y	N	Y	N
Pressler	Y	Y	N	Y	N	Y	Y	Y
TENNESSEE								
Gore	N	N	Y	N	Y	Y	Y	?
Sasser	N	Y	Y	N	Y	N	Y	N
TEXAS								
Bentsen	N	Y	Y	N	Y	N	Y	Y
Gramm	Y	Y	N	Y	N	Y	Y	Y
UTAH								
Garn	+	Y	N	N	N	N	Y	?
Hatch	Y	Y	N	Y	N	N	Y	+
VERMONT								
Leahy	N	N	Y	N	Y	N	Y	N
Jeffords	N	N	N	N	Y	N	Y	N
VIRGINIA								
Robb	N	N	N	N	Y	N	Y	N
Warner	Y	Y	N	N	N	N	?	Y
WASHINGTON								
Adams	N	N	Y	N	Y	Y	Y	N
Gorton	+	Y	N	N	N	N	Y	Y
WEST VIRGINIA								
Byrd	N	N	Y	N	Y	Y	Y	N
Rockefeller	N	N	Y	N	Y	N	Y	N
WISCONSIN								
Kohl	N	N	Y	N	Y	Y	Y	N
Kasten	Y	N	N	Y	N	Y	Y	+
WYOMING								
Simpson	Y	Y	N	N	N	N	Y	Y
Wallop	Y	Y	N	Y	N	Y	Y	Y

KEY

Y	Voted for (yea).
#	Paired for.
+	Announced for.
N	Voted against (nay).
X	Paired against.
-	Announced against.
P	Voted "present."
C	Voted "present" to avoid possible conflict of interest.
?	Did not vote or otherwise make a position known.

Democrats *Republicans*

ND Northern Democrats SD Southern Democrats

Southern states - Ala., Ark., Fla., Ga., Ky., La., Miss., N.C., Okla., S.C., Tenn., Texas, Va.

1. S 2. Elementary and Secondary Education/School Choice. Hatch, R-Utah, amendment to authorize $30 million for six demonstration projects to give low-income parents money to pay for enrolling a child at the public or private school of their choice, including religiously affiliated schools. Rejected 36-57: R 33-6; D 3-51 (ND 2-35, SD 1-16), Jan. 23, 1992. A "yea" was a vote supporting the president's position.

2. S 2166. National Energy Policy/NRC Hearings. Johnston, D-La., motion to table (kill) the Graham, D-Fla., amendment to the Johnston amendment, to require the Nuclear Regulatory Commission (NRC) to conduct full adjudicatory hearings on serious new safety issues or major construction deficiencies before operation of new power reactors. Motion agreed to 52-43: R 31-11; D 21-32 (ND 9-27, SD 12-5), Feb. 6, 1992.

3. S 2399. Eliminate Budget Walls/Cloture. Mitchell, D-Maine, motion to invoke cloture (thus limiting debate) on the motion to proceed to the bill to modify the 1990 Budget Enforcement Act to knock down the walls that prohibit shifting funds between defense and domestic appropriations. Motion rejected 50-48: R 3-40; D 47-8 (ND 35-3, SD 12-5), March 26, 1992. A three-fifths majority vote (60) of the total Senate is required to invoke cloture. A "nay" was a vote supporting the president's position.

4. HR 2507. National Institutes of Health Reauthorization/Fetal Tissue Research. Hatch, R-Utah, amendment to replace provisions that lift the ban on fetal tissue transplant research, including tissue from induced abortions, with provisions to establish a registry for a non-profit bank of tissue from spontaneous abortions and ectopic pregnancies. Rejected 23-77: R 20-23; D 3-54 (ND 1-39, SD 2-15), March 31, 1992. A "yea" was a vote supporting the president's position.

5. S 3. Campaign Finance/Veto Override. Passage, over President Bush's May 9 veto, of the bill to limit spending in congressional campaigns by providing incentives to candidates to agree to voluntary spending limits, restricting money from political action committees (PACs) and restricting "soft money" raised by state parties in federal elections. Rejected 57-42: R 3-40; D 54-2 (ND 39-0, SD 15-2), May 13, 1992. A two-thirds majority of those present and voting (66 in this case) is required to override a veto. A "nay" was a vote supporting the president's position.

6. S 2532. Aid for Former Soviet Republics/Russian Troops in Baltic States. Pressler, R-S.D., motion to table (kill) the Pell, D-R.I., amendment to the DeConcini, D-Ariz., amendment to give a one-year grace period before imposing DeConcini provisions to suspend aid until the president certifies that Russia has significantly withdrawn armed forces from the Baltic States. Motion rejected 35-60: R 11-30; D 24-30 (ND 14-24, SD 10-6), July 1, 1992. A "nay" was a vote supporting the president's position. (The Pell amendment subsequently was adopted by voice vote.)

7. HR 5260. Extended Unemployment Benefits/Conference Report. Adoption of the conference report to provide 20 or 26 weeks of extended unemployment benefits between July 4, 1992, and March 6, 1993, if the national unemployment rate stays above 7 percent. After March 6, 1993, states could use a new 6.5 percent unemployment rate to trigger 13 weeks of extended benefits. Passed 93-3: R 37-3; D 56-0 (ND 40-0, SD 16-0), July 2, 1992. A "yea" was a vote supporting the president's position.

8. S 3114. Fiscal 1993 Defense Authorization/Strategic Defense Initiative. Warner, R-Va., motion to table (kill) the Sasser, D-Tenn., amendment to cut the strategic defense initiative by $1 billion from the committee level of $4.3 billion. Motion rejected 43-49: R 34-5; D 9-44 (ND 4-33, SD 5-11), Aug. 7, 1992. A "yea" was a vote supporting the president's position.

1. HR 4210. 1992 Tax Bill/Democratic Substitute. Rostenkowski, D-Ill., substitute to give workers a temporary tax credit worth up to $400 for couples and $200 for individuals a year to be paid for with a 10 percent surtax on millionaires and a new top income tax rate of 35 percent for individuals with taxable income higher than $85,000 and couples with more than $145,000. The package includes indexing of capital gains and other provisions designed to spur economic growth. Adopted 221-210: R 1-164; D 219-46 (ND 156-27, SD 63-19); I 1-0, Feb. 27, 1992. A "nay" was a vote supporting the president's position.

2. H Res 396. Further Disclosure of House Bank Abuses/Adoption. Adoption of the resolution to disclose the name of any member or former member who wrote a check that exceeded his balance at the House bank and the number of insufficient funds checks written by each from July 1, 1988, to Oct. 3, 1991. Adopted 426-0: R 165-0; D 260-0 (ND 178-0, SD 82-0); I 1-0, in the session that began, and the *Congressional Record* dated, March 12, 1992.

3. HR 3732. Eliminate Budget Walls/Passage. Passage of the bill to modify the 1990 Budget Enforcement Act to knock down the walls that prohibit shifting funds between defense, international and domestic appropriations. Rejected 187-238: R 0-162; D 186-76 (ND 151-28, SD 35-48); I 1-0, March 31, 1992. A "nay" was a vote supporting the president's position.

4. HR 4704. RTC Financing/Passage. Passage of the bill to provide the Resolution Trust Corporation with about $17 billion to resolve failed savings and loan institutions by eliminating the April 1, 1992, expiration date on $25 billion provided in November 1991. Rejected 125-298: R 45-117; D 80-180 (ND 47-130, SD 33-50); I 0-1, April 1, 1992. A "yea" was a vote supporting the president's position.

5. S 3. Campaign Finance Reform/Conference Report. Adoption of the conference report to limit spending in congressional campaigns by providing incentives to candidates to agree to voluntary spending limits, restricting contributions from political action committees (PACs) and restricting "soft money" raised and spent by state parties in federal elections. The bill would create a separate system for House and Senate campaigns. Adopted 259-165: R 19-145; D 239-20 (ND 171-6, SD 68-14); I 1-0, April 9, 1992. A "nay" was a vote supporting the president's position.

6. HR 3090. Family Planning Reauthorization/Passage. Passage of the bill to reauthorize Title X of the Public Health Service Act for five years through fiscal 1997. The bill would overturn the administration's ban on abortion counseling at federally funded family planning clinics. Passed 268-150: R 55-105; D 212-45 (ND 146-28, SD 66-17); I 1-0, April 30, 1992. A "nay" was a vote supporting the president's position. (The text of HR 3090 was subsequently inserted into a Senate bill, S 323.)

7. HR 776. National Energy Policy/Passage. Passage of the bill to promote increased domestic energy production and conservation; promote the wider use of alternative motor fuels; streamline the nuclear plant licensing process; restrict state powers to regulate gas production; ban certain new offshore oil and gas drilling; overhaul federal laws governing electric utilities; and provide tax incentives for renewable energy. Passed 381-37: R 135-23; D 245-14 (ND 173-2, SD 72-12); I 1-0, May 27, 1992.

8. HR 5006. Fiscal 1993 Defense Authorization/Strategic Defense Initiative. Durbin, D-Ill., amendment to reduce funding for the strategic defense initiative by $937.5 million — from the $4.3 billion in the bill to $3.3 billion. Rejected 161-211: R 11-134; D 149-77 (ND 125-31, SD 24-46); I 1-0, June 5, 1992. A "nay" was a vote supporting the president's position.

KEY

Y	Voted for (yea).
#	Paired for.
+	Announced for.
N	Voted against (nay).
X	Paired against.
-	Announced against.
P	Voted "present."
C	Voted "present" to avoid possible conflict of interest.
?	Did not vote or otherwise make a position known.

Democrats ***Republicans***
Independent

ND Northern Democrats
SD Southern Democrats

Southern states - Ala., Ark., Fla., Ga., Ky., La., Miss., N.C., Okla., S.C., Tenn., Texas, Va.

	1	2	3	4	5	6	7	8
ALABAMA								
1 ***Callahan***	N	Y	N	N	N	N	Y	N
2 ***Dickinson***	X	Y	N	N	N	Y	Y	N
3 Browder	Y	Y	N	N	Y	Y	Y	N
4 Bevill	Y	Y	Y	N	Y	Y	Y	N
5 Cramer	Y	Y	Y	N	Y	Y	Y	N
6 Erdreich	Y	Y	N	N	Y	Y	Y	N
7 Harris	Y	Y	N	N	Y	Y	Y	N
ALASKA								
AL ***Young***	N	Y	N	N	N	N	Y	N
ARIZONA								
1 ***Rhodes***	N	Y	N	Y	N	N	Y	N
2 Pastor	Y	Y	Y	N	Y	Y	Y	Y
3 ***Stump***	N	Y	N	N	N	N	N	N
4 ***Kyl***	N	Y	N	Y	N	N	Y	N
5 ***Kolbe***	N	Y	N	N	N	Y	Y	N
ARKANSAS								
1 Alexander	Y	Y	Y	Y	Y	Y	Y	N
2 Thornton	Y	Y	Y	N	Y	Y	Y	N
3 ***Hammerschmidt***	N	Y	N	Y	N	N	N	N
4 Anthony	Y	Y	N	Y	Y	Y	?	?
CALIFORNIA								
1 ***Riggs***	N	Y	N	N	N	Y	Y	N
2 ***Herger***	N	Y	N	N	N	N	N	X
3 Matsui	Y	Y	Y	Y	Y	Y	Y	Y
4 Fazio	Y	Y	Y	Y	Y	Y	Y	Y
5 Pelosi	Y	Y	Y	N	Y	Y	Y	?
6 Boxer	Y	Y	#	N	Y	Y	?	Y
7 Miller	Y	?	Y	N	Y	Y	Y	?
8 Dellums	N	Y	Y	N	Y	Y	Y	Y
9 Stark	Y	Y	Y	N	Y	Y	Y	Y
10 Edwards	Y	Y	Y	Y	Y	Y	Y	Y
11 Lantos	Y	Y	Y	N	Y	Y	Y	N
12 ***Campbell***	N	Y	N	N	N	Y	?	?
13 Mineta	Y	Y	Y	Y	Y	Y	Y	Y
14 ***Doolittle***	N	Y	N	N	N	N	N	N
15 Condit	N	Y	N	N	Y	Y	Y	Y
16 Panetta	Y	Y	Y	Y	Y	Y	Y	Y
17 Dooley	Y	Y	N	N	Y	?	Y	Y
18 Lehman	N	Y	Y	N	Y	Y	Y	?
19 ***Lagomarsino***	N	Y	N	N	N	N	#	N
20 ***Thomas***	N	Y	N	Y	N	Y	Y	?
21 ***Gallegly***	N	Y	N	N	N	N	Y	N
22 ***Moorhead***	N	Y	N	N	N	N	Y	N
23 Beilenson	N	Y	Y	Y	Y	Y	Y	#
24 Waxman	Y	Y	Y	N	Y	Y	Y	Y
25 Roybal	Y	Y	Y	Y	Y	Y	Y	Y
26 Berman	Y	Y	Y	Y	Y	Y	Y	Y
27 Levine	Y	Y	#	?	?	Y	?	?
28 Dixon	Y	Y	Y	?	Y	Y	Y	?
29 Waters	Y	Y	Y	N	Y	+	Y	Y
30 Martinez	Y	Y	Y	N	Y	Y	?	Y
31 Dymally	Y	Y	Y	?	Y	Y	Y	?
32 Anderson	Y	Y	Y	Y	Y	Y	Y	N
33 ***Dreier***	N	Y	N	N	N	N	Y	N
34 Torres	Y	Y	Y	Y	Y	Y	Y	Y
35 ***Lewis***	N	Y	?	Y	N	Y	Y	N
36 Brown	Y	Y	Y	Y	Y	Y	Y	?
37 ***McCandless***	N	Y	N	N	N	Y	Y	N
38 ***Dornan***	N	Y	X	N	N	N	Y	N
39 ***Dannemeyer***	N	+	N	-	?	?	?	?
40 ***Cox***	N	Y	N	N	N	N	Y	N
41 ***Lowery***	N	Y	N	N	N	N	Y	N
42 ***Rohrabacher***	N	Y	N	N	N	N	Y	N
43 ***Packard***	N	Y	N	N	N	N	X	N
44 ***Cunningham***	N	Y	N	N	N	N	Y	N
45 ***Hunter***	N	Y	N	N	N	N	N	N
COLORADO								
1 Schroeder	N	Y	Y	N	Y	Y	Y	Y
2 Skaggs	Y	Y	Y	Y	Y	Y	Y	Y
3 Campbell	Y	Y	N	N	Y	?	Y	N
4 ***Allard***	N	Y	N	N	N	N	Y	N
5 ***Hefley***	N	Y	N	N	N	N	Y	N
6 ***Schaefer***	N	Y	N	N	N	N	Y	N
CONNECTICUT								
1 Kennelly	Y	Y	Y	N	Y	Y	Y	N
2 Gejdenson	Y	Y	N	N	Y	Y	Y	Y
3 DeLauro	Y	Y	Y	N	Y	#	Y	Y
4 ***Shays***	N	Y	N	Y	Y	Y	Y	Y
5 ***Franks***	N	Y	N	Y	N	Y	Y	N
6 ***Johnson***	N	Y	N	Y	N	Y	Y	N
DELAWARE								
AL Carper	N	Y	N	Y	Y	Y	Y	Y
FLORIDA								
1 Hutto	N	Y	N	N	N	N	Y	N
2 Peterson	Y	Y	Y	N	Y	Y	Y	Y
3 Bennett	Y	Y	N	N	N	N	Y	Y
4 ***James***	N	Y	N	N	N	N	Y	N
5 ***McCollum***	N	Y	N	N	N	N	Y	N
6 ***Stearns***	N	Y	N	N	N	N	Y	N
7 Gibbons	Y	Y	Y	N	Y	Y	Y	Y
8 ***Young***	N	Y	N	N	N	N	Y	N
9 ***Bilirakis***	N	Y	N	N	N	N	Y	N
10 ***Ireland***	N	Y	N	Y	N	N	Y	?
11 Bacchus	Y	Y	Y	N	Y	Y	Y	N
12 ***Lewis***	N	Y	N	N	N	N	Y	N
13 ***Goss***	N	Y	N	N	N	N	Y	N
14 Johnston	Y	Y	Y	Y	Y	Y	Y	Y
15 ***Shaw***	N	Y	N	Y	N	N	Y	N
16 Smith	Y	Y	Y	Y	Y	#	Y	Y
17 Lehman	Y	?	Y	Y	Y	Y	Y	?
18 ***Ros-Lehtinen***	N	Y	N	N	N	N	Y	N
19 Fascell	Y	Y	Y	Y	Y	Y	Y	N
GEORGIA								
1 Thomas	N	Y	N	N	Y	Y	Y	N
2 Hatcher	Y	Y	Y	N	Y	Y	Y	?
3 Ray	?	Y	N	N	Y	N	Y	X
4 Jones	Y	Y	Y	N	Y	Y	Y	?
5 Lewis	Y	Y	Y	Y	Y	Y	Y	?
6 ***Gingrich***	N	Y	N	Y	N	N	Y	N
7 Darden	Y	Y	N	N	Y	Y	Y	N
8 Rowland	N	Y	N	N	Y	Y	Y	N
9 Jenkins	Y	Y	N	Y	Y	Y	Y	N
10 Barnard	N	Y	N	Y	?	?	Y	N
HAWAII								
1 Abercrombie	Y	Y	Y	N	Y	Y	Y	Y
2 Mink	Y	Y	Y	N	Y	Y	Y	?
IDAHO								
1 LaRocco	Y	Y	N	N	Y	Y	Y	Y
2 Stallings	N	Y	N	N	Y	Y	Y	Y
ILLINOIS								
1 Hayes	Y	Y	Y	N	Y	Y	Y	Y
2 Savage	Y	?	Y	N	Y	Y	Y	Y
3 Russo	N	Y	Y	N	?	Y	Y	Y
4 Sangmeister	Y	Y	Y	N	Y	Y	Y	Y
5 Lipinski	Y	Y	Y	N	Y	N	Y	N
6 ***Hyde***	N	Y	N	N	N	N	Y	N
7 Collins	Y	?	Y	N	Y	Y	#	#
8 Rostenkowski	Y	Y	Y	N	Y	Y	Y	?
9 Yates	Y	Y	Y	Y	?	Y	Y	Y
10 ***Porter***	N	Y	N	Y	N	Y	Y	#
11 Annunzio	Y	Y	Y	Y	Y	N	Y	N
12 ***Crane***	N	Y	N	N	N	N	N	N
13 ***Fawell***	N	Y	N	Y	N	Y	Y	N
14 ***Hastert***	N	Y	N	N	N	N	Y	N
15 ***Ewing***	N	Y	N	N	N	N	Y	N
16 Cox	Y	Y	Y	N	Y	Y	Y	Y
17 Evans	Y	Y	Y	N	Y	Y	Y	Y
18 ***Michel***	N	Y	N	Y	N	N	?	N
19 Bruce	Y	Y	Y	N	Y	Y	+	Y
20 Durbin	Y	Y	Y	N	Y	Y	Y	Y
21 Costello	Y	Y	Y	N	?	N	Y	N
22 Poshard	Y	Y	Y	N	Y	N	Y	Y
INDIANA								
1 Visclosky	Y	Y	N	N	Y	Y	Y	Y
2 Sharp	Y	Y	N	N	Y	Y	Y	N
3 Roemer	N	Y	N	N	Y	Y	Y	N

	1	2	3	4	5	6	7	8
4 Long	N	Y	N	N	Y	Y	N	Y
5 Jontz	Y	Y	Y	N	Y	Y	Y	Y
6 ***Burton***	N	Y	N	N	N	N	Y	N
7 ***Myers***	N	Y	N	N	N	N	Y	N
8 McCloskey	Y	Y	Y	N	Y	Y	Y	N
9 Hamilton	N	Y	N	N	Y	Y	Y	N
10 Jacobs	Y	Y	N	N	Y	Y	Y	Y
IOWA								
1 ***Leach***	N	Y	N	Y	Y	Y	Y	Y
2 ***Nussle***	N	Y	N	N	N	N	Y	Y
3 Nagle	Y	Y	Y	N	N	Y	Y	Y
4 Smith	Y	Y	Y	N	?	Y	Y	N
5 ***Lightfoot***	N	Y	N	N	N	N	Y	N
6 ***Grandy***	N	Y	N	Y	N	N	Y	N
KANSAS								
1 ***Roberts***	N	Y	N	N	N	N	Y	N
2 Slattery	Y	Y	N	N	Y	Y	Y	Y
3 ***Meyers***	N	Y	N	Y	N	Y	Y	N
4 Glickman	Y	Y	N	N	Y	Y	Y	Y
5 ***Nichols***	N	Y	N	N	N	Y	Y	?
KENTUCKY								
1 Hubbard	Y	Y	N	N	Y	Y	Y	?
2 Natcher	Y	Y	Y	N	Y	Y	Y	N
3 Mazzoli	Y	Y	N	N	Y	N	Y	Y
4 ***Bunning***	N	Y	?	N	N	N	Y	N
5 ***Rogers***	N	Y	N	N	N	N	Y	N
6 ***Hopkins***	N	Y	N	N	N	N	Y	N
7 Perkins	Y	Y	Y	?	N	N	Y	Y
LOUISIANA								
1 ***Livingston***	N	Y	N	N	N	N	N	?
2 Jefferson	Y	Y	Y	N	Y	Y	Y	Y
3 Tauzin	N	Y	N	N	N	N	Y	N
4 ***McCrery***	N	Y	N	Y	N	N	Y	N
5 Huckaby	Y	Y	N	N	N	Y	Y	N
6 ***Baker***	N	Y	N	Y	N	N	N	N
7 Hayes	N	Y	N	N	N	N	Y	N
8 ***Holloway***	N	Y	N	N	N	N	Y	N
MAINE								
1 Andrews	Y	Y	Y	N	Y	Y	Y	Y
2 ***Snowe***	Y	Y	N	N	Y	Y	Y	N
MARYLAND								
1 ***Gilchrest***	N	Y	N	Y	N	Y	Y	N
2 ***Bentley***	?	Y	N	N	N	?	?	N
3 Cardin	Y	Y	Y	Y	Y	Y	Y	Y
4 McMillen	N	Y	N	Y	Y	Y	Y	N
5 Hoyer	Y	Y	Y	Y	Y	Y	Y	N
6 Byron	Y	Y	N	N	Y	Y	Y	?
7 Mfume	Y	Y	Y	N	Y	Y	Y	Y
8 ***Morella***	N	Y	N	Y	Y	Y	Y	#
MASSACHUSETTS								
1 Olver	Y	Y	Y	N	Y	Y	Y	Y
2 Neal	Y	Y	Y	N	Y	Y	Y	Y
3 Early	N	Y	Y	N	Y	Y	Y	Y
4 Frank	Y	Y	Y	N	Y	Y	Y	Y
5 Atkins	Y	Y	Y	N	Y	Y	Y	Y
6 Mavroules	Y	Y	Y	Y	Y	N	Y	Y
7 Markey	Y	Y	Y	Y	Y	Y	Y	Y
8 Kennedy	Y	Y	Y	Y	Y	Y	Y	Y
9 Moakley	Y	Y	Y	Y	Y	Y	Y	Y
10 Studds	Y	Y	Y	N	Y	Y	Y	Y
11 Donnelly	Y	Y	Y	N	Y	N	?	Y
MICHIGAN								
1 Conyers	Y	+	Y	N	Y	Y	Y	Y
2 ***Pursell***	N	Y	N	?	N	Y	Y	?
3 Wolpe	Y	Y	Y	N	Y	Y	Y	?
4 ***Upton***	N	Y	N	N	N	Y	Y	N
5 ***Henry***	N	Y	N	N	N	N	Y	N
6 Carr	N	Y	Y	N	N	Y	Y	Y
7 Kildee	Y	Y	Y	N	Y	N	Y	Y
8 Traxler	Y	Y	Y	Y	Y	?	Y	?
9 ***Vander Jagt***	N	Y	N	N	N	N	Y	?
10 ***Camp***	N	Y	N	N	N	N	Y	N
11 ***Davis***	N	Y	N	N	N	N	Y	N
12 Bonior	Y	Y	Y	Y	Y	Y	Y	Y
13 Collins	Y	?	Y	N	Y	+	Y	Y
14 Hertel	Y	Y	Y	Y	Y	Y	Y	?
15 Ford	Y	Y	Y	Y	Y	Y	Y	Y
16 Dingell	Y	Y	Y	?	Y	Y	Y	?
17 Levin	Y	Y	Y	Y	Y	Y	Y	Y
18 ***Broomfield***	N	Y	N	N	N	N	Y	?
MINNESOTA								
1 Penny	Y	Y	N	N	Y	Y	N	Y
2 ***Weber***	N	Y	N	N	N	N	Y	N
3 ***Ramstad***	N	Y	N	N	N	Y	Y	N
4 Vento	Y	Y	Y	Y	Y	Y	Y	Y

	1	2	3	4	5	6	7	8
5 Sabo	N	Y	Y	Y	Y	Y	Y	Y
6 Sikorski	Y	Y	Y	N	Y	Y	Y	Y
7 Peterson	N	Y	Y	N	Y	N	Y	Y
8 Oberstar	Y	Y	Y	Y	Y	N	Y	Y
MISSISSIPPI								
1 Whitten	?	?	Y	Y	?	N	Y	?
2 Espy	Y	Y	N	N	Y	Y	Y	Y
3 Montgomery	N	Y	N	Y	Y	N	N	N
4 Parker	N	Y	N	Y	Y	N	Y	N
5 Taylor	N	Y	N	N	N	N	Y	N
MISSOURI								
1 Clay	Y	Y	Y	N	Y	Y	Y	Y
2 Horn	Y	Y	Y	N	Y	Y	Y	Y
3 Gephardt	Y	Y	Y	Y	Y	Y	Y	Y
4 Skelton	N	Y	X	N	Y	N	Y	N
5 Wheat	Y	Y	Y	N	Y	Y	Y	Y
6 ***Coleman***	N	Y	N	N	N	Y	Y	N
7 ***Hancock***	N	Y	N	N	N	N	N	N
8 ***Emerson***	N	Y	N	N	N	N	Y	N
9 Volkmer	Y	Y	N	N	Y	N	Y	Y
MONTANA								
1 Williams	Y	Y	Y	N	Y	Y	Y	?
2 ***Marlenee***	N	Y	N	N	Y	X	N	Y
NEBRASKA								
1 ***Bereuter***	N	Y	N	Y	N	Y	Y	N
2 Hoagland	Y	Y	N	Y	Y	Y	Y	N
3 ***Barrett***	N	Y	N	Y	N	N	Y	N
NEVADA								
1 Bilbray	Y	Y	N	N	Y	Y	Y	N
2 ***Vucanovich***	N	Y	N	N	N	N	N	?
NEW HAMPSHIRE								
1 ***Zeliff***	N	Y	N	N	N	Y	Y	N
2 Swett	N	Y	Y	N	Y	Y	Y	N
NEW JERSEY								
1 Andrews	N	Y	Y	N	Y	Y	Y	N
2 Hughes	N	Y	Y	N	Y	Y	Y	Y
3 Pallone	N	Y	Y	N	Y	Y	Y	Y
4 ***Smith***	N	Y	N	?	Y	N	Y	N
5 ***Roukema***	N	Y	N	Y	N	Y	Y	Y
6 Dwyer	N	Y	Y	N	Y	Y	Y	Y
7 ***Rinaldo***	N	Y	N	N	Y	N	Y	N
8 Roe	N	Y	Y	N	Y	N	Y	N
9 Torricelli	N	Y	Y	N	Y	Y	Y	N
10 Payne	Y	Y	Y	N	Y	Y	Y	Y
11 ***Gallo***	N	Y	N	Y	N	Y	Y	N
12 ***Zimmer***	N	Y	N	N	Y	Y	Y	N
13 ***Saxton***	N	Y	N	?	N	N	Y	N
14 Guarini	Y	Y	Y	N	Y	Y	Y	N
NEW MEXICO								
1 ***Schiff***	N	Y	N	N	N	Y	Y	N
2 ***Skeen***	N	Y	N	Y	N	Y	Y	N
3 Richardson	Y	Y	N	N	Y	Y	Y	N
NEW YORK								
1 Hochbrueckner	Y	Y	Y	N	Y	Y	Y	Y
2 Downey	Y	Y	Y	N	Y	Y	Y	Y
3 Mrazek	N	Y	Y	?	Y	Y	Y	Y
4 ***Lent***	N	Y	N	N	N	N	Y	?
5 ***McGrath***	N	Y	N	N	N	N	Y	N
6 Flake	Y	Y	Y	N	Y	Y	Y	?
7 Ackerman	Y	Y	Y	Y	Y	Y	Y	?
8 Scheuer	Y	Y	Y	N	Y	Y	Y	?
9 Manton	Y	Y	Y	Y	Y	N	Y	Y
10 Schumer	Y	Y	Y	Y	Y	Y	Y	Y
11 Towns	Y	Y	Y	N	Y	Y	Y	Y
12 Owens	Y	Y	Y	N	Y	Y	Y	Y
13 Solarz	Y	Y	Y	Y	Y	Y	Y	Y
14 ***Molinari***	N	Y	N	N	N	Y	Y	N
15 ***Green***	N	Y	N	Y	Y	Y	Y	?
16 Rangel	Y	Y	Y	N	Y	Y	Y	Y
17 Weiss	Y	Y	Y	Y	Y	Y	Y	Y
18 Serrano	Y	Y	Y	N	Y	Y	Y	Y
19 Engel	Y	Y	Y	N	Y	Y	Y	Y
20 Lowey	Y	Y	Y	N	Y	Y	Y	Y
21 ***Fish***	N	Y	N	N	Y	Y	Y	N
22 ***Gilman***	N	Y	N	Y	Y	Y	Y	N
23 McNulty	Y	Y	Y	N	Y	Y	Y	Y
24 ***Solomon***	N	Y	N	N	N	N	Y	N
25 ***Boehlert***	N	Y	N	Y	Y	Y	Y	N
26 ***Martin***	N	Y	N	N	?	Y	Y	N
27 ***Walsh***	N	Y	N	Y	N	N	Y	N
28 McHugh	Y	Y	Y	Y	Y	Y	Y	Y
29 ***Horton***	N	Y	N	N	N	Y	Y	N
30 Slaughter	Y	Y	Y	N	Y	Y	Y	Y
31 ***Paxon***	N	Y	N	N	N	N	Y	N

	1	2	3	4	5	6	7	8
32 LaFalce	Y	Y	Y	N	Y	N	Y	Y
33 Nowak	Y	Y	Y	N	Y	N	Y	Y
34 ***Houghton***	N	Y	N	Y	N	Y	Y	N
NORTH CAROLINA								
1 Jones	Y	Y	Y	Y	Y	Y	Y	Y
2 Valentine	Y	Y	N	?	Y	Y	Y	Y
3 Lancaster	N	Y	N	N	Y	Y	Y	N
4 Price	Y	Y	Y	Y	Y	Y	Y	Y
5 Neal	Y	Y	?	Y	Y	Y	Y	Y
6 ***Coble***	N	Y	N	N	N	N	Y	N
7 Rose	Y	Y	Y	Y	Y	Y	Y	Y
8 Hefner	Y	Y	Y	N	Y	Y	Y	?
9 ***McMillan***	N	Y	N	N	Y	N	Y	N
10 ***Ballenger***	N	Y	N	N	N	Y	X	N
11 ***Taylor***	N	Y	-	N	N	N	Y	N
NORTH DAKOTA								
AL Dorgan	Y	Y	N	N	Y	Y	Y	Y
OHIO								
1 Luken	Y	Y	N	N	Y	N	Y	?
2 ***Gradison***	N	Y	N	Y	N	Y	Y	N
3 Hall	Y	Y	Y	N	Y	N	Y	Y
4 ***Oxley***	N	Y	N	N	N	N	Y	N
5 ***Gillmor***	N	Y	N	Y	N	N	Y	N
6 ***McEwen***	N	Y	N	N	N	X	Y	N
7 ***Hobson***	N	Y	N	N	N	Y	Y	N
8 ***Boehner***	N	Y	N	N	N	N	Y	N
9 Kaptur	Y	Y	Y	N	Y	Y	Y	Y
10 ***Miller***	N	Y	N	N	N	N	Y	N
11 Eckart	Y	Y	Y	N	Y	Y	Y	Y
12 ***Kasich***	N	Y	N	N	N	N	Y	N
13 Pease	Y	Y	Y	Y	Y	Y	Y	Y
14 Sawyer	Y	Y	Y	N	Y	Y	Y	Y
15 ***Wylie***	N	Y	N	Y	N	N	Y	N
16 ***Regula***	N	Y	N	N	N	Y	Y	N
17 Traficant	N	Y	Y	N	N	Y	Y	Y
18 Applegate	Y	Y	Y	N	N	N	Y	Y
19 Feighan	Y	Y	Y	Y	Y	Y	Y	?
20 Oakar	Y	Y	Y	N	Y	N	?	Y
21 Stokes	Y	Y	Y	N	Y	Y	Y	Y
OKLAHOMA								
1 ***Inhofe***	N	Y	N	N	N	N	N	N
2 Synar	Y	Y	Y	Y	Y	Y	N	Y
3 Brewster	Y	Y	N	N	Y	Y	Y	N
4 McCurdy	N	Y	N	Y	Y	Y	Y	N
5 ***Edwards***	N	Y	N	N	N	N	N	N
6 English	N	Y	N	N	Y	Y	N	N
OREGON								
1 AuCoin	Y	Y	Y	N	Y	Y	Y	Y
2 ***Smith***	N	Y	N	N	N	N	N	N
3 Wyden	Y	Y	Y	N	Y	Y	Y	Y
4 DeFazio	Y	Y	Y	N	Y	Y	Y	Y
5 Kopetski	Y	Y	Y	N	Y	Y	Y	+
PENNSYLVANIA								
1 Foglietta	Y	Y	Y	N	Y	Y	Y	Y
2 Blackwell	Y	Y	Y	N	Y	Y	Y	Y
3 Borski	Y	Y	Y	N	Y	N	Y	N
4 Kolter	Y	Y	Y	N	Y	?	Y	?
5 ***Schulze***	N	Y	N	N	N	N	Y	N
6 Yatron	Y	Y	N	N	Y	N	Y	N
7 ***Weldon***	N	Y	N	N	N	N	Y	N
8 Kostmayer	Y	Y	Y	N	Y	Y	Y	Y
9 ***Shuster***	N	Y	N	N	N	N	Y	N
10 ***McDade***	N	Y	N	Y	N	?	?	?
11 Kanjorski	Y	Y	Y	N	Y	N	Y	Y
12 Murtha	Y	Y	N	Y	Y	N	Y	N
13 ***Coughlin***	N	Y	N	Y	N	Y	Y	N
14 Coyne	Y	Y	Y	Y	Y	Y	Y	Y
15 ***Ritter***	N	Y	N	N	N	N	Y	N
16 ***Walker***	N	Y	N	N	N	N	Y	N
17 ***Gekas***	N	Y	N	N	N	Y	Y	N
18 ***Santorum***	N	Y	N	N	N	N	Y	N
19 ***Goodling***	N	Y	N	N	N	N	Y	Y
20 Gaydos	Y	Y	Y	N	N	?	Y	?
21 ***Ridge***	N	Y	N	N	Y	Y	Y	Y
22 Murphy	Y	Y	Y	N	N	N	Y	Y
23 ***Clinger***	N	Y	N	Y	N	Y	N	-
RHODE ISLAND								
1 ***Machtley***	N	Y	N	N	Y	Y	Y	N
2 Reed	Y	Y	Y	N	Y	Y	Y	Y
SOUTH CAROLINA								
1 ***Ravenel***	N	Y	N	N	N	Y	Y	N
2 ***Spence***	N	Y	N	N	N	N	Y	N
3 Derrick	Y	Y	N	Y	Y	Y	Y	Y
4 Patterson	N	Y	N	N	Y	Y	Y	-
5 Spratt	Y	Y	N	Y	Y	Y	Y	N
6 Tallon	Y	Y	Y	N	Y	N	Y	Y

	1	2	3	4	5	6	7	8
SOUTH DAKOTA								
AL Johnson	Y	Y	Y	Y	Y	Y	Y	N
TENNESSEE								
1 ***Quillen***	N	Y	N	N	N	N	Y	N
2 ***Duncan***	N	Y	N	N	Y	N	N	Y
3 Lloyd	N	Y	N	N	Y	Y	Y	N
4 Cooper	N	Y	N	N	Y	Y	Y	N
5 Clement	Y	Y	N	N	Y	Y	Y	N
6 Gordon	Y	Y	N	N	Y	Y	Y	Y
7 ***Sundquist***	N	Y	N	N	N	N	Y	N
8 Tanner	Y	Y	N	N	Y	Y	Y	N
9 Ford	Y	Y	Y	N	Y	Y	Y	Y
TEXAS								
1 Chapman	Y	Y	Y	N	Y	Y	N	N
2 Wilson	Y	Y	N	N	?	Y	Y	N
3 ***Johnson***	N	Y	N	N	N	N	N	N
4 Hall	N	Y	N	N	N	N	N	N
5 Bryant	Y	Y	Y	N	Y	Y	Y	Y
6 ***Barton***	N	Y	N	N	N	N	Y	N
7 ***Archer***	N	Y	N	N	N	N	N	N
8 ***Fields***	N	Y	N	N	N	?	N	-
9 Brooks	Y	Y	?	Y	Y	Y	Y	?
10 Pickle	Y	Y	N	Y	Y	Y	Y	N
11 Edwards	Y	Y	N	N	Y	Y	Y	N
12 Geren	N	Y	N	Y	N	Y	Y	N
13 Sarpalius	N	Y	N	Y	N	N	N	N
14 Laughlin	N	Y	N	N	Y	Y	Y	?
15 de la Garza	#	Y	Y	N	Y	N	N	?
16 Coleman	Y	Y	Y	Y	Y	Y	Y	N
17 Stenholm	Y	Y	N	Y	Y	N	N	N
18 Washington	Y	Y	Y	N	Y	Y	Y	Y
19 ***Combest***	N	Y	N	N	N	N	N	N
20 Gonzalez	Y	Y	Y	Y	Y	Y	N	Y
21 ***Smith***	N	Y	N	N	N	Y	N	N
22 ***DeLay***	N	Y	N	N	N	N	N	N
23 Bustamante	Y	Y	Y	N	Y	Y	N	X
24 Frost	Y	Y	Y	N	N	Y	Y	N
25 Andrews	Y	Y	N	N	Y	Y	N	N
26 ***Armey***	N	Y	N	N	N	N	N	N
27 Ortiz	Y	Y	N	N	Y	N	N	N
UTAH								
1 ***Hansen***	N	Y	N	Y	N	N	Y	N
2 Owens	Y	Y	N	N	Y	Y	Y	Y
3 Orton	Y	Y	N	N	Y	N	Y	Y
VERMONT								
AL *Sanders*	Y	Y	Y	N	Y	Y	Y	Y
VIRGINIA								
1 ***Bateman***	N	Y	N	Y	N	N	Y	N
2 Pickett	N	Y	N	Y	N	Y	Y	N
3 ***Bliley***	N	Y	N	Y	N	N	Y	N
4 Sisisky	Y	Y	N	Y	N	Y	Y	N
5 Payne	Y	Y	N	Y	Y	Y	Y	N
6 Olin	Y	Y	N	Y	N	Y	Y	?
7 ***Allen***	N	Y	N	N	N	N	Y	N
8 Moran	Y	?	Y	Y	Y	Y	Y	Y
9 Boucher	Y	Y	Y	N	Y	Y	Y	Y
10 ***Wolf***	N	Y	N	Y	N	N	Y	N
WASHINGTON								
1 ***Miller***	N	Y	N	Y	Y	Y	Y	?
2 Swift	Y	Y	Y	Y	Y	Y	Y	Y
3 Unsoeld	Y	Y	Y	N	Y	Y	Y	?
4 ***Morrison***	N	Y	N	Y	Y	Y	Y	?
5 Foley	Y	Y						
6 Dicks	Y	Y	Y	Y	Y	Y	Y	N
7 McDermott	Y	Y	Y	N	Y	Y	Y	Y
8 ***Chandler***	N	Y	N	Y	N	Y	Y	N
WEST VIRGINIA								
1 Mollohan	Y	Y	Y	N	Y	N	Y	N
2 Staggers	Y	Y	Y	N	Y	N	Y	Y
3 Wise	Y	Y	Y	N	Y	Y	Y	Y
4 Rahall	Y	Y	Y	N	Y	N	Y	Y
WISCONSIN								
1 Aspin	Y	Y	Y	Y	Y	Y	Y	N
2 ***Klug***	N	Y	N	N	Y	Y	Y	Y
3 ***Gunderson***	N	Y	N	N	N	N	Y	N
4 Kleczka	Y	Y	Y	Y	Y	Y	Y	Y
5 Moody	Y	Y	Y	N	Y	Y	Y	Y
6 ***Petri***	N	Y	N	N	Y	N	Y	N
7 Obey	N	Y	Y	Y	Y	Y	Y	Y
8 ***Roth***	N	Y	N	N	N	Y	Y	X
9 ***Sensenbrenner***	N	Y	N	N	N	N	Y	Y
WYOMING								
AL ***Thomas***	N	Y	N	Y	N	Y	Y	Y

9. H J Res 290. Balanced Budget Constitutional Amendment/Passage. Passage of the joint resolution to propose a constitutional amendment that would prohibit deficit spending unless a three-fifths majority of both chambers of Congress approved a specific deficit amount or there was a declaration of war (or national military emergency) enacted into law; require the president to submit a balanced budget each fiscal year; and require a three-fifths majority of both chambers of Congress to increase the public debt. The amendment would take effect in fiscal 1998 or the second year after ratification, whichever is later. Rejected 280-153: R 164-2; D 116-150 (ND 52-130, SD 64-20); I 0-1, June 11, 1992. A two-thirds majority of those present and voting of both chambers (289 in this case) is required to propose an amendment to the Constitution. A "yea" was a vote supporting the president's position.

10. HR 5373. Fiscal 1993 Energy and Water Appropriations/Superconducting Supercollider. Eckart, D-Ohio, amendment to cut $450 million of the $483.7 million provided for the superconducting supercollider, leaving approximately $34 million to shut down the project. Adopted 232-181: R 79-79; D 152-102 (ND 126-49, SD 26-53); I 1-0, June 17, 1992. A "nay" was a vote supporting the president's position.

11. HR 5132. Fiscal 1992 Disaster Relief Supplemental Appropriations/Conference Report. Adoption of the conference report to provide $1,075,510,000 in new budget authority in fiscal 1992 for disaster assistance and loans to respond to the Los Angeles riots and Chicago flooding, with $500 million allocated for Summer Youth Employment. The funds are designated as emergency spending, thus exempt from the spending caps of the 1990 Budget Enforcement Act. Adopted 249-168: R 43-117; D 205-51 (ND 158-17, SD 47-34); I 1-0, June 18, 1992. A "yea" was a vote supporting the president's position.

12. HR 4850. Cable Television Reregulation/Program Access. Tauzin, D-La., amendment to give satellite distributors and other potential cable competitors lower-priced access to cable programming. Adopted 338-68: R 116-45; D 221-23 (ND 152-18, SD 69-5); I 1-0, July 23, 1992.

13. HR 5679. Fiscal 1993 VA, Housing and Urban Development, Independent Agencies Appropriations/Space Station Cuts. Traxler, D-Mich., amendment to cut $1.2 billion of the $1.73 billion in the bill for NASA's space station *Freedom*, leaving $525 million to close down the program. Rejected 181-237: R 38-127; D 142-110 (ND 115-59, SD 27-51); I 1-0, July 29, 1992. A "nay" was a vote supporting the president's position.

14. HR 4547. Russian Aid/Passage. Passage of the bill to provide aid to the former republics of the Soviet Union. The bill also increases the U.S. contribution to the International Monetary Fund by $12.3 billion and includes numerous other measures to boost aid to the former republics. Passed 255-164: R 94-68; D 161-95 (ND 115-63, SD 46-32); I 0-1, Aug. 6, 1992. A "yea" was a vote supporting the president's position.

15. HR 5368. Fiscal 1993 Foreign Operations Appropriations/Conference Report. Adoption of the conference report to provide $26.26 billion for foreign aid in fiscal 1993. The administration requested $27.43 billion. The bill would provide $10 billion in loan guarantees for Israel and increase the U.S. contribution to International Monetary Fund by $12.3 billion. Adopted 312-105: R 104-58; D 208-46 (ND 152-20, SD 56-26); I 0-1, Oct. 5, 1992.

16. HR 429. Western Water Bill/Central Valley Project. Thomas, R-Calif., motion to recommit to conference the conference report with instructions to report it back after deleting the reform of the Central Valley Project in California. Motion rejected 159-244: R 117-41; D 42-202 (ND 15-152, SD 27-50); I 0-1, in the session that began, and the *Congressional Record* dated, Oct. 5, 1992. (The conference report subsequently was adopted by voice vote.)

---

[1] *Rep. Ted Weiss, D-N.Y., died Sept. 14, 1992.*
[2] *Rep. Walter B. Jones, D-N.C., died Sept. 15, 1992.*

KEY

Y	Voted for (yea).
#	Paired for.
+	Announced for.
N	Voted against (nay).
X	Paired against.
-	Announced against.
P	Voted "present."
C	Voted "present" to avoid possible conflict of interest.
?	Did not vote or otherwise make a position known.

Democrats ***Republicans***
Independent

ND	Northern Democrats
SD	Southern Democrats

Southern states - Ala., Ark., Fla., Ga., Ky., La., Miss., N.C., Okla., S.C., Tenn., Texas, Va.

	9	10	11	12	13	14	15	16
ALABAMA								
1 ***Callahan***	Y	N	N	Y	N	N	N	Y
2 ***Dickinson***	Y	N	N	Y	N	?	N	?
3 Browder	Y	N	N	Y	N	Y	Y	Y
4 Bevill	Y	N	Y	Y	N	?	N	Y
5 Cramer	Y	N	N	Y	N	Y	Y	N
6 Erdreich	Y	N	N	Y	N	N	Y	N
7 Harris	Y	N	N	Y	N	N	Y	Y
ALASKA								
AL ***Young***	Y	N	?	Y	N	Y	Y	Y
ARIZONA								
1 ***Rhodes***	Y	N	N	N	N	Y	Y	N
2 Pastor	N	Y	Y	N	Y	N	Y	N
3 ***Stump***	Y	N	N	N	N	N	N	Y
4 ***Kyl***	Y	N	N	N	N	N	Y	N
5 ***Kolbe***	Y	N	N	N	Y	Y	Y	N
ARKANSAS								
1 Alexander	N	N	Y	Y	?	Y	Y	?
2 Thornton	N	N	Y	Y	N	Y	Y	N
3 ***Hammerschmidt***	Y	N	N	Y	N	Y	N	Y
4 Anthony	Y	N	Y	?	Y	Y	Y	N
CALIFORNIA								
1 ***Riggs***	Y	N	N	Y	N	Y	Y	N
2 ***Herger***	Y	Y	N	N	N	N	N	Y
3 Matsui	N	N	Y	Y	N	Y	Y	N
4 Fazio	N	N	Y	Y	N	Y	Y	Y
5 Pelosi	N	Y	Y	Y	Y	Y	Y	N
6 Boxer	N	Y	Y	Y	?	N	#	?
7 Miller	N	Y	Y	Y	Y	N	Y	N
8 Dellums	N	Y	Y	Y	Y	N	Y	N
9 Stark	N	Y	Y	Y	Y	N	N	N
10 Edwards	N	Y	Y	Y	N	Y	Y	N
11 Lantos	N	Y	Y	Y	Y	Y	Y	N
12 ***Campbell***	Y	Y	Y	Y	N	Y	Y	Y
13 Mineta	N	N	Y	Y	N	Y	Y	Y
14 ***Doolittle***	Y	Y	N	N	Y	N	N	Y
15 Condit	Y	Y	Y	Y	Y	N	N	Y
16 Panetta	N	Y	Y	Y	Y	Y	Y	Y
17 Dooley	Y	Y	Y	Y	Y	N	N	Y
18 Lehman	N	Y	Y	N	Y	N	N	Y
19 ***Lagomarsino***	Y	N	N	N	N	Y	Y	Y
20 ***Thomas***	Y	Y	N	Y	N	Y	Y	Y
21 ***Gallegly***	Y	N	N	Y	N	N	N	Y
22 ***Moorhead***	Y	N	N	Y	N	N	N	Y
23 Beilenson	N	Y	Y	Y	Y	Y	Y	N
24 Waxman	N	Y	Y	Y	N	Y	Y	N
25 Roybal	N	Y	Y	Y	Y	N	?	N
26 Berman	N	Y	Y	N	N	Y	Y	N
27 Levine	N	N	Y	?	N	Y	Y	Y
28 Dixon	N	N	Y	N	N	N	Y	N
29 Waters	N	Y	Y	Y	N	N	Y	N
30 Martinez	N	Y	Y	Y	N	Y	Y	N
31 Dymally	N	?	Y	?	N	N	Y	N
32 Anderson	Y	N	Y	Y	N	Y	Y	N
33 ***Dreier***	Y	N	N	Y	N	N	N	Y
34 Torres	N	N	Y	N	N	Y	Y	N
35 ***Lewis***	Y	Y	Y	Y	N	Y	Y	Y
36 Brown	N	N	Y	Y	N	Y	Y	N
37 ***McCandless***	Y	Y	N	Y	N	N	N	Y
38 ***Dornan***	Y	N	N	N	N	N	N	Y
39 ***Dannemeyer***	Y	N	N	N	N	N	N	Y
40 ***Cox***	Y	N	N	N	N	N	Y	Y
41 ***Lowery***	Y	Y	Y	Y	N	Y	Y	Y
42 ***Rohrabacher***	Y	Y	N	N	N	N	N	Y
43 ***Packard***	Y	N	N	N	N	N	N	Y
44 ***Cunningham***	Y	N	N	Y	N	N	Y	Y
45 ***Hunter***	Y	N	N	Y	N	Y	Y	Y
COLORADO								
1 Schroeder	N	Y	Y	N	Y	Y	Y	N
2 Skaggs	N	N	Y	N	Y	Y	Y	N
3 Campbell	Y	Y	Y	N	?	N	Y	Y
4 ***Allard***	Y	N	N	N	N	Y	Y	Y
5 ***Hefley***	Y	Y	N	N	N	N	Y	Y
6 ***Schaefer***	Y	N	N	N	N	N	Y	Y
CONNECTICUT								
1 Kennelly	N	Y	Y	Y	N	Y	Y	N
2 Gejdenson	N	Y	Y	Y	N	Y	Y	N
3 DeLauro	N	Y	Y	Y	N	N	Y	N
4 ***Shays***	Y	Y	N	Y	Y	Y	Y	N
5 ***Franks***	Y	N	Y	N	N	Y	Y	Y
6 ***Johnson***	Y	Y	Y	Y	N	Y	Y	Y
DELAWARE								
AL Carper	Y	Y	N	Y	N	Y	Y	N
FLORIDA								
1 Hutto	Y	Y	N	Y	Y	N	N	Y
2 Peterson	Y	Y	N	+	N	Y	Y	N
3 Bennett	Y	Y	Y	Y	Y	Y	N	N
4 ***James***	Y	Y	N	Y	N	Y	N	Y
5 ***McCollum***	Y	Y	N	Y	N	Y	Y	Y
6 ***Stearns***	Y	Y	N	Y	N	N	?	?
7 Gibbons	Y	N	Y	Y	N	Y	Y	N
8 ***Young***	Y	N	N	Y	N	N	N	Y
9 ***Bilirakis***	Y	N	N	N	Y	N	Y	Y
10 ***Ireland***	Y	N	Y	Y	N	Y	?	Y
11 Bacchus	Y	N	N	Y	N	Y	Y	N
12 ***Lewis***	Y	Y	N	Y	N	N	N	Y
13 ***Goss***	Y	Y	N	Y	N	N	N	Y
14 Johnston	Y	Y	Y	Y	Y	Y	Y	N
15 ***Shaw***	Y	Y	N	Y	N	Y	Y	Y
16 Smith	N	Y	Y	Y	N	Y	Y	N
17 Lehman	N	N	Y	?	Y	Y	Y	?
18 ***Ros-Lehtinen***	Y	Y	Y	Y	Y	N	Y	N
19 Fascell	N	N	Y	Y	N	Y	Y	N
GEORGIA								
1 Thomas	Y	N	Y	?	?	Y	Y	Y
2 Hatcher	Y	?	Y	?	?	?	Y	?
3 Ray	Y	N	N	?	Y	N	N	Y
4 Jones	Y	#	?	Y	Y	Y	Y	?
5 Lewis	N	Y	Y	Y	N	N	Y	N
6 ***Gingrich***	Y	N	Y	Y	N	Y	Y	Y
7 Darden	Y	N	N	Y	N	N	N	N
8 Rowland	Y	N	N	Y	Y	N	N	N
9 Jenkins	Y	N	?	Y	N	Y	Y	N
10 Barnard	Y	N	Y	N	N	?	?	?
HAWAII								
1 Abercrombie	N	Y	Y	Y	Y	N	Y	N
2 Mink	N	Y	Y	N	Y	Y	Y	N
IDAHO								
1 LaRocco	Y	N	Y	Y	Y	Y	Y	N
2 Stallings	Y	N	Y	Y	?	Y	Y	Y
ILLINOIS								
1 Hayes	N	Y	Y	Y	Y	N	Y	N
2 Savage	N	Y	Y	Y	?	N	N	N
3 Russo	N	Y	Y	Y	Y	Y	Y	N
4 Sangmeister	Y	Y	Y	Y	Y	N	N	N
5 Lipinski	Y	Y	Y	Y	N	N	?	?
6 ***Hyde***	Y	N	?	?	?	Y	Y	Y
7 Collins	N	Y	Y	N	Y	N	Y	N
8 Rostenkowski	N	Y	Y	Y	Y	Y	?	N
9 Yates	N	Y	Y	?	Y	Y	Y	?
10 ***Porter***	Y	Y	Y	Y	Y	Y	Y	N
11 Annunzio	N	Y	Y	Y	N	Y	Y	?
12 ***Crane***	Y	?	?	N	Y	N	N	Y
13 ***Fawell***	Y	N	N	N	Y	Y	Y	Y
14 ***Hastert***	Y	Y	N	Y	Y	N	Y	N
15 ***Ewing***	Y	Y	N	Y	Y	Y	Y	N
16 Cox	Y	Y	Y	Y	Y	Y	Y	N
17 Evans	N	Y	Y	Y	Y	N	Y	N
18 ***Michel***	Y	?	Y	Y	N	Y	Y	Y
19 Bruce	Y	Y	Y	Y	Y	Y	Y	N
20 Durbin	N	Y	Y	Y	Y	N	Y	N
21 Costello	Y	Y	Y	Y	Y	N	Y	N
22 Poshard	Y	Y	Y	Y	Y	N	Y	N
INDIANA								
1 Visclosky	N	Y	N	Y	Y	Y	Y	N
2 Sharp	Y	Y	Y	Y	Y	Y	Y	?
3 Roemer	Y	N	N	Y	Y	N	N	N

	9	10	11	12	13	14	15	16
4 Long	Y	Y	Y	Y	Y	Y	Y	N
5 Jontz	Y	Y	Y	Y	Y	N	N	N
6 ***Burton***	Y	Y	N	N	Y	N	Y	Y
7 ***Myers***	Y	N	N	N	N	N	N	Y
8 McCloskey	Y	N	Y	Y	Y	Y	Y	N
9 Hamilton	N	Y	Y	Y	Y	Y	Y	N
10 Jacobs	Y	Y	Y	Y	Y	N	N	N
IOWA								
1 ***Leach***	Y	Y	Y	Y	Y	Y	Y	N
2 ***Nussle***	Y	Y	N	Y	Y	Y	N	Y
3 Nagle	N	N	Y	Y	N	Y	Y	N
4 Smith	N	N	Y	Y	Y	Y	Y	N
5 ***Lightfoot***	Y	N	N	Y	N	Y	Y	Y
6 ***Grandy***	Y	Y	N	Y	Y	Y	Y	Y
KANSAS								
1 ***Roberts***	Y	Y	N	Y	N	Y	N	Y
2 Slattery	N	Y	?	Y	N	Y	Y	N
3 ***Meyers***	Y	Y	N	Y	N	Y	Y	N
4 Glickman	Y	Y	?	Y	N	Y	Y	N
5 ***Nichols***	Y	Y	?	Y	N	Y	N	Y
KENTUCKY								
1 Hubbard	Y	?	?	Y	N	N	N	Y
2 Natcher	Y	N	Y	Y	N	Y	Y	N
3 Mazzoli	Y	N	Y	Y	Y	N	Y	N
4 ***Bunning***	Y	Y	N	Y	N	N	N	Y
5 ***Rogers***	Y	N	N	Y	Y	N	N	Y
6 ***Hopkins***	Y	N	N	N	N	Y	N	N
7 Perkins	N	N	Y	Y	N	N	N	Y
LOUISIANA								
1 ***Livingston***	Y	N	N	Y	N	Y	Y	Y
2 Jefferson	N	Y	Y	Y	?	N	Y	N
3 Tauzin	Y	N	N	Y	?	N	N	Y
4 ***McCrery***	Y	N	N	Y	N	Y	Y	Y
5 Huckaby	Y	N	N	Y	N	N	N	Y
6 ***Baker***	Y	N	N	Y	N	N	N	Y
7 Hayes	Y	N	N	Y	?	N	N	N
8 ***Holloway***	Y	N	N	Y	N	N	N	Y
MAINE								
1 Andrews	N	Y	Y	Y	Y	Y	Y	N
2 ***Snowe***	Y	Y	N	Y	Y	N	Y	N
MARYLAND								
1 ***Gilchrest***	Y	N	Y	Y	N	N	Y	N
2 ***Bentley***	Y	N	N	Y	N	Y	Y	Y
3 Cardin	N	?	Y	Y	N	Y	Y	N
4 McMillen	Y	N	Y	Y	N	Y	Y	N
5 Hoyer	Y	N	Y	Y	Y	Y	Y	N
6 Byron	Y	N	Y	Y	N	Y	Y	Y
7 Mfume	N	Y	Y	Y	Y	N	Y	N
8 ***Morella***	Y	Y	Y	Y	N	Y	Y	N
MASSACHUSETTS								
1 Olver	N	Y	Y	Y	Y	Y	Y	N
2 Neal	N	Y	Y	Y	N	N	Y	N
3 Early	Y	Y	Y	?	Y	N	Y	N
4 Frank	N	Y	Y	Y	Y	Y	Y	N
5 Atkins	N	Y	Y	Y	Y	N	?	N
6 Mavroules	N	N	Y	Y	N	Y	Y	N
7 Markey	N	Y	Y	Y	Y	Y	Y	N
8 Kennedy	Y	Y	Y	Y	Y	Y	Y	N
9 Moakley	N	Y	Y	Y	Y	Y	Y	N
10 Studds	N	Y	Y	Y	Y	Y	Y	N
11 Donnelly	Y	Y	Y	Y	Y	N	N	N
MICHIGAN								
1 Conyers	N	Y	Y	?	?	N	Y	N
2 ***Pursell***	Y	N	N	Y	Y	N	Y	Y
3 Wolpe	N	Y	Y	Y	Y	Y	Y	N
4 ***Upton***	Y	Y	Y	Y	Y	Y	Y	N
5 ***Henry***	Y	Y	N	Y	Y	Y	N	Y
6 Carr	Y	Y	N	Y	N	N	Y	N
7 Kildee	N	Y	Y	Y	Y	Y	Y	N
8 Traxler	?	?	?	?	Y	?	Y	?
9 ***Vander Jagt***	Y	N	N	Y	N	Y	Y	Y
10 ***Camp***	Y	Y	N	Y	Y	N	Y	Y
11 ***Davis***	Y	N	Y	Y	N	Y	?	?
12 Bonior	N	?	?	N	N	Y	Y	N
13 Collins	N	Y	Y	Y	?	N	Y	N
14 Hertel	N	N	Y	Y	Y	Y	Y	N
15 Ford	N	Y	Y	?	Y	Y	Y	N
16 Dingell	N	Y	Y	Y	Y	Y	Y	N
17 Levin	N	Y	Y	Y	Y	Y	Y	N
18 ***Broomfield***	Y	?	N	Y	N	Y	Y	Y
MINNESOTA								
1 Penny	Y	Y	N	Y	Y	Y	Y	N
2 ***Weber***	Y	?	Y	Y	N	Y	Y	Y
3 ***Ramstad***	Y	Y	N	Y	Y	N	Y	N
4 Vento	N	Y	Y	Y	Y	Y	Y	N
5 Sabo	N	Y	Y	Y	Y	Y	Y	N
6 Sikorski	Y	Y	Y	Y	Y	Y	?	N
7 Peterson	Y	Y	N	Y	Y	Y	Y	N
8 Oberstar	N	Y	Y	Y	Y	Y	Y	N
MISSISSIPPI								
1 Whitten	Y	N	Y	Y	N	Y	Y	N
2 Espy	Y	?	Y	Y	Y	N	Y	Y
3 Montgomery	Y	N	N	Y	Y	Y	N	N
4 Parker	Y	Y	N	N	Y	Y	Y	Y
5 Taylor	Y	Y	N	Y	N	N	N	Y
MISSOURI								
1 Clay	N	Y	Y	Y	Y	N	Y	N
2 Horn	N	Y	Y	Y	Y	Y	Y	N
3 Gephardt	N	N	Y	Y	N	Y	Y	N
4 Skelton	Y	N	N	Y	Y	Y	Y	Y
5 Wheat	N	Y	Y	Y	Y	N	Y	N
6 ***Coleman***	Y	Y	N	Y	N	Y	N	Y
7 ***Hancock***	Y	Y	N	N	N	N	N	Y
8 ***Emerson***	Y	N	N	Y	N	Y	Y	Y
9 Volkmer	Y	N	N	Y	N	N	N	Y
MONTANA								
1 Williams	N	Y	Y	Y	Y	N	N	N
2 ***Marlenee***	Y	Y	N	Y	Y	N	N	Y
NEBRASKA								
1 ***Bereuter***	Y	Y	N	Y	Y	Y	Y	Y
2 Hoagland	Y	Y	Y	Y	Y	Y	Y	N
3 ***Barrett***	Y	Y	N	Y	N	Y	N	Y
NEVADA								
1 Bilbray	Y	Y	Y	Y	Y	Y	Y	N
2 ***Vucanovich***	Y	N	Y	Y	N	Y	Y	N
NEW HAMPSHIRE								
1 ***Zeliff***	Y	Y	Y	N	N	Y	Y	Y
2 Swett	Y	Y	N	Y	Y	Y	Y	N
NEW JERSEY								
1 Andrews	Y	N	Y	N	N	N	Y	N
2 Hughes	N	Y	N	Y	Y	N	Y	N
3 Pallone	Y	Y	Y	Y	Y	Y	Y	N
4 ***Smith***	Y	N	Y	Y	N	Y	Y	N
5 ***Roukema***	Y	Y	N	N	Y	Y	Y	N
6 Dwyer	N	N	Y	Y	Y	#	Y	?
7 ***Rinaldo***	Y	Y	Y	N	Y	Y	Y	N
8 Roe	N	N	Y	Y	N	Y	Y	N
9 Torricelli	Y	N	Y	Y	N	Y	Y	N
10 Payne	N	Y	Y	Y	Y	N	Y	N
11 ***Gallo***	Y	N	Y	Y	N	Y	Y	Y
12 ***Zimmer***	Y	Y	N	Y	Y	N	Y	N
13 ***Saxton***	Y	Y	N	Y	N	Y	Y	Y
14 Guarini	N	Y	Y	Y	N	Y	X	N
NEW MEXICO								
1 ***Schiff***	Y	N	Y	Y	N	Y	Y	Y
2 ***Skeen***	Y	N	Y	Y	N	Y	Y	Y
3 Richardson	Y	N	Y	Y	N	Y	Y	N
NEW YORK								
1 Hochbrueckner	N	N	Y	Y	N	Y	Y	Y
2 Downey	N	Y	Y	Y	N	Y	Y	N
3 Mrazek	N	Y	Y	Y	N	Y	?	N
4 ***Lent***	Y	Y	Y	N	N	Y	Y	Y
5 ***McGrath***	Y	Y	Y	N	N	Y	Y	N
6 Flake	N	Y	Y	Y	Y	N	Y	N
7 Ackerman	N	Y	Y	Y	Y	Y	Y	N
8 Scheuer	N	Y	Y	Y	Y	Y	Y	N
9 Manton	N	N	Y	Y	N	Y	Y	N
10 Schumer	N	?	#	Y	Y	Y	Y	N
11 Towns	N	Y	Y	Y	?	N	Y	N
12 Owens	N	Y	Y	Y	Y	N	Y	N
13 Solarz	N	Y	Y	?	?	Y	Y	?
14 ***Molinari***	Y	Y	N	N	Y	Y	Y	Y
15 ***Green***	N	N	Y	Y	Y	Y	Y	N
16 Rangel	N	N	Y	Y	Y	N	Y	N
17 Weiss [1]	N	Y	Y	C	Y	Y		
18 Serrano	N	Y	Y	Y	Y	N	Y	N
19 Engel	N	N	Y	Y	N	Y	Y	N
20 Lowey	N	N	Y	Y	Y	Y	Y	N
21 ***Fish***	Y	Y	Y	N	Y	Y	Y	Y
22 ***Gilman***	N	Y	Y	Y	N	Y	Y	N
23 McNulty	N	N	Y	Y	N	Y	Y	N
24 ***Solomon***	Y	Y	N	Y	Y	N	N	N
25 ***Boehlert***	Y	Y	Y	Y	N	Y	Y	N
26 ***Martin***	Y	Y	Y	Y	N	Y	Y	Y
27 ***Walsh***	Y	N	Y	Y	N	N	Y	Y
28 McHugh	N	N	Y	Y	Y	Y	Y	N
29 ***Horton***	Y	Y	Y	N	N	Y	Y	N
30 Slaughter	N	Y	Y	Y	Y	Y	Y	N
31 ***Paxon***	Y	Y	N	Y	N	N	Y	Y
32 LaFalce	N	Y	Y	Y	Y	Y	Y	N
33 Nowak	N	Y	Y	Y	Y	Y	Y	N
34 ***Houghton***	Y	N	Y	Y	N	Y	Y	N
NORTH CAROLINA								
1 Jones [2]	Y	?	Y	?	N	N		
2 Valentine	Y	Y	N	Y	-	N	N	Y
3 Lancaster	Y	Y	N	Y	Y	Y	Y	N
4 Price	Y	Y	Y	Y	Y	Y	Y	N
5 Neal	Y	Y	Y	Y	Y	N	N	N
6 ***Coble***	Y	Y	N	Y	Y	N	Y	Y
7 Rose	N	Y	Y	Y	N	Y	Y	?
8 Hefner	?	?	?	Y	Y	N	N	N
9 ***McMillan***	Y	Y	N	Y	N	?	Y	Y
10 ***Ballenger***	Y	Y	N	Y	Y	N	N	Y
11 ***Taylor***	Y	N	N	Y	N	Y	Y	Y
NORTH DAKOTA								
AL Dorgan	Y	Y	N	Y	Y	N	Y	N
OHIO								
1 Luken	Y	Y	Y	N	Y	?	Y	Y
2 ***Gradison***	Y	Y	N	N	N	Y	Y	Y
3 Hall	Y	Y	Y	N	N	Y	Y	?
4 ***Oxley***	Y	N	N	N	N	Y	N	Y
5 ***Gillmor***	Y	Y	N	Y	N	Y	Y	Y
6 ***McEwen***	Y	N	N	Y	N	?	N	Y
7 ***Hobson***	Y	N	N	N	N	Y	Y	Y
8 ***Boehner***	Y	N	N	N	N	Y	Y	Y
9 Kaptur	N	N	Y	Y	Y	N	Y	N
10 ***Miller***	Y	N	N	N	N	Y	N	Y
11 Eckart	Y	Y	Y	Y	Y	Y	Y	?
12 ***Kasich***	Y	N	Y	Y	Y	N	Y	N
13 Pease	N	Y	N	Y	Y	Y	Y	N
14 Sawyer	N	Y	Y	Y	Y	Y	Y	N
15 ***Wylie***	Y	Y	N	Y	N	Y	Y	Y
16 ***Regula***	Y	Y	N	Y	N	Y	Y	Y
17 Traficant	N	N	Y	Y	N	N	N	N
18 Applegate	N	Y	N	Y	N	N	N	N
19 Feighan	Y	Y	?	?	N	Y	Y	N
20 Oakar	N	N	Y	Y	N	N	Y	N
21 Stokes	N	N	Y	Y	Y	N	Y	N
OKLAHOMA								
1 ***Inhofe***	Y	Y	N	Y	N	N	Y	Y
2 Synar	N	Y	Y	Y	Y	Y	Y	N
3 Brewster	Y	N	N	Y	N	Y	Y	N
4 McCurdy	Y	Y	Y	Y	N	Y	Y	Y
5 ***Edwards***	Y	Y	N	Y	N	N	Y	?
6 English	Y	Y	Y	Y	N	N	N	Y
OREGON								
1 AuCoin	N	Y	Y	Y	Y	N	Y	N
2 ***Smith***	Y	N	N	Y	N	N	N	Y
3 Wyden	N	Y	Y	Y	Y	Y	Y	N
4 DeFazio	Y	N	Y	Y	Y	N	N	N
5 Kopetski	N	N	Y	N	N	Y	Y	N
PENNSYLVANIA								
1 Foglietta	N	Y	Y	Y	Y	N	Y	?
2 Blackwell	N	Y	Y	?	Y	N	Y	N
3 Borski	N	N	Y	Y	N	Y	Y	N
4 Kolter	Y	?	?	?	N	Y	Y	?
5 ***Schulze***	Y	?	Y	Y	N	?	N	?
6 Yatron	Y	N	Y	Y	N	Y	Y	?
7 ***Weldon***	Y	Y	N	Y	N	Y	N	N
8 Kostmayer	N	Y	Y	N	Y	Y	Y	N
9 ***Shuster***	Y	Y	N	Y	Y	N	N	Y
10 ***McDade***	Y	X	Y	Y	N	Y	Y	?
11 Kanjorski	N	Y	Y	Y	Y	N	N	N
12 Murtha	N	N	Y	Y	Y	Y	Y	N
13 ***Coughlin***	Y	Y	Y	?	N	Y	Y	Y
14 Coyne	N	N	Y	Y	Y	Y	Y	N
15 ***Ritter***	Y	Y	N	Y	N	Y	Y	Y
16 ***Walker***	Y	N	N	Y	N	Y	N	Y
17 ***Gekas***	Y	N	N	Y	N	Y	Y	Y
18 ***Santorum***	Y	N	N	Y	N	N	Y	N
19 ***Goodling***	Y	Y	N	N	Y	N	N	?
20 Gaydos	N	Y	Y	Y	N	?	N	?
21 ***Ridge***	Y	?	N	Y	N	N	Y	Y
22 Murphy	N	#	N	Y	Y	X	N	N
23 ***Clinger***	Y	N	Y	Y	N	Y	Y	Y
RHODE ISLAND								
1 ***Machtley***	Y	Y	Y	Y	Y	N	Y	N
2 Reed	N	Y	Y	Y	Y	N	Y	N
SOUTH CAROLINA								
1 ***Ravenel***	Y	Y	N	Y	Y	Y	Y	N
2 ***Spence***	Y	N	N	Y	N	N	N	Y
3 Derrick	Y	N	Y	Y	Y	Y	Y	N
4 Patterson	Y	Y	N	Y	Y	N	N	N
5 Spratt	Y	Y	Y	Y	Y	Y	Y	N
6 Tallon	N	Y	Y	?	N	Y	Y	Y
SOUTH DAKOTA								
AL Johnson	Y	N	N	Y	Y	Y	Y	N
TENNESSEE								
1 ***Quillen***	Y	X	X	Y	N	N	Y	N
2 ***Duncan***	Y	Y	N	Y	Y	N	N	Y
3 Lloyd	Y	N	Y	Y	N	N	N	N
4 Cooper	Y	N	Y	Y	N	Y	Y	N
5 Clement	Y	Y	Y	Y	Y	?	?	?
6 Gordon	Y	Y	Y	Y	Y	?	Y	N
7 ***Sundquist***	Y	Y	N	Y	N	N	Y	Y
8 Tanner	Y	Y	Y	Y	N	N	N	Y
9 Ford	N	Y	Y	Y	Y	?	Y	N
TEXAS								
1 Chapman	Y	N	N	Y	N	N	N	N
2 Wilson	Y	N	Y	?	N	?	Y	N
3 ***Johnson***	Y	N	N	N	N	Y	Y	Y
4 Hall	Y	N	N	Y	N	N	N	Y
5 Bryant	Y	N	Y	Y	N	N	Y	N
6 ***Barton***	Y	N	N	N	N	N	N	Y
7 ***Archer***	Y	N	N	N	N	N	N	Y
8 ***Fields***	Y	N	N	N	N	N	N	Y
9 Brooks	N	N	Y	Y	N	Y	N	N
10 Pickle	Y	N	Y	Y	N	Y	Y	N
11 Edwards	Y	N	N	Y	N	Y	Y	Y
12 Geren	Y	N	N	Y	N	N	Y	Y
13 Sarpalius	Y	N	N	Y	N	N	N	N
14 Laughlin	Y	N	N	?	N	Y	Y	N
15 de la Garza	Y	N	Y	Y	N	Y	Y	N
16 Coleman	N	N	Y	N	N	Y	Y	Y
17 Stenholm	Y	N	N	Y	N	Y	Y	Y
18 Washington	N	Y	N	Y	Y	N	Y	N
19 ***Combest***	Y	N	N	Y	N	N	N	N
20 Gonzalez	N	N	Y	Y	Y	N	N	N
21 ***Smith***	Y	N	Y	Y	N	Y	Y	Y
22 ***DeLay***	Y	N	N	?	N	N	N	Y
23 Bustamante	N	N	Y	Y	N	Y	Y	N
24 Frost	Y	N	Y	?	N	Y	Y	N
25 Andrews	Y	N	N	Y	N	Y	Y	N
26 ***Armey***	Y	N	N	N	N	N	N	Y
27 Ortiz	Y	N	Y	Y	N	N	Y	N
UTAH								
1 ***Hansen***	Y	N	N	?	N	Y	N	N
2 Owens	Y	Y	Y	Y	Y	Y	Y	N
3 Orton	Y	Y	N	N	Y	Y	Y	N
VERMONT								
AL *Sanders*	N	Y	Y	Y	Y	N	N	N
VIRGINIA								
1 ***Bateman***	Y	N	Y	Y	N	Y	Y	Y
2 Pickett	N	N	N	N	N	Y	Y	Y
3 ***Bliley***	Y	N	N	N	N	Y	Y	Y
4 Sisisky	Y	Y	N	Y	N	Y	Y	Y
5 Payne	Y	N	N	Y	Y	Y	Y	Y
6 Olin	N	N	N	N	Y	Y	Y	Y
7 ***Allen***	Y	N	N	Y	N	N	N	Y
8 Moran	Y	N	Y	Y	N	Y	Y	N
9 Boucher	N	N	N	Y	N	Y	N	N
10 ***Wolf***	Y	Y	N	Y	N	Y	Y	Y
WASHINGTON								
1 ***Miller***	Y	N	N	N	N	Y	Y	N
2 Swift	N	Y	Y	Y	N	Y	Y	N
3 Unsoeld	N	Y	Y	Y	Y	Y	Y	N
4 ***Morrison***	Y	N	Y	Y	N	Y	Y	Y
5 Foley	N					Y		
6 Dicks	N	N	Y	Y	N	Y	Y	N
7 McDermott	N	Y	Y	Y	Y	Y	Y	N
8 ***Chandler***	Y	N	?	Y	N	Y	?	?
WEST VIRGINIA								
1 Mollohan	N	N	Y	Y	N	Y	Y	N
2 Staggers	N	Y	Y	Y	Y	N	?	Y
3 Wise	Y	Y	Y	Y	N	Y	Y	N
4 Rahall	N	Y	Y	Y	N	N	N	N
WISCONSIN								
1 Aspin	N	N	Y	N	N	Y	Y	N
2 ***Klug***	Y	Y	Y	N	N	N	Y	N
3 ***Gunderson***	Y	Y	N	Y	N	Y	Y	N
4 Kleczka	N	Y	Y	Y	Y	N	N	N
5 Moody	Y	Y	N	Y	Y	N	Y	N
6 ***Petri***	Y	Y	N	Y	N	N	N	N
7 Obey	N	Y	Y	Y	Y	Y	Y	N
8 ***Roth***	Y	Y	N	Y	N	N	N	Y
9 ***Sensenbrenner***	Y	Y	N	Y	N	N	N	Y
WYOMING								
AL ***Thomas***	Y	N	N	?	N	Y	N	Y

	9	10	11	12	13	14	15
ALABAMA							
Heflin	N	N	N	Y	Y	Y	Y
Shelby	N	N	Y	Y	Y	N	Y
ALASKA							
Murkowski	Y	Y	?	Y	Y	Y	?
Stevens	N	N	Y	Y	Y	N	Y
ARIZONA							
DeConcini	Y	Y	N	Y	Y	N	Y
McCain	N	Y	Y	N	Y	Y	Y
ARKANSAS							
Bumpers	Y	Y	N	Y	N	Y	Y
Pryor	Y	Y	N	Y	N	Y	Y
CALIFORNIA							
Cranston	Y	Y	?	Y	Y	N	Y
Seymour	?	?	?	Y	Y	N	N
COLORADO							
Wirth	?	Y	N	Y	Y	N	Y
Brown	N	N	Y	Y	Y	N	N
CONNECTICUT							
Dodd	Y	Y	N	Y	Y	Y	Y
Lieberman	Y	Y	N	Y	Y	Y	Y
DELAWARE							
Biden	Y	Y	N	Y	Y	Y	Y
Roth	N	Y	N	Y	N	Y	Y
FLORIDA							
Graham	Y	Y	N	Y	Y	Y	Y
Mack	N	N	Y	N	Y	P	Y
GEORGIA							
Fowler	Y	Y	N	Y	Y	N	Y
Nunn	N	Y	N	Y	Y	Y	Y
HAWAII							
Akaka	Y	Y	N	Y	Y	Y	Y
Inouye	Y	Y	N	Y	Y	Y	Y
IDAHO							
Craig	N	N	Y	N	N	N	N
Symms	N	N	Y	N	N	N	Y
ILLINOIS							
Dixon	N	Y	N	Y	Y	Y	Y
Simon	Y	Y	N	Y	Y	Y	Y
INDIANA							
Coats	N	Y	Y	N	Y	Y	Y
Lugar	N	N	Y	Y	Y	N	Y
IOWA							
Harkin	Y	Y	N	Y	Y	Y	Y
Grassley	Y	N	N	N	Y	Y	Y
KANSAS							
Dole	N	N	Y	N	Y	N	Y
Kassebaum	Y	N	Y	Y	Y	Y	N
KENTUCKY							
Ford	Y	Y	N	N	Y	Y	Y
McConnell	N	N	N	Y	Y	Y	Y
LOUISIANA							
Breaux	N	Y	N	N	Y	Y	Y
Johnston	N	Y	N	N	Y	Y	Y
MAINE							
Mitchell	Y	Y	N	Y	Y	Y	Y
Cohen	N	Y	N	Y	Y	Y	N
MARYLAND							
Mikulski	Y	Y	N	Y	Y	Y	Y
Sarbanes	Y	Y	N	Y	Y	Y	Y
MASSACHUSETTS							
Kennedy	Y	Y	N	Y	Y	Y	Y
Kerry	Y	Y	N	Y	Y	Y	Y
MICHIGAN							
Levin	Y	Y	N	Y	Y	Y	Y
Riegle	Y	Y	N	Y	Y	Y	Y
MINNESOTA							
Wellstone	Y	Y	N	Y	Y	Y	Y
Durenberger	N	Y	Y	N	Y	Y	Y
MISSISSIPPI							
Cochran	N	N	Y	N	Y	Y	Y
Lott	N	N	Y	N	Y	N	Y
MISSOURI							
Bond	Y	Y	?	Y	Y	Y	?
Danforth	Y	Y	N	N	Y	Y	Y
MONTANA							
Baucus	Y	Y	N	Y	Y	Y	Y
Burns	N	N	Y	N	N	N	Y
NEBRASKA							
Exon	Y	Y	N	Y	Y	Y	C
Kerrey	Y	Y	N	Y	Y	Y	Y
NEVADA							
Bryan	N	Y	N	Y	Y	Y	Y
Reid	N	Y	N	Y	Y	N	Y
NEW HAMPSHIRE							
Rudman	N	N	Y	Y	Y	N	N
Smith	N	N	Y	N	N	N	N
NEW JERSEY							
Bradley	Y	Y	N	Y	Y	Y	Y
Lautenberg	Y	Y	N	Y	Y	Y	Y
NEW MEXICO							
Bingaman	?	Y	N	Y	Y	Y	Y
Domenici	N	N	Y	N	Y	Y	Y
NEW YORK							
Moynihan	Y	Y	Y	Y	Y	Y	Y
D'Amato	Y	Y	Y	Y	Y	Y	Y
NORTH CAROLINA							
Sanford	Y	Y	N	Y	Y	Y	?
Helms	N	N	Y	N	N	N	?
NORTH DAKOTA							
Burdick [1]	N	Y	Y	N	Y	N	Y
Conrad	Y	Y	N	Y	Y	Y	Y
OHIO							
Glenn	Y	Y	N	Y	Y	Y	Y
Metzenbaum	Y	Y	N	Y	Y	Y	Y
OKLAHOMA							
Boren	?	Y	?	Y	Y	N	Y
Nickles	N	N	N	N	Y	N	Y
OREGON							
Hatfield	Y	Y	Y	Y	Y	Y	Y
Packwood	Y	Y	N	Y	Y	N	Y
PENNSYLVANIA							
Wofford	Y	Y	N	Y	Y	Y	Y
Specter	Y	Y	N	Y	Y	Y	Y
RHODE ISLAND							
Pell	Y	Y	N	Y	Y	Y	Y
Chafee	Y	Y	Y	Y	Y	N	Y
SOUTH CAROLINA							
Hollings	N	N	Y	Y	N	Y	Y
Thurmond	N	N	Y	N	Y	Y	N
SOUTH DAKOTA							
Daschle	Y	Y	N	Y	Y	Y	Y
Pressler	Y	N	Y	N	Y	Y	Y
TENNESSEE							
Gore	?	Y	?	?	?	Y	?
Sasser	Y	Y	N	Y	Y	Y	Y
TEXAS							
Bentsen	N	Y	N	Y	Y	Y	Y
Gramm	N	N	Y	N	Y	N	Y
UTAH							
Garn	N	N	Y	N	N	N	Y
Hatch	N	N	Y	N	Y	Y	Y
VERMONT							
Leahy	Y	Y	N	Y	Y	Y	?
Jeffords	Y	Y	Y	Y	Y	Y	?
VIRGINIA							
Robb	N	Y	N	Y	Y	Y	Y
Warner	N	N	Y	Y	Y	Y	Y
WASHINGTON							
Adams	Y	Y	N	Y	Y	Y	Y
Gorton	N	N	Y	Y	Y	Y	Y
WEST VIRGINIA							
Byrd	Y	Y	N	Y	N	Y	Y
Rockefeller	Y	Y	N	Y	Y	Y	Y
WISCONSIN							
Kohl	Y	Y	N	Y	Y	Y	Y
Kasten	Y	N	?	N	Y	Y	?
WYOMING							
Simpson	N	N	Y	Y	Y	Y	Y
Wallop	N	N	Y	N	N	N	Y

KEY

- Y Voted for (yea).
- # Paired for.
- + Announced for.
- N Voted against (nay).
- X Paired against.
- \- Announced against.
- P Voted "present."
- C Voted "present" to avoid possible conflict of interest.
- ? Did not vote or otherwise make a position known.

Democrats ***Republicans***

ND Northern Democrats SD Southern Democrats

Southern states - Ala., Ark., Fla., Ga., Ky., La., Miss., N.C., Okla., S.C., Tenn., Texas, Va.

[1] *Sen. Jocelyn Birch Burdick, D-N.D., was sworn in Sept. 16, 1992, to succeed Quentin N. Burdick, D, who died Sept. 8, 1992.*

9. S 3114. Fiscal 1993 Defense Authorization/Nuclear Testing Moratorium. Hatfield, R-Ore., amendment to the Cohen, R-Maine, amendment, to impose a nine-month moratorium on nuclear testing until July 1, 1993; allow limited testing between July 1, 1993, and Jan. 1, 1997; require reports to Congress on the remaining weapons in the U.S. stockpile, proposed safety improvements and tests, and plans for a comprehensive test ban by Sept. 30, 1996; and, contingent on certain factors, prohibit nuclear tests after Sept. 30, 1996, unless a foreign state conducts a test. The Cohen amendment would impose a three-month testing moratorium, allow limited testing until 1998, and impose a test ban in 1998; the president could waive that ban for one year to negotiate a comprehensive test ban. Adopted 55-40: R 13-29; D 42-11 (ND 35-3, SD 7-8), Sept. 18, 1992. The Cohen amendment, as amended by the Hatfield amendment, subsequently was adopted by voice vote. A "nay" was a vote supporting the president's position.

10. S 5. Family and Medical Leave/Veto Override. Passage, over President Bush's Sept. 22 veto, of the bill to require companies with more than 50 employees to provide workers with up to 12 weeks of unpaid leave for family emergencies. Passed (thus cleared for House action) 68-31: R 14-28; D 54-3 (ND 40-0, SD 14-3), Sept. 24, 1992. A two-thirds majority of those present and voting (66 in this case) is required to override a veto. A "nay" was a vote supporting the president's position.

11. HR 11. Tax Bill/Enterprise Zones. Dole, R-Kan., amendment to eliminate provisions making permanent the existing cap on itemized deductions and the phaseout of the personal exemption for upper-income taxpayers; to cut the number of tax enterprise zones from 125 to 30; and to limit the individual retirement account deduction. Rejected 34-59: R 31-8; D 3-51 (ND 1-38, SD 2-13), Sept. 25, 1992. A "yea" was a vote supporting the president's position.

12. S 323. Family Planning Amendments/Veto Override. Passage, over President Bush's Sept. 25 veto, of the bill to reauthorize Title X of the Public Health Service Act for five years through fiscal 1997. The bill would overturn the administration's ban on abortion counseling at federally funded family planning clinics. Passed (thus cleared for House action) 73-26: R 20-23; D 53-3 (ND 40-0, SD 13-3), Oct. 1, 1992. A two-thirds majority of those present and voting (66 in this case) is required to override a veto. A "nay" was a vote supporting the president's position.

13. HR 5368. Fiscal 1993 Foreign Operations Appropriations/Passage. Passage of the bill to provide $26.4 billion in new budget authority for foreign assistance and related programs in fiscal 1993. The administration requested $27.3 billion. Passed 87-12: R 35-8; D 52-4 (ND 39-1, SD 13-3), Oct. 1, 1992.

14. S 12. Cable Television Reregulation/Veto Override. Passage, over President Bush's Oct. 3 veto, of the bill to improve competition in the cable industry by giving the Federal Communications Commission authority over basic rates and giving broadcasters the right to charge cable operators for the use of over-the-air signals. Passed (thus cleared for House action) 74-25: R 24-18; D 50-7 (ND 36-4, SD 14-3), Oct. 5, 1992. A two-thirds majority of those present and voting (67 in this case) is required to override a veto. A "nay" was a vote supporting the president's position.

15. HR 429. Western Water Bill/Conference Report. Adoption of the conference report to reauthorize Bureau of Reclamation construction programs, including authorization for completing the Central Utah Project and reforms for the Central Valley Project in California. Adopted (thus clearing the bill for the president) 83-8: R 30-8; D 53-0 (ND 38-0, SD 15-0), Oct. 8, 1992.

Congress and Its Members

Membership Lists 1107
Members of Congress 1115
Congressional Committees 1125
Post-Election Sessions 1137
Senate Cloture Votes 1139

Senate Membership in the 101st Congress

Lineup as of Jan. 3, 1989: Democrats 55, Republicans 45

ALABAMA
Howell Heflin (D)
Richard C. Shelby (D)

ALASKA
Frank H. Murkowski (R)
Ted Stevens (R)

ARIZONA
Dennis DeConcini (D)
John McCain (R)

ARKANSAS
Dale Bumpers (D)
David Pryor (D)

CALIFORNIA
Alan Cranston (D)
Pete Wilson (R)

COLORADO
Tim Wirth (D)
William L. Armstrong (R)

CONNECTICUT
Christopher J. Dodd (D)
Joseph I. Lieberman (D)

DELAWARE
Joseph R. Biden Jr. (D)
William V. Roth Jr. (R)

FLORIDA
Bob Graham (D)
Connie Mack (R)

GEORGIA
Wyche Fowler Jr. (D)
Sam Nunn (D)

HAWAII
Daniel K. Inouye (D)
Spark M. Matsunaga (D)
(died April 15, 1990)
Daniel K. Akaka (D)[a]
(sworn in May 16, 1990)

IDAHO
James A. McClure (R)
Steve Symms (R)

ILLINOIS
Alan J. Dixon (D)
Paul Simon (D)

INDIANA
Daniel R. Coats (R)
Richard G. Lugar (R)

IOWA
Tom Harkin (D)
Charles E. Grassley (R)

KANSAS
Bob Dole (R)
Nancy Landon Kassebaum (R)

KENTUCKY
Wendell H. Ford (D)
Mitch McConnell (R)

LOUISIANA
John B. Breaux (D)
J. Bennett Johnston (D)

MAINE
George J. Mitchell (D)
William S. Cohen (R)

MARYLAND
Barbara A. Mikulski (D)
Paul S. Sarbanes (D)

MASSACHUSETTS
Edward M. Kennedy (D)
John Kerry (D)

MICHIGAN
Carl Levin (D)
Donald W. Riegle Jr. (D)

MINNESOTA
Rudy Boschwitz (R)
Dave Durenberger (R)

MISSISSIPPI
Thad Cochran (R)
Trent Lott (R)

MISSOURI
Christopher S. Bond (R)
John C. Danforth (R)

MONTANA
Max Baucus (D)
Conrad Burns (R)

NEBRASKA
Jim Exon (D)
Bob Kerrey (D)

NEVADA
Richard H. Bryan (D)
Harry Reid (D)

NEW HAMPSHIRE
Warren B. Rudman (R)
Gordon J. Humphrey (R)
(resigned Dec. 4, 1990)
Robert C. Smith (R)[b]
(sworn in Dec. 7, 1990)

NEW JERSEY
Bill Bradley (D)
Frank R. Lautenberg (D)

NEW MEXICO
Jeff Bingaman (D)
Pete V. Domenici (R)

NEW YORK
Daniel Patrick Moynihan (D)
Alfonse M. D'Amato (R)

NORTH CAROLINA
Terry Sanford (D)
Jesse Helms (R)

NORTH DAKOTA
Quentin N. Burdick (D)
Kent Conrad (D)

OHIO
John Glenn (D)
Howard M. Metzenbaum (D)

OKLAHOMA
David L. Boren (D)
Don Nickles (R)

OREGON
Mark O. Hatfield (R)
Bob Packwood (R)

PENNSYLVANIA
John Heinz (R)
Arlen Specter (R)

RHODE ISLAND
Claiborne Pell (D)
John H. Chafee (R)

SOUTH CAROLINA
Ernest F. Hollings (D)
Strom Thurmond (R)

SOUTH DAKOTA
Tom Daschle (D)
Larry Pressler (R)

TENNESSEE
Al Gore (D)
Jim Sasser (D)

TEXAS
Lloyd Bentsen (D)
Phil Gramm (R)

UTAH
Jake Garn (R)
Orrin G. Hatch (R)

VERMONT
Patrick J. Leahy (D)
James M. Jeffords (R)

VIRGINIA
Charles S. Robb (D)
John W. Warner (R)

WASHINGTON
Brock Adams (D)
Slade Gorton (R)

WEST VIRGINIA
Robert C. Byrd (D)
John D. Rockefeller IV (D)

WISCONSIN
Herb Kohl (D)
Bob Kasten (R)

WYOMING
Alan K. Simpson (R)
Malcolm Wallop (R)

[a] Appointed April 28, 1990, and then elected to complete the remaining four years of Matsunaga's term in a special election Nov. 6, 1990.
[b] Smith, who was elected to a six-year term in the Senate Nov. 6, 1990, resigned from the House Dec. 7 to be appointed for the remainder of Humphrey's term, which expired Jan. 3, 1991.

Appendix

House Membership in the 101st Congress

Lineup as of Jan. 3, 1989: Democrats 259, Republicans 174, Vacancies 2

ALABAMA
1. Sonny Callahan (R)
2. Bill L. Dickinson (R)
3. Glen Browder (D)[a]
   (sworn in April 18, 1989)
4. Tom Bevill (D)
5. Ronnie G. Flippo (D)
6. Ben Erdreich (D)
7. Claude Harris (D)

ALASKA
AL Don Young (R)

ARIZONA
1. John J. Rhodes III (R)
2. Morris K. Udall (D)
3. Bob Stump (R)
4. Jon Kyl (R)
5. Jim Kolbe (R)

ARKANSAS
1. Bill Alexander (D)
2. Tommy F. Robinson (D)[b]
3. John Paul Hammerschmidt (R)
4. Beryl Anthony Jr. (D)

CALIFORNIA
1. Douglas H. Bosco (D)
2. Wally Herger (R)
3. Robert T. Matsui (D)
4. Vic Fazio (D)
5. Nancy Pelosi (D)
6. Barbara Boxer (D)
7. George Miller (D)
8. Ronald V. Dellums (D)
9. Pete Stark (D)
10. Don Edwards (D)
11. Tom Lantos (D)
12. Tom Campbell (R)
13. Norman Y. Mineta (D)
14. Norman D. Shumway (R)
15. Tony Coelho (D)
    (resigned June 15, 1989)
    Gary Condit (D)
    (sworn in Sept. 20, 1989)
16. Leon E. Panetta (D)
17. Charles "Chip" Pashayan Jr. (R)
18. Richard H. Lehman (D)
19. Robert J. Lagomarsino (R)
20. Bill Thomas (R)
21. Elton Gallegly (R)
22. Carlos J. Moorhead (R)
23. Anthony C. Beilenson (D)
24. Henry A. Waxman (D)
25. Edward R. Roybal (D)
26. Howard L. Berman (D)
27. Mel Levine (D)
28. Julian C. Dixon (D)
29. Augustus F. Hawkins (D)
30. Matthew G. Martinez (D)
31. Mervyn M. Dymally (D)
32. Glenn M. Anderson (D)
33. David Dreier (R)
34. Esteban E. Torres (D)
35. Jerry Lewis (R)
36. George E. Brown Jr. (D)
37. Al McCandless (R)
38. Robert K. Dornan (R)
39. William E. Dannemeyer (R)
40. C. Christopher Cox (R)
41. Bill Lowery (R)
42. Dana Rohrabacher (R)
43. Ron Packard (R)
44. Jim Bates (D)
45. Duncan Hunter (R)

COLORADO
1. Patricia Schroeder (D)
2. David E. Skaggs (D)
3. Ben Nighthorse Campbell (D)
4. Hank Brown (R)
5. Joel Hefley (R)
6. Dan Schaefer (R)

CONNECTICUT
1. Barbara B. Kennelly (D)
2. Sam Gejdenson (D)
3. Bruce A. Morrison (D)
4. Christopher Shays (R)
5. John G. Rowland (R)
6. Nancy L. Johnson (R)

DELAWARE
AL Thomas R. Carper (D)

FLORIDA
1. Earl Hutto (D)
2. Bill Grant (D)[c]
3. Charles E. Bennett (D)
4. Craig T. James (R)
5. Bill McCollum (R)
6. Cliff Stearns (R)
7. Sam M. Gibbons (D)
8. C. W. Bill Young (R)
9. Michael Bilirakis (R)
10. Andy Ireland (R)
11. Bill Nelson (D)
12. Tom Lewis (R)
13. Porter J. Goss (R)
14. Harry A. Johnston (D)
15. E. Clay Shaw Jr. (R)
16. Lawrence J. Smith (D)
17. William Lehman (D)
18. Claude Pepper (D)
    (died May 30, 1989)
    Ileana Ros-Lehtinen (R)
    (sworn in Sept. 6, 1989)
19. Dante B. Fascell (D)

GEORGIA
1. Lindsay Thomas (D)
2. Charles Hatcher (D)
3. Richard Ray (D)
4. Ben Jones (D)
5. John Lewis (D)
6. Newt Gingrich (R)
7. George "Buddy" Darden (D)
8. J. Roy Rowland (D)
9. Ed Jenkins (D)
10. Doug Barnard Jr. (D)

HAWAII
1. Patricia Saiki (R)
2. Daniel K. Akaka (D)
   (resigned May 16, 1990)
   Patsy T. Mink (D)
   (sworn in Sept. 27, 1990)

IDAHO
1. Larry E. Craig (R)
2. Richard Stallings (D)

ILLINOIS
1. Charles A. Hayes (D)
2. Gus Savage (D)
3. Marty Russo (D)
4. George E. Sangmeister (D)
5. William O. Lipinski (D)
6. Henry J. Hyde (R)
7. Cardiss Collins (D)
8. Dan Rostenkowski (D)
9. Sidney R. Yates (D)
10. John Porter (R)
11. Frank Annunzio (D)
12. Philip M. Crane (R)
13. Harris W. Fawell (R)
14. Dennis Hastert (R)
15. Edward R. Madigan (R)
16. Lynn Martin (R)
17. Lane Evans (D)
18. Robert H. Michel (R)
19. Terry L. Bruce (D)
20. Richard J. Durbin (D)
21. Jerry F. Costello (D)
22. Glenn Poshard (D)

INDIANA
1. Peter J. Visclosky (D)
2. Philip R. Sharp (D)
3. John Hiler (R)
4. Jill L. Long (D)[d]
   (sworn in April 5, 1989)
5. Jim Jontz (D)
6. Dan Burton (R)
7. John T. Myers (R)
8. Frank McCloskey (D)
9. Lee H. Hamilton (D)
10. Andrew Jacobs Jr. (D)

IOWA
1. Jim Leach (R)
2. Tom Tauke (R)
3. Dave Nagle (D)
4. Neal Smith (D)
5. Jim Ross Lightfoot (R)
6. Fred Grandy (R)

KANSAS
1. Pat Roberts (R)
2. Jim Slattery (D)
3. Jan Meyers (R)
4. Dan Glickman (D)
5. Bob Whittaker (R)

KENTUCKY
1. Carroll Hubbard Jr. (D)
2. William H. Natcher (D)
3. Romano L. Mazzoli (D)
4. Jim Bunning (R)
5. Harold Rogers (R)
6. Larry J. Hopkins (R)
7. Carl L. Perkins (D)

LOUISIANA
1. Robert L. Livingston (R)
2. Lindy (Mrs. Hale) Boggs (D)
3. W. J. "Billy" Tauzin (D)
4. Jim McCrery (R)
5. Jerry Huckaby (D)
6. Richard H. Baker (R)
7. Jimmy Hayes (D)
8. Clyde C. Holloway (R)

MAINE
1. Joseph E. Brennan (D)
2. Olympia J. Snowe (R)

MARYLAND
1. Roy Dyson (D)
2. Helen Delich Bentley (R)
3. Benjamin L. Cardin (D)
4. Tom McMillen (D)
5. Steny H. Hoyer (D)
6. Beverly B. Byron (D)
7. Kweisi Mfume (D)
8. Constance A. Morella (R)

MASSACHUSETTS
1. Silvio O. Conte (R)
2. Richard E. Neal (D)
3. Joseph D. Early (D)
4. Barney Frank (D)
5. Chester G. Atkins (D)
6. Nicholas Mavroules (D)
7. Edward J. Markey (D)
8. Joseph P. Kennedy II (D)
9. Joe Moakley (D)
10. Gerry E. Studds (D)
11. Brian Donnelly (D)

MICHIGAN
1. John Conyers Jr. (D)
2. Carl D. Pursell (R)
3. Howard Wolpe (D)
4. Fred Upton (R)
5. Paul B. Henry (R)
6. Bob Carr (D)
7. Dale E. Kildee (D)
8. Bob Traxler (D)
9. Guy Vander Jagt (R)
10. Bill Schuette (R)
11. Robert W. Davis (R)
12. David E. Bonior (D)
13. George W. Crockett Jr. (D)
14. Dennis M. Hertel (D)
15. William D. Ford (D)
16. John D. Dingell (D)
17. Sander M. Levin (D)
18. William S. Broomfield (R)

MINNESOTA
1. Timothy J. Penny (D)
2. Vin Weber (R)
3. Bill Frenzel (R)
4. Bruce F. Vento (D)
5. Martin Olav Sabo (D)
6. Gerry Sikorski (D)
7. Arlan Stangeland (R)
8. James L. Oberstar (D)

MISSISSIPPI
1. Jamie L. Whitten (D)
2. Mike Espy (D)
3. G. V. "Sonny" Montgomery (D)
4. Mike Parker (D)
5. Larkin Smith (R)
   (died Aug. 13, 1989)
   Gene Taylor (D)
   (sworn in Oct. 24, 1989)

MISSOURI
1. William L. Clay (D)
2. Jack Buechner (R)
3. Richard A. Gephardt (D)
4. Ike Skelton (D)
5. Alan Wheat (D)
6. E. Thomas Coleman (R)
7. Mel Hancock (R)

8. Bill Emerson (R)
9. Harold L. Volkmer (D)

MONTANA
1. Pat Williams (D)
2. Ron Marlenee (R)

NEBRASKA
1. Doug Bereuter (R)
2. Peter Hoagland (D)
3. Virginia Smith (R)

NEVADA
1. James Bilbray (D)
2. Barbara F. Vucanovich (R)

NEW HAMPSHIRE
1. Robert C. Smith (R)
   (resigned Dec. 7, 1990)
2. Chuck Douglas (R)

NEW JERSEY
1. James J. Florio (D)
   (resigned Jan. 16, 1990)
   Robert E. Andrews (D)
   (sworn in Jan. 3, 1991)
2. William J. Hughes (D)
3. Frank Pallone Jr. (D)
4. Christopher H. Smith (R)
5. Marge Roukema (R)
6. Bernard J. Dwyer (D)
7. Matthew J. Rinaldo (R)
8. Robert A. Roe (D)
9. Robert G. Torricelli (D)
10. Donald M. Payne (D)
11. Dean A. Gallo (R)
12. Jim Courter (R)
13. H. James Saxton (R)
14. Frank J. Guarini (D)

NEW MEXICO
1. Steven H. Schiff (R)
2. Joe Skeen (R)
3. Bill Richardson (D)

NEW YORK
1. George J. Hochbrueckner (D)
2. Thomas J. Downey (D)
3. Robert J. Mrazek (D)
4. Norman F. Lent (R)
5. Raymond J. McGrath (R)
6. Floyd H. Flake (D)
7. Gary L. Ackerman (D)
8. James H. Scheuer (D)
9. Thomas J. Manton (D)
10. Charles E. Schumer (D)
11. Edolphus Towns (D)
12. Major R. Owens (D)
13. Stephen J. Solarz (D)
14. Guy V. Molinari (R)
    (resigned Jan. 1, 1990)
    Susan Molinari (R)
    (sworn in March 27, 1990)
15. Bill Green (R)
16. Charles B. Rangel (D)
17. Ted Weiss (D)
18. Robert Garcia (D)
    (resigned Jan. 7, 1990)
    Jose E. Serrano (D)
    (sworn in March 28, 1990)
19. Eliot L. Engel (D)
20. Nita M. Lowey (D)
21. Hamilton Fish Jr. (R)
22. Benjamin A. Gilman (R)
23. Michael R. McNulty (D)
24. Gerald B. H. Solomon (R)
25. Sherwood Boehlert (R)
26. David O'B. Martin (R)
27. James T. Walsh (R)
28. Matthew F. McHugh (D)
29. Frank Horton (R)
30. Louise M. Slaughter (D)
31. Bill Paxon (R)
32. John J. LaFalce (D)
33. Henry J. Nowak (D)
34. Amo Houghton (R)

NORTH CAROLINA
1. Walter B. Jones (D)
2. Tim Valentine (D)
3. H. Martin Lancaster (D)
4. David E. Price (D)
5. Stephen L. Neal (D)
6. Howard Coble (R)
7. Charlie Rose (D)
8. W. G. "Bill" Hefner (D)
9. Alex McMillan (R)
10. Cass Ballenger (R)
11. James McClure Clarke (D)

NORTH DAKOTA
AL Byron L. Dorgan (D)

OHIO
1. Thomas A. Luken (D)
2. Bill Gradison (R)
3. Tony P. Hall (D)
4. Michael G. Oxley (R)
5. Paul E. Gillmor (R)
6. Bob McEwen (R)
7. Mike DeWine (R)
8. Donald E. "Buz" Lukens (R)
   (resigned Oct. 24, 1990)
9. Marcy Kaptur (D)
10. Clarence E. Miller (R)
11. Dennis E. Eckart (D)
12. John R. Kasich (R)
13. Don J. Pease (D)
14. Thomas C. Sawyer (D)
15. Chalmers P. Wylie (R)
16. Ralph Regula (R)
17. James A. Traficant Jr. (D)
18. Douglas Applegate (D)
19. Edward F. Feighan (D)
20. Mary Rose Oakar (D)
21. Louis Stokes (D)

OKLAHOMA
1. James M. Inhofe (R)
2. Mike Synar (D)
3. Wes Watkins (D)
4. Dave McCurdy (D)
5. Mickey Edwards (R)
6. Glenn English (D)

OREGON
1. Les AuCoin (D)
2. Bob Smith (R)
3. Ron Wyden (D)
4. Peter A. DeFazio (D)
5. Denny Smith (R)

PENNSYLVANIA
1. Thomas M. Foglietta (D)
2. William H. Gray III (D)
3. Robert A. Borski (D)
4. Joe Kolter (D)
5. Richard T. Schulze (R)
6. Gus Yatron (D)
7. Curt Weldon (R)
8. Peter H. Kostmayer (D)
9. Bud Shuster (R)
10. Joseph M. McDade (R)
11. Paul E. Kanjorski (D)
12. John P. Murtha (D)
13. Lawrence Coughlin (R)
14. William J. Coyne (D)
15. Don Ritter (R)
16. Robert S. Walker (R)
17. George W. Gekas (R)
18. Doug Walgren (D)
19. Bill Goodling (R)
20. Joseph M. Gaydos (D)
21. Tom Ridge (R)
22. Austin J. Murphy (D)
23. William F. Clinger Jr. (R)

RHODE ISLAND
1. Ronald K. Machtley (R)
2. Claudine Schneider (R)

SOUTH CAROLINA
1. Arthur Ravenel Jr. (R)
2. Floyd D. Spence (R)
3. Butler Derrick (D)
4. Liz J. Patterson (D)
5. John M. Spratt Jr. (D)
6. Robin Tallon (D)

SOUTH DAKOTA
AL Tim Johnson (D)

TENNESSEE
1. James H. Quillen (R)
2. John J. "Jimmy" Duncan Jr. (R)
3. Marilyn Lloyd (D)
4. Jim Cooper (D)
5. Bob Clement (D)
6. Bart Gordon (D)
7. Don Sundquist (R)
8. John Tanner (D)
9. Harold E. Ford (D)

TEXAS
1. Jim Chapman (D)
2. Charles Wilson (D)
3. Steve Bartlett (R)
4. Ralph M. Hall (D)
5. John Bryant (D)
6. Joe L. Barton (R)
7. Bill Archer (R)
8. Jack Fields (R)
9. Jack Brooks (D)
10. J. J. Pickle (D)
11. Marvin Leath (D)
12. Jim Wright (D)
    (resigned June 30, 1989)
    Pete Geren (D)
    (sworn in Sept. 20, 1989)
13. Bill Sarpalius (D)
14. Greg Laughlin (D)
15. E. "Kika" de la Garza (D)
16. Ronald D. Coleman (D)
17. Charles W. Stenholm (D)
18. Mickey Leland (D)
    (died Aug. 7, 1989)
    Craig Washington (D)
    (sworn in Jan. 23, 1990)
19. Larry Combest (R)
20. Henry B. Gonzalez (D)
21. Lamar Smith (R)
22. Tom DeLay (R)
23. Albert G. Bustamante (D)
24. Martin Frost (D)
25. Michael A. Andrews (D)
26. Dick Armey (R)
27. Solomon P. Ortiz (D)

UTAH
1. James V. Hansen (R)
2. Wayne Owens (D)
3. Howard C. Nielson (R)

VERMONT
AL Peter Smith (R)

VIRGINIA
1. Herbert H. Bateman (R)
2. Owen B. Pickett (D)
3. Thomas J. Bliley Jr. (R)
4. Norman Sisisky (D)
5. Lewis F. Payne Jr. (D)
6. Jim Olin (D)
7. D. French Slaughter Jr. (R)
8. Stan Parris (R)
9. Rick Boucher (D)
10. Frank R. Wolf (R)

WASHINGTON
1. John Miller (R)
2. Al Swift (D)
3. Jolene Unsoeld (D)
4. Sid Morrison (R)
5. Thomas S. Foley (D)
6. Norm Dicks (D)
7. Jim McDermott (D)
8. Rod Chandler (R)

WEST VIRGINIA
1. Alan B. Mollohan (D)
2. Harley O. Staggers Jr. (D)
3. Bob Wise (D)
4. Nick J. Rahall II (D)

WISCONSIN
1. Les Aspin (D)
2. Robert W. Kastenmeier (D)
3. Steve Gunderson (R)
4. Gerald D. Kleczka (D)
5. Jim Moody (D)
6. Thomas E. Petri (R)
7. David R. Obey (D)
8. Toby Roth (R)
9. F. James Sensenbrenner Jr. (R)

WYOMING
AL Dick Cheney (R)
   (resigned March 17, 1989)
   Craig Thomas (R)
   (sworn in May 2, 1989)

Note: Members of the 101st Congress also included delegates Ben Blaz, R-Guam; Ron de Lugo, D-Virgin Islands; Eni F. H. Faleomavaega, D-Am. Samoa; Walter E. Fauntroy, D-D.C.; and resident commissioner Jaime B. Fuster, Pop. Dem.-Puerto Rico.

[a] Bill Nichols, D, was re-elected Nov. 8, 1988, but died Dec. 13, 1988, before the start of the 101st Congress and was not sworn in. Glen Browder was elected to fill the vacant seat in a special election held April 4, 1989.
[b] Tommy Robinson switched to the Republican Party on July 28, 1989.
[c] Bill Grant switched to the Republican Party on Feb. 21, 1989.
[d] Daniel R. Coats, R, was re-elected Nov. 8, 1988. However, he resigned Jan. 1, 1989, to assume the Senate seat vacated by Dan Quayle, R, who was elected vice president. Jill L. Long was elected to fill the vacant seat in a special election held March 28, 1989.

Membership Changes, 101st and 102nd Congresses

101st Congress

Senate

Party	Member	Died	Resigned	Successor	Party	Appointed	Sworn In
R	Dan Quayle, Ind.		1/3/89	Daniel R. Coats	R	1/3/89	1/3/89
D	Spark M. Matsunaga, Hawaii	4/15/90		Daniel K. Akaka[a]	D	4/28/90	5/16/90
R	Gordon J. Humphrey, N.H.		12/4/90	Robert C. Smith[b]	R	12/7/90	12/7/90

House

Party	Member	Died	Resigned	Successor	Party	Elected	Sworn In
D	Bill Nichols, Ala.	12/13/88		Glen Browder	D	4/4/89	4/18/89
R	Daniel R. Coats, Ind.		1/1/89	Jill L. Long	D	3/28/89	4/5/89
D	Bill Grant, Fla.	Grant switched to the Republican Party on Feb. 21, 1989.					
R	Dick Cheney, Wyo.		3/17/89	Craig Thomas	R	4/26/89	5/2/89
D	Claude Pepper, Fla.	5/30/89		Ileana Ros-Lehtinen	R	8/29/89	9/6/89
D	Tony Coelho, Calif.		6/15/89	Gary Condit	D	9/12/89	9/20/89
D	Jim Wright, Texas		6/30/89	Pete Geren	D	9/12/89	9/20/89
D	Tommy F. Robinson, Ark.	Robinson switched to the Republican Party on July 28, 1989.					
D	Mickey Leland, Texas	8/7/89		Craig Washington	D	12/9/89	1/23/90
R	Larkin Smith, Miss.	8/13/89		Gene Taylor	D	10/17/89	10/24/89
R	Guy V. Molinari, N.Y.		1/1/90	Susan Molinari	R	3/20/90	3/27/90
D	Robert Garcia, N.Y.		1/7/90	Jose E. Serrano	D	3/20/90	3/28/90
D	James J. Florio, N.J.		1/16/90	Robert E. Andrews[c]	D	11/6/90	1/3/91
D	Daniel K. Akaka, Hawaii		5/16/90	Patsy T. Mink	D	9/22/90	9/27/90
R	Donald E. "Buz" Lukens, Ohio		10/24/90				
R	Robert C. Smith, N.H.		12/7/90				

102nd Congress

Senate

Party	Member	Died	Resigned	Successor	Party	Appointed	Sworn In
R	Pete Wilson, Calif.		1/7/91	John Seymour	R	1/7/91	1/10/91
R	John Heinz, Pa.	4/4/91		Harris Wofford[d]	D	5/8/91	5/9/91
D	Quentin N. Burdick, N.D.	9/8/92		Jocelyn Birch Burdick	D	9/12/92	9/16/92
R	John Seymour, Calif.		11/3/92	Dianne Feinstein[e]	D		11/10/92
D	Kent Conrad, N.D.		12/14/92	Byron L. Dorgan[f]	D	12/14/92	12/15/92
D	Jocelyn Birch Burdick, N.D.		12/14/92	Kent Conrad	D	12/4/92[g]	12/14/92
D	Al Gore, Tenn.		1/2/93				

House

Party	Member	Died	Resigned	Successor	Party	Elected	Sworn In
R	Silvio O. Conte, Mass.	2/8/91		John Olver	D	6/4/91	6/18/91
R	Edward R. Madigan, Ill.		3/8/91	Thomas W. Ewing	R	7/2/91	7/10/91
R	Steve Bartlett, Texas		3/11/91	Sam Johnson	R	5/18/91	5/22/91
D	Morris K. Udall, Ariz.		5/4/91	Ed Pastor	D	9/24/91	10/3/91
D	William H. Gray III, Pa.		9/11/91	Lucien E. Blackwell	D	11/5/91	11/13/91
R	D. French Slaughter Jr., Va.		11/5/91	George F. Allen	R	11/5/91	11/12/91
D	Ted Weiss, N.Y.	9/14/92		Jerrold Nadler[h]	D	11/3/92	
D	Walter B. Jones, N.C.	9/15/92		Eva Clayton[i]	D	11/3/92	

[a] Elected to complete the remaining four years of Matsunaga's term in a special election Nov. 6, 1990.
[b] Smith, who was elected to a six-year Senate term on Nov. 6, 1990, resigned from the House on Dec. 7 to serve the remainder of Humphrey's term, which expired Jan 3, 1991.
[c] Elected to complete the remainder of Florio's term and to the 102nd Congress on Nov. 6, 1990.
[d] Elected to complete the remaining three years of Heinz's term in a special election Nov. 5, 1991.
[e] Elected Nov. 3, 1992, to complete the remaining two years of Wilson's term, succeeding Seymour, an interim appointment.
[f] Elected Nov. 3, 1992, to the 103rd Congress, to the Senate seat Kent Conrad had planned to vacate at the end of the 102nd Congress. Upon Conrad's Dec. 14 resignation, Dorgan was appointed to fill Conrad's remaining term in the 102nd Congress.
[g] On this date, Conrad won a special election to serve the remaining two years of Quentin N. Burdick's term.
[h] Elected to complete the remainder of Weiss' term and to the 103rd Congress on Nov. 3, 1992.
[i] Elected to complete the remainder of Jones' term and to the 103rd Congress on Nov. 3, 1992.

Senate Membership in the 102nd Congress

Lineup as of Jan. 3, 1991: Democrats 56, Republicans 44

ALABAMA
Howell Heflin (D)
Richard C. Shelby (D)

ALASKA
Frank H. Murkowski (R)
Ted Stevens (R)

ARIZONA
Dennis DeConcini (D)
John McCain (R)

ARKANSAS
Dale Bumpers (D)
David Pryor (D)

CALIFORNIA
Alan Cranston (D)
Pete Wilson (R)
(resigned Jan. 7, 1991)
John Seymour (R)
(sworn in Jan. 10, 1991; resigned Nov. 3, 1992)
Dianne Feinstein (D)[a]
(sworn in Nov. 10, 1992)

COLORADO
Tim Wirth (D)
Hank Brown (R)

CONNECTICUT
Christopher J. Dodd (D)
Joseph I. Lieberman (D)

DELAWARE
Joseph R. Biden Jr. (D)
William V. Roth Jr. (R)

FLORIDA
Bob Graham (D)
Connie Mack (R)

GEORGIA
Wyche Fowler Jr. (D)
Sam Nunn (D)

HAWAII
Daniel K. Akaka (D)
Daniel K. Inouye (D)

IDAHO
Larry E. Craig (R)
Steve Symms (R)

ILLINOIS
Alan J. Dixon (D)
Paul Simon (D)

INDIANA
Daniel R. Coats (R)
Richard G. Lugar (R)

IOWA
Tom Harkin (D)
Charles E. Grassley (R)

KANSAS
Bob Dole (R)
Nancy Landon Kassebaum (R)

KENTUCKY
Wendell H. Ford (D)
Mitch McConnell (R)

LOUISIANA
John B. Breaux (D)
J. Bennett Johnston (D)

MAINE
George J. Mitchell (D)
William S. Cohen (R)

MARYLAND
Barbara A. Mikulski (D)
Paul S. Sarbanes (D)

MASSACHUSETTS
Edward M. Kennedy (D)
John Kerry (D)

MICHIGAN
Carl Levin (D)
Donald W. Riegle Jr. (D)

MINNESOTA
Paul Wellstone (D)
Dave Durenberger (R)

MISSISSIPPI
Thad Cochran (R)
Trent Lott (R)

MISSOURI
Christopher S. Bond (R)
John C. Danforth (R)

MONTANA
Max Baucus (D)
Conrad Burns (R)

NEBRASKA
Jim Exon (D)
Bob Kerrey (D)

NEVADA
Richard H. Bryan (D)
Harry Reid (D)

NEW HAMPSHIRE
Warren B. Rudman (R)
Robert C. Smith (R)

NEW JERSEY
Bill Bradley (D)
Frank R. Lautenberg (D)

NEW MEXICO
Jeff Bingaman (D)
Pete V. Domenici (R)

NEW YORK
Daniel Patrick Moynihan (D)
Alfonse M. D'Amato (R)

NORTH CAROLINA
Terry Sanford (D)
Jesse Helms (R)

NORTH DAKOTA
Quentin N. Burdick (D)
(died Sept. 8, 1992)
Jocelyn Birch Burdick (D)
(sworn in Sept. 16, 1992; resigned Dec. 14, 1992)
Kent Conrad (D)[b]
Byron L. Dorgan (D)
(sworn in Dec. 15, 1992)

OHIO
John Glenn (D)
Howard M. Metzenbaum (D)

OKLAHOMA
David L. Boren (D)
Don Nickles (R)

OREGON
Mark O. Hatfield (R)
Bob Packwood (R)

PENNSYLVANIA
John Heinz (R)
(died April 4, 1991)
Harris Wofford (D)[c]
(sworn in May 9, 1991)
Arlen Specter (R)

RHODE ISLAND
Claiborne Pell (D)
John H. Chafee (R)

SOUTH CAROLINA
Ernest F. Hollings (D)
Strom Thurmond (R)

SOUTH DAKOTA
Tom Daschle (D)
Larry Pressler (R)

TENNESSEE
Al Gore (D)
(resigned Jan. 2, 1993)
Jim Sasser (D)

TEXAS
Lloyd Bentsen (D)
Phil Gramm (R)

UTAH
Jake Garn (R)
Orrin G. Hatch (R)

VERMONT
Patrick J. Leahy (D)
James M. Jeffords (R)

VIRGINIA
Charles S. Robb (D)
John W. Warner (R)

WASHINGTON
Brock Adams (D)
Slade Gorton (R)

WEST VIRGINIA
Robert C. Byrd (D)
John D. Rockefeller IV (D)

WISCONSIN
Herb Kohl (D)
Bob Kasten (R)

WYOMING
Alan K. Simpson (R)
Malcolm Wallop (R)

[a] Elected Nov. 3, 1992, to complete the remaining two years of Wilson's term, replacing Seymour, an interim appointment.
[b] Conrad did not run for re-election in November 1992 to the 103rd Congress. His seat was won by Byron L. Dorgan, D. Upon the death of Quentin N. Burdick, D, Conrad decided to run in a special election to fill Burdick's remaining term. Conrad won the election Dec. 4, 1992, resigned his own seat Dec. 14 and assumed Burdick's seat the same day. Dorgan was appointed to fill Conrad's remaining term in the 102nd Congress.
[c] Appointed May 8, 1991, and then elected to complete the remaining three years of Heinz's term in a special election Nov. 5, 1991.

House Membership in the 102nd Congress

Lineup as of Jan. 3, 1991: Democrats 267, Republicans 167, Independent 1

ALABAMA
1. Sonny Callahan (R)
2. Bill Dickinson (R)
3. Glen Browder (D)
4. Tom Bevill (D)
5. Bud Cramer (D)
6. Ben Erdreich (D)
7. Claude Harris (D)

ALASKA
AL Don Young (R)

ARIZONA
1. John J. Rhodes III (R)
2. Morris K. Udall (D)
   (resigned May 4, 1991)
   Ed Pastor (D)
   (sworn in Oct. 3, 1991)
3. Bob Stump (R)
4. Jon Kyl (R)
5. Jim Kolbe (R)

ARKANSAS
1. Bill Alexander (D)
2. Ray Thornton (D)
3. John Paul Hammerschmidt (R)
4. Beryl Anthony Jr. (D)

CALIFORNIA
1. Frank Riggs (R).
2. Wally Herger (R)
3. Robert T. Matsui (D)
4. Vic Fazio (D)
5. Nancy Pelosi (D)
6. Barbara Boxer (D)
7. George Miller (D)
8. Ronald V. Dellums (D)
9. Pete Stark (D)
10. Don Edwards (D)
11. Tom Lantos (D)
12. Tom Campbell (R)
13. Norman Y. Mineta (D)
14. John T. Doolittle (R)
15. Gary Condit (D)
16. Leon E. Panetta (D)
17. Calvin Dooley (D)
18. Richard H. Lehman (D)
19. Robert J. Lagomarsino (R)
20. Bill Thomas (R)
21. Elton Gallegly (R)
22. Carlos J. Moorhead (R)
23. Anthony C. Beilenson (D)
24. Henry A. Waxman (D)
25. Edward R. Roybal (D)
26. Howard L. Berman (D)
27. Mel Levine (D)
28. Julian C. Dixon (D)
29. Maxine Waters (D)
30. Matthew G. Martinez (D)
31. Mervyn M. Dymally (D)
32. Glenn M. Anderson (D)
33. David Dreier (R)
34. Esteban E. Torres (D)
35. Jerry Lewis (R)
36. George E. Brown Jr. (D)
37. Al McCandless (R)
38. Robert K. Dornan (R)
39. William E. Dannemeyer (R)
40. C. Christopher Cox (R)
41. Bill Lowery (R)
42. Dana Rohrabacher (R)
43. Ron Packard (R)
44. Randy "Duke" Cunningham (R)
45. Duncan Hunter (R)

COLORADO
1. Patricia Schroeder (D)
2. David E. Skaggs (D)
3. Ben Nighthorse Campbell (D)
4. Wayne Allard (R)
5. Joel Hefley (R)
6. Dan Schaefer (R)

CONNECTICUT
1. Barbara B. Kennelly (D)
2. Sam Gejdenson (D)
3. Rosa DeLauro (D)
4. Christopher Shays (R)
5. Gary Franks (R)
6. Nancy L. Johnson (R)

DELAWARE
AL Thomas R. Carper (D)

FLORIDA
1. Earl Hutto (D)
2. Pete Peterson (D)
3. Charles E. Bennett (D)
4. Craig T. James (R)
5. Bill McCollum (R)
6. Cliff Stearns (R)
7. Sam M. Gibbons (D)
8. C.W. Bill Young (R)
9. Michael Bilirakis (R)
10. Andy Ireland (R)
11. Jim Bacchus (D)
12. Tom Lewis (R)
13. Porter J. Goss (R)
14. Harry A. Johnston (D)
15. E. Clay Shaw Jr. (R)
16. Lawrence J. Smith (D)
17. William Lehman (D)
18. Ileana Ros-Lehtinen (R)
19. Dante B. Fascell (D)

GEORGIA
1. Lindsay Thomas (D)
2. Charles Hatcher (D)
3. Richard Ray (D)
4. Ben Jones (D)
5. John Lewis (D)
6. Newt Gingrich (R)
7. George "Buddy" Darden (D)
8. J. Roy Rowland (D)
9. Ed Jenkins (D)
10. Doug Barnard Jr. (D)

HAWAII
1. Neil Abercrombie (D)
2. Patsy T. Mink (D)

IDAHO
1. Larry LaRocco (D)
2. Richard Stallings (D)

ILLINOIS
1. Charles A. Hayes (D)
2. Gus Savage (D)
3. Marty Russo (D)
4. George E. Sangmeister (D)
5. William O. Lipinski (D)
6. Henry J. Hyde (R)
7. Cardiss Collins (D)
8. Dan Rostenkowski (D)
9. Sidney R. Yates (D)
10. John Porter (R)
11. Frank Annunzio (D)
12. Philip M. Crane (R)
13. Harris W. Fawell (R)
14. Dennis Hastert (R)
15. Edward R. Madigan (R)
    (resigned March 8, 1991)
    Thomas W. Ewing (R)
    (sworn in July 10, 1991)
16. John W. Cox Jr. (D)
17. Lane Evans (D)
18. Robert H. Michel (R)
19. Terry L. Bruce (D)
20. Richard J. Durbin (D)
21. Jerry F. Costello (D)
22. Glenn Poshard (D)

INDIANA
1. Peter J. Visclosky (D)
2. Philip R. Sharp (D)
3. Tim Roemer (D)
4. Jill L. Long (D)
5. Jim Jontz (D)
6. Dan Burton (R)
7. John T. Myers (R)
8. Frank McCloskey (D)
9. Lee H. Hamilton (D)
10. Andrew Jacobs Jr. (D)

IOWA
1. Jim Leach (R)
2. Jim Nussle (R)
3. Dave Nagle (D)
4. Neal Smith (D)
5. Jim Ross Lightfoot (R)
6. Fred Grandy (R)

KANSAS
1. Pat Roberts (R)
2. Jim Slattery (D)
3. Jan Meyers (R)
4. Dan Glickman (D)
5. Dick Nichols (R)

KENTUCKY
1. Carroll Hubbard Jr. (D)
2. William H. Natcher (D)
3. Romano L. Mazzoli (D)
4. Jim Bunning (R)
5. Harold Rogers (R)
6. Larry J. Hopkins (R)
7. Carl C. Perkins (D)

LOUISIANA
1. Robert L. Livingston (R)
2. William J. Jefferson (D)
3. W. J. "Billy" Tauzin (D)
4. Jim McCrery (R)
5. Jerry Huckaby (D)
6. Richard H. Baker (R)
7. Jimmy Hayes (D)
8. Clyde C. Holloway (R)

MAINE
1. Thomas H. Andrews (D)
2. Olympia J. Snowe (R)

MARYLAND
1. Wayne T. Gilchrest (R)
2. Helen Delich Bentley (R)
3. Benjamin L. Cardin (D)
4. Tom McMillen (D)
5. Steny H. Hoyer (D)
6. Beverly B. Byron (D)
7. Kweisi Mfume (D)
8. Constance A. Morella (R)

MASSACHUSETTS
1. Silvio O. Conte (R)
   (died Feb. 8, 1991)
   John Olver (D)
   (sworn in June 18, 1991)
2. Richard E. Neal (D)
3. Joseph D. Early (D)
4. Barney Frank (D)
5. Chester G. Atkins (D)
6. Nicholas Mavroules (D)
7. Edward J. Markey (D)
8. Joseph P. Kennedy II (D)
9. Joe Moakley (D)
10. Gerry E. Studds (D)
11. Brian Donnelly (D)

MICHIGAN
1. John Conyers Jr. (D)
2. Carl D. Pursell (R)
3. Howard Wolpe (D)
4. Fred Upton (R)
5. Paul B. Henry (R)
6. Bob Carr (D)
7. Dale E. Kildee (D)
8. Bob Traxler (D)
9. Guy Vander Jagt (R)
10. Dave Camp (R)
11. Robert W. Davis (R)
12. David E. Bonior (D)
13. Barbara-Rose Collins (D)
14. Dennis M. Hertel (D)
15. William D. Ford (D)
16. John D. Dingell (D)
17. Sander M. Levin (D)
18. William S. Broomfield (R)

MINNESOTA
1. Timothy J. Penny (D)
2. Vin Weber (R)
3. Jim Ramstad (R)
4. Bruce F. Vento (D)
5. Martin Olav Sabo (D)
6. Gerry Sikorski (D)
7. Collin C. Peterson (D)
8. James L. Oberstar (D)

MISSISSIPPI
1. Jamie L. Whitten (D)
2. Mike Espy (D)
3. G.V. "Sonny" Montgomery (D)
4. Mike Parker (D)
5. Gene Taylor (D)

MISSOURI
1. William L. Clay (D)
2. Joan Kelly Horn (D)

3. Richard A. Gephardt (D)
4. Ike Skelton (D)
5. Alan Wheat (D)
6. E. Thomas Coleman (R)
7. Mel Hancock (R)
8. Bill Emerson (R)
9. Harold L. Volkmer (D)

MONTANA
1. Pat Williams (D)
2. Ron Marlenee (R)

NEBRASKA
1. Doug Bereuter (R)
2. Peter Hoagland (D)
3. Bill Barrett (R)

NEVADA
1. James Bilbray (D)
2. Barbara F. Vucanovich (R)

NEW HAMPSHIRE
1. Bill Zeliff (R)
2. Dick Swett (D)

NEW JERSEY
1. Robert E. Andrews (D)
2. William J. Hughes (D)
3. Frank Pallone Jr. (D)
4. Christopher H. Smith (R)
5. Marge Roukema (R)
6. Bernard J. Dwyer (D)
7. Matthew J. Rinaldo (R)
8. Robert A. Roe (D)
9. Robert G. Torricelli (D)
10. Donald M. Payne (D)
11. Dean A. Gallo (R)
12. Dick Zimmer (R)
13. H. James Saxton (R)
14. Frank J. Guarini (D)

NEW MEXICO
1. Steven H. Schiff (R)
2. Joe Skeen (R)
3. Bill Richardson (D)

NEW YORK
1. George J. Hochbrueckner (D)
2. Thomas J. Downey (D)
3. Robert J. Mrazek (D)
4. Norman F. Lent (R)
5. Raymond J. McGrath (R)
6. Floyd H. Flake (D)
7. Gary L. Ackerman (D)
8. James H. Scheuer (D)
9. Thomas J. Manton (D)
10. Charles E. Schumer (D)
11. Edolphus Towns (D)
12. Major R. Owens (D)
13. Stephen J. Solarz (D)
14. Susan Molinari (R)
15. Bill Green (R)
16. Charles B. Rangel (D)
17. Ted Weiss (D)
    (died Sept. 14, 1992)
18. Jose E. Serrano (D)
19. Eliot L. Engel (D)
20. Nita M. Lowey (D)
21. Hamilton Fish Jr. (R)
22. Benjamin A. Gilman (R)
23. Michael R. McNulty (D)
24. Gerald B. H. Solomon (R)
25. Sherwood Boehlert (R)
26. David O'B. Martin (R)
27. James T. Walsh (R)
28. Matthew F. McHugh (D)
29. Frank Horton (R)
30. Louise M. Slaughter (D)
31. Bill Paxon (R)
32. John J. LaFalce (D)
33. Henry J. Nowak (D)
34. Amo Houghton (R)

NORTH CAROLINA
1. Walter B. Jones (D)
    (died Sept. 15, 1992)
2. Tim Valentine (D)
3. H. Martin Lancaster (D)
4. David E. Price (D)
5. Stephen L. Neal (D)
6. Howard Coble (R)
7. Charlie Rose (D)
8. W. G. "Bill" Hefner (D)
9. Alex McMillan (R)
10. Cass Ballenger (R)
11. Charles H. Taylor (R)

NORTH DAKOTA
AL Byron L. Dorgan (D)

OHIO
1. Charles Luken (D)
2. Bill Gradison (R)
3. Tony P. Hall (D)
4. Michael G. Oxley (R)
5. Paul E. Gillmor (R)
6. Bob McEwen (R)
7. David L. Hobson (R)
8. John A. Boehner (R)
9. Marcy Kaptur (D)
10. Clarence E. Miller (R)
11. Dennis E. Eckart (D)
12. John R. Kasich (R)
13. Don J. Pease (D)
14. Thomas C. Sawyer (D)
15. Chalmers P. Wylie (R)
16. Ralph Regula (R)
17. James A. Traficant Jr. (D)
18. Douglas Applegate (D)
19. Edward F. Feighan (D)
20. Mary Rose Oakar (D)
21. Louis Stokes (D)

OKLAHOMA
1. James M. Inhofe (R)
2. Mike Synar (D)
3. Bill Brewster (D)
4. Dave McCurdy (D)
5. Mickey Edwards (R)
6. Glenn English (D)

OREGON
1. Les AuCoin (D)
2. Bob Smith (R)
3. Ron Wyden (D)
4. Peter A. DeFazio (D)
5. Mike Kopetski (D)

PENNSYLVANIA
1. Thomas M. Foglietta (D)
2. William H. Gray III (D)
    (resigned Sept. 11, 1991)
    Lucien E. Blackwell (D)
    (sworn in Nov. 13, 1991)
3. Robert A. Borski (D)
4. Joe Kolter (D)
5. Richard T. Schulze (R)
6. Gus Yatron (D)
7. Curt Weldon (R)
8. Peter H. Kostmayer (D)
9. Bud Shuster (R)
10. Joseph M. McDade (R)
11. Paul E. Kanjorski (D)
12. John P. Murtha (D)
13. Lawrence Coughlin (R)
14. William J. Coyne (D)
15. Don Ritter (R)
16. Robert S. Walker (R)
17. George W. Gekas (R)
18. Rick Santorum (R)
19. Bill Goodling (R)
20. Joseph M. Gaydos (D)
21. Tom Ridge (R)
22. Austin J. Murphy (D)
23. William F. Clinger Jr. (R)

RHODE ISLAND
1. Ronald K. Machtley (R)
2. John F. Reed (D)

SOUTH CAROLINA
1. Arthur Ravenel Jr. (R)
2. Floyd D. Spence (R)
3. Butler Derrick (D)
4. Liz J. Patterson (D)
5. John M. Spratt Jr. (D)
6. Robin Tallon (D)

SOUTH DAKOTA
AL Tim Johnson (D)

TENNESSEE
1. James H. Quillen (R)
2. John J. "Jimmy" Duncan Jr. (R)
3. Marilyn Lloyd (D)
4. Jim Cooper (D)
5. Bob Clement (D)
6. Bart Gordon (D)
7. Don Sundquist (R)
8. John Tanner (D)
9. Harold E. Ford (D)

TEXAS
1. Jim Chapman (D)
2. Charles Wilson (D)
3. Steve Bartlett (R)
    (resigned March 11, 1991)
    Sam Johnson (R)
    (sworn in May 22, 1991)
4. Ralph M. Hall (D)
5. John Bryant (D)
6. Joe L. Barton (R)
7. Bill Archer (R)
8. Jack Fields (R)
9. Jack Brooks (D)
10. J. J. Pickle (D)
11. Chet Edwards (D)
12. Pete Geren (D)
13. Bill Sarpalius (D)
14. Greg Laughlin (D)
15. E. "Kika" de la Garza (D)
16. Ronald D. Coleman (D)
17. Charles W. Stenholm (D)
18. Craig Washington (D)
19. Larry Combest (R)
20. Henry B. Gonzalez (D)
21. Lamar Smith (R)
22. Tom DeLay (R)
23. Albert G. Bustamante (D)
24. Martin Frost (D)
25. Michael A. Andrews (D)
26. Dick Armey (R)
27. Solomon P. Ortiz (D)

UTAH
1. James V. Hansen (R)
2. Wayne Owens (D)
3. Bill Orton (D)

VERMONT
AL Bernard Sanders (I)

VIRGINIA
1. Herbert H. Bateman (R)
2. Owen B. Pickett (D)
3. Thomas J. Bliley Jr. (R)
4. Norman Sisisky (D)
5. Lewis F. Payne Jr. (D)
6. Jim Olin (D)
7. D. French Slaughter Jr. (R)
    (resigned Nov. 5, 1991)
    George F. Allen (R)
    (sworn in Nov. 12, 1991)
8. James P. Moran Jr. (D)
9. Rick Boucher (D)
10. Frank R. Wolf (R)

WASHINGTON
1. John Miller (R)
2. Al Swift (D)
3. Jolene Unsoeld (D)
4. Sid Morrison (R)
5. Thomas S. Foley (D)
6. Norm Dicks (D)
7. Jim McDermott (D)
8. Rod Chandler (R)

WEST VIRGINIA
1. Alan B. Mollohan (D)
2. Harley O. Staggers Jr. (D)
3. Bob Wise (D)
4. Nick J. Rahall II (D)

WISCONSIN
1. Les Aspin (D)
2. Scott L. Klug (R)
3. Steve Gunderson (R)
4. Gerald D. Kleczka (D)
5. Jim Moody (D)
6. Thomas E. Petri (R)
7. David R. Obey (D)
8. Toby Roth (R)
9. F. James Sensenbrenner Jr. (R)

WYOMING
AL Craig Thomas (R)

Note: Members of the 102nd Congress also included delegates Ben Blaz, R-Guam; Ron de Lugo, D-Virgin Islands; Eni F. H. Faleomavaega, D-Am. Samoa; Eleanor Holmes Norton, D-D.C.; and resident commissioner Jaime B. Fuster, Pop. Dem.-Puerto Rico.

Members of Congress: 1989-92

The names in this list include, alphabetically, all senators, representatives, resident commissioners and territorial delegates who served in the 101st and 102nd Congresses — from 1989 to 1992.

The material is organized as follows: name; relationship to other members and presidents and vice presidents; party; state (of service); date of birth; date of death (if applicable); congressional service; service as president, vice president, member of the Cabinet or Supreme Court, governor, Speaker of the House, president pro tempore of the Senate, majority leader, minority leader and chairman of the Democratic or Republican National Committee.

If the member changed parties during his or her congressional service, the party designation appearing after the member's name is that which applied at the end of such service and further breakdown is included after the dates of congressional service. Where the service date is left open, the member was still serving in the 103rd Congress (as of August 1993).

Dates of service are inclusive, starting in year of service and ending when service ends. Under the Constitution, terms of service since 1934 have been from Jan. 3 to Jan. 3. In actual practice, members often have been sworn in on other dates at the beginning of a Congress. The exact date is shown (where available) if a member began or ended his or her service in mid-term.

The major sources for the following list were the *Congressional Directory* and Congressional Quarterly's *Almanac, Guide to Congress, Guide to U.S. Elections* and *Weekly Report.*

In the list, D stands for Democrat; I, Independent; Pop. Dem., Popular Democrat; and R, Republican.

A

ABERCROMBIE, Neil (D Hawaii) June 26, 1938-—; House Sept. 23, 1986-87, 1991-—.

ACKERMAN, Gary L. (D N.Y.) Nov. 19, 1942-—; House March 1, 1983-—.

ADAMS, Brock (D Wash.) Jan. 13, 1927-—; House 1965-Jan. 22, 1977; Senate 1987-93; Secy. of Transportation 1977-79.

AKAKA, Daniel K. (D Hawaii) Sept. 11, 1924-—; House 1977-May 16, 1990; Senate May 16, 1990-—.

ALEXANDER, Bill (D Ark.) Jan. 16, 1934-—; House 1969-93.

ALLARD, Wayne (R Colo.) Dec. 2, 1943-—; House 1991-—.

ALLEN, George F. (R Va.) March 8, 1952-—; House Nov. 12, 1991-93.

ANDERSON, Glenn M. (D Calif.) Feb. 21, 1913-—; House 1969-93.

ANDREWS, Michael A. (D Texas) Feb. 7, 1944-—; House 1983-—.

ANDREWS, Robert E. (D N.J.) Aug. 4, 1957-—; House 1991-—.

ANDREWS, Thomas H. (D Maine) March 22, 1953-—; House 1991-—.

ANNUNZIO, Frank (D Ill.) Jan. 12, 1915-—; House 1965-93.

ANTHONY, Beryl Jr. (D Ark.) Feb. 21, 1938-—; House 1979-93.

APPLEGATE, Doug (D Ohio) March 27, 1928-—; House 1977-—.

ARCHER, Bill (R Texas) March 22, 1928-—; House 1971-—.

ARMEY, Dick (R Texas) July 7, 1940-—; House 1985-—.

ARMSTRONG, William L. (R Colo.) March 16, 1937-—; House 1973-79; Senate 1979-91.

ASPIN, Les (D Wis.) July 21, 1938-—; House 1971-Jan. 21, 1993; Secy. of Defense 1993-—.

ATKINS, Chester G. (D Mass.) April 14, 1948-—; House 1985-93.

AuCOIN, Les (D Ore.) Oct. 21, 1942-—; House 1975-93.

B

BACCHUS, Jim (D Fla.) June 21, 1949-—; House 1991-—.

BAKER, Richard H. (R La.) May 22, 1948-—; House 1987-—.

BALLENGER, Cass (great-great grandson of Lewis Cass) (R N.C.) Dec. 6, 1926-—; House Nov. 4, 1986-—.

BARNARD, Doug Jr. (D Ga.) March 20, 1922-—; House 1977-93.

BARRETT, Bill (R Neb.) Feb. 9, 1929-—; House 1991-—.

BARTLETT, Steve (R Texas) Sept. 19, 1947-—; House 1983-March 11, 1991.

BARTON, Joe L. (R Texas) Sept. 15, 1949-—; House 1985-—.

BATEMAN, Herbert H. (R Va.) Aug. 7, 1928-—; House 1983-—.

BATES, Jim (D Calif.) July 21, 1941-—; House 1983-91.

BAUCUS, Max (D Mont.) Dec. 11, 1941-—; House 1975-Dec. 14, 1978; Senate Dec. 15, 1978-—.

BEILENSON, Anthony C. (D Calif.) Oct. 26, 1932-—; House 1977-—.

BENNETT, Charles E. (D Fla.) Dec. 2, 1910-—; House 1949-93.

BENTLEY, Helen Delich (R Md.) Nov. 28, 1923-—; House 1985-—.

BENTSEN, Lloyd (D Texas) Feb. 11, 1921-—; House Dec. 4, 1948-55; Senate 1971-Jan. 20, 1993; Secy. of Treasury 1993-—.

BEREUTER, Doug (R Neb.) Oct. 6, 1939-—; House 1979-—.

BERMAN, Howard L. (D Calif.) April 15, 1941-—; House 1983-—.

BEVILL, Tom (D Ala.) March 27, 1921-—; House 1967-—.

BIDEN, Joseph R. Jr. (D Del.) Nov. 20, 1942-—; Senate 1973-—.

BILBRAY, James (D Nev.) May 19, 1938-—; House 1987-—.

BILIRAKIS, Michael (R Fla.) July 16, 1930-—; House 1983-—.

BINGAMAN, Jeff (D N.M.) Oct. 3, 1943-—; Senate 1983-—.

BLACKWELL, Lucien E. (D Pa.) Aug. 1, 1931-—; House Nov. 13, 1991-—.

BLAZ, Ben (R Guam) Feb. 14, 1928-—; House (Delegate) 1985-93.

BLILEY, Thomas J. Jr. (R Va.) Jan. 28, 1932-—; House 1981-—.

BOEHLERT, Sherwood (R N.Y.) June 28, 1936-—; House 1983-—.

BOEHNER, John A. (R Ohio) Nov. 17, 1949-—; House 1991-—.

BOGGS, Lindy (Mrs. Hale) (widow of Thomas Hale Boggs Sr.) (D La.) March 13, 1916-—; House March 20, 1973-91.

BOND, Christopher S. "Kit" (R Mo.) March 6, 1939-—; Senate 1987-—; Gov. 1973-77, 1981-85.

BONIOR, David E. (D Mich.) June 6, 1945-—; House 1977-—.

BOREN, David L. (son of Lyle H. Boren) (D Okla.) April 21, 1941-—; Senate 1979-—; Gov. 1975-79.

BORSKI, Robert A. (D Pa.) Oct. 20, 1948-—; House 1983-—.

BOSCHWITZ, Rudy (R Minn.) Nov. 7, 1930-—; Senate Dec. 30, 1978-91.

BOSCO, Douglas H. (D Calif.) July 28, 1946-—; House 1983-91.

BOUCHER, Rick (D Va.) Aug. 1, 1946-—; House 1983-—.

BOXER, Barbara (D Calif.) Nov. 11, 1940-—; House 1983-93; Senate 1993-—.

BRADLEY, Bill (D N.J.) July 28, 1943-—; Senate 1979-—.

BREAUX, John B. (D La.) March 1, 1944-—; House Sept. 30, 1972-87; Senate 1987-—.

BRENNAN, Joseph E. (D Maine) Nov. 2, 1934-—; House 1987-91; Gov. 1979-87.

BREWSTER, Bill (D Okla.) Nov. 8, 1941-—; House 1991-—.

BROOKS, Jack (D Texas) Dec. 18, 1922-—; House 1953-—.

BROOMFIELD, William S. (R Mich.) April 28, 1922-—; House 1957-93.

BROWDER, Glen (D Ala.) Jan. 15, 1943-—; House April 18, 1989-—.

BROWN, George E. Jr. (D Calif.) March 6, 1920-—; House 1963-71, 1973-—.

BROWN, Hank (R Colo.) Feb. 12, 1940-—; House 1981-91; Senate 1991-—.

BRUCE, Terry L. (D Ill.) March 25, 1944-—; House 1985-93.

BRYAN, Richard H. (D Nev.) July 16, 1937-—; Senate 1989-—; Gov. 1983-89.

BRYANT, John (D Texas) Feb. 22, 1947-—; House 1983-—.

BUECHNER, Jack (R Mo.) June 6, 1940-—; House 1987-91.

BUMPERS, Dale (D Ark.) Aug. 12, 1925-—; Senate 1975-—; Gov. 1971-75.

BUNNING, Jim (R Ky.) Oct. 23, 1931-—; House 1987-—.

BURDICK, Jocelyn Birch (widow of Quentin N. Burdick, daughter-in-law of Usher Lloyd Burdick) (D N.D.) Feb. 6, 1922-—; Senate Sept. 16-Dec. 14, 1992.

BURDICK, Quentin N. (son of Usher Lloyd Burdick, brother-in-law of Robert Woodrow Levering) (D N.D.) June 19, 1908-Sept. 8, 1992; House 1959-Aug. 8, 1960; Senate Aug. 8, 1960-Sept. 8, 1992.

BURNS, Conrad (R Mont.) Jan. 25, 1935-—; Senate 1989-—.

BURTON, Dan (R Ind.) June 21, 1938-—; House 1983-—.

BUSTAMANTE, Albert G. (D Texas) April 8, 1935-—; House 1985-93.

BYRD, Robert C. (D W.Va.) Nov. 20, 1917-—; House 1953-59; Senate 1959-—; Senate minority leader, 1981-87; Senate majority leader 1977-81, 1987-89; Pres. pro tempore 1989-—.

BYRON, Beverly B. (widow of Goodloe Edgar Byron) (D Md.) July 26, 1932-—; House 1979-93.

C

CALLAHAN, Sonny (R Ala.) Sept. 11, 1932-—; House 1985-—.

CAMP, Dave (R Mich.) July 9, 1953-—; House 1991-—.

CAMPBELL, Ben Nighthorse (D Colo.) April 13, 1933-—; House 1987-93; Senate 1993-—.

CAMPBELL, Tom (R Calif.) Aug. 14, 1952-—; House 1989-93.

CARDIN, Benjamin L. (D Md.) Oct. 5, 1943-—; House 1987-—.

CARPER, Thomas R. (D Del.) Jan. 23, 1947-—; House 1983-93; Gov. 1993-—.

CARR, Bob (D Mich.) March 27, 1943-—; House 1975-81, 1983-—.

CHAFEE, John H. (R R.I.) Oct. 22, 1922-—; Senate Dec. 29, 1976-—; Gov. 1963-69.

CHANDLER, Rod (R Wash.) July 13, 1942-—; House 1983-93.

CHAPMAN, Jim (D Texas) March 8, 1945-—; House Sept. 4, 1985-—.

CHENEY, Dick (R Wyo.) Jan. 30, 1941-—; House 1979-March 17, 1989; Secy. of Defense 1989-93.

CLARKE, James McClure (D N.C.) June 12, 1917-—; House 1983-85, 1987-91.

CLAY, William L. (D Mo.) April 30, 1931-—; House 1969-—.

CLEMENT, Bob (D Tenn.) Sept. 23, 1943-—; House Jan. 25, 1988-—.

CLINGER, William F. Jr. (R Pa.) April 4, 1929-—; House 1979-—.

COATS, Daniel R. (R Ind.) May 16, 1943-—; House 1981-Jan. 1, 1989; Senate Jan. 3, 1989-—.

COBLE, Howard (R N.C.) March 18, 1931-—; House 1985-—.

COCHRAN, Thad (R Miss.) Dec. 7, 1937-—; House 1973-Dec. 26, 1978; Senate Dec. 27, 1978-—.

COELHO, Tony (D Calif.) June 15, 1942-—; House 1979-June 15, 1989.

COHEN, William S. (R Maine) Aug. 28, 1940-—; House 1973-79; Senate 1979-—.

COLEMAN, E. Thomas (R Mo.) May 29, 1943-—; House Nov. 2, 1976-93.

COLEMAN, Ronald D. (D Texas) Nov. 29, 1941-—; House 1983-—.

COLLINS, Barbara-Rose (D Mich.) April 13, 1939-—; House 1991-—.

COLLINS, Cardiss (widow of George Washington Collins) (D Ill.) Sept. 24, 1931-—; House June 5, 1973-—.

COLORADO, Antonio J. (Pop. Dem. Puerto Rico) Aug. 8, 1939-—; House (Res. Comm.) March 4, 1992-93.

COMBEST, Larry (R Texas) March 20, 1945-—; House 1985-—.

CONDIT, Gary (D Calif.) April 21, 1948-—; House Sept. 20, 1989-—.

CONRAD, Kent (D N.D.) March 12, 1948-—; Senate 1987-Dec. 14, 1992, Dec. 14, 1992-—.

CONTE, Silvio O. (R Mass.) Nov. 9, 1921-Feb. 8, 1991; House 1959-Feb. 8, 1991.

CONYERS, John Jr. (D Mich.) May 16, 1929-—; House 1965-—.

COOPER, Jim (D Tenn.) June 19, 1954-—; House 1983-—.

COSTELLO, Jerry F. (D Ill.) Sept. 25, 1949-—; House Aug. 11, 1988-—.

COUGHLIN, Lawrence (nephew of Clarence Dennis Coughlin) (R Pa.) April 11, 1929-—; House 1969-93.

COURTER, Jim (R N.J.) Oct. 14, 1941-—; House 1979-91.

COX, C. Christopher (R Calif.) Oct. 16, 1952-—; House 1989-—.

COX, John W. Jr. (D Ill.) July 10, 1947-—; House 1991-93.

COYNE, William J. (D Pa.) Aug. 24, 1936-—; House 1981-—.

CRAIG, Larry E. (R Idaho) July 20, 1945-—; House 1981-91; Senate 1991-—.

CRAMER, Bud (D Ala.) Aug. 22, 1947-—; House 1991-—.

CRANE, Philip M. (brother of Daniel Bever Crane) (R Ill.) Nov. 3, 1930-—; House Nov. 25, 1969-—.

CRANSTON, Alan (D Calif.) June 19, 1914-—; Senate 1969-93.

CROCKETT, George W. Jr. (D Mich.) Aug. 10, 1909-—; House Nov. 12, 1980-91.

CUNNINGHAM, Randy "Duke" (R Calif.) Dec. 8, 1941-—; House 1991-—.

D

D'AMATO, Alfonse M. (R N.Y.) Aug. 1, 1937-—; Senate 1981-—.

DANFORTH, John C. (R Mo.) Sept. 5, 1936-—; Senate Dec. 27, 1976-—.

DANNEMEYER, William E. (R Calif.) Sept. 22, 1929-—; House 1979-93.

DARDEN, George "Buddy" (D Ga.) Nov. 22, 1943-—; House Nov. 8, 1983-—.

DASCHLE, Thomas A. (D S.D.) Dec. 9, 1947-—; House 1979-87; Senate 1987-—.

DAVIS, Robert W. (R Mich.) July 31, 1932-—; House 1979-93.

DeCONCINI, Dennis (D Ariz.) May 8, 1937-—; Senate 1977-—.

DeFAZIO, Peter A. (D Ore.) May 27, 1947-—; House 1987-—.

de la GARZA, E. "Kika" (D Texas) Sept. 22, 1927-—; House 1965-—.

DeLAURO, Rosa (D Conn.) March 2, 1943-—; House 1991-—.

DeLAY, Thomas D. (R Texas) April 8, 1947-—; House 1985-—.

DELLUMS, Ronald V. (D Calif.) Nov. 24, 1935-—; House 1971-—.

de LUGO, Ron (D V.I.) Aug. 2, 1930-—; House (Delegate) 1973-79, 1981-—.

DERRICK, Butler (D S.C.) Sept. 30, 1936-—; House 1975-—.

DeWINE, Michael (R Ohio) Jan. 5, 1947-—; House 1983-91.

DICKINSON, William L. (R Ala.) June 5, 1925-—; House 1965-93.

DICKS, Norman D. (D Wash.) Dec. 16, 1940-—; House 1977-—.

DINGELL, John D. (son of John David Dingell) (D Mich.) July 8, 1926-—; House Dec. 13, 1955-—.

DIXON, Alan J. (D Ill.) July 7, 1927-—; Senate 1981-93.

DIXON, Julian C. (D Calif.) Aug. 8, 1934-—; House 1979-—.

DODD, Christopher J. (son of Thomas Joseph Dodd) (D Conn.) May 27, 1944-—; House 1975-81; Senate 1981-—.

DOLE, Robert (R Kan.) July 22, 1923-—; House 1961-69; Senate 1969-—; Chrmn. Rep. Nat. Comm. 1971-73; Senate majority leader 1985-87; Senate minority leader 1987-—.

DOMENICI, Pete V. (R N.M.) May 7, 1932-—; Senate 1973-—.

DONNELLY, Brian J. (D Mass.) March 2, 1946-—; House 1979-93.

DOOLEY, Calvin (D Calif.) Jan. 11, 1954-—; House 1991-—.

DOOLITTLE, John T. (R Calif.) Oct. 30, 1950-—; House 1991-—.

DORGAN, Byron L. (D N.D.) May 14, 1942-—; House 1981-93; Senate Dec. 15, 1992-—.

DORNAN, Robert K. (R Calif.) April 3, 1933-—; House 1977-83, 1985-—.

DOUGLAS, Chuck (R N.H.) Dec. 2, 1942-—; House 1989-91.

DOWNEY, Thomas J. (D N.Y.) Jan. 28, 1949-—; House 1975-93.

DREIER, David (R Calif.) July 5, 1952-—; House 1981-—.

DUNCAN, John J. "Jimmy" Jr. (son of John J. Duncan) (R Tenn.) July 21, 1947-—; House Nov. 8, 1988-—.

DURBIN, Richard J. (D Ill.) Nov. 21, 1944-—; House 1983-—.

DURENBERGER, Dave (R Minn.) Aug. 19, 1934-—; Senate Nov. 8, 1978-—.

DWYER, Bernard J. (D N.J.) Jan. 24, 1921-—; House 1981-93.

DYMALLY, Mervyn M. (D Calif.) May 12, 1926-—; House 1981-93.

DYSON, Roy (D Md.) Nov. 15, 1948-—; House 1981-91.

E

EARLY, Joseph D. (D Mass.) Jan. 31, 1933-—; House 1975-93.

ECKART, Dennis E. (D Ohio) April 6, 1950-—; House 1981-93.

EDWARDS, Chet (D Texas) Nov. 24, 1951-—; House 1991-—.

EDWARDS, Don (D Calif.) Jan. 6, 1915-—; House 1963-—.

EDWARDS, Mickey (R Okla.) July 12, 1937-—; House 1977-93.

EMERSON, Bill (R Mo.) Jan. 1, 1938-—; House 1981-—.

ENGEL, Eliot L. (D N.Y.) Feb. 18, 1947-—; House 1989-—.

ENGLISH, Glenn (D Okla.) Nov. 30, 1940-—; House 1975-—.

ERDREICH, Ben (D Ala.) Dec. 9, 1938-—; House 1983-93.

ESPY, Mike (D Miss.) Nov. 30, 1953-—; House 1987-Jan. 22, 1993; Secy. of Agriculture 1993-—.

EVANS, Lane (D Ill.) Aug. 4, 1951-—; House 1983-—.

EWING, Thomas W. (R Ill.) Sept. 19, 1935-—; House July 10, 1991-—.

EXON, J. James (D Neb.) Aug. 9, 1921-—; Senate 1979-—; Gov. 1971-79.

F

FALEOMAVAEGA, Eni F. H. (D Am. Samoa) Aug. 15, 1943-—; House (Delegate) 1989-—.

FASCELL, Dante B. (D Fla.) March 9, 1917-—; House 1955-93.

FAUNTROY, Walter E. (D D.C.) Feb. 6, 1933-—; House (Delegate) March 23, 1971-91.

FAWELL, Harris W. (R Ill.) March 25, 1929-—; House 1985-—.

FAZIO, Vic (D Calif.) Oct. 11, 1942-—; House 1979-—.

FEIGHAN, Edward F. (nephew of Michael Aloysius Feighan) (D Ohio) Oct. 22, 1947-—; House 1983-93.

FEINSTEIN, Dianne (D Calif.) June 22, 1933-—; Senate Nov. 10, 1992-—.

FIELDS, Jack (R Texas) Feb. 3, 1952-—; House 1981-—.

FISH, Hamilton Jr. (son of Hamilton Fish Jr. born in 1888, grandson of Hamilton Fish born in 1849, great grandson of Hamilton Fish born in 1808) (R N.Y.) June 3, 1926-—; House 1969-—.

FLAKE, Floyd H. (D N.Y.) Jan. 30, 1945-—; House 1987-—.

FLIPPO, Ronnie G. (D Ala.) Aug. 15, 1937-—; House 1977-91.

FLORIO, James J. (D N.J.) Aug. 29, 1937-—; House 1975-Jan. 16, 1990; Gov. 1990-—.

FOGLIETTA, Thomas M. (D Pa.) Dec. 3, 1928-—; House 1981-— (1981-82, Independent).

FOLEY, Thomas S. (D Wash.) March 6, 1929-—; House 1965-—; House majority leader 1987-June 6, 1989; Speaker June 6, 1989-—.

FORD, Harold E. (D Tenn.) May 20, 1945-—; House 1975-—.

FORD, Wendell H. (D Ky.) Sept. 8, 1924-—; Senate Dec. 28, 1974-—; Gov. 1971-74.

FORD, William D. (D Mich.) Aug. 6, 1927-—; House 1965-—.

FOWLER, Wyche Jr. (D Ga.) Oct. 6, 1940-—; House April 6, 1977-87; Senate 1987-93.

FRANK, Barney (D Mass.) March 31, 1940-—; House 1981-—.

FRANKS, Gary (R Conn.) Feb. 9, 1953-—; House 1991-—.

FRENZEL, Bill (R Minn.) July 31, 1928-—; House 1971-91.

FROST, Martin (D Texas) Jan. 1, 1942-—; House 1979-—.

FUSTER, Jaime B. (Pop. Dem. Puerto Rico) Jan. 12, 1941-—; House (Res. Comm.) 1985-March 3, 1992.

G

GALLEGLY, Elton (R Calif.) March 7, 1944-—; House 1987-—.

GALLO, Dean A. (R N.J.) Nov. 23, 1935-—; House 1985-—.

GARCIA, Robert (D N.Y.) Jan. 9, 1933-—; House Feb. 21, 1978-Jan. 7, 1990.

GARN, Jake (R Utah) Oct. 12, 1932-—; Senate Dec. 21, 1974-93.

GAYDOS, Joseph M. (D Pa.) July 3, 1926-—; House Nov. 5, 1968-93.

GEJDENSON, Sam (D Conn.) May 20, 1948-—; House 1981-—.

GEKAS, George W. (R Pa.) April 14, 1930-—; House 1983-—.

GEPHARDT, Richard A. (D Mo.) Jan. 31, 1941-—; House 1977-—; House majority leader June 14, 1989-—.

GEREN, Pete (D Texas) Jan. 29, 1952-—; House Sept. 20, 1989-—.

GIBBONS, Sam (D Fla.) Jan. 20, 1920-—; House 1963-—.

GILCHREST, Wayne T. (R Md.) April 15, 1946-—; House 1991-—.

GILLMOR, Paul E. (R Ohio) Feb. 1, 1939-—; House 1989-—.

GILMAN, Benjamin A. (R N.Y.) Dec. 6, 1922-—; House 1973-—.

GINGRICH, Newt (R Ga.) June 17, 1943-—; House 1979-—.

GLENN, John (D Ohio) July 18, 1921-—; Senate Dec. 24, 1974-—.

GLICKMAN, Dan (D Kan.) Nov. 24, 1944-—; House 1977-—.

GONZALEZ, Henry B. (D Texas) May 3, 1916-—; House Nov. 4, 1961-—.

GOODLING, Bill (son of George Atlee Goodling) (R Pa.) Dec. 5, 1927-—; House 1975-—.

GORDON, Bart (D Tenn.) Jan. 24, 1949-—; House 1985-—.

GORE, Albert Jr. (son of Albert Arnold Gore) (D Tenn.) March 31, 1948-—; House 1977-85; Senate 1985-Jan. 2, 1993; Vice President 1993-—.

GORTON, Slade (R Wash.) Jan. 8, 1928-—; Senate 1981-87, 1989-—.

GOSS, Porter J. (R Fla.) Nov. 26, 1938-—; House 1989-—.

GRADISON, Bill (R Ohio) Dec. 28, 1928-—; House 1975-Jan. 31, 1993.

GRAHAM, Bob (D Fla.) Nov. 9, 1936-—; Senate 1987-—; Gov. 1979-87.

GRAMM, Phil (R Texas) July 8, 1942-—; House 1979-Jan. 5, 1983, Feb. 22, 1983-85 (1979-Jan. 5, 1983, Democrat); Senate 1985-—.

GRANDY, Fred (R Iowa) June 29, 1948-—; House 1987-—.

GRANT, Bill (R Fla.) Feb. 21, 1943-—; House 1987-91 (1987-Feb. 21, 1989, Democrat).

GRASSLEY, Charles E. (R Iowa) Sept. 17, 1933-—; House 1975-81; Senate 1981-—.

GRAY, William H. III (D Pa.) Aug. 20, 1941-—; House 1979-Sept. 11, 1991.

GREEN, Bill (R N.Y.) Oct. 16, 1929-—; House Feb. 21, 1978-93.

GUARINI, Frank J. (D N.J.) Aug. 20, 1924-—; House 1979-93.

GUNDERSON, Steve (R Wis.) May 10, 1951-—; House 1981-—.

H

HALL, Ralph M. (D Texas) May 3, 1923-—; House 1981-—.

HALL, Tony P. (D Ohio) Jan. 16, 1942-—; House 1979-—.

HAMILTON, Lee H. (D Ind.) April 20, 1931-—; House 1965-—.

HAMMERSCHMIDT, John Paul (R Ark.) May 4, 1922-—; House 1967-93.

HANCOCK, Mel (R Mo.) Sept. 14, 1929-—; House 1989-—.

HANSEN, James V. (R Utah) Aug. 14, 1932-—; House 1981-—.

HARKIN, Tom (D Iowa) Nov. 19, 1939-—; House 1975-85; Senate 1985-—.

HARRIS, Claude (D Ala.) June 29, 1940-—; House 1987-93.

HASTERT, Dennis (R Ill.) Jan. 2, 1942-—; House 1987-—.

HATCH, Orrin G. (R Utah) March 22, 1934-—; Senate 1977-—.

HATCHER, Charles (D Ga.) July 1, 1939-—; House 1981-93.

HATFIELD, Mark O. (R Ore.) July 12, 1922-—; Senate Jan. 10, 1967-—; Gov. 1959-67.

HAWKINS, Augustus F. (D Calif.) Aug. 31, 1907-—; House 1963-91.

HAYES, Charles A. (D Ill.) Feb. 17, 1918-—; House Aug. 23, 1983-93.

HAYES, Jimmy (D La.) Dec. 21, 1946-—; House 1987-—.

HEFLEY, Joel (R Colo.) April 18, 1935-—; House 1987-—.

HEFLIN, Howell (D Ala.) June 19, 1921-—; Senate 1979-—.

HEFNER, W. G. "Bill" (D N.C.) April 11, 1930-—; House 1975-—.

HEINZ, John (R Pa.) Oct. 23, 1938-April 4, 1991; House Nov. 2, 1971-77; Senate 1977-April 4, 1991.

HELMS, Jesse (R N.C.) Oct. 18, 1921-—; Senate 1973-—.

HENRY, Paul B. (R Mich.) July 9, 1942-July 31, 1993; House 1985-July 31, 1993.

HERGER, Wally (R Calif.) May 20, 1945-—; House 1987-—.

HERTEL, Dennis M. (D Mich.) Dec. 7, 1938-—; House 1981-93.

HILER, John (R Ind.) April 24, 1953-—; House 1981-91.

HOAGLAND, Peter (D Neb.) Nov. 17, 1941-—; House 1989-—.

HOBSON, David L. (R Ohio) Oct. 17, 1936; House 1991-—.

HOCHBRUECKNER, George J. (D N.Y.) Sept. 20, 1938-—; House 1987-—.

HOLLINGS, Ernest F. (D S.C.) Jan. 1, 1922-—; Senate Nov. 9, 1966-—; Gov. 1959-63.

HOLLOWAY, Clyde C. (R La.) Nov. 28, 1943-—; House 1987-93.

HOPKINS, Larry J. (R Ky.) Oct. 25, 1933-—; House 1979-93.

HORN, Joan Kelly (D Mo.) Oct. 18, 1936-—; House 1991-93.

HORTON, Frank (R N.Y.) Dec. 12, 1919-—; House 1963-93.

HOUGHTON, Amo (grandson of Alanson Bigelow Houghton) (R N.Y.) Aug. 7, 1926-—; House 1987-—.

HOYER, Steny H. (D Md.) June 14, 1939-—; House June 3, 1981-—.

HUBBARD, Carroll Jr. (D Ky.) July 7, 1937-—; House 1975-93.

HUCKABY, Jerry (D La.) July 19, 1941-—; House 1977-93.

HUGHES, William J. (D N.J.) Oct. 17, 1932-—; House 1975-—.

HUMPHREY, Gordon J. (R N.H.) Oct. 9, 1940-—; Senate 1979-Dec. 4, 1990.

HUNTER, Duncan (R Calif.) May 31, 1948-—; House 1981-—.

HUTTO, Earl (D Fla.) May 12, 1926-—; House 1979-—.

HYDE, Henry J. (R Ill.) April 18, 1924-—; House 1975-—.

I

INHOFE, James M. (R Okla.) Nov. 17, 1934-—; House 1987-—.

INOUYE, Daniel K. (D Hawaii) Sept. 7, 1924-—; House Aug. 21, 1959-63; Senate 1963-—.

IRELAND, Andy (R Fla.) Aug. 23, 1930-—; House 1977-93 (1977-July 5, 1984, Democrat).

J

JACOBS, Andrew Jr. (son of Andrew Jacobs Sr., husband of Martha Elizabeth Keys) (D Ind.) Feb. 24, 1932-—; House 1965-73, 1975-—.

JAMES, Craig T. (R Fla.) May 5, 1941-—; House 1989-93.

JEFFERSON, William J. (D La.) March 14, 1947-—; House 1991-—.

JEFFORDS, James M. (R Vt.) May 11, 1934-—; House 1975-89; Senate 1989-—.

JENKINS, Ed (D Ga.) Jan. 4, 1933-—; House 1977-93.

JOHNSON, Nancy L. (R Conn.) Jan. 5, 1935-—; House 1983-—.

JOHNSON, Sam (D Texas) Oct. 11, 1930-—; House May 22, 1991-—.

JOHNSON, Tim (D S.D.) Dec. 28, 1946-—; House 1987-—.

JOHNSTON, Harry A. (D Fla.) Dec. 2, 1931-—; House 1989-—.

JOHNSTON, J. Bennett (father-in-law of Tim Roemer) (D La.) June 10, 1932-—; Senate Nov. 14, 1972-—.

JONES, Ben (D Ga.) Aug. 30, 1941-—; House 1989-93.

JONES, Walter B. (D N.C.) Aug. 19, 1913-Sept. 15, 1992; House Feb. 5, 1966-Sept. 15, 1992.

JONTZ, Jim (D Ind.) Dec. 18, 1951-—; House 1987-93.

K

KANJORSKI, Paul E. (D Pa.) April 2, 1937-—; House 1985-—.

KAPTUR, Marcy (D Ohio) June 17, 1946-—; House 1983-—.

KASICH, John R. (R Ohio) May 13, 1952-—; House 1983-—.

KASSEBAUM, Nancy Landon (R Kan.) July 29, 1932-—; Senate Dec. 23, 1978-—.

KASTEN, Bob (R Wis.) June 19, 1942-—; House 1975-79; Senate 1981-93.

KASTENMEIER, Robert W. (D Wis.) Jan. 24, 1924-—; House 1959-91.

KENNEDY, Edward M. (brother of John Fitzgerald Kennedy and Robert Francis Kennedy, grandson of John Francis Fitzgerald, uncle of Joseph P. Kennedy II) (D Mass.) Feb. 22, 1932-—; Senate Nov. 7, 1962-—.

KENNEDY, Joseph P. II (son of Robert Francis Kennedy, great grandson of John Francis Fitzgerald, nephew of Edward Moore Kennedy and John Fitzgerald Kennedy) (D Mass.) Sept. 24, 1952-—; House 1987-—.

KENNELLY, Barbara B. (D Conn.) July 10, 1936-—; House Jan. 25, 1982-—.

KERREY, Bob (D Neb.) Aug. 27, 1943-—; Senate 1989-—; Gov. 1983-89.

KERRY, John (D Mass.) Dec. 22, 1943-—; Senate 1985-—.

KILDEE, Dale E. (D Mich.) Sept. 16, 1929-—; House 1977-—.

KLECZKA, Gerald D. (D Wis.) Nov. 26, 1943-—; House April 10, 1984-—.

KLUG, Scott L. (R Wis.) Jan. 16, 1953-—; House 1991-—.

KOHL, Herb (D Wis.) Feb. 7, 1935-—; Senate 1989-—.

KOLBE, Jim (R Ariz.) June 28, 1942-—; House 1985-—.

KOLTER, Joe (D Pa.) Sept. 3, 1926-—; House 1983-93.

KOPETSKI, Mike (D Ore.) Oct. 27, 1949-—; House 1991-—.

KOSTMAYER, Peter H. (D Pa.) Sept. 27, 1946-—; House 1977-81, 1983-93.

KYL, Jon (son of John Henry Kyl) (R Ariz.) April 25, 1942-—; House 1987-—.

L

LaFALCE, John J. (D N.Y.) Oct. 6, 1939-—; House 1975-—.

LAGOMARSINO, Robert J. (R Calif.) Sept. 4, 1926-—; House March 5, 1974-93.

LANCASTER, H. Martin (D N.C.) March 24, 1943-—; House 1987-—.

LANTOS, Tom (father-in-law of Dick Swett) (D Calif.) Feb. 1, 1928-—; House 1981-—.

LaROCCO, Larry (D Idaho) Aug. 25, 1946-—; House 1991-—.

LAUGHLIN, Greg (D Texas) Jan. 21, 1942-—; House 1989-—.

LAUTENBERG, Frank R. (D N.J.) Jan. 23, 1924-—; Senate Dec. 27, 1982-—.

LEACH, Jim (R Iowa) Oct. 15, 1942-—; House 1977-—.

LEAHY, Patrick J. (D Vt.) March 31, 1940-—; Senate 1975-—.

LEATH, Marvin (D Texas) May 6, 1931-—; House 1979-91.

LEHMAN, Richard H. (D Calif.) July 20, 1948-—; House 1983-—.

LEHMAN, William (D Fla.) Oct. 4, 1913-—; House 1973-93.

LELAND, Mickey (D Texas) Nov. 27, 1944-Aug. 7, 1989; House 1979-Aug. 7, 1989.

LENT, Norman F. (R N.Y.) March 23, 1931-—; House 1971-93.

LEVIN, Carl (brother of Sander M. Levin) (D Mich.) June 28, 1934-—; Senate 1979-—.

LEVIN, Sander M. (brother of Carl Levin) (D Mich.) Sept. 6, 1931-—; House 1983-—.

LEVINE, Mel (D Calif.) June 7, 1943-—; House 1983-93.

LEWIS, Jerry (R Calif.) Oct. 21, 1934-—; House 1979-—.

LEWIS, John (D Ga.) Feb. 21, 1940-—; House 1987-—.

LEWIS, Tom (R Fla.) Oct. 26, 1924-—; House 1983-—.

LIEBERMAN, Joseph I. (D Conn.) Feb. 24, 1942-—; Senate 1989-—.

LIGHTFOOT, Jim Ross (R Iowa) Sept. 27, 1938-—; House 1985-—.

LIPINSKI, William O. (D Ill.) Dec. 22, 1937-—; House 1983-—.

LIVINGSTON, Robert L. (R La.) April 30, 1943-—; House Sept. 7, 1977-—.

LLOYD, Marilyn (D Tenn.) Jan. 3, 1929-—; House 1975-—.

LONG, Jill L. (D Ind.) July 15, 1952-—; House April 5, 1989-—.

LOTT, Trent (R Miss.) Oct. 9, 1941-—; House 1973-89; Senate 1989-—.

LOWERY, Bill (R Calif.) May 2, 1947-—; House 1981-93.

LOWEY, Nita M. (D N.Y.) July 5, 1937-—; House 1989-—.

LUGAR, Richard G. (R Ind.) April 4, 1932-—; Senate 1977-—.

LUKEN, Charles (son of Thomas A. Luken) (D Ohio) July 18, 1951-—; House 1991-93.

LUKEN, Thomas A. (father of Charles Luken) (D Ohio) July 9, 1925-—; House March 5, 1974-75, 1977-91.

LUKENS, Donald E. "Buz" (R Ohio) Feb. 11, 1931-—; House 1967-71, 1987-Oct. 24, 1990.

M

MACHTLEY, Ronald K. (R R.I.) July 13, 1948-—; House 1989-—.

MACK, Connie (R Fla.) Oct. 29, 1940-—; House 1983-89; Senate 1989-—.

MADIGAN, Edward R. (R Ill.) Jan. 13, 1936-—; House 1973-March 8, 1991; Secy. of Agriculture March 8, 1991-93.

MANTON, Thomas J. (D N.Y.) Nov. 3, 1932-—; House 1985-—.

MARKEY, Edward J. (D Mass.) July 11, 1946-—; House Nov. 2, 1976-—.

MARLENEE, Ron (R Mont.) Aug. 8, 1935-—; House 1977-93.

MARTIN, David O'B. (R N.Y.) April 26, 1944-—; House 1981-93.

MARTIN, Lynn (R Ill.) Dec. 26, 1939-—; House 1981-91; Secy. of Labor Feb. 22, 1991-93.

MARTINEZ, Matthew G. (D Calif.) Feb. 14, 1929-—; House July 15, 1982-—.

MATSUI, Robert T. (D Calif.) Sept. 17, 1941-—; House 1979-—.

MATSUNAGA, Spark M. (D Hawaii) Oct. 8, 1916-April 15, 1990; House 1963-77; Senate 1977-April 15, 1990.

MAVROULES, Nicholas (D Mass.) Nov. 1, 1929-—; House 1979-93.

MAZZOLI, Romano L. (D Ky.) Nov. 2, 1932-—; House 1971-—.

McCAIN, John (R Ariz.) Aug. 29, 1936-—; House 1986-87; Senate 1987-—.

McCANDLESS, Al (R Calif.) July 23, 1927-—; House 1983-—.

McCLOSKEY, Frank (D Ind.) June 12, 1939-—; House 1983-85; May 1, 1985-—.

McCLURE, James A. (R Idaho) Dec. 27, 1924-—; House 1967-73; Senate 1973-91.

McCOLLUM, Bill (R Fla.) July 12, 1944-—; House 1981-—.

McCONNELL, Mitch (R Ky.) Feb. 20, 1942-—; Senate 1985-—.

McCRERY, Jim (R La.) Sept. 18, 1949-—; House April 26, 1988-—.

McCURDY, Dave (D Okla.) March 30, 1950-—; House 1981-—.

McDADE, Joseph M. (R Pa.) Sept. 29, 1931-—; House 1963-—.

McDERMOTT, Jim (D Wash.) Dec. 28, 1936-—; House 1989-—.

McEWEN, Bob (R Ohio) Jan. 12, 1950-—; House 1981-93.

McGRATH, Raymond J. (R N.Y.) March 27, 1942-—; House 1981-93.

McHUGH, Matthew F. (D N.Y.) Dec. 6, 1938-—; House 1975-93.

McMILLAN, J. Alex (R N.C.) May 9, 1932-—; House 1985-—.

McMILLEN, Tom (D Md.) May 26, 1952-—; House 1987-93.

McNULTY, Michael R. (D N.Y.) Sept. 16, 1947-—; House 1989-—.

METZENBAUM, Howard M. (D Ohio) June 4, 1917-—; Senate Jan. 4-Dec. 23, 1974, Dec. 29, 1976-—.

MEYERS, Jan (R Kan.) July 20, 1928-—; House 1985-—.

MFUME, Kweisi (D Md.) Oct. 24, 1948-—; House 1987-—.

MICHEL, Robert H. (R Ill.) March 2, 1923-—; House 1957-—; House minority leader 1981-—.

MIKULSKI, Barbara A. (D Md.) July 20, 1936-—; House 1977-87; Senate 1987-—.

MILLER, Clarence E. (R Ohio) Nov. 1, 1917-—; House 1967-93.

MILLER, George (D Calif.) May 17, 1945-—; House 1975-—.

MILLER, John R. (R Wash.) May 23, 1938-—; House 1985-93.

MINETA, Norman Y. (D Calif.) Nov. 12, 1931-—; House 1975-—.

MINK, Patsy T. (D Hawaii) Dec. 6, 1927-—; House 1965-77, Sept. 27, 1990-—.

MITCHELL, George J. (D Maine) Aug. 20, 1933-—; Senate May 19, 1980-—; Senate majority leader 1989-—.

MOAKLEY, Joe (D Mass.) April 27, 1927-—; House 1973-— (elected as an Independent Democrat; changed affiliation to Democrat Jan. 2, 1973).

MOLINARI, Guy V. (father of Susan Molinari) (R N.Y.) Nov. 23, 1928-—; House 1981-Jan. 1, 1990.

MOLINARI, Susan (daughter of Guy V. Molinari) (R N.Y.) March 27, 1958-—; House March 27, 1990-—.

MOLLOHAN, Alan B. (son of Robert Homer Mollohan) (D W.Va.) May 14, 1943-—; House 1983-—.

MONTGOMERY, G. V. "Sonny" (D Miss.) Aug. 5, 1920-—; House 1967-—.

MOODY, Jim (D Wis.) Sept. 2, 1935-—; House 1983-93.

MOORHEAD, Carlos J. (R Calif.) May 6, 1922-—; House 1973-—.

MORAN, James P. Jr. (D Va.) May 16, 1945-—; House 1991-—.

MORELLA, Constance A. (R Md.) Feb. 12, 1931-—; House 1987-—.

MORRISON, Bruce A. (D Conn.) Oct. 8, 1944-—; House 1983-91.

MORRISON, Sid (R Wash.) May 13, 1933-—; House 1981-93.

MOYNIHAN, Daniel Patrick (D N.Y.) March 16, 1927-—; Senate 1977-—.

MRAZEK, Robert J. (D N.Y.) Nov. 6, 1945-—; House 1983-93.

MURKOWSKI, Frank H. (R Alaska) March 28, 1933-—; Senate 1981-—.

MURPHY, Austin J. (D Pa.) June 17, 1927-—; House 1977-—.

MURTHA, John P. (D Pa.) Jan. 17, 1932-—; House Feb. 5, 1974-—.

MYERS, John T. (R Ind.) Feb. 8, 1927-—; House 1967-—.

N

NAGLE, David R. (D Iowa) April 15, 1943-—; House 1987-93.

NATCHER, William H. (D Ky.) Sept. 11, 1909-—; House Aug. 1, 1953-—.

NEAL, Richard E. (D Mass.) Feb. 14, 1949-—; House 1989-—.

NEAL, Stephen L. (D N.C.) Nov. 7, 1934-—; House 1975-—.

NELSON, Bill (D Fla.) Sept. 29, 1942-—; House 1979-91.

NICHOLS, Dick (R Kan.) April 29, 1926-—; House 1991-93.

NICKLES, Don (R Okla.) Dec. 6, 1948-—; Senate 1981-—.

NIELSON, Howard C. (R Utah) Sept. 12, 1924-—; House 1983-91.

NORTON, Eleanor Holmes (D D.C.) June 13, 1937-—; House (Delegate) 1991-—.

NOWAK, Henry J. (D N.Y.) Feb. 21, 1935-—; House 1975-93.

NUNN, Sam (D Ga.) Sept. 8, 1938-—; Senate Nov. 8, 1972-—.

NUSSLE, Jim (R Iowa) June 27, 1960-—; House 1991-—.

O

OAKAR, Mary Rose (D Ohio) March 5, 1940-—; House 1977-93.

OBERSTAR, James L. (D Minn.) Sept. 10, 1934-—; House 1975-—.

OBEY, David R. (D Wis.) Oct. 3, 1938-—; House April 1, 1969-—.

OLIN, Jim (D Va.) Feb. 28, 1920-—; House 1983-93.

OLVER, John W. (D Mass.) Sept. 3, 1936-—; House June 18, 1991-—.

ORTIZ, Solomon P. (D Texas) June 3, 1937-—; House 1983-—.

ORTON, Bill (D Utah) Sept. 22, 1949-—; House 1991-—.

OWENS, Major R. (D N.Y.) June 28, 1936-—; House 1983-—.

OWENS, Wayne (D Utah) May 2, 1937-—; House 1973-75, 1987-93.

OXLEY, Michael G. (R Ohio) Feb. 11, 1944-—; House June 25, 1981-—.

P

PACKARD, Ron (R Calif.) Jan. 19, 1931-—; House 1983-—.

PACKWOOD, Bob (R Ore.) Sept. 11, 1932-—; Senate 1969-—.

PALLONE, Frank Jr. (D N.J.) Oct. 30, 1951-—; House Nov. 8, 1988-—.

PANETTA, Leon E. (D Calif.) June 28, 1938-—; House 1977-Jan. 21, 1993.

PARKER, Mike (D Miss.) Oct. 31, 1949-—; House 1989-—.

PARRIS, Stan (R Va.) Sept. 9, 1929-—; House 1973-75, 1981-91.

PASHAYAN, Charles "Chip" Jr. (R Calif.) March 27, 1941-—; House 1979-91.

PASTOR, Ed (D Ariz.) June 28, 1943-—; House Oct. 3, 1991-—.

PATTERSON, Liz J. (daughter of Olin D. Johnston) (D S.C.) Nov. 18, 1939-—; House 1987-93.

PAXON, Bill (R N.Y.) April 29, 1954-—; House 1989-—.

PAYNE, Donald M. (D N.J.) July 16, 1934-—; House 1989-—.

PAYNE, Lewis F. Jr. (D Va.) July 9, 1945-—; House June 21, 1988-—.

PEASE, Don J. (D Ohio) Sept. 26, 1931-—; House 1977-93.

PELL, Claiborne (son of Herbert Claiborne Pell Jr.) (D R.I.) Nov. 22, 1918-—; Senate 1961-—.

PELOSI, Nancy (daughter of Thomas D'Alesandro Jr.) (D Calif.) March 26, 1940-—; House June 9, 1987-—.

PENNY, Timothy J. (D Minn.) Nov. 19, 1951-—; House 1983-—.

PEPPER, Claude (D Fla.) Sept. 8, 1900-May 30, 1989; Senate Nov. 4, 1936-51; House 1963-May 30, 1989.

PERKINS, Carl C. (son of Carl Dewey Perkins) (D Ky.) Aug. 6, 1954-—; House 1985-93.

PETERSON, Collin C. (D Minn.) June 29, 1944-—; House 1991-—.

PETERSON, Pete (D Fla.) June 26, 1935-—; House 1991-—.

PETRI, Thomas E. (R Wis.) May 28, 1940-—; House April 3, 1979-—.

PICKETT, Owen B. (D Va.) Aug. 31, 1930-—; House 1987-—.

PICKLE, J. J. (D Texas) Oct. 11, 1913-—; House Dec. 21, 1963-—.

PORTER, John Edward (R Ill.) June 1, 1935-—; House Jan. 22, 1980-—.

POSHARD, Glenn (D Ill.) Oct. 30, 1945-—; House 1989-—.

PRESSLER, Larry (R S.D.) March 29, 1942-—; House 1975-79; Senate 1979-—.

PRICE, David E. (D N.C.) Aug. 17, 1940-—; House 1987-—.

PRYOR, David (D Ark.) Aug. 29, 1934-—; House Nov. 8, 1966-73; Senate 1979-—; Gov. 1975-79.

PURSELL, Carl D. (R Mich.) Dec. 19, 1932-—; House 1977-93.

Q

QUILLEN, James H. (R Tenn.) Jan. 11, 1916-—; House 1963-—.

R

RAHALL, Nick J. II (D W.Va.) May 20, 1949-—; House 1977-—.

RAMSTAD, Jim (R Minn.) May 6, 1946-—; House 1991-—.

RANGEL, Charles B. (D N.Y.) June 1, 1930-—; House 1971-—.

RAVENEL, Arthur Jr. (R S.C.) March 29, 1927-—; House 1987-—.

RAY, Richard (D Ga.) Feb. 2, 1927-—; House 1983-93.

REED, Jack (D R.I.) Nov. 12, 1949-—; House 1991-—.

REGULA, Ralph (R Ohio) Dec. 3, 1924-—; House 1973-—.

REID, Harry (D Nev.) Dec. 2, 1939-—; House 1983-87; Senate 1987-—.

RHODES, John J. III (son of John Jacob Rhodes) (R Ariz.) Sept. 8, 1943-—; House 1987-93.

RICHARDSON, Bill (D N.M.) Nov. 15, 1947-—; House 1983-—.

RIDGE, Tom (R Pa.) Aug. 26, 1945-—; House 1983-—.

RIEGLE, Donald W. Jr. (D Mich.) Feb. 4, 1938-—; House 1967-Dec. 30, 1976 (1967-Feb. 27, 1973, Republican); Senate Dec. 30, 1976-—.

RIGGS, Frank (R Calif.) Sept. 5, 1950-—; House 1991-93.

RINALDO, Matthew J. (R N.J.) Sept. 1, 1931-—; House 1973-93.

RITTER, Don (R Pa.) Oct. 21, 1940-—; House 1979-93.

ROBB, Charles S. (D Va.) June 26, 1939-—; Senate 1989-—; Gov. 1982-86.

ROBERTS, Pat (R Kan.) April 20, 1936-—; House 1981-—.

ROBINSON, Tommy F. (R Ark.) March 7, 1942-—; House 1985-91 (1985-July 28, 1989, Democrat).

ROCKEFELLER, John D. IV (nephew of Nelson Aldrich Rockefeller and great-grandson of Nelson Aldrich) (D W.Va.) June 18, 1937-—; Senate Jan. 15, 1985-—; Gov. 1977-85.

ROE, Robert A. (D N.J.) Feb. 28, 1924-—; House Nov. 4, 1969-93.

ROEMER, Tim (son-in-law of J. Bennett Johnston) (D Ind.) Oct. 30, 1956-—; House 1991-—.

ROGERS, Harold (R Ky.) Dec. 31, 1937-—; House 1981-—.

ROHRABACHER, Dana (R Calif.) June 21, 1947-—; House 1989-—.

ROSE, Charlie (D N.C.) Aug. 10, 1939-—; House 1973-—.

ROS-LEHTINEN, Ileana (R Fla.) July 15, 1952-—; House Sept. 6, 1989-—.

ROSTENKOWSKI, Dan (D Ill.) Jan. 2, 1928-—; House 1959-—.

ROTH, Toby (R Wis.) Oct. 10, 1938-—; House 1979-—.

ROTH, William V. Jr. (R Del.) July 22, 1921-—; House 1967-Dec. 31, 1970; Senate Jan. 1, 1971-—.

ROUKEMA, Marge (R N.J.) Sept. 19, 1929-—; House 1981-—.

ROWLAND, J. Roy (D Ga.) Feb. 3, 1926-—; House 1983-—.

ROWLAND, John G. (R Conn.) May 24, 1957-—; House 1985-91.

ROYBAL, Edward R. (D Calif.) Feb. 10, 1916-—; House 1963-93.

RUDMAN, Warren B. (R N.H.) May 13, 1930-—; Senate Dec. 29, 1980-93.

RUSSO, Marty (D Ill.) Jan. 23, 1944-—; House 1975-93.

S

SABO, Martin Olav (D Minn.) Feb. 28, 1938-—; House 1979-—.

SAIKI, Patricia F. (R Hawaii) May 28, 1930-—; House 1987-91.

SANDERS, Bernard (I Vt.) Sept. 8, 1941-—; House 1991-—.

SANFORD, Terry (D N.C.) Aug. 20, 1917-—; Senate Dec. 10, 1987-93; Gov. 1961-65.

SANGMEISTER, George E. (D Ill.) Feb. 16, 1931-—; House 1989-—.

SANTORUM, Rick (R Pa.) May 10, 1958-—; House 1991-—.

SARBANES, Paul S. (D Md.) Feb. 3, 1933-—; House 1971-77; Senate 1977-—.

SARPALIUS, Bill (D Texas) Jan. 10, 1948-—; House 1989-—.

SASSER, Jim (D Tenn.) Sept. 30, 1936-—; Senate 1977-—.

SAVAGE, Gus (D Ill.) Oct. 30, 1925-—; House 1981-93.

SAWYER, Thomas C. (D Ohio) Aug. 15, 1945-—; House 1987-—.

SAXTON, H. James (R N.J.) Jan. 22, 1943-—; House 1985-—.

SCHAEFER, Dan (R Colo.) Jan. 25, 1936-—; House April 7, 1983-—.

SCHEUER, James H. (D N.Y.) Feb. 6, 1920-—; House 1965-73, 1975-93.

SCHIFF, Steven H. (R N.M.) March 18, 1947-—; House 1989-—.

SCHNEIDER, Claudine (R R.I.) March 25, 1947-—; House 1981-91.

SCHROEDER, Patricia (D Colo.) July 30, 1940-—; House 1973-—.

SCHUETTE, Bill (R Mich) Oct. 13, 1953-—; House 1985-91.

SCHULZE, Richard T. (R Pa.) Aug. 7, 1929-—; House 1975-93.

SCHUMER, Charles E. (D N.Y.) Nov. 23, 1950-—; House 1981-—.

SENSENBRENNER, F. James Jr. (R Wis.) June 14, 1943-—; House 1979-—.

SERRANO, Jose E. (D N.Y.) Oct. 24, 1943-—; House March 28, 1990-—.

SEYMOUR, John (R Calif.) Dec. 3, 1937-—; Senate Jan. 10, 1991-Nov. 3, 1992.

SHARP, Philip R. (D Ind.) July 15, 1942-—; House 1975-—.

SHAW, E. Clay Jr. (R Fla.) April 19, 1939-—; House 1981-—.

SHAYS, Christopher (R Conn.) Oct. 18, 1945-—; House Sept. 9, 1987-—.

SHELBY, Richard C. (D Ala.) May 6, 1934-—; House 1979-87; Senate 1987-—.

SHUMWAY, Norman D. (R Calif.) July 28, 1934-—; House 1979-91.

SHUSTER, Bud (R Pa.) Jan. 23, 1932-—; House 1973-—.

SIKORSKI, Gerry (D Minn.) April 26, 1948-—; House 1983-93.

SIMON, Paul (D Ill.) Nov. 29, 1928-—; House 1975-85; Senate 1985-—.

SIMPSON, Alan K. (son of Milward Lee Simpson) (R Wyo.) Sept. 2, 1931-—; Senate Jan. 1, 1979-—.

SISISKY, Norman (D Va.) June 9, 1927-—; House 1983-—.

SKAGGS, David E. (D Colo.) Feb. 22, 1943-—; House 1987-—.

SKEEN, Joe (R N.M.) June 30, 1927-—; House 1981-—.

SKELTON, Ike (D Mo.) Dec. 20, 1931-—; House 1977-—.

SLATTERY, Jim (D Kan.) Aug. 4, 1948-—; House 1983-—.

SLAUGHTER, D. French Jr. (R Va.) May 20, 1925-—; House 1985-Nov. 5, 1991.

SLAUGHTER, Louise M. (D N.Y.) Aug. 14, 1929-—; House 1987-—.

SMITH, Christopher H. (R N.J.) March 4, 1953-—; House 1981-—.

SMITH, Denny (cousin of Steve Symms) (R Ore.) Jan. 19, 1938-—; House 1981-91.

SMITH, Lamar (R Texas) Nov. 19, 1947-—; House 1987-91.

SMITH, Larkin (R Miss.) June 26, 1944-Aug. 13, 1989; House 1989-Aug. 13, 1989.

SMITH, Lawrence J. (D Fla.) April 25, 1941-—; House 1983-93.

SMITH, Neal (D Iowa) March 23, 1920-—; House 1959-—.

SMITH, Peter (R Vt.) Oct. 31, 1945-—; House 1989-91.

SMITH, Robert C. (R N.H.) March 30, 1941-—; House 1985-Dec. 7, 1990; Senate Dec. 7, 1990-—.

SMITH, Robert F. (R Ore.) June 16, 1931-—; House 1983-—.

SMITH, Virginia (R Neb.) June 30, 1911-—; House 1975-91.

SNOWE, Olympia J. (wife of John R. McKernan Jr.) (R Maine) Feb. 21, 1947-—; House 1979-—.

SOLARZ, Stephen J. (D N.Y.) Sept. 12, 1940-—; House 1975-93.

SOLOMON, Gerald B. H. (R N.Y.) Aug. 14, 1930-—; House 1979-—.

SPECTER, Arlen (R Pa.) Feb. 12, 1930-—; Senate 1981-—.

SPENCE, Floyd D. (R S.C.) April 9, 1928-—; House 1971-—.

SPRATT, John M. Jr. (D S.C.) Nov. 1, 1942-—; House 1983-—.

STAGGERS, Harley O. Jr. (son of Harley Orrin Staggers) (D W.Va.) Feb. 22, 1951-—; House 1983-93.

STALLINGS, Richard H. (D Idaho) Oct. 7, 1940-—; House 1985-93.

STANGELAND, Arlan (R Minn.) Feb. 8, 1930-—; House March 1, 1977-91.

STARK, Fortney H. "Pete" (D Calif.) Nov. 11, 1931-—; House 1973-—.

STEARNS, Cliff (R Fla.) April 16, 1941-—; House 1989-—.

STENHOLM, Charles W. (D Texas) Oct. 26, 1938-—; House 1979-—.

STEVENS, Ted (R Alaska) Nov. 18, 1923-—; Senate Dec. 24, 1968-—.

STOKES, Louis (D Ohio) Feb. 23, 1925-—; House 1969-—.

STUDDS, Gerry E. (D Mass.) May 12, 1937-—; House 1973-—.

STUMP, Bob (R Ariz.) April 4, 1927-—; House 1977-— (1977-June 11, 1982, Democrat).

SUNDQUIST, Don (R Tenn.) March 15, 1936-—; House 1983-—.

SWETT, Dick (son-in-law of Tom Lantos) (D N.H.) May 1, 1957-—; House 1991-—.

SWIFT, Al (D Wash.) Sept. 12, 1935-—; House 1979-—.

SYMMS, Steve (cousin of Denny Smith) (R Idaho) April 23, 1938-—; House 1973-81; Senate 1981-93.

SYNAR, Mike (D Okla.) Oct. 17, 1950-—; House 1979-—.

T

TALLON, Robin (D S.C.) Aug. 8, 1946-—; House 1983-93.

TANNER, John (D Tenn.) Sept. 22, 1944-—; House 1989-—.

TAUKE, Tom (R Iowa) Oct. 11, 1950-—; House 1979-91.

TAUZIN, W. J. "Billy" (D La.) June 14, 1943-—; House May 17, 1980-—.

TAYLOR, Charles H. (R N.C.) Jan. 23, 1941-—; House 1991-—.

TAYLOR, Gene (D Miss.) Sept. 17, 1953-—; House Oct. 24, 1989-—.

THOMAS, Craig (R Wyo.) Feb. 17, 1933-—; House May 2, 1989-—.

THOMAS, Robert Lindsay (D Ga.) Nov. 20, 1943-—; House 1983-93.

THOMAS, William M. (R Calif.) Dec. 6, 1941-—; House 1979-—.

THORNTON, Ray (D Ark.) July 16, 1928-—; House 1973-79, 1991-—.

THURMOND, Strom (R S.C.) Dec. 5, 1902-—; Senate Dec. 24, 1954-April 4, 1956, Nov. 7, 1956-— (1947-Sept. 16, 1964, Democrat); Pres. pro tempore 1981-87; Gov. 1947-51.

TORRES, Esteban Edward (D Calif.) Jan. 27, 1930-—; House 1983-—.

TORRICELLI, Robert G. (D N.J.) Aug. 26, 1951-—; House 1983-—.

TOWNS, Edolphus (D N.Y.) July 21, 1934-—; House 1983-—.

TRAFICANT, James A. Jr. (D Ohio) May 8, 1941-—; House 1985-—.

TRAXLER, Bob (D Mich.) July 21, 1931-—; House April 16, 1974-93.

U

UDALL, Morris K. (brother of Stewart Lee Udall) (D Ariz.) June 15, 1922-—; House May 2, 1961-May 4, 1991.

UNSOELD, Jolene (D Wash.) Dec. 3, 1931-—; House 1989-—.

UPTON, Fred (R Mich.) April 23, 1953-—; House 1987-—.

V

VALENTINE, Tim (D N.C.) March 15, 1926-—; House 1983-—.

VANDER JAGT, Guy (R Mich.) Aug. 26, 1931-—; House Nov. 8, 1966-93.

VENTO, Bruce F. (D Minn.) Oct. 7, 1940-—; House 1977-—.

VISCLOSKY, Peter J. (D Ind.) Aug. 13, 1949-—; House 1985-—.

VOLKMER, Harold L. (D Mo.) April 4, 1931-—; House 1977-—.

VUCANOVICH, Barbara F. (R Nev.) June 22, 1921-—; House 1983-—.

W

WALGREN, Doug (D Pa.) Dec. 28, 1940-—; House 1977-91.

WALKER, Robert S. (R Pa.) Dec. 23, 1942-—; House 1977-—.

WALLOP, Malcolm (R Wyo.) Feb. 27, 1933-—; Senate 1977-—.

WALSH, James T. (R N.Y.) June 19, 1947-—; House 1989-—.

WARNER, John W. (R Va.) Feb. 18, 1927-—; Senate Jan. 2, 1979-—.

WASHINGTON, Craig (D Texas) Oct. 12, 1941-—; House Jan. 23, 1990-—.

WATERS, Maxine (D Calif.) Aug. 31, 1938-—; House 1991-—.

WATKINS, Wes (D Okla.) Dec. 15, 1938-—; House 1977-91.

WAXMAN, Henry A. (D Calif.) Sept. 12, 1939-—; House 1975-—.

WEBER, Vin (R Minn.) July 24, 1952-—; House 1981-93.

WEISS, Ted (D N.Y.) Sept. 17, 1927-Sept. 14, 1992; House 1977-Sept. 14, 1992.

WELDON, Curt (R Pa.) July 22, 1947-—; House 1987-—.

WELLSTONE, Paul (D Minn.) July 21, 1944-—; Senate 1991-—.

WHEAT, Alan (D Mo.) Oct. 16, 1951-—; House 1983-—.

WHITTAKER, Bob (R Kan.) Sept. 18, 1939-—; House 1979-91.

WHITTEN, Jamie L. (D Miss.) April 18, 1910-—; House Nov. 4, 1941-—.

WILLIAMS, Pat (D Mont.) Oct. 30, 1937-—; House 1979-—.

WILSON, Charles (D Texas) June 1, 1933-—; House 1973-—.

WILSON, Pete (R Calif.) Aug. 23, 1933-—; Senate 1983-Jan. 7, 1991; Gov. 1991-—.

WIRTH, Timothy E. (D Colo.) Sept. 22, 1939-—; House 1975-87; Senate 1987-93.

WISE, Bob (D W.Va.) Jan. 6, 1948-—; House 1983-—.

WOFFORD, Harris (D Pa.) April 9, 1926-—; Senate May 9, 1991-—.

WOLF, Frank R. (R Va.) Jan. 30, 1939-—; House 1981-—.

WOLPE, Howard (D Mich.) Nov. 2, 1939-—; House 1979-93.

WRIGHT, Jim (D Texas) Dec. 22, 1922-—; House 1955-June 30, 1989; House majority leader 1977-87; Speaker 1987-June 6, 1989.

WYDEN, Ron (D Ore.) May 3, 1949-—; House 1981-—.

WYLIE, Chalmers P. (R Ohio) Nov. 23, 1920-—; House 1967-93.

Y

YATES, Sidney R. (D Ill.) Aug. 27, 1909-—; House 1949-63, 1965-—.

YATRON, Gus (D Pa.) Oct. 16, 1927-—; House 1969-93.

YOUNG, C. W. Bill (R Fla.) Dec. 16, 1930-—; House 1971-—.

YOUNG, Don (R Alaska) June 9, 1933-—; House March 6, 1973-—.

Z

ZELIFF, Bill (R N.H.) June 12, 1936-—; House 1991-—.

ZIMMER, Dick (R N.J.) Aug. 16, 1944-—; House 1991-—.

Congressional Committees, 101st and 102nd Congresses

Following is a list of congressional committees and subcommittees as of the start of the 101st and 102nd Congresses. Committee jurisdictions, party ratios, committee chairmen and the dates of their service in that capacity, ranking minority members (in italics) and subcommittee chairmen are included. Political and joint committees also are listed.

In both the Senate and House, committee and subcommittee chairmen are Democrats and ranking minority members are Republicans in the 101st and 102nd Congresses. Ranking minority members and subcommittee chairmen served during both Congresses unless otherwise noted. Party ratios for House committees do not include delegates or the resident commissioner.

Senate Committees

Agriculture, Nutrition and Forestry

Agriculture in general; animal industry and diseases; crop insurance and soil conservation; farm credit and farm security; food from fresh waters; food stamp programs; forestry in general; home economics; human nutrition; inspection of livestock, meat and agricultural products; pests and pesticides; plant industry, soils and agricultural engineering; rural development, rural electrification and watersheds; school nutrition programs; matters relating to food, nutrition, hunger and rural affairs.

D 10 - R 9 *(101st Congress)*
D 10 - R 8 *(102nd Congress)*

Patrick J. Leahy, Vt. (1987-93)
Richard G. Lugar, Ind.

Agricultural Credit — Kent Conrad, N.D.
Agricultural Production and Stabilization of Prices — David Pryor, Ark.
Agricultural Research and General Legislation — Tom Daschle, S.D.
Conservation and Forestry — Wyche Fowler Jr., Ga.
Domestic and Foreign Marketing and Product Promotion — David L. Boren, Okla.
Nutrition and Investigations — Tom Harkin, Iowa
Rural Development and Rural Electrification — Howell Heflin, Ala.

Appropriations

Appropriation of revenue; rescission of appropriations; new spending authority under the Congressional Budget Act.

D 16 - R 13

Robert C. Byrd, W.Va. (1989-93)
Mark O. Hatfield, Ore.

Agriculture, Rural Development and Related Agencies — Quentin N. Burdick, N.D. (died Sept. 8, 1992); Dale Bumpers, Ark. (through 102nd Congress)
Commerce, Justice, State and Judiciary (102nd Congress) — Ernest F. Hollings, S.C.
Commerce, Justice, State, the Judiciary and Related Agencies (101st Congress) — Ernest F. Hollings, S.C.
Defense — Daniel K. Inouye, Hawaii
District of Columbia — Brock Adams, Wash.
Energy and Water Development — J. Bennett Johnston, La.
Foreign Operations — Patrick J. Leahy, Vt.
HUD - Independent Agencies (101st Congress) — Barbara A. Mikulski, Md.
Interior (102nd Congress) — Robert C. Byrd, W.Va.
Interior and Related Agencies (101st Congress) — Robert C. Byrd, W.Va.
Labor, Health and Human Services, Education (102nd Congress) — Tom Harkin, Iowa
Labor, Health and Human Services, Education and Related Agencies (101st Congress) — Tom Harkin, Iowa
Legislative Branch — Harry Reid, Nev.
Military Construction — Jim Sasser, Tenn.
Transportation (102nd Congress) — Frank R. Lautenberg, N.J.

References

The names and dates of terms of chairmen of standing committees for the years 1947-65 may be found in *Congress and the Nation Vol. I*, pp. 32a-35a; for the years 1947-69, *Congress and the Nation Vol. II*, pp. 46a-50a; for the years 1947-73, *Congress and the Nation Vol. III*, p. 52a-56a; for the years 1947-77, *Congress and the Nation Vol. IV*, pp. 1068-1072; for the years 1977-81, *Congress and the Nation Vol. V*, pp. 1069-1078; for the years 1981-84, *Congress and the Nation Vol. VI*, pp. 963-974; and for the years 1985-88, *Congress and the Nation Vol. VII*, pp. 1019-1033.

Transportation and Related Agencies (101st Congress) — Frank R. Lautenberg, N.J.
Treasury, Postal Service and General Government — Dennis DeConcini, Ariz.
VA, HUD and Independent Agencies (102nd Congress) — Barbara A. Mikulski, Md.

Armed Services

Defense and defense policy generally; aeronautical and space activities peculiar to or primarily associated with the development of weapons systems or military operations; maintenance and operation of the Panama Canal, including the Canal Zone; military research and development; national security aspects of nuclear energy; naval petroleum reserves (except Alaska); armed forces generally; Selective Service System; strategic and critical materials.

D 11 - R 9

Sam Nunn, Ga. (1987-93)
John W. Warner, Va.

Conventional Forces and Alliance Defense — Carl Levin, Mich.
Defense Industry and Technology — Jeff Bingaman, N.M.
Manpower and Personnel — John Glenn, Ohio
Projection Forces and Regional Defense — Edward M. Kennedy, Mass.
Readiness, Sustainability and Support — Alan J. Dixon, Ill.
Strategic Forces and Nuclear Deterrence — Jim Exon, Neb.

Banking, Housing and Urban Affairs

Banks, banking and financial institutions; price controls; deposit insurance; economic stabilization and growth; defense production; export and foreign trade promotion; export controls; federal monetary policy, including Federal Reserve System; financial aid to commerce and industry; issuance and redemption of notes; money and credit, including currency and coinage; nursing home construction; public and private housing, including veterans' housing; renegotiation of government contracts; urban development and mass transit; international economic policy.

D 12 - R 9

Donald W. Riegle Jr., Mich. (1989-93)
Jake Garn, Utah

Consumer and Regulatory Affairs — Alan J. Dixon, Ill.
Housing and Urban Affairs — Alan Cranston, Calif.
International Finance and Monetary Policy — Paul S. Sarbanes, Md.
Securities — Christopher J. Dodd, Conn.

Budget

Federal budget generally; concurrent budget resolutions; Congressional Budget Office.

D 13 - R 10 *(101st Congress)*
D 12 - R 9 *(102nd Congress)*

Jim Sasser, Tenn. (1989-93)
Pete V. Domenici, N.M.

No standing subcommittees.

Commerce, Science and Transportation

Interstate commerce and transportation generally; Coast Guard; coastal zone management; communications; highway safety; inland waterways, except construction; marine fisheries; Merchant Marine and navigation; non-military aeronautical and space sciences; oceans, weather and atmospheric activities; interoceanic canals generally; regulation of consumer products and services; science, engineering and technology research, development and policy; sports; standards and measurement; transportation and commerce aspects of Outer Continental Shelf lands.

D 11 - R 9

Ernest F. Hollings, S.C. (1987-93)
John C. Danforth, Mo.

Aviation — Wendell H. Ford, Ky.
Communications — Daniel K. Inouye, Hawaii
Consumer — Richard H. Bryan, Nev.
Foreign Commerce and Tourism — John D. Rockefeller IV, W.Va.
Merchant Marine — John B. Breaux, La.
National Ocean Policy Study — Ernest F. Hollings, S.C.
Science, Technology and Space — Al Gore, Tenn.
Surface Transportation — Jim Exon, Neb.

Energy and Natural Resources

Energy policy, regulation, conservation, research and development; coal; energy-related aspects of deep-water ports; hydroelectric power, irrigation and reclamation; mines, mining and minerals generally; national parks, recreation areas, wilderness areas, wild and scenic rivers, historic sites, military parks and battlefields; naval petroleum reserves in Alaska; non-military development of nuclear energy; oil and gas production and distribution; public lands and forests; solar energy systems; territorial possessions of the United States.

D 10 - R 9 *(101st Congress)*
D 11 - R 9 *(102nd Congress)*

J. Bennett Johnston, La. (1987-93)
James A. McClure, Idaho (101st Congress)
Malcolm Wallop, Wyo. (102nd Congress)

Energy Regulation and Conservation — Howard M. Metzenbaum, Ohio (101st Congress); Tim Wirth, Colo. (102nd Congress)

Energy Research and Development — Wendell H. Ford, Ky.

Mineral Resources Development and Production — Jeff Bingaman, N.M.

Public Lands, National Parks and Forests — Dale Bumpers, Ark.

Water and Power — Bill Bradley, N.J.

Environment and Public Works

Environmental policy, research and development; air, water and noise pollution; construction and maintenance of highways; environmental aspects of Outer Continental Shelf lands; environmental effects of toxic substances, other than pesticides; fisheries and wildlife; flood control and improvements of rivers and harbors; non-military environmental regulation and control of nuclear energy; ocean dumping; public buildings and grounds; public works, bridges and dams; regional economic development; solid waste disposal and recycling; water resources.

D 9 - R 7

Quentin N. Burdick, N.D. (1987-92; died Sept. 8, 1992)
Daniel Patrick Moynihan, N.Y. (through 102nd Congress)
John H. Chafee, R.I.

Environmental Protection — Max Baucus, Mont.

Gulf Pollution (102nd Congress) — Joseph I. Lieberman, Conn.

Nuclear Regulation — John B. Breaux, La. (101st Congress); Bob Graham, Fla. (102nd Congress)

Superfund, Ocean and Water Protection — Frank R. Lautenberg, N.J.

Toxic Substances, Environmental Oversight, Research and Development — Harry Reid, Nev.

Water Resources, Transportation and Infrastructure — Daniel Patrick Moynihan, N.Y.

Finance

Revenue measures generally; taxes; tariffs and import quotas; foreign trade agreements; customs; revenue sharing; federal debt limit; Social Security; health programs financed by taxes or trust funds.

D 11 - R 9

Lloyd Bentsen, Texas (1987-93)
Bob Packwood, Ore.

Deficits, Debt Management and International Debt (102nd Congress) — Bill Bradley, N.J.

Energy and Agricultural Taxation — David L. Boren, Okla. (101st Congress); Tom Daschle, S.D. (102nd Congress)

Health for Families and the Uninsured — Donald W. Riegle Jr., Mich.

International Debt (101st Congress) — Bill Bradley, N.J.

International Trade — Max Baucus, Mont.

Medicare and Long-Term Care — John D. Rockefeller IV, W.Va.

Private Retirement Plans and Oversight of the Internal Revenue Service — David Pryor, Ark.

Social Security and Family Policy — Daniel Patrick Moynihan, N.Y.

Taxation (102nd Congress) — David L. Boren, Okla.

Taxation and Debt Management (101st Congress) — Spark M. Matsunaga, Hawaii (died April 15, 1990); Tom Daschle, S.D. (through 101st Congress)

Foreign Relations

Relations of the United States with foreign nations generally; treaties; foreign economic, military, technical and humanitarian assistance; foreign loans; diplomatic service; International Red Cross; international aspects of nuclear energy; International Monetary Fund; intervention abroad and declarations of war; foreign trade; national security; oceans and international environmental and scientific affairs; protection of U.S. citizens abroad; United Nations; World Bank and other development assistance organizations.

D 10 - R 9 *(101st Congress)*
D 10 - R 8 *(102nd Congress)*

Claiborne Pell, R.I. (1987-93)
Jesse Helms, N.C.

African Affairs — Paul Simon, Ill.

East Asian and Pacific Affairs — Alan Cranston, Calif.

European Affairs — Joseph R. Biden Jr., Del.

International Economic Policy, Trade, Oceans and Environment — Paul S. Sarbanes, Md.

Near Eastern and South Asian Affairs — Daniel Patrick Moynihan, N.Y. (101st Congress); Terry Sanford, N.C. (102nd Congress)

Terrorism, Narcotics and International Operations — John Kerry, Mass.

Western Hemisphere and Peace Corps Affairs — Christopher J. Dodd, Conn.

Governmental Affairs

Budget and accounting measures; census and statistics; federal civil service; congressional organization; intergovernmental relations; government information; District of Columbia; organization and management of nuclear export policy; executive branch reorganization; Postal Service; efficiency, economy and effectiveness of government.

D 8 - R 6

John Glenn, Ohio (1987-93)
William V. Roth Jr., Del.

Federal Services, Post Office and Civil Service — David Pryor, Ark.

General Services, Federalism and the District of Columbia — Jim Sasser, Tenn.

Government Information and Regulation — Jeff Bingaman, N.M. (101st Congress); Herb Kohl, Wis. (102nd Congress)

Oversight of Government Management — Carl Levin, Mich.

Permanent Investigations (102nd Congress) — Sam Nunn, Ga.
Permanent Subcommittee on Investigations (101st Congress) — Sam Nunn, Ga.

Judiciary

Civil and criminal judicial proceedings generally; penitentiaries; bankruptcy, mutiny, espionage and counterfeiting; civil liberties; constitutional amendments; apportionment of representatives; government information; immigration and naturalization; interstate compacts generally; claims against the United States; patents, copyrights and trademarks; monopolies and unlawful restraints of trade; holidays and celebrations.

D 8 - R 6

Joseph R. Biden Jr., Del. (1987-93)
Strom Thurmond, S.C.

Antitrust, Monopolies and Business Rights — Howard M. Metzenbaum, Ohio
Constitution — Paul Simon, Ill.
Courts and Administrative Practice — Howell Heflin, Ala.
Immigration and Refugee Affairs — Edward M. Kennedy, Mass.
Juvenile Justice (102nd Congress) — Herb Kohl, Wis.
Patents, Copyrights and Trademarks — Dennis DeConcini, Ariz.
Technology and the Law — Patrick J. Leahy, Vt.

Labor and Human Resources

Education, labor, health and public welfare generally; aging; arts and humanities; biomedical research and development; child labor; convict labor; American National Red Cross; equal employment opportunity; handicapped individuals; labor standards and statistics; mediation and arbitration of labor disputes; occupational safety and health; private pension plans; public health; railway labor and retirement; regulation of foreign laborers; student loans; wages and hours.

D 9 - R 7 *(101st Congress)*
D 10 - R 7 *(102nd Congress)*

Edward M. Kennedy, Mass. (1987-93)
Orrin G. Hatch, Utah

Aging — Spark M. Matsunaga, Hawaii (101st Congress; died April 15, 1990); Brock Adams (through 102nd Congress)
Children, Family, Drugs and Alcoholism — Christopher J. Dodd, Conn.
Disability Policy (102nd Congress) — Tom Harkin, Iowa
Education, Arts and the Humanities — Claiborne Pell, R.I.
Employment and Productivity — Paul Simon, Ill.
Handicapped (101st Congress) — Tom Harkin, Iowa
Labor — Howard M. Metzenbaum, Ohio

Rules and Administration

Senate administration generally; corrupt practices; qualifications of senators; contested elections; federal elections generally; Government Printing Office; *Congressional Record;* meetings of Congress and attendance of members; presidential succession; the Capitol, congressional office buildings, the Library of Congress, the Smithsonian Institution and the Botanic Garden.

D 9 - D 7

Wendell H. Ford, Ky. (1987-93)
Ted Stevens, Alaska

No standing subcommittees.

Select Ethics

Studies and investigates standards and conduct of Senate members and employees and may recommend remedial action.

D 3 - R 3

Howell Heflin, Ala. (1987-91)
Terry Sanford, N.C. (1991-93)
Warren B. Rudman, N.H. (vice chairman)

No standing subcommittees.

Select Indian Affairs

Problems and opportunities of Indians, including Indian land management and trust responsibilities, education, health, special services, loan programs and Indian claims against the United States.

D 5 - R 3 *(101st Congress)*
D 9 - R 7 *(102nd Congress)*

Daniel K. Inouye, Hawaii (1987-93)
John McCain, Ariz. (vice chairman)

No standing subcommittees.

Select Intelligence

Legislative and budgetary authority over the Central Intelligence Agency, the Defense Intelligence Agency, the National Security Agency and intelligence activities of the Federal Bureau of Investigation and other components of the federal intelligence community.

D 8 - R 7

David L. Boren, Okla. (1987-93)
William S. Cohen, Maine (vice chairman, 101st Congress)
Frank H. Murkowski, Alaska (vice chairman, 102nd Congress)

No standing subcommittees.

Select POW/MIA Affairs

All messages, petitions, memorials and other matters relating to United States military personnel unaccounted for from military conflicts.

D 6 - R 6 *(102nd Congress)*

John Kerry, Mass. (1991-93)
Robert C. Smith, N.H. (vice chairman)

No standing subcommittees.

Small Business

Problems of small business; Small Business Administration.

D 10 - R 9 *(101st Congress)*
D 10 - R 8 *(102nd Congress)*

Dale Bumpers, Ark. (1987-93)
Rudy Boschwitz, Minn. (101st Congress)
Bob Kasten, Wis. (102nd Congress)

Competition and Antitrust Enforcement (101st Congress) — Tom Harkin, Iowa
Competitiveness and Economic Opportunity (102nd Congress) — Joseph I. Lieberman, Conn.
Export Expansion — Barbara A. Mikulski, Md.
Government Contracting and Paperwork Reduction — Alan J. Dixon, Ill.
Innovation, Technology and Productivity — Carl Levin, Mich.
Rural Economy and Family Farming — Max Baucus, Mont.
Urban and Minority-Owned Business Development — John Kerry, Mass.

Special Aging

Problems and opportunities of older people including health, income, employment, housing and care and assistance. Reports findings and makes recommendations to the Senate but cannot report legislation.

D 10 - R 9 *(101st Congress)*
D 11 - R 10 *(102nd Congress)*

David Pryor, Ark. (1989-93)
John Heinz, Pa. (died April 4, 1991)
William S. Cohen, Maine (through 102nd Congress)

No standing subcommittees.

Veterans' Affairs

Veterans' measures generally; compensation; armed forces life insurance; national cemeteries; pensions; readjustment benefits; veterans' hospitals, medical care and treatment; vocational rehabilitation and education.

D 6 - D 5 *(101st Congress)*
D 7 - R 5 *(102nd Congress)*

Alan Cranston, Calif. (1977-81, 1987-93)
Frank H. Murkowski, Alaska (101st Congress)
Arlen Specter, Pa. (102nd Congress)

No standing subcommittees.

Political Committees

Democratic Policy Committee (schedules legislation; reviews legislative proposals and provides recommendations) — George J. Mitchell, Maine
Democratic Senatorial Campaign Committee (provides campaign support for Democratic senatorial candidates) — John B. Breaux, La. (101st Congress); Charles S. Robb, Va. (102nd Congress)
Democratic Steering Committee (makes Democratic committee assignments) — Daniel K. Inouye, Hawaii
Republican Committee on Committees (makes Republican committee assignments) — Larry Pressler, S.D. (101st Congress); Trent Lott, Miss. (102nd Congress)
Republican Policy Committee (advises on party action and policy in the 101st Congress; schedules legislation, reviews legislative proposals and provides recommendations in the 102nd Congress) — William L. Armstrong, Colo. (101st Congress); Don Nickles, Okla. (102nd Congress)
National Republican Senatorial Committee (provides campaign support for Republican senatorial candidates) — Don Nickles, Okla. (101st Congress); Phil Gramm, Texas (102nd Congress)

House Committees

Agriculture

Agriculture generally; production, marketing and stabilization of agricultural prices; animal industry and diseases of animals; crop insurance and soil conservation; dairy industry; farm credit and security; forestry in general; human nutrition; home economics; inspection of livestock and meat products; plant industry, soils and agricultural engineering; rural electrification; commodities exchanges; rural development.

D 27 - R 18

E. "Kika" de la Garza, Texas (1981-93)
Edward R. Madigan, Ill. (resigned March 8, 1991)
Tom Coleman, Mo. (through 102nd Congress)

Conservation, Credit and Rural Development — Glenn English, Okla.
Cotton, Rice and Sugar — Jerry Huckaby, La.
Department Operations, Research and Foreign Agriculture — George E. Brown Jr., Calif. (101st Congress); Charlie Rose, N.C. (102nd Congress)
Domestic Marketing, Consumer Relations and Nutrition — Charles Hatcher, Ga. (101st Congress); Robin Tallon, S.C. (102nd Congress)
Forests, Family Farms and Energy — Harold L. Volkmer, Mo.
Livestock, Dairy and Poultry — Charles W. Stenholm, Texas
Peanuts and Tobacco (102nd Congress) — Charles Hatcher, Ga.
Tobacco and Peanuts (101st Congress) — Charlie Rose, N.C.
Wheat, Soybeans and Feed Grains — Dan Glickman, Kan.

Appropriations

Appropriation of revenue for support of the federal government; rescissions of appropriations; transfers of unexpended balances; new spending authority under the Congressional Budget Act.

D 35 - R 22 *(101st Congress)*
D 37 - R 22 *(102nd Congress)*

Jamie L. Whitten, Miss. (1979-93)
Silvio O. Conte, Mass. (died Feb. 8, 1991)
Joseph M. McDade, Pa. (through 102nd Congress)

Commerce, Justice and State, the Judiciary and Related Agencies (101st Congress) — Neal Smith, Iowa
Commerce, Justice, State and Judiciary (102nd Congress) — Neal Smith, Iowa
Defense — John P. Murtha, Pa.
District of Columbia — Julian C. Dixon, Calif.
Energy and Water Development — Tom Bevill, Ala.
Foreign Operations (101st Congress) — David R. Obey, Wis.
Foreign Operations, Export Financing and Related Programs (102nd Congress) — David R. Obey, Wis.
Interior (102nd Congress) — Sidney R. Yates, Ill.
Interior and Related Agencies (101st Congress) — Sidney R. Yates, Ill.
Labor, Health and Human Services and Education (102nd Congress) — William H. Natcher, Ky.
Labor, Health and Human Services, Education and Related Agencies (101st Congress) — William H. Natcher, Ky.
Legislative (102nd Congress) — Vic Fazio, Calif.
Legislative Branch (101st Congress) — Vic Fazio, Calif.
Military Construction — W. G. "Bill" Hefner, N.C.
Rural Development, Agriculture and Related Agencies — Jamie L. Whitten, Miss.
Transportation (102nd Congress) — William Lehman, Fla.
Transportation and Related Agencies (101st Congress) — William Lehman, Fla.
Treasury, Postal Service and General Government — Edward R. Roybal, Calif.
VA, HUD and Independent Agencies (101st Congress) — Bob Traxler, Mich.
Veterans Affairs, Housing and Urban Development and Independent Agencies (102nd Congress) — Bob Traxler, Mich.

Armed Services

Common defense generally; Department of Defense; ammunition depots; forts; arsenals; Army, Navy and Air Force reservations and establishments; naval petroleum and oil shale reserves; scientific research and development in support of the armed services; Selective Service System; strategic and critical materials; military applications of nuclear energy; soldiers' and sailors' homes.

D 31 - R 20 *(101st Congress)*
D 33 - R 21 *(102nd Congress)*

Les Aspin, Wis. (1985-93)
Bill Dickinson, Ala.

Investigations — Nicholas Mavroules, Mass. (indicted Aug. 27, 1992, and required to step down from chairmanship); Dennis M. Hertel, Mich. (acting chairman through the 102nd Congress)
Military Installations and Facilities — Patricia Schroeder, Colo.
Military Personnel and Compensation — Beverly B. Byron, Md.
Procurement and Military Nuclear Systems — Les Aspin, Wis.
Readiness — Earl Hutto, Fla.
Research and Development — Ronald V. Dellums, Calif.
Seapower and Strategic and Critical Materials — Charles E. Bennett, Fla.

Banking, Finance and Urban Affairs

Banks and banking including deposit insurance and federal monetary policy; money and credit; currency; issuance and redemption of notes; gold and silver; coinage, valuation and revaluation of the dollar; urban development; private and public housing; economic stabilization; defense production; renegotiation; price controls; international finance; financial aid to commerce and industry.

D 30 - R 20 *(101st Congress)*
D 31 - R 20 - I 1 *(102nd Congress)*

Henry B. Gonzalez, Texas (1989-93)
Chalmers P. Wylie, Ohio

Consumer Affairs and Coinage — Richard H. Lehman, Calif. (101st Congress); Esteban E. Torres, Calif. (102nd Congress)
Domestic Monetary Policy — Stephen L. Neal, N.C.
Economic Stabilization — Mary Rose Oakar, Ohio (101st Congress); Thomas R. Carper, Del. (102nd Congress)
Financial Institutions Supervision, Regulation and Insurance — Frank Annunzio, Ill.
General Oversight (102nd Congress) — Carroll Hubbard Jr., Ky.
General Oversight and Investigations (101st Congress) — Carroll Hubbard Jr., Ky.
Housing and Community Development — Henry B. Gonzalez, Texas
International Development, Finance, Trade and Monetary Policy — Walter E. Fauntroy, D.C. (101st Congress); Mary Rose Oakar, Ohio (102nd Congress)
Policy Research and Insurance* — Ben Erdreich, Ala. (acting chairman until Jan. 7, 1990; chairman through 102nd Congress)

* Robert Garcia, N.Y., was required to step down from the chairmanship upon being indicted Nov. 21, 1988. He resigned from the House Jan. 7, 1990.

Budget

Federal budget generally; concurrent budget resolutions; Congressional Budget Office.

D 21 - R 14 *(101st Congress)*
D 23 - R 14 *(102nd Congress)*

Leon E. Panetta, Calif. (1989-93)
Bill Frenzel, Minn. (101st Congress)
Bill Gradison, Ohio (102nd Congress)

Task Forces

Budget Process, Reconciliation and Enforcement — Marty Russo, Ill. (101st Congress); Anthony C. Beilenson, Calif. (102nd Congress)
Community Development and Natural Resources — Ed Jenkins, Ga. (101st Congress); Mike Espy, Miss. (102nd Congress)
Defense, Foreign Policy and Space — Marvin Leath, Texas (101st Congress); Richard J. Durbin, Ill. (102nd Congress)
Economic Policy, Projections and Revenues — Jim Slattery, Kan. (101st Congress); Dale E. Kildee, Mich. (102nd Congress)
Human Resources — Barbara Boxer, Calif. (101st Congress); James L. Oberstar, Minn. (102nd Congress)
Urgent Fiscal Issues — Charles E. Schumer, N.Y. (101st Congress); Frank J. Guarini, N.J. (102nd Congress)

District of Columbia

Municipal affairs of the District of Columbia.

D 7 - R 4

Ronald V. Dellums, Calif. (1979-93)
Stan Parris, Va. (101st Congress)
Thomas J. Bliley Jr., Va. (102nd Congress)

Fiscal Affairs and Health — Walter E. Fauntroy, D.C. (101st Congress); Pete Stark, Calif. (102nd Congress)
Government Operations and Metropolitan Affairs — Alan Wheat, Mo.
Judiciary and Education — Mervyn M. Dymally, Calif.

Education and Labor

Education and labor generally; child labor; convict labor; labor standards and statistics; mediation and arbitration of labor disputes; regulation of foreign laborers; school food programs; vocational rehabilitation; wages and hours; welfare of miners; work incentive programs; Indian education; juvenile delinquency; human services programs; Gallaudet College; Howard University.

D 21 - R 13 *(101st Congress)*
D 23 - R 14 *(102nd Congress)*

Augustus F. Hawkins, Calif. (1984-91)
William D. Ford, Mich. (1991-93)
Bill Goodling, Pa.

Elementary, Secondary and Vocational Education — Augustus F. Hawkins, Calif. (101st Congress); Dale E. Kildee, Mich. (102nd Congress)
Employment Opportunities — Matthew G. Martinez, Calif. (101st Congress); Carl C. Perkins, Ky. (102nd Congress)
Health and Safety — Joseph M. Gaydos, Pa.
Human Resources — Dale E. Kildee, Mich. (101st Congress); Matthew G. Martinez, Calif. (102nd Congress)
Labor-Management Relations — William L. Clay, Mo. (101st Congress); Pat Williams, Mont. (102nd Congress)
Labor Standards — Austin J. Murphy, Pa.
Postsecondary Education — Pat Williams, Mont. (101st Congress); William D. Ford, Mich. (102nd Congress)
Select Education — Major R. Owens, N.Y.

Energy and Commerce

Interstate and foreign commerce generally; national energy policy generally; exploration, production, storage, supply, marketing, pricing and regulation of energy resources; nuclear energy; solar energy; energy conservation; generation and marketing of power; inland waterways; railroads and railway labor and retirement; communications generally; securities and exchanges; consumer affairs; travel and tourism; public health and quarantine; health care facilities; biomedical research and development.

D 26 - R 17 *(101st Congress)*
D 27 - R 16 *(102nd Congress)*

John D. Dingell, Mich. (1981-93)
Norman F. Lent, N.Y.

Commerce, Consumer Protection and Competitiveness — James J. Florio, N.J. (resigned House Jan. 16, 1990); Doug Walgren, Pa. (through 101st Congress); Cardiss Collins, Ill. (102nd Congress)
Energy and Power — Philip R. Sharp, Ind.
Health and the Environment — Henry A. Waxman, Calif.
Oversight and Investigations — John D. Dingell, Mich.
Telecommunications and Finance — Edward J. Markey, Mass.
Transportation and Hazardous Materials — Thomas A. Luken, Ohio (101st Congress); Al Swift, Wash. (102nd Congress)

Foreign Affairs

Relations of the United States with foreign nations generally; foreign loans; international conferences and congresses; intervention abroad and declarations of war; diplomatic service; foreign trade; neutrality; protection of Americans abroad; Red Cross; United Nations; international economic policy; export controls including non-proliferation of nuclear technology and hardware; international commodity agreements; trading with the enemy; international financial and monetary organizations.

D 26 - R 17

Dante B. Fascell, Fla. (1984-93)
William S. Broomfield, Mich.

Africa — Howard Wolpe, Mich. (101st Congress); Mervyn M. Dymally, Calif. (102nd Congress)

Arms Control, International Security and Science — Dante B. Fascell, Fla.

Asian and Pacific Affairs — Stephen J. Solarz, N.Y.

Europe and the Middle East — Lee H. Hamilton, Ind.

Human Rights and International Organizations — Gus Yatron, Pa.

International Economic Policy and Trade — Sam Gejdenson, Conn.

International Narcotics Control (102nd Congress) — Edward F. Feighan, Ohio

International Operations — Mervyn M. Dymally, Calif. (101st Congress); Howard L. Berman, Calif. (102nd Congress)

Western Hemisphere Affairs — George W. Crockett Jr., Mich. (101st Congress); Robert G. Torricelli, N.J. (102nd Congress)

Government Operations

Budget and accounting measures; overall economy and efficiency in government including federal procurement; executive branch reorganization; general revenue sharing; intergovernmental relations; National Archives.

D 24 - R 15 *(101st Congress)*
D 25 - R 15 - I 1 *(102nd Congress)*

John Conyers Jr., Mich. (1989-93)
Frank Horton, N.Y.

Commerce, Consumer and Monetary Affairs — Doug Barnard Jr., Ga.

Employment and Housing — Tom Lantos, Calif.

Environment, Energy and Natural Resources — Mike Synar, Okla.

Government Activities and Transportation — Cardiss Collins, Ill. (101st Congress); Barbara Boxer, Calif. (102nd Congress)

Government Information, Justice and Agriculture — Bob Wise, W.Va.

Human Resources and Intergovernmental Relations — Ted Weiss, N.Y. (died Sept. 14, 1992); Donald M. Payne, N.J. (through 102nd Congress)

Legislation and National Security — John Conyers Jr., Mich.

House Administration

House administration generally; contested elections; federal elections generally; corrupt practices; qualifications of members of the House; *Congressional Record;* the Capitol; Library of Congress; Smithsonian Institution; Botanic Garden.

D 13 - R 8 *(101st Congress)*
D 15 - R 9 *(102nd Congress)*

Frank Annunzio, Ill. (1985-91)
Charlie Rose, N.C. (1991-93)
Newt Gingrich, Ga. (resigned post April 10, 1989
Bill Thomas, Calif. (through 102nd Congress)

Accounts — Joseph M. Gaydos, Pa.

Campaign Finance Reform (102nd Congress) — Sam Gejdenson, Conn.

Elections — Al Swift, Wash.

Libraries and Memorials — William L. Clay, Mo.

Office Systems — Charlie Rose, N.C. (101st Congress); Sam Gejdenson, Conn. (102nd Congress)

Personnel and Police — Mary Rose Oakar, Ohio

Procurement and Printing — Jim Bates, Calif. (101st Congress); Frank Annunzio, Ill. (102nd Congress)

Interior and Insular Affairs

Public lands; parks and natural resources generally; U.S. Geological Survey; interstate water compacts; irrigation and reclamation; Indian affairs; minerals, mines and mining; petroleum conservation on public lands; regulation of domestic nuclear energy industry, including waste disposal; territorial affairs of the United States.

D 23 - R 14 *(101st Congress)*
D 26 - R 16 *(102nd Congress)*

Morris K. Udall, Ariz. (1977-91; resigned House May 4, 1991)
George Miller, Calif. (through 102nd Congress)
Don Young, Alaska

Energy and the Environment — Morris K. Udall, Ariz. (resigned House May 4, 1991); Peter H. Kostmayer, Pa. (through 102nd Congress)

General Oversight and California Desert Lands (102nd Congress) — Richard H. Lehman, Calif.

General Oversight and Investigations (101st Congress) — Peter H. Kostmayer, Pa.

Insular and International Affairs — Ron de Lugo, Virgin Islands

Mining and Natural Resources — Nick J. Rahall II, W.Va.

National Parks and Public Lands — Bruce F. Vento, Minn.

Water, Power and Offshore Energy Resources (101st Congress) — George Miller, Calif.

Water, Power and Offshore Energy (102nd Congress) — George Miller, Calif.

Judiciary

Civil and criminal judicial proceedings generally; federal courts and judges; bankruptcy, mutiny, espionage and counterfeiting; civil liberties; constitutional amendments; immigration and naturalization; interstate compacts; claims against the United States; apportionment of representatives; meetings of Congress and attendance of members; penitentiaries; patents, copyrights and trademarks; presidential succession; monopolies and unlawful restraints of trade; internal security.

D 21 - R 14 *(101st Congress)*
D 21 - R 13 *(102nd Congress)*

Jack Brooks, Texas (1989-93)
Hamilton Fish Jr., N.Y.

Administrative Law and Governmental Relations — Barney Frank, Mass.
Civil and Constitutional Rights — Don Edwards, Calif.
Courts, Intellectual Property and the Administration of Justice (101st Congress) — Robert W. Kastenmeier, Wis.
Crime (101st Congress) — William J. Hughes, N.J.
Crime and Criminal Justice (102nd Congress) — Charles E. Schumer, N.Y.
Criminal Justice (101st Congress) — Charles E. Schumer, N.Y.
Economic and Commercial Law — Jack Brooks, Texas
Immigration, Refugees and International Law (101st Congress) — Bruce A. Morrison, Conn.
Intellectual Property and Judicial Administration (102nd Congress) — William J. Hughes, N.J.
International Law, Immigration and Refugees (102nd Congress) — Romano L. Mazzoli, Ky.

Merchant Marine and Fisheries

Merchant marine generally; oceanography and marine affairs including coastal zone management; Coast Guard; fisheries and wildlife; regulation of common carriers by water and inspection of merchant marine vessels, lights and signals, lifesaving equipment and fire protection; navigation; Panama Canal, Canal Zone and interoceanic canals generally; registration and licensing of vessels; rules and international arrangements to prevent collisions at sea; international fishing agreements; Coast Guard and Merchant Marine academies and state maritime academies.

D 26 - R 17 *(101st Congress)*
D 28 - R 17 *(102nd Congress)*

Walter B. Jones, N.C. (1981-92; died Sept. 15, 1992)
Gerry E. Studds, Mass. (through 102nd Congress)
Robert W. Davis, Mich.

Coast Guard and Navigation — W. J. "Billy" Tauzin, La.
Fisheries and Wildlife Conservation and the Environment — Gerry E. Studds, Mass.
Merchant Marine — Walter B. Jones, N.C. (died Sept. 15, 1992); Carroll Hubbard Jr., Ky. (through 102nd Congress)
Oceanography and Great Lakes (101st Congress) — Dennis M. Hertel, Mich.
Oceanography, Great Lakes and Outer Continental Shelf (102nd Congress) — Dennis M. Hertel, Mich.
Oversight and Investigations — Thomas M. Foglietta, Pa. (101st Congress); William O. Lipinski, Ill. (102nd Congress)
Panama Canal/Outer Continental Shelf (101st Congress) — Roy Dyson, Md.

Post Office and Civil Service

Postal and federal civil services; census and the collection of statistics generally; Hatch Act; holidays and celebrations.

D 14 - R 8

William D. Ford, Mich. (1981-91)
William L. Clay, Mo. (1991-93)
Benjamin A. Gilman, N.Y.

Census and Population — Thomas C. Sawyer, Ohio
Civil Service — Gerry Sikorski, Minn.
Compensation and Employee Benefits — Gary L. Ackerman, N.Y.
Human Resources —Paul E. Kanjorski, Pa.
Investigations — William D. Ford, Mich. (101st Congress); William L. Clay, Mo. (102nd Congress)
Postal Operations and Services — Mickey Leland, Texas (died Aug. 7, 1989); Frank McCloskey, Ind. (through 102nd Congress)
Postal Personnel and Modernization — Frank McCloskey, Ind. (resigned post Oct. 16, 1989); Charles A. Hayes, Ill. (through 102nd Congress)

Public Works and Transportation

Flood control and improvement of rivers and harbors; construction and maintenance of roads; oil and other pollution of navigable waters; public buildings and grounds; public works for the benefit of navigation including bridges and dams; water power; transportation, except railroads; Botanic Garden; Library of Congress; Smithsonian Institution.

D 30 - R 20 *(101st Congress)*
D 34 - R 21 *(102nd Congress)*

Glenn M. Anderson, Calif. (1988-91)
Robert A. Roe, N.J. (1991-93)
John Paul Hammerschmidt, Ark.

Aviation — James L. Oberstar, Minn.
Economic Development — Gus Savage, Ill. (101st Congress); Joe Kolter, Pa. (102nd Congress)
Investigations and Oversight — Glenn M. Anderson, Calif. (101st Congress); Robert A. Borski, Pa. (102nd Congress)
Public Buildings and Grounds — Douglas H. Bosco, Calif. (101st Congress); Gus Savage, Ill. (102nd Congress)
Surface Transportation — Norman Y. Mineta, Calif.
Water Resources — Henry J. Nowak, N.Y.

Rules

Rules and order of business of the House; emergency waivers under the Congressional Budget Act of required reporting date for bills and resolutions authorizing new budget authority; recesses and final adjournments of Congress.

D 9 - R 4

Claude D. Pepper, Fla. (1983-89; died May 30, 1989)
Joe Moakley, Mass. (through 102nd Congress)
James H. Quillen, Tenn. (101st Congress)
Gerald B. H. Solomon, N.Y. (102nd Congress)

Legislative Process — Butler Derrick, S.C.
Rules of the House — Joe Moakley, Mass. (101st Congress); Anthony C. Beilenson, Calif. (102nd Congress)

Science, Space and Technology

Astronautical research and development, including resources, personnel, equipment and facilities; Bureau of Standards, standardization of weights and measures and the metric system; National Aeronautics and Space Administration; National Aeronautics and Space Council; National Science Foundation; outer space, including exploration and control; science scholarships; scientific research, development and demonstration; federally owned or operated non-military energy laboratories; civil aviation research and development; environmental research and development; energy research, development and demonstration; National Weather Service.

D 30 - R 19 *(101st Congress)*
D 32 - R 19 *(102nd Congress)*

Robert A. Roe, N.J. (1987-91)
George E. Brown Jr., Calif. (1991-93)
Robert S. Walker, Pa.

Energy (102nd Congress) — Marilyn Lloyd, Tenn.
Energy Research and Development (101st Congress) — Marilyn Lloyd, Tenn.
Environment (102nd Congress) — James H. Scheuer, N.Y.
International Scientific Cooperation (101st Congress) — Ralph M. Hall, Texas
Investigations and Oversight — Robert A. Roe, N.J. (101st Congress); Howard Wolpe, Mich. (102nd Congress)
Natural Resources, Agriculture Research and Environment (101st Congress) — James H. Scheuer, N.Y.
Science (102nd Congress) — Rick Boucher, Va.
Science, Research and Technology (101st Congress) — Doug Walgren, Pa. (resigned post March 6, 1990); Tim Valentine, N.C. (through 101st Congress)
Space (102nd Congress) — Ralph M. Hall, Texas
Space Science and Applications (101st Congress) — Bill Nelson, Fla.
Technology and Competitiveness (102nd Congress) — Tim Valentine, N.C.
Transportation, Aviation and Materials (101st Congress) — Tim Valentine, N.C. (resigned post March 6, 1990); Robert G. Torricelli, N.J. (through 101st Congress)

Select Aging

Problems of older Americans including income, housing, health, welfare, employment, education, recreation and participation in family and community life. Studies and reports findings to the House but cannot report legislation.

D 39 - R 26 *(101st Congress)*
D 42 - R 26 *(102nd Congress)*

Edward R. Roybal, Calif. (1983-93)
Matthew J. Rinaldo, N.J.

Health and Long-Term Care — Claude Pepper, Fla. (died May 30, 1989); Edward R. Roybal, Calif. (through 102nd Congress)
Housing and Consumer Interests — James J. Florio, N.J. (resigned House Jan. 16, 1990); Marilyn Lloyd, Tenn. (through 102nd Congress)
Human Services — Thomas J. Downey, N.Y.
Retirement, Income and Employment — Edward R. Roybal, Calif. (resigned post July 1989); William J. Hughes, N.J. (through 102nd Congress)

Select Children, Youth and Families

Problems of children, youth and families including income maintenance, health, nutrition, education, welfare, employment and recreation. Studies and reports finding to the House but cannot report legislation.

D 18 - R 12 *(101st Congress)*
D 22 - R 14 *(102nd Congress)*

George Miller, Calif. (1983-91)
Patricia Schroeder, Colo. (1991-93)
Thomas J. Bliley Jr., Va. (101st Congress)
Frank R. Wolf, Va. (102nd Congress)

No standing subcommittees.

Select Hunger

Comprehensive study and review of hunger and malnutrition, including U.S. development and economic assistance programs; U.S. trade relations with less-developed nations; food production and distribution; agribusiness efforts to further international development; policies of development banks and international development institutions; and food assistance programs in the United States. Review of executive branch recommendations relating to programs affecting hunger and malnutrition, and recommend legislation or other action with respect to such programs to the appropriate committees of the House.

D 18 - R 12 *(101st Congress)*
D 21 - R 12 *(102nd Congress)*

Mickey Leland, Texas (1984-89; died Aug. 7, 1989)
Tony P. Hall, Ohio (through 102nd Congress)
Bill Emerson, Mo. (vice chairman)

Task Forces

Domestic — Mike Espy, Miss.
International — Tony P. Hall, Ohio (resigned post Sept. 28, 1989); Byron L. Dorgan, N.D. (through 102nd Congress)

Select Intelligence

Legislative and budgetary authority over the Central Intelligence Agency, the Defense Intelligence Agency, the National Security Agency, intelligence activities of the Federal Bureau of Investigation and other components of the federal intelligence community.

D 12 - R 7

Anthony C. Beilenson, Calif. (1989-91)
Dave McCurdy, Okla. (1991-93)
Henry J. Hyde, Ill. (101st Congress)
Bud Shuster, Pa. (102nd Congress)

Legislation — Matthew F. McHugh, N.Y. (101st Congress); Barbara B. Kennelly, Conn. (102nd Congress)
Oversight and Evaluation — Dave McCurdy, Okla. (101st Congress); Charles Wilson, Texas (102nd Congress)
Program and Budget Authorization — Anthony C. Beilenson, Calif. (101st Congress); Dave McCurdy, Okla. (102nd Congress)

Select Narcotics Abuse and Control

Problems of narcotics, drug and polydrug abuse and control including opium and its derivatives, other narcotic drugs, psychotropics and other controlled substances; trafficking, manufacturing and distribution; treatment, prevention and rehabilitation; narcotics-related violations of tax laws; international treaties and agreements relating to narcotics and drug abuse; role of organized crime in narcotics and drug abuse; abuse and control in the armed forces and in industry; criminal justice system, narcotics and drug law violations and crimes related to drug abuse. Studies and reports findings to the House but cannot report legislation.

D 18 - R 12 *(101st Congress)*
D 20 - R 14 *(102nd Congress)*

Charles B. Rangel, N.Y. (1983-93)
Lawrence Coughlin, Pa.

No standing subcommittees.

Small Business

Assistance to and protection of small business including financial aid; participation of small business enterprises in federal procurement and government contracts.

D 27 - R 17

John J. LaFalce, N.Y. (1987-93)
Joseph M. McDade, Pa. (101st Congress)
Andy Ireland, Fla. (102nd Congress)

Antitrust, Impact of Deregulation and Ecology (102nd Congress) — Dennis E. Eckart, Ohio
Antitrust, Impact of Deregulation and Privatization (101st Congress) — Dennis E. Eckart, Ohio
Environment and Employment (102nd Congress) — Jim Olin, Va.
Environment and Labor (101st Congress) — Esteban E. Torres, Calif.
Exports, Tax Policy and Special Problems — Norman Sisisky, Va.
Procurement, Tourism and Rural Development — Ike Skelton, Mo.
Regulation, Business Opportunity and Energy — Ron Wyden, Ore.
SBA, the General Economy and Minority Enterprise Development — John J. LaFalce, N.Y.

Standards of Official Conduct

Measures relating to the Code of Official Conduct; conduct of House members and employees; Ethics in Government Act.

D 6 - R 6 *(101st Congress)*
D 7 - R 7 *(102nd Congress)*

Julian C. Dixon, Calif. (1985-91)
Louis Stokes, Ohio (1991-93)
John T. Myers, Ind. (101st Congress)
James V. Hansen, Utah (102nd Congress)

No standing subcommittees.

Veterans' Affairs

Veterans' measures generally; compensation, vocational rehabilitation and education of veterans; armed forces life insurance; pensions; readjustment benefits; veterans' hospitals, medical care and treatment.

D 21 - R 13

G. V. "Sonny" Montgomery, Miss. (1981-93)
Bob Stump, Ariz.

Compensation, Pension and Insurance — Douglas Applegate, Ohio
Education, Training and Employment — Timothy J. Penny, Minn.
Hospitals and Health Care — G. V. "Sonny" Montgomery, Miss.
Housing and Memorial Affairs — Harley O. Staggers Jr., W.Va.
Oversight and Investigations — Lane Evans, Ill.

Ways and Means

Revenue measures generally; reciprocal trade agreements; customs, collection districts and ports of entry and delivery; bonded debt of the United States; deposit of public moneys; transportation of dutiable goods; tax-exempt foundations and charitable trusts; Social Security.

D 23 - R 13

Dan Rostenkowski, Ill. (1981-93)
Bill Archer, Texas

Health — Pete Stark, Calif.
Human Resources† — Thomas J. Downey, N.Y. (acting chairman)
Oversight — J. J. Pickle, Texas
Select Revenue Measures — Charles B. Rangel, N.Y.
Social Security — Andrew Jacobs Jr., Ind.
Trade — Sam M. Gibbons, Fla.

† Harold E. Ford, Tenn., was required to step down from the chairmanship upon being indicted April 24, 1987. He was acquitted April 9, 1993.

Political Committees

Democratic Congressional Campaign Committee (provides campaign support for Democratic House candidates) — Beryl Anthony Jr., Ark. (101st Congress); Vic Fazio, Calif. (102nd Congress)
Democratic Personnel Committee (selects, appoints and supervises Democratic patronage positions) — Jack Brooks, Texas
Democratic Steering and Policy Committee (schedules legislation and makes Democratic committee assignments) — Jim Wright, Texas (resigned post June 6, 1989); Thomas S. Foley, Wash. (through 102nd Congress)
National Republican Congressional Committee (provides campaign support for Republican House candidates) — Guy Vander Jagt, Mich.
Republican Committee on Committees (makes Republican committee assignments) — Robert H. Michel, Ill.
Republican Policy Committee (advises on party action and policy) — Mickey Edwards, Okla.
Republican Research Committee (at leadership's request, provides information and recommendations on specific policy issues likely to come before Congress) — Duncan Hunter, Calif.

Joint Committees

Joint committees are set up to examine specific questions and are established by public law. Membership is drawn from both chambers and both parties. When a senator serves as chairman, the vice chairman usually is a representative, and vice versa. The chairmanship traditionally rotates from one chamber to the other at the beginning of each Congress (except for the Taxation chairmanship, which rotates at the start of each session).

Economic

Studies and investigates all recommendations in the president's annual *Economic Report to Congress.* Reports findings and recommendations to the House and Senate.

Rep. Lee H. Hamilton, D-Ind., chairman (1989-91)
Sen. Paul S. Sarbanes, D-Md., chairman (1987-89, 1991-93)
Sen. Paul S. Sarbanes, D-Md., vice chairman (101st Congress)
Rep. Lee H. Hamilton, D-Ind., vice chairman (102nd Congress)

Economic Goals and Intergovernmental Policy — Rep. Lee H. Hamilton, D-Ind.
Economic Growth, Trade and Taxes — Sen. Lloyd Bentsen, D-Texas
Economic Resources and Competitiveness — Rep. David R. Obey, D-Wis.
Education and Health — Rep. James H. Scheuer, D-N.Y.
Fiscal and Monetary Policy — Sen. Edward M. Kennedy, D-Mass.
International Economic Policy — Sen. Paul S. Sarbanes, D-Md.
Investment, Jobs and Prices — Rep. Augustus F. Hawkins, D-Calif. (101st Congress); Rep. Pete Stark, D-Calif. (102nd Congress)
National Security Economics (101st Congress) — Sen. Jeff Bingaman, D-N.M.
Technology and National Security (102nd Congress) — Sen. Jeff Bingaman, D-N.M.

Library

Management and expansion of the Library of Congress; receipt of gifts for the benefit of the library; development and maintenance of the Botanic Garden; placement of statues and other works of art in the Capitol.

Rep. Frank Annunzio, D-Ill., chairman (1985-87, 1989-91)
Sen. Claiborne Pell, D-R.I., chairman (1987-89, 1991-93)
Sen. Claiborne Pell, D-R.I., vice chairman (101st Congress)
Rep. Charlie Rose, D-N.C., vice chairman (102nd Congress)

No standing subcommittees.

Printing

Probes inefficiency and waste in the printing, binding and distribution of federal government publications. Oversees the arrangement and style of the *Congressional Record.*

Sen. Wendell H. Ford, D-Ky., chairman (1989-91)
Rep. Charlie Rose, D-N.C., chairman (1991-93)
Rep. Frank Annunzio, D-Ill., vice chairman (101st Congress)
Sen. Wendell H. Ford, D-Ky., vice chairman (102nd Congress)

No standing subcommittees.

Taxation

Operation, effects and administration of the federal system of internal revenue taxes; measures and methods for simplification of taxes.

Rep. Dan Rostenkowski, D-Ill., chairman (1981, 1983, 1985, 1987, 1989, 1991)
Sen. Lloyd Bentsen, D-Texas, chairman (1988, 1990, 1992)
Sen. Lloyd Bentsen, D-Texas, vice chairman (1989, 1991)
Rep. Dan Rostenkowski, D-Ill., vice chairman (1982, 1984, 1986, 1988, 1990, 1992)

No standing subcommittees.

Post-Election Sessions

Congress has held seven post-election sessions since 1945.

1948. The 1948 post-election session of the 80th Congress lasted only two hours. Both chambers swore in new members, approved several minor resolutions and received last-minute reports from committees.

In addition to final floor action, several committees resumed work. The most active was the House Un-American Activities Committee, which continued its investigation of alleged communist espionage in the federal government.

1950. After the 1950 elections, President Harry S. Truman sent a "must" agenda to the lame-duck session of the 81st Congress. The president's list included supplemental defense appropriations, an excess profits tax, aid to Yugoslavia, a three-month extension of federal rent controls and statehood for Hawaii and Alaska. During a marathon session that lasted until only a few hours before its successor took over, the 81st Congress acted on all of the president's legislative items except the statehood bills, which were blocked by a Senate filibuster.

1954. Only one chamber of the 83rd Congress convened after the 1954 elections. The Senate returned Nov. 8 to hold what has been called a "censure session," a continuing investigation into the conduct of Sen. Joseph R. McCarthy, R-Wis. (1947-57). By a 67-22 roll call, the Senate Dec. 2 voted to "condemn" McCarthy for his behavior.

In other post-election floor action, the Senate passed a series of miscellaneous and administrative resolutions and swore in new members.

1970. President Richard Nixon criticized the lame-duck Congress as one that had "seemingly lost the capacity to decide and the will to act." Filibusters and intense controversy contributed to inaction on the president's request for trade legislation and welfare reform.

Congress nevertheless claimed some substantive results during the session, which ended Jan. 2, 1971. Several major appropriations bills were cleared for presidential signature. Congress also approved foreign aid to Cambodia, provided interim funding for the supersonic transport (SST) plane and repealed the Tonkin Gulf Resolution that had been used as a basis for American military involvement in Vietnam.

1974. In a session that ran from Nov. 18 to Dec. 20, 1974, the 93rd Congress cleared several important bills for presidential signature, including a mass transit bill, a Labor-Health, Education and Welfare appropriations bill and a foreign assistance package. A House-Senate conference committee reached agreement on a major strip-mining bill, but President Gerald R. Ford vetoed it.

Congress approved the nomination of Nelson A. Rockefeller as vice president. It also overrode presidential vetoes of two bills — one broadening the Freedom of Information Act, a second authorizing educational benefits for Korean War and Vietnam-era veterans.

Recent Lame-Duck Sessions

Year	Congress	Dates
1948	80th	Dec. 31, 1948 (2-hour session)
1950	81st	Nov. 27, 1950 — Jan. 2, 1951
1954	83rd	Nov. 8, 1954 — Dec. 2, 1954
1970	91st	Nov. 16, 1970 — Jan. 2, 1971 (Senate)
1974	93rd	Nov. 18, 1974 — Dec. 20, 1974
1980	96th	Nov. 12, 1980 — Dec. 16, 1980
1982	97th	Nov. 29, 1982 — Dec. 23, 1982 (Senate) Nov. 29, 1982 — Dec. 21, 1982 (House)

1980. The lame-duck session of the 96th Congress was productive, at least until Dec. 5, the original adjournment date set by congressional leaders. By that date a budget had been approved, along with a budget reconciliation measure. Ten regular appropriations bills had cleared, though one subsequently was vetoed. Congress had approved two major environmental measures — an Alaskan lands bill and toxic waste "superfund" legislation — as well as a three-year extension of general revenue sharing.

After Dec. 5, however, the legislative pace slowed noticeably. Action on a continuing appropriations resolution for those departments and agencies whose regular funding had not been cleared was delayed, first by a filibuster on a fair housing bill and later by more than 100 "Christmas tree" amendments, including a $10,000-a-year pay raise for members. After the conference report failed in the Senate and twice was rewritten, the bill was shorn of virtually all its "ornaments" and finally cleared by both chambers on Dec. 16.

1982. Despite the reluctance of congressional leaders, President Ronald Reagan urged the convening of a post-election session at the end of the 97th Congress, principally to pass remaining appropriations bills.

Rising unemployment — and Democratic election gains in the House — made job creation efforts the focus of the lame-duck Congress, however. Overriding the objections of Republican conservatives, Congress passed Reagan-backed legislation raising the federal gasoline tax from 4 cents to 9 cents a gallon to pay for highway repairs and mass transit. Supporters said the legislation would help alleviate unemployment by creating 300,000 jobs.

Congress eventually cleared four additional appropriations bills, packaging the remaining six in a continuing appropriations resolution that also included a pay raise for House members. Conferees dropped funding for emergency jobs programs to avert a threatened veto of the resolution.

The lame-duck session also was highlighted by Congress' refusal to fund production and procurement of the first five MX intercontinental missiles. This was the first time in recent history that either house of Congress had denied a president's request to fund production of a strategic weapon.

Senate Cloture Votes, 1917-92

The Senate's ultimate check on the filibuster is the provision for cloture, or limitation on debate, contained in Rule 22 of its Standing Rules. The original Rule 22 was adopted in 1917 following a furor over the "talking to death" of a proposal by President Woodrow Wilson for arming American merchant ships before the United States entered World War I. The new cloture rule required the votes of two-thirds of all of the senators present and voting to invoke cloture. In 1949, during a parliamentary skirmish preceding scheduled consideration of a Fair Employment Practices Commission bill, the requirement was raised to two-thirds of the entire Senate membership.

A revision of the rule in 1959 provided for limitation of debate by a vote of two-thirds of the senators present and voting, two days after a cloture petition was submitted by 16 senators. If cloture was adopted by the Senate, further debate was limited to one hour for each senator on the bill itself and on all amendments affecting it. No new amendments could be offered except by unanimous consent. Amendments that were not germane to the pending business and dilatory motions were out of order. The rule applied both to regular legislation and to motions to change the Standing Rules.

Rule 22 was revised significantly in 1975 by lowering the vote needed for cloture to three-fifths of the Senate membership (60, if there were no vacancies). That revision applied to any matter except proposed rules changes, for which the old requirement of a two-thirds majority of senators present and voting still applied.

In a further revision of the rule, the Senate in 1979 limited post-cloture delaying tactics by providing that once cloture was invoked, a final vote had to be taken after no more than 100 hours of debate. All time spent on quorum calls, roll-call votes and other parliamentary procedures was to be included in the 100-hour limit.

When the Senate decided to televise its floor proceedings in 1986, it further tightened up the time on post-cloture debate. Rule 22 was revised to reduce to 30 hours, from 100, the time allowed for debate, procedural moves and roll-call votes after the Senate had invoked cloture to end a filibuster.

Following is a list of the 345 cloture votes taken between 1917, when Senate Rule 22 was adopted, and the end of 1992; 126 of the votes (in **bold type**) were successful.

Issue	Date	Vote	Yeas Needed
Versailles Treaty	Nov. 15, 1919	78-16	63
Emergency tariff	Feb. 2, 1921	36-35	48
Tariff bill	July 7, 1922	45-35	54
World Court	Jan. 25, 1926	68-26	63
Migratory birds	June 1, 1926	46-33	53
Branch banking	Feb. 15, 1927	65-18	56
Disabled officers	Feb. 26, 1927	51-36	58
Colorado River	Feb. 26, 1927	32-59	61
D.C. buildings	Feb. 28, 1927	52-31	56
Prohibition Bureau	Feb. 28, 1927	55-27	55
Banking Act	Jan. 19, 1933	58-30	59
Anti-lynching	Jan. 27, 1938	37-51	59
Anti-lynching	Feb. 16, 1938	42-46	59
Anti-poll tax	Nov. 23, 1942	37-41	52
Anti-poll tax	May 15, 1944	36-44	54
Fair Employment Practices Commission	Feb. 9, 1946	48-36	56
British loan	May 7, 1946	41-41	55
Labor disputes	May 25, 1946	3-77	54
Anti-poll tax	July 31, 1946	39-33	48
Fair Employment	May 19, 1950	52-32	64
Fair Employment	July 12, 1950	55-33	64
Atomic Energy Act	July 26, 1954	44-42	64
Civil Rights Act	March 10, 1960	42-53	64
Amend Rule 22	Sept. 19, 1961	37-43	54
Literacy tests	May 9, 1962	43-53	64
Literacy tests	May 14, 1962	42-52	63
Comsat Act	Aug. 14, 1962	63-27	60
Amend Rule 22	Feb. 7, 1963	54-42	64
Civil Rights Act	June 10, 1964	71-29	67
Legislative reapportionment	Sept. 10, 1964	30-63	62
Voting Rights Act	May 25, 1965	70-30	67
Right-to-work repeal	Oct. 11, 1965	45-47	62
Right-to-work repeal	Feb. 8, 1966	51-48	66
Right-to-work repeal	Feb. 10, 1966	50-49	66
Civil Rights Act	Sept. 14, 1966	54-42	64
Civil Rights Act	Sept. 19, 1966	52-41	62
D.C. Home Rule	Oct. 10, 1966	41-37	52
Amend Rule 22	Jan. 24, 1967	53-46	66
Open Housing	Feb. 20, 1968	55-37	62
Open Housing	Feb. 26, 1968	56-36	62
Open Housing	March 1, 1968	59-35	63
Open Housing	March 4, 1968	65-32	65
Fortas Nomination	Oct. 1, 1968	45-43	59
Amend Rule 22	Jan. 16, 1969	51-47	66
Amend Rule 22	Jan. 28, 1969	50-42	62
Electoral College	Sept. 17, 1970	54-36	60
Electoral College	Sept. 29, 1970	53-34	58
Supersonic transport	Dec. 19, 1970	43-48	61
Supersonic transport	Dec. 22, 1970	42-44	58
Amend Rule 22	Feb. 18, 1971	48-37	57
Amend Rule 22	Feb. 23, 1971	50-36	58
Amend Rule 22	March 2, 1971	48-36	56
Amend Rule 22	March 9, 1971	55-39	63
Military Draft	June 23, 1971	65-27	62
Lockheed Loan	July 26, 1971	42-47	60
Lockheed Loan	July 28, 1971	59-39	66
Lockheed Loan	July 30, 1971	53-37	60
Military Draft	Sept. 21, 1971	61-30	61
Rehnquist nomination	Dec. 10, 1971	52-42	63
Equal Job Opportunity	Feb. 1, 1972	48-37	57
Equal Job Opportunity	Feb. 3, 1972	53-35	59
Equal Job Opportunity	Feb. 22, 1972	71-23	63

Appendix

Issue	Date	Vote	Yeas Needed
U.S.-Soviet Arms Pact	Sept. 14, 1972	76-15	61
Consumer Agency	Sept. 29, 1972	47-29	51
Consumer Agency	Oct. 3, 1972	55-32	58
Consumer Agency	Oct. 5, 1972	52-30	55
School Busing	Oct. 10, 1972	45-37	55
School Busing	Oct. 11, 1972	49-39	59
School Busing	Oct. 12, 1972	49-38	58
Voter Registration	April 30, 1973	56-31	58
Voter Registration	May 3, 1973	60-34	63
Voter Registration	May 9, 1973	67-32	66
Public Campaign Financing	Dec. 2, 1973	47-33	54
Public Campaign Financing	Dec. 3, 1973	49-39	59
Rhodesian Chrome Ore	Dec. 11, 1973	59-35	63
Rhodesian Chrome Ore	Dec. 13, 1973	62-33	64
Legal Services Program	Dec. 13, 1973	60-36	64
Legal Services Program	Dec. 14, 1973	56-29	57
Rhodesian Chrome Ore	Dec. 18, 1973	63-26	60
Legal Services Program	Jan. 30, 1974	68-29	65
Genocide Treaty	Feb. 5, 1974	55-36	61
Genocide Treaty	Feb. 6, 1974	55-38	62
Government Pay Raise	March 6, 1974	67-31	66
Public Campaign Financing	April 4, 1974	60-36	64
Public Campaign Financing	April 9, 1974	64-30	63
Public Debt Ceiling	June 19, 1974	50-43	62
Public Debt Ceiling	June 19, 1974	45-48	62
Public Debt Ceiling	June 26, 1974	48-50	66
Consumer Agency	July 30, 1974	56-42	66
Consumer Agency	Aug. 1, 1974	59-39	66
Consumer Agency	Aug. 20, 1974	59-35	63
Consumer Agency	Sept. 19, 1974	64-34	66
Export-Import Bank	Dec. 3, 1974	51-39	60
Export-Import Bank	Dec. 4, 1974	48-44	62
Trade Reform	Dec. 13, 1974	71-19	60
Fiscal 1975 Supplemental Funds	Dec. 14, 1974	56-27	56
Export-Import Bank	Dec. 14, 1974	49-35	56
Export-Import Bank	Dec. 16, 1974	54-34	59
Social Services Programs	Dec. 17, 1974	70-23	62
Tax Law Changes	Dec. 17, 1974	67-25	62
Rail Reorganization Act	Feb. 26, 1975	86-8	63
Amend Rule 22	March 5, 1975	73-21	63
Amend Rule 22	March 7, 1975	73-21	63
Tax Reduction	March 20, 1975	59-38	60
Tax Reduction	March 21, 1975	83-13	60
Agency for Consumer Advocacy	May 13, 1975	71-27	60
Senate Staffing	June 11, 1975	77-19	64
New Hampshire Senate Seat	June 24, 1975	57-39	60
New Hampshire Senate Seat	June 25, 1975	56-41	60
New Hampshire Senate Seat	June 26, 1975	54-40	60
New Hampshire Senate Seat	July 8, 1975	57-38	60
New Hampshire Senate Seat	July 9, 1975	57-38	60
New Hampshire Senate Seat	July 10, 1975	54-38	60
Voting Rights Act	July 21, 1975	72-19	60
Voting Rights Act	July 23, 1975	76-20	60
Oil Price Decontrol	July 30, 1975	54-38	60
Labor-HEW Appropriations	Sept. 23, 1975	46-48	60
Labor-HEW Appropriations	Sept. 24, 1975	64-33	60
Common-Site Picketing	Nov. 11, 1975	66-30	60
Common-Site Picketing	Nov. 14, 1975	58-31	60
Common-Site Picketing	Nov. 18, 1975	62-37	60
Rail Reorganization	Dec. 4, 1975	61-27	60
New York City Aid	Dec. 5, 1975	70-27	60
Rice Production Act	Feb. 3, 1976	70-19	60
Antitrust Amendments	June 3, 1976	67-22	60
Antitrust Amendments	Aug. 31, 1976	63-27	60
Civil Rights Attorneys' Fees	Sept. 23, 1976	63-26	60

Issue	Date	Vote	Yeas Needed
Draft Resisters Pardons	Jan. 24, 1977	53-43	60
Campaign Financing	July 29, 1977	49-45	60
Campaign Financing	Aug. 1, 1977	47-46	60
Campaign Financing	Aug. 2, 1977	52-46	60
Natural Gas Pricing	Sept. 26, 1977	77-17	60
Labor Law Revision	June 7, 1978	42-47	60
Labor Law Revision	June 8, 1978	49-41	60
Labor Law Revision	June 13, 1978	54-43	60
Labor Law Revision	June 14, 1978	58-41	60
Labor Law Revision	June 15, 1978	58-39	60
Labor Law Revision	June 22, 1978	53-45	60
Revenue Act of 1978	Oct. 9, 1978	62-28	60
Energy Taxes	Oct. 14, 1978	71-13	60
Windfall Profits Tax	Dec. 12, 1979	53-46	60
Windfall Profits Tax	Dec. 13, 1979	56-40	60
Windfall Profits Tax	Dec. 14, 1979	56-39	60
Windfall Profits Tax	Dec. 17, 1979	84-14	60
Lubbers Nomination	April 21, 1980	46-60	60
Lubbers Nomination	April 22, 1980	62-34	60
Rights of Institutionalized	April 28, 1980	44-39	60
Rights of Institutionalized	April 29, 1980	56-34	60
Rights of Institutionalized	April 30, 1980	53-35	60
Rights of Institutionalized	May 1, 1980	60-34	60
Bottlers' Antitrust Immunity	May 15, 1980	86-6	60
Draft Registration Funding	June 10, 1980	62-32	60
Zimmerman Nomination	Aug. 1, 1980	51-35	60
Zimmerman Nomination	Aug. 4, 1980	45-31	60
Zimmerman Nomination	Aug. 5, 1980	63-31	60
Alaska Lands	Aug. 18, 1980	63-25	60
Vessel Tonnage/ Strip Mining	Aug. 21, 1980	61-32	60
Fair Housing Amendments	Dec. 3, 1980	51-39	60
Fair Housing Amendments	Dec. 4, 1980	62-32	60
Fair Housing Amendments	Dec. 9, 1980	54-43	60
Breyer Nomination	Dec. 9, 1980	68-28	60
Justice Department Authorization	July 10, 1981	38-48	60
Justice Department Authorization	July 13, 1981	54-32	60
Justice Department Authorization	July 29, 1981	59-37	60
Justice Department Authorization	Sept. 10, 1981	57-33	60
Justice Department Authorization	Sept. 16, 1981	61-36	60
Justice Department Authorization	Dec. 10, 1981	64-35	60
State, Justice, Commerce, Judiciary Appropriations	Dec. 11, 1981	59-35	60
Justice Department Authorization	Feb. 9, 1982	63-33	60
Broadcast Senate Proceedings	April 20, 1982	47-51	60
Criminal Code Reform Act	April 27, 1982	45-46	60
Urgent Supplemental Appropriations, Fiscal 1982	May 27, 1982	95-2	60
Voting Rights Act	June 15, 1982	86-8	60
Debt Limit Increase	Sept. 9, 1982	41-47	60
Debt Limit Increase	Sept. 13, 1982	45-35	60
Debt Limit Increase	Sept. 15, 1982	50-44	60
Debt Limit Increase	Sept. 20, 1982	50-39	60
Debt Limit Increase	Sept. 21, 1982	53-47	60
Debt Limit Increase	Sept. 22, 1982	54-46	60
Debt Limit Increase	Sept. 23, 1982	53-45	60
Antitrust Equal Enforcement Act	Dec. 2, 1982	38-58	60
Antitrust Equal Enforcement Act	Dec. 2, 1982	44-51	60
Transportation Assistance Act	Dec. 13, 1982	75-13	60
Transportation Assistance Act	Dec. 16, 1982	48-50	60
Transportation Assistance Act	Dec. 16, 1982	5-93	60

Issue	Date	Vote	Yeas Needed
Transportation Assistance Act	Dec. 19, 1982	89-5	60
Transportation Assistance Act	Dec. 20, 1982	87-8	60
Transportation Assistance Act	Dec. 23, 1982	81-5	60
Emergency Jobs Appropriations/ Interest Withholding	March 16, 1983	50-48	60
Emergency Jobs Appropriations/ Interest Withholding	March 16, 1983	59-39	60
International Trade and Investment/ Interest Withholding	April 19, 1983	34-53	60
International Trade and Investment/ Interest Withholding	April 19, 1983	39-59	60
Defense Authorizations, 1984	July 21, 1983	55-41	60
Radio Broadcasting to Cuba	Aug. 3, 1983	62-33	60
National Gas Policy Act	Nov. 3, 1983	86-7	60
Capital Punishment	Feb. 9, 1984	65-26	60
Hydroelectric Power Plants	July 30, 1984	60-28	60
Wilkinson Nomination	July 31, 1984	57-39	60
Agriculture Appropriations, Fiscal 1985	Aug. 6, 1984	54-31	60
Agriculture Appropriations, Fiscal 1985	Aug. 8, 1984	68-30	60
Wilkinson Nomination	Aug. 9, 1984	65-32	60
Financial Services Competitive Equity Act	Sept. 10, 1984	89-3	60
Financial Services Competitive Equity Act	Sept. 13, 1984	92-6	60
Broadcasting of Senate Procedures	Sept. 18, 1984	73-26	60
Broadcasting of Senate Procedures	Sept. 21, 1984	37-44	60
Surface Transportation and Uniform Relocation Assistance Act	Sept. 24, 1984	70-12	60
Continuing Appropriations	Sept. 29, 1984	92-4	60
Anti-Apartheid	July 10, 1985	88-8	60
Line-item veto	July 18, 1985	57-42	60
Line-item veto	July 23, 1985	57-41	60
Line-item veto	July 24, 1985	58-40	60
Anti-Apartheid	Sept. 9, 1985	53-34	60
Anti-Apartheid	Sept. 11, 1985	57-41	60
Anti-Apartheid	Sept. 12, 1985	11-88	60
Debt Limit/Balanced Budget	Oct. 6, 1985	57-38	64
Debt Limit/Balanced Budget	Oct. 9, 1985*	53-39	62
Conrail Sale	Jan. 23, 1986	90-7	60
Conrail Sale	Jan. 30, 1986	70-27	60
Fitzwater Nomination	March 18, 1986	64-33	60
Washington Airports Transfer	March 21, 1986	50-39	60
Washington Airports Transfer	March 25, 1986	66-32	60
Hobbs Act Amendments	April 16, 1986	44-54	60
Defense Authorization, Fiscal 1987	Aug. 6, 1986	53-46	60
Military Construction Appropriations, Fiscal 1987 (Aid to Contras)	Aug. 13, 1986	59-40	60
South Africa Sanctions	Aug. 13, 1986	89-11	60
Military Construction Appropriations, Fiscal 1987 (Aid to Contras)	Aug. 13, 1986	62-37	60
Rehnquist Nomination	Sept. 17, 1986	68-31	60
Product Liability Reform	Sept. 25, 1986	97-1	60
Omnibus Drug Bill	Oct. 15, 1986	58-38	60
Immigration Reform	Oct. 17, 1986	69-21	60
Contra Aid Moratorium	March 23, 1987	46-45	60
Contra Aid Moratorium	March 24, 1987	50-50	60
Contra Aid Moratorium	March 25, 1987	54-46	60
Relief for the Homeless	April 9, 1987	68-29	60
Defense Authorization, Fiscal 1988	May 15, 1987	52-36	60
Defense Authorization, Fiscal 1988	May 19, 1987	58-41	60
Defense Authorization, Fiscal 1988	May 20, 1987	59-39	60
Campaign Finance	June 9, 1987	52-47	60
Campaign Finance	June 16, 1987	49-46	60
Campaign Finance	June 17, 1987	51-47	60
Campaign Finance	June 18, 1987	50-47	60
Campaign Finance	June 19, 1987	45-43	60
Trade (Kuwaiti tanker reflagging)	July 9, 1987	57-42	60
Trade (Kuwaiti tanker reflagging)	July 14, 1987	53-40	60
Trade (Kuwaiti tanker reflagging)	July 15, 1987	54-44	60
Wells Nomination	Sept. 9, 1987	65-24	60
Campaign Finance	Sept. 10, 1987	53-42	60
Campaign Finance	Sept. 15, 1987	51-44	60
Defense Authorization, Fiscal 1988 (Kuwaiti tanker escort)	Oct. 1, 1987	54-45	60
Defense Authorization, Fiscal 1988	Oct. 1, 1987	41-58	60
Verity Nomination	Oct. 13, 1987	85-8	60
War Powers Compliance	Oct. 20, 1987	67-28	60
Energy and Water Appropriations (Nuclear Waste Depository)	Nov. 10, 1987	87-0	60
Campaign Finance	Feb. 26, 1988	53-41	60
Polygraph Protection	March 3, 1988	77-19	60
Intelligence Oversight	March 15, 1988	73-18	60
Risk Notification	March 23, 1988	33-59	60
Risk Notification	March 24, 1988	2-93	60
Risk Notification	March 28, 1988	41-44	60
Risk Notification	March 29, 1988	42-52	60
Campaign Spending Limitations	April 21, 1988	52-42	60
Campaign Spending Limitations	April 22, 1988	53-37	60
Extension of Immigration Legalization Program	April 28, 1988	40-56	60
Death Penalty for Drug-Related Killings	June 9, 1988	70-26	60
Great Smoky Mountain Wilderness Act	June 20, 1988	49-35	60
Great Smoky Mountain Wilderness Act	June 21, 1988	54-42	60
Plant-Closing Notification	June 29, 1988	58-39	60
Plant-Closing Notification	July 6, 1988	88-5	60
Textile Import Quotas	Sept. 7, 1988	68-29	60
Minimum Wage Restoration	Sept. 22, 1988	53-43	60
Minimum Wage Restoration	Sept. 23, 1988	56-35	60
Parental and Medical Leave	Oct. 3, 1988	85-6	60
Parental and Medical Leave	Oct. 7, 1988	50-46	60
Defense Authorization, Fiscal 1990	Aug. 2, 1989	84-13	60
Airline Smoking Ban	Sept. 14, 1989	77-21	60
Eastern Airlines Strike Commission	Oct. 3, 1989	61-36	60
Nicaraguan Election Aid	Oct. 13, 1989	52-42	60
Nicaraguan Election Aid	Oct. 17, 1989	74-25	60
Eastern Airlines Strike Commission	Oct. 26, 1989	62-38	60
Capital Gains Tax Cut	Nov. 14, 1989	51-47	60
Capital Gains Tax Cut	Nov. 15, 1989	51-47	60
Government Pay-and-Ethics Package	Nov. 17, 1989	90-9	60
Armenian Genocide Day of Remembrance	Feb. 22, 1990	49-49	60
Armenian Genocide Day of Remembrance	Feb. 27, 1990	48-51	60

Appendix

Issue	Date	Vote	Yeas Needed
Hatch Act Revisions	May 1, 1990	70-28	60
AIDS Emergency Relief	May 15, 1990	95-3	60
Chemical Weapons Sanctions	May 17, 1990	87-4	60
Omnibus Crime Package	June 5, 1990	54-37	60
Omnibus Crime Package	June 7, 1990	57-37	60
Air Travel Rights for the Blind	June 12, 1990	56-44	60
Civil Rights Act of 1990	July 17, 1990	62-38	60
Fiscal 1991 Defense Authorization	Aug. 3, 1990	58-41	60
Motor Vehicle Fuel Efficiency Act	Sept. 14, 1990	68-28	60
Motor Vehicle Fuel Efficiency Act	Sept. 25, 1990	57-42	60
Title X Family Planning Amendments	Sept. 26, 1990	50-46	60
National Motor-Voter Registration	Sept. 26, 1990	55-42	60
Fiscal 1991 Foreign Operations Appropriations	Oct. 12, 1990	51-38	60
Vertical Price Fixing	May 7, 1991	61-37	60
Vertical Price Fixing	May 8, 1991	63-35	60
Crime Bill	June 28, 1991	41-58	60
Crime Bill	July 10, 1991	56-43	60
Crime Bill	July 10, 1991	71-27	60
National Motor-Voter Registration	July 18, 1991	57-41	60
Fiscal 1992 VA-HUD Appropriations	July 18, 1991	57-40	60
National Motor-Voter Registration	July 18, 1991	59-40	60
Foreign Aid Authorization	July 24, 1991	87-10	60
Foreign Aid Authorization	July 25, 1991	52-44	60
Foreign Aid Authorization	July 25, 1991	63-33	60
Extended Unemployment Benefits	July 29, 1991	96-1	60
Fiscal 1992 Defense Authorization	Aug. 2, 1991	58-40	60
Fiscal 1992 Interior Appropriations	Sept. 19, 1991	55-41	60
Federal Facility Compliance Act	Oct. 17, 1991	85-14	60
Civil Rights Act	Oct. 22, 1991	93-4	60
National Energy Policy	Nov. 1, 1991	50-44	60
Banking Reform	Nov. 13, 1991	76-19	60
Iranian Hostage Release Investigation	Nov. 22, 1991	51-43	60
Crime Conference Report	Nov. 27, 1991	49-38	60
School Improvement Bill	Jan. 21, 1992	93-0	60
National Energy Strategy	Feb. 4, 1992	90-5	60
Joint Ventures Antitrust	Feb. 25, 1992	98-0	60
Lumbee Tribe Recognition	Feb. 27, 1992	58-39	60
Corp. for Public Broadcasting	March 3, 1992	87-7	60
Crime Bill	March 19, 1992	54-43	60
Defense/Domestic Spending Walls	March 26, 1992	50-48	60
NIH Reauthorization/ Fetal Tissue Research	March 31, 1992	98-2	60
Motor-Voter Bill	May 7, 1992	61-38	60
Motor-Voter Bill	May 12, 1992	58-40	60
Drug Abuse Mental Health	June 9, 1992	84-9	60
Striker Replacement	June 11, 1992	55-41	60
Striker Replacement	June 16, 1992	57-42	60
Gov't Sponsored Enterprises/ Balanced Budget Amendment	June 30, 1992	56-39	60
Gov't Sponsored Enterprises/ Balanced Budget Amendment	July 1, 1992	56-39	60
National Energy Strategy	July 23, 1992	58-33	60
National Energy Strategy	July 28, 1992	93-3	60
Edward Carnes Nomination	Sept. 9, 1992	66-30	60
Product Liability	Sept. 10, 1992	57-39	60
Product Liability	Sept. 10, 1992	58-38	60
School Improvement Bill	Sept. 15, 1992	85-6	60
Labor/HHS/ Education Appropriations	Sept. 16, 1992	56-38	60
START Treaty	Sept. 29, 1992	87-6	60
School Improvement Bill	Oct. 2, 1992	59-40	60
Crime Bill	Oct. 2, 1992	55-43	60
NIH Reauthorization/ Fetal Tissue Research	Oct. 2, 1992	85-12	60
National Energy Strategy	Oct. 8, 1992	84-8	60
Tax Bill	Oct. 8, 1992	80-10	60

* Vote was taken after midnight in the session that began Oct. 8, 1985.

Congressional Reapportionment

Redistricting for the 1990s 1145

Reapportionment History 1151

Redistricting for the 1990s

The U.S. Bureau of the Census, a division of the Department of Commerce, spent much of 1990 in the throes of counting the U.S. population for the 21st time since the founding of the Union. Its efforts, however, were called into question when a significant undercount became apparent.

Despite the problems with the original census, it was used to determine the distribution of House seats among the states for the 1990s. The redrawn congressional districts that resulted had a noticeable effect on the 1992 general election.

Census Undercount

The official 1990 census pegged the national population at 249,632,692 — an increase of more than 23 million (10.2 percent) over the 1980 total. The final tally, released Dec. 26, 1990, added about 4 million to the preliminary tally announced Aug. 29, 1990. After their release, the preliminary figures were subjected to four months of tabulation, review and legal challenges. They were mailed by the Census Bureau to 39,000 state and local governments, which had three weeks to provide evidence of error or omission by census enumerators.

The results of the first-ever "post-enumeration survey," released April 18, 1991, indicated that the 1990 census missed as many as 6.3 million people. Census Bureau officials made public June 13, 1991, new estimates that showed a net national undercount of 5.27 million or 2.1 percent. Furthermore, blacks were undercounted by 4.8 percent, American Indians by 5 percent and Hispanics by 5.2 percent.

Commerce Secretary Robert A. Mosbacher said July 15, 1991, however, that the Bush administration would not adjust the 1990 census to correct the undercount.

The General Accounting Office (GAO), an investigative arm of Congress, released a report Aug. 22, 1991, estimating that the 1990 census contained "a minimum of 14.1 million gross errors and perhaps as many as 25.7 million errors." These numbers included approximately 9.7 million persons uncounted altogether.

Response Problems

Census Bureau Director Barbara Everitt Bryant told Congress on April 19, 1990, that of the 106 million census questionnaires sent out by the bureau, only 63 percent were completed and returned. Census enumerators on April 26 began visiting households — many more than had been expected — that did not respond. The mail-in response rate for the 1980 count was 75 percent. Bryant said the dropoff generally seemed to be across the board, not confined to certain areas.

The bureau budgeted for a 70 percent response rate in 1990. Bryant estimated that each 1 percentage point shortfall in the targeted mail response rate increased follow-up costs by $10 million. For each percentage point of the population that failed to send back the questionnaire, enumerators had to visit 950,000 households, meaning census workers would have had to knock on 35.2 million doors to complete their constitutional mandate.

To improve the accuracy of the 1990 count, the Census Bureau said it put 90 percent of its promotional effort into reaching the 10 percent of the population that was most difficult to count. The bureau said it was involving more organizations, cities and people than ever before in determining the count.

Critics, however, pointed to numerous incidents and tactics to explain some of the bureau's problems. Rep. Charles E. Schumer, D-N.Y., for example, said the bureau refused to use New York City data to find residents who were doubled-up in public housing against regulations and might have been eager to avoid census-takers. He also complained that many residents who did not speak English probably did not respond because they had received questionnaires written in English and had to call a toll-free number to get one in another language.

State and Local Interests

State and local governments arguably had the greatest stake in an accurate count of each person within their borders. Apart from determining political representation, the head count fit into sometimes complex formulas for the distribution of federal funds, which totaled about $40 billion in the early 1990s.

After a decade of cuts in federal aid for housing, employment and other programs, no state wanted to be short shrifted in a national reckoning that would provide the basis for federal allocations over the next 10 years. As a result, local officials were the most critical of the 1990 census effort. Big-city mayors such as New York's David N. Dinkins and Houston's Kathy Whitmire worried that undercounting, particularly of hard-to-reach minority groups, would mean big losses in federal funds to the areas they represented.

The GAO estimated that 100 federal programs were doled out in part on the basis of census population data, including job training funds, Community Development Block Grants and Head Start. The Medicaid Assistance Program relied on per capita income data from the census to distribute 50 percent of its funds.

Members of Congress expected federal funds to follow population shifts from the Northeast and Midwest to the Sun Belt states. With undercounts in inner-city areas, that drop in funds could be exacerbated. Schumer said New

York City could lose more than $1 billion in federal aid because the census enumerators passed by many people, particularly illegal aliens.

Other followers of the census, though, said the problem was overstated. "There tends to be an exaggerated view of the importance of census data for federal aid," said Richard P. Nathan, provost of Rockefeller College of Public Affairs at the State University of New York and a researcher on state and local census issues. "Most of the big federal programs are open-ended matching grants." States that lost population would gain money under other programs, such as Community Development Block Grants, he said.

In addition, some federal programs offset population data with other factors, such as per capita income, or, in the case of transportation funding, a state's share of public road mileage. These factors could mitigate the impact of population losses on federal funds.

Winners and Losers

If Mosbacher had chosen adjustment, the House would have been reapportioned according to the totals released in June 1991. The survey results had been broken down by 1,392 combinations of demographic information, including age, gender, race and region. This processing eventually produced figures that could be projected to totals for each geographic area.

The states where the undercount was apparently worst corresponded with states with large immigration rates in the 1980s: California, Arizona, New Mexico and Texas. Among the eight cities with more than 1 million people, the final estimate showed the census to have been least accurate in Los Angeles. Adjustment would have set that city's population 5.1 percent higher than the original count. Philadelphia, however, would have found itself even worse off, proportionately, under adjustment. It was the city the survey found to have been undercounted the least (1.3 percent) among cities larger than 1 million. Philadelphia officials argued that about 130,000 people were missed, but the bureau estimated it missed only about 20,000. The revision found that the count in Washington, Baltimore, Dallas and Houston was off by about 5 percent; in San Diego and San Jose, Calif., by about 4 percent; in New York City and Phoenix, by 3 percent; and in Chicago, by 2.6 percent.

The new data were rife with political contradictions. The states that had gained most in the actual census — such as California, Texas, Florida and Arizona — would generally be even better off under an adjustment. Many of the states that wanted to force an adjustment — such as New York, Pennsylvania, Illinois and Michigan — would do worse if one were ordered.

Further complications developed because urban, suburban and rural jurisdictions within individual states would not fare the same under an adjustment. Generally speaking, cities would have done better under an adjustment and rural areas would have done worse.

If the census were adjusted, Pennsylvania would lose three House seats instead of the two it was slated to lose at the end of 1990. Wisconsin, which expected to stand pat with nine seats on the basis of the census, stood to lose one. The Pennsylvania seat would, in effect, go to Arizona, which was to gain a seat on the basis of the census. The new seat would bring the state's total to seven. Wisconsin's ninth seat would go to California, bringing that state's gain to eight seats for a delegation total of 53.

Census Adjustment

An undercount was nothing new. In 1980, the Census Bureau estimated that it counted about 99 percent of the white population but only about 94 percent of blacks. Calls for an adjusted count were not new either. Several cities with large minority populations sought but failed to win adjustment of the 1980 census count.

In 1987, the Commerce Department announced that it would not adjust the 1990 count, which fueled charges that the Republican administration was undercounting a Democratic constituency. A lawsuit was brought by New York City (along with other cities, states and civil rights groups) calling on the Census Bureau to make a statistical adjustment of the tally to account for people who were missed. In response to the lawsuit, the Commerce Department in 1989 agreed to defer a final judgment on the adjustment question until as late as mid-July 1991.

Early in 1990, the plaintiffs in the New York City case reopened their lawsuit to get the Commerce Department to draft new guidelines that would require the department to adjust the count in 1991, unless it could demonstrate that a statistical change would not be more accurate than the actual tally. In something of a split decision, a federal district court in New York ruled June 7 that an adjustment would be constitutional and that the Commerce Department would "clearly incur a heavier burden" to explain an anti-adjustment decision in 1991. But Judge Joseph M. McLaughlin also ruled that the Commerce Department's guidelines on the matter were not inadequate or biased.

The Census Bureau had agreed to do the post-enumeration survey as part of a 1989 settlement of a lawsuit brought against the Commerce Department by the nation's four largest cities (New York, Los Angeles, Chicago and Houston) and by New York state and Dade County (Miami), Fla. The plaintiffs alleged an undercount and asked for a post-census evaluative survey of 300,000 households, which could have provided enough detail at the local level to substitute for the full census count. The bureau, however, won agreement to a sample of 165,000. The case for adjusting the 1990 census thus became poised on whether 165,000 constituted an adequate sample size for evaluation.

Republicans generally opposed any deviation from the traditional, Constitution-based head count. They were buttressed by Democrats from states that stood to lose a House seat if the 1990 reapportionment were adjusted for the undercount. Furthermore, since the first census was taken, the federal government preferred the original head count over any later revision.

Democrats generally, however, sought to cast the question as a conflict between good and bad numbers. "The post-enumeration survey is telling us that the original census numbers are demonstrably wrong," said Tom Sawyer, D-Ohio, chairman of the Subcommittee on Census and Population.

Although characterizing himself as "deeply troubled" by the disproportionate undercount of racial minorities, Commerce Secretary Mosbacher decided that sticking with the original head count would be "fairest for all Americans." Mosbacher did not attempt to dispute the difference between minority and white undercounts, but he said he did not believe the census was "the appropriate vehicle" for addressing that inequity. In addition, he said the adjusted figures would not be accurate in the block-by-block detail needed for redistricting.

Status of Redistricting

As a result of the 1990 census, 43 of the 50 states were required to draw new House district boundaries. The number of House seats assigned for the 1990s appears after the name of the state, and the number of seats gained or lost in 1990 reapportionment is in parenthesis.

Alabama 7
Map issued by federal court Jan. 27, 1992; that map became law March 27, after a map passed by the legislature was rejected by the Justice Department.

Arizona 6 (+1)
Map issued by federal court May 6, 1992.

Arkansas 4
Map passed legislature March 26, 1991; governor signed April 10. Federal court upheld map Nov. 15; Supreme Court upheld map June 1, 1992.

California 52 (+7)
Map drawn by a special panel of retired judges approved by state Supreme Court Jan. 27, 1992; federal court Jan. 28 rejected an effort to block use of that map in 1992 pending appeal. A federal appeals court March 3 dismissed a challenge to the map.

Colorado 6
Map passed legislature March 19, 1992; governor signed March 24.

Connecticut 6
Redistricting commission filed map with secretary of state Nov. 27, 1991; governor's signature not required.

Florida 23 (+4)
Federal court approved map May 29, 1992.

Georgia 11 (+1)
Map passed legislature March 31, 1992; governor signed March 31; Justice Department approved April 2.

Hawaii 2
Map adopted by commission July 19, 1991; governor's signature not required.

Idaho 2
Map passed legislature Jan. 21, 1992; governor signed Jan. 28.

Illinois 20 (−2)
Legislature failed to act by June 30, 1991, deadline. Federal court approved map Nov. 6.

Indiana 10
Map passed legislature June 13, 1991; governor signed June 14.

Iowa 5 (−1)
Map passed legislature May 11, 1991; governor signed May 30.

Kansas 4 (−1)
Map passed legislature May 7, 1992; governor signed May 11. Federal court finalized map with minor changes June 3.

Kentucky 6 (−1)
Map passed legislature Dec. 18, 1991; governor signed Dec. 20.

Louisiana 7 (−1)
Map passed legislature May 26, 1992; governor signed June 1. Justice Department approved July 6.

Maine 2
Legislature to consider redistricting in its 1993 session; the 1992 House elections ran under the existing map.

Maryland 8
Map passed legislature Oct. 22, 1991; governor signed Oct. 23.

Massachusetts 10 (−1)
Map passed legislature July 8, 1992; governor signed July 9.

Michigan 16 (−2)
Federal court issued map March 23, 1992.

Minnesota 8
Map passed legislature Jan. 9, 1992; vetoed by governor Jan. 10. Federal court issued map Feb. 19.

Mississippi 5
Map passed legislature Dec. 20, 1991; governor signed Dec. 20. Justice Department approved Feb. 21, 1992.

Missouri 9
Map passed legislature May 16, 1991; governor signed July 8.

Nebraska 3
Map passed legislature June 5, 1991; governor signed June 10.

Nevada 2
Map passed legislature June 11, 1991; governor signed June 20.

New Hampshire 2
Map passed legislature March 24, 1992; governor signed March 27. Justice Department approved June 12.

New Jersey 13 (−1)
Legislature established bipartisan commission Jan. 13, 1992; commission issued map March 20.

New Mexico 3
Map passed legislature Sept. 18, 1991; governor signed Oct. 4.

New York 31 (−3)
Map passed legislature June 9, 1992; governor signed June 11. Justice Department approved July 2.

North Carolina 12 (+1)
Map passed legislature Jan. 24, 1992; Justice Department approved Feb. 6.

Ohio 19 (−2)
Map passed legislature March 26, 1992; governor signed March 27.

Oklahoma 6
Map passed legislature May 24, 1991; governor signed May 27.

Oregon 5
Federal court approved map Dec. 2, 1991; map became law Dec. 16, after legislature failed to act.

Pennsylvania 21 (−2)
Commonwealth court judge issued map Feb. 24, 1992; state Supreme Court approved it March 10.

Rhode Island 2
Map passed legislature May 14, 1992; no action taken by governor; map became law May 22.

South Carolina 6
Federal court issued map May 1, 1992.

Tennessee 9
Map passed legislature May 6, 1992; governor signed May 7.

Texas 30 (+3)
Map passed legislature Aug. 25, 1991; governor signed Aug. 29. Justice Department approved Nov. 18. Federal court upheld map Dec. 24.

Utah 3
Map passed legislature Oct. 31, 1991; governor signed Nov. 8.

Virginia 11 (+1)
Map passed legislature Dec. 9, 1991; governor signed Dec. 11. Justice Department approved Feb. 18, 1992.

Washington 9 (+1)
Redistricting commission map became law Feb. 12, 1992.

West Virginia 3 (−1)
Map passed legislature Oct. 11, 1991; governor signed Oct. 12. Federal court upheld map Jan. 7, 1992.

Wisconsin 9
Map passed legislature April 14, 1992; governor signed April 28.

Note: Summary reflects redistricting action taken as of Oct. 24, 1992. The states with one House seat are Alaska, Delaware, Montana, North Dakota, South Dakota, Vermont and Wyoming. The remaps of Alabama, Arizona, California, Florida, Georgia, Louisiana, Michigan, Mississippi, New Hampshire, New York, North Carolina, South Carolina, Texas and Virginia must be reviewed by the Justice Department under Voting Rights Act provisions. Federal court-drawn maps, however, are not subject to Justice review.

Mosbacher's political task was made no easier when Census Director Bryant announced that her recommendation to him had been in favor of adjustment. That news came after it was learned that the bureau's internal panel, the Undercount Steering Committee, had voted 7-2 in favor of adjusting. Bryant made clear that she saw every flaw in the post-census survey data that Mosbacher did, but she said her judgment was that the minority undercount was severe enough to require redress.

Beyond seeking judicial recourse, states and communities sought to increase their share of federal funds by altering the census-based formulas by which the funds were distributed. Mosbacher said the administration might support some adjustment to census figures for distributing federal dollars.

States and communities tried to obtain the figures Commerce would have used for an adjustment had Mosbacher ordered one. For example, a lawsuit was filed under the Freedom of Information Act by California state legislators. Possession of the numbers could enable states to perform their own internal census adjustment before distributing funds within their states. Depending on their constitutions, some states also could have used adjusted numbers in their own redistricting. But the Commerce Department refused to release the figures.

In trying to obtain the figures for his subcommittee, Sawyer gave Mosbacher a deadline of Sept. 30, 1991. On that day, Sawyer got a letter from Mosbacher reiterating the secretary's opposition to adjustment and asking why Sawyer thought the subcommittee had any use for the numbers. Mosbacher's letter said the revised numbers were only useful for redrawing district lines for congressional and legislative elections. "The department has already released the official figures intended for redistricting," Mosbacher wrote. "Release of the rejected adjusted figures would serve no useful purpose and would only confuse the public and disrupt and distort the redistricting process."

The confrontation led Sawyer's subcommittee to issue a subpoena Nov. 19 ordering Mosbacher to release all the Census Bureau's computer tapes relating to adjustment. When Mosbacher did not comply, he was ordered to appear before the subcommittee Dec. 10 and explain himself.

Mosbacher did not show up, sending a deputy who said the subcommittee's subpoena had been issued improperly. In the meantime, a court in New York had ordered a partial release of the adjustment data, and Commerce officials had offered to release half of all the data to the subcommittee if that data could be kept confidential.

On Jan. 9, 1992, Sawyer announced that he had reached an agreement with Commerce that called for the release of half the data. Sawyer said Mosbacher had dropped his insistence on confidentiality. "With all due respect to the secretary," Sawyer said, "he was just plain wrong in trying to withhold these numbers."

Court Action

The pro-adjustment lawsuit filed by New York City and 31 other plaintiffs in 1987 was still pending in federal court in Brooklyn when Mosbacher refused to adjust on July 15, and fresh briefs were being filed in that case before the week was out. Suits also were filed in federal courts in Georgia and Illinois.

The federal judge in the New York case, McLaughlin, had been elevated from the district bench to the Federal Court of Appeals for the Second Circuit (also in New York). But he chose to carry the census case with him. Justice Department lawyers representing Mosbacher asked McLaughlin not to hold a new trial but to rule on the evidence and record already accumulated. Without a trial, the plaintiffs' attorneys would not be entitled to dig through the most recent Commerce and Census Bureau files and records under pretrial discovery rules.

The governments suing along with New York City to gain a correction were Chicago; Cleveland; Denver; Houston; Inglewood, Calif.; Los Angeles; New Orleans; Oakland, Calif.; Pasadena, Calif.; Philadelphia; Phoenix; San Antonio; San Francisco; Broward and Dade counties in Florida; and five states: California, Florida, New Jersey, New York and Texas. Also suing were the U.S. Conference of Mayors, the League of United Latin American Citizens, the National League of Cities, the National Association for the Advancement of Colored People and several individuals.

On April 13, 1993, McLaughlin let stand the unadjusted Census Bureau count as the official basis for apportioning House seats. He said Mosbacher probably erred in refusing to adjust the count, but it was too late to overturn the decision. McLaughlin said no evidence existed that Mosbacher acted in an "arbitrary and capricious" manner.

Besides judicial relief, another potential recourse for advocates of adjustment was in legislative remedies. Legislation was enacted in 1991 that called for a study of the census-taking process to determine more timely and accurate methods of counting the population in the future. However, congressional efforts to force a census adjustment went nowhere. *(102nd Congress action, p. 895)*

1992 General Election

Compared with other issues that affected the 1992 House elections — the economy, the House bank scandal, the widespread anti-incumbent sentiment, the presidential election — redistricting received little attention. However, in dozens of districts across the country, the once-a-decade redrawing of House boundary lines had a direct and substantial impact on the outcome Nov. 3 — shaping not only which party won a district but also, in numerous cases, which racial or ethnic group prevailed.

Partisan Impact

At the outset of the 1992 campaign cycle, national Republican strategists counted on remap ripple effects to boost their efforts to cut into — and perhaps even overturn — the 38-year hold Democrats had on the House majority. Their hopes were predicated on two presumptions:

(1) The national reapportionment, based on the 1990 census, took 19 House seats away from 13 slow-growing states — mostly in strong Democratic areas of the Northeast and Midwest. Those seats were shifted to eight states, mainly in the conservative-leaning South and West, where population soared in the 1980s. This movement, Republicans reasoned, could not help but benefit them.

(2) Beyond the incumbents who saw their districts disappear because of population trends, others were displaced by the state-by-state effort to comply with the Voting Rights Act (as amended in 1982), which required increased minority-group representation in the House. The fashioning of new black- and Hispanic-majority districts from the constituencies of urban Democrats would force incumbents to seek re-election in mostly white suburban

districts where they would be vulnerable to Republican challenge and where many voters would be new to them.

The GOP's hopes for major gains resulting from redistricting were frustrated, however. The party's failure to capitalize on the redrawn boundaries was a factor in its meager nine-seat House pickup, which hardly put a dent in the Democrats' 100-seat majority. Furthermore, the presidential campaign proved to be a negative backdrop for many Republican House candidates, particularly in high-growth Western states, where President George Bush scored poorly and Democratic challenger Bill Clinton ran well — a reverse of the top-of-the-ticket situation that prevailed for nearly a generation.

Pre-Emptive Strikes

In several states, Republicans were thwarted in their desire to benefit from redistricting in the mapmaking process, long before any votes were cast.

In Texas, for example, the state's three-seat gain was earmarked for expanding minority representation. Republicans were certain this would hurt at least a few Democratic incumbents who relied on the Democratic voting habits of minority-group constituents. But state Democrats, who controlled the legislature and governorship, enacted an intricate map that created two new Hispanic-majority districts and one new black-majority seat and still managed to maintain Democratic voter advantages for the party's remaining incumbents. Several Texas Democrats faced tough general election contests, but for reasons other than redistricting.

In North Carolina, Republican strategists outsmarted themselves. The Democratic-controlled legislature passed a plan that ceded the state's new House seat to the Republicans while creating a black-majority 1st District. But GOP officials backed successful efforts by minority activists to persuade the Justice Department to order the state to create a second majority-minority district. Given a second shot, the legislature kept the black-majority 1st and crafted an oddly shaped, black-majority 12th District — in the process eliminating the hoped-for new Republican seat.

In California, Republicans thought they had scored a coup: GOP Gov. Pete Wilson vetoed a Democratic-drawn redistricting plan, arguing that it did not go far enough in undoing a gerrymandered map that gave Democrats a decade of unshakable dominance in the delegation. As a result, the remap fell to the Republican-dominated state Supreme Court, which said its mandate was to restore partisan competition to the state's House elections.

The district boundaries were drastically revised, but the judges may have provided more competition than Republicans would have wished. While three of the new districts (the 10th, 25th and 41st) clearly were in the Republican fold and one district — the Hispanic-majority 33rd — would go securely for the Democratic candidate, the remaining three (the 11th, 43rd, and 49th) could not easily be assigned to one party or the other. On election day, Democrats took the 49th and appeared to have won the 43rd, but the Republican candidate was named the winner on a recount. Republicans had set their sights on taking at least five of the new seats, which they did, but not without a struggle.

In addition, the court reshaped the map so that some incumbents of both parties were put at risk. Democrats Vic Fazio, Anthony C. Beilenson and Richard H. Lehman were in challenging races mainly because of redistricting, as was Republican Elton Gallegly. (All won re-election.) Republican Rep. Robert J. Lagomarsino lost much of his political base in the remap, then lost a GOP primary to businessman Michael Huffington, who won narrowly in November.

Incumbents Displaced

As the GOP anticipated, most of the incumbents displaced by redistricting were Democrats. But even as party strategists and media pundits trumpeted predictions of an anti-incumbent mood that would "clean House," the advantages of incumbency still proved strong for most members seeking re-election — even those who had to run on new playing fields because of redistricting changes. Just a handful of unseated members could blame their defeats directly on redistricting.

For instance, in Illinois — which lost two House seats and created a new Hispanic-majority district — Democratic Reps. Marty Russo and Terry L. Bruce lost redistricting-forced primary matchups with other Democratic incumbents (William O. Lipinski and Glenn Poshard, respectively); veteran Democratic Rep. Frank Annunzio retired, thus avoiding having to run against a colleague, Ways and Means Committee Chairman Dan Rostenkowski. Georgia Democratic Rep. Richard Ray, facing thousands of new voters in a drastically revamped 3rd District, lost to Republican Mac Collins. Alabama's new map made Ben Erdreich, D, an instant re-election underdog. Most of the city of Birmingham was transferred to the new black-majority 7th District, leaving Erdreich with the suburban-exurban 6th, which was mainly white and more conservative. He was defeated at the polls. Joan Kelly Horn, D-Mo., winner by a razor-thin margin in 1990, lost just a little Democratic turf in redistricting, but she had none to spare. She lost by nearly 9,000 votes.

In all, there were four incumbent-incumbent primary matchups: Democrats Russo and Bruce faced Lipinski and Poshard in Illinois; Democrat Harley O. Staggers Jr. lost to Democrat Alan B. Mollohan in West Virginia; and Ohio Republican Clarence E. Miller narrowly lost to Republican Bob McEwen. The McEwen-Miller primary in Ohio's 6th District was a bitter fight in which Miller harped on McEwen's 166 House bank overdrafts. McEwen survived but was badly weakened and lost Nov. 3 to Democrat Ted Strickland. Another incumbent brought down by a combination of unfavorable new lines and House bank overdrafts was Massachusetts Democrat Joseph D. Early, who lost to GOP state Rep. Peter I. Blute.

Five members were victims in incumbent-incumbent general election matchups. In Maryland's 1st District, Democratic Rep. Tom McMillen lost to GOP Rep. Wayne T. Gilchrest in a face-off forced when their districts were merged to make way for a new black-majority seat in the Washington, D.C., suburbs. In Louisiana, creation of the new black-majority 4th District resulted in Democrat Jerry Huckaby entering into a campaign against Republican Rep. Jim McCrery in the 5th District; Huckaby lost. Iowa Democrat Dave Nagle lost to GOP Rep. Jim Nussle in the 2nd District; Republican Ron Marlenee lost to Democrat Pat Williams in Montana's at-large district; and Republican Clyde C. Holloway was defeated by GOP colleague Richard H. Baker in Louisiana's 6th District.

Incumbents undone by redistricting were outnumbered by those (mostly Democrats) who survived even though remapping dealt them a bad hand. Democrats Richard H. Lehman of California's 19th District, Bob Carr of Michigan's 8th District and Gary L. Ackerman of New York's 5th District all eked out re-election victories; Iowa

Republican Rep. Jim Ross Lightfoot, at a disadvantage throughout his campaign in the drastically redrawn 3rd District, also won narrowly.

Other seemingly map-threatened members won by more comfortable margins. This group included Maryland Democratic Rep. Steny H. Hoyer, the chairman of the House Democratic Caucus. Hoyer lost most of his black constituent base to the new black-majority 4th District; much of the redrawn 5th District where he ran was new to him and more conservative than his old territory. But Hoyer fended off a strong challenge from Republican Lawrence J. Hogan Jr.

Another House Democratic leader put at risk by redistricting was Vic Fazio, chairman of the Democratic Congressional Campaign Committee. He took 51 percent in California's conservative-leaning 3rd District.

Minority Districts

In compliance with the Voting Rights Act, seventeen new "majority-minority" districts were created in the 1990 reapportionment. They were made from the dramatically reshaped districts of white incumbents — mainly Democrats who had large black or Hispanic constituencies. Those incumbents largely were left running in less Democratic (and often more suburban) districts where they appeared more vulnerable to Republican challenge.

But the GOP fell short of expectations for picking off white Democrats wounded in the process of drawing new minority districts. Only three Democratic incumbents had defeats directly attributable to the creation of new majority-minority districts: Alabama's Erdreich, Maryland's McMillan and Louisana's Huckaby.

Republicans also were thwarted in other states where they hoped for ripple-effect gains. In most of these, Democrats had controlled the redistricting process and skillfully crafted new black- and Hispanic-majority districts in ways that did not ruin the re-election prospects of white Democratic incumbents.

In North Carolina, the Democratic House delegation added two new black members, Eva Clayton and Melvin Watt, who won in districts designed to their advantages. However, all six of the state's white Democratic incumbents also won re-election, including Tim Valentine and Stephen L. Neal. They were considered at risk because redistricting deprived them of so many black constituents.

In Texas, the Democratic-controlled state legislature protected the partisan interests of Democratic House incumbents while creating three new majority-minority districts. Democratic Rep. Martin Frost was expected to be hurt by the drafting of a new black-majority district in Dallas and its environs, but Frost — who helped design the redistricting plan — won re-election with 60 percent of the vote. Of 19 Democratic House incumbents in Texas, the only loser was Albert G. Bustamante, who was burdened by allegations of ethical misconduct.

Sometimes map-drawers went to extraordinary lengths to meet the goal of greater minority empowerment, abandoning the traditional approach of drawing compact districts made up of contiguous territory. Under that approach, districts with majorities of minority-group residents tended to be confined within black or Hispanic urban concentrations. But in the 1990s round of redistricting, numerous states, following the direction of the federal courts and the Justice Department, created majority-minority districts in rough proportion to a state's minority-group population. Several states achieved that by tortuously connecting territory from districts held by several House incumbents to link widely separated communities of minority residents.

In New York City, for example, the new 12th District meandered from the Lower East Side of Manhattan through parts of Brooklyn until it terminated in Queens; Hispanic residents were a majority of the 12th. Democratic Rep. Stephen J. Solarz, whose Brooklyn district was cut up in the process, ran in the 12th but lost the primary to Puerto Rican activist Nydia M. Velazquez, who went on to win the general election commandingly. At the Queens end, Rep. Gary L. Ackerman — who had an urbanized, safely Democratic district for the past decade — lost most of his Hispanic constituency. He ran, and won, in a partisan "swing" district, the mainly suburban 5th.

GOP Bright Spots

Although nationally the GOP failed to make the redistricting-related House gains it expected in 1992, some bright spots existed for the party.

Republicans cracked the longtime Democratic hegemony in Georgia's House delegation with the unexpected help of a Democratic-drawn redistricting plan. The remap's author, state House Speaker Thomas B. Murphy, sought primarily to displace House Minority Whip Newt Gingrich. But in dismantling Gingrich's old district, the new map also disadvantaged Democratic Rep. Ray and left another suburban Atlanta district up for grabs. Ray lost; Republican John Linder narrowly won the redrawn 4th District; and Gingrich, despite tough primary and general election competition, won again. Republicans also picked up the open 1st District, which lost black voters to the new, black-majority 11th (won by Democrat Cynthia McKinney).

Republicans also have reason to hope for a "timed-release" effect in some districts over the course of the next decade. Some Democratic incumbents clearly find themselves in politically marginal districts and are likely to be targeted in coming years. California's Fazio and Lehman fall into this category.

Despite creation of new majority-minority districts, some voters re-elected white incumbents. In Texas' 29th District, for example, Democrats narrowly nominated popular Anglo state Sen. Gene Green over a Hispanic opponent in the primary. But if Hispanic voter registration grows, Green could find fending off Hispanic candidates difficult.

In California, three new Hispanic-majority districts were created in addition to the 33rd. Partly because Hispanics as a group had a low voter-participation rate, these districts re-elected Anglo Democratic incumbents Howard L. Berman and Calvin Dooley, and Republican Robert K. Dornan, one of Congress' most outspoken white conservatives. But if political participation by Hispanics grows during the 1990s, so too will the chances for Hispanic candidates to win those districts.

Also, some redistricting maneuvers that looked like shrewd partisanship could bring unintended consequences in future elections. While the Democratic-drawn map in North Carolina elected two new black Democrats in 1992, it deprived Democratic Reps. Valentine and Neal of large portions of their overwhelmingly Democratic black constituent bases. Their now conservative-leaning districts could turn over if the national political pendulum swings back to favor Republicans, or if the seats become open sometime during the 1990s.

Reapportionment History

Reapportionment, the redistribution of the 435 seats in the U.S. House of Representatives among the states to reflect shifts in population, and redistricting, the redrawing of congressional district boundaries within the states, are among the most important processes in the U.S. political system. They help to determine whether the House will be dominated by Democrats or Republicans, liberals or conservatives, and whether racial or ethnic minorities receive fair representation.

Reapportionment and redistricting occur every 10 years on the basis of the decennial population census. States where populations grew quickly during the previous 10 years gain congressional seats, while those that lost population or grew much more slowly than the national average lose seats. The number of House members for the rest of the states remains the same.

The states that gain or lose seats must usually make extensive changes in their congressional maps. Even those states with stable delegations must make modifications that account for population shifts within their boundaries, in accordance with Supreme Court "one-person, one-vote" rulings.

Despite their importance to the political process, reapportionment and redistricting draw little interest from the general public. In most states, the state legislatures are responsible for drawing up and enacting the new district map. The majority party in each state legislature is thus often in a position to draw a congressional district map that enhances the fortunes of its incumbents and candidates at the expense of the opposing party. Partisan interests are enhanced, personal ambitions of powerful politicians are furthered. Incumbents are protected or politically crippled.

Among the many unique features of the Constitution, as fashioned in 1787, was a national legislative body whose membership was to be elected by the people and apportioned on the basis of population. In keeping with the nature of the document, however, only fundamental rules and regulations were provided. The interpretation and implementation of the instructions were left to future generations.

Within this flexible framework many questions soon arose. How large was the House of Representatives to be? What mathematical formula was to be used in calculating the distribution of seats among the various states? Were the representatives to be elected at large or by districts? If by districts, what standards should be used in fixing their boundaries? Congress and the courts have been wrestling with these questions for more than 200 years.

Until the mid-20th century, such questions generally remained in the hands of the legislators. But with the population increasingly concentrated in urban areas, variations in populations among rural and urban districts in a single state grew more and more pronounced. Efforts to persuade Congress to address the issue of heavily populated but underrepresented areas proved unsuccessful. Legislators from rural areas were so intent on preventing power from slipping from their hands that they managed to block reapportionment of the House after the 1920 census.

Not long afterward, litigants tried to persuade the Supreme Court to order the states to revise congressional district boundaries in line with population shifts. A breakthrough finally occurred in 1964 in the case of *Wesberry v. Sanders,* when the Court declared that the Constitution required that "as nearly as practicable, one man's vote in a congressional election is to be worth as much as another's."

In the years that followed, the Court repeatedly reaffirmed its one-person, one-vote requirement. Following the 1980 census, several states adopted new maps that had districts of nearly equal population but that disregarded other traditional factors — such as the compactness of the district or the integrity of county and city lines. In *Karcher v. Daggett* in 1983 the Court held that no deviation from the one-person, one-vote principle was permissible unless the state proved that the population variation was necessary to achieve some legitimate goal. So long as they were equal in population, these districts — drawn to serve political interests — seemed unassailable in the courts until 1986, when a slim majority of the Supreme Court held in *Davis v. Bandemer* that redistricting was subject to constitutional review by federal courts.

Early History

Modern legislative bodies are descended from the councils of feudal lords and gentry that medieval kings summoned for the purpose of raising revenues and armies. The councils represented only certain groups of people, such as the nobility, the clergy, the landed gentry and town merchants; the notion of equal representation for equal numbers of people or even for all groups of people had not yet begun to develop.

Beginning as little more than administrative and advisory arms of the throne, royal councils in time developed into lawmaking bodies and acquired powers that eventually eclipsed those of the monarchs they served. In England, the king's council became Parliament, with the higher nobility and clergy making up the House of Lords and representatives of the gentry and merchants making up the House of Commons. The power struggle between king and council climaxed in the mid-1600s, when the king was executed and a "benevolent" dictatorship was set up under Oliver Cromwell. Although the monarchy was soon restored, by 1800 Parliament was clearly the more powerful branch of government.

During the 18th and early 19th centuries, as the power of Parliament grew, the English became increasingly concerned about the "representativeness" of their system of apportionment. Newly developing industrial cities had no more representation in the House of Commons than almost deserted country towns. Small constituencies were bought and sold. Men from these "rotten boroughs" often were sent to Parliament representing a single "patron" landowner or clique of wealthy men. It was not until the Reform Act of 1832 that Parliament curbed such excesses and turned toward a representative system based on population.

The growth of the powers of Parliament, as well as the development of English ideas of representation during the 17th and 18th centuries, had a profound effect on the colonists in America. Representative assemblies were unifying forces behind the breakaway of the colonies from England and the establishment of the newly independent nation.

Colonists in America generally modeled their legislatures after England's, using both population and land units as bases for apportionment. Patterns of early representation varied. "Nowhere did representation bear any uniform relation to the number of electors. Here and there the factor of size had been crudely recognized," Robert Luce noted in his book *Legislative Principles.*

The Continental Congress, with representation from every colony, proclaimed in the Declaration of Independence in 1776 that governments derive "their just powers from the consent of the governed" and that "the right of representation in the legislature" is an "inestimable right" of the people. The Constitutional Convention of 1787 included representatives from all the states. However, in neither of these bodies were the state delegations or voting powers proportional to population.

In New England, the town was usually the basis for representation. In the Middle Atlantic region, the county frequently was used. Virginia used the county with additional representation for specified cities. In many areas, towns and counties were fairly equal in population, and territorial representation afforded roughly equal representation for equal numbers of people. Delaware's three counties, for example, were of almost equal population and had the same representation in the legislature. But, in Virginia, the disparity was enormous (from 951 people in one county to 22,015 in another). Thomas Jefferson criticized the state's constitution on the ground that "among those who share the representation, the shares are unequal."

Intentions of the Founding Fathers

In the book *Congressional Districting,* Andrew Hacker said that to understand what the framers of the Constitution had in mind when they drew up the section concerning the House of Representatives, it was necessary to study closely several sources: the Constitution itself, the recorded discussions and debates at the Constitutional Convention, *The Federalist Papers* (essays written by Alexander Hamilton, John Jay and James Madison in defense of the Constitution) and the deliberations of the states' ratifying conventions.

The Constitution declares only that each state is to be allotted a certain number of representatives. It does not state specifically that congressional districts must be equal or nearly equal in population. Nor does it explicitly require that a state create districts at all. However, it seems clear that the first clause of Article I, Section 2, providing that House members should be chosen "by the people of the several states," indicates that the House of Representatives, in contrast to the Senate, was to represent people instead of states. "It follows," Hacker wrote, "that if the states are to have equal representation in the upper chamber, then individuals are to be equally represented in the lower body."

The third clause of Article I, Section 2 provided that congressional apportionment among the states must be according to population. "There is little point in giving the states congressmen 'according to their respective numbers' if the states do not redistribute the members of their delegations on the same principle," Andrew Hacker argued. "For representatives are not the property of the states, as are the senators, but rather belong to the people who happen to reside within the boundaries of those states. Thus, each citizen has a claim to be regarded as a political unit equal in value to his neighbors."

The issue of unequal representation arose only once during debate in the Constitutional Convention. The occasion was Madison's defense of Article I, Section 4 of the proposed Constitution, giving Congress the power to override state regulations on "the times ... and manner" of holding elections for members of Congress. Madison's argument related to the fact that many state legislatures of the time were badly malapportioned: "The inequality of the representation in the legislatures of particular states would produce a like inequality in their representation in the national legislature, as it was presumable that the counties having the power in the former case would secure it to themselves in the latter."

The implication was that states would create congressional districts and that unequal districting was undesirable and should be prevented.

Madison made this interpretation even more clear in his contributions to the *Federalist*. Arguing in favor of the relatively small size of the projected House of Representatives, he wrote in No. 56: "Divide the largest state into 10 or twelve districts and it will be found that there will be no peculiar local interests ... which will not be within the knowledge of the Representative of the district."

In the same paper, Madison said, "The Representatives of each state will not only bring with them a considerable knowledge of its laws, and a local knowledge of their respective districts, but will probably in all cases have been members, and may even at the very time be members, of the state legislature, where all the local information and interests of the state are assembled, and from whence they may easily be conveyed by a very few hands into the legislature of the United States." And, finally, in the *Federalist* No. 57, Madison stated that "each Representative of the United States will be elected by five or six thousand citizens." In making these arguments, Madison seems to have assumed that all or most representatives would be elected by districts, not at large.

In the states' ratifying conventions, the grant to Congress by Article I, Section 4 of ultimate jurisdiction over the "times, places and manner of holding elections" (except the places of choosing senators) held the attention of many delegates. There were differences over the merits of this section, but no justification of unequal districts was prominently used to attack the grant of power. Further evidence that individual districts were the intention of the Founding Fathers was given in the New York ratifying convention, when Alexander Hamilton said, "The natural and proper mode of holding elections will be to divide the state into districts in proportion to the number to be elected. This state will consequently be divided at first into six."

From his study of the sources relating to the question of congressional districting, Hacker concluded: "There is, then, a good deal of evidence that those who framed and ratified the Constitution intended that the House of Representatives have as its constituency a public in which the votes of all citizens were of equal weight. . . . The House of Representatives was designed to be a popular chamber, giving the same electoral power to all who had the vote. And the concern of Madison . . . that districts be equal in size was an institutional step in the direction of securing this democratic principle."

Reapportionment of Seats

Article I, Section 2, Clause 3 of the Constitution laid down the basic rules for apportionment and reapportionment of seats in the House of Representatives: "Representatives . . . shall be apportioned among the several States which may be included in the Union, according to their respective Numbers, which shall be determined by adding to the whole Number of free Persons, including those Bound to Service for a Term of Years, and excluding Indians not taxed, three-fifths of all other Persons. The actual Enumeration shall be made within three Years after the first Meeting of the Congress of the United States, and within every subsequent Term of Ten years, in such manner as they shall by Law direct. The number of Representatives shall not exceed one for every thirty Thousand, but each state shall have at least one Representative."

The Constitution made the first apportionment, which was to remain in effect until the first census was taken. No reliable figures on the population were available at the time. The Constitution's apportionment yielded a sixty-five member House. The seats were allotted among the 13 states as follows: New Hampshire, three; Massachusetts, eight; Rhode Island and Providence Plantations, one; Connecticut, five; New York, six; New Jersey, four; Pennsylvania, eight; Delaware, one; Maryland, six; Virginia, 10; North Carolina, five; South Carolina, five; and Georgia, three. This apportionment remained in effect during the 1st and 2nd Congresses (1789-93).

Apparently realizing that apportionment of the House was likely to become a major bone of contention, the 1st Congress submitted to the states a proposed constitutional amendment containing a formula to be used in future reapportionments. The amendment, which was not ratified, provided that following the taking of a decennial census one representative would be allotted for every 30,000 people until the House membership reached 100. Once that level was reached, there would be one representative for every 40,000 people until the House membership reached 200, when there would be one representative for every 50,000 people.

First Apportionment by Congress

The states' refusal to ratify the reapportionment formula amendment forced Congress to enact apportionment legislation after the first census was taken in 1790. The first apportionment bill was sent to the president in March 1792. President George Washington sent the bill back to Congress without his signature — the first presidential veto.

The bill had incorporated the constitutional minimum of 30,000 as the size of each district. But the population of each state was not a simple multiple of 30,000; significant fractions were left over. For example, Vermont was found to be entitled to 2.851 representatives, New Jersey to 5.98, and Virginia to 21.018. A formula had to be found that would deal in the fairest possible manner with unavoidable variations from exact equality.

Accordingly, Congress proposed in the first apportionment bill to distribute the members on a fixed ratio of one representative for each 30,000 inhabitants and to give an additional member to each state with a fraction exceeding one-half. Washington's veto was based on the belief that eight states would receive more than one representative for each 30,000 people under this formula.

A motion to override the veto was unsuccessful. A new bill meeting the president's objections, approved on April 14, 1792, provided for a ratio of one member for every 33,000 inhabitants and fixed the exact number of representatives to which each state was entitled. The total membership of the House was to be 105. In dividing the population of the various states by 33,000, all remainders were to be disregarded. Thomas Jefferson devised the solution, known as the method of rejected fractions.

Jefferson's Method

Jefferson's method of reapportionment resulted in great inequalities among districts. A Vermont district would contain 42,766 inhabitants, a New Jersey district 35,911, and a Virginia district only 33,187. Emphasis was placed on what was considered the ideal size of a congressional district instead of on what the size of the House ought to be.

The reapportionment act based on the census of 1800 continued the ratio of 33,000, which provided a House of 141 members. The third apportionment bill, enacted in 1811, fixed the ratio at 35,000, yielding a House of 181 members. Following the 1820 census Congress set the ratio at 40,000 inhabitants per district, which produced a House of 213 members. The act of May 22, 1832, fixed the ratio at 47,700, resulting in a House of 240 members.

Dissatisfaction with inequalities produced by the method of rejected fractions grew. Launching a vigorous attack against it, Daniel Webster urged adoption of a method that would assign an additional representative to each state with a large fraction. Webster outlined his reasoning in a report he submitted to Congress in 1832: "The Constitution, therefore, must be understood not as enjoining an absolute relative equality — because that would be demanding an impossibility — but as requiring of Congress to make the apportionment of Representatives among the several states according to their respective numbers, *as near as may be*. That which cannot be done perfectly must be done in a manner as near perfection as can be. . . . In such a case approximation becomes a rule."

Following the 1840 census, Congress adopted a reapportionment method similar to that advocated by Webster. The method fixed a ratio of one representative for every 70,680 people. This figure was reached by deciding on a fixed size of the House in advance (223), dividing that figure into the total national "representative population" and using the result (70,680) as the fixed ratio. The population of each state was then divided by this ratio to find the number of its representatives and the states were assigned an additional representative for each fraction over one-half. Under this method the actual size of the House dropped.

The modified reapportionment formula adopted by Congress in 1842 was more satisfactory than the previous method, but another change was made following the census of 1850. Proposed by Rep. Samuel F. Vinton of Ohio, the new system became known as the Vinton method.

Vinton Apportionment Formula

Under the Vinton formula, Congress first fixed the size of the House and then distributed the seats. The total qualifying population of the country was divided by the desired number of representatives, and the resulting number became the ratio of population to each representative. The population of each state was divided by this ratio, and each state received the number of representatives equal to the whole number in the quotient for that state. Then, to reach the required size of the House, additional representatives were assigned based on the remaining fractions, beginning with the state having the largest fraction. This procedure differed from the 1842 method only in the last step, which assigned one representative to every state having a fraction larger than one-half.

Proponents of the Vinton method pointed out that it had the distinct advantage of fixing the size of the House in advance and taking into account at least the largest fractions. The concern of the House turned from the ideal size of a congressional district to the ideal size of the House itself.

Under the 1842 reapportionment formula, the exact size of the House could not be fixed in advance. If every state with a fraction over one-half were given an additional representative, the House might wind up with a few more or a few less than the desired number. However, under the Vinton method, only states with the largest fractions were given additional House members and only up to the desired total size of the House.

Apportionment by the Vinton Method

Six reapportionments were carried out under the Vinton method. The 1850 census act contained three provisions not included in any previous law. First, it required reapportionment not only after the census of 1850 but also after all the subsequent censuses; second, it purported to fix the size of the House permanently at 233 members; and third, it provided in advance for an automatic apportionment by the secretary of the interior under the method prescribed in the act.

Following the census of 1860, an automatic reapportionment was to be carried out by the Interior Department. However, because the size of the House was to remain at the 1850 level, some states faced loss of representation and others were to gain fewer seats than they expected. To avert that possibility, an act was approved in 1862 increasing the size of the House to 241 and giving an extra representative to eight states — Illinois, Iowa, Kentucky, Minnesota, Ohio, Pennsylvania, Rhode Island and Vermont.

Apportionment legislation following the 1870 census contained several new provisions. The act fixed the size of the House at 283, with the proviso that the number should be increased if new states were admitted. A supplemental act assigned one additional representative each to Alabama, Florida, Indiana, Louisiana, New Hampshire, New York, Pennsylvania, Tennessee and Vermont.

Another section of the 1872 act provided that no state should thereafter be admitted "without having the necessary population to entitle it to at least one representative fixed by this bill." That provision was found to be unenforceable because no Congress can bind a succeeding Congress. Moreover, no ration was fixed by the act, although the basis on which the representatives were assigned was 131,425. In 1890, Idaho was admitted with a population of 84,385 and Wyoming with a population of 60,705.

With the Reconstruction era at its height in the South, the reapportionment legislation of 1872 reflected the desire of Congress to enforce Section 2 of the new 14th Amendment. That section attempted to protect the right of blacks to vote by providing for reduction of representation in the House of a state that interfered with the exercise of that right. The number of representatives of such a state was to be reduced in proportion to the number of inhabitants of voting age whose right to go to the polls was denied or abridged. The reapportionment bill repeated the language of Section 2, but the provision never was put into effect because of the difficulty of determining the exact number of people whose right to vote was being abridged.

The reapportionment act of Feb. 25, 1882, provided for a House of 325 members, with additional members for any new states admitted to the Union. No new apportionment provisions were added. The acts of Feb. 7, 1891, and Jan. 16, 1901, were routine as far as apportionment was concerned. The 1891 measure provided for a House of 356 members, and the 1901 statute increased the number to 386.

Problems with the Vinton Method

Despite the apparent advantages of the Vinton method, certain difficulties revealed themselves as the formula was applied. Zechariah Chafee Jr. of the Harvard Law School summarized these problems in an article in the *Harvard Law Review* in 1929. The method, he pointed out, suffered from what he called the "Alabama paradox." Under that aberration, an increase in the total size of the House might be accompanied by an actual loss of a seat by some states, even though there had been no corresponding change in population. This phenomenon first appeared in tables prepared for Congress in 1881, which gave Alabama eight members in a House of 299 but only seven members in a House of 300. It could even happen that the state that lost a seat was the one state that had expanded in population, while all the others had fewer people.

Chafee concluded from his study of the Vinton method: "Thus, it is unsatisfactory to fix the ratio of population per Representative before seats are distributed. Either the size of the House comes out haphazard, or, if this be determined in advance, the absurdities of the "Alabama paradox" vitiate the apportionment. Under present conditions, it is essential to determine the size of the House in advance; the problem thereafter is to distribute the required number of seats among the several states as nearly as possible in proportion to their respective populations so that no state is treated unfairly in comparison with any other state."

Maximum Membership of House

On Aug. 8, 1911, the membership of the House was fixed at 433. Provision was made for the addition of one representative each from Arizona and New Mexico, which

Congressional Apportionment, 1789-1990

Year of Census[a]

	1789[b]	1790	1800	1810	1820	1830	1840	1850	1860	1870	1880	1890	1900	1910	1930[c]	1940	1950	1960	1970	1980	1990
Ala.				1[d]	3	5	7	7	6	8	8	9	9	10	9	9	9	8	7	7	7
Alaska																	1[d]	1	1	1	1
Ariz.														1[d]	1	2	2	3	4	5	6
Ark.						1[d]	1	2	3	4	5	6	7	7	7	7	6	4	4	4	4
Calif.							2[d]	2	3	4	6	7	8	11	20	23	30	38	43	45	52
Colo.										1[d]	1	2	3	4	4	4	4	4	5	6	6
Conn.	5	7	7	7	6	6	4	4	4	4	4	4	5	5	6	6	6	6	6	6	6
Del.	1	1	1	2	1	1	1	1	1	1	1	1	1	1	1	1	1	1	1	1	1
Fla.							1[d]	1	1	2	2	2	3	4	5	6	8	12	15	19	23
Ga.	3	2	4	6	7	9	8	8	7	9	10	11	11	12	10	10	10	10	10	10	11
Hawaii																	1[d]	2	2	2	2
Idaho											1[d]	1	1	2	2	2	2	2	2	2	2
Ill.				1[d]	1	3	7	9	14	19	20	22	25	27	27	26	25	24	24	22	20
Ind.				1[d]	3	7	10	11	11	13	13	13	13	13	12	11	11	11	11	10	10
Iowa							2[d]	2	6	9	11	11	11	11	9	8	8	7	6	6	5
Kan.									1	3	7	8	8	8	7	6	6	5	5	5	4
Ky.		2	6	10	12	13	10	10	9	10	11	11	11	11	9	9	8	7	7	7	6
La.				1[d]	3	3	4	4	5	6	6	6	7	8	8	8	8	8	8	8	7
Maine				7[d]	7	8	7	6	5	5	4	4	4	4	3	3	3	2	2	2	2
Md.	6	8	9	9	9	8	6	6	5	6	6	6	6	6	6	6	7	8	8	8	8
Mass.	8	14	17	13[e]	13	12	10	11	10	11	12	13	14	16	15	14	14	12	12	11	10
Mich.						1[d]	3	4	6	9	11	12	12	13	17	17	18	19	19	18	16
Minn.								2[d]	2	3	5	7	9	10	9	9	9	8	8	8	8
Miss.				1[d]	1	2	4	5	5	6	7	7	8	8	7	7	6	5	5	5	5
Mo.					1	2	5	7	9	13	14	15	16	16	13	13	11	10	10	9	9
Mont.											1[d]	1	1	2	2	2	2	2	2	2	1
Neb.									1[d]	1	3	6	6	6	5	4	4	3	3	3	3
Nev.									1[d]	1	1	1	1	1	1	1	1	1	1	2	2
N.H.	3	4	5	6	6	5	4	3	3	3	2	2	2	2	2	2	2	2	2	2	2
N.J.	4	5	6	6	6	6	5	5	5	7	7	8	10	12	14	14	14	15	15	14	13
N.M.														1[d]	1	2	2	2	2	3	3
N.Y.	6	10	17	27	34	40	34	33	31	33	34	34	37	43	45	45	43	41	39	34	31
N.C.	5	10	12	13	13	13	9	8	7	8	9	9	10	10	11	12	12	11	11	11	12
N.D.											1[d]	1	2	3	2	2	2	2	1	1	1
Ohio			1[d]	6	14	19	21	21	19	20	21	21	21	22	24	23	23	24	23	21	19
Okla.													5[d]	8	9	8	6	6	6	6	6
Ore.								1[d]	1	1	1	2	2	3	3	4	4	4	4	5	5
Pa.	8	13	18	23	26	28	24	25	24	27	28	30	32	36	34	33	30	27	25	23	21
R.I.	1	2	2	2	2	2	2	2	2	2	2	2	2	3	2	2	2	2	2	2	2
S.C.	5	6	8	9	9	9	7	6	4	5	7	7	7	7	6	6	6	6	6	6	6
S.D.											2[d]	2	2	3	2	2	2	2	2	1	1
Tenn.		1[d]	3	6	9	13	11	10	8	10	10	10	10	10	9	10	9	9	8	9	9
Texas							2[d]	2	4	6	11	13	16	18	21	21	22	23	24	27	30
Utah												1[d]	1	2	2	2	2	2	2	3	3
Vt.		2	4	6	5	5	4	3	3	3	2	2	2	2	1	1	1	1	1	1	1
Va.	10	19	22	23	22	21	15	13	11	9	10	10	10	10	9	9	10	10	10	10	11
Wash.											1[d]	2	3	5	6	6	7	7	7	8	9
W.Va.										3	4	4	5	6	6	6	6	5	4	4	3
Wis.							2[d]	3	6	8	9	10	11	11	10	10	10	10	9	9	9
Wyo.											1[d]	1	1	1	1	1	1	1	1	1	1
Total	65	106	142	186	213	242	232	237	243	293	332	357	391	435	435	435	437[f]	435	435	435	435

[a] Apportionment effective with congressional election two years after census.
[b] Original apportionment made in Constitution, pending first census.
[c] No apportionment was made in 1920.
[d] These figures are not based on any census but indicate the provisional representation accorded newly admitted states by Congress, pending the next census.
[e] Twenty members were assigned to Massachusetts, but seven of these were credited to Maine when that area became a state.
[f] Normally 435, but temporarily increased two seats by Congress when Alaska and Hawaii became states.

Sources: *Biographical Directory of the American Congress* and Bureau of the Census.

were expected to become states in the near future. Thus, the size of the House reached 435, where it has remained with the exception of a brief period (1959-63) when the admission of Alaska and Hawaii raised the total temporarily to 437.

Limiting the size of the House amounted to recognition that the body soon would expand to unmanageable proportions if Congress continued the practice of adding new seats every 10 years to match population gains without depriving any state of its existing representation. Agreement on a fixed number made the task of reapportionment all the more difficult when the population not only increased but also became much more mobile. Population shifts brought Congress up against the politically painful necessity of taking seats away from slow-growing states to give the fast-growing states adequate representation.

A new mathematical calculation was adopted for the reapportionment following the 1910 census. Devised by W. F. Willcox of Cornell University, the new system established a priority list that assigned seats progressively, beginning with the first seat above the constitutional minimum of at least one seat for each state. When there were 48 states, this method was used to assign the 49th member, the 50th member, and so on, until the agreed upon size of the House was reached. The method was called major fractions and was used after the censuses of 1910, 1930 and 1940. There was no reapportionment after the 1920 census.

1920s Struggle

The results of the 14th decennial census were announced on Dec. 17, 1920, just after the short session of the 66th Congress convened. The 1920 census showed that for the first time in history most Americans were urban residents. This came as a profound shock to people accustomed to emphasizing the nation's rural traditions and the virtues of life on farms and in small towns. Rural legislators immediately mounted an attack on the census results and succeeded in postponing reapportionment for almost a decade.

Thomas Jefferson once wrote: "Those who labor in the earth are the chosen people of God, if ever He had a chosen people, whose breasts He had made His peculiar deposit for substantial and genuine virtue.... The mobs of great cities add just as much to the support of pure government as sores do to the strength of the human body.... I think our governments will remain virtuous for many centuries as long as they are chiefly agricultural: and this shall be as long as there shall be vacant lands in any part of America. When they get piled up upon one another in large cities as in Europe, they will become corrupt as in Europe."

As their power waned throughout the latter part of the 19th century and the early part of the 20th, farmers clung to the Jeffersonian belief that somehow they were more pure and virtuous than the growing number of urban residents. When finally faced with the fact that they were in the minority, these country residents put up a strong rearguard action to prevent the inevitable shift of congressional districts to the cities.

Rural representatives insisted that, because the 1920 census was taken as of Jan. 1, the farm population had been undercounted. In support of this contention, they argued that many farm laborers were seasonally employed in the cities at that time of year. Furthermore, midwinter road conditions probably had prevented enumerators from visiting many farms, they said, and other farmers were said to have been uncounted because they were absent on winter vacation trips. The change of the census date to Jan. 1 in 1920 had been made to conform to recommendations of the U.S. Department of Agriculture, which had asserted that the census should be taken early in the year if an accurate statistical picture of farming conditions was to be obtained.

Another point raised by rural legislators was that large numbers of unnaturalized aliens were congregated in northern cities, with the result that these cities gained at the expense of constituencies made up mostly of citizens of the United States. Rep. Homer Hoch, R-Kan., submitted a table showing that in a House of 435 representatives, exclusion from the census count of people not naturalized would have altered the allocation of seats in sixteen states. Southern and western farming states would have retained the number of seats allocated to them in 1911 or would have gained, while northern industrial states and California would have lost or at least would have gained fewer seats.

A constitutional amendment to exclude all aliens from the enumeration for purposes of reapportionment was proposed during the 70th Congress (1927-29) by Hoch, Sen. Arthur Capper, R-Kan., and others. But nothing further came of the proposals.

Reapportionment Bills Opposed

The first bill to reapportion the House according to the 1920 census was drafted by the House Census Committee early in 1921. Proceeding on the principle that no state should have its representation reduced, the committee proposed to increase the total number of representatives from 435 to 483. But the House voted 267-76 to keep its membership at 435. Eleven states would have lost seats and eight would have gained. The bill then was blocked by a Senate committee, where it died when the 66th Congress expired March 4, 1921.

Early in the 67th Congress, the House Census Committee again reported a bill, this time fixing the total membership at 460, an increase of 25. Two states — Maine and Massachusetts — would have lost one representative each and 16 states would have gained. On the House floor, an unsuccessful attempt was made to fix the number at the existing 435, and the House sent the bill back to committee.

During the 68th Congress (1923-25), the House Census Committee failed to report any reapportionment bill. On April 8, 1926, midway through the 69th Congress (1925-27), it became apparent that the committee would not produce a reapportionment measure. A motion to discharge a reapportionment bill from the committee failed, however, and the matter once again was put aside.

Intervention by Coolidge

President Calvin Coolidge, who previously had made no reference to reapportionment in his communications to Congress, announced in January 1927 that he favored passage of a new apportionment bill during the short session of the 69th Congress, which would end in less than two months. The House Census Committee refused to act. Its chairman, Rep. E. Hart Fenn, R-Conn., therefore moved in the House to suspend the rules and pass a bill he had introduced authorizing the secretary of commerce to reapportion the House immediately after the 1930 census. The motion was voted down 183-197.

The Fenn bill was rewritten early in the 70th Congress (1927-29) to give Congress itself a chance to act before the proposed reapportionment by the secretary of commerce would go into effect. The House passed an amended version of the Fenn bill on Jan. 11, 1929, and it was quickly reported by the Senate Commerce Committee. Repeated efforts to bring it up for floor action ahead of other bills failed. Its supporters gave up the fight when it became evident that senators from states slated to lose representation were ready to carry on a filibuster that would have blocked reapportionment as well as all other measures.

Intervention by Hoover

As the date of the next census became imminent, President Herbert Hoover listed provision for the 1930 census and reapportionment as "matters of emergency legislation" that should be acted upon in the special session of the 71st Congress, which was convened on April 15, 1929. In response to this urgent request, the Senate June 13 passed, 48-37, a combined census-reapportionment bill that had been approved by voice vote of the House two days earlier.

The 1929 law established a permanent system of reapportioning the 435 House seats following each census. It provided that immediately after the convening of the 71st Congress for its short session in December 1930, the president was to transmit to Congress a statement showing the population of each state together with an apportionment of representatives to each state based on the existing size of the House. Failing enactment of new apportionment legislation, that apportionment would go into effect without further action and would remain in effect for ensuing elections to the House of Representatives until another census had been taken and another reapportionment made.

Because two decades had passed between reapportionments, a greater shift than usual took place following the 1930 census. California's House delegation was almost doubled, rising from 11 to 20. Michigan gained four seats, Texas three, and New Jersey, New York and Ohio two each. Twenty-one states lost a total of 27 seats; Missouri lost three, and Georgia, Iowa, Kentucky and Pennsylvania each lost two.

To test the fairness of two allocation methods — the familiar major fractions and the new equal proportions system — the 1929 act required the president to report the distribution of seats by both methods. But, pending legislation to the contrary, the method of major fractions was to be used.

The two methods gave an identical distribution of seats based on 1930 census figures. However, in 1940, the two methods gave different results: under major fractions, Michigan would gain a seat lost by Arkansas; under equal proportions, no change would occur in either state. The automatic reapportionment provisions of the 1929 act went into effect in January 1941. But the House Census Committee moved to reverse the result, favoring the method of equal proportions and the certain Democratic seat in Arkansas over a possible Republican gain if the seat were shifted to Michigan. The Democratic-controlled Congress went along, adopting equal proportions as the method to be used in reapportionment calculations after the 1950 and subsequent censuses, and making this action retroactive to January 1941 to save Arkansas its seat.

While politics doubtless played a part in the timing of the action taken in 1941, the method of equal proportions had come to be accepted as the best available. It had been worked out by Edward V. Huntington of Harvard in 1921. At the request of the Speaker of the House, all known methods of apportionment were considered in 1929 by the National Academy of Sciences Committee on Apportionment. The committee expressed its preference for equal proportions.

Method of Equal Proportions

The method of equal proportions involves complicated mathematical calculations. In brief, each of the 50 states is initially assigned the one seat to which it is entitled by the Constitution. Then "priority numbers" for states to receive second seats, third seats and so on are calculated by dividing the state's population by the square root of n(n-1), where "n" is the number of seats for that state. The priority numbers are then lined up in order and the seats given to the states with priority numbers until 435 are awarded.

The method is designed to make the proportional difference in the average district size in any two states as small as possible. After the 1981 reapportionment, for example, South Dakota's single district was the most populous, with 690,768 residents, while Montana's two districts, each with slightly fewer than 400,000 people, were the least populous. Under the 1990 apportionment, Montana lost one of its two seats; its remaining district became the most populous, with 799,065 residents. With 453,588 people, Wyoming's single district was the least populous. The mean population per district nationwide was about 572,500.

Montana protested the reapportionment decision on the grounds that the method of equal proportions was unconstitutional because it violated the one-person, one-vote guarantee by creating districts with populations that vary too widely between states. Montana urged that another formula more favorable to small states be adopted. On March 31, 1992, the Supreme Court unanimously upheld the method of equal proportion in *United States Department of Commerce v. Montana.* The Court acknowledged that the established formula does not fully conform to the principle of one-person, one-vote, but it said that was impossible to do because the Constitution mandates that each state be assigned at least one representative and that congressional districts stay within state boundaries.

Redistricting: Drawing the Lines

Although the Constitution contained provisions for the apportionment of U.S. House seats among the states, it was silent about how the members should be elected. From the beginning, most states divided their territory into geographic districts, permitting only one member of Congress to be elected from each district.

But some states allowed would-be House members to run at large, with voters able to cast as many votes as there were seats to be filled. Still other states created what were known as multi-member districts, in which a single geographic unit would elect two or more members of the House. At various times, some states used combinations of these methods. For example, a state might elect 10 representatives from 10 individual districts and two at large.

In the first few elections to the House, New Hampshire, Pennsylvania, New Jersey and Georgia elected their

Origins of the Gerrymander

The practice of "gerrymandering" — the excessive manipulation of the shape of a legislative district to benefit a certain incumbent or party — is probably as old as the Republic, but the name originated in 1812.

In that year, the Massachusetts legislature carved out of Essex County a district that historian John Fiske said had a "dragonlike contour." When the painter Gilbert Stuart saw the misshapen district, he penciled in a head, wings and claws and exclaimed: "That will do for a salamander!" — to which editor Benjamin Russell replied: "Better say a Gerrymander" — after Elbridge Gerry, then governor of Massachusetts.

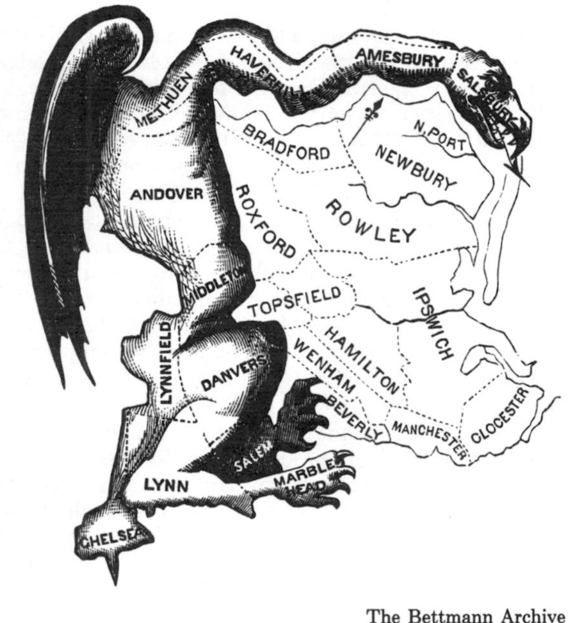

The Bettmann Archive

representatives at large, as did Rhode Island and Delaware, the two states with only a single representative. Districts were used in Massachusetts, New York, Maryland, Virginia and South Carolina. In Connecticut, a preliminary election was held to nominate three times as many people as the number of representatives to be chosen at large in the subsequent election. In 1840, 22 of the 31 states elected their representatives by districts. New Hampshire, New Jersey, Georgia, Alabama, Mississippi and Missouri, with a combined representation of 33 House seats, elected their representatives at large. Three states, Arkansas, Delaware and Florida, had only one representative each.

Those states that used congressional districts quickly developed what came to be known as the gerrymander. The term refers to the practice of drawing district lines so as to maximize the advantage of a political party or interest group. The name originated from a salamander-shaped congressional district created by the Massachusetts legislature in 1812 when Elbridge Gerry was governor. *(Box, this page)*

Constant efforts were made during the early 1800s to lay down national rules, by means of a constitutional amendment, for congressional districting. The first resolution proposing a mandatory division of each state into districts was introduced in Congress in 1800. In 1802, the legislatures of Vermont and North Carolina adopted resolutions in support of such action. From 1816 to 1826, 22 states adopted resolutions proposing the election of representatives by districts.

In Congress, Sen. Mahlon Dickerson, R-N.J., proposed such an amendment regularly almost every year from 1817 to 1826. It was adopted by the Senate three times, in 1819, 1820 and 1822, but each time it failed to reach a vote in the House. Although the constitutional amendment was unsuccessful, a law passed in 1842 required continuous single-member congressional districts. That law required representatives to be "elected by districts composed of contiguous territory equal in number to the representatives to which said state may be entitled, no one district electing more than one Representative."

When President John Tyler signed the bill, he appended to it a memorandum voicing doubt as to the constitutionality of the districting provisions. The memorandum precipitated a minor constitutional crisis. The House, urged on by Rep. John Quincy Adams of Massachusetts, appointed a select committee to consider the action of the president. Chaired by the aging former president, the committee drew up a resolution protesting Tyler's action as "unwarranted by the Constitution and laws of the United States, injurious to the public interest, and of evil example for the future; and this House do hereby solemnly protest against the said act of the President and against its ever being repeated or adduced as a precedent hereafter." The House took no action on the resolution; several attempts to call it up under suspension of the rules failed to receive the necessary two-thirds vote.

Districting Legislation, 1850-1910

The districting provisions of the 1842 act were not repeated in the legislation that followed the 1850 census. But in 1862 legislation separate from the reapportionment act revived the provisions of the 1842 act requiring districts to be composed of contiguous territory.

The 1872 reapportionment act repeated the districting provisions and went even further by adding that districts should contain "as nearly as practicable an equal number of inhabitants." Similar provisions were included in the acts of 1881 and 1891. In the districting legislation of Jan. 16, 1901, the words "compact territory" were added, and the clause then read "contiguous and compact territory and containing as nearly as practicable an equal number of inhabitants." This requirement appeared also in the legislation of Aug. 8, 1911. The "contiguous and compact" provisions of the act subsequently lapsed, and Congress never replaced them.

Several unsuccessful attempts were made to enforce redistricting provisions. Despite the districting requirements of the act of June 25, 1842, New Hampshire, Georgia, Mississippi and Missouri elected their representatives at large that autumn. When the new House convened for its first session, on Dec. 4, 1843, objection was made to seating the representatives of the four states. The dispute was referred to the Committee on Elections. The majority report to the committee, submitted by its chairman, Rep. Stephen A. Douglas, D-Ill., asserted that the act of 1842 was not binding upon the states and that the representatives in question were entitled to their seats. An amendment to the majority report deleted all reference to the apportionment law. A minority report by Rep. Garrett Davis, Whig-Ky., contended that the members had not been elected according to the Constitution and the laws and thus were not entitled to their seats.

The House debated the matter Feb. 6-14, 1844. With the Democratic Party holding a majority of more than 60, and with 18 of the 21 challenged members being Democrats, the House decided to seat the members. However, by 1848 all four states had come around to electing their representatives by districts.

The next challenge a representative encountered over federal districting laws occurred in 1901. A charge was leveled that the existing Kentucky redistricting law did not comply with the reapportionment law of Jan. 16, 1901; the charge aimed at preventing the seating of Rep. George G. Gilbert, D, of Kentucky's 8th District. The committee assigned to investigate the matter turned aside the challenge, asserting that the federal act was not binding on the states. The reasons given were practical and political: "Your committee are therefore of opinion that a proper construction of the Constitution does not warrant the conclusion that by that instrument Congress is clothed with power to determine the boundaries of Congressional districts, or to revise the acts of a State Legislature in fixing such boundaries; and your committee is further of opinion that even if such power is to be implied from the language of the Constitution, it would be in the last degree unwise and intolerable that it should exercise it. To do so would be to put into the hands of Congress the ability to disfranchise, in effect, a large body of the electors. It would give Congress the power to apply to all the States, in favor of one party, a general system of gerrymandering. It is true that the same method is to a large degree resorted to by the several states, but the division of political power is so general and diverse that notwithstanding the inherent vice of the system of gerrymandering, some kind of equality of distribution results."

In 1908, the Virginia legislature transferred Floyd County from the 5th District to the 6th District. As a result, the population of the 5th was reduced from 175,579 to 160,191 and that of the 6th was increased from 181,571 to 196,959. The average for the state was 185,418.

When the newly elected representative from the 5th District, Edward W. Saunders, D, was challenged by his opponent in the election, the majority of the congressional investigating committee upheld the challenge. They concluded that the Virginia law of 1908 was null and void because it did not conform with the federal reapportionment law of Jan. 16, 1901, or with the constitution of Virginia, and that the district should be regarded as including the counties that were a part of it before enactment of the 1908 state legislation. In that case, Saunders's opponent would have had a majority of the votes, so the committee recommended that he be seated. Thus, for the first time, it appeared that the districting legislation would be enforced, but the House did not take action on the committee's report and Saunders's challenger was not seated.

Court Action on Redistricting

After the long and desultory battle over reapportionment in the 1920s, those who were unhappy over the inaction of Congress and the state legislatures began taking their cases to court. At first, the protesters had no luck. But as the population disparities grew in both federal and state legislative districts and the Supreme Court began to show a tendency to intervene, the objectors were more successful.

Finally, in a series of decisions beginning in 1962 with *Baker v. Carr* (369 U.S. 186), the Court exerted great influence over the redistricting process, ordering that congressional districts as well as state and local legislative districts be drawn so that their populations would be as nearly equal as possible.

Supreme Court's 1932 Decision

Baker v. Carr essentially reversed the direction the Court had taken in 1932. *Wood v. Broom* (287 U.S. 1) was a case challenging the constitutionality of a Mississippi redistricting law because it violated the standards of the 1911 federal redistricting act. The question was whether the act was still in effect. That law, which required that districts be separate, compact, contiguous and equally populated, had been neither specifically repealed nor reaffirmed in the 1929 reapportionment act.

Speaking for the Court, Chief Justice Charles Evans Hughes ruled that the 1911 act, in effect, had expired with the approval of the 1929 apportionment act and that the standards of the 1911 act therefore were no longer applicable. The Court reversed the decision of a lower federal court, which had permanently enjoined elections under the new Mississippi redistricting act because it violated the standards of the 1911 act.

That the Supreme Court upheld a state law that failed to provide for districts of equal population was almost less important than the minority opinion that the Court should not have heard the case. Four justices — Louis D. Brandeis, Harlan F. Stone, Owen J. Roberts and Benjamin N. Cardozo — while concurring in the majority opinion, said they would have dismissed the Wood suit for "want of equity." The "want of equity" phrase in this context suggested a policy of judicial self-limitation with respect to the entire question of judicial involvement in essentially "political" questions.

'Political Thicket'

Not until 1946, in *Colegrove v. Green* (328 U.S. 549), did the Court again rule in a significant case dealing with congressional redistricting. The case was brought by Kenneth Colegrove, a political science professor at Northwestern University, who alleged that congressional districts in Illinois, which varied between 112,116 and 914,053 in population, were so unequal that they violated the 14th Amendment's guarantee of equal protection of the laws. A seven-member Supreme Court divided 4-3 in dismissing the suit.

Justice Felix Frankfurter gave the opinion of the Court, speaking for himself and Justices Stanley F. Reed and Harold H. Burton. Frankfurter's opinion cited *Wood v. Broom* to indicate that Congress had deliberately removed the standard set by the 1911 act. He also said that he, Reed and Burton agreed with the minority that the Court should have dismissed the case. The issue, Frankfurter said, was "of a peculiarly political nature and therefore not meant for judicial interpretation.... The short of it is that the Constitution has conferred upon Congress exclusive authority to secure fair representation by the states in the popular House and has left to that House determination whether states have fulfilled their responsibility. If Congress failed in exercising its powers, whereby standards of fairness are offended, the remedy lies ultimately with the people.... To sustain this action would cut very deep into the very being of Congress. Courts ought not to enter this political thicket. The remedy for unfairness in districting is to secure state legislatures that will apportion properly, or to invoke the ample powers of Congress." Frankfurter also said that the Court could not affirmatively remap congressional districts and that elections at large would be politically undesirable.

Justice Hugo L. Black, joined by Justices William O. Douglas and Frank Murphy, in a dissenting opinion maintained that the district court did have jurisdiction over congressional redistricting. The three justices cited as evidence a section of the *U.S. Code* that allowed district courts to redress deprivations of constitutional rights occurring through action of the states. Black's opinion also rested on an earlier case in which the Court had indicated that federal constitutional questions, unless "frivolous," fall under the jurisdiction of the federal courts. Black asserted that the appellants had standing to sue and that the population disparities violated the equal protection clause of the 14th Amendment.

With the Court split 3-3 on whether the judiciary had or should exercise jurisdiction, Justice Wiley B. Rutledge cast the deciding vote in *Colegrove v. Green.* On the question of justiciability, Rutledge agreed with Black, Douglas and Murphy that the issue could be considered by the federal courts. Thus a majority of the court participating in the *Colegrove* case felt that congressional redistricting cases were justiciable.

Yet on the question of granting relief in this specific instance, Rutledge agreed with Frankfurter, Reed and Burton that the case should be dismissed. He pointed out that four of the nine justices in *Wood v. Broom* had felt that dismissal should be for want of equity. Rutledge saw a "want of equity" situation in *Colegrove v. Green* as well. "I think the gravity of the constitutional questions raised [are] so great, together with the possibility of collision [with the political departments of the government], that the admonition [against avoidable constitutional decision] is appropriate to be followed here," Rutledge said. Jurisdiction, he thought, should be exercised "only in the most compelling circumstances." He thought that "the shortness of time remaining [before the forthcoming election] makes it doubtful whether action could or would be taken in time to secure for petitioners the effective relief they seek." Rutledge warned that congressional elections at large would deprive citizens of representation by districts, "which the prevailing policy of Congress demands." In the case of at-large elections, he said, "the cure sought may be worse than the disease." For all these reasons he concluded that the case was "one in which the court may properly, and should, decline to exercise its jurisdiction."

Changing Views

In the ensuing years, law professors, political scientists and other commentators increasingly criticized the *Colegrove* doctrine and grew impatient with the Supreme Court's reluctance to intervene in redistricting disputes. At the same time, the membership of the Court was changing, and the new members were more inclined toward judicial action on redistricting.

In the 1950s, the Court decided two cases that laid some groundwork for its subsequent reapportionment decisions. The first was *Brown v. Board of Education* (347 U.S. 483), the historic 1954 school desegregation case, in which the Court decided that an individual citizen could assert a right to equal protection of the laws under the 14th Amendment, contrary to the "separate but equal" doctrine of public facilities for white and black citizens. Six years later, in *Gomillion v. Lightfoot* (364 U.S. 339), the Court held that the Alabama legislature could not draw the city limits of Tuskegee so as to exclude nearly every black vote. In his opinion, Justice Frankfurter drew a clear line between redistricting challenges based on the 14th Amendment, such as *Colegrove,* and challenges to discriminatory redistricting based on the 15th Amendment's voting rights protections, as in *Gomillion.* But Justice Charles E. Whittaker said that the equal protection clause was the proper constitutional basis for the decision. One commentator later remarked that *Gomillion* amounted to a "dragon" in the "political thicket" of *Colegrove.*

By 1962 only three members of the Court that ruled in *Colegrove* remained: Justices Black and Douglas, dissenters in that case, and Justice Frankfurter, aging spokesman for restraint in the exercise of judicial power.

By then it was clear that malapportionment within the states no longer could be ignored. By 1960 not a single state legislative body existed in which there was not at least a 2-to-1 population disparity between the most and the least heavily populated districts. For example, the disparity was 242-1 in the Connecticut House, 223-1 in the Nevada Senate, 141-1 in the Rhode Island Senate and 9-1 in the Georgia Senate. Studies of large and small counties in state legislatures between 1910 and 1960 showed that, on the one hand, the effective vote of the most populous counties had slipped while their percentage of the national population had more than doubled. The most lightly populated counties, on the other hand, advanced from a position of slight over-representation to one of extreme over-representation, holding almost twice as many seats as they would be entitled to by population size alone. Predictably, the rural-dominated state legislatures resisted every move toward reapportioning state legislative districts to reflect new population patterns.

Population imbalance among congressional districts was substantially lopsided but by no means so gross. In Texas, the 1960 census showed the most heavily populated district had four times as many inhabitants as the most lightly populated. Arizona, Maryland and Ohio each had at least one district with three times as many inhabitants as the least populated. In most cases, rural areas benefited from the population imbalance in congressional districts. As a result of the postwar population movement out of central cities to the surrounding areas, the suburbs were the most under-represented.

Baker v. Carr

Against this background, a group of Tennessee city dwellers successfully broke the longstanding precedent against federal court involvement in legislative apportionment problems. For more than half a century, since 1901, the Tennessee legislature had refused to reapportion itself, even though a decennial reapportionment based on population was specifically required by the state's constitution. In the meantime, Tennessee's population had grown and shifted dramatically to urban areas. By 1960 the House legislative districts ranged from 3,454 to 36,031 in population, while the Senate districts ranged from 39,727 to 108,094. Appeals by urban residents to the rural-controlled Tennessee legislature proved fruitless. A suit brought in the state courts to force reapportionment was rejected on grounds that the courts should stay out of legislative matters.

City dwellers then appealed to the federal courts, stating that they had no redress: The legislature had refused to act for more than half a century, the state courts had refused to intervene and Tennessee had no referendum or initiative laws. They charged that there was "a debasement of their votes by virtue of the incorrect, obsolete and unconstitutional apportionment" to such an extent that they were being deprived of their right to equal protection of the laws under the 14th Amendment. (The 14th Amendment reads, in part: "No state shall . . . deny to any person within its jurisdiction the equal protection of the laws.")

The Supreme Court on March 26, 1962, handed down its historic decision in *Baker v. Carr,* ruling in favor of the Tennessee city dwellers by a 6-2 margin. In the majority opinion, Justice William J. Brennan Jr. emphasized that the federal judiciary had the power to review the apportionment of state legislatures under the 14th Amendment's equal protection clause. "The mere fact that a suit seeks protection as a political right," Brennan wrote, "does not mean that it presents a political question" that the courts should avoid.

In a vigorous dissent, Justice Frankfurter said the majority decision constituted "a massive repudiation of the experience of our whole past" and was an assertion of "destructively novel judicial power." He contended that the lack of any clear basis for relief "catapults the lower courts" into a "mathematical quagmire." Frankfurter insisted that "there is not under our Constitution a judicial remedy for every political mischief." Appeal for relief, Frankfurter maintained, should not be made in the courts, but "to an informed civically militant electorate."

The Court had abandoned the view that malapportionment questions were outside its competence. But it stopped there and in *Baker v. Carr* did not address the merits of the challenge to the legislative districts.

Gray v. Sanders

The one-person, one-vote rule was set out by the Court almost exactly one year after its decision in *Baker v. Carr.* But the 1963 case in which the announcement came did not involve congressional districts.

In *Gray v. Sanders* (372 U.S. 368) the Court found that Georgia's county-unit primary system for electing state officials — a system that weighted votes to give advantage to rural districts in statewide primary elections — denied voters equal protection of the laws.

All votes in a statewide election must have equal weight, the Court held: "How then can one person be given twice or 10 times the voting power of another person in a statewide election merely because he lives in a rural area or because he lives in the smallest rural county? Once the geographical unit for which a representative is to be chosen is designated, all who participate in the election are to have an equal vote — whatever their race, whatever their sex, whatever their occupation, whatever their income, and wherever their home may be in that geographical unit. This is required by the Equal Protection Clause of the Fourteenth Amendment. The concept of 'we the people' under the Constitution visualizes no preferred class of voters but equality among those who meet the basic qualification. The idea that every voter is equal to every other voter in his State, when he casts his ballot in favor of one of several competing candidates, underlies many of our decisions. . . . The conception of political equality from the Declaration of Independence to Lincoln's Gettysburg Address, to the Fifteenth, Seventeenth, and Nineteenth Amendments can mean only one thing — one person, one vote."

The Rule Applied

The Court's rulings in *Baker* and *Gray* concerned the equal weighting and counting of votes cast in state elections. In 1964, deciding the case of *Wesberry v. Sanders,* the Court applied the one-person, one-vote principle to congressional districts and set equality as the standard for congressional redistricting.

Shortly after the *Baker* decision was handed down, James P. Wesberry Jr., an Atlanta resident and a member of the Georgia Senate, filed suit in federal court in Atlanta claiming that gross disparity in the population of Georgia's congressional districts violated 14th Amendment rights of equal protection of the laws. At the time, Georgia districts ranged in population from 272,154 in the rural 9th District in the northeastern part of the state to 823,860 in the 5th District in Atlanta and its suburbs. District lines had not been changed since 1931. The state's number of House seats remained the same in the interim, but Atlanta's district population — already high in 1931 compared with the others — had more than doubled in 30 years, making a 5th District vote worth about one-third that of a vote in the 9th.

On June 20, 1962, the three-judge federal court divided 2-1 in dismissing Wesberry's suit. The majority reasoned that the precedent of *Colegrove* still controlled in congressional district cases. The judges cautioned against federal judicial interference with Congress and against "depriving others of the right to vote" if the suit should result in at-large elections. They suggested that the Georgia legislature (under court order to reapportion itself) or the U.S. Congress might better provide relief. Wesberry then appealed to the Supreme Court.

On February 17, 1964, the Supreme Court ruled in *Wesberry v. Sanders* (376 U.S. 1) that congressional districts must be substantially equal in population. The Court, which upheld Wesberry's challenge by a 6-3 decision, based its ruling on the history and wording of Article I, Section 2 of the Constitution, which states that representatives shall be apportioned among the states according to their respective numbers and be chosen by the people of the several states. This language, the Court stated, meant that "as nearly as is practicable, one man's vote in a congressional election is to be worth as much as another's."

The majority opinion, written by Justice Black and supported by Chief Justice Earl Warren and Justices Brennan, Douglas, Arthur J. Goldberg and Byron R. White, said: "While it may not be possible to draw congressional districts with mathematical precision, that is no excuse for ignoring our Constitution's plain objective of making equal representation for equal numbers of people the fundamental goal for the House of Representatives."

Malapportionment and Gerrymandering

The prevalence of malapportionment in the creation of U.S. congressional districts was, to many observers, one of the chief evils in the American system before the "one-person, one-vote" ruling by the Supreme Court in 1964. On Feb. 17 of that year, the Court, in the case of *Westberry v. Sanders,* declared that "as nearly as is practicable, one man's vote in a congressional election is to be worth as much as another's."

Malapportionment

Malapportionment occurred when districts of grossly unequal populations were created — either through actions of state legislatures in establishing new districts or, as was the more frequent practice in America, simply by failing to redistrict despite major population shifts.

Within a single state, populations in some congressional districts varied by as much as 8-to-1. Generally, growing urban areas were under-represented, to the advantage of rural areas.

Examples of great disparity in congressional district sizes in modern U.S. history included: New York (1930), 776,425 residents in the largest district and 90,671 in the smallest; Ohio (1946), 698,650 and 163,561; Texas (1962), 951,527 and 216,371; and Michigan (1962), 802,994 and 177,431.

The decennial census and ensuing reapportionment of House seats eventually forced redistricting in most states, although some resorted to electing members at large (this occurred in Texas, Hawaii, Ohio, Michigan and Maryland in 1962) instead of redrawing district lines. A 1967 law (PL 90-196) banned at-large elections in states with more than one representative. However, that law has been interpreted variously by the states. Where divided states' legislatures have been unable to agree on a redistricting plan, the courts have had to impose their own plan.

Although sizes vary somewhat because of apportionment and inequalities that build between censuses, generally the districts start out nearly equal in population.

In *Congress and Its Members,* published in 1990, political scientists Roger H. Davidson and Walter J. Oleszek noted: "Population equality has thus been achieved at the expense of other goals. Parity in numbers of residents makes it hard to respect political divisions such as county lines. It also makes it hard to follow economic, social, or geographic boundaries. The congressional district, therefore, tends to be an artificial creation with little relationship to real communities of interest — economic or geographic or political. This heightens the congressional district's isolation, forcing candidates to forge their own unique factions and alliances. It also aids incumbents, who have ways of reaching voters without relying on commercial communications media."

Gerrymandering

Gerrymandering was the name given to excessive manipulation of the shape of legislative districts to benefit a particular politician or political party. The gerrymander was named after Democrat Elbridge Gerry, the governor of Massachusetts in 1812 when the legislature created a peculiar salamander-shaped district to benefit his party. *(Sketch of district, box, p. 1158)*

Unlike malapportionment, gerrymandering has not been prohibited by law. It was still in use in the 20th century by both political parties. In 1961, Republican legislators in New York created one gerrymander-like creature stretching across the greater part of upstate New York, his head hanging over Albany in the east and his tail reaching for Rochester in the west. In North Carolina after the 1960 census, Democratic redistricters formed an almost perfect gerrymander shape to throw the state's sole Republican representative in with a strong Democratic opponent.

After the 1980 census, Democrats in control of California's legislature drew a district in the San Francisco Bay area in which two segments were linked only by a body of water. New Jersey's map was a gerrymander that boasted some of the most bizarrely shaped districts in the nation. The Supreme Court threw those districts out in 1983 but on the grounds of population inequality, not because they were gerrymandered.

Davidson and Oleszek cite two kinds of gerrymandering: "packing" and "cracking." In the first case, a district line is drawn so as to encompass as many of one party's voters as possible, thus "packing" it with supporters." "Cracking" entails diluting one party's strength by dispersing it among two or more districts.

The intent of practically every gerrymander is political — to create a maximum number of districts that would elect the party candidates or types of candidates favored by the controlling group in the state legislature that did the redistricting, thus increasing, or maintaining, the political power of the already politically dominant group. Concluded Davidson and Oleszek: "The effects of gerrymanders are not easily measured. Marginal or competitive districts (those where the winner gains less than 55 percent of the votes) are tougher for a party to capture and hold, but they have the advantage of yielding legislative seats with a modest number of voters (that is, a minimal winning coalition). Safe districts, while naturally preferred by the incumbents, can waste the majority party's votes by furnishing outsized victories."

In a strongly worded dissent, Justice John M. Harlan asserted that the Constitution did not establish population as the only criterion of congressional districting but left the subject to the discretion of the states, subject only to the supervisory power of Congress. "The constitutional right which the court creates is manufactured out of whole cloth," Harlan concluded.

The *Wesberry* opinion established no precise standards for districting beyond declaring that districts must be as nearly equal in population "as is practicable." In his dissent, Harlan suggested that a disparity of more than 100,000 between a state's largest and smallest districts would "presumably" violate the equality standard enunciated by the majority. On that basis, Harlan estimated, the districts of 37 states with 398 representatives would be unconstitutional, "leaving a constitutional House of 37 members now sitting."

Neither did the Court's decision make any reference to gerrymandering, since it discussed only the population, not the shape of districts. In a separate opinion handed down the same day as *Wesberry,* the Court dismissed a challenge to congressional districts in New York City, which had been brought by voters who charged that Manhattan's "silk-stocking" 17th District had been gerrymandered to exclude blacks and Puerto Ricans.

Strict Equality

Five years elapsed between *Wesberry v. Sanders* and the Court's next application of constitutional standards to congressional districting. In 1967, the Court hinted at the strict stance it would adopt two years later. With two unsigned opinions, the Court sent back to Indiana and Missouri for revision those two states' congressional redistricting plans because they allowed variations of as much as 20 percent from the average district population.

Two years later, Missouri's revised plan returned to the Court for full review. By a 6-3 vote, the Court rejected the plan. It was unacceptable, the Court held in *Kirkpatrick v. Preisler* (385 U.S. 450), because it allowed a variation of as much as 3.1 percent from perfectly equal population districts. Thus the Court made clear its stringent application of the one-person, one-vote rule to congressional districts. Minor deviations from the strict equal-population principle were permissible only when the state provided substantial evidence that the variation was unavoidable.

There was no "fixed numerical or percentage population variance small enough to be considered *de minimis* and to satisfy without question the 'as nearly as practicable' standard," Justice Brennan wrote for the Court. "Equal representation for equal numbers of people is a principle designed to prevent debasement of voting power and diminution of access to elected Representatives. Toleration of even small deviations detracts from these purposes."

The only permissible variances in population, the Court ruled, were those that were unavoidable despite the effort to achieve absolute equality or those that could be legally justified. The variances in Missouri could have been avoided, the Court said.

None of Missouri's arguments for the plan qualified as "legally acceptable" justifications. The Court rejected the argument that population variance was necessary to allow representation of distinct interest groups. It said that acceptance of such variances to produce districts with specific interests was "antithetical" to the basic purpose of equal representation.

Justice White dissented from the majority opinion, which he characterized as "an unduly rigid and unwarranted application of the Equal Protection Clause which will unnecessarily involve the courts in the abrasive task of drawing district lines." White added that some "acceptably small" population variance could be established. He indicated that considerations of existing political boundaries and geographical compactness could justify to him some variation from "absolute equality" of population.

Justice Harlan, joined by Justice Potter Stewart, dissented, saying that "whatever room remained under this court's prior decisions for the free play of the political process in matters of reapportionment is now all but eliminated by today's Draconian judgments."

Practical Results

As a result of the Court's decisions of the 1960s, nearly every state was forced to redraw its congressional district lines — sometimes more than once. By the end of the decade, 39 of the 45 states with more than one representative had made the necessary adjustments.

However, the effect of the one-person, one-vote standard on congressional districts did not bring about immediate population equality in districts. Most of the new districts were far from equal in population, because the only official population figures came from the 1960 census. Massive population shifts during the decade rendered most post-*Wesberry* efforts to achieve equality useless.

But redistricting based on the 1970 census resulted in districts that differed only slightly in population from the state average. Among House members elected in 1972, 385 of 435 represented districts that varied by less than 1 percent from the state average district population.

By contrast, only nine of the districts in the 88th Congress (elected in 1962) deviated less than 1 percent from the state average; 81 were between 1 and 5 percent; 87 from 5 to 10 percent; and in 236 districts the deviation was 10 percent or greater. Twenty-two House members were elected at large.

In 1973, the Supreme Court declared the Texas congressional districts, as redrawn in 1971, unconstitutional because of excessive population variance among districts. The variance between the largest and smallest districts was 4.9872 percent. The Court returned the case to a three-judge federal panel, which adopted a new congressional district plan effective Oct. 17, 1973.

Precise Equality

Following the 1980 census, several federal courts accepted or imposed redistricting maps that achieved population equality but were drawn for blatant partisan purposes. In Missouri, a federal court accepted the Democrats' remap proposal over the Republican plan because its districts were more nearly equal in population. The Democratic map obtained population equality by dismantling a district in a part of the state where population was growing and by preserving a district in inner-city St. Louis that had been losing population. The plan cost one Republican incumbent his seat.

A state may never come closer to precise population equality than Michigan did in 1982, when a court-imposed map created 16 congressional districts with exactly equal populations — 514,560. The state's two other districts each had a population of just one person fewer — 514,559. To achieve that equality, however, the line for many districts cut through many small cities and towns, dividing their residents between two or three different districts.

Although maps such as these raised the question whether partisan gerrymandering was also a violation of an individual's voting rights, the Supreme Court in 1983 appeared to make it even more difficult to challenge a redistricting map on grounds other than population deviation. In a 5-4 decision, the Court ruled on June 22 in *Karcher v. Daggett* (462 U.S. 725) that states must adhere as closely as possible to the one-person, one-vote standard and bear the burden of proving that deviations from precise population equality were made in pursuit of a legitimate goal. The decision overturned New Jersey's congressional map because the variation between the most populated and the least populated districts was 0.69 percent.

Brennan, who wrote the Court's opinion in *Baker* and *Kirkpatrick,* also wrote the opinion in *Karcher,* contending that population differences between districts "could have been avoided or significantly reduced with a good-faith effort to achieve population equality."

Brennan continued: "Adopting any standard other than population equality, using the best census data available, would subtly erode the Constitution's ideal of equal representation. In this case, appellants argue that a maximum deviation of approximately 0.7 percent should be considered *de minimis.* If we accept that argument, how are we to regard deviations of 0.8 percent, 0.95 percent, 1.0 percent or 1.1 percent? ... To accept the legitimacy of unjustified, though small population deviations in this case would mean to reject the basic premise of *Kirkpatrick* and *Wesberry.*"

Brennan said that "any number of consistently applied legislative policies might justify" some population variation. These included "making districts compact, respecting municipal boundaries, preserving the cores of prior districts, and avoiding contests between incumbent Representatives." However, he cautioned, the state must show "with some specificity that a particular objective required the specific deviations in its plan, rather than simply relying on general assertions."

In his dissent, Justice White criticized the majority for its "unreasonable insistence on an unattainable perfection in the equalizing of congressional districts." He warned that the decision would invite "further litigation of virtually every congressional redistricting plan in the nation."

Partisan Gerrymandering

In *Karcher,* the Court did not address the underlying political issue in the New Jersey case, which was that its map had been drawn to serve Democratic interests. As a partisan gerrymander, the map had few peers, boasting some of the most oddly shaped districts in the country. One constituency, known as the "fishhook" by its detractors, twisted through central New Jersey's industrial landscape, picking up Democratic voters along the way. Another stretched from the eastern suburbs of New York to the western fringes of Trenton.

In separate dissents, Justices Lewis F. Powell Jr. and John Paul Stevens broadly hinted that they were willing to hear constitutional challenges to instances of partisan gerrymandering. "A legislator cannot represent his constituents properly — nor can voters from a fragmented district exercise the ballot intelligently — when a voting district is nothing more than an artificial unit divorced from, and indeed often in conflict with, the various communities established in the State," wrote Powell.

The Court's opportunity to address that issue came in *Davis v. Bandemer* (478 U.S. 109). On June 30, 1986, the Court ruled that political gerrymanders are subject to constitutional review by federal courts, even if the disputed districts meet the one-person, one-vote test. The case arose from a challenge by Indiana Democrats who argued that the Republican-drawn map so heavily favored the Republican party that Democrats were denied appropriate representation. But the Court rejected the Democrats' challenge to the alleged gerrymander, saying that one election was insufficient to prove unconstitutional discrimination. Left unclear were what standards the Court would use to find a partisan gerrymander legally unacceptable.

National Republicans expressed delight with the *Bandemer* decision. The GOP had long held that Democratic control over most state legislatures had allowed them to draw congressional and legislative districts to their partisan advantage. In particular, Republicans expressed confidence that the *Bandemer* decision lay the groundwork for overturning California's congressional district map, created by Democratic Rep. Phillip Burton in the early 1980s.

Widely recognized as a classic example of a partisan gerrymander, the California map featured a number of oddly shaped districts, drawn neither compactly nor with respect to community boundaries, but all with nearly equal populations. As one commentator described it, "Burton carefully stretched districts from one Democratic enclave to another — sometimes joining them with nothing but a bridge, a stretch of harbor, or a spit of land ... — avoiding Republicans block for block and household for household." Before the 1982 elections, Democrats held 22 congressional districts, Republicans 21. With the Burton map in place for the 1982 elections, Democrats held 28 seats, Republicans only 17.

Republican Rep. Robert E. Badham filed a lawsuit against the Burton plan in federal district court in 1983. In the wake of the *Bandemer* decision, that court held a hearing on *Badham v. Eu* but dismissed the Republican complaint by a 2-1 vote. The court in essence ruled that a party seeking to overturn a gerrymandered map must show a general pattern of exclusion from the political process, which the California Republican Party, in control of the governorship, a Senate seat and 40 percent of the House seats, could not do. The Republicans appealed to the Supreme Court, but the Court refused to become involved, voting 6-3 in 1989 to reaffirm the lower court's decision without comment.

Minority Representation

One form of gerrymandering is expressly forbidden by law: redistricting for the purpose of racial discrimination. The Voting Rights Act of 1965, extended in 1970, 1975 and 1982, banned redistricting that diluted the voting strength of black communities. Other minorities, including Hispanics, Asian-Americans, American Indians and native Alaskans, subsequently were brought under the protection of the law.

In 1980, the Supreme Court for the first time narrowed the reach of the Voting Rights Act in the case of *Mobile v. Bolden,* a challenge to the at-large system of electing city commissioners used in Mobile, Ala. By a vote of 6-3, the Court ruled that proof of discriminatory intent by the commissioners was necessary before a violation could be found; the fact that no black had ever been elected under the challenged system was not proof enough.

The *Mobile* decision set off an immediate reaction on Capitol Hill. In extending the Voting Rights Act in 1982, Congress amended it to outlaw any practice that had the effect of discriminating against blacks or other minorities — regardless of the lawmakers' intent.

The Justice Department later adopted a similar "results test" for another part of the act (Section 5), which required certain states and localities with a history of discrimination to have their electoral plans "precleared" by the department. In 1986, the Supreme Court applied this test in *Thornburg v. Gingles* (478 U.S. 30), ruling that six of North Carolina's multi-member legislative districts impermissibly diluted black voting strength. Sharply departing from *Mobile,* the Court held that because very few blacks had been elected from these districts, the system must be in violation of the law.

The Court also used the *Thornburg* decision to develop three criteria that, if met, should lead to the creation of a minority legislative district: The minority group must be large and geographically compact enough to constitute a majority in a single-member electoral district, the group must be politically cohesive and the white majority must vote as a bloc to the degree that it usually can defeat candidates preferred by the minority. Thus, within a period of 10 years, the burden of proof was shifted from minorities, who had been required to show that lines were being drawn to dilute their voting strength, to lawmakers, who had to show that they had done all they could to maximize minority voting strength.

Another important ruling came in 1989, when a special three-judge federal panel ordered Arkansas to redraw its state legislative districts to create almost as many black majority districts as was mathematically possible. The *Jeffers v. Clinton* decision was left intact by the Supreme Court, which declined to hear the case.

Further, in 1990, a federal district judge ruled in *Garza v. County of Los Angeles* that the Los Angeles County Board of Supervisors had violated the Voting Rights Act by gerrymandering its districts to dilute the Hispanic vote. The judge ordered the creation of a majority-Hispanic district.

In the 1990s round of redistricting, for the first time, states operated under federal legal mandates to draw lines that maximized the number of "majority-minority" districts — constituencies where blacks and Hispanics made up a majority of the population. Redistricting experts also argued about how to draw lines in areas where the minority population was sizable but not large or compact enough to make up a majority in a new district. Some advocated "minority-influence" districts, which might be as much as 40 percent black or Hispanic, but others feared these districts could become polarized, with white representatives unconcerned about their minority constituents.

In the first lower court ruling on this matter, a three-judge panel in *Armour v. Ohio* ordered the pooling of blacks in the Youngstown area into a state House district whose population would be one-third black. The court said that minority voters then would have "the ability to elect the candidate of their choice" — though not necessarily a black candidate. In *Turner v. Arkansas,* a three-judge

The Voting Rights Act

In 1965, President Lyndon B. Johnson asked Congress to pass a voting rights measure to close legal loopholes that enabled local officials to stall black voter registration. Within months, Congress approved the sweeping Voting Rights Act of 1965, which was later extended in 1970, 1975 and 1982. The law suspended literacy tests, provided for the appointment of federal supervisors of voting registration in all states where literacy testing or qualifying devices had been in effect and established criminal penalties for persons found guilty of interfering with the voting rights of others.

The law originally was aimed at those Southern states where blacks had long been targets of discrimination. When the original law was passed, racial redistricting was not a great problem given that black voting strength was minimal. However, with the enhancement of registration and voting rights for blacks, lawmakers feared that affected states would, through gerrymandering, divide black communities among several congressional districts and lower the chances of electing black representatives. That concern resulted in Section 5, the preclearance provisions of the act under which states with histories of racial discrimination must receive Justice Department approval of any changes in their election laws and procedures.

The Supreme Court has repeatedly backed and broadly interpreted the act. In its 1976 *Beers v. United States* decision, the Court said that if a minority district existed, it was to be protected in redistricting, but affirmative action was not necessary to create new districts. Early 1980s redistricting maps were judged by this standard.

The 1982 Voting Rights Act amendments and later court decisions established a broader mandate: Under Section 2 of the act, any state law that had the effect of diluting minority voting strength, regardless of legislative intent, was deemed illegal. A key Supreme Court ruling in 1986, *Thornburg v. Gingles*, signaled states to create minority districts wherever possible. In 1987, the Justice Department issued new regulations prohibiting preclearance of laws that clearly violated Section 2, even if they complied with the Section 5 non-retrogression standard.

The Voting Rights Act is widely regarded as the most effective civil rights measure ever enacted. The voter registration provisions have been highly successful, with black registration in Mississippi increasing from 6.7 percent in 1964 to 67.4 percent in 1976. It has also effected the numbers of blacks winning elective office. When the act was first passed in 1965, there were six black members of Congress; in 1993 there were 39 black and 19 Hispanic House members and one black senator.

panel ruled against black and Republican plaintiffs who wanted Arkansas to create a 42 percent black minority-influence congressional district, maintaining that the criteria established in *Thornburg* required only the creation of majority-minority districts.

The Supreme Court on June 28, 1993, invited a new wave of lawsuits challenging the constitutionality of districts drawn to ensure the election of minorities. In a 5-4 ruling in *Shaw v. Reno,* the Court reinstated a suit by five white North Carolinians who contended that the state's congressional district map, which created in 1992 two sinuous majority-black districts, violated their 14th Amendment right to "equal protection under law." The Court, however, did not invalidate North Carolina's map or rule in favor of the plaintiffs' 14th Amendment complaint.

The ruling's implications extended well beyond the narrow action taken in *Shaw.* By calling into question the constitutionality of the amorphous computer-generated entities that wriggled through areas to collect a majority of minority voters, the Court gave legal standing to challenges to any congressional map with an oddly shaped majority-minority district that may not be defensible on grounds other than race, such as shared community interest or geographical compactness.

The decision triggered a debate among constitutional scholars, civil rights advocates and minority-group representatives over how effective majority-minority districts were in helping minorities attain equal representation. It also raised questions about the viability and constitutionality of the Voting Rights Act of 1965 and its 1982 amendments. More than anything, though, *Shaw* appeared to breed confusion over what, if any, new standards needed to be applied to a redistricting plan. For some, the case established a contradictory set of criteria for a state, subject to the Voting Rights Act, to win federal approval of a map. While the Justice Department or a federal court must approve the state's redistricting plans, *Shaw* raised the possibility that Justice Department insistence on creating the maximum number of minority districts may be challenged on constitutional grounds.

In her majority opinion, Justice Sandra Day O'Connor decried the creation of districts based solely on racial composition. She wrote, "[W]e believe that reapportionment is one area in which appearances do matter. A reapportionment plan that includes in one district individuals . . . who may have little in common with one another but the color of their skin bears an uncomfortable resemblance to political apartheid." O'Connor's opinion was regarded as signaling dissatisfaction with the broad interpretation of the Voting Rights Act's mandate, as expressed in *Thornburg,* for states to create minority districts wherever possible.

Congress and Redistricting

Congress considered several proposals in the post-World War II period concerning redistricting. Only one of these efforts was successful — enactment of a measure barring at-large elections in states with more than one House seat.

On Jan. 9, 1951, President Harry S. Truman, upon presentation of the official state population figures of the 1950 census, asked for a ban on gerrymandering, an end to at-large seats in states having more than one representative and a sharp reduction in the huge differences in size among congressional districts within most states. On behalf of the administration, Emanuel Celler, D-N.Y., chairman of the House Judiciary Committee, introduced a bill reflecting these requests, but the committee took no action.

Rep. Celler regularly introduced the bill throughout the 1950s and early 1960s, but it made no headway until the Supreme Court handed down the *Wesberry* decision in 1964. The House passed a version of the Celler bill in 1965, largely to discourage the Supreme Court from imposing even more rigid criteria. The Senate, however, took no action and the measure died.

In 1967, after defeating a conference report that would have prevented the courts from ordering a state to redistrict or to hold at-large elections until after the 1970 census, Congress approved a measure to ban at-large elections in all states entitled to more than one representative. Exceptions were made for New Mexico and Hawaii, which had a tradition of electing their representatives at large. Both states, however, soon passed districting laws, New Mexico for the 1968 elections and Hawaii for 1970.

Bills to increase the size of the House to prevent states from losing seats as a result of population shifts have been introduced after most recent censuses, but Congress has given little consideration to any of them.

The Presidency

Bush Appointments 1169
Presidential Vetoes 1181
Presidential Texts 1183

Bush Appointments to Major Posts

Despite Democratic control of Congress, President George Bush began his term with a high level of support for his Cabinet nominations. All but one of his 11 original selections were confirmed by the Senate, nine unanimously. The one defeat was the bitter battle over the nomination of John Tower to be secretary of defense.

Three Cabinet members were holdovers from the Reagan administration and did not need to be reconfirmed: Treasury Secretary Nicholas F. Brady, Education Secretary Lauro F. Cavazos and Attorney General Dick Thornburgh. In addition, James A. Baker III, who served as Reagan's Treasury secretary, was confirmed as Bush's secretary of state.

Bush selected Edward J. Derwinski to become the first secretary of veterans affairs. The Veterans Administration was upgraded to the new Cabinet-level Department of Veterans Affairs effective March 15, 1989.

No Cabinet position had more than one turnover during Bush's tenure, and six Cabinet members remained at their posts throughout Bush's four-year term. As the 1992 election drew near, several members resigned to take positions in the campaign or to remove themselves as potential liabilities to the president. *(Bush Cabinet, box, p. 1171)*

Bush chose about one-fourth of the federal bench. He continued Reagan's policy of appointing conservative jurists who kept to a narrow reading of the Constitution and federal law and who held a restrictive view of individual rights. Bush appointed a record level of females to the federal district courts, but blacks and Hispanics were under-represented in his judicial choices. Bush named two justices to the U.S. Supreme Court: David L. Souter and Clarence Thomas. *(Bush judicial appointments, box, p. 776; Souter, Thomas nominations, p. 801)*

As during Reagan's term, Sen. Jesse Helms, R-N.C., held up ambassadorial nominees whose positions did not agree with his conservative agenda. Other Bush diplomatic nominees were criticized for lacking foreign policy experience, and the president was accused of offering appointments as political rewards for large campaign donations.

Below are profiles of Cabinet members and others who served in key executive branch positions during the Bush administration, followed by brief accounts of major controversial nominations made from 1989 to 1992.

Cabinet, 1989-92

Agriculture

A farmer-rancher from Nebraska, **Clayton Yeutter** on Feb. 8, 1989, won unanimous 100-0 approval from the Senate to be secretary of agriculture. The day before, his nomination received unanimous support from the Senate Agriculture Committee.

During the confirmation hearing, Yeutter preached a message broadly popular in Congress: Boosting U.S. agriculture required hard-nosed efforts to expand its share of the international market. He made clear his basic philosophical approach when he criticized government programs for giving farmers "little or no flexibility," which he said created "distortions in production patterns for the nation as a whole." One of his goals, Yeutter said, was "to loosen the bonds between government and farmers." He added that the budget deficit also made that imperative.

Yeutter's appointment returned him to the federal agency where he got his start in 1970 as administrator of the Consumer and Marketing Service. He subsequently served as assistant secretary of agriculture for marketing and consumer services from 1973 to 1974, then assistant secretary of agriculture for international affairs and commodity programs from 1974 to 1975. He was deputy to the U.S. trade representative from 1975 through 1977, after which he took a hiatus from government service to become president of the Chicago Mercantile Exchange. In 1985, President Ronald Reagan selected Yeutter to be U.S. trade representative.

Edward R. Madigan was confirmed 99-0 by the Senate March 7, 1991, as secretary of agriculture. He succeeded Yeutter, who resigned March 1, 1991, to become chairman of the Republican National Committee.

Madigan's selection culminated an unusually public campaign by the Illinois Republican to join the Cabinet. Madigan had engaged in an all-out lobbying effort to persuade Bush and his chief of staff, John H. Sununu, to appoint him to the post. He made entreaties directly to the White House seeking to replace Yeutter after Republicans told him President Bush needed to build a better relationship with the agriculture community as the 1992 election drew closer. And fellow House GOP members circulated letters on his behalf, one signed by 132 members.

A House member for 19 years, Madigan served for two years as chief deputy whip. He was the ranking Republican member of the House Agriculture Committee and of the Energy and Commerce Subcommittee on Health and the Environment. Madigan had a reputation as a steady and thoughtful lawmaker who worked well with all members of Congress. His hope of moving up in the leadership, however, was dashed in 1989 when he lost by two votes to Newt Gingrich of Georgia to become minority whip.

During confirmation hearings by the Senate Agriculture Committee, Democrats and Republicans heaped accolades on Madigan. Committee Chairman Patrick J. Leahy, D-Vt., said, "He is a tough but fair and open-minded legislator." The committee approved Madigan's nomination by voice vote on March 6.

Attorney General

Attorney General **Dick Thornburgh** was a holdover from the Reagan administration. Confirmed unanimously by the Senate on Aug. 11, 1988, Thornburgh succeeded the controversial Edwin Meese III. Thornburgh had held several positions at the Justice Department, was a two-term governor of Pennsylvania and served as director of Harvard University's John F. Kennedy School of Government. *(Congress and the Nation Vol. VII, p. 1044)*

Thornburgh resigned as attorney general on Aug. 9, 1991, to run for the U.S. Senate; he lost.

Acting Attorney General **William P. Barr** won easy voice vote approval by the Senate Nov. 21, 1991, to succeed Thornburgh.

The Senate Judiciary Committee on Nov. 15 had unanimously approved, 14-0, Barr's nomination. Committee Chairman Joseph R. Biden Jr., D-Del., said that, although Barr held conservative views similar to those of Thornburgh and Meese, "he's a throwback to the days when we had an attorney general who would actually talk to you." Barr's predecessors often jousted with Congress over the Justice Department's operations and ideological focus.

In his testimony, Barr defended Justice's role in the investigation of the Bank of Credit and Commerce International (BCCI), boldly stated his opposition to legalized abortion and said a special counsel was reviewing allegations that Justice Department officials conspired to force a computer software company into bankruptcy.

The only concern raised in committee was by Dennis DeConcini, D-Ariz., who questioned whether the department's Nov. 14 indictments against two Libyan intelligence officers in the 1988 bombing of a Pan Am jumbo jet over Lockerbie, Scotland, was timed to coincide with Barr's confirmation. The allegation was denied.

Barr was assistant attorney general in the Office of Legal Counsel from 1989 to 1991, deputy assistant director at the Domestic Policy Council under President Reagan and a midlevel professional at the CIA from 1973 to 1977.

Commerce

Robert A. Mosbacher, a multimillionaire Houston oilman and longtime friend of President Bush, was confirmed 100-0 by the Senate to be secretary of commerce on Jan. 31, 1989. Earlier in the day, he received unanimous support from the Senate Commerce, Science and Transportation Committee.

Mosbacher had come under fire from Common Cause, the self-styled citizens' lobby, and other groups for failing to provide full disclosure about his efforts to solicit "soft money" contributions for George Bush outside of the federal campaign finance reporting system. Senate Commerce Chairman Ernest F. Hollings, D-S.C., said that Mosbacher did nothing illegal and chided Congress for not enacting stricter campaign finance laws. Questions also were raised about Mosbacher's involvement in an oil-drilling joint venture in the Philippines in which then-president Ferdinand E. Marcos was a secret partner.

During his confirmation hearings, Mosbacher vowed to promote American business aggressively and enforce laws against unfair foreign competition. He said trade was a "two-way street" that required countries selling products in the United States to open their markets to U.S. exporters. Mosbacher promised to give high priority to furthering private sector high-technology initiatives and to efforts to clean up the oceans and coastal environment.

Mosbacher was chief fund-raiser for Gerald R. Ford's 1976 presidential re-election campaign and Bush's 1980 and 1988 campaigns. In addition, he served as director of the Aspen Institute and on the advisory board of the Center for Strategic and International Studies. He graduated from Washington and Lee University and garnered international yachting championships. In 1986, he married Georgette Paulsin, principal owner of a cosmetics company, La Prairie. The Mosbachers were favorite subjects for society and style pages in New York and Houston.

Barbara H. Franklin was confirmed by the Senate by voice vote on Feb. 27, 1992, to be secretary of commerce. She replaced Mosbacher, who resigned Jan. 15, 1992, to join Bush's re-election team.

The only opposition to Franklin was raised by Commerce Chairman Hollings and panel member John D. Rockefeller IV, D-W.Va., who feared that she would not sufficiently challenge Bush's free-trade policies. Rockefeller argued that the administration's trade policy needed drastic changes and that Franklin would be only a "capable steward of the status quo." Her nomination was approved by the Commerce Committee on Feb. 18 with Rockefeller casting the lone "nay" vote.

Franklin headed her own management consulting firm and served as a member of the Consumer Product Safety Commission during the 1970s. She was appointed by Presidents Reagan and Bush to the President's Advisory Commission on Trade Negotiations (1982-86, 1989-92).

Defense

Dick Cheney was confirmed by the Senate March 17, 1989, to be secretary of defense by a vote of 92-0. His confirmation came after a quick and amicable review, which was a bold contrast to the long, drawn-out battle and ultimate rejection of President Bush's first choice for the post: former Texas senator John Tower. *(Controversial nominations, p. 1177)*

The Senate Armed Services Committee's one open hearing on the nomination, held March 14, was replete with tributes to Cheney's personal integrity and close-knit family life. Cheney assured the panel that he would squeeze Pentagon spending into the overall totals projected by the administration but added that he would underscore the consequences of substantial reductions from earlier budget plans.

During his confirmation hearings, Cheney expressed doubts that Mikhail S. Gorbachev would succeed in making serious changes in the Soviet government. If reforms were instituted, Cheney was inclined to believe the Soviet state would be rendered less centralized and less militaristic. He thought, however, that the West should not seize on hopeful signs of changes in Moscow to rationalize imprudent reductions in military preparedness.

Cheney shied away from answering most questions about specific issues. He did urge restraint in expanding the military's role in keeping illegal drugs out of the United States and backed a controversial agreement under which U.S. and Japanese firms would collaborate to develop a new jet fighter for Japan, designated FS-X.

The committee took a particularly close look at Cheney's medical status because of his history of coronary artery disease. He had heart attacks in 1978, 1984 and

Bush Administration Cabinet

Following is a list of Cabinet officers who served in the Bush administration from the time President Bush took office on Jan. 20, 1989, until the end of his term on Jan. 20, 1993. President Bush retained three Cabinet members from the Reagan administration (Treasury Secretary Nicholas F. Brady, Education Secretary Lauro F. Cavazos and Attorney General Dick Thornburgh); they did not have to be reconfirmed.

Dates given are for actual service in office, which may vary from dates of confirmation by the Senate. *(Presidents and their Cabinets, 1933-80, Congress and the Nation Vol. V, p. 1111; Reagan Cabinet, 1981-89, Congress and the Nation Vol. VII, p. 1045)*

Secretary of State

James A. Baker III—Jan. 27, 1989-Aug. 23, 1992
Lawrence S. Eagleburger[a]—Dec. 8, 1992-Jan. 19, 1993

Secretary of the Treasury

Nicholas F. Brady—Sept. 16, 1988-Jan. 20, 1993

Secretary of Defense

Dick Cheney—March 21, 1989-Jan. 20, 1993

Attorney General

Dick Thornburgh—Aug. 12, 1988-Aug. 9, 1991
William P. Barr—Nov. 26, 1991-Jan. 20, 1993

Secretary of the Interior

Manuel Lujan Jr.—Feb. 8, 1989-Jan. 20, 1993

Secretary of Agriculture

Clayton Yeutter—Feb. 16, 1989-March 1, 1991
Edward R. Madigan—March 12, 1991-Jan. 20, 1993

Secretary of Commerce

Robert A. Mosbacher—Feb. 3, 1989-Jan. 15, 1992
Barbara H. Franklin—Feb. 27, 1992-Jan. 20, 1993

Secretary of Labor

Elizabeth H. Dole—Jan. 30, 1989-Nov. 23, 1990
Lynn M. Martin—Feb. 22, 1991-Jan. 20, 1993

Secretary of Health and Human Services

Louis W. Sullivan—March 10, 1989-Jan. 20, 1993

Secretary of Education

Lauro F. Cavazos—Sept. 20, 1988-Dec. 12, 1990
Lamar Alexander—March 22, 1991-Jan. 20, 1993

Secretary of Housing and Urban Development

Jack F. Kemp—Feb. 13, 1989-Jan. 20, 1993

Secretary of Transportation

Samuel K. Skinner—Feb. 6, 1989-Dec. 16, 1991
Andrew H. Card Jr.—Feb. 21, 1992-Jan. 20, 1993

Secretary of Energy

James D. Watkins—March 9, 1989-Jan. 20, 1993

Secretary of Veterans Affairs

Edward J. Derwinski—March 15, 1989-Sept. 26, 1992

[a] Eagleburger served as a recess appointment. His name was never submitted to the Senate for confirmation.

1988, and he underwent coronary bypass surgery in 1988. Panel members were reassured by Cheney's cardiologist.

Cheney received a series of draft deferments in the 1960s; he thus became the fifth secretary of defense without prior military service.

Cheney was deputy assistant to President Gerald R. Ford in 1974-75 and White House chief of staff in 1975-76. He was elected to the House in 1978 as the at-large representative of Wyoming. He won his first leadership post in 1981 as chairman of the Republican Policy Committee and moved up in 1987 to chairman of the House Republican Conference. He served on the House Intelligence Committee since 1985 and became House minority whip at the start of the 101st Congress in 1989.

During the Reagan years, Cheney was an active behind-the-scenes player on foreign policy, sometimes offering the administration private advice that differed with stated policy. In late 1983 and early 1984, for example, he urged Reagan to pull the U.S. Marines from Lebanon. In 1987, Cheney was the senior Republican on the House select committee probing the Iran-contra affair. While an ardent supporter of Reagan's backing of the contras, he said that Lt. Col. Oliver L. North and others were "stupid" to lie to Congress.

Historian Lynne V. Cheney, Cheney's wife, chaired the National Endowment for the Humanities from 1986 to 1992.

Education

President Bush retained **Lauro F. Cavazos** in the top spot at the Department of Education. Cavazos, a Ph.D. in psychology who was president of Texas Tech University, succeeded William J. Bennett in September 1988. The White House asked Cavazos to resign in December 1990, citing frustration with the lack of progress in education reform. On Capitol Hill, where Bush's education proposals died at the hands of Senate Republicans during the 101st Congress, lawmakers and education aides described Cavazos as a dolphin among sharks — an ineffective spokesman and lobbyist for education. *(Congress and the Nation Vol. VII, p. 1046)*

Replacing Cavazos at the Education Department was **Lamar Alexander**, governor of Tennessee from 1979 to 1987. He was confirmed by the Senate on March 14, 1991, by voice vote. The day before, the Senate Labor and Human Resources Committee approved his nomination 16-0, with Tom Harkin, D-Iowa, voting "present."

Concerns over Alexander's financial dealings surfaced in committee hearings. Revelations that Alexander had earned large sums of money with little investment of his own while governor prompted members to scrutinize his financial statements. His net worth jumped from about $321,000 in 1984 to between $2 million and $3 million in 1991, according to the committee. In the end, members said they felt Alexander's potential to improve the nation's education system outweighed doubts about his finances.

His only detractor, Harkin, commented, "Frankly the whole thing sounds to me like someone paying a lot of attention to making money while in public service."

Alexander was considered a determined and savvy politician. As governor, he pushed through the Democratic-controlled legislature a major education package, which would be financed with a 1-cent sales tax increase. As chairman of the National Governors' Association, Alexander encouraged other governors to examine their states' education systems. In January 1988, he became president of the University of Tennessee system.

Energy

On March 1, 1989, the Senate Energy and Natural Resources Committee voted 19-0 to report favorably to the Senate the nomination of **James D. Watkins** as energy secretary. Later the same day, the full Senate confirmed him on a 99-0 vote.

Watkins served in the Navy from 1949 to 1986, retiring with the rank of admiral. A U.S. Naval Academy graduate, he worked for the Atomic Energy Commission in 1962-64 and was executive officer of the USS *Long Beach,* the Navy's first nuclear-powered surface ship, in 1967-69. Watkins was chief of naval personnel in 1975-78, commander of the Sixth Fleet (Mediterranean) in 1978-79, commander in chief of the U.S. Pacific Fleet in 1981-82 and chief of naval operations in 1982-86. He was the recipient of the Distinguished Service Medal, Legion of Merit, Navy Commendation Medal and Vietnam Service Medal.

In October 1987, President Reagan asked Watkins to step in as chairman of the Presidential Commission on the Human Immunodeficiency Virus (HIV) Epidemic. (HIV is the virus that causes AIDS — acquired immune deficiency syndrome.) He was credited with quickly bringing leadership and direction to the faltering commission. On June 24, 1988, the commission issued a report containing nearly 600 recommendations, including the widely publicized call for federal legislation to prevent discrimination against those infected with HIV.

No opposition to Watkins was expressed throughout the confirmation proceedings. During the hearings, Watkins pledged to shake up management of the troubled nuclear weapons production program and make safety its "bedrock." He vowed tighter controls over the private contractors who performed much of the weapons production work. He also said he would try to forge an "integrated energy strategy" to reduce dependence on oil imports and avert the risk of global warming.

Health and Human Services

Louis W. Sullivan won Senate confirmation as secretary of health and human services (HHS) on March 1, 1989, by a vote of 98-1. Jesse Helms, R-N.C., cast the lone "nay" vote "as a matter of conscience," he said, because of Sullivan's "failure or refusal ... to take positions on a number of extremely important issues" concerning abortion-related matters within the purview of the department.

The nomination of Sullivan, a physician and director of Atlanta's Morehouse School of Medicine, caused a furor among anti-abortion groups, who accused him of coming down on both sides of the abortion issue.

In appearances before the Finance Committee, which approved his nomination 19-0 on Feb. 23, and before the Labor and Human Resources Committee, Sullivan appeared to allay the fears of senators opposed to abortion. He insisted that his views were identical to President Bush's: He opposed abortion except in cases of rape, incest or danger to the life of the mother, and he favored reversal of *Roe v. Wade*, the landmark 1973 Supreme Court decision that legalized abortion nationwide.

Controversy also arose over whether Sullivan would have to forgo several hundred thousand dollars in accrued sabbatical and severance pay from Morehouse. After consulting with federal ethics officials, Sullivan voluntarily agreed not to accept any of the money at issue. However, members of both the Finance and Labor committees questioned whether Sullivan needed to give up the payments. They voiced concern that if he relinquished payments that did not violate ethics rules, others from academia might be reluctant to serve in the government in the future. On March 28, 1989, a compromise was reached: Sullivan was allowed to accept his severance pay but would be placed on an unpaid leave of absence from the college while he served as secretary.

Questions were raised about the financial arrangements that Morehouse's medical school had with Reginald Eaves, a former Fulton County, Ga., commissioner convicted of extortion. Eaves' situation, however, did not warrant withdrawal of Sullivan's nomination.

In his testimony, Sullivan said that as HHS secretary he would emphasize preventative medicine, particularly given budget constraints. He also warned that his fellow practitioners should be prepared to share in the effort to restrain medical costs.

Sullivan, a specialist in blood disorders related to vitamin deficiencies, had served as chairman of the National Leukemia Association. He was the only African-American to serve in the Bush Cabinet.

Housing and Urban Development

Jack F. Kemp was confirmed by a vote of 100-0 by the Senate on Feb. 2, 1989, to be secretary of housing and urban development (HUD).

Kemp served nine terms in the House, from 1971 to 1989, as a representative for a district in the Buffalo area of western New York and established himself as an effective and outspoken advocate of conservative causes. In 1981, he became chairman of the House Republican Conference. He unsuccessfully challenged Vice President George Bush for the 1988 Republican presidential nomination. Kemp was a professional football quarterback from 1957 to 1970 and was once named the American Football League most valuable player.

Kemp was expected to have to field a number of questions from the Banking, Housing and Urban Affairs Committee relating to his 1988 outside earned income. He reported income of $93,950 in speaking fees — substantially above the $26,850 limit imposed by the House. Aides to Kemp said that, when he filed his financial disclosure form Jan. 19, 1989, he had not yet received much of the money. Furthermore, they said it was unclear whether limits applied to pay for 1988 events received after Kemp left office Jan. 3, 1989. He subsequently decided to follow rules and laws as they applied to sitting members. Thus, he returned or refused to accept some fees and deferred accepting other payments until 1989, which House rules allowed. After a corrected disclosure form was sent to the U.S. Office of Government Ethics, the subject was dropped and not mentioned in the hearings.

Kemp testified that as HUD secretary he would give the problem of homelessness "the highest priority." He extolled the virtues of enterprise zones and tenant ownership of public housing and endorsed the low-income housing tax credit and the mortgage revenue bond program for first-time home buyers. Kemp was approved by the committee 21-0 on Feb. 2.

Interior

Manuel Lujan Jr., a ten-term member of the U.S. House (1969-89) from New Mexico, won unanimous approval by the Senate on Feb. 2, 1989, to be secretary of the interior.

The Senate Energy and Natural Resources Committee approved his nomination Feb. 1 without a dissenting vote. Chairman J. Bennett Johnston, D-La., began the hearing by quipping, "I look forward to voting for your confirmation, almost no matter what you say." That tone pervaded the remainder of the session, despite some contentious issues that were raised. Western senators, in particular, reminded Lujan how important his decisions were to their states. They went on to warn him not to allow eastern lawmakers to dictate western land use policy.

While his description of his agenda included little detail, Lujan stressed more attention to U.S. territories, to Indian schools, to the federal war on drugs and to minority appointments at the Department of the Interior. In the House, Lujan, like many Westerners, tended to favor development over conservation of oil, water and other natural resources. He also advocated more state control over federal lands.

Business groups praised Lujan's nomination, while environmentalists were more reserved. Although none of them flatly opposed him, they were concerned by his House voting record. Between 1973 and 1988, according to the League of Conservation Voters, he voted with environmentalists only 18 percent of the time.

While in the House, Lujan served as the ranking Republican on the Interior and Insular Affairs Committee and later on the Science, Space and Technology Committee.

Labor

Elizabeth H. Dole was confirmed by the Senate Jan. 25, 1989, by a vote of 99-0 to be secretary of labor.

Dole had won approval Jan. 19 from the Labor and Human Resources Committee on a 16-0 vote. At the confirmation hearing, her husband, Senate Minority Leader Robert Dole, R-Kan., introduced her as "an exceptional nominee . . . who can and will make a difference for America." Panel chairman Edward M. Kennedy, D-Mass., echoed the praise, calling Dole "an excellent choice . . . [with] a remarkable record of achievement."

Dole demurred as committee members pressed her to get specific on certain issues. While she did not state the administration's position on raising the minimum wage, she did reiterate Bush's support for a subminimum training wage. Dole also said that government should give business incentives to offer benefits such as job-protected unpaid parental leave and universal health insurance.

Only Howard M. Metzenbaum, D-Ohio, alluded to problems Dole faced as secretary of transportation during the Reagan administration. A group of women had criticized her for failing to follow through on anti-discrimination legislation; and a similar barrage of complaints came from transportation groups on safety issues.

Dole, a graduate of Duke University with a law degree from Harvard, was transportation secretary from 1983 to 1987. She resigned to work full time on her husband's bid for the 1988 Republican presidential nomination. She worked from 1968 to 1971 as the executive director of the Presidential Commission for Consumer Interests, from 1971 to 1973 as deputy director of the White House Office of Consumer Affairs under President Richard Nixon, from 1973 to 1979 as a member of the Federal Trade Commission and from 1981 to 1983 as assistant to President Reagan for public liaison. *(Congress and the Nation Vol. VI, p. 1024)*

On a 94-0 vote Feb. 7, 1991, the Senate confirmed **Lynn M. Martin** as secretary of labor to succeed Dole, who resigned Nov. 23, 1990, to become head of the American Red Cross. Martin's nomination had been approved 17-0 the day before by the Senate Labor and Human Resources Committee.

Martin had longstanding ties to George Bush, having backed him in his first presidential bid in 1980 and served as national co-chair of his 1988 campaign. Her policy positions did not always match his, however. For example, she favored legislation mandating unpaid leave for workers caring for newborn children or seriously ill family members. She emphasized to the committee, though, that as labor secretary she would back whatever position Bush took.

Martin served five terms as a Republican representative from Illinois (1981-91). She made an unsuccessful run for the Senate in 1990 against incumbent Democrat Paul Simon. While in the House, she served on the Rules Committee and was co-chair of a bipartisan panel formed by House leaders in February 1989 to review House ethics standards. She began her political career in the Illinois Senate, where she served from 1979 to 1981.

State

James A. Baker III won unanimous approval, 99-0, by the Senate Jan. 25, 1989, to be secretary of state. He won a 19-0 endorsement Jan. 19 from the Senate Foreign Relations Committee amid praise from both Republicans and Democrats, especially for his call for bipartisanship. He was lauded for his political savvy and negotiating skills.

What little in the way of persistent questioning that Baker faced from the committee came from Republicans — particularly the ranking minority member, Jesse Helms of North Carolina. Helms pressed Baker on El Salvador, Angola and other issues. Often reading from briefing papers prepared by the State Department, Baker rarely departed from foreign policy positions of the Reagan administration. He did admit that Reagan's policy toward Nicaragua failed because of lack of support on Capitol Hill. On many points, Baker simply told senators that he had no answers to their questions.

Baker graduated from Princeton, received his law degree from the University of Texas and spent two years in the Marine Corps. While working as a corporate attorney in Houston, Baker got involved in politics in 1970 by running George Bush's unsuccessful Senate campaign. He went on to head Gerald R. Ford's 1976 re-election campaign, Bush's bid for the 1980 Republican presidential nomination and Bush's 1988 presidential campaign.

Baker served as undersecretary of commerce in the Ford administration. From 1981 to 1985, he was White House chief of staff, and in 1985, he took over as Ronald Reagan's Treasury secretary. *(Congress and the Nation Vol. VII, p. 1047)*

Baker resigned Aug. 23, 1992, as secretary of state to become President Bush's chief of staff. He replaced Samuel K. Skinner. Deputy Secretary of State **Lawrence S. Eagleburger** was named acting secretary of state. On Dec. 8, 1992, Eagleburger was sworn in as secretary of state to handle affairs until the change of administrations. As a recess appointment, Eagleburger's selection did not require Senate approval.

A career foreign service officer for 27 years, Eagleburger served during the Reagan administration as assistant secretary of state for European affairs from 1981 to 1982 and as undersecretary of state for political affairs from 1982 to 1984. After retiring from the State Department in 1984, he joined Kissinger Associates, a New York-based consulting firm for U.S. and foreign businesses that was headed by former secretary of state Henry A. Kissinger.

Eagleburger had come under close scrutiny during his 1989 confirmation hearings to become deputy secretary of state because of possible conflicts of interest between his former clients at Kissinger Associates and the duties of the No. 2 official at the State Department.

Transportation

Samuel K. Skinner was unanimously confirmed by the Senate on Jan. 31, 1989, to become secretary of transportation. He won unanimous support from the Senate Commerce, Science and Transportation Committee earlier the same day.

Skinner's familiarity with transportation issues — not a characteristic of all transportation secretaries — won him backing from transportation lobbyists. During his confirmation hearings, he described himself as a problem-solver able to work with both parties. As transportation secretary, he said, his principal goal would be to develop a national policy to account for transportation needs into the 21st century. He opposed proposals to raise the federal gasoline tax to reduce the budget deficit.

At the time of his nomination, Skinner was chairman of the Regional Transportation Authority of Northeastern Illinois, the nation's second largest mass transportation system. He served as U.S. attorney for Illinois from 1975 to 1977 and later as chairman of the Illinois Capitol Development Board. He also earned an all-weather pilot's license.

The Senate confirmed **Andrew H. Card Jr.** as transportation secretary by voice vote on Feb. 21, 1992. He succeeded Skinner, who resigned Dec. 16, 1991, to become President Bush's chief of staff, replacing John H. Sununu. Card was deputy chief of staff and was one of Bush's most trusted political advisers. He did not have extensive experience with transportation issues, and his nomination was widely viewed as a reward for years of loyal service to the president.

The Senate Commerce, Science and Transportation Committee approved Card's nomination by voice vote on Feb. 18 after minimal debate.

A Massachusetts native, Card served in the state House of Representatives from 1974 to 1983 and unsuccessfully ran for governor in 1982. He managed Bush's crucial primary victory in New Hampshire in 1988. An engineer, Card also had been vice president of the CMIS Corp., a computer software company in Vienna, Va.

Treasury

Upon assuming the presidency, George Bush kept on his longtime associate **Nicholas F. Brady** as Treasury secretary. Brady had been confirmed on Sept. 14, 1988, to succeed James A. Baker III; Baker had resigned to run Bush's 1988 presidential campaign.

Brady had been an investment banker and was appointed in 1982 to fill the remaining Senate term of Harrison A. Williams Jr., D-N.J. He served on several presidential commissions during the Reagan administration, before being tapped for Treasury. *(Congress and the Nation Vol. VII, p. 1048)*

Veterans Affairs

Edward J. Derwinski was confirmed 94-0 by the Senate on March 2, 1989, and was thereby designated the first secretary of veterans affairs (VA). Earlier that day, the Senate Veterans' Affairs Committee approved his nomination 11-0.

The new Cabinet position was created when President Reagan signed HR 3471 (PL 100-527) on Oct. 25, 1988, transforming the Veterans Administration into the 14th executive department. The law became effective on March 15, 1989.

Derwinski was widely regarded as an expert in foreign policy and the civil service. A veteran of World War II, Derwinski served in the House, representing Illinois, from 1959 to 1983. He twice before had gone through the Senate confirmation process — in 1983 to be counselor at the State Department and in 1987 to be undersecretary of state for security assistance, science and technology.

His nomination as VA secretary had been delayed by allegations that in 1977 he tipped off South Korea about the impending defection of one of its officials. During hearings, Veterans' Affairs Committee Chairman Alan Cranston, D-Calif., said the Korean incident "raises serious ethical questions" about Derwinski.

Derwinski admitted that at the height of the investigation into "Koreagate" — an alleged conspiracy by Korea to influence U.S. legislation by bribing members of Congress — he inadvertently told a South Korean embassy official that a South Korean intelligence officer was about to defect to the United States. He said "no motive other than frustration" that Koreagate was overblown and would endanger U.S.-Korean relations was at work. He conceded, however, that "it was a rather stupid thing for me to do."

Cranston repeatedly quizzed the nominee on whether he had any other contact with the South Korean embassy. Published reports alleged that Derwinski telephoned the embassy; the conversation reportedly was taped by U.S. intelligence. Testifying under oath, Derwinski told the panel he was "absolutely sure" no other communications were made.

Derwinski's slip was the focus of a 1977 federal grand jury investigation as well as one conducted by the House Committee on Standards of Official Conduct (ethics committee). Both probes were dropped without implicating Derwinski in any wrongdoing.

Derwinski resigned on Sept. 26, 1992, as a result of increased criticism from veterans organizations and a fear that President Bush was losing support from those groups. Deputy VA Secretary Anthony J. Principi was named acting secretary. Derwinski became deputy chairman for ethnic coalitions on the 1992 Bush/Quayle campaign.

Other Key Positions

Office of Management and Budget

By a vote of 99-0, **Richard G. Darman** on Jan. 25, 1989, won Senate approval to head the Office of Management and Budget.

Two days earlier, Darman won unanimous support from the Senate Governmental Affairs Committee. In his appearance before the committee, he stuck firmly to President Bush's "Read my lips; no new taxes" pledge and essentially ruled out any administration effort to reduce the deficit by raising taxes, even if they were called by another name.

Democrats repeatedly tried to pin Darman down on the administration's fiscal plans, but he refused to give specifics in advance of Bush's fiscal 1990 recommendations.

Darman previously held a variety of government positions, including assistant secretary of commerce for policy in the Ford administration and deputy Treasury secretary under James A. Baker III from 1985 to 1987. He graduated from Harvard University and Harvard Business School and later taught at Harvard's John F. Kennedy School of Government.

Office of U.S. Trade Representative

Carla A. Hills was confirmed by the Senate Jan. 31, 1989, to be U.S. trade representative by a vote of 100-0.

After a swift confirmation hearing on Jan. 27, the Senate Finance Committee voted 19-0 to approve Hills' nomination as the chief U.S. negotiator on trade issues. Hills, an attorney in Washington, D.C., graduated from Stanford University and Yale Law School. She previously had served as secretary of housing and urban development in the Ford administration and as assistant attorney general, civil division, at the Justice Department.

Hills' main obstacle heading into her confirmation hearings was her husband's position as chairman of an international trade consulting firm. He promised not to advise his wife on specific issues and to keep the counsel of the U.S. trade representative's office abreast of his business activities.

The hearing focused almost exclusively on trade matters, with Hills demonstrating a command of both broad trade policy and complex, narrower issues. Hills quashed conflict-of-interest objections by promising to recuse herself from any cases in which she previously represented a firm involved in a trade dispute. She pledged routine consultations with Congress and tough negotiations with trade partners and vowed to open foreign markets "with a crowbar or a handshake."

Council of Economic Advisers

Michael J. Boskin was unanimously confirmed by the Senate Feb. 2, 1989, to head the Council of Economic Advisers (CEA). A former director of the Center for Economic Policy Research at Stanford University and one of Bush's chief economic advisers during his 1988 campaign, Boskin described himself as a staunch advocate of the "flexible-freeze" plan for reducing the deficit. He called for reduced government spending coupled with steady economic growth and a reduction in interest rates as opposed to a tax hike to curb the deficit. Although only 43 at the time of his nomination, he was widely recognized for studies on taxation, saving and the Social Security program, and on the effect of government policy on the economy.

One of Boskin's chief goals as administrator was to restore credibility to the CEA, which, under Beryl W. Sprinkel, received criticism for its rosy view of the economy's potential for growth.

Environmental Protection Agency

William K. Reilly was confirmed, 100-0, by the Senate Feb. 2, 1989, to be administrator of the Environmental Protection Agency (EPA) after winning unanimous committee support earlier in the day.

The Senate Environment and Public Works Committee hearings were a honeymoon for Reilly, the first officer of an environmental group to be named to the top EPA slot. He had spent 16 years as president of the Conservation Foundation, a small environmental policy think tank, and of the U.S. affiliate of the World Wildlife Fund, an activist group devoted to saving the natural resources of developing nations. Reilly also had served as a senior staff member of the President's Council on Environmental Quality from 1970 to 1972.

Several senators, including Max Baucus, D-Mont., chairman of the Environmental Protection Subcommittee, hoped Reilly would be a tough enforcer of environmental laws. Committee members complained that the Office of Management and Budget in the past had denied EPA the funds needed to do its job and muzzled its regulatory and legislative initiatives.

Reilly supported giving EPA Cabinet status. Bush was reluctant to elevate the agency because he was trying to achieve a "more manageable Cabinet" by limiting its size. Bush, however, had assured Reilly that he would sit on the Domestic Policy Council and that he would "be in the Cabinet room whenever issues touch on the environment."

United Nations

The Senate on March 7, 1989, confirmed, by a vote of 99-0, the nomination of **Thomas R. Pickering** to the post of U.S. ambassador to the United Nations. In contrast to many of his predecessors, Bush selected a foreign service officer for the post instead of installing a political appointee. Bush relegated the U.N. position to the jurisdiction of the State Department, as opposed to its former role in the Cabinet.

Pickering served as ambassador to Israel, El Salvador and Nigeria under President Ronald Reagan. In addition, he was assistant secretary of state for oceans and international environmental and scientific affairs under President Jimmy Carter and ambassador to Jordan in the mid-1970s.

Pickering breezed through confirmation hearings despite admitting to the special Iran-contra committees in July 1987 that while in El Salvador he had helped arrange one shipment of military supplies to the contras in late 1984 or early 1985.

National Drug Control Policy

The often controversial **William J. Bennett** passed quietly through the confirmation process and was approved by the Senate March 9, 1989, as director of the new Office of National Drug Control Policy. The position, often referred to as the "drug czar," was created as a Cabinet-level post in the 1988 anti-drug abuse law (PL 100-690).

The Senate voted 97-2 to confirm Bennett, a former college professor of law and philosophy, who was described by proponents as honorable, capable and indefatigable. Earlier in the day, the Senate Judiciary Committee approved his nomination 13-1, the lone "nay" vote belonging to Sen. Paul Simon, D-Ill., who criticized Bennett's leadership ability while secretary of education in the Reagan administration.

Sen. Howard M. Metzenbaum, D-Ohio, and Simon also questioned his commitment to hiring minorities and his ability to work with other officials. Sen. Edward M. Kennedy, D-Mass., bristled when Bennett refused to take a stand on banning or restricting semiautomatic assault rifles, which had become a weapon of choice in the illegal drug trade.

At his hearing, Bennett would say only that as the director of national drug policy he would look into curbs on assault weapons. He said he had always been sensitive to minorities, including at the Education Department and at the National Endowment for the Humanities, where he was chairman from 1981 to 1985.

On March 21, 1991, the Senate 88-12 confirmed **Bob Martinez** to succeed Bennett despite concern over his qualifications for the post. The Senate Judiciary Committee had endorsed the nomination 11-3 on March 7.

Bennett resigned Nov. 30, 1990, to head the Republican National Committee but later withdrew to write a book and do public speaking. Democrats in Congress criticized Bennett for his combativeness and partisanship as drug czar.

Many Democratic committee members were critical of Martinez's performance while governor of Florida from 1987 to 1991. Kennedy pointed to Florida's high crime rate and poor anti-drug policy as reasons to oppose Martinez. Chairman Joseph R. Biden Jr., D-Del., objected to the low regard Martinez placed on drug education programs. Simon derided Martinez for not promising to stay away from partisan politics.

Proponents claimed that Martinez was responsible for stiffening penalties for drug dealers and was a strong backer of increased use of U.S. military force in fighting international drug activities. Martinez headed the task force on drug trafficking and substance abuse at the National Governors' Association.

Martinez was defeated in 1990 in his bid for a second term as governor of Florida.

Federal Reserve Board

Alan Greenspan was confirmed by the Senate on Feb. 27, 1992, for a second four-year term as chairman of the Federal Reserve Board.

Senators gave their approval — by voice vote and without debate — despite the unhappiness that many expressed over high unemployment, higher-than-desired long-term interest rates and the general course of the Fed's monetary policy over his first four years.

The Senate Banking, Housing and Urban Affairs Committee recommended Greenspan's reconfirmation on Feb. 20 by a 20-1 vote. Republican Alfonse M. D'Amato, N.Y., cast the only "nay" vote.

Before being confirmed as chairman in 1987, Greenspan was a private consultant with the firm of Townsend-Greenspan and Co., which he founded in 1953. He had served as chairman of the Council of Economic Advisers during the Ford administration and as an adviser on economic matters to President Richard Nixon. *(Congress and the Nation Vol. VII, p. 1049)*

Federal Deposit Insurance Corporation

William Taylor was confirmed by the Senate by voice vote Oct. 22, 1991, to replace L. William Seidman as chairman of the Federal Deposit Insurance Corporation (FDIC). Taylor's term was to expire Feb. 28, 1993. Seidman, appointed by President Ronald Reagan in 1985, was praised by members of the House and Senate Banking Committees as a tough and respected regulator who acquired his reputation by openly disagreeing with members of the Bush administration. He stepped down Oct. 16.

The Senate Banking, Housing and Urban Affairs Committee recommended Taylor's confirmation by a 21-0 vote on Oct. 18. Taylor had been director of the Division of Banking Supervision and Regulation of the Federal Reserve Board, where he had spent most of his professional career.

As top regulator at the Fed, Taylor was questioned in 1991 about an international scandal involving the Bank of Credit and Commerce International (BCCI), which involved allegations of fraud, money laundering, loss of perhaps $10 billion by BCCI depositors worldwide and the secret, decade-long, illegal ownership of several large U.S. banks. He and other Fed officials maintained that they were misled about BCCI's ownership of those banks. His nomination ultimately was not hurt by the investigation.

As FDIC chairman, Taylor also assumed charge of one of the two boards that ran the Resolution Trust Corporation (RTC), the agency created in 1989 to bail out the savings and loan industry. To enhance RTC leadership, Treasury officials Sept. 23, 1991, announced that former American Airlines chairman Albert V. Casey would assume the newly created post of RTC chief executive officer. Congress subsequently made the post a presidentially appointed, Senate-confirmed position, pursuant to a thrift financing bill (HR 3435 — PL 102-233) signed into law Dec. 12, 1991.

Central Intelligence Agency

Robert M. Gates was confirmed as director of central intelligence on Nov. 5, 1991, nearly six months after President Bush nominated his deputy national security adviser to replace retiring director William H. Webster. The 64-31 vote came after weeks of heated testimony.

President Ronald Reagan in 1987 had nominated Gates as CIA director, but Gates withdrew his name from consideration in response to opposition in the Senate about his involvement in the Iran-contra affair. Gates had been deputy director of the CIA, then became acting director upon the death of William J. Casey. *(Congress and the Nation Vol. VII, p. 1050)*

Supporters said Gates was the best man for the job because of his extensive CIA experience and his close relationship with Bush. But opponents pointed to his background as the primary reason for not confirming him. Testimony by former colleagues indicated that Gates may have had more knowledge of the Iran-contra scandal than he previously admitted. Others countered, however, that Casey had intentionally kept Gates out of the loop so as not to harm his future with the agency.

Gates' analytical ability also was questioned. Harold P. Ford, a veteran of the CIA, said that Gates, a Soviet expert, was "dead wrong" in not predicting the demise of the Soviet Union and its influence in the Third World. Former Soviet affairs analyst Melvin A. Goodman also alleged that Gates had slanted various analyses to exaggerate the Soviet threat while at the CIA.

Gates dismissed the charges and others in a 20-point rebuttal and stated that, if confirmed, one of his goals would be to bury the cloak-and-dagger administrative techniques employed by Casey and improve relations with the congressional intelligence committees.

Controversial Nominations

1989

John Tower. After weeks of bitter debate, the Senate on a 47-53 vote March 9 rejected Tower's nomination to be secretary of defense. Only eight times before had the Senate turned down a Cabinet nominee; never had it denied a president a Cabinet nominee at the start of his first term. *(Story, p. 339)*

Tower, a long-time political ally of President Bush, served in the Senate from 1961 to 1985 and chaired the Armed Services Committee from 1981 to 1985. He was chief U.S. negotiator at the strategic arms reduction talks (START) with the Soviet Union in 1985-86.

Tower's nomination ran into trouble largely because of his personal life. He had a reputation for being a womanizer and for abusing alcohol. Concern also was raised about consulting work he did from 1986 to 1988 for major defense contractors.

The Armed Services Committee Feb. 23 recorded a straight 9-11 party-line vote against the nomination.

Robert B. Fiske Jr. Although he had the support of Attorney General Dick Thornburgh, Fiske withdrew his nomination as deputy attorney general in July following intense criticism from conservative Republicans.

At issue was Fiske's tenure as chairman of the American Bar Association (ABA) Standing Committee on the Federal Judiciary. For more than 30 years, the Justice Department confidentially provided the names of potential nominees for federal judgeships to the bar association, a private, voluntary professional group that screened candidates before their nominations were made public by the president or sent to the Senate for confirmation. The 15-member screening committee examined the legal writings of a prospective nominee and interviewed judges, law professors and lawyers in his or her community. The ABA said its investigation was intended to provide information on professional competence, integrity and temperament. Critics contended that the committee often displayed political bias against conservative nominees.

Fiske was charged with heading a screening committee that had been unduly critical of some Reagan judicial nominees and had passed on the names of some White House choices to liberal groups that then tried to derail the nominations. He subsequently said the committee would no longer furnish lists of nominees to any organization.

William Lucas. The Senate Judiciary Committee on Aug. 1 killed the nomination of Lucas to be assistant attorney general for civil rights. Civil rights organizations generally opposed the nomination, citing Lucas' lack of experience. *(Story, p. 763)*

By a 7-7 vote, the committee rejected a motion to report Lucas' nomination favorably. By the same vote, members then refused to send the nomination to the floor without a recommendation. All six committee Republicans and Democrat Dennis DeConcini, Ariz., voted for Lucas. The decisive vote, and the only one in doubt when the hearings began, was cast by Howell Heflin, D-Ala.

Republicans argued that Lucas, who was black, was the victim of racism; Democrats, including Joseph R. Biden Jr., Del., accused the Bush administration of engineering the "perfect cynical setup" in nominating Lucas, who had

Legal Services Corporation

The Bush administration, unlike the preceding Reagan administration, did not seek to abolish the Legal Services Corporation (LSC) or significantly cut its funding. However, President Bush did support restrictions on the types of services LSC lawyers could provide; for example, barring them from handling abortion cases.

Throughout the 1980s, Congress kept the LSC alive through the regular, annual appropriations bills for the Departments of Commerce, State and Justice and the judiciary. Congress had not cleared an authorization bill for the agency since 1977. Debate over the LSC in the Reagan years boiled down to whether participating local attorneys should represent the poor only in specific civil cases, such as divorces and landlord/tenant disputes, or also in broader political and social causes.

The LSC was established in 1974 as a quasi-independent corporation that provided federal funds for civil legal aid for the poor. Clients were represented through local, non-profit Legal Services programs funded primarily by the federal corporation in Washington. The LSC was run by an appointed 11-member board of directors, with two of the seats designated for client-eligible members.

At first, Ronald Reagan appointed members opposed, in varying degrees, to the LSC. Eventually, he named some liberal members, but the board was still controlled by conservatives.

Bush inherited a bitterly divided board. He left the members in place for 10 months, even though the terms of all but one had expired. Bush made all recess appointments to the LSC board. The members thus were not confirmed by the Senate and were able to sit until the end of the session of Congress following their nomination.

101st Congress. In September 1989, the White House abandoned its plan to name former representative M. Caldwell Butler, R-Va. (1972-83), to be chairman of the LSC board, despite the written endorsement of more than 30 House Republicans. Conservatives fought the nomination because Butler said that he did not oppose LSC lawyers counseling women seeking abortions.

In November 1989, when a resignation threatened to tip the balance of power on the board, Bush used recess appointments to name former representative John N. Erlenborn, R-Ill. (1965-85), to the vacancy and renamed J. Blakeley Hall (son of Rep. Ralph M. Hall, D-Texas), whose previous recess appointment had expired.

The day before Congress returned from recess — on Jan. 22, 1990 — Bush filled out the board by naming nine new members. Senate Labor and Human Resources Committee Chairman Edward M. Kennedy, D-Mass., was critical. "President Bush has had a year to choose these nominees," Kennedy said. "He should have waited another 18 hours and sent them to the Senate for confirmation, as the Constitution provides."

The nine appointees were: Luis Guinot Jr., a Washington lawyer and Bush campaign supporter who was later named ambassador to Costa Rica; Penny L. Pullen, Republican leader of the Illinois House; Xavier L. Suarez, Miami mayor; Howard H. Dana Jr., a Maine lawyer who had been a liberal dissenter on an early Reagan-era board; George W. Wittgraf, an Iowa lawyer and Bush's 1988 campaign manager in that state; former representative Guy V. Molinari, R-N.Y. (1981-90); John F. Collins, former mayor of Boston and a Bush campaign supporter; Jo Betts Love, of Mississippi, the only black chosen, named to a client-eligible seat; and Jeanine E. Wolbeck, of Minnesota, an anti-abortion activist chosen for the second client-eligible seat. Administration officials designated Wittgraf as chairman.

In April 1990, the board asked for the resignation of LSC President Terrance J. Wear, a former aide to Sen. Jesse Helms, R-N.C. The board charged that Wear had conducted what legal aid supporters viewed as a distorted campaign against wasteful spending by LSC-funded programs.

Erlenborn resigned from the board in June 1990 when the American Farm Bureau Federation complained that his service posed a conflict of interest. Erlenborn was a partner in a Washington law firm that dealt with agricultural concerns. While legal experts saw no problems, Erlenborn decided to quit to avoid embarrassing the firm. In August, Bush picked Tom Rath, a former New Hampshire attorney general, to succeed Erlenborn. With Congress in session, Rath could not be named as a recess appointment. No Senate confirmation hearings were held before adjournment, so the board was reduced to 10 members for the remainder of the congressional session.

On Aug. 9, 1990, the LSC board voted 8-2 for David H. Martin, a Reagan administration official with no legal aid experience, as the new LSC president.

102nd Congress. Bush failed to renew the board members' recess appointments after the 101st Congress adjourned Oct. 28, 1990, so the LSC went without a board until Bush made new recess appointments on Jan. 2, 1991 — again skirting Senate confirmation.

Included on Bush's new slate were eight of the 10 members who had served on the last board, plus Rath. The two new appointees were Basile J. Uddo, a law professor at Loyola University, and William Lee Kirk Jr., a former law partner of Rep. Bill McCollum, R-Fla. They replaced Suarez and Collins.

virtually no background in civil rights law. When questioned about 1989 Supreme Court rulings that civil rights activists considered a setback for their cause, Lucas stated that he did not feel the decisions were significant but conceded, "I'm new to the law."

Other points of concern were a contempt-of-court citation Lucas received when he was Wayne County, Mich., sheriff and a fine Lucas had to pay for failing to declare several thousands of dollars in goods purchased on a trip to the Far East.

Donald P. Gregg. After a lengthy debate, the Senate on Sept. 12 confirmed Gregg to be U.S. ambassador to South Korea by a vote of 66-33. The nomination had been held up for six months by the Senate Foreign Relations Committee over questions of Gregg's involvement in the Iran-contra scandal. Gregg had served as Vice President Bush's national security adviser.

Gregg underwent a lengthy committee hearing on May 12, when he insisted that neither he nor Bush was aware of ex-White House aide Oliver L. North's secret aid program at the time it was in operation. Democratic committee members grilled Gregg about several documents — some of which surfaced in the North trial — that appeared to indicate Gregg was aware of North's activities in 1984-86 and that he had apprised Bush of them. Gregg, however, testified that he never saw those memos until December 1986, after North's operation became public, and that he immediately took them to the House Intelligence Committee.

Republicans accused the Democrats of waging a "character assassination" and of using the Gregg nomination as a means of reviving questions of Bush's involvement in the scandal. They cited Gregg's willingness to turn over controversial memos instead of shredding or hiding them as an indication of his cooperation.

The committee on June 20 approved his nomination, 12-7.

James E. Cason. Senate Republicans Nov. 17 gave up on Cason's nomination to be assistant secretary of agriculture with jurisdiction over the Forest Service and the Soil Conservation Service, after it became apparent that he would be rejected by the full Senate. Senate Minority Leader Bob Dole of Kansas asked that the nomination not come to a vote, and it was sent back to the president.

Cason had been criticized for repeatedly siding with private industry when setting land-use and environmental policy while a Reagan administration official in the Interior Department. Cason allegedly suppressed a 1986 Bureau of Land Management report suggesting that logging in the Pacific Northwest was endangering the survival of the northern spotted owl.

Many environmental groups made opposition to him a test of senators' support for their agenda. Republicans, in particular, wanted to avoid having to choose between supporting the president or ignoring the environmentalists.

The Senate Agriculture Committee voted 12-7 to report the nominee favorably to the floor, but support for Cason began to wane shortly after.

Frederick M. Bush. Bush, a major GOP fund-raiser and former aide to President Bush, withdrew his name from consideration for ambassador to Luxembourg.

Bush and his consulting firm, which went out of business in 1989, reportedly shared more than $600,000 in fees for lobbying on Department of Housing and Urban Development (HUD) projects being investigated by the House. Bush testified that he had only occasional dealings with a former top HUD aide, Deborah Gore Dean, the main target of the investigation. Later, after a personal thank-you letter to Dean from Bush and his wife was found, Bush clarified his statements and said that he had met with her many times and that a social relationship had developed.

1990

Joy A. Silverman. After receiving complaints that President Bush was handing out ambassadorships to major campaign donors who had little or no relevant experience in foreign policy, in late January the White House dropped the nomination of Silverman to be ambassador to Barbados. Silverman, of New York City, had given $299,360 to GOP causes from 1987 to 1989, according to the Senate Foreign Relations Committee.

Following hearings in the fall of 1989, the Senate sent the nomination back to the president as Congress was ending its session in late November. The Senate had received the nomination July 11; under Senate rules, all unapproved nominations automatically are returned to the president at the end of a session unless the Senate acts to keep them.

Silverman's detractors pointed out that she had no experience in foreign policy and had little paid employment. As a qualification for the ambassadorship, she wrote that she had "assisted husband . . . by planning and hosting corporate functions."

Victor Stello Jr. On April 24, President Bush fulfilled Stello's request to withdraw his nomination to be assistant secretary of energy in charge of defense programs.

A coalition of environmentalists and anti-nuclear activists charged that Stello was too cozy with the industry during his 24-year career as a nuclear regulator and repeatedly impeded criminal investigations of wrongdoing within the industry.

Concerns also were raised about his conduct while at the Nuclear Regulatory Commission (NRC). Stello had been accused of helping to orchestrate an effort to have another top NRC official, Roger Fortuna, fired for being too aggressive in his efforts to uncover industry wrongdoing. Stello admitted sitting on significant safety-related allegations about a nuclear plant in New York in his zeal to pursue his investigation of Fortuna.

After receiving testimony from the inspector general of the NRC, including allegations that Stello may have lied to Congress, the Senate Armed Services Committee announced Jan. 31 that it would delay action on the nomination indefinitely. The House Interior Investigations Subcommittee subsequently ended its yearlong probe and issued a report April 5 that was highly critical of Stello's performance.

Stello steadfastly denied any wrongdoing.

Frederick Vreeland. On Oct. 4, the State Department announced that President Bush would withdraw the nomination of Vreeland to be ambassador to Myanmar (formerly Burma), citing a decision by that country not to accept him because of criticisms he had made of human rights violations there.

His nomination had run into difficulties in the Senate as well. The Foreign Relations Committee was upset that Vreeland misrepresented his career by submitting a biography that listed him as a career foreign service officer instead of a career CIA official. His nomination, however, was withdrawn before extensive debate could occur.

George Fleming Jones. Ranking Republican on the Senate Foreign Relations Committee Jesse Helms, N.C., on Oct. 19 successfully derailed the nomination of Jones to be ambassador to Guyana.

Helms reportedly believed that Jones, a career foreign service officer, was involved in the 1986 leak of a secret Chilean report about the death of an American in Santiago. Helms reportedly was angered that his office was blamed for the leak.

Jones' appointment remained pending before the Foreign Relations Committee and was not acted upon again before Congress adjourned.

John Bushnell. President Bush submitted the nomination of Bushnell to be ambassador to Costa Rica on Oct. 26, two days before the 101st Congress adjourned. The Senate failed to take up the nomination in its waning hours.

Bushnell's nomination had been stalled for months by Jesse Helms, who had concerns about Bushnell's performance as deputy chief of the U.S. Embassy in Panama during the U.S. invasion of that country in December 1989 and about Bushnell's role in the State Department 10 years earlier when the leftist Sandinistas came to power in Nicaragua.

1991

Robert L. Clarke. After charging Clarke with allowing hundreds of banks to sink into insolvency, the Senate Banking, Housing and Urban Affairs Committee killed his appointment to a second five-year term as comptroller of the currency.

In back-to-back party-line votes of 9-12 on Nov. 6, the committee rejected motions to approve Clarke's reconfirmation and to send the nomination to the floor with an unfavorable recommendation.

Committee Chairman Donald W. Riegle Jr., D-Mich., argued that Clarke brought a deregulatory philosophy to the post that said, "Industry had to regulate itself." As a consequence, investments in real estate and other risky ventures increased.

Republicans, in response, accused Riegle of blaming the banking crisis on the Reagan and Bush administrations, while Congress and other regulators were largely to blame.

Even though Clarke's term expired in 1990, no successor was named in 1991, and he remained in office until February 1992.

Bernadine P. Healy. The Senate on March 21 approved by voice vote the nomination of Cleveland cardiologist Healy to head the National Institutes of Health (NIH). Healy's nomination breezed through the Senate Labor and Human Resources Committee the day before, also by voice vote.

Healy's selection by the Bush administration followed a yearlong search. Several candidates had backed away from the job complaining about White House questioning of their views on abortion.

The nomination of Healy, a former Reagan administration official, had stirred controversy because she twice had voted to overturn an administration ban on funding of research using tissue from aborted fetuses. But at her confirmation hearing, Healy defused potential opposition from abortion opponents by pledging to support the ban.

Healy became the first woman to head NIH.

1992

George J. Terwilliger III. Late on the night of April 9, the Senate confirmed Terwilliger as deputy attorney general, despite a sexual harassment allegation.

After the fiasco that surrounded Clarence Thomas' nomination to the Supreme Court, the all-male Senate Judiciary Committee was careful to give a full hearing to suggestions of harassment from a woman formerly employed by Terwilliger.

Following President Bush's nomination of Terwilliger, a former U.S. attorney in Vermont, an FBI investigation uncovered a conflict between him and Sandra Strempel, a former deputy. Strempel and others said that when she arrived at a staff meeting and announced she had some information to share, Terwilliger jokingly asked if she were pregnant. Terwilliger, questioned by Biden on April 2, said he did not remember the exchange but added: "If I said this, I failed as a manager."

The committee April 9 approved the nomination 12-1, with Paul Simon, D-Ill., voting "nay."

Presidential Vetoes, 1989-92

President Bush vetoed a total of 43 public bills during his term in office. He also pocket-vetoed one private bill. Bush's predecessor, Republican Ronald Reagan, vetoed 71 public bills during his two terms (34 in the first and 37 in the second). Reagan's predecessor, Democrat Jimmy Carter, vetoed 29 public bills during his four-year tenure.

Grover Cleveland issued the most vetoes in one term — 414. Franklin D. Roosevelt, who served as president for three full terms, vetoed the most measures — 635. Seven presidents issued no vetoes.

Congress made nine override attempts in 1989-92; only one was successful. Veto overrides require a two-thirds majority vote of both houses. Only four presidents who vetoed more than 10 bills never had a veto overridden. William McKinley Jr. (1897-1901) had the most vetoes without an override, 42. He was followed by Lyndon B. Johnson (1963-69), with 30; John F. Kennedy (1961-63), 21; and Andrew Jackson (1829-37), 12.

The record for veto overrides — 15 — was held by Andrew Johnson. Harry S. Truman and Gerald Ford was both had 12 vetoes overridden.

Fourteen of Bush's public bill vetoes were pocket vetoes. When Congress is in session, a bill becomes a law without the president's signature if he does not act upon it within 10 days, excluding Sundays, from the time he receives it. But if Congress adjourns within that 10-day period, the bill is killed, or pocket-vetoed, without the president's signature.

Following is a list of public and private bills vetoed by Bush in 1989-92. Pocket-veto dates reflect dates of presidential memorandums of disapproval.

1989

1. HR 2 (Minimum Wage)
   Vetoed: June 13, 1989
   House sustained June 14: 247-178
   (Story, p. 705)
2. S J Res 113 (FS-X Fighter Plane)
   Vetoed: July 31, 1989
   Senate sustained Sept. 13: 66-34
   (Story, p. 351)
3. HR 2990 (Labor, HHS, Education Fiscal 1990 Appropriations)
   Vetoed: Oct. 21, 1989
   House sustained Oct. 25: 231-191
   (Story, p. 594)
4. HR 3026 (District of Columbia Fiscal 1990 Appropriations)
   Vetoed: Oct. 27, 1989
   No override attempt
   (Story, p. 594)
5. HR 2939 (Foreign Aid Fiscal 1990 Appropriations)
   Vetoed: Nov. 19, 1989
   No override attempt
   (Story, p. 228)
6. HR 3610 (District of Columbia Fiscal 1990 Appropriations)
   Vetoed: Nov. 20, 1989
   No override attempt
   (Story, p. 594)
7. HR 1231 (Eastern Airlines Strike)
   Vetoed: Nov. 21, 1989
   House sustained March 7, 1990: 261-160
   (Story, p. 712)
8. HR 1487 (State Department Authorization)
   Vetoed: Nov. 21, 1989
   No override attempt
   (Story, p. 247)
9. HR 2712[a] (Chinese Immigration Relief)
   Vetoed: Nov. 30, 1989
   House: 390-25, Jan. 24, 1990
   Senate sustained Jan. 25, 1990: 62-37
   (Story, p. 755)

1990

10. HR 2364 (Amtrak Authorization)
    Vetoed: May 24, 1990
    House: 294-123, June 7
    Senate sustained June 12: 64-36
    (Story, p. 424)
11. HR 20 (Hatch Act Amendments)
    Vetoed: June 15, 1990
    House: 327-93, June 20
    Senate sustained June 21: 65-35
    (Story, p. 859)
12. HR 770 (Family and Medical Leave)
    Vetoed: June 29, 1990
    House sustained July 25: 232-195
    (Story, p. 710)
13. HR 4328 (Textile Import Quotas)
    Vetoed: Oct. 5, 1990
    House sustained Oct. 10: 275-152
    (Story, p. 174)
14. H J Res 660 (Continuing Resolution)
    Vetoed: Oct. 6, 1990
    House sustained Oct. 6: 260-138
    (Story, p. 73)
15. S 2104 (Civil Rights Act of 1990)
    Vetoed: Oct. 22, 1990
    Senate sustained Oct. 24: 66-34
    (Story, p. 757)
16. HR 4638 (Orphan Drug Amendments)
    Pocket-vetoed: Nov. 8, 1990
    (Story, p. 585)

17. S 321 (Indian Preference Act)
    Pocket-vetoed: Nov. 16, 1990
    (Story, p. 884)
18. HR 4653 (Export Controls Authorization)
    Pocket-vetoed: Nov. 16, 1990
    (Story, p. 175)
19. HR 3134 (Relief of Joan R. Daronco)
    Pocket-vetoed: Nov. 16, 1990
20. S 2834 (Intelligence Authorization)
    Pocket-vetoed: Nov. 30, 1990
    (Story, p. 242)

1991

21. HR 2699[a] (District of Columbia Fiscal 1992 Appropriations)
    Vetoed: Aug. 17, 1991
    (Story, p. 597)
22. S 1722 (Unemployment Benefits)
    Vetoed: Oct. 11, 1991
    Senate sustained Oct. 16: 65-35
    (Story, p. 721)
23. HR 2707 (Labor, HHS, Education Fiscal 1992 Appropriations)
    Vetoed: Nov. 19, 1991
    House sustained Nov. 19: 276-156
    (Story, p. 597)

1992

24. HR 2212 (Conditional MFN Status for China)
    Vetoed: March 2, 1992
    House: 357-61, March 11
    Senate sustained March 18: 60-38
    (Story, p. 190)
25. HR 4210 (Tax Bill)
    Vetoed: March 20, 1992
    House sustained March 25: 211-215
    (Story, p. 100)
26. S 3 (Campaign Finance)
    Vetoed: May 9, 1992
    Senate sustained May 13: 57-42
    (Story, p. 959)
27. S 2342 (Sioux Indian Claims)
    Vetoed: June 16, 1992
    No override attempt
28. HR 2507 (Fetal Tissue Research)
    Vetoed: June 23, 1992
    House sustained June 24: 271-156
    (Story, p. 597)
29. S 250 ('Motor Voter' Registration)
    Vetoed: July 2, 1992
    Senate sustained Sept. 22: 62-38
    (Story, p. 893)
30. S 5 (Family and Medical Leave)
    Vetoed: Sept. 22, 1992
    Senate: 68-31, Sept. 24
    House sustained Sept. 30: 258-169
    (Story, p. 730)
31. S 323 (Family Planning)
    Vetoed: Sept. 25, 1992
    Senate: 73-26, Oct. 1
    House sustained Oct. 2: 266-148
    (Story, p. 597)
32. HR 5318 (Conditional MFN Status for China)
    Vetoed: Sept. 28, 1992
    House: 345-72, Sept. 30
    Senate sustained Oct. 1: 59-40
    (Story, p. 190)
33. HR 5517 (District of Columbia Fiscal 1993 Appropriations)
    Vetoed: Sept. 30, 1992
    No override attempt
    (Story, p. 597)
34. S 12 (Cable TV Reregulation)
    Vetoed: Oct. 3, 1992
    Veto overridden Oct. 5
    Senate: 74-25, Oct. 5
    House: 308-114, Oct. 5
    (Story, p. 451)
35. S 3095 (Jena Band of Choctaws)
    Pocket-vetoed: Oct. 21, 1992
36. HR 5452 (Delaware River Port Authority)
    Pocket-vetoed: Oct. 27, 1992
37. HR 2859 (Lynn, Mass., Study Authorization)
    Pocket-vetoed: Oct. 27, 1992
38. HR 5021 (Wild and Scenic Rivers Amendments)
    Pocket-vetoed: Oct. 27, 1992
39. HR 5061 (Dry Tortugas National Park)
    Pocket-vetoed: Oct. 27, 1992
40. HR 2109 (Revere Beach Study Authorization)
    Pocket-vetoed: Oct. 28, 1992
41. HR 6185 (Federal Courts)
    Pocket-vetoed: Oct. 30, 1992
42. HR 6138 (Farm Loan/Grant Eligibility Rules Amendments)
    Pocket-vetoed: Oct. 31, 1992
43. S 3144 (Abortion at Military Hospitals)
    Pocket-vetoed: Oct. 31, 1992
    (Story, p. 597)
44. HR 11 (Tax Bill)
    Pocket-vetoed: Nov. 4, 1992
    (Story, p. 103)

Note: President Bush also claimed to have pocket-vetoed H J Res 390 on Aug. 16, 1989, and S 1176 on Dec. 20, 1991. The first came during a congressional recess (Aug. 4-Sept. 6, 1989) and the second following adjournment of the first session of the 102nd Congress (Nov. 27, 1991-Jan. 3, 1992). In both cases, Bush issued a memorandum of disapproval, asserting that the recesses prevented the return of the bills and therefore he had pocket-vetoed the legislation. Congressional experts claimed that a true pocket veto could occur only after final adjournment of a Congress and not during recesses or between sessions if Congress had taken certain steps allowing it to receive any veto message the president might send. Congress considered H J Res 390 and S 1176 enacted into law without the president's signature because of his failure to return the legislation. Neither measure, however, was assigned a public law number.

[a] Bush said he pocket-vetoed the bill but sent it back to Congress, where it was treated as a regular veto.

President Reagan's Fiscal 1990 Budget Message

Following is the White House text of President Reagan's fiscal 1990 budget message sent to Congress Jan. 9, 1989.

TO THE SPEAKER OF THE HOUSE OF REPRESENTATIVES AND THE PRESIDENT OF THE SENATE:

Eight years ago many in this country were concerned about the future of our economy, our government and, indeed, the Nation itself. Unemployment was high and rising. Inflation and interest rates were reaching record levels. Our Nation's defense capabilities had been weakened by neglect. The international prestige of the U.S. was at a low ebb.

To resolve the economic problems then facing us, our administration proposed a recovery program centering on four fundamental principles:

- Reduce personal and business tax rates.
- Reduce the rate of growth of Federal spending.
- Reduce the Federal regulatory burden by eliminating unnecessary restrictions while protecting the public's interest and safety.
- Support a moderate and steady monetary policy to bring inflation under control.

To rebuild our defense capabilities and restore America's standing in the world we proposed expanded national security and international programs.

We also initiated the largest management improvement program ever attempted in order to restore the proper relationships among the Federal, State and local governments, and the private sector; to eliminate waste in Federal programs; and to introduce management controls and efficiencies, while improving services.

Today, the American people can be proud of the progress that has been made on each of these fronts. As a result of this progress, America is internally stronger, internationally more secure, and stands taller in the eyes of the world than it did eight years ago.

Eight Years of Accomplishment

Working together, we have accomplished much over the last eight years.

The Economy. The current economic expansion, now in its seventy-fourth month, has outlasted all previous peacetime expansions in U.S. history. Business investment and exports are rising, and economic growth is expected to continue into the 1990's.

- Since this expansion began, 19 million new jobs have been created, while the unemployment rate has fallen by more than 5 percentage points — to 5.4 percent, the lowest level in 14 years.
- Inflation, which averaged 10.4 percent annually during the four years before our administration began, has averaged less than a third of that during the past six years.
- Real after-tax personal income has risen 24 percent since 1982, increasing our overall standard of living.

Taxes and Regulations. Between 1981 and 1987, changes in the Federal tax code have made the tax laws more equitable, cut income tax rates, and eliminated Federal income taxes for 4.3 million low-income individuals and families.

- Since 1981, the time spent by the public filling out forms required by the Federal Government has been cut by 600 million hours annually, and the number of pages of regulations published annually in the *Federal Register* has been reduced by over 45 percent.

Budget. The growth in domestic spending has been slowed, and the budget priorities have been shifted to those functions the Federal Government should provide, such as national defense, basic scientific research, and protecting the rights of all citizens.

- The social security system has been rescued from the brink of insolvency and made sound into the next century.
- The runaway growth of spending for means-tested entitlement programs that occurred in the 1970's has been curbed. Eligibility rules have been tightened to retarget benefits to the needy. Basic benefits for the poor, the elderly, and others in need of Federal assistance have been maintained.
- We have begun the process of putting other entitlement programs on a more rational basis, including medicare hospital insurance, which was converted to a system that encourages efficiency and lower costs.

Defense and International Affairs. Our defenses have been strengthened. Weapons systems have been modernized and upgraded. We are recruiting and retaining higher caliber military personnel. The readiness, training, and morale of our troops have been improved significantly.

- As a result of our greater strength, we were able to negotiate with the Soviet Union a verifiable treaty that completely eliminates an entire class of nuclear missiles.
- We began the Strategic Defense Initiative research and technology program that offers our best hope of a safer world in which our security, and that of our allies, no longer rests on deterrence through the threat of nuclear retaliation, but on defenses that threaten no one.
- Our willingness to defend freedom throughout the world has met with success in the spread of democracy and in turning back the tide of communist expansion.

Management of the Government. Federal agencies undertook a major management improvement program, "Reform '88," to carry out the cash, credit, and financial operations of the Federal Government in a more business-like manner, and to reduce waste, fraud, and abuse.

- Functions that were pre-empted by the Federal Government are being transferred back to the private sector or to State and local governments.
- Greater use is being made of cost sharing and user fees, shifting the cost of projects and programs where appropriate to those who benefit from them.

The Federal Deficit. The one area in which I have been persistently disappointed throughout my term of office has been in the efforts to bring the budget under control. Time and again I have proposed measures to help curb Federal domestic program spending. Time and again these proposals have been rejected by Congress.

The reasons for the rise in the Federal deficit in the early 1980's are simple. First, we experienced one of the most severe recessions of the post-war period. It has been estimated that 81 percent — over $640 billion — of the growth of the deficit over the 1981-1986 levels originally projected in my March 1981 budget was attributable to that recession. The second reason is that, even after including necessary increases for defense, my March 1981 budget called for net spending reductions totalling $331 billion over five years; but Congress approved less than 40 percent of those reductions. Wasteful programs continued to be funded. The necessary reductions have still not been made.

If the deficit is not curbed by continuing to limit the appetite of government, we put in jeopardy all that we worked so hard over the years to achieve. Large deficits brought on by excessive domestic spending undercut the incentives to work and save by absorbing the savings that would otherwise lead to productive investment. We cannot allow this to happen.

I am proud of America's accomplishments. Our economy is booming, our defenses are stronger, and our standing in the world is again second to none.

This Budget Reduces the 1990 Deficit Below the G-R-H Target and Achieves Balance in 1993

The fiscal year 1990 budget, my last, represents a continuation of my efforts to reduce the Federal budget deficit through restraint in domestic spending.

The budget I am submitting today complies with the deficit targets set in the Gramm-Rudman-Hollings (G-R-H) Act, by proposing measures that meet the 1990 deficit target of $100 billion and assure a steady reduction in the deficit leading to a balanced budget in 1993.

Under my proposals, the deficit would decline to less than 3 percent of GNP in 1990, and the Federal debt held by the public would also decline as a proportion of GNP.

This budget shows that a gradual elimination of the deficit is possible without raising taxes, without cutting into essential social programs, without devastating defense, and without neglecting other national priorities. It can be done in a reasonable, responsible way — with discipline and fairness. New taxes are not required. Receipts will grow dramatically between 1989 and 1990 because our economy is growing. This budget simply proposes to increase spending by less than the increase in revenues, and therefore, reduce the deficit. The proposed reforms will yield additional deficit reductions in future years. We have an opportunity this year to put the worst of the deficit problem behind us and enable the next Administration to begin its term of office with a clean slate and with the promise of continuing prosperity.

Funding National Priorities

To address urgent national priorities within the deficit limit set by the G-R-H Act, my budget proposes that some programs — such as those for AIDS research and prevention, drug enforcement, and technology development — receive significant funding increases, while others are reduced, reformed, or, in some cases, terminated.

Defense. Maintaining peace and protecting our country are the foremost responsibilities of the Federal government. Defense budget authority declined in real (inflation-adjusted) terms for the fourth straight year with funding of $299 billion for 1989. This trend cannot continue without severe impact on combat readiness. Therefore, my budget requests defense funding of $315 billion in budget authority and $303 billion in outlays for 1990, and $331 billion in budget authority and $314 billion in outlays in 1991. These amounts provide 2 percent annual real growth in budget authority over the 1989 level, bringing it back up to the 1984 level in inflation-adjusted terms by 1991. The budget also projects 2 percent real growth in these programs in future years.

We must continue to maintain our nuclear deterrent. For 1990, the budget proposes $9.0 billion for atomic energy defense programs, a $0.9 billion increase over 1989. A total of $2.8 billion is dedicated to the modernization of the nuclear materials production complex and to increase environmental clean-up and waste management efforts.

International. To consolidate and build on the foreign policy gains of the past eight years, additional funds are needed for international affairs that would promote our foreign policy and national security interests in the Middle East, Central America, and elsewhere. A special program is proposed to foster strong economic growth in the Philippines to support that country's return to democracy. Other increases in foreign aid would pay arrearages on contributions to multilateral lending institutions and make payments to the United Nations and related agencies.

Drug Abuse and Law Enforcement. Our fight against drug abuse must continue, as well as our efforts to protect the individual against crime:

- For drug law enforcement, prevention, and treatment programs, I propose $5.7 billion in 1990, an increase of $164 million over 1989. This funding, together with the new authorities and sanctions contained in the Anti-Drug Abuse Act of 1988, will enable us to move toward our goal of a drug-free America.
- To relieve prison overcrowding and adequately house a growing inmate population, I would provide $1.6 billion for prison construction and operation, $193 million more than was devoted to this purpose in 1989.

AIDS Research and Education. This budget reflects my belief that addressing the problem of AIDS must remain a top priority:

- Preventing and alleviating suffering from the Human Immunodeficiency Virus (HIV), which causes AIDS, is our highest public health priority. Federal support for research, prevention, and treatment exceeds $2.1 billion in 1989, and will approach $2.8 billion in 1990. This budget asks for $1.6 billion, or 24 percent over 1989, for Public Health Service HIV funding.

Research. One of our highest priorities is to strengthen U.S. technology and make America more competitive. For example:

- I propose a continued increase in federally supported basic research aimed at longer-term improvements in the Nation's productivity and global competitiveness. This budget continues the commitment to double National Science Foundation support for academic basic research by 1993, increases support for training future scientists and engineers, and expedites transfer of the results of Government-funded basic research to industry.
- Our space program will provide $13.1 billion for continued development of America's first permanently manned space station; for increased support for improving the performance and reliability of the space shuttle; for initiation of two major new international planetary space science missions; and for support to encourage the commercial development of space.
- Also included in the budget is $250 million in 1990 as the Federal share of support for initiating construction of the Superconducting Super Collider (SSC). Non-Federal cost sharing will be required to support one-third of the project's costs. The SSC as currently envisaged will be the largest pure science project ever undertaken. It will help keep this country on the cutting edge of high energy physics research well into the next century.

Other Priorities. Other areas of Federal responsibility receive priority funding in this budget:

- To continue the Federal Aviation Administration's multi-year program to increase its controller and inspector workforces and to modernize the Nation's air traffic control systems, the budget provides $7.7 billion — a 17 percent increase over the 1989 level.
- To alleviate the problems facing our savings institutions, I propose that the Federal Savings and Loan Insurance Corporation (FSLIC) spend $16 billion in 1989 and $9 billion in 1990 to address the most serious thrift institution problems. The Secretary of the Treasury is developing a comprehensive plan to resolve the savings industry's problems, and reform the financial institution regulatory structure and deposit insurance system to prevent a reoccurrence of these problems. I expect the Secretary to submit his proposals to the new President shortly.
- To improve coordination of Federal rural development programs and to redirect funding toward needy rural areas and program recipients, I am continuing support of the rural development initiative coordinated by the Secretary of Agriculture.
- By emphasizing housing vouchers, I would provide housing assistance to 132,000 additional low-income households in 1990, 5 percent more than the 126,124 additional households receiving housing subsidies in 1989. Housing vouchers can serve more low-income households at a lower Federal cost and provide greater

opportunity for these families to rent housing of their own choosing.

• To maintain the progress we have been making in fostering State and local education reform, I would sustain the present level of spending on discretionary education programs at $18.5 billion, but refocus those funds to put more money where the needs of the disadvantaged and students with handicaps are greatest.

• To continue the significant progress we have made in cleaning up the environment, I recommend a $153 million increase for the Environmental Protection Agency's regulatory, research and enforcement programs. I also recommend an increase of $315 million for the Superfund hazardous waste cleanup program in order to maintain the program's momentum and support a stronger enforcement role.

• Because changes in the earth's natural systems can have tremendous economic and social effects, global climate change is becoming a critical concern. Our ability to understand and predict these changes is currently limited, and a better understanding is essential for developing policies. The budget proposes a coordinated and effective Federal research program on global change. This budget is accompanied by a report by the Committee on Earth Sciences that describes this program and its strategy.

• Last year's fires on Federal forestlands indicated the need for more timely funding for annual fire-fighting costs. I therefore propose that two new Federal wild land firefighting accounts be established in the Departments of Agriculture and Interior.

• To further strengthen our energy security, I propose legislation authorizing the sale of the naval petroleum reserves to the private sector in exchange for cash and oil to be added to the strategic petroleum reserve. I also propose the establishment of a separate 10 million barrel defense petroleum inventory.

• To provide for the timely completion of my Reform '88 management improvement program I propose an additional $103 million for 1990, to further improve our management and credit systems.

Major Programs Are Reformed to Achieve Deficit Reduction

The program structure and incentives underlying many domestic Federal programs need to be altered to promote greater efficiency and cost-effectiveness.

• Current farm price support programs are far too costly. For the period 1986-89 an estimated $130 billion in Federal spending for farm-related assistance programs provided an average of nearly $600,000 per farmer. Much of this assistance goes to farmers with high incomes — more than twice the U.S. family average. I therefore propose outlay reductions for the price and income support programs of $2 billion in 1990 and additional annual reductions of between $2 and $2.5 billion in each year from 1991 through 1994. In addition, I urge reform of the counterproductive sugar price support program.

• The rapidly rising costs of the medicare program need to be moderated. I propose a reasonable increase in the medicare prospective payment system rate and reductions in hospital capital payments and special graduate medical education payments. Also, in an effort to restrain excessive growth in supplementary medical insurance (SMI) costs, I propose extension of the current law SMI premiums, limitations on physician payments, reductions in payments for certain overpriced procedures, and reforms in the durable medical equipment payment system. Medicare spending would still grow by 9 percent between 1989 and 1990 under these proposals — but not by the 13 percent that would occur under current law.

• I also propose reforms in the medicaid program to reduce spending growth between 1989 and 1990 to $1.7 billion, or 5 percent, rather than the $3.3 billion, or 9 percent, that would occur under current law. These reforms reinstate successful incentives employed in the early 1980's. My budget also proposes restructuring Federal financing of administrative expenses to give States greater incentives to operate their administrative systems as efficiently as possible.

• The Government often continues programs at the Federal level that are either duplicative or are no longer needed, or more appropriately undertaken by other levels of government or the private sector. This is the case with the Economic Development Administration, Amtrak, urban mass transit discretionary grants, and most operating subsidies for the Postal Service. Efforts to reverse this situation have been undertaken by prior administrations as well as my own. These programs should be eliminated. The budget proposes termination of 82 programs that are not needed to satisfy national priorities.

• Under current law, outlays for Federal employee retirement and health benefits are estimated to grow from $51.3 billion in 1989 to $55.9 billion in 1990. I propose freezing retirement cost-of-living allowances (COLAs) and other reforms to hold the 1990 level to slightly above that for 1989, reducing the growth that would otherwise occur by $4.4 billion.

Achieving a Proper Federal Role and Improving Management

As the Federal Government grew, it took on improper responsibilities, and managed its programs inefficiently. We undertook to return the Federal Government to its proper role. We also initiated a major program to improve the management of the remaining programs. These priorities are continued and expanded in this budget.

Privatization. The Government and the private sector should each do what it does best. The Federal Government should not be involved in providing goods and services where private enterprise can do the job cheaper and better.

Accordingly, my budget proposes that a number of Federal enterprises be opened to the private sector, through public offerings or outright sales. Following our success in the sale of Conrail and the sale of $21 billion in selected loan portfolios, I am proposing sale of the naval petroleum reserves, the Alaska Power Administration, and the Southeastern Power Administration. I also propose sale of the Federal Government's helium-processing assets, excess real property, and a further $4.3 billion in loan portfolios. In addition, my budget proposes legislation to establish a government corporation for the uranium enrichment enterprise, as the first step towards eventual privatization.

The Federal Government should also depend more on the private sector to provide ancillary and support services for activities that remain in Federal hands. Therefore, I propose a number of pilot projects and studies in areas such as the private delivery of advertising materials and urgent mail, and the Department of Justice's prison hospitals.

Improved Management. In 1981, I made a promise to the American people "to limit Government to its proper role and make it the servant, not the master, of the people." My "Management Improvement Program: Reform '88" has helped make Government more efficient and more responsive. We reduced waste and fraud in Federal programs by combining the efforts of the inspectors general into the President's Council on Integrity and Efficiency, resulting in over $110 billion saved or put to better use — and their efforts are continuing.

I saw that the Federal Government did not have effective cash management practices for dealing with what is now a $2 trillion annual cash flow, nor did it have a government-wide credit management program for what is now a $1 trillion portfolio. This resulted in the waste of billions of dollars each year. We built the necessary government-wide controls in both areas and stopped the drain.

Moreover, we began the establishment of the first government-wide financial accounting system, consolidating and making uniform over 400 previously incompatible individual agency systems. This was essential for any well-managed government, and is presently being implemented.

The Federal Government has a major effect on our daily lives through the collection of taxes and fees, the direct provisions of services, the payment of financial assistance through various entitlement programs, and the regulation of commercial enterprises. Through modernization, improved administration, and automated services the Government has made substantial reductions in the time it takes to provide services to the public. As the 21st century approaches, the Federal Government must adapt its role in our society to changing conditions and changing technology. At the turn of the century, the U.S. population will exceed 268 million, with a larger proportion of elderly citizens. Changes in technology and communication will increasingly link the world's economies, trade, capital flows, and travel as never before.

The 1990 *Management Report,* which is being forwarded to the Congress as part of the 1990 budget submission, reflects the highlights of OMB's report to me on "Government of the Future." That *Management Report* has been expanded as a beginning to a planning process that has, in part, shaped the proposals in this budget and should become a part of the annual budget process.

Budget Process Reform Is Desperately Needed to Continue Deficit Reduction

The persistence of the budget deficit is overwhelming evidence that the Federal budget process is fundamentally flawed. Past efforts at "reform" have been directed largely toward protecting a large portion of domestic spending from real fiscal discipline. Fourteen years after passage of the Congressional Budget Act and three years after enactment of the Balanced Budget and Emergency Deficit Control Act, the Federal budget process remains unwieldy and undisciplined. The American people expect better of their political system, and they deserve it.

Under the Congressional Budget Act, Congressional budget resolutions — Congress' proposed budgets — are passed each year. They are not sent to the President for approval and, therefore, are not law. They provide guidance to the committees of Congress, but the guidance is often late and ambiguous. The resolutions are usually passed well after the dates required by law, and well after they are needed by the finance, authorizing, and appropriations committees. Moreover, there is little agreement within Congress on the guidance provided. The House of Representatives and the Senate do not agree, except in the most general terms, on the priorities implied by resolutions both have approved.

Except for last year's on-time performance, Congress' self-imposed budget deadlines have usually been missed, and massive continuing resolutions and reconciliation bills have been the rule rather than the exception. These large, cumbersome bills provide cozy hiding places for hundreds of special interest add-ons, which line-item veto authority would permit the President to challenge.

A number of changes in the budget process — most of which I have recommended before — are needed to instill budget discipline throughout the legislative process. I urge Congress to adopt the following measures:

Balanced budget amendment. I remain committed to and urge approval of a constitutional amendment requiring a balanced budget. The amendment should require a super-majority vote (at least 60 percent) in the Congress to increase taxes.

Line-item veto. My successors should be given the authority, subject to Congressional override, to veto line-items in annual appropriations bills, in authorizing legislation that provides or mandates funding for programs, and in revenue bills. Such authority would permit the elimination of substantial waste and would be an effective instrument for enforcing budget discipline.

Enhanced rescission authority. To enhance the President's ability to control Government spending, I recommend that line-item veto authority be complemented by a change in law that would require the Congress to vote "yea" or "nay" on any rescission proposed by the President. Current law allows the Congress to duck responsibility by simply ignoring proposed rescissions for 45 days.

Biennial budgeting. The annual budget process consumes too much time and energy. A biennial budget would reduce the repetitive budget tasks, allow more time for considering key spending and revenue decisions, provide less scope for gimmicks that give the illusion of "savings," such as shifting spending from one year to another without affecting the underlying programs, and permit the realization of real savings that would be possible with a more assured availability of funds. For these reasons, I recommend that biennial budgeting be adopted.

Joint budget resolution. To ensure the broader scrutiny and stricter discipline that is needed in the congressional budget process, I propose that Congress be required to prepare a budget resolution covering a minimum of two years showing revenue proposals individually and showing spending priorities. The Congress should also be required to submit its budget resolution to the President for his signature or veto. Subsequent legislation which exceeds these allocations should not be considered without super-majority approval.

Individual transmittal of appropriations bills. The practice of transmitting full-year continuing resolutions covering a number of appropriations bills does not permit the Legislative or Executive Branches to exercise proper scrutiny of those bills. Too often in the past, such continuing resolutions have provided convenient cover for special-interest spending that would not survive close scrutiny. To minimize this risk, I propose that appropriations bills be transmitted individually to the President.

Credit reform. The effects of credit activities are recorded imperfectly under current budget accounting. The subsidy component of Federal lending programs remains hidden.

To correct this major fault in the budget system, I recommended credit reform legislation two years ago. This legislation, which I am recommending again, would measure the true cost — the present value — of the subsidies provided by Federal credit programs and put that cost on an expenditure basis equivalent to the cost of other Federal programs. This change must be an integral part of the reform of the budget process.

Measuring the effects of budget proposals. Budget discipline and lasting deficit reduction would be facilitated if the Legislative and Executive Branches were to use a common set of principles for scoring budget proposals and actions on them. I urge that the Congressional Budget Office and the Office of Management and Budget be charged with the responsibility to develop, in consultation with the budget, finance, authorizing, and appropriations committees, a common set of budget scoring principles for use by the Legislative and Executive Branches.

Adoption of these reforms should enable the Federal Government to make informed decisions in a deliberate fashion that fosters rational priorities. The American people deserve no less from their elected representatives.

Conclusion

The accomplishments of the American people in the past eight years will always be for me a source of pride. However, we must continue our recent progress in reducing the Federal deficit.

Deficit reduction is a key national priority, written into law by the G-R-H Act, which, despite its defects, legislated a process to achieve a balanced budget.

This budget achieves the 1990 target of the amended Act, and projects a budget balance in 1993. It preserves legitimate programs for the aged and needy, provides for adequate national security, devotes more resources to other high-priority activities, and accomplishes all this without raising taxes. Tax increases are not needed. History shows that they would simply be used by the Congress to increase spending. Tax increases have been overwhelmingly voted down in the last three Presidential elections.

I call upon the Congress to enact this budget. Higher taxes are not needed — as this budget demonstrates — but genuine deficit reduction through moderating the growth in spending is essential to enable the next Administration and Congress to address the Nation's agenda for the future.

Over the past eight years, we Americans have made our world a safer place for freedom because we had the will to reinvigorate our economy, rebuild our defenses, and provide for the less fortunate among us. Together, we achieved a new beginning for our country and prepared the way for the next Administration to build on our accomplishments.

RONALD REAGAN

January 9, 1989

George Bush's Inaugural Address

Following is the White House text of President Bush's inaugural address as delivered Jan. 20, 1989.

Mr. Chief Justice, Mr. President, Vice President Quayle, Senator Mitchell, Speaker Wright, Senator Dole, Congressman Michel, and fellow citizens, neighbors and friends.

There is a man here who has earned a lasting place in our hearts — and in our history. President Reagan, on behalf of our nation I thank you for the wonderful things that you have done for America.

I have just repeated word-for-word the oath taken by George Washington 200 years ago; and the Bible on which I placed my hand is the Bible on which he placed his.

It is right that the memory of Washington be with us today, not only because this is our Bicentennial Inauguration, but because Washington remains the father of our country. And he would, I think, be gladdened by this day. For today is the concrete expression of a stunning fact: Our continuity these 200 years since our government began.

We meet on democracy's front porch. A good place to talk as neighbors, and as friends. For this is a day when our nation is made whole, when our differences, for a moment, are suspended.

And my first act as President is a prayer and I ask you to bow your heads:

"Heavenly Father, we bow our heads and thank you for your love. Accept our thanks for the peace that yields this day and the shared faith that makes its continuance likely. Make us strong to do your work, willing to heed and hear your will, and write on our hearts these words: 'Use power to help people.' For we are given power not to advance our own purposes, nor to make a great show in the world, nor a name. There is but one just use of power, and it is to serve people. Help us to remember, Lord. Amen."

I come before you and assume the presidency at a moment rich with promise. We live in a peaceful, prosperous time, but we can make it better.

For a new breeze is blowing, and a world refreshed by freedom seems reborn; for in man's heart, if not in fact, the day of the dictator is over. The totalitarian era is passing, its old ideas blown away like leaves from an ancient lifeless tree.

A new breeze is blowing — and a nation refreshed by freedom stands ready to push on: There is new ground to be broken, and new action to be taken.

There are times when the future seems thick as a fog; you sit and wait, hoping the mists will lift and reveal the right path.

But this is a time when the future seems a door you can walk right through — into a room called Tomorrow.

Great nations of the world are moving toward democracy — through the door to freedom.

Men and women of the world move toward free markets — through the door to prosperity.

The people of the world agitate for free expression and free thought — through the door to the moral and intellectual satisfactions that only liberty allows.

We know what works: Freedom works. We know what's right: Freedom is right. We know how to secure a more just and prosperous life for man on earth: through free markets, free speech, free elections, and the exercise of free will unhampered by the state.

For the first time in this century — for the first time in perhaps all history — man does not have to invent a system by which to live. We don't have to talk into the night about which form of government is better. We don't have to wrest justice from the kings — we only have to summon it from within ourselves.

We must act on what we know. I take as my guide the hope of a saint: In crucial things, unity — in important things, diversity — in all things, generosity.

America today is a proud, free nation, decent and civil — a place we cannot help but love. We know in our hearts, not loudly and proudly, but as a simple fact, that this country has meaning beyond what we see, and that our strength is a force for good.

But have we changed as a nation even in our time? Are we enthralled with material things, less appreciative of the nobility of work and sacrifice?

My friends, we are not the sum of our possessions. They are not the measure of our lives. In our hearts we know what matters. We cannot hope only to leave our children a bigger car, a bigger bank account. We must hope to give them a sense of what it means to be a loyal friend a loving parent, a citizen who leaves his home, his neighborhood and town better than he found it.

And what do we want the men and women who work with us to say when we are no longer there? That we were more driven to succeed than anyone around us? Or that we stopped to ask if a sick child had gotten better, and stayed a moment there to trade a word of friendship.

No President, no government, can teach us to remember what is best in what we are. But if the man you have chosen to lead this government can help make a difference; if he can celebrate the quieter, deeper successes that are made not of gold and silk, but of better hearts and finer souls; if he can do these things, then he must.

Kinder and Gentler

America is never wholly herself unless she is engaged in high moral principle. We as a people have such a purpose today. It is to make kinder the face of the nation and gentler the face of the world.

My friends, we have work to do. There are the homeless, lost and roaming — there are the children who have nothing, no love, no normalcy — there are those who cannot free themselves of enslavement to whatever addiction — drugs, welfare, the demoralization that rules the slums. There is crime to be conquered, the rough crime of the streets. There are young women to be helped who are about to become mothers of children they can't care for and might not love. They need our care, our guidance, and our education; though we bless them for choosing life.

The old solution, the old way, was to think that public money alone could end these problems. But we have learned that that is not so. And in any case, our funds are low. We have a deficit to bring down. We have more will than wallet; but will is what we need.

We will make the hard choices, looking at what we have, perhaps allocating it differently, making our decisions based on honest need and prudent safety.

And then we will do the wisest thing of all: We will turn to the only resource we have that in times of need always grows: the goodness and the courage of the American people.

And I am speaking of a new engagement in the lives of others — a new activism, hands-on and involved, that gets the job done. We must bring in the generations, harnessing the unused talent of the elderly and the unfocused energy of the young. For not only leadership is passed from generation to generation, but so is stewardship. And the generation born after the Second World War has come of age.

I have spoken of a thousand points of light — of all the community organizations that are spread like stars throughout the nation, doing good.

We will work hand in hand, encouraging, sometimes leading, sometimes being led, rewarding. We will work on this in the White House, in the Cabinet agencies. I will go to the people and the programs that are the brighter points of light, and I will ask every member of my government to become involved.

The old ideas are new again because they're not old, they are timeless: duty, sacrifice, commitment, and a patriotism that finds its expression in taking part and pitching in.

We need a new engagement, too, between the Executive and the Congress.

An Offered Hand

The challenges before us will be thrashed out with the House and Senate. We must bring the federal budget into balance. And we must ensure that America stands before the world united: strong, at peace, and fiscally sound. But, of course, things may be difficult.

We need compromise; we've had dissension. We need harmony; we've had a chorus of discordant voices.

For Congress, too, has changed in our time. There has grown a certain divisiveness. We have seen the hard looks and heard the statements in which not each other's ideas are challenged, but each other's motives. And our great parties have too often been far apart and untrusting of each other.

It's been this way since Vietnam. That war cleaves us still. But, friends, that war began in earnest a quarter of a century ago; and surely the statute of limitations has been reached. This is a fact: The final lesson of Vietnam is that no great nation can long afford to be sundered by a memory.

A new breeze is blowing — and the old bipartisanship must be made new again.

To my friends — and yes, I do mean friends — in the loyal opposition — and yes, I mean loyal: I put out my hand.

I am putting out my hand to you, Mr. Speaker.

I am putting out my hand to you, Mr. Majority Leader.

For this is the thing: This is the age of the offered hand.

And we can't turn back clocks, and I don't want to. But when our fathers were young, Mr. Speaker, our differences ended at the water's edge. And we don't wish to turn back time, but when our mothers were young, Mr. Majority Leader, the Congress and the Executive were capable of working together to produce a budget on which this nation could live. Let us negotiate soon — and hard. But in the end, let us produce.

The American people await action. They didn't send us here to bicker. They ask us to rise above the merely partisan. "In crucial things, unity" — and this, my friends, is crucial.

To the world, too, we offer new engagement and a renewed vow: We will stay strong to protect the peace. The "offered hand" is a reluctant fist; once made strong, it can be used with great effect.

There are today Americans who are held against their will in foreign lands, and Americans who are unaccounted for. Assistance can be shown here, and will be long remembered. Good will begets good will. Good faith can be a spiral that endlessly moves on.

"Great nations like great men must keep their word." When America says something, America means it, whether a treaty or an agreement or a vow made on marble steps. We will always try to speak clearly, for candor is a compliment. But subtlety, too, is good and has its place.

While keeping our alliances and friendships around the world strong, ever strong, we will continue the new closeness with the Soviet Union, consistent both with our security and with progress. One might say that our new relationship in part reflects the triumph of hope and strength over experience. But hope is good. And so is strength. And vigilance.

Here today are tens of thousands of our citizens who feel the understandable satisfaction of those who have taken part in democracy and seen their hopes fulfilled.

But my thoughts have been turning the past few days to those who would be watching at home —

To an older fellow who will throw a salute by himself when the flag goes by, and the woman who will tell her sons the words of the battle hymns. I don't mean this to be sentimental. I mean that on days like this, we remember that we are all part of a continuum, inescapably connected by the ties that bind —

Our children are watching in schools throughout our great land. And to them I say, thank you for watching democracy's big day. For democracy belongs to us all, and freedom is like a beautiful kite that can go higher and higher with the breeze. . . .

And to all I say: No matter what your circumstances or where you are, you are part of this day, you are part of the life of our great nation.

A President is neither prince nor pope, and I don't seek "a window on men's souls." In fact, I yearn for a greater tolerance, an easy-goingness about each other's attitudes and way of life.

There are few clear areas in which we as a society must rise up united and express our intolerance. And the most obvious now is drugs. And when that first cocaine was smuggled in on a ship, it may as well have been a deadly bacteria, so much has it hurt the body, the soul of our country. There is much to be done and to be said, but take my word for it: This scourge will stop.

And so, there is much to do; and tomorrow the work begins.

And I do not mistrust the future; I do not fear what is ahead. For our problems are large, but our heart is larger. Our challenges are great, but our will is greater. And if our flaws are endless, God's love is truly boundless.

Some see leadership as high drama, and the sound of trumpets calling. And sometimes it is that. But I see history as a book with many pages — and each day we fill a page with acts of hopefulness and meaning.

The new breeze blows, a page turns, the story unfolds — and so today a chapter begins: a small and stately story of unity, diversity, and generosity — shared, and written, together.

Thank you.

God bless you.

And God bless the United States of America.

President Bush's Economic Proposals

Following is the White House text of President Bush's budget proposals as delivered to a joint session of Congress Feb. 9, 1989.

Less than three weeks ago, I joined you on the West Front of this very building and — looking over the monuments to our proud past — offered you my hand in filling the next page of American history with a story of extended prosperity and continued peace. Tonight, I am back, to offer you my plans as well. The hand remains extended, the sleeves are rolled up, America is waiting, and now we must produce. Together, we can build a better America.

It is comforting to return to this historic chamber. Here, 22 years ago, I first raised my hand to be sworn into public life. So tonight, I feel as if I am returning home to friends. And I intend, in the months and years to come, to give you what friends deserve: frankness, respect, and my best judgment about ways to improve America's future.

In return, I ask for an honest commitment to our common mission of progress. If we seize the opportunities on the road before us, there will be praise enough for all. The people didn't send us here to bicker. It's time to govern.

Many Presidents have come to this chamber in times of great crisis. War. Depression. Loss of national spirit.

Eight years ago, I sat in that chair as President Reagan spoke of punishing inflation and devastatingly high interest rates, people out of work, American confidence on the wane. Our challenge is different.

We are fortunate — a much-changed landscape lies before us tonight. So I don't propose to reverse direction. We are headed the right way. But we cannot rest. We are a people whose energy and drive have fueled our rise to greatness. We are a forward-looking nation — generous, yes, but ambitious as well — not for ourselves, but for the world. Complacency is not in our character — not before, not now, not ever.

So tonight, we must take a strong America — and make it even better. We must address some very real problems. We must establish some very clear priorities. And we must make a very substantial cut in the Federal budget deficit.

Some people find that agenda impossible. But I am presenting to you tonight a realistic plan for tackling it. My plan has four broad features: attention to urgent priorities, investment in the future, an attack on the deficit, and no new taxes.

This budget represents my best judgment of how we can address our priorities, consistent with the people's view. There are many areas in which we would all like to spend more than I propose, but we cannot until we get our fiscal house in order.

Next year alone, thanks to economic growth, without any change in the law, the Federal Government will take in over $80 billion more than it does this year. That's right — over $80 billion in new revenues, with no increase in taxes. Our job is to allocate those new resources wisely.

We can afford to increase spending — by a modest amount, but enough to invest in key priorities and still cut the deficit by almost 40 percent in one year. That will allow us to meet the targets set forth in the Gramm-Rudman-Hollings law.

But to do that, we must recognize that growth above inflation in Federal programs is not preordained, that not all spending initiatives were designed to be immortal.

I make this pledge tonight. My team and I are ready to work with the Congress, to form a special leadership group, to negotiate in good faith, to work day and night — if that's what it takes — to meet the budget targets, and to produce a budget on time.

We cannot settle for business as usual. Government by Continuing Resolution — or government by crisis — will not do.

The Budget Process

I ask the Congress tonight to approve several measures which will make budgeting more sensible. We could save time and improve efficiency by enacting two-year budgets. Forty-three Governors have the line-item veto. Presidents should have it, too.

At the very least, when a President proposes to rescind Federal spending, the Congress should be required to vote on that proposal — instead of killing it by inaction.

And I ask for Congress to honor the public's wishes by passing a constitutional amendment to require a balanced budget. Such an amendment, once phased in, will discipline both Congress and the Executive branch.

Several principles describe the kind of America I hope to build with your help in the years ahead.

We will not have the luxury of taking the easy, spendthrift approach to solving problems — because higher spending and higher taxes put economic growth at risk.

Economic growth provides jobs and hope. Economic growth enables us to pay for social programs. Economic growth enhances the security of the Nation. And low tax rates create economic growth.

I believe in giving Americans greater freedom and greater choice — and I will work for choice for American families, whether in the housing in which they live, the schools to which they send their children, or the child care they select for their young.

I believe that we have an obligation to those in need, but that Government should not be the provider of first resort for things that the private sector can produce better.

I believe in a society that is free from discrimination and bigotry of any kind. I will work to knock down the barriers left by past discrimination, and to build a more tolerant society that will stop such barriers from ever being built again.

I believe that family and faith represent the moral compass of the nation — and I will work to make them strong, for as Benjamin Franklin said: "If a sparrow cannot fall to the ground without His notice, [can] a [great nation] rise without His aid?"

And I believe in giving people the power to make their own lives better through growth and opportunity. Together, let's put power in the hands of people.

Three weeks ago, we celebrated the Bicentennial Inaugural, the 200th anniversary of the first Presidency. And if you look back, one thing is so striking about the way the Founding Fathers looked at America. They didn't talk about themselves. They talked about posterity. They talked about the future.

We, too, must think in terms bigger than ourselves.

'A Better Tomorrow'

We must take actions today that will ensure a better tomorrow. We must extend American leadership in technology, increase long-term investment, improve our education system, and boost productivity. These are the keys to building a better future.

Here are some of my recommendations:

- I propose almost $2.2 billion for the National Science Foundation to promote basic research;
- I propose to make permanent the tax credit for research and development;
- I have asked Vice President Quayle to chair a new Task Force on Competitiveness;
- I request funding for NASA and a strong space program — an increase of almost $2.4 billion over the current fiscal year. We must have a manned space station; a vigorous, safe space shuttle program; and more commercial development in space. The space program should always go "full throttle up" — that's not just our ambition; it's our destiny.

I propose that we cut the maximum tax rate on capital gains to increase long-term investment. History is clear: This will increase revenues, help savings, and create new jobs.

We won't be competitive if we leave whole sectors of America behind. This is the year we should finally enact urban enterprise zones, and bring hope to our inner cities.

Education: Top Priority

But the most important competitiveness program of all is one which improves education in America. When some of our students actually have trouble locating America on a map of the world, it is time for us to map a new approach to education.

We must reward excellence, and cut through bureaucracy. We must help those schools that need help most. We must give choice to parents, students, teachers and principals. And we must hold all concerned accountable. In education, we cannot tolerate mediocrity.

I want to cut the drop-out rate, and make America a more literate nation. Because what it really comes down to is this: The longer our graduation lines are today, the shorter our unemployment lines will be tomorrow.

So tonight I am proposing the following initiatives:

- the beginning of a $500-million program to reward America's best schools — "merit schools";
- the creation of special Presidential awards for the best teachers in every State — because excellence should be rewarded;
- the establishment of a new program of National Science Scholars, one each year for every Member of the House and Senate, to give this generation of students a special incentive to excel in science and mathematics;
- the expanded use of magnet schools which give families and students greater choice;
- and a new program to encourage "alternative certification" — which will let talented people from all fields teach in the classroom.

I have said I'd like to be "the Education President." Tonight, I ask you to join me by becoming "the Education Congress."

The War on Drugs

Just last week, as I settled into this new office, I received a letter from a mother in Pennsylvania, who had been struck by my message in the Inaugural address. "Not 12 hours before," she wrote, "my husband and I received word that [our] son was addicted to cocaine. [He] had the world at his feet. Bright, gifted, personable . . . he could have done anything with his life. [Now] he has chosen cocaine."

"Please," she wrote, "find a way to curb the supply of cocaine. Get tough with the pushers. [Our son] needs your help."

My friends, that voice crying out for help could be the voice of your own neighbor. Your own friend. Your own son. Over 23 million Americans used illegal drugs last year — at a staggering cost to our Nation's well-being.

Let this be recorded as the time when America rose up and said "No" to drugs. The scourge of drugs must be stopped. I am asking tonight for an increase of almost a billion dollars in budget outlays to escalate the war against drugs. The war will be waged on all fronts.

Our new "drug czar," Bill Bennett, and I will be shoulder to shoulder leading the charge.

Some money will be used to expand treatment to the poor, and to young mothers. This will offer the helping hand to the many innocent victims of drugs — like the thousands of babies born addicted, or with AIDS, because of the mother's addiction.

Some will be used to cut the waiting time for treatment. Some money will be devoted to those urban schools where the emergency is now the worst. And much of it will be used to protect our borders, with help from the Coast Guard, the Customs Service, the departments of State and Justice, and yes, the U.S. military.

I mean to get tough on the drug criminals. Let me be clear: This President will back up those who put their lives on the line every day — our local police officers.

My budget asks for beefed-up prosecution, for a new attack on organized crime, and for enforcement of tough sentences — and for the worst kingpins, that means the death penalty.

I also want to make sure that when a drug dealer is convicted, there is a cell waiting for him. He should not go free because prisons are too full.

Let the word go out: If you are caught and convicted, you will do time.

But for all we do in law enforcement, in interdiction and treatment, we will never win this war on drugs unless we stop demand for drugs.

So some of this increase will be used to educate the young about the dangers of drugs. We must involve parents. We must involve teachers. We must involve communities. And my friends, we must involve ourselves.

One problem related to drug use demands our urgent attention and our continuing compassion. That is the terrible tragedy of AIDS. I am asking for $1.6 billion for education to prevent the disease — and for research to find a cure.

Environmental Protection

If we're to protect our future, we need a new attitude about the environment. We must protect the air we breathe. I will send to you shortly legislation for a new, more effective Clean Air Act. It will include a plan to reduce, by date certain, the emissions which cause acid rain — because the time for study alone has passed, and the time for action is now.

We must make use of clean coal. My budget contains full funding, on schedule, for the clean-coal technology agreement we have made with Canada. We intend to honor that agreement.

We must not neglect our parks. So I am asking to fund new acquisitions under the land and water conservation fund.

We must protect our oceans. I support new penalties against those who would dump medical waste and other trash in the oceans. The age of the needle on the beach must end.

In some cases, the gulfs and oceans off our shores hold the promise of oil and gas reserves which can make our Nation more secure and less dependent on foreign oil. When those with the most promise can be tapped safely, as with much of the Alaska National Wildlife Refuge, we should proceed. But we must use caution and we must respect the environment.

So tonight I am calling for the indefinite postponement of three lease sales which have raised troubling questions — two off the coast of California, and one which could threaten the Everglades in Florida. Action on these three lease sales will await the conclusions of a special task force set up to measure the potential for environmental damage.

I am directing the Attorney General and the Administrator of the Environmental Protection Agency to use every tool at their disposal to speed and toughen the enforcement of our laws against toxic waste dumpers. I want faster cleanups and tougher enforcement of penalties against polluters.

A Compassionate Society

In addition to caring for our future, we must care for those around us. A decent society shows compassion for the young, the elderly, the vulnerable, and the poor.

Our first obligation is to the most vulnerable — infants, poor mothers, children living in poverty — and my proposed budget recognizes this. I ask for full funding of Medicaid — an increase of over $3 billion — and an expansion of the program to include coverage of pregnant women who are near the poverty line.

I believe we should help working families cope with the burden of child care. Our help should be aimed at those who need it most — low-income families with young children. I support a new child care tax credit that will aim our efforts at exactly those families — without discriminating against mothers who choose to stay at home.

Now, I know there are competing proposals. But remember this: The overwhelming majority of all preschool child care is now provided by relatives and neighbors, churches and community groups. Families who choose these options should remain eligible for help. Parents should have choice.

And for those children who are unwanted or abused, or whose parents are deceased, I believe we should encourage adoption. I propose to re-enact the tax deduction for adoption expenses, and to double it to $3,000. Let's make it easier for these kids to have parents who love them.

We have a moral contract with our senior citizens. In this budget, Social Security is fully funded, including a full cost-of-living adjustment. We must honor our contract.

We must care about those in "the shadows of life," and I, like many Americans, am deeply troubled by the plight of the homeless. The causes of homelessness are many, the history is long, but the moral imperative to act is clear.

Thanks to the deep well of generosity in this great land, many organizations already contribute. But we in Government cannot stand on the sidelines. In my budget, I ask for greater support for emergency food and shelter, for health services and measures to prevent substance abuse, and for clinics for the mentally ill — and I propose a new initiative involving the full range of Government agencies. We must confront this national shame.

There is another issue I decided to mention here tonight. I have long believed that the people of Puerto Rico should have the right to determine their own political future. Personally, I favor statehood. But I ask the Congress to take the necessary steps to let the people decide in a referendum.

Certain problems, the result of decades of unwise practices, threaten the health and security of our people. Left unattended, they will only get worse — but we can act now to put them behind us.

Earlier this week, I announced my support for a plan to restore the financial and moral integrity of our savings system. I ask Congress to enact our reform proposals within 45 days. We must not let this situation fester.

Certainly, the savings of Americans must remain secure — insured depositors will continue to be fully protected. But any plan to refinance the system must be accompanied by major reform. Our proposals will prevent such a crisis from recurring. The best answer is to make sure that a mess like this will never happen again.

The majority of thrifts in communities across this Nation have been honest; they have played a major role in helping families achieve the American dream of home ownership. But make no mistake: Those who are corrupt, those who break the law, must be kicked out of the business; and they should go to jail.

We face a massive task in cleaning up the waste left from decades of environmental neglect at America's nuclear weapons plants. Clearly, we must modernize these plants and operate them safely. That is not at issue — our national security depends on it.

But beyond that, we must clean up the old mess that's been left behind — and I propose in this budget to more than double our current effort to do so. This will allow us to identify the exact nature of the various problems so we can clean them up — and clean them up we will.

The Pentagon Budget

We have been fortunate during these past eight years. America is a stronger nation today than it was in 1980. Morale in our Armed Forces is restored. Our resolve has been shown. Our readiness has been improved. And we are at peace. There can no longer be any doubt that peace has been made more secure through strength. When America is stronger, the world is safer.

Most people don't realize that after the successful restoration of our strength, the Pentagon budget has actually been reduced in real terms for each of the last four years. We cannot tolerate further reductions.

In light of the compelling need to reduce the deficit, however, I support a one-year freeze in the military budget — something I proposed last fall in my flexible freeze plan.

This freeze will apply for only one year — after that increases above inflation will be required. I will not sacrifice American preparedness; and I will not compromise American strength.

I should be clear on the conditions attached to my recommendation for the coming year:

- the savings must be allocated to those priorities for investing in our future that I have spoken about tonight;
- this defense freeze must be part of a comprehensive budget agreement which meets the targets spelled out in the Gramm-Rudman-Hollings law without raising taxes, and which incorporates reforms in the budget process.

I have directed the National Security Council to review our national security and defense policies and report back to me within 90 days to ensure that our capabilities and resources meet our commitments and strategies.

I am also charging the Department of Defense with the task of developing a plan to improve the defense procurement process and management of the Pentagon — one which will fully implement the Packard Commission report. Many of the changes can only be made with the participation of the Congress — so I ask for your help.

We need fewer regulations. We need less bureaucracy. We need multi-year procurement and two-year budgeting. And frankly, we need less congressional micromanagement of our Nation's military policy.

America and the World

Securing a more peaceful world is perhaps the most important priority I'd like to address tonight. We meet at a time of extraordinary hope. Never before in this century have our values of freedom, democracy, and economic opportunity been such a powerful political and intellectual force around the globe.

Never before has our leadership been so crucial, because while America has its eyes on the future, the world has its eyes on America.

It is a time of great change in the world — and especially in the Soviet Union. Prudence and common sense dictate that we try to understand the full meaning of the change going on there, review our policies carefully, and proceed with caution. But I have personally assured General Secretary Gorbachev that, at the conclusion of such a review, we will be ready to move forward. We will not miss any opportunity to work for peace.

The fundamental fact remains that the Soviets retain a very powerful military machine, in the service of objectives which are still too often in conflict with ours. So let us take the new openness seriously. Let us step forward to negotiate. But let us also be realistic. And let us always be strong.

There are some pressing issues we must address: I will vigorously pursue the Strategic Defense Initiative. The spread and even use of sophisticated weaponry threatens global stability as never before.

Chemical weapons must be banned from the face of the Earth, never to be used again. This won't be easy. Verification will be difficult. But civilization and human decency demand that we try.

And the spread of nuclear weapons must be stopped. I will work to strengthen the hand of the International Atomic Energy Agency. Our diplomacy must work every day against the proliferation of nuclear weapons.

And, around the globe, we must continue to be freedom's best friend. We must stand firm for self-determination and democracy in Central America — including in Nicaragua. For when people are given the chance, they inevitably will choose a free press, freedom of worship, and certifiably free and fair elections.

We must strengthen the alliance of industrial democracies — as solid a force for peace as the world has ever known. This is an alliance forged by the power of our ideals, not the pettiness of our differences. So let us lift our sights — to rise above fighting about beef hormones to building a better future, to move from protectionism to progress.

I have asked the Secretary of State to visit Europe next week and to consult with them on the wide range of challenges and opportunities we face together — including East-West relations. And I look forward to meeting with our NATO partners in the near future.

I, too, shall begin a trip shortly — to the far reaches of the Pacific Basin, where the winds of democracy are creating new hope, and the power of free markets is unleashing a new force.

When I served as our representative in China just 14 years ago, few would have predicted the scope of the changes we've witnessed since then. But in preparing for this trip, I was struck by something I came across from a Chinese writer. He was speaking of his country, decades ago — but his words speak to each of us, in America, tonight.

"Today," he said, "we are afraid of the simple words like goodness and mercy and kindness."

My friends, if we're to succeed as a Nation, we must rediscover those words.

In just three days, we mark the birthday of Abraham Lincoln — the man who saved our Union, and gave new meaning to the word opportunity. Lincoln once said: "I hold that while man exists, it is his duty to improve not only his own condition, but to assist in ameliorating [that of] mankind."

It is this broader mission to which I call all Americans. Because the definition of a successful life must include serving others.

To the young people of America, who sometimes feel left out — I ask you tonight to give us the benefit of your talent and energy through a new program called "YES," for Youth Entering Service to America.

To those men and women in business — remember the ultimate end of your work — to make a better product, to create better lives. I ask you to plan for the longer term and avoid the temptation of quick and easy paper profits.

To the brave men and women who wear the uniform of the United States of America — thank you. Your calling is a high one — to be the defenders of freedom and the guarantors of liberty. And I want you to know that the Nation is grateful for your service.

To the farmers of America, we appreciate the bounty you provide. We will work with you to open foreign markets to American agricultural products.

To the parents of America, I ask you to get involved in your child's schooling. Check on their homework. Go to school, meet the teachers, care about what is happening there. It is not only your child's future on the line, it is America's.

To kids in our cities — don't give up hope. Say no to drugs. Stay in school. And yes, "Keep hope alive."

To those 37 million Americans with some form of disability — you belong in the economic mainstream. We need your talents in America's work force. Disabled Americans must become full partners in America's opportunity society.

To the families of America watching tonight in your living rooms: Hold fast to your dreams, because ultimately America's future rests in your hands.

And to my friends in this Chamber, I ask for your cooperation to keep America growing while cutting the deficit. That is only fair to those who now have no vote — the generations to come.

Let them look back and say that we had the foresight to understand that a time of peace and prosperity is not a time to rest, but a time to push forward. A time to invest in the future.

And let all Americans remember that no problem of human making is too great to be overcome by human ingenuity, human energy, and the untiring hope of the human spirit. I believe this. I would not have asked to be your President if I didn't.

Reaching Out to Congress

Tomorrow, the debate on the plan I have put forward begins. I ask the Congress to come forward with your proposals, if they are different. Let us not question each other's motives. Let us debate. Let us negotiate. But let us solve the problem.

Recalling anniversaries may not be my specialty in speeches . . . but tonight is one of some note. On February 9, 1941, just 48 years ago tonight, Sir Winston Churchill took to the airwaves during Britain's hour of peril.

He had received from President Roosevelt a hand-carried letter quoting Longfellow's famous poem: "Sail on, O Ship of State! Sail on, Oh Union, strong and great! Humanity with all its fears, with all the hopes of future years, Is hanging breathless on thy fate!"

Churchill responded on this night by radio broadcast to a nation at war, but he directed his words to Roosevelt. "We shall not fail or falter," he said. "We shall not weaken or tire. Give us the tools, and we will finish the job."

Tonight, almost a half-century later, our peril may be less immediate, but the need for perseverance and clear-sighted fortitude is just as great.

Now, as then, there are those who say it can't be done. There are voices who say that America's best days have passed. That we are bound by constraints, threatened by problems, surrounded by troubles which limit our ability to hope.

Well, tonight I remain full of hope. We Americans have only begun on our mission of goodness and greatness. And to those timid souls, I repeat the plea —give us the tools; and we will do the job.

Thank you, and God bless you, and God bless America.

GEORGE BUSH

February 9, 1989

Bush Address on Panama Invasion

Following is the Reuter transcript of President Bush's Dec. 20, 1989, televised address to the American people about the decision to send U.S. troops to Panama.

My fellow citizens. Last night, I ordered U.S. military forces to Panama. No president takes such action lightly. This morning, I want to tell you what I did and why I did it.

For nearly two years, the United States, the nations of Latin America and the Caribbean have worked together to resolve the crisis in Panama. The goals of the United States have been to safeguard the lives of Americans, to defend democracy in Panama, to combat drug trafficking and to protect the integrity of the Panama Canal treaty.

Many attempts have been made to resolve this crisis through diplomacy and negotiations. All were rejected by the dictator of Panama, General Manuel Noriega, an indicted drug trafficker.

Last Friday, Noriega declared his military dictatorship to be in a state of war with the United States and publicly threatened the lives of Americans in Panama. The very next day, forces under his command shot and killed an unarmed American serviceman, wounded another, arrested and brutally beat a third American serviceman, and then brutally interrogated his wife, threatening her with sexual abuse. That was enough.

General Noriega's reckless threats and attack upon Americans in Panama created an imminent danger to the 35,000 American citizens in Panama. As president, I have no higher obligation than to safeguard the lives of American citizens.

And that is why I directed our armed forces to protect the lives of American citizens in Panama and to bring General Noriega to justice in the United States.

I contacted the bipartisan leadership of Congress last night and informed them of this decision. And after taking this action, I also talked with leaders in Latin America, the Caribbean and those of other U.S. allies.

At this moment U.S. forces, including forces deployed from the United States last night, are engaged in action in Panama. The United States intends to withdraw the forces newly deployed to Panama as quickly as possible.

Our forces have conducted themselves courageously and selflessly. And as commander-in-chief, I salute every one of them and thank them on behalf of our country. Tragically, some Americans have lost their lives in defense of their fellow citizens, in defense of democracy. And my heart goes out to their families. We also regret and mourn the loss of innocent Panamanians.

The brave Panamanians elected by the people of Panama in the elections last May, President Guillermo Endara and Vice Presidents Calderon and Ford, have assumed the rightful leadership of their country.

You remember those horrible pictures of newly elected Vice President Ford, covered head to toe with blood, beaten mercilessly by so-called dignity battalions. Well, the United States today recognizes the democratically elected government of President Endara. I will send our ambassador back to Panama immediately.

Key military objectives have been achieved. Most organized resistance has been eliminated. But the operation is not over yet, General Noriega is in hiding. And nevertheless, yesterday a dictator ruled Panama and today constitutionally elected leaders govern.

I've today directed the secretary of the Treasury and the secretary of state to lift the economic sanctions with respect to the democratically elected government of Panama and, in cooperation with that government, to take steps to effect an orderly unblocking of Panamanian government assets in the United States.

I am fully committed to implement the Panama Canal Treaties and turn over the Canal to Panama in the year 2000. The actions we have taken and the cooperation of a new democratic government in Panama will permit us to honor those commitments. As soon as the new government recommends a qualified candidate — Panamanian — to be administrator of the canal as called for in the treaties, I will submit this nominee to the Senate for expedited consideration.

I am committed to strengthening our relationship with the democratic nations in this hemisphere. I will continue to seek solutions to the problems of this region through dialogue and multilateral diplomacy. I took this action only after reaching the conclusion that every other avenue was closed and the lives of American citizens were in grave danger.

I hope that the people of Panama will put this dark chapter of dictatorship behind them and move forward together as citizens of a democratic Panama with this government that they themselves have elected. The United States is eager to work with the Panamanian people in partnership and friendship to rebuild their economy.

The Panamanian people want democracy, peace and the chance for a better life in dignity and freedom. The people of the United States seek only to support them in pursuit of these noble goals.

Thank you very much.

President Bush's 1990 State of the Union Address

Following is the Reuter transcript of President Bush's first State of the Union address to a joint session of Congress Jan. 31, 1990.

Mr. President, Mr. Speaker, members of the United States Congress: I return as a former president of the Senate and a former member of this great House. And now, as president, it is my privilege to report to you on the State of the Union.

Tonight, I come not to speak about the "state of the government," not to detail every new initiative we plan for the coming year, nor describe every line in the budget. I'm here to speak to you and to the American people about the State of the Union, about our world, the changes we've seen, the challenges we face — and what that means for America.

There are singular moments in history, dates that divide all that goes before from all that comes after. Many of us in this chamber have lived much of our lives in a world whose fundamental features were defined in 1945. And the events of that year decreed the shape of nations, the pace of progress, freedom or oppression for millions of people around the world.

1945 provided the common frame of reference — the compass points of the postwar era we've relied upon to understand ourselves. And that was our world — until now. The events of the year just ended — the revolution of '89 — have been a chain reaction, change so striking that it marks the beginning of a new era in the world's affairs.

Think back — think back just 12 short months ago to the world we knew as 1989 began.

One year ago, the people of Panama lived in fear, under the thumb of a dictator. Today democracy is restored — Panama is free. Operation "Just Cause" has achieved its objective. The number of military personnel in Panama is now very close to what it was before the operation began. And tonight, I am announcing that well before the end of February the additional numbers of American troops, the brave men and women of our armed forces who made this mission a success, will be back home.

A year ago in Poland, Lech Walesa declared that he was ready to open a dialogue with the communist rulers of that country. And today, with the future of a free Poland in their own hands, members of Solidarity lead the Polish government.

A year ago, freedom's playwright, Vaclav Havel, languished as a prisoner in Prague. And today, it's Vaclav Havel — president of Czechoslovakia.

And one year ago, Erich Honecker of East Germany claimed history as his guide. He predicted the Berlin Wall would last another hundred years. Today, less than one year later, it's the wall that's history.

Remarkable events, events that fulfill the long-held hopes of the American people — events that validate the longstanding goals of American policy, a policy based on a single, shining principle: the cause of freedom.

America — not just the nation, but an idea, alive in the minds of people everywhere. As this new world takes shape, America stands at the center of a widening circle of freedom — today, tomorrow and into the next century.

Our nation is the enduring dream of every immigrant who ever set foot on these shores and the millions still struggling to be free. This nation, this idea called America, was and always will be a new world. Our new world.

At a workers' rally — in a place called Branik on the outskirts of Prague — the idea called America is alive. A worker, dressed in grimy overalls, rises to speak at the factory gates. He begins his speech to his fellow citizens with these words, words of a distant revolution:

"We hold these truths to be self-evident: that all men are created equal, that they are endowed by their Creator with certain unalienable rights, that among these are life, liberty and the pursuit of happiness."

Goals for America

It's no secret that, here at home, freedom's door opened long ago. The cornerstones of this free society have already been set in place: Democracy. Competition. Opportunity. Private investment. Stewardship. And, of course, leadership.

And our challenge today is to take this democratic system of ours — a system second to none — and make it better — a better America.

Where there's a job for everyone who wants one.

Where women working outside the home can be confident their children are in safe and loving care, and where government works to expand child-care alternatives for parents.

Where we reconcile the needs of a clean environment and a strong economy.

Where "Made in the U.S.A." is recognized around the world as the symbol of quality and progress. And where every one of us enjoys the same opportunities to live, to work and to contribute to society. And where, for the first time, the American mainstream includes all of our disabled citizens.

Where everyone has a roof over his head — and where the homeless get the help they need to live in dignity.

Where our schools challenge and support our kids and our teachers — and where all of them make the grade.

Where every street, every city, every school and every child is drug-free.

And, finally, where no American is forgotten. Our hearts go out to our hostages, our hostages who are ceaselessly on our minds and in our efforts.

That's part of the future we want to see, the future we can make for ourselves. But dreams alone won't get us there. We need to extend our horizon, commit to the long view. Our plans for the future start today.

In the tough competitive markets around, America faces great challenges and great opportunities. We know that we can succeed in the global economic arena of the '90s, but to meet that challenge we must make some fundamental changes — some crucial investment in ourselves.

Yes, we are going to invest in America. This administration is determined to encourage the creation of capital — capital of all kinds. Physical capital — everything, from our farms and factories to our workshops and production lines, all that is needed to produce and deliver quality goods and quality services.

Intellectual capital — the source of ideas that spark tomorrow's products. And, of course, our human capital — the talented work force we'll need to compete in the global market. And let me tell you: If we ignore human capital, we lose the spirit of American ingenuity, the spirit that is the hallmark of the American worker. That would be bad. The American worker is the most productive worker in the world.

We need to save more. We need to expand the pool of capital for the new investments that mean more jobs and more growth. And that's the idea behind a new initiative I call the Family Savings Plan, which I will send to Congress tomorrow.

We need to cut the tax on capital gains. Encourage risk-takers — especially those in our small businesses — to take those steps that translate into economic reward, jobs and a better life for all of us.

We'll do what it takes to invest in America's future. The budget commitment is there. The money is there. It's there for Research and Development, R&D — a record high. It's there for our housing initiative — HOPE — to help everyone from first-time home buyers to the homeless.

The money's there to keep our kids drug-free: 70 percent more than when I took office in 1989. It's there for space exploration. And it's there for education — another record high.

And one more thing. Last fall at the education summit, the governors and I agreed to look for ways to help make sure kids are ready to learn — the very first day they walk into that classroom. And I've made good on that commitment — by proposing a record increase in funds, an extra half a billion dollars, for something near and dear to all of us: Head Start.

America's Education Goals

Education is the one investment that means more for our future because it means the most for our children. Real improvement in our schools is not simply a matter of spending more. It is a matter of asking more — expecting more — of our schools, our teachers, of our kids and our parents and ourselves. That's why tonight I am announcing America's education goals — goals developed with the nation's governors. And, if I might, I'd like to say I'm very pleased that Governor [Booth] Gardner [D-Wash.] and Governor [Bill] Clinton [D-Ark.], Governor [Terry E.] Branstad [R-Iowa], Governor [Carroll A.] Campbell [Jr., R-S.C.], all of whom were very key in these discussions, these deliberations, are with us here tonight.

- By the year 2000, every child must start school ready to learn.
- The United States must increase the high school graduation rate to no less than 90 percent.
- And we're going to make sure our schools' diplomas mean something. In critical subjects — at the fourth, eighth and 12th grades — we must assess our students' performance.
- By the year 2000, U.S. students must be first in the world in math and science achievement.
- Every American adult must be a skilled, literate worker and citizen.
- Every school must offer the kind of disciplined environment that makes it possible for our kids to learn — and every school in America must be drug-free.

Ambitious aims? Of course. Easy to do? Far from it. But the future's at stake. This nation will not accept anything less than excellence in education.

These investments will keep America competitive. And I know this about the American people: We welcome competition. We'll match our ingenuity and energy, our experience and technology, our spirit and enterprise, against anyone. Let the competition be free — but let it also be fair. America is ready.

Controlling the Deficit

Since we really mean it, and since we are serious about being ready to meet that challenge, we're getting our own house in order. We've made real progress. Seven years ago, the federal deficit was 6 percent of our gross national product — 6 percent. In the new budget I sent up two days ago, the deficit is down to 1 percent of gross national product.

That budget brings federal spending under control. It meets the Gramm-Rudman target, brings that deficit down further, and balances the budget by 1993 — with no new taxes.

And let me tell you, there's still more than enough federal spending. For most of us, $1.2 trillion is still a lot of money. And once the budget is balanced, we can operate the way every family must when it has bills to pay. We won't leave it to our children and our grandchildren. Once it's balanced, we will start paying off the national debt.

Protecting the Environment

And there's something more. There's something more we owe the generations of the future: stewardship, the safekeeping of America's precious environmental inheritance. As just one sign of how serious we are, we will elevate the Environmental Protection Agency to Cabinet rank. Not more bureaucracy, not more red tape — but the certainty that here at home, and especially in our dealings with other nations, environmental issues have the status they deserve.

This year's budget provides over $2 billion in new spending to protect our environment, with over $1 billion for global change research. And a new initiative I call "America the Beautiful," to expand our national parks and wildlife preserves and improve recreational facilities on public lands. And something else — something that will help keep this country clean, from our forest land to the inner cities, and keep America beautiful for generations to come: the money to plant a billion trees a year.

And tonight — tonight, let me say again to all the members of the Congress: The American people did not send us here to bicker. There is work to do, and they sent us here to get it done. And once again, in a spirit of cooperation, I offer my hand to all of you, and let's work together to do the will of the people. Clean air. Child care. The Educational Excellence Act. Crime and drugs. It's time to act. The farm bill. Transportation policy. Product-liability reform. Enterprise zones. It's time to act together.

Social Security, Health Care

And there's one thing I hope we will be able to agree on. It's about our commitments. And I'm talking about Social Security. To every American out there on Social Security, to every American supporting that system today and to everyone counting on it when they retire: We made a promise to you, and we are going to keep it.

We rescued the system in 1983 — and it's sound again. Bipartisan arrangement. Our budget fully funds today's benefits, and it assures that future benefits will be funded as well. And the last thing we need to do is mess around with Social Security.

There's one more problem we need to address. We must give careful consideration to the recommendations of the health care studies under way now, and that's why tonight, I am asking Dr. Sullivan, Lou Sullivan, secretary of health and human services, to lead a Domestic Policy Council review of recommendations on the quality, accessibility and cost of our nation's health care system. I am committed to bring the staggering costs of health care under control.

The "state of the government" — the "state of the government" does indeed depend on many of us in this very chamber. But the State of the Union depends on all Americans. We must maintain the democratic decency that makes a nation out of millions of individuals. And I have been appalled at the recent mail bombings across this country. Every one of us must confront and condemn racism, anti-Semitism, bigotry and hate. Not next week, not tomorrow, but right now. Every single one of us.

'The Idea We Call America'

The State of the Union depends on whether we help our neighbor — claim the problems of our community as our own. We've got to step forward when there's trouble, lend a hand, be what I call a point of light to a stranger in need. We've got to take the time after a busy day to sit down and read with our kids, help them with their homework, pass along the values we learned as children. And that's how we sustain the State of the Union.

Every effort is important. It all adds up — it's doing the things that give democracy meaning. It all adds up to who we are — and who we will be.

And let me say that so long as we remember the American idea, so long as we live up to the American ideal, the State of the Union will remain sound and strong.

And to those who worry that we've lost our way, well, I want you to listen to parts of a letter written by James Markwell, Private First Class James Markwell, a 20-year-old Army medic of the 1st Battalion, 75th Rangers. It's dated December 18th, the night before our Armed Forces went into action in Panama. It's a letter servicemen write — and hope will never be sent. And sadly, Private Markwell's mother did receive this letter. She passed it along to me out there in Cincinnati.

And here is some of what he wrote: "I have never been afraid of death, but I know he is waiting at the corner. I have been trained to kill and to save, and so has everyone else. I am frightened of what lays beyond the fog, and yet, do not mourn for me — revel in the life that I have died to give you. But most of all, don't forget the Army was my choice — something that I wanted to do. Remember I joined the Army to serve my country and insure that you are free to do what you want and live your lives freely."

Let me add that Private Markwell was among the first to see battle in Panama and one of the first to fall. But he knew what he believed in. He carried the idea we call America in his heart.

I began tonight speaking about the changes we've seen this past year. There is a new world of challenges and opportunities before us. And there is a need for leadership that only America can provide.

Nearly 40 years ago, in his last address to the Congress, President Harry Truman predicted such a time would come. He said: "As our world grows stronger, more united, more attractive to men on both sides of the Iron Curtain, then inevitably there will come a time of change within the communist world."

Today, that change is taking place.

For more than 40 years, America and its allies held communism in check and ensured that democracy would continue to exist. Today, with communism crumbling, our aim must be to ensure democracy's advance, to take the lead in forging peace and freedom's best hope, a great and growing commonwealth of free nations.

And to the Congress and to all Americans, I say it is time to acclaim a new consensus at home and abroad, a common vision of the peaceful world we want to see.

Here in our own hemisphere, it's time for all the people of the Americas, North and South, to live in freedom.

In the Far East and Africa, it is time for the full flowering of free governments and free markets that have served as the engine of progress.

It is time to offer our hand to the emerging democracies of Eastern Europe, so that continent, for too long a continent divided, can see a future whole and free.

It's time to build on our new relationship with the Soviet Union, to endorse and encourage a peaceful process of internal change toward democracy and economic opportunity.

Troop Reduction in Europe

We are in a period of great transition, great hope, yet great uncertainty. We recognize that the Soviet military threat in Europe is diminishing, but we see little change in Soviet strategic modernization. Therefore, we must sustain our own strategic offense modernization and the strategic defense initiative. But the time is right to move forward on a conventional arms control agreement to move us to more appropriate levels of military forces in Europe, a coherent defense program that ensures the U.S. will continue to be a catalyst for peaceful change in Europe. I've consulted with leaders of NATO — and in fact I spoke by phone with [Soviet] President [Mikhail S.] Gorbachev just today.

And I agree with our European allies that an American military presence in Europe is essential — and that it should not be tied solely to the Soviet military presence in Eastern Europe. But our troop levels can still be lower. So tonight I am announcing a major new step, for a further reduction in U.S. and Soviet manpower in Central and Eastern Europe to 195,000 on each side. This number — this number, this level — reflects the advice of our senior military advisers. It is designed to protect American and European interests and sustain NATO's defense strategy. A swift conclusion to our arms control talks — conventional, chemical and strategic — must now be our goal. And that time has come.

Still, we must recognize an unfortunate fact: In many regions of the world tonight, the reality is conflict, not peace. Enduring animosities and opposing interests remain. Thus the cause of peace must be served by an America strong enough and sure enough to defend our interests and our ideals. It's this American idea that for the past four decades helped inspire this Revolution of '89.

And here at home and in the world, there is history in the making and history to be made. Six months ago, early in this season of change, I stood at the gates of the Gdansk Shipyard in Poland at the monument to the fallen workers of Solidarity. It's a monument of simple majesty. Three tall crosses rise up from the stones. And atop each cross, an anchor, an ancient symbol of hope. The anchor in our world today is freedom — holding us steady in times of change, a symbol of hope to all the world. And freedom is at the very heart of the idea that is America.

Giving life to that idea depends on every one of us. Our anchor has always been faith and family. In the last few days of this past momentous year, our family was blessed once more, celebrating the joy of life when a little boy became our 12th grandchild. When I held the little guy for the first time, the troubles at home and abroad seemed manageable and totally in perspective.

Now, I know you're thinking: That's a grandfather talking. Well, maybe you're right. But I've met a lot of children this past year, across this country and everywhere from the Far East to Eastern Europe. All kids are unique. Yet all kids are alike: the budding young environmentalists I met this month, who joined me exploring the Florida Everglades; the Little Leaguers I played catch with in Poland, ready to go from Warsaw to the World Series. Even the kids who are ill or alone — and God bless those boarder babies, born addicted to drugs, coping with problems no child should have to face.

But, you know, when it comes to hope and the future, every kid is the same — full of dreams, ready to take on the world, all special because they are the very future of freedom. To them belongs this new world I've been speaking about.

And so tonight I'm going to ask something of every one of you. Let me start with my generation, with the grandparents out there. You are our living link to the past. Tell your grandchildren the story of struggles waged at home and abroad, of sacrifices freely made for freedom's sake. And tell them your own story as well — because every American has a story to tell.

Parents, your children look to you for direction and guidance. Tell them of faith and family. Tell them we are one nation under God. Teach them that of all the many gifts they can receive, liberty is their most precious legacy. And of all the gifts they can give, the greatest — the greatest — is helping others.

And to the children and young people out there tonight: With you rests our hope, all that America will mean in the years and decades ahead. Fix your vision on a new century, your century. On dreams we cannot see. On the destiny that is yours — and yours alone.

And, finally, let all Americans — all of us together here in this chamber, the symbolic center of democracy — affirm our allegiance to this idea we call America. And let us all remember that the State of the Union depends on each and every one of us.

God bless all of you, and may God bless this great nation, the United States of America.

President Bush's Fiscal 1991 Budget Message

Following is the Congressional Record *text of President Bush's fiscal 1991 budget message sent to Congress Jan. 29, 1990.*

TO THE CONGRESS OF
THE UNITED STATES:

I have the honor to present the *Budget of the United States Government for Fiscal Year 1991.*

The American economy is now in its eighth consecutive year of expansion and growth. It is essential that the growth of the economy continue and increase in the future. The budget is designed to achieve that goal.

The budget has five broad themes:

- **Investing in Our Future**. With an eye toward future growth, and expansion of the human frontier, the budget's chief emphasis is on investment in the future. It proposes: a capital gains incentive for long-term private investment and new incentives for family savings; record-high amounts for research and development, space, education, and Head Start; a major investment in civil aviation; and a large increase in spending to attack the scourge of drugs. At the same time, the budget maintains a strong national defense while reflecting the dramatic changes in the world political situation that are taking place; and it fulfills responsibilities to protect the environment, and preserve America's cultural heritage.

- **Advancing States as Laboratories.** The budget recognizes the emergence of new ideas and initiatives originating at the State and local level. The Federal Government will foster such innovation and experimentation in numerous fields, from transportation to health, through waivers of certain rules and regulations, and through demonstration grants.
- **Reforming Mandatory Programs.** Entitlement and other mandatory spending now constitutes nearly half the budget, not counting an additional 14 percent for interest. The budget provides for full payment of social security benefits and funds growth in health, low income and other mandatory programs. However, it proposes reforms where warranted to slow the growth in some of these programs and thus leave more room in the budget for priority initiatives.
- **Acknowledging Inherited Claims.** The budget faces up to such inherited claims as the cleanup of decades old environmental damage at nuclear weapons facilities. It analyzes potential claims from unfunded annuities and Federal insurance programs. It assesses the growing volume of defaults in Federal credit programs and proposes essential credit reforms.
- **Managing for Integrity and Efficiency.** The budget contains suggestions for reforms in the way Congress deals with the budget. It provides more resources and suggests improved methods for managing the vast Federal enterprise better. It identifies low-return domestic discretionary programs where a smaller investment of budgetary resources is warranted.

The budget meets the deficit target of $64 billion for 1991 established by the Gramm-Rudman-Hollings law without raising taxes. It would balance the budget by 1993 as required by the law, begin reducing debt, and protect the integrity of Social Security.

Each of the themes outlined above is discussed in more detail in Section One of the budget, the Overview. The customary tabular and appendix material is contained in Section Two.

I look forward to working with the Congress in the weeks and months ahead to produce a budget that meets the Gramm-Rudman-Hollings target, advances the Nation's essential interests, and keeps the economy on the path of continued growth.

GEORGE BUSH

January 29, 1990

Texts Regarding the Persian Gulf War

Following are texts of President Bush's addresses, statements, press briefings and letters regarding the Persian Gulf War, from the invasion of Kuwait in the summer of 1990 to the defeat of Iraq in the spring of 1991.

Bush Address on U.S. Troop Deployment

Following is White House text of President Bush's address to the nation from the Oval Office on Aug. 8, 1990, on his decision to send U.S. air and ground forces to Saudi Arabia to help it defend against possible aggressive actions by Iraq.

In the life of a nation, we're called upon to define who we are and what we believe. Sometimes, these choices are not easy. But today, as president, I ask for your support in a decision I've made to stand up for what's right and condemn what's wrong, all in the cause of peace.

At my direction, elements of the 82nd Airborne Division, as well as key units of the United States Air Force, are arriving today to take up defensive positions in Saudi Arabia. I took this action to assist the Saudi Arabian government in the defense of its homeland. No one commits American armed forces to a dangerous mission lightly, but after perhaps unparalleled international consultation and exhausting every alternative, it became necessary to take this action.

Let me tell you why. Less than a week ago in the early morning hours of Aug. 2, Iraqi armed forces, without provocation or warning, invaded a peaceful Kuwait. Facing negligible resistance from its much smaller neighbor, Iraq's tanks stormed in blitzkrieg fashion through Kuwait in a few short hours. With more than 100,000 troops, along with tanks, artillery and surface-to-surface missiles, Iraq now occupies Kuwait.

This aggression came just hours after [Iraqi President] Saddam Hussein specifically assured numerous countries in the area that there would be no invasion. There is no justification whatsoever for this outrageous and brutal act of aggression.

A puppet regime, imposed from the outside, is unacceptable. The acquisition of territory by force is unacceptable.

No one, friend or foe, should doubt our desire for peace, and no one should underestimate our determination to confront aggression.

Four simple principles guide our policy.

First, we seek the immediate, unconditional and complete withdrawal of all Iraqi forces from Kuwait.

Second, Kuwait's legitimate government must be restored to replace the puppet regime.

And third, my administration, as has been the case with every president from President [Franklin D.] Roosevelt to President [Ronald] Reagan, is committed to the security and stability of the Persian Gulf.

And fourth, I am determined to protect the lives of American citizens abroad.

Immediately after the Iraqi invasion, I ordered an embargo of all trade with Iraq, and together with many other nations, announced sanctions that both froze all Iraqi assets in this country and protected Kuwait's assets.

The stakes are high. Iraq is already a rich and powerful country that possesses the world's second-largest reserves of oil and over a million men under arms. It's the fourth-largest military in the world.

Our country now imports nearly half the oil it consumes and could face a major threat to its economic independence. Much of the world is even more dependent on imported oil and is even more vulnerable to Iraqi threats.

We succeeded in the struggle for freedom in Europe because we and our allies remain stalwart. Keeping the peace in the Middle East will require no less.

We're beginning a new era. This new era can be full of promise, an age of freedom, a time of peace for all peoples. But if history teaches us anything, it is that we must resist aggression, or it will destroy our freedoms.

Appeasement does not work. As was the case in the 1930s, we see in Saddam Hussein an aggressive dictator threatening his neighbors. Only 14 days ago, Saddam Hussein promised his friends he would not invade Kuwait. And four days ago, he promised the world he would withdraw. And twice we have seen what his promises mean. His promises mean nothing.

In the last few days I've spoken with political leaders from the Middle East, Europe, Asia, the Americas, and I've met with [British] Prime Minister [Margaret] Thatcher, [Canadian] Prime Minister [Brian] Mulroney, and NATO Secretary General [Manfred] Wöerner. And all agree that Iraq cannot be allowed to benefit from its invasion of Kuwait.

We agree that this is not an American problem or a European problem or a Middle East problem. It is the world's problem, and that's why soon after the Iraqi invasion, the United Nations Security Council, without dissent, condemned Iraq, calling for the immediate and unconditional withdrawal of its troops from Kuwait.

The Arab world, through both the Arab League and the Gulf Cooperation Council, courageously announced its opposition to Iraqi aggression. Japan, the United Kingdom and France, and other governments around the world have imposed severe sanctions. The Soviet Union and China ended all arms sales to Iraq, and this past Monday, the United Nations Security Council approved for the first time in 23 years mandatory sanctions under Chapter 7 of the United Nations Charter.

These sanctions, now enshrined in international law, have the potential to deny Iraq the fruits of aggression, while sharply limiting its ability to either import or export anything of value, especially oil.

I pledge here today that the United States will do its part to see that these sanctions are effective and to induce Iraq to withdraw without delay from Kuwait. But we must recognize that Iraq may not stop using force to advance its ambitions.

Iraq has massed an enormous war machine on the Saudi border, capable of initiating hostilities with little or no additional preparation. Given the Iraqi government's history of aggression against its own citizens as well as its neighbors, to assume Iraq will not attack again would be unwise and unrealistic. And therefore, after consulting with [Saudi] King Fahd, I sent Secretary of Defense Dick Cheney to discuss cooperative measures we could take.

Following those meetings, the Saudi government requested our help and I responded to that request by ordering U.S. air and ground forces to deploy to the kingdom of Saudi Arabia.

Let me be clear: The sovereign independence of Saudi Arabia is of vital interest to the United States. This decision, which I shared with the congressional leadership, grows out of the longstanding friendship and security relationship between the United States and Saudi Arabia. U.S. forces will work together with those of Saudi Arabia and other nations to preserve the integrity of Saudi Arabia and to deter further Iraqi aggression.

Through their presence, as well as through their training and exercises, these multinational forces will enhance the overall capability of Saudi armed forces to defend the kingdom.

I want to be clear about what we are doing and why. America does not seek conflict, nor do we seek to chart the destiny of other nations. But America will stand by her friends. The mission of our troops is wholly defensive. Hopefully, they will not be needed long.

They will not initiate hostilities, but they will defend themselves, the kingdom of Saudi Arabia and other friends in the Persian Gulf.

We are working around the clock to deter Iraqi aggression and to enforce U.N. sanctions. I'm continuing my conversations with world leaders. Secretary of Defense Cheney has just returned from valuable consultations with President [Hosni] Mubarak of Egypt and King Hassan of Morocco. Secretary of State [James A.] Baker [III] has consulted with his counterparts in many nations, including the Soviet Union. And today he heads for Europe to consult with President [Turgut] Ozal of Turkey, a staunch friend of the United States. And he'll then consult with the NATO foreign ministers.

I will ask oil-producing nations to do what they can to increase production in order to minimize any impact that oil-flow reductions will have on the world economy. And I will explore whether we and our allies should draw down our strategic petroleum reserves. Conservation measures can also help. Americans everywhere must do their part.

And one more thing: I'm asking the oil companies to do their fair share. They should show restraint and not abuse today's uncertainties to raise prices. Standing up for our principles will not come easy. It may take time and possibly cost a great deal, but we are asking no more of anyone than of the brave young men and women of our armed forces and their families, and I ask that in the churches around the country prayers be said for those who are committed to protect and defend America's interests.

Standing up for our principles is an American tradition. As it has so many times before, it may take time and tremendous effort, but most of all, it will take unity of purpose. As I've witnessed throughout my life in both war and peace, America has never wavered when her purpose is driven by principle, and on this August day, at home and abroad, I know she will do no less.

Thank you, and God bless the United States of America.

Bush Briefing to Members of Congress

Following are President Bush's public comments to about 150 members of Congress on Aug. 28, 1990, preceding an executive session to brief the lawmakers on the situation in the Middle East.

Meeting the challenge in the Persian Gulf is not something that I or this administration can do by ourselves. We can only succeed if all of us, executive and legislative, Republican and Democrat, work together. And that was one of the reasons I wanted you to come here today.

Let no one at home doubt that my commitment to work with the Congress — and let no one abroad doubt our national unity or our staying power.

Let me begin by providing some background to the unfolding drama in the gulf, and then later, I want to hear from you, and as I say, respond to — respond to questions.

First, the background. When this administration began, we sought to strengthen the cease-fire between Iran and Iraq, and to improve relations with Iraq. While we held no illusions about that, we hoped, along with many in the Congress, that Iraqi behavior might be moderated.

But even before the current crisis, though, Iraq was moving at odds to our interest, and to the interests of many around the world. And so we suspended the provisions of the CCC [Commodity Credit Corporation] agricultural credits; stopped the export of furnaces that had the potential to contribute to Iraq's nuclear capabilities.

And you all know the events of the last several weeks. Iraq threatened Kuwait, lied about its intentions and, finally, invaded.

And in three days Iraq had 120,000 troops and 850 tanks in Kuwait moving south toward the Saudi border. And it was this clear and rapidly escalating threat that led King Fahd of Saudi Arabia to ask for our assistance. And we knew that an Iraq that had the most powerful military machine in the gulf and controlled 20 percent of the world's proven reserves of oil would pose a threat to the Persian Gulf, to the Middle East and to the entire world.

We responded to this quickly, without hesitation. And our objectives were obvious from the start: the immediate, complete and unconditional withdrawal of all Iraqi forces from Kuwait, the restoration of Kuwait's legitimate government, security and stability of Saudi Arabia and the Persian Gulf, and the protection of American citizens abroad. Our actions to achieve these objectives have been equally clear.

Within hours of the assault, the United States moved to freeze Iraq's assets in this country and to protect those of Kuwait. I asked Dick Cheney, [Defense] Secretary Cheney, to go to Saudi Arabia, Egypt and Morocco to arrange for military cooperation between us and key Arab states. And I asked Jim Baker, Secretary [of State James A.] Baker [III], to go to Turkey and to Brussels to rally the support of our NATO allies. Both of these missions were extraordinarily successful.

The world response to Iraq was a near-unanimous chorus of condemnation, and with great speed the United Nations Security Council passed five resolutions. These resolutions condemned Iraq's invasion of Kuwait, demanded Iraq's immediate and unconditional withdrawal and rejected Iraq's annexation of Kuwait. The U.N. has also mandated sanctions against Iraq —

those Chapter 7 sanctions — and endorsed all measures that may be necessary to enforce these sanctions. And the United Nations has demanded that Iraq release all foreign nationals being held against their will without delay.

The United Nations sanctions are in effect and have been working remarkably well, even on a voluntary basis. Iraqi oil no longer flows through pipelines to ports in Turkey and Saudi Arabia, and again I want to thank both the Saudis and the Turks for their lead role in all of this.

And today, reports indicate that traffic through Aqaba [Jordanian port] has come virtually to a halt. U.S. military forces stand shoulder to shoulder with forces of many Arab and European states to deter, and, if need be, defend Saudi Arabia against attack, and U.S. naval forces sail with the navies of many other states to make the sanctions as watertight as possible.

This is not, as [Iraqi President] Saddam Hussein claims, the United States against Iraq. It is truly Iraq against a majority in the Arab world, Iraq against the rest of the world.

And so the basic elements of our strategy are now in place, and where do we want to go? Well, our intention, and indeed the intention of almost every country in the world is to persuade Iraq to withdraw, that it cannot benefit from this illegal occupation, that it will pay a stiff price by trying to hold on, and an even stiffer price by widening the conflict.

And of course we seek to achieve these goals without further violence. The United States supports the U.N. secretary-general [Javier Pérez de Cuéllar] and other leaders working to promote a peaceful resolution of this crisis on the basis of Security Council Resolution 660.

I also remain deeply concerned about the American and other foreign nationals held hostage by Iraq. As I've said before, when it comes to the safety and well-being of American citizens held against their will, I will hold Baghdad responsible.

Bush Address on Iraqi Invasion of Kuwait

Following is an excerpt of the White House text of President Bush's address to a joint session of Congress on Sept. 11, 1990, on the U.S. response to Iraq's Aug. 2 invasion of Kuwait.

Mr. President, Mr. Speaker, members of the Congress, distinguished guests, fellow Americans, thank you very much for that warm welcome.

We gather tonight witness to events in the Persian Gulf as significant as they are tragic. In the early morning hours of Aug. 2, following negotiations and promises by Iraq's dictator Saddam Hussein not to use force, a powerful Iraqi army invaded its trusting and much weaker neighbor, Kuwait. Within three days, 120,000 Iraqi troops with 850 tanks had poured into Kuwait and moved south to threaten Saudi Arabia. It was then I decided to act to check that aggression.

At this moment, our brave servicemen and women stand watch in that distant desert and on distant seas, side by side with the forces of more than 20 other nations. They are some of the finest men and women of the United States of America, and they're doing one terrific job.

These valiant Americans were ready at a moment's notice to leave their spouses, their children, to serve on the front line halfway around the world. And they remind us who keeps America strong — they do.

In the trying circumstances of the gulf, the morale of our servicemen and women is excellent. In the face of danger, they are brave, they're well-trained and dedicated.

A soldier, Pfc. Wade Merritt of Knoxville, Tenn., now stationed in Saudi Arabia, wrote his parents of his worries, his love of family, and his hopes for peace. But Wade also wrote: "I am proud of my country and its firm stand against inhumane aggression. I am proud of my army and its men. I am proud to serve my country."

Well, let me just say, Wade, America is proud of you and is grateful to every soldier, sailor, marine, and airman serving the cause of peace in the Persian Gulf.

I also want to thank the chairman of the Joint Chiefs of Staff, Gen. [Colin L.] Powell [Jr.], the chiefs here tonight, our commander in the Persian Gulf, Gen. [H. Norman] Schwarzkopf, and the men and women of the Department of Defense.

What a magnificent job you all are doing, and thank you very, very much from a grateful country.

I wish I could say that their work is done, but we all know it is not.

So if ever there was a time to put country before self and patriotism before party, the time is now. And let me thank all Americans, especially those here in this chamber tonight, for your support for our armed forces and their mission. That support will be even more important in the days to come.

So tonight, I want to talk to you about what's at stake, what we must do together to defend civilized values around the world and maintain our economic strength at home. Our objectives in the Persian Gulf are clear, our goals defined and familiar:

Iraq must withdraw from Kuwait completely, immediately and without condition. Kuwait's legitimate government must be restored. The security and stability of the Persian Gulf must be assured, and American citizens abroad must be protected.

These goals are not ours alone. They've been endorsed by the United Nations Security Council five times in as many weeks. Most countries share our concern for principle. And many have a stake in the stability of the Persian Gulf. This is not, as Saddam Hussein would have it, the United States against Iraq. It is Iraq against the world.

As you know, I've just returned from a very productive meeting with Soviet President [Mikhail S.] Gorbachev. And I am pleased that we are working together to build a new relationship. In Helsinki [Finland], our joint statement affirmed to the world our shared resolve to counter Iraq's threat to peace. Let me quote: "We are united in the belief that Iraq's aggression must not be tolerated. No peaceful international order is possible if larger states can devour their smaller neighbors. Clearly, no longer can a dictator count on East-West confrontation to stymie concerted United Nations action against aggression."

A new partnership of nations has begun, and we stand today at a unique and extraordinary moment. The crisis in the Persian Gulf, as grave as it is, also offers a rare opportunity to move toward an historic period of cooperation. Out of these troubled times, our fifth objective — a new world order — can emerge: a new era — freer from the threat of terror, stronger in the pursuit of justice, and more secure in the quest for peace, an era in which the nations of the world, East and West, North and South, can prosper and live in harmony.

A hundred generations have searched for this elusive path to peace, while a thousand wars raged across the span of human endeavor. And today that new world is struggling to be born, a world quite different from the one we've known, a world where the rule of law supplants the rule of the jungle, a world in which nations recognize the shared responsibility for freedom and justice, a world where the strong respect the rights of the weak. This is the vision I shared with President Gorbachev in Helsinki. He, and other leaders from Europe, the gulf and around the world, understand that how we manage this crisis today could shape the future for generations to come.

The test we face is great and so are the stakes. This is the first assault on the new world that we seek, the first test of our mettle. Had we not responded to this first provocation with clarity of purpose, if we do not continue to demonstrate our determination, it would be a signal to actual and potential despots around the world.

America and the world must defend common vital interests, and we will.

America and the world must support the rule of law, and we will.

America and the world must stand up to aggression. And we will.

And one thing more — in the pursuit of these goals — America will not be intimidated.

Vital issues of principle are at stake. Saddam Hussein is literally trying to wipe a country off the face of the Earth. We do not exaggerate. Nor do we exaggerate when we say Saddam Hussein will fail.

Vital economic interests are at risk as well. Iraq itself controls some 10 percent of the world's proven oil reserves. Iraq plus Kuwait controls twice that.

An Iraq permitted to swallow Kuwait would have the economic and military power, as well as the arrogance, to intimidate and coerce its neighbors, neighbors who control the lion's share of the world's remaining oil reserves. We cannot permit a resource so vital to be dominated by one so ruthless — and we won't.

Recent events have surely proven that there is no substitute for American leadership. In the face of tyranny, let no one doubt American credibility and reliability.

Let no one doubt our staying power. We will stand by our friends. One way or another, the leader of Iraq must learn this fundamental truth.

From the outset, acting hand in hand with others, we've sought to fashion the broadest possible international response to Iraq's aggression. The level of world cooperation and condemnation of Iraq is unprecedented. Armed forces from countries spanning four continents are there at the request of King Fahd of Saudi Arabia to deter and, if need be, to defend against attack. Muslims and non-Muslims, Arabs and non-Arabs, soldiers from many nations stand shoulder to shoulder, resolute against Saddam Hussein's ambitions.

And we can now point to five United Nations Security Council resolutions that condemn Iraq's aggression. They call for Iraq's immediate and unconditional withdrawal, the restoration of Kuwait's legitimate government, and categorically reject Iraq's cynical and self-serving attempt to annex Kuwait.

Finally, the United Nations has demanded the release of all foreign nationals held hostage against their will and in contravention of international law. It is a mockery of human decency to call these people "guests." They are hostages, and the whole world knows it.

[British] Prime Minister Margaret Thatcher, our dependable ally, said it all: "We do not bargain over hostages. We will not stoop to the level of using human beings as bargaining chips — ever."

Of course — of course our hearts go out to the hostages and their families. But our policy cannot change. And it will not change. America and the world will not be blackmailed by this ruthless policy.

We're now in sight of a United Nations that performs as envisioned by its founders. We owe much to the outstanding leadership of Secretary-General Javier Pérez de Cuéllar. The United Nations is backing up its words with action. The Security Council has imposed mandatory economic sanctions on Iraq, designed to force Iraq to relinquish the spoils of its illegal conquest. The Security Council has also taken the decisive step of authorizing the use of all means necessary to ensure compliance with these sanctions.

Together with our friends and allies, ships of the United States Navy are today patrolling Mideast waters, and they've already intercepted more than 700 ships to enforce the sanctions.

Three regional leaders I spoke with just yesterday told me that these sanctions are working. Iraq is feeling the heat. We continue to hope that Iraq's leaders will recalculate just what their aggression has cost them. They are cut off from world trade, unable to sell their oil, and only a tiny fraction of goods gets through.

The communiqué with President Gorbachev made mention of what happens when the embargo is so effective that children of Iraq literally need milk or the sick truly need medicine. Then, under strict international supervision that guarantees the proper destination, then food will be permitted.

At home, the material cost of our leadership can be steep. And that's why Secretary of State [James A.] Baker [III] and Treasury Secretary [Nicholas F.] Brady have met with many world leaders to underscore that the burden of this collective effort must be shared.

We are prepared to do our share and more to help carry the load; we insist others do their share as well.

The response of most of our friends and allies has been good. To help defray costs, the leaders of Saudi Arabia, Kuwait and the UAE, the United Arab Emirates, have pledged to provide our deployed troops with all the food and fuel they need. And generous assistance will also be provided to stalwart front-line nations, such as Turkey and Egypt.

And I'm also heartened to report that this international response extends to the neediest victims of this conflict — those refugees. For our part, we have contributed $28 million for relief efforts. And this is but a portion of what is needed. I commend, in particular, Saudi Arabia, Japan, and several European nations who have joined us in this purely humanitarian effort.

There's an energy-related cost to be borne as well. Oil-producing nations are already replacing lost Iraqi and Kuwaiti output. More than half of what was lost has been made up, and we're getting superb cooperation.

If producers, including the United States, continue steps to expand oil and gas production, we can stabilize prices and guarantee against hardship. Additionally, we and several of our allies always have the option to extract oil from our Strategic Petroleum Reserves, if conditions warrant. As I've pointed out before, conservation efforts are essential to keep our energy needs as low as possible.

And we must then take advantage of our energy sources across the board: coal, natural gas, hydro and nuclear. Our failure to do these things has made us more dependent on foreign oil than ever before.

And finally, let no one even contemplate profiteering from this crisis. We will not have it.

And I cannot predict just how long it will take to convince Iraq to withdraw from Kuwait. Sanctions will take time to have their full intended effect. We will continue to review all options with our allies, but let it be clear: We will not let this aggression stand.

Our interest, our involvement in the gulf, is not transitory. It predated Saddam Hussein's aggression and will survive it. Long after all our troops come home — and we all hope it's soon, very soon — there will be a lasting role for the United States in assisting the nations of the Persian Gulf. Our role then, is to deter future aggression. Our role is to help our friends in their own self-defense and something else: to curb the proliferation of chemical, biological, ballistic missiles and, above all, nuclear technologies.

And let me also make clear that the United States has no quarrel with the Iraqi people. Our quarrel is with Iraq's dictator and with his aggression. Iraq will not be permitted to annex Kuwait. And that's not a threat, it's not a boast — it's just the way it's going to be. . . .

Bush Press Conference on Persian Gulf

Following is the Reuter transcript of President Bush's opening statement at a White House news conference on Nov. 30, 1990, along with answers to the first two questions dealing with the Persian Gulf crisis.

We're in the gulf because the world must not and cannot reward aggression. And we're there because our vital interests are at stake. And we're in the gulf because of the brutality of Saddam Hussein.

We're dealing with a dangerous dictator all too willing to use force, who has weapons of mass destruction and is seeking new ones and desires to control one of the world's key resources, all at a time in history when the rules of the post-Cold War world are being written.

Our objectives remain what they were at the outset. We seek Iraq's immediate and unconditional withdrawal from Kuwait. We seek the restoration of Kuwait's legitimate government. We seek the release of all hostages, and the free functioning of all embassies. And we seek the stability and security of this critical region of the world.

We are not alone in these goals and objectives. The United Nations, invigorated with a new sense of purpose, is in full agreement. The United Nations Security Council has endorsed 12 resolutions to condemn Iraq's unprovoked invasion and occupation of Kuwait; implement tough economic sanctions to stop all trade in and out of Iraq; and authorize the use of force to compel Saddam to comply.

Saddam Hussein has tried every way he knows how to make this a fight between Iraq and the United States, and clearly he has failed. Forces of 26 other nations are standing shoulder to shoulder with our troops in the gulf. The fact is that it is not the United States against Iraq; it is Iraq against the world. And there's never been a clearer demonstration of a world united against appeasement and aggression. Yesterday's United Nations Security Council resolution was historic. Once again, the Security Council has enhanced the legitimate peacekeeping function of the United Nations.

Until yesterday, Saddam may not have understood what he's up against in terms of world opinion, and I'm hopeful that now he will realize that he must leave Kuwait immediately.

I am continually asked how effective are the U.N. sanctions, those put into effect on Aug. 6. I don't know the answer to that question. Clearly, the sanctions are having some effect, but I can't tell you that the sanctions alone will get the job done, and thus, I welcome yesterday's United Nations action. The fledgling democracies in Eastern Europe are being severely damaged by the economic effects of Saddam's actions. The developing countries of Africa and in our hemisphere are being victimized by this dictator's rape of his neighbor, Kuwait.

Those who feel that there is no downside to waiting months and months must consider the devastating damage being done every day to the fragile economies of those countries that can afford it the least.

As [Federal Reserve] Chairman Alan Greenspan testified just the other day, the increase in oil prices resulting directly from Saddam's invasion is hurting our country, too, and our economy, as I said the other day, is at best in a serious slowdown, and if uncertainty remains in the energy markets the slowdown will get worse.

I've spelled out, once again, our reasons for sending troops to the gulf. Let me tell you the things that concern me most.

First, I put the immorality of the invasion of Kuwait itself. No nation should rape, pillage and brutalize its neighbor. No nation should be able to wipe a member state of the United Nations and the Arab League off the face of the Earth.

And I'm deeply concerned about all the hostages — innocent people held against their will in direct contravention of international law. And then there's this cynical and brutal policy of forcing people to beg for their release, parceling out human lives to families and traveling emissaries like so much chattel.

I'm deeply concerned about our own embassy in Kuwait. The flag is still flying there. A handful of beleaguered Americans remain inside the embassy, unable to come and go. . . .

This treatment of our embassy violates every civilized principle of diplomacy and it demeans our people. It demeans our country. And I am determined that this embassy, as called for under Security Council resolution 674, be fully replenished and our people free to come home. . . .

I'm deeply concerned about Saddam's efforts to acquire nuclear weapons. Imagine his ability to blackmail his neighbors should he possess a nuclear device. We've seen him use chemical weapons on his own people. We've seen him take his own country, one that should be wealthy and prosperous, and turn it into a poor country, all because of an insatiable appetite for military equipment and conquest. . . .

In our country I know that there are fears about another Vietnam. Let me assure you, should military action be required, this will not be another Vietnam. This will not be a protracted, drawn-out war.

The forces arrayed are different. The opposition is different. The resupply of Saddam's military would be very different. The countries united against him in the United Nations are different. The topography of Kuwait is different. And the motivation of our all-volunteer force is superb.

I want peace. I want peace, not war. But if there must be war, we will not permit our troops to have their hands tied behind their backs, and I pledge to you there will not be any murky ending. If one American soldier has to go into battle, that soldier will have enough force behind him to win and then get out as soon as possible, as soon as the U.N. objectives have been achieved. . . .

Many people have talked directly to Saddam Hussein and to his foreign minister, Tariq Aziz. All have been frustrated by Iraq's ironclad insistence that it will not leave Kuwait.

However, to go the extra mile for peace, I will issue an invitation to Foreign Minister Tariq Aziz to come to Washington at a mutually convenient time during the latter part of the week of Dec. 10 to meet with me. And I'll invite ambassadors of several of our coalition partners in the gulf to join me at that meeting.

In addition, I'm asking Secretary [of State] Jim [James A.] Baker [III] to go to Baghdad to see Saddam Hussein, and I will suggest to Iraq's president that he receive the secretary of State at a mutually convenient time between Dec. 15 and Jan. 15 of next year.

Within the mandate — within the mandate of the United Nations resolutions, I will be prepared, and so will Secretary Baker, to discuss all aspects of the gulf crisis. However, to be very clear about these efforts to exhaust all means for achieving, all means for a diplomatic and political solution, I am not suggesting discussions that will result in anything less than Iraq's complete withdrawal from Kuwait, restoration of Kuwait's legitimate government, and freedom for all hostages.

Q: Mr. President, now that you have a clear-cut U.N. resolution on use of force . . . doesn't this force you into the position of having to use force on Jan. 15 if Saddam Hussein hasn't left?

P: No, the date was not a date that — at which point force had to be used.

Q: Are you going to ask Congress for approval of this resolution? Would you like to see Congress pass the same kind of resolution as the U.N.?

P: I'd love to see Congress pass a resolution enthusiastically endorsing what the United Nations has done, yes. But we're in consultation on that, and I have no plans to call a special session. I'm not opposed to it, but we're involved in consultations right now.

I've talked to several members of Congress. I've talked to the leaders in the House. I've talked to several on the Republican side and Democratic side in the Senate. And I want to be sure that these consultations are complete.

Some feel a lame-duck session is not good, that the new members should have a right to have a say. Others feel that we ought to move right now.

The Congress, as you know, in their adjournment resolution, had a provision in there that they could come back and take this up; they are a coequal branch of government. They can do that if they want to. . . .

Bush's Letter to Congress Regarding the Use of Force

Following is the White House text of President Bush's letter to Congress on Jan. 8, 1991, requesting passage of a resolution authorizing the use of force in the Persian Gulf.

The current situation in the Persian Gulf, brought about by Iraq's unprovoked invasion and subsequent brutal occupation of Kuwait, threatens vital U.S. interests. The situation also threatens the peace. It would, however, greatly enhance the chances for peace if Congress were now to go on record supporting the position adopted by the U.N. Security Council on twelve separate occasions. Such an action would underline that the United States stands with the international community and on the side of law and decency; it also would help dispel any belief that may exist in the minds of Iraq's leaders that the United States lacks the necessary unity to act decisively in response to Iraq's continued aggression against Kuwait.

Secretary of State [James A.] Baker [III] is meeting with Iraq's Foreign Minister [Tariq Aziz] on January 9. It would have been most constructive if he could have presented the Iraqi government a Resolution passed by both houses of Congress supporting the U.N. position and in particular Security Council Resolution 678. As you know, I have frequently stated my desire for such a Resolution. Nevertheless, there is still opportunity for Congress to act to strengthen the prospects for peace and safeguard this country's vital interests.

I therefore request that the House of Representatives and the Senate adopt a Resolution stating that Congress supports the use of all necessary means to implement U.N. Security Council Resolution 678. Such action would send the clearest possible message to Saddam Hussein that he must withdraw without condition or delay from Kuwait. Anything less would only encourage Iraqi intransigence; anything else would risk detracting from the international coalition arrayed against Iraq's aggression.

I am determined to do whatever is necessary to protect America's security. I ask Congress to join with me in this task. I can think of no better way than for Congress to express its support for the President at this critical time. This truly is the last best chance for peace.

Bush's Letter, Report on Failed Diplomacy

Following is the White House text of President Bush's letter and his report to Congress complying with Congress' Jan. 12, 1991, resolution (H J Res 77 — PL 102-1), which authorized the use of force in the Persian Gulf once the president certified that efforts to resolve the problem without force had been unsuccessful.

Dear Mr. Speaker: (Dear Mr. President:)

Pursuant to Section 2(b) of the Authorization for Use of Military Force Against Iraq Resolution (H J Res 77, PL 102-1), I have concluded that:

1. the United States has used all appropriate diplomatic and other peaceful means to obtain compliance by Iraq with U.N. Security Council Resolutions 660, 661, 662, 664, 665, 666, 667, 669, 670, 674, 677 and 678; and

2. that those efforts have not been and would not be successful in obtaining such compliance.

Enclosed is a report that supports my decision.

Sincerely,
GEORGE BUSH

Attachment

Report for Use in Connection with Section 2(b) of the Joint Congressional Resolution Authorizing the Use of Military Force Against Iraq.

The report that follows is a summary of diplomatic and other peaceful means used in an attempt to obtain compliance by Iraq with the 12 U.N. Security Council resolutions relating to its invasion and occupation of Kuwait.

It is not a definitive rendition of these means, because the administration cannot, of necessity, include at this time all the factual data that would support a complete historical record. This report, therefore, should be considered in light of formal and informal information already provided to the Congress and that which will be provided in the future.

1. Background. For over 5½ months, the international community has sought with unprecedented unity to reverse Iraq's brutal and unprovoked aggression against Kuwait. The United States and the vast majority of governments of the world, working together through the United Nations, have been united both in their determination to compel Iraq's withdrawal from Kuwait and in their strong preference for doing so through peaceful means.

Since Aug. 2, we have sought to build maximum diplomatic and economic pressure against Iraq. Regrettably, Iraq has given no sign whatever that it intends to comply with the will of the international community; nor is there any indication that diplomatic and economic means alone would ever compel Iraq to do so. Instead, Iraq has continued to reject the relevant U.N. Security Council resolutions and refuses to recognize them.

From the beginning of the gulf crisis, the United States has consistently pursued four basic objectives: 1) the immediate, complete and unconditional Iraqi withdrawal from Kuwait; 2) the restoration of the legitimate government of Kuwait; 3) the protection of U.S. citizens abroad; and 4) the security and stability of a region vital to U.S. national security. In pursuit of these objectives, we have sought and obtained action by the U.N. Security Council, resulting in 12 separate resolutions that have been fully consistent with U.S. objectives.

The last of these 12 resolutions, U.N. Security Council Resolution 678 of 29 November 1990, authorizes U.N. member states to use "all necessary means" to implement Resolution 660 and all subsequent relevant resolutions of the Security Council, and to restore international peace and security in the area, unless Iraq fully implements those resolutions on or before Jan. 15, 1991.

The nearly seven week "pause of goodwill" established in U.N. Security Council Resolution 678 has now passed. Iraq has taken no steps whatever to fulfill these requirements.

Iraq has forcefully stated that it considers the Security Council's resolutions invalid and has no intention of complying with them at any time.

Iraqi forces remain in occupation of Kuwait and have been substantially reinforced in recent weeks rather than withdrawn. Iraq has strongly and repeatedly reiterated its annexation of Kuwait and stated its determination that Kuwait will remain permanently a part of Iraq.

The Iraqi closure of diplomatic and consular missions in Kuwait has in no way been rescinded.

In short, the Government of Iraq remains completely intransigent in rejecting the U.N. Security Council's demands — despite the exhaustive use by the United States and the United Nations of all appropriate diplomatic, political and economic measures to persuade or compel Iraq to comply.

This has been a truly international effort. More than two dozen other countries have sent their own military forces to the gulf region, including more than 250,000 troops. They have given or pledged substantial funds and other assistance to us for our operations, including over $8 billion in calendar year 1990 alone. They have taken on the responsibility for assisting those nations that have suffered the most from the effects of international sanctions against Iraq and higher energy prices.

As additional costs are incurred during 1991, we will look to our allies to shoulder their fair share of our military expenses and exceptional economic assistance efforts.

2. Diplomatic and Political Actions. The extensive diplomatic and political efforts undertaken by the United States, other countries, regional organizations including the Arab League and the European Community and the United Nations to persuade or compel Iraq to withdraw from Kuwait have not succeeded.

The U.N. Security Council and General Assembly have overwhelmingly and repeatedly condemned the Iraqi invasion and demanded Iraq's immediate and unconditional withdrawal from Kuwait.

The Security Council has invoked its extraordinary authority under Chapter VII of the U.N. Charter, not only to order comprehensive economic sanctions, but to authorize the use of all other means necessary, including the use of force.

The Security Council has directed other U.N. organizations (e.g., the International Atomic Energy Agency) to take appropriate actions toward the same and within their areas of competence, and they have done so where relevant.

The president, the secretary of State and other U.S. officials have engaged in an exhaustive process of consultation with other governments and international organizations. The secretary of State alone has, since Aug. 2 of last year, held more than 250 meetings with foreign heads of state, foreign ministers and other high foreign officials. He has traveled over 125,000 miles in the course of these contacts.

While this extensive diplomacy has been very successful in maintaining international solidarity in support of our objectives, it has not caused the government of Iraq to withdraw from Kuwait.

Most recently, on Jan. 9, the secretary of State met at length in Geneva with the Iraqi foreign minister, who in 6½ hours of talks demonstrated no readiness whatever to implement the U.N. Security Council resolutions. The Iraqi foreign minister even refused to receive a diplomatic communication from the president intended for Saddam Hussein.

On Jan. 13, the U.N. secretary general was rebuffed by Iraq for a second time, in this case in a direct attempt to persuade Saddam Hussein to withdraw from Kuwait peacefully. Many other heads of state, foreign ministers and private persons have made similar attempts. In short, the international community has in an unprecedented way directed the full scope and vigor of its political and diplomatic means to produce an Iraqi withdrawal.

These exhaustive efforts have produced not the slightest indication of any intention by Saddam Hussein to meet the demands of the international community for immediate and unconditional withdrawal from Kuwait.

For our part, the administration made clear that there could be no reward for aggression lest we undermine prospects for an expanded constructive role for the U.N. Security Council and for a new, more peaceful world order. Attempts to link resolution of Iraq's aggression against Kuwait with other issues were rejected on the grounds that these issues were unrelated to Iraq's aggression and that such efforts would only serve to divert attention from the immediate challenge posed by Iraq.

3. Economic Sanctions. Since Aug. 2 (in the case of the United States) and Aug. 9 (in the case of the Security Council and the other U.N. member states), comprehensive economic sanctions have been imposed on Iraq, prohibiting all trade and financial transactions with Iraq, with the exception of goods for a very limited category of essential humanitarian purposes.

These sanctions have since Aug. 25 been backed by an extensive maritime interception effort involving warships of many states, and since Sept. 25 by rigorous controls on air traffic to and from Iraq. The United States and other countries have engaged in tireless efforts during this period to uncover and defeat attempted evasions of these sanctions around the world, whether by direct attempts to pass through the allied interception cordon or by the use of financial and trade intermediaries.

Our efforts have resulted in a very substantial reduction of the volume of trade to and from Iraq and significant shortages in Iraq's financial resources. The most serious impact on Iraq thus far has been on the financial sector, where hard currency shortages have led Baghdad to take a variety of unusual steps to conserve or obtain foreign exchange.

The sanctions have shut off 97 percent of Iraq's exports and more than 90 percent of its imports and have prevented Baghdad from reaping the proceeds of higher oil prices or its seizure of Kuwaiti oil fields. The departure of foreign workers and the cutoff of imported industrial inputs has caused problems for a variety of industries.

Notwithstanding the substantial economic impact of sanctions to date, and even if sanctions were to continue to be enforced for an additional six to 12 months, economic hardship alone is highly unlikely to compel Saddam to retreat from Kuwait or cause regime-threatening popular discontent in Iraq.

Due to a reduction of domestic consumption, cannibalization of Kuwaiti facilities, smuggling and use of existing stockpiles, the most vital Iraqi industries do not appear to be threatened.

The price of foodstuffs for the Iraqi population has sharply increased and rations have been reduced, but there is still access to sufficient staple foods, and new supplies are being injected from the fall harvest and smuggling.

While we might succeed in substantially reducing the overall Iraqi supply of food and other essential consumer commodities, Saddam Hussein has made clear his willingness to divert such supplies to his military forces, even at the cost of severe deprivation of his civilian population.

Even if the international community were prepared to deprive the Iraqi civilian population of food, there is no reason to believe that this would change Saddam Hussein's policies.

The ability of Iraqi armed forces to defend Kuwait and southern Iraq is unlikely to be eroded substantially over the next six to 12 months even if effective sanctions could be maintained. Iraq's infantry and artillery forces probably would not suffer significantly, since Iraq could maintain the relatively simple Soviet-style weaponry of these forces. Low-technology defensive preparations could also be expanded.

Iraq's armored and mechanized forces would be degraded somewhat, but Iraq has large stocks of spare parts and other supplies that would ameliorate this effect.

Iraqi air forces and air defenses would likely be hit far more severely by continued effective sanctions, but in any case, Iraqi air defense and air forces would play a limited role — in relation to the ground forces — with respect to Iraq's ability to hold Kuwait.

In short, while sanctions might degrade to some extent the operational readiness of some portion of the Iraqi armed forces, it is clear that Iraq would still retain very large and powerful land and air forces, as well as substantial capability to replace ammunition and other essential replacement items.

Delay would also have important military consequences that might make any eventual military action more costly and increase U.S. and coalition casualties.

Iraq has already exploited its five-month occupation of Kuwait to increase significantly its ability to resist coalition efforts to restore that country's sovereignty and to increase further its already formidable military capability.

Iraq has increased the size of its forces in the Kuwait theater of operations by 450,000 personnel and has increased the overall size of its armed forces by mobilizing many thousands of combat veterans and reservists.

Additional time has already permitted the Iraqis to extend and reinforce their fortifications along the Saudi border; more time would only make these defenses more formidable. Delay also would give the Iraqis more time to further develop, produce and weaponize weapons of mass destruction, thus making any eventual conflict more destructive and strengthening Iraq's ability to coerce other nations with the threat of mass destruction. Delay may also degrade the readiness of coalition forces.

In short, international sanctions have not caused Iraq to comply with the Jan. 15, 1991, deadline in U.N. Security Council Resolution 678 or to retreat from its insistence that its annexation of Kuwait is permanent.

Even if the world community were to maintain the current high level of success in sanctions enforcement, these economic results would not produce such compliance.

Further, the longer the sanctions continue, the more likely it is that leaks in the sanctions enforcement system will develop, that intermediaries will devise ways to circumvent sanctions, and that Iraq will find means of using its own resources to fill critical shortfalls.

Even more important, if the coalition fails now to carry through on the U.N. Security Council's demands for immediate Iraqi withdrawal from Kuwait, there will be strong pressures and temptations on various countries to ease their enforcement of sanctions and to compromise on demands that Iraq meet existing objectives fully and unconditionally.

In summary, diplomatic and economic pressures have not diminished Iraq's intransigence despite 5½ months of unparalleled international effort, and continued reliance upon them alone could risk achieving the basic objective of bringing about Iraq's complete and unconditional withdrawal from Kuwait.

Bush Announcement on Start of War

Following is the White House text of President Bush's address to the nation Jan. 16, 1991, from the Oval Office shortly after the beginning of a multinational military effort to force Iraq to withdraw from Kuwait.

Just two hours ago, allied air forces began an attack on military targets in Iraq and Kuwait. These attacks continue as I speak. Ground forces are not engaged.

This conflict started Aug. 2 when the dictator of Iraq invaded a small and helpless neighbor. Kuwait, a member of the Arab League and a member of the United Nations, was crushed, its people brutalized.

Five months ago, Saddam Hussein started this cruel war against Kuwait. Tonight the battle has been joined.

This military action, taken in accord with United Nations resolutions and with the consent of the United States Congress, follows months of constant and virtually endless diplomatic activity on the part of the United Nations, the United States and many, many other countries.

Arab leaders sought what became known as an Arab solution, only to conclude that Saddam Hussein was unwilling to leave Kuwait. Others traveled to Baghdad in a variety of efforts to restore peace and justice.

Our Secretary of State James [A.]

Baker [III] held an historic meeting in Geneva, only to be totally rebuffed.

This past weekend, in a last ditch effort, the secretary-general of the United Nations went to the Middle East with peace in his heart — his second such mission. And he came back from Baghdad with no progress at all in getting Saddam Hussein to withdraw from Kuwait.

Now, the 28 countries with forces in the gulf area have exhausted all reasonable efforts to reach a peaceful resolution [and] have no choice but to drive Saddam from Kuwait by force. We will not fail.

As I report to you, air attacks are under way against military targets in Iraq. We are determined to knock out Saddam Hussein's nuclear bomb potential. We will also destroy his chemical weapons facilities. Much of Saddam's artillery and tanks will be destroyed. Our operations are designed to best protect the lives of all the coalition forces by targeting Saddam's vast military arsenal.

Initial reports from Gen. [H. Norman] Schwarzkopf are that our operations are proceeding according to plan. Our objectives are clear: Saddam Hussein's forces will leave Kuwait, the legitimate government of Kuwait will be restored to its rightful place, and Kuwait will once again be free.

Iraq will eventually comply with all relevant United Nations resolutions, and then, when peace is restored, it is our hope that Iraq will live as a peaceful and cooperative member of the family of nations, thus enhancing the security and stability of the gulf.

Some may ask, why act now? Why not wait? The answer is clear. The world could wait no longer. Sanctions, though having some effect, showed no signs of accomplishing their objective. Sanctions were tried for well over five months, and we and our allies concluded that sanctions alone would not force Saddam from Kuwait.

While the world waited, Saddam Hussein systematically raped, pillaged and plundered a tiny nation, no threat to his own. He subjected the people of Kuwait to unspeakable atrocities, and among those maimed and murdered, innocent children.

While the world waited, Saddam sought to add to the chemical weapons arsenal he now possesses an infinitely more dangerous weapon of mass destruction, a nuclear weapon. And while the world waited, while the world talked peace and withdrawal, Saddam Hussein dug in and moved massive forces into Kuwait. While the world waited, while Saddam stalled, more damage was being done to the fragile economies of the Third World, the emerging democracies of Eastern Europe, to the entire world, including to our own economy. The United States, together with the United Nations, exhausted every means at our disposal to bring this crisis to a peaceful end. However, Saddam clearly felt that by stalling and threatening and defying the United Nations, he could weaken the forces arrayed against him. While the world waited, Saddam Hussein met every overture of peace with open contempt. While the world prayed for peace, Saddam prepared for war.

I had hoped that when the United States Congress, in historic debate, took its resolute action, Saddam would realize he could not prevail and would move out of Kuwait in accord with the United Nations resolutions. He did not do that. Instead, he remained intransigent, certain that time was on his side. Saddam was warned over and over again to comply with the will of the United Nations, leave Kuwait or be driven out. Saddam has arrogantly rejected all warnings. Instead he tried to make this a dispute between Iraq and the United States of America. Well, he failed.

Tonight 28 nations, countries from five continents — Europe and Asia, Africa and the Arab League — have forces in the gulf area standing shoulder to shoulder against Saddam Hussein. These countries had hoped the use of force could be avoided. Regrettably, we now believe that only force will make him leave.

Prior to ordering our forces into battle, I instructed our military commanders to take every necessary step to prevail as quickly as possible and with the greatest degree of protection possible for American and allied servicemen and women.

I've told the American people before that this will not be another Vietnam, and I repeat this here tonight. Our troops will have the best possible support in the entire world, and they will not be asked to fight with one hand tied behind their back.

I'm hopeful that this fighting will not go on for long and that casualties will be held to an absolute minimum. This is an historic moment. We have in this past year made great progress in ending the long era of conflict and cold war. We have before us the opportunity to forge for ourselves and for future generations a new world order, a world where the rule of law, not the law of the jungle, governs the conduct of nations.

When we are successful — and we will be — we have a real chance at this new world order, an order in which a credible United Nations can use its peacekeeping role to fulfill the promise envisioned of the U.N.'s founders. We have no argument with the people of Iraq; indeed, for the innocents caught in this conflict, I pray for their safety. Our goal is not the conquest of Iraq; it is the liberation of Kuwait. It is my hope that somehow the Iraqi people can even now convince their dictator that he must lay down his arms, leave Kuwait and let Iraq itself rejoin the family of peace-loving nations.

Thomas Paine wrote many years ago, "These are the times that try men's souls." Those well-known words are so very true today, but even as planes of the multinational forces attack Iraq, I prefer to think of peace, not war. I am convinced not only that we will prevail, but that out of the horror of combat will come the recognition that no nation can stand against a world united, no nation will be permitted to brutally assault its neighbor.

No president can easily commit our sons and daughters to war. They are the nation's finest. Ours is an all-volunteer force, magnificently trained, highly motivated. The troops know why they're there, and listen to what they say, for they've said it better than any president or prime minister ever could. Listen to Hollywood Huddleston, Marine lance corporal. He says: "Let's free these people so we can go home and be free again."

He's right. The terrible crimes and tortures committed by Saddam's henchmen against the innocent people of Kuwait are an affront to mankind and a challenge to the freedom of all.

Listen to one of our great officers out there, Marine Lt. Gen. Walter Boomer. He said: "There are things worth fighting for. A world in which brutality and lawlessness are allowed to go unchecked isn't the kind of world we're going to want to live in."

Listen to Master Sgt. J. P. Kendall of the 82nd Airborne: "We're here for more than just the price of a gallon of gas. What we're doing is going to chart the future of the world for the next 100 years. It's better to deal with this guy now than five years from now."

And finally we should all sit up and listen to Jackie Jones, an Army lieutenant, when she says: "If we let him get away with this, who knows what's going to be next."

I have called upon Hollywood and Walter and J. P. and Jackie and all their courageous comrades in arms to do what must be done. Tonight, America and the world are deeply grateful to them and to their families. And let me say to everyone listening or watching tonight, when the troops we've sent in finish their work, I am determined to bring them home as soon as possible.

Tonight, as our forces fight, they and their families are in our prayers. May God bless each and every one of them, and the coalition forces at our side in the gulf, and may he continue to bless our nation, the United States of America.

Bush Address on Cease-Fire in Gulf War

Following is the Reuter text of President Bush's televised speech from the White House Feb. 27, 1991, announcing the liberation of Kuwait and a cease-fire in the Persian Gulf War.

Kuwait is liberated. Iraq's army is defeated. Our military objectives are met. Kuwait is once more in the hands of Kuwaitis, in control of their own destiny. We share in their joy, a joy tempered only by our compassion for their ordeal.

Tonight, the Kuwaiti flag once again flies above the capital of a free and sovereign nation, and the American flag flies above our embassy.

Seven months ago, America and the world drew a line in the sand. We declared that the aggression against Kuwait would not stand, and tonight America and the world have kept their word.

This is not a time of euphoria, certainly not a time to gloat. But it is a time of pride: pride in our troops, pride in the friends who stood with us in the crisis, pride in our nation and the people whose strength and resolve made victory quick, decisive, and just. And soon, we will open wide our arms to welcome back home to America our magnificent fighting forces.

No one country can claim this victory as its own. It was not only a victory for Kuwait, but a victory for all the coalition partners.

This is a victory for the United Nations, for all mankind, for the rule of law, and for what is right.

After consulting with Secretary of Defense [Dick] Cheney, the chairman of the Joint Chiefs of Staff [Gen. Colin L.] Powell [Jr.], and our coalition partners, I am pleased to announce that at midnight tonight, Eastern Standard Time, exactly one hundred hours since ground operations commenced, and six weeks since the start of Operation Desert Storm, all United States and coalition forces will suspend offensive combat operations.

It is up to Iraq whether this suspension on the part of the coalition becomes a permanent cease-fire. Coalition political and military terms for a formal cease-fire include the following requirements:

Iraq must release immediately all coalition prisoners of war, third-country nationals, and the remains of all who have fallen.

Iraq must release all Kuwaiti detainees. Iraq also must inform Kuwaiti authorities of the location and nature of all land and sea mines.

Iraq must comply fully with all relevant United Nations Security Council resolutions. This includes a rescinding of Iraq's August decision to annex Kuwait and acceptance in principle of Iraq's responsibility to pay compensation for the loss, damage, and injury its aggression has caused.

The coalition calls upon the Iraqi government to designate military commanders to meet within forty-eight hours with their coalition counterparts, at a place in the theater of operations to be specified, to arrange for military aspects of the cease-fire.

Further, I have asked Secretary of State [James A.] Baker [III] to request that the United Nations Security Council meet to formulate the necessary arrangements for this war to be ended.

This suspension of offensive combat operations is contingent upon Iraq's not firing upon any coalition forces, and not launching Scud missiles against any other country. If Iraq violates these terms, coalition forces will be free to resume military operations.

At every opportunity, I have said to the people of Iraq that our quarrel was not with them, but instead with their leadership, and above all with Saddam Hussein. This remains the case. You, the people of Iraq, are not our enemy. We do not seek your destruction. We have treated your POWs with kindness. Coalition forces fought this war only as a last resort, and looked forward to the day when Iraq is led by people prepared to live in peace with their neighbors.

We must now begin to look beyond victory and war. We must meet the challenge of securing the peace. In the future, as before, we will consult with our coalition partners. We've already done a good deal of thinking and planning for the postwar period.

And Secretary Baker has already begun to consult with our coalition partners on the region's challenges. There can be and will be no solely American answer to all these challenges, but we can assist and support the countries of the region and be a catalyst for peace.

In this spirit, Secretary Baker will go to the region next week to begin a new round of consultations.

This war is now behind us. Ahead of us is the difficult task of securing a potentially historic peace. Tonight, though, let us be proud of what we have accomplished. Let us give thanks to those who risked their lives. Let us never forget those who gave their lives.

May God bless our valiant military forces and their families, and let us all remember them in our prayers. Good night, and may God bless the United States of America.

Bush Speech on Victory in the Persian Gulf War

Following is the Reuter transcript of President Bush's speech to a joint session of Congress on March 6, 1991, on the allied victory in the Persian Gulf War.

Five short weeks ago I came to this House to speak to you about the state of the union. We met then in time of war. Tonight, we meet in a world blessed by the promise of peace.

From the moment Operation Desert Storm commenced on January 16th until the time the guns fell silent at midnight one week ago, this nation has watched its sons and daughters with pride, watched over them with prayer.

As commander in chief, I can report to you: Our armed forces fought with honor and valor. And as president, I can report to the nation: Aggression is defeated; the war is over.

This is a victory for every country in the coalition, for the United Nations. A victory for unprecedented international cooperation and diplomacy, so well led by our Secretary of State James A. Baker III. It is a victory for the rule of law and for what is right.

Desert Storm's success belongs to the team that so ably leads our armed forces, our secretary of Defense and our chairman of the Joint Chiefs: Dick Cheney and Gen. Colin L. Powell Jr..

And while you're standing — this military victory also belongs to the one the British call the "Man of the Match," the tower of calm at the eye of Desert Storm, Gen. H. Norman Schwarzkopf.

And let us, recognizing this was a coalition effort, let us not forget Saudi Gen. Khalid, or Britain's Gen. de la Billiere, or Gen. Roquejoffre of France, and all the others whose leadership played such a vital role. And, most importantly, most importantly of all, those who served in the field.

I thank the members of this Congress: Support here for our troops in battle was overwhelming. And above all, I thank those whose unfailing love and support sustained our courageous men and women: I thank the American people.

Tonight, I come to this House to speak about the world, the world after war.

The recent challenge could not have been clearer. Saddam Hussein was the villain, Kuwait the victim. To the aid of this small country came nations from North America and Europe, from Asia, South America, from Africa and the Arab world — all united against aggression.

Our uncommon coalition must now work in common purpose to forge a future that should never again be held hostage to the darker side of human nature.

Tonight in Iraq, Saddam walks amidst ruin. His war machine is crushed. His ability to threaten mass destruction is itself destroyed. His people have been lied to, denied the truth. And when his defeated legions come home, all Iraqis will see and feel the havoc he has wrought. And this I promise you: For all that Saddam has done to his own people, to the Kuwaitis and to the entire world, Saddam and those around him are accountable.

All of us grieve for the victims of war, for the people of Kuwait and the suffering that scars the soul of that proud nation. We grieve for all our fallen soldiers and their families, for all the innocents caught up in this conflict. And, yes, we grieve for the people of Iraq, a people who have never been our enemy. My hope is that one day we will once again welcome them as friends into the community of nations.

Our commitment to peace in the Middle East does not end with the liberation of Kuwait. So tonight let me outline four key challenges to be met:

First, we must work together to create shared security arrangements in the region. Our friends and allies in the Middle East recognize that they will bear the bulk of the responsibility for regional security. But we want them to know that just as we stood with them to repel aggression, so now America stands ready to work with them to secure the peace.

This does not mean stationing U.S. ground forces on the Arabian peninsula, but it does mean American participation in joint exercises involving both air and ground forces. It means maintaining a capable U.S. naval presence in the region, just as we have for over 40 years. Let it be clear: Our vital national interests depend on a stable and secure gulf.

Second, we must act to control the proliferation of weapons of mass destruction and the missiles used to deliver them. It would be tragic if the nations of the Middle East and Persian Gulf were now, in the wake of war, to embark on a new arms race. Iraq requires special vigilance. Until Iraq convinces the world of its peaceful intentions, that its leaders will not use new revenues to rearm and rebuild its menacing war machine, Iraq must not have access to the instruments of war.

And, third, we must work to create new opportunities for peace and stability in the Middle East. On the night I announced Operation Desert Storm, I expressed my hope that out of the horrors of war might come new momentum for peace. We have learned in the modern age [that] geography cannot guarantee security, and security does not come from military power alone.

All of us know the depth of bitterness that has made the dispute between Israel and its neighbors so painful and intractable. Yet in the conflict just concluded, Israel and many of the Arab states have for the first time found themselves confronting the same aggressor. By now it should be plain to all parties that peacemaking in the Middle East requires compromise. At the same time, peace brings real benefits to everyone. We must do all that we can to close the gap between Israel and the Arab states, and between Israelis and Palestinians. The tactics of terror lead absolutely nowhere. There can be no substitute for diplomacy.

A comprehensive peace must be grounded in United Nations Security Council Resolutions 242 and 338 and the principle of territory for peace. This principle must be elaborated to provide for Israel's security and recognition, and at the same time for legitimate Palestinian political rights. Anything else would fail the twin tests of fairness and security. The time has come to put an end to Arab-Israeli conflict.

The war with Iraq is over. The quest for solutions to the problems in Lebanon, in the Arab-Israeli dispute and in the gulf must go forward with new vigor and determination. And I guarantee you: No one will work harder for a stable peace in the region than we will.

Fourth, we must foster economic development for the sake of peace and progress. The Persian Gulf and Middle East form a region rich in natural resources, with a wealth of untapped human potential. Resources once squandered on military might must be redirected to more peaceful ends. We are already addressing the immediate economic consequences of Iraq's aggression. Now, the challenge is to reach higher, to foster economic freedom and prosperity for all people of the region.

By meeting these four challenges, we can build a framework for peace. I have asked Secretary of State Baker to go to the Middle East to begin the process. He will go to listen, to probe, to offer suggestions, to advance the search for peace and stability. I have also asked him to raise the plight of the hostages held in Lebanon. We have not forgotten them, and we will not forget them.

To all the challenges that confront this region of the world, there is no single solution, no solely American answer. But we can make a difference. America will work tirelessly as a catalyst for positive change.

But we cannot lead a new world abroad if, at home, it's politics as usual on American defense and diplomacy. It's time to turn away from the temptation to protect unneeded weapons systems and obsolete bases.

It's time to put an end to micro-management of foreign- and security-assistance programs, micro-management that humiliates our friends and allies, and hamstrings our diplomacy.

It's time to rise above the parochial and the pork barrel to do what is necessary, what's right and what will enable this nation to play the leadership role required of us.

The consequences of the conflict in the gulf reach far beyond the confines of the Middle East. Twice before in this century, an entire world was convulsed by war. Twice this century, out of the horrors of war, hope emerged for enduring peace. Twice before, those hopes proved to be a distant dream, beyond the grasp of man.

Until now, the world we've known has been a world divided, a world of barbed wire and concrete block, conflict and Cold War.

Now, we can see a new world coming into view. A world in which there is the very real prospect of a new world order. In the words of Winston Churchill: "a world order in which the principles of justice and fair play protect the weak against the strong." A world where the United Nations, freed from Cold War stalemate, is poised to fulfill the historic vision of its founders. A world in which freedom and respect for human rights find a home among all nations.

The gulf war put this new world to its first test. And, my fellow Americans, we passed that test.

For the sake of our principles, for the sake of the Kuwaiti people, we stood our ground. Because the world would not look the other way, Ambassador Al-Sabah, tonight Kuwait is free.

Tonight, as our troops begin to come home, let us recognize that the hard work of freedom still calls us forward. We've learned the hard lessons of history. The victory over Iraq was not waged as a war to end all wars. Even the new world order cannot guarantee an era of perpetual peace. But enduring peace must be our mission.

Our success in the gulf will shape not only the new world order we seek but our mission here at home.

In the war just ended, there were clear-cut objectives, timetables and, above all, an overriding imperative to achieve results. We must bring that same sense of self-discipline, that same sense of urgency, to the way we meet challenges here at home.

In my State of the Union address and in my budget, I defined a comprehensive agenda to prepare for the next American century.

Our first priority is to get this economy rolling again. The fear and uncertainty caused by the gulf crisis were understandable. But now that the war is over, oil prices are down, interest rates are down, and confidence is rightly coming back. Americans can move forward to lend, spend, and invest in this, the strongest economy on earth.

We must also enact the legislation that is key to building a better America. For example, in 1990, we enacted an historic Clean Air Act. And now we've proposed a national energy strategy. We passed a child-care bill that put power in the hands of parents. And today we're ready to do the same thing with our schools, and expand choice in education. We passed a crime bill that made a useful start in fighting crime and drugs. This year we're sending to Congress our comprehensive crime package to finish the job. We passed the landmark Americans with Disabilities Act. And now we've sent forward our civil rights bill. We also passed the aviation bill. This year we've sent up our new highway bill.

And these are just a few of our pending proposals for reform and renewal.

So tonight I call on Congress to move forward aggressively on our domestic front. Let's begin with two initiatives we should be able to agree on quickly: transportation and crime. And then let's build on success with those and enact the rest of our agenda. If our forces could win the ground war in 100 hours, then surely the Congress can pass this legislation in 100 days.

Let that be a promise we make tonight to the American people.

When I spoke in this House about the state of our union, I asked all of you: If we can selflessly confront evil for the sake of good in a land so far away, then surely we can make this land all that it should be. In the time since then, the brave men and women of Desert Storm accomplished more than even they may realize. They set out to confront an enemy abroad and in the process, they transformed a nation at home.

Think of the way they went about their mission: with confidence and quiet pride. Think about their sense of duty, about all they taught us about our values, about ourselves.

We hear so often about our young people in turmoil, how our children fall short, how our schools fail us, how American products and American workers are second-class. Well, don't you believe it. The America we saw in Desert Storm was first-class talent.

And they did it using America's state-of-the-art technology. We saw the excellence embodied in the Patriot missile and the patriots who made it work.

And we saw soldiers who know about honor and bravery and duty and country and the world-shaking power of these simple words.

There is something noble and majestic about the pride, about the patriotism, that we feel tonight.

So to everyone here and everyone watching at home, think about the men and women of Desert Storm. Let us honor them with our gratitude. Let us comfort the families of the fallen and remember each precious life lost.

Let us learn from them as well. Let us honor those who have served us by serving others.

Let us honor them as individuals — men and women of every race, all creeds and colors — by setting the face of this nation against discrimination, bigotry and hate. Eliminate them.

I'm sure many of you saw on television the unforgettable scene of four terrified Iraqi soldiers surrendering. They emerged from their bunker broken, tears streaming from their eyes, fearing the worst. And then there was an American soldier. Remember what he said? He said: "It's okay, you're all right now, you're all right now."

That scene says a lot about America, a lot about who we are. Americans are a caring people. We are a good people, a generous people. Let us always be caring and good and generous in all we do.

Soon, very soon, our troops will begin the march we've all been waiting for: their march home. And I have directed Secretary Cheney to begin the immediate return of American combat units from the gulf.

Less than two hours from now, the first plane-load of American soldiers will lift off from Saudi Arabia headed for the U.S.A.

That plane will carry men and women of the 24th Mechanized Infantry Division bound for Ft. Stewart, Ga. This is just the beginning of a steady flow of American troops coming home.

Let their return remind us that all those who have gone before are linked with us in the long line of freedom's march.

Americans have always tried to serve, to sacrifice nobly for what we believe to be right.

Tonight, I ask every community in this country to make this coming Fourth of July a day of special celebration for our returning troops. They may have missed Thanksgiving and Christmas, but I can tell you this: For them and for their families, we can make this a holiday they'll never forget.

In a very real sense, this victory belongs to them: to the privates and the pilots, to the sergeants and the supply officers, to the men and women in the machines, and the men and women who made them work. It belongs to the regulars, to the reserves, to the National Guard. This victory belongs to the finest fighting force this nation has ever known in its history.

We went halfway around the world to do what is moral and just and right. We fought hard, and, with others, we won the war. We lifted the yoke of aggression and tyranny from a small country that many Americans had never even heard of, and we ask nothing in return.

We're coming home now — proud, confident, heads high. There is much we must do at home and abroad. And we will do it. We are Americans.

May God bless this great nation, the United States of America. Thank you all very, very much.

President Bush's 1991 State of the Union Address

Following is the Reuter transcript of President Bush's State of the Union address to a joint session of Congress Jan. 29, 1991.

Mr. President, Mr. Speaker, members of the United States Congress. I come to this House of the people, to speak to you and all Americans, certain that we stand at a defining hour. Halfway around the world, we are engaged in a great struggle in the skies and on the seas and sands. We know why we're there. We are Americans: part of something larger than ourselves.

For two centuries, we've done the hard work of freedom. And tonight we lead the world in facing down a threat to decency and humanity. What is at stake is more than one small country; it is a big idea: a new world order, where diverse nations are drawn together in common cause to achieve the universal aspirations of mankind: peace and security, freedom and the rule of law. Such is a world worthy of our struggle and worthy of our children's future.

The community of nations has resolutely gathered to condemn and repel lawless aggression. [Iraqi President] Saddam Hussein's unprovoked invasion, his ruthless, systematic rape of a peaceful neighbor, violated everything the community of nations holds dear. The world has said this aggression would not stand — and it will not stand.

Together, we have resisted the trap of appeasement, cynicism and isolation that gives temptation to tyrants. The world has answered Saddam's invasion with 12 United Nations resolutions, starting with a demand for Iraq's immediate and unconditional withdrawal — and backed up by forces from 28 countries of six continents. With few exceptions, the world now stands as one.

The end of the Cold War has been a victory for all humanity. A year and a half ago, in Germany, I said that our goal was a Europe whole and free. Tonight, Germany is united. Europe has become whole and free — and America's leadership was instrumental in making it possible.

Our relationship with the Soviet Union is important, not only to us but to the world. That relationship has helped to shape these and other historic changes. But like many other nations, we have been deeply concerned by the violence in the Baltics, and we have communicated that concern to the Soviet leadership.

The principle that has guided us is simple: Our objective is to help the Baltic peoples achieve their aspirations, not to punish the Soviet Union.

In our recent discussions with the Soviet leadership, we have been given representations, which, if fulfilled, would result in the withdrawal of some Soviet forces, a reopening of dialogue with the republics and a move away from violence. We will watch carefully as the situation develops. And we will maintain our contact with the Soviet leadership to encourage continued commitment to democratization and reform.

Victory over Tyranny

If it is possible, I want to continue to build a lasting basis for U.S.-Soviet cooperation, for a more peaceful future for all mankind. The triumph of democratic ideas in Eastern Europe and Latin America — and the continuing struggle for freedom elsewhere all around the world — all confirm the wisdom of our nation's founders. Tonight, we work to achieve another victory, a victory over tyranny and savage aggression.

We in this union enter the last decade of the 20th century thankful for our blessings, steadfast in our purpose, aware of our difficulties and responsive to our duties at home and around the world.

For two centuries, America has served the world as an inspiring example of freedom and democracy. For generations, America has led the struggle to preserve and extend the blessings of liberty. And today, in a rapidly changing world, American leadership is indispensable. Americans know that leadership brings burdens and sacrifices.

But we also [know] why the hopes of humanity turn to us.

We are Americans: We have a unique responsibility to do the hard work of freedom. And when we do — freedom works.

The conviction and courage we see in the Persian Gulf today is simply the American character in action. The indomitable spirit that is contributing to this victory for world peace and justice is the same spirit that gives us the power and the potential to meet our toughest challenges at home.

We are resolute and resourceful. If we can selflessly confront the evil for the sake of good in a land so far away, then surely we can make this land all that it should be.

If anyone tells you that America's best days are behind her, they're looking the wrong way.

An Appeal for Renewal

Tonight, I come before this House and the American people with an appeal for renewal. This is not merely a call for new government initiatives, it is a call for new initiative in government, in our communities and from every American to prepare for the next American century.

America has always led by example. So who among us will set the example? Which of our citizens will lead us in this American century? Everyone who steps forward today to get one addict off drugs, to convince one troubled teenager not to give up on life, to comfort one AIDS patient, to help one hungry child.

We have within our reach the promise of a renewed America. We can find meaning and reward by serving some higher purpose than ourselves — a shining purpose, the illumination of a thousand points of light. And it is expressed by all who know the irresistible force of a child's hand, of a friend who stands by you and stays there, a volunteer's generous gesture, an idea that is simply right.

The problems before us may be different, but the key to solving them remains the same: It is the individual — the individual — who steps forward. And the state of our union is the union of each of us, one to the other; the sum of our friendships, marriages, families and communities.

We all have something to give. So if you know how to read, find someone who can't. If you've got a hammer, find a nail. If you're not hungry, not lonely, not in trouble — seek out someone who is.

Join the community of conscience. Do the hard work of freedom. And that will define the state of our union.

Since the birth of our nation, "We, the people" has been the source of our strength. What government can do alone is limited, but the potential of the American people knows no limits.

We are a nation of rock-solid realism and clear-eyed idealism. We are Americans: We are the nation that believes in the future; we are the nation that can shape the future.

And we've begun to do just that — by strengthening the power and choice of individuals and families.

Together, these last two years, we've put dollars for child care directly in the hands of parents, instead of bureaucracies. Unshackled the potential of Americans with disabilities. Applied the creativity of the marketplace in the service of the environment, for clean air. And made home ownership possible for more Americans.

The strength of a democracy is not in bureaucracy, it is in the people and their communities. In everything we do, let us unleash the potential of our most precious resource — our citizens, our citizens themselves. We must return to families, communities, counties, cities, states and institutions of every kind the power to chart their own destiny, and the freedom and opportunity provided by strong economic growth. And that's what America is all about.

I know, tonight, in some regions of our country, people are in genuine economic distress. And I hear them.

'My Heart Is Aching'

Earlier this month, Kathy Blackwell of Massachusetts wrote me about what can happen when the economy slows down, saying, "My heart is aching, and I think that you should know: Your people out here are hurting badly."

I understand. And I'm not unrealistic about the future. But there are reasons to be optimistic about our economy.

First, we don't have to fight double-digit inflation. Second, most industries won't have to make big cuts in production, because they don't have big inventories piled up. And, third, our exports are running solid and strong. In fact, American businesses are exporting at a record rate.

So let's put these times in perspective. Together, since 1981, we've created almost 20 million jobs, cut inflation in half and cut interest rates in half.

And, yes, the largest peacetime economic expansion in history has been temporarily interrupted. But our economy is still over twice as large as our closest competitor.

We will get this recession behind us and return to growth soon.

We will get on our way to a new record of expansion and achieve the competitive strength that will carry us into the next American century.

We should focus our efforts today on encouraging economic growth, investing in the future, and giving power and opportunity to the individual.

We must begin with control of federal spending.

And that's why I'm submitting a budget that holds the growth in spending to less than the rate of inflation. And that's why, amid all the sound and fury of last year's budget debate, we put into law new enforceable spending caps so that future spending debates will mean a battle of ideas, not a bidding war.

Though controversial, the budget agreement finally put the government on a pay-as-you-go plan — and cut the growth of debt by nearly $500 billion. And that frees funds for saving and job-creating investment.

Now, let's do more. My budget again includes tax-free family savings accounts; penalty-free withdrawals from IRA's for first-time home buyers; and, to increase jobs and growth, a reduced tax for long-term capital gains.

I know there are differences among us about the impact and the effects of a capital gains incentive. So tonight I am asking the congressional leaders and the Federal Reserve to cooperate with us in a study, led by Chairman Alan Greenspan, to sort out our technical differences so that we can avoid a return to unproductive partisan bickering.

But just as our efforts will bring economic growth now and in the future, they must also be matched by long-term investments for the next American century.

Investment in the Future

And that requires a forward-looking plan of action — and that's exactly what we will be sending to the Congress. We have prepared a detailed series of proposals that include:

A budget that promotes investment in America's future — in children, education, infrastructure, space and high technology.

Legislation to achieve excellence in education — building on the partnership forged with the 50 governors at the Education Summit, enabling parents to choose their children's schools and helping to make America No. 1 in math and science.

A blueprint for a new national highway system, a critical investment in our transportation infrastructure.

A research and development agenda that includes record levels of federal investment and a permanent tax credit to strengthen private R&D and to create jobs.

A comprehensive national energy strategy that calls for energy conservation and efficiency, increased development and greater use of alternative fuels.

A banking reform plan to bring America's financial system into the 21st century so that our banks remain safe and secure and can continue to make job-creating loans for our factories, businesses and home buyers. You know, I do think there has been too much pessimism. Sound banks should be making sound loans, now — and interest rates should be lower, now.

In addition to these proposals, we must recognize that our economic strength depends upon being competitive in world markets. We must continue to expand American exports. A successful Uruguay Round of world trade negotiations will create more real jobs and more real growth — for all nations. You and I know that if the playing field is level, America's workers and farmers can outwork and outproduce anyone, any time, anywhere.

And with a Mexican free trade agreement and our Enterprise for the Americas Initiative, we can help our partners strengthen their economies and move toward a free trade zone throughout this entire hemisphere.

The budget also includes a plan of action right here at home to put more power and opportunity in the hands of the individual. And that means new incentives to create jobs in our inner cities by encouraging investment through enterprise zones. It also means tenant control and ownership of public housing. Freedom and the power to choose should not be the privilege of wealth. They are the birthright of every American.

Civil rights are also crucial to protecting equal opportunity.

Every one of us has a responsibility to speak out against racism, bigotry and hate.

We will continue our vigorous enforcement of existing statutes, and I will once again press the Congress to strengthen the laws against employment discrimination without resorting to the use of unfair preferences.

We're determined to protect another fundamental civil right — freedom from crime and the fear that stalks our cities. The attorney general will soon convene a crime summit of our nation's law enforcement officials. And to help us support them, we need tough crime-control legislation, and we need it now.

And as we fight crime, we will fully implement our national strategy for combating drug abuse. Recent data show we are making progress, but much remains to be done. We will not rest until the day of the dealer is over forever.

Good health care is every American's right and every American's responsibility. And so we are proposing an aggressive program of new prevention initiatives — for infants, for children, for adults and for the elderly — to promote a healthier America and to help keep costs from spiraling.

Eliminating PACs

It's time to give people more choice in government by reviving the ideal of the citizen politician who comes not to stay but to serve. And one of the reasons there is so much support for term limitations is that the American people are increasingly concerned about big-money influence in politics. So we must look beyond the next election to the next generation. And the time has come to put the national interest above the special interest and totally eliminate political action committees [PACs].

And that would truly put more competition in elections and more power in the hands of individuals. And where power cannot be put directly in the hands of the individual, it should be moved closer to the people — away from Washington. The federal government too often treats government programs as if they are of Washington, by Washington and for Washington. Once established, federal programs seem to become immortal. It's time for a more dynamic program life cycle: Some programs should increase, some should decrease, some should be terminated, and some should be consolidated and turned over to the states.

My budget includes a list of programs for potential turnover totaling more than $20 billion. Working with Congress and the governors, I propose we select at least $15 billion in such programs and turn them over to the states in a single consolidated grant, fully funded, for flexible management by the states.

The value of this turnover approach is straightforward. It allows the federal government to reduce overhead. It allows states to manage more flexibly and more efficiently. It moves power and decision-making closer to the people. And it reinforces a theme of this administration: appreciation and encouragement of the innovative power of "states as laboratories."

This nation was founded by leaders who understood that power belongs in the hands of people. And they planned for the future. And so must we, here and all around the world. As Americans, we know there are times when we must step forward and accept our responsibility to lead the world away from the dark chaos of dictators toward the brighter promise of a better day. Almost 50 years ago we began a long struggle against aggressive totalitarianism. Now we face another defining hour for America and the world.

There is no one more devoted, more committed to the hard work of freedom, than every soldier and sailor, every Marine, airman, and Coast Guardsman, every man and woman now serving in the Persian Gulf.

[Bush interrupted by extended applause.]

What a wonderful fitting tribute to them. Each of them has volunteered, volunteered to provide for this nation's defense — and now they bravely struggle, to earn for America, for the world, and for future generations a just and lasting peace.

Our commitment to them must be the equal of their commitment to their country. They are truly America's finest.

War in the Gulf

The war in the gulf is not a war we wanted. We worked hard to avoid war. For more than five months we, along with the Arab League, the European Community, and the United Nations, tried every diplomatic avenue. U.N. Secretary General Perez de Cuellar; Presidents [Mikhail S.] Gorbachev [of the Soviet Union], [François] Mitterrand [of France], [Turgut] Ozal [of Turkey], [Hosni] Mubarak [of Egypt], and [Chadli] Benjedid [of Algeria]; Kings Fahd [of Saudi Arabia] and Hassan [of Morocco]; Prime Ministers [John] Major [of Britain] and [Giulio] Andreotti [of Italy] — just to name a few — all worked for a solution. But time and again, Saddam Hussein flatly rejected the path of diplomacy and peace. The world well knows how this conflict began and when: It began on Aug. 2nd, when Saddam invaded and sacked a small, defenseless neighbor. And I am certain of how it will end. So that peace can prevail, we will prevail.

Tonight, I am pleased to report that we are on course. Iraq's capacity to sustain war is being destroyed. Our investment, our training, our planning — all are paying off. Time will not be Saddam's salvation. Our purpose in the Persian Gulf remains constant: to drive Iraq out of Kuwait, to restore Kuwait's legitimate government and to ensure the stability and security of this critical region. Let me make clear what I mean by the region's stability and security. We do not seek the destruction of Iraq, its culture or its people. Rather, we seek an Iraq that uses its great resources not to destroy, not to serve the ambitions of a tyrant, but to build a better life for itself and its neighbors. We seek a Persian Gulf where conflict is no longer the rule, where the strong are neither tempted nor able to intimidate the weak.

Most Americans know instinctively why we are in the gulf. They know we had to stop Saddam now, not later. They know that this brutal dictator will do anything, will use any weapon, will commit any outrage, no matter how many innocents must suffer. They know we must make sure that control of the world's oil resources does not fall into his hands, only to finance further aggression. They know that we need to build a new, enduring peace — based not on arms races and confrontation, but on shared principles and the rule of law. And we all realize that our responsibility to be the catalyst for peace in the region does not end with the successful conclusion of this war.

Democracy brings the undeniable value of thoughtful dissent — and we have heard some dissenting voices here at home — some, a handful, reckless; most responsible. But the fact that all voices have the right to speak out is one of the reasons we've been united in purpose and principle for 200 years.

A Strong Defense

Our progress in this great struggle is the result of years of vigilance and a steadfast commitment to a strong defense. Now, with remarkable technological advances like the Patriot missile, we can defend against ballistic missile attacks aimed at innocent civilians.

Looking forward, I have directed that the SDI [strategic defense initiative] program be refocused on providing protection from limited ballistic missile strikes — whatever their source.

Let us pursue an SDI program that can deal with any future threat to the United States, to our forces overseas, and to our friends and allies. The quality of American technology, thanks to the American worker, has enabled us to successfully deal with difficult military conditions and help minimize precious loss of life. We have given our men and women the very best. And they deserve it.

We all have a special place in our hearts for the families of our men and women serving in the gulf. They are represented here tonight by Mrs. Norman Schwarzkopf.

We are all very grateful to Gen. [H. Norman] Schwarzkopf [commander of U.S. troops in the Persian Gulf] and to all those serving with him. And I might also recognize one who came with Mrs. Schwarzkopf, Alma Powell, wife of the distinguished chairman of the Joint Chiefs.

And to the families, let me say our forces in the gulf will not stay there one day longer than is necessary to complete their mission.

The courage and success of the R.A.F. [Royal Air Force] pilots — of the Kuwaiti, Saudi, French, the Canadians, the Italians, the pilots of Qatar and Bahrain — all are proof that for the first time since World War II, the international community is united. The leadership of the United Nations, once only a hoped-for ideal, is now confirming its founders' vision.

And I am heartened that we are not being asked to bear alone the financial burden of this struggle. Last year, our friends and allies provided the bulk of the economic costs of Desert Shield, and now, having received commitments of over $40 billion for the first three months of 1991, I am confident they will do no less as we move through Desert Storm.

The Dictator of Iraq

But the world has to wonder what the dictator of Iraq is thinking. If he thinks that by targeting innocent civilians in Israel and Saudi Arabia, that he will gain advantage, he is dead wrong.

And if he thinks that he will advance his cause through tragic and despicable environmental terrorism — he is dead wrong.

And if he thinks that by abusing the coalition prisoners of war, he will benefit — he is dead wrong.

We will succeed in the gulf. And when we do, the world community will have sent an enduring warning to any dictator or despot, present or future, who contemplates outlaw aggression. The world can therefore seize this opportunity to fulfill the long-held promise of a new world order — where brutality will go unrewarded and aggression will meet collective resistance.

Yes, the United States bears a major share of leadership in this effort. Among the nations of the world, only the United States of America has had both the moral standing and the means to back it up. We are the only nation on this Earth that could assemble the forces of peace. This is the burden of leadership — and the strength that has made America the beacon of freedom in a searching world. This nation has never found glory in war. Our people have never wanted to abandon the blessings of home and work for distant lands and deadly conflict. If we fight in anger, it is only because we have to fight at all. And all of us yearn for a world where we will never have to fight again.

Each of us will measure, within ourselves, the value of this great struggle. Any cost in lives, any cost, is beyond our power to measure. But the cost of closing our eyes to aggression is beyond mankind's power to imagine. This we do know: Our cause is just, our cause is moral, our cause is right.

Let future generations understand the burden and the blessings of freedom. Let them say, we stood where duty required us to stand. Let them know that together, we affirmed America and the world as a community of conscience.

The winds of change are with us now. The forces of freedom are together and united. And we move toward the next century more confident than ever that we have the will at home and abroad to do what must be done — the hard work of freedom.

May God bless the United States of America. Thank you very, very much.

President Bush's Fiscal 1992 Budget Message

Following is the Congressional Record *text of President Bush's fiscal 1992 budget message sent to Congress Feb. 4, 1991.*

TO THE CONGRESS OF
THE UNITED STATES:

I am pleased to present the *Budget of the United States Government for Fiscal Year 1992.*

The budget is consistent with the 5-year deficit reduction law enacted last fall. It recommends discretionary spending levels that fall within the statutory caps for defense, international, and domestic discretionary programs. It implements the entitlement savings and reforms enacted in the Budget Agreement. It conforms to the new pay-as-you-go-requirements.

By holding the overall rate of growth of Federal Government spending to approximately 2.6 percent — below the inflation rate — the budget puts into effect the concept of a "flexible freeze," which is an essential means of bringing the budget into long-term balance.

The longest period of peacetime economic expansion in history has been temporarily interrupted. We can, however, return to growth soon — and proceed on the path to a new era of expansion. With that goal in mind, the budget places special priority on policies that will enhance America's potential for long-term economic growth, and that will give individuals the power to take advantage of the opportunity America uniquely offers.

To this end, I am again proposing tax incentives to increase savings and long-term investment.

On the spending side of the budget, the existence of a cap on domestic discretionary outlays rightly creates a competition for resources. Priorities must be set. This budget proposes that domestic investment be increased in the following key areas:

Education and Human Capital. The budget proposes investments to prepare children better for school, to promote choice and excellence in our educational system, to improve math and science education, and to increase the access of low-income Americans to higher education.

Prevention and the Next Generation. The budget includes proposals to help reduce illness and death from preventable diseases, and to reverse the long-term trend of underinvestment in children.

Research and Development and the Human Frontier. The budget recommends an increase of $8.4 billion in the Federal investment in research and development, with special emphasis on basic research, high performance computing, and energy research and development. It proposes to extend permanently the tax credit for research and experimentation to encourage private sector R&D investment. In addition, the budget reflects the Administration's continued commitment to expanding human frontiers in space and biotechnology.

Transportation Infrastructure. The budget supports an expansion of the Federal Government's investment in highways and bridges to over $20 billion within 5 years, and proposes substantial increases to improve the condition of the Nation's airports, to modernize the air traffic control system, and to continue to develop the transportation infrastructure for exploration and use of space.

America's Heritage and Environmental Protection. The budget includes increased funds for the expansion and improvement of America's treasury of parks, forests, wildlife refuges, and other public lands; for the implementation of the Clean

Air Act and other key environmental statutes; for the cleanup of pollution at various Federal facilities and at Superfund sites; and for protection and enhancement of coastal areas and wetlands.

Choice and Opportunity. The budget provides: funds to help give parents greater choice in child care, health care, education, and housing; the resources to allow all Americans, especially those with low incomes, to seize the opportunities that such choice provides; and a proposal to establish Enterprise Zones to bring hope to our inner cities and distressed rural areas.

Drugs and Crime. The budget further increases the Administration's investment in drug prevention, treatment, and law enforcement. And the budget substantially increases the resources available to help the Federal Bureau of Investigation fight crime, the Federal prosecutors prosecute criminals, and the Federal prison system accommodate those convicted of crimes.

To make such investments possible, the budget includes recommendations to terminate or reduce Federal investment in certain low-return programs, and proposes reforms to slow the continuing growth of mandatory entitlement programs and to increase fairness in the distribution of the benefits these programs provide.

In addition, the budget contains a new proposal to fund various programs now carried out by the States through a comprehensive block grant. The States are continuing to develop new and innovative ways to deliver services more effectively. The budget not only highlights several of these innovations; it proposes to reinforce and build upon them.

The budget contains several proposals that reflect my commitment to managing government better. These include measures to improve accountability, to reduce waste, to reform regulation, to employ risk management budgeting in addressing threats to health and safety, and to set clear objectives and measure performance in meeting them.

Finally, consistent with the statutory caps enacted last year, the budget provides the resources necessary to maintain national security, and to better advance American interests abroad. As the budget goes to press, the timing of the resolution of the multinational coalition's efforts to reverse the aggression in the Persian Gulf is uncertain. For this reason, the budget reflects only a placeholder for Operation Desert Shield. A supplemental request for the incremental costs of Desert Shield, which includes Desert Storm, will be forwarded to the Congress in the coming weeks.

The priority investments embodied in this budget will help America prepare for the requirements and opportunities presented by a rapidly changing world. I look forward to working with the Congress in developing a budget that lays the groundwork for a brighter future, protects our national interests, and helps create the conditions for long-term economic growth and prosperity.

GEORGE BUSH

February 4, 1991

Bush and Gorbachev on START Treaty

Following is the Reuter transcript of the remarks by President Bush and Soviet President Mikhail S. Gorbachev July 31, 1991, on signing the strategic arms reduction treaty (START) in the Kremlin's St. Vladimir's Hall.

PRESIDENT GORBACHEV (through interpreter): In a few moments, President Bush and I will put our signatures under the treaty on the reduction of strategic offensive arms.

This completes many years of efforts that required hard work and patience on the part of government leaders, diplomats and military officials. They required will, courage and the rejection of outdated perceptions of each other. They required trust.

This is also a beginning, the beginning of voluntary reduction of the nuclear arsenals of the U.S.S.R. and the United States, a process with unprecedented scope and objectives. It is an event of global significance that we, imparting to the dismantling of the infrastructure of fear that has ruled the world, and momentum which is so powerful that it will be hard to stop.

In both countries we face the complex process of the ratification of the new treaty. There will be critics. Here in Moscow some will point to our unilateral concessions, while in Washington there will be talk about concessions made to the Soviet Union.

Some will say the new treaty does not really fulfill the promise of a peace dividend, since considerable resources will be required to destroy the missiles. And if the missiles are not destroyed, critics will say they are obsolete and must be replaced with new ones. And that will be even more expensive.

Sharp criticism is to be expected also from those who want to see faster and more ambitious steps toward abolishing nuclear weapons. In other words, the treaty will have to be defended. I'm sure we have achieved the best that is now possible, and that is required to continue progress. Tremendous work has been done, and unique experience has been gained of cooperating in this enormously complex area.

It is important that there is a growing realization of the absurdity of armament, now that the world has started to move toward an era of economic interdependence and that the information revolution is making the indivisibility of the world ever more evident.

But the policy-makers have to bear in mind that as we move toward that era we will have to make new immense efforts to remove the dangers inherited from the past and newly emerging dangers. To overcome various physical, intellectual and psychological obstacles, normal human thinking will have to replace the kind of militarized political thinking that has taken root in the minds of men. That will take time.

A new conceptual foundation of security will be of great help. Doctrines of all fighting must be abandoned in favor of concepts of preventing war. Plans calling for a crushing defeat of the perceived enemy must be replaced with joint projects of strategic stability and defense sufficiency.

The document before us marks a moral achievement and a major breakthrough in our country's thinking and behavior.

Our next goal is to make full use of this breakthrough to make disarmament an irreversible process. So as we give credit to what has been achieved, let us express our appreciation to those who have contributed to this treaty their talent and their intellectual and numerous resources, and let us get down to work again for the sake of our own and global security.

Mr. President, we can congratulate each other. We can congratulate the Soviet and American people and the world community on the conclusion of this agreement. Thank you.

PRESIDENT BUSH: Thank you, Mr. President.

To President Gorbachev and to members of the Soviet government and all the honored guests here, may I salute you. The treaty that we sign today is most — is a most complicated one. The most complicated contract governing the most serious of concerns. Its 700 pages stand as a monument to several generations of U.S. and Soviet negotiators, for their tireless efforts to carve out common ground from a thicket of contentious issues, and it represents a major step forward for our mutual security and the cause of world peace.

And may I, too, thank everybody who worked on this treaty, military and State Department, arms control negotiators, really on both sides, and I would like to say that many are here today, some like my predecessor, President Reagan, is not here, but I think all of us realize that there are many who are not in this room that deserve an awful lot of credit on both the Soviet side and the United States' side.

The START treaty vindicates an approach to arms control that guided us for almost a decade: the belief that we could do more than merely halt the growth of our nuclear arsenals. We could seek more than limits on the number of arms. In our talks we sought stabilizing reductions in our strategic arsenals.

START makes that a reality. In a historic first for arms control we will actually reduce U.S. and Soviet strategic nuclear arsenals. But reductions alone are not enough. So START requires even deeper cuts of the most dangerous and destabilizing weapons.

The agreement itself is exceedingly complex. But the central idea at the heart of this treaty can be put simply: Stabilizing reductions in our strategic nuclear forces reduce the risk of war.

But these promises to reduce arms levels cannot automatically guarantee success. Just as important are the treaty's monitoring mechanisms, so that we know that the commitments made are being translated into real security. In this area, START builds on the experience of earlier agreements but goes far beyond them in provisions to ensure that we can verify this treaty effectively.

Mr. President, in the warming relations between our nations, this treaty stands as both cause and consequence. Many times during the START talks, reaching agreement seemed all but impossible.

In the end, the progress that we made in the past year's time, progress in easing tensions and ending the Cold War, change the atmosphere at the negotiating table and pave the way for START's success.

Neither side won unilateral advantage over the other. Both sides committed themselves instead to achieving a strong effective treaty and securing the mutual stability that a good agreement would provide.

Mr. President, by reducing arms, we reverse a half-century of steadily growing strategic arsenals. But more than that, we take a significant step forward in dispelling a half-century of mistrust. By building trust, we pave a path to peace.

We sign the START treaty as testament to the new relationship emerging between our two countries and the promise of further progress toward lasting peace.

Thank you very much.

Bush's Speech at Middle East Peace Conference

Following is the Reuter transcript of President Bush's address Oct. 30, 1991, to the Middle East Peace Conference in Madrid, Spain.

Let me begin by thanking the government of Spain for hosting this historic gathering. With short notice, the Spanish people and their leaders stepped forward to make available this magnificent setting. And let us hope that this conference of Madrid will mark the beginning of a new chapter in the history of the Middle East.

I also want to express at the outset my pleasure at the presence of our fellow cosponsor, President [Mikhail S.] Gorbachev. At a time of momentous challenges at home, President Gorbachev and his senior associates have demonstrated their intent to engage the Soviet Union as a force for positive change in the Middle East. And this sends a powerful signal to all those who long for peace.

We come to Madrid on a mission of hope, to begin work on a just, lasting and comprehensive settlement to the conflict in the Middle East.

We come here to seek peace for part of the world that in the long memory of man has known far too much hatred, anguish and war. I can think of no endeavor more worthy or more necessary. Our objective must be clear and straightforward. It is not simply to end the state of war in the Middle East and replace it with a state of nonbelligerency. This is not enough. This would not last. Rather we seek peace, real peace. And by real peace I mean treaties, security, diplomatic relations, economic relations, trade, investment, cultural exchange, even tourism.

What we seek is a Middle East where vast resources are no longer devoted to armaments. A Middle East where young people no longer have to dedicate and all too often give their lives to combat. A Middle East no longer victimized by fear and terror. A Middle East where normal men and woman lead normal lives.

Hope vs. History

Let no one mistake the magnitude of this challenge. The struggle we seek to end has a long and painful history. Every life lost, every outrage, every act of violence, is etched deep in the hearts and history of the people of this region.

There is a history that weighs heavily against hope, and yet history need not be man's master.

I expect that some will say that what I'm suggesting is impossible. But think back. Who back in 1945 would have thought that France and Germany, bitter rivals for nearly a century, would become allies in the aftermath of World War II? And who, two years ago, would have predicted that the Berlin Wall would come down? And who in the early 1960s would have believed that the Cold War would come to a peaceful end, replaced by cooperation, exemplified by the fact that the United States and the Soviet Union are here today, not as rivals, but as partners, as Prime Minister [Felipe] González pointed out.

Peace Is Possible

No, peace in the Middle East need not be a dream. Peace is possible. The Egyptian-Israeli peace treaty is striking proof that former adversaries can make and sustain peace. And moreover, parties in the Middle East have respected agreements, not only in the Sinai, but on the Golan Heights as well.

The fact that we are all gathered here today for the first time attests to a new potential for peace. Each of us has taken an important step toward real peace by meeting here in Madrid.

All the formulas on paper, all the pious declarations in the world won't bring peace if there is not a practical mechanism for moving ahead.

Peace will only come as the result of direct negotiations, compromise, give-and-take. Peace cannot be imposed from the outside by the United States or anyone else. And while we will continue to do everything possible to help the parties overcome obstacles, peace must come from within.

We come here to Madrid as realists. We don't expect peace to be negotiated in a day or a week or a month or even a year. It will take time. Indeed, it should take time: time for parties so long at war to learn to talk to one another, to listen to one another; time to heal old wounds and build trust.

In this quest, time need not be the enemy of progress. What we envision is a process of direct negotiations proceeding along two tracks: one between Israel and the Arab states, the other between Israel and the Palestinians. Negotiations are to be conducted on the basis of U.N. Security Council resolutions 242 and 338. The real work will not happen here in this — in the plenary sessions, but in direct, bilateral negotiations.

This conference cannot impose a settlement on the participants or veto agreements. And just as important, the conference can only be reconvened with the consent of every participant.

Progress is in the hands of the parties who must live with the consequences. Soon after the bilateral talks commence, parties will convene as well to organize multilateral negotiations. These will focus on issues that cross national boundaries and are common to the region: arms control, water, refugee concerns, economic development.

Progress in these four is not intended as a substitute for what must be decided in the bilateral talks. To the contrary, progress in the multilateral issues can help create an atmosphere in which long-standing bilateral disputes can more easily be settled.

For Israel and the Palestinians, a framework already exists for diplomacy. Negotiations will be conducted in phases, beginning with talks on interim self-government arrangements.

We aim to reach agreement within one year, and once agreed, interim self-government arrangements will last for five years. Beginning the third year, negotiations will commence on permanent status.

No one can say with any precision what the end result will be. In our view, something must be developed, something acceptable to Israel, the Palestinians and Jordan that gives the Palestinian people meaningful control over their own lives and fate and provides for the acceptance and security of Israel.

Israeli-Palestinian Compromise

We can all appreciate that both Israelis and Palestinians are worried about compromise, worried about compromising even the smallest point for fear it becomes a precedent for what really matters.

But no one should avoid compromise on interim arrangements for a simple reason: Nothing agreed to now will prejudice permanent status negotiations. To the contrary, these subsequent negotiations will be determined on their own merits.

Peace cannot depend upon promises alone. Real peace, lasting peace, must be based upon security for all states and people, including Israel. For too long, the Israeli people have lived in fear surrounded by an unaccepting Arab world. And now is the ideal moment for the Arab world to demonstrate that attitudes have changed, that the Arab world is willing to live in peace with Israel and make allowances for Israel's reasonable security needs.

We know that peace must also be based on fairness. In the absence of fairness, there will be no legitimacy, no stability. And this applies above all to the Palestinian people, many of whom have known turmoil and frustration above all else.

Israel now has an opportunity to demonstrate that it is willing to enter into a new relationship with its Palestinian neighbors, one predicated upon mutual respect and cooperation. Throughout the Middle East we seek a stable and enduring settlement. We've not defined what this means. Indeed, I make these points with no map showing where the final borders are to be drawn. And nevertheless, we believe that territorial compromise is essential for peace. Boundaries should reflect the quality of both security and political arrangements, and the United States is prepared to accept whatever the parties themselves find acceptable.

What we seek, as I said on March 6th, is a solution that meets the twin tests of fairness and security.

Focus on a Vision

I know, I expect we all know, that these negotiations will not be easy. I know too that these negotiations will not be smooth. There will be disagreement and criticism. Setbacks. Who knows, possibly interruptions. Negotiation and compromise are always painful. Success will escape us if we focus solely upon what is being given up. We must fix our vision on what real peace would bring. Peace, after all, means not just avoiding war and the costs of preparing for it. The Middle East is blessed with great resources, physical, financial and, yes, above all, human. And new opportunities are within reach, if we only have the vision to embrace them.

To succeed, we must recognize that peace is in the interest of all parties — war, the absolute advantage of none. The alternative to peace in the Middle East is a future of violence and waste and tragedy.

In any future wars lurk the dangers of weapons of mass destruction. As we learned in the gulf war, modern arsenals make it possible to attack urban areas, to put the lives of innocent men, women and children at risk, to transform city streets, schools, children's playgrounds, into battlefields.

Today we can decide to take a different path to the future, to avoid conflict. And I call upon all parties to avoid unilateral acts, be they words or deeds, that would invite retaliation, or worse yet, prejudice or even threaten the process itself.

I call upon all parties to consider taking measures that will bolster mutual confidence and trust, steps that signal a sincere commitment to reconciliation.

U.S. Guarantees

I want to say something about the role of the United States of America. We played an active role in making this conference possible. And both the secretary of State, Jim Baker, and I will play an active role in helping the process succeed.

Toward this end we've provided written assurances to Israel, to Syria, to Jordan, Lebanon and the Palestinians, and in the spirit of openness and honesty, we will brief all parties on assurances that we have provided to the others.

We're prepared to extend guarantees, provide technology and support, if that is what peace requires. And we will call upon our friends and allies in Europe and in Asia to join with us in providing resources so that peace and prosperity go hand in hand.

Seize the Moment

Outsiders can assist, but in the end, it is up to the peoples and the governments of the Middle East to shape the future of the Middle East. It is their opportunity and it is their responsibility to do all that they can to take advantage of this gathering, this historic gathering, and what it symbolizes and what it promises.

No one should assume that the opportunity before us to make peace will remain if we fail to seize the moment.

Ironically, this is an opportunity born of war, the destruction of past wars, the fear of future wars. The time has come to put an end to war. The time has come to choose peace.

And speaking for the American people, I want to reaffirm that the United States is prepared to facilitate the search for peace, to be a catalyst as we have been in the past, and as we've been very recently.

We seek only one thing, and this we seek not for ourselves, but for the peoples of the area, and particularly the children: that this and future generations of the Middle East may know the meaning and blessing of peace.

We have seen too many generations of children whose haunted eyes show only fear. Too many funerals for the brothers and sisters — the mothers and fathers who died too soon. Too much hatred, too little love.

And if we cannot summon the courage to lay down the past for ourselves, let us resolve to do it for the children.

May God bless and guide the work of this conference and may this conference set us on the path of peace.

Thank you.

President Bush's 1992 State of the Union Address

Following is the Reuter transcript of President Bush's State of the Union address to a joint session of Congress Jan. 28, 1992.

Mr. Speaker, Mr. President, distinguished members of Congress, honored guests and fellow citizens: Thank you very much for that warm reception.

You know, the big buildup this address has had, I wanted to make sure it would be a big hit, but I couldn't convince Barbara to deliver it for me.

I see the Speaker and the vice president are laughing. They saw what I did in Japan, and they're just happy they're sitting behind me.

I mean to speak tonight of big things, of big changes and the promises they hold, and of some big problems and how together we can solve them and move our country forward as the undisputed leader of the age.

We gather tonight at a dramatic and deeply promising time in our history and in the history of man on Earth.

'Communism Died'

For in the past 12 months, the world has known changes of almost biblical proportions. And even now, months after the failed coup that doomed a failed system, I am not sure we have absorbed the full impact, the full import of what happened. But communism died this year.

Even as president, with the most fascinating possible vantage point, there were times when I was so busy helping to manage progress and helping to lead change, that I didn't always show the joy that was in my heart.

But the biggest thing that has happened in the world in my life — in our lives — is this: By the grace of God, America won the Cold War.

I mean to speak this evening of the changes that can take place in our country now that we can stop making the sacrifices we had to make when we had an avowed enemy that was a superpower. Now we can look homeward even more and move to set right what needs to be set right.

And I will speak of those things.

But let me tell you something I've been thinking these past few months. It's a kind of roll call of honor. For the Cold War didn't "end" — it was won.

And I think of those who won it, in places like Korea and Vietnam. And some of them didn't come back. And back then, they were heroes; but this year they were victors.

The long roll call — all the G.I. Joes and Janes, all the ones who fought faithfully for freedom, who hit the ground and sucked the dust and knew their share of horror.

This may seem frivolous — I don't mean it so — but it's moving to me how the world saw them.

The world saw not only their special valor but their special style — their rambunctious, optimistic bravery, their do-or-die unity unhampered by class or race or region. What a group we've put forth, for generations now — from the ones who wrote "Kilroy was here" on the walls of German stalags to those who left signs in the Iraq desert that said "I saw Elvis." What a group of kids we've sent out into the world.

And there's another to be singled out — though it may seem inelegant. I mean a mass of people called "the American taxpayer." No one ever thinks to thank the American people who pay a country's bills or an alliance's bills. But for half a century now the American people have shouldered the burden and paid taxes that were higher than they would have been to support a defense that was bigger than it would have been if imperial communism had never existed.

But it did. Doesn't anymore.

And here is a fact that I wouldn't mind the world acknowledging: The American taxpayer bore the brunt of the burden and deserves a hunk of the glory.

Plans for Peace

And so now, for the first time in 35 years, our strategic bombers stand down. No longer are they on round-the-clock alert. Tomorrow our children will go to school and study history and how plants grow. And they won't have, as my children did, air raid drills in which they crawl under their desks and cover their heads in case of nuclear war. My grandchildren don't have to do that and won't have the bad dreams children had once in decades past. There are still threats. But the long, drawn-out dread is over.

A year ago tonight I spoke to you at a moment of high peril. American forces had just unleashed Operation Desert Storm. And after 40 days in the desert skies and four days on the ground, the men and women of America's armed forces and our allies accomplished the goals that I declared and you endorsed: We liberated Kuwait.

Soon after, the Arab world and Israel sat down to talk seriously and comprehensively about peace — an historic first. And soon after that, at Christmas, the last American hostages came home. Our policies were vindicated.

Much good can come from the prudent use of power. And much good can come of this: A world once divided into two armed camps now recognizes one sole and preeminent power — the United States of America.

And they regard this with no dread. For the world trusts us with power — and the world is right. They trust us to be fair and restrained; they trust us to be on the side of decency. And they trust us to do what's right.

I use those words advisedly. A few days after the war began, I received a telegram from Joanne Speicher, the wife of the first pilot killed in the gulf, Lt. Cmdr. Scott Speicher. Even in her grief, she wanted me to know that some day when her children were old enough, she would tell them "that their father went away to war because it was the right thing to do."

And she said it all: It was the right thing to do.

And we did it together. There were honest differences here in this chamber. But when the war began, you put partisanship aside and we supported our troops.

This is still a time for pride — but this is no time to boast. For problems face us, and we must stand together once again and solve them — and not let our country down.

Two years ago, I began planning cuts in military spending that reflected the changes of the new era. But now, this year, with imperial communism gone, that process can be accelerated.

Tonight I can tell you of dramatic changes in our strategic nuclear force. These are actions we are taking on our own — because they are the right thing to do.

After completing 20 planes for which we have begun procurement, we will shut down further production of the B-2 bomber.

We will cancel the small ICBM [intercontinental ballistic missile] program. We will cease production of new warheads for our sea-based ballistic missiles. We will stop all new production of the Peacekeeper missile. And we will not purchase any more advanced cruise missiles.

This weekend I will meet at Camp David with Boris Yeltsin of the Russian Federation. I have informed President Yeltsin that if the Commonwealth — the former Soviet Union — will eliminate all land-based multiple warhead ballistic missiles, I will do the following:

We will eliminate all Peacekeeper missiles. We will reduce the number of warheads on Minuteman missiles to one and reduce the number of warheads on our sea-based missiles by about one-third. And we will convert a substantial portion of our strategic bombers to primarily conventional use.

President Yeltsin's early response has been very positive, and I expect our talk at Camp David to be fruitful.

I want you to know that for half a century, American presidents have longed to make such decisions and say such words. But even in the midst of celebration we must keep caution as a friend.

For the world is still a dangerous place. Only the dead have seen the end of conflict. And though yesterday's challenges are behind us, tomorrow's are being born.

The secretary of Defense recommended these cuts after consultation with the Joint Chiefs of Staff. And I make them with confidence. But do not misunderstand me.

The reductions I have approved will save us an additional $50 billion over the next five years. By 1997 we will have cut defense by 30 percent since I took office. These cuts are deep and you must know my resolve: this deep and no deeper.

To do less would be insensible to progress — but to do more would be ignorant of history.

We must not go back to the days of "the hollow army." We cannot repeat the mistakes made twice in this century, when armistice was followed by recklessness and defense was purged as if the world were permanently safe.

I remind you this evening that I have asked for your support in funding a program to protect our country from limited nuclear missile attack. We must have this protection because too many people in too many countries have access to nuclear arms.

And I urge you again to pass the Strategic Defense Initiative — SDI.

There are those who say that now we can turn away from the world, that we have no special role, no special place.

But we are the United States of America, the leader of the West that has become the leader of the world.

As long as I am president, I will continue to lead in support of freedom everywhere — not out of arrogance, not out of altruism, but for the safety and security of our children.

This is a fact: Strength in the pursuit of peace is no vice; isolationism in the pursuit of security is no virtue.

Setting the Economy Free

Now to our troubles at home. They are not all economic, but the primary problem is our economy. And there are some good signs: Inflation, that thief, is down; and interest rates are down. But unemployment is too high, some industries are in trouble, and growth is not what it should be.

Let me tell you right from the start and right from the heart: I know we're in hard times, but I know something else — this will not stand.

My friends in this chamber, we can bring the same courage and sense of common purpose to the economy that we brought to Desert Storm. And we can defeat hard times together.

I believe you will help. One reason is that you're patriots, and you want the best for your country. And I believe that in your hearts you want to put partisanship aside and get the job done — because it's the right thing to do.

The power of America rests in a stirring but simple idea — that people will do great things if only you set them free.

Well, we're going to set the economy free, for if this age of miracles and wonders has taught us anything, it's that if we can change the world, we can change America.

We must encourage investment. We must make it easier for people to invest money and create new products, new industries and new jobs. We must clear away the obstacles to growth — high taxes, high regulation, red tape and, yes, wasteful government spending.

None of this will happen with a snap of the fingers — but it will happen. And the test of a plan isn't whether it's called new or dazzling. The American people aren't impressed by gimmicks; they're smarter on this score than all of us in this room. The only test of a plan is, is it sound and will it work.

We must have a short-term plan to address our immediate needs and heat up the economy. And we need a longer-term plan to keep the combustion going and to guarantee our place in the world economy.

There are certain things that a president can do without Congress — and I am going to do them.

I have this evening asked major Cabinet departments and federal agencies to institute a 90-day moratorium on any new federal regulations that could hinder growth.

In those 90 days, major departments and agencies will carry out a top-to-bottom review of all regulations, old and new, to stop the ones that will hurt growth and speed up those that will help growth.

Further, for the untold number of hard-working, responsible American workers and businessmen and women who've been forced to go without needed bank loans — the banking credit crunch must end.

I won't neglect my responsibility for sound regulations that serve the public good, but regulatory overkill must be stopped.

And I have instructed our government regulators to stop it.

I have directed Cabinet departments and federal agencies to speed up progrowth expenditures as quickly as possible. This should put an extra $10 billion into the economy in the next six months. And our new transportation bill provides more than $150 billion for construction and maintenance projects that are vital to our growth and well-being. That means jobs building roads, jobs building bridges and jobs building railways.

And I have this evening directed the secretary of the Treasury to change the federal tax withholding tables. With this change, millions of Americans from whom the government withholds more than necessary can now choose to have the government withhold less from their paychecks. Something tells me a number of taxpayers may take us up on this one. This initiative could return about $25 billion back into our economy over the next 12 months — money people can use to help pay for clothing, college or to get a new car.

And, finally, working with the Federal Reserve, we will continue to support monetary policy that keeps both interest rates and inflation down.

These are the things that I can do.

Congress' Responsibilities

And now, members of Congress, let me tell you what you can do for your country.

You must pass the other elements of my plan to meet our economic needs. Everyone knows that investment spurs recovery. And I am proposing this evening a change in the alternative minimum tax and the creation of a new 15 percent investment tax allowance.

This will encourage businesses to accelerate investment and bring people back to work.

Real estate has led our economy out of almost all the tough times we've ever had. Once building starts, carpenters and plumbers work, people buy homes and take out mortgages.

My plan would modify the passive-loss rule for active real estate developers.

And it would make it easier for pension plans to purchase real estate.

For those Americans who dream of buying a first home and who can't quite afford it, my plan would allow first-time buyers to withdraw savings from IRA without penalty — and provide a $5,000 tax credit for the first purchase of that home.

And, finally, my immediate plan calls on Congress to give crucial help to people who own a home, to everyone who has a business, or a farm, or a single investment.

This time, at this hour, I cannot take no for an answer. You must cut the capital gains tax on the people of our country.

Never has an issue been more demagogued by its opponents.

But the demagogues are wrong — and they know it. Sixty percent of the people who benefit from lower capital gains have incomes under $50,000. A cut in the capital gains tax increases jobs and helps just about everyone in our country.

And so I'm asking you to cut the capital gains tax to a maximum of 15.4 percent.

And I'll tell you, those of you who say, oh, no, someone who's comfortable may benefit from this. You kind of remind me of the old definition of the Puritan, who wouldn't sleep at night worrying that somehow someone somewhere was out having a good time.

The opponents of this measure — and those who've authored various so-called soak-the-rich bills that are floating around this chamber — should be reminded of something: When they aim at the big guy they usually hit the little guy. And maybe it's time that stopped.

This then is my short-term plan. Your part, members of Congress, requires enactment of these common-sense proposals that will have a strong effect on the economy without breaking the budget agreement and without raising tax rates.

While my plan is being passed and kicking in, we've got to care for those in trouble today. I have provided up to $4.4 billion in my budget to extend federal unemployment benefits. I ask for congressional action right away. And I thank the committee —

Well, at last.

And let's be frank — let me level with you. I know, and you know, that my plan is unveiled in a political season. And I know, and you know, that everything I propose will be viewed by some in merely partisan terms. But I ask you to know what is in my heart: And my aim is to increase our nation's good. And I am doing what I think is right; I am proposing what I know will help.

I pride myself that I am a prudent man, and I believe that patience is a virtue. But I understand that politics is for some a game — and that sometimes the game is to stop all progress and then decry the lack of improvement.

But let me tell you: Far more important than my political future — and far more important than yours — is the well-being of our country.

And members of this chamber are practical people, and I know you won't resent some practical advice: When people put their party's fortunes, whatever the party, whatever side of this aisle, before the public good, they court defeat not only for their country, but for themselves. And they will certainly deserve it.

And I submit my plan tomorrow. And I am asking you to pass it by March 20. And I ask the American people to let you know they want this action by March 20.

From the day after that, if it must be: The battle is joined.

And you know when principle is at stake, I relish a good fair fight.

I said my plan has two parts, and it does. And it is the second part that is the heart of the matter. For it's not enough to get an immediate burst. We need long-term improvement in our economic position.

We all know that the key to our economic future is to ensure that America continues as the economic leader of the world. We have that in our power.

Plan for the Future

Here, then, is my long-term plan to guarantee our future.

First, trade: We will work to break down the walls that stop world trade. We will work to open markets everywhere. And in our major trade negotiations, I will continue pushing to eliminate tariffs and subsidies that damage America's farmers and workers.

And we'll get more good American jobs within our own hemisphere through the North American Free Trade Agreement and through the Enterprise for the Americas Initiative.

But changes are here, and more are coming. The workplace of the future will demand more highly skilled workers than ever — more people who are computer literate, highly educated.

And we must be the world's leader in education. And we must revolutionize America's schools.

My America 2000 education strategy will help us reach that goal. My plan will give parents more choice, give teachers more flexibility and help communities create New American schools.

Thirty states across the nation have established America 2000 programs. Hundreds of cities and towns have joined in.

And now Congress must join this great movement: Pass my proposals for New American schools.

That was my second long-term proposal.

And here's my third: We must make common-sense investments that will help us compete long term in the marketplace. We must encourage research and development. And my plan is to make the R&D [research and development] tax credit permanent and to provide record levels of support — over $76 billion this year alone — for people who will explore the promise of emerging technologies.

Fourth, we must do something about crime and drugs.

And it is time for a major renewed investment in fighting violent street crime. It saps our strength and hurts our faith in our society and in our future together.

Surely a tired woman on her way to work at 6 in the morning on a subway deserves the right to get there safely.

And surely it's true that everyone who changes his or her life because of crime — from those afraid to go out at night to those afraid to walk in the parks they pay for — surely these people have been denied a basic civil right.

It is time to restore it.

Congress, pass my comprehensive crime bill.

It is tough on criminals and supportive of police — and it has been languishing in these hallowed halls for years now. Pass it. Help your country.

And, fifth, I ask you tonight to fund our HOPE housing proposal and to pass my enterprise zone legislation, which will get businesses into the inner city. We must empower the poor with the pride that comes from owning a home, getting a job, becoming a part of things.

My plan would encourage real estate construction by extending tax incentives for mortgage revenue bonds and low-income housing.

And I ask tonight for record expenditures for the program that helps children born into want move into excellence: Head Start.

Step six: We must reform our health-care system.

For this, too, bears on whether or not we can compete in the world. American health costs have been exploding. This year America will spend over $800 billion on health. And that's expected to grow to 1.6 trillion by the end of the decade. We simply cannot afford this.

The cost of health care shows up not only in your family budget but in the price of everything we buy and everything we sell. When health coverage for a fellow on an assembly line costs thousands of dollars, the cost goes into the products he makes — and you pay the bill.

We must make a choice.

Now, some pretend we can have it both ways. They call it "play or pay." But that expensive approach is unstable. It will mean higher taxes, fewer jobs and eventually a system under complete government control.

Really, there are only two options: We can move toward a nationalized system — which will restrict patient choice — a system which will restrict patient choice in picking a doctor and force the government to ration services arbitrarily — and what we'll get is patients in long lines, indifferent service and a huge new tax burden; or we can reform our own private health-care system, which still gives us, for all its flaws, the best-quality health care in the world.

Well, let's build on our strengths.

My plan provides insurance security for all Americans — while preserving and increasing the idea of choice. We make basic health insurance affordable for all low-income people not now covered. And we do it by providing a health insurance tax credit of up to $3,750 for each low-income family.

And the middle class gets new help too. And, by reforming the health insurance market, my plan assures that Americans will have access to basic health insurance even if they change jobs or develop serious health problems.

We must bring costs under control, preserve quality, preserve choice and reduce the people's nagging daily worry about health insurance. My plan, the details of which I will announce very shortly, does just that.

And, seventh, we must get the federal deficit under control.

We now have in law enforceable spending caps and a requirement that we pay for the programs we create.

There are those in Congress who would ease that discipline now. But I cannot let them do it — and I won't.

My plan would freeze all domestic discretionary budget authority — which means "no more next year than this year."

I will not tamper with Social Security.

But I would put real caps on the growth of uncontrolled spending. And I would also freeze federal domestic government employment.

And with the help of Congress, my plan will get rid of 246 programs that don't deserve federal funding.

Some of them have noble titles, but none of them is indispensable. We can get rid of each and every one of them.

You know, it's time we rediscovered a "home truth" the American people have never forgotten: This government is too big and spends too much.

I call upon Congress to adopt a measure that will help put an end to the annual ritual of filling the budget with pork-barrel appropriations. Every year the press has a field day making fun of outrageous examples — Lawrence Welk museum, research grant for Belgian endive.

We all know how these things get into the budget. And maybe you need someone to help you say no. I know how to say it. And I know what I need to make it stick. Give me the same thing 43 governors have — the line item veto and let me help you control spending.

We must put an end to unfinanced federal government mandates. These are the requirements Congress puts on our cities, counties and states — without supplying the money.

And if Congress passes a mandate, it should be forced to pay for it and balance the cost with savings elsewhere. After all, a mandate just increases someone else's burden — and that means higher taxes at the state and local level.

Step eight: Congress should enact the bold reform proposals that are still awaiting congressional action — bank reform, civil justice reform, tort reform and my national energy strategy.

Finally, we must strengthen the family — because it is the family that has the greatest bearing on our future.

When Barbara holds an AIDS baby in her arms and reads to children, she's saying to every person in this country: Family matters.

New Commission on Families

And I am announcing tonight a new Commission on America's Urban Families. I've asked Missouri's governor, John Ashcroft, to be chairman, former Dallas Mayor Annette Strauss to be co-chair. You know, I had mayors from the League of Cities in the other day at the White House, and they told me something striking. They said that every one of them, Republicans and Democrats, agreed on one thing: that the major cause of the problems of the cities is the dissolution of the family.

And they asked for this commission, and they were right to ask, because it's time to determine what we can do to keep families together, strong and sound.

There's one thing we can do right away: Ease the burden of rearing a child. I ask you tonight to raise the personal exemption by $500 per child for every family.

For a family with four kids, that's an increase of $2,000. And this is a good start in the right direction, and it's what we can afford.

It's time to allow families to deduct the interest they pay on student loans.

I am asking you to do just that. And I'm asking you to allow people to use money from their IRAs to pay medical and education expenses — all without penalties.

And I'm asking for more. Ask American parents what they dislike about how things are in our country and chances are good that pretty soon they'll get to welfare. Americans are the most generous people on earth. But we have to go back to the insight of [President] Franklin Roosevelt who, when he spoke of what became the welfare program, warned that it must not become "a narcotic" and a "subtle destroyer" of the spirit.

Welfare was never meant to be a lifestyle; it was never meant to be a habit; it was never supposed to be passed from generation to generation like a legacy.

It's time to replace the assumptions of the welfare state and help reform the welfare system.

States throughout the country are beginning to operate with new assumptions: that when able-bodied people receive government assistance, they have responsibilities to the taxpayer, a responsibility to seek work, education or job training; a responsibility to get their lives in order; a responsibility to hold their families together and refrain from having children out of wedlock — and a responsibility to obey the law.

We are going to help this movement.

Often, state reform requires waiving certain federal regulations. I will act to make that process easier and quicker for every state that asks our help.

And I want to add, as we make these changes, we work together to improve this system, that our intention isn't scapegoating or fingerpointing. If you can read the papers or watch TV, you know there's been a rise these days in a certain kind of bitterness, racist comments, anti-Semitism, an increased sense of division.

Really, this is not us — this is not who we are. And this is not acceptable.

'Move on Together'

And so you have my plan for America. And I am asking for big things — but I believe in my heart you will do what's right.

And, you know, it's kind of an American tradition to show a certain skepticism toward our democratic institutions. I myself have sometimes thought the aging process could be delayed if it had to make its way through Congress.

You will deliberate, and you will discuss, and that is fine. But, my friends, the people cannot wait. They need help now.

And there is a mood among us. People are worried, there has been talk of decline. Someone even said our workers are lazy and uninspired.

And I thought, really, you go tell Neil Armstrong standing on the moon, tell the men and women who put him there, tell the American farmer who feeds his country and the world. Tell the men and women of Desert Storm.

Moods come and go, but greatness endures. Ours does. And maybe for a moment it's good to remember what, in the dailiness of our lives, we forget:

We are still and ever the freest nation on earth — the kindest nation on earth — the strongest nation on earth — and we have always risen to the occasion.

And we are going to lift this nation out of hard times inch by inch and day by day, and those who would stop us had better step aside — because I look at hard times and I make this vow: This will not stand.

And so we move on together, a rising nation, the once and future miracle that is still, this night, the hope of the world.

Thank you. God bless you. And God bless our beloved country. Thank you very, very much.

President Bush's Fiscal 1993 Budget Message

Following is the Congressional Record *text of President Bush's fiscal 1993 budget message sent to Congress Jan. 29, 1992.*

TO THE CONGRESS OF
THE UNITED STATES:

I am pleased to present the *Budget of the United States Government for Fiscal Year 1993.*

In the State of the Union message, which I delivered yesterday, I presented to the Congress and the Nation a comprehensive agenda for economic growth. I stated that we must not only get the economy moving again in the short term, but also set America firmly on the path toward long-term economic growth and competitiveness.

I emphasized in that message the importance of: stimulating the investment necessary to create jobs, addressing problems related to real estate and health care, improving America's capacity to compete in a global economy, eliminating unnecessary

Federal regulation, and accomplishing these objectives in a way that brings the deficit under control. I outlined specific incentives for investment, savings, and homeownership; tax relief for families; investments in the future; and proposals for reform in areas ranging from health to education.

This document translates the agenda for growth into a set of specific budget and policy recommendations. These are summarized in the Introduction and presented in detail in the chapters and appendices which follow.

I have asked the Congress to lay aside partisanship and to join me in enacting this growth agenda promptly. To that end, I pledge my full cooperation.

GEORGE BUSH

January 29, 1992

Bush Speech on Aid to Soviets

Following is the Reuter transcript of the statement President Bush made April 1, 1992, at the White House after presenting his assistance package for the nations of the former Soviet Union to the congressional leadership.

I have a statement that is a little longer than the normal, but let me just say that I have just met with the congressional leadership to request their bipartisan backing for a new, comprehensive and integrated program to support the struggle of freedom under way in Russia, Ukraine and the other new states that have replaced the Soviet Union.

The revolution in these states is a defining moment in history, with profound consequences for America's own national interest. The stakes are as high for us now as any that we have faced in this century, and our adversary for 45 years, the one nation that posed a worldwide threat to freedom and peace, is now seeking to join the community of democratic nations. A victory for democracy and freedom in the former U.S.S.R. creates the possibility of a new world of peace for our children and grandchildren.

But if this democratic revolution is defeated, it could plunge us into a world more dangerous in some respects than the dark years of the Cold War.

America must meet this challenge, joining with those who stood beside us in the battle against imperial communism: Germany, the United Kingdom, Japan, France, Canada, Italy and other allies. Together, we won the Cold War, and today we must win the peace.

This effort will require new resources from the industrial democracies, but nothing like the price we would pay if democracy and reform failed in Russia and Ukraine and Belarus and Armenia and the states of central Asia.

It will require the commitment of a united America strengthened by a consensus that transcends even the heated partisanship of a presidential election campaign.

And today I call upon Congress, Republicans and Democrats alike, and the American people, to stand behind this united effort. Our national effort must be part of a global effort. I've been in contact with [German] Chancellor [Helmut] Kohl, [British] Prime Minister [John] Major, [French] President [François] Mitterrand, other key allies, to discuss our plans and to assure them of the high priority I place on the success of this endeavor.

Supporting Democracy

To this end, I would like to announce today a plan to support democracy in the states of the former Soviet Union. This is a complex set of issues which took months to sort out, working within the administration, working with our major allies and with the leaders of the new independent states of the former Soviet Union. A number of things had to come together to make sure we got it right. Let me give you a little bit of the history.

I asked Secretary [of State James A.] Baker [III] to outline our fundamental approach in his Dec. 12 speech at Princeton. I spoke again on the need to embrace Russia and the other new states of the former Soviet Union in my Jan. 22 speech at the Washington conference to coordinate the humanitarian assistance. On Feb. 1, [Russian President] Boris [N.] Yeltsin and I discussed these issues at Camp David, and that same day [Treasury] Secretary [Nicholas F.] Brady met with Boris Yeltsin's key economic adviser, Yegor Gaidar, to discuss how we could support Russian reforms.

A week later Jim Baker followed up during his meeting with Kozyrev, [Russian] Foreign Minister [Andrei V.] Kozyrev and Boris Yeltsin in Moscow. And just yesterday the IMF [International Monetary Fund] reached tentative agreement with Russia on its market reform program.

After weeks of intensive consultations in the G-7 [group of seven leading industrial nations], Chancellor Kohl currently serving as chairman of the G-7, has announced today G-7 support for an IMF program for Russia. The program that I'm announcing today builds on this progress and includes three major components.

First, the United States has been working with its Western allies and the international financial institutions on an unprecedented multilateral program to support reform in the newly independent states. The success of this program will depend upon their commitment to reform and their willingness to work with the international community.

Russia is exhibiting that commitment, and I'm announcing today that the U.S. is prepared to join in a substantial multilateral financial assistance package in support of Russia's reforms. We're working to develop, with our allies and the IMF, a $6 billion currency stabilization fund, to help maintain confidence in the Russian ruble.

The U.S. will also join in a multilateral effort to marshal roughly $18 billion in financial support in 1992 to assist Russian efforts to stabilize and restructure their economy. We've been working with the Russian government for three months to help it develop an economic reform plan to permit the major industrialized countries to provide support.

We will work to complete action on this approximately $24 billion package by the end of April, and I pledge the full cooperation of the United States in this effort.

Second, the United States will also act to broaden its own capacity to extend assistance to the new states. I am transmitting to Congress a comprehensive bill — the Freedom Support Act — to mobilize the executive branch, the Congress, and indeed, our private sector, around a comprehensive and integrated package of support for the new states.

Now, this package will authorize a U.S. quota increase of $12 billion for the IMF, which is critical to supporting Russia and the other new states. The IMF and World Bank will be the primary sources of funding for the major financial assistance needs of the new governments.

The U.S. quota increase for the IMF was specifically assumed in the budget agreement and does not require a budget outlay.

Support my existing authority to work with the G-7 and the IMF to put together this stabilization program for Russia, and support possible subsequent programs for other states of the former Soviet Union, as they embark on landmark reforms, including up to $3 billion for stabilization funds.

It would also repeal restrictive Cold War legislation so that American business can compete on an even footing in these new markets. And I'm determined that American business be given the chance to invest in trade with the new states, and to that end, I've also directed that the United States negotiate trade and bilateral investment in tax treaties with these countries just as soon as possible.

Significant new trade relationships can create jobs right here in this country.

The package will broaden the use of $500 million appropriated by Congress last year to encompass not only the safe dismantling and destruction of nuclear weapons but also the broader goals of nuclear plant safety, demilitarization and defense conversion.

It will also establish a major people-to-people program between the United States and the states of the former Soviet Union to create the type of lasting personal bonds among our peoples and Russian understanding of democratic institutions so critical to long-term peace.

This effort will complement our existing programs to bring hundreds of businessmen to the United States from the Commonwealth [of Independent States] and then send hundreds of Peace Corps volunteers to the new states.

In sending this authorization legislation to Congress, I call upon the Congress to act concurrently to provide the appropriations necessary to make these authorizations a reality.

Third, in the addition to the $3.75 billion already extended by the [United States] since January 1991, I am announcing today $1.1 billion in new Commodity Credit Corporation credit guarantees for the purchase of American agricultural products; $600 million of that will go for U.S. sales to Russia and an additional $500 million for U.S. sales to Ukraine and other states.

Supporting Yeltsin

Now, let me close on a personal note. I think every day about the challenge of securing a peaceful future for the American future. And I believe very strongly that President Yeltsin's reform program holds the greatest hope for the future of the Russian people, and for the security of the American people, as we define a new relationship with that great country.

President Yeltsin has taken some very courageous steps for democracy and free markets. And I am convinced that it is in our own national interest to support him strongly.

For more than 45 years, the highest responsibility of nine American presidents, Democrats and Republicans, was to wage and win the Cold War. It was my privilege to work with [former President] Ronald Reagan on these broad programs, and now, to lead the American people in winning the peace by embracing the people so recently freed from tyranny, to welcome them into the community of democratic nations.

I know there are those who say we should pull back, concentrate our energies, our interest and our resources on our pressing domestic problems, and they are, they are very important.

But I ask them to think of the consequences here at home of peace in the world. We've got to act now.

And if we turn away, if we do not do what we can to help democracy succeed in the lands of the old Soviet Union, our failure to act will carry a far higher price, and if we face up to the challenge, matching the courage of President Yeltsin, of Ukrainian President [Leonid M.] Kravchuk, of Armenian President [Levon A.] Ter-Petrosyan.

And many other future generations of Americans will thank us for having had the foresight and the conviction to stand up for democracy and work for peace in this decade and into the next century.

That is the end of this statement. I'll be glad to take just a handful of questions, and then Jim Baker and Secretary Brady will — I think Secretary Brady will go into more detail on the legislation, and Secretary Brady and others will be available. I think [Agriculture Secretary Edward R.] Madigan will talk to you about the agricultural sector of it.

Bush, Yeltsin on Arms Reductions and POWs

Following is the Reuter transcript of the joint announcement June 16, 1992, by President Bush and Russian President Boris N. Yeltsin on the new strategic arms agreement and on the POW/MIA question. Yeltsin spoke through an interpreter.

PRESIDENT BUSH: ... Let me just say that I'm pleased to announce that President Yeltsin and I have just reached an extraordinary agreement on two areas of vital importance to our countries and to the world. First, we have agreed on far-reaching new strategic arms reductions, building on the agreement reached with Russia, Ukraine, Kazakhstan and Belarus. Our two countries are now agreeing to even further dramatic strategic arms reductions substantially below the levels determined by START [strategic arms reduction treaty].

We have agreed to eliminate the world's most dangerous weapons, heavy ICBMs [intercontinental ballistic missiles], and all other multiple-warhead ICBMs, and dramatically reduce our total strategic nuclear weapons.

Those dramatic reductions will take place in two phases. They will be completed no later than the year 2003 and may be completed as early as the year 2000 if the United States can assist Russia in the required destruction of ballistic missile systems.

With this agreement, the nuclear nightmare recedes more and more for ourselves, for our children and for our grandchildren.

Just a few years ago, the United States was planning a strategic nuclear stockpile of about 13,000 warheads. Now President Yeltsin and I have agreed that both sides will go down to 3,000 to 3,500 warheads, with each nation determining its own force structure within that range.

And I'd like to point out that this fundamental agreement, which in earlier years could not have been completed even in a decade, has been completed in only five months.

Our ability to reach this agreement so quickly is a tribute to the new relationship between the United States and Russia and to the personal leadership of our guest, Boris Yeltsin.

In the near future, the United States and Russia will record our agreement in a brief treaty document that President Yeltsin and I will sign and submit for ratification in our countries.

President Yeltsin and I have also agreed to work together, along with the allies and other interested states, to develop a concept for a global protection system against limited ballistic missile attack.

And we will explore a senior group — or we will establish a senior group — to explore practical steps toward that end, including the sharing of early warning and cooperation in developing ballistic missile defense capabilities and technologies.

This group will also explore the development of a legal basis for cooperation, including new treaties and agreements, and possible changes to existing treaties and agreements necessary to implement the global protection system.

That group is headed by [Policy Planning State Director] Dennis Ross for the United States [and] will first meet in Moscow within the next 30 days.

In conclusion, these are remarkable steps for our two countries, a departure from the tensions and the suspicions of the past, and a tangible, important expression of our new relationship. They also hold major promise for a future world protected against the danger of limited ballistic missile attack.

Yeltsin Responds

PRESIDENT YELTSIN: Mr. President, ladies and gentlemen, I'd like to add a few words to what President Bush has just announced here.

What we have achieved is an unparalleled and probably an unexpected thing for you and for the whole world. You are the first to hear about this historic decision, which has been reached today after just five months of negotiations. We are in fact meeting a sharp, dramatic reduction in the total number for the two sides of the number of nuclear warheads, from 21,000 to 6,000 or 7,000 for the United States of America and Russia.

Indeed, we have been able to cut over those five months of negotiations the total number of nuclear warheads to one-third, while it took 15 years under the START treaty to make some reductions.

This is an expression of the fundamental change in the political and economic relations between the United States of America and Russia.

It is also an expression and a proof of the personal trust and confidence that has been established between the presidents of these countries, President Bush of the United States of America and [the] president of Russia, and these things have been achieved without deception, without anybody wishing to gain unilateral advantages.

This is a result of the trust entertained by the president of democratic Russia toward America and by the president of the United States toward the new Russia.

This is the result of a carefully measured balance of security. We were not going in for numbers, for just 1,000, 2,000 or 3,000 pieces. Rather we have established a record for each country to elect the number, the figure that it will consider appropriate for its own defense and security.

As I have told you, the total number will go down from 21,000 to 6,000 for the two sides. Under the first phase, the reductions for the two sides will be down to the 3,800-to-4,250 bracket: including ICBMs, 1,250; and heavy missiles, 650; SLBMs [submarine-launched ballistic missiles], 2,250. Under the second phase we shall go down to, respectively, 3,000 and 3,500, including total reduction and destruction of heavy missiles.

Land-based MIRVs [multiple independently targetable reentry vehicles] will be reduced as well. SLBMs will go down to 1,750.

Each country will elect the figure that it will consider appropriate to ensure its defense and security.

Thus we are departing from the ominous parity where each country was exerting every effort to stay in line, which has led Russia, for instance, to have half of its population living below the poverty line. We cannot afford it, and therefore we must have a minimum-security level to deal with any possible eventuality which might arise anywhere in the world and threaten our security.

But we know one thing: We shall not fight against each other. This is a solemn undertaking that we are taking today, and it will be reflected as a matter of partnership and friendship in the charter that we are going to sign.

Our proposal is to cut the process of destruction from the proposed 13 years down to nine years. So the things that I have been mentioning before will materialize by the year 2000.

I am happy to be involved here in this historic occasion, and I will also hope that I will be as happy when this thing materializes and President Bush and I will be celebrating together the implementation of that agreement in the year 2000.

I thank you.

I want to add that these figures have been agreed with and ratified by the secretary for Defense, Mr. [Dick] Cheney, and the defense minister, Pavel Grachev, of the Russian Federation.

I thank you.

P: And I would only add to that my gratitude to the secretary of State, to Mr. [Andrei V.] Kozyrev, his counterpart, and also to Gen. [Brent] Scowcroft and others that have worked on this and accomplished all this in record time....

Q: Would you explain for people who might not understand why friends who trust each other and who do not plan to attack would still need 7,000 nuclear warheads —

P: What I'm saying is, we've moved dramatically down from 13,000. It's going to be a — this will be seen as an enormous move forward toward the relaxation of tension and toward the friendship that we feel for each other.

The elimination of these — the most destabilizing of weapons — is extraordinarily positive. And the fact that each country at this juncture in history retains some nuclear weapons speaks for itself.

Who knows what lies out there ahead? But certainly I agree with what President Yeltsin said, that there is no animosity. The Cold War days are over, and he came here in a spirit of forward movement on these arms control agreements, and that speaks for itself.

YELTSIN: I would like to amplify on that.

I would say that in response to your question that the technical and financial resources that are required in order to destroy, dismantle and reduce the total number of warheads and missiles from 21,000 to 6,000 or 7,000 is enormous, and this is the only thing that conditions this figure.

American POWs

Q: [Question on the status of possible American POWs in Russia].

P: .... President Yeltsin and I discussed this morning the issue that is of the highest priority for our administration and, I know, for every American — the fate of American POWs and MIAs from World War II, Korea, the Cold War period and Vietnam.

President Yeltsin informed me for the first time that Russia may have information about the fate of some of our servicemen from Vietnam. And he said the Russian government is pursuing this information vigorously, just as we speak.

And with us today are President Yeltsin's adviser, Dmitri Volkogonov over here, and our able former ambassador to the U.S.S.R., Ambassador Malcolm Toon. Now they are the co-chairs of the Joint U.S.-Russian Commission on POW-MIAs, and they've met during the last few months along with the members of the United States Congress who are also part of this bipartisan U.S. delegation to unearth information on American POWs and MIAs from 1945 on, and Russian POWs and MIAs from the Afghan war.

President Yeltsin and I have instructed both of these gentlemen to begin immediately a joint U.S.-Russian pursuit of the latest information — it was given to me today.

I have asked Ambassador Toon to return immediately to Moscow to work on this issue, and I want to assure all Americans, and particularly those families of the American POWs and MIAs, that we will spare no effort in working with our Russian colleagues to investigate all information in the Russian archives concerning our servicemen.

And while we do not have any specific information to make public today, I pledge to keep the American people informed of developments on this issue as we find out more about these latest leads.

And let me just point out that the forthcoming comments by President Yeltsin are just one more sign of this improved new relationship between Russia and the United States of America. For him to go back and dig into these records, without fear of embarrassment, is of enormous consequence to the people of the United States of America.

And I salute him for this. He has told me he will go the last mile to find whatever ... [information exists about] American POWs and MIAs, and to clear this record once and for all, and in so many other fields this demonstrates his leadership and the period of change that we are saluting and I saluted here today on the South Lawn of the White House. So we're very grateful to you, Mr. President.

YELTSIN: I will only add a couple of points, Mr. President.

Our commission, headed and chaired by Dmitri Volkogonov, has been meeting for several months now, and it has already met with some success, and I can promise that the joint commission which will be established following this press conference will be working hard and will report to the American public all the information that will be found in the archives that we are going to open for it, in . . . [opening] the archives in the KGB, in the Central Committee of the Communist Party, regarding the fate of American POWs and MIAs.

Q: Do you agree it's possible some of those Americans may still be alive?

P: I would simply say that this — I have no evidence of that, but the cooperation that is, has been extended, and again is being extended by the president of Russia will guarantee to the American people that if anyone's alive, that person, those people would be found. And equally as important to the loved ones is the accounting for any possible MIA.

And so we have no evidence of anyone being alive, but I would simply say again that this, this is the best way to get to the bottom of it, and this new approach by the president of Russia to go into these archives and to try to find missing records will be the best assurance that I can give the American people that the truth will, will be revealed, finally.

Q: Is there a danger of raising false hopes?

P: You got to be careful of that, yeah.

Bush Address on Sending Forces to Somalia

Following is the Reuter transcript of President Bush's Dec. 4, 1992, address to the nation announcing troop deployments to Somalia.

I want to talk to you today about the tragedy in Somalia, and about a mission that can ease suffering and save lives. Every American has seen the shocking images from Somalia; the scope of suffering there is hard to imagine. Already, over a quarter-million people, as many people as live in Buffalo, New York, have died in the Somali famine. In the months ahead, five times that number — 1.5 million people — could starve to death.

For many months now, the United States has been actively engaged in the massive international relief effort to ease Somalia's suffering. All told, America has sent Somalia 200,000 tons of food, more than half the world total. This summer, the distribution system broke down. Truck convoys from Somalia's ports were blocked. Sufficient food failed to reach the starving in the interior of Somalia.

And so in August we took additional action in concert with the United Nations. We sent in the U.S. Air Force to help fly food to the towns. To date, American pilots have flown over 1,400 flights, delivering over 17,000 tons of food aid. And when the U.N. authorized 3,500 U.N. guards to protect the relief operation, we flew in the first of them, 500 soldiers from Pakistan.

But in the months since then, the security situation has grown worse. The U.N. has been prevented from deploying its initial commitment of troops. In many cases, food from relief flights is being looted upon landing. Food convoys have been hijacked, aid workers assaulted, ships with food have been subject to artillery attacks that prevented them from docking.

There is no government in Somalia. Law and order have broken down. Anarchy prevails. One image tells the story: Imagine 7,000 tons of food aid literally bursting out of a warehouse on a dock in Mogadishu while Somalis starve less than a kilometer away because relief workers cannot run the gauntlet of armed gangs roving the city.

Confronted with these conditions, relief groups called for outside troops to provide security so they could feed people. It's now clear that military support is necessary to ensure the safe delivery of the food Somalis need to survive.

It was this situation which led us to tell the United Nations that the United States would be willing to provide more help to enable relief to be delivered. Last night the United Nations Security Council, by unanimous vote and after the tireless efforts of Secretary-General [Boutros] Boutros-Ghali, welcomed the United States' offer to lead a coalition to get the food through.

After consulting with my advisers, with world leaders and the congressional leadership, I have today told Secretary-General Boutros-Ghali that America will answer the call. I have given the order to [Defense] Secretary [Dick] Cheney to move a substantial American force into Somalia. As I speak, a Marine amphibious ready group, which we maintain at sea, is offshore Mogadishu. These troops will be joined by elements of the First Marine Expeditionary Force based out of Camp Pendleton, California, and by the Army's 10th Mountain Division out of Fort Drum, New York.

These and other American forces will assist in Operation Restore Hope. They are America's finest. They will perform this mission with courage and compassion and they will succeed.

The people of Somalia, especially the children of Somalia, need our help. We're able to ease their suffering. We must help them live. We must give them hope. America must act.

In taking this action I want to emphasize that I understand the United States alone cannot right the world's wrongs, but we also know that some crises in the world cannot be resolved without American involvement. That American action is often necessary as a catalyst for broader involvement in the community of nations. Only the United States has the global reach to place a large security force on the ground in such a distant place, quickly and efficiently, and thus save thousands of innocents from death. We will not, however, be acting alone.

I expect forces from about a dozen countries to join us in this mission. When we see Somalia's children starving, all of America hurts. We've tried to help in many ways, and make no mistake about it — now we and our allies will ensure that aid gets through. And here is what we and our coalition partners will do.

First, we will create a secure environment in the hardest-hit parts of Somalia, so that food can move from ships overland to the people in the countryside now devastated by starvation. And second, once we have created that secure environment, we will withdraw our troops, handing the security mission back to a regular U.N. peacekeeping force.

Our mission has a limited objective — to open the supply routes, to get the food moving and to prepare the way for a U.N. peacekeeping force to keep it moving.

This operation is not open-ended. We will not stay one day longer than is absolutely necessary. And let me be very clear. Our mission is humanitarian, but we will not tolerate armed gangs ripping off their own people, condemning them to death by starvation. General [Joseph P.] Hoar and his troops have the authority to take whatever military action is necessary to safeguard the lives of our troops and the lives of Somalia's people.

The outlaw elements in Somalia must understand this is serious business. We will accomplish our mission. We have no intent to remain in Somalia with fighting forces, but we are determined to do it right, to secure an environment that will allow food to get to the starving people of Somalia. To the people of Somalia I promise this: We do not plan to dictate political outcomes. We respect your sovereignty and independence.

Based on my conversations with other coalition leaders, I can state with confidence we come to your country for one reason only: to enable the starving to be fed.

And let me say to the men and women of our armed forces, we're asking you to do a difficult and dangerous job. As commander in chief, I assure you you will have our full support to get the job done. And we will bring you home as soon as possible.

And finally, let me close with a message to the families of the men and women who take part in this mission.

I understand it is difficult to see your loved ones go, to send them off knowing they will not be home for the holidays. But the humanitarian mission they undertake is in the finest traditions of service.

And so to every sailor, soldier, airman and Marine who is involved in this mission, let me say, you're doing God's work. We will not fail.

Thank you and may God bless the United States of America.

Bush Proclamation Granting Iran-Contra Pardons

Following is the White House text of President Bush's Dec. 24, 1992, proclamation granting a pardon to six people indicted in the Iran-contra affair.

Today I am exercising my power under the Constitution to pardon former Secretary of Defense Caspar Weinberger and others for their conduct related to the Iran-Contra affair.

For more than 6 years now, the American people have invested enormous resources into what has become the most thoroughly investigated matter of its kind in our history. During that time, the last American hostage has come home to freedom, worldwide terrorism has declined, the people of Nicaragua have elected a democratic government, and the Cold War has ended in victory for the American people and the cause of freedom we championed.

In the mid 1980's, however, the outcome of these struggles was far from clear. Some of the best and most dedicated of our countrymen were called upon to step forward. Secretary Weinberger was among the foremost.

Caspar Weinberger is a true American patriot. He has rendered long and extraordinary service to our country. He served for 4 years in the Army during World War II where his bravery earned him a Bronze Star. He gave up a lucrative career in private life to accept a series of public positions in the late 1960's and 1970's, including Chairman of the Federal Trade Commission, Director of the Office of Management and Budget, and Secretary of Health, Education and Welfare. Caspar Weinberger was one of the principal architects of the downfall of the Berlin Wall and the Soviet Union. He directed the military renaissance in this country that led to the breakup of the communist bloc and a new birth of freedom and democracy. Upon his resignation in 1987, Caspar Weinberger was awarded the highest civilian medal our Nation can bestow on one of its citizens, the Presidential Medal of Freedom.

Secretary Weinberger's legacy will endure beyond the ending of the Cold War. The military readiness of this Nation that he in large measure created could not have been better displayed than it was 2 years ago in the Persian Gulf and today in Somalia.

As Secretary Weinberger's pardon request noted, it is a bitter irony that on the day the first charges against Secretary Weinberger were filed, Russian President Boris Yeltsin arrived in the United States to celebrate the end of the Cold War. I am pardoning him not just out of compassion or to spare a 75-year-old patriot the torment of lengthy and costly legal proceedings, but to make it possible for him to receive the honor he deserves for his extraordinary service to our country.

Moreover, on a somewhat more personal note, I cannot ignore the debilitating illnesses faced by Caspar Weinberger and his wife. When he resigned as Secretary of Defense, it was because of his wife's cancer. In the years since he left public service, her condition has not improved. In addition, since that time, he also has become ill. Nevertheless, Caspar Weinberger has been a pillar of strength for his wife; this pardon will enable him to be by her side undistracted by the ordeal of a costly and arduous trial.

I have also decided to pardon five other individuals for their conduct related to the Iran-Contra affair: [former Assistant Secretary of State] Elliott Abrams, [former CIA official] Duane Clarridge, [former CIA official] Alan Fiers, [former CIA official] Clair George, and [former National Security Adviser] Robert McFarlane. First, the common denominator of their motivation —whether their actions were right or wrong — was patriotism. Second, they did not profit or seek to profit from their conduct. Third, each has a record of long and distinguished service to this country. And finally, all five have already paid a price — in depleted savings, lost careers, anguished families — grossly disproportionate to any misdeeds or errors of judgment they may have committed.

The prosecutions of the individuals I am pardoning represent what I believe is a profoundly troubling development in the political and legal climate of our country: the criminalization of policy differences. These differences should be addressed in the political arena, without the Damocles sword of criminality hanging over the heads of some of the combatants. The proper target is the President, not his subordinates; the proper forum is the voting booth, not the courtroom.

In recent years, the use of criminal processes in policy disputes has become all too common. It is my hope that the action I am taking today will begin to restore these disputes to the battleground where they properly belong.

In addition, the actions of the men I am pardoning took place within the larger Cold War struggle. At home, we had a long, sometimes heated debate about how that struggle should be waged. Now the Cold War is over. When earlier wars have ended, Presidents have historically used their power to pardon to put bitterness behind us and look to the future. This healing tradition reaches at least from James Madison's pardon of Lafitte's pirates after the War of 1812, to Andrew Johnson's pardon of soldiers who had fought for the Confederacy, to Harry Truman's and Jimmy Carter's pardons of those who violated the selective service laws in World War II and Vietnam.

In many cases, the offenses pardoned by these Presidents were at least as serious as those I am pardoning today. The actions of those pardoned and the decisions to pardon them raised important issues of conscience, the rule of law, and the relationship under our Constitution between the government and the governed. Notwithstanding the seriousness of these issues and the passions they aroused, my predecessors acted because it was time for the country to move on. Today I do the same.

Some may argue that this decision will prevent full disclosure of some new key fact to the American people. That is not true. This matter has been investigated exhaustively. The Tower Board, the Joint Congressional Committee charged with investigating the Iran-Contra affair, and the Independent Counsel have looked into every aspect of this matter. The Tower Board interviewed more than 80 people and reviewed thousands of documents. The Joint Congressional Committee interviewed more than 500 people and reviewed more than 300,000 pages of material. Lengthy committee hearings were held and broadcast on national television to millions of Americans. And as I have noted, the Independent Counsel investigation has gone on for more than 6 years, and it has cost more than $31 million.

Moreover, the Independent Counsel stated last September that he had completed the active phase of his investigation. He will have the opportunity to place his full assessment of the facts in the public record when he submits his final report. While no impartial person has seriously suggested that my own role in this matter is legally questionable, I have further requested that the Independent Counsel provide me with a copy of my sworn testimony to his office, which I am prepared to release immediately. And I understand Secretary Weinberger has requested the release of all of his notes pertaining to the Iran-Contra matter.

For more than 30 years in public service, I have tried to follow three precepts: honor, decency, and fairness. I know, from all those years of service, that the American people believe in fairness and fair play. In granting these pardons today, I am doing what I believe honor, decency, and fairness require.

NOW, THEREFORE, I, George Bush, President of the United States of America, pursuant to my power under Article II, Section 2, of the Constitution, do hereby grant a full, complete, and unconditional pardon to Elliott Abrams, Duane R. Clarridge, Alan Fiers, Clair George, Robert C. McFarlane, and Caspar Weinberger for all offenses charged or prosecuted by Independent Counsel Lawrence E. Walsh or other members of his office, or committed by these individuals and within the jurisdiction of that office.

IN WITNESS WHEREOF, I have hereunto set my hand this twenty-fourth day of December, in the year of our Lord nineteen hundred and ninety-two, and of the Independence of the United States of America the two hundred and seventeenth.

Political Charts

Victorious Party in Presidential Races	*1225*
Presidential Elections, 1860-1992	*1226*
1988 Presidential Election	*1228*
1992 Presidential Election	*1229*
1992 Electoral Votes	*1230*
Republican Convention Balloting	*1231*
Democratic Convention Balloting	*1232*
House Seats and Electoral Votes	*1233*
Political Party Affiliations	*1234*
House Election Results, 1948-92	*1236*
101st Congress Special Elections	*1238*
1990 Election Returns	*1240*
102nd Congress Special Elections	*1248*
1992 Election Returns	*1250*
Governors, 1989-92	*1259*

Victorious Party in Presidential Races, 1860-1992

State	1860	1864	1868	1872	1876	1880	1884	1888	1892	1896	1900	1904	1908	1912	1916	1920	1924	1928	1932	1936	1940	1944	1948	1952	1956	1960	1964	1968	1972	1976	1980	1984	1988	1992	Number of Times Parties Won: Dem.	Rep.	Other
Ala.	SD	[b]	R	R	D	D	D	D	D	D	D	D	D	D	D	D	D	D	D	D	D	D	SR	D	D[r]	D[s]	R	AI	R	D	R	R	R	R	22	8	3
Alaska																										R	D	R	R	R	R	R	R	R	1	8	0
Ariz.														D	D	R	R	R	D	D	D	D	D	R	R	R	R	R	R	R	R	R	R	R	7	14	0
Ark.	SD	[b]	R	[d]	D	D	D	D	D	D	D	D	D	D	D	D	D	D	D	D	D	D	D	D	D	D	D	AI	R	D	R	R	R	D	25	5	2
Calif.	R	R	R	R	R	D[f]	R	R	D[g]	R[l]	R	R	R	PR	D	R	R	R	D	D	D	D	D	R	R	R	D	R	R	R	R	R	R	D	10	23	1
Colo.					R	R	R	R	PP	D	D	R	D	D	D	R	R	R	D	D	R	R	D	R	R	R	D	R	R	R	R	R	R	D	10	19	1
Conn.	R	R	R	R	D	R	D	D	D	R	R	R	R	D	R	R	R	R	R	D	D	D	R	R	R	D	D	D	R	R	R	R	R	D	12	22	0
Del.	SD	D	D	R	D	D	D	D	D	R	R	R	R	D	R	R	R	R	R	D	D	D	R	R	R	D	D	R	R	D	R	R	R	D	15	18	1
D.C.																											D	D	D	D	D	D	D	D	8	0	0
Fla.	SD	[b]	R	R	R	D	D	D	D	D	D	D	D	D	D	D	D	R	D	D	D	D	D	R	R	R	D	R	R	D	R	R	R	R	19	13	1
Ga.	SD	[b]	D	D[e]	D	D	D	D	D	D	D	D	D	D	D	D	D	D	D	D	D	D	D	D	D	D	R	AI	R	D	D	R	R	D	27	4	2
Hawaii																										D	D	D	R	D	D	R	D	D	7	2	0
Idaho									PP	D	D	R	R	D	D	R	R	R	D	D	D	D	D	R	R	R	D	R	R	R	R	R	R	R	10	15	1
Ill.	R	R	R	R	R	R	R	R	D	R	R	R	R	D	R	R	R	R	D	D	D	D	D	R	R	D	D	R	R	R	R	R	R	D	10	24	0
Ind.	R	R	R	R	D	R	D	R	D	R	R	R	R	D	R	R	R	R	D	D	R	R	R	R	R	R	D	R	R	R	R	R	R	R	7	27	0
Iowa	R	R	R	R	R	R	R	R	R	R	R	R	R	D	R	R	R	R	D	D	R	R	D	R	R	R	D	R	R	R	R	R	D	D	7	27	0
Kan.		R	R	R	R	R	R	R	PP	D	R	R	R	D	D	R	R	R	D	D	R	R	R	R	R	R	D	R	R	R	R	R	R	R	6	26	1
Ky.	CU	D	D	D	D	D	D	D	D	R[m]	D	D	D	D	D	D	R	R	D	D	D	D	D	D	R	R	D	R	R	D	R	R	R	D	23	10	1
La.	SD	[b]	D	[d]	R	D	D	D	D	D	D	D	D	D	D	D	D	D	D	D	D	D	SR	D	R	D	R	AI	R	D	R	R	R	D	22	7	3
Maine	R	R	R	R	R	R	R	R	R	R	R	R	R	D	R	R	R	R	R	R	R	R	R	R	R	R	D	D	R	R	R	R	R	D	4	30	0
Md.	SD	R	D	D	D	D	D	D	D	R	R	D[n]	D[o]	D	D	R	R	R	D	D	D	D	R	R	R	D	D	D	R	D	D	R	R	D	21	12	1
Mass.	R	R	R	R	R	R	R	R	R	R	R	R	R	D	R	R	R	D	D	D	D	D	D	R	R	D	D	D	D	D	R	R	D	D	14	20	0
Mich.	R	R	R	R	R	R	R	R	R[h]	R	R	R	R	PR	R	R	R	R	D	D	R	D	R	R	R	D	D	D	R	R	R	R	R	D	7	26	1
Minn.	R	R	R	R	R	R	R	R	R	R	R	R	R	PR	R	R	R	R	D	D	D	D	D	R	R	D	D	D	R	D	D	D	D	D	13	20	1
Miss.	SD	[b]	[c]	R	D	D	D	D	D	D	D	D	D	D	D	D	D	D	D	D	D	D	SR	D	D	[t]	R	AI	R	D	R	R	R	R	21	7	3
Mo.	D	R	R	D	D	D	D	D	D	D	D	R	R	D	D	R	R	R	D	D	D	D	D	R	D	D	D	R	R	D	R	R	R	D	21	13	0
Mont.									R	D	D	R	R	D	D	R	R	R	D	D	D	D	D	R	R	R	D	R	R	R	R	R	R	D	11	15	0
Neb.			R	R	R	R	R	R	R	D	R	R	D	D	D	R	R	R	D	D	R	R	R	R	R	R	D	R	R	R	R	R	R	R	7	25	0
Nev.		R	R	R	R	D	R	R	PP	D	D	R	D	D	D	R	R	R	D	D	D	D	D	R	R	D	D	R	R	R	R	R	R	D	14	18	1
N.H.	R	R	R	R	R	R	R	R	R	R	R	R	R	D	D	R	R	R	R	D	D	D	R	R	R	R	D	R	R	R	R	R	R	D	7	27	0
N.J.	R[a]	D	D	R	D	D	D	D	D	R	R	R	R	D	R	R	R	R	D	D	D	D	R	R	R	D	D	R	R	R	R	R	R	D	15	19	0
N.M.														D	D	R	R	R	D	D	D	D	D	R	R	D	D	R	R	R	R	R	R	D	10	11	0
N.Y.	R	R	D	R	D	R	D	R	D	R	R	R	R	D	R	R	R	R	D	D	D	D	R	R	R	D	D	D	R	D	R	R	D	D	15	19	0
N.C.	SD	[b]	R	R	D	D	D	D	D	D	D	D	D	D	D	D	D	R	D	D	D	D	D	D	D	D	D	R[v]	R	D	R	R	R	R	23	9	1
N.D.									[i]	R	R	R	R	D	D	R	R	R	D	D	R	R	R	R	R	R	D	R	R	R	R	R	R	R	5	20	1
Ohio	R	R	R	R	R	R	R	R	R[j]	R	R	R	R	D	D	R	R	R	D	D	D	R	D	R	R	R	D	R	R	D	R	R	R	D	9	25	0
Okla.													D	D	D	R	D	R	D	D	D	D	D	R	R	R[u]	D	R	R	R	R	R	R	R	10	12	0
Ore.	R	R	D	R	R	R	R	R	R[k]	R	R	R	R	D	R	R	R	R	D	D	D	D	R	R	R	R	D	R	R	R	R	R	D	D	9	25	0
Pa.	R	R	R	R	R	R	R	R	R	R	R	R	R	PR	R	R	R	R	R	D	D	D	R	R	R	D	D	D	R	D	R	R	R	D	8	25	1
R.I.	R	R	R	R	R	R	R	R	R	R	R	R	R	D	R	R	R	D	D	D	D	D	D	R	R	D	D	D	R	D	D	R	D	D	14	20	0
S.C.	SD	[b]	R	R	R	D	D	D	D	D	D	D	D	D	D	D	D	D	D	D	D	D	SR	D	D	D	R	R	R	D	R	R	R	R	21	10	2
S.D.									R	D	R	R	R	PR	R	R	R	R	D	D	R	R	R	R	R	R	D	R	R	R	R	R	R	R	4	21	1
Tenn.	CU	[b]	R	D	D	D	D	D	D	D	D	D	D	D	D	R	D	R	D	D	D	D	D[q]	R	R	R	D	R	R	D	R	R	R	D	21	11	1
Texas	SD	[b]	[c]	D	D	D	D	D	D	D	D	D	D	D	D	D	D	R	D	D	D	D	D	R	R	D	D	D	R	D	R	R	R	R	23	8	1
Utah										D	R	R	R	R	D	R	R	R	D	D	D	D	D	R	R	R	D	R	R	R	R	R	R	R	8	17	0
Vt.	R	R	R	R	R	R	R	R	R	R	R	R	R	R	R	R	R	R	R	R	R	R	R	R	R	R	D	R	R	R	R	R	R	D	2	32	0
Va.	CU	[b]	[c]	R	D	D	D	D	D	D	D	D	D	D	D	D	D	R	D	D	D	D	D	R	R	R	D	R	R[w]	R	R	R	R	R	19	12	1
Wash.									R	D	R	R	R	PR	D	R	R	R	D	D	D	D	D	R	R	R	D	D	R	R[x]	R	R	D	D	11	14	1
W.Va.		R	R	R	D	D	D	D	D	R	R	R	R	D	R[p]	R	R	R	D	D	D	D	D	D	R	D	D	D	R	D	D	R	D[y]	D	19	14	0
Wis.	R	R	R	R	R	R	R	R	D	R	R	R	R	D	R	R	PR	R	D	D	D	R	D	R	R	R	D	R	R	D	R	R	D	D	10	23	1
Wyo.									R	D	R	R	R	D	D	R	R	R	D	D	D	R	D	R	R	R	D	R	R	R	R	R	R	R	8	18	0
Winning Party	R	R	R	R	R	R	D	R	D	R	R	R	R	D	D	R	R	R	D	D	D	D	D	R	R	D	D	R	R	D	R	R	R	D	13	21	0

Note: With the exception of the District of Columbia, blanks indicate states not yet admitted to the Union. The District of Columbia received the presidential vote in 1961.

Key: A—American Party; AI—American Independent Party; CU—Constitutional Union Party; D—Democratic Party; PP—People's Party; PR—Progressive (Bull Moose) Party; R—Republican Party; SD—Southern Democratic Party; SR—States' Rights Party.

[a] Four electors voted Republican; three, Democratic.
[b] Confederate states did not vote in 1864.
[c] Did not vote in 1868.
[d] Votes were not counted.
[e] Three votes for Greeley not counted.
[f] Five electors voted Democratic; one, Republican.
[g] Eight electors voted Democratic; one, Republican.
[h] Nine electors voted Republican; five, Democratic.
[i] One vote each for Democratic, Republican and People's party.
[j] Twenty-two electors voted Republican; one, Democratic.
[k] Three electors voted Republican; one, People's Party.
[l] Eight electors voted Republican; one, Democratic.
[m] Twelve electors voted Republican; one, Democratic.
[n] Seven electors voted Democratic; one, Republican.
[o] Six electors voted Democratic; two, Republican.
[p] Seven electors voted Republican; one, Democratic.
[q] Eleven electors voted Democratic; one, States' Rights.
[r] One elector voted for Walter B. Jones.
[s] Six of eleven electors voted for Harry F. Byrd.
[t] Eight independent electors voted for Byrd.
[u] One vote cast for Byrd.
[v] Twelve electors voted Republican; one, American Independent.
[w] One elector voted Libertarian.
[x] One elector voted for Ronald Reagan.
[y] One elector voted for Lloyd Bentsen.

Summary of American...

YEAR	NO. OF STATES	CANDIDATES		ELECTORAL VOTE		POPULAR VOTE	
		DEM.	GOP	DEM.	GOP	DEM.	GOP
1860[a]	33	Stephen A. Douglas Herschel V. Johnson	Abraham Lincoln Hannibal Hamlin	12 4%	180 59%	1,380,202 29.5%	1,865,908 39.8%
1864[b]	36	George B. McClellan George H. Pendleton	Abraham Lincoln Andrew Johnson	21 9%	212 91%	1,812,807 45.0%	2,218,388 55.0%
1868[c]	37	Horatio Seymour Francis P. Blair Jr.	Ulysses S. Grant Schuyler Colfax	80 27%	214 73%	2,708,744 47.3%	3,013,650 52.7%
1872[d]	37	Horace Greeley Benjamin Gratz Brown	Ulysses S. Grant Henry Wilson	(d)	286 78%	2,834,761 43.8%	3,598,235 55.6%
1876	38	Samuel J. Tilden Thomas A. Hendricks	Rutherford B. Hayes William A. Wheeler	184 50%	185 50%	4,288,546 51.0%	4,034,311 47.9%
1880	38	Winfield S. Hancock William H. English	James A. Garfield Chester A. Arthur	155 42%	214 58%	4,444,260 48.2%	4,446,158 48.3%
1884	38	Grover Cleveland Thomas A. Hendricks	James G. Blaine John A. Logan	219 55%	182 45%	4,874,621 48.5%	4,848,936 48.2%
1888	38	Grover Cleveland Allen G. Thurman	Benjamin Harrison Levi P. Morton	168 42%	233 58%	5,534,488 48.6%	5,443,892 47.8%
1892[e]	44	Grover Cleveland Adlai E. Stevenson	Benjamin Harrison Whitelaw Reid	277 62%	145 33%	5,551,883 46.1%	5,179,244 43.0%
1896	45	William J. Bryan Arthur Sewall	William McKinley Garret A. Hobart	176 39%	271 61%	6,511,495 46.7%	7,108,480 51.0%
1900	45	William J. Bryan Adlai E. Stevenson	William McKinley Theodore Roosevelt	155 35%	292 65%	6,358,345 45.5%	7,218,039 51.7%
1904	45	Alton B. Parker Henry G. Davis	Theodore Roosevelt Charles W. Fairbanks	140 29%	336 71%	5,028,898 37.6%	7,626,593 56.4%
1908	46	William J. Bryan John W. Kern	William H. Taft James S. Sherman	162 34%	321 66%	6,406,801 43.0%	7,676,258 51.6%
1912[f]	48	Woodrow Wilson Thomas R. Marshall	William H. Taft James S. Sherman	435 82%	8 2%	6,293,152 41.8%	3,486,333 23.2%
1916	48	Woodrow Wilson Thomas R. Marshall	Charles E. Hughes Charles W. Fairbanks	277 52%	254 48%	9,126,300 49.2%	8,546,789 46.1%
1920	48	James M. Cox Franklin D. Roosevelt	Warren G. Harding Calvin Coolidge	127 24%	404 76%	9,140,884 34.2%	16,133,314 60.3%
1924[g]	48	John W. Davis Charles W. Bryant	Calvin Coolidge Charles G. Dawes	136 26%	382 72%	8,386,169 28.8%	15,717,553 54.1%
1928	48	Alfred E. Smith Joseph T. Robinson	Herbert C. Hoover Charles Curtis	87 16%	444 84%	15,000,185 40.8%	21,411,991 58.2%
1932	48	Franklin D. Roosevelt John N. Garner	Herbert C. Hoover Charles Curtis	472 89%	59 11%	22,825,016 57.4%	15,758,397 39.6%
1936	48	Franklin D. Roosevelt John N. Garner	Alfred M. Landon Frank Knox	523 98%	8 2%	27,747,636 60.8%	16,679,543 36.5%
1940	48	Franklin D. Roosevelt Henry A. Wallace	Wendell L. Willkie Charles L. McNary	449 85%	82 15%	27,263,448 54.7%	22,336,260 44.8%
1944	48	Franklin D. Roosevelt Harry S. Truman	Thomas E. Dewey John W. Bricker	432 81%	99 19%	25,611,936 53.4%	22,013,372 45.9%
1948[h]	48	Harry S. Truman Alben W. Barkley	Thomas E. Dewey Earl Warren	303 57%	189 36%	24,105,587 49.5%	21,970,017 45.1%
1952	48	Adlai E. Stevenson John J. Sparkman	Dwight D. Eisenhower Richard M. Nixon	89 17%	442 83%	27,314,649 44.4%	33,936,137 55.1%
1956[i]	48	Adlai E. Stevenson Estes Kefauver	Dwight D. Eisenhower Richard M. Nixon	73 14%	457 86%	26,030,172 42.0%	35,585,245 57.4%
1960[j]	50	John F. Kennedy Lyndon B. Johnson	Richard M. Nixon Henry Cabot Lodge	303 56%	219 41%	34,221,344 49.7%	34,106,671 49.5%
1964	50*	Lyndon B. Johnson Hubert H. Humphrey	Barry Goldwater William E. Miller	486 90%	52 10%	43,126,584 61.1%	27,177,838 38.5%
1968[k]	50*	Hubert H. Humphrey Edmund S. Muskie	Richard M. Nixon Spiro T. Agnew	191 36%	301 56%	31,274,503 42.7%	31,785,148 43.4%

...Presidential Elections, 1860-1992

YEAR	NO. OF STATES	CANDIDATES		ELECTORAL VOTE		POPULAR VOTE	
		DEM.	GOP	DEM.	GOP	DEM.	GOP
1972[l]	50*	George McGovern Sargent Shriver	Richard M. Nixon Spiro T. Agnew	17 3%	520 97%	29,171,791 37.5%	47,170,179 60.7%
1976[m]	50*	Jimmy Carter Walter F. Mondale	Gerald R. Ford Robert Dole	297 55%	240 45%	40,830,763 50.1%	39,147,793 48.0%
1980	50*	Jimmy Carter Walter F. Mondale	Ronald Reagan George Bush	49 9%	489 91%	35,483,883 41.0%	43,904,153 50.7%
1984	50*	Walter F. Mondale Geraldine Ferraro	Ronald Reagan George Bush	13 2%	525 98%	37,577,137 40.6%	54,455,074 58.8%
1988[n]	50*	Michael S. Dukakis Lloyd Bentsen	George Bush Dan Quayle	111 21%	426 79%	41,809,074 45.6%	48,886,097 53.4%
1992	50*	Bill Clinton Al Gore	George Bush Dan Quayle	370 69%	168 31%	44,908,233 43.0%	39,102,282 37.4%

[a] 1860: John C. Breckinridge, Southern Democrat, polled 72 electoral votes. John Bell, Constitutional Union, polled 39 electoral votes.
[b] 1864: 81 electoral votes were not cast.
[c] 1868: 23 electoral votes were not cast;
[d] 1872: Horace Greeley, Democrat, died after election. In the electoral college, Democratic electoral votes went to Thomas Hendricks, 42 votes; B. Gratz Brown, 18 votes; Charles J. Jenkins, 2 votes; and David Davis, 1 vote. Seventeen electoral votes were not cast.
[e] 1892: James B. Weaver, People's Party, polled 22 electoral votes.
[f] 1912: Theodore Roosevelt, Progressive Party, polled 86 electoral votes.
[g] 1924: Robert M. LaFollette, Progressive Party, polled 13 electoral votes.
[h] 1948: J. Strom Thurmond, States' Rights Party, polled 39 electoral votes.
[i] 1956: Walter B. Jones, Democrat, polled 1 electoral vote.
[j] 1960: Harry Flood Byrd, Democrat, polled 15 electoral votes.
[k] 1968: George C. Wallace, American Independent, polled 46 electoral votes.
[l] 1972: John Hospers, Libertarian Party, polled 1 electoral vote.
[m] 1976: Ronald Reagan, Republican, polled 1 electoral vote.
[n] 1988: Lloyd Bentsen, the Democratic vice presidential nominee, polled 1 electoral vote for president.
*Fifty states plus District of Columbia.

Official 1988 Presidential Election Results

(Based on reports from the secretaries of state for the fifty states and the District of Columbia)

State	Total Vote	George Bush (Republican) Votes	%	Michael S. Dukakis (Democrat) Votes	%	Ron Paul (Libertarian) Votes	%	Lenora B. Fulani (New Alliance) Votes	%	Other * Votes	%	Plurality	
Alabama	1,378,476	815,576	*59.2*	549,506	*39.9*	8,460	*0.6*	3,311	*0.2*	1,623	*0.1*	266,070	R
Alaska	200,116	119,251	*59.6*	72,584	*36.3*	5,480	*2.7*	1,024	*0.5*	1,773	*0.9*	46,667	R
Arizona	1,171,873	702,541	*60.0*	454,029	*38.7*	13,351	*1.1*	1,662	*0.1*	290	—	248,512	R
Arkansas	827,738	466,578	*56.4*	349,237	*42.2*	3,297	*0.4*	2,161	*0.2*	6,465	*0.8*	117,341	R
California	9,887,065	5,054,917	*51.1*	4,702,233	*47.6*	70,105	*0.7*	31,181	*0.3*	28,629	*0.3*	352,684	R
Colorado	1,372,394	728,177	*53.1*	621,453	*45.3*	15,482	*1.1*	2,539	*0.2*	4,743	*0.3*	106,724	R
Connecticut	1,443,394	750,241	*52.0*	676,584	*46.9*	14,071	*1.0*	2,491	*0.1*	7	—	73,657	R
Delaware	249,891	139,639	*55.9*	108,647	*43.5*	1,162	*0.5*	443	*0.2*			30,992	R
D.C.	192,877	27,590	*14.3*	159,407	*82.6*	554	*0.3*	2,901	*1.5*	2,425	*1.3*	131,817	D
Florida	4,302,313	2,618,885	*60.9*	1,656,701	*38.5*	19,796	*0.5*	6,655	*0.2*	276	—	962,184	R
Georgia	1,809,672	1,081,331	*59.8*	714,792	*39.5*	8,435	*0.5*	5,099	*0.3*	15	—	366,539	R
Hawaii	354,461	158,625	*44.8*	192,364	*54.3*	1,999	*0.6*	1,003	*0.3*	470	*0.1*	33,739	D
Idaho	408,968	253,881	*62.1*	147,272	*36.0*	5,313	*1.3*	2,502	*0.6*			106,609	R
Illinois	4,559,120	2,310,939	*50.7*	2,215,940	*48.6*	14,944	*0.3*	10,276	*0.2*	7,021	*0.2*	94,999	R
Indiana	2,168,621	1,297,763	*59.8*	860,643	*39.7*			10,215	*0.5*			437,120	R
Iowa	1,225,614	545,355	*44.5*	670,557	*54.7*	2,494	*0.2*	540	—	6,668	*0.5*	125,202	D
Kansas	993,044	554,049	*55.8*	422,636	*42.6*	12,553	*1.3*	3,806	*0.4*			131,413	R
Kentucky	1,322,517	734,281	*55.5*	580,368	*43.9*	2,118	*0.2*	1,256	*0.1*	4,494	*0.3*	153,913	R
Louisiana	1,628,202	883,702	*54.3*	717,460	*44.1*	4,115	*0.3*	2,355	*0.1*	20,570	*1.3*	166,242	R
Maine	555,035	307,131	*55.3*	243,569	*43.9*	2,700	*0.5*	1,405	*0.3*	230	—	63,562	R
Maryland	1,714,358	876,167	*51.1*	826,304	*48.2*	6,748	*0.4*	5,115	*0.3*	24	—	49,863	R
Massachusetts	2,632,805	1,194,635	*45.4*	1,401,415	*53.2*	24,251	*0.9*	9,561	*0.4*	2,943	*0.1*	206,780	D
Michigan	3,669,163	1,965,486	*53.6*	1,675,783	*45.7*	18,336	*0.5*	2,513	*0.1*	7,045	*0.2*	289,703	R
Minnesota	2,096,790	962,337	*45.9*	1,109,471	*52.9*	5,109	*0.2*	1,734	*0.1*	18,139	*0.9*	147,134	D
Mississippi	931,527	557,890	*59.9*	363,921	*39.1*	3,329	*0.4*	2,155	*0.2*	4,232	*0.5*	193,969	R
Missouri	2,093,713	1,084,953	*51.8*	1,001,619	*47.8*	434	—	6,656	*0.3*	51	—	83,334	R
Montana	365,674	190,412	*52.1*	168,936	*46.2*	5,047	*1.4*	1,279	*0.3*			21,476	R
Nebraska	661,465	397,956	*60.2*	259,235	*39.2*	2,534	*0.4*	1,743	*0.3*			138,721	R
Nevada	350,067	206,040	*58.9*	132,738	*37.9*	3,520	*1.0*	835	*0.2*	6,934	*2.0*	73,302	R
New Hampshire	451,074	281,537	*62.4*	163,696	*36.3*	4,502	*1.0*	790	*0.2*	549	*0.1*	117,841	R
New Jersey	3,099,553	1,743,192	*56.2*	1,320,352	*42.6*	8,421	*0.3*	5,138	*0.2*	22,449	*0.7*	422,840	R
New Mexico	521,287	270,341	*51.9*	244,497	*46.9*	3,268	*0.6*	2,237	*0.4*	944	*0.2*	25,844	R
New York	6,485,683	3,081,871	*47.5*	3,347,882	*51.6*	12,109	*0.2*	15,845	*0.2*	27,976	*0.4*	266,011	D
North Carolina	2,134,370	1,237,258	*58.0*	890,167	*41.7*	1,263	*0.1*	5,682	*0.3*			347,091	R
North Dakota	297,261	166,559	*56.0*	127,739	*43.0*	1,315	*0.4*	396	*0.1*	1,252	*0.4*	38,820	R
Ohio	4,393,699	2,416,549	*55.0*	1,939,629	*44.1*	11,989	*0.3*	12,017	*0.3*	13,515	*0.3*	476,920	R
Oklahoma	1,171,036	678,367	*57.9*	483,423	*41.3*	6,261	*0.5*	2,985	*0.3*			194,944	R
Oregon	1,201,694	560,126	*46.6*	616,206	*51.3*	14,811	*1.2*	6,487	*0.5*	4,064	*0.3*	56,080	D
Pennsylvania	4,536,251	2,300,087	*50.7*	2,194,944	*48.4*	12,051	*0.3*	4,379	*0.1*	24,790	*0.5*	105,143	R
Rhode Island	404,620	177,761	*43.9*	225,123	*55.6*	825	*0.2*	280	*0.1*	631	*0.2*	47,362	D
South Carolina	986,009	606,443	*61.5*	370,554	*37.6*	4,935	*0.5*	4,077	*0.4*			235,889	R
South Dakota	312,991	165,415	*52.8*	145,560	*46.5*	1,060	*0.3*	730	*0.2*	226	*0.1*	19,855	R
Tennessee	1,636,250	947,233	*57.9*	679,794	*41.5*	2,041	*0.1*	1,334	*0.1*	5,848	*0.4*	267,439	R
Texas	5,427,410	3,036,829	*56.0*	2,352,748	*43.3*	30,355	*0.6*	7,208	*0.1*	270	—	684,081	R
Utah	647,008	428,442	*66.2*	207,343	*32.0*	7,473	*1.2*	455	*0.1*	3,295	*0.5*	221,099	R
Vermont	243,328	124,331	*51.1*	115,775	*47.6*	1,000	*0.4*	205	*0.1*	2,017	*0.8*	8,556	R
Virginia	2,191,609	1,309,162	*59.7*	859,799	*39.2*	8,336	*0.4*	14,312	*0.7*			449,363	R
Washington	1,865,253	903,835	*48.5*	933,516	*50.0*	17,240	*0.9*	3,520	*0.2*	7,142	*0.4*	29,681	D
West Virginia	653,311	310,065	*47.5*	341,016	*52.2*			2,230	*0.3*			30,951	D
Wisconsin	2,191,608	1,047,499	*47.8*	1,126,794	*51.4*	5,157	*0.2*	1,953	*0.1*	10,205	*0.5*	79,295	D
Wyoming	176,551	106,867	*60.5*	67,113	*38.0*	2,026	*1.1*	545	*0.3*			39,754	R
	91,594,809	48,886,097	*53.4*	41,809,074	*45.6*	432,179	*0.5*	217,219	*0.2*	250,240	*0.3*	7,077,023	R

* Others receiving votes: David E. Duke (Populist), 47,047; Eugene Joseph McCarthy (Consumer), 30,905; James C. Griffin (American Independent), 27,818; Lyndon H. LaRouche Jr. (Independent), 25,562; William A. Marra (Right to Life), 20,504; Edward Winn (Workers League), 18,693; James Mac Warren (Socialist Workers), 15,604; Herbert Lewin (Peace and Freedom), 10,370; Earl F. Dodge (Prohibition), 8,002; Larry Holmes (Workers World), 7,846; Willa Kenoyer (Socialist), 3,882; Delmar Dennis (American), 3,475; Jack E. Herer (Grassroots), 1,949; Louie G. Youngkeit (Independent), 372; John G. Martin (Third World Assembly), 236; "None of these candidates," 6,934; scattered write-in votes, 21,041.

Official 1992 Presidential Election Results

(Based on reports from the secretaries of state for the fifty states and the District of Columbia)

State	Total Vote	Bill Clinton (Democrat) Votes	%	George Bush (Republican) Votes	%	Ross Perot (Independent) Votes	%	Other* Votes	%	Plurality	
Alabama	1,688,060	690,080	*40.9*	804,283	*47.6*	183,109	*10.8*	10,588	*0.6*	114,203	R
Alaska	258,506	78,294	*30.3*	102,000	*39.5*	73,481	*28.4*	4,731	*1.8*	23,706	R
Arizona	1,486,975	543,050	*36.5*	572,086	*38.5*	353,741	*23.8*	18,098	*1.2*	29,036	R
Arkansas	950,653	505,823	*53.2*	337,324	*35.5*	99,132	*10.4*	8,374	*0.9*	168,499	D
California	11,131,722	5,121,325	*46.0*	3,630,575	*32.6*	2,296,006	*20.6*	83,816	*0.8*	1,490,750	D
Colorado	1,569,180	629,681	*40.1*	562,850	*35.9*	366,010	*23.3*	10,639	*0.7*	66,831	D
Connecticut	1,616,332	682,318	*42.2*	578,313	*35.8*	348,771	*21.6*	6,930	*0.4*	104,005	D
Delaware	289,735	126,054	*43.5*	102,313	*35.3*	59,213	*20.4*	2,155	*0.7*	23,741	D
D.C.	227,572	192,619	*84.6*	20,698	*9.1*	9,681	*4.3*	4,574	*2.0*	171,921	D
Florida	5,311,219	2,071,651	*39.0*	2,171,781	*40.9*	1,052,481	*19.8*	15,306	*0.3*	100,130	R
Georgia	2,321,125	1,008,966	*43.5*	995,252	*42.9*	309,657	*13.3*	7,250	*0.3*	13,714	D
Hawaii	372,842	179,310	*48.1*	136,822	*36.7*	53,003	*14.2*	3,707	*1.0*	42,488	D
Idaho	482,142	137,013	*28.4*	202,645	*42.0*	130,395	*27.0*	12,089	*2.5*	65,632	R
Illinois	5,050,157	2,453,350	*48.6*	1,734,096	*34.3*	840,515	*16.6*	22,196	*0.4*	719,254	D
Indiana	2,305,871	848,420	*36.8*	989,375	*42.9*	455,934	*19.8*	12,142	*0.5*	140,955	R
Iowa	1,354,607	586,353	*43.3*	504,891	*37.3*	253,468	*18.7*	9,895	*0.7*	81,462	D
Kansas	1,157,236	390,434	*33.7*	449,951	*38.9*	312,358	*27.0*	4,493	*0.4*	59,517	R
Kentucky	1,492,900	665,104	*44.6*	617,178	*41.3*	203,944	*13.7*	6,674	*0.4*	47,926	D
Louisiana	1,790,017	815,971	*45.6*	733,386	*41.0*	211,478	*11.8*	29,182	*1.6*	82,585	D
Maine	679,499	263,420	*38.8*	206,504	*30.4*	206,820	*30.4*	2,755	*0.4*	56,600	D
Maryland	1,984,878	988,571	*49.8*	707,094	*35.6*	281,414	*14.2*	7,799	*0.4*	281,477	D
Massachusetts	2,773,664	1,318,639	*47.5*	805,039	*29.0*	630,731	*22.7*	19,255	*0.7*	513,600	D
Michigan	4,274,673	1,871,182	*43.8*	1,554,940	*36.4*	824,813	*19.3*	23,738	*0.6*	316,242	D
Minnesota	2,347,947	1,020,997	*43.5*	747,841	*31.9*	562,506	*24.0*	16,603	*0.7*	273,156	D
Mississippi	981,793	400,258	*40.8*	487,793	*49.7*	85,626	*8.7*	8,116	*0.8*	87,535	R
Missouri	2,391,565	1,053,873	*44.1*	811,159	*33.9*	518,741	*21.7*	7,792	*0.3*	242,714	D
Montana	410,611	154,507	*37.6*	144,207	*35.1*	107,225	*26.1*	4,672	*1.1*	10,300	D
Nebraska	737,546	216,864	*29.4*	343,678	*46.6*	174,104	*23.6*	2,900	*0.4*	126,814	R
Nevada	506,318	189,148	*37.4*	175,828	*34.7*	132,580	*26.2*	8,762	*1.7*	13,320	D
New Hampshire	537,943	209,040	*38.9*	202,484	*37.6*	121,337	*22.6*	5,082	*0.9*	6,556	D
New Jersey	3,343,594	1,436,206	*43.0*	1,356,865	*40.6*	521,829	*15.6*	28,694	*0.9*	79,341	D
New Mexico	569,986	261,617	*45.9*	212,824	*37.3*	91,895	*16.1*	3,650	*0.6*	48,793	D
New York	6,926,560	3,444,450	*49.7*	2,346,649	*33.9*	1,090,721	*15.7*	44,740	*0.6*	1,097,801	D
North Carolina	2,611,850	1,114,042	*42.7*	1,134,661	*43.4*	357,864	*13.7*	5,283	*0.2*	20,619	R
North Dakota	308,133	99,168	*32.2*	136,244	*44.2*	71,084	*23.1*	1,637	*0.5*	37,076	R
Ohio	4,939,967	1,984,942	*40.2*	1,894,310	*38.3*	1,036,426	*21.0*	24,289	*0.5*	90,632	D
Oklahoma	1,390,359	473,066	*34.0*	592,929	*42.6*	319,878	*23.0*	4,486	*0.3*	119,863	R
Oregon	1,462,643	621,314	*42.5*	475,757	*32.5*	354,091	*24.2*	11,481	*0.8*	145,557	D
Pennsylvania	4,959,810	2,239,164	*45.1*	1,791,841	*36.1*	902,667	*18.2*	26,138	*0.5*	447,323	D
Rhode Island	453,365	213,299	*47.0*	131,601	*29.0*	105,045	*23.2*	3,420	*0.8*	81,698	D
South Carolina	1,202,527	479,514	*39.9*	577,507	*48.0*	138,872	*11.5*	6,634	*0.6*	97,993	R
South Dakota	336,254	124,888	*37.1*	136,718	*40.7*	73,295	*21.8*	1,353	*0.4*	11,830	R
Tennessee	1,982,638	933,521	*47.1*	841,300	*42.4*	199,968	*10.1*	7,849	*0.4*	92,221	D
Texas	6,154,018	2,281,815	*37.1*	2,496,071	*40.6*	1,354,781	*22.0*	21,351	*0.3*	214,256	R
Utah	743,999	183,429	*24.7*	322,632	*43.4*	203,400	*27.3*	34,538	*4.6*	119,232	R
Vermont	289,701	133,592	*46.1*	88,122	*30.4*	65,991	*22.8*	1,996	*0.7*	45,470	D
Virginia	2,558,665	1,038,650	*40.6*	1,150,517	*45.0*	348,639	*13.6*	20,859	*0.8*	111,867	R
Washington	2,288,230	993,037	*43.4*	731,234	*32.0*	541,780	*23.7*	22,179	*1.0*	261,803	D
West Virginia	683,677	331,001	*48.4*	241,974	*35.4*	108,829	*15.9*	1,873	*0.3*	89,027	D
Wisconsin	2,531,114	1,041,066	*41.1*	930,855	*36.8*	544,479	*21.5*	14,714	*0.6*	110,211	D
Wyoming	200,617	68,160	*34.0*	79,347	*39.6*	51,263	*25.6*	1,847	*0.9*	11,187	R
	104,420,995	44,908,233	*43.0*	39,102,282	*37.4*	19,741,048	*18.9*	669,324	*0.6*	5,805,912	D

* Others receiving votes: Andre Marrou (Libertarian), 291,612; James "Bo" Gritz (Populist), 106,968; Lenora B. Fulani (New Alliance), 73,707; Howard Phillips (U.S. Taxpayers), 43,396; John Hagelin (Natural Law), 39,155; Ron Daniels (Independent), 27,440; Lyndon H. LaRouche Jr. (Independent), 26,321; James Mac Warren (Socialist Workers), 23,087; Drew Bradford (Independent), 4,749; Jack Herer (Grassroots), 3,875; Helen Halyard (Workers League), 3,050; John Quinn Brisben (Socialist), 2,909; John Yiamouyiannis (Independent), 2,199; Delbert Ehlers (Independent), 1,149; Jim Doren (Apathy), 956; Earl F. Dodge (Prohibition), 935; Eugene Hem (Third Party), 405; Isabelle Masters (Looking Back Group), 327; Robert J. Smith (American), 292; Gloria Estella La Riva (Workers World), 181; "None of these candidates," 2,537; scattered write-in votes, 13,909.

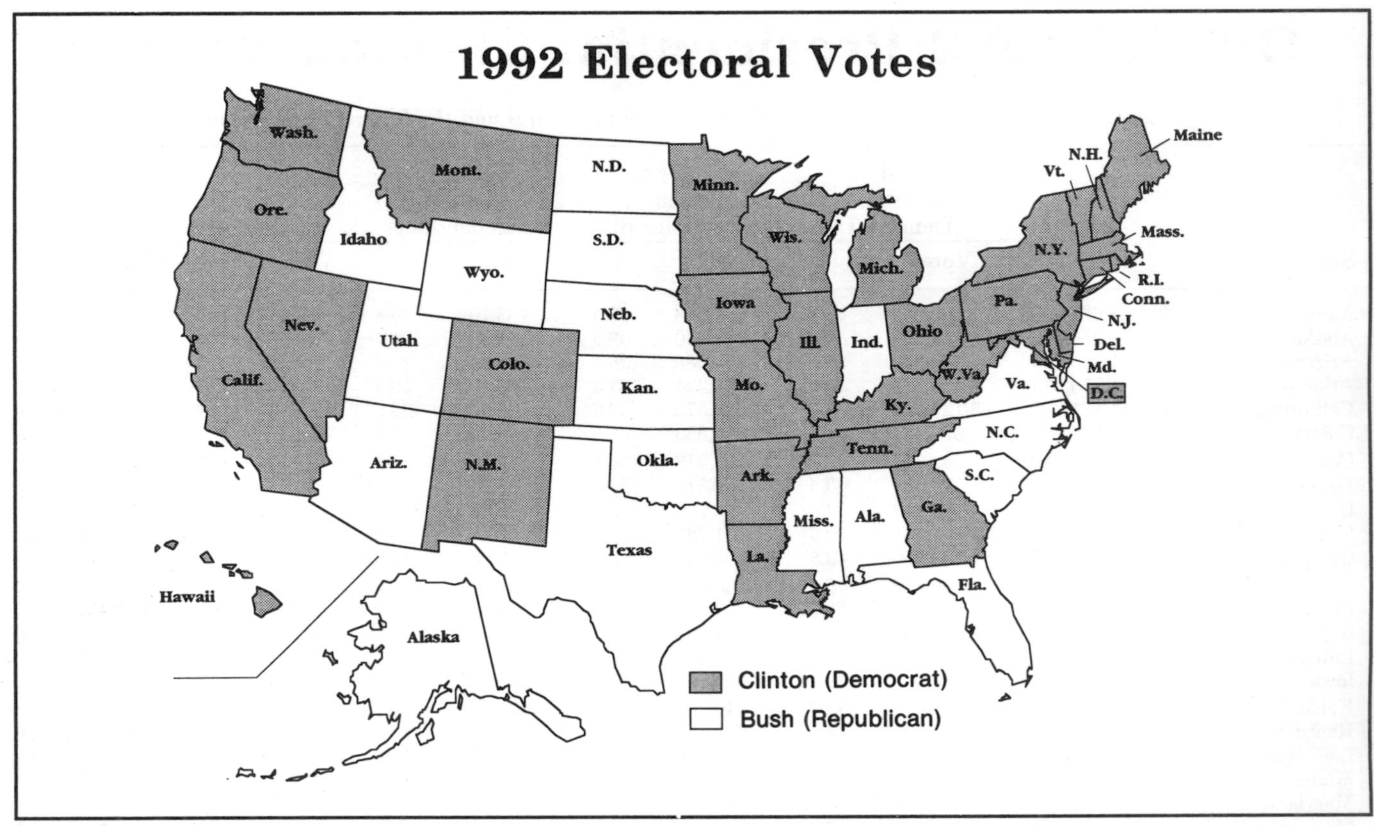

States	Electoral Votes	Clinton	Bush
Alabama	(9)	-	9
Alaska	(3)	-	3
Arizona	(8)	-	8
Arkansas	(6)	6	-
California	(54)	54	-
Colorado	(8)	8	-
Connecticut	(8)	8	-
Delaware	(3)	3	-
District of Columbia	(3)	3	-
Florida	(25)	-	25
Georgia	(13)	13	-
Hawaii	(4)	4	-
Idaho	(4)	-	4
Illinois	(22)	22	-
Indiana	(12)	-	12
Iowa	(7)	7	-
Kansas	(6)	-	6
Kentucky	(8)	8	-
Louisiana	(9)	9	-
Maine	(4)	4	-
Maryland	(10)	10	-
Massachusetts	(12)	12	-
Michigan	(18)	18	-
Minnesota	(10)	10	-
Mississippi	(7)	-	7
Missouri	(11)	11	-

States	Electoral Votes	Clinton	Bush
Montana	(3)	3	-
Nebraska	(5)	-	5
Nevada	(4)	4	-
New Hampshire	(4)	4	-
New Jersey	(15)	15	-
New Mexico	(5)	5	-
New York	(33)	33	-
North Carolina	(14)	-	14
North Dakota	(3)	-	3
Ohio	(21)	21	-
Oklahoma	(8)	-	8
Oregon	(7)	7	-
Pennsylvania	(23)	23	-
Rhode Island	(4)	4	-
South Carolina	(8)	-	8
South Dakota	(3)	-	3
Tennessee	(11)	11	-
Texas	(32)	-	32
Utah	(5)	-	5
Vermont	(3)	3	-
Virginia	(13)	-	13
Washington	(11)	11	-
West Virginia	(5)	5	-
Wisconsin	(11)	11	-
Wyoming	(3)	-	3
Total	(538)	370	168

1992 Republican Convention: Presidential Ballot

Delegation	Total Votes	Bush	Buchanan	Others[a]	Abstentions
Alabama	38	38	0	0	0
Alaska	19	19	0	0	0
Arizona	37	37	0	0	0
Arkansas	27	27	0	0	0
California	201	201	0	0	0
Colorado	37	31	5	1	0
Connecticut	35	35	0	0	0
Delaware	19	19	0	0	0
Florida	97	97	0	0	0
Georgia	52	52	0	0	0
Hawaii	14	14	0	0	0
Idaho	22	22	0	0	0
Illinois	85	85	0	0	0
Indiana	51	51	0	0	0
Iowa	23	23	0	0	0
Kansas	30	30	0	0	0
Kentucky	35	35	0	0	0
Louisiana	38	38	0	0	0
Maine	22	22	0	0	0
Maryland	42	42	0	0	0
Massachusetts	38	35	1	2	0
Michigan	72	72	0	0	0
Minnesota	32	32	0	0	0
Mississippi	34	34	0	0	0
Missouri	47	47	0	0	0
Montana	20	20	0	0	0
Nebraska	24	24	0	0	0
Nevada	21	21	0	0	0
New Hampshire	23	—	0	0	23[b]
New Jersey	60	60	0	0	0
New Mexico	25	25	0	0	0
New York	100	100	0	0	0
North Carolina	57	57	0	0	0
North Dakota	17	17	0	0	0
Ohio	83	83	0	0	0
Oklahoma	34	34	0	0	0
Oregon	23	23	0	0	0
Pennsylvania	91	90	1	0	0
Rhode Island	15	15	0	0	0
South Carolina	36	36	0	0	0
South Dakota	19	19	0	0	0
Tennessee	45	34	11	0	0
Texas	121	121	0	0	0
Utah	27	27	0	0	0
Vermont	19	19	0	0	0
Virginia	55	55	0	0	0
Washington	35	35	0	0	0
West Virginia	18	18	0	0	0
Wisconsin	35	35	0	0	0
Wyoming	20	20	0	0	0
District of Columbia	14	14	0	0	0
Puerto Rico	14	14	0	0	0
Virgin Islands	4	4	0	0	0
American Samoa	4	4	0	0	0
Guam	4	4	0	0	0
Total	2,210	2,166	18	3	23

[a] Details on the votes for other candidates: Colorado—Howard Phillips, 1; Massachusetts—Howard Phillips, 1, Alan Keyes, 1.
[b] Never voted.

Appendix

1992 Democratic Convention: Key Ballots

Delegates	Presidential Balloting						Balloting on Tax Fairness Platform Plank		
	Total Votes	Clinton	Brown	Tsongas	Others[a]	Abstentions	Y	N	A
Alabama	67	67	0	0	0	0	0	67	0
Alaska	18	18	0	0	0	0	0	16	0
Arizona	49	23	12	14	0	0	29	15	1
Arkansas	48	48	0	0	0	0	0	48	0
California	406	211	160	0	0	35	96	176	0
Colorado	58	26	19	13	0	0	31	23	4
Connecticut	66	45	21	0	0	0	23	30	0
Delaware	21	17	3	1	0	0	8	8	0
Florida	167	141	3	15	0	8[b]	50	71	0
Georgia	96	96	0	0	0	0	14	50	32
Hawaii	28	24	2	0	0	2	5	17	6
Idaho	26	22	0	1	1	2[b]	5	17	4
Illinois	195	155	9	29	0	2[c]	51	76	0
Indiana	93	73	20	0	0	0	21	68	4
Iowa	59	55	2	0	0	2	7	43	9
Kansas	44	43	0	0	0	1	5	38	0
Kentucky	64	63	0	0	0	1	3	53	2
Louisiana	75	75	0	0	0	0	0	75	0
Maine	31	14	13	4	0	0	18	2	0
Maryland	85	83	0	2	0	0	27	23	0
Massachusetts	119	109	6	1	0	3[b]	97	0	22
Michigan	159	120	35	0	0	4[d]	43	82	34
Minnesota	92	61	8	2	20	1	23	43	0
Mississippi	46	46	0	0	0	0	0	46	0
Missouri	92	91	1	0	0	0	6	46	0
Montana	24	21	2	0	0	1[b]	0	19	1
Nebraska	33	24	9	0	0	0	10	14	0
Nevada	27	23	4	0	0	0	0	25	2
New Hampshire	24	17	0	7	0	0	10	10	0
New Jersey	126	102	24	0	0	0	12	76	0
New Mexico	34	30	3	0	1	0	3	27	0
New York	290	155	67	64	0	4[b]	116	109	1
North Carolina	99	95	1	0	0	3	0	64	0
North Dakota	22	18	0	0	1	3[b]	3	14	5
Ohio	178	144	34	0	0	0	37	141	0
Oklahoma	58	56	2	0	0	0	0	53	5
Oregon	57	38	19	0	0	0	14	38	0
Pennsylvania	194	139	43	4	2	6[b]	21	78	0
Rhode Island	29	27	2	0	0	0	7	9	0
South Carolina	54	54	0	0	0	0	7	40	7
South Dakota	21	21	0	0	0	0	1	16	4
Tennessee	85	85	0	0	0	0	6	38	0
Texas	232	204	4	20	0	4	33	112	0
Utah	29	20	9	0	0	0	25	0	4
Vermont	21	14	7	0	0	0	11	6	0
Virginia	97	94	3	0	0	0	11	43	0
Washington	84	49	18	14	0	3[b]	30	29	25
West Virginia	41	41	0	0	0	0	0	13	0
Wisconsin	94	46	30	18	0	0	29	61	4
Wyoming	19	18	1	0	0	0	5	8	0
District of Columbia	31	31	0	0	0	0	0	30	1
Puerto Rico	58	57	0	0	0	1[b]	0	58	0
Virgin Islands	5	5	0	0	0	0	0	5	0
American Samoa	5	5	0	0	0	0	0	5	0
Guam	4	4	0	0	0	0	0	4	0
Democrats Abroad	9	9	0	0	0	0	0	8.75	0
Total	4,288	3,372	596	209	25	86	953.00	2,286.75	177.00

Note: Y—Yes; N—No; A—Abstain.

[a] Details on the votes for other candidates: Idaho—Larry Agran, D-Calif., 1; Minnesota—Gov. Robert P. Casey, D-Pa., 10, Rep. Patricia Schroeder, D-Colo., 8, Agran, 2; New Mexico—other, 1; North Dakota—other, 1; Pennsylvania—Sen. Albert Gore Jr., D-Tenn., 1, Joseph Simonetti, 1.

[b] No vote.

[c] One no vote.

[d] One uncommitted.

Distribution of House Seats and Electoral Votes

(Based on Censuses of 1950, 1960, 1970, 1980 and 1990)

State	U.S. House Seats									Electoral Votes				
	1953-1963	1960 Census Changes	1963-1973	1970 Census Changes	1973-1983	1980 Census Changes	1983-1993	1990 Census Changes	1993-2003	1952, 1956, 1960	1964, 1968	1972, 1976, 1980	1984, 1988	1992
Alabama	9	−1	8	−1	7	—	7	—	7	11	10	9	9	9
Alaska	1	—	1	—	1	—	1	—	1	3	3	3	3	3
Arizona	2	+1	3	+1	4	+1	5	—	6	4	5	6	7	8
Arkansas	6	−2	4	—	4	—	4	—	4	8	6	6	6	6
California	30	+8	38	+5	43	+2	45	+7	52	32	40	45	47	54
Colorado	4	—	4	+1	5	+1	6	—	6	6	6	7	8	8
Connecticut	6	—	6	—	6	—	6	—	6	8	8	8	8	8
Delaware	1	—	1	—	1	—	1	—	1	3	3	3	3	3
District of Columbia	—	—	—	—	—	—	—	—	—	—	3	3	3	3
Florida	8	+4	12	+3	15	+4	19	+4	23	10	14	17	21	25
Georgia	10	—	10	—	10	—	10	+1	11	12	12	12	12	13
Hawaii	1	+1	2	—	2	—	2	—	2	3	4	4	4	4
Idaho	2	—	2	—	2	—	2	—	2	4	4	4	4	4
Illinois	25	−1	24	—	24	−2	22	−2	20	27	26	26	24	22
Indiana	11	—	11	—	11	−1	10	—	10	13	13	13	12	12
Iowa	8	−1	7	−1	6	—	6	−1	5	10	9	8	8	7
Kansas	6	−1	5	—	5	—	5	−1	4	8	7	7	7	6
Kentucky	8	−1	7	—	7	—	7	−1	6	10	9	9	9	8
Louisiana	8	—	8	—	8	—	8	−1	7	10	10	10	10	9
Maine	3	−1	2	—	2	—	2	—	2	5	4	4	4	4
Maryland	7	+1	8	—	8	—	8	—	8	9	10	10	10	10
Massachusetts	14	−2	12	—	12	−1	11	−1	10	16	14	14	13	12
Michigan	18	+1	19	—	19	−1	18	−2	16	20	21	21	20	18
Minnesota	9	−1	8	—	8	—	8	—	8	11	10	10	10	10
Mississippi	6	−1	5	—	5	—	5	—	5	8	7	7	7	7
Missouri	11	−1	10	—	10	−1	9	—	9	13	12	12	11	11
Montana	2	—	2	—	2	—	2	−1	1	4	4	4	4	3
Nebraska	4	−1	3	—	3	—	3	—	3	6	5	5	5	5
Nevada	1	—	1	—	1	+1	2	—	2	3	3	3	4	4
New Hampshire	2	—	2	—	2	—	2	—	2	4	4	4	4	4
New Jersey	14	+1	15	—	15	−1	14	−1	13	16	17	17	16	15
New Mexico	2	—	2	—	2	+1	3	—	3	4	4	4	5	5
New York	43	−2	41	−2	39	−5	34	−3	31	45	43	41	36	33
North Carolina	12	−1	11	—	11	—	11	+1	12	14	13	13	13	14
North Dakota	2	—	2	−1	1	—	1	—	1	4	4	3	3	3
Ohio	23	+1	24	−1	23	−2	21	−2	19	25	26	25	23	21
Oklahoma	6	—	6	—	6	—	6	—	6	8	8	8	8	8
Oregon	4	—	4	—	4	+1	5	—	5	6	6	6	7	7
Pennsylvania	30	−3	27	−2	25	−2	23	−2	21	32	29	27	25	23
Rhode Island	2	—	2	—	2	—	2	—	2	4	4	4	4	4
South Carolina	6	—	6	—	6	—	6	—	6	8	8	8	8	8
South Dakota	2	—	2	—	2	−1	1	—	1	4	4	4	3	3
Tennessee	9	—	9	−1	8	+1	9	—	9	11	11	10	11	11
Texas	22	+1	23	+1	24	+3	27	+3	30	24	25	26	29	32
Utah	2	—	2	—	2	+1	3	—	3	4	4	4	5	5
Vermont	1	—	1	—	1	—	1	—	1	3	3	3	3	3
Virginia	10	—	10	—	10	—	10	+1	11	12	12	12	12	13
Washington	7	—	7	—	7	+1	8	+1	9	9	9	9	10	11
West Virginia	6	−1	5	−1	4	—	4	−1	3	8	7	6	6	5
Wisconsin	10	—	10	−1	9	—	9	—	9	12	12	11	11	11
Wyoming	1	—	1	—	1	—	1	—	1	3	3	3	3	3

Party Affiliations in Congress . . .

Year	Congress	House: Majority Party	House: Principal Minority Party	Senate: Majority Party	Senate: Principal Minority Party	President
1789-1791	1st	Ad-38	Op-26	Ad-17	Op-9	F (Washington)
1791-1793	2nd	F-37	DR-33	F-16	DR-13	F (Washington)
1793-1795	3rd	DR-57	F-48	F-17	DR-13	F (Washington)
1795-1797	4th	F-54	DR-52	F-19	DR-13	F (Washington)
1797-1799	5th	F-58	DR-48	F-20	DR-12	F (John Adams)
1799-1801	6th	F-64	DR-42	F-19	DR-13	F (John Adams)
1801-1803	7th	DR-69	F-36	DR-18	F-13	DR (Jefferson)
1803-1805	8th	DR-102	F-39	DR-25	F-9	DR (Jefferson)
1805-1807	9th	DR-116	F-25	DR-27	F-7	DR (Jefferson)
1807-1809	10th	DR-118	F-24	DR-28	F-6	DR (Jefferson)
1809-1811	11th	DR-94	F-48	DR-28	F-6	DR (Madison)
1811-1813	12th	DR-108	F-36	DR-30	F-6	DR (Madison)
1813-1815	13th	DR-112	F-68	DR-27	F-9	DR (Madison)
1815-1817	14th	DR-117	F-65	DR-25	F-11	DR (Madison)
1817-1819	15th	DR-141	F-42	DR-34	F-10	DR (Monroe)
1819-1821	16th	DR-156	F-27	DR-35	F-7	DR (Monroe)
1821-1823	17th	DR-158	F-25	DR-44	F-4	DR (Monroe)
1823-1825	18th	DR-187	F-26	DR-44	F-4	DR (Monroe)
1825-1827	19th	Ad-105	J-97	Ad-26	J-20	C (John Q. Adams)
1827-1829	20th	J-119	Ad-94	J-28	Ad-20	C (John Q. Adams)
1829-1831	21st	D-139	NR-74	D-26	NR-22	D (Jackson)
1831-1833	22nd	D-141	NR-58	D-25	NR-21	D (Jackson)
1833-1835	23rd	D-147	AM-53	D-20	NR-20	D (Jackson)
1835-1837	24th	D-145	W-98	D-27	W-25	D (Jackson)
1837-1839	25th	D-108	W-107	D-30	W-18	D (Van Buren)
1839-1841	26th	D-124	W-118	D-28	W-22	D (Van Buren)
1841-1843	27th	W-133	D-102	W-28	D-22	W (W. Harrison) W (Tyler)
1843-1845	28th	D-142	W-79	W-28	D-25	W (Tyler)
1845-1847	29th	D-143	W-77	D-31	W-25	D (Polk)
1847-1849	30th	W-115	D-108	D-36	W-21	D (Polk)
1849-1851	31st	D-112	W-109	D-35	W-25	W (Taylor) W (Fillmore)
1851-1853	32nd	D-140	W-88	D-35	W-24	W (Fillmore)
1853-1855	33rd	D-159	W-71	D-38	W-22	D (Pierce)
1855-1857	34th	R-108	D-83	D-40	R-15	D (Pierce)
1857-1859	35th	D-118	R-92	D-36	R-20	D (Buchanan)
1859-1861	36th	R-114	D-92	D-36	R-26	D (Buchanan)
1861-1863	37th	R-105	D-43	R-31	D-10	R (Lincoln)
1863-1865	38th	R-102	D-75	R-36	D-9	R (Lincoln)
1865-1867	39th	U-149	D-42	U-42	D-10	R (Lincoln) R (A. Johnson)
1867-1869	40th	R-143	D-49	R-42	D-11	R (A. Johnson)
1869-1871	41st	R-149	D-63	R-56	D-11	R (Grant)
1871-1873	42nd	R-134	D-104	R-52	D-17	R (Grant)
1873-1875	43rd	R-194	D-92	R-49	D-19	R (Grant)
1875-1877	44th	D-169	R-109	R-45	D-29	R (Grant)
1877-1879	45th	D-153	R-140	R-39	D-36	R (Hayes)
1879-1881	46th	D-149	R-130	D-42	R-33	R (Hayes)
1881-1883	47th	R-147	D-135	R-37	D-37	R (Garfield) R (Arthur)
1883-1885	48th	D-197	R-118	R-38	D-36	R (Arthur)
1885-1887	49th	D-183	R-140	R-43	D-34	D (Cleveland)
1887-1889	50th	D-169	R-152	R-39	D-37	D (Cleveland)
1889-1891	51st	R-166	D-159	R-39	D-37	R (B. Harrison)
1891-1893	52nd	D-235	R-88	R-47	D-39	R (B. Harrison)
1893-1895	53rd	D-218	R-127	D-44	R-38	D (Cleveland)
1895-1897	54th	R-244	D-105	R-43	D-39	D (Cleveland)

... and the Presidency, 1789-1993

Year	Congress	House Majority Party	House Principal Minority Party	Senate Majority Party	Senate Principal Minority Party	President
1897-1899	55th	R-204	D-113	R-47	D-34	R (McKinley)
1899-1901	56th	R-185	D-163	R-53	D-26	R (McKinley)
1901-1903	57th	R-197	D-151	R-55	D-31	R (McKinley) R (T. Roosevelt)
1903-1905	58th	R-208	D-178	R-57	D-33	R (T. Roosevelt)
1905-1907	59th	R-250	D-136	R-57	D-33	R (T. Roosevelt)
1907-1909	60th	R-222	D-164	R-61	D-31	R (T. Roosevelt)
1909-1911	61st	R-219	D-172	R-61	D-32	R (Taft)
1911-1913	62nd	D-228	R-161	R-51	D-41	R (Taft)
1913-1915	63rd	D-291	R-127	D-51	R-44	D (Wilson)
1915-1917	64th	D-230	R-196	D-56	R-40	D (Wilson)
1917-1919	65th	D-216	R-210	D-53	R-42	D (Wilson)
1919-1921	66th	R-240	D-190	R-49	D-47	D (Wilson)
1921-1923	67th	R-301	D-131	R-59	D-37	R (Harding)
1923-1925	68th	R-225	D-205	R-51	D-43	R (Coolidge)
1925-1927	69th	R-247	D-183	R-56	D-39	R (Coolidge)
1927-1929	70th	R-237	D-195	R-49	D-46	R (Coolidge)
1929-1931	71st	R-267	D-167	R-56	D-39	R (Hoover)
1931-1933	72nd	D-220	R-214	R-48	D-47	R (Hoover)
1933-1935	73rd	D-310	R-117	D-60	R-35	D (F. Roosevelt)
1935-1937	74th	D-319	R-103	D-69	R-25	D (F. Roosevelt)
1937-1939	75th	D-331	R-89	D-76	R-16	D (F. Roosevelt)
1939-1941	76th	D-261	R-164	D-69	R-23	D (F. Roosevelt)
1941-1943	77th	D-268	R-162	D-66	R-28	D (F. Roosevelt)
1943-1945	78th	D-218	R-208	D-58	R-37	D (F. Roosevelt)
1945-1947	79th	D-242	R-190	D-56	R-38	D (F. Roosevelt) D (Truman)
1947-1949	80th	R-245	D-188	R-51	D-45	D (Truman)
1949-1951	81st	D-263	R-171	D-54	R-42	D (Truman)
1951-1953	82nd	D-234	R-199	D-49	R-47	D (Truman)
1953-1955	83rd	R-221	D-211	R-48	D-47	R (Eisenhower)
1955-1957	84th	D-232	R-203	D-48	R-47	R (Eisenhower)
1957-1959	85th	D-233	R-200	D-49	R-47	R (Eisenhower)
1959-1961	86th	D-283	R-153	D-64	R-34	R (Eisenhower)
1961-1963	87th	D-263	R-174	D-65	R-35	D (Kennedy)
1963-1965	88th	D-258	R-177	D-67	R-33	D (Kennedy) D (L. Johnson)
1965-1967	89th	D-295	R-140	D-68	R-32	D (L. Johnson)
1967-1969	90th	D-247	R-187	D-64	R-36	D (L. Johnson)
1969-1971	91st	D-243	R-192	D-57	R-43	R (Nixon)
1971-1973	92nd	D-254	R-180	D-54	R-44	R (Nixon)
1973-1975	93rd	D-239	R-192	D-56	R-42	R (Nixon) R (Ford)
1975-1977	94th	D-291	R-144	D-60	R-37	R (Ford)
1977-1979	95th	D-292	R-143	D-61	R-38	D (Carter)
1979-1981	96th	D-276	R-157	D-58	R-41	D (Carter)
1981-1983	97th	D-243	R-192	R-53	D-46	R (Reagan)
1983-1985	98th	D-269	R-165	R-54	D-46	R (Reagan)
1985-1987	99th	D-252	R-182	R-53	D-47	R (Reagan)
1987-1989	100th	D-258	R-177	D-55	R-45	R (Reagan)
1989-1991	101st	D-259	R-174	D-55	R-45	R (Bush)
1991-1993	102nd	D-267	R-167	D-56	R-44	R (Bush)
1993-1995	103rd	D-258	R-176	D-57	R-43	D (Clinton)

Key: Ad—Administration; AM—Anti-Masonic; C—Coalition; D—Democratic; DR—Democratic-Republican; F—Federalist; J—Jacksonian; NR—National Republican; Op—Opposition; R—Republican; U—Unionist; W—Whig.

Note: Figures are for the beginning of the first session of each Congress.

Results of Elections in . . .

	48	50	52	54	56	58	60	62	64	66	68	70	72	74	76	78	80	82	84	86	88	90	92
National Totals																							
Democrats	263	235	213	232	234	283	263	259	295	248	243	255	243	291	292	277	243[g]	269	253	258	260	268[i]	259[i]
Republicans	171	199	221	203	201	153	174	176	140	187	192	180	192	143	143	158	192	166	182	177	175	167	176
Alabama																							
Democrats	9	9	9	9	9	9	9	8[b]	3	5	5	5	4[b]	4	4	4	4	5	5	5	5	5	4
Republicans	0	0	0	0	0	0	0	0	5	3	3	3	3	3	3	3	3	2	2	2	2	2	3
Alaska																							
Democrats	—	—	—	—	—	1	1	1	1	0	0	1	1[d]	0	0	0	0	0	0	0	0	0	0
Republicans	—	—	—	—	—	0	0	0	0	1	1	0	0	1	1	1	1	1	1	1	1	1	1
Arizona																							
Democrats	2	2	1	1	1	1	1	2[a]	2	1	1	1	1[a]	1	2	2	2	2[a]	1	1	1	1	3[a]
Republicans	0	0	1	1	1	1	1	1	1	2	2	2	3	3	2	2	2	3	4	4	4	4	3
Arkansas																							
Democrats	7	7	6	6	6	6	6	4[b]	4	3	3	3	3	3	3	2	2	2	3	3	3	3	2
Republicans	0	0	0	0	0	0	0	0	0	1	1	1	1	1	1	2	2	2	1	1	1	1	2
California																							
Democrats	10	10	11	11	13	16	16	25[a,d]	23	21	21	20	23[a]	28	29	26	22	28[a]	27	27	27	26	30[a]
Republicans	13	13	19	19	17	14	13	15	17	17	18	20	15	14	17	21	17	17	18	18	18	19	22
Colorado																							
Democrats	3	2	2	2	2	3	2	2	4	3	3	2	2[a]	3	3	3	3	3[a]	2	3	3	3	2
Republicans	1	2	2	2	2	1	2	2	0	1	1	2	3	2	2	2	2	3	4	3	3	3	4
Connecticut																							
Democrats	3	2	1	1	0	6	4	5	6	5	4	4	3	4	4	5	4	4	3	3	3	3	3
Republicans	3	4	5	5	6	0	2	1	0	1	2	2	3	2	2	1	2	2	3	3	3	3	3
Delaware																							
Democrats	0	0	0	1	0	1	1	1	1	0	0	0	0	0	0	0	0	1	1	1	1	1	0
Republicans	1	1	1	0	1	0	0	0	0	1	1	1	1	1	1	1	1	0	0	0	0	0	1
Florida																							
Democrats	6	6	8	7	7	7	7	10[a]	10	9	9	9	11[a]	10	10	12	11	13[a]	12	12	10	9	10[a]
Republicans	0	0	0	1	1	1	1	2	2	3	3	3	4	5	5	3	4	6	7	7	9	10	13
Georgia																							
Democrats	10	10	10	10	10	10	10	10	9	8	8	8	9	10	10	9	9	9	8	8	9	9	7[a]
Republicans	0	0	0	0	0	0	0	0	1	2	2	2	1	0	0	1	1	1	2	2	1	1	4
Hawaii																							
Democrat	—	—	—	—	—	—	1	2[a]	2	2	2	2	2	2	2	2	2	2	2	1	1	2	2
Republicans	—	—	—	—	—	—	0	0	0	0	0	0	0	0	0	0	0	0	0	1	1	0	0
Idaho																							
Democrats	1	0	1	1	1	1	2	2	1	0	0	0	0	0	0	0	0	0	1	1	1	2	1
Republicans	1	2	1	1	1	1	0	0	1	2	2	2	2	2	2	2	2	2	1	1	1	0	1
Illinois																							
Democrats	12	8	9	12	11	14	14	12[b]	13	12	12	12	10	13	12	11	10	12[b]	13	13	14	15	12[b]
Republicans	14	18	16	13	14	11	11	12	11	12	12	12	14	11	12	13	14	10	9	9	8	7	8
Indiana																							
Democrats	7	2	1	2	2	8	4[c]	4	6	5	4	5	4	9	8	7	6	5[b]	5[h]	6	6	8	7
Republicans	4	9	10	9	9	3	7	7	5	6	7	6	7	2	3	4	5	5	5	4	4	2	3
Iowa																							
Democrats	0	0	0	0	1	4	2	1[b]	6	2	2	2	3[b]	5	4	3	3	3	2	2	2	2	1[b]
Republicans	8	8	8	8	7	4	6	6	1	5	5	5	3	1	2	3	3	3	4	4	4	4	4
Kansas																							
Democrats	0	0	1	0	1	3	1	0[b]	0	0	0	1	1	1	2	1	1	2	2	2	2	2	2[b]
Republicans	6	6	5	6	5	3	5	5	5	5	5	4	4	4	3	4	4	3	3	3	3	3	2
Kentucky																							
Democrats	7	7	6	6	6	7	7	5[b]	6	4	4	5	5	5	5	4	4	4	4	4	4	4	4[b]
Republicans	2	2	2	2	2	1	1	2	1	3	3	2	2	2	2	3	3	3	3	3	3	3	2
Louisiana																							
Democrats	8	8	8	8	8	8	8	8	8	8	8	8	7[d]	6[f]	6	5	6	6	6	5	4	4	4[b]
Republicans	0	0	0	0	0	0	0	0	0	0	0	0	1	1	2	3	2	2	2	3	4	4	3
Maine																							
Democrats	0	0	0	0	1	2	0	0[b]	1	2	2	2	1	0	0	0	0	0	0	1	1	1	1
Republicans	3	3	3	3	2	1	3	2	1	0	0	0	1	2	2	2	2	2	2	1	1	1	1
Maryland																							
Democrats	4	3	3	4	4	7	6	6[a]	6	5	4	5	4	5	5	6	7	7	6	6	6	5	4
Republicans	2	3	4	3	3	0	1	2	2	3	4	3	4	3	3	2	1	1	2	2	2	3	4
Massachusetts																							
Democrats	6	6	6	7	7	8	8	7[b]	7	7	7	8	9[e]	10	10	10	10	10[b]	10	10	10	10	8[b]
Republicans	8	8	8	7	7	6	6	5	5	5	5	4	3	2	2	2	2	1	1	1	1	1	2
Michigan																							
Democrats	5	5	5	7	6	7	7	8[a]	12	7	7	7	7	12	11	13	12	12[b]	11	11	11	11	10[b]
Republicans	12	12	13	11	12	11	11	11	7	12	12	12	12	7	8	6	7	6	7	7	7	7	6
Minnesota																							
Democrats	4	4	4	5	5	4	3	4[b]	4	3	3	4	4	5	5	4	3	5	5	5	5	6	6
Republicans	5	5	5	4	4	5	6	4	4	5	5	4	4	3	3	4	5	3	3	3	3	2	2
Mississippi																							
Democrats	7	7	6	6	6	6	6	5[b]	4	5	5	5	3	3	3	3	3	3	3	4	4	5	5
Republicans	0	0	0	0	0	0	0	0	1	0	0	0	2	2	2	2	2	2	2	1	1	0	0
Missouri																							
Democrats	12	10	7	9	10	10	9	8[b]	8	8	9	9	9	9	8	8	6	6[b]	6	5	5	6	6
Republicans	1	3	4	2	1	1	2	2	2	2	1	1	1	1	2	2	4	3	3	4	4	3	3
Montana																							
Democrats	1	1	1	1	2	2	1	1	1	1	1	1	1	2	1	1	1	1	1	1	1	1	1[b]
Republicans	1	1	1	1	0	0	1	1	1	1	1	1	1	0	1	1	1	1	1	1	1	1	0
Nebraska																							
Democrats	1	0	0	0	0	2	0	0[b]	1	0	0	0	0	0	1	1	0	0	0	0	1	1	1
Republicans	3	4	4	4	4	2	4	3	2	3	3	3	3	3	2	2	3	3	3	3	2	2	2

. . . House of Representatives, 1948-92

	48	50	52	54	56	58	60	62	64	66	68	70	72	74	76	78	80	82	84	86	88	90	92
Nevada																							
Democrats	1	1	0	0	1	1	1	1	1	1	1	1	0	1	1	1	1	1[a]	1	1	1	1	1
Republicans	0	0	1	1	0	0	0	0	0	0	0	0	1	0	0	0	0	1	1	1	1	1	1
New Hampshire																							
Democrat	0	0	0	0	0	0	0	0	1	0	0	0	0	1	1	1	1	1	0	0	0	1	1
Republicans	2	2	2	2	2	2	2	2	1	2	2	2	2	1	1	1	1	1	2	2	2	1	1
New Jersey																							
Democrat	5	5	5	6	4	5	6	7[a]	11	9	9	9	8	12	11	10	8	9[b]	8	8	8	8	7[b]
Republicans	9	9	9	8	10	9	8	8	4	6	6	6	7	3	4	5	7	5	6	6	6	6	6
New Mexico																							
Democrat	2	2	2	2	2	2	2	2	2	2	0	1	1	1	1	1	0	1[a]	1	1	1	1	1
Republicans	0	0	0	0	0	0	0	0	0	0	2	1	1	1	1	1	2	2	2	2	2	2	2
New York																							
Democrats	24	23	16	17	17	19	22	20[b]	27	26	26	24	22[b]	27	28	26	22	20[b]	19	20	21	21	18[b]
Republicans	20	22	27	26	26	24	21	21	14	15	15	17	17	12	11	13	17	14	15	14	13	13	13
North Carolina																							
Democrat	12	12	11	11	11	11	11	9[b]	9	8	7	7	7	9	9	9	7	9	6	8	8	7	8[a]
Republicans	0	0	1	1	1	1	1	2	2	3	4	4	4	2	2	2	4	2	5	3	3	4	4
North Dakota																							
Democrats	0	0	0	0	0	1	0	0	1	0	0	1	0[b]	0	0	0	1	1	1	1	1	1	1
Republicans	2	2	2	2	2	1	2	2	1	2	2	1	1	1	1	1	0	0	0	0	0	0	0
Ohio																							
Democrats	12	7	6	6	6	9	7	6[a]	10	5	6	7	7[b]	8	10	10	11	10[b]	11	11	11	11	10[b]
Republicans	11	15	16	17	17	14	16	18	14	19	18	17	16	15	13	13	12	11	10	10	10	10	9
Oklahoma																							
Democrats	8	6	5	5	5	5	5	5	5	4	4	4	5	6	5	5	5	5	5	4	4	4	4
Republicans	0	2	1	1	1	1	1	1	1	2	2	2	1	0	1	1	1	1	1	2	2	2	2
Oregon																							
Democrats	0	0	0	1	3	3	2	3	3	2	2	2	2	4	4	4	3	3[a]	3	3	3	4	4
Republicans	4	4	4	3	1	1	2	1	1	2	2	2	2	0	0	0	1	2	2	2	2	1	1
Pennsylvania																							
Democrats	16	13	11	14	13	16	14	13[b]	15	14	14	14	13[b]	14	17	15	13[g]	13[b]	13	12	12	11	11[b]
Republicans	17	20	19	16	17	14	16	14	12	13	13	13	12	11	8	10	12	10	10	11	11	12	10
Rhode Island																							
Democrats	2	2	2	2	2	2	2	2	2	2	2	2	2	2	2	2	1	1	1	1	0	1	1
Republicans	0	0	0	0	0	0	0	0	0	0	0	0	0	0	0	0	1	1	1	1	2	1	1
South Carolina																							
Democrats	6	6	6	6	6	6	6	6	6	5	5	5	4	5	5	4	2	3	3	4	4	4	3
Republicans	0	0	0	0	0	0	0	0	0	1	1	1	2	1	1	2	4	3	3	2	2	2	3
South Dakota																							
Democrats	0	0	0	0	1	1	0	0	0	0	0	2	1	0	0	1	1	1[b]	1	1	1	1	1
Republicans	2	2	2	2	1	1	2	2	2	2	2	0	1	2	2	1	1	0	0	0	0	0	0
Tennessee																							
Democrats	8	8	7	7	7	7	7	6	6	5	5	5	3[b]	5	5	5	5	6[a]	6	6	6	6	6
Republicans	2	2	2	2	2	2	2	3	3	4	4	4	5	3	3	3	3	3	3	3	3	3	3
Texas																							
Democrats	21	21	22	21	21	21	21	21[a]	23	21	20	20	20[a]	21	22	20	19	22[a]	17	17	19	19	21[a]
Republicans	0	0	0	1	1	1	1	2	0	2	3	3	4	3	2	4	5	5	10	10	8	8	9
Utah																							
Democrats	2	2	0	0	0	1	2	0	1	0	0	1	2	2	1	1	0	0[a]	0	1	1	2	2
Republicans	0	0	2	2	2	1	0	2	1	2	2	1	0	0	1	1	2	3	3	2	2	1	1
Vermont																							
Democrats	0	0	0	0	0	1	0	0	0	0	0	0	0	0	0	0	0	0	0	0	0	1[i]	1[i]
Republicans	1	1	1	1	1	0	1	1	1	1	1	1	1	1	1	1	1	1	1	1	1	0	0
Virginia																							
Democrats	9	9	7	8	8	8	8	8	8	6	5	4	3	5	4	4	1	4	4	5	5	6	7[a]
Republicans	0	0	3	2	2	2	2	2	2	4	5	6	7	5	6	6	9	6	6	5	5	4	4
Washington																							
Democrats	2	2	1	1	1	1	2	1	5	5	5	6	6	6	6	6	5	5[a]	5	5	5	5	8[a]
Republicans	4	4	6	6	6	6	5	6	2	2	2	1	1	1	1	1	2	3	3	3	3	3	1
West Virginia																							
Democrats	6	6	5	6	4	5	5	4[b]	4	4	5	5	4[b]	4	4	4	2	4	4	4	4	4	3[b]
Republicans	0	0	1	0	2	1	1	1	1	1	0	0	0	0	0	0	2	0	0	0	0	0	0
Wisconsin																							
Democrats	2	1	1	3	3	5	4	4	5	3	3	5	5[b]	7	7	6	5	5	5	5	5	4	4
Republicans	8	9	9	7	7	5	6	6	5	7	7	5	4	2	2	3	4	4	4	4	4	5	5
Wyoming																							
Democrats	0	0	0	0	0	0	0	0	1	0	0	1	1	1	1	0	0	0	0	0	0	0	0
Republicans	1	1	1	1	1	1	1	1	0	1	1	0	0	0	0	1	1	1	1	1	1	1	1

[a] State gained seats due to reapportionment.

[b] State lost seats due to reapportionment.

[c] Indiana 1960: Figures include final outcome of disputed election in 5th District where a Republican was at first certified the winner but the House decided to seat the Democrat. The 7-4 figure reflects the seating of the Democrat.

[d] California 1962, Alaska and Louisiana 1972: Total includes one Democratic candidate who died before the election but his name remained on the ballot and he was re-elected. A special election was held the next year to fill the vacancy.

[e] Massachusetts 1972: Democratic total includes Rep. Joe Moakley, elected as an Independent but served as a Democrat.

[f] Louisiana 1974: One vacancy. There was no declared winner in the 6th District. A special election was held the next year to fill the vacancy.

[g] Pennsylvania 1980: Includes Rep. Thomas M. Foglietta, elected as an Independent.

[h] Indiana 1984: Figures include final outcome of disputed election in 8th District where a Republican was at first certified the winner but the House decided to seat the Democrat. The 5-5 figure reflects the seating of the Democrat.

[i] Vermont 1990, 1992: Includes Rep. Bernard Sanders, elected as an Independent.

101st Congress Special, 1989 Gubernatorial Returns

1989 Gubernatorial Elections

VIRGINIA — Nov. 7, 1989

	Vote Total	Percent
L. Douglas Wilder (D)	896,936	50.1
J. Marshall Coleman (R)	890,195	49.8

NEW JERSEY — Nov. 7, 1989

	Vote Total	Percent
James J. Florio (D)	1,379,937	61.2
Jim Courter (R)	838,553	37.2
Daniel M. Karlan (LIBERT)	11,878	0.5
Michael Ziruolo (I)	10,210	0.5
Tom Suscaldo (I)	6,989	0.3
Catherine Renee Sedwick (SW)	6,162	0.3

Special House Elections, 101st Congress

INDIANA 4th District — March 28, 1989

	Vote Total	Percent
Jill L. Long (D)	65,272	50.7
Dan Heath (R)	63,494	49.3

ALABAMA 3rd District — April 4, 1989

	Vote Total	Percent
Glen Browder (D)	47,294	65.3
John Rice (R)	25,142	34.7

WYOMING At Large District — April 26, 1989

	Vote Total	Percent
Craig Thomas (R)	74,384	52.5
John P. Vinich (D)	60,845	43.0
Craig Alan McCune (LIBERT)	5,825	4.1
Daniel Johnson (I)	507	0.4

Abbreviations

C	—	Conservative
D	—	Democrat
I	—	Independent
L	—	Liberal
LIBERT	—	Libertarian
R	—	Republican
SW	—	Socialist Worker

FLORIDA 18th District — Aug. 29, 1989

	Vote Total	Percent
Ileana Ros-Lehtinen (R)	9,298	53.2
Gerald Richman (D)	43,274	46.8

TEXAS 12th District — Sept. 12, 1989

	Vote Total	Percent
Pete Geren (D)	40,210	51.0
Bob Lanier (R)	38,590	49.0

CALIFORNIA 15th District — Sept. 12, 1989

	Vote Total	Percent
Gary Condit (D)	51,543	57.1
Clare Berryhill (R)	1,592	35.0
Robert J. Weimer (R)	2,939	3.3
Cliff Burris (R)	2,385	2.6
Roy Shimp (LIBERT)	781	0.9
Dave Williams (R)	381	0.4
Chris Patterakis (R)	344	0.4
Jack McCoy (R)	225	0.3

MISSISSIPPI 5th District — Oct. 17, 1989

	Vote Total	Percent
Gene Taylor (D)	83,296	65.2
Tom Anderson Jr. (R)	44,494	34.8

TEXAS 18th District — Dec. 9, 1989

	Vote Total	Percent
Craig Washington (D)	24,140	56.6
Anthony Hall (D)	18,484	43.4

NEW YORK 14th District — March 20, 1990

	Vote Total	Percent
Susan Molinari (R)	29,336	59.0
Robert Gigante (D)	17,302	34.8
Barbara Bollaert (RTL)	2,649	5.3
Carl Grillo (L)	427	0.9

NEW YORK 18th District — March 20, 1990

Jose E. Serrano (D, L)	26,928	92.4
Simeon Golar (R)	2,079	7.1
Kevin Brawley (C)	126	0.5

HAWAII 2nd District — Sept. 22, 1990

	Vote Total	Percent
Patsy T. Mink (D)	51,841	37.4
Mufi F. Hannemann (D)	50,164	36.1
Ron Menor (D)	23,629	17.0
Andy Poepoe (R)	8,872	6.4
Stanley Monsef (R)	2,264	1.6
Duane A. Black (D)	1,242	0.9
Lloyd J. Mallan (LIBERT)	791	0.6

NEW JERSEY 1st District — Nov. 6, 1990

Robert E. Andrews (D)	72,324	55.3
Daniel J. Mangini (R)	58,671	44.7

Note: Robert E. Andrews, D-N.J., was elected Nov. 6, 1990, to fill the remaining House term of James J. Florio, who resigned Jan. 16, 1990, and to the 102nd Congress. Results of the balloting to fill the vacancy are listed above. *(See 1990 returns for 102nd Congress vote tallies, p. 1240)*

Daniel K. Akaka, D-Hawaii, was elected Nov. 6, 1990, to complete the remaining four years of the Senate term of Spark M. Matsunaga, who died April 15, 1990. *(See 1990 returns for 102nd Congress vote tallies, p. 1240)*

1990 Elections Returns for Governors, Senate and House

Following are the final, official 1990 vote returns for the governorships, Senate and House compiled by Congressional Quarterly from figures supplied by each state's election agency. The box below provides a key to party designation. Also included are write-in candidates that received at least 0.1 percent of the vote. Because of rounding and because scattered write-in votes are not listed, percentages do not always add to 100.

An asterisk (*) indicates incumbents.

An X denotes candidates without major-party opposition and no votes were cast.

A dagger (†) indicates that a runoff election was required because no candidate received a majority.

ALABAMA

		Vote Total	Percent
Governor			
	Guy Hunt (R) *	633,520	52.1
	Paul Hubbert (D)	582,106	47.9
Senate			
	Howell Heflin (D) *	717,814	60.6
	Bill Cabaniss (R)	467,190	39.4
House			
1	Sonny Callahan (R) *	82,185	99.6
	(No Democratic candidate)		
2	Bill Dickinson (R) *	87,649	51.3
	Faye Baggiano (D)	83,243	48.7
3	Glen Browder (D) *	101,923	73.7
	Don Sledge (R)	36,317	26.3
4	Tom Bevill (D) *	129,872	99.7
	(No Republican candidate)		
5	Bud Cramer (D)	113,047	67.1
	Albert McDonald (R)	55,326	32.9
6	Ben Erdreich (D) *	134,412	92.8
	David A. Alvarez (I)	8,640	6.0
	Nathaniel Ivory (I)	1,745	1.2
7	Claude Harris (D) *	127,490	70.5
	Michael D. Barker (R)	53,258	29.5

ALASKA

		Vote Total	Percent
Governor			
	Walter J. Hickel (I)	75,721	38.9
	Tony Knowles (D)	60,201	30.9
	Arliss Sturgulewski (R)	50,991	26.2
	Jim Sykes (Green)	6,563	3.4
	Michael O'Callaghan (P)	942	0.5
Senate			
	Ted Stevens (R) *	125,806	66.2
	Michael Beasley (D)	61,152	32.2
House			
AL	Don Young (R) *	99,003	51.7
	John E. Devens (D)	91,677	47.8

ARIZONA

		Vote Total	Percent
Governor †			
	Fife Symington (R)	523,984	49.6
	Terry Goddard (D)	519,691	49.2
	Max Hawkins (write-in)	10,983	1.0
House			
1	John J. Rhodes III (R) *	166,223	99.5
	(No Democratic candidate)		
	Tim Rose (write-in)	621	0.4
	Betsy McDonald (write-in)	172	0.1
2	Morris K. Udall (D) *	76,549	65.9
	Joseph D. Sweeney (R)	39,586	34.1
3	Bob Stump (R) *	134,279	56.6
	Roger Hartstone (D)	103,018	43.4
4	Jon Kyl (R) *	141,843	61.3
	Mark Ivey Jr. (D)	89,395	38.7
5	Jim Kolbe (R) *	138,975	64.8
	Chuck Phillips (D)	75,642	35.2

ARKANSAS

		Vote Total	Percent
Governor			
	Bill Clinton (D) *	400,386	57.5
	Sheffield Nelson (R)	295,925	42.5
Senate			
	David Pryor (D) *	493,910	99.8
	(No Republican candidate)		
	Betty White (write-in)	825	0.2
House			
1	Bill Alexander (D) *	101,026	64.3
	Terry Hayes (R)	56,071	35.7
2	Ray Thornton (D)	103,471	60.4
	Jim Keet (R)	67,800	39.6
3	John Paul Hammerschmidt (R) *	129,876	70.5
	Dan Ivy (D)	54,332	29.5
4	Beryl Anthony Jr. (D) *	110,365	72.4
	Roy Rood (R)	42,130	27.6

CALIFORNIA

		Vote Total	Percent
Governor			
	Pete Wilson (R)	3,791,904	49.2
	Dianne Feinstein (D)	3,525,197	45.8
	Dennis Thompson (LIBERT)	145,628	1.9
	Jerome "Jerry" McCready (AMI)	139,661	1.8
	Maria Elizabeth Munoz (PF)	96,795	1.3
House			
1	Frank Riggs (R)	99,782	43.3
	Douglas H. Bosco (D) *	96,468	41.9
	Darlene G. Comingore (PF)	34,011	14.8
2	Wally Herger (R) *	133,315	63.7
	Erwin E. "Bill" Rush (D)	65,333	31.2
	Ross Crain (LIBERT)	10,753	5.1
3	Robert T. Matsui (D) *	132,143	60.3
	Lowell P. Landowski (R)	76,148	34.8
	David M. McCann (LIBERT)	10,797	4.9
4	Vic Fazio (D) *	115,090	54.7
	Mark Baughman (R)	82,738	39.3
	Bryce Bigwood (LIBERT)	12,626	6.0
5	Nancy Pelosi (D) *	120,633	77.2
	Alan Nichols (R)	35,671	22.8

Abbreviations for Party Designations

AC — Anti-corruption
AM — American
AMI — American Independent
ACP — A Connecicut Party
AM — American Party
ASI — American Systems Independent
BAG — Better Affordable Government
BB — Back to Basics
C — Conservative
CC — Concerned Citizens
COP — Concerns of People
D — Democratic
ER — Earth Rights
GR — Grass Roots
GWT — God We Trust
I — Independent
I-C — Independent Conservative
IHT — Independent High-Tech
IS — Illinois Solidarity
L — Liberal
LIBERT — Libertarian
LU — Liberty Union
NA — New Alliance
P — Political
PB — Colorado Prohibition
PF — Peace and Freedom
PH — Pride & Honesty
POP — Populist
R — Republican
RTL—Right to Life
SIS — Sataten Island Secession
SW — Socialist Workers
TIC — Tisch Independent Citizens
UC — United Citizens
WW — Workers World
WWW — World Without War

		Vote Total	Per-cent
6	Barbara Boxer (D) *	137,306	68.1
	Bill Boerum (R)	64,402	31.9
7	George Miller (D) *	121,080	60.5
	Roger A. Payton (R)	79,031	39.5
8	Ronald V. Dellums (D) *	119,645	61.3
	Barbara Galewski (R)	75,544	38.7
9	Pete Stark (D) *	94,739	58.4
	Victor Romero (R)	67,412	41.6
10	Don Edwards (D) *	81,875	62.7
	Mark Patrosso (R)	48,747	37.3
11	Tom Lantos (D) *	105,029	65.9
	G. M. "Bill" Quraishi (R)	45,818	28.8
	June R. Genis (LIBERT)	8,518	5.3
12	Tom Campbell (R) *	125,157	60.8
	Robert Palmer (D)	69,270	33.7
	Chuck Olson (LIBERT)	11,271	5.5
13	Norman Y. Mineta (D) *	97,286	58.0
	David E. Smith (R)	59,773	35.7
	John H. Webster (LIBERT)	10,587	6.3
14	John T. Doolittle (R)	128,309	51.5
	Patricia Malberg (D)	120,742	48.5
15	Gary Condit (D) *	97,147	66.2
	Cliff Burris (R)	49,634	33.8
16	Leon E. Panetta (D) *	134,236	74.2
	Jerry M. Reiss (R)	39,885	22.0
	Brian H. Tucker (LIBERT)	6,881	3.8
17	Calvin Dooley (D)	82,611	54.5
	Charles "Chip" Pashayan Jr. (R) *	68,848	45.5
18	Richard H. Lehman (D) *	98,804	100
	(No Republican candidate)		
19	Robert J. Lagomarsino (R) *	94,599	54.6
	Anita Perez Ferguson (D)	76,991	44.4
	Mindy Lorenz (write-in)	1,655	1.0
20	Bill Thomas (R) *	112,962	59.8
	Michael A. Thomas (D)	65,101	34.4
	William H. Dilbeck (LIBERT)	10,555	5.6
	Lita Martin Reid (write-in)	307	0.2
21	Elton Gallegly (R) *	118,326	58.4
	Richard D. Freiman (D)	68,921	34.0
	Peggy Christensen (LIBERT)	15,364	7.6
22	Carlos J. Moorhead (R) *	108,634	60.0
	David Bayer (D)	61,630	34.1
	William H. Wilson (LIBERT)	6,702	3.7
	Jan B. Tucker (PF)	3,963	2.2
23	Anthony C. Beilenson (D) *	103,141	61.7
	Jim Salomon (R)	57,118	34.2
	John Honigsfeld (PF)	6,834	4.1
24	Henry A. Waxman (D) *	71,562	68.9
	John N. Cowles (R)	26,607	25.6
	Maggie Phair (PF)	5,706	5.5
25	Edward R. Roybal (D) *	48,120	70.0
	Steven J. Renshaw (R)	17,021	24.8
	Robert H. Scott (LIBERT)	3,576	5.2
26	Howard L. Berman (D) *	78,031	61.1
	Roy Dahlson (R)	44,492	34.8
	Bernard Zimring (LIBERT)	5,268	4.1
27	Mel Levine (D) *	90,857	58.2
	David Barrett Cohen (R)	58,140	37.2
	Edward E. Ferrer (PF)	7,101	4.5
28	Julian C. Dixon (D) *	69,482	72.7
	George Z. Adams (R)	21,245	22.2
	William R. Williams (PF)	2,723	2.8
	Bob Weber (LIBERT)	2,150	2.2
29	Maxine Waters (D)	51,350	79.4
	Bill DeWitt (R)	12,054	18.6
	Waheed R. Boctor (LIBERT)	1,268	2.0
30	Matthew G. Martinez (D) *	45,456	58.2
	Reuben D. Franco (R)	28,914	37.0
	G. Curtis Feger (LIBERT)	3,713	4.8
31	Mervyn M. Dymally (D) *	56,394	67.1
	Eunice A. Sato (R)	27,593	32.9
32	Glenn M. Anderson (D) *	68,268	61.5
	Sanford W. Kahn (R)	42,692	38.5
33	David Dreier (R) *	101,336	63.7
	Georgia Houston Webb (D)	49,981	31.4
	Gail Lightfoot (LIBERT)	7,840	4.9
34	Esteban E. Torres (D) *	55,646	60.7
	John Eastman (R)	36,024	39.3
35	Jerry Lewis (R) *	121,602	60.6
	Barry Norton (D)	66,100	32.9
	Jerry Johnson (LIBERT)	13,020	6.5
36	George E. Brown Jr. (D) *	72,409	52.7
	Robert Hammock (R)	64,961	47.3
37	Al McCandless (R) *	115,469	49.7
	Ralph Waite (D)	103,961	44.8
	Gary R. Odom (AMI)	6,474	2.8
	Bonnie Flickinger (LIBERT)	6,178	2.7
38	Robert K. Dornan (R) *	60,561	58.1
	Barbara Jackson (D)	43,693	41.9
39	William E. Dannemeyer (R) *	113,849	65.3
	Francis X. Hoffman (D)	53,670	30.8
	Maxine B. Quirk (PF)	6,709	3.9
40	C. Christopher Cox (R) *	142,299	67.6
	Eugene C. Gratz (D)	68,087	32.4
41	Bill Lowery (R) *	105,723	49.2
	Dan Kripke (D)	93,586	43.6
	Karen S. R. Works (PF)	15,428	7.2
42	Dana Rohrabacher (R) *	109,353	59.3
	Guy C. Kimbrough (D)	67,189	36.5
	Richard Gibb Martin (LIBERT)	7,744	4.2
43	Ron Packard (R) *	151,206	68.1
	(No Democratic candidate)		
	Doug Hansen (PF)	40,212	18.1
	Richard L. Arnold (LIBERT)	30,720	13.8
44	Randy "Duke" Cunningham (R)	50,377	46.3
	Jim Bates (D) *	48,712	44.8
	Donna White (PF)	5,237	4.8
	John Wallner (LIBERT)	4,385	4.0
45	Duncan Hunter (R) *	123,591	72.8
	(No Democratic candidate)		
	Joe Shea (LIBERT)	46,068	27.2

COLORADO

Governor

	Vote Total	Per-cent
Roy Romer (D) *	626,032	61.9
John Andrews (R)	358,403	35.4
David Aitken (LIBERT)	18,932	1.9
Wm. David Livingston (PB)	7,907	0.8

Senate

	Vote Total	Per-cent
Hank Brown (R)	569,048	55.7
Josie Heath (D)	425,746	41.7
John Heckman (COP)	15,432	1.5
Earl F. Dodge (PB)	11,801	1.1

House

		Vote Total	Per-cent
1	Patricia Schroeder (D) *	82,176	63.7
	Gloria Gonzales Roemer (R)	46,802	36.3
2	David E. Skaggs (D) *	105,248	60.7
	Jason Lewis (R)	68,226	39.3
3	Ben Nighthorse Campbell (D) *	124,487	70.2
	Bob Ellis (R)	49,961	28.2
	Howard E. Fields (POP-Colo)	2,859	1.6
4	Wayne Allard (R)	89,285	54.1
	Dick Bond (D)	75,901	45.9
5	Joel Hefley (R) *	127,740	66.4
	Cal Johnston (D)	57,776	30.0
	Keith L. Hamburger (LIBERT)	6,761	3.5
6	Dan Schaefer (R) *	105,312	64.5
	Don Jarrett (D)	57,961	35.5

CONNECTICUT

Governor

	Vote Total	Per-cent
Lowell P. Weicker Jr. (ACP)	460,576	40.4
John G. Rowland (R)	427,840	37.5
Bruce A. Morrison (D)	236,641	20.7
Joseph A. Zdonczyk (CC)	16,044	1.4

House

		Vote Total	Per-cent
1	Barbara B. Kennelly (D) *	126,566	71.4
	James M. Garvey (R)	50,690	28.6
2	Sam Gejdenson (D) *	105,085	59.7
	John M. Ragsdale (R)	70,922	40.3
3	Rosa DeLauro (D)	90,772	52.1
	Thomas Scott (R)	83,440	47.9
4	Christopher Shays (R) *	105,682	76.5
	Al Smith (D)	32,352	23.4
5	Gary Franks (R)	93,912	51.7
	Toby Moffett (D)	85,803	47.2
	William G. Hare (Liberty)	1,888	1.0
6	Nancy L. Johnson (R) *	141,105	74.4
	Paul Kulas (D)	48,628	25.6

DELAWARE

Senate

	Vote Total	Per-cent
Joseph R. Biden Jr. (D) *	112,918	62.7
M. Jane Brady (R)	64,554	35.8
Lee Rosenbaum (LIBERT)	2,680	1.5

House

		Vote Total	Per-cent
AL	Thomas R. Carper (D) *	116,274	65.5
	Ralph O. Williams (R)	58,037	32.7
	Richard A. Cohen (LIBERT)	3,121	1.8

FLORIDA

Governor

	Vote Total	Per-cent
Lawton Chiles (D)	1,995,206	56.5
Bob Martinez (R) *	1,535,068	43.5

House

		Vote Total	Per-cent
1	Earl Hutto (D) *	88,416	52.2
	Terry Ketchel (R)	80,851	47.8
2	Pete Peterson (D)	103,032	56.9
	Bill Grant (R) *	77,939	43.1
3	Charles E. Bennett (D) *	84,280	72.7
	Rod Sullivan (R)	31,727	27.3
4	Craig T. James (R) *	120,895	55.9
	Reid Hughes (D)	95,320	44.1
5	Bill McCollum (R) *	94,453	59.9
	Bob Fletcher (D)	63,253	40.1
6	Cliff Stearns (R) *	138,588	59.2
	Art Johnson (D)	95,421	40.8
7	Sam M. Gibbons (D) *	99,464	67.6
	Charles D. Prout (R)	47,765	32.4
8	C. W. Bill Young (R) *	X	X
	(No Democratic candidate)		
9	Michael Bilirakis (R) *	142,163	58.1
	Cheryl Davis Knapp (D)	102,503	41.9
10	Andy Ireland (R) *	X	X
	(No Democratic candidate)		
11	Jim Bacchus (D)	120,991	51.9
	Bill Tolley (R)	111,970	48.1
12	Tom Lewis (R) *	X	X
	(No Democratic candidate)		
13	Peter J. Goss (R) *	X	X
	(No Democratic candidate)		
14	Harry A. Johnston (D) *	156,055	66.0
	Scott Shore (R)	80,249	34.0
15	E. Clay Shaw Jr. (R) *	104,295	97.8
	(No Democratic candidate)		
	Charles Goodmon (write-in)	2,374	2.2
16	Lawrence J. Smith (D) *	X	X
	(No Republican candidate)		
17	William Lehman (D) *	79,569	78.3
	Earl Rodney (R)	22,029	21.7
18	Ileana Ros-Lehtinen (R) *	56,364	60.4
	Bernard Anscher (D)	36,978	39.6
19	Dante B. Fascell (D) *	87,696	62.0
	Bob Allen (R)	53,796	38.0

GEORGIA

Governor

	Candidate	Vote Total	Per-cent
	Zell Miller (D)	766,662	52.9
	Johnny Isakson (R)	645,625	44.5
	Carole Ann Rand (LIBERT)	37,365	2.6

Senate

	Candidate	Vote Total	Per-cent
	Sam Nunn (D) *	1,033,439	100
	(No Republican candidate)		

House

	Candidate	Vote Total	Per-cent
1	Lindsay Thomas (D) *	80,515	71.2
	Chris Meredith (R)	32,532	28.8
2	Charles Hatcher (D) *	77,910	73.0
	Jonathan Perry Waters (R)	28,781	27.0
3	Richard Ray (D) *	72,961	63.2
	Paul Broun (R)	42,561	36.8
4	Ben Jones (D) *	96,526	52.4
	John Linder (R)	87,569	47.6
5	John Lewis (D) *	86,037	75.6
	J. W. Tibbs Jr. (R)	27,781	24.4
6	Newt Gingrich (R) *	78,768	50.3
	David Worley (D)	77,794	49.7
7	George "Buddy" Darden (D) *	95,817	60.1
	Al Beverly (R)	63,588	39.9
8	J. Roy Rowland (D) *	81,344	68.7
	Robert F. Cunningham (R)	36,980	31.3
9	Ed Jenkins (D) *	96,197	55.8
	Joe Hoffman (R)	76,121	44.2
10	Doug Barnard Jr. (D) *	89,683	58.3
	Sam Jones (R)	64,184	41.7

HAWAII

Governor

	Candidate	Vote Total	Per-cent
	John Waihee III (D) *	203,491	59.8
	Fred Hemmings (R)	131,310	38.6
	Triaka-Don Smith (LIBERT)	2,885	0.8
	Peggy Ha'o Ross (Nonpartisan)	2,446	0.7

Senate[a]

	Candidate	Vote Total	Per-cent
	Daniel K. Akaka (D) *	188,901	54.0
	Patricia Saiki (R)	155,978	44.6
	Ken Schoolland (LIBERT)	4,787	1.4

House

	Candidate	Vote Total	Per-cent
1	Neil Abercrombie (D)	97,622	60.0
	Mike Liu (R)	62,982	38.7
	Roger Lee Taylor (LIBERT)	2,107	1.3
2	Patsy T. Mink (D) *	118,155	66.3
	Andy Poepoe (R)	54,625	30.6
	Lloyd Jeffrey Mallan (LIBERT)	5,508	3.1

IDAHO

Governor

	Candidate	Vote Total	Per-cent
	Cecil D. Andrus (D) *	218,673	68.2
	Roger Fairchild (R)	101,937	31.8

Senate

	Candidate	Vote Total	Per-cent
	Larry E. Craig (R)	193,641	61.3
	Ron J. Twilegar (D)	122,295	38.7

House

	Candidate	Vote Total	Per-cent
1	Larry LaRocco (D)	85,054	53.0
	C. A. "Skip" Smyser (R)	75,406	47.0
2	Richard Stallings (D) *	98,008	63.6
	Sean McDevitt (R)	56,044	36.4

ILLINOIS

Governor

	Candidate	Vote Total	Per-cent
	Jim Edgar (R)	1,653,126	50.7
	Neil F. Hartigan (D)	1,569,217	48.2
	Jessie Fields (IS)	35,067	1.1

Senate

	Candidate	Vote Total	Per-cent
	Paul Simon (D) *	2,115,377	65.1
	Lynn Martin (R)	1,135,628	34.9

House

	Candidate	Vote Total	Per-cent
1	Charles A. Hayes (D) *	100,890	93.8
	Babette Peyton (R)	6,708	6.2
2	Gus Savage (D) *	80,245	78.2
	William T. Hespel (R)	22,350	21.8
3	Marty Russo (D) *	110,512	70.9
	Carl L. Klein (R)	45,299	29.1
4	George E. Sangmeister (D) *	77,290	59.2
	Manny Hoffman (R)	53,258	40.8
5	William O. Lipinski (D) *	73,805	66.3
	David J. Shestokas (R)	34,440	31.0
	Ronald Bartos (IS)	3,001	2.7
6	Henry J. Hyde (R) *	96,410	66.7
	Robert J. Cassidy (D)	48,155	33.3
7	Cardiss Collins (D) *	80,021	79.9
	Michael Dooley (R)	20,099	20.1
8	Dan Rostenkowski (D) *	70,151	79.1
	(No Republican candidate)		
	Robert Marshall (LIBERT)	18,529	20.9
9	Sidney R. Yates (D) *	96,557	71.2
	Herbert Sohn (R)	39,031	28.8
10	John Porter (R) *	104,070	67.7
	Peg McNamara (D)	47,286	30.8
	Herbert L. Gorrell (IS)	2,243	1.5
11	Frank Annunzio (D) *	82,703	53.6
	Walter W. Dudycz (R)	68,850	44.6
	Larry Saska (IS)	2,692	1.7
12	Philip M. Crane (R) *	113,081	82.2
	(No Democratic candidate)		
	Steve Pedersen (IS)	24,450	17.8
13	Harris W. Fawell (R) *	116,048	65.8
	Steven Thomas (D)	60,305	34.2
14	Dennis Hastert (R) *	112,383	66.9
	Donald J. Westphal (D)	55,592	33.1
15	Edward Madigan (R) *	119,812	100
	(No Democratic candidate)		
16	John W. Cox Jr. (D)	83,061	54.6
	John W. Hallock Jr. (R)	69,105	45.4
17	Lane Evans (D) *	102,062	66.5
	Dan Lee (R)	51,380	33.5
18	Robert H. Michel (R) *	105,693	98.4
	(No Democratic candidate)		
	Walter Gillin (write-in)	1,524	1.4
	Alan J. Port (write-in)	153	0.1
19	Terry L. Bruce (D) *	113,958	66.3
	Robert F. Kerans (R)	55,680	32.4
	Brian James O'Neill II (IS)	2,250	1.3
20	Richard J. Durbin (D) *	130,114	66.2
	Paul E. Jurgens (R)	66,433	33.8
21	Jerry F. Costello (D) *	95,208	66.0
	Robert H. Gaffner (R)	48,949	34.0
22	Glenn Poshard (D) *	138,425	83.7
	(No Republican candidate)		
	Jim Wham (Jim Wham Party)	26,896	16.3

INDIANA

Senate

	Candidate	Vote Total	Per-cent
	Daniel R. Coats (R) *	806,048	53.6
	Baron P. Hill (D)	696,639	46.4

House

	Candidate	Vote Total	Per-cent
1	Peter J. Visclosky (D) *	68,920	66.0
	William B. Costas (R)	35,450	34.0
2	Philip R. Sharp (D) *	93,495	59.4
	Mike Pence (R)	63,980	40.6
3	Tim Roemer (D)	80,740	50.9
	John Hiler (R) *	77,911	49.1
4	Jill Long (D) *	99,347	60.7
	Rick Hawks (R)	64,415	39.3
5	Jim Jontz (D) *	81,373	53.1
	John A. Johnson (R)	71,750	46.9
6	Dan Burton (R) *	116,470	63.5
	James P. Fadely (D)	67,024	36.5
7	John T. Myers (R) *	88,598	57.6
	John W. Riley Sr. (D)	65,248	42.4
8	Frank McCloskey (D) *	97,465	54.7
	Richard E. Mourdock (R)	80,645	45.3
9	Lee H. Hamilton (D) *	107,526	69.0
	Floyd Eugene Coates (R)	48,325	31.0
10	Andrew Jacobs Jr. (D) *	69,362	66.4
	Janos Horvath (R)	35,049	33.6

IOWA

Governor

	Candidate	Vote Total	Per-cent
	Terry E. Branstad (R) *	591,852	60.6
	Donald D. Avenson (D)	379,372	38.9
	Nan Bailey (SW)	4,263	0.4

Senate

	Candidate	Vote Total	Per-cent
	Tom Harkin (D) *	535,975	54.5
	Tom Tauke (R)	446,869	45.4

House

	Candidate	Vote Total	Per-cent
1	Jim Leach (R) *	90,042	99.8
	(No Democratic candidate)		
2	Jim Nussle (R)	82,650	49.8
	Eric Tabor (D)	81,008	48.8
	Jan J. Zonneveld (I)	2,325	1.4
3	Dave Nagle (D) *	100,947	99.2
	(No Republican candidate)		
4	Neal Smith (D) *	127,812	97.9
	(No Republican candidate)		
5	Jim Ross Lightfoot (R) *	99,978	68.0
	Rod Powell (D)	47,022	32.0
6	Fred Grandy (R) *	112,333	71.8
	Mike D. Earll (D)	44,063	28.2

KANSAS

Governor

	Candidate	Vote Total	Per-cent
	Joan Finney (D)	380,609	48.6
	Mike Hayden (R) *	333,589	42.6
	Christina Campbell-Cline (I)	69,127	8.8

Senate

	Candidate	Vote Total	Per-cent
	Nancy Landon Kassebaum (R) *	578,605	73.6
	Dick Williams (D)	207,491	26.4

House

	Candidate	Vote Total	Per-cent
1	Pat Roberts (R) *	102,974	62.6
	Duane West (D)	61,396	37.4
2	Jim Slattery (D) *	99,093	62.8
	Scott Morgan (R)	58,643	37.2
3	Jan Meyers (R) *	88,725	60.1
	Leroy Jones (D)	58,923	39.9
4	Dan Glickman (D) *	112,015	70.8
	Roger M. Grund (R)	46,283	29.2
5	Dick Nichols (R)	90,555	59.3
	George Wingert (D)	62,244	40.7

KENTUCKY

Senate

	Candidate	Vote Total	Per-cent
	Mitch McConnell (R) *	478,034	52.2
	Harvey Sloane (D)	437,976	47.8

House

	Candidate	Vote Total	Per-cent
1	Carroll Hubbard Jr. (D) *	85,323	86.9
	(No Republican candidate)		
	Marvin H. Seat (POP)	12,879	13.1
2	William H. Natcher (D) *	77,057	66.0
	Martin A. Tori (R)	39,624	34.0
3	Romano L. Mazzoli (D) *	84,750	60.6
	Al Brown (R)	55,188	39.4
4	Jim Bunning (R) *	101,680	69.3
	Galen Martin (D)	44,979	30.7

		Vote Total	Percent
5	Harold Rogers (R) *	64,660	100
	(No Democratic candidate)		
6	Larry J. Hopkins (R) *	76,859	100
	(No Democratic candidate)		
7	Carl C. Perkins (D) *	61,330	50.8
	Will T. Scott (R)	59,377	49.2

LOUISIANA

		Vote Total	Percent
Senate			
	J. Bennett Johnston (D) *	X	X
House			
1	Bob Livingston (R) *	X	X
2	William J. Jefferson (D)	55,621	52.5
	Marc H. Morial (D)	50,232	47.5
3	W. J. "Billy" Tauzin (D) *	X	X
4	Jim McCrery (R) *	X	X
5	Jerry Huckaby (D) *	X	X
6	Richard H. Baker (R) *	X	X
7	Jimmy Hayes (D) *	X	X
8	Clyde C. Holloway (R) *	X	X

MAINE

		Vote Total	Percent
Governor			
	John R. McKernan Jr. (R) *	243,766	46.7
	Joseph E. Brennan (D)	230,038	44.0
	Andrew Adam (Unenrolled)	48,377	9.3
Senate			
	William S. Cohen (R) *	319,167	61.3
	Neil Rolde (D)	201,053	38.6
House			
1	Thomas H. Andrews (D)	167,623	60.1
	David F. Emery (R)	110,836	39.7
2	Olympia J. Snowe (R) *	121,704	51.0
	Patrick K. McGowan (D)	116,798	49.0

MARYLAND

		Vote Total	Percent
Governor			
	William Donald Schaefer (D) *	664,015	59.8
	William S. Shepard (R)	446,980	40.2
House			
1	Wayne T. Gilchrest (R)	88,920	56.8
	Roy Dyson (D) *	67,518	43.2
2	Helen Delich Bentley (R) *	115,398	74.4
	Ronald P. Bowers (D)	39,785	25.6
3	Benjamin L. Cardin (D) *	82,545	69.7
	Harwood Nichols (R)	35,841	30.3
4	Tom McMillen (D) *	85,601	58.9
	Robert P. Duckworth (R)	59,846	41.1
5	Steny H. Hoyer (D) *	84,747	80.7
	Lee F. Breuer (R)	20,314	19.3
6	Beverly B. Byron (D) *	106,502	65.3
	Christopher P. Fiotes Jr. (R)	56,479	34.7
7	Kweisi Mfume (D) *	59,628	85.0
	Kenneth Kondner (R)	10,529	15.0
8	Constance A. Morella (R) *	130,059	73.5
	James Walker Jr. (D)	39,343	22.2
	Sidney Altman (I)	7,485	4.2

MASSACHUSETTS

		Vote Total	Percent
Governor			
	William F. Weld (R)	1,175,817	50.2
	John Silber (D)	1,099,878	46.9
	Leonard Umina (IHT)	62,703	2.7
Senate			
	John Kerry (D) *	1,321,712	57.1
	Jim Rappaport (R)	992,917	42.9
House			
1	Silvio O. Conte (R) *	150,748	77.5
	John R. Arden (D)	43,611	22.4
2	Richard E. Neal (D) *	134,152	99.8
	(No Republican candidate)		
3	Joseph D. Early (D) *	150,992	99.4
	(No Republican candidate)		
4	Barney Frank (D) *	143,473	65.5
	John R. Soto (R)	75,454	34.5
5	Chester G. Atkins (D) *	110,232	52.2
	John F. MacGovern (R)	101,017	47.8
6	Nicholas Mavroules (D) *	149,284	65.0
	Edgar L. Kelley (R)	80,177	34.9
7	Edward J. Markey (D) *	155,380	99.9
	(No Republican candidate)		
8	Joseph P. Kennedy II (D) *	125,479	72.2
	Glenn W. Fiscus (R)	39,310	22.6
	Susan C. Davies (NA)	8,806	5.1
9	Joe Moakley (D) *	124,534	70.3
	(No Republican candidate)		
	Robert Horan (I)	52,660	29.7
10	Larry E. Studds (D) *	137,805	53.4
	Jon L. Bryan (R)	120,217	46.6
11	Brian Donnelly (D) *	145,480	99.7
	(No Republican candidate)		

MICHIGAN

		Vote Total	Percent
Governor			
	John Engler (R)	1,276,134	49.8
	James J. Blanchard (D) *	1,258,539	49.1
	William Roundtree (WW)	28,091	1.1
Senate			
	Carl Levin (D) *	1,471,753	57.5
	Bill Schuette (R)	1,055,695	41.2
	Susan Farquhar (WW)	32,796	1.3
House			
1	John Conyers Jr. (D) *	76,556	89.3
	Ray Shoulders (R)	7,298	8.5
	Robert Mays (No affiliation)	1,134	1.3
	Jonathan Paul Flint (LIBERT)	764	0.9
2	Carl D. Pursell (R) *	95,962	64.1
	Elmer White (D)	49,678	33.2
	Paul S. Jensen (TIC)	4,119	2.7
3	Howard Wolpe (D) *	82,376	57.9
	Brad Haskins (R)	60,007	42.1
4	Fred Upton (R) *	75,850	57.8
	JoAnne McFarland (D)	55,449	42.2
5	Paul B. Henry (R) *	126,308	75.4
	Thomas Trzybinski (D)	41,170	24.6
6	Bob Carr (D) *	97,547	99.8
	(No Republican candidate)		
7	Dale E. Kildee (D) *	90,307	68.4
	David J. Morrill (R)	41,759	31.6
8	Bob Traxler (D) *	98,903	68.6
	James White (R)	45,259	31.4
9	Guy Vander Jagt (R) *	89,078	54.8
	Geraldine Greene (D)	73,604	45.2
10	Dave Camp (R)	99,952	65.0
	Joan Louise Dennison (D)	50,923	33.1
	Charles Congdon (LIBERT)	2,496	1.6
11	Robert W. Davis (R) *	94,555	61.3
	Marcia Gould (D)	59,759	38.7
12	David E. Bonior (D) *	98,232	64.7
	Jim Dingeman (R)	51,119	33.7
	Robert W. Roddis (LIBERT)	2,472	1.6
13	Barbara-Rose Collins (D)	54,345	80.1
	Carl R. Edwards Sr. (R)	11,203	16.5
	Joyce Ann Griffin (WW)	1,090	1.6
	Jeff J. Hampton (LIBERT)	649	1.0
	Cleve Andrew Pulley (none)	530	0.8
14	Dennis M. Hertel (D) *	78,506	63.6
	Kenneth C. McNealy (R)	40,499	32.8
	Robert John Gale (TIC)	2,692	2.2
	Kenneth G. Morris (LIBERT)	1,721	1.4
15	William D. Ford (D) *	68,742	61.2
	Burl C. Adkins (R)	41,092	36.6
	David R. Hunt (LIBERT)	2,497	2.2
16	John D. Dingell (D) *	88,962	66.6
	Frank Beaumont (R)	42,629	31.9
	Roger Conant Pope (LIBERT)	2,019	1.5
17	Sander M. Levin (D) *	92,205	69.7
	Blaine L. Lankford (R)	40,100	30.3
18	William S. Broomfield (R) *	126,629	66.4
	Walter O. Briggs IV (D)	64,185	33.6

MINNESOTA

		Vote Total	Percent
Governor			
	Arne Carlson (R)	895,988	49.6
	Rudy Perpich (D) *	836,218	46.3
	Heart Warrior (Judith Ann) Chosa (ER)	21,139	1.2
	Ross S. Culverhouse (GR)	17,176	1.0
	Jon Grunseth (originally GOP nominee)	10,941	0.6
	Wendy Lyons (SW)	6,701	0.4
Senate			
	Paul Wellstone (D)	911,999	50.4
	Rudy Boschwitz (R) *	864,375	47.8
	Russell B. Bentley (GR)	29,820	1.6
House			
1	Timothy J. Penny (D) *	156,749	78.1
	Doug Andersen (R)	43,856	21.9
2	Vin Weber (R) *	126,367	61.8
	Jim Stone (D)	77,935	38.1
3	Jim Ramstad (R)	195,833	66.9
	Lewis DeMars (D)	96,395	32.9
4	Bruce F. Vento (D) *	143,353	64.7
	Ian Maitland (R)	77,639	35.1
5	Martin Olav Sabo (D) *	144,682	72.9
	Raymond C. "Buzz" Gilbertson (R)	53,720	27.1
6	Gerry Sikorski (D) *	164,816	64.6
	Bruce D. Anderson (R)	90,138	35.3
7	Collin C. Peterson (D)	107,126	53.5
	Arlan Stangeland (R) *	92,876	46.4
8	James L. Oberstar (D) *	151,145	72.9
	Jerry Shuster (R)	56,068	27.0

MISSISSIPPI

		Vote Total	Percent
Senate			
	Thad Cochran (R) *	274,244	100
	(No Democratic candidate)		
House			
1	Jamie L. Whitten (D) *	43,668	64.9
	Bill Bowlin (R)	23,650	35.1
2	Mike Espy (D) *	59,393	84.1
	Dorothy Benford (R)	11,224	15.9
3	G. V. "Sonny" Montgomery (D) *	49,162	100
	(No Republican candidate)		
4	Mike Parker (D) *	57,137	80.6
	Jerry "Rev" Parks (R)	13,754	19.4
5	Gene Taylor (D) *	89,926	81.4
	Sheila Smith (R)	20,588	18.6

MISSOURI

		Vote Total	Percent
House			
1	William L. Clay (D) *	62,550	60.9
	Wayne G. Piotrowski (R)	40,160	39.1
2	Joan Kelly Horn (D)	94,378	50.0
	Jack Buechner (R) *	94,324	50.0
3	Richard A. Gephardt (D) *	88,950	56.8
	Malcolm L. Holekamp (R)	67,659	43.2

		Vote Total	Percent
4	Ike Skelton (D) *	105,527	61.8
	David Eyerly (R)	65,095	38.2
5	Alan Wheat (D) *	71,890	62.1
	Robert H. Gardner (R)	43,897	37.9
6	E. Thomas Coleman (R) *	78,956	51.9
	Bob McClure (D)	73,093	48.1
7	Mel Hancock (R) *	83,609	52.1
	Thomas Patrick Deaton (D)	76,725	47.9
8	Bill Emerson (R) *	81,452	57.3
	Russ Carnahan (D)	60,751	42.7
9	Harold L. Volkmer (D) *	94,156	57.5
	Don Curtis (R)	69,514	42.5

MONTANA

Senate

		Vote Total	Percent
	Max Baucus (D) *	217,563	68.1
	Allen C. Kolstad (R)	93,836	29.4
	Westley F. Deitchler (LIBERT)	7,937	2.5

House

		Vote Total	Percent
1	Pat Williams (D) *	100,409	61.1
	Brad Johnson (R)	63,837	38.9
2	Ron Marlenee (R) *	96,449	63.0
	Don Burris (D)	56,739	37.0

NEBRASKA

Governor

		Vote Total	Percent
	Ben Nelson (D)	292,771	49.9
	Kay A. Orr (R) *	288,741	49.2
	Mort Sullivan (write-in)	1,887	0.3

Senate

		Vote Total	Percent
	Jim Exon (D) *	349,779	58.9
	Hal Daub (R)	243,013	40.9

House

		Vote Total	Percent
1	Doug Bereuter (R) *	129,654	64.7
	Larry Hall (D)	70,587	35.2
2	Peter Hoagland (D) *	111,903	57.9
	Ally Milder (R)	80,845	41.8
3	Bill Barrett (R)	98,607	51.1
	Sandra K. Scofield (D)	94,234	48.8

NEVADA

Governor

		Vote Total	Percent
	Bob Miller (D) *	207,878	64.8
	Jim Gallaway (R)	95,789	29.9
	None of these	9,017	2.8
	James Frye (LIBERT)	8,059	2.5

House

		Vote Total	Percent
1	James Bilbray (D) *	84,650	61.4
	Bob Dickinson (R)	47,377	34.4
	William Moore (LIBERT)	5,825	4.2
2	Barbara F. Vucanovich (R) *	103,508	59.1
	Jane Wisdom (D)	59,581	34.0
	Dan Becan (LIBERT)	12,120	6.9

NEW HAMPSHIRE

Governor

		Vote Total	Percent
	Judd Gregg (R) *	177,611	60.2
	J. Joseph Grandmaison (D)	101,886	34.6
	Miriam F. Luce (LIBERT)	14,348	4.9

Senate

		Vote Total	Percent
	Robert C. Smith (R)	189,630	65.1
	John A. Durkin (D)	91,262	31.3
	John Elsnau (LIBERT)	9,717	3.3

House

		Vote Total	Percent
1	Bill Zeliff (R)	81,684	55.1
	Joseph F. Keefe (D)	66,176	44.6
2	Dick Swett (D)	74,829	52.7
	Chuck Douglas (R) *	67,063	47.2

NEW JERSEY

Senate

		Vote Total	Percent
	Bill Bradley (D) *	977,810	50.4
	Christine Todd Whitman (R)	918,874	47.4
	John L. Kucek (POP)	19,978	1.0
	Louis M. Stefanelli (LIBERT)	13,988	0.7
	Don Mackle (SW)	7,804	0.4

House

		Vote Total	Percent
1	Robert E. Andrews (D)	73,522	54.3
	Daniel J. Mangini (R)	57,801	42.7
	Jerry Zeldin (LIBERT)	1,599	1.2
	Walter E. Konstanty (PH)	1,431	1.0
	William Henry Harris (POP)	1,078	0.8
2	William J. Hughes (D) *	98,734	88.2
	(No Republican candidate)		
	William A. Kanengiser (POP)	13,246	11.8
3	Frank Pallone Jr. (D) *	77,709	49.1
	Paul A. Kapalko (R)	73,451	46.4
	Richard D. McKean (I)	4,390	2.8
	William Stewart (LIBERT)	1,875	1.2
	Joseph A. Plonski (POP)	867	0.5
4	Christopher H. Smith (R) *	101,508	62.9
	Mark Setaro (D)	55,454	34.4
	Carl Peters (LIBERT)	2,168	1.3
	Joseph J. Notarangelo (POP)	1,219	0.8
	J. M. Carter (GWT)	1,029	0.6
5	Marge Roukema (R) *	118,101	75.7
	Lawrence Wayne Olsen (D)	35,010	22.4
	Mark Richards (POP)	2,998	1.9
6	Bernard J. Dwyer (D) *	63,696	50.5
	Paul Danielczyk (R)	58,209	46.2
	Randolph Waller (POP)	2,364	1.9
	Howard F. Schoen (LIBERT)	1,784	1.4
7	Matthew J. Rinaldo (R) *	100,274	74.6
	Bruce H. Bergen (D)	31,114	23.2
	Thomas V. Sarnowski (POP)	2,929	2.2
8	Robert A. Roe (D) *	55,212	76.9
	(No Republican candidate)		
	Stephen Sibilia (I-C)	13,239	18.4
	Bruce Eden (POP)	3,347	4.7
9	Robert G. Torricelli (D) *	82,736	57.0
	Peter J. Russo (R)	59,759	41.2
	Chester Grabowski (POP)	2,573	1.8
10	Donald M. Payne (D) *	42,616	81.5
	Howard E. Berkeley (R)	9,072	17.3
	George Mehrabian (SW)	617	1.2
11	Dean A. Gallo (R) *	95,198	64.9
	Michael Gordon (D)	47,782	32.6
	Jasper Gould (POP)	3,610	2.5
12	Dick Zimmer (R)	108,173	64.0
	Marguerite Chandler (D)	52,498	31.1
	Joan I. Bottcher (BB)	4,443	2.6
	C. Max Kortepeter (I-Reform)	2,442	1.4
	Michael A. Notarangelo (POP)	1,408	0.8
13	H. James Saxton (R) *	100,537	58.1
	John H. Adler (D)	68,286	39.5
	Howard Scott Pearlman (WWW)	4,178	2.4
14	Frank J. Guarini (D) *	57,581	66.1
	Fred J. Theemling Jr. (R)	25,473	29.2
	Michael Ziruolo (BAG)	1,897	2.2
	Jane E. Harris (SW)	1,355	1.5
	Donald K. Stoveken Sr. (POP)	519	0.6
	Louis Vernotico (Right to Vote)	324	0.4

NEW MEXICO

Governor

		Vote Total	Percent
	Bruce King (D)	224,564	54.6
	Frank M. Bond (R)	185,692	45.2
	Joseph E. Knight (write-in)	788	0.2

Senate

		Vote Total	Percent
	Pete V. Domenici (R) *	296,712	72.9
	Tom R. Benavides (D)	110,033	27.1

House

		Vote Total	Percent
1	Steven H. Schiff (R) *	97,375	70.2
	Rebecca Vigil-Giron (D)	41,306	29.8
2	Joe Skeen (R) *	80,677	100
	(No Democratic candidate)		
3	Bill Richardson (D) *	104,225	74.5
	Phil T. Archuletta (R)	35,751	25.5

NEW YORK

Governor

		Vote Total	Percent
	Mario M. Cuomo (D, L) *	2,157,087	53.2
	Pierre A. Rinfret (R)	865,948	21.3
	Herbert I. London (C)	827,614	20.4
	Louis P. Wein (RTL)	137,804	3.4
	Lenora B. Fulani (NA)	31,089	0.8
	W. Gary Johnson (LIBERT)	24,611	0.6
	Craig Gannon (SW)	12,743	0.3

House

		Vote Total	Percent
1	George J. Hochbrueckner (D, Tax Break) *	75,211	56.3
	Francis W. Creighton (R)	46,380	34.7
	Clayton Baldwin Jr. (C)	6,883	5.2
	Peter J. O'Hara (RTL)	5,111	3.8
2	Thomas J. Downey (D) *	56,722	55.8
	John W. Bugler (R, RTL, Tax Cut)	36,859	36.2
	Dominic A. Curcio (C)	8,150	8.0
3	Robert J. Mrazek (D, L) *	73,029	53.3
	Robert Previdi (R, C)	59,089	43.1
	Francis A. Dreger (RTL)	4,915	3.6
4	Norman F. Lent (R, C) *	79,304	61.2
	Francis T. Goban (D)	41,308	31.8
	John J. Dunkle (RTL)	6,706	5.2
	Ben-Zion J. Heyman (L)	2,343	1.8
5	Raymond J. McGrath (R, C) *	71,948	54.6
	Mark S. Epstein (D, L)	53,920	40.9
	Edward K. Kitt (RTL)	6,000	4.5
6	Floyd H. Flake (D, L) *	44,306	73.1
	William Sampol (R)	13,224	21.8
	John Cronin (RTL)	3,111	5.1
7	Gary L. Ackerman (D, L) *	51,091	100
	(No Republican candidate)		
8	James H. Scheuer (D, L) *	56,396	72.3
	Gustave Reifenkugel (R)	21,646	27.7
9	Thomas J. Manton (D) *	35,177	64.4
	Ann Pfoser Darby (R, AC)	13,330	24.4
	Thomas V. Ognibene (C)	6,137	11.2
10	Charles E. Schumer (D, L) *	61,468	80.4
	Patrick J. Kinsella (R, C)	14,963	19.6
11	Ed Towns (D, L) *	36,286	92.9
	(No Republican candidate)		
	Ernest Johnson (C)	1,676	4.3
	Lorraine Stevens (NA)	1,094	2.8
12	Major R. Owens (D, L) *	40,570	94.9
	(No Republican candidate)		
	Joseph N. O. Caesar (C)	1,159	2.7
	Mamie Moore (NA)	1,021	2.4
13	Stephen J. Solarz (D, L) *	47,446	80.4
	Edwin Ramos (R, C)	11,557	19.6
14	Susan Molinari (R, C) *	58,616	60.0
	Anthony J. Pocchia (D, L, SIS)	34,625	35.5
	Christine Sacchi (RTL)	4,370	4.5
15	Bill Green (R) *	52,919	58.8
	Frances L. Reiter (D)	33,464	37.2
	Michael T. Berns (C)	3,654	4.0
16	Charles B. Rangel (D, R, L) *	55,882	97.2
	Alvaader Frazier (NA)	1,592	2.8
17	Ted Weiss (D, L) *	79,161	80.4
	William W. Koeppel (R)	15,219	15.5
	Mark Goret (C)	2,928	3.0
	John Patterson (NA)	1,087	1.1
18	Jose E. Serrano (D, L) *	38,024	93.2
	Joseph Chiavaro (R)	1,189	2.9

		Vote Total	Percent
	Mary Rivera (NA)	866	2.1
	Anna Johnson (C)	717	1.8
19	Eliot L. Engel (D, L) *	45,758	61.2
	William J. Gouldman (R)	17,135	22.9
	Kevin Brawley (C, RTL)	11,868	15.9
20	Nita M. Lowey (D) *	82,203	62.8
	Glenn D. Belitto (R)	35,575	27.2
	John M. Schafer (C, RTL)	13,030	10.0
21	Hamilton Fish Jr. (R, C) *	99,866	71.4
	Richard L. Barbuto (D)	34,128	24.4
	Richard S. Curtin II (RTL)	5,925	4.2
22	Benjamin A. Gilman (R) *	95,495	68.6
	John G. Dow (D)	37,034	26.6
	Margaret M. Beirne (RTL)	6,656	4.8
23	Michael R. McNulty (D, C) *	117,239	64.1
	Margaret B. Buhrmaster (R)	65,760	35.9
24	Gerald B. H. Solomon (R, C, RTL) *	121,206	68.1
	Bob Lawrence (D)	56,671	31.9
25	Sherwood Boehlert (R) *	91,348	83.9
	(No Democratic candidate)		
	William L. Griffen (L)	17,481	16.1
26	David O'B. Martin (R, C) *	97,340	100
	(No Democratic candidate)		
27	James T. Walsh (R, C) *	95,220	63.2
	Peggy L. Murray (D, L)	52,438	34.8
	Stephen K. Hoff (RTL)	3,097	2.0
28	Matthew F. McHugh (D) *	97,815	64.8
	Seymour Krieger (R)	53,077	35.2
29	Frank Horton (R) *	89,105	63.0
	Alton F. Eber (D)	34,835	24.6
	Peter DeMauro (C)	12,599	8.9
	Donald M. Peters (RTL)	4,878	3.4
30	Louise M. Slaughter (D) *	97,280	59.0
	John M. Regan Jr. (R, C, RTL)	67,534	41.0
31	Bill Paxon (R, C, RTL) *	90,237	56.6
	Kevin P. Gaughan (D, L)	69,328	43.4
32	John J. LaFalce (D, L) *	68,367	55.0
	Michael T. Waring (R)	39,053	31.4
	Kenneth J. Kowalski (C, RTL)	16,853	13.6
33	Henry J. Nowak (D, L) *	84,905	77.5
	Thomas K. Kepfer (R)	18,181	16.6
	Louis P. Corrigan Jr. (C)	6,460	5.9
34	Amo Houghton (R, C) *	89,831	69.6
	Joseph P. Leahey (D)	37,421	29.0
	Nevin K. Eklund (L)	1,807	1.4

NORTH CAROLINA

Senate

		Vote Total	Percent
	Jesse Helms (R) *	1,088,331	52.6
	Harvey B. Gantt (D)	981,573	47.4

House

		Vote Total	Percent
1	Walter B. Jones (D) *	105,832	64.8
	Howard D. Moye (R)	57,526	35.2
2	Tim Valentine (D) *	130,979	74.7
	Hal C. Sharpe (R)	44,263	25.3
3	H. Martin Lancaster (D) *	83,930	59.3
	Don Davis (R)	57,605	40.7
4	David E. Price (D) *	139,396	58.1
	John Carrington (R)	100,661	41.9
5	Stephen L. Neal (D) *	113,814	59.1
	Ken Bell (R)	78,747	40.9
6	Howard Coble (R) *	125,392	66.6
	Helen R. Allegrone (D)	62,913	33.4
7	Charlie Rose (D) *	94,946	65.6
	Robert C. Anderson (R)	49,681	34.4
8	W. G. "Bill" Hefner (D) *	98,700	55.0
	Ted Blanton (R)	80,852	45.0
9	Alex McMillan (R) *	131,936	62.0
	David P. McKnight (D)	80,802	38.0
10	Cass Ballenger (R) *	106,400	61.8
	Daniel R. Green Jr. (D)	65,710	38.2
11	Charles H. Taylor (R)	101,991	50.7
	James McClure Clarke (D) *	99,318	49.3

NORTH DAKOTA

House

		Vote Total	Percent
AL	Byron L. Dorgan (D) *	152,530	65.2
	Edward T. Schafer (R)	81,443	34.8

OHIO

Governor

		Vote Total	Percent
	George V. Voinovich (R)	1,938,103	55.7
	Anthony J. Celebrezze Jr. (D)	1,539,416	44.3

House

		Vote Total	Percent
1	Charles Luken (D)	83,932	51.1
	J. Kenneth Blackwell (R)	80,362	48.9
2	Bill Gradison (R) *	103,817	64.4
	Tyrone K. Yates (D)	57,345	35.6
3	Tony P. Hall (D) *	116,797	100
	(No Republican candidate)		
4	Michael G. Oxley (R) *	103,897	61.7
	Thomas E. Burkhart (D)	64,467	38.3
5	Paul E. Gillmor (R) *	113,615	68.5
	P. Scott Mange (D)	41,693	25.1
	John E. Jackson (I)	10,612	6.4
6	Bob McEwen (R) *	117,220	71.2
	Ray Mitchell (D)	47,415	28.8
7	David L. Hobson (R)	97,123	62.1
	Jack Schira (D)	59,349	37.9
8	John A. Boehner (R)	99,955	61.1
	Gregory V. Jolivette (D)	63,584	38.9
9	Marcy Kaptur (D) *	117,681	77.7
	Jerry D. Lammers (R)	33,791	22.3
10	Clarence E. Miller (R) *	106,009	63.2
	John M. Buchanan (D)	61,656	36.8
11	Dennis E. Eckart (D) *	111,923	65.7
	Margaret Mueller (R)	58,372	34.3
12	John R. Kasich (R) *	130,495	72.0
	Mike Gelpi (D)	50,784	28.0
13	Don J. Pease (D) *	93,431	56.7
	William D. Nielsen (R)	60,925	36.9
	John Michael Ryan (I)	10,506	6.4
14	Thomas C. Sawyer (D) *	97,875	59.6
	Jean E. Bender (R)	66,460	40.4
15	Chalmers P. Wylie (R) *	99,251	59.1
	Thomas V. Erney (D)	68,510	40.8
	William L. Buckel (write-in)	158	0.1
16	Ralph Regula (R) *	101,097	58.9
	Warner D. Mendenhall (D)	70,516	41.1
17	James A. Traficant Jr. (D) *	133,207	77.7
	Robert R. DeJulio Jr. (R)	38,199	22.3
18	Doug Applegate (D) *	120,782	74.3
	John A. Hales (R)	41,823	25.7
19	Edward F. Feighan (D) *	132,951	64.8
	Susan M. Lawko (R)	72,315	35.2
20	Mary Rose Oakar (D) *	109,390	73.3
	Bill Smith (R)	39,749	26.7
21	Louis Stokes (D) *	103,338	80.0
	Franklin H. Roski (R)	25,906	20.0

OKLAHOMA

Governor

		Vote Total	Percent
	David Walters (D)	523,196	57.4
	Bill Price (R)	297,584	32.7
	Thomas D. Ledgerwood II (I)	90,534	9.9

Senate

		Vote Total	Percent
	David L. Boren (D) *	735,684	83.2
	Stephen Jones (R)	148,814	16.8

House

		Vote Total	Percent
1	James M. Inhofe (R) *	75,618	56.0
	Kurt G. Glassco (D)	59,521	44.0
2	Mike Synar (D) *	90,820	61.3
	Terry M. Gorham (R)	57,331	38.7
3	Bill Brewster (D)	107,641	80.4
	Patrick K. Miller (R)	26,261	19.6
4	Dave McCurdy (D) *	100,879	73.6
	Howard Bell (R)	36,232	26.4
5	Mickey Edwards (R) *	114,608	69.6
	Bryce Baggett (D)	50,086	30.4
6	Glenn English (D) *	110,100	80.0
	Robert Burns (R)	27,540	20.0

OREGON

Governor

		Vote Total	Percent
	Barbara Roberts (D)	508,749	45.7
	Dave Frohnmayer (R)	444,646	40.0
	Al Mobley (I)	144,062	12.9
	Fred Oerther (LIBERT)	14,583	1.3

Senate

		Vote Total	Percent
	Mark O. Hatfield (R) *	590,095	53.7
	Harry Lonsdale (D)	507,743	46.2

House

		Vote Total	Percent
1	Les AuCoin (D) *	150,292	63.1
	Earl Molander (R)	72,382	30.4
	Rick Livingston (I)	15,585	6.5
2	Bob Smith (R) *	127,998	68.0
	Jim Smiley (D)	60,131	32.0
3	Ron Wyden (D) *	169,731	80.8
	Philip E. Mooney (R)	40,216	19.1
4	Peter A. DeFazio (D) *	162,494	85.8
	(No Republican candidate)		
	Tonie Nathan (LIBERT)	26,432	14.0
5	Mike Kopetski (D)	124,610	55.0
	Denny Smith (R) *	101,650	44.9

PENNSYLVANIA

Governor

		Vote Total	Percent
	Robert P. Casey (D) *	2,065,244	67.7
	Barbara Hafer (R)	987,516	32.3

House

		Vote Total	Percent
1	Thomas M. Foglietta (D) *	73,423	79.4
	James Love Jackson (R)	19,018	20.6
2	William H. Gray III (D) *	94,584	92.1
	Donald Bakove (R)	8,118	7.9
3	Robert A. Borski (D) *	89,908	60.0
	Joseph Marc McColgan (R)	59,901	40.0
4	Joe Kolter (D) *	74,114	55.9
	Gordon R. Johnston (R)	58,469	44.1
5	Richard T. Schulze (R) *	75,097	57.1
	Samuel C. Stretton (D)	50,597	38.5
	Lewis Dupont Smith (ASI)	5,795	4.4
6	Gus Yatron (D) *	74,394	57.0
	John F. Hicks (R)	56,093	43.0
7	Curt Weldon (R) *	105,868	65.3
	John Innelli (D)	56,292	34.7
8	Peter H. Kostmayer (D) *	85,015	56.6
	Audrie Zettick Schaller (R)	65,100	43.4
9	Bud Shuster (R, D) *	106,632	100
10	Joseph M. McDade (R, D) *	113,490	100
11	Paul E. Kanjorski (D) *	88,219	100
	(No Republican candidate)		
12	John P. Murtha (D) *	80,686	61.7
	William Choby (R)	50,007	38.3
13	Lawrence Coughlin (R) *	89,577	60.3
	Bernard Tomkin (D)	58,967	39.7
14	William J. Coyne (D) *	77,636	71.8
	Richard Edward Caligiuri (R)	30,497	28.2
15	Don Ritter (R) *	77,178	60.6
	Richard J. Orloski (D)	50,233	39.4
16	Robert S. Walker (R) *	85,596	66.1
	Ernest Eric Guyll (D)	43,849	33.9
17	George W. Gekas (R, D) *	110,317	100
18	Rick Santorum (R)	85,697	51.4
	Doug Walgren (D) *	80,880	48.6

		Vote Total	Percent
19	Bill Goodling (R) *	96,336	100
	(No Democratic candidate)		
20	Joseph M. Gaydos (D) *	82,080	65.6
	Robert C. Lee (R)	43,054	34.4
21	Tom Ridge (R) *	92,732	100
	(No Democratic candidate)		
22	Austin J. Murphy (D) *	78,375	63.3
	Suzanne Hayden (R)	45,509	36.7
23	William F. Clinger Jr. (R) *	78,189	59.4
	Daniel J. Shannon (D)	53,465	40.6

RHODE ISLAND

Governor

	Vote Total	Percent
Bruce Sundlun (D)	264,411	74.2
Edward D. DiPrete (R) *	92,177	25.8

Senate

	Vote Total	Percent
Claiborne Pell (D) *	225,105	61.8
Claudine Schneider (R)	138,947	38.2

House

		Vote Total	Percent
1	Ronald K. Machtley (R) *	89,963	55.2
	Scott Wolf (D)	73,131	44.8
2	John F. Reed (D)	108,818	59.2
	Gertrude M. "Trudy" Coxe (R)	74,953	40.8

SOUTH CAROLINA

Governor

	Vote Total	Percent
Carroll A. Campbell Jr. (R) *	528,831	69.5
Theo Mitchell (D)	212,034	27.9
John Peeples (AM)	17,302	2.3

Senate

	Vote Total	Percent
Strom Thurmond (R) *	482,032	64.2
Bob Cunningham (D)	244,112	32.5
William H. Griffin (LIBERT)	13,805	1.8
Marion C. Metts (AM)	10,317	1.4

House

		Vote Total	Percent
1	Arthur Ravenel Jr. (R) *	80,839	65.5
	Eugene Platt (D)	42,555	34.5
2	Floyd D. Spence (R) *	90,054	88.7
	(No Democratic candidate)		
	Geb Sommer (LIBERT)	11,101	10.9
3	Butler Derrick (D) *	72,561	58.0
	Ray Haskett (R)	52,419	41.9
4	Liz J. Patterson (D) *	81,927	61.4
	Terry E. Haskins (R)	51,338	38.4
5	John M. Spratt Jr. (D) *	91,775	99.9
	(No Republican candidate)		
6	Robin Tallon (D) *	94,121	99.6
	(No Republican candidate)		

SOUTH DAKOTA

Governor

	Vote Total	Percent
George S. Mickelson (R) *	151,198	58.9
Bob L. Samuelson (D)	105,525	41.1

Senate

	Vote Total	Percent
Larry Pressler (R) *	135,682	52.4
Ted Muenster (D)	116,727	45.1
Dean L. Sinclair (I)	6,567	2.5

House

		Vote Total	Percent
AL	Tim Johnson (D) *	173,814	67.6
	Don Frankenfeld (R)	83,484	32.4

TENNESSEE

Governor

	Vote Total	Percent
Ned McWherter (D) *	480,885	60.8
Dwight Henry (R)	289,348	36.6
W. Curtis Jacox (I)	10,993	1.4
David Brandon Shepard (I)	9,109	1.2

Senate

	Vote Total	Percent
Al Gore (D) *	530,898	67.7
William R. Hawkins (R)	233,703	29.8
Bill Jacox (I)	11,191	1.4
Charles Gordon Vick (I)	8,021	1.0

House

		Vote Total	Percent
1	James H. Quillen (R) *	47,796	99.9
	(No Democratic candidate)		
2	John J. "Jimmy" Duncan Jr. (R) *	62,797	80.6
	(No Democratic candidate)		
	Peter Hebert (I)	15,127	19.4
3	Marilyn Lloyd (D) *	49,662	53.0
	Grady L. Rhoden (R)	36,855	39.3
	Peter T. Melcher (I)	5,598	6.0
	George E. Googe (I)	1,546	1.7
4	Jim Cooper (D) *	52,101	67.4
	Claiborne "Clay" Sanders (R)	22,890	29.6
	Gene M. Bullington (I)	2,281	3.0
5	Bob Clement (D) *	55,607	72.4
	(No Republican candidate)		
	Tom Stone (I)	13,577	17.7
	Al Borgman (I)	5,383	7.0
	Maurice C. Kuttab (I)	2,192	2.9
6	Bart Gordon (D) *	60,538	66.7
	Gregory Cochran (R)	26,424	29.1
	Ken Brown (I)	3,793	4.2
7	Don Sundquist (R) *	66,141	62.0
	Ken Bloodworth (D)	40,516	38.0
8	John Tanner (D) *	62,241	100
	(No Republican candidate)		
9	Harold E. Ford (D) *	48,629	58.1
	Aaron C. Davis (R)	25,730	30.8
	Thomas M. Davidson (I)	7,249	8.7
	Isaac Richmond (I)	2,032	2.4

TEXAS

Governor

	Vote Total	Percent
Ann W. Richards (D)	1,925,670	49.5
Clayton Williams (R)	1,826,431	46.9
Jeff Daiell (LIBERT)	129,157	3.3
Bubbles Cash (write-in)	3,275	0.1

Senate

	Vote Total	Percent
Phil Gramm (R) *	2,302,357	60.2
Hugh Parmer (D)	1,429,986	37.4
Gary Johnson (LIBERT)	89,089	2.3

House

		Vote Total	Percent
1	Jim Chapman (D) *	89,241	61.0
	Hamp Hodges (R)	56,954	39.0
2	Charles Wilson (D) *	76,974	55.6
	Donna Peterson (R)	61,555	44.4
3	Steve Bartlett (R) *	153,857	99.6
	(No Democratic candidate)		
	Noel Kopala (write-in)	617	0.4
4	Ralph M. Hall (D) *	108,300	99.6
	(No Republican candidate)		
	Tim J. McCord (write-in)	394	0.4
5	John Bryant (D) *	65,228	59.6
	Jerry Rucker (R)	41,307	37.7
	Kenneth Ashby (LIBERT)	2,939	2.7
6	Joe L. Barton (R) *	125,049	66.5
	John E. Welch (D)	62,344	33.1
	Michael Worsham (write-in)	737	0.4
7	Bill Archer (R) *	114,254	100
	(No Democratic candidate)		
8	Jack Fields (R) *	60,603	100
	(No Democratic candidate)		
9	Jack Brooks (D) *	79,786	57.7
	Maury Meyers (R)	58,399	42.3
10	J. J. "Jake" Pickle (D) *	152,784	64.9
	David Beilharz (R)	73,766	31.3
	Jeff Davis (LIBERT)	8,905	3.8
11	Chet Edwards (D)	73,810	53.5
	Hugh D. Shine (R)	64,269	46.5
12	Pete Geren (D) *	98,026	71.3
	Mike McGinn (R)	39,438	28.7
13	Bill Sarpalius (D) *	81,815	56.5
	Dick Waterfield (R)	63,045	43.5
14	Greg Laughlin (D) *	89,251	54.3
	Joe Dial (R)	75,098	45.7
15	E. "Kika" de la Garza (D) *	72,461	100
	(No Republican candidate)		
16	Ronald D. Coleman (D) *	62,455	95.6
	(No Republican candidate)		
	William Burgett (write-in)	2,854	4.4
17	Charles W. Stenholm (D) *	104,100	100
	(No Republican candidate)		
18	Craig Washington (D) *	54,477	99.6
	(No Republican candidate)		
	Timothy John Hattenbach (write-in)	166	0.3
	Shirley Fobbs (write-in)	38	0.1
19	Larry Combest (R) *	83,795	100
	(No Democratic candidate)		
20	Henry B. Gonzalez (D) *	56,318	100
	(No Republican candidate)		
21	Lamar Smith (R) *	144,570	74.8
	Kirby J. Roberts (D)	48,585	25.2
22	Tom DeLay (R) *	93,425	71.2
	Bruce Director (D)	37,721	28.8
23	Albert G. Bustamante (D) *	71,052	63.5
	Jerome L. "Jerry" Gonzales (R)	40,856	36.5
24	Martin Frost (D) *	86,297	100
	(No Republican candidate)		
25	Michael A. Andrews (D) *	67,427	100
	(No Republican candidate)		
26	Dick Armey (R) *	147,856	70.4
	John Wayne Caton (D)	62,158	29.6
27	Solomon P. Ortiz (D) *	62,822	100
	(No Republican candidate)		

UTAH

House

		Vote Total	Percent
1	James V. Hansen (R) *	82,746	52.1
	Kenley Brunsdale (D)	69,491	43.8
	Reva Marx Wadsworth (AM)	6,429	4.1
2	Wayne Owens (D) *	85,167	57.6
	Genevieve Atwood (R)	58,869	39.8
	Lawrence Rey Topham (I-Utah)	3,424	2.3
	Eleanor Garcia (SW)	411	0.3
3	Bill Orton (D)	79,163	58.3
	Karl Snow (R)	49,452	36.4
	Robert J. Smith (AM)	6,542	4.8
	Anthony Melvin Dutrow (SW)	519	0.4

VERMONT

Governor

	Vote Total	Percent
Richard A. Snelling (R)	109,540	51.8
Peter Welch (D)	97,321	46.0
David Atkinson (LIBERT)	2,777	1.3
Richard F. Gottlieb (LU)	1,389	0.7

	Vote Total	Percent
House		
AL Bernard Sanders (I)	117,522	56.0
Peter Smith (R) *	82,938	39.5
Dolores Sandoval (D)	6,315	3.0
Peter Diamondstone (LU)	1,965	0.9

VIRGINIA

	Vote Total	Percent
Senate		
John W. Warner (R) *	876,782	80.9
(No Democratic candidate)		
Nancy B. Spannaus (I)	196,755	18.2
House		
1 Herbert H. Bateman (R) *	72,000	51.0
Andrew H. Fox (D)	69,194	49.0
2 Owen B. Pickett (D) *	55,179	75.0
(No Republican candidate)		
Harry G. Broskie (I)	15,915	21.6
3 Thomas J. Bliley Jr. (R) *	77,125	65.3
Jay Starke (D)	36,253	30.7
Rose L. Simpson (I)	4,317	3.7
4 Norman Sisisky (D) *	71,051	78.3
(No Republican candidate)		
Don L. Reynolds (I)	12,295	13.6
Loretta F. Chandler (I)	7,102	7.8
5 Lewis F. Payne Jr. (D) *	66,532	99.4
(No Republican candidate)		
6 Jim Olin (D) *	92,968	82.7
(No Republican candidate)		
Gerald E. "Laser" Berg (I)	18,148	16.1
7 D. French Slaughter Jr. (R) *	81,688	58.1
David M. Smith (D)	58,684	41.7
8 James P. Moran Jr. (D)	88,475	51.7
Stan Parris (R) *	76,367	44.6
Robert T. Murphy (I)	5,958	3.5
9 Rick Boucher (D) *	67,215	97.1
(No Republican candidate)		
10 Frank R. Wolf (R) *	103,761	61.5
N. MacKenzie Canter III (D)	57,249	33.9

	Vote Total	Percent
Barbara S. Minnich (I)	5,273	3.1
Lyndon H. LaRouche Jr. (I)	2,293	1.4

WASHINGTON

	Vote Total	Percent
House		
1 John Miller (R) *	100,339	52.0
Cynthia Sullivan (D)	92,447	48.0
2 Al Swift (D) *	92,837	50.5
Doug Smith (R)	75,669	41.2
William L. McCord (LIBERT)	15,165	8.3
3 Jolene Unsoeld (D) *	95,645	53.8
Bob Williams (R)	82,269	46.2
4 Sid Morrison (R) *	106,545	70.7
Ole Hougen (D)	44,241	29.3
5 Thomas S. Foley (D) *	110,234	68.8
Marlyn A. Derby (R)	49,965	31.2
6 Norm Dicks (D) *	79,079	61.4
Norbert Mueller (R)	49,786	38.6
7 Jim McDermott (D) *	106,761	72.3
Larry Penberthy (R)	35,511	24.1
Robbie Scherr (SW)	5,370	3.6
8 Rod Chandler (R) *	96,323	56.2
David E. Giles (D)	75,031	43.8

WEST VIRGINIA

	Vote Total	Percent
Senate		
John D. Rockefeller IV (D) *	276,234	68.3
John Yoder (R)	128,071	31.7
House		
1 Alan B. Mollohan (D) *	72,849	67.1
Howard K. Tuck (R)	35,657	32.9
2 Harley O. Staggers Jr. (D) *	63,174	55.5
Oliver Luck (R)	50,708	44.5
3 Bob Wise (D) *	75,327	100
(No Republican candidate)		
4 Nick J. Rahall II (D) *	39,948	52.0
Marianne R. Brewster (R)	36,946	48.0

WISCONSIN

	Vote Total	Percent
Governor		
Tommy G. Thompson (R) *	802,321	58.2
Thomas Loftus (D)	576,280	41.8
House		
1 Les Aspin (D) *	93,961	99.4
(No Republican candidate)		
2 Scott L. Klug (R)	96,938	53.2
Robert W. Kastenmeier (D) *	85,156	46.8
3 Steve Gunderson (R) *	94,509	61.0
James L. Ziegeweid (D)	60,409	39.0
4 Gerald D. Kleczka (D) *	96,981	69.2
Joseph L. Cook (R)	43,001	30.7
5 Jim Moody (D) *	77,557	68.0
Donalda Arnell Hammersmith (R)	31,255	27.4
Nathaniel J. Stampley (I)	4,968	4.4
6 Thomas E. Petri (R) *	111,036	99.5
(No Democratic candidate)		
7 David R. Obey (D) *	100,069	62.1
John L. McEwen (R)	60,961	37.9
8 Toby Roth (R) *	95,902	53.5
Jerome Van Sistine (D)	83,199	46.4
9 F. James Sensenbrenner Jr. (R) *	117,967	99.7
(No Democratic candidate)		

WYOMING

	Vote Total	Percent
Governor		
Mike Sullivan (D) *	104,638	65.4
Mary Mead (R)	55,471	34.6
Senate		
Alan K. Simpson (R) *	100,784	63.9
Kathy Helling (D)	56,848	36.1
House		
AL Craig Thomas (R) *	87,078	55.1
Pete Maxfield (D)	70,977	44.9

[a] Election to fill the remaining four years of Democrat Spark Matsunaga's Senate term.

102nd Congress Special, 1991 Gubernatorial Returns

1991 Gubernatorial Elections

ARIZONA (runoff) — Feb. 16, 1991

	Vote Total	Percent
Fife Symington (R)	492,569	52.4
Terry Goddard (D)	448,168	47.6

KENTUCKY — Nov. 5, 1991

	Vote Total	Percent
Brereton Jones (D)	540,468	64.7
Larry J. Hopkins (R)	294,452	35.3

MISSISSIPPI — Nov. 5, 1991

	Vote Total	Percent
Kirk Fordice (R)	361,500	50.8
Ray Mabus (D)	338,435	47.6
Shawn O'Hara (I)	11,253	1.6

Special House Elections, 102nd Congress

TEXAS 3rd District — May 18, 1991

	Vote Total	Percent
Sam Johnson (R)	24,004	52.6
Tom Pauken (R)	21,647	47.4

MASSACHUSETTS 1st District — June 4, 1991

	Vote Total	Percent
John Olver (D)	70,022	49.6
Steven D. Pierce (R)	68,052	48.2
Patrick Joseph Armstrong (I)	1,859	1.3
Dennis Kelly (I)	880	0.6
Thomas Boynton (I)	250	0.2

ILLINOIS 15th District — July 2, 1991

	Vote Total	Percent
Thomas W. Ewing (R)	25,675	66.4
Gerald Bradley (D)	13,011	33.6

Abbreviations

D	—	Democrat
I	—	Independent
L	—	Liberal
LIBERT	—	Libertarian
R	—	Republican

ARIZONA 2nd District — Sept. 24, 1991

	Vote Total	Percent
Ed Pastor (D)	32,289	55.5
Pat Conner (R)	25,814	44.4

PENNSYLVANIA 2nd District — Nov. 5, 1991

	Vote Total	Percent
Lucien E. Blackwell (D)	51,820	39.2
Chaka Fattah (D)	37,068	28.0
John F. White Jr. (D)	36,469	27.6
Nadine G. Smith-Bulford (R)	6,928	5.2

VIRGINIA 7th District — Nov. 5, 1991

	Vote Total	Percent
George F. Allen (R)	106,745	62.0
Kay Slaughter (D)	59,655	34.7
John Torrice (I)	5,566	3.3

NEW YORK 8th District — Nov. 3, 1992

	Vote Total	Percent
Jerrold Nadler (D, L)	151,122	100.0

NORTH CAROLINA 1st District — Nov. 3, 1992

	Vote Total	Percent
Eva Clayton (D)	118,324	56.7
Ted Tyler (R)	86,273	41.3
C. Barry Williams (LIBERT)	4,121	2.0

Special Senate Elections, 102nd Congress

PENNSYLVANIA — Nov. 5, 1991

	Vote Total	Percent
Harris Wofford (D)	1,860,760	55.0
Dick Thornburgh (R)	1,521,986	45.0

NORTH DAKOTA — Dec. 4, 1992

	Vote Total	Percent
Kent Conrad (D)	102,887	63.3
Jack Dalrymple (R)	54,726	33.7
Darold Larson (I)	4,839	3.0

Note: Jerrold Nadler, D-N.Y., was elected Nov. 3, 1992, to fill the remaining House term of Ted Weiss, who died Sept. 14, 1992, and to the 103rd Congress. Eva Clayton, D-N.C., was elected Nov. 3, 1992, to fill the remaining House term of Walter B. Jones, who died Sept. 15, 1992, and to the 103rd Congress. Results of the balloting to fill the vacancies are listed above. *(See 1992 returns for 103rd Congress vote tallies, p. 1250)*

1992 Elections Returns for Governors, Senate and House

Following are the final, official 1992 vote returns for the governorships, Senate and House compiled by Congressional Quarterly from figures supplied by each state's election agency. The box below provides a key to party designation. Also included are write-in candidates that received at least 0.1 percent of the vote. Because of rounding and because scattered write-in votes are not listed, percentages do not always add to 100.

An asterisk (*) indicates incumbents.

An X denotes candidates without major-party opposition and no votes were cast.

A dagger (†) indicates that a runoff election was required because no candidate received a majority.

ALABAMA

		Vote Total	Percent
Senate			
	Richard C. Shelby (D) *	1,022,698	64.9
	Richard Sellers (R)	522,015	33.1
	Jerome Shockley (LIBERT)	31,811	2.0
House			
1	Sonny Callahan (R) *	128,874	60.2
	William A. Brewer (D)	78,742	36.8
	John R. Garrett (LIBERT)	6,548	3.1
2	Terry Everett (R)	112,906	49.5
	George C. Wallace Jr. (D)	109,335	47.9
	Glynn Reeves (LIBERT)	3,150	1.4
	Malcolm S. Brassell (I)	1,426	.6
	Richard C. Boone (I)	1,330	.6
3	Glen Browder (D) *	119,175	60.3
	Don Sledge (R)	73,800	37.4
	Rodric D. Templeton (LIBERT)	4,570	2.3
4	Tom Bevill (D) *	157,907	68.5
	Mickey Strickland (R)	66,934	29.0
	Robert P. King (LIBERT)	5,646	2.4
5	Robert E. "Bud" Cramer (D) *	160,060	65.6
	Terry Smith (R)	77,951	31.9
	C. Michael Seibert (LIBERT)	6,006	2.5
6	Spencer Bachus (R)	146,599	52.4
	Ben Erdreich (D) *	126,062	45.0
	Carla Cloum (I)	4,521	1.6
	Mark Bodenhausen (LIBERT)	2,836	1.0
7	Earl F. Hilliard (D)	144,320	69.5
	Kervin Jones (R)	36,086	17.4
	James M. Lewis (I)	12,461	6.0
	James Chambliss (I)	11,466	5.5
	Michael Todd Mayer (LIBERT)	2,135	1.0
	John Hawkins (SW)	1,165	.6

ALASKA

		Vote Total	Percent
Senate			
	Frank H. Murkowski (R) *	127,163	53.0
	Tony Smith (D)	92,065	38.4
	Mary E. Jordan (GREEN)	20,019	8.4
House			
AL	Don Young (R) *	111,849	46.8
	John S. Devens (D)	102,378	42.8
	Michael A. States (Alaskan Independence)	15,049	6.3
	Mike Milligan (GREEN)	9,529	4.0

ARIZONA

		Vote Total	Percent
Senate			
	John McCain (R) *	771,395	55.8
	Claire Sargent (D)	436,321	31.6
	Evan Mecham (I)	145,361	10.5
	Kiana Delamare (LIBERT)	22,613	1.6
	Ed Finkelstein (NA)	6,335	.5
House			
1	Sam Coppersmith (D)	130,715	51.3
	John J. Rhodes III (R) *	113,613	44.6
	Ted Goldstein (NL)	10,461	4.1
2	Ed Pastor (D) *	90,693	66.0
	Don Shooter (R)	41,257	30.0
	Dan Detaranto (LIBERT)	5,423	3.9
3	Bob Stump (R) *	158,906	61.5
	Roger Hartstone (D)	88,830	34.4
	Pamela Volponi (NL)	10,767	4.2
4	Jon Kyl (R) *	156,330	59.2
	Walter R. Mybeck II (D)	70,572	26.7
	Debbie Collings (I)	25,553	9.7
	Tim McDermott (LIBERT)	11,611	4.4
5	Jim Kolbe (R) *	172,867	66.5
	Jim Toevs (D)	77,256	29.7
	Perry Willis (LIBERT)	9,690	3.7
6	Karan English (D)	124,251	53.0
	Doug Wead (R)	97,074	41.4
	Sarah Stannard (I)	13,047	5.6

ARKANSAS

		Vote Total	Percent
Senate			
	Dale Bumpers (D) *	553,635	60.2
	Mike Huckabee (R)	366,373	39.8
House			
1	Blanche Lambert (D)	149,558	69.8
	Terry Hayes (R)	64,618	30.2
2	Ray Thornton (D) *	154,946	74.2
	Dennis Scott (R)	53,978	25.8
3	Tim Hutchinson (R)	125,295	50.2
	John VanWinkle (D)	117,775	47.2
	Ralph Forbes (I)	6,329	2.5
4	Jay Dickey (R)	113,009	52.3
	W. J. "Bill" McCuen (D)	102,918	47.7

CALIFORNIA

		Vote Total	Percent
Senate[a]			
	Dianne Feinstein (D)	5,853,651	54.3
	John Seymour (R) *	4,093,501	38.0
	Gerald Horne (PFP)	305,697	2.8
	Paul Meeuwenberg (AMI)	281,973	2.6
	Richard B. Boddie (LIBERT)	247,799	2.3

Abbreviations for Party Designations

ACP — A Connecticut Party
AFP — America First Populist
AM — American
AMI — American Independent
C — Conservative
CC — Concerned Citizens
D — Democratic
ECR — Economic Recovery
EJ — Economic Justice
FFL — Freedom for LaRouche
GR — Grassroots
GREEN — Green
I — Independent
IA — Independent American
IFC — Independents for Change
IP — Independent Party
IV — Independent Voters
L — Liberal
LIBERT — Libertarian
LIF — Long Island First
LU — Liberty Union
NA — New Alliance
NJC — New Jersey Conservative Party
NJI — New Jersey Independents
NL — Natural Law
PFP — Peace and Freedom
POP — Populist
R — Republican
RTL — Right to Life
SW — Socialist Worker
TCP-LI — Tax Cut Party-Long Island
TIC — Tisch Independent Citizens
WL — Workers League

	Candidate	Vote Total	Per-cent
Senate			
	Barbara Boxer (D)	5,173,467	47.9
	Bruce Herschensohn (R)	4,644,182	43.0
	Jerome McCready (AMI)	373,051	3.5
	Genevieve Torres (PFP)	372,817	3.5
	June R. Genis (LIBERT)	235,919	2.2
House			
1	Dan Hamburg (D)	119,676	47.6
	Frank Riggs (R) *	113,266	45.1
	Phil Baldwin (PFP)	10,764	4.3
	Matthew L. Howard (LIBERT)	7,500	3.0
2	Wally Herger (R) *	167,247	65.2
	Elliot Roy Freedman (D)	71,780	28.0
	Harry H. Pendery (LIBERT)	17,529	6.8
3	Vic Fazio (D) *	122,149	51.2
	H. L. "Bill" Richardson (R)	96,092	40.3
	Ross Crain (LIBERT)	20,444	8.6
4	John T. Doolittle (R) *	141,155	49.8
	Patricia Malberg (D)	129,489	45.7
	Patrick McHargue (LIBERT)	12,705	4.5
5	Robert T. Matsui (D) *	158,250	68.6
	Robert S. Dinsmore (R)	58,698	25.5
	Gordon D. Mors (AMI)	4,745	2.1
	Chris Rufer (LIBERT)	4,547	2.0
	Tian Harter (GREEN)	4,316	1.9
6	Lynn Woolsey (D)	190,322	65.2
	Bill Filante (R)	98,171	33.6
	Claude Heater (write-in)	3,141	1.1
	Louis G. Beary (write-in)	152	.1
7	George Miller (D) *	153,320	70.3
	Dave Scholl (R)	54,822	25.1
	David L. Franklin (PFP)	9,840	4.5
8	Nancy Pelosi (D) *	191,906	82.5
	Marc Wolin (R)	25,693	11.0
	Cesar G. Cadabes (PFP)	7,572	3.3
	James R. Elwood (LIBERT)	7,511	3.2
9	Ronald V. Dellums (D) *	164,265	71.9
	G. William Hunter (R)	53,707	23.5
	Dave Linn (PFP)	10,472	4.6
10	Bill Baker (R)	145,702	52.0
	Wendell H. Williams (D)	134,635	48.0
11	Richard W. Pombo (R)	94,453	47.6
	Patricia Garamendi (D)	90,539	45.6
	Christine Roberts (LIBERT)	13,498	6.8
12	Tom Lantos (D) *	157,205	68.8
	Jim Tomlin (R)	53,278	23.3
	Mary Weldon (PFP)	10,142	4.4
	George L. O'Brien (LIBERT)	7,782	3.4
13	Pete Stark (D) *	123,795	60.2
	Verne Teyler (R)	64,953	31.6
	Roslyn A. Allen (PFP)	16,768	8.2
14	Anna G. Eshoo (D)	146,873	56.7
	Tom Huening (R)	101,202	39.0
	Chuck Olson (LIBERT)	7,220	2.8
	David Wald (PFP)	3,912	1.5
15	Norman Y. Mineta (D) *	168,617	63.5
	Robert Wick (R)	82,875	31.2
	Duggan Dieterly (LIBERT)	13,293	5.0
	Bill Futrell (write-in)	585	.2
16	Don Edwards (D) *	96,661	62.0
	Ted Bundesen (R)	49,843	32.0
	Amani S. Kuumba (PFP)	9,370	6.0
17	Leon E. Panetta (D) *	151,565	72.0
	Bill McCampbell (R)	49,947	23.7
	Maureen Smith (PFP)	4,804	2.3
	John D. Wilkes (LIBERT)	4,051	1.9
18	Gary Condit (D) *	139,704	84.7
	(No Republican candidate)		
	Kim R. Almstrom (LIBERT)	25,307	15.3
19	Richard H. Lehman (D) *	101,619	46.9
	Tal L. Cloud (R)	100,590	46.4
	Dorothy L. Wells (PFP)	13,334	6.2
	James E. Williams Jr. (write-in)	1,097	.5
20	Calvin Dooley (D) *	72,679	64.9
	Ed Hunt (R)	39,388	35.1
21	Bill Thomas (R) *	127,758	65.2
	Deborah A. Vollmer (D)	68,058	34.7
	Michael David Hodges (write-in)	149	.1
22	Michael Huffington (R)	131,242	52.5
	Gloria Ochoa (D)	87,328	34.9
	Mindy Lorenz (GREEN)	23,699	9.5
	W. Howard Dilbeck (LIBERT)	7,553	3.0
23	Elton Gallegly (R) *	115,504	54.3
	Anita Perez Ferguson (D)	88,225	41.4
	Jay C. Wood (LIBERT)	9,091	4.3
24	Anthony C. Beilenson (D) *	141,742	55.5
	Tom McClintock (R)	99,835	39.1
	John Paul Lindblad (PFP)	13,690	5.4
25	Howard P. "Buck" McKeon (R)	113,611	51.9
	James H. "Gil" Gilmartin (D)	72,233	33.0
	Rick Pamplin (I)	13,930	6.4
	Peggy Christensen (LIBERT)	6,932	3.2
	Charles Wilken (GREEN)	6,919	3.2
	Nancy Lawrence (PFP)	5,090	2.3
26	Howard L. Berman (D) *	73,807	61.0
	Gary Forsch (R)	36,453	30.1
	Margery Hinds (PFP)	7,180	5.9
	Bernard Zimring (LIBERT)	3,468	2.9
27	Carlos J. Moorhead (R) *	105,521	49.7
	Doug Kahn (D)	83,805	39.4
	Jesse A. Moorman (GREEN)	11,003	5.2
	Margaret L. Edwards (PFP)	7,329	3.4
	Dennis Decherd (LIBERT)	4,790	2.3
28	David Dreier (R) *	122,353	58.4
	Al Wachtel (D)	76,525	36.5
	Walter Sheasby (GREEN)	6,233	3.0
	Thomas J. Dominy (LIBERT)	4,271	2.0
29	Henry A. Waxman (D) *	160,312	61.3
	Mark A. Robbins (R)	67,141	25.7
	David Davis (I)	15,445	5.9
	Susan C. Davies (PFP)	13,888	5.3
	Felix Tsvi Rogin (LIBERT)	4,699	1.8
30	Xavier Becerra (D)	48,800	58.4
	Morry Waksberg (R)	20,034	24.0
	Blase Bonpane (GREEN)	6,315	7.6
	Elizabeth A. Nakano (PFP)	6,173	7.4
	Andrew Consalvo (LIBERT)	2,221	2.7
31	Matthew G. Martinez (D) *	68,324	62.6
	Reuben D. Franco (R)	40,873	37.4
32	Julian C. Dixon (D) *	150,644	87.2
	(No Republican candidate)		
	Bob Weber (LIBERT)	12,384	7.2
	William R. Williams (PFP)	9,782	5.7
33	Lucille Roybal-Allard (D)	32,010	63.0
	Robert Guzman (R)	15,428	30.4
	Tim Delia (PFP)	2,135	4.2
	Dale S. Olvera (LIBERT)	1,206	2.4
34	Esteban E. Torres (D) *	91,738	61.3
	J. "Jay" Hernandez (R)	50,907	34.0
	Carl M. Swinney (LIBERT)	7,072	4.7
35	Maxine Waters (D) *	102,941	82.5
	Nate Truman (R)	17,417	14.0
	Alice Mae Miles (PFP)	2,797	2.2
	Carin Rogers (LIBERT)	1,618	1.3
36	Jane Harman (D)	125,751	48.4
	Joan Milke Flores (R)	109,684	42.2
	Richard H. Greene (GREEN)	13,297	5.1
	Owen Staley (PFP)	5,519	2.1
	Marc F. Denny (LIBERT)	5,504	2.1
37	Walter R. Tucker (D)	97,159	85.7
	(No Republican candidate)		
	B. Kwaku Duren (PFP)	16,178	14.3
38	Steve Horn (R)	92,038	48.6
	Evan Anderson Braude (D)	82,108	43.4
	Paul Burton (PFP)	8,391	4.4
	Blake Ashley (LIBERT)	6,756	3.6
39	Ed Royce (R)	122,472	57.3
	Molly McClanahan (D)	81,728	38.2
	Jack Dean (LIBERT)	9,484	4.4
40	Jerry Lewis (R) *	129,563	63.1
	Donald M. Rusk (D)	63,881	31.1
	Margie Akin (PFP)	11,839	5.8
41	Jay C. Kim (R)	101,753	59.6
	Bob Baker (D)	58,777	34.4
	Mike Noonan (PFP)	10,136	5.9
42	George E. Brown Jr. (D) *	79,780	50.7
	Dick Rutan (R)	69,251	44.0
	Fritz R. Ward (LIBERT)	8,424	5.4
43	Ken Calvert (R)	88,987	46.7
	Mark A. Takano (D)	88,468	46.4
	Gary R. Odom (AMI)	6,095	3.2
	Gene L. Berkman (LIBERT)	4,989	2.6
	John Schwab (write-in)	2,100	1.1
44	Al McCandless (R) *	110,333	54.2
	Georgia Smith (D)	81,693	40.1
	Phil Turner (LIBERT)	11,515	5.7
45	Dana Rohrabacher (R) *	123,731	54.5
	Patricia McCabe (D)	88,508	39.0
	Gary D. Copeland (LIBERT)	14,777	6.5
46	Robert K. Dornan (R) *	55,659	50.2
	Robert John Banuelos (D)	45,435	41.0
	Richard G. Newhouse (LIBERT)	9,712	8.8
47	C. Christopher Cox (R) *	165,004	64.9
	John F. Anwiler (D)	76,924	30.3
	Maxine B. Quirk (PFP)	12,297	4.8
48	Ron Packard (R) *	140,935	61.1
	Michael Farber (D)	67,415	29.2
	Donna White (PFP)	13,396	5.8
	Ted Lowe (LIBERT)	8,749	3.8
49	Lynn Schenk (D)	127,280	51.1
	Judy Jarvis (R)	106,170	42.7
	John Wallner (LIBERT)	10,706	4.3
	Milton Zaslow (PFP)	4,738	1.9
50	Bob Filner (D)	77,293	56.6
	Tony Valencia (R)	39,531	28.9
	Barbara Hutchinson (LIBERT)	15,489	11.3
	Roger B. Batchelder (PFP)	4,250	3.1
51	Randy "Duke" Cunningham (R) *	141,890	56.1
	Bea Herbert (D)	85,148	33.7
	Bill Holmes (LIBERT)	10,309	4.1
	Miriam E. Clark (PFP)	10,307	4.1
	Richard L. Roe (GREEN)	5,328	2.1
52	Duncan Hunter (R) *	112,995	52.9
	Janet M. Gastil (D)	88,076	41.2
	Joe Shea (LIBERT)	6,977	3.3
	Dennis P. Gretsinger (PFP)	5,734	2.7

COLORADO

	Candidate	Vote Total	Per-cent
Senate			
	Ben Nighthorse Campbell (D)	803,725	51.8
	Terry Considine (R)	662,893	42.7
	Richard O. Grimes (Perot's Independents)	42,455	2.7
	Matt Noah (Christian Pro-Life)	22,846	1.5
	Dan Winters (I)	20,347	1.3
House			
1	Patricia Schroeder (D) *	156,629	68.8
	Raymond Diaz Aragon (R)	70,902	31.2
2	David E. Skaggs (D) *	164,790	60.7
	Bryan Day (R)	88,470	32.6

		Vote Total	Percent
	Vern Tharp (American Grassroots Alternative)	18,101	6.7
3	Scott McInnis (R)	143,293	54.7
	Mike Callihan (D)	114,480	43.7
	Ki R. Nelson (Colorado Populist)	4,189	1.6
4	Wayne Allard (R) *	139,884	57.8
	Tom Redder (D)	101,957	42.2
5	Joel Hefley (R) *	173,096	71.1
	Charles A. Oriez (D)	62,550	25.7
	Keith L. Hamburger (LIBERT)	7,769	3.2
6	Dan Schaefer (R) *	142,021	60.9
	Tom Kolbe (D)	91,073	39.1

CONNECTICUT

Senate

		Vote Total	Percent
	Christopher J. Dodd (D, ACP) *	882,569	58.8
	Brook Johnson (R)	572,036	38.1
	Richard D. Gregory (CC)	35,315	2.4
	Howard A. Grayson Jr. (LIBERT)	10,741	.7

House

		Vote Total	Percent
1	Barbara B. Kennelly (D, ACP) *	164,735	67.1
	Philip L. Steele (R)	75,113	30.6
	Gary R. Garneau (CC)	5,577	2.3
2	Sam Gejdenson (D, ACP) *	123,291	50.8
	Edward W. Munster (R)	119,416	49.2
3	Rosa DeLauro (D, ACP) *	162,568	65.7
	Tom Scott (R)	84,952	34.3
4	Christopher Shays (R) *	147,816	67.3
	Dave Schropfer (D)	58,666	26.7
	Al Smith (ACP)	11,679	5.3
	Ronald M. Fried (NL)	1,445	.7
5	Gary Franks (R) *	104,891	43.7
	James J. Lawlor (D)	74,791	31.1
	Lynn H. Taborsak (ACP)	54,022	22.5
	Rosita Rodriguez (CC)	5,090	2.1
	Bernard A. Nevas (NL)	864	.4
	David G. LaPointe (I)	625	.3
6	Nancy L. Johnson (R) *	166,967	69.7
	Eugene F. Slason (D)	60,373	25.2
	Daniel W. Plawecki (CC)	9,544	4.0
	Charles Pearl (I)	1,677	.7
	Ralph C. Economu (I)	1,036	.4

DELAWARE

Governor

		Vote Total	Percent
	Thomas R. Carper (D)	179,365	64.7
	B. Gary Scott (R)	90,725	32.7
	Floyd E. McDowell (A Delaware Party)	3,779	1.4
	Richard A. Cohen (LIBERT)	3,165	1.1

House

		Vote Total	Percent
AL	Michael N. Castle (R)	153,037	55.4
	S. B. Woo (D)	117,426	42.5
	Peggy Schmitt (LIBERT)	5,661	2.1

FLORIDA

Senate

		Vote Total	Percent
	Bob Graham (D) *	3,244,299	65.4
	Bill Grant (R)	1,715,156	34.6

House

		Vote Total	Percent
1	Earl Hutto (D) *	118,753	52.0
	Terry Ketchel (R)	100,136	43.9
	Barbara Ann Rodgers-Hendricks (GREEN)	9,320	4.1
2	Pete Peterson (D) *	167,151	73.4
	Ray Wagner (R)	60,378	26.5
3	Corrine Brown (D)	91,877	59.3
	Don Weidner (R)	63,070	40.7
4	Tillie Fowler (R)	135,772	56.7
	Mattox Hair (D)	103,484	43.2
5	Karen L. Thurman (D)	129,678	49.2
	Tom Hogan (R)	114,331	43.4
	Cindy Munkittrick (I)	19,459	7.4
6	Cliff Stearns (R) *	144,120	65.4
	Phil Denton (D)	76,396	34.6
7	John L. Mica (R)	125,790	56.4
	Dan Webster (D)	96,926	43.5
	Ken McCarthy (write-in)	213	.1
8	Bill McCollum (R) *	141,925	68.5
	Chuck Kovaleski (D)	65,132	31.5
9	Michael Bilirakis (R) *	157,822	58.9
	Cheryl Davis Knapp (D)	110,023	41.1
10	C. W. Bill Young (R) *	149,347	56.6
	Karen Moffitt (D)	114,637	43.4
11	Sam M. Gibbons (D) *	100,962	52.8
	Mark Sharpe (R)	77,625	40.6
	Joe De Minico (I)	12,729	6.7
12	Charles T. Canady (R)	100,468	52.1
	Tom Mims (D)	92,333	47.9
13	Dan Miller (R)	158,836	57.8
	Rand Snell (D)	115,741	42.2
14	Porter J. Goss (R) *	220,324	82.1
	(No Democratic candidate)		
	James H. King (I)	48,156	17.9
15	Jim Bacchus (D) *	132,385	50.7
	Bill Tolley (R)	128,830	49.3
16	Tom Lewis (R) *	157,253	60.8
	John P. Comerford (D)	101,217	39.2
17	Carrie Meek (D)	102,732	100.0
	(No Republican candidate)		
18	Ileana Ros-Lehtinen (R) *	104,715	66.8
	Magda Montiel Davis (D)	52,095	33.2
19	Harry A. Johnston (D) *	177,411	63.1
	Larry Metz (R)	103,848	36.9
20	Peter Deutsch (D)	130,946	55.1
	Beverly Kennedy (R)	91,573	38.5
	James M. Blackburn (I)	15,340	6.4
21	Lincoln Diaz-Balart (R)	X	X
22	E. Clay Shaw Jr. (R) *	128,376	52.0
	Gwen Margolis (D)	91,605	37.1
	Richard "Even" Stephens (I)	15,467	6.3
	Michael F. Petrie (I)	6,311	2.6
	Bernard Anscher (I)	5,272	2.1
23	Alcee L. Hastings (D)	84,232	58.5
	Ed Fielding (R)	44,800	31.1
	Al Woods (I)	14,873	10.3

GEORGIA

Senate †

		Vote Total	Percent
	Wyche Fowler Jr. (D) *	1,108,416	49.2
	Paul Coverdell (R)	1,073,282	47.7
	Jim Hudson (LIBERT)	69,878	3.1

Senate *(Nov. 24, 1992, runoff)*

		Vote Total	Percent
	Paul Coverdell (R)	635,114	50.6
	Wyche Fowler Jr. (D) *	618,877	49.4

House

		Vote Total	Percent
1	Jack Kingston (R)	103,932	57.8
	Barbara Christmas (D)	75,808	42.2
2	Sanford Bishop (D)	95,789	63.7
	Jim Dudley (R)	54,593	36.3
3	Mac Collins (R)	114,107	54.8
	Richard Ray (D) *	94,271	45.2
4	John Linder (R)	126,495	50.5
	Cathey Steinberg (D)	123,819	49.5
5	John Lewis (D) *	147,445	72.1
	Paul R. Stabler (R)	56,960	27.9
6	Newt Gingrich (R) *	158,761	57.7
	Tony Center (D)	116,196	42.3
7	George "Buddy" Darden (D) *	111,374	57.3
	Al Beverly (R)	82,915	42.7
8	J. Roy Rowland (D) *	108,472	55.7
	Bob Cunningham (R)	86,220	44.3
9	Nathan Deal (D)	113,024	59.2
	Daniel Becker (R)	77,919	40.8
10	Don Johnson (D)	108,426	53.8
	Ralph Hudgens (R)	93,059	46.2
11	Cynthia McKinney (D)	120,168	73.1
	Woodrow Lovett (R)	44,221	26.9

HAWAII

Senate

		Vote Total	Percent
	Daniel K. Inouye (D) *	208,266	57.3
	Rick Reed (R)	97,928	26.9
	Linda B. Martin (GREEN)	49,921	13.7
	Richard O. Rowland (LIBERT)	7,547	2.1

House

		Vote Total	Percent
1	Neil Abercrombie (D) *	129,332	72.9
	Warner C. Kimo Sutton (R)	41,575	23.4
	Rockne Hart Johnson (LIBERT)	6,569	3.7
2	Patsy T. Mink (D) *	131,454	72.6
	Kamuela Price (R)	40,070	22.1
	Lloyd "Jeff" Mallan (LIBERT)	9,431	5.2

IDAHO

Senate

		Vote Total	Percent
	Dirk Kempthorne (R)	270,468	56.5
	Richard Stallings (D)	208,036	43.5

House

		Vote Total	Percent
1	Larry LaRocco (D) *	140,985	58.1
	Rachel S. Gilbert (R)	90,983	37.5
	John Abel (I)	6,255	2.6
	Henry "Sonny" Kinsey (I)	4,567	1.9
2	Michael D. Crapo (R)	139,783	60.8
	J. D. Williams (D)	81,450	35.4
	Steven L. Kauer (I)	4,917	2.1
	David William Mansfield (I)	3,807	1.7

ILLINOIS

Senate

		Vote Total	Percent
	Carol Moseley-Braun (D)	2,631,229	53.3
	Richard S. Williamson (R)	2,126,833	43.1
	Chad Koppie (Conservative Party of Illinois)	100,422	2.0
	Andrew B. Spiegel (LIBERT)	34,527	.7
	Charles A. Winter (NL)	15,118	.3
	Alan J. Port (NA)	12,689	.3
	Kathleen Kaku (SW)	10,056	.2
	John Justice (POP)	8,656	.2

House

		Vote Total	Percent
1	Bobby L. Rush (D)	209,258	82.8
	Jay Walker (R)	43,453	17.2
2	Mel Reynolds (D)	182,614	78.1
	Ron Blackstone (R)	31,957	13.7
	Louanner Peters (Louanner Peters Party)	19,293	8.2
3	William O. Lipinski (D) *	162,165	63.5
	Harry C. Lepinske (R)	93,128	36.5
4	Luis V. Gutierrez (D)	90,452	77.6
	Hildegarde Rodriguez-Schieman (R)	26,154	22.4

		Vote Total	Per-cent
5	Dan Rostenkowski (D) *	132,889	57.3
	Elias R. "Non-Incumbent" Zenkich (R)	90,738	39.1
	Blaise C. Grenke (LIBERT)	8,456	3.6
6	Henry J. Hyde (R) *	165,009	65.5
	Barry W. Watkins (D)	86,891	34.5
7	Cardiss Collins (D) *	182,811	81.1
	Norman G. Boccio (R)	35,346	15.7
	Rose-Marie Love (ECR)	4,711	2.1
	Geri Knoll McLauchlan (NL)	2,413	1.1
8	Philip M. Crane (R) *	132,887	55.7
	Sheila A. Smith (D)	96,419	40.4
	Joe M. Dillier (Independent Congressional)	9,327	3.9
9	Sidney R. Yates (D) *	162,942	68.0
	Herb Sohn (R)	64,760	27.0
	Sheila A. Jones (ECR)	12,001	5.0
10	John Edward Porter (R) *	155,230	64.5
	Michael J. Kennedy (D)	85,400	35.5
11	George E. Sangmeister (D) *	135,387	55.7
	Robert T. Herbolsheimer (R)	107,860	44.3
12	Jerry F. Costello (D) *	168,762	71.2
	Mike Starr (R)	68,115	28.8
13	Harris W. Fawell (R) *	179,257	68.4
	Dennis Michael Temple (D)	82,985	31.6
14	Dennis Hastert (R) *	155,271	67.3
	Jonathan Abram Reich (D)	75,294	32.6
15	Thomas W. Ewing (R) *	142,167	59.3
	Charles D. Mattis (D)	97,190	40.6
	Gerard Archibald (write-in)	229	.1
16	Donald Manzullo (R)	142,388	55.6
	John W. Cox Jr. (D) *	113,555	44.4
17	Lane Evans (D) *	156,233	60.1
	Ken Schloemer (R)	103,719	39.9
18	Robert H. Michel (R) *	156,533	57.8
	Ronald C. Hawkins (D)	114,413	42.2
19	Glenn Poshard (D) *	187,156	69.1
	Douglas E. Lee (R)	83,526	30.9
20	Richard J. Durbin (D) *	154,869	56.5
	John M. Shimkus (R)	119,219	43.5

INDIANA

Governor

		Vote Total	Per-cent
	Evan Bayh (D) *	1,382,151	62.0
	Linley E. Pearson (R)	822,533	36.9
	Mary Catherine Barton (NA)	24,378	1.1

Senate

		Vote Total	Per-cent
	Daniel R. Coats (R) *	1,267,972	57.3
	Joseph H. Hogsett (D)	900,148	40.7
	Steve Dillon (LIBERT)	35,733	1.6
	Raymond Tirado (NA)	7,474	.3

House

		Vote Total	Per-cent
1	Peter J. Visclosky (D) *	147,054	69.4
	David J. Vucich (R)	64,770	30.6
2	Philip R. Sharp (D) *	130,881	57.1
	William G. Frazier (R)	90,593	39.5
	Theodore Shaver (I)	7,821	3.4
3	Tim Roemer (D) *	121,269	57.4
	Carl H. Baxmeyer (R)	89,834	42.6
4	Jill L. Long (D) *	134,907	62.1
	Charles W. Pierson (R)	82,468	37.9
5	Steve Buyer (R)	112,492	51.0
	Jim Jontz (D) *	107,973	49.0
6	Dan Burton (R) *	186,499	72.2
	Natalie M. Bruner (D)	71,952	27.8
7	John T. Myers (R) *	129,189	59.5
	Ellen E. Wedum (D)	88,005	40.5
8	Frank McCloskey (D) *	125,244	52.5
	Richard E. Mourdock (R)	108,054	45.3
	John W. Taylor (I)	3,098	1.3
	Jimmy Gale Funkhouser Jr. (LIBERT)	2,001	.8
9	Lee H. Hamilton (D) *	160,980	69.7
	Michael E. Bailey (R)	70,057	30.3
10	Andrew Jacobs Jr. (D) *	117,604	64.0
	Janos Horvath (R)	64,378	35.0
	Carolyn P. Sackett (NA)	1,849	1.0

IOWA

Senate

		Vote Total	Per-cent
	Charles E. Grassley (R) *	899,761	69.6
	Jean Lloyd-Jones (D)	351,561	27.2
	Stuart Zimmerman (NL)	16,403	1.3
	Sue Atkinson (I)	6,277	.5
	Mel Boring (I)	5,508	.4
	Rosanne Freeburg (I)	4,999	.4
	Carl Eric Olsen (GR)	3,404	.3
	Richard O'Dell Hughes (I)	2,918	.2
	Cleve Andrew Pulley (SW)	1,370	.1

House

		Vote Total	Per-cent
1	Jim Leach (R) *	178,042	68.1
	Jan J. Zonneveld (D)	81,600	31.2
2	Jim Nussle (R) *	134,536	50.2
	Dave Nagle (D) *	131,570	49.1
	Albert W. Schoeman (GR)	1,757	.7
3	Jim Ross Lightfoot (R) *	125,931	48.9
	Elaine Baxter (D)	121,063	47.1
	Larry Chroman (NL)	10,181	4.0
4	Neal Smith (D) *	158,610	61.6
	Paul Lunde (R)	94,045	36.5
	Jerry Yellin (NL)	2,427	.9
	William C. Oviatt (GR)	2,359	.9
5	Fred Grandy (R) *	196,942	99.3
	(No Democratic candidate)		

KANSAS

Senate

		Vote Total	Per-cent
	Bob Dole (R) *	706,246	62.7
	Gloria O'Dell (D)	349,525	31.0
	Christina Campbell-Cline (I)	45,423	4.0
	Mark B. Kirk (LIBERT)	25,253	2.2

House

		Vote Total	Per-cent
1	Pat Roberts (R) *	194,912	68.3
	Duane West (D)	83,620	29.3
	Steven A. Rosile (LIBERT)	6,765	2.4
2	Jim Slattery (D) *	151,019	56.2
	Jim Van Slyke (R)	109,801	40.8
	Arthur L. Clack (LIBERT)	7,986	3.0
3	Jan Meyers (R) *	169,929	58.0
	Tom Love (D)	110,076	37.6
	Frank Kaul (LIBERT)	12,791	4.4
4	Dan Glickman (D) *	143,671	51.7
	Eric R. Yost (R)	117,070	42.1
	Seth L. Warren (LIBERT)	17,275	6.2

KENTUCKY

Senate

		Vote Total	Per-cent
	Wendell H. Ford (D) *	836,888	62.9
	David L. Williams (R)	476,604	35.8
	James A. Ridenour (LIBERT)	17,366	1.3

House

		Vote Total	Per-cent
1	Tom Barlow (D)	128,524	60.5
	Steve Hamrick (R)	83,088	39.1
	Marvin Seat (Reform)	962	.5
2	William H. Natcher (D) *	126,894	61.4
	Bruce R. Bartley (R)	79,684	38.6
3	Romano L. Mazzoli (D) *	148,066	52.7
	Susan B. Stokes (R)	132,689	47.3
4	Jim Bunning (R) *	139,634	61.6
	Dr. Floyd G. Poore (D)	86,890	38.4
5	Harold Rogers (R) *	115,255	54.6
	John Doug Hays (D)	95,760	45.4
6	Scotty Baesler (D)	135,613	60.7
	Charles W. Ellinger (R)	87,816	39.3

LOUISIANA

Senate

		Vote Total	Per-cent
	John B. Breaux (D) *	X	X

House

		Vote Total	Per-cent
1	Robert L. Livingston (R) *	X	X
2	William J. Jefferson (D) *	X	X
3	W. J. "Billy" Tauzin (D) *	X	X
4	Cleo Fields (D)	143,980	73.9
	Charles Jones (D)	50,851	26.1
5	Jim McCrery (R) *	153,501	63.0
	Jerry Huckaby (D) *	90,079	37.0
6	Richard H. Baker (R) *	123,953	50.6
	Clyde C. Holloway (R) *	121,225	49.4
7	Jimmy Hayes (D) *	X	X

MAINE

House

		Vote Total	Per-cent
1	Thomas H. Andrews (D) *	232,696	65.0
	Linda Bean (R)	125,236	35.0
2	Olympia J. Snowe (R) *	153,022	49.1
	Patrick K. McGowan (D)	130,824	42.0
	Jonathan K. Carter (GREEN)	27,526	8.8

MARYLAND

Senate

		Vote Total	Per-cent
	Barbara A. Mikulski (D) *	1,307,610	71.0
	Alan L. Keyes (R)	533,688	29.0

House

		Vote Total	Per-cent
1	Wayne T. Gilchrest (R) *	120,084	51.6
	Tom McMillen (D) *	112,771	48.4
2	Helen Delich Bentley (R) *	165,443	65.1
	Michael C. Hickey Jr. (D)	88,658	34.9
3	Benjamin L. Cardin (D) *	163,354	73.5
	William T.S. Bricker (R)	58,869	26.5
4	Albert R. Wynn (D)	136,902	75.2
	Michele Dyson (R)	45,166	24.8
5	Steny H. Hoyer (D) *	118,312	53.0
	Lawrence J. Hogan Jr. (R)	97,982	43.9
	William D. Johnston III (I)	6,990	3.1
6	Roscoe G. Bartlett (R)	125,564	54.2
	Thomas H. Hattery (D)	106,224	45.8
7	Kweisi Mfume (D) *	152,689	85.3
	Kenneth Kondner (R)	26,304	14.7
8	Constance A. Morella (R) *	203,377	72.5
	Edward J. Heffernan (D)	77,042	27.5

MASSACHUSETTS

House

		Vote Total	Per-cent
1	John W. Olver (D) *	135,049	51.5
	Patrick Larkin (R)	113,828	43.4
	Louis R. Godena (Peace Jobs Justice)	7,162	2.7
	Dennis M. Kelly (Pro-Democracy Reform)	4,355	1.7
	Jeffrey W. Rebello (FFL)	1,598	.6
2	Richard E. Neal (D) *	131,215	53.1
	Anthony W. Ravosa Jr. (R)	76,795	31.1
	Thomas R. Sheehan (For the People)	38,963	15.8
3	Peter I. Blute (R)	131,473	50.4
	Joseph D. Early (D) *	115,587	44.3
	Leonard J. Umina (IV)	9,691	3.7
	Michael T. Moore (NL)	4,130	1.6
4	Barney Frank (D) *	182,633	67.7
	Edward J. McCormick III (R)	70,665	26.2
	Luke Lumina (IV)	13,670	5.1
	Dennis J. Ingalls (FFL)	2,797	1.0

		Vote Total	Per-cent
5	Martin T. Meehan (D)	133,844	52.2
	Paul W. Cronin (R)	96,206	37.5
	Mary J. Farinelli (I)	19,077	7.4
	David E. Coleman (I)	7,214	2.8
6	Peter G. Torkildsen (R)	159,165	54.8
	Nicholas Mavroules (D) *	130,248	44.9
7	Edward J. Markey (D) *	174,837	62.1
	Stephen A. Sohn (R)	78,262	27.8
	Robert B. Antonelli (I)	28,421	10.1
8	Joseph P. Kennedy II (D) *	149,903	83.1
	(No Republican candidate)		
	Alice Harriett Nakash (I)	30,402	16.8
9	Joe Moakley (D) *	175,550	69.2
	Martin D. Conboy (R)	54,291	21.4
	Lawrence C. Mackin (I)	15,637	6.2
	Robert W. Horan (I)	8,084	3.2
10	Gerry E. Studds (D) *	189,342	60.8
	Daniel W. Daly (R)	75,887	24.4
	Jon L. Bryan (I)	39,265	12.6
	Michael P. Umina (IV)	6,020	1.9
	Robert W. Knapp (FFL)	1,106	.4

MICHIGAN

House

		Vote Total	Per-cent
1	Bart Stupak (D)	144,857	53.9
	Philip E. Ruppe (R)	117,056	43.6
	Gerald Aydlott (LIBERT)	4,094	1.5
	Lyman Clark (NL)	2,570	1.0
2	Peter Hoekstra (R)	155,577	63.0
	John H. Miltner (D)	86,265	35.0
	Dick Jacobs (LIBERT)	4,840	2.0
3	Paul B. Henry (R) *	162,451	61.3
	Carol S. Kooistra (D)	95,927	36.2
	Richard Whitelock (LIBERT)	3,232	1.2
	Susan Normandin (NL)	3,228	1.2
4	Dave Camp (R) *	157,337	62.5
	Lisa A. Donaldson (D)	87,573	34.8
	Joan Dennison (TIC)	3,344	1.3
	Gary R. Bradley (LIBERT)	2,027	.8
	Thomas E. List (NL)	1,247	.5
5	James A. Barcia (D)	147,618	60.3
	Keith Muxlow (R)	93,098	38.0
	Lloyd Clarke (Workers World)	4,270	1.7
6	Fred Upton (R) *	144,083	61.8
	Andy Davis (D)	89,020	38.2
7	Nick Smith (R)	133,972	87.6
	(No Democratic candidate)		
	Kenneth Proctor (LIBERT)	18,751	12.3
8	Bob Carr (D) *	135,517	47.6
	Dick Chrysler (R)	131,906	46.3
	Frank D. McAlpine (I)	12,155	4.3
	Michael E. Marotta (LIBERT)	5,115	1.8
9	Dale E. Kildee (D) *	133,956	53.7
	Megan O'Neill (R)	111,798	44.8
	Key Halverson (NL)	1,891	.8
	Jerome White (WL)	1,872	.8
10	David E. Bonior (D) *	138,193	53.1
	Douglas Carl (R)	114,918	44.2
	David A. Weidner (LIBERT)	7,098	2.7
11	Joe Knollenberg (R)	168,940	57.6
	Walter Briggs (D)	117,725	40.2
	Brian R. Wright (LIBERT)	4,144	1.4
	Henry Ogden Clark (NL)	2,269	.8
12	Sander M. Levin (D) *	137,514	52.6
	John Pappageorge (R)	119,357	45.7
	Charles Hahn (LIBERT)	2,751	1.1
	R.W. Montgomery (NL)	1,724	.7
13	William D. Ford (D) *	127,642	51.9
	R. Robert Geake (R)	105,169	42.8
	Randall F. Roe (I)	8,626	3.5
	Paul Steven Jensen (TIC)	3,314	1.3
	Larry Roberts (WL)	1,127	.5
14	John Conyers Jr. (D) *	165,496	82.4
	John W. Gordon (R)	32,036	15.9
	Richard R. Miller (NL)	2,043	1.0
	D'Artagnan Collier (WL)	1,296	.6
15	Barbara-Rose Collins (D) *	148,908	80.5
	Charles C. Vincent (R)	31,849	17.2
	James E. Harris Jr. (I)	2,704	1.5
	Jane Walker Meade (NL)	1,496	.8
16	John D. Dingell (D) *	156,964	65.1
	Frank Beaumont (R)	75,694	31.4
	Max J. Siegle (TIC)	4,048	1.7
	Jeff Hampton (LIBERT)	2,387	1.0
	Martin P. McLaughlin (WL)	1,842	.8

MINNESOTA

House

		Vote Total	Per-cent
1	Timothy J. Penny (D) *	206,369	73.9
	Timothy R. Droogsma (R)	72,367	25.9
2	David Minge (D)	132,156	47.8
	Cal R. Ludeman (R)	131,587	47.6
	Stan Bentz (I)	12,146	4.4
3	Jim Ramstad (R) *	200,240	63.6
	Paul Mandell (D)	104,606	33.2
	Dwight Fellman (GR)	9,164	2.9
4	Bruce F. Vento (D) *	159,796	57.5
	Ian Maitland (R)	101,744	36.6
	James L. Willess (I)	6,732	2.4
	Dan R. Vacek (GR)	4,418	1.6
	Lynn Marvin Johnson (NL)	3,602	1.3
	Jo Rothenberg (SW)	1,236	.4
5	Martin Olav Sabo (D) *	174,139	62.8
	Stephen A. Moriarty (R)	77,093	27.8
	Russell B. Bentley (GR)	6,786	2.4
	Sandra Coleman (NA)	5,927	2.1
	Mary Mellen (NL)	5,499	2.0
	Glenn Mesaros (I)	4,809	1.7
	Christopher Nisan (SW)	2,062	.7
6	Rod Grams (R)	133,564	44.4
	Gerry Sikorski (D) *	100,016	33.2
	Dean Barkley (I)	48,329	16.1
	James H. Peterson (Independents for Perot)	16,411	5.5
	Tom Firnstahl (NL)	2,400	.8
7	Collin C. Peterson (D) *	133,886	50.4
	Bernie Omann (R)	130,396	49.1
8	James L. Oberstar (D) *	167,104	59.0
	Phil Herwig (R)	83,823	29.6
	Harry Robb Welty (Perot Choice)	22,619	8.0
	Floyd A. Henspeter (Term Limits Candidate)	8,602	3.0

MISSISSIPPI

House

		Vote Total	Per-cent
1	Jamie L. Whitten (D) *	121,664	59.5
	Clyde E. Whitaker (R)	82,952	40.5
2	Mike Espy (D) *	133,361	76.4
	Dorothy Benford (R)	41,248	23.6
3	G. V. "Sonny" Montgomery (D) *	162,864	81.2
	Michael E. Williams (R)	37,710	18.8
4	Mike Parker (D) *	130,927	67.3
	Jack L. McMillan (R)	43,705	22.5
	Liz Gilchrist (I)	10,523	5.4
	James H. Meredith (I)	9,389	4.8
5	Gene Taylor (D) *	120,766	63.2
	Paul Harvey (R)	67,619	35.4
	Shawn O'Hara (I)	2,673	1.4

MISSOURI

Governor

	Vote Total	Per-cent
Mel Carnahan (D)	1,375,425	58.7
William L. Webster (R)	968,574	41.3

Senate

	Vote Total	Per-cent
Christopher S. Bond (R) *	1,221,901	51.9
Geri Rothman-Serot (D)	1,057,967	44.9
Jeanne F. Bojarski (LIBERT)	75,048	3.2

House

		Vote Total	Per-cent
1	William L. Clay (D) *	158,693	68.1
	Arthur S. Montgomery (R)	74,482	31.9
2	James M. Talent (R)	157,594	50.4
	Joan Kelly Horn (D) *	148,729	47.6
	Jim Higgins (LIBERT)	6,119	2.0
3	Richard A. Gephardt (D) *	174,000	64.0
	Mack Holekamp (R)	90,006	33.1
	Robert Stockhausen (LIBERT)	7,828	2.9
4	Ike Skelton (D) *	176,977	70.4
	John Carley (R)	74,475	29.6
5	Alan Wheat (D) *	151,014	59.1
	Edward "Gomer" Moody (R)	93,562	36.6
	Tom Danaher (GREEN)	6,107	2.4
	Grant Stauffer (LIBERT)	4,629	1.8
6	Pat Danner (D)	148,887	55.4
	Tom Coleman (R) *	119,637	44.6
7	Mel Hancock (R) *	160,303	61.6
	Thomas Patrick Deaton (D)	99,762	38.4
8	Bill Emerson (R) *	147,398	62.9
	Thad Bullock (D)	86,730	37.0
	Harold Reed (write-in)	282	.1
9	Harold L. Volkmer (D) *	124,694	47.7
	Rick Hardy (R)	118,811	45.5
	Jeff Barrow (GREEN)	10,565	4.0
	Duane Neil Burghard (I)	7,265	2.8

MONTANA

Governor

	Vote Total	Per-cent
Marc Racicot (R)	209,401	51.3
Dorothy Bradley (D)	198,421	48.7

House

		Vote Total	Per-cent
AL	Pat Williams (D) *	203,711	50.5
	Ron Marlenee (R) *	189,570	47.0
	Jerome J. Wilverding (LIBERT)	10,454	2.6

NEBRASKA

House

		Vote Total	Per-cent
1	Doug Bereuter (R) *	142,713	59.7
	Gerry Finnegan (D)	96,309	40.3
2	Peter Hoagland (D) *	119,512	51.2
	Ronald L. Staskiewicz (R)	113,828	48.8
3	Bill Barrett (R) *	170,857	71.7
	Lowell Fisher (D)	67,457	28.3

NEVADA

Senate

	Vote Total	Per-cent
Harry Reid (D) *	253,150	51.0
Demar Dahl (R)	199,413	40.2
"None of these candidates"	13,154	2.7
Joe S. Garcia Jr. (IA)	11,240	2.3
Lois Avery (NL)	7,279	1.5
H. Kent Cromwell (LIBERT)	7,222	1.5
Harry Tootle (POP)	4,429	.9

House

		Vote Total	Per-cent
1	James Bilbray (D) *	128,278	57.9
	J. Coy Pettyjohn (R)	84,217	38.0
	Scott A. Kjar (LIBERT)	8,993	4.1
2	Barbara F. Vucanovich (R) *	129,575	47.9
	Pete Sferrazza (D)	117,199	43.3
	Daniel M. Hansen (IA)	13,285	4.9
	Dan Becan (LIBERT)	7,552	2.8
	Don Golden (POP)	2,850	1.1

NEW HAMPSHIRE

Governor

	Candidate	Vote Total	Percent
	Steve Merrill (R)	289,170	56.0
	Deborah Arnie Arnesen (D)	206,232	40.0
	Miriam F. Luce (LIBERT)	20,663	4.0

Senate

	Candidate	Vote Total	Percent
	Judd Gregg (R)	249,591	48.1
	John Rauh (D)	234,982	45.3
	Katherine M. Alexander (LIBERT)	18,214	3.5
	Larry Brady (I)	9,340	1.8
	Kenneth E. Blevens Sr. (I)	4,752	.9
	David Haight (NL)	1,284	.2

House

	Candidate	Vote Total	Percent
1	Bill Zeliff (R) *	135,936	53.1
	Bob Preston (D)	108,578	42.4
	Knox Bickford (LIBERT)	5,633	2.2
	Richard P. Bosa (I)	3,537	1.4
	Linda Spitzfaden (NL)	1,997	.8
2	Dick Swett (D) *	157,328	61.7
	Bill Hatch (R)	91,126	35.7
	John A. Lewicke (LIBERT)	5,977	2.3
	James J. Bingham (NL)	657	.3

NEW JERSEY

House

	Candidate	Vote Total	Percent
1	Robert E. Andrews (D) *	153,525	67.3
	Lee A. Solomon (R)	65,123	28.6
	James E. Smith (Pro-Life Pro-Family Veteran)	3,761	1.6
	Jerry Zeldin (LIBERT)	2,641	1.2
	Kenneth L. Lowndes (Pro-Life Independent Conservative)	2,163	.9
	Nicholas Pastuch (AFP)	859	.4
2	William J. Hughes (D) *	132,465	55.9
	Frank A. LoBiondo (R)	98,315	41.5
	Roger W. Bacon (LIBERT)	2,575	1.1
	Joseph Ponczek (Anti-Tax)	2,067	.9
	Andrea Lippi (Freedom Equality Prosperity)	1,605	.7
3	H. James Saxton (R) *	151,368	59.2
	Timothy E. Ryan (D)	94,012	36.8
	Helen L. Radder (LIBERT)	2,711	1.1
	Joseph A. Plonski (AFP)	2,309	.9
	Michael S. Permuko (NJC)	1,728	.7
	James Reilly (I)	915	.4
	William Donald McMahon ("Donald of Moorestown")	901	.4
	Anthony J. Verderese (The Independent Party)	749	.3
	Martin T. King (I)	593	.2
	Frank Burke (Basic Reformed Government)	512	.2
4	Christopher H. Smith (R) *	149,095	61.8
	Brian M. Hughes (D)	84,514	35.0
	Benjamin Grindlinger (LIBERT)	2,984	1.2
	Patrick C. Pasculli (I)	2,137	.9
	Agnes A. James (NJC)	1,630	.7
	Joseph J. Notarangelo (AFP)	865	.4
5	Marge Roukema (R) *	196,198	71.5
	Frank R. Lucas (D)	67,579	24.6
	William J. Leonard (I)	6,182	2.3
	Michael V. Pierone (LIBERT)	2,636	1.0
	George Lahood (Equality Brotherhood Justice)	994	.4
	Stuart Bacha (AFP)	782	.3
6	Frank Pallone Jr. (D) *	118,266	52.3
	Joseph M. Kyrillos (R)	100,949	44.6
	Joseph Spalletta (The People's Candidate)	2,153	1.0
	Bill Stewart (LIBERT)	1,404	.6
	Peter Cerrato (Independent for Freedom)	1,073	.5
	George P. Predham (You Gotta Believe)	951	.4
	Simone Berg (SW)	613	.3
	Kenneth Matto (AFP)	411	.2
	Charles H. Dickson (Capitalist)	273	.1
7	Bob Franks (R)	132,174	53.3
	Leonard R. Sendelsky (D)	105,761	42.6
	Eugene J. Gillespie Jr. (I)	4,043	1.6
	Bill Campbell (No Nonsense Government)	2,612	1.1
	Spencer Layman (LIBERT)	1,964	.8
	John L. Kucek (AFP)	844	.3
	Kevin Michael Criss (People's Congressional Preference)	684	.3
8	Herbert C. Klein (D)	96,742	47.0
	Joseph L. Bubba (R)	84,674	41.1
	Gloria J. Kolodziej (IFC)	16,170	7.9
	Thomas Caslander (IFC)	2,916	1.4
	Carmine O. Pellosie (Independent People's Network)	2,135	1.0
	Louis M. Stefanelli (LIBERT)	1,109	.5
	Rob Dominianni (Restore Public Trust)	1,099	.5
	Jason Redrup (SW)	392	.2
	Gregory E. Dzula (AFP)	316	.2
	Neal A. Gorfinkle (NJI)	275	.1
9	Robert G. Torricelli (D) *	139,188	58.3
	Patrick J. Roma (R)	88,179	36.9
	Peter J. Russo (Clean Up Congress)	4,491	1.9
	Gary Novosielski (NJI)	2,257	.9
	Joseph D'Alessio (AFP)	1,606	.7
	Herbert H. Shaw (Politicians Are Crooks)	1,369	.6
	Daniel M. Karlan (LIBERT)	1,099	.5
	Shel Haas (An Independent Voice)	515	.2
10	Donald M. Payne (D) *	117,287	78.4
	Alfred D. Palermo (R)	30,160	20.2
	Roberto Caraballo (LIBERT)	1,272	.9
	William T. Leonard (SW)	913	.6
11	Dean A. Gallo (R) *	188,165	70.1
	Ona Spiridellis (D)	68,871	25.7
	Richard S. Roth (LIBERT)	3,538	1.3
	Barry J. Fitzpatrick (Time for Change)	3,127	1.2
	David C. Karlen (I)	1,882	.7
	Howard Safier (Howard Safier-Independent)	1,711	.6
	Richard E. Hrazanek (AFP)	1,142	.4
12	Dick Zimmer (R) *	174,216	63.9
	Frank Abate (D)	83,035	30.4
	Carl J. Mayer (I)	11,051	4.1
	Carl Peters (LIBERT)	1,906	.7
	Edward F. Eggert (I)	1,804	.7
	Compton C. Pakenham (AFP)	745	.3
13	Robert Menendez (D)	93,670	64.3
	Fred J. Theemling Jr. (R)	44,525	30.6
	Joseph D. Bonacci (Stop Tax Increases)	2,363	1.6
	Len Flynn (LIBERT)	1,539	1.1
	John E. Rummel (Communist)	1,525	1.0
	Jane Harris (SW)	1,406	1.0
	Donald K. Stoveken (AFP)	682	.5

NEW MEXICO

House

	Candidate	Vote Total	Percent
1	Steven H. Schiff (R) *	128,426	62.6
	Robert J. Aragon (D)	76,600	37.3
	Orlin G. Cole (write-in)	188	.1
2	Joe Skeen (R) *	94,838	56.4
	Dan Sosa Jr. (D)	73,157	43.5
	David Lee Pilley (write-in)	175	.1
3	Bill Richardson (D) *	122,850	67.4
	F. Gregg Bemis Jr. (R)	54,569	29.9
	Ed Nagel (LIBERT)	4,798	2.6

NEW YORK

Senate

	Candidate	Vote Total	Percent
	Alfonse M. D'Amato (R, C, RTL) *	3,166,994	49.0
	Robert Abrams (D, L)	3,086,200	47.8
	Norma Segal (LIBERT)	108,530	1.7
	Mohammad T. Mehdi (NA)	56,631	.9
	Stanley Nelson (NL)	23,747	.4
	Ed Warren (SW)	16,724	.3

House

	Candidate	Vote Total	Percent
1	George J. Hochbrueckner (D, LIF) *	117,940	51.7
	Edward P. Romaine (R, C, RTL, TCP-LI)	110,043	48.3
2	Rick A. Lazio (R, C, TCP-LI)	109,386	53.2
	Thomas J. Downey (D, LIF) *	96,328	46.8
3	Peter T. King (R, C)	124,727	49.6
	Steve A. Orlins (D)	116,915	46.5
	Louis P. Roccanova (RTL)	6,888	2.7
	Ben-Zion J. Heyman (L)	3,092	1.2
4	David A. Levy (R, C)	110,710	50.2
	Philip Schiliro (D, L)	100,386	45.5
	Vincent P. Garbitelli (RTL)	9,548	4.3
5	Gary L. Ackerman (D, L) *	110,476	52.4
	Allan E. Binder (R, C)	94,907	45.0
	Andrew J. Duff (RTL)	5,448	2.6
6	Floyd H. Flake (D) *	96,972	81.0
	Dianand D. Bhagwandin (R, C)	22,687	19.0
7	Thomas J. Manton (D) *	72,280	56.9
	Dennis C. Shea (R, C)	54,639	43.1
8	Jerrold Nadler (D, L)	138,296	81.2
	David L. Askren (R)	25,548	15.0
	Margaret V. Byrnes (C)	5,180	3.0
	Arthur R. Block (NA)	1,224	.7
9	Charles E. Schumer (D, L) *	116,545	88.6
	(No Republican candidate)		
	Alice E. Gaffney (C)	14,985	11.4
10	Edolphus Towns (D, L) *	97,509	95.8
	(No Republican candidate)		
	Owen Augustin (C)	4,315	4.2
11	Major R. Owens (D, L) *	80,028	93.6
	(No Republican candidate)		
	Michael Gaffney (C)	4,287	5.0
	Ernest N. Foster (NA)	1,179	1.4
12	Nydia M. Velázquez (D)	55,926	76.5
	Angel Diaz (R, C, RTL)	14,976	20.5
	Ruben Franco (L)	1,556	2.1
	Rafael Mendez (NA)	609	.8
13	Susan Molinari (R, C) *	107,903	56.1
	Sal F. Albanese (D, L)	73,520	38.2
	Kathleen M. Murphy (RTL)	10,825	5.6
14	Carolyn B. Maloney (D, L)	101,652	50.4
	Bill Green (R, Independent Neighbors) *	97,215	48.2
	Abraham J. Hirschfeld (Better East Side)	2,970	1.5
15	Charles B. Rangel (D) *	105,011	94.9
	(No Republican candidate)		
	Jose A. Suero (C, Independent Fusion)	4,345	3.9
	Jessie Fields (NA)	1,337	1.2
16	Jose E. Serrano (D, L) *	85,222	91.4
	Michael Walters (R, C)	7,975	8.6
17	Eliot L. Engel (D, L) *	98,068	80.1
	Martin Richman (R)	16,511	13.5
	Kevin Brawley (C)	3,143	2.6

		Vote Total	Percent
	Martin J. O'Grady (RTL)	3,067	2.5
	Nana LaLuz (NL)	1,592	1.3
18	Nita M. Lowey (D) *	115,841	55.6
	Joseph J. DioGuardi (R, C, RTL)	92,687	44.4
19	Hamilton Fish Jr. (R, C) *	139,610	60.1
	Neil McCarthy (D)	92,854	39.9
20	Benjamin A. Gilman (R) *	150,301	66.1
	Jonathan L. Levine (D)	66,826	29.4
	Robert F. Garrison (RTL)	10,204	4.5
21	Michael R. McNulty (D, C) *	166,371	62.7
	Nancy Norman (R, L)	91,184	34.4
	William J. Donnelly (RTL)	7,723	2.9
22	Gerald B. H. Solomon (R, C, RTL) *	164,436	65.4
	David Roberts (D)	86,896	34.6
23	Sherwood Boehlert (R) *	139,774	63.6
	Paula DiPerna (D)	61,835	28.2
	Randall A. Terry (RTL)	8,688	4.0
	Geoffrey P. Grace (C)	8,011	3.6
	Ted F. Janowski (NL)	1,354	.6
24	John M. McHugh (R, Voter Rights)	122,257	60.8
	Margaret M. Ravenscroft (D)	47,675	23.7
	Morrison J. Hosley Jr. (C, RTL)	26,763	13.3
	Stephen Burke (L)	4,374	2.2
25	James T. Walsh (R, C) *	135,076	55.7
	Rhea Jezer (D, Common Sense)	107,310	44.3
26	Maurice D. Hinchey (D, L)	119,557	50.4
	Bob Moppert (R, C)	110,738	46.7
	Mary C. Dixon (RTL)	6,821	2.9
27	Bill Paxon (R, C, RTL) *	156,596	63.5
	W. Douglas Call (D)	89,906	36.5
28	Louise M. Slaughter (D) *	140,908	55.2
	William P. Polito (R, C)	112,273	44.0
	Keith R.T. Perez (EJ)	1,897	.7
29	John J. LaFalce (D, L) *	128,230	54.5
	William E. Miller Jr. (R, C)	98,031	41.6
	Kenneth J. Kowalski (RTL)	7,367	3.1
	John A. Basar Jr. (EJ)	1,830	.8
30	Jack Quinn (R, Change Congress)	125,734	51.7
	Dennis Gorski (D, C)	111,445	45.8
	Mary F. Refermat (RTL)	6,025	2.5
31	Amo Houghton (R, C) *	150,696	70.6
	Joseph P. Leahey (D)	52,010	24.4
	Gretchen S. McManus (RTL)	10,848	5.1

NORTH CAROLINA

Governor

		Vote Total	Percent
	James B. Hunt Jr. (D)	1,368,246	52.7
	Jim Gardner (R)	1,121,955	43.2
	Scott McLaughlin (LIBERT)	104,983	4.0

Senate

		Vote Total	Percent
	Lauch Faircloth (R)	1,297,892	50.3
	Terry Sanford (D) *	1,194,015	46.3
	Bobby Yates Emory (LIBERT)	85,948	3.3

House

		Vote Total	Percent
1	Eva Clayton (D)	116,078	67.0
	Ted Tyler (R)	54,457	31.4
	C. Barry Williams (LIBERT)	2,727	1.6
2	Tim Valentine (D) *	113,693	53.7
	Don Davis (R)	93,893	44.4
	Dennis Bryant Lubahn (LIBERT)	3,983	1.9
3	H. Martin Lancaster (D) *	101,739	54.4
	Tommy Pollard (R)	80,759	43.2
	Mark Jackson (LIBERT)	4,552	2.4
4	David Price (D) *	171,299	64.6
	LaVinia "Vicky" Rothrock Goudie (R)	89,345	33.7
	Eugene Paczelt (LIBERT)	4,416	1.7
5	Stephen L. Neal (D) *	117,835	52.7
	Richard M. Burr (R)	102,086	45.6
	Gary Albrecht (LIBERT)	3,758	1.7
6	Howard Coble (R) *	162,822	70.8
	Robin Hood (D)	67,200	29.2
7	Charlie Rose (D) *	92,414	56.7
	Robert C. Anderson (R)	66,536	40.8
	Marc Kelley (LIBERT)	4,151	2.5
8	W. G. "Bill" Hefner (D) *	113,162	59.3
	Coy C. Privette (R)	71,842	37.6
	J. Wendell Drye (LIBERT)	5,947	3.1
9	Alex McMillan (R) *	153,650	67.3
	Rory Blake (D)	74,583	32.7
10	Cass Ballenger (R) *	149,033	63.4
	Ben Neill (D)	79,206	33.7
	Jeffrey Clayton Brown (LIBERT)	6,888	2.9
11	Charles H. Taylor (R) *	130,158	54.7
	John S. Stevens (D)	108,003	45.3
12	Melvin Watt (D)	127,262	70.4
	Barbara Gore Washington (R)	49,402	27.3
	Curtis W. Krumel (LIBERT)	4,160	2.3

NORTH DAKOTA

Governor

		Vote Total	Percent
	Edward T. Schafer (R)	176,398	57.9
	Nicholas Spaeth (D)	123,845	40.6
	Harley McLain (I)	2,614	.9
	Michael O. DuPaul (I)	2,004	.7

Senate

		Vote Total	Percent
	Byron L. Dorgan (D)	179,347	59.0
	Steve Sydness (R)	118,162	38.9
	Tom Asbridge (I)	6,448	2.1

House

		Vote Total	Percent
AL	Earl Pomeroy (D)	169,273	56.8
	John T. Korsmo (R)	117,442	39.4
	Anna Belle Bourgois (I)	7,394	2.5
	Grady Blount (I)	3,789	1.3

OHIO

Senate

		Vote Total	Percent
	John Glenn (D) *	2,444,419	51.0
	Mike DeWine (R)	2,028,300	42.3
	Martha Kathryn Grevatt (I)	321,234	6.7

House

		Vote Total	Percent
1	David Mann (D)	120,190	51.3
	(No Republican candidate)		
	Steve Grote (I)	101,498	43.3
	James A. Berns (I)	12,734	5.4
2	Bill Gradison (R) *	177,720	70.1
	Thomas R. Chandler (D)	75,924	29.9
3	Tony P. Hall (D) *	146,072	59.7
	Peter W. Davis (R)	98,733	40.3
4	Michael G. Oxley (R) *	147,346	61.3
	Raymond M. Ball (D)	92,608	38.5
	James R. Stahl (write-in)	486	.2
5	Paul E. Gillmor (R) *	187,860	100.0
6	Ted Strickland (D)	122,720	50.7
	Bob McEwen (R) *	119,252	49.3
7	David L. Hobson (R) *	164,195	71.3
	Clifford S. Heskett (D)	66,237	28.7
8	John A. Boehner (R) *	176,362	74.0
	Fred Sennet (D)	62,033	26.0
9	Marcy Kaptur (D) *	178,879	73.6
	Ken D. Brown (R)	53,011	21.8
	Ed Howard (I)	11,162	4.6
10	Martin R. Hoke (R)	136,433	56.8
	Mary Rose Oakar (D) *	103,788	43.2
11	Louis Stokes (D) *	154,718	69.2
	Beryl E. Rothschild (R)	43,866	19.6
	Edmund Gudenas (I)	19,773	8.8
	Gerald C. Henley (I)	5,267	2.4
12	John R. Kasich (R) *	170,297	71.2
	Bob Fitrakis (D)	68,761	28.8
13	Sherrod Brown (D)	134,486	53.3
	Margaret R. Mueller (R)	88,889	35.2
	Mark Miller (I)	20,320	8.1
	Tom Lawson (I)	4,719	1.9
	Werner J. Lange (I)	3,844	1.5
14	Tom Sawyer (D) *	165,335	67.8
	Robert Morgan (R)	78,659	32.2
15	Deborah Pryce (R)	110,390	44.1
	Richard Cordray (D)	94,907	37.9
	Linda S. Reidelbach (I)	44,906	17.9
16	Ralph Regula (R) *	158,489	63.7
	Warner D. Mendenhall (D)	90,224	36.3
17	James A. Traficant Jr. (D) *	216,503	84.2
	Salvatore Pansino (R)	40,743	15.8
18	Douglas Applegate (D) *	166,189	68.3
	Bill Ress (R)	77,229	31.7
19	Eric D. Fingerhut (D)	138,465	52.6
	Robert A. Gardner (R)	124,606	47.4

OKLAHOMA

Senate

		Vote Total	Percent
	Don Nickles (R) *	757,876	58.5
	Steve Lewis (D)	494,350	38.2
	Roy V. Edwards (I)	21,225	1.6
	Thomas D. Ledgerwood II (I)	20,972	1.6

House

		Vote Total	Percent
1	James M. Inhofe (R) *	119,211	52.8
	John Selph (D)	106,619	47.2
2	Mike Synar (D) *	118,542	55.5
	Jerry Hill (R)	87,657	41.1
	William S. Vardeman (I)	7,314	3.4
3	Bill Brewster (D) *	155,934	75.1
	Robert W. Stokes (R)	51,725	24.9
4	Dave McCurdy (D) *	140,841	70.7
	Howard Bell (R)	58,235	29.3
5	Ernest Jim Istook (R)	123,237	53.4
	Laurie Williams (D)	107,579	46.6
6	Glenn English (D) *	134,734	67.8
	Bob Anthony (R)	64,068	32.2

OREGON

Senate

		Vote Total	Percent
	Bob Packwood (R) *	717,455	52.1
	Les AuCoin (D)	639,851	46.5
	Harry Lonsdale (write-in)	5,793	.4

House

		Vote Total	Percent
1	Elizabeth Furse (D)	152,917	52.0
	Tony Meeker (R)	140,986	47.9
2	Bob Smith (R) *	184,163	67.1
	Denzel Ferguson (D)	90,036	32.8
3	Ron Wyden (D) *	208,028	77.1
	Al Ritter (R)	50,235	18.6
	Blair Bobier (LIBERT)	11,413	4.2
4	Peter A. DeFazio (D) *	199,372	71.4
	Richard L. Schulz (R)	79,733	28.5
5	Mike Kopetski (D) *	174,443	63.9
	Jim Seagraves (R)	97,984	35.9

PENNSYLVANIA

Senate

		Vote Total	Percent
	Arlen Specter (R) *	2,358,125	49.1
	Lynn Yeakel (D)	2,224,966	46.3
	John F. Perry III (LIBERT)	219,319	4.6

House

		Vote Total	Per-cent
1	Thomas M. Foglietta (D) *	150,172	80.9
	Craig Snyder (R)	35,419	19.1
2	Lucien E. Blackwell (D) *	164,355	76.8
	Larry Hollin (R)	47,906	22.4
	Mark Wyatt (SW)	1,666	.8
3	Robert A. Borski (D) *	130,828	58.9
	Charles F. Dougherty (R)	86,787	39.1
	John J. Hughes (I)	4,356	2.0
4	Ron Klink (D)	186,684	78.5
	Gordon R. Johnston (R)	48,484	20.4
	Drew Ley (I)	2,754	1.2
5	William F. Clinger (R, D) *	188,911	100.0
6	Tim Holden (D)	108,312	52.1
	John E. Jones (R)	99,694	47.9
7	Curt Weldon (R) *	180,648	66.0
	Frank Daly (D)	91,623	33.5
	William Alan Hickman (NL)	1,627	.6
8	Jim Greenwood (R)	129,593	51.9
	Peter H. Kostmayer (D) *	114,095	45.7
	William H. Magerman (Magerman for Congress)	5,850	2.3
9	Bud Shuster (R, D) *	182,406	100.0
10	Joseph M. McDade (R, D) *	189,414	90.4
	Albert A. Smith (LIBERT)	20,134	9.6
11	Paul E. Kanjorski (D) *	138,875	67.1
	Michael A. Fescina (R)	68,112	32.9
12	John P. Murtha (D) *	166,916	100.0
	(No Republican candidate)		
13	Marjorie Margolies-Mezvinsky (D)	127,685	50.3
	Jon D. Fox (R)	126,312	49.7
14	William J. Coyne (D) *	165,633	72.3
	Byron W. King (R)	61,311	26.8
	Joanne S. Kuniansky (SW)	1,300	.6
	Paul Scherrer (WL)	794	.3
15	Paul McHale (D)	111,419	52.2
	Don Ritter (R) *	99,520	46.7
	Eugene A. Nau (NL)	2,385	1.1
16	Robert S. Walker (R) *	137,823	64.8
	Robert Peters (D)	74,741	35.2
17	George W. Gekas (R) *	150,158	69.5
	Bill Sturges (D)	65,881	30.5
18	Rick Santorum (R) *	154,024	60.6
	Frank A. Pecora (D)	96,655	38.0
	Denise Winebrenner Edwards (New Independent)	3,650	1.4
19	Bill Goodling (R) *	98,599	45.3
	Paul V. Kilker (D)	74,798	34.4
	Thomas M. Humbert (I)	44,190	20.3
20	Austin J. Murphy (D) *	114,898	50.7
	Bill Townsend (R)	111,591	49.3
21	Tom Ridge (R) *	150,729	68.0
	John C. Harkins (D)	70,802	32.0

RHODE ISLAND

Governor

		Vote Total	Per-cent
	Bruce Sundlun (D) *	261,484	61.6
	Elizabeth Ann Leonard (R)	145,590	34.3
	Joseph F. Devine (Reform '92)	14,511	3.4
	Jack D. Potter (POP)	1,698	.4
	John J. Staradumsky (I)	1,535	.4

House

		Vote Total	Per-cent
1	Ronald K. Machtley (R) *	135,982	70.1
	David R. Carlin Jr. (D)	48,092	24.8
	Frederick E. Dick (Ross Perot Independent)	6,012	3.1
	Norman J. Jacques (I)	4,003	2.1
2	Jack Reed (D) *	144,450	70.7
	James W. Bell (R)	49,998	24.5
	Thomas J. Ricci (I)	6,715	3.3
	John Turnbull (Independent Thinking)	3,250	1.6

SOUTH CAROLINA

Senate

		Vote Total	Per-cent
	Ernest F. Hollings (D) *	591,030	50.1
	Thomas F. Hartnett (R)	554,175	46.9
	Mark Johnson (LIBERT)	22,962	1.9
	Robert B. Clarkson II (AM)	11,568	1.0

House

		Vote Total	Per-cent
1	Arthur Ravenel Jr. (R) *	121,938	66.1
	Bill Oberst Jr. (D)	59,908	32.5
	John R. Peeples (AM)	2,608	1.4
2	Floyd D. Spence (R) *	148,667	87.6
	(No Democratic candidate)		
	Geb Sommer (LIBERT)	20,816	12.3
3	Butler Derrick (D) *	119,119	61.1
	Jim Bland (R)	75,660	38.8
4	Bob Inglis (R)	99,879	50.3
	Liz J. Patterson (D) *	94,182	47.5
	Jo Jorgensen (LIBERT)	4,286	2.2
5	John M. Spratt Jr. (D) *	112,031	61.2
	Bill Horne (R)	70,866	38.7
6	James E. Clyburn (D)	120,647	65.3
	John Chase (R)	64,149	34.7

SOUTH DAKOTA

Senate

		Vote Total	Per-cent
	Tom Daschle (D) *	217,095	64.9
	Charlene Haar (R)	108,733	32.5
	Gus Hercules (LIBERT)	4,353	1.3
	Kent Hyde (NL)	4,314	1.3

House

		Vote Total	Per-cent
AL	Tim Johnson (D) *	230,070	69.1
	John Timmer (R)	89,375	26.8
	Ronald Wieczorek (I)	6,746	2.0
	Robert J. Newland (LIBERT)	3,931	1.2
	Ann Balakier (I)	2,780	.8

TENNESSEE

House

		Vote Total	Per-cent
1	James H. Quillen (R) *	114,797	67.5
	J. Carr "Jack" Christian (D)	47,809	28.1
	Don Fox (I)	4,126	2.4
	Fred A. Hartley (I)	3,416	2.0
2	John J. "Jimmy" Duncan Jr. (R) *	148,377	72.2
	Troy Goodale (D)	52,887	25.7
	Randon J. Krieg (I)	4,134	2.0
3	Marilyn Lloyd (D) *	105,693	48.8
	Zach Wamp (R)	102,763	47.5
	Carol Hagan (I)	4,433	2.0
	Pete Melcher (I)	2,048	.9
	Marjorie M. Martin (I)	1,593	.7
4	Jim Cooper (D) *	98,984	64.1
	Dale Johnson (R)	50,340	32.6
	Ginnia C. Fox (I)	3,970	2.6
	Kieven Parks (I)	1,210	.8
5	Bob Clement (D) *	125,233	66.8
	Tom Stone (R)	49,417	26.3
	Steven L. Edmondson (I)	6,724	3.6
	Richard H. Wyatt (I)	3,507	1.9
	John D. Haury (I)	1,685	.9
	Ben Tomeo (I)	1,002	.5
6	Bart Gordon (D) *	120,177	56.6
	Marsha Blackburn (R)	86,285	40.6
	H. Scott Benson (I)	5,952	2.8
7	Don Sundquist (R) *	125,101	61.7
	David R. Davis (D)	72,062	35.5
	Rickey Boyette (I)	2,290	1.1
	Jim Osburn (I)	1,83[illegible]	.9
	Francis Fredrick Tapp (I)	1,573	.8
8	John Tanner (D) *	136,852	83.7
	(No Republican candidate)		

		Vote Total	Per-cent
	Lawrence J. Barnes (I)	9,605	5.9
	David L. Ward (I)	6,930	4.2
	John E. Vinson (I)	5,435	3.3
	Millard J. McKissack II (I)	4,600	2.8
9	Harold E. Ford (D) *	123,276	57.9
	Charles L. Black (R)	60,606	28.5
	Richard Liptock (I)	14,075	6.6
	James Vandergriff (I)	12,265	5.8
	William Rolen (I)	2,517	1.2

TEXAS

House

		Vote Total	Per-cent
1	Jim Chapman (D) *	152,209	100.0
2	Charles Wilson (D) *	118,625	56.1
	Donna Peterson (R)	92,176	43.6
	Roger Northen (write-in)	549	.3
3	Sam Johnson (R) *	201,569	86.1
	(No Democratic candidate)		
	Noel Kopala (LIBERT)	32,570	13.9
4	Ralph M. Hall (D) *	128,008	58.1
	David L. Bridges (R)	83,875	38.1
	Steven Rothacker (LIBERT)	8,450	3.8
5	John Bryant (D) *	98,567	58.9
	Richard Stokley (R)	62,419	37.3
	William H. Walker (LIBERT)	6,344	3.8
6	Joe L. Barton (R) *	189,140	71.9
	John Dietrich (D)	73,933	28.1
7	Bill Archer (R) *	169,407	100.0
8	Jack Fields (R) *	179,349	77.0
	Chas. Robinson (D)	53,473	23.0
9	Jack Brooks (D) *	118,690	53.6
	Steve Stockman (R)	96,270	43.5
	Billy Joe Crawford (LIBERT)	6,401	2.9
10	J.J. Pickle (D) *	177,233	67.7
	Herbert Spiro (R)	68,646	26.2
	Terry Blum (LIBERT)	6,353	2.4
	Jeff Davis (I)	6,056	2.3
	Stephen Hopkins (write-in)	3,510	1.3
11	Chet Edwards (D) *	119,999	67.4
	James W. Broyles (R)	58,033	32.6
12	Pete Geren (D) *	125,492	62.8
	David Hobbs (R)	74,432	37.2
13	Bill Sarpalius (D) *	117,892	60.3
	Beau Boulter (R)	77,514	39.7
14	Greg Laughlin (D) *	135,930	68.1
	Humberto J. Garza (R)	54,412	27.3
	Vic Vreeland (I)	9,329	4.7
15	E. "Kika" de la Garza (D) *	86,351	60.4
	Tom Haughey (R)	56,549	39.6
16	Ronald D. Coleman (D) *	66,731	51.9
	Chip Taberski (R)	61,870	48.1
17	Charles W. Stenholm (D) *	136,213	66.1
	Jeannie Sadowski (R)	69,958	33.9
18	Craig Washington (D) *	111,422	64.7
	Edward Blum (R)	56,080	32.6
	Gregg Lassen (LIBERT)	4,706	2.7
19	Larry Combest (R) *	162,057	77.4
	Terry Lee Moser (D)	47,325	22.6
20	Henry B. Gonzalez (D) *	103,755	100.0
21	Lamar Smith (R) *	190,979	72.2
	James M. Gaddy (D)	62,827	23.7
	William E. Grisham (LIBERT)	10,847	4.1
22	Tom DeLay (R) *	150,221	68.9
	Richard Konrad (D)	67,812	31.1
23	Henry Bonilla (R)	98,259	59.1
	Albert G. Bustamante (D) *	63,797	38.4
	David Alter (LIBERT)	4,291	2.6
24	Martin Frost (D) *	104,174	59.8
	Steve Masterson (R)	70,042	40.2
25	Michael A. Andrews (D) *	98,975	56.0
	Dolly Madison McKenna (R)	73,192	41.4
	Richard Mauk (LIBERT)	4,710	2.7

		Vote Total	Per-cent
26	Dick Armey (R) *	150,209	73.1
	John Wayne Caton (D)	55,237	26.9
27	Solomon P. Ortiz (D) *	87,022	55.5
	Jay Kimbrough (R)	66,853	42.6
	Charles Henry Schoonover (LIBERT)	2,969	1.9
28	Frank Tejeda (D)	122,457	87.1
	(No Republican candidate)		
	David C. Slatter (LIBERT)	18,128	12.9
29	Gene Green (D)	64,064	64.9
	Clark Kent Ervin (R)	34,609	35.1
30	Eddie Bernice Johnson (D)	107,831	71.5
	Lucy Cain (R)	37,853	25.1
	Ken Ashby (LIBERT)	5,063	3.4

UTAH

Governor

		Vote Total	Per-cent
	Mike Leavitt (R)	321,713	42.2
	Merrill Cook (IP)	255,753	33.5
	Stewart Hanson (D)	177,181	23.2
	Rita Gum (POP)	3,593	.5
	Gary R. Van Horn (AM)	1,492	.2
	Eleanor Garcia (SW)	1,158	.2
	Linda Metzger-Agin (I)	917	.1
	Frank W. Richins (IA)	729	.1

Senate

		Vote Total	Per-cent
	Robert F. Bennett (R)	420,069	55.4
	Wayne Owens (D)	301,228	39.7
	Anita R. Morrow (POP)	17,549	2.3
	Maury Modine (LIBERT)	14,341	1.9
	Patricia Grogan (SW)	5,292	.7

House

		Vote Total	Per-cent
1	James V. Hansen (R) *	160,037	65.3
	Ron Holt (D)	68,712	28.0
	William J. Lawrence (IP)	16,505	6.7
2	Karen Shepherd (D)	127,738	50.5
	Enid Greene (R)	118,307	46.8
	A. Peter Crane (IP)	6,274	2.5
	Eileen Koschak (SW)	650	.3
3	Bill Orton (D) *	135,029	58.9
	Richard R. Harrington (R)	84,019	36.7
	Wayne L. Hill (IP)	5,764	2.5
	Charles M. Wilson (I)	2,068	.9
	Doug Jones (LIBERT)	1,797	.8
	Nels J'Anthony (SW)	384	.2

VERMONT

Governor

		Vote Total	Per-cent
	Howard Dean (D) *	213,523	74.7
	John McClaughry (R)	65,837	23.0
	Richard F. Gottlieb (LU)	3,120	1.1
	August "Gus" Jaccaci (NL, NA)	2,834	1.0

Senate

		Vote Total	Per-cent
	Patrick J. Leahy (D) *	154,762	54.2
	James H. Douglas (R)	123,854	43.3
	Jerry Levy (LU)	5,121	1.8
	Michael B. Godeck (FFL)	1,780	.6

House

		Vote Total	Per-cent
AL	Bernard Sanders (I) *	162,724	57.8
	Tim Philbin (R)	86,901	30.9
	Lewis E. Young (D)	22,279	7.9
	Pete Diamondstone (LU)	3,660	1.3
	John Dewey (NL, NA)	3,549	1.3
	Douglas M. Miller (FFL)	2,049	.7

VIRGINIA

House

		Vote Total	Per-cent
1	Herbert H. Bateman (R) *	133,537	57.5
	Andrew H. Fox (D)	89,814	38.7
	Donald L. Macleay Jr. (I)	8,677	3.7
2	Owen B. Pickett (D) *	99,253	56.0
	J.L. "Jim" Chapman IV (R)	77,797	43.9
3	Robert C. Scott (D)	132,432	78.6
	Daniel Jenkins (R)	35,780	21.2
4	Norman Sisisky (D) *	147,649	68.4
	A.J. "Tony" Zevgolis (R)	68,286	31.6
5	Lewis F. Payne Jr. (D) *	133,031	68.9
	W. A. "Bill" Hurlburt (R)	60,030	31.1
6	Robert W. Goodlatte (R)	127,309	60.0
	Stephen Alan Musselwhite (D)	84,618	39.9
7	Thomas J. Bliley Jr. (R) *	211,618	82.9
	(No Democratic candidate)		
	Gerald E. Berg (I)	43,267	16.9
8	James P. Moran Jr. (D) *	138,542	56.1
	Kyle E. McSlarrow (R)	102,717	41.6
	Alvin O. West (I)	5,601	2.3
9	Rick Boucher (D) *	133,284	63.1
	L. Garrett Weddle (R)	77,985	36.9
10	Frank R. Wolf (R) *	144,471	63.6
	Raymond E. Vickery (D)	75,775	33.4
	Alan R. Ogden (I)	6,874	3.0
11	Leslie L. Byrne (D)	114,172	50.0
	Henry N. Butler (R)	103,119	45.2
	A.T. "Art" Narro (I)	6,681	2.9
	Perry J. Mitchell (I)	4,155	1.8

WASHINGTON

Governor

		Vote Total	Per-cent
	Mike Lowry (D)	1,184,315	52.2
	Ken Eikenberry (R)	1,086,216	47.8

Senate

		Vote Total	Per-cent
	Patty Murray (D)	1,197,973	54.0
	Rod Chandler (R)	1,020,829	46.0

House

		Vote Total	Per-cent
1	Maria Cantwell (D)	148,844	54.9
	Gary Nelson (R)	113,897	42.0
	Patrick L. Ruckert (I)	4,322	1.6
	Anne Fleming (NL)	4,211	1.6
2	Al Swift (D) *	133,207	52.1
	Jack Metcalf (R)	107,365	42.0
	R. M. "Robin" Dexter (I)	8,702	3.4
	Karen Leibrant (NL)	6,646	2.6
3	Jolene Unsoeld (D) *	138,043	56.0
	Pat Fiske (R)	108,583	44.0
4	Jay Inslee (D)	106,556	50.8
	Richard "Doc" Hastings (R)	103,028	49.2
5	Thomas S. Foley (D) *	135,965	55.2
	John Sonneland (R)	110,443	44.8
6	Norm Dicks (D) *	152,933	64.2
	Lauri J. Phillips (R)	66,664	28.0
	Tom Donnelly (I)	14,490	6.1
	Jim Horrigan (LIBERT)	4,075	1.7
7	Jim McDermott (D) *	222,604	78.4
	Glenn C. Hampson (R)	54,149	19.1
	Paul Glumaz (I)	7,197	2.5
8	Jennifer Dunn (R)	155,874	60.4
	George O. Tamblyn (D)	87,611	33.9
	Bob Adams (I)	14,686	5.7
9	Mike Kreidler (D)	110,902	52.1
	Pete von Reichbauer (R)	91,910	43.2
	Brian Wilson (I)	6,585	3.1
	Timothy J. Brill (I)	3,522	1.7

WEST VIRGINIA

Governor

		Vote Total	Per-cent
	Gaston Caperton (D) *	368,302	56.0
	Cleve Benedict (R)	240,390	36.6
	Charlotte Jean Pritt (write-in)	48,501	7.4

House

		Vote Total	Per-cent
1	Alan B. Mollohan (D) *	172,924	100.0
2	Bob Wise (D) *	143,988	70.9
	Samuel A. Cravotta (R)	59,102	29.1
3	Nick J. Rahall II (D) *	122,279	65.6
	Ben Waldman (R)	64,012	34.4

WISCONSIN

Senate

		Vote Total	Per-cent
	Russell D. Feingold (D)	1,290,662	52.6
	Bob Kasten (R) *	1,129,599	46.0
	Patrick W. Johnson (I)	16,513	.7
	William Bittner (LIBERT)	9,147	.4
	Mervin A. Hanson Sr. (I)	3,264	.1
	Robert L. Kundert (I)	2,747	.1
	Joseph Selliken (I)	2,733	.1

House

		Vote Total	Per-cent
1	Les Aspin (D) *	147,495	57.6
	Mark Neumann (R)	104,352	40.7
	John Graf (I)	4,391	1.7
2	Scott L. Klug (R) *	183,366	62.6
	Ada E. Deer (D)	108,291	37.0
	Joseph E. Schumacher (I)	1,140	.4
3	Steve Gunderson (R) *	146,903	56.4
	Paul Sacia (D)	108,664	41.7
	Jay B. Evenson (I)	4,736	1.8
4	Gerald D. Kleczka (D) *	173,482	65.8
	Joseph L. Cook (R)	84,872	32.2
	Daniel Slak (I)	2,803	1.1
	John Washburn (LIBERT)	2,488	.9
5	Thomas M. Barrett (D)	162,344	69.3
	Donalda Hammersmith (R)	71,085	30.4
6	Tom Petri (R) *	143,875	52.9
	Peggy A. Lautenschlager (D)	128,232	47.1
7	David R. Obey (D) *	166,200	64.4
	Dale R. Vannes (R)	91,772	35.6
8	Toby Roth (R) *	191,704	70.1
	Catherine L. Helms (D)	81,792	29.9
9	F. James Sensenbrenner Jr. (R) *	192,898	69.7
	Ingrid K. Buxton (D)	77,362	28.0
	David E. Marlow (I)	4,619	1.7
	Jeffrey H. Millikin (LIBERT)	1,881	.7

WYOMING

House

		Vote Total	Per-cent
AL	Craig Thomas (R) *	113,882	57.8
	Jon Herschler (D)	77,418	39.3
	Craig A. McCune (LIBERT)	5,677	2.9

[a] Election to fill the remaining two years of Republican Pete Wilson's Senate term.

Governors, 1989-92

Following is a list of governors who served during the period of President Bush's term, 1989-92. All governors serve four-year terms except those representing New Hampshire, Rhode Island and Vermont; they serve two-year terms.

Party designation appears in parentheses following the governor's name. D stands for Democrat; R, Republican; I, Independent. *(Governors, 1981-84, Congress and the Nation Vol. VI, p. 1122; 1985-88, Congress and the Nation Vol. VII, p. 1143)*

	Dates of Service
Alabama	
Guy Hunt (R)	1987-
Alaska	
Steve Cowper (D)	1986-90
Walter J. Hickel (I)	1966-69 (D), 1990-
Arizona	
Rose Mofford (D)	1988-91
Fife Symington (R)	1991-
Arkansas	
Bill Clinton (D)	1979-81, 1983-93
California	
George Deukmejian (R)	1983-91
Pete Wilson (R)	1991-
Colorado	
Roy R. Romer (D)	1987-
Connecticut	
William A. O'Neill (D)	1980-91
Lowell P. Weicker Jr. (I)	1991-
Delaware	
Michael N. Castle (R)	1985-93
Florida	
Bob Martinez (R)	1987-91
Lawton Chiles (D)	1991-
Georgia	
Joe Frank Harris (D)	1983-91
Zell Miller (D)	1991-
Hawaii	
John Waihee III (D)	1986-
Idaho	
Cecil D. Andrus (D)	1971-77, 1987-
Illinois	
James R. Thompson (R)	1977-91
Jim Edgar (R)	1991-
Indiana	
Evan Bayh (D)	1989-
Iowa	
Terry E. Branstad (R)	1983-
Kansas	
Mike Hayden (R)	1987-91
Joan Finney (D)	1991-

	Dates of Service
Kentucky	
Wallace G. Wilkinson (D)	1987-91
Brereton Jones (D)	1991-
Louisiana	
Buddy Roemer (D)	1988-92
Edwin W. Edwards (D)	1972-80, 1984-88, 1992-
Maine	
John R. McKernan Jr. (R)	1987-
Maryland	
William Donald Schaefer (D)	1987-
Massachusetts	
Michael S. Dukakis (D)	1975-79, 1983-91
William F. Weld (R)	1991-
Michigan	
James J. Blanchard (D)	1983-91
John Engler (R)	1991-
Minnesota	
Rudy Perpich (D)	1976-79, 1983-91
Arne Carlson (R)	1991-
Mississippi	
Ray Mabus (D)	1988-92
Kirk Fordice (R)	1992-
Missouri	
John Ashcroft (R)	1985-93
Montana	
Stan Stephens (R)	1989-93
Nebraska	
Kay A. Orr (R)	1987-91
Ben Nelson (D)	1991-
Nevada	
Bob Miller (D)	1989-
New Hampshire	
Judd Gregg (R)	1989-93
New Jersey	
Thomas H. Kean (R)	1982-90
James J. Florio (D)	1990-
New Mexico	
Garrey Carruthers (R)	1987-91
Bruce King (D)	1971-75, 1979-83, 1991-
New York	
Mario M. Cuomo (D)	1983-

	Dates of Service
North Carolina	
James G. Martin (R)	1985-93
North Dakota	
George Sinner (D)	1985-93
Ohio	
Richard F. Celeste (D)	1983-91
George V. Voinovich (R)	1991-
Oklahoma	
Henry Bellmon (R)	1963-67, 1987-91
David Walters (D)	1991-
Oregon	
Neil Goldschmidt (D)	1987-91
Barbara Roberts (D)	1991-
Pennsylvania	
Robert P. Casey (D)	1987-
Rhode Island	
Edward D. DiPrete (R)	1985-91
Bruce Sundlun (D)	1991-
South Carolina	
Carroll A. Campbell Jr. (R)	1987-
South Dakota	
George S. Mickelson (R)	1987-
Tennessee	
Ned McWherter (D)	1987-

	Dates of Service
Texas	
William P. Clements Jr. (R)	1979-83, 1987-91
Ann W. Richards (D)	1991-
Utah	
Norman H. Bangerter (R)	1985-93
Vermont	
Madeleine M. Kunin (D)	1985-91
Richard A. Snelling (R)	1977-85, 1991
Howard Dean (D)	1991-
Virginia	
Gerald L. Baliles (D)	1986-90
L. Douglas Wilder (D)	1990-
Washington	
Booth Gardner (D)	1985-93
West Virginia	
Gaston Caperton (D)	1989-
Wisconsin	
Tommy G. Thompson (R)	1987-
Wyoming	
Mike Sullivan (D)	1987-

Index

Index

A

A-6 bombers
A-12 cancellation, 379 (box)
appropriations, 350, 352
authorization, 344, 347
A-12 attack aircraft
appropriations, 364
authorization, 357, 362, 378
cancellation (box), 379
A-X bombers
A-12 cancellation, 379 (box)
appropriations, 409
authorization
FY 1992, 372, 378
FY 1993, 396, 401, 405
A&P Co., 719
AAAM missiles, 362
AAWS-M missiles, 347, 378
Abandoned Infants Assistance Act, 622
Abandoned Mine Reclamation Fund, 63, 511
Abbott Laboratories, 623
ABC bill. *See Act for Better Child Care*
Abercrombie, Neil D-Hawaii
civil rights/job bias, 784
House elections, 1990, 11
ABM. *See Anti-ballistic missile treaty*
Abortion
action
1989-90, 594-595
1991-92, 597-600
appropriations, 52, 74, 78
family planning authorization, 592-593
fetal tissue research, 591
foreign aid
appropriations, 230, 234, 274-276
authorization, 267-269
U.N. fund controversy (box), 235
infertility research, 591
Legal Services authorization, 795
Mexico City policy, 235 (box), 267-269, 600
military hospitals, personnel, 358, 359, 376, 381, 397, 400-401
New Jersey governor's race, 8
NIH authorization, 590-591, 602-603
Supreme Court decisions, 838-839
summary, 801, 804
Abrams, Elliott, 286
Accounting
corporate fraud reporting, 160
Accreditation of Health Organizations, Joint Committee on the, 572
Acid rain
Clean Air Act, 473-483
Ackerman, Gary L. D-N.Y.
ethics committee reorganization, 947
House bank scandal (chart), 934
parental leave, 731
ACM missiles, 350, 404
Acquired immune deficiency syndrome (AIDS)
abandoned infants, 622
Americans with Disabilities Act, 743-747
Bush term summary, 997
housing authorization, 658, 675
immigration exclusion policy, 753 (box)
Medicaid demonstration projects, 582
presidential election, 1992, 19, 20
prevention, treatment programs, 588-590
drug abusers, 604
rape victims, 778
women's disability benefits, 623-624
Act for Better Child Care, 611-613
ACTION, 619
ADA. *See Americans with Disabilities Act*
ADAMHA. *See Alcohol, Drug Abuse and Mental Health Administration*
Adams, Arlin M., 684
Adams, Brock D-Wash.
ethics case, 944
Adams, Paul A., 676-685
ADATS weapon
appropriations, 351, 364
authorization, 347, 361
Administrative Conference of the United States, 864
Administrative law judges, 774
Administrative Procedures Act of 1946, 599, 774, 864
Adolescent Family Life Program, 595
Adolescents and youth
employment
hazardous occupations, 733
Job Training Partnership Act, 704, 713-714, 728-730
subminimum wage, 705-708
summer jobs, 722 (box)
targeted jobs tax credit, 94
foster care program, 615, 616
health
drug abuse prevention, 789
Indian alcohol abuse services, 905
mental health services, 592
parental notice of abortion, 593, 594-595, 598-599
sexual behavior survey, 602
juvenile delinquency prevention, 797-798
Adoption. *See also Foster care*
children's Social Security benefits, 51, 62
human services reconciliation, 615, 616
Advanced Communication Technology Satellite, 876
Advanced cruise missiles, 360
Advanced manufacturing, 880, 891-892
Advanced oil recovery, 510
Advanced Solid Rocket Motor (ASRM), 874-875, 876, 898, 899
Advanced tactical fighter (ATF) planes. *See also F-22 fighter planes*
appropriations
FY 1990, 350, 351, 352
FY 1991, 364
authorization
FY 1990, 341, 347
FY 1991, 357, 362
F-14 cancellation, 348
Advanced Technology Program, 880, 902
Advancement of Women in the Science and Engineering Work Forces, Commission on the, 732
Adult education
literacy programs, 652, 657, 658-659
Adult Education Act, 659
Advertising
children's TV, 429
corporate sponsors of athletic events, 111
deceptive mail curbs, 870
highway billboards, 439, 444
political advertising, 957-958
sexually explicit mail, 870
telemarketing controls, 432, 459-460
AFDC. *See Aid to Families with Dependent Children*
Affirmative action
civil rights/job bias, 781, 785
race preference ban, 787
Supreme Court decisions, 839, 758
FCC minority preference, 431 (box)
Affordable Housing Preservation, Office of, 667
Afghanistan
rebel, refugee aid, 233, 243, 244
AFL-CIO. *See American Federation of Labor-Congress of Industrial Organizations*
Africa
food aid, 256, 257
Somalia relief, 278-280
African-Americans. *See Blacks*
African Development Bank and Fund, 185, 186, 238
African Elephant Conservation Act, 522
African National Congress, 253-254
Age discrimination
lawsuit waivers, 716-717
pensions, 705, 714-716
Supreme Court decisions, 839
Age Discrimination in Employment Act of 1967, 714, 716
Agency for Health Care Policy and Research, 572, 608-609
Agency for International Development (AID)
Caribbean Basin Initiative, 183
Enterprise for the Americas, 179, 200
foreign aid
appropriations, 230, 232, 271, 274, 276
authorization, 227
Food for Peace, 256-258
global warming initiatives, 505-506
Nicaragua policy, 221
Poland, Hungary aid, 213
South Africa policy, 254
U.S. business relocation, 276
Agent Orange
compensation, 632-633
Medicaid eligibility, 615
controversy summary (box), 628
omnibus veterans bill, 625
veterans' COLA increase, 631
Aging research, 592
Agricultural Credit Insurance Fund, 547
Agricultural equipment
drivers' licenses, 424
emissions standards, 483
Agricultural exports and imports
China trade status, 192
cotton, 543
credit guarantees, 545
Latin American debt relief, 195
prewar Iraq policy, 300
Soviet Union, 209-210, 262, 267, 276, 330, 555
dairy products, 544
export aid, promotion, 541, 545, 548, 554-555
farm bill, 545
foreign food aid, 256-258
NAFTA highlights, 188 (box)
Soviet-U.S. trade, 171, 330
sugar prices, 540, 543
summary, 166-167, 536, 537, 551
trade expansion act, 196-197
trade programs, 541
Agricultural price supports and income subsidies
Agriculture Department streamlining, 556 (box)
crop yield reporting, 550-551
flexibility, 544-545
glossary (box), 538
omnibus farm bill, 537-547
changes, 548, 555-556
payments cap, 540, 541, 545
summary, 535
triple-base allotment plan, 537, 547
Agricultural Resources Conservation Program, 546
Agricultural workers
child labor, 733
income tax withholding, 49
legal aid, 774
minimum wage, 708
rural housing authorization, 674-675
unemployment taxes, 728

Agriculture and farming. *See also Agricultural exports and imports; Agricultural price supports and income subsidies; Agricultural workers; Farm Credit System; Rural development*
biomass fuels, 109
chemicals reduction, 529, 541
chronology of action
1989-90, 537-551
1991-92, 551-557
conservation, 546
disaster relief, 557
farm economics
cooperatives tax, 110, 111
credit, 546-547
crop insurance, 549 (box)
foreclosure acquisition, 551
new-farmer loans, 553-554
Indian lands management, 907
irrigation subsidies, 495-496, 513-518
pesticide regulation, 522-523
Poland, Hungary aid, 213
research, 545-546
Agriculture Department, U.S.
crop insurance, 549 (box)
crop yield reporting, 551
dairy production, 553 (box)
exports
enhancement, 554-555
Soviet credit guarantees, 555
farm bill provisions, 542-547
food and nutrition
assistance programs, 618
fish inspection, 434-435
food pyramid (box), 554
food stamps, 618-619
foreign food aid, 256-257
labels, 604 (box)
nutrition monitoring, 593
leadership (box), 539
rural development, 548
screwworm eradication, 550
streamlining (box), 556
wetlands preservation, 557
Agriculture Stabilization and Conservation Service, 556 (box)
AHIP equipment, 346, 350, 351, 401
Aid to Families with Dependent Children (AFDC), 615, 616
AIDS. *See Acquired immune deficiency syndrome*
Air defense initiative, 346
Air Force, U.S.
appropriations
FY 1990, 350-352
FY 1991, 363-365
FY 1992, 380-382
FY 1993, 409
military construction, 365
defense authorization
FY 1990, 340-350
FY 1991, 355-363
FY 1992, 369-380
FY 1993, 395-407
military base closings, 394 (chart)
MX missile continuation, 343
women in combat, 374-375 (box)
Air Line Pilots Association, 713
Air National Guard, 351
Air pollution
auto fuel efficiency, 501
Clean Air Act, 473-483
toxic pollutants (list), 481
indoor pollution, 531
Air safety
accident compensation, 446
aging aircraft, 420, 436
blind passengers, 422
congested area maps, 447
de-icing, 446-447
guidelines, 420
Air traffic control
aviation package, 417-418
FAA authorization, 422, 446
FAA maps, 447
Air transportation. *See also Air safety; Air traffic control; Aircraft; Federal Aviation Administration*
airline buyouts, 421
chronology of action
1989-90, 417-423
1991-92, 445-447
customs collection, 65
employees
drug testing, 425, 448
Eastern Airlines strike, 712-713
FAA civil fees, 445-446
flight attendants' workday, 446
pilot pension plans, 107
noise abatement, 419, 446, 447
reservations system, 445
security
authorization, 421
research, 421
procedures, 420
smoking ban, 419-420
Soviet-U.S. service, 209
summary, 415, 436
Supreme Court decisions, 808
ticket taxes, 67, 92, 96
collection period, 49
international passengers, 49
passenger facility charges, 417-418, 445
trust fund surplus, 417
war insurance, 447
Wright brothers national landmarks, 526
Airai Airfield, 259
Aircraft. *See also Aircraft, military; National Aerospace Plane*
exit row seating, 422
fastener standards, 436
liability insurance, 422
noise abatement, 447
safety inspections, 420, 436
Aircraft carriers
appropriations, 364, 409
defense authorization
FY 1990, 341, 347
FY 1992, 378-379
FY 1993, 405-406
Aircraft, military
appropriations
FY 1990, 350-352
FY 1991, 364
FY 1992, 381-382
FY 1993, 409
cancelled programs
A-12, 379 (box)
B-2, 398-399 (box)
F-14, Osprey, 348 (box)
CFE treaty, 385
defense authorization
FY 1990, 341, 347, 349
FY 1991, 361-362
FY 1992, 378
FY 1993, 395, 396, 405, 406
defense policy summary, 337
Japan plane deal, 354-355
Airport and Airway Trust Fund, 49, 96, 417-419, 422, 446
Airport Improvement Program, 418, 446
Akaka, Daniel K. D-Hawaii
Senate seat, 12
al-Assad, Hafez, 302
al-Sabah, Jaber Ahmed, 300
Alabama
Clean Air Act, 474
Madison amendment, 972
water projects, 493 (box)
Alaska
Arctic wildlife refuge, 499, 512
governor's race, 1990, 11-12
Native issues, programs
home loans, 636
housing study, 689
land sale dividends tax, 908
language preservation, 907-908
offshore drilling ban, 491
public broadcasting, 458
Tongass National Forest, 492-493
water projects, 493 (box)
Alaska Lands Conservation Act of 1980, 492
Alaska Native Claims Settlement Act of 1971, 111, 908
Albania
U.S. trade agreement, 194
Alcohol abuse and alcoholism
ADAMHA authorization, 604-605
Americans with Disabilities Act, 743-752
impaired driving, 443
boat operators, 449
Indian health services, 883, 905
testing, background checks
merchant marine applicants, 425
transportation workers, 425, 439, 448
veterans benefits limits, 627
workplace bans
oil-spill liability, 491
Alcohol, Drug Abuse and Mental Health Administration (ADAMHA), 604-605
Alcohol, Drug Abuse and Mental Health block grants, 604
Alcohol fuels
alternative fuels, 487 (box), 506
tax incentives, 69, 96
Alcoholic beverages
Caribbean Basin Initiative, 182
domestic air flights, 420
excise taxes, 67, 95
producers, retailers tax, 112
Alexander, Bill D-Ark.
ethics case, 945
Gingrich ethics case, 925-926
House bank scandal, 932
members with overdrafts (chart), 934
Alexander, Debra, 945
Alexander, Lamar
biographical profile, 1172
Bush term summary, 997
Education Department leadership, 645 (box)
higher education aid, 654, 655
race-exclusive scholarships, 655 (box)
school reform, 657-658
Aliens. *See also Deportation; Illegal aliens*
Chinese students, 252-253
military base civilian employees, 362
torture victims suits, 797
travel, tourism fees, 65
U.S. military service, 779-780, 793-794
All-terrain vehicles, 433
Allegheny National Forest, 512
Allen African Methodist Episcopal Church, 927
Allen, George F. R-Va.
House elections, 1991, 14
Allen, Richard V., 288
Allred, Gloria, 943
Aloha-Rigolette, La., 493 (box)
Alternative agriculture, 545-546
Alternative dispute resolution, 865
Alternative energy, 486
Alternative fuels and vehicles
Clean Air Act, 475-476, 477-478, 483
energy bill, 500, 502, 503, 506
tax provisions, 108-109
gasoline substitutes (box), 487
hydrogen fuel research, 486-487
Alternative minimum tax
appreciated property, 103
budget reconciliation
FY 1990, 50
FY 1991, 66, 69
corporations, 100, 103
energy bill, 108, 109
individuals, 66
oil, gas producers, 69, 96
small insurance companies, 111
Altus, Okla., 518
Alzheimer's disease, 576, 592, 608
Amaral, Annelle, 944
America 2000, 657
America the Beautiful Foundation, 546
American Academy for the Advancement of Science, 651
American Airlines, 421, 445
American Arts Alliance, 866
American Association of Retired Persons, 960
American Bar Association, 771
American Civil Liberties Union
Hatch Act revision, 860
political advertising, 958
RICO limits, 771
TV violence, 428
American Continental Corp., 976, 980-984
American Council on Education, 655 (box)
American Farm Bureau Federation, 501
American Federation of Government Employees, 858, 860
American Federation of Labor-Congress of Industrial Organizations (AFL-CIO)
age discrimination, 715
minimum wage, 707
motor voter bill, 871
NAFTA, 189
National Endowment for Democracy, 247
pension reversions, 719
Poland, Hungary aid, 213
striker replacements, 733-734
American Financial Corp., 976
American Home Products, 623, 793
American Institute of Certified Public Accountants, 772
American-Israel Public Affairs Committee, 230
American Medical Association, 568
American Postal Workers Union, 860
American Samoa
House voting privileges, 948
American Schools and Hospitals, 232
American Technology Pre-Eminence Act of 1992, 903
Americans for Generational Equity, 922
Americans to Limit Congressional Terms, 959
Americans with Disabilities Act of 1990 (ADA)
action, 743-752
Bush term summary, 997
closed-captioned congressional TV, 949
mass transit, 443
Oregon health plan, 597 (box)
remedies, 782
AMRAAM missiles
appropriations, 352, 382, 409
authorization, 347, 362, 378

Amtrak
Americans with Disabilities Act, 745, 749
authorization, 424, 447
rail strikes, 448
waste disposal, 424
Anabolic steroids, 768
Anadromous fish, 427, 515, 521-522
Andean region
Caribbean Basin Initiative, 183
narcotics control, 238, 255-256, 749
U.S. trade, 193-194, 296-297
Anderson, Glenn M. D-Calif.
House leadership, 13, 929
water projects, 494
Anderson, Terence, 775-776
Anderson, Tom Jr., 8
Andrews, Michael A. D-Texas
civil rights/job bias, 759
House bank scandal (chart), 934
Andrews, Robert E. D-N.J.
higher education aid, 654
House elections, 1990, 12
Anesthesiology, 570, 575, 576
Angola
covert rebel aid, 243, 244-245, 283
Animal rights
research lab protections, 881, 904
Anniston, Ala., Army Depot, 411
Annunzio, Frank D-Ill.
banking overhaul, 138
House leadership, 13, 929
money laundering, 156
savings and loan bailout, 119-121, 153
Annunzio-Wylie Anti-Money-Laundering Act, 698
Ansaid, 793
Antarctic Marine Living Resources Convention Act, 489
Antarctica
mining ban, 489, 529-530
Anthony, Beryl Jr. D-Ark.
House bank scandal (chart), 934
House leadership, 916, 928
term limits, 958
Anti-ballistic missile (ABM) treaty
congressional-executive relations, 386
defense authorization
FY 1990, 341, 346
FY 1992, 373, 375-377
START treaty, 389
strategic defense initiative, 370-371 (box)
Anti-Drug Abuse Act of 1988, 344
Antigua and Barbuda
Caribbean Basin Initiative, 180
Anti-satellite (ASAT) weapons
appropriations, 364
defense authorization
FY 1990, 345, 346
FY 1991, 358, 360
FY 1992, 377
Antitrust law
Baby Bells restrictions, 461-462
cable TV regulation, 457
insurance exemption, 435, 463
interlocking directorates, 772
joint ventures, 772, 890-891
penalties, 772
Supreme Court decisions, 807-808
TV violence guidelines, 428
vertical price fixing, 770-771, 791
Apache helicopters
appropriations, 350, 351, 409
authorization, 346, 347, 361, 378, 405
Apache Indians, 517
Apartheid, 253-254, 294-295
Appeals courts. *See Federal courts*
Applied Agricultural Research Commercialization Center, 545-546
Appointments. *See Nominations and appointments*
Apprentices
ERISA reforms, 738
high-tech training, 892
non-traditional jobs for women, 732
Appropriations
expedited rescissions, 85-86
FY 1990, 52-53
FY 1991, 73-75
FY 1992, 77-79
defense rescissions, 383
FY 1993, 81-84
Appropriations Committee, Senate
authorization-appropriations process, 381
Aqua Fria River, 517
Aquatic Nuisance Species Task Force, 497
Aquatic Resources Trust Fund, 67
Aquifers, 517
Aquino, Corazon C., 231, 411-412
Arab countries. *See also specific countries*
"Israel only" passports, 292
Middle East peace talks, 277-278
Persian Gulf War, 299-317
Arafat, Yasir, 248
Arbitrage, 50
Arbitration, 814
Archer, Bill R-Texas
catastrophic medical costs insurance, 565
energy bill tax provisions, 108
foreign ship subsidies, 449
highway authorization, 440
unemployment benefits, 723, 724, 726
urban aid tax bill, 104
Architectural and Transportation Barriers Compliance Board, 752
Architecture and buildings. *See also Construction industry; Federal buildings; Housing*
Americans with Disabilities Act, 743-752
energy efficiency standards, 507
indoor air pollution, 531
Archives and records-keeping
acid-free paper, 869
Archivist of the United States. *See National Archives*
Arctic islands, 209
Arctic National Wildlife Refuge (ANWR), 499, 500, 502-504
ARENA. *See National Republican Alliance*
Argentina
Persian Gulf War, 316 (box)
Aristide, Jean-Bertrand, 296
Arizona
bankruptcy judges, 799
governor's election, 1990, 11
Indian electric project, 530
Mexican border housing aid, 675
military base closings, 353
Navajo-Hopi relocation, 908
radiation victims compensation, 586
term limits, 10 (box), 963
water projects, 493 (box), 517
wilderness area, 496
Arkansas
term limits, 10 (box), 963
Arkansas River, 516, 908
***Arleigh Burke*-class destroyers**
appropriations, 352, 382
authorization, 347, 362, 378, 406
Armed Services Committee, Senate
authorization-appropriations process, 381
Armenia
ethnic violence, 331
genocide resolution, 259-260
refugee asylum, 756
U.S. aid to post-Soviet republics, 266
Armey, Dick R-Texas
banking overhaul, 141
farm bill, 540
highway authorization, 440
House bank scandal (chart), 934
NEA funding, 865
Arms control. *See also Anti-ballistic missile (ABM) treaty; Conventional forces in Europe (CFE) treaty; Nuclear non-proliferation; Strategic arms reduction talks (START) treaty*
biological weapons, 780
chemical weapons, 328, 366-367 (box)
chronology of action
1989-90, 366-367 (box)
1991-92, 383-393
comprehensive test ban, 392-393, 400, 401, 523-524
defense authorization
FY 1990, 342, 346, 347
FY 1991, 358
FY 1992, 372
nuclear test treaties, 366-368
reconnaissance overflights treaty, 390, 392
Soviet arsenal
emigrating scientists, 794
non-Russian republics, 322, 329
U.S. aid for dismantling, 260-262, 266, 330-331, 382, 407
Soviet Union dissolution, 328-329
Soviet-U.S. relations, 205-208
summary (box), 366-367
troop reduction proposals (box), 387
unilateral U.S. cutbacks, 391
Arms sales and transfers
CFE "cascading," 386
China
sanctions, 251, 252
trade status, 191-192
El Salvador aid, 214-219, 268
export controls, 175-177
Export-Import Bank financing, 176-177
foreign military aid
Andean narcotics control, 255-256
appropriations, 229-231, 238, 269-271, 274, 276
authorization, 268
loan guarantees, 291
Middle East proliferation, 291
Pakistan, 293-294
sanctions
Persian Gulf War, 301
post-Yugoslav republics, 275, 278
terrorism, 238
Saudi planes, 294
Stinger missiles, 231
third-party transfers, 238
Armstrong, William L. R-Colo.
abortion, 594
family planning authorization, 593
oil shale claims, 499
Senate leadership, 915
Social Security earnings test, 718
Army Corps of Engineers, U.S.
reorganization, 395
Sonoma Baylands management, 517
water projects, 493-494, 528
wetlands preservation, 529
Army National Guard, 407
Army, U.S.
appropriations
FY 1990, 350, 351
FY 1991, 363-365
FY 1992, 380-382
FY 1993, 407-409
defense authorization
FY 1990, 343-350
FY 1991, 355-363
FY 1992, 369-380
FY 1993, 395-407
magnetic levitation, 444
military base closings, 394 (chart)
Persian Gulf War, 313
Rocky Mountain arsenal, 527
Aroostook Band of Micmac Indians, 885, 908-909
Arts
copyright, 773-774
immigration law, 794
NEA funding, 865-867
Aruba
Caribbean Basin Initiative, 180
ASAT. *See Anti-satellite weapons*
Asbra, Donald, 882
Asia. *See also specific countries*
food aid, 256
Asian-Americans
civil rights/job bias, 784
immigration reform, 752
Aspin, Les D-Wis.
defense authorization
FY 1990, 341, 345
FY 1991, 356-358
FY 1992, 372, 373, 376
FY 1993, 396-397
Defense budget reprogramming, 356 (box)
defense policy summary, 337
Iran-contra pardons, 287
MX continuation, 343
Persian Gulf War, 302, 305, 307, 310, 314
Soviet aid, 262, 264, 330
unilateral U.S. arms cutbacks, 391
ASPJ radar jammer, 362
ASRM. *See Advanced Solid Rocket Motor*
ASROC missile, 362
Assault weapons, 764-768, 788, 896
ATA attack plane, 341, 347
ATACMS missiles
appropriations, 351, 364
authorization, 347, 361, 377, 405
ATF. *See Advanced tactical fighter planes*
Atkins, Chester G. D-Mass.
House bank scandal (chart), 934
Atlantic Ocean
barrier islands, 497
drift net fishing, 528
offshore drilling ban, 491
Atlantic Striped Bass Conservation Act of 1984, 521-522
Atlas-Centaur rockets, 404
Atomic Vapor Laser Isotope Separation (AVLIS), 508, 509
Attorneys. *See Law profession and practice*
Attorneys, U.S.
health care fraud, 609
Atwater, Lee, 6, 965, 993
AuCoin, Les D-Ore.
House bank scandal, 938
members with overdrafts (chart), 934
Auerbach, Arnold "Red," 790
Austin, Richard, 890
Australia
Persian Gulf War, 316 (box)
Automobiles and auto industry. *See also Alternative fuels and vehicles*
carjacking penalties, 790
emissions standards, 473-483
deadlines, 477 (box)
fuel-efficiency standards, 95, 478, 484
energy bill summary (box), 501
gas-guzzler tax, 67
Japanese import limits, 196-197
minivan tariffs, 197-198
NAFTA highlights, 188 (box)

parts origin labels, 445
safety, 443, 501
air bags, 437, 439, 443, 444
AVLIS. *See Atomic Vapor Laser Isotope Separation*
Azerbaijan
Commonwealth withdrawal, 322
ethnic violence, 331
U.S. aid to post-Soviet republics, 266
Aziz, Tariq, 299, 308, 310, 314-315

B

B-1 bombers
appropriations, 409
authorization, 346, 377, 404
B-2 bomber, 398
B-2 bombers
appropriations
FY 1990, 350, 351
FY 1991, 74, 363, 364
FY 1992, 380, 381
FY 1992 defense rescissions, 383
FY 1993, 408, 409
authorization
FY 1990, 341, 342, 344, 346
FY 1991, 355-360
FY 1992, 369, 372-374, 376-377
FY 1993, 395-404
Defense budget reprogramming, 356 (box)
defense policy summary, 337, 339, 369
program closure (box), 398-399
B-52 bombers, 346, 404
Babies. *See Infants*
Baby Bells, 432, 461-462
Backfire bombers, 388 (box)
Badham, Robert E., 934 (chart)
Bahamas
Caribbean Basin Initiative, 180
Bahrain
Persian Gulf War, 302, 316 (box)
Stinger missile sales, 231
Bail, 817
Baker, James A. III
biographical profile, 1174
Bush term summary, 993, 995, 998
Cambodia aid, 246
chemical weapons accord, 367 (box)
China policy, 251
Chinese student visas, 756
El Salvador aid, 218
foreign aid
appropriations, 231
authorization, 227
covert aid programs, 245
"leveraging," 239
foreign trade summary, 167
irrigation subsidies, 515
Middle East peace talks, 277
Nicaragua policy, 219-222
Pakistan arms sales, 293
Panama policy, 224
Persian Gulf War, 299, 305, 307-310
Soviet Union dissolution, 325
Soviet-U.S. relations, 207-208, 209
Moscow Embassy, 263
aid, 264
START, 387, 389
State Department leadership, 207 (box)
Baker, Richard H. R-La.
House bank scandal, 938
Balanced budget amendment
action
1989-90, 75
1991-92, 15, 84-85
superconducting supercollider, 901
Ballenger, Cass R-N.C.
age discrimination, 715
job training programs, 713
Baltic republics
CFE treaty, 386
Soviet Union dissolution, 320, 322, 331
Soviet-U.S. relations, 205, 208, 210
U.S. aid to Soviet republics, 261-262, 265, 275, 276
Soviet-U.S. trade, 169, 192-193
U.S. aid, 269, 270, 276
U.S. trade, 193
export controls, 196
Bangladesh
Persian Gulf War, 303, 316 (box)
Bani-Sadr, Abol Hassan, 288
Bank Insurance Fund, 124-125 (box), 126, 136, 138, 142-143
Bank of Credit and Commerce International (BCCI), 156, 285 (box)
Bank of New England, 137
Bank Secrecy Act of 1970, 134
Bankruptcy
Eastern Airlines strike, 712-713
judgeships, 798-799
pension fund responsibility, 720 (box)
renegotiated corporate debt, 111
Supreme Court decisions, 808-809
trucking firms, 445
Banks and banking. *See also Deposit insurance; Farm Credit System; Federal Deposit Insurance Corporation; Federal Reserve System; Home loans and mortgages; House bank scandal; Savings and loan associations; World Bank*
brokered deposits, 128, 145
capital requirements, 118, 127, 143
consumer issues
credit card interest rate cap (box), 137
credit reporting safeguards, 157
fees, 128
telemarketing controls, 432
truth-in-savings, 134, 142, 147, 161
corporate auditors, 160
disaster areas, 161
financial institution fraud, 133-134, 764-768
FmHA loan guarantees, 553-554
international banking
fair trade in financial services, 142, 187, 198, 368, 412
foreign deposits, 146
foreign-owned banks in United States, 147
NAFTA highlights, 188 (box)
Panama bank secrecy, 227
Third World debt, 184
interstate branches, 139, 142
loan limits, 128
money laundering, 134-135, 156
overhaul, 113-116, 136-148
regulators (box), 114
regulatory relief, 160-161
securities affiliates, 137, 139
student loans, 653-657
summary, 12
Supreme Court decisions, 808
systemic risk, 144
Barbados
Caribbean Basin Initiative, 180
Barco, Virgilio, 256
Barksdale, Maurice, 683
Barnard, Doug Jr. D-Ga.
banking overhaul, 140
House bank scandal (chart), 934
savings and loan bailout refinancing, 151
Barr, William P.
biographical profile, 1170
INSLAW case, 792 (box)
Iran-contra pardons, 286
law leadership, 745 (box)
Barreto, Hector, 685
Barrett, Bill R-Neb.
Niobrara River, 525
Barrier islands, 497
Barry, Marion S., 873, 895
Bartlett, Steve R-Texas
Americans with Disabilities Act, 745
education for disabled, 648
House bank scandal (chart), 934
House leadership, 916
housing authorization, 668
HUD reforms, 686
job training programs, 714
minimum wage, 705
mortgage prepayments, 692-693
parental leave, 711
Section 89 tax rules, 709
successor, 14
Barton, Joe L. R-Texas
caller ID, 462
Medicaid, 580
Base Realignment and Closure, Commission on, 353-354, 393
Bass, Gary, 868 (box)
Bates, Jim D-Calif.
ethics case, 913, 924
House bank scandal, 932
members with overdrafts (chart), 934
House elections, 1990, 11
Battered women. *See Domestic violence*
Baucus, Max D-Mont.
China trade status, 191
Clean Air Act, 476, 478
farm bill, 541
Montana wilderness, 526
motor voter bill, 871
Soviet-U.S. trade, 171
Bayou La Batre, Ala., 493 (box)
BCCI. *See Bank of Credit and Commerce International*
Becerra, Xavier, 27
Beilenson, Anthony C. D-Calif.
highway authorization, 440-441
House leadership, 917, 929
Belarus
arms control, 328, 329, 336
reconnaissance overflights, 392
START, 387-390
Soviet Union dissolution, 322
Belgium
Persian Gulf War, 316 (box)
Belize
Caribbean Basin Initiative, 180
Bell telephone companies, 432, 461-462
Benavides, Guillermo Alfredo, 218
Bennett, Robert S., 921-922, 977-986
Bennett, William J.
biographical profile, 1176
drug czar post, 745 (box), 768, 789
Quayle nominating speech, 21
student loan defaults, 649
Bentsen, Lloyd D-Texas
Americans with Disabilities Act, 744
budget policy
budget walls, 83 (box)
debt ceiling extensions, 44 (box)
reconciliation, FY 1990, 46
summary, 38
campaign finance, 955
catastrophic medical costs insurance, 565-566
child care, 612, 613
child welfare overhaul, 621
congressional pay, 968
health reform, 597
highway authorization, 439
NAFTA, 189
Senate election, 1970, 998
tax policy
capital gains tax cut, 98
middle-class tax cut, 101-102
Section 89 tax rules, 709-710
Social Security earnings test, 718, 736
urban aid tax bill, 103, 105, 106
unemployment benefits, 722-724, 727, 728
Bereuter, Doug R-Neb.
House bank scandal (chart), 934
housing authorization, 695
HUD reforms, 687
Berlin Wall, 324
Berman, Howard L. D-Calif.
abortion, 600
cable TV regulation, 452 (box)
House bank scandal (chart), 934
Persian Gulf War, 310
Berne Convention, 170
Berryessa Creek, Calif., 493 (box)
Berryhill, Clare, 8
Besharov, Douglas, 991
Bevill, Tom D-Ala.
superconducting supercollider, 878, 901
Bexar County, Texas, 616
Bicycles
helmet safety standards, 462
paths, 442
Biden, Joseph R. D-Del.
crime bills, 764-767, 786-787, 789
flag desecration, 761-762
joint ventures, 891
judicial nominating process, 796
Lucas nomination, 764
Ryskamp nomination, 796
violence against women, 778
Bilby, Richard, 976
Bilirakis, Michael R-Fla.
catastrophic medical costs insurance, 565
Bill of Rights. *See also specific amendments*
commemorative coins, 161
Billiere, Peter de la, 314
Binary weapons, 367 (box)
Bingaman, Jeff D-N.M.
defense authorization, FY 1992, 375
ethics committee reorganization, 947
Keating Five investigation, 985-986
OMB regulatory review, 869
striker replacements, 734
Biological diversity
BLM authorization, 520
Earth Summit, 277, 529, 997
South Dakota trust, 517
Biological weapons
ban, 780
non-proliferation program authorization, 407
sanctions, 291, 292-293
Biomass fuels, 108, 507
Biotechnology
guidelines, 903 (box)
Bipartisan Commission on Comprehensive Health Care, U.S., 919, 572-573, 584 (box)
Birds
exotic pets, 522
northern spotted owl, 494-495, 520-521
wetlands preservation, 494
Birth control. *See also Abortion*
family planning authorization, 592-593, 595, 598-599
international family planning, 234, 267-269, 594, 600
NIH authorization, 591
Black colleges
education for disabled, 648

higher education aid, 653, 656
housing authorization, 676
student loan defaults, 650
Black lung disease benefits, 734, 845
Black, Manafort, Stone & Kelly, 678-679 (box)
Black, William, 980-981
Blackhawk helicopters, 379, 382
Blackmun, Harry A.
pension fund responsibility, 720 (box)
Supreme Court summary, 801
Blacks
Bush relations, 780
capital punishment, 787
congressional elections, 1990, 11
congressional elections, 1992, 17, 23, 27
Gray House leadership, 5
judicial appointments, 776 (box)
Lucas nomination, 763-764
members of Congress, 1947-95 (table), 18
motor voter bill, 871, 894
presidential election, 1992, 22
race-exclusive scholarships, 655 (box)
Ryskamp nomination, 796
Virginia governor's race, 6-7
women in business, 464
Blackwell, Lucien E. D-Pa.
House elections, 1991, 14
Blanchard, James J., 11
Blaz, Ben R-Guam
House bank scandal (chart), 934
Bliley, Thomas J. Jr. R-Va.
abortion, 599
ADAMHA authorization, 604
House leadership, 917, 929
lead poisoning prevention, 607
Blind persons
air passenger seating, 422
Supplemental Security Income, 615, 616
BLM. *See Land Management, Bureau of*
Block III tanks, 364, 377
Block grant programs
housing authorization, 665, 666, 669, 670-671
motor voter bill, 894
Bloodworth-Thomason, Linda, 19
Blumstein, James, 869
Board for International Broadcasting, 247
"Boarder babies," 622
Boats and boating
Coast Guard user fees, 65, 110, 425, 449
fuel tax, 67
luxury taxes, 67, 722
pipeline inspections, 488
Boehlert, Sherwood R-N.Y.
superconducting supercollider, 878-879, 901
Boeing Corp., 252
Boland amendment, 221 (box)
Bolivia
Andean import duties, 296-297
U.S. aid
appropriations, 228, 232-233
narcotics control, 255-256, 769
Bolton, John R., 279
Bombers. *See also B-2 bombers*
air defense initiative, 346
short-range missiles, 360
START, 387-389
unilateral U.S. arms cutbacks, 391
Bond, Christopher S. R-Mo.
airline passenger seating, 422
export controls, 176
housing authorization, 667
parental leave, 730
Persian Gulf War, 310
Senate leadership, 928
Bond, Rich, 20
Bonior, David E. D-Mich.
House bank scandal, 933
members with overdrafts (chart), 934
House elections, 1992, 27
House leadership, 7 (chart), 13, 916, 928
Persian Gulf War, 303
Bonneville Power Administration, 510, 522
Bonneville Unit water project, 516
Borders, William, 775-777
Boren, David L. D-Okla.
campaign finance, 953, 960-961
capital gains tax cut, 98
civil rights/job bias, 759
intelligence authorization, 281, 283
intelligence reorganization plans, 284-285 (box)
job training, 730
Persian Gulf War, 302
Soviet aid, 264
Bork, Robert H., 801
Borski, Robert A. D-Pa.
House bank scandal (chart), 934
Boschwitz, Rudy R-Minn.
civil rights/job bias, 760
immigration reform, 754
Senate elections, 1990, 10, 11
Senate leadership, 915, 928
Bosco, Douglas H. D-Calif.
airline buyouts, 421
aviation taxes, 418
House bank scandal, 932
members with overdrafts (chart), 934
House elections, 1990, 11
Boskin, Michael J., 32 (box), 167, 1175
Bosnia
foreign aid appropriations, 271, 275, 276
U.S. aid, 278
Yugoslav-U.S. trade, 194
Bosque del Apache National Wildlife Refuge, 517
Boston, Mass.
harbor project, 493 (box)
Boucher, Rick D-Va.
cable TV regulation, 427
NSF authorization, 903
Boutros-Ghali, Boutros, 278, 279, 280
Bowsher, Charles A., 60 (box)
Boxer, Barbara D-Calif.
abortion, 594
House bank scandal, 938
members with overdrafts (chart), 934
Senate elections, 1992, 23, 24
Bradley, Bill D-N.J.
Bush education initiative, 644
farm bill, 541
foreign trade summary, 168
higher education aid, 654
irrigation subsidies, 496, 513-514
Keating Five investigation, 987
natural gas decontrol, 485
presidential election, 1992, 19
Senate elections, 1990, 10, 11
Soviet-U.S. relations, 210
student athletes "right to know," 647
tax policy summary, 88
Bradley troop carriers
appropriations, 351, 364, 407-409
authorization, 346, 361, 373, 377, 404
Brady bill, 765 (box), 785, 787, 789
Brady, James S., 765 (box), 786
Brady, Nicholas F.
banking overhaul, 115, 140
biographical profile, 1174
budget action, FY 1992, 76
Bush economic team, 32-33 (box)
credit card rate cap, 137 (box)
debt ceiling extensions, 44 (box)
deficit commission, 38
economic policy summary, 34
Enterprise for the Americas, 179
foreign trade summary, 167
savings and loan bailout, 120-122
refinancing, 149, 150, 153
Section 89 tax rules, 709
securities market reforms, 130
Third World debt, 179, 184, 166
unemployment benefits, 724
Brady plan, 179, 184, 166
Brady, Sarah, 765 (box), 786
Brandt, Werner W., 931, 937
Branson, Mo., 445
Brazil
U.S. trade, 167
Breast cancer
Army research appropriations, 408, 409
Medicare coverage for mammography, 573, 577
Pacific yew harvest, 527
screening programs authorization, 593, 608
tracking registry, 608
Breaux, John B. D-La.
highway authorization, 439
Persian Gulf War, 310
Senate elections, 1992, 24
Senate leadership, 915
Breeden, Richard C., 114, 419 (box)
Brennan, William J. Jr.
Bush term summary, 994
FCC minority preference, 431 (box)
flag desecration, 762
Supreme Court summary, 801, 803, 805
Brezhnev Doctrine, 324
Bridges
highway authorization, 442, 445
"Brilliant pebbles"
arms control action, 391
authorization, 357, 371, 377, 396, 400, 404
Briscoe, Leonard E. Sr., 678 (box), 685
Bristol Bay, 491
Bristol-Myers Squibb Co., 527
British Virgin Islands
Caribbean Basin Initiative, 180
Brodhead, William M., 952
Bromley, D. Allan, 881
Brook, Edward, 679 (box)
Brooks, Jack D-Texas
Baby Bells restrictions, 461-462
banking overhaul, 139
cable TV regulation, 452 (box)
civil rights/job bias, 760
crime bill, 767-768
gun control summary, 765 (box)
federal employee honoraria, 858, 886
federal judgeships, 774
flag desecration, 761
House leadership, 916
HUD scandal, 684
immigration reform, 754
insurance antitrust exemption, 435, 463
JFK assassination documents, 893
Brother Industries, 106
Browder, Glen D-Ala.
campaign finance, 961
election, 8
Brown, Edmund G. "Jerry," 17, 19
Brown Foundation, 111
Brown, George E. Jr. D-Calif.
competitiveness bills, 892
House bank scandal (chart), 934
House leadership, 929
superconducting supercollider, 901
Brown, Hank R-Colo.
campaign finance, 961
congressional pay, 967
House bank scandal, 936
members with overdrafts (chart), 934
term limits, 964
unemployment benefits, 725-726
Brown, Ronald H., 871
Brown, William H., 924
Bruner, Lynn, 863
Bryan, Richard H. D-Nev.
air bags, 444
Clean Air Act, 478
CPSC authorization, 433
energy bill, 501, 505
ethics committee reorganization, 947
fuel-efficiency standards, 484, 501
NASA authorization, 1992-94, 898
political advertising, 958
Yucca Mountain nuclear dump, 513
Bryant, John D-Texas
foreign investment data, 177-178
Hastings impeachment, 775
House bank scandal (chart), 934
Persian Gulf War, 310
Bua, Nicholas, 792 (box)
Buchanan, Patrick J., 20, 458, 998
Buck, Marilyn J., 922 (box)
Budapest, Hungary, 213
Budget, U.S. *See also Balanced budget amendment; Congressional Budget Office; Gramm-Rudman-Hollings law; Management and Budget, Office of; Taxes and taxation*
administration budget requests
FY 1990, 41-42
FY 1991, 53-54
FY 1992, 76
FY 1993, 79-80
budget process
miscellaneous tax bills, 110
rules changes, 1990, 37-38, 56-57 (box), 70-72
budget reconciliation
FY 1990, 43-52
FY 1991, 55-73
budget resolutions
FY 1990, 42-43
FY 1991, 54-55
FY 1992, 76-77
FY 1993, 80-81
totals, FY 1990-93 (chart), 40
budget summits
FY 1990, 38, 41-42
FY 1991, 38-39, 53
budget "walls"
defense authorizations, 372
summary, 15
test (box), 82-83
debt ceiling extensions, 70, 74
1989-90 (box), 44-45
debt collection
IRS matching, 890
uniform procedures, 768, 779
uranium enrichment, 508
deficit reduction
proposals, 84-86
summary, 31-32
taxpayer designation, 892
IRS pie charts, 69
off-budget plans
Postal Service, 869-870
savings and loan bailout, 118, 122, 123
presidential messages (texts)
FY 1990, 1183-1186, 1188-1192
FY 1991, 1195-1196
FY 1992, 1209-1210
FY 1993, 1216-1217
summary, 9, 15, 37-40, 41, 75 79, 995
Buena Vista Lake, Va., 493 (box)
Buffalo Bayou, Texas, 493 (box)
Buffalo Bill Dam, 514

Bulgaria
Persian Gulf War, 316 (box)
U.S. trade, 194
Bumpers, Dale D-Ark.
flag desecration, 762
Gulf War veterans benefits, 630
mining law overhaul, 519
Senate elections, 1992, 24
space station, 900
superconducting supercollider, 901-902
Bunning, Jim R-Ky.
ethics committee reorganization, 947
Burdick, Quentin N. D-N.D.
death, successor, 26
Senate leadership, 928
Burials
Indian remains, 884-885
veterans benefits, 627
Burma. *See Myanmar*
Burns, Conrad R-Mont.
Montana wilderness, 526
Burton, Dan R-Ind.
AIDS programs, 589
Bus transportation
air bags, 444
Americans with Disabilities Act, 743, 746, 749
drug testing, 425
emissions standards deadlines, 477 (box)
highway authorization, 442, 443
Bush, Barbara, 21, 992
Bush, Frederick M., 679-680, 681, 1179
Bush, George
abortion, 594, 597-600, 235 (box)
agriculture
farm policy, 537, 539
Soviet credit guarantees, 555
appropriations
FY 1990, 52
FY 1991, 74
FY 1992, 77
defense rescissions, 383 (box)
FY 1993, 81
arms control
CFE treaty, 384
chemical weapons sanctions, 292
nuclear test treaties, 366-368
reconnaissance overflights, 390
Soviet Union dissolution, 328-329
START treaty, 387, 390
summary, 366-367 (box), 383
troop reductions, 387 (box)
unilateral cutbacks (box), 391
biography, 991-993
profile (box), 992
budget policy
administration budget requests
FY 1990, 41-42
FY 1991, 53-54
FY 1992, 76
FY 1993, 79-80
budget process changes, 56
budget "walls," 83 (box)
congressional budget action
FY 1990, 47
FY 1991, 54-55, 58
FY 1993, 80-83
credit reform, 60 (box)
debt ceiling extension, 44 (box)
debt reduction, 892
summary, 9, 38-39, 41, 53
business and labor
dislocated workers, 714
Eastern Airlines strike, 712-713
Indian preference, 884
job training, 730
minimum wage, 705-708
parental leave, 710-712, 730-732
product liability, 435
striker replacements, 733
summary, 703-704, 705, 720-721
unemployment benefits, 721-725, 725-728
vertical price fixing, 791
communications
cable TV regulation, 416, 451-454
children's TV, 429
fairness doctrine, 430
telemarketing controls, 432
congressional relations
congressional pay, 965-966
covert actions, 237 (box), 242-247, 280-281
House bank scandal, 931
judicial nominating process, 796
news leaks investigations, 947
Pepper legacy, 919
pocket-veto power, 927
State Department authorization, 247-249
summary, 10, 12, 16, 997-998
Udall Foundation, 527
D.C. appropriations, 895
defense policy
appropriations, 350-351, 380-381, 407-409
B-2 bomber, 399
defense authorization
FY 1990, 341, 342, 344
FY 1991, 355-359
FY 1992, 369-380
FY 1993, 395-396, 400
FS-X aircraft deal, 354-355
military base closings, 394-395
military construction appropriations, 365, 411
MX, Midgetman missiles, 343
Seawolf submarine, 410
strategic defense initiative, 371
summary, 335-338, 339, 369
Tower nomination, 339-340
economic policy
advisers (box), 32-33
summary, 31-36, 995
education
education initiative, 643-644
higher education aid, 655
math, science education, 651
school reform, 657-658
summary, 643, 653
vocational education, 646
elections and politics
campaign finance, 951, 953, 956, 959-963
congressional term limits, 959
fund raising (box), 962
House candidates, 26
motor voter bill, 893-895
"October surprise" probe, 287-288
presidential election, 1992, 17-23, 998
energy policy
energy bill, 470, 500, 502
Strategic Petroleum Reserve, 488-489
summary, 467
tax breaks, 484
environment
Clean Air Act, 468, 473-482
Earth Summit, 528-529
EPA Cabinet status, 498
global warming treaty, 297
irrigation subsidies, 514
offshore drilling ban, 491
summary, 467
wetlands preservation, 494
federal government
Hatch Act revision, 859-861, 886-887
pay overhaul, 858
regulatory review, 891
whistleblowers protection, 862
financial regulation
banking overhaul, 136, 141
credit card rate cap, 137 (box)
savings and loan bailout, 117-123, 150
summary, 117
foreign aid
Angola rebel aid, 244
appropriations, 228-231, 235-236, 269-270
authorization, 267-269
El Salvador, 214-219
former Soviet republics, 260-266, 330-331
Hungary, Poland, 210-211, 324
Israel, 272-273 (box)
Pakistan, 232
Somalia relief, 278-280
foreign policy
Andean narcotics control, 255-256
Armenian genocide resolution, 259
chemical weapons sanctions, 254-255
China, 250-253
German unification treaty, 214
intelligence authorization, 281, 283
Iran-contra pardons, 284-287
Middle East peace talks, 277
Nicaragua policy, 219-223
Panama policy, 223-226
Persian Gulf War, 299-317
POW/MIA investigation, 289, 290
Saudi arms sales, 294
South Africa policy, 253, 294-295
Soviet Union dissolution, 325, 331
Soviet-U.S. relations, 205-210
State Department authorization, 247-249
summary, 8-9, 205, 260, 995-997
foreign trade
China status, 173, 190-192
Enterprise for the Americas, 179, 194-195
export controls, 175-177
NAFTA, 187-190
Soviet, East bloc trade, 169-173, 192-193, 330
steel import quotas, 186
summary, 165-166
textile import quotas, 174-175
health
AIDS programs, 588
health reform, 596
Medicaid, 600-602
NIH authorization, 602-603
Oregon health plan, 597 (box)
orphan drug marketing, 585, 604
housing
authorization, 665-666, 669
FHA insurance fund, 691
HOPE, HOME funding, 696 (box)
HUD reforms, 686
HUD scandal, 685
law and judiciary
Americans with Disabilities Act, 743, 744
Chinese student visas, 755-756
civil rights/job bias, 757-760, 780-785
crime bills, 764, 765, 786, 788-789
customs damage liability, 798
drug legislation, 768-770
flag desecration, 761
judicial appointments, 774, 776 (box), 777-778
Legal Services authorization, 773-774, 795
Lucas nomination, 763-764
Supreme Court appointments, 801, 804, 994-995
messages (texts), 1187-1222
inaugural, 1187-1188
State of the Union, 1193, 1195, 1206-1209, 1213-1216
nominations and appointments, 993-994, 1169-1180
Persian Gulf War, 299-317
veterans benefits, 630-631
Puerto Rico plebiscite, 873-874
science programs
NASA authorization, 876, 897-898
space station, 877, 899
superconducting supercollider, 878, 901-902
taxes
budget reconciliation, 91, 92, 94
capital gains tax cut, 96-97, 99
middle-class tax cut, 100-103
summary, 87-90, 91, 99-100
urban aid tax bill, 103-106, 699
term overview, 991-998
press review (box), 994
transportation
airline buyouts, 421
Amtrak authorization, 424
aviation package, 417
highway authorization, 436, 437, 440-441
rail strikes, 448
summary, 415
urban aid, 103, 664
vetoes (list), 1181-1182
welfare and social services
child care, 611
child welfare, 621
community service, 617
reform, 623
Bush, Neil, 120, 133, 995, 997
Bushnell, John, 1180
Business and industry. *See also Advertising; Antitrust law; Banks and banking; Business interest groups; Business taxes; Competition and monopoly; Defense contractors; Employment and unemployment; Employment and working conditions; Enterprise zones; Federal contractors; Foreign trade and business; Labor unions and interests; Minority-owned business; Small business; Stocks, bonds and securities; Women-owned business; specific industries*
airline buyouts, 421
corporate campaign spending (box), 955
education partnership programs, 647
energy efficiency standards, 507
high-technology programs, 879-880, 891-892, 902
job training, 728-730
RICO limits, 771-772
Soviet aid, 267
Supreme Court decisions, 807-813
toxic air pollutants, 473, 474, 475, 477 (box)
Business Coalition for RICO Reform, 772
Business interest groups
Americans with Disabilities Act, 743-744
auto fuel efficiency, 484, 501
banking overhaul, 136, 139, 141
cable lobbying, 452 (box)
civil rights/job bias, 758, 782, 784
Clean Air Act, 478-479
CPSC authorization, 433
ERISA reforms, 737-738
immigration reform, 752
Indonesia aid, 276
mandated health benefits, 595
northern spotted owl, 494-495, 520
parental leave, 710-712, 730

pension reversions, 719-720
pesticide regulation, 522-523
product liability, 435, 463
RICO limits, 771-772, 791
savings and loan bailout, 118
Section 89 tax rules, 708-710
striker replacements, 734
vertical price fixing, 791
Business taxes
Americans with Disabilities Act, 744
budget reconciliation
FY 1990, 47-51
FY 1991, 68-69, 93, 96
energy bill, 109, 484, 500
environmental tax, 68
expiring provisions, 68-69, 109-110 (box), 94
foreign workers, 754
incentives, 69
middle-class tax cut, 100-103
miscellaneous tax bills, 110-112
pension reversions, 70, 719-720
percentage of GDP, 90 (chart)
Puerto Rico plebiscite, 873-874
savings and loan bailout, 117, 122, 129
Section 89 provisions, 703, 705, 708-710
South Africa policy, 294
Supreme Court decisions, 812-813
unemployment benefits, 728
urban aid tax bill, 103-107, 699
Bustamante, Albert G. D-Texas
House bank scandal, 938
members with overdrafts (chart), 934
House elections, 1992, 26
Butane, 487 (box)
Butter. *See Milk and dairy products*
"Buy American" provisions
Baby Bells restrictions, 461
foreign aid authorization, 268, 269
naval cargo ships, 406
supercomputers, 889
Buy Indian Act, 907
Buzenberg, Bill, 946
Byrd, Robert C. D-W.Va.
appropriations, FY 1990, 52
balanced budget amendment, 15, 85
budget "walls," 83 (box)
campaign finance, 960
CIA relocation, 282 (box)
Clean Air Act, 474, 478-479
congressional pay, 970-971
D.C. appropriations, 895
defense policy summary, 338
dislocated workers, 714
federal employee honoraria, 886
foreign aid appropriations, 234, 236, 275
Israel, 272
highway authorization, 439
HUD reforms, 685
intelligence authorization, 282
joint ventures, 891
Keating Five investigation, 987
lobbying curbs, 862
Madison amendment, 972
middle-class tax cut, 102
NEA funding, 865, 867
public broadcasting, 458
Senate leadership, 5, 7 (chart), 915, 928
Byrd rule, 98
Byrd scholarships, 656

C

C-17 aircraft
appropriations, 352, 364, 382, 407, 409
authorization, 349, 362, 379, 395, 396, 406
C-135 tanker planes, 404, 405
Cabinet
Bush appointments
biographical profiles, 1169-1180
chart, 1171
term summary, 993-994
EPA status, 498, 529
Cable Telecommunications Act of 1984, 427, 454
Cable television
Baby Bells restrictions, 461
chronology of action
1989-90, 427-428
1991-92, 451-457
FCC user fees, 458
lobbying (box), 452
must-carry requirements, 455
retransmission consent, 455
summary, 16, 416, 436
California
auto emissions control, 473, 475, 480
bankruptcy judges, 799
cable TV regulation, 452 (box)
coastal zone management, 491
desert protection, 522
disaster relief, 549
endangered species, 521
northern spotted owl, 495
governor's race, 1990, 12
highway authorization, 442
Indian tribal recognition, 908
irrigation subsidies, 495, 513-515
Mexican border housing aid, 675
military base closings, 353
offshore drilling ban, 491, 504
presidential election, 1992, 22
term limits, 10 (box), 958, 963
water projects, 493 (box), 494, 517, 518, 528
California gnatcatcher, 521
California Indian Policy Council, 908
Cambodia
refugee asylum, 756
U.S. aid, 234, 237, 243, 245, 247
Vietnam War POW/MIAs, 277, 289-290, 291
Campaign finance
corporate limits, 955 (box)
ethics code rewrite, 920
federal employee honoraria, 886
franking privilege, 969
Gingrich ethics case, 926
Hatch Act revision, 860-861
House Post Office scandal, 939-942
Keating Five investigation, 975-988
presidential "checkoff" fund (box), 954
reform action
1989-90, 951-957
1991-92, 959-963
retirement conversion (box), 952
state reforms (box), 956
summary, 9
Campaign Finance Task Force, House, 951, 956
Campbell, Ben Nighthorse D-Colo.
Senate elections, 1992, 23, 24
Campbell, Tom R-Calif.
Americans with Disabilities Act, 746
civil rights/job bias, 759
Canada
Great Lakes pollution control, 492
NAFTA, 187-190
natural gas exports, 509
Persian Gulf War, 303, 316 (box)
space station, 877, 900
wetlands preservation, 494
Cancer. *See also Breast cancer*
Agent Orange controversy, 628 (box), 632
DES research, 607
indoor air pollution, 531
Medicare coverage
Pap tests, 570
research hospitals, 571
Pacific yew harvest, 527
radiation exposure compensation, 636
radon abatement, 530
toxic air pollutants, 473, 477, 478
tracking registries, 508
Canola, 549
Capital gains tax
budget proposal, FY 1991, 53
budget reconciliation
FY 1990, 91, 43, 46, 47
FY 1991, 66, 92-93, 95
cut proposals, 96-99
history (box), 98
home sales, 111
middle-class tax cut, 100, 103
Poland, Hungary aid, 212
summary, 6, 36, 88
technology programs, 902
unemployment benefits, 723
urban aid tax bill, 104, 105, 699
Capital punishment
Carnes nomination, 797
federal death penalty, 764-768, 786-788
habeas corpus appeals, 764-768, 786-789
racial justice, 764-768, 787, 797
Supreme Court decisions, 817-818
summary, 805
Capitol Police
House Post Office scandal, 939
Capitol, U.S.
bombing, 922 (box)
Carbon dioxide
Clean Air Act, 473
global warming, 297, 495, 505, 529
Carbon monoxide, 473, 474, 482
Card, Andrew H.
biographical profile, 1174
Transportation leadership, 419 (box)
Cardin, Benjamin L. D-Md.
ethics committee reorganization, 947
unemployment benefits, 724
Cardin, Shoshana S., 270
Caribbean area. *See also specific countries*
U.S. trade
Caribbean Basin Initiative, 180-184
Enterprise for the Americas, 179-180
ethanol, 186
Caribbean Basin Economic Recovery Act of 1983, 180
Caribbean Basin Initiative
action, 1989-90, 180-184
footwear imports, 107
Carl D. Perkins Vocational and Applied Technology Education Act, 645, 646
Carley, James E., 943
Carley, L. David, 943
Carnes, Edward Earl Jr., 796
Carney, William, 952
Carper, Thomas R. D-Del.
mortgage prepayments, 693
Cars. *See Automobiles and auto industry*
Cassini space mission, 875, 876, 898
Carter, Jimmy
Nicaragua policy, 222, 223
"October surprise" probe, 287-288
Panama elections, 224
presidential election, 1992, 19
Soviet aid, 266
Carville, James, 998
Casey, William J., 288
Cason, James E., 1179
Catholic Church
Jesuit murders in El Salvador, 217
Nicaragua policy, 221
Panama policy, 224, 225
Poland agricultural aid, 213
Cavazos, Lauro F.
biographical profile, 1172
Bush term summary, 993
Education Department leadership, 645 (box)
school reform, 657
CDBGs. *See Community Development Block Grants*
CDC. *See Centers for Disease Control*
Ceausescu, Nicolae, 336
Cellular phones, 49, 458
Censorship
TV violence guidelines, 428
Census Bureau
census reform study, 895
foreign investment data, 177
temporary employees, 182
Centennial Wash, 517
Center for Democracy, 222
Center for Resource Development, 678 (box)
Center for Tobacco Products, 591
Center for Training and Election Promotion, 222
Center on Budget and Policy Priorities, 723
Centers for Disease Control (CDC)
Agent Orange controversy, 628 (box)
childhood vaccines, 587
disabilities prevention, 595, 610
injury research, 591-592
TB prevention, 587
Central America. *See also specific countries*
immigration reform, 754
refugee asylum, 756
regional peace accords, 219-223
U.S. business relocation, 276
Central Arizona Project, 517
Central Europe. *See Eastern Europe; specific countries*
Central Intelligence Agency (CIA)
Afghan aid, 233
arms sales controls, 238
covert actions
aid programs, 244-245
notification (box), 237
intelligence authorizations, 239-242, 280-284
intelligence reorganization plans, 284-285 (box)
JFK assassination documents, 893
leadership (box), 261
Nicaragua policy, 221, 222
Panama policy, 224, 225
relocation plan, 282 (box)
State Department authorization, 247
watchdog inspector general, 238-239
Central Utah Project, 514, 516
Central Valley Project, 513-514, 515-516
***Centurion*-class submarines**, 406, 409, 410

Cervical cancer
Medicare coverage of Pap tests, 570
screening programs authorization, 593
women with AIDS, 623-624
CFCs. *See Chlorofluorocarbons*
CFE. *See Conventional forces in Europe treaty*
CFIUS. *See Foreign Investment in the United States, Committee on*
CFM Development Corp., 678-679 (box)
CFTC. *See Commodity Futures Trading Commission*
CH-53 helicopters, 344, 379, 382
Chafee, John H. R-R.I.
Clean Air Act, 476, 478
family planning authorization, 592
farm bill, 541
highway authorization, 439
Senate leadership, 7 (chart), 13-14, 915, 928
Chamber of Commerce, U.S.
age discrimination, 715
Hatch Act revision, 860
National Endowment for Democracy, 247
parental leave, 711
Section 89 tax rules, 709
Chamorro, Violeta, 219, 222, 223, 224, 257
CHAMPUS, 600, 635
Channell, Carl R. "Spitz," 287 (box)
Chapman, Jim D-Tex.
Americans with Disabilities Act, 746, 747
superconducting supercollider, 879
Chapter 1 education aid, 652
Chapter 2 education aid, 659
Charities and non-profit organizations
campaign finance, 955
congressional honoraria, 971
donations for federal programs
environmental education, 495
food assistance programs, 618
Food for Peace, 257
housing authorization, 666, 668, 670, 697
miscellaneous tax bills, 110-111
VA leases for homeless, 635
Cheese. *See Milk and dairy products*
Chemical weapons
disposal facility, 411
non-proliferation
defense authorization, 407
economic sanctions, 254-255, 291, 292-293, 367 (box)
export controls, 175-176, 177, 195-196
Soviet-U.S. accord, 328, 366-367 (box)
Persian Gulf War, 300, 314
Rocky Mountain arsenal, 527
Chemicals and chemical industry. *See also Ozone-layer depleting chemicals; Pesticides*
hazardous chemicals tax, 68
pollution prevention, 64, 529
transportation safety, 422
Cheney, Dick R-Wyo.
B-2 bomber, 398
biographical profile, 1170-1172
defense appropriations
FY 1990, 350-351
FY 1993, 408
defense authorization
FY 1990, 340-350
FY 1991, 355-363
FY 1992, 372, 373, 379
FY 1993, 396
Defense budget reprogramming, 356 (box)
Defense leadership, 339, 341 (box)
defense policy summary, 337, 339, 369
House bank scandal, 933, 936
members with overdrafts (chart), 934
House leadership, 5, 916
intelligence reorganization plans, 285 (box)
military base closings, 353-354, 393-394
Persian Gulf War, 300, 302, 304, 310, 311, 315
strategic defense initiative, 371
strategic materials, 368
successor, 8
weapons programs cancellation (box), 348
A-12 bomber, 379 (box)
V-22 Osprey aircraft, 406 (box)
Cheraw Indians, 909
Chernobyl nuclear accident, 329
Cherokee Indians, 883, 908
Chicago & North Western railroad, 424
Chicago Board of Trade, 550, 551
Chicago, Ill.
aviation package, 418
urban aid, 84, 699
Chicago Mercantile Exchange, 550
Chickasaw Indians, 908
Child abuse
child welfare overhaul, 621
court personnel training, 798
crime bill, 764, 768
Indian health, human services, 883
prevention, treatment, 619, 622
respite care, 619, 623
Child Abuse Prevention and Treatment Act of 1974, 622
Child care
child care centers
food assistance programs, 618
lead-poisoning prevention, 607
military families, 349
parental leave, 710-712, 730-732
public, Indian housing authorization, 673
state grants, 613
state referral programs, 614
tax credit, 44-45, 46, 100, 102, 611-613
workers' Social Security earnings test, 718
Child Care Block Grant, 613
Child custody law, 798
Child health and nutrition. *See also Women, Infants and Children (WIC) program*
abandoned children, 622
block grant, 579-580
food assistance programs, 617-618, 623
human services reconciliation, 615, 616
immunization program authorization, 587
lead-poisoning prevention, 530, 606-607, 608, 697-698
mandated benefits, 595
Medicaid coverage, 578-579, 581
mental health services, 592
national commission, 573
respite care, 619, 623
safety
airline seating, 422
bicycle helmet standards, 462
child-resistant packaging, 870
hazardous occupations, 733
Somalia relief, 278-279
tobacco sales ban, 799
vaccine injury compensation, 572, 587
Child labor law
constitutional amendment, 972
OPIC authorization, 199
regulation action, 733
violations penalties, 61
Child pornography
crime bill, 768
NEA funding, 866, 867
Child sexual abuse
Indian programs, 882, 883
Child support
custody law, 798
enforcement, 615-616, 790
Medicaid eligibility, 615
Child welfare
abandoned children, 622
authorization, 621
comprehensive centers, 614
human services reconciliation, 614-616, 616
urban aid tax bill, 107
Children. *See also Adolescents and youth; Adoption; Child abuse; Child care; Child health and nutrition; Child welfare; Elementary and secondary education; Foster care; Infants; Parental rights and issues*
earned income tax credit, 66
900-number regulation, 460
Supreme Court decisions, 840-841
television
advertising, 429
cable TV regulation, 457
educational programming grants, 429
violence, 428
Children's Defense Fund, 85
Chiles, Lawton, 915
China
development bank authorization, 185, 186
Persian Gulf War, 304, 305
population control policies, 230, 234, 269, 274, 594, 600, 755-756
summary (box), 235
U.S. relations, 250-253
broadcasting commission, 292
immigration issues, 753, 755-756, 794
State Department authorization, 250
U.S. trade
Export-Import Bank authorization, 184
MFN summary, 172 (box), 269
satellite launches, 875
trade status, 173-174, 190-192
U.S. World Bank contributions, 238
Chinook helicopters, 379
Chloracne, 628 (box), 632
Chlorofluorocarbons (CFCs)
production phaseout, 476, 483
tax, 49, 67, 505
Choctaw Indians, 908
Choice in Management Program, 697, 698
Chrysler Corp., 484
Church-state separation
Supreme Court decisions, 834
summary, 805
Church Universal and Triumphant, 526
Churches and religious groups
Americans with Disabilities Act, 748, 750
child care, 612-613
domestic partners benefits, 897
Social Security exemption, 51
student group access to schools, 647 (box)
Supreme Court summary, 805
Cigarettes. *See Tobacco*
Citizen Action, 960
Citizens' Commission on Public Service Compensation, 967, 972-973
Citizens for Congressional Reform, 959
Citizenship, U.S.
marital tax deduction, 51
naturalization process, 779, 794
Philippine war veterans, 779-780
Civil rights and liberties. *See also First Amendment; Habeas corpus appeals; Search and seizure*
Americans with Disabilities Act, 743-752
Carnes nomination, 796-797
coerced confessions, 788
job bias protections, 757-760, 780-785
Lucas nomination, 763-764
Supreme Court decisions, 838-844, 757-758
summary, 806
Civil Rights Act of 1964
damage awards, 757-760, 780-785
Civil Rights Commission, U.S., 762-763, 785-786
Civil rights groups
Americans with Disabilities Act, 743
civil rights/job bias, 757-760, 782
crime bill, 787
motor voter bill, 871
Civil service. *See Federal employees*
Civilian Health and Medical Program of the Uniformed Services (CHAMPUS), 600, 635
Claims Court, U.S., 572
Clark Air Base, 353, 411-412
Clarke, James McClure D-N.C.
House elections, 1990, 11
Clarke, Robert L., 114, 1180
Clarridge, Duane R., 286
Classification Act of 1923, 857
Clay, William L. D-Mo.
age discrimination, 716
civil rights/job bias, 759
defense workers relief, 888
House bank scandal, 932
members with overdrafts (chart), 934
House leadership, 929
parental leave, 711
pension reversions, 719-720
Clayton Antitrust Act of 1914, 772
Clean Air Act of 1970
amendment, 1990, 473-493
deadlines (box), 477
summary, 9, 468-469, 997
toxic air pollutants (list), 481
dislocated workers, 483, 714
EPA fees, 64
fuel-efficiency mandates, 501
highway authorization, 438-444
nuclear power, 503
Clean-coal technology
energy bill, 511
Poland, Hungary aid, 213
Clean Water Act, 64, 492, 529
Climate. *See Global climate change; Weather*
Climsat Earth probe, 899
Clines, Thomas G., 287 (box)
Clinton, Bill
budget-control efforts, 86
business and labor
Competitiveness Council, 891
parental leave, 732
defense policy
V-22 Osprey aircraft, 406
foreign, trade policy
Cuba embargo, 295
Haitian refugees, 296
NAFTA, 187, 190
Somalia relief, 279, 280
Soviet aid, 264
government ethics, 887
health, human services
abortion, 600

health reform, 596
Medicaid, 578
Iran-contra pardons, 286
motor voter bill, 895
presidential election, 1992, 17-23
Clinton "firsts" (box), 24
congressional candidates, 24, 26-27
space station, 899
Supreme Court summary, 804
Clothing and apparel
Caribbean Basin Initiative, 180-181
footwear imports, 107
NAFTA highlights, 188 (box)
textile import quotas, 174-175
tuxedo taxes, 110
Cloture votes
Senate cloture votes, 1917-92, 1139-1142
CNW Corp., 424
Coal
abandoned mine reclamation, 63
acid rain reduction, 473-483
black lung trust fund, 734
clean-coal technology, 213, 511
dislocated workers, 478-479, 714
energy bill, 511
miners' benefits fund, 108, 505, 511, 735 (box)
Coalition for Vehicle Choice, 501
Coalition to End the Permanent Congress, 973
Coast Guard, U.S.
appropriations, 409
authorization, 425, 448-449
foreign ship inspection, 449
user fees, 65, 110, 425, 449
vessel appropriations, 352
zebra mussels control, 497
Coastal areas
barrier islands protection, 497
beach pollution, 492, 531
environmental protection, 63-64, 491
flood insurance, 697
offshore oil drilling, 504
water pollution control, 492
zebra mussels control, 496
Coastal Barrier Resources Act of 1982, 497
Coastal Energy Impact Program, 64
Coastal Zone Management Act of 1972, 63-64, 491
Coats, Daniel R. R-Ind.
abortion, 598
House bank scandal, 936
NEA funding, 866
NIH authorization, 591
Senate elections, 1992, 26
Senate seat, House successor, 8
Cocaine, 232, 255-256, 296
Cochran, Thad R-Miss.
airline smoking ban, 420
fish inspection, 434
Older Americans Act, 620
Senate leadership, 7 (chart), 13-14, 915, 928
CoCom. *See Coordinating Committee on Multilateral Export Controls*
Coelho, Tony D-Calif.
Americans with Disabilities Act, 745
ethics case, resignation, 5, 913, 918
House bank scandal, 932
members with overdrafts (chart), 934
House leadership, 5, 916
savings and loan bailout, 121
Cohen, William S. R-Maine
nuclear test ban, 524
Senate leadership, 928
textile import quotas, 174
Coins
commemorative coins, 161
redesign, 135, 161
Soviet gold coin imports, 193
Coldwater Creek, Mo., 493 (box)
Coleman, E. Thomas R-Mo.
higher education aid, 654
House bank scandal, 932, 938
House elections, 1992, 26-27
House leadership, 929
NEA funding, 866-867
Taft Institute authorization, 652
Coleman, J. Marshall, 6
Coleman, Ronald D. D-Texas
census study, 895
House bank scandal, 938
members with overdrafts (chart), 934
Coleman, William T., 760
Colleges and universities
athletes "right to know," 648-649
campus crime, 648-649, 656
community service, 616
copyright, 773
corporate sponsors of athletic events, 111
defense bills, 364, 409
faculty tenure, 650 (box)
high-tech training, 892
higher education aid, 653-657
Indian education, 883
mining research, 880
NSF grant overhead, 902
patent infringement, 792
Collier, Bill, 925
Collins, Barbara-Rose D-Mich.
House elections, 1990, 11
Collins, Cardiss D-Ill.
banking overhaul, 139
House bank scandal (chart), 934
Colombia
Andean import duties, 296-297
U.S. aid
Andean narcotics control, 255-256, 769
appropriations, 228, 232-233
Colonias, 675
Colorado
oil shales, 499, 530
radiation victims compensation, 586
Rocky Mountain arsenal, 527
term limits, 10 (box), 958
water projects, 517-518
wilderness area, 526
Colorado River
Grand Canyon erosion, 496, 516
irrigation subsidies, 513-514
Columbia Savings and Loan, 918
Columbus, Christopher
commemorative coins, 161
Comanche helicopters
appropriations, 382, 409
authorization, 372, 378, 405
Comet Rendezvous Asteroid Flyby (CRAF), 875, 876, 898
Commerce Department, U.S.
census study, 895
economic statistics
foreign investment data, 166, 177-179
GDP v. GNP (box), 36
environmental protection
Antarctica mining ban, 489
endangered species, 521
fish conservation, 426, 427
Florida Keys, 497
Landsat, 900
export controls, 175-177, 196
export promotion, 200
fish inspection, 434-435
FS-X aircraft deal, 355
high-tech programs, 879-880, 891-892, 902
high-tech training, 892
leadership, 419 (box)
radio spectrum allocation, 459
tourism promotion, 462
Commercial-Military Integration Partnerships, 403
Commercial Space Launch Act, 65
Commercial speech, 835
Commercial State Bank (St. Paul), 922
Committee Against Torture, 259
Committee on Committees, House, 916
Committees. *See Congressional committees; specific committees*
Commodity Credit Corporation
Food for Peace, 258
Latin American debt relief, 195
surplus food distribution, 619
Commodity Distribution Program, 617
Commodity futures trading
market abuses, regulation, 550, 552
Commodity Futures Trading Commission (CFTC)
authorization, 550, 551-553
securities market reforms, 130-132
Commodity Supplemental Food Program, 619
Common Cause
balanced budget amendment, 85
campaign finance, 957, 960, 961
Coelho resignation, 918
congressional pay, 968
Hatch Act revision, 860
Keating Five investigation, 977
political advertising, 957
Wright resignation, 917
Communications. *See Telecommunications*
Communications Act of 1934, 430, 751
Communism and communist countries. *See also specific countries*
Jackson-Vanik amendment, 172 (box)
Soviet Union dissolution, 319-332
Community-based health care
Medicaid coverage, 581
mental health services, 592
veterans programs, 625
Community colleges
high-tech training, 892
Indian education, 883
vocational education, 645
Community development. *See also Community Development Block Grants; Enterprise zones; Rural development*
bank incentives, 147
defense conversion aid, 402-403
neighborhood revitalization programs, 670
Community Development Block Grants (CDBGs)
housing authorization, 675-676
HUD reforms, 685, 687, 688
HUD scandal, 680
Indian environmental quality, 884
Community Development Corporations, 147
Community Food and Nutrition Program, 614
Community health centers
authorization, 588
malpractice suits, 609
Community hospitals
Medicare budget reconciliation, 1989, 571
Community Housing Partnership, 666, 668, 669, 671
Community mental health centers, 576
Community policing, 873
Community Reinvestment Act of 1977, 128, 152
Community service
authorization, 616-617
student aid, 656
Community Services Block Grant, 614
Compact of Free Association, 258-259
Compensated Work Therapy program, 628
Compensatory education aid, 652
Competition and monopoly. *See also Antitrust law*
airline reservations, 445
alternative power, 486
Baby Bells restrictions, 432, 461-462
cable TV regulation, 427-428, 453-457
electric utilities, 500
naval shipyards, 379
oil service stations, 530
orphan drugs, 585
vertical price fixing, 771, 791
Competitiveness
Americans with Disabilities Act, 744
Baby Bells restrictions, 432, 461
cruise ships, 450
export controls, 176
FS-X aircraft deal, 354-355
fuel-efficiency standards, 501
high-tech programs, 879, 891-892, 902
high-tech training, 892
math, science education, 651
product liability, 463
radio spectrum allocation, 430
supercomputers, 889
superconducting supercollider, 901
Competitiveness Council, 435, 891, 996
Comprehensive Anti-Apartheid Act of 1986, 294
Comprehensive Child Development Centers, 614
Comprehensive Homeless Assistance Plan, 675
Comptroller of the Currency, 114, 126
Computers
high-speed network, 903-904
INSLAW software theft case, 792 (box)
rural development, 548
software copyright, 773
supercomputers, 889
Condit, Gary D-Calif.
election, 8
Conejos Water Conservancy District, 518
Conference of Presidents of Major American Jewish Organizations, 270
Conference on Security and Cooperation in Europe, 207
Conflict of interest. *See Congressional ethics*
Congress, U.S. *See also Campaign finance; Congressional committees; Congressional elections; Congressional employees and staff; Congressional ethics; Congressional-executive relations; Congressional pay and benefits; House of Representatives, U.S.; Incumbents; Redistricting; Senate, U.S.*
closed-captioned TV coverage, 949
leadership, 1989-92 (chart), 7
members
age structure (table), 27
blacks, 1947-95 (table), 18
list, 1989-92, 1115-1123
women, 1947-95 (table), 18
nuclear bunker, 973
organization
101st, 915-917
102nd, 928-929
party affiliations, 1789-1993 (chart), 1234-1235
post-election sessions, 1137-1138
public opinion, 8, 15, 913, 929
reform study, 948

session statistics (boxes)
1989, 6
1990, 9
1991, 13
1992, 15
Supreme Court decisions, 834
Congressional Black Caucus
budget alternatives, 42, 54, 80
South Africa policy, 295
Congressional Budget and Impoundment Control Act of 1974, 56, 83, 85
Congressional Budget Office (CBO)
Agent Orange compensation, 632
bank deposit insurance, 124-125 (box)
banking overhaul, 136-137
budget policy
budget process changes, 70, 71, 72
credit reform, 60 (box), 72, 73
deficit estimates, 38
economic forecasts, 43, 54, 80
government-sponsored enterprises, 73, 154
tax, entitlement bill estimates, 631
campaign finance, 955, 963
defense authorization, 1990, 345
economic summary, 33-34
federal employee performance standards, 888
federal pensions, 859
flood insurance, 699
housing authorization, 669
HUD scandal, 683
Israel aid, 272
Medicaid, 578, 601
Micmac Indian settlement, 885
pension reversions, 720
Puerto Rico plebiscite, 874
Soviet aid, 265
unemployment benefits, 724, 725-726, 728
uniform poll closing time, 872
VA nurses pay, 627
WIC authorization, 617
Congressional committees. *See also specific committees*
jurisdiction, subcommittees, 1125-1136
leadership
101st Congress, 915, 916-917
102nd Congress, 928, 929
rules, 916
Congressional elections. *See also Campaign finance*
franking privilege, 968
House bank scandal, 937-938
pre-election ethics complaints, 947
returns
1990, 1240-1247
1992, 1250-1258
special elections, 8, 12, 1238-1239, 1248-1249
summary
1990, 9-11
1992, 23-27
term limits, 958-959, 963-964
Congressional employees and staff
Americans with Disabilities Act, 743-747, 751
civil rights/job bias, 759, 784, 785
congressional ethics cases, 926
federal employee honoraria, 886
House administrator, 947-948
House Post Office scandal, 939-942
pay, 970
Congressional ethics. *See also House bank scandal; Keating Five investigation*
"appearance standard" (box), 978
code rewrite, 920-921
House election results, 11, 26
House leadership turmoil, 5
Coelho resignation, 918
Wright resignation, 917-918
House Post Office scandal, 939-942
investigations
1989-90, 921-927
1991-92, 942-946
lobbying curbs, 862
pre-election complaints, 947
"revolving door," 861
summary, 913-914
Congressional-executive relations
appointments
judicial nominating process, 795-796
Udall Foundation, 527
budget policy
appropriations lapses, 72
balanced budget amendment, 75
budget submission, 57, 73
expedited rescissions, 85-86
summary, 41
Bush term summary, 997-998
foreign policy
arms sales controls, 238
chemical weapons, 292, 367 (box)
covert actions notification, 237 (box), 242-247, 280-281
export controls, 175
foreign aid "leveraging," 239
foreign aid policy, 267
FS-X aircraft deal, 355
Nicaragua policy, 219-220
queries to State Department, 292
State Department authorization, 247-249
summary, 204
pocket-veto power, 927
separation of powers issues
aging conference, 620
Americans with Disabilities Act, 744, 746
House bank scandal, 936-937
housing program, 680
JFK assassination documents, 893
Micmac Indians, 908-909
OMB review authority, 645-646, 867-869
Rose ethics case, 946
treaty ratification
"authoritative" testimony, 386
"treaty form" v. executive agreement, 367 (box)
war powers
Panama policy, 225
Persian Gulf War, 12-13, 308
Somalia relief, 280
Congressional mail
action
1989-90, 968-970
1991-92, 973
campaign finance, 951, 955
out-of-district mailings, 973
pre-election mailing limits, 968
stamp allowance (box), 940
Congressional pay and benefits
action
1989-90, 965-968
1991-92, 970-972
cost-of-living adjustments, 972
gifts, travel ethics, 920
honoraria, outside income, 967, 968, 970-971
Madison amendment, 972
pay raise history (box), 971
restaurant bills, 942
stamp allowance (box), 940
summary, 5-6
Wright resignation, 917
Congressional Record
text changes, 924-925
Congressional Research Service
D.C., territorial House voting, 948
mining law overhaul, 520
motor voter bill, 894
Congressional votes
D.C., territorial House voting, 948-949
key votes, 1989-92, 1021-1104
recorded vote totals, 1950-92 (table), 16
Senate cloture votes, 1917-92, 1139-1142
Speaker's votes, 246
teller votes, 411
treaty ratification, 367 (box)
vice president's, 996
Connecticut
bankruptcy judges, 799
governor's race, 1990, 11
highway authorization, 442
Seawolf submarine, 410
Conrad, Kent D-N.D.
budget resolutions, 43, 77
Keating Five investigation, 987
Senate elections, 1992, 23, 26
Conservation. *See Energy conservation and efficiency; Soil conservation*
Conservation Law Foundation, 530
Conservation Reserve Program, 539, 541, 546
Conservative Democratic Forum
campaign finance, 961
health reform, 597
Conservative Opportunity Society, 925
Consistency provision, 63-64, 674
Constellation, 347
Constituent service
Keating Five investigation, 975-988
Constitution, U.S. *See also Congressional-executive relations; Constitutional amendments; Federal-state relations; specific amendments*
commemorative coins, 161
congressional term limits, 958-959, 963
D.C. political issues, 872, 896
D.C., territorial House voting, 948-949
education about, 659
interstate garbage, 523
legislative vetoes, 171
militia clauses, 361 (box)
severability provisions
Americans with Disabilities Act, 744, 752
sovereignty proviso in treaty ratification, 259
Speech or Debate Clause, 945
Constitutional amendments. *See also Balanced budget amendment*
Madison amendment ratification, 972-973
proposed, suggested amendments
congressional term limits, 959
flag desecration ban, 6, 760-762
invalidated proposals, 972
Construction industry
Davis-Bacon Act revision, 732
earthquake hazards, 881
safety, 736
tax accounting, 49
urban aid, 700
Youthbuild, 697, 698
Construction Safety, Health and Education, Office of, 736
Consumer Federation of America, 452 (box)
Consumer interest groups
aircraft liability insurance, 422
Baby Bells restrictions, 432
banking overhaul, 139, 141
cable TV regulation, 452 (box)
CPSC authorization, 433, 462
credit reporting safeguards, 157
dairy production, 553 (box)
food labeling, 585, 901
fuel efficiency mandates, 501
Medigap insurance regulation, 583
pesticide regulation, 522-523
product liability, 463
Consumer issues and protection
banking, 128, 137, 147-148
CPSC authorization, 433, 462
credit reporting safeguards, 157-158
deceptive mail curbs, 870
fastener standards, 436
fuel efficiency mandates, 501
insurance antitrust, 435
manufactured housing, 668
natural gas decontrol, 484-485
octane labeling, 487
product liability, 435
summary, 416
telephone service
Baby Bells restrictions, 461-462
caller ID, 462
900-number regulation, 460
telemarketing controls, 459
Consumer Product Safety Commission (CPSC)
authorization, 432-433, 462
cigarette safety, 436, 591
members, 419 (box)
Consumers Union, 691
Conte, Silvio O. R-Mass.
farm bill, 540
House leadership, 929
legislative summary, 1990, 8
NEA funding, 867
successor, 14
Continental Airlines, 421, 712
Convention Against Torture and Other Cruel, Inhuman or Degrading Treatment or Punishment, 259
Conventional forces in Europe (CFE) treaty
action, 1991-92, 383-386
weapons effects (chart), 385
congressional observers, 249
Soviet-U.S. relations, 328, 366 (box)
Conyers, John Jr. D-Mich.
EPA Cabinet status, 529
federal financial centralization, 862
federal-state fund transfers, 865
GSA overhaul, 889
Hastings impeachment, 775
House bank scandal, 932
members with overdrafts (chart), 934
House leadership, 916
motor voter bill, 871
OMB regulatory review, 868
RICO limits, 772, 791
South Africa policy, 294
urban aid, 700
Cook, Charles E., 943
Cook, Dorothy, 943
Cooper, Jim D-Tenn.
cable TV regulation, 427
Coordinating Committee on Multilateral Export Controls (CoCom), 175-176, 195-196
Coors, Joseph, 683
Copyright
artists' rights, 772-773
cable TV regulation, 452 (box), 453, 456
computer software, 773
fair use, 791-792
fees, 773
home digital recording, 459
renewal, 793
royalty tribunal, 773
Soviet-U.S. trade, 170
state, university coverage, 773
Supreme Court decisions, 809-810
Copyright Office, U.S., 773
Copyright Royalty Tribunal, 773
Coral reefs, 497
Corn, 555

Corporal punishment, 648
Corporation for Public Broadcasting, 457-458
CORRTEX, 368
Corwin Springs, 526
Costa Rica
Caribbean Basin Initiative, 180
Nicaragua policy, 222
Cotton
import quotas, 543
price supports, 542-543
warehouse accounting, 111
Coughlin, Lawrence R-Pa.
House leadership, 917
Council of Freely Elected Heads of Government, 222
Council on Competitiveness, 435, 891, 996
Counterfeiting, 134
Courter, Jim
New Jersey governor's race, 7-8
Coverdell, Paul, 23, 24
Cox, C. Christopher R-Calif.
airline buyouts, 421
Coyle, Jim, 959
Coyote Creek, Calif., 493 (box)
CPSC. *See Consumer Product Safety Commission*
Craig, Larry E. R-Idaho
House bank scandal, 936
Yucca Mountain nuclear dump, 513
Crane, Philip M. R-Ill.
NEA funding, 866
Cranston, Alan D-Calif.
California desert protection, 522
coin redesign, 135, 161
FHA insurance fund, 691
housing authorization, 666, 670
HUD reforms, 685, 687
Keating Five investigation, 975-988
mortgage prepayments, 692-693
Pakistan arms sales, 293
savings and loan bailout, 122-123
Senate leadership, 7 (chart), 13, 915, 928
veterans' COLA increase, 631
veterans leadership, 67 (box)
Cranston-Gonzalez National Affordable Housing Act, 665-676
Credit cards
Bush term summary, 993
interest rate cap (box), 137
telemarketing controls, 432
Credit reports, 157-158
Credit Union National Association, 129
Credit unions
banking overhaul, 142, 148
deposit insurance, 129
money laundering, 156
Crime and criminals. *See also Capital punishment; Drug trafficking; Fraud; Habeas corpus appeals; Police and law enforcement agencies; Prisons and prisoners; Sex crimes*
anti-crime bills, 764-768, 786-789
campus crime, 648-649, 656
carjacking penalties, 790
D.C. police hirings, 873
DNA testing, 798
hate crimes, 778, 797
Indian jurisdiction, 906
Indian programs investigations, 882
juvenile delinquency prevention, 797-798
money laundering, 134-135
RICO limits, 771-772
Supreme Court decisions, 817-819
summary, 805
torture treaty, 259
victims' compensation, 616
Crime insurance, 52, 61, 694
Cristiani, Alfredo, 215-218, 229, 234, 268
Critical technologies, 891-892, 902
Croatia
refugee aid, 276, 278
U.S. trade, 194
Crockett, George W. Jr. D-Mich.
Hastings impeachment, 775
Crop insurance
farm bill, 539, 546
program revision (box), 549
Crowe, William, 305-306
Cruise missiles
appropriations, 364
START treaty, 387-389
Cruse, Victor R., 678 (box)
CSX Corp., 448, 973
Cuba
Bay of Pigs documents, 285 (box)
economic embargo, 295
Soviet aid, 268
TV Marti, 250
Cuba Democracy Act, 295
Cuban-Americans
Cuba embargo, 295
Ros-Lehtinen election, 8
Ryskamp nomination, 796
Cultural exchange programs
Poland, Hungary aid, 213
Soviet-U.S. relations, 209, 267, 276
Cuomo, Mario M., 17, 19
Currency. *See Money*
Cushing, R. Hunter, 680-681
Custer Battlefield National Monument, 525
Customs and Trade Act of 1990, 65
Customs duties. *See also Tariffs*
budget reconciliation, FY 1991, 64-65
Caribbean Basin Initiative, 181-182
electronic filing, 108, 197, 198
Customs Forfeiture Fund, 65, 182
Customs Service, U.S.
Caribbean Basin Initiative, 181, 183
customs law revisions, 198-199
drug interdiction, 788
minivan tariffs, 197-198
modernization, 108
overtime pay, 609
property damage liability, 798
Czechoslovakia
communism downfall, 328
Persian Gulf War, 316 (box)
U.S. trade
agreement, 171, 193-194
duty rates, 182
export controls, 196

D

Dairy cattle, 541
Dairy products. *See Milk and dairy products*
Damage suits
Supreme Court decisions, 841-842
D'Amato, Alfonse M. R-N.Y.
banking overhaul, 142
Bush economic team, 33 (box)
credit card rate cap, 137 (box)
crime bill, 787
ethics case, 923, 943-944
FHA insurance, 691
Hatch Act revision, 861
housing authorization, 666-667, 669, 697
HUD scandal, 681-682
irrigation subsidies, 515
Senate elections, 1992, 24, 26
urban aid tax bill, 106
D'Amato, Armand, 923, 944
Danforth, John C. R-Mo.
cable TV regulation, 427, 451, 453
civil rights/job bias, 758, 783-784
expiring tax provisions, 109
foreign trade summary, 168
NASA authorization, 875
news leaks investigations, 947
political advertising, 957-958
Daniels, Anthony E., 882
Daniels Cablevision Inc., 451
Dannemeyer, William E. R-Calif.
AIDS programs, 588-589
budget resolutions, 54, 77, 80
congressional pay, 956
House bank scandal (chart), 934
House leadership, 916
housing authorization, 669
Indian health services, 905
vocational education, 646
Darden, George "Buddy" D-Ga.
ethics committee reorganization, 947
House bank scandal (chart), 934
Darman, Richard G.
biographical profile, 1175
budget action
FY 1990, 41
FY 1991, 53
mini-sequester, 78 (box)
budget process changes, 56
budget "walls," 82 (box)
Bush economic team, 32 (box)
credit reform, 60 (box)
deficit commission, 38
foreign trade summary, 167
Gulf War veterans benefits, 630, 631
OMB regulatory review, 868
Soviet-U.S. trade, 193
superconducting supercollider, 878
unemployment benefits, 724-725
Daschle, Tom D-S.D.
congressional pay, 971
election day holiday, 895
farm bill, 541
Indian programs
health services, 905
investigations, 882
lands management, 907
welfare services, 883
Senate elections, 1992, 26
Senate leadership, 915, 928
unemployment benefits, 726
d'Aubuisson, Roberto, 215, 216
Davies, John, 367
Davis-Bacon Act of 1931, 732
Davis, Mendel J., 952
Davis, Robert W. R-Mich.
House bank scandal, 932
members with overdrafts (chart), 934
Dayton, Ohio, 526
D.C. *See District of Columbia*
Deaf and hearing-impaired persons
Americans with Disabilities Act, 743, 745, 751
close-captioned TV, 428-429, 949
education programs authorization, 660
Pepper scholarships, 653
Dean, Deborah Gore, 663, 676-685
Death penalty. *See Capital punishment*
Death Valley National Monument, 522
De Bartolomeis, Silvio, 677-678, 679 (box)
Declassification. *See Information access and classification*
DeConcini, Dennis D-Ariz.
bankruptcy judges, 798
crime bill, 766
federal pay overhaul, 857
immigration reform, 754
Indian programs investigation, 881-882
Keating Five investigation, 975-988
Lucas nomination, 764
Soviet aid, 265
DeFazio, Peter A. D-Ore.
airline buyouts, 421
farm bill, 540
food labeling, 540
Defense Base Closure and Realignment Commission, 353-354, 393
Defense burden sharing
defense appropriations, 363-365
defense authorization
FY 1990, 345, 349
FY 1991, 358, 362-363
FY 1992, 373
FY 1993, 397, 407
Soviet-U.S. relations, 206
Defense contractors
D'Amato ethics case, 944
defense conversion aid, 402-403
Dickinson ethics case, 925
displaced workers, 358
foreign ownership, 407
Tower nomination, 339-340
Defense conversion aid
action, 1992 (box), 402-403
appropriations, 408, 409
defense authorization, 358, 395, 397, 400, 401
military airports, 419
workers relief, 888-889
Defense Department, U.S.
aircraft and weapons
A-12 bomber cancellation, 379 (box)
B-2 bomber, 398-399
FS-X aircraft deal, 354-355
roles and missions study, 405
appropriations
FY 1990, 350-352
military construction, 352-353
FY 1991, 363-365
military construction, 365-366
FY 1992, 380-382
military construction, 382-383
rescissions, 383 (box), 410 (box)
FY 1993, 407-409
military construction, 409, 411
summary, 13
authorization
FY 1990, 340-350
FY 1991, 355-363
FY 1992, 369-380
FY 1993, 395-407
budget reprogramming (box), 356
coastal zone management, 491
defense conversion aid, 402-403
employees, 888-889
export controls, 176-177, 195
foreign policy
arms sales controls, 238
foreign aid appropriations, 229
Nicaragua policy, 221
post-Yugoslav conflict, 278
Soviet aid, 260, 266
intelligence authorization, 239, 243, 283
intelligence reorganization plans, 284-285 (box)
leadership, 341 (box)
Tower nomination, 338, 339-340
military base closings, 353-354, 393-395
Philippines, 412
personnel
POW/MIA investigation, 289, 290
women in combat, 374-375 (box)
procurement
"revolving door," 861
strategic materials, 368
radio spectrum allocation, 459
research, 403, 900

Defense Intelligence Agency, 284
Defense policy. *See also Arms control; Defense burden sharing; Military personnel; Military posts; Strategic materials*
chronology of action
1989-90, 339-368
1991-92, 369-412
summary, 335-338, 339, 369
Defense Production Act, 187, 198, 368-369, 412, 694
Deficit. *See Budget, U.S.*
de Klerk, F. W., 253-254, 294
de la Garza, E. "Kika" D-Texas
farm bill, 540
fish inspection, 435
FmHA loans, 553
House bank scandal, 933
members with overdrafts (chart), 934
pesticides exports, 540
DeLauro, Rosa D-Conn.
House elections, 1990, 11
Delaware
offshore drilling ban, 491
sports lottery ban, 790
Delaware River Channel, 528
DeLay, Tom R-Texas
Section 89 tax rules, 710
Dellenback, John, 943
Dellums, Ronald V. D-Calif.
covert aid programs, 244
defense authorizations, 357, 373
domestic partners benefits, 897
House bank scandal, 936
members with overdrafts (chart), 934
South Africa policy, 254
de Lugo, Ron D-Virgin Islands
House bank scandal (chart), 934
Puerto Rico plebiscite, 897
Delvalle, Eric, 224
Demery, Thomas T., 676, 679 (box), 681, 685
Democracy Corps, 267
"Democracy Day," 895
Democratic Caucus, House
campaign finance, 961
D.C., territorial voting, 948-949
defense authorization, FY 1991, 356
defense policy summary, 337
leadership, 916, 928, 929
unemployment benefits, 722
Democratic Conference, Senate, 915, 928
Democratic Congressional Campaign Committee, 916, 918, 928
Democratic National Committee
motor voter bill, 871
Democratic Party
National Endowment for Democracy, 247
presidential election, 1992
convention, 18-20, 1232
primaries, 17-18
South Africa policy, 254
Democratic Policy Committee, Senate, 915, 928
Democratic Senatorial Campaign Committee, 915, 928, 944
Democratic Steering Committee, Senate, 915, 928
Denmark
Persian Gulf War, 316 (box)
Dennig Tract, 525
Dentists and dental care
Medicare budget reconciliation, 1989, 571
VA pay, 628, 633-634
veterans services, 634
Department of Housing and Urban Development Reform Act of 1989, 687
Deportation
Chinese deferrals, 253
immigration reform, 753, 755
terrorism, 786
Deposit insurance
banking overhaul, 136-148
budget reconciliation, FY 1991, 59
FDIC premium increase (box), 124-125
pass-through insurance, 129, 145-146
private reinsurance, 148
Derrick, Butler D-S.C.
House leadership, 916, 928
pocket-veto power, 927
Derwinski, Edward J.
Agent Orange, 628 (box), 632
biographical profile, 1174-1175
tobacco, smoking bans, 635
VA leadership, 627 (box)
DES. *See Diethylstibestrol*
Desalination, 903
Developing countries. *See also Foreign aid; Third World debt*
chemical weapons sanctions, 255
Enterprise for the Americas, 179-180
environmental protection, 529
exports promotion, 199-200
Food for Peace, 256-258
multilateral authorizations, 184, 185-186
textile import quotas, 174
war victims aid, 232
Development Coordination Committee, 257
Developmental disabilities.
community living services, 581-582
nursing home regulation, 573
services authorization, 593
DeWine, Mike R-Ohio
House bank scandal, 938
Diamond Fork River, 516
Diaz-Balart, Lincoln, 27
Dickinson, Bill R-Ala.
ethics case, 925
export controls, 176
Diesel fuel taxes, 95, 112
Diet. *See Food and nutrition*
"Dietary Guidelines for Americans," 593
Diethylstibestrol (DES), 607
Digital audio technology, 459
Dingell, John D. D-Mich.
Americans with Disabilities Act, 745
auto fuel efficiency, 484
Baby Bells restrictions, 461
banking overhaul, 137, 139-140, 142
cable TV regulation, 453, 454
carjacking penalties, 790
Clean Air Act, 468, 473-480
drug testing, 448
energy bill, 504
energy policy summary, 470
fairness doctrine, 430
fish inspection, 435
health reform, 597
House bank scandal (chart), 934
natural gas decontrol, 485
Persian Gulf War, 310
political advertising, 957
radio spectrum allocation, 430
railroad safety, 447
RICO limits, 791
tourism promotion, 462
Dinkins, David N., 7
DiPrete, Edward D., 11
Direct-broadcast satellite service, 456
Disabled persons. *See also Blind persons; Deaf and hearing-impaired persons; Developmental disabilities; Disabled veterans*
Americans with Disabilities Act, 743-752
disabilities prevention research, 595, 610
early intervention for children, 622
educational programs
authorization, 647-648, 659
math, science education, 651
vocational education, 645, 647
employment
human services reconciliation, 616
Rehabilitation Act authorization, 607
trial period with Social Security, 62
health insurance continuation, 572
housing authorization, 675
mixed housing, 695-698
Medicare buy-in, 571, 579
Oregon health plan, 597 (box)
Supplementary Security Income, 615, 616
Supreme Court decisions, 842
transit programs, 443
women with AIDS, 623
Disabled veterans
benefits limits for alcohol, drug abuse, 627
budget reconciliation, 626
COLA increases, 631
dependents' benefits, 632
hiring preference, 628, 629
omnibus veterans bill, 625
retirement pay, 629
services, 634
vocational rehabilitation, 633
Disaster relief
appropriations, 53, 79, 84, 409
eased bank regulation, 161
emergency employment, 713
farm aid, 537, 539, 544, 548-549, 557
fishermen, 409
flood insurance, 694
forestry, 546
insurance proceeds reinvestment, 111
sub-Saharan Africa, 276
urban aid, 699
Discrimination in employment. *See also Affirmative action*
age-based discrimination, 714-717
Americans with Disabilities Act, 743-752
cable TV regulation, 457
civil rights bill, 757-760, 780-785
federal employee complaints, 888
Section 89 benefit tax rules, 705, 708-710
Supreme Court decisions, 757-758, 842-843
faculty tenure, 650 (box)
patronage jobs, 861 (box)
summary, 9, 806
veterans, 636-637
Discrimination in housing
neighborhood accountability, 672
redlining, 128
Supreme Court decisions, 842
District courts. *See Federal courts*
District of Columbia
abortion funding, 594, 600
appropriations, 895-896
assault weapons liability, 896
budget autonomy, 896
congressional parking tickets, 923, 942
domestic partners benefits, 896-897
drug-crime death penalty, 787
federal payment formula, 896
House voting privileges, 948-949
Metro aid, 873
police hirings, 873
statehood, shadow delegation, 872-873, 896
Diversity jurisdiction, 815
Divorce. *See Marriage and divorce*
Dixon, Alan J. D-Ill.
Keating Five investigation, 987
Senate leadership, 915, 928
Dixon, Julian C. D-Calif.
D.C. appropriations, 895-896
House leadership, 929
Dixon, Sharon Pratt. *See Kelly, Sharon Pratt*
DNA testing, 798
Dodd, Christopher J. D-Conn.
budget resolution, FY 1993, 80
campaign finance, 955
congressional pay, 967-968, 970
Cuba embargo, 295
export controls, 176
federal employee honoraria, 886
foreign aid authorization, 268
housing authorization, 666-667, 670
investment advisers regulation, 159
parental leave, 730-731
partnership roll-ups, 159
securities market reforms, 130
Senate elections, 1992, 26
Dole, Bob R-Kan.
defense, foreign, and trade issues
Armenian genocide resolution, 259-260
China trade status, 191, 192
Chinese student visas, 756
foreign aid appropriations, 234
Iran-contra pardons, 287
Persian Gulf War, 308
Soviet credit guarantees, 555
Tower nomination, 339-340
domestic issues
budget reconciliation, FY 1991, 58
child care, 612
civil rights/job bias, 759, 784
Clean Air Act, 477
coal miners' health fund, 735 (box)
crime bills, 766, 787, 789
disaster relief, 557
flag desecration, 761-762
Hatch Act revision, 860
judicial appointments, 776 (box)
independent counsel law, 795
minimum wage, 706, 707
motor voter bill, 894
Pepper scholarships, 646
public broadcasting, 458
student loan defaults, 650
Supreme Court summary, 802
unemployment benefits, 722-725, 728
urban aid tax bill, 105
whistleblowers protection, 863
presidential election, 1992, 21
Senate leadership
campaign finance, 954-955, 961
congressional pay, 965, 971
election, 1992, 26
House bank scandal, 931
news leaks investigations, 946
summary, 7 (chart), 915, 928
Dole, Elizabeth H.
biographical profile, 1173
Bush term summary, 993
Labor Department leadership, 707 (box)
minimum wage, 705, 707, 708
Dolphins, 433-434, 528
Domenici, Pete V. R-N.M.
budget resolution
FY 1990, 42-43
FY 1993, 81
campaign finance, 955
Hatch Act revision, 860, 861
homeless aid, 693
middle-class tax cut, 102
Section 89 tax rules, 710
Senate leadership, 928

Domestic violence
expert witnesses for battered women, 797
prevention, 622
Indian programs, 883
Domestic Volunteer Service Act of 1973, 619
Dominica
Caribbean Basin Initiative, 180
Dominican Republic
Caribbean Basin Initiative, 180
Donnelly, Brian D-Mass.
catastrophic medical costs insurance, 565-566
House bank scandal (chart), 934
Dorgan, Byron L. D-N.D.
House bank scandal, 938
members with overdrafts (chart), 934
Senate elections, 1992, 26
urban aid tax bill, 104
dos Santos, José Eduardo, 244
Double jeopardy, 818-819, 925
Douglas, Chuck R-N.H.
bank fraud penalties, 133
Dowd, John M., 980, 982, 984
Downey, Thomas J. D-N.Y.
child welfare overhaul, 621
farm bill, 540
House bank scandal, 938
members with overdrafts (chart), 934
House elections, 1992, 26
Soviet-U.S. trade, 171
unemployment benefits, 717, 721, 726-727
Drake, David, 925
Drexel Burnham Lambert, 918, 923
DRG Funding Corp., 681, 683
Drinking. *See Alcohol abuse and alcoholism*
Drinking water
desalination, 903
Indian health services, 906
lead-poisoning prevention, 607
Drivers' licenses
agricultural machinery, 424
drug offense suspensions, 444
forgery-proof license, 755
motor voter bill, 871, 893
Dropouts and dropout prevention
authorization, 652, 659
Bush education initiative, 644
high-tech training, 892
student loan defaults, 649
Taft Institute, 652
vocational education, 646
Drought
agriculture disaster relief, 537, 548-549
desalination, 903
irrigation subsidies, 513-514
livestock sale taxes, 110
Drug abuse. *See also Employee drug tests*
ADAMHA authorization, 604-605
addicted mothers treatment, 358
AIDS prevention, 589, 604
impaired driving, 443
license suspensions, 444
Indian health services, 883, 905, 906
prevention, treatment
authorization, 619, 789
drug legislation, 769-770
religious practices, 805
statistical decline, 789
student aid ban, 654
veterans benefits limits, 627
workplace prohibitions
Americans with Disabilities Act, 743-752
civil rights/job bias, 758
oil-spill liability, 491
Drug Enforcement Administration, 768, 770
Drug-Free Schools and Communities Act of 1986, 768, 769
Drug-Free Work Place Act of 1988, 749
Drug trafficking
asset forfeiture, 769
drug-related crime
D.C. death penalty, 787
housing issues, 673, 674
enforcement
appropriations, 52-53
crime bill, 766, 768
drug legislation, 769-770
highway truck stops, rest areas, 424
House Post Office scandal, 939
interdiction
crime bill, 788
defense appropriations, FY 1990, 352
defense authorization, 1990, 344, 350
international narcotics control
Andean nations, 232-233, 238, 255-256, 296, 769
foreign aid appropriations, 233, 238
money laundering, 134, 156
Panama bank secrecy, 227
Noriega arrest, 223
steroids, 768
Drugs and pharmaceutical industry
biodiversity treaty, 997
FDA consolidation, 586
FDA user fees, 603
generic drug regulation, 606
licensing regulation, 608
Medicaid provisions, 580-581
Medicaid, VA discounts, 605-606
Medicare coverage, 576
opium imports, 788
organ transplant patients, 590
orphan drugs
marketing rules, 585, 603-604
tax credit, 94
Pacific yew harvest, 527
patent extensions, 793
vaccine injury compensation, 572, 587
women, minorities in clinical trials, 591
Drunk driving
boat operators, 449
highway authorization, 443
DSP satellites, 360
Dual-use critical technologies, 403
Duarte, José Napoleón, 215, 219
Due process
Supreme Court decisions, 815
Dukakis, Michael S., 225
Duke, David, 20, 760, 780-781
Dunbar, Lawrence, 526
Duncan, John J., 952
Dunne, John R., 764
Durbin, Richard J. D-Ill.
abortion, 599
airline smoking ban, 420
House bank scandal (chart), 934
superconducting supercollider, 901
veterans' health care, 635
Durenberger, Dave R-Minn.
campaign finance, 953
catastrophic medical costs insurance, 566
civil rights/job bias, 758
ethics case, 913, 921-923, 978
higher education aid, 654
highway authorization, 439
parental leave, 730-731
vocational education, 646
Dwight D. Eisenhower Mathematics and Science Education Act, 651
Dymally, Mervyn M. D-Calif.
census study, 895
Dyson, Roy D-Md.
ethics case, 926
House elections, 1990, 11

E

E-2 aircraft, 347
Eagleburger, Lawrence S.
biographical profile, 1174
Bush term summary, 997
foreign aid appropriations, 270
State Department leadership, 207 (box)
Early childhood development grants, 673
Early, Joseph D. D-Mass.
House bank scandal, 932, 933, 938
members with overdrafts (chart), 934
House elections, 1992, 26
Earmarks and pork-barrel politics
Brooklyn courthouse, 438 (box)
defense appropriations, 364, 407
federal judgeships, 774
foreign aid
appropriations, 229, 230, 276
authorization, 227
highway authorization, 440
HUD reforms, 685, 687
national parks projects, 526
superconducting supercollider, 878
veterans medical projects, 636
Earned-income tax credit
budget reconciliation, FY 1991, 66
child care, 611-613
deficit reduction, FY 1990, 95
middle-class tax bill, 103
minimum wage, 706, 707
Persian Gulf War veterans benefits, 630
Earth Charter, 529
Earth Day 90, 467
Earth Observing System, 876, 898,899
Earth Summit. *See United Nations Conference on Environment and Development*
Earthquakes
bridge, highway improvements, 442
disaster relief, 53, 549-550
research, preparedness, 880-881
East Germany. *See also Germany*
communism downfall, 324, 328, 336
U.S. duty rates, 1[illegible]2
East Mojave Desert, 522
East Timor, 274
Eastern Airlines, 421, 705, 712-713
Eastern Europe. *See also specific countries*
communism downfall, 323-324
development bank authorization, 185-186
Poland, Hungary aid, 212
Soviet-U.S. relations, 206-207
troop reduction proposals, 387 (box)
U.S. aid, 186
appropriations, 233-237, 274, 276
SEED program, 267
U.S. trade, 169, 193-194
export controls, 195
nuclear cooperation, 293
EC. *See European Community*
ECHO. *See Elder cottage housing opportunity*
Eckart, Dennis E. D-Ohio
Amtrak authorization, 424
federal facilities cleanup, 498
SEC/CFTC merger plan, 550
superconducting supercollider, 878, 901
Economic Adjustment, Office of, 403
Economic Analysis, Bureau of, 166, 177-179
Economic conditions. *See also Business and industry; Employment and unemployment; Foreign trade and business*
Bush term summary, 995
GDP v. GNP (box), 36
presidential election, 1992, 17, 20
summary, 4, 31-36, 703
Economic development. *See also Community development; Developing countries; Enterprise zones; Rural development*
barrier islands, 497
coastal zone management, 491
wilderness areas, 496
Economic Development Administration, 403
Economic Support Fund, 229, 236, 273, 274, 276
Economically Dislocated Workers Assistance Act, 714
Ecorse Creek, Mich., 493 (box)
Ecuador
Andean import duties, 296-297
Education. *See also Colleges and universities; Cultural exchange programs; Elementary and secondary education; Literacy programs; Preschool education; Student aid; Veterans education programs; Vocational education*
Bush term summary, 997
chronology of action
1989-90, 643-653
1991-92, 653-660
environmental education, 495
Education Department, U.S.
adult literacy, 659
drug legislation, 769-770
higher education aid, 653-657
leadership (box), 645
math, science education, 651
research authorization, 660
school reform, 657-658
student loan defaults, 649-650
Education Excellence Act of 1989, 997
Education of the Handicapped Act of 1975, 647
Educational Opportunity Centers, 655
Educational Research and Improvement, Office of, 660
Edwards, Don D-Calif.
Americans with Disabilities Act, 746
Civil Rights Commission, 763, 785
House bank scandal (chart), 934
Madison amendment, 972
Nixon impeachment, 777
TV violence, 428
Edwards, Mickey R-Okla.
foreign aid appropriations, 236
House bank scandal, 932, 933
members with overdrafts (chart), 934
House leadership, 7 (chart), 916, 929
Egypt
Persian Gulf War, 302, 313-314, 316 (box)
U.S. aid
appropriations, 228, 231, 234-236, 271, 276
debt relief, 74
Eicher, Thomas J., 938
Eighth Amendment, 805
Eisenhower math, science education program, 651
El Paso County Water Improvement District, 518
El Salvador
Caribbean Basin Initiative, 180
human rights, 74
immigration reform, 752, 754, 755
Nicaragua policy, 219, 222

refugee asylum, 756
U.S. aid
action, 1989-90, 214-219
appropriations, 228, 229, 231, 234-237, 270, 271, 276
authorization, 268
budget action, 74
summary (box), 216
Elder cottage housing opportunity (ECHO) units, 675
Elderly persons. *See also Medicare; Pensions; Senior citizens' interest groups; Social Security*
deceptive mail curbs, 870
health
aging research, 592
catastrophic medical costs insurance, 565-567
home health care, 581, 592
Medigap insurance regulation, 582-585
housing authorization, 675
mixed housing, 695-698
job training, 730
presidential election, 1992, 22
transit programs, 443
welfare and social services
food stamps, 618
Older Americans Act, 620-621
Election law
Supreme Court decisions, 829-830
Elections. *See also Congressional elections; Presidential elections*
political advertising, 957-958
Electric Boat, 410
Electric cars
alternative fuels, 487 (box)
energy bill, 109, 506
research, development, 904
Electric power. *See also Hydroelectric power; Nuclear power plants*
acid rain reduction, 473-483
deadlines, 477 (box)
alternative power, 486
appliance efficiency standards, 507
biomass fuels, 109
energy bill, 500, 503-505, 509-510
fuel cells, 511
Indian project, 530
Electromagnetic fields, 511
Electronic publishing, 432
Elementary and secondary education. *See also Dropouts and dropout prevention; Literacy programs; Math education; Science education; Schools*
Bush education initiative, 643-644
children's TV, 429
civics, public service, 859 (box)
compensatory education aid, 652
disabled students, 647-648
drug-free schools, 768, 769-770
federal role summary, 641-642
high-tech training, 892
longer school year, 659
Native American languages, 907-908
readiness videos, 659-660
research, 660
rural telecommunications, 461
school choice, 657-658
school reform, 657-658
teacher training, 402, 653, 656
vocational education, 646
Elephant Butte Irrigation District, 518
11th Amendment, 647, 751, 773, 792
Ellacuria, Ignacio, 217
Emergency and rescue work
earthquake preparedness, 880
hazardous materials transport, 423
oil-spill response, 490-491
telemarketing controls, 432, 460
Emergency Food Assistance Program, 618, 619
Emergency Low Income Housing Preservation Act of 1989, 61
Emergency medical care
patient dumping ban, 572, 575
trauma services, 590
triage demonstration, 572
Emergency Shelter Grants, 675
Emergency Unemployment Compensation Act of 1991, 193
Emerson, Bill R-Mo.
House bank scandal (chart), 935
Employee Benefit Research Institute, 719
Employee drug tests
CIA employees, 242, 281
Coast Guard employees, 449
merchant seamen, 450
NASA employees, 898
Pentagon employees, 373
State Department employees, 291
Supreme Court decisions, 845
transportation workers, 425, 439, 448, 748, 752, 770
Employee Retirement Income Security Act (ERISA) of 1974, 47, 720, 737-738, 897
Employee stock ownership plans, 48-49, 92, 111
Employment and unemployment. *See also Employment and working conditions; Job training programs; Labor unions and interests; Unemployment insurance; Vocational education*
dislocated workers
Clean Air Act compliance, 478-479, 482, 483
defense conversion aid, 358, 402-403, 888-889
summary, 705
trade adjustment aid, 190
electoral effects, 31
immigration reform, 754, 757
jobs as legislative issue
Clean Air Act, 474
defense bills, 372, 395
Seawolf submarine, 410
endangered species, 521, 721
northern spotted owl, 494-495, 520-521
highway authorization, 437, 439, 440
NAFTA, 189
minimum wage, 705
summary, 703
summer youth jobs, 722 (box)
targeted jobs tax credit, 94
unemployment statistics, 722, 724, 725
urban aid, 700
welfare reform, 623
Employment and working conditions. *See also Congressional employees and staff; Discrimination in employment; Employee drug tests; Federal employees; Health insurance; Military pay and benefits; Occupational health and safety; Pensions; Whistleblowers and whistleblower protections*
adult literacy, 658, 659
child labor, 733
FAA civil fees, 445-446
flight attendants' workday, 446
housing trust funds, 717
legal services, 47, 68-69, 94
military reservists protections, 634
minimum wage, 705-708
parental leave, 710-712, 730-732
Section 89 tax provisions, 45-46, 703, 705, 708-710
Social Security wage base, 91, 92 (box)
striker replacements, 733-734
transportation benefits, 108
tuition aid, 47, 68, 94
workers' rights
Caribbean Basin Initiative, 182
End-stage renal disease, 570, 577
Endangered species
exotic birds, 522
northern spotted owl, 494-495, 520-521
preservation act authorization, 521
salmon, trout, 522
striped bass protection, 521-522
unemployment benefits, 721
Endangered Species Act of 1973, 494-495, 520-521
Endangered Species Committee, 520-521
Endara, Guillermo, 223
Energy conservation and efficiency
energy bill, 500-511
energy policy summary, 471
federal facilities, 508, 890
promotion programs, 486
utility rebates, 108
Energy Department, U.S.
advanced reactors, 508
alternative fuels, 487 (box)
defense programs
appropriations, 365
authorizations, 341, 345, 395
energy bill, 500
energy conservation, 486
global warming, 505
high-tech labs, 532
hydrogen fuel research, 486-487
leadership, 475 (box)
nuclear waste
federal facilities cleanup, 498, 509, 525
future needs report, 509
uranium enrichment, 509
WIPP, 524
Yucca Mountain dump, 513
Poland, Hungary aid, 213
renewable energy, 507
research, 510-511
Strategic Petroleum Reserve, 488
superconducting supercollider, 878-879
uranium enrichment, 489
user fee study, 65
Energy Policy Act of 1992, 108-110, 469-472, 500-512
Energy Policy and Conservation Act of 1975, 486
Energy resources. *See Alternative fuels and vehicles; Coal; Electric power; Energy conservation and efficiency; Nuclear energy; Oil and natural gas; Renewable energy*
chronology of action
1989-90, 473-500
1991-92, 500-532
research, 500, 503, 510-511
summary, 467-472
Energy taxes. *See also Fuel taxes; Gasoline taxes*
business energy tax credits, 94, 96
energy bill tax provisions, 108-109, 500
Engel, Eliot L. D-N.Y.
House bank scandal (chart), 934
Engineering education, 650-651
English, Glenn D-Okla.
House bank scandal (chart), 935
English language
immigration reform, 753, 754
limited proficiency
closed-captioned TV, 429
vocational education, 647
Enhanced Structural Adjustment Facility, 185
Enterprise for the Americas, 179-180, 194-195, 200, 274, 276
Enterprise zones
second mortgages, 697
summary, 15
urban aid tax bill, 103-106, 699
Entertainers
immigration law, 794
Entrapment, 819
Environmental Education Foundation, 495
Environmental Education, Office of, 495
Environmental interest groups
Arctic wildlife refuge, 499, 512
barrier islands, 497
Clean Air Act, 478-480
endangered species, 521
northern spotted owl, 494-495, 520
energy bill, 502-504
fuel-efficiency mandates, 501
Grand Canyon erosion, 496
oil-spill liability, 490
pesticide regulation, 522-523
Tongass forest protection, 492
Environmental protection. *See also Air pollution; Endangered species; Energy conservation and efficiency; Global climate change; Hazardous substances; Soil conservation; U.N. Conference on Environment and Development; Water resources; Wetlands preservation; Wilderness areas; Wildlife*
BLM authorization, 520
budget authority, outlays (chart), 469
chronology of action
1989-90, 473-500
1991-92, 500-532
educational foundations, 495, 527
Enterprise for the Americas, 179
farm bill, 537-538, 539, 540, 542
foreign aid appropriations, 277
NAFTA, 187-190
oil-spill liability, 490-491
pipeline safety, 531-532
special areas
Antarctica, 489, 529-530
California desert, 522
coastal areas, 63-64, 491
Florida Keys, 497
Grand Canyon, 496, 513-514, 516
Indian reservations, 884, 906
old-growth forest, 520
Poland, Hungary aid, 211, 213
tall-grass prairie, 527
Yellowstone Park, 526
summary, 467-472
Supreme Court decisions, 830-831
taxes, 68
Environmental Protection Agency (EPA)
alternative fuels, 487 (box)
beach pollution, 492, 531
budget reconciliation, FY 1991, 64, 65
Cabinet status, 498-499, 529
Clean Air Act, 473-483
environmental education, 495
federal RCRA compliance, 497, 525
food
pesticide residues, 498
transportation safety, 423-424
Great Lakes cleanup, 492
indoor air pollution, 531
lead-poisoning prevention, 530, 606-607, 697-698
leadership, 475 (box)
nuclear waste
WIPP, 524

Yucca Mountain dump, 505, 509, 513
ocean dumping, 531
pesticide regulation, 523
Poland, Hungary aid, 213
water quality, 529
Environmental Statistics, Bureau of, 498, 529
Environmental summit. *See United Nations Conference on Environment and Development*
EPO. *See Erythropoietin*
Equal Access Act of 1984, 647 (box)
Equal Employment Opportunity Commission (EEOC)
age discrimination, 715-716
civil rights/job bias, 781
faculty tenure, 650 (box)
federal employee complaints, 888
whistleblowers protection, 863
Erdreich, Ben D-Ala.
flood insurance, 699
House elections, 1992, 26
Ergonomic hazards, 734
ERISA. *See Employee Retirement Income Security Act*
Erythropoietin (EPO), 570, 577
Eskimos, 512
Espionage
Moscow, Washington embassies, 248, 263 (box)
reconnaissance overflights treaty, 390, 392
State Department authorization, 248, 249
Espy, Mike D-Miss.
House bank scandal (chart), 934
Estate taxes, 69, 107, 111
Estonia. *See Baltic republics*
Ethanol
alternative fuels, 487 (box)
Caribbean imports, 186
Caribbean Basin Initiative, 180, 182-183
Clean Air Act, 473
tax breaks for gas blends, 109
Ethics. *See Congressional ethics; Ethics in government; Medical ethics*
Ethics committee, House. *See Standards of Official Conduct Committee*
Ethics Committee, Senate
membership changes, 947
Ethics in government. *See also Congressional ethics; Waste, fraud and abuse in government programs*
federal employee honoraria, 858, 886
revolving door, 861, 887
Tower nomination, 339-340
Ethics in Government Act of 1978, 207 (box), 686 (box), 937 (box), 943
Ethics Reform Act of 1989, 633, 858, 886
Ethnic groups. *See Minorities; specific groups*
Etpison, Ngiratkel, 259
Europe. *See also Conventional forces in Europe (CFE) treaty; Eastern Europe; European Community; North Atlantic Treaty Organization (NATO); specific countries*
immigration reform, 752, 753
troop reduction proposals, 387 (box)
U.S. troops
appropriations, 74, 351
authorizations, 349, 357, 362, 373, 376, 397, 401, 407
Soviet-U.S. relations, 208
European Bank for Reconstruction and Development
appropriations, 236, 237, 275
authorization, 185-186
European Community (EC)
agricultural subsidies, 166-167, 554-555
environmental summit, 529
high-tech programs, 879
joint ventures, 891
Persian Gulf War, 308
South Africa policy, 253, 294
European Space Agency, 877, 900
Evangelical Christians, 613, 756
Evans, Daniel J., 915
Evans, Lane D-Ill.
Agent Orange controversy, 628 (box), 633
House bank scandal (chart), 935
veterans' COLA increase, 631
Evans, Linda S., 922 (box)
Evidence
Supreme Court decisions, 815, 819-820
Ewing, Thomas W. R-Ill.
House elections, 1991, 14
Excise taxes
budget reconciliation
FY 1990, 49
FY 1991, 67, 95-96
cigarettes, 591
miscellaneous tax bills, 110, 111
pension reversions, 719-720
percentage of GDP, 90 (chart)
superfund, 186
telephone service, 611
urban aid tax bill, 107
Exclusionary rule, 764, 766, 786-789
Executive, Legislative and Judicial Salaries, Commission on, 965, 967
Exon, Jim D-Neb.
budget resolution, FY 1993, 81
campaign finance, 961
defense authorization, 376
foreign investment data, 177-178
highway authorization, 439
Expedited rescissions, 85-86
Export Administration Act of 1979, 175-177, 195-196, 293
Export controls
action
1989-90, 175-177
1992, 195-196
chemical weapons, 175-176
China, 252
pesticides, 540, 541, 542
timber, 181
Export Enhancement Program, 545, 551, 554-555
Export-Import Bank
authorization, 184, 199
China sanctions, 252
Eastern Europe, 237
foreign aid appropriations, 228, 232, 269-271
Latin American debt relief, 195
military sales financing, 176-177, 670
Poland, Hungary aid, 213, 214
Poland-U.S. trade agreement, 172
Soviet-U.S. trade, 170, 171, 193, 330
tied aid, 184, 185, 186
Exports. *See Foreign trade and business*
Extraterrestrial life, 898, 899
***Exxon Valdez* oil spill**, 425, 467, 490, 499

F

F-14 fighter planes
appropriations, 350-352, 364, 382, 408, 409
cancellation battle, 348
defense authorization
FY 1990, 340, 341, 342, 344, 347
FY 1991, 361, 362
FY 1992, 372, 373, 378
F-15 fighter planes
appropriations, 350-352, 364, 380, 382
defense authorization
FY 1990, 341, 344, 347
FY 1991, 361
Saudi sales, 294
F-16 fighter planes
appropriations, 352, 364, 382, 409
authorization
FY 1990, 344, 347
FY 1991, 362
FY 1992, 372, 374, 378
FY 1993, 396, 400, 401, 405
FS-X aircraft deal, 354-355
F-22 fighter planes. *See also Advanced tactical fighter planes*
appropriations, 382, 407, 409
authorization, 372, 378, 400, 401, 405
F-117 Nighthawk aircraft
appropriations, 381
authorization, 374, 376, 378
B-2 bomber, 399
Persian Gulf War success, 337
F/A-18 aircraft
A-12 cancellation, 379 (box)
appropriations, 352, 364, 382, 409
authorization
FY 1990, 344, 347
FY 1991, 357, 358, 361-362
FY 1992, 378
FY 1993, 395, 400, 401, 405
FAA. *See Federal Aviation Administration*
Fair Credit Reporting Act of 1970, 157
Fair Employment Office, Senate, 785
Fair housing. *See Discrimination in housing*
Fair Labor Standards Act of 1938, 61, 705, 706
Fair Trade in Financial Services Act, 142, 187, 198, 412
Fair trial, 828
Fairchild, Drew, 777
Fairchild, Lauch, 24
Fairchild, Wiley, 777
Fairness doctrine, 46, 430
Faleomavaega, Eni F. H. D-Am. Samoa
House bank scandal (chart), 934
Family and Medical Leave Act, 732
Family Educational Rights and Privacy Act, 648
Family Investment Centers, 673
Family issues. *See also Birth control; Children; Domestic violence; Marriage and divorce; Parental rights and issues*
domestic partners benefits, 896-897
immigration reform, 752-755
parental leave, 710-712, 730-732
public housing programs, 673
Supreme Court decisions, 831
Family Medical Leave Coalition, 711
Family Preservation Act, 107
Family Support Act of 1988, 615-616, 623
Family violence. *See Domestic violence*
Fannie Mae. *See Federal National Mortgage Association*
Fannin, Paul, 517
Farabundo Marti Front for National Liberation (FMLN), 215, 218-219
Farm Credit Administration, 547, 556
Farm Credit System
bailout debt retirement, 548, 554
government-sponsored enterprises, 154
rural development, 548
Farmer Mac. *See Federal Agricultural Mortgage Corporation*
Farmer-Owned Reserve, 544
Farmers Home Administration (FmHA)
Agriculture Department streamlining, 556 (box)
farm bill, 539, 546-547
housing authorization, 674
HUD reforms, 689
new-farmer loans, 553-554
rural development, 548
Farming. *See Agriculture and farming*
Fascell, Dante F. D-Fla.
barrier islands, 497
environmental summit, 528
Florida Keys, 497
Foreign Affairs Committee clout, 268 (box)
foreign aid authorization, 227-228
House bank scandal (chart), 935
Persian Gulf War, 317
State Department authorization, 247
Fauntroy, Walter E. D-D.C.
D.C. statehood, 872
ethics case, 926
House bank scandal (chart), 934
Third World debt, 184
Fawell, Harris W. R-Ill.
ERISA reforms, 738
Fazio, Vic D-Calif.
abortion, 594
congressional pay, 966
franking privilege, 968, 969-970
House bank scandal, 933
House elections, 1992, 27
House leadership, 928
FBI. *See Federal Bureau of Investigation*
FCC. *See Federal Communications Commission*
FDA. *See Food and Drug Administration*
FDIC. *See Federal Deposit Insurance Corporation*
Federal Agricultural Mortgage Corporation (Farmer Mac), 547, 556
Federal Aviation Administration (FAA)
aging aircraft, 420, 446
airport noise abatement, 419
authorization, 422, 446-447
aviation package, 417
aviation safety guidelines, 420
aviation security, 420, 421
aviation worker fines, 445-446
blind passengers, 422
employees drug testing, 448
maps, 447
radio spectrum allocation, 459
Federal buildings
earthquake hazards, 881
energy efficiency standards, 507
fire safety, 904
Federal Bureau of Investigation (FBI)
animal research labs, 881
carjacking penalties, 790
congressional ethics cases, 943, 945
House bank scandal, 937-939
Indian gambling, 882
Indian law enforcement, 883-884
money laundering, 156
news leaks investigations, 946-947
Federal Communications Commission (FCC)
Americans with Disabilities Act, 751
authorization, 429-430, 458-459
Baby Bells restrictions, 462
cable TV regulation, 427-428, 451-457
children's TV advertising, 429
fairness doctrine, 430
minority preference, 431 (box)
900-number regulation, 460

political advertising, 957
radio spectrum allocation, 430-431, 459
telemarketing controls, 432, 459-460
telephone rates, 431-432
user fees, 47, 458-459
Federal contractors. *See also Defense contractors*
Davis-Bacon Act revision, 732
high-tech small business, 464
Indian preference, 884
INSLAW case, 792 (box)
Federal courts. *See also Supreme Court*
administrative improvements, 798
cases and decisions
abortion counseling ban, 599
Baby Bells restrictions, 432, 461
Brooklyn courthouse, 438 (box)
congressional pay, 972-973
congressional term limits, 963
copyright, 773
D.C., territorial House voting, 949
ERISA reforms, 738
federal employee honoraria, 858, 886
flag desecration, 762
Flake trial, 945
franking privilege, 973
Garcia extortion case, 925
House bank scandal, 937
HUD scandal, 684
HUD subsidy calculations, 688
North conviction, 240-241 (box)
northern spotted owl, 495, 520-521
nuclear waste, 524
obscenity in art, 867
pesticide residue in food, 522
Rose ethics case, 946
Speech or Debate Clause, 945
judges
bankruptcy judges, 798
Bush appointments, 776 (box)
Carnes nomination, 796-797
impeachments, 775-777
new judgeships, 774
nominating process, 795-796
Ryskamp nomination, 796
Thomas nomination, 777-778
jurisdiction
habeas corpus appeals, 766-767, 787
naturalization process, 794
vaccine injury compensation, 572
legislative intent, 784
procedures
suit consolidation, 779, 798
Supreme Court decisions, 813-817
Federal Courts Study Committee, 774, 798
Federal Crop Insurance Corporation, 549 (box)
Federal debt. *See Budget, U.S.*
Federal Deposit Insurance Corporation (FDIC)
banking overhaul, 136-148
summary, 115-116
budget reconciliation, FY 1991, 59, 73
leadership, 114
premium increase (box), 124-125
savings and loan bailout, 117, 122-128
refinancing, 151
Federal Election Campaign Act, 954 (box), 960
Federal Election Commission (FEC)
campaign finance, 951, 954 (box), 956 (box), 960
federal employee honoraria, 886
Federal Emergency Management Agency
crime insurance, 694
earthquake preparedness, 880
Federal employees
age discrimination, 716
census workers, 182
displaced defense workers, 889
drug testing
CIA, 242, 281
Coast Guard, 449
Defense Department, 373
NASA, 898
State Department, 291
election day holiday, 895
Hatch Act revision, 859-861, 886-887
job bias complaints, 888
pay and benefits
Defense, Energy scientists, 349
FDA salaries, 586
graduate recruiting, 858
Gulf War compensation, 889
honoraria, 633, 858, 886, 967
lump-sum pension payments, 858-859
overtime, 858
parental leave, 712
pay overhaul, 857-858, 967
pensions, 858
Postal Service off-budget plan, 870
Volcker Commission (box), 859
performance standards, 887-888
"revolving door," 349, 861-862, 887
Supreme Court decisions, 832
veterans preference, 629
waste-buster awards, 888
whistleblowers protection, 862-864
Federal Employees Health Benefits Program, 859
Federal Energy Regulatory Commission (FERC)
electric utilities, 507, 509-510
natural gas decontrol, 485
Federal Executive Institute Alumni Association, 887
Federal Express, 107
Federal Financial Management, Office of, 862
Federal Financing Bank
FDIC borrowing, 59, 142-143
RTC borrowing, 151, 152
Federal government (general). *See also Budget, U.S.; Federal employees; Federal-state relations; specific agency or program*
acid-free paper, 869
administrative law judges, 775
alternative-fuel vehicles, 478, 500, 506
Columbus Day shutdown, 1990, 55, 74
credit reform, 60 (box), 72-73
debt collection, 768, 779
energy efficiency, 890, 502, 508
financial centralization, 862
GSA overhaul, 889-890
hazardous waste cleanup, 497-498, 515
paperwork reduction, 890
procurement rules, 890
radio spectrum allocation, 430
regulatory negotiation, 864-865
Federal Highway Administration, 444
Federal Home Loan Bank System
consumer, housing issues, 128
government-sponsored enterprises, 154, 155
Keating Five investigation, 976, 979-984
leadership, 114
savings and loan bailout, 117-130
Federal Home Loan Mortgage Corporation (Freddie Mac)
flood insurance, 698-699
oversight, 129-130, 154-156
Federal Housing Administration (FHA)
comptroller, 688
housing authorization, 665-672
HUD reforms, 685, 688
insurance fund, 690-692
mortgage limit, premiums, 59-61, 689-690, 694-698
Federal Housing Finance Board, 126, 128, 154
Federal Insecticide, Fungicide and Rodenticide Act (FIFRA), 522-523
Federal lands. *See also Forests and national forests; National parks*
BLM authorization, 500, 520
grazing fees, 518-519
highway authorization, 442
hydroelectric power, 507
mining law overhaul, 519-520
mining restrictions, 531
oil, gas leases, 511, 518
oil shale claims, 499
Pacific yew harvest, 527
timber exports, 181, 183-184
Federal Maritime Commission
authorization, 426, 450
tariff data base user fees, 448
Federal National Mortgage Association (Fannie Mae)
executive compensation, 155
flood insurance, 698-699
oversight, 129-130, 154-156
Federal Railroad Administration, 447
Federal Railroad Safety Act of 1970, 65
Federal Reserve System
bank fees, 128
banking overhaul, 138, 144-148
Bush economic team, 32-33 (box)
economic policy summary, 34
government securities market regulation, 158
money laundering, 134
securities market reforms, 131-132
stock index futures regulation, 551, 552
Federal Robert T. Stafford Student Loan Program, 656
Federal Savings and Loan Insurance Corporation (FSLIC)
Keating Five investigation, 976-981
savings and loan bailout, 117, 119, 124-126
Federal-state relations
consistency provision
coastal zone protection, 63-64, 491
mortgage prepayments, 674
constitutional amendment, 972
fund transfers, 865, 890
motor voter bill, 871, 893-894
oil-spill liability, 490
National Guard exercises, 361 (box)
sovereign immunity concept, 498, 525, 792
water rights, 526
Federal Supplemental Educational Opportunity Grants, 656
Federal Tort Claims Act, 609, 780, 798
Federal Trade Commission (FTC)
credit reporting safeguards, 157
energy efficiency labeling, 507-508
telemarketing controls, 432, 460
Federal Transit Administration, 443
Federal Water Pollution Control Act of 1972, 64, 492, 529
Federated States of Micronesia
PCB cleanup, 512
Federation for American Immigration Reform, 752
Feighan, Edward F. D-Ohio
credit reporting safeguards, 158
House bank scandal, 932
members with overdrafts (chart), 934
House Post Office scandal, 941
Feingold, Russell, 24
Feinstein, Dianne, 23, 24
Fenwick, Millicent, 683
FERC. *See Federal Energy Regulatory Commission*
Fermi National Accelerator Laboratory, 901
Fernald, Ohio, 525
Fernandez, Joseph, 287 (box)
Fertilizer, 529
Fetal alcohol syndrome, 883, 905
Fetal tissue research
Clinton policy, 1993, 600
NIH authorization action
1990, 590-591
1991-92, 599, 602-603
FHA. *See Federal Housing Administration*
Fields, Jack R-Texas
Clean Air Act, 475
House bank scandal (chart), 934
Fiers, Alan D. Jr., 286
FIFRA. *See Federal Insecticide, Fungicide and Rodenticide Act*
Fifth Amendment
Supreme Court decisions, 818-819, 825-826
Financial Democracy Campaign, 149
Financial disclosure
congressional ethics code, 920
Financial institutions. *See Banks and banking; Credit unions; Savings and loan associations*
Financial Institutions Reform, Recovery and Enforcement Act, 117-130
Financial planners, 159-160
Fire Administration, U.S., 889
Firearms
ammunition taxes, 110
crime bills, 764-768, 786-789
criminal use, 764, 766, 786, 787, 788
D.C. weapons liability law, 896
gun control summary (box), 765
handgun wait period, 765 (box), 786, 787, 789
revenue from registration violations, 788
Fires and firefighting
cigarette safety, 436
fire prevention, 889
fire safety in federal buildings, 904
Franklin commemorative coin, 161
hotel safety equipment, 436
First Amendment
cable TV regulation, 451
campaign finance, 963
children's TV, 429
federal employee honoraria, 886
flag desecration, 761-762
NEA funding, 866, 867
patronage jobs, 861 (box)
political advertising, 958
pornography victims, 797
sexually explicit ads, 870
Supreme Court decisions, 834-838
corporate campaign spending, 955 (box)
summary, 805-806
TV violence guidelines, 428
Fish and fisheries
conservation, environmental protection
"dolphin-safe" tuna, 433-434
drift net ban, 434, 528
federal-state programs, 426
marine die-off, 531
New England ground fish, 530-531
salmon, 427, 522
striped bass, 521-522
water projects, 515, 516
disaster relief, 409

food inspection, 434-435
Japan-U.S. agreement, 426
taxes, 110
Fish and Wildlife Service, U.S.
endangered species, 521
irrigation subsidies, 515
northern spotted owl, 495
Fish, Hamilton Jr. R-N.Y.
Americans with Disabilities Act, 746
civil rights/job bias, 759
sports lottery ban, 791
Fisher, Mary, 20, 997
Fisher, William F., 877
Fiske, Robert B., 763, 1177
Fitzwater, Marlin
export controls, 176
Hatch Act revision, 860-861
Persian Gulf War, 310
savings and loan bailout, 121
Soviet-U.S. trade, 169
urban aid, 664
Flag desecration
action, 760-762
Supreme Court summary, 805
whistleblowers protection bill, 863
Flag Protection Act of 1989, 761
Flake, Floyd H. D-N.Y.
ethics case, 927, 945
House bank scandal (chart), 935
housing authorization, 667-668
Flake, Margaret, 927
Fleming, Peter E. Jr., 946-947
Fletcher, Arthur A., 786
Fletcher, James C., 875 (box)
Flint Hills, Kan., 527
Flippo, Ronnie G. D-Ala.
House bank scandal (chart), 934
Flood insurance
authorization, 694
barrier island protection, 497
budget action, 52, 61
program revision, 697, 698-699
Floods and flood control
flood prevention programs, 557
water projects authorization, 493-494, 517, 528
Florida
ADAMHA authorization, 604
bankruptcy judges, 799
barrier islands, 497
coastal zone management, 491
disaster relief, 84
governor's election, 1990, 11, 12
Keys, 497
offshore drilling ban, 491, 504
refugee asylum, 756
term limits, 10 (box), 963
water projects, 493 (box), 494
Florio, James J. D-N.J.
Bradley Senate race, 1990, 10
New Jersey governor's race, 6, 7-8
successor, 12
FmHA. *See Farmers Home Administration*
FMLN. *See Farabundo Marti Front for National Liberation*
FMS. *See Foreign Military Sales*
Foley, Heather, 939
Foley, Thomas S. D-Wash.
defense, foreign and trade issues
China policy, 251
defense authorization, FY 1991, 356
defense policy summary, 337
El Salvador aid, 217, 218
intelligence authorization, 246
Iran-contra pardons, 287
NAFTA, 189
Persian Gulf War, 12-13, 308, 310, 311
domestic issues
Americans with Disabilities Act, 746
appropriations, FY 1990, 52
budget-control efforts, 36
budget reconciliation, FY 1990, 46
budget resolution, FY 1993, 81
capital gains tax cut, 97
census study, 895
civil rights/job bias, 785
Clean Air Act, 480
credit card interest cap, 137 (box)
energy bill, 504
gun control, 765 (box)
Hatch Act revision, 887
motor voter bill, 894
northern spotted owl, 521
savings and loan bailout refinancing, 149, 150
unemployment benefits, 722, 724
urban aid, 664
floor votes, 81, 86, 246
House leadership
adjournment, 1991, 12
bank scandal, 930-937
campaign finance, 956, 962
Coelho resignation, 918
congressional pay, 5, 966
congressional reform study, 948
elections, 1992, 27
ethics committee reorganization, 947
flag desecration, 761-762
Madison amendment, 972
nuclear bunker, 973
Post Office scandal, 939, 941
restaurant bills, 942
summary, 5, 7 (chart), 913, 914, 916, 928
term limits, 963
traffic tickets, 942
Follow Through, 614
Food and Drug Administration (FDA)
agency consolidation, 586
enforcement powers, 610
fish inspection, 434-435
food labels, 604 (box)
generic drug regulation, 606
medical device regulation, 586, 607
pharmaceutical licensing, 608
user fees, 603
Food and nutrition
communicable disease in food-workers, 743, 746, 747, 749
dietary guidelines, 593
fish inspection, 434-435
food pyramid (box), 554
labeling
fat, daily diet, 604 (box)
food supplements, vitamins, 603
nutrition, 585
"organic" food, 540, 546
nutrition monitoring, 593
pesticide residues, 498, 522-523
transportation safety, 423-424
Food assistance programs. *See also Food stamps; Women, Infants and Children (WIC) program*
authorization, 614, 617, 618, 619
Food for Peace, 256-258
Poland, Hungary aid, 213
Somalia relief, 278-280
surplus commodity distribution, 617, 619
wheat reserve, 545
Food for Peace, 256-258
Food for Progress, 267
Food Security Wheat Reserve, 545
Food stamps
authorization, 618-619
farm bill, 539
Football, 111
Ford, Gerald
Panama elections, 224
pocket-veto power, 927
Soviet aid, 266
Volcker Commission, 859 (box)
Ford, Guillermo, 224
Ford, Harold E. D-Tenn.
ethics case, 927
House bank scandal, 932
members with overdrafts (chart), 934
Ford Motor Co., 484
Ford, Wendell H. D-Ky.
airline smoking ban, 420
Americans with Disabilities Act, 744
aviation package, 418
cable TV regulation, 451
civil rights/job bias, 759
FAA authorization, 446
franking privilege, 970
House bank scandal (chart), 935
motor voter bill, 894
news leaks investigation, 946
Senate elections, 1992, 24
Senate leadership, 7 (chart), 13, 915, 928
uniform poll closing time, 872
uranium enrichment, 489
Ford, William D. D-Mich.
budget resolution, 76
civil rights/job bias, 782
higher education aid, 654-655
House leadership, 929
occupational safety, 734
school reform, 657-658
student loan defaults, 649
student "right to know," 648
Fordice, Kirk, 14
Foreign Affairs Committee, House
prestige (box), 268
Foreign aid. *See also Tied aid; specific countries*
abortion, 600
appropriations
FY 1990, 228-233
FY 1991, 74, 233-238
FY 1992, 269-271
FY 1993, 82, 271-277
authorization
FY 1990-91, 227-228
FY 1992-93, 267-269
communism downfall, 324, 325, 330-331
Food for Peace, 256-258
foreign policy "leveraging," 228, 230-231, 239, 248
global warming initiatives, 505-506
prohibitions, 233
Foreign Assistance Act of 1961, 267
Foreign Assistance Act of 1985, 293
Foreign Investment in the United States, Committee on (CFIUS), 178-179
Foreign languages. *See also English language*
bilingual voting aid, 793
Native American languages, 907-908
student aid, 282-283
Foreign Military Financing (FMF), 273, 276
Foreign Military Sales (FMS), 229
Foreign policy. *See also Arms control; Defense policy; Foreign aid; Foreign service and diplomacy; Foreign trade and business; Immigration and emigration; Intelligence activities; State Department, U.S.; Treaties and international agreements; United Nations*
Bush term summary, 203-204, 995, 997
chronology of action
1989-90, 205-260
1991-92, 260-297
foreign aid "leveraging," 228, 230-231, 239, 248
military incursions since 1903 (box), 226
Foreign Relations Committee, Senate
prestige, 227-228, 268 (box)
subcommittee powers, 928
Foreign service and diplomacy
Moscow Embassy, 209 (box), 248, 263 (box), 290-291
political appointees, 248
security, 240-241
Soviet republics, 267
State Department authorization, 292
Foreign trade and business. *See also Agricultural exports and imports; "Buy American" provisions; Customs duties; Export controls; Export-Import Bank; General Agreement on Tariffs and Trade; Oil and natural gas; Overseas Private Investment Corporation; Ships and shipping; Tariffs; Third World debt; Trade agreements; Trade representative, U.S.; specific countries*
anti-dumping rules, 197
chronology of action
1989-90, 169-187
1991-92, 187-200
Bush term summary, 995
civil rights/job bias, 782, 785
defense contracts, 407
embargoes, sanctions and limits
chemical weapons, 254-255, 291, 292-293, 367 (box)
China, 251-252
Cuba, 295
drift net fishing, 528
exotic birds, 522
Iraq, Persian Gulf War, 238, 301-304, 307
nuclear arms technology, 293
South Africa policy, 253-254, 294-295
Vietnam POW/MIA cooperation, 289, 291
exports promotion, 199-200
foreign investment in United States, 147, 166, 177-179, 454
import quotas
steel, 186
textiles, footwear, 174-175
joint manufacturing ventures, 891
most-favored-nation status (box), 172
PAC contributions, 955
products and services
banking, securities, 129, 142, 146, 147, 187, 198, 412
futures trading, 552-553
money laundering, 157, 768
securities fraud, 132-133
coal, 511
electric utilities, 510
high-tech programs, 879
satellite launches, 875, 876
semiconductor chips, 793
space station, 900
strategic minerals, 880
superconducting supercollider, 878-879
tobacco products, 591
uranium imports, 509
space inventions patents, 869
Structural Impediments Initiative, 168
summary, 33, 165-168, 169, 187
Super 301 provisions, 167-168, 197
taxes, 49, 50, 51
U.S. business relocation, 276
Forest Service, U.S.
hydroelectric power, 507
Missouri tract purchase, 525-526
northern spotted owl, 494, 520
Pacific yew harvest, 527
scenic trails, 526
Tongass National Forest, 492

Forests and national forests
farm bill, 546
Indian lands, 884
Missouri tract purchase, 525-526
northern spotted owl, 494-495, 520-521
oil, gas development, 512
Pacific yew harvest, 527
timber exports, 181, 183-184
Tongass National Forest, 492-493
wilderness areas, 496
Fort Berthold Reservation, 517
Fort Wayne River, Ind., 493 (box)
Foster care
abandoned children, 622
adolescent transition program, 615, 616
child welfare overhaul, 621
rental assistance, 669, 673
Foster Grandparents program, 619
Foundation for Future Choices, 922
Fountain, L. H., 952
14th Amendment, 815
Fourth Amendment, 824-825
Fowler, Battle, 683
Fowler, Wyche Jr. D-Ga.
cable TV regulation, 453
NEA funding, 866
Senate elections, 1992, 23, 24
France
Persian Gulf War, 302-304, 308, 311, 313-317
Frank, Barney D-Mass.
defense authorization, 376
Eastern Airlines strike, 712
ethics case, 913, 923-924
federal employee honoraria, 886
housing authorization, 695-696
HUD reforms, 686-687
HUD scandal, 677, 681
mortgage prepayments, 692-693
Savage ethics case, 924
Social Security notch babies, 737
Franking privilege
action
1989-90, 968-970
1992, 973
campaign finance, 951, 955, 963
stamp allowance, 940 (box)
Franklin, Barbara Hackman
biographical profile, 1170
Bush term summary, 993
Commerce leadership, 419 (box)
Franklin, Benjamin, 161
Franks, Gary R-Conn.
House bank scandal (chart), 935
House elections, 1990, 11
House elections, 1992, 27
Fraud. *See also Waste, fraud and abuse in government programs*
corporate auditors, 160
counterfeit ID, 755, 757
deceptive mail curbs, 870
farm foreclosure sales ban, 551
financial institution fraud
crime bill, 764-768
penalties, 133-134
savings and loan bailout, 121, 128-129
Flake, Ford ethics cases, 927
generic drug regulation, 606
health care, 609
infertility clinics, 606
Keating Five investigation, 976, 981
Medigap insurance regulation, 582
octane labeling, 487-488
RICO limits, 771-772
securities market reforms, 132-133
telemarketing controls, 432, 460
Freddie Mac. *See Federal Home Loan Mortgage Corporation*
Frederick, Okla., 518
Free Congress Federation, 959
Freedom National Bank, 148
Freedom of Choice Act, 598, 599
Freedom of Information Act
securities fraud, 132
Supreme Court decisions, 833
Freedom of speech, press. *See First Amendment*
***Freedom* space station**
action
1989-90, 877-878
1991-92, 899-900
appropriations, 77, 81
NASA authorization
FY 1990, 874
FY 1991, 876
FY 1992-94, 897-898
FY 1993, 898-899
Freedom Support Act, 265-267, 331
Freeman Diversion Dam, 518
Frenzel, Bill R-Minn.
franking privilege, 968, 969, 970
House bank scandal (chart), 935
House leadership, 917, 929
Fried, Charles, 761, 778
FSLIC. *See Federal Savings and Loan Insurance Corporation*
FSLIC Resolution Fund, 125, 151
FS-X fighter plane, 354-355
FTC. *See Federal Trade Commission*
Fuel cells, 403, 511
Fuel taxes. *See also Gasoline taxes*
budget reconciliation, 67, 96
diesel, 95, 112
pollution, spill liability funds, 49, 52, 92, 490
recreational fuels, 444
superfund, 68, 186
Fujimori, Alberto, 256, 276
Fund for the Improvement of Postsecondary Education, 657
Fuqua, Don, 952
Fuster, Jaime B. Pop. Dem.-Puerto Rico
House bank scandal (chart), 935

G

Gaffney, Frank J. Jr., 208
Gallaudet University, 660
Gallegly, Elton R-Calif.
House bank scandal (chart), 935
Gallo, Dean A. R-N.J.
House bank scandal (chart), 935
Gambling
cruise ships, 450
Indian programs investigation, 882
passenger ships, 111
sports lottery ban, 790-791
tax withholding, 109, 111
"Gang of Seven," 930
Gangs, 766, 789
Gantt, Harvey B., 11
GAO. *See General Accounting Office*
Garbage. *See Waste products*
Garcia, Alan, 256
Garcia, Jane Lee, 925
Garcia, Robert D-N.Y.
House bank scandal (chart), 934
resignation, 925
successor, 12
Garn, Jake R-Utah
banking overhaul, 141
fair trade in financial services, 187
irrigation subsidies, 515
savings and loan bailout, 114, 122-123
Garrison Dam, 517
Gasohol, 183, 506
Gasoline
ethanol blends, 109
fuel-efficiency mandates, 501
lead use restrictions, 530
octane labeling, 487-488, 510
reformulated gas, 483, 487 (box)
Gasoline taxes
budget reconciliation, 49, 67
deficit reduction bill, 1990, 95
energy bill, 502
highway bill, 110, 437, 439, 440, 441, 442
summary, 415
Gates, Robert M.
biographical profile, 1177
CIA leadership, 261 (box)
CIA relocation, 282 (box)
intelligence authorization, 282, 283
intelligence reorganization plans, 284-285 (box)
GATT. *See General Agreement on Tariffs and Trade*
Gawthrop, Robert S. III, 945
Gaydos, Joseph M. D-Pa.
construction safety, 736
House bank scandal (chart), 935
House leadership, 929
Gejdenson, Sam D-Conn.
campaign finance, 961
export controls, 176
House bank scandal (chart), 934
Gekas, George W. R-Pa.
crime bill, 788
federal employee honoraria, 886
Section 89 tax rules, 710
General Accounting Office (GAO)
abandoned barges, 449
age discrimination waivers, 717
Agriculture Department streamlining, 556 (box)
banking overhaul, 136-137
deposit insurance, 124-125 (box), 129
FDIC oversight, 143, 144-145
commodity futures trading fees, 552
congressional ethics issues
House bank scandal, 930, 932, 938
House Post Office scandal, 939
news leaks investigation, 946-947
restaurant bills, 942
crop insurance, 549 (box)
Fannie Mae audits, 130
federal credit reform, 60 (box)
FHA loan ceiling, 690
foreign investment data, 177-179
FS-X aircraft deal, 355
government-sponsored enterprises, 129
Hatch Act revision, 860
highway authorization, 439
hospitals, nursing facilities, 572
HUD ethics, 686 (box)
HUD scandal, 682
job training, 729
long-term care insurance, 572
Medicare administrative costs, 570
Medigap insurance regulation, 583
military base closings, 353, 411
mining law overhaul, 519-520
National Endowment for Democracy, 291
octane labeling, 487-488
OMB review authority, 646
parental leave, 711
physician hospital ownership, 569
savings and loan bailout, 117, 129
RTC audits, 150
Social Security notch babies, 719
supercomputers, 889
superconducting supercollider, 879
VA-IRS tax information, 70
General Agreement on Tariffs and Trade (GATT)
Caribbean Basin Initiative, 181-182, 183
customs adjustment authority, 64
farm subsidies, 547, 555
fast-track procedures, 188-189
foreign trade summary, 165, 166-167
MFN summary, 172 (box)
Soviet observer, 169
steel import limits, 186
textile import quotas, 174-175
General Dynamics Corp.
A-12 cancellation, 379 (box)
F-16 authorization, 378, 396
FS-X aircraft deal, 354
Seawolf submarine, 410
General Services Administration (GSA)
Brooklyn courthouse, 438 (box)
energy efficiency, 890
overhaul, 889-890
Generalized System of Preferences, 182, 211-212, 213
Genetic engineering
biotech rules, 903 (box)
mutant mice lab, 595
Genetics
DNA testing, 798
Geological Survey, U.S.
earthquake research, 880
national map project, 532
Western water policy review, 517
Geology. *See Mineral resources and mining*
George, Clair E., 286
George Washington University, 908
Georgia (republic)
reconnaissance overflights, 392
Soviet Union dissolution, 322, 331
Georgia
bankruptcy judges, 799
Geothermal energy
alternative power, 486
research, development, 507
tax credit, 47, 69, 94
Yellowstone Park, 526
Gephardt, Richard A. D-Mo.
budget resolution, FY 1990, 42
capital gains tax cut, 97
debt ceiling extensions, 44 (box)
defense authorization, FY 1991, 358
House bank scandal, 930, 933
members with overdrafts (chart), 934
House leadership, 5, 7 (chart), 916, 928
Iran-contra pardons, 287
middle-class tax cut, 100-101
NAFTA, 189, 190
parental leave, 712
Persian Gulf War, 308, 310
supercomputers, 889
tax policy summary, 88
trade expansion act, 196-197
unemployment benefits, 726
urban aid tax bill, 104
Gerasimov, Gennady, 324
Geren, Pete D-Texas
election, 8
House bank scandal (chart), 935
Germany. *See also East Germany*
arms control, 328
troop reduction proposals, 387 (box)
Persian Gulf War, 303, 316 (box)
Soviet aid, 330
Soviet-U.S. relations, 206
unification treaty, 214
U.S. trade
duty rates, 182
Gesell, Gerhard A., 241 (box)
GI Bill, 629

Gibbons, Sam M. D-Fla.
Caribbean Basin Initiative, 180-181
chemical weapons sanctions, 292
China trade status, 190-191
Persian Gulf War, 301-302
savings and loan bailout, 122
textile import quotas, 175
Gilchrest, Wayne T. R-Md.
Dyson ethics case, 926
Gillen, Craig, 286
Gilliam, DuBois R., 678 (box), 684-685
Gillmor, Paul E. R-Ohio
motor voter bill, 871
Gilman, Benjamin A. R-N.Y.
foreign aid authorization, 227
House leadership, 917
Gingrich, Marianne, 925-926
Gingrich, Newt R-Ga.
adult literacy, 659
budget summary, 9
congressional pay, 966
ethics case, 913, 925-926
Frank ethics case, 924
House bank scandal, 930, 931, 933
members with overdrafts (chart), 934
House elections
1990, 10
1992, 27
House leadership, 5, 7 (chart), 916, 917, 928-929
motor voter bill, 871
Section 89 tax rules, 709-710
unemployment benefits, 723
urban aid tax bill, 104
Wright resignation, 917
Ginnie Mae. *See Government National Mortgage Association*
Ginsburg, Ruth Bader
Supreme Court summary, 804
Giugni, Henry A., 916 (box)
Glaspie, April C., 300
Glass Ceiling Commission, 782, 784, 785
Glass-Steagall Act of 1933, 137
Glen Canyon Dam, 496, 513, 516
Glen Canyon National Recreation Area, 516
Glenn, John D-Ohio
Competitiveness Council, 891
federal employee honoraria, 886
federal financial centralization, 862
federal pay overhaul, 857
Gulf War veterans benefits, 629
Hatch Act revision, 860, 887
House bank scandal, 938
JFK assassination documents, 893
Keating Five investigation, 975-988
nuclear arms proliferation, 293
Pakistan arms sales, 293-294
Senate elections, 1992, 24
VA medical salaries, 633
Glickman, Dan D-Kan.
Agriculture Department streamlining, 556 (box)
budget summary, 9
House bank scandal, 938
members with overdrafts (chart), 934
insurance antitrust exemption, 463
pizza for school lunches, 556
SEC/CFTC merger plan, 550
Global climate change
Clean Air Act, 78, 483
energy bill, 505-506
environmental summit, 528-529
foreign aid appropriations, 277
"Greenhouse Conspiracy" documentary, 458
NASA authorizations, 876, 898, 899
NOAA authorization, 426
research authorization, 495
summary, 467-468, 471
U.N. emissions control treaty, 297, 506
Global Environmental Facility, 277
Global protection against limited strikes (GPALS), 371, 391
Gobie, Steve, 923-924
"God squad," 520-521
Gold
Soviet coin imports, 193
Goldin, Daniel S., 875 (box), 900, 996
Gonzalez, Henry B. D-Texas
banking overhaul, 138-142
coin redesign, 135
credit reporting safeguards, 157-158
FHA insurance fund, 691
FHA loan ceiling, 690
government securities market regulation, 158
House bank scandal, 937
House leadership, 916, 929
housing authorization, 665-670, 695, 697
HUD reforms, 685-687
HUD scandal, 685
mortgage prepayments, 692
RICO limits, 772
savings and loan bailout, 119, 121-123
refinancing, 150, 153
urban aid, 700
Goodling, Bill R-Pa.
age discrimination, 715-716
community service, 617
House bank scandal, 932, 933, 938
members with overdrafts (chart), 934
House leadership, 917
job training programs, 713
minimum wage, 707
occupational safety, 735
striker replacements, 733
vocational education, 646
Gorbachev, Mikhail S.
arms control, 328-329, 366-367 (box), 383
CFE treaty, 384
nuclear test treaties, 368
START treaty, 387-389
troop cuts, 205-210, 328, 335-336, 384, 387 (box)
unilateral U.S. cutbacks, 391
German unification, 214
Nobel prize, 8
Persian Gulf War, 314
Soviet Union dissolution, 319-332
coup attempt, 321 (box), 336
resignation (text), 322-323
Soviet-U.S. relations, 205-210
U.S. aid, 260-264
Soviet-U.S. trade, 169, 192
Gordon, Bart D-Tenn.
higher education aid, 655
House bank scandal (chart), 935
parental leave, 711, 731
Gore, Al D-Tenn.
cable TV regulation, 427-428
congressional pay, 966
earthquake research, 881
environmental summit, 528
food-waste transport, 424
Medicare budget reconciliation, 1990, 574
NASA authorization, 876, 899
NASA leadership, 875 (box)
parental leave, 732
Persian Gulf War, 310
presidential election, 1992, 17-23
space inventions patents, 879
State Department authorization, 248
striker replacements, 734
supercomputers, 889
Gorton, Slade R-Wash.
ethics committee reorganization, 947
food-waste transport, 424
highway authorization, 439
Keating Five investigation, 985
Goss, Porter J. R-Fla.
ethics committee reorganization, 947
Governing International Fishery Agreement, 426
Government ethics. *See Congressional ethics; Ethics in government; Waste, fraud and abuse in government programs*
Government Ethics, Office of, 686 (box), 858, 888
Government National Mortgage Association (Ginnie Mae), 672
Government securities
accounting rules, 44 (box)
market regulation, 113, 158
Social Security tax changes, 718-719, 737
Government Securities Act of 1986, 158
Government-sponsored enterprises (GSEs), 73, 129, 153-156, 698
Governors
Bush education initiative, 643
gubernatorial races
1989, 6-7, 1238-1239
1990, 11-12, 1240-1247
1991, 14, 1248-1249
1992, 28, 1250-1258
list, 1989-92, 1259-1260
Medicaid, 578
GPALS. *See Global protection against limited strikes*
Grachev, Pavel, 321 (box)
Gradison, Bill R-Ohio
budget resolution, 76-77
catastrophic medical costs insurance, 566
flood insurance, 699
higher education aid, 655
House bank scandal (chart), 935
House leadership, 929
Medicaid, 601
savings and loan bailout, 122
Graduate education, 625, 657
Graham, Anne, 419 (box)
Graham, Bob D-Fla.
ADAMHA authorization, 604
bank deposit insurance, 125 (box)
cable TV regulation, 453
Caribbean Basin Initiative, 181
crime bills, 766-767, 787
Cuba embargo, 295
energy bill, 503, 504
Florida Keys, 497
highway authorization, 439
middle-class tax cut, 102
minimum wage, 706
Persian Gulf War, 310, 312
political advertising, 958
Ryskamp nomination, 796
Senate elections, 1992, 24
textile import quotas, 175
unemployment benefits, 728
Grain. *See Wheat and feed grains*
Gramm, Phil R-Texas
Baby Bells restrictions, 461
budget-control efforts, 85
caller ID, 462
community service, 617
crime bills, 766, 789
government-sponsored enterprises, 155-156
housing authorization, 669
investment advisers regulation, 159
minimum wage, 708
motor voter bill, 894
partnership roll-ups, 158-159
presidential election, 1992, 21
savings and loan bailout, 123
Senate leadership, 928
student loan defaults, 650
superconducting supercollider, 901
Thomas confirmation, 803
unemployment benefits, 723
Gramm-Rudman-Hollings law
background, 44 (box)
budget policy summary, 37-40, 41
budget process changes, 56-57
sequesters
budget process changes, 57, 70-72, 73
Defense budget reprogramming, 356 (box)
mini-sequester, 78 (box), 193
spending cuts
FY 1990, 43, 47
FY 1991, 55
update efforts, 84
Grand Canyon, 496, 513-514, 516
Grand juries, 129, 820
Grandy, Fred R-Iowa
ethics committee reorganization, 947
NEA funding, 866-867
unemployment benefits, 727
Grant, Bill R-Fla.
House bank scandal (chart), 934
party switch, 6
Grant Foundation, 645
Grassley, Charles E. R-Iowa
Americans with Disabilities Act, 744, 747
budget resolution, FY 1991, 54
Persian Gulf War, 310
POW/MIA investigation, 290
Senate elections, 1992, 26
State Department authorization, 248
Gray, C. Boyden, 785, 869
Gray, Edwin J., 976, 979-984
Gray, Kenneth J.
House bank scandal (chart), 934
Gray, William H. D-Pa.
capital gains tax cut, 97
Coelho resignation, 918
House bank scandal (chart), 934
House leadership, 5, 7 (chart), 13, 916, 928
motor voter bill, 871
successor, 14
Grazing fees, 78, 518-519
Great Britain
Persian Gulf War, 301-304, 311, 313-317
Great Lakes
barrier islands, 497
fish die-off, 531
foreign food aid shipments, 257, 258
pollution control, 491-492
water projects authorization, 493 (box)
zebra mussels control, 496-497
Greece
CFE weapons cascading, 386
Persian Gulf War, 316 (box)
U.S. aid, 274, 275, 276
Green, Bill R-N.Y.
House bank scandal (chart), 935
House elections, 1992, 27
Green, Mark, 923
Green, Thomas C., 980
Greenbrier bunker, 973
Greene, Harold H., 461, 949
"Greenhouse Conspiracy," 458
Greenhouse gases
energy bill, 505
environmental summit, 528-529
global warming treaty, 297
Greenspan, Alan
banking overhaul, 138
biographical profile, 1176
Bush economic team, 32-33 (box)

economic policy summary, 34
Keating Five investigation, 976
Third World debt relief, 184
Gregg, Donald P., 1179
Grenada
Caribbean Basin Initiative, 180
Grogan, James J., 982-983
Groundwater
farm bill protection, 539
research, 517
Group Health of New York, 111
Group of Seven, 330
Grumman Corp., 347, 348
GSEs. *See Government-sponsored enterprises*
Guam
disaster relief, 84
food stamps, 618
Guantanamo Naval Base, 296
Guatemala
Caribbean Basin Initiative, 180
Gulf Cooperation Council, 316 (box)
Gulf of Mexico
barrier islands, 497
offshore drilling ban, 491
pipeline inspections, 488
Gulf War. *See Persian Gulf War*
Gunderson, Steve R-Wis.
age discrimination waivers, 717
civil rights/job bias, 759
higher education aid, 654
House bank scandal (chart), 934
Section 89 tax rules, 710
Gutierrez, Luis V., 27
Guyana
Caribbean Basin Initiative, 180
Gynecology, 591

H

Habeas corpus appeals
crime bills, 764-768, 786-789
Supreme Court decisions, 820-822
summary, 805
Haidle Irrigation Project, 518
Haiti
Caribbean Basin Initiative, 180
refugees, 296
Hakim, Albert, 287 (box)
Hale, Janet, 680
Hall, Ralph M. D-Texas
House bank scandal (chart), 934
superconducting supercollider, 878
Hall, Sam B. Jr., 952
Hall, Tony P. D-Ohio
House leadership, 917
Hamilton, James, 984
Hamilton, Lee H. D-Ind.
congressional reform study, 948
covert actions notification, 237 (box)
covert aid programs, 244
Foreign Affairs Committee clout, 268 (box)
foreign aid authorization, 227
foreign investment data, 178
House leadership, 916
Iran-contra pardons, 286
Middle East peace talks, 277
"October surprise" probe, 288
Persian Gulf War, 300, 310, 312
Somalia relief, 279
Soviet-U.S. relations, 208
Hammerschmidt, John Paul R-Ark.
House bank scandal, 933
members with overdrafts (chart), 934
Hammond Irrigation District, 518
Hampton, Lionel, 683
Hampton University, 684
Handgun Control, 765 (box)
Hansen, James V. R-Utah
ethics committee reorganization, 947
House leadership, 929
Harbor Maintenance Trust Fund, 67
Harkin, Tom D-Iowa
Americans with Disabilities Act, 744
appropriations, FY 1992, 78
defense appropriations, 408
education for disabled, 647
flag desecration, 762
foreign investment data, 178
Keating Five investigation, 987
Nicaragua policy, 222
NIH authorization, 591
Persian Gulf War, 309
presidential election, 1992, 17
Soviet credit guarantees, 555
Harlow, Bryce, 998
HARM missiles, 405
Harpoon missiles, 378
Harrell, Marilyn Louise, 678 (box)
Harrier aircraft, 350, 352
Hassayampa River, 517
Hastert, Dennis R-Ill.
Americans with Disabilities Act, 746
House bank scandal (chart), 934
Hastings, Alcee L., 775-777
Hatch Act, 859-861, 886-887
Hatch, Orrin G. R-Utah
age discrimination, 716, 717
Americans with Disabilities Act, 744
Amtrak waste disposal, 424
campaign finance, 955
child care, 611-612
civil rights/job bias, 758-759
community service, 617
computer software copyright, 773
crime bills, 766, 787
election day holiday, 895
FDA user fees, 603
fetal tissue research, 599, 602
hate crime statistics, 778
immigration reform, 755
mandated health benefits, 595
minimum wage, 706, 708
NEA funding, 866, 867
parental leave, 731
school reform, 658
striker replacements, 734
superconducting supercollider, 878
violence against women, 778
Hatcher, Charles D-Ga.
House bank scandal, 930, 932
members with overdrafts (chart), 934
Hate crimes, 778, 797
"Hate speech," 805
Hatfield, Mark O. R-Ore.
crime bill, 767
ethics case, 914, 942-943
Gulf War veterans benefits, 630
motor voter bill, 871, 894
nuclear test ban, 524
Persian Gulf War, 310
Senate elections, 1990, 11
Havel, Vaclav, 171
Hawaii
congressional elections, 1990, 11, 12
disaster relief, 84
Native health care, 906
Hawkins, Augustus F. D-Calif.
Bush education initiative, 644
child care, 613
civil rights/job bias, 757-760
House leadership, 929
minimum wage, 707
Hayden, Mike, 11
Hayden-Rhodes Aqueduct, 517
Hayes, Charles A. D-Ill.
House bank scandal, 932, 933
members with overdrafts (chart), 934
Hazardous Materials Transportation Act, 422-423
Hazardous substances. *See also Acid rain; Air pollution; Hazardous waste cleanup; Lead poisoning prevention; Nuclear waste; Pesticides; Radiation; Sewers and sewage treatment; Waste products; Water pollution*
agricultural chemicals, 541, 542
child-resistant packaging, 870
electromagnetic fields, 511
radon abatement, 530
selenium contamination, 517
source pollution reduction, 64
transportation safety law, 422-423
backhauling, 423-424
pipeline safety, 531-532
Hazardous waste cleanup. *See also Superfund*
abandoned mines, 63
bank liability protection, 141
federal facilities, 497-498, 525
military bases, 349
national map project, 532
oil spills, 448, 490-491
Pacific island PCBs, 512
Rocky Mountain arsenal, 527
Head Start
authorization, 613-614
child care, 611-612
program changes, 621
Health and Human Services Department, U.S. (HHS)
abortion counseling ban, 599
aging research, 592
anti-smoking bills, 591
cancer-tracking registries, 608
child welfare overhaul, 621
communicable disease in food workers, 747, 749
FDA user fees, 603
fetal tissue research, 591
food assistance programs, 618
food labeling, 585
food transport safety, 423-424
generic drug regulation, 606
Head Start, 614
health care fraud, 609
Indian health services, 905
infertility clinics, 606
leadership (box), 567
Medicaid, 579-582, 601
Medicare budget reconciliation
1989, 571-573
1990, 574-578
Medicare physician payments, 568-570
Medigap insurance regulation, 583-585
minority health programs, 588
NIH authorization, 602
nursing home regulation, 587
nutrition monitoring, 593
organ donor registries, 590
Social Security Administration independence, 718, 736, 737
Social Security earnings, benefits statements, 51
welfare tracking, 623
Health and medical care. *See also Community-based health care; Dentists and dental care; Health and Human Services Department, U.S. ; Health insurance; Home health care; Hospitals and medical facilities; Immunization; Indian Health Service; Infant mortality; Medical devices and equipment; Medical research and technology; Mental health and illness; Nurses and nursing; Nursing homes; Physicians; Primary medical care; Veterans health care; Women's health issues; specific diseases*
case-management demonstrations, 577-578
chronology of action
1989-90, 565-595
1991-92, 595-610
disease prevention, 608
food workers, 743, 746, 747, 749
foreign aid, 213, 232
fraud, 609
Indians, native Hawaiians, 883, 905-906
living wills, 577
minority programs, 588
rural development, 548
state planning grants, 593
summary, 561-564, 565, 595
treatment effectiveness, 567, 572
Health Care Financing Administration, 572, 601
Health Care Policy and Research, Agency for, 572, 608-609
Health care workers. *See also Dentists and dental care; Nurses and nursing; Physicians*
Health Service Corps authorization, 587-588
VA facilities, 625, 629
Health Education Assistance Loans, 609
Health insurance. *See also Health maintenance organizations; Medicaid; Medicare*
catastrophic costs insurance repeal, 43, 46, 51, 565-567
child care, 611-613
disabled workers, 572
domestic partners benefits, 896-900
ERISA reforms, 738
federal employees, 859
health reform, 596-597
long-term care standards, 572, 609
mandated benefits, 595
Medicaid alternative, 579, 582
Medigap policies regulation, 582-585, 609
military benefits, 363, 634
Oregon health plan, 597 (box)
parental leave, 711
pension funds, 49, 70
coal miners, 505, 511, 735 (box)
reversions, 719-720
Pepper Commission, 584 (box)
Persian Gulf crisis, 238
secondary payer provisions, 570, 577
Section 89 tax rules, 708-710
tax treatment, 66
self-employed persons, 47, 69, 94
uninsurable children, 580
workers' plan continuation, 582
Health Insurance Claims Fairness Act, 738
Health maintenance organizations (HMOs)
Medicare budget reconciliation, 1990, 577
Medicare physician payments, 570
Healthy People 2000, 905
Healy, Bernadine P.
biographical profile, 1180
HHS leadership, 567 (box)
Heath, Dan, 8
Hefley, Joel R-Colo.
House bank scandal (chart), 935
Heflin, Howell D-Ala.
animal research labs, 881, 904
ethics committee reorganization, 947
Keating Five investigation, 975-988
Lucas nomination, 764

motor voter bill, 871
Persian Gulf War, 310
Senate leadership, 928
Hefner, W. G. "Bill" D-N.C.
House elections, 1992, 27
Heinz, John R-Pa.
civil rights/job bias, 758
HUD scandal, 683
Persian Gulf War, 634
savings and loan bailout, 122
Senate leadership, 928
successor, 14
textile import quotas, 174
Helicopter carriers, 406, 407, 409
Helicopters
appropriations, 351, 382, 409
CFE treaty, 385
defense authorization
FY 1990, 346-347, 349
FY 1991, 361
FY 1992, 378, 379, 380
FY 1993, 401
Osprey cancellation controversy, 348
Hellfire missiles, 347
Helms, Jesse R-N.C.
abortion, 600
AIDS immigration exclusion, 753 (box)
AIDS programs, 588-589
airline smoking ban, 420
Americans with Disabilities Act, 747
Bush education initiative, 643-644
cable TV regulation, 453
chemical weapons sanctions, 255
civil rights/job bias, 781
crime bill, 787
ethics committee reorganization, 947
flag desecration, 762
foreign aid authorization, 228
Gulf War veterans benefits, 630
hate crime statistics, 778
House bank scandal, 931
Keating Five investigation, 977, 985-986
NEA funding, 52, 865-867, 519
Nicaragua policy, 222
NIH authorization, 602
Panama policy, 225
Poland, Hungary aid, 212
public broadcasting, 458
school reform, 658
Senate elections, 1990, 11
South Africa policy, 254
Soviet-U.S. relations, 208
State Department authorization, 248
textile import quotas, 174
torture treaty, 259
TV violence, 428
uniform poll closing time, 872
Henry, Paul B. R-Mich.
ERISA reforms, 738
House bank scandal (chart), 934
NEA funding, 866
occupational safety, 735
student "right to know," 648
Hercules cargo planes, 406
Heritage Foundation, 244
Herres, Robert T., 375 (box)
Hertel, Dennis M. D-Mich.
House bank scandal (chart), 934
House Post Office scandal, 941
Herzegovina, 194, 275, 278
Heye Foundation, 885
Hickel, Walter J., 11-12
High-definition television, 880
High Energy Physics Advisory Panel, 878
High Plains groundwater program, 517
High-speed rail
highway authorization, 442, 444
research, development, 904
state bonds, 111-112
Higher Education Act Amendments of 1980, 652
Higher Education Act of 1965, 653-657
Highway Beautification Act of 1965, 439
Highway Trust Fund, 67, 437-443
Highways and roads
authorization, 437-444
technical corrections, 445
billboard advertising, 439, 444
historic roadways, 444
recycled materials, 445
research, 444
safety, 441, 442, 443
scenic trails, 526
speed limits, 444
summary, 415
truck stop, rest area drug traffic, 425
Hiler, John R-Ind.
House bank scandal (chart), 935
House elections, 1990, 11
housing authorization, 668
Hill, Anita F.
Thomas confirmation, 802-803, 804, 994
effect on women candidates, 13, 24, 26
news leaks investigation, 946-947
Hills, Carla A.
biographical profile, 1175
Bush economic team, 32 (box)
Bush term summary, 993
foreign trade summary, 167-168
HUD scandal, 681, 683
NAFTA, 189, 190
Hispanic Chamber of Commerce, U.S., 685
Hispanic Trade Center, 685
Hispanics
Bush judicial appointments, 776 (box)
congressional elections, 1992, 17, 27
higher education aid, 656
House elections, 1991, 14
immigration reform, 752, 755
presidential election, 1992, 22
women in business, 464
Historic preservation
acid-free paper, 869
act amendment, 518
ADA exemptions for buildings, vehicles, 749, 752
rehabilitation tax credit, 111
Historic sites and monuments
Little Bighorn battlefield, 525
Mimbres archeology, 909
roadways, 444
Wright brothers landmarks, 526
HIV. *See Acquired immune deficiency syndrome (AIDS)*
HMOs. *See Health maintenance organizations*
Hoagland, Peter D-Neb.
high-tech training, 892
insurance antitrust exemption, 463
mortgage prepayments, 693
Hobson, David L. R-Ohio
ethics committee reorganization, 947
Hochbrueckner, George J. D-N.Y.
House bank scandal (chart), 934
HoDAG. *See Housing development action grants*
Holderman, James B., 943
Holland, Ken, 952
Hollings Centers, 880
Hollings, Ernest F. D-S.C.
airline smoking ban, 420
Baby Bells restrictions, 461
blind airline passengers, 422
budget resolution, FY 1990, 43
cable TV regulation, 451
Coast Guard authorization, 449
high-tech programs, 880
Keating Five investigation, 982
Moscow Embassy, 263
political advertising, 957-958
Senate elections, 1992, 24
Holloway, Clyde C. R-La.
domestic partners benefits, 897
House bank scandal, 938
members with overdrafts (chart), 935
House elections, 1992, 26
Holmes, Paul, 777
HOME Corporation, 566, 667
Home health care. *See also Respite care*
elderly programs authorization, 592, 620
kidney dialysis, 577
Medicaid coverage, 581
Medicare coverage, 577, 578
veterans programs, 625
HOME Investment Partnerships
authorization, 665, 670-671, 694-698
funding (box), 696
Home loans and mortgages
farms, 546-547, 553-554
FHA insurance, 59-61, 671-672, 689-690, 690-692, 694-698
first-time buyer aid, 666, 671
flood insurance, 698-699
FmHA authorization, 675-676
HUD scandal, 678-679
neighborhood accountability, 672
prepayment, 674
redlining, 128
savings and loan regulation, bailout, 127, 153, 688
second, vacation homes, 672, 685, 687
tax reporting
loan fees, 50
seller financing, 109
VA programs, 625, 626, 627, 635-636
Home Mortgage Disclosure Act of 1975, 128
Home shopping channels, 453, 454, 456
Home Shopping Network, 453
Homefront Budget Initiative, 77
Homeless persons
aid authorization, 675, 693-694, 698
food assistance for children, 618, 623
food stamps, 618
housing authorization, 675
veterans, 625, 629, 634-635, 636
youth drug prevention, 789
Homeownership and Opportunity for People Everywhere (HOPE) program
authorization, 665, 666, 668, 694-698
funding (box), 696
mortgage prepayments, 692
Homer Spit, Alaska, 493 (box)
Homosexuality
Americans with Disabilities Act, 747
Frank ethics case, 923-924
hate crime statistics, 778
homoerotic art, 865-867
Honduras
Caribbean Basin Initiative, 180
military construction appropriations, 353
National Guard exercises, 361 (box)
Nicaragua policy, 220
Honecker, Erich, 214
Honey, 541, 544
Hong Kong
immigration reform, 753, 755
Honoraria
congressional pay, 965, 967, 970-971
federal employees, 858, 886
Hoover Dam, 516
HOP. *See Housing Opportunity Partnerships*
HOPE. *See Homeownership and Opportunity for People Everywhere*
Hopi Indians, 908
Hopkins, Larry J. R-Ky.
B-2 bomber, 398
governor's election, 1991, 14
House bank scandal (chart), 934
Horn, Joan Kelly D-Mo.
House bank scandal (chart), 935
House elections, 1990, 11
House elections, 1992, 26
Horton, Frank R-N.Y.
federal-state fund transfers, 865
House bank scandal (chart), 935
OMB regulatory review, 868
whistleblowers protection, 863
Hospices
Medicare budget reconciliation, 571, 575
veterans pilot program, 637
Hospitals and medical facilities. *See also Hospices; Military hospitals; Nursing homes; Veterans hospitals*
abandoned infants, 622
AIDS programs, 588
catastrophic medical costs insurance, 565-567
disproportionate share of poor patients, 571, 574, 601
infertility clinics, 606
Medicaid, 579, 600-602
Medicare budget reconciliation
1989, 571-572
1990, 574-576
patient dumping ban, 572, 575
physician ownership, referrals, 569
sole, essential community access, 571
trauma services, 590
triage demonstrations, 572
Hostages
Iran-contra legacy, 238
"October surprise" probe, 287-288
Persian Gulf War, 304
Hotels
Americans with Disabilities Act, 743-752
fire safety, 436
telephone rates, 431
House Administration Committee
House professional administrator, 948
House bank scandal
action, 1991-92, 929-939
election effects, 26
financial disclosure reports (box), 937
members with overdrafts (charts)
abusers, 932
complete list, 934-935
summary, 13, 15-16, 913-914
House of Representatives, U.S. *See also House bank scandal; Redistricting*
characteristics, 103rd Congress, 27
committees, 1129-1136
debate record, 924-925
elections
1989, 8
1990, 11, 12
1991, 14
1992, 26-28
results, 1948-92, 1236-1237
members
101st Congress, 1108-1109
102nd Congress, 1112-1113
changes, 1110
organization, leadership
101st Congress, 5, 915-917
102nd Congress, 13, 928-929
professional administrator, 947-948
House Post Office scandal
action, 939-942
summary, 16, 914
House Progressive Caucus, 80

House-Senate relations
House bank scandal, 931
immigration reform, 754
Housing. *See also Home loans and mortgages; Housing assistance and public housing*
budget reconciliation, FY 1991, 59-61, 69
capital gains tax, 111
employer trust funds, 717
energy conservation, efficiency, 486, 507
lead poisoning prevention, 606-607, 697-698
mobile home standards, 668
rental income taxes, 110
savings and loan bailout, 119
tax credits
construction, rehab, 94
first-time buyers, 100, 102
low-income investments, 47, 69
Housing and Urban Development Department, U.S. (HUD)
D'Amato ethics case, 923, 944
FHA insurance fund, 690-691
fraud, mismanagement scandal, 676-685
bending the rules (box), 682
court action (box), 678-679
ethics program (box), 686
reform proposals, 685-689
summary, 663
government-sponsored enterprises, 154, 155
homeless veterans, 629
housing authorization, 665-676, 694-698
Indian programs investigation, 882
leadership (box), 667
mortgage auction, 61
mortgage insurance premiums, 59-61
prepayment of subsidized mortgages, 692-693
Housing assistance and public housing
authorization, 665-676, 694-698
block grants, 666-667, 669, 670-671, 675-676
government-sponsored enterprises, 155
health, social services, 666
AIDS patients, 675
congregate services, 675
disabled, 675, 695-698
drug-crime control, 674
elderly, 675, 695-698
family support, 669, 673
perinatal care, 673
home ownership aid
banking bills, 128, 147
community-based programs, 666, 668
prepayment of subsidized mortgages, 692
public housing tenants, 666, 672, 695-698
RTC operations, 150, 152-153
Indian programs, 672
Israel loan guarantees, 234
prepayment of subsidized mortgages, 666, 668, 674, 689, 692-693
public housing
authorization, 666, 672-673
management choices, 697, 698
mixed housing, 695-698
older tenants ombudsmen, 620
severely distressed projects, 689
rental aid, 666, 667-669, 673-674, 692-693
rural programs, 674-675
Section 8 Moderate Rehabilitation, 663, 676, 680, 682
summary, 663-664
Housing development action grants (HoDAGs), 667, 671
Housing Opportunity Partnerships (HOP), 666, 667, 668-669
Housing Opportunity Zones, 666
Howard, A. E. Dick, 959
Hoyer, Steny D-Md.
Americans with Disabilities Act, 745
House bank scandal, 933
members with overdrafts (chart), 935
House elections, 1992, 27
House leadership, 5, 7 (chart), 916, 928
Hubbard, Carroll Jr. D-Ky.
House bank scandal (chart), 934
HUD reforms, 686
Hubble Space Telescope, 876
Huckaby, Jerry D-La.
farm bill, 540
House bank scandal, 938
members with overdrafts (chart), 934
House elections, 1992, 26
Hughes Aircraft, 252
Hughes, William J. D-N.J.
cable TV regulation, 452 (box)
legislative summary, 1991, 12
RICO limits, 791
Human immunodeficiency virus. *See Acquired immune deficiency syndrome (AIDS)*
Human rights
agricultural export credits, 545
Cambodia, 245
China, 173, 185, 190-192, 250-253
El Salvador, 74, 214-219
Haitian refugees, 296
Indonesia, 274
Kenya, 233 (box)
Myanmar trade sanctions, 182
Romania-U.S. trade, 194
South Africa, 294-295
Soviet republics, 266
torture treaty, 259
torture victims suits, 797
Yugoslavia, 194
Humphrey, Gordon J. R-N.H.
franking privilege, 968, 969
Hungary
U.S. aid, 186, 210-214
appropriations, 230, 231
U.S. trade
export controls, 196
status, 173, 193-194
Hunger. *See Food assistance programs*
Hunger Protection Act of 1988, 623
Hunter, Duncan R-Calif.
export controls, 196
House bank scandal, 933
members with overdrafts (chart), 934
House leadership, 916, 929
Soviet-U.S. relations, 208
Hurricane relief
appropriations, 53, 557
eased bank regulation, 161
fishermen, 409
flood insurance, 694
Hussein, King, 277
Hutto, Earl D-Fla.
House bank scandal (chart), 935
Hyde, Henry J. R-Ill.
civil rights/job bias, 759, 783
crime bill, 767, 768
flag desecration, 762
House bank scandal (chart), 935
parental leave, 731
savings and loan bailout, 122
Soviet aid, 264
Hydrocarbon emissions, 473, 480, 487 (box)
Hydroelectric power
dam improvement financing, 109
federal lands, 507
fish protection, 522
Grand Canyon erosion, 496, 513-514, 516
licensing, 507
Hydrogen fuel, 486-487

I

Ichord, Richard H., 952
Iliesco, Ion, 194
Illegal aliens
Haitian refugee policy, 296
immigration reform, 752-755
Legal Services aid ban, 795
refugee asylum, 756
Social Security fraud amnesty, 62-63
Illinois
Clean Air Act, 483
congressional elections, 1990, 11
highway authorization, 442
military base closings, 353
motor voter bill, 871
wilderness areas, 496
Immigration and emigration. *See also Illegal aliens*
AIDS exclusion, 753 (box)
Chinese nationals, 251, 252-253, 755-756, 794
Israel housing loan guarantees, 270, 272-273 (box)
naturalization process changes, 779, 794
nurses, 757
reform, 752-755
refugee admissions, 233
asylum, 756-757
Soviet-U.S. trade, 169-171
Supreme Court decisions, 838
Immigration and Naturalization Service (INS)
AIDS exclusion policy, 753 (box)
naturalization process, 779, 794
Philippine war veterans, 779
refugee asylum, 756
visa exemptions, 795
Immigration Reform and Control Act of 1986, 752, 757
Immunity
North conviction, appeal, 240-241 (box)
Supreme Court decisions, 816, 849
Immunization
Indian health services, 883
program authorization, 587
vaccine injury compensation, 572, 587
Impeachments
judicial cases, 775-777
Imports. *See Foreign trade and business*
Inaugural address, Bush, 1187-1188
Income taxes
budget reconciliation, FY 1991, 58, 66-67, 92, 93-96
expiring provisions (box), 94
campaign finance
contributions credit, 951, 953, 961, 962
presidential fund "checkoff," 954 (box)
child care credit, 611-613
estimated payments, 107, 110
health reform, 596
middle-class relief, 36, 89-90, 100-103
miscellaneous tax bills, 110, 111
penalties, 50-51
percentage of GDP, 90 (chart)
Section 89 tax rules, 708-710
Social Security, 92 (box), 718-719
top-bracket increase, 102
unemployment benefits, 727, 728
urban aid tax bill, 105, 107
withholding requirements, 40, 49, 109
Incumbents
campaign finance, 951-957
congressional elections
1990, 9-10
1991, 14
1992, 15, 23-24, 26, 27
term limits, 958-959, 963-964
Independent counsel
House bank scandal, 936-937
HUD scandal, 684
independent counsel law, 795
INSLAW case, 792 (box)
JFK documents bill, 893
news leaks investigation, 946-947
whistleblowers protection, 862-864
Independent Counsel Act of 1978, 684, 795
Independent Living Initiatives, 615, 616
Independent Television Service, 458
India
U.S. aid, 267, 269, 274
U.S. trade, 167-168
Indian Affairs, Bureau of (BIA)
Arizona electric project, 530
Indian health, human services, 883
Indian preference, 884
Indian programs investigation, 882-883
land management, 907
law enforcement, 883
tribal courts, 906-907
tribal self-governance, 906
Indian Alcohol and Substance Abuse Prevention and Treatment Act of 1986, 905
Indian Claims Commission, 885, 908
Indian Energy Resource Commission, 512
Indian Health Care Improvement Act of 1976, 905
Indian Health Service
authorization, 905-906
program abuse, 882
tribal self-governance, 906
Indian lands and reservations
Alaska dividends tax, 908
Arkansas River waterway, 908
criminal jurisdiction, 906
energy resource development, 512
enterprise zones, 106
environmental quality, 884
forest management, 884
Isleta claim, 908
land management programs, 907
law enforcement, 883-884
Micmac recognition, 908-909
Navajo-Hopi relocation, 908
Puyallup settlement, 885
right-to-sue, 908
Seminole claims settlement, 885
water rights, 516, 517
welfare services eligibility, 883
Indian Self-Determination and Education Assistance Act of 1988, 906
Indiana
Clean Air Act, 479, 483
highway authorization, 442
military base closings, 353
solid waste, 523
water projects, 493 (box)
Indians
Arizona electric power project, 530
Bighorn battlefield, 525
business contract preference, 884, 907
Campbell Senate election, 23, 24
community colleges, 650, 883

criminal jurisdiction, 906
federal programs investigation, 881-883
health care, 883, 905-906
home loans, 636
housing, 672, 689, 882
job training, 907
language preservation, 907
museum of history, culture, 885
Older Americans Act, 620
policy research institute, 908
radiation victims compensation, 586
recognition
Lumbees, 909
Micmacs, 885-886, 908-909
unacknowledged tribes, 908
right-to-sue, 908
Supreme Court decisions, 833-834
tax-deferred savings plans, 111
tribal courts, 906-907
tribal remains, 884-885
tribal self-governance, 906
veterans memorial, 908
Individual retirement accounts (IRAs)
capital gains tax cut, 97-98
middle-class tax cut, 100-103
unemployment benefits, 728
urban aid tax bill, 103, 105, 106
Individual rights
Supreme Court decisions, 838-844
Individuals with Disabilities Act of 1975, 647-648, 622
Indonesia
U.S. aid, 274, 276
Indoor Radon Abatement Act of 1988, 530
Industrial policy
technology programs, 902
INF. *See Intermediate-range nuclear force treaty*
Infant formula, 623
Infant mortality
fetal alcohol syndrome, 905
Medicaid data link, 580
Infants
abandoned children, 622
early intervention in disabilities, 622
Gulf War veterans benefits, 630
maternal, child block grant, 579-580
Medicaid coverage, 578-579, 581
model projects, 968
parental leave, 710-712, 730-732
Information access and classification
CIA budget, 281-282, 284
CIA documents declassification, 285 (box)
congressional news leaks, 947-948
Keating Five investigation, 982
Defense Department POW/MIA files, 380
failed banks, 148
foreign investment data, 177-179
House Speaker, 243 (box)
Intelligence Committee secrecy oath, 281, 283
JFK assassination documents, 892-893
Medicare secondary payer provisions, 570
POW/MIA investigation, 289, 290
Supreme Court decisions, 833
VA-IRS tax information, 70
Information Agency, U.S., 247, 267
Information and Regulatory Affairs, Office of (OIRA), 867-869
Information services
Baby Bells restrictions, 432, 461-462
Information Technology and Paperwork Commission, 890
Inhalant abuse, 906
Inkatha, 254
Inland Waterways Trust Fund, 493 (box)
Inouye, Daniel K. D-Hawaii
cable TV regulation, 451
children's TV grants, 429
defense appropriations, 331
ethics case, 944
Indian programs investigation, 882
Iran-contra pardons, 286
Keating Five investigation, 982
political advertising, 957
radio spectrum allocation, 430
Senate elections, 1992, 26
Senate leadership, 915, 928
INS. *See Immigration and Naturalization Service*
INSLAW, 792 (box)
Institute of Museum Services, 867
Institute of Peace, U.S., 943
Insurance. *See also Health insurance*
antitrust exemption, 435, 463
banking overhaul, 131-142, 145
miscellaneous tax bills, 111
NAFTA highlights, 188 (box)
war use of aircraft, 447
Intellectual property rights. *See also Copyright; Patents*
Czech trade agreement, 171
NAFTA highlights, 188 (box)
Soviet-U.S. trade, 170 (box), 193
Intelligence activities
authorizations, 239-242, 242-247, 280-281, 281-283, 283-284
military uses, 301, 374
reconnaissance overflights treaty, 390, 392
reorganization plans, 284-285 (box)
surveillance aircraft, 405
Intelligence Committee, House
secrecy oaths, 281, 283
Specker's access, 243 (box)
Intelligence Community Staff, 285 (box)
Interagency Council, 699
Inter-American Development Bank, 184-185
Intercontinental ballistic missiles (ICBMs). *See also Midgetman missiles; MX missiles*
START treaty, 387-390
unilateral U.S. cutbacks, 391
Intergovernmental Panel on Climate Change, 468
Interior Department, U.S.
Arctic wildlife refuge, 512
barrier islands, 497
BLM authorization, 500
coastal zone management, 491
Endangered Species Act, 521
fish conservation, 427, 522
Indians
job training, 907
lands management, 907
law enforcement, 883
irrigation subsidies, 515-518
leadership, 475 (box)
National Park Service autonomy, 499
northern spotted owl, 520-524
oil shale claims, 499
Rocky Mountain arsenal, 527
wetlands preservation, 494
Intermediate-range nuclear force (INF) treaty
Soviet Union dissolution, 323, 325
U.S. troop cuts, 349
Intermodalism, Office of, 441, 444
Internal Revenue Service (IRS)
child support, 615
debt/refund "matching," 890
Medicare secondary payer provisions, 570, 577
penalties, 50-51
reporting requirements, 48, 50
Section 89 tax rules, 709
tax compliance, 68
urban aid tax bill, 104
International Association of Machinists and Aerospace Workers, 448, 713
International Banking Act of 1978, 147, 187
International Development Association (IDA), 185-186, 238
International Emergency Economic Powers Act of 1976, 175
International Fund for Ireland, 232, 238
International law
Supreme Court decisions, 844
International Monetary Fund (IMF)
appropriations, 269, 271, 275, 276
authorization, 185, 331
U.S. aid to Egypt, 230
U.S. aid to Soviet republics, 264, 265, 266
International Narcotics, Bureau of, 238
International Planned Parenthood Federation, 234, 235 (box)
International Red Cross, 278
International Trade Commission, U.S.
authorization, 181, 199
minivan tariffs, 198
Interstate Child Support Commission, 615-616
Interstate Commerce Commission
railroad acquisitions, 424
trucking bankruptcies, 445
Interstate highways
authorization, 437, 439, 441, 442
Inupiat Eskimos, 512
Iowa
congressional elections, 1990, 11
Iran
"October surprise" probe, 288
Persian Gulf War, 304, 312, 316-317
Russian arms sales, 275
Iran-contra affair
arms sales controls, 238
CIA watchdog provision, 238-239
contra aid, 221 (box)
covert actions notification, 237 (box)
foreign aid "leveraging," 230, 239, 248
independent counsel law, 795
indictments (box), 287
North conviction, appeal (box), 240-241
pardons, 284-287, 997
proclamation (text), 1221-1222
Iraq. *See also Persian Gulf War*
agricultural credits, 257
chemical weapons sanctions, 175-176
Export-Import Bank ban, 232
postwar aid, 630
prewar relations, 300
refugees, 79, 297, 316-317
Soviet relations, 324
Iraqi Kurdistan Front, 316
IRAs. *See Individual retirement accounts*
Ireland
U.S. aid, 232, 238
Ireland, Andy R-Fla.
House bank scandal (chart), 934
Irrigation
water subsidies, 495-496, 513-518
IRS. *See Internal Revenue Service*
Isleta Pueblo, 908
Israel
Middle East peace talks, 277-278
Persian Gulf War, 312
U.S. aid
appropriations, 228, 231, 234, 236, 271-276
authorization, 227
housing loan guarantees, 269-271
summary (box), 272-273
petroleum reserve, 364
port facilities upgrade, 365
radio transmitter, 250
refugees, 233
summary, 260, 273
U.S. trade
customs fees, 182
Italy
Persian Gulf War, 303, 311, 316 (box)
Iyad, Abu, 248
Izetbegovic, Alija, 278

J

Jackrabbit Wash, 517
Jackson, Jesse
civil rights/job bias, 760
D.C. political issues, 872-873
motor voter bill, 871
presidential election, 1992, 17, 18-19
Jackson, Thomas Penfield, 886, 946
Jackson-Vanik amendment
Caribbean Basin Initiative, 180-181, 182
China trade status, 173, 190-192
joint resolution requirement, 171
MFN summary, 172 (box)
Soviet-U.S. relations, 210
Soviet-U.S. trade, 169-171, 192
Jacobs, Andrew Jr., D-Ind.
congressional pay, 967
House bank scandal (chart), 935
Jacobson, Joy, 979, 981-982, 983
Jail. *See Prisons and prisoners*
Jamaica
Caribbean Basin Initiative, 180
Japan
environmental summit, 529
Persian Gulf War, 303
U.S. trade
drift net fishing, 528
fisheries agreement, 426
FS-X aircraft deal, 354-355
fuel-efficient cars, 484
high-tech programs, 879
investments in United States, 177
minivan tariffs, 197-198
semiconductor chips, 793
space station, 877, 900
summary, 165-168
Tongass forest timber, 492, 493
trade expansion act, 196-197
U.S. troop deployments
appropriations, 364
defense burden-sharing, 349, 358, 363
military construction appropriations, 353
Japanese-Americans
World War II internee compensation, 794
Jaruzelski, Wojciech, 211
Javelin missiles, 378
Jefferson, William J. D-La.
House bank scandal (chart), 935
House elections, 1990, 11
school reform, 658
Jeffords, James M. R-Vt.
age discrimination, 715
civil rights/job bias, 758
energy bill, 503
grazing fees, 519
House bank scandal, 936
members with overdrafts (chart), 935
mandated health benefits, 595

Jenkins, Ed D-Ga.
capital gains tax cut, 97-99
House leadership, 916
Jesuits, 217
Jews
Israel aid appropriations, 270
Ryskamp nomination, 796
Soviet emigration, 170-171, 272
"JFK" (film), 892-893
Job discrimination. *See Discrimination in employment*
Job Opportunities and Basic Skills (JOBS) program
urban aid tax bill, 107
welfare reform, 623
Job Training Partnership Act of 1982
dislocated workers, 402, 714
displaced homemakers, 715 (box)
non-traditional jobs for women, 732
revision, 705, 713-714, 728-730
summary, 704, 720
Job training programs
disadvantaged youth, 704, 713-714, 728-730
dislocated workers, 714
defense conversion aid, 402
displaced homemakers, 715 (box)
high-tech training, 892
Indians, 907
Rehabilitation Act programs, 607
veterans programs, 629, 633
women's employment, 732
JOBS. *See Job Opportunities and Basic Skills program*
Jobs Corps, 730
John F. Kennedy, 364, 378-379
Johnson, Earvin "Magic," 997
Johnson, Frank M., 797
Johnson, Nancy L. R-Conn.
child welfare, 621
ethics committee reorganization, 947
foreign investment data, 178
House bank scandal (chart), 935
Medicare physician payments, 568
Johnson, Sam R-Texas
House elections, 1991, 14
housing authorization, 695
Johnston, Harry A. D-Fla.
House bank scandal (chart), 935
Johnston, J. Bennett D-La.
alternative power, 486
Arctic wildlife refuge, 512
budget resolution, FY 1990, 43
energy bill, 500, 502-503, 505
energy policy summary, 470, 472
FHA loan ceiling, 690
irrigation subsidies, 514
natural gas decontrol, 485
Persian Gulf War, 301, 310
Puerto Rico plebiscite, 873-874
Senate leadership, 915
superconducting supercollider, 879
wetlands preservation, 529
Yucca Mountain nuclear dump, 513
Joint committees. *See also other part of name*
membership, 1136
Joint Understanding on Nuclear Arms Reductions, 329
Jones, Ben D-Ga.
House bank scandal (chart), 935
Jones, Brereton, 14
Jones coastal zone management awards, 64
Jones, Ed, 952
Jones, George Fleming, 1180
Jones-Smith, Jacqueline, 419 (box)
Jones, Walter B. D-N.C.
House bank scandal (chart), 934
House leadership, 929
Jontz, Jim D-Ind.
House bank scandal (chart), 935
House elections, 1992, 26
wetlands preservation, 557
Jordan
Middle East peace talks, 277
Persian Gulf War, 304
U.S. aid, 231, 238, 268, 269
Jordan, Barbara C., 19
Jordan, Carolyn, 981-982, 983
Jordan, Hamilton, 25
Jordan River, Utah, 493 (box)
Joshua Tree National Monument, 522
JSTARS radar, 361, 364, 378, 382, 405, 409
Judicial Conference of the United States, 774
Judicial Improvements Act of 1990, 798
Judiciary Committee, House
cable TV regulation, 452 (box)
Junk bonds
thrift regulation, 127-128
Jury selection
Supreme Court decisions, 816, 822
Justice Department, U.S.
Americans with Disabilities Act, 745, 751
animal research labs, 881
antitrust
joint ventures, 891
Chinese student visas, 755-756
congressional ethics, 914, 926, 943, 945, 946
House bank scandal, 929, 936-939
House Post Office scandal, 939-942
election day holiday, 895
financial institution fraud, 121, 129, 133, 764
flag desecration, 762
Hatch Act revision, 861
hate crime statistics, 778
HUD scandal, 676, 678, 681
independent counsel law, 795
Indian law enforcement, 884
INSLAW case, 792 (box)
JFK assassination documents, 893
judicial appointments, 776 (box)
juvenile violence, 797-798
lobbying rules, 887
Lucas nomination, 762-763
reorganization plan, 766
vertical price fixing, 771
Juvenile delinquency
prevention, 797-798
Juvenile Justice and Delinquency Prevention, Office of, 797-798

K

Kanjorski, Paul E. D-Pa.
House bank scandal (chart), 935
Kansas
disaster relief, 549
tall-grass prairie monument, 527
Karnes, David K., 683
Kasich, John R. R-Ohio
B-2 bomber, 398
budget resolutions
FY 1990, 42
FY 1991, 54
FY 1992, 77
defense authorization, FY 1991, 357
export controls, 196
Kassebaum, Nancy Landon R-Kan.
abortion, 598
adult literacy, 659
Bush education initiative, 644
civil rights/job bias, 759
higher education aid, 654
Keating Five investigation, 987
Kasten, Bob R-Wis.
abortion, 235 (box)
expiring tax provisions, 109-110
high-tech programs, 880
Israel aid, 272
motor voter bill, 894
product liability, 435, 463
Section 89 tax rules, 709, 710
Senate elections, 1992, 23, 24
Senate leadership, 7 (chart), 928
Kastenmeier, Robert W. D-Wis.
House bank scandal (chart), 935
space inventions patents, 879
Kazakhstan
arms control, 328, 329, 336
START treaty, 387-390
U.S. relations, 331
KC-135 tanker planes, 377
Kean, Thomas H., 6, 7-8
Keating, Charles H. Jr., 123, 133, 960, 975-988, 772
Keating Five investigation
"appearance standard" (box), 978
campaign finance, 953, 960
Ethics Committee findings (box), 987
Keating and Lincoln Savings (box), 976
news leaks investigation, 946
Senate elections, 1992, 24
special report, 975-988
summary, 13, 913
Kelley, Edward W. Jr., 33 (box)
Kelly, John H., 300
Kelly, Virginia, 19
Kelly, Sharon Pratt, 895-896
Kemp, Jack F.
abortion, 235 (box)
biographical profile, 1173
Bush term summary, 994
economic policy summary, 36
FHA insurance fund, 690-691
HOPE, HOME funding, 696 (box)
House bank scandal, 936
members with overdrafts (chart), 935
housing authorization, 665-670, 694-698
housing leadership, 667 (box)
HUD ethics, 686 (box)
HUD reforms, 685-687
HUD scandal, 663, 676-681
presidential election, 1992, 21
urban aid tax bill, 104
Kennedy, Anthony M.
Supreme Court summary, 801, 804, 805
Kennedy, Edward M. D-Mass.
adult literacy, 658
AIDS programs, 589
Americans with Disabilities Act, 747
artists' copyright, 772-773
child labor, 733
civil rights/job bias, 757-760, 783, 785
community service, 617
congressional pay, 971
crime bills, 767, 787
D.C. political issues, 872
Eastern Airline strikes, 705, 712
family planning authorization, 593
fetal tissue research, 599
health reform, 596
immigration reform, 753-755
Labor Department leadership, 707 (box)
mandated health benefits, 595
minimum wage, 706
parental leave, 730
Persian Gulf War, 304-305, 308
pesticide residues, 498
pocket-veto power, 927
South Africa policy, 294
striker replacements, 734
Kennedy, John F.
assassination documents, 892-893
Bay of Pigs documents, 285 (box)
Kennedy, Joseph P. II D-Mass.
government-sponsored enterprises, 155
housing authorization, 668
HUD reforms, 686
mortgage prepayments, 692
savings and loan bailout, 119
VA nurses, 627
Kennelly, Barbara B. D-Conn.
House bank scandal (chart), 934
House leadership, 916, 928
Kentucky
governor's election, 14
water projects, 493 (box)
Kenya
U.S. aid, 233 (box)
Kerrey, Bob D-Neb.
Agent Orange controversy, 628 (box)
Keating Five investigation, 987
presidential election, 1992, 17, 19
Kerry, John F. D-Mass.
Agent Orange controversy, 628 (box)
cable TV regulation, 452
campaign finance, 955, 961
environmental summit, 528
money laundering, 135
POW/MIA investigation, 289-290
Senate leadership, 928
Keswick Dam, 515
Khmer Rouge, 234, 245, 247
Kidney disease, 570, 577
Kildee, Dale E. D-Mich.
House bank scandal (chart), 934
King, Coretta Scott, 757
Kiowa helicopters, 378
Kirkland, Lane, 707
Kissimmee River, Fla., 494
Kissinger, Henry A., 289
Kleczka, Gerald D. D-Wis.
House bank scandal (chart), 935
housing authorization, 695, 696
Klug, Scott L. R-Wis.
higher education aid, 654
House bank scandal, 930
members with overdrafts (chart), 935
Knapp, John J., 682 (box)
Koblick, Ian, 945
Koch, Charles, 963
Koch, David, 963
Koch, Edward I., 7
Kohl, Helmut, 206, 214, 303, 330
Kohl, Herb D-Wis.
middle-class tax cut, 102
Kohrs, Richard, 877
Kolter, Joe D-Pa.
House Post Office scandal, 940-942
Koop, E. Everett, 881
Korean War
POW/MIA investigation, 289, 290
Kosovo, 278
Kostmayer, Peter H. D-Pa.
abortion, 600
House bank scandal, 938
members with overdrafts (chart), 934
House elections, 1992, 26
Kozyrev, Andrei V., 263
Krakow, Poland, 211, 213
Krasnoyarsk radar station, 389
Kravchuk, Leonid, 331
Kristol, William, 996
Kurds
Gulf War aftermath, 316-317
refugee aid, 233, 297
Kuwait
immigration reform, 754
Persian Gulf War, 299-317
Kwajalein Atoll, 383

Kyl, Jon R-Ariz.
ethics committee reorganization, 947
export controls, 196

L

Labeling
auto parts origin, 445
energy efficiency of lighting, 507-508
food
"dolphin-safe" tuna, 433-434
fat, daily diet information, 604 (box)
health claims of supplements, 603
nutrition information, 585
"organic" food, 540, 546
gasoline octane levels, 487-488, 510
metric packaging, 903
Labor Department, U.S.
adult literacy, 659
black lung trust fund, 734
child labor, 733
defense conversion aid, 402
ERISA reforms, 737-738
homeless veterans, 634
job training programs, 714, 729-730
leadership, 707 (box)
occupational safety, 734-735
pension law penalties, 47
Poland, Hungary aid, 213
unemployment reports, 722, 724, 725, 726
veterans rehabilitation, 629
wage equity, 782
women's employment, 732
Labor law. *See also Child labor law*
Supreme Court decisions, 845-848
Labor Statistics, Bureau of
foreign investment data, 177
occupational safety, 735
unemployment reports, 722
Labor unions and interests
adult literacy, 659
age discrimination, 715
airline buyouts, 421
Baby Bells restrictions, 461
balanced budget amendment, 85
Bush education initiative, 643-644
campaign finance, 951-957
child care, 611
coal miners' health fund, 735 (box)
Davis-Bacon Act revision, 732
Eastern Airlines strike, 712-713
federal employee honoraria, 858
Hatch Act revision, 860
labor policy summary, 703-704
NAFTA, 189
non-traditional apprenticeships for women, 732
parental leave, 711
pension reversions, 719-720
Postal Service off-budget plan, 869
rail strikes, 447-449
Section 89 tax rules, 708
striker replacements, 733-734
Supreme Court decisions, 845-846, 847-848
trucking bankruptcies, 445
LaFalce, John J. D-N.Y.
civil rights/job bias, 760
parental leave, 731
Section 89 tax rules, 709
small business loans, 463
Third World debt, 184
Lagomarsino, Robert J. R-Calif.
House bank scandal (chart), 935
House leadership, 916
Laird, Melvin R., 289
Lake Andes-Wagner Unit, 517
Lake Francis Case, 517
Lake Gaston, 494
Lake Mendocino, 518
Lake Meredith, 516-517
Lancaster, H. Martin D-N.C.
House bank scandal (chart), 935
House elections, 1992, 27
Lance missiles, 347
Land Development Mortgage Insurance Program, 678-679, 680, 688
Land Management, Bureau of (BLM)
authorization, 499-500, 520
grazing fees, 518-519
hydroelectric power, 507
Indian programs investigation, 882
mining law overhaul, 519
northern spotted owl, 520
Pacific yew harvest, 527
Landsat Remote-Sensing Satellite Program, 900
Lanier, Bob, 8
Lantos, Tom D-Calif.
HUD scandal, 676-685
Romanian trade agreement, 194
Laos
refugee asylum, 756
Vietnam War MIAs, 277, 289-290
Las Vegas, Nev., 528
Latin America. *See also Central America; specific countries*
debt-for-science swaps, 903
development bank authorization, 184
Enterprise for the Americas, 179-180, 194-195, 200
appropriations, 274, 275, 276
immigration reform, 752
Latta, Delbert L., 917, 935 (chart)
Latvia. *See Baltic republics*
Laughlin, Greg D-Texas
House bank scandal (chart), 935
Lautenberg, Frank R. D-N.J.
abortion, 599
airline smoking ban, 420
Clean Air Act, 478
CPSC authorization, 433
highway authorization, 439
"Israel only" passports, 292
rural telecommunications, 461
LAV armored vehicles, 405
Law profession and practice
aircraft liability, 422
attorneys' fees
civil rights/job bias, 758, 759
Social Security proceedings, 62
Supreme Court decisions, 839-840
group legal services, 47, 68-69, 94
lawsuit consolidation, 779, 798
Supreme Court decisions, 814
Lawlor, James, 27
LCAC barges, 349
Leach, Jim R-Iowa
Middle East peace talks, 277
Philippine base closings, 412
savings and loan bailout, 119
Lead poisoning prevention
block grant, 608
EPA restrictions, 530
housing bills, 606-607, 697-698
Leadership Conference on Civil Rights, 744
Leadville Mine drainage, 516
League of Women Voters, 85, 871, 961
Leahy, Patrick J. D-Vt.
agricultural exports enhancement, 555
Agriculture Department streamlining, 556 (box)
cable TV regulation, 453
dairy production, 553 (box)
farm bill, 541
food pyramid, 554 (box)
foreign aid
appropriations, 274
authorization, 268
Israel, 272
Persian Gulf War, 315
rural development, 547-548
Senate elections, 1992, 26
Senate leadership, 915
wetlands preservation, 556
Leaking Underground Storage Tank Trust Fund, 67
Leath, Marvin D-Texas
House bank scandal (chart), 935
Leather goods, 182
Lebanon
immigration reform, 754
Lee, Rex, 778
Legal Services Corporation
authorization, 773-774, 795
Bush appointments (box), 1178
Legislative Initiative Mandating Incumbent Terms (LIMIT), 963
Legislative intent, 784
Legislative process
budget process changes (box), 56-57
fast-track procedures
NAFTA, 187-189
glossary, 1001-1012
how a bill becomes a law (chart), 1017
legislative process in brief, 1013-1016
Legislative veto
Jackson-Vanik amendment, 171, 172 (box), 180-181
Lehman, Richard H. D-Calif.
House bank scandal (chart), 935
Leland, Mickey D-Texas
death, successor, 8
House leadership, 917
Lend-Lease, 170 (box), 330
Lenoir, William, 877
Lent, Norman F. R-N.Y.
Americans with Disabilities Act, 745
cable TV regulation, 453
Clean Air Act, 475
foreign investment data, 178
Leukemia, 634
Leveraged buyouts
airlines, 421
Levin, Carl D-Mich.
lobbying rules, 837
middle-class tax cut, 102
regulatory negotiation, 865
whistleblowers protection, 862-863
Levin, Sander M. D-Mich.
minivan tariffs, 198
trade expansion act, 197
Levy, David, 234
Lewis, Drew, 38
Lewis, Jerry R-Calif.
franking privilege, 968
House bank scandal, 933
House leadership, 7 (chart), 916, 929
Lewis, John D-Ga.
civil rights/job bias, 783
House bank scandal (chart), 934
House leadership, 928
Lewis, Tom R-Fla.
House bank scandal (chart), 935
LH helicopters, 357, 361, 354
LHX helicopters, 347, 351
Liability issues
aircraft, 422, 446
damage suits
Customs searches, 798
law enforcement agents, 778-779
medical malpractice, 609, 780, 798
Supreme Court decisions, 841-842
nuclear accidents, 509
oil spills, 490-491
product liability, 435, 462-463
RTC asset sales, 149
toxic real estate, 141
Liaison Services, Office of, 764
Liberia
immigration reform, 754
Libraries
federal aid authorization, 652
higher education aid, 653
Library of Congress
acid-free paper, 869
Libya
U.S. aid to Kenya, 233 (box)
Lieberman, Joseph I. D-Conn.
Persian Gulf War, 309, 310
Life insurance
taxes, 50, 68, 96
Lightfoot, Jim Ross R-Iowa
House bank scandal, 938
members with overdrafts (chart), 934
LIMIT. *See Legislative Initiative Mandating Incumbent Terms*
Lincoln Savings and Loan Association, 114, 120, 123, 133, 975-988
Linder, Carl H., 976
Lindsey, Lawrence B., 33 (box)
Line-item veto
expedited rescissions, 85-86
joint ventures bill, 891
Lipinski, William O. D-Ill.
House bank scandal (chart), 935
Literacy programs
adult literacy, 657, 658-659
Bush education initiative, 643, 644
close-captioned TV, 429
Head Start parents, 621
library aid authorization, 652
prison programs, 659
trucker safety, 659
VISTA authorization, 619
Lithuania. *See Baltic republics*
Little Bighorn Battlefield National Monument, 525
Livestock and ranching
dairy herd buy-up limits, 541
drought sale, 110
grazing fees, 78, 518-519
mining restrictions, 531
Living wills, 573, 577
Lloyd, Marilyn D-Tenn.
House bank scandal (chart), 935
House leadership, 929
Loan Management Set Aside program, 680
Lobbying Registration and Public Disclosure, Office of, 887
Lobbyists and lobbying
cable TV regulation, 452 (box)
campaign finance, 955, 957
congressional ethics code, 921
fuel efficiency mandates, 501
HUD reforms, 688
Israel housing loan guarantees, 270
Legal Services ban, 795
lobbying curbs, 862, 887
"revolving door," 861-862, 887
Local Rail Assistance Program, 424-425
Lochner, Philip R. Jr., 419 (box)
Lodine, 793
Logging. *See Forests and national forests*
Long, Jill D-Ind.
election, 8
House bank scandal (chart), 934
Long, Russell B., 952
Long-term health care
insurance regulation, 609
Pepper Commission, 584 (box), 919
social health maintenance organizations, 577
Longbow helicopters, 378, 382, 405, 409
Lord, Winston, 289
Lorenzo, Frank, 421, 712-713

Los Angeles, Calif., riots
housing authorization, 698
summary, 15
urban aid, 84, 699-700
Los Angeles County, Calif., 493 (box), 494
***Los Angeles*-class submarines**
appropriations, 350, 352
rescissions, 383 (box)
authorization, 1990, 341, 344, 349
Seawolf submarine, 410
LOSAT vehicles, 378
Lott, Trent R-Miss.
B-2 bomber, 399
Hatch Act revision, 861
highway authorization, 439
Keating Five investigation, 977, 980, 984-985
public broadcasting, 458
Section 89 tax rules, 709
Louisiana
Clean Air Act, 474
congressional elections, 1990, 11
disaster relief, 84
water projects, 493 (box)
wetlands restoration, 67
Low-Income Home Energy Assistance Program, 614
Low-Income Housing Preservation and Resident Home Ownership Act of 1990, 674
Lowery, Bill R-Calif.
House bank scandal (chart), 934
Lowery, Mike, (chart), 935
Lowey, Nita M. D-N.Y.
House bank scandal (chart), 935
Loyola University of Chicago, 78 (box), 193
LSD landing ships, 349, 379
LTV Corp., 720
Lucas, William, 763-764, 1177-1179
Lugar, Richard R-Ind.
Agriculture Department streamlining, 556 (box)
congressional pay, 971
farm bill, 541
Persian Gulf War, 314
South Africa policy, 253, 295
Soviet aid, 262, 330
Lujan, Manuel Jr.
biographical profile, 1173
BLM authorization, 520
Bush term summary, 993
campaign funds, 952
Interior leadership, 475 (box)
irrigation subsidies, 514
northern spotted owl, 521
Luken, Thomas A. D-Ohio
food labeling, 585
hazardous materials transport, 423
House bank scandal (chart), 935
Lukens, Donald E. "Buz" R-Ohio
ethics case, 913, 925
House bank scandal (chart), 934
House elections, 1990, 11
Lumbee Tribe of Cheraw Indians, 909
Luxury taxes, 67, 96, 103, 107, 109-110, 722

M

M-1 tanks
appropriations, 351, 364, 382, 407-409
authorization
FY 1990, 344, 346
FY 1991, 360-361
FY 1992, 372, 376, 377, 380
FY 1993, 396, 404
M-88 tractors, 346
Mabus, Ray, 14
MacDonald, Peter Sr., 882
Machine tools, 197
Machtley, Ronald K. R-R.I.
House bank scandal (chart), 934
Mack, Connie R-Fla.
housing authorization, 668-669, 697
Mack, John P., 918
Madigan, Edward R. R-Ill.
Agriculture Department streamlining, 556 (box)
Agriculture leadership, 539 (box)
biographical profile, 1169
food pyramid, 554 (box)
Health Service Corps, 588
House bank scandal, 933, 936
members with overdrafts (chart), 934
House leadership, 5, 916, 929
irrigation subsidies, 514
successor, 14
Madison amendment, 972-973
Madison, James, 161
Magic Lantern defenses, 379, 406
Magnetic levitation, 904, 437, 438, 442, 444
Magnuson Fishery Conservation and Management Act, 434
Mahe, Eddie, 959
Maine
bridge repairs, 445
wilderness areas, 496
Maine Indian Claims Settlement Act of 1980, 909
Make Democracy Work Fund, 962
Malakai Harbor, Palau, 259
Mallick, George, 917-918
Malta summit, 1989, 169, 205, 206-207, 328, 330, 389
Mammography
cancer screening authorization, 593, 608
Medicare coverage, 573, 577
Manafort, Paul J., 679 (box)
Management and Budget, Office of (OMB)
Brooklyn courthouse, 438 (box)
budget policy
accounting standards, 858
budget process changes, 70, 71, 72
credit reform, 60 (box), 72, 73
deficit forecasts, 39, 43
federal financial centralization, 862
mini-sequester, 78 (box)
tax, entitlement bill estimates, 631
Bush economic team, 32 (box)
defense authorization, 1990, 345
energy bill, 502
EPA Cabinet status, 498
federal energy efficiency, 890
federal pensions, 859
FHA insurance fund, 691
flood insurance, 699
foreign aid, 271
food aid, 257
Israel loan guarantees, 272
government-sponsored enterprises, 155
Gulf War veterans benefits, 630-631
Hatch Act revision, 860
Head Start, 614
highway authorization, 438 (box), 441
housing authorization, 669, 670
Indian law enforcement, 884
Medicaid, 601
motor voter bill, 894
regulatory review authority, 645-646, 867-869, 891
Social Security earnings test, 736
Soviet, East bloc trade, 193
unemployment benefits, 723-725, 725-726
whistleblowers protection, 862
Mandel, Ruth, 24
Mandela, Nelson, 8, 253-254, 294-295
Mankiller, Wilma P., 883
Manley, Michael, 232
Manton, Thomas J. D-N.Y.
cable TV regulation, 454
House bank scandal (chart), 934
Mapplethorpe, Robert, 865
Marine Corps, U.S.
appropriations, 350, 352, 363-365, 380-382, 407-409
defense authorization, 340-350, 355-363, 369-380, 395-407
Persian Gulf War, 313
V-22 Osprey controversy, 348
Marine Resources Development Foundation, 945
Maritime Administration, 426, 450
Mark torpedoes, 349
Mark Twain National Forest, 525-526
Market Promotion Program, 545
Markey, Edward J. D-Mass.
cable TV regulation, 428, 453, 454
children's TV, 429
corporate auditors, 160
House bank scandal (chart), 934
radio spectrum allocation, 459
securities market reforms, 130
Marlenee, Ron R-Mont.
House bank scandal, 938
members with overdrafts (chart), 934
House elections, 1992, 26
Marriage and divorce
domestic partners health benefits, 896-897
Gulf War veterans counseling, 636
Social Security benefits, 62, 63
tax deduction, 51
Marron, Donald B., 684
Mars space mission, 876, 898, 899
Marshall Islands
PCB cleanup, 512
Marshall, Thurgood
Bush term summary, 994
Supreme Court summary, 801, 804, 805
Martin-Baro, Ignacio, 217
Martin County, Fla., 493 (box)
Martin, David O'B. R-N.Y.
House bank scandal (chart), 935
Martin, Lynn R-Ill.
biographical profile, 1173-1174
Bush term summary, 993
child labor law, 733
congressional pay, 966
ERISA reforms, 737-738
House bank scandal, 933, 936
members with overdrafts (chart), 934
House leadership, 916
Labor Department leadership, 707 (box)
occupational safety, 735
presidential election, 1992, 21
striker replacements, 733-734
unemployment benefits, 726
Martinez, Bob, 11, 745 (box), 768, 789, 1176
Martinez, Matthew G. D-Calif.
age discrimination, 716
lawsuit waivers, 716
displaced homemakers, 715 (box)
Head Start, 621
House bank scandal (chart), 934
Older Americans Act, 620
Marty II Unit, 517
Maryland
D.C. retrocession offer, 872
highway authorization, 442
offshore drilling ban, 491
Mass transit
authorization, 437-443
D.C. Metro aid, 873
employee benefits, 108
employee drug testing, 448
summary, 417
Massachusetts
bankruptcy judges, 799
highway authorization, 442
offshore drilling ban, 491
water projects, 493 (box)
Maternal and Child Health Block Grant, 579
Math education
Bush education initiative, 643
high-tech training, 892
program authorization, 650-651
student aid, 770
Matsui, Robert T. D-Calif.
House bank scandal (chart), 934
Matsunaga, Spark M. D-Hawaii
hydrogen fuel research, 486-487
Senate leadership, 915
successor, 12
Maumee River, Ind., 493 (box)
Maverick missiles, 344
Mavroules, Nicholas D-Mass.
ethics case, 914, 945
House bank scandal (chart), 935
House Post Office scandal, 941
Maxwell National Wildlife Refuge, 517
Mazowiecki, Tadeusz, 171, 324
McAlpine Dam, Ind., 493 (box)
McCafferty, Phillip, 679 (box)
McCain, John R-Ariz.
campaign finance, 955
catastrophic medical costs insurance, 566-567
community service, 617
Gulf War veterans benefits, 630
Indians
health, human services, 883, 905
lands management, 907
programs investigation, 882
irrigation subsidies, 515
joint ventures, 891
Keating Five investigation, 975-988
motor voter bill, 894
Older Americans Act, 620
Persian Gulf War, 312
political advertising, 958
Senate elections, 1992, 24
Senate leadership, 915
Social Security earnings test, 736-737
State Department authorization, 291
superconducting supercollider, 878
unemployment benefits, 723
McCandless, Al R-Calif.
coin redesign, 161
McCarran-Ferguson Act of 1945, 435, 463
McCarran-Walter Act of 1952, 247, 250, 753 (box)
McCloskey, Frank D-Ind.
deceptive mail curbs, 870
House bank scandal (chart), 934
McClure, Frederick D., 706
McClure, James A. R-Idaho
age discrimination, 716
CPSC authorization, 433
natural gas decontrol, 485
Puerto Rico plebiscite, 873-874
Senate leadership, 928
McCollum, Bill R-Fla.
Americans with Disabilities Act, 746
civil rights/job bias, 782
House bank scandal, 933
House leadership, 916
immigration reform, 754

McConnell, Mitch R-Ky.
campaign finance, 953, 955, 960-961
Hatch Act revision, 860
motor voter bill, 894
political advertising, 957
Senate elections, 1990, 11
Senate leadership, 928
uniform poll closing time, 872
McCrery, Jim R-La.
House bank scandal, 938
McCurdy, Dave D-Okla.
community service, 617
House bank scandal (chart), 935
House leadership, 929
intelligence authorization, 239, 283
intelligence reorganization plans, 284-285 (box)
Soviet Union dissolution, 321
McDade, Joseph M. R-Pa.
ethics case, 914, 917-945
House leadership, 916, 929
McDermott, Jim D-Wash.
ethics committee reorganization, 947
unemployment benefits, 721
McDonnell Douglas Corp., 294, 379
McEwen, Bob R-Ohio
House bank scandal, 938
members with overdrafts (chart), 934
House elections, 1992, 26
Persian Gulf War, 315
McFarland, Ernest, 517
McFarlane, Robert C., 241 (box), 286
McGlotten, Robert, 734
McGrath, Raymond J. R-N.Y.
House bank scandal (chart), 935
savings and loan bailout, 122
McHugh, Matthew F. D-N.Y.
ethics committee reorganization, 947
House bank scandal, 930-931, 936
members with overdrafts (chart), 935
Savage ethics case, 924
McKinney Homeless Assistance Act, 675, 693-694, 698
McMillan, J. Alex R-N.C.
House bank scandal (chart), 935
McMillen, Tom D-Md.
House elections, 1992, 26
McNulty, Michael R. D-N.Y.
House bank scandal (chart), 934
Mead Johnson & Co., 623
Meals on Wheels, 620
Measles, 587
Meat
food pyramid, 554 (box)
Medal of Freedom, 919
Mediation
rail strikes, 448
striker replacements, 734
Medicaid
action
1989, 578-580
1990, 580-582
budget reconciliation, FY 1990, 43-44
drug discounts, 605-606
human services reconciliation, 615
Oregon health plan, 597 (box)
Medigap insurance regulation, 583
Pepper Commission, 584 (box)
summary, 578, 580
Medical care. *See Health and medical care*
Medical devices and equipment
Medicare payments, 570, 576
regulation, 586, 607
Medical education
Health Service Corps, 587-588
Indian health services, 905
student loan defaults, 650
training authorization, 609
Medical ethics
fetal tissue research, 591
living wills, 573, 577
Medical malpractice
community, migrant health centers, 609
health reform, 596
military reservists protections, 634
military suits, 780, 798
Medical Recoveries Fund, 626
Medical research and technology
aging, 592
Alzheimer's disease, 592, 608
animal research labs, 881, 904
cancer-tracking registries, 608
defense appropriations, 408, 409
disabilities prevention, 595, 610
disease prevention, 608
fetal tissue, 591, 602-603
injury prevention, treatment, 591-592
mutant mice lab, 595
treatment effectiveness, 567, 572
VA grants, 629
women's health needs, 590-591
Medicare
budget reconciliation
FY 1990, 43, 571-573
FY 1991, 71, 573-578
fraud, abuse prevention, 609
Indian health services, 905
Medigap insurance regulation, 582-585
physician payments, physician referrals, 567-571
state, local employees, 68
tax wage base, 68, 92 (box), 96
urban aid tax bill, 107-108
Medicare Catastrophic Coverage Act of 1988
Medigap insurance regulation, 582-583
preserved, re-enacted provisions
case management, 577-578
hospice care, 575
Medicaid, 578
repeal, 43, 46, 51, 565-567
Medigap insurance policies, 582-585, 609
Melcher, John, 915
Membrane technology, 903
Mendocino County, Calif., 518
Menendez, Robert, 27
Mental health and illness
ADAMHA authorization, 604-605
Americans with Disabilities Act, 743
education for disabled, 647
Indian health services, 883
Medicare
budget reconciliation, 1989, 571-572
budget reconciliation, 1990, 576
physician payments, 570
nursing home regulation, 573, 587
protection, advocacy, 622
services authorization, 592
veterans programs, 625
homeless vets, 635
post-traumatic stress disorder, 636
Mental Health Block Grant, 604
Mental retardation. *See Developmental disabilities*
Merit Systems Protection Board, 862-864
Methane
coal-bed extraction, 511
global warming, 297, 483
Methanol
alternative fuels, 487 (box)
Clean Air Act, 473, 475
Metric system, 442, 903
Metzenbaum, Howard M. D-Ohio
age discrimination, 715-716
Eastern Airlines strike, 712
federal judgeships, 774
highway authorization, 439
intelligence authorization, 282
joint ventures, 891
natural gas decontrol, 485
news leaks investigation, 947
Older Americans Act, 620
pension reversions, 720
savings and loan bailout, 119, 149
striker replacements, 734
vertical price fixing, 771
Mexico
agricultural debt relief, 195
NAFTA, 187-190
screwworm eradication, 550
wetlands preservation, 494
Mexico City policy, 235 (box), 267-269, 600
Mexico-U.S. border
housing authorization, 675
Meyers, John T. R-Kan.
House leadership, 917
MFN. *See Most-favored-nation trading status*
Mfume, Kweisi D-Md.
House bank scandal (chart), 934
Miami, Fla., 493 (box)
Miccousukee Tribe of Indians, 885
Michel, Robert H. R-Ill.
budget action
FY 1990 reconciliation, 46
FY 1991 resolution, 55
campaign finance, 956, 962
congressional pay, 965-966
D.C., territorial voting, 949
defense authorization, 373
Gulf War veterans benefits, 631
Hatch Act revision, 861
legislative summary, 1991, 12
House bank scandal, 930, 933, 936
House elections, 1992, 27
House leadership, 5, 7 (chart), 914, 916, 928-929
McDade ethics case, 945
motor voter bill, 871, 894
Persian Gulf War, 310
Poland, Hungary aid, 211
savings and loan bailout refinancing, 150
unemployment benefits, 724, 725
Michigan
congressional elections, 1990, 11
highway authorization, 442
Madison amendment, 972
term limits, 10 (box), 963
unemployment benefits, 726
water projects, 493 (box)
Micmac Indians, 885-886, 908-909
Mid-Dakota Rural Water System Inc., 517
Middle East. *See also specific countries*
arms proliferation, 291
foreign aid appropriations, 269, 271, 276
foreign aid authorization, 268, 269
Madrid peace talks, 277-278
Bush address (text), 1211
State Department authorization, 248
Midgetman missiles
appropriations, 351, 364, 382
continued development (box), 343
defense authorization
FY 1990, 341-346
FY 1991, 358-359, 360
FY 1992, 373, 377
unilateral U.S. arms cutbacks, 391
Midwestern states
Clean Air Act, 474, 479, 482, 483
Migrant health centers, 588
Migrant workers
higher education aid, 656
housing authorization, 675
minimum wage, 708
Migratory Bird Conservation Commission, 494
Mikulski, Barbara A. D-Md.
Medicare budget reconciliation, 1990, 574
Senate elections, 1992, 24
Mildred and Claude Pepper Scholarship Act, 653
Military aid. *See Arms sales and transfers*
Military base closings
action
1989-90, 353-354
1991, 393-395
airport conversion, 419
appropriations, 382-383, 409, 411
authorization
FY 1990, 350
FY 1991, 357, 358, 359, 363
FY 1992, 380
closed, realigned bases, 1992-97 (chart), 394
community turnover, 376, 380
displaced workers, 402, 888-889
environmental cleanup, 365-366, 380
NATO training site, 357
overseas bases, 395
summary, 339
unemployment benefits, 721
Military dependents
abortion, 359, 376, 381, 397, 400, 401, 599-600
child care, 349
medical services, 635
Military hospitals
abortion
FY 1991 defense authorization, 358, 359, 594
FY 1992 appropriations, 381
FY 1992 defense authorization, 376, 599-600
FY 1993 defense authorization, 397, 400, 401
malpractice suits, 780, 798
Military pay and benefits
budget reprogramming, 356 (box)
hardship post bonuses, 380
pay raise, 379
recruiting bonuses, 349
retirement, 380, 401, 409
defense conversion aid, 402
early-out payments, 363, 407
lump-sum pension payments, 859
VA nurses, 625
Military personnel. *See also Veterans*
abortion
FY 1991 defense authorization, 359, 594
FY 1992 appropriations, 381
FY 1992 defense authorization, 376, 599-600
FY 1993 defense authorization, 397, 400, 401
aliens, 779-780, 793-794
appropriations, 352, 364, 382, 408-409
family separation prevention, 634
Gulf War mail service, 969
malpractice suits, 780, 798
manpower authorization
FY 1990, 349
FY 1991, 356, 359-360
FY 1992, 369, 372, 379-380
FY 1993, 395, 406-407
sexual harassment, rape counseling, 635
U.S. troops overseas, 372, 407
El Salvador, 219
Europe
appropriations, 74, 351

authorizations, 357, 362, 373, 376, 397, 401, 407
Soviet-U.S. relations, 208
incursions since 1903 (box), 226
Japan, 358, 363, 364
military construction appropriations, 352-353, 365, 382-383
Panama invasion, 223-225
Philippine base closings, 411-412
reduction proposals, 387 (box)
Somalia relief, 260, 278-280
South Korea, 345, 349, 351, 373
women (box), 374-375
Military posts. *See also Military base closings; Military hospitals*
construction appropriations, 352-353, 365-366, 382-383, 409, 411
construction authorization, 349-350
environmental cleanup, 349
overseas bases, 407
NATO countries aid, 274
Palau autonomy, 258-259
Philippines, 411-412
Military reserves
appropriations, 364, 381, 382, 407, 409
availability period, 364
defense authorization
FY 1990, 349
FY 1991, 356, 363
FY 1992, 369, 373, 376, 380
FY 1993, 396, 404, 406, 407
foreign civilian employees, 362
job protections, 634
military construction appropriations, 352, 365, 382-383, 411
Persian Gulf War, 302
veterans benefits, 629, 630
radiation exposure compensation, 634
veterans benefits, 625
job, education aid, 633
home loans, 635-636
Milk and dairy products
exports, 544
price supports, 544, 548, 555
production limits (box), 553
Miller, Clarence E. R-Ohio
foreign aid appropriations, 234
Miller, George D-Calif.
House bank scandal, 936
members with overdrafts (chart), 934
House leadership, 929
irrigation subsidies, 496, 513-514
minimum wage, 706
Tongass forest, 492
Miller, John R. R-Wash.
House bank scandal (chart), 934
Miller, Richard R., 287 (box)
Miller, Zell, 19
Milstar communications satellite, 350, 357
Mimbres Indians, 909
Mine sweepers
apppropriations, 352, 364, 382, 409
authorization, 349, 379, 406
Mineral Leasing Act of 1920, 499
Mineral Management Service, 518
Mineral resources and mining. *See also Coal; Oil and natural gas; Uranium*
environmental protection
Antarctica, 489, 529-530
Arizona wilderness, 496
California desert, 522
Nevada wilderness, 496
federal rangelands, 531
health, safety violations penalties, 61
mining law overhaul, 519-520
research institute, 880
Mineta, Norman Y. D-Calif.
highway authorization, 440, 441
House bank scandal (chart), 935
Minimum wage, 703, 705-708
Mining Law of 1872, 499, 519-520
Mink, Patsy T. D-Hawaii
civil rights/job bias, 784
House elections, 1990, 12
Minnesota
campaign finance reform, 957 (box)
Medicaid alternative, 579, 582
water projects, 493 (box)
welfare alternative, 615
Minnesota National Guard, 361 (box)
Minorities. *See also Asian-Americans; Blacks; Hispanics; Indians; Japanese-Americans; Jews; Kurds; Minority-owned business*
broadcast license preference, 431 (box)
civil rights/job bias, 757-760, 780-785
education
education for disabled, 648
higher education aid, 657
housing authorization, 676
math, science education, 651
race-exclusive scholarships, 655 (box)
health programs, 588, 591
disabled children, 622
housing opportunity, 671
immigration reform, 752
international issues
Bosnian conflict, 278
Soviet ethnic unrest, 320, 331
VA post, 636
Minority Health, Office of, 588
Minority-owned business
Davis-Bacon Act revision, 732
highway contracts, 440, 441
Indian preference, 884, 907
RTC contracts, 150, 152
superconducting supercollider, 877
Mint, U.S.
coin redesign, 135, 161
director, 161
Minuteman missiles, 377
MIRACL, 346, 360
Missing-in-action (MIA) servicemen
Defense Department files, 380
foreign aid appropriations, 276, 277
Gulf War veterans benefits, 630
investigation, 288-290
State Department authorization, 291
Mission to Planet Earth, 876, 898, 899
Mississippi
ASRM plant, 874, 876
governor's election, 1991, 14
military construction appropriations, 411
Missouri
Clean Air Act, 474
Madison amendment, 972
national forest, 525-526
term limits, 10 (box), 963
water projects, 493 (box)
Missouri River
water projects, 517, 518
wild, scenic river designation, 525
Mitchell, George J. D-Maine
defense, trade and foreign policy
arms control, 329, 391
China trade, 173-174, 191
covert aid, 245
Iran-contra pardons, 287
Persian Gulf War, 304-305, 307-311
Soviet aid, 265
Soviet-U.S. trade, 171
domestic issues
abortion, 598
age discrimination, 716
Arctic wildlife refuge, 512
budget-control efforts, 85
budget reconciliation, 46, 58
budget "walls," 83 (box)
cable TV regulation, 427-428
capital gains tax cut, 5, 97-99
child care, 612
civil rights/job bias, 758
Clean Air Act, 468, 474, 476-478
crime bills, 766, 787, 789
Eastern Airlines strike, 713
expiring tax provisions, 110
federal employee honoraria, 886
federal facilities cleanup, 525
Hatch Act revision, 860, 887
health reform, 596
highway authorization, 439
housing authorization, 697
Medicare physician payments, 568
middle-class tax cut, 102
minimum wage, 706
motor voter bill, 894
oil-spill liability, 490
Pepper scholarships, 653
product liability, 463
Section 89 tax rules, 710
transportation corrections, 445
unemployment benefits, 723-725
Senate leadership
campaign finance, 953-955
congressional pay, 965, 967, 970-971
judicial nominating process, 796
Keating Five investigation, 985
news leaks investigation, 946
Souter nomination, 801
summary, 5, 7 (chart), 914, 915, 928
Thomas confirmation, 802-803
Mitchell, John, 679 (box)
Mitsubishi, 354
Mitterand, François, 207
MLRS rockets
appropriations, 351
authorization, 347, 374, 378, 405
Moakley, Joe D-Mass.
Caribbean Basin Initiative, 180
coin redesign, 135
El Salvador aid, 218
Gulf War veterans benefits, 630
House bank scandal, 936
members with overdrafts (chart), 934
House leadership, 917
immigration reform, 754, 755
Mobile homes
rental assistance, 673
safety standards, 668
Model Projects for Pregnant and Post Partum Women and Their Infants, 968
Mofford, Rose, 982
Mohair, 544
Moi, Daniel arap, 233 (box)
Mojave Desert, 522
Moldova, 331
Molinari, Guy V. R-N.Y.
House elections, 1990, 12
Molinari, Susan R-N.Y.
House bank scandal (chart), 935
House elections, 1990, 12
Mollohan, Alan B. D-W.Va.
House bank scandal (chart), 934
Mondale, Walter D., 859 (box)
Money
coin redesign, 135, 161
commemorative coins, 161
dollar value, 165-166
Russian currency stabilization, 264, 266
Soviet gold coin imports, 193
Money laundering, 134-135, 156-157, 766, 768
Mongolia
U.S. trade, 194
Monney, Neil, 945
Monopoly. *See Competition and monopoly*
Montana
irrigation subsidies, 518
sports lottery ban, 790
term limits, 10 (box), 963
wilderness area, 526
Montenegro
U.S. trade, 194
Montgomery GI bill, 625
Montgomery, G.V. "Sonny" D-Miss.
Agent Orange controversy, 628 (box), 633
Gulf War veterans' benefits, 630-631
VA medical salaries, 633
veterans' COLA increase, 631-632
veterans' dependents' benefits, 632
veterans leadership, 627 (box)
Monticciolo, Joseph D., 682
Montreal Protocols, 446
Montserrat
Caribbean Basin Initiative, 180
Monuments. *See Historic sites and monuments*
Moody, Jim D-Wis.
House Post Office scandal, 941
unemployment benefits, 724
Moon
space exploration, 876, 898, 899
Moore, W. Henson, 488
Moorefield, W.Va., 493 (box)
Moran, James P. Jr. D-Va.
House bank scandal (chart), 935
Moreland, Charles, 872
Morella, Constance A. R-Md.
women's employment, 732-733
Morgan, Robert, 982
Morocco
Persian Gulf War, 302, 316 (box)
U.S. aid, 275, 276
Morrison, Alan B., 937
Morrison, Bruce A. D-Conn.
governor's elections, 1990, 11
House bank scandal (chart), 935
HUD scandal, 683, 684
immigration reform, 754
Mortgage Bankers Association, 691
Mortgage revenue bonds, 47, 69, 94
Mortgages. *See Home loans and mortgages*
Mosbacher, Robert A.
biographical profile, 1170
Bush term summary, 993
Commerce leadership, 419 (box)
foreign trade summary, 167
FS-X aircraft deal, 355
Moscow Embassy, 209 (box), 248, 263 (box), 290-291
Mosely-Braun, Carol, 23, 24
Most-favored-nation trading status
China, 173-174
Poland, Hungary aid, 211-212
summary (box), 172
Motion Picture Association of America, 452 (box)
Motion pictures and movie industry
cable TV regulation, 451, 452 (box), 454
transportation infrastructure film, 444
Motor vehicles. *See Automobiles and auto industry; Fuel taxes; Trucks and trucking*
Motorcycle safety, 443
Mount Pinatubo, 411-412
Mountain Park Master Conservancy District, 518
Moving to Opportunity, 698
Moynihan, Daniel Patrick D-N.Y.
Brooklyn courthouse, 438 (box)
budget resolution, FY 1992, 77
campaign finance, 955

congressional pay, 968
foreign aid appropriations, 230
highway authorization, 437-439, 441
Iran-contra legacy, 239
Persian Gulf War, 304
Senate leadership, 928
Social Security tax changes, 718-719, 736, 737
State Department authorization, 248-249
tax policy summary, 89-90
welfare dependency research, 623
Mrazek, Robert L. D-N.Y.
House bank scandal, 932, 933
members with overdrafts (chart), 934
Mubarak, Hosni, 236, 299
Mujahedeen, 246
Mullins, David W. Jr., 33 (box)
Mulroney, Brian, 187, 188 (box)
Multi-Fiber Arrangement of 1973, 167, 174-175
Murkowski, Frank H. R-Alaska
Arctic wildlife refuge, 499
civil rights/job bias, 784-785
congressional pay, 968
energy bill, 504
foreign investment data, 178
Indian health service, 905
Senate elections, 1992, 24, 25
Senate leadership, 915, 928
Tongass forest, 493
Murphy, Austin J. D-Pa.
House bank scandal (chart), 935
House Post Office scandal, 940-942
minimum wage, 706
Murphy, Richard W., 300
Murray, Patty, 24
Murthra, John P. D-Pa.
House bank scandal (chart), 935
Persian Gulf War, 310
Somalia relief, 279
Museums
Indian remains, 884-885
Music industry
home digital recording, 459
Muslims
Iraqi Shi'ites, 316-317
Yugoslav conflict, 278
Mussels, 496-497
Mutual Mortgage Insurance Fund, 60, 669, 672, 690
Mutual funds, 48
MX missiles
appropriations, 351, 364, 381
continued development (box), 343
defense authorization
FY 1990, 341-346
FY 1991, 358-359, 360
FY 1992, 373, 376, 377
defense policy summary, 337
unilateral U.S. arms cutbacks, 391
Myanmar
U.S. trade sanctions, 182
Myers, John T. R-Ind.
House bank scandal (chart), 934
superconducting supercollider, 878
Myrtle Beach, S.C., 493 (box)

N

NAACP. *See National Association for the Advancement of Colored People*
Nader, Ralph, 959, 965, 967
NAFTA. *See North American Free Trade Agreement*
Nagle, Dave D-Iowa
farm bill, 540
House bank scandal, 938
members with overdrafts (chart), 935
House elections, 1992, 26
NASA authorization, 875
Nagorno-Karabakh, 266, 331
Namibia
peace accord, 247
Natcher, William H. D-Ky.
House leadership, 929
National Academy of Sciences
Agent Orange study, 632
census study, 895
nuclear waste disposal, 505, 509, 513
space station, 877
National Academy of Social Insurance, 719
National Aeronautics and Space Administration (NASA)
aircraft noise abatement, 447
authorizations
1990, 874-876
1991, 876-877
1992-94, 897-898
1993, 898-899
Landsat program, 900
leadership (box), 876
Quayle vice presidency, 996
"revolving door," 861
satellite launchers, 404
space station, 877-878, 899-900
National Aerospace Plane
defense authorizations, 346, 404
NASA authorizations, 875, 898, 899
National Archives
JFK assassination documents, 893
Madison amendment, 972
POW/MIA investigation, 289
National Association for the Advancement of Colored People (NAACP), 871
National Association of Broadcasters
cable TV regulation, 452 (box)
children's television, 429
FCC user fees, 458
radio spectrum allocation, 431
National Association of Evangelicals, 613
National Association of Home Builders, 691
National Association of Insurance Commissioners, 583
National Association of Manufacturers, 772
National Association of Realtors
FHA insurance fund, 691, 696
lead poisoning prevention, 607
National Association of Theatre Owners, 744
National Association of Wholesaler-Distributors, 710
National Bank of Washington, 937
National Basketball Association, 790
National Board for Professional Teaching Standards, 643, 656-657
National Bone Marrow Donor Registry, 590
National Bureau of Economic Research, 33
National Cable Television Association, 427, 452 (box), 453
National Campground Owners Association, 501
National Cancer Institute
authorization, 590, 602
cancer registries, 608
Pacific yew harvest, 527
Pepper legacy, 919
National Center for Health Services Research and Health Care Technology Assessment, 572
National Center for Rehabilitation Research, 590
National Clearinghouse for Science, Mathematics, and Technology Education, 651
National Collegiate Athletic Association, 648
National Commission on a Longer School Year, 659
National Commission on AIDS, 997
National Commission on American Indian and Alaska Native Housing, 689
National Commission on Children, 573, 616
National Commission on Severely Distressed Public Housing, 689
National Commission on the Public Service, 857, 858, 859 (box)
National Commission on Violent Crime Against Women, 778
National Committee to Preserve Social Security and Medicare, 565, 870
National Conference on Aging, 620
National Cooperative Research Extension Act of 1984, 891
National Council on the Arts, 867
National Council on the Handicapped, 744
National debt. *See Budget, U.S.*
National Defense Reserve Fleet, 426
National Drug Control Policy, Office of, 745 (box), 789
National Earthquake Hazards Reduction Act of 1977, 880, 881
National Economic Commission, 38
National Endowment for Children's Educational Television, 429
National Endowment for Democracy (NED), 222, 247, 291, 292
National Endowment for the Arts (NEA), 52, 865-867
National Endowment for the Humanities, 866, 867
National Energy Strategy, 470, 502
National Federation of Independent Business
ERISA reforms, 738
Section 89 tax rules, 709, 710
National Federation of the Blind, 422
National Flood Insurance Program, 697, 698-699
National Football League, 790-791
National forests. *See Forests and national forests*
National Foundation for Biomedical Research, 590
National Guard
appropriations, 352, 364, 381, 382, 407, 409
availability period, 364
defense authorization
FY 1991, 356, 363
FY 1992, 369, 373, 376, 380
FY 1993, 396-397, 401, 404, 406-407
Gulf War veterans benefits, 629
home loan programs, 635
military construction appropriations, 352, 365, 382-383, 411
overseas training exercises, 361 (box)
veterans education benefits, 625
National Governors' Association
housing authorization, 667
National Health Service Corps, 587-588
National Heart, Lung and Blood Institute, 590, 602
National Highway System, 415, 437-442
National Highway Traffic Safety Administration, 443
National Historic Preservation Act, 518
National Homeownership Trust, 671
National Housing Act of 1949, 665
National Housing Advisory Board, 152
National Housing Trust, 665, 666
National Imagery Agency, 283, 284 (box)
National Indian Policy Research Institute, 908
National Institute for Literacy, 658, 659
National Institute of Mental Health, 592, 604
National Institute of Standards and Technology
fastener standards, 436
high-tech programs, 880, 902
National Institute on Aging, 602
National Institute on Alcohol Abuse and Alcoholism, 604
National Institute on Child Health and Human Development, 590
National Institute on Drug Abuse, 604, 770, 789
National Institutes of Health (NIH)
ADAMHA authorization, 604
animal research labs, 881
authorization, 590-591, 602-603
DES research, 607
fetal tissue research, 599
HHS leadership, 567 (box)
Pepper legacy, 919
research lab, 595
National Intelligence Center, 284 (box)
National Intelligence Council, 283, 285 (box)
National Labor Relations Board, 733, 864
National Manufactured Housing Construction and Safety Standards Act of 1974, 668
National Marine Fisheries Service, 426, 521, 522, 530-531
National Mediation Board, 705, 712
National Milk Producers Federation, 553
National Nutrition Monitoring Advisory Council, 593
National Ocean Service, 426
National Oceanic and Atmospheric Administration (NOAA)
authorization, 425-426, 450
fish inspection, 434-435
Landsat management, 900
undersea research, 531
user fees, 65
National Opposition Union, 222, 223
National Park Service
autonomy plan, 499
hydroelectric power, 507
scenic trails, 526
unauthorized projects, 526
National parks
action, 1991-92, 525-527
California desert protection, 522
National Public Radio, 458
National Recreational Trails Fund, 444
National Republican Alliance (ARENA), 214, 215-216
National Republican Congressional Committee, 916, 929
National Republican Senatorial Committee, 915, 928
National Research Council, 651, 899
National Rifle Association, 765 (box), 766, 787-789
National Safety Council, 735
National School Boards Association, 658
National Science Foundation (NSF)
authorization, 902-903
earthquake research, 880
high-speed computer network, 903-904
high-tech training, 892

inter-American research cooperation, 903
math, science education, 651
water desalination, 903
National Science Scholars Programs, 651
National Security Act of 1947, 243, 246
National Security Council
foreign food aid, 257
National Security Education Trust Fund, 282-283
National service
community service, 616-617
higher education aid, 656
National Small Business United, 710
National Space Council, 875 (box), 996
National Student Loan Data System, 650
National Taxpayers Union, 149, 959, 973
National Technical Institute for the Deaf, 660
National Treasury Employees Union, 858, 859 (box)
National Urban League, 871
National Vaccine Program, 587
National Weather Service, 426, 450
National Wildlife Federation, 501
National Women's Business Council, 464
Native Americans. *See Indians*
Native Americans, Administration for, 907-908
NATO. *See North Atlantic Treaty Organization*
Natural disasters. *See Disaster relief; Drought; Earthquakes*
Natural gas. *See Oil and natural gas*
Natural Gas Policy Act of 1978, 484-485
Naturalization, 779, 794
Navajo Community College, 650
Navajo-Hopi Relocation Housing Program, 908
Navajo Indians
health services, 905
Indian programs investigation, 882
radiation victims compensation, 586
relocation aid, 908
Naval bases
closures, 378-379
Philippines, 411-412
Israeli port upgrade, 364
Naval ships
amphibious landing ships, 409
appropriations, 352, 363, 364, 382, 407, 409
defense authorization
FY 1990, 347, 349
FY 1991, 362
FY 1992, 378-379
FY 1993, 405-406
defense policy summary, 336
high-speed cargo ships, 349, 362, 364, 380, 406
Navy, U.S.
A-12 bomber cancellation, 379 (box)
appropriations, 350-352, 363-365, 380-382, 407-409
defense authorization
FY 1990, 341, 342, 347
FY 1991, 355-363
FY 1992, 369-380
FY 1993, 395-407
F-14 cancellation, 348
military base closings, 394 (chart)
oil shale reserves, 530
Persian Gulf War, 302, 303-304
Tailhook scandal, 374-375 (box)
women in combat, 374-375 (box)
Nazarbayev, Nursultan, 331
NEA. *See National Endowment for the Arts*
Neal, Richard E. D-Mass.
House bank scandal (chart), 934
Neal, Stephen L. D-N.C.
civil rights/job bias, 759
House bank scandal (chart), 935
House elections, 1992, 27
housing authorization, 695
Nebraska
congressional elections, 1990, 11
Niobrara River, 525
term limits, 10 (box), 963
NED. *See National Endowment for Democracy*
NEH. *See National Endowment for the Humanities*
Nehemiah grants, 671
Neighborhood Reinvestment Corporation, 676
Neighborhood revitalization programs, 670
Neighborhood Schools Improvement Act, 657
Nelson, Bill D-Fla.
NASA authorization, 875
Nerve gas, 347
Nessi, Dom, 882
Netherlands
Persian Gulf War, 316 (box)
Netherlands Antilles
Caribbean Basin Initiative, 180
Neutral Buoyancy Laboratory, 876, 877
Nevada
radiation victims compensation, 586
sports lottery ban, 790
wilderness area, 496
Yucca Mountain nuclear waste dump, 504, 505, 509, 512-513
New American Schools, 657-658
New Columbia, 872, 896
New England Fishery Management Council, 531
New Hampshire
bankruptcy judges, 799
campaign finance reform, 957 (box)
presidential election, 1992, 24 (box)
New Jersey
bankruptcy judges, 799
congressional elections, 1990, 10, 11
governor's election, 1989, 6, 7-8
highway authorization, 442
Madison amendment, 972
military base closings, 353
offshore drilling ban, 491, 504
pharmaceutical licensing, 608
rail transit, 443
respite care project, 582
sports lottery ban, 791
water projects, 493 (box), 494
New Mexico
Mexican border housing aid, 675
Mimbres historic sites, 909
nuclear waste, 524
radiation victims compensation, 586
water projects, 517, 518
New River, Ariz., 517
New School of Social Research, 867
New York
bankruptcy judges, 799
congressional elections, 1990, 12
highway authorization, 442
water projects, 493 (box), 494
weapons programs cancellation, 345, 348
New York, N.Y.
mayor's race, 7
U.N. offices financing, 111
New Zealand
Persian Gulf War, 316 (box)
Newspapers
Baby Bells restrictions, 461-462
Nicaragua
Caribbean Basin Initiative, 183
intelligence authorization, 240
refugee asylum, 756
U.S. aid, 74, 224
contra aid (box), 221
food aid, 257
U.S. policy, 219-223
Nichols, Bill D-Ala.
House bank scandal (chart), 935
successor, 8
Nickerson, Eugene H., 945
Nickles, Don R-Okla.
abortion, 598
campaign finance, 955, 961
FHA loan ceiling, 690
franking privilege, 970
motor voter bill, 894
Puerto Rico plebiscite, 873
school reform, 658
Senate elections, 1992, 26
Senate leadership, 915, 928
Nielson, Howard C. R-Utah
House bank scandal (chart), 935
Niger
Persian Gulf War, 316 (box)
Nighthawk bombers. *See F-117 Nighthawk aircraft*
NIH. *See National Institutes of Health*
Niobrara River, 525
Nitrogen oxides, 473-474, 483
Nixon, Richard
POW/MIA investigation, 289
Soviet aid, 266
Nixon, Walter L. Jr., 775, 777
NOAA. *See National Oceanic and Atmospheric Administration*
Nogales Wash, Ariz., 493 (box)
Noise abatement
airports, 418, 419
Nominations and appointments
Bush appointments, 1169-1180
Cabinet (chart), 1171
controversial nominations, 1177-1180
judicial appointments, 776 (box)
confirmation process, 795-796, 803
confirmation requirement
CIA posts, 282
Indian health director, 905, 906
Non-Indigenous Aquatic Nuisance Act of 1990, 496-497
Noriega, Manuel Antonio, 8, 223-225, 248
North American Free Trade Agreement (NAFTA)
action, 1991-92, 187-190
highlights (box), 188
summary, 165-166, 995
North American Waterfowl Management Plan, 494
North American Wetlands Conservation Council, 494
North Atlantic Treaty Organization (NATO)
arms control summary, 366 (box)
CFE treaty, 328, 384-386
Crotone air base, 349, 353, 357, 358, 365, 380, 382-383
defense authorization, 380
defense policy summary, 336
infrastructure fund, 365, 382-383, 411
reconnaissance overflights, 392
Soviet-U.S. relations, 206
training at U.S. base, 357
U.S. troops in Europe, 351
appropriations, 352-353, 365
reduction proposals, 387 (box)
North Carolina
congressional elections, 1990, 11
water projects, 494
North Dakota
Lawrence Welk birthplace, 526
term limits, 10 (box), 963
North, Oliver L., 240-241 (box), 286, 287 (box)
Northern Ireland
U.S. aid, 232
Northern spotted owl, 494-495, 520-521
Northrop Corp., 399
Norton, Eleanor Holmes D-D.C.
D.C. appropriations, 895-896
D.C. statehood, 896
D.C., territorial House voting, 948
highway authorization, 441
Norway
Persian Gulf War, 316 (box)
NRC. *See Nuclear Regulatory Commission*
NSF. *See National Science Foundation*
NSFnet, 903-904
Nuclear energy
cooperation agreements
China, 252
Soviet Union, 209
Fermi Lab upgrade, 901
Soviet scientists and immigration, 794
superconducting supercollider, 878-879, 901-902
Nuclear non-proliferation
defense authorization, 407
export controls, 196
foreign aid authorization, 267
Pakistan aid limits, 232, 293
Soviet republics, 266, 329, 387-390
trade sanctions, 293
Nuclear power plants
advanced reactors, 508
decommissioning fund, 109
energy policy summary, 470-472
fastener standards, 436
fuel recovery, 345
licensing, 500, 503, 504, 508
NRC fees, 489-490
Nuclear Regulatory Commission (NRC)
plant licensing, 503, 508
regulatory fees, 47, 64, 489-490
Yucca Mountain nuclear waste dump, 509
Nuclear Suppliers Group, 293
Nuclear test treaties
Senate approval, 366-368
summary, 366 (box)
Nuclear waste
federal facilities cleanup, 498, 504, 509
uranium enrichment sites, 509
future needs report, 509
national map project, 531
nuclear negotiator, 509
research, 511
transuranic facility (WIPP), 524-525
Yucca Mountain dump, 504, 505, 509, 512-513
Nuclear Waste Policy Act of 1982, 509, 513
Nuclear weapons. *See also Arms control; Strategic defense initiative*
comprehensive test ban, 392-393, 400, 401, 523-524
Energy Department appropriations, 365
Gulf War aftermath, 315
radiation exposure compensation, 586, 634
Nunn, Sam D-Ga.
arms control

CFE treaty, 384
nuclear test ban, 392-393
unilateral U.S. arms cutbacks, 391
B-2 bomber, 398
community service, 617
defense appropriations, 364, 381
defense authorization
FY 1990, 342-345
FY 1991, 357-359
FY 1992, 374-377
FY 1993, 397, 400
defense conversion aid, 402
defense policy summary, 337-338
Gulf War veterans benefits, 630
intelligence authorization, 281
MX, Midgetman continuation, 343
OMB regulatory review, 869
Persian Gulf War, 307, 310
Somalia relief, 279
Soviet aid, 262, 330
Soviet-U.S. relations, 208
strategic defense initiative, 370-371
Tower nomination, 339-340
Nurse anesthetists, 575, 576, 627
Nurse midwives, 588
Nurse practitioners, 576, 579, 588
Nurses and nursing
immigration, 757
Medicare, 570, 576
nursing home regulation, 587
student aid, 656, 609, 625
VA hospital pay, 625
Nursing homes
Medicaid, 600-602
Medicare, 570, 572, 575
regulation, 573, 586-587
Nutrition. *See Food and nutrition*
Nutrition Education and Training Program, 617
Nutrition Labeling and Education Act of 1990, 603, 604 (box)

O

Oahe Dam, 517
Oakar, Mary Rose D-Ohio
House bank scandal, 932, 938
members with overdrafts (chart), 934
House elections, 1992, 26
House leadership, 916
House Post Office scandal, 939-940, 941
Oakley, Robert, 232
OAS. *See Organization of American States*
Oberstar, James L. D-Minn.
airline smoking ban, 419
aviation package, 417-418
House bank scandal (chart), 935
Obey, David R. D-Wis.
campaign finance, 956-957
foreign aid appropriations, 229, 231, 234, 236, 269, 271, 274
House bank scandal (chart), 934
Iran-contra legacy, 239
Israel aid, 272
Persian Gulf War, 307
stamp allowance, 940 (box)
Obscenity and pornography
cable TV regulation, 453, 457
caller ID, 462
NEA funding, 865-867
public broadcasting, 458
rape victims' suits, 797
sexually explicit mail ads, 870
Supreme Court decisions, 837-838
telephone pornography, 431
Observational Instrument Laboratory, 876
Obstetrics, 579
Occupational health and safety
child labor, 733
communicable disease in food-workers, 743, 746, 747, 749
construction industry, 736
Gulf War environmental conditions, 635
OMB regulatory review, 868 (box)
OPIC authorization, 199
OSHA changes, 734-735
violations penalties, 61
whistleblowers protection, 864
Occupational Safety and Health Act, 734
Occupational Safety and Health Administration (OSHA)
construction safety, 736
lead poisoning prevention, 607, 697-698
revision, 734-735
Occupational therapy, 570
Ocean thermal energy
tax credit, 47, 69, 94
Oceans. *See also Coastal areas; Fish and fisheries; Ships and shipping*
desalination, 903
marine mammal die-off, 531
NOAA research, 426, 531
ocean dumping, 531
Soviet-U.S. research cooperation, 209
Oceanside Harbor, Calif., 493 (box)
O'Connor, Sandra Day
abortion, 598
Supreme Court summary, 801, 804
Odom, James B., 877
Off-road vehicles
all-terrain vehicle safety, 433
California desert protection, 522
drivers' licenses, 424
emissions standards, 483
Offshore Oil Pollution Compensation Fund, 52
Ohio
Clean Air Act, 483
highway authorization, 442
solid waste, 523
term limits, 10 (box), 963
Ohio Republican Party, 977
Oil and natural gas
advanced recovery, 510
alternative fuels, 487 (box), 503
environmental issues
Antarctica, 529
Arctic wildlife refuge, 499, 504, 512
cleanup research, 425
coastal zone protection, 64
offshore drilling
ban, 491, 500, 504, 505
emissions controls, 474
Florida Keys, 497
pipeline safety, 531-532
pollution, spill liability, 448, 490-491
funds, 49, 52, 92
superfund tax, 68, 186
tanker safety, 448
federal leases, 511
royalties, 518
foreign imports, 502
Israel petroleum reserve, 364
natural gas
Canadian imports, 509
decontrol, 484-486
extraction research, 510
power plants, 504
pro-rationing, 504, 505, 509
pipelines
inspections, 488
rates, 511
safety, 531-532
Persian Gulf War, 299-304, 306-307, 314
refined products reserve, 488
service station competition, 530
Strategic Petroleum Reserve, 488-489, 509
stripper wells, 512
taxes
drillers' alternative minimum tax, 69, 96, 108, 109
depletion, 69, 95
energy bill, 502, 505
enhanced recovery, 69
Oil Pollution Act of 1990, 448
Oil seeds, 548, 549
Oil shales, 499, 511, 530
Oil-Spill Liability Trust Fund, 49, 92
OIRA. *See Information and Regulatory Affairs, Office of*
Oklahoma
term limits, 958
water projects, 518
Older Americans Act of 1965
authorization, 620-621
Social Security earnings test, 736
Olestra, 793
Olin, Jim D-Va.
House bank scandal (chart), 935
Ols, John M. Jr., 632
Olver, John D-Mass.
House elections, 1991, 14
Olympic Games, 111, 294
Oman
Persian Gulf War, 302, 316 (box)
OMB Watch, 868 (box)
Omnibus Budget Reconciliation Act of 1989, 47-52
Omnibus Budget Reconciliation Act of 1990, 59-73
O'Neill, Thomas P. Jr., 952
O'Neill, William, 11
Open Skies treaty, 390, 392
Operation Bootstrap, 666
Operation Desert Shield/Storm. *See Persian Gulf War*
Operation Restore Hope. *See Somalia relief*
OPIC. *See Overseas Private Investment Corporation*
Opium, 788
Oregon
endangered species, 521
northern spotted owl, 495
health care plan, 597 (box)
offshore oil drilling, 504
sports lottery ban, 790
term limits, 10 (box), 963
Oregon Coalition Against Domestic and Sexual Violence, 943
Organ Transplantation, Office of, 590
Organ transplants
donor registries, 590
fetal research, 591
immunosuppressive drugs, 590
Organic food, 540, 546
Organization for Economic Cooperation and Development, 199
Organization of American States (OAS)
Nicaragua policy, 222
Panama policy, 224
Organization of Congress, Joint Committee on, 948
Organization of Petroleum Exporting Countries (OPEC)
Persian Gulf War, 299, 301
O'Rourke, Joanna G., 942
Orphan drugs
marketing rights, 585, 603-604
tax credit, 50, 69, 94
Orr, Kay A., 11
Ortega, Daniel, 219, 222
Ortiz, Solomon P. D-Texas
House bank scandal (chart), 934
OSHA. *See Occupational Safety and Health Administration*
Osprey. *See V-22 Osprey aircraft*
***Osprey*-class mine sweepers**, 379
Osteoporosis, 576
Oswald, Lee Harvey, 892-893
Ovarian cancer, 527
Overseas Private Investment Corporation (OPIC)
appropriations, 230, 231
authorization, 199-200
China sanctions, 252
Eastern Europe, 237
Latin American debt relief, 195
Poland, Hungary aid, 211, 212, 214
Soviet-U.S. trade, 170, 330
Owen, Stephen F. Jr., 744
Owens, Jesse, 135
Owens, Major R. D-N.Y.
education for disabled, 648
House bank scandal (chart), 934
vocational education, 645
Owens, Wayne D-Utah
foreign aid appropriations, 270
House bank scandal (chart), 934
Middle East peace talks, 277
Oxley, Michael G. R-Ohio
House bank scandal (chart), 935
Oxnard Plain, Calif., 518
Ozone
pollution control, 473-476, 482
Ozone-layer depleting chemicals
tax
budget reconciliation, FY 1990, 49, 92
budget reconciliation, FY 1991, 67, 96
energy bill, 109, 505
production phase-out, 476, 483

P

P-3 aircraft, 405
Pacific-Americans
civil rights/job bias, 784
Pacific Northwest
fish protection, 522
northern spotted owl, 494-495, 520-521
Pacific Ocean
barrier islands, 497
drift net fishing, 528
Palau autonomy, 258-259
Pacific yew, 527
Packaging
child-resistant packaging, 870
metric labeling, 903
Packard, Ron R-Calif.
airline buyouts, 421
House bank scandal (chart), 935
Packwood, Bob R-Ore.
budget reconciliation, 58, 91
cable TV regulation, 428, 452
capital gains tax cut, 98, 99
Caribbean Basin Initiative, 181
ERISA reforms, 738
ethics case, 914, 943
foreign trade summary, 168
House bank scandal, 938
motor voter bill, 871
Section 89 tax rules, 708
Senate elections, 1992, 24, 26
striker replacements, 734

PaineWebber, 678 (box), 684
Pakistan
arms sales, 293-294
Persian Gulf War, 302, 303, 316 (box)
U.S. aid
appropriations, 275, 276, 277
limits (box), 232
Palau
autonomy charter, 258-259
Palestine Liberation Organization (PLO)
Middle East peace talks, 277
State Department authorization, 248, 249, 250
Pan Am Flight 103, 446
Panama
Caribbean Basin Initiative, 180
military construction appropriations, 352, 353
U.S. aid, 74, 223-227
U.S. military invasion, 223, 225
Bush message (text), 1192
summary, 8
Panama Canal
maintenance, 426
U.S. troop defenses, 224
Panama Canal Commission, 426
Panetta, Leon E. D-Calif.
budget-control efforts, 84
budget process changes, 56
budget reconciliation, FY 1990, 46
budget resolution, FY 1992, 76
capital gains tax cut, 97-98
higher education aid, 654
House bank scandal (chart), 935
House leadership, 916
urban aid tax bill, 106
Pap tests, 570, 593
Papa Ola Lokahi, 906
Paper industry
Tongass forest, 492
Paperwork Reduction Act of 1980, 867-869
Pappas, Tom, 926
Parent Loans for Undergraduate Students, 655, 656
Parental leave
action
1990, 710-712
1991-92, 730-732
1993, 732
summary, 703, 705, 720-721
Parental rights and issues. *See also Adoption; Child support; Foster care; Parental leave*
abortion notification, 593, 594-595, 598-599
child care, 613
Head Start education programs, 621
military deployment, 634
Parker, Mike D-Miss.
House bank scandal (chart), 934
Parris, Stan R-Va.
D.C. political issues, 872-873
House elections, 1990, 11
Participating Physician Program, 568-569
Pashayan, Charles "Chip" R-Calif.
House bank scandal (chart), 935
House elections, 1990, 11
Passaic River, 493 (box), 494
Passports and visas
Chinese student visas, 251, 252-253, 755-756
exemptions, 794-795
"Israel only" passports, 292
political exclusions, 250, 292
Pastor, Ed D-Ariz.
House elections, 1991, 14
Patent and Trademark Office, U.S.
user fees, 65, 792
Patents
drug companies, 793
generic drug regulation, 606
maintenance fees, 792
semiconductor chips, 792-793
space inventions, 879
state infringements, 792
Supreme Court decisions, 810
Pathology, 575
Patriarca, Michael, 981
Patriot missiles
defense authorization
FY 1990, 347
FY 1992, 372, 374, 380
Persian Gulf War, 312, 337
Patronage
diplomatic posts, 248
House administrator, 948
House Post Office scandal, 939-942
Supreme Court decisions, 861 (box)
Patterson, Liz J. D-S.C.
House bank scandal (chart), 935
House elections, 1992, 26
mortgage prepayments, 693
Pauken, Tom, 14
Paxon, Bill R-N.Y.
House bank scandal (chart), 934
Payne, Donald M. D-N.J.
House bank scandal (chart), 935
PCBs. *See Polychlorinated biphenyls*
Peace Corps
Poland, Hungary aid, 213
Peaceful Nuclear Explosions Treaty, 366-368
Peanuts, 541, 544
Pearce, Trudy, 959
Pease, Don J. D-Ohio
China trade, 173
Foreign Affairs Committee clout, 268 (box)
taxation, 95
unemployment benefits, 727
Pediatric medical care, 579
Pell, Claiborne D-R.I.
chemical weapons sanctions, 255, 292
foreign aid authorization, 228
Foreign Relations Committee clout, 268 (box)
German unification treaty, 214
global warming treaty, 297
higher education aid, 654
House leadership, 928
Persian Gulf War, 301
Poland, Hungary aid, 211
Soviet aid, 265
vocational education, 646
Pell grants, 653-657
Pelletreau, Robert, 248
Pelosi, Nancy D-Calif.
ethics committee reorganization, 947
House bank scandal (chart), 934
Pelvic inflammatory disease, 623
Pendleton, Florence, 872
Penn, John Garrett, 937
Pennsylvania
bankruptcy judges, 799
defense authorizations, 356, 372, 379
highway authorization, 442
pharmaceutical licensing, 608
Senate election, 1991, 14, 596
solid waste, 523
weapons programs cancellation, 345, 406 (box)
Penny, Timothy J. D-Minn.
franking privilege, 968
House bank scandal (chart), 935
parental leave, 711, 731
veterans health programs, 635
Pension Guaranty Benefit Corporation
fund responsibility, 720 (box)
Older Americans Act, 620
premiums, 70, 96
Pensions. *See also Social Security*
budget reconciliation, FY 1990, 47
age discrimination, 714-716
lawsuit waivers, 716-717
airline pilots, 107
ERISA reforms, 737-738
federal employees, 858
lump-sum payments, 858-859
fund responsibility, 720 (box)
health benefits, 49, 70
pass-thru deposit insurance, 129
portable pensions, 720, 737
real estate investments, 100
reversions, 70, 96, 719-720
summary, 704
Supreme Court decisions, 846
Pentagon. *See Defense Department, U.S.*
Pentecostals, 756
People for the American Way, 866
Pepper, Claude D-Fla.
death, legacy, 919 (box)
House leadership, 917
successor, 8
Pepper Commission, 572-573, 584 (box), 919
Pepper research centers, 592
Pepper scholarship program, 652-653
Pérez de Cuéllar, Javier, 218, 258, 308
Performance Management and Recognition System, 858, 888
Perito, Paul L., 683, 685
Perkins act, 645, 646
Perkins, Carl C. D-Ky.
House bank scandal, 932
members with overdrafts (chart), 934
job training, 729
student "right to know," 648
Perkins loans, 656
Perot, Ross
NAFTA, 190
POW/MIA investigation, 289
presidential election, 1992, 17-23, 25 (box)
Perpich, Rudy, 11, 361 (box)
Persian Gulf War. *See also Persian Gulf War veterans*
appropriations
FY 1991, 363, 365
FY 1992, 79, 382
budget for Desert Shield, 71
Bush messages (texts), 1196-1206
defense authorization, FY 1991, 355, 357, 358
defense policy summary, 336-337
energy policy, 470, 500, 502
Middle East peace talks, 277
military mail, 969
Soviet policy, 324
special report, 299-317
joint resolution on use of force (box), 309
maps, 301, 311, 313
U.N. Resolution 678 (box), 305
Strategic Petroleum Reserve, 488
summary, 8-9, 12-13, 203-204, 997
women in combat, 374 (box)
Persian Gulf War veterans
benefits, 629-631
family counseling, 636
federal employee compensation, 889
job, education aid, 633
unemployment benefits, 722
health registry, 635
medals, 161
Personal exemption phase-outs, 727, 728
Personnel Management, Office of
age discrimination, 716
displaced defense workers, 889
election day holiday, 895
Hatch Act revision, 887
performance standards, 888
Volcker Commission, 859 (box)
whistleblowers protection, 863
Peru
Andean import duties, 296-297
U.S. aid
Andean narcotics control, 255-256, 769
appropriations, 228, 232-233, 276
Pesticides
export controls, 540, 542
farm recordkeeping, 541, 542, 546
food residues, 498, 522-523
registration, 522-523
Pests
screwworm eradication, 550
zebra mussels control, 496-497
Petersburg, W.Va., 493 (box)
Peterson, Colin C. D-Minn.
Stangeland ethics case, 926
Peterson, Pete D-Fla.
striker replacements, 733-734
Petri, Thomas E. R-Wis.
age discrimination, 716
House bank scandal (chart), 934
minimum wage, 706
parental leave, 731
Phalanx weapons, 347
Phase One missile defense, 370, 373
Phelan, Pope & John, 926
Phelan, Richard J., 917
Phelps, Timothy, 946-947
Philadelphia Naval Shipyard, 378-379
Philippines
military construction appropriations, 352, 353
U.S. aid appropriations, 231
U.S. base closings, 411-412
war veterans citizenship, 779-780
Phillips, Kevin, 93
Phillips, Susan Meredith, 33 (box)
Phoenix missiles
appropriations, 350, 352
authorization, 347, 362
Photovoltaic energy, 507
Physical therapy, 570
Physician Payment Review Commission, 569
Physicians
Health Service Corps, 587-588
lab referrals, 567-570
Medicaid qualifications, 582
medical training, 609
Medicare payments, 43, 567-571, 575-576, 578
VA pay, 628, 633-634
Pick-Sloan water project, 518
Pickering, Thomas R., 1176
Pickett, Owen B. D-Va.
House bank scandal (chart), 935
Pickle, J.J. D-Texas
coal miners' health fund, 735 (box)
higher education aid, 655
Pierce, Samuel R. Jr., 663, 676-685, 686 (box)
Pipelines. *See Oil and natural gas*
Piranha Press, 921-922
Pizza Hut, 556
Plager, S. Jay, 869
Planned Parenthood, 234, 235 (box)
Plant Variety Protection Act, 792
Platoro Dam, 517-518
PLO. *See Palestine Liberation Organization*
PLO Commitments Compliance Act of 1989, 250
Plotkin, Robert, 683
Plutonium
nuclear waste, 524
weapons recovery, 360

PM Group Inc., 679 (box)
Pocket-veto power, 927
Poindexter, John M., 240-241 (box), 286, 287 (box)
Points of Light Initiatives Foundation, 617
Poland
communism downfall, 324
Persian Gulf War, 316 (box)
U.S. aid, 186, 210-214
appropriations, 230, 231, 237
U.S. trade
agreement, 171-173
export controls, 196
Police and law enforcement agencies. *See also Federal Bureau of Investigation*
crime bill, 764-768
D.C. hirings, 873
drug legislation, 769-770
foreign aid
Andean narcotics control, 255-256
El Salvador, 216
Panama, 226
Indian lands, 883-884
police brutality, 796
property damage liability, 778-779
public housing rent waiver, 673
Supreme Court summary, 805
Political action committees (PACs)
campaign finance, 951-957, 960-963
Hatch Act revision, 860-861
leadership PACs, 953
Political advertising
broadcasting rates, 957
campaign finance, 961
negative ads, 957-958
Political Broadcasting Disclosure Act, 958
Political parties
affiliation of public employees, 805
affiliations, Congress and presidency, 1789-1993 (chart), 1234-1235
campaign finance, 951-957
Hatch Act revision, 859-861, 887
independent, 3rd-party candidates (table), 21
patronage jobs, 861 (box)
Pollution. *See also Air pollution; Hazardous waste cleanup; Water pollution*
selenium contamination, 517
source reduction, 64
Pollution Prevention Act of 1990, 64
Polychlorinated biphenyls (PCBs), 512
Pope, Martha S., 916 (box)
Pork-barrel. *See Earmarks and pork-barrel politics*
Pornography. *See Obscenity and pornography*
Porter, John R-Ill.
abortion, 598
House bank scandal (chart), 935
Porter, Roger B., 477, 644, 715
Ports. *See Ships and shipping*
Portugal
Persian Gulf War, 316 (box)
U.S. aid, 274, 275, 276
Postal Inspection Service, 939
Postal Service, U.S. *See also House Post Office scandal*
child-resistant packaging, 870
deceptive mail curbs, 870
off-budget status, 869-870
retired employees, 859
sexually explicit ads, 870
Postsecondary education. *See also Colleges and universities*
trade school loan defaults, 649-650
vocational education, 644-647
Post-traumatic stress disorder, 636
Poverty. *See also Homeless persons; Housing assistance and public housing; Student aid; Welfare and social services*
cancer screening, 593
child care, 611-613
compensatory education, 652
Head Start, 613-614
health care costs, 582
higher education aid, 655
home health care, 592
Indian programs investigation, 881-882
job training programs, 713-714, 728-730
legal aid, 773-774, 795
Medicare hospital payments, 571, 574
school reform, 658
vocational education, 644-647
Powell, Adam Clayton Jr., 958-959
Powell, Colin L. Jr., 314, 337
Powell, Lewis F. Jr.
habeas corpus appeals, 766
Practicing Physicians Advisory Council, 575-576
Prairie County, Mont., 518
Prairie Potholes, 517
Pregnancy. *See also Abortion; Birth control*
adolescent family life, 595
DES research, 607
fetal alcohol syndrome, 883
health insurance, 579
hospital patient-dumping ban, 572, 575
infertility
clinic regulation, 606
research, 591
maternal, child health grants, 579-580
model projects, 968
Medicaid coverage, 578-579, 581
public housing perinatal services, 673
Preschool education. *See also Head Start*
early childhood development, 673
school readiness videos, 659-660
Prescription Drug Marketing Act of 1988, 608
Presidential Access Scholarships, 656
Presidential election, 1992
Clinton "firsts" (box), 24
electoral votes, 1230
official results (chart), 1229
Perot factor (box), 25
State Department leadership, 207 (box)
summary, 17-23, 998
vote by region (table), 23
Presidential elections. *See also Presidential election, 1992*
campaign finance, 961
independent, 3rd-party candidates (table), 21
official results, 1988 (chart), 1228
summary, 1860-1992 (chart), 1226-1227
tax return "checkoff" fund (box), 954, 960
unemployment rates, 31
uniform poll closing time, 872
victorious party, 1860-1992 (chart), 1225
Presidential Public Service Scholarship program, 890
President's Council on Academic Excellence, 643
President's Council on Competitiveness, 435, 891, 996
President's Dinner, 962 (box)
Presidents, U.S. *See also Congressional-executive relations; Presidential elections; specific presidents*
party affiliations, 1789-1993, 1234-1235
Supreme Court decisions, 832
travel, White House expenses, 888
Pressler, Larry R-S.D.
Baby Bells restrictions, 461
congressional pay, 966
Pakistan aid, arms sales, 232 (box), 293
Soviet aid, 265
Preventive Health Services Block Grant, 608
Preventive medical care
disease prevention, 608
Indian services, 883
Price-Anderson Act, 509
Price, Charles R., 877
Price, David D-N.C.
House bank scandal (chart), 935
mortgage prepayments, 693
Price Waterhouse, 690-691
Primary medical care
medical training authorization, 609
Medicare physician payments, 567, 570
rural community hospitals, 571
Prince William County, Va., 282 (box)
Principi, Anthony J., 627 (box)
Prisoners of war (POWs)
Persian Gulf War, 312
veterans benefits, 630
Vietnam War POW/MIAs
Bush, Yeltsin statements (text), 1218-1220
Defense Department files, 380
investigation, 288-290, 291
Prisons and prisoners
alternatives
boot camp, 768
house arrest, 764
juveniles, 797
construction, 765
drug legislation, 769
habeas corpus appeals, 764-768
literacy programs, 659
Pell grant eligibility, 655
Supreme Court decisions, 823
WIC eligibility, 618
Prisons, Bureau of, 768
Privacy
caller ID, 462
DNA testing, 798
Supreme Court decisions, 843
summary, 806
Privatization
space programs, 875-876
uranium enrichment, 508
Proctor & Gamble Co., 793
Product liability
action, 435, 462-463
D.C. weapons law, 896
motor voter bill, 894
technology programs bill, 880
Propane, 487 (box)
Property rights
damage liability
Customs searches, 798
law enforcement agents, 778-779
highway authorization, 439
Supreme Court decisions, 848-849
summary, 806
wetlands preservation, 529
wild, scenic rivers, 525
Property taxes, 111
Prospective Payment System, 571, 574, 575
Prospective Payment Assessment Commission, 571
Prostitution
Frank ethics case, 923
Provo River, 516
Prowler aircraft, 405
Proxmire, William, 130, 915, 982, 983
Pryor, David D-Ark.
age discrimination, 714
civil rights/job bias, 759
ethics committee reorganization, 947
Keating Five investigation, 977, 982, 985-986
minimum wage, 706
Section 89 tax rules, 709-710
Senate leadership, 7 (chart), 915, 928
Public broadcasting
cable TV regulation, 456, 457
children's TV grants, 429
CPB authorization, 457-458
summary, 436-437
transportation infrastructure film, 444
Public Broadcasting Service, 457
Public Citizen
blanced budget amendment, 85
campaign finance, 960, 961
franking privilege, 973
term limits, 959
Public Citizen Litigation Group, 937
Public Health Service Act
family planning authorization, 592-593, 598-599
medical training, 609
Public Health Service, U.S. *See also Centers for Disease Control; Indian Health Service*
Medicaid drug discounts, 605
minority health programs, 588
treatment effectiveness research, 567, 572
Public housing. *See Housing assistance and public housing*
Public Integrity Section, 676, 681
Public Interest Research Group, U.S., 501
Public laws
totals, 1975-92 (box), 14
Public Utilities Regulatory Policies Act of 1978, 486
Public Utility Holding Company Act of 1935 (PUHCA), 131, 500, 502-505, 509-510
Pueblo of Isleta tribe, 908
Puerto Rico
barrier islands, 497
Caribbean Basin Initiative, 182, 183
D'Amato ethics case, 944
House voting privileges, 948-949
nutrition block grants, 619
pharmaceuticals licensing, 608
plebiscite, 873-874, 897
thrift regulation, 127
water projects, 493 (box)
Pursell, Carl D. R-Mich.
House bank scandal (chart), 934
House leadership, 929
Puyallup Indians, 885

Q

Qaddafi, Muammar el-, 233 (box)
Qatar
Persian Gulf War, 302, 316 (box)
U.S. aid, 238
Quadrennial Commission, 965, 967
Quayle, Dan
biographical profile (box), 998
Competitiveness Council, 891, 996
crime bill, 766
El Salvador aid, 215
NASA leadership, 875 (box)
presidential election, 1992, 20
product liability, 435
Senate successor, 8
space station, 899

term limits, 959
vice presidency overview (box), 996
Quayle, Marilyn, 20
Quillen, James H. R-Tenn.
House leadership, 929
QVC Shopping Network, 453

R

Rabin, Yitzhak, 272, 277
Racial discrimination
death penalty, 764-768, 787
hate crime statistics, 778
job bias, 757-760, 780-785
juror challenges, 806
mortgage redlining, 128
NIH authorization, 590
Ryskamp nomination, 796
scholarships, 655 (box)
Racial harassment, 757-758, 781, 785
Racial quotas, 757-760, 780-781, 783
Racism
Ford ethics case, 927
Hastings impeachment, 775
Savage ethics case, 924-925
Thomas confirmation, 802-803
Racketeer Influenced and Corrupt Organizations (RICO) Act
financial institution fraud, 129
limitations, 771-772, 791
McDade investigation, 945
Racketeering
Supreme Court decisions, 816
Radar jammers, 362, 405
Radiation
exposure compensation, 586
veterans, 633, 634, 636
nuclear waste disposal, 505, 509
Radiation-Exposed Veterans Compensation Act of 1988, 636
Radiation Exposure Trust Fund, 586
Radio
China broadcasting commission, 292
CPB authorization, 457-458
fairness doctrine, 430
FCC minority preference, 431 (box)
FCC user fees, 458
Israel transmitter, 250
political advertising, 957-958
spectrum allocation, 430-431, 459
Radio Act of 1927, 430
Radio Free Europe, 250
Radio Liberty, 250
Radiology, 570, 575
Radon, 65, 530
Rahall, Nick J. II D-W.Va.
mining law overhaul, 519
oil, gas royalties, 518
Railroads. *See also Amtrak; High-speed rail*
Americans with Disabilities Act, 743, 746, 749
corporate acquisitions, 424
electric vehicles, 506
employees
drug testing, 425
retirement trust fund, 51-52, 63
strikes, 447-448
unemployment benefits, 726
food-waste transport, 423
fuels tax, 95
highway authorization, 443
MX missile development, 343
safety, 447
small community freight service, 424-425
user fees, 65
Ramstad, Jim R-Minn.
House bank scandal (chart), 935
Rancheria Termination Act of 1958, 908
Ranching. *See Livestock and ranching*
Rangel, Charles B. D-N.Y.
House bank scandal (chart), 934
minority veterans affairs, 636
urban aid tax bill, 104
Raven aircraft, 405
Ray, Richard D-Ga.
House bank scandal (chart), 935
House elections, 1992, 26
Ray Roberts Lake, Texas, 493 (box)
RCRA. *See Resources Conservation and Recovery Act*
Ready Reserve Force, 426
Ready to Learn Act, 659-660
Reagan, Ronald
Americans with Disabilities Act, 744
arms control, 387-389
budget message, FY 1990 (text), 1183-1186
budget policy, 41
Bush term summary, 991
Civil Rights Commission, 762
congressional pay, 965
defense policy, 341
economic policy, 31
HUD scandal, 683
Iran-contra affair, 284-287
Nicaragua policy, 219-220
"October surprise" probe, 287-288
OMB regulatory review, 868
pocket-veto power, 927
presidential election, 1992, 20
Soviet aid, 266
strategic defense initiative, 370 (box)
Supreme Court appointments, 801
torture treaty, 259
whistleblowers protection, 862
Real estate
appraisal standards, 129
bank regulatory relief, 160
banking overhaul, 141, 146, 147
depreciation, 107
direct investments by thrifts, 979
lead poisoning prevention, 607
passive-loss tax deductions, 100, 103, 106
pension fund investments, 100
Reclamation, Bureau of
irrigation subsidies, 495-496, 515-518
Western water policy review, 517
Recorded votes. *See Congressional votes*
Recreation. *See also Sports*
trails, 444
Recycling
highway construction, 445
lead batteries, 530
solid waste, 523
Red Cross, 278
Redistricting
campaign finance, 951
franking privilege, 973
gerrymanders
history (box), 1162
origins (box), 1158
House elections, 1992, 26, 27
Legal Services aid ban, 795
malapportionment (box), 1162
reapportionment history, 1151-1166
apportionment, 1789-1990 (chart), 1155
Voting Rights Act (box), 1165
redistricting for the 1990s, 1145-1150
states' status (chart), 1147
Redlining, 128
Redwood Valley, Calif., 518
Reed Act of 1954, 616
Reed, Rick, 944
RefCorp. *See Resolution Funding Corporation*
Refugee Act of 1980, 757
Refugees
appropriations, 79, 233, 276
asylum, 756-757
Gulf War aftermath, 297, 316-317
Haitians, 296
State Department authorization, 290
Yugoslav conflict, 278
Regional Technology Alliances, 403
Regula, Ralph R-Ohio
abortion, 599
D.C. political issues, 872
House bank scandal (chart), 934
NEA funding, 867
Regulated investment companies, 48
Regulation and deregulation
alternative power, 486
banking, 113-116, 160-161
Bush appointments (box), 114
biotech rules, 903 (box)
cable TV, 427-428, 451-457
Competitiveness Council, 891
CPSC authorization, 433
electric utilities, 509-510
government-sponsored enterprises, 153-156
investment advisers, 159-160
natural gas pricing, 484-486
negotiation guidelines, 864-865
OMB review authority, 867-869
partnership roll-ups, 158-159
savings and loan bailout, 117-130
securities markets, 117, 130-133
Supreme Court decisions
federal powers, 810-811, 832-833
OMB powers, 868 (box)
state powers, 849-850
Rehabilitation Act of 1973, 607
Rehnquist, William H.
crime bill, 788
federal judgeships, 774
habeas corpus appeals, 766
House bank scandal, 937
Supreme Court summary, 801
Reid, Harry D-Nev.
energy bill, 505
farm bill, 541
highway authorization, 439
Keating Five investigation, 986
Nevada wilderness, 496
Persian Gulf War, 310
political advertising, 957
Senate elections, 1992, 26
Yucca Mountain nuclear dump, 513
Reid, Inez Smith, 683
Reilly, William K.
biographical profile, 1175-1176
EPA leadership, 475 (box)
Reischauer, Robert D., 60 (box), 124 (box)
Religious Action Center of Reform Judaism, 85
Religious discrimination
child care, 612-613
Religious issues. *See also Church-state separation; Churches and religious groups*
sacrilegious art, 865-867
Renewable energy
alternative power, 486
energy bill, 500, 502, 507
tax provisions, 109
summary, 471
Renovo, Pa., 945
Republican Conference, House, 916, 929, 945
Republican Conference, Senate, 915, 928
Republican National Committee
Bush term summary, 993
congressional pay, 965
Republican Party
National Endowment for Democracy, 247
presidential election, 1992, 20-21, 1231
South Africa policy, 254
Republican Policy Committee, House, 916, 929
Republican Policy Committee, Senate, 915, 928
Republican Research Committe, House, 916
Rescissions
appropriations, FY 1993, 82-84
defense rescissions, 383 (box)
expedited rescissions, 85-86
Seawolf submarine, 410
Resolution Funding Corporation (RefCorp), 118, 123-125, 129
Resolution Trust Corporation (RTC)
low-income housing, 128
savings and loan bailout, 117, 119-129
refinancing, 148-153
summary, 15, 116
urban homesteading, 676
Resources Conservation and Recovery Act of 1976 (RCRA), 497, 523, 525
Respite care
chronically ill children, 619, 623
N.J. project for elderly, 582
veterans programs, 625
Restaurants
Americans with Disabilities Act, 743-752
food stamps, 618
House restaurant, 930, 942
Retired Senior Volunteer Program (RSVP), 619
Revenue. *See Budget, U.S.; Taxes and taxation*
Revenue Act of 1971, 954 (box), 960
Revenue Reconciliation Act of 1989, 69-70
Reverse discrimination, 781
Reynolds, Mel, 925
Rhode Island
bank deposit insurance, 148
congressional elections, 1990, 11
Seawolf submarine, 410
Rhodes, John J. III R-Ariz.
House bank scandal (chart), 934
House elections, 1992, 26
Indian law enforcement, 883
Rice
price supports, 543
trade expansion act, 196
Richardson, Bill D-N.M.
House bank scandal (chart), 935
Richardson, Elaine, 679 (box)
RICO. *See Racketeer Influenced and Corrupt Organizations Act*
Ridge, Tom R-Pa.
FHA insurance fund, 691
franking privilege, 969
House bank scandal (chart), 935
housing authorization, 667-669
minimum wage, 706
sexually explicit mail ads, 870
Riegle, Donald W. Jr. D-Mich.
bank regulatory relief, 160
banking overhaul, 138, 141-142
disaster area banking, 161
fair trade in financial services, 187
foreign trade summary, 168
government-sponsored enterprises, 155
Keating Five investigation, 975-988
minivan tariffs, 198
money laundering, 157

savings and loan bailout, 118-119, 122, 123
Senate leadership, 915
Riggs, Frank R-Calif.
House bank scandal (chart), 935
House elections, 1992, 26
housing authorization, 695
Right to counsel, 823-824
Right to die, 573, 577
Rinaldo, Matthew J. R-N.J.
banking overhaul, 139
cable TV regulation, 428
House bank scandal (chart), 935
Rio de la Plata, Puerto Rico, 493 (box)
Rio Grande Floodway, 517
Rio summit. *See United Nations Conference on Environment and Development*
Ritter, Don R-Pa.
House bank scandal, 938
House elections, 1992, 27
public broadcasting, 458
River Des Peres, Mo., 493
Rivers. *See Waterways*
Rivlin, Alice M., 36
Robb, Charles S. D-Va.
ethics case, 944
Hatch Act revision, 860
middle-class tax cut, 102
Persian Gulf War, 310
Senate leadership, 928
Robert C. Byrd Scholarships, 656
Roberts, Pat R-Kan.
House bank scandal (chart), 935
House Post Office scandal, 940
Roberts, Ray, 952
Roberts, Richard Y., 419 (box)
"Robin HUD," 678 (box)
Robinson, Tommy F. R-Ark.
House bank scandal, 932
members with overdrafts (chart), 934
minimum wage, 706
party switch, 6
Rockefeller, John D. IV D-W.Va.
coal miners' health fund, 505, 735 (box)
energy bill tax provisions, 108
motor voter bill, 894
Pepper Commission, 584 (box)
Rockfish, 521-522
Rocky Flats, Colo., nuclear plant, 360
Rocky Mountain arsenal, 527
Rodino, Peter W. Jr., 916
Rodriguez, Paul M., 946
Roe, Robert A. D-N.J.
highway authorization, 415, 440
House bank scandal (chart), 935
House leadership, 13, 929
NASA authorization, 874
superconducting supercollider, 878-879
Roemer, Buddy, 11
Rohrabacher, Dana R-Calif.
House bank scandal (chart), 935
NEA funding, 865, 866
Roll Call, 924, 930, 939
Rollins, Edward J., 25
Romania
communism downfall, 336
U.S. trade, 194
Romano, Frank, 775, 777
Romano, Thomas, 775, 777
Roosevelt, James, 565
Ros-Lehtinen, Ileana R-Fla.
election, 8
Rose, Charlie D-N.C.
campaign finance, 961
ethics case, 946
House bank scandal, 936
House leadership, 13, 929
House Post Office scandal, 940
Rosebud County, Mont., 518
Ross, Steven R., 927, 939-941
Rostenkowski, Dan D-Ill.
budget policy summary, 38
budget reconciliation, FY 1990, 46
campaign finance, 956
catastrophic medical costs insurance, 566
congressional pay, 966
crime bill, 788
ethics case, 914
foreign trade
Baltic trade, 193
chemical weapons sanctions, 292-293
China trade status, 190-191
NAFTA, 189
Romanian trade status, 194
steel import limits, 186
textile import quotas, 175
trade expansion act, 196-197
House bank scandal, 936
House elections, 1992, 27
House Post Office scandal, 16, 940-942
mini-sequester, 78 (box)
Persian Gulf War, 310
Poland, Hungary aid, 210
savings and loan bailout, 122
Social Security earnings test, 736
taxation
budget reconciliation, FY 1990, 91
budget reconciliation, FY 1991, 93
capital gains tax cut, 97
expiring provisions, 94 (box), 109
middle-class tax cut, 100-102
miscellaneous tax bills, 110, 112
Section 89 provisions, 708-710
urban aid tax bill, 103, 104, 106
unemployment benefits, 722-724, 725, 726
Rota, Robert V., 939-942
Roth, Toby R-Wis.
Foreign Affairs Committee clout, 268 (box)
Roth, William V. R-Del.
campaign finance, 961
capital gains tax cut, 98
farm bill, 541
federal employee honoraria, 886
federal pay overhaul, 857
Hatch Act revision, 860, 887
Social Security earnings test, 718
urban aid tax bill, 105
Roukema, Marge R-N.J.
age discrimination, 716
higher education aid, 655
House bank scandal (chart), 935
housing authorization, 695
HUD reforms, 686-687
Rowland, J. Roy D-Ga.
AIDS programs, 589
Rowland, John G. R-Conn.
governor's election, 1990, 11
House bank scandal (chart), 934
Roybal, Edward R. D-Calif.
age discrimination, 714
House bank scandal (chart), 935
immigration reform, 755
Roybal-Allard, Lucille, 27
RSVP. *See Retired Senior Volunteer Program*
RTC. *See Resolution Trust Corporation*
RU 486, 591, 600
Ruder, David S., 419 (box)
Rudman, Warren B. R-N.H.
Iran-contra pardons, 286
Keating Five investigation, 975, 977, 984-988
middle-class tax cut, 102
Ruff, Charles F.C., 984
Rules Committee, House
energy bill, 504
Rumsey Indian Rancheria, 883
Rural areas. *See also Rural development; Rural health care*
cable TV regulation, 453
drug enforcement, 768
Rural Business Incubator fund, 548
Rural development
authorization, 547-548
banking overhaul, 139
housing authorization, 674-675
small business grants, 435-436
telecommunications, 460-461
tourism promotion, 462
transit systems, 443
Rural Development Administration, 548
Rural Electrification Act of 1936, 460
Rural Electrification Administration, 548
Rural Electrification and Telephone Revolving Fund, 547
Rural health care
ADAMHA authorization, 605
disabled children, 622
hospitals, 571, 574
nurse practitioners, 576
physician referrals, 569, 570
telecommunications, 461
VA hospital patients, 627 (box)
Russ, Jack, 916 (box), 930, 931
Russia
arms control, 328, 336
nuclear test ban, 393
reconnaissance overflights, 392
START treaty, 387-390
Moscow Embassy, 263
Soviet Union dissolution, 319, 322, 331
U.S. aid, 260, 264-267
appropriations, 271, 275, 276
Russo, Marty D-Ill.
health reform, 597
House bank scandal (chart), 935
House leadership, 928
Rutskoy, Aleksandr, 331
Ryan, T. Timothy, 114
Ryan White Comprehensive AIDS Resources Emergency Act of 1990, 589
Ryder, David J., 161
Ryskamp, Kenneth L., 796

S

S corporations, 48
Sacramento, Calif., 517, 528
Saddam Hussein
Iraq aid ban, 630
Persian Gulf War, 299-317
Safe Havens for the Homeless, 698
Safety. *See also Air safety; Emergency and rescue work; Occupational health and safety*
cigarettes, 591
injury research, 591-592
medical device regulation, 586, 607
Safire, William, 930, 992, 998
Salinas de Gortari, Carlos
NAFTA, 187, 188 (box), 189
Sallie Mae. *See Student Loan Marketing Association*
Salmon, 515, 522
Salomon Brothers Inc., 113, 158
Salt-Gila Aqueduct, 517
Salt River, 517
Samuelson, Paul A., 36
San Antonio, Texas, 616
San Carlos Apache Indians, 517
San Carlos Indian Irrigation Project, 530
San Francisco, Calif.
Bay Area rail transit, 443
water reclamation, 517
San Francisco Federal Home Loan Bank, 976, 980, 983
San Joaquin River, 515, 517
San Juan Suburban Water District, 518
Sanctions
Supreme Court decisions, 817
Sand, Leonard, 925
Sanders, Bernard I-Vt.
foreign aid authorization, 269
House bank scandal (chart), 935
House elections, 1990, 11
Sandinistas, 219-223
Sanford, Terry D-N.C.
congressional pay, 966
ethics committee reorganization, 947
housing authorization, 697
Keating Five investigation, 977, 980
Senate elections, 1992, 23, 24
Senate leadership, 928
Social Security notch babies, 737
Santa Clara River, 518
Sarajevo, Bosnia, 278
Saratoga, 409
Sarbanes, Paul S. D-Md.
foreign aid authorization, 269
State Department authorization, 291
Sarpalius, Bill D-Texas
House bank scandal (chart), 935
Sasser, Jim D-Tenn.
budget process changes, 56
budget resolutions
FY 1990, 42-43
FY 1991, 54-55
FY 1993, 80
budget "walls," 83 (box)
community service, 617
debt/tax refund "matching," 890
defense authorization, 400
Medicaid, 601
military construction appropriations, 411
Senate leadership, 915
Satellites and satellite communications
ASAT weapons, 346, 404
cable TV regulation, 427, 451, 453, 456
China sanctions, 252
defense appropriations
FY 1990, 350
FY 1991, 364
defense authorization, 357, 360, 404
FCC user fees, 458
foreign launches, 875, 876
intelligence coordination, 283, 285 (box)
Landsat, 900
launch vehicles authorization, 346, 404
national launch system, 404, 897-898, 899
Saturn space mission, 875
Saudi Arabia
arms sales, 294
Nicaraguan contra aid, 221 (box), 286
Persian Gulf War, 299-317
Savage, Gus D-Ill.
ethics case, 913, 924-925
Fauntroy ethics case, 926
highway authorization, 440
House bank scandal (chart), 935
Savage, Thomas John, 926
Savimbi, Jonas, 244-245
Savings and loan associations
bailout, 117-130
funding, 116, 120-121
government-sponsored enterprises, 154

refinancing, 148-153
summary, 6, 15, 113, 995
bank regulatory relief, 160
banking overhaul, 148
corporate auditors, 160
direct investments in real estate, 979
financial institution fraud, 121, 128-129
crime bill, 764-768
penalties, 133-134
RICO limits, 772
frozen accounts, 111
Keating Five investigation, 975-988
money laundering, 156
tax benefits for thrift purchasers, 51, 107
Savings Association Insurance Fund, 124 (box), 126
Saxton, H. James R-N.J.
House bank scandal (chart), 935
SBA. *See Small Business Administration*
Scalia, Antonin
Supreme Court summary, 801, 805
Scanlon, Terrence M., 419 (box)
Scavo, Carmine, 995
Scenic rivers, 525
Scenic roads, 444
Schaefer, Dan R-Colo.
House bank scandal (chart), 935
Schaefer, William Donald, 872
Scherer, Roger, 922
Scheuer, James H. D-N.Y.
House bank scandal, 933
members with overdrafts (chart), 934
Schiff, Steven H. R-N.M.
House bank scandal (chart), 935
Schlesinger, James R., 289
Schneider, Claudine R-R.I.
House bank scandal (chart), 935
School breakfast program, 618
School desegregation
Supreme Court decisions, 843-844
summary, 806
School lunch program, 556, 617
School prayer
school reform, 658
Supreme Court summary, 801
vocational education, 646
Schools. *See also Elementary and secondary education*
access by religious groups, 647 (box)
community service, 616
lead poisoning prevention, 607
Schroeder, Patricia D-Colo.
House bank scandal (chart), 935
House leadership, 929
parental leave, 711
Rocky Mountain arsenal, 527
Savage ethics case, 924
whistleblowers protection, 863
Schuelke, Henry F. III, 923, 944
Schulze, Richard T. R-Pa.
House bank scandal (chart), 935
Schumer, Charles E. D-N.Y.
farm bill, 540
housing authorization, 667-670
HUD scandal, 677, 678, 684
savings and loan bailout, 121
Schussheim, Morton J., 683
Schwarzkopf, H. Norman, 310, 315
Science and technology. *See also Computers; Medical research and technology; Nuclear energy; Space programs; Technology transfer; Telecommunications*
competitiveness bills, 891-892
defense conversion aid, 403
Defense, Energy salaries, 349
export controls, 175-177, 195-196
FDA salaries, 586
high-tech programs, 879-880, 892, 902
Energy Department labs, 532
highway research, 444
Poland, Hungary aid, 213
small business research contracts, 464
Soviet scientists immigration, 794
women's employment, 732-733
Science education
Bush education initiative, 643
high-tech training, 892
program authorization, 650-651
student aid, 770
Scout helicopters
appropriations, 351, 409
authorization
FY 1990, 346-347
FY 1991, 361
FY 1992, 372, 376, 378
FY 1993, 405
Scowcroft, Brent, 251, 343, 389, 995
Screwworm eradication, 550
Scud missiles, 312, 337
SDI. *See Strategic defense initiative*
Sea Lance missiles, 362, 364
Sea Stallion helicopters, 349
Seafood. *See Fish and fisheries*
Seahawk helicopters, 382
Search and seizure
Customs damage liability, 798
exclusionary rule, 764, 766, 786-789
firearms, 786
Supreme Court decisions, 824-825
***Seawolf*-class submarines**
action (box), 410
appropriations, 352, 364, 381, 382, 409
rescissions, 83-84, 383 (box)
authorization
1990, 341, 344, 347, 349
1991, 357, 362
1992, 379
budget resolution, FY 1993, 80
SEC. *See Securities and Exchange Commission*
Secondary schools. *See Elementary and secondary education*
Secord, Richard V., 287 (box)
Section 8 Moderate Rehabilitation Program, 663, 676-685, 689
Section 89 tax provisions
action, 708-710
budget reconciliation, FY 1990, 45-46
summary, 703, 705
Securities and Exchange Commission (SEC)
foreign electric utilities, 510
government securities market regulation, 158
investment advisers regulation, 159-160
Keating Five investigation, 976
leadership, 114, 419 (box)
partnership roll-ups, 159
securities market reforms, 130-133
stock index futures regulation, 550, 551-552
Securities Exchange Act of 1934, 158
Securities Industry Association, 772
Securities Market Reform Act of 1990, 130, 131-132
Sedlmayr, Laurie, 980
SEED. *See Support for Eastern European Democracies*
Seidman, L. William, 114, 120-121, 124 (box), 149, 150
Selenium, 517
Self-employed persons
health insurance, 47, 69, 94
Self-incrimination, 825-826
Semiconductors, 197, 792-793
Seminole Indians, 885
Senate, U.S.
committees, 1125-1129
elections
1990, 11
1991, 14
1992, 23-26
franking privilege, 969
members
101st Congress, 1107
102nd Congress, 1111
changes, 1110
news leaks investigation, 946-947
organization, leadership
101st Congress, 7, 915
102nd Congress, 7, 13-14, 928
Senegal
Persian Gulf War, 316 (box)
Senior citizens. *See Elderly persons*
Senior citizens' interest groups
catastrophic medical costs insurance, 565-566
Medicare budget reconciliation, 1990, 574
Social Security earnings test, 718
Senior Companion Program, 619
Senior Executive Service, 921
Sensenbrenner, F. James Jr. R-Wis.
Americans with Disabilities Act, 746, 747
civil rights/job bias, 759, 782
House bank scandal (chart), 934
superconducting supercollider, 879
Sentelle, David B., 241
Sentencing
Supreme Court decisions, 826-827
Separation of powers. *See Congressional-executive relations*
Sequesters
budget process changes, 57, 70-72, 73
Defense budget reprogramming, 356 (box)
mini-sequester, (box) 78, 193
Serbia
U.S. aid to Bosnia, 275, 278
U.S. trade, 194
Sergeant-at-Arms, House, 916 (box), 930
Sergeant-at-Arms, Senate, 916 (box)
Serrano, Andres, 865
Serrano, Jose E. D-N.Y.
House bank scandal (chart), 935
House elections, 1990, 12
Service America Corp., 942
Service Learning Program, 619
Sessions, William S.
JFK assassination documents, 893
Sewers and sewage treatment
Indian health services, 906
rural development, 548
storm runoff, 529
wastewater research, 517
Sex crimes
campus crime, 656
military counseling, 635
penalties, 797
pornography victims' suits, 797
Sex discrimination
job bias, 757-760, 780-785
Supreme Court decisions, 844
summary, 806
Sexual behavior
survey authorization, 602
TV guidelines, 428
Sexual harassment
congressional ethics cases
Bates, 924
Inouye, 944
Lukens, 925
Packwood, 943
Savage, 924
federal employee complaints, 888
military personnel
counseling, 635
Tailhook scandal, 374-375 (box)
State Department authorization, 292
Thomas confirmation, 802-803, 994
Sexual misconduct
congressional ethics cases
Adams, 944
Frank, 923-924
Lukens, 925
Tower nomination, 339-340
Sexually transmitted diseases. *See also Acquired immune deficiency syndrome (AIDS)*
prevention programs, 608
Seymour, John R-Calif.
California desert protection, 522
irrigation subsidies, 514, 515
news leaks investigation, 946
Senate elections, 1992, 23
Shamir, Yitzhak, 272, 277
Shapiro, Mary L., 419 (box)
Shaposhnikov, Yevgeny, 321 (box)
Sharp, Philip R. D-Ind.
Clean Air Act, 476, 479
energy bill, 503
foreign investment data, 178
House bank scandal (chart), 934
natural gas decontrol, 485
Shasta Dam, 515
Shaw, E. Clay R-Fla.
child care, 612
Shawnee National Forest, 496
Shays, Christopher R-Conn.
House bank scandal (chart), 934
HUD scandal, 676-677, 682 (box)
Shelby, Richard, 680-681
Shelby, Richard C. D-Ala.
Persian Gulf War, 310
Senate elections, 1992, 24
Shell Oil Co., 527
Shelter Plus Care, 665, 666, 675
Sherman Antitrust Act, 772
Shevardnadze, Eduard A.
chemical weapons accord, 367 (box)
Persian Gulf War, 301
reconnaissance overflights, 390, 392
Soviet-U.S. relations, 205, 209
START, 389
Shi'ite Muslims, 316-317
Shinay, Michael J., 939
Ships and shipping. *See also Boats and boating; Customs duties; Fish and fisheries; Naval ships*
cargo preference, 212
foreign aid, 267-268
foreign food aid, 257, 258
employees
crew documents, 450
substance abuse, 425, 491
environment
abandoned barges, 449
double-hull tankers, 490
Florida Keys, 497
zebra mussels control, 496-497
foreign cruise ships, 450
foreign ship inspections, 449
foreign ship subsidies, 449
gambling control taxes, 111
maritime authorization, 426
river, harbor projects authorization, 493 (box)
Soviet-U.S. relations, 209
Supreme Court decisions, 810
taxes, 65, 67, 96
tonnage duties, 425
Shoes, 107, 174, 180, 181
Shumway, Norman D. R-Calif.
House bank scandal (chart), 935
Shuster, Bud R-Pa.
El Salvador aid, 218
highway authorization, 440
House bank scandal (chart), 934
House leadership, 929
intelligence authorization, 281

Sick, Gary, 288
Sierra Club, 501
Sierra Research, 487 (box)
Sihanouk, Norodom, 247
Sikorski, Gerry D-Minn.
ethics case, 926
House bank scandal, 938
members with overdrafts (chart), 934
House elections, 1992, 26
Sikorsky helicopters, 670
Silberman, Laurence H., 241 (box)
Silverado Banking, Savings and Loan Association, 120, 133, 995
Silverman, Joy A., 1179
Simon, Paul D-Ill.
abortion, 600
adult literacy, 659
budget-control efforts, 85
budget resolution, FY 1990, 43
crime bill, 787
D.C. political issues, 872
higher education aid, 654
immigration reform, 753-754
job training programs, 713, 729-730
Keating Five investigation, 982
NIH authorization, 602
Thomas confirmation, 803
TV violence, 428
Simpson, Alan K. R-Wyo.
Bush judicial appointments, 776 (box)
congressional pay, 966, 971
immigration reform, 752-745
refugee asylum, 756
Senate leadership, 7 (chart), 915, 928
veterans' COLA increase, 631
Single parents, 646, 630, 634
Singletary, Samuel P., 678 (box)
Sioux Indians, 517
Sixth Amendment
Supreme Court decisions, 828
Skaggs, David E. D-Colo.
D.C., territorial House voting, 948
House bank scandal (chart), 934
Skelton, Ike D-Mo.
House bank scandal (chart), 935
Skinner, Samuel K.
aviation package, 417-418
biographical profile, 1174
Bush term summary, 993
fuel-efficiency standards, 484
highway bill, 415, 437, 440, 441
Transportation leadership, 419 (box)
unemployment benefits, 725
Slattery, Jim D-Kan.
House bank scandal (chart), 934
superconducting supercollider, 901
Slaughter, D. French Jr. R-Va.
House bank scandal (chart), 935
successor, 14
Slovenia
refugee aid, 276, 278
Small business
adult literacy, 659
Americans with Disabilities Act, 744, 746
bank loan reporting, 147-148
civil rights/job bias, 760
ERISA reforms, 737-738
federal research contracts, 464, 403
Gulf War veterans benefits, 629
health reform, 596-597
high-tech programs, 880
mandated health benefits, 595
minimum wage, 705-708
parental leave, 711
RTC contracts, 152
taxes, 93, 96, 110
incentives, 69
Section 89 provisions, 708-710
venture capital program, 463-464
vertical price fixing, 791
welfare reform, 623
Small Business Administration (SBA)
authorization, 435-436, 463-464
Gulf War veterans benefits, 629, 630
IRS regulations, 69
parental leave, 730
women-owned business loans, 464
Small Business Innovative Research Program, 464, 403
Smith, Christopher H. R-N.J.
abortion, 600
Smith-Corona, 106
Smith, Denny R-Ore.
House bank scandal (chart), 934
House elections, 1990, 11
Smith, James C., 940-941
Smith, Lamar R-Texas
House bank scandal (chart), 935
Smith, Larkin R-Miss.
death, successor, 8
Smith, Lawrence J. D-Fla.
House bank scandal (chart), 934
Smith, Neal D-Iowa
House bank scandal (chart), 935
Moscow Embassy, 263
Smith, Peter R-Vt.
child care, 612
civil rights/job bias, 759
House bank scandal (chart), 934
House elections, 1990, 11
Smith, Robert C. R-N.H.
House bank scandal, 936
members with overdrafts (chart), 935
POW/MIA investigation, 289-290
Senate leadership, 928
unemployment benefits, 725
Smith, Virginia R-Neb.
House bank scandal (chart), 935
Niobrara River, 525
Smithsonian Institution
Indian museum, 885
tribal remains, 884, 885
Smog, 482
Smoking. *See Tobacco*
Snake River, 522
Snowe, Olympia J. R-Maine
House bank scandal (chart), 935
middle-class tax cut, 102
Snyder, Gene, 952
Snyder, Okla., 518
Soccer, 161
Social health maintenance organizations, 577
Social Security
budget action
FY 1990, 51
FY 1991, 61-63
FY 1993, 77
budget process changes, 73
earnings, benefits statements, 51, 62
earnings test, 718, 736-737, 620
notch babies, 719, 736, 737
payroll taxes
changes, 77, 718-719, 736, 737
fishermen, 110
summer camp workers, 111
Pepper legacy, 919
representative payee reforms, 62
state, local employees, 68
summary, 704, 705, 717
Supreme Court decisions, 834
tax policy summary, 89-90
telephone service, 62
wage base increase, 50, 91, 92 (box), 96
Social Security Act
child care, 611
child welfare, 621
human services reconciliation, 615
Social Security Administration
agency independence, 718, 736, 737
beneficiary protections, 51
Medicare secondary payer provisions, 570, 577
SSI eligibility, 616
women with AIDS, 623
Social services. *See Welfare and social services*
Social Services Block Grant, 612, 614
"Sodbuster" program, 546
Soil conservation
farm bill, 539, 546
Grand Canyon erosion, 496, 513-514, 516
selenium pollution prevention, 517
Soil Conservation Service, 556 (box)
Solar energy
alternative power, 486
hydrogen fuel research, 487
research, development, 507
tax credit, 47, 69, 94
Solarz, Stephen J. D-N.Y.
Foreign Affairs Committee clout, 268 (box)
foreign aid appropriations, 234
House bank scandal, 932
members with overdrafts (chart), 934
intelligence authorization, 246
Persian Gulf War, 310
Soldiers' and Sailors' Civil Relief Act of 1940, 634, 637
Solidarity, 211, 213
Solomon, Gerald B.H. R-N.Y.
banking overhaul, 141
China trade status, 173
House bank scandal (chart), 934
House leadership, 929
NASA authorization, 1992-94, 898
Somalia relief
action, 278-280
appropriations, 276
Bush address (text), 1220-1221
summary, 260, 997
Sonoma Baylands, 517
Sony Corp., 459
Source Reduction Clearinghouse, 64
Souter, David H.
Supreme Court
nomination, 801, 994
summary, 801, 804
South Africa
U.S. policy, 253-254, 294-295
South Carolina
bankruptcy judges, 799
water projects, 493 (box)
South Carolina, University of, 943
South Dakota
biological diversity trust, 517
rural water systems, 517
selenium contamination, 517
term limits, 10 (box), 963
South Korea
defense burden-sharing, 349
military construction appropriations, 352, 353
U.S. trade, 197
U.S. troop deployments, 345, 351, 373
Southeast Asia
refugee aid, 233
Southern states
Senate elections, 1992, 24
Sovereign immunity concept, 498, 525, 792
Soviet Union and Commonwealth of Independent States. *See also Arms control; Soviet-U.S. trade*
emigration, 233, 272-273
nuclear scientists, 794
refugee asylum, 756-757
European development bank, 185
German unification, 214
Middle East peace talks, 277
Nicaragua policy, 220
Persian Gulf War, 301, 303-304, 314, 316 (box)
strategic defense initiative, 370-371
U.S. aid, 260-267, 330-331, 372, 376
appropriations, 269, 271, 274, 275, 276
authorization, 268
Bush statement (text), 1217-1218
nuclear weapons dismantling, 382, 407
State Department authorization, 291
U.S. relations, 205-210, 324-331
CIA documents declassification, 285
covert aid programs, 244-245 (box)
defense policy summary, 335-336, 369
diplomatic missions, 249, 267
Moscow Embassy, 209 (box), 248, 263 (box), 290-291
POW/MIA investigation, 289
USSR dissolution, 319-332
coup attempt (box), 321
Gorbachev resignation (text), 322-323
summary, 260
Soviet-U.S. trade
export controls, 176, 195-196
Export-Import Bank authorization, 199
grain sales, credit guarantees, 262, 267, 551, 555
MFN summary, 172 (box)
OPIC authorization, 200
satellite launches, 875, 876
Soviet Union dissolution, 329-330
space program cooperation, 899
summary, 209
trade agreement, 169-171, 192-193
highlights (box), 170
Sowell, David, 684-685
Soybeans, 543
Space Exploration Initiative, 899
Space programs
commercial activities, 65, 898, 902
inventions patents, 879
NASA authorizations
1990, 874-876
1991, 876-877
1992-94, 897-898
1993, 898-899
space station, 877-878
Space shuttle, 876, 897-899
Space station. *See Freedom space station*
Space Station Processing Facility, 876
Spain
CFE weapons cascading, 386
Persian Gulf War, 316 (box)
Speaker of the House
House administrator, 948
Intelligence Committee access, 243 (box)
Special Counsel, Office of the, 862-864, 886
Special education, 647-648
Special Isotope Separation plant, 345
Special Masters, Office of, 572
Special prosecutors. *See Independent counsel.*
Special Supplemental Food Program for Women, Infants and Children. *See Women, Infants and Children (WIC) program*
Special Volunteer Programs, 619

Specter, Arlen R-Pa.
crime bill, 766-767
Hatch Act revision, 861
immigration reform, 754
Persian Gulf War, 315
Senate elections, 1992, 24, 25
Senate leadership, 928
textile import quotas, 174
torture victims, 797
Spector, Leonard S., 232
Spence, Floyd D. R-S.C.
House bank scandal (chart), 935
Spiegel, Thomas, 918
Sporkin, Stanley, 972-973
Sports
cable TV regulation, 454, 457
colleges
athletic scholarships, 656
student "right to know," 648-649
lottery ban, 790-791
tobacco company sponsors, 591
Sports Fish Restoration Account, 67
Spratt, John M. Jr. D-S.C.
House bank scandal (chart), 934
SRAM II missiles, 360, 377
SRAM-T missiles, 360, 364, 376, 377
SSI. *See Supplemental Security Income*
St. Christopher and Nevis
Caribbean Basin Initiative, 180
St Germain, Fernand J., 916
St. Lucia
Caribbean Basin Initiative, 180
St. Mary's River, Ind., 493 (box)
St. Paul, Minn.
Port Authority bonds, 111
St. Vincent and the Grenadines
Caribbean Basin Initiative, 180
Staff Development Activities, 655
Stafford loans, 655, 656
Stafford, Robert T., 915
Staggers, Harley O. D-W.Va.
campaign funds conversion, 952
veterans health programs, 635
Stallings, Richard D-Idaho
House bank scandal (chart), 935
Standard & Poor's Corp., 154
Standard missiles, 347, 378
Standards of Official Conduct Committee, House
ethics code rewrite, 920
reorganization, 947
Standing Rock Indian Reservation, 517, 905
Stanford University, 903
Stangeland, Arlan R-Minn.
ethics case, 926
House bank scandal (chart), 934
House elections, 1990, 11
Stanislaus River, 515
Star Schools, 659
Star wars. *See Strategic defense initiative*
Stark, Pete D-Calif.
catastrophic medical costs insurance, 566
energy bill tax provisions, 108
House bank scandal (chart), 934
Medicare physician payments, 567
Starr, Kenneth W., 778
START. *See Strategic arms reduction talks treaty*
State and local government. *See also Federal-state relations*
border disputes, 849
business and labor
bank powers, 145
cable TV regulation, 453
credit reporting safeguards, 157-158
ERISA reforms, 738
job training programs, 713, 728-730
savings and loan bailout, 118-119, 127
timber exports, 183
unemployment benefits, 717, 721, 724-725, 725-728
constitutional amendment, 972
education
adult literacy, 658, 659
disabled students, 647-648
school reform, 657-658
vocational education, 644-647
elections and politics
campaign finance (box), 956
legislative elections, 1990, 12
term limits, 10 (box), 958, 963-964
employees
age discrimination, 715-716
Social Security, Medicare coverage, 68, 96
energy policy
electric utilities, 509
energy conservation, 486, 508
natural gas pro-rationing, 509
octane labeling, 487
oil, gas royalties, 518
environmental protection
alternative fuel, cars, 500, 506
beach pollution, 531
Clean Air Act, 473-483
coastal zone management, 491
federal facilities cleanup, 497-498, 525
oil-spill liability, 490
solid waste, 523
health
ADAMHA authorization, 604-605
AIDS programs, 588-590
cancer screening, 593
developmental disabilities, 593
food labeling, 585
mandated benefits, 595
Medicaid, 578-582, 600-602
Medigap insurance regulation, 583
nursing home regulation, 586-587
planning grants, 593
preventive health services, 607
housing, 670-671, 694-698
law and judiciary
copyright, 773
courts, 798
patent infringement, 792
tobacco sales to minors, 799
Supreme Court decisions, 849-851
taxation and finance
Medicaid funding, 600-602
hedge bonds, 50
high-speed rail, 111-112
hydropower improvements, 109
mortgage revenue bonds, 47, 69, 94
sports lottery ban, 790-791
U.N. offices, 111
transportation
hazardous materials, 422
highway authorization, 437-444
water projects cost sharing, 494
welfare and social services
child care, 611-613
Older Americans Act, 620
welfare reform, 623
State Department, U.S.
AIDS immigration exclusion, 753 (box)
Antarctica mining ban, 489
authorizations, 247-250, 290-292
China policy, 252
foreign aid
appropriations, 229, 232, 270
El Salvador aid, 218
Enterprise for the Americas, 195
Food for Peace, 257
foreign policy "leveraging," 239
Somalia relief, 279
Soviet republics, 267
Kurdish refugee aid, 297
leadership (box), 207
money laundering, 768
Moscow Embassy, 263
narcotics control, 233, 238
Nicaragua policy, 220, 222
Persian Gulf War, 300
political appointees, 248
POW/MIA investigation, 289
State Dependent Care Development Grants, 614
State Justice Institute
authorization, 798
child abuse prevention, 798
State Literacy Resource Centers, 658, 659
State of the Union addresses
election-year proposals, 997-998
product liability, 435
Soviet Union dissolution, 261-262
texts
1990, 1193-1195
1991, 1206-1209
1992, 1213-1216
withholding tax, 40
State Student Incentive Grants, 656
State taxes, 94, 850-851
Statehood
D.C. proposals, 872-873, 896
Puerto Rico plebiscite, 873-874, 897
Stealth bombers. *See B-2 bombers; F-117 Nighthawk aircraft*
Stealth cruise missiles, 350, 360, 377, 382, 404, 409
Stearns, Cliff R-Fla.
House bank scandal (chart), 935
NEA funding, 865
Steel industry
Clean Air Act, 473
import limits, 186
Steel Trade Liberalization Act of 1989, 182
Steelhead trout, 522
Steier, Maurice, 678 (box)
Stello, Victor Jr., 1179
Stenholm, Charles W. D-Texas
animal research labs, 881, 904
budget-control efforts, 84, 85
budget reconciliation, FY 1990, 46
budget "walls," 82 (box)
child care, 612
House bank scandal (chart), 934
House leadership, 916
NEA funding, 865
parental leave, 711
pizza for school lunch, 556
Stennis, John C., 915
Stephens, Jay B., 942
Steroids, 768
Stevens, David, 982
Stevens, John Paul
National Guard exercises, 361 (box)
Supreme Court summary, 801
Stevens, Ted R-Alaska
cable TV regulation, 452
civil rights/job bias, 784
congressional pay, 970
energy bill, 504
franking privilege, 969
motor voter bill, 894
news leaks investigations, 946
political advertising, 958
public broadcasting, 458
regulation negotiation, 865
Social Security tax changes, 719
Tongass forest, 493
Stevenson amendment, 170, 171
Stewart, Rosemary, 983
Stinger missiles
appropriations, 408
authorization, 347, 372, 378, 405
Persian Gulf sales ban, 231
Stock Raising Homestead Act of 1916, 531
Stockdale, James B., 289
Stockman, David A., 952
Stocks, bonds and securities
arbitrage rebate rules, 50
banking overhaul, 130-142, 148
dealer taxes, 107
debt-equity whipsaw, 111
employee stock ownership plans, 48-49
fair trade in financial services, 187, 198
government securities market regulation, 158
hybrid instruments, 551, 552
index futures regulation, 550, 551
investment advisers regulation, 159-160
junk bonds, 48, 127
market regulation, 113, 130-133
mutual funds, 48
non-recognition, 48
partnership roll-ups, 158-159
small issues, 47, 69, 94
state, local hedge bonds, 50
Supreme Court decisions, 811-812
swaps, 551, 552
wasting stock, 48
Stockpile. *See Strategic materials*
Stokes, Louis D-Ohio
ethics committee reorganization, 947
House bank scandal, 930, 936
members with overdrafts (chart), 934
House leadership, 917, 929
JFK assassination, 892
superconducting supercollider, 879
Stone, Oliver, 892, 893
Strategic and Critical Minerals Act, 880
Strategic arms reduction talks (START) treaty
action, 1991-92, 384, 387-390
Bush, Gorbachev remarks (text), 1210-1211
provisions (box), 388
warhead allotments (chart), 392
arms control summary, 366 (box)
B-2 bomber, 398
MX missile continuation, 343
Soviet-U.S. relations, 205, 328-329
START II, 329, 390, 392 (chart), 997
Strategic defense initiative (SDI)
appropriations, 350, 351, 363, 364, 380-382, 407-409
rescissions, 383 (box)
defense authorization
FY 1990, 340, 341, 342, 344, 346
FY 1991, 355-360
FY 1992, 369-377
FY 1993, 395-397, 400, 404
Defense budget reprogramming, 356 (box)
defense policy summary, 337, 338, 339
START treaty, 389
summary (box), 370-371
unilateral U.S. arms cutbacks, 391
Strategic materials
Defense Production Act, 368-369, 412
mining research, 880
oil reserves, 488-489
uranium reserve, 509
Strategic Petroleum Reserve
appropriations, 409
energy bill, 504, 509
expansion, sales, 488-489
Stratton, Sam, 952
Strauss, Joseph A., 677
Strauss, Robert S., 38, 262
Strawberry River, 516
Strikes
Eastern Airlines, 712-713
railroads, 447-448
replacement workers, 733-734

Striped bass, 521-522
Structural Impediments Initiative, 168
Studds, Gerry E. D-Mass.
endangered species, 521
fish inspection, 435
House bank scandal (chart), 935
House leadership, 929
New England ground fish, 531
Student aid. *See also Veterans education programs*
athletes "right to know," 647-648
authorization, 653-657
Caribbean Basin Initiative, 183
community development, service, 616-617, 675-676
defense conversion aid, 402
direct loans, 654, 656
drug user ban, 654, 770
employer-provided aid, 47, 68, 94
federal employee recruiting, 858
foreign languages, 282-283
loan defaults, 649-650, 724
math, science education, 650-651, 770
medical training, 587-588, 609
Indian health services, 905
Poland, Hungary aid, 213
Sallie Mae regulation, 156
Vietnamese scholarships, 292
vocational education, 644-647
Student Loan Marketing Association (Sallie Mae), 154, 156, 655
Student Support Services, 655
Stump, Bob R-Ariz.
House leadership, 917
Sturgulewski, Arliss, 12
Subic Bay Naval Base, 353, 411-412
Submarines and submarine warfare
appropriations
FY 1990, 351, 352
FY 1991, 364
FY 1992, 381, 382, 383 (box)
FY 1993, 409
defense authorization
FY 1990, 341-349
FY 1991, 360, 362
FY 1992, 379
FY 1993, 404, 406
Seawolf action, 410
Subminimum wage, 705-708
Substance abuse. *See Alcohol abuse and alcoholism; Drug abuse*
Substance Abuse and Mental Health Services Administration, 604
Substance Abuse Block Grant, 604
Substance Abuse Prevention, Office for, 770
Suburban areas
presidential election, 1992, 22
Subways. *See Mass transit*
Sugar
allotment process, 557
imports, 543, 180-181
price supports, 540, 541, 543-544
Sulfur dioxide, 473-483
Sullivan, Louis W.
AIDS exclusion policy, 753 (box)
Americans with Disabilities Act, 746
animal research labs, 881
biographical profile, 1172-1173
Bush term summary, 993-994
child welfare, 621
fetal tissue research, 591, 602
Head Start, 614
HHS leadership, 567 (box)
Medicaid, 601
VA hospitals, 627 (box)
Summer Food Program, 617, 618
Sundquist, Don R-Tenn.
House bank scandal (chart), 935
House leadership, 929
Sunkist Growers, 555
Sunia, Fofō I.F., 935
Sunnyside, Wash., 517
Sununu, John H.
Bush term summary, 993
campaign finance, 953
Hatch Act revision, 861
minimum wage, 707
OMB regulatory review, 869
Souter appointment, 994
Super 301 trade provisions, 167-168, 197
Superconducting supercollider
action
1989-90, 878-879
1991-92, 901-902
appropriations, 78, 81
Superconductivity
high-tech programs, 880
Superfund
charitable organizations, 111
extension, 68
oil tax, 64, 186
Supplemental Assistance for Facilities to Assist the Homeless, 675
Supplemental Loans for Students, 649, 655, 656
Supplemental Security Income (SSI)
human services reconciliation, 615, 616
women with AIDS, 623
Support for Eastern European Democracies (SEED) program, 186, 267
Supportive Housing Demonstration Program, 675
Supreme Court cases
Adams Fruit Co. Inc. v. Barrett, 848
Air Courier Conference of America v. American Postal Workers Union, 832
Air Line Pilots Association v. O'Neil, 847
Alabama v. Smith, 826
Alabama v. White, 825
Allegheny County v. American Civil Liberties Union, Greater Pittsburgh Chapter, 835
Allegheny Pittsburgh Coal Co. v. County Commission of Webster County, 850
Allied-Signal Inc. v. Director, Division of Taxation, 850-851
Amerada Hess Corp. v. Director, Division of Taxation, New Jersey Department of the Treasury, 812
American Foreign Service Association v. Garfinkel, 832
American Hospital Association v. National Labor Relations Board, 846
American National Red Cross v. S. G., 816
American Trucking Associations Inc. v. Smith, 812-813
Ankenbrandt v. Richards, 815
Arcadia v. Ohio Power Co., 811
Ardestani v. Immigration and Naturalization Service, 838
Argentine Republic v. Amerada Hess Shipping, 844
Arizona v. Fulminante, 788, 826
Arizona v. Youngblood, 819
Arkansas v. Oklahoma, 831
Arrington v. Wilks, 842
ASARCO v. Kadish, 849
Astoria Federal Savings and Loan Association v. Solimino, 839
Astroline Communications Co. Ltd. Partnership v. Shurberg Broadcasting of Hartford Inc., 839
Atlantic Richfield Co. v. USA Petroleum Corp., 807
Austin v. Michigan State Chamber of Commerce, 955 (box), 829
Ayers v. Fordice, 843-844
Baltimore City Department of Social Services v. Bouknight, 825
Barker v. Kansas, 850
Barnard v. Thorstenn, 814
Barnes v. Glen Theatre Inc., 836
Barnhill v. Johnson, 809
Beech Aerospace Services Inc. v. Rainey, 815
Beech Aircraft Corp. v. Rainey, 815
Begier v. Internal Revenue Service, 808
Berry v. City of Dallas, 836
Blanchard v. Bergeron, 839
Blanton v. City of North Las Vegas, 828
Blatchford v. Native Village of Noatak, 849
Blystone v. Pennsylvania, 817-818
Board of Education of Oklahoma City Public Schools v. Dowell, 843
Board of Education of the Westside Community Schools v. Mergens, 647 (box), 835
Board of Estimate of City of New York v. Morris, 829
Board of Governors of the Federal Reserve System v. MCorp Financial Inc., 833
Board of Trustees of State University of New York v. Fox, 835
Boeing Co. v. United States, 832
Bonito Boats Inc. v. Thunder Craft Boats Inc., 810
Bonjorno v. Kaiser Aluminum & Chemical Corp., 816
Bowen v. Georgetown University Hospital, 834
Boyde v. California, 818
Braxton v. United States, 827
Breininger v. Sheet Metal Workers International Association, Local Union No. 6, 847
Brendale v. Confederated Tribes and Bands of the Yakima Indian Nation, 834
Brower v. Inyo County, 824
Browning-Ferris Industries of Vermont Inc. v. Kelco Disposal Inc., 851
Buckley v. Valeo, 960
Burdick v. Takushi, 830
Burlington Northern Railroad Co. v. Ford, 816
Burnham v. Superior Court, 816
Burns v. Reed, 816
Burns v. United States, 827
Burson v. Freeman, 830
Business Guides Inc. v. Chromatic Communications Enterprises Inc., 817
Butler v. McKellar, 821
Butterworth v. Smith, 836
California v. Acevedo, 825
California v. American Stores Co., 807
California v. ARC America Corp., 807
California v. Federal Energy Regulatory Commission, 849
California v. Hodari D., 825
California v. United States, 833
California State Board of Equalization v. Sierra Summit Inc., 850
Caplin & Drysdale, Chartered v. United States, 824
Carden v. Arkoma Associates, 815
Carella v. California, 828
Carlucci v. Doe, 832
Carnival Cruise Lines Inc. v. Shute, 816
Casey v. Planned Parenthood of Southeastern Pennsylvania, 839
Castille v. Peoples, 821
Chambers v. NASCO Inc., 840
Chan v. Korean Air Lines Ltd., 808
Chapman v. United States, 827
Chauffeurs, Teamsters and Helpers, Local No. 391 v. Terry, 847
Cheek v. United States, 828-829
Chema v. United States, 842
Chemical Waste Management, Inc. v. Hunt, 523, 831
Chesapeake & Ohio Railway Co. v. Schwalb, 848
Chisom v. Roemer, 844
Cipollone v. Liggett Group Inc., 851
Citibank, N.A. v. Wells Fargo Asia Ltd., 808
City of Burlington v. Dague, 840
City of Canton v. Harris, 841
City of Columbia v. Omni Outdoor Advertising Inc., 807
City of Dallas v. Stanglin, 836
City of Richmond v. J.A. Croson Co., 839
Clark v. Roemer, 844
Clemons v. Mississippi, 818
Clinchfield Coal Co. v. Director, Office of Workers' Compensation Programs, Department of Labor, 845
Cohen v. Cowles Media Inc., 837
Coit Independence Joint Venture v. Federal Savings and Loan Insurance Corp., 810
Coleman v. Thompson, 821-822
Collins v. City of Harker Heights, 842
Collins v. Youngblood, 827
Colonial American Life Insurance Co. v. Commissioner of Internal Revenue, 812
Commissioner, Immigration and Naturalization Service v. Jean, 840
Commissioner of Internal Revenue v. Clark, 812
Commissioner of Internal Revenue v. Indianapolis Power & Light Co., 812
Committee on Legal Ethics of the West Virginia State Bar v. Triplett, 845
Community for Creative Non-Violence v. Reid, 809
Confederated Tribes and Bands of the Yakima Indian Nation v. County of Yakima, 850
Connecticut v. Doehr, 815
Connecticut National Bank v. Germain, 809
Consolidated Coal Co. v. Director, Office of Workers' Compensation Programs, Department of Labor, 845
Consolidated Rail Corp. v. Railway Labor Executives' Association, 845
Cook County Officers Electoral Board v. Reed, 829-830
Cooter & Gell v. Hartmarx Corp., 817
Cottage Savings Association v. Commissioner of Internal Revenue, 813
Cotton Petroleum Corp. v. New Mexico, 833
County of Riverside v. McLaughlin, 825
County of Yakima v. Confederated Tribes and Bands of the Yakima Indian Nation, 834-850
Crandon v. United States, 832
Crawford Fitting Co. v. J.T. Gibbons Inc., 785
Cruzan v. Director, Missouri Department of Health, 573, 843
CSX Transportation Inc. v. Brotherhood of Railway Carmen, 807
Dallas Independent School District v. Jett, 841
Davis v. Michigan Department of Treasury, 850
Davis v. United States, 835
Dawson v. Delaware, 827
Dellmuth v. Muth, 647, 842
Demarest v. Manspeaker, 828
Dennis v. Higgins, 841
Denton v. Hernandez, 815

Department of Commerce v. Montana, 830
Department of Energy v. Ohio, 831
Department of Justice v. Tax Analysts, 833
Department of State v. Ray, 833
De Shaney v. Winnebago County Department of Social Services, 840-841
Dewsnup v. Timm, 809
Director, Office of Workers' Compensation Programs, United States Department of Labor v. Broyles, 845
Doggett v. United States, 828
Dole v. United Steelworkers of America, 832, 868 (box)
Dowling v. United States, 819
Duckworth v. Egan, 825
Dugger v. Adams, 821
Duquesne Light Co. v. Barasch, 810
Duro v. Reina, 828, 906
East Kentucky Energy Corp. v. County Commission of Webster County, 850
Eastern Airlines Inc. v. Floyd, 808
Eastman Kodak Co. v. Image Technical Services Inc., 807-808
Edmonson v. Leesville Concrete Co. Inc., 816
Eli Lilly & Co. v. Medtronic Inc., 810
Employment Division, Department of Human Resources of Oregon v. Smith, 835
English v. General Electric Co., 848
Environmental Protection Agency v. Oklahoma, 831
Equal Employment Opportunity Commission v. Arabian American Oil Co., 785, 843
Estate of Cowart v. Nicklos Drilling Co., 848
Estelle v. McGuire, 820
Eu v. San Francisco County Democratic Central Committee, 829
Evans v. United States, 829
Exxon Corp. v. Central Gulf Lines Inc., 810
Farrey v. Sanderfoot, 809
Federal Communications Commission v. Sable Communications of California Inc., 838
Federal Election Commission v. Massachusetts Citizens for Life, 955 (box)
Federal Energy Regulatory Commission v. United States Distribution Cos., 811
Federal Savings and Loan Insurance Corp. v. Ticktin, 810
Federal Trade Commission v. Superior Court Trial Lawyers Association, 807
Federal Trade Commission v. Ticor Title Insurance Co., 808
Feist Publications Inc. v. Rural Telephone Service Co. Inc., 810
Ferens v. John Deere Co., 815
Firstier Mortgage Co. v. Investors Mortgage Insurance Co., 814
Firestone Tire & Rubber Co. v. Bruch, 846
Finley v. United States, 851
Florida v. Bostick, 825
Florida v. Jimeno, 825
Florida v. Riley, 824
Florida v. Wells, 824
Florida Star v. B.J.F., 837
FMC Corp. v. Holliday, 851
Ford v. Georgia, 822
Forsyth County v. Nationalist Movement, 836-837
Fort Gratiot Landfill Inc. v. Michigan Department of Natural Resources, 523, 831
Fort Stewart Schools v. Federal Labor Relations Authority, 832
Fort Wayne Books Inc. v. Indiana, 837
Foucha v. Louisiana, 827
Franchise Tax Board of California v. Alcan Aluminium Ltd., 812
Frank v. Minnesota Newspaper Association, 835
Franklin v. Gwinnett County Public Schools, 844
Franklin v. Massachusetts, 830
Frazee v. Illinois Department of Employment Security, 834-835
Frech v. Rutan, 836
Freeman v. Pitts, 843
Freytag v. Commissioner of Internal Revenue, 817
FW/PBS Inc. v. City of Dallas, 836
Gade v. National Solid Wastes Management Association, 831
General Motors Corp. v. Romein, 848
General Motors Corp. v. United States, 830-831
Gentile v. State Bar of Nevada, 814
Georgia v. McCollum, 823
Georgia v. South Carolina, 849
Gilmer v. Interstate/Johnson Lane Corp., 839
Goldberg v. Sweet, 812
Golden State Transit Corp. v. City of Los Angeles, 846
Gollust v. Mendell, 811
Golzon-Peretz v. United States, 827
Gomez v. United States, 828
Grady v. Corbin, 819
Graham v. Commissioner of Internal Revenue, 835
Graham v. Conor, 841
Granfinanciera S.A. v. Nordberg, 808
Green v. Bock Laundry Machine Co., 815
Gregory v. Ashcroft, 839
Griffen v. United States, 820
Griggs v. Duke Power Co., 758, 781, 784
Grogan v. Garner, 808-809
Groves v. Ring Screw Works, 846
GTE Sprint Communications Corp. v. Sweet, 812
Guidry v. Sheet Metal Workers National Pension Fund, 846
Hafer v. Melo, 841-842
Hallstrom v. Tillamook County, 830
Hardin v. Straub, 841
Harmelin v. Michigan, 827
Harris v. Reed, 820-821
Harte-Hanks Communications Inc. v. Connaughton, 837
Healy v. Beer Institute Inc., 849
Hernandez v. Commissioner of Internal Revenue, 835
Hernandez v. New York, 822-823
Hildwin v. Florida, 817
Hilton v. South Carolina Public Railways Commission, 848
H. J., Inc. v. Northwestern Bell Telephone Co., 816, 772
Hodgson v. Minnesota, 595, 838
Hoffman v. Connecticut Income Maintenance, 808
Hoffman-La Roche Inc. v. Sperling, 843
Holland v. Illinois, 822
Holmes v. Securities Investor Protection Corporation, 812
Holywell Corp. v. Smith, 809
Horton v. California, 825
Houston Lawyers' Association v. Attorney General of Texas, 844
Howlett v. Rose, 841
Hudson v. McMillian, 823
Hughey v. United States, 826
Idaho v. Wright, 819
Illinois v. Kentucky, 849
Illinois v. Perkins, 826
Illinois v. Rodriquez, 825
Immigration and Naturalization Service v. Chadha, 171, 172 (box)
Immigration and Naturalization Service v. Doherty, 838
Immigration and Naturalization Service v. Elias-Zacarias, 838
Immigration and Naturalization Service v. National Center for Immigrants' Rights Inc., 838
Independent Federation of Flight Attendants v. Zipes, 758, 782, 840
INDOPCO v. Commissioner of Internal Revenue, 850
Ingersoll-Rand Co. v. McClendon, 847
Internal Revenue Service v. Federal Labor Relations Authority, 832
International Organization for Masters, Mates & Pilots v. Brown, 847
International Primate Protection League v. Administrators of Tulane Educational Fund, 816
International Society for Krishna Consciousness Inc. v. Lee, 837
International Union, United Automobile, Aerospace & Agricultural Implement Workers of America, UAW v. Johnson Controls Inc., 844
Interstate Commerce Commission v. Boston & Maine Corp., 848
Irwin v. Veterans Administration, 844
Jacobson v. United States, 819
James v. Illinois, 819
James B. Beam Distilling Co. v. Georgia, 850
Jett v. Dallas Independent School District, 841
Jimmy Swaggart Ministries v. Board of Equalization of California, 835
John Doe Agency v. John Doe Corp., 833
Johnson v. Home State Bank, 809
Jones v. Thomas, 819
Kaiser Aluminum & Chemical Corp. v. Bonjorno, 816
Kamen v. Kemper Financial Services Inc., 811
Kansas v. Utilicorp United Inc., 807
Karahalios v. National Federation of Federal Employees, Local 1263, 832
Kay v. Ehrler, 840
Keeney v. Tamayo-Reyes, 822
Keller v. State Bar of California, 814
Kentucky Department of Corrections v. Thompson, 823
King v. St. Vincent's Hospital, 848
Kraft General Foods Inc. v. Iowa Department of Revenue and Finance, 851
Lampf, Pleva, Lipkind, Prupis, & Petigrow v. Gilbertson, 148, 811
Lankford v. Idaho, 818
Lauro Lines s.r.l. v. Chasser, 813-814
League of United Latin American Citizens v. Attorney General of Texas, 844
Leathers v. Medlock, 837
Lechmere Inc. v. National Labor Relations Board, 846
Lee v. Weisman, 835
Lehnert v. Ferris Faculty Association, 847
Lewis v. Continental Bank Corp., 811
Lewis v. Jeffers, 821
Library of Congress v. Shaw, 785
Litton Financial Printing Division v. National Labor Relations Board, 846
Lockhard v. Nelson, 818
Longo v. United States, 842
Lorance v. AT&T Technologies Inc., 758, 781-782, 785, 842
Lucas v. South Carolina Coastal Council, 849
Lujan v. Defenders of Wildlife, 831
Lujan v. National Wildlife Federation, 831
Lytle v. Household Manufacturing Inc., 843
Maislin Industries, U.S. Inc. v. Primary Steel Inc., 811
Maleng v. Cook, 821
Mallard v. U.S. District Court for the Southern District of Iowa, 814
Mansell v. Mansell, 831
Marsh v. Oregon National Resources Council, 830
Martin v. Occupational Safety and Health Review Commission, 832
Martin v. Wilks, 758, 781, 784, 785, 842
Maryland v. Buie, 824
Maryland v. Craig, 819-820
Massachusetts v. Morash, 846
Massachusetts v. Oakes, 836
Masson v. The New Yorker, 837
McCarthy v. Bronson, 844
McCarthy v. Madigan, 842
McCleskey v. Zant, 821
McCormick v. United States, 829
McDernott International Inc. v. Wilander, 810
McKesson Corporation v. Division of Alcoholic Beverages and Tobacco, Department of Business Regulation of Florida, 813
McKoy v. North Carolina, 818
McLaughlin v. Sebben, 845
McNary v. Haitian Refugee Center, 838
McNeil v. Wisconsin, 826
MCorp v. Board of Governors of the Federal Reserve System, 833
Mead Corp. v. Tilley, 846
Medina v. California, 820
Medlock v. Leathers, 837
Melkonyan v. Sullivan, 840
Mesa v. California, 816
Metro Broadcasting Inc. v. Federal Communications Commission, 431 (box), 839
Metropolitan Washington Airports Authority v. Citizens for the Abatement of Aircraft Noise Inc., 834
Michael H. v. Gerald D., 831
Michigan v. Harvey, 825-826
Michigan v. Lucas, 820
Michigan Citizens for an Independent Press v. Thornburgh, 807
Michigan Department of State Police v. Sitz, 825
Midland Asphalt Corp. v. United States, 820
Miles v. Apex Marine Corp., 810
Milkovich v. Lorain Journal Co., 837
Minnesota v. Olson, 824
Minnick v. Mississippi, 826
Mississippi Band of Choctaw Indians v. Holyfield, 833
Missouri v. Jenkins, 840, 843
Mistretta v. United States, 826
M. J. R. Inc. v. City of Dallas, 836
Mobil Oil Exploration & Producing Southeast Inc. v. United Distribution Cos., 811
Molzof v. United States, 851
Morales v. Trans World Airlines Inc., 811
Morgan v. Illinois, 823
Moskal v. United States, 828
Mu'min v. Virginia, 823
Murray v. Giarratano, 821

National Collegiate Athletic Association v. Tarkanian, 815
National Labor Relations Board v. Curtin Matheson Scientific Inc., 846
National Railroad Passenger Corporation v. Boston & Maine Corp., 848
National Treasury Employees Union v. Von Raab, 845
Nationwide Mutual Insurance Co. v. Darden, 847
Neitzke v. Williams, 814-815
New Orleans Public Service Inc. v. New Orleans City Council, 810-811
New York v. Harris, 819
New York v. United States, 831
Newman-Green Inc. v. Alfonzo-Larrain, 815
Ngiraingas v. Sanchez, 841
Nordlinger v. Hahn, 851
Norfolk & Western Railway Co. v. American Train Dispatchers Association, 807
Norfolk & Western Railway Co. v. Goode, 848
Norman v. Reed, 829-830
North Dakota v. United States, 849
Northbrook National Insurance Co. v. Brewer, 815
Northwest Central Pipeline Corp. v. State Coporation Commission of Kansas, 810
Office of Personnel Management v. Richmond, 832
Ohio v. Akron Center for Reproductive Health, 595, 838
Ohio v. Department of Energy, 831
Oklahoma v. New Mexico, 849
Oklahoma Tax Commission v. Citizen Band Potawatomi Indian Tribe of Oklahoma, 850
Oklahoma Tax Commission v. Graham, 833
Osborne v. Ohio, 838
Osterneck v. Ernst & Whinney, 813
Owen v. Owen, 809
Owens v. Okure, 841
Pacific Mutual Life Insurance Co. v. Haslip, 851
Parker v. Dugger, 818
Patterson v. McLean Credit Union, 757, 781, 784, 785, 842-843
Patterson v. Shumate, 809
Pauley v. Bethenergy Mines Inc., 845
Pavelic & LeFlore v. Marvel Entertainment Group, 817
Payne v. Tennessee, 818
Peel v. Attorney Registration and Disciplinary Commission of Illinois, 814
Pennsylvania v. Bruder, 825
Pennsylvania v. Muniz, 826
Pennsylvania v. Union Gas Co., 830
Pennsylvania Department of Public Welfare v. Davenport, 808
Penry v. Lynaugh, 817
Pension Benefit Guaranty Corporation v. LTV Corp., 720 (box), 846
Penson v. Ohio, 823
Peretz v. United States, 829
Perpich v. Department of Defense, 361 (box), 832
Perry v. Leeke, 823
Personnel Board of Jefferson County v. Wilks, 842
Pilot Life Insurance Co. v. Dedeaux, 738
Pittsburgh & Lake Erie Railroad Co. v. Railway Labor Executives' Association, 845-846
Pittston Coal Corp v. Sebben, 845
Planned Parenthood of Southeastern Pennsylvania v. Casey, 598, 839
Port Authority Trans-Hudson Corp. v. Feeney, 849
Port Authority Trans-Hudson Corp. v. Foster, 849
Portland Golf Club v. Commissioner of Internal Revenue, 813
Powell v. McCormack, 958-959
Powell v. Texas, 824
Powers v. Ohio, 822
Presecult v. Interstate Commerce Commission, 848
Presley v. Etowah County Commission, 844
Price Waterhouse v. Hopkins, 758, 781, 784, 785, 842
Public Citizen v. Department of Justice, 833
Public Employees Retirement System of Ohio v. Betts, 714-716, 839
Quill Corp. v. North Dakota, 850
Quinn v. Millsap, 829
Rapone v. Inmates of the Suffolk County Jail, 844
R.A.V. v. City of St. Paul, 837
Reed v. United Transportation Union, 847
Renne v. Geary, 829
Republic of Argentina v. Weltover Inc., 845
Reves v. Ernst & Young, 811
Rhodes v. Stewart, 839
Riggins v. Nevada, 829
Robertson v. Methow Valley Citizens Council, 830
Robertson v. Seattle Audubon Society, 831
Rodriguez de Quijas v. Shearson/American Express Inc., 814
Roe v. Wade, 598, 801, 804
Rowan Companies v. United States, 51
Rufo v. Inmates of the Suffolk County Jail, 844
Rust v. Sullivan, 598, 838-839
Rutan v. Republican Party of Illinois, 835, 861 (box)
Sable Communications of California Inc. v. Federal Communications Commission, 431, 838
Saffle v. Parks, 821
Salve Regina College v. Russell, 814
Sapenfield v. Indiana, 837
Sawyer v. Smith, 821
Sawyer v. Whitley, 822
Schad v. Arizona, 818
Schmuck v. United States, 828
Secretary of the Interior v. California, 63
Sheet Metal Workers v. Lynn, 847
Shell Oil Co. v. Iowa Department of Revenue, 812
Siegert v. Gilley, 841
Simon & Schuster Inc. v. Members of New York State Crime Victims Board, 836
Sisson v. Ruby, 810
Skinner v. Mid-America Pipeline Co., 810
Skinner v. Railway Labor Executives' Association, 845
Smith v. Barry, 814
Sochor v. Florida, 828
South Carolina v. Gathers, 826
Southwest Marine Inc. v. Gizoni, 848
Spallone v. United States, 842
Stanford v. Kentucky, 817
Stevens v. Department of the Treasury, 839
Stewart v. Abend, 809-810
Stringer v. Black, 822
Sullivan v. Everhart, 834
Sullivan v. Finkelstein, 834
Sullivan v. Hudson, 840
Sullivan v. Stroop, 834
Sullivan v. Zebley, 834
Summit Health Ltd. v. Pinhas, 807
Suter v. Artist M., 841
Tafflin v. Levitt, 816
Taylor v. Freeland & Kronz, 809
Taylor v. United States, 826-827
Teague v. Lane, 788, 821
Texaco v. Hasbrouck, 807
Texas v. Johnson, 760, 836
Texas Monthly Inc. v. Bullock, 837
Texas State Teachers Association v. Garland Independent School District, 840
Thornburgh v. Abbott, 823
Toibb v. Radloff, 809
Tompkins v. Texas, 822
Touby v. United States, 829
Town of Huntington v. Huntington Branch, NAACP, 842
Trans World Airlines Inc. v. Independent Federation of Flight Attendants, 845
Trinova Corp. v. Michigan Departmet of Treasury, 813
Two Pesos Inc. v. Taco Cabana Inc., 813
Union Bank v. Wolas, 809
United States v. Alaska, 850
United States v. Alvarez-Machain, 845
United States v. Broce, 818
United States v. Burke, 843
United States v. Centennial Savings Bank FSB, 813
United States v. Dalm, 812
United States v. Eichman, 836, 761
United States v. Energy Resources Co. Inc., 808
United States v. Felix, 819
United States v. Fordice, 843-844
United States v. Gaubert, 833
United States v. Goodyear Tire & Rubber Co., 812
United States v. Halper, 818
United States v. Kokinda, 836
United States v. Monsanto, 823
United States v. Montalvo-Murillo, 817
United States v. Munoz-Flores, 834
United States v. Nordic Village Inc., 809
United States v. Ojeda Rios, 824
United States v. R. Enterprises Inc., 820
United States v. R.L.C., 827
United States v. Roemer, 844
United States v. Ron Pair Enterprises Inc., 808
United States v. Salerno, 820
United States v. Smith, 809
United States v. Smith, 851
United States v. Sokolow, 824
United States v. Sperry Corp., 848
United States v. Stuart, 812
United States v. Thompson/Center Arms Co., 813
United States v. Verdugo-Urquidez, 824
United States v. Williams, 820
United States v. Wilson, 827
United States v. Zolin, 815
United States Department of Justice v. Reporters Committee for Freedom of the Press, 833
United States Department of Labor v. Triplett, 845
United Steelworkers of America v. Rawson, 847
University of Pennsylvania v. Equal Employment Opportunity Commission, 650 (box), 843
Venegas v. Mitchell, 840
Virgin Islands Bar Association v. Thornstenn, 814
Virginia Bankshares Inc. v. Sandberg, 811-812
Volt Information Sciences Inc. v. Board of Trustees of Leland Stanford Junior University, 814
Wade v. United States, 827-828
Walton v. Arizona, 818
Ward v. Rock Against Racism, 836
Wards Cove Packing Co. v. Atonio, 757-759, 781-785, 842
Washington v. Harper, 823
Washington Legal Foundation v. Department of Justice, 833
Webster v. Reproductive Health Services, 7, 52, 594, 838
West Virginia University Hospitals Inc. v. Casey, 785, 840
White v. Illinois, 820
Whitmore v. Arkansas, 818
Wilder v. Virginia Hospital Association, 834
Wilkins v. Missouri, 817
Wilkinson v. Confederated Tribes and Bands of the Yakima Indian Nation, 834
Will v. Michigan Department of State Police, 841
Williams v. United States, 827
Willy v. Coastal Corp., 817
Wilson v. Seiter, 823
Wine and Spirits Wholesalers of Connecticut Inc. v. Beer Institute Inc., 849
Wisconsin Department of Revenue v. William Wrigley Jr. Co., 851
Wisconsin Public Intervenor v. Mortier, 849
Wooddell v. International Brotherhood of Electrical Workers, Local 71, 847-848
Wright v. West, 822
W.S. Kirkpatrick & Co. Inc. v. Environmental Tectonics Corp., 845
Wyatt v. Cole, 816
Wyoming v. Oklahoma, 850
Wyoming v. United States, 833-834
Yates v. Evatt, 829
Yee v. City of Escondido, 848-849
Yellow Freight System Inc. v. Donnelly, 843
Ylst v. Nunnemaker, 822
Zant v. Moore, 821
Zinermon v. Burch, 841

Supreme Court decisions
abortion, 7, 52, 594, 595, 598, 838-839
affirmative action, 431 (box), 839
age discrimination, 714, 839
antitrust law, 807-808
appeals, 813
arbitration, 814
attorneys, 814
attorneys' fees, 839-840
aviation, 808
Baby Bells, 461-462
bail, 817
banking, 808
bankruptcy, 808-809
black lung benefits, 845
business law, 807-813
capital punishment, 817-818, 767
children, 840-841
church-state separation, 834-835
civil rights and liberties, 838-844
commercial speech, 835
Congress
campaign finance, 960
congressional powers, 834

corporate campaign spending, 955 (box)
qualifications of members, 958-959
copyright, 809-810
court procedures, 813-817
criminal law, 817-829
damage suits, 841-842
disabled persons, 647, 842
dismissals, 814-815
diversity jurisdiction, 815
double jeopardy, 818-819
drug testing, 448, 845
due process, 815
election law, 829-830
entrapment, 819
environmental law, 830-831
evidence, 815, 819-820
executive power, 832
faculty tenure, 650 (box)
fair trial, 828
family law, 831
federal employees, 832
federal government, 832-834
federal regulation, 810-811, 832-833
federal-state relations, 361 (box)
First Amendment, 834-838
flag desecration, 760-761
forum selection, 816
freedom of information, 833
freedom of speech, 835-837
freedom of the press, 837
grand juries, 820
habeas corpus appeals, 820-822
housing discrimination, 842
immigration law, 838
immunity, 816
Indians, 833-834, 906
individual rights, 838-844
international law, 844-845
interstate garbage, 523
job discrimination, 757-760, 780-785, 842-843
judgments, 816
jurisdiction, 816
jury selection, 816, 822-823
labor law, 845-848
labor unions, 847-848
legislative veto, 171, 172 (box)
living wills, 573
maritime law, 810
North conviction, appeal, 240-241 (box)
obscenity, 431, 837
OMB regulatory review, 868 (box)
patents, 810
patronage jobs, 861 (box)
pensions, 720 (box), 738, 846
prisons, 823
privacy, 843
property law, 848-849
racketeering, 816, 772
removal, 816
right to counsel, 823-824
sanctions, 817
school desegregation, 843-844
search and seizure, 824-825
self-incrimination, 825-826
sentencing, 826-828
sex discrimination, 844
Social Security, 834
state powers, 849-851
stocks, bonds and securities, 811-812
striker replacements, 733
student religious groups, 647
Tax Court, 817
taxes, 812-813, 850-851
torts, 851
trademarks, 813
vertical price fixing, 771
voting rights, 844
welfare services, 834

Supreme Court, U.S.
caseload, 801, 805 (box)
justices
Bush appointments, 994-995
list, 1993 (box), 804
Thomas confirmation (box), 802-803
solicitor general, 778
term summary, 801-806
Surface Transportation Efficiency Act of 1991, 437-444
Surface Transportation Program, 437, 441, 442
Susman, Stephen D., 918
Sustainable agriculture, 545
"Swampbuster" program, 541, 546
Sweden
Persian Gulf War, 316 (box)
Swett, Dick D-N.H.
House bank scandal (chart), 935
Swezy Realty Inc., 681
Swift, Al D-Wash.
Amtrak authorization, 447
motor voter bill, 871
solid waste, 523
Symington, Fife, 11
Symms, Steve R-Idaho
Clean Air Act, 476
CPSC authorization, 433
crime bill, 787
highway authorization, 439
Keating Five investigation, 987
minimum wage, 708
Synar, Mike D-Okla.
campaign finance, 956-957
grazing fees, 518-519
House bank scandal (chart), 935
House leadership, 916
Synthetic fuels, 109
Syria
Middle East peace talks, 277
Persian Gulf War, 302, 313-314, 316 (box)

T

Taborsak, Lynn, 27
Taft-Hartley Labor-Management Act of 1947, 717
Taft Institute, 651-652
Tagliabue, Paul, 790
Tailhook scandal, 374-375 (box)
Taiwan
Nicaraguan contra aid, 221 (box)
U.S. trade
trade expansion act, 197
Tajikistan, 331
Take the Boards Off, 697
Talent Search, 655
Tallon, Robin D-S.C.
House bank scandal (chart), 935
Tanks and tank warfare
appropriations, 351, 364, 382, 409
CFE treaty, 385, 386
defense authorization
FY 1990, 344, 346-347
FY 1991, 360-361
FY 1992, 373-374, 377-378
FY 1993, 404-405
Tanner, John D-Tenn.
House bank scandal (chart), 935
Targeted Export Assistance program, 545
Targeted jobs tax credit, 47, 69, 94
Tariffs. *See also Customs duties; General Agreement on Tariffs and Trade*
Andean products, 296-297
Caribbean Basin Initiative, 180-184
footwear, 107
Generalized System of Preference, 182, 211-212, 213
MFN status (box), 172
minivans, 197-198
NAFTA, 187-190
trade expansion act, 197
Tauke, Tom R-Iowa
House bank scandal (chart), 934
Tauzin, W.J. "Billy" D-La.
cable TV regulation, 453-454
House bank scandal (chart), 935
pipeline inspections, 488
Tax Court, U.S., 817
Tax Reform Act of 1986, 182
Taxation, Joint Committee on
capital gains tax cut, 97, 99
deficit-reduction bill, 1990, 93
ERISA reforms, 738
pension reversions, 720
Section 89 tax rules, 708
unemployment benefits, 728
Taxes and taxation. *See also Business taxes; Capital gains tax; Customs duties; Earned-income tax credit; Excise taxes; Fuel taxes; Income taxes; Internal Revenue Service; Tariffs; User fees*
budget action, 77, 80
chronology of action
1989-90, 91-99
1991-92, 99-112
energy bill, 505
expiring provisions, 94 (box), 103, 107, 109-110
percentage of GDP, 90 (chart)
state powers, 850-851
summary, 36, 87-90, 91, 99-100, 995
Taxol, 527
Taylor, Gene D-Miss.
election, 8
House bank scandal (chart), 934
Taylor, Gene R-Mo.
campaign funds conversion, 952
Taylor, William, 114, 1176-1177
Taylor, William M., 681
Taylor, William W. III, 977, 981, 983, 984
Teachers
Bush education initiative, 643-644
defense conversion aid, 402
higher education aid, 653, 656
Teamsters union, 445
Technology Administration, 880
Technology Assessment, Office of
Americans with Disabilities Act, 746
math, science education, 651
Technology transfer
clean-coal technology, 511
global warming initiatives, 505-506
high-tech programs, 880
nuclear arms proliferation, 293
Telecommunications. *See also Satellites and satellite communications*
Americans with Disabilities Act, 743, 745, 751
Baby Bells restrictions, 432, 461-462
export controls, 196
NAFTA highlights, 188 (box)
rural development, 548
Star Schools, 659
summary, 416
tax treatment of equipment, 49
Telemarketing
commodity futures trading regulation, 552
controls, 432, 459
Telephone communications
alternative operator rates, 431-432
Americans with Disabilities Act, 745, 751
Baby Bells restrictions, 432, 461-462
cable TV regulation, 427, 453
caller ID, 462
Cuba-U.S. links, 295
excise taxes, 67, 91, 96, 611
FCC user fees, 458
900-number regulation, 460
rural cooperatives loans, 460-461
telephone pornography, 431
Television. *See also Cable television*
campaign finance, 953, 955, 961
children's programming
advertising, 429
educational TV grants, 429
closed-captioning, 428-429, 751, 949
CPB authorization, 457-458
fairness doctrine, 430
FCC minority preference, 431 (box)
FCC user fees, 458
high-definition television, 880
low-power stations, 456
political advertising, 957-958
uniform poll closing time, 872
violence guidelines, 428
Teller votes, 411
Temporary Emergency Food Assistance Program, 619
Tennessee Valley Authority, 510
Term limits, 10 (box), 958-959, 963-964
Territories, U.S.
House voting privileges, 948-949
insular energy resources, 512
Puerto Rico plebiscite, 873-874
Terrorism
arms sales ban, 238
aviation security, 420, 421
Capitol bombing, 922 (box)
death penalty, 766
deportation, 786
State Department authorization, 248
Terwilliger, George J. Jr., 1180
Texas
bankruptcy judges, 799
child support enforcement, 616
Clean Air Act, 474
defense contracts
FY 1991, 345
FY 1992, 372, 378, 379
FY 1993, 396
V-22 Osprey aircraft, 406 (box)
governor's election, 1990, 12
federal judgeships, 774
highway authorization, 442
housing authorization, 669
Mexican border area, 675
irrigation subsidies, 516-517
presidential election, 1992, 24 (box)
refugee asylum, 756
superconducting supercollider, 878-879, 901
water projects, 493 (box)
Yucca Mountain nuclear dump, 513
Texas Air Corp., 421, 712
Textile industry
Caribbean Basin Initiative, 180
foreign trade summary, 167
import quotas, 174-175
NAFTA highlights, 188 (box)
Thailand
POW/MIA investigation, 289
Thatcher, Margaret, 301
Third World debt
budget reconciliation, FY 1990, 49
debt-for-science swaps, 903
development banks authorization, 184, 185, 186
drug legislation, 769
Egypt aid, 74, 235-236
Enterprise for the Americas, 179-180, 194-195
foreign aid appropriations, 229, 230, 274, 275, 276

summary, 166
Thomas, Bill R-Calif.
campaign finance, 961-962
franking privilege, 968, 973
House bank scandal (chart), 934
House leadership, 917
irrigation subsidies, 515
motor voter bill, 871, 894
Thomas, Clarence
appeals court nomination, 777-778
effects of confirmation hearings
civil rights/job bias, 780
Keating Five investigation, 986
news leaks investigation, 946-947
nominating process changes, 795-796
Senate elections, 1992, 24, 26
summary, 13
Supreme Court
confirmation, 802-803 (box), 994-995
term summary, 801, 804
Thomas, Craig R-Wyo
election, 8
irrigation subsidies, 514
Thomas, Lindsay D-Ga.
House bank scandal (chart), 935
Thompson, Bruce, 944
Thompson, Frank Jr., 940 (box)
Thompson, James R., 871
Thompson, Robert J., 995
Thorium mill cleanup, 509
Thornburgh, Dick
Americans with Disabilities Act, 745
biographical profile, 1170
civil rights/job bias, 758
crime bill, 767
Gray ethics case, 5
Hatch Act revision, 861
HUD scandal, 681, 683, 684, 685
law leadership, 745 (box)
Lucas nomination, 763
Senate elections, 1991, 14, 596
whistleblowers protection, 863
Thornton, Ray D-Ark.
House bank scandal (chart), 935
House elections, 1990, 11
Three Affiliated Tribes, 517
Threshold Test Ban Treaty, 366-368
Thrift Depositor Protection Oversight Board, 152
Thrift Supervision, Office of
Keating Five investigation, 981, 983
leadership, 114
savings and loan bailout, 117, 122-123, 126-127
refinancing, 152
Thrifts. *See Savings and loan associations*
Thurber, James A., 15
Thurmond, Strom R-S.C.
crime bills, 765-767, 786-788
displaced homemakers, 715 (box)
Keating Five investigation, 982
NEA funding, 866
news leaks investigation, 947
textile import quotas, 174
vertical price fixing, 771
Tied aid
Export-Import Bank authorization, 184, 185, 186, 199
foreign aid appropriations, 236
Poland trade aid, 172
Timber. *See Forests and national forests*
Titan IV rockets, 404
Title X, 592-593, 598-599
Tobacco
anti-smoking bills, 591, 604
airline flights, 419-420
excise taxes, 49, 67, 96
exports
health warnings, 591
market promotion, 555
"fire-safe" cigarettes, 436
quota change, 557
sales bans
minors, 604, 799
VA hospitals, 627 (box), 635
Tom Steed Resevoir, Okla., 518
Tomahawk missiles
appropriations, 364, 409
authorization, 378, 406
START treaty, 388 (box)
Tongass National Forest, 492-493
Torres, Esteban E. D-Calif.
credit reporting safeguards, 157-158
House leadership, 916
immigration reform, 755
Torricelli, Robert G. D-N.J.
environmental summit, 528
House bank scandal (chart), 934
Soviet-U.S. trade, 171
Torts. *See also Liability issues*
Supreme Court decisions, 851
Torture
treaty, 259
victims' suits, 797
Totenberg, Nina, 946-947
TOW missiles, 347
Tower, John
biographical profile, 1177
Defense nomination, 6, 338, 339-340, 917, 993
Iran-contra investigation, 286
Towns, Edolphus D-N.Y
airline smoking ban, 419
House bank scandal, 932
members with overdrafts (chart), 934
Toxic substances. *See Hazardous substances*
Toxic Substances Control Act, 64
Toys, 462
Trade. *See Foreign trade and business*
Trade Act of 1988, 189
Trade adjustment assistance, 190
Trade agreements
compliance review, 197
fisheries, 426, 434, 528
MFN status (box), 172
NAFTA, 165-166, 187-190
semiconductor chips, 793
Soviet, East bloc, 169-171, 192-194, 209
textiles, 167
Trade and Development Program, U.S., 199, 200
Trade Credit Insurance Program, 213
Trade representative, U.S.
authorization, 181, 199
Bush economic team, 32 (box)
foreign trade summary, 167-168
trade expansion act, 197
Trade schools, 649-650, 655
Trademarks
Supreme Court decisions, 813
tax treatment, 49
Trading with the Enemy Act, 295
Traficant, James A. D-Ohio
superconducting supercollider, 879
Trans-Alaska Pipeline, 49, 491
Transport Workers Union of America, 713
Transportation. *See also Air transportation; Automobiles and auto industry; Bus transportation; Highways and roads; Railroads; Ships and shipping; Travel and tourist trade; Trucks and trucking*
city, state planning, 442-443
employee drug testing, 770
energy conservation research, 510
Transportation Department, U.S.
aviation, 418
airline buyouts, 421
flight attendants' workday, 446
reservations systems, 445
security procedures, 420
drug testing, 425, 439, 448, 748, 752, 770
highways and motor vehicles
air bags, 444
food-waste backhauling, 423-424
fuel-efficiency mandates, 501
hazardous materials, 422-423
highway authorization, 439
leadership, 419 (box)
pipeline safety, 532
user fees, 65
Transportation Statistics, Bureau of, 444
Travel and Tourism Administration, U.S., 462
Travel and tourist trade. *See also Passports and visas*
airline, cruise taxes, 65
airline reservations system, 445
Caribbean Basin Initiative, 183
cruise ships, 450
Florida Keys, 497
promotion bill, 462
telephone rates, 431-432
Traxler, Bob D-Mich.
House bank scandal (chart), 934
space station, 900
Treadway, James C. Jr., 684
Treasury Department, U.S.
banking
bank deposit insurance, 124 (box), 129
banking overhaul, 136-148
disaster areas, 161
fair trade in financial services, 187, 198, 412
money laundering, 134, 156
savings and loan bailout, 117-126
Bush economic team, 32 (box)
capital gains tax cut, 97, 99
foreign food aid, 257
government securities market regulation, 158
government-sponsored enterprises, 73, 129, 154-156
gun registration violations, 788
minivan tariffs, 193
pension reversions, 719-720
Puerto Rico plebiscite, 873-874
Section 89 tax rules, 708-710
securities market reforms, 131-132
state fund transfers, 865, 890
stock index futures regulation, 550
Third World debt, 184, 185, 274
unemployment benefits, 724
Treasury securities. *See Government securities*
Treaties and international agreements. *See also Arms control; Trade agreements*
environmental protection
Antarctica mining ban, 489, 529-530
global warming, 297
Great Lakes water quality, 492
ocean studies, 209
U.N. conference, 528-529
waterfowl management, 494
executive branch powers, 249
German unification, 214
nuclear energy cooperation, 209
ratification issues, 367, 386
refugee protocol, 296
torture treaty, 259
Treatment Improvement, Office for, 770
Treverton, Gregory F., 243
Tribal Judicial Conference, 906
Tribal Justice Support, Office of, 906-907
Trident II missiles
appropriations, 351, 364, 382, 409
authorization, 341, 342, 346, 360, 373, 377, 404
START treaty, 388 (box)
Trident missile-launching submarines, 341, 342, 346, 364
Trinidad and Tobago
Caribbean Basin Initiative, 180
Trucks and trucking
air bags, 444
alternative-fuel vehicles, 108-109
bankrupt firms, 445
defense authorization, 377, 380
emissions standards, 475, 482-483
deadlines, 477 (box)
food-waste backhauling, 423-424
fuel-efficiency mandates, 500, 501
hazardous materials, 422-423
length, weight limits, 439, 444
minivan tariffs, 197-198
NAFTA highlights, 188 (box)
truck drivers
drug testing, 425
highway rest area drug trafficking, 425
literacy skills, 659
Truly, Richard H., 875 (box), 899, 996
Truman, Margaret, 991
Trump, Donald J., 421
Trust Indenture Act of 1939, 132-133
Trust Territory of the Pacific Islands, 258-259
Truth-in-savings, 134, 142, 147, 161
Tsongas, Paul E., 17, 19
Tuberculosis prevention, 587
Tupper, Kari, 944
Turkey
Armenian genocide resolution, 259
CFE weapons cascading, 386
Persian Gulf War, 301, 303, 304, 316 (box), 317
Saratoga accident compensation, 409
U.S. aid, 274, 275-276
Turner Broadcasting System, 451
Tutwiler, Margaret D., 300
TV Marti, 250
27th Amendment, 972-973

U

UDAG. *See Urban Development Action Grants*
Udall, Morris K. D-Ariz.
environmental foundation, 527
House bank scandal (chart), 934
House leadership, 929
successor, 14
Ueberroth, Peter V., 713
Uintah Basin, 516
Ukraine
arms control, 328, 329, 336
CFE treaty, 386
reconnaissance overflights, 392
START treaty, 387-390
Soviet Union dissolution, 322
U.S. relations, 331
Unemployment insurance
benefits extension
1990 action, 717
1991 action, 721-725
1992 action, 725-728
dislocated workers, 714
summary, 703-704, 720
tax action, 110
trade bill, 193

census workers, 182
federal payroll tax
budget reconciliation, 68, 96
excess revenues, 616
wage base increase, 717
Gulf War veterans benefits, 630
UNICEF. *See United Nations Children's Fund*
Union of Concerned Scientists, 501
Unisys Corp., 944
United Airlines, 421, 445
United Arab Emirates
Persian Gulf War, 299, 300, 302-303, 316 (box)
United Auburn Indian Community, 908
United Auto Workers, 715
United ChemCon Corp., 945
United Nations
drift net fishing, 528
El Salvador civil war, 218
Middle East conference, 250
Nicaragua policy, 222
office building financing, 111
Security Council
Middle East peace talks, 277
Persian Gulf War, 299-317
Resolution 678 (box), 305
Somalia relief, 278-279
Yugoslav conflict, 278
torture treaty, 259
U.S. contributions, 247, 258, 271
United Nations Children's Fund (UNICEF), 232
United Nations Conference on Environment and Development (Earth Summit)
Bush participation, 528-529, 997
global warming treaty, 297
United Nations Development Program, 232
United Nations Framework Convention on Climate Change, 297, 506
United Nations Fund for Population Activities
abortion action, 594, 600
controversy summary (box), 235
foreign aid appropriations
FY 1990, 228, 229-230
FY 1991, 234
FY 1992, 269
FY 1993, 274, 275, 276
foreign aid authorization
FY 92-93, 267
United Nations Refugee Convention and Protocol, 296
United Negro College Fund, 148
United Technologies, 295
United We Stand, America, 25
Unsoeld, Jolene D-Wash.
House bank scandal, 937
members with overdrafts (chart), 935
Upjohn Co., 793
Upton, Fred R-Mich.
House bank scandal (chart), 935
Upward Bound, 655
Uranium
enrichment program
plant licenses, 486
revision, 489, 500, 504, 508-509
nuclear waste, 509, 525
radiation victims compensation, 586
strategic reserve, 509
Urban areas
Clean Air Act, 473, 478-480, 482
deadlines, 477 (box)
crime insurance, 694
federal aid, 15, 103, 664, 699-700
hospitals, 574
irrigation subsidies, 513
job training programs, 713
summer youth jobs, 722 (box)
transportation planning, 438, 442-443
Urban Development Action Grants (UDAGs), 680, 684
Urban homesteading, 676
Urban Mass Transportation Administration, 443
Uruguay Round. *See General Agreement on Tariffs and Trade*
U.S.-Canada Great Lakes Water Quality Agreement, 492
U.S. Term Limits, 963
User fees
budget reconciliation, FY 1991, 64-65
Coast Guard services, 425
FCC services, 47, 430, 458-459
FDA drug review, 603
Medicare compliance certification, 578
Nuclear Regulatory Commission, 47, 489-490
Patent Office, 792
radio spectrum allocation, 430-431
shipping data base, 448, 449
Utah
irrigation subsidies, 516
radiation victims compensation, 586
water projects, 493 (box)
Utah Lakes Wetlands Preserve, 516
Ute Indians, 516

V

V-22 Osprey aircraft
appropriations, 350, 352, 364, 382, 407-409
cancellation controversy, 348, 406 (box)
defense authorization
FY 1990, 341-342, 344, 349
FY 1991, 355-357, 362
FY 1992, 372, 373, 376, 379
FY 1993, 396
summary, 339
Vaccines. *See Immunization*
Valenti, Jack, 452 (box)
Valentine, Tim D-N.C.
competitiveness bills, 892
House bank scandal (chart), 935
House elections, 1992, 27
NASA authorization, 875
Value-added tax, 596
van Paasschan, Gwendolyn, 980
Vander Jagt, Guy R-Mich.
House bank scandal, 933
House leadership, 916, 929
Vento, Bruce F. D-Minn.
FHA insurance fund, 691
House bank scandal (chart), 935
House leadership, 929
housing authorization, 669
Ventura Harbor, Calif., 493 (box)
Vermejo Water Conservancy District, 517
Vermont
credit reporting safeguards, 157
House elections, 1990, 11
Veterans. *See also Disabled veterans; Persian Gulf War veterans; Veterans education programs; Veterans health care; Vietnam War veterans*
chronology of action
1989-90, 625-629
1991-92, 629-637
flag desecration, 762
hiring preference, 625, 629
home loans and housing programs, 625-627, 628-629, 635-636
RTC operations, 153
Indian veterans memorial, 908
job discrimination, 636-637
job training, 629
minority veteran affairs, 636
Philippine veterans citizenship, 779-780
rehabilitation certificates, 629
Veterans Affairs Department, U.S. (VA)
drug discounts, 605
homeless veterans, 634-635
housing loans, 626, 627, 628-629, 635-636
leadership, 627 (box)
minority affairs, 636
nurses pay, 627-628
omnibus veterans bill, 625
physicians, dentists salaries, 633-634
tax information, 70
veterans' COLA increase, 632
Veterans education programs
buy-in option, 363
Persian Gulf War benefits, 629-631
reservists, 633
reservist benefits for nursing, 625
services extension, 629
Veterans health care
budget reconciliation, 626-627
drug discounts, 605, 635
hospice care pilot project, 637
omnibus bills, 625, 635
post-traumatic stress disorder, 636
radiation exposure compensation, 636
research grants, 629
substance abuse housing aid, 628
Veterans hospitals
non-veteran patients, 627 (box)
nurses pay, 625, 627-628
personnel retention, 629
physicians, dentists salaries, 633-634
tobacco sales, smoking ban, 627 (box), 635
Veterans Readjustment Appointment authority, 625
Veterans Recruitment Authority, 629
Vetoes
Bush vetoes, 1989-92
list, 1181-1182
summary, 998
pocket-veto power, 927
Victims compensation, 616
Vietnam
POW-MIA issue, 289-290, 627 (box), 291
refugee asylum, 756
student aid, 291
U.S. aid to Cambodia, 245, 247
Vietnam War
POW/MIAs
Defense files, 380
investigation, 288-290
foreign aid appropriations, 276, 277
State Department authorization, 291
Vietnam War veterans
Agent Orange controversy, 628 (box)
hiring priority, 625
job aid, 633
post-traumatic stress disorder, 636
Violence. *See also Domestic violence*
animal research labs, 881, 904
cable TV regulation, 457
TV programming, 428
violence against women, 778, 797
Virgin Islands
barrier islands, 497
food stamps, 618
Virginia
governor's race, 6-7
solid waste, 523
water projects, 493 (box), 494
Virginia Beach, Va., 494
Visas. *See Passports and visas*
Visclosky, Peter J. D-Ind.
pension reversions, 719
VISTA. *See Volunteers in Service to America*
VISTA Literacy Corps, 619
Vocational and Applied Technology Education Act
Vocational education
program overhaul, 644-647
veterans benefits, 625, 627
Vocational rehabilitation
disabled veterans, 633
human services reconciliation, 616
Social Security beneficiaries, 62
Volcker Commission, 857, 858, 859 (box)
Volcker, Paul A., 34, 857, 859 (box)
Volkmer, Harold L. D-Mo.
House bank scandal (chart), 935
Volunteers
community service, 616-617
programs authorizations, 619
Volunteers in Service to America (VISTA), 619
Von Raab, William, 982
Voter participation
bilingual aid, 793
election day holiday, 895
get-out-the-vote drives, 960
motor voter bill, 894
presidential campaign fund, 954 (box)
presidential election, 1992, 22-23
uniform poll-closing time, 872
Voter registration drives
campaign finance, 960
Keating Five investigation, 981
motor voter bill, 871, 893-895
Voting rights
D.C. political issues, 872
Supreme Court decisions, 844
Voting Rights Act of 1965, 793, 1165
Vreeland, Frederick, 1179-1180
Vucanovich, Barbara F. R-Nev.
BLM authorization, 520
energy bill, 505
House bank scandal (chart), 935
Nevada wilderness, 496

W

Wald, Patricia M., 241 (box)
Walesa, Lech, 171, 211, 212, 707
Walgren, Doug D-Pa.
House bank scandal, 932
members with overdrafts (chart), 934
Walker, Robert S. R-Pa.
competitiveness bills, 891-892
Hatch Act revision, 861
high-tech programs, 902
highway authorization, 441
House leadership, 917
Savage ethics case, 925
Wall, M. Danny, 114, 117, 122-123, 126, 981
Wallop, Malcolm R-Wyo.
AIDS programs, 589
cable TV regulation, 428
defense authorization, 400
energy bill, 503, 505
housing authorization, 697
irrigation subsidies, 515
oil, gas royalties, 518
Puerto Rico plebiscite, 874
Senate leadership, 928
START treaty, 390
unilateral U.S. arms cutbacks, 391
Walsh, James T.
House bank scandal (chart), 934

Walsh, Lawrence E., 240, 286, 287, 997
War Powers Resolution of 1973, 224, 225, 280, 308
Wards Cove Packing Co., 784-785
Warner, John R-Va.
CIA relocation, 282 (box)
civil rights/job bias, 784
defense authorization
FY 1990, 344
FY 1992, 374-375
Hatch Act revision, 860
highway authorization, 439
START treaty, 390
Warren Commission, 892-893
Warsaw Pact
arms control summary, 366 (box)
CFE treaty, 328, 384-385
defense policy summary, 336
dissolution, 323-324
reconnaissance overflights, 392
troop reduction proposals, 387 (box)
Wasatch County, Utah, 516
Washington
endangered species, 521
northern spotted owl, 495
offshore oil drilling, 504
Puyallup Indian settlement, 885
term limits, 10 (box), 963
Yucca Mountain nuclear dump, 513
Washington, Craig D-Texas
civil rights/job bias, 780-781
election, 8
House bank scandal, 937
members with overdrafts (chart), 935
Washington, D.C. *See District of Columbia*
Washington summit, 1990, 209, 328, 366 (box), 368
Washington summit, 1992, 169, 329, 330
Waste, fraud and abuse in government programs
A-12 bomber cancellation, 379 (box)
financial centralization, 862
food assistance programs, 618
food stamps, 618, 619
HUD reforms, 685-689
HUD scandal, 663, 676-685
Indian programs investigation, 881-883
infant formula price fixing, 623
lobbying curbs, 862
Medicare fraud, 609
motor voter bill, 871, 893
Social Security fraud by illegal aliens, 62-63
Tower nomination, 339-340
waste-buster awards, 888
whistleblowers, 779, 862-864
Waste Isolation Pilot Project (WIPP), 524-525
Waste products. *See also Hazardous waste cleanup; Nuclear waste; Recycling; Sewers and sewage treatment*
alternative power, 486
Amtrak disposal, 424
debris in outer space, 876
food-waste backhauling, 423-424
interstate garbage, 523
ocean dumping, 531
RCRA authorization, 523
Water conservation, 516
Water pollution
abandoned mine seepage, 63
beach pollution, 531
clean water revision, 529
coastal non-point pollution control, 64
farm programs, 546
fish inspection, 434
Great Lakes cleanup, 491-492
groundwater contamination, 539
ocean dumping, 531
reclamation projects, 516, 517
salinity control, 516-517
Water Pollution Control Act, 64
Water projects
authorization, 493-494, 513-518, 528
new projects (box), 493
irrigation subsidies, 513-516
Water Quality Incentives Program, 546
Water resources. *See also Drinking water; Water pollution; Waterways; Wetlands preservation*
desalination, 903
irrigation subsidies, 495-496, 513-518
plumbing energy efficiency, 507
Western water policy review, 517
Water Resources Development Act of 1990, 493-494
Water rights
Colorado wilderness, 526
Indian settlements, 516, 517
Nevada wilderness, 496
Water supply projects
mine pollution abatement, 63
Oklahoma systems, 518
rural development, 548
South Dakota, 517
Waterfowl, 494
Waters, Maxine D-Calif.
higher education aid, 655
House bank scandal (chart), 935
House elections, 1990, 11
Waterways. *See also Water projects*
non-point source pollution, 529
wild, scenic rivers, 525
zebra mussels control, 496-497
Watkins, James D.
biographical profile, 1172
energy bill, 470, 502
energy leadership, 475 (box)
federal facilities cleanup, 498
fuel-efficiency standards, 484
superconducting supercollider, 878
Watkins, Wes D-Okla.
House bank scandal (chart), 935
Watt, James G., 663, 676, 677, 683
Waxman, Henry A. D-Calif.
ADAMHA authorization, 604-605
animal research labs, 881
Clean Air Act, 468-469, 474-476, 479
fish inspection, 434
health reform, 597
House bank scandal, 936
members with overdrafts (chart), 934
Medicare physician payments, 568
NAFTA, 190
NIH authorization, 591
Waxman, Margery, 983
Weather. *See also Drought*
disaster relief, 548-549
emergency information services, 65
NOAA authorization, 426, 450
Weaver, Gerald R. III, 942
Weber, Vin R-Minn.
abortion, 598
House bank scandal, 933
members with overdrafts (chart), 934
House leadership, 916, 929
Webster, William H.
CIA leadership, 261 (box)
intelligence authorization, 239-241
Persian Gulf War, 307
Wedtech Corp., 923, 925
"Weed and Seed" program, 699
Weicker, Lowell P. Jr., 11, 915
Weidenfeld, Edward, 681
Weinberger, Caspar W., 284, 286, 795, 997
Weingarten, Reid, 288
Weiss, Ted D-N.Y.
House bank scandal, 937
members with overdrafts (chart), 935
HUD scandal, 677
Weldon, Curt R-Pa.
coin redesign, commemoratives, 161
House bank scandal (chart), 935
parental leave, 711
Welfare and social services. *See also Child welfare; Food assistance programs; Homeless persons; Housing assistance and public housing; Medicaid*
child school attendance, 658
chronology of action
1989-90, 611-619
1991-92, 620-624
Indian programs, 883
job training, 730
motor voter bill, 894
Puerto Rico plebiscite, 873-874
reform proposals, 623
summary, 611, 620
Supreme Court decisions, 834
welfare dependency research, 623
Welk, Lawrence, birthplace, 526
Wellington Convention, 528
Wellstone, Paul D-Minn.
campaign finance, 961
health reform, 597
Senate elections, 1990, 11
West Germany. *See Germany*
West Virginia
CIA relocation, 282 (box)
water projects, 493 (box)
Western states
BLM authorization, 520
grazing fees, 518-519
highway authorization, 442
irrigation subsidies, 495-496, 513-518
water policy review, 517
mining law overhaul, 519
uniform poll-closing time, 872
Wetlands preservation
authorization, 494
barrier islands, 497
clean water revision, 529
farm bill, 539, 541, 542, 546
funding, 556-557
irrigation subsidies, 515-517
restoration program, 67
water projects bill, 494
Wetlands Reserve Program, 546
Wheat, Alan D-Mo.
House bank scandal (chart), 934
Wheat and feed grains
China trade status, 192
commodity reserve, 545
disaster relief, 549, 557
export enhancement, 554-555
foreign food aid, 257
price supports, 541, 542
quality improvement, 541
Soviet sales, 330, 551, 555
Whistleblowers and whistleblower protections
Americans with Disabilities Act, 751
animal research labs, 904
awards, 779, 888
banking, 134, 148
emergency physicians, 572
federal workers, 862-864
fish inspection, 434
health, safety violations, 864
intelligence analysts, 285 (box)
White, Byron R.
Supreme Court summary, 801, 804
White House. *See also Presidents, U.S.*
commemorative coins, 161
White House Conference on Aging, 620
White Mountain National Forest, 496
Whitehorn, Laura J., 922 (box)
Whitley, Charles, 952
Whitman, Christine Todd, 11
Whitten, Jamie L. D-Miss.
agricultural exports, 554-555
crop insurance, 549 (box)
D.C. appropriations, 895
franking privilege, 969
House bank scandal, 936
House leadership, 929
jobs bill, 14
mini-sequester, 78 (box)
NASA authorization, 874, 898
NEA funding, 867
service record, 929 (box)
Whole, House Committee of the, 948-949
WIC. *See Women, Infants and Children (WIC) program*
Wild and scenic rivers, 525
Wilder, L. Douglas, 6-7, 17, 944
Wilderness areas
Americans with Disabilities Act, 752
Arizona, 496
California desert protection, 522
Colorado, 526
Montana, 526
national forest areas, 496
Nevada, 496
scenic trails, 526
Wildlife. *See also Endangered species; Fish and fisheries; Wildlife refuges*
biological resources inventory, 522
irrigation subsidies, 515, 516
marine mammal die-off, 531
wetlands preservation, 494
Wildlife refuges
Arctic National Wildlife Refuge, 499, 512
irrigation subsidies, 512, 517
Rocky Mountain arsenal, 527
Wilensky, Gail R., 601
Wilkey, Malcolm R., 933, 936-937
Williams, Griff, 941
Williams, Michael, 655 (box)
Williams, Pat D-Mont.
House bank scandal, 938
members with overdrafts (chart), 934
House Post Office scandal, 941
job training programs, 713-714
NEA funding, 866-867
striker replacements, 733
vocational education, 645
Wilson, Charles D-Texas
House bank scandal, 933, 938
members with overdrafts (chart), 934
Wilson, Don W., 972
Wilson, Lance H., 678 (box), 684
Wilson, Pete R-Calif.
California desert protection, 522
Clean Air Act, 478
flag desecration, 761
franking privilege, 968-969
governor's election, 1990, 12
Hatch Act revision, 860
irrigation subsidies, 495, 514
Wind energy
alternative power, 486
energy bill tax provisions, 108, 109, 507
Winn, Philip, 679 (box)
WIPP. *See Waste Isolation Pilot Project*
Wirth, Tim D-Colo.
abortion, 594, 599
Arctic wildlife refuge, 512
budget resolution, FY 1992, 77
cable TV regulation, 428, 452 (box)
California desert protection, 522
Clean Air Act, 478
energy policy summary, 470, 472
Persian Gulf War, 305
school reform, 658
striker replacements, 734

Wise, Bob D-W.Va.
dislocated workers, 714
veterans health care, 635
Wiseman, Shirley McVay, 679, 680, 684
Wishart, Leonard P., 948
Wofford, Harris D-Pa.
Senate elections, 1991, 14, 596
Wolf, Diane, 135
Wolpe, Howard D-Mich.
House bank scandal (chart), 935
superconducting supercollider, 878
Women. *See also Women-owned business; Women's health issues*
education
higher education aid, 657
math, science education, 651
vocational education, 646-647
elections and politics
congressional elections, 17
House elections, 1990, 11
House elections, 1992, 27
judicial appointments, 776 (box)
members of Congress, 1947-95 (table), 18
presidential election, 1992, 22
Senate elections, 1992, 19, 23, 24
state elections, 1992, 28
employment
child care, 611
displaced homemakers, 715 (box)
job bias, 757-760, 780-785
non-traditional job training, 732
science, engineering, 732-733
housing opportunity, 671
military service, 369, 373, 380
summary (box), 374-375
Thomas-Hill hearings, 802
violent crime, 778, 797
expert witnesses in domestic violence, 797
Women, Infants and Children (WIC) program
authorization, 617-618
farmers' markets, 622-623
infant formula price fixing, 623
Medicaid action, 579
Women-owned business
highway contracts, 440, 441
RTC operations, 150, 152
SBA loans, 464
Women's Equal Rights Legal Defense and Education Fund, 943, 944
Women's health issues. *See also Pregnancy; Women, Infants and Children (WIC) program*
AIDS disability benefits, 623-624
cancer screening, 593, 608
DES research, 607
drug treatment, 358, 968-969
Indian programs, 905
maternal, child health block grant, 579-580
Medicare coverage
mammography, 577
osteoporosis therapy, 576
Pap tests, 570
NIH authorization, 590-591, 602
Women's Health Research and Development, Office of, 591
Women's interest groups
abortion, 594
parental leave, 711
Women's Legal Defense Fund, 711
Woods, Alan, 227
Wool, 544
Work incentive (WIN) credit, 49
Work-study programs, 625, 656, 675-676
Workers' compensation
Supreme Court decisions, 848
Workplace Literacy Partnerships, 659
World Bank
China loans, 238, 251, 252
Japanese-American compensation, 794
U.S. aid appropriations, 229, 230, 274, 277
World War II
missing-in-action servicemen, 289-290
Philippine veterans citizenship, 779-780
Wrangel Island, 209
Wright, Betty, 917
Wright, Jim D-Texas
congressional pay, 965-966
Eastern Airlines strike, 712
House bank scandal (chart), 934
House leadership
Coelho resignation, 918
resignation, 917-918
summary, 5, 913, 915, 916
Keating Five investigation, 984
savings and loan bailout, 121
successor, 8
Wright, Orville and Wilbur, 526
Wyden, Ron D-Ore.
election day holiday, 895
Wylie, Chalmers P. R-Ohio
banking overhaul, 138, 141
FHA loan ceiling, 690
House bank scandal (chart), 934
housing authorization, 669
HUD reforms, 686-687
savings and loan bailout refinancing, 150, 151, 153
Wyngaarden, James, 567 (box)
Wyoming
radiation victims compensation, 586
term limits, 10 (box), 963

Y

Yakovlev, Aleksandr, 320
Yankton Sioux Reservation, 517
Yates, Sidney R. D-Ill.
House bank scandal, 937
members with overdrafts (chart), 935
NEA funding, 865-867
superconducting supercollider, 901
Yatron, Gus D-Pa.
environmental summit, 528
Yazov, Dmitri T., 392
Yeakel, Lynn, 26
Yellowstone National Park, 526-527
Yeltsin, Boris N.
address to Congress, 265, 324
text, 326-327
arms control, 328-329
B-2 bomber, 399
nuclear test ban, 392
START II, 390, 997
Gorbachev coup, 321 (box), 336
Russia-U.S. relations, 324-325, 330, 331
Moscow Embassy, 263
POWs statement (text), 1218-1220
U.S. aid, 262-265
Soviet Union dissolution, 319-322, 331-332
YES program. *See Youth Engaged in Service to America*
Yeutter, Clayton
Agriculture appointment, 539 (box)
biographical profile, 1169
farm bill, 539
"revolving door," 887
sugar price supports, 541
Young, Don R-Alaska
House bank scandal (chart), 934
Youth. *See Adolescents and youth*
Youth Engaged in Service to America, 617
Youthbuild, 697, 698
Yucca Mountain nuclear waste dump
action, 512-513
energy bill, 504, 505, 509
WIPP, 524
Yugoslavia and successor republics
U.S. aid, 271, 275, 278
U.S. relations summary, 260
U.S. trade, 194

Z

Zaire
U.S. aid, 232, 238
Zamora, Jaime Paz, 256
Zebra mussels, 496-497
Zimmer, Dick, R-N.J.
NASA authorization, 1992-94, 897-898